All Music Guide to Jazz

3RD EDITION

The Experts' Guide to the Best Jazz Recordings

EDITED BY
Michael Erlewine, Executive Editor
Vladimir Bogdanov, Database Design
Chris Woodstra, Editor-In-Chief
Stephen Thomas Erlewine, Senior Editor
Scott Yanow, Senior Jazz Editor

MF Miller Freeman Books

San Francisco

Published in 1998 by Miller Freeman Books, 600 Harrison Street, San Francisco, CA 94107
Publishers of *Guitar Player*, *Bass Player*, and *Keyboard* magazines
A member of the United Newspapers Group

 Miller Freeman
A United News & Media company

Distributed to the book trade in the U.S. and Canada by
Publishers Group West, 1700 Fourth St., Berkeley, CA 94710
Distributed to the music trade in the U.S. and Canada by
Hal Leonard Publishing, P.O. Box 13819, Milwaukee, WI 53213

ISBN 0-87930-530-4

Cover photo: Charles Mingus, Thelonious Monk, Roy Haynes, and Charlie Parker.
Used with permission from the Bob Parent Photo Archive, Copyright © 1998 Dale Parent.
Production: Dorothy Cox, Jan Hughes, Amy Conroy

Printed in the United States of America
98 99 00 01 02 9 8 7 6 5 4 3 2 1

Table of Contents

All Music Guide Website

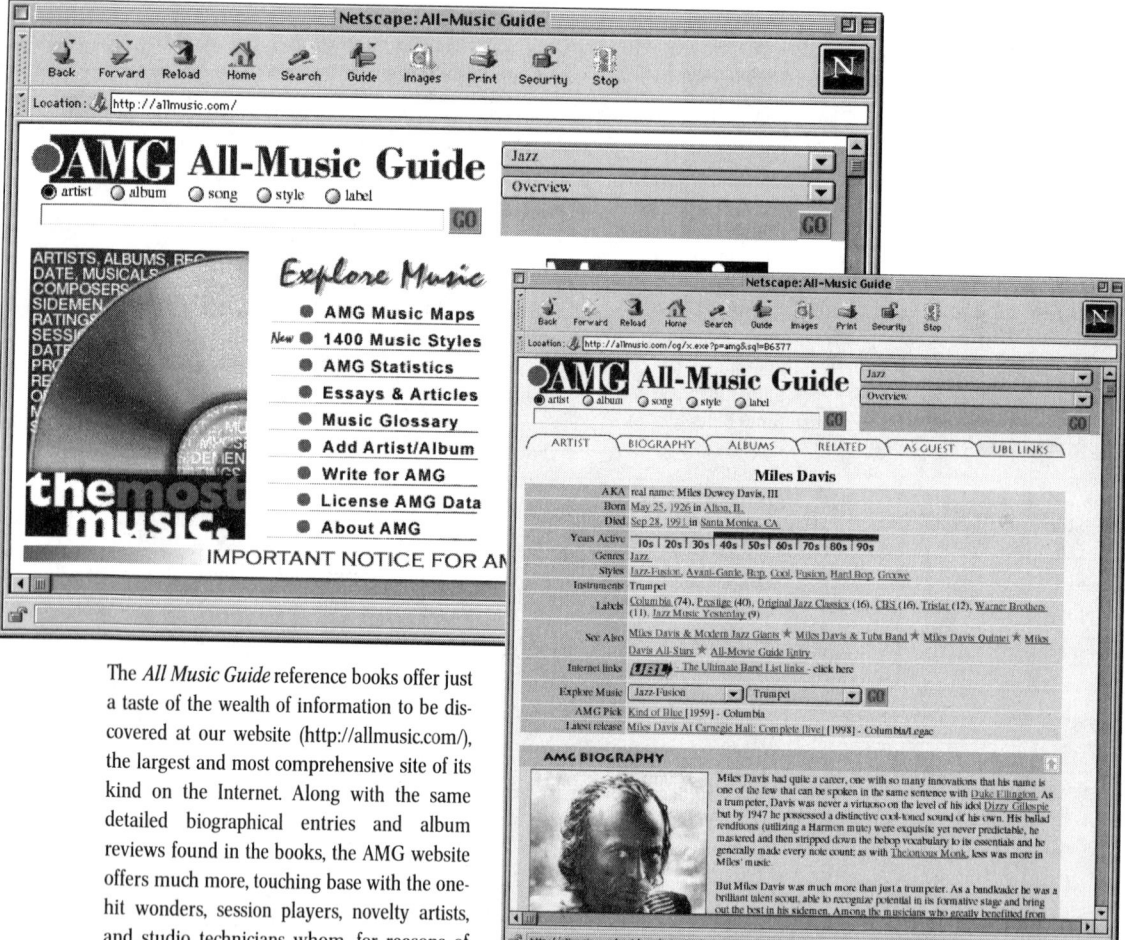

The *All Music Guide* reference books offer just a taste of the wealth of information to be discovered at our website (http://allmusic.com/), the largest and most comprehensive site of its kind on the Internet. Along with the same detailed biographical entries and album reviews found in the books, the AMG website offers much more, touching base with the one-hit wonders, session players, novelty artists, and studio technicians whom, for reasons of space, the book cannot.

Of course, the site doesn't replace the books, it complements them; while the books compile overviews of the superstars, the cult heroes and the true innovators into one handy volume, the AMG homepage fills in the gaps, taking full advantage of the seemingly boundless scope of the web to offer exhaustive coverage of thousands of other, more obscure artists and albums. In addition, it features even more detailed information on music's landmark performers and records, including recording information and hyperlinks to related artists. At the same time, the site affords one luxury that the print format cannot; while published books cannot be updated until the next edition, the AMG website evolves and changes along with the music industry; if your favorite band releases a new album, or their drummer quits, you'll find it noted on-line long before you'll see it mentioned in book form. Information can be accessed through the All Music Guide site in one of three easy ways: to find what you're looking for, simply type the name of the particular artist, album or song in the appropriate space, click on the "search" button, and the available data will appear. You can also click on regular features like our music maps, essays and glossaries, or even help us grow by suggesting new artists and albums to cover.

Foreword

The third edition of the *All Music Guide to Jazz* is the most complete consumer guide to jazz recordings ever made available. It includes biographies of 1,700 jazz artists and groups with more than 18,000 of their finest recordings rated and/or reviewed. For this new edition, all sections have been re-examined, reworked, and we have included a great many more Music Maps and historical essays. In addition, we have broadened the scope of the book to take in some artists not previously covered. We hope the increased coverage will make it easier for more people to find their way to enjoying jazz.

Thanks to the efforts of guest editor Scott Yanow and the unflagging work of the *AMG* editorial staff Chris Woodstra, Vladimir Bogdanov, and Stephen Thomas Erlewine, this revised edition of the *All Music Guide to Jazz* contains a number of enhancements including more (and longer) reviews and artist biographies, plus additional Music Maps and essays.

And special thanks to *AMG* jazz editor Scott Yanow for his hard work. Yanow is a frequent contributor to *DOWN BEAT, Cadence, Jazz Times,* and a contributor to the *New Grove Dictionary of Jazz* and Leonard Feather's *Encyclopedia of Jazz.*

Aside from this volume, the *All Music Guide* series includes our main guide (*All Music Guide*) and the *All Music Guide to Rock, All Music Guide to the Blues*, and the *All Music Guide to Country Music.* The complete *AMG* guide is also available on CD-ROM from Corel Corporation. Also, be sure to visit our home page on the World-Wide Web at http://AllMusic.com. The *All-Music Guide* is an ongoing database project, the largest collection of substantive album reviews ever assembled. We welcome your feedback.

Perhaps we have left out some of your favorite albums, and/or included ones that you don't consider essential. Let us know about it. We welcome criticism, suggestions, and additions. Perhaps you are an expert on the complete output of a particular artist or group and would like to participate in future editions of this book and/or our larger computer database. We would be glad to hear from you.

Michael Erlewine, executive editor

All-Music Guide
407 N. State Street
Big Rapids, MI 49307
Phone (616) 796 3437
Fax (616) 796 1244
E-mail: AMG@AllMusic.com

Contributors

All Music Guide to Jazz, 3rd Edition

Special thanks to Charlie Lourie and Michael Cuscuna of Mosaic Recordings for setting the standard for jazz reissues.

Editors
Michael Erlewine, Executive Editor
Vladimir Bogdanov, Database Design
Chris Woodstra, Editor-In-Chief
Stephen Thomas Erlewine,
    Senior Editor
Scott Yanow, Senior Jazz Editor

AMG Production Staff
Jason Akeny
Jackie Baldwin
Jonathan Ball
Sherry Batchelder
Nancy Beilfuss
Julie Bloem
John Bush
Julie Clark
Dave Datta
M. Sharkey Donkers
Brandy Ellison
Jamie Erler
Elizabeth Carey Erlewine
Margaret J. Erlewine
Margaret Louise Erlewine
Kevin Fowler
Doug Gabert
Yelena German
Tanya Guild
Brenda Haney
April Hinkley
Will Holmes
Steve Huey
Jennifer Hughes
Mike King
Debbie Kirby
Forest Ray
Danielle Ruppert
Shey Ryans
Bob Smith
Mike Tinnes
Reuben Tucker

Matrix Software/
All-Movie Guide Staff
Kyle Alexander
Sandra Brennan
Irene Baldwin
Richard Batchelder
Susan Brownlee
Stephanie Clement
Walter Crockett
Tricia Davis
Yuri German
Richard Gilliam
Thomas Goyett
Mary E. King
Madeline Koperski
Teresa Swift-Eckert
Phillip Erlewine
Stephen Erlewine
Dan Pavlides
Frank Piechoski

Contributors
Steve Aldrich
Jason Ankeny
Lee Bloom
Myles Boisen
Ross Boissoneau
Rob Bowman
John Bush
Bil Carpenter
Kenneth M. Cassidy
Sean Cooper
Joanna Curzon
Bill Dahl
Hank Davis
Michael P. Dawson
John Dougan
Ken Dryden
Bruce Eder
Michael Erlewine
Stephen Thomas Erlewine
Frank Federico
Milo Fine
Richard S. Ginell
Bob Gottlieb
Thom Granger

Mark C. Gridley
Scot Hacker
Alex Henderson
Terri Hinte
Larry Hoffman
Steve Huey
Ken Hunt
Michael Katz
Chris Kelsey
Cub Koda
Linda Kohanov
Paul Kohler
Stuart Kremsky
Richard Lieberson
Les Line
Brian Mansfield
David Nelson McCarthy
Steven McDonald
Alex Merck
David A. Milberg
Dan Morgenstern
Michael G. Nastos
Buz Overbeck
Thom Owens
Douglas Payne
Barry Lee Pearson
Bob Porter
Bruce Boyd Raeburn
Joel Roberts
John Storm Roberts
William Ruhlmann
Bob Rusch
Tim Sheridan
Richard Skelly
Chris Slawecki
Leo Stanley
Ned Sublette
David Szatmary
Bob Tarte
"Blue" Gene Tyranny
Richie Unterberger
Tony Wilds
Charles S. Wolfe
Chris Woodstra
Ron Wynn
Scott Yanow

Michael Erlewine

All Music Guide editor Michael Erlewine helped form the Prime Movers Blues Band in Ann Arbor, Michigan in 1965. He was the lead singer and played amplified harmonica in this pace-setting band (the first of its kind). The original band included a number of now well-known musicians including Iggy Pop (drums), "Blue" Gene Tyranny (piano; now a well-known avant-garde classical composer); Jack Dawson (bass; became bass player for Siegel-Schwall Blues Band); and Michael's brother Dan Erlewine (lead guitar; now monthly columnist for *Guitar Player* magazine). Michael has extensively interviewed blues per-formers, both in video and audio, and, along with his band, helped to shape the first few Ann Arbor Blues festivals. Today Michael is a systems programmer and director of Matrix Software. Aside from the company's work in music and film data, Matrix is the largest center for astrological programming and research in North America. Michael has been a practicing astrologer for more than 30 years and has an international reputation in that field.

Michael is also very active in Tibetan Buddhism and serves as the director of the Heart Center Karma Thegsum Choling, one of the main centers in North America for the translation, transcription, and publication of psychological texts and teach-ings of the Karma Kagyu Lineage of Tibetan Buddhism. Michael has been married for 25 years, and he and his wife Margaret live in Big Rapids, Michigan. They have four children.

Vladimir Bogdanov

Russian mathematician and programmer Vladimir Bogdanov has been involved in the design and development of *All Music Guide* databases since 1991. Having experience in many different fields such as nuclear physics, psychology, social studies and ancient chronology he now applies his knowledge to the construction of unique music reference tools utilizing the latest computer technologies. His personal interest lies in applying artificial intelligence and other mathematical methods to areas with complex semantic structures, like music, film, literature. Vladimir's ultimate goal is to provide people with the means to find what they need, even if they don't know what they are looking for.

Chris Woodstra

Chris Woodstra has had a lifelong obsession with music and is an avid record collector. He has worked many years in music retail, he was a DJ, hosting programs in every genre of music, and has been a contributing editor for several local arts and entertainment magazines. Working as an editor for the *All Music Guide* database has given him the opportunity to combine his technical skills, a B.S. in Physics and Mathematics, and his love of music for the first time in his life. Being a perfectionist by nature, Chris makes sure that that any information that goes into the database has been carefully researched and verified.

Stephen Thomas Erlewine

Stephen Thomas Erlewine studied English at the University of Michigan and was the arts editor of the school's newspaper, The Michigan Daily. In addition to editing the *All Music Guide*, Erlewine is a freelance writer and musician.

Scott Yanow

Scott Yanow has been writing about jazz since 1975. He was the jazz editor of *Record Review* during its entire existence (1976-84), has been a freelancer since 1983, and has written for *Down Beat, Jazz Times* and *Jazz Forum.* He is currently a reg-ular contributor to ten magazines including *Jazziz, Cadence, Coda,* the *L.A. Jazz Scene,* the *Mississippi Rag* and the *Jazz Report.* In addition, he has written over 100 liner notes, was a contributor to the *New Grove Dictionary* and assisted on the fourth edition of Leonard Feather and Ira Gitler's *Encyclopedia of Jazz.* It is his goal to collect every good jazz record ever made and to have time to listen to them.

How to Use This Book

ARTIST NAME   (Alternate name in parentheses)

VITAL STATISTICS   For groups, **f.** indicates date (and place) of formation; **db.** indicates date disbanded. For individual performers, date and place of birth (**b.**) and death (**d.**) are given, if known.

INSTRUMENT(S) / STYLE   For individual performers, major instruments are listed here, followed by one or more styles of music associated with each performer or group.

BIOGRAPHY   A quick view of the artist's life and musical career. For major performers, proportionately longer biographies are provided.

MAJOR ALBUMS   These are the albums selected and reviewed by our editors and contributors.

KEY TO SYMBOLS   ● ★ ☆

☆ ESSENTIAL COLLECTIONS   Albums marked with a star should be part of any good collection of the genre. Often, these are also a good first purchase (filled star). By hearing these albums, you can get a good overview of the entire genre. These are must-hear and must-have recordings. You can't go wrong with them.

● ★ FIRST PURCHASE   Albums marked with either a filled circle or a filled star should be your first purchase. This is where to begin to find out if you like this particular artist. These albums are representative of the best this artist has to offer. If you don't like these picks, chances are this artist is not for you. In the case of an artist who has a number of distinct periods, you will find an essential pick marked for each period. Albums are listed chronologically by recording session date when possible.

ALBUM RATINGS: ✦ TO ✦✦✦✦✦   In addition to the stars and circles used to distinguish exceptionally noteworthy albums, as explained above, all albums are rated on a scale from one to five diamonds.

ALBUM TITLE   The name of the album is listed in bold as it appears on the original when possible. Very long titles have been abbreviated, or repeated in full as part of the review, where needed.

DATE   The date of an album's first release, if known.

RECORD LABEL   Record labels indicate the current (or most recent) release of this recording. Label numbers are not given because they change frequently.

REVIEWERS   The name of each review's author are given at the end of the review. "AMG" indicates a review written by the *All Music Guide* staff.

Charlie Parker

b. Aug. 29, 1920, Kansas City, KS **d.** Mar. 12, 1955, New York, NY
Alto Saxophone, Composer, Leader / Bop

One of a handful of musicians who can be said to have permanently changed jazz, Charlie Parker was arguably the greatest saxophonist of all time. He could play remarkably fast lines that, if slowed down to half speed, would reveal that every note made sense. Bird, along with his contemporaries Dizzy Gillespie and Bud Powell, is considered a founder of bebop; in reality he was an intuitive player who simply was expressing himself. Rather than basing his improvisations closely on the melody as was done in swing, he was a master of chordal improvising, creating new melodies that were based on the structure of a song. In fact, Bird wrote several future standards (such as "Anthropology," "Ornithology," "Scrapple from the Apple," and "Ko Ko" along with such blues as "Now's the Time" and "Parker's Mood") that "borrowed" and modernized the chord structures of earlier tunes. Parker's remarkable technique, fairly original sound and ability to come up with harmonically advanced phrases that could be both logical and whimsical were highly influential. By 1950 it was impossible to play "modern jazz" with credibility without closely studying Charlie Parker. —*Scott Yanow*

☆ **Complete Savoy Studio Sessions** / Sep. 15, 1944-Sep. 24, 1948 / Savoy ✦✦✦✦✦

This three CD box set contains all of the recordings Charlie Parker made for the Savoy label and it is overflowing with gems and an almost countless number of alternate takes. Bird was one of the most important jazzmen of all time and nearly every note he recorded (in the studios if not live) is well worth hearing. This box starts off with his sideman date with Tiny Grimes in 1944, contains Parker's famous "Ko Ko" session of 1945 (with a young Miles Davis on trumpet and highlighted by "Now's the Time" and "Billie's Bounce") and continues through his 1947-48 quintet sessions with a more mature Miles Davis, either Bud Powell, John Lewis or Duke Jordan on piano, bassists Tommy Potter, Curly Russell or Nelson Boyd and drummer Max Roach. Together they recorded such classics as "Donna Lee," "Chasin' the Bird," "Milestones" and "Parker's Mood." Every scrap that the great altoist cut for Savoy is in this box. —*Scott Yanow*

● **Yardbird Suite: The Ultimate Collection** / Feb. 28, 1945-Sep. 26, 1952 / Rhino ✦✦✦✦✦

Subtitled "The Ultimate Charlie Parker Collection," this two-CD set from 1997 is highly recommended to listeners who wish to become acquainted with the immortal bebop altoist's music, although veteran collectors will find no previously unissued gems among the 38 selections. Bird is featured as a sideman on six classic performances with Dizzy Gillespie in 1945 and on most of his greatest studio sides as a leader; the program draws its music from the Savoy, Dial and Verve catalogs. In addition, Parker is heard on a 1951 radio broadcast with Gillespie and Bud Powell and for a few numbers from his 1952 Rockland Palace concert. Missing are examples of his early work with Jay McShann, broadcasts from the Royal Roost during 1948-49, the original string version of "Just Friends" and an example from his 1953 Massey Hall Concert, but perhaps a third CD would have been needed for all that! Perfect for beginners. —*Scott Yanow*

★ **Charlie Parker and the Stars of Modern Jazz at Carnegie Hall** (Christmas 1949) / Dec. 25, 1949 / Jass ✦✦✦✦

This Carnegie Hall concert can be considered the height of the bebop era. Among the top young modernists heard near their early peaks are pianist Bud Powell, trumpeter Miles Davis, baritonist Serge Chaloff, altoist Sonny Stitt, trombonist Kai Winding, tenor saxophonists Stan Getz and Warne Marsh, pianist Lennie Tristano, altoist Lee Konitz and Sarah Vaughan. But while their performances are consistently outstanding, Charlie Parker and his quintet (which includes trumpeter Red Rodney, pianist Al Haig, bassist Tommy Potter and drummer Roy Haynes) steals the show. Bird and Rodney rarely sounded more fiery than on their five songs and Parker's incredible solo on this version of "Ko Ko" might very well be his best. This CD is highly recommended for all collections. —*Scott Yanow*

The 2nd edition of the *All Music Guide To Jazz*, which came out in the fall of 1996, contained more reviews than any other jazz book in history.

The 3rd edition is an expanded version, including hundreds of additional biographical entries, new essays, updated information and thousands of additional CD reviews. Because there are so many new recordings and reissues being released each week, and because there is a very strong interest in this project, it is planned that future editions of the jazz book will be compiled and released every two years.

The *All Music Guide* is always a work-in-progress because the music world is a constantly evolving and active force. It is our goal that every recording from each field will be reviewed, rated and evaluated by our team of experts. While this book contains the most significant jazz recordings, the enormous All Music Guide database has an endless amount of information, including reviews of out-of-print LPs and sessions led by artists (both up-and-coming and lesser-known figures) who are not in this edition of the book. Please refer to the All-Music Guide website—www.allmusic.com—for the complete database which is updated monthly.

The basic definition of jazz that is followed for our purposes (and outlined in greater detail in the essays) is that jazz is music that emphasizes improvisation and always has the feeling of the blues. An inclusive approach is used because we prefer to err on the side of including too much rather than too little. For example, readers have asked why Frank Sinatra, Tony Bennett and Kenny G. are included in this book since the first two are not really jazz singers in the strict sense of the term while Kenny G. is outside of jazz. Sinatra has influenced jazz singers, Bennett utilizes a jazz rhythm section and Kenny G., although an instrumental pop musician, symbolizes jazz in the minds of many listeners. Since the trio best fit into this genre (as opposed to being in the rock or country books) and are indirectly important to the jazz world, they are included.

Why are some musicians given biographical entries and others left out?

Since the majority of this book is taken up by recording reviews, the emphasis is on significant jazz artists who recorded as leaders. There are obvious exceptions made for historically important sidemen who did not lead their own sessions (no jazz book would be complete without including the likes of Buddy Bolden and Jimmy Blanton) but no attempt has been made to have the *AMG* become the *Encyclopedia Of Jazz*, listing every talented player (including supportive bassists and drummers, section players in big bands and studio musicians). The publisher would probably not stand for the *All Music Guide To Jazz* being twice as big as it already is. However virtually every major (and most minor) jazz player is represented somewhere along the way, for most reviews include a mention of the key sidemen. The biographies are purposely concise and to-the-point, giving listeners a lot of information in a small amount of space. While Duke Ellington and the other major giants have the longest bios, in general one should not evaluate the importance of the artist by the length of their bio; some players had lengthier resumes!

Each review is written with hopes of giving listeners a good idea what the music sounds like, how it compares to the artist's other work and it relates to the jazz mainstream in general. Most importantly, the reviews are designed to give enough clues so readers will know whether they would be interested in acquiring the recording or not. The star ratings should be used as a general guide; they compare the artist's work to his or her other recordings rather than those of other players. For example, a 3 star Duke Ellington release is not necessarily inferior to a 4 star Ornette Coleman recording; it depends on the reader's musical tastes and interests.

In general, five stars given to a recording means that it is among the artist's finest work and is a gem. Four stars signify that the release is very good, easily recommended to fans of the artist and a worthy addition to one's jazz collection. Three stars are given to decent recordings that may contain some flaws but are still quite worthwhile. Two stars denote that the music is a bit disappointing but not without value and is still of some interest to collectors of the artist's music. One star means that the recording is essentially a dud and should be passed by. Because the quality of jazz recordings and reissues is on the average quite high, most releases fall into the 3-5 star range, with some exceptions. We have been careful never to condemn music because it is too advanced or unpredictable but only if it did not live up to its potential.

The question arose with the previous edition as to why some recordings were given full reviews, others were just listed and some were left out altogether. Time limitations affected that decision to an extent but it is much less a factor with the new book. For the 3rd edition, the emphasis is first on CDs that are in-print, then the cut-out CDs and finally important LPs whose music will probably be reissued in time.

I've been a jazz fanatic since discovering Dixieland in August 1970. By early 1972 I was exploring all eras of jazz and haven't been bored since! I've written about jazz since late-1975 and I hope that my enthusiasm for the remarkable music and all of its styles translates well into this book. I believe that because jazz is so vast, it can be forbidding to the average person. They should remember three basic things: (1) There are so many different jazz styles that nearly everyone could become a fan of some area of jazz if properly exposed. (2) One does not need a degree or musical ability to be able to appreciate jazz (even though it tends to be more complex than the average pop music). (3) Jazz thrives on unpredictability, adventure and a touch of danger. Listeners who explore jazz with open ears and an open mind will be amazed at what they can discover from this "underground" music.

Many people deserve thanks for their assistance on this project: Brian Ashley (who got me started in the jazz writing business with *Record Review*), the many publicists who make life easier for jazz journalists (in particular Lori Hehr, Terri Hinte, Monica Petty and Ann Braithwaite), Bob Rusch of *Cadence* for giving me permission to adapt some of my *Cadence* reviews for the *All Music Guide*, Carlos Iramain for his assistance in coming up with some of the proper birthdates and deathdates, all of the writers who have contributed directly or indirectly to the book (in particular Richard Ginell whose expertise was greatly appreciated) and the overburdened but skilled in-house staff run by *AMG* Editor-In-Chief Chris Woodstra. I also want to personally thank *AMG* Executive Editor Michael Erlewine for having the wisdom to found this project and for his confidence and trust in allowing me to shape so much of the book. And lastly my personal thanks to my wife Kathy and daughter Melody.

—*Scott Yanow*

Acid Jazz

The music played by a generation raised on jazz as well as funk and hip-hop, Acid Jazz used elements of all three; its existence as a percussion-heavy, primarily live music placed it closer to jazz and Afro-Cuban than any other dance style, but its insistence on keeping the groove allied it with funk, hip-hop and dance music. The term itself first appeared in 1988 as both an American record label and the title of an English compilation series which reissued jazz-funk music from the '70s, called rare groove by the Brits during a major mid-'80s resurgence. A variety of acid jazz artists emerged during the late '80s and early '90s: live bands such as Stereo MC's, James Taylor Quartet, the Brand New Heavies, Groove Collective, Galliano and Jamiroquai as well as studio projects like Palmskin Productions, Mondo Grosso, Outside and United Future Organization. — *John Bush*

Acoustic Blues

A general catch-all term describing virtually every type of blues that can be played on a non-electric musical instrument. It embraces a wide range of guitar and musical styles including folk, the songster tradition, slide, fingerpicking, ragtime, and all of the myriad regional strains (Chicago, Delta, Louisiana, Mississippi, Texas, Piedmont, etc.) that thrived in the early days of the musics' gestation. But Acoustic Blues is not limited to merely guitar music; its "acoustic" appellation being an elastic enough term to also include mandolin, banjo, piano, harmonica, jug bands, and other non-electric instruments including home made ones, like the one string monochord bottleneck diddleybow. — *Cub Koda*

Acoustic Chicago Blues

This describes the version of music emanating from the Windy City in the years before the twin arrivals of Muddy Waters and electric guitars changed everything. Chicago was recording central for most blues recording artists of the 1930s and 1940s and most performers were plugged into was became known as "the Blue-bird Beat," an acoustic based progenitor of the later electric Chicago blues band lineup. Its music is earmarked by what is usually described as a "hokum style," heavy on lyrics that promote a light hearted atmosphere, propelled by a jazz influenced beat and a more city derived slant to it. — *Cub Koda*

Afro-Cuban Jazz

Afro-Cuban jazz is a combination of jazz improvising and rhythms from Cuba and Africa; it is also known as Latin Jazz although several of its practioners prefer the former term. There were some hints of Afro-Cuban jazz in isolated cases during the 1920s and '30s (Jelly Roll Morton's "Spanish tinge" in some of his more rhythmic piano solos, a few Gene Krupa performances where he sought to include South American rhythms and even in the Latin pop music of Xavier Cugat) but one can really trace its birth to trumpeter-arranger Mario Bauza. Bauza introduced trumpeter Dizzy Gillespie to the masterful Cuban percussionist Chano Pozo (they teamed up during 1947-48 to create innovative music before Pozo's death) and also persuaded Latin bandleader Machito to use jazz soloists. During the late '40s Stan Kenton began to integrate Latin rhythms in his music and, with the rise in popularity during the 1950s of Tito Puente and Cal Tjader, Afro-Cuban jazz caught on as one of the most popular jazz styles. In more recent times some groups have developed Afro-Cuban jazz beyond its boppish roots, performing Monk and Coltrane tunes, adding funk to the mixture and having more adventurous solos. The spirit of the music (a true fusion between North, South and Central America) and an emphasis on infectious rhythms are the keys. — *Scott Yanow*

Avant-Garde

Avant-garde Jazz differs from Free Jazz in that it has more structure in the ensembles (more of a "game plan") although the individual improvisations are generally just as free of conventional rules. Obviously there is a lot of overlap between Free Jazz and Avant-Garde; most players in one idiom often play in the other "style,"

too. In the best Avant-Garde performances it is difficult to tell when compositions end and improvisations begin; the goal is to have the solos be an outgrowth of the arrangement. As with Free Jazz, the Avant-Garde came of age in the 1960s and has continued almost unnoticed as a menacing force in the jazz underground, scorned by the mainstream that it influences. Among its founders in the mid- to late 1950s were pianist Cecil Taylor, altoist Ornette Coleman and keyboardist-bandleader Sun Ra. John Coltrane became the avant-garde's most popular (and influential) figure and from the mid-1960s on the avant-garde innovators made a major impact on jazz, helping to push the music beyond bebop. — *Scott Yanow*

Ballads

The word "ballad" often has two meanings: a lyrical and melodic piece that can be sung, or simply any selection taken at a slow tempo. In the *AMG* we generally use the former definition while the latter can be said to be played at a "ballad tempo." Although there were sentimental ballads in the 1800s, the idiom came of age with the rise of the great American popular song and such composers as Jerome Kern, Irving Berlin, George Gershwin and Cole Porter among others. Even if there have been some standard ballads written since 1970 (only a few from the pop and rock fields are easily transferable to jazz), the majority of the repertoire of jazz-influenced ballad singers tends to date from the 1920-60 period. — *Scott Yanow*

Big Band

Big Band refers to a jazz group of ten or more musicians, usually featuring at least three trumpets, two or more trombones, four or more saxophones and a "rhythm section" of accompanists playing some combination of piano, guitar, bass, and drums. "Big band music" as a concept for music fans is identified most with the swing era, although there were large, jazz-oriented, dance bands before the swing era of the 1930s and 1940s, and large jazz-oriented concert bands after the swing era.

Classification difficulties occur when music stores shelve recordings by all large jazz ensembles as though it were a single style, despite the shifting harmonic and rhythmic approaches employed by new ensembles of similar instrumentation that have formed since the swing era. By lumping the music of all large jazz bands together, marketers overlook the different kinds of jazz that large groups have performed: swing (Duke Ellington and Count Basie), bebop (Dizzy Gillespie), cool (Gerry Mulligan, Shorty Rogers, Gil Evans), hard bop (Gerald Wilson), free jazz (some of Sun Ra's work after the 1950s), and jazz-rock fusion (Don Ellis' and Maynard Ferguson's groups of the 1970s). Not all of them are "swing bands."

Many listeners consider "big band" to denote an idiom, not just an instrumentation. For them, the strategies of arranging and soloing that were established during the 1930s link all large jazz ensembles more than the different rhythmic and harmonic concepts distinguish those of one era, for example bebop, from those of another, for example those of jazz-rock.

Another important consideration is that journalists and jazz fans of the 1930s and 1940s drew distinctions between bands that conveyed the most hard-driving rhythmic qualities and frequent solo improvisations and those that conveyed less pronounced swing feeling and improvisation. The former were called "swing bands" or "hot bands" (for example, Count Basie's and Duke Ellington's). The latter were called "sweet bands" (for example, Glenn Miller's, Wayne King's, Freddy Martin's, and Guy Lombardo's). Although the big band era ended by 1946, there have been some large orchestras used in jazz ever since even if virtually none (other than the Count Basie ghost band) operate on a full-time basis. Nearly all are led by arrangers. — *Mark Gridley*

Boogie-Woogie

Boogie-woogie is a jazz piano style using two pulses stated by the left hand for every beat and the 12-bar blues chord progression as its repertory. The brief, continuously repeating patterns from the left hand give the style its identity. It's jazz flavor comes from rhythmically and melodically playful phrases improvised by the pianist's right hand.

First popularized during the late 1920s by Pinetop Smith, boogie-woogie experienced a strong revival during the late 1930s and early 1940s through the recordings of Meade Lux Lewis, Albert Ammons, Pete Johnson, Jimmy Yancey, Cripple Clarence Lofton, and Cow Cow Davenport. This genre had considerable influence on accompaniment styles in the popular music called rhythm & blues, as well as the beginnings of rock 'n' roll. —*Mark Gridley*

Bop

Also known as bebop, bop was a radical new music that developed gradually in the early 1940s and seemed to explode in 1945. The main difference between bop and swing is that the soloists engaged in chordal (rather than melodic) improvisation, often discarding the melody altogether after the first chorus and using the chords as the basis for the solo. Ensembles tended to be unisons, most jazz groups were under seven pieces and the soloist was free to get as adventurous as possible as long as the overall improvisation fit into the chord structure. Since the musicians were getting away from using the melodies as the basis for their solos (leading some listeners to ask "Where's the melody?"), the players were generally virtuosos and some of the tempos were very fast, bop divorced itself during the early years of bop from popular music and a dancing audience, uplifting jazz to an art music but cutting deeply into its potential commercial success. Ironically the once-radical bebop style has become the foundation for all of the innovations that followed and now can be almost thought of as establishment music. Among its key innovators were altoist Charlie Parker, trumpeter Dizzy Gillespie, pianist Bud Powell, drummer Max Roach and pianist-composer Thelonious Monk. —*Scott Yanow*

Bossa Nova

Influenced by West Coast jazz, in the 1950s composer Antonio Carlos Jobim helped to form a new music that blended together gentle Brazilian rhythms and melodies with cool-toned improvising; the rhythms are usually played lightly as 3-3-4-3-3 with beats 1, 4, 7, 11 and 14 being accented during every two-bars (played in 8/4 time). Joao Gilberto's soothing voice perfectly communicated the beauty of Jobim's music. The late '50s film *Black Orpheus* helped to introduce Jobim's compositions to an American audience and other important early exponents of bossa nova were guitarist Charlie Byrd, tenor saxophonist Stan Getz (Byrd and Getz teamed up for the highly influential Jazz/Samba) and housewife-turned-singer Astrud Gilberto who, along with her husband Joao and Getz, made "The Girl from Ipanema" a huge hit. The very appealing bossa nova's popularity peaked in the mid-'60s but it has remained a viable music up to the present time. —*Scott Yanow*

Cabaret

As a musical style cabaret refers to two different aspects of music. The "night clubs" were initially opened to provide a place for painters, writers, musicians and other artists to gather, talk, perform and experiment. The key to understanding cabaret as a style is that the music was all experimental. Avant-garde styles, reactions to (or against) current trends and conventions were formulated in the cabarets. Other styles include the music that was performed in the cabarets when these clubs received their repute for being associated with vice. Cabaret music was considered bawdy, vampish, rhythmic and often lewd considering the numerous lyrical double entendres. Melodic lines could be smooth and soft when that form of stimulation was wanted from and for the audience but most of the time lines were memorable, filled with motions and extended interval leaps. There were few soft curves to these musical phrases. Cabaret music was intended as an energized form of entertainment. —*Keith Johnson*

Classic Female Blues

This is the earliest aurally documented form of the blues. The classic female blues singers of the 1920s were the first to get on record and the first to have hits in the genre, subsequently reaching a national audience and starting the first great push in recording blues music of all styles. This strain generally features big voiced female vocalists singing material with close connections to pop music of the period (mid-'20s to early '30s), utilizing primarily jazz backings, giving even the most gutbucket of performances a more uptown air to them. The style of these women singers is loud, brassy, sassy, and assertive with the occasional nascent feminist sentiment being inserted into the lyrics from time to time. —*Cub Koda*

Classic Jazz

Not all jazz from the 1920s can be described as "New Orleans Jazz" or "Dixieland." The 1920s were a rich decade musically with jazz-influenced dance bands and a gradual emphasis on solo (as opposed to collective) improvisations. Whether it be

the stride pianists, the increasingly adventurous horn soloists or the arranged music that predates swing, much of the jazz from this decade can be given the umbrella title of "Classic Jazz." Some of the modern-day revivalists (many who can be heard on the Stomp Off label) who look beyond the Dixieland repertoire into the music of Fletcher Henderson, Clarence Williams and Bix Beiderbecke (to name a few) can be said to be playing in this open-ended style. —*Scott Yanow*

Contemporary Funk

Contemporary funk refers to a kind of jazz from the 1970s and 1980s in which accompanists perform in the Black pop style of soul and funk music while extensive solo improvisations ride atop. Instead of using standard vocabularies of any modern jazz saxophonists (Charlie Parker, Lee Konitz, John Coltrane, Ornette Coleman), most saxophone improvisations in this style use their own repertory of simple phrases that include bluesy wails and moans. They draw upon traditions illustrated by sax solos on rhythm & blues vocal recordings, such as those of King Curtis with the Coasters, Junior Walker with the Motown vocal groups, and Dave Sanborn with the Paul Butterfield Blues Band.

A prominent figure in this genre is Grover Washington, Jr., who often solos in a Hank Crawford-like style over funk accompaniments. These instances comprise his best-known recordings, though he is also capable of playing other styles of jazz. The Jazz Crusaders (Wilton Felder, Joe Sample) achieved wide popularity when they changed their repertory to this approach during the 1970s and dropped "Jazz" from their band name. A considerable portion of music by Michael Brecker, Tom Scott, and their disciples uses this approach, though they can also play in the jazz styles of John Coltrane and Joe Henderson. Najee, Richard Elliott, and their contemporaries also perform in this "contemporary funk" style. From approximately 1971 to 1992, Miles Davis led bands in a sophisticated variation of this style, though his saxophone soloists also drew upon the methods of John Coltrane, and his guitarists also showed modern jazz thinking and Jimi Hendrix influence. Much of contemporary funk can also be classified as "crossover." —*Mark Gridley*

Contemporary Jazz

Contemporary jazz refers to mainstream jazz performed in the '80s and '90s. Usually, it is either a variation on classic, small-group hard-bop or slick fusion that concentrates on rhythms instead of improvisation. Often, Contemporary jazz exhibits more rock and pop influences than traditional hard-bop, but its bop origins are still quite evident. —*Stephen Thomas Erelwine*

Cool

In the late 1940s and 1950s cool jazz evolved directly from bop. Essentially it was a mixture of bop with certain aspects of swing that had been overlooked or temporarily discarded. Dissonances were smoothed out, tones were softened, arrangements became important again and the rhythm section's accents were less jarring. Because some of the key pacesetters of the style (many of whom were studio musicians) were centered in Los Angeles, it was nicknamed "West Coast Jazz." Some of the recordings were experimental in nature (hinting at classical music), while some overarranged sessions were bland but in general this was a viable and popular style. By the late 1950s hard bop from the East Coast had succeeded cool jazz although many of the style's top players had long and productive careers. Among the many top artists who were important in the development of Cool Jazz were Lester Young, Miles Davis, Gerry Mulligan, Stan Getz, Shorty Rogers and Howard Rumsey (leader of the Lighthouse All-Stars). —*Scott Yanow*

Country Blues

A catch-all term that delineates the depth and breadth of the first flowering of guitar-driven blues, embracing both solo, duo, and string band performers. The term also provides a convenient general heading for all the multiple regional styles and variations (Piedmont, Atlanta, Memphis, Texas, acoustic Chicago, Delta, ragtime, folk, songster, etc.) of the form. It is primarily—but not exclusively—a genre filled with acoustic guitarists, embracing a multiplicity of techniques from elaborate fingerpicking to the early roots of slide playing. But some country-blues performers like Lightnin' Hopkins and John Lee Hooker were to later switch over to electric guitars without having to drastically change or alter their styles. —*Cub Koda*

Crossover Jazz

With the gradual decline of rock (from an artistic standpoint) starting in the early 1970s, fusion (a mixture of jazz improvisations with rock rhythms) began to become more predictable since there was less input and inspiration from the rock world. At the same time, now that it was proven that electric jazz could sell records, producers and some musicians searched for other combinations of styles in order to have big sellers. They were quite successful in making their brand of jazz more accessible to the average consumer. Many different combinations have been tried during the past two decades and promoters and publicists enjoy using the phrase "Ccontemporary jazz" to describe these "fusions" of jazz with elements of pop music, R&B and world music. However, the word "crossover" (which describes the intent of the performances as well as the usual results) is more accurate. Crossover and fusion have been quite valuable in increasing the jazz audience (many of whom end up exploring other styles). In some cases the music is quite worthwhile, while in other instances the jazz content is a relatively small part of the ingredients. When the style is actually pop music with only an insignificant amount of improvisation (meaning that it is largely outside of jazz), the term "instrumental pop" applies best of all. Examples of crossover range from Al Jarreau and George Benson vocal records to Kenny G., Spyro Gyra and the Rippingtons. All contain the influence of jazz but tend to fall as much (if not more) into the pop field. —*Scott Yanow*

Dance Bands

Although virtually all jazz groups prior to the rise of bebop in the early to mid-'40s played for dancers, the term "dance bands" is used to describe orchestras of the 1920s and '30s whose primary function was to play background music for dancers rather than to serve as vehicles for jazz improvisations. The more progressive dance bands of the early to mid-'20s (such as those led by Paul Whiteman, Isham Jones and Ben Selvin) left some room for short solos and by the late '20s most of the less commercial dance bands had brief spots in their arrangements for trumpeters or reed players to solo after the vocal refrain. The dance bands, although emphasizing the melody and vocalists, were generally influenced by jazz and incorporated elements of swing after the emergence of Benny Goodman in 1935 although they were often classified as "sweet" bands. After 1945, dance orchestras became less common, were often tied to nostalgia and were much less relevant to jazz. —*Scott Yanow*

Dixieland

Because the Dixieland revival (one could say fad) of the 1950s was eventually overrun by amateurs, corny trappings (such as straw hats and suspenders) and clichés, many musicians playing in that idiom grew to dislike the term and wanted it to be changed to "traditional" or "classic." But rather than blame the term or the style, it seems more justifiable to separate the professionals from the poor imitators. Dixieland, a style that overlaps with New Orleans jazz and classic jazz, has also been called "Chicago jazz" because it developed to an extent in Chicago in the 1920s. Most typically the framework involves collective improvisation during the first chorus (or, when there are several themes, for several choruses), individual solos with some riffing by the other horns, and a closing ensemble or two with a four bar tag by the drummer being answered by the full group. Although nearly any song can be turned into Dixieland, there is a consistent repertoire of forty or so songs that have proven to be consistently reliable. Despite its decline in popularity since the 1950s, Dixieland (along with the related classic jazz and New Orleans jazz idioms) continues to flourish as an underground music. —*Scott Yanow*

East Coast Blues

This genre combines two basic schools under one general heading. The first and most notable consists of disciples of the Piedmont school (primarily of the East Coast area's main Piedmont practitioner, Blind Boy Fuller—also see separate listing on the Piedmont style) who had relocated along the East Coast by the early to mid 1950s and ended up comprising much of that city's early blues revival scene in the mid 1960s. The second consists of both electric R&B artists and modern performers hailing from the area working in a variety of styles indigenous to the overall genre itself. —*Cub Koda*

Folk-Jazz

This term is used for musicians from the 1950s on who often utilize strong folk melodies as vehicles for solos. They tend to keep their ears open to musical developments in other countries (world music), emphasize quieter volumes and break down boundaries between jazz and seemingly unrelated genres. Examples of folk-jazz include some of the music of Jimmy Giuffre, Tony Scott (post-1959), Paul Horn, Paul Winter and Oregon. Folk-jazz was a direct influence on new age. —*Scott Yanow*

Free Funk

Free Funk is a mixture of avant-garde jazz with funky rhythms. When Ornette Coleman formed Prime Time in the early '70s, he had a "double quartet" (comprising two guitars, two electric bassists and two drummers plus his alto) performing with freedom tonally but over eccentric funk rhythms. Three of Ornette's sidemen (guitarist James "Blood" Ulmer, bassist Jamaaladeen Tacuma and drummer

Ronald Shannon Jackson) have since led free funk groups of their own and free funk has been a major influence on the music of the M-Base players including altoists Steve Coleman and Greg Osby. —*Scott Yanow*

Free Jazz

Dixieland and swing stylists improvise melodically and bop, cool and hard bop players follow chord structures in their solos. Free jazz was a radical departure from past styles for typically after playing a quick theme, the soloist does not have to follow any progression or structure and can go in any unpredictable direction. When Ornette Coleman largely introduced Free jazz to New York audiences (although Cecil Taylor had preceded him with less publicity), many of the bop musicians and fans debated about whether what was being played would even qualify as music; the radicals had become conservatives in less than 15 years. Free jazz, which overlaps with the avant-garde (the latter can utilize arrangements and sometimes fairly tight frameworks), remains a controversial and mostly underground style, influencing the modern mainstream while often being ignored. Having dispensed with many of the rules as far as pitch, rhythm and development are concerned (although it need not be atonal or lack a steady pulse to be Free jazz), the success of a Free jazz performance can be measured by the musicianship and imagination of the performers, how colorful the music is and whether it seems logical or merely random. —*Scott Yanow*

Fusion

The word "fusion" has been so liberally used during the past quarter-century as to become almost meaningless. Fusion's original definition was best: a mixture of jazz improvisation with the power and rhythms of rock. Up until around 1967 the worlds of jazz and rock were nearly completely separate. But as rock became more creative and its musicianship improved, and as some in the jazz world became bored with hard bop and did not want to play strictly avant-garde music, the two different idioms began to trade ideas and occasionally combine forces. By the early 1970s, fusion had its own separate identity as a creative jazz style (although sneered upon by many purists) and such major groups as Return to Forever, Weather Report, the Mahavishnu Orchestra and Miles Davis' various bands were playing high-quality fusion that mixed together some of the best qualities of both jazz and rock. Unfortunately as it became a moneymaker and as rock declined artistically from the mid-'70s on, much of what was labelled fusion was actually a combination of jazz with easy-listening pop music and lightweight R&B crossover. The promise of fusion to an extent went unfulfilled although it continues to exist today in groups such as Tribal Tech and Chick Corea's Elektric Band. —*Scott Yanow*

Groove

Groove is a sub-set of soul-jazz, one that is injected with the blues and concentrates on the rhythm. It is a funky, joyous music, where everything in the performance is there to establish and maintain the groove. There's a steady beat to the music, whether it's uptempo funk or slow blues. Usually, groove is performed by small combos that feature guitar, organ, bass and drums. Horns, especially saxophones, can be featured, but sometimes the presence of too many horns moves the music too close to hard-bop, which tends to be cerebral. Groove is emotional and physical, hitting your soul. In many ways, it's almost spiritual, since everyone is working collectively for the greater good, and, at its best, it locks into rhythms that are nearly hypnotic. Groove always has funky rhythms, bluesy vamps and, usually, gospel overtones to the playing. There are solos, but they are worked into the overall feeling, the overall groove of the music, and in the end, that's what counts with groove. —*Stephen Thomas Erlewine*

Hard Bop

Although some history books claim that hard bop arose as a reaction to the softer sounds featured in cool jazz, it was actually an extension of bop that largely ignored West Coast jazz. The main differences between hard bop and bop are that the melodies tend to be simpler and often more "soulful," the rhythm section is usually looser with the bassist not as tightly confined to playing four-beats-to-the-bar as in bop, a gospel influence is felt in some of the music, and quite often the saxophonists and pianists sound as if they are familiar with early rhythm and blues. Since the prime time period of hard bop (1955-70) was a decade later than bop, these differences were a logical evolution and one can think of hard bop as bop of the '50s and '60s. By the second half of the 1960s, the influence of the avant-garde was being felt and some of the more adventurous performances of the hard bop stylists (such as Jackie McLean and Lee Morgan) fell somewhere between the two styles. With the rise of fusion and the sale of Blue Note (hard bop's top label) in the late 1960s, the style fell upon hard times although it was revived to a certain extent in the 1980s. Much of the music performed by the so-called Young Lions during the latter decade (due to other influences altering their style) can be said to play modern mainstream, although some groups (such as the Harper Brothers and T.S. Monk's Sextet) have kept the 1960s idiom alive. —*Scott Yanow*

Instrumental Pop

Music classified under this style is commercially-oriented music with minimal improvisation or creative risks. The music is characterized as generic and short in duration with simplified themes with little or no development. Major proponents of instrumental pop are Herb Alpert, Chuck Mangione, Kenny G., Acker Bilk, Boots Randolph and George Benson.

Jazz Blues

While seemingly self explanatory, the jazz blues genre is somewhat misleading. Many jazz musicians have roots in the blues, with several of them providing their own interesting hybrids of the form. Its major proponents are blues performers who have integrated jazz stylings into their work, with surprisingly successful results. Some of these artists work both sides of the fence (vacillating between hard blues and jazzier sounds), while others utilize the genre as their principal stylistic distinction. Embracing everything from honking tenor saxophonists to big band singers to cocktail piano stylings, the style still has room to grow and enter a more contemporary phase. —*Cub Koda*

Jazz-Rock

Unlike fusion—which is jazz played with rock influences—jazz-rock is essentially rock-based songs palyed with jazz flourishes and jazzy improvisations. When the two genres first developed in the late '60s, the genres were nearly identical; during the early '70s they began to branch away from each other and jazz-rock became known as a slightly more commercial version of fusion.

Jive

Jive, a slang word meaning nonsense (as in "don't jive me," or don't mess with me), also became associated with a type of vocalizing popularized in the 1930s and '40s by Cab Calloway, Fats Waller, Slim Gaillard, Leo Watson and Harry "The Hipster" Gibson, among others. Connected musically to swing, jive featured its singers making up nonsense syllables and humorous words, some of which were adopted by the youth of the swing era. —*Scott Yanow*

Jump Blues

This form refers to an uptempo, jazz-tinged style of blues that first came to prominence in the mid- to late '40s. Usually featuring a vocalist in front of a large horn-driven orchestra or medium sized combo with multiple horns, the style is earmarked by a driving rhythm, intensely shouted vocals, and honking tenor saxophone solos— elements now associated with rock 'n' roll. The lyrics are almost always celebratory in nature, full of braggadocio and swagger. With less reliance on guitar work (which was usually confined to the rhythm section) than other styles, jump blues was the bridge between the older styles of blues—primarily those in a small band context—and the big band jazz sound of the 1940s. —*Cub Koda*

Latin Jazz

Of all the post-swing styles, Latin jazz has been the most consistently popular and it is easy to see why. The emphasis on percussion and Cuban rhythms make the style quite danceable and accessible. Essentially it is a mixture of bop-oriented jazz with Latin percussion. Among the pioneers in combining the two styles in the 1940s were the big bands of Dizzy Gillespie and Machito, and the music (which has never gone out of style) has remained a viable force through the 1990s, played most notably by the bands of Tito Puente and Poncho Sanchez. The style has not changed much during the past 40 years but it still communicates to today's listeners. Latin Jazz is also sometimes called Afro-Cuban Jazz, a term preferred by Mario Bauza and Ray Barretto. —*Scott Yanow*

M-Base

Short for "macro-basic array of structured extemporization," M-Base was developed by altoists Steve Coleman and Greg Osby, tenor saxophonist Gary Thomas and various other young associates (including singer Cassandra Wilson) in the 1980s. An extension of Ornette Coleman's free funk (although with a greater use of space and dynamics), M-Base often features crowded and noisy ensembles, unpredictable funk rhythms and an entirely new logic in soloing that owes little to bebop. Although the leaders of M-Base have since gone their separate ways (occasionally regrouping in different combinations), the influence of the music can be

heard in the playing of some of the more adventurous young musicians. —*Scott Yanow*

Mainstream Jazz

The term "mainstream" was coined by critic Stanley Dance to describe the type of music that trumpeter Buck Clayton and his contemporaries (veterans of the swing era) were playing in the 1950s. Rather than modernize their styles and play bop or join Dixieland bands (which some did on a part-time basis in order to survive), the former big band stars (which included such players as Coleman Hawkins, Lester Young, Harry "Sweets" Edison and Roy Eldridge, among many others) jammed standards and riff tunes in smaller groups. Mainstream, which was fairly well documented in the 1950s, was completely overshadowed by other styles in the '60s and its original players gradually passed away. However, with the rise of tenor saxophonist Scott Hamilton and trumpeter Warren Vache in the 1970s and the beginning of the Concord label (which emphasized the music), mainstream has made a comeback that, with its hints of both bop and Dixieland, survives up to this day. —*Scott Yanow*

Modern Electric Blues

Modern electric blues is an eclectic mixture, a subgenre embracing both the old, the new and something that falls between the two. Some forms copy the older styles of urban blues—primarily offshoots of the electric Chicago band style—right down to playing the music on vintage instruments and using replications of amplifiers from the period. It also a genre that pays homage to those vintage styles while simultaneously recasting them in contemporary fashion. It can also be the most forward looking of all blues styles, embracing rock beats and pyrotechnics, and enlivening the form with funk rhythms and chord progressions that expand beyond the standard three usually heard in blues. —*Cub Koda*

New Orleans R&B

Primarily a piano and horn-driven style, New Orleans R&B is the next step over from its more bluesier practitioners. There's a cheerful good naturedness to the style that infuses the music with a good time feel, no matter how somber the lyrical text may be. The music itself utilizes a distinctively "lazy" feel, with all of its somewhat complex rhythms falling just a hair behind the beat, making for what is known as "the sway." The vocals can run the full emotional gamut from laid back crooning to full throated gospel shouting, while the horn lines provide a perfect droning backdrop. Enlivened by Caribbean rhythms, an unrelenting party atmosphere, and the distinctive "second-line" strut of the Dixieland music so indigenous to the area, there's nothing quite as intoxicating as the sound of Crescent City R&B. —*Cub Koda*

New Orleans Jazz

The earliest style of jazz, the music played in New Orleans from about the time that Buddy Bolden formed his first band in 1895 until Storyville was closed in 1917 unfortunately went totally unrecorded. However, with the success of the Original Dixieland Jazz Band in 1917 and the many performances documented in the 1920s, it became possible to hear what this music sounded like in later years. Ensemble-oriented with fairly strict roles for each instrument, New Orleans jazz generally features a trumpet or cornet providing a melodic lead, harmonies from the trombone, countermelodies by the clarinet and a steady rhythm stated by the rhythm section (which usually consists of piano, banjo or guitar, tuba or bass and drums). This music is a direct descendant of marching brass bands, and although overlapping with Dixieland, tends to de-emphasize solos in favor of ensembles featuring everyone playing and improvising together. Due to its fairly basic harmonies and the pure joy of the ensembles, it is consistently the happiest and most accessible style of jazz. —*Scott Yanow*

Piano Blues

A genre that runs through the entire history of the music itself, this embraces everything from ragtime, barrelhouse, boogie-woogie, and smooth West Coast jazz stylings to the hard-rocking rhythms of Chicago blues. —*Cub Koda*

Piedmont Blues

Piedmont blues refers to a regional substyle characteristic of African-American musicians of the southeastern United States. Geographically, Piedmont refers to the foothills of the Appalachians west of the tidewater region and the Atlantic coastal plain stretching roughly from Richmond, VA, to Atlanta, GA. Musically, Piedmont blues describes the shared style of musicians from Georgia, the Carolinas and Virginia, as well as others from as far afield as Florida, West Virginia, Maryland and Delaware. It refers to a wide assortment of aesthetic values, performance techniques, and shared repertoire rooted in common geographical, historical, and sociological circumstances. The Piedmont guitar style employs a complex fingerpicking method in which a regular, alternating thumb bass pattern supports a melody on treble strings. The guitar style is highly syncopated and is closely related to an earlier string-band tradition integrating ragtime, blues, and country dance songs. It's excellent party music with a full, rock-solid sound. —*Barry Lee Pearson*

Post-Bop

It has become increasingly difficult to categorize modern jazz. A large segment of the music does not fit into any historical style, is not as rock-oriented as fusion or as free as the avant-garde. Starting with the rise of Wynton Marsalis in 1979, a whole generation of younger players chose to play an updated variety of hard bop that was also influenced by the mid-'60s Miles Davis Quintet and aspects of free jazz. Since this music (which often features complex chordal improvisation) has become the norm for jazz in the 1990s, the terms "modern mainstream" or "post-bop" are used for everything from Wallace Roney to John Scofield and symbolize the eclectic scene as jazz enters its second century. —*Scott Yanow*

Progressive Big Band

Progressive big band music is music for listening, with denser, more modernistic arrangements than the earlier, more dance-oriented big-band styles, with more room to improvise. Major proponents of this style were Gil Evans, Stan Kenton, Toshiko Akiyoshi, Cal Massey, Frank Foster, Carla Bley, George Gruntz, David Amram, Sun Ra, and Duke Ellington.

R&B

Evolving out of jump blues in the late '40s, R&B laid the groundwork for rock 'n' roll. R&B kept the tempo and the drive of jump blues, but its instrumentation was more sparse and the emphasis was on the song, not improvisation. It was blues chord changes played with an insistent backbeat. During the '50s, R&B was dominated by vocalists like Ray Charles and Ruth Brown, as well as vocal groups like the Drifters and the Coasters. Eventually, R&B metamorphosed into soul, which was funkier and looser than the pile-driving rhythms of R&B.

Ragtime

Although not really jazz (ragtime does not have improvisation or the feeling of the blues), this early style (which was at its prime during 1899-1915) was a strong influence on the earlier forms of jazz. Best-known as a piano music, ragtime (which is totally written-out) was also performed by orchestras. Its syncopations and structure (blending together aspects of classical music and marches) hinted strongly at jazz and many of its melodies (most notably "Maple Leaf Rag") would be played in later years by jazz musicians in a dixieland context. —*Scott Yanow*

Soul-Jazz

Soul-jazz, which was the most popular jazz style of the 1960s, differs from bebop and hard bop (from which it originally developed) in that the emphasis is on the rhythmic groove. Although soloists follow the chords as in bop, the basslines (often played by an organist if not a string bassist) dance rather than stick strictly to a four-to-the-bar walking pattern. The musicians build their accompaniment around the bassline and, although there are often strong melodies, it is the catchiness of the groove and the amount of heat generated by the soloists that determine whether the performance is successful. Soul-jazz's roots trace back to pianist Horace Silver whose funky style infused bop with the influence of church and gospel music along with the blues. Other pianists who followed and used similar approaches were Bobby Timmons, Junior Mance, Les McCann, Gene Harris (with his Three Sounds) and Ramsey Lewis. With the emergence of organist Jimmy Smith in 1956 (who has dominated his instrument ever since), soul-jazz organ combos (usually also including a tenor, guitarist, drummer and an occasional bassist) caught on and soulful players including Brother Jack McDuff, Shirley Scott, Jimmy McGriff, Charles Earland and Richard "Groove" Holmes, along with such other musicians as guitarists Grant Green, George Benson and Kenny Burrell, tenors Stanley Turrentine, Willis "Gator" Jackson, Eddie "Lockjaw" Davis, David "Fathead" Newman, Gene "Jug" Ammons, Houston Person, Jimmy Forrest, King Curtis, Red Holloway and Eddie Harris and altoist Hank Crawford were soul-jazz stars. Despite its eclipse by fusion and synthesizers in the 1970's, sou- jazz has stayed alive and made a healthy comeback in recent years. —*Scott Yanow*

Standards

During the golden age of the American popular song (dating from around 1915-60), a couple dozen very talented composers wrote a countless number of flexible songs that were adopted (and often transformed) by creative jazz musicians and singers. Often originally written for Broadway shows and Hollywood films, many of these works (generally 32-bars in length) have been performed and recorded a seemingly infinite number of times including "Body and Soul," "Stardust" and "All the Things You Are." Such composers as Jerome Kern, Irving Berlin, George Gershwin, Harold Arlen, Hoagy Carmichael, Cole Porter, Richard Rodgers, Harry Warren, Fats Waller and Duke Ellington along with other talents supplied the jazz and pop music worlds with what must have seemed like an endless supply of gems. Called standards (which means that they caught on as a permanent part of the jazz and pop music repertoire), the songs differ from less flexible "originals" that are often put together for a record date and then quickly forgotten. Since the rise of rock, the pop music world has been a much less fertile area for jazz players to "borrow" material from and, although many of the old standards are still performed, jazz musicians and singers have had to rely much more on original material during the past three decades. —*Scott Yanow*

Stride

Stride is a style of jazz piano playing in which the pianist's left hand maintains a continuous pulse in groups of four beats by percussively playing a bass note on the first and third beats and a chord on the second and fourth beats. The right hand improvises melodies and harmonies, and the result resembles a very energetic one-man band. It was performed by immensely talented pianists who were able to control the piano with a power and virtuosic force previously unknown in popular music.

The style originated in New York before the 1920s, as pianists took ragtime and began developing new, more swinging styles. Major proponents were James P. Johnson, Willie "The Lion" Smith, and Luckey Roberts. They influenced Fats Waller, Duke Ellington, Count Basie, and Joe Sullivan, who, in turn, went on to be influential themselves. Art Tatum and Ralph Sutton, for instance, were both influenced by Fats Waller. —*Mark Gridley*

Swing

While New Orleans jazz has improvised ensembles, when jazz started becoming popular in the 1920s and demand was growing for larger dance bands, it became necessary for ensembles to be written down, particularly when a group included more than three or four horns. Although swing largely began when Louis Armstrong joined Fletcher Henderson's Orchestra in 1924 and Don Redman began writing arrangements for the band that echoed the cornetist's relaxed phrases, the swing era officially started in 1935 when Benny Goodman's Orchestra caught on. Swing was a major force in American popular music until the big band era largely ended in 1946. Swing differs from New Orleans jazz and Dixieland in that the ensembles (even for small groups) are simpler and generally filled with repetitious riffs while in contrast the solos are more sophisticated. Individual improvisations still paid close attention to the melody but due to the advance in musicianship, the solo flights were more adventurous. The swing-oriented musicians who continued performing in the style after the end of the big band era (along with later generations who adopted this approach) can also be said to be playing "mainstream." Among the many stars of swing during the big band era were trumpeters Louis Armstrong, Bunny Berigan, Harry James and Roy Eldridge, trombonists Tommy Dorsey and Jack Teagarden, clarinetists Benny Goodman and Artie Shaw, tenor saxophonists Coleman Hawkins, Lester Young and Ben Webster, altoists Johnny Hodges and Benny Carter, pianists Teddy Wilson, Art Tatum, Earl Hines, Count Basie and Nat King Cole, guitarist Charlie Christian, drummers Gene Krupa and Chick Webb, vibraphonist Lionel Hampton, bandleader Glenn Miller and singers Billie Holiday, Ella Fitzgerald and Jimmy Rushing. —*Scott Yanow*

Texas Blues

A geographical subgenre earmarked by a more relaxed, swinging feel than other styles of blues, Texas Blues encompasses a number of style variations and has a long, distinguished history. Its earliest incarnation occurred in the mid-'20s, featuring acoustic guitar work rich in filigree patterns, almost an extension of the vocals rather than merely a strict accompaniment to it. This version of Texas blues embraced both the songster and country-blues traditions, with its lyrics relying less on affairs of the heart than in other forms. The next stage of development in the region's sound came after World War II, bringing forth a fully electric style that featured jazzy, single-string soloing over predominantly horn-driven backing. The style stays current with a raft of regional performers primarily working in a small combo context. —*Cub Koda*

Third Stream

Third stream (a term invented by composer Gunther Schuller in 1957) essentially means a mixture of jazz and classical music.

Most attempts at fusing the two very different idioms have been at best mixed successes with string sections weighing down jazz soloists. Paul Whiteman in the

1920s, tried to (in his own words) "make a lady out of jazz" and alternated between symphonic string sections and classic jazz solos. Strings were used in some swing bands in the 1940s (most inventively by Artie Shaw and Stan Kenton's dissonant works of 1950-51), but in all cases the added musicians were merely reading their parts and backing the improvisers. Starting with Charlie Parker in 1949 jazz players recorded now and then while joined by strings but it was not until the mid- to late '50s that more serious experiments began to take place. Schuller, John Lewis, J.J. Johnson and Bill Russo were some of the more significant composers attempting to bridge the gap between jazz and classical musics. Most musical forecasters in the mid-'50s would have predicted that jazz's next phase would involve a fusion of sorts with classical music but the rise of the avant-garde (which has a spontaneity and an extrovertism that most pseudo-classical works lack) largely ended the Third Stream movement before it came close to catching on beyond academic circles. Since its heyday in the late 1950s, there have been occasional Third Stream projects ranging from significant successes (such as Eddie Daniels' *Breakthrough* CD for GRP) to some that sound closer to pompous muzak. Although the movement never really became a major force, it still has potential. —*Scott Yanow*

Trad Jazz

Although the term "traditional jazz" has been used for everything from Dixieland to the current straightahead jazz scene, "trad" was the name for the form of New Orleans jazz that flourished in the United Kingdom during the 1950s and '60s. Similar in style and sound to Dixieland, the best trad bands developed their own repertoire and distinctive approach to playing the happy music. The most popular bands were led by trumpeter Kenny Ball (who had a major hit in "Midnight in Moscow") and trombonist Chris Barber and such stars as Humphrey Lyttelton, Ken Colyer and Monty Sunshine kept the scene alive and well, at least until the Beatles caught on. —*Scott Yanow*

Traditional Pop

Traditional pop refers to post-big band and pre-rock 'n' roll pop music. Traditional pop drew from a repertoire of songs written by professional songwriters and were performed by a vocalist that was supported by either an orchestra or a small-combo. In Traditional pop, the song is the key, and although the singer is the focal point, this style of singing doesn't rely on vocal improvisations like jazz singing does. Traditional pop can also refer to the orchestra leaders and arrangers that provided the instrumental settings for vocalists.

Urban Blues

The descriptive phrase, urban blues, was first used starting in the early part of the 20th century to differentiate between the more uptown sentiments pervasive to the style and the cruder, more rural stylings of "country" blues artists. This term was later used in the 1940s to describe a type of sophisticated blues written about the vagaries of city life, its lyrics alternately dealing with romantic strife and the innumerable good times to be easily obtained in an urban area. Always city derived, the music is always earmarked by a pronounced "uptown" emphasis, embracing everything from jump blues to jazz influenced stylings to smooth supper club style vocals. —*Cub Koda*

Vocal-Pop

Vocal-pop is considerably different than Traditional pop, which is largely comprised of standards and performed by skilled singers like Sinatra and Bennett. Vocal-pop is considerably lighter, falling somewhere between pop and easy listening. Vocal-pop's heyday was in the late '50s and early '60s, before rock 'n' roll had completely infiltrated all areas of popular record making. In those days, clean-cut groups like the Four Freshmen sang sweet, romantic and innocent songs that were given lush productions and arrangements. Vocal-pop primarily consisted of similar groups and sounds, the material lighter than Traditional pop, but sonically it had more in common with those standards than it did with rock.

Vocalese

Vocalese is the art of writing lyrics to fit recorded instrumental solos, many of which end up being tongue twisters. Eddie Jefferson was the first important vocalese lyricist in the late '40s, although a 1929 record released for the first time in 1996 finds Bee Palmer singing words set to Bix Beiderbecke's solo on "Singing the Blues." Jefferson's words to Gene Ammons' "Red Top" and Charlie Parker's "Parker's Mood" resulted in a pair of hits for King Pleasure (who also wrote some fine vocalese of his own). Vocalese reached its highest peak with Lambert, Hendricks & Ross during 1957-62, a group featuring the genius of vocalese Jon Hendricks, Annie Ross (famous for "Twisted") and Dave Lambert. In later years Hendricks led the Hendricks Family (which revived many of the Lambert, Hendricks & Ross classics) and Manhattan Transfer sometimes used vocalese. Although it has rarely advanced beyond bop (other than Eddie Jefferson's successful transformations of "Freedom Jazz Dance" and "Bitches Brew"), vocalese is still used as an option by today's jazz singers. —*Scott Yanow*

West Coast Blues

More piano-based and jazz-influenced than anything else, the West Coast style of blues is, in actuality, the California style, with all of the genre's main practitioners coming to prominence there, if not actual natives of the state in particular. In fact, the state and the style played host to a great many post-war Texas guitar expatriates and their jazzy, T-Bone Walker style of soloing would become an earmark of the genre. The genre also features smooth, honey toned vocals, frequently crossing into "urban blues" territory. The West Coast style was also home to numerous jump-blues practitioners, as many traveling bands of the 1940s ended up taking permanent residence there. Its current practitioners work almost exclusively in the standard small West Coast Jazz. Main proponents: Charles Brown, Pee Wee Crayton, Lowell Fulson, and Percy Mayfield.

World Fusion

World fusion refers to a fusion of Third World music, or just "world music" with jazz, specifically: 1) Ethnic music that has incorporated jazz improvisations (for example, Latin-jazz). Frequently, only the solos are improvised jazz. The accompaniments and compositions are essentially the same as the ethnic music. 2) Jazz that has incorporated limited aspects of a particular non-Western music. Examples include performances of Dizzy Gillespie's "A Night in Tunisia"; music on some of the 1970s quartet recordings by Keith Jarrett's quartet and quintet on Impulse, in which Middle Eastern instruments and harmonic methods are modified and used; some of Sun Ra's music from the 1950s into the 1990s, in which African rhythms are incorporated; some of Yusef Lateef's recordings that feature traditional Islamic instruments and methods. 3) New musical styles that result from distinctly original ways of combining jazz improvisation with original ideas and the instruments, harmonies, compositional practices, and rhythms of an existing ethnic tradition. The product is original, but its flavor still reflects some aspects of a non-jazz, ethnic tradition. Examples include Don Cherry's bands Codona and Nu, some of John McLaughlin's music from the 1970s and the 1990s that drew heavily on the traditions of India, some of Don Ellis' music of the 1970s that drew upon the music of India and Bulgaria, work by Andy Narrell in the 1990s that melds the music and instruments of Trinidad with jazz improvisations and funk styles.

World fusion jazz did not first occur with modern jazz, and its trends are not exclusive to American jazz. For instance, Polynesian music was fusing with Western pop styles at the beginning of the twentieth century, and its feeling attracted some of the earliest jazz musicians. Caribbean dance rhythms have been a significant part of American pop culture throughout the twentieth century, and, since jazz musicians frequently improvised when performing in pop music contexts, blends have been occurring almost continuously. Django Reinhardt was melding the traditions of Gypsy music with French impressionist concert music and jazz improvisation during the 1930s in France. —*Mark C. Gridley*

Greg Abate

b. May 31, 1947, Fall River, MA
Alto Saxophone, Tenor Saxophone / Bop, Big Band
A superior bop player who finally emerged on records as a leader in the 1990s, Abate had picked up experience playing with the Ray Charles Orchestra (starting in 1973 when he succeeded David "Fathead" Newman) and the Artie Shaw band when it was headed by clarinetist Dick Johnson during 1985-87. Based in Rhode Island, Abate has played at many festivals and club dates, mostly on the East Coast and in Europe. Although he also plays tenor, flute and soprano, alto is his main ax. Abate, who considers Charlie Parker, Paul Desmond and Phil Woods to be among his most important influences, has recorded as a leader for Seaside, Candid and Blue Chip Jazz (*Bop Lives!*). —*Scott Yanow*

● **Bop City: Live at Birdland** / Jul. 28, 1991 / Candid ✦✦✦✦✦
Journeyman saxophonist Greg Abate makes a decent hard bop recording on this '92 session. His playing is solid and sometimes frenetic, but also derivative. The compositions are straightforward and long enough for Abate and cast to make effective solos, yet short enough not to become tiring. He has a first-rate rhythm section with pianist James Williams, bassist Rufus Reid, and drummer Kenny Washington. —*Ron Wynn*

Straight Ahead / Sep. 21, 1992 / Candid ✦✦✦✦
The title perfectly summarizes this quintet date—hard bop and standards delivered professionally and competently by an experienced band. Greg Abate is a fluid alto and tenor saxophonist who executes the chord changes, progressions, and solos efficiently, while trumpeter Claudio Roditi adds some Afro-Latin spice and hot licks, and pianist Hilton Ruiz, bassist George Mraz, and drummer Kenny Washington keep the rhythmic center together. Mraz's bass sounds undermiked at times, but otherwise this date does exactly what it set out to do: showcase jazz professionals comfortable in their environment and with their material. —*Ron Wynn*

Dr. Jeckyll & Mr. Hyde / Jun. 20, 1995 / Candid ✦✦✦

Bop Lives! / May 6, 1996 / Blue Chip Jazz ✦✦✦✦
With a title such as *Bop Lives!*, it is a bit surprising to realize that there are actually no bop standards on this CD. However, the playing by altoist Greg Abate (whose sound recalls Phil Woods and Richie Cole) is certainly in the bop tradition; he is a heated and frequently exciting improviser. Trumpeter Claudio Roditi is aboard for five of the nine selections and is a perfect front line partner for Abate. Of the repertoire, three tunes are by the leader and there is one apiece from Roditi, pianist Kenny Barron (who leads a rhythm section also including bassist Rufus Reid and drummer Ben Riley), Mark Morganelli, Hank Mobley ("This I Dig of You"), Thelonious Monk and Kurt Weill (a nearly 11-minute rendition of "Speak Low"). The well-rounded program features Greg Abate at his best and this uncomplicated but generally chance-taking bop set is easily recommended. —*Scott Yanow*

Ahmed Abdul-Malik

b. Jan. 30, 1927, New York, NY, d. Oct. 2, 1993, Long Branch, NJ
Bass, Oud / Hard Bop, World Fusion
Ahmed Abdul-Malik was one of the first musicians to integrate non-Western musical elements with jazz. In addition to being a hard-bop bassist of some distinction, he also played the oud—a double-stringed, unfretted Middle-Eastern lute, played with a plectrum. Abdul-Malik recorded on the instrument in the '50s with Johnny Griffin, and in 1961 with John Coltrane, contributing to one of the several albums that resulted from the latter's *Live at the Village Vanguard* sessions.

Abdul-Malik was born and raised in Brooklyn, NY. In his 20s and 30s he worked as a bassist with Art Blakey, Randy Weston, and Thelonious Monk, among others. He played the oud on a tour of South America under the aegis of the US State Department, and performed at one of the first major African jazz festivals in Morocco in 1972. From 1970 he taught at New York University, and later, Brooklyn College. In 1984 he received BMI's "Pioneer in Jazz" award in recognition of his work in melding Middle-Eastern musics and jazz. —*Chris Kelsey*

● **Jazz Sahara** / Oct. 1958 / Original Jazz Classics ✦✦✦✦
This CD reissue is an early example of fusing jazz with world music. Abdul-Malik switches between bass and oud, interacts closely with the droning violin of Naim Karacand, Jack Ghanaim's kanoon (a 72-string instrument) and Mike Hamway's darabeka (a percussive drum), and mixes in Al Harewood's drums and (on three of the four selections) the tenor of Johnny Griffin. The music is a qualified success, essentially Middle Eastern folk music with Griffin added in. This set is interesting and in its own way innovative but not essential. —*Scott Yanow*

Ahmed Abdullah

b. May 10, 1947, New York, NY
Trumpet / Avant-Garde
An exciting but still little-known trumpeter, Ahmed Abdullah began playing music when he was 13. He started to get notice during the 1970s, performing in New York's loft scene. Since then he has played with Chico Freeman, Charles Brackeen and Marion Brown, led his own Solomonic Quintet, and recorded for Silkheart and Cadence Jazz. This powerful avant-garde trumpeter deserves much greater recognition. —*Scott Yanow*

● **Live at Ali's Alley** / Apr. 24, 1978 / Cadence ✦✦✦✦✦
Trumpeter Ahmed Abdullah featured French horn and cello in his instrumental configuration, while also working alongside tenor saxophonist Chico Freeman on this 1978 date. It's symbolic of the decade's "loft" jazz, a free-wheeling date with uneven, but often compelling solos as well as periods of rambling, unproductive and ragged ensemble work. Freeman's blistering tenor sax is uniformly inspired, while Abdullah's solos are also aggressive and energetic. Vincent Chancey's French horn and Muneer Abdul Fataah's cello contributions provide interesting contrast, while bassist Jerome Hunter and drummer Rashied Sinan are competent and effective, though not memorable. —*AMG*

Life's Force / 1978-1979 / About Time ✦✦✦✦
The short-lived About Time label started off with this stimulating release from trumpeter Ahmed Abdullah. Abdullah, who has an appealing tone and an adventurous style, heads a sextet also including the French horn of Vincent Chancey, vibraphonist Jay Hoggard, cellist Muneer Abdul Fataah, bassist Jerome Hunter and drummer Rashied Sinan for explorations of five of his compositions plus Cal Massey's "Assunata." The unusual blend of colorful instruments is the prime reason to pick up this obscure LP. —*Scott Yanow*

Liquid Magic / Feb. 16, 1987 / Silkheart ✦✦✦✦
Trumpeter Abdullah's debut for Silkheart resulted in him sometimes being eclipsed on his session. That wasn't due so much to Abdullah lacking verve or skill, but to the brilliance exhibited by tenor saxophonist Charles Brackeen and bassist Malachi Favors, whose acrobatics threaten to stretch and pull some songs beyond their harmonic fabric. —*Ron Wynn*

And the Solomonic Quintet / Dec. 3, 1987+Dec. 4, 1987 / Silkheart ✦✦✦✦
Trumpeter Ahmed Abdullah sprays around dissonant solos and spearheads an often frenzied set that was his second release for Silkheart. The lineup was exceptional, notably the powerful tenor saxophonist David S. Ware, dynamic bassist Fred Hopkins, and underrated drummer Charles Moffett. —*Ron Wynn*

Michael Abene

b. Jul. 2, 1942, New York, NY
Piano / Hard Bop
A staff producer, arranger and pianist for the GRP label, to date Michael Abene has led only one solo recording session, 1984's *You Must Have Been a Beautiful Baby*. A noted modern mainstream player, he was instead better known for his work outside of the limelight, accompanying singers ranging from Esther Phillips to Liza Minnelli and performing with countless top-flight jazz players; as an arranger, Abene also earned a number of Grammy nominations. —*Jason Ankeny*

You Must Have Been A Beautiful Baby / Dec. 1984 / Stash ✦✦✦✦
It seems strange that pianist Michael Abene did not have an opportunity to lead his own record date until he was already 42 in 1984, and that he has not led one since. A flexible and talented modern mainstream player, Abene has accompanied

a wide variety of singers throughout his career and both written and played for a strong who's-who listing of top jazz players. For his set of unaccompanied solos, Abene interprets two songs apiece by Billy Strayhorn and Thelonious Monk, an obscure Fats Waller tune ("When the Nylons Bloom Again"), Steve Swallow's "Hullo, Bolinas," two originals, and the standard "You Must Have Been a Beautiful Baby." The performances are both exploratory and melodic; well worth several listens. This Stash LP has not yet been reissued on CD. —*Scott Yanow*

John Abercrombie

b. Dec. 16, 1944, Port Chester, NY
Guitar / Post-Bop

John Abercrombie's tying together of jazz's many threads made him one of the most influential acoustic and electric guitarists of the 1970s and early '80s; his recordings for ECM have helped define that label's progressive chamber-jazz reputation. More recently his star has faded somewhat, due largely to the general conservatism that's come to dominate jazz, though he has remained a vital creative personality. Abercrombie's style draws upon all manner of contemporary improvised music; his style is essentially jazz-based, but he also displays a more-than-passing familiarity with forms that range from folk and rock to Eastern and Western art music.

Abercrombie attended Boston's Berklee College of Music from 1962 to 1966. While at Berklee, the guitarist toured with bluesman Johnny Hammond. After relocating to New York in 1969, Abercrombie spent time in groups led by drummers Chico Hamilton and Billy Cobham. It was with the latter's Spectrum group that Abercrombie first received widespread attention. Abercrombie's first album as leader was *Timeless*, a trio album with drummer Jack DeJohnette and keyboardist Jan Hammer. That was followed by *Gateway*, another trio with DeJohnette and bassist Dave Holland replacing Hammer. Abercrombie's subtle and lyrical style is heard to best effect in small, intimate settings—with the recurring *Gateway* trio, or as captured in duos with fellow guitarist Ralph Towner. —*Chris Kelsey*

● **Timeless** / Jun. 21, 1974-Jun. 22, 1974 / ECM ✦✦✦✦✦

Guitarist John Abercrombie's first in a long line of recordings for ECM was also his debut as a leader. Teamed up with Jan Hammer (who here plays organ, synthesizer and piano) and drummer Jack DeJohnette, Abercrombie plays four of his originals plus two by Hammer. This performance differs from many of the guitarist's later ECM dates in that Hammer injects a strong dose of fusion into the music and there is plenty of spirited interplay between those two with fine support by DeJohnette. Thought-provoking and occasionally exciting music that generally defies categorization. —*Scott Yanow*

Works / 1974-1991 / ECM ✦✦✦

A good 1989 compilation of past Abercrombie selections on various ECM releases, spotlighting his versatility and proficiency. Songs featuring his fluid guitar in introspective, mainstream, and free contexts, as well as playing everything from new age-tinged originals to covers of standards, are presented. —*Ron Wynn*

Gateway / Mar. 1975 / ECM ✦✦✦✦✦

Guitarist John Abercrombie was one of the stars of ECM in its early days. His playing on this trio set with bassist Dave Holland and drummer Jack DeJohnette is really beyond any simple categorization. Abercrombie's improvisations are sophisticated yet, because his sound is rockish and sometimes quite intense (particularly on the nearly 11-minute "Sorcery 1"), there is really no stylistic name for the music. Holland contributed four of the six originals while DeJohnette brought in the other two (one of which was co-written with Abercrombie). The interplay between the three musicians is quite impressive although listeners might find some of the music to be quite unsettling. It takes several listens for one to digest all that is going on, but it is worth the struggle. —*Scott Yanow*

Sargasso Sea / May 1976 / ECM ✦✦✦

A nice, though not as spectacular a session as anticipated, matches guitarists John Abercrombie and Ralph Towner, who also plays piano. Towner's 12-string solos are stronger than his classical ones, which are frequently beautiful but don't make much of an impression contrasted to Abercrombie's more energetic improvisations. The title track's the best cut on the sessions; the others are more decorative than intriguing. —*AMG*

Gateway 2 / Jul. 1977 / ECM ✦✦✦✦

Unlike the first Gateway album, this CD reissue puts more of an emphasis on the rockish side of guitarist John Abercrombie's style. Abercrombie (who also plays some electric mandolin) still indulges in close interplay with bassist Dave Holland and drummer Jack DeJohnette (who doubles a bit on piano) but the playing on the five group originals is generally more fiery than introspective. None of the individual selections are all that memorable but the group improvising does have plenty of surprising moments. —*Scott Yanow*

Pictures / 1977 / ECM ✦✦✦

Arcade / Dec. 1978 / ECM ✦✦✦

Straight Flight / Mar. 19, 1979-Mar. 20, 1979 / JAM ✦✦✦✦

Abercrombie Quartet / Nov. 1979 / ECM ✦✦✦

M / Nov. 1980 / ECM ✦✦✦✦

Five Years Later / Mar. 1981 / ECM ✦✦✦

It was recorded with Ralph Towner (g). Abercrombie is more electric in this duet setting. Three pieces were co-written by the duo. Two vastly different sounds mesh nicely. —*Michael G. Nastos*

Solar / May 1982 / Palo Alto ✦✦✦

Night / Apr. 1984 / ECM ✦✦✦✦

This spirited original features Jan Hammer (k). It's a favorable group setting for guitarist Abercrombie and timeless trio. Michael Brecker (ts). —*Michael G. Nastos*

Current Events / Sep. 1985 / ECM ✦✦✦✦

Excellent trio date featuring Abercrombie playing with bassist Marc Johnson and drummer Peter Erskine. The three take chances, converge, collide, alternate time in the spotlight, and make emphatic, unpredictable music while never staying locked into one groove or style. —*Ron Wynn*

Witchcraft / Jun. 24, 1986-Jun. 25, 1986 / Justin Time ✦✦✦✦

Getting There / Apr. 1987 / ECM ✦✦✦

John Abercrombie, Marc Johnson & Peter Erskine / Apr. 21, 1988 / ECM ✦✦✦✦✦

An excellent trio outing with Abercrombie, inventive bassist Marc Johnson, and careening drummer Peter Erskine. The trio sometimes unite for piercing interpretations as on "Stella By Starlight," and other times collide and interact on furious rhythm dialogues and extended improvisations. —*Ron Wynn*

Animato / Oct. 1989 / ECM ✦✦

Vince Mendoza (who wrote six of the eight pieces on this John Abercrombie CD) sets the mood of each selection on his synthesizers, either playing long tones, drones, minimalistic chordings, or (in rare cases) a repetitive rhythm. Drummer Jon Christensen contributes some rhythms and percussive sounds while guitarist Abercrombie solos on top, either adding to the downbeat mood or displaying his technique. Despite the talent involved, overall the results are a bit of a bore —*Scott Yanow*

While We're Young / Jun. 1992 / ECM ✦✦✦

November / Nov. 1992 / ECM ✦✦✦✦

Speak of the Devil / Jul. 1993 / ECM ✦✦✦

Nosmo King / Aug. 1, 1994 / Steeple Chase ✦✦✦

● **Gateway: Homecoming** / Dec. 1994 / ECM ✦✦✦✦✦

The trio heard on this CD (guitarist John Abercrombie, bassist Dave Holland and drummer Jack DeJohnette) recorded *Gateway* and *Gateway 2* for ECM back in 1975 and 1977. Although each of the musicians has grown musically since that time and has piled up plenty of accomplishments, the style of music that they perform when they come together as Gateway has remained largely unchanged. One could call it creative fusion or post-bop; whatever the name, the music's success depends on a great deal of intuitive interplay between the talented players. John Abercrombie's often-distorted tone and use of color show hints of Bill Frisell (who must have learned from the example of the older guitarist). Dave Holland's bass is never predictable nor subservient to Abercrombie and, even if the other musicians were allowed to coast, Jack DeJohnette's constantly rumbling drumming would keep the performances from ever getting too comfortable. Although the original music (which concludes with a quiet piece for DeJohnette's piano) is not for all jazz fans (Abercrombie's rockish sound may scare some off), the high improvisational level makes this a set deserving of close listens. —*Scott Yanow*

In the Moment / Dec. 1994 / ECM ✦✦✦

The group Gateway (a trio comprising guitarist John Abercrombie, bassist Dave Holland and drummer Jack DeJohnette, who also plays the Korg wave-drum, a Turkish frame drum and piano) certainly covers a lot of ground. The interplay between the musicians is the main reason to acquire this set. The five group originals sound freely improvised, and they include the Indian-flavored "In the Moment," a full-scale Abercrombie guitar freakout on "Shrubberies" and some quieter moments. Intriguing and atmospheric music. —*Scott Yanow*

Now It Can Be Played / Jan. 17, 1995 / Steeple Chase ✦✦✦

Tactics / Jul. 13, 1996-Jul. 15, 1996 / ECM ✦✦✦✦

This set is a little different than most ECM releases, because the trio (guitarist John Abercrombie, organist Dan Wall and drummer Adam Nussbaum) performs a couple of fairly straightahead standards—"You and the Night and the Music" and "Long Ago and Far Away"—in addition to six originals, including Wall's rhythmic "Bo Diddy." Not sounding at all like a typical soul-jazz organ group, these musicians take more advanced improvisations, with Wall (whose accompaniment of Abercrombie is quite atmospheric) emerging as the top soloist. —*Scott Yanow*

Muhal Richard Abrams

b. Sep. 19, 1930, Chicago, IL
Piano / Avant-Garde

Although somewhat underrated through the years due to his behind-the-scenes work, Muhal Richard Abrams was one of the most important figures to emerge from the Association for the Advancement of Creative Musicians (AACM), an organization whose successes would have been much fewer without his participation. Influential as an avant-garde pianist who bridged the gap between hard bop, free jazz and (to a certain extent) contemporary classical music, Abrams' additional significance as a composer, arranger and bandleader has long put him near the top of the avant-garde field. Although he went to music college when he was 17, Muhal Richard Abrams was essentially self-taught, learning his craft on the job and through his own explorations. Influenced early on by pianist Bud Powell, Abrams performed at a wide variety of jobs during the 1950s, gained some early attention for his playing on the MJT+3's album *Branching Out*, and through the years gigged and/or recorded with such musicians as Max Roach, Sonny Stitt, Dexter Gordon, Eddie Harris, Ruth Brown and Woody Shaw. In 1961 Abrams formed a short-lived orchestra (the Experimental Band) and then on May 8, 1965, he was a major force in the founding of the AACM, a still-active Chicago-based organization that emphasizes self-reliance by performing original compositions, organizing one's own concerts and educating the community (including younger musicians) about the new music. The innovators who emerged from the AACM (including the Art Ensemble of Chicago, Anthony Braxton and Henry Threadgill) invigorated the avant-garde, taking the music out of the potential dead-end of consistently intense improvisations into an appreciation of the value of space and silence and a logical mix of compositions with individual expression. As the AACM's first president, Abrams established the organization as a vital force on the Chicago jazz scene. Fortunately he did not neglect his own playing and through the years, most notably on Delmark (starting with the groundbreaking *Levels and Degrees of Light* in 1967) and continuing on India Navigation, Arista/Freedom and Black Saint, Abrams (who moved to New York in 1977) has recorded in a wide variety of settings, from solo piano to leader of his own innovative big band. He has stuck consistently to his principles (which became the philosophy of the AACM) and forged his own singular path in jazz. —*Scott Yanow*

Levels and Degrees of Light / Jun. 7, 1967+Dec. 21, 1967 / Delmark ✦✦✦✦
This was one of Muhal Richard Abrams' early gems, a 1967 session that included him playing both piano and synthesizer and heading a quartet with Anthony Braxton on clarinet, Thurman Barker on drums and Gordon Emmanuel on vibes. Abrams superbly interspersed free, hard bop, and blues elements, while Braxton's solos and the intriguing front line and contrasts provided by vibes and drums rather than bass resulted in some unusual and striking compositions. This has been reissued on CD. —*AMG*

Young at Heart, Wise in Time / Jul. 2, 1969+Aug. 20, 1969 / Delmark ✦✦✦
Muhal Richard Abrams, as the founder of the AACM in Chicago, has been one of the unsung leaders of the avant-garde ever since the mid-'60s. A versatile pianist, Abrams is heard in two different settings on this, his second session as a leader. "Young at Heart" finds him stretching out on a solo piano performance that hints at earlier styles while exploring the potential sounds and silence of free jazz. *Wise in Time* has Abrams functioning as part of an explorative quintet with trumpeter Leo Smith and altoist Henry Threadgill, both of whom were unknown youngsters at the time. Fascinating music, it is recommended strictly for the open-eared listener who does not demand that all jazz swing conventionally. —*Scott Yanow*

Things to Come from Those Now Gone / Oct. 10, 1972 / Delmark ✦✦✦✦
A masterpiece and one of the finest works in the contemporary (post-'50s free) jazz vernacular. Muhal Richard Abrams' compositions and piano solos illuminate multiple traditions, from stride and ragtime to the percussive style of the '50s and '60s. —*Ron Wynn*

Afrisong / Sep. 9, 1975 / India Navigation ✦✦✦
Muhal Richard Abrams seamlessy blended elements of stride, bebop, blues, and free music on this collection of solo piano pieces originally recorded in 1975 for the Japanese label Trio/Whynot. It was also available briefly on India Navigation. Top numbers included "Hymn to the East," "Blues For M" and the title track. It was also a chance for Abrams to display his instrumental facility and underrated keyboard skills, which often take a back seat to his arranging, compositions and bandleading. —*AMG*

Sightsong / Oct. 13, 1975-Oct. 14, 1975 / Black Saint ✦✦✦
Fine duets with Malachi Favors (b); first Black Saint date. —*Ron Wynn*

Duets 1976 / Aug. 1, 1976-Aug. 2, 1976 / Black Saint ✦✦
This was not Muhal Richard Abrams' session, but Anthony Braxton's, and was issued on Arista under his name. The duo teamed for intriguing, sometimes intense and other times more introspective performances on material ranging from Braxton's numerical compositions to their unusual version of "Maple Leaf Rag." Braxton played alto and soprano saxophones, plus contrabass clarinet and sax and standard clarinet, while Abrams concentrated on piano and added everything from bop riffs to stride accents, ragtime and blues lines. —*AMG*

1-OQA+19 / Nov. 1977-Dec. 1977 / Black Saint ✦✦✦
Muhal Richard Abrams hasn't presided over many small combos with a more imposing lineup than on this 1977 session. Anthony Braxton and Henry Threadgill played numerous instruments from alto, tenor and soprano saxes to flutes and clarinets, even adding background vocals. Fiery percussionist Steve McCall and bassist Leonard Jones, who also added some vocals, completed the lineup. The unit made demanding, harmonically dense and rhythmically unpredictable material, with Braxton's scurrying solos ably matched by Threadgill's bluesier lines and Abrams' leadership and inventive blend of jazz, blues, and other sources holding things together. —*AMG*

Lifea Blinec / Feb. 1978 / Novus ✦✦✦
Muhal Richard Abrams headed one of his finest small combos on this intense quintet session from 1978. Joseph Jarman provided riveting bass saxophone and bassoon contributions in addition to playing alto clarinet, flute, soprano sax, percussion and vocals. His multiple contributions were matched by Douglas Ewart on an equal array of reed instruments, including bass and soprano clarinet, bassoon, alto and tenor sax and percussion. Abrams divided his time between keyboards, conducting and percussion, while Amina Claudine Myers was also on hand adding vibrant, bluesy riffs and statements. Thurman Barker took care of drum duties and doubled on percussion. —*AMG*

Spiral Live at Montreux 1978 / Jul. 22, 1978 / Novus ✦✦✦✦
Muhal Richard Abrams performs unaccompanied throughout this concert appearance from the 1978 Montreux Jazz Festival. The relatively brief "String Song" features some odd sound explorations as Abrams plays the strings from inside the piano along with gongs. "D Song" and "Voice Song" find Abrams sticking to the piano and offering a slightly mellower alternative to Cecil Taylor in exploring new music. Abrams' occasional use of devices from earlier styles (including a bit of dissonant stride and basslines à la Lennie Tristano) make this music a bit more accessible than one might expect at times, but in general this set is for listeners who enjoy hearing new approaches to musical freedom. —*Scott Yanow*

Spihumonesty / Jul. 1979 / Black Saint ✦✦✦

Mama and Daddy / Jun. 16, 1980+Jun. 19, 1980 / Black Saint ✦✦✦
This was a first-rate big band/large group session from 1980, with Muhal Richard Abrams' compositions being played by a masterful ensemble which included French horn and tuba in its instrumental mix. There were wonderful solos, dashing arrangements and fiery rhythm support from Thurman Barker on drums, marimba and percussion, with Andrew Cyrille adding additional percussive assistance. The group also featured Baikida Carroll on trumpet and fluegelhorn, Wallace McMillan on various reeds, violinist Leroy Jenkins, bassist Brian Smith, Abrams on keyboards, trombonist George Lewis, Bob Stewart on tuba and Vincent Chancey on French horn. They presented adventurous, disciplined, frequently exciting music. —*AMG*

Duet / May 12, 1981 / Black Saint ✦✦✦✦
Muhal Richard Abrams recorded several memorable and successful duet sessions during the 1970s and '80s. Few covered more territory or were as invigorating as the album with Amina Claudine Myers, a capable player on either organ or piano. Myers discarded the organ for this date, as both she and Abrams used Yamaha C3D pianos. While Myers displayed her gospel and blues influences, Abrams' muscular riffs and solos resulted in exciting dialogues and marvelous complementary, contrasting and dueling passages. This was an intense, yet also swinging, enjoyable session, one in which Abrams displayed the mastery of multiple genres that's distinguished his music, and Myers her distinctive mix of secular and spiritual elements. —*Ron Wynn*

Blues Forever / Jul. 20, 1981-Jul. 27, 1981 / Black Saint ✦✦✦✦
Tremendous large orchestra session, with Abrams heading a crew that includes the cream of '70s and '80s improvisers, plus some '60s survivors. Although every arrangement doesn't click, the band successfully romps and stomps through enough cuts to show that the big band sound doesn't just mean "ghost" groups recreating dusty numbers from the '30s and '40s. —*Ron Wynn*

● **Rejoicing with the Light** / Jan. 8, 1983-Jan. 25, 1983 / Black Saint ✦✦✦✦✦
Muhal Richard Abrams blended vintage and progressive sensibilities on this outstanding 1984 session. It was a large band outing, and Abrams assembled many of the finest active improvisers. His orchestra did not include just saxophones and

trumpets but also French horns, bass clarinets, cello, guitar, vibes and timpani. This assured Abrams a varied, rich sound with multiple options. He led the orchestra through pieces that were sometimes introspective and other times jubilant and swinging, but never simple or predictable. This session was a challenging, instructive and entertaining lesson in modern big-band writing, arranging and performing. —*Ron Wynn*

View from Within / Sep. 22, 1984+Sep. 27, 1984 / Black Saint ✦✦✦✦

Abrams' work for mid-sized groups varies markedly from his solo, trio, or large orchestra material. Compositions are even more unpredictable, there's more emphasis on mood and less on rhythm, and solos are crisper and shorter. This '84 date included some intriguing instrumental configurations at times (vibes/flute/percussion, piano/clarinet/bass clarinet) and ranked among his best '80s dates. —*Ron Wynn*

Roots of Blue / Jan. 7, 1986 / RPR ✦✦✦✦

Colours in Thirty-Third / Dec. 19, 1986 / Black Saint ✦✦✦✦

Muhal Richard Abrams constantly varied the lineups for the seven numbers that this 1986 session comprised, alternating between trio, quartet, quintet and sextet pieces. The title track and "Introspection" featured the entire group, and were the most striking works, though the trio tunes offered the most musically challenging material. John Purcell on soprano and tenor sax and bass clarinet provided several stirring solos, while violinist John Blake was a solid contributor on several selections and the rhythm tandem of bassist Fred Hopkins and drummer Andrew Cyrille were also consistent and engaging, particularly Cyrille. Abrams as usual was an inspiring force as an instrumentalist and conceptualist. —*AMG*

The Hearinga Suite / Jan. 17, 1989-Jan. 18, 1989 / Black Saint ✦✦✦✦✦

Pianist Muhal Richard Abrams leads an 18-piece orchestra on his seven originals that make up the *Hearinga Suite*. Much of the music is quite adventurous although "Oldfotalk" is fairly conventional. Although the personnel includes such fine players as trumpeters Jack Walrath and Cecil Bridgewater and saxophonists John Purcell and Marty Ehrlich, the emphasis is on group interplay and the colorful arrangements. Throughout this very interesting set, Abrams shows how a big band can logically be utilized in freer forms of jazz. —*Scott Yanow*

Blu Blu Blu / Nov. 9, 1990-Nov. 10, 1990 / Black Saint ✦✦✦✦

His finest pure big band date. Abrams leads a surging, eclectic aggregation through numbers that are mostly uptempo and aggressive. Whistler Joel Brandon gets honors as the most distinctive stylist, but the entire crew is showcased favorably in this '90 session. Things were further enhanced by some of Abrams' most intense pieces, especially "One For The Whistler" and "Stretch Time." —*Ron Wynn*

Family Talk / 1993 / Black Saint ✦✦✦

Muhal Richard Abrams' compositions are never structured in a usual manner. This is a quintet outing that pairs trumpeter Jack Walraith and multi-reed player Patience Higgins in the front line, with Abrams on piano and synthesizer, Warren Smith on vibes, marimba, gongs and timpani and bassist Brad Jones. Over the album, Abrams varies the moods, instrumentation, voicings and solo order, with lengthy numbers that have both carefully crafted sections and places that allow the musicians to soar. His music does not have catchy hooks; it is rewarding and captivating but requires some effort and attention, the kind of thing that separates great fare from merely good material. —*Ron Wynn*

Think All, Focus One / Jul. 1994 / Black Saint ✦✦✦✦

The seven compositions by Muhal Richard Abrams on this release can be considered part of a suite. Although there are no memorable melodies, the music flows from one piece to another and stays consistently stimulating; the only exception is the closing "Think All, Focus One" which has Abrams on synthesizer and seems quite directionless. Otherwise many moods are covered, from a dirge-like "The Harmonic Veil" and the complex but often exuberant "Crossbeams" to the swinging (in its own fashion) "Scaledance" and a funky jam on "Encore." The highly expressive trumpeter Eddie Allen (who is masterful with a wa-wa mute) is often the lead voice, although guitarist David Gilmore also makes a strong impression and the leader's piano (which often drops out) keeps the musicians on track; tenorman Eugene Ghee, trombonist Alfred Patterson, bassist Brad Jones and drummer Reggie Nicholson complete the unit. Due to the frequently dense ensembles of the septet and the complexity of the music, this set will take several listens to fully absorb, but it is well worth the effort. —*Scott Yanow*

Song For All / Apr. 26, 1995-Apr. 29, 1995 / Black Saint ✦✦✦✦

One Line, Two Views / Jun. 23, 1995-Jun. 24, 1995 / New World ✦✦✦✦

Open Air Meeting / Aug. 11, 1996 / New World ✦✦✦

George Adams

b. Apr. 29, 1940, Covington, GA, **d.** Nov. 14, 1992, New York, NY
Tenor Saxophone, Flute / Avant-Garde, Post-Bop

A passionate tenor and flute player who was not shy to break up chordal improvising with an unexpected scream or roar, George Adams was an original voice who (like his friend Don Pullen) crossed over several stylistic boundaries. He started on piano but by the time he was in high school he was playing tenor in funk bands. In 1961 he toured with Sam Cooke and in 1963 Adams moved to Ohio where he played with organ groups for the next few years. In 1968 he relocated to New York where he played with Roy Haynes, Gil Evans and Art Blakey, among others. However it was his association with Charles Mingus (1973-76) that gave him his initial fame. After playing a bit with McCoy Tyner, Adams co-led a stimulating quartet with Don Pullen that made many records. Late in life Adams (who enjoyed taking an occasional raspy blues vocal) teamed up with James "Blood" Ulmer in the group Phalanx and occasionally played with Mingus Dynasty. —*Scott Yanow*

Suite for Swingers / Jul. 28, 1976 / Horo ✦✦✦

These extended compositions, with Don Pullen, feature one of the great jazz quartets of the last two decades. All of their albums are worthwhile. —*Michael G. Nastos*

Sound Suggestions / May 1979 / ECM ✦✦✦✦

Tenor saxophonist George Adams' third recording as a leader (following two obscure releases for the Italian Horo label) is a little unusual in that the extroverted soloist is heard on the usually introverted ECM label. Adams is teamed with fellow tenor Heinz Sauer (who has a cooler sound), trumpeter Kenny Wheeler, pianist Richard Beirach, bassist Dave Holland and drummer Jack DeJohnette for five group originals. The playing is advanced but not as fiery as most of Adams' later sets. —*Scott Yanow*

Don't Lose Control / Nov. 2, 1979-Nov. 3, 1979 / Soul Note ✦✦✦

Tenor saxophonist George Adams and pianist Don Pullen first joined forces in Charles Mingus' band of the 1970s and, upon the great bassist's death, they formed their own dynamic quartet, resulting in many recordings (mostly for European labels). *Don't Lose Control*, although their fourth time together, was the first to gain much recognition. On the five originals (all written by either Adams or Pullen), the two principals are in fine form with bassist Cameron Brown and drummer Dannie Richmond contributing stimulating support. Adams' raspy vocal on the title track is fun. This set is not quite as essential as some of the Adams-Pullen Quartet's later releases, but worth picking up. —*Scott Yanow*

Paradise Space Shuttle / Dec. 21, 1979 / Timeless ✦✦✦

Hand to Hand / Feb. 13, 1980-Feb. 14, 1980 / Soul Note ✦✦✦

Earth Beams / Aug. 3, 1981-Aug. 5, 1981 / Timeless ✦✦✦✦

The usual spinning, chaotic, yet coherent George Adams tenor solos, contrasted by Don Pullen's ever-striding, attacking piano solos, were the attraction on this 1981 session. Bassist Cameron Brown, now comfortable in the quartet setting, and drummer Dannie Richmond filled their roles admirably as the Adams-Pullen foursome continued a great string of top-flight '80s releases. —*Ron Wynn*

Melodic Excursions / Jun. 6, 1982+Jun. 9, 1982 / Timeless ✦✦✦

Gentleman's Agreement / Jan. 11, 1983-Jan. 12, 1983 / Soul Note ✦✦✦

Live at the Village Vanguard, Vol. 1 / Aug. 19, 1983 / Soul Note ✦✦✦✦✦

The George Adams-Don Pullen Quartet was one of the top jazz groups of the 1980s, although it tended to be overlooked in the US. Tenor saxophonist Adams and pianist Pullen (who were assisted by bassist Cameron Brown and drummer Dannie Richmond) were both flexible players easily capable of playing both inside and outside music, sometimes simultaneously. This first of two volumes from a night at the Village Vanguard has four lengthy performances: a tune apiece by Adams, Pullen, Charles Mingus and Duke Ellington ("Solitude"). Passionate music. —*Scott Yanow*

Live at the Village Vanguard, Vol. 2 / Aug. 19, 1983 / Soul Note ✦✦✦✦✦

The second album taken from a strong performance by the George Adams-Don Pullen Quartet, this set features three compositions by pianist Pullen (including his catchy "Big Alice") and tenorman Adams' "City Gates." The music swings in its own way while being quite unpredictable, intense and sometimes avant-garde. There is nothing sleepy or routine about the chance-taking (and frequently exciting) music. —*Scott Yanow*

Decisions / Feb. 2, 1984-Feb. 3, 1984 / Timeless ✦✦✦✦

Although one of the most stimulating groups of the first half of the 1980s, the George Adams-Don Pullen Quartet (which could play both inside or completely outside) was largely ignored by American labels. Fortunately, European companies (most notably Soul Note and Timeless) kept the important band from being completely undocumented. This particular album features the quartet (consisting of Adams on tenor, pianist Pullen, bassist Cameron Brown and drummer Dannie Richmond) playing five group originals, plus a tender rendition of "His Eye Is on the Sparrow," with passion and power. —*Scott Yanow*

More Sightings / Sep. 9, 1984 / Enja ◆◆◆

The intense tenor saxophonist George Adams teams up with trumpeter Marvin "Hannibal" Peterson, guitarist John Schofield and an alert rhythm section (pianist Ron Burton, bassist Walter Schmocker and drummer Allen Nelson) during this 1984 concert to explore five originals by the three principals, plus the standard "Don't Take Your Love From Me." The music has its strong moments, although nothing all that memorable occurs, except perhaps for Adams' eccentric vocal on "I Could Really Go for You." —*Scott Yanow*

Nightingale / Aug. 1988 / Blue Note ◆◆

This is an odd session that should have been much more successful. George Adams (on tenor with one appearance apiece on flute and soprano) is joined by pianist Hugh Lawson, bassist Sirone and drummer Victor Lewis for a set of ballads and spirituals. Adams puts plenty of feeling into the melodies, but some (particularly "Bridge Over Troubled Water," "What a Wonderful World" and "Moon River") really cannot be saved. —*Scott Yanow*

● **America** / May 24, 1989-Jul. 18, 1989 / Blue Note ◆◆◆◆◆

This is one of tenor saxophonist George Adams' most fun records. He takes eight songs, all of which now qualify as American folk songs (along with two originals) and gives them melodic but inventive treatments. "America the Beautiful" starts out with a Sousa march before Adams takes a chorus fairly straight, leading to interesting tonal variations. "Georgia" is treated as a tasteful ballad," "You Are My Sunshine" is given a funky background, and, best of all, "Take Me Out to the Ballgame" becomes an unaccompanied tenor solo; at one point Adams makes clicking sounds that are very similar to a ball hitting a mitt. He sings three numbers, the rhythm section (comprising pianist Hugh Lawson, bassist Cecil McBee and drummer Mark Johnson) is fine in support and Adams (who plays both his humming flute and tenor on "Old Folks at Home") is heard in top form. This CD is accessible, patriotic and a highly recommended and continually surprising set. —*Scott Yanow*

Old Feeling / Mar. 11, 1991-Mar. 12, 1991 / Blue Note ◆◆◆◆

Old Feeling ranks as one of George Adams' most exciting and eccentric sessions. Unlike some other avant-gardists who seem to lose their personality and purpose when they play standard material, Adams turns even overplayed songs into his own inventive devices; three standards get the Adams treatment on this CD. —*Scott Yanow*

Pepper Adams (Pepper Park Adams III)

b. Oct. 8, 1930, Highland Park, MI, **d.** Sep. 10, 1986, New York, NY

Baritone Saxophone / Hard Bop

Pepper Adams was one of the all-time great baritonists, ranking at the top with Harry Carney, Serge Chaloff and Gerry Mulligan. But Mulligan overshadowed Adams throughout virtually his entire career, which is a little strange because Pepper had a much different sound (heavier and more intense) than the light-toned and playful Mulligan.

Adams grew up in Rochester, NY, and when he was 16 he moved to Detroit where he became an important part of the very fertile local jazz scene. Other than a period in the military (1951-53), Adams was a major fixture in Detroit, playing with such up-and-coming musicians as Donald Byrd, Kenny Burrell, Tommy Flanagan, Barry Harris and Elvin Jones. Adams had opportunities to tour with Stan Kenton, Maynard Ferguson and Chet Baker and he moved to New York in 1958. In addition to recording both as a leader and a sideman, Adams played with Benny Goodman (1958-59) and Charles Mingus (off and on between 1959-63) and co-led a quintet with Donald Byrd (1958-62). He was a longtime member of the Thad Jones/Mel Lewis Orchestra (1965-78) and a major stylist up until his death. —*Scott Yanow*

Pepper Adams Quintet / Jul. 12, 1957 / V.S.O.P. ◆◆◆◆

Pepper Adams ranked among modern jazz's finest baritone saxophonists. His mastery of the middle and lower registers and technical acumen enabled him to play the cumbersome baritone with a speed, facility, and style usually restricted to smaller horns. This '57 quintet date featured him in a more relaxed context with West Coast jazz types like trumpeter Stu Williamson and pianist Carl Perkins. Bassist Leroy Vinnegar added his famous "walking" lines and drummer Mel Lewis provided a steady, smooth rhythmic pace, while Adams contributed two originals and did three standards in his usual impeccable fashion. —*Ron Wynn*

Pure Pepper / Nov. 19, 1957 / Savoy ◆◆◆

Originally titled *The Cool Sound of Pepper Adams*, this 1984 reissue LP features the great baritonist on an early session as a leader with the euphonium of Bernard McKinney, pianist Hank Jones, bassist George Duvivier and drummer Elvin Jones.

The unusual front line blends together better than expected and the often-explosive baritonist (who brought a new sound to his instrument) is heard in his early prime on the straightahead material. —*Scott Yanow*

● **10 to 4 at the Five-Spot** / Apr. 5, 1958 / Original Jazz Classics ◆◆◆◆◆

Most of the recordings by the Donald Byrd-Pepper Adams Quintet were released under the trumpeter's name but this near-classic (reissued on CD) is an exception. With pianist Bobby Timmons, bassist Doug Watkins and drummer Elvin Jones completing (and inspiring) the group, Adams and Byrd make for a potent team on "You're My Thrill" and some originals; hard bop at its best. —*Scott Yanow*

Stardust / 1960 / Bethlehem ◆◆◆

Baritonist Pepper Adams and trumpeter Donald Byrd teamed up on a regular basis during the late 1950s–early '60s. For this Bethlehem LP, they utilize an all-star sextet that also includes guitarist Kenny Burrell, pianist Tommy Flanagan, bassist Paul Chambers and a drummer identified as "Hey" Lewis who was actually Louis Hayes. The unit stretches out on Erroll Garner's rarely-performed but rewarding "Trio," a pair of Adams originals, Thad Jones' "Bitty Ditty" and a memorable rendition of "Stardust." Well worth searching for. —*Scott Yanow*

Out of This World / 1961 / Fresh Sound ◆◆◆

Plays Compositions of Charles Mingus / Sep. 9, 1963 / Fresh Sound ◆◆◆◆

This adventurous outing builds on Adams' bebop base. —*David Szatmary*

Encounter! / Dec. 11, 1968-Dec. 12, 1968 / Original Jazz Classics ◆◆◆◆

Baritonist Pepper Adams and tenor saxophonist Zoot Sims (who rarely performed together) make a surprisingly compatible team on this CD reissue of a 1968 Prestige session. With pianist Tommy Flanagan, bassist Ron Carter and drummer Elvin Jones forming a fairly adventurous rhythm section, Pepper and Sims sound inspired on material that includes obscurities by Flanagan, Thad Jones and Adams in addition to the Ellington-Strayhorn ballad "Star-Crossed Lovers" and a pair of Joe Henderson songs. The setting is more advanced than usual for Sims, who rises to the challenge. —*Scott Yanow*

Ephemera / Sep. 10, 1973 / Spotlite ◆◆◆◆

On tour with the Thad Jones-Mel Lewis Orchestra in England, baritonist Pepper Adams took time off to record a fine straightahead quartet session with the big band's rhythm section: pianist Roland Hanna, bassist George Mraz and drummer Mel Lewis. Adams performs four of his obscure originals (most memorable is the melodic title cut), Thad Jones' "Quiet Lady," "Jitterbug Waltz" and a romping version of Bud Powell's classic "Bouncing with Bud." A fine example of the deep-toned baritonist at his best. —*Scott Yanow*

Julian / Aug. 13, 1975 / Inner City ◆◆◆◆

Recorded five days before Julian "Cannonball" Adderley's death, the title cut of this out-of-print LP was retitled and dedicated to the late altoist. The powerful baritonist Pepper Adams is well showcased with a quartet comprising pianist Walter Norris, bassist George Mraz and drummer Makaya Ntshoko on three of his originals, one by Norris and two ("Three and One" and "'Tis") by Thad Jones. Adams is in typically excellent form, playing intense solos that push but stay within the boundaries of hard bop. —*Scott Yanow*

Pepper / Aug. 13, 1975+Feb. 25, 1986 / Enja ◆◆◆◆

This CD reissue has the four numbers recorded by baritone great Pepper Adams for an obscure 1975 Enja quartet LP with pianist Walter Norris, bassist George Mraz and drummer Makaya Ntshoko plus one number apiece from Adams' two Justin Time albums with Denny Christianson's big band in 1986. Although Pepper was seriously ill by the mid-'80s, he plays quite well on his features with the orchestra ("Osage Autumn" and "My Funny Valentine"). However, it is for his numbers with Norris (two originals, "A Child Is Born" and a powerful version of "Well You Needn't") that this fine hard bop-oriented CD is most highly recommended. —*Scott Yanow*

Live / Sep. 18, 1977 / Just Jazz ◆◆◆◆

Baritonist Pepper Adams had a rare chance to really stretch out on this live set from Half Moon Bay, CA. The music, released for the first time on this 1995 CD, really showcases Adams since pianist John Marabuto, bassist Bob Maize and drummer Ron Marabuto are subtle and quite supportive. Adams performs three standards (including versions of "Dewey Square" and "How Long Has This Been Going On" that are over 13 minutes apiece) plus a couple of original blues. A good showcase. —*Scott Yanow*

Reflectory / Jun. 14, 1978 / Muse ◆◆◆◆

Excellent hard-bop vehicle. —*Ron Wynn*

The Master / Mar. 11, 1980 / Muse ◆◆◆◆

A brilliant example of bebop on the baritone sax, it also featured Tommy Flanagan (p), George Mraz (b), and Leroy Williams (d). —*David Szatmary*

Urban Dreams / Sep. 30, 1981 / Palo Alto ◆◆◆◆

It is a real pity that this session from baritonist Pepper Adams was for a now-defunct label for it is one of his best recordings. Adams, accompanied quite tastefully by pianist Jimmy Rowles, bassist George Mraz and drummer Billy Hart, sticks primarily to straightahead material and he often roars through such songs as "Dexter Rides Again," "Three Little Words" and "Pent Up House"; the ballad "Time On My Hands" and his title cut are fine changes of pace. —*Scott Yanow*

Conjuration: Fat Tuesday's Session / Aug. 19, 1983-Aug. 20, 1983 / Reservoir ✦✦✦✦✦

The great baritonist Pepper Adams is teamed up with the adventurous trumpeter Kenny Wheeler and veteran pianist Hank Jones for this live quintet date. Wheeler, although often associated with the avant-garde, has never had any difficulty playing changes and his strong style clearly inspired Adams. Together they perform three of the baritonist's originals, Thad Jones' "Tis," Wheeler's "Old Ballad" and the standard "Alone Together." —*Scott Yanow*

Generations / Jan. 25, 1985 / Muse ✦✦✦

Baritonist Pepper Adams gets first billing on this record but he is actually on only four of the seven cuts. James L. Dean (who is heard on tenor, alto and clarinet) organized the session and it is largely his date, despite the presence of Adams, tenor saxophonist Frank Foster and a fine (if obscure) rhythm section. Bud Powell's "Dance of the Infidels," "Stablemates" and "Titter Pipes" are jams for the entire group, as is Dean's modal "Generations" (which has Vinnie Cutro guesting on trumpet). "Mood In Question" is an Artie Shaw classical piece that Dean plays as a clarinet-piano duet with Noreen Grey while Foster and Dean head the quintet (without Pepper) on "Milestones" and Dean's "Inventory." Overall the modern hard bop music is quite successful, but this album should have come out under Dean's name. —*Scott Yanow*

Adams Effect / Jun. 25, 1985-Jun. 26, 1985 / Uptown ✦✦✦

Baritonist Pepper Adams' final album as a leader (he died 14 months later) matches him with tenor saxophonist Frank Foster, pianist Tommy Flanagan, bassist Ron Carter and drummer Billy Hart for five of his straightahead if occasionally complex originals plus Foster's "How I Spent The Night." Adams still sounded in prime form at the time and, even if none of his tunes became standards, they served as strong and diverse vehicles for the musicians' improvisations. A fine effort by a classic baritone-saxophonist. —*Scott Yanow*

Cannonball Adderley (Julian Edwin Adderley)

b. Sep. 15, 1928, Tampa, FL, **d.** Aug. 8, 1975, Gary, IN
Alto Saxophone / Hard Bop, Soul Jazz, Groove

One of the great alto saxophonists, Cannonball Adderley had an exuberant and happy sound (as opposed to many of the more serious stylists of his generation) that communicated immediately to listeners. His intelligent presentation of his music (often explaining what he and his musicians were going to play) helped make him one of the most popular of all jazzmen.

Adderley already had an established career as a high school band director in Florida when during a 1955 visit to New York he was persuaded to sit in with Oscar Pettiford's group at the Cafe Bohemia. His playing created such a sensation that he was soon signed to Savoy and persuaded to play jazz full-time in New York. With his younger brother cornetist Nat, Cannonball formed a quintet that struggled until its breakup in 1957. Adderley then joined Miles Davis, forming part of his super sextet with John Coltrane and participating on such classic recordings as *Milestones* and *Kind of Blue*. Adderley's second attempt to form a quintet with his brother was much more successful for in 1959 with pianist Bobby Timmons he had a hit recording of "This Here." From then on, Cannonball always was able to work steadily with his band.

During its Riverside years (1959-63) the Adderley Quintet primarily played soulful renditions of hard bop and Cannonball really excelled in the straightahead settings. During 1962-63 Yusef Lateef made the group a sextet and pianist Joe Zawinul was an important new member. The collapse of Riverside resulted in Adderley signing with Capitol and his recordings became gradually more commercial. Charles Lloyd was in Lateef's place for a year (with less success) and then with his departure the group went back to being a quintet. Zawinul's 1966 composition "Mercy, Mercy, Mercy" was a huge hit for the group, Adderley started doubling on soprano and the Quintet's later recordings emphasized long melody statements, funky rhythms and electronics. However during his last year, Cannonball Adderley was revisiting the past a bit and on *Phenix* he recorded new versions of many of his earlier numbers. But before he could evolve his music any further, Cannonball Adderley died suddenly from a stroke. —*Scott Yanow*

The Adderleys: Cannonball & Nat / Jun. 26, 1955-Jul. 26, 1955 / Savoy ✦✦✦

This CD features altoist Cannonball Adderley and his brother Nat at the beginning of their recording careers, starting just seven days after Cannonball caused a sensation when he sat in with Oscar Pettiford's group at the Cafe Bohemia. Actually, a close look at the recording details show that the first six selections are alternate takes taken from their first sessions and that the remainder of this set features Nat without Cannonball, mostly in a quintet with Jerome Richardson (who doubles on

flute and tenor). Collectors who already have the original Cannonball recordings will find these alternates of great interest. In general the music is high-powered bop by two fine musicians in the early stages of developing their own styles. —*Scott Yanow*

Spontaneous Combustion / Jun. 28, 1955-Jul. 14, 1955 / Savoy ✦✦✦✦

This valuable two-LP set features altoist Cannonball Adderley's first recordings, cut just days after the unknown had greatly impressed musicians when he sat in with Oscar Pettiford's group at the Cafe Bohemia. He is quite impressive throughout, holding his own in an all-star octet led by drummer Kenny Clarke with trumpeter Donald Byrd, brother Nat on cornet, Jerome Richardson on reeds and pianist Horace Silver. The second half of this two-fer is the first of many quintet dates he led with Nat. This near-classic music is highlighted by "Bohemia After Talk," Nat's feature on "We'll Be Together Again," "A Little Taste" and the title cut. —*Scott Yanow*

Cannonball / Jul. 21, 1955 / EmArcy ✦✦✦

Compact Jazz: Cannonball Adderley / Jul. 1955-Jan. 1962 / EmArcy ✦✦

Decent anthology of Cannonball Adderley's mid- and late-period material, weighted toward both recognizable, popular soul-jazz material and shorter, less involved songs, with plenty of hard-charging solos by Cannonball, Nat, and the crew. Like most compilations, it provides a good introduction to his work, and works best for those with limited knowledge. —*Ron Wynn*

With Strings/Jump for Joy / Oct. 27, 1955-Aug. 21, 1958 / Polygram ✦✦✦✦

This CD reissues two complete LPs from near the beginning of altoist Cannonball Adderley's career. The first session is quite unusual for Adderley (who was completely unknown just a few months earlier) was given a very early opportunity to record with strings and Terry Gibbs' "Lonely Dreams" but mostly sticks near the melody while Richard Hayman's Orchestra sounds rather anonymous. The 1958 sessions finds him performing ten songs from the early-'40s Duke Ellington show *Jump for Joy* (including "Just Squeeze Me," "I Got It Bad" and "Jump for Joy") while accompanied by a string quartet, a rhythm section and trumpeter Emmett Berry; Bill Russo provided the generally stimulating arrangements. The formerly rare music on this CD is enjoyable but not as essential as Adderley's slightly later Riverside albums. —*Scott Yanow*

In the Land of Hi-Fi / Jun. 8, 1956+Jun. 18, 1956 / EmArcy ✦✦✦

Sophisticated Swing: The EmArcy Small Group Sessions / Jul. 12, 1956-Mar. 6, 1958 / EmArcy ✦✦✦✦✦

Reissued in this two-CD set are all of the recordings from the first Cannonball Adderley Quintet, a group that despite its talents failed commercially. With Cannonball on alto, cornetist Nat Adderley, pianist Junior Mance, bassist Sam Jones and drummer Jimmy Cobb, it is surprising that the group did not make it but the Adderleys were fairly unknown at the time. The music is quite bop-oriented, bluesy but not as soulful as it would be when Cannonball put together a new group in 1959. This set reissues all of the music originally included on Nat Adderley's *To the Ivy League from Nat*, and Cannonball's *Sophisticated Swing, Cannonball Enroute* and *Sharpshooters* (except for one trio feature without the horns) plus a few cuts not released until the CD era. The generous reissue not only gives one a fine sampling of the first Cannonball Adderley Quintet but everything they recorded. Highly recommended to bop fans. —*Scott Yanow*

Verve Jazz Masters, Vol. 31 / 1956-1958 / Polygram ✦✦✦

★ **Somethin' Else** / Mar. 9, 1958 / Blue Note ✦✦✦✦✦

Shortly after Adderley broke up his original quintet and joined Miles Davis' sextet, he recorded this LP with Davis in the rare role of a sideman. Actually Davis dominates several of the selections (including "Autumn Leaves," "Love for Sale" and "One for Daddy-O") but both hornmen (backed by pianist Hank Jones, bassist Sam Jones and drummer Art Blakey) sound quite inspired by each other's presence. —*Scott Yanow*

Jazz Profile / Mar. 9, 1958-Oct. 20, 1966 / Capitol ✦✦✦

Cannonball Adderley only recorded once as a leader for Blue Note, but this sampler manages to cover most of his prime years. There are cuts taken from the Riverside catalog ("Au Privave" with Wes Montgomery, "Sack o' Woe" and "Gemini"), plus Adderley's big Capitol hit "Mercy, Mercy, Mercy," "One for Daddy-O" (taken from the Blue Note set with Miles Davis as a sideman), and a previously unreleased "Bohemia After Dark" from 1966. The latter (a hot uptempo version taken from a Japanese concert) will drive completists mad, since they will undoubtedly already own all of the rest of the material. For beginners, this is an excellent overview of the exuberant altoist's bop-oriented years, before he gradually switched to funkier sounds. —*Scott Yanow*

Portrait of Cannonball / Jul. 1, 1958 / Original Jazz Classics ✦✦✦✦

Adderley's first album for Riverside, recorded while he was working as a sideman in Miles Davis' classic sextet. W/ Blue Mitchell (tpt), Bill Evans (p), Sam Jones (b), and Philly Joe Jones (d). —*Michael Erlewine*

Alabama Concerto / Jul. 28, 1958-Aug. 2, 1958 / Original Jazz Classics ✦✦✦

This is one of the more unusual sessions that altoist Cannonball Adderley recorded during his career. Originally released under composer John Benson Brooks' name and now available as an Adderley CD, the nine-part four-movement suite has original folk melodies interpreted by a quartet comprising Adderley, trumpeter Art Farmer, guitarist Barry Galbraith and bassist Milt Hinton; Brooks briefly plays piano on one piece. Although not essential, the music is thought-provoking and quite melodic, and looks backwards toward folk music of the 1800s while giving the pieces a 1950s jazz sensibility. —*Scott Yanow*

★ **Things Are Getting Better** / Oct. 28, 1958 / Original Jazz Classics ✦✦✦✦✦

Cannonball Adderley teams up with vibraphonist Milt Jackson, pianist Wynton Kelly, bassist Percy Heath and drummer Art Blakey for a jubilant and often-explosive session on this CD reissue. On tunes such as "Things Are Getting Better," "Just One of Those Things" and a memorable "Sidewalks of New York," the altoist-leader is quite joyful in his solos, really ripping into the material. This set is a very good example of early Cannonball Adderley, recorded a year before his quintet caught on. —*Scott Yanow*

● **Cannonball and Coltrane** / Feb. 3, 1959 / EmArcy ✦✦✦✦✦

This LP (whose contents have been reissued many times) features the Miles Davis Sextet of 1959 without the leader. Altoist Cannonball Adderley and tenor saxophonist John Coltrane really push each other on these six selections with this version of "Limehouse Blues" really burning. Coltrane's very serious sound is a striking contrast to the jubilant Adderley alto; the latter is showcased on "Stars Fell on Alabama." With pianist Wynton Kelly, bassist Paul Chambers and drummer Jimmy Cobb playing up to their usual level, this gem is highly recommended. —*Scott Yanow*

Cannonball Adderley Collection, Vol. 6: Cannonball Takes Charge / Apr. 23, 1959-May 12, 1959 / Landmark ✦✦✦

Adderley was on the verge of leaving Miles Davis' Sextet when he recorded the seven titles and two alternates that this LP comprises, the sixth in a seven-volume series of Riverside dates reissued by producer Orrin Keepnews. Accompanied by pianist Wynton Kelly and alternating bassists and drummers, Adderley is in fine form on these standards with the emphasis leaning a bit toward ballads and blues. Highlights include "Serenata," "Poor Butterfly" and two versions of "I Remember You." —*Scott Yanow*

● **Cannonball Adderley Quintet in San Francisco** / Oct. 18, 1959+Oct. 20, 1959 / Original Jazz Classics ✦✦✦✦✦

Cannonball Adderley had struggled unsuccessfully with a quintet during 1955-57, giving up for a time to play with Miles Davis' group. In 1959 his new quintet suddenly caught on with the release of this very exciting live album, which has been reissued on CD in the Original Jazz Classics series. With cornetist Nat Adderley, pianist Bobby Timmons, bassist Sam Jones and drummer Louis Hayes, Cannonball had the top new jazz group of 1959. Their version of Timmons' "This Here" was a major hit and the other numbers on this famous date (which include "Spontaneous Combustion," "Hi-Fly," "You Got It," "Bohemia After Dark" and "Straight, No Chaser") are also quite enjoyable, showing why Cannonball Adderley's group was a pacesetter in funky soul jazz and proving that they could outswing most of their competition. This gem is essential for all jazz collections. —*Scott Yanow*

Cannonball Adderley Collection, Vol. 1: Them Dirty Blues / Feb. 1, 1960 / Landmark ✦✦✦✦

The first of seven LPs that reissue recordings from his period with Riverside contains several notable selections. The first side (which has pianist Bobby Timmons well-featured with bassist Sam Jones, drummer Louis Hayes, cornetist Nat Adderley and the leader/altoist) includes the original versions of Timmons' "Dat Dere" (his follow-up to "This Here" which is heard here in two takes), Sam Jones' "Del Sasser" and Nat's "Work Song"; the latter was previously unissued. On the flip side (with Barry Harris in Timmons' place), the quintet performs the initial "official" version of "Work Song," a heated "Jeannine," "Easy Living" and "Them Dirty Blues." Lots of classic music comes from this influential soul-jazz band. —*Scott Yanow*

Cannonball Adderley Collection, Vol. 4: The Poll Winners / May 21, 1960-Jun. 5, 1960 / Landmark ✦✦✦✦

The "Poll-Winners" at the time of this recording were Adderley, guitarist Wes Montgomery and bassist Ray Brown; together with Victor Feldman doubling on piano and vibes and drummer Louis Hayes they cut this excellent quintet date. This was the only meeting on records by Adderley and Montgomery and, although not quite a classic encounter, the music (highlighted by "The Chant," "Never Will I Marry" and two takes of "Au Privave") swings hard and is quite enjoyable. —*Scott Yanow*

Cannonball Adderley Collection, Vol. 5: The Quintet at The Lighthouse / Oct. 16, 1960 / Landmark ✦✦✦✦

This is a fine all-around set from the Cannonball Adderley Quintet of 1960 with the altoist/leader, cornetist Nat Adderley, pianist Victor Feldman, bassist Sam Jones and drummer Louis Hayes. The fifth of seven LPs reissued by Orrin Keepnews and taken from Adderley's Riverside years finds his band in top form on the original version of "Sack o' Woe," a previously unissued "Our Delight," Jimmy Heath's "Big 'P'" and "Blue Daniel" among others. It's a strong introduction to the music of this classic hard bop group. —*Scott Yanow*

What Is This Thing Called Soul? / Nov. 22, 1960-Nov. 23, 1960 / Original Jazz Classics ✦✦✦✦

Cannonball Adderley's 1960 Quintet (with cornetist Nat Adderley and pianist Victor Feldman) was in top form during their tour of Europe. Norman Granz did not release the music heard on this CD until almost 25 years after the fact but the strong solos and enthusiastic ensembles had not dated nor faded with time. These versions of "The Chant," "What Is This Thing Called Love?" and "Big 'P'" make for interesting comparisons with the better-known renditions. Adderley fans will want this set. —*Scott Yanow*

Paris 1960 / Nov. 25, 1960 / Pablo ✦✦✦

Norman Granz was on hand to record music from Cannonball Adderley's first European tour in 1960, but he and the Adderley estate have been parsimonious in dealing out the goods. It took 24 years for Part One, *What Is This Thing Called Soul?* to emerge, and another 13 years passed before this follow-up album came out. But better late than never, as they say, and the reward is hearing Cannonball's alto in full ecstatic flight, lots of fighting work from brother Nat on cornet and the prized rhythm section of Victor Feldman (piano), Sam Jones (bass) and Louis Hayes (drums) in a state of complete rapport. Only "The Chant" is duplicated from the earlier album, and Cannonball's solo is a model of Parker-derived hard bop laced with his own highly rhythmic personality. Other than an overlong drum solo on "Bohemia After Dark," this is a most enjoyable slice of what, alas, is now history. —*Richard S. Ginell*

African Waltz / Feb. 8, 1961-May 15, 1961 / Original Jazz Classics ✦✦

The music on this CD reissue is better than it should be. Cannonball Adderley had a fluke hit with "African Waltz," so a full album was recorded with the hope of coming up with additional hits. These 11 selections (which include "African Waltz") feature altoist Adderley backed by an 18-piece big band with arrangements provided by Ernie Wilkins and Bob Brookmeyer. The tunes clock in between two-five minutes and leave little room for much improvising by anyone other than Cannonball, his brother Nat on cornet and pianist Wynton Kelly. There is some strong material on the set (including "West Coast Blues," "Stockholm Sweetnin'" and a remake of "This Here") but the results are not too substantial and this was not that big a seller. A lesser but still reasonably enjoyable effort. —*Scott Yanow*

The Quintet Plus / May 11, 1961 / Original Jazz Classics ✦✦✦✦

For this CD reissue of a Riverside date, altoist Cannonball Adderley's 1961 Quintet (which includes cornetist Nat Adderley, pianist Victor Feldman, bassist Sam Jones and drummer Louis Hayes) is joined by guest pianist Wynton Kelly on five of the eight selections, during which Feldman switches quite effectively to vibes. The music falls between funky soul-jazz and hard bop, and each of the performances (particularly "Star Eyes" and "Well You Needn't") is enjoyable. The CD adds a new alternate take of "Lisa" and the previously unissued "O.P." to the original program. —*Scott Yanow*

In New York / Jan. 12, 1962+Jan. 14, 1962 / Original Jazz Classics ✦✦✦✦

This album (reissued on CD) was the recording debut of altoist Cannonball Adderley's strongest group, his sextet with brother Nat on cornet, Yusef Lateef on tenor, oboe and flute, pianist Joe Zawinul, bassist Sam Jones and drummer Louis Hayes. All of Lateef's 1962-63 recordings with Adderley are well worth acquiring. This live set (recorded at the Village Vanguard) has plenty of variety and is highlighted by "Gemini," the boppish "Dizzy's Business" and "Scotch and Water." —*Scott Yanow*

Cannonball Adderley Collection, Vol. 7: Cannonball in Europe / Aug. 5, 1962 / Landmark ✦✦✦✦

Adderley led what was arguably his finest group during 1962-63, a sextet with brother Nat on cornet, Yusef Lateef on flute, oboe and tenor, pianist Joe Zawinul, bassist Sam Jones and drummer Louis Hayes. This excellent LP (whose contents were never previously available in the US) is highlighted by Jimmy Heath's "Gemini," "Work Song," a lengthy "Trouble in Mind" and the exciting "Dizzy's Business." Lateef fit into this band perfectly, giving the unit a fresh and distinctive voice. All of his recordings with Adderley are easily recommended. —*Scott Yanow*

The Sextet / Sep. 21, 1962-Jul. 19, 1963 / Milestone ✦✦✦
This excellent LP features the Cannonball Adderley Sextet (with cornetist Nat Adderley and Yusef Lateef on tenor and flute) of 1962-63. Because most of this material had been recorded just a couple years earlier, these versions of such songs as "This Here," "Bohemia After Dark" and "New Delhi" were unissued until the 1980s. The music remains quite exciting and fresh for, although somewhat overshadowed at the time, this was one of the great jazz groups of the 1960s. —Scott Yanow

Cannonball Adderley Collection, Vol. 3: Jazz Workshop Revisited / Sep. 22, 1962-Sep. 23, 1962 / Landmark ✦✦✦✦
Three years after having a surprise hit ("This Here") recorded live at The Jazz Workshop in San Francisco, Cannonball Adderley and his sextet (featuring cornetist Nat Adderley and Yusef Latef on tenor, flute and oboe) returned to the club and recorded this particularly rewarding LP, reissued by Orrin Keepnews on his Landmark label. The material was challenging but hard-swinging, including "Primitivo," "Jessica's Days," "Mellow Buno" and Nat Adderley's new composition "The Jive Samba." A previously unknown version of the classic "Unit 7" was substituted for the Sam Jones ballad "Lillie" with this issue. Every recording by this particular unit is well worth acquiring. —Scott Yanow

Cannonball Adderley Collection, Vol. 2: Bossa Nova / Dec. 7, 1962-Dec. 11, 1962 / Landmark ✦✦✦
Recorded when the bossa nova craze was generating steam, this was one of the better albums of the genre. Cannonball Adderley wisely cut his lone bossa nova record with South American musicians, a group called the Bossa Rio Sextet that included pianist Sergio Mendes and future Weather Report member Dom Um Romao on drums. Adderley's sound on alto was well attuned to this music (as was his upbeat musical personality), as can be heard on "Once I Loved" and two versions of "Corcovado." —Scott Yanow

The Best of Cannonball Adderley / 1962-1969 / Blue Note ✦✦
It contains "Mercy, Mercy, Mercy" and Adderley's most successful jazz/gospel/pop fusion work with Joe Zawinul (k). —Hank Davis

Lugano, 1963 / Mar. 24, 1963 / TCB ✦✦✦✦✦
This Italian concert (broadcast by Swiss radio) features the 1963 Cannonball Adderley Sextet which was arguably the altoist's finest band. In addition to the leader, the performance features cornetist Nat Adderley, the versatile Yusef Lateef on tenor, flute and oboe, pianist Joe Zawinul, bassist Sam Jones and drummer Louis Hayes. Highlights include "Jive Samba," "Dizzy's Business," a lengthy "Trouble in Mind" and "Work Song" but all seven selections are quite rewarding. Cannonball Adderley fans can consider every recording by this classic unit to be essential. —Scott Yanow

Dizzy's Business / July 9, 1963 / Milestone ✦✦✦
Although the nine songs on this new Cannonball Adderley reissue were originally done live at concerts in Japan and San Francisco in 1963, they nevertheless make a nice tribute to recently departed jazz giant Dizzy Gillespie. The assembled group was among the finest Adderley ever led, with Yusef Lateef providing a dynamic, unpredictable third solo voice on flute, tenor sax and oboe contrasting with Cannonball's pungent alto sax and Nat Adderley's pithy cornet solos. Bassist Sam Jones and drummer Louis Hayes were a top-flight tandem, while Joe Zawinul was then playing bluesy, funky piano in his pre-synthesizer, Miles Davis/Weather Report phase. Everything is illustrative of a prime band enjoying some great nights. —Ron Wynn

Japanese Concerts / Jul. 9, 1963-Jul. 15, 1963 / Milestone ✦✦✦✦✦
Cannonball Adderley's finest group (his sextet with cornetist Nat Adderley, Yusef Lateef on tenor, flute and oboe, pianist Joe Zawinul, bassist Sam Jones and drummer Louis Hayes) is heard at the peak of their powers on this two-LP set. The first half was previously released as Nippon Soul while the second LP was only issued for the first time in 1975. After a period of stable personnel (all but Zawinul and Lateef had been in the band since 1959), these musicians were very familiar with each other's playing and they had grown together. The enthusiastic Japanese crowds inspired the all-star band to some of their most rewarding playing, which can be heard on such standouts as "Nippon Soul," "Come Sunday," "Work Song," "Dizzy's Business" and "Jive Samba" among others. It's a definitive portrait of a classic group. —Scott Yanow

Nippon Soul / Jul. 14, 1963+Jul. 15, 1963 / Original Jazz Classics ✦✦✦
First live jazz album. Recorded in Tokyo by Cannonball Adderley, with Yusef Lateef (ts). —Michael G. Nastos

Cannonball Adderley—Live! / Aug. 1, 1964-Aug. 2, 1964 / Capitol ✦✦✦
When Riverside Records went into bankruptcy, Adderley signed with Capitol, a label whose interest in jazz tended to be short-lived. As a result, Cannonball's recordings would become more commercial as the 1960s developed, but this early Capitol effort is quite good. Charles Lloyd had just joined Adderley's Sextet and

his tenor and flute were major assets; he contributed two of the four songs ("Sweet Georgia Bright" and "The Song My Lady Sings") to this fine session, which also includes Nat Adderley's "Little Boy with the Sad Eyes" and yet another version of "Work Song." —Scott Yanow

Fiddler on the Roof / Oct. 19, 1964-Oct. 21, 1964 / Capitol ✦✦✦✦
It is a bit strange that none of the eight songs performed on this LP found their way into Adderley's permanent repertoire, for the altoist is quite inspired throughout this surprising set. With strong assists from cornetist Nat Adderley, Charles Lloyd on tenor and flute, pianist Joe Zawinul, bassist Sam Jones and drummer Louis Hayes, Cannonball plays near his peak; this is certainly the finest album by this particular sextet. —Scott Yanow

Domination / Apr. 26, 1965 / Capitol ✦✦
Cannonball and Nat Adderley are joined by an unidentified orchestra arranged by Oliver Nelson for this decent outing. None of the eight performances are all that memorable (and pale next to Cannonball's earlier recordings with Gil Evans), but the music is enjoyable enough. This LP has been out of print for years. —Scott Yanow

Cannonball Live in Japan / Aug. 26, 1966 / Capitol ✦✦
Performing some of their finest songs ("Work Song," "Mercy, Mercy, Mercy," "This Here," "Money in the Pocket, "The Sticks" and "Jive Samba"), the Cannonball Adderley Quintet is strangely uninspired during this Japanese concert, just going through the motions. Perhaps they were already tired of this material or maybe it was jet lag. In any case, this CD is a disappointment. —Scott Yanow

Mercy, Mercy, Mercy / Oct. 20, 1966 / Capitol ✦✦✦✦✦
This set (reissued on CD) is one of Cannonball Adderley's finest albums of his last decade. "Mercy, Mercy, Mercy," a soulful Joe Zawinul melody that is repeated several times without any real improvisation, became a surprise hit, but the other selections on this live date ("Fun," "Games," "Sticks," "Hippodelphia" and "Sack o' Woe") all have plenty of fiery solos from the quintet (which comprises the leader on alto, cornetist Nat Adderley, pianist Joe Zawinul, bassist Victor Gaskin, and drummer Roy McCurdy). Cannonball sounds quite inspired (his expressive powers had expanded due to the unacknowledged influence of the avant-garde) and Nat shows just how exciting a player he was back in his prime. "Sack o' Woe" is particularly memorable. This CD, which is far superior to most of Cannonball's later Capitol recordings, is highly recommended. —Scott Yanow

Why Am I Treated So Bad? / 1967 / Capitol ✦✦
The follow-up album to Cannonball Adderley's major hit Mercy, Mercy, Mercy is surprisingly forgettable. The group originals are run-of-the-mill and the solos by the altoist/leader, cornetist Nat Adderley and keyboardist Joe Zawinul, although decent enough, are hardly inspiring. This LP has been out of print for quite some time. —Scott Yanow

Radio Nights / 1967-1968 / Night ✦✦✦
This CD contains private recordings of Cannonball Adderley's groups during 1967-68 playing at the Half Note in New York City. The music is quite worthy with altoist Cannonball Adderley featured in a quartet setting on "Stars Fell on Alabama," performing three songs with his quintet (including "Fiddler on the Roof") and playing three other pieces (highlighted by "Work Song" and "Unit Seven") with the sextet he had that featured Charles Lloyd on tenor. This music is generally superior to Adderley's commercial Capitol recordings of the period. —Scott Yanow

Accent on Africa / Jun. 13, 1968-Jun. 14, 1968 / Capitol ✦✦✦
Though labeled as a Cannonball Adderley Quintet session, this is actually a workout with a percussion section loaded with African drums, a big band, and spots, voices—all unidentified. Nevertheless, this is one of the best and most overlooked of the Cannonball Adderley Capitols, a rumbling session that bursts with the joy of working in an unfamiliar yet vital rhythmic context. Cannonball turns in one of his swinging-est solos through a Varitone electronic attachment on Caiphus Semenya's "Gumba Gumba" and "Marabi" is a real hip-jiggler; you can't sit still through it. Other highlights include Cannon preaching blue smoke in his own Afro-Cuban-blues-flavored "Hamba Nami," a dignified trip through Wes Montgomery's "Up and At It," and Nat Adderley's commanding work on cornet at all times. —Richard S. Ginell

Cannonball Adderley and His Quintet / Mar. 27, 1969 / RTE ✦✦
This concert recording, released for the first time in the US in 1994, features Cannonball Adderley's 1969 quintet, a unit that also included cornetist Nat Adderley, keyboardist Joe Zawinul, bassist Victor Gaskin and drummer Roy McCurdy. Cannonball, whose music had gradually moved beyond bop as it became influenced by rock, funk and the avant-garde, is actually booed a bit on this set by the French audience who expected him to be playing the same songs as a decade earlier. Actually the altoist is in excellent form and the music (which includes "Black Orpheus" and "Work Song" along with newer material by Zawinul) is generally

superior to his Capitol studio recordings of the era. Despite the mixed reaction (which makes Cannonball's usually enthusiastic talks to the audience a bit downbeat), this is an excellent example of late-period Adderley. —*Scott Yanow*

Country Preacher / Oct. 1969 / Capitol ✦✦
This live benefit for Jesse Jackson's Operation Breadbasket in 1969 has been reissued as a CD. There are some decent moments (particularly "Walk Tall" and the original version of "Hummin'"), but there are also quite a few weak spots including cornetist Nat Adderley's vocal on "Oh Babe," the unmemorable four-part Afro-Spanish "Omlet" and the title cut (which is in a similar vein as the then-recent hit "Mercy, Mercy, Mercy"). Cannonball Adderley, although fine in his brief alto and soprano spots, at this point in his career was delegating far too much solo space to his rhythm section, making this a lesser effort. —*Scott Yanow*

The Price You Got to Pay to Be Free / Sep. 14, 1970-Sep. 19, 1970 / Capitol ✦✦✦
Jazz was undergoing a sea change in 1970 thanks to Miles Davis' electronic and structural breakthroughs, and his former sideman Cannonball Adderley was right in the thick of things (the two leaders shared musicians and traded influences during this period). Like Miles, the Adderleys expanded their canvas to double LPs—this live album being the first of a series in the double-pocket format—and each side would be organized into nearly continuous medleys. Not only that, Cannonball still had Joe Zawinul on board, who greatly altered the texture of Cannonball's music with his floating electric piano and science-fiction interludes with a ring modulator (this would be his last album with the Quintet). Still, Cannonball was a populist at heart, and his generosity of spirit shines through this often deliciously diverse album, which ranges wildly from flat-out soul to Brazilian music to a cautious toedip into the avant-garde. Along the way, we hear vocals from both Adderleys (including an exceedingly rare yet oddly charming one from Cannon on Milton Nascimento's challenging "Bridges"), a stunningly touching Cannonball testament on soprano in "Some Time Ago" and alto solos that definitely show that Cannonball had absorbed the Coltrane vocabulary. One can do without guest Nat Adderley, Jr.'s cliched anti-Nixon sloganeering on the title tune (granted, he was only 15 years old) but again, his presence testifies to the close-knit, liberal family atmosphere that Cannonball encouraged. This is a fascinating contemporary snapshot of the Quintet, whose later recordings are too casually dismissed these days. —*Richard S. Ginell*

Black Messiah / 1972 / Capitol ✦✦
This is an odd double LP in that the music, which sounded so contemporary in 1972, now comes across as a bit dated. The Cannonball Adderley Quintet (which at the time featured George Duke on keyboards) was joined by percussionist Airto and on some tracks tenor saxophonist Ernie Watts, guitarist/vocalist Mike Deasy, clarinetist Alvin Batiste and percussionist Buck Clark. The rhythm section is excessively funky at times and the many stylists clash a bit (Batiste in particular is out of place). The strongest performances are "The Black Messiah," "Dr. Honouris Cousa" and "The Chocolate Nuisance," but there is a lot of fat on this rather loose two-fer. —*Scott Yanow*

Inside Straight / Jun. 4, 1973 / Original Jazz Classics ✦✦✦
After seven years with Capitol, Cannonball Adderley switched labels to Fantasy where he reunited with producer Orrin Keepnews and the quality of his music immediately improved. With Hal Galper as the band's keyboardist (he contributed three of the seven group originals to this LP), this version of the Quintet (actually Sextet with the addition of percussionist King Errison) was more jazz-oriented than previously, while remaining modern and funky. —*Scott Yanow*

Pyramid / 1974 / Original Jazz Classics ✦✦✦
Cannonball Adderley is in generally good form on this 1974 recording. His Quintet at the time featured cornetist Nat Adderley, keyboardist Hal Galper, bassist Walter Booker and drummer Roy McCurdy. Guests on some selections include guitarist Phil Upchurch, keyboardist George Duke and (on "Bess, Oh Where's My Bess") veteran pianist Jimmy Jones. The emphasis is on recent group originals including the three-part "Suite Cannon," two Galper compositions and Cannonball's "Pyramid." Nothing too earthshattering occurs, but this is an improvement over many of Adderley's Capitol recordings. —*Scott Yanow*

Big Man / 1975 / Fantasy ✦✦
Few had any idea of how large Cannonball Adderley's ambitions were until the release of this project shortly after his sudden death in 1975. Helped by his brother Nat, the big man composed music for a full-blown, nearly-hour-long theatre piece, which he called a "folk musical." The subject is John Henry, the mythical black hero who is inflated here by librettists Diane Lampert and Peter Farrow into a God-like behemoth who singlehandedly built most of the universe himself before descending to earth in his spare time to compete against a mere steam drill. Alas, it's too bad there wasn't a John Henry on hand here to repair this score, for *Big Man* is an eclectic hash almost completely devoid of any memorable passages and textures. There is a good-sized orchestra as well as a rhythm section on hand, but the Adderleys feed them watered-down gospel, lackluster tunes, and some pale

second-hand grooves from the Quintet's electronic-tinged period. Jazz content is surprisingly scarce; Cannonball's alto doesn't surface until Side 4, and then only briefly. As per the script, Joe Williams is a truly heroic, soulful, almost larger-than-life John Henry and Randy Crawford makes a sexy debut on records in the role of Big John's woman Carolina. Yet this is a case of ambition greatly outrunning inspiration, an intended monument that became only a footnote in the great alto player's career. —*Richard S. Ginell*

Phenix / Feb. 1975-Apr. 1975 / Fantasy ✦✦✦✦
Adderley's next-to-last recording (cut just four months before he died of a stroke at age 46) was ironically a retrospective of his career. While his then-current group (with cornetist Nat Adderley, keyboardist Mike Wolff, bassist Walter Booker and drummer Roy McCurdy) was featured on half of this two-fer (highlighted by "Stars Fell on Alabama," "74 Miles Away" and a medley of "Walk Tall" and "Mercy, Mercy, Mercy"), on the remainder of this two-LP set the Adderleys welcome back several alumni (keyboardist George Duke, bassist Sam Jones and drummer Louis Hayes) for new versions of "High Fly," "Work Song," "Sack o' Woe," "Jive Samba," "This Here" and "The Sidewalks of New York." A recommended set with plenty of excellent music, it serves as a fine overview of Cannonball Adderley's career. —*Scott Yanow*

Lovers / Jun. 24, 1975-Oct. 31, 1975 / Fantasy ✦✦
Cannonball Adderley's death on Aug. 8, 1975 was a major surprise to the jazz world because, although he had long been overweight, he was only 46 when he died from a stroke. This LP was already more than half completed when Adderley taking his last solos on three of the selections. The group he had utilized was quite unusual with Cannonball and cornetist Nat Adderley joined by Alvin Batiste (on electric clarinet, flute and tenor), keyboardist George Duke, bassist Alphonso Johnson, drummer Jack DeJohnette and percussionist Airto. Batiste and Nat have individual features but unfortunately none of the music is all that memorable; Hermeto Pascoal's "Nascente" comes the closest. After Cannonball's death "Lovers" (which had been planned for the album) was recorded as a memorial with Flora Purim on the vocal, Nat Adderley, Batiste, Duke and Nat Adderley Jr. on keyboards, bassists Johnson and Ron Carter, DeJohnette and Airto. The intentions were honorable but the music is fairly forgettable. —*Scott Yanow*

Nat Adderley

b. Nov. 25, 1931, Tampa, FL
Cornet / Hard Bop, Soul Jazz, Groove

Nat Adderley's cornet (which in its early days was strongly influenced by Miles Davis) was always a complementary voice to his brother Cannonball in their popular quintet. His career ran parallel to his older brother's for quite some time. Nat took up trumpet in 1946, switched to cornet in 1950 and spent time in the military, playing in an Army band during 1951-53. After a period with Lionel Hampton (1954-55), Nat made his recording debut in 1955, joined Cannonball's unsuccessful quintet of 1956-57 and then spent periods with the groups of J.J. Johnson and Woody Herman before hooking up with Cannonball again in Oct. 1959. This time the group became a major success and Nat remained in the quintet until Cannonball's death in 1975, contributing such originals as "Work Song," "Jive Samba" and "The Old Country" along with many exciting hard bop solos. Nat Adderley, who was at the peak of his powers in the early to mid-'60s and became adept at playing solos that dipped into the subtone register of his horn, has led his own quintets since Cannonball's death; his most notable sidemen were altoists Sonny Fortune (in the early '80s) and Vincent Herring. Although his own playing has declined somewhat (Adderley's chops no longer have the endurance of his earlier days), Nat has continued recording worthwhile sessions. Many but not all of his recordings through the years (for such labels as Savoy, EmArcy, Riverside, Jazzland, Atlantic, Milestone, A&M, Capitol, Prestige, Steeple Chase, Galaxy, Theresa, In & Out, Landmark, Evidence, Enja, Timeless, Jazz Challenge and Chiaroscuro) are currently available. —*Scott Yanow*

That's Nat Adderley / Jul. 26, 1955 / Savoy ✦✦✦
Early material from Nat Adderley. His pithy, pungent trumpet and cornet work is effective in a hard bop context, although his own work outside his brother's group has never seemed quite as effective, plus his backing group included Kenny Clarke in a non-Modern Jazz Quartet role, plus pianist Hank Jones, bassist Wendell Marshall, and Jerome Richardson on tenor sax and flute, playing with more punch than on either his Quincy Jones or Oliver Nelson large group dates. —*Ron Wynn*

Introducing Nat Adderley / Sep. 6, 1955 / EmArcy ✦✦✦
To the Ivy League from Nat / Jul. 12, 1956 / EmArcy ✦✦✦✦
Branching Out / Sep. 1958 / Original Jazz Classics ✦✦✦✦
Cornetist Nat Adderley's debut for Riverside (reissued on CD in the OJC series) was recorded about a year before he permanently rejoined his brother Cannonball Adderley's quintet. Teamed with tenor saxophonist Johnny Griffin and the Three

Sounds (the popular soul jazz rhythm section comprising pianist Gene Harris, bassist Andy Simpkins and drummer Bill Dowdy), Nat is in excellent form on such tunes as "Well You Needn't," "Don't Get Around Much Anymore" and "I Never Knew" in addition to two of his lesser-known originals. Adderley and Griffin made for an exciting front line. —*Scott Yanow*

Much Brass / Mar. 23, 1959+Mar. 27, 1959 / Original Jazz Classics ✦✦✦✦

● **Work Song** / Jan. 25, 1960-Jan. 27, 1960 / Original Jazz Classics ✦✦✦✦✦
This CD reissue brings back a near-classic by cornetist Nat Adderley. Utilizing a cornet-cello-guitar front line (with Sam Jones and Wes Montgomery) along with a top-notch rhythm section (pianist Bobby Timmons, Percy Heath or Keter Betts on bass and drummer Louis Hayes), Adderley performs a fine early version of his greatest hit ("Work Song") and helps introduce Cannonball Adderley's "Sack o' Woe." Four songs use a smaller group, with Timmons absent on "My Heart Stood Still" (which finds Keter Betts on cello and Jones on bass), "Mean to Me" featuring Nat backed by Montgomery, Betts and Hayes and two ballads ("I've Got a Crush on You" and "Violets for Your Furs") interpreted by the Adderley-Montgomery-Jones trio. No matter the setting, Nat Adderley is heard throughout in peak form, playing quite lyrically. Highly recommended. —*Scott Yanow*

That's Right! Nat Adderley & the Big Sax Section / Aug. 9, 1960+Sep. 15, 1960 / Original Jazz Classics ✦✦✦✦✦
Nat Adderley has seldom played with more fire, verve and distinction than he did on *That's Right!* It placed him in the company of an expanded sax section that included his brother Cannonball on alto, Yusef Lateef on tenor, flute and oboe, Jimmy Heath and Charlie Rouse on tenor and baritone saxophonist Tate Houston. Solos crackled, the backing was tasty and stimulating, and the eight songs ranged from brisk standards to delightful originals. This CD reissue, despite lacking any new or alternate material, is most welcome due to the full, striking sound that the big reed section provided. —*Ron Wynn*

Naturally! / Jun. 20, 1961 / Jazzland ✦✦✦

In the Bag / May 9, 1962 / Original Jazz Classics ✦✦
This CD reissue (which as an earlier LP reissue came out under Cannonball Adderley's name with the title of *The Adderley Brothers In New Orleans*) was a bit unusual, for cornetist Nat Adderley and altoist Cannonball (along with bassist Sam Jones) teamed up with three of the more significant modern New Orleans musicians of the 1960s: Nat Perrilliat on tenor, drummer James Black and the then-unknown pianist Ellis Marsalis. The repertoire they perform is quite fresh, but there is less excitement than one might hope and the musicians do not really form a unified group sound despite some strong individual moments. —*Scott Yanow*

Natural Soul / Sep. 23, 1963 / Milestone ✦✦✦
With Kenny Burrell (g) and Junior Mance (p). —*Michael Erlewine*

Autobiography / Dec. 21, 1964-Jan. 7, 1965 / Atlantic ✦✦✦✦
Cornetist Nat Adderley's first album as a leader after the collapse of Riverside found him switching to Atlantic and performing eight of his most rewarding compositions. With several brass players, Seldon Powell on tenor and flute, pianist Joe Zawinul (who provided the arrangements), bassist Sam Jones, Grady Tate or Bruno Carr on drums and guest spots by Victor Pantoja and Willie Bobo on Latin percussion, Nat performs such numbers as his greatest hit "Work Song," "Sermonette," "The Old Country," "Little Boy with the Sad Eyes" and "Jive Samba." It is a pity that the music on this valuable LP has yet to be reissued on CD. —*Scott Yanow*

Sayin' Somethin' / Feb. 16, 1966 / Atlantic ✦✦✦
Cornetist Nat Adderley was at the peak of his powers in the mid-1960s. This Atlantic LP (which has not yet been reissued on CD) has four quintet numbers with tenor saxophonist Joe Henderson (three also feature pianist Herbie Hancock) plus four tunes in which Nat is part of an 11-piece group. He plays quite well on such songs as "Cantaloupe Island," "Hippodelphia," "Gospellete" and even the then-current pop tune "Call Me," making this out-of-print set one to search for. —*Scott Yanow*

Live at Memory Lane / Oct. 30, 1966 / Atlantic ✦✦✦

The Scavenger / Jan. 18, 1968-Jan. 19, 1968 / Milestone ✦✦

You Baby / Mar. 26, 1968-Apr. 4, 1968 / A&M ✦✦✦✦✦
As Cannonball Adderley moved with the times in the late '60s, so did brother Nat on his own. While Adderley generally buys into Creed Taylor's A&M mixture of top-flight jazz talent, pop tunes and originals, and orchestrations packaged in bite-sized tracks, this album has its own pleasingly veiled yet soulful sound quite apart from its neighbors in the A&M/CTI series. Give credit to Adderley's successful use of a Varitone electronic attachment on his cornet, giving the horn an "electric blue" sound that he handles with marvelous rhythmic dexterity. Add Joe Zawinul's lively, funky electric piano from Cannonball's quintet, as well as the brooding, genuinely classically-inspired orchestrations of Bill Fischer that only use violas, cellos and flutes. While not always technically perfect, Adderley's solos have soul and

substance; his brief, catchy bop licks on "Halftime" are some of the best he ever played. and on Zawinul's "Early Minor" he evokes a sense of loneliness that Miles would have admired. A lovely, intensely musical album, well worth seeking out. —*Richard S. Ginell*

Calling out Loud / Nov. 19, 1968-Dec. 4, 1968 / A&M ✦✦✦✦✦
For his second and, alas, last album for A&M, Nat Adderley reunites with Joe Zawinul and the greatly underrated arranger Bill Fischer, this time with a tight, often surprisingly progressive concept in mind. All the tunes are by the above three, all are linked by classical arrangements for winds to form a suite, yet both Adderley and Zawinul are given plenty of room to burn. Nat's "Biafra," clearly written with the then-raging Nigerian civil war in mind, sets the thoughtful mood, contrasting a moving dirge with buoyant extended solos by Adderley and Zawinul. Adderley plays both acoustic and electric Varitone cornet; it's amazing how the latter alters his boppish personality into something more sensitive and soulful. Fischer's charts are always intriguing, brooding even when the music is joyous, and already Zawinul is displaying some of the freedom on electric piano that would soon emerge with Miles Davis and Weather Report. Indeed, Zawinul's "Grey Moss" and Fischer's "Nobody Knows" sound like cautious prototypes for portions of Miles' *Bitches Brew*. A fascinating album, beautifully produced, with mordant cover art (firecrackers). —*Richard S. Ginell*

Love, Sex and the Zodiac / 1970 / Fantasy ✦

The Soul Zodiac / 1972 / Capitol ✦✦✦✦
A few seconds of spacy echo loops and you know where this album is coming from—the early jazz-rock era, the Age of Aquarius and all that. Yet this crazy amalgam of jazz, rock, electronics, and spoken astrological advice by the popular Los Angeles DJ Rick Holmes actually works, for the music behind the soulfully intoned words is very inventive and Holmes plays effectively off its rhythms. Basically this is the Cannonball Adderley group (Nat, cornet; George Duke, electric piano; Walter Booker, bass; Roy McCurdy, drums), with the young eloquent Ernie Watts sitting in for Cannonball (who appears only on "Libra" and "Aries") on tenor and flute and Mike Deasy contributing wild psychedelic guitar at times. Indeed Nat seems like just the nominal leader of the session—Cannonball actually gets top billing as co-producer—though he plays spiritedly at all times. The music is very eclectic, ranging from mainstream jazz to freeform freakouts and even hilarious heavy-metal rock on the stomping 14-minute "Taurus." Actually these were expansions of the directions the Adderley group was exploring at the time, and one wonders how they determined the idiom for each sign. Whether or not you accept astrology, this double set is a lot of fun. —*Richard S. Ginell*

Soul of the Bible / Oct. 14, 1972 / Capitol ✦✦
In the predictable tradition of sequels, this quick two-LP followup to *Soul Zodiac* is not nearly as much fun. The concept is scattered, without the imposed order of 12 zodiac signs, and DJ Rick Holmes sounds uncomfortable quoting scripture, his charisma muted. Again, this is Cannonball's quintet in action, augmented by four percussionists (including Airto Moreira) and some unnecessary gospel singers. This time, top-billed Cannonball is heard frequently, often probing the outside on soprano sax. Nat skillfully plays his usual Quintet sidekick role and George Duke has a lot to do on acoustic and electric pianos, often determining the idiom with each change of keyboard. While the group rambles through an adventurous series of acoustic and electric jazz, Latin and funk episodes—"Fun in the Church" sounds like someone had been into the James Brown sauce—the music strikes fire only intermittently. —*Richard S. Ginell*

Double Exposure / 1974 / Prestige ✦✦✦

Don't Look Back / Aug. 9, 1976 / Inner City ✦✦✦

Hummin' / Oct. 1976 / Little David ✦✦✦
Cornetist Nat Adderley's second recording after his brother Cannonball's death features him in a sextet with tenor saxophonist John Stubblefield, keyboardist Onaje Gumbs, bassist Fernando Gumbs, drummer Buddy Williams and percussionist Victor See Yuen. In addition, Nat Adderley Jr. provides vocal arrangements that use his voice plus those of two other singers on a pair of the seven selections. However, the music on this LP (other than the memorable "Hummin'") is somewhat dated and often a bit commercial; not one of Nat Adderley's more significant releases. —*Scott Yanow*

A Little New York Midtown Music / Sep. 18, 1978-Sep. 19, 1978 / Galaxy ✦✦✦✦
Cornetist Nat Adderley is heard with an all-star quintet also featuring tenor saxophonist Johnny Griffin and keyboardist Victor Feldman on this enjoyable set. Except for "Come Rain or Come Shine," all of the melodies are group originals (including four by Nat). The music is essentially modern hard bop and is as well played as one would expect from this strong personnel. —*Scott Yanow*

Blue Autumn / Oct. 1982 / Evidence ✦✦✦
This '83 live set at the Keystone Korner was certainly an uneven, sometimes curious event. The opening number is a solo alto workout for Sonny Fortune, who

seems to amble through midway before he becomes recharged by the end. The last track, "The Tallahassee Kid," fades out early and Adderley provides a rundown of band personnel until the disc ends. There are some fine cuts with punchy, snappy melodies, taut solos, and nice rhythm section interaction between pianist Larry Willis, drummer Jimmy Cobb and bassist Walter Booker. But overall, this proves a good but not essential Nat Adderley date. —*Ron Wynn*

On the Move / Oct. 1982 / Theresa ✦✦✦

Nat Adderley teamed with alto saxophonist Sonny Fortune on two albums for Theresa in the mid-'80s, including this six-cut outing. Fortune, capable of playing with as much invention, energy, and drive as any contemporary alto player, was uniformly aggressive and intense. He dominated the proceedings, followed closely by the outstanding rhythm section duo of underrated bassist Walter Booker and drummer Jimmy Cobb. But neither Adderley nor pianist Larry Willis, who supplied half the date's songs, were in top form. Willis played some nice melodies but did not offer much during his solos, while Adderley was plagued by sloppy articulation. However, the work of Fortune, who has not recorded nearly often enough, salvages things somewhat. —*Ron Wynn*

We Remember Cannon / Nov. 18, 1989 / In & Out ✦✦✦

Autumn Leaves / May 12, 1990-May 13, 1990 / Evidence ✦✦✦✦✦

Cornetist Nat Adderley is in excellent form on his live sextet set but he is somewhat overshadowed by his two altoists: Vincent Herring and especially the explosive Sonny Fortune. With pianist Rob Bargad, bassist Walter Booker and drummer Jimmy Cobb offering stimulating support, Adderley and his men perform a pair of lengthy standards (a 15-minute "Yesterdays" and an over-20-minute "Autumn Leaves") plus Jimmy Heath's "Big 'P'" and Fortune's "For Duke and Cannon." The long solos are consistently inventive and colorful, making this an easily recommended Nat Adderley CD. —*Scott Yanow*

Talkin' About You / Nov. 8, 1990-Nov. 9, 1990 / Landmark ✦✦✦

A '90 date that found Nat Adderley sometimes struggling to maintain his tone, but holding things together anyhow. The star proved to be young lion Vincent Herring, whose interaction with Adderley was sometimes reminiscent of how the brothers used to mesh. Former Adderley combo bassist Walter Booker and drummer Jimmy Cobb were peerless in their support, while pianist Rob Bargad was effective, but not outstanding. —*Ron Wynn*

The Old Country / Dec. 5, 1990-Dec. 6, 1990 / Enja ✦✦✦

Adderley has evidently found a soul mate in alto saxophonist Vince Herring, with whom he works once more on this 1990 date. Herring's voice has grown more impressive with each release, and he now offers more than just dazzling lines and phrases; he's constructing and completing confident statements. Pianist Rob Bargad, another regular, is on board, with bassist James Genus and drummer Billy Drummond. —*Ron Wynn*

Workin' / Mar. 26, 1992 / Timeless ✦✦

Good Company / Jun. 20, 1994-Jun. 21, 1994 / Jazz Challenge ✦✦✦

Live at the 1994 Floating Jazz Festival / Oct. 25, 1994-Oct. 27, 1994 / Chiaroscuro ✦✦✦✦

Nat Adderley and his quintet (with altoist Vincent Herring, pianist Rob Bargad, bassist Walter Booker and drummer Jimmy Cobb) are heard on this double CD in particularly fine form, playing eight lengthy selections; all but "Mercy, Mercy, Mercy" are over nine minutes long. Herring often takes solo honors, the rhythm section (which includes two survivors from the Cannonball Adderley days plus young pianist Bargad) is excellent and Nat's chops are in better than usual shape. The music overall is very much in the tradition of Cannonball's quintet. But actually the main reason to acquire this set is for Nat's storytelling; there are 38 minutes of talking in addition to the 84 minutes of music. Nat's monologues between songs have been left intact and he talks about the origin of the title of Sam Jones' "Unit Seven" and the reason why "Work Song" is his favorite tune, and tells some other interesting tales. Adderley (who competes well with his late brother Cannonball at contributing intelligent commentary) also is heard on the closing "Jazzspeak" (which clocks in at 13:44) remembering a humorous but important lesson that he learned from Cannonball. Recommended. —*Scott Yanow*

Mercy, Mercy, Mercy / Dec. 18, 1995-Dec. 19, 1995 / Evidence ✦✦✦

Cornetist Nat Adderley's music has not developed much since his years with Cannonball Adderley, but the playing on this CD is of such a high level that one really does not mind. Adderley's chops sound better than usual for the period as he teams up with altoist Antonio Hart (who hints at Cannonball while giving the music his own approach), pianist Rob Bargad, bassist Walter Booker and drummer Jimmy Cobb. The nine songs include six from the Cannonball days, including a version of the title cut that gets beyond the melody for some fine solos, as well as a catchy original apiece by Hart and Bargad, and the standard "On the Sunny Side of the Street." Excellent hard bop. —*Scott Yanow*

Larry Adler

b. Feb. 10, 1914, Baltimore, MD
Harmonica / Classical, Swing, Pop
Larry Adler, who can play jazz but has spent most of his career in other fields, did more than anyone else to make the harmonica accepted as a legitimate instrument, playing everything from classical music to pop. A virtuoso musician, Adler's most interesting jazz-related recordings were with Django Reinhardt and Stephane Grappelli in 1938 and John Kirby's Sextet in 1944, and on later sessions with pianist Ellis Larkins. Adler has remained active into the mid-'90s. —*Scott Yanow*

● **Live at the Ballroom** / 1986 / Newport Classics ✦✦✦✦✦

Ron Affif

b. Dec. 30, 1965, Pittsburgh, PA
Guitar / Hard Bop
The nephew of guitarist Ron Anthony (who played with George Shearing and Frank Sinatra), Ron Affif received his first guitar lesson from his uncle when he was 12. After high school he moved to Los Angeles in 1984, playing with Dick Berk, Dave Pike, Pete Christlieb and Jack Sheldon and recording a quartet date for the R.A. label in 1987. Two years later he moved to New York, and has worked since mostly as a leader. Affif, an excellent bop-based guitarist whose style was influenced a bit by Joe Pass and George Benson (both of whom in turn enjoyed his playing), has recorded several impressive albums for Pablo. —*Scott Yanow*

Ron Affif / Oct. 20, 1992-Oct. 22, 1992 / Pablo ✦✦✦

Guitarist Ron Affie's debut recording offers bright, often impressive performances done in vintage swing/mainstream form from the 27-year-old Pittsburgh native. It's heavy on standards, and his renditions of shopworn numbers like "Time After Time," "Blues in the Closet," and "How Deep Is The Ocean" are respectful, cleanly played, and efficiently delivered. The rhythm section featuring pianist Brian O'Rourke, bassist Andy Simpkins, and drummer Colin Bailey likewise is effective. This serves as a fine introduction to a good, potentially outstanding player, who shows a thorough knowledge of the idiom and its traditions. —*Ron Wynn*

Vierd Blues / Dec. 28, 1993 / Pablo ✦✦✦

52nd Street / Oct. 10, 1995-Oct. 12, 1995 / Pablo ✦✦✦✦

The cool-toned guitarist Ron Affif recalls Kenny Burrell a bit in this outing with a pianoless trio also including bassist Essiet Essiet and drummer Jeff "Tain" Watts. Although the program is dedicated to 52nd Street, the opening number ("Bohemia After Dark") was not even written when Swing Street was functioning. The setting and Affif's improvising style recall Kenny Burrell in spots, but the guitarist does have a voice of his own. Highlights include "Stompin' at the Savoy," "Yardbird Suite" and "Steeple Chase." —*Scott Yanow*

● **Ringside** / Feb. 13, 1997+Feb. 15, 1997 / Pablo ✦✦✦✦

Recorded live before a hand-picked audience at Fantasy Records' Studio A, guitarist Affif blows through eight selections with Essiet Essiet on string bass and Colin Bailey on drums giving solid support. The opener, "If I Were a Bell," sets the tone of this performance, with Affif swapping solos with Essiet, and Bailey dropping bop-approved bombs in the background. Selections include several tunes written by the guitarist, including the bluesy "Don't Make Me Pull That Tongue Out," "Farewell," "Uncle Joe" and the set closer "Holly." On the standard side of things, Gershwin's "Love Walked In," "Alone Together" and Sammy Cahn's "I Should Care" complete the song lineup. The interplay between the three players is strong and empathetic (even without a rhythm instrument providing underpinning), making this album delightful listening all the way. —*Cub Koda*

Affinity

f. 1992
Group / Avant-Garde, Post-Bop
Comprising soprano saxophonist Joe Rosenberg (the quartet's leader), tenor saxophonist Rob Sudduth, bassist Michael Silverman (who succeeded Richard Saunders) and drummer Bobby Lurie, Affinity has recorded several very interesting sets for the Music & Arts label. The versatile group (based in Northern California) in 1993 on their first recording (*Plays Nine Modern Jazz Classics*) interpreted works by such diverse jazz masters as Lee Morgan, Lee Konitz, Ornette Coleman and Anthony Braxton. Later sets included tributes to Coleman (with guest Dewey Redman) and Eric Dolphy (using Buddy Collette as a fifth member). Ranging from bebop to free bop, Affinity has been one of the more stimulating (if underrated) groups of the mid- to late '90s. —*Scott Yanow*

Plays Nine Modern Jazz Classics / 1993 / Music & Arts ✦✦✦✦✦

Affinity consists of Joe Rosenberg on soprano, Rob Sudduth playing tenor, bassist Richard Saunders and drummer Bobby Lurie. They have a very inclusive approach in picking out "nine modern jazz classics," so this inventive CD ranges in repertoire from Lee Morgan and Thelonious Monk to Ornette Coleman and Anthony Braxton (two compositions, including his infamous march). Affinity's playful interplay is a bit reminiscent of Steve Lacy's early recordings, and the versatile solos fit into the mood of each piece. —*Scott Yanow*

A Tribute to Eric Dolphy / Mar. 24, 1995+Mar. 25, 1995 / Music & Arts ◆◆◆◆
Affinity's tribute to Ornette Coleman (which featured Dewey Redman on tenor as guest soloist) was a major success. Their Eric Dolphy set is not quite on that level. Affinity (Joe Rosenberg on soprano, tenor saxophonist Rob Sudduth, bassist Michael Silverman and drummer Bobby Lurie) welcomes Dolphy's old friend Buddy Collette on alto and flute. Although the material (six songs recorded by Dolphy, but only "Booker's Waltz" written by him) does push the bop-based Collette to play more advanced solos than usual, the overall interpretations are still more conservative than Dolphy's from over 30 years before. The solos during such songs as "Bee Vamp," "Fire Waltz" and "So Long Eric" by the quintet are fine, but are generally overshadowed by the original versions. —*Scott Yanow*

This is Our Lunch / Apr. 4, 1995 / Music & Arts ◆◆◆◆
● **A Tribute to Ornette Coleman** / May 6, 1995 / Music & Arts ◆◆◆◆◆
This is a consistently exciting set. Affinity (Joe Rosenberg on soprano, bassist Michael Silverman and drummer Bobby Lurie) welcomes tenor saxophonist Dewey Redman to a San Francisco concert and performs six Ornette Coleman compositions from Ornette's early Quartet days. Redman, who played regularly with Coleman during the late 1960s/early '70s, always had a different sound than Ornette (and plays tenor rather than alto), but his improvising style fit in perfectly with Coleman during the era and their musical relationship was mutually beneficial. With Rosenberg's soprano sometimes sounding like Ornette, Silverman and Lurie contributing very alert support and Redman playing with a great deal of fire, this is a very successful project. Such rarely performed Coleman tunes as "Blues Connotation," "The Sphinx" and "Beauty Is A Rare Thing" serve as perfect vehicles for lengthy free bop improvisations full of fresh melodies. Highly recommended. —*Scott Yanow*

Air

f. 1971, db. 1986
Group / Modern Creative, Avant-Garde, Free Jazz
Originally comprising Henry Threadgill on reeds, bassist Fred Hopkins and drummer Steve McCall, Air emphasized equality of roles by the instruments (without any clear-cut leader) and a smooth mixture of advanced arrangements and free improvisations. In 1971 Threadgill was asked to arrange some of Scott Joplin's songs for a production at Columbia College in Chicago. He teamed up with Hopkins and McCall as the trio Reflection. A few years later in 1975 the musicians came together again as Air, touring Europe, Japan and America and recording 11 records for such labels as Nessa, India Navigation, Black Saint, Novus and Antilles. By far their most popular release was 1979's *Air Lore* which found the group performing abstract versions of tunes by Joplin and Jelly Roll Morton. In 1982 when McCall returned to Chicago and was replaced by Pheeroan AkLaff, the group changed its name to New Air. A year before their breakup in 1986 Andrew Cyrille took over the drum slot. Since then all of the musicians (other than McCall who passed away in 1989) have had very productive careers. —*Scott Yanow*

Air Song / Sep. 10, 1975 / India Navigation ◆◆◆◆
Air Song was the first recording by Air, a trio comprising altoist Henry Threadgill (who also plays tenor, baritone and flute on this date), bassist Fred Hopkins and drummer Steve McCall. The idea behind this unit was always to have all three members on an equal footing and, although Threadgill consistently comes across as the lead voice, their advanced interplay and consistently strong solos on these four lengthy performances make this a rather successful outing. —*Scott Yanow*

Live Air / Jul. 1, 1976+Oct. 28, 1977 / Black Saint ◆◆◆
1976 New York/1977 Ann Arbor. Bass, drums, and sax. —*Michael G. Nastos*

Air Raid / Jul. 15, 1976 / India Navigation ◆◆◆◆
Air's third recording (following two others recorded during the previous ten months) once again features Henry Threadgill (who contributed all four compositions) as the main lead voice, switching between alto, tenor, Chinese musette, flute, and hubkaphone (a percussive instrument that he put together made of hubcaps). Threadgill's close interaction with bassist Fred Hopkins and drummer Steve McCall should make this obscure album of strong interest to avant-garde collectors. —*Scott Yanow*

Air Time / Nov. 17, 1977-Nov. 18, 1977 / Nessa ◆◆◆◆
The trio Air aimed to have close interplay between three musical equals. This Nessa release (their first recording for an American label) has plenty of explorative solos and is highlighted by Threadgill's three extended compositions; check out his hubkaphone feature on "G.V.E." —*Scott Yanow*

Open Air Suit / Feb. 21, 1978-Feb. 22, 1978 / Novus ◆◆◆◆
Although in actuality a suite, this LP is called *Open Air Suit* with the five compositions supposedly approximating a five-piece suit. The music played by this talented trio is complex yet ultimately logical. The talented musicians seem to communicate instantly with each other and they consistently develop their music in the same direction on this stimulating set. —*Scott Yanow*

Live at Montreux 1978 / Jul. 22, 1978 / Novus ◆◆◆
The last recording by the original lineup of Air (Henry Threadgill on alto, tenor, baritone and hubkaphone, bassist Fred Hopkins and drummer Steve McCall) finds the group stretching out on a pair of Threadgill originals ("Let's All Go Down to the Footwash" and "Abra"), plus the group improv "Suisse Air" at the 1978 Montreux Jazz Festival. McCall would soon depart (replaced in New Air by Pheeroan AkLaff). One of the more notable avant-garde groups of the era, Air's music frequently takes several listens to appreciate, and that is true of this passionate yet thoughtful outing. —*Scott Yanow*

● **Air Lore** / May 11, 1979-May 12, 1979 / RCA/Bluebird ◆◆◆◆◆
This was the most unusual and accessible recording ever made by Air. Instead of performing their complex originals as usual, this group stretches out on two songs apiece by Jelly Roll Morton and Scott Joplin (in addition to Threadgill's brief "Paille Street"). Most memorable is their investigation of Joplin's "The Ragtime Dance." Threadgill's solos in particular really fit the mood of these classic pieces. —*Scott Yanow*

Air Mail / Dec. 28, 1980 / Black Saint ◆◆◆◆
The Chicago trio Air was at a high point on this 1980 date, thanks in part to remarkable percussive foundations provided by the late Steve McCall and his interaction with bassist Fred Hopkins, plus the amazing solos and versatility of nominal leader Henry Threadgill. Besides alto and tenor sax, flute, and bass flute, Threadgill plays his own unique instrument called the hubkaphone and makes it just as memorable a weapon as the other horns. —*Ron Wynn*

80 Degrees Below '82 / Jan. 23, 1982-Jan. 24, 1982 / Antilles ◆◆◆
This was Air's ninth LP and the final one featuring drummer Steve McCall. The avant-garde trio stretches out on three of the saxophonist's originals and Jelly Roll Morton's "Chicago Breakdown." This blues-oriented set is more accessible than many of Air's previous recordings without watering down the explorative nature of this always-interesting group. —*Scott Yanow*

New Air: Live at the Montreux Int'l Jazz Festival / Jul. 1983 / Black Saint ◆◆◆
New drummer Pheeroan AkLaff brought a fresh approach and crackling edge to the trio Air on this 1983 live date, done at the Montreux Festival. Hopkins didn't mesh as smoothly with AkLaff on this date, although they found a comfortable meeting place by mid-album. Henry Threadgill, as always, was a compelling soloist, especially on alto sax. —*Ron Wynn*

Air Show No. 1 / Jun. 2, 1986-Jun. 3, 1986 / Black Saint ◆◆◆◆
The second and final Air recording after drummer/percussionist Pheeroan AkLaff took Steve McCall's place is a bit unusual, for vocalist Cassandra Wilson is heard on three of the six selections. She does an expert job of fitting into this complex music, giving a strong blues feeling to some of altoist Henry Threadgill's originals; bassist Fred Hopkins is also in top form on these unpredictable and dynamic performances. —*Scott Yanow*

Toshiko Akiyoshi

b. Dec. 12, 1929, Dairen, China
Piano, Arranger, Leader / Bop, Hard Bop, Post Bop
As an arranger Toshiko Akiyoshi (influenced originally by Gil Evans and Thad Jones) has been particularly notable for incorporating elements of traditional Japanese music into her otherwise boppish charts. A strong (and underrated) pianist in the Bud Powell tradition, Akiyoshi was born in China but moved to Japan in 1946. She played locally (Sadao Watanabe was among her sidemen) and, after being noticed and encouraged by Oscar Peterson, studied at Berklee during 1956-59. Married for a time to altoist Charlie Mariano, she co-led the Toshiko-Mariano quartet in the early '60s. After working with Charles Mingus in 1962 (including participating in his ill-fated Town Hall concert), Toshiko returned to Japan for three years. Back in New York by 1965, she did a radio series and formed a quartet with her second husband Lew Tabackin in 1970. After moving to Los Angeles in 1972, Toshiko Akiyoshi put together her very impressive big band, which featured such fine soloists as Bobby Shew, Gary Foster and Tabackin. They recorded several notable albums before Akiyoshi decided in 1981 to move to New York. Since their relocation, Akiyoshi and Tabackin have both been quite active although her reformed big band has actually received less publicity than it did in L.A. She ranks as one of the top jazz arrangers of the past 25 years. —*Scott Yanow*

Toshiko & Modern Jazz / Jul. 16, 1964 / Denon ◆◆
Kogun / Apr. 3, 1974+Apr. 4, 1974 / RCA ◆◆◆◆

Long Yellow Road / Apr. 4, 1974-Mar. 4, 1975 / RCA ✦✦✦✦✦

Toshiko Akiyoshi's second big-band album (closely following *Kogun*) is a hard-swinging and consistently exciting set that has strong solos from the likes of trumpeter Don Rader, fluegelhornist Bobby Shew, altoist Gary Foster and Toshiko's husband Lew Tabackin on tenor in addition to the pianist-leader. Akiyoshi draws on her culture successfully on "Children in the Temple Ground" and shows throughout this memorable set (which deserves to be reissued on CD) that she had by this early point already developed into one of the most distinctive big-band arrangers around. —*Scott Yanow*

Tales of a Courtesan / Dec. 1, 1975-Dec. 3, 1975 / RCA ✦✦✦✦✦

Virtually every Toshiko Akiyoshi big-band recording is well worth acquiring—not only does Akiyoshi have a highly appealing and original arranging style, but her orchestra always boasts top soloists. In addition to Lew Tabackin on tenor and flute, *Tales of a Courtesan* features worthy improvisations by altoists Gary Foster and Dick Spencer, trombonist Britt Woodman, trumpeter Bobby Shew and pianist Akiyoshi. "Road Time Shuffle" and "Strive for Jive" are particulary memorable. —*Scott Yanow*

Road Time / Jan. 30, 1976-Feb. 8, 1976 / RCA ✦✦✦✦✦

This two-LP set, which, like most of the Toshiko Akiyoshi Orchestra's recordings, is currently out of print, gives one a definitive look at her 1970s orchestra. Akiyoshi's arrangements are colorful and swinging; the best charts on this two-fer are "Tuning Up," the nearly 23-minute "Henpecked Old Man," "Kogun" (which pays tribute to her Japanese heritage) and "Road Time Shuffle." This edition of the orchestra includes such major players as trumpeter Steve Huffstetter and Bobby Shew, trombonist Jimmy Knepper, altoists Dick Spencer and Gary Foster and Lew Tabackin on tenor and flute. It's highly recommended, if it can be found. —*Scott Yanow*

Insights / Jun. 22, 1976-Jun. 24, 1976 / Novus ✦✦✦✦

Dedications / Apr. 25, 1977-Apr. 27, 1977 / Inner City ✦✦✦
One of her few trio recordings. —*Michael Erlewine*

Tribute to Billy Strayhorn / Apr. 3, 1978-Apr. 4, 1978 / Jazz America ✦✦✦✦

Finesse / May 8, 1978 / Concord Jazz ✦✦✦
The material on *Finesse* was mostly ballads interspersed with a few things done at medium tempo; although this had been pianist-bandleader-composer Toshiko Akiyoshi's domain in the past, this time she brought to it a dirge-like sound that bred impatience in the listener. In her writing for big band, alongside the drama created by her unusual horn voicings, there was an emotionalism, at turns humorous or reflective, introduced by her sense of rhythmic juxtaposition. It was this later feature that was lacking in all but three of the selections on "Finesse." Akiyoshi was not the only culprit, as bassist Monty Budwig, who shared much of the solo space, plodded through most of his solos as if his bass strings were coated with molasses. The three tunes that broke out of this somber pattern were "Mr. Jelly Lord," an original from the Akiyoshi-Tabackin band book, "Warning," and an arrangement of a Grieg piece, "Solvejg's Song." The Jelly Roll Morton tune was played as a ballad, but this time instead of a facile explication of the melody, Akiyoshi explored the emotional beauty of the notes, pausing in reflection before continuing. "Warning" and "Solvejg's Song" were both taken at a medium tempo. —*Bob Rusch, Cadence*

European Memoirs / Sep. 21, 1978-Sep. 22, 1978 / Ascent ✦✦✦

Notorious Tourist from the East / Dec. 5, 1978-Dec. 6, 1978 / Inner City ✦✦✦
Fine set showcasing the tasty Akiyoshi piano in a non-big band setting. Akiyoshi is a good ballad interpreter, excellent composer, and accomplished soloist, qualities that have been obscured by her conducting and arranging skills. This album put those talents in the forefront. —*Ron Wynn*

Farewell to Mingus / Jan. 10, 1980-Jan. 11, 1980 / Jazz America ✦✦✦✦

Tanuki's Night Out / Mar. 24, 1981-Mar. 25, 1981 / JAM ✦✦✦✦✦

Wishing Peace / Jul. 21, 1986-Jul. 22, 1986 / Ken Music ✦✦✦

Interlude / Feb. 1987 / Concord Jazz ✦✦✦
A nice trio outing from 1987, with Akiyoshi displaying more accomplished pianistic skills than she was generally given credit for while heading the Akiyoshi-Tabackin big band. She emerges as the dominant instrumentalist among the three, with bassist Dennis Irwin and drummer Eddie Marshall content to let her set the pace and work off her leads, rather than seek to influence the sound themselves. —*Ron Wynn*

Remembering Bud: Cleopatra's Dream / Jul. 31, 1990-Aug. 1, 1990 / Evidence ✦✦✦
Bandleader and pianist Toshiko Akiyoshi is a far better player than she claims, and she demonstrates her abilities on these 10 tracks recorded in 1990. Akiyoshi displays an accomplished rhythmic style, nice harmonic sense and good command of the keyboard. While her touch and volume are not as emphatic as those of

some other pianists, Akiyoshi's melodic sense and her floating lines are strong enough to express what is necessary within each song. For those unaccustomed to hearing Akiyoshi outside the big band arena, this will be a pleasant departure. —*Ron Wynn*

● **Carnegie Hall Concert** / Sep. 20, 1991 / Columbia ✦✦✦✦✦

Desert Lady-Fantasy / Dec. 1, 1993-Dec. 3, 1993 / Columbia ✦✦✦

Live at Maybeck Recital Hall, Vol. 36 / Jul. 10, 1994 / Concord Jazz ✦✦✦✦

Manny Albam (Emmanuael Albam)

b. Jun. 24, 1922, Samana, Dominican Republic
Arranger / Progressive Big Band, Cool, Bop

A top arranger whose peak years in jazz were during the 1950s and early '60s, Manny Albam grew up in New York and played reed instruments, mostly settling on baritone. He gigged as a player and arranger with such big bands as Muggsy Spanier (1941), Bob Chester (1942), Georgie Auld, Charlie Spivak and Boyd Raeburn (1943-45). After spending 1945-46 in the army, Albam worked for Sam Donohue, Charlie Barnet (1948-49) and Jerry Wald. He eventually gave up playing to become a full-time freelance arranger-composer. During 1955-62 Albam recorded as a leader for RCA, Coral, Dot, United Artists and Impulse and in 1966 led a couple of albums for Solid State, in addition to contributing charts to dates by such jazzmen as Dizzy Gillespie, Gerry Mulligan, Terry Gibbs, Stan Getz, Count Basie, Woody Herman, Stan Kenton and Buddy Rich. Starting in 1964, Manny Albam became quite active in jazz education, teaching at the Eastman School and at Glassboro State College. —*Scott Yanow*

● **The Jazz Greats of Our Time, Vol. 1** / Apr. 2, 1957-Apr. 4, 1957 / MCA ✦✦✦✦
All-star set with Art Farmer, Zoot Sims, Al Cohn, Phil Woods, Gerry Mulligan, Hank Jones, and Milt Hinton among the participants. Albam's role is in the background as arranger-conductor. —*Ron Wynn*

Joe Albany (Joseph Albani)

b. Jan. 24, 1924, Atlantic City, NJ, **d.** Jan. 12, 1988, New York, NY
Piano / Bop

Looking at pianist Joe Albany's life in hindsight, it is miraculous that he lived to almost reach 64. Serious problems with drugs and alcohol resulted in a series of harrowing incidents and his domestic life would never be described as tranquil (his second wife committed suicide while his third almost died from a drug overdose). Albany's life was so erratic that he only recorded once during 1947-71. However, Joe Albany's real importance is as one of the early bop pianists. After playing accordion as a child, he switched to piano in high school and in 1942 joined Leo Watson's group. He had short-term associations with Benny Carter, Georgie Auld, Boyd Raeburn and most significantly Charlie Parker. Albany's live recordings with Parker and some brilliant studio sides with Lester Young in 1946 (the latter later reissued on Blue Note) were the high points of his career. Decades of struggle followed (which he frankly described in the excellent 1980 documentary *Joe Albany . . . A Jazz Life*) with Riverside's *The Right Combination* (a rehearsal session with tenor saxophonist Warne Marsh) being the only documentation from the lost years. Other than a short stint with Charles Mingus in the mid-'60s, it was not until 1972 that Albany started to have a comeback. He recorded a set with violinist Joe Venuti and was a leader on albums for Revelation, Horo, Inner City, Sea Breeze and Interplay. The excellent 1982 Elektra/Musician set *Portrait of an Artist* was the final statement from the troubled but talented pianist. —*Scott Yanow*

● **Right Combination** / Sep. 1957 / Original Jazz Classics ✦✦✦✦✦
Although he was a pioneer of the bebop era and made a few isolated sides with Georgie Auld and Lester Young in 1945-46, pianist Joe Albany can be heard on extremely few recordings before 1971. This CD reissue, which was actually a rehearsal, was Albany's only recorded date as a leader before the 1970s. The set of trios with tenor saxophonist Warne Marsh and bassist Bob Whitlock consists of seven jazz standards and, although not flawless, is of generally high quality. Marsh and Albany worked together quite well (their conceptions were similar) and these versions of such songs as Clifford Brown's "Daahoud," "Body and Soul" and "All The Things You Are" are quite rewarding. From the historical standpoint, this release is essential. —*Scott Yanow*

At Home / Aug. 31, 1971+Sep. 5, 1971 / Spotlite ✦✦✦✦
This release was quite important for a couple of reasons. It was the first LP put out by the British Spotlite label and only the second date led by the legendary (and until then largely forgotten) bop pianist Joe Albany; the earlier session was actually a 1957 rehearsal! Recorded at home on his own piano, this solo set has Albany performing 11 standards and bop tunes, plus his own "Birdtown Blues." The recording quality is decent if not state-of-the-art, but the playing is quite excellent and fortunately led to the rediscovery of this important "missing link." —*Scott Yanow*

Proto Bopper / Feb. 14, 1972-Oct. 10, 1972 / Revelation ✦✦✦✦
Joe Albany came very close to being one of the lost legends, a pioneering bebop pianist who barely recorded until Spotlite released a private solo recital of his in 1971. The follow-up LP (which also came out domestically on the Revelation label) has Albany playing five unaccompanied solos (including "You Don't Know What Love Is" and "Like Someone in Love") plus six trio numbers with bassist Bob Whitlock and either Jerry McKenzie or Nick Martinis on drums; best of the latter is "When Lights Are Low" and "Yardbird Suite." Despite an out-of-tune piano on a few of the songs, this is a worthy and historical set. —*Scott Yanow*

Birdtown Birds / Apr. 25, 1973-Apr. 30, 1973 / Steeple Chase ✦✦✦

Two's Company / Feb. 17, 1974 / Steeple Chase ✦✦✦✦
After being poorly documented during the first 30 years of his career, pianist Joe Albany made quite a few records (mostly for European labels) during 1971-77. This duet set with bassist Niels-Henning Orsted Pedersen (reissued on CD) finds Albany in particularly good form on six veteran standards, including "Out of Nowhere," "Lover Man" and "Star Eyes." His lyrical and boppish style was still very much intact and Albany is heard in prime form on the thoughtful yet swinging set. —*Scott Yanow*

Albany Touch / Jun. 25, 1977-Jul. 5, 1977 / Sea Breeze ✦✦✦
The legendary pianist Joe Albany, whose career was largely fouled up by drugs, recorded several rewarding sets during 1977-82. This solo album (originally recorded for the Japanese Trio label before being made available domestically on an obscure Sea Breeze LP) is relaxed, thoughtful and shows off Albany's roots in the bop era, although the pianist generally sounded at his best in a trio setting. Highlights include "A.B. (After Bird) Blues II," "You Stepped out of a Dream" and "A Night in Tunisia." —*Scott Yanow*

Bird Lives / Jan. 4, 1979 / Storyville ✦✦✦✦✦
Joe Albany's next-to-last recording features the veteran bop pianist performing seven Charlie Parker compositions, his own "Charlie Parker Blues" and the standard "They Can't Take That Away from Me" in a superb trio that also includes bassist Art Davis and drummer Roy Haynes. This was the perfect setting for Albany and he comes up with fresh ideas on such familiar classics as "Yardbird Suite," "Little Suede Shoes" and "Confirmation." The CD is easily recommended to bop lovers. —*Scott Yanow*

Portrait of an Artist / 1982 / Elektra ✦✦✦✦
This mostly ballad-oriented trio set with bassist George Duvivier and drummer Charlie Persip was pianist Joe Albany's final recording. Albany, whose career (especially on records) did not really get going until his final decade, is in generally good form on such tunes as "Autumn in New York," "They Say It's Wonderful" and "Confirmation." The album concludes with a brief interview that sums up some aspects of his episodic life. —*Scott Yanow*

Gerald Albright

b. 1957, Los Angeles, CA
Tenor Saxophone, Alto Saxophone / Instrumental Pop, Crossover Jazz
Gerald Albright has occasionally shown the ability to play jazz (most notably on his Atlantic set *Live at Birdland West*) but has chosen to make his career as an R&B saxophonist. Originally he studied piano before switching to tenor, and in college he began doubling on electric bass. Through the years Albright has performed in a variety of R&Bish settings (with Patrice Rushen, Anita Baker, Quincy Jones, the Temptations, etc.), content to play simplistic music and disappointingly little jazz. —*Scott Yanow*

Just Between Us / 1988 / Atlantic ✦✦

Bermuda Nights / 1989 / Atlantic ✦✦✦

Dream Come True / Nov. 6, 1990 / Atlantic ✦✦
A talented saxman whose influences range from John Coltrane to soul jazz/hard bop players like David "Fathead" Newman and Hank Crawford, Gerald Albright showed just how much potential he has on 1991's superb *Live at Birdland West.* Sadly, most of his commercial recordings offer little evidence of his considerable improvisatory skills—*Dream Come True* being among the offenders. Designed primarily for commercial radio airplay, this pop/R&B/jazz CD is, for the most part, as dull as it is contrived. Instead of taking risks, Albright embraces a tired, cliché-ridden Najee-meets-George Howard formula on such forgettable cuts as "Say Yes," "Sweet Dreams" and the title song. Instead of interpreting Johnny Gill's 1990 R&B hit "My My My," Albright offers a pointless, robotic note-for-note cover. The only decent cut here is the uplifting "Growing with Each Other," which boasts a heartfelt vocal by gospel singer BeBe Winans. Albright is too strong a player to be recording albums this weak. —*Alex Henderson*

● **Live at Birdland West** / 1991 / Atlantic ✦✦✦✦
Virtually all of saxophonist Gerald Albright's previous recordings were in the pop/R&B field, making this mostly straightahead session a major surprise. Albright,

alternating between alto and tenor, plays quite well throughout this set, which is highlighted by versions of "Impressions," "Georgia on My Mind" and "Limehouse Blues." Tenorman Kirk Whalum helps out on three tracks and Eddie Harris makes a guest appearance on "Bubblehead McDaddy." This is easily Gerald Albright's most rewarding session to date. —*Scott Yanow*

Smooth / Feb. 22, 1994 / Atlantic ✦✦
The title to *Smooth* is appropriate—the album is a collection of slick fusion, drawing more from urban R&B than jazz. However, smooth can be good, as Gerald Albright proves throughout the album. The saxophonist is a proficient, graceful player and he can create a romantic atmosphere rather effortlessly. Jazz purists may disdain it, but *Smooth* would please any of the saxist's fans. —*Stephen Thomas Erlewine*

Giving Myself to You / 1995 / Atlantic ✦✦

Live to Love / 1997 / Atlantic ✦✦✦
Live to Love finds Gerald Albright returning to urban R&B, turning in an album of laidback, polished soul and smooth jazz. Several vocalists, including Albright's daughter Selina, his longtime partner Will Downing, and the Whispers' Walter and Wallace Scott, contribute their skills to these well-crafted tracks. The vocal cuts form the core of *Live to Love,* making it of more interest to an urban audience than to fusion jazz fans, although there are a few instrumental interludes as well. However, the key thing distinguishing *Live to Love* is focus—Albright hasn't had such a consistently engaging set of songs in years, and that's what makes the album such a pleasure for fans of his work. —*Leo Stanley*

Alvin Alcorn (Alvin Elmore Alcorn)

b. Sep. 7, 1912, New Orleans, LA
Trumpet / New Orleans Jazz
Alvin Alcorn's playing with Kid Ory's Creole Jazz Band during 1954-56 (which was well documented by Good Time Jazz and has been reissued in the Original Jazz Classics series) was simple but frequently superb. He was an expert at leading ensembles, had an attractive tone and was both subtle and occasionally powerful, building up ensembles to an explosive level. Taught music theory by his brother, Alcorn's early years were active if now cloaked in obscurity. He freelanced in New Orleans (playing with Armand J. Piron's Sunny South Syncopators during 1930-31) and toured with Don Albert's Texas-based swing band during 1932-37, making one recording date but probably not taking any solos. Alcorn worked in New Orleans from 1937 on, playing with many groups including those led by Paul Barbarin, Sidney Desvignes, Oscar Celestin (1951) and Octave Crosby. Alcorn moved to Los Angeles in 1954 to join Ory, and their four records were easily the best of his career. After returning to New Orleans in 1956, Alcorn played steadily into the 1980s with local groups, touring Europe a few times (including with Chris Barber in 1978). Unfortunately, all of his post-Ory recordings (other than a Verve date with George Lewis) were for small labels, and they tend to be disappointing due to the erratic recording quality and the trumpeter's gradual decline, but his work with Kid Ory assures him a place in history as a New Orleans legend. —*Scott Yanow*

● **Sounds of New Orleans, Vol. 5** / 1952-1953 / Storyville ✦✦✦✦
New Orleans trumpeter Alvin Alcorn is best known for his association with Kid Ory and did not lead that many sessions of his own. This Storyville CD has some rare live performances by Alcorn with a variety of top Dixielanders during three occasions in 1952-53. The repertoire mostly has typical standards, but Alcorn sounds in fine form, and his sidemen (which include clarinetist Raymond Burke, trombonist Jack Delaney and pianist Stan Mendelson) are spirited in their solos and ensemble playing. Highlights include "Original Dixieland One Step," "Royal Garden Blues," "Over the Waves" and "Roses of Picardy." —*Scott Yanow*

New Orleans Jazz Brunch / 1976 / Sandcastle ✦✦✦✦

Howard Alden

b. Oct. 17, 1958, Newport Beach, CA
Guitar / Swing, Mainstream Jazz
Howard Alden is to the guitar what Scott Hamilton, Warren Vache, Dan Barrett and Ken Peplowski are to the tenor, trumpet, trombone and clarinet. Part of a youthful swing movement that gained momentum in the 1980s, Alden plays the earlier pre-bop styles quite effectively but also has the ability to perform the music of Thelonious Monk and Bill Evans and he is equally talented on electric guitar, acoustic guitar and his rarely played banjo. Alden began playing guitar at age ten and he counts as his early influences guitarists Barney Kessel, Charlie Christian and George Van Eps in addition to Louis Armstrong, Benny Goodman and Count Basie. He began gigging professionally in Los Angeles as a teenager and became good friends with trombonist Dan Barrett. In 1979 Alden played with vibraphonist Red Norvo and in 1982 he followed Barrett to New York where he quickly became established as a major guitarist. He performed and recorded with the who's who of

mainstream jazz (including Joe Bushkin, Ruby Braff, Joe Williams, Woody Herman, Benny Carter, Flip Phillips, Bud Freeman, Clark Terry and Dizzy Gillespie) and by the mid-'80s was one of the most popular artists on the Concord label. A very consistent and inventive musician, Alden has been in great demand for recording sessions, jazz parties and festivals for the past 15 years. His many recordings (which include a quintet co-led with Barrett, sessions on the seven-string guitar with his idol George Van Eps and duets with Peplowski) are all enjoyable and perfect examples of modern swing. —*Scott Yanow*

No Amps Allowed / 1985 / Chiaroscuro ✦✦✦

● **Swing Street** / Sep. 1986 / Concord Jazz ✦✦✦✦✦
This is a remarkable record by the Howard Alden-Dan Barrett Quintet. Although the group has an instrumentation of guitarist Alden, trombonist Barrett, Chuck Wilson on alto and clarinet, bassist Frank Tate and drummer Jackie Williams, its arrangements (some by Buck Clayton) often make the band sound a bit like the John Kirby Sextet, a classic unit comprising trumpet, alto, clarinet, piano, bass and drums. The delightful unit uplifts such tunes as "Lullaby in Rhythm," "I May Be Wrong," Charlie Shavers' "Dawn on the Desert," "Stompin' at the Savoy" and even Thelonious Monk's "Pannonica," revitalizing small-group swing. Highly recommended. —*Scott Yanow*

Plays the Music of Harry Reser / Dec. 7, 1988+Dec. 21, 1988 / Stomp Off ✦✦✦
Although one thinks of the banjo as being primarily a background chordal instrument played rhythmically in Dixieland bands, Harry Reser in the 1920s showed that it could be used creatively by virtuosos (although virtually no one followed in his shadow). In 1988 guitarist Howard Alden for a change of pace switched to banjo and performed 15 of Reser's compositions that were written during 1922-35. These duets (with supportive piano supplied by Dick Hyman) are often remarkable, for Reser's wholly-composed music (which was influenced by novelty piano ragtime) is quite tricky and difficult, yet very rewarding to hear. Performing such numbers as "Crackerjack," "Lollipops," "Wampum" and "The Cat and the Dog," Howard Alden makes the obscure vintage music come alive and does not sound as if he were playing his "second" instrument. A gem. —*Scott Yanow*

The Howard Alden Trio Plus Special Guests Ken Peplowski & Warren Vache / Jan. 1989 / Concord Jazz ✦✦✦✦
The emphasis of this excellent session is on lesser-known swing standards. Guitarist Howard Alden (in a trio with bassist Lynn Seaton and drummer Mel Lewis) welcomes either Ken Peplowski (doubling on tenor and clarinet) or cornetist Warren Vache on eight of the 11 selections. It is particularly rewarding to hear such songs as "You Showed Me the Way," Duke Ellington's "Purple Gazelle," Charlie Parker's "Back Home Blues" and Django Reinhardt's "Tears" getting revived. —*Scott Yanow*

The ABQ Salutes Buck Clayton / Jun. 1989 / Concord Jazz ✦✦✦✦✦
It is surprising that the Alden-Barrett Quintet (ABQ) has recorded relatively little for the group (comprising guitarist Howard Alden, trombonist Dan Barrett, Chuck Wilson on alto and clarinet, bassist Frank Tate and drummer Jackie Williams) was one of the top small swing groups of the late 1980s, creating an unusual sound that often recalled the John Kirby Sextet despite the difference in instrumentation. For this CD, the Quintet performs 11 songs written by Buck Clayton (who contributed most of the arrangements for the band) plus two standards ("Way Down Yonder in New Orleans" and "Dickie's Dream") that the swing trumpeter had recorded near the beginning of his career. The very enjoyable music, which includes many rewarding obscurities, is easily recommended; the success of the group helped inspire Buck Clayton to put together a big band of his own. —*Scott Yanow*

Snowy Morning Blues / Apr. 1990 / Concord Jazz ✦✦✦✦
Guitarist Howard Alden welcomes bassist Lynn Seaton, drummer Dennis Mackrel and on most selections pianist Monty Alexander to this rewarding Concord CD. The repertoire ranges from James P. Johnson's "Snowy Morning Blues" and Django Reinhardt's "Swing 39" to a couple of lesser-known Duke Ellington songs and Thelonious Monk's "Bye-Ya" and "Ask Me Now"; the latter is a particularly beautiful ballad. Highlights include an Alden-Alexander duet on "I'm Through with Love" and a guitar-bass feature on Duke's "Melancholia." This generally relaxed set gives one a strong sampling of Howard Alden's artistry. —*Scott Yanow*

Thirteen Strings / Feb. 1991 / Concord Jazz ✦✦✦
Howard Alden and George Van Eps always make for a perfect team. Van Eps, the inventor of the seven-string guitar, has played beautiful chordal solos since the early 1930s, while Alden is a masterful modern swing stylist. On this quartet set with bassist Dave Stone and drummer Jake Hanna, the two guitarists are easy to tell apart and complement each other very well. Several songs are taken as guitar duets with Van Eps having two solo numbers and Alden has one. Of the veteran swing standards, the highlights include "Just You, Just Me," "Ain't Misbehavin'," "Love Walked In" and "Emaline" but all 13 melodic renditions are quite pretty in their own way. —*Scott Yanow*

Misterioso / Apr. 1991 / Concord Jazz ✦✦✦✦
This Concord CD serves as a particularly strong showcase for guitarist Howard Alden who is featured in a trio with bassist Frank Tate and drummer Keith Copeland. Alden's repertoire contains plenty of unusual but superior choices (including Bud Freeman's "Song of the Dove," "Flying Down to Rio," Duke Ellington's "Black Beauty" and "Ghost of Yesterday") and he excels on all dozen selections. Whether it be a couple of Thelonious Monk tunes, Jelly Roll Morton's "The Pearls" or his own "Waltz for Julie," this is an excellent all-round set with plenty of variety for the swing-based guitarist. Recommended. —*Scott Yanow*

Hand-Crafted Swing / Jun. 11, 1991-Jun. 12, 1991 / Concord Jazz ✦✦✦

Good Likeness / Aug. 1992 / Concord Jazz ✦✦✦✦

Your Story: the Music of Bill Evans / May 19-20, 1994 / Concord Jazz ✦✦✦

Encore! / Aug. 15, 1994 / Concord Jazz ✦✦✦✦✦

Concord Jazz Guitar Collective / May 23, 1995-May 24, 1995 / Concord Jazz ✦✦✦

Take Your Pick / Mar. 16, 1996-Mar. 18, 1996 / Concord Jazz ✦✦✦✦

Oscar Alemán

b. Feb. 20, 1909, Restencia, Argentina, d. Oct. 10, 1980, Buenos Aires, Argentina
Guitar / Swing
Oscar Alemán, one of the finest jazz guitarists of the 1930s, is a difficult player to evaluate because he sounded like a near-exact duplicate of Django Reinhardt. Since Django was a year younger, some have speculated that he developed his style from Alemán, although the opposite is just as likely. Alemán began playing guitar as a teenager in Argentina, and in the late '20s he moved to Europe, Spain at first. By 1931 he was living in Paris, and during 1933-35 he was a regular member of Freddy Taylor's Swing Men from Harlem. Alemán appeared on records with trumpeter Bill Coleman and clarinetist Danny Polo and was the leader on eight selections from 1938-39. He moved back to Argentina in 1941 and, although he recorded as late as 1974, few outside of his native country have ever heard of him. Strangely enough, Oscar Alemán does not seem to have ever visited the US, and none of his many recordings of swing tunes in his post-Europe years (except for a few titles put out by the collectors TOM label) have ever been released domestically. —*Scott Yanow*

● **Swing Guitar Legend** / Dec. 5, 1938-Jan. 22, 1945 / Rambler ✦✦✦✦
Because his style was very similar to Django Reinhardt's and because he spent most of his last few decades living in his native Argentina, guitarist Oscar Alemán has often been overlooked in jazz history books. One of the finest swing guitarists of the late '30s and still active up until his death in 1980, Alemán deserved better. This highly recommended (but hard-to-find) LP has Alemán's eight European recordings of 1938-39 (which range from unaccompanied solos and trios to two sextet numbers with violinist Svend Asmussen) and a sampling of his Buenos Aires sides of 1941-45. Rewarding (and rare) swing music. —*Scott Yanow*

The Guitar of Oscar Alemán, Vol. 2 / Nov. 4, 1942-1957 / The Old Masters ✦✦✦
After having made a bit of an impression in Europe during the late 1930s, the Django Reinhardt-influenced guitarist Oscar Alemán returned home to Argentina, where he played in obscurity for the last four decades of his life. Alemán's Buenos Aires recordings are quite rare, so swing collectors will want to search for this LP, which has a dozen little-known titles (none of which duplicate the music on an Alemán Rambler LP). The talented guitarist is heard in small groups which sometimes include violins, clarinet and a full rhythm section. —*Scott Yanow*

Eric Alexander

b. 1968, Illinois
Tenor Saxophone / Hard Bop, Post-Bop
A fine hard bop player who grows a bit in individuality each year, Eric Alexander grew up in the state of Washington. He initially attended Indiana University, studying classical music as an altoist. However, Alexander soon discovered jazz, switched to the tenor, and transferred to William Paterson College in New Jersey. After graduating, he moved to Chicago and soon gained important experience touring with Charles Earland while also becoming a fixture in local clubs. In 1991, Alexander placed second at the Thelonious Monk Institute's saxophone competition, finishing just behind Joshua Redman. In 1992, he relocated to New York and that year made his recording debut as a leader with a set for Criss Cross. Alexander was set to join Art Taylor's Wailers in 1995 when the drummer passed away. Influenced by Dexter Gordon and George Coleman, but gradually developing a more original sound, Alexander has also worked with Mel Rhyne, Cecil Payne, Kenny Barron, and Eddie Henderson, among others. Eric Alexander recorded two additional sets as a leader for Criss Cross, was part of their *Tenor Triangle* session, and has cut a pair of heated CDs for Delmark, including one that he co-leads with veteran tenor Lin Halliday. —*Scott Yanow*

Straight Up / 1992 / Delmark ✦✦✦✦

Tenor saxophonist Eric Alexander finished second in the 1991 Thelonious Monk sax competition, and shows why throughout these eight tracks. He has a full, bright, impressive tone, and excellent facility and command of the instrument and is steadily developing a personal sound. While the tracks vary in quality, most are at worst competent and at best outstanding. Alexander is more interesting on uptempo tunes than ballads, where he concentrates more on melodic presentation than thematic exposition. —*Ron Wynn*

New York Calling / Dec. 20, 1992 / Criss Cross ✦✦✦✦

Up, Over & Out / Aug. 18, 1993-Aug. 19, 1993 / Delmark ✦✦✦✦

Full Range / Jan. 3, 1994 / Criss Cross ✦✦✦✦

● **Stablemates** / 1995 / Delmark ✦✦✦✦✦

Eric Alexander in Europe / Apr. 10, 1995 / Criss Cross ✦✦✦✦

Two of a Kind / Dec. 15, 1996 / Criss Cross ✦✦✦✦

Monty Alexander (Montgomery Bernard)

b. Jun. 6, 1944, Kingston, Jamaica
Piano / Bop, Hard Bop

Monty Alexander long ago combined the influence of Oscar Peterson with the soul of Gene Harris and Nat King Cole to form his own appealing and personable style. Long a bit underrated (due to the shadow of Peterson), Alexander has recorded more than a score of excellent albums. Monty Alexander began piano lessons when he was six and he played professionally in Jamaica clubs while still a teenager; his band, Monty and the Cyclones, was quite popular locally during 1958-60. He first played in the US when he appeared in Las Vegas with Art Mooney's Orchestra. Soon he was accompanying a variety of top singers, formed a friendship with vibraphonist Milt Jackson and began gigging with bassist Ray Brown. With the recording of a pair of Pacific Jazz albums in 1965, an RCA date in 1967 and a Verve session in 1969, Alexander began to gain a strong reputation. His series of exciting albums for MPS during 1971-77 found him in prime form and later recordings (most notably on Pablo and Concord) found him building on his original style. Alexander, who often pays tribute to his Jamaican heritage, performs regularly with his own trio and swings hard in his own voice. —*Scott Yanow*

Live! Montreux Alexander / Jun. 10, 1976 / Verve ✦✦✦

Pianist Monty Alexander did some of his finest recordings for the MPS label. This live trio set with bassist John Clayton and drummer Jeff Hamilton (reissued on CD) features Alexander playing his usual repertoire of the period with blues, standards ("Satin Doll," "Work Song" and "Battle Hymn of the Republic") and a version of "Feelings" that uplifts the song a bit (although not enough). His soulful approach to the generally familiar melodies makes them sound fresh and swinging. —*Scott Yanow*

Jamento: The Monty Alexander 7 / Jun. 15, 1978-Jun. 16, 1978 / Original Jazz Classics ✦✦✦✦

Monty Alexander's Jamaican heritage is combined with his bop-oriented piano on this date to create some enjoyable music. This was his first recording to make use of a steel drummer (Vince Charles), and Alexander also uses an oversized rhythm section with Jamaican guitarist Ernest Ranglin, bassist Andy Simpkins, both Duffy Jackson and Roger Bethelmy on drums and percussionist Larry McDonald. The repertoire (which includes four Alexander originals and George Benson's poppish "Weekend In L.A.") is mostly obscure, but the interpretations are lively and full of spirit. —*Scott Yanow*

Monty Alexander in Tokyo / Jan. 22, 1979 / Pablo ✦✦✦✦

A straightforward outing with his trio (which also includes bassist Andy Simpkins and drummer Frank Gant), this excellent studio set features pianist Monty Alexander displaying his bop chops and creativity in a straightahead setting. Highlights include "Broadway," Oscar Pettiford's "Tricotism" and "Never Let Me Go." The fine music on this LP has yet to be reissued on CD. —*Scott Yanow*

Facets / Aug. 1979 / Concord Jazz ✦✦✦✦

Pianist Monty Alexander teams up with bassist Ray Brown and drummer Jeff Hamilton on this spirited and fairly definitive set. While the emphasis is on straightahead bop, Alexander plays soulfully on "When Johnny Comes Marching Home" and shows off his calypso roots on "Hold 'Em Joe"; other highlights include the ballad "Lost April," "I'm Walkin'" and "Tune Up." —*Scott Yanow*

Ivory & Steel / Mar. 1980 / Concord Jazz ✦✦✦✦

This well-rounded set features Monty Alexander exploring his West Indian heritage by utilizing the steel drum of Othello Molineaux and performing both straightahead jazz and calypsos. The music is often quite joyous and even the more familiar material (such as "Work Song," "Stella By Starlight" and a medley of

"Impressions" and "So What") sounds fresh. Whether it be the Milt Jackson blues "S.K.J." or the Crusaders' hit "Street Life," this is a very successful outing that is quite enjoyable. —*Scott Yanow*

Trio / Aug. 1980 / Concord Jazz ✦✦✦

Just Friends / Dec. 17, 1980-Dec. 18, 1980 / Pausa ✦✦✦✦

Originally released on MPS and then released domestically by the now-defunct Pausa label, this is a subtle and fairly creative duet set featuring pianist Monty Alexander and the Jamaican guitarist Ernest Ranglin. On seven standards (including "Just Friends," "If I Should Lose You" and "Fly Me to the Moon") and three originals, Alexander and Ranglin listen closely to each other and indulge in some tight musical interaction. Although boppish, the music is not overly predictable; the musicians' mutual respect is obvious. Well worth searching for. —*Scott Yanow*

Overseas Special / Mar. 1982 / Concord Jazz ✦✦✦✦

This is a very good live recording. —*Michael G. Nastos*

● **Triple Treat, Vol. 1** / Mar. 1982 / Concord Jazz ✦✦✦✦✦

One can excuse pianist Monty Alexander if his playing on this Concord set recalls Oscar Peterson, for his sidemen in the trio are O.P.-alumni guitarist Herb Ellis and bassist Ray Brown. The combination lives up to its potential with the group romping on such songs as "The Flintstones," Blue Mitchell's "Fungi Mama" and an uptempo "Small Fry." —*Scott Yanow*

Duke Ellington Songbook / Mar. 29, 1983 / Verve ✦✦✦✦

This is an outstanding duo rendition of Ellington standards. —*AMG*

Reunion in Europe / Mar. 1983 / Concord Jazz ✦✦✦✦

During 1976-77, the Monty Alexander Trio included bassist John Clayton and drummer Jeff Hamilton. In 1983 they had a reunion tour, resulting in this recording for Concord. Clayton and Hamilton had both grown in the interim although pianist Alexander naturally dominates the well-rounded trio set. The material is sometimes quite offbeat with the high points including the straightahead "Two Bass Hit," a funky "Got My Mojo Working," Clayton's arco bass solo on Charlie Chaplin's "Smile," the bassist's catchy "Blues For Stephanie" and Alexander's "Eleuthra." A typically excellent Monty Alexander recording. —*Scott Yanow*

Full Steam Ahead / 1985 / Concord Jazz ✦✦✦

For his seventh Concord recording, all of which are easily recommended, pianist Monty Alexander teams up with bassist Ray Brown and drummer Frank Gant for four bop standards, a pair of bossa nova tunes, and such unusual jazz vehicles as "Because You're Mine" (taken from a Mario Lanza movie), "Happy Talk," and "I Can't Get No Satisfaction." No matter what its source, the music is all turned into an entertaining and joyous brand of rhythmically exciting straightahead jazz, showing off Monty Alexander in good form. —*Scott Yanow*

The River / Oct. 1985 / Concord Jazz ✦✦✦

On this Concord CD, pianist Monty Alexander performs religious hymns plus a few of his originals that also fit comfortably in that tradition. Accompanied by bassist John Clayton and drummer Ed Thigpen, Alexander's sensitive, but generally swinging, interpretations of these timeless melodies communicate very well. —*Scott Yanow*

Threesome / Nov. 30, 1985-Dec. 1, 1985 / Soul Note ✦✦✦

For this fairly obscure Soul Note album, pianist Monty Alexander is joined by the virtuosic bassist Niels Pedersen and drummer Grady Tate who contributes warm baritone ballad vocals to "A Weaver of Dreams" and "All Blues." Alexander gets in his best playing on his own "Renewal" and "I'll Remember April"; in addition the trio plays a composition apiece by Wes Montgomery and Milt Jackson. The music is what one would expect from Monty Alexander: Oscar Peterson-style bop with some chance-taking and hints of his Jamaican heritage. A tasteful effort. —*Scott Yanow*

Triple Treat, Vol. 3 / Jun. 1987 / Concord Jazz ✦✦✦✦

Recorded at the sessions that resulted in *Triple Treat, Vol 2*, this Concord release follows the same format, with the trio of pianist Monty Alexander, guitarist Herb Ellis and bassist Ray Brown being joined by violinist John Frigo for around half of the selections. The music consists of boppish interpretations of standards ranging from "I Told You I Love You, Now Get Out," and "High Heel Sneakers" to "Corcovado." Fans of these veteran players will be very satisfied with the results. —*Scott Yanow*

Triple Treat, Vol. 2 / Jun. 1987 / Concord Jazz ✦✦✦✦✦

Five years after the original *Triple Treat*, pianist Monty Alexander has a reunion with guitarist Herb Ellis and bassist Ray Brown in a program that is in the tradition of both Oscar Peterson and Nat King Cole. A special bonus is violinist John Frigo who sits in on four of the eight songs. High points include Ray Brown's "Lined with a Groove," "Straighten up and Fly Right," "Seven Come Eleven" and "Lester Leaps In." —*Scott Yanow*

Jamboree: Monty Alexander's Ivory and Steel / Feb. 1988-Mar. 1988 / Concord Jazz ✦✦✦✦✦

Pianist Monty Alexander's "Ivory nnd Steel" group combines together bop-based jazz with Jamaican calypsoes and West Indian rhythms. On this quite enjoyable set, Alexander utilizes both Othello and Len "Boogsie" Sharpe on steel drums, either Marshall Wood or Bernard Montgomery on bass, drummer Marvin "Smitty" Smith and the hand drums of Robert Thomas Jr. Alexander contributed four of the rhythmic originals, which are joined by some Jamaican folk songs (including "Sly Mangoose"), Joni Mitchell's "Big Yellow Taxi" and a couple of obscurities. The accessible results are often memorable. —*Scott Yanow*

Caribbean Circle / Jun. 3, 1992-Jun. 4, 1992 / Chesky ✦✦✦✦

First-rate example of connecting diverse styles and traditions. Alexander, a solid soloist well versed in Caribbean music, integrates rhythms from the islands into his solos, yet retains the jazz edge and drive. A great supporting cast as well, which includes Slide Hampton and Jon Faddis. —*Ron Wynn*

Steamin' / Sep. 14, 1994 / Concord Jazz ✦✦✦

Pianist Monty Alexander, with the exception of "Make Believe," sticks to offbeat material on his trio session with bassist Ira Coleman and drummer Dion Parson. In addition to his original "Dear Diz," Alexander performs such songs as Anthony Newley's "Pure Imagination," Bob Marley's "Lively up Yourself," the "Theme from *The Pawnbroker*" and "Young at Heart." The emphasis is on medium-tempos and the results are consistently swinging and colorful. —*Scott Yanow*

Maybeck Recital Hall Series, Vol. 40 / Sep. 20, 1994 / Concord Jazz ✦✦✦✦

To the Ends of the Earth / May 8, 1996-May 9, 1996 / Concord Picante ✦✦✦

Echoes of Jilly's / Dec. 20, 1996-Dec. 21, 1996 / Concord Jazz ✦✦✦✦

From 1963-67, pianist Monty Alexander played regularly at Jilly's in New York City, a popular hangout where Frank Sinatra would occasionally drop in and, on very rare occasions, sing a song or two. This trio set with bassist John Patitucci and drummer Troy Davis gives Alexander an opportunity to pay tribute to both Jilly's and Sinatra. Performing 13 of the many hundreds of songs associated with the singer, Alexander plays melodic and swinging versions of such tunes as "I've Got You Under My Skin," "Just One of Those Things," "Fly Me to the Moon," "Come Fly With Me" and "Here's That Rainy Day," among others. The songs are mostly familiar, and Alexander does not stretch himself all that much (the only real departure is his haunting unaccompanied melodica solo on "Strangers In the Night"), but his renditions are quite enjoyable and accessible. —*Scott Yanow*

Lorez Alexandria (Lorez Nelson [née Turner])

b. Aug. 14, 1929, Chicago, IL

Vocals / Standards

A solid singer who is superior at interpreting lyrics, gives a soulful feeling to each song and improvises with subtlety, Lorez Alexandria has been a popular attraction for several decades. She sang gospel music with her family at churches starting in the mid-'40s and worked in Chicago nightclubs in the 1950s. With the release of several albums for King during 1957-59, Alexandria became popular beyond her hometown and by the early '60s she was living and working in Los Angeles. Despite a long period off records (only a few private recordings during the 1965-76 period), Alexandria has survived through the many changes in musical styles and in the 1990s can be heard in excellent form. In addition to King, her earlier recording sessions were for Argo and Impulse, while her later albums have been for Discovery and Muse. —*Scott Yanow*

The Band Swings / Feb. 25, 1957+Mar. 5, 1957/ King ✦✦✦

Lorez Alexandria displayed more conventional jazz phrasing and style on this release, which was supported by fine charts and solid production. Although not the strongest or most dynamic vocalist, Alexandria did attract attention with her often sensual leads and sound. —*Ron Wynn*

Singing Songs Everyone Knows / 1960 / Deluxe ✦✦✦

Stylish vocals and pre-rock interpretative standards done by a singer whose delivery, tone, and approach skirted the boundary between jazz-tinged pop and pop-oriented show biz material. —*Ron Wynn*

● **Alexandria the Great/More of the Great Lorez Alexandria** / 1964 / MCA ✦✦✦✦✦

Recorded in 1964, this two-fer features fine jazz vocal stylings and combines two Impulse albums. —*Hank Davis*

How Will I Remember You? / Jan. 16, 1978+Jan. 23, 1978 / Discovery ✦✦✦

Late '70s material with Alexandria essentially sounding the same as she did in the late '50s and early '60s, except that her voice has a weary, wavering quality. She still does pre-rock pop and is backed by another good group of session professionals. —*Ron Wynn*

Music Map

Accordion

Early Uses of the Accordion in Jazz

Buster Moten (1929-31 with Bennie Moten orchestra)
Jack Cornell (1929-30, Irving Mill's Hotsy-Totsy Gang)
Cornell Smelser (recorded "Accordion Joe" with Duke Ellington 1930)
Charles Melrose (1930-31, Cellar Boys)

Accordion Popular in Europe

Nisse Lind (1935-36, Sweden)
Kamil Behounek (1936-46, Czechoslovakia)
Buddy Bertinat (1940-48, Switzerland)
Erik Frank

Pianists Occasionally Doubling on Accordion

George Shearing
Pete Jolly

Bop and Beyond

Joe Mooney
Mat Mathews (1953-54, group with Herbie Mann)
Art Van Damme
Leon Sash (1957, recorded at Newport Jazz Festival)
Tommy Gumina (1960-63, group with Buddy DeFranco)
Gordie Fleming (1977, recorded with Buddy DeFranco)

Frank Morocco
(1980s-90s, featured with Most Brothers)

Guy Klucevsek (1993, recorded with Bill Frisell)
Pete Selvaggio

A Woman Knows / Dec. 19, 1978 / Discovery ✦✦✦

Another late '70s album with Alexandria doing more upbeat, varied material, supported by a sextet with Charles Owens and Brian Atkinson. Things range from pleasant to tepid, with most performances falling somewhere in between. —*Ron Wynn*

Sings the Songs of Johnny Mercer, Vol. 1 / Dec. 5, 1980 / Discovery ✦✦✦✦

This excellent recent work features jazz vocals and classy material with solid four-piece backing. —*Hank Davis*

Sings the Songs of Johnny Mercer, Vol. 2: Harlem Butterfly / Mar. 27, 1984 / Discovery ✦✦✦✦

Sings the Songs of Johnny Mercer, Vol. 3: Tangerine / Nov. 13, 1984 / Trend ✦✦✦✦

With the Mike Wofford Quartet, this excellent recent work features jazz vocals. It's classy material with a solid four-piece backing. —*Hank Davis*

Dear to My Heart / Mar. 24, 1987-Apr. 14, 1987 / Trend ✦✦✦

May I Come In? / Aug. 16, 1990-Aug. 17, 1990 / Muse ✦✦✦

Recent sides with Houston Person on sax. —*Hank Davis*

I'll Never Stop Loving You / Mar. 14, 1992 / Muse ✦✦✦✦✦

This is one of singer Lorez Alexandria's finest recordings of her later years. Alexandria has an expressive style and improvises thorugh her phrasing and placing of words. Backed by a particularly attentive quintet featuring Herman Riley (on tenor and flute) and pianist Gildo Mahones, Alexandria is in particularly fine form on nine superior standards that are highlighted by "Love Walked In," "No Moon at All" and a ten-minute version of "For All We Know." —*Scott Yanow*

Star Eyes / Jun. 6, 1993 / Muse ✦✦✦

Alexandria is backed by tenor saxman Houston Person, guitarist Bruce Forman and drummer Michael Carvin on this outing. The material includes Cole Porter's "Where Have You Been?" and Jerome Kern's "Long Ago and Far Away." —*Jason Ankeny*

Rashied Ali (Robert Patterson)

b. Jul. 1, 1935, Philadelphia, PA

Drums / Free Jazz, Avant-Garde

The task of following Elvin Jones as drummer with John Coltrane must have been one of the most daunting situations ever entered into by a jazz musician. In the mid-'60s, most jazz listeners would have assumed that Jones was the only drummer alive who possessed the requisite imagination, intensity, and powerful sense of swing necessary to drive Coltrane's passions. As it turned out, even Elvin had limitations, and since Coltrane was all about transcending limitations, it seems proper that he would complement Jones' polymetric intractability with the addition of Rashied Ali's skittish, asymmetrical flexibility. The two drummers shared the bandstand briefly, before Jones, reportedly disgusted, left the band. It's not difficult to understand why the pairing proved ill-fated. Jones was an innovator, but he was bound to tradition—specifically, the tradition of ground-beat swing. He was the last stage in the evolution of the drummer as timekeeper; he reiterated swing's primal importance, even as he extended the drummer's role in terms of interaction with the ensemble. For his part, Ali almost completely abandoned a steady pulse, adopting instead a rhythmically irregular, textural, hyperactive approach that propelled the music in a manner at odds with Jones' more literal style. The addition of Ali and the departure of Jones marked Coltrane's last and most extreme step away from the jazz tradition. The removal of a steady beat, and the multitude of implied meters set by Ali and bassist Jimmy Garrison freed Coltrane to an unprecedented extent. Indeed, it was with the addition of Ali to his group that Coltrane's free jazz period truly began.

Ali studied at Philadelphia's Granoff School of Music. He gained early experience with local jazz and R&B bands around Philadelphia. In 1963, he toured Japan with Sonny Rollins, before moving to New York, where he became involved in the free jazz scene there. Associations with Pharoah Sanders, Albert Ayler, Bill Dixon, and Sunny Murray preceded his tenure with Coltrane, which began in 1965 and lasted until the latter's death in 1967. For a time, Ali continued playing with pianist Alice Coltrane, before going off on his own as a bandleader and musical organizer. In 1972, he helped coordinate the New York Musicians Festival. The next year, he formed his own record label, Survival, and opened his own performance venue, Ali's Alley, a New York City loft space that presented free jazz performances until the summer of 1979. In the '80s and '90s, his presence on the scene was sporadic; he performed on occasion with saxophonist Makanda Ken McIntyre, and recorded with multi-instrumentalist Zusaan Kali Fasteau and tenor saxophonist David Murray. In 1987 he recorded as a member of the group Phalanx, with guitarist James "Blood" Ulmer, tenor saxophonist George Adams, and bassist Sirone. In 1991, he made the critically acclaimed album *Touchin' on Trane* with bassist William Parker and tenor saxophonist Charles Gayle. The '90s found Ali at the helm of the band Prima Materia (initially co-led with Parker), an ensemble dedicated to interpreting the late works of Coltrane and Albert Ayler. —*Chris Kelsey*

Rashied Ali Quintet / 1973 / Survival ✦✦✦

Carl Allen

b. 1957, Milwaukee, WI

Drums / Hard Bop

Carl Allen, a fine drummer who has worked with Freddie Hubbard, Jackie McLean, George Coleman, Art Farmer and Bennie Green, fit right in with the band The Message: A Tribute to Art Blakey in the late '80s. He has since led his own sessions for Timeless, Atlantic and Evidence in addition to working on producing albums by other top Young Lions. —*Scott Yanow*

Piccadilly Square / Dec. 6, 1989-Dec. 7, 1989 / Timeless ✦✦✦

The Dark Side of Dewey / Jan. 21, 1992-Jan. 22, 1992 / Evidence ✦✦✦✦

Pursuer / Sep. 26, 1993-Sep. 27, 1993 / Atlantic ✦✦✦✦

Drummer Carl Allen welcomed some of the Young Lions to his Atlantic CD including altoist Vincent Herring, Teodross Avery on tenor and trumpeter Marcus Printup. The music, essentially modern mainstream jazz circa 1967, comprises mostly Allen's originals. Printup sounds like a mixture of Freddie Hubbard and Wynton Marsalis, Herring is content to emulate Cannonball Adderley and Avery looks towards early John Coltrane; in other words, the soloists are generally fairly derivative. Despite that fault, the performances (which have colorful guest appearances from tenor saxophonist George Coleman and trombonist Steve Turre) are generally enjoyable and hard-swinging. —*Scott Yanow*

● **Testimonial** / Dec. 6, 1994-Dec. 7, 1994 / Atlantic ✦✦✦✦

Allen's a decent though hardly extraordinary mainstream drummer who here leads an all-star neo-bop contingent in a set of standards and originals. Nothing surprising about the general conservatism of the date, given the personnel—Vincent Herring on alto sax, Nicholas Payton on trumpet, Cyrus Chestnut on organ, to name a few. There's also nothing in particular wrong with the music, which is heartily played and deeply felt. Nothing, that is, except for the fact that it's covering ground that's been pretty much trampled into dust. It's a pleasant-enough listen, however, and since Cannonball Adderley isn't around to make albums like this anymore, maybe it's a good thing that musicians like these are. On the other hand, as long as guys like Johnny Griffin, Joe Henderson, and Phil Woods still walk the planet, I think the need is somewhat diminished. —*Chris Kelsey*

Geri Allen

b. Jun. 12, 1957, Pontiac, MI

Piano / Post-Bop

Geri Allen is the quintessence of what a late-'90s mainstream jazz musician should be. Well versed in a variety of modern jazz styles, from bop to free, Allen steers a middle course in her own music, speaking in a cultivated and moderately distinctive voice, respectful of, but not overly impressed with the doctrine of conservatism that rules the scene at the end of jazz's first century. There is little conceptually that separates her from her most obvious models—Keith Jarrett, Herbie Hancock and Bill Evans primary among them—yet Allen plays with a spontaneity and melodic gift that greatly transcends rote imitation. Her improvisational style is at various times both spacious and dense, rubato and swinging, blithe and percussive. It's a genuinely expressive, personal voice; her music is an amalgam—honestly conceived, intelligently accessible, and well within the bounds of what is popularly expected from a jazz musician of her generation.

Allen received her early jazz education at the famed Cass Technical High School in Detroit, where her mentor was the highly regarded trumpeter/teacher Marcus Belgrave. In 1979, Allen earned her bachelor's degree in jazz studies from Howard University in Washington, D.C. After graduation, she moved to New York City, where she studied with the veteran bop pianist Kenny Barron. From there, at the behest of the jazz educator Nathan Davis, Allen attended the University of Pittsburgh, earning a master's degree in ethnomusicology, and returning to New York in 1982. In the mid-'80s, Allen formed an association with the Brooklyn "MBase" crowd that surrounded alto saxophonist Steve Coleman. Allen played on several of Coleman's albums, including his first, 1985's *Motherland Pulse*. Allen's own first album, *The Printmakers*, with Anthony Cox and Andrew Cyrille, from a year earlier, showcased the pianist's more avant-garde tendencies. In 1988 came perhaps her first mature group statement, *Etude*, a cooperative trio effort with Charlie Haden and Paul Motian. Allen's loose-limbed lyricism and off-center linearity are perfectly complemented by the innate tunefulness of bassist Haden and the unerring timbral sense of drummer Motian. In the '90s, Allen signed first with Blue Note, then Verve. Her subsequent records placed her in ever more conventional contexts, supported by the cream of the mainstream Young Lion crop. As a soloist, however, Allen continued to push the improvisational envelope, as evidenced by *Sound Museum*, a 1996 recording made under the leadership of Ornette Coleman. Allen was named the top Talent Deserving Wider Recognition among pianists in the 1993 and 1994 *Down Beat* magazine Critics' Polls. Her significant collaborators have included saxophonists Oliver Lake, Arthur Blythe, and Julius Hemphill, trumpeter Lester Bowie, and singer Betty Carter. —*Chris Kelsey*

The Printmakers / Feb. 8, 1984-Feb. 9, 1984 / Minor Music ✦✦✦✦

The pianist's first album is a beauty, with Anthony Cox (b), Andrew Cyrille (d). —*Michael G. Nastos*

Homegrown / Jan. 1985 / Minor Music ✦✦✦

Geri Allen's second recording, a solo effort for the German Minor Music label, finds her already displaying a fairly original style (which occasionally has hints of Herbie Nichols). Allen performs a pair of Thelonious Monk tunes ("Bemsha Swing" and "'Round Midnight"), plus six of her diverse and usually rhythmic originals. A fine early set. —*Scott Yanow*

Open on All Sides in the Middle / Dec. 1987 / Minor Music ✦✦

One of the lesser items in Geri Allen's discography, this erratic set features such soloists as David McMurray on soprano and flute, trombonist Robin Eubanks, altoist Steve Coleman, and on one song, fluegelhornist Marcus Belgrave. Unfortunately, vocalist Shahita Nurallah is also well showcased and the material is comparatively lightweight for a Geri Allen recording, often only bordering on jazz. She can do (and has done) much better than this so-so affair. —*Scott Yanow*

Twylight / 1989 / Verve ✦✦✦✦

Although this CD appears from its cover to be possibly a reggae session, it is actually a strong example of jazz pianist Geri Allen's originality. In addition to playing with her trio of the time (which included bassist Jaribu Shahid and drummer Tani

Tabbal), Allen (who adds synthesizer for color on several numbers) also utilizes percussionists Sadiq Bey and Eli Fountain on some tunes and backs vocalist Clarice Taylor Bell on two songs. All of the 11 selections (which cover a wide variety of moods and are generally quite advanced) are Geri Allen's originals. Worth investigating. —*Scott Yanow*

In the Year of the Dragon / Mar. 1989 / Verve ✦✦✦✦
Throughout *In the Year of the Dragon*, whether the music is classic bop or very free, this trio (comprising pianist Geri Allen, bassist Charlie Haden and drummer Paul Motian) is creative, colorful and unpredictable but logical. The musical communication between the three musicians on their originals, Bud Powell's "Oblivion" and Ornette Coleman's "Invisible" seems telepathic. —*Scott Yanow*

Segments / Apr. 6, 1989-Apr. 8, 1989 / DIW ✦✦✦

The Nurturer / Jan. 5, 1990-Jan. 6, 1990 / Blue Note ✦✦✦✦✦
A fine example of Geri Allen's advanced music (which holds onto tradition without merely recreating the past), this CD matches the talented pianist with veteran trumpeter Marcus Belgrave, altoist Kenny Garrett, bassist Robert Hurst, drummer Jeff Watts and percussionist Eli Fountain on group originals and two obscurities. Everyone is in fine form, and the Belgrave-Garrett combination works quite well. —*Scott Yanow*

● **Maroons** / Feb. 11, 1992-Feb. 14, 1992 / Blue Note ✦✦✦✦✦
Allen has developed into one of the major voices of the modern jazz piano. On *Maroons* she brings out the best in trumpeter Wallace Roney, welcomes her mentor, trumpeter Marcus Belgrave on a few tracks and performs 15 fresh compositions, 13 of them her originals. The music is unpredictable and explorative but still tied enough to the tradition to make the results quite coherent. This is a strong example of Allen's playing and compositional talents. —*Scott Yanow*

Twenty One / Mar. 23, 1994-Mar. 24, 1994 / Blue Note ✦✦✦✦
Pianist Geri Allen has thus far been a very consistent performer and all of her recordings are easily recommended. This particular set finds her in a trio with bassist Ron Carter and drummer Tony Williams performing six of her originals along with six jazz standards. Allen's style is fairly original (with hints of Herbie Nichols) and her chance-taking but logical solos are generally quite stimulating. —*Scott Yanow*

Eyes in the Back of Your Head / Dec. 14, 1995-Mar. 1, 1996 / Blue Note ✦✦✦✦✦
This is possibly pianist Geri Allen's most advanced release. Always a pianist with her own voice, the increasingly original Allen performs three atmospheric piano solos, including a version of Ron Carter's "Little Waltz," during which she adds a little bit of synthesizer. There is a duet with percussionist Cyro Baptista, two duets with altoist Ornette Coleman (who through the years has almost never recorded as a sideman), and four numbers in which Allen is joined by her husband, trumpeter Wallace Roney (two of which also include Baptista). Except for the Ornette pieces, Allen is the dominant force throughout the intriguing set, which includes the very haunting "Windows to the Soul" (dedicated to the recently departed drummer Tony Williams). The music is mostly avant-garde, but purposeful and logical in its own fashion. Well worth several listens. —*Scott Yanow*

Some Aspects of Water / Mar. 15, 1996+Mar. 17, 1996 / Storyville ✦✦✦✦

Harry Allen

b. Oct. 12, 1966, Washington, DC
Tenor Saxophone / Swing
A swing revivalist in the tradition of Scott Hamilton and Ken Peplowski, Harry Allen started playing tenor and clarinet while in high school. Since graduating from Rutgers he has worked with Bucky Pizzarelli, John Colliani, Keith Ingham and as a leader, showing great potential for the future. —*Scott Yanow*

How Long Has This Been Going On? / Jun. 30, 1988 / Progressive ✦✦✦✦

A Night at Birdland, Vol. 1 / Nov. 19, 1993-Nov. 20, 1993 / Nagel-Heyer ✦✦✦✦✦
A glance at this CD's cover might cause collectors to do a double take for it looks similar to the original *A Night at Birdland* album by Horace Silver and the Jazz Messengers from the mid-'50s. The Birdland in this case is a jazz club in Hamburg, Germany and the music is not hard bop but hard-driving swing. The excellent young tenor Harry Allen is heard leading a quintet that also includes trumpeter Randy Sandke, pianist Brian Dee, bassist Len Skeat and (in one of his final sessions) drummer Oliver Jackson. Allen has an attractive and passionate tone and is heard in excellent form throughout the nine standards; he and Sandke make for a very effective team. A rewarding release (as is the second volume) from the German Nagel-Heyer label. —*Scott Yanow*

A Night at Birdland, Vol. 2 / Nov. 19, 1993-Nov. 20, 1993 / Nagel-Heyer ✦✦✦✦✦
On the second of two volumes, Harry Allen plays not at New York's Birdland but a club with the same name in Hamburg. A talented young tenor whose swing style and hard tone make for an appealing mix, Harry Allen swings through 11 standards with the assistance of trumpeter Randy Sandke, pianist Brian Dee, bassist

Len Skeat and drummer Oliver Jackson. Highlights include "Isn't This a Lovely Day," "The Song Is You," "Stardust" and "Lover Come Back to Me." A very enjoyable set of modern swing/mainstream made available by the German Nagel-Heyer label. —*Scott Yanow*

Blue Skies / May 13, 1994 / John Marks ✦✦✦✦
The young tenor Harry Allen, assisted by pianist John Bunch, bassist Dennis Irwin and drummer Duffy Jackson, is in excellent form on a variety of swing standards. Allen seems poised at this point to follow in the footsteps of Scott Hamilton, for he also has a warm tone, and a melodic approach to improvising, and swings at any tempo. —*Scott Yanow*

● **Jazz im Amerika Haus, Vol. 1** / May 28, 1994 / Nagel-Heyer ✦✦✦✦✦
Following a generation after the Concord All-Stars and such fine swing stylists as Scott Hamilton, Warren Vache and Ken Peplowski, the young tenor Harry Allen has become a fixture on the German Nagel-Heyer label. His appealing sound and solid sense of swing are well showcased on this live set from Hamburg's Amerika Haus club in a quartet with pianist John Bunch, bassist Dennis Irwin and drummer Duffy Jackson. Among the highlights of the ten standards are "'Deed I Do," Count Basie's "The King," "Honeysuckle Rose" and "Limehouse Blues." Recommended. —*Scott Yanow*

Celebration of Billy Strayhorn's Music, Vol. 1 / Aug. 26, 1994 / Progressive ✦✦✦✦
Billy Strayhorn's impressive work as a composer was often overshadowed by that of Duke Ellington. On two CDs, pianist Keith Ingham (who provided the arrangements), promising young tenor Harry Allen, guitarist Chris Flory, bassist Dennis Irwin and drummer Chuck Riggs perform 32 Strayhorn originals, including 16 on this first disc. In addition to such well-known pieces as "Satin Doll," "Take the 'A' Train" and "Daydream," the musicians (who are heard in a variety of combinations) also revive such rarely performed tunes as "Violet Blue," "Smada," "Noir Blue" and "Newport Up." Both of these well-conceived releases are easily recommended. —*Scott Yanow*

Celebration of Billy Strayhorn's Music, Vol. 2 / Aug. 26, 1994 / Progressive ✦✦✦✦
The second of two CDs once again finds pianist-arranger Keith Ingham teaming up in various combinations with tenor saxophonist Harry Allen (26 at the time), guitarist Chris Flory, bassist Dennis Irwin and drummer Chuck Riggs to perform 16 Billy Strayhorn selections. Some of these tunes ("Jazz Festival Jazz," "Balcony Serenade," "After All," "Snibor" and "Midriff") had not been played much, if ever, in recent years. Somehow the quintet manages to convey the power of the Duke Ellington Orchestra on this very successful (and welcome) tribute. —*Scott Yanow*

Henry "Red" Allen

b. Jan. 7, 1908, New Orleans, LA, d. Apr. 17, 1967, New York, NY
Trumpet, Vocals / New Orleans Jazz, Dixieland, Swing
One of the last great New Orleans trumpeters to emerge during the post-Louis Armstrong era, Henry "Red" Allen has long been overshadowed by Satch and his successors but actually had a fresh new approach of his own to offer. Allen sounded modern no matter what the setting and the rhythmic freedom he achieved made his solos consistently unpredictable and exciting. The son of Henry Allen, Sr. (a famous New Orleans brass band leader), he learned trumpet early on and played in his father's parade band along with other local groups. After working on the riverboats with Fate Marable and with Fats Pichon the following year, Allen joined King Oliver in Chicago. He recorded in New York with Oliver and Clarence Williams and then Red Allen joined Luis Russell's superb orchestra and began his own solo recording career. Signed by Victor as an alternative to OKeh's Louis Armstrong, Allen's solos were original and brilliant from the start (particularly "It Should Be You"); throughout the 1930s his trumpet and gruff vocals would be heard on dozens of recordings, and even when the material was indifferent Allen was usually able to uplift the music. After notable stints with Luis Russell (1929-32), Fletcher Henderson (1933-34) and the Mills Blue Rhythm Band (1934-37), Allen became part of Louis Armstrong's backup band for three years, secure but somewhat anonymous work. However, starting in 1940 Red Allen led a series of impressive combos that were Dixieland-based but also open to certain aspects of rhythm & blues. Trombonist J.C. Higginbotham (a lifelong friend) and altoist Dan Stovall were on many of his recordings. From 1954-65 Allen's frequently riotous group played regularly at New York's Metropole (Coleman Hawkins was occasionally among his sidemen); he visited Europe several times (including in 1959 with Kid Ory's band), and was one of the most memorable participants in the Dec. 1957 CBS TV special *The Sound of Jazz*. Red Allen remained very active up until his death and was proclaimed in the 1960s by Don Ellis as "the most creative and avant-garde trumpeter in New York." The European Classics label documents his recordings of the 1930s and many (but not all) of his later performances are also available on CD. —*Scott Yanow*

The Henry Allen Collection, Vol. 1 (1929-1930) / Jul. 16, 1929-Dec. 17, 1930 / JSP ✦✦✦✦
The program on this excellent CD reissues the first recordings led by the great trumpeter Henry "Red" Allen. The music (which has also been reissued in the Classics series) includes such exciting numbers as "It Should Be You," "Biff'ly Blues," "Sugar Hill Function," "Pleasin' Paul" and "You Might Get Better, But You'll Never Get Well" plus songs in which Allen is prominent in the backup group that accompanies singers Victoria and Addie Spivey. With sidemen drawn from the Luis Russell Orchestra (including trombonist J.C. Higginbotham, clarinetist Albert Nicholas, and altoist Charlie Holmes), the performances are timeless and these sessions are essential to all classic jazz collections in one form or another. *Vol. 2* in the JSP series has the alternate takes from the same dates. —*Scott Yanow*

The Henry Allen Collection, Vol. 2 (1929-1930) / Jul. 16, 1929-Dec. 17, 1930 / JSP ✦✦✦
This English import is a perfect complement to the Classics series, for the CD consists of all of the alternate takes from Red Allen's 1929-30 sessions (including two very different versions of "It Should Be You") and his meetings with singers Victoria and Addie Spivey. In addition, Luis Russell's rare recordings from Oct. 24 and Dec. 17, 1930 (which feature Allen's trumpet) wrap up this gap-filling CD. —*Scott Yanow*

1929-1933 / Jul. 16, 1929-Nov. 9, 1933 / Classics ✦✦✦✦✦
The first of a five-volume CD series released by the European Classics label that reissues all of the recordings led by trumpeter Red Allen during 1929-41 is one of the best. The great trumpeter is first heard fronting the Luis Russell Orchestra for such classics as "It Should Be You" and "Biff'ly Blues," he interacts with blues singer Victoria Spivey, and on the selections from 1933 (two of which were previously unreleased) he co-leads a group with tenor saxophonist Coleman Hawkins. Not all of the performances are gems but there are many memorable selections including "How Do They Do It That Way," "Pleasin' Paul," "Sugar Hill Function," and "Patrol Wagon Blues." Other soloists include trombonists J.C. Higginbotham and Dicky Wells, clarinetist Albert Nicholas and altoist Charlie Holmes. —*Scott Yanow*

Henry "Red" Allen [Time-Life] / Jul. 16, 1929-Jul. 19, 1959 / Time-Life ✦✦✦
This attractive three-LP set gives one a good overview of the early recordings of trumpeter Red Allen with the first two records covering just a six-year period (1929-35); unfortunately only four selections are from after 1940. Completists will want to pick up the Classics CDs instead, but this reissue does have a large and informative booklet (with notes by Richard Sudhalter) and serves as a fine introduction to the great trumpeter. —*Scott Yanow*

A Recorded Documentary 1933-1941 / Aug. 18, 1933-Jul. 22, 1941 / Meritt ✦✦✦✦
This hard-to-find double LP from the collectors label Meritt has a great deal of valuable material. Allen and a variety of All-Stars are heard on previously unissued alternate takes by Fletcher Henderson's Orchestra in 1933 (including a version of "King Porter Stomp"), bands led by trombonist Benny Morton, clarinetist Buster Bailey and blues singer Victoria Spivey in 1937 and a few numbers with singers Ruby Smith and Ida Cox. In addition, the complete Red Allen sessions of April 17 and July 22, 1941 (including all alternate takes and breakdowns) wrap up the two-fer with many fine solos from trombonist J.C. Higginbotham, clarinetist Edmond Hall and pianist Ken Kersey. Vintage jazz collectors and Red Allen fans are advised to search for this memorable set of heated swing music. —*Scott Yanow*

1933-1935 / Nov. 9, 1933-Jul. 19, 1935 / Classics ✦✦✦✦
The second of five CDs put out by the European Classics label that document trumpeter Red Allen's 1929-41 recordings has three titles from a session co-led with tenor saxophonist Coleman Hawkins, eight songs from 1934 and a dozen from the following year. Allen takes vocals on most of the tracks and, even if not all of the songs are gems, there are many highlights including "Pardon My Southern Accent," "Rug Cutter Swing," "Believe It, Beloved," "Rosetta" and "Truckin'." The strong supporting cast includes trombonists Dickie Wells and J.C. Higginbotham, clarinetists Buster Bailey and Cecil Scott, and, on one date, tenorman Chu Berry. All five of the Red Allen Classics CDs are recommended. —*Scott Yanow*

1935-1936 / Nov. 8, 1935-Aug. 31, 1936 / Classics ✦✦✦✦
The third of five Classics CDs that cover Red Allen's recordings of the 1930s has the contents of six complete sessions from a ten-month period. Allen (who has vocals on all but one of the 24 selections) is assisted by such classic players as trombonist J.C. Higginbotham, Cecil Scott (on tenor and clarinet), and altoist Tab Smith, plus several strong rhythm sections. Among the more memorable swing performances are "On Treasure Island," "Take Me Back to My Boots and Saddle," "Lost," "Algiers Stomp" and "I'll Sing You a Thousand Love Songs." The fairly obscure recordings (cut during an era when the big bands really ruled) have long been underrated. —*Scott Yanow*

1936-1937 / Oct. 12, 1936-Apr. 29, 1937 / Classics ✦✦✦
The fourth in the Classics label's five-CD series of Red Allen recordings reissues 20 obscure performances from a seven-month period. Although Red Allen was mostly playing with big bands during the 1930s, these small-group sides gave him a chance to be showcased quite a bit more than usual. Allen takes vocals on each of the tunes and, although many of the songs are long forgotten, his trumpet solos and the improvisations of altoist Tab Smith, clarinetist Buster Bailey and Ted McRae on tenor keep one's interest. This is actually the weakest of the five CDs but all are worth picking up. —*Scott Yanow*

1937-1941 / Jun. 19, 1937-Jul. 22, 1941 / Classics ✦✦✦✦✦
The final of the five Classics CDs that document the early recordings of trumpeter Henry "Red" Allen covers music from three very different bands. Allen is first heard singing and playing trumpet on eight pop tunes he uplifts with a recording group in 1937 that features altoist Tab Smith. Allen also plays four Dixieland standards with a hot septet in 1940 that includes trombonist Benny Morton, clarinetist Edmond Hall and pianist Lil Armstrong. The final eight numbers (four of which were previously unreleased) showcases his regular band from 1941 (with trombonist J.C. Higginbotham and clarinetist Edmond Hall) really romping through some hard-swinging performances, including "K.K. Boogie" and a two-part version of "Sometimes I'm Happy." All five of these Classics CDs are easily recommended; this is one of the better ones. —*Scott Yanow*

The Very Great / Apr. 17, 1941-Jul. 16, 1946 / Rarities ✦✦✦
The valuable music on this now-rare European LP is well-deserving to be reissued on CD. Trumpeter Red Allen is heard on four numbers with his 1941 sextet (which also features trombonist J.C. Higginbotham, clarinetist Edmond Hall and pianist Ken Kersey) and on 12 heated jams with his band of 1944-46, an ensemble that found Higginbotham and the underrated altoist Don Stovall holding their own with Allen. The latter group combined the excitement and drive of R&B with the spontaneity and hot solos of Dixieland. "The Crawl" is a classic and several of the other performances are close behind. It's well worth the search. —*Scott Yanow*

Nice / 1946-Feb. 1963 / Phoenix ✦✦✦✦
This long out-of-print LP has seven titles (two previously unreleased) from Red Allen's exciting 1946 band with trombonist J.C. Higginbotham and altoist Don Stovall), the two selections ("Wild Man Blues" and "Rosetta") performed by Allen with an all-star group on *The Sound of Jazz* television broadcast and four Dixieland standards played in 1963 with a sextet including trombonist Cutty Cutshall, clarinetist Tony Parenti and pianist Ralph Sutton. Red Allen collectors (and listeners who enjoy the spirit of classic jazz) will enjoy this fine LP. —*Scott Yanow*

Jazz from Bill Green's Rustic Lodge, 1949-1951 / 1949-1951 / Jass ✦✦✦

★ **World on a String** / Mar. 21, 1957-Apr. 10, 1957 / Bluebird ✦✦✦✦✦
This CD is a true classic. Trumpeter Red Allen is heard at the peak of his creative powers with a remarkable octet also featuring trombonist J.C. Higginbotham, clarinetist Buster Bailey and the great tenor Coleman Hawkins. "I Cover the Waterfront" has a wonderfully abstract statement from Allen, "Love Is Just Around the Corner" is joyous Dixieland, "Let Me Miss You, Baby" is a particularly strong blues (featuring Allen's vocal) and the simple blues line that serves as a melody on "Algiers Bounce" is quite catchy. The other seven selections from the classic veterans are also quite enjoyable. Although the music has its basis in Dixieland and swing, the solos of Allen and Hawkins in particular look ahead toward the future. There is nothing dated about these essential performances; highly recommended. —*Scott Yanow*

Red Allen, Jack Teagarden & Kid Ory at Newport / Jul. 4, 1957 / Verve ✦✦
When confronted with a variety of his alumni from his past at the 1957 Newport Jazz Festival, Louis Armstrong preferred instead to play his standard show with his regular group. The veterans had their own separate set, and that is what is heard on this LP. Trumpeter Red Allen, trombonist J.C. Higginbotham, and clarinetist Buster Bailey play spirited versions of "Struttin' with Some Barbecue" and "St. James Infirmary"; trombonist Jack Teagarden joins up for "China Boy" and an overly loose "Basin Street Blues"; trombonist Kid Ory struts and sings on "Muskrat Ramble"; and Ory, Teagarden and Higginbotham perform a somewhat incoherent "High Society." An upbeat, if somewhat streaky affair, this historic encounter has its strong moments, but at 27 minutes, it is all over much too soon. —*Scott Yanow*

Henry Red Allen Quartet "Live" / Sep. 15, 1961+Sep. 22, 1961 / Fanfare ✦✦✦
On this LP trumpeter Red Allen is heard during two performances at Chicago's London House in 1961. Assisted by pianist Sammy Price (who is featured on James P. Johnson's "Snowy Morning Blues"), bassist Frank Skeete and drummer Jerry Potter, Allen is in excellent form. Although he sticks to Dixieland-oriented standards, his trumpet playing is surprisingly modern with many hints of advanced harmonies and surprising placements of notes. This LP is becoming difficult to find and has yet to surface on CD. —*Scott Yanow*

Rare Red Allen Trio Performances / Mar. 1962-Mar. 22, 1963 / Flutegroove ◆◆◆
Trumpeter Red Allen is heard with his quartets of 1962-63 (which include either Sammy Price or Lannie Scott on piano, bassist Frank Skeete and drummer Jerry Potter) playing an odd variety of material ranging from "That's a Plenty" and a remake of "Biff'ly Blues" to "I've Grown Accustomed to Her Face" and "Hava Nagila." Throughout, Allen's New Orleans-based but unclassifiable solos are much more modern than expected in spots while still being accessible enough to the audience at Chicago's London House. —*Scott Yanow*

Henry Red Allen Memorial Album / Jun. 5, 1962 / Prestige ◆◆◆
This very enjoyable if brief (under 29 minutes) LP gives one a definitive look at Red Allen in his later years. Allen (who is accompanied by pianist Lannie Scott, bassist Franklin Skeete and drummer Jerry Potter) plays melodic yet advanced trumpet solos on six standards, "There's a House in Harlem" and his "Bif'ly Blues." His solos are unpredictable and he has expressive vocals on "I Ain't Got Nobody" and "Cherry." This LP (the material has not yet been reissued on CD) is worth searching for. —*Scott Yanow*

Feeling Good / Jun. 29, 1965-Aug. 18, 1965 / Columbia ◆◆◆

Marshall Allen

b. May 25, 1924, Louisville, KY
Alto Saxophone / Avant-Garde, Free Jazz
Marshall Allen's name will always be closely linked with that of Sun Ra. Although he was 32 when he started playing regularly with Ra (and had performed previously with pianist Art Simmons in Paris during 1949-50 and toured Europe with James Moody), the altoist was a virtual unknown at the time. However, from 1956 up until Sun Ra's death in 1993 (with only brief periods off, such as to record with Paul Bley in the mid-'60s), Allen was an integral part of Ra's sound. On alto, flute, piccolo and oboe Marshall Allen's intense flights could be quite violent and out of tune (sounding like Johnny Hodges from a different dimension) but there was no doubting his sincerity and passion or the directness of his musical message. —*Scott Yanow*

Steve Allen (Stephen Valentine Patrick William Allen)

b. Dec. 21, 1921, New York, NY
Piano / Bop, Swing
For someone of Steve Allen's versatility and staggering capacity for work, jazz occupies a small yet significant portion of his biography. Yet despite his crowded agenda, Allen can still spin out facile, competent, bop-and-cocktail-flavored piano in fast jazz company—nothing particularly original but always pleasurable to hear. He started to play the piano while a child—his parents were traveling vaudeville performers—but the keyboard soon had to take a back seat to his media career, first on radio and then on television. Best known as a comedian and the first host of the American TV institution, the *Tonight Show* (1954-57), Allen frequently played piano and sang on his shows and used them as a forum to present guests from the jazz world. He also played the lead role in the film *The Benny Goodman Story* in 1955, produced the TV series *Jazz Scene USA* in 1962, and narrated a history of jazz on records, *The Jazz Story* (Coral). Allen recorded frequently for Coral, Dot, Roulette, EmArcy, and Decca during the peak of his TV fame and as late as 1992, taped an enjoyable mainstream set for Concord Jazz, *Plays Jazz Tonight.*. In addition to some 43 books (and counting), Allen claims to have written (as of 1994) more than 4,700 songs, of which only a bare handful—"This Could Be The Start of Something (Big)," "Gravy Waltz," "Impossible"—have staked claims in the repertoire. Ultimately Allen's most valuable contribution to jazz has been as a cheerleader in the mass media. —*Richard S. Ginell*

Plays Hi-Fi Music for Influentials / 1957-1966 / Varese ◆◆◆◆◆
Sixteen tracks selected from various albums released between 1957 and 1966. Allen distributes the material fairly evenly between his own compositions and interpretations of standards by the likes of Cole Porter, Johnny Mercer, and Irving Berlin. As cocktail jazz goes, it's very straightahead (though some cuts take a bossa nova approach), and perhaps not eccentric enough to appeal to the lounge revival crowd. —*Richie Unterberger*

● **Steve Allen Plays Jazz Tonight** / Nov. 18, 1982 / Concord Jazz ◆◆◆◆◆

Eric Allison

b. Mar. 7, 1951, South Bend, IL
Tenor Saxophone, Clarinet / Hard Bop, Bop
Although he has been a professional since he was 15, Eric Allison did not make his recording debut as a leader until he was 45 and cut the highly enjoyable *Mean Streets Beat* (Contemporary). Allison became interested in jazz while in junior high school and was originally mostly self-taught on alto. After attending Northwestern University and the University of Miami, he settled in Florida, working

steadily in clubs since the mid-1970s, gigging with pianist Eddie Higgins and the New Gene Krupa Orchestra and gaining a strong local reputation. A versatile player whose gigs have ranged from Dixieland to funk, Allison is at his best on cooking bop-oriented jazz. —*Scott Yanow*

● **Mean Streets Beat** / Mar. 1996 / Contemporary ◆◆◆◆◆
This is a fun recording that succeed both as a goodtime party record and as a set well worth several close listens. Eric Allison (who plays tenor, alto, clarinet and flute) leads a varied program that features among his sidemen on various cuts the very compatible Turk Mauro (an impressive baritonist who also plays tenor), trumpeter Melton Mustafa, four different pianists (including an effective Dr. Lonnie Smith, normally an organist), three bassists and two drummers. The music ranges from "Mean Streets Beat" (which utilizes an infectious New Orleans parade rhythm), a couple of mellow features for Allison's clarinet, and the cheerful bop melody "Here I Go Again" (which deserves to become a standard) to "Improvisation for Unaccompanied Saxophones," a rhythmic duet with Mauro that was originally recorded several decades ago by Zoot Sims and Al Cohn. Each of the ten selections has its own purpose and musical identity, and all but the saxophone duet are Allison originals. It is surprising that the 45-year-old Allison had only led one previous recording, and that for a local label in 1985, but perhaps it takes a lot of living to come up with so much good material. In any case, this highly enjoyable set was certainly worth the wait. —*Scott Yanow*

After Hours / 1997 / Contemporary ◆◆◆◆
Taking Avery Parrish's "After Hours," a blues classic that was a hit for the Erskine Hawkins band in the 1940s, and using it as a blueprint for an entire concept is what fuels this interesting and effective album by saxman Eric Allison. Writing a batch of tunes in the same Saturday night smoky-old-bar mold, Allison put together a crack small band that could swing and still manage to sound like they were playing the last set of the night in some dingy little jazz club. The ambience is sensational, the soloing is cathartic, and the groove is wide and deep, making this one concept album that truly works on every level. —*Cub Koda*

Mose Allison

b. Nov. 11, 1927, Tippo, MS
Piano, Vocals, Lyricist / Hard Bop, Folk-Jazz, Jazz Blues, Country Blues
Not unlike his namesake, Luther Allison, pianist Mose Allison has suffered from "categorization problem," given his equally brilliant career. Although his boogie woogie and bebop-laden piano style is innovative and fresh sounding when it comes to blues and jazz, it is as a songwriter that Allison really shines. Allison's songs have been recorded by The Who ("Young Man Blues"), Leon Russell ("I'm Smashed"), and Bonnie Raitt ("Everybody's Cryin' Mercy"). Other admirers include Tom Waits, John Mayall, Georgie Fame, the Rolling Stones and Van Morrison. But because he's always played both blues and jazz, and not one to the exclusion of the other, his career has suffered. As he himself admits, he has a "category" problem that lingers to this day. "There's a lot of places I don't work because they're confused about what I do," he explained in a 1990 interview in *Goldmine* magazine. Despite the lingering confusion, Allison remains one of the finest songwriters in 20th century blues.

Mose Allison's first exposure to blues on record was through Louis Jordan recordings, including "Outskirts of Town" and "Pinetop Blues." Allison credits Jordan as being a major influence on him, and also credits Nat King Cole, Louis Armstrong and Fats Waller. He started out on trumpet but later switched to piano. In his youth, he had easy access, via the radio, to the music of Pete Johnson, Albert Ammons and Meade Lux Lewis. Allison also credits the songwriter Percy Mayfield, the "Poet Laureate of the Blues," as being a major inspiration on his songwriting.

After a stint in college and the army, Allison's first professional gig was in Lake Charles, LA, in 1950. He returned to college to finish up at Louisiana State University in Baton Rouge, where he studied English and Philosophy, a far cry from his initial path as a chemical engineering major.

Allison began his recording career with the Prestige label in 1956, shortly after he moved to New York City. He recorded an album with Al Cohn and Bob Brookmeyer, and then in 1957 got his own record contract. A big break was the opportunity to play with Cohn and Zoot Sims shortly after his arrival in New York, but he later became more well known after playing with saxophonist Stan Getz. After leaving Prestige Records, where he recorded now classic albums like *Back Country Suite* (1957), *Young Man Mose* (1958), and *Seventh Son* (1958-59), he moved to Columbia for two years before meeting up with Neshui Ertegun of Atlantic Records. He recalled that he signed his contract with Atlantic after about ten minutes in Neshui's office. Allison spent a big part of his recording career at Atlantic Records, where he became most friendly with Ertegun. After the company saw substantial growth and Allison was no longer working directly with Ertegun, he became discouraged and left.

Allison's discography is a lengthy one, and there are gems to be found on all of his albums, many of which can be found in vinyl shops. His output since 1957 has averaged at least one album a year until 1976, when he finished up at Atlantic with the classic *Your Mind Is on Vacation*. There was a gap of six years before he recorded again, this time for Elektra's Musician subsidiary in 1982, when he recorded *Middle Class White Boy*. Since 1987, he's been with Blue Note/Capitol. His debut for that label was *Ever Since the World Ended*. Allison has recorded some of the most creative material of his career on the Blue Note subsidiary of Capitol Records, including *My Backyard* (1992) and *The Earth Wants You* (1994), both produced by Ben Sidran. Also in 1994, Rhino Records released a boxed set, *Allison Wonderland*. —*Richard Skelly*

Back Country Suite / Mar. 7, 1957 / Original Jazz Classics ✦✦✦✦
Mose Allison's very first recording finds the 29-year-old pianist taking just two vocals (on his "Young Man Blues" and "One Room Country Shack") but those are actually the most memorable selections. The centerpiece of this trio outing with bassist Taylor LaFargue and drummer Frank Isola (which has been reissued on CD) is Allison's ten-part "Back Country Suite," a series of short concise folk melodies that puts the focus on his somewhat unique piano style that, although boppish, also looked back towards the country blues tradition. Very interesting music. —*Scott Yanow*

● Greatest Hits / Mar. 7, 1957-Feb. 13, 1959 / Original Jazz Classics ✦✦✦✦✦
Basic, no-frills anthology of 13 of his better late-'50s Prestige sides, all of which feature his vocals. It has most of his most famous songs, particularly to listeners from a rock background, including his versions of "The Seventh Son," "Eyesight to the Blind" (covered by the Who on *Tommy*, though Sonny Boy Williamson did it before Allison), "Parchman Farm" (done by John Mayall), and "Young Man's Blues" (also covered by the Who). Were it not for the significant omission of "I'm Not Talking" (retooled by the Yardbirds), this would qualify as the basic collection for most listeners, although more thorough retrospectives are available (particularly Rhino's *Anthology*). *Greatest Hits* does include liner notes by Pete Townshend, originally penned for a 1972 collection. —*Richie Unterberger*

Local Color / Nov. 8, 1957 / Original Jazz Classics ✦✦✦
This CD reissue brings back Mose Allison's second of six Prestige recordings. Allison performs eight instrumentals in a trio with bassist Addison Farmer and drummer Nick Stabulas, displaying his unusual mixture of country blues and bebop and even taking an effective trumpet solo on "Trouble In Mind." However it is his vocals on "Lost Mind" and particularly the classic "Parchman Farm" that are most memorable. —*Scott Yanow*

● Allison Wonderland: Anthology / 1957-1989 / Rhino ✦✦✦✦✦
Only Dave Frishberg and possibly Mark Murphy can rival Mose Allison when it comes to creative use of irony in lyric writing and neither compares as an instrumentalist. He's a fine bop pianist able to play challenging instrumentals and eclectic enough to integrate country blues and gospel elements into his style. Allison's unique mix of down-home and uptown styles has made him a standout since the '50s. He's one of the few jazz musicians on Atlantic's roster ideally suited for Rhino's two-disc anthology format. Allison recorded so many different kinds of songs and was always as much, if not more, a singles than an album artist. In addition, Rhino thankfully sequenced the selected songs—which span over 40 years, from 1957 to 1989, and include all of his best-known songs—chronologically. Allison does reflective duo and trio pieces, moves into uptempo combo numbers with a jump beat, then returns to the intimate small group sound. His ability to highlight key lyrics, and his delivery, timing and packing are superb. The set includes such classics as "Back Country Blues," "Parchman Farm," "Western Man," and "Ever Since the World Ended," plus definitive covers of of Willie Dixon's "The Seventh Son" and Sonny Boy Williamson II's "Eyesight to the Blind." It's an essential introduction to Allison's catalog. —*Ron Wynn*

Creek Bank / Jan. 24, 1958+Aug. 15, 1958 / Prestige ✦✦✦✦
When Mose Allison recorded his six early albums for Prestige, he was best known as a bop-based pianist who occasionally sang. This single CD (which reissues in full *Young Man Mose* and *Creek Bank*) has 15 instrumentals—including a rare appearance by Allison on trumpet ("Stroll")—but it is his five typically ironic vocals that are most memorable, particularly Allison's classic "The Seventh Son" and "If You Live." His piano playing, even with the Bud Powell influence, was beginning to become original and he successfully performs both revived swing songs and moody originals. —*Scott Yanow*

Autumn Song / Feb. 13, 1959 / Original Jazz Classics ✦✦✦✦
Mose Allison recorded six albums as a leader for Prestige during 1957-59, an era when he was better known as a jazz pianist than as a folk-country blues vocalist and masterful lyricist. On this CD reissue of his final Prestige date, Allison (in a trio with bassist Addison Farmer and drummer Ronnie Free) performs seven instrumentals (including "It's Crazy," "Autumn Song" and "Groovin' High") but it is the three vocals ("Eyesight to the Blind," "That's All Right" and Duke Ellington's

"Do Nothin' Till You Hear from Me") that are most memorable. One realizes why Allison was soon emphasizing his vocals; he was a much more distinctive singer than pianist, although his piano playing was actually fairly inventive. This is an excellent all-round set. —*Scott Yanow*

Mose Allison Trilogy: High Jinks! / Dec. 21, 1959-May 23, 1961 / Columbia/Legacy ✦✦✦✦
Three formerly rare Mose Allison albums originally cut for Columbia and Epic (*Transfiguration of Hiram Brown, I Love the Life I Live* and *V-8 Ford Blues*) are reissued in full on this attractive three-CD set plus six previously unreleased numbers. During this period (which dates between his associations with the Prestige and Atlantic labels), Mose Allison was making the transition from being a pianist-vocalist to a vocalist-pianist. He sings on roughly half the selections including "Baby, Please Don't Go," "'Deed I Do," "Fool's Paradise" and "I Love the Life I Live." The instrumentals (which also feature Addison Farmer, Henry Grimes, Bill Crow or Aaron Bell on bass and Jerry Segal, Paul Motian, Gus Johnson or Osie Johnson on drums) are highlighted by the interesting eight-song "Hiram Brown Suite." Mose Allison fans will want to go out of their way to get this set. —*Scott Yanow*

I Don't Worry About a Thing / Mar. 15, 1962 / Rhino ✦✦✦✦✦
Mose Allison was already 34 and had recorded nine records as a leader before cutting his debut for Atlantic (which has been reissued on CD by Rhino), but this was his breakthrough date. One of jazz's greatest lyricists, at the time, Allison was making the transition from being a pianist who occasionally sang to becoming a vocalist who also played his own unusual brand of piano. In addition to such originals as "Your Mind Is on Vacation," "I Don't Worry About a Thing (Because I Know Nothing Will Turn out Right)" and "It Didn't Turn out That Way," he sings bluish versions of two standards ("Meet Me at No Special Place" and "The Song Is Ended") and plays five instrumentals with his trio. There are only thirty-three-and-a-half minutes of music on this straight reissue of the orignal LP, but the set is one of Mose Allison's most significant recordings. —*Scott Yanow*

Your Mind Is on Vacation / Apr. 5, 1976-Apr. 9, 1976 / Atlantic ✦✦✦✦✦
It seems strange to realize that this was Mose Allison's only recording during the 1973-81 period. In addition to his trio with bassist Jack Hannah and drummer Jerry Granelli, such guests as altoist David Sanborn, Al Cohn and Joe Farrell on tenors and trumpeter Al Porcino pop up on a few selections. However Mose Allison is easily the main star, performing ten of his originals (including a remake of the famous title cut, "What Do You Do After You Ruin Your Life" and "Swingin' Machine") plus renditions of the standards "Foolin' Myself" and "I Can't See For Lookin'." This excellent LP has unfortunately not been reissued yet. —*Scott Yanow*

Pure Mose / 1978 / 32 Jazz ✦✦✦

Middle Class White Boy / Feb. 2, 1982 / Elektra/Musician ✦✦✦✦
This Elektra LP finds the unique Mose Allison well featured in a sextet also including Joe Farrell on tenor and flute and guitarist Phil Upchurch. Allison's unusual mixture of bop and country-blues, and his own eccentric personality have long given him a distinctive sound on piano, but it is his ironic vocals and superb lyric-writing abilities that make him a major figure. In addition to such originals as "How Does It Feel? (To Be Good Looking)," "I Don't Want Much" and "I'm Nobody Today," Allison brings new life to such standards as "When My Dreamboat Comes Home," "I'm Just a Lucky So-and-So" and "The Tennessee Waltz." —*Scott Yanow*

Lesson in Living / Jul. 21, 1982 / Elektra ✦✦✦
On the second of two albums cut in 1982 (which were his only recordings from the 1977-86 period), vocalist-pianist Mose Allison is saddled with an unnecessary and not always complementary all-star group consisting of guitarist Eric Gale, bassist Jack Bruce, drummer Billy Cobham and (on "You Are My Sunshine") altoist Lou Donaldson. However, for this live set (recorded at the Montreux Jazz Festival), Mose is in fine form performing mostly remakes of his songs. Highlights include "Your Mind on Vacation," "Lost Mind," "Seventh Son," "I Don't Worry About a Thing" and the definitive rendition of his unusual minor-toned version of "You Are My Sunshine." —*Scott Yanow*

Ever Since the World Ended / May 11, 1987-Jun. 2, 1987 / Blue Note ✦✦✦
Mose Allison, who was a musical institution long before 1987, had not run out of creative juices after 30 years of major league performances. This set finds him introducing such ironically truthful songs as "Ever Since the World Ended," "Top Forty," "I Looked in the Mirror" and "What's Your Movie." The many guest artists (including altoist Arthur Blythe, tenor saxophonist Bennie Wallace, Bob Malach on both alto and tenor and guitarist Kenny Burrell) are unnecessary frivolities, but Allison's trio (with bassist Dennis Irwin and drummer Tom Whaley) is tight and ably backs the unique singer-pianist. —*Scott Yanow*

Jazz Profile / May 11, 1987-Sep. 1993 / Blue Note ✦✦✦
This single CD has highlights from Mose Allison's three Blue Note albums of 1987-93 (*Ever Since the World Ended, My Backyard* and *The Earth Wants You*).

Although it would be preferable to acquire the complete records instead (and Allison's greatest material was actually recorded in earlier years), there are plenty of gems on this set, including "Ever Since the World Ended," "I Looked in the Mirror," "Ever Since I Stole the Blues" and "Certified Senior Citizen." Joined by a variety of all-star players (including Bennie Wallace on tenor, altoist Arthur Blythe and guitarist John Scofield), Allison's singing, witty delivery, piano playing and insightful (yet humorous) lyrics easily steal the show. —*Scott Yanow*

My Backyard / Dec. 5, 1989-Dec. 7, 1989 / Blue Note ✦✦✦

For this New Orleans session, vocalist-pianist-lyricist Mose Allison utilized several top local but world-class musicians: tenor saxophonist Tony Dagradi, guitarist Steve Masakowski, bassist Bill Huntington and drummer John Vidacovich. Among the new songs introduced at the session were "Ever Since I Stole the Blues," "You Call It Joggin'," "The Gettin' Paid Waltz" and "My Backyard." Allison, who is heard in top form, revived "That's Your Red Wagon" and "Sleepy Lagoon" and sounds in good spirits throughout this enjoyable and typically philosophical outing. —*Scott Yanow*

The Earth Wants You / Sep. 8, 1993-Sep. 9, 1993 / Blue Note ✦✦✦✦

Mose Allison, one of the top lyricists of the '90s, shows throughout this entertaining CD that his powers as a pianist and singer are also very much intact. The album introduces a few new classics in "Certified Senior Citizen," "This Ain't Me" and "Who's In, Who's Out." His voice is still in prime form and his piano playing remains quite unique. It is true that the guests on the set (guitarist John Scofield, altoist Joe Lovano, Bob Malach on tenor and trumpeter Randy Brecker) are not all that necessary, but Allison's performance makes this an excellent showcase for his music. —*Scott Yanow*

Gimcracks and Gewgaws / May 17, 1997-May 18, 1997 / Blue Note ✦✦✦

Gimcracks and Gewgaws is a typically stylish, tasteful and witty affair from Mose Allison. Supported again by his rhythm section of bassist Ratzo Harris and drummer Paul Motian, Allison plays a set of wry originals highlighted by "Old Man Blues," a knowing jibe at his standard "Young Man Blues." Allison remains a supple, engaging vocalist, and his humor is as sardonic as ever; similarly, his piano playing hasn't diminished over the years, and he sounds remarkably vigorous for a 70-year-old man. Guest appearances by saxophonist Mark Shim and guitarist Russell Malone do nothing to diminish the fact that this is Mose's show. Once again, he has turned in an album that does justice to his place as a jazz elder statesman. —*Stephen Thomas Erlewine*

Bill Allred

b. Nov. 19, 1936

Trombone / Dixieland

A solid Dixieland trombonist who is a fixture at classic jazz festivals, Bill Allred started playing in bands while in high school. He worked locally with the Dixie Lads, the Davenport Jazz Band and the Reedy Creek Jazz Band. In 1971 he settled in Florida and has often played at Disney World. Allred, who toured with Wild Bill Davison, has recorded as a leader for several small labels (including Fat Cat Jazz, World Jazz, and in 1995, Nagel-Heyer), and his son John Allred (who plays in a similar style and sometimes teams up with his father) had a quartet date for Arbors in 1993. —*Scott Yanow*

Allred Hot and Blue / 1984 / World Jazz ✦✦✦✦

Trombonist Bill Allred, who has mostly recorded for very small labels throughout his career, gained some exposure with this World Jazz LP. Teamed up with some of the best trad jazz musicians who happened to live in Florida at the time (cornetist David Jones, clarinetist Jack Matese, Terry Myers on reeds and pianist Eddie Higgins), plus two ringers (bassist Milt Hinton and drummer Butch Miles), Allred and his sidemen perform eight Dixieland and swing standards. Highlights include "Singing the Blues," "Oh Baby," "Sugar" and "St. Louis Blues." Mainstream fans will want to search for this one. —*Scott Yanow*

● **Absolutely** / Sep. 28, 1995 / Nagel-Heyer ✦✦✦✦

Bill Allred and his English counterpart Roy Williams are very complementary veteran trombonists who share this swinging date. With fine support from pianist Johnny Varro, bassist Isla Eckinger and drummer Butch Miles, the two trombonists take turns soloing on a variety of standards and obscurities, with highlights including Vic Dickenson's "Constantly," a lengthy "Satin Doll," "Gypsy In My Soul," a calypso-flavored "It's Only a Paper Moon" and a driving rendition of "Sometimes I'm Happy." While there are fine individual features for Williams ("Isn't It a Pity"), Varro ("If There Is Someone Lovelier") and Allred ("Makin' Whoopee"), it is the interaction between the co-leaders that is most memorable on their spirited outing. —*Scott Yanow*

Karrin Allyson

b. Great Bend, KS

Vocals, Piano / Standards, Bop

One of the more impressive jazz singers to emerge in the 1990s, Karrin Allyson is a great scat singer but also highly expressive on ballads. She grew up in Omaha, NE, and the San Francisco Bay Area and graduated from the University of Nebraska in 1987. After performing regularly at a Minneapolis club, Allyson moved to Kansas City which has been her home base ever since. All of Karrin Allyson's Concord recordings are highly recommended and she has the potential to be an important pacesetter for decades to come. —*Scott Yanow*

I Didn't Know About You / 1992 / Concord Jazz ✦✦✦✦

This CD was the debut of the talented singer Karrin Allyson, a creative scat singer also very capable of holding her own on ballads. She primarily utilizes top Kansas City musicians (including pianists Paul Smith, Russ Long and Joe Cartwright, guitarists Danny Embrey and Rod Fleeman, bassists Bob Bowman and Gerald Spaits, drummer Todd Strait, cornetist Gary Sivils and fluegelhornist Mike Metheny) on a variety of bop-based material. Among the highlights are "Nature Boy," Karrin's chance-taking duet with drummer Strait on "What a Little Moonlight Can Do," a rapid version of "'S Wonderful" and a bossa nova-tized "It Might As Well Be Spring." Karrin Allyson, who also plays piano on three numbers, shows a great deal of potential throughout her rewarding debut. —*Scott Yanow*

● **Sweet Home Cookin'** / Jun. 9, 1993-Jun. 10, 1993 / Concord Jazz ✦✦✦✦✦

Karrin Allyson has a small and sometimes hoarse voice but she does so much with it that her bop session is easily recommended. Her all-star sextet (comprising trumpeter Randy Sandke, the late tenor Bob Cooper, guitarist Danny Embrey, pianist Alan Broadbent, bassist Putter Smith and drummer Sherman Ferguson) has plenty of short solos on colorful charts by Alan Broadbent. Allyson sounds perfectly at ease, whether scatting on "No Moon at All," finding fresh melodic variations on "I Cover the Waterfront" or singing her original blues "Sweet Home Cookin' Man." She always swings. —*Scott Yanow*

Azure-Te / Nov. 14, 1994-Nov. 16, 1994 / Concord Jazz ✦✦✦✦

Karrin Allyson is one of the best jazz singers to emerge in the 1990s. She is a masterful scatter, as she shows on some of these selections (including "How High the Moon" and "Yardbird Suite"), but she is also quite expressive on ballads (including "Blame It on My Youth" and "Some Other Time"). The strong backup musicians (a variety of top Kansas City players with guest spots for violinist Claude Williams and fluegelhornist Mike Metheny) keep the music swinging. Highly recommended. —*Scott Yanow*

Collage / Jan. 5, 1996-Jan. 10, 1996 / Concord Jazz ✦✦✦✦✦

Vocalist Karrin Allyson stretches herself during this diverse set. A superior jazz singer, Allyson scats quite well during "It Could Happen to You/Fried Bananas" and "Cherokee," sings lyrics in English, French ("Autumn Leaves") and Italian, interprets some fairly current pop tunes, is touching on Thelonious Monk's "Ask Me Now" and is quite memorable on "Joy Spring" and "All of You." With assistance from her fine Kansas City-based rhythm section (led by pianist Paul Smith) and with some worthy guests (including altoist Kim Park, violinist Claude Williams and fluegelhornist Mike Metheny), Karrin Allyson shows just how versatile and talented a singer she is. Recommended. —*Scott Yanow*

Daydream / Jan. 5, 1996-Apr. 25, 1997 / Concord Jazz ✦✦✦✦

Karrin Allyson has a beautiful voice that is also quite flexible, as she shows throughout this consistently interesting release. The emphasis is a little more on ballads than usual, but there are some heated moments too. Joined by some of her favorite Kansas City-based musicians, plus a few guests (trumpeter Randy Brecker, vibraphonist Gary Burton and altoist Kim Park), Allyson sounds both lyrical and enthusiastic. High points include a touching rendition of "Everything Must Change" (a solo performance in which she accompanies herself on piano), "Daydream," "My Foolish Heart" and "So Danco Samba." —*Scott Yanow*

Laurindo Almeida

b. Sep. 2, 1917, São Paulo, Brazil, d. Jul. 26, 1995, Van Nuys, CA

Guitar / Brazilian Jazz, Afro-Cuban Jazz

Laurindo Almeida helped introduce the Brazilian guitar to jazz, and in his 1954 recordings with Bud Shank was essentially playing bossa nova seven years before Stan Getz! After spending time as a staff guitarist in Brazil, Almeida moved to Los Angeles and was a member of Stan Kenton's Orchestra (1947-48). A studio guitarist in L.A. from 1950 on, Almeida also continued playing jazz along with classical music. A decade after the Shank sessions, Almeida recorded some best-selling bossa nova dates for Capitol. He co-founded the L.A. Four in the mid-'70s (which reunited him with Bud Shank), collaborated on recordings with Charlie Byrd and made several worthwhile sessions for Concord. —*Scott Yanow*

● **Brazilliance, Vol. 1** / Apr. 15, 1953-Apr. 22, 1953 / World Pacific ✦✦✦✦✦
More than seven years before Stan Getz and Charlie Byrd introduced the bossa nova of Antonio Carlos Jobim to American audiences, guitarist Laurindo Almeida and altoist Bud Shank (in a quartet with bassist Harry Babasin and drummer Roy Harte) recorded the intriguing music heard on this CD reissue. The performances are very close to bossa nova in their combination of cool-toned jazz and Brazilian rhythms; in fact these are arguably the first bossa nova recordings, long before even Jobim and Joao Gilberto initially recorded. Only four of the 14 tunes ("Speak Low" is heard in two versions) are not based on Brazilian folk songs and many of the songs (particularly "Carinoso") are quite memorable. This historically significant, very accessible and highly recommended release is a gem. — *Scott Yanow*

Brazilliance, Vol. 2 / Mar. 1958 / World Pacific ✦✦✦✦
Five years after guitarist Laurindo Almeida and altoist Bud Shank had a regular quartet, documented what could be considered the first bossa nova records (*Brazilliance, Vol. 1*) and then disbanded, they had a reunion. This CD reissue features Almeida, Shank (now doubling on flute), bassist Gary Peacock and drummer Chuck Flores once again combining Brazilian rhythms and folk melodies with cool bop improvising. This time around the arrangements are not as restrictive, Shank's solos are longer and the jazz content sometimes overrides the Brazilian elements. The music is still quite enjoyable (the very complementary Almeida and Shank would join together again in the 1970s as the L.A. Four) if not as historical; both volumes are highly recommended. — *Scott Yanow*

The Best of Laurindo Almeida / 1962-1965 / Curb ✦✦✦✦
Best of Laurindo Almeida is a ten-track budget-priced collection that features some of his biggest hits, including "Desafinado," "More," "Lisbon Antigua," "Satin Doll" and "I Left My Heart in San Francisco." Although this isn't a bad budget-priced disc, there are better collections available, offering more songs and better sound for not much more money. — *Stephen Thomas Erlewine*

Concierto de Aranjuez / Mar. 27, 1978-Mar. 28, 1978 / Inner City ✦✦✦
Originally recorded for the Japanese East Wind label, this LP features the great Brazilian guitarist Laurindo Almeida on a peaceful and inwardly passionate unaccompanied set of music. There are medleys from "Black Orpheus" and Gershwin, four standards (including "Holiday For Strings"), one original and the nine-and-a-half-minute title cut. Almeida's classically-oriented guitar sounds beautiful throughout. — *Scott Yanow*

Chamber Jazz / Sep. 1978 / Concord Jazz ✦✦✦
For this CD reissue, the Brazilian acoustic guitarist Laurindo Almeida (in a trio with bassist Bob Magnusson and drummer Jeff Hamilton) performs music that straddles the boundary between melodic jazz and classical music. Tasteful renditions of Brazilian melodies alternate with classical themes by Bach, Debussy and Chopin and the results are well-played and quite likable. — *Scott Yanow*

First Concerto for Guitar & Orchestra / Nov. 1979 / Concord Jazz ✦✦✦
Guitarist Laurindo Almeida spins delicate melodies and frequently beautiful riffs and solos, backed by the Los Angeles Orchestra de Camera under the direction of Elmer Ramsey. The program on this 1979 set included both classical and Afro-Latin compositions. — *Ron Wynn*

Brazilian Soul / Dec. 1980 / Concord Jazz ✦✦✦
The first of at least four meetings on record between the great Brazilian-styled guitarists Laurindo Almeida and Charlie Byrd, this very logical matchup (in a quartet with bassist Bob Magnusson and percussionist Milt Holland) is quite succesful. The music is tightly arranged with very little improvisation but the beauty of the two guitarist's distinctive tones and the colorful melodies makes this a rewarding set. From "Carioca" and Jobim's "Stone Flower" to several Brazilian classical pieces and even "Don't Cry for Me, Argentina," everything works. — *Scott Yanow*

Latin Odyssey / Dec. 1982 / Concord Jazz ✦✦✦
The second meeting on records by Brazilian-styled guitarists Laurindo Almeida and Charlie Byrd is similar to their first in that the emphasis is on melodies and arrangements with only subtle improvising in spots. The quartet is completed by Joe Byrd or Bob Magnusson on bass and Chuck Redd or Jeff Hamilton playing drums. Almeida and Byrd perform works from several South American composers (including Astor Piazzola) plus the current show tune "Memory" and the peaceful music holds one's interest. — *Scott Yanow*

Artistry in Rhythm / Apr. 1983 / Concord Jazz ✦✦✦✦✦
Most of guitarist Laurindo Almeida's recordings for Concord during the late 1970s and '80s were classically-oriented; *Artistry in Rhythm* and the earlier *Chamber Jazz* were the only real exceptions. On this set with bassist Bob Magnusson and percussionist Milt Holland, Almeida does display his classical training but he also improvises a bit on a diverse repertoire that includes "Chariots of Fire," "Artistry in Rhythm," "Liza" and "Slaughter on Tenth Avenue!" Actually there is a strong unity to this music with Almeida as usual emphasizing the melody and his beautiful sound. — *Scott Yanow*

Tango: Laurindo Almeida and Charlie Byrd / Aug. 1985 / Concord Jazz ✦✦✦✦
This unusual CD finds guitarists Laurindo Almeida and Charlie Byrd (who have both mastered bop and Brazilian music) performing 11 tangoes with the assistance of bassist Joe Byrd and drummer Chuck Redd. Although the two acoustic guitarists have their short solos, the emphasis in this delightful set is on their ensemblework, respectful interpretations of the melodies and those infectious tango rhythms. — *Scott Yanow*

Music of the Brazilian Masters / May 1989 / Concord Jazz ✦✦✦
The great Brazilian guitarists Laurindo Almeida, Charlie Byrd and Carlos Barbosa-Lima team up for a tightly arranged set that (even with a Jobim tune and an original apiece by Byrd and Almeida) is mostly composed of Brazilian classical music. The guitarists' distinctive but complementary tones add a great deal of beauty to the quiet but often-complex music. Fans of the acoustic guitar will find this CD well worth acquiring. — *Scott Yanow*

● **Outra Vez** / Oct. 5, 1991 / Concord Jazz ✦✦✦✦✦

Herb Alpert

b. Mar. 31, 1935, Los Angeles, CA
Trumpet / Instrumental Pop, Pop-Jazz
One of the most successful instrumental performers in pop history, trumpeter Herb Alpert was also one of the entertainment industry's shrewdest businessmen: A&M, the label he cofounded with partner Jerry Moss, ranks among the most prosperous artist-owned companies ever established. Born March 31, 1935 in Los Angeles, Alpert began playing the trumpet at the age of eight. After serving in the army, he attempted to forge an acting career, but soon returned to music, recording under the name Dore Alpert for RCA.

With Lou Adler, Alpert co-wrote a number of Sam Cooke's most enduring hits, including "Wonderful World" and "Only Sixteen." Under the name Dante and the Evergreens, he and Adler also recorded a cover of the Hollywood Argyles' "Alley Oop"; additionally, Alpert produced tracks for the surf duo Jan and Dean. In 1962 he teamed with Moss to found A&M Records, scoring a Top Ten hit with the single "The Lonely Bull."

From its humble origins as a company run out of Alpert's garage, A&M grew to become the world's largest independent label; among its greatest successes were the Carpenters, Cat Stevens, Joe Cocker and Sergio Mendes & Brasil '66. Nevertheless, Alpert and his backing unit the Tijuana Brass remained the label's flagship act: on the strength of the hit "A Taste of Honey," his 1965 LP *Whipped Cream and Other Delights* topped the charts, popularizing his Latin-influenced style (dubbed "Ameriachi"). The follow-up, 1965's *Going Places*, also hit No. 1, launching the hit "Spanish Flea."

After 1966's *What Now My Love*—his most popular effort, remaining at No. 1 for nine weeks—Alpert continued to dominate the charts with records including 1966's *S.R.O.* and the following year's *Sounds Like* and *Herb Alpert's Ninth*. In 1968, he scored his first No. 1 single by taking a rare vocal turn on a rendition of Burt Bacharach's "This Guy's in Love With You"; the album *The Best of the Brass* followed the hit to the top of the charts, becoming Alpert's fifth and final No. 1 LP.

1969's *Warm* was the first of Alpert's 11 albums not to crack the Top 20; by 1971's *Summertime*, his commercial fates had fallen to the point where he no longer reached the Top 100. As A&M continued to thrive, he moved his primary focus from music to industry, although he regularly recorded throughout the early 1970s; 1974's *You Smile—The Song Begins* was his most successful outing in several years, but subsequent releases like 1975's *Coney Island* and 1976's *Just You and Me* met with greater chart resistance.

In 1979, Alpert staged a major comeback with *Rise;* not only did the album reach the Top Ten, but the title track topped the singles charts and became the biggest hit of his career. The follow-up, 1980s *Beyond*, was a Top 40 success, but subsequent efforts like 1982's *Fandango* and 1985's *Wild Romance* fared poorly. In 1987 Alpert enjoyed another renaissance with the album *Keep Your Eye on Me;* the lead single "Diamonds" hit the Top Five and featured a guest vocal from Janet Jackson, one of A&M's towering successes of the late 1980s.

Alpert continued recording throughout the 1990s, producing work like 1991's *North on South Street*, 1992's *Midnight Sun* and 1997's *Passion Dance*. After selling A&M to PolyGram in 1990 for a sum in excess of $500 million, he and Moss founded a new label, Almo Sounds, in 1994; among the imprint's hit artists was the group Garbage. Alpert also tackled other forms of media, exhibiting his abstract expressionist paintings and co-producing a number of Broadway successes including *Angels in America* and *Jelly's Last Jam*. He also established the Herb Alpert Foundation, a philanthropic organization dedicated to establishing educational, arts, and environmental programs for children. — *Jason Ankeny*

The Lonely Bull / Dec. 1962 / A&M ✦✦✦
The colossus that is A&M Records starts right here with the first album by the 1960s instrumental juggernaut known as the Tijuana Brass. True, there was no

"Tijuana Brass" per se at this time; just Herb Alpert and a coterie of Los Angeles sessionmen, with Alpert overdubbing himself on trumpet to get that bullring effect. Also, Alpert was just getting the TJB concept underway; the textures are leaner, the productions less polished, and the accent more consciously on a Mexican mariachi ambience—the relatively square rhythms, the mandolins, the mournful, wistful siesta feeling—than the records down the road. The hit title track (originally a tune called "Twinkle Star"!) is a cleverly structured, exciting and haunting piece of record-making—and its composer, Sol Lake, becomes the charter member of Alpert's team of TJB tunesmiths with several more ethnic-flavored numbers. In accordance with the newly emerging bossa nova movement, Alpert does a nice, straightforward, authentic cover of "Desafinado," even departing a bit from the tune with some spare jazz-inspired licks, and "Crawfish" pleasingly adapts the mariachi horn sound to a bossa beat. Still a charming record, still in print on CD. —*Richard S. Ginell*

● **Classics, Vol. 1** / 1962-1972 / A&M ✦✦✦✦✦
All the high points from the ten-year dominance of Alpert and the Tijuana Brass; includes "A Taste of Honey," "Spanish Flea," and others. —*Cub Koda*

● **Classics, Vol. 20** / 1964-1972 / A&M ✦✦✦✦✦
This set features Alpert's solo hits, from "This Guy's in Love with You" to "Rise."
—*Cub Koda*

Tijuana Brass Featuring Herb Alpert, Vol. 2 / May 1963 / A&M ✦✦
The follow-up LP to *The Lonely Bull*, in the great tradition of follow-ups, tries to duplicate its appeal right off the bat with another leadoff track featuring bullfight sounds and an authentic bullring tune, "The Great Manolete." Yet Alpert is beginning to expand his reach beyond Baja California without losing the ambience of "The Lonely Bull," sharpening his skills as a producer and exploring other moods and rhythms. In doing so, he comes up with the greatest stripper record this side of David Rose, "Swinger from Seville," a mocking version of Leonard Bernstein's "America" to a lively guajira beat in a wild simulated nightclub, and covers of '60s standards like "More" and "Spanish Harlem." He also receives some more haunting contributions from Sol Lake, including the wistful "Winds of Barcelona" (later recorded by Wes Montgomery) and a marvelously produced, Spanish-tinged tone poem, "Marching Through Madrid." Though released in 1963, this record didn't really start selling until 1966, when TJB albums were monopolizing the upper reaches of the charts en masse. —*Richard S. Ginell*

South of the Border / Oct. 1964 / A&M ✦✦
A comeback from the relatively disappointing initial sales of *Herb Alpert's Tijuana Brass, Volume 2*, *South of the Border* was helped considerably by the selection of the tune "Mexican Shuffle" by the Clark Teaberry Gum Company as its commercial theme. The album became Alpert's first Top Ten hit and fifth gold record. Despite that success, however, for the most part it found Alpert simply applying his double-tracked-trumpet-and-Mexican-band style to a series of disparate pop favorites, from Antonio Carlos Jobim's "The Girl from Ipanema" to the Beatles' "All My Loving." He did impart a warm melancholy to "I've Grown Accustomed to Her Face," but did you ever really want to hear "Hello, Dolly!" sung with a Spanish accent? —*William Ruhlmann*

Whipped Cream & Other Delights / Apr. 1965 / A&M ✦✦✦✦✦
We'll never know exactly what made this album Herb Alpert's big commercial breakthrough—the music or the LP jacket's luscious nude model covered almost entirely with simulated whipped cream. Probably both. In any case, Alpert's most famous album is built around a coherent concept; every song has a title with food in it. Within this concept, Alpert's musical tastes are still refreshingly eclectic; he uses Brazilian rhythms on "Green Peppers" and "Bittersweet Samba," reaches back to the big-band era for the haunting "Tangerine," uses Dixieland jazz on "Butterball," and goes to New Orleans for the Allen Toussaint-penned title track (familiar to viewers of TV's *The Dating Game*). He also has developed a unique sense of timing as a producer, using pauses for humorous effect, and managing to score his second Top Ten hit with a complex, tempo-shifting version of "A Taste of Honey." No wonder Alpert drew such a large, diverse audience at his peak; his choices of tunes spanned eras and generations, his arrangements were energetic enough for the young and melodic enough for older listeners. This album, No. 1 in the nation for eight weeks, is still available on CD, though the cover obviously doesn't make as alluring an impression as it did on LP. —*Richard S. Ginell*

Going Places / Sep. 1965 / A&M ✦✦✦
Herb Alpert and the Tijuana Brass were rolling right down the middle of the American pop scene like a locomotive in 1966—and this LP captures them at the peak of their exuberance. By now, there really was a live, touring edition of the Tijuana Brass, and there was an easily identifiable TJB sound, with its strummed Latin American guitars, twin trumpet leads, delicate marimba or vibes (played by Julius Wechter of Baja Marimba Band fame in the studio), and strong grooves rooted in Latin American music, jazz and rock. Alpert's family of sidemen and composers were busy generating their own catchy hits, like Wechter's deadly infec-

tious "Spanish Flea," and the tragically short-lived Ervan Coleman's wonderfully goofy "Tijuana Taxi." The bossman's trumpet could be joyous, mocking and melancholy in turns, and his choices of tunes totally unpredictable; who else would dare juxtapose "The Third Man Theme," "Walk, Don't Run," "I'm Getting Sentimental Over You" and "Zorba the Greek" on one record? No other TJB record has as much unbuttoned fun and humor as this one—and, not surprisingly, it spent six weeks at No. 1 in 1966. —*Richard S. Ginell*

What Now My Love / Apr. 1966 / A&M ✦✦✦
With this album, Herb Alpert and the Tijuana Brass settle into their hitmaking groove, the once strikingly eclectic elements of Dixieland, pop, rock, and mariachi becoming more smoothly integrated within Alpert's infectious "Ameriachi" blend. They sound more like a band now; along with Alpert's now-indelibly stamped trumpet sound, we can recognize other elements such as guitarist John Pisano's distinctive rhythm guitar, Lou Pagani's piano, the droll Bob Edmondson's dulcet trombone. Pisano, who debuted as a composer on *Going Places*, comes up with a memorably whistleable song "So What's New," and the rest of Alpert's songwriting brigade (Ervan Coleman, Julius Wechter and Sol Lake) chime in with some lively, catchy tunes. There is also an assortment of pop, film, and Broadway standards of the day, all impeccably arranged by Alpert, whose production instincts grew sharper and surer with every release. Result: another hugely entertaining hit LP, one that stayed at No. 1 longer than any other TJB album (nine weeks). —*Richard S. Ginell*

S.R.O. / Nov. 1966 / A&M ✦✦✦
By late 1966, it seemed as if every TV commercial and every pop arranger had latched onto the Herb Alpert "Ameriachi" sound—at which point the resourceful originator of that sound began to pare it down and loosen it up a bit. *S.R.O.* (Standing Room Only), referring to the Tijuana Brass' string of sold-out concerts, is an accurate title, for this LP is about a seven-piece band loaded with experienced jazzers who groove and swing together to a greater degree than on their previous albums. Sure, the arrangements are very tightly knit and don't allow much room for spontaneity, but they still sound fresh and uninhibited, and Alpert often allows the flavor of jazz to come through more clearly. Indeed, two of the album's three hit singles, "The Work Song" and "Flamingo," are jazz tunes—the former nervous and driving, the latter joyously kicking—and the third, "Mame," gets a nifty Dixieland treatment à la Louis Armstrong, with Alpert singing one verse. The sleeping gem of the record is guitarist John Pisano's "Freight Train Joe," a wistfully evocative tune that won't quit the memory, and the mournful Alpert/Pisano/Nick Ceroli tune "For Carlos" later became Wes Montgomery's "Wind Song." Though *S.R.O.* only went to No. 2 on the LP charts, Alpert's creativity and popularity were still peaking. —*Richard S. Ginell*

Sounds Like / May 1967 / A&M ✦✦✦
For one week in June 1967, *Sounds Like* was able to break the Monkees' 31-week hammerlock on the No. 1 slot on the charts—just two weeks before the Beatles' *Sgt. Pepper* took over and changed the world. This shows, lest we forget—and many have—just how popular the Tijuana Brass were, still spanning the generations during the Summer of Love, still putting out records as fresh and musical and downright joyous as this one. Though not as jazz-flavored as *S.R.O.*, *Sounds Like* does preserve the feeling, particularly in the extended vamps on an updated slave song, "Wade In the Water" (a hit single). "Gotta Lotta Livin' to Do" settles us into the record with nothing but a long vamp—a daring production decision. Yet Alpert was on a roll; everything he tried in the TJB's heyday seemed to work. The lesser-known tunes back-loaded on Side Two are a string of pearls—John Pisano's appropriately titled bossa nova "The Charmer," Roger Nichols' tense "Treasure of San Miguel," Ervan Coleman's catchy "Miss Frenchy Brown." Finally, Alpert takes a flyer and concludes the LP with an extravagant Burt Bacharach orchestration of his theme from the film *Casino Royale*—an artifact of '60s pop culture, to be sure, but still a perfectly structured record. —*Richard S. Ginell*

Herb Alpert's Ninth / Dec. 1967 / A&M ✦✦✦
The cover art of this LP is hilarious—a bust of grim old Beethoven wearing a Herb Alpert sweatshirt, a parody of the pop icon fad going around at the time and maybe a comment on the rock world's newfound pretensions in the wake of the Beatles' *Sgt. Pepper*. In any case, *Herb Alpert's Ninth* does introduce some highbrow pretensions of sorts to Alpert's Ameriachi sound—some very subtly applied strands of strings on several numbers and a madcap, multi-sectioned fantasy of tunes from Bizet's *Carmen* that is full of in-jokes from the opera and the TJB's hits. Alpert is also quite aware of the brave new world around him; he does a spare, lazy, yet entirely novel-sounding cover version of *Sgt. Pepper's* "With a Little Help from My Friends" and gives the Supremes' "The Happening" a bouncy workout. There is also a touching memorial to the late Ervan Coleman ("Bud") and another underrated contribution from the Alpert songwriting team, Sol Lake's swinging "Cowboys and Indians." The TJB still churns out the Latin American rhythms, but sometimes with a shade less exuberance. —*Richard S. Ginell*

Beat of the Brass / Apr. 1968 / A&M ✦✦✦

Meant as the companion album to a Herb Alpert and the Tijuana Brass television special of the same name and packaged in a fancy double-fold LP jacket, *The Beat of the Brass* came out amid signs that Alpert's hot streak was finally beginning to run out. Not quite. Viewer requests for a new Burt Bacharach song, "This Guy's in Love with You"—featuring an Alpert vocal—were so strong that A&M released it as a single, which shot up to No. 1 and took *The Beat of the Brass* with it to the top. Herb's vocal is touching in its strained naiveté; he sounds sincere, and that overrides the lush, overbearing Bacharach orchestral arrangement. The rest of the album generated an often nostalgic quality then and still does; the tunes by John Pisano and Sol Lake are exquisite, and Alpert's arrangements of songs like "Thanks for the Memory" seem autumnal in quality, as if an era was about to close. The band still has the ability to groove; the vamp on Julius Wechter's bossa nova "Panama," with Wechter's jazzy vibes and Pisano's strong rhythm guitar, could have been stretched to half an hour. Yet Alpert's trumpet sounds a bit withered at times, and we can do without the band vocals and cloying children's chorus on "Talk to the Animals." —*Richard S. Ginell*

Warm / Jun. 1969 / A&M ✦✦✦

Herb Alpert and the Tijuana Brass shed almost all of the dust of Tijuana on this mellow, richly textured album; one reviewer at the time wrote that Alpert seemed to have exchanged bullrings for wedding rings. Lest one think that the TJB came down with a terminal case of the warm fuzzies, though, there are some selections here that sizzle—particularly the old standard "The Continental"—and in terms of arrangements and song selection, the accent falls on Brazil more than on any other TJB album. Shorty Rogers again was called in to provide voices and orchestrations, but he is more tasteful here than on the *Christmas Album*, the extreme dynamic range on Harry Nilsson's "Without Her" notwithstanding. A different take of "To Wait for Love"—the lovely, Bacharach-penned, Alpert-sung follow-up to "This Guy's In Love With You" from 1968—is included here, as is the fine single "Zazueira." Yet *Warm* was the first non-seasonal TJB album in some time that couldn't crack the Top 20, for the Brass' cross-generational appeal was fading fast. —*Richard S. Ginell*

The Brass Are Comin' / Nov. 1969 / A&M ✦✦

The Western motif on the double-fold album jacket—with Herb Alpert and the Tijuana Brass in costume—signals this as another companion album to a TV special. But there is a deeper significance to this LP, for shortly after its release, a burned-out, personally troubled Alpert disbanded the Brass and retired from music for awhile. Indeed, stretches of this record reveal a tired group and a leader whose trumpet has lost much of its old zip. Even so, as on all TJB albums, there are several gems—the stunning shifts in texture and tempo that enliven the worn-out "Moon River," the chugging bluegrass-tinged arrangement of Villa-Lobos' "The Little Train of the Caipira" that masquerades under the name of the title track, a haunting rendition of the Beatles' "I'll Be Back," the fast samba treatment of "Anna." Dave Grusin and Shorty Rogers contribute an occasional orchestration, and Alpert does a modest vocal turn on the lush "You Are My Life." But this time, the old sales magic was gone; the Tijuana Brass had suddenly become unhip in polarized 1969. —*Richard S. Ginell*

Greatest Hits / Mar. 1970 / A&M ✦✦✦

Released in 1970, a bit too late to capitalize on the Tijuana Brass at the peak of their appeal, this early hits collection compounded the error of its tardy timing by only including selections from the TJB's first five albums. Still, since the CDs of three of the five albums are currently out of print, this can serve as a decent, if brief, overview of the development of Herb Alpert's vehicle from its clever ethnic novelty beginnings into a cosmopolitan septet that could actually bridge the yawning generation gap of the 1960s. But for a more sweeping look at the TJB, there are better, more economical packages around. —*Richard S. Ginell*

Summertime / Jul. 1971 / A&M ✦✦

Though Herb Alpert was technically taking a sabbatical from music in the early 1970s, he wasn't entirely inactive, recording in dribs and drabs. So A&M assembled this brief collection of singles and stray cuts in the summer of 1971; it went nowhere on the charts but added some pleasing entries to the Alpert discography. The two best cuts, taken from a 1970 single, are as good as anything from the Tijuana Brass' heyday—Alpert's own haunting tone poem "Jerusalem" and a great, strutting arrangement of "Strike Up the Band." The title track, with a dual vocal by Alpert and his new wife Lani Hall, is also intriguing, drawing inspiration from the famous Miles Davis/Gil Evans version, while Alpert pulls off a really good jazz trumpet solo on "The Nicest Things Happen." Otherwise, most of the tracks on this LP lack energy, and even vigorous arrangements like that of the Beach Boys' "Darlin'" drift off distractedly into the ozone. Clearly, Alpert wasn't quite ready to re-emerge full-blown into the performing world. —*Richard S. Ginell*

Four Sider / Nov. 1973 / A&M ✦✦✦

When Herb Alpert wound down activity with the Tijuana Brass at the end of the 1960s and the beginning of the 1970s, his record label, A&M, began releasing hits collections and compilations culled from the group's catalog. First came *Greatest Hits*, then *Solid Brass*, then *Greatest Hits, Volume 2*, and then this 21-track album, originally released as a double LP (hence the title). Twelve of Alpert's 27 pop chart hits up to this point were included (which was twice as many as you would find on *Greatest Hits*), among them the Top Tens "The Lonely Bull" and "A Taste of Honey," and the chart-topping "This Guy's in Love with You." But most of these songs had turned up on one of the earlier compilations already, not to mention the original albums on which they were featured. The major exception was Alpert's most recent hit at the time, a minor chart entry with Gato Barbieri's theme from the movie *Last Tango in Paris*, which was making its first LP appearance. The music was, as always, pleasant, but the repeated cannibalization of Alpert's catalog was beginning to become a consumer concern. —*William Ruhlmann*

You Smile, the Song Begins / May 1974 / A&M ✦✦

His four-year sabbatical over, Herb Alpert returned to the studio creatively refreshed, his trumpet sounding more soulful and thoughtful, his ears attuned more than ever to jazz. The name of his studio group has been shortened to just the initials T.J.B., in whose ranks one hears the familiar mallets of Julius Wechter and the lazy trombone of Bob Edmondson, and the old Mexican flavors still come through now and then. But Alpert was definitely still in a pensive mood, and his evocative self-penned title track and choice of tunes like "Alone Again (Naturally)" and "Save the Sunlight" reinforce the LP's mellow, '70s contemporary pop atmosphere. Even the upbeat remake of the TJB's "Up Cherry Street" is filtered through a phase-shifted gauze, a wistful rose-colored vision of the past. Left over from a 1973 single is a terrific, subtle, Latin-jazz-tinged arrangement of "Last Tango in Paris," with a distinctive orchestral helping hand from Quincy Jones. —*Richard S. Ginell*

Coney Island / Apr. 1975 / A&M ✦✦✦

Encouraged by his comeback album, Herb Alpert assembled a new version of the TJB—including a hotshot second trumpeter, Bob Findley, and jazz piano whiz Dave Frishberg—and hit the studio and road in 1975. Yet *Coney Island* was a brave, nearly complete departure from the old Tijuana Brass; the jazzers were given carte blanche and the rhythm section encouraged to do more complex things. As a signal of independence, the new Brass tackle Chick Corea's "Senor Mouse" head-on, in which Frishberg runs wild and even longtime marimbist Julius Wechter is affected by the adventurous spirit. Alpert's own playing on trumpet (and now fluegelhorn and piano) is a bit freer as well, and he goes out on a limb as a composer with the experimental, not-quite-coherent "Carmine." TJB tradition is also served by a loose, swinging version of "I Have Dreamed," and an older legacy pops up in the Alpert/Frishberg duet on Jelly Roll Morton's "The Crave." But this edition of the Brass was short-lived; the public didn't get it and Alpert soon moved on to solo projects, leaving this sole LP as its legacy. —*Richard S. Ginell*

Just You and Me / 1976 / A&M ✦✦

After all of those years fronting the Tijuana Brass or studio equivalents thereof, this was actually Herb Alpert's first album under his name alone, and as if to proclaim his independence, he wrote all of the tunes himself, played all the trumpet parts, sang, and even handled the piano too. For all of that enterprise, though, this is a spotty, intermittently pleasing collection in which the pop-jazz-oriented music often still has the distinctive melancholy tinge of the TJB (the death of Alpert's father in 1976 no doubt influenced the album's tone). The opening track, "Promenade," is a great tune, an upbeat, Latin-flavored update of the TJB style, but nothing else in the set is in that class, and Alpert even has to resort to an earnest rewrite of "Yankee Doodle" to fill space. Frankly, Alpert is no great shakes as a pianist—his playing plods tonelessly along—and there is a lot of it, which tends to put a damper on the record the further one pursues it. Ultimately, few record buyers noticed anyway. —*Richard S. Ginell*

Herb Alpert/Hugh Masekela / Jan. 1978 / A&M ✦✦✦

A mustachioed Herb Alpert breaks out of his '70s blue funk to fuse himself with fellow horn player Hugh Masekela and producer-pianist Caiphus Semenya in a magnificent LP (later issued on CD) of South African/American pop-jazz. From the joyous opening strains of the South African oldie "Skokiaan," continuing with the haunting groove of "Moonza," Alpert wholeheartedly melts into Masekela's distinctive idiom, his trumpet a relaxed foil for the South African exile's blazing fluegelhorn. But Masekela can also lean the other way, joining Alpert in TJB-like dual harmony on "Ring Bell." The band is mostly a coterie of L.A. sessionmen, but they can swing along to the township jive fairly well, and they get some excellent musical material (mostly by Semenya) to work with. Alpert sounded like he was having more fun making music than he had in a long time. —*Richard S. Ginell*

Rise / Sep. 1979 / A&M ✦✦✦✦✦

Fresh from his Masekela experience and hoping to dabble in the then-raging disco movement, Herb Alpert recorded a soaring dance-beat tune composed by his nephew Randy Badazz and friend Andy Armer, slowed the tempo way down, and put it out as a 12-inch disco single. Hardly anyone except Alpert and Badazz thought it would sell, but almost as if on command, "Rise" inexorably rose up the charts, landing at No. 1 to provide Alpert with the biggest hit of his life. Faced with following up a sudden huge hit, Alpert quickly put together an album brimming with renewed confidence and an instinct for the contemporary jugular, assimilating then-current dance beats and electronic backing instruments. He even goes beyond the contemporary with the avant-garde, electronic loop stunt piece "Rotation," which still sounds fascinating today. And Alpert's trumpet playing has new-found authority and power; a No. 1 hit can do wonders for your adrenaline level. *Rise* brought Alpert back to the upper reaches (No. 6) of the album charts, and discophobes will always be grateful to the laidback beat of "Rise" for having the ironic effect of letting the hot air out of the disco craze, which soon faded from sight. —*Richard S. Ginell*

Beyond / Jul. 1980 / A&M ✦✦

Naturally, the wild success of "Rise" would lead anyone to the temptation of repeating oneself, and at first, this follow-up LP does plenty of that, grafting the same slow, hand-clapping beat onto several numbers. But Alpert won't sit still for long, and he comes through with some startling things that wake up the record midway through. The funky, percolating party beat of "Red Hot" starts the engine, which is pushed to an electrifying degree by the sequencer-driven, Echoplexed, hard-charging title track, on which we hear Alpert's distinctive horn through a metallic electronic buffer. The most amazing track is the finale, "The Factory," a terrifying, relentlessly grinding depiction of a soulless foundry that must have shocked sedate former TJB fans who bought this album on a lark, expecting happy music from the past. Bold stuff indeed, and it did make some impact on the charts, though not nearly to the degree of *Rise*. —*Richard S. Ginell*

Magic Man / Aug. 1981 / A&M ✦✦

The high-flying confidence of *Rise* and the experimental bent of *Beyond* began to wear off by 1981, giving way to the more relaxed but musically weaker ministrations of *Magic Man*. With Michael Stokes, then A&M's director of Black Product/A&R, co-producing, Alpert came up with a pleasant collection of mostly forgettable, mild-mannered R&B-pop-slanted tunes, plus a fairly uneventful rendition-at-length of "Besame Mucho" and a redundant cha-cha/disco remake of his own "You Smile, the Song Begins." Alpert's haunting trumpet still reflects his post-"Rise" sense of command, but he doesn't have much to say this time; the material holds him back. —*Richard S. Ginell*

Fandango / May 1982 / A&M ✦✦

Challenged and fired up by some new Mexican colleagues, Herb Alpert set out to make a record specifically for the Latin American market and ended up producing a masterpiece—the equal of the best Tijuana Brass albums, and in some ways maybe better than any of them. *Fandango* has a more authentically Latin American sound than the cosmopolitan TJB records, using rhythms from Mexico to South America, adding a coating of strings or synthesizers and Alpert's soaring trumpets. More importantly, with the help of co-producer Jose Quintana, Alpert lined up some incredibly beautiful material from then-little-known writers like Juan Carlos Calderon, Diego Verdaguer and Roberto Carlos. Some of these tracks are spine-chilling in their emotional pull and uncanny sense of structure; Alpert the master of the studio working at his peak. Alpert's magnificent renderings of Calderon's high-flying "Route 101" (a Top 40 hit single) and aching "Margarita" are perfect records; you wouldn't want to change a note. He also has a ball with Verdaguer's driving "Coco Loco," and the concluding track is a fast-moving medley of Latin American hits, starting with Mexico's "Frenesi" and rambling through Brazil's "Bahia" and Spain's "Moliendo Cafe" before riding off with the irresistible Venezuelan "Porompompero." As much as one hates to limit the horizons of an adventurous musician like Herb Alpert, one must admit that Latin influences inspire his best work—and whether working in a Latin framework or not, he has yet to equal this CD. —*Richard S. Ginell*

Blow Your Own Horn / Sep. 1983 / A&M ✦✦✦

Blow Your Own Horn is an anthology of concepts and production teams that mostly retrace the steps Herb Alpert had taken since "Rise," reflecting the steady hand of a seasoned pop instrumental pro. "Blow Your Own Horn," "The Midnight Tango" and "Garden Party" all try to emulate the laidback, high-tech groove of "Rise"—with the inimitable help of the latter's co-composer Randy Badazz—and *Beyond* is given an extra tweaking by a hotter remix of the album's "Red Hot." The Motown triumvirate of Holland-Dozier-Holland shares the production chair with Alpert on two tracks; Jose Quintana of Fandango drops in for three more—though the accent here is high-tech North America this time and not as inspired—and there is a pleasant L.A.-session-flavored encounter with Lee Ritenour on "Paradise

Cove." Not knowing which way to turn, Alpert refines and consolidates, awaiting the next flash of creative fire. —*Richard S. Ginell*

Bullish / Aug. 1984 / A&M ✦✦

Yes, Herb Alpert did indeed record an album in 1984 under the name Tijuana Brass for the first time in nine years—and in fact, he took a Tijuana Brass contingent on tour that year with four of the original band members on hand. But this album has nothing to do with the old TJB, for the music is the same high-tech pop of the 1980s that Alpert had been mostly purveying since "Rise," with synths galore, a frantic electronic dance beat on many numbers, and none of the original Brass on the sessions. No wonder, for the arranger is John Barnes, who had worked for the Jacksons (Alpert was no fool; the Jacksons' sound was never hotter). About all that remains of the TJB is Alpert's familiar trumpet, which often hearkens back to his '60s manner in this gleaming setting. The best moments are the whomping title track, the hyperactive "Struttin' on Five," and the optimistic "Life Is My Song." But to call this a "Tijuana Brass" album was bordering on consumer fraud for the faithful—though on its own terms, it is a fairly live slice of '80s pop. —*Richard S. Ginell*

Wild Romance / Jul. 1985 / A&M ✦✦

With his sights aimed squarely at the R&B charts, where he had become a regular visitor in the 1980s, Herb Alpert continued to collaborate with keyboardist John Barnes and bassist Romeo Williams on an album of mostly R&B-flavored dance music. Alpert sounds exactly the same as he had throughout most of the '80s thus far, merely grafting his spare, gently dancing trumpet onto drum machines and electronic keyboard textures, with Brenda Russell adding soul vocals at times. The most evocative track is the relatively reflective "African Flame" (later the B-side for "Cantare, Cantaras," the Latin American answer to "We Are the World"), and Alpert still exercises his vocal cords on a couple of tracks. Otherwise, this is mostly routine high-tech club music for the 1980s. —*Richard S. Ginell*

Keep Your Eye on Me / Feb. 1987 / A&M ✦✦✦

The unbelievable sales success of this record is a testament to Herb Alpert's extraordinary ability to keep his ear to the ground—no doubt aided by his position as vice-chairman and co-owner of A&M Records—and adapt to the times. At a time when A&M's Janet Jackson was blazing up the charts, Alpert journeyed to Minneapolis and cut some tracks with Jackson's producers Jimmy Jam and Terry Lewis, producing the others himself in a mostly similar techno-pop vein. Presto! Three Top Ten R&B singles came out of the album, "Keep Your Eye on Me," "Making Love in the Rain," and the No. 1 hit "Diamonds." The flashy, trashy "Diamonds" no doubt was aided on its rush up the charts by Jackson and Lisa Keith's bouncy lead vocals; it's really their record and that of Jam and Lewis, despite Alpert's top billing. Jackson and Keith also take the lead in the simple-minded lyrics of "Making Love in the Rain," which nevertheless has a haunting effect accented by Alpert's muted musings through an electronic gauze. At first, this seems like a gleaming digital machine of a record, loaded with repetitive sampling effects and drum machines churning out that ubiquitous '80s backbeat. But the techno stuff gradually gives way to Alpert's humane trumpet, which in a touching valentine to the '60s on Acker Bilk's "Stranger on the Shore," is eventually allowed to soar unimpeded over the electronics. —*Richard S. Ginell*

Under a Spanish Moon / 1988 / A&M ✦✦

Again, as in the case of *Rise*, Herb Alpert courageously followed a megahit album with a bold one that took big chances. The centerpiece of the album is "Under a Spanish Moon," an ambitious three-movement trumpet concerto commissioned by Alpert from the Argentinian-born composer Jorge del Barrio. A neo-classical, sometimes dissonant piece combining the Pacific Symphony Orchestra with electronic textures, "Under a Spanish Moon" successfully evokes the neo-classical period of Manuel de Falla and hauntingly captures the lonely Alpert muted-trumpet persona in the slow movement "Lamento." It's a fine piece of music, although difficult to perform (as the L.A. Philharmonic found out in a disastrous live performance at the Hollywood Bowl in 1988). The rest of the brief (34 minutes) CD clearly revolves around the concerto, with Alpert pursuing a moody, synth-laden direction, covering tunes by Sting ("Fragile") and Keith Jarrett ("My Song"), and hooking up with another del Barrio, Eddie, on four others. Admittedly, it's easier to experiment when you co-own the record company, but Alpert's willingness to continually risk his artistic capital and grow is laudable and rare among pop musicians. —*Richard S. Ginell*

My Abstract Heart / 1989 / A&M ✦✦

My Abstract Heart was the disappointing followup to the hugely successful *Keep Your Eye on Me*. There's no Janet Jackson to sing along, just associate producer Eddie del Barrio providing a battery of synthesized strings, keyboards, bass, and percussion. Much of the album is somewhat melancholy, and the lack of any pop vocal connection (there is a laconic duet between Alpert and Lani Hall on "When the Lights Go Down Low") kept it from finding much of an audience, although "3 O'Clock Jump" got to No. 59 in the Black singles chart. —*William Ruhlmann*

North on South Street / 1991 / A&M ♦♦

This was the next-to-last album trumpeter Herb Alpert did before leaving the label he founded (A&M). Alpert tried the same formula that worked in the late '80s—contemporary arrangements with a light beat and occasional trumpet solos. He used a hip-hop and dance pop sound, but didn't achieve the favorable results of '87's "Keep Your Eye On Me." —*Ron Wynn*

Midnight Sun / Jun. 9, 1992 / A&M ♦♦

Second Wind / Apr. 1996 / Geffen ♦♦

They finally couldn't keep the man away from the recording studio, or from owning a record label. Alpert is back in fine playing form on this part-mellow, part-funky set, blowing his trumpety heart out over a steady set of radio-ready grooves built up by keyboards player Jeff Lorber. It's intriguing to listen to the set, in fact, because there's a tendency for flourishes to come slapping out of left field, unexpected little touches that belie the formality of the construction and structure. —*Steven McDonald*

Passion Dance / Apr. 29, 1997 / Almo ♦♦♦

Herb Alpert led the *tres chic* Tijuana Brass in the sixties, and produced classic albums by Sergio Mendes and Gato Barbieri, so why not a Latin album—or, to be more precise, why not an album of "urban Latin groove?" *Passion Dance* is wonderfully, appropriately titled; this album really *does* make you feel romantic and want to samba, cha-cha, mambo, and all the rest. It opens with the fervently swinging "TKO" (co-written with, and one of the best things to ever drop from the pen of, fusion keyboard whiz Jeff Lorber); the motif continues with "Baila Conmigo (Dance with Me)," which spotlights salsa singers Johnny Rivera, Domingo Quinones and Jerry Medina, as well as an authentically slinky cover of Stevie Wonder's "Creepin'" and another uptempo toe-tapper called "Slinky." Alpert probably couldn't release an album without at least one killer ballad on it; on *Passion Dance*, the honors go to the title track and "Until We Meet Again," as tender and sweet as oven-fresh pastry, melting in your ears rather than your mouth. —*Chris Slawecki*

Barry Altschul

b. Jan. 6, 1943, New York, NY

Drums, Percussion / Avant-Garde

In the early '70s, Altschul was the drummer for Circle—a band that (with a membership that also included Chick Corea, Dave Holland, and Anthony Braxton) might possibly have been the most technically adept free jazz ensemble ever. Altschul's drumming with that band was stylistically all-encompassing—in his own words, "from ragtime to no time"—thanks to his background in traditional jazz styles, which gave him a solid grounding on which to build his free playing. From his days with Circle to his more recent work as a leader of his own ensembles, Altschul has demonstrated a notable consistency, especially in the way he inevitably manages to generate an enormous momentum without overpowering the ensemble. Much of his power as a rhythm player stems from the subtlety of his touch; Altschul's sound is very tight and exceedingly well-defined. A strict attention to rhythmic and tonal detail has always characterized his playing.

Altschul was largely self-taught until 1960, when he began study with Charlie Persip. From 1964 until 1970, Altschul played regularly with pianist Paul Bley; their relationship continued intermittently through the '70s and '80s. In 1969, he studied with Sam Ulano. Altschul was a member of the Jazz Composers' Guild and the Jazz Composers' Orchestra Association from 1964-68. He spent a portion of the '60s playing mainstream jazz in Europe. In the '70s, he recorded with the individual members of Circle. In '72, under Holland's leadership, Altschul recorded the classic album *Conference of the Birds*, with Braxton and saxophonist Sam Rivers. Around this time, he also made records with Bley, bassist Alan Silva, and pianist Andrew Hill, among others. In the '80s, Altschul made records of his own for Soul Note and continued his sideman work with such musicians as the Russianborn pianist Simon Nabotov and Kenny Drew, Sr. Altschul's 1985 album, *That's Nice*, shows him to be an exciting and good-humored bandleader in a rather modern-mainstream vein. Unfortunately, since that album was made, little has been heard from him as a leader. —*Chris Kelsey*

Virtuosi / Jun. 28, 1967 / IAI ♦♦♦

Drummer Barry Altschul, pianist Paul Bley and bassist Gary Peacock perform two lengthy improvisations based on Annette Peacock compositions on this CD which is a straight reissue of an earlier IAI LP. Although Altschul gets first billing, this is really an outing by Bley's trio. With its many wandering sections, the somewhat aimless and often-boring set is definitely a lesser effort and is far from essential. —*Scott Yanow*

● **You Can't Name Your Own Tune** / Feb. 8, 1977-Feb. 9, 1977 / Muse ♦♦♦♦♦

Although Barry Altschul is showcased on a solo performance on "Hey Toots!" and there is a trio piece with pianist Muhal Richard Abrams and bassist Dave Holland, the highlights of this excellent LP are the other selections, which feature interplay

between Sam Rivers (on tenor, flute and soprano) and trombonist George Lewis. Lewis in particular has rarely been heard in this type of relatively straightforward (if still adventurous) setting and really excels. —*Scott Yanow*

Another Time, Another Place / Mar. 13, 1978-Mar. 14, 1978 / Muse ♦♦♦♦

There is certainly plenty of variety on avant-garde drummer Barry Altschul's Muse set. Although only recorded on two separate occasions, each of the five performances uses very different instrumentation. The three-part "Suite for Monk" matches Altschul with altoist Arthur Blythe, trombonist Ray Anderson, the legendary guitarist Bill DeArango, pianist Anthony Davis and bassist Brian Smith for a well-conceived medley. Altschul teams up with pianist Davis and cellist Abdul Wadud for the fairly free "Chael"; bassist Dave Holland's complex "Pentacle" utilizes two basses and two cellists (plus the leader); trombonist Ray Anderson joins Davis, Smith and Altschul for the spirited and sometimes humorous "Another Time/Another Place"; and Barry Altschul takes it alone on the brief "Traps." All five selections work in their own unpredictable way. —*Scott Yanow*

For Stu / Feb. 18, 1979 / Soul Note ♦♦♦

This is a well-rounded set featuring drummer/leader Barry Altschul, pianist Anthony Davis, rambunctious trombonist Ray Anderson and bassist Rick Rozie. The four lengthy performances include a solo feature for Altschul ("Drum Role"), the intriguing title cut, an Anthony Davis ballad ("Sleepwalker") and a fine thirteen-and-a-half-minute interpretation of Charles Mingus' "Orange Was the Color of Her Dress, Then Silk Blues." A continually interesting set. —*Scott Yanow*

Brahma / Jan. 23, 1980 / Sackville ♦♦♦

Barry Altschul's 1980 trio (which had recorded a live set for Moers Music in 1979) consisted of trombonist Ray Anderson, bassist Mark Helias and the leader/drummer. In general, the music on this Sackville release is quite spontaneous and exploratory, but Anderson's playing sometimes hints strongly at earlier styles, particularly on "Lism" and the ballad "Irina." —*Scott Yanow*

Irina / Feb. 12, 1983 / Soul Note ♦♦♦♦

That's Nice / Nov. 25, 1985+Nov. 26, 1985 / Soul Note ♦♦♦

Drummer Barry Altschul gets to show off his versatility and talents throughout this interesting quartet/quintet set with trombonist Glen Ferris, Sean Bergin (doubling on alto and tenor), bassist Andy McKee and (on two of the five pieces) pianist Mike Melillo. All of the quirky pieces are group originals (Altschul contributed three), with the leader's "For Papa Jo, Klook and Philly Too" being a fine tribute to three drummers. In general, the music has many free moments, yet is not afraid to swing or to include melodies. A stimulating set. —*Scott Yanow*

Franco Ambrosetti

b. Dec. 10, 1941, Lugano, Switzerland

Trumpet, Fluegelhorn / Hard Bop

Franco Ambrosetti has had dual careers as a very successful businessman and as a fine trumpeter and fluegelhornist inspired by Freddie Hubbard and Miles Davis. His father, Flavio Ambrosetti, was an excellent saxophonist. Franco had piano lessons for eight years but is self-taught on trumpet, which he did not take up until he was 17. In 1972 he was one of the founders of the George Gruntz Concert Jazz Band and through the years he has recorded quite a few worthy hard-boppish albums for Enja in addition to leading his own groups. —*Scott Yanow*

Close Encounter / Mar. 21, 1978 / Enja ♦♦♦

Franco Ambrosetti's debut for Enja (his previous releases were all for Italian labels) finds the talented cool-toned fluegelhornist holding his own with the notable sidemen (Bennie Wallace on tenor and soprano, pianist George Gruntz, bassist Mike Richmond and drummer Bob Moses). The sometimes episodic repertoire (two Ambrosetti originals and one apiece by his father Flavio, Gruntz and Kuhn) is quite obscure and generally hard bop-oriented. Everyone plays well on this lesser-known but enjoyable effort. —*Scott Yanow*

Heartbop / Feb. 10, 1981-Feb. 11, 1981 / Enja ♦♦♦

Although fluegelhornist Franco Ambrosetti is only a part-time musician (making his main living as a businessman), his playing has always been at a high level. On this colorful set (which includes three of his originals, plus Hal Galper's "Triple Play" and the standard "My Funny Valentine"), Ambrosetti makes a strong team with altoist Phil Woods (who also plays a bit of clarinet), pianist Galper, bassist Mike Richmond and drummer Billy Hart. Advanced hard bop. —*Scott Yanow*

Wings / Dec. 1, 1983-Dec. 2, 1983 / Enja ♦♦♦♦

Also released as *Gin & Penatonic*, fluegelhornist Franco Ambrosetti's third in a series of consistently rewarding recordings for Enja has a particularly strong group (including tenor saxophonist Michael Brecker, John Clark on French horn, pianist Kenny Kirkland, bassist Buster Williams and drummer Daniel Humair) stretching out on three originals (two by Franco and one from his father Flavio), plus a brief rendition of George Gruntz's "More Wings for Wheelers." The music is solid post-bop, and Clark's French horn is a major plus in the ensembles. —*Scott Yanow*

Tentets / Mar. 13, 1985-Mar. 14, 1985 / Enja ◆◆◆◆

Movies / Nov. 24, 1986-Nov. 25, 1986 / Enja ◆◆◆◆
When one considers the repertoire—eight songs from movies. including the theme from *The Magnificent Seven* and the Beatles' "Yellow Submarine"—this recording may not seem to have much potential. But actually, the set list includes four well-known standards (including "That Old Black Magic" and "Falling in Love Again"), and all of the music is transformed into creative and consistently exciting jazz. Trumpeter/fluegelhornist Franco Ambrosetti is the lead voice, but gives plenty of solo space to his illustrious sidemen (guitarist John Scofield, pianist Geri Allen, bassist Michael Formanek, drummer Daniel Humair and percussionist Jerry Gonzalez), and the performances are generally quite memorable. Recommended. —*Scott Yanow*

Movies, Too / Mar. 22, 1988-Mar. 23, 1988 / Enja ◆◆◆◆◆
This second CD of movie themes once again finds fluegelhornist Franco Ambrosetti transforming some unpromising themes into jazz (including "Theme from Superman," "Theme from Peter Gunn" and "What's New, Pussycat," in addition to better-known standards such as "My Man," "Angel Eyes" and "God Bless the Child." The inventive arrangements feature excellent solos from Ambrosetti, altoist Greg Osby (doubling on soprano), guitarist John Scofield and pianist Geri Allen, with fine support from bassist Michael Formanek and drummer Daniel Humair. Well worth checking out. —*Scott Yanow*

★ **Music for Symphony & Jazz Band** / Oct. 1, 1990-Oct. 6, 1990 / Enja ◆◆◆◆◆
This CD is a classic, one of the all-time best examples of Third Stream music (a combination of jazz and classical music). Trumpeter-fluegelhornist Franco Ambrosetti's sextet is joined by the NDR Radio Orchestra Hannover, and together they perform nine of Daniel Schnyder's very complex and continually surprising arrangements of six standards, two of his originals and Ambrosetti's "Close Encounter." The leader, altoist Greg Osby, and Schnyder himself on soprano have some superior solos, but it is the unusual charts that take honors; the transformations of Duke Ellington's "C Jam Blues" and Thelonious Monk's "Well You Needn't" are among the many high points of this essential set. —*Scott Yanow*

Live at the Blue Note / Jul. 13, 1992 / Enja ◆◆◆

Albert Ammons

b. Sep. 23, 1907, Chicago, IL, **d.** Dec. 2, 1949, Chicago, IL
Piano / Boogie-Woogie, Swing
Albert Ammons was one of the big three of late-'30s boogie-woogie along with Pete Johnson and Meade Lux Lewis. Arguably the most powerful of the three, Ammons was also flexible enough to play swing music. Ammons played in Chicago clubs from the 1920s on, although he also worked as a cab driver for a time. Starting in 1934 he led his own band in Chicago and he made his first records in 1936. In 1938 Ammons appeared at Carnegie Hall with Pete Johnson and Meade Lux Lewis, an event that really helped launch the boogie-woogie craze. Ammons recorded with the other pianists in duets and trios, fit right in with the Port of Harlem Jazzmen on their Blue Note session, appeared regularly at Cafe Society, recorded as a sideman with Sippie Wallace in the 1940s, and even cut a session with his son, the great tenorman Gene Ammons. Albert Ammons worked steadily throughout the 1940s, playing at President Harry Truman's inauguration in 1949; he died later that year. Many of his recordings are currently available on CD. —*Scott Yanow*

☆ **The Complete Blue Note Recordings of Albert Ammons and Meade Lux Lewis** / Nov. 21, 1935-Apr. 22, 1944 / Mosaic ◆◆◆◆◆
This magnificent three-LP box set was issued as part of the first release by the Mosaic label. The out-of-print collection has all of the music recorded during Blue Note's first session (nine piano solos by Albert Ammons, eight including a five-part "The Blues" by Meade Lux Lewis and a pair of Ammons-Lewis duets) plus Lewis' 1935 version of "Honky Tonk Train Blues" and his complete sessions of Oct. 4, 1940, Apr. 9, 1941 (four songs on harpsichord) and Aug. 22, 1944. The music emphasizes boogie-woogie and both Ammons (quite memorable on "Boogie Woogie Stomp") and Lewis are heard in prime form. Incidentally, one of their duets (which is mistakenly titled "The Sheik of Araby") is actually "Nagasaki." This box is well worth bidding on at an auction. —*Scott Yanow*

1936-1939 / Feb. 13, 1936-Apr. 8, 1939 / Classics ◆◆◆◆◆

Master of Boogie / Dec. 23, 1938-May 1939 / Milan ◆◆
This is the type of CD that frustrates completists and veteran collectors; the 13 selections are taken from a variety of sessions and the recording dates that are given are often incorrect. The great boogie-woogie pianist Albert Ammons is heard on five of the nine piano solos he recorded at Blue Note's debut session in 1939, along with a solo number apiece that were cut for Columbia and Storyville.

In addition, Ammons plays "Two and Fews" in duet with Meade Lux Lewis (from the Blue Note date), leads a hot group on two of the four numbers from his relatively rare debut session (dating from 1936, not 1939 as it states on the back cover) and is heard at the famous Spirituals to Swing concert of 1938 backing blues singer-guitarist Big Bill Broonzy and jamming with Meade Lux Lewis and Pete Johnson on three pianos. Great music, inexcusably lousy packaging. —*Scott Yanow*

● **The First Day** / Jan. 6, 1939 / Blue Note ◆◆◆◆◆
Producer Alfred Lion, who had attended John Hammond's Spiritual to Swing concert of Dec. 23, 1938 which had introduced boogie-woogie pianists Albert Ammons and Meade Lux Lewis to New York audiences, was very impressed. Two weeks later he started the Blue Note label by recording nine Ammons solos, eight by Lewis and a pair of heated duets during a single day. All of the music (except an untitled original by Meade Lux Lewis slated to be issued by Blue Note in the future) is on this single CD. Ammons, the more forceful (relatively speaking) of the two pianists, generally takes honors but there are plenty of rewarding performances including Lewis' five-part "The Blues," Ammons' "Boogie Woogie Stomp" and their duet on "Nagasaki." Highly recommended to collectors who do not already own Mosaic's more extensive three-LP limited-edition Ammons/Lewis set. —*Scott Yanow*

King of Boogie Woogie (1939-1949) / Jan. 6, 1939-Jan. 4, 1948 / Blues Classics ◆◆◆
Albert Ammons is featured on six piano solos from two sessions in 1939, leading a quartet in 1946 and jamming with his sextet during 1947-48 on this LP sampler. His boogie-woogie music is consistently exciting in all the formats even if one regrets that these performances have been reissued in a somewhat hodgepodge fashion; the selections are drawn from the catalogs of Blue Note, Solo Art and Mercury. Highlights include "Boogie Woogie Stomp," "Boogie Woogie at the Civic Opera," "Baltimore Breakdown" and "Swanee River Boogie." —*Scott Yanow*

1939-1946 / Apr. 8, 1939-Apr. 2, 1946 / Classics ◆◆◆◆

Gene Ammons

b. Apr. 14, 1925, Chicago, IL, **d.** Aug. 6, 1974, Chicago, IL
Tenor Saxophone / Bop, Hard Bop, Soul Jazz, Groove
Gene Ammons, who had a huge and immediately recognizable tone on tenor, was a very flexible player who could play bebop with the best (always battling his friend Sonny Stitt to a tie) yet was an influence on the R&B world. Some of his ballad renditions became hits and, despite two unfortunate interruptions in his career, Ammons remained a popular attraction for 25 years.

Son of the great boogie-woogie pianist Albert Ammons, Gene Ammons (who was nicknamed "Jug") left Chicago at age 18 to work with King Kolax's band. He originally came to fame as a key soloist with Billy Eckstine's orchestra during 1944-47, trading off with Dexter Gordon on the famous Eckstine record *Blowing the Blues Away*. Other than a notable stint with Woody Herman's Third Herd in 1949 and an attempt at co-leading a two tenor group in the early '50s with Sonny Stitt, Ammons worked as a single throughout his career, recording frequently (most notably for Prestige) in settings ranging from quartets and organ combos to all-star jam sessions. Drug problems kept him in prison during much of 1958-60 and, due to a particularly stiff sentence, 1962-69. When Ammons returned to the scene in 1969 he opened up his style a bit, including some of the emotional cries of the avant-garde while utilizing funky rhythm sections, but he was still able to battle Sonny Stitt on his own terms. Ironically, the last song that he ever recorded (just a short time before he was diagnosed with terminal cancer) was "Goodbye." —*Scott Yanow*

Young Jug / Oct. 12, 1948-Mar. 24, 1952 / Chess ◆◆◆◆
This is a CD that will most likely frustrate Gene Ammons collectors a bit. From 1948-51, the great tenor recorded 24 titles for Chess and its related labels, and all were reissued on the double LP *Early Visions*. This best-of CD has 16 of the songs, plus a very rare four-song session from 1952 for Decca that had not been reissued previously; completists are therefore stuck acquiring both sets. But discographical details aside, the music on the Chess CD is excellent, with Ammons sounding quite lyrical on the ballads (which showcase his huge tone), quoting a dozen Christmas songs on "Swingin' for Xmas," and romping with his combos on the jump material. This CD is recommended to those listeners not already owning the two-fer. —*Scott Yanow*

All Star Sessions / Mar. 5, 1950-Jun. 16, 1955 / Original Jazz Classics ◆◆◆◆
This enjoyable and frequently exciting CD contains a variety of performances mostly featuring the tenors of Gene Ammons and Sonny Stitt. The two combative saxophonists battle it out on "Blues Up and Down" (heard in three takes), the superior "New Blues Up and Down" and two versions of "You Can Depend on Me." In addition, Ammons has a few ballad features and there are a pair of extended jams from 1955 matching him in a sextet with trumpeter Art Farmer, altoist Lou

Donaldson, pianist Freddie Redd, bassist Addison Farmer and drummer Kenny Clarke. The music is perhaps not essential but has enough exciting moments to fully satisfy bebop collectors. —Scott Yanow

The Gene Ammons Story: The 78 Era / Mar. 5, 1950-Nov. 4, 1955 / Prestige ✦✦✦✦

This CD contains 26 of the 30 selections included on the two-LP set of the same name (and catalog number). Although mostly cut during an era when Ammons co-led a two-tenor group with Sonny Stitt, the focus is almost entirely on Ammons. All but the final five titles are from the 1950-51 period and these concise performances were originally on 78s. Even at this early stage Ammons' tone was quite distinctive and he was able to combine the innovations of bop with the simplicity of R&B in his forceful and direct solos; also, few could play ballads with the passion he possessed. This CD is recommended to listeners who do not already own the two-fer. —Scott Yanow

☆ **The Happy Blues** / Apr. 23, 1956 / Original Jazz Classics ✦✦✦✦✦

This is one of the great studio jam sessions. Tenor saxophonist Gene Ammons is teamed up with trumpeter Art Farmer, altoist Jackie McLean, pianist Duke Jordan, bassist Addison Farmer, drummer Art Taylor and the congas of Candido for four lengthy selections. Best is "The Happy Blues," which has memorable solos and spontaneous but perfectly fitting riffing by the horns behind each others' solos. The other numbers ("The Great Lie," "Can't We Be Friends" and "Madhouse") are also quite enjoyable, making this a highly recommended set. —Scott Yanow

Jammin' with Gene / Jul. 13, 1956 / Original Jazz Classics ✦✦✦✦

The tenor saxophonist led a series of excellent all-star jam sessions for the Prestige label during the mid-'50s that took advantage of the extra time available on LPs (as opposed to the three-minute 78). This CD is a straight reissue of the original LP and features versions of "Jammin' with Gene" (a blues), "We'll Be Together Again" (which evolves from being an Ammons ballad feature into a group jam and then back again) and "Not Really the Blues" that clocks in between ten and over 16 minutes. With such sidemen as trumpeters Art Farmer and Donald Byrd, altoist Jackie McLean, pianist Mal Waldron, bassist Doug Watkins and drummer Art Taylor, this is an excellent (and rather spontaneous) straightahead session. —Scott Yanow

Funky / Jan. 11, 1957 / Original Jazz Classics ✦✦✦✦

The Gene Ammons all-star jam session recordings of the 1950s are all quite enjoyable and this one is no exception. The great tenor is matched with trumpeter Art Farmer, altoist Jackie McLean, guitarist Kenny Burrell, pianist Mal Waldron, bassist Doug Watkins and drummer Art Taylor for lengthy versions of "Stella By Starlight," the Burrell blues "Funky" and a pair of numbers by arranger Jimmy Mundy. All of the horns plus Burrell and Waldron get ample solo space and Ammons seems to really inspire his sidemen on these soulful bop jams. —Scott Yanow

Jammin' in Hi-Fi with Gene Ammons / Apr. 12, 1957 / Original Jazz Classics ✦✦✦✦

Tenorman Gene Ammons headed a series of notable studio jam session in the 1950s and this is one of the better ones. With such fine young players as trumpeter Idrees Sulieman, altoist Jackie McLean, pianst Mal Waldron, guitarist Kenny Burrell, bassist Paul Chambers and drummer Art Taylor, Ammons and his friends jam through four numbers all of which clock in between 11:59 and 13:01. The results are an accessible and often exciting brand of bebop. —Scott Yanow

Big Sound / Jan. 3, 1958 / Original Jazz Classics ✦✦✦✦

Along with its fellow CD *Groove Blues*, this reissue fully documents all of the music recorded by tenor saxophonist Gene Ammons on the busy day of Jan. 3, 1958. Although there were many guest soloists, only one of the four songs on this half of the set (Mal Waldron's "The Real McCoy") has appearances by John Coltrane (on alto) and the tenor of Paul Quinichette. However, baritonist Pepper Adams is aboard for two of the performances and flutist Jerome Richardson (along with pianist Mal Waldron, bassist George Joyner and drummer Art Taylor) is on all four. Ammons is easily the main star (he really excelled in this setting) and he is in generally fine form on the two standards ("That's All" and "Cheek to Cheek"), his own "Blue Hymn" and the Waldron original. —Scott Yanow

Groove Blues / Jan. 3, 1958 / Original Jazz Classics ✦✦✦✦

On Jan. 3, 1958, Gene Ammons led one of his last all-star jam sessions for Prestige. The most notable aspect to this date (which resulted in two albums of material) is that it featured among its soloists John Coltrane, on alto. This CD, a straight reissue of one of the original LPs, includes baritonist Pepper Adams, the tenor of Paul Quinichette and Coltrane on two of the four selections and Jerome Richardson's flute during three of the songs, in addition to a fine rhythm section (pianist Mal Waldron, bassist George Joyner and drummer Art Taylor). This set consists of three of Waldron's originals in addition to the standard ballad "It Might as Well Be

Spring" and it (along with the CD *The Big Sound*) fully documents the productive day. —Scott Yanow

Blue Gene / May 3, 1958 / Original Jazz Classics ✦✦✦

The final of his series of jam sessions for Prestige features an excellent septet (the leader on tenor, trumpeter Idrees Sulieman, baritonist Pepper Adams, pianist Mal Waldron, bassist Doug Watkins, drummer Art Taylor and Ray Barretto on congas) stretching out on three original blues and the ballad "Hip Tip"; all four pieces were written by Waldron. Few surprises occur but everyone plays up to their usual high level. This enjoyable straightahead CD is a reissue of the original LP. —Scott Yanow

Boss Tenor / Jun. 16, 1960 / Original Jazz Classics ✦✦✦✦✦

There are many Gene Ammons recordings currently available on CD in Fantasy's Original Jazz Classics since the versatile tenorman was a longtime Prestige recording artist. Unlike his earlier jam sessions, this particular outing finds Ammons as the only horn, fronting a talented rhythm section (pianist Tommy Flanagan, bassist Doug Watkins, drummer Art Taylor and Ray Barretto on congas). Jug explores standards (including a near-classic version of "Canadian Sunset"), blues and ballads in his usual warm, soulful and swinging fashion. This is a fine outing by one of the true "bosses" of the tenor. —Scott Yanow

The Gene Ammons Story: Organ Combos / Jun. 17, 1960+Nov. 28, 1961 / Prestige ✦✦✦✦

Gene Ammons recorded frequently for Prestige during the 1950s and early '60s and virtually all of the tenor's dates were quite rewarding. This two-LP set reissues *Twistin' the Jug* plus part of *Angel Eyes* and *Velvet Soul*. Ammons, a bop-based but very versatile soloist, sounds quite comfortable playing a variety of standards and lesser-known material in groups featuring Jack McDuff or Johnny "Hammond" Smith on organ and either trumpeter Joe Newman or Frank Wess on tenor and flute. This version of "Angel Eyes" became a surprise hit. —Scott Yanow

The Gene Ammons Story: Gentle Jug / Jan. 26, 1961+Apr. 14, 1962 / Prestige ✦✦✦

This single CD reissues the two-LP set of the same name. Included are two sessions originally cut for Prestige's subsidiary Moodsville (*Nice an' Cool* and *The Soulful Mood of Gene Ammons*), which are purposely relaxed and strictly at ballad tempos. Fortunately, Ammons (who had a distinctive, huge tone) was long a master at interpreting ballads, and although these performances do not quite reach the heights of his greatest recordings, the lyrical music is quite enjoyable. Accompanied by either Richard Wyands or Patti Bown on piano, Doug Watkins or George Duvivier on bass and J.C. Heard or Ed Shaughnessy on drums, Ammons is tasteful and creative in a subtle way throughout these successful dates. —Scott Yanow

Jug / Jan. 27, 1961 / Original Jazz Classics ✦✦✦

Tenor saxophonist Gene Ammons recorded many albums during 1961-62, a busy period that was brought to an abrupt halt by his arrest for narcotics abuse. *Jug* finds the great tenor in excellent form, interpreting six standards and two of his originals with the assistance of pianist Richard Wyands, bassist Doug Watkins, drummer J.C. Heard and the congas of Ray Barretto; Sleepy Anderson replaces Wyands on two songs, one of which he takes on organ. Few surprises occur but fans will not be disappointed by his soulful and lyrical playing. —Scott Yanow

Late Hour Special / Jun. 13, 1961-Apr. 13, 1962 / Original Jazz Classics ✦✦✦

Originally released by Prestige while tenor saxophonist Gene Ammons was serving a long prison sentence for possession of drugs (the label effectively kept Ammons' name alive by regularly coming out with "new" material), this album was reissued on CD in 1997. The distinctive tenor is heard on three numbers with a quartet/quintet also including pianist Patti Bown, bassist George Duvivier, drummer Walter Perkins and sometimes Ray Barretto on conga, and on four cuts as part of a ten-piece group arranged by Oliver Nelson. Fluegelhornist Clark Terry gets a couple of choruses on "Things Ain't What They Used to Be," and Bown has several solos, but Ammons is the main star throughout. In addition to performing his own "Lascivious" (a blues), Jug sticks to standards, infusing each tune with soul and swing. A fine outing, although with brief (thirty-five-and-a-half minutes) playing time. —Scott Yanow

Soul Summit / Jun. 13, 1961-Apr. 13, 1962 / Prestige ✦✦✦✦

This single CD reissues all of the music from two LPs titled *Soul Summit* and *Soul Summit, Vol. 2*. The latter session is one of the lesser known of the many collaborations of tenors Gene Ammons and Sonny Stitt, who are joined by organist Jack McDuff and drummer Charlie Persip. Their six performances are primarily riff tunes with "When You Wish upon a Star" taken at a medium pace and "Out in the Cold Again" the lone ballad. The second half of this CD features Ammons on two songs ("Love I've Found You" and a swinging "Too Marvelous for Words") with a big band arranged by Oliver Nelson, jamming "Ballad for Baby" with a quintet, sitting out of "Scram" (which stars McDuff and the tenor of Harold Vick) and backing singer Etta Jones on three numbers, of which, "Cool, Cool Daddy" is the most memorable. Overall, this is an interesting and consistently swinging set that adds to the large quantity of recordings that the great Ammons did during the early '60s. —*Scott Yanow*

We'll Be Together Again / Aug. 26, 1961 / Original Jazz Classics ✦✦✦✦
The title of this exciting meeting between the tenors of Gene Ammons and Sonny Stitt was rather poignant, because this recording was released in the late '60s, when Ammons was serving a long jail sentence for possession of heroin, and it appeared that he and Stitt might never meet up again. Backed by pianist John Houston, bassist Buster Williams and drummer George Brown, Ammons and Stitt (who had co-led a regular group a decade before) proved once again to be a perfect team, jamming on a variety of standards, blues and ballads while also revisiting "New Blues Up and Down." The two tenors always brought out the best in each other, and luckily, they would get back together in the early '70s. This is high-quality bebop. —*Scott Yanow*

★ **Boss Tenors: Straight Ahead from Chicago 1961** / Aug. 27, 1961 / Verve ✦✦✦✦✦
There are perhaps no better tenors, no better jazz. This is definitive. With Sonny Stitt. —*Michael G. Nastos*

Live! in Chicago / Aug. 29, 1961 / Original Jazz Classics ✦✦✦✦
The tenor saxophonist is heard in a surprisingly sparse setting for this live set, in a trio with organist Eddie Buster and drummer Gerald Donovan, two Chicago-based musicians. Ammons performs standards, blues and ballads, sounding at his best on an emotional "Please Send Me Someone to Love" and a hard-charging "Sweet Georgia Brown." This is one of many Gene Ammons recordings from the 1961-62 period; virtually all are worth getting. The CD reissue adds two previously unreleased selections to the original program. —*Scott Yanow*

Up Tight / Oct. 17, 1961-Oct. 18, 1961 / Prestige ✦✦✦✦
Gene Ammons recorded many albums for Prestige but this CD is a good start for listeners unfamiliar with his playing. A reissue of two LPs (*Up Tight* and *Boss Soul*) recorded during the same two-day period, these performances find Ammons backed by a pair of four-piece rhythm sections (with either Walter Bishop or Patti Bown on piano and Ray Barretto's congas a major asset) and taking the lion's share of the solo space. Ammons sounds particularly warm and emotional throughout this CD, particularly on such numbers as "The Breeze and I," "I'm Afraid the Masquerade Is Over," a cooking "Lester Leaps In" and "Song of the Islands." His sound and style effectively bridged the gap between bop and soul jazz. —*Scott Yanow*

Preachin' / May 3, 1962 / Original Jazz Classics ✦✦✦✦
This is a most unusual session. The great tenor performs 11 religious hymns with accompaniment by organist Clarence "Sleepy" Anderson (along with bassist Sylvester Hickman and drummer Dorral Anderson) that is straight from the church. Ammons mostly sticks very closely to the themes, but gives such melodies as "Abide with Me," "You'll Never Walk Alone," "What a Friend" and "Holy Holy" passion, soul and honest feelings. This little-known album (now available on CD) is a rather touching and emotional outing and quite unique. —*Scott Yanow*

Jug and Dodo / May 1962 / Prestige ✦✦✦
This CD (which completely reissues a double LP with the same title) is a bit unusual, for it teams together the great tenor Gene Ammons with the very talented (but now obscure) bop pianist Dodo Marmarosa whose mental problems kept him from pursuing his career. Actually Ammons is only half of this set (which also includes bassist Sam Jones and drummer Marshall Thompson) but Marmarosa is in top form; it's strange that the music was not released for the first time until the mid-'70s. This historical curiosity contains plenty of hard-swinging performances (including two versions apiece of "Yardbird Suite" and "Falling in Love with Love") and is worth picking up. —*Scott Yanow*

Nothin' But Soul / May 1962 / Up Front ✦✦
This budget LP (which has also been reissued by some other semilegitimate labels) contains four similar and lengthy blues that match tenor saxophonist Gene Ammons and trumpeter Howard McGhee with an obscure and pianoless rhythm section. The music is surprisingly forgettable and there are many more valuable Ammons recordings around although completists might want to get this one anyway. —*Scott Yanow*

Bad! Bossa Nova / Sep. 9, 1962 / Original Jazz Classics ✦✦✦
This was Ammons' final recording before "being made an example of" and getting a lengthy jail sentence for possession of heroin; his next record would be cut over seven years later. Surprisingly the music is upbeat with Ammons joined by two guitars (Bucky Pizzarelli and Kenny Burrell), a fine rhythm section (pianist Hank Jones, bassist Norman Edge and drummer Oliver Jackson) and the bongos of Al Hayes for a set of Latin-flavored jazz that was masquerading as bossa nova. The music is offbeat if not all that memorable, a decent effort but not essential. —*Scott Yanow*

The Boss Is Back / Nov. 10, 1969-Nov. 11, 1969 / Prestige ✦✦✦✦
The executives at Prestige must have been ecstatic when they heard Gene Ammons first play after his release from a very severe seven-year jail sentence. The great tenor proved to still be in his prime, his huge sound was unchanged and he was hungry to make new music. This CD, which completely reissues the first two LPs Ammons cut after his return (*The Boss Is Back!* and *Brother Jug!*) rewards repeated listenings. The first date (in an acoustic quintet with pianist Junior Mance) hints at his earlier bop-based music, while the numbers from the following day (with organist Sonny Phillips) find Ammons playing over a couple of boogaloo vamps very much of the period. Actually, it is his ballad statements (particularly "Here's That Rainy Day," "Feeling Good" and even "Didn't We") that really make this CD memorable, although on "He's a Real Gone Guy" Ammons shows that he had not forgotten how to jam the blues either. —*Scott Yanow*

My Way / 1970 / Prestige ✦✦
Few of Gene Ammons' recordings from his final period (1969-74) have been reissued on CD and it is doubtful that many people are waiting anxiously for this one. The great tenor is heard mostly tackling commercial material such as "What's Going On," "A House Is Not a Home" and "My Way" on this R&B-ish effort. While Ammons sounds fine (his tone was never to be denied), the dated arrangements and unimaginative playing by the rhythm section (what is Roland Hanna doing on electric piano?) largely sink this effort. —*Scott Yanow*

Night Lights / Feb. 2, 1970 / Prestige ✦✦✦
One of his first recording sessions after he returned to the scene following a rather severe jail sentence was this tribute to Nat King Cole. As it turned out, the quartet date with pianist Wynton Kelly, bassist George Duvivier and drummer Rudy Collins was quickly forgotten as Ammons recorded some more commercial material and this set was not released for the first time until 1985. Ammons is in excellent form on such ballads as "Nature Boy," "Lush Life," "Sweet Lorraine" and "The Christmas Song," making one wish that the contents of this LP were available on CD. —*Scott Yanow*

The Chase / Jul. 26, 1970 / Prestige ✦✦✦
Although Gene Ammons received first billing, his fellow tenor Dexter Gordon is an equal partner on this exciting live bebop set. Expanded from the original LP with a previously unissued ballad medley and a full-length 17-minute rendition of "Wee Dot," this CD is highly recommended to fans of tenor battles and straightahead jazz. "Wee Dot" and the ballad "Polka Dots and Moonbeams" are Gordon's features, while Ammons gets to revive "The Happy Blues," and the two tenors take a pair of songs apiece on the lengthy ballad medley. However, it is their all-out battles on "Lonesome Lover Blues" (which has a spontaneous vocal by Vi Redd) and "The Chase" that are most memorable. With a pair of fine Chicago-based rhythm sections taking turns (pianists John Young and Jodie Christian, bassists Cleveland Eaton and Rufus Reid, and drummers Steve McCall and Wilbur Campbell), Jug and Gordon (who had last recorded together in 1944) are heard in prime, combative form. —*Scott Yanow*

Legends of Acid Jazz / Nov. 11, 1970-Feb. 8, 1971 / Prestige ✦✦✦✦
As is often the case in this CD reissue series, the music has little to do with acid jazz, but it does feature a few organists. Tenor saxophonist Gene Ammons is heard on music that formerly comprised two complete LPs from 1970-71 (*The Black Cat* and *As You Talk That Talk*), plus a pair of titles from a 1962 date only previously out on a sampler. *The Black Cat* is an interesting if erratic set that finds Ammons (along with guitarist George Freeman, Harold Mabern on electric piano, bassist Ron Carter and drummer Idris Muhammad) playing everything from the pop tune "Long Long Time" and George Harrison's "Something" (both of those tunes have unimaginative strings) to "Jug Eyes" and the boppish blues "Hi Ruth." *As You Talk That Talk* is a reunion with fellow tenor Sonny Stitt (they are joined by Freeman, Muhammad and organist Leon Spencer), but it has a major problem. Stitt uses the electrified Varitone saxophone throughout the date, and his horn sounds even stranger than on his other Varitone dates, like a cross between an electric guitar and a dated keyboard; very eerie and odd. Ammons plays well enough (including on two throwaway numbers from 1962 with organist Don Patterson, guitarist Paul Weeden and drummer Billy James), but overall, the music on this CD is dated and very much of the period. There are many more rewarding Gene Ammons reissues currently available. —*Scott Yanow*

Chicago Concert / Nov. 21, 1971 / Prestige ✦✦✦
This meeting between Gene Ammons and James Moody is not as memorable as one might hope. Backed by pianist Jodie Christian, bassist Cleveland Eaton and drummer Marshall Thompson, the two tenors square off on "Just in Time," "Have You Met Miss Jones?," "C-Jam Blues" and Ammons' "Jim-Jam-Jug." Although there are a few sparks, they do not blend together that well and the results are surprisingly workmanlike. Ammons is actually best on his two features "Work Song" and "I'll Close My Eyes." This set has not yet been reissued on CD. —*Scott Yanow*

Big Bad Jug / Oct. 28, 1972-Nov. 1, 1972 / Prestige ♦♦

After he made his comeback, Gene Ammons recorded a series of somewhat commercial albums for Prestige on which he was backed by electric R&B rhythm sections. This particular set finds the veteran tenor joined by electric piano, organ, guitar (either Maynard Parker or Joe Beck), Ron Carter (mostly on electric bass) and drums (Billy Cobham, Idris Muhammad or Mickey Roker). The repertoire, which includes a couple of funky originals, Dave Grusin's "Fuzz" and "Papa Was a Rolling Stone," is not too inspiring on this LP (as of yet not reissued on CD) but Ammons makes the best of it. —*Scott Yanow*

Got My Own / Oct. 28, 1972-Nov. 1, 1972 / Prestige ♦♦♦

Recorded at the same sessions that resulted in the more commercial *Big Bad Jug,* this LP (whose contents have not yet been reissued on CD) is the better of the two, thanks to the inclusion of four Billie Holiday-associated songs. Ammons (even with the electric rhythm section) is in strong form on "Lady Sings the Blues," "God Bless the Child," "Strange Fruit" and "Fine and Mellow." The other three pieces (which include the theme from *Ben* and a Neal Diamond tune) are not as inspiring, but Ammons' huge sound makes the music worthwhile. —*Scott Yanow*

Gene Ammons and Friends at Montreux / Jul. 7, 1973 / Prestige ♦♦♦♦

This is a Prestige LP well-deserving of being reissued on CD. Ammons, whose studio recordings of the period were somewhat commercial, is heard in excellent form playing a blues and three standards with the backing of a fine rhythm section: Hampton Hawes (who unfortunately sticks to electric piano), electric bassist Bob Cranshaw, drummer Kenny Clarke and Kenneth Nash on congas. Best of all is a 17-minute blues on which Ammons welcomes fellow tenor Dexter Gordon, cornetist Nat Adderley and altoist Cannonball Adderley; the four horns all get to trade off with each other. This is one of the better late-period Gene Ammons records. —*Scott Yanow*

In Sweden / Jul. 14, 1973 / Enja ♦♦♦

Lesser-known, but still interesting, concert dates featuring Ammons heading a group with pianist Horace Parlan, bassist Red Mitchell, and drummer Ed Jones during appearance at the 1973 Abus Jazz Festival. It's not that well recorded, but Ammons' playing is furious, funky, and riveting. —*Ron Wynn*

Brasswind / Oct. 30, 1973 / Prestige ♦♦

Veteran tenor saxophonist Ammons is accompanied by a funky 12-piece band arranged by David Axelrod on this commercial but interesting release, one of his last recordings. The repertoire consists of a couple of Ammons originals, two by Axelrod, Wes Montgomery's "Cariba," Antonio Carlos Jobim's "Once I Loved" and the Monk standard "'Round Midnight." Ammons plays well and even if the arrangements are somewhat dated (George Duke's keyboards do not help), this set has its strong moments. —*Scott Yanow*

Together Again for the Last Time / Nov. 20, 1973-Dec. 10, 1973 / Prestige ♦♦♦♦

Gene Ammons and Sonny Stitt had a longtime musical partnership and friendship. The two tenors first teamed up on a regular basis in 1950 and they recorded together on an irregular basis over the next two decades. Their similar styles and combative approach made their musical encounters quite exciting and this Prestige LP, their last joint recording, has some strong tradeoffs. Actually, the two saxophonists only appear together on three of the six selections (all Ammons originals) while Gene takes "The More I See You" and "I'll Close My Eyes" as his ballad features and Stitt is the only horn on "For All We Know." With pianist Junior Mance leading the rhythm section, this is a fine date (which has yet to be reissued on CD) that is recommended to fans of the two tenors. —*Scott Yanow*

Goodbye / Mar. 18, 1974-Mar. 20, 1974 / Prestige ♦♦♦♦

It is ironic that on tenor saxophonist Gene Ammons' final recording date, the last song he performed was the standard "Goodbye." That emotional rendition is the high point of this LP (which has not been reissued on CD yet) a septet date with cornetist Nat Adderley, altoist Gary Bartz, pianist Kenny Drew, bassist Sam Jones, drummer Louis Hayes, and Ray Barretto on congas. In contrast to the somewhat commercial studio albums he had recorded during the past couple of years, this set was much more freewheeling, for Ammons was clearly happy to perform the material (which included "It Don't Mean a Thing," "Alone Again [Naturally]" and "Jeannine") without any tight arrangements, in the spirit of his Prestige jam sessions of the 1950s. It's a fine ending to a colorful career. —*Scott Yanow*

David Amram

b. Nov. 17, 1930, Philadelphia, PA

French Horn / Bop, World Fusion, Classical

Musical compartments mean nothing to David Amram, whose compositions and activities have crossed fearlessly back and forth between the classical and jazz worlds, as well as those of Latin jazz, folk, and television and film music. In addition to his rare (to jazz) specialty, the French horn, Amram has also recorded on piano, recorder, Spanish guitar and various percussion instruments.

Amram spent a year at the Oberlin College Conservatory (1948) but graduated from George Washington University with a BA in history in 1952. His long association with Latin music began in 1951 in D.C. when he played horn and percussion in the Buddy Rowell Latin band while also serving as a classical horn player in the National Symphony Orchestra. Stationed with the Seventh Army in Europe, Amram recorded with Lionel Hampton in Paris in 1955, and then returned to New York later that year to join Charles Mingus' Jazz Workshop, performing with Mingus and Oscar Pettiford. Amram led a quartet with tenor saxophonist George Barrow that made an album for Decca in 1957 and later played regularly at New York's Five Spot in 1963-65. However, Amram's career gravitated mostly over to the classical side after the 1950s, producing orchestral and instrumental pieces, incidental music (his score for Archibald MacLeish's *J.B.* won a Pulitzer prize), and other works that attracted enough respect to have the New York Philharmonic sign him on as its first composer-in-residence (1966-67).

In 1977, Amram sailed on the cruise ship Daphne from New Orleans to Havana with Dizzy Gillespie, Stan Getz and Earl "Fatha" Hines, who were among the first US citizens to legally visit Cuba in 16 years. An exciting live recording of Amram's "En Memoria de Chano Pozo" was made in Havana with members of Irakere (including Arturo Sandoval and Paquito D'Rivera) and several visiting Americans, which can be heard on the album *Havana/New York* (Flying Fish). Amram's Cuban visit received extensive news coverage at the time and also provided many Americans with their first glimpse of Irakere.

Most of Amram's available recordings can also be found on Flying Fish. In addition, the open-minded Amram can be heard playing bouncy French horn, recorder and piano obligatos on some bizarre 1971 tracks by beat poet Allen Ginsberg (sample titles: "Vomit Express," "Going to San Diego"), later released on John Hammond's eponymous label. —*Richard S. Ginell*

Triple Concerto / 1977 / Flying Fish ♦♦♦

This album finds Amram playing his own compositions with the assistance of his jazz quintet, featuring Pepper Adams, and with the Rochester Philharmonic. —*AMG*

● **Havana/New York** / Jun. 1977-Jul. 1977 / Flying Fish ♦♦♦♦

A very versatile player interested in combining folk music from other countries with jazz, David Amram has recorded surprisingly few records through the years as a leader. In fact, this excellent Flying Fish set was only his third album, and first since 1957. In 1977, several American musicians were able to travel to Cuba for a short visit, resulting in the lengthy "En Memoria De Chano Pozo," which matches Amram (on guitar, piano, flute, penny whistle, French horn, xylophone and percussion) with an American rhythm section and two then-unknown Cubans: altoist Paquito D'Rivera and 20-year-old trumpeter Arturo Sandoval. Two other selections on the set mostly feature Americans (including trumpeter Thad Jones, baritonist Pepper Adams and the tenor of Billy Mitchell) with some expatriate Cubans (including Candido and Ray Mantilla among the percussionists), while "Broadway Reunion" has Amram on flute sitting in with a visiting Cuban band on the streets of New York. This little-known album crosses several musical boundaries and is well worth searching for. —*Scott Yanow*

No More Walls / 1978 / Flying Fish ♦♦♦♦

The "walls" referred to in this album's title are the artificial boundaries between jazz, classical and world music. David Amram (heard here on piano, French horn, guitar, flutes and percussion) has long been a pioneer in crossing between genres. With altoist Jerry Dodgion, baritonist Pepper Adams, and an oversized rhythm section, plus an oud, viola, dumbeg and five percussionists (including Candido), Amram performs seven of his diverse compositions, two of which also have vocalists. Intriguing music. —*Scott Yanow*

At Home/Around the World / 1980 / Flying Fish ♦♦

Amram plays an eclectic mix of styles from all over the world. —*AMG*

Latin-Jazz Celebration / Jan. 1982 / Elektra/Musician ♦♦♦♦

David Amram, who has played and composed in several different areas of music, has always had a special love for Latin jazz. This out-of-print LP finds Amram (on French horn, piano, guitar and various flutes and whistles) playing six of his compositions, plus "Take the 'A' Train," with an impressive 14-piece group that features such notables as altoist Paquito D'Rivera, altoist Jerry Dodgion, David "Fathead" Newman on tenor, baritonist Pepper Adams, trumpeter Joe Wilder, trombonist Jimmy Knepper and many percussionists, including Machito and Candido. Frequently explosive and always infectious music. —*Scott Yanow*

Autobiography / May 8, 1990 / Flying Fish ♦♦♦♦

Arild Anderson

b. Oct. 27, 1945, Lillestrom, Norway

Bass / Post-Bop

Arild Andersen is best-known in the US for his duet album with Sheila Jordan which preceded the singer's collaborations with Harvie Swartz. Andersen studied with George Russell and during 1967-73 played regularly with both Jan Garbarek and Karin Krog. While in the US during 1973-74, Andersen worked with Sam Rivers and Paul Bley. In addition to leading his own groups, Andersen has played with Kenny Wheeler and Paul Motian (1979), Bill Frisell (1981) and a group he co-led in the mid-'80s, Masqualero. He has recorded frequently for the ECM label through the years. — *Scott Yanow*

● **If You Look Far Enough** / Sept. 1988-Feb. 1992 / ECM ✦✦✦✦

Kristin Lavransdatter / Apr. 1995-Jun. 1995 / FXCD ✦✦

In the '70s and '80s, bassist Andersen made a number of albums for ECM. I remember then liking one in particular — *Green Shading into Blue* — though I might feel differently if I heard it today. This music was written to accompany a play based on the 1928 Nobel Prize-winning novel of the same name, and it does indeed sound like incidental music. Andersen's pastoral, synthesizer- and reverb-laden jazz/fusion is evocative, but hardly provocative, which means that it probably served its original purpose well. Asking it to stand alone as a work unto itself is unfair to the composer's intent (though I doubt the record was put out against his will). Listen to this music without referring to the personnel listings, and you'll swear the saxophonist is Jan Garbarek. It's not — just an amazingly lifelike facsimile. Pretty music, but its charms are ephemeral and ultimately negligible. — *Chris Kelsey*

Cat Anderson (William Alonzo Anderson)

b. Sep. 12, 1916, Greenville, SC, d. Apr. 29, 1981, Norwalk, CA

Trumpet / Swing

Cat Anderson was arguably the greatest high note trumpeter of all time. His solo on "Satin Doll" from Duke Ellington's *70th Birthday Concert* is a perfectly coherent chorus consisting of notes that are so high that it is doubtful if another trumpeter from all of jazz history could hit more than one or two! He first learned trumpet while at the Jenkins Orphanage in Charleston and toured with the Carolina Cotton Pickers, a group in which he made his recording debut. During 1935-44 Andeson played with many groups including those of Claude Hopkins, Lucky Millinder, Erskine Hawkins and Lionel Hampton. Hampton loved his high-note mastery although Hawkins reportedly fired Cat out of jealousy. In 1944 Cat Anderson was first hired by Duke Ellington and it ended up being the perfect setting for him. Duke enjoyed writing impossible parts for Cat to play and Anderson received publicity and a steady income. He was more than just a high-note player, being a master with mutes and having a fine tone in lower registers, but no one could really challenge him in the stratosphere (although Maynard Ferguson, Jon Faddis and Arturo Sandoval have come close!). Anderson was with Ellington during 1944-47, 1950-59 and off and on during 1961-71. Occasionally he would go out on his own to lead his own bands but he always came back. After Ellington's death, Cat Anderson settled on the West Coast where he often played with local big bands including an exciting one led by Bill Berry. — *Scott Yanow*

Cat on a Hot Tin Horn / Aug. 23, 1958 / EmArcy ✦✦✦

Cat Anderson, taking a day off from the Duke Ellington Orchestra, is heard on this out-of-print LP playing on his first full album as a bandleader (he had previously cut eight selections during two sessions in 1947 and 1949). With arrangements by Anderson (who contributed six of the nine tunes) and (on two songs) Ernie Wilkins, the all-star big band has plenty of opportunities to blow even if only one piece exceeds four minutes. In addition to Cat's powerful trumpet, other soloists include tenor saxophonist Jimmy Forrest, baritonist Sahib Shihab and trombonist Jimmy Cleveland. Hopefully this swinging session will get reissued on CD eventually by Polygram. — *Scott Yanow*

Cat Anderson & the Ellington All Stars in Paris / Oct. 30, 1958-Mar. 20, 1964 / Disques Swing ✦✦✦✦

Arguably the greatest high-note trumpeter of all time, Cat Anderson was also quite handy with a plunger mute and capable of playing a creative swing solo without any flights into the stratosphere. This swing LP has a pair of sessions that Cat led while touring Europe with Duke Ellington in 1958 and 1964. Anderson mostly used Duke Ellington sidemen (including either Quentin Jackson or Buster Cooper on trombone, the underrated Russell Procope on alto and clarinet, tenorman Paul Gonsalves on the later date, bassist Jimmy Woode on the earlier session, drummer Sam Woodyard and French musicians in the remaining spots); the great stride pianist Joe Turner (an expatriate) guests on three selections. The music is generally in the world of Duke Ellington although there are also a few spirited Dixieland jams (including "Ain't Misbehavin'," an Anderson quartet feature on "I'm

Confessin'" and "Muskrat Ramble"). This is a particularly strong collection that was last available as a DRG LP. — *Scott Yanow*

Cat Speaks / Jun. 4, 1977 / Classic Jazz ✦✦✦✦

Cat Anderson, 60 at the time of this session, was still at the height of his power. Heading a quintet with fellow former Ellington member Sam Woodyard on drums plus Frenchmen Gerard Badini on tenor and clarinet, pianist Raymond Fol and bassist Michel Gaudry, Cat not only blasts out a few high notes but displays his expertise in the lower registers and with the plunger mute; he even takes a vocal on "The Cat Hums." This small group swing LP (which is among its more memorable performances spirited renditions of "Stompy Jones" and "The Jeep Is Jumpin'") is one of Cat Anderson's finest and is well worth searching for. — *Scott Yanow*

● **Plays W.C. Handy** / Jun. 1977+May 1978 / Black & Blue ✦✦✦✦

Clifton Anderson

b. Oct. 5, 1957, New York, NY

Trombone / Hard Bop

Clifton Anderson, the nephew of Sonny Rollins and a longtime member of his band, has long been in the awkward position of sharing the stage with his uncle, standing motionless while Rollins takes extended solos. In 1996 on his own excellent *Landmarks* recording (Milestone), Anderson finally had the opportunity to step out from his uncle's giant shadow. Anderson started on trombone at age seven, when Sonny Rollins bought him his first instrument. He attended the High School of Music and Art in New York City, graduated from the Manhattan School of Music, and worked with Slide Hampton's World of Trombones, Frank Foster's Loud Minority, McCoy Tyner's Orchestra, Lester Bowie's Brass Fantasy and Abdullah Ibrahim before joining Rollins' band in 1983. Influenced most by J.J. Johnson, Clifton Anderson remains quite underrated. — *Scott Yanow*

Landmarks / Jan. 30, 1995-Jan. 31, 1995 / Milestone ✦✦✦✦

After many years in the thankless role of being the regular trombonist with his uncle Sonny Rollins' group, Clifton Anderson finally made his recording debut with this CD. Strongly influenced by J.J. Johnson, Anderson is a fine bop-based player with a warm tone and an underrated improvising style. The trombonist is featured with pianist Monty Alexander, bassist Bob Cranshaw, drummer Al Foster and percussionist Victor See Yuen on five straightahead originals, two standards, and a calypso. There is one guest appearance apiece for trumpeter Wallace Roney and altoist Kenny Garrett, but the focus is very much on Anderson's fluid horn. Recommended. — *Scott Yanow*

Ernestine Anderson

b. Nov. 11, 1928, Houston, TX

Vocals / Standards

Positioned squarely in the mainstream camp, at home in the worlds of jazz and pop standards as well as the blues, comfortable with small groups and big bands, Ernestine Anderson regularly receives a lot of airplay on traditional jazz radio stations these days. She fits those demographics well with her tasteful, slightly gritty, moderately swinging contralto, someone who doesn't probe too deeply into emotional quagmires (and thus doesn't disturb the dispositions of those who use the radio as background) but always gives you an honest, musical account.

Anderson's career actually got rolling in the embryonic R&B field at first; as a teenager, she sang with Russell Jacquet's band in 1943, and she moved on to the Johnny Otis band from 1947 to 1949, making her first recording with Shifty Henry's Orchestra in 1947 for the Black-And-White label. In the 1950s, however, she converted over to the jazz side, working with Lionel Hampton in 1952-53 and recording with a band featuring Jacquet, Milt Jackson, and Quincy Jones in 1953 and with Gigi Gryce in 1955. Upon hearing the latter record, Rolf Ericson booked Anderson on a three-month Scandinavian tour; while in Sweden, she made a recording called *Hot Cargo* that ironically established her reputation in America. Once back in the US, she signed with Mercury and made a number of albums for that label until the early 1960s, when her career went into a decline. She moved to England in 1965 and remained largely invisible on the American radar screen until 1975, when Ray Brown heard her sing at the Turnwater Festival in Canada. Brown became her manager, got her to appear at the 1976 Concord Jazz Festival, and that led to a Concord contract, which immediately bore fruit with the albums *Live From Concord to London* and *Hello Like Before*. These and other comeback albums made her a top-flight jazz attraction in the US again — this time for the long haul — and in the 1980s, she was recording with the Hank Jones Trio, George Shearing, Benny Carter, the Capp-Pierce Juggernaut, the Clayton-Hamilton Jazz Orchestra, and her own quartet. By 1992, she had attracted major-label attention once again, signing with Quincy Jones' Qwest outfit. — *Richard S. Ginell*

Ernestine Anderson / 1958 / Polygram ✦✦✦
This CD brings back singer Ernestine Anderson's first full-length US recording session. The program only clocks in at thirty-one-and-a-half minutes and some of the performances are remarkably brief (including a 59-second version of "There Will Never Be Another You"). Backed by an orchestra arranged by Pete Rugolo, Anderson (who was at the time influenced by Dinah Washington) is in good voice and swings without getting very far from the melodies. The highlights are "Stardust," "Social Call," "A Sleepin' Bee" and particularly a touching "My Ship." Although this brief program should have been combined with another Mercury release for this reissue, the music should please Ernestine Anderson's fans. —*Scott Yanow*

● **Live from Concord to London** / Aug. 1, 1976+Oct. 11, 1977 / Concord Jazz ✦✦✦✦✦
The first half of this CD is quite historic—17 minutes from Ernestine Anderson's comeback concert at the 1976 Concord Jazz Festival. One can feel excitement throughout the performance as the audience rediscovers the talented singer, who had not recorded in a decade. Four songs ("Don't Get Around Much Anymore," "Days of Wine and Roses," "Stormy Monday" and a soulful "Am I Blue") have swinging and stimulating accompaniment by pianist Hank Jones, bassist Ray Brown and drummer Jake Hanna, while a brief "Take the 'A' Train" has Anderson joined by Bill Berry's Big Band. The "London" half of the disc is from a year later and is more laidback and routine, although enjoyable. Backed by an English rhythm section, the singer interprets "My Romance," a four-song Duke Ellington medley, and "Love for Sale" in winning fashion. Overall, this is one of the best in Ernestine Anderson's string of Concord recordings. —*Scott Yanow*

Hello Like Before / Oct. 8, 1976-Oct. 10, 1976 / Concord Jazz ✦✦✦✦
Ernestine Anderson's first official Concord recording (which was predated by part of *Live From Concord to London*) launched her "comeback" after years of neglect (and a decade off of records). Accompanied by pianist Hank Jones, bassist Ray Brown and drummer Jimmie Smith, Anderson mixes together veteran standards (such as "Yes Sir That's My Baby," "It Don't Mean a Thing" and "Tain't Nobody's Bizness") with more recent songs from Johnny Mandel, Stevie Wonder ("Bird of Beauty"), and Ray Brown ("Soft Shoe"), and even "Send In the Clowns" on this CD reissue. The singer's enthusiasm comes across throughout this fine studio set. —*Scott Yanow*

Sunshine / Aug. 1979 / Concord Jazz ✦✦✦✦
For this set, Ernestine Anderson (who is joined by pianist Monty Alexander, bassist Ray Brown and drummer Jeff Hamilton) mostly sings overly familiar songs, doing her best to uplift such tunes as "Summertime," "God Bless the Child," "Satin Doll" and even "You Are My Sunshine" and "Sunny." Ernestine's voice sounds fine and her interpretations reasonably fresh, but some of the tunes really did not need to be revived again. —*Scott Yanow*

● **Never Make Your Move Too Soon** / Aug. 1980 / Concord Jazz ✦✦✦✦✦
The title cut of this near-classic album became a sort of theme song for Ernestine Anderson, but it is not the only high point. The singer sounds in top form on such fine material as "As Long as I Live," a touching "Old Folks," "My Shining Hour" and "Poor Butterfly." With fine assistance from pianist Monty Alexander, bassist Ray Brown and drummer Frank Gant, Ernestine Anderson is heard throughout in prime form, sounding quite enthusiastic and powerful. Highly recommended. —*Scott Yanow*

Big City / Feb. 1983 / Concord Jazz ✦✦✦
This well-rounded set features vocalist Ernestine Anderson on a few classics (including "Street of Dreams," "All Blues" and "I Didn't Know What Time It Was"), plus some newer material (including a surprisingly successful version of "The 59th Street Bridge Song"). She is accompanied by pianist Hank Jones, bassist Monty Budwig and drummer Jeff Hamilton, giving listeners a strong example of her singing. —*Scott Yanow*

When the Sun Goes Down / Aug. 1984 / Concord Jazz ✦✦✦✦
On one of her best Concord recordings, Ernestine Anderson (who is joined by tenorman Red Holloway, pianist Gene Harris, bassist Ray Brown and drummer Gerryck King) is quite soulful and bluesy throughout this strong program. She makes such tunes as "Someone Else Is Steppin' In," "In the Evening When the Sun Goes Down" and "I Love Being Here with You" sound as if they were written for her, while "Mercy, Mercy, Mercy" is heard in a very rare vocal version. Actually, all eight songs (which also include "Goin' to Chicago Blues" and "Down Home Blues") are well worth hearing. Recommended. —*Scott Yanow*

Be Mine Tonight / Dec. 1986 / Concord Jazz ✦✦✦✦
Backed by a fine rhythm section (pianist Marshall Otwell deserves a date of his own) and assisted by Benny Carter's alto on several selections, Anderson sounded as if she really enjoyed this session. Best were a rare vocal version of "In a Mellotone" and a Dinah Washington-inspired treatment of "Christopher Columbus," the two most jazz-oriented tracks on this well-rounded album. —*Scott Yanow*

Boogie Down / Sep. 1989 / Concord Jazz ✦✦✦
A solid but unspectacular effort, this CD matches singer Ernestine Anderson with the Clayton-Hamilton Jazz Orchestra. The big band is mostly heard in the background (except on the instrumental "Le Blues"), with the spotlight otherwise totally on the vocalist. Anderson sounds fine, but the material (which ranges from Al Jarreau's "Boogie Down" to "Love Walked In" and "One Mint Julep") offers few surprises, and she is not really smoothly integrated into the big band. However, the music still has its enjoyable moments. —*Scott Yanow*

Now & Then / Sep. 24, 1992-Feb. 12, 1993 / Qwest ✦✦✦

Blues, Dues & Love News / Nov. 27, 1995-Nov. 28, 1995 / Warner Brothers ✦✦✦
Ernestine Anderson's *Blues Dues & Love News* was recorded live at B.B. King's Blues Club, where she was supported by a cast of highly accomplished session musicians. At times the sound of the album is too slick, but Anderson's powerful vocals have enough grit to make the record a worthwhile listen. —*Stephen Thomas Erlewine*

Ivie Anderson

b. Jul. 10, 1905, Gilroy, CA, **d.** Dec. 28, 1949, Los Angeles, CA
Vocals / Swing
Ivie Anderson was a classy yet swinging singer, the best that Duke Ellington ever had. Early on she worked at the Cotton Club in shows and sang with Anson Weeks, Curtis Mosby, Paul Howard's Quality Serenaders and Earl Hines (1930). And then from February 1931 until 1942, Ivie Anderson was an integral part of the Duke Ellington Orchestra, introducing "It Don't Mean a Thing" and singing such numbers as "Stormy Weather," "I'm Checkin' Out Goombye" and a variety of pop tunes. When she left Ellington it was because of asthma. She opened a restaurant in Los Angeles and recorded eight songs in 1946 but her illness eventually struck her down. —*Scott Yanow*

● **With Duke Ellington** / 1932-1942 / Epm Musique ✦✦✦✦

Ray Anderson

b. Oct. 16, 1952, Chicago, IL
Trombone / Avant-Garde, Post-Bop
A boisterous trombonist who has greatly expanded the range of the trombone and is masterful at multiphonics, Ray Anderson's playing is often hilarious. His main fault is a tendency to repeat the same joke over and over again, namely "Look how high I can play!" Anderson began playing the trombone when he was eight and early on had a wide variety of experience including classical lessons, enjoying Dixieland, playing blues and funk and going to some concerts by the AACM. After spending some time in California, he moved to New York in 1972 and freelanced. In 1977 Anderson joined Anthony Braxton's Quartet (replacing George Lewis) and started working with Barry Altschul's group. From this point forward he started ranking high in polls and became influential himself. In addition to leading his own groups since the late '70s (including the funk-oriented Slickaphonics), Anderson has worked with George Gruntz's Concert Jazz Band. In recent times he has begun taking an occasional good-humored vocal, during which he shows the ability to sing two notes at the same time (a minor third apart). —*Scott Yanow*

Harrisburg Half Life / Jun. 1980 / Moers ✦✦✦✦

Right Down Your Alley / Feb. 3, 1984 / Soul Note ✦✦✦
Trombonist Ray Anderson's third set as a leader (following fairly obscure efforts for the Auricle and Moers Music labels) uses the same trio that was on his first release. Anderson interacts closely with bassist Mark Helias and drummer Gerry Hemingway. The occasional infectious rhythms and the trombonist's often wild humor keep the music (all originals by band members) from ever getting dull or predictable. —*Scott Yanow*

Old Bottles, New Wine / Jun. 14, 1985-Jun. 15, 1985 / Enja ✦✦✦✦✦
Trombonist Ray Anderson, best known for his avant-garde recordings, surprised many with these explorations of standards. His high-note outbursts are often hilarious, yet on this program he really digs into the material. "Love Me or Love Me," "La Rosita" and "In a Mellotone" are among the high points and Anderson takes an interesting vocal on "Wine." The all-star rhythm section (pianist Kenny Barron, bassist Cecil McBee and drummer Dannie Richmond) is also a strong asset to this memorable date. —*Scott Yanow*

You Be / Nov. 1985 / Minor Music ✦✦✦✦
The third of three sets to team the trio of trombonist Ray Anderson, bassist Mark Helias and drummer Gerry Hemingway has plenty of advanced group improvising; all three of the musicians contributed at least two originals apiece. Some listeners may get bored with the sparse setting, but Anderson's unpredictable humor generally keeps the proceedings quite stimulating and eccentric. —*Scott Yanow*

Music Map

Arrangers

Pioneers Jelly Roll Morton Don Redman (with Fletcher Henderson and his own groups) Bill Challis (with Jean Goldkette and Paul Whiteman)	**1950s** Gil Evans • Neal Hefti (with Count Basie) Ernie Wilkins • Frank Foster • Jimmy Heath Benny Golson • Slide Hampton • Melba Liston Quincy Jones
Most Significant Arranger Duke Ellington	**Third Stream** John Lewis • Gunther Schuller • J.J. Johnson
Other Important Arrangers of the 1930s and '40s Fletcher Henderson Benny Carter Gene Gifford (with the Casa Loma Orchestra) Sy Oliver (with Jimmy Lunceford and Tommy Dorsey) Edgar Sampson (with Chick Webb) Mary Lou Williams (with Andy Kirk) Horace Henderson • Jimmy Mundy • Glenn Miller Bill Finegan (with Glenn Miller) Eddie Sauter (with Red Norvo and Benny Goodman) Billy May (with Charlie Barnet)	**1960s** Oliver Nelson Hank Levy (with Stan Kenton and Don Ellis) Thad Jones Bob Brookmeyer
	Avant-Garde Bob Graettinger George Russell Sun Ra Muhal Richard Abrams Julius Hemphill Carla Bley Maria Schneider George Gruntz Willem Breuker
Bop Innovator Tadd Dameron	
Other Top Bop Arrangers Ralph Burns (with Woody Herman) George Handy (with Boyd Raeburn) Gil Fuller (with Dizzy Gillespie) Gerry Mulligan • Shorty Rogers	**Crossover** Don Sebesky • Bob James • Eumir Deodato
The Great Stan Kenton Arrangers Pete Rugolo Bill Russo Bill Holman Marty Paich Johnny Richards	**Modern Mainstream** Gerald Wilson Francy Boland Rob McConnell Bob Florence John Clayton Toshiko Akiyoshi Wynton Marsalis

It Just So Happens / Jan. 31, 1987-Feb. 1, 1987 / Enja ♦♦♦
Although trombonist Ray Anderson sounded fine on his earlier trio and quartet dates, he really comes into his own when joined by other horns. This spirited (and sometimes jubilant) CD matches Anderson with trumpeter Stanton Davis, clarinetist Perry Robinson, Bob Stewart on tuba, bassist Mark Dresser and drummer Ronnie Burrage. "Fishin' With Gramps" (which was also recorded by Anderson with George Gruntz's Concert Jazz Band) is a crackup; the two versions of "Once in a While" are full of spirit; this interpretation of "La Vie En Rose" is unique; and the trombonist's many originals cover plenty of ground (including "Raven's Jolly Jump-Up" and "Ross the Boss"). An excellent example of the innovative Ray Anderson's work. —*Scott Yanow*

Blues Bred in the Bone / Mar. 27, 1988-Mar. 28, 1988 / Gramavision ♦♦
Unlike on his previous *Old Bottles, New Wine* recording, trombonist Ray Anderson's high-note technique gets the better of him on this set. He often comes across as a one-line Las Vegas comedian who constantly exclaims, "Look how high I can play!" Whether it be a rather absurd version of "Mona Lisa" or a potentially sensitive ballad such as "A Flower Is a Lonesome Thing," the results are consistently silly if colorful. Even with a supporting cast that includes guitarist John Scofield and pianist Anthony Davis, this has to be considered one of Anderson's lesser efforts. —*Scott Yanow*

What Because / Nov. 15, 1989-Nov. 22, 1989 / Gramavision ♦♦♦♦♦
If you don't like Ray Anderson, then you probably just don't like trombone players in general, for there's not a more engaging trombonist in jazz—certainly not one who communicates greater love for life. He invests so much genuine good humor and enthusiasm in every note he plays. And that's to say nothing of his extraordinary chops and imagination, and his wonderful compositional ability. Anderson's got the total package. He plays "in" every bit as strongly as he does "out"; for Anderson, there seems to be no separation between the two. This album, with guitarist Allan Jaffe, pianist John Hicks, bassist Mark Dresser, and drummer Pheeroan AkLaff, is quintessential Anderson, from the funky, goofy intelligence of "Alligatory Crocodile," to the theremin-like expressivity of his playing on the ballad "Let's Fall in Love," and the noirish formal complexities of "Off Peak." It's a marvelous album, one that, when all the musical politics get sorted out (who knows when that will be), should take its place as one of the very finest works of the last decade. —*Chris Kelsey*

Wishbone / Dec. 1990 / Gramavision ♦♦♦
This is a good effort from distinctive trombonist Ray Anderson, who is joined by pianist Fumio Itabashi, bassist Mark Helias, drummer Dion Parson, percussionist Don Alias and (on two songs) violinist Mark Feldman. Anderson takes an eccentric vocal on "Comes Love," debuts his three-part "Wishbone Suite" and shows off

his high-note talents whenever possible. Not essential but enjoyable. *—Scott Yanow*

Every One of Us / 1992 / Gramavision ✦✦✦

Trombonist Ray Anderson is in top form throughout this well-rounded set. Assisted by pianist Simon Nabatov, bassist Charlie Haden and drummer Ed Blackwell, Anderson gets lowdown on "Funkalific," comes up with fresh renditions of Wayne Shorter's "Lady Day" (during which he emulates Tricky Sam Nanton a bit) and John Coltrane's "Dear Lord," contributes four diverse originals, takes a typically odd vocal on "Brother, Can You Spare a Dime" and adds plenty of humor and high-note acrobatics to the spirited date. *—Scott Yanow*

● **Big Band Record** / 1994 / Gramavision ✦✦✦✦✦

Ray Anderson has nine of his originals performed by the 17-piece George Gruntz Concert Jazz Band on this Gramavision CD and the results are quite spirited and very satisfying. The often riotous trombonist is fortunate to have his complex but always lively music interpreted by quite an all-star group and Gruntz's arrangements give each musician at least one opportunity to solo. When one considers that the orchestra contains such individualists as trumpeters Lew Soloff, Ryan Kisor, John D'Earth and Herb Robertson, altoist Tim Berne, Marty Ehrlich on several reeds, Ellery Eskelin on tenor and violinist Mark Feldman, it is little surprise that this was one of the top jazz albums released in 1994. *—Scott Yanow*

Don't Mow Your Lawn / Mar. 23, 1994-Mar. 25, 1994 / Enja ✦✦✦✦

Trombonist Ray Anderson is typically uninhibited throughout this joke-filled set. His high-note screams are well-matched by trumpeter Lew Soloff and some of the vocals (most notably on the title cut) are memorable. There is some strong playing by the two horns (who are joined by the funky rhythm section of guitarist Jerome Harris, bassist Gregory Jones, drummer Tommy Campbell and percussionist Frank Colon) but, with titles like "Damaged but Good," "Alligatory Pecadillo" and "What'cha Gonna Do with That?," the humor and philosophizing are often dominant. *—Scott Yanow*

Azurety / Apr. 21, 1994-Apr. 22, 1994 / Hat Art ✦✦✦

Cheer Up / Mar. 15, 1995-Mar. 16, 1995 / Hat Art ✦✦✦

As is usual on most Ray Anderson albums, a lot of joking around takes place on this trio outing as the trombonist constantly shows off his huge range. With guitarist Christy Doran and drummer Han Bennink completing the group, Anderson engages in a variety of mostly concise but very uninhibited flights; all but Horace Silver's "Melancholy Moods" are group originals. The music is colorful but far from essential. *—Scott Yanow*

Heads & Tales / May 17, 1995-May 19, 1995 / Enja ✦✦✦✦

Wessell Anderson

b. 1966

Alto Saxophone, Soprano Saxophone / Hard Bop, Swing, Post-Bop

A fine altoist, Wessell Anderson gained his initial recognition as a member of Wynton Marsalis' mid-'90s septet. He started on piano when he was 12, switching to alto after hearing a Charlie Parker record. He attended Southern University in Baton Rouge, LA, and played with Betty Carter for two months before being discovered by Marsalis. Anderson became a member of Marsalis' group in 1988 and has since worked with the trumpeter as part of the Lincoln Center Jazz Orchestra, in addition to leading his own sessions for Atlantic. *—Scott Yanow*

● **Warmdaddy in the Garden of Swing** / 1994 / Atlantic ✦✦✦✦

Ways of Warmdaddy / Jun. 20, 1995-Jun. 22, 1995 / Atlantic ✦✦✦

Wessell Anderson is a big-toned alto saxophonist of generous spirit and above-average skill, who obviously admires the late Cannonball Adderley a great deal. This album's opening track, "Sunday Souful Supper," comes off as virtual Cannonball, with the equally rotund younger altoist serving heaping portions of red beans and rice, Adderley-style. The record as a whole is a hard-bop (re)hash, well-played, yet tasting a bit like it's been microwaved back to life—a moderately tasty and almost immediately forgettable side dish. *—Chris Kelsey*

Ernie Andrews

b. Dec. 25, 1927, Philadelphia, PA

Vocals / Swing, Bop, West Coast Blues, Standards

Ernie Andrews has managed to be both popular and underrated throughout his lengthy career. After his family moved to Los Angeles he sang in a church choir and while still attending high school had a few hits for the G&G label. Billy Eckstine and Al Hibbler were early influences and, after reaching maturity, Andrews was somewhat in the shadow of Joe Williams (who has a similar style). He recorded for Aladdin, Columbia and London in the late '40s, spent six years singing with the Harry James Orchestra and cut a couple of big band dates for GNP/

Crescendo during 1958-59. Despite his unchanging style, Andrews was mostly in obscurity during the 1960s and '70s, just making a couple of albums for Dot during 1965-66. A 1980 Discovery date found him in excellent form and in the '80s he was rediscovered. Andrews recorded with the Capp/Pierce Juggernaut, Gene Harris' Superband, Jay McShann and the Harper Brothers in addition to making a few sets in the 1990s for Muse. He is also prominent in the documentary *Blues for Central Avenue*. *—Scott Yanow*

Travelin' Light / Mar. 1959 / GNP ✦✦✦

Prototype big band and jazz-based vocals by Ernie Andrews cut in the late '50s for GNP. Andrews was a fine blues, ballad, and standards stylist, with big sound and excellent phrasing. He was backed on these dates by a polished orchestra that sometimes included Benny Carter on alto sax. The sessions have been reissued on CD. *—Ron Wynn*

From the Heart / Nov. 18, 1980 / Discovery ✦✦✦✦

● **No Regrets** / Aug. 2, 1992 / Muse ✦✦✦✦✦

The Great City / Feb. 16, 1995 / Muse ✦✦✦

Lori Andrews

b. Jan. 23, 1958, Philadelphia, PA

Harp / Bop, Crossover Jazz

The harp is rarely thought of as a jazz instrument, but in the 1990s Lori Andrews and Deborah Henson-Conant have proved that their instrument is not restricted to producing pretty backgrounds. Lori Andrews graduated from Temple University in 1979, played regularly in Atlantic City during 1980-85, moved to Los Angeles in 1985 and from 1992 on has had a regular gig at the Warehouse in Marina Del Rey in addition to working in the studios and touring with John Tesh. She had brief on-camera appearances in such films as *Bird*, *The Mambo Kings* and *In the Line of Fire*. More importantly from the jazz standpoint, she founded her own label JazHarp Records and has documented her music since 1993, showing that the harp (at least when played by her) is a viable jazz instrument. *—Scott Yanow*

Suspended / 1993 / JazHarp ✦✦✦

Jazz harpist Lori Andrews' first recording as a leader finds the talented musician showing that the electric harp can be adapted to play jazz. Her music on this CD (which features groups ranging from a sextet to the unaccompanied title track) is often quite funky but also explorative and it features plenty of variety. The local players who are heard as sidemen do a fine job of complementing the colorful harpist. *—Scott Yanow*

● **Bossame Mucho** / 1994 / JazHarp ✦✦✦✦✦

Jazz harpists are a real rarity, but even if they were plentiful, Lori Andrews would rank near the top of her field. On this set of unaccompanied solos, Andrews performs selections from the likes of Kenny Dorham ("Blue Bossa"), Sting, Grover Washington, Jr., Jobim, Clare Fischer ("Morning"), and Michael Franks, among others. No matter the source, she turns all of the music into swinging and sometimes funky jazz. Her playing is very self-sufficient, often with two independent lines and rhythm being heard, yet there was no overdubbing on this date. Listeners who think of the harp as only capable of producing pretty background music are in for a surprise, particularly when hearing the harder-swinging performances. *—Scott Yanow*

A Jazz Harp Christmas / 1994 / JazHarp ✦✦✦

Swinging Strings / 1995 / JazHarp ✦✦✦✦

This is a very impressive outing. Lori Andrews plays solo harp throughout this disc and, without using overdubbing, she sounds very much like a full orchestra. Her creative treatments of such standards as "Popsicle Toes," "Take Five" and a delightful "Is You Is or Is You Ain't My Baby" are high points but her original material is also quite enjoyable. Andrews de-emphasizes the prettiness of her instrument and digs in with some soulful statements. *—Scott Yanow*

No Strings Attached / 1996-1997 / JazHarp ✦✦✦

Lori Andrews is one of the world's greatest jazz harpists, which would probably be true even if there were more than half a dozen currently active. This particular CD, though, is a bit of a mixed bag. The dominance of Sean Holt's rather average pop vocals on three selections is unfortunate, for they put the harpist in the role of a mere supporting player, and they take away from the set's jazz content. However, most of the other nine selections are on a much higher level, featuring the harpist with a fine rhythm section and occasionally saxophonist George Shelby and flutist Doug Norwine. Flute great Hubert Laws makes a guest appearance on "Smilin' Again." As for Lori Andrews, whether it be on "The Pluckin' Blues," "Song for My Father," "Alice in Wonderland" or especially Clare Fischer's "Morning," she is in top form, playing her harp with the power of a pianist and the facility of a horn player. *—Scott Yanow*

Peter Apfelbaum

b. 1960

Tenor Saxophone / Avant-Garde, World Fusion

Best known as the leader of the Hieroglyphics Ensemble, Peter Apfelbaum is most comfortable when playing with musicians who mix avant-garde explorations with folk music from other cultures. He began playing drums when he was three and switched to piano and saxophone when he was nine. He played locally in Berkeley as a teenager, formed the Berkeley Arts Company (a quartet) in 1975, and played with the Berkeley High Jazz Ensemble. Apfelbaum formed the Hieroglyphics Ensemble for the first time in 1977. He was in New York during 1979-81, working with Eddie Jefferson, Carla Bley and Karl Berger. He returned to the Bay Area in 1981 and during the late 1980s often played with Don Cherry in various ensembles. Apfelbaum, who made several records with his 1990s version of the Hieroglyphics Ensemble (for Antilles and Gramavision), has also worked with (among others) Cecil Taylor, Nana Vasconcelos and Jim Pepper. —*Scott Yanow*

Signs of Life / Nov. 23, 1990-Nov. 26, 1990 / Antilles ✦✦✦

This set by saxophonist Peter Apfelbaum's Hieroglyphics Ensemble features an odd mixture of styles, including avant-garde jazz, African roots music, rock, funk and folk music. Due to the amount of improvising that takes place in the frequently dense ensembles, the music should be considered jazz despite the other influences. Apfelbaum is the strongest soloist (particularly on tenor), and there are some good spots for Paul Hanson's bassoon, Will Bernard's rockish guitar, Tony Jones' violent tenor, and Jeff Cressman's spirited trombone, among others. The ten Apfelbaum originals set moods rather than state melodies and have an unfinished and unsettling quality about them. Although not a total success, *Signs of Life* shows signs of innovation. —*Scott Yanow*

● **Jodoji Brightness** / Jan. 25, 1992-Jan. 28, 1992 / Antilles ✦✦✦✦

A fine outing from Apfelbaum and his Hieroglyphics Ensemble, a West Coast collective that blends international and American elements, influences, and instruments. They add plenty of fresh sounds and rhythms to the proceedings and keep things from ever sounding routine. —*Ron Wynn*

Luminous Charms / 1996 / Gramavision ✦✦✦✦

Peter Appleyard

b. Aug. 26, 1928, Cleethorpes, England

Vibes / Swing

A versatile vibraphonist capable of doing close musical and verbal imitations of Lionel Hampton, Red Norvo, Milt Jackson and Terry Gibbs, Appleyard is a superior swing player. His wide-ranging career has included playing drums in English dance bands, a period spent living in Bermuda (before settling in Canada in 1951) and a busy career in the studios. He was with Calvin Jackson's quartet in the mid-1950s, toured with Benny Goodman in the early 1970s, and hosted a musical television series in Canada during 1977-79 (*Peter Appleyard Presents*). Appleyard, who has appeared at many festivals through the years, has led his own record dates since 1956, including sets for Canadian RCA, Audio Fidelity, Dauntless and two 1990 albums for Concord. —*Scott Yanow*

● **Barbados Cool** / Feb. 17, 1990-Feb. 18, 1990 / Concord Jazz ✦✦✦✦

On this quintet set, vibraphonist Peter Appleyard often sounds like Lionel Hampton (with touches of Milt Jackson and Red Norvo), tenor saxophonist Rick Wilkins plays like a close relative of Zoot Sims, Butch Miles' hard-driving drums owe obvious debts to Gene Krupa and Buddy Rich, and the repertoire is far from inspired. But Appleyard & Co. (which also includes guitarist Bucky Pizzarelli and bassist Major Holley) sound so enthusiastic (as if they were thoroughly enjoying themselves as they come up with new variations on the ancient material) that the swinging results are quite infectious. Whether it be "Tangerine," "Stompin' at the Savoy," "Air Mail Special" or "Cherokee," the talented veterans sound like they just invented the songs. —*Scott Yanow*

Barbados Heat / Feb. 17, 1990-Feb. 18, 1990 / Concord Jazz ✦✦✦✦

Lil Armstrong

b. Feb. 3, 1898, Memphis, TN, d. Aug. 27, 1971, Chicago, IL

Piano, Vocals / New Orleans Jazz, Swing

Lil Harden Armstrong will always be best-known for her influence in shaping Louis Armstrong's career (persuading him to leave King Oliver's band and accept Fletcher Henderson's offer in New York) and for her work with Louis' Hot Five and Seven, but she actually had an interesting career after she parted with Armstrong. Early on she worked in Chicago, demonstrating new songs at a music store. She worked with Sugar Johnny's Creole Orchestra and then Freddie Keppard's Original Creole Orchestra before becoming a member of King Oliver's Creole Jazz Band. Lil's rhythmic piano helped keep the ensembles solid and she made her recording debut with Oliver in 1923. She met Louis Armstrong while in the band and their

marriage lasted from 1924-38 although they separated in 1931. Lil played piano and occasionally sang on Louis' famous Hot Five and Seven recordings and she composed "Struttin' with Some Barbecue." During the latter half of the 1930s she was house pianist at Decca, recording 26 titles as a leader (mostly as a vocalist) during 1936-40 including her "Just for a Thrill." Although she rarely recorded during the remainder of her career (12 titles during 1945-47, six songs in 1953-54, two selections in 1959 and an album in 1961), Lil remained active during her last 30 years in Chicago. She recorded a talking record in 1959 on which she reminisced about her days with Louis Armstrong and ironically she died of a heart attack while playing "St. Louis Blues" at an Armstrong tribute concert less than two months after Louis himself had passed away. —*Scott Yanow*

Born to Swing 1936-1937 / Oct. 27, 1936-Jul. 23, 1937 / Harlequin ✦✦✦

The 14 selections that Lil Armstrong recorded during her three sessions of 1936-37 are reissued in full on this British LP; however all of the music (plus a dozen other cuts) is more readily available on a Classics CD. Lil Armstrong, whose life and career did not end when she broke up with Louis Armstrong in the early 1930s, sings on all of the songs and does not play piano at all. However her sidemen (which include Joe Thomas or Shirley Clay on trumpet, clarinetist Buster Bailey, Chu Berry, Robert Carroll or Prince Robinson on tenor and Teddy Cole or James Sherman on piano) are quite talented and give her consistently strong support along with some short solos. Lil's "Just for a Thrill" is best-known among these generally overlooked sides and some of the better selections are "Brown Gal," "Doin' the Suzy-Q," "Born to Swing" and "Bluer than Blue." —*Scott Yanow*

● **1936-1940** / Oct. 27, 1936-Mar. 18, 1940 / Classics ✦✦✦✦✦

Lil Harden Armstrong will always be best remembered for her association/marriage with Louis Armstrong and for her recordings with King Oliver's Creole Jazz Band and Armstrong's Hot Five and Seven in the 1920s. However she also led a series of high-quality small-group swing dates in the mid- to late 1930s, all of which are on this single CD. Lil takes spirited vocals on the first 22 of these 26 selections ("Brown Gal," "It's Murder" and particularly "Just For A Thrill" are quite memorable) and only actually plays piano on the final eight songs. Many top sidemen of the period make contributions to the swinging performances including trumpeters Joe Thomas, Shirley Clay and Jonah Jones, clarinetist Buster Bailey, trombonist J.C. Higginbotham and tenorman Chu Berry. Although it seems strange that only two of the songs are instrumentals, these very underrated cuts are consistently enjoyable, including "My Hi-De-Ho Man," "Born to Swing," "Oriental Swing" and "Harlem on Saturday Night." Recommended. —*Scott Yanow*

Chicago: The Living Legends / Sep. 7, 1961 / Original Jazz Classics ✦✦✦

Despite being active up until her death in 1971, Lil Armstrong only recorded a handful of numbers in the 1950s. This CD reissue has her final recording (other than the soundtrack of a slightly later television special), a jam session from 1961. On three Dixieland warhorses, some blues, a few basic originals and "Bugle Blues," the pianist (who sings on "Clip Joint") leads a spirited if overcrowded band comprising three trumpets, two trombones, two clarinetists (Darnell Howard and Franz Jackson), bassist Pops Foster and drummer Booker Washington; "Boogie Me" gives her a chance to perform a duet with Washington. The ensembles of the other songs are often riotous and this rather spontaneous and undisciplined outing is generally exciting if erratic. This is fun music by a pianist who should have been documented much more extensively in her later years. —*Scott Yanow*

Louis Armstrong

b. Aug. 4, 1901, New Orleans, LA, d. Jul. 6, 1971, New York, NY

Trumpet, Vocals / New Orleans Jazz, Swing, Dixieland, Traditional Pop, Classic Jazz, Traditional Jazz

Louis Armstrong was the most important and influential musician in jazz history. Although he is often thought of by the general public as a lovable, clowning personality, a gravel-voiced singer who played simple but dramatic trumpet in a New Orleans-styled Dixieland setting, Armstrong was much much more.

One of the first soloists on record (although he was preceded by Sidney Bechet), Louis was more responsible than anyone else for jazz changing from an ensemble-oriented folk music into an art form that emphasized inventive solo improvisations. His relaxed phrasing was a major change from the staccato style of the early '20s (helping set the stage for the swing era) and Armstrong demonstrated that it was possible to have both impressive technique and a strong feeling for the blues. One of jazz's first true virtuosos, his influence over his contemporaries was so powerful that nearly every trumpeter to record between 1927 and 1940 sounded to an extent like one of his followers!

Louis Armstrong's unique singing voice was imitated by a countless number of listeners through the years; he popularized scat singing (using nonsense syllables rhythmically rather than words) and his phrasing (carried over from his horn playing) affected virtually every singer to emerge after 1930, including Bing Crosby, Billie Holiday and Frank Sinatra. In addition, Louis Armstrong's accessible humor and sunny stage personality were major assets in popularizing jazz with larger audiences. Many youngsters were inspired to take up the trumpet after hearing or seeing him and millions more were introduced to jazz through Armstrong; in later years Louis Armstrong's worldwide tours resulted in his being widely known as "America's goodwill ambassador."

Few would have predicted greatness for Louis Armstrong based on his humble beginnings. Born in New Orleans on Aug. 4, 1901 (until his birth certificate was discovered in the late '80s, Armstrong's birth date was believed to have been July 4, 1900), Louis grew up in the poorest part of the city, sometimes singing in a vocal quartet on the street for pennies. On New Year's Eve of 1912 he got his hands on a pistol, shot it in the air in celebration and was quickly arrested and sent to live in a waifs' home that functioned as a type of juvenile hall. This would be the turning point of his life for it was at the waifs' home that he learned to play the cornet. Released after two years, Armstrong began playing with jazz groups and brass bands in New Orleans, developing quickly. When King Oliver, who had befriended Louis, left New Orleans in 1918 he recommended the young player as his replacement in a popular band led by trombonist Kid Ory. Four years later, Oliver sent for his protégé to join his Creole Jazz Band in Chicago as second cornetist.

During 1922-24 King Oliver led the top classic jazz orchestra of the era, an octet that although emphasizing group improvisation, also left room for short solos. While Oliver was a fine cornetist (more an inspiration than a direct influence on Louis' playing), it soon became obvious that Armstrong was surpassing him. Fortunately this very significant band recorded 41 tracks in 1923 for four labels, for by the following year pianist Lil Harden (who became Louis' second of four wives) talked him into leaving Oliver and joining Fletcher Henderson's big band in New York.

Although considered the top jazz orchestra of the time, Henderson's band had not yet learned how to swing, really improvise, or play the blues; at the time New York musicians were generally behind those from Chicago. However, Armstrong's playing soon inspired the musicians and it was at this point that his impact was first really felt. Armstrong also began to record as an accompanist to blues singers (including Bessie Smith and Ma Rainey) teamed up with Sidney Bechet in Clarence Wiliams' Blue Five and in 1925 (after he left Henderson and moved back to Chicago) began his remarkable series of Hot Five and Hot Seven recordings.

With clarinetist Johnny Dodds, trombonist Kid Ory, pianist Lil Armstrong and banjoist Johnny St. Cyr, Armstrong recorded one classic after another during 1925-27, music that can be thought of as both the height of New Orleans jazz and the death of it due to the increasing emphasis on Armstrong's virtuosity. "Cornet Chop Suey" amazed fellow trumpeters (Louis switched from cornet to the similar-sounding trumpet in 1927), "Heebies Jeebies" was a hit that greatly popularized scat singing and both "Potato Head Blues" and "Struttin' with Some Barbecue" had perfectly constructed and thrilling solos. In 1928 Armstrong led a completely different group in the studio, the Savoy Ballroom Five, that used the trombone and clarinet more as color than as competing voices and put the emphasis on the interplay between the trumpeter and the remarkable pianist Earl Hines. "West End Blues," with its remarkable opening trumpet cadenza, was considered by many (including Louis himself) to be his greatest recording, while "Weather Bird" is a duet between Armstrong and Hines that found the two taking many chances with time; Louis' classic versions of "St. James Infirmary" and "Basin Street Blues" (which helped to introduce the two future standards) are almost afterthoughts next to these other remarkable records.

The odd part is that, with the exception of one appearance at a function put on by OKeh Records, the Hot Five and Seven (the latter added tubaplayer Pete briggs and drummer Baby Dodds to the original quintet) never played in public. Louis Armstrong was actually featured on a nightly basis in Chicago with big bands led by Erskine Tate and Carrol Dickerson and he was rapidly developing his talents as a showman. Starting in 1929 he began recording almost exclusively as the head of a variety of big bands, emphasizing superior pop standards of the era (such as "I Can't Give You Anything but Love"). During the next decade he became a household name, making two acclaimed visits to Europe during 1932-34, appearing in small but memorable roles in movies and leading a swing-oriented big band that mostly functioned as a backdrop for his vocals and trumpet solos. Although the most advanced playing of his career took place with Earl Hines in 1928 and his Decca recordings of 1935-44 often involved novelties and commercial material, Armstrong provided some musical magic to nearly all of the records and his singing voice was at its peak in the early '40s.

Still, by the mid-'40s Louis Armstrong was considered out of style. His orchestra had declined and his own solos and clowning sounded at odds with his younger more bop-oriented sidemen. But after appearing with a variety of veteran players in the interesting if flawed Hollywood film New Orleans and having success playing with a small group at an acclaimed Town Hall concert in 1947, Armstrong broke up his big band and formed the All-Stars. His sextet (which originally

included trombonist Jack Teagarden and clarinetist Barney Bigard and soon had Earl Hines) was an immediate success playing Dixieland and swing standards along with some comedy numbers, and Armstrong began a schedule of nearly nonstop traveling that lasted until his death.

After a few years the routines became fairly predictable and critics tired of them, while some in the civil rights community thought of Armstrong as an Uncle Tom. However, they all missed the point. While Armstrong was quick to make fun of himself and his nickname of "Satchmo" (short for "Satchelmouth") could be considered objectionable, Armstrong always stood up for his race (most notably during the struggle to integrate schools in the South) and spread more goodwill than anyone; his brilliant trumpet playing set an example that busted stereotypes. Audiences the world over loved the joy of Louis Armstrong's music; his main concern was always to please the people who paid to see him. And although Armstrong's music did not evolve much after the 1940s, neither did the playing of Johnny Hodges and Thelonious Monk!

In the 1950s Hines left the All-Stars and Teagarden and Bigard were replaced by Trummy Young and Edmond Hall, but the basic sound of the group did not change. Armstrong, who also occasionally recorded with larger orchestras and with Ella Fitzgerald, found his celebrity status continuing to grow. He had major hits in "Blueberry Hill," "Mack the Knife" and "Hello Dolly" and when he died on July 6, 1971, there was no jazz musician who could approach him in popularity. With all of the reissues and continued acclaim (including a postage stamp), there is little chance that Louis Armstrong will ever be forgotten! —*Scott Yanow*

Portrait of the Artist as a Young Man / Apr. 6, 1923-Oct. 1934 / Columbia ✦✦✦✦
This very attractive four-CD box set has definitive liner notes from Dan Morgenstern and draws its 81 selections from Louis Armstrong's prime period. Why then does it not receive the highest rating? Armstrong's immortal *Hot Five* and *Hot Seven* recordings, along with his early big-band sides, had already been reissued complete and in chronological order on seven Columbia CDs and his less interesting performances as an accompanist to various blues singers (some of which are on this set) have also been reissued in similar fashion. Therefore this box is of no real interest to veteran collectors and, although a good introduction to beginners just starting to explore Satch's classic music, they too will eventually be moved to duplicate many of these recordings by getting the more complete series. As for the music, this set has literally dozens of influential classics and 19 performances that actually predate The Hot Fives but, since everything is available elsewhere, this box is recommended only for the informative booklet. —*Scott Yanow*

Highlights from His Decca Years / Oct. 10, 1924-Feb. 4, 1958 / Decca ✦✦
Music aside (and there are many fine moments here), this two-CD sampler is a real mess. Rather than reissue complete sessions or at least repackage the music in chronological order, the 36 selections are divided into four overlapping sections ("In the Beginning," "The Decca Sessions, Part l," "The Collaborations," and "The Decca Sessions, Part 2," and range from sideman stints in the 1920s with clarinetist Johnny Dodds and Fletcher Henderson ("Shanghai Shuffle") to streaky big-band performances from the swing era, five vocal duets and commercial performances (including "Your Cheatin' Heart") from the 1950s. It is a real mishmash (with some classics like "I Double Dare You" being overlooked) and Armstrong's important Decca recordings deserve much better. Get the CD releases from the European Classics label instead. —*Scott Yanow*

Louis Armstrong and the Blues Singers / Oct. 16, 1924-Jul. 16, 1930 / Affinity ✦✦✦✦
During 1924-26 (and to a lesser extent 1927-30), Louis Armstrong appeared as a sideman on a series of sessions by a variety of blues-oriented singers. All of these recordings are included on this attractive six-CD set issued by the English Affinity label (which also includes a lengthy booklet). Armstrong's cornet and, by 1928, trumpet) is heard backing and occasionally taking solos on record dates led by singers Ma Rainey, Virginia Liston, Eva Taylor, Alberta Hunter, Margaret Johnson, Sippie Wallace, Maggie Jones, Clara Smith, Bessie Smith, Trixie Smith, Billy Jones, Grant and Wilson, Perry Bradford, Chippie Hill, Blanche Calloway, Hociel Thomas, Baby Mack, Nolan Welsh, Butterbeans and Susie, Lillie Delk Christian, Seger Ellis, Victoria Spivey and even the country pioneer Jimmie Rodgers ("Blue Yodel No. 9"). The Bessie Smith recordings are the most powerful but there are other memorable selections including those with the remarkably nasal Lillie Delk Christian (Armstrong even joins in and scats during "Too Busy"), Eva Taylor (during "Mandy Make up Your Mind" soprano-great Sidney Bechet switches to the remarkable sarrusophone), Eva Taylor (Armstrong's solo on "Cake Walking Babies from Home" was one of his first great ones), Chippie Hill (the original version of "Trouble in Mind") and Ma Rainey (the earliest recording of "See See Rider"). These recordings on a whole are not as essential as his own classic sessions from the 1920s, so this perfectly packaged set is recommended mostly to the more fanatical early jazz and blues collectors rather than the more general listeners, who are advised to get Armstrong's Hot Five recordings first. —*Scott Yanow*

★ **Hot Fives, Vol. 1** / Nov. 12, 1925-Jun. 23, 1926 / Columbia ✦✦✦✦✦

To say that the performances on this CD (plus the ones on Vols. 2-4) are classic would be an extreme understatement. With these first 16 recordings by Louis Armstrong's Hot Five, the trumpeter revolutionized jazz, changing it from an ensemble-oriented music into an art form dominated by virtuoso soloists. The most powerful jazz improviser of the 1920s, Louis Armstrong's beautiful tone, his sense of swing (which set the stage for the big band era) and his chance-taking yet melodic improvisations amazed his contemporaries and permanently altered the future of jazz. Among the many gems on this first volume are "Come Back, Sweet Papa," "Heebies Jeebies" (which is highlighted by Armstrong's highly influential scat vocal), the brilliant "Cornet Chop Suey," the debut of Kid Ory's "Muskrat Ramble" and the joyous "Don't Forget to Mess Around." With clarinetist Johnny Dodds (the pacesetter on his instrument), trombonist Kid Ory, pianist Lil Armstrong and banjoist Johnny St. Cyr all making strong contributions, the music is consistently memorable and innovative. —*Scott Yanow*

★ **Hot Fives and Sevens, Vol. 2** / Jun. 28, 1926-May 13, 1927 / Columbia ✦✦✦✦✦

Eight apiece from Louis Armstrong's Hot Five and Seven, with some stunning trumpet on "Willie the Weeper" and "Potato Head Blues" and Johnny Dodds' very distinctive clarinet at its best during "Weary Blues." Classic and very influential New Orleans jazz. —*Scott Yanow*

★ **The Louis Armstrong Collection, Vol. 4: Louis Armstrong and Earl Hines** / May 9, 1927-Dec. 12, 1928 / Columbia ✦✦✦✦✦

It can easily be argued that Louis Armstrong was at his most advanced during the 1928 recordings that featured him with the Savoy Ballroom Five. Constantly challenged by the equally adventurous pianist Earl Hines, Armstrong is consistently remarkable throughout the 18 selections that are on this CD. First there are three tracks with big bands during 1927-28 ("Chicago Breakdown," "Symphonic Raps" and "Savoyagers' Stomp") that also include Hines; then the chronology picks up where Vol. 3 left off. The startling "West End Blues" (with its classic trumpet cadenza) was always Armstrong's personal favorite recording, "Weather Bird" is a hair-raising duet with Hines and other highlights include "Sugar Foot Strut," "Beau Koo Jack" and the earliest recorded versions of "Basin Street Blues" and "St. James Infirmary." Although the other musicians in the Savoy Ballroom Five (trombonist Fred Robinson, Jimmy Strong on clarinet and tenor, banjoist Mancy Cara and, for some selections, Don Redman on clarinet and alto) are excellent, it is the interplay between Hines, drummer Zutty Singleton and Satch that really makes the music classic. The first four volumes in this series are essential for all serious jazz collections. —*Scott Yanow*

☆ **Hot Fives and Sevens, Vol. 3** / May 13, 1927-Jun. 28, 1928 / Columbia ✦✦✦✦✦

Louis Armstrong's 1925-28 recordings with his Hot Fives and Hot Sevens belong in every serious jazz collection, even those owned by listeners who otherwise do not listen to music before bebop. Armstrong's remarkable trumpet solos of the 1920s were so advanced that they indirectly led the way towards not only swing but bop of 20 years later. On the third of seven CD volumes that have all of Louis' earliest records, Armstrong is featured with three separate groups. His Hot Seven (with the brilliant clarinetist Johnny Dodds, trombonist John Thomas, pianist Lil Armstrong, banjoist Johnny St. Cyr, Pete Briggs on tuba and drummer Baby Dodds) plays three numbers (including the humorous "That's When I'll Come Back to You"). There are nine of the greatest Hot Five performances (with Dodds, trombonist Kid Ory, Lil on piano and St. Cyr), including a perfectly constructed Louis Armstrong solo on the original version of "Struttin' with Some Barbecue," "Once in a While," and exciting guest appearances by guitarist Lonnie Johnson on three numbers (most notably "Hotter Than That"). This set concludes in 1928 with Louis Armstrong's new recording group, the Savoy Ballroom Five (a sextet with pianist Earl Hines, drummer Zutty Singleton, trombonist Fred Robinson, Jimmy Strong on clarinet and tenor and banjoist Mancy Cara); their four songs include the initial version of Hines' "A Monday Date" and the tricky "Fireworks." Essential music. —*Scott Yanow*

Louis Armstrong Collection, Vol. 5: Louis in New York / Mar. 5, 1929-Nov. 26, 1929 / Columbia/Legacy ✦✦✦✦✦

By 1929, Louis Armstrong had switched from New Orleans jazz to fronting a variety of larger orchestras, widening his repertoire to include pop tunes but always leaving room for closing trumpet solos. This set includes all known versions (including a few new alternates) of his recordings of this era, including appearances by backing singers Seger Ellis and Victoria Spivey. High points include "Mahogany Hall Stomp" and "Ain't Misbehavin'." —*Scott Yanow*

Louis Armstrong Collection, Vol. 6: St. Louis Blues / Dec. 10, 1929-Oct. 9, 1930 / Columbia/Legacy ✦✦✦✦✦

19 of Louis Armstrong's early big band performances have been reissued complete and in chronological order on the sixth CD in this very valuable Columbia series. Armstrong, whose virtuosity and showmanship by the late 1920s could no longer be confined to a New Orleans jazz format, is heard supported by several

different big bands (including Luis Russell's Orchestra) on these classic recordings. And while trombonist J.C. Higginbotham, clarinetist Albert Nicholas and drummer Lionel Hampton are in the supporting cast, they are completely overshadowed by the leader. "St. Louis Blues," "Song of the Islands," "Dinah," "Tiger Rag," "I'm Confessin'" and "Body and Soul" are given memorable treatment, "Dear Old Southland" is a showcase in which Louis is backed just by pianist Buck Washington and "I'm a Ding Dong Daddy" is a real tour-de-force. The latter piece has Armstrong forgetting the words in perfect rhyme and then scatting up a storm before constructing an absolutely perfect trumpet solo. Collectors will want to note that this CD has four previously unheard alternate takes including two of "St. Louis Blues." A gem. —*Scott Yanow*

Louis Armstrong Collection, Vol. 7: You're Driving Me Crazy / Oct. 16, 1930-Nov. 3, 1931 / Columbia/Legacy ✦✦✦✦✦

It took domestic Columbia until the late 1980s before the label finally started a program reissuing, complete and in chronological order, all of Louis Armstrong's earliest recordings as a leader; only 60 years after the classic music was originally recorded. The series reached its seventh CD by 1992 but thus far an eighth and final album has not been compiled to complete the essential task of making Louis' greatest recordings available. Vol. 7 has 17 big band selections from 1930-31 (plus an alternate take of "You're Drivin' Me Crazy") and, even if the first six volumes are a bit more essential, this one contains plenty of gems. Lionel Hampton made his first recorded appearance on vibes during "Memories of You" and "Shine" and the other memorable selections include "Sweethearts on Parade," Armstrong's theme song "When It's Sleepy Time Down South," "I'll Be Glad When You're Dead, You Rascal You," "Lazy River" and "Chinatown, My Chinatown." Recommended. —*Scott Yanow*

From the Big Band to the All-Stars (1946-56) / Aug. 12, 1932-Jan. 8, 1956 / RCA ✦✦✦✦

With the exception of the alternate take of "Hobo, You Can't Ride This Train" from 1932 and a couple of numbers with a big band in 1956, this two-CD set (a straight reissue of the RCA Jazz Tribune two-LP release of the same name) concentrates on the 1946-47 period. Most of the music has been reissued several times by RCA (including in their Bluebird series), but it is still quite valuable and enjoyable. The great trumpeter-vocalist Louis Armstrong is heard on a couple of numbers with the Esquire All-Americans, on his final dozen recordings with his swing big band, with trombonist Kid Ory for a few songs (highlighted by the earliest version of "Do You Know What It Means to Miss New Orleans"), with "The Leader's Band" (a group taken from the film *A Song Is Born*) and with trombonist Jack Teagarden in a couple of all-star bands; their version of "Jack-Armstrong Blues" is a real classic while "Please Stop Playing Those Blues" and "A Song Was Born" are close behind. Very enjoyable music, highly recommended in one form or another. —*Scott Yanow*

Laughin' Louis (1932-1933) / Dec. 8, 1932-Apr. 26, 1933 / Bluebird ✦✦✦

This single CD, unlike the more comprehensive Classics series, has just some of the highlights from Louis Armstrong's Victor recordings of 1932-33. The backup big band generally sounds under-rehearsed and occasionally out of tune but Armstrong is the dominant star anyway. Although not of the consistent high level of Louis' 1929-31 orchestra records, there are quite a few gems on this set including the touching "That's My Home," "I've Got the World on a String," "Hustlin' and Bustlin' for Baby," remakes of "Basin Street Blues," "Mahogany Hall Stomp" and "St. Louis Blues," and the somewhat bizarre "Laughin' Louie." In addition there are two three-song medleys of "Armstrong Hits." This CD is worth picking up by those not already owning the Classics releases although it is advisable to get Louis Armstrong's earlier Columbia CDs first. —*Scott Yanow*

Complete RCA Victor Recordings / Dec. 8, 1932-Aug. 1, 1956 / RCA ✦✦✦✦✦

Most of the music on this four-CD set from 1997 has been reissued many times, both on LP and CD, but this is the most "complete" set thus far. Louis Armstrong recorded for RCA during two separate times. During 1932-33, he led an erratic (and under-rehearsed) big band on a series of numbers, but all of the selections have their moments of interest. Although not up to the level of his Hot Five and Seven recordings of five years earlier, these spirited tracks find Armstrong mostly in excellent form both instrumentally and vocally, and the reissue has four alternate takes never before released. Highlights include the two-part "Hits Medley," "That's My Home," "I've Got the World on a String," "There's a Cabin in the Pines," "Hustlin' and Bustlin' for Baby," a unique 1930 collaboration with country singer Jimmie Rodgers, and the two bizarre versions of "Laughin' Louis." The second half of the reissue features Armstrong during 1946-47, including appearances with the Esquire poll winners (Louis takes a surprisingly modern solo on "Snafu," the last titles by his big band, a few wonderful combo performances (including the classic "Jack-Armstrong Blues") and the first songs by Armstrong's All-Stars (co-starring Jack Teagarden); this collection concludes with two unrelated 1956 orchestral tracks. Overall, this is wonderful music, although collectors who already have everything other than the alternates have a right to hesitate. —*Scott Yanow*

1932-1933 / Dec. 21, 1932-Apr. 26, 1933 / Classics ✦✦✦
The European Classics label may or may not be a "legitimate" record label but it currently has the best reissue series for those listeners wanting the complete output of vintage jazz artists. These 24 selections, as with the less-complete *Laughin' Louie* set, find Armstrong mostly overcoming an inferior big band to play some pacesetting trumpet. —*Scott Yanow*

Greatest Hits / Jan. 27, 1933-May 27, 1970 / RCA Victor ✦✦
This CD is part of RCA's extensive *Greatest Hits* jazz program, a beginner's series designed to introduce listeners to jazz, specifically RCA's jazz catalog. The 13 selections on this somewhat confusing CD jump back and forth between three different periods: 1933 (highlighted by "St. Louis Blues"), 1946-47 (the best music on the set) and Armstrong's next-to-last session in 1970 (including the definitive version of "What a Wonderful World"). Serious collectors will want to skip this series entirely and even novices may wonder why the music was not programmed in chronological order and why no personnel listing was included. The well-intentioned release (which does contain some worthwhile material but none of Armstrong's "Hits") is rather lightweight and all of the material is currently available elsewhere. —*Scott Yanow*

1934-1936 / Oct. 1934-Feb. 4, 1936 / Classics ✦✦✦✦
This valuable CD includes Armstrong's often riotous Paris session from 1934 ("St. Louis Blues" and "Tiger Rag" almost get out of control) and then Satch's first 17 Decca recordings, smooth renditions of pop tunes that he turns into classic jazz. It duplicates and exceeds Decca's *Rhythm Saved the World*. —*Scott Yanow*

Rhythm Saved the World / Oct. 3, 1935-Feb. 4, 1936 / GRP ✦✦✦
This is the first domestic volume on CD of Armstrong's swing-era recordings for Decca in chronological order. Joined by the musical, but by then somewhat anonymous, Luis Russell Orchestra, Armstrong's melodic variations turn these pop tunes into fine jazz, even "La Cucaracha." —*Scott Yanow*

Pocketful of Dreams, Vol. 3 / Oct. 3, 1935-Jun. 21, 1938 / GRP ✦✦✦✦
The current Decca reissue program (produced by Orrin Keepnews) has long been frustrating for completists, with incomplete sessions and previously unreleased music often being included on the same CD, forcing collectors to either skip music or duplicate many selections from previous issues. This CD, in contrast, is actually better than most of the sets for four of Louis Armstrong's 1938 recording dates are reissued in full (with the exception of the master take of "The Trumpet Player's Lament") plus two takes of "Got a Brand New Suit" from 1935. Backed up but the June 24, 1938 performances by the remnants of the Luis Russell Orchestra, Armstrong's trumpet playing is fairly basic while his vocalizing was entering its peak period. Most memorable are "I Double Dare You" (a near-classic), "The Saints" and the remakes of "I Can't Give You Anything but Love" and "Ain't Misbehavin'," but even the lesser material has its strong moments. Although nothing significant is heard from trumpeter Red Allen or clarinetist Albert Nicholas, there are some fine spots by altoist Charlie Holmes, Bingie Madison on tenor and particularly trombonist J.C. Higginbotham. —*Scott Yanow*

The Composer / Nov. 21, 1935-Jan. 28, 1957 / Decca ✦
Louis Armstrong had many talents, but he was not a great or a prolific composer. This hodgepodge set has some fine examples of his playing from both the '30s and the '50s, but it is somewhat pointless compared to the more complete collections available elsewhere, particularly when it lists "Struttin' with Some Barbecue" (a Lil Armstrong composition) as Louis'. —*Scott Yanow*

1936-1937 / Feb. 4, 1936-Apr. 7, 1937 / Classics ✦✦✦✦
Continuing the complete chronological reissue of Louis Armstrong's output for Decca during the swing era, this set finds Satch at his most exhibitionistic (hitting dozens of high notes on "Swing That Music"), fronting Jimmy Dorsey's orchestra, doing a "Pennies from Heaven" medley with Bing Crosby, joining in for two collaborations with the Mills Brothers and, on four selections, even making charming (if weird) music with a group of Hawaiians. Not essential but quite enjoyable. —*Scott Yanow*

Louis Armstrong & His Orchestra, Vol. 2 (1936-1938): Heart Full of Rhythm / Apr. 28, 1936-Jan. 15, 1938 / GRP/Decca ✦✦✦✦
Some of Louis Armstrong's better Decca recordings from the 1936-38 period are reissued on this CD. Inferior to the much more "complete" series undertaken by the European Classics label, this set nevertheless does have some classics from Satch including two versions of "Swing That Music," a remake of "Mahogany Hall Stomp," "Once in a While," "On the Sunny Side of the Street," "Jubilee" and "Struttin' with Some Barbecue." The backup band (the remains of Luis Russell's Orchestra) does not have a great deal to do although trombonist J.C. Higginbotham gets in a few solos. But this is largely Armstrong's show (both instrumentally and vocally) and he comes up with some masterful statements. —*Scott Yanow*

New Discoveries / Apr. 16, 1937-Dec. 17, 1961 / Pumpkin ✦✦✦
This unusual LP should greatly interest collectors. Included is a variety of previously unreleased material spanning a 24-year period in the great trumpeter's career. Armstrong is featured on broadcast versions of "Dinah" and "Twelfth Street Rag" with his big band, singing "Flat Foot Floogie" with the Mills Brothers, backing Frank Sinatra on "Blue Skies," rehearsing a couple of songs in 1947 with the all-star cast of the film *A Song Was Born*, performing five numbers at his famous Town Hall concert (including four on which he is backed only by a rhythm section) and playing two songs in a small group with Duke Ellington recorded a few months after their famous joint recording. Most of this music still has not surfaced on CD. —*Scott Yanow*

1937-1938 / Jun. 29, 1937-May 13, 1938 / Classics ✦✦✦✦
22 of Armstrong's big-band recordings and a couple of selections with the Mills Brothers are taken in chronological order. A few ("I Double Dare You," "On the Sunny Side of the Street" and his first version of "The Saints") are classics but mostly it is a matter of Armstrong joyfully uplifting mundane material, often higher up than it deserves. —*Scott Yanow*

1938-1939 / May 18, 1938-Apr. 5, 1939 / Classics ✦✦✦
A mixed bag of Armstrong, these 23 selections, if taken complete and in chronological order, include routine swing, three enjoyable numbers with the Mills Brothers, a few spirituals, an odd two-part sermon and some remakes of Armstrong's earlier classics. His career was drifting a bit but there is enough enjoyable music to make this a worthwhile acquisition. —*Scott Yanow*

Live in 1943: On the Sunny Side of the Street / Jun. 13, 1938-Aug. 4, 1946 / Jass ✦✦
Other than the soundtrack version of "Jeepers Creepers" and two other items, all of this CD is taken from broadcasts of Armstrong's little-known and unrecorded orchestra of 1943. Much of the music is fairly routine swing, but the Armstrong trumpet (which always sounds so enthusiastic) and features for the Mills Brothers ("Paper Doll") and clarinetist Barney Bigard make this rarity of some interest. —*Scott Yanow*

1939-1940 / Apr. 5, 1939-May 1, 1940 / Classics ✦✦✦
Armstrong's Decca years by the late '30s found him treading water, playing well on these orchestra recordings (four songs find him having a good time with the Mills Brothers), but the remakes are generally more interesting than the newer novelty material from the swing era. —*Scott Yanow*

1940-1942 / May 1, 1940-Apr. 17, 1942 / Classics ✦✦✦✦
While MCA continues to release incomplete samplers of his Decca recordings, the European Classics series has reissued the great trumpeter's performances the best possible way: complete and in chronological order. This final CD has 18 mostly rare big-band selections from 1940-42 (highlighted by "I Cover the Waterfront," a remake of "When It's Sleepy Time down South," "Coquette" and "I Never Knew") along with the four songs recorded by Armstrong during a reunion session with the great soprano saxophonist Sidney Bechet (including a heated "Down in Honky Tonk Town"). Ignore the better publicized MCA Louis Armstrong reissues and get this series instead. —*Scott Yanow*

Now You Has Jazz: Louis Armstrong at MGM / Aug. 28, 1942-Jul. 26, 1965 / Rhino ✦✦✦
More than any other jazz musician before or since, Louis Armstrong had a propensity for entertaining that stood him in good stead when it came time for the cameras to roll. It helped that he had a one-of-a-kind singing and speaking voice and could handle dialogue like a champ and mug shamelessly, but Louis' presence on film was every bit as much a musical one as it was that of an comic entertainer. Working with the Turner Classic Movie network, Rhino has compiled 25 tracks taken from Armstrong's appearances in the MGM movies *The Strip, Cabin in the Sky, Glory Alley, High Society* and *When the Boys Meet the Girls*. Five of the selections ("It's a Most Unusual Day," "One O'Clock Jump," "I'm Coming Virginia," "I Got Rhythm" and "Ain't It the Truth") are compiled from alternate takes and unissued material. While some see Pops as a clown in these films (those unable to connect the dots between extraordinary musicianship and fine comedic talent, thus making one legendary entertainer), the music reveals that his strong jazz roots were always close to the surface, making for great music to listen to when you can't watch all the mugging that went with it. Nobody put more real jazz into the movies than Louis Armstrong, and here's a solid collection of some of the very best of it. —*Cub Koda*

Pops: 1940s Small Band Sides / Sep. 6, 1946-Oct. 16, 1947 / RCA/Bluebird ✦✦✦✦
Recorded at the time Armstrong was in the film *New Orleans*, broke up his orchestra and formed his very popular "All-Stars," these 20 tracks feature Satch in prime form, whether playing relaxed standards, New Orleans gems, or duetting with trombonist/vocalist Jack Teagarden. High points include a reunion with his

old boss trombonist Kid Ory, five selections from his classic 1947 Town Hall concert (including definitive versions of "Ain't Misbehavin'," "Rockin' Chair" and "Back O'Town Blues"), sharing the spotlight with Jack T. on "A Song Was Born" and "Please Stop Playing Those Blues, Boy" and taking one of his greatest-ever solos on "Jack-Armstrong Blues." An outstanding set. —*Scott Yanow*

The Complete Town Hall Concert / May 17, 1947 / RCA ✦✦✦✦
One of the key turning points of Louis Armstrong's career occurred at the Town Hall concert fully documented on this two-CD set, a reissue of the earlier two-LP release. Armstrong, who had been leading a big band for 18 years, was showcased with some musical friends who were all very complementary players (including trombonist Jack Teagarden, clarinetist Peanuts Hucko and cornetist Bobby Hackett), and the results were so exciting that Armstrong soon broke up his orchestra to form a similar all-star sextet. The recording quality of some of the numbers from this concert is erratic but the magic of the music definitely comes through. Highlights include a few tunes on which Louis is backed by just a rhythm section (including "Cornet Chop Suey" and an emotional "Dear Old Southland"), definitive versions of "Ain't Misbehavin'" and "Back O'Town Blues" and a memorable feature for Jack Teagarden on "St. James Infirmary." Recommended for all Louis Armstrong fans who wish to hear the real birth of his All-Stars. —*Scott Yanow*

Satchmo at Symphony Hall / Nov. 30, 1947 / GRP ✦✦✦✦✦
Louis Armstrong's concert at Symphony Hall with his All-Stars in 1947 was a major success, featuring the trumpeter-vocalist, trombonist Jack Teagarden, clarinetist Barney Bigard, pianist Dick Cary, bassist Arvell Shaw and drummer Big Sid Catlett in particularly inspired form. This single CD reissues 15 of the 18 selections from the earlier two-LP set, dropping "How High the Moon" (which was mostly a bass solo), singer Velma Middleton's feature on "I Cried for You" and, most regrettably, a definitive comedy vocal duet by Middleton and Armstrong on "That's My Desire." Otherwise the music (whose order has been partly shuffled around without any explanation) is intact. Highlights include Satch's superb vocal on "Black and Blue," heated jams on "Royal Garden Blues," "Muskrat Ramble" and "High Society," and Teagarden's feature on "Lover Man." Joyous music. —*Scott Yanow*

The Complete Decca Studio Louis Armstrong All-Stars / Apr. 26, 1950-Oct. 8, 1958 / Mosaic ✦✦✦✦
This attractive limited-edition six-CD set features all of the studio small-group sides done by Armstrong in the 1950s for Decca. The first disc in particular is quite rewarding, for it contains a full program by his 1950 sextet with trombonist Jack Teagarden, clarinetist Barney Bigard and pianist Earl Hines. While the second disc has a variety of odds and ends (including the first version of "A Kiss to Build a Dream On" and two vocal duets with Gary Crosby), most of the final four CDs are from an ambitious project (originally titled "A Musical Autobiography") in which the great trumpeter-vocalist revisited many of the songs that he had recorded in the 1920s and '30s; some of the newer versions are actually better than the earlier ones. The one fault is that Mosaic's decision to reissue the latter in strict chronological order mixes up the original program with some of the '30s selections preceding the ones from the decade before; also, Armstrong's verbal introductions (which are often charming) have been deleted. But musically this excellent box set serves as proof that Louis Armstrong was still a very vital trumpeter in the 1950s. —*Scott Yanow*

The California Concerts / Jan. 30, 1951-Jan. 21, 1955 / GRP ✦✦✦✦
Armstrong's All-Stars, giving one a very good idea of the type of performance the great trumpeter-vocalist put on every night. Some dated comedy aside, Satch is in exciting form, assisted by trombonists Jack Teagarden and Trummy Young, clarinetist Barney Bigard and, for the earlier concert, pianist Earl Hines. Actually, it is the later session (which takes up most of the last three CDs) that is quite spirited and lively, with Armstrong enthusiastically leading his All-Stars through time-worn but fresh Dixieland standards. —*Scott Yanow*

Louis Armstrong & His All-Stars [Storyville] / 1954 / Storyville ✦✦✦✦
This Storyville CD has two radio broadcasts that emanated from San Francisco's Club Hangover by Louis Armstrong's 1954 All-Stars. The first 15 minutes are from a New Year's Eve celebration and the five selections (which includes a very brief "Auld Lang Syne") are highlighted by a delightful version of "Big Butter and Egg Man" that finds Satch scatting some beautiful harmony behind Velma Middleton's vocal. The remainder of the release is from earlier in the year, featuring trombonist Trummy Young and clarinetist Barney Bigard joining Armstrong on such numbers as "Back O'Town Blues," "12th Street Rag" and "West End Blues." Easily recommended to Louis Armstrong fans. —*Scott Yanow*

☆ **Louis Armstrong Plays W.C. Handy** / Jul. 12, 1954-Jul. 14, 1954 / Columbia ✦✦✦✦✦
This recording was not only Louis Armstrong's finest record of the 1950s but one of the truly classic jazz sets. Out of print for years, it was reissued quite shoddily in 1986 on a Columbia CD with alternates in place of many of the original versions

and no real explanation. It was a complete and inexcusable mess and should be avoided by all but completists. Ten years later, Columbia finally got around to bringing back the original gem, and the music is at last available on CD. Armstrong and his All-Stars (trombonist Trummy Young, clarinetist Barney Bigard, pianist Billy Kyle, bassist Arvell Shaw, drummer Barrett Deems and singer Velma Middleton), were clearly inspired by the fresh repertoire, 11 songs written by W.C. Handy. Their nearly nine-minute version of "St. Louis Blues" (with witty vocals, roaring Young trombone and a couple of long majestic trumpet solos) is arguably the greatest version of the oft-recorded song. Other highlights include "Loveless Love," "Beale Street Blues" and a romping version of "Ole Miss Blues." This CD also includes rehearsal versions of three songs, Louis Armstrong telling a joke and a brief George Avakian interview with W.C. Handy. Essential music for all serious jazz collections. —*Scott Yanow*

Satch Plays Fats: The Music of Fats Waller / Apr. 26, 1955-May 3, 1955 / Columbia ✦✦
Six of the nine songs heard here are actually alternate takes inferior to the original releases. The music is still decent but only a shadow of the real version. Wait until this important music is properly reissued! —*Scott Yanow*

Satchmo the Great / 1955-1956 / Columbia ✦✦✦
This CD reissues the former LP of the same name. In 1956 Edward R. Murrow narrated a feature film, *Satchmo the Great*, that contained highlights from some of Louis Armstrong's world tours. This soundtrack has some narration by Murrow between songs plus an interview with Armstrong. Musically there are renditions of "When It's Sleepy Time Down South," "Indiana," "Oh Didn't He Ramble," "Mack the Knife," "Mahogany Hall Stomp" and "Black and Blue" that add little to the more familiar versions. Most interesting is a lengthy "St. Louis Blues" that teams Armstrong and his All-Stars with Leonard Bernstein and a symphony orchestra. —*Scott Yanow*

Great Chicago Concert 1956 / Jun. 1, 1956 / Sony ✦✦✦✦
Originally out on a double LP, this is a definitive set of the Louis Armstrong All-Stars of 1956. The music and many of the solos will be familiar to longtime Armstrong fans, but whether it be "Struttin' with Some Barbecue," "Basin Street" or his new hit "Mack the Knife," the spirit and enthusiasm of this music is irresistible. This is his best live set in the '50s. The CD reissue, a two-CD set, is slightly more complete than the two-fer LP in that it adds a version of Armstrong's theme song "When It's Sleepy Time Down South," a closing "Saints" that allows Satch to introduce his band and a straightforward rendition of "The Star Spangled Banner." —*Scott Yanow*

The Sullivan Years: Louis Armstrong / Jul. 15, 1956-Sep. 11, 1966 / TVT ✦✦
Louis Armstrong was always a welcome guest on *The Ed Sullivan Show*, where his bright renditions of Dixieland tunes and pop songs were consistent crowd-pleasers. This CD has 18 selections from nine of his appearances, performing everything from "Hello Dolly" and "Mack the Knife" to "Muskrat Ramble" and "Basin Street." Although one cannot see these performances (at least until they are released on videotape), one can certainly feel the joy. —*Scott Yanow*

Basin Street Blues / Jul. 1956-Oct. 17, 1957 / Black Lion ✦✦✦
This release consists of highlights from two concerts by Louis Armstrong's All-Stars. His front line (which at the time boasted the very distinctive sounds of trombonist Trummy Young and clarinetist Edmond Hall) was always a major asset and singer Velma Middleton helps out on a funny vocal duet version of "Baby, It's Cold Outside." The typical program (which includes such songs as Satch's perennial opener "Indiana," "Basin Street Blues" and "Tiger Rag") offers few surprises, but there are also no disappointments from the master of joyful New Orleans jazz. —*Scott Yanow*

Louis and the Angels / 1957 / Decca ✦✦✦
This obscure set by Louis Armstrong (not yet reissued on CD) has its strange appeal. The great trumpeter/vocalist performs a dozen songs, all of which have "heaven" or "angel" in their title or lyrics, while backed by the Sy Oliver Orchestra plus a heavenly female choir. Satch gets off a few good trumpet solos and is quite cheerful throughout, even joking during "The Prisoner's Song" when the word "angel" finally shows up. Among the highlights are "When Did You Leave Heaven," "I Married An Angel" and "I'll String Along With You." Although more commercial than Armstrong's usual recordings of the era, this set is more memorable than one would expect and is worth searching for. —*Scott Yanow*

Mack the Knife / Jul. 4, 1957 / Pablo ✦✦✦
Before his appearance at the 1957 Newport Jazz Festival, Louis Armstrong learned that the promoters planned to shunt aside his regular band in favor of a group of his historical associates. Never a pushover and always protective of his sidemen, Armstrong threw a major temper tantrum that resulted in his regular show going on as usual. No hint of the turmoil can be heard during this swinging concert appearance, which features the trumpeter, trombonist Trummy Young, and clari-

netist Edmund Hall romping through their usual program, highlighted by "Now You Has Jazz" (from the movie *High Society*), "Mahogany Hall Stomp," some individual features, and Armstrong's recent hit "Mack the Knife." —*Scott Yanow*

Porgy and Bess / Aug. 18, 1957 / Verve ✦✦✦
Louis Armstrong and Ella Fitzgerald, great mutual admirers, team up for 16 songs from the famous George Gershwin opera. Although this would not be considered either's finest moment on record, it is worthwhile. Russ Garcia's arrangements for the large orchestra work very well with the two singers. —*Scott Yanow*

Louis Armstrong Meets Oscar Peterson / Oct. 14, 1957 / Verve ✦✦✦
An unusual set with Louis Armstrong singing a variety of popular standards in a relaxed and easy-going manner, he is backed by the Oscar Peterson trio and drummer Louis Bellson. Few fireworks occur but the change of pace for Armstrong (who also contributes some brief trumpet solos) is refreshing. —*Scott Yanow*

Happy Birthday, Louis! Armstrong & His All-Stars / Jul. 1, 1960 / Omega ✦✦✦
Armstrong and the 1960 version of his All-Stars (which included trombonist Trummy Young, clarinetist Barney Bigard, pianist Billy Kyle, bassist Mort Herbert, drummer Danny Barcelona and singer Velma Middleton) are heard putting on their usual show at that year's Newport Jazz Festival. The repertoire (which includes "Indiana," a slapdash "Tiger Rag," two songs from the film *High Society*, individual features for the musicians and "Mack the Knife") offers no real surprises but Armstrong's enthusiasm and beautiful tone on the trumpet make this joyful CD (whose contents were released for the first time in 1994) worth having. —*Scott Yanow*

Blueberry Hill / 1961 / Milan ✦✦
An obscure concert performance, probably from around 1961-63 (no date is given), the erratic recording quality and somewhat typical repertoire keep this from being highly recommended but it has its strong moments, most notably a beautiful version of "That's My Home" and a relaxed run-through of "Jazz Me Blues." —*Scott Yanow*

Armstrong/Ellington: Together for the First Time/The Great Reunion / Apr. 3, 1961-Apr. 5, 1961 / Mobile Fidelity ✦✦✦✦✦
Formerly available as a two-LP set and also released on CD by Roulette, these 17 selections are the entire results of the only meeting in the studios by Louis Armstrong and Duke Ellington. Although it might have been preferable to have Armstrong perform with Duke Ellington's orchestra, Ellington's performance as pianist with Satch's All-Stars is quite satisfying. The all-Ellington program gave Armstrong a rest from his usual repertoire and permitted him an opportunity to work his magic on fresh material. Lots of surprises, some sensitive vocalizing and fine supporting work from trombonist Trummy Young and clarinetist Barney Bigard make this a gem. —*Scott Yanow*

Armstrong and His All-Stars / Apr. 24, 1962 / RTE ✦✦✦
Louis Armstrong and his All-Stars are heard during a typical concert performance in 1962. There are no real surprises in the repertoire or the solos, but the enthusiasm shown by Armstrong, trombonist Trummy Young, and clarinetist Joe Darensbourg (somehow Armstrong makes this music sound quite fresh and timely) and the excellent recording quality result in an infectious Dixieland set that should be of interest to Satch's many fans. —*Scott Yanow*

Masters of Jazz, Vol. 1 / Aug. 1, 1962 / Storyville ✦✦✦
This concert in Chicago by Louis Armstrong's All-Stars in 1962 featured the usual repertoire being played with swing and subtlety. Armstrong was beyond his playing prime but made the most of every note and his singing remained quite individual and personable. —*Scott Yanow*

Hello, Dolly! / Dec. 3, 1963-Apr. 18, 1964 / Kapp ✦✦✦✦
Not only does this wonderful LP have the original hit version of "Hello Dolly" but a great rendition of "A Kiss to Build a Dream On" and Louis Armstrong's last extended trumpet solo during a hot version of "Jeepers Creepers." No matter how many times one hears "Hello Dolly" it is still a joy. —*Scott Yanow*

The Essential Louis Armstrong / Jun. 4, 1965 / Verve ✦✦✦✦
Maybe it is not "essential," but this two-CD set is a definitive look at the Louis Armstrong All-Stars in their later years, when Tyree Glenn was on trombone and the group was riding high from the success of "Hello Dolly." Armstrong's trumpet solos were briefer and stuck closer to the melody (age was taking its toll), yet were still full of beauty and feeling. —*Scott Yanow*

Disney Songs the Satchmo Way / Mar. 1968 / Walt Disney ✦✦✦
This is a delightful set, a straight CD reissue of an LP featuring Louis Armstrong in 1968 (not 1966 as it states in the liners) performing ten tunes associated with Disney films. One may not expect much from such songs as "Zip-A-Dee-Doo-Dah," "Whistle While You Work" and "The Ballad of Davy Crockett" but Armstrong's joyful vocals and occasional emotional trumpet really uplift the material. His rendition of "When You Wish upon a Star" is touching and few of the songs (including

"The Bare Necessities" and "Heigh-Ho") have ever sounded livelier and more fun. —*Scott Yanow*

Louis Armstrong's Greatest Hits Live / Jul. 3, 1968-Jul. 4, 1968 / Brunswick ✦✦✦
Louis Armstrong's performance on this live set (which was actually recorded in England for a television show) was one of the last in which he played trumpet. The CD reissue unfortunately does not list recording dates or personnel (inexcusable omissions). Armstrong's 1968 band included trombonist Tyree Glenn (who sings with Satch on "Rockin' Chair" and takes Velma Middleton's vocal on a humorous "That's My Desire") and clarinetist Joe Muranyi. Armstrong runs through his standard repertoire of the period (including his hits "Mame," "Mack the Knife" and of course "Hello, Dolly") and on trumpet makes every note count. A fine late release although this set pales next to Louis Armstrong's work of even just a few years earlier. —*Scott Yanow*

Louis Armstrong and His Friends / May 26, 1970-May 29, 1970 / Flying Dutchman ✦✦✦
Louis Armstrong's next-to-last recording (his final one was a few months later singing country songs in front of a Nashville rhythm section) has its touching moments. Backed by a large orchestra, Armstrong (who was too ill to play trumpet) sings some unlikely material including "The Creator Has a Master Plan" (which also features Leon Thomas' yodelling), "We Shall Overcome," "Everybody's Talkin'" and "Give Peace a Chance." The high points occur during "Mood Indigo," "Boy From New Orleans" (during which Louis sums up his life story over the chords of "When the Saints Go Marching In") and the definitive version of "What A Wonderful World." This historic LP is overdue to be reissued on CD. —*Scott Yanow*

Greatest Hits / Columbia/Legacy ✦✦✦
Columbia's *Greatest Hits* is good sampling of Louis Armstrong's most popular hits, capturing familiar versions of such staples as "A Theme from the Threepenny Opera (Mack the Knife)," "(What Did I Do to Be So) Black and Blue," "Ain't Misbehavin'," "Basin Street Blues," "All of Me," "West End Blues" and "Struttin' with Some Barbecue." Jazz purists won't be satisfied by this sampler, but for casual fans, it's good collection of some of Louis' best-known material. —*Stephen Thomas Erlewine*

Lynne Arriale

b. Milwaukee, WI
Piano / Post-Bop
Lynne Arriale gained her initial fame when she won the 1993 International Great American Jazz Piano competition and was immediately signed to DMP. A fine advanced bop pianist, Arriale graduated from the Wisconsin Conservatory of Music and toured Japan in 1991 with "100 Golden Fingers" which matched her along with nine veteran pianists, an honor that preceded her contest victory by two years. Lynne Arriale has strong potential for the future. —*Scott Yanow*

The Eyes Have It / Nov. 16, 1993 / DMP ✦✦✦✦
Winner of the 1993 International Great American Jazz Piano Competition, Lynne Arriale makes her recording debut on this CD. Her style at this early point fell easily into the modern mainstream (with the usual influences of Bill Evans, McCoy Tyner, Chick Corea and Herbie Hancock). Arriale does take some chances, opening her release with a moody version of "My Funny Valentine," taking "Yesterdays" at a rapid pace and having the tempo purposely speed up during the early part of "Witchcraft." With attentive support from bassist Jay Anderson and drummer Steve Davis, Lynne Arriale (who contributes four diverse originals) shows a great deal of potential and this CD is a strong start to her career. —*Scott Yanow*

When You Listen / Dec. 16, 1994+Dec. 17, 1994 / DMP ✦✦✦✦

● **With Words Unspoken** / May 20, 1996 / DMP ✦✦✦✦✦
With sympathetic support from bassist Drew Gress and drummer Steve Davis, pianist Lynne Arriale's third DMP release is the equal of her first two. A sensitive and lyrical player who fits into jazz's modern mainstream, Arriale is also able to swing hard ("Windswept" is a good example) and excels on both ballads and medium-tempo romps throughout this superior trio set. In addition to three of her originals, Arriale performs five jazz standards, including most notably Thelonious Monk's "Think of One" and Jimmy Rowles' "The Peacocks." Recommended. —*Scott Yanow*

Long Road Home / Apr. 1997 / TCB ✦✦✦✦
Pianist Lynne Arriale shows increasing individuality on this set, growing away from her roots in Bill Evans and developing her own voice. Joined by bassist Jon Patitucci and drummer Steve Davis, Arriale performs four modern mainstream originals and five renditions of jazz standards, including Thelonious Monk's "Bye-Ya" and Dizzy Gillespie's "Con Alma." Her playing is sometimes introspective and impressionistic, at other times harder-swinging, and always worth investigating. Recommended. —*Scott Yanow*

Art Ensemble of Chicago

f. 1966
Group / Avant-Garde, Free Jazz

The Art Ensemble of Chicago has long been one of the most significant avant-garde jazz groups and the most famous band to come out of the AACM. At a time when most musicians involved with the free jazz movement were playing at a consistently intense level, the Art Ensemble showed how to use space and dynamics creatively and to mix together free-form passages with arranged sections. Not shy to hint at earlier styles while playing originals, the Art Ensemble also helped introduce the concept of "little instruments" (such as bicycle horns, gongs, sirens and unusual percussive devices) to jazz. The group began as saxophonist Roscoe Mitchell's band. After trumpeter Lester Bowie, saxophonist Joseph Jarman and bassist Malachi Favors joined, it became a co-op. Its original drummer was Phillip Wilson but, when he departed to tour with the Butterfield Blues Band, the Art Ensemble continued for a time as a drumless quartet. During the early part of a two-year period spent in Paris (1969-71) Don Moye permanently took over the drum slot. The Art Ensemble was in its prime during the 1970s but by the '80s individual projects began to result in fewer performances. The group has continued on a part-time basis into the mid-'90s and has remained influential. *—Scott Yanow*

Art Ensemble: 1967/68 / May 18, 1967-Mar. 11, 1968 / Nessa ◆◆◆◆

This limited-edition five-CD set available directly from Nessa not only reissues the important free jazz albums *Old/Quartet, Numbers 1 & 2* and *Congliptious* but contains quite a bit of music taken from rehearsals by the members of the group that would by 1969 become known as the Art Ensemble of Chicago. With such advanced improvisers as trumpeter Lester Bowie, Roscoe Mitchell and Joseph Jarman on reeds, bassist Malachi Favors, and drummer Phillip Wilson, and appearances from bassist Charles Clark, drummers Robert Crowder and Thurman Barker, the music is usually very emotional and sometimes quite scary. There are meandering sections and individual performances that do not work all that well but in general the music is quite colorful, adventurous and innovative: in many ways the beginning of the modern avant-garde. Open-eared listeners are advised to search for this important historical set. *—Scott Yanow*

Jackson in Your House / Jun. 23, 1969-Aug. 1969 / Affinity ◆◆◆

Vitality was the key to the success of the Art Ensemble of Chicago's *Jackson in Your House*, which reissued the material from the BYG LP of the same name. This was recorded with just the quartet of Lester Bowie, Roscoe Mitchell, Joseph Jarman and bassist Malachi Favors (drummer Philip Wilson had left and Don Moye had yet to link up). *—Bob Rusch, Cadence*

Tutankhamun / Jun. 26, 1969 / Black Lion ◆◆◆

This CD reissue starts off so weird (with verbal sound explorations by Malachi Favors) that it might scare away some listeners. It is best to skip "Tutankhamun" altogether and put on "The Ninth Room" which has fine solos from altoist Roscoe Mitchell, trumpeter Lester Bowie and Joseph Jarman on alto over the walking bass of Favors. The other selection ("Tthinitthedalen Parts 1 and 2") consists of a pair of free improvisations by Mitchell and Favors that are passionate and sometimes a bit violent. Recorded during a period when the Art Ensemble of Chicago was between drummers, each of the musicians plays "little instruments" and percussion at times to fill in the gap. Due to the weak opener and the LP-length playing time, this is one of the Art Ensemble's lesser efforts despite "The Ninth Room." *—Scott Yanow*

People in Sorrow / Jul. 7, 1969 / Nessa ◆◆◆

In 1969, the Art Ensemble of Chicago (which had recorded just one official record, *Congliptious,* as a group at that point in time) moved to Paris for two years and recorded eight albums during their first year overseas alone. This particular LP has the innovative band (which was then a quartet consisting of trumpeter Lester Bowie, bassist Malachi Favors and both Roscoe Mitchell and Joseph Jarman on multiple reeds) performing the 40-minute group original "People in Sorrow." The still-startling music, which uses space, dynamics and a wide range of emotions expertly, is not for everyone's taste (the high-energy tenors of the mid-'60s are actually easier to get into), but worth the struggle. *—Scott Yanow*

Reese and the Smooth Ones / Aug. 12, 1969 / Freedom ◆◆◆

Recorded when the Art Ensemble of Chicago was in Paris and between drummers (Don Moye would not join up until 1970), this English imported LP has a continuous piece featuring trumpeter Lester Bowie, reed players Roscoe Mitchell and Joseph Jarman and bassist Malachi Favors all playing plenty of "little instruments" (which include various horns, gongs, logs, bells, sirens, whistles, steel drums, marimba, and banjo, among others) in addition to their mainstays. The episodic music continually holds one's interest, and overall, it makes a unified (if unpredictable) statement. *—Scott Yanow*

● Live at Mandel Hall / Jan. 15, 1972 / Delmark ◆◆◆◆◆

The Art Ensemble of Chicago had just returned to Chicago after several years in Europe when they recorded this continuous 76-minute concert. Drummer Don Moye (who had recently joined the classic avant-garde group) was proving to be a major asset, holding his own with trumpeter Lester Bowie, the reeds of Joseph Jarman and Roscoe Mitchell and bassist Malachi Favors. Although there are some meandering moments during their lengthy set, the music almost always holds onto one's interest (a humorous drunken march is a high point) and gives listeners a very good idea of how the Art Ensemble sounded in its early days when it was not at all shy about exploring music's outer limits. *—Scott Yanow*

Fanfare for the Warriors / Sep. 6, 1973 / Atlantic ◆◆◆◆

The Art Ensemble of Chicago's first (and arguably most significant) period concluded with this high-quality studio session. The quintet (trumpeter Lester Bowie, Roscoe Mitchell and Joseph Jarman on reeds, bassist Malachi Favors and drummer Don Moye) provides concise but adventurous performances. High points include Mitchell's "Nonnaah," Bowie's humorous "Barnyard Scuffel Shuffle" and "Tnoona," but all of the selections have their own musical personality. It's a fine showcase for this important avant-garde unit. *—Scott Yanow*

Nice Guys / May 1978 / ECM ◆◆◆◆

The Art Ensemble of Chicago's first studio album in six years finds the dynamic quintet incorporating elements of other musics into their own style, including earlier forms of jazz. "Dreaming of the Master" is an expert tribute to the Miles Davis Sextet of 1958, "Ja" hints strongly at reggae and "Nice Guys" is spacey in a humorous way. This fairly accessible set serves as a fine introduction to this important band's legacy. *—Scott Yanow*

Full Force / Jan. 1980 / ECM ◆◆

Not quite up to the level of their previous *Nice Guys, Full Force* is nevertheless a decent effort from the Art Ensemble of Chicago. Although there is one composition apiece from each of the band members except drummer Don Moye, trumpeter Lester Bowie emerges as the most memorable soloist and his "Charlie M" (a tribute to Charles Mingus) is the most interesting performance. It's not essential but is worth picking up. *—Scott Yanow*

Urban Bushmen / May 1980 / ECM ◆◆◆

This is arguably the greatest avant-garde jazz band of the 60s and 70s. *—Ron Wynn*

The Third Decade / Jun. 1984 / ECM ◆◆◆

Good set; extensive compositions. *—Ron Wynn*

Art Ensemble of Soweto / Dec. 1989-Jan. 1990 / DIW ◆◆

Dreaming of the Masters Suite / Jan. 12, 1990-Mar. 24, 1990 / DIW ◆◆◆◆

America South Africa / 1991 / Columbia ◆◆◆

Welcome return to American recording scene for the premier Chicago outside band. This mixes African rhythms, township melodies, and the Ensemble's usual array of blistering solos, vocal effects, percussive colors, and furious collective improvisations. *—Ron Wynn*

Thelonious Sphere Monk: Dreaming of the Masters, Vol. 2 / May 6, 1992 / DIW ◆◆

This CD promises much more than it delivers, appearing to be a tribute to Thelonious Monk that features the Art Ensemble of Chicago and guest pianist Cecil Taylor. As it turns out, Taylor is not on the two Monk pieces ("'Round Midnight" and "Nutty"), which, although reasonably enjoyable, do not contain any new revelations. The four collaborations between the Art Ensemble (trumpeter Lester Bowie, Roscoe Mitchell and Joseph Jarman on reeds, bassist Malachi Favors and drummer Don Moye) and Taylor (which have nothing to do with Thelonious) find the group mostly in a subsidiary role behind the pianist's volcanic waves of sound. So overall, this set is more significant historically than it is musically. *—Scott Yanow*

Dorothy Ashby (Dorothy Jeanne Ashby)

b. Aug. 6, 1932, Detroit, MI, **d.** Apr. 13, 1986, Santa Monica, CA
Harp / Cool, Hard Bop

There have been very few jazz harpists in history and Dorothy Ashby was one of the greats. Somehow she was able to play credible bebop on her instrument. As a pianist she studied at Wayne University and in 1952 she switched to harp. Within two years Ashby was gigging in jazz and in 1956 she made her first recording as a leader. Between 1956-70 she led ten albums for such labels as Savoy, Prestige, New Jazz, Argo, Jazzland, Atlantic and Cadet, guested on many records and was firmly established as a top studio and session player. She moved to the West Coast in the 1970s and was active up until her death. *—Scott Yanow*

● In a Minor Groove / 1958 / Prestige ◆◆◆◆◆

Dorothy Ashby, the top jazz harpist during the 1950s, '60s and '70s, recorded just a few albums as a leader during her career. This CD reissue has the complete contents of her Prestige and New Jazz albums, *Hip Harp* and *In a Minor Groove*. In both cases, Ashby (who really could improvise) was joined by flutist Frank Wess, bassist Gene Wright and either Art Taylor or Roy Haynes on drums. The bop-oriented program is naturally at a low volume, but Dorothy Ashby shows that she could swing hard too. Her definitive reissue. —*Scott Yanow*

The Fantastic Jazz Harp of Dorothy Ashby / May 3, 1965-May 4, 1965 / Atlantic ✦✦✦

Detroiter Ashby is the premier player on her instrument. With horns and percussion from Richard Davis (b), Grady Tate (d), Willie Bobo (per). —*Michael G. Nastos*

Afro Harping / Apr. 1968 / Chess ✦✦✦✦

The best and most complete album done by jazz harpist Dorothy Ashby. She didn't approach her instrument as if it were a gimmick, and she wasn't content to be a background/mood specialist. She turned the harp into a lead instrument, and offered solos that were as tough and memorable as those done by any reed, brass, or percussion player. —*Ron Wynn*

Harold Ashby

b. Mar. 27, 1925, Kansas City, MO
Tenor Saxophone / Swing
An excellent Ben Webster-inspired tenor saxophonist, Harold Ashby fit right in during his period with Duke Ellington. He had played in Kansas City (starting in 1946) and from the early '50s in Chicago. While most of his previous work was in R&B and blues bands, he was always a fine swing-based improviser. In 1957 Ashby moved to New York, met Ben Webster and through the older tenor was introduced to Duke Ellington. During the next decade he was on the periphery of Duke's world, playing with Mercer Ellington's short-lived band, recording with Ellington stars and appearing in Duke's *My People* show. Ashby was more than ready when he joined Ellington in 1968 and he was a major asset to the band up until the leader's death. He continued with Mercer Ellington into 1975, gigged with Benny Goodman and Sy Oliver and since then has performed often in Europe and led occasional record dates, keeping the Ellington swing tenor legacy alive. —*Scott Yanow*

● **Born to Swing** / Oct. 9, 1959+Feb. 27, 1960 / Master Jazz ✦✦✦✦✦

Presenting Harold Ashby / Aug. 7, 1978 / Progressive ✦✦✦✦
Considering that he was a major soloist with Duke Ellington's band of the early 1970s, it is surprising that the warm-toned tenor saxophonist Harold Ashby has not led more record sessions. This excellent quartet date with pianist Don Friedman, bassist George Mraz and drummer Ronnie Bedford finds Ashby featured on four standards and four of his basic originals. Excellent modern swing with the highlights including "Candy," the ironically titled uptempo number "Dainty" and the heated "Cous Cous." —*Scott Yanow*

The Viking / Aug. 4, 1988 / Gemini ✦✦✦✦
Tenor saxophonist Harold Ashby has relatively few opportunities to record as a leader, making this date for the Norwegian Gemini label a notable effort. Ashby, who is heavily influenced by Ben Webster, gets to stretch out while accompanied by the Norman Simmons Trio (with Simmons on piano, bassist Paul West and drummer Gerryck King). The repertoire includes four mostly basic Ashby originals plus a quartet of swing standards; "I Got It Bad" and "Whispering" are highlights. A strong effort by the very underrated veteran tenor. —*Scott Yanow*

What Am I Here For? / Nov. 30, 1990 / Criss Cross ✦✦✦✦

I'm Old Fashioned / Jul. 25, 1991 / Stash ✦✦✦✦✦

Svend Asmussen

b. Feb. 28, 1916, Copenhagen, Denmark
Violin / Swing
It seems strange that Svend Asmussen is not better known in the US for he has been a top swing violinist since the mid-'30s. He started playing violin when he was seven and in 1933 made his professional debut. Always based in Scandinavia (hence his obscurity in the US), Asmussen made his first records as a leader in 1935 and has been consistently popular in his homeland ever since. He played with the Mills Brothers and Fats Waller in the 1930s when they passed through Denmark, but when Benny Goodman tried to get him in the mid-'50s for his small group, strict immigration laws made it impossible for him to get to the US. Asmussen recorded with John Lewis (1962), Duke Ellington (as part of a 1963 violin summit), Toots Thielemans, Lionel Hampton (1978) and on a few occasions with Stephane Grappelli, in addition to many dates with his own groups. —*Scott Yanow*

● **Musical Miracle Vol. 1, 1935-1940** / Nov. 6, 1935-Dec. 4, 1940 / Phontastic ✦✦✦✦✦

Svend Asmussen was (and is still) one of the great swing violinists but, because he has spent most of his life in Scandinavia, his talents have often been overlooked through the years. This Phontastic CD is a very welcome release, for it features

Asmussen on 11 selections from 1935-40; all but the first seven date from 1940. Although this is not a "complete" reissue, it does give one a fine overview of the violinist's better swing sides, usually featuring him in a sextet/septet with one or two other horns and tripling on vocals and occasional vibes. Until a more comprehensive series comes out, this sampler is essential for listeners who think that Stephane Grappelli did not have any competitors in the 1930s. —*Scott Yanow*

Two of a Kind / Jan. 23, 1965-Jan. 24, 1965 / Storyville ✦✦✦✦
Frenchman Stephane Grappelli and the Great Dane Svend Asmussen had had parallel careers as jazz violinists for over 30 years when they finally met up for this Storyville session in 1965; they had only previously recorded together as part of Duke Ellington's Violin Summit a couple years earlier. Since they both have similar swing-based styles, it is not at all surprising that Grappelli and Asmussen consistently complement and inspire each other throughout this fine set. In addition to two Asmussen songs, Grappelli's "Love Is Back" and Toots Theielmans' "Blue Lady," the sextet (with guitarists Ole Molin and Jorn Grauengaard, bassist Niels Pedersen and drummer William Schiopffe) plays four joyful standards. Recommended. —*Scott Yanow*

Prize/Winners / Feb. 12, 1978+Feb. 17, 1978 / Matrix ✦✦✦
Kenny Drew's Matrix label debuted with this excellent session from violinist Svend Asmussen, an underrated but talented swing stylist. Asmussen, pianist Drew, bassist Niels Pedersen and drummer Ed Thigpen mix together swing with some more modern material including "Django," "Donna Lee" and "You Are the Sunshine of My Life" on the enjoyable program. This hard-to-find LP is worth picking up by fans of the jazz violin. —*Scott Yanow*

String Swing / Feb. 12, 1983-Feb. 13, 1983 / Sonet ✦✦✦✦
Records by Danish swing violinist Svend Asmussen tend to be hard to find in the US despite his 60 years of productive playing. This Sonet import matches Asmussen in 1983 with three guitarists (including soloist Ulf Wakenius), bassist Hugo Rasmussen and (on two of the eight numbers) drummer Bjarne Rostvold. The repertoire is quite wide-ranging, including two Duke Ellington pieces from the 1920s ("East St. Louis Toodle-oo" and "The Mooche"), a few traditional pieces (such as "Two Guitars" and "Prelude In C-Minor") and Jimmy Rowles' haunting ballad "The Peacocks." Worth searching for. —*Scott Yanow*

June Night / Aug. 18, 1983-Aug. 19, 1983 / Doctor Jazz ✦✦✦✦
Of Danish swing violinist Svend Asmussen's many recordings, this session for Bob Thiele's Doctor Jazz label should be one of the easier ones to find. Asmussen (teamed with pianist Derek Smith, guitarist Bucky Pizzarelli, bassist Milt Hinton and drummer Oliver Jackson for a rare American date) mostly sticks to swing standards and is heard throughout in top form. Age 67 at the time, Asmussen was still very much in his musical prime, as his versions of "Sweet Georgia Brown," "Lazy River," "A Pretty Girl Is Like a Melody" and "Careless Love" fully display. Recommended. —*Scott Yanow*

Phenomenal Fiddler / Aug. 27, 1996 / Phontastic ✦✦✦✦
The second of two Phontastic CDs that trace violinist Svend Asmussen's early years has a sampling of his recordings from the 1941-50 period. Despite the rise of bop during the era, the music is essentially all small-group swing, with a few novelty numbers (some of which use a rather average vocal group). Due to his spending virtually his entire life in Europe, Asmussen has long been greatly underrated. His playing on such numbers included on this set as "Ring Dem Bells," "Exactly Like You," "I've Found a New Baby" and "Dinah" shows that he was actually on the level of Stephane Grappelli; his backup musicians were also quite talented, if obscure. Easily recommended to swing collectors. —*Scott Yanow*

Fred Astaire (Frederick Austerlitz)

b. May 10, 1899, Omaha, NE, d. Jun. 22, 1987, Los Angeles, CA
Vocals, Dancer / Swing, Standards
Without question, one of the greatest all-around performers in motion picture history, though his vocal skills were among the least of his talents. Indeed, to overstate Astaire's average musical ability (as has become inexplicably common lately among certain jazz critics) only serves to demean his genius as a dancer. The extreme athleticism and rhythmic sophistication of his dance was masked by an air of off-handed suaveness that emphasized an utter control of his medium. That same delivery, transposed to song, revealed a genial, somewhat rhythmically astute, but ultimately unexceptional vocalist, whose limitations could not be hidden by strong material and/or a winning personality. Astaire's warbling mezzo tenor was little more than a slightly melodicized extension of his speaking voice—charming, perhaps, and certainly effective given the relatively low artistic standards of the run-of-the-mill Hollywood film, yet no more profound than one of their typically threadbare plots. Astaire himself had no illusions about his singing, either.

Astaire was practically born into vaudeville; he began on stage at the age of five with his sister Adele. Their collaboration produced a significant success on Broadway. It lasted into the '30s, when she gave up show business for marriage. An infamous screen test from 1932 (the evaluation of the studio functionary responsible supposedly read, "can't act, slightly bald, can dance a little") led to Astaire's teaming with Ginger Rogers. In the '30s they co-starred in a series of superficial but often quite witty musical comedies, such as *Roberta, Top Hat,* and *Shall We Dance?* Astaire's career as an actor continued fairly steadily until the early '80s. Astaire had (and continues to have) a great many admirers as a singer. Irving Berlin purportedly preferred Astaire's renditions of his tunes to those of any other vocalist. The most important songwriters of the '30s and '40s wrote songs especially for him—Berlin, Johnny Mercer, Cole Porter, and George Gershwin among them. He was often the first to sing songs that would become jazz standards, hence his tangential importance to jazz. Throughout his career, Astaire made recordings of pop material, often in the company of top-notch jazz instrumentalists. His 1950s album *Swings and Sings Irving Berlin* featured as sidemen pianist Oscar Peterson, trumpeter Charlie Shavers, and bassist Ray Brown. Astaire, however—to the extent that he was a musician—was a pop singer. The art of improvisation played a negligible role in his work, reason enough not to consider him a jazz musician. —*Chris Kelsey*

★ **Fred Astaire & Ginger Rogers at RKO** / 1933-1943 / Rhino ✦✦✦✦✦
Fred Astaire & Ginger Rogers is a stunning double-disc set featuring 35 tracks (including ten previously unreleased songs) culled from 11 musicals the pair made for RKO between 1933 and 1943, including *The Gay Divorcee, Swing Time, Flying Down to Rio, Top Hat* and *The Sky's the Limit.* The duo were at the height of their popularity and creativity during this era, and many of the songs that appeared in these films became standards including "A Needle in a Haystack," "Night and Day," "The Continental," "Top Hat, White Tie and Tails," "Cheek to Cheek," "Let's Begin," "I'll Be Hard to Handle," "I'm Putting All My Eggs in One Basket," "Let's Face the Music and Dance," "Pick Yourself Up," "The Way You Look Tonight," "A Fine Romance," "A Foggy Day," "Nice Work if You Can Get It," "Let's Call the Whole Thing Off," "They Can't Take That Away From Me" and "One for My Baby (And One More for the Road)." These are the versions that became popular through their appearances in movies, and while Astaire was limited as a singer, his voice was charming and helped make these songs the standards they are. And there is no better way to get his best, original versions than *Fred Astaire & Ginger Rogers at RKO.* —*Stephen Thomas Erlewine*

Fred Astaire at MGM / Oct. 16, 1933-Feb. 15, 1957 / Rhino ✦✦✦✦

● **Starring Fred Astaire** / Jun. 26, 1935-Sep. 22, 1940 / Columbia ✦✦✦✦✦
This 36-track double album traces Fred Astaire's recordings from June 1935 to September 1940, including his No.1 hits with "Cheek to Cheek," "I'm Putting All My Eggs in One Basket," "The Way You Look Tonight," "A Fine Romance," "They Can't Take That Away From Me," "Nice Work if You Can Get It," and "Change Partners." In addition to his movie stardom, Astaire was a major recording success in the second half of the '30s, introducing songs that would become standards by some of the great songwriters of the era—Irving Berlin, Jerome Kern and Dorothy Fields, and the Gershwins, especially. These recordings, which are studio efforts, not identical to the same songs in the movies, show Astaire to be as effortless a singer as he is a dancer (and you get to hear the tapping of those famous feet now and then, too). —*William Ruhlmann*

The Astaire Story / Dec. 1952 / Verve ✦✦✦✦✦
Because he was world renowned as a dancer and quite popular as a movie actor, Fred Astaire has tended to be underrated (if not completely overlooked) as a jazz singer. Although not really an improviser, Astaire's phrasing always swung and his occasional vocals on record were usually a joy. This two-CD set is something special for it features Astaire with six members of Jazz at the Philharmonic: tenor saxophonist Flip Phillips, trumpeter Charlie Shavers, pianist Oscar Peterson, guitarist Barney Kessel, bassist Ray Brown and drummer Alvin Stoller. Astaire sings 34 swing standards (many of which he had originally introduced in movies), dances on three ad-lib numbers and sits out on the instrumental "Jam Session"; the musicians have plenty of opportunities to stretch out. The biggest surprise to this classic deluxe box (which was originally four LPs) is that Fred Astaire did not do similar projects more often throughout his career. Highly recommended. —*Scott Yanow*

Eden Atwood

b. 1970, Memphis, TN
Vocals / Standards
A fine interpreter of lyrics, Eden Atwood started off her jazz career with a series of excellent recordings for Concord. Raised in Montana, Atwood studied drama and musical theater at college but became interested in jazz and at 19 she began singing locally. Although she worked as a model and an actress, Atwood has focused her attentions on singing; she made her debut in New York in 1992 and sings in a style somewhere between jazz and cabaret. —*Scott Yanow*

No One Ever Tells You / 1992 / Concord Jazz ✦✦✦✦
An excellent singer who swings and is at her best when interpreting superior lyrics (she does not improvise much), Eden Atwood's recording debut is quite impressive. Featured in a variety of settings ranging from duets with pianist Laurence Hobgood and Eldee Young to a nonet arranged by Jim Martin, Atwood excels on each of the 11 songs. High points include "I Didn't Know What Time It Was," "Is You Is or Is You Ain't My Baby," "Ballad of the Sad Young Men" and her own "Nothing's Changed." —*Scott Yanow*

Cat on a Hot Tin Roof / Oct. 1993 / Concord Jazz ✦✦✦✦
Eden Atwood is a young singer whose appeal sometimes compensates on her second Concord release for a few shortcomings. She has a clear and attractive voice and is at her best on ballads but occasionally (as on "Not While I'm Around") borders on being a cabaret singer. In contrast, on the uptempo mateiral her scatting and improvising skills are not fully mature nor all that adventurous. To her credit, she gives her sidemen (particularly Ken Peplowski on clarinet and tenor) plenty of solo space on the more cooking material. Atwood does write intelligent lyrics (best are "Silent Movie" and "Cat on a Hot Tin Roof"), is quite expressive on the ballads, and shows versatility, but at this point she does not stand apart from the crowd of young jazz vocalists. Her future progress should be worth watching though. —*Scott Yanow*

There Again / Dec. 7, 1994-Jan. 9, 1995 / Concord Jazz ✦✦
Eden Atwood has a lovely voice but this CD (which is dominated by ballads) features little improvising and much of the material has been overdone through the years. Her versions of "It Never Entered My Mind" (a song she is too young to sing) and "The Nearness of You" are far from definitive, Atwood interprets "Sonny Boy" with such seriousness that one wonders if she ever heard Al Jolson's version, and by speeding up "You're My Thrill" she drains that song of all its sensuality. Her rhythm section (pianist Dave Berkman, bassist Michael Moore and drummer Ron Vincent) is supportive without making an impression, while the guest appearances of pianist Marian McPartland and tenorman Chris Potter are not enough to uplift this set. Eden Atwood, 26 at the time of this recording (her third Concord CD) is fine as a middle-of-the-road pop singer but she will have to work on her improvising abilities before she can be taken all that seriously by the jazz world. —*Scott Yanow*

● **A Night in the Life** / Apr. 8, 1996-Apr. 22, 1996 / Concord Jazz ✦✦✦✦✦
Eden Atwood is occasionally reminiscent of Lee Wiley in her ability to bring jazz feeling to lyrics without actually improvising all that much. Atwood really understands the words that she interprets, and even when interpreting well-known tunes (as on this CD, when she sings "When the Sun Comes Out," "The Folks Who Live on the Hill" and "Spring Can Really Hang You up the Most"), she makes the music sound quite fresh and timely. Assisted by pianist Jeremy Kahn, bassist Larry Kohut, drummer Joel Spencer and (on four songs) the fiery tenor of Chris Potter, the young singer shows a great deal of maturity on this session; she takes a song apiece as a duet with each of her rhythm section mates, and even "Moon River" (which has her joined by just bassist Kohut) is a success. Recommended. —*Scott Yanow*

Georgie Auld (John Altwerger)

b. May 19, 1919, Toronto, Canada, **d.** Jan. 8, 1990, Palm Springs, CA
Tenor Saxophone / Swing, Bop
Georgie Auld had a long and varied career, changing his tenor sound gradually with the times and adapting to many different musical situations. He moved from Canada to the US in the late '20s and, although originally an altoist, he switched to tenor after hearing Coleman Hawkins. While with Bunny Berigan during 1937-8, Auld sounded like a dead ringer for Charlie Barnet. After spending a year with Artie Shaw in 1939 (including leading the band briefly after Shaw ran away to Mexico), Auld sounded much closer to Lester Young when he joined Benny Goodman. With BG, Auld was a major asset, jamming with a version of Goodman's Sextet that also included Cootie Williams and Charlie Christian. He was back with Shaw in 1942 and then led his own big band (1943-46), an excellent transitional unit between swing and bop that at various times included such young modernists as Dizzy Gillespie, Erroll Garner and Freddie Webster; Sarah Vaughan also guested on a couple of his recordings. After the band's breakup, Auld led some smaller groups that tended to be bop-oriented. He was with Count Basie's octet in 1950 and then freelanced for the remainder of his career, maintaining a lower profile but travelling frequently overseas and not losing his enthusiasm for jazz. Some may remember that in 1977 he had a small acting role as a bandleader and played Robert De Niro's tenor solos in the otherwise forgettable Liza Minelli movie *New York, New York.* —*Scott Yanow*

Jump, Georgie, Jump / Jan. 1940-Jul. 1945 / Hep ✦✦✦✦✦
This CD features the talented but underrated saxophonist Georgie Auld (heard on tenor, alto and soprano) during three different periods. When Artie Shaw tempo-

rarily fled from success to Mexico in late 1939, Auld took over his big band and tried his best to keep it together. In Jan. and Feb. 1940, the remnants of the Shaw Orchestra recorded ten titles (formerly quite obscure), and eight of those decent but not overly memorable dance band performances are included on this reissue. In addition, Auld is heard in 1944 at an extensive radio transcription session with his new big band (which features some rare solos from the ill-fated trumpeter Sonny Berman) and at a live date with his orchestra in 1945. The music from the later occasions is transitional, falling between swing and bop, and of consistently high quality. Well worth picking up. —*Scott Yanow*

Big Band Jazz 1945-1946 / Feb. 7, 1945-Oct. 23, 1945 / Musicraft ◆◆◆◆
The Georgie Auld big band of 1944-46 has generally been totally overlooked in jazz history books, due to its formation during the period when the swing era was ending. This first of two LPs put out by Discovery on their Musicraft subsidiary has 14 valuable performances by the fine orchestra. Among Auld's many interesting sidemen are Dizzy Gillespie (who guests on the first two sessions and takes notable solos on "In the Middle" and "Co-Pilot"), Al Killian, Errol Garner, Joe Albany, Serge Chaloff and Al Porcino (excellent on "Jump Georgie"). Auld (playing tenor, alto and soprano) consistently distinguishes himself, and even with a few forgettable vocals by Patti Powers, Lynn Stevens and one by Auld himself, the music (based in swing but looking toward bop) is quite enjoyable. —*Scott Yanow*

Georgie Auld Aand His Orchestra with Sarah Vaughan, Vol. 2 / Oct. 23, 1945-Jun. 14, 1946 / Musicraft ◆◆◆◆
The second of two Georgie Auld Musicraft LPs features his regular band of 1945-46, an interesting (and generally overlooked) outfit that included such sidemen as trumpeter Al Porcino, tenorman Al Cohn and baritonist Serge Chaloff. The modern orchestra features two early vocals by Sarah Vaughan (on "A Hundred Years from Today" and "You're Blasé") and a pair by Auld, who otherwise contributes many warm tenor solos. Fine transitional music between swing and bop. —*Scott Yanow*

● **In the Land of Hi-Fi** / Sep. 29, 1955-Nov. 11, 1955 / EmArcy ◆◆◆◆
For this set, tenor saxophonist Georgie Auld (whose last regular big band broke up in 1946) had a rare opportunity to front a larger group for a studio session. Using some of the West Coast's top players (including high-note trumpeter Maynard Ferguson, trumpet soloist Ray Linn, trombonist Frank Rosolino and pianist Arnold Ross), Auld sounds fine on a set of swing-based tunes. The music mixes together swing, bop and cool jazz in winning fashion; unfortunately, this LP (which is one in a series of "In the Land of Hi-Fi" releases by various artists) has not been reissued on CD yet. —*Scott Yanow*

Hawaii On the Rocks / 1959 / Jaro ◆◆◆◆
This is one of the best and most interesting "Hawaiian" records—actually exotic rock with an emphasis on Hawaiian standards—for a variety of reasons. First, George Auld is otherwise known as an orchestra leader and soloist. Second, records on the Jaro label are very rare, at least for this type of pop music. Third, personnel includes two steel guitarists, Candido Dimanlig and Dennis Regor; both men performed regularly at New York's Hawaiian Room in the Hotel Lexington. The twin steel players contribute heavily to a unique sound, but the arrangements, excellent performances, and mild rock tempo really set this album apart. "Song of India" and "The Sheik of Araby" can be considered exotic rock of a sort. Finally, the group has a little fun with "My Little Grass Shack in Kealakekua Hawaii," the fun-but-embarassing warhorse of tourist records in the 1950s. —*Tony Wilds*

Homage / Sep. 5, 1959 / Xanadu ◆◆◆◆
Tenor saxophonist Georgie Auld's career went through several phases. He was a member of one of Benny Goodman's finest small groups (his 1940-41 sextet with Charlie Christian and Cootie Williams), and on this fine session, he paid tribute to those days. Auld is heard teamed with the excellent trumpeter Don Fagerquist, guitarist Howard Roberts, pianist Lou Levy, vibraphonist Larry Bunker, bassist Leroy Vinnegar and drummer Mel Lewis on a dozen swing songs, most of which he originally recorded with the Benny Goodman Sextet. The treatments are a bit more modern (as much West Coast jazz as swing), and Benny Goodman's clarinet is replaced by vibes, but the musicians sometimes quote the original recordings in subtle ways. Highlights include "I Found a New Baby," "Seven Come Eleven," "Benny's Bugle" and "Flying Home." —*Scott Yanow*

Lovie Austin

b. Sep. 19, 1887, Chattanooga, TN, **d.** Jul. 10, 1972, Chicago, IL
Piano / Classic Jazz
One of the first important female bandleaders in jazz, Lovie Austin deserves to be much better known. After studying music in college, she toured on the vaudeville circuit, settling in Chicago in 1923. During 1924-26, she recorded frequently with her Blues Serenaders, a group that at various times had Tommy Ladnier, Bob Shoffner, Natty Dominique or Shirley Clay on cornet, Kid Ory or Albert Wynn on trombone and Jimmy O'Bryant or Johnny Dodds on clarinet along with banjo and

occasional drums. Fortunately, a Classics CD has collected together all of those recordings. Austin (as house pianist for Paramount) also backed many blues singers (including Ida Cox, Ma Rainey and Alberta Hunter). But after 1926, her recording activity largely came to a halt. Austin worked for 20 yers as the musical director for the Monogram Theatre and later on as a pianist at a dancing school, only returning to record in 1961 as part of Riverside's "Living Legends" series. Although mostly an ensemble pianist, Lovie Austin was a skilled arranger. —*Scott Yanow*

● **1924-1926** / Sep. 1924-Aug. 1926 / Classics ◆◆◆◆◆

Sil Austin

b. Sep. 17, 1929, Dunnellon, FL
Tenor Saxophone / Groove, East Coast Blues, Jump Blues
R&B tenor saxman and band leader Sil (Silvester) Austin won a talent show in 1946 at the Apollo theater in New York City for a version of "Danny Boy." In 1949, he worked with Roy Eldridge and then with Cootie Williams from 1949 to 1952. From 1953 to 1954 he was with Tiny Bradshaw. Ella Fitzgerald recorded Austin's composition "Ping Pong" and then gave him the title as a nickname. He later signed with Mercury and recorded with his own band. His R&B hits include "Slow Walk." —*Michael Erlewine*

Slow Rock Rock / Oct. 15, 1956-Oct. 19, 1956 / Wing ◆◆◆◆
● **Sil Austin Plays Pretty for the People** / 1960 / Mercury ◆◆◆◆

Teodross Avery

b. Jul. 2, 1973, Fairfield, CA
Tenor Saxophone / Hard Bop
A promising young tenor saxophonist, Teodross Avery made his recording debut as a leader on GRP when he was a few days short of turning 21. He had studied classical guitar when he was ten, switched to alto at 13, and a few years later took up the tenor. Avery studied with Joe Henderson, attended Berklee, and soon was leading his own group. In 1993 he appeared on a Carl Allen record and then utilized his quartet on his GRP debut. —*Scott Yanow*

In Other Words / Jun. 27, 1994-Jun. 29, 1994 / GRP ◆◆◆
Teodross Avery, a few days shy of turning 21 at the time of his GRP release, sounds quite mature on his debut as a leader. His tenor tone is attractive, his style is very influenced by Joe Henderson and John Coltrane and he is surprisingly relaxed on the ballads. Avery contributed nine of the 11 selections (all but "What's New" and Wayne Shorter's "Edda"). Three of the songs find trumpeter Roy Hargrove making the group a quintet. The music is very much in the hard bop vein and nothing too innovative or unexpected occurs, but this is an impressive initial effort from Teodross Avery who will hopefully have a long and productive career. —*Scott Yanow*

● **My Generation** / Oct. 10, 1995-Oct. 12, 1995 / Impulse! ◆◆◆◆
Young saxophonist Teodross Avery's latest recording covers a lot of ground, from explorative improvisations that sound as if they really belong on Impulse to selections that use a funky (and even a light hip-hop) rhythm and a straightforward ("Mr. Wonsey") boppish blues. Avery has strong technique and his sound, particularly on tenor (where he hints at Stanley Turrentine and to a lesser extent Sonny Stitt), is gradually becoming personal. He is joined by bassist Rodney Whitaker and drummer Greg Hutchinson on every selection along with either John Scofield, Mark Whitfield, or Peter Bernstein on guitar or pianist Charles Craig. Of the supporting crew, only Scofield (who creates some very unusual and distorted sounds on his guitar during "Theme for Malcolm") makes much of an impression and Avery seems to be most comfortable with the pianist (who is on four of the 11 selections). "Lover Man" sounds surprisingly passionless (showing that Avery is not yet mature enough to uplift veteran ballads) and there is an annoying (and meaningless) 35-second rap on the title cut that lowers the quality of the record. The overall results are generally enjoyable if not all that memorable or unique. —*Scott Yanow*

Roy Ayers

b. Sep. 10, 1940, Los Angeles, CA
Vibes / Instrumental Pop, Soul Jazz
Once one of the most visible and winning jazz vibraphonists of the 1960s, then an R&B bandleader in the 1970s and '80s, Roy Ayers' reputation in the 1990s is now that of one of the prophets of acid jazz, a man decades ahead of his time. A tune like 1972's "Move to Groove" by the Roy Ayers Ubiquity has a crackling backbeat that serves as the prototype for the shuffling hip-hop groove that became, shall we say, ubiquitous on acid jazz records—and his relaxed 1976 song "Everybody Loves the Sunshine" has been frequently sampled. Yet Ayers' own playing has always been rooted in hard bop—crisp, lyrical, rhythmically resilient. His own reaction to

being canonized by the hip-hop crowd as the "Icon Man" is tempered with the detachment of a survivor in a rough business. "I'm having fun laughing with it," he has said. "I don't mind what they call me, that's what people do in this industry."

Growing up in a musical family—his father played trombone, his mother taught him the piano—the five-year-old Ayers was given a set of vibe mallets by Lionel Hampton, but didn't start on the instrument until he was 17. He got involved in the West Coast jazz scene in his early 20s, recording with Curtis Amy (1962), Jack Wilson (1963-67), and the Gerald Wilson Orchestra (1965-66), and playing with Teddy Edwards, Chico Hamilton, Hampton Hawes and Phineas Newborn. A session with Herbie Mann at the Lighthouse in Hermosa Beach led to a four-year gig with the versatile flutist (1966-70), an experience that gave Ayers tremendous exposure and opened his ears to styles of music other than the bebop that he had grown up with.

After being featured prominently on Mann's hit *Memphis Underground* album and recording three solo albums for Atlantic under Mann's supervision, Ayers left the group in 1970 to form the Roy Ayers Ubiquity, which recorded several albums for Polydor and featured such players as Sonny Fortune, Billy Cobham, Omar Hakim and Alphonse Mouzon. An R&B-jazz-rock band influenced by electric Miles Davis and the Herbie Hancock Sextet at first, the Ubiquity gradually shed its jazz component in favor of R&B/funk and disco. Though Ayers' pop records were commercially successful, with several charted singles on the R&B charts in Polydor and Columbia, they became increasingly, perhaps correspondingly, devoid of musical interest.

In the 1980s, besides leading his bands and recording, Ayers collaborated with Nigerian musician Fela Anikulapo-Kuti, formed Uno Melodic Records, and produced and/or co-wrote several recordings for various artists. As the merger of hip-hop and jazz took hold in the early '90s, Ayers made a guest appearance on Guru's seminal *Jazzmatazz* album in 1993 and played at New York clubs with Guru and Donald Byrd. Though most of his solo records have been out of print for years, Verve has recently issued a two-CD anthology of his work with Ubiquity and the first US release of a live gig at the 1972 Montreux Jazz Festival that finds the group playing excellent straightahead jazz, as well as jazz-rock and R&B. —*Richard S. Ginell*

Virgo Vibes / Jan. 18, 1967-Mar. 6, 1967 / Atlantic ♦♦♦
Long before he switched to playing disco and pop music, Roy Ayers was considered a promising young jazz vibraphonist. This LP, his second as a leader, was one of his finest. On four of the five selections (obscurities and pieces by group members), Ayers teams up with trumpeter Charles Tolliver, tenor saxophonist Joe Henderson, bassist Reggie Workman, drummer Bruno Carr and the mysterious pianist Ronnie Clark (Herbie Hancock under a disguised name). On "Glow Flower," Ayers and Tolliver are joined by Harold Land on tenor, pianist Jack Wilson, bassist Buster Williams and drummer Donald Bailey. The music is primarily advanced hard bop with some freer moments on Tolliver's "The Ringer." This underrated music is long overdue to be reissued on CD and displays Roy Ayers' lost potential. —*Scott Yanow*

Daddy Bug & Friends / Mar. 6, 1967-Dec. 11, 1969 / Atlantic ♦♦♦♦
During 1967-69, vibraphonist Roy Ayers (a few years before he turned to disco music) recorded three excellent albums for Atlantic. This 1976 LP has selections from two of the records, plus a pair of selections ("In the Limelight" and "Virgo Vibes") that were previously unreleased. On this fine sampler, Ayers' sidemen include Herbie Hancock, Joe Henderson, Charles Tolliver and Ron Carter. "Slow Motion," the latest selection (from Dec. 1969), hints at the commercial direction that Ayers would be emphasizing from 1970 on. —*Scott Yanow*

● **Evolution: the Polydor Anthology** / 1970-1978 / Polydor Chronicles ♦♦♦♦
Containing several first-rate cuts of funky soul jazz, *Evolution* captures many of the highlights from Roy Ayers' stint with Polydor Records during the '70s. —*Stephen Thomas Erlewine*

The Best Of . . . Love Fantasy / 1970-1979 / Polydor ♦♦♦♦
Vibist Roy Ayers' proto-acid jazz is collected on this best-of-compilation, which features performances of "Running Away," "Don't Stop the Feeling," "What You Won't Do for Love" and "Mystic Voyage." —*Jason Ankeny*

Ubiquity / 1971 / Polydor ♦♦♦
Start of Ubiquity phase; best of funk with R&B-jazz. —*Ron Wynn*

Live at the Montreux Jazz Festival / Jun. 20, 1972 / Verve ♦♦♦
This is a session that crosses a lot of musical boundaries. Roy Ayers is best known for being a promising hard bop vibraphonist in the 1960s and for his disco/funk records of the mid- to late '70s (many of which have been sampled in recent times). His 1972 Montreux appearance is somewhere in between. The music ranges from lightly funky grooves that could have fit well on Pharoah Sanders' records of the period to a couple of lightweight vocals and interesting explorations of "In a Silent Way" and "Raindrops Keep Fallin' on My Head." Ayers' vibes are a pleasing element of the music and he gets off some strong solos although nothing

all that substantial occurs during the generally dated effort, a quartet outing with keyboardist Harry Whitaker, bassist Clint Houston and drummer David Lee. —*Scott Yanow*

● **Mystic Voyage** / 1975 / Polydor ♦♦♦♦
Nice outing, although there's minimal jazz content. Ayers, once a Downbeat New Star winner, decided at end of the '60s to forego the rigors of straight jazz life and investigate the world of funk and R&B. He would (and still does) dabble back into light soul-jazz, but has become far more known for his funk and R&B releases like this one. —*Ron Wynn*

Albert Ayler

b. Jul. 13, 1936, Cleveland, OH, d. Nov. 5, 1970, New York, NY
Tenor Saxophone, Alto Saxophone / Free Jazz, Avant-Garde
One of the giants of free jazz, Albert Ayler was also one of the most controversial. His huge tone and wide vibrato were difficult to ignore and his 1966 group sounded like a runaway New Orleans brass band from 1910. It could be said of Ayler's music that he was so far advanced that he came in at jazz's beginning!

Unlike John Coltrane or Eric Dolphy, Albert Ayler was not a virtuoso who had come up through the bebop ranks. His first musical jobs were in R&B bands, including one led by Little Walter, although oddly enough he was nicknamed "Little Bird" in his early days because of a similarity in sound on alto to Charlie Parker. During his period in the army (1958-61) he played in a service band and switched to tenor. Unable to find work in the US after his discharge due to his uncompromising style, Ayler spent time in Sweden and Denmark during 1962-63, making his first recordings (which reveal a tone with roots in Sonny Rollins) and working a bit with Cecil Taylor. Ayler's prime period was during 1964-67. In 1964 he toured Europe with a quartet that included Don Cherry and was generally quite free and emotional. The following year he had a new band with his brother Donald Ayler on trumpet and Charles Tyler on alto, and the emphasis in his music began to change. Folk melodies (which had been utilized a bit with Cherry) had a more dominant role as did collective improvisation and yet, despite the use of spaced-out marches, Irish jigs and brass-band fanfares, tonally Ayler remained quite free. His ESP recordings from this era and his first couple of Impulses find Ayler at his peak and were influential; John Coltrane's post-1964 playing was definitely affected by Ayler's innovations. However, during his last couple of years Albert Ayler's career seemed to become a bit aimless and his final Impulse sessions, although experimental (with the use of vocals, rock guitar and R&Bish tunes), were at best mixed successes. A 1970 live concert that was documented features him back in top form, but in November 1970 Ayler was found drowned in New York's East River under mysterious circumstances. —*Scott Yanow*

Albert Ayler: The First Recordings, Vol. 1 / Oct. 25, 1962 / GNP Crescendo ♦♦
The problem with the trio recordings heard on this LP is that bassist Torbjorn Hultcrantz and drummer Sune Spangberg sound as if they are completely ignoring what tenor saxophonist Albert Ayler is playing. While Ayler improvises quite freely on a lengthy "I'll Remember April" and versions of "Rollins' Tune," "Tune Up" and his original "Free," Ayler's sidemen just play conventionally, never reacting to the tenor's flights or any of his ideas. It is a pity, for the lack of interplay weighs down what could have been an innovative outing. The second half of this interesting but flawed session has been released on CD by the Japanese DIW label. —*Scott Yanow*

Albert Ayler: The First Recordings, Vol. 2 / Oct. 25, 1962 / DIW ♦♦
This should have been a memorable and possibly innovative session since this CD reissue features the avant-garde tenor saxophonist Albert Ayler interpreting four standards ("Softly as in a Morning Sunrise," "I Didn't Know What Time It Was," "Moanin'" and "Good Bait"). Unfortunately, the Swedish sidemen (bassist Torbjorn Hultcrantz and drummer Sune Spangberg) completely ignore what Ayler is playing and just act as if they were backing a conventional bop musician. The lack of communication between the musicians defeats this effort, although Ayler collectors will find the results quite interesting. —*Scott Yanow*

My Name Is Albert Ayler / Jan. 14, 1963 / Fantasy ♦♦♦
This Black Lion CD reissue brings back a session originally on Fantasy, Albert Ayler's second recording. The avant-garde tenor saxophonist is featured in Copenhagen with a quartet consisting of pianist Niels Bronsted, bassist Niels Pedersen (who was 16 at the time) and drummer Ronnie Gardiner. The set definitely has its interesting aspects even though the rhythm section essentially sticks to bebop; one is reminded of Eric Dolphy jamming with the Latin Jazz Quintet or Anthony Braxton performing with Tete Montoliu, in that Ayler's sidemen mostly seem to be ignoring what he is playing. The opening introduction (which lasts just 75 seconds) gives listeners a rare chance to hear Ayler's voice as he talks briefly about his background. "Bye Bye Blackbird" is hurt a bit by Ayler's out-of-tune soprano (otherwise he sticks to tenor) but on "Billie's Bounce" he shows off his roots in Sonny Rollins, "Summertime" finds him breaking boundaries in his willingness to

display intense emotions and he fares well on an explorative version of "On Green Dolphin Street." On "CT" (dedicated to Cecil Taylor), Ayler, Pedersen and Gardiner (Bronsted sits this one out) play quite freely and the musical communication between the players for once is strong. This may not be one of Albert Ayler's most significant sessions but the historic reissue should interest collectors of early avant-garde jazz. —*Scott Yanow*

Goin' Home / Feb. 24, 1964 / Black Lion ✦✦✦
1964 was a busy year on records for avant-garde tenor Albert Ayler and it began with this unusual set. Imagine hearing Ayler play "When the Saints Go Marching In"; did Wild Bill Davison ever record "Ghosts"? Assisted by pianist Call Cobbs, bassist Henry Grimes and drummer Sonny Murray, Ayler plays seven unlikely folk melodies including an overly emotional "Ol' Man River," "Swing Low, Sweet Chariot" and "Nobody Knows the Trouble I've Seen." The high point is a jubilant "Down by the Riverside" on which Ayler sounds surprisingly close to Rahsaan Roland Kirk both in tone and ideas. This CD reissue adds the two versions of "Riverside" plus a pair of other alternate takes to the original program and is certainly more accessible than most of Ayler's recordings. —*Scott Yanow*

Witches and Devils / Feb. 24, 1964 / Freedom ✦✦✦✦
This album was recorded the same day as a lyrical spiritual album, and on this session, tenor saxophonist Albert Ayler really lets his emotions loose. Teamed with primitive trumpeter Norman Howard, Henry Grimes and/or Earle Henderson on bass and drummer Sunny Murray, Ayler plays quite freely on his four originals, "Witches and Devils" (a dirge), "Spirits," the melodic "Holy Holy" and "Saints." The often-intense music (which has been reissued on CD) is not for everyone, and this is one of Ayler's more forbidding releases, but open-eared listeners will find these radical explorations quite colorful. —*Scott Yanow*

Prophecy / Jun. 14, 1964 / ESP ✦✦✦
The first of Albert Ayler's ESP recordings (but one of the last to be released) is this live session with bassist Gary Peacock and drummer Sunny Murray. The tenor is heard on the earliest versions of his most famous theme "Ghosts" (two renditions are included), along with such melodies as "Spirits," "Wizard" and "Prophecy." Ayler alternated the simple march-like themes with wild and very free improvisations that owe little if anything to the bop tradition or even his contemporaries in the avant-garde. Ayler always had his own individual message and his ESP sessions find him in consistently explorative form. —*Scott Yanow*

Spiritual Unity / Jul. 10, 1964 / ESP ✦✦✦✦
Tenor saxophonist Albert Ayler seemed to burst onto the scene in 1964, playing heated free-form solos that put an emphasis on emotion over melodic development. Ironically, many of his themes (particularly "Ghosts," which is heard twice on this brief set) were quite catchy, reminiscent of pre-1910 folk music, but his improvisations need an open mind for one to fully appreciate them. On this ESP date (reissued on CD but under a half hour long), Ayler also performs "The Wizard" and "Spirits" with bassist Gary Peacock and drummer Sunny Murray. The intense music has not lost any of its fire through the decades. —*Scott Yanow*

New York Eye and Ear Control / Jul. 17, 1964 / ESP ✦✦✦
This is a very interesting set, music that was freely improvised and used as the soundtrack for the 34-minute short film *New York Eye and Ear Control*. Tenor saxophonist Albert Ayler leads the all-star sextet (which also includes trumpeter Don Cherry, altoist John Tchicai, trombonist Roswell Rudd, bassist Gary Peacock and drummer Sunny Murray) on two lengthy jams. The music is fiery but with enough colorful moments to hold one's interest throughout. —*Scott Yanow*

Vibrations / Sep. 14, 1964 / Freedom ✦✦✦✦
1964 was a busy year for Albert Ayler, who recorded at least seven albums worth of material. This particular session, a quartet date with trumpeter Don Cherry, bassist Gary Peacock and drummer Sunny Murray, was probably his most significant of the period. Switching between tenor and alto, Ayler is often ferocious on the six performances, jumping from simple melodies (of which "Ghosts" is the most memorable) to intense sound explorations overflowing with emotion; he even makes Cherry seem conservative. It helps greatly to have open ears to appreciate this music, although Ayler's jams would become a bit more accessible the following year. Recommended. —*Scott Yanow*

The Hilversum Session / Nov. 9, 1964 / Osmosis ✦✦✦
The first part of Albert Ayler's career found the tenor saxophonist playing rather violent solos and searching for the right sidemen to interact with. This set (recorded in the Netherlands) features Ayler with a fairly ideal group: a quartet with cornetist Don Cherry, bassist Gary Peacock and drummer Sunny Murray. Together they perform five of Ayler's themes (including "Ghosts") along with Cherry's "Infant Happiness." It's not for the faint of heart. —*Scott Yanow*

Bells: At Town Hall / May 1, 1965 / ESP ✦✦✦
Albert Ayler teamed up with his brother, trumpeter Donald Ayler, on this record for the first time, with the exception of one slightly earlier track issued on an

Impulse sampler. The concert performance with both Aylers, Charles Tyler on alto, bassist Lewis Worrell and drummer Sunny Murray is their entire 20-minute set from a Town Hall concert and originally came out as a one-sided LP (with the flip-side being blank). What is here is quite interesting, with some ferocious ensembles, military-like themes (most of the music is taken up by "Holy Ghost") and a couple of tenor solos from Albert. This music should have been combined with some other dates so the release would not be so ridiculously brief, but it's worth getting (if found at a budget price) anyway. —*Scott Yanow*

Spirits Rejoice / Sep. 1965 / ESP ✦✦✦✦
Tenor saxophonist Albert Ayler's 1965 group (with trumpeter Donald Ayler, altoist Charles Tyler, both Henry Grimes and Gary Peacock on basses, drummer Sunny Murray and an appearance by Call Cobbs on harpsichord) is a fairly strong and sometimes riotous effort. As is often true of the ESP releases, the playing time is brief (32 minutes), but the quality of the free-form improvisations is high and the music is somewhat groundbreaking while always being stimulating. —*Scott Yanow*

At Slug's Saloon, Vol. 1 / May 1, 1966 / ESP ✦✦✦✦
One of two CDs that originated from the Albert Ayler Quintet's May Day 1966 appearance at Slug's in New York, this is the better of the pair although Ayler fans will want both. The leader's tenor is both melodic and ferocious in spots and his group (with trumpeter Donald Ayler, violinist Michel Sampson, bassist Lewis Worrell and drummer Ronald Shannon Jackson was one of his finest. The adventurous performances of lengthy versions of "Truth Is Marching In," "Our Prayer" and "Bells" often sound a bit like a runaway turn-of-the-century marching band and, although the droning violin sometimes gets in the way, the spirit of this rambunctious and often-wild set is memorable. —*Scott Yanow*

At Slug's Saloon, Vol. 2 / May 1, 1966 / ESP ✦✦✦
The second of two CDs from the Albert Ayler Quintet's engagement at Slug's on May 1, 1966 has long versions of "Ghosts" (over 23 minutes) and "Initiation" performed by the tenor-leader, trumpeter Donald Ayler, violinist Michel Sampson, bassist Lewis Worrell and drummer Ronald Shannon Jackson. The music is both futuristic (with extroverted emotions expressed in free improvisations) and ancient (New Orleans marching band rhythms, group riffing and folkish melodies). Although *Vol. 1* gets the edge, most avant-garde collectors will want both releases. —*Scott Yanow*

Live at Lorrach: Paris, 1966 / Nov. 7, 1966+Nov. 13, 1966 / Hat Art ✦✦✦✦✦
Originally released as a double LP (with the second half being a 45), this single CD finds tenor saxophonist Albert Ayler in top form in 1966. At the time, his music could be considered to have been so advanced that it came in at the beginning of jazz. The folk melodies and some of the ensembles sound very much like an out-of-control New Orleans brass band circa 1900, yet the individual improvisations are as explorative as any heard in free jazz. Ayler heads a quintet with his brother Donald on trumpet, violinist Michel Sampson (whose sawing often sets a drone effect), bassist William Folwell and drummer Beaver Harris. Together they perform two versions of "Ghosts" and such group originals as "Bells," "Jesus," "Our Prayer," "Spirits," "Holy Ghost" and "Holy Family." Due to the accessible nature of some of the melodies, this is the perfect place for open-eared listeners unfamiliar with Albert Ayler's unique music to start. —*Scott Yanow*

In Greenwich Village / Dec. 18, 1966+Feb. 26, 1967 / Impulse! ✦✦✦✦
During 1967-69 avant-garde innovator Albert Ayler recorded a series of albums for Impulse that started on a high level and gradually declined in quality. This LP, Ayler's first Impulse set, was probably his best for that label. There are two selections apiece from a pair of live appearances with Ayler having a rare outing on alto on the emotional "For John Coltrane" and the more violent "Change Has Come" while backed by cellist Joel Friedman, both Alan Silva and Bill Folwell on basses and drummer Beaver Harris. The other set (with trumpeter Donald Ayler, violinist Michel Sampson, Folwell and Henry Grimes on basses and Harris) has a strong contrast between the simple childlike melodies and the intense solos. However this LP (which was augmented later on by the two-LP set *The Village Concerts*) will be difficult to find. —*Scott Yanow*

Albert Ayler: The Village Concerts, Vol. 7 / Dec. 18, 1966-Feb. 26, 1967 / ABC/ Impulse! ✦✦✦✦
On this two-LP set, the avant-garde innovator Albert Ayler is heard in top form. The tenor saxophonist, teamed with his brother trumpeter Donald Ayler, violinist Michel Sampson, two bassists, drummer Beaver Harris and sometimes cellist Joel Freedman, really stretches out on these often-melodic and occasionally violent improvisations. Ayler stretched free jazz to the breaking point, yet his use of simple melodies during this phase of his career, in conjunction with Donald Ayler's primitive trumpet, often recalled the sound of a very early New Orleans brass band. Sampson's violin does not really fit in and sounds a bit jarring, but otherwise this is one of Ayler's strongest recordings. —*Scott Yanow*

Love Cry / Aug. 31, 1967 / Impulse! ✦✦✦✦

The strongest of his Impulse recordings (all of which are from the last part of his career), this set avoids the weak attempts at commercialism that plagued most of Ayler's other Impulses. The CD reissue, in addition to the eight original tracks (all but one four minutes long and "Universal Indians" now restored to its unedited full length) also adds three additional tracks. Ayler's three vocals are a bit difficult to sit through, but his tenor and alto solos (along with those of trumpeter Donald Ayler) are worthwhile even if the use of Call Cobbs on harpsichord comes across as merely eccentric. —*Scott Yanow*

New Grass / Sep. 5, 1968+Sep. 6, 1968 / Impulse! ✦✦

This LP (which has not yet been reissued on CD) attempts to combine the avant-garde tenor of Albert Ayler with R&B and the results are quite a mess. Ayler himself sings a bit, over half of the selections feature an unidentified vocal group called the Soul Singers, and the use of a horn section on several tracks sounds very dated. There are a few moments of interest (particularly "New Ghosts," a remake of "Ghosts"), but in general, this attempt at commercialism flops. —*Scott Yanow*

The Last Album / Aug. 26, 1969 / Impulse! ✦✦

Despite the title, this was not Albert Ayler's final album. *Music Is the Healing Force* was recorded at the same sessions (although it came out first) and a concert from a year later was released on two albums. In any case this date is a bit infamous due to the R&Bish material and a few throwaway tracks. Albert Ayler, an important avant-garde tenor innovator, plays bagpipes on a weird duet with the rock guitarist Henry Vestine, takes an odd vocal on "Desert Blood," backs Mary Maria's singing on "Again Comes the Rising of the Sun" and does what he can on a few passionate but weak instrumentals; Ayler sounds as if he had definitely lost his way. This album is of more interest for its novelty value and historical importance than it is musically. —*Scott Yanow*

Music Is the Healing Force of the Universe / Aug. 26, 1969-Aug. 29, 1969 / Impulse! ✦✦

At a peak of experimentation, Ayler used bagpipes, blues instrumentals, and vocals to expand his challenging sound and keep his music at the center of controversy. —*Myles Boisen*

● **Fondation Maeght Nights, Vol. 1** / Jul. 25, 1970-Jul. 27, 1970 / Jazz View ✦✦✦✦✦

A little over three months before he was found drowned, Ayler was caught performing in concert at the height of his powers. Unlike his Impulse releases which often featured him trying to incorporate commercial elements into his music, the release from the European label Jazz View (the first of two CDs) allows Ayler to stretch out and "preach" in his emotional and unique style with just sparse backing (pianist Call Cobbs, bassist Steve Tintweiss and drummer Allen Blairman). This and the second volume would be Albert Ayler's final recordings and are quite memorable. —*Scott Yanow*

Fondation Maeght Nights, Vol. 2 / Jul. 27, 1970 / Jazz View ✦✦✦✦

While the avant-gardist's later Impulse albums were erratic and half-hearted attempts at commercialism, his final recordings (two CDs recorded live in concert) feature him in peak form. Ayler, one of the most controversial of free jazz players of the 1960s, has rarely sounded more viable or creative than on these special recordings. *Vol. 2*, as with the first set, finds him stretching out on four of his free yet melodic originals. Both sets are recommended. —*Scott Yanow*

Azymuth

f. 1971, Brazil

Group / Contemporary Funk, Brazilian Jazz, Fusion

Azymuth is an electrified trio from Brazil who call their music *samba doido*, which means "crazy samba." The actual sounds, though, are not so crazy—an intelligent, high-voltage blend of Brazilian rhythms, jazz and funk with occasional acoustic episodes that gained a sizable following in the 1980s. The members of the group included Jose Roberto Bertrami (b. Feb. 21, 1946, Tatui, Brazil) on acoustic piano and keyboards, Alex Malheiros (b. Aug. 19, 1946, Niteroi, Brazil) on bass, and Ivan Conti (b. Aug. 16, 1946, Rio de Janeiro, Brazil) on drums.

Classically trained and originally influenced by pianists Bill Evans and Luiz Eca (of the Tamba 4), Bertrami worked with Flora Purim and Robertinho Silva before meeting Conti at a Rio nightclub. Upon a visit to a bowling alley/club in 1972, they heard Malheiros and decided to join forces to form Azymuth. Their first album, the soundtrack for the film *O Fabuloso Fittipaldi*, was released in Brazil in 1973. After spending a number of years as sessionmen in Rio recording studios and touring South America, a successful appearance at the 1977 Montreux Jazz Festival led to a 1978 US tour with Airto and Purim. A contract with Milestone in 1979 resulted in a long string of eclectic albums—some of which are still available on

CD—that established the group in the American and European markets. All three members also recorded solo albums for Milestone (now out of print). Bertrani left the group around 1988, after which Malheiros and Conti carried on for a while with keyboardist Jota Moraes. In the '90s, Bertrami rejoined Azymuth for sporadic appearances, though their profile isn't as high in the US as it once was. —*Richard S. Ginell*

Light As a Feather / 1979 / Black Sun ✦✦✦

A 1990 release that is good; close to retaining the spirit of the original *Return to Forever*. —*Ron Wynn*

Outubro / 1980 / Black Sun ✦✦✦

Telecommunication / 1982 / Milestone ✦✦✦

A mixed bag that has more strengths than weaknesses, *Telecommunication* demonstrates Azymuth's ability to occasionally get into trouble when resorting to high-tech gimmickry for its own sake, but also illustrates how rewarding the Brazilian trio can be. With its vocoder-ish gimmickry, the funk-influenced "May I Have This Dance" is a dated and corny bit of silliness unworthy of Azymuth. But there's also much to admire on this CD, including the haunting "The House I Lived In," the sensuous "Country Road," and the sentimental "Last Summer in Rio." Though keyboardist/pianist Jose Roberto Bertrami and bassist/guitarist Alex Malheiros don't always stretch out enough, the results are quite appealing when they do. —*Alex Henderson*

Cascades / Aug. 1982 / Milestone ✦✦✦

One of their better numbers. —*Ron Wynn*

Rapid Transit / 1983 / Milestone ✦✦✦

1983 session, better than usual. —*Ron Wynn*

● **Flame** / Mar. 1984+Apr. 1984 / Milestone ✦✦✦✦✦

The one to get. Flora Purim (v) joins them and things move up a notch. —*Ron Wynn*

Spectrum / Feb. 1985-May 1985 / Milestone ✦✦

1985 date, some good playing. —*Ron Wynn*

Tightrope Walker / Apr. 1986+May 1986 / Milestone ✦✦

1987 session, standard stuff. —*Ron Wynn*

Crazy Rhythm / Jan. 1987-Oct. 1987 / Milestone ✦✦✦✦✦

With *Crazy Rhythm*, Azymuth may well have recorded its best album ever by rejecting any type of gimmickry and focusing on what it does best—sensuous, understated yet rhythmically exciting Brazilian jazz/pop/R&B. Brazilian artists have often been quite adept at creating music that has light and delicate qualities, but never degenerates into "elevator muzak." Like the bossa nova of the '60s, *Crazy Rhythm* is "easy listening" music with a difference—some of it was soft enough for airplay on "quiet storm" and "smooth jazz" radio, but nothing on this CD comes across as contrived or calculated. Jose Roberto Bertrami delivers one of the finest solos of his career on the beautiful and enchanting "Diza," and special guest Joe Pass (guitar) is in fine form on "Tropical Horizon" and "Hobalala." —*Alex Henderson*

Carioca / Nov. 1987+Dec. 1988 / Milestone ✦✦✦

Carioca would be a swan song of sorts for Azymuth—the last album for keyboardist/leader Jose Roberto Bertrami, who left the group around this time, and their last album for Milestone, which spelled the beginning of the end for them as players in the US music scene. Indeed, Bertrami doesn't even include his longtime cohorts Alex Malheiros and Ivan Conti on the lovely waltz tune "Valsa Se Uma Cidade," or the smooth showcase for Hammond organ, "Guaratiba," preferring the solid, mobile work of guests Paulo Russo (bass) and Jurim Moreira (drums). The selections with Malheiros and Conti are often more reflective than much of Azymuth's past work, with a few references to American funk ("Toque De Cuica") and fewer overtly Brazilian rhythmic influences (Malheiros' nicely soft-focused "Bom Tempo" being a nice exception). In sum, a handsome if diffuse farewell performance right down to Bertrami's brief solo piano postlude and the cryptic inscription at the bottom of the list of credits—"P.S. The End." —*Richard S. Ginell*

Carumim / Jan. 1990 / Intima ✦✦

Though not a bad album, *Curumim* was far from Azymuth's finest hour. Longtime keyboardist Jose Roberto Bertrami is gone, replaced by the less imaginative Jota Moraes—and his contributions as a composer, soloist and producer are sorely missed. While the CD contains some attractive melodies, heartfelt improvisation is in short supply this time. For the most part, this material never really soars. *Curumim* does have its moments—including the somewhat Return to Forever-ish "Homem" and the tender title song. But for those checking out Azymuth for the first time, *Crazy Rhythm* would be a much wiser investment. —*Alex Henderson*

B

B Sharp Jazz Quartet

f. 1990
Group / Post-Bop
The B Sharp Jazz Quartet made a strong impression with their recordings for the MAMA Foundation label. Consisting of drummer Herb Graham, Jr., Randall Willis on reeds, pianist Eliot Douglass (later replaced by Rodney Lee) and bassist Reggie Carson, the L.A.-based group plays advanced hard bop that looks towards the avant-garde but always swings. This group has a lot of potential. —*Scott Yanow*

● **B Sharp Jazz Quartet** / 1994 / MAMA ♦♦♦♦
The 1994 debut by the B Sharp Jazz Quartet is quite impressive. The L.A.-based group, whose roots are in hard bop while being very open to the influences of the avant-garde, performs nine originals plus John Coltrane's "Naima." Comprising drummer Herb Graham, Jr., saxophonist Randall Willis, pianist Eliot Douglass and bassist Reggie Carson, the quartet creates a wide-ranging and colorful set that is well worth picking up. —*Scott Yanow*

Mirage / Jun. 3, 1995-Jun. 4, 1995 / MAMA ♦♦♦
The second recording by the B Sharp Jazz Quartet, one of the more creative regularly working jazz units based in Los Angeles, is as interesting for its departures as for the bulk of its performances. Three of the nine selections are a bit unusual. On "The Velvet Touch" guest singer Carmen Bradford vocalizes wordlessly and matches wits quite favorably with the tenor of Randall Willis. Joe Henderson's "Inner Urge" is given a light funk rhythm along with some atmospheric organ from Rodney Lee and, although it does not live up to its potential, it hints at possible innovations. Also the closing "C.R.S." has an African-flavored group vocal by the band along with Carmen Bradford. Otherwise the music is more conventional. Best are the driving "Beside Jo'Self," "Mirage" and Freddie Hubbard's "Intrepid Fox." In contrast "Spirit of J.C." is a disappointment, lacking the passion one would expect from a song with its title. In general this is an excellent session even though some of the music sounds as if the B Sharp Quartet (which also includes drummer Herb Graham, Jr. and bassist Reggie Carson) is treading water a bit. —*Scott Yanow*

Searching for the One / May 14, 1996-May 16, 1996 / MAMA ♦♦♦♦
On their third release for the MAMA Foundation, the B Sharp Jazz Quartet was clearly looking to stretch their appeal beyond a jazz audience. The opening and closing verbal narrations are rather forgettable if harmless and a few of the numbers are more groove-oriented than one might expect. However the band has not given up its left-of-center nature and there are plenty of stirring improvisations by Randall Willis (doubling on tenor and soprano) and pianist-organist Rodney Lee while bassist Osama Afifi and drummer Herb Graham, Jr. (who co-leads the group with Willis) offer fine support. Most memorable are such originals as "Twelve Tone Blue," "How Dare You," "Church Bells" and the brooding "Nami." —*Scott Yanow*

Tha Go 'Round / May 27, 1997-May 29, 1997 / MAMA ♦♦♦♦
The strongest recording by B Sharp to date, this outing finds the quartet (Randall Willis on tenor and soprano, pianist Rodney Lee, bassist Osama Afifi and drummer Herb Graham, Jr.) performing eight originals by the drummer/leader (two of which were co-written with Lee), Thelonious Monk's "Brilliant Corners," and an unusual version of "Confirmation." Although the latter is a bit routine, lightly funky and mostly dropping out the chord changes, the other selections are very rewarding; the brooding "Mujeres" and the title cut have the best chances of catching on. Willis has grown quite a bit as an improviser, particularly on tenor; Lee is also a strong soloist, and the group sounds quite tight throughout the post-bop set. Recommended. —*Scott Yanow*

Harry Babasin

b. Apr. 19, 1921, Dallas, TX, d. May 2, 1988, Los Angeles, CA
Bass, Cello / Bop, Cool
Harry Babasin's main significance to jazz is that he was its first soloing cellist, pre-dating Oscar Pettiford by a couple of years. After playing bass with territory bands

in the Midwest, he spent 1945 with the orchestras of Gene Krupa, Boyd Raeburn and Charlie Barnet. Moving to the West Coast, Babasin worked again with Raeburn and with Benny Goodman (1946-47). In 1947 he first recorded on cello, taking jazz solos in a bop setting. In 1948 he was with Woody Herman and then became a busy studio musician in Los Angeles. Occasionally through the years Babasin would appear in a jazz setting, as when he formed his own label Nocturne and recorded his group in 1954. In 1956 he recorded on cello with his Jazzpickers and he was briefly with Harry James in 1959. —*Scott Yanow*

Jazz in Hollywood / Sep. 23, 1954 / Original Jazz Classics ♦♦♦

● **Harry Babasin and the Jazz Pickers** / Terry Gibbs / Jul. 1957 / V.S.O.P. ♦♦♦♦
Harry Babasin was (along with Oscar Pettiford) probably the first bassist to play jazz cello. This LP reissue of a set originally for the MOD (Music of the Day) label features Babasin's Jazz Pickers (a quartet with guitarist Dempsey Wright, bassist Ben Tucker and drummer Bill Douglas) plus guest vibraphonist Terry Gibbs. The music (five Babasin originals and three veteran standards) swings hard but lightly, with Babasin's cello solos being the date's most unusual feature. —*Scott Yanow*

Alice Babs

b. Jan. 26, 1924, Kalmar, Sweden
Vocals / Swing, Standards
A popular singer when she was still a young teenager, Alice Babs has had a long and varied career. She made her recording debut in 1939 at the age of 15 and, although her yodelling made her initially popular and the novelty "Swing It, Mr. Teacher" was her first hit, Babs even at the start had a highly appealing voice and a lightly swinging style. She mostly recorded in jazz and swing-oriented settings throughout the years of World War II. Babs remained active throughout the 1950s and '60s in Europe, singing everything from jazz (recording with Duke Ellington in 1963 and performing the classic "Heaven" at his second spiritual concert) and pop to a bit of classical music. By the late '70s Alice Babs had become less active, but into the mid-'90s she has occasionally performed on special occasions. Although her important first set with Duke Ellington (on Reprise) remains out of print, a Phontastic CD (*Swing It!*) does a fine job of summing up her first 15 years on records. —*Scott Yanow*

● **Swing It!** / May 31, 1939-Apr. 1, 1953 / Phontastic ♦♦♦♦♦
Alice Babs was one of the most famous jazz singers to come out of Sweden. Only 15 at the time of her recording debut, Babs became initially well-known for her yodelling but soon became a superior swing singer. This definitive CD, which has 25 selections, gives listeners the highlights from her first 14 years on record and features Babs being accompanied by some of Sweden's top jazz musicians. High points include "Some of These Days," "Minnie the Moocher's Wedding Day," "Lady Be Good," "Truckin'," "Opus in Scat" and even "Yodel in Swing." —*Scott Yanow*

Benny Bailey (Ernest Harold Bailey)

b. Aug. 13, 1925, Cleveland, OH
Trumpet / Bop, Hard Bop
It is a bit ironic that Benny Bailey is best known for his contributions to the famous Eddie Harris/Les McCann *Swiss Movement* album, since he admitted later on that he did not care for the funky music. An extroverted and highly expressive player who has mostly appeared in boppish settings, Bailey's longtime residence in Europe has resulted in him gaining less fame (although probably more work) than if he had spent more time in the US.

Bailey had some training on piano and flute early in his career, switched permanently to trumpet, and studied at the Cleveland Conservatory of Music. In the early 1940s, he played with groups led by Bull Moose Jackson and Scatman Crothers. After gigging with Jay McShann, he was with Dizzy Gillespie's big band from 1947-48, and then became a key member of the Lionel Hampton Orchestra (1948-53). The trumpeter left Hampton during a European tour, settling overseas. He spent a long period in Sweden, working with Harry Arnold's big band (1957-59), recording with Stan Getz and touring with Quincy Jones (1959). A brief visit to the US in 1960 (during which he recorded a near-classic album for Candid, *Big Brass*) was followed by his relocation to Germany. Bailey has worked steadily during the past four decades, recording with Eric Dolphy in 1961, being featured with the Kenny Clarke-Francy Boland Big Band, touring with George Gruntz's Concert Jazz band, and in 1986 becoming a member of the Paris Reunion Band. In addition to the Candid date, Bailey has led sessions for many European labels, including Sonet, Metronome, Saba, Freedom, Enja, Ego, Hot House and Gemini, plus an American set in 1978 for Jazzcraft. But it is his explosive solos on "Cold Duck Time" and "Compared to What" from the Harris/McCann concert (now also available on video) that made him most famous. —*Scott Yanow*

● **Big Brass** / Nov. 25, 1960 / Candid ✦✦✦✦✦

Trumpeter Benny Bailey has had an on-and-off recording career and due to his longtime residency in Europe has been underrated through the years. This CD reissue of his Candid date is one of the high points of his career. Bailey is joined by an all-star septet including altoist Phil Woods, Julius Watkins on French horn and pianist Tommy Flanagan, and the high-quality arrangements (some by Quincy Jones) give a lot of variety to this highly recommended set. —*Scott Yanow*

Grand Slam / Oct. 14, 1978 / Jazzcraft ✦✦✦✦

Trumpeter Benny Bailey was teamed with veteran tenor saxophonist Charlie Rouse on this hard-blowing quintet date. The fresh material (two songs by Fritz Pauer who arranged the date, a pair from Bailey and one by Pepper Adams) inspires the soloists to play near their peak. With a fine rhythm section (pianist Richard Wyands, bassist Sam Jones and drummer Billy Hart) pushing the horns, this set is even better than expected. —*Scott Yanow*

While My Lady Sleeps / Apr. 22, 1990-Apr. 23, 1990 / Gemini ✦✦✦

Buster Bailey (William C. Bailey)

b. Jul. 19, 1902, Memphis, TN, **d.** Apr. 12, 1967, New York, NY
Clarinet / Big Band, Swing, Classic Jazz

Buster Bailey was a brilliant clarinetist who, although known for his smooth and quiet playing with John Kirby's Sextet, occasionally really cut loose with some wild solos (including on a recording called "Man with a Horn Goes Berserk!"). Expertly trained by the classical teacher Franz Schoepp (who also taught Benny Goodman), Bailey worked with W.C. Handy's band in 1917. He moved to Chicago in 1919 and was soon working with Erskine Tate and King Oliver's Creole Jazz Band. He gained some fame in 1924 when he joined Fletcher Henderson's Orchestra in New York. Bailey was with Henderson off and on during 1924-34 and 1936-37, also playing with Noble Sissle and the Mills Blue Rhythm Band (1934-35). Next up was the cool-toned swing of John Kirby's Sextet (1937-46), a role he fit perfectly. With the end of the Kirby band, Bailey was mostly employed in Dixieland settings with Wilbur DeParis (1947-49), Big Chief Russell Moore (1952-53), Henry "Red" Allen (1950-51 and 1954-60), Wild Bill Davison (1961-63) and the Saints and Sinners (1963-65), finishing up with the Louis Armstrong All-Stars (1965-67). One of the most technically skilled of the clarinetists to emerge during the 1920s, Buster Bailey never modernized his style or became a leader, but he contributed his talents and occasional wit to a countless number of rewarding and important recordings. —*Scott Yanow*

● **1925-1940** / May 20, 1925-Jun. 1940 / Classics ✦✦✦✦✦

Other than four titles from 1959 and an obscure 1958 LP, all of clarinetist Buster Bailey's recordings as a leader are on this definitive CD from the European Classics label. Bailey, a virtuoso whose occasional display of a wild sense of humor (best heard on "Man with a Horn Goes Berserk") was always a surprise when one considered his cool and subtle tone, starts off the reissue with two rare (and scratchy) performances from 1925. Otherwise, he heads an all-star group filled with fellow Fletcher Henderson sidemen in 1934, backs singer Jerry Kruger, and heads several overlapping combos mostly consisting of members of John Kirby's Sextet; Kirby's influence is strongly felt throughout the later selections. Highlights overall include "Shanghai Shuffle," "Dizzy Debutante," "The Blue Room" and "Pine Top's Boogie Woogie." Highly recommended. —*Scott Yanow*

All About Memphis / Feb. 13, 1958-Feb. 27, 1958 / Felsted ✦✦✦✦

Buster Bailey was one of the top clarinetists to emerge during the 1920s, but he led relatively few sessions throughout his long career. This LP features Bailey with a quartet (along with pianist Red Richards, bassist Gene Ramey and drummer Jimmie Crawford) and, with the horns of trumpeter Herman Autrey, trombonist Vic Dickenson and altoist Hilton Jefferson added, a septet. In addition to W.C. Handy tunes, the other five songs are Bailey originals that mix together swing and the flavor of New Orleans jazz. It's a fine outing for the classic clarinetist. —*Scott Yanow*

Craig Bailey

b. Feb. 3, 1960, Cincinnati, OH
Alto Saxophone, Flute / Post-Bop, Hard Bop

Although already in his mid-30s at the time, Craig Bailey emerged in the mid-'90s to become one of the most consistently inventive and potentially significant reed players of his generation. He had played in his native Cincinnati and studied at the University of Miami, graduating in 1984. After moving to New York, Bailey worked with big bands led by Charlie Persip (1985-86), Slide Hampton and Ray Charles (1987-91) along with Panama Francis' swing combos and recorded with the Nancy Banks Orchestra and Bobby Watson's short-lived big band. Bailey joined the Tana Reid Quintet in 1991 and had his recording debut as a leader with 1995's impressive Candid CD *A New Journey*. —*Scott Yanow*

● **A New Journey** / Mar. 7, 1995-Apr. 13, 1995 / Candid ✦✦✦✦✦

This is a consistently memorable date with some rather special moments. "What Would I Do Without You" has a catchy soulful melody very reminiscent of David Newman's "Hard Times," "Laura" features a beautiful blend between Craig Bailey's flute and violinist Mark Feldman, and "Cherokee" is conventional except that it is played by a trio consisting of altoist Bailey, trumpeter Patrick Rickman and drummer Bruce Cox. Other numbers on this colorful set (which revitalizes the hard bop tradition through an inventive use of frameworks and instrumental colors) include a driving tribute to Art Blakey, a reharmonized "Li'l Darlin'" and the blues "No Hip Hop" which alternates between straightahead and hip hop rhythms. Despite the constantly changing personnel (with three different trumpeters and a choice of four pianists), every selection is successful on the highly recommended disc. If only every jazz artist would put as much planning into their studio sessions as Craig Bailey. —*Scott Yanow*

Derek Bailey

b. Jan. 29, 1932, Sheffield, England
Guitar / Free Jazz, Avant-Garde

At first glance, Derek Bailey possesses almost none of the qualities one expects from a jazz musician—his music does not swing in any appreciable way, it lacks a discernible sense of blues feeling—yet there's a strong connection between his amelodic, arhythmic, atonal, uncategorizable free-improvisatory style, and much free jazz of the post-Coltrane era. His music draws upon a vast array of resources, including indeterminacy, rock 'n' roll, and various world musics. Indeed, this catholic acceptance of any and all musical influences is arguably what sets Bailey's art outside the strict bounds of "jazz." The essential element of his work, however, is the type of spontaneous musical interrelation that evolved from the '60s jazz avant-garde. Sound, not ideology, is Bailey's medium. He differs in approach to almost any other guitarist who preceded him. Bailey uses the guitar as a sound-making, rather than a "music"-making, device. Meaning, he rarely plays melodies or harmonies in a conventional sense, but instead pulls out of his instrument every conceivable type of sound using every imaginable technique. His timbral range is quite broad. On electric guitar, Bailey is capable of the most gratingly harsh, distortion-laden heavy-metalisms; unamplified, he's as likely to mimic a set of wind chimes. Bailey's guitar is much like John Cage's prepared piano; both innovations enhanced the respective instrument's percussive possibilities. As a group player, Bailey is an exquisitely sensitive respondent to what goes on around him. He has the sort of quick reflexes and complementary character that can meld random musical events into a unified whole.

Bailey came from a musical family; his grandfather and uncle were musicians. As a youngster living in Sheffield in the '40s, Bailey studied music with C.H.C. Biltcliffe and guitar with George Wing and John Duarte. Bailey began playing conventional jazz and commercial music professionally in the '50s. In the early '60s, Bailey played in a trio called Joseph Holbrooke, with drummer Tony Oxley and bassist (and later renowned classical composer) Gavin Bryars. In the course of its existence, from 1963-66, the group evolved from playing relatively traditional jazz with tempo and chord changes, to playing totally free. In 1966 Bailey moved to London; there, he formed a number of important musical associations with, among others, drummer John Stevens, saxophonist Evan Parker, trumpeter Kenny Wheeler, and bassist Dave Holland. This specific collection of players recorded as the Spontaneous Music Ensemble, which served as a crucible for the sort of egalitarian, collective improvisation that Bailey was to pursue from then on. In 1968, Bailey joined Oxley—another musician interested in new possibilities of sound generation—in whose sextet he remained until 1973. In 1970, Bailey formed the trio Iskra with bassist Barry Guy and trombonist Paul Rutherford. Also that year, Bailey started (with Parker and Oxley) the Incus record label, for which he would continue to record into the '90s. In 1976, Bailey founded Company, a long-lived free improv ensemble with ever-shifting personnel, which has included, at various times, Anthony Braxton, Han Bennink, Steve Lacy, and George Lewis, among others.

The 1980s saw Bailey collaborating with many of the aforementioned, along with newer figures on the scene such as John Zorn and Joelle Leandre. Solo playing has always been a particular specialty, as have (especially in recent years, it seems) ad hoc duos with a variety of associates. Most recently, Bailey recorded an uncompromising three-disc set with a group that included the usually more pop-oriented guitarist Pat Metheny. Bailey's extreme radicalism makes for a difficult music, yet there's no doubting his influence; his methods and aesthetic have significantly impacted the downtown New York free scene, though many (if not most) of his disciples are little known to the general public. In 1980, Bailey wrote *Improvisation: Its Nature and Practice*, an informative and undervalued volume on various traditions of improvised music. —*Chris Kelsey*

Improvisations for Cello and Guitar / Jan. 1971 / ECM ✦✦✦

Solo Guitar / Feb. 1971 / Incus ✦✦✦✦
Substance abounds in Derek Bailey's *Solo Guitar Vol. 1*. This reissue consolidates material on two Incus LPs. His linear conception is given weight and counter-balanced by unusual intervallic concerns linking the guitarist to the Viennese 12-tone school (an encounter with Franz Koglmann seems inevitable) as well as Thelonious Monk. The regular utilization of harmonic overtones, all manner of overdubbing, chopping and scraping of chordal clusters and, on electric, feedback and volume pedal phasing are supportively interwoven with grace and finesse. Compared to later a cappella documents, *Vol. 1* is attractively austere, purposefully ragged and, on the first four cuts, effectively random in approach. Also of interest here is the hardcore improvising guitarist's meeting with three compositions: Misha Mengelberg's shuffling "Police" augmented by synthesizer enhancement, the fretboard tapping of Gavin Bryars' "Squirrel," and the intricate linearisms of Willem Breuker's "Eddy", where the struggle between score and interpreter IS the piece, and hilariously so. —*Milo Fine, Cadence*

Royal, Vol. 1 / Jul. 2, 1974 / Incus ✦✦✦

London Concert / Feb. 14, 1975 / Incus ✦✦✦

Diverso N. 2 / Sep. 16, 1975-Sep. 18, 1975 / Cramps ✦✦✦
Throughout his career, Derek Bailey has primarily been involved with atonal sound explorations on his guitar. This solo session (available as an Italian LP) features Bailey on 14 sketches getting a wide variety of noises and sounds out of his instrument. All but the most open-eared listeners will probably think of these performances as random noise but there is a method to Derek Bailey's apparent madness. —*Scott Yanow*

Time / Apr. 1979 / Incus ✦✦✦

Dart Drug / Aug. 1981 / Incus ✦✦

● **Yankees** / 1982 / Celluloid ✦✦✦✦

Cyro / Oct. 1982 / Incus ✦✦

Han / Mar. 15, 1986-Mar. 22, 1986 / Incus ✦✦✦✦

Wireforks / 1995 / Shanachie ✦✦✦✦

Moments Précieux / 1996 / Victo ✦✦✦✦

Mildred Bailey

b. Feb. 27, 1907, Tekoa, WA, **d.** Dec. 12, 1951, Pougakeepsie, WA
Vocals / Swing, Standards, Traditional Pop, Classic Female Blues
Although her high-pitched childlike voice (which contrasted with her plump body) takes a bit of getting used to for some, Mildred Bailey was one of the finest jazz singers to emerge during the 1930s. She learned from her predecessors Ethel Waters, Bessie Smith and Connie Boswell, and developed her own lightly swinging style. After singing locally, Bailey sent a demonstration record to Paul Whiteman in 1929; he immediately added her to his band. During her four years with Whiteman, Bailey mostly sang ballads and became identified with "Rockin' Chair" and "Georgia on My Mind." In 1933 she married Red Norvo and they eventually were known as "Mr. and Mrs. Swing." Mildred Bailey was famous and well-paid throughout the 1930s, appearing regularly on radio and recording some superb small-group jazz dates. She was well-featured with Red Norvo's distinctive big band during 1936-39, a group that often found her vocals enhanced by Eddie Sauter's arrangements. Unfortunately her insecurities about her appearance made her an erratic personality. Bailey's marriage ended in divorce in 1943 although she worked with Norvo on and off in the '40s. After 1945 her health faded and the singer died in 1951 when she was 44. Many of Mildred Bailey's records are currently available and she would probably be shocked to know that she is on a postage stamp! —*Scott Yanow*

Volume One / Oct. 5, 1929-Mar. 2, 1932 / TOM ✦✦✦
The first of two Mildred Bailey CDs from the TOM label contains 21 of the vocalist's first 23 recordings; the two bypassed selections are included on the second volume. The superior swing singer is mostly heard on ballads (some of which are

a bit dated) with orchestras led by Eddie Lang ("What Kind o' Man Is You?"), Frankie Trumbauer ("I Like to Do Things for You"), Jimmie Noone, Glen Gray and Paul Whiteman in addition to her initial sessions as a leader; this release is accurately subtitled "Sweet Beginnings" and the jazz content is generally not all that high. Although there are fairly long liner notes (the same ones are used on both volumes), the personnel for these early recordings are not included. Despite that inexcusable omission, fans of Mildred Bailey should be delighted to have these interesting sides reissued; highlights include "Concentratin' on You," "Home," "All of Me" and her original version of "Georgia on My Mind." —*Scott Yanow*

★ **Her Greatest Performances (1929-1946)** / 1929-1946 / Columbia ✦✦✦✦✦
This three-LP box set (which deserves to be reissued on CD) lives up to its name. Bailey was one of the top singers of the 1930s and this package, which features highlights from her career (mostly dating from 1933-39), shows why. She holds her own with a variety of all-star groups which include such classic players as trumpeters Bunny Berigan, Buck Clayton, Charlie Shavers and Roy Eldridge (the latter is great on "I'm Nobody's Baby"), trombonist Tommy Dorsey, clarinetist Benny Goodman, altoist Johnny Hodges, tenors Coleman Hawkins and Chu Berry, pianists Teddy Wilson and Mary Lou Williams, and her husband, xylophonist Red Norvo. There are lots of gems on this definitive set. —*Scott Yanow*

The Rockin' Chair Lady / Sep. 15, 1931-Apr. 25, 1950 / Decca ✦✦✦✦
The superior swing singer is heard on 20 studio performances throughout this diverse CD which spans virtually her entire recording career. The best selections are the first four, a complete session from 1935 that has Bailey joined by an all-star quartet comprising trumpeter Bunny Berigan, altoist Johnny Hodges, pianist Teddy Wilson and bassist Grachan Moncur. In addition she sings four ballads from 1931 with the Casa Loma Orchestra and is accompanied on ten songs by the Delta Rhythm Boys, a quartet led by pianist Herman Chittison or Harry Sosnick's octet in 1941-42. This interesting CD concludes with Mildred Bailey's final studio session, two numbers ("Cry, Cry, Cry" and "Blue Prelude") from 1950. Some of the material was formerly rare, making this an essential CD for swing collectors. —*Scott Yanow*

Volume 2 / Dec. 1, 1931-Feb. 2, 1934 / TOM ✦✦✦
The second of two CDs from the TOM ("The Old Masters") label finishes the documentation of singer Mildred Bailey's earliest recordings. Bailey is featured with Paul Whiteman, the Dorsey Brothers Big Band, the Casa Loma Orchestra ("Heat Wave"), an all-star group with Benny Goodman (and tenor-great Coleman Hawkins), and on a few of her own sessions. Although the emphasis is on ballads, the program generally holds on to one's interest (despite a few songs with racist lyrics, notably "Snowball") and the Goodman session (which is rounded off with an instrumental version of "Georgia Jubilee") is a near-classic. Other highlights include "I'll Never Be the Same," "Love Me Tonight," a touching "There's a Cabin in the Pines" and Bailey's earliest version of her future theme song "Rockin' Chair." —*Scott Yanow*

Legendary V-Disc Series / 1940-1951 / Vintage Jazz ✦✦✦✦
Mildred Bailey fans will find this to be a very interesting CD for the talented swing singer is heard on some previously unavailable V-Disc sessions from the war years (including a few false starts) along with some radio appearances. There is a complete radio show with her guests the Delta Rhythm Boys, four duets with pianist Teddy Wilson, three selections with vibraphonist Red Norvo's quintet, a few songs with either Paul Baron's studio orchestra or the Ellis Larkins Trio, one number ("There'll Be a Jubilee") with Benny Goodman's big band, and two selections ("Lover, Come Back to Me" and "It's So Peaceful in the Country") from a 1951 radio aircheck that ended up being her last recordings. Any listener who wonders why Mildred Bailey was awarded her own postage stamp should be required to get this CD. —*Scott Yanow*

Mildred Bailey Radio Show / Nov. 24, 1944-Jan. 1945 / Sunbeam ✦✦✦
These radio performances, taken from three different shows, find singer Mildred Bailey in particularly stirring form. While she sticks mostly to ballads, there are also instrumentals featuring trombonist Trummy Young, the Teddy Wilson Sextet and the Paul Baron Orchestra; in addition Woody Herman drops by to sing a blues. This hard-to-find LP is easily recommended to those who can find it. —*Scott Yanow*

All of Me / Dec. 1945 / Monmouth Evergreen ✦✦✦
This difficult-to-find LP features Bailey singing 16 songs recorded during 1945-47 when she is still in her prime. Some feature her former husband, vibraphonist Red Norvo, while the selections on side two include some of her most mature ballad statements. High points include "I've Got the World on a String," "I'm Glad There Is You," "Me and the Blues" and the title cut. —*Scott Yanow*

Majestic Mildred Bailey / Mar. 5, 1946-Nov. 1947 / Savoy ✦✦✦
During 1946-47 Mildred Bailey recorded four sessions for the Majestic record label; these late sides were among her finest recordings. This Savoy LP reissues

Music Map

Bass (acoustic)

Pioneers
Bill Johnson (first to develop plucked string style)
Ed Garland
Steve Brown
John Lindsay
Wellman Braud (with Duke Ellington 1927-35)
Pops Foster

Swing Era
Israel Crosby (1935 solo on "Blues of Israel")
Walter Page (with Count Basie)
John Kirby
Bob Haggart
Gene Ramey
Milt Hinton

Three Great Innovators
Jimmy Blanton (with Duke Ellington 1939-41)
Oscar Pettiford
Charles Mingus

1940s
Slam Stewart	Tommy Potter
Curly Russell	Red Callender

Bop to Modern Mainstream
Ray Brown	Percy Heath
George Duvivier	Major Holley
Wendell Marshall	Ed Safranski
Red Mitchell	Monty Budwig
Leroy Vinnegar	Eugene Wright
Paul Chambers	Doug Watkins
Sam Jones	Wilbur Ware
Richard Davis	Ron Carter
Buster Williams	Miroslav Vitous
George Mraz	Harvie Swartz
Dave Friesen	Brian Torff
Glen Moore	John Clayton
Christian McBride	Reginald Veal
Robert Hurst	Charnett Moffett
John Patitucci	Charles Fambrough
Niels Henning-Orsted Pedersen	

Bill Evan's Bassists
Scott LaFaro
Chuck Israels
Eddie Gomez
Marc Johnson

Avant-Garde
Buell Neidlinger (with Cecil Taylor 1955-61)
Charlie Haden
Gary Peacock
Reggie Workman
Art Davis
Jimmy Garrison
Henry Grimes
David Izenzon (with Ornette Coleman 1961-68)
Malachi Favors
(a founder of the Art Ensemble Of Chicago)
Dave Holland
Sirone
Johnny Dyani
Barre Phillips
Cecil McBee
Fred Hopkins
Mark Helias
Anthony Cox
John Lindberg
William Parker
Barry Guy

most of the music from these sessions, including cuts with bassist Neil Swainson and drummer Jerry Fuller. This Montreal recording features four of Ballantyne's originals along with the standard "You and the Night and the Music" and is a strong example of modern straightahead jazz. It's well worth picking up. *—Scott Yanow*

American Legends #4 / LaserLight ◆◆◆
The almost complete lack of documentation on this low-priced disc (which nevertheless manages to state both the artist's claimed year of birth, 1907, and her actual one, 1901) makes it difficult to place in Mildred Bailey's discography, but the performances, on many of which Bailey is backed by Red Norvo or Ellis Larkins, are typically accomplished. Her hit "Thanks for the Memory" (now remembered as Bob Hope's theme song) is included, as are some excellent off-beat

arrangements of such songs as "The Lamp Is Low" and "Smoke Dreams" (the latter featuring a delightful Norvo xylophone solo). Sound quality is adequate, and with a running time for the 12 tracks of over 36 minutes, you will get what you pay for if you only pay in the vicinity of $5 for this disc. *— William Ruhlmann*

Chet Baker (Chesney Henry Baker)

b. Dec. 23, 1929, Yale, OK, **d.** May 13, 1988, Amsterdam, Netherlands
Trumpet, Vocals / Cool, West Coast Jazz
A popular cool-toned trumpeter and a fragile singer whose charisma made up for his limited voice, with his good looks Chet Baker probably could have been a movie star. Instead he became a drug addict in the mid-'50s and had an extremely erratic lifestyle with horrific episodes alternating with some wonderful musical moments.

Chet Baker certainly started out on top. After getting out of the Army, he gigged with Charlie Parker on the West Coast in 1952 and then joined the Gerry Mulligan Quartet, a pianoless unit that soon became among the most popular in jazz. After Mulligan was jailed for his own drug problems, Baker (who had helped make "My Funny Valentine" into a hit) formed a quartet with pianist Russ Freeman. He began to win polls on both trumpet and vocals, toured Europe in 1955 and seemed on his way to a lucrative career. But by 1960 Baker was in an Italian jail and, although he made a few worthy recordings in the '60s, by the end of the decade his teeth had been knocked out after a botched drug deal and he was out of music.

Against all odds Chet Baker made a gradual comeback in the 1970s. Although Baker recorded far too much during his final 15 years, his nomadic lifestyle (never kicking drugs and essentially wandering all over Europe) was unstable and his occasional vocals (always an acquired taste) were generally poor, his trumpet playing actually improved as the decade progressed. In fact despite everything, Chet Baker was still in his musical prime when he fell out of a second story window (pushed or slipped?) to his death in 1988. He remains one of the great cult figures of jazz. —*Scott Yanow*

Live at the Trade Winds / Mar. 24, 1952-Aug. 4, 1952 / Fresh Sound ✦✦✦

Pacific Jazz Years / Oct. 15, 1952-Dec. 9, 1957 / Pacific Jazz ✦✦✦
This attractive four-CD box set gives one a good overview of trumpeter Chet Baker's 1952-57 recordings, a period when he became unexpectedly popular. Baker is heard on four numbers with Gerry Mulligan, with his own quartet (which featured pianist Russ Freeman), in quintets with either altoist Art Pepper or tenor saxophonist Phil Urso and with larger groups that also include altoist Herb Geller, valve trombonist Bob Brookmeyer, and altoist Bud Shank among others. Perfect as an introduction for those just beginning to appreciate Chet Baker, this set will also interest veteran collectors for, in addition to its attractive booklet, it contains four previously unissued selections with Stan Getz (including a 17-minute version of "All the Things You Are") and four selections from what was thought to be a long-lost session in which the trumpeter is backed on some Bob Zieff arrangements by French horn, bass clarinet, bassoon, cello and bass. —*Scott Yanow*

West Coast Live / Jun. 12, 1953-Aug. 17, 1954 / Blue Note ✦✦✦✦✦
This two-CD set, released in 1997, has 20 formerly rare selections (seven previously unreleased and the remainder mostly put out in Europe) that feature trumpeter Chet Baker and/or tenor saxophonist Stan Getz. The Baker-Getz relationship was never too friendly, but they teamed up on at least four occasions, two of which are represented here. The bulk of the set is taken from June 12, 1953, and features the Gerry Mulligan Quartet with Getz in place of the jailed baritonist. With bassist Carson Smith and drummer Larry Bunker offering quiet support, the tenor tries his best to fit into the ensembles but is much more comfortable when taking solos, with Baker sometimes playing background harmonies. Actually, the trumpeter steals the show and has rarely sounded better, coming up with consistently inventive improvisations on such tunes as "Strike Up the Band," "Winter Wonderland," "Move," "Bernie's Tune" and "Whispering." The second date is from a year later and has Getz sitting in with Chet's regular quartet (which also includes pianist Russ Freeman, bassist Carson Smith and drummer Shelly Manne). A seventeen-and-a-half-minute version of "All the Things You Are" holds one's interest, while Baker is absent on the two other Getz features. It is a pity that Baker and Getz disliked each other, for their cool-toned sounds and bop/swing styles were potentially very complementary. In any case, this two-fer is essential for all serious bop collectors. —*Scott Yanow*

☆ **The Complete Pacific Jazz Studio Recordings of the Chet Baker Quartet with Ross Freeman** / Jul. 24, 1953-Nov. 6, 1956 / Mosaic ✦✦✦✦✦
This essential four-LP box set features trumpeter Chet Baker leading his own group during the 1953-56 period (shortly after the breakup of the Gerry Mulligan Quartet) with pianist Russ Freeman, either Bob Whitlock, Carson Smith, Joe Mondragon, Jimmy Bond or Leroy Vinnegar on bass, and Bobby White, Larry Bunker, Shelly Manne, Bob Neel, Peter Littman or Lawrence Marable on drums. Baker is heard at his coolest (mostly before he became influenced by Miles Davis); some of the later selections also feature his first recorded vocals. Because the Mosaic box sets are limited editions, they should be acquired as soon as possible. —*Scott Yanow*

Witch Doctor / Sep. 13, 1953-1985 / Original Jazz Classics ✦✦
This album features Baker sitting in at the legendary Lighthouse with some of the top exponents of West Coast jazz. In addition to Baker, the lineup is quite impressive: trumpeter Rolf Ericson, Bud Shank on alto and baritone, Jimmy Guiffre and Bob Cooper alternating on tenors, either Russ Freeman or Claude Williamson on piano, bassist Howard Rumsey, and Max Roach or Shelly Manne on drums. The recording quality of these live performances is so-so but the music ("I'll Remember

April", "Winter Wonderland" and three originals) is full of spirit and excitement. —*Scott Yanow*

Jazz Profile / Dec. 14, 1953-Oct. 31, 1956 / Blue Note ✦✦✦
The first in Blue Note's *Jazz Profile* CD series, this sampler features trumpeter/vocalist Chet Baker, who never actually recorded for Blue Note; his Pacific Jazz recordings, however, are also owned by Blue Note's parent company EMI. All 11 selections on this set have been reissued on CD; although they are not quite definitive (no "My Funny Valentine" here), there is a great deal of fine music to be heard. Baker is featured in settings ranging from his quartet with Russ Freeman (taking four vocals) to medium-size groups with altoist Herb Geller and tenor/arranger Jack Montrose; plus, there is one appearance apiece for valve trombonist Bob Brookmeyer, altoist Art Pepper and tenorman Phil Urso. A good introduction to the cool-toned trumpeter in his early days, when he was also considered to be a heartthrob as a singer. —*Scott Yanow*

Grey December / Dec. 22, 1953-Feb. 28, 1955 / Pacific Jazz ✦✦✦✦
This excellent CD reissues two Chet Baker sessions. The trumpeter is heard in a septet from 1953 with tenor saxophonist Jack Montrose (who contributed the arrangements), altoist Herb Geller, baritonist Bob Gordon and pianist Russ Freeman, and backed by strings on four vocal numbers from 1955. The latter cuts are passable but the former session (which is augmented by five alternate takes, two being issued for the first time) is frequently superb, West Coast jazz at its best. —*Scott Yanow*

Chet Baker with Strings / Dec. 30, 1953-Feb. 20, 1954 / Columbia ✦✦✦
Trumpeter Chet Baker (who fortunately does not sing on this CD) is heard backed by a string section on these generally enjoyable selections from his early period. In addition to the strings, Zoot Sims (and on some tracks altoist Bud Shank) sits in with Baker's quartet, resulting in an enjoyable easy-listening set. —*Scott Yanow*

● **The Best of Chet Baker Sings: Let's Get Lost** / 1953-1956 / Capitol/Pacific Jazz ✦✦✦
To much of the pop (as opposed to the jazz) audience, Chet Baker was known not as an able cool jazz trumpeter, but as a romantic balladeer. The two classifications were not mutually exclusive; Baker's vocal numbers would also feature his trumpet playing, as well as fine instrumental support from West Coast cool jazzers. For those who prefer the vocal side of the Baker canon, this is an excellent compilation of his best vintage material in that mode. The 20 tracks draw from sessions covering the era when he was generally conceded to be at his vocal peak (1953-56), and are dominated by standards from the likes of Rodgers & Hart, Carmichael, Gershwin, and Kern. Baker's singing was white and naive in both senses, with a quavering, uncertain earnestness that embodied a certain (safe) strain of mid-'50s bohemianism. That's the Chet we hear on this collection, which contains some his most famous interpretations, including "My Funny Valentine," "Time After Time," "There Will Never Be Another You," and "Let's Get Lost." —*Richie Unterberger*

Young Chet / Feb. 15, 1954-Jul. 31, 1956 / Blue Note ✦✦✦
This CD brings together some leftover tracks from trumpeter Chet Baker's Pacific Jazz sessions. The first five songs originally featured Baker's overdubbed vocals, but Richard Bock had a change of heart and also had "alternate" versions made with either tenor saxophonist Bill Perkins or (on one song) clarinetist Jimmy Giuffre overdubbed where Baker's vocals had been. It is those renditions that form the first half of this CD. The remainder is from a 1956 session by Baker with his quintet when it included tenor saxophonist Phil Urso and pianist Bobby Timmons. Baker plays well on five songs from this set but is actually not present on "It's Only a Paper Moon" (an Urso feature) and "Autumn in New York" (which is played by the trio). Although there is some good music on the CD, this release is mostly for Baker completists since there are many more essential Chet Baker albums currently available. —*Scott Yanow*

Boston / Mar. 16, 1954-Oct. 19, 1954 / Uptown ✦✦✦✦
Released for the first time in the early '90s, this CD consists of three radio broadcasts by the Chet Baker Quartet from the Storyville Club in Boston. In each case the trumpeter/leader is joined by pianist Russ Freeman, bassist Carson Smith and drummer Bob Neel. Baker, who takes a vocal on "Time After Time," is in excellent form performing his standard repertoire of the period. It's easily recommended to all Chet Baker fans. —*Scott Yanow*

Complete Pacific Jazz Live Recordings / May 9, 1954-Oct. 1954 / Mosaic ✦✦✦✦
Chet Baker and his popular Quartet (pianist Russ Freeman, bassist Carson Smith and drummer Bob Neel) recorded live for Pacific Jazz on three different occasions in 1954. While their appearance at Ann Arbor was released, less than half of the music recorded in Los Angeles and none of the five selections cut in Santa Cruz, CA, were issued until this limited-edition four-LP box set was put out by Mosaic. Throughout this instrumental set Baker and Freeman are in their early peak form,

showing that their variation of bop was not as cool as the stereotype of West Coast jazz might lead one to expect. Get this gem while you can. —*Scott Yanow*

Chet Baker Big Band / Sep. 9, 1954-Oct. 26, 1954 / Pacific Jazz ◆◆◆◆
Despite the title, only four of the 16 titles that comprise this CD are actually performed by a big band. Trumpeter Chet Baker is featured with an 11-piece group for those selections, plays in a nonet for six others, and with a sextet for the remainder. The arrangements of Jimmy Heath, Jack Montrose, Johnny Mandel, Bill Holman, Christian Chevallier, Pierre Michelot and Phil Urso really bring out the best in Baker, making this a highly enjoyable and varied set. —*Scott Yanow*

Chet in Paris, Vol. 1 / Oct. 11, 1955-Oct. 25, 1955 / EmArcy ◆◆◆◆
The first of four CDs documenting Baker's first visit to Europe has nine selections on which the trumpeter is heard in a quartet with the ill-fated pianist Dick Twardzik and four other numbers with a fine French sextet. Baker shows that his "cool" style actually had plenty of fire. All of the sets in this valuable series contain rewarding music. —*Scott Yanow*

Chet in Paris, Vol. 2: Everything Happens to Me / Oct. 24, 1955-Nov. 28, 1955 / EmArcy ◆◆◆◆
The second in a four-CD series that documents his first trip to Europe has the studio sides from two separate sessions in which the trumpeter was teamed with French rhythm sections. The music (all but one are standards) finds Baker in top early form, making this cool-toned bop music well worth hearing. —*Scott Yanow*

Chet in Paris, Vol. 3: Cheryl / Dec. 26, 1955-Mar. 15, 1956 / EmArcy ◆◆◆◆
The third of four CDs in this valuable series continues the documentation of Baker's first trip to Europe with three interesting sessions. Baker is teamed with tenor saxophonist Bobby Jaspar and pianist Rene Urtreger for four selections, interacts with the tenor of Jean-Louis Chautemps and pianist Francy Boland on the next four songs, and is finally heard with a fine French octet. Throughout this entire series, the trumpeter is in fine form. —*Scott Yanow*

Chet in Paris, Vol. 4: Alternate Takes / Oct. 25, 1955-Feb. 10, 1956 / EmArcy ◆◆◆
The final CD in this four-volume series features alternate versions of the many selections recorded by Chet Baker while in Europe for his first visit. Taken from four different sessions, he is heard with a quartet, a sextet and two different quintets (including one with the fine tenor saxophonist Bobby Jaspar). Each of these sets is essential for true Chet Baker fans. —*Scott Yanow*

Quartet: Russ Freeman and Chet Baker / Jan. 6, 1956 / Pacific Jazz ◆◆◆
On this 1997 CD release, the final recordings by trumpeter Chet Baker's quartet with pianist Russ Freeman are reissued. The music was originally issued under Freeman's name, but has been repackaged as the trumpeter's date ever since. With bassist Leroy Vinnegar and drummer Shelly Manne the music (which had also been reissued as part of a Chet Baker limited-edition LP box on Mosaic) often swings hard. Baker's appealing soft-toned trumpet (no vocals this time around) is well showcased during the program, which consists of "Love Nest," "Lush Life" and six Freeman originals. —*Scott Yanow*

Chet Baker & Crew / Jul. 24, 1956-Jul. 31, 1956 / Pacific Jazz ◆◆◆◆
This CD brings back one of his lesser-known bands, the quintet with tenor saxophonist Phil Urso and pianist Bobby Timmons. Urso's cool tenor blended in perfectly with Baker's relaxed trumpet while Timmons's funky piano (which in three years would make him famous with Art Blakey and Cannonball Adderley) inspired the soloists. The fresh repertoire heard on this consistently enjoyable set contains many songs begging to be revived. —*Scott Yanow*

The Route / Jul. 26, 1956 / Pacific Jazz ◆◆◆◆
One of two CDs that team Baker and altoist Art Pepper, this one also features tenor saxophonist and pianist Pete Jolly; all four players get their own showcases. The often-heated results make it obvious that there was no strict borderline between artists associated with West Coast jazz and hard bop for some of these performances burn. It's strange that both Baker and Pepper could play such consistent music while conducting chaotic lifestyles. —*Scott Yanow*

Playboys / Oct. 31, 1956 / Pacific Jazz ◆◆◆◆
This is the second CD (following *The Route*) to team trumpeter Chet Baker and altoist Art Pepper, two masterful players who had similar (and rather strange) life stories, with so many ups and downs as to be almost unbelievable. None of the chaos of their lives appears in the fine music they created. This sextet session (which has five Jimmy Heath compositions in addition to two originals from Pepper) also contains spots for excellent solos by tenor saxophonist Phil Urso and pianist Carl Perkins. —*Scott Yanow*

Embraceable You / Dec. 9, 1957 / Pacific Jazz ◆◆
This is a ballad CD that puts the emphasis on Chet Baker's vulnerable vocals. Only one selection ("Trav'lin' Light") was previously released when this set came out in 1995, all of the songs (with the exception of the two versions of "Little Girl

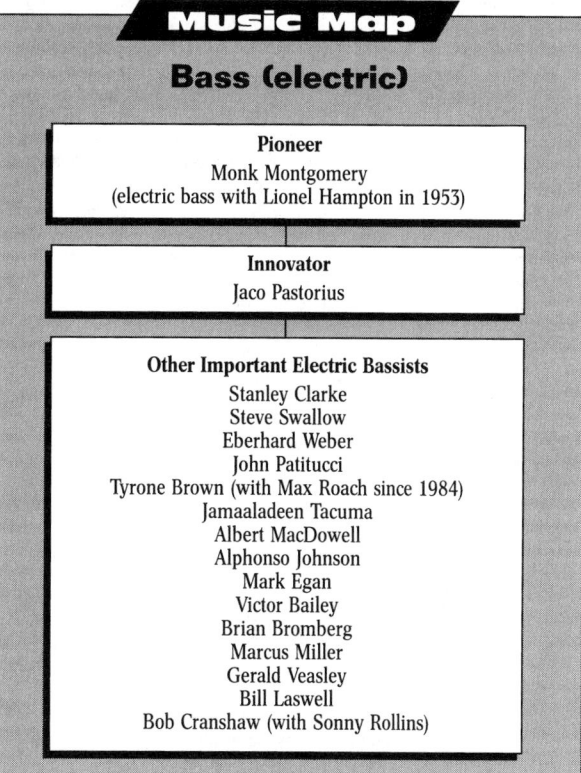

Music Map

Bass (electric)

Pioneer
Monk Montgomery
(electric bass with Lionel Hampton in 1953)

Innovator
Jaco Pastorius

Other Important Electric Bassists
Stanley Clarke
Steve Swallow
Eberhard Weber
John Patitucci
Tyrone Brown (with Max Roach since 1984)
Jamaaladeen Tacuma
Albert MacDowell
Alphonso Johnson
Mark Egan
Victor Bailey
Brian Bromberg
Marcus Miller
Gerald Veasley
Bill Laswell
Bob Cranshaw (with Sonny Rollins)

Blue") clock in around the three-minute mark and just six of the 13 tunes (five of which are instrumentals) have any of Baker's trumpet. Backed by guitarist David Wheat and bassist Ross Savakus, Baker largely sticks to the melodies (both instrumentally and vocally) with the main improvisations taking place in his phrasing rather than his notes. Although he was rarely in better voice than during this period, those listeners who think of Chet Baker as chiefly a trumpeter are advised to look elsewhere. —*Scott Yanow*

Chet Baker Sings It Could Happen to You / Aug. 1958 / Original Jazz Classics ◆◆◆
Baker's singing has always been an acquired taste. Completely untrained, his high voice sometimes sounded similar to Chris Connor's low tones, and his interpretations of innocent lyrics almost seem absurd when one considers his lifestyle. Still, it has its charm and remains popular among a select audience. This vocal-dominated session finds Baker (who is backed by trios led by pianist Kenny Drew) interpreting ten songs plus two that were only discovered in 1987. —*Scott Yanow*

Chet Baker Introduces Johnny Pace / Sep. 1958 / Original Jazz Classics ◆◆
One of the more obscure Chet Baker dates, this LP (which has since been reissued on CD in the OJC series) finds the trumpeter and a quintet that includes Herbie Mann on tenor and flute and pianist Bill Evans backing a young singer on his debut session. Johnny Pace, although he sounds fine on these superior standards, seems to have since disappeared and this is probably his only recording in a jazz setting. It's worth picking up. —*Scott Yanow*

Chet Baker in New York / Sep. 1958 / Original Jazz Classics ◆◆◆◆
This audiophile CD is a straight reissue of an Original Jazz Classics CD that is also very much available. Trumpeter Baker performs with a quartet/quintet including pianist Al Haig, bassist Paul Chambers, drummer Philly Joe Jones and (on four of the seven selections) tenor saxophonist Johnny Griffin. Highlights of this decent if not essential session include "Polka Dots and Moonbeams," "Solar" and "When Lights Are Low." The CD reissue adds a quintet version of "Soft Winds" from the same sessions formerly released on a sampler. —*Scott Yanow*

Chet (The Lyrical Trumpet of Chet Baker) / Dec. 30, 1958-Jan. 19, 1959 / Original Jazz Classics ◆◆◆
The shifting personnel on this excellent CD finds Baker joined by such players as baritonist Pepper Adams, flutist Herbie Mann, pianist Bill Evans and guitarist Kenny Burrell. This reissue of an LP adds one selection ("Early Morning Mood")

formerly only avilable on a sampler. Fine straightahead music comes from the tailend of the West Coast jazz era. —*Scott Yanow*

Chet Baker Plays the Best of Lerner and Loewe / Jul. 21, 1959-Jul. 22, 1959 / Original Jazz Classics ✦✦✦

Chet Baker is featured on eight Lerner and Loewe tunes (including four from *My Fair Lady*) along with a front line that includes flutist Herbie Mann, Zoot Sims on alto and tenor, and baritonist Pepper Adams. Although not up to the historical level of his slightly earlier Pacific Jazz dates, this Riverside date is a fine example of the modern mainstream jazz scene of 1959. —*Scott Yanow*

Chet Baker with Fifty Italian Strings / Oct. 1959 / Original Jazz Classics ✦✦

In 1959 while in Italy, Baker was showcased playing trumpet and (on five of the ten songs) singing a set of ballads while backed by a large string section. Fans will want this set but, due to the mundane string arrangements and the lack of variety, more general collectors should acquire his earlier jazz-oriented dates first. —*Scott Yanow*

● **The Italian Sessions** / Jan. 5, 1962 / RCA/Bluebird ✦✦✦✦✦

Throughout the 1950s Chet Baker gained fame as a quiet low-register trumpeter with a cool tone and a relaxed style. This CD therefore should be a major surprise to listeners who believe he was incapable of playing heated material or of utilizing the upper register of his horn. Assisted by a fine European sextet (including Bobby Jaspar on tenor and flute and guitarist Rene Thomas), Baker is heard in peak form throughout this memorable and frequently exciting bop date. —*Scott Yanow*

Baker's Holiday: Plays & Sings Billie Holiday / May 1965 / PSM ✦✦✦

This CD finds him effectively paying tribute to Billie Holiday with mellow trumpet solos and occasional vocals. Baker is backed by a full sax section and a four-piece rhythm section that includes pianist Hank Jones; Jimmy Mundy contributed the colorful arrangements. His performance of ten songs associated with Lady Day (most of which he had not recorded previously) is often exquisite. —*Scott Yanow*

● **Lonely Star** / Aug. 23, 1965-Aug. 25, 1965 / Prestige ✦✦✦✦✦

In 1964, trumpeter Chet Baker returned to the US after five sometimes-traumatic years spent overseas (which included a long stay in an Italian jail for drug abuse). Baker recorded prolifically during his first 14 months back in the States, including a set for Colpix, two records for Limelight and, in a busy three-day period, five albums for Prestige titled *Groovin', Comin' On, Cool Burnin', Smokin'* and *Boppin' with the Chet Baker Quintet*. The Prestige sets have been long overlooked and only partially reissued in the past, but in 1997 they reappeared as three CDs. Teamed up with tenorman George Coleman (fresh from his notable period with Miles Davis), the young pianist Kirk Lightsey (who sometimes takes solo honors) and the supportive bass-drums team of Herman Wright and Roy Brooks, Chet Baker (sticking exclusively to fluegelhorn) is heard throughout in top form. Although his cool style was very much intact (sometimes hinting strongly at both Miles Davis and Shorty Rogers), Baker also plays with surprising fire in spots. Of the trio of CDs, this particular one has a slight edge due to a well-rounded repertoire (two standards, Tadd Dameron's appealing blues "So Easy," and seven often-catchy Richard Carpenter originals), but all three sets (which also include *On a Misty Night* and *Stairway to the Stars*) are easily recommended to straightahead jazz fans. —*Scott Yanow*

On a Misty Night / Aug. 23, 1965-Aug. 25, 1965 / Prestige ✦✦✦✦

Chet Baker was quite busy during three days in August 1965, recording five LPs worth of material with tenor saxophonist George Coleman (formerly with Miles Davis), pianist Kirk Lightsey, bassist Herman Wright and drummer Roy Brooks. Baker, sticking to fluegelhorn, is heard in fine form on this CD reissue which (along with *Stairway to the Stars* and *Lonely Star*) brings back all of the music in full; each CD also contains all of the liner notes from the five original albums. For this particular reissue, the quintet performs six likable originals by Richard Carpenter, Jimmy Mundy's "Sleeping Susan," three Tadd Dameron tunes, and a Sonny Stitt blues. Most of the selections are taken at relaxed tempos, but it is the hottest number, "Go-Go," that is most memorable. Considering that Baker's records of the next few years were consistent commercial turkeys (including *A Taste of Tequila*, *In the Mood*, the infamous *Albert's House* and *Blood, Chet and Tears*), it can accurately be stated that the Prestige sets are Chet Baker's last worthwhile recordings before his comeback began in 1974. —*Scott Yanow*

● **Stairway to the Stars** / Aug. 23, 1965-Aug. 25, 1965 / Prestige ✦✦✦✦

During a three-day period in 1965, trumpeter Chet Baker (who during the era was exclusively playing fluegelhorn) recorded five albums for Prestige that were soon forgotten, despite their quality. In 1997, the entire program was reissued on three CDs (which also include *Lonely Star* and *On a Misty Night*), showing that Baker was in excellent form at the time. Chet is teamed with tenor saxophonist George Coleman, pianist Kirk Lightsey (in top form), bassist Herman Wright and drummer Roy Brooks; the one-time gathering group on the whole sometimes recalls

the Miles Davis Quintet of 1956. There are some occasional missteps (Baker gets a bit lost during the rapid rendition of "Cherokee" that opens this CD), but overall, the music (some light swingers and a few more heated tracks) is quite rewarding. Producer Richard Carpenter (Baker's manager at the time and best known for writing "Walkin'") contributed three songs to this set (and 13 others to the other two CDs), which also includes three jazz standards, a few obscurities, and three Tadd Dameron originals. Enjoyable straightahead music. —*Scott Yanow*

Live at Pueblo, Colorado 1966 / 1966 / Baker ✦✦

This CD features the trumpeter with his good friend tenor saxophonist Phil Urso and pianist Dave MacKay in a quintet performing live in his hometown. The playing is excellent but the recording quality is a bit disappointing, making this potentially valuable set (a straightahead session performed at a time when Baker's studio recordings were very commercial) of greatest interest to Chet Baker completists. —*Scott Yanow*

Albert's House / 1969 / Par ✦

In 1968 Baker had his teeth knocked out by a group of thugs. In 1969 he recorded this remarkably bad set of music. Of the dozen songs, 11 are forgettable melodies by Steve Allen. Baker, who sounds as if he is struggling to get any air at all out of his horn, rarely ventures out of the lower register or away from the themes. He sounds in sad shape, so why does this music repeatedly get reissued? —*Scott Yanow*

Blood, Chet & Tears / 1970 / Verve ✦

She Was Too Good to Me / Jul. 19, 1974-Nov. 1974 / Columbia ✦✦✦

Baker began his comeback after five years of musical inactivity with this excellent CTI date. Highlights include "Autumn Leaves," "Tangerine" and "With a Song in My Heart." Altoist Paul Desmond is a major asset on two songs and the occasional strings give variety to this fine session. —*Scott Yanow*

The Best Thing for You / Feb. 16, 1977-May 13, 1977 / A&M ✦✦✦✦

This CD features previously unissued material from the same sessions that resulted in *You Can't Go Home Again* and, if anything, the music is a touch better. While an alternate take of Don Sebesky's "El Morro" uses a larger group, the other five performances find Baker accompanied just by a rhythm section (pianist Kenny Barron, bassist Ron Carter, drummer Tony Williams and, on one song, guitarist Gene Bertoncini). As a special bonus, altoist Paul Desmond makes memorable appearances on three songs during what would be his final recording session. Throughout, Chet Baker shows that his playing during his much documented final period would be equal if not superior to his more acclaimed recordings of the 1950s. —*Scott Yanow*

You Can't Go Home Again / Feb. 16, 1977-May 13, 1977 / A&M ✦✦✦

Against all odds, Baker made a successful comeback in the mid-'70s after several years totally outside of music. This LP from A&M Horizon features him with a large group on three selections playing Don Sebesky arrangements. Tenor saxophonist Michael Brecker and guitarist John Scofield are among the all-star supporting cast on "Love for Sale," "Un Poco Loco" and "El Morro." The fourth selection has altoist Paul Desmond (on his very last recording) interacting with the trumpeter/leader on a small group version of Sebesky's "You Can't Go Home Again." This is worth searching for. —*Scott Yanow*

Once upon a Summertime / Feb. 20, 1977 / Original Jazz Classics ✦✦✦✦

Artists House, a classy if short-lived label, released this attractive Chet Baker LP, a quintet date with tenor saxophonist Gregory Herbert, pianist Harold Danko, bassist Ron Carter and drummer Mel Lewis. The challenging material ("The Song Is You" is the only one of the five songs that is a standard) inspires the musicians to play creative solos. It is particularly interesting to hear Baker interpret the Wayne Shorter tune "ESP." This set has been reissued on CD in the OJC series. —*Scott Yanow*

Live at Nick's / Nov. 30, 1978 / Criss Cross ✦✦✦✦

Considering his erratic lifestyle, it is surprising how many good records Chet Baker made during his final 15 years. This quartet outing with pianist Phil Markowitz, bassist Scott Lee and drummer Jeff Brillinger has been greatly expanded in its CD reissue. Four songs (including a 17-minute version of Wayne Shorter's obscure "Beautiful Black Eyes") are joined by previously unreleased and fairly long versions of "I Remember You" and "Love for Sale." The quiet but swinging music is quite enjoyable and finds Baker in fine form. —*Scott Yanow*

Broken Wing / Dec. 28, 1978 / Inner City ✦✦

Trumpeter Chet Baker is in above average form on this Paris date, using a quartet that includes pianist Phil Markowitz, bassist Jean-Francois Jenny Clark and drummer Jeff Brillinger. Originally recorded for the obscure French label Sonopresse and leased for the US by the now-defunct Inner City company, this little-known outing finds Baker taking an ok vocal on "Oh You Crazy Moon" and stretching out musically on five selections including the title tune (an original by Richard Beirach), Wayne Shorter's "Black Eyes" and the standard "How Deep Is the Ocean."

Chet Baker completists and fanatics will want this one but more general collectors have at least 100 more readily available recordings to choose from. —*Scott Yanow*

Ballads for Two / Jan. 8, 1979-Jan. 9, 1979 / Sandra ✦✦✦

Chet Baker often sounded at his best during his later years when playing with a quiet trio consisting of himself, guitar and a bassist. For this reissue from the German Inak label, the trumpeter is joined in 1979 not only by guitarist Larry Coryell and bassist Buster Williams but by the mellow-toned vibraphonist Wolfgang Lackerschmid (who gets co-leadership) and a very restrained Tony Williams on drums. Although the CD only has 36 minutes of music, the mostly little-known material (five originals by the sidemen plus "Here's That Rainy Day") suits Baker fine. The emphasis is on slower tempos (other than Buster Williams' closing blues) including a pair of jazz waltzes and Baker's chops sound fine within the limited scope that he plays. The overall results are not essential but are worthwhile. —*Scott Yanow*

The Touch of Your Lips / Jun. 21, 1979 / Steeple Chase ✦✦✦✦

This was the perfect setting during his later years. The trumpeter (who also sings on two of the six songs) sounds very relaxed and comfortable while accompanied by the duo of guitarist Doug Raney and bassist Niels Pedersen, taking some consistently lyrical solos on the six standards. —*Scott Yanow*

No Problem / Oct. 2, 1979 / Steeple Chase ✦✦✦

Pianist Duke Jordan's presence adds some punch and spark to this quartet session, which is further helped along by bassist Niels Henning-Orsted Pedersen and selections that are suited for Baker's increasingly mellow and wavering playing. —*Ron Wynn*

Day Break / Oct. 4, 1979 / Steeple Chase ✦✦✦

This follow-up to *The Touch of Your Lips* also has the trumpeter/vocalist joined by guitarist Doug Raney and bassist Niels Pedersen but differs in that the repertoire (Jimmy Heath's "For Minor's Only," Hoagy Carmichael's "Daybreak," Richard Beirach's "Broken Wing" and Miles Davis' "Down") avoids standards in favor of lesser-known pieces. Baker is in fine form stretching out on these six- to eleven-minute performances. —*Scott Yanow*

Live in Montmartre, Vol. 2 / Oct. 4, 1979 / Steeple Chase ✦✦✦✦✦

The perfect setting for trumpeter Chet Baker in his later years was in an intimate trio with guitar and bass. Such is the case for this Steeple Chase CD reissue which adds a fifth song (Phil Urso's "Way to Go Out") to the original four-tune LP program. With fine support and solowork from guitarist Doug Raney and bassist Niels Pedersen, Baker is heard in top form on such tunes as "How Deep Is the Ocean," Wayne Shorter's "House of Jade" and "This Is Always." —*Scott Yanow*

Someday My Prince Will Come / Oct. 4, 1979 / Steeple Chase ✦✦✦

Chet Baker with Wolfgang Lackerschmid / Nov. 1979 / Inakustik ✦✦✦

This was a record not so much of rhythm as of tonal coloring, pitch and reverberation. This was also an avant-garde Chet Baker, without gimmicks, just meeting an interest to expand and further develop: to invent, expand, create. This was also very beautiful creativity, art for art's sake. Wolfgang Lackerschmid played vibes in a manner owing itself more to Red Norvo and Gary Burton than Milt Jackson, and proved himself to be a creator and artist in his ebb and flow with the trumpeter. Bravos for both artists. —*Bob Rusch, Cadence*

And the Boto Brasilian Quartet / Jul. 21, 1980-Jul. 23, 1980 / Dreyfus ✦✦

Chet Baker is in lyrical form throughout this Dreyfus CD, performing six of keyboardist Rique Pentoja's compositions plus two other obscure pieces. None of the laidback performances are all that memorable and Baker's vocal on "Forgetful" lives up to that piece's title. It is unusual to hear Baker joined by both an electric keyboardist and an accordion player although Richard Galliano (who is on the latter instrument) is only heard from occasionally. The results are quite musical and not without their moments of charm but fall very much into the easy-listening vein and are overly sleepy. —*Scott Yanow*

Live at Fat Tuesday's / Apr. 1981 / Fresh Sound ✦✦✦

In Concert / 1982 / India Navigation ✦✦✦

The matchup of the cool-toned trumpeter Chet Baker with the advanced but equally mellow-toned altoist Lee Konitz (in a pianoless quartet with bassist Michael Moore and drummer Beaver Harris) was a very logical combination. This CD reissues the original five-song LP program while adding three more selections from the same concert, all of them jazz standards. Baker and Konitz very much inspired each other on this frequently superb and exciting set. —*Scott Yanow*

Peace / Feb. 2, 1982 / Enja ✦✦

This one is a bit unusual since the trumpeter is accompanied by David Friedman (on vibes and marimba), bassist Buster Williams and drummer Joe Chambers. The music (which includes two takes of "3+15") is somewhat challenging ("The Song Is You" is the only standard) and it inspires Baker to come up with some lyrical

statements. There are many recordings from his final decade and his true fans will want to pick up this one. —*Scott Yanow*

Studio Trieste / Mar. 1982-Apr. 1982 / CTI ✦✦✦✦

Baker's CTI recordings (which were usually arranged by Don Sebesky) always came off well. For what would be his final CTI date, he was matched with guitarist Jim Hall, flutist Hubert Laws, and a fine rhythm section for two jazz standards ("Django" and "All Blues") and a pair of unusual pieces ("Malaguena" and "Swan Lake"). Throughout, Sebesky's charts favorably showcase Baker's lyrical trumpet, making this a recommended LP that deserves to be reissued on CD. —*Scott Yanow*

Out of Nowhere / Dec. 24, 1982 / Milestone ✦✦✦

Baker made a rare appearance in his home state of Oklahoma for this live gig with a group of local players. The trumpeter (who sings "There Will Never Be Another You") is in good form on these jazz standards and the other musicians (which include Frank Adams on alto and flute and guitarist Frank Brown) are inspired by his presence. This posthumously issued set should satisfy Chet Baker's many fans. —*Scott Yanow*

Mr. B / May 25, 1983 / Timeless ✦✦✦

Baker recorded many albums (mostly in Europe) during his final decade and it is surprising how consistent his trumpet playing generally was (as opposed to his singing) despite a very hectic and disorganized life. This Timeless set finds him accompanied by pianist Michel Graillier and bassist Ricardo del Fra for a variety of modern material including "Beatrice" (although the liners state that it is Baker's original, this was actually composed by Sam Rivers), Horace Silver's "Strollin'" and Dave Brubeck's "In Your Own Sweet Way." —*Scott Yanow*

The Improviser / Aug. 15, 1983-Aug. 30, 1983 / Cadence ✦✦✦

Baker recorded this Cadence LP in Norway, backed by a pair of fine Norwegian trios that in both cases include pianist Per Husby. In addition to Sam Rivers' "Beatrice" (a song that the trumpeter recorded numerous times) and the standard "Polka Dots and Moonbeams," this fine set includes interpretations of two Hal Galper songs ("Margarine" and "Night Bird") and Tadd Dameron's lesser-known "Gnid." Although a little loose in spots, this is an excellent date by the colorful trumpeter. —*Scott Yanow*

Live in Sweden with Åke Johansson Trio / Sep. 29, 1983 / Dragon ✦✦✦

At Capolinea / Oct. 1983 / Red ✦✦✦

For this Italian session, the trumpeter was joined by a flute-soprano-piano-bass-drums quintet of Italians. Although four of the six straightahead songs are group originals, Baker somehow sounds comfortable playing the new music, an impressive feat when one considers that he barely read music. It's not essential but enjoyable. —*Scott Yanow*

Blues for a Reason / Sep. 30, 1984 / Criss Cross ✦✦✦✦✦

This combination works quite well. For what might have been the only time in their careers, trumpeter Chet Baker and tenor saxophonist Warne Marsh were teamed together in a quintet (which also includes pianist Hod O'Brien, bassist Cecil McBee and drummer Eddie Gladden) for this Criss Cross session. The CD reissue adds two alternate takes to the original six songs which consist of "If You Could See Me Now," "Imagination," Marsh's "Well Spoken" and three Baker originals. Recommended. —*Scott Yanow*

Diane: Chet Baker and Paul Bley / Feb. 27, 1985 / Steeple Chase ✦✦✦

On first glance this duet session between Chet Baker and pianist Paul Bley should not have worked. Bley is primarily interested in freer improvising while Baker loved playing melodies but for this encounter the pianist compromised and laid down a fairly solid foundation for the veteran trumpeter. The results contain some chance-taking moments but sound more comfortable than one might have expected. —*Scott Yanow*

Chet's Choice / Jun. 6, 1985-Jun. 25, 1985 / Criss Cross ✦✦✦✦

One of the best settings for trumpeter Chet Baker was when he was accompanied by a guitar-bass duo. On this excellent Criss Cross CD, Baker is joined by guitarist Philip Catherine and bassist Jean-Louis Rassinfosse on a variety of high-quality standards that include such songs as "If I Should Lose You," Horace Silver's "Doodlin'," "Conception" and "Love for Sale." A special treat is hearing the talented but forgotten Bob Zieff's "Sad Walk." This is one of Baker's better albums from his later period. —*Scott Yanow*

Candy / Jun. 30, 1985 / Gazell ✦✦✦✦

Trumpeter Chet Baker, accompanied by pianist Michel Graillier and bassist Jean Louis Rassinfosse, covers a lot of emotional ground on this European date. This LP is highlighted by a passionate version of "Love for Sale," a surprisingly melancholy "Bye, Bye Blackbird," and a relatively upbeat rendition of "Tempus Fugit." —*Scott Yanow*

Strollin' / Jun. 1985 / Enja ✦✦✦✦

Baker always sounded at his best when performing in a trio with guitar and bass. Guitarist Philip Catherine and bassist Jean Louis Rassinfosse (both of whom had recorded with the trumpeter previously) are major assets to the subtle but swinging session. Each of the performances (Bob Zieff's "Sad Walk," Horace Silver's "Strollin'," "Love for Sale," "But Not for Me" and a 15-minute version of Richard Beirach's "Leaving") are extended versions but there are no rambling or wandering moments during this set of lyrical jazz. —*Scott Yanow*

Symphonically / Jul. 1985 / Soul Note ✦✦✦

When Sunny Gets Blue / Feb. 1986 / Steeple Chase ✦✦✦

Chet Baker in Tokyo / Jun. 14, 1987 / Evidence ✦✦✦

The Legacy, Vol. 1 / Nov. 14, 1987 / Enja ✦✦✦✦

On first glance, this CD might be mistaken for the pair of Enja releases titled *The Last Great Concert* which took place April 28, 1988. A few of the songs are the same and in both cases Baker was accompanied by the German NDR Big Band, but this particular set is taken from a previously unreleased concert from five months earlier and should delight his followers. Although Baker's singing voice had greatly declined through the years, his trumpet playing experienced a renaissance starting in the late '70s and he is in fine form throughout this purely instrumental set, a rare opportunity for the trumpeter to be showcased with a big band. Altoist Herb Geller and pianist Walter Norris (two of Baker's old friends) have occasional solos but the focus is almost entirely on Baker's horn and he proves up to the task, particularly on songs such as "In Your Own Sweet Way," "All of You" and "Look for the Silver Lining." —*Scott Yanow*

In Memory Of / Mar. 13, 1988-Mar. 14, 1988 / Optimism ✦✦

This is one of the odder releases of the 1980s. For the first and only times, trumpeter Chet Baker and tenor saxophonist Archie Shepp teamed up for a pair of concerts in a quintet which also included pianist Horace Parlan, bassist Herman Wright and drummer Clifford Jarvis. That Shepp is an emotional avant-gardist and Baker a cool-toned, lyrical trumpeter, and that both have radically different singing styles (they take a vocal apiece) results in the obvious: these two individualists do not blend together very well. Other than Shepp's "Dedication to Bessie Smith's Blues," the repertoire is all standards. Baker plays prettily, while Shepp sounds sloppy and heavy. This CD is definitely a historical curiosity, but does not need to be listened to more than once. —*Scott Yanow*

● **My Favourite Songs, Vols. 1-2: The Last Great Concert** / Apr. 28, 1988 / Enja ✦✦✦✦✦

Despite a rough up-and-down life, Baker remained an excellent trumpeter to the end of his career. This concert, performed two weeks before his mysterious fall out of an Amsterdam hotel window (and his last known recording), is a near-perfect summation of his career. The emphasis is on his trumpet playing and Baker, whether backed by a symphony orchestra, a big band or playing in a small group with altoist Herb Geller, is in inspired form. This double-CD set is also available as two separate CDs and, in one form or another, is highly recommended. —*Scott Yanow*

Ginger Baker

b. Aug. 19, 1939, London, England

Drums / Post-Bop, Hard Rock, Fusion, Art-Rock/Progressive-Rock, Jazz-Rock, Blues-Rock

Peter "Ginger" Baker is one of the most prominent drummers in popular music. He was born in Lewisham, London, and joined Alexis Korner's Blues, Incorporated in mid-1962, then moved on to the Graham Bond Trio (later the Graham Bond Organization) in February 1963, where he played with bassist Jack Bruce. The two then joined guitarist Eric Clapton in the summer of 1966 to form Cream, one of the most successful and influential British blues-rock groups of the late '60s. Cream broke up in November 1968 and was succeeded by Blind Faith, featuring Baker, Clapton, Steve Winwood, and Rick Grech, which lasted for one album and tour in 1969. In January 1970, Baker formed the loosely organized Ginger Baker's Air Force, which recorded two albums. He formed the Baker Gurvitz Army with Adrian and Paul Gurvitz in late 1974, and they made three albums. At the end of the decade, he had such groups as Energy and Ginger Baker's Nutters and played with Hawkwind and Atomic Rooster, before retiring to play polo. In 1982, he moved to an olive farm in Italy. But he was wooed back to music by producer Bill Laswell and made a number of instrumental albums before reuniting with Jack Bruce in BBM in 1994. The power-trio of BBM was shortlived and Baker returned to jazz-fusion by the end of the year with the worldbeat-tinged record *Going Back Home*. Two years later, he released *Falling off the Roof*, which was recorded with Charlie Haden and Bill Frisell. —*William Ruhlmann*

Horses & Trees / 1986 / Celluloid ✦✦✦✦✦

This instrumental percussion album mixes rock with various world musics, especially African influences, creating a stimulating soundscape. An impressive return from one of popular music's most distinctive drummers. —*William Ruhlmann*

● **Middle Passage** / 1990 / Axiom ✦✦✦✦✦

With producer Bill Laswell, mixing African drummers (Ayib Dieng, Mar Gueye, Magette Fall) with fusioneers (Bernie Worrell, Jonas Hellborg, Nicky Skopelitis) and bassists (Jah Wobble and Laswell) to land in a "middle passage" of worldbeat. Not bad at all. —*Michael G. Nastos*

Unseen Rain / 1992 / Day Eight ✦✦✦

This is an instrumental trio album with drummer Ginger Baker as leader and also featuring bassist Jonas Hellborg and pianist Jens Johansson. Baker is characteristically busy at the drum kit, but the three play off each other well, creating what is in essence a free-form jazz date. —*William Ruhlmann*

Going Back Home / 1994 / Atlantic ✦✦✦✦✦

Drummer Ginger Baker (who will always be best known for being one-third of the creative rock group Cream) followed a long period of retirement with an exploration of world music and then this CD, his first real jazz album. A trio set with the remarkable guitarist Bill Frisell and the great bassist Charlie Haden, the often-eccentric music could fit comfortably on one of Frisell's releases. The performances (all originals except Ornette Coleman's "Ramblin'" and the standard "Straight, No Chaser") are quite unpredictable and showcase each of the musician's large ears, quick reactions and continual creativity. The results of this unexpected matchup are quite stimulating. —*Scott Yanow*

Falling off the Roof / Dec. 12, 1995-Dec. 16, 1995 / Atlantic ✦✦✦

The second project to match drummer Ginger Baker with guitarist Bill Frisell and bassist Charlie Haden does not reach the heights of the first effort. Guest appearances by banjoist Béla Fleck on three songs and guitarist Jerry Hahn on one are welcome, but the diversity and wide scope of the first Baker trio set are not reached. The music often leans towards country (Frisell was probably preparing mentally for his *Nashville* project), the originals are less memorable than before, and the element of danger is mostly absent. A bit of a disappointment. —*Scott Yanow*

Shorty Baker (Harold J. Baker)

b. May 26, 1914, St. Louis, MO, **d.** Nov. 8, 1966, New York, NY

Trumpet / Swing

Harold "Shorty" Baker had a mellow sound and a lyrical style that was the modern successor to Arthur Whetsol in the Duke Ellington Orchestra. Originally a drummer, Baker switched to trumpet as a teenager. A fine section player and a warm soloist, Baker played with Fate Marable on riverboats, Erskine Tate, Don Redman (1936-38), Teddy Wilson's Orchestra (1939-1940) and Andy Kirk (1940-42). He married Mary Lou Williams (Kirk's pianist at the time). Baker was with Duke Ellington's Orchestra off and on during 1942-62 (particularly 1943-51 and 1957-59) during which he was well-featured despite being in a trumpet section that at times also included Ray Nance, Clark Terry, Taft Jordan, Willie Cook and Cat Anderson among others. He was with Johnny Hodges' group in the early '50s and after the Ellington years primarily led a quartet. Baker also recorded in later years with Bud Freeman and Doc Cheatham. —*Scott Yanow*

Shorty & Doc / Jan. 17, 1961 / Original Jazz Classics ✦✦✦✦

This CD reissue brings back a rare Swingville session that matches together the trumpets of Harold "Shorty" Baker and Doc Cheatham. At the time Baker, a veteran of Duke Ellington's Orchestra, was much better known and his soft tone and lyrical style often takes honors on this blowing date with pianist Walter Bishop, Jr., bassist Wendell Marshall and drummer J.C. Heard. For Doc Cheatham, then 55 and (unknown to everyone) only at the halfway mark of his career, this was just his second opportunity to lead a record date, 11 years after an obscure session in France. The results of this meeting are generally quite friendly rather than combative with Cheatham's Dixielandish phrasing sounding slightly old-fashioned next to Baker. They perform appealing swing-oriented material and sound fine in their many trade-offs. —*Scott Yanow*

Burt Bales

b. Apr. 20, 1916, Stevensville, MO, **d.** Oct. 26, 1989, San Francisco, CA

Piano / Ragtime, Stride

Overshadowed through the years by his contemporary Wally Rose, Burt Bales was a talented stride and ragtime pianist in his own right. He started playing piano when he was 12 and worked in California in the 1930s in various hotel and dance bands. Bales became part of the 1940s San Francisco jazz movement when he started playing with Lu Watters' Yerba Buena Jazz Band, but he was soon drafted (1943) and never officially recorded with the group (other than a session in which they were joined by Bunk Johnson). Poor eyesight resulted in his discharge from the service, and Bales led a band during 1943-46 before becoming the solo pianist at the 1018 Club in San Francisco for several years. After stints with Turk Murphy (1949-50), Bob Scobey and Marty Marsala, Bales mostly performed as a solo pianist (1954-66), often at Pier 23 in San Francisco. Although he spent a period outside of music working with electronics, Bales was active on at least a part-time basis until near his death. Bales recorded as a leader for Good Time Jazz (1949-50), Arhoolie, ABC-Paramount, Euphonic (1975), and in a pickup group for the Sacramento Jazz Society. —*Scott Yanow*

● **They Tore My Playhouse Down** / Oct. 22, 1949-Feb. 11, 1952 / Good Time Jazz ◆◆◆◆

Burt Bale's testament to Jelly Roll Morton has numbers such as "Wild Man Blues," "New Orleans Joys," and "Midnight Mama," backed with Paul Lingle's mixed bag of W.C. Handy and Morton's blues and stomps, including "Memphis Blues" and "Black Bottom Stomp" (1953). —*Bruce Raeburn*

New Orleans Ragtime / 1974 / Euphonic ◆◆◆

Burt Bales, a superior trad jazz pianist best-known for his associations with Turk Murphy and Bob Scobey, did not record enough during his career. This Euphonic LP might well fill the gap a bit. The set of solos leans heavily on Jelly Roll Morton with some Scott Joplin and early jazz classics also included. Lovers of pre-bop piano will enjoy this hard-to-find album. —*Scott Yanow*

Kenny Ball (Kenneth Daniel Ball)

b. May 22, 1930, Ilford, Essex, England
Trumpet / Dixieland

Kenny Ball will always be associated with his huge 1961 hit "Midnight in Moscow," cut in the days when it was possible for a Dixieland song to make it on to the charts. He started playing trumpet at age 15 and gained experience playing in the bands of Charlie Galbraith, Eric Delaney and Sid Phillips. In 1958 he formed his own group and quickly became a leader in Britain's trad jazz movement. "I Love You Samantha," his first hit and after "Midnight in Moscow" and "So Do I," Ball was set. He has remained active into the mid-'90s (touring the Soviet Union in 1985) and remains a household name in England. —*Scott Yanow*

Midnight in Moscow / Apr. 1961-Sep. 1961 / Kapp ◆◆◆◆

Kenny Ball's surprise hit of "Midnight in Moscow" in 1961 helped accelerate the trad jazz movement in England. Already a popular trumpeter, Ball's hit briefly made him an internationally known figure. This LP mostly has infectious versions of Dixieland standards featuring Ball, trombonist Johnny Bennett and clarinetist Dave Jones. —*Scott Yanow*

It's Trad / 1962 / Kapp ◆◆◆

Kenny Ball's follow-up album to *Midnight in Moscow* did not result in any new pop hits but the results do contain a great deal of joyous Dixieland. Trumpeter Ball (who is also a fine singer) formed an excellent front line with trombonist John Bennett and clarinetist Dave Jones as can be heard on a diverse set highlighted by "Cornet Chop Suey," "Potato Head Blues," "I Shall Not Be Moved," "The Green Leaves of Summer" and a tune called "My Old Man Said Follow the Van." —*Scott Yanow*

● **In Concert in the U.S.A., Vol. 1** / May 9, 1965 / Jazzology ◆◆◆◆

In 1965 Engligh trad trumpeter Kenny Ball was still riding high from the unexpected success of his 1961 hit "Midnight in Moscow." This LP (the first of two) features a rather definitive concert showcasing all of the members of Ball's band on some of their favorite songs. Highly recommended to fans of Dixieland, this set features Kenny Ball at his best. —*Scott Yanow*

In Concert in the U.S.A., Vol. 2 / May 9, 1965 / Jazzology ◆◆◆◆

The second of two LPs taken from a 1965 concert holds its own with the first half, highlighted by versions of "Midnight in Moscow," "I Shall Not Be Moved" and "Tiger Rag." The popular Kenny Ball has long been a talented trumpeter and an enjoyable singer and his sidemen have always been quite musical. —*Scott Yanow*

Gabe Baltazar

b. Nov. 1, 1929, Hilo, HI
Alto Saxophone / Bop, Hard Bop

Gabe Baltazar was one of the last great graduates from the Stan Kenton Orchestra but, because he lives in Hawaii, he is greatly underrated. Baltazar moved to the Mainland from Hawaii in the mid-'50s, recording with Paul Togawa in 1957 and spending a brief unrecorded period in 1960 with the Lighthouse All-Stars. He gained recognition for his years with Kenton (1960-65) during which he recorded quite a few rewarding solos. Baltazar worked with Terry Gibbs (1965) and recorded with Gil Fuller and Oliver Nelson before returning to Hawaii in 1969. In recent times he has visited California fairly often and recorded as a leader for the

Fresh Sound and V.S.O.P. labels, showing the jazz world just how strong a soloist he is. —*Scott Yanow*

Stan Kenton Presents Gabe Baltazar / Jan. 9, 1979-Jan. 11, 1979 / Creative World ◆◆◆

Gabe Baltazar was one of the last significant soloists to graduate from the Stan Kenton Orchestra. Because he has spent much of his career living in Hawaii and has recorded relatively little, he has been underrated for the past 30 years. This out-of-print LP, his debut as a leader, features Baltazar's alto in front of a big band with strings, playing a program mostly arranged by Don Menza. It is a good but not quite definitive showcase for Gabe Baltazar, one of the few he has had on record as a leader to date. —*Scott Yanow*

● **Back in Action** / Oct. 18, 1992-Oct. 1992 / V.S.O.P. ◆◆◆◆◆

Gabe Baltazar has long been one of the most underrated alto saxophonists in jazz. Because he long ago chose to live in Hawaii, his talents (which were earlier heard with the Stan Kenton Orchestra) have been overlooked but this V.S.O.P. CD signalled a higher profile on the Mainland when it was released. Backed by pianist Tom Rainier, bassist Richard Simon and drummer Steve Houghton, Baltazar is in brilliant form, interpreting standards and blues in his bop-oriented style. His reshapings of "Is It True What They Say About Dixie?" and "The Birth of the Blues" are among the high points. —*Scott Yanow*

Birdology / Oct. 24, 1992-Oct. 25, 1992 / Fresh Sound ◆◆◆◆◆

Considering his talent, it is surprising that altoist Gabe Baltazar has recorded so infrequently through the years. Much of it is due to him living in Hawaii, but fortunately, Baltazar's visits to the Mainland have become more common in the 1990s. This quartet set with pianist Frank Strazzeri, bassist Andy Simpkins and drummer Nick Martinis finds the boppish altoist in peak form. His heated "Birdology 101" mixes together excerpts of several Charlie Parker lines into a coherent song, Baltazar digs into some ballads (including the haunting "Autumn Nocturne," Hoagy Carmichael's "One Morning in May" and a rare outing on clarinet on "Memories of You") and cooks hard on most of the other selections. His definitive CD, this set is available from the Spanish Fresh Sound label. —*Scott Yanow*

Billy Bang

b. Sep. 20, 1947, Mobile, AL
Violin / Avant-Garde

One of the most stimulating, bluish and accessible violinists in the avant-garde, Billy Bang had a false start on his instrument as a youth and then became serious in 1968. Along the way he studied with Leroy Jenkins and by 1972 he was gigging. In 1977 Bang helped form the co-op group the String Trio of New York with guitarist James Emery and bassist John Lindberg, leaving in 1986. Bang, who has played with Ronald Shannon Jackson's Decoding Society and Material, has recorded frequently as a leader (including an intriguing Stuff Smith tribute set with Sun Ra in a quartet). —*Scott Yanow*

Changing Seasons / Dec. 28, 1980 / Bellows ◆◆◆

This is a difficult record to find, out of print but worth looking for. The opening track, "Summer Night (With Crickets)" lays down an irresistibly funky groove—not in the fusion sense of the word, but in the acoustic sense. Tsuchitori brings an almost Asian rhythmic influence to the setting, though this is strictly jazz. At 13 minutes, there is plenty of elbow room for everyone to stretch out in, and they do take advantage of that fact. The proceedings have an organic, woody feel to them, as if they are playing deep within forest. After the first track, things grow somewhat denser, and more complex. The closing "Winter Rains" brings everything back down to earth. This particular group did not stay together long, which is a shame. There is the feeling that they are just beginning to become family. —*Scot Hacker*

Rainbow Gladiator / Jun. 10, 1981-Jun. 1981 / Soul Note ◆◆◆◆

Ever since his emergence in the late '70s, Billy Bang has been one of the top violinists in the jazz avant-garde (along with his predecessor Leroy Jenkins), a musician not shy to play either melodies or sound explorations. This set, his first as a leader, finds Bang holding his own with a strong cast of players including Charles Tyler on alto and baritone and pianist Michele Rosewoman. All six compositions are Bang's, making this a good introduction to his music for those who have an open mind towards adventurous jazz. —*Scott Yanow*

Invitation / Apr. 13, 1982-Apr. 14, 1982 / Soul Note ◆◆◆

Outline, No. 12 / Jul. 1982 / Celluloid ◆◆◆

Fine, animated, but tough-to-find album featuring violinist Billy Bang, arguably the most striking to emerge on the jazz scene since Leroy Jenkins. The songs on this set weren't gentle, demure or bluesy; they were explosive, searching, and combative and, as such, were ideal for Bang's sawing effects and sweeping solos. —*Ron Wynn*

The Fire from Within / Sep. 19, 1984-Sep. 29, 1984 / Soul Note ✦✦✦

Billy Bang, one of the top violinists of the avant-garde, combines a classical technique with a rough rural sound. On this release he performs seven of his diverse originals with a sextet that also features trumpeter Ahmed Abdullah, guitarist Oscar Sanders, Thurman Barker on marimbas, bassist William Parker and drummer John Betsch. The music is abstract but often melodic and more accessible than one might expect. —*Scott Yanow*

● **Live at Carlos 1** / Nov. 23, 1986 / Soul Note ✦✦✦✦✦

Violinist Billy Bang uses the same instrumentation on this set as on his previous *The Fire from Within* although his sextet had two new members: trumpeter Roy Campbell and drummer Zen Matsuura. A more rhythmic album, this melodic avant-garde set rewards repeated listenings and has an impressive amount of variety. —*Scott Yanow*

Valve, No. 10 / Mar. 8, 1988-Mar. 9, 1988 / Soul Note ✦✦✦

This very intriguing set finds the adventurous jazz violinist Billy Bang leading a quartet that includes tenor saxophonist Frank Lowe, bassist Sirone and drummer Dennis Charles. The music is often quite melodic (particularly Lowe's relaxed solos) yet is utterly unpredictable. Bang combines a strong technique with a primitive sound and it may take listeners a little while to get used to his tone. —*Scott Yanow*

Tribute to Stuff Smith / Sep. 1992 / Soul Note ✦✦✦

The connections to the past are worth pointing out here: Sun Ra and violinist Stuff Smith once played together, back in 1953 or 1954. Bassist John Ore has also been a staple in Ra's bands, and Andrew Cyrille is no stranger to any of this crew. That said, those who like their violin "inside" will want to start their Bang collections with this recording: it is the last avant-garde of his oeuvre. For Sun Ra lovers, this recording will be important for being probably the very last thing he did before passing on to the interplanetary spaceways. The entire date is relaxed and highly structured. Like Smith, Bang plays here well within established boundaries, but still manages to place his notes somewhere just out of reach, in a place that's difficult to put a finger on, and all the more rewarding because of this enigma. —*Scot Hacker*

Spirits Gathering / Feb. 28, 1996 / CIMP ✦✦✦✦

Paul Barbarin (Adolphe Paul Barbarin)

b. May 5, 1899, New Orleans, LA, d. Feb. 17, 1969, New Orleans, LA
Drums / New Orleans Jazz

One of the top New Orleans drummers, Paul Barbarin was also quite significant as both a bandleader (his groups almost always boasted high musicianship) and as a composer (he wrote "Bourbon Street Parade" and "The Second Line"). Part of a large musical family, Paul's father Isadore played brass instruments; three of his brothers were musicians (including Louis, who was also a fine drummer), and his nephew was banjoist Danny Barker. Paul started on clarinet before saving up enough money to buy a set of drums. He played in many important New Orleans groups, including the Silver Leaf Orchestra and the Young Olympia Band, and early on developed a basic, straightforward style that was perfectly suitable for both parades and dances; the press roll was his specialty. In 1917, Barbarin moved to Chicago, playing with local groups (including some that he led) and with Freddie Keppard and Jimmie Noone. From 1923-24, he returned to New Orleans, where he performed with the Onward and Excelsior bands, before moving back to Chicago late in 1924 to join King Oliver (1925-27). After more time back in New Orleans, Barbarin relocated to New York in 1928, where he joined Luis Russell's notable band, staying until 1932 and anchoring one of the top jazz groups of the era. After leaving Russell, Barbarin freelanced in both New York and New Orleans and then rejoined Russell in 1935, staying with the pianist when the orchestra became Louis Armstrong's backup band. In 1938 he left to lead his own group in New Orleans, and after a short stint back with Armstrong in 1941, he became a member of Red Allen's sextet (1942-43). Other than a period with Sidney Bechet in 1944 and some work with Art Hodes in Chicago (1953), Barbarin mostly led his own bands from this point on (including the Onward Brass Band, which he founded in 1955), staying based in his hometown. It was somehow fitting that, when he passed away, it was while taking part in a New Orleans street parade. Through the years, Paul Barbarin recorded with King Oliver, Luis Russell, Jelly Roll Morton, Louis Armstrong and Sidney Bechet, in addition to leading many sessions of his own (starting in 1950) for 504, Circle, GHB, Jazztone, Atlantic, Good Time Jazz, Southland and Nobility. —*Scott Yanow*

Paul Barbarin and Percy Humphrey / 1951 / Storyville ✦✦✦

The first of ten volumes put out by the Storyville label (all of which consist of live performances of New Orleans jazz bands from the early to mid-'50s), this CD has excellent performances from drummer Paul Barbarin's group (which features trumpeter Ernie Cagnolatti, clarinetist Albert Burbank and trombonist Eddie Pier-

son) and a decent outing from what was billed as "Percy Humphrey's Jam Session" (with solo space divided between the trumpeter-leader, clarinetist Raymond Burke, trombonist Joe Avery and pianist Sweet Emma Barrett). New Orleans jazz fans will want to acquire the entire series which has more than its share of spirited and fun music. —*Scott Yanow*

New Orleans Jamboree / Dec. 1954 / Jazztone ✦✦✦✦

This hard-to-find LP showcases drummer Paul Barbarin's excellent New Orleans jazz group of the 1950s, a band featuring trumpeter John Brunious, trombonist Bobby Thomas, clarinetist Willie Humphrey and Danny Barker on banjo. They romp on such tunes as "Gettysburg March," "Tiger Rag," "L'il Liza Jane" and "The Second Line," not to mention "The Saints." This set is long overdue to be reissued. —*Scott Yanow*

● **And His New Orleans Jazz** / Jan. 7, 1955 / Atlantic ✦✦✦✦✦

Drummer Paul Barbarin (a fine composer whose "Bourbon Street Parade" is included on this set) always had New Orleans bands that played in tune, knew how to solo, and could jam in coherent and often exciting ensembles. This Atlantic release features his 1955 septet (with trumpeter John Brunious, clarinetist Willie Humphreys, trombonist Bob Thomas, pianist Lester Santiago, Danny Barker on banjo and guest bassist Milt Hinton) playing a variety of traditional and ancient themes. These performances, ranging from three to nine minutes, find the band really stretching out and creating memorable and enjoyable music. —*Scott Yanow*

Paul Barbarin and Punch Miller / Jul. 5, 1962 / Atlantic ✦✦✦

Recorded with Punch Miller, this album offers a mixed bag featuring Paul Barbarin's Band/Punch Miller's Bunch & George Lewis (cl). It's worth acquiring for the Barbarin composition "The Second Line" alone, but offers much more. —*Bruce Raeburn*

Paul Barbarin's Bourbon Street / 1962 / Southland ✦✦✦

Paul Barbarin's 1962 band was a particularly strong one, featuring trumpeter/vocalist Thomas Jefferson and clarinetist Louis Cottrell. Unfortunately this LP has an excess of vocals by Blanche Thomas and a version of "Just a Little While to Stay Here" completely given to Sister Elizabeth Eustis and her choir, so the musicians are not heard from as much as one might like. However, the spirit of their brand of New Orleans jazz is quite infectious and this LP is still worth searching for. —*Scott Yanow*

Chris Barber

b. Apr. 17, 1930, Welwyn Garden City, Hertfordshire, England
Trombone / Dixieland

One of the leaders of England's early-'60s trad jazz movement, Chris Barber (a solid trombonist) has been leading his own bands since 1948. In 1954 trumpeter Pat Halcox joined Barber and with the later additions of clarinetist Monty Sunshine, banjoist/singer Lonnie Donegan and blues singer Ottilie Patterson, Barber had an all-star crew. Sunshine's hit version of "Petite Fleur" made both Barber and the clarinetist into big names. Although his group was based in Dixieland, Barber has long been open-minded towards ragtime, swing, mainstream, blues, R&B and rock. He has collaborated with many artists including Louis Jordan, Russell Procope, Wild Bill Davis and Dr. John and has toured the US several times since 1959. —*Scott Yanow*

Petite Fleur / Apr. 12, 1953-Sep. 12, 1957 / Hallmark ✦✦✦

This long out-of-print LP gives one a good overview of trombonist Chris Barber's recordings of the mid-'50s. His English trad band had an unexpected hit with their version of Sidney Bechet's "Petite Fleur," a feature for clarinetist Monty Sunshine. That recording is included on this LP along with hot versions of a variety of well-known (such as "The Saints" and "Sweet Georgia Brown") and obscure (including "Olga" and "Thriller Rag") tunes from the 1920s. Pat Halcox's trumpet solos and Ottilie Patterson's vocals are major assets. —*Scott Yanow*

Barber/Bue Bestsellers / Oct. 8, 1954+1963 / Storyville ✦✦✦✦

Despite the title, this CD reissue does not contain the "greatest hits" or most-requested numbers by the Chris Barber and Papa Bue bands. What is contained on the release is a couple of worthwhile sessions by these two popular European Dixieland bands. Trombonist Barber and the 1954 edition of his group (a sextet that includes trumpeter Pat Halcox, clarinetist Monty Sunshine and the banjo and vocals of Lonnie Donegan) jam through five joyous numbers (including "Ice Cream" and "Tiger Rag") in a style that helped lead to the British trad jazz craze of the early '60s. Papa Bue's Viking Jazz Band (with the leader on trombone and trumpeter Finn Otto Hansen) performs less interesting material including a couple of Swedish folk songs, "Listen to the Mockingbird," and even the theme from *Bonanza!* Papa Bue does his best to Dixiefy the tunes but it is a bit of a struggle. —*Scott Yanow*

Guest Artist Lonnie Donegan / Oct. 9, 1954-Jan. 9, 1956 / Everest ✦✦✦
This budget LP from the obsolete Everest label features Chris Barber's Dixieland band of 1954 and 1956. Barber's output was fairly consistent through the years although his group was still in its formative stage. Trombonist Barber, trumpeter Pat Halcox and clarinetist Monty Sunshine are the main soloists while Lonnie Donegan contributes three spirited vocals including his hit "Rock Island Line." However this album is rather chintzy with under 30 minutes of music. —*Scott Yanow*

Original Copenhagen Concert / Oct. 10, 1954 / Storyville ✦✦✦
In 1954, trombonist Chris Barber became a full-time bandleader, and he has had his own group ever since. The original unit, one of the first English trad bands, is well featured on a wide-ranging show at this concert, which has been reissued along with three previously unreleased tracks on a 1995 Storyville CD. The Barber band (with trumpeter Pat Halcox, clarinetist Monty Sunshine, who is showcased on "St. Philip Street Breakdown," and Lonnie Donegan on banjo, guitar and vocals) was more primitive than it would become, often looking at the time towards George Lewis' group for inspiration. A change of pace is heard on two selections that have Donegan singing folk songs ("Over in the New Burying Ground" and "Leavin' Blues") with Barber forming a duet by switching to bass. A historic release, although there are better Chris Barber CDs currently available. —*Scott Yanow*

In Budapest / Jul. 7, 1962 / Storyville ✦✦✦✦
The 1962 Chris Barber English trad band (featuring trumpeter Pat Halcox, Ian Wheeler on clarinet and alto, and singer Ottilie Patterson) shows a lot of versatility on this CD, playing everything from Duke Ellington's "Mood Indigo" and Ruth Brown's "Mama, He Treats Your Daughter Mean" to the ancient "Whistling Rufus" and a spirited "Ice Cream." It's an enjoyable set of Dixieland and blues. —*Scott Yanow*

Live in East Berlin / Nov. 26, 1968 / Black Lion ✦✦✦✦
This CD features the 1968 Chris Barber band playing music that ranges from English trad to early Duke Ellington and even some gospel numbers. The trombonist/leader, his longtime trumpeter Pat Halcox and John Crocker (on clarinet and alto) form a potent front line for spirited renditions of such numbers as "Royal Garden Blues," "Saratoga Swing," "Wild Cat Blues" and Johnny Hodges' "Sweet as Bear Meat." —*Scott Yanow*

Echoes of Ellington, Vol. 1 / Jun. 3, 1976 / Timeless ✦✦✦✦
Trombonist Chris Barber was one of the most popular British bandleaders of the early 1960s "trad" boom. During this 1976 concert of Duke Ellington-associated tunes (which has been released on CD by Timeless), Barber and his septet (which includes trumpeter Pat Halcox and the reeds of John Crocker) actually only perform five of the nine numbers (highlighted by "Stevedore Stomp" and "Shout 'Em Aunt Tilly"). Ellington alumnus Russell Procope is well featured on the four other numbers, doubling on alto and clarinet while backed by a rhythm section that also includes organist Wild Bill Davis (who sticks exclusively to piano); this date gave Procope (who also sits in with Barber's band on "Mood Indigo") a rare opportunity to stretch out. Recommended. —*Scott Yanow*

Take Me Back to New Orleans / Apr. 4, 1980-Apr. 9, 1980 / Black Lion ✦✦
Although Chris Barber gets first billing on this CD, singer/pianist Dr. John dominates much of the music which attempts to depict several scenes in New Orleans including a funeral, a concert on Canal Street and visits to Bourbon Street and Basin Street. In general the music is merely routine and the jazz content is not as strong as one might hope. Chris Barber has recorded many better albums. —*Scott Yanow*

Barbican Blues / Apr. 20, 1982 / Black Lion ✦✦✦
This two-LP set from the British Black Lion label features Chris Barber's Jazz and Blues Band during a London concert in 1982. The trombonist-leader is joined by his longtime trumpeter Pat Halcox, both John Crocker and Ian Wheeler on reeds, guitarist Roger Hill, banjoist Johnny McCallum, bassist Vic Pitt and drummer Norman Emberson. While the program emphasizes 1920s tunes and Dixieland standards (including "Bourbon Street Parade," "Bugle Boy March," "Wild Cat Blues" and "Ice Cream"), there are also some swing tunes (such as Johnny Hodges' "Good Queen Bess"), an ad-lib blues and George Gruntz's "Spanish Castles." A fine example of Barber's popular trad band in the early 1980s although this two-fer will be difficult to find. —*Scott Yanow*

● **Copulatin Jazz** / 1993 / Great Southern ✦✦✦✦✦
The repertoire performed by Chris Barber's band on this CD may be full of warhorses but the hot Dixieland performances are full of such enthusiasm and high musicianship that this set is highly recommended. With trumpeter Pat Halcox and the reeds of John Crocker and Ian Wheeler joining trombonist Barber on the front line, this band infuses such songs as "Down by the Riverside," "Swanee River,"

"My Old Kentucky Home" and even "The Saints" with new life. Dixieland fans should consider this CD to be essential for their collections. —*Scott Yanow*

Patricia Barber

b. , Chicago, IL
Vocals, Piano / Post-Bop, Cabaret
Patricia Barber is a difficult performer to easily categorize. A singer with an unusual voice and a talented jazz pianist, Barber has sought to expand the repertoire that singers have today by not only taking obscurities from the pop world but writing her own material. A fixture at Chicago's Gold Star Sardine Bar since 1984 (switching in more recent years to the Green Mill), Barber is the daughter of a saxophonist who played with Glenn Miller (Floyd Barber). She studied classical piano, played saxophone in her high-school band, and mostly stuck to classical while at the University of Iowa before switching permanently to jazz. She worked locally in Iowa, moved back to Chicago and formed a regular trio. Beginning in 1989 Barber started appearing regularly at the North Sea Jazz Festival. Thus far she has recorded for her own Floyd label (1989's *Split*), Antilles (1992's *A Distortion of Love*) and more recently for Premonition. —*Scott Yanow*

A Distortion of Love / Nov. 25, 1991-Nov. 29, 1991 / Antilles ✦✦✦✦
Patricia Barber's debut finds the vocalist-pianist performing moody originals, a couple of standards (including an eerie version of "Summertime") and a few oddities (including Smokey Robinson's "My Girl"). She is assisted by guitarist Wolfgang Muthepiel, bassist Marc Johnson and drummer Adam Nussbaum in a set of challenging and thought-provoking music that has plenty of subtle surprises. —*Scott Yanow*

● **Cafe Blue** / 1994 / Premonition ✦✦✦✦
Patricia Barber, who is both a fine keyboardist and an atmospheric singer, contributes roughly half of the material to her Premonition debut. Her dark voice and the generally esoteric program takes awhile to get used to (listeners will have to be patient) but after two or three listens this thought-provoking and rather moody set becomes more accessible. The music ranges stylewise from sophisticated pop sensitivities to the avant-garde and even touches of minimalism while not fitting securely into any category. Barber gives a new slant to "The Thrill Is Gone," "Ode to Billy Joe" and even "A Taste of Honey" and her vocals are all quite haunting and contemporary. An added plus to this unusual music is the adventurous guitarist John McLean. —*Scott Yanow*

Gato Barbieri (Leandro J. Barbieri)

b. Nov. 28, 1934, Rosario, Argentina
Tenor Saxophone / Avant-Garde, Latin Jazz, Pop
Gato Barbieri is the second Argentinian musician to make a significant impact upon jazz—the first being Lalo Schifrin, in whose band Barbieri played as a teenager. His story has been that of an elongated zigzag odyssey between his homeland and North America. He started out playing traditional Latin rhythms in his early years, turning his back on his heritage to explore the jazz avant-garde in the '60s, reverting to South American influences in the early '70s, playing pop and fusion in the late '70s, only to go back and forth again in the '80s. North American audiences first heard Barbieri when he was a wild bull, sporting a coarse, wailing, John Coltrane/Pharoah Sanders-influenced tone. Yet by the mid-'70s, his approach and tone began to mellow somewhat in accordance with ballads like "What a Diff'rence a Day Makes" (which he always knew as the vintage bolero "Cuando Vuelva a tu Lado") and Carlos Santana's "Europa." Still, regardless of the idiom in which he works, the warm-blooded Barbieri has always been one of the most overtly emotional tenor sax soloists on records, occasionally driving the voltage ever higher with impulsive vocal cheerleading.

Though Barbieri's family included several musicians, he did not take up an instrument until the age of 12 when a hearing of Charlie Parker's "Now's the Time" encouraged him to study the clarinet. Upon moving to Buenos Aires in 1947, he continued private music lessons, picked up the alto sax, and by 1953 had become a prominent national musician through exposure in the Schifrin orchestra. Later in the '50s, Barbieri started leading his own groups, switching to tenor sax. After moving to Rome in 1962 with his Italian-born wife, he met Don Cherry in Paris the following year and, upon joining his group, became heavily absorbed in the jazz avant-garde. Barbieri also played with Mike Mantler's Jazz Composers' Orchestra in the late '60s; you can hear his fierce tone unleashed in the "Hotel Overture" of Carla Bley's epic work "Escalator over the Hill."

Yet after the turn of the next decade, Barbieri experienced a slow change of heart and began to re-incorporate and introduce South American melodies, instruments, harmonies, textures and rhythm patterns into his music. Albums such as the live *El Pampero* on Flying Dutchman and the four-part *Chapter* series on Impulse—the latter of which explored Brazilian and Afro-Cuban rhythms and textures, as well as Argentinian—brought Barbieri plenty of acclaim in the jazz world and gained him a following on American college campuses.

However, it was a commercial accident, his sensuous theme and score for the controversial film *Last Tango in Paris* in 1972, that made Barbieri an international star and a draw at festivals in Montreux, Newport, Bologna and other locales. A contract with A&M in the US led to a series of softer pop-jazz albums in the late 1970s, including the brisk-selling *Caliente!* He returned to a more intense, rock-influenced, South American-grounded sound in 1981 with the live *Gato... Para Los Amigos* under the aegis of producer Teo Macero, before doubling back to pop-jazz on *Apasionado*. Yet his profile in the US was diminished later in the decade in the wake of the buttoned-down neo-bop movement.

Beset by triple-bypass surgery and bereavement over the death of his wife Michelle, who was his closest musical confidant, Barbieri was inactive through much of the 1990s. But he returned to action in 1997, playing with most of his impassioned intensity, if limited in ideas, at the Playboy Jazz Festival in Los Angeles and recording a somewhat bland album, *Que Pasa,* for Columbia. —*Richard S. Ginell*

Gato Barbieri and Don Cherry / 1965 / Inner City ✦✦✦
This LP features tenor saxophonist Gato Barbieri (at the beginning of his career) and trumpeter Don Cherry teaming up with a French rhythm section for the trumpeter's five-part "Togetherness." While Cherry plays fairly free, he sounds conservative next to the often-violent wails of Barbieri. This interesting set (long out-of-print) is for the open-minded only. —*Scott Yanow*

In Search of Mystery / Mar. 15, 1967 / ESP ✦✦✦
Gato Barbieri's ESP album finds the Argentine tenor playing some ferocious solos on four of his originals. Joined by cellist Calo Scott, bassist Sirone and drummer Bobby Kapp, Barbieri is virtually the whole show so this set is mainly interesting for listeners who enjoy the intense tone he had in his early days. —*Scott Yanow*

Obsession / May 1967-Jun. 1967 / Affinity ✦✦✦
Backed by bassist Jean-Francois Jenny Clark and drummer Aldo Romano on this LP, tenor saxophonist Gato Barbieri plays with great intensity and fire during these lengthy performances (two versions of "Obsession" and "Michelle"; the latter has no relation to the Beatles' tune). Barbieri's playing would become, if not more mellow, much more melodic a few years later, but at this early stage he was in his avant-garde stage, playing with ferocious energy. —*Scott Yanow*

Confluence / Mar. 16, 1968 / Arista ✦✦✦✦
In 1968 tenor saxophonist Gato Barbieri and pianist Abdullah Ibrahim (then known as Dollar Brand) recorded a surprisingly successful set of duets. Although their collaboration was unexpected (Barbieri at the time was mostly known for his intense solos and Brand for his melodic qualities), they seemed to bring out the best in each other, performing two originals apiece and finding a great deal of common ground. —*Scott Yanow*

The Third World / Nov. 24, 1969+Nov. 25, 1969 / Flying Dutchman ✦✦✦
Spectacular frenetic tenor solos, daring Afro-Latin concept. —*Ron Wynn*

● **Fenix** / Apr. 27, 1971-Apr. 28, 1971 / Flying Dutchman ✦✦✦✦✦
The manic album that won him fame on college campuses in the early '70s. —*Ron Wynn*

El Pampero / Jun. 18, 1971 / RCA ✦✦✦✦
After making his initial reputation as a passionate avant-gardist in Europe, Gato Barbieri rediscovered his Third World roots in the early 1970s. *El Pampero* finds him at a transitional point in his career. Performing with a percussion-filled sextet live at the 1971 Montreux Jazz Festival, Barbieri's playing is as intense as previously but there is more of an emphasis on melody, particularly on his version of "Brasil." —*Scott Yanow*

Under Fire / 1971 / Flying Dutchman ✦✦✦
Superb solos, great bass work from Stanley Clarke. —*Ron Wynn*

Last Tango in Paris / Nov. 20, 1972-Nov. 25, 1972 / United Artists ✦✦✦✦
An incredibly popular soundtrack, dreamy and lush. Still sounds great 20 years later. Grammy winning, sensual soundtrack to the controversial film. —*Ron Wynn*

Latino America / Apr. 18, 1973-Oct. 17, 1973 / Impulse! ✦✦✦✦✦
Tenor saxophonist Gato Barbieri made some of his definitive recordings during 1973-75, rediscovering his Argentinian heritage and combining folky melodies with his own passionate, often screaming sound. During this era, he recorded the albums *Chapter One, Chapter Two, Chapter Three, Chapter Four* and *Yesterdays.* This two-CD set from 1997 has the complete *Chapter One* and *Chapter Two* sessions, including five previously unreleased recordings and four that had only been out in shortened form. Recorded in both Buenos Aires and Los Angeles, the music features Gato and a variety of mostly South American musicians performing highly rhythmic music with lots of lengthy vamps. Barbieri's jubilant playing,

punctuated with his eccentric vocal outbursts, is the main reason to acquire this strong release. —*Scott Yanow*

The Third World Revisited / 1974 / Bluebird ✦✦✦✦
Tenor saxophonist Gato Barbieri is in particularly fine form on this release, stretching out on four selections which include "Yesterdays," "Carinoso" and a song simply titled "A John Coltrane Blues." Backed by a six-piece rhythm section that includes Jorge Dalto's keybaords and guitarist Paul Metzke, Barbieri is often exuberant on this spirited and emotional set. —*Scott Yanow*

Chapter 3: Viva Emiliano Zapata / Jun. 25, 1974 / Impulse! ✦✦✦✦✦
On the third of four "Chapters," the intense tenor saxophonist Gato Barbieri is accompanied by a big band playing Chico O'Farrill arrangements. The charts really showcase Barbieri at his peak, performing four of his melodic originals, "Milonga Triste" and "What a Difference a Day Makes." This CD (a straight reissue of the original LP) is highly recommended. —*Scott Yanow*

Yesterday / 1974 / Flying Dutchman ✦✦✦

Chapter 4: Alive in New York / Feb. 20, 1975-Feb. 23, 1975 / ABC/Impulse! ✦✦✦
As with the first three "Chapters" in this series, this LP (which has not yet been reissued on CD) is easily recommended. Gato Barbieri was frequently heard at his best in the mid-'70s, featuring his very emotional tenor in melodic and highly rhythmic settings. This live set matches Barbieri with multi-instrumentalist Howard Johnson (who on this date plays the unusual triple of fluegelhorn, tuba and bass clarinet) and a strong rhythm section for four extended workouts. —*Scott Yanow*

Caliente / 1976 / A&M ✦✦✦
Large band. His best Latin jazz-pop recording. —*Ron Wynn*

Ruby, Ruby / Feb. 1978 / A&M ✦✦✦
An overproduced, but at times hypnotic, release from Barbieri. He achieved success with *Caliente*, an album filled with lush, sentimental material, so he copied that formula for *Ruby, Ruby*. It didn't yield any big hit, but did get consistent airplay on Adult Contemporary stations. —*Ron Wynn*

Tropico / May 1978 / A&M ✦✦

Euphoria / Mar. 1979 / A&M ✦✦
Good playing, lightweight material. —*Ron Wynn*

Para Los Amigos!! / Jun. 1981 / Doctor Jazz ✦✦✦

Apasionado / Oct. 1982 / Doctor Jazz ✦✦✦✦
After his successes of the mid-'70s, Barbieri, on the heels of his hit "Last Tango in Paris," went the commercial route for awhile. This Doctor Jazz LP was one of his better recordings of the '80s, a spirited workout with a large Latin rhythm section during which he interprets six lesser-known tunes (four written by Gato) plus a remake of "Last Tango." —*Scott Yanow*

Que Pasa / 1997 / Sony ✦✦
Gato Barbieri's first recording in a decade finds his distinctive (and always passionate) tenor tone still mostly intact. However, he does little other than state the 11 melodies (which range from catchy to completely forgettable), and the backing is quite anonymous, overproduced and obviously geared for potential radio airplay. In fact, if Gato's tenor were replaced by a vocalist, this would be a pop record. It is nice to have Gato Barbieri back on the scene again, but he is capable of much better than this run-of-the-mill effort. —*Scott Yanow*

Eddie Barefield (Eddie Emmanuel Barefield)

b. Dec. 12, 1909, Scandia, IA, d. Jan. 4, 1991, New York, NY
Clarinet, Tenor Saxophone, Alto Saxophone / Swing

A fine journeyman saxophonist and arranger, Eddie Barefield never gained much fame but he had a productive 60-year career. Barefield came to musical maturity in the 1930s, playing with Bernie Young (1930) in Chicago and then with Bennie Moten (1932), Zack Whyte (1933), the McKinney's Cotton Pickers (1933), Cab Calloway (1933-36), Les Hite (1937), Fletcher Henderson (1938) and Don Redman (1938). Barefield recorded with several orchestras, most notably Moten, Calloway and Henderson.

He supplied arrangements during the swing era to several top big bands (including Calloway, Glenn Miller, Benny Goodman and Jimmy Dorsey), was a staff musician for ABC in the 1940s and also was briefly with Benny Carter (1941), Ella Fitzgerald (1942) and Duke Ellington (1947). After playing with Fletcher Henderson's final band in 1950, Barefield mostly worked in the studios during the '50s and on Broadway in addition to returning now and then to Cab Calloway. He also played with Sammy Price (1958), Wilbur DeParis and the Saints and Sinners before joining the circus band of Ringling Brothers (1971-82). Barefield freelanced in many situations during his last two decades and recorded a fine 1977 album as a leader for Famous Door. —*Scott Yanow*

The Indestructible Eddie Barefield / 1977 / Famous Door ✦✦✦✦

A respected journeyman throughout his long career, Eddie Barefield led relatively few small-group sessions. For this rare outing, he teamed together the contrasting trumpets of Jon Faddis and Warren Vache in a septet with pianist John Bunch and guitarist Bucky Pizzarelli and performed six of his swinging originals. It's an unusual album well worth searching for. —*Scott Yanow*

Blue Lu Barker

b. Nov. 13, 1913, New Orleans, LA, **d.** May 14, 1998, New Orleans, LA

Vocals / Swing, Blues

Blue Lu Barker was a reluctant singer with a limited range who had a huge hit with "Don't You Make Me High" in 1938. She married Danny Barker in 1930 (a marriage that lasted until his death in 1994) and made a series of popular recordings for Decca in the late '30s (all of which are currently available on a Classics CD). Because she disliked singing in public (although she felt more comfortable in the recording studio), Barker only performed on a rare basis after the 1940s. —*Scott Yanow*

● **1938-1939** / Aug. 11, 1938-Dec. 13, 1939 / Classics ✦✦✦✦

This is one of the lesser entries put out by the European Classics label. Blue Lou Barker was a so-so singer who had the novelty hit "Don't You Make Me High"; all 21 of her prewar recordings are included on this CD. The more memorable moments are provided by the sidemen which include trumpeters Red Allen and Charlie Shavers, clarinetist Buster Bailey, tenor saxophonist Chu Berry, and her husband, guitarist Danny Barker. —*Scott Yanow*

Danny Barker

b. Jan. 13, 1909, New Orleans, LA, **d.** Mar. 13, 1994, New Orleans, LA

Banjo, Guitar, Vocals / New Orleans Jazz, Swing

A humorous personality as important for his storytelling and teaching as for his playing, Danny Barker had a long and colorful career. He played with the Boozan Kings early on in New Orleans and toured Mississippi with Little Brother Montgomery. In 1930 he moved to New York, switching from banjo to guitar and working with Dave Nelson, Sidney Bechet, Fess Williams, Albert Nicholas, James P. Johnson, Lucky Millinder (1937-38), Benny Carter (1938) and Cab Calloway (1939-46). He wrote "Don't You Feel My Leg" for his wife Blue Lu Barker (with whom he recorded frequently) and also had a hit with "Save the Bones for Henry Jones" (recorded by Nat King Cole). By 1947 Barker was fully involved in the Dixieland revival (he never cared for bebop), appearing on the *This Is Jazz* radio series, recording with Bunk Johnson and returning to the banjo. He performed at Ryan's throughout the 1950s (often with Conrad Janis or Wilbur DeParis) and then returned to New Orleans in 1965 where he worked as the assistant curator of the New Orleans Jazz Museum (1965-75), led the Onward Brass Band, encouraged younger players and wrote about his experiences. Danny Barker, who appeared at the 1993 Monterey Jazz Festival with Milt Hinton, penned his memoirs (*A Life in Jazz*) in 1986 and was active in keeping New Orleans jazz alive up until to the end. His definitive recording is a solo set for Orleans; Barker can also be heard late in life on records by Wynton Marsalis and the Dirty Dozen Brass Band. —*Scott Yanow*

● **Save the Bones** / 1988 / Orleans ✦✦✦✦✦

Veteran guitarist Danny Barker made a countless number of sessions through a five-decade period as a sideman but only two full-length dates as a leader. This CD is quite definitive, for Barker is heard singing and playing guitar unaccompanied on a variety of ancient standards and obscurities. Barker's version of "St. James Infirmary" (which contains many of his own lyrics and asides) is classic. —*Scott Yanow*

Emile Barnes

b. Feb. 18, 1892, New Orleans, LA, **d.** Mar. 2, 1970, New Orleans, LA

Clarinet / New Orleans Jazz

A respected New Orleans clarinetist, Emile Barnes made relatively few recordings during his career but can be heard on sessions for Folkways in 1951 and 1952 (which were issued in the 1970s on LPs) and for Jazzology during 1961 and 1963. He was the brother of Polo Barnes and learned from the early clarinetists including Lorenzo Tio, Jr. and Alphonse Picou. Barnes worked with Buddy Petit and Chris Kelly (the latter throughout the 1920s). He spent much of the 1930s and '40s outside of music but by the late '40s was gigging with Kid Howard and he remained fairly active in the 1950s and '60s. —*Scott Yanow*

Emile Barnes' Harmony Four / Jul. 1946-Aug. 7, 1954 / American Music ✦✦✦

Clarinetist Emile Barnes' relatively few recordings and strong reputation have made him a legend. This 1997 CD starts off with four selections featuring Barnes in 1946 (his recording debut) with trumpeters De De Pierce and Lawrence Tocca,

pianist Billie Pierce, and drummer Willie Wilson. The music, which includes "High Society" and "Walking the Dog," is better than the recording quality. The bulk of the release is from a pair of 1954 sessions by clarinetist Israel Gorman's quintet (which also includes trumpeter Charlie Love, trombonist Joe Avery, pianist Sweet Emma Barrett and drummer Albert Jiles) jamming both standards and some off-beat material, including "Kinklets," "Marine's Hymn" and "Grace & Beauty." The set concludes with a couple numbers from De De and Billie Pierce in 1953. Although the overall music is not essential—there are some flaws along the way that are sometimes compensated for by the spirit and joy—and Barnes himself is only on the opening session, collectors interested in historic New Orleans postwar trad jazz will find these performances to be of strong interest. —*Scott Yanow*

● **Early Recordings, Vol. 1** / Jul. 11, 1951 / Folkways ✦✦✦

During a period of time when there were not that many recordings being made in New Orleans, the legendary (and at that point unrecorded) clarinetist Emile Barnes was documented playing with a fine pickup group that also included trumpeter Lawrence Toca and trombonist Harrison Brazlee. On this LP, the first of two volumes, Barnes is in good form on ten standards (including two versions of "St. Louis Blues"), playing a style of New Orleans jazz rarely heard anymore. There are some rough moments from the other players but the spontaneity and joy of this music should win most New Orleans jazz fans over. —*Scott Yanow*

Early Recordings, Vol. 2 / Jul. 11, 1951-Sep. 8, 1952 / Folkways ✦✦✦

The second of two LPs documenting the earliest recordings of the legendary New Orleans clarinetist Emile Barnes contains six alternate takes from his 1951 sextet session with trumpeter Lawrence Toca and trombonist Harrison Brazlee heard in *Volume 1* plus six selections from the following year that feature a quintet with Barnes and trumpeter Charlie Love. Even with some erratic moments from the band, these two sets are recommended to New Orleans jazz fans; Barnes in particular is in good form. —*Scott Yanow*

George Barnes

b. Jul. 17, 1921, South Chicago Heights, IL, **d.** Sep. 5, 1977, Concord, CA

Guitar / Swing

A major player who has always been underrated, George Barnes was one of the first to record on electric guitar (accompanying blues singers) and was a top studio guitarist during much of his career. His style was very much based in the 1930s, and his single-note lines predated Charlie Christian, although he had much less of an impact. A professional by the time he was 13, Barnes was working on the staff of NBC by 1938. Based in Chicago, he recorded with Big Bill Broonzy, Washboard Sam and other blues performers. After a stint in the military during World War II, Barnes resumed his studio work and recorded radio transcriptions with his unusual octet. Although he performed in many types of settings in the 1950s, Barnes did not gain much recognition until he teamed up with fellow guitarist Carl Kress (whose sophisticated chord voicings perfectly complemented Barnes' solos) in the early '60s. After Kress' death in 1965, Barnes often collaborated with the younger guitarist Bucky Pizzarelli, but it was his period as co-leader of a quartet with cornetist Ruby Braff (1973-75) that gave Barnes his greatest fame, shortly before his death. He recorded as a leader for OKeh (two numbers in 1940), Wolf, Keynote (with his octet on a posthumously released Hindsight LP), commercial sides for Decca and Mercury, with Kress (and in one instance Bud Freeman) for Stash, United Artists and Audiophile, with Pizzarelli for Columbia and A&R, and in the 1970s for Famous Door and Concord. —*Scott Yanow*

The Uncollected: George Barnes and His Octet 1946 / 1946 / Hindsight ✦✦✦

George Barnes, a pioneering electric guitarist, was a very valuable studio musician during the 1940s and '50s. This Hindsight LP of previously unissued transcriptions made for radio has an unusual instrumentation. In addition to Barnes and a standard four-piece rhythm section (with drummer Frank Rullo doubling on vibes), there are four woodwind players utilizing clarinets, bass clarinets, an English horn, an oboe, flutes and a piccolo. Barnes is pretty much the only soloist on these 15 selections but his colorful and unpredictable arrangements give the other studio musicians plenty to do. The unusual set is quite enjoyable and somewhat unique. —*Scott Yanow*

Two Guitars / 1962 / Stash ✦✦✦

In the early '60s, the two great guitarists Carl Kress and George Barnes teamed up for a Town Hall concert and some rare recordings. This Stash LP finds Barnes playing single-note lines over Kress' sophisticated chordings. Their collaborations on this easily recommended set find the duo interpreting a variety of superior veteran standards along with Kress' "Golden Retriever Puppy Dog Blues" and an original by Barnes. —*Scott Yanow*

● **Two Guitars (And a Horn)** / 1962 / Stash ✦✦✦✦✦

On the follow-up to *Two Guitars*, the great guitarists George Barnes (who emphasizes single-note lines) and Carl Kress (whose chord voicings were unique) once again team up, this time for seven additional standards. The second side of this LP has the duo becoming a trio with the addition of tenor saxophonist Bud Freeman who contributes the colorfully titled originals "The Eel's Nephew" and "Disenchanted Trout." Timeless small-group swing music, it is well worth acquiring. Both of these sets should be reissued on CD. —*Scott Yanow*

Guitars Anyone / 1964 / Audiophile ✦✦✦
George Barnes and Carl Kress often teamed up to play guitar duets from 1962-65, although they made relatively few recordings. This Audiophile LP was their last meeting on record, and it finds the pair in high spirits on a dozen selections—11 standards and their collaboration "Don't Be Nervous." Highlights of this enjoyable set include "Blue Moon," "Undecided" and "Tea for Two." —*Scott Yanow*

Swing Guitar / Aug. 3, 1972 / Famous Door ✦✦✦
This hard-to-find LP from the now-dormant Famous Door catalog features the great swing guitarist George Barnes in a pair of all-star quartets with either Dick Hyman or Hank Jones on piano, bassist Milt Hinton and drummer Jo Jones. A few traditional themes are mixed in with the swing standards and Barnes is in top form throughout. —*Scott Yanow*

Plays So Good / Apr. 17, 1977 / Concord Jazz ✦✦✦
Guitarist George Barnes' final recording is rather brief (32 minutes) but this LP (which contains fine versions of nine standards) has its enjoyable moments. Accompanied by rhythm guitarist Duncan James, bassist Dean Reilly and drummer Benny Barth, George Barnes shows that he never did decline. His hornlike lines are always a joy to hear. —*Scott Yanow*

Charlie Barnet

b. Oct. 26, 1913, New York, NY, d. Sep. 4, 1991, San Diego, CA
Tenor Saxophone, Alto Saxophone, Soprano Saxophone / Swing, Big Band
Charlie Barnet was unusual in several ways. One of the few jazzmen to be born a millionaire, Barnet was a bit of a playboy throughout his life, ending up with a countless number of ex-wives and anecdotes. He was one of the few White big band leaders of the swing era to openly embrace the music of Duke Ellington (he also greatly admired Count Basie), Barnet was a pioneer in leading integrated bands (as early as 1935) and, although chiefly a tenor saxophonist (where he developed an original sound out of the style of Coleman Hawkins), Barnet was an effective emulator of Johnny Hodges on alto in addition to being virtually the only soprano player (other than Sidney Bechet) in the 1930s and '40s.

And yet Charlie Barnet was only significant in jazz for about a decade (1939-49). Although his family wanted him to be a lawyer, he was a professional musician by the time he was 16 and ironically in his career made more money than he would have in business! Barnet arrived in New York in 1932 and started leading bands on records the following year but his career was quite erratic until 1939. Many of Barnet's early records are worthy but some are quite commercial as he attempted to find a niche. Best is a sideman appearance on a 1934 Red Norvo date that also includes Artie Shaw and Teddy Wilson.

In 1939, with the hit recording of "Cherokee" and a very successful run at the Famous Door in New York, Charlie Barnet soon became a household name. In addition to the fine trumpeter Bobby Burnet (who soloed on many of Barnet's Bluebird records), such sidemen as guitarist Bus Etri, drummer Cliff Leeman, singers Lena Horne, Francis Wayne and Kay Starr, pianist Dodo Marmarosa, clarinetist Buddy DeFranco, guitarist Barney Kessel and even trumpeter Roy Eldridge spent time with Barnet's bands. Although at the height of his popularity during 1939-42 (when his orchestra could often play a close imitation of Ellington's), Barnet's recordings for Decca during 1942-46 were also of great interest with "Skyliner" being a bestseller.

By 1947 Barnet was starting to look towards bop. Clark Terry was his star trumpeter that year and in 1949 his screaming trumpet section included Maynard Ferguson, Doc Severinsen, Rolf Ericson and Ray Wetzel. Barnet however soon lost interest and near the end of 1949 he broke up his band. Semi-retired throughout the remainder of his life, Charlie Barnet occasionally led swing-oriented big bands during short tours and appearances, making his last recording in 1966. —*Scott Yanow*

Complete Charlie Barnet, Vol. 1 (1939-1942) / Jan. 21, 1935-Jan. 20, 1939 / Bluebird ✦✦
Charlie Barnet's entire output for Bluebird has been reissued on six two-LP sets. The first two-fer is actually the weakest for it finds Barnet during five sessions in 1936-37 searching for a sound of his own. There are a few hot swing numbers ("Growlin'," "Nagasaki," Benny Carter's arrangement of "Devil's Holiday" and a fine feature for the modernaires on "Make Believe Ballroom") but there is also an excess of sweet sides, erratic vocals (including eight by Barnet himself) and dull arrangements. It is not until the final two numbers on this set (both from early 1939) that the familiar Barnet sound emerges. Historically significant, Barnet collectors may want to acquire this initial volume last. —*Scott Yanow*

Complete Charlie Barnet, Vol. 2 / 1939 / Bluebird ✦✦✦
In 1939 Charlie Barnet, after several years of struggling and cutting a variety of erratic recordings, found his sound. His orchestra, featuring trumpeter Bobby Burnet and the leader's tenor, quickly became one of the better swing bands of the era. This second of six two-fers that reissue all of Barnet's Bluebird recordings has among its many highlights "Knockin' at the Famous Door," "The Gal from Joe's," "Jump Session," "Scotch and Soda," "Miss Annabelle Lee," "I Never Knew" and the band's big hit, "Cherokee." —*Scott Yanow*
essential as *Volumes 2-5*, this final set is still well worth picking up, especially by Charlie Barnet completists. —*Scott Yanow*

Complete Charlie Barnet, Vol. 3 / Jul. 17, 1939-Feb. 7, 1940 / Bluebird ✦✦✦
The third of six two-fers that reissue all of Charlie Barnet's Bluebird recordings finds the Duke Ellington-influenced orchestra progressing into 1940. Bobby Burnet contributes many fine trumpet solos, Barnet is generally memorable on tenor, and even on the slower numbers the band always swings. With such hot performances as "The Last Jump," "The Duke's Idea," "The Count's Idea," "The Right Idea" and "Clap Hands Here Comes Charlie," the Charlie Barnet band shows that it could hold its own with its top contemporaries. And, with the inclusion of the hilarious "The Wrong Idea" (a satire of sweet bands with a remarkable vocal from Billy May), this set is essential for swing fans. —*Scott Yanow*

Complete Charlie Barnet, Vol. 4 (1940) / Feb. 27, 1940-Jun. 19, 1940 / Bluebird ✦✦✦
The fourth of six two-LP sets in this perfectly done reissue series contains all of the Charlie Barnet big band's recordings from a busy four-month period. High points include "Leapin' at the Lincoln," "Afternoon of a Moax," "Flying Home," "No Name Jive" and "Rockin' in Rhythm." The brief electric guitar solos of Bus Etri are quite interesting and, even if there are an excess of vocals, those of Mary Ann McCall are generally worth hearing. —*Scott Yanow*

Complete Charlie Barnet, Vol. 5 (1940-1941) / Jul. 15, 1940-Jan. 23, 1941 / Bluebird ✦✦✦
The fifth of six two-LP sets that reissue all of Charlie Barnet's Bluebird recordings from 1935-42 finds his "Cherokee" big band at its prime on such memorable numbers as "Pompton Turnpike," "Ring Dem Bells," "Southern Fried," "Redskin Rumba," "Charleston Alley" and "Little John Ordinary." With Bobby Burnet taking some fine trumpet solos, Bernie Privin impressive as lead trumpeter, the forgotten electric guitarist Bus Etri getting some spots and Barnet adding his distinctive voices on tenor, alto and soprano, this was one of the top swing bands of the era. All six volumes of this superb series are worth searching for, particularly *Vols. 2, 3* and *5*. —*Scott Yanow*

Complete Charlie Barnet, Vol. 6 (1941-1942) / Jan. 20, 1939-Jan. 20, 1942 Bluebird ✦✦✦
The sixth and final two-LP set in this very valuable Bluebird series has all of Charlie Barnet's recordings from Jan. 23, 1941 through Jan. 20, 1942, plus early alternate takes of two numbers from 1939. Barnet had one of the finest White swing bands and this set contains a few real gems, including three Duke Ellington numbers ("Merry Go Round," "Birmingham Breakdown" and "Harlem Speaks"). Not as essential as *Volumes 2-5*, this final set is still well worth picking up, especially by Charlie Barnet completists. —*Scott Yanow*

Transcription Performances 1941 / Jan. 27, 1941 / Hep ✦✦✦
The Charlie Barnet Orchestra was busy on Jan. 27, 1941, waxing no less than 25 titles as radio transcriptions. There is one vocal apiece for Lena Horne ("It's a Haunted Town") and Bob Carroll, but otherwise it is a purely instrumental date. The popular Barnet band, which often looked towards Duke Ellington and Count Basie for inspiration, had few major soloists (trumpeter Bobby Burnet, pianist Bill Miller, guitarist Bus Etri and Barnet himself on tenor, soprano and alto) and a spirited ensemble sound. Many of the charts on this CD were provided by Horace Henderson, and the band swings hard on such numbers as "Charleston Alley," "Redskin Rhumba," "Little John Ordinary" and "Dutch Kitchen Stomp." —*Scott Yanow*

● **Drop Me Off in Harlem** / Apr. 30, 1942-Jun. 16, 1946 / Decca ✦✦✦✦✦
Charlie Barnet reached his greatest popularity during his years with Bluebird (1939-42) but the orchestra he led during his period with Decca (1942-46) was even more powerful. This CD contains 20 of their best recordings and, even if "Skyliner" was their only commercial hit, such top soloists as trumpeters Peanuts Holland, Al Killian and Roy Eldridge, clarinetist Buddy DeFranco, pianists Dodo Marmarosa and Al Haig, guitarist Barney Kessel and singer Kay Starr (not to mention Barnet himself) make strong appearances on this well-conceived and hard-swinging set. —*Scott Yanow*

1949 / Jun. 22, 1949-Oct. 1949 / Alamac ✦✦✦
This budget LP features Charlie Barnet's 1949 bop big band, a short-lived unit that featured a screaming trumpet section (with Maynard Ferguson, Doc Severinsen

and Ray Wetzel), modern arrangements and hot solos from the likes of altoist Vinnie Dean, tenor saxophonist Dick Hafer, pianist Claude Williamson, bassist Eddie Safranski and Barnet himself on tenor, alto and soprano. These broadcasts increase the slim discography of this forgotten but talented band. —*Scott Yanow*

Cherokee / Aug. 5, 1958 / Bluebird ✦✦✦
Charlie Barnet's band spurned conventional wisdom when they issued this set of rousing stompers and vintage standards in 1958. As the theory went, big bands had been dead for years and there was no interest among modern fans in these old numbers. That may or may not have been true then or now, but it was true enough that the band came out roaring on the title track and did not stop through 11 quick, often blistering numbers. The ensemble playing was furious but well disciplined, while solos were, out of necessity, quick, terse, and hot. Here is a disc proving that great material never goes out of style. —*Ron Wynn*

More / Sep. 3, 1958-Sep. 29, 1958 / Evidence ✦✦
This CD reissue brings back an Everest session that was one of Charlie Barnet's odder recordings. For this big-band set the distinctive swing tenor sticks exclusively to alto and soprano where his personality is much less unique. Actually, except for some moments from trumpeter Charlie Shavers, little memorable happens during these dozen performances which are mostly updates of swing hits. Bill Holman contributed the arrangements but his charts are much less interesting than usual and, although Phil Woods is in the sax section, the altoist does not have a single solo. Also, the sound quality on a few of the pieces (particularly "Evergreens") is a bit distorted. —*Scott Yanow*

Charlie Barnet Big Band: 1967 / Nov. 21, 1966 / Mobile Fidelity ✦✦✦
This LP was not only Charlie Barnet's final recording before he retired but is also the last album that veteran altoist Willie Smith ever made. With arrangements for the orchestra from Billy Byers and Bill Holman, solos by Barnet (on alto and soprano), Smith, pianist Jack Wilson and trumpeter Conte Candoli, and a fine Ruth Price vocal on "Something to Live For," this set wraps up Charlie Barnet's 32-year recording career quite nicely. —*Scott Yanow*

Joey Baron

b. Jun. 26, 1955, Richmond, VA
Drums / Avant-Garde
Joey Baron is chiefly associated with the avant-garde but he is versatile enough to fit into a wide variety of jazz-oriented settings. He has had a longtime association with Bill Frisell, co-led a group with Tim Berne and Hank Roberts, led an unusual trio (Barondown) with trombonist Steve Swell and tenorman Ellery Eskelin, and recorded with John Zorn but was also quite comfortable supporting Jim Hall and Toots Thielemans. —*Scott Yanow*

Tongue in Groove / May 1, 1991 / Polygram ✦✦✦
Joey Baron does the near-impossible on this CD, making music in a trio comprising his drums, trombonist Steve Swell and tenor saxophonist Ellery Eskelin; no piano, guitar or bass. Some of the originals find the unusual group resembling a high school band a bit while other pieces are quite explorative and interesting. The fact that the spirited group sounds complete much of the time is particularly notable. —*Scott Yanow*

● **Raised Pleasure Dot** / 1993 / New World ✦✦✦
Drummer Joey Baron has played with such unorthodox types as John Zorn, Wayne Horvitz and Tim Berne, so it's not surprising that his own sessions are equally diverse and ambitious. This date presents an unusual instrumental lineup and a free-wheeling, constantly changing musical menu. Baron heads a trio with trumpet and trombone; the absence of bass, keyboards, or guitar results in intriguing voicings, and the pieces are solely dependent on the interaction of his drumming with Ellery Eseklin's saxophone and Steve Sewell's trombone contributions. Elements of free jazz, contemporary funk, Afro-Latin, and even modern classical are incorporated into the mix, and it's an outstanding example of Joey Baron's scope and range as a composer, bandleader and player. —*Ron Wynn*

Down Home / 1997 / Intuition ✦✦✦✦

Dan Barrett

b. Dec. 14, 1955, Pasadena, CA
Trombone / Swing, Dixieland
A major player in the small-group swing movement of the 1980s and '90s, Dan Barrett's trombone is equally at home in Dixieland and swing settings. He started on trombone in high school and played in California with the South Frisco Jazz Band and the Golden Eagle Jazz Band, two fine trad groups. At the urging of Howard Alden, Barrett moved to New York in 1983 where he worked with the Widespread Depression Orchestra, played at Eddie Condon's club and in 1985 was with Benny Goodman's Orchestra. Barrett came to fame through his series of recordings (both as a leader and as a sideman) with Concord; among his many

projects were co-leading a quintet with Howard Alden that was reminiscent of John Kirby's band of the 1940s despite having very different instrumentation. Dan Barrett, who also played with Buck Clayton's Big Band, switched to the Arbors label in the 1990s where he became musical director and has recorded frequently. —*Scott Yanow*

● **Strictly Instrumental** / Jun. 1987 / Concord Jazz ✦✦✦✦✦
Trombonist Dan Barrett utilizes some of the top younger players of pre-bop in this delightful octet session. In addition to Barrett, the lineup includes cornetist Warren Vache, Ken Peplowski on clarinet and tenor, altoist Chuck Wilson, the late great pianist Dick Wellstood, guitarist Howard Alden, bassist Jack Lesberg and drummer Jackie Williams. Together they play a variety of high-quality standards including relative obscurities such as "No Regrets," Hoagy Carmichael's "Moon Country" and "There's Honey on the Moon Tonight." The concise solos and Barrett's clever arrangements make this a particularly memorable release. —*Scott Yanow*

Jubilesta / Dec. 3, 1991-Feb. 17, 1992 / Arbors ✦✦✦✦
Dan Barrett, probably the top young trombonist currently playing classic jazz, is very well featured on this quartet set with pianist Ray Sherman (himself in superior form), bassist David Stone and drummer Jake Hanna. Barrett revives such songs as "Why Can't You Behave?," "Then I'll Be Happy," "Wherever There's Love," "Wait 'Til You See 'Ma Cherie,'" and "Little Jazz," making one wonder why such attractive pieces are not performed more often. —*Scott Yanow*

Reunion with Al / Mar. 5, 1993-Mar. 6, 1993 / Arbors ✦✦✦✦
Trombonist Al Jenkins, who recorded with Doc Evans in the late 1940s and Art Hodes in 1956, spent much of his career playing either in the Midwest or in Los Angeles and never achieved much fame. He was an early influence on Dan Barrett's style, so in 1993, the younger trombonist persuaded Jenkins to join him on his record date. As it turned out, this would be Jenkins' final recording, since he passed away Nov. 15, 1996, at the age of 82. In deference to Jenkins, Barrett sticks to cornet exclusively on this CD (it is a pity they did not both play trombone on a song or two). With pianist Ray Sherman (always a marvelous soloist), bassist David Stone and drummer Jeff Hamilton contributing tasteful and swinging support, Barrett, Jenkins and Rick Fay (who switches between clarinet, soprano and tenor) make for an appealing front line. Jenkins was 80-90% in his prime at the time, and one excuses the occasional blurry note due to the rare experience of hearing him stretch out. Barrett's crisp cornet solos put him near the top of his field, despite it being his second instrument, while on this set Fay tends to sound at his best on tenor. The repertoire generally sticks to familiar tunes, but even the warhorses, such as "Sugar Blues," "After You've Gone" (a feature for Sherman's sparkling piano) and "I Can't Give You Anything But Love" (sung by Jenkins), sound quite fresh and enthusiastic. A definite highlight is the exuberant playing heard throughout "Do You Ever Think of Me." —*Scott Yanow*

Two Sleepy People / Jan. 2, 1994-Jan. 3, 1994 / Arbors ✦✦✦✦
The word that best sums up this set of duets by Dan Barrett and John Sheridan is "delightful." Trombonist Barrett (who doubles quite effectively on cornet) and the stride/swing pianist Sheridan match together quite well, inspiring each other on a set of older swing standards and obscurities. Although the emphasis is on melodic improvising, there are enough chances taken to make this music slightly unpredictable. The program begins and ends with different versions of "Two Sleepy People." Other highlights include an unusual jazz treatment of Hank Williams' "Hey, Good Lookin'," a four-song Billie Holiday medley that avoids the more obvious tunes, Louis Armstrong's rarely performed "Heah Me Talkin' to Ya," "All My Love" and "You Can't Lose a Broken Heart." Actually each of the 14 performances are quite enjoyable and this set is easily recommended to fans of Dixieland, swing and mainstream jazz. There is nothing sleepy about the music. —*Scott Yanow*

Sweet Emma Barrett

b. Mar. 25, 1897, New Orleans, LA, **d.** Jan. 28, 1983, New Orleans, LA
Piano, Vocals / New Orleans Jazz
Sweet Emma Barrett, who was at her most powerful in the early '60s, became a symbolic figure with the Preservation Hall Jazz Band, playing in a joyous but obviously weakened and past-her-prime style on world tours. Barrett spent most of her career living and playing in New Orleans, including gigs with Oscar "Papa" Celestin in the 1920s and later with Armand Piron. Sweet Emma, who gained the nickname of "the bell gal" because she wore red garters with bells that made sounds while she played, was purely a local figure until 1961, when she made her finest recording, a Riverside set with the future members of the Preservation Hall Jazz Band. Ironically, as Barrett (through the group's well-received tours) became better known, her playing and singing swiftly declined due to her age, and after a 1967 stroke, she continued to perform, despite having a largely paralyzed left hand. In addition to the recommended Riverside set (reissued on CD), Barrett led less significant sessions for GHB (1963-64), Preservation Hall, Nobility and a 1978 album for Smoky Mary. —*Scott Yanow*

● **Sweet Emma—New Orleans: The Living Legends** / Jan. 1961 / Original Jazz
Classics ✦✦✦✦✦

This CD reissue of the future members of the Preservation Hall Jazz Band is at
such a high level it makes one wonder why this group had so many erratic recordings. Pianist Emma Barrett (who also takes four vocals) is in fine form and trombonist Jim Robinson was always a major asset to any New Orleans jazz band but
it is the performances of trumpeter Percy Humphrey (who never sounded better
on record) and his brother, clarinetist Willie, that really makes this music special.
Together the septet plays such songs as "Bill Bailey," "Just a Little While to Stay
Here" and "The Saints" with drive, enthusiasm and surprising musicianship. It's
essential music for all New Orleans jazz fans. —*Scott Yanow*

Sweet Emma and Her Preservation Hall Jazz Band / Oct. 18, 1964 / Preservation Hall ✦✦✦

This LP features the Preservation Hall Jazz Band in its early days, when pianist/
vocalist Sweet Emma Barrett was the leader. Clarinetist Willie Humphrey and
trumpeter Percy Humphrey, although not up to the level they attained on the Riverside CD, are in better than usual form, and trombonist Jim Robinson is his usual
consistent self. This band clearly enjoys themselves jamming mostly on warhorses, making this a high-spirited set of New Orleans jazz. —*Scott Yanow*

Ray Barretto

b. Apr. 29, 1929, New York, NY
Percussion, Conga / Latin Jazz, Afro-Cuban Jazz, Salsa

While Ray Barretto's congas have graced more recording sessions than virtually
any other conguero of his time, he has also led some refreshingly progressive
Latin jazz bands over the decades. His records often have a more tense, more
adventurously eclectic edge than those of most conventional salsa groups,
unafraid to use electronics and novel instrumental or structural combinations,
driven hard by his rock-steady, endlessly flexible percussion work. This no doubt
reflects Barretto's wide range of musical interests and also the fact that he came to
Latin music from jazz, rather than the usual vice-versa route for Latin-descended
musicians. Indeed, he has said that he learned how to play swing-style before he
came to master Latin grooves. Puerto Rican by extraction, Barretto took up the
congas while stationed in Germany during an Army hitch. He began working
with American jazz musicians upon his return to New York, eventually replacing
Mongo Santamaria in the Tito Puente band for four years, beginning in the late
1950s. Barretto made his debut as a leader for Riverside in 1962 and scored a
crossover hit (No. 17 on the pop charts) the following year on Tico with "El Watusi"
(in tandem with a dance craze of the time). He tried to modernize the charanga
sound with injections of brass, covering rock and pop tunes of the time as several
Latin artists did then. However, Barretto made his main mark in the '60s as a
super session player, playing on albums by Gene Ammons, Cannonball Adderley,
Kenny Burrell, Lou Donaldson, Red Garland, Dizzy Gillespie, Freddie Hubbard,
Wes Montgomery, Cal Tjader and several other jazz and pop albums. In moving
over to the Fania label in 1967, Barretto began to achieve recognition as one of the
leading Latin jazz artists of the day, eventually becoming music director of the
Fania All-Stars. In the '70s, he was incorporating rock and funk influences into his
music—with only limited success—while recording for Atlantic, and in 1981, he
made a highly regarded album for CTI La Cuna, with Puente, Joe Farrell and
Charlie Palmieri as guest players. He became music director of the "Bravisimo"
television program and took part in the multi-idiom, all-star, anti-apartheid *Sun
City* recording and video in 1985. In 1992, he unveiled a new Latin jazz sextet
New World Spirit, which made some absorbingly unpredictable albums for Concord Picante. —*Richard S. Ginell*

Carnaval / 1962 / Fantasy ✦✦✦

These tough, energetic Afro-Latin and Latin jazz sessions were originally cut in
1962, when Barretto organized his first band as a leader and made albums in different styles. One was a charanga date, the other a surging jam session. This was
subsequently reissued in a two-record vinyl package, and now are available as a
single-disc set. —*Ron Wynn*

Fiesta en El Barrio / 1968 / Polydor ✦✦✦✦

If you wonder (a) why Barretto suddenly has such a hot band, (b) what the two
hokey Mexicali cuts are doing mixed in with all the other fine stuff, and (c) why
there are zippo notes, one explanation fits all. This CD, copyright 1994, is a re-
release of one of Barretto's long-lost 1960s United Artists recordings. But the
music is terrific: a hell of a swing, great solo trumpet. —*John Storm Roberts, Original Music*

Hard Hands / 1968 / Charly ✦✦✦

A 1968 album with Barretto in the midst of his most productive period. He had
made inroads into pop and jazz markets and was a dominant figure on the Latin
jazz and salsa circuit. The album not only provided the great conga player and
percussionist with a nickname, it yielded hit single "Abidjan" and also brought

personnel changes. Joseph Roman replaced Rene Lopez on trumpet (he'd been
drafted), and Tony Fuentes joined the group on bongos. —*Ron Wynn*

Eye of the Beholder / 1977 / Atlantic ✦✦

Percussionist Ray Barretto has been a valuable sideman for a couple of decades.
This Atlantic LP, however, finds Barretto's brand of Latin-jazz somewhat overshadowed by funk rhythms and commercial elements with a lot of faceless solos. There
are some worthwhile moments, but in general this set is a bit of a disappointment.
—*Scott Yanow*

Cuna / Aug. 1979 / Sony ✦✦✦✦

Producer Creed Taylor has inspired everything from praise to anger among jazz
fans. His work has been brilliant at times, detrimental at others (his worst flaw
being a tendency to overproduce). Taylor plays a mostly positive role on *La Cuna*,
a jazz-oriented effort uniting Ray Barretto with such first-class talent as Tito
Puente (timbales) and the late Joe Farrell (tenor & soprano sax, flute). As slick as
things get at times on *La Cuna* (originally released on vinyl by Taylor's CTI label
and reissued on CD in 1995), Taylor wisely gives the players room to blow on
everything from the haunting "Doloroso" and the driving "Cocinando" (a piece by
Carlos Franzetti that shouldn't be confused with Barretto's major salsa/cha-cha hit)
to a somewhat Gato Barbieri-ish take on Mussorgsky's "The Old Castle." Barretto
successfully moves into soul territory on Stevie Wonder's "Pastime Paradise"
(which rapper Coolio recast as his hit "Gangsta's Paradise" in 1994). Barretto may
hate the term "Latin jazz," but make no mistake: *La Cuna* is one of his most memorable contributions to that genre. —*Alex Henderson*

Aqui Se Puede / 1987 / Fania ✦✦✦

Barretto has a long history of producing a series of faintly disappointing albums
followed by a blockbuster. This one doesn't really bust any blocks, but it works the
classic trumpet/trombone expanded conjunto sound to fresher effect than he has
contrived for a while, helped by a very gutty trombonist in Jimmy Bosch. —*John
Storm Roberts, Original Music*

● **Handprints** / Mar. 1991 / Concord Picante ✦✦✦✦

Percussionist Ray Barretto, best-known as a sideman, had a rare chance to lead a
session in 1991 and his Concord Picante debut is quite impressive. With saxophonist Steve Slagle, trumpeter Tim Ouimette and trombonist Barry Olson leading the front line of this septet, Barretto mostly sticks to group originals for an
infectious Latin jazz session. —*Scott Yanow*

Live in New York / 1992 / Messidor ✦✦✦

Recent release by Messidor of the still-dynamic Ray Barretto heading a group for a
live New York concert. He ranks alongside Mongo Santamaria for consistency,
staying power, and impact in both jazz and jazz circles, and his conga playing
and presence drive a band like almost no other. —*Ron Wynn*

Ancestral Messages / Dec. 1992-Jan. 1993 / Concord Picante ✦✦✦

Although overshadowed during this era by Tito Puente and Poncho Sanchez, veteran percussionist Ray Barretto led one of the top Latin-jazz groups around a two-
horn septet. This fine release includes a few standards (including "Freedom Jazz
Dance" and "Killer Joe") along with a variety of excellent group originals, all of
them both stimulating and danceable. —*Scott Yanow*

Taboo / 1994 / Concord Picante ✦✦✦✦

Ray Barretto's group New World Spirit quickly became one of the top Latin jazz
bands of the mid-'90s. Trumpeter Ray Vega, saxophonist Adam Kolker and pianist
Hector Martignon create some worthy solos, Barretto takes some strong improvisations on congas and the band's repertoire finds the middle ground between salsa
and jazz. —*Scott Yanow*

My Summertime / Jul. 1, 1995-Jul. 3, 1995 / Owl ✦✦✦✦✦

Ray Barretto (a master of the congas) has effectively fused together bop-oriented
jazz with Latin rhythms to form a particularly viable version of Afro-Cuban jazz;
he hates the term "Latin jazz." Rather than sounding like two forms of music, Barretto's group New World Spirit shows that Latin rhythms can uplift all types of
jazz songs, even ballads such as "When You Wish upon a Star." Barretto's sextet is
quite strong with Michael Philip Mossman's trumpet recalling Freddie Hubbard at
times, Adam Kolker showing versatility and hard-driving swing during his tenor
and soprano solos, and the leader constantly cooking in the rhythm section.
Whether it be Duke Jordan's "No Problem," "While My Lady Sleeps" or "Summertime" (which has Barretto partly talking his way through a vocal), the music is
both creative and easily accessible. Recommended. —*Scott Yanow*

Contact! / Apr. 3, 1997-Apr. 9, 1997 / Blue Note ✦✦✦✦

Leading his longtime backing group New World Spirit, Ray Barretto assembled
another first-rate record with *Contact*. As usual, the music seamlessly shifts
between Latin jazz and bop, concentrating this time on straightahead jazz—the
Latin flourishes are there for coloring. It's one of his most bop-oriented dates and
it proves that Barretto is an excellent bop player, as well as one of the leaders of
Latin jazz. —*Stephen Thomas Erlewine*

Bill Barron

b. Mar. 27, 1927, Philadelphia, PA, d. Sep. 21, 1989, Middletown, CT

Tenor Saxophone, Soprano Saxophone / Hard Bop, Post-Bop

Bill Barron was an advanced and adventurous tenor saxophonist (doubling on soprano) who never compromised his music or received much recognition. He spent his formative years and beyond in Philadelphia, not moving to New York until 1958. Barron first came to the jazz world's attention through his participation on a Cecil Taylor date in 1959. After recording with Philly Joe Jones, Barron co-led a fine post-bop quartet with Ted Curson. However, Barron spent much of the remainder of his career as an educator, directing a jazz workshop at the Children's Museum in Brooklyn, teaching at City College of New York, and becoming the chairman of the music department at Wesleyan University. His "day job" made it possible for him to consistently record noncommercial music for Savoy (in 1972 he made that label's last jazz record), Dauntless and Muse. Every one of Bill Barron's recordings as a leader uses brother Kenny Barron (16 years his junior) on piano. — *Scott Yanow*

Nebulae / Feb. 21, 1961 / Savoy ✦✦✦

Originally titled *The Tenor Stylings of Bill Barron*, this set was tenor saxophonist Barron's debut as a leader after recently leaving Cecil Taylor's band. Teamed up with trumpeter Ted Curson, younger brother Kenny Barron (then just 17 but already talented) on piano, bassist Jimmy Garrison (just prior to joining John Coltrane), and drummer Frankie Dunlop, Bill Barron plays music that falls between advanced hard bop and the free jazz of Ornette Coleman. His seven originals (which include the previously unreleased "Desolation") are often complex, but consistently swing and contain plenty of unpredictable solos. Excellent music. — *Scott Yanow*

Hot Line / Mar. 31, 1962 / Savoy ✦✦✦✦

Tenors Bill Barron and Booker Ervin team up on this frequently exciting quintet outing with pianist Kenny Barron, bassist Larry Ridley and drummer Andrew Cyrille. Barron's five advanced originals alternate with three standards (including "Now's the Time," "Work Song" and a previously unissued "Billie's Bounce") that give the two tenors an opportunity to display their contrasting but complementary inside/outside styles. This fine release has been reissued on CD. — *Scott Yanow*

Jazz Caper / Aug. 1978 / Muse ✦✦✦

Bill Barron was always a bit overlooked during his career, and after 1968, he spent most of his time as an educator. This set was only his second date as a leader in 15 years, and it shows how the always adventurous tenorman (who doubled on soprano) had continued to advance through the years. Heading a quintet with trumpeter Jimmy Owens, his brother pianist Kenny Barron, bassist Buster Williams and drummer Ed Blackwell, Barron performs seven of his complex but thoughtful originals, including such titles as "Until Further Notice," One for Bird" and "Flip Flop." Intriguing music that rewards repeated listenings. — *Scott Yanow*

● **Variations in Blue** / Aug. 23, 1984-Aug. 24, 1984 / Muse ✦✦✦✦

Bill Barron, who spent much of his life as a music educator, played inventive solos that sounded both spontaneous and well thought out. Barron, who was underrated throughout his career, cut three records for Muse during 1978-87, of which this set was the second. Barron, his brother, pianist Kenny Barron, trumpeter Jimmy Owens, bassist Ray Drummond and drummer Ben Riley perform five of the leader's complex originals (including "Swingin' in Bushness Park," which finds the tenorman switching to soprano) and Gigi Gryce's "Minority." — *Scott Yanow*

The Next Plateau / Mar. 1987 / Muse ✦✦✦✦

Bill Barron's final album (which has been reissued on CD) finds the distinctive but underrated tenorman (then about to turn 60 and two years before his death) playing five of his obscure but superior originals, including "This One's for Monk" and "Travelin' on the Freeway," plus pianist Kenny Barron's blues "Row House." The two brothers are joined by bassist Ray Drummond and drummer Ben Riley for a consistently stimulating advanced post-bop outing, one of Bill Barron's finest recordings. — *Scott Yanow*

Kenny Barron

b. Jun. 9, 1943, Philadelphia, PA

Piano / Hard Bop, Post-Bop

In recent years Kenny Barron has been recognized as one of the giants of modern mainstream piano. The younger brother of the late saxophonist Bill Barron (who was 16 years older), he started on piano when he was 12 and played with Mel Melvin's R&B band in 1957. Barron moved to New York in 1961 where he worked briefly with James Moody, Lee Morgan, Roy Haynes and Lou Donaldson. Most significant were his four years (1962-66) playing and recording with Dizzy Gillespie. Barron followed that important association with periods in the groups of Freddie Hubbard (1966-70), Yusef Lateef (1970-75) and Ron Carter's two-bass quartet (1976-80). Barron was a co-leader of the group Sphere in the 1980s and since then has

generally been the leader of his own trios. The pianist was on Stan Getz's final session (a series of brilliant duets) and has recorded many dates as a leader. In the 1990s Barron received long overdue recognition for his talents. — *Scott Yanow*

Sunset at Dawn / Apr. 2, 1973 / Muse ✦✦✦

Kenny Barron could easily go unidentified if some of the selections on this CD reissue were played for a listener during a "blindfold test" for he sounds quite unrecognizable on the three numbers on which he plays electric piano. Barron, who is joined by electric bassist Bob Cranshaw, drummer Freddie Waits and the colorful percussion of both Richard Landrum and Warren Smith on his five originals and one by Waits, utilizes electricity with intelligence and creativity. His songs are moody and complex yet somewhat accessible and this underrated set would certainly surprise some of his current fans. Barron is the main soloist on every selection while Landrum and Smith's versatile colors add a lot to the unusual session's value. — *Scott Yanow*

Soft Spoken Here / Apr. 2, 1973-Apr. 18, 1980 / 32 Jazz ✦✦✦✦✦

Two of pianist Kenny Barron's earlier LPs (*Sunset to Dawn* and *Golden Lotus*) are reissued in full on this double CD from 1997. The 1973 date has its moments of interest, with Barron doubling on electric piano as part of a five-piece rhythm section, performing five of his originals and a song by drummer Freddie Waits. Those post-bop sides hint a bit at fusion and funk while still remaining reasonably creative. However, it is the later set (a quintet outing with John Stubblefield on tenor and soprano, vibraphonist Steve Nelson, bassist Buster Williams and drummer Ben Riley) that is of greatest interest; the group performs four Barron tunes, including "Golden Lotus," plus "Darn That Dream." Nelson's playing at that early stage showed great potential that he has since largely realized. An excellent two-fer. — *Scott Yanow*

Peruvian Blue / Mar. 14, 1974 / Muse ✦✦✦

A more experimental, diverse album than Barron has made in quite some time. This 1974 date saw him playing in varied settings and alternating the size and personnel according to the song. There were solos, duos, tunes with bass and drums, then one with multiple percussion. Barron's playing has grown since then, but his albums, while beautifully played, aren't anywhere as unusual. — *Ron Wynn*

Golden Lotus / Apr. 4, 1980 / Muse ✦✦✦

Solid 1980 session with the always vibrant, challenging pianist Kenny Barron and the underrated saxophonist John Stubblefield in fiery form. Steve Nelson began generating interest on vibes with his playing on this session. It has been reissued on CD. — *Ron Wynn*

Green Chimneys / Jul. 9, 1983 / Criss Cross ✦✦✦✦

Fine trio date, as Barron, bassist Buster Williams, and drummer Ben Riley prove you can inject life into warhorses and constantly played standards. They recorded this for the Criss Cross label in Holland. — *Ron Wynn*

1 + 1 + 1 / Apr. 23, 1984-Apr. 24, 1984 / Black Hawk ✦✦✦

This out-of-print LP finds the talented if underrated pianist Kenny Barron in excellent form during duets with either Ron Carter or Michael Moore on bass. The one exception is a creative solo version of "'Round Midnight." Barron has never recorded a bad record and this set is above average with seven standards and Carter's "United Blues" all receiving favorable and subtly swinging treatment. — *Scott Yanow*

Scratch / Mar. 11, 1985 / Enja ✦✦✦✦

Kenny Barron, one of those talented pianists who always seems to be underrated, breaks away from playing standards and conventional bebop on this frequently exciting trio date. Matched up with bassist Dave Holland and drummer Daniel Humair, Barron explores five of his originals and Carmen Lundy's "Quiet Times." The fresh material and close interplay between the musicians make this set one of Barron's best trio recordings to date. — *Scott Yanow*

What If? / Feb. 17, 1986 / Enja ✦✦✦✦

Live at Fat Tuesday's / Jan. 15, 1988-Jan. 16, 1988 / Enja ✦✦✦

Barron stretches out and plays both flashy and hot and cool, on this 1988 set cut at Fat Tuesday's in New York. Bassist Cecil McBee and drummer Victor Lewis drive the rhythms a bit harder than the Riley/Drummond team, while Eddie Henderson and John Stubblefield on trumpet and tenor sax add some welcome intensity and contrasting solo voices. — *Ron Wynn*

Rhythm-A-Ning / Sep. 3, 1989 / Candid ✦✦✦✦

Kenny Barron and John Hicks are both well-respected veteran pianists whose styles fall well within the modern mainstream of jazz, initially influenced by Bud Powell but today much closer to McCoy Tyner. They join forces for this two-piano quartet date with bassist Walter Booker and drummer Jimmy Cobb. Only the 5:35 "Ghost of Yesterday" (a feature for Booker's bowed bass) and "Rhythm-A-Ning" at 9:50 clock in under 12 minutes. Although it can be fun to figure out who is playing what when, Barron and Hicks have such complementary styles that they often sound like one pianist with four hands. Their riotous version of "Rhythm-A-Ning" is the high point of this successful collaboration. —*Scott Yanow*

The Only One / Jun. 6, 1990 / Reservoir ♦♦♦
Standards galore, each played with care, artistry, and brilliance by the Kenny Barron trio. If there must be continued recording of "Love for Sale" and "Surrey with the Fringe on Top," then these are the people to do it. —*Ron Wynn*

● **Live at Maybeck Recital Hall, Vol. 10** / Dec. 3, 1990 / Concord Jazz ♦♦♦♦♦
Wonderful Kenny Barron solo set. Bonus cuts in disc. —*Ron Wynn*

Invitation / Dec. 20, 1990 / Criss Cross ♦♦♦

Lemuria-Seascape / Jan. 17, 1991 / Candid ♦♦♦
The Barron/Drummond/Riley trio step forward into the '90s and churn out another impressive collection, this one containing mostly either Barron or group originals rather than tons of standards. Exacting, carefully constructed, and consistently brilliant playing all around. —*Ron Wynn*

Quickstep / Feb. 18, 1991 / Enja ♦♦♦

Wanton Spirit / Feb. 22, 1994-Feb. 23, 1994 / Verve ♦♦♦♦

Things Unseen / 1997 / Verve ♦♦♦♦
Things Unseen is a lovely set of swinging jazz, finding pianist Kenny Barron supported by a stellar combo of saxophonist John Stubblefield, trumpeter Eddie Henderson, guitarist John Scofield, bassist David Williams, drummer Victor Lewis, violinist Naoko Terai and percussionist Mino Cinelu. Barron's playing, alternately graceful and kinetic, confirms his status as one of the finest pianists of the '90s, and *Things Unseen* is another welcome addition to his canon. —*Stephen Thomas Erlewine*

Gary Bartz

b. Sep. 26, 1940, Baltimore, MD
Alto Saxophone, Soprano Saxophone / Post-Bop
When Gary Bartz burst upon the scene in the late '60s and particularly when he led his Ntu Troop in the early '70s, he showed the potential of becoming one of the important leaders of jazz. Although he spent an aimless period in commercialism and never quite fulfilled the initial potential, by the late '80s Bartz had returned to jazz in prime form. He had started on alto at age 11 and, after studying at Juilliard and the Peabody Conservatory, Bartz worked with the Max Roach-Abbey Lincoln group in 1964. He followed that up by stints with Art Blakey's Jazz Messengers (1965-66), McCoy Tyner and Blue Mitchell. Bartz made a strong impression with Miles Davis' 1970-71 fusion group, emerging as perhaps the strongest soloist on the recording *Live/Evil*. The altoist, who had recorded as a leader for Milestone and Prestige fairly regularly since 1967, did some of his finest work at the 1973 Montreux Jazz Festival (released on Prestige as *I've Known Rivers and Other Bodies*). From that point on his recordings became funkier and more commercial; 1978's *Love Affair* on Capitol (which featured a discofied version of "Giant Steps") was an obvious lowpoint. However by 1987 Bartz started recording stronger albums for Mapleshade, Steeple Chase and Candid. Now, instead of being a potential giant, Gary Bartz is an underrated (and often totally overlooked) jazz great. —*Scott Yanow*

Libra / May 31, 1967+Jun. 15, 1967 / Milestone ♦♦♦
Featured are excellent compositions and playing in mainstream mode. It includes Kenny Barron on piano and Jimmy Owens on trumpet. This is the more lyrical side of Bartz. —*Michael G. Nastos*

Another Earth / Jun. 19, 1968-Jun. 25, 1968 / Milestone ♦♦♦♦
This out-of-print LP (one of several from the Prestige and Milestone catalog that are long overdue to be reissued on CD) was one of the finest of altoist Gary Bartz's early years. The 24-minute multimovement "Another Earth" is a stormy affair matching Bartz with trumpeter Charles Tolliver, the fiery tenor Pharoah Sanders, pianist Stanley Cowell, bassist Reggie Workman and drummer Freddy Waits. The flip side of the record has three quartet outings by Bartz, Cowell, Workman and Waits, including the mysterious ballad "Dark Nebula" and an uptempo blues, "UFO," plus a Bartz-Workman duet on "Lost in the Stars." Well worth searching for, this adventurous music is quite colorful and always holds one's interest. —*Scott Yanow*

Home / Mar. 30, 1969 / Milestone ♦♦♦

Juju Street Songs / Follow, the Medicine Man / Oct. 1972 / Prestige/Ace ♦♦♦
Juju Street Songs / Follow, the Medicine Man combines two early '70s albums Gary Bartz recorded with his NTU Troop onto one CD. Both of the albums are excursions into African music, with hard-bop and soul-jazz foundations and while that very conceit sounds dated today, there's some moments that stand out particularly well. You either love or hate keyboardist Andy Bey's vocals, which usually are about some mystical spirit, but the music itself is often a heady fusion of jazz-

rock, worldbeat and hard-bop that sounds surprisingly fresh decades after it was recorded, even if the end result is a little uneven. —*Stephen Thomas Erlewine*

Follow the Medicine Man / Oct. 1972 / Prestige ♦♦♦
Gary Bartz's NTU Troop played an interesting brand of music, mixing together the influences of the avant-garde, hard bop, African folk songs and early fusion and funk. This album features Bartz (on alto, soprano and sopranino) with singer/keyboardist Andy Bey, bassist Stafford James and drummer Howard King; two songs have Hubert Eaves in Bey's place and add guitarist Hector Centeno. The emphasis is mostly on group originals, plus the pop tune "Betcha by Golly, Wow," and is generally atmospheric and (with its dated electronics) very much of the period, but it still sounds good. —*Scott Yanow*

I've Known Rivers and Other Bodies / Jul. 7, 1973 / Prestige ♦♦♦♦♦
At the time of this Montreux Festival concert (which has been released almost complete), altoist Gary Bartz was one of the most promising players in jazz. Already a veteran of the Miles Davis and McCoy Tyner bands, Bartz's future appeared limitless. Although he has not quite lived up to his potential and maintained a rather low profile since the 1970s, Bartz is still playing well over 20 years after this impressive effort. His 1974 quartet (which consisted of pianist Hubert Eaves, bassist Stafford James and drummer Howard King) is in top form on this lengthy two-LP set of original music, creating a new modern mainstream of fresh material that never really caught on. —*Scott Yanow*

Singerella: A Ghetto Fairy Tale / Nov. 1973+Feb. 1974 / Prestige ♦

Music Is My Sanctuary / 1975 / Capitol ♦♦

Jujuman / Oct. 1976 / Catalyst ♦♦♦
Although altoist Gary Bartz's career was beginning to become a bit aimless during this period (as if he were searching for commercial success), and his recordings tended to be erratic, this mostly straightahead outing was a major exception. Bartz teams up with pianist Charles Mims, bassist Curtis Robertson and drummer Howard King for a stimulating set of music. While "Ju Ju Man" effectively uses voices in a tribute of sorts to John Coltrane's "A Love Supreme," "My Funny Valentine" is a feature for the warm vocal of Syreeta, 'Trane's "Straight Street" and Bartz's "Pisces Daddy Blue" are both swinging, and "Chelsea Bridge" finds the leader taking rare solos on soprano and clarinet. This was Gary Bartz's best jazz session as a leader until he re-emerged on Mapleshade in 1987; it is a pity that the Catalyst label's LPs are difficult to find. —*Scott Yanow*

Love Song / May 1978 / VJ International ♦♦♦
A reasonably enjoyable but not essential release, this album features altoist Gary Bartz (doubling on soprano) performing some originals and older R&B tunes with a four-piece rhythm section (which includes George Cables on electric piano and guitarist Carl McDaniels); three songs have soulful vocalists. The music overall is generally danceable and funky, sounding a bit dated despite some decent solos. Not Gary Bartz's worst (from a jazz standpoint), but also far from his best. —*Scott Yanow*

Bartz / 1980 / Arista ♦♦

Monsoon / Apr. 1988 / Steeple Chase ♦♦♦

Reflections of Monk / Nov. 1988 / Steeple Chase ♦♦♦♦

● **West 42nd Street** / Mar. 31, 1990 / Candid ♦♦♦♦♦
After a long period of indifferent recordings, altoist Gary Bartz started to fulfill his potential in the early 1990s. Joined by a superb rhythm section (comprising pianist John Hicks, bassist Ray Drummond and drummer Al Foster) and trumpeter Claudio Roditi (whose restrained power complements than competes with Bartz), the altoist really stretches out, particularly on "Speak Low" and "The Night Has a Thousand Eyes" which both clock in at within seven seconds of 19 minutes apiece. Bartz is quite lyrical on a superior version of "It's Easy to Remember" and also takes inventive solos on his modal blues "Cousins" and Wilbur Harden's "West 42nd Street." A highly recommended gem. —*Scott Yanow*

There Goes the Neighborhood / Nov. 11, 1990-Nov. 12, 1990 / Candid ♦♦♦♦
Although he dismissed notions about a comeback, this 1990 album was the triumphant, exuberant vehicle Gary Bartz hadn't made in quite a while. His rippling solos and dominant presence were welcome for fans who wondered if he had squandered the potential he'd shown in the '60s. —*Ron Wynn*

Shadows / Jun. 11, 1991-Jun. 12, 1991 / Timeless ♦♦♦

Episode One: Children of Harlem / Jan. 20, 1994 / Jazz Challenge ♦♦
Although the theme of this CD is ostensibly supposed to be nostalgia for Harlem, the music (which includes the "Amos n' Andy Theme") actually has little to do with the subject. However Bartz (who is heard on alto and soprano) is in fine form playing with a top-notch quartet that also includes pianist Larry Willis, bassist Buster Williams and drummer Ben Riley. The hard-bop oriented music includes a few standards (including "Tico Tico" and "Crazy She Calls me") and three originals by either Bartz or Willis. It's not essential but enjoyable. —*Scott Yanow*

Red & Orange Poems / Sep. 24, 1994-Sep. 25, 1994 / Atlantic ✦✦✦

Alto veteran Gary Bartz may not have made it as big as originally predicted but, as shown on this 1994 studio date, he developed a sound of his own and was always capable of coming out with exciting yet thoughtful music. Joined by such associates as trumpeter Eddie Henderson, John Clark on French horn, pianist Mulgrew Miller, bassist Dave Holland, drummer Greg Bandy and percussionist Steve Kroon, Bartz is in excellent form on a variety of standards (including "By Myself" and "But Not for Me") and originals. —Scott Yanow

Blues Chronicles: Tales of Life / 1996 / Atlantic ✦✦✦✦

A decent, sometimes quite excellent, album of (mostly) Bartz tunes. The record suffers only from the saxophonist's occasionally too-pronounced debt to John Coltrane, especially in the sustained modal passages, yet Bartz is nonetheless an exciting and expressive player. His compositions are varied and imaginative, and his rhythm section is fabulous; pianist George Colligan is an in-the-pocket blues player of the first magnitude, and drummer Greg Bandy is swinging, exciting, and tasteful. Bassist James King is a fine supporting player, and trumpeter Tom Williams—despite owing more than a little to Bartz's most prominent former employer—fills out the ensemble passages nicely. Although there's plenty here that's overly familiar, the obvious commitment of the artists effectively mitigates the sporadic cliché. —Chris Kelsey

Paul Bascomb

b. Feb. 12, 1912, Birmingham, AL, **d.** Dec. 2, 1986, Chicago, IL
Tenor Saxophone / Swing, Early R&B

It is easy to divide Paul Bascomb's career into two for he was a top soloist with Erskine Hawkins' swing orchestra and later on recorded a popular series of early rhythm & blues records. The brother of trumpeter Dud Bascomb (another star of the Hawkins band), the tenorman was one of the founding members of the 'Bama State Collegians (which eventually became the Erskine Hawkins Big Band) in the early '30s and, except for a period in 1938-39 when he replaced the late Herschel Evans with Count Basie's Orchestra, he was with Hawkins until 1944. Bascomb co-led groups with Dud (1944-47) and in the early '50s recorded extensively for the United label; the accessible performances have been partially reissued by Delmark. Paul Bascomb was active (if maintaining a low profile) into the mid-'80s. —Scott Yanow

● **Bad Bascomb!** / Mar. 3, 1952-Aug. 30, 1952 / Delmark ✦✦✦✦✦

This CD collects together tenor saxophonist Paul Bascomb's United recordings of 1952. The material is fairly basic and R&Bish but fun with the highlights including "Blues and the Beat," "Pink Cadillac," "Soul and Body" and "Indiana." The backup group includes trumpeter Eddie Lewis and pianist Duke Jordan and the CD reissue adds four alternate takes to the original 13 selections. Recommended. —Scott Yanow

Count Basie (William Basie)

b. Aug. 21, 1904, Red Bank, NJ, **d.** Apr. 26, 1984, Hollywood, CA
Piano / Swing

Throughout his career the name of Count Basie was synonymous with swing. Basie, whose influence remains huge over a decade after his death, not only led two of the finest jazz orchestras ever but he redefined the role of the piano in the rhythm section. Originally a stride pianist in the vein of his idol Fats Waller, Basie had such a strong rhythm section in the mid-'30s that he pared down his style drastically, eliminating the oom-pah timekeeping function of his left hand. With bassist Walter Page, rhythm guitarist Freddie Green and drummer Jo Jones filling in the spaces, Count stuck to simple phrases that were strategically placed to add momentum to the ensembles and he unwittingly acted as a transitional figure towards the bop of Bud Powell.

But Count Basie was really an institution by himself. Born as William Basie, he played for silent movies (under the tutelage of Waller), learned from the great stride pianists of New York, and played the vaudeville circuit. Stranded in Kansas City in 1927 he soon joined Walter Page's Blue Devils (the best small group in the city) and eventually when Bennie Moten (himself a pianist) made Basie a better offer, he became the main pianist with Moten's Kansas City Orchestra, recording with Moten during 1929-32. The final session of Moten's band sounds very much like a predecessor of Count Basie's Orchestra.

After Moten's premature death in 1935, Basie formed his own group (known originally as the Barons of Rhythm) and was based in Kansas City's Reno Club. The nine-piece band had a regular radio program and in 1936 producer John Hammond happened to hear them on his car radio. He was so impressed that he quickly travelled to Kansas City in hopes of signing up Basie to Columbia. However his articles (which raved about the great unknown band) alerted Decca and scouts from the rival label beat Hammond to it (although Basie would switch to Columbia in 1939).

After a period of struggle in which the orchestra (which was immediately expanded) had some rough moments, by late 1937 the Count Basie band had caught on. With such important soloists as the cool-toned tenor Lester Young (whose sound was an alternative to Coleman Hawkins), trumpeters Buck Clayton and Harry "Sweets" Edison, trombonist Dicky Wells, vocalist Jimmy Rushing (and for a period Billie Holiday) and the classic rhythm section, Basie's orchestra could hold its own against any other swing band. Its theme "One O'Clock Jump" soon became widely recorded (almost serving as an anthem for the era) and "Jumpin' at the Woodside" became a standard.

In the 1940s the band's arrangements (many of which were originally thought up by sidemen while on the bandstand) became more formalized. While Lester Young's departure in late 1940 left a hole, such other fine soloists as tenors Don Byas, Illinois Jacquet, Lucky Thompson and Paul Gonsalves, altoist Tab Smith, trumpeters Joe Newman and Clark Terry, and trombonist Vic Dickenson kept the band's music swinging. Bad money management and the change in the public's musical taste led Basie to reluctantly break up his orchestra at the end of 1949 and use a small group (ranging from a sextet to a nonet) for the next two years; it often featured Terry, Wardell Gray on tenor and clarinetist Buddy DeFranco.

In 1952, during a period when very few jazz orchestras were being formed, Count Basie put together what became known as his "New Testament" (as opposed to the earlier "Old Testament") band. Against all odds, Basie's orchestra caught on, especially after recording "April in Paris" in 1954 and after singer Joe Williams signed on the following year. Although it featured more than its share of top soloists including trumpeters Joe Newman and Thad Jones, and tenors Frank Wess (who helped introduce the flute to jazz) and Frank Foster, it was the arrangements (particularly those of Neal Hefti, Ernie Wilkins, Wess, Foster, Thad Jones and later on Sammy Nistico) and the sound of the swinging ensembles (along with the distinctive rhythm section) that were emphasized.

Although there was a lot of turnover in the 1960s, the Basie sound never changed and the orchestra did not decline nor stop travelling. A series of indifferent commercial records in the mid- to late '60s (which often found famous singers using the Basie band as a prop) were far inferior to the band's live performances, but when Basie renewed ties with producer Norman Granz in the 1970s and signed with Pablo Records, his recordings (which by then often featured Jimmy Forrest on tenor and trombonist Al Grey) were greatly improved. Count Basie's health gradually failed in the 1980s and his death was greatly mourned. However his orchestra (under the direction first of Thad Jones, then Frank Foster and most recently Grover Mitchell) became the only viable ghost band in jazz history. —Scott Yanow

Basie's Basement / Oct. 23, 1929-Dec. 13, 1932 / Bluebird ✦✦✦✦

The genesis of the Count Basie band can be heard in these recordings by Bennie Moten's Kansas City Orchestra. With Basie on piano, trumpeter Hot Lips Page, tenor saxophonist Ben Webster and such future Basieites as trombonist/guitarist Eddie Durham, baritonist Jack Washington, bassist Walter Page and the great singer Jimmy Rushing, there are times when Moten's orchestra almost sounds like Basie's. Eight selections from the 1929-30 period are followed by eight numbers recorded at Moten's last and greatest sesssion (from Dec. 13, 1932). Such tunes as "Moten's Swing," "Lafayette" and "Blue Room" are prime examples of early swing. —Scott Yanow

The Essential Count Basie, Vol. 1 / Oct. 9, 1936-Jun. 24, 1939 / Columbia ✦✦✦

Rather than release all of Count Basie's studio recordings (as Decca recently has or as French Columbia did in two large LP sets over a decade ago), CBS has put together three samplers that contain some (but not all) of the essential Basie recordings from the 1939-41 period. This first volume has Lester Young's great solo on 1936's "Lady Be Good," the classics "Rock-A-Bye Basie" and "Taxi War Dance," and fine examples of the Basie orchestra throughout 1939. —Scott Yanow

Super Chief / Oct. 9, 1936-Jul. 24, 1942 / Columbia ✦✦✦

This very interesting two-LP set has quite a variety of material from the 1936-42 period, including a few airchecks, small-group sessions led by Mildred Bailey, Harry James, Glenn Harriman and Teddy Wilson (all feature Basie sidemen), and some studio sessions by both Basie's orchestra and small groups from his big band. Along with the rarities is the very first post-Bennie Moten session, a quintet date (under the pseudonym of Jones-Smith Incorporated) from 1936 that served as the recording debut of Lester Young; "Lady Be Good" was one of his greatest solos. This two-LP set is highly recommended, if you can find it. —Scott Yanow

At the Chatterbox: 1937 / Jan. 10, 1937-Feb. 12, 1937 / Jazz Archives ✦✦✦

This historic LP features broadcasts by Count Basie's orchestra in Pittsburgh during its first visit to the East Coast. The music is primarily head arrangements and charts borrowed from other bands. Two of the soloists (trumpeter Carl "Tatti" Smith and violinist/guitarist Claude Williams) would eventually be replaced. It is fascinating to hear what this orchestra sounded like at this early stage. Tenor saxophonist Lester Young and trumpeter Buck Clayton (along with Basie) quickly emerge as the most impressive soloists. —*Scott Yanow*

☆ **The Complete Decca Recordings (1937-1939)** / 1937-Feb. 4, 1939 / GRP ♦♦♦♦♦
This magnificent three-disc set has the first 63 recordings by Count Basie's Orchestra, all of his Deccas. The consistency is remarkable (with not more than two or three turkeys) and the music is the epitome of swing. With such soloists as Lester Young and Herschel Evans on tenors, trumpeters Buck Clayton and Harry "Sweets" Edison, the great blues singer Jimmy Rushing and that brilliant rhythm section of Basie, guitarist Freddie Green, bassist Walter Page and drummer Jo Jones, the music is timeless. It's all here: "One O'Clock Jump," "Sent for You Yesterday," "Blue and Sentimental," "Jumpin' at the Woodside," "Jive at Five" and many others. This is the first Count Basie collection to acquire and should be in every jazz collection. —*Scott Yanow*

Rock-A-Bye Basie, Vol. 2 / Aug. 9, 1938-Mar. 7, 1940 / Vintage Jazz Classics ♦♦♦
These broadcasts (all but one selection from 1938-39) capture Count Basie's orchestra live from the Famous Door. This CD contains 24 performances, a few of which are incomplete or poorly recorded. However the enthusiastic solos of Lester Young, fellow tenors Herschel Evans and Buddy Tate, trumpeters Buck Clayton and Harry "Sweets" Edison and Basie himself are fresh and creative, and the ensembles are consistently swinging. These are the best pre-World War II live recordings of the Count Basie Orchestra and well worth acquiring. —*Scott Yanow*

The Essential Count Basie, Vol. 2 / Aug. 4, 1939-May 31, 1940 / Columbia ♦♦♦
A fine sampler of the 1939-40 Count Basie orchestra, it features such classic performances as "Dickie's Dream," "Lester Leaps In" and "Tickle Toe." Lester Young and fellow tenor Buddy Tate, trumpeters Buck Clayton and Harry Edison, and trombonist Dickie Wells all have their chances to star; they can't help swinging with that light but solid Basie rhythm section. Count's Columbia recordings deserve to be reissued in full (with all of the alternate takes), but until CBS gets around to it, this is a good introduction to that period. —*Scott Yanow*

Blues by Basie / 1939-1950 / Columbia ♦♦♦
Because Basie streamlined his piano style down to the bare basics, it is often forgotten how strong a pianist he could be when he was inspired. This intriguing LP features live performances taken from a variety of settings and time periods (dating from 1941-67), all of which put the focus on Basie's piano. Not too surprisingly, most of the numbers are blues but he is in consistently fine form, and there is enough variety to keep one's interest throughout this excellent set. —*Scott Yanow*

The Essential Count Basie, Vol. 3 / Aug. 8, 1940-Apr. 10, 1941 / Columbia ♦♦♦
This is the third and thus far final volume in a sampler series picking out some of the high points of Count Basie's 1939-42 period on Columbia. Lester Young's departure in December 1940 robbed the orchestra of their top soloist but the band still outswung all of its competitors and the personnel was consistently outstanding. Coleman Hawkins' guest appearance on "9:20 Special" and "Feedin' the Bean" round out this enjoyable set, but when is Columbia going to reissue all of their Count Basie recordings instead of always recycling the same ones? —*Scott Yanow*

Count Basie V Discs, Vol. 2: 1943-1945 / Jun. 1943-May 14, 1945 / Jazz Society ♦♦♦♦
This second volume of V Discs almost reaches the great heights of the first LP. Covering a slightly wider span of time, the Basie band is heard during one of its peak periods, the otherwise poorly documented war years. The music is consistently exciting and tops much of what Basie would record during the following five years. —*Scott Yanow*

Old Manuscripts, Broadcast Transcriptions (1944-45) / Jul. 1943-1945 / Music & Arts ♦♦♦♦♦
This CD contains 25 selections featuring the Count Basie Orchestra taken from radio broadcasts. Ten numbers are from an April 1944 session in which tenor great Lester Young (who had rejoined the band the following year) is well featured. In addition there is one number ("G.I. Stomp) from 1943 while the remainder are from several sessions during 1944-45. In addition to Young, the main soloists include trumpeter Harry "Sweets" Edison, trombonist Dickie Wells, Buddy Tate on tenor, clarinetist Rudy Rutherford and the pianist/leader; plus there are occasional vocals from Jimmy Rushing, Thelma Carpenter, Maxine Johnson and Earl Warren. This underrated version of Basie's big band was one of his best and the 76 minutes on this CD contains many high points. —*Scott Yanow*

Count Basie (1944) / Jan. 10, 1944 / Circle ♦♦♦
This is the first of two LPs of transcriptions recorded by Count Basie's orchestra during a time when the musicians union was on strike and no commercial recordings were being made. These 11 performances are particularly valuable because they document Lester Young's all-too-brief return to the Basie band and also feature fine moments by trumpeter Harry Edison and the tenor of Buddy Tate. A few too many Earle Warren vocals and the skimpy playing time are the only drawbacks. —*Scott Yanow*

1944-1945 / Jan. 10, 1944-May 25, 1944 / Circle ♦♦♦
The second LP of transcriptions from a period when the musicians union strike resulted in no commercial recordings being made, this set (which is actually superior to the first volume) features Lester Young back with Count Basie in 1944. Trumpeter Harry Edison, trombonist Dickie Wells, Buddy Tate on tenor and Basie all have their strong moments and it is nice to hear the orchestra playing such fresh material, some of which they never got around to recording commercially. —*Scott Yanow*

Count Basie V Discs, Vol. 1: 1944-1945 / May 27, 1944-Jan. 11, 1945 / Jazz Society ♦♦♦♦
Among the very best recordings cut by Count Basie's orchestra in the '40s are the V Discs they recorded exclusively for distribution to servicemen. The first of two volumes, the 11 performances on this LP are quite inspired with Harry Edison, Dickie Wells, Lester Young (during the half when he is present), Buddy Tate and Lucky Thompson taking heated solos. This version of "Taps Miller" is a real classic; there are no weak cuts on this excellent set. —*Scott Yanow*

Beaver Junction (1944-1946) / May 27, 1944-Nov. 12, 1947 / Vintage Jazz ♦♦♦♦
A worthy CD full of Basie rarities, it includes unissued and alternate versions of V Discs and two radio broadcasts; the one from 1944 features drummer Buddy Rich filling in for the recently drafted Jo Jones. Rich had so much fun being part of the swing machine that when Basie handed him a blank check for his services, he tore it up; the music throughout this CD will be equally fun for the listener. —*Scott Yanow*

Count Basie and His Orchestra (1944) / 1944 / Hindsight ♦♦♦
Taken from radio broadcasts, this LP comprises live performances including some fine vocals by Jimmy Rushing and Thelma Carpenter, two numbers that feature guest Artie Shaw on clarinet, and Lester Young (temporarily back with Basie) being well showcased on "Jumpin' at the Woodside" and "Every Tub." Considering the high quality of the Basie orchestra during the war years, virtually every broadcast of theirs is worth acquiring. —*Scott Yanow*

Count Basie: The Orchestra and the Octet / Jan. 9, 1946-Apr. 10, 1951 / Columbia France ♦♦♦♦
This French CBS two-LP set has 13 recordings by the 1946 edition of Count Basie's orchestra (including several features for the exciting tenor of Illinois Jacquet), 12 performances by Basie's octet in 1950 (which starred trumpeter Clark Terry, clarinetist Buddy DeFranco and tenor great Wardell Gray among others), and Basie's first session with his new big band in 1951 (Wardell Gray's showcase "Little Pony" is considered a classic). The music throughout this two-fer is consistently memorable and the octet performances are so swinging that it makes one regret that he could not keep it going along with his new orchestra. —*Scott Yanow*

Brand New Wagon: Count Basie 1947 / Jan. 3, 1947-Dec. 12, 1947 / Bluebird ♦♦♦
While French RCA put out a three-LP set documenting 48 of Count Basie's recordings for that label during 1947-50, its American counterpart instead just reissued 21 of those sides (all from 1947) on this highly enjoyable CD. Best are the octet and nonet recordings of May 20-21 but none of these tracks are weak. Trumpeter Harry "Sweets" Edison, the tenors of Paul Gonsalves and Buddy Tate and the long underrated baritonist Jack Washington star, along with vocalist Jimmy Rushing and the rhythm section. Even during what is sometimes written off as a declining period, the Basie orchestra was near the top in quality, if not popularity. —*Scott Yanow*

Count Basie, Vols. 1-3 / Jan. 3, 1947-Feb. 2, 1950 / RCA ♦♦♦♦
This three-LP box set from French RCA skips around a bit and fails to give complete personnel information but it is a gem. 95% of Count Basie's studio recordings for RCA during the 1947-50 period are included and, even during the weaker and more commercial numbers, the band always swings. There are quite a few obscure gems (Basie's orchestra was not getting much publicity during this era) including features for baritonist Jack Washington and the tenor of Paul Gonsalves, a nonet date from 1947 and Basie's octet session of February 2, 1950, cut shortly after economics forced him to disband his classic orchestra. This box is becoming increasingly difficult to locate but it far exceeds anything put out thus far by its American counterpart. —*Scott Yanow*

Greatest Hits [RCA] / Jan. 3, 1947-Feb. 6, 1950 / RCA Victor ♦♦♦
There are actually no "hits" on this reissue from Count Basie, part of RCA Victor's erratic introduction to jazz program that resulted in ten CDs in 1996. Basie was only with Victor during 1947-50 and, although his band still swung, it was falling on hard times financially. Due to the complete lack of personnel given to these 15 recordings, purchasers will probably not realize that the main soloists are trumpeters Harry "Sweets" Edison and Emmett Berry, tenors Buddy Tate and Paul Gonsalves. The music is consistently excellent, late-period swing with the slight influence of bop and a rare small-group side ("If You See My Baby") from 1950. The

recordings are available in more complete form elsewhere but this is a good sampling of Basie's Victor period. —*Scott Yanow*

1949: Shoutin' Blues / Apr. 11, 1949-Feb. 6, 1950 / RCA ✦✦✦
The cuts on this anthology were recorded with Count Basie's legendary 1940s band nearing the end. These cuts were mostly unissued and show a band still capable of playing joyous blues and vigorous swing, but also close to exhausting its creative juices. Most cuts are entertaining; some, like "Hit That Ball," are enjoyable period pieces, but none of them equal the vitality or drive in the great music Basie made earlier in the decade. The really intriguing numbers are the three tunes by Basie with a sextet, but J. August's forgettable vocals mar "If You See My Baby," and "Sweets" offers crackling trumpet solos from Harry Edison contrasted by highly derivative tenor solos from George Auld. This disc isn't great or classic Basie, but it provides insight into a critical and seldom-evaluated period in his legacy. —*Ron Wynn*

Paradise Squat / Jul. 22, 1952-Dec. 12, 1952 / Verve ✦✦✦✦
In 1952 Count Basie put together his second big band after two years of work with six to eight-piece units. This double LP documents his recordings of that year and it is very interesting to hear the beginnings of his second great orchestra. The soloists are mostly different than he would feature during the remainder of the '50s with the most impressive voices being the two contrasting tenors of Eddie "Lockjaw" Davis and Paul Quinichette. With new charts by Neal Hefti and Ernie Wilkins, it seems apparent that the band was on its way even if Al Hibbler was at this point Basie's vocalist; his version of "Goin' to Chicago" sounds a bit odd. This two-fer also has a pair of combo performances that are Count Basie's first matchup with pianist Oscar Peterson. —*Scott Yanow*

Sixteen Men Swinging / Dec. 12, 1953-Jun. 1954 / Verve ✦✦✦
The second Count Basie Orchestra stabilized its sound and its personnel on the two solid sessions from 1953-54 featured on this two-LP set. With Joe Newman and Thad Jones in the trumpet section and the two tenors of Frank Foster and Frank Wess, the band had more than its share of talented soloists, but it was the clean ensemble sound, the lightly but firmly swinging rhythm section and the inventive and uncluttered arrangements of Ernie Wilkins and Neal Hefti that made this band a surprise success in 1954. This two-fer (which includes "Blues Backstage" and "Down for the Count") has 25 examples of '50s Basie swing. —*Scott Yanow*

Class of '54 / Sep. 2, 1954-Sep. 7, 1954 / Black Lion ✦✦✦
This fine CD consists of two radio airchecks from 1954, featuring Count Basie with a nonet and his full orchestra. The smaller group also has trumpeter Joe Newman, trombonist Henry Coker and the tenors of Frank Wess and Frank Foster well-featured while the big-band tracks (which mostly sport Neal Hefti arrangements) find the orchestra on the brink of great success. —*Scott Yanow*

Count Basie, Lester Young & the Stars of Birdland / Feb. 1955 / Jass ✦✦✦✦
This live CD documents a tour by top performers who appeared regularly at Birdland. Count Basie's orchestra backs Basie alumnus Lester Young on three tracks, welcomes Stan Getz to sit in for four numbers (including an exciting version of "Little Pony"), accompanies Sarah Vaughan during eight songs and performs seven tunes by itself, four of which feature Joe Williams (who had just recently joined the band). The historic set will be prized by collectors. —*Scott Yanow*

★ **Count Basie Swings, Joe Williams Sings** / Jul. 17, 1955-Jul. 26, 1955 / Verve ✦✦✦✦✦
Joe Williams' debut as the featured vocalist in Count Basie's band was one of those landmark moments that even savvy observers don't fully appreciate when it occurs, then realize years later how momentous an event they witnessed. Williams brought a different presence to the great Basie orchestra than the one Jimmy Rushing provided; he couldn't shout like Rushing, but he was more effective on romantic and sentimental material, while he was almost as spectacular on surging blues, uptempo wailers, and stomping standards. Basie's band maintained an incredible groove behind Williams, who moved from authoritative statements on "Every Day I Have the Blues" and "Please Send Me Someone to Love" to brisk workouts on "Roll 'Em Pete" and his definitive hit, "All Right, OK, You Win." —*Ron Wynn*

☆ **April in Paris** / Jul. 26, 1955-Jan. 5, 1956 / Verve ✦✦✦✦✦
A true classic, this studio album includes Count Basie's hit versions of "April in Paris," "Shiny Stockings" and "Corner Pocket"; these three tunes have remained in the Basie band's repertoire ever since. Actually all ten selections are very enjoyable, and this exciting and of course swinging record is definitive of '50s Count Basie. With such soloists as trumpeters Joe Newman and Thad Jones, the tenors of Frank Foster and Frank Wess (who doubles on flute) and the leader-pianist, the Basie Orchestra was well on its way to exceeding the success of its earlier counterpart. This CD reissue adds seven alternate takes to the original program, showing that Thad Jones' famous "Pop Goes the Whistle" quote on "April in Paris" was planned in advance! —*Scott Yanow*

The Greatest! Count Basie Plays...Joe Williams Sings Standards / Apr. 28, 1956 / Verve ✦✦✦
Joe Williams never wanted to be typecast as just a blues singer, so on his second full album with Count Basie he concentrated on standards. The swinging treatments given to songs such as "Thou Swell," "My Baby Just Cares for Me" and even "Singin' in the Rain" work quite well even if the band is mostly confined to a supporting role. —*Scott Yanow*

Count Basie in London / Sep. 7, 1956 / Verve ✦✦✦
The origin of this session's title is a bit of a mystery since this album was actually recorded live in Sweden. The Count Basie Orchestra plays its usual repertoire (including "Jumpin' at the Woodside," "Shiny Stockings" and "Corner Pocket") with enthusiasm, concise solos and typical Basie swing. Joe Williams takes a few vocals and this CD is rounded by three previously unreleased performances. —*Scott Yanow*

● **Count Basie at Newport** / Sep. 7, 1957 / Verve ✦✦✦✦✦
At the 1957 Newport Jazz Festival the music was consistently inspired and often historic. Count Basie welcomed back tenor-great Lester Young and singer Jimmy Rushing for part of a very memorable set highlighted by "Boogie Woogie" and "Evenin'"; Young plays beautifully throughout and Rushing is in prime form. An exciting full-length version of "One O'Clock Jump" features Young, Illinois Jacquet and trumpeter Roy Eldridge; the Basie band stretches out on "Swingin' at Newport"; and five previously unreleased selections (put out for the first time on this CD) include four Joe Williams vocals. It's a great set of music. —*Scott Yanow*

Atomic Mr. Basie / Oct. 21, 1957-Oct. 22, 1957 / Roulette ✦✦✦✦✦
Known as the "Atomic" album due to the cover picture of an A-bomb exploding, this is one of the great Count Basie records, ranking with *April in Paris*. The 1957 edition of the Basie orchestra romps through "The Kid from Red Bank" (a superlative feature for its leader), "Whirly Bird" and "Lil' Darlin'" among others; everything works on this essential album. —*Scott Yanow*

The Complete Roulette Studio Count Basie / Oct. 21, 1957-Jul. 26, 1962 / Mosaic ✦✦✦✦✦
Some of Count Basie's finest recordings were cut for the Roulette label during 1957-62 and all of his studio performances are included on this massive Mosaic ten-CD box set. Among the classic former LPs that are reissued here are *The Atomic Mr. Basie*, *Basie Plays Hefti*, *Chairman of the Board*, *Everyday I Have the Blues* and *Kansas City Suite*. With such soloists as trumpeters Thad Jones and Joe Newman, the tenors of Frank Foster and Eddie Lockjaw Davis and Frank Wess on alto and flute, vocals by Joe Williams and the timeless arrangements of Neal Hefti, Thad Jones, Frank Foster, Ernie Wilkins and Frank Wess among others, this essential (but unfortunately limited-edition) set features the second Count Basie Orchestra at its very best. —*Scott Yanow*

The Best of the Roulette Years / 1957-1962 / Roulette ✦✦✦
Compilation gathering prime Basie material from his years on Roulette, a period that includes songs cut with Lambert, Hendricks & Ross, Joe Williams, Tony Bennett, and a lineup with Thad Jones, Eddie "Lockjaw" Davis, Frank Foster, and Joe Newman, among others, in the band. —*Ron Wynn*

Basie Plays Hefti / Apr. 3, 1958-Apr. 14, 1958 / Roulette ✦✦✦✦
The Count Basie Orchestra was in top form for this set of Neal Hefti arrangements. Hefti had been one of the main architects of the new Basie sound of the '50s and on this memorable date he utilizes the flute of Frank Wess prominently. "Cute" (heard here in its initial recording) became a standard. —*Scott Yanow*

Sing Along with Basie / May 26, 1958-Sep. 3, 1958 / Roulette ✦✦✦✦
The extraordinary jazz vocal group Lambert, Hendricks and Ross had debuted in 1957 with *Sing a Song of Basie* during which they recreated his orchestra with their overdubbed voices. That album was so successful that the following year they were able to actually team up with the Basie band. Frank Foster put down on paper the original head arrangements of the '30s and '40s for the orchestra, leaving space for the vocalists to recreate the original solos. The result is a colorful and swinging set. Best is a version of "Goin' to Chicago Blues" that has Joe Williams taking his original vocal while L.H. & Ross sing around him. —*Scott Yanow*

One More Time / Dec. 18, 1958-Jan. 24, 1959 / Roulette ✦✦✦
For this studio album from late 1958 and early 1959, the Count Basie Orchestra performs ten Quincy Jones compositions; he also contributed all of the arrangements. "I Needs to Be Beed With," "For Lena and Lennie" and "The Midnight Sun Never Sets" all caught on and Jones' charts helped expand the Basie sound without altering it. An excellent CD. —*Scott Yanow*

The Complete Roulette Live Recordings of Count Basie and His Orchestra (1958-1962) / 1958 / Mosaic ✦✦✦✦
This consistently exciting eight-CD set features the Count Basie Orchestra at three different locations and time periods: at a convention in Florida in 1959, at Bird-

land on two nights in 1961 and in Stockholm during a four-day period. Of the 133 selections, only 28 were released before, making these hard-swinging performances (which would be essential for Basie fans on the basis of the music alone) of even greater interest. During this era Basie had such top soloists as Frank Wess on alto and flute, the tenors of Frank Foster and Billy Mitchell, trumpeters Thad Jones and Joe Newman and trombonists Al Grey and Quentin Jackson. In addition, drummer Louis Bellson is featured throughout the Stockholm engagement and such guests as trumpeter Harry "Sweets" Edison and singers Joe Williams, Sarah Vaughan and Jon Hendricks are heard from. But it is the swinging Basie rhythm section and the enthusiasm of the ensembles that make this a truly classic and somewhat historic set. —*Scott Yanow*

1959 / Apr. 24, 1959 / Jazz Unlimited ✦✦✦
The Count Basie Orchestra is heard on this set playing live in Fresno in 1959 during the peak of their "atomic period." The purely instrumental set (released for the first time on this 1993 CD) features such fine soloists as trumpeters Thad Jones and Joe Newman, trombonist Al Grey, altoist-flutist Frank Wess and the tenors of Frank Foster and Billy Mitchell. However, it is the arrangements by Neal Hefti, Foster, Jones and Quincy Jones that gave the band its personality. Most of the selections were recorded at other times, but these spirited versions, with their very different solos, will be savored by Basie's fans. Highlights include "A Little Tempo Please," "Whirly-Bird," "Jessica's Day" and "Corner Pocket." —*Scott Yanow*

Basie and Eckstine, Inc. / May 22, 1959-Jul. 28, 1959 / Roulette ✦✦✦✦✦
This rare big band outing for singer Billy Eckstine (which has been reissued on CD) is one of Mr. B's best ever recordings. Heard in prime voice, Eckstine was clearly inspired by the Count Basie Orchestra on the jazz-oriented set and he can be heard swinging in top form on such numbers as "Stormy Monday Blues," a remake of his early hit "Jelly Jelly," "I Want A Little Girl" and "Song of the Wanderer." This is arguably Billy Eckstine's best post-1950 album. —*Scott Yanow*

Breakfast Dance and Barbecue / Sep. 24, 1959 / Roulette ✦✦✦
The Count Basie Orchestra is heard on this album playing live at a disc-jockey convention in Miami. Their first of three sets took place at 2 a.m. but the late hour if anything kept the band loose. Most of the selections on this record were not recorded during that era, including fine charts on "In a Mellow Tone" and "Moten Swing." —*Scott Yanow*

Everyday I Have the Blues / Sep. 24, 1959 / Roulette ✦✦✦
One of Joe Williams' most rewarding recordings with Count Basie came on this set of blues-oriented material. Williams does a fine remake of "Everyday I Have the Blues" and a classic version of "Going to Chicago," but all ten selections are quite enjoyable. —*Scott Yanow*

Paris Jazz Concert / Mar. 29, 1960+May 5, 1962 / RTE ✦✦✦
This two-CD set documents a pair of hour-long performances by the Count Basie big band that are quite complementary despite being recorded two years apart. No real surprises occur (the Basie Orchestra was nothing if not predictably swinging) but neither are there any low points. Most of the material was recorded elsewhere at least once during this productive period and the repertoire alternates Basie standards with dance music and blues. Singers O.C. Smith ("All Right, OK, You Win") and Irene Reid ("The Blues") only have one vocal apiece and fail to make much of an impression. With such soloists (who are unfortunately unidentified in the liner notes) as Thad Jones, Joe Newman, Al Grey, Quentin Jackson, Frank Wess, Frank Foster and Basie himself (among others), this is a well-recorded and enjoyable set that Basie fanatics and completists will want. —*Scott Yanow*

Count Basie & Sarah Vaughan / Jul. 1960-Jan. 1961 / Roulette ✦✦✦✦
Although Count Basie gets top billing, he actually does not appear on this CD reissue. Basie's Orchestra (other than a couple of short spots for trumpeter Joe Newman and Frank Foster's tenor) and pianist Kirk Stuart are purely in a supporting role behind the magnificent voice of Sarah Vaughan. Sometimes she gets overly mannered and seems to give little weight to the words she is singing but Vaughan's wide range and impeccable musicianship carry the day. In addition to such numbers as "Perdido," "Mean to Me" and "You Go to My Head," this CD is rounded out by two charming Vaughan duets with Joe Williams ("Teach Me Tonight" and "If I Were a Bell") that were originally released as a single plus a "new" alternate take of "Until I Met You" that is a bit tentative. The set is much more recommended to Sarah Vaughan fans than to Count Basie collectors. —*Scott Yanow*

Kansas City Suite: The Music of Benny Carter / Sep. 1960 / Roulette ✦✦✦
These two 1960 sessions gave Benny Carter a unique chance to write a full program for Count Basie's orchestra. Arranged as a type of suite, the ten originals pay tribute to the various Kansas City clubs that were active in the '30s when Basie

was a resident. The band swings throughout as usual, with concise solos adding color to this memorable modern session. —*Scott Yanow*

The Count Basie Story / 1961 / Roulette ✦✦
These sessions found Count Basie's orchestra remaking the repertoire of his first band's arrangements from 1936-45. Although this 1960 two-LP box set is well done, one misses the great soloists of the earlier orchestra like Lester Young, Buck Clayton and Dickie Wells, so this hi-fi revival is a bit pointless. —*Scott Yanow*

First Time! The Count Meets the Duke / Jul. 6, 1961 / Columbia ✦✦✦✦
This session was an impossible dream come true, the teaming of the entire Count Basie and Duke Ellington orchestras, including the principals on joint pianos. Whether it be "Take the 'A' Train," "Jumpin' at the Woodside," or "Until I Met You," everything works on this album and somehow the ensembles avoid sounding overcrowded. This version of "Segue in C" is the outstanding performance of a unique and highly enjoyable set. —*Scott Yanow*

Basie at Birdland / Jul. 28, 1961 / Roulette ✦✦✦✦✦
The Count Basie orchestra was very much at home in New York's Birdland in the '50s and early '60s, frequently playing there several months a year. This spirited set has swinging versions of such Basie classics as "Segue in C," "Blues Backstage" and "Little Pony" with Jon Hendricks' guest vocal on "Whirly Bird" taking honors. —*Scott Yanow*

Count Basie in Sweden / 1962 / Roulette ✦✦✦✦

Count Basie and the Kansas City 7 / Mar. 21, 1962 / MCA ✦✦✦✦
One of Count Basie's few small-group sessions of the '60s was his best. With trumpeter Thad Jones and tenors Frank Foster and Eric Dixon filling in the septet, Basie is in superlative form on a variety of blues, standards and two originals apiece from Thad Jones and Frank Wess. Small-group swing at its best. —*Scott Yanow*

Live in Sweden / Aug. 10, 1962-Aug. 12, 1962 / Roulette ✦✦✦
All of the music on this CD reissue plus a great deal more was previously released on a Mosaic eight-CD box set. Count Basie's final Roulette recordings before his band would drift artistically throughout the troublesome 1960s, these Stockholm concerts feature Basie's orchestra still in peak form with such soloists as trumpeter Thad Jones, trombonists Quentin Jackson and Benny Powell, Frank Wess on flute and tenor, tenorman Frank Foster and guest trumpeter Benny Bailey. Highlights include "Good Time Blues," "Blues Backstage" and Irene Reid's outing on "Backwater Blues." This CD is easily recommended to Basie collectors who do not already own the limited-edition Mosaic box. —*Scott Yanow*

Frankly Basie: Count Basie Plays the Hits of Frank Sinatra / Apr. 8, 1963-Jan. 14, 1965 / Verve ✦✦
Originally titled *More Hits of the '50s and '60s*, this salute to Frank Sinatra by Count Basie's Orchestra is mostly closer to dance music than jazz. Billy Byers' arrangements are pleasing enough but in general the music is rather easy-listening with few exciting moments and most solos being quite brief. The original 12-song program is augmented by a "new" alternate take of "Hey, Jealous Lover" and two selections ("My Kind of Town" and "Come Rain or Come Shine") taken from the LP *Basie Picks the Winners*. Considering the personnel and the material, the results are disappointingly sleepy; only "All of Me" is at all memorable. —*Scott Yanow*

Basie Land / Apr. 25, 1963 / Verve ✦✦✦
Billy Byers was given the task of writing ten numbers for the Count Basie Orchestra to interpret, and he proved very much up to the job. None of these originals became standards, but with the tenors of Frank Foster and Eric Dixon and trumpeter Al Aarons taking solo honors, and the classic Basie rhythm section swinging lightly but with passion, this album succeeds easily. —*Scott Yanow*

Ella and Basie! / Jul. 15, 1963-Jul. 16, 1963 / Verve ✦✦✦
Surprisingly enough this 1963 LP was the first time (other than a couple songs) that Ella Fitzgerald and Count Basie recorded together. The matchup was so logical that it would be repeated many times over the next 20 years. Fitzgerald sounds fine and, even if Quincy Jones' arrangements did not give the Basie musicians much space for solos (two songs do feature a bit of trumpeter Joe Newman, trombonist Urbie Green and Frank Foster on tenor), this is an enjoyable effort. High points include "Honeysuckle Rose," "Them There Eyes" and "Shiny Stockings." —*Scott Yanow*

Basie's Beat / Oct. 7, 1965-Feb. 15, 1967 / Verve ✦✦✦✦
During an era when the Count Basie Orchestra was often being used as a mere prop behind other singers, this album was quite refreshing. With the exception of trombonist Richard Boone's two eccentric vocals, this is an instrumental date with arrangements provided by band members past and present, and concise solos contributed by quite a few talented players. —*Scott Yanow*

Live in Antibes (1968) / Jul. 1968 / Esoldun ✦✦✦

The late-'60s Count Basie Band, featuring the frenetic, surging tenor sax of Eddie "Lockjaw" Davis, was spotlighted on this 17-cut CD reissue, part of a series issued by the French Esoldun label and available as an import. The band stuck to its predictable pattern of alternating mid-tempo and fast-paced numbers, blues and vocal change-of-pace items, plus slower treatments, all done in a relaxed, highly professional fashion. The menu included "Going to Chicago Blues," "In a Mellow Tone," "Lil' Darlin," "Stormy Monday Blues" and "Cherokee," as well as the expected closer "Jumping at the Woodside." The arrangements, ensemble interaction and general performances were good, if not exceptional, and Basie's customary sparse piano licks were timely and right in the groove. —*Ron Wynn*

Jazz Fest Masters: Count Basie / Jun. 1969 / Scotti Bros. ✦✦✦✦

If one judged them by their studio albums of the 1963-70 period, it would seem that Count Basie's orchestra was in its decline, but this recently released live CD proves otherwise. Recorded at the 1969 New Orleans Jazz Festival, the Basie band swings such tunes as "Whirlybird," "Corner Pocket," "Cherokee" (an Eddie "Lockjaw" Davis feature) and "April in Paris" with enthusiasm and power. A fine session. —*Scott Yanow*

High Voltage / Feb. 23, 1970-Feb. 25, 1970 / Verve ✦✦✦

A dozen generally excellent standards are given overly brief interpretations by the Count Basie Orchestra. Chico O'Farrill was responsible for the arrangements and he should have given the band more space in which to explore these tunes. Since only one number exceeds four minutes in length, none get much beyond the melody. —*Scott Yanow*

Afrique / Dec. 22, 1970-Dec. 23, 1970 / Doctor Jazz ✦✦✦✦

Possibly the most unusual album by Count Basie, it's certainly the most modern. For this session Oliver Nelson arranged eight recent songs including avant-gardist Albert Ayler's "Love Flower" and Pharoah Sanders' "Japan," giving the Basie band a more "contemporary" setting (utilizing electric bass on half the songs) while not altering its basic sound. Nelson's "Kilimanjaro" and "Hobo Flats" are highlights of this very successful but never repeated "experiment." —*Scott Yanow*

The Golden Years / Apr. 17, 1972-Dec. 14, 1983 / Pablo ✦✦✦✦

Count Basie spent the last decade of his life recording regularly for Norman Granz's Pablo label. This four-CD set, which does not contain any material not available elsewhere, has "the best of" Basie's final period, 61 selections in all. Each disc covers a different (although sometimes overlapping) aspect of Basie's career: live performances, small groups, his big band and working behind vocalists. The Who's Who of Pablo's roster is featured with such soloists as various Basie members (including tenor saxophonist Jimmy Forrest and Eric Dixon, trombonist Al Grey and trumpeter Pete Minger), vibraphonist Milt Jackson, altoist Benny Carter, tenors Johnny Griffin, Zoot Sims and Eddie "Lockjaw" Davis, trumpeters Roy Eldridge, Harry "Sweets" Edison, Clark Terry, Dizzy Gillespie and Freddie Hubbard, trombonists Vic Dickenson and J.J. Johnson, guitarist Joe Pass, bassists Niels Pedersen and Ray Brown, drummer Louie Bellson, pianist Oscar Peterson, and singers Ella Fitzgerald, Sarah Vaughan, Big Joe Turner, Eddie "Cleanhead" Vinson (who also plays alto), and band vocalist Bill Caffey. This well-conceived set is easily recommended to Count Basie fans who do not already own too many of his individual Pablo recordings. —*Scott Yanow*

Loose Walk / Apr. 24, 1972 / Pablo ✦✦✦

Ironically, the earliest recording by Count Basie for Norman Granz's Pablo label was one of the most recent to be released. This jam session features trumpeter Roy Eldridge, trombonist Al Grey and tenor saxophonist Eddie "Lockjaw" Davis on a set of jammable standards. The results are quite fun. —*Scott Yanow*

Basie Jam, Vol. 1 / Dec. 10, 1973 / Pablo ✦✦

The official start of Count Basie's decade-long association with Norman Granz's Pablo label was a bit disappointing, an all-star cast (with trumpeter Harry "Sweets" Edison, trombonist J.J. Johnson and tenors Eddie Davis and Zoot Sims) playing one blues after another. Reasonably pleasing but uninspired, there would be many better Basie dates coming up. —*Scott Yanow*

The Bosses / Dec. 11, 1973 / Original Jazz Classics ✦✦✦✦

Count Basie and an all-star band (including trumpeter Harry Edison, trombonist J.J. Johnson and the tenors of Eddie Davis and Zoot Sims) back up veteran Kansas City blues singer Big Joe Turner on one of his better later albums. The many fine solos inspire Turner, who is in top form on such tunes as "Night Time Is the Right Time," "Wee Baby Blues" and "Roll 'Em Pete." —*Scott Yanow*

For the First Time / May 22, 1974 / Pablo ✦✦✦

Throughout his career, Count Basie was modest about his own abilities as a pianist, and his success at streamlining his style to the bare essentials often made listeners underrate his playing talents. This 1974 session was a rarity, an opportunity for Basie to be featured in a trio setting (with bassist Ray Brown and drummer

Louie Bellson), during which he provides enough variety to hold one's interest and enough technique to lead many to reassess his piano skills. —*Scott Yanow*

Satch and Josh / Dec. 2, 1974 / Pablo ✦✦✦

Producer Norman Granz occasionally got carried away with the quantity of his recording projects. In 1974 he recorded a full album teaming fellow pianists Count Basie and Oscar Peterson in a rhythm quintet; little did anyone realize that this then-unique matchup would eventually result in five albums. This first one, which finds Basie doubling on organ, is among the best. Peterson's virtuosic style somehow worked very well with Basie's sparse playing and these ten numbers really swing. —*Scott Yanow*

Basie and Friends / Dec. 2, 1974-Nov. 1, 1981 / Pablo ✦✦

This is a hodgepodge collection focusing on Basie's piano-playing from four different sessions. Five selections find him in trios while the other three numbers are meetings with Oscar Peterson during which they both double on organ. All of these performances are unavailable elsewhere and are enjoyable if not too unique. —*Scott Yanow*

The Last Decade / 1974-1980 / Artistry ✦✦✦

The well-recorded live performances on this two-LP set date from three different periods: Count Basie's pre-Pablo 1974 band with tenor-great Eddie "Lockjaw" Davis, the star-studded 1977 orchestra (featuring Jimmy Forrest's tenor, trombonist Al Grey and drummer Butch Miles) and the very solid 1980 group. Throughout, the various Basie orchestras are consistently exciting and swinging. —*Scott Yanow*

Basie and Zoot / Apr. 9, 1975 / Original Jazz Classics ✦✦✦✦✦

This is a classic encounter that has been reissued on CD in the Original Jazz Classics series. Pianist Count Basie (in his best-small group outing of the 1970s) and tenor saxophonist Zoot Sims were mutually inspired by each other's presence and, with the tasteful assistance of bassist John Heard and drummer Louie Bellson, they can be heard playing at the peak of their creative powers. Every listener interested in swinging jazz should pick up this disc, if only to hear these hard-charging versions of "I Never Knew," "It's Only a Paper Moon" and "Honeysuckle Rose." A gem, essential music. —*Scott Yanow*

Basie Jam at Montreux '75 / Jul. 19, 1975 / Pablo ✦✦✦

On one of the earliest and best of the Count Basie jams for Pablo, Basie sounds very high-spirited pushing the combative trumpeter Roy Eldridge, tenor saxophonist Johnny Griffin and vibraphonist Milt Jackson on two blues and a lengthy version of "Lester Leaps In." Plenty of sparks fly. —*Scott Yanow*

Fun Time: Count Basie Big Band at Montreux '75 / Jul. 19, 1975 / Pablo ✦✦✦

This big-band performance from the 1975 Montreux Jazz Festival introduces what could be called Count Basie's third great orchestra (although in style it was a continuation of the second one he formed in 1952). With trombonist Al Grey, Jimmy Forrest on tenor and the fiery drummer Butch Miles giving this early Pablo version of the band its own personality, the Basie orchestra is in top form for a strong set. Of special note are two fine vocals by Bill Caffey, who would quickly drift into obscurity. —*Scott Yanow*

The Basie Big Band / Aug. 16, 1975-Aug. 27, 1975 / Pablo ✦✦

The Count Basie Orchestra's initial studio album for Pablo mostly features pleasant but lightweight arrangements by Sammy Nestico. The music is quite recognizable as Basie's but the results are somewhat forgettable and predictable. —*Scott Yanow*

For the Second Time / Aug. 28, 1975 / Original Jazz Classics ✦✦✦

On Count Basie's second trio album for Pablo, he is reunited with bassist Ray Brown and drummer Louie Bellson. In addition to the expected blues, the main joy of this set is hearing Basie stretch out on such numbers as "If I Could Be with You," "On the Sunny Side of the Street" and "The One I Love," tunes he did not play much with his orchestra in this later period. —*Scott Yanow*

I Told You So / Jan. 12, 1976-Jan. 14, 1976 / Original Jazz Classics ✦✦✦✦

This is one of Count Basie's best big-band studio recordings for Norman Granz during his Pablo years. The arrangements by Bill Holman are both challenging and swinging, containing enough surprises to make this session a real standout. —*Scott Yanow*

Basie Jam, Vol. 2 / May 6, 1976 / Original Jazz Classics ✦✦✦

For this enjoyable jam session, Count Basie heads up a very impressive cast of players, including altoist Benny Carter, Eddie "Lockjaw" Davis on tenor, trumpeter Clark Terry, trombonist Al Grey and guitarist Joe Pass. The four lengthy performances give each of the principals plenty of solo space and the results are predictably exciting. It's a big improvement over the first *Basie Jam*. —*Scott Yanow*

Basie Jam, Vol. 3 / May 6, 1976 / Original Jazz Classics ✦✦✦

From the same recording session that resulted in *Basie Jam—Vol. 2*, these four performances of standards also feature Count Basie, guitarist Joe Pass, trumpeter Clark Terry, altoist Benny Carter, trombonist Al Grey and tenorman Eddie Lockjaw Davis, all in fine form. Norman Granz always preferred Basie in a small group and the success of these jams helped bolster his argument. —*Scott Yanow*

Basie in Europe / 1977 / LRC ✦✦✦

A fine collection by the Count Basie Orchestra, it was taken from concerts in France and Germany. Dating from the period when the band featured trombonist Al Grey and tenor saxophonist Jimmy Forrest (not to mention the exciting drummer Butch Miles), the orchestra plays their usual repertoire from the '70s (including "Freckle Face," "Whirly Bird" and "Basie!") but manages to sound fresh and creative within the boundaries of the Basie tradition. —*Scott Yanow*

Prime Time / Jan. 18, 1977-Jan. 20, 1977 / Pablo ✦✦✦✦

One of arranger Sammy Nestico's most enjoyable sessions for Count Basie, these eight selections (six composed by Nestico, including the title cut and "Ya Gotta Try") are performed by an inspired Basie orchestra. Tenor saxophonist Jimmy Forrest and trombonist Al Grey star among the soloists. —*Scott Yanow*

Kansas City, Vol. 5 / Jan. 26, 1977 / Original Jazz Classics ✦✦✦

This studio session from 1977 features Count Basie in a quintet with vibraphonist Milt Jackson and guitarist Joe Pass. The predictably excellent group performs spirited versions of some of Basie's "hits" (including "Jive at Five" and "One O'Clock Jump"), some blues and a few standards. It is always interesting to hear Basie in a hornless setting like this one where he gets opportunities to stretch out on the piano. —*Scott Yanow*

The Gifted Ones / Feb. 3, 1977 / Original Jazz Classics ✦✦✦

Norman Granz got this one backwards. Instead of featuring Dizzy Gillespie with the Count Basie Orchestra, he put Gillespie and Basie together in a quartet which the trumpeter naturally dominates. The music is generally quite rewarding, including an unusual version of "St. James Infirmary," but never reaches the great heights one might have expected. —*Scott Yanow*

Basie Jam: Montreux '77 / Jul. 14, 1977 / Original Jazz Classics ✦✦✦✦

From Norman Granz's marathon series of performances recorded at the 1977 Montreux Jazz Festival, this set finds Count Basie fronting a jam session featuring trumpeter Roy Eldridge, altoist Benny Carter, Zoot Sims on tenor and the trombones of Vic Dickenson and Al Grey. Despite the possibility of being overcrowded, a bit of planning by Basie made this into a very coherent set with a blues, a long ballad medley and the closing "Jumpin' at the Woodside." Lots of nice moments. —*Scott Yanow*

Basie Big Band: Montreux '77 / Jul. 15, 1977 / Original Jazz Classics ✦✦✦

The Count Basie Orchestra is heard performing a fine set, recorded at the 1977 Montreux Jazz Festival. There are no surprises in the repertoire (which includes tunes by Sammy Nestico, Neal Hefti and some Basie standards) but the band seems inspired by the surroundings and tenor saxophonist Jimmy Forrest is in particularly solid form. —*Scott Yanow*

Satch and Josh....Again / Sep. 20, 1977 / Original Jazz Classics ✦✦✦

Recorded three years after their first full album together, this second encounter between Count Basie and Oscar Peterson on twin pianos (this time with a quartet) is as strong as the original, alternating standards with blues. Both Peterson and Basie have one number apiece on electric piano, making this album historic as well as quite musical. —*Scott Yanow*

Yessir, That's My Baby / Feb. 21, 1978 / Pablo ✦✦✦

From the same week that resulted in *Night Rider* and *Timekeepers,* this is the fifth album that documents the matchup of Count Basie and Oscar Peterson. The two pianists (backed by bassist John Heard and drummer Louis Bellson) play five standards and three blues with predictable swing, finding much more in common with each other than one might have originally suspected. —*Scott Yanow*

Night Rider / Feb. 21, 1978-Feb. 22, 1978 / Original Jazz Classics ✦✦✦

When they first met up for a full album in 1974, the two-piano team of Count Basie and Oscar Peterson must have seemed like an unlikely matchup. After all, Peterson is known for filling up his rapid solos with virtuosic passages while Basie is the master of the "less-is-more" approach, making every note count. But because Peterson has such high respect for Basie, he showed great self-restraint and left room for Basie's percussive solos. *Night Rider,* like their two previous joint albums, emphasizes the similarities rather than the differences in these two masters' styles. —*Scott Yanow*

The Timekeepers / Feb. 21, 1978-Feb. 22, 1978 / Original Jazz Classics ✦✦✦

From the same sessions that resulted in *Night Rider* and *Yessir,* this quartet date also features the two pianos of Oscar Peterson and Count Basie collaborating and interacting on swing standards and blues. Any of their five albums together are worth acquiring. —*Scott Yanow*

Live in Japan (1978) / May 21, 1978 / Pablo ✦✦✦

By 1978 the Count Basie Orchestra no longer had trombonist Al Grey and tenor saxophonist Jimmy Forrest as their stars, but this superb ensemble band was also

no longer dependent on famous names. In fact, one does not miss their presence on this superior live performance which features such Basie standbys as "Freckle Face," "All of Me," "Shiny Stockings" and "Jumpin' at the Woodside." Although the soloists were no longer household names, they all fare well, particularly Eric Dixon on tenor and flute. —*Scott Yanow*

On the Road / Jul. 12, 1979 / Original Jazz Classics ✦✦✦✦

This release gives one a definitive look at the Count Basie Orchestra during its final years. Trumpeter Pete Minger, trombonist Booty Wood and Eric Dixon on tenor and flute are the main soloists, but it is the classic Basie ensemble sound (which never seems to get dated or lose its charm and power) that carries the day. Whether it is "Wind Machine," "Splanky" or "In a Mellow Tone," this is a highly enjoyable set. —*Scott Yanow*

Get Together / Sep. 4, 1979 / Pablo ✦✦✦✦

This typically enjoyable Basie all-star jam is particularly noteworthy because it includes the great (but underrated) tenor of Budd Johnson along with Eddie "Lockjaw" Davis and trumpeters Clark Terry and Harry "Sweets" Edison. The music is quite delightful, topped by a fine ballad medley. —*Scott Yanow*

Kansas City Shout / Apr. 7, 1980 / Pablo ✦✦✦✦

This session from 1980 helps to recreate the atmosphere of '30s Kansas City. Featured are the great blues singer Joe Turner and the strong singer and altoist Eddie "Cleanhead" Vinson, along with the Count Basie Orchestra. "Just a Dream," "Everyday I Have the Blues," "Cherry Red" and "Stormy Monday" receive very spirited renditions, as do some newer blues. Since all of the principals are no longer with us, Norman Granz deserves special thanks for organizing this special session. —*Scott Yanow*

Kansas City, Vol. 7 / Apr. 10, 1980 / Original Jazz Classics ✦✦✦

Norman Granz recorded Count Basie in many different settings during his decade with Granz's Pablo label. This jam session set was a little unusual in that, along with the tenor of Eddie "Lockjaw" Davis, guitarist Joe Pass and trombonist J.J. Johnson, trumpeter Freddie Hubbard is in the cast along with Basie; pity he never recorded with the Count Basie Orchestra. This spirited session is a strong consolation prize, with plenty of fine solos taking over familiar chord changes. —*Scott Yanow*

Warm Breeze / Sep. 1, 1981-Sep. 2, 1981 / Pablo ✦✦✦

This big-band album finds Count Basie (at age 77) and his orchestra performing seven charts by longtime friend Sammy Nestico, including six originals and "Satin Doll." Trumpeter Harry "Sweets" Edison sits in on "How Sweet It Is" and trumpeter Willie Cook has a couple of strong spots, but it is the classic Basie ensemble sound that is this enjoyable studio session's strongest asset. —*Scott Yanow*

Kansas City, Vol. 6 / Nov. 1, 1981 / Original Jazz Classics ✦✦✦

This is one of many small-group jam sessions organized by Norman Granz to feature pianist Count Basie. This time around the proceedings (utilizing a sextet) have plenty of solo space for trumpeter Willie Cook, altoist Eddie "Cleanhead" Vinson (who also takes a vocal) and guitarist Joe Pass. As usual, when Basie had his way, the emphasis is on the blues and the music always swings. —*Scott Yanow*

Farmers Market Barbecue / May 1982 / Original Jazz Classics ✦✦✦✦

This was an excellent outing by the Count Basie Orchestra during its later years. Actually, half of this album features a medium-sized group from Basie's big band, but his orchestra usually had the feel of a small group anyway. Soloists at this late stage include Eric Dixon and Kenny Hing on tenors, trombonist Booty Wood, altoist Danny Turner and four different trumpeters. The rhythm section is of course instantly recognizable and the music is very much in the Basie tradition. —*Scott Yanow*

Me and You / Feb. 22, 1983-Feb. 28, 1983 / Original Jazz Classics ✦✦✦

Five big-band selections (including a remake of the half-century-old "Moten Swing") and four songs featuring an octet from the orchestra comprise this excellent outing by Count Basie recorded only a little more than a year before his death. However, the spirit of this music (helped out by some Ernie Wilkins arrangements) makes Count Basie seem ageless. —*Scott Yanow*

88 Basie Street / May 11, 1983-May 12, 1983 / Original Jazz Classics ✦✦✦✦

One of Basie's final albums, the very appealing title cut seems to sum up his career, a lightly swinging groove with a strong melody. Two small-group performances with guest Joe Pass on guitar and the tenor of Kenny Hing add variety to a particularly strong set. —*Scott Yanow*

Mostly Blues...and Some Others / Jun. 22, 1983 / Pablo ✦✦✦

Count Basie's final small-group studio session (one of a countless number for Norman Granz during Basie's last decade), this outing features trumpeter Snooky Young (who was last with the orchestra in the early '60s), tenor great Eddie "Lockjaw" Davis and the dependable guitarist Joe Pass (along with rhythm guitarist

Freddie Green). The repertoire lives up to the album's title: blues and swing standards all played with joy and spirit. —*Scott Yanow*

Fancy Pants / Dec. 1983 / Pablo ✦✦✦

Count Basie's last-known album (recorded four months before his death), this big-band record gives no hints of the end nearing; in fact the music is quite upbeat and typically spirited. The Count Basie Orchestra never declined and its leader (who remained in his musical, if not physical prime) went out swinging. —*Scott Yanow*

Live at Manchester Craftsmen's Guild / Feb. 10, 1996 / Blue Jackel ✦✦✦

Basin Street Six

f. 1950, **db.** 1953
Group / Dixieland

The New Orleans-based Basin Street Six was most notable for featuring clarinetist Pete Fountain and trumpeter/vocalist George Girard at the beginning of their careers. A Dixieland sextet that also included trombonist Joe Rotis and pianist Roy Zimmerman among the soloists, the Basin Street Six worked steadily for a time in New Orleans and recorded for 504, Circle and Mercury; the Circle recordings have been reissued on CD by GHB. —*Scott Yanow*

● **Complete Circle Recordings** / Aug. 20, 1950-Nov. 3, 1950 / GHB ✦✦✦✦

Django Bates (Leon Bates)

b. Oct. 2, 1960, Beckenham, England
Piano, Tenor Horn, Keyboards / Avant-Garde

A talented chance-taking improviser with a wicked sense of humor, Django Bates had extensive musical training. In 1979 he started the group Human Chain and Bates was in the quartet Borderline during 1981-84. In 1983 he joined Dudu Pukwana's band and became a founding member of the unusual English big band Loose Tubes. Bates played and recorded with Bill Bruford's Earthworks from the mid-'80s until 1994 when he decided that he preferred to lead his own bands. In addition to heading the big band Human Precipice, working with George Russell and George Gruntz and fulfilling commissions, Django Bates has recorded as a leader for JMT and as a sideman for ECM. —*Scott Yanow*

Music for the Third Policeman / Jan. 1990-Feb. 1990 / Ah Um ✦✦✦

● **Autumn Fires (And Green Shoots)** / Feb. 15, 1994-Feb. 16, 1994 / JMT ✦✦✦✦

English pianist Django Bates has a crazy sense of humor, the ability to use dissonance and noise as a logical part of his music and a fresh approach to group playing. On this CD, a solo piano outing, he is more subtle than on his group albums and the music takes a little while to cut loose. Bates plays with great reverence on "Solitude," tears conventionally into "Giant Steps," and does a close imitation of Keith Jarrett on "Hollyhock." However, Bates' unusual take on the world eventually comes to the surface on the overcrowded "Rat King" and a wonderfully titled piece called "The Loneliness of Being Right." He often displays a classical technique that is bent a bit to his purposes and, although his previous JMT group recording ("Summer Fruits") is recommended first, this solo set rewards repeated listenings. —*Scott Yanow*

Alvin Batiste

b. 1937, New Orleans, LA
Clarinet / Avant-Garde

Although sometimes called a "New Orleans clarinetist" (his Columbia album even billed him as a "Legendary Pioneer of Jazz"), in reality Alvin Batiste is an avant-garde player who does not fit easily into any classification. Underrecorded throughout his career, Alvin Batiste was a childhood friend of Ed Blackwell and he spent time in Los Angeles in 1956 playing with Ornette Coleman. However Batiste chose the life of an educator in Louisiana. He did make some little-known records with the AFO ("all for one") quintet in New Orleans, popped up on a couple of Cannonball Adderley dates and toured with Ray Charles in 1958 but was an obscure legend until he made three albums with Clarinet Summit in the 1980s (a quartet also including John Carter, David Murray and Jimmy Hamilton). Batiste recorded as a leader for India Navigation and made the 1993 Columbia album *Late*. He remains a very explorative (and under-recognized) player. —*Scott Yanow*

● **Musique D'afrique Nouvell Oreans** / 1984 / India Navigation ✦✦✦✦

Bayou Magic / 1988 / India Navigation ✦✦✦

Late / 1993 / Columbia ✦✦✦

Alvin Batiste spent much of his career as an educator so he tends to get overlooked when one thinks of the top jazz clarinetists. He has a conventional and pleasing tone that he utilizes to improvise in an unusual and harmonically advanced style. Most of this CD teams the avant-gardist with a bop-based trio led by Kenny Barron and the clarinetist is constantly bending the material. The well-

paced set (only a dumb modal version of "The Saints" is a disappointment) has among its high points a slow atmospheric New Orleans blues ("Late"), a relative of Coltrane's "Giant Steps" ("Imp and Perry"), a Ray Charles lick ("Ray's Segue") and the lengthy vamp-filled "Kinshasa." It's a strong introduction to the rarely recorded clarinetist. —*Scott Yanow*

Ray Bauduc (Raymond Bauduc)

b. Jun. 18, 1909, New Orleans, LA, **d.** Jan. 8, 1988, Houston, TX
Drums / Dixieland, Swing

Ray Bauduc was a trend setter in traditional jazz circles. His precise, disciplined, yet fiery patterns and syncopated fills helped New Orleans drummers make the transition into swing from the rigid, clipped progressions that had defined the previous era. The son of the great cornetist Jules Bauduc, his brother Jules Jr. taught Bauduc drums. His sister was also a musician, a pianist. Bauduc's first professional job came with a band that accompanied films. Later, though still in school, he worked with cornetist Emmett Hardy and also the Six Nola Jazzers. Bauduc toured in 1924 with Johnny Bayersdorffer, then worked with the Scranton Sirens; this group included Billy Lustig in 1925 and Joe Venuti and Eddie Lang in 1926. He spent two years with a vaudevillian band led by Fred Rich playing drums and doing tap, and played with Miff Mole in 1927. During the '30s he became a star. Bauduc spent six years (1928-1934) with Ben Pollack's orchestra, and also found time for sessions with Red Nichols, Jack Teagarden, Benny Goodman, Wingy Manone, Louis Prima and Glenn Miller. A year after leaving Pollack, in 1935, Bauduc joined the Bob Crosby Orchestra and remained with him until 1942. "South Rampart Street Parade" and "The Big Noise from Winnetka," both of which he co-wrote with Bob Haggart, became standards. He spent some time in the army during the '40s, briefly co-led a band with Gil Rodin, then headed his own groups. There were recording reunions with Manone and Crosby later in the '40s, plus stints with Jimmy Dorsey (1948-1950) and Teagarden (1951-1955). Bauduc and Nappy Lamare headed a band from 1956-1959, and he worked as a freelance player on the West Coast in the '60s, finally moving to Bellaire, TX, where he occasionally performed. —*Ron Wynn*

Billy Bauer

b. Nov. 14, 1915, New York, NY
Guitar / Cool

Billy Bauer will always be best known for his late-'40s association with Lennie Tristano, playing clean-toned lines that perfectly fit in with the pianist, Lee Konitz and Warne Marsh. He originally started out on banjo, switching to guitar in the early '30s. Bauer worked with Jerry Wald's Orchestra, Woody Herman's First Herd (1944-46), Chubby Jackson (1947) and then (on several occasions) Benny Goodman. With Tristano during his most significant years (1946-49), Bauer participated in the first recorded free improvisations and the classic early Konitz-Marsh dates. He won *Downbeat* and *Metronome* polls during 1949-53. Bauer spent most of the 1950s as a busy studio musician although he did find time to record with the popular J.J. Johnson-Kai Winding Quintet (1954), Bobby Hackett (1957), Cootie Williams (1957) and Lee Konitz (1955 and 1957). In 1961 he opened his own jazz club in Long Island, NY, and then worked in lounges. In 1970 Bauer opened up his own guitar school. He cut back drastically on his freelancing after a serious ear infection hit in 1975 but has remained active as a teacher. —*Scott Yanow*

● **Anthology** / 1959-Dec. 1969 / Interplay ✦✦✦✦

Guitarist Billy Bauer, best known for his early associations with Lennie Tristano and Woody Herman, only recorded three albums as a leader. While his first dates were in 1953 and 1956, this Interplay LP collects together private solo performances from 1959, 1960 and 1969 and a trio gig in 1969 (with bassist John Sherin and drummer Charles Kay) that were taped but originally not planned for release. Fortunately they were saved and in 1987 (when it finally came out) this album showed that Bauer's creative abilities had not diminished with time even though he lacked the drive to have a full time performing career. Most of the music is introspective but there are some swinging moments (most notably on the trio's rendition of "I'll Remember April"). Guitarists and bop historians will be most interested in this quiet set. —*Scott Yanow*

Mario Bauza

b. Apr. 28, 1911, Havana, Cuba, **d.** Jul. 11, 1993, New York, NY
Trumpet / Afro-Cuban Jazz, Latin Jazz

A talented section player who rarely soloed, Mario Bauza's main importance to music was behind the scenes as one of the main instigators of Afro-Cuban jazz, the potent mixture of Latin rhythms with jazz improvisation. A multi-instrumentalist, Bauza played clarinet and oboe with the Havana Philharmonic before moving to New York in 1930. During a stint with Noble Sissle in 1932 he switched to trumpet. As musical director with Chick Webb (1933-38), Bauza helped convince the drummer of the potential greatness of Ella Fitzgerald. He was with Don Redman during 1938-39 and then Cab Calloway (1939-41). Bauza was largely responsible for Calloway hiring Dizzy Gillespie and in 1947 he would introduce Dizzy to Chano Pozo. Bauza became the longtime musical director of his brother-in-law Machito's orchestra (1941-76), encouraging Machito to add jazz solos to his music. In the 1980s and early '90s as the head of his own Afro-Cuban Orchestra, Mario Bauza (who had long since given up playing trumpet) recorded three excellent albums of his arrangements and finally received some recognition for his important contributions to music. —Scott Yanow

● **The Tanga Suite** / Jul. 29, 1992 / Messidor ✦✦✦✦✦
Mario Bauza's place as one of the key founders of Latin-jazz was overlooked for decades until he formed the exciting orchestra found on this Messidor CD. His 23-piece big band, along with a variety of singers, performs a full set of Bauza's originals including the five movements of his Afro-Cuban jazz suite "Tanga." Victor Paz's lead trumpet drives the ensembles and Paquito D'Rivera has a strong appearance sitting in on alto. —Scott Yanow

944 Columbus / 1993 / Messidor ✦✦✦✦
During his final two years, Mario Bauza and his newly formed Afro-Cuban Jazz Orchestra recorded three albums of which *944 Columbus* (made just two months before his death) was the last. Three of the ten selections on the CD are dominated by vocals but jazz is a very strong element throughout these sessions with a variety of fine solos, particularly from trumpeter Michael Mossman. The percussion section blends in well with the horns in this 19-piece orchestra and the final statement from the Father of Afro-Cuban Jazz is a memorable one. —Scott Yanow

Beachfront Property

f. 1990
Vocal Group / Bop, Standards

Jazz vocal groups (at least worthwhile ones) are a rare species. Beachfront Property differs from their predecessors due to its size, originally starting out with nine singers (Jeff Dolan, Wendy Abeling, Stan Castongia, Renee Kerr, Tom & Jennifer Dustman, Alyce Ohl and Bill & Jill Mumaw) in 1990 and cutting back to eight (Michelle Carroll took the places of both Wendy Abeling and Renee Kerr) by 1993. The group, which sometimes sounds like an enlarged jazz-oriented version of Manhattan Transfer, has recorded several sets for Cexton and can be relied upon to put on a swinging and very musical show. —Scott Yanow

● **Straight Up** / 1993 / Cexton ✦✦✦✦✦
The eight-voice (four male/four female) Beachfront Property romps through a variety of loop-oriented material on this bright session. Backed by a trio (with pianist Kevin Kearney, bassist Tom Warrington and drummer Steve Houghton), the group performs such material as "Straighten Up & Fly Right," "Tenor Madness," "Stompin' at the Savoy," "Pick Yourself Up" and "Linus & Lucy" with swing and honest feeling. This is their definitive release to date. —Scott Yanow

A Beachfront Christmas / 1995 / Cexton ✦✦
Beachfront Property, which at the time of this recording was a seven-voice vocal ensemble, performs Christmas-related songs on this set with the assistance of a trio led by pianist/organist Dave Loeb, plus guests Bob Sheppard on reeds and guitarist Frank Potenza. Unlike their previous release, much of the material on the set is taken fairly straight without much improvising. Although there are a couple of celebratory tunes (such as "Santa Claus Is Coming to Town" and "Rudolph the Red-Nosed Reindeer"), most of the renditions are borderline sacred, overly respectful and predictable. A sincere but forgettable effort. —Scott Yanow

Jeff Beal

b. 1963, San Francisco, CA
Piano, Composer , Trumpet, Fluegelhorn / Post-Bop

A superior trumpeter, Jeff Beal is thus far most notable for his advanced writing abilities. While studying at the Eastman School of Music, Beal won 11 *Downbeat* student awards. He also received three Exxon/Meet the Composer Grants during 1986-87. Beal moved to New York after graduating, recorded his debut *Liberation* for Antilles and then moved to the West Coast to work on film scores. He has since recorded a second date for Antilles (*Perpetual Motion*) and three sets for Triloka. Beal's writing has been featured on albums by Spyro Gyra, Dave Samuels and John Patitucci but he has not neglected his unpredictable trumpet playing, gigging often in the Los Angeles area. —Scott Yanow

Perpetual Motion / Jul. 1986-Nov. 4, 1986 / Antilles ✦✦✦✦
Trumpeter Jeff Beal, who has very impressive technique, displays obvious love for both jazz and classical music during his nine compositions included on this release. On "Exit Only" Beal's tone might immediately recall Chuck Mangione but his solo is much more advanced. The gospelish "Crossing the River" (which has a colorful trade-off between Beal and tenorman Bob Mintzer) is reminiscent of Keith

Jarrett while the colorful funk of "Meshugenah Man" would have fit in perfectly in the repertoire of Miles Davis' 1980s band. The second half of the set really puts the focus on Jeff Beal's playing for he is the only horn (except for two appearances by Larry Schneider on tenor) in addition to being the keyboardist (via overdubbing). Highlights include Beal's playful interaction with Mary Corbett-Laven's violin during "Zarzuela" and his solo on the funky "Round A'bout." Stimulating and thought-provoking music. —Scott Yanow

Liberation / Apr. 1988 / Antilles ✦✦✦
Always much more than a trumpeter, Jeff Beal on his debut as a leader plays trumpet, piccolo trumpet, fluegelhorn, keyboards and contributed all eight of the compositions. Mixing acoustic and electric instruments and the post-bop tradition with aspects of fusion and funk, the music on this set is quite unclassifiable. Beal is joined by guitarist Jay Azzolina, bassist Ned Mann, drummer Larry Aberman on five of the numbers (two of which also include saxophonist David Mann), while three songs are overdubbed showcases for Beal's keyboards, drum programming and horns, and Joan Beal sings "Skylight." An impressive beginning for the potentially significant musician. —Scott Yanow

Objects in the Mirror / Feb. 1990-Jun. 25, 1991 / Triloka ✦✦✦
This CD is a rather mixed bag, alternating between spacy electronic jazz and pop vocals to more challenging structures. Trumpeter Jeff Beal and tenorman Bob Sheppard have some worthwhile solos ("Improvisation No. 2" and "Waiting Game" are among the high points of the trumpeter's recording career), but there are also a few throwaway tracks (particularly "A Different Shade of Blue"). A rather unpredictable set that is generally worthwhile and certainly takes chances. —Scott Yanow

● **Three Graces** / Jan. 1993 / Triloka ✦✦✦✦
Trumpeter Jeff Beal's compositions do not contain catchy melodies but instead set mysterious and often melancholy moods with interesting frameworks, using occasional funklines creatively. Much of the music builds logically to unexpected heights with surprising turns. Beal's fine trumpet playing is generally quite original (even if he hints strongly at Miles Davis' sound when he is muted) and his sextet (with Steve Tavaglione's tenor, pianist John Beasley and bassist John Patitucci) is flexible enough to interpret his complex compositions. —Scott Yanow

Contemplations / Aug. 1993-Dec. 1993 / Triloka ✦✦✦
Contemplations is not about contemplation, but are themselves contemplations. Inspired by the writings of Thomas Merton, especially his "Seeds of Contemplation," Jeff Beal wrote *Contemplations* after his own self-imposed isolation . . . The piano improvisations evolve from a simple theme that is explored and expanded upon. Like Merton's writings, where simple and graceful words were used to make a point, Beal uses only the essential elements of music in a jazz medium to create a spiritual motive force . . . —MusD

Alternate Route / Mar. 6, 1994+Jan. 30, 1996 / Unit ✦✦✦
Performed in conjunction with the Berkeley Symphony Orchestra and the Metropole Orchestra of Holland, Jeff Beal's *Alternate Route* is an intriguing classical/jazz crossover outing; highlighted by an engaging trumpet concerto, the record utilizes its orchestral players primarily as a rhythmic accompaniment for the jazz soloists, but occasionally allows for symphonic solos of sorts which successfully bridge the gap between the two musical forms. —Jason Ankeny

The Gathering / Nov. 1995+Dec. 1995 / Triloka ✦✦✦

Bebop & Beyond

f. 1984
Group / Bop, Hard Bop

Bebop & Beyond is a repertory ensemble devoted to interpreting works from the modern jazz canon, and one of the few working jazz bands that is also a not-for-profit corporation (Benny Carter, Jimmy Heath, and Orrin Keepnews sit on its board of advisors). Founded and led by San Francisco-based tenor saxophonist Mel Martin, the band has, since its inception, concentrated on updates of classic bebop tunes by such as Charlie Parker, Tadd Dameron, and Charles Mingus. Their record, *Bebop & Beyond Plays Dizzy Gillespie*, was the trumpet innovator's final studio date. —Chris Kelsey

Bebop and Beyond / Feb. 1984 / Concord Jazz ✦✦✦✦✦
This debut record of Mel Martin's Bebop and Beyond is a very impressive effort so it is surprising that six years would pass before their first encore. Martin (playing tenor and soprano) teams up wih the great altoist John Handy, trumpeter Warren Gale, pianist George Gables, bassist Frank Tusa and drummer Eddie Marshall for four group originals, Tadd Dameron's "On a Misty Night" and two Thelonious Monk songs. The exciting "Longhorn" (dedicated to Art Blakey) and Monk's "Evidence" are among the high points of this inventive straightahead set. Recommended. —Scott Yanow

● **Plays Thelonious Monk** / Feb. 13, 1990+Feb. 15, 1990 / Blue Moon ✦✦✦✦✦
This CD contains one of the best Thelonious Monk tributes that have come out since the pianist/composer's death in 1982. Mel Martin (heard here in top form on tenor, soprano and flute) leads Bebop & Beyond through nine of Monk's most difficult originals and his arrangements (which use the versatile guitarist Randy Vincent in Monk's place) are consistently inventive. Pianist George Cables, tenor saxophonist Joe Henderson and Howard Johnson (on baritone and tuba) make important guest appearances while trumpeter Warren Gale contributes many fine solos. —*Scott Yanow*

Plays Dizzy Gillespie / May 23, 1991-May 24, 1991 / Blue Moon ✦✦✦
Bebop & Beyond's third recording was particularly special, because for their performances of six Dizzy Gillespie tunes (plus Ray Brown's "That's Earl, Brother" and leader Mel Martin's "Rhythm Man"), the group has as guest artist on six of the eight numbers—Dizzy himself. 73 at the time and way past his musical prime, Dizzy does get off a few good solos and takes a touching vocal on "I Waited for You." Martin (switching between soprano, alto, tenor and flute), trumpeter Warren Gale, pianist George Cables, the distinctive and creative guitarist Randy Vincent, bassist Jeff Chambers, drummer Donald Bailey, Vince Lateano on drums and timbales and guest percussionist John Santos are all in fine form on fresh versions of such numbers as "Wheatleigh Hall," "Manteca" and "Diddy-Wa-Diddy." —*Scott Yanow*

Sidney Bechet

b. May 14, 1897, New Orleans, LA, d. May 14, 1959, Paris, France
Clarinet, Soprano Saxophone / New Orleans Jazz, Dixieland, Traditional Jazz
Sidney Bechet was the first important jazz soloist on records in history (beating Louis Armstrong by a few months). A brilliant soprano saxophonist and clarinetist with a wide vibrato that listeners either loved or hated, Bechet's style did not evolve much through the years but he never lost his enthusiasm or creativity. A master at both individual and collective improvisation within the genre of New Orleans jazz, Bechet was such a dominant player that trumpeters found it very difficult to play with him. Bechet wanted to play lead and it was up to the other horns to stay out of his way!
Sidney Bechet studied clarinet in New Orleans with Lorenzo Tio, Big Eye Louis Nelson and George Baquet and he developed so quickly that as a child he was playing with some of the top bands in the city. He even taught clarinet and one of his students (Jimmie Noone) was actually two years older than him! In 1917 he travelled to Chicago and in 1919 he joined Will Marion Cook's Orchestra, touring Europe with Cook and receiving a remarkably perceptive review from Ernst Ansermet. While overseas he found a soprano sax in a store and from then on it was his main instrument. Back in the US, Bechet made his recording debut in 1923 with Clarence Williams and during the next two years he appeared on records backing blues singers, interacting with Louis Armstrong and playing some stunning solos. He was with Duke Ellington's early orchestra for a period and at one point hired a young Johnny Hodges for his own band. However from 1925-29 Bechet was overseas, travelling as far as Russia but getting in trouble (and spending jail time) in France before being deported.
Most of the 1930s were comparatively lean times for Bechet. He worked with Noble Sissle on and off and had a brilliant session with his New Orleans Feetwarmers in 1932 (featuring trumpeter Tommy Ladnier). But he also ran a tailor's shop which was more notable for its jam sessions than for any money it might make. However in 1938 he had a hit recording of "Summertime," Hugues Panassie featured Bechet on some records and soon he was signed to Bluebird where he recorded quite a few classics during the next three years. Bechet worked regularly in New York, appeared on some of Eddie Condon Town Hall concerts and in 1945 he tried unsuccessfully to have a band with the veteran trumpeter Bunk Johnson (whose constant drinking killed the project). Jobs began to dry up about this time and Bechet opened up what he hoped would be a music school. He only had one main pupil but Bob Wilber became his protégé.
Sidney Bechet's fortunes changed drastically in 1949. He was invited to the Salle Pleyel Jazz Festival in Paris, caused a sensation, and decided to move permanently overseas. Within a couple years he was a major celebrity and a national hero in France even though the general public in the US never did know who he was! Bechet's last decade was filled with exciting concerts, many recordings and infrequent visits back to the US before his death from cancer. His colorful (if sometimes fanciful) memoirs *Treat It Gentle* and John Chilton's magnificent Bechet biography *The Wizard of Jazz* (which traces his life nearly week-by-week) are both highly recommended. Many of Sidney Bechet's recordings are currently available on CD. —*Scott Yanow*

The Chronological Sidney Bechet, 1923-1936 / Oct. 1923-Mar. 1936 / Classics ✦✦✦✦
The first in a series of Classics CDs focusing on the recordings of Sidney Bechet,

this disc features the clarinetist/soprano saxophonist on two early titles with blues singer Rosetta Crawford, his torrid 1932 session with the New Orleans Feetwarmers (which also features trumpeter Tommy Ladnier and is highlighted by "Shag" and "Maple Leaf Rag") and sides from Noble Sissle's somewhat commercial orchestra. Fortunately Sissle was wise enough to give Bechet plenty of solo space on some of his selections, most notably "Polka Dot Rag." Even with a few indifferent vocals, this CD is recommended to those not already owning this music. —*Scott Yanow*

● **1924-1938** / 1924-1938 / DRG ✦✦✦
Decent sampler of vintage Bechet performances culled from various sessions and issued on a single disc. This is neither the best sequenced nor remastered Bechet set around, but the playing is wonderful, even when the sound isn't. —*Ron Wynn*

Sidney Bechet (1924-1938) / 1924-1938 / Pearl Flapper ✦✦✦
A compendium of Bechet sides with the Blue Five, Red Onion Jazz Babies, Noble Sissle & His International Orchestra, and Noble Sissle's Swingsters, provides good coverage of the clarinetist in differing musical formats (especially on sarrusophone on "Mandy, Make Up Your Mind!"). —*Bruce Raeburn*

The Complete, Vols. 1-2 / Sep. 15, 1932-Jan. 8, 1941 / RCA ✦✦✦✦✦
Of all the overlapping Bechet reissue series, this series of two-LP sets released by French RCA is easily the best, with all of the Victor sides by the great soprano saxophonist and clarinetist (including the valuable alternate takes) being issued complete and in chronological order. The first two-fer is highlighted by the blazing session by the New Orleans Feetwarmers from 1932, four selections from the "Really the Blues" date with trumpeter Tommy Ladnier and clarinetist Mezz Mezzrow, and such Bechet classics as "Indian Summer," "Old Man Blues" and "Nobody Knows the Way I Feel 'Dis Mornin'." —*Scott Yanow*

☆ **Master Takes: Victor Sessions (1932-1943)** / Sep. 15, 1932-Dec. 8, 1943 / Bluebird ✦✦✦✦✦
This three-CD set has most of the finest recordings ever made by soprano saxophonist and clarinet master Sidney Bechet. Although the alternate takes have unfortunately been left out (making the three sadly out-of-print French RCA double-LPs the absolute best way to acquire this timeless music), there are a remarkable amount of exciting performances in this box. Bechet jams with trumpeter Tommy Ladnier and the New Orleans Feetwarmers on a 1932 session (including torrid versions of "I've Found a New Baby," "Maple Leaf Rag" and "Shag") and then is heard mostly during 1940-41 on his other Victor recordings. Among the highlights are "Indian Summer," "One O'Clock Jump," Duke Ellington's "Old Man Blues," an emotional and definitive "Nobody Knows the Way I Feel 'Dis Mornin'," "Blues in Thirds," "Stompy Jones," "Egyptian Fantasy," Bechet's one-man band version of "The Sheik of Araby," "Swing Parade," "The Mooche" and "What Is This Thing Called Love." Although the supporting cast (17 different combinations of musicians are utilized) is quite impressive, it is Sidney Bechet who makes these performances quite classic. This music is essential (in one form or another) for every serious jazz collection. —*Scott Yanow*

The Chronological Sidney Bechet, 1937-1938 / Apr. 1937-Nov. 1938 / Classics ✦✦✦
The second in a series of CD reissues featuring Sidney Bechet has quite a bit of variety. The unique soprano saxophonist is heard with Noble Sissle's showband, dominating a small group sponsored by Sissle, backing blues singer Trixie Smith and the team of Grant & Wilson, and leading his own sextet with a sextet that includes baritonist Ernie Caceres, and on "Hold Tight," a vocal by "The Two Fish Mongers." Enjoyable if not quite essential music. —*Scott Yanow*

The Complete, Vols. 5-6 / Nov. 21, 1938-Dec. 8, 1943 / RCA ✦✦✦✦✦
The third and final two-fer in this definitive series concludes the reissuance of every Sidney Bechet recording on Victor (including the alternate takes) with sessions from 1941 (highlighted by a classic rendition of "What Is This Thing Called Love?") and a quintet set from two years later with trombonist Vic Dickenson. Filling out this two-LP set are what was known as the "Panassie sessions," the recordings organized by French critic Hugues Panassie during a visit to New York in 1938-39. Mezz Mezzrow is heard at length on performances with trumpeters Tommy Ladnier and Sidney DeParis, but it is the six progressive swing tracks from trumpeter Frankie Newton's septet (with pianist James P. Johnson) that are most memorable, particularly a brilliant version of "Rosetta." —*Scott Yanow*

1938-1939 / Nov. 28, 1938-Feb. 5, 1940 / Classics ✦✦✦
This entry in Classics' chronological reissue of the master takes of Bechet's early recordings finds the soprano great playing with trumpeter Tommy Ladnier and Mezz Mezzrow on the famous "Really the Blues" session, performing a hit version of "Summertime," overshadowing the other members of the all-star Port of Harlem Seven and recording "Indian Summer" and a hot version of "One O'Clock

Jump" in a 1940 session for Victor. However, half of this CD is taken up by an odd and surprisingly restrained marathon date with pianist Willie "The Lion" Smith in which they perform Haitian folk songs. —*Scott Yanow*

☆ **Complete Blue Note Recordings** / 1939-1953 / Mosaic ✦✦✦✦✦

Mosaic, a mail-order company, has compiled a series of remarkable box sets that feature the complete recordings of various immortal musicians at the peak of their careers. This limited-edition six-LP set (get it while you can) has all of Sidney Bechet's recordings for Blue Note including three songs with the Port of Harlem Seven (climaxed by his hit version of "Summertime"), two blues with guitarist Josh White, and Bechet's sessions from 1940, 1944, 1945, 1946, 1949, 1950, 1951 and 1953 in which he shares the front line with such cornetists as Sidney DeParis, Max Kaminsky, Bunk Johnson, Wild Bill Davison and Jonah Jones. The music ranges from hot swing to exuberant Dixieland, and Bechet somehow always sounds inspired. —*Scott Yanow*

1940 / Mar. 7, 1940-Jun. 4, 1940 / Classics ✦✦✦✦

Classics' chronological reissue of Bechet's recordings (at least the regular takes) continues with a pair of songs made with blues singer Josh White, eight very enjoyable performances cut with a quartet consisting of cornetist Muggsy Spanier, guitarist Carmen Mastren and bassist Wellman Braud, and a pair of Bechet's Victor sessions. This is one of the strongest entries in this valuable series. —*Scott Yanow*

1940-1941 / Sep. 6, 1940-Oct. 14, 1941 / Classics ✦✦✦✦

Classics' Sidney Bechet series continues with this CD, a generous set full of the soprano's prime Victor recordings, including appearances by cornetist Rex Stewart and pianist Earl Hines, Bechet's guest shot with the Chamber Music Society of Lower Basin Street, and his innovative "one-man-band" recordings of "The Sheik of Araby" and "Blues of Bechet." —*Scott Yanow*

The Complete, Vols. 3-4 / Jan. 8, 1941-Oct. 24, 1941 / RCA ✦✦✦✦✦

The second of three two-LP sets released by French RCA continues the complete chronological repackaging (including alternate takes) of all of Bechet's Victor recordings. During the ten-month period covered in this valuable set, he recorded such classics as "Egyptian Fantasy," "Swing Parade," "The Mooche" and even the odd "Laughin' in Rhythm." Bechet, a remarkable soprano saxophonist who made traditional jazz sound modern, also is heard on six instruments during his innovative overdubbed "one-man-band" performances of a blues and "The Sheik of Araby." This series is highly recommended but is becoming increasingly difficult to find. —*Scott Yanow*

Masters of Jazz, Vol. 4 / Aug. 29, 1945-Dec. 20, 1947 / Storyville ✦✦✦

The dozen performances on this CD are all taken from Sidney Bechet's famous sessions for Mezz Mezzrow's King Jazz label; in fact the CD (along with four other Storyville releases titled *The King Jazz Story, Vols. 1-4*) is part of the complete reissuance of that label's output. Since this is by far the briefest of the five CDs (at around 41 minutes), this one can be acquired last. However the music (hot quintet/sextets featuring Bechet, Mezzrow and sometimes trumpeter Hot Lips Page) is often quite exciting with the emphasis on blues and heated ensembles. —*Scott Yanow*

La Legende de Sidney Bechet / Oct. 14, 1949-Jul. 4, 1958 / Vogue ✦✦✦

This CD features a cross-section of soprano great Bechet's '50s European recordings. A national hero in France during this time, although relatively unknown to the general public in the US, Bechet really dominates this set. The music ranges from his 1949 hit "Les Oignons," an early version of "Petite Fleur" and a passionate "Summertime" to romping jams on "Royal Garden Blues" and "When the Saints Go Marchin' In." A fine introduction to late-period Bechet, one of the true giants of jazz history. —*Scott Yanow*

Live in New York, 1950-51 / Apr. 1, 1950-Oct. 19, 1951 / Storyville ✦✦✦✦

Neglected in his homeland, the great soprano saxophonist Sidney Bechet first moved to France (where he quickly became known as a national hero) in 1949 but made a couple of trips back to the US during the next few years. His Storyville CD features Bechet in the US during two occasions, leading a quartet/quintet with only a trombone joining him in the front line; at least he was not compelled to battle for the lead with a trumpeter. There are eight selections with trombonist Vic Dickenson, pianist Ken Kersey, bassist Herb Ward and drummer Cliff Leeman that include individual features for Dickenson and Kersey along with spirited renditions of "Muskrat Ramble," "High Society" and "Royal Garden Blues"; in addition Bechet caresses the melody of "Laura" and romps through "Just One of Those Things." However it is the other 11 numbers (which were only previously released on LP by Pumpkin) that are most notable for these are probably the finest recordings of the underrated trombonist Big Chief Russell Moore. With pianist Red Richards and drummer Art Trappier functioning quite well as the entire rhythm section (without a bassist), the trombonist stays out of Bechet's way and adds some robust and humorous solos of his own. During memorable versions of "I Found a

New Baby," "Bugle Call Rag," "Panama" and even "Casey Jones," Bechet never runs out of infectious riffs and is in consistently exciting form. —*Scott Yanow*

Salle Pleyel: 31 January 52 / Jan. 31, 1952 / Vogue ✦✦✦

Bechet is heard on this CD in concert with Claude Luter's orchestra before a semi-hysterical audience. The crowd shows one just how popular Bechet was in France during the '50s; if only America treated its jazzmen as well. The music is generally rewarding if without many surprises, a variety of standards and Dixieland tunes with Bechet's soprano rightfully dominating the proceedings. —*Scott Yanow*

Sidney Bechet in Paris, Vol. 1 / May 18, 1953+1964 / Vogue ✦✦

This Vogue CD is a bit unusual for, rather than featuring the masterful soprano saxophonist Sidney Bechet in his usual Dixieland settings, it contains his original music for two ballets as performed by a pair of symphony orchestras. "La Nuit Est Une Sorciere" from 1953, after some narration in French, has the orchestra playing dramatic themes with a few token appearances by Bechet himself. "La Colline du Delta," a lively tribute to Louisiana, was recorded posthumously in 1964 with Claude Luter (a close Sidney Bechet disciple) in Bechet's place; Luter gets to stretch out a bit. Overall this is an interesting, but not essential, set. —*Scott Yanow*

Jazz at Storyville / Oct. 1953 / Black Lion ✦✦✦

Taken from Sidney Bechet's last major tour of the US, this live session teams his passionate soprano with the subtle wit of trombonist Vic Dickenson and a fine rhythm section (including George Wein on piano). This set may only contain familiar standards, but the general enthusiasm and the interplay between Bechet and Dickenson makes the music enjoyable and well worth hearing. —*Scott Yanow*

Olympia Concert, October 19, 1955 / Oct. 19, 1955 / Vogue ✦✦✦✦

Bechet is heard on this CD at a 1955 concert held before an adoring crowd in Paris where he was continually honored as a national hero. Backed by a pair of alternating French trad bands, Bechet plays some fresher material than usual, bringing back such classics as "Wild Man Blues," "Wild Cat Rag" and "Viper Mad." —*Scott Yanow*

Back to Memphis / May 16, 1956 / Vogue ✦✦✦✦✦

While in France during the 1950s, soprano saxophonist Sidney Bechet recorded many exciting sessions. In most cases he was the dominant soloist since he was joined by local groups full of younger players. But for this LP, Bechet meets up with a band of American all-stars. Pianist Sammy Price, trumpeter Emmett Berry, trombonist George Stevenson (who is in particularly good form), clarinetist Herbert Hall, bassist Pops Foster and drummer Freddie Moore all collaborate with Bechet in some very hot performances. Highlights include "St. Louis Blues" and up-tempo "Darktown Strutters Ball," a charming and hard-swinging "Yes We Have No Bananas Today" and "Dinah." Although Bechet is clearly the leader, Berry (who rarely played Dixieland), Stevenson and Hall (along with the driving rhythm section) make strong contributions to the overheated moments. By the way, the song listed as "Back Home" is actually the standard "One Sweet Letter from You." This out-of-print French LP is well worth the search and will hopefully reappear on CD someday. —*Scott Yanow*

When a Soprano Meets a Piano / Mar. 12, 1957 / Inner City ✦✦✦✦

One of Sidney Bechet's final recordings was this relatively modern quartet session which also features pianist Martial Solal. This LP finds Bechet playing melodically and with invention on superior swing (rather than Dixieland) standards, meeting the modern 25-year-old pianist halfway. Bechet's sound was still beautiful, even at this late stage. —*Scott Yanow*

Paris Jazz Concert / May 27, 1957-Aug. 3, 1958 / RTE ✦✦✦

This Sidney Bechet CD comprises previously unreleased material taken from three Paris concerts that was fortunately broadcast over the radio and properly preserved through the years. The classic master of the soprano sax is heard in reasonably inspired form quite late in his career. The first two sets feature Bechet being accompanied by French groups that, although not overly distinctive, offer contrasting solos that do not get in the way; both Guy Lognon and Roland Hug are fine on trumpet. The other band has much bigger names including trumpeter Buck Clayton, trombonist Vic Dickenson and pianist George Wein but, even with Clayton being showcased on "All of Me," there is no doubt that Sidney Bechet is the leader. It's easily recommended to Dixieland fans. —*Scott Yanow*

Parisian Encounter / Jul. 4, 1958 / Vogue ✦✦✦✦

One of the most competitive of all jazzmen, Bechet was well teamed with the Louis Armstrong-influenced trumpet of Teddy Buckner on this spirited set from late in Bechet's life. Buckner is reasonably respectful but gets in plenty of hot licks during this Dixielandish session; a concert shortly afterward by the two would be very combative. This fine CD shows that Sidney Bechet never did decline or lose any of his formidable power. —*Scott Yanow*

Bix Beiderbecke

b. Mar. 10, 1903, Davenport, IA, **d.** Aug. 6, 1931, New York, NY

Cornet / Classic Jazz

Bix Beiderbecke was one of the greatest jazz musicians of the 1920s. His colorful life, quick rise and fall, and eventual status as a martyr made him a legend even before he died and he has long stood as proof that not all the innovators in jazz history were black. Possessor of a beautiful distinctive tone and a strikingly original improvising style, Bix's only competitor among cornetists in the '20s was Louis Armstrong and (due to their different sounds and styles) one really could not compare them.

Beiderbecke was a bit of a child prodigy, picking out tunes on the piano when he was three. While he had conventional training on the piano, he taught himself the cornet. Influenced by the original Dixieland Jazz Band, Beiderbecke craved the freedom of jazz but his straight-laced parents felt he was being frivolous. He was sent to Lake Forest Military Academy in 1921 but by coincidence it was located fairly close to Chicago, the center of jazz at the time. Bix was eventually expelled he missed so many classes! After a brief period at home he became a full-time musician. In 1923 Beiderbecke became the star cornetist of the Wolverines and a year later this spirited group made some classic recordings.

In late 1924 Bix left the Wolverines to join Jean Goldkette's Orchestra but his inability to read music resulted in him losing the job. In 1925 he spent time in Chicago and worked on his reading abilities. The following year he spent time with Frankie Trumbauer's Orchestra in St. Louis. Although already an alcoholic, 1927 would be Beiderbecke's greatest year. He worked with Jean Goldkette's Orchestra (most of their records are unfortunately quite commercial), recorded his piano masterpiece "In a Mist" (one of his four Debussy-inspired originals), cut many classic sides with a small group headed by Trumbauer (including his greatest solos: "Singin' the Blues," "I'm Comin' Virginia" and "Way Down Yonder in New Orleans") and then signed up with Paul Whiteman's huge and prosperous orchestra. Although revisionist historians would later claim that Whiteman's wide mixture of repertoire (much of it outside of jazz) drove Bix to drink, he actually enjoyed the prestige of being with the most popular band of the decade. Beiderbecke's favorite personal solo was his written-out part on George Gershwin's "Concerto in F."

With Whiteman, Bix's solos tended to be short moments of magic, sometimes in odd settings; his brilliant chorus on "Sweet Sue" is a perfect example. He was productive throughout 1928 but by the following year his drinking really began to catch up with him. Beiderbecke had a breakdown, made a comeback and then in September 1929 was reluctantly sent back to Davenport to recover. Unfortunately Bix made a few sad records in 1930 before his death at age 28. The bad liquor of the Prohibition era did him in.

For the full story, *Bix: Man & Legend* is a remarkably detailed book. Beiderbecke's recordings (even the obscure ones) are continually in print for his followers believe that every note he played was special. This writer agrees. —*Scott Yanow*

And the Chicago Cornets / Feb. 18, 1924-Jan. 26, 1925 / Milestone ♦♦♦♦

Not only does this superior double-LP set contain all of cornetist Bix Beiderbecke's recordings with the Wolverines in 1924 (much of which is classic), but it features him with the Sioux City Six and his Rhythm Jugglers (highlighted by the original version of "Davenport Blues"), the two titles cut by the Wolverines after Beiderbecke departed (with Jimmy McPartland in his spot) and seven performances by the Bucktown Five in 1924 (the recording debut of cornetist Muggsy Spanier). Collectors of '20s jazz should be familiar with most of this music, especially the Wolverines sides. Bix Beiderbecke, although only 21 years old at the time, already demonstrated the lyricism, inventiveness and beautiful tone that one asociates with him. —*Scott Yanow*

Singin' the Blues / Jun. 2, 1924-Sep. 15, 1930 / Drive Archives ♦♦♦

Cornetist Bix Beiderbecke's recordings have been reissued in more complete fashion elsewhere but this single budget CD contains 14 of his greatest performances. Highlights include "Singin' the Blues," "I'm Comin' Virginia," "Riverboat Shuffle" and early versions (with the Wolverines in 1924) of "Royal Garden Blues" and "Tiger Rag." This set does a good job of introducing newer listeners to the classic music. —*Scott Yanow*

The Indispensable / Nov. 24, 1924-Sep. 15, 1930 / RCA ♦♦♦♦

This double-CD from French RCA in their Jazz Tribune series (a reissue of an earlier double-LP) gives one a good overview of cornetist Bix Beiderbecke's Victor recordings. More serious collectors will want to acquire this music as part of a more complete series (since all of his solos are significant) while beginning collectors are advised to pick up his Columbia reissue CDs (which feature Beiderbecke in smaller groups) first. The 36 performances on this two-fer mostly focus on his sideman appearances with the large dance orchestras of Jean Goldkette and Paul

Whiteman during 1926-28 although there is one 1924 track ("I Didn't Know") with Goldkette and a few later sessions from 1930. Highlights include "Clementine," "San," "There Ain't No Sweet Man," "From Monday On" and "You Took Advantage of Me." —*Scott Yanow*

★ **Bix Beiderbecke, Vol. 1: Singin' the Blues** / Feb. 4, 1927-Sep. 30, 1927 / Columbia ♦♦♦♦♦

At the Jazz Band Ball, Vol. 2 / Oct. 1927-Apr. 3, 1928 / Columbia ♦♦♦♦♦

Bix Lives / 1927-1930 / RCA ♦♦♦♦

This album includes Jean Goldkette and Whiteman material. It's a nice complement to the Columbia Records compilations (*Vols. 1 & 2*). —*Richard Lieberson*

Richie Beirach

b. May 23, 1947, New York, NY

Piano / Post-Bop

Although somewhat underrated, Richie Beirach is a consistently inventive pianist whose ability to play both free and with lyricism makes him an original. After studying classical piano, Beirach switched to jazz. He studied at Berklee and the Manhattan School of Music and took lessons with Stan Getz, Dave Holland and Jack DeJohnette. Beirach played electric piano while with Dave Liebman's Lookout Farm in 1974 but has mostly stuck to acoustic piano ever since. He has teamed up with Liebman on many occasions (including the early-'80s group Quest) and has recorded frequently during the past 20 years. Among his many jobs as a sideman were important stints with Getz, Lee Konitz, John Abercrombie and Chet Baker, and Beirach has played music ranging from hard bop to totally free. His classical training can sometimes be heard in his more advanced improvisations, along with the sensitivity of a Bill Evans. —*Scott Yanow*

Leaving / Aug. 17, 1976-Aug. 18, 1976 / Storyville ♦♦♦

This CD reissue has a set of introspective and quiet duets by pianist Richie Beirach and flutist Jeremy Steig. Eight of the ten selections were composed by Beirach while the other two cuts (which sound like free improvisations) are collaborations. In general the music is peaceful with some dissonances. Steig provides long tones while Beirach creates light rhythmic patterns and, although it does not entirely stay at the same emotional level, the music is generally quite dry and uneventful. —*Scott Yanow*

Eon / Nov. 1976 / ECM ♦♦♦

Hubris / Jun. 1977 / ECM ♦♦♦

Merta / Jun. 9, 1978 / Storyville ♦♦♦♦

Pianist Richie Beirach and saxophonist Dave Liebman have teamed up on many record dates through the years starting in 1973. This CD reissue, taken from the Japanese Trio label, is a set of duets that are primarily introspective and thoughtful. However, the melodies (mixing together originals and standards) are strong, Liebman's reeds (tenor, soprano and alto flute) provide some variety, and the musical communication is very tight. The date is a sleeper, but listeners who have the patience will find much to enjoy, with the highlights including "Spring Is Here" (featuring Liebman's soprano), Beirach's "Eden," Liebman's tonal distortions on tenor during "Cadeques," and his unaccompanied tenor on "In a Sentimental Mood." —*Scott Yanow*

Elm / May 1979 / ECM ♦♦♦♦

Rendevous / Jan. 24, 1981-Jan. 25, 1981 / IPI ♦♦♦

Elegy for Bill Evans / May 12, 1981 / Palo Alto ♦♦♦

This tribute to Beirach's good friend and influence has trio jazz with Al Foster on drums and George Mraz on bass. It includes three songs co-written by Evans and Miles Davis, two other standards, and Evans' immortal "Peace Piece." —*Michael G. Nastos*

Breathing of Statues / Sep. 1982 / Magenta ♦♦♦

Continuum / Jul. 5, 1983 / Eastwind ♦♦♦♦

Another in the solo piano series Bierach cranked out in the '80s. This was done for the Japanese Baybridge label, and like its predecessors and successors, it was mostly originals, although this time he did the title track (Tadd Dameron) and also covered "Some Other Time" and "Round Midnight." —*Ron Wynn*

Antarctica / Sep. 12, 1985-Sep. 14, 1985 / Pathfinder ♦♦♦♦

Ambitious, erratic but interesting concept album by pianist Beirach for the Pathfinder label. It's a solo piano suite with all original pieces. He hits sometimes and misses at other times, but it's certainly good to hear something besides standards and hard bop, even when it's more mood than substance. —*Ron Wynn*

Emerald City / Feb. 23, 1987-Feb. 25, 1987 / Pathfinder ♦♦♦

Depending on how you choose to define "jazz," this duet session linking pianist Richie Beirach with John Abercrombie (playing guitar synthesizer) may or may not fit your criteria. There are certainly passages with a rock sensibility, and Abercrombie's use of a guitar synthesizer may distress those who instinctively distrust electronics in any improvising context. But if you rank jazz pedigree on skills, individuality, and the willingness to take chances, then this date qualifies on all counts. Bierach and Abercrombie don't fall into quickly identifiable patterns. If you aren't appalled by Abercrombie's embrace of technology and want to hear material that doesn't fit any rigid definition, here's something right up your alley. —*Ron Wynn*

Common Heart / Sep. 28, 1987-Sep. 29, 1987 / Owl ✦✦✦
Alternately stunning and uneven solo piano work from 1987, with Bierach covering originals, spinning out melodies, pacing the set, and trying something different from conventional theme/solo/theme arrangements. This has been reissued on CD. —*Ron Wynn*

Some Other Time / Apr. 1989 / Triloka ✦✦✦✦
When one thinks of pianist Richie Beirach, tenor saxophonist Michael Brecker, bassist George Mraz and guitarist John Scofield, the name of Chet Baker is not the first one to come to mind, but each of the musicians played regularly with the trumpeter at one time or another. Beirach, who arranged the ten selections (including five of his originals) performed on this Chet Baker tribute CD, organized the project and is the only musician on every track. Most of the performances are brooding and introspective ballads. Michael Brecker's two appearances include a duet with Beirach on the moody "Sunday Song" and a trio with the pianist and Mraz for "Inborn" while Scofield's three appearances are close to cameos. Trumpeter Randy Brecker emerges as the co-star along with Beirach, performing on the only two uptempo tracks ("Alone Together" and "In Your Own Sweet Way"), playing sensitively on a melodic "My Funny Valentine," and displaying the frequently melancholy mood of Chet Baker throughout the disc. A sincere and successful effort overall. —*Scott Yanow*

● **Convergence** / Nov. 10, 1990-Nov. 11, 1990 / Triloka ✦✦✦✦
Pianist Richie Beirach and saxophonist George Coleman interpret a collection of standards, with a few Beirach originals thrown in for good measure. Beirach's a world-class jazz romantic; his soft touch makes it sound as if there's a pillow underneath the keyboard. Which is not to say he's an imprecise player, or needlessly docile. He's really quite the opposite, but there's an underlying gentleness to his work that imparts an air of vulnerability to everything he plays, even when he's at his most aggressive. Coleman is similar, in a way, though the saxophonist's sensitivity is occasionally camouflaged by a good-natured surliness that we know is just a front. On this album, Coleman can't help but put his heart on his sleeve—Beirach's accompaniments demand it. The music that results is a nice blend of the bucolic and the temperamental; the pianist's pastoral tranquility combines with the saxophonist's restless urbanity to good ends. —*Chris Kelsey*

Snow Leopard / Jun. 16, 1996-Jun. 17, 1996 / Evidence ✦✦✦✦

Bob Belden

b. Oct. 31, 1956, Charleston, SC
Arranger, Tenor Saxophone / Post-Bop
One of the most adventurous arrangers of the 1990s, Bob Belden has taken the music of Puccini, Prince and (with the most success) Sting and turned it into jazz. After graduating from the University of North Texas in 1978 he was with Woody Herman's Orchestra for 18 months, worked with Donald Byrd off and on during 1981-85, played with the Mel Lewis Orchestra, and produced a couple of Red Rodney records. In 1983 Belden settled in New York as a writer for studio sessions. Influenced by Gil Evans, Belden debuted on Sunnyside with *Treasure Island* before working on transforming nonjazz material into jazz. Belden has also been assisting with Columbia Records' Miles Davis reissue program. —*Scott Yanow*

● **Treasure Island** / Aug. 12, 1989+Aug. 13, 1989 / Sunnyside ✦✦✦✦✦
For his recorded debut as a leader, Bob Belden put together an adventurous and thought-provoking set of highly original music. The tenor saxophonist's six-part 34-minute *Treasure Island Suite* reads in the liner notes like a fantasy novel with overtones of *The Twilight Zone*. The gradually evolving music (which explores many moods) fits the narrative and contains excellent solos from Belden (who is most influenced by Wayne Shorter), the plaintive trumpet of Tim Hagans, pianist Marc Cohen, altoist Mike Migliore and Craig Handy's tenor. Belden also composed three of the other seven selections, arranging all of them including Joe Zawinul's rarely performed but still modern "Directions," the Wayne Shorter ballad "Face on the Barroom Floor," the driving Bobby Watson piece "Country Cornflakes" (which has some intense Glenn Wilson baritone) and a modern rendition of "Basin Street Blues." Even with the fine solos, it is the variety of moods set by the colorful arrangements of Bob Belden that make *Treasure Island* a very impressive debut. —*Scott Yanow*

Straight to My Heart: The Music of Sting / Dec. 1, 1989-May 9, 1991 / Blue Note ✦✦✦✦✦
This project, interpretations of ten songs written by Sting, would not seem to have much potential from a jazz standpoint. But by reharmonizing the tunes and contributing inventive charts for a notable group of jazz players, arranger Bob Belden put together a very memorable set, turning pop material into creative jazz. Belden (who takes a tenor solo on "Children's Crusade") allocated solo space to such players as guitarists John Scofield, John Hart and Fareed Haque, pianists Billy Childs, Bennie Green, Joey Calderazzo, Marc Copland and Kevin Hays, trumpeter Tim Hagans, tenors Rick Margitza and Kirk Whalum and altoist Bobby Watson. In addition, there is a vocal apiece by Dianne Reeves ("Wrapped Around Your Finger"), Phil Perry ("Sister Moon"), Mark Ledford ("Every Breath You Take") and Jimi Tunnell ("I Burn for You"), but the emphasis is on jazz improvizing. A surprise success; highly recommended. —*Scott Yanow*

When the Doves Cry: The Music of Prince / May 5, 1993-Sep. 27, 1993 / Metro Blue ✦✦
Shades of Blue / Nov. 9, 1994-Jan. 5, 1995 / Blue Note ✦✦✦
In 1994 producer-tenor saxophonist Bob Belden received the unusual assignment of putting together a variety of all-star groups to revisit tunes associated with the Blue Note legacy. From Nov. 1994 to Mar. 1995 he recorded most of Blue Note's current roster, documenting 39 compositions of which 12 are on this CD while many of the others have been released in Japan. Each of the dozen numbers uses a different group and they are generally consistent if not filled with surprises. Dianne Reeves, Cassandra Wilson, Holly Cole and Kurt Elling are heard on vocal features (Reeves and Elling fare best), trumpeter Marcus Printup shows off his warm tone on "You've Changed" and, in a performance that brings back the "Bitches Brew" era (and is both the most modern and the most dated of these interpretations), Belden, trumpeter Tim Hagans and three keyboardists explore Andrew Hill's "Siete Ocho." Of the many pianists who are featured on this set (including Geri Allen, Jacky Terrasson, Renee Rosnes and Eliane Elias), Geoff Keezer's fairly free improvisation on Herbie Nichols' "2300 Skidoo" is the most memorable. Quite unusual are the complete absence of any of the quintet or sextet lineups that were almost a trademark of Blue Note in the 1950s and '60s and the relatively few trumpet and saxophone solos. Sure to be a collector's item, this CD is not essential but it has enough variety to keep the interest of most jazz listeners. —*Scott Yanow*

Marcus Belgrave

b. Jun. 12, 1936, Chester, PA
Trumpet, Fluegelhorn / Post-Bop
Because he has spent most of his career in Detroit and has not recorded enough, Marcus Belgrave has often been overlooked. A flexible and talented trumpeter able to play both hard bop and free, Belgrave was tutored by Clifford Brown a bit when he was 17. He toured with Ray Charles during 1954-1959 and had opportunitites to play with the groups of Charles Mingus and Max Roach. In 1963 Belgrave moved to Detroit where he has been continually active as an educator and a studio player. He has recorded with (among others) McCoy Tyner, David Newman, Art Hodes (duets), David Murray, Geri Allen (one of his former students), swing tenor Franz Jackson and Sammy Price, mostly since the 1980s. Belgrave has also been featured with the Lincoln Center Jazz Orchestra. Among his other former students are Bob Hurst, Kenny Garrett and James Carter, so at least indirectly Marcus Belgrave is making a strong impact on jazz. —*Scott Yanow*

Gemini II / 1975 / Tribe ✦✦✦
The nonet with the master trumpeter is sometimes funky, spacy, or swinging, but always potent. On this LP with Roy Brooks, Wendell Harrison, Harold McKinney, and Phil Ranelin, the band sounds twice its size due to the expansive compositional stance of the leader. —*Michael G. Nastos*

Graeme Bell (Graeme Emerson Bell)

b. Sep. 7, 1914, Melbourne, Australia
Piano / Classic Jazz, Dixieland
A pioneering Australian jazzman, Graeme Bell recorded an extensive series of hot jazz performances (particularly during 1947-52) that were quite influential in the Australian trad jazz scene. Bell worked professionally from the late '30s but it was after he formed his Australian Jazz Band and toured in Europe for a full year (1947-48) that his brand of freewheeling jazz (mixing together standards and obscurities) made its impact, recording in Czechoslovakia, Paris and London before returning home. Back home, Bell in 1949 helped found the Swaggie label, he revisited Europe several times in the 1950s and recorded extensively up until 1967. Among his more significant sidemen were cornetist Roger Bell (his talented brother), Lazy Ade Monsborough on clarinet, trumpet and trombone, clarinetist Don Roberts and in the early '60s trumpeter Bob Barnard. Graeme Bell remained active on a part-time basis in the 1980s and '90s. —*Scott Yanow*

Louie Bellson (Luigi Paulino Alfredo Francesco Antonion Balassoni)

b. Jul. 6, 1924, Rock Falls, IL
Drums / Swing, Bop

One of the great drummers of all time (and one of the few whose name can be said in the same sentence with Buddy Rich), Louie Bellson has the rare ability to continually hold one's interest throughout a 15-minute solo. He became famous in the 1950s for using two bass drums simultaneously, but Bellson was never a gimmicky or overly bombastic player. In addition to being able to drive a big band to exciting effect, Bellson can play very quietly with a trio and sound quite satisfied.

Winner of a Gene Krupa talent contest while a teenager, Bellson was with the big bands of Benny Goodman (1943 and 1946), Tommy Dorsey (1947-49) and Harry James (1950-51) before replacing Sonny Greer with the Duke Ellington Orchestra. A talented writer, Bellson contributed "Skin Deep" and "The Hawk Talks" to Duke's permanent repertoire. He married Pearl Bailey in 1952 and the following year left Ellington to be her musical director. Bellson toured with Jazz at the Philharmonic (1954-55), recorded many dates in the 1950s for Verve and was with the Dorsey Brothers (1955-56), Count Basie (1962), Duke Ellington (1965-66) and Harry James (1966). He has been continually active up to the present day, leading big bands (different ones on the East and West Coasts), putting together combos for record dates, giving clinics for younger drummers and writing new music. Bellson has recorded extensively for Roulette (early '60s), Concord, Pablo and most recently Music Masters. —*Scott Yanow*

Louie in London / May 21, 1970-May 23, 1970 / DRG ♦♦
This CD reissue of a Louie Bellson big band recording that was originally out on the PYE label is surprisingly forgettable. The British big band (mostly a no-name outfit other than trumpeter Kenny Wheeler who has a short solo on "Limehouse Blues") is fairly anonymous, Bellson's six compositions (including his three-part "London Suite") are far from catchy and, other than the leader's drum solos, nothing significant or memorable takes place. There are many more interesting Louie Bellson recordings currently available. —*Scott Yanow*

150 M.P.H. / May 25, 1974 / Concord Jazz ♦♦♦
One of the better Louie Bellson big band albums, this set features arrangements by Bill Holman and the drummer-leader. The orchestra boasts such fine soloists as the tenors of Menza and Pete Christlieb, trumpeters Bobby Shew, Conte Candoli, Harry "Sweets" Edison and Blue Mitchell, trombonist Frank Rosolino and either Nat Pierce or Ross Tompkins on piano. High points include "Time Check," "Inferno," "Back Home" and Holman's reworking of "Hello Young Lovers." —*Scott Yanow*

The Louis Bellson Explosion / May 21, 1975-May 22, 1975 / Pablo ♦♦♦
A fine mid-'70s date that was both a showcase for Bellson's bombastic drumming and also a nice straightahead date with great contributions from Blue Mitchell, Snookey Young, Dick Mitchell and others. It's been reissued on CD. —*Ron Wynn*

Louie Bellson's 7 / Jul. 25, 1976 / Concord Jazz ♦♦♦
Louie Bellson led a strong group for the 1976 Concord Jazz Fesitival that comprised trumpeter Blue Mitchell, tenor saxophonist Pete Christlieb, trombonist Dick Nash, pianist Ross Tompkins, the young guitarist Grant Geissman and bassist John Williams. The septet's wide-ranging set included an original apiece by Christlieb and Mitchell (both of whom consistently took solo honors), a five-song ballad medley, a showcase for Bellson on "Roto Blues" and a lengthy jam on "Dig." Fine straightahead music played with spirit. —*Scott Yanow*

Ecue Ritmos Cubanos / Jan. 21, 1977-Jan. 21, 1977 / Original Jazz Classics ♦♦
Drummer Louis Bellson is co-leader on this CD reissue of a Pablo set with percussionist Walfredo De Los Reyes, but it is very much Reyes' set. Actually, there are eight percussionists on this date and, even with the presence of keyboards, two bassists (including the legendary Cachao) and up to three horns (Cat Anderson and Alejandro Vivar on trumpets and Lew Tabackin contributing some flute and tenor), the five selections are essentially percussion displays. This would have been a fun date to see live with all of the colorful sounds being made but, as a pure listening experience, the lack of variety and the emphasis on fairly simple (if dense) rhythmic vamps makes this a surprisingly forgettable affair. —*Scott Yanow*

Prime Time / Nov. 4, 1977 / Concord Jazz ♦♦♦♦
For this set (reissued on CD), drummer Louie Bellson teamed up with some of his favorite West Coast players of the era: tenor saxophonist Pete Christlieb, trumpeter Blue Mitchell, pianist Ross Tompkins, and bassist John Williams, plus, on the last four of the eight numbers, guitarist Bob Bain and percussionist Emil Richards. The first half of the program is essentially straightahead bop, including a three-song ballad medley and a rousing "Cottontail," while the other four numbers (originals by Bellson, Christlieb, and Mitchell, plus Dizzy Gillespie's "And Then She Stopped") are a little funkier but still swinging. An excellent effort overall, with the tenorman often taking solo honors. —*Scott Yanow*

Sunshine Rock / Dec. 21, 1977-Dec. 23, 1977 / Pablo ♦♦♦
Louie Bellson's various big bands (this one is called "The Explosion Orchestra") have always been notable for passionate swinging, if not subtlety. This particular edition was full of top names, including altoist Ted Nash, both Pete Christlieb and Don Menza on tenors, trumpeters Cat Anderson, Bobby Shew and Conte Candoli, either Nat Pierce or Ross Tompkins on piano, and guitarist Grant Geissman. An ironic aspect to the mostly hard-driving set is that Geissman gets to play on a Bellson original called "Feels So Good" (a reworking of "Sweet Georgia Brown") that predated Chuck Mangione's famous version (for which he contributed a well-known guitar solo). Fine big-band music (two tunes by Bill Holman and six, including a remake of "The Hawk Talks," by Bellson) that lives up to the group's name. —*Scott Yanow*

Intensive Care / Mar. 17, 1978-Mar. 18, 1978 / Voss ♦♦
Unlike his contemporary Buddy Rich, drummer Louie Bellson could be perfectly happy playing quietly in a trio setting. This out-of-print direct-to-disc LP (originally put out by Discwasher) is not all that sleepy, for Paul Smith was always a powerhouse pianist. The group (which also includes bassist Ray Brown) explores eight standards, alternating stomps and ballads and displaying plenty of energy. Highlights include "The Lady Is a Tramp," "On a Clear Day" and "Lover." —*Scott Yanow*

Raincheck / May 3, 1978-May 4, 1978 / Concord Jazz ♦♦♦
At the time of its release, it seemed that the main significance of this album (which has been reissued on CD) was to introduce the fine solo skills of alto and tenor saxophonist Ted Nash. However Nash, while having a respectable career, never did become a major star or stylist. Drummer Louie Bellson's fine straightahead quintet also features trumpeter Blue Mitchell, pianist Ross Tompkins and bassist Joel DiBartolo on a program consisting of two basic originals, five standards (including "Raincheck" and "Oleo") and a three-song ballad medley. —*Scott Yanow*

Note Smoking / Aug. 14, 1978-Aug. 15, 1978 / Voss/Allegiance ♦♦♦

Louis Bellson Jam / Sep. 28, 1978-Sep. 29, 1978 / Pablo ♦♦♦
This CD reissue brings back one of Louie Bellson's better small-group dates for Pablo. In addition to the drummer/leader, his septet includes trumpeter Blue Mitchell (still in good form on one of his last recordings), the underrated but great tenor Pete Christlieb, pianist Ross Tompkins, guitarist Bob Bain, bassist Gary Pratt and percussionist Emil Richards. Most intriguing about the date (which mostly sticks to group originals) is that there is a three-song ballad medley comprised not of standards but of Bellson tunes. "Shave Tail" (an older song co-composed by Bellson and Charlie Shavers) is a highlight. —*Scott Yanow*

Side Track / Jun. 1979 / Concord Jazz ♦♦♦♦
Drummer Louie Bellson plays a smaller role on this set than on his usual dates, only contributing one original ("I See You") and taking but a single (and brief) solo. However, his band—comprising the great tenor Don Menza, trumpeter Sam Noto, pianist Frank Collett, bassist John Heard and Walfredo De Los Reyes on congas—is particularly strong, and the repertoire is well-rounded. A three-song ballad medley, "Caravan" (which has Bellson's solo), and Collett's "Fat's Blues" are among the highlights of the superior straightahead set. —*Scott Yanow*

Dynamite / Aug. 1979 / Concord Jazz ♦♦♦
Recordings by Louie Bellson's various big bands tend to be a slight disappointment, full of fire and explosive moments but sometimes lacking in subtlety and surprises. This effort finds the classic drummer at the head of a 14-horn, 19-piece orchestra that is certainly full of power. Bellson, his tenor star Don Menza and altoist Matt Catingub wrote all of the six songs, and among the key soloists are Menza, Catingub, trumpeter Bobby Shew, altoist Dick Spencer and guitarist John Chiodini (featured on "Where Did You Go") Nothing all that unusual occurs (although Don Menza's "Sambandrea Swing" is exciting), but modern big-band fans will enjoy the effort. —*Scott Yanow*

Live at Ronnie Scott's / Oct. 28, 1979-Oct. 29, 1979 / DRG ♦♦♦
Although drummer Louie Bellson is the leader of the big band heard on this 1979 set (reissued by DRG on CD), tenor saxophonist Don Menza is the main star. Not only does the fiery saxophonist solo on four of the six songs (which also include features for trumpeter Bobby Shew and altoist Joe Romano) but he contributed four originals and most of the arrangements. Trumpeter Bill Berry and pianist Nat Pierce are also heard from (unfortunately the full personnel is not given) as is tenorman Larry Covelli (who successfully battles Menza to a draw on "Time Check") and the drummer-leader, but it is for the playing and writing of the underrated Don Menza that this disc is most highly recommended. —*Scott Yanow*

London Scene / Oct. 13, 1980 / Concord Jazz ♦♦♦
Sticking to group originals (five of the seven by the drummer/leader) plus Duke Ellington's ballad "Don't You Know I Care," this is a solid outing by Louie Bellson's 17-piece big band. The arrangements were contributed by Tommy Newsom, Don Menza, Gordon Brisker and Alan Downey, and they leave space for solos by trum-

peter Bobby Shew, altoists Arnie Lawrence and Andy Mackintosh, pianist Frank Strazzeri and tenors Joe Romano and Don Menza. Romps alternate with ballads, and the music, although not all that memorable or unique, is well executed and swinging. —*Scott Yanow*

The London Gig / Nov. 1, 1982 / Original Jazz Classics ✦✦✦
Drummer Louie Bellson's 1982 big band performs five of his originals and one song apiece by Matt Catingub ("My Mother the Jazz Singer" is dedicated to Mavis Rivers), Hale Rood and Bob Florence ("Drum Squad"). The mostly young band features talented soloists in trumpeter John Eckert, altoist Catingub, pianist Frank Strazzeri and tenorman Ted Nash, making this an album worth searching for by big-band collectors. —*Scott Yanow*

Cool Cool Blue / Nov. 9, 1982 / Original Jazz Classics ✦✦✦
This Pablo set (reissued on CD) was a change of pace from drummer Louie Bellson's many big-band dates of the period. He performs "Wanderlust" in a trio with pianist Frank Strazzeri and bassist George Duvivier (who wrote the song); features tenor saxophonist Ted Nash (one of his main discoveries) on four quartet tunes; and has Matt Catingub make the group a quintet on three numbers, taking one song apiece on alto, tenor and soprano. Several of the pieces—either group originals or obscurities—are blues-based; a few are more complex, and all of them swing in a spirited fashion, as one would expect from a Louie Bellson date. Good modern mainstream music. —*Scott Yanow*

Loose Walk / Jun. 23, 1983-Jun. 24, 1983 / Chonto Lope ✦✦✦✦
A true obscurity, this 1983 LP matches the great drummer Louie Bellson and bassist George Duvivier with a pair of little-known veterans: altoist Jack Scott and pianist Warren Parrish. Scott displays a pretty tone and a lyrical style that are quite complementary to Parrish's mainstream style. The quartet performs six jazz standards, including "Blues Walk," "Ruby, My Dear," "Stolen Moments" and "Prelude to a Kiss" in winning fashion. Straight-ahead collectors will want to pick up this release, despite the unfamiliar lead voices and label. —*Scott Yanow*

Don't Stop Now! / 1984 / Bosco ✦✦✦
Recorded in 1984 for Pete Christlieb's Bosco label, this outing by the Louie Bellson Orchestra has plenty of power, more variety than usual, and swings up a storm; half of the selections actually feature a small group from the orchestra. The big band tracks have spots for trumpeters Conte Candoli and Ron King, trombonists Carl Fontana and Andy Martin, tenor great Christlieb and drummer Bellson (who is showcased on Thad Jones' "With Bells On"), while the combo tracks put the focus on trumpeters Conte Candoli and Steve Huffsteter, trombonist Fonanta (featured on "Indian Summer") and Christlieb. This is a rather obscure and hard-to-find release, but is worth the search, for the musicians sound consistently inspired. —*Scott Yanow*

Classics in Jazz / Oct. 14, 1986-Oct. 15, 1986 / Music Masters ✦✦✦✦
This early Music Masters release features drummer Louie Bellson on six big-band numbers (with some fine trumpet solos by Brian O'Flaherty) and four songs on which he heads a sextet that includes tenorman Ted Nash, trumpeter Glenn Drewes and pianist Derek Smith. Other than three originals, the emphasis throughout is on modernized versions of swing standards, including "It Don't Mean a Thing" (which has a tenor battle by Nash and Ken Hitchcock), "Flyin' Home," and Bellson's showcase on "Caravan." Swinging music. —*Scott Yanow*

East Side Suite / Dec. 7, 1987-Dec. 9, 1987 / Music Masters ✦✦✦✦
Don Menza emerges as the main star of *East Side Suite,* taking four tenor solos, as well as "My One and Only Love" as a ballad feature, and contributing arragements for three pieces plus "Tenor Time," his sax battle with Ken Hitchcock. Drummer Louie Bellson also has a strong role on his big-band CD and has three full-fledged solos, including breaks on "Blues for Uncommon Kids," that serve as transitions for the shifts between three different tempos. Fluegelhornist Clark Terry is in his usual spirited form during his two guest appearances. The title suite's three parts were based on sketches of Bellson's that Tommy Newsom developed for the 17-piece orchestra, paying tribute to three aspects of New York City. The suite and the six shorter pieces hold one's interest throughout, and although somewhat conventional, this is one of Louie Bellson's most satisfying big-band releases. —*Scott Yanow*

Hot / Dec. 7, 1987-Dec. 9, 1987 / Music Masters ✦✦✦
Louie Bellson's big bands are always hot and explosive, if not all that surprising. This 1987 CD features four originals by the drummer, three obscurities, and an opening "Caravan" that has solo space for guest fluegelhornist Clark Terry, the great tenor Don Menza and Bellson. The other selections feature such talented soloists as trumpeters Brian O'Flaherty and Glenn Drewes, George Young on alto and soprano, altoist Joe Roccisano, Kenny Hitchcock on tenor, and pianist John Bunch. The 17-piece big band mixes together veterans with comparative youngsters and has many names familiar to followers of Bellson's orchestras. An above-average effort from the swinging crew. —*Scott Yanow*

Jazz Giants / Apr. 30, 1989 / Music Masters ✦✦✦
For this all-star gathering, drummer Louie Bellson and five fellow veterans (tenor saxophonist Don Menza, clarinetist Buddy DeFranco, trumpeter Conte Candoli, pianist Hank Jones and bassist Keter Betts) perform "Allen's Alley" and five basic originals, all of which have chord changes fertile for hot solos. The musicians all play up to par, Bellson's spots are as exciting as usual, and the music should certainly please bop fans. —*Scott Yanow*

Peaceful Thunder / Sep. 24, 1991-Sep. 25, 1991 / Music Masters ✦✦✦
Good combo date from a veteran drummer with substantial swing and big-band credentials. Bellson's recent records adhere to established musical values, yet seem to have a freshness that escapes some of the recent traditional dates. Marvin Stamm and Derek Smith are examples of critically unheralded players who seldom fail to elevate a session. —*Ron Wynn*

Live at the Jazz Showcase / Jan. 25, 1992 / Concord Jazz ✦✦✦
For this quartet set, drummer Louie Bellson is teamed up with the underrated but great tenor Don Menza, pianist Larry Novak and bassist John Heard. Each of the musicians has their features, with Menza hard-driving on "Sonny Side" and switching for flute for the waltz "3 P.M.," Heard stretching out on "Jam for Your Bread," Novak taking several spots and Bellson tearing into "Cherokee." Few surprises occur, but there are some fireworks on this mixture of familiar standards and obscure tunes. —*Scott Yanow*

Black Brown & Beige / Oct. 20, 1992-Oct. 22, 1992 / Music Masters ✦✦✦
Rather than try to recreate Duke Ellington's famous "Black, Brown & Beige," Louie Bellson's big band does a reinterpretation of the 50-minute work on this CD that takes a lot of liberties with the composition. A little more space is allocated to solos, Johnny Hodges' famous "Come Sunday" melody statement is given to Clark Terry, Joe Williams sings "The Blues," and such players as trumpeter Barrie Lee Hall, Art Baron on plunger trombone, pianist Harold Danko and baritonist Joe Temperley are heard from. This version does give some new life to the classic suite. In addition, Bellson's band plays five of the drummer's originals including the boppish "Hawk Talks" and "Skin Deep." The shorter orchestral pieces fit into the general mood of the respectful but fairly creative tribute. —*Scott Yanow*

● **Live from New York** / Jan. 20, 1994 / Telarc ✦✦✦✦
At 71 Louie Bellson on this CD displays more energy than most drummers half his age. Bellson not only takes solos on more than half the selections (including a lengthy workout on "Santos") but he composed all seven originals; the only surprise is that Bellson decided to let some of his musical friends (including Matt Catingub, Tommy Newsom and Bob Florence) arrange the charts instead of writing them himself. With concise solos from such sidemen as trumpeters Marvin Stamm and Glenn Drewes, tenorman Ted Nash, altoists Joe Roccisano and Steve Wilson and trombonist Keith O'Quinn, Bellson's music is given perfectly suitable interpretations. But just in case, the equally ageless fluegelhornist Clark Terry (at 75) stars on two songs including the exquisite ballad "Blow Your Horn." With Louie Bellson constantly driving the ensembles, this is a big-band disc well worth acquiring. —*Scott Yanow*

Salute / Apr. 4, 1994-Apr. 7, 1994 / Chiaroscuro ✦✦✦✦
This two-CD set has its interesting moments. Drummer Louie Bellson and his quintet (which also includes trumpeter Bobby Shew, George Young on tenor, pianist Willie Pickens and bassist Keter Betts) perform seven selections including Horace Silver's "Blowin' the Blues Away," George Young's "For Diz" and "When You Wish upon a Star." The second CD has a 27-minute medley that pays tribute to drummers Gene Krupa, Buddy Rich, Art Blakey, Jo Jones, Shelly Manne and Chick Webb. In addition there is a nearly 34-minute "Jazzspeak" in which Bellson talks about the drummers, the many bandleaders that he has worked with and a variety of miscellaneous music-related subjects. Although interesting, much of it is probably not worth hearing twice. —*Scott Yanow*

Air Bellson / Aug. 21, 1996-Aug. 22, 1996 / Concord ✦✦✦✦

Sathima Bea Benjamin

b. Oct. 17, 1936, Cape Town, South Africa
Vocals / Post-Bop

An enchanting, evocative vocalist, Satima Bea Benjamin has made several recordings as a leader since establishing herself in Abdullah Ibrahim's (her husband) band during the '70s. Benjamin has performed and recorded show tunes and standards, traditional South African and African music, and improvised on her originals and other jazz pieces. Benjamin and Ibrahim (then known as Dollar Brand) met in South Africa at the end of the '50s. After leaving their homeland and emigrating to Europe, they met Duke Ellington in Switzerland in 1962. He sponsored recordings for the two; Benjamin's was unfortunately not released for the first time until 1996. She eventually sang with Duke's orchestra at Newport (1965) and her first full recorded set as a leader (1979) was an Ellington tribute. Sathima Bea

Benjamin, who has since led dates for Ekapa, BlackHawk and Enja, has used such fine musicians as Ricky Ford, Kenny Barron, Buster Williams and Billy Higgins. —*Ron Wynn & Scott Yanow*

● **Morning in Paris** / Feb. 23, 1963 / Enja ♦♦♦♦♦
In 1963, singer Sathima Bea Benjamin persuaded Duke Ellington to see her future husband Abdullah Ibrahim (then known as Dollar Brand) play in a club in Europe. Ellington was impressed by both of the recent South African emigres and arranged with Reprise to record them. While Brand's record came out within a year, Benjamin's debut was lost and not heard for decades, even by the singer. As it turned out, engineer Gerhard Lehner had made a second copy and kept it for all of these years, so the initial 1997 release of this important session was possible. Backed by pianist Ibrahim, bassist Johnny Gertze, drummer Makaya Ntshoko and (on two songs apiece) Duke Ellington or Billy Strayhorn, and occasionally joined by violinist Svend Asmussen (who here plays exclusively pizzicato, as if he were using a high-pitched guitar), Benjamin's love sounds quite beautiful. She performs two Ellington tunes, Strayhorn's "Your Love Has Faded" and nine standards, with the emphasis on slow ballads. The moody music is often haunting and quite memorable. —*Scott Yanow*

Sathima Sings Ellington / Apr. 1979 / Ekapa ♦♦♦

Memories and Dreams / Oct. 7, 1983 / Ekapa ♦♦♦♦
Although Sathima Bea Benjamin had sung with her husband Abdullah Ibrahim (then known as Dollar Brand) before they left South Africa in the early '60s and had recorded with Duke Ellington on a set shortly after settling in Europe (a date not released until 1997), she did not make her first recording as a leader until 1976, when she was already nearing 40. Finally, in 1979, Benjamin began to record regularly for the Ekapa label (which was made available domestically through the now-defunct Black Hawk record company). This fine LP features the singer performing three of her moody originals (as the "Liberation Suite"), along with emotional versions of four standard ballads, including "Till There Was You" and "In a Sentimental Mood." With pianist Onaje Allan Gumbs, bassist Buster Williams, either Billy Higgins or Ben Riley on drums and altoist Carlos Ward (doubling on flute), Benjamin has strong support for an excellent all-round set of lyrical music. —*Scott Yanow*

Windsong / Jun. 17, 1985 / Black Hawk ♦♦♦
Sathima Bea Benjamin mostly emphasizes spiritual-sounding ballads on this date (which are leavened by a couple of more swinging tracks), giving plenty of emotion to her intelligent lyrics. On the out-of-print LP (which was made available in the US by Black Hawk), she is accompanied by pianist Kenny Barron, bassist Buster Williams and drummer Billy Higgins for three originals (including "Lady Day") and a trio of standards ("Sometimes I Feel Like a Motherless Child," "Indian Summer" and "Song of Songs"). One of her better albums. —*Scott Yanow*

Love Light / Sep. 5, 1987 / Enja ♦♦♦♦
An emotional singer with a great deal of credibility, Sathima Bea Benjamin is heard at her peak on this set, a quartet outing with tenor saxophonist Ricky Ford, pianist Larry Willis, bassist Buster Williams and drummer Billy Higgins. Her "Winnie Mandela—Beloved Heroine" is heartfelt, the vocalist puts plenty of feeling into "You Are My Heart's Delight" and Noel Coward's "I'll See You Again," and her other originals (dedicated to Duke Ellington, Africa and music in general) are intelligent, sincere and passionate in a subtle way. This CD is recommended. —*Scott Yanow*

Southern Touch / Dec. 14, 1989 / Enja ♦♦♦
Evocative, expressive ballads and love songs done by wonderful vocalist Satima Bea Benjamin, wife of Abdullah Ibrahim. She sings without a trace of self-indulgence and has the right touch to make even the most sentimental lyric seem convincing and genuine. —*Ron Wynn*

Tony Bennett (Anthony Dominick Benedetto)

b. Aug. 3, 1926, Queens, NY
Vocals / Show Tunes, Traditional Pop, Ballads
Any discussion of Tony Bennett within the context of a book on jazz ought to start with the disclaimer that he is not, never was, and doesn't claim to be, a "jazz singer" per se. However, there isn't any question that Bennett has always felt a kinship with jazz musicians and has collaborated with them several times in his long career, often with delightful results. Though not an improviser, Bennett could always follow the contours of a jazz rhythm section with confidently jazzy inflections; indeed, he sounds absolutely ebullient whenever he records with jazzers. Bennett's pianist and musical director since the 1950s, Ralph Sharon, is a solid, dependable jazzman in his own right, and has occasionally steered his boss away from the all-American easy-listening ballad into a more jazz-oriented setting. Bennett counts among his influences Art Tatum, from whom he drew ideas on phrasing and breathing, Mildred Bailey for her relaxed delivery, and of course, the inev-

itable Billie Holiday and Frank Sinatra, who once proclaimed Bennett to be the best singer in the business. Indeed, as Sinatra's voice aged, Bennett found himself in the position of being the leading purveyor of American popular songs by 1990.

The jazz influence on Bennett was inevitable for a child of the big-band era, and his teacher Miriam Spier urged him to listen to instrumentalists instead of singers for inspiration. He worked as a singing waiter as a teenager, sang with military bands during the war, and appeared on *Arthur Godfrey's Talent Scouts*. Bob Hope heard him performing at a New York nightclub with Pearl Bailey in 1950 and booked him into his show at the Paramount Theatre, where his rendition of "Boulevard of Broken Dreams" attracted the attention of Columbia Records head honcho Mitch Miller. After some early setbacks, Bennett started to put together a string of hit singles like "Because of You," "Rags to Riches" and a pioneering pop cover of a Hank Williams tune, "Cold, Cold Heart"—all of which went to No. 1. With his commercial flanks covered, Bennett was occasionally allowed to use the LP format to experiment with jazz in the 1950s, recording with the likes of the Count Basie Orchestra, Ralph Burns, Bobby Hackett, Stan Getz and Zoot Sims. Perhaps his most successful and unusual experiment was a lively 1957 album called *The Beat of My Heart,* dominated by the drums of Chico Hamilton, Art Blakey and Jo Jones and populated by the likes of Nat Adderley, Herbie Mann, Al Cohn, Kai Winding and Milt Hinton.

Bennett got through the first decade and a half of the rock 'n' roll invasion mostly unscathed, thanks in part to an occasional smash hit like "I Left My Heart in San Francisco" that would thrust his name back into the public consciousness. But the pressures of resisting the rock trend drove Bennett away from Columbia in 1972, and after a brief period with MGM, he made several albums for his own Improv label, DRG and Fantasy, collaborating with Ruby Braff and Marian and Jimmy McPartland and making two now-revered duet albums with Bill Evans. From 1979 to 1986, however, he was unable to secure a recording contract on his terms, and interviews from the period found him quite bitter about the dominance of rock in the music business.

However, once his son Danny took over his management and started to sell him to a younger audience, Bennett's career underwent a remarkable resurrection. Upon re-signing with Columbia in 1986, Bennett started a new carefully produced and planned series of albums, beginning with the ostentatiously titled *The Art of Excellence.* In 1987, a fascinating compilation from the '50s and '60s entitled *Jazz* helped remind jazz fans of his old ties, and the new album *Bennett/Berlin* was graced by the presence of George Benson, Dizzy Gillespie and Dexter Gordon. Next, he became an unlikely favorite of Generation X, more perhaps for his stubborn refusal to conform to fashion than for his music, and an appearance on *MTV Unplugged* in 1993 was turned into a hit album. Bennett still appears frequently at jazz festivals in tandem with big bands or the Ralph Sharon Trio, and his current reputation as an artiste is buttressed by the fact that he is also a skilled painter, signing his works with his original name, Anthony Benedetto. —*Richard S. Ginell*

★ **All-Time Greatest Hits** / 1950-1972 / Columbia ♦♦♦♦♦
Tony Bennett's departure from Columbia Records after 22 years in 1972 inspired the label to put together a one-volume hits compilation (originally released on two LPs) of 20 songs covering his entire Columbia output, from "Boulevard of Broken Dreams" and the early hits like "Because of You" and "Rags to Riches," through the early to mid-'60s hit period of "I Left My Heart in San Francisco" and "I Wanna Be Around," to the more problematic late '60s and early '70s of "Something" and "Love Story." The selection sacrifices quality to achieve breadth; it represents all phases of Bennett's career up to this point, but doesn't really include his 20 best performances or even his 20 biggest hits. Nevertheless, it's a good place for the complete novice to start. (Note, however, that several selections are in fake stereo and several are re-recorded versions, not the original recordings.) —*William Ruhlmann*

★ **40 Years: The Artistry of Tony Bennett** / 1950-1972 / Columbia/Legacy ♦♦♦♦♦
When this impressive box set was released in 1991, it put the capstone upon Tony Bennett's remarkable return to prominence by looking back at a legacy that had been overshadowed by that of the colossus Sinatra. The collection methodically traces his career from his first Columbia record, "Boulevard of Broken Dreams," in 1950, through the hit singles and key or capriciously selected album tracks up until 1972. Then, after borrowing three tracks from Fantasy's 1975 Tony Bennett/Bill Evans project (including an exquisite "Some Other Time" with a "Peace Piece" introduction from Evans), the box leaps 11 years ahead to contemplate Bennett's unlikely resurrection as an icon of the cynical young. Bennett's early records are almost operatic in feeling, a honey-smooth Italian tenor building toward histrionic climaxes, but the voice eventually busts loose into an outgoing, life-celebrating baritone, and by the 1980s, re-emerges as a darker, softer, even somewhat raspy replica of itself. There isn't much for the jazz listener here other than an occasional session with Count Basie (dig their ebullient "Lullaby of Broadway" together), a few cameos by jazz names, the Evans tracks, or some upbeat charts by Ralph

Sharon, Ralph Burns and a few others. Ultimately, the most striking difference between Bennett's records and Sinatra's is the sheer, unbeatably high quality of arrangements that Sinatra was able to get. Yet despite the abundance of period MOR treacle, many of these records are more interesting than memory recalls; for example, it's difficult to resist such a naively joyous track as Frank DeVol's rendering of "Put on a Happy Face" that has the Mitch Miller era written all over it. There is no better Tony Bennett retrospective at any price, although jazz specialists might be better served by the *Jazz* compilation. —*Richard S. Ginell*

Tony's Greatest Hits / 1951-1958 / Columbia ✦✦✦✦✦

Tony Bennett's first hits collection chronicles his initial seven years as a recording artist, during which he frequently was found in the singles charts. Among this album's 12 selections are nine chart songs: "Because of You" (No. 1 for ten weeks, 1951), "Cold, Cold Heart" (No. 1 for six weeks, 1951), "Rags to Riches" (No. 1 for eight weeks, 1953), "Stranger in Paradise" (No. 2, 1954), "There'll Be No Teardrops Tonight" (No. 7, 1954), "Just in Time" (No. 46, 1956), "In the Middle of an Island" (No. 9, 1957), "Ca, C'est L'amour" (No. 22, 1957), and "Young and Warm and Wonderful" (No. 23, 1958). Also featured is Bennett's non-charting debut single, "Boulevard of Broken Dreams," a tango complete with castanets that first gained him notice. In retrospect, early Bennett is not Bennett at his best—the song selection and arrangements are often so idiosyncratic and gimmicky they border on being novelty material, and Bennett often oversings in a mock-operatic style. But his intonation is always clear, his confidence always apparent. And there remains a historical interest—this is Tony Bennett as pop idol, and he carries it off. —*William Ruhlmann*

☆ Jazz / 1954-1967 / Columbia ✦✦✦✦✦

What a wonderful idea. This is a compilation album ranging across Tony Bennett's early career, from 1954 to 1967, highlighting some of his more adventurous sessions with jazz musicians, including Count Basie, Herbie Hancock, Herbie Mann, Art Blakey, Stan Getz, and others, and featuring jazz standards like "Green Dolphin Street," along with a healthy dose of Duke Ellington compositions. Bennett not only holds his own, he sounds delighted on every track. The ironic thing, of course, is that Columbia frowned on these kinds of side excursions from his pop career in the '50s. Now, all is forgiven, and this proves an unusually imaginative repackaging that illuminates an important part of Bennett's talent and further contributes to his '80s renaissance. (The album contains a previously unreleased 1964 performance of "Danny Boy" featuring Stan Getz. Originally released as a two-LP set, *Jazz* was compressed to a 68-minute CD by excising two tracks.) —*William Ruhlmann*

The Beat of My Heart / 1957 / Columbia ✦✦✦✦✦

On only his third full-length, 12-inch LP, Tony Bennett comes up with a concept album, singing against novel percussion arrangements, backed by drummers like Art Blakey, Jo Jones, Chico Hamilton, Billy Exiner, Candido, and Sabu. Several songs feature only drums and flutes. Over this unusual instrumentation, Bennett sings beautifully, giving his usual full-voiced emotion to songs like "Lullaby of Broadway," "Let's Face the Music and Dance," and "Just One of Those Things." This was the first album to give notice that Bennett was more than just another near-operatic, melodramatic pop singer of the early 1950s. Here was a man who had jazz chops, musical imagination, and a sense of swing. He was practically a hipster! —*William Ruhlmann*

More Tony's Greatest Hits / 1958-1960 / Columbia ✦✦

It had been only two years since Tony Bennett's first hits collection when Columbia released this, his second. In that time, he hadn't scored many hits. In fact, he'd had only three chart entries: "Firefly" (No. 20, 1958), "Smile" (No. 73, 1959), and "Climb Ev'ry Mountain" (No. 74, 1960). So, the album's title was a misnomer, but it signalled that here was a collection of Bennett performances of either contemporary songs or older songs in contemporary arrangements, intended for the hit parade even if they didn't get there. There is a light, optimistic tone to much of the material—"Smile," "Put on a Happy Face," "You'll Never Get Away from Me"—and although much is also slight, Bennett brings his trademark warmth to the settings. —*William Ruhlmann*

Strike Up the Band / 1959 / Roulette ✦✦✦

Chicago / 1959 / DCC ✦✦✦

Tony Bennett recorded two albums with Count Basie and His Orchestra under a contractual agreement giving one of the records to Bennett's label, Columbia, and the other to Basie's, Roulette. The Columbia album, *In Person!*, was released once, while the Roulette album, initially issued under the title *Strike Up The Band*, has been re-released by various labels under various titles endlessly. This is one of those reissues, and while one may deplore the duplicitous marketing scheme, the pairing between Bennett and Basie remains impressive. The band raves through tunes like "With Plenty of Money and You," and Bennett matches them, drawing strength from the bravura arrangements, while band and singer achieve a know-

ing tenderness on "Growing Pains." This is an album well worth owning; just make sure you don't buy it twice. —*William Ruhlmann*

To My Wonderful One / 1960 / Columbia ✦✦✦

Working with arranger/conductor Frank DeVol, Tony Bennett here recorded a string-filled ballad session featuring standards like "September Song" and "Autumn Leaves." In so doing, he demonstrated how far he had come in controlling his instrument in his ten years of recording. There was none of the oratorical style of his early hits. The restraint was especially noticeable on a song like "Till," which could have allowed for some of the old bel canto belting. Instead, Bennett's interpretations now had a detail and a nuance that marked him as a master interpreter. —*William Ruhlmann*

★ Tony's Greatest Hits, Vol. 3 / 1960-1965 / Columbia ✦✦✦✦✦

Tony Bennett's third hits collection isn't only the best of his best-ofs, it's a classic "classic pop" album. Bennett's career hit its second and highest artistic peak in the first half of the 1960s, starting with "I Left My Heart In San Francisco" and continuing through a series of magnificent ballad hits—"I Wanna Be Around," "The Good Life," "This Is All I Ask," "When Joanna Loved Me," "Who Can I Turn To," "If I Ruled The World"—all of which are here, along with such equally impressive album tracks as "Once Upon A Time" and "The Best Is Yet to Come." As a result, this album became Bennett's second gold seller, and it remains the definitive statement of a major pop singer at his zenith. A complete understanding of his work requires a listen to his 1991 box set, *Forty Years: The Artistry of Tony Bennett*. But this 12-song set, covering the years 1962-1965, remains the brightest jewel in his crown. —*William Ruhlmann*

☆ I Left My Heart in San Francisco / 1962 / Columbia ✦✦✦✦✦

Along with his producer, Ernest Altschuler, and his arranger/pianist Ralph Sharon, Tony Bennett had been searching for a repertoire and a musical approach beyond his long-gone pop work with Mitch Miller of the early 1950s and his artistically pleasing but commercially dicey jazz work of the mid- to late '50s. It seemed to be a combination of Broadway songs and other contemporary material, carefully selected and arranged to show off Bennett's now-burnished vocals, which, as he approached the end of his thirties, were starting to be located in a more comfortable range closer to a baritone than a tenor. With this album, they found the key, not only by happening across a signature song in the title track, but also in the approach to songs like "Once upon a Time," a gem from the flop musical *All American*, and Cy Coleman and Carolyn Leigh's "The Best Is Yet to Come," which Bennett helped make a standard. (Frank Sinatra didn't do it until two years later.) From here on until the world changed again toward the late '60s, Bennett would not have to feel that he had to compromise his art for popularity, making uptempo singles in an attempt to meet the marketplace while longing to do ballads and swing material instead. *I Left My Heart in San Francisco*, a gold-selling Top Ten hit that stayed in the charts almost three years, demonstrated that he could have it all. (Tony Bennett won two 1962 Grammy Awards for the title song: Record of the Year and Best Solo Vocal Performance, Male.) —*William Ruhlmann*

Mr. Broadway / 1962 / Columbia ✦✦

In the search for new, non-rock material in the late 1950s and early 1960s, Tony Bennett had turned increasingly to Broadway shows. His second greatest hits collection, for example, found him singing songs from *The Sound of Music, Gypsy, Bye Bye Birdie*, and *Flower Drum Song*. On this compilation, subtitled "Tony's Greatest Broadway Hits," Columbia Records culled those tracks, plus others taken from shows like *Bells Are Ringing* and *Kismet* that had been chart singles for Bennett. It's a fair idea, but doesn't make for an essential Bennett release. —*William Ruhlmann*

● At Carnegie Hall / Jun. 9, 1962 / Columbia ✦✦✦✦✦

Recorded on June 9, 1962, one week before the release of the *I Left My Heart in San Francisco* album that would catapult Tony Bennett's career into the stratosphere, this concert album effectively sums up his accomplishments so far. Some of the hits—"Stranger in Paradise," "Rags to Riches," "Because of You"—are still on the set list (although drastically rearranged), but clearly he has found his true repertoire in reinventions of older material like "All the Things You Are" (the version here is exquisite) and good choices of new songs—he champions the team of Cy Coleman and Carolyn Leigh, and introduces "San Francisco," which some in the audience already know. (Released as a single in advance of the *San Francisco* album, it was in the charts already.) And on the album's original four LP sides, Bennett managed to find time for such experiments as an uptempo "Ol' Man River" featuring percussionist Candido, a throwback to his innovative *Beat of My Heart* album. As a consistent demonstration of Bennett's strengths, the album earns its designation as a "pick." More than his greatest-hits collections of the '50s and early '60s, it gives a broad sense of Bennett's work, and it does so in the format with which he's most comfortable—live in concert. —*William Ruhlmann*

I Wanna Be Around / 1963 / Columbia ✦✦✦✦✦

As the studio album follow-up to Tony Bennett's breakthrough record, *I Left My Heart in San Francisco, I Wanna Be Around* had a lot to live up to, but since *San Francisco* was a culmination of Bennett's development, not a fluke, *I Wanna Be Around* turned out to be almost on a par with its predecessor. "The Good Life" and "I Wanna Be Around" became Top 20 hits, showing that Bennett had somehow found a line into good new pop material, and there were also some excellent arrangements, courtesy of Marty Manning, including a percussion-and-flute reading of "Let's Face the Music and Dance" that echoed the *Beat of My Heart* album and a nod to the South American trend with Antonio Carlos Jobim's "Quiet Nights (Corcovado)." A worthy successor. —*William Ruhlmann*

This Is All I Ask / 1963 / Columbia ✦✦✦

Tony Bennett got a No. 70 hit out of the title track, a warm ballad written by Gordon Jenkins, and elsewhere he turned to old standbys like Cy Coleman and Carolyn Leigh, pulling another song from their show *Little Me,* in this case "On the Other Side of the Tracks" ("I've Got Your Number" had appeared on *I Wanna Be Around*), and included a duet track, "Tricks," with Chico Hamilton. If you hadn't heard Bennett's previous two albums, *I Left My Heart in San Francisco* and *I Wanna Be Around, This Is All I Ask* would sound like a varied, satisfying collection, but if you had, you recognized the formula and realized it had been done slightly better before. —*William Ruhlmann*

Tony & Gene—Fascinatin' Rhythm / 1963/ Columbia ✦✦

This is a 1963 radio show by drummer Gene Krupa and His Orchestra, with vocals on some tracks by Tony Bennett. Bennett trades remarks with disc jockey Martin Block and then sounds overjoyed to be fronting a big band, especially on the frantic title track. It's an energetic session with modest fidelity, a minor addition to the Bennett catalog. —*William Ruhlmann*

The Many Moods of Tony / 1964 / Columbia ✦✦

Tony Bennett's Columbia Records contract in the 1960s called for three albums a year, and the result was occasional releases like this one, whose title gives away the truth: it's a hodgepodge of previously released singles ("Spring in Manhattan," "Don't Wait Too Long," "The Little Boy") and sessions held at various times with various arrangers and musicians, all stitched together to meet the release schedule. What rescues it is a remarkable new ballad, "When Joanna Loved Me," that immediately went onto the Bennett concert short list. He even named his daughter after it. Other highlights are a delicate arrangement of "A Taste of Honey" and one of Bennett's patented drum duets with Chico Hamilton on "Caravan." But on the whole, this album does not meet the standard Bennett had set with recent releases. —*William Ruhlmann*

Who Can I Turn To / 1964 / Columbia ✦✦✦

Tony Bennett returned to the Top 40 in late 1964 with his version of the Leslie Bricusse-Anthony Newley anthem "Who Can I Turn To (When Nobody Needs Me)," from Newley's Broadway show *The Roar of the Greasepaint, The Smell of the Crowd.* That song, like the rest of this album, was arranged and conducted by George Siravo, who made detailed ballad arrangements, using individual instruments and groups to echo and counterpoint the Bennett vocals. Still searching for new material, and finding it in works by Cy Coleman and Carolyn Leigh, as well as Mel Tormé (whose "Got the Gate on the Golden Gate" recalled Bennett's musical connection to San Francisco), Bennett didn't discover anything to match the title track, and he re-recorded "Autumn Leaves" in a more uptempo framework. But the match of singer and arranger made for a consistent and effective album. —*William Ruhlmann*

If I Ruled the World: Songs for the Jet Set / 1965 / Columbia ✦✦✦

Employing Sinatra arranger Don Costa, Tony Bennett put together a concept album similar to Sinatra's *Come Fly with Me.* Travel was the loose theme that united Antonio Carlos Jobim's "Song of the Jet" (set in Rio de Janeiro, a photograph of which graces the album cover), "Fly Me to the Moon," and the title song, a Leslie Bricusse-Cyril Ornadel tune from the show *Pickwick* that was Bennett's latest hit single. There were also two songs from the Richard Rodgers-Stephen Sondheim musical *Do I Hear a Waltz?,* which was set in Venice. Other sections might not justify the flight theme—Duke Ellington's "Love Scene" was given a "destination" of Harlem on the back cover, and that neighborhood is on no known flight plan—but with such high-quality material, it was hard to complain. —*William Ruhlmann*

Tony Bennett's Greatest Hits, Vol. 4 / 1965-1969 / Columbia ✦✦

The fourth and final volume of Columbia's series of Tony Bennett hits (although the label would issue many compilations after be left in 1972), covering the years 1965-1969, traces the gradual decline in his popularity over the period. None of the hits got higher than No. 84 in the Hot 100, although seven got into the Easy Listening charts. These are mid-level standards—"The Shadow of Your Smile," "Fly

Me to the Moon"; respectable efforts, but not on a par with the best pop songwriting or the best of Bennett. —*William Ruhlmann*

Movie Song Album / 1966 / Columbia ✦✦✦

By the mid-1960s, retreating from the rock 'n' roll onslaught, that old-time staple of the pre-rock days, the big romantic ballad, had been relegated to Hollywood, where it turned up in the opening and closing credits of movies. Like other classic pop singers, Tony Bennett had sought it out there, and with this album, coincident with his first (and last) acting role in *The Oscar,* he devoted himself exclusively to movie themes, everything from "The Trolley Song" (*Meet Me in St. Louis*) to "Days of Wine and Roses." Some of the tunes were not first-rate, but in "The Shadow of Your Smile" and "The Second Time Around" (previously recorded by Frank Sinatra), Bennett found material worthy of him, and even when he was faced with minor material, he sang movingly. —*William Ruhlmann*

A Time for Love / 1966 / Columbia ✦✦

A couple of movie themes, a few standards, and some new songs, this mixed selection, which featured four different arranger/conductors, had some nice moments here and there—a good duet with cornetist Bobby Hackett on "The Very Thought of You," a late-night trio version of "In the Wee Small Hours of the Morning"—but was not one of Tony Bennett's more outstanding efforts. Also notable was that it marked a commercial marginalization for Bennett that all non-rock recording artsts were experiencing. Thus began the pressures Columbia would apply to Bennett to contemporize his image and his music. —*William Ruhlmann*

For Once in My Life / 1967 / Columbia ✦✦

Those of you who think of "For Once in My Life" as a Stevie Wonder song, reconsider. True, Wonder took it to No. 2 in 1968, but Tony Bennett's ballad version was a pop chart entry (his last) and an Easy Listening Top Ten more than a year earlier. On the accompanying album Bennett made his by-now usual selections of standards ("They Can't Take That Away from Me"), Broadway and Hollywood material, and choices from the catalogs of songwriter favorites such as Leslie Bricusse and Cy Coleman. He was a faithful friend and a dependable talent, but, while maintaining his usual standard, this album didn't feature any standout performances to lift it to higher grade. —*William Ruhlmann*

I've Gotta Be Me / 1969 / Columbia ✦✦

Bennett, whose sales had nosedived in recent years, was coming under pressure from his record label to take a more contemporary approach. This album demonstrated that he was willing to bend, but not break. The title song, a hit earlier in the year for Sammy Davis, Jr., "What the World Needs Now Is Love" (in a ludicrous swing arrangement), and "Alfie" were current pop material, which Bennett covered gamely, but it was songs like the Gershwins' "They All Laughed" that he obviously felt more comfortable with. Bennett's real failure to deal with contemporary pop was most apparent on his version of Andre and Dory Previn's "Theme from *Valley of the Dolls,*" on which he just sang his way through the hesitant, fragmented, uncertain lyric as though it was a dramatic ballad on the scale of "Who Can I Turn To." —*William Ruhlmann*

Tony Bennett's Something / 1970 / Columbia ✦✦

Columbia Records took Tony Bennett's recording of the Beatles' "Something," which had appeared on the previous year's *Tony Sings the Great Hits of Today!* and been a No. 23 Easy Listening hit the previous spring, and put it at the top of his 1970 album, which otherwise was a collection arranged and conducted by Peter Matz (who handled the early Barbra Streisand albums) and produced by Teo Macero (who handled jazz artists like Miles Davis). While Bennett still wasn't comfortable with songs like "The Long and Winding Road" and "Everybody's Talkin'," he did manage to place favorites like Antonio Carlos Jobim ("Wave") and Cy Coleman on the songlist, and Matz's tasteful arrangements assured that this record wouldn't be the debacle *Great Hits* had been. Not that Bennett was out of the woods yet. —*William Ruhlmann*

Tony Sings the Great Hits of Today! / 1970 / Columbia ✦

Disaster strikes. Accompanied by a sleeve note from company president Clive Davis, who forced this record down his throat, Tony Bennett is presented on the album cover in a garish illustration, wearing bellbottoms and a psychedelic tie. On the record, he sings "MacArthur Park" (well, some of it, anyway), "Eleanor Rigby" (most of which he recites instead of singing), "Something," and other "great hits of today." You'd think he might make peace at least with numbers like "The Look of Love," but the only song he shows any real enthusiasm for is "Is That All There Is?," and even that is too cynical for his style. —*William Ruhlmann*

The Best of Tony Bennett / 1972-1973 / Capitol ✦✦

This is not the best of Tony Bennett by any stretch of the imagination, but it is an interesting record from the collector's point of view, because it contains a set of recordings that are not otherwise available. In 1972, after 22 years with Columbia Records, Bennett left for MGM/Verve, where he stayed for only a year or so. This album presents some of the recordings he made then, recordings that were out of print on LP for a long time. It's not great stuff, unless your idea of great Tony Bennett includes hearing him sing George Harrison's "Give Me Love (Give Me Peace on Earth)," and no one looking for a Bennett hits collection should touch it. But fans curious about this small, previously hard-to-find area of Bennett's catalog will want to seek it out. — *William Ruhlmann*

Rodgers & Hart Songbook / Sept. 1973 / DRG ✦✦✦

In sessions recorded in September 1973, Tony Bennett cut a series of songs by Richard Rodgers and Lorenz Hart, backed by the Ruby Braff-George Barnes Quartet. Originally, they resulted into two albums on Bennett's Improv Records, each containing ten selections. The 20-track DRG disc brings the entire collection together. Bennett is a sterling interpreter, and the backup is sympathetic. — *William Ruhlmann*

The Tony Bennett Bill Evans Album / 1975 / Columbia ✦✦✦

Tony Bennett has always had an affinity for good pianists, and many of his best performances have been with trios or solo piano, so when he got the chance to make the kind of records he wanted to in the mid-1970s, a pairing with jazz pianist Bill Evans was a natural. This is a true duet, with Evans getting considerable solo time. A low-key effort, but an effective one. — *William Ruhlmann*

Tony Bennett Sings . . . "Life is Beautiful" / 1975 / Columbia ✦✦✦

After 22 years with Columbia Records and a brief sojourn on MGM, Tony Bennett launched his own record label with this release. The title track was co-written by Fred Astaire, and the album also features such Bennett favorites as Duke Ellington, Cole Porter, Richard Rodgers and Lorenz Hart, and Irving Berlin, plus a Bennett reading of Herman Hupfield's "As Time Goes By." The result was a record that had nothing to do with pop music trends in 1975, which was exactly the way that Bennett wanted it. Decades later, it sounds fresher than many of his late '60s/early '70s attempts to be contemporary. — *William Ruhlmann*

Together Again / 1976 / DRG ✦✦✦

The second Tony Bennett-Bill Evans duet album was recorded a year after the first and took an essentially similar approach, mixing Bennett's warm, relaxed vocals with the reflective, melodic, and spare piano work of Evans. If anything, Evans dominates this encounter more than he did the first, but it's still a good showcase for Bennett, too. (Originally released on Bennett's own Improv Records label, *Together Again* was reissued on CD by DRG.) — *William Ruhlmann*

Tony Bennett/The McPartlands and Friends Make Magic / May 13, 1977-May 14, 1977 / DRG ✦✦✦

"Sit down, make yourselves comfortable," Tony Bennett says near the beginning of this album, as he introduces an entertaining live club performance, taped in May 1977. Note, however, that the co-billing in the title indicates that different songs are given over to Marian and Jimmy McPartland and their jazz band, or to Bennett and his trio. The McPartland material is fine, but unremarkable; Bennett shines as usual, but there isn't enough of him. — *William Ruhlmann*

The Special Magic of Tony Bennett / 1979 / DRG ✦✦

On the last of his independent albums before he gave up recording for seven years, Tony Bennett puts together a 12-song medley of Cole Porter songs (it's okay, but why not just devote the whole album to complete versions?) and adds songs drawn from his *Life Is Beautiful* album, plus a couple of new numbers. — *William Ruhlmann*

Art of Excellence / 1986 / Columbia ✦✦✦✦✦

This album marked Tony Bennett's return to recording after half a dozen years, his return to Columbia Records after 14 years, and the beginning of the third stage in his career. Back with the Ralph Sharon Trio and backed by the UK Orchestra, Bennett demonstrated that he had spent his time off from recording gathering a bunch of good songs and refining his singing. The older material, such as "A Rainy Day" and "I Got Lost in Her Arms," were better than the new discoveries, like "How Do You Keep the Music Playing?" and "Everybody Has the Blues," but the new ones weren't bad, and with this album Bennett joined and helped to lead the swelling trend toward classic pop. It became his best-selling album in 15 years. — *William Ruhlmann*

Bennett/Berlin / 1987 / Columbia ✦✦✦

With his warmth and upbeat attitude, Tony Bennett makes an excellent interpreter of Irving Berlin, whose songs share exactly those qualities. This was Bennett's second newly recorded album in his return to recording and to Columbia Records, and it's a classy collection, with Bennett breathing life into songs like "Isn't This a Lovely Day" and "Cheek to Cheek." He stuck to the backing of his regular piano-bass-drums trio, led by Ralph Sharon, with extra colors provided by guests Dexter Gordon, Dizzy Gillespie, and George Benson. The result is an understated, informal session that brings out the best in the already impressive material. The only real criticism of the album is that it's too short—just over 30 minutes—which, in the emerging CD era, seems fairly skimpy. — *William Ruhlmann*

Astoria: Portrait of the Artist / 1990 / Columbia ✦✦✦✦✦

Like *The Art of Excellence*, the album that marked Tony Bennett's return to recording in 1986, *Astoria: A Portrait of the Artist* was a non-thematic collection of new and old songs on which Bennett was backed both by his regular trio, led by pianist Ralph Sharon, and the UK Orchestra. Bennett's new songwriting discovery was Charles DeForest, three of whose songs—"When Do the Bells Ring for Me," "Where Do You Go from Love," and "I've Come Home Again"—were included, along with songs by the Gershwins and Jerome Kern, standards like "Body and Soul," and even a re-recording of Bennett's initial Columbia recording, "The Boulevard of Broken Dreams." That recording had come in 1950, and the point of *Astoria* (which featured a cover photo of the young Bennett in the old neighborhood, with Bennett today standing in the same spot on the back) was to celebrate that 40-year anniversary while looking into both the past and the future, a task it accomplished admirably. — *William Ruhlmann*

Perfectly Frank / 1992 / Columbia ✦✦✦✦✦

Think no one can touch the Chairman on his own turf? Think again. Bennett's tribute is such an obvious move, it's odd that it's taken this long to materialize. Sinatra made no secret of his admiration of Bennett, who puts his spin on this collection of Francis Albert classics. In the process, we wind up with Bennett's best in years. — *Steve Aldrich*

MTV Unplugged / 1994 / Columbia ✦✦✦

Of course, Tony Bennett never was "plugged," so the concept here is redundant, but what the hell. It's been a while since a Tony Bennett live album, and he's always terrific in concert. Certainly, he is here, singing 22 pop standards, including many of his hits and many other songs he's made his own. Elvis Costello and k.d. lang drop by, but they're feeding off Bennett's energy and star power, not the other way around. The album may be part of a successful marketing plan, but forget that and revel in the singing of a masterful song interpreter still, after 40 years, at the top of his game. — *William Ruhlmann*

Here's to the Ladies / 1995 / Columbia ✦✦✦

For years, it was rumored that Frank Sinatra was going to record an album called *Here's to the Ladies*, but the Chairman of the Board never got around to actually making the record. However, Tony Bennett did and his record covers a wider range of artists and styles than Sinatra's scheduled record. Naturally, Bennett turns in a thoroughly entertaining, professional performance. It's a solid contribution to his impressively assured and diverse comeback. — *Stephen Thomas Erlewine*

Tony Bennett on Holiday: A Tribute to Billie Holiday / 1996 / Sony ✦✦✦

Bennett tackles the Billie Holiday songbook in an intimate trio setting, augmented by the occasional use of a string section. Though much of the collection is lovely, Bennett's "duet" with Holiday on "God Bless the Child" is both creepy and unnecessary. — *Jason Ankeny*

Han Bennink

b. Apr. 17, 1942, Zaandam, Netherlands
Drums / Free Jazz, Avant-Garde

In the niche-oriented world of major-league jazz, it's almost unfashionable to be so multifaceted a player as Han Bennink. Bennink is one of the unfortunately rare musicians whose abilities and interests span the music's entire spectrum, from Dixieland to free. His straightahead playing is absolutely convincing—his time is solid, his sense of swing strong, and his technique flawless. He also possesses the requisite qualities of a free jazz virtuoso; Bennink's ability to interact quickly and creatively with horn players and pianists is great, as is his ear for timbral contrasts. What ultimately makes Bennink special is his manifest love for the music—a love that inclines him to tear down the cardboard walls that too often separate different schools of jazz. At his best, with colleagues who share his all-encompassing stylistic embrace, Bennink plays the continuum of jazz as an instrument unto itself.

Bennink began playing drums while in his teens, under the influence of his father, a classical percussionist. He played with hometown musicians in the early '60s. Between 1962 and 1969, Bennink backed local American jazz greats like Dexter Gordon, Sonny Rollins, and Eric Dolphy on their visits to Holland (he was the drummer on Dolphy's *Last Date* album, from 1964). In 1963, he formed a quartet that included the pianist Misha Mengelberg, which played the Newport Jazz Festival in 1966. In the mid-'60s, Bennink began to play free jazz with the likes of Mengelberg and Willem Breuker. In 1967, those three founded the Instant Composer's Pool, a not-for-profit organization designed to promote the Dutch jazz avant-garde. Around that same period, Bennink began continuing associations with the saxophonist Peter Brotzman, guitarist Derek Bailey, trombonist Alex Schlippenbach, trumpeter Don Cherry, and the Globe Unity Orchestra. In the '70s and '80s, Bennink led and played as sideman on a number of sessions on the FMP, Incus, and Soul Note labels; he made a notable contribution to Steve Lacy's Herbie Nichols tribute album, *Regeneration*, with Mengelberg, bassist Kent Carter, and trombonist Roswell Rudd. In the late '80s Bennink started, with the cellist Ernst Reijseger and saxophonist Michael Moore, the Clusone Trio, which has since become perhaps the percussionist's most ideal performance vehicle. Both Reijseger and Moore share Bennink's extraordinarily wide range of musical interests, to say nothing of his absurdist sense of humor. It is, in fact, Bennink's rather whimsical theatricality that mitigates—for some, at least—the seriousness and depth of his art. —*Chris Kelsey*

Solo / Oct. 1978 / FMP ✦✦✦

● **Serpentine** / Jan. 30, 1996 / Songlines ✦✦✦

David Benoit

b. 1953, Bakersfield, CA
Piano, Keyboards / Crossover Jazz
One of the more popular performers in the idiom somewhat inaccurately called "contemporary jazz," David Benoit has mostly performed light melodic background music, what critic Alex Henderson has dubbed "new age with a beat." Benoit has done a few fine jazz projects (including a tribute to Bill Evans and a collaboration with Emily Remler) but most of his output for GRP has been aimed clearly at the charts. He studied composition and piano at El Camino College and in 1975 played on the soundtrack of the film *Nashville*. After recording with Alphonse Mouzon and accompanying singer Gloria Lynne, he was signed to the AVI label when he was 24, recording sets that paved the way towards his later output. Benoit has been been a solo artist for GRP since 1986. —*Scott Yanow*

Heavier than Yesterday / 1977 / Blue Moon ✦✦✦
Before being signed to GRP and hitting it big in pop-jazz and crossover, pianist David Benoit recorded several albums for the tiny AVI label. Blue Moon in the early '90s reissued these sets on CD including this early date. Benoit, on piano, electric piano and synthesizer, performs seven of his more obscure originals along with a faceless rhythm section that includes occasional solos from guitarist Michael Miller plus a string section. The music alternates lightweight and jazzy background music with pop tunes including one number dominated by some forgotten vocalists. Little of significance occurs and David Benoit had not yet developed his musical personality, so there is no real reason for anyone but Benoit completists to search out this lesser effort. —*Scott Yanow*

Freedom at Midnight / 1987 / GRP ✦✦✦
Pianist David Benoit's debut for GRP was a big seller and set the tone for the next decade of his career. In general, Benoit's piano is heard in the forefront, joined by oversized rhythm sections (including the Rippingtons' Russ Freeman) and a string section. A strictly boppish quartet rendition of "Del Sasser" (with altoist Sam Riney) is a nice change of pace, but otherwise, the music is melodic, lightweight and better for backgrounds than for close listening. Overall, this program is pleasant and not at all objectionable, but difficult to remember once the CD is finished. —*Scott Yanow*

Every Step of the Way / 1987 / GRP ✦✦✦

The Best of David Benoit 1987-1995 / 1987-1995 / GRP ✦✦
During his years with the GRP label, pianist David Benoit became very popular among listeners who enjoy hearing melodic jazz-influenced pop instrumentals that groove in a generally quiet manner. This sampler has 14 selections including two previously unreleased numbers and tunes taken from ten of Benoit's earlier releases. Unfortunately the exact personnel is only given for the new tracks (a rather inexcusable omission). The music overall (which includes a couple of straightahead performances recorded for tributes to Bill Evans and Vince Guaraldi) is lightly funky and enjoyable if somewhat lightweight. Highlights include "Cast Your Fate to the Wind," "Linus and Lucy," "Freedom at Midnight," "Letter to Evan" and "Urban Daydreams." —*Scott Yanow*

Urban Daydreams / 1988 / GRP ✦✦
David Benoit's third release for GRP has some pretty melodies and Benoit's appealing piano, but no real surprises. Jennifer Warnes takes a forgettable vocal, Eric Marienthal (on alto and soprano) generates a little derivative heat, Don Grusin adds additional keyboards and electronic programming, and most of the other backup musicians (which on two numbers include the Warfield Avenue Symphony Orchestra) sound fairly anonymous. The overall results on this popular CD are actually quite routine and predictable, lightweight crossover music. —*Scott Yanow*

● **Waiting for Spring** / Feb. 5, 1989+May 25, 1989 / GRP ✦✦✦✦
After making so many forgettable albums with commercial radio in mind, David Benoit took a break from the type of "smooth jazz" fluff he usually records and delivered a respectable straightahead CD with *Waiting for Spring*. Instead of shamelessly wasting his improvisatory skills, he actually lets loose on the acoustic piano and makes some meaningful statements. Bill Evans is obviously a great influence on Benoit, whose vulnerability makes his love of the late piano legend

obvious on originals as well as lyrical interpretations of standards like "My Romance" and "Secret Love." Benoit has a fine soloist in the late guitarist Emily Remler, who is consistently warm, melodic and inviting. Though the album isn't breathtaking, it's satisfying and heartfelt. —*Alex Henderson*

Inner Motion / Apr. 1990-May 1990 / GRP ✦✦
"Lightweight" is a word seemingly invented to describe most of keyboardist David Benoit's music. Benoit's piano always sounds attractive, his originals are upbeat and usually pretty and (to use a cliché) many people would consider *Inner Motion* perfect music to wash dishes by. The melodies are pleasant but vacuous and the countless number of background musicians sound as if they are more concerned with counting their money then playing creative music. Instantly dated performances. —*Scott Yanow*

Shadows / 1991 / GRP ✦✦
David Benoit found himself enjoying orchestral support on *Shadows*. But in many respects, it is the quintessential Benoit album—overproduced, formulaic and defined by commercial motives more than creative or artistic ones. Some of the material isn't bad—the obvious winner being "Saudade," a poetic, Brazilian-influenced piece featuring Freddie Hubbard on fluegelhorn. But all too often, Benoit is content to offer bland and lightweight elevator muzak. Making sure he doesn't offend or alienate timid commercial radio programmers, Benoit either sees to it that improvisation is kept to a minumum or avoids it altogether. *Shadows* has its moments, but overall, underscores everything that's wrong with David Benoit's commercialism. —*Alex Henderson*

Letter to Evan / 1992 / GRP ✦✦✦
David Benoit had a slight departure with this 1992 release, performing two previously unheard Bill Evans compositions ("Letter to Evan" and "Knit for Mary F."), Dave Brubeck's "Kathy's Waltz" and a mixture of standards and originals. Most of the tunes are played with small groups (duets to quartets) and such fine players as bassist John Patitucci, drummer Peter Erskine and guitarists Larry Carlton and Peter Sprague make strong contributions. The melodic and mostly straightahead music is pleasing, pretty and sometimes swinging, if not all particularly innovative. Worth checking out by jazz listeners. —*Scott Yanow*

Shaken Not Stirred / 1994 / GRP ✦✦
The popular pianist's release is supposed to be a series of tributes to aspects of the 1960s but the music is essentially crossover jazz-pop of the 1990s. As usual Benoit plays reasonably well but few of the melodies are all that memorable and there is little to distinguish this set from his last few. Benoit is heard in a variety of settings from the solo "Jacqueline" and a few quartets (including two songs with Eric Marienthal on alto and tenor) to a string orchestra, but jazz listeners will find little of interest here. —*Scott Yanow*

American Landscape / 1997 / GRP ✦✦✦
In the 1990s, David Benoit has fluctuated between acoustic, Bill Evans-influenced post-bop dates stressing improvisation, and overproduced, fluffy commercial albums that left little or no room for improvisation. *American Landscape* definitely falls into the latter category. The heavily arranged, extremely slick CD isn't as bad as some of the other pop-jazz and instrumental pop releases that came out in 1997 and does have a few worthwhile tracks, including "Mom's Boogie" (a perky tune that brings to mind Vince Guaraldi) and "Lost in Tokyo," which sounds a bit like something Joe Sample might do. But for the most part, *American Landscape* is a mundane offering that functions mainly as innocuous background music. As the pianist demonstrated on 1989's *Waiting for Spring*, he can do better. —*Alex Henderson*

George Benson

b. Mar. 22, 1943, Pittsburgh, PA
Guitar, Vocals / Hard Bop, Crossover Jazz, Pop, R&B
George Benson is simply one of the greatest guitarists in jazz history, but he is also an amazingly versatile musician—and that frustrates critics to no end who would paint him into a narrow bop box. He can play in just about any style—from swing to bop to R&B to pop—with supreme taste, a beautiful rounded tone, terrific speed, a marvelous sense of logic in building solos, and always, an unquenchable urge to swing. His inspirations may have been Charlie Christian and Wes Montgomery—and he can do dead-on impressions of both—but his style is completely his own. Not only can he play lead brilliantly, he is also one of the best rhythm guitarists around, supportive to soloists and a dangerous swinger, particularly in a soul-jazz format. Yet Benson can also sing in a lush soulful tenor with mannerisms similar to those of Stevie Wonder and Donny Hathaway—and it is his voice that has proved to be more marketable to the public than his guitar. Benson is the guitar-playing equivalent of Nat Cole—a fantastic pianist whose smooth way with a pop vocal eventually eclipsed his instrumental prowess in the marketplace—but

unlike Cole, Benson has been granted enough time after his fling with the pop charts to reaffirm his jazz guitar credentials, which he still does at his concerts.

Benson actually started out professionally as a singer, performing in nightclubs at eight, recording four sides for RCA's "X" label in 1954 and forming a rock band at 17 while using a guitar that his stepfather made for him. Exposure to records by Christian, Montgomery and Charlie Parker got him interested in jazz, and by 1962, the teenaged Benson was playing in Brother Jack McDuff's band. After forming his own group in1965, Benson became another of talent scout John Hammond's major discoveries, recording two highly regarded albums of soul jazz and hard bop for Columbia and turning up on several records by others, including Miles Davis' *Miles in the Sky.* He switched to Verve in 1967, and shortly after the death of Montgomery in June 1968, producer Creed Taylor began recording Benson with larger ensembles on A&M (1968-69) and big groups and all-star combos on CTI (1971-1976).

While the A&M and CTI albums certainly earned their keep and made Benson a guitar star in the jazz world, the mass market didn't catch on until he began to emphasize vocals after signing with Warner Bros. in 1976. His first album for WB, *Breezin',* became a Top Ten hit on the strength of its sole vocal track "This Masquerade," and this led to a string of hit albums in an R&B-flavored pop mode, culminating with the Quincy Jones-produced *Give Me the Night.* As the '80s wore on, though, Benson's albums became riddled with commercial formulas and inferior material, with his guitar almost entirely relegated to the background. Perhaps aware of the futility of chasing the charts (after all, "This Masquerade" was a lucky accident), Benson reversed his field late in the '80s to record a fine album of standards, *Tenderly,* and another with the Basie band, his guitar now featured more prominently. His pop-flavored work also improved noticeably in the '90s. Benson retains the ability to spring surprises on his fans and critics, like his dazzlingly idiomatic TV appearance and subsequent record date with Benny Goodman in 1975 in honor of John Hammond, and his awesome command of the moment at several Playboy Jazz Festivals in the 1980s. —*Richard S. Ginell*

The New Boss Guitar / May 1, 1964 / Original Jazz Classics ✦✦✦✦
A definitive early album, it features Brother Jack McDuff (organ). —*Michael G. Nastos*

George Benson/Jack McDuff / May 1, 1964+Oct. 19, 1965 / Prestige ✦✦✦✦✦
Guitarist George Benson spent an important period early in his career as a sideman with organist Jack McDuff. This two-LP set brings back two albums that they recorded together; one was originally under Benson's name while the other was led by McDuff. With tenor saxophonist Red Holloway adding his distinctive solo voice, this quartet/quintet (depending on whether they use a bassist) was an exciting, blues-oriented unit that was rightfully popular in the mid-'60s. The two-fer gives one a valuable look at George Benson in his early years. —*Scott Yanow*

It's Uptown / 1965 / Columbia ✦✦✦
While George Benson's solid jazz reputation supposedly rests on his early John Hammond-produced Columbia albums, one listen to this disc will reveal that his interests roamed widely from the beginning. Yes, there is plenty of straight-forward bop playing here, with Benson stretching his technical chops on "Hello Birdie" and "Myna Bird Blues" and ruminating thoughtfully on "Willow Weep for Me." But Benson also had an interest in quasi-rock 'n' roll, producing Wes-like octaves on "Young Jaguar," and some Bo Diddley-in-Spain rhythm chording on "Bullfight." The young George sounds pure and mellifluous on three vocal numbers, the basic elements of his later successes mostly in place. Yet Benson's backing combo doesn't click on all cylinders; Lonnie Smith is reliable on organ but Ronnie Cuber's blunt baritone sax is rather cumbersome here. —*Richard S. Ginell*

Benson Burner / 1965-1966 / Columbia ✦✦✦
Some but not all of guitarist George Benson's Columbia records (plus some unreleased songs and other tunes that he recorded under organist Lonnie Smith's name) are included on this out-of-print double-LP. Fitting into the soul-jazz/hard bop idiom, Benson (who at the time was heavily influenced by Wes Montgomery and Charlie Christian, but already had his own approach) is mostly heard in a quartet with organist Smith, baritonist Ronnie Cuber and drummer Jimmy Lovelace, although some selections add horns (including trumpeter Blue Mitchell) and more players in the rhythm section. The majority of the songs are basic originals by Benson or Smith, and the emphasis is on soulful swinging. Fine music. —*Scott Yanow*

This Is Jazz / 1965-Jan. 11, 1975 / Columbia ✦✦✦
Taken from Columbia's multivolume jazz primer, this is not bad for a single-company compilation. The selections split down the middle between Benson's early 1965-66 Columbia albums and his 1971-76 CTI output that Columbia now controls; the gaps are obvious but the title of the series neatly narrows the scope of the survey. We hear the young, eager Benson in four cuts from *It's Uptown* and only two from the superior *Cookbook* including the spectacular "The

Cooker"—before sampling a cut apiece from CTI's *Beyond the Blue Horizon, Bad Benson, Good King Bad,* and *At Carnegie Hall.* In addition, the outtake solo "From Now On" is reprised from CTI/CBS's *Best of Benson,* as is "I Remember Wes." Throughout, there are plenty of examples that explain why Benson is so esteemed as a jazz guitarist —the unerring selection of notes, the churning rhythms, melting lyricism and sheer ability to swing. This, coupled with Warner Bros.' *Collection,* will give the casual Benson browser an adequate idea of his multiple talents. —*Richard S. Ginell*

The George Benson Cookbook / Aug. 1, 1966-Oct. 19, 1966 / Columbia ✦✦✦✦✦
The second of Benson's John Hammond-produced albums is far and away the superior of the pair, mixing down-to-basics, straightahead jazz with soul-drenched grooving. Suddenly Benson's backup group—same as that of *Uptown,* with Bennie Green added on trombone now and then—has found its bearings and apropos to the title, they can cook, even sizzle. The effect upon Benson's own playing is striking; with something to react against, his sheer ability to swing advances into the realm of awesome. The rapid-fire work on "The Cooker" and "Ready and Able" will make you gasp. Only one vocal here, an exuberant "All of Me." —*Richard S. Ginell*

Giblet Gravy / Feb. 1967 / Verve ✦✦✦✦
No, we're not in Creed Taylor country yet but we might as well be, for many of the ingredients that would garnish Benson's albums with Taylor are already present in this often enjoyable prototype. The immediate goal was to groom Benson as the next Wes Montgomery (who was about to leave Verve)—and so he covers hit tunes of the day ("Sunny," "Along Comes Mary," "Groovin'"), playing either with a big band plus voices or a neat quintet anchored by Herbie Hancock, and the sound is contoured to give his guitar a warm mellow ambience. But the eclectic Benson is his own man, as his infectious repeated-interval rhythm trademark tells us on his self-composed title track, and despite Tom McIntosh's mostly lame arrangements, George's work is always tasty and irresistibly melodic. —*Richard S. Ginell*

The Silver Collection / Feb. 1967-Nov. 1968 / Verve ✦✦✦
Most of the tracks from Benson's two Verve albums, *Giblet Gravy* and *Goodies,* were deposited here in one of the label's earliest CDs. As such, it exists to plug a small hole in the collections of Benson fans, for it is hardly a prime choice if you want a representative Benson sampler. —*Richard S. Ginell*

Talkin' Verve / Feb. 5, 1968-Nov. 19, 1968 / Verve ✦✦✦

☆ **Shape of Things to Come** / Aug. 27, 1968-Oct. 22, 1968 / A&M ✦✦✦✦✦
Upon Wes Montgomery's sudden death on June 15, 1968, Creed Taylor signed Benson up and immediately thrust him onto the master's pedestal—or so the line has it. While this smashing debut for A&M has some of the Wes trappings—Don Sebesky's charts, Herbie Hancock and Ron Carter in the rhythm team—Benson triumphantly stamps his own image on the sessions with his infectious riffing, R&B slant, and solid jazz licks, propelled by Wes Covington's soulful organ and Leo Morris' driving drums. Just once, Benson tries a Varitone hookup with multi-speed overdubbings à la Les Paul on the title track; he would never use it again on discs but it is a great, futuristic electronic guitar trip, driven hard by a sizzling rhythm section and decorated sparingly by Sebesky. This superbly produced record made Benson a formidable pop-jazz guitar star, not a mere Montgomery clone. —*Richard S. Ginell*

Goodies / Nov. 1968 / Verve ✦✦
Verve needed one more album from Benson after he signed with A&M/CTI, and ended up with a strange grab-bag in which Benson plays superbly throughout, whatever the odd goulash of sounds in back of him. Horace Ott's string arrangements are overbearing in scope and undernourished in tone; at times they don't even seem in sync with Benson's group. The big band tracks—"Song for My Father" in particular—are more tolerable, and the gospel singing of the Sweet Inspirations is harmless. There is one high-spirited Benson vocal, "That Lucky Old Sun," and it strikes fire. Perversely perhaps, the choice cut is a surprisingly hard-driven "Windmills of Your Mind," in which Benson fights off the cheesy arrangement with some powerfully rhythmic work (watch out for the shattering psychedelic ending!). —*Richard S. Ginell*

Verve Jazz Masters 21 / 1968-1969 / Polygram ✦✦✦
This is a more satisfactory summary of George Benson's late-'60s recordings than the early CD era's *Silver Collection* because it includes a pair of the later A&M recordings and a couple of guest spots on a Jimmy Smith album from that period. At this time, Benson, still in his mid-20s, was solidifying his reputation as a tremendously fluent and powerful guitar soloist, with plenty of hard bop facility and a genuine taste for R&B riffing and swinging. The eloquent slow blues of "Low Down and Dirty," the wild, weird use of a Varitone octave multiplier on "The Shape of Things to Come," and the gutsy if occasionally scattered bop licks as a foil for the smoldering Smith (with drummer Donald Bailey) on "The Boss" go a long way toward illustrating Benson's range here. —*Richard S. Ginell*

The Best of George Benson [A&M] / 1968-1970 / A&M ✦✦✦

Anthology aimed at his earlier soul-jazz years. It includes some strong tunes, but isn't comprehensive enough to provide a full portrait. It's good as an introduction and also fine for casual listeners. —*Ron Wynn*

I Got a Woman & Some Blues / 1969 / A&M ✦✦

This mysterious album was supposed to be A&M/CTI's last release but it lay fallow until 1984 when it came out on A&M's Audio Master series along with a bunch of A&M/CTI reissues. Why was it shelved? A subjective guess is that it just isn't that good; it's as patchy and disjointed as *The Other Side of Abbey Road* is brilliantly unified. Even the title seems like an afterthought 15 years after the fact. No personnel or arrangers are listed, but some of the tracks sound like outtakes from *Tell It Like It Is;* the charts have the same sharp reeds/trumpet attack. Best cut by far is Benson's own Latin-flavored instrumental "Durham's Turn." "Out of the Blue" has a rare acoustic/electric guitar duet under Benson's romantic vocal, and the great guitarist always comes through with something worth hearing when asked. Still, as Yul Brynner puts it in *The King and I,* a puzzlement. —*Richard S. Ginell*

Tell It Like It Is / Apr. 29, 1969-May 20, 1969 / A&M ✦✦✦

Trying to shake things up, producer Creed Taylor brought in arranger Marty Sheller from Mongo Santamaria's Afro-Cuban band, reduced the sizes of the servings (no track is longer than 3:45), cranked up the decibels to a raucous level, and presented Benson in what he hoped would be a radio-friendly setting. The wonder is that Benson manages to transcend the blasting Latin-percussion-spiced production, the tight time limits, and all with often brilliantly tasty guitar fills and brief solos in many styles and three reverb-heavy vocals. The most attractive—and most frustrating—track is Eumir Deodato's lovely "Jackie, All"; George states the tune twice and just as he starts a beautiful solo, the faders go down at the 2:15 mark! Damn. Worth hearing despite the long production knives. —*Richard S. Ginell*

The Other Side of Abbey Road / Oct. 22, 1969-Nov. 9, 1969 / A&M ✦✦✦✦✦

Just three weeks after the US release of the Beatles' swan song *Abbey Road,* Creed Taylor ushered Benson into the studio to begin a remarkably successful pop-jazz translation of the record (complete with a parody of the famous cover, showing George with guitar crossing an Eastern urban street). It is a lyrical album, with a hint of the mystery and a lot of the cohesive concept of the Beatles' original despite the scrambled order of the tunes. Benson is given some room to stretch out on guitar, sometimes in a bluesy groove, and there are more samples of his honeyed vocals than ever before (oddly, his voice would not be heard again by record-buyers until he signed with Warner Bros.). Don Sebesky's arrangements roam freely from Baroque strings to a full-throated big band, and Freddie Hubbard, Sonny Fortune and Hubert Laws get some worthy solo space. Yet for all its diversity, the record fits together as a whole more tightly than any other George Benson project, thanks to his versatile talents and the miraculous overarching unity of the Beatles' songs. One wonders if the Fab Four liked it, too. —*Richard S. Ginell*

☆ **Beyond the Blue Horizon** / Feb. 2, 1971-Feb. 3, 1971 / Columbia ✦✦✦✦✦

Having taken Benson along with him when he founded CTI, Creed Taylor merely leaves the guitarist alone with a small group on his first release. The payoff is a superb jazz session where Benson rises to the challenge of the turbulent rhythm section of Jack DeJohnette and Ron Carter, with Clarence Palmer ably manning the organ. Benson is clearly as much at home with DeJohnette's advanced playing as he was in soul-jazz (after all, he did play on some Miles Davis sessions a few years before), and his tone is edgier, with more bite, than it had been for awhile. The lyrical Benson is also on eloquent display in "Ode to a Kudu" (heard twice on the CD, as is "All Clear"), and there is even a somewhat experimental tilt toward Afro-Cuban-Indian rhythms in "Somewhere to the East." A must-hear for all aficionados of Benson's guitar. —*Richard S. Ginell*

White Rabbit / Nov. 23, 1971-Nov. 30, 1971 / Columbia ✦✦✦✦

For Benson's second CTI project, producer Creed Taylor and arranger Don Sebesky successfully place the guitarist in a Spanish-flavored setting full of flamenco flourishes, brass fanfares, moody woodwinds and such. The idea works best on "California Dreamin'" (whose chords are based on Andalusian harmonies), where, driven by Jay Berliner's exciting Spanish rhythm guitar, Benson comes through with some terrifically inspired playing. On "El Mar," Berliner is replaced by Benson's protege Earl Klugh (then only 17) in an inauspicious—though at the time, widely heralded—recorded debut. The title track is another winner, marred only by the out-of-tune brasses at the close, and in a good example of the CTI classical/jazz formula at work, Heitor Villa-Lobos' "Little Train of the Caipira" is given an attractive early-'70s facelift. Herbie Hancock gets plenty of nimble solo space on Rhodes electric piano, Airto Moreira contributes percussion and atmospheric wordless vocals, and Ron Carter and Billy Cobham complete the high-energy rhythm section. In this prime sample of the CTI idiom, everyone wins. —*Richard S. Ginell*

The Best of George Benson [CBS] / 1971-1976 / Columbia ✦✦✦✦

Released in 1989, this anthology is a generous cross-section of tracks from Benson's CTI period, where he consolidated his jazz-soul guitar credentials just before striking gold with Warner Bros. All of the albums except *Benson & Farrell* are touched upon with one or two tracks, and CBS is enterprising enough to reach a bit further for "I Remember Wes" (from the anthology *CTI Masters of the Guitar*)—an octave-laden theme that soon enough turns into pure Benson—and a gentle solo outtake from *Bad Benson,* "From Now On." The only "unrepresentative" track per se is the vocal on "Summertime," in the sense that there were hardly any vocal tracks to pick from in the CTI catalogue. —*Richard S. Ginell*

Jazz on a Sunday Afternoon, Vol. 1 / Apr. 1973 / Accord ✦✦✦✦

Although probably released only semi-legally (since guitarist George Benson was at the time signed to CTI), this first of two LPs finds Benson really stretching out and sounding at his best. Joined by pianist Mickey Tucker, bassist George Duvivier and drummer Al Harewood for four straightahead standards, the guitarist takes long solos on "Love for Sale," "There Will Never Be Another You" and "All Blues" (all of which are over 10 minutes long) and takes a pleasing vocal on "The Masquerade Is Over." One wishes that Benson, having become famous, would still allow himself the luxury to stretch out like this now and then. Worth searching for; fortunately the music has been reissued on a Jazz Hour CD (titled *This Masquerade*). —*Scott Yanow*

Jazz on a Sunday Afternoon, Vol. 2 / Apr. 1973 / Accord ✦✦✦✦

The second of two live LPs featuring the quartet of guitarist George Benson, pianist Mickey Tucker, bassist George Duvivier and drummer Al Harewood, this instrumental set (which has been reissued along with the first volume on a Jazz Hour CD) showcases the leader's guitar on lengthy versions of "Witchcraft," "Blue Bossa," "Oleo" and "Lil' Darlin'." Benson could always play creative hard bop, and this superior set (which might have originally been a bootleg) will be enjoyed by his jazz fans. —*Scott Yanow*

Body Talk / Jul. 17, 1973-Jul. 18, 1973 / Columbia ✦✦✦✦

With an eye and ear on what was happening on the soul charts—James Brown in particular—Benson made a decided swerve toward R&B on this release. Indeed the JB's Pee Wee Ellis turns up as a big-band arranger on three tracks, and he no doubt had a direct influence on the distinct JB groove of one of the non-big-band tunes, "Dance." It should come as no surprise by now that this formidable guitarist has no problem handling any kind of groove, although the mixed rhythm section of Jack DeJohnette, Ron Carter, electric pianist Harold Mabern, and percussionist Mobutu sometimes sends mixed messages. Earl Klugh has a few tasty moments on his own, and there are some reconnaissance flights back to the jazz side of George, which he handles with his usual confident aplomb. —*Richard S. Ginell*

Bad Benson / May 1974 / Columbia ✦✦✦

The CTI formula of long tracks tastefully decorated and shaped takes firm hold here, though Benson, apropos the title, makes sure that the flavor of funky soul-jazz is the dominant one. With the help of the relentless rhythm guitar of Phil Upchurch, Benson produces some relentless riffing of his own on "Take Five"; indeed on several cuts, he flaunts his prowess as a rhythm soloist. Alas, arranger Don Sebesky is not in one of his more inventive moods; "Summer Wishes, Winter Dreams" is an outright attempt to evoke Wes Montgomery's last albums, and it falls flat—and there are a few times when George himself seems to be on automatic pilot. Nice, but there's better Benson out there. (The CD reissue offers two extra numbers.) —*Richard S. Ginell*

In Concert at Carnegie Hall / Jan. 11, 1975 / Columbia ✦✦✦

Recorded in NYC. —*AMG*

Good King Bad / Jul. 1975 / Columbia ✦✦✦✦✦

The R&B elements get stronger, the sound and mix are more attuned to the dance floor, yet this brings out the best in George Benson's funky side. Thanks in part to the more rigid beat, Benson pares down his style to its rhythmic essentials, refusing to spray notes all over the place at random and as a result, the record cooks and dances. His treatment of Vince Guaraldi's "Cast Your Fate to the Wind," hugely complemented by Joe Farrell's wistfully prancing flute, is a mini-masterpiece in the use of space, of hitting exactly the right stabbing note right in the pocket. Again, Creed Taylor turns to a James Brown alumnus, David Matthews, for arrangements, and he discreetly and wisely stays out of Bad George's way. Buy this one for "Cast Your Fate" but there is plenty more to savor here (the CD also includes "Hold On, I'm Comin'" as a bonus!). —*Richard S. Ginell*

Breezin' / Jan. 6, 1976-Jan. 9, 1976 / Warner Brothers ✦✦✦

All of a sudden, George Benson became a pop superstar with this album, thanks to its least representative track. Most of *Breezin'* is a softer-focused variation of Benson's R&B/jazz-flavored CTI work, his guitar as assured and fluid as ever with Claus Ogerman providing the suave orchestral backdrops and his crack then-working band (including Ronnie Foster on keyboards and sparkplug Phil

Upchurch on rhythm guitar) pumping up the funk element. Yet it is the sole vocal track (his first in many years), Leon Russell's "This Masquerade"—where George unveiled his new trademark, scatting along with a single-string guitar solo—that reached No. 10 on the pop singles charts and drove the album all the way to No. 1 on the pop (!) LP charts. The attractive title track also became a minor hit single, although Gabor Szabo's 1971 recording with composer Bobby Womack is even more fetching. In the greater scheme of Benson's career, this is really not so much a breakthrough as it is a transition album; the guitar is still the core of his identity. —*Richard S. Ginell*

The Best of George Benson [Warner Brothers] / Jan. 1976-1986 / Warner Brothers ++

Warner Bros.' second Benson compilation, unlike *Collection*, only draws from the label's own catalogue, so by definition, it is a less representative sampler. And even then, it does not give a thorough overview of Benson's 17-year tenure at Warner Bros. Understandably for a Best Of album, it concentrates on such hot-selling Benson vocal hits as "This Masquerade," "Give Me the Night," "Turn Your Love Around" and "On Broadway." Yet there is not so much as a single instrumental—which borders upon the criminal—nor anything from Benson's last five Warners albums, the last three of which (*Tenderly, Big Boss Band, Love Remembers*) contain a good deal of his best mature work, if not any hits. For those only interested in George Benson, chartmaker, this will do. Otherwise, pass right by. —*Richard S. Ginell*

Benson & Farrell / Mar. 1976-Sep. 1976 / Columbia +++

This little-known CTI recording matches guitarist George Benson and Joe Farrell, a multi-reed player who mostly sticks to flute. Joined by a large rhythm section and sometimes two other flutists (including Eddie Daniels), Benson and Farrell play four originals by session arranger Dave Matthews, plus the standard "Old Devil Moon." This pleasing if not all that memorable instrumental date was recorded right after Benson's *Breezin'* (and before its release), ending the guitarist's CTI period right before he became a vocal star. —*Scott Yanow*

In Flight / Aug. 1976-Nov. 1976 / Warner Brothers +++

In the wake of "This Masquerade," the balance of power now shifts for the first time toward Benson's suddenly marketable side; four of the six tracks are vocals. By this time, Benson was tailoring his tenor toward soulful pitch-bending à la Stevie Wonder on tunes as diverse as "Nature Boy" and "The World Is a Ghetto," and the unison scatting with the guitar that caught fire with the public on "Masquerade" is now pulled out whenever possible. Benson's backing band from *Breezin'*, still set in its funk mode, is intact, and Claus Ogerman again contributes gentle orchestral cushions. The two instrumentals, particularly Donny Hathaway's "Valdez in the Country," prove that Benson remained a brilliantly inventive melodist on guitar, in full possession of his powers. Yet there is every indication here that Benson was set upon becoming primarily a pop star. —*Richard S. Ginell*

The George Benson Collection / 1976-1981 / Warner Brothers +++

In order to produce what it thought would be a definitive two-LP retrospective on Benson, Warner Bros. raided not only its own archives but also those of A&M, Arista and CTI. For added sales appeal, Warners inserted two new recordings, one of which ("Turn Your Love Around") became another huge hit single, rising to No. 5 on the pop charts. Today, *Collection* remains the most inclusive Benson sampler, though far from a definitive one due in part to the scarcity of instrumentals. Of course, the big Warner Bros. vocal hits are here ("This Masquerade," "On Broadway," "Give Me the Night"), plus an artistic triumph like "Moody's Mood," but only one WB instrumental ("Breezin'") can be heard. From Arista, it's strictly pop—"The Greatest Love of All" and the duet with Aretha Franklin, "Love All the Hurt Away." The A&M choices "Last Train to Clarksville" and "Here Comes the Sun," could have been better but the two CTIs, "White Rabbit" and the great "Cast Your Fate to the Wind," are excellent representatives. Unfortunately, when it came time to squeeze *Collection* onto one CD, Warners in its corporate wisdom chose to delete one cut—and wouldn't you know, it was "Cast Your Fate"! In other words, hunt for the LPs. —*Richard S. Ginell*

The Best of George Benson: The Instrumentals / 1976-1993 / Warner Brothers ++++

Anyone who despaired about the total lack of instrumentals on Warner's unrepresentative *The Best of George Benson* will be overjoyed by this sequel, which contains nothing but instrumentals (that may have been the game plan all along). Admittedly, the instrumental pickings in the Warner catalog are slimmer than, say, those for Benson's pre-"This Masquerade" recordings on CBS/CTI and A&M/Verve, and the style is often slanted toward the kind of easy jazz heard on *The Wave* radio format. But Benson could still create funky fireworks with his guitar on tunes like "Dinorah, Dinorah," "Affirmation," and "Weekend In L.A.," and Benson's off-the-cuff fluency is shown off to stunning effect all alone on "Tenderly." The range of albums is more inclusive than that of the earlier set, spanning Ben-

son's long Warner period and even reaching out to the funky-butt title track from his first GRP album, *That's Right*. If you combine this album and the vocal *Best Of* collection, you'll get an excellent summary of George Benson over a span of 20 years. —*Richard S. Ginell*

Livin' Inside Your Love / Feb. 1, 1977 / Warner Brothers +++

The success of *Weekend in L.A.* no doubt prompted producer Tommy LiPuma and Warner Bros. to give Benson another double album (now on one CD)—and this, like its three Warners predecessors, also went Top Ten. It is also, alas, slicker, more romantic in mood and more bound by perceptions of formula than the others, fussed over in three different studios in earnest search of another hit single (the dance-tempo cover of L.T.D.'s "Love Ballad"). Most of the touring band, including Ronnie Foster, Ralph MacDonald and Phil Upchurch, is back, and Claus Ogerman's soft symphonic touch provides most of the backdrops, with Mike Mainieri supplying the orchestra on three tracks. Even at this point, the great guitarist is still given much room to burn—the balance between instrumentals and vocals remains close—and George comes up with some tasty stuff when the rhythm section pushes him on "Nassau Day" and "You're Never Too Far from Me." Ultimately there is just enough jazz content amidst the velvet soul to keep guitar buffs interested. —*Richard S. Ginell*

Weekend in L A / Sep. 30, 1977-Oct. 2, 1977 / Warner Brothers ++++

Recording live at Los Angeles' Roxy club—then a showcase for many of the hottest acts in pop—was just the tonic that Benson and his *Breezin'* band needed on this often jumping double LP set (reissued on one CD). With unusually lively crowds (for a record industry watering hole) shouting encouragement, the band gets deep into the four-on-the-floor funk and Benson digs in hard, his rhythmic instincts on guitar sharp as ever. The balance between vocals and instrumentals is about even—George's voice sounds more throaty and soul oriented than before—and amidst the new material, there is a revisit to a favored CTI-era instrumental, the lovely "Ode to a Kudu." This album also introduced "On Broadway," an extended stomping version of the Drifters' hit that has become Benson's climactic showstopper to this day. The only superfluous element is the after-the-fact addition of Nick De Caro's string synthesizer backdrop; the real Claus Ogerman-arranged thing would have been preferable if we must have strings. —*Richard S. Ginell*

In Your Eyes / 1978 / Warner Brothers ++

In search of more platinum, Benson turns to one time Atlantic Records ace producer Arif Mardin for support. Yet Mardin's best days seemed to be behind him, as this mostly routine package of period R&B backbeats, synthesizer rhythm tracks and love songs indicates. Any competent soul vocalist could have fit in comfortably here. For jazz fans, Benson's albums at this point become a search for buried treasure, for his guitar time is extremely limited. But when you do encounter a Benson solo, hang on tight. "Love Will Come Again," otherwise a routine soul bumper, concludes with a magnificent solo in octaves that Wes Montgomery would have envied, breathtaking in its economy and swing. Also, check out the instrumental "In Search of a Dream" for proof that George could still burn. —*Richard S. Ginell*

● **Give Me the Night** / 1980 / Warner Brothers +++++

This is the peak of Benson's courtship of the mass market—a superbly crafted and performed pop album with a large supporting cast—and wouldn't you know that Quincy Jones, the master catalyst, is the producer. Q's regular team, including the prolific songwriter Rod Temperton and the brilliant engineer Bruce Swedien, is in control, and Benson's voice, caught beautifully in the rich, floating sound, had never before been put to such versatile use. On "Moody's Mood," Benson really exercises his vocalese chops and proves that he is technically as fluid as just about any jazz vocalist, and he becomes a credible rival to Al Jarreau on the joyous title track. Benson's guitar now plays a subsidiary role—only two of the ten tracks are instrumentals—but Q has him play terrific fills behind the vocals and in the gaps, and the engineering gives his tone a variety of striking, new, full-sounding timbres. The instrumentals themselves are marvelous. "Off Broadway" is a kick driving, danceable and Ivan Lins' "Dinorah, Dinorah" grows increasingly seductive with each play. Benson should have worked with Quincy Jones from this point on, but this would be their only album together. —*Richard S. Ginell*

20/20 / 1984 / Warner Brothers ++

George Benson certainly is a good soul vocalist, fervently turning every phrase as if he meant every lovelorn syllable. Here, though, he is shackled by stale pop-soul sentiments and one hack arrangement after another, assembled in no less than 17 studios! Russ Titelman, who shows only a flickering awareness of George's huge talent, is the producer, spelled twice by the even more commercial Michael Masser. The only bright spots are the tense high-tech title track and—surprise—an elegant Basie-like treatment of "Beyond the Sea," with several jazz luminaries in the all-star band and Frank Foster and Ralph Burns handling the chart. Only one instrumental, "Stand Up," and it ain't much. —*Richard S. Ginell*

While the City Sleeps / 1986 / Warner Brothers ♦♦

The transformation of George Benson, guitar icon, into George Benson, pop singer, is completed here, for there are no instrumentals at all on this hard-sell, synth-laden series of ballads and dance tunes. This is marginally better than *20/20*, for at least Narada Michael Walden's high-tech production (with added tracks by Kashif and Tommy LiPuma) has more punch, and the material, though still mostly lame, is easier to take. There is very little guitar to be heard, and what little there is can usually be found hidden behind Benson's scatting or the pulsating electronics. The best bet for ferreting out some strong guitar is on "Love Is Here Tonight," but it's deep within the mix. For those who care, an animated Kenny G. turns up on "Did You Hear Thunder." —*Richard S. Ginell*

Collaboration / 1987 / Warner Brothers ♦♦♦

Benson rebels against the machine and comes out with an all-instrumental album, his first in 11 years and also his first full teaming with onetime protege, acoustic guitarist Earl Klugh. Klugh sounds much more mature and forthcoming here than he did as a teenager in Benson's CTI days. Yet George still blows him away with his effortless swing, endless invention (within the constraints of the carefully controlled arrangements, though) and totally assured placement of the notes. "Mimosa" has some especially fluid work by Benson, with Klugh serving as an effective foil. The backing is mostly an electronic wash, though underpinned by solid funk support from former Benson band members Harvey Mason and Paulinho Da Costa. The biggest hangup are the so-so tunes, which both guitarists gratefully transcend whenever they solo. While *Collaboration* disappointed many guitar fans back in 1987 who were hoping for a more energetic session, time has underlined and strengthened its musical virtues. —*Richard S. Ginell*

Twice the Love / 1988 / Warner Brothers ♦♦

In what Benson claimed was a risk, he works with six different production teams, but if diversity was the goal, the result is just the same homogenized, synth/electronic-drum-laden, pop-soul sound geared toward someone's perception of what the market would bear. Benson sings well as always but again, the biggest problem, as has been the case from *In Your Eyes* onward, is crummy song material. Without Benson's improvising guitar to take the music somewhere else, all you have left are the so-called tunes—and brother, that's not a lot. The one blast of fresh air is Curtis Mayfield's oldie "Let's Do It Again," which has a nice groove, and "You're Still My Baby," the sole instrumental, finds the Benson guitar in good shape, if not terribly challenged. "Everybody does it but that don't make it right," sing the voices on one cut—a fitting epitaph for this album's attempt to chase the charts. —*Richard S. Ginell*

Tenderly / 1989 / Warner Brothers ♦♦♦♦♦

Apparently Benson got the message. Giving up the fruitless search for decent contemporary material, he switched gears and recorded an album of old standards with top-grade jazz musicians (including pianist McCoy Tyner and bassist Ron Carter) and Marty Paich's classy string and brass charts. With good songs to sing, Benson gives some moving performances, particularly on "This Is All I Ask," and there is a lovely reminder of his affinity for the Beatles, "Here There and Everywhere." Moreover, his jazz instincts were fully at his command; you'll hear some remarkable Latin-slanted guitar work on "At the Mambo Inn," some brilliant bebop on "Stella by Starlight" and "I Could Write a Book," and a stunning solo performance of "Tenderly" itself. One could read a bit of calculation into all of this; a Benson riposte to all those critics who thought he'd never play bebop again, an attempt by his record company to pander to an aging fan base. But don't. Enjoy the music, some of the best Benson has made in the last decade. —*Richard S. Ginell*

Big Boss Band / 1990 / Warner Brothers ♦♦♦♦

This project had its genesis back in 1983 with a Benson promise to Count Basie that he would record an album in his style, a promise partially fulfilled the following year with *20/20*'s "Beyond the Sea." Focusing on standards that steer commendably clear from tunes normally associated with Basie, Benson takes on the dual challenge of big-band singer and lead guitarist and succeeds with authority in both roles. The robust playing of the Basie band under Frank Foster poses absolutely no problems for Benson's muscular guitar, for he punches out the notes and octaves in irresistibly swinging fashion (for prime mature Benson, check out "Basie's Bag"). As a vocalist, he sounds solid and debonair, blending well with Basie vocalist Carmen Bradford on "How Do You Keep the Music Playing." There are two deviations from the format, though. "Baby Workout" starts out as an electronic dance number, augmented by horns, that harkens back to his run of routine '80s albums. The sole Robert Farnon-arranged track, a lush orchestral treatment of "Portrait of Jennie" recorded in London, was salvaged from an aborted project that was promised back in 1988. Clearly Benson had wrestled control of his music from the accountants, and though the direction is conservative, it makes better use of his talents. —*Richard S. Ginell*

Love Remembers / 1993 / Warner Brothers ♦♦

There is no significant jazz on this effort from guitarist/singer George Benson, just rather routine R&B vamps and ballads. Benson uses his guitar mostly as a prop and an occasional contrast to the rather dull grooves. Even the instrumentals are forgettable and this music, even when rated as pop or R&B, deserves a low rating for its lack of originality and strong melodies. —*Scott Yanow*

That's Right / 1996 / GRP ♦♦♦

George Benson may have changed labels with *That's Right*, but he didn't change his approach. Like his other '90s albums, *That's Right* is jazz-inflected quiet-storm soul. It's quietly funky and always grooving, whether he's playing a light uptempo number or a silky ballad. As always, Benson's tone is smooth and supple—it's a pleasure to hear him play, even if the material he has selected doesn't always showcase his ample skills. In fact, the unevenness in material is the very thing that keeps *That's Right* from being on par with Benson's early '80s contemporary soul records. Although the sound is right, and Benson's heart is clearly in it, he just doesn't have quite enough memorable melodies to make the album thoroughly engaging. Still, the joy that is readily apparent within his performance makes *That's Right* a worthy acquisition for fans of Benson's latter-day recordings. —*Thom Owens*

Bob Berg

b. Apr. 7, 1951, New York, NY
Tenor Saxophone, Soprano Saxophone / Hard Bop, Post-Bop

A fine tenor and soprano saxophonist most influenced by Wayne Shorter, Bob Berg studied at the High School of Performing Arts and Juilliard. Although he was originally attracted to free jazz, by 1969 (when he joined Jack McDuff), Berg was more intrigued by bop. He had stints with Horace Silver (1974-76) and Cedar Walton (1976-81), spent a couple years (1981-83) in Europe and then was with Miles Davis' electric group during 1984-86. Associated on an occasional basis with Chick Corea, Berg has mostly appeared in hard bop settings, recording as a leader early on for Xanadu, Red and more recently for Denon, Red and Stretch. —*Scott Yanow*

New Birth / May 12, 1978 / Xanadu ♦♦♦♦

Tenor saxophonist Bob Berg's debut as a leader is mostly in the bop vein although he does his best to break down the boundaries a bit. With trumpeter Tom Harrell sharing the front line and Cedar Walton (on both acoustic and electric piano) heading the fine rhythm section, Berg performs four group originals, the classic ballad "You're My Thrill" and a reworking of "This Masquerade." It's an impressive debut for the young tenor. —*Scott Yanow*

Steppin': Live in Europe / Dec. 8, 1982 / Red ♦♦♦

Short Stories / Mar. 1987 / Denon ♦♦♦

Bob Berg's third release as a leader (released on a Japanese Denon CD) was his first fairly commercial date. Doubling on tenor and soprano but not sounding too distinctive on either, Berg performs eight funky group originals with a sextet also including keyboardist Don Grolnick, guitarist Mike Stern, bassist Will Lee, drummer Peter Erskine and Robby Kilgore on additional keyboards; altoist David Sanborn drops by to add some heat to "Kalimba." The R&B-ish music is very much of the period and sounds a bit dated now, but has its moments of interest due to the high musicianship of the players. —*Scott Yanow*

Cycles / Jun. 17, 1988-Jun. 26, 1988 / Denon ♦♦♦

The follow-up recording to Berg's first Denon release, *Short Stories*, *Cycles* carries on the legacy with even more convincing results. Featured are Mike Stern (g) and Dennis Chambers (d). —*Paul Kohler*

In the Shadows / 1990 / Denon ♦♦

On his third Denon release Berg ventures into a few jazz standards while maintaining a strong hold on his fusion roots. Jim Beard is featured on keyboards. —*Paul Kohler*

Back Roads / 1991 / Denon ♦♦♦♦

One of the Bobs who has been greatly influenced by Michael Brecker—the others include Bob Shepherd, Bob Mintzer and Bob Malach—Bob Berg has one of his strongest and most inspired efforts in *Back Roads*. Although Jim Beard is heard on synthesizers in addition to acoustic piano and electric guitarist Mike Stern doesn't shy away from rock elements, the album isn't really fusion per se so much as "straightahead" post-bop with electric references. Varied and unpredictable, this CD ranges from the intense ("Silverado") to the haunting ("Travelin' Man") to the congenial ("American Gothic"). Whatever the mood, Berg's inspired tenor has sympathetic and flexible support in the ubiquitous drummer Dennis Chambers. —*Alex Henderson*

Virtual Reality / Aug. 1992 / Denon ♦♦

This CD is a disappointment. Many of the selections use unimaginative funk rhythms and Berg (on tenor and soprano) comes across as an anonymous blending of Ernie Watts and Michael Brecker. In addition, this has to be about the dumbest version of "Can't Help Lovin' That Man" that has ever been recorded. There are some good solos from Berg here and there but not enough to justify the purchase of this set. —*Scott Yanow*

● **Enter the Spirit** / 1993 / Stretch ✦✦✦✦
Although Bob Berg has still not developed a strikingly original tone, his talents on tenor and soprano are so consistent as to be taken for granted. With either Chick Corea, David Kikoski or Jim Beard on keyboards, Berg is in fine form on this quartet session which is highlighted by two of Corea's tunes, "Sometime Ago" and Sonny Rollins' "No Moe," the latter a duet with drummer Dennis Chambers. —*Scott Yanow*

Riddles / Apr. 29, 1994-May 10, 1994 / GRP ✦✦✦
Bob Berg, whose tenor playing often hints at Michael Brecker, is heard leading a medium-sized group (ranging from five to seven pieces) that often includes Gil Goldstein's accordion and Jim Beard's keyboards on this CD. The music is a bit poppish in spots but the solos are of a generally high caliber with Berg sounding most original on soprano. —*Scott Yanow*

Unchained / Aug. 1, 1995 / ITM ✦✦✦

Another Standard / 1997 / Stretch ✦✦✦✦

Shelly Berg

Piano / Hard Bop
Although he has achieved some recognition as the president of the International Association of Jazz Educators and as a teacher, Shelly Berg's powerhouse piano playing has thus far been generally overlooked due to him not recording often enough. Inspired by his father, trumpeter Jay Berg, Shelly at the age of six was accepted at the Cleveland Institute of Music. He started playing professionally when he was 13, playing both classical music and jazz. Moving to Houston with his family when he was 15, Berg played regularly with Arnett Cobb and various all-stars passing through town. He turned down a job with Woody Herman to finish his education. After graduating from the University of Houston, Berg played locally with a variety of groups including with the Brass Connection. He became a respected music educator at San Jacinto College in Texas before moving to Los Angeles in 1991 to teach at USC. Shelly Berg appears occasionally in Los Angeles clubs, often playing with Bill Watrous' groups, and in 1996 he recorded a fine trio set for DMP. —*Scott Yanow*

The Joy / 1995 / DMP ✦✦✦✦
For this fine straightahead trio set, the talented if somewhat obscure pianist Shelly Berg performs five standards and seven originals with bassist Lou Fischer and either Randy Drake or Steve Houghton on drums. The music swings in conventional fashion with the high points including "Star Eyes," "How Deep Is the Ocean" and "Here's That Rainy Day." —*Scott Yanow*

Karl Berger

b. Mar. 30, 1935, Heidelberg, Germany
Piano, Vibes / Avant-Garde, Post-Bop
Karl Berger cites Ornette Coleman as a close friend and mentor; Coleman's ways of playing jazz are certainly reflected in Berger's concept, more so than any other vibist one could name. Berger eschews four-mallet technique; his style is all single-line, with little (if any) chordal playing. Berger's compositions are brief, songlike free-bop heads in the manner of Ornette, with free/modal solo sections sandwiched in between the theme statements. At his best, Berger's improvisations have much in common with his tunes; they are strongly and logically rhythmic, played over a swinging pulse, and mostly tied to tonal centers. Like Coleman, Berger is not as radical in the hearing as one might expect; both their musics are based on the core elements of swing and coherent melody. Although his fleet melodic sense carries over from the vibes, Berger's piano work is not as interesting, if only because his technique is less sure—the firm touch and solid time that characterizes his vibe playing are not as apparent.

Berger began playing piano in his native Germany at the age of ten. As a young adult, he landed a gig as house pianist for jam sessions at Club 54 in Heidelberg. There he accompanied such visiting American players as Leo Wright, Lex Humphries, and Don Ellis—learning, in the process, the complexities of modern jazz. Eventually, he took up vibes and in the early '60s developed an interest in free jazz. Berger earned a Ph.D. in musicology in 1963; two years later, he joined Don Cherry's Paris-based quintet. The group traveled to New York in 1966 to record *Symphony for Improvisers* on Blue Note. Berger stayed in the US and recorded his first album under his own name for ESP later that year. From 1967-71, Berger played educational demonstrations in public schools with the pianist Horace Arnold's group, and led his own ensembles. In 1972, he and Coleman formed the Creative Music Studio in Woodstock, NY. The school was geared toward encouraging young students to explore their own creative ideas, rather

than imposing traditional jazz concepts upon them. Teachers at the school at various times included Jack DeJohnette, Sam Rivers, and Anthony Braxton, among many other prominent musicians. In the summer of 1982, Berger led a 28-piece big band at a "Jazz and World Music" concert as part of that year's Kool Jazz Festival in New York. Berger cut back on his teaching, shutting down the Creative Music School in the mid-'80s. Consequently, he seemed to become more active as a player, embarking on a world tour in 1985-86, during which he served as a guest conductor and composer for the West German Radio Orchestra in Cologne. Berger also participated in percussion festivals in New Delhi and Bombay, and served as a pianist in a duo with the African percussionist Baba Olatunji. Berger has not recorded prolifically, though he has worked as a sideman on sessions with guitarist John McLaughlin, saxophonist Lee Konitz, and bassist Alan Silva. He also played on Carla Bley's late-'60s recording of "Escalator over the Hill." Berger's recordings as leader are scarce, though 1987's *Transit* (with Ed Blackwell and Dave Holland), and 1990s *Around*—both on Black Saint—are available and worth seeking out. —*Chris Kelsey*

Karl Berger Quartet / Dec. 8, 1966 / ESP ✦✦✦

All Kinds of Time / Apr. 26, 1976 / Sackville ✦✦✦
Relatively few of Karl Berger's recordings have been made available in the US (he has lived most of his life in his native Germany), but this Sackville release has generally been one of the easier ones to acquire. A set of rather dry duets with bassist Dave Holland, Berger is heard interpreting five of his originals on vibes, piano and balafon, showing originality and taking chances on each of his instruments. —*Scott Yanow*

Live at the Donaueschingen Festival / Oct. 1979 / MPS ✦✦✦✦✦
Definitive Berger originals are done live in Germany with the Woodstock Workshop Orchestra, a combination of Creative Music Studio students and instructors. —*Michael G. Nastos*

● **Transit** / Aug. 25, 1988-Aug. 16, 1988 / Black Saint ✦✦✦✦✦
An innovative vibraphonist who has traveled his own musical path throughout his career, Karl Berger is heard on this Black Saint release performing seven of his diverse pieces in trios with bassist Dave Holland and the colorful drummer Ed Blackwell. Many moods are explored, there is a feature for Blackwell and also a tribute piece for Ornette Coleman. Recommended as an excellent example of Karl Berger's inside/outside playing. —*Scott Yanow*

Around / May 9, 1990-May 10, 1990 / Black Saint ✦✦✦

Crystal Fire / Apr. 4-5, 1991 / Enja ✦✦✦✦

Borah Bergman

Piano / Avant-Garde, Free Jazz
Early in his career, it was typical for jazz critics to compare the extraordinary free jazz pianist Borah Bergman to Cecil Taylor. Lately, however, critics now regularly point out the folly in such comparisons, perpetuating the very same juxtaposition, instead of listening to Bergman abstracted from such concerns. Though Bergman himself claims Tristano, Monk, and Powell as influences, he rates comparison with nobody, so singular is his ability as an improvising pianist. Bergman has perhaps the most comprehensive technique of any jazz musician on any instrument. His facility is nonpareil with both hands. Bergman can improvise spontaneous free counterpoint at unfathomable speeds and with remarkable precision. His utterly personal style is due in no small part to his own technical innovations; no pianist in the history of jazz has ever developed more speed and agility in his left hand. Additionally, Bergman has refined a technique of playing with crossed hands that augments his fluency to an even greater degree. Bergman's greatest attributes are, however, the staggering quality and quantity of his ideas, and the ineffable intensity with which he executes those ideas. Bergman is of a kind with the very greatest jazz musicians in terms of originality and inspiration. The only reason now to weigh him against Cecil Taylor is to place the two artists on the same level of creative accomplishment.

Bergman played clarinet as a child, but didn't begin on piano until in his twenties. Bergman determined right away that he wanted to develop an individual voice. As he told the writer Francis Davis, "I knew there was no point in sounding almost as good as Bud Powell." The right-handed Bergman worked for years in strengthening his left hand. For a time, he practiced playing left-handed almost exclusively. Eventually—as a pianist, at least—he became ambidextrous.

Bergman began recording late as well. His first four albums were solo efforts; the first, *Discovery*, was released in 1975 on the Chiaroscuro label. Three more would follow, including 1983's *A New Frontier* and 1985's *Upside Down Visions*, both on Soul Note. In 1992, the pianist began a series of successful duo collaborations. The first was *Inversions* on the Muworks label, with the young free-bop altoist Thomas Chapin. Following that came a pair of Soul Note albums that cemented Bergman's reputation, 1993's *The Human Factor* with drummer Andrew

Cyrille, and 1994's *The Fire Tale,* with soprano saxophonist Evan Parker. The latter album was especially powerful, matching as it did two of the most formidable improvisers in jazz. Recent albums include a duo/trio recording with saxophonist Roscoe Mitchell and vocalist Thomas Buckner, a trio with saxophonists Peter Brotzman and Thomas Borgmann, and another trio with Brotzman and Cyrille. As the '90s draw to a close, Bergman's recorded output continues to rise substantially, as does his profile as one of the music's major contributors. —*Chris Kelsey*

Bursts of Joy / 1976 / Chiaroscuro ✦✦✦

A New Frontier / Jan. 1983 / Soul Note ✦✦✦

The similarities in style between pianist Borah Bergman and Cecil Taylor cannot be denied. Bergman, like Taylor, assaults, cajoles, and fully explores the instrument; there's nothing mild or polite about the way he rips through chords, develops spiraling, teeming two-handed statements, or barrels through the octaves with each hand making its own furious phrases. This contains two lengthy pieces, each broken into movements. This is intense solo piano that requires just as committed and concentrated an effort from the audience as the performer in order to appreciate and follow the direction. —*Ron Wynn*

The Fire Tale / Mar. 18, 1990-Mar. 20, 1990 / Soul Note ✦✦✦✦

A showdown between the two players with the most comprehensive techniques in jazz—Borah Bergman and Evan Parker. As a pianist, Bergman breaks down all distinctions between the left and right hands; his style is a multilayered counterpoint of extreme sophistication and complexity. The equally hyper-dextrous Parker comes as close as any saxophonist ever has to playing counterpoint on a single-line instrument. At full steam, Parker's soprano lines are a continuous, mercuric flow, covering all registers of the horn, segmented by his incredibly fleet and precise articulations. These players do not really complement one another—in many ways, they're just too much alike—but neither is likely to find another so technically advanced. Scary and brilliant music. —*Chris Kelsey*

● **The Human Factor** / Jun. 1992 / Soul Note ✦✦✦✦✦

Borah Bergman is perhaps the most technically accomplished pianist in jazz—and if he's not at the top, then he's certainly on a short list of two. Bergman's probably best known for his extreme ambidexterity; his left hand is as melodically active as his right, to the point that the pianist frequently crosses them, one over the other, as he plays. Of course, Bergman's incredible technique sets him apart, but more of what makes him such a consummate improviser is his sense of organization within a free context. Bergman plays with a rhythmic insistence that's unlike virtually any other improviser on any instrument. He has an almost obsessive manner of motivic development that both holds together the music and moves it forward. On this set of duets with the very able percussionist Andrew Cyrille, Bergman's treatment of "Chasin' the Trane" is a quintessential example. Throughout his densely percussive improvisation, the pianist interpolates fragments of Coltrane's melody, using them concurrently as a point of reference, and as source material for further elaboration. The result is an unusually well-balanced music that sounds almost as if it could have been composed, were it not for the essential spontaneity and intensity lent by the improvising's reflexive nature. It seems as if most of Bergman's recorded performances have been duos; this one with Cyrille is as good as any, which is to say that it's quite marvelous. The drummer is everything a Bergman foil needs to be—sensitive and reactive, with an almost boundless range. Cyrille complements Bergman's various guises, whether it be the rather blunt, slightly skewed romanticism of the pianist's ballad, "When Autumn Comes," or the fervent tumult of the two "Chasin' the Trane'"s. A superb teaming, and a terrific album. —*Chris Kelsey*

First Meeting / Dec. 19, 1994 / Knitting Factory ✦✦✦✦

This duo meeting between Borah Bergman and saxophonist Roscoe Mitchell (vocalist Thomas Buckner joins in on the last few tracks) is, on its face, a meeting of opposites. Bergman is usually thought of in terms of his emphatic statements; Mitchell is known for the restrained hesitancy of his work. Preconceptions get the shaft on this record, however, especially where Bergman's concerned. The pianist shows that he's just as comfortable in stressing the use of space as he is in obliterating it. The title track's opening minutes are a paradigm of the creative use of silence. Inevitably, the two cut loose, with Mitchell unleashing his cascades of unbroken chromaticism, and Bergman engaging in his characteristic two-handed intervallic gymnastics. The resulting music is fraught with contrasts—the strength and agility of Bergman's bass lines underneath the diffident simplicity of Mitchell's barely sounded alto on "Deep Delta," for instance. A most thoughtful album marked by episodes of laconic austerity. —*Chris Kelsey*

Reflections on Ornette Coleman and the Stone House / Mar. 23, 1995 / Soul Note ✦✦✦✦✦

Jerry Bergonzi

b. 1950, Boston, MA

Tenor Saxophone / Post-Bop, Bop

A fine high-powered tenor saxophonist with a tone influenced by John Coltrane, a mastery of chord changes, and a strong musical imagination, Jerry Bergonzi has long had an underground following in the Boston area. He started on clarinet when he was eight, switching to alto at 12 and finally to tenor two years later. Bergonzi was inspired early on by Sonny Rollins, Coltrane and Hank Mobley. He attended Lowell University and then after graduation played electric bass in local bands behind singers and strippers, saving up enough money to move to New York in 1972. After struggling in the Big Apple for seven years and gaining some recognition as a member of Two Generations of Brubeck and of the Dave Brubeck Quartet (with whom he appeared on several Concord albums during 1979-81), Bergonzi moved back to Boston in 1981, where he developed a strong career both as a tenorman and as an educator. He has since led several groups (including two called Con Brio and Gonz) and recorded for the Plug, Not Fat, Red and Blue Note labels. —*Scott Yanow*

Con Brio / Oct. 1982+Mar. 1983 / Plug ✦✦✦✦

Tenor saxophonist Jerry Bergonzi's debut as a leader finds him heading a particularly strong group that also features guitarist Mick Goodrick, bassist Bruce Gertz and drummer Jeff Williams. Bergonzi was starting to shed his John Coltrane influence, his interplay with the sidemen is impressive (hearing Goodrick in this setting is a treat), and the six originals (four by Bergonzi and two by Gertz) are diverse and challenging enough to make this small-label LP worth searching for by post-bop collectors. —*Scott Yanow*

● **Featuring Bruce Gertz** / 1984-1985 / Not Fat ✦✦✦✦✦

Uranian Undertow / May 1986 / Plug ✦✦✦✦

Jerry Bergonzi has long had an underground reputation among saxophonists due to his brilliant technique and ability to build on some of the ideas of John Coltrane. His set finds his group of the era, Gonz, performing as a stripped-down trio also including bassist Bruce Gertz and drummer Gullotti. Bergonzi contributed six of the seven pieces, some of which get into an eccentric and catchy groove; all serve as strong vehicles for impressive musical communication between the three musicians. —*Scott Yanow*

Caught in the Act! / Mar. 1988 / Not Fat ✦✦✦✦

From 1982-88, Jerry Bergonzi and his groups (Con Brio and Gonz) recorded frequently for first the Plug and then the Not Fat label; the former releases were reissued by the latter company. This live set (recorded in Australia) was the final album before the underrated tenor began making records for Red. Bergonzi, bassist Bruce Gertz and drummer Bob Gullotti were joined by Gonz's newest member, the talented young pianist Salvatore Bonafede. They perform Bergonzi's sly "Arbonius Unt" (dedicated to you-know-who), John Coltrane's "Moment's Notice," and a lengthy version of "Softly, As in a Morning Sunrise." Despite the length of the renditions, the soloing (particularly by the fiery Bergonzi) holds one's interest throughout. —*Scott Yanow*

On Red / May 1988 / Red ✦✦✦

Inside Out / 1989 / Red ✦✦✦

Lineage / Oct. 15, 1989 / Red ✦✦✦

Standard Gonz / Oct. 19, 1989-Apr. 5, 1990 / Blue Note ✦✦✦✦✦

Jerry Bergonzi has always been strongly influenced by the sound of John Coltrane circa 1960-63. But despite the derivative nature of his style, this is an enjoyable CD. Bergonzi really has 'Trane down, and he tears into the pieces with all of his fire and creativity. "If I Were a Bell," normally a lighthearted song, is here quite dissonant, the tenorman's "McCoy" has a melody reminiscent of "Bessie's Blues" and a groove closer to "Dahomey's Dance," and "Night and Day" was altered to accommodate the chord changes of "Giant Steps." Even Bergonzi's originals sound to certain degrees like they are taken from the John Coltrane songbook. The rhythm section (pianist Joey Calderazzo, bassist Dave Santoro and drummer Adam Nussbaum) is fine in support (McCoy Tyner is one of Calderazzo's influences), but this is essentially Bergonzi's show. —*Scott Yanow*

Tilt / May 1990 / Red ✦✦✦

Etc Plus One / Mar. 15, 1991 / Red ✦✦✦

Peek a Boo / Oct. 9, 1992-Oct. 10, 1992 / Evidence ✦✦✦

Just Within / Dec. 29, 1996-Dec. 30, 1996 / Double-Time ✦✦✦✦

Bunny Berigan (Rowland Bernart Berrigan)

b. Nov. 2, 1908, Hilbert, WI, d. Jun. 2, 1942, New York, NY
Trumpet, Vocals / Swing

Bunny Berigan during 1935-39 was arguably the top trumpeter in jazz (with his main competition being Louis Armstrong and Roy Eldridge). Blessed with a beautiful tone and a wide range (Berigan's low notes could be as memorable as his upper register shouts), Bunny brought excitement to every session he appeared on. He was not afraid to take chances during his solos and could be a bit reckless but Berigan's successes and occasional failures were always colorful to hear, at least until he drank it all away.

Bunny Berigan played in local bands and then college groups in the Midwest. He tried out for Hal Kemp's Orchestra unsuccessfully in 1928 (rejected because of his thin tone!) but showed tremendous improvement by 1930 when he was hired. After a few recordings and a trip to Europe, Bunny joined Fred Rich's CBS studio band in 1931 where (except for a few months with Paul Whiteman) he would remain up to 1935. Berigan soon gained a strong reputation as a hot jazz soloist and he appeared on quite a few records with studio bands, the Boswell Sisters and the Dorsey Brothers. In 1935 he spent a few months with Benny Goodman's Orchestra but that was enough to launch the swing era. Berigan had classic solos on Goodman's first two hit records ("King Porter Stomp" and "Sometimes I'm Happy") and was with BG as he went on his historic tour out West, climaxing in the near-riot at the Palomar Ballroom in Los Angeles.

Berigan soon returned to the more lucrative studio scene, making his only film appearance in 1936 with Fred Rich. In 1937 he joined Tommy Dorsey's band and was once again largely responsible for two hits: "Marie" and "Song of India." Bunny's solos on these tunes became so famous that in future years Dorsey had them written out and orchestrated for the full trumpet section! After leaving Dorsey, Bunny Berigan finally put together his own orchestra. He scored early on with his biggest hit "I Can't Get Started." With Georgie Auld on tenor and Buddy Rich on drums, Berigan had a potentially strong band. Unfortunately he was already an alcoholic and a reluctant businessman. By 1939 there had been many lost opportunities and the following year Bunny (who was bankrupt) was forced to break up his band. He rejoined Tommy Dorsey for a few months but never stopped drinking and was not happy being a sideman again. Soon Berigan formed a new orchestra but his health began declining and on June 2, 1942, he died when he was just 33. What would this brilliant swing trumpeter have done in the bop era?

Bunny Berigan's life is definitively profiled in Robert Dupuis' book *Elusive Legend of Jazz*. —*Scott Yanow*

Unknown Band 1939: The Sideman 1931-1933 / Jun. 15, 1931-Sep. 26, 1939 / Meritt ✦✦✦

This LP from the collector's label Meritt allows one to hear the great trumpeter Bunny Berigan at the beginning of his career and near its conclusion, a span of only eight years. The bulk of this set consists of two radio broadcasts from Sept. 20 and 26, 1939, shortly before the alcoholic Berigan was forced to break up his no-name big band. Despite the problems facing him, Berigan is in reasonable form on these airchecks, typically putting his heart into each solo. This set concludes with early solos by Berigan with recording groups led by Fred Rich, Chick Bullock and Lee Wiley. Berigan collectors will want to search for this hard-to-find LP. —*Scott Yanow*

Great Soloists / Feb. 24, 1932-Feb. 17, 1937 / Biograph ✦✦✦✦✦

The great swing trumpeter Bunny Berigan is heard in a variety of studio settings on this excellent LP. Bunny takes a hot solo with the Boswell Sisters in 1932 on "Everybody Loves My Baby," is the star of performances with the Dorsey Brothers, the Mound City Blowers and Dick McDonough, and is also heard leading his own recording groups during 1936-37. Of the latter, highlights include "It's Been So Long," "In a Little Spanish Town" and an early version of "I Can't Get Started" that contains a similar framework and trumpet solo to Bunny's famous recording. This is a good all-around set from the exciting if ill-fated trumpeter. —*Scott Yanow*

Portrait of Bunny Berigan / 1932-1936 / ASV/Living Era ✦✦✦

1992 reissue covering some mid-'30s Bunny Berigan sessions with the Dorsey Brothers, Artie Shaw, and Connie Boswell, among others. This set is weighted towards his most popular tunes, not necessarily the most jazz-oriented although everything presented rates as prime Berigan. —*Ron Wynn*

Bunny and Red / May 9, 1935-Feb. 5, 1936 / Jazz Archives ✦✦✦

During 1935-36 trumpeter Bunny Berigan made a series of little-known recordings with Red McKenzie's Mound City Blue Blowers. McKenzie, a decent singer and a hot comb player, was wise enough to give Berigan plenty of space on these 16 selections which also include some clarinet and tenor solos from Eddie Miller, Forrest Crawford and Babe Russin. Hot, if obscure, swing. —*Scott Yanow*

● The Pied Piper / Jul. 1, 1935-Aug. 3, 1940 / Bluebird ✦✦✦✦✦

This is the best single-CD compilation of Bunny Berigan recordings issued to date. Although all of the trumpeter's big-band sides for Bluebird have come out on three double LPs, this set gives more general collectors a better overview of his talents. One of the top trumpeters active during the 1935-39 period (only Louis Armstrong and the up and coming Roy Eldridge were on his level), Berigan was largely responsible for the success of important hit records for Benny Goodman ("King Porter Stomp" and "Sometimes I'm Happy") and Tommy Dorsey ("Marie" and "Song of India"), in addition to having a bestseller of his own ("I Can't Get Started"). Unfortunately, Berigan's alcoholism eventually did him in, but this CD has all of the hits, plus appearances with Gene Gifford's Orchestra (a majestic solo on "Nothin' But the Blues"), Frankie Trumbauer, jamming with Fats Waller, and with the Metronome All-Stars, plus more titles as a leader, with BG, and with Dorsey (including a radio broadcast version of "I've Found a New Baby" from 1940). This is a well-conceived reissue of important and often exciting swing by one of the greats. —*Scott Yanow*

Bunny Berigan: Leader & Sideman / 1935-Apr. 10, 1940 / Meritt ✦✦✦

The collector's label Meritt is responsible for this very interesting LP. The great swing trumpeter Bunny Berigan is heard on a broadcast version of "Sometimes I'm Happy" with Benny Goodman's Orchestra, during a short aircheck with Paul Whiteman in 1938 (with two vocals from Mildred Bailey), on an alternate take of "No Regrets" with Billie Holiday, alternates with his own big band (two of "Dixieland Shuffle" and a "new" version of "I Cried for You") and on a lengthy aircheck from April 9, 1939. Concluding this excellent set, which collectors will love, is an alternate version of "I'm Nobody's Baby" from 1940 with Tommy Dorsey's Orchestra. Every solo that Berigan (who died at age 33) took was worth hearing. —*Scott Yanow*

Sing! Sing! Sing!, Vol. 1: 1936-1938 / Jul. 20, 1936-Jun. 27, 1938 / Jass ✦✦✦✦

The first of CDs reissuing all of Bunny Berigan's radio transcriptions, this set features him with a studio orchestra on 20 selections in 1936 and with his 1938 big band for the last five numbers. In addition to Berigan (who is generally in superb form), the early tracks feature some vocals by Peggy Lawson and spots for tenor saxophonist Artie Drelinger and a clarinetist who might be Artie Shaw. The later performances give one brief glimpses of tenor saxophonist Georgie Auld and trombonist Ray Coniff. —*Scott Yanow*

Down by the Old Mill Stream / Oct. 22, 1936-1939 / Jazz Archives ✦✦✦✦

This set of radio appearances by Bunny Berigan finds the great swing trumpeter at his best. On "Down by the Old Mill Stream" he shows off his entire (and very impressive) range and the other selections (mostly from 1938) find him romping with his big band. The music on this collector's LP has not been reissued elsewhere and is well worth searching for. Hopefully it will appear on CD eventually. —*Scott Yanow*

The Complete Bunny Berigan, Vol. 1 / Apr. 1, 1937-Oct. 7, 1937 / Bluebird ✦✦✦✦✦

This two-LP set is the first of three reissues that contained all of the Victor studio recordings of the Bunny Berigan Orchestra. This initial two-fer covers a six-month period when there seemed to be a great deal of potential for this big band. Berigan's hit "I Can't Get Started" is on this set as are such near-classics as "The Prisoner's Song," "Mahogany Hall Stomp," "A Study in Brown" and "Mama I Wanna Make Rhythm." Since this is a "complete" series, there are also some turkey songs mixed in, but in general the music is swinging and very enjoyable. —*Scott Yanow*

The Complete Bunny Berigan, Vol. 2 / Oct. 7, 1937-Jun. 8, 1938 / Bluebird ✦✦

At the tail end of RCA's two-fer LP reissue series, they managed to sneak in all of Bunny Berigan's Victor recordings on three volumes. *Vol. 2* is by far the weakest (although the packaging here is beyond criticism) for, during the eight months covered by this set, Berigan's band was being given some of the worst possible material to record: tunes such as "An Old Straw Hat," "Never Felt Better, Never Had Less," "'Round the Old Deserted Farm," "I Dance Alone" and "Rinka Tinka Man." Truth be told, there are only around five or six worthwhile songs on this set of 28, but completists will want to acquire this two-fer anyway, for it will fill many gaps. —*Scott Yanow*

● The Complete Bunny Berigan, Vol. 3 / Jun. 8, 1938-Nov. 28, 1939 / RCA/Bluebird ✦✦✦✦✦

The third and final volume of two-fers that reissue all of the Bunny Berigan big band's Victor recordings is a large improvement over *Vol. 2*. Covering a chaotic 17-month period in Berigan's life (the orchestra had several disasters before collapsing completely), strangely enough, their output in 1938 seemed to improve as they went along. At one point, Berigan had strong soloists in trombonist Ray Coniff and tenor saxophonist Georgie Auld and a young Buddy Rich (who is heard here prior to joining Artie Shaw's orchestra) really propelled the ensembles. "Livery Stable Blues," "High Society," "Sobbin' Blues," "I Cried for You," "Night Song" and a six-song Bix Beiderbecke tribute set are among the high points of this excellent reissue. —*Scott Yanow*

Devil's Holiday, Vol. 2: 1938 / Jun. 27, 1938-Aug. 9, 1938 / Jass ✦✦✦✦
The second of three Jass CDs that reissue all of Berigan's radio transcriptions, this set has 15 numbers from June 27 (a consistently strong session) and 12 from August 8-9, 1938. Even with a few dull vocal numbers, the emphasis here is on hard-driving swing with his mighty trumpet, trombonist Ray Coniff, clarinetist Joe Dixon and tenor saxophonist Georgie Auld—all in fine form. It's recommended as a fine example of his exciting chance-taking style. —*Scott Yanow*

Dick Berk (Richard Alan Berk)

b. May 22, 1939, San Francisco, CA
Drums / Bop, Hard Bop
Leader of the Jazz Adoption Agency since the early '80s, Dick Berk has been important both as a stimulating drummer and as a talent scout. After attending the Berklee College of Music and playing with bands in Boston in the early '60s, he moved to New York where he performed with a quintet that included Ted Curson and Bill Barron (1962-64) plus with Charles Mingus, Mose Allison, Freddie Hubbard and Walter Bishop, Jr., among others. Relocating to Los Angeles in the late '60s, Berk worked and recorded with many top musicians including Milt Jackson, George Duke, Cal Tjader, Jean-Luc Ponty and Blue Mitchell. Berk, who eventually moved to the Pacific Northwest, has recorded sets for Discovery, Trend, 9 Winds and Reservoir; among the sidemen he has featured with his Jazz Adoption Agency have been trombonists Andy Martin and Mike Fahn, baritonist Nick Brignola, vibraphonist Jon Nagorney, pianists Keith Saunders and Tad Weed and bassist John Patitucci. —*Scott Yanow*

More Birds Less Feathers / Jan. 18, 1986 / Discovery ✦✦✦

Let's Cool One / Sep. 26, 1991 / Reservoir ✦✦✦✦

● **East Coast Stroll** / Feb. 3, 1993 / Reservoir ✦✦✦✦✦

One by One / Oct. 26, 1995 / Reservoir ✦✦✦✦

Tim Berne

b. 1954, Syracuse, NY
Alto Saxophone / Avant-Garde
One of the top avant-garde saxophonists of the 1980s and '90s, Tim Berne was even able to keep his noncompromising music intact during a short association with Columbia Records. After moving to New York in 1974 and studying with Julius Hemphill, Berne recorded a few records for his own Empire label. He later recorded for Soul Note, Columbia and JMT. Although he participated in John Zorn's Ornette Coleman tribute (*Spy vs. Spy*), Berne has mostly played as a leader, carving out his own unique path in improvised music. —*Scott Yanow*

The Five Year Plan / Apr. 25, 1979 / Empire ✦✦✦

7X / Jan. 8, 1980 / Empire ✦✦✦✦
Ever since his debut, altoist Tim Berne has pursued his own musical vision, forming an original style that is very much in the avant-garde yet not derivative of any of his predecessors. On this, his second session as a leader, Berne teams up with some of the West Coast's top musicians (including Vinnie Golia on a variety of reeds, guitarist Nels Cline and bassist Robert Miranda) to perform some very creative music that deserves more than one close listen. —*Scott Yanow*

Songs and Rituals in Real Time / Jul. 1, 1981 / Empire ✦✦✦

Ancestors / Feb. 1983 / Soul Note ✦✦✦
Tim Berne's playing on *Ancestors* is fluid, warm and conveys a relaxed levity. For this live recording Berne enlarges his regular quartet (Mack Goldsburg, tenor sax, soprano sax; Ed Schuller, bass; Paul Motian, percussion) to include Herb Robertson (trumpet) and Ray Anderson, perhaps the finest trombonist of the past five years. As usual, the tunes are all Berne originals and display the sectional and harmonic structures that so much of his music seems to exhibit. —*Bob Rusch, Cadence*

Mutant Variations / Mar. 5, 1983-Mar. 6, 1983 / Soul Note ✦✦✦✦
Definitely not part of the new traditional scene, alto saxophonist Tim Berne keeps moving forward. This 1983 quartet set of all originals is reminiscent at times of mid-'50s Ornette Coleman, notably due to Herb Robertson's pocket trumpet solos and the dynamics generated by Berne and Robertson's interaction with bassist Ed Schuller and percussionist Paul Motian. —*Ron Wynn*

Theoretically / Aug. 1983-1984 / Empire ✦✦✦✦

Fulton Street Maul / 1986 / Columbia ✦✦✦✦
How did avant-gardist Tim Berne get signed to Columbia? During his relatively brief alliance with that media giant, the passionate altoist was somehow able to continue recording his uncompromising music with apparently no real interference. On this set, he teams up with the amazing guitarist Bill Frisell, cellist Hank

Roberts and percussionist Alex Cline for five explorative pieces that one can safely bet did not receive much airplay. —*Scott Yanow*

Sanctified Dreams / Jun. 1988 / Columbia ✦✦✦
Alto saxophonist Tim Berne ranks among the more progressive players around, someone who keeps looking ahead rather than behind. This 1988 set was no different; it contains odd passages, moments of indecision, and segments where Berne and associates blazed away. —*Ron Wynn*

Fractured Fairy Tales / Jun. 1989 / JMT ✦✦✦✦
Tim Berne's music on his CD sometimes looks a little towards Anthony Braxton's free bop lines but also incorporates some electronics, unusual instrumental textures and some just plain weird sounds. Among the miscellaneous instruments listed are Mark Dresser's giffus and bungy, Herb Robertson's laryngeal crowbar and Joey Baron's shacktronics; obviously these performances are not devoid of humor. The "medley" of "Hong Kong Sad Song" and "More Coffee" features Robertson's passionate wa-wa trumpet over exotic rhythms and Tim Berne on a staccatoish alto solo. "Now Then" recalls the original Chico Hamilton Quintet. The first half of "The Telex Blues" is a good joke with a distorted nonsensical voice almost drowned out by feedback (as if it were a long-distance call that did not quite connect) although the performance does go on too long. An episodic "SEP" and the 19-minute multisectioned "Evolution of a Pearl" (which ranges from sound explorations to avant-funk) wrap up this esoteric yet listenable set. —*Scott Yanow*

Pace Yourself: Tim Berne's Caos Totale / Nov. 1990 / JMT ✦✦
Some outstanding playing; erratic songs. —*Ron Wynn*

● **Diminutive Mysteries** / Sep. 1992 / JMT ✦✦✦✦
This is certainly the most unusual David Sanborn recording to date. Avant-gardist Tim Berne (heard here on alto and baritone) and the popular R&B star Sanborn (mostly leaving his trademark alto behind to play sopranino) share a great respect for altoist Julius Hemphill and the St. Louis free jazz movement. Along with guitarist Marc Ducret, cellist Hank Roberts and drummer Joey Baron, they perform seven often-emotional Hemphill pieces plus Berne's "The Maze." Sanborn is to be congratulated for successfully stretching himself although this is very much Berne's date. —*Scott Yanow*

Nice View / Aug. 1993 / JMT ✦✦✦

Lowlife / Sep. 22, 1994-Sep. 25, 1994 / JMT ✦✦✦

Poisoned Minds / Sep. 22, 1994-Sep. 25, 1994 / JMT ✦✦✦

Warren Bernhardt

b. Nov. 1938, Wausau, WI
Piano, Keyboards / Fusion, Post-Bop
A fine soloist who is influenced by Bill Evans but has his own musical identity, Warren Bernhardt has appeared in many different settings through the years. He studied classical piano, played in Chicago while attending college and was with Paul Winter's sextet during 1961-64. After moving to New York, Bernhardt was with Gerry Mulligan, Clark Terry, George Benson and Jeremy Steig in addition to doubling as a studio musician on many pop dates. He was with Jack DeJohnette's Directions (1976) and Steps Ahead (1984-85) and has frequently led his own trios. Bernhardt has recorded several fine dates for DMP. —*Scott Yanow*

Free Smiles / Jul. 22, 1978 / Arista/Novus ✦✦✦

Floating / 1979 / Arista/Novus ✦✦✦
Warren Bernhardt's second recording as a leader (not counting the all-star *Blue Montreux* sessions) is a mostly introspective set of piano solos (six by the pianist, along with Mike Mainieri's "Song to My Father") that work equally well as background music and for close listening. —*Scott Yanow*

Trio '83 / Jan. 17, 1983-Jan. 19, 1983 / DMP ✦✦✦✦

Hands On / Oct. 17, 1986-Oct. 18, 1986 / DMP ✦✦

Heat of the Moment / Mar. 1, 1989-Mar. 5, 1989 / DMP ✦✦✦
Performing standards (such as "Love Walked In" and "In a Sentimental Mood"), obscurities, and originals, Warren Bernhardt shows off his Bill Evans influence in spots during this enjoyable DMP. Teamed with bassist Jay Anderson, drummer Peter Erskine, percussionist Gordon Gottlieb and guitarist Mike DeMicco, Bernhardt is heard throughout in excellent form playing high-quality modern mainstream jazz. —*Scott Yanow*

● **Ain't Life Grand** / Apr. 1990 / DMP ✦✦✦✦

Reflections / Dec. 1, 1991-Dec. 3, 1991 / DMP ✦✦✦
A 1991 quintet set alternating between good renditions of shopworn jazz standards and some extended blowing on original numbers. Bernhardt plays in a steady, sometimes vibrant manner while heading a group with tenor saxophonist

and clarinetist Bob Mintzer, guitarist Chuck Loeb, bassist Jay Anderson, and drummer Jeff Hirshfield. It was cut live at Carriage House in Stamford, CT. —*Ron Wynn*

Bill Berry (William R. Berry)

b. Sep. 14, 1930, Benton Harbor, MI
Trumpet / Swing

Bill Berry has been leading big bands in the Los Angeles area since the early '70s, still inspired by his years with Duke Ellington. After being discharged from the Air Force in 1955 he studied at the Cincinnati College of Music and Berklee. Berry worked in the big bands of Woody Herman and Maynard Ferguson before joining Ellington (1961-64). After leaving Duke he was with the Thad Jones/Mel Lewis Orchestra (1966-68), led his own New York Big Band and did studio work. After he moved to Los Angeles in 1971, Berry formed the L.A. Big Band which he has continued leading on a part-time basis up to the present time. He has also toured with Louie Bellson and been involved in the jazz education program run by the Monterey Jazz Festival. Bill Berry is an excellent veteran mainstream trumpet player who has recorded several sets (with both small groups and his big band) for Concord. —*Scott Yanow*

● **Hello Rev** / Aug. 1976 / Concord Jazz ✦✦✦✦✦

Although a bit overlooked at the time (especially on the East Coast), Bill Berry's L.A. Big Band was one of the finest jazz orchestras of the mid- to late 1970s. The all-star unit unfortunately recorded much too little, just one album for cornetist Berry's Beez label and this lone Concord set. The power and joyful swing of the all-star unit can certainly be heard on the latter which was recorded at the 1976 Concord Jazz Festival. Solo space is allocated to Berry, trumpeters Jack Sheldon (who also sings "Tulip or Turnip"), Blue Mitchell and Cat Anderson, trombonists Tricky Lofton, Jimmy Cleveland and Britt Woodman, tenor saxophonists Richie Kamuca and Don Menza, and pianist Dave Frishberg among others and one should not overlook the lead alto work by Marshall Royal; this was certainly a remarkable unit. Berry modelled the band after Duke Ellington's and his rendition of "Cottontail" (with high note blasts in the "background" by Cat Anderson) is a classic. Highly recommended. —*Scott Yanow*

The Ellington All-Stars / Jan. 11, 1978-Jan. 12, 1978 / Drive Archives ✦✦✦

This CD reissues an award-winning (for sound quality) Real Time direct-to-disc album, adding alternate takes of "Mood Indigo" and "I Got It Bad" to the original program. Cornetist Bill Berry gathered together a variety of veterans (altoist Marshall Royal, trombonist Britt Woodman, pianist Nat Pierce, bassist Ray Brown and drummer Frankie Capp) along with the young tenor Scott Hamilton to perform eight numbers associated with Duke Ellington. Each of the horns get some solo space with Royal's feature on "I Got It Bad" and the full group's jamming on "Perdido" and "Cottontail" being high points. —*Scott Yanow*

Shortcake / Mar. 3, 1978 / Concord Jazz ✦✦✦✦

This album, one of Bill Berry's few to fully showcase his cornet playing, is really two in one. On five selections he is featured in a quintet also including pianist Dave Frishberg, guitarist Mundell Lowe, bassist Monty Budwig and drummer Frankie Capp; "Avalon" and "I Didn't Know About You" are highlights. The remaining five selections (Berry's ballad "Betty" and two romps) use a different rhythm section (pianist Alan Broadbent, bassist Chuck Berghofer and drummer Nick Ceroli) and add the exciting horns of trombonist Bill Watrous, altoist Marshall Royal and Lew Tabackin on tenor and flute. An excellent outing, well worth picking up by mainstream jazz fans. —*Scott Yanow*

Chu Berry (Leon Brown Berry)

b. Sep. 13, 1910, Wheeling, WV, d. Oct. 30, 1941, Conneaut, OH
Tenor Saxophone / Swing

Chu Berry was considered one of the top tenor saxophonists of the 1930s, just below Coleman Hawkins (his main influence), Lester Young and Ben Webster. Particularly strong on uptempo numbers (although his ballad statements could be overly sentimental), Berry might have become an influential force if he had not died prematurely. After playing alto in college, he switched to tenor in 1929 when he joined Sammy Stewart's band. In 1930 he moved to New York, playing with Benny Carter's band and Charlie Johnson's Orchestra. He was prominently featured in Spike Hughes 1933 recording sessions, was a star with the bands of Teddy Hill (1933-35) and Fletcher Henderson (1936) (to whom he contributed his song "Christopher Columbus") and then found a permanent home with Cab Calloway in 1937. Berry was used on many sessions including with his friend Roy Eldridge, Lionel Hampton (a classic version of "Sweethearts on Parade"), Teddy Wilson and Calloway (his version of "Ghost of a Chance" became well known); in addition he led a couple of his own fine dates. Chu Berry died from the effects of a car crash when he was just 31. —*Scott Yanow*

Chu / May 14, 1936-Jul. 3, 1941 / Columbia ✦✦✦✦✦

One of the finest tenor saxophonists of the 1930s (he died in a car crash in late 1941), Leon "Chu" Berry made a lot of exciting music during his 31 years. He only led five sessions in his career (including two for Commodore and a rare date with Charlie Ventura). The first two four-song dates lead off this well-conceived LP (which will hopefully be reissued by Columbia in the future). Berry is heard jamming with trumpeter Hot Lips Page (who sings "Too Marvelous for Words") and clarinetist Buster Bailey on the first date, and with trumpeter Irving Randolph and trombonist Keg Johnson on the later session; highlights include "Indiana," "Limehouse Blues" and "Chuberry Jam." Rounding off the album of hot swing is 1936's "Warmin' Up" (from a Teddy Wilson date on which Berry teams up with trumpeter Roy Eldridge) and seven of his feature numbers with Cab Calloway's Orchestra, including Chu's most famous ballad recording, "Ghost of a Chance." A definitive set. —*Scott Yanow*

★ **Indispensable** / 1936-1939 / RCA ✦✦✦✦✦

A wide variety of sessions (1936-39) from an immortal stylist are included. With Gene Krupa (d), Lionel Hampton (vib), Cab Calloway (v), Fletcher Henderson (leader), and Wingy Manone's bands. —*Michael G. Nastos*

Eddie Bert

b. May 16, 1922, Yonkers, NY
Trombone / Bop

Eddie Bert has had a rather long career in jazz and in the studios, managing to go almost unnoticed by all but his fellow musicians. A fine and flexible soloist, Bert has also played a large part behind the scenes, performing his parts quite capably in orchestras. Among his early teachers were fellow trombonists Benny Morton and Trummy Young. In 1940, when he was 18, Bert joined Sam Donahue's Orchestra, and two years later cut his first solo on record, "Jersey Bounce," with Red Norvo's band. Bert gigged with the orchestras of Charlie Barnet (1943) and Woody Herman, performed at a well-recorded Town Hall concert with Norvo in 1944, where he was extensively featured, and, after a stint in the military, he worked during the next decade with such orchestras as Herbie Fields, Stan Kenton (1947-48 and 1950-51), Benny Goodman (1948-49), Woody Herman again, and Les Elgart. From 1952-55, Bert recorded several dates as a leader for Discovery, Savoy, Jazztone and Trans-World, showing that he could be a personable bop-based improviser in small groups too. He worked and recorded with Charles Mingus in late 1955, rejoined Benny Goodman in 1957, was part of the ensembles on the various Miles Davis-Gil Evans projects, and performed with Thelonious Monk at his famed big band concerts of 1959 and 1963. In addition to his extensive studio work, Bert was associated with Elliot Lawrence, Chubby Jackson and again with Mingus; he was part of Dick Cavett's TV big band from 1968-72 and toured Europe with the Thad Jones-Mel Lewis Orchestra. In 1976, he led an obscure effort for the Danish Backbone label and has since headed sessions for Molshajala (a duo album with bassist Steve Roane), Keybone, and Fresh Sound (1987), in addition to recording as a sideman with Lionel Hampton, Sal Salvador and Teo Macero, among others. In 1997, Eddie Bert toured with T.S. Monk's "Monk on Monk" ensemble. —*Scott Yanow*

Kaleidoscope / Jul. 29, 1953 / Savoy ✦✦✦

Other than an earlier four-song date, trombonist Eddie Bert's first three sessions as a leader are on this valuable LP (put out in 1987); some of the music has reappeared on CD, but not with as much coherence. The fine bop-oriented trombonist is heard at the head of quintets that include either altoist Vinnie Dean or guitarist Sal Salvador, pianist Duke Jordan, bassist Clyde Lombardi and either Mel Zelnick, Art Mardigan or Joe Morello (during his first studio session) on drums. In addition, Bert takes a rare vocal on "He Ain't Got Rhythm." Highlights of the swinging set include "Love Me or Leave Me," "Conversation Piece," "Broadway" and an extended "Cherokee." —*Scott Yanow*

● **Encore** / Sep. 1, 1955 / Savoy ✦✦✦✦✦

Trombonist Eddie Bert has had a long and honorable musical career but relatively few opportunities to record as a leader. He is heard in two different settings on this CD reissue; with a pianoless quartet that includes guitarist Joe Puma and a quintet that includes pianist Hank Jones and the complementary tenor of J.R. Monterose. The repertoire comprises originals by either Bert or Puma but the style is very much of the era: cool-toned and lightly swinging bop. Despite the extreme brevity of this CD (under 35 minutes), the music is worth exploring. —*Scott Yanow*

Gene Bertoncini

b. Apr. 6, 1937, New York, NY
Guitar / Cool

One of the more elegant, tasteful and senstive guitarists, Gene Bertoncini has perfected the art of playing soft, sentimental music and presenting it in a light, fluid fashion, yet retaining a degree of feeling and spontaneity. He began on guitar at nine, and was a professional at 16, playing on a children's television show. Bertoncini took architecture at Notre Dame rather than music, though he later returned to full-time playing. He played with a group led by Buddy Rich that also included Mike Mainieri and Sam Most. Bertoncini worked with Clark Terry, Paul Winter, Nancy Wilson and in the television orchestras of Merv Griffin and Skitch Henderson in the '60s. He also backed Tony Bennett and worked with the Metropolitan Opera House orchestra. During the '70s, Bertoncini played with Wayne Shorter and Charles McPherson, then formed a duo with Mike Moore. They've played and recorded together over parts of two decades, with Bertoncini selecting the material and writing arrangments. Their performances blend classical, light (not "lite") jazz, Latin and popular material. Bertoncini and Moore were joined by Michal Urbaniak in a trio date in 1981, and he's also led workshops and taught at the Eastman School. Bertoncini has recorded for Stash, Chiaroscuro and Omisound. He and Moore have several releases available on CD. —*Ron Wynn*

O Grande Amor / 1986 / Stash ✦✦✦

Strollin' / 1987 / Stash ✦✦✦

Art of the Duo / 1987-1987 / Stash ✦✦✦

● **Two in Time** / Mar. 10, 1989+Mar. 20, 1989 / Chiaroscuro ✦✦✦✦

Jobim: Someone to Light Up My Life / Oct. 16, 1995-Nov. 2, 1995 / Chiaroscuro ✦✦✦

The veteran guitarist's collection of bossa novas by the late Antonio Carlos Jobim demonstrate his gift for counterpoint and improvisation in this all-acoustic masterpiece. Accompanied only by the Latin percussion of John Arruci and Jon Bates, Bertoncini plays an astonishingly uptempo "Corcavado" that seems to have overdubbed guitar lines but doesn't. Also remarkable is his soft, understated version of "Double Rainbow." Any guitar student or jazz fan will be mesmerized by Bertoncini's crisp playing on "Zingaro." —*Ken Dryden*

Ed Bickert

b. Nov. 29, 1932, Hochfeld, Manitoba, Canada
Guitar / Cool
Ed Bickert, a cool-toned guitarist with a boppish style, has been a fixture in Toronto since the 1950s. While he played steadily in the studios from 1956 on and had associations with Moe Koffman and (more importantly) Rob McConnell, it was not until he performed and recorded with Paul Desmond during 1974-75 that Ed Bickert received much recognition in the US. He has since been featured on records with Rob McConnell's Boss Brass and small groups, Oscar Peterson (1980), Rosemary Clooney, Benny Carter and on his own Concord and Sackville dates. —*Scott Yanow*

Ed Bickert / Jun. 1975 / PM ✦✦✦

42 at the time, guitarist Ed Bickert (who had been a top Canadian studio musicians since the late '50s) finally had an opportunity to lead his own record date in 1975; fortunately, there would be many more. The cool-toned guitarist sounds fine on six sophisticated standards (including "Come Rain or Come Shine," "When Sunny Gets Blue" and "It Might as Well Be Spring") with two other versatile Canadian players, bassist Don Thompson and drummer Terry Clarke. Subtle and lightly swinging music. —*Scott Yanow*

Ed Bickert/Don Thompson / Jan. 22, 1978 / Sackville ✦✦✦✦

After years in the Canadian studios, guitarist Ed Bickert began to gain some recognition in the mid-'70s for his work with altoist Paul Desmond. This exquisite duo album with bassist Don Thompson finds Bickert exploring six standards plus Victor Feldman's "A Face Like Yours." The melodic but explorative improvisations reward repeated listenings. —*Scott Yanow*

Mutual Street / Mar. 1982-May 1984 / Innovation ✦✦✦✦

When one thinks of jazz duos, the combination of valve trombone and guitar rarely comes to mind. Back in the early '80s, Rob McConnell (leader of the Boss Brass) and his regular guitarist Ed Bickert cut ten duets that are full of wit, swing and creative ideas despite the lack of variation in the instrumental colors. One rarely notices the absence of other musicians on this CD reissue, since Bickert is an expert chorder and McConnell plays bass notes behind the guitar solos. A fun session and an unexpected success. —*Scott Yanow*

● **At Toronto's Bourbon Street** / Jan. 1983 / Concord Jazz ✦✦✦✦✦

After years of being underrated and overlooked, guitarist Ed Bickert's association with Concord made him a household name in the jazz world. Bickert is pushed on this set by tenor saxophonist Scott Hamilton, cornetist Warren Vache, bassist Steve Wallace and drummer Jake Hanna and such numbers as Buck Clayton's relaxed "Swingin' Along on Broadway," a cooking "Limehouse Blues" and Coleman Hawkins' "The Walker" find the normally cool guitarist swinging hard. Even the inclusion of a couple of trio numbers ("I'll Wait and Pray" and "Walk It Off") and a few

ballads does not take away from the heat. One of the best Ed Bickert recordings. —*Scott Yanow*

Bye Bye Baby / Aug. 1983 / Concord Jazz ✦✦✦

The sophisticated guitar soloist Ed Bickert can be overly relaxed when playing with a trio, so it is a joy to hear him matched up on this quartet date with the driving swing pianist Dave McKenna. Their unaccompanied duet version of "Bye Bye Baby" is a delight. The other particularly memorable performances include "You're in Love with Someone," "Barbados," "Nobody Else But Me" and "Things Are Getting Better." Recommended. —*Scott Yanow*

I Wished on the Moon / Jun. 1985 / Concord Jazz ✦✦✦

The cool-toned guitarist Ed Bickert sounds in fine form on this quartet set with fellow Canadians Rick Wilkins on tenor, bassist Steve Wallace and drummer Terry Clarke. Sticking mostly to swing standards (plus Jimmy Heath's "C.T.A.," a Milt Jackson blues and "Somewhere Along the Way"), Bickert varies the tempos while always sounding relaxed and lightly swinging; Rick Wilkins gets in some good spots too. —*Scott Yanow*

Third Floor Richard / Jan. 1989 / Concord Jazz ✦✦✦✦

The appearance of pianist Dave McKenna on an Ed Bickert record is a guarantee that the quiet guitarist will be playing at his most passionate. Actually, McKenna is on just around half of this Concord set, but Bickert (heard in the company of fellow Canadians Neil Swainson on bass and drummer Terry Clarke) sounds generally inspired on such numbers as Duke Ellington's "Band Call," "Louisiana," "Tonight I Shall Sleep" and "This Can't Be Love." Fine straightahead jazz. —*Scott Yanow*

This Is New / Dec. 1989 / Concord Jazz ✦✦✦

Barney Bigard (Albany Leon Bigard)

b. Mar. 3, 1906, New Orleans, LA, d. Jun. 27, 1980, Culver City, CA
Clarinet, Tenor Saxophone / Swing, New Orleans Jazz
Barney Bigard was one of the most distinctive clarinetists in jazz and a longtime asset to Duke Ellington's Orchestra. Although he took clarinet lessons with Lorenzo Tio, Bigard's initial reputation was made as a tenor saxophonist; in fact, based on a few of his recordings (particularly those with Luis Russell), Bigard was number two behind Coleman Hawkins in the mid-'20s. After working with several groups in New Orleans, Bigard moved to Chicago in 1924 where he played with King Oliver during 1925-27. He would also record with Jelly Roll Morton, Johnny Dodds and future boss Louis Armstrong in the 1920s but, after short stints with Charles Elgar and Luis Russell, Bigard found his true home with Duke Ellington's Orchestra, with whom he almost exclusively played clarinet. Between 1927-42 he was well featured on a countless number of recordings with Ellington who understood Bigard's musical strengths and wrote to showcase him at his best. From "Mood Indigo" (which he co-composed) to "Harlem Air Shaft," Bigard was an important fixture of the Ellington Orchestra.

When he quit the band in 1942 (due to tiring of the road) Bigard played with Freddie Slack's big band, Kid Ory's New Orleans group and appeared in the 1946 film *New Orleans*. Bigard then joined the Louis Armstrong All-Stars, constantly travelling the world during 1947-55 and 1960-61; he spent 1958-59 with Cozy Cole's band. Bigard became largely semi-retired after 1962 but still played now and then, recording with Art Hodes, Earl Hines and as a leader. However Barney Bigard, whose swing style was sometimes out-of-place with Armstrong, really sounded at his best during his Duke Ellington years. —*Scott Yanow*

Barney Bigard-Albert Nicholas / Aug. 26, 1935-Sep. 29, 1941 / RCA ✦✦✦✦

This long out-of-print LP from the legendary RCA Vintage series has unrelated sessions featuring clarinetists Barney Bigard and Albert Nicholas. The Bigard sides (two dates from 1940-41 with fellow Duke Ellington sidemen that have since been reissued on CD) feature such fine players as cornetist Ray Nance, tenor saxophonist Ben Webster, valve trombonist Juan Tizol, baritonist Harry Carney, Duke himself on piano, bassist Jimmy Blanton and drummer Sonny Greer. Most notable among the eight numbers is the original version of "C Jam Blues" which here is called "'C' Blues." However it is the Albert Nicholas recordings with Bernard Addison's Rhythm and the Little Ramblers (both in 1935) that are most memorable and quite rare. Guitarist Addison takes a brilliant chordal solo on "Toledo Shuffle," trumpeter Freddy Jenkins is heard at his best with the former group and the Little Ramblers' feature two rewarding but obscure solos from trumpeter Ward Pinkett. Classic small-group swing. —*Scott Yanow*

Barney Bigard-Claude Luter / Dec. 14, 1960-Dec. 15, 1960 / Vogue ✦✦✦✦✦

This CD from the French Vogue label has one of Barney Bigard's most exciting recordings. Teamed with fellow clarinetist Claude Luter and a fine French rhythm section, Bigard and Luter romp on two Sidney Bechet tunes, a variety of swing and Dixieland standards (including "Struttin' With Some Barbecue," "Royal Garden Blues," "China Boy" and "'S Wonderful") and a pair of colorfully-titled originals ("Doo Boo Loo Blues" and two takes of "Double Gin Stomp"). The clarinetists really push and inspire each other and their ensemblework is consistently exciting. Well worth searching for. —*Scott Yanow*

● **Bucket's Got a Hole in It** / Jan. 1968 / Delmark ✦✦✦✦
This is one of clarinetist Barney Bigard's best recordings of his later period. On four of the eight selections he is well-featured on swing standards with a quartet that also includes the great pianist Art Hodes. The other four tracks are more in the Dixieland vein with trumpeter Nappy Trottier and the veteran trombonist George Brunis making the band a sextet. Throughout, Bigard (whose tone was instantly recognizable) is the main star and in splendid form. —*Scott Yanow*

Clarinet Gumbo / Jun. 25, 1973+Jul. 18, 1973 / RCA ✦✦✦
Clarinetist Barney Bigard only led one album during the 1961-72 period but, during 1973-76 (starting with this RCA LP), he recorded a bit more often. The veteran swing stylist is matched with a top-notch rhythm section (pianist Ray Sherman, guitarist Dave Koonse, bassist Eddie Safranski and drummer Nick Fatool) for the Los Angeles date. However it is the underrated Dick Cary (heard on trumpet, piano and/or alto horn) who is the most impressive of the supporting players. Cary also arranged the 11 selections and contributed two tricky originals. The material in general is fairly obscure with only three conventional standards and Bigard (not really known as a composer) performing five of his own little-known songs. The music is therefore fresher than one might expect, containing a few subtle surprises and consistently strong playing from the great Barney Bigard. —*Scott Yanow*

Barney Bigard & The Pelican Trio / 1976 / Jazzology ✦✦✦
Clarinetist Barney Bigard's final recording (cut four years before his death) is perhaps more notable for the name of his group and the cover drawing (of three pelicans playing jazz) than it is for the music. The performances of mostly swing standards (along with three standards) is fine, but the group (consisting of Bigard, pianist Duke Burrell and drummer Barry Martyn) would have certainly benefited from the inclusion of a bassist, while the three vocals (two by Burrell and one by Martyn) do not help much. In general, Bigard is in good form and, despite the lack of any real adventure, the music is pleasing and swinging. —*Scott Yanow*

Acker Bilk (Bernard Stanley Bilk)

b. Jan. 28, 1929, Pensford, Somerset, England
Clarinet / Trad Jazz, Pop
Acker Bilk—or Mr. Acker Bilk, as he was billed—has won immortality on rock oldies radio for his surprise 1962 hit "Stranger on the Shore," an evocative ballad featuring his heavily quavering low-register clarinet over a bank of strings. To the jazz world, though, he has a longer-running track record as one of the biggest stars of Britain's trad jazz boom, playing in a distinctive early New Orleans manner. After learning his instrument in the British Army, Bilk joined Ken Colyer's trad band in 1954 before stepping out on his own in 1956. By 1960, a record of his, "Summer Set"—a pun on the name of his home county—landed on the British pop charts, and Bilk was on his way, clad in the Edwardian clothing and bowler hats that his publicist told his Paramount Jazz Band to wear. Several other British hits followed, but none bigger than "Stranger," which Bilk wrote for his daughter Jenny. The single stayed 55 weeks on the British charts and crossed the sea to America, where it hit No. 1 in an era when radio was open to oddball records of all idioms (Bilk gratefully called "Stranger" "my old-age pension"). Released on English Columbia in Britain, several Bilk albums came out in America on the Atco label, and he continued to have hits until the British rock invasion of 1964 made trad seem quaint. With that, Bilk moved into cabaret and continued to have some success in Europe, leading jazz bands, recording with lush string ensembles, and even scoring another hit, "Aria" (No. 5 in Britain), in 1976. Continuing to perform through the 1990s, Bilk slackened his pace recently so that he could pursue, like Miles Davis, a hobby of painting. —*Richard S. Ginell*

Stranger on the Shore / 1962 / Philips ✦✦✦
Clarinetist Acker Bilk, who started recording extensively in London back in 1955 (mostly Dixieland-oriented trad jazz), made this LP in 1961 and had a major hit in "Stranger on the Shore," a song he had written for a children's show two years earlier. As on virtually all of the other tunes on the set (all ballads), the lower register of Bilk's clarinet was emphasized as he stuck closely to the melody and was joined by the Muzak-ish Leon Young String Chorale. Whether it be "Sentimental Journey," "Brahms' Lullaby," "Carolina Moon" or his own "Is This the Blues," all of the selections are given similar dreamy arrangements. The jazz content is not all that strong, but the title cut did succeed in making Acker Bilk a household name for a time. —*Scott Yanow*

Acker Bilk and His Paramount Jazz Band / Nov. 9, 1971-Nov. 25, 1975 / Dixieland Jubilee ✦✦✦✦
Although best known for his pop hit "Stranger on the Shore," Acker Bilk was

always a fine Dixieland-oriented clarinetist. This GNP/Crescendo album features Bilk's 1971 band (except for two cuts from 1975), which had such fine British soloists as trumpeter Rod Mason, trombonist John Mortimer and pianist Barney Bates. Highlights of this set include "South Rampart Street Parade," "Honeysuckle Rose," "Wolverine Blues" and "Rose of the Rio Grande," plus three standards with good-time vocals by Bilk. —*Scott Yanow*

Acker Bilk in Holland / Feb. 1983 / Timeless ✦✦✦✦

● **It Looks Like a Big Time Tonight** / Jul. 14, 1985 / Stomp Off ✦✦✦✦✦
Clarinetist Acker Bilk and cornetist Ken Colyer had first played together in the early '50s, so this Stomp Off set was a reunion. The music is essentially New Orleans jazz in the Bunk Johnson/George Lewis tradition, and both Colyer and Bilk are heard in top form in a septet also including trombonist Les Handscombe, pianist Pat Hawes, banjoist Brian Mitchell, bassist Julian Davies and drummer Pete Lay. Listeners who only associate the clarinetist with his fluke pop hit "Stranger on the Shore" will be surprised at his passionate playing on such numbers as "Down Among the Sheltering Palms," "It Looks Like a Big Time Tonight" and "Mabel's Dream." Highly recommended. —*Scott Yanow*

Blaze Away / Jan. 1987 / Timeless ✦✦✦

Walter Bishop, Jr.

b. Apr. 10, 1927, New York, NY, d. Jan. 24, 1998, New York, NY
Piano / Bop
Walter Bishop, Jr., was a valuable utility pianist on many a modern jazz session during the bebop era, remaining an active performer until his death at the age of 70 in early 1998. The son of composer Walter Bishop, Sr., he grew up in Harlem's Sugar Hill area, and as a teen counted among his friends Sonny Rollins, Kenny Drew and Art Taylor; acknowledging Art Tatum, Bud Powell and Nat King Cole as important influences, Bishop first attracted notice on the Manhattan club circuit around 1947, going on to play and record in bands led by Art Blakey, Charlie Parker, Oscar Pettiford, Kai Winding, and Miles Davis in the years to follow. In 1960, he played in trombonist Curtis Fuller's group before forming his own trio the next year with bassist Jimmy Garrison and drummer G.T. Hogan. In 1964, Bishop toured with vibist Terry Gibbs, and in the late '60s, he studied at Juilliard with composer/pianist Hall Overton. He moved to Los Angeles in 1969, where he continued to study and work as a freelancer with local groups, including Supersax and trumpeter Blue Mitchell's band. From 1972-1975, Bishop taught jazz theory, both privately and in local colleges. He returned to New York in 1975. The next year, Bishop authored an insightful if neglected book on jazz theory, *A Study in Fourths*, in which he proffered a technique of chromatic improvisation based on the use of cycles of fourths and fifths. Bishop played in trumpeter Clark Terry's big and small bands in 1977. He continued to lead his own groups, and in the early '80s began teaching at the University of Hartford; in 1983, he played a solo concert at Carnegie Hall. In the mid-'90s, Bishop appeared to great acclaim at the Charlie Parker Jazz Festival on New York City's Lower East Side. —*Chris Kelsey*

Milestones / Mar. 14, 1961 / Black Lion ✦✦✦
Although pianist Walter Bishop had played earlier with Charlie Parker and was quite active throughout the 1950s, this Black Lion session was his first as a leader. Teamed with bassist Jimmy Garrison in his pre-Coltrane period (Garrison's bowed solos sound a bit like Paul Chambers) and drummer G.T. Hogan, Bishop performs six jazz standards which are augmented by three previously unreleased alternate takes; both of these versions of "Speak Low" were released for the first time on this 1989 CD. Nothing all that remarkable occurs but fans of bebop-oriented piano trios will enjoy this music. Highlights include "Blues in the Closet," "Speak Low" and one of the first "cover" versions of "Milestones." —*Scott Yanow*

Speak Low / Mar. 14, 1961 / Muse ✦✦✦
This was Bishop's first as a leader. —*David Szatmary*

● **The Walter Bishop Trio** / 1962-Oct. 1963 / Original Jazz Classics ✦✦✦✦
This CD reissue brings back the music that pianist Walter Bishop, Jr., recorded on two occasions with bassist Butch Warren and either Jimmy Cobb (on a dozen numbers) or Granville T. Hogan (four other songs). Perhaps for potential airplay reasons, all of the selections are under four minutes apiece (only three exceed three minutes), but as in the days of the 78, Bishop plays a great deal of music in a short period of time. The performances are essentially classic bebop, although 11 of the 16 tunes (five by Bishop) can be considered obscurities. An underrated gem. —*Scott Yanow*

Bish Bash / Aug. 1964+May 1968 / Xanadu ✦✦✦✦
Released for the first time in 1977, the two obscure sessions on this Xanadu set were pianist Walter Bishop, Jr.'s only dates as a leader during the 1964-70 period. The earlier set is particularly valuable, since it offers rare glimpses of the short-

lived tenor saxophonist Frank Haynes, who gets to really stretch out on "Days of Wine and Roses" and a medium-tempo waltz version of "Willow Weep for Me." "Summertime" is taken by Bishop's trio (with bassist Eddie Khan and drummer Dick Berk) and acts as a prelude to five numbers from four years later (including four of the pianist's originals), which Bishop performed with bassist Reggie Johnson and drummer Idris Muhammed. Throughout, Walter Bishop, Jr., plays at his most creative, extending the bebop tradition during the enjoyable performances. —*Scott Yanow*

Valley Land / Dec. 30, 1974 / Muse ✦✦✦
Bishop demonstrates his proficiency with rapid-fire bop tunes and standards, playing superbly throughout this trio date, backed by bassist Sam Jones and drummer Billy Hart. —*Ron Wynn*

Soliloquy / Oct. 21, 1976 / Sea Breeze ✦✦✦
Walter Bishop, Jr.'s first (and thus far only) full set of unaccompanied piano solos sounds fine. Bishop explores six standards (including "Up Jumped Spring," "I Got Rhythm" and "All the Things You Are") in mostly swinging fashion, taking thoughtful solos, although one often wishes that the bop-oriented pianist had been joined by bass and drums (which might have inspired him to play with more passion on this occasion). Worthwhile but not essential music. —*Scott Yanow*

Soul Village / Jun. 1977 / Muse ✦✦✦
Interesting, often intriguing work that plays off a village concept on the title track, but is otherwise a fairly standard, although expertly performed, batch of standards and bop originals. Bishop utilizes the classic Messenger three-horn lineup, except that he substitutes a second saxophonist for a trombonist and uses Randy Brecker as trumpeter. —*Ron Wynn*

Hot House / Dec. 14, 1977-Mar. 14, 1988 / Muse ✦✦✦
Excellent bebop session by this pianist, assisted by Junior Cook (ts) and Bill Hardman (tpt). —*David Szatmary*

Cubicle / Jun. 21, 1978 / Muse ✦✦✦✦✦
The fine bop pianist heads a large group of distinguished stars, among them Curtis Fuller, Pepper Adams, Randy Brecker, and Billy Hart, plus vocalist Carmen Lundy on this 1978 session. It's a different atmosphere for Bishop, usually featured in small combos or trios. The songs are nicely played, and there are several sparkling solos. —*Ron Wynn*

Just in Time / Aug. 10, 1988 / Interplay ✦✦✦

What's New / Oct. 25, 1990 / DIW ✦✦✦✦✦
This Japanese CD (which for a time was made available through Columbia) features veteran pianist Walter Bishop, Jr., in top form in a trio with bassist Peter Washington and drummer Kenny Washington. The repertoire (mostly standards, including "Crazy She Calls Me," and Kenny Dorham's "Una Mas," plus one Bishop original, "Waltz Zweetie") is superior, the communication between the players is strong, and the hard bop renditions are inventive within the tradition. —*Scott Yanow*

Midnight Blue / Dec. 1991 / Red ✦✦✦

Big Bill Bissonnette
b. Feb. 5, 1937, Bridgeport, CT
Trombone / New Orleans Jazz
A strong advocate of New Orleans jazz as played by the veteran Black musicians, Big Bill Bissonnette in the 1960s ran his own group (the Easy Riders Jazz Band), formed his own label (Jazz Crusade) and organized Northern tours for such veteran players as Kid Thomas Valentine, George Lewis and Jim Robinson. After a period off the scene, with the successful publication of his 1992 memoirs *The Jazz Crusade* (which has many stories about the New Orleans musicians), Bissonnette reactivated his label and began to play again. Although a somewhat primitive trombonist, Bissonnette (whose idol is Jim Robinson) is a boisterous player with plenty of spirit. —*Scott Yanow*

Rhythm Is Our Business / Sep. 1985-Nov. 1986 / Jazz Crusade ✦✦✦

Trambone Moan / 1985-1986 / Jazz Crusade ✦✦✦✦
Big Bill Bissonnette, a trombonist greatly influenced by Jim Robinson and a crusader for New Orleans revival jazz during the 1960s, had been out of music for a decade when he put together a new version of his Easy Riders Jazz Band in the mid-1980s. He has since returned to playing full-time and his Jazz Crusade label has been quite successful at documenting his favorite type of mouldy jazz. Bissonnette would never claim to be a virtuoso (he sounds quite rough on "What Am I Living For?") but he has a lot of feeling in his playing and his sense of rhythm is strong. His partner in the front line of this quintet is a real powerhouse, Paul Boehmke. Some of the tempos on this set are killers but Boehmke (whether on his 1920s style clarinet or romping tenor) has no trouble playing heated doubletime lines. With either Bill Sinclair or Bob Shallue on piano, bassist Jim Tutunjian (who

takes several enjoyable slap bass solos) and drummer Bob Lasprogato, this is a fun date and one never misses the trumpet. Oh there are mistakes, occasional missteps and out-of-tune sections (the spontaneous music comprises first takes) and some of the musician vocals are unnecessary, but the drive of the band, especially on the uptempo tunes such as a blistering "Bugle Call Rag," "Girl of My Dreams" and "Chicago Rhythm" (to name three), is quite memorable. Recommended to New Orleans revival collectors. —*Scott Yanow*

● **Big Bill's British Band** / Oct. 9, 1993 / Jazz Crusade ✦✦✦✦
Trombonist Big Bill Bissonnette has stated that his goal is "to lead the mouldiest jazz band in the world" and, from the evidence of this often-riotous set, he may well have succeeded. A partisan of New Orleans jazz as performed by Kid Thomas Valentine and Captain John Handy in the 1960s, Bissonnette's trombone is heard as a part of a spirited octet/nonet jamming such unusual swing tunes as "Smile Darn You Smile," "On Moonlight Bay" and "On a Coconut Island." The slightly out-of-tune ensembles make up in color and spontaneity for the rough moments. Trumpeter Ken Pye has a clipped, almost staccato style that recalls Valentine while Bissonnette harks back to his idol Jim Robinson, but this band's unusual personality is actually formed by its saxophonists. Norman Field (who doubles on clarinet) also plays a lot of alto as does guest John R.T. Davies while Sarah Bissonnette's tenor emerges as the most impressive solo voice. Although this ensemble-oriented band does not boast any virtuosos, its extroverted emotions and boisterous spirit should make it of strong interest to fans of New Orleans jazz. —*Scott Yanow*

Black/Note
f. 1991
Group / Hard Bop, Post-Bop
In 1990, bassist Mark Shelby heard about a performance space in Los Angeles called the World Stage that was funded by drummer Billy Higgins and often featured open jam sessions. In August of that year, Shelby met trumpeter Richard Grant at the World Stage, and a couple months later they were joined by drummer Willie Jones III and altoist James Mahone. Jamming each night at the World Stage from 8 p.m. to 4 a.m. gave the musicians an opportunity to form and solidify a group sound. They played their first gigs in Jan. 1991, and among their first pianists were Eric Reed and Kenneth Crouch. However, by the time the group recorded its first set, *43rd and Degnan* (for the World Stage label), Ark Sano was Black/Note's regular pianist. When Grant received a scholarship to Rutgers in Feb. 1992, he left the band. After a period as a quartet, Gilbert Castellanos became the group's new trumpeter.

Along with the B Sharp Quartet, Black/Note gained some recognition in the mid-1990s as a fine hard bop and post-bop group comprising young Black players in Los Angeles who wanted to explore acoustic jazz. Black/Note has since recorded for Columbia (*Jungle Music*) and Impulse (*Nothin' But the Swing*) but lost some of its personality when Castellanos left the band, which made it a less distinctive (and part-time) quartet. —*Scott Yanow*

43rd & Degnan / May 16, 1991 / World Stage ✦✦✦
Although the Los Angeles-based group Black/Note has recorded for Columbia and Impulse, their debut was actually made for the tiny World Stage label, which (like the club) is run by drummer Billy Higgins. At the time the group was a quintet (trumpeter Richard Grant would eventually depart), and while sticking to originals, Black/Note essentially played modern hard bop. With the Jackie McLean-inspired altoist James Mahone, pianist Ark Sano, bassist Mark Shelby and drummer Willie Jones III (who has thus far had the most significant individual career) joining Grant in the band, the music is well played, spirited and swinging in its own fashion. Worth searching for. —*Scott Yanow*

● **L.A. Underground** / Mar. 31, 1993 / Red ✦✦✦✦
The Los Angeles hard bop group Black/Note was expanded a bit for this excellent recording. The core members (altoist James Mahone, pianist Ark Sano, bassist Mark Shelby and drummer Willie Jones III) are joined by trumpeter of the time Gilbert Castellanos (Richard Grant substitutes for him on two cuts) and local tenor Phil Vieux. They perform five Shelby originals, three by Mahone, a rapid "All the Things You Are" and "The Ancient Rome Suite," which comprises "One Up One Down," "All Blues," "Impressions" and Shelby's "Fourth Grade." Mahone's Jackie McLean-inspired alto works well with the other horns, while Jones consistently drives the band. This particular edition of Black/Note displays plenty of fire on what is their definitive release. —*Scott Yanow*

● **Jungle Music** / Nov. 10, 1993-Nov. 11, 1993 / Columbia ✦✦✦✦✦
Black/Note initially created a stir partly because many on the East Coast have a stereotyped view of music from Los Angeles and were not expecting a young sextet of superior musicians dedicated towards revitalizing jazz to emerge from L.A. Although this group does stick to originals throughout their second release (their debut for Columbia), the often hard-driving music is not all that innovative but

instead is a logical extension of the hard bop tradition. Lovers of classic Blue Note albums should enjoy this dynamic set. — *Scott Yanow*

Nothin' But the Swing / Sep. 18, 1995-Sep. 20, 1995 / Impulse! ◆◆◆
Although comprising four fine young musicians (there is no trumpeter in the band's regular lineup), the lack of originality or any hint of innovation in Black/Note's compositions and solos is unfortunate. The music on this CD could have been recorded in 1963. There is nothing inherently wrong with reviving older styles, as long as one does not claim (as the liner notes seem to) that that is the only way to play creative jazz. James Mahone's alto style comes straight from Jackie McLean, pianists Greg Kurstin and Ark Sano both recall early Herbie Hancock, and the "original" compositions could have been played by the Jazz Messengers 35 years earlier. Guest trumpeters Nicholas Payton (who plays in a Freddie Hubbard groove on four songs) and Gilbert Castellanos (on seven) help fill out the group while Teodross Avery makes one appearance apiece on tenor and soprano. The results are a pleasing variety of spirited but derivative hard bop that rewrites the past a bit without hinting at the future; nothing less, nothing more. — *Scott Yanow*

Cindy Blackman

b. Nov. 18, 1959, Yellow Springs, OH
Drums / Hard Bop
An accomplished, yet not flamboyant or showy drummer, Cindy Blackman has become a well-respected drummer and occasional bandleader in a short time. Both her mother and grandmother were classical musicians, and her uncle a vibist. Blackman began playing drums as a child, and studied classical percussion at the University of Hartford and Berklee. Alan Dawson and Lennie Nelson were two of her instructors. Blackman moved to New York in the early '80s and played with Freddie Hubbard and Sam Rivers. She became Jackie McLean's regular drummer in 1987 and began recording as a leader that year for Muse. Blackman was a big attraction at jam sessions organized at the Blue Note by Ted Curson and played with Don Pullen's trio in 1990 at several festivals. She has a few sessions available on CD. — *Ron Wynn*

Arcane / Aug. 1987-Dec. 1987 / Muse ◆◆◆◆
Cindy Blackman's debut as a leader finds the talented drummer showing a great deal of confidence and holding her own with her illustrious sidemen: trumpeter Wallace Roney, either altoist Kenny Garrett or (on two songs) tenor saxophonist Joe Henderson, pianist Larry Willis, and Buster Williams or Clarence Seay on bass. The music (which includes an unaccompanied drum solo by Blackman on "Incindyary") is modern hard bop, and all of the musicians play up to par in their concise solos; Blackman, Willis, Williams and Henderson ("Teeter Totter") provided all of the songs. A strong start to Cindy Blackman's productive recording career. — *Scott Yanow*

Code Red / Oct. 1990 / Muse ◆◆◆
● **Telepathy** / 1992 / Muse ◆◆◆◆
Drummer Cindy Blackman's third Muse album shows a maturity, confidence and assertiveness that her two previous sessions lacked. She is the unquestioned leader, sparkling in her playing and punctuating the songs with the vigor you'd expect from a veteran percussionist. This is an ensemble sound, with Blackman's drums prominent but no less important than any other element on the 11 numbers; among them are sharp readings of "Tune Up" and "Well You Needn't," plus her own "Persuasion," "Spank," "Missing You" and the title cut. While hard bop, as well as some funk tinges, are present, Cindy Blackman shows signs of being much more than another neobop follower on this date. — *Ron Wynn*

The Oracle / Jan. 23, 1995 / Muse ◆◆◆
Blackman took time off from touring with rocker Lenny Kravitz to cut her fourth record, on which she leads a band including bassist Ron Carter, pianist Kenny Barron and Gary Bartz on alto sax. — *Jason Ankeny*

Ed Blackwell

b. Oct. 10, 1929, New Orleans, LA, **d.** Oct. 8, 1992, Hartford, CT
Drums / Avant-Garde, Free Jazz
Ed Blackwell made his reputation as a member of Ornette Coleman's band in the early '60s; without that association, one wonders whether he would be considered one of the great jazz percussionists. That's to take nothing away from his considerable ability, but Blackwell's unfashionably arcane and somewhat unpolished approach to playing time was perhaps too melodic, too subtle to attract attention independently, especially amidst the heavy-handed Art Blakey/Elvin Jones zeitgeist that prevailed throughout much of his career. The multiplicity of musics to be heard in Blackwell's hometown of New Orleans played an unmistakable role in his peculiar evolution, yet what separated Blackwell from other modern jazz drummers was his personal interpretation of swing. Like every other post-Kenny

Clarke jazz percussionist, Blackwell kept time on his ride cymbal. However, far more than most jazz drummers, Blackwell initiated his accents on the one and three of a four-beat measure. Consequently, Blackwell's style was more martial in character, his rhythmic counterpoint to the soloist more overtly songlike. Additionally, he infused his music with a multiplicity of non-Western elements, and incorporated mannerisms of pre-modern jazz. There was a certain rather endearing quaintness to Blackwell's playing, though he swung as hard and as imaginatively as anybody.

Blackwell's incongruous "squareness" was come by honestly, for one of his earliest influences was the traditional New Orleans percussion style of Paul Barbarin. As a young player, Blackwell spent time in the rhythm & blues band of Plas and Raymond Johnson. He moved to Los Angeles in 1951, where he met his future employer, Ornette Coleman, though it would be some time before their collaboration would capture the attention of the jazz public. In 1953 he moved to Texas, then in 1956 returned to New Orleans. In 1960, he moved to New York, where he replaced Billy Higgins in the by-now-famous Coleman quartet. With Coleman over the next several years, Blackwell made a series of important records for Atlantic (*This Is Our Music, Free Jazz, Ornette on Tenor*). He also worked and recorded with Eric Dolphy's great quintet with Booker Little, recording *At the Five Spot* in 1961. In 1965, he began playing with Randy Weston (with whom he toured Africa two years later) and Archie Shepp. Blackwell was named an Artist in Residence at Connecticut's Wesleyan University in 1975. The next year he joined with ex-Coleman mates Don Cherry, Dewey Redman, and Charlie Haden to form the collective Old and New Dreams, a band dedicated in the main to playing tunes from Ornette's book. Old and New Dreams served as Blackwell's best showcase throughout the '80s. For a variety of reasons—ill health significant among them—Blackwell had often been unable to record and publicly perform with Coleman's early bands, even as he contributed so greatly to their development. Hence, Old and New Dreams' well-distributed albums and intermittent tours exposed him to an audience that might have been otherwise unfamiliar with his work. The band recorded a tribute to Blackwell in 1987, "One for Blackwell," which features the drummer, giving him a bit more solo space than usual.

Until his death from kidney disease in 1992, Blackwell would continue to perform with colleagues from his Ornette days, as well as New Orleans contemporaries like Ellis Marsalis and Alvin and Harold Batiste. Blackwell recorded very seldom as a leader, though just before his death he made *Walls*, a posthumously released trio recording with Dewey Redman and bassist Cameron Brown that showed—especially given his deteriorating physical condition—he was still a voice to reckon with. — *Chris Kelsey*

● **Boogie Live...1958** / 1958 / AFO ◆◆◆◆
When Ed Blackwell returned to New Orleans after a brief early stint with Ornette Coleman in Los Angeles, he joined the American Jazz Quintet which on this CD also includes clarinetist Alvin Batiste, Nat Perrillat on tenor, pianist Ellis Marsalis and bassist Otis Deverney. This live concert, performed at a high school in 1958, was previously unissued until 1994 and features these strong players in top early form. Alvin Batiste shows that, although he would be buried in the jazz education field (and would therefore be greatly underrated), he was an excellent hard bop clarinetist early in his career. Nat Perilliat is a bit of a revelation because he had already absorbed John Coltrane's sheets of sound style at this early period and was developing his own sound. Ellis Marsalis and Otis Deverney are fine while Ed Blackwell (who has several colorful solos) shows that he was already a giant. The group's six originals are generally based on earlier standards, most obviously Batiste's "Fourth Month" (which uses the chords of "I Remember April"). An excellent set. — *Scott Yanow*

Walls-Bridges / Feb. 27, 1992 / Black Lion ◆◆◆◆◆
Ed Blackwell Project / Aug. 8, 1992 / Enja ◆◆◆
What It Is / Aug. 8, 1992 / Enja ◆◆◆

Eubie Blake (James Hubert Blake)

b. Feb. 7, 1883, Baltimore, MD, **d.** Feb. 12, 1983, New York, NY
Piano, Composer / Ragtime
Eubie Blake had a rather unique career. Although his main importance was as a songwriter for Broadway shows in the 1920s, late in life he became known as the last living link to ragtime. Blake always had a colorful life. He wrote his first rag "The Charleston Rag" in 1899, spent years playing in medicine shows and in sporting houses and by 1915 was teaming up with singer Noble Sissle in vaudeville. Sissle and Blake wrote for the 1921 hit show *Shuffle Along* (the first all-Black musical) and it was followed by *Revue Negre, Plantation Review, Rhapsody in Black* and *Bamville Review*. The team of Sissle and Blake, in addition to making recordings, were filmed for some early experimental sound shorts. Among Blake's hit songs of the 1920s were "I'm Just Crazy About Harry," "You're Lucky to Me" and "Memories of You."

Although he made some recordings in 1931, Eubie Blake generally had a lower profile for the next three decades. He worked with Sissle now and then and earned a degree from New York University but was largely forgotten until 1969. That year he recorded a double-LP for Columbia (*The Eighty-Six Years of Eubie Blake*) that amazed listeners who had never heard of him. During his remaining 14 years, Eubie Blake was a very popular performer, playing and singing ragtime-era pieces, charming audiences, making new records, appearing on Broadway in the 1978 show *Eubie* (he was 95 at the time) and running his own label Eubie Blake Music. He continued performing until he was 98 and Eubie Blake made it to his 100th birthday with five days to spare. —*Scott Yanow*

● **Blues and Ragtime (1917-1921)** / 1917-1921 / Biograph ◆◆◆
Piano roll collection featuring vintage tunes done by ragtime and early jazz great Eubie Blake. The feeling and energy he generates is tremendous, and even when the solos aren't impressive, Blake's attitude and personality keep things moving. —*Ron Wynn*

Blues & Spirituals (1921) / Mar. 1921-Dec. 1921 / Biograph ◆◆◆
More classic piano rolls from pianist Eubie Blake, whose 100-year lifespan kept him in the public eye through much of the 20th century. He reflected that experience through his playing, which rocks, sways, and rips at times, and then is appropriately mournful or reverent. —*Ron Wynn*

Rags to Classics / Jul. 1921+1971 / Stash ◆◆◆◆◆
Originally released on Eubie Blake's own label, this set of solo performances features the 88-year-old pianist in fine form. Recently rediscovered after decades in obscurity, Eubie was enjoying a renaissance and was on his way to becoming more famous than he had ever been. He performs a dozen piano solos on this 1971 program including seven of his originals (a couple of which had been recently composed). In addition, his 1921 recording of "Charleston Rag" (which Blake composed in 1899) is reissued side-by-side with his rendition of a half-century later. Other highlights include "You're Lucky to Me," "You Do Something to Me," Luckey Roberts' "Pork and Beans" and "Classical Rag." This Stash LP, one of Eubie Blake's best all-round recordings, is recommended and deserves to be reissued on CD. —*Scott Yanow*

Eubie Blake/Frank Tanner / Apr. 1931-Oct. 24, 1936 / Harrison ◆◆◆
Until he was "discovered" in 1968 when he was 86, pianist-composer Eubie Blake had a rather occasional recording career. He recorded a lot of titles during 1921-22 (some were duets with singer Noble Sissle), just a few other songs later in the decade and then, with the exception of 15 dance band recordings in 1931, a couple of piano solos in 1933 and one title in 1951, did not appear on a commercial record again until 1958. This LP from the collector's label Harrison has seven of Blake's 1931 orchestra sides plus seven by the obscure San Antonio octet Frank Tanner's Rhythm Kings. Blake, other than his own occasional piano, did not have any major soloists in his dance band and the most dominant voice is actually singer Dick Robertson. Blake's Sept. 1931 rendition of Benny Carter's "Blues in My Heart" was one of the first on record but surprisingly he does not play any of his own compositions. Tanner's band has unidentified personnel and, although spirited, tends to be a bit erratic. This LP is therefore primarily for collectors rather than for more general listeners. —*Scott Yanow*

● **The 86 Years of Eubie Blake** / Dec. 25, 1968-Mar. 12, 1969 / Columbia ◆◆◆◆◆
After he went through decades of semi-obscurity, this two-LP set (which is long overdue to be reissued on CD) launched an unlikely comeback by Eubie Blake, the last surviving ragtime composer and performer. Blake revisits some of his finest compositions (including "I'm Just Wild About Harry," "Memories of You," "Charleston Rag" and a medley from "Shuffle Along"), has a reunion with singer Dick Robertson (who he had last recorded with in the mid-1920s) and splits the solo program between rags and theatre songs. Blake's rendition of the "Stars and Stripes Forever" is particularly delightful and he displays a great deal of energy, enthusiasm and joy throughout this classic (and historic) set. —*Scott Yanow*

Eubie Blake Introducing Jim Hession / 1973 / Eubie Blake Music ◆◆◆
This LP from Eubie Blake's label features the 90-year old pianist taking five solos and allocating the second half of the program to Jim Hession, an L.A.-based pianist who is a few years younger. Blake's remake of "Troublesome Ivories" and Scott Joplins' "Elite Syncopations" are highlights while Hession's stride performances range from James P. Johnson and Duke Ellington to Dave Brubeck and the Beatles ("Martha My Dear"). This is an interesting if now hard-to-find set. —*Scott Yanow*

Live Concert / May 22, 1973 / Eubie Blake Music ◆◆◆
Pianist/singer/composer Eubie Blake (who was 90 years old at the time) is in fairly good shape on this LP, telling stories and playing piano continuously for 37 minutes before an enthusiastic audience. Some of his stories (and playing) might be a bit fanciful, but it is all quite enjoyable. In addition to performing some of his own tunes (including "Tricky Fingers" and "Memories of You"), Blake sounds fine on a James P. Johnson medley. —*Scott Yanow*

Eubie Blake & His Proteges / Mar. 18, 1974 / Eubie Blake Music ◆◆◆◆
For this colorful concert hosted by Eubie Blake, four different pianists (three of whom take vocals) have opportunities to display their ragtime/classic jazz styles. Terry Waldo, Mike Lipskin and Jim Hession all fare well but it is naturally Blake's performance of three obscurities (he was 91 at the time) that serves as the climax. This LP, as with most of the other sets on Eubie's short-lived label, will be a bit difficult to find but is worth the search. —*Scott Yanow*

Wild About Eubie / 1976 / Columbia ◆◆◆
Pianist William Bolcom and soprano Joan Morris (a semi-opera singer) perform a variety of Eubie Blake compositions on this fairly straight but reasonably entertaining outing. In addition to the eight Bolcom-Morris duets, the pianist takes "Capricious Harlem" as an instrumental, Blake himself (93 at the time) steals the show with his solo renditions of "Eubie's Classical Rag" (a classic) and "Boogie Woogie Beguine," and also duets with Bolcom behind Morris on "Dixie Moon." Of particular significance is that this LP has the recording debut of Blake's "I'd Give a Dollar for a Dime," which Joe Williams would soon add to his repertoire. —*Scott Yanow*

An American Classic: Eubie Blake / 1981 / Music Masters ◆◆◆
This rather unusual album features the classical Amherst Saxophone Quartet (which consists of a soprano, alto, tenor and baritone saxophonist) performing wholly written-out arrangements of 14 Eubie Blake compositions. Blake, who was 98 at the time, greatly appreciated the gesture. In addition to renditions of "Charleston Rag," "Troublesome Ivories" and "I'm Just Wild About Harry," the group plays many lesser-known Blake tunes. While most of the pieces date from 1899-1924, four are from more recent times including a pair from the 1970s. The high musicianship of the classical musicians plus the colorful arrangements make this album of interest to jazz listeners despite the lack of improvisation. —*Scott Yanow*

Tricky Fingers / Quicksilver ◆◆◆
This Eubie Blake CD is a difficult one to rate. The music (a dozen piano solos) finds the ancient pianist in prime form but the packaging frankly stinks. Not only are there no recording dates given (these selections are probably taken from a few previously released sessions) and a complete lack of liner notes, but the back cover of the CD lists six selections apiece on side one and side two, and the order is reversed. In other words, cuts 7-12 are actually 1-6 and vice versa. If one can overlook those flaws, the music is actually quite wonderful. Blake sounds very much at the peak of his powers not only during such familiar pieces as "Charleston Rag," "Stars and Stripes Forever," "You're Lucky to Me" (during which he takes a vocal) and "Memories of You" but eight of his lesser-known rags and songs. In fact, if the packaging were decent, this would rank (along with his classic two-LP set *The 87 Years of Eubie Blake*) as the ancient ragtime pianist's definitive release. —*Scott Yanow*

John Blake

b. Jul. 3, 1947, Philadelphia, PA
Violin / Post-Bop, Crossover Jazz

Throughout his career, John Blake has veered back and forth between R&B-ish sets and more adventurous dates. A pleasing if not overly distinctive violinist, the versatile Blake has played in a wide variety of settings. After advanced classical study, he first gained recognition for his early-'70s recordings with Archie Shepp. During the next decade Blake recorded with McCoy Tyner, James Newton, Cecil McBee, Jay Hoggard and Grover Washington, Jr., touring extensively with Tyner and Washington. He made a series of generally interesting if diverse sets for Gramavision in the 1980s (including a fascinating 1986 date with fellow violinists Michal Urbaniak and Didier Lockwood) and one CD for Sunnyside in 1992, showing a lot of potential but thus far not becoming a pacesetter. —*Scott Yanow*

Maiden Dance / Dec. 1983 / Gramavision ◆◆
With his diverse experience (playing with everyone from McCoy Tyner to Grover Washington, Jr.), it is not surprising that violinist John Blake's debut as a leader covers a wide area of music, from post-bop jazz to more R&B-ish tracks. The level of the musicianship is quite impressive, helped out by alternating pianists McCoy Tyner and Kenny Barron and bassist Cecil McBee; two members of the Blake family (Alan and Lita) take some vocals. But on a whole, none of the originals (which are joined by the date's lone standard, "Beautiful Love") are all that memorable by themselves. Good music, but not essential. —*Scott Yanow*

Twinkling of an Eye / Jan. 1985 / Gramavision ◆◆◆
Violinist John Blake's second Gramavision set is generally a bit R&B-oriented, with the talented violinist (who doubles on synthesizer) being joined by an over-sized rhythm section (which includes either electric bassist Gerald Veasley or acoustic bassist Avery Sharpe) for a variety of melodic and danceable numbers. Blake's solos (and the inclusion of "Dat Dere" and "Con Alma" to balance out the

originals) make this into a worthwhile session, but the next project (*Rhythm & Blu*) is the John Blake set to get. —*Scott Yanow*

● **Rhythm and Blu** / Jun. 1986 / Gramavision ✦✦✦✦✦
Three top jazz violinists (John Blake, Didier Lockwood and Michal Urbaniak) who have shown versatility throughout their careers perform a variety of straightahead and funky originals on this consistently enjoyable effort. Assisted by keyboardist Bernard Wright, Marcus Miller or Carl James on bass and drummer Lenny White, the trio of fiddlers match wits and trade off on such numbers as "Romance," "Va Va Voom" "Serenade" and "Fiddle Funk." Highly recommended. —*Scott Yanow*

Adventures of the Heart / Feb. 1987 / Gramavision ✦✦

A New Beginning / Mar. 1988 / Gramavision ✦✦✦✦✦
The compositions by violinist John Blake on this Gramavision set are more complex than usual, sometimes using funky grooves but obviously challenging the leader. Blake is heard throughout in top form, accompanied by electric keyboardist James Simmons, acoustic pianist Sumi Tonooka, electric bassist Gerald Veasley, drummer Leon Jordon and percussionist Leonard "Doc" Gibbs. The blend of the two keyboards and the inventive use of African and Brazilian elements in the music uplift the date and make this an intriguing set worth acquiring. —*Scott Yanow*

Quest / Mar. 31, 1992-Apr. 1, 1992 / Sunnyside ✦✦✦

Ran Blake

b. Apr. 20, 1935, Springfield, MA
Piano / Avant-Garde
A champion of "Third Stream" music (mixing together aspects of jazz and classical music), Ran Blake has long had a very individual and unusual piano style. His solos are generally very dramatic, making inventive use of explosive outbursts and silence. When performing standards he often keeps the melody intact but drops the chord structure, creating fresh new music. Blake graduated from Bard College, attended the Lenox School of Jazz during several summers and starting in 1957 had an association with singer Jeanne Lee; they toured Europe in 1963 and performed some fairly free piano-vocal duets. Blake, who recorded for ESP in 1965, became very involved in jazz education at the New England Conservatory of Music where he has worked since 1967. He has recorded on an infrequent basis throughout his career including solo dates on several labels and collaborations with Ricky Ford, Jaki Byard, Houston Person and Jeanne Lee. —*Scott Yanow*

The Newest Sound Around / Nov. 15, 1961-Dec. 7, 1961 / Bluebird ✦✦✦✦✦

Blue Potato / Apr. 9, 1969-Apr. 10, 1969 / Milestone ✦✦✦✦
Ran Blake has always had such an unusual piano style that it is not surprising that he is far from a household name. A very emotional improviser (whose unexpected explosions of sound sometimes punctuate otherwise introspective performances), Blake is a true original. This Milestone LP, only his third recording in eight years, shows Ran Blake really finding unusual things to say on a variety of standards (highlighted by "God Bless the Child," "Chicago," "Stars Fell on Alabama" and even "Never on Sunday") in addition to some originals. On this solo piano date, Blake makes political (if nonverbal) statements on many of these pieces, improvising off of the titles rather than the chord changes. —*Scott Yanow*

Breakthru / Dec. 2, 1975+Dec. 5, 1975 / IAI ✦✦✦✦
The unique pianist Ran Blake is heard on this album performing brief versions (all but one of the 14 songs are under four minutes) of a colorful variety of standards and originals. Blake's emotional playing (which emphasizes the contrast between silence and explosive sounds) is both witty and unpredictable. Among the many short sketches are versions of "You Stepped Out of a Dream," "If Dreams Come True," "Drop Me Off in Harlem," "All About Ronnie," "Tea for Two" and even "Spinning Wheel." Intriguing music. —*Scott Yanow*

Third Stream Recompositions / Jun. 23, 1977 / Owl ✦✦✦

Portfolio of Doktor Mabuse / Oct. 1977 / Owl ✦✦✦

Rapport / Apr. 30, 1978-May 3, 1978 / Novus ✦✦
Ran Blake has been primarily known as a highly individual solo pianist, so this Novus album (put out by Arista in 1978 and overdue to be reissued on CD) was a change of pace in instrumentation, if not in style. Four pieces are duets with the talented hard bop tenor saxophonist Ricky Ford, and a fifth number adds bassist Rufus Reid. In addition, the innovative altoist Anthony Braxton duets with Blake on "Vanguard," Eleni Odoni sings an obscurity, there are three piano solos, and on "Wende," Blake gets to accompany one of his favorite singers, Chris Connor. In general, the music is fairly sparse and very much in the pianist's unique style, a strong addition to his discography. —*Scott Yanow*

Film Noir / Jan. 23, 1980+Jan. 27, 1980 / Novus ✦✦✦✦✦
Ran Blake's dark piano style and dramatic improvisations make for a perfect match with the mood of film noir. This memorable set not only has Blake per-

forming vivid explorations of six songs from films (including melodies from *All About Eve, Pinky, A Streetcar Named Desire* and *The Pawnbroker*), but five originals that somehow musically sum up the plots of other films (including *Spiral Staircase* and *Touch of Evil*). Blake is heard in a variety of settings ranging from solo and a duet with trumpeter Ted Curson to an 11-piece band. Utterly fascinating interpretations that add up to a memorable gem. —*Scott Yanow*

● **Duke Dreams** / May 29, 1981-Jun. 2, 1981 / Soul Note ✦✦✦✦✦
Although Ran Blake plays nine Duke Ellington and Billy Strayhorn songs on this set (plus his own "Duke Dreams," Dave Brubeck's "The Duke," and the ancient and rather delightful "Animal Crackers," which Ellington recorded in 1926), he does not try to emulate the masters; instead, Blake interprets their music on his own terms, making each note count and each performance into a dramatic solo recital. While hinting at Duke's piano style, Ran Blake often reharmonizes and greatly reinvents his music, including such pieces as "Drop Me Off in Harlem," "It Don't Mean a Thing" and "Take the 'A' Train." Highly recommended. —*Scott Yanow*

Improvisations / Jun. 1981 / Soul Note ✦✦✦
This very interesting release matches together Ran Blake and Jaki Byard in a set of piano duets. Because Byard (who can play credibly in virtually every jazz style) is highly flexible, he was able to meet Blake on his own terms and inspire him to play more extrovertedly than usual. Their seven collaborations (a pair of standards, one recent obscurity, Blake's "Wende" and three songs co-written by the pianists) have their playful moments, are quite exploratory, and always hold one's interest. In other words, this matchup works. —*Scott Yanow*

Suffield Gothic / Sep. 28, 1983-Sep. 29, 1983 / Soul Note ✦✦✦
On four of the nine selections of this otherwise solo piano set, Ran Blake duets with the warm and soulful tenor of Houston Person. Rather than playing some blues or standards (all of the solo pieces are well known), Person and Blake surprisingly explore four of the pianist's quirky originals, and the unusual matchup turns out quite well. Other highlights include Blake's transformations of "Pete Kelly's Blues," "Old Man River" and "Stars and Stripes Forever," plus a medley of tunes played in tribute to Mahalia Jackson. No Ran Blake record is ever dull. —*Scott Yanow*

Vertigo / Nov. 15, 1984 / Owl ✦✦✦✦✦
Ran Blake's follow-up to his *Film Noir* Novus album of 1980 is just as extraordinary. Half of the selections on this set are his reinterpretations of themes from moody films, including *The Wild One, Rosemary's Baby*, and a remarkable suite from *Vertigo* in which he musically depicts the movie in a different light. The other selections are originals based on the plots of films (including the Alfred Hitchcock films *Marnie, Wrong Man* and *Strangers on a Train*). One can almost see the action occuring during these new "soundtracks." The set makes for fascinating listening and is particularly recommended to movie fans. —*Scott Yanow*

Painted Rhythms: The Compleat Ran Blake, Vol. 1 / Dec. 1985 / GM ✦✦✦✦
The first of two Ran Blake solo albums cut for the GM label, this CD may not offer the "compleat" Blake, but it does feature the dramatic pianist (who constantly improvises while making every note count) in particularly inventive form and is a strong introduction to his unique playing. With one exception ("Impresario of Death"), the pianist sticks to standards, but he makes them sound unlike any previous rendition. He interprets three very different versions of "Maple Leaf Rag" (a fourth is on the second volume), three Duke Ellington songs (including "Drop Me Off in Harlem"), and numbers by Mary Lou Williams, George Russell, Pete Rugolo, Stan Kenton and Jerome Kern, plus the standard "Moonlight on the Ganges." Highly recommended, as are most of Ran Blake's unique recordings. —*Scott Yanow*

Painted Rhythms: The Compleat Ran Blake, Vol. 2 / Dec. 1985 / GM ✦✦✦
The first volume of *Painted Rhythms*, from the same sessions as its partner, was an excellent introduction to pianist Ran Blake's style, for it included his reharmonizations of a variety of jazz standards and obscurities. The second volume ranges from Blake's often-scary originals ("Shoah!/Babbit/Storm Warning") to 1,000-year-old melodies written by Spanish Jews and a fourth re-interpretation of "Maple Leaf Rag" (the first three were on the first volume). Throughout, Blake was quite concise (only "Shoah!" exceeded four minutes and seven other sketches were under two), very expressive and, as usual, totally individual. —*Scott Yanow*The first volume of *Painted Rhythms*, from the same sessions as its partner, was an excellent introduction to pianist Ran Blake's style, for it included his reharmonizations of a variety of jazz standards and obscurities. The second volume ranges from Blake's often-scary originals ("Shoah!"/Babbit/Storm Warning) to 1,000-year-old melodies written by Spanish Jews and a fourth re-interpretation of "Maple Leaf Rag" (the first three were on the first volume). Throughout, Blake was quite concise (only "Shoah!" exceeded four minutes and seven other sketches were under two), very expressive and, as usual, totally individual. —*Scott Yanow*

Short Life of Barbara Monk / Aug. 26, 1986 / Soul Note ✦✦✦
Ran Blake has recorded fairly often during his career, but this was his first full set with a standard quartet. Tenor saxophonist Ricky Ford works surprisingly well with Blake, whose phrasing and use of space are unusual, while his interpretations are sometimes based on the feeling he gets from song titles rather than the chord changes. Bassist Ed Felson and drummer Jon Hazilla (former students) were very familiar with Blake's music. The repertoire is as unusual as usual for a Ran Blake date, including "I've Got You Under My Skin," "Artistry in Rhythm," obscurities, and originals including the emotional "Short Life of Barbara Monk." Another intriguing Ran Blake set. —*Scott Yanow*

A Memory of Vienna / Nov. 19, 1988 / Hatology ✦✦✦✦
In 1988, both pianist Ran Blake and multireedist Anthony Braxton happened to be in Vienna, Austria, at the same time. Braxton dropped by the studio where Blake was finishing up a recording project, and producer Art Lange noticed that there were still a couple hours of paid-for studio time remaining. Within minutes, it was decided that Blake and Braxton (sticking to alto) would record a set of jazz standards, and a tune list was put together very quickly. Released for the first time on this 1997 CD, the spontaneous duets find Braxton playing fairly melodically (he pays respect to each of the veteran themes before getting more abstract) and with lyricism. Blake, who has always been an expert at contrasting sound with silence in dramatic fashion, keeps an implied beat going during most of the songs, but throws in plenty of surprising curves, consistently stimulating Braxton. On such songs as "'Round Midnight," "Yardbird Suite," "Just Friends" and "I'm Getting Sentimental over You," the pair of avant-garde masters show that they are well acquainted with the jazz tradition. They swing whenever they feel it best serves the music; however, they do not let the tradition restrain their improvising and creativity. This fairly accessible CD is most highly recommended to listeners not yet familiar with the remarkable playing of Anthony Braxton (who has recorded dozens of more forbidding but equally rewarding releases) and Ran Blake. —*Scott Yanow*

You Stepped Out of a Cloud / Aug. 11, 1989 / Owl ✦✦✦✦✦
In 1961, both pianist Ran Blake and singer Jeanne Lee (helped out on two cuts by bassist George Duvivier) made their recording debut with a set of coolly emotional duets. Nearly 28 years later, they had a reunion for this Owl CD, showing the musical growth they had experienced while still sounding quite recognizable; both had found their own musical paths early on. Half of the numbers on the set are originals (including Lee's "I Like Your Style"), but it is generally the fresh renditions of standards that are most memorable, including a haunting "You Stepped Out of a Dream," "Where Are You," "You Go to My Head" and "Alone Together." Blake and Lee should work together more often. —*Scott Yanow*

Masters from Different Worlds / Dec. 26, 1989-Dec. 30, 1989 / Mapleshade ✦✦✦

That Certain Feeling / Jul. 3, 1990-Jul. 4, 1990 / Hat Art ✦✦✦
More rhythmic and beat-oriented than the usual Blake release, as he displays his love for gospel and spiritual rhythms, as well as the familiar Third Stream and film noir sounds. Blake has been among jazz's least acclaimed players for years, and that probably won't change, but this should refute the notion that his work is too obsessed with cerebral concerns rather than emotions. —*Ron Wynn*

Epistrophy / Apr. 19, 1991+Apr. 20, 1991 / Soul Note ✦✦✦
Ran Blake's re-interpretations of 12 Thelonious Monk songs and four standards that Monk enjoyed playing are quite different than everyone else's. He states the basic melody but, rather than improvising off the chord changes, Blake's flights on these solo piano performances stay close to the mood of the melodies, alternating silence with unexpected emotional flurries. —*Scott Yanow*

Round About / Dec. 19, 1992+Sep. 29, 1993 / Music & Arts ✦✦✦✦
Ran Blake has long been a very emotional pianist whose use of space and sometimes-thunderous outbursts are always stimulating if unpredictable. For this set he performs solos and duets with the straightforward but very effective vocalist Christine Correa, alternating stirring versions of standards with five of his songs. Among the more memorable selections are "Angel Eyes," "Drop Me Off in Harlem," "The Short Life of Barbara Monk," "Long As You're Living" and "I Get a Kick Out of You." Thought-provoking music. —*Scott Yanow*

Unmarked Van: Tribute to Sarah Vaughan / Dec. 14, 1995-Dec. 17, 1995 / Soul Note ✦✦✦✦
This is certainly an off-the-wall tribute. Ran Blake, a very individual pianist who often emphasizes the melodies and emotions of standards while stripping the songs of their chord sequences, pays homage to Sarah Vaughan. While Blake is an introverted improviser prone to surprise explosions at the piano, Sassy was extroverted and never shy about showing off her incomparable technique. Blake simply plays in his own distinctive style, giving such songs as "Sometimes I Feel Like a Motherless Child," "My Man's Gone Now," "Whatever Lola Wants," "Moonlight on the Ganges," "Stompin' at the Savoy" and four versions of "Tenderly" very unusual

and haunting treatments; drummer Tiziano Tononi, although listed as only being on one song, actually helps out on several tracks. This moody and melancholy yet strangely celebratory set will stay in one's memory long after the CD has been played. —*Scott Yanow*

Seamus Blake

b. 1969, England
Tenor Saxophone / Hard Bop, Post-Bop
Seamus Blake is an up-and-coming saxophonist who thus far has mostly worked as a sideman. Raised in Vancouver, British Columbia, Blake played violin at the age of nine, but it was not until he was 14 and started playing alto in his high school stage band that he became serious about music. Soon switching to tenor, Blake attended Berklee College in Boston a few years later, where he had the opportunity to interact with many of the Young Lions. After moving to New York in Sept. 1992, Blake recorded with Victor Lewis (for Red), Franco Ambrosetti, Billy Drummond, Darrell Grant (the latter two for Criss Cross), and Kevin Hayes (Blue Note), and led his own Criss Cross sets. Seamus Blake has in recent times toured with John Scofield, worked regularly with the Mingus Big Band, and headed his own electronic group, the Bloomdaddies. —*Scott Yanow*

● **The Call** / Dec. 24, 1993 / Criss Cross ✦✦✦✦

Bloomdaddies / Apr. 16, 1996 / Criss Cross ✦✦✦
Criss Cross is famous as one of the top European bop-oriented labels, so this particular release was a real departure. The music uses electronics a bit; the playing is open to the influences of the avant-garde and funk, and the instrumentation is a bit different: Seamus Blake and Chris Creek on tenors, Jesse Murphy on electric bass and both Jorge Rossy and Dan Reiser on drums. With the exception of an eccentric version of "Sing, Sing, Sing," all of the tunes are originals by either Blake or Creek, including such titles as "Hick As Heck," "Final Sauna" and "To Be Ornette to Be." An intriguing, if not essential set. —*Scott Yanow*

Four Track Mind / 1997 / Criss Cross ✦✦✦

Art Blakey

b. Oct. 11, 1919, Pittsburgh, **d.** Oct. 16, 1990, New York, NY
Drums / Hard Bop
In the '60s, when John Coltrane and Ornette Coleman were defining the concept of a jazz avant-garde, few knowledgeable observers would have guessed that in another 30 years, the music's mainstream would virtually bypass their innovations, in favor of the hard bop style that free jazz had apparently supplanted. As it turned out, many listeners who had come to love jazz as a sophisticated manifestation of popular music were unable to accept the extreme esotericism of the avant-garde; their tastes were rooted in the core elements of "swing" and "blues," characteristics found in abundance in the music of the Jazz Messengers, the quintessential hard bop ensemble led by drummer Art Blakey. In the '60s, '70s, and '80s, when artists on the cutting edge were attempting to transform the music, Blakey continued to play in more or less the same bag he had since the '40s, when his cohorts included the likes of Charlie Parker, Miles Davis, and Fats Navarro. By the '80s, the evolving mainstream consensus had reached a point of overwhelming approval in regard to hard bop: this is what jazz is, and Art Blakey—as its longest-lived and most eloquent exponent—was its master.

The Jazz Messengers had always been an incubator for young talent. A list of the band's alumni is a who's-who of straightahead jazz from the '50s on—Lee Morgan, Wayne Shorter, Freddie Hubbard, Johnny Griffin, Jackie McLean, Donald Byrd, Bobby Timmons, Cedar Walton, Benny Golson, Joanne Brackeen, Billy Harper, Valery Ponomarev, Bill Pierce, Branford Marsalis, James Williams, Freddie Hubbard, Keith Jarrett and Chuck Mangione, to name several of the most well known. In the '80s, precocious graduates of Blakey's School for Swing would continue to number among jazz's movers and shakers, foremost among them being trumpeter Wynton Marsalis. Marsalis became the most visible symbol of the '80s jazz mainstream; through him, Blakey's conservative ideals came to dominate the public's perception of the music. At the time of his death in 1990, the Messenger aesthetic dominated jazz, and Blakey himself had arguably become the most influential jazz musician of the past 20 years.

Blakey's first musical education came in the form of piano lessons; he was playing professionally as a seventh grader, leading his own commercial band. He switched to drums shortly thereafter, learning to play in the hard-swinging style of Chick Webb and Sid Catlett. In 1942, he played with pianist Mary Lou Williams in New York. He toured the South with Fletcher Henderson's band in 1943-44. From there, he briefly led a Boston-based big band before joining Billy Eckstine's new group, with which he would remain from 1944-47. Eckstine's big band was the famous "cradle of modern jazz," and included (at different times) such major figures of the forthcoming bebop revolution as Dizzy Gillespie, Miles Davis, and Charlie Parker. When Eckstine's group disbanded, Blakey started a rehearsal ensemble called the Seventeen Messengers. He also recorded with an octet, the first of his bands to be called the Jazz Messengers. In the early '50s, Blakey began an association with Horace Silver, a particularly like-minded pianist, with whom he recorded several times. In 1955, they formed a group with Hank Mobley and Kenny Dorham, calling themselves "Horace Silver and the Jazz Messengers." The Messengers typified the growing hard bop movement—hard, funky, and bluesy, the band emphasized the music's primal rhythmic and harmonic essence. A year later, Silver left the band, and Blakey became its leader. From that point, the Messengers were Blakey's primary vehicle, though he would continue to freelance in various contexts. Notable was a 1963 Impulse record date with McCoy Tyner, Sonny Stitt, and Art Davis; a 1971-72 world tour with "The Giants of Jazz," an all-star venture with Thelonious Monk, Dizzy Gillespie, Sonny Stitt, and Al McKibbon; and an epochal drum battle with Max Roach, Elvin Jones, and Buddy Rich at the 1964 Newport Jazz Festival. Blakey also frequently recorded as a sideman under the leadership of ex-Messengers.

Blakey's influence as a bandleader could not have been nearly so great had he not been such a skilled instrumentalist. No drummer ever drove a band harder; none could generate more sheer momentum in the course of a tune; and probably no drummer had a lower boiling point—Blakey started every performance full-bore and went from there. His accompaniment style was relentless, and woe to the young saxophonist who couldn't keep up, for Blakey would run him over like a fullback. Blakey differed from other bop drummers in that his style was almost wholly about the music's physical attributes. Where his contemporary Max Roach dealt extensively with the drummer's relationship to melody and timbre, for example, Blakey showed little interest in such matters. To him, jazz percussion wasn't about tone color; it was about rhythm—first, last, and in between. Blakey's drumset was the engine that propelled the music. To the extent that he exhibited little conceptual development over the course of his long career, either as a player or as a bandleader, Blakey was limited. He was no visionary by any means. But Art Blakey did one thing exceedingly well, and he did it with genius, spirit, and generosity until the very end of his life. —*Chris Kelsey*

New Sounds / Dec. 22, 1947-1948 / Blue Note ✦✦✦✦
This historically significant CD collects together two sessions led by tenor saxophonist James Moody in 1948 (when he was a member of Dizzy Gillespie's big band) along with drummer Art Blakey's first recording date as a leader. Moody's music features boppish arrangements by Gil Fuller and solos by trumpeter Dave Burns, altoist Ernie Henry and baritonist Cecil Payne while the Blakey set (originally released under the title of *Art Blakey's Messengers*) features an octet that includes trumpeter Kenny Dorham, altoist Sahib Shihab and pianist Walter Bishop. Classic and formerly rare music. —*Scott Yanow*

A Night at Birdland, Vols. 1-3 / Feb. 21, 1954 / Blue Note ✦✦✦✦✦
Art Blakey Quintet. 1987 CD reissue of early editions of the group. How can you overlook the sets with Horace Silver (p) and others? Many feel they are his best live dates. I agree. —*Michael G. Nastos*

Jazz Profile / Feb. 21, 1954-Feb. 1977 / Capitol ✦✦✦
A good single-CD sampler of drummer Art Blakey's Blue Note years is an impossibility, for he recorded dozens of gems for the label. There is nothing wrong with the six numbers on this set (a 1954 version of "Wee Dot" with Clifford Brown, the classics "Moanin'," "Along Came Betty" and "Up Jumped Spring," Freddie Hubbard's lesser-known "Down Under," and the only post-1962 number, "Jodi") but it barely hints at the Art Blakey story. Only three versions of the Jazz Messengers are represented (along with the Brownie cut, which is out of place), making the release a bit frivolous. —*Scott Yanow*

The History of Jazz Messengers / 1954-1964 / Blue Note ✦✦✦✦✦
Three-disc anthology that covers various editions of the Messengers from the beginning to the end. It contains such classics as "Moanin'" and does a good job of showing how much talent passed through the Blakey organization over the decades. It's particularly valuable as an introductory tool, but is not comprehensive enough to substitute for what should come from the label: a true multi-disc boxed set featuring his full recordings for Blue Note. —*Ron Wynn*

At the Cafe Bohemia, Vol. 1 / Nov. 11, 1955 / Blue Note ✦✦✦✦
This first of two LP volumes features the original version of the Jazz Messengers, the quintet co-led by drummer Art Blakey and pianist Horace Silver that also featured trumpeter Kenny Dorham, Hank Mobley on tenor and bassist Doug Watkins. Caught live, the band stretches out on such numbers as "Soft Winds,'" "Minor's Holiday," "Alone Together" and Dorham's "Prince Albert." Highly enjoyable and still timeless music. —*Scott Yanow*

At the Cafe Bohemia, Vol. 2 / Nov. 11, 1955 / Blue Note ✦✦✦✦
The second of two LP volumes showcasing the 1955 Jazz Messengers features Art Blakey, Horace Silver, Kenny Dorham, Hank Mobley and Doug Watkins digging into such strong material as Mobley's "Sportin' Crowd" and "Avila and Tequila" and

three standards. This band has influenced jazz up to the present day and was in fine form for this live appearance. —*Scott Yanow*

Art Blakey with the Original Jazz Messengers / Apr. 5, 1956-May 4, 1956 / Columbia ✦✦✦
The original version of the Jazz Messengers only lasted around a year, cutting four albums before the departure of pianist and chief composer Horace Silver. This LP (which also features trumpeter Donald Byrd, Hank Mobley's tenor and bassist Doug Watkins) is highlighted by the earliest recordings of two of Silver's songs, "Nica's Dream" and "Ecaroh," and plenty of typically hard swinging from the band. —*Scott Yanow*

The Jazz Messengers [Columbia] / Apr. 15, 1956+May 4, 1956 / Columbia ✦✦✦
This CD reissue brings back the music on the earlier LP titled *Art Blakey with the Original Jazz Messengers*, plus five other selections (just one of which is an alternate) from the same two sessions that were formerly out on imported sets; "Deciphering the Message" was previously unreleased altogether. These were the last recordings by the Art Blakey-Horace Silver Jazz Messengers before pianist Silver went out on his own and the first edition disbanded. Trumpeter Donald Byrd, tenor saxophonist Hank Mobley and bassist Doug Watkins (along with Silver and Blakey) are in excellent form. Silver's "Nica's Dream" is heard here in the original version, and the band is typically hard-swinging throughout the 76-minute-plus program. —*Scott Yanow*

Originally / May 4, 1956+Jun. 25, 1956 / Columbia ✦✦
This LP contains valuable performances by the early Jazz Messengers that sat unissued until decades later. Four selections feature the band when drummer Art Blakey and pianist Horace Silver were co-leaders; trumpeter Donald Byrd, Hank Mobley on tenor and bassist Doug Watkins were also in that quintet. Two numbers from June 1956 find Blakey as sole leader of the Messengers for the first time, heading an otherwise unrecorded unit with Byrd and multi-instrumentalist Ira Sullivan. This LP concludes with a humorous Gershwin medley from later in the year with altoist Jackie McLean and trumpeter Bill Hardman in prominent roles. Although not an essential set, Art Blakey fans will find this album to be a valuable gapfiller in the history of the Jazz Messengers. —*Scott Yanow*

The Jazz Messenger / May 4, 1956-Dec. 13, 1956 / Columbia ✦✦
This CD is a sampler of Art Blakey's 1956 recordings and will be frustrating for Jazz Messengers' collectors. None of the eight selections were previously unissued and they are taken from three separate sessions, none of which are offered here complete. Four selections feature the Art Blakey-Horace Silver quintet during their final recording dates (including "Ecaroh" and "Carol's Interlude"), one has multi-instrumentalist Ira Sullivan joining trumpeter Donald Byrd in the front line and the remaining selections feature altoist Jackie McLean and trumpeter Bill Hardman. A good sampler for beginners, but Blakey fans should try to acquire the complete sessions instead. —*Scott Yanow*

Hard Bop / Dec. 12, 1956+Dec. 13, 1956 / Columbia ✦✦✦
This LP features the Jazz Messengers shortly after pianist Horace Silver departed to form his own band. With altoist Jackie McLean and trumpeter Bill Hardman as the key soloists (pianist Sam Dockery and bassist Spanky DeBrest completed the quintet), this group was already a potentially great outfit although its most glorious days were still in the future. Three group originals (including McLean's "Little Melonae") and two standards are performed during this fine set. —*Scott Yanow*

Hard Drive / Dec. 12, 1956-Dec. 13, 1956 / Bethlehem ✦✦✦
The final recording by the second version of Art Blakey's Jazz Messengers features trumpeter Bill Hardman, tenor saxophonist Johnny Griffin, either Junior Mance or Sam Dockery on piano and bassist Spanky DeBrest along with leader/drummer Blakey performing four group originals, two Jimmy Heath compositions and the obscure "Late Spring." Although this was not the most famous edition of the Messengers, it set a standard that its successors would uphold, training its members to be bandleaders in their own right. The music on this LP is typical hard bop of the period, well played and full of enthusiasm and fire. —*Scott Yanow*

Second Edition 1957 / 1957 / Bluebird ✦✦✦✦
This is an interesting CD reissue of formerly rare material from the second version of Art Blakey's Jazz Messengers. The first six selections are the full contents of a long-out-of-print VIK LP which find the Messengers (with tenor saxophonist Johnny Griffin, trumpeter Bill Hardman, pianist Sam Dockery, bassist Spanky DeBrest and the drummer/leader) playing six songs by Lerner and Loewe including "Almost Like Being in Love," "On the Street Where You Live" and "I Could Have Danced All Night." In addition, the same group is heard on two previously unreleased alternate takes with altoist Jackie McLean (who was actually Griffin's predecessor) making the band a sextet, and there are three numbers (including two "new" takes) from an expanded unit (called "The Jazz Messengers Plus Two") which features such players as a very young Lee Morgan (making his debut with Blakey a year before he joined the group), Hardman, trombonist Melba Liston,

Griffin and pianist Wynton Kelly. But rarity aside, the performances should please straightahead jazz fans. —*Scott Yanow*

Once upon a Groove / Jan. 14, 1957+Feb. 11, 1957 / Blue Note ✦✦✦
Following the original all-star version of the Jazz Messengers and preceding the Lee Morgan-Benny Golson band of late 1958, the group that drummer Art Blakey led in 1957 has tended to be overlooked. Featuring altoist Jackie McLean and trumpeter Bill Hardman, this particular outfit soon set the standard for the many versions of the Jazz Messengers that would follow, featuring originals by Blakey's young sidemen, hard-swinging ensembles and increasingly distinctive solos. This hard-to-find LP is worth a search. —*Scott Yanow*

Ritual: The Modern Jazz Messengers / Jan. 14, 1957+Feb. 11, 1957 / Blue Note ✦✦✦
Interesting, uneven 1957 date that contains a lengthy drum piece by Blakey. This was not his greatest group, although alto saxophonist Jackie McLean was among the hardest blowers he ever employed. Bassist Spanky Debrest and trumpeter Bill Hardman were good musicians, but a notch below the others who filled their roles in future Messenger editions. —*Ron Wynn*

Orgy in Rhythm, Vols. 1-2 / Mar. 7, 1957 / Blue Note ✦✦✦✦
This CD reissues one of the first percussion-oriented jazz records, although it was preceded two weeks earlier by Art Blakey's obscure Columbia set *Drum Suite*. For the Blue Note date, which was originally released as two LPs and is now available as a single CD, Blakey enlisted quite a lineup—the leader, Art Taylor, Jo Jones, and Specs Wright on drums (with the latter two doubling on tympani), five percussionists, flutist Herbie Mann, pianist Ray Bryant and bassist Wendell Marshall. Mann plays a variety of African wood flutes, except on the final number, a conventional blues featuring his regular flute. With percussionist Sabu leading the chanting and taking three vocals (Blakey himself sings a little on "Toffi"), the music is quite African-oriented and generally holds one's interest, preceding Max Roach's *M'Boom* by over 20 years. Mostly for specialized tastes, this is a set that drummers should consider essential. —*Scott Yanow*

Mirage / Mar. 8, 1957-Mar. 9, 1957 / Savoy ✦✦✦
The 1957 edition of the Jazz Messengers heard throughout this enjoyable LP features altoist Jackie McLean, trumpeter Bill Hardman, pianist Sam Dockery, bassist Spanky DeBrest and leader/drummer Art Blakey. Already at this early stage, the band was the epitome of hard bop and just beginning to become an influential force. Although none of these six selections (three by tuba player Ray Draper) would become standards, the music is consistently excellent and typically hard swinging. —*Scott Yanow*

Jazz Messengers Play Lerner and Loewe / Mar. 13, 1957 / VIK ✦✦✦✦
One of the rarest of all Art Blakey records, this LP finds the Jazz Messengers (featuring new member Johnny Griffin on tenor and trumpeter Bill Hardman) performing jazz versions of six show tunes by Lerner and Loewe including three ("Almost Like Being in Love," "I Could Have Danced All Night" and "On the Street Where You Live") that would soon become standards. Despite some of the musicians' unfamiliarity with the songs, this date is quite successful and should be reissued on CD someday. —*Scott Yanow*

Theory of Art / Apr. 2, 1957 / RCA ✦✦✦
This CD contains two unique sessions in the history of Art Blakey's Jazz Messengers. Five numbers feature a sextet that includes both altoist Jackie McLean, who had recently left the band, and his replacement, tenor saxophonist Johnny Griffin along with trumpeter Bill Hardman; "A Night in Tunisia" best shows off this short-lived group. The remaining two numbers were unissued until this CD came out and feature Blakey heading a nonet that included future Messenger Lee Morgan, trombonist Melba Liston and Griffin. The music is consistently excellent and also succeeds as a historical curiosity that should greatly interest Blakey collectors. —*Scott Yanow*

Art Blakey/John Handy: Messages / May 13, 1957 / Roulette ✦✦✦
This double LP combines together two totally unrelated sessions that happened to be recorded on the same day for Roulette. Art Blakey's Jazz Messengers (with tenor great Johnny Griffin, trumpeter Bill Hardman and guest Sabu Martinez on congas) stretches out on four numbers which include "Woodyn' You" and Charlie Shavers' "Dawn on the Harvest" while altoist John Handy (heard in his first session as a leader), who would join Charles Mingus the following year, mostly sounds fairly individual on his six selections with a quartet. Enjoyable if not essential music, hard bop from the late '50s. —*Scott Yanow*

Art Blakey's Jazz Messengers with Thelonious Monk / May 14, 1957+May 15, 1957 / Atlantic ✦✦✦✦
This was an ideal matchup, one that should have been repeated in future years. Art Blakey was always one of the perfect drummers for Thelonious Monk's music, matching the innovative pianist's percussive excitement while leaving him plenty of space. Blakey's tenorman Johnny Griffin also proved to have a perfect under-

standing of Monk's music, joining Monk's quartet the following year. With trumpeter Bill Hardman and bassist Spanky DeBrest completing the quintet, five of Monk's finest compositions plus Griffin's "Purple Shades" are explored on this LP. —*Scott Yanow*

Art Blakey and the Jazz Messengers [Bethlehem] / Oct. 11, 1957 / Bethlehem ✦✦
Des Femmes Disparaissent / Jan. 5, 1958-Dec. 19, 1958 / Fontana ✦✦✦
The bulk of this CD has the soundtrack of a 1958 French film titled *Des Femmes Disparaissent*. Art Blakey's Jazz Messengers (which at the time consisted of the drummer-leader, trumpeter Lee Morgan, tenor saxophonist Benny Golson, pianist Bobby Timmons and bassist Jymie Merritt) perform 18 mostly brief sketches that were co-written by Golson and Blakey. Although the music is generally inconclusive and fragmented, fans of the Jazz Messengers will find these performances of some interest. The last five selections are from a different French film of the period, *Les Tricherus*. One number has Lionel Hampton (on drums) jamming in a quartet with clarinetist Mezz Mezzrow. The other songs have pianist Oscar Peterson, guitarist Herb Ellis, bassist Ray Brown and drummer Gus Johnson joined on one tune apiece by tenor saxophonist Coleman Hawkins, trumpeters Roy Eldridge and Dizzy Gillespie and tenorman Stan Getz; Eldridge is also part of the Getz track. Of these, Dizzy on "Mic's Jump" fares best. But overall the historical curiosities on this CD are not all that essential. —*Scott Yanow*

★ **Moanin' [Blue Note]** / Oct. 30, 1958 / Blue Note ✦✦✦✦✦
The third version of Art Blakey's Jazz Messengers debuted with this stunning LP which has since been reissued (along with an alternate version of "Moanin'") on CD. Tenor saxophonist Benny Golson helped give the quintet its own personality with his compositions and arrangements (contributing "Blues March," "Along Came Betty," "Are You Real" and "The Drum Thunder Suite" to this set), 20-year-old trumpeter Lee Morgan quickly emerged as a powerful soloist and the funky pianist Bobby Timmons' "Moanin'" became the Messengers' first real hit. This classic album, a major influence on hard bop, is highly recommended. —*Scott Yanow*

Holiday for Skins, Vol. 1 / Nov. 9, 1958 / Blue Note ✦✦✦
Holiday for Skins, Vol. 2 / Nov. 9, 1958 / Blue Note ✦✦✦
Olympia Concert: Art Blakey's Jazz Messengers / Nov. 22, 1958+Dec. 17, 1958 / Polygram ✦✦✦
With the Jazz Messengers, this is prototype Blakey on a 1988 reissue. Lee Morgan (tpt), Benny Golson (ts), and Bobby Timmons (p). —*Michael G. Nastos*

Paris 1958 / Dec. 18, 1958-Dec. 19, 1958 / Bluebird ✦✦✦✦
Originally part of an 11-song three-LP set, this six-song CD (not counting the 28-second "Theme") features the Lee Morgan-Benny Golson-Bobby Timmons version of the Jazz Messengers stretching out on their "hits" (including "Blues March," "Moanin'" and "Whisper Not"), giving one alternate versions of their studio recordings. This was one of the finest bands of the period, and this CD serves as a perfect introduction to the exciting music of the Jazz Messengers. —*Scott Yanow*

Au Club Saint-Germain, Vols. 1-3 / Dec. 21, 1958 / RCA ✦✦✦✦
This three-LP box set from French RCA (part of which was reissued on the CD *Paris 1958*) features the 1958 Jazz Messengers live in Paris stretching out on 11 songs. Trumpeter Lee Morgan, tenor saxophonist Benny Golson and pianist Bobby Timmons formed a potent team, backed up by bassist Jymie Merritt and the powerful drumming of leader Art Blakey. This hard-to-find set gives one a definitive look at the influential band. —*Scott Yanow*

1958: Paris Olympia / 1958 / Fontana ✦✦✦
The 1958 version of the Jazz Messengers was widely recorded during their stay in Paris, but this CD does not duplicate any of the other recordings previously released. This band (with trumpeter Lee Morgan, Benny Golson on tenor and pianist Bobby Timmons) was particularly strong, and it is quite enjoyable to hear them stretch out on such songs as "I Remember Clifford," "Moanin'," "Blues March" and "Whisper Not." Hard bop at its best, all of it propelled by the powerful drumming of Art Blakey. —*Scott Yanow*

At the Jazz Corner of the World: Vols. 1 & 2 / Apr. 15, 1959 / Blue Note ✦✦✦✦✦
This two-CD set is a logical reissue, combining both volumes (formerly LPs) of a live performance by Art Blakey and his 1959 Jazz Messengers. Recorded shortly after tenor saxophonist Benny Golson had left the group, this particular version of Blakey's classic band featured trumpeter Lee Morgan, Hank Mobley on tenor (his only recordings with the band), pianist Bobby Timmons, bassist Jymie Merritt and the drummer-leader. Surprisingly Morgan, Timmons and the departed Golson did not contribute any compositions to the set although there are three Hank Mobley songs. In addition, the band performs songs by Thelonious Monk ("Justice"), Ray Bryant, Randy Weston ("Hi-Fly") and Gildo Mahones plus the standard "Close Your

Eyes" and two versions of "The Theme." The music falls short of being essential but hard bop collectors will find much to savor on the two-fer. —*Scott Yanow*

Les Liaisons / Jul. 8, 1959-Jul. 9, 1959 / Polygram ◆◆◆
An interesting set of music originally recorded as the soundtrack for the French film *Les Liaisons Dangereuses*, the majority of these tracks feature Art Blakey's Jazz Messengers of mid-1959 with trumpeter Lee Morgan, tenorman Barney Wilen, pianist Boby Timmons and bassist Jymie Merritt joining the explosive drummer/leader. In general, the music manages to stand on its own with the ensemble getting to stretch out a bit on the rare material. —*Scott Yanow*

Africaine / Nov. 10, 1959 / Blue Note ◆◆◆◆
Not released until over 20 years after it was recorded, this LP features tenor saxophonist Wayne Shorter in his first recording with the Jazz Messengers. The quintet at the time also featured the great trumpeter Lee Morgan, pianist Walter Davis, Jr., bassist Jymie Merritt and the drummer/leader Art Blakey. The high point is easily Shorter's memorable composition "Lester Left Town" (written after Lester Young's passing). Overall, this forgotten session contains plenty of excellent hard bop. —*Scott Yanow*

Live in Stockholm (1959) / Nov. 23, 1959 / Dragon ◆◆◆◆◆
The version of Art Blakey's Jazz Messengers heard on this CD differs from most from the period because pianist Bobby Timmons had just departed to join Cannonball Adderley so Walter Davis, Jr., is in the piano chair. Otherwise the lineup (with trumpeter Lee Morgan, tenor saxophonist Wayne Shorter, bassist Jymie Merritt and drummer Blakey) is familiar. Performing three standards (including "Night in Tunisia") and two group originals (best known is one of the earliest versions of Shorter's "Lester Left Town," the Jazz Messengers are up to their usual high standards; both Morgan and Shorter are in particularly strong form while Davis fits in quite well. —*Scott Yanow*

Paris Jam Session / Dec. 18, 1959 / EmArcy ◆◆◆◆
This very interesting CD features Art Blakey's Jazz Messengers (with trumpeter Lee Morgan and their new tenor saxophonist Wayne Shorter) on fine versions of Morgan's "The Midget" and "A Night in Tunisia" but is highlighted by the guest appearances of altoist Barney Wilen and particularly pianist Bud Powell on two Powell classics ("Dance of the Infidels" and "Bouncing with Bud"). Exciting music, most highly recommended to veteran Art Blakey collectors. —*Scott Yanow*

☆ **The Complete Blue Note Recordings of Art Blakey's 1960 Messengers** / 1960 / Mosaic ◆◆◆◆◆
This six-CD limited-edition box set from Mosaic is quite remarkable. It includes all of the music from the Jazz Messenger albums *The Big Beat, A Night in Tunisia,* the two volumes of *Meet You at the Jazz Corner of the World, The Freedom Rider, Like Someone in Love, The Witch Doctor, Roots and Herbs* and *Pisces* (the latter was originally issued only in Japan) along with two previously unissued alternate takes. More importantly, the music is consistently brilliant, featuring one of the great editions of Art Blakey's band, the group with trumpeter Lee Morgan, tenor saxophonist Wayne Shorter, pianist Bobby Timmons and bassist Jymie Merritt. —*Scott Yanow*

Lausanne 1960, 2nd Set / 1960 / TCB ◆◆◆◆
The 1960 version of Art Blakey's Jazz Messengers (which consisted of the drummer/leader, trumpeter Lee Morgan, tenor saxophonist Wayne Shorter, pianist Bobby Timmons, and bassist Jymie Meritt) was very well documented. This 1996 CD releases for the first time music from the second half of a Geneva concert by the band. One can argue that these performances of "It's Only a Paper Moon," "'Round Midnight," Wayne Shorter's "The Summit," "A Night In Tunisia" and Timmons' "This Here" do not add that much to the Messengers' vast legacy, but the music is really too good for hard bop fans (even those with many other versions) to pass up. —*Scott Yanow*

Lausanne 1960, Pt. 1 / 1960 / TCB ◆◆◆◆
Nearly every recording by Art Blakey's Jazz Messengers, particularly during the 1958-61 period, is well worth acquiring by fans of hard bop. This 1995 CD from the Swiss label TCB features a particularly strong edition of Blakey's group, with trumpeter Lee Morgan, tenor saxophonist Wayne Shorter, pianist Bobby Timmons, bassist Jymie Merritt and the drummer/leader. Together they perform "Now's the Time," two of Shorter's tunes ("Lester Left Town" and "Noise in the Attic"), Morgan's "Kozo's Waltz" and Timmons' recent hit "Dat Dere." Recommended. —*Scott Yanow*

The Big Beat / Mar. 6, 1960 / Blue Note ◆◆◆◆
In 1960, Art Blakey led one of the greatest versions of his Jazz Messengers. The particular edition heard on this CD features three distinctive soloists (trumpeter Lee Morgan, tenor saxophonist Wayne Shorter and pianist Bobby Timmons). Highlights of *The Big Beat* include Timmons' "Dat Dere" and Shorter's "Lester Left Town" in addition to a colorful arrangement of "It's Only a Paper Moon," heard in two versions. A gem. —*Scott Yanow*

Like Someone in Love / Aug. 7, 1960 / Blue Note ◆◆◆◆
Taken from the same sessions that resulted in *A Night in Tunisia*, this fine CD features the 1960 version of the Jazz Messengers starring trumpeter Lee Morgan, tenor saxophonist Wayne Shorter and pianist Bobby Timmons. The title cut is the most impressive performance, but this excellent program of high-quality hard bop also allows listeners to hear three obscure Wayne Shorter compositions and Lee Morgan's forgotten "Johnny's Blue." —*Scott Yanow*

Night in Tunisia / Aug. 14, 1960 / Blue Note ◆◆◆◆
The lengthy title track on this CD easily overshadows the rest of the program for it is one of the most exciting versions ever recorded of Dizzy Gillespie's "A Night in Tunisia." Trumpeter Lee Morgan (then only in his early 20s), tenor saxophonist Wayne Shorter, pianist Bobby Timmons and bassist Jymie Merritt formed one of the strongest of the many versions of Art Blakey's Jazz Messengers and are actually in fine form during the remainder of the satisfying (if anticlimatic) set. The CD augments the LP by adding a version of "When Your Lover Has Gone" and an alternate take of "Sincerely Diana" to the original program. —*Scott Yanow*

Meet You at the Jazz Corner of the World, Vol. 1 / Sep. 14, 1960 / Blue Note ◆◆◆
Art Blakey's 1960 Jazz Messengers recorded so many excellent records that the "good" rating given this LP is relative. With trumpeter Lee Morgan, tenor saxophonist Wayne Shorter and pianist Bobby Timmons all receiving plenty of solo space, the band is in fine form on Hank Mobley's "The Opener," Lee Morgan's "What Know" and two standards. Little unexpected occurs, but fans of hard-swinging jazz will want to pick up both volumes in this series. —*Scott Yanow*

Meet You at the Jazz Corner of the World, Vol. 2 / Sep. 14, 1960 / Blue Note ◆◆◆
The much-recorded 1960 Jazz Messengers are in fine form for both of the LP volumes in this series of "Live at Birdland" recordings. Trumpeter Lee Morgan, tenor saxophonist Wayne Shorter and pianist Bobby Timmons all take excellent solos on Wayne Shorter's "The Summit," a standard ("The Things I Love") and two Hank Mobley songs. Not essential hard bop music but quite enjoyable in its own right. —*Scott Yanow*

Live in Stockholm (1960) / Dec. 6, 1960 / Dragon ◆◆◆◆
Recorded from a radio broadcast in Sweden, this LP finds the Jazz Messengers near their peak. This edition of the band (with trumpeter Lee Morgan, Wayne Shorter on tenor and pianist Bobby Timmons) was the most celebrated and most frequently recorded of all the versions of the Jazz Messengers. This album (which includes strong versions of "Blues March," "Lester Left Town," "Along Came Betty," "A Night in Tunisia" and Wayne Shorter's lesser-known "The Summit") is easily recommended as a strong example of their legacy. —*Scott Yanow*

Pisces / Feb. 12, 1961 / Blue Note ◆◆◆

Roots & Herbs / Feb. 18, 1961 / Blue Note ◆◆◆

The Witch Doctor / Mar. 14, 1961 / Blue Note ◆◆◆
The 1960-61 Jazz Messengers featured three distinctive soloists (trumpeter Lee Morgan, Wayne Shorter on tenor and pianist Bobby Timmons), perfectly suitable accompaniment by bassist Jymie Merritt and typically powerful drumming from its leader, Art Blakey. *Witch Doctor* has two compositions apiece from Morgan and Shorter in addition to Timmons' "A Little Busy" and Clifford Jordan's "Lost and Found." None of these songs became standards, but the fine solos and strong group sound make this LP worth picking up. —*Scott Yanow*

Paris Jazz Concert / May 13, 1961 / RTE ◆◆◆

The Freedom Rider / May 27, 1961 / Blue Note ◆◆◆◆◆
The final recording by this edition of the Jazz Messengers (featuring trumpeter Lee Morgan, tenor saxophonist Wayne Shorter, pianist Bobby Timmons, bassist Jymie Merritt and drummer/leader Art Blakey) finds the group consolidating their year-and-a-half of experience into yet another exciting document. Blakey's unaccompanied drum feature on "The Freedom Rider" is full of drama while the rest of the program (two compositions apiece by Morgan and Shorter) makes this last chapter for this particular band quite memorable. —*Scott Yanow*

Art Blakey!!!!! Jazz Messengers!!!!! / Jun. 13, 1961-Jun. 14, 1961 / Impulse! ◆◆◆
An absolutely wonderful 1961 set from Blakey and company, who demonstrate here how to be note-perfect without leeching away the emotion of a performance. Aside from Blakey's divine drum work, the standouts include Jaymie Merritt's trippy bass fingerwork, and Wayne Shorter blowing his heart out on tenor sax. Beautifully remastered, well worth having in this edition. —*Steven McDonald*

Mosaic / Oct. 1, 1961 / Blue Note ◆◆◆◆
The first studio recording by Art Blakey's all-star Messengers of 1961-64 features five group originals (including "Mosaic," "Arabia" and "Crisis") and exciting solos from the great front line (trumpeter Freddie Hubbard, trombonist Curtis Fuller and tenor saxophonist Wayne Shorter). All of the recordings by this classic hard bop group are well worth acquiring. —*Scott Yanow*

Buhaina's Delight / Nov. 28, 1961+Dec. 18, 1961 / Blue Note ✦✦✦✦
There have been several classic editions of Art Blakey's Jazz Messengers including the sextet heard on this CD which adds four alternate takes to the original LP's program. With trumpeter Freddie Hubbard, tenor saxophonist Wayne Shorter, trombonist Curtis Fuller and pianist Cedar Walton (all of whom would be major names in jazz for the next 30 years) taking consistently excellent solos, it is not surprising that this CD (which is highlighted by "Moon River," "Bu's Delight" and "Backstage Sally"), as with all of the other recordings by this group, is easily recommended to lovers of hard bop. —*Scott Yanow*

The African Beat / Jan. 24, 1962 / Blue Note ✦✦✦

Three Blind Mice, Vol. 1 / Mar. 9,1962+Mar. 18, 1962/ Blue Note ✦✦✦
The first of two volumes in this brief CD series greatly expands upon the original LP, adding Wayne Shorter's "Children of the Night" and an alternate version of Freddie Hubbard's "Up Jumped Spring" to an already strong set of memorable material. Other highlights by this all-star sextet (featuring trumpeter Hubbard, Shorter's tenor and trombonist Curtis Fuller) include Fuller's reworking of "Three Blind Mice," "Blue Moon" and "When Lights Are Low." —*Scott Yanow*

Three Blind Mice, Vol. 2 / Mar. 9, 1962-Mar. 18, 1962 / Blue Note ✦✦✦
The second of two CDs that greatly expand the original *Three Blind Mice* LP captures the all-star Jazz Messengers sextet of 1961-62 at two separate concerts. The five extended performances, which consist of four group originals (including "Mosaic" and "Ping Pong") and "It's Only a Paper Moon," include many strong solos from trumpeter Freddie Hubbard, trombonist Curtis Fuller, tenor saxophonist Wayne Shorter and pianist Cedar Walton, all future bandleaders. Both of the CD volumes are highly recommended. —*Scott Yanow*

Caravan / Oct. 23, 1962-Oct. 24, 1962 / Original Jazz Classics ✦✦✦✦
Art Blakey led many strong versions of his Jazz Messengers over a 30-year period. This particular unit featured five young greats: trumpeter Freddie Hubbard, tenor saxophonist Wayne Shorter, trombonist Curtis Fuller, pianist Cedar Walton and bassist Reggie Workman. On the CD reissue (which adds a pair of alternate takes to the original LP program), the group is heard in prime form with the highlights including "Caravan," "Thermo" (two versions are included) and "Skylark." —*Scott Yanow*

Ugetsu / Jun. 16, 1963 / Original Jazz Classics ✦✦✦✦
Art Blakey's 1963 Jazz Messengers (which included trumpeter Freddie Hubbard, tenor saxophonist Wayne Shorter, trombonist Curtis Fuller, pianist Cedar Walton and bassist Reggie Workman in addition to the drummer-leader) was one of his finest. The CD reissue (which adds two songs to the seven on the original LP) has plenty of strong moments, particularly on "Ping-Pong," Shorter's feature ("I Didn't Know What Time It Was") and the memorable "One by One." This high-quality hard bop session is recommended. —*Scott Yanow*

A Jazz Message / Jul. 16, 1963 / MCA ✦✦✦
Drummer Art Blakey took time off from his busy schedule as leader of the Jazz Messengers to participate in this quartet session with saxophonist Sonny Stitt, pianist McCoy Tyner and bassist Art Davis. Although this session was under Blakey's leadership, Stitt (on both tenor and alto) emerges as the main soloist, playing his trademark bebop lines with creativity and typical enthusiasm. —*Scott Yanow*

Blues Bag / 1964 / Affinity ✦✦✦
This LP is a real curiosity in the history of Art Blakey's Jazz Messengers, for it found his band utilizing two trumpets (Lee Morgan and Freddie Hill) and welcoming Buddy DeFranco as the only reed player, with the clarinetist sticking exclusively to bass clarinet. Even the repertoire, which includes John Coltrane's "Cousin Mary," Ornette Coleman's "Blues Connotation" and Leonard Feather's "Twelve Tone Blues," is unusual. DeFranco is the main soloist throughout this unique (if consistently swinging) set. —*Scott Yanow*

Free for All / Feb. 10, 1964 / Blue Note ✦✦✦✦
During most of 1961-64 Art Blakey's Jazz Messengers (except for bassist Reggie Workman replacing Spanky DeBrest) managed to keep the same personnel, a remarkable feat when one considers the strong talent (which included trumpeter Freddie Hubbard, trombonist Curtis Fuller, Wayne Shorter on tenor and pianist Cedar Walton). *Free for All* was this particular group's last recording before Freddie Hubbard went out on his own, and it includes lengthy versions of two Shorter tunes, Hubbard's "The Core" and the standard "Pensativa." Fine music. —*Scott Yanow*

Kyoto / Feb. 20, 1964 / Original Jazz Classics ✦✦✦
Reissued on Fantasy's OJC series, this LP (also available as a CD) finds Art Blakey's Jazz Messengers paying tribute to Japan (where they had toured to great acclaim) on two selections, featuring Art Blakey's cousin as a vocalist on "Wellington's Blues" (a real rarity in the Jazz Messengers' discography) and debuting Curtis Fuller's "The High Priest." With trumpeter Freddie Hubbard and tenorman Wayne

Shorter and trombonist Fuller in fine form, this is one of literally dozens of recommended Jazz Messengers recordings. —*Scott Yanow*

Indestructible / Apr. 24, 1964+May 15, 1964 / Blue Note ✦✦✦✦
In 1964, trumpeter Lee Morgan rejoined the Jazz Messengers, replacing his original replacement, Freddie Hubbard. The hard-swinging style of this influential unit remained unchanged with drummer/leader Art Blakey still insisting on distinctive solos and constant new material. Typically, the music on this fine LP consists of five then-recent compositions by band members, one apiece from Morgan, pianist Cedar Walton ("When Love Is New") and tenor saxophonist Wayne Shorter and two from trombonist Curtis Fuller. Enjoyable music. —*Scott Yanow*

Soul Finger / May 12, 1965-May 13, 1965 / Limelight ✦✦✦
After six years of very consistent personnel (with only a few gradual changes), Art Blakey's Jazz Messengers in 1965 were in a state of transition. This particular LP found both Lee Morgan and Freddie Hubbard making farewell appearances on trumpet, pianist John Hicks and bassist Victor Sproles joining up as short-term members and veteran Lucky Thompson being well featured on both tenor and soprano sax. The music is more relaxed than usual but still contains some of that distinctive Jazz Messengers fire. This rare set is worth searching for. —*Scott Yanow*

Buttercorn Lady / Jan. 1, 1966-Jan. 9, 1966 / Limelight ✦✦✦
Few jazz followers would think of trumpeter Chuck Mangione and pianist Keith Jarrett as former members of Art Blakey's Jazz Messengers, but in 1966, they both worked in the drummer's classic hard bop unit and the stint gave them needed exposure and helped the pair to develop their own individual voices. With tenor saxophonist Frank Mitchell and bassist Reggie Workman completing the quintet, this particular version of the Jazz Messengers only had the opportunity to record this one excellent live LP (which is currently out of print) but proved to be a worthy successor to their more acclaimed predecessors. —*Scott Yanow*

Hold On, I'm Coming / May 27, 1966 / Limelight ✦✦
One of the few out-and-out commercial recordings made by drummer Art Blakey during his long career, this attempt at jazzing up some pop tunes features so-so arrangements by Tom McIntosh and Melba Liston on such songs as "Hold On, I'm Coming," "Secret Agent Man," "Mame" and "Monday, Monday." A real curiosity (finding Blakey using organist Malcom Bass as a particularly unlikely sideman), it would not be an understatement to say that this is not one of the more essential Art Blakey recordings. —*Scott Yanow*

Moanin' [LaserLight] / 1968 / LaserLight ✦✦✦✦
This is a particularly obscure live set by Art Blakey's Jazz Messengers, one not even listed in most discographies. The 1968 edition of Blakey's band was a strong if underrated unit consisting of the drummer/leader, trumpeter Bill Hardman, trombonist Julian Priester, tenor saxophonist Billy Harper, pianist Ronnie Mathews and bassist Lawrence Evans. This CD is well-recorded and is highlighted by "Slide's Delight," Harper's ballad feature on "You Don't Know What Love Is," and a spirited remake of "Moanin'." —*Scott Yanow*

Art Blakey and the Jazz Messengers [Catalyst] / Feb. 19, 1970 / Catalyst ✦✦✦
One of only two albums recorded by Art Blakey's Jazz Messengers during 1967-71, this LP is quite unusual, for not only does it feature veteran trumpeter Bill Hardman, but the avant-garde tenor of Carlos Garnett and pianist Joanne Brackeen (the first female member of the Jazz Messengers). Mostly performing durable standards such as "Moanin'," "Whisper Not" and "A Night in Tunisia," the quintet casts new light on these tunes, making them sound fresh and flexible. This unusual set is recommended to longtime followers of Art Blakey; it deserves to be reissued on CD. —*Scott Yanow*

Child's Dance, Vol. 1 / May 23, 1972-Mar. 27, 1973 / Prestige ✦✦✦✦
Art Blakey's three albums for Prestige from 1972-73 have been reissued with additional material on two CDs. For this volume the four songs that originally comprised *Child's Dance* are joined by a previously unissued "Kaku Aka" and two tunes from *Anthenagin*. The different instrumentation featured on some of these numbers was a real change-of-pace for Blakey; on "Song for the Lonely Woman" and "Kaku Aka" he utilizes several percussionists, a flute-soprano front line and electric piano. The great trumpeter Woody Shaw is on the other five numbers and is showcased on a memorable version of "I Can't Get Started;" other sidemen include Carter Jefferson on tenor, keyboardists Cedar Walton and George Cables and bassist Stanley Clarke (20 at the time). Even with some funky and electrified moments, the music definitely holds onto one's interest throughout. —*Scott Yanow*

Mission Eternal, Vol. 2 / May 26, 1973-May 29, 1973 / Prestige ✦✦✦✦
The second of two CDs that reissue the music from three Art Blakey LPs plus additional material (reshuffling the order to make it more logical), this set features trumpeter Woody Shaw, Carter Jefferson on tenor and soprano, Cedar Walton on keyboards, bassist Mickey Bass, Tony Waters on congas and the drummer/leader plus three guests: guitarist Michael Howell, trombonist Steve Turre and (on "Moa-

nin'" and "Along Came Betty"), singer Jon Hendricks. Shaw is in excellent form and Blakey propels and inspires his sidemen as usual. In addition to the two vocals, the nine instrumentals (which had originally been divided between the LPs *Buhaina* and *Athenagin*) are consistently swinging and well worth hearing. —*Scott Yanow*

Gypsy Folk Tales: Art Blakey and the Jazz Messengers / Feb. 14, 1977-Mar. 1, 1977 / Roulette ✦✦✦

The 1977 version of the Jazz Messengers introduced two new voices to jazz (altoist Bobby Watson and the Russian trumpeter Valeri Ponomarev) in addition to featuring tenor saxophonist Dave Schnitter, veteran pianist Walter Davis and bassist Dennis Irwin. This Roulette LP includes six fairly recent originals in addition to a pair of numbers co-written by drummer Art Blakey with saxophonist Bob Mintzer. Davis' "Gypsy Folk Tales" and "Jodi" are the best-known songs and the hard-bop oriented solos are consistently fresh. —*Scott Yanow*

In My Prime, Vol. 1 / Dec. 29, 1977 / Timeless ✦✦✦

Leader of the Jazz Messengers at the time of this recording for over 22 years, drummer Art Blakey was still discovering new talent. In addition to altoist Bobby Watson, trumpeter Valeri Ponomarev and David Schnitter on tenor, this particular session introduced the great pianist James Williams to the Messenger fold. Despite the changes in musical fashions, Art Blakey and his hard-bop institution were still turning out new material and solos in the late '70s that sound fresh and alive today. —*Scott Yanow*

In This Korner / May 8, 1978 / Concord Jazz ✦✦✦✦

Although one of the lesser-known editions of the Jazz Messengers, the sextet featured on this Concord LP (trumpeter Valeri Ponomarev, altoist Bobby Watson, tenor saxophonist David Schnitter, pianist James Williams and bassist Dennis Irwin in addition to the leader/drummer) could hold its own with its more acclaimed predecessors and successors. Blakey always encouraged his sidemen to write new music, so on this set Williams, Watson and Ponomarev contributed fresh material for the hard-bop ensemble. Blakey fans should enjoy this underrated set. —*Scott Yanow*

Reflections in Blue / Dec. 4, 1978 / Timeless ✦✦✦

The 1978 Jazz Messengers was one of Art Blakey's strongest groups in years, although it would soon be overshadowed by its successor (which introduced a young Wynton Marsalis). With trumpeter Valerie Ponomarev, altoist Bobby Watson and a tenor saxophonist forming a potent front line and new material from each of the principals (plus pianist James Williams) in addition to a lengthy ballad medley, this is a fine all-around set, last available on LP. —*Scott Yanow*

And the Jazz Messengers Big Band / Jul. 13, 1980-Jul. 17, 1980 / Timeless ✦✦✦✦

Art Blakey, leader of the highly influential hard-bop group the Jazz Messengers (which was usually a quintet or a sextet), made a rare tour with an 11-piece little big band in mid-1980. Included among the personnel were such unknown youngsters as trumpeter Wynton Marsalis (then age 18), Branford Marsalis on baritone and alto, trombonist Robin Eubanks and guitarist Kevin Eubanks. The remarkable group also included the regular members of the Jazz Messengers (trumpeter Valeri Ponomarev, altoist Bobby Watson, tenor saxophonist Billy Pierce and pianist James Williams) and even a second drummer, John Ramsey. The music (three Bobby Watson compositions, the standard "Stairway to the Stars" and Williams' blues "Minor Thesis") is consistently excellent and all of the musicians get their chance to solo. A historically significant and rather enjoyable release. —*Scott Yanow*

Live at Bubba's / Oct. 11, 1980 / Who's Who In Jazz ✦✦✦

The teenage trumpeter Wynton Marsalis (then most heavily influenced by Freddie Hubbard) made his recording debut as a member of Art Blakey's Jazz Messengers on this fine LP and, as his feature on "My Funny Valentine" shows, he was more than ready for the spotlight. This version of the Messengers was particularly strong with such future bandleaders as altoist Bobby Watson, tenor saxophonist Billy Pierce, pianist James Williams and bassist Charles Fambrough (along with the leader/drummer) rompin' on such pieces as "Moanin'," "Soulful Mr. Timmons" and "Free for All." —*Scott Yanow*

Art Blakey in Sweden / Mar. 9, 1981 / Evidence ✦✦✦✦✦

On this 1981 live session, the teenage trumpeter Wynton Marsalis is in fine form on "How Deep Is the Ocean," Bobby Watson makes the most of his feature on "Skylark" and the full sextet (which also includes tenor saxophonist Billy Pierce and pianist James Williams) romps on "Webb City" and "Gypsy Folk Tales." The contents of this excellent LP have since been reissued on CD by Evidence. Recommended in either form. —*Scott Yanow*

In Sweden / Mar. 9, 1981 / Evidence ✦✦✦

This CD (a straight reissue of an Amigo LP) documents a live appearance by Art Blakey's Jazz Messengers in 1981 at a period when he was featuring quite an all-

star lineup (although its young members were then fairly unknown): trumpeter Wynton Marsalis (showcased on "How Deep Is the Ocean"), altoist Bobby Watson (heard throughout "Skylark"), tenorman Billy Pierce, pianist James Williams and bassist Charles Fambrough. This CD gives one classic hard bop and a chance to hear Wynton Marsalis at the beginning of his productive career. —*Scott Yanow*

Album of the Year / Apr. 12, 1981 / Timeless ✦✦✦✦

The 1981 edition of the Jazz Messengers featured more than its share of young greats (trumpeter Wynton Marsalis, altoist Bobby Watson, tenor saxophonist Billy Pierce, pianist James Williams and bassist Charles Fambrough), reinforcing drummer Art Blakey's recognition as jazz's greatest talent scout. This high-quality set, recorded in Paris, includes new material (highlighted by James Williams' "Soulful Mister Timmons"), Wayne Shorter's "Witch Hunt" and the Charlie Parker blues "Cheryl." —*Scott Yanow*

Straight Ahead / Jun. 1981 / Concord Jazz ✦✦✦✦✦

One of the best recordings by Art Blakey's 1981 Jazz Messengers, this set features Wynton Marsalis (then 19) on "How Deep Is the Ocean" and other illustrious sidemen (including altoist Bobby Watson, tenor saxophonist Bill Pierce and pianist James Williams) playing such group pieces as "Falling in Love with Love," "My Romance" and Watson's "E.T.A." Highly recommended. —*Scott Yanow*

Killer Joe: Art Blakey & George Kawaguchi / Dec. 4, 1981 / Storyville ✦✦✦

This unusual LP finds Art Blakey and the Jazz Messengers adding a second drummer, the fine Japanese player George Kawaguchi, to a set featuring three standards and two Kawaguchi pieces. Recorded at a time when Wynton Marsalis was on leave (touring with Herbie Hancock), this date showcases such players as trumpeter Wallace Roney, altoist Branford Marsalis and veteran trombonist Slide Hampton. Fine music, although a bit of an oddity. —*Scott Yanow*

Keystone 3 / Jan. 1982 / Concord Jazz ✦✦✦✦✦

Wynton Marsalis' final recording as a member of Art Blakey's Jazz Messengers finds his brother Branford taking Bobby Watson's place on alto. The remainder of this superb sextet includes tenor saxophonist Bill Pierce, pianist Donald Brown, bassist Charles Fambrough and the veteran drummer/leader. All concerned sound in top form on both new (Wynton's "Waterfalls" and Watson's "Fuller Love") and old ("In Walked Bud" and "In a Sentimental Mood") material alike. Mostly high-powered hard bop in the best tradition of the Jazz Messengers. —*Scott Yanow*

Art Blakey and the All Star Messengers / Apr. 11, 1982 / RCA ✦✦

Drummer Art Blakey could have formed quite a few all-star groups drawn exclusively from the alumni of his Jazz Messengers. One of his few one-shot bands of that nature sounds fine on this LP featuring trumpeter Freddie Hubbard, trombonist Curtis Fuller, Benny Golson's tenor, pianist Cedar Walton and bassist Buster Williams. In addition to newer Golson tunes, this unit clearly enjoys themselves playing such classics as "Moanin'," "Blues March," "A Night in Tunisia" and "I Remember Clifford." Few surprises occur, but the music should satisfy Blakey's many fans. —*Scott Yanow*

Oh, by the Way / May 20, 1982 / Timeless ✦✦✦

When the Marsalis Brothers left the Jazz Messengers in early 1982, Wynton suggested that Art Blakey take a close listen to trumpeter Terence Blanchard (then 19) and 21-year-old altoist Donald Harrison. The drummer took his advice, and after also adding young pianist Johnny O'Neal, Blakey soon had an exciting new version of the Jazz Messengers. Tenor saxophonist Bill Pierce and bassist Charles Fambrough were still present from the older band for this excellent LP. In the Blakey tradition, this set has five new compositions from band members in addition to Wayne Shorter's "One by One" and the standard "My Funny Valentine"; the music is a fine example of high-quality hard bop. —*Scott Yanow*

New York Scene / May 1984 / Concord Jazz ✦✦✦✦

Nearly 30 years after forming the first version of the Jazz Messengers, drummer Art Blakey was still jazz's top talent scout. For this Concord LP such new members as tenor saxophonist Jean Toussaint, pianist Mulgrew Miller and bassist Lonnie Plaxico joined the team of trumpeter Terence Blanchard and altoist Donald Harrison (who had hooked up with Blakey two years earlier) to create a fine set of hard bop. Miller has a ballad medley to himself, Blanchard is well featured on "Tenderly" and the rest of the program features the full band on stimulating group originals. —*Scott Yanow*

Blue Night / Mar. 17, 1985 / Timeless ✦✦✦

The last time that drummer Art Blakey was able to keep a consistent personnel in his Jazz Messengers together for a lengthy period of time was the version he had with trumpeter Terence Blanchard and altoist Donald Harrison in the mid-'80s (a band which also included Jean Toussaint on tenor, pianist Mulgrew Miller and bassist Lonnie Plaxico). This excellent Timeless CD has a version of "Body and Soul" along with seven stimulating (if not overly memorable) recent originals by band members. Fine modern hard bop. —*Scott Yanow*

Live at Sweet Basil: Art Blakey and the Jazz Messengers / Mar. 24, 1985 / GNP
♦♦♦

This excellent all-around session showcases the 1985 edition of Art Blakey's Jazz Messengers, a band that boasted such fine young soloists as trumpeter Terence Blanchard, altoist Donald Harrison, tenor saxophonist Jean Toussaint and pianist Mulgrew Miller. In addition to Harrison's "Mr. Babe" and Walter Davis' "Jodi," the ensemble successfully updates two Jazz Messenger classics: "Blues March" and "Moanin'." —*Scott Yanow*

Live at Kimball's / Apr. 1985 / Concord Jazz ♦♦♦♦

Art Blakey's mid-1980s version of the Jazz Messengers made many recordings, but since the group (featuring trumpeter Terence Blanchard, altoist Donald Harrison, tenor saxophonist Jean Toussaint, pianist Mulgrew Miller, bassist Lonnie Plaxico and the leader/drummer) was particularly talented, all of its sessions are well worth acquiring by lovers of modern hard bop. This particular LP has ballad features for Blanchard ("Polka Dots and Moonbeams"), Toussaint ("I Love You") and Miller ("Old Folks" and "You and the Night and the Music") along with three flag-wavers for the full ensemble. —*Scott Yanow*

Hard Champion: Art Blakey and the Jazz Messengers / May 24, 1985 / Evidence ♦♦

Three of the four selections on this CD are taken from the same session as *Live at Sweet Basil*, but despite some fine playing, the music is not all that memorable or unique. Trumpeter Terence Blanchard, altoist Donald Harrison and tenor saxophonist Jean Toussaint did make a potent front line so completists may want to pick up this reissue of Paddle Wheel material that was only previously released in Japan. A final throwaway track (the three-minute "Theme of 'Hard Champion'") was actually recorded two years later by a different version of the Jazz Messengers. —*Scott Yanow*

Dr. Jeckyle / Dec. 30, 1985 / Evidence ♦♦♦

The second of two CDs documenting one of the last appearances by the Jazz Messengers before trumpeter Terence Blanchard and altoist Donald Harrison decided to go out on their own finds Blakey's group expanded temporarily to a septet with the addition of trombonist Tim Williams. The ensemble is in particularly strong form on Bobby Watson's "Fuller Love," Jackie McLean's "Dr. Jeckyle," Wayne Shorter's "One by One" and the advanced Ron Carter tune "81." —*Scott Yanow*

New Year's Eve at Sweet Basil: Art Blakey and His Jazz Messengers / Dec. 30, 1985 / Evidence ♦♦♦♦

One of two CDs recorded by the Jazz Messengers during the last two days of 1985 documents one of the final appearances by the Terence Blanchard-Donald Harrison version of this jazz institution. With trombonist Tim Williams (along with tenor saxophonist Jean Toussaint, pianist Mulgrew Miller and bassist Lonnie Plaxico) added on, the Messengers were temporarily a septet, but their blend of hard bop and youthful enthusiasm was unchanged. Three group originals and Billy Eckstine's "I Want to Talk About You" are performed by this fine group. The Evidence CD is a reissue of music formerly issued by the Japanese Paddle Wheel label. —*Scott Yanow*

Feeling Good / Sep. 8, 1986-Sep. 9, 1986 / Delos ♦♦♦

After nearly a decade of relative stability, the turnover in Art Blakey's Jazz Messengers greatly increased during the veteran drummer's last four years. This was not due to dissatisfaction with his dedication to hard bop and hard-swinging but to Blakey's desire to play with as many of the promising young jazzmen as possible. The CD *Feeling Good*, the Jazz Messengers' only recording from 1986-87, features a septet with trumpeter Wallace Roney, altoist Kenny Garrett and holdovers Jean Toussaint (on tenor), trombonist Tim Williams and pianist Donald Brown. The repertoire includes both new originals and a few Messenger standbys; the music is consistently enjoyable. —*Scott Yanow*

Not Yet / Mar. 19, 1988 / Soul Note ♦♦♦♦

The 1988 edition of the Jazz Messengers, which drummer Art Blakey had been leading for 33 years, showed a great deal of promise. Comprising trumpeter Phillip Harper (soon to form the Harper Brothers), trombonist Robin Eubanks, the tenor of Javon Jackson, pianist Bennie Green and bassist Peter Washington, this band (whose average age without counting Blakey was around 25) performs one original apiece by Green and Jackson along with five older songs on this enjoyable release. The music may not have contained too many surprises or been startlingly new, but the results are quite pleasing. —*Scott Yanow*

I Get a Kick Out of Bu / Nov. 11, 1988 / Soul Note ♦♦♦

Even after heading the Jazz Messengers for over three decades, drummer Art Blakey kept true to his original vision, using the band as a forum for talented young players to swing hard and grow rapidly. Certainly his crop of players in 1988 (which included trumpeter Phillip Harper, trombonist Robin Eubanks, tenor saxophonist Javon Jackson and pianist Bennie Green) could compete favorably with many of his earlier bands. This Soul Note release, which includes a nine-

minute drum solo by the leader, mostly sticks to inventive reworkings of standards along with a song apiece from Eubanks and Harper. Excellent music. —*Scott Yanow*

The Art of Jazz: Live in Leverkusen / Oct. 9, 1989 / In & Out ♦♦♦

Drummer Art Blakey and the 1989 version of his Jazz Messengers (with trumpeter Brian Lynch, tenor saxophonist Javon Jackson, trombonist Frank Lacy, pianist Geoff Keezer and bassist Buster Williams) celebrated the leader's 70th birthday by welcoming back several notable alumni: trumpeters Freddie Hubbard and Terence Blanchard, altoists Jackie McLean and Donald Harrison, tenors Wayne Shorter and Benny Golson, pianist Walter Davis, Jr., and trombonist Curtis Fuller. This single CD has some of the highlights of the British concert, although one wishes that the entire date had been released, for some of the musicians only make cameo appearances. Highlights include the opportunities to hear Shorter in this setting (he is well featured on "Lester Left Town") and versions of "Along Came Betty" and "Blues March" that contain short solos from many of the players. In addition, Michele Hendricks sings Horace Silver's words to "Mr. Blakey"; drummer Roy Haynes plays second drums on "Blues March"; and the CD concludes with a nearly 13-minute interview that Mike Hennessey conducted with Blakey in 1976 in which the drummer reminisces about the Jazz Messengers' early days. Well worth picking up. —*Scott Yanow*

Chippin' In: Art Blakey and His Jazz Messengers / Feb. 1, 1990-Feb. 2, 1990 / Timeless ♦♦♦

35 years after first officially forming the Jazz Messengers, drummer Art Blakey entered his final year still at it. Due to the many promising young players around at the time, Blakey expanded the Messengers from its usual quintet or sextet into a septet for this fine recording session. In addition to trumpeter Brian Lynch, pianist Geoff Keezer and bassist Essiet Okon Essiet, this version of the Messengers had two tenors (Javon Jackson and Dale Barlow) and a pair of alternating trombonists (Frank Lacy and Steve Davis). Quite typically, other than Wayne Shorter's obscure "Hammerhead" and two standards, all of the material on this CD was new and composed by Blakey's sidemen. Because Blakey constantly persuaded his musicians to write music, the Jazz Messengers stayed young in spirit, just like its leader. A fine effort. —*Scott Yanow*

One for All / Apr. 10, 1990-Apr. 11, 1990 / A&M ♦♦♦

The final recording by Art Blakey's Jazz Messengers found the 70-year-old drummer (just months before his death) doing what he loved best, leading a group of young players through hard-swinging and generally new music in the hard-bop style. The last edition of the Jazz Messengers (a septet with trumpeter Brian Lynch, trombonist Steve Davis, the tenors of Dale Barlow and Javon Jackson, pianist Geoffrey Keezer and bassist Essiet O. Essiet) was comprised, as usual, of future bandleaders and stylists. Blakey, although fairly well deaf by this time, still pushed the ensembles and the individual players to play above their heads. A satisfying final effort from an irreplaceable drummer and bandleader. —*Scott Yanow*

Terence Blanchard

b. Mar. 13, 1962, New Orleans, LA
Trumpet / Hard Bop, Post-Bop

Although he originally rose to prominence in the shadow of Wynton Marsalis, Terence Blanchard was one of the first Young Lions to develop his own sound, mixing in elements of Freddie Hubbard and Marsalis. He studied piano from the age of five and took up trumpet in 1976. Blanchard was with Lionel Hampton during 1980-82 and then replaced Marsalis with Art Blakey's Jazz Messengers. He found fame while with Blakey during 1982-86 and then co-led a group with Donald Harrison. After taking time off to work on his embouchure (and returning with a greatly increased range), Blanchard became active writing film scores for Spike Lee. He played in the films *Do the Right Thing* and *Mo' Better Blues* and then wrote for *Jungle Fever* and *Malcolm X*, launching a potentially lucrative second career. Fortunately Blanchard has not neglected his own playing and in the 1990s he has recorded several superior sets of advanced hard-bop music. —*Scott Yanow*

New York Second Line / Oct. 15, 1983-Oct. 16, 1983 / George Wein Collection ♦♦♦♦

Trumpeter Terence Blanchard and altoist Donald Harrison were both still members of Art Blakey's Jazz Messengers when they co-led this colorful set; they would break away to form their own group in early 1986. "New York Second Line," which sounds like a crazy marching band and is an eccentric tribute to the co-leaders' New Orleans heritage, is the most memorable selection but all of the group originals plus "I Can't Get Started" are given inventive treatment. With pianist Mulgrew Miller, bassist Lonnie Plaxico and drummer Marvin "Smitty" Smith, this was a particularly strong early effort by Blanchard and Harrison. —*Scott Yanow*

Discernment / Dec. 1984 / George Wein Collection ✦✦✦

The second recording co-led by trumpeter Terence Blanchard and altoist Donald Harrison (both of whom had become stars with Art Blakey's Jazz Messengers) mixes together the influences of New Orleans (they even perform a somber version of "When the Saints Go Marching In"), hard bop and the avant-garde. With pianist Mulgrew Miller, bassist Phil Bowler and the colorful drummer Ralph Peterson, Jr., making strong contributions, the quintet performs spirited renditions of four Blanchard originals, two Harrison songs, "The Saints" and the ballad "When I Fall in Love." —*Scott Yanow*

Nascence / Jan. 28, 1986-Jan. 31, 1986 / Columbia ✦✦✦

This Columbia album was recorded shortly after trumpeter Terence Blanchard and altoist Donald Harrison left Art Blakey's Jazz Messengers to form their own group although it was their third recording project together co-leading a quintet. Pianist Mulgrew Miller, bassist Phil Bowler and drummer Ralph Peterson, Jr., give the horns solid and stimulating support on two Blanchard pieces, three Harrison originals, "Alabama" and "She's Out of My Life." Harrison has rarely sounded as advanced and as distinctive as he did in this group while Blanchard shows a great deal of potential that he later realized. —*Scott Yanow*

Eric Dolphy & Booker Little Remembered Live at Sweet Basil / Oct. 1986 / Evidence ✦✦✦

On one night at the Five Spot Cafe in 1961, multi-reedist Eric Dolphy, trumpeter Booker Little, pianist Mal Waldron, bassist Richard Davis and drummer Ed Blackwell recorded seven lengthy selections (six originals and the standard "Like Someone in Love"), enough music to fill up three LPs. 25 years and a couple of months later, trumpeter Terence Blanchard and altoist Donald Harrison used the same rhythm section and performed new versions of the six obscure Dolphy, Little and Waldron compositions. The results were released on two CDs, this one and *Fire Waltz*. While the rhythm section had grown through the years, Blanchard was not in 1986 as original a player as Little had been, and Harrison was not a match for Dolphy; nobody is. But if one can put the original versions of "The Prophet," "Aggression" and "Booker's Waltz" out of one's mind, these two CDs (which were made available domestically by Intersound) are quite enjoyable. They do document the development of Blanchard and Harrison and are strong examples of modern hard bop. If only Eric Dolphy's name was not misspelled on the front cover as "Erich." —*Scott Yanow*

Fire Waltz: Eric Dolphy and Booker Little Remembered / Oct. 3, 1986-Oct. 4, 1986 / Projazz ✦✦✦

This is the second of two King CDs (the other is *Eric Dolphy & Booker Little Remembered Live at Sweet Basil*) from the same sessions. On the tribute to the Dolphy-Little marathon Five Spot recording session of 1961, trumpeter Terence Blanchard and altoist Donald Harrison 35 years later utilized the original rhythm section (pianist Mal Waldron, bassist Richard Davis and drummer Ed Blackwell) and performed the same six compositions that had resulted in three LPs, leaving out the lone standard "Like Someone in Love." These renditions are of course quite different than the earlier versions with Blanchard and Harrison (who doubles on bass clarinet) sounding like themselves rather than their predecessors. On this CD they perform lengthy renditions of "Number Eight," "Fire Waltz" and "Bee Vamp." The advanced modern mainstream music is stimulating without reaching the heights of the original performances. —*Scott Yanow*

Crystal Stair / Apr. 1, 1987-Apr. 3, 1987 / Columbia ✦✦✦✦

The fourth of five albums co-led by trumpeter Terence Blanchard and altoist Donald Harrison, this quintet session (with pianist Cyrus Chestnut, bassist Reginald Veal and drummer Carl Allen) has seven originals by the co-leaders plus "God Bless the Child" and "Softly as in a Morning Sunrise." Although an outgrowth of Art Blakey and hard bop, the stimulating music contains more than its share of surprises and chance-taking, stretching the boundaries of the mainstream a bit. —*Scott Yanow*

Black Pearl / Jan. 22, 1988-Jan. 30, 1988 / Columbia ✦✦✦✦

The fifth and final recording by the Terence Blanchard-Donald Harrison Quintet uses the same notable rhythm section that was on their previous Crystal Stair release: pianist Cyrus Chestnut, bassist Reginald Veal and drummer Carl Allen. In addition, two songs add vibraphonist Monte Croft and percussionist Steve Thornton while guitarist Mark Whitfield sits in on "Infinite Heart." With the exception of Leonard Bernstein's "Somewhere," the repertoire is split between compositions by the co-leaders. Harrison (who contributed tributes to two notable trumpeters ("Selim Sivad" and "Dizzy Gillespie's Hands") was heard at his best during his period with this group. All five of the Quintet's releases (two for the George Wein Collection on Concord and three for Columbia) are worth picking up for this was one of the most stimulating acoustic jazz groups of the mid- to late 1980s. —*Scott Yanow*

Terence Blanchard / 1992 / Columbia ✦✦✦✦

During the four years since he last led a record date, trumpeter Terence Blanchard had broken up his quintet with altoist Donald Harrison, worked with Spike Lee on *Mo' Better Blues* and rebuilt his trumpet technique, emerging as a truly outstanding player. For this excellent "comeback" album, Blanchard uses a sympathetic rhythm section (pianist Bruce Barth, bassist Rodney Whitaker and either Jeff Watts or Troy Davis on drums) and welcomes guest tenors Branford Marsalis and Sam Newsome to three songs apiece. On the varied program, Blanchard opens and closes the set with a hymn ("Motherless Child" and "Amazing Grace"), performs four originals and comes up with personal interpretations of three standards ("Goodbye," "Au Privave" and "I'm Getting Sentimental over You"). By the time this recording came out in 1992, Terence Blanchard was ready to take his place as one of the trumpet giants of the 1990s. —*Scott Yanow*

● **The Malcolm X Jazz Suite** / Dec. 10, 1992-Dec. 14, 1992 / Columbia ✦✦✦✦✦

Trumpeter Terence Blanchard continues to grow and develop with each year. He wrote the score for *Malcolm X* and this set finds him exploring 11 of his themes from the movie with his quintet (which also includes Sam Newsome on tenor, pianist Bruce Bath, bassist Tarus Matten and drummer Troy Davis). Many moods are explored and the fresh material really invigorates the quintet. Newsome's Traneisms blend well with Blanchard (whose range has become quite impressive) and the performances (which easily stand apart from the film) are quite memorable. It's one of Terence Blanchard's finest recordings. —*Scott Yanow*

Simply Stated / 1993 / Columbia ✦✦✦✦

Terence Blanchard is in top form throughout this highly enjoyable outing. The trumpeter is most memorable on "Dear Old Stockholm" (a song from the 1950s that he helped revive), an emotional "When It's Sleepy Time Down South" and a medley of his "Glass J," the theme from *Mo' Better Blues*, and Ornette Coleman's "Lonely Woman." Blanchard, who also plays "Detour Ahead" and four of his originals, is joined by tenor saxophonist Sam Newsome, pianist Bruce Barth, bassist Rodney Whitaker, either Troy Davis or Billy Kilson on drums and (on "Dear Old Stockholm") the up-and-coming altoist Antonio Hart. The music is tied to the hard-bop tradition yet is quite fresh and open to more modern influences. Recommended. —*Scott Yanow*

The Billie Holiday Songbook / Oct. 20, 1993-Oct. 29, 1993 / Columbia ✦✦

Trumpeter Terence Blanchard's tribute to Billie Holiday is a rather melancholy and often downbeat affair. Sounding less original than usual (he displays a strong Wynton Marsalis influence and also hints at times at both Miles Davis and Thad Jones), there is little joy to these renditions of Lady Day material other than the second half of "I Cried for You." The trumpeter's arrangements for the unswinging string section is occasionally oppressive, sometimes borders on Muzak and tends to weigh down the music. The only bright spots are the five fine vocals by Jeanie Bryson, who wisely does not try to sound like Holiday and comes across quite well. Otherwise this is a disappointing outing. —*Scott Yanow*

Romantic Defiance / Dec. 12, 1994-Dec. 15, 1994 / Columbia ✦✦✦✦

The Heart Speaks / Aug. 28, 1995-Aug. 31, 1995 / Columbia ✦✦✦✦

Jimmy Blanton

b. Oct. 5, 1918, Chattanooga, TN, d. Jul. 30, 1942, Los Angeles, CA
Bass / Swing

There is an unbelievably tragic symmetry between the lives of Jimmy Blanton and Charlie Christian. Both were string players who broke into a major big band in the fall of 1939, completely rewrote the vocabularies of their instruments, never led recording sessions of their own, played at the prophetic birth-of-bop jam sessions at Minton's Playhouse in Harlem, and died from the same illness in their late 20s in the same year. In Blanton's case, he fractured the 4/4 meter straitjacket that had shackled bass players before him. With his big rounded tone, flexible technique, superb sense of swing and fluent imagination with both a bow and fingers, Blanton's bass could dance freely around the band and phrase like a horn, all without undermining the music's bass foundation.

Blanton started to play the bass professionally in local Chattanooga groups led by his mother, a pianist. After attending Tennessee State College briefly, he moved to St. Louis where he joined the Jeter-Pillars Orchestra and Fate Marable's riverboat bands, where Duke Ellington heard him and added him to his band. Blanton's arrival helped spur the Ellington band into a major creative phase, and the young bassist created some of the first important bass solos in jazz in such Ellington compositions as "Ko Ko," "Jack the Bear" and "Concerto for Cootie." In addition, Blanton recorded a series of duets with Ellington on piano, the most astounding of which is the playful "Pitter Panther Patter." In 1941, having been diagnosed with congenital tuberculosis, Blanton was forced to retire to a California sanatorium, where he died a few months later. Blanton's legacy became the model for bass players over the next 20 years—Charles Mingus, Oscar Pettiford and Ray

Brown all reflect his influence—and he can be heard to excellent advantage on the two-CD *The Indispensable Duke Ellington, Vols. 5 & 6 1940* (RCA Black and White Series). —*Richard S. Ginell*

Carla Bley

b. May 11, 1938, Oakland, CA

Piano, Arranger, Composer, Leader / Post-Bop

Post-bop jazz has produced only a few first-rate composers of larger forms; Carla Bley ranks high amongst them. Bley possesses an unusually wide compositional range; she combines an acquaintance with and love for jazz in all its forms with great talent and originality. Her music is a peculiarly individual type of hyper-modern jazz. Bley is capable of writing music of great drama and profound humor, often within the confines of the same piece.

Born Carla Borg, Bley learned the fundamentals of music as a child from her father, a church musician. Thereafter, she was mostly self-taught. Bley moved to New York around 1955, where she worked as a cigarette girl and occasional pianist. She married pianist Paul Bley, for whom she began to write tunes (she also wrote for George Russell and Jimmy Giuffre). In 1964, with her second husband, trumpeter Michael Mantler, Bley formed the Jazz Composers Guild Orchestra, which a year later became known simply as the Jazz Composers' Orchestra. Two years later, Bley helped found the Jazz Composers' Orchestra Association, a non-profit organization designed to present, distribute, and produce unconventional forms of jazz. In 1967, vibist Gary Burton's quartet recorded Bley's cycle of tunes *A Genuine Tong Funeral*, which brought her to the attention of the general public for the first time. In 1969, Bley composed and arranged music for Charlie Haden's Liberation Music Orchestra. In 1971, Bley completed the work that cemented her reputation, the jazz opera *Escalator over the Hill*. In the '70s and '80s, Bley continued to run the JCOA and compose and record for her own Watt label. The JCOA essentially folded in the late '80s, but Bley's creative life has continued mostly unabated. For much of the past two decades, she's maintained a mid-sized big band with fairly stable personnel to tour and record. She's also worked a great deal with the bassist Steve Swallow, in duo and in ensembles of varying size.

Bley wrote the music for the soundtrack to the 1985 film *Mortelle Randone*. She also contributed new compositions to the Liberation Music Orchestra's second incarnation in 1983. As an instrumentalist, Bley makes a fine composer; she plays piano and/or organ with most of her bands, and while her playing is always quite musical, it's clear that her strengths lie elsewhere. Bley's asymmetrical compositional structures subvert jazz formula to wonderful effect, and her unpredictable melodies are often as catchy as they are obscure. In the tradition of jazz's very finest composers and improvisers, Bley has developed a style of her very own, and the music as a whole is the better for it. —*Chris Kelsey*

Escalator over the Hill / Nov. 1968-Jun. 1971 / ECM ♦♦

At the time, this was probably the longest jazz-generated work in existence (its length has since been exceeded by recent pieces like Wynton Marsalis' *Blood on the Fields*), a massive, messy, all-encompassing, all-star ego trip that nevertheless gave Carla Bley an immense cachet of good will among the avant-garde. Bley and librettist Paul Haines called it a "chronotransduction," whatever that means. The critics called it a jazz opera—which it isn't. *Escalator* is, however, very much of its time, a late-'60s attempt to let a thousand flowers bloom and indulge in every trendy influence that Bley could conceive. There is rock music, early synthesizer and ring modulator experiments, the obligatory Indian section, repeated outbreaks of Weimar Republic cabaret in 3/4 time that both mock and revere European tradition. The incomprehensible "libretto" and a good deal of the lugubrious writing for big band amount to a textbook of avant-garde pretension. And yet sometimes this unwieldy hash pulls itself together—the woolly, somber, sectional "Hotel Overture" with avant-squeal solos from clarinetist Perry Robinson and the young Gato Barbieri in all his Wild Bull of the Pampas glory, the clear voice of Linda Ronstadt brightening up a song called "Why," Don Cherry's clarion trumpet work, the power trio of John McLaughlin, Jack Bruce and Paul Motian rumbling energetically away amidst the Indian structures of "Rawalpindi Blues." Originally released on three LPs, an almost unheard-of extravagance in 1971, today this giant relic fits comfortably on two CDs. Yet the hard-to-find LP version does have an advantage, for the work concludes with an endless windy drone via one of those locked run-out grooves, an effect that obviously cannot be transferred to a CD, which shuts off automatically. —*Richard S. Ginell*

Tropic Appetites / Sep. 1973-Feb. 1974 / Watt ♦♦♦

The music for this was composed by Carla Bley, the words by Paul Haines. —*AMG*

● **Dinner Music** / Jul. 1976-Sep. 1976 / ECM ♦♦♦♦♦

First excursion on a funky trail, executed immaculately. Near essential. —*Michael G. Nastos*

● **European Tour (1977)** / Sep. 1977 / Watt ♦♦♦♦♦

One of Carla Bley's most rewarding recordings, this set features her tentet playing such numbers as "Wrong Key Donkey," "Drinking Music" and the 19-minute "Spangled Banner Minor and Other Patriotic Songs." Bley's wry humor is often felt and she utilizes such colorful players as trumpeter Michael Mantler, Gary Windo on tenor, trombonist Roswell Rudd and Bob Stewart on tuba in this unusual, somewhat innovative and always fun music. —*Scott Yanow*

Musique Mecanique / Aug. 1978-Nov. 1978 / Watt ♦♦♦♦

Carla Bley's tentet performs some of her most colorful themes on this often-humorous and generally stimulating set. "Jesus Maria and Other Spanish Strains" and the three-part "Musique Mecanique" are particularly memorable. This is the perfect setting for Bley's music, with such musicians as trumpeter Michael Mantler, Gary Windo on tenor and bass clarinet, trombonist Roswell Rudd and Bob Stewart on tuba making their presence felt. —*Scott Yanow*

Social Studies / Sep. 1980-Dec. 1980 / ECM ♦♦♦♦♦

Not everything Carla Bley has done has been artistically successful, but much of it has—and the imaginative, good-humored pianist/organist/composer certainly deserves credit for daring to take so many risks. Bley's risk-taking serves her quite well on *Social Studies*, an unorthodox and adventurous pearl that is as rewarding as it is cerebral. Highlights of this CD range from "Reactionary Tango" (an abstract take on Argentinean music) to the melancholy "Utviklingssang" to the angular quasi-hard bop number "Walking Batteriewoman." This time, Bley leads a nonet, and the star soloists include Carlos Ward (soprano and alto sax), Tony Dagradi (tenor sax, clarinet), Gary Valente (trombone) and frequent allies Michael Mantler (trumpet) and Steve Swallow (electric bass). Bley doesn't allot herself much solo space, but the results are appealing when she does. —*Alex Henderson*

Live! / Aug. 1981 / Watt ♦♦♦

Heavy Heart / Sep. 1983-Oct. 1983 / ECM ♦♦♦

I Hate to Sing / 1984 / ECM ♦♦♦

Night-Glo / Jun. 1985-Aug. 1985 / ECM ♦♦♦

As usual, Carla Bley's albums offer provocative arrangements, unorthodox playing, and interesting guest musicians. Randy Brecker and Paul McCandless are among those who provide interesting solos, while ECM's patented lush, overwhelming production adds atmosphere and color. —*Ron Wynn*

Sextet / Dec. 1986-Jan. 1987 / Watt ♦♦

Fleur Carnivore / Nov. 1988 / ECM ♦♦♦

Duets: Carla Bley and Steve Swallow / 1988 / Watt ♦♦♦♦♦

Despite the coy packaging of this set, there was more *music* here than Carla Bley had offered in many a document, including a healthy revisit to "Batteriewoman" from her investigative days of yesteryear. With the exceptions of the static "Utviklingssang" and "Tango," her work throughout showed a mature voice embracing spare lyricism, sly subtle dissonance and inventive phrasing. —*Milo Fine, Cadence*

The Very Big Carla Bley Band / Oct. 29, 1990-Oct. 30, 1990 / ECM ♦♦♦

Her best LP of the last decade. Best cut is the Latin-tinged "Lo Ultimo." —*Michael G. Nastos*

Go Together / 1992 / ECM ♦♦♦♦

After years spent emphasizing her compositions and bandleading abilities, in the late '80s, Carla Bley finally started featuring her own piano playing to a much greater degree. A melodic but explorative player, Bley (whose use of space sometimes recalls Thelonious Monk) interacts closely with the electric bass of Steve Swallow on this excellent duet session, performing six of her originals and two of Swallow's. —*Scott Yanow*

Big Band Theory / Jul. 2, 1993-Jul. 3, 1993 / Watt ♦♦♦

Songs with Legs / Dec. 1995 / Watt ♦♦♦

Goes to Church / Jul. 19, 1996-Jul. 21, 1996 / ECM ♦♦♦♦♦

This unusual set (recorded live in Italy) features Carla Bley's 17-piece big band playing a set of her originals that hint at times at church hymns without getting particularly somber. Most memorable is the complex "Beads," but all of the music is full of colorful surprises and often rambunctious solos; the nearly 24-minute "Setting Calvin's Waltz" is episodic and frequently fascinating. The key soloists include tenor saxophonist Andy Sheppard, trumpeter Lew Soloff, altoist Wolfgang Puschnig and the extroverted trombonist Gary Valente, while the ensembles are both loose and tight. One of Carla Bley's finest recordings of the 1990s. —*Scott Yanow*

Paul Bley

b. Nov. 10, 1932, Montreal, Canada

Piano, Keyboards / Avant-Garde, Free Jazz

Paul Bley has long offered avant-garde pianists an alternative approach to improvising than that of Cecil Taylor. Bley has been able to use melody and space in inventive ways while performing fairly free improvisations. He started on piano at age eight, studied at Juilliard during 1950-52 and in 1953 played with Charlie Parker on a Canadian television show; the soundtrack serves as his recording debut. After recording for Charles Mingus' Debut label in 1953, Bley moved to New York. Following a stint with Jackie McLean's quintet, he relocated to Los Angeles. Bley played with Chet Baker and then in 1958 played at the Hillcrest with musicians who would soon form the Ornette Coleman Quartet: Coleman, Don Cherry, Charlie Haden and Billy Higgins. Bley soon returned to New York, played and recorded with Charles Mingus and Don Ellis, was part of the Jimmy Giuffre Three (which also included Steve Swallow) and was married to the talented up-and-coming pianist/composer Carla Bley. After leading his own trio, Paul Bley spent much of 1963 with Sonny Rollins' group. He participated in the famous October Revolution in Jazz in 1964 and was a founding member of the Jazz Composers Guild. He recorded frequently with his trios, for a few years experimented with electronics with his second wife Annette Peacock, and then in 1974 founded his Improvising Artists label. Virtually all of that short-lived label's output has been reissued on CD by Black Saint/Soul Note. Since the mid-'70s Paul Bley has recorded a countless number of albums for literally dozens of labels (once cutting two albums in the same day, in two different countries!). A key link between Bill Evans and Keith Jarrett, Bley's adventurous yet thoughtful playing sounds like no one else. —*Scott Yanow*

Introducing Paul Bley / Nov. 30, 1953 / Original Jazz Classics ✦✦✦
Pianist Paul Bley's debut as a leader features the 21-year-old in a trio with bassist Charles Mingus and drummer Art Blakey for Mingus' Debut label. The CD reissue, which adds four performances to the original program, finds Bley developing his voice within the bebop tradition. Mixing together stimulating originals such as "Opus 1" and "Spontaneous Combustion" with a few standards, Horace Silver's "Split Kick" and a surprisingly effective version of "Santa Claus Is Coming to Town," Paul Bley may not have been distinctive this early on but he clearly had a potentially strong future. —*Scott Yanow*

Paul Bley [EmArcy] / Feb. 3, 1954 Aug. 27, 1954 / EmArcy ✦✦✦

Solemn Meditation / 1958 / GNP ✦✦✦
This early quartet date from pianist Paul Bley is somewhat historic because it was the recording debut of both bassist Charlie Haden and vibraphonist Dave Pike. With drummer Lennie McBrowne completing the group, Bley explores a lot of unlikely material in an early post-bop manner including Bill Harris' "Everywhere," Roy Eldridge's "I Remember Harlem" and some group originals. The liner notes by Carla Borg (soon to be Carla Bley), who has her "O Plus One" recorded by the group, are also noteworthy. —*Scott Yanow*

Live at the Hillcrest Club (1958) / Oct. 1958 / Inner City ✦✦✦✦
This out-of-print LP is quite valuable, for it features altoist Ornette Coleman live in concert shortly after making his first studio sessions. Musicians from what would be the Coleman Quartet (with trumpeter Don Cherry, bassist Charlie Haden and drummer Billy Higgins) are heard at a live gig in Los Angeles under the leadership of pianist Paul Bley. Bley's piano is mostly sparse and Coleman is the dominant force, particularly on his melodic "The Blessing" and the well-titled "Free." It is particularly interesting to hear Coleman and Cherry improvising freely on Charlie Parker's "Klactoveesedstene" and Roy Eldridge's "I Remember Harlem." The recording quality is decent for the period, and avant-garde collectors will want to search for this pioneering effort. —*Scott Yanow*

Footloose / Aug. 17, 1962 / Savoy ✦✦✦

The Floater / Aug. 17, 1962+Sep. 12, 1963 / Savoy ✦✦✦✦
Paul Bley's Savoy recordings of 1962-63 were an extension of the innovations of Bill Evans and served as a transition to the avant-garde. Bley, who would offer other pianists a more lyrical alternative to Cecil Taylor in playing free music, engaged in very close interaction with bassist Steve Swallow and drummer Pete La Roca on these influential recordings; so close in fact that it is surprising to realize that this particular trio only really existed in the recording studios! This LP (which, as with its companion *Syndrome*, is long overdue to be fully reissued on CD) features the trio on three of Bley's originals plus two songs apiece from a pair of composers whose work was rarely "covered" this early on: Ornette Coleman and Carla Bley. With such strong yet challenging melodies as "When Will the Blues Leave," "Floater" and "The Circle with the Hole in the Middle," Bley and his sidemen were free to engage in advanced and intuitive improvisations that barely held on to the idea of chord structures but were quite logical and generally fairly melodic. Highly recommended. —*Scott Yanow*

Paul Bley with Gary Peacock / Apr. 13, 1963 / ECM ✦✦✦
Good '60s session with bassist Gary Peacock, Paul Motian on drums. —*Ron Wynn*

Syndrome / Sep. 12, 1963 / Savoy ✦✦✦✦
Paul Bley's 1962-63 trio (which only officially came together during a couple of Savoy recording sessions) has long been underrated, partly because half of its recordings were unreleased at the time. The next logical step beyond the Bill Evans Trio, Bley's group with bassist Steve Swallow and drummer Pete La Roca featured the three musicians often functioning as equals during group improvisations that were generally melodic but never too predictable. On this LP (which is a companion to their other Savoy album *Floater*), the group performs three of Paul Bley's tunes plus five by his then-wife Carla Bley (who at the time was quite unknown). Although these songs (such as "Cousins," "King Korn" and "Vashkar") never caught on, the music is quite innovative and occupies its own niche in jazz history. —*Scott Yanow*

Paul Bley Quartet / Feb. 9, 1964 / ECM ✦✦✦✦✦
Paul Bley Quartet. One of his stronger groups. John Surman (sax) and Bill Frisell (g) especially sharp. —*Ron Wynn*

Turning Point / Mar. 9, 1964 / Improvising Artists ✦✦✦
When this album was released in 1975 by Paul Bley's Improvising Artists label, the seven selections had been previously unheard. The five pieces from Mar. 9, 1964 (which feature pianist Bley, tenor saxophonist John Gilmore, bassist Gary Peacock and drummer Paul Motian) were later released in a more complete form on the Savoy LP *Turns*. This was a unique onetime encounter between the innovative Bley (whose lyrical approach to free-form improvising was quite different than that used by the high-energy players of the time) and Sun Ra's longtime tenor John Gilmore; "Ida Lupino" is the most memorable of these tracks. In addition there are a couple of trio performances ("Mr. Joy" and "Kid Dynamite") from a May 10, 1964, concert with bassist Peacock and drummer Billy Elgart that have not been released elsewhere. Very interesting if not quite essential music. —*Scott Yanow*

Turns / Mar. 9, 1964 / Savoy ✦✦✦✦
On this unusual album, pianist Paul Bley's 1964 trio (with bassist Gary Peacock and drummer Paul Motian) is joined by tenor saxophonist John Gilmore during his brief hiatus from Sun Ra's Arkestra. Unissued at the time (five of the eight numbers made their debut on Bley's IAI label), the music is explorative but not as free as one might expect. Best known among the six Carla Bley originals (which are joined by Paul's "Turns") is the lyrical "Ida Lupino" which is heard in two versions. The music overall is quite stimulating and a bit offbeat, a reflection of Paul Bley's adventurous spirit. —*Scott Yanow*

Barrage / Oct. 15, 1964 / ESP ✦✦✦
This CD reissue of Paul Bley's first of two ESP sessions does not even sound like a Bley recording. Instead of utilizing lyricism and melodic improvisation, pianist Bley is heard as part of a high-energy and often violent quintet comprising altoist Marshall Allen (on a brief vacation from Sun Ra), trumpeter Dewey Johnson, bassist Eddie Gomez and drummer Milford Graves. The barely 29 minutes of music comprises very abstract and intense renditions of six obscure Carla Bley originals. The lack of variety and development are definite minuses although this set is a historical curiosity. —*Scott Yanow*

Copenhagen and Harlem / Nov. 5, 1965+Nov. 4, 1966 / Arista ✦✦✦
This out-of-print double LP from Arista's *Freedom* series features Paul Bley with his trios (either Kent Carter or Mark Levenson on bass along with drummer Barry Altschul) at two different sessions recorded in Scandinavia during 1965-66. Cut during a time when Bley's style was becoming progressively freer, the improvisations (on melodies by Bley, Carla Bley and Annette Peacock) are fairly loose and abstract but perfectly coherent. As has been stated elsewhere, Bley's groups were a logical extension of the Bill Evans Trio, venturing into freer areas than Evans ever chose to travel. —*Scott Yanow*

Touching / Nov. 5, 1965+Nov. 4, 1966 / Black Lion ✦✦✦
With the exception of a lengthy version of "Blood" (which is from a year later and has bassist Mark Levinson), this Paul Bley reissue CD features the pianist with bassist Ken Carter and drummer Barry Altschul in 1965. "Pablo" is a free improvisation but otherwise the compositions (by Bley, his wife at the time Carla Bley and Annette Peacock) contrast thoughtful moments with fiery group interaction. Although not all that memorable, the playing by the trio is at a high level and it is interesting to hear Paul Bley's mid-'60s avant-garde improvising style which offered a contrast to the more dense playing of Cecil Taylor. —*Scott Yanow*

Closer / Dec. 12, 1965 / ESP ✦✦✦
Pianist Paul Bley's second of two ESP albums features his superb 1965 trio which also includes bassist Steve Swallow and drummer Barry Altschul. Only the brief playing time of the ESP CD reissue (twenty-eight-and-a-half minutes) keeps it from deserving a higher rating, for the trio's interpretations of seven Carla Bley

compositions (including the memorable "Ida Lupino"), along with one apiece by Ornette Coleman, Annette Peacock and Paul Bley, are quite original and intriguing. The telepathic interplay between these musicians would become much more influential as time passed; worth checking out. —*Scott Yanow*

● **Open for Love** / Sep. 11, 1972 / ECM ✦✦✦✦✦
This set is one of Paul Bley's finest solo outings which, considering how often he has recorded during the past 30 years, is really saying something. His rendition of "Ida Lupino" is classic and his other interpretations (of originals by Carla Bley and Annette Peacock in addition to his own "Harlem") are close to definitive. Loose yet logical, these piano solos (which make expert use of space) always hold one's interest. —*Scott Yanow*

Solo Piano / Sep. 1972-Apr. 1988 / Steeple Chase ✦✦✦

Scorpio: Paul Bley & Scorpio / Oct. 22, 1972-Oct. 24, 1972 / Milestone ✦✦

Paul Bley [Improvising Artists] / Jun. 16, 1974 / Improvising Artists ✦✦✦

Alone Again / Aug. 8, 1974-Aug. 9, 1974 / Improvising Artists ✦✦✦
Bley is an engaging, thoughtful and highly individualistic player who doesn't fit any rigid category. At the time, he was returning to acoustic music after having worked almost exclusively on electric keyboards for several years. This seven-song session (recently reissued on CD) was done on two days in Oslo, Norway, in 1974. Bley wrote four numbers, with two others by his ex-wife and frequent collaborator Carla Bley and one by Annette Peacock. No composition was that rhythmically arresting, as Bley stayed mainly in the piano's center, creating nimble melodies, working off them and crafting alternate directions or intriguing counterpoints. It was intellectual, occasionally stiff, but never dull or detached. —*Ron Wynn*

Quiet Song / Nov. 14, 1974 / Improvising Artists ✦✦✦
This is a surprisingly introspective session featuring Paul Bley (on piano and electric piano), guitarist Bill Connors (who had recently left Return to Forever) and Jimmy Giuffre (who mostly plays clarinet). The music consists of nine group originals (many of which were freely improvised) and an abstract rendition of the standard "Goodbye." Although there are some interesting instrumental colors, much of the music rambles and wanders without much purpose and the results are rather inconclusive and slightly disappointing considering the talent involved. —*Scott Yanow*

Japan Suite / Jul. 25, 1976 / IAI ✦✦
Due to a long delay which resulted in this concert starting very late, the Japanese audience was in an obviously surly mood. Paul Bley (on piano and electric keyboards), bassist Gary Peacock and drummer Barry Altschul reacted by playing with as much intensity as possible, gradually winning over the crowd. This 33-minute continuous performance (which has been reissued on CD) is certainly more fiery than many of the other recordings by the trio and has its colorful moments. —*Scott Yanow*

Axis/Solo Piano / Jul. 1, 1977-Jul. 3, 1977 / Improvising Artists ✦✦✦✦
An excellent solo date by Paul Bley, his improvisations on three brief pieces (including George Gershwin's "Porgy") and a 16-minute version of his own "Axis" are thoughtful and sometimes introspective explorations. Bley has long given the avant-garde an alternative approach to piano from Cecil Taylor's and this is a good example of his artistry. —*Scott Yanow*

Hot / Mar. 10, 1985 / Soul Note ✦✦✦
Excellent playing by Bley keeps things moving on this 1985 date. The songs vary in quality, but Bley's moving, teeming solos are consistently impressive, and the production and sound are excellent. —*Ron Wynn*

My Standard / Dec. 8, 1985 / Steeple Chase ✦✦✦✦
When one considers that Paul Bley is a constant improviser, the repertoire he chose for this set (ten standards, most of which are from the '40s and '50s) is rather surprising. But even on tunes such as "Santa Claus Is Coming to Town," "Long Ago and Far Away" and "I Can't Get Started," pianist Bley (accompanied by bassist Jesper Lundgaard and drummer Billy Hart) avoids the obvious and comes up with something new to say. —*Scott Yanow*

Notes / Jul. 3, 1987-Jul. 4, 1987 / Soul Note ✦✦✦

Solo / Dec. 1987 / Justin Time ✦✦✦✦

Live at Sweet Basil / May 1, 1988-May 6, 1988 / Soul Note ✦✦✦

The Nearness of You / Nov. 1988 / Steeple Chase ✦✦✦

Life of a Trio: Saturday and Sunday / Dec. 17, 1989 / Owl ✦✦✦

Bebopbebopbebopbebop / Dec. 22, 1989 / Steeple Chase ✦✦✦✦
A surprising album from Bley, long considered an outside player with little, if any, affinity for straight bop. He shatters that myth on this set, going through a dozen songs, including such anthems as "Ornithology" and "The Theme," with vigor, har-

monic distinction, and rhythmic edge. He's brilliantly backed by bassist Bob Cranshaw, providing some of his best, least detached playing in quite a while, and drummer Keith Copeland, navigating the tricky changes with grace. —*Ron Wynn*

In a Row / May 23, 1990-May 24, 1990 / Hat Art ✦✦✦

Paul Bley/NHOP / Jun. 24, 1990+Jul. 1, 1990 / Steeple Chase ✦✦✦

Memoirs / Jul. 1990 / Soul Note ✦✦✦✦

● **Paul Plays Carla** / Dec. 1991 / Steeple Chase ✦✦✦✦✦

If We May / Apr. 1993 / Steeple Chase ✦✦✦✦
Paul Bley has long enjoyed engaging in fairly free improvising, making this set of standards (along with the title cut, an original blues) a bit of a surprise. With bassist Jay Anderson and drummer Adam Nussbaum, Bley plays such songs as "Long Ago and Far Away," "All the Things You Are" and "Confirmation" fairly straight at first, almost as if he were normally a bop-based improviser. The music is quite accessible to straightahead fans even if Bley gives these warhorses some new twists, and he shows that he can swing with the best of them (not that anyone really doubted it). —*Scott Yanow*

Synth Thesis / Aug. 23, 1993-Aug. 24, 1993 / Postcards ✦✦
Paul Bley is such an undeniably fine player, it's hard for me to imagine myself having a strongly negative response to his work. There's no getting around the fact, however, that this is a seriously flawed album, fatally compromised throughout by Bley's use of a cheesy-sounding digital synthesizer. The inherent artificiality of the synth patches is inimical to Bley's usual steadfast aesthetic honesty. Not that there's any deception intended on his part, but the timbral fakery of the electronics intrude rather roughly on the sincerity of Bley's acoustic piano sound. Perhaps if he had attempted to use the synthesizer in a less orthodox way, Bley could have redeemed the concept, but he simply uses the instrument as it came out of the box. It's commendable that an older artist like Bley still sees fit to experiment, but, as any high-school chemistry student can tell us, not all experiments are successful. —*Chris Kelsey*

Time Will Tell / Jan. 1994 / ECM ✦✦✦
This CD contains a series of mostly thoughtful free improvisations featuring three of the giants of the idiom: pianist Paul Bley, Evan Parker (doubling on tenor and soprano) and bassist Barre Phillips. Surprisingly enough, Bley and Parker had never played together before (although Phillips had performed often with both musicians), but they communicate very well including on the lengthy "Poetic Justice," their initial meeting. Nothing was preplanned for the set, and in general, it is very much a Paul Bley session. The emphasis is on free ballads and mood pieces with Parker sounding somewhat restrained. He actually cuts loose much more on his two duets with Phillips than he does on the trios. Although the results overall are not classic, the music never fails to hold on to one's interest as the three musicians continually think and evolve together. —*Scott Yanow*

Outside In / Jul. 8, 1994 / Justin Time ✦✦✦
This duet set by pianist Paul Bley and guitarist Sonny Greenwich, after two melodic solos by Greenwich and Bley's feature on "Arrival," becomes a loose bop session. "Meandering" is a blues and, in the tradition of Lennie Tristano, the origins of the originals "Willow" and "You Are" are not too difficult to figure out. The music does meander a bit but mostly swings in a floating way. Although there are some freer moments, this is as straight as Paul Bley has played on records in years and Sonny Greenwich also sounds fairly conservative, at least if one does not listen too closely. It's a relaxed and very interesting set. —*Scott Yanow*

Modern Chant: Inspiration from Gregorian Chant / Sep. 17, 1994 / Music Masters ✦✦✦
Can it be a coincidence that this CD, subtitled "Inspiration from Gregorian Chant," was recorded right around the time that chant music was reaching its improbable peak on the album charts? In any case, this enjoyable, offbeat trio album featuring the unusual combination of Bley's piano, David Eyges' electric cello and Bruce Ditmas' drums seems to have very little to do with Gregorian chant per se. Indeed, such numbers as "Wisecracks" and "Loose Change" are definitely based on the blues, "Decompose" has an M-base funk foundation, and "Funhouse" is a nasty, down-home bit of grooving that eventually becomes engulfed in a swirling maelstrom (so this is from whom Keith Jarrett may have picked up some of his group concepts). Only "Digitant" seems to breathe some of the ambience of chant in its thematic material. Eyges' cello usually fills in the traditional function of a bass—albeit a very light-toned bass—while occasionally forming dissonant arco (bowed) counterlines around the piano. Bley's playing is often brilliantly unpredictable, difficult to categorize, and thus, able to stand out from the pack. —*Richard S. Ginell*

Jane Ira Bloom

b. 1955, Newton, MA

Soprano Saxophone / Avant-Garde, Post-Bop

One of the great soprano saxophonists, Jane Ira Bloom studied at Berklee and Yale. She recorded two albums for her own Outline label and then around 1980 moved to New York. Bloom has since that time recorded for JMT, Columbia, Enja and Arabesque. Notable for sometimes using live electronics on stage, Bloom has a distinctive tone and an adventurous style. —*Scott Yanow*

Second Wind / Jun. 1980 / Outline ✦✦✦

Mighty Lights / Nov. 17, 1982-Nov. 18, 1982 / Enja ✦✦✦

This was, in a way, soprano saxophonist Jane Ira Bloom's debut, in that it was the first of her albums to be put out by a label she did not herself own—her first two records were self-produced. Even at such an early stage in her development one can hear the attention to craft that would always characterize her work, though her skills at this point were not what they would later become. Bloom's control over the horn was occasionally dubious, but she evidenced an attractive tone and a coherent (if a bit immature and self-conscious) manner of phrasing. Her tunes were already quite sophisticated and distinctive, pointing to the even more ambitious composer into which she evolved. On the other hand, her band for this album will probably not be excelled for the rest of her career. Charlie Haden and Ed Blackwell are very heavy company for such a callow young musician to be keeping, and pianist Fred Hersch is certainly no slouch. Obviously, the rhythm section's work raises this music to a higher plane than it would have reached had not Bloom the wherewithal to engage the services of these gentlemen. —*Chris Kelsey*

As One / Sep. 1984 / JMT ✦✦✦

The inventive soprano saxophonist Jane Ira Bloom performs a set of duets with the adaptable and complementary pianist Fred Hersch. They play two originals apiece (including Hersch's "Janeology"), collaborate on "Inside," and perform a song apiece by Wayne Shorter ("Miyako") and Alec Wilder. The improvisations are generally melodic but unpredictable, coherent but fairly free. Worth several listens. —*Scott Yanow*

Modern Drama / Feb. 9, 1987-Feb. 13, 1987 / Columbia ✦✦✦✦

Jane Ira Bloom, one of the finest soprano saxophonists of the past decade, is in fine form on this Columbia LP. In addition to her soprano and a bit of alto, Bloom makes creative use of live electronics. Key among her sidemen on these nine originals is keyboardist Fred Hersch. The music is explorative yet generally melodic and worth searching for. —*Scott Yanow*

Slalom / Jun. 6, 1988-Jun. 9, 1988 / Columbia ✦✦✦✦

Jane Ira Bloom is teamed with pianist Fred Hersch in a quartet that explores a variety of melodic material in unexpected ways. Bloom, one of the top soprano saxophonists around and a creative user of electronics, has a fairly original tone and her improvisations are consistently full of surprises. Check out her transformations of "I Loves You Porgy" and "If I Should Lose You" on this Columbia LP. —*Scott Yanow*

● **Art & Aviation** / Jul. 22, 1992-Jul. 23, 1992 / Arabesque ✦✦✦✦✦

Nearness / Jul. 12, 1995-Jul. 14, 1995 / Arabesque ✦✦✦

If forced to choose between this eminently thoughtful soprano saxophonist's writing and improvising, I'd have to say it's her original tunes that might keep me coming back. Not that there's anything wrong with her playing. Quite the contrary. She gets a full, gently inflected, well-centered sound on her finicky horn—the kind that only a full-time soprano player can produce with consistency. In the past I've found her improvising somewhat mannered; here, however, she's as spontaneous as one could ask. Her ballad playing is especially effective. But I think it's the sophistication of her contexts that fixes her among the modern mainstream's elite. "Flat6 Bop" is typically intriguing; a harmonically ambiguous, medium-tempo ostinato tune with an intervallically irregular melody, it's the product of a methodical and highly creative intellect. Bloom's arrangements of familiar material—she does heavily re-arranged versions of standards like "Summertime" and "'Round Midnight"—are just as meticulously conceived, but somehow seem a bit precious to my ears. They are very skillfully done, however. Bloom's collaborators are almost perfectly chosen. Trumpeter Kenny Wheeler, trombonist Julian Priester, bassist Rufus Reid, drummer Bobby Previte, and (particularly) pianist Fred Hersch are well attuned to the saxophonist's subtle musical gestures. —*Chris Kelsey*

Blue Wisp Big Band

f. 1981, **db.** 1985

Big Band/Bop, Hard Bop

In the 1980s, the Blue Wisp Big Band was certainly one of the top jazz orchestras active in Cincinnati. The hard bop-oriented big band recorded four albums for the Mopro label; all of the music was reissued in the mid-'90s on two Sea Breeze CDs

and one of the sets was recorded in Los Angeles during a West Coast tour. Among the group's more notable members were trumpeter Tim Hagans, bassist Lynn Seaton and leader-drummer John Von Ohlen. —*Scott Yanow*

● **Butterfly/The Smooth One** / 1982 / Sea Breeze ✦✦✦✦✦

During 1981-85, the Cincinnati-based Blue Wisp Big Band recorded four albums for the Mopro label; all of the music has since been reissued on a pair of Sea Breeze CDs. This first disc features the straightahead orchestra in excellent form on a mixture of standards and originals. Best-known among the soloists is trumpeter Tim Hagens (who is on the second date), but also impressive are trumpeter Al Kiger, baritonist Larry Dickson, pianist Steve Schmidt, and tenors Herb Aronoff and Joe Guadio. Actually, the musicianship throughout the big band is impressive, and fans of conventional jazz orchestras will enjoy both of the Blue Wisp's discs. Among the highlights on this reissue are "Love for Sale," Oscar Pettiford's "Tricrotism," "I Won't Dance," Thelonious Monk's "Evidence," and "The Bull and a Big Band." —*Scott Yanow*

Rollin' with Von Ohlen/Live at Carmelo's / Feb. 1984-Sep. 1984 / Sea Breeze ✦✦✦✦✦

The second of two Sea Breeze CDs that reissue the Blue Wisp Big Band's four Mopro albums only has a few "names" in the orchestra (trumpeter Tim Hagans, bassist Lynn Seaton and drummer/leader John Von Ohlen), but the group always had strong unity and plenty of spirit. One of the two albums heard in this disc was recorded when the band was on a rare road trip, playing at Carmelo's near Los Angeles, while the other set was cut at their home base in Cincinnati. Among the many enjoyable selections are "Manteca," "Footprints," "Rockin' in Rhythm," "Bolivia," and Hagans' "Rollin' with Von Ohlen." —*Scott Yanow*

Hamiet Bluiett

b. Sep. 16, 1940, Lovejoy, IL

Baritone Saxophone / Avant-Garde

The most prominent baritone saxophonist of his generation, Bluiett combines a blunt, modestly inflected attack with a fleet, aggressive technique, and (maybe most importantly) a uniform hugeness of sound that extends from his horn's lowest reaches to far beyond what is usually its highest register. Probably no other baritonist has played so high, with so much control; Bluiett's range travels upward into an area usually reserved for the soprano or even sopranino. His technical mastery aside, Bluiett's solo voice is unlikely to be confused with any other. Enamored with the blues, brusque and awkwardly swinging—in his high-energy playing, Bluiett makes a virtue out of tactlessness; on ballads, he assumes a considerably more lush, romantic guise. Like his longtime collaborator, tenor saxophonist David Murray, Bluiett incorporates a great deal of conventional bebop into his free playing. In truth, Bluiett's music is not free jazz at all, but rather a plain-spoken extension of the mainstream tradition.

Bluiett was first taught music as a child by his aunt, a choral director. He began playing clarinet at the age of nine. He took up the flute and bari sax while attending Southern Illinois University. Bluiett left college before graduating. He joined the Navy, in which he served for several years. He moved to St. Louis in the mid-'60s, where he met and played with many of the musicians who would become the musicians' collective known as the Black Artists Group—Lester Bowie, Charles "Bobo" Shaw, Julius Hemphill, and Oliver Lake, among others. Bluiett moved to New York in 1969; there he joined Sam Rivers' large ensemble, and worked freelance with a variety of musicians. In 1972, Bluiett's avant-garde garrulousness and his competency as a straightahead player gained him a place in one of Charles Mingus' last great bands, which also included pianist Don Pullen. Bluiett stayed with Mingus until 1975. In 1976, he recorded the material that would comprise his first two albums as a leader, *Endangered Species* and *Birthright*.

In December of 1976, Bluiett played a one-shot concert in New Orleans with Murray, Lake, and Hemphill. That supposedly ad-hoc group continued to perform and record as the World Saxophone Quartet, which in the '80s became arguably the most popular free jazz band ever. The WSQ's early free-blowing style eventually transformed into a sophisticated and largely composed melange of bebop, Dixieland, funk, free, and various world musics, its characteristic style anchored and largely defined by Bluiett's enormous sound. Bluiett continued to record and tour with the WSQ through the '80s and '90s; he also led his own ensembles and recorded a number of strong, progressive-mainstream albums for Black Saint/Soul Note. By the mid-'90s, Bluiett was recording and supervising sessions for Mapleshade records. —*Chris Kelsey*

Endangered Species / Jun. 19, 1976 / India Navigation ✦✦✦✦

Baritonist Hamiet Bluiett's first full album as a leader is quite impressive. His style on baritone, even at this early point, owed little to his predecessors. In a quintet with trumpeter Olu Dara and Jumma Santos on balafon, Bluiett takes a lot of chances during this adventurous performance. The four selections (three are fairly lengthy) are his originals and fit firmly in the avant-garde mainstream of the day. —*Scott Yanow*

Resolution / Nov. 1977 / Black Saint ✦✦✦

Orchestra Duo and Septet / Nov. 1977-Dec. 1977 / Chiaroscuro ✦✦✦✦
Array of pieces by Bluiett. Excellent duet with Pullen, good sextet numbers, interesting orchestral piece. —*Ron Wynn*

Birthright / Jun. 1978 / India Navigation ✦✦✦✦✦
This concert performance is quite unusual: an unaccompanied recital by the great baritonist Hamiet Bluiett. Although its subtitle is "A Solo Blues Concert," the "blues" refers to the feeling that Bluiett puts into his music rather than the structure of his originals itself. "In Tribute to Harry Carney" is a high point. Bluiett is in top form during this adventurous but fairly melodic performance. —*Scott Yanow*

S.O.S. / Mar. 1980 / India Navigation ✦✦✦✦
This India Navigation LP (which will hopefully be reissued in the near future) has a continuous 37-minute three-song medley of Hamiet Bluiett originals. The masterful avant-garde baritonist is clearly inspired by the playing of the powerful pianist Don Pullen, bassist Fred Hopkins and drummer Don Moye, and the adventurous music is consistently colorful and driving. A strong effort. —*Scott Yanow*

Dangerously Suite / Apr. 9, 1981-Apr. 17, 1981 / Soul Note ✦✦✦
This session was recorded on April 9 and 17, 1981, and tried a bit too hard to cover all the "Black music" bases from ballads to swing to blues to gospel to funk. The group played well, but only a few surface levels of feeling/commitment seemed to be explored. —*Milo Fine, Cadence*

The Clarinet Family / Nov. 1984 / Black Saint ✦✦✦
There's a big problem in the old play of presenting a group's most gripping work at the beginning of an album—the listener can only feel let down as the music plays on. That it happens here was almost inevitable. What could, after all, possibly follow the heady arrangements and hot solo work of the first two tunes? (Their width and depth almost made for lessons in jazz history swirling from Africa and South America to the avant-garde.) The next cut, "Nioka," a lush ballad (which, because of its voicings, sounded like a swing standard and thus garnered misplaced applause) almost succeeded due to a heart rending reading and the effective change of pace. But from there, the program mainly consisted of inconclusive snippets culled from the remainder of this concert. —*Milo Fine, Cadence*

Ebu / 1984 / Soul Note ✦✦✦
As a founding member of the World Saxophone Quartet, baritone saxophonist Hamiet Bluiett acquired a well-deserved reputation as an avant-gardist. However, as this album proved in 1984 (and others have proven countless times since), his talents also run to the more conventional. Though Ebu has a taste of the arcane, it is mostly a collection of relatively straightahead Bluiett-penned blowing vehicles done with fire and invention. Bluiett has the biggest sound in town; his phrasing and articulation is a little heavy, as one would expect, but he plays with a strength and conviction that's rarely equalled by other baritonists. And, of course, he has an immediately identifiable style. His band—John Hicks, piano; Fred Hopkins, bass; Marvin "Smitty" Smith, drums—is well attentive to the music's needs, and ambitious enough to take it to places not commonly explored. An interesting album, given the perspective of the years that have passed since it was made. It's very straightahead; however, it's wildly different from the mannered product that's usually presented as mainstream jazz in the late '90s. This music has a manifest unruliness, a spirit of adventure; it leaps outrageously into the unknown and usually lands square on its feet—unlike its contemporary equivalent, which can rarely be bothered to scuff its polished Gucci loafers. If jazz remains content to continually re-examine its past, this would be a great place to revisit. —*Chris Kelsey*

Live at Carlos I / 1986 / Just a Memory ✦✦✦✦

Sankofa/Rear Garde / Oct. 1992 / Soul Note ✦✦✦

Live at the Village Vanguard / Feb. 20, 1994 / Soul Note ✦✦✦✦

● **Young Warrior, Old Warrior** / Mar. 1, 1995-Mar. 3, 1995 / Mapleshade ✦✦✦✦

Bluiett's Barbeque Band / Jun. 22, 1995-Jan. 16, 1996 / Mapleshade ✦✦✦✦

Arthur Blythe

b. Jul. 5, 1940, Los Angeles, CA
Alto Saxophone / Post-Bop, Avant-Garde
For a time in the late '70s and early '80s, it seemed as if jazz's avant-garde was on the verge of a popular breakthrough in the person and music of Arthur Blythe. Blythe was signed by Columbia Records; the label's hype-heavy promotion of the saxophonist almost made him a star. It didn't work; Blythe was too "out" for the masses. Columbia realized that it had made a mistake by expecting too much of the public, and threw its promotional weight behind a more malleable, less threatening young prince by the name of Wynton Marsalis. And the rest is history.

Arthur Blythe grew up in San Diego. He began playing music in school bands at the age of nine. In his teens he studied with a former member of Jimmie Lunceford's sax section, Kirtland Bradford. After moving to Los Angeles in 1960, he began playing with pianist/bandleader Horace Tapscott. In 1961, the two became founding members of the Union of God's Musicians and Artist's Ascension. Blythe recorded under Tapscott's leadership in 1969 and worked regularly with the pianist until 1974.

After moving to New York, Blythe worked and recorded as a sideman with Chico Hamilton (1974-77) and Gil Evans (1976-80). Blythe first recorded as a leader in 1977. He was no young lion—Blythe was 37 years old when his first records, *The Grip* and *Metamorphosis*, were released on the independent India Navigation label. By then, Blythe was a fully developed, mature artist, a free-influenced player who was also capable of playing older styles in an utterly personal and borderline iconoclastic way. When Blythe played a standard, he imbued it with all that had happened in jazz since it was written, up to and including the free techniques that were integral to his concept; one can hear traces of his predecessors, but as an affectionate remembrance, not an affectation. Blythe's style varied mostly in the form of his contexts. His earliest recordings feature unusual instrumentations; 1977's *Bush Baby* featured the saxophonist in a transmogrified version of the sax-bass-drums trio, with Bob Stewart on tuba and Muhamed Abdullah on conga. During his Columbia days, Blythe maintained two separate-but-equal performing units. One was the so-called "electric band," a free-funk-oriented quintet with Stewart, cellist Abdul Wadud, drummer Bobby Battle, and, at various times, electric guitarists James "Blood" Ulmer and Kelvyn Bell. The other was an acoustic jazz quartet that took its name from its first Columbia release—1979's *In the Tradition*. The band included bassist Fred Hopkins, drummer Steve McCall, and pianist Stanley Cowell. That album gained Blythe a great deal of critical and popular attention. In retrospect, *In the Tradition* can be seen as a forerunner to the hard-bop revival that dominated major-label jazz in the '80s and into the late '90s—a development that ultimately consigned progressive jazzers like Blythe to the margins. Blythe made several records for Columbia of varying quality—*Lennox Avenue Breakdown* and *Illusions* were very strong; others were not. By 1984's *Put Sunshine in It*—a disturbingly inane (and perhaps last-ditch) effort at grabbing a portion of the expanding jazz fusion market—Blythe's welcome at Columbia had just about worn out. He did rebound a bit with 1987's *Basic Blythe*, an *In the Tradition*-type album that was unnecessarily cluttered by a string section. The record was his last for Columbia.

Blythe recorded less frequently in the late '80s and '90s. He and David Murray comprised a state-of-the-art sax section on one of the most highly praised albums of the '80s, Jack DeJohnette's *Special Edition*. Blythe also joined Lester Bowie, Chico Freeman, Don Moye, Kirk Lightsey, and Cecil McBee in a band rather presumptuously called the Leaders, which recorded a pair of well-received albums for Black Hawk and Black Saint. Blythe briefly replaced Julius Hemphill in the World Saxophone Quartet in 1990. He recorded for Enja in the '90s—1991's *Hipmotism* featured a revamped version of his "electric" group; 1993's *Retroflection* was an acoustic effort.

Blythe possesses one of the most easily recognizable alto sax sounds in jazz—big and round, with a fast, wide vibrato and an aggressive, precise manner of phrasing. His lines are frequently quite baroque and always well defined; Blythe's playing has been criticized (unfairly, some would say) as being overly ornamental, but he is certainly capable of improvising melodies of great character and originality. —*Chris Kelsey*

In Concert / Feb. 26, 1977 / India Navigation ✦✦✦✦
Altoist Arthur Blythe's first two recordings as a leader, *The Grip* and *Metamorphosis*, were recorded at the same concert; all of the two LPs' contents are on this single CD. Blythe was already quite distinctive and an impressive improviser at this early stage, a year before he signed with Columbia. His sextet (which consists of trumpeter Ahmed Abdullah, cellist Abdul Wadud, tuba player Bob Stewart, drummer Steve Reid and percussionist Muhamad Abdullah) performs seven of Blythe's challenging originals and "Spirits in the Field" while the 18-minute "Duet for Two" is a free collaboration by the leader and Wadud. —*Scott Yanow*

Bush Baby / Dec. 1977 / Adelphi ✦✦✦
During this outstanding and challenging recital, altoist Arthur Blythe (who at the time went by the title of "Black Arthur") stretches out on four originals in a sparse trio with Bob Stewart on tuba and Ahkmed Abdullah on conga. Blythe had an original sound from the start and his soulful yet adventurous and intense style is heard in its early prime on what was his second recording session as a leader, cut just before he was surprisingly signed to Columbia. —*Scott Yanow*

Lenox Avenue Breakdown / 1978 / Columbia ✦✦✦✦
The signing of Arthur Blythe to Columbia in 1978 received a great deal of attention. Fortunately, the adventurous altoist was able to record for that giant label for a few years without being pressured to water down his sound or his music. This

set matches Blythe with such talents as flutist James Newton, guitarist James "Blood" Ulmer, bassist Cecil McBee, drummer Jack DeJohnette, tuba player Bob Stewart and percussionist Guillermo Franco; no weak spots to this group. The band performs four of Blythe's diverse originals with creativity and a strong bluesy feeling. —*Scott Yanow*

In the Tradition / Oct. 1978 / Columbia ✦✦✦✦✦
Sometimes the easiest way to get "in" to someone's music is to see how they handle standards. Altoist Arthur Blythe, who—although he has been associated somewhat with the avant-garde—does not fit easily into any category, is heard on this 1978 studio session exploring four veteran songs plus two of his originals. The instrumentation of his quartet is conventional but the musicianship is exceptionally high (pianist Stanley Cowell, bassist Fred Hopkins and drummer Steve McCall), and it is quite interesting to hear how they stretch such songs as "In a Sentimental Mood," "Jitterbug Waltz" and "Caravan," making them sound fresh and original. —*Scott Yanow*

Illusions / Apr. 1980-May 1980 / Columbia ✦✦✦✦
It is surprising how artistically productive altoist Arthur Blythe was during his period on Columbia. Despite the hype and Columbia's reputation for pressuring artists to play mass appeal music, Blythe's recordings for that label are inventive and creative. For this, his third Columbia release, Blythe uses two different groups: an "in the tradition" quartet with pianist John Hicks, bassist Fred Hopkins and drummer Steve McCall, and a more eccentric unit with guitarist James "Blood" Ulmer, cellist Abdul Wadud, tuba player Bob Stewart and drummer Bobby Battle. No matter the setting, the distinctive alto of Blythe is heard in top form on six of his unusual originals. It's recommended and well deserving of reissue on CD. —*Scott Yanow*

Blythe Spirit / 1981 / Columbia ✦✦✦✦
This is one of the most well-rounded Arthur Blythe records from his Columbia period. The distinctive altoist performs three passionate originals and an unlikely version of "Strike Up the Band" with a quintet also including cellist Abdul Wadud, guitarist Kelvyn Bell, Bob Stewart on tuba and drummer Bobby Battle. In addition he is featured on "Misty" with a more conventional trio (pianist John Hicks, bassist Fred Hopkins and drummer Steve McCall), plays his "Spirits in the Field" with Wadud and Stewart, and is quite effective on a reverent but swinging rendition of "Just aCloser Walk with Thee" with Stewart and organist Amina Claudine Myers. One of many Columbia LPs long overdue to be reissued on CD, this is a fairly definitive Arthur Blythe recording, showing off his links to hard bop, R&B and the avant-garde. —*Scott Yanow*

Elaboration / 1982 / Columbia ✦✦✦
With only one or two exceptions, all of altoist Arthur Blythe's recordings for Columbia during 1978-87 are surprisingly rewarding; he avoided the temptations of commercialism and generally kept true to his musical vision. Blythe's unusual quintet (with guitarist Kelvyn Bell, cellist Abdul Wadud, Bob Stewart on tuba and drummer Bobby Battle) is well featured on five of his originals (most memorable is "The Lower Nile") and "One Mint Julep." This post-bop music (which falls between advanced hard bop and the avant-garde) is well worth several listens but unfortunately the recommended LP (as with all of Blythe's Columbia albums) has yet to be reissued on CD. —*Scott Yanow*

Light Blue: Arthur Blythe Plays Thelonious Monk / Jan. 27, 1983 / Columbia ✦✦✦✦
This out-of-print Columbia LP will be difficult to locate but it is worth the search. Altoist Arthur Blythe and his unique quintet (comprising guitarist Kelvyn Bell, cellist Abdul Wadud, Bob Stewart on tuba and drummer Bobby Battle) perform six underplayed Thelonious Monk songs ("We See," "Light Blue," "Off Minor," "Epistrophy," "Coming on the Hudson" and "Nutty") and these creative players (and the unusual instrumentation) put a fresh slant on Monk's music. Blythe's passionate sound throughout this inspired set is consistently memorable. —*Scott Yanow*

Put Sunshine in It / 1984 / Columbia ✦✦
In the nine projects that altoist Arthur Blythe recorded for Columbia during 1978-87, he avoided performing inferior commercial material, except on this occasion. Blythe's musical personality is unfortunately somewhat lost during this misfire with the synthesizers and drum machines of Todd Cochran being the dominant voice. It is to Blythe's credit that this was the only weak set of his Columbia period, and fortunately this dud has not been reissued on CD. —*Scott Yanow*

Da-Da / 1986 / Columbia ✦✦✦
Altoist Arthur Blythe is featured in a variety of settings on this fairly obscure Columbia LP. "Splain Thang," with its electronic rhythms, is a bit commercial but Bob Stewart's crazy electric tuba solo holds one's interest. "Esquinas" also uses electronics but fairly effectively as a pretty ballad. Otherwise, Blythe is heard in all-star groups that include cornetist Olu Dara, pianist John Hicks, bassist Cecil McBee and drummer Bobby Battle; Geri Allen guests on electric piano during

"Break Tune." The post-bop music overall is not essential but should interest Arthur Blythe collectors. —*Scott Yanow*

Basic Blythe / 1987 / Columbia ✦✦✦✦
Altoist Arthur Blythe's final Columbia album is a varied set that includes the two-part "Autumn In New York," Thelonious Monk's "Ruby My Dear," John Hicks' "Heart to Heart" and three Blythe originals including a remake of "Lennox Avenue Breakdown." Blythe's quartet (with pianist John Hicks, bassist Anthony Cox and drummer Bobby Battle) is excellent although the use of eight strings does not add much to the music and is sometimes a bit distracting. However the altoist's playing makes the project (not yet reissued on CD) quite worthwhile. —*Scott Yanow*

Hipmotism / Mar. 15, 1991-Mar. 17, 1991 / Enja ✦✦✦✦
Altoist Arthur Blythe is heard in various settings on this CD, ranging from a full septet with baritonist Hamiet Bluiett, guitarist Kelvin Bell, vibraphonist Gust William Tsilis, Bob Stewart on tuba, drummer Don Moye and percussionist Arto Tuncboyaci to different trios and quartets with the same musicians and an unaccompanied display on "My Son Ra." All nine compositions are Blythe's and he shows that not only did he survive his unexpectedly long stay on the roster of Columbia Records, but he had continued to grow in power and creativity. This set gives a strong example of his talents. —*Scott Yanow*

● **Retroflection** / Jun. 25, 1993-Jun. 26, 1993 / Enja ✦✦✦✦✦
Arthur Blythe, whose alto tone has been quite original ever since the start of his career, is joined by pianist John Hicks, bassist Cecil McBee and drummer Bobby Battle on this superior quartet date from Enja. Blythe really stretches out at this "Live at the Village Vanguard" set, with six of the seven songs being over nine minutes long. "Jana's Delight" (which is based on a five-note pattern), "JB Blues," a remake of Blythe's "Lenox Avenue Breakdown" and one of the best versions ever of Thelonious Monk's "Light Blue" are the high points of the explorative program. Arthur Blythe fans are strongly advised to pick up this particularly strong effort. —*Scott Yanow*

Calling Card / Jun. 26, 1993 / Enja ✦✦✦

Synergy / Jul. 24, 1996 / In & Out ✦✦✦✦
Throughout his career, Arthur Blythe has appeared with a wide variety of instrumentation, always willing to try new ensemble sounds. On this date, Blythe is teamed in a trio with the talented cellist David Eyges and the flexible drummer Bruce Ditmas. Blythe's bluesy and soulful tone, along with his ability to caress a melody, makes his adventurous flights more accessible than one might expect. David Eyges holds the group together by playing both supportive bass lines (although obviously in a higher register) and soloing along with Blythe, while Bruce Ditmas keeps the momentum of the music flowing. All nine selections on the date were co-composed by the three musicians, so it is quite possible that they are largely free improvisations. However, the interplay between the players, the gradual development of the often fiery performances, and the strong (and sometimes joyful) melodies that pop up are so coherent that the music sounds as if it were more planned in advance than it probably was. Well worth checking out. —*Scott Yanow*

Night Song / 1997 / Clarity ✦✦✦

Jimmy Blythe

b. Jan. 1901, Louisville, KY, **d.** Jun. 21, 1931, Chicago, IL
Piano / Classic Jazz
Considering how many fine recording sessions he was on in Chicago in the 1920s (particularly with Johnny Dodds), it is surprising how little is known about the mysterious Jimmy Blythe. He was raised in Kentucky, moved to Chicago in 1918, and studied with pianist Clarence Jones. Blythe recorded dozens of piano rolls in the early '20s. He began cutting records in 1924 (Blythe's "Chicago Stomp" from that year is considered by some to be the first full-length boogie-woogie recording) and during the next seven years made a few piano solos, backed singers Viola Bartlette and Alexander Robinson, teamed up with Dodds in several settings, led Blythe's Sinful Five, recorded with the Midnight Rounders, Jimmy Bertrand's Washboard Wizards, Lonnie Johnson and the State Street Ramblers, and cut piano duets with Buddy Burton and Charlie Clark. Jimmy Blythe died at the age of 30 from meningitis. A decent soloist and a superior accompanist, nearly all of Blythe's recordings are available on an RST CD. —*Scott Yanow*

● **Jimmy Blythe [RST]** / Apr. 1924-Mar. 20, 1931 / RST ✦✦✦✦✦
From his first recordings to his last, the short musical life of Jimmy Blythe is fully covered on this imported CD from the Austrian RST label. All of his sessions as a leader (with the exception of his duets with Buddy Burton) are on this very definitive CD. The music ranges from piano solos (early examples of boogie-woogie and stride) to blues records with singers Viola Bartlette and Alexander Robinson, combo performances with Blythe's Sinful Five, the Midnight Rounders and Jimmy Bertrand's Washboard Wizards and piano duets with Charlie Clark. There is plenty

of variety on this excellent program of early jazz and blues, highly recommended to 1920s collectors. —*Scott Yanow*

Willie Bobo (William Correa)

b. Feb. 28, 1934, New York, NY, d. Sep. 15, 1983, Los Angeles, CA
Percussion, Timbales / Latin Jazz, Salsa

Willie Bobo was one of the great Latin percussionists of his time, a relentless swinger on the congas and timbales, a flamboyant showman onstage, and an engaging if modestly endowed singer. He also made serious inroads into the pop, R&B and straight jazz worlds, and he always said that his favorite song was Antonio Carlos Jobim's "Dindi." Growing up in Spanish Harlem, Bobo began on the bongos at age 14, only to find himself performing with Perez Prado a year later, studying with Mongo Santamaria while serving as his translator, and joining Tito Puente for a four-year stint at age 19. Mary Lou Williams gave Correa his nickname Bobo when they recorded together in the early '50s. After working with Cal Tjader, Herbie Mann and Santamaria—with whom he recorded the evergreen Latin standard "Afro-Blue"—Bobo stepped forward in 1963 with his first recording as a leader, with Clark Terry and Joe Farrell as sidemen. Recording for Verve in the mid-'60s, Bobo achieved his highest solo visibility with albums that enlivened pop hits of the day with Latin rhythms, spelled by sauntering originals like "Spanish Grease" and "Fried Neck Bones and Some Home Fries." In addition, Bobo played on innumerable sessions in New York, recording with artists like Miles Davis, Cannonball Adderley, Herbie Hancock, Wes Montgomery, Chico Hamilton and Sonny Stitt. In 1969, he moved to Los Angeles where he led jazz and Latin jazz combos, appeared on Bill Cosby's first comedy series (1969-1971) and short-lived 1976 variety show, and recorded on his own for Sussex, Blue Note and Columbia. One of Bobo's last appearances, only three months before his death from cancer, was at the 1983 Playboy Jazz Festival where he reunited with Santamaria for the first time in 15 years. —*Richard S. Ginell*

Spanish Grease / Aug. 20, 1965-Sep. 8, 1965 / Verve ✦✦✦✦

One pass through the title cut, and you know that Carlos Santana was listening. The easy R&B-Latin-jazz shuffle on this Bobo original, with its mix of Spanish and English vocals, is an obvious touchstone of cuts like "Evil Ways" on Santana's first two albums. What a shame, then, that the rest of the record primarily comprises covers of pop hits of the day like "It's Not Unusual" (a vocal AND an instrumental version!) and "Our Day Will Come." The timbales player and his band lay down respectable grooves, but "Spanish Grease" is the only original on the album, and by far the most rewarding number. *Spanish Grease* has been combined with the 1966 LP *Uno Dos Tres 1-2-3* on one CD reissue. —*Richie Unterberger*

● Uno, Dos, Tres/Spanish Grease / Oct. 8, 1965-Apr. 26, 1966 / Verve ✦✦✦✦✦

Talkin' Verve / 1965-1968 / Verve ✦✦✦✦

Whatever the meaning of the word "talkin'," this is still a most valuable release because it succinctly sums up Willie Bobo's Verve recordings, most of which have yet to see the light of the laser. By this time, Bobo had followed Mongo Santamaria into the marketplace as an energetic exponent of the Latin boogaloo, even scoring a minor hit with "Spanish Grease." But Bobo went even further than Mongo toward an accommodation with the '60s scene, adding the R&B-oriented electric rhythm guitar of Sonny Henry, dropping the piano, incorporating strings and even an occasional graceful vocal now and then. While there are a few covers of '60s standards here, like "The Look of Love" and "Grazing in the Grass"—and he had the great sense to seek out and record a hip-shaking version of Eddie Harris' "Sham Time"—Bobo's biggest contribution on these tracks was in providing the inspiration for the Latin rock boom to come. "Evil Ways" is almost an exact blueprint for Carlos Santana's career-launching hit version; "Spanish Grease" reappeared uncredited six years later as Santana's "No One to Depend On," and Santana also played Bobo's lowdown "Fried Neck Bones and Some Homefries" in the band's early days. With Bobo's galvanic congas and timbales swinging at all times, few CDs by a single artist capture the ambience of late-'60s jazz radio in the evening as well as this one. —*Richard S. Ginell*

Uno, Dos, Tres / Jan. 1966 / Verve ✦✦✦

As with his previous album *Spanish Grease,* the toughest and most memorable track is the one Bobo original, "Fried Neck Bones and Some Home Fries." Its creeping Latin soul groove was, like "Spanish Grease," an obvious inspiration for Carlos Santana. But on most of the rest of the recording, Bobo coasts through interpretations of period hits like "Michelle," "Goin' Out of My Head," and Jay & the Americans' (!) "Come a Little Bit Closer," with some jazz and pop standards as well. *Uno Dos Tres* has been combined with the 1965 LP *Spanish Grease* on one CD reissue. —*Richie Unterberger*

A New Dimension / Dec. 1968 / Verve ✦✦✦✦✦

Tomorrow Is Here / 1977 / Blue Note ✦✦✦

Willie Bobo's only LP for Blue Note came at a point well past the label's heyday, when crossover was its primary focus. Hence *Tomorrow Is Here* has a pronounced '70s R&B/funk feel, with synthesizers, envelope followers, electric pianos, guitars and occasional strings interwoven with Bobo's steady Latin congas, timbales and self-effacing vocals. But there are a few gems to be found here—one in particular. The leadoff track "Suitcase Full of Dreams" is a great, haunting, Latin-accented song about a journeyman musician's life on the road that should have become a standard but is now almost completely forgotten. Karma's Reggie Andrews sits in on keyboards to give the record its contemporary sound; the other participants are L.A. sessionmen. Bobo's engaging personality, the injected Latin element, and "Suitcase" are what makes this otherwise dated record come alive. —*Richard S. Ginell*

Phil Bodner (Philip L. Bodner)

b. Jun. 13, 1919, Waterbury, CT
Clarinet / Swing

Essentially a swing-based clarinetist, Phil Bodner has spent most of his career as a studio musician. Among his more notable jazz gigs have been with Benny Goodman (1955), the Gil Evans Orchestra with Miles Davis (1958), Oliver Nelson (1962), J.J. Johnson (1965-68) and Bill Evans (1974). He has recorded just a few sets as a leader (most recently for Stash and Jazz Mania), making one regret that he could not have spent a larger portion of his career playing jazz. —*Scott Yanow*

Fine and Dandy / 1980-1981 / Stash ✦✦✦

A longtime studio musician, clarinetist Phil Bodner has led relatively few jazz sessions throughout his lengthy career. Other than a couple of obscure dates for Camden during 1964-65, this Stash album was his first as a leader, and he was already 61 at the time. Although a multireedist, Bodner sticks to his favorite instrument (the clarinet) on the ten standards. Six are with pianist Marty Napoleon, bassist Rick Laird and drummer Butch Miles while the other four utilize pianist Tony Monte, bassist George Duvivier and drummer Mel Lewis; Don Elliot makes one of his last recordings on mellophone during a cooking rendition of "It Had to Be You." This is a pleasing swing set. —*Scott Yanow*

● Jammin' at Phil's Place / Jan. 25, 1990 / JazzMania ✦✦✦✦

Phil Bodner has long been known as a flexible studio musician, so this outing for JazzMania (on which Bodner is joined by pianist Derek Smith, bassist Milt Hinton and drummer Bob Rosengarden) was a special event. Sticking to clarinet, Bodner jams his way through 11 familiar standards, sounding quite individual and occasionally heated in the swing idiom. The strong supporting cast and the attractive (if familiar) chord changes of songs such as "Them There Eyes," "After You've Gone" and "Bill Bailey" make this an enjoyable set. —*Scott Yanow*

Buddy Bolden

b. Sep. 6, 1877, New Orleans, LA, d. Nov. 4, 1931, Jackson, LA
Cornet / Classic New Orleans Jazz

Although no one knows when jazz music was "invented," a good starting point is when cornetist Buddy Bolden formed his first band in 1895. The first important name in jazz history, Bolden's career has long been buried in legend but Donald Marquis' definitive book *In Search of Buddy Bolden* successfully pieced together a factual and coherent biography. Bolden left school in 1890, learned cornet and originally played dance music. Because he never recorded (a legendary 1898 cylinder has never been found), one can only guess how Bolden sounded but according to reports he was very blues-oriented. He was the most popular musician in New Orleans by 1900 and an influence on later cornetists but by 1906 he was going slowly insane. The following year Bolden was committed to Jackson Mental Institute where he remained completely forgotten for his final 24 years. —*Scott Yanow*

Claude Bolling

b. Apr. 10, 1930, Cannes, France
Piano, Leader / Swing, Pop

Claude Bolling has found his greatest fame in the US for his jazzy classical collaborations with Jean-Pierre Rampal, Maurice Andre, Elena Duran and Yo Yo Ma while in Europe he is best known as the leader of various swing big bands. Bolling formed his first group when he was 14 in 1944. In 1948 he recorded with Rex Stewart and accompanied blues singer Chippie Hill at a jazz festival. Bolling also recorded with Roy Eldridge (1951) and Lionel Hampton (1953 and 1956), led big bands since the 1950s and recorded ragtime, tributes to Duke Ellington and his own original music. Although not an innovator, Claude Bolling has been an important fixture in the French jazz scene since the 1950s. —*Scott Yanow*

Nuances / May 28, 1956-May 29, 1956 / DRG ✦✦✦
Claude Bolling has had a long and multifaceted career in his native France. It is as a leader of a series of big bands that Bolling is most significant. This LP features Bolling's arrangements in three different settings: with an octet also including trombonist Benny Vasseur and tenor saxophonist Guy Lafitte; in a quintet with trumpeter Christian Bellest and the reeds of Pierre Gosssez (Bernard Verstraete guests on one song on accordion); and, surprisingly, in a septet with Martial Solal taking over for Bolling on piano. The music is often influenced by Duke Ellington, although none of the songs (which include five Bolling originals) are Duke's. Mixing together swing and bop, this is one of Claude Bolling's best jazz sessions, and it was for a time in the late '80s readily available in the US. —*Scott Yanow*

Original Ragtime / Mar. 16, 1966-Mar. 18, 1966 / Columbia ✦✦✦
The first of four piano solo albums recorded by Claude Bolling during the 1966-70 period (Bolling is much better known for his classical/jazz pop records and as a leader of big bands), this date finds Bolling showing off his technique on both famous and unfamiliar rags, including "Maple Leaf Rag," James P. Johnson's "Harlem Strut," Tom Turpin's "Saint Louis Rag" and Jelly Roll Morton's "Perfect Rag." In addition, Bolling romps through "Waiting for the Robert E. Lee" and Zez Confrey's novelty ragtime classic "Kitten on the Keys." Although the album was released domestically in 1976 after the brief ragtime craze caused by the movie *The Sting*, the music was actually recorded ten years earlier in France when ragtime was considered extinct. Fine interpretations. —*Scott Yanow*

Original Bolling Boogie / Oct. 1, 1968-Oct. 2, 1968 / Mercury ✦✦✦
Claude Bolling has appeared in many roles throughout his career, but this album was a bit unusual, a set of boogie-woogie-oriented piano solos. In addition to numbers by Pete Johnson, Pine Top Smith and Meade Lux Lewis ("Honky Tonk Train Blues"), Bolling plays spirited versions of some standards ("Weary Blues," "Cow Cow Boogie," and "Dardanella") and contributed a couple of originals in the boogie tradition. Fun music, very much out of style in 1968. —*Scott Yanow*

● **Suite for Flute and Jazz Piano** / 1975 / CBS Masterworks ✦✦✦✦
This was a very popular album of jazz/classical fusion. —*Myles Boisen*

Vintage Bolling / 1975-1985 / Milan ✦✦✦✦
Vintage Bolling compiles a selection of Claude Bolling's most popular recordings, culled from performances with Jean-Pierre Rampal, Pinchas Zukerman, and Alexandre Lagoya. It's a fair, if incomplete, introduction to the pianist and is primarily of interest to neophytes or casual fans; dedicated listeners will prefer the original albums. —*Stephen Thomas Erlewine*

Live at the Meridien / 1984 / Columbia ✦✦✦
In 1984, Claude Bolling's 18-piece orchestra performed eight of his originals during a recorded live concert in Paris. The music is influenced by Duke Ellington, although Bolling's own musical personality often peeks through during his arrangements. The music is not overly memorable as a whole, but there are some good moments, particularly from such soloists as trumpeter Fernand Verstraete, trombonist Benny Vasseur, tenorman Andre Villeger and pianist Bolling himself. —*Scott Yanow*

First Class / 1991 / RCA ✦✦✦
According to this CD's liner notes (and they seem to be accurate), violinist Stephane Grappelli had never recorded with a jazz big band prior to these 1991 sessions (although he did have a couple of dates with large orchestras). Other soloists are heard from (Bolling on piano, trombonist Andre Paquinet, Carl Schlosser on tenor, Philipe Portejoie on soprano and altoist Claude Tissendier, who sounds a bit like Johnny Hodges on "Moon Mist"), but the emphasis is on Grappelli and his interplay with the orchestra. There are no real surprises in the repertoire, which is mostly swing standards (including "Minor Swing," the haunting "Tears," "Crazy Rhythm" and "Lady Be Good"), and the two Bolling originals that open the set (including one called "Stephane") are in the swing tradition, but, as usual for a Grappelli recording, the results are delightful. —*Scott Yanow*

Bolling Plays Ellington, Vol. 1 / Nov. 12, 1991 / Columbia ✦✦✦
Claude Bolling leads his big band through ten Duke Ellington compositions (mostly from the 1930s and '40s), plus Mercer Ellington's "Blue Serge," on this mid-'80s release. Although Bolling's orchestra does closely emulate Duke's in the ensembles (many of the arrangements are close adaptations of Ellington's recordings), one does miss the distinctive soloists. Vaneese Thomas takes a pair of vocals (on "Sophisticated Lady" and "It Don't Mean a Thing"), and the French musicians do their best, but why get this release when so many Duke Ellington records are currently available? —*Scott Yanow*

Bolling Plays Ellington, Vol. 2 / Nov. 18, 1991 / Columbia ✦✦✦
Black, Brown & Beige / 1993 / Milan ✦✦✦
Claude Bolling brings back Duke Ellington's classic "Black, Brown and Beige" on this enjoyable CD. Since Ellington's three-part suite did not feature extensive solos

by his unique sidemen, Bolling is able to hint at their presence in his adaptation of Ellington's arrangements for the big band. Forgiving a slightly cutesy interpretation of "Sugar Hill Penthouse," this is a fine recreation of a much-neglected work. —*Scott Yanow*

With the Help of My Friends / Apr. 1993 / Who's Who In Jazz ✦✦✦
This is an unusual record. In 1977, Dick Hyman played the standard "A Child Is Born" in the styles of a wide variety of players, but few realize that two years earlier Claude Bolling (in a quartet) paid tribute to a dozen top pianists by writing and performing an original piece that found him doing close impressions of his predecessors. This is a mostly successful effort that finds Bolling sounding close to Oscar Peterson, Count Basie, Scott Joplin, George Shearing, Dave Brubeck, Thelonious Monk, Duke Ellington, Fats Waller, Ramsey Lewis, Art Tatum, Jelly Roll Morton and Erroll Garner. Not every stylist is covered (among the missing are James P. Johnson, Teddy Wilson, Bud Powell, McCoy Tyner and Bill Evans), but Bolling does show off his versatility and impressive pianistic skills; the results are quite fun. —*Scott Yanow*

Cross Over U.S.A. / Jun. 8, 1993 / Milan ✦
The music on this fluffy release is so sweet that it's surprising the number of calories are not listed. Classical players are added to Bolling's regular rhythm section in different pairs for three numbers apiece (including flutist Jean-Pierre Rampal) but the results are consistently insipid and saccharine with very little improvisation by anyone but the pianist/leader. There is not much here to interest jazz listeners. —*Scott Yanow*

Victory Concert / Jun. 5, 1994-Jun. 7, 1994 / Milan ✦✦
Claude Bolling's big band has been performing at some World War II anniversary tributes and it is this orchestra which performs a dozen 1940s favorites on this CD. The problem is that, other than Bolling and trumpeter Charles Martinez, none of the soloists are all that impressive and quite a few were expected to play note-for-note recreations of the original recorded solos. This then is essentially predictable dance music laced with nostalgia and falls far short of its potential. —*Scott Yanow*

Sharkey Bonano (Joseph Gustaf Bonano)

b. Apr. 9, 1902, New Orleans, LA, **d.** Mar. 27, 1972, New Orleans, LA
Trumpet / Dixieland
In the early '20s, New Orleans native Bonano played locally with the bands of Chink Martin and Freddie Newman, among others. Later, he moved to New York, where he unsuccessfully auditioned for a spot with the Wolverines. In 1924, he landed a spot with pianist Jimmy Durante. The next year, he returned home to lead his own band. In 1927, he joined the famous Jean Goldkette Orchestra, which then featured Bix Beiderbecke and Frankie Trumbauer. From 1928-30, Bonano led his own group, the Melody Masters, with Leon Prima. After playing in California with Original Dixieland Jazz Band clarinetist Larry Shields, Bonano once again returned to New Orleans, where he stayed from 1930-36. In 1936, Bonano worked with Ben Pollack before forming his own New York-based group, the Sharks of Rhythm, with which he recorded much of his finest work. Around that time, he also played sporadically with the ODJB. After a military stint in the '40s, Bonano played around and about New Orleans, where his outgoing musical personality gained him a large following. From 1949 on, he led his own groups; Bonano remained active around New Orleans, Chicago, and New York until the 1960s, when ill health forced him to retire. —*Chris Kelsey*

● **Sharkey Bonano** / Apr. 25, 1928-Apr. 22, 1937 / Timeless ✦✦✦✦✦
Sharkey Bonano was a straightforward New Orleans trumpeter who could be relied upon to lead driving ensembles and play hot, melodic solos. This definitive CD features Bonano in 1928 on two numbers with Johnnie Miller's New Orleans Frolickers and on four songs from the same year with Monk Hazel's Bienville Roof Orchestra; both of the early sessions were recorded in New Orleans and feature plenty of strong solos and memorable melodies. The bulk of this reissue contains the 14 numbers recorded by Sharkey and his Sharks of Rhythm during 1936-37 in New York. Bonano's recording band changes personnel a lot during the four sessions and includes such top players as pianists Armand Hug, Clyde Hart and Joe Bushkin, trombonists Santo Pecora and George Brunis, clarinetists Irving Fazola and Joe Marsala, drummers Ben Pollack and George Wettling and even the rhythm guitar of Eddie Condon. Dixieland standards mix in with jumping originals and, during an era dominated by swing-oriented big bands, these combo jams were a bit unusual. The CD is rounded out by four selections (including "I Never Knew What a Gal Could Do") by trombonist Santo Pecora's Back Room Boys, which are similar in feel to the Bonano numbers, although Shorty Sherock is on trumpet. Since Sharkey's next recordings as a leader would not be until 1949, this is a particularly valuable reissue for trad and Dixieland fans. —*Scott Yanow*

A Night in Old New Orleans / Jan. 28, 1950-Jul. 27, 1950 / Capitol ✦✦✦
During the 1949-53 period, trumpeter Sharkey Bonano recorded several albums worth of material for Capitol. This LP is drawn from six different sessions, but has similar-styled personnel, with Bonano joined by either Santa Pecora, Charles Miller, Jack Delaney or Jimmy Blount on trombone, Lester Bouchon or Bujie Centobie on clarinet, and a fine rhythm section with either Jeff Riddick or Stan Mendelson on piano. Co-leading the album is veteran singer Lizzie Miles, who is on five of the 12 numbers, including "A Good Man Is Hard to Find" and "Salty Dog." Bonano is in fine form on a set mostly consisting of Dixieland standards. Unfortunately, Capitol has yet to really exploit the many Dixieland-oriented sessions in its catalog and bring enjoyable music like this set back in print. —*Scott Yanow*

Midnight on Bourbon Street / 1951-1952 / Capitol ✦✦✦

At Lenfant's Lounge / Aug. 17, 1952-Sep. 7, 1952 / Storyville ✦✦✦✦
Volume eight in Storyville's *Sounds of New Orleans*, this CD features the spirited Dixieland sextet of trumpeter Sharkey Bonano (which includes trombonist Jack Delaney, clarinetist Bujie Centobie, pianist Stanley Mendelsohn, bassist Arnold Loyacano and drummer Abbie Brunies) along with guest singer Lizzie Miles. The performances are taken from three radio broadcasts and feature such typical Dixieland songs as "Tin Roof Blues," "High Society," "The Saints" and "Weary Blues" along with Bonano's "North Rampart Street Parade" and "She's Crying for Me" among others. Fun music that Dixieland fans should like. —*Scott Yanow*

Live at the Perez Club / Dec. 7, 1952 / Storyville ✦✦✦
One of two live sets (originally aired on the radio) by Dixieland trumpeter Sharkey Bonano that have been released by Storyville in their *Sounds of New Orleans* CD series (this is Vol. 4), the date features Bonano heading his usual sextet of the time: trombonist Jack Delaney, clarinetist Bujie Centobie, pianist Stanley Mendelsohn, bassist Arnold Loyacano and drummer Abbie Brunies. The band romps through their repertoire with plenty of rambunctious Dixieland tunes (including "Chinatown, My Chinatown," "Royal Garden Blues" and "Tiger Rag") plus Bonano's slightly tasteless vocal on "Stick Out Your Can." —*Scott Yanow*

Sharkey & His Kings of Dixieland / Sep. 9, 1958 / Southland ✦✦
A fixture in New Orleans from the 1920s up until his death in 1972, Sharkey Bonano made quite a few recordings in the 1950s. This 1958 set (originally on Southland) was his next-to-last recording and features him with an all-star group of Crescent City greats: trombonist Bob Havens, clarinetist Harry Shields (brother of Larry), pianist Armand Hug, banjoist Joe Capraro, either Emile Christian (doubling on bass trombone) or Chink Martin on bass, and drummer Monk Hazel. A couple of New Orleans favorites ("The Buzzard's Parade" and "Mad") are joined by "The Eyes of Texas" (a song Bonano enjoyed playing), a swinging "It's a Sin to Tell a Lie" and four Dixieland standards. Bonano's no-nonsense trumpet leads the ensembles and is featured on basic but very effective solos. A good example of Sharkey Bonano's playing. —*Scott Yanow*

Joe Bonner

b. Apr. 20, 1948, Rocky Mount, NC
Piano / Post-Bop
A fine pianist who was originally heavily influenced by McCoy Tyner, Joe Bonner is an excellent interpreter of modal-based music and advanced hard bop. He studied music at Virginia State College and early on played with Roy Haynes (1970-71), Freddie Hubbard (1971-72), Pharoah Sanders (1972-74) and Billy Harper (late '70s). Bonner, who recorded as a leader for Muse, Theresa and most prominently Steeple Chase, has been based in Colorado since the 1980s and remains a talented improviser. —*Scott Yanow*

Angel Eyes / Oct. 1974 / Muse ✦✦✦
This is a solo piano recording. —*AMG*

The Lifesaver / Nov. 1974 / Muse ✦✦✦✦
Although Joe Bonner's *Angel Eyes* was actually recorded a month earlier, *Lifesaver* was his first album to be released. This solo piano date is still one of Bonner's best. The influence of McCoy Tyner is strong but Bonner's six originals give the set an impressive amount of diversity and even at the relatively young age of 26, Joe Bonner had a lot to say. It is surprising that he has not become very wellknown. —*Scott Yanow*

Parade / Feb. 8, 1979 / Steeple Chase ✦✦✦

● **Impressions of Copenhagen** / 1981 / Evidence ✦✦✦✦✦
Originally released by Theresa and reissued on CD by Evidence in 1992, this frequently exquisite set features the McCoy Tyner-inspired piano of Joe Bonner on four originals, Cal Massey's "Quiet Dawn" and (released for the first time on the CD) "Lush Life." Bonner and a rhythm section are joined by a string quartet, trumpet, trombone and flutist Holly Hofmann (the leader provided the arrangements) for music that is both lyrical and often passionate. Bonner is an underrated talent, and this is one of his finest recordings. —*Scott Yanow*

Music Map

Bassoon

1920s
Frankie Trumbauer
Garvin Bushell

Later Bassoonists
Ken McIntyre
Yusef Lateef
Illinois Jacquet
Frank Tiberi

Virtually the Only Full-time Jazz Bassoonists
Karen Borca (free jazz)
Janet Grice (crossover)
Michael Rabinowitz

Suburban Fantasies / Feb. 18, 1983 / Steeple Chase ✦✦✦

Devotion / Feb. 20, 1983 / Steeple Chase ✦✦✦

Suite for Chocolate / Aug. 1986 / Steeple Chase ✦✦✦✦
Pianist Joe Bonner made a series of rewarding sets for the Danish Steeple Chase label during 1979-88 without achieving all that much fame, despite his talent. This set teams the modal-oriented Bonner with vibraphonist Khan Jamal, bassist Jesper Lundgaard and drummer Leroy Lowe for six of his diverse originals, all of which display passion (either overtly or inwardly). Although the songs fit together well as a suite, they also stand alone as fine individual pieces, and the interplay between Bonner and Jamal gives this fine date its own personality. —*Scott Yanow*

The Lost Melody / Mar. 1987 / Steeple Chase ✦✦✦

New Beginnings / 1988 / Theresa ✦✦✦
A Colorado-based legend, pianist Joe Bonner (joined by an unidentified bassist on two of the six songs) for the first time is heard doubling on electric piano. The music (five originals, including "Primal Scream" and "Ode to Trane," plus Thad Jones' "A Child Is Born") is intense at times and displays Bonner's roots in 1960s-type modal music and his association with Pharoah Sanders. This out-of-print LP from the now-defunct Theresa label has not yet appeared on CD. —*Scott Yanow*

Earl Bostic

b. Apr. 25, 1913, Tulsa, OK, **d.** Oct. 28, 1965, Rochester, NY
Alto Saxophone / R&B, Swing, Groove
Earl Bostic's roots and foundation were steeped in jazz and swing, but he later became one of the most prolific R&B bandleaders. His searing, sometimes bluesy, sometimes soft and moving, alto sax style influenced many players, including John Coltrane. His many King releases, which featured limited soloing and basic melodic and rhythmic movements, might have fooled novices into thinking Bostic possessed minimal skills, but Art Blakey once said, "Nobody knew more about the saxophone than Bostic, I mean technically, and that includes Bird." Bostic worked in several Midwest bands during the early '30s, then studied at Xavier University. He left school to tour with various groups, among them a band co-led by Charlie Creath and Fate Marable. He moved to New York in the late '30s, where he was a soloist in the bands of Don Redman, Edgar Hayes, and Lionel Hampton. Bostic also led his own combos, whose members included Jimmy Cobb, Al Casey, Blue Mitchell, Stanley Turrentine, Benny Golson and Coltrane. Bostic toured extensively through the '50s, while cutting numerous sessions for King. His recording of "Flamingo" in 1951 was a huge hit, as were the songs "Sleep," "You Go to My Head," "Cherokee," and "Temptation." Bostic recorded for Allegro, Gotham and King from the late '40s to the mid-'60s. He made more than 400 selections for King; the label would use stereo remakes of songs with different personnel, then use the same album numbers. After a heart attack, Bostic became a part-time player. His mid-'60s albums were more soul-jazz than R&B. Several of his King LPs are available on CD. —*Ron Wynn and Michael Erlewine*

That's Earl, Brother / 1943-Dec. 1945 / Spotlite ✦✦✦✦

Earl Bostic was one of the most technically gifted of all saxophonists, having complete control of his alto including a huge range. Because he became famous for his R&B hits of the 1950s, Bostic has tended to be underrated in jazz circles, but this set from the British Spotlite label shows how powerfully he could play in swing settings. Bostic is featured on four rare numbers apiece with Lionel Hampton's big band (broadcasts from 1943-44), a studio set with an octet headed by cornetist Rex Stewart in 1945, and with his own ensemble in concert in late 1945; the latter numbers are the earliest documented examples of Bostic leading a band. This set is highly recommended to swing and bop collectors and even to fans of R&B; Bostic's brilliant playing crossed many musical boundaries. —*Scott Yanow*

● **14 Hits** / Jul. 1946-Jul. 17, 1964 / King ✦✦✦✦✦

This definitive LP is not entirely made of altoist Earl Bostic's "hits"; in fact, "Arrividerci Roma" was never previously released. However, virtually all of Bostic's best-selling numbers are here, including the two-part "That's the Groovy Thing," "Flamingo," "Sleep," and "845 Stomp," plus later tunes taken from albums. 1964's "Walk on the Wild Side" is from Bostic's final King record, cut a year before his death. Listeners wanting to be introduced to Earl Bostic's popular R&B-ish music cannot do better than picking up this album. —*Scott Yanow*

Wild, Man / 1946-1948 / Grand Prix ✦✦✦

Prior to signing with King, the brilliant altoist Earl Bostic recorded 33 selections as a leader, most for Gotham; some of these titles would later be acquired by King. At this relatively early point, Bostic (who was in his mid-30s) had his sound and technique down, along with a melodic and showy way of interpreting standards and jam tunes. Mostly ignoring the harmonic innovations of bebop, Bostic opted to extend his swing playing into R&B. Although this budget LP does not give the personnel or even the recording dates, most of the selections are relatively rare and quite enjoyable. Highlights include the two-part "Let's Ball," "Barfly Baby," "Tippin' In" and "Temptation," which was very much in the style of Bostic's upcoming King hits. —*Scott Yanow*

Earl Blows a Fuse / 1946-Jan. 30, 1958 / Charly ✦✦✦✦

This English import has a fine cross-section of altoist Earl Bostic's recordings for King, starting with 1946's two-part "That's the Groovy Thing" and his huge hit version of "Flamingo" and continuing up until 1958. Although Bostic generally had impressive names in his backup groups (including on this set clarinetist Tony Scott, pianist Jaki Byard, guitarist Al Casey, trumpeter Blue Mitchell, tenors Stanley Turrentine and Benny Golson and even John Coltrane on "Moonglow"), the spotlight is entirely on the altoist. Romps alternate with ballads, and the repertoire ranges from jumping originals to swing-era standards. A fine sampling of Earl Bostic's music. —*Scott Yanow*

● **The Best of Earl Bostic** / 1951-1956 / Deluxe ✦✦✦✦

A nice cross-section of this fiery alto saxist's '50s output, it includes his hits "Sleep" and "Flamingo." —*Bill Dahl*

The Boswell Sisters

f. 1925, USA, **db.** 1936

Group / Classic Jazz, Swing, Traditional Pop

The Boswell Sisters were the greatest jazz vocal group prior to Lambert, Hendricks and Ross 30 years later. Consisting of Connee (1907-76), Martha (1908-58) and Helvetia (1909-88), the trio (which often used Martha on piano) featured hard-swinging choruses and group scatting with numerous key and tempo changes. Connee received all of the solos but Martha and Helvetia both had very appealing voices too. The Boswells grew up in New Orleans where they all learned how to play numerous instruments. They recorded "Nights When I'm Lonely" (and Connee cut "I'm Gonna Cry") in 1925 and they soon were appearing regularly on Los Angeles radio. The group really got going in 1930 with four recordings for OKeh. They were soon signed to Brunswick where they recorded regularly during 1931-35. Their records usually featured top jazz soloists (including Bunny Berigan, the Dorsey Brothers and Joe Venuti) and were often quite exciting. During this period the Boswell Sisters appeared in several films (both shorts and full-length movies) and were a popular radio attraction. They recorded four numbers for Decca in 1936 but by that year all three sisters were married. Martha and Helvetia retired and Connee Boswell (who had been recording solo sides on an occasional basis for several years) went out on her own. A high point was her recordings with Bob Crosby but otherwise Connee's career (although reasonably satisfying) did not live up to its potential. In the 1950s for a time she had a major role on the television series *Pete Kelly's Blues*. Ella Fitzgerald always stated that Connee Boswell was her main influence. —*Scott Yanow*

Syncopating Harmonists from New Orleans / 1930-1935 / Take Two ✦✦✦

The Boswell Sisters were the premiere jazz vocal group (along with the early Mills Brothers) of the 1930s. This Take Two CD not only has nine enjoyable (but mostly fairly common) studio recordings from the 1932-35 period but nine numbers from a 1930 radio show and two ("I'll Never Say 'Never Again' Again" and "Lullaby of Broadway") that are taken from a 1935 program. Unfortunately the personnel are not given for the studio sides but the rarity of the 1930 show (which exclusively features songs not recorded elsewhere by this very appealing group) will make classic jazz collectors want to get this release anyway. —*Scott Yanow*

● **That's How Rhythm Was Born** / 1931-1934 / Sony ✦✦✦✦

That's How Rhythm Was Born compiles 20 of the Boswell Sisters' greatest hits of the '30s, including "The Darktown Strutters' Ball" and "Between the Devil and the Deep Blue Sea." All of the tracks feature musical support from the Dorsey Brothers Orchestra. —*Stephen Thomas Erlewine*

★ **The Boswell Sisters Collection, Vol. 1: 1931-1932** / Mar. 19, 1931-Apr. 9, 1932 / Collector's Classics ✦✦✦✦✦

Most vocal groups that attempt to sing jazz instead end up in the genre of middle-of-road pop music. The Boswell Sisters (comprising Connee, Vet and Martha) were a strong exception, always swinging and, by changing tempos and keys frequently while including some other surprises, performing creative jazz of the early '30s. This Collector's Classics CD unfortunately skips their first seven recordings but then reissues complete and in chronological order 24 of the Boswells finest performances. With a supporting cast frequently including trumpeters Bunny Berigan and Manny Klein, trombonist Tommy Dorsey and clarinetist Jimmy Dorsey (all of whom receive a generous amount of solo space), the sisters are heard at their best throughout this consistently exciting set. Highlights include "Roll On Mississippi, Roll On," "Shine On, Harvest Moon," "Heebies Jeebies," "River Stay 'Way from My Door," "Put That Sun Back in the Sky" and "There'll Be Some Changes Made." This is an essential acquisition. —*Scott Yanow*

Okay America!: Alternate Takes and Rarities / May 25, 1931-Jul. 19, 1935 / Vintage Jazz ✦✦✦✦

An expansion of the earlier LP, this valuable CD features a lot of rare performances by one of the premiere jazz vocal groups, the Boswell Sisters. The many alternate takes should appeal to longtime collectors familiar with the Boswells better-known recordings. Connee Boswell is featured on guest appearances with Red Nichols and the Casa Loma Orchestra, and there are some unusual medleys. Classic jazz fans will want to get this one. —*Scott Yanow*

Sand in My Shoes / Oct. 8, 1935-Jun. 28, 1941 / MCA ✦✦✦✦✦

This superior LP from British MCA has the final six recordings by the Boswell Sisters and 14 selections by Connee Boswell from the 1936-40 period after the group broke up. While the Boswell sides are a bit tame by their standards, Connee Boswell sounds at her very best on such solo numbers as "Yes Indeed," "Martha," "Mama Don't Allow It" and a swinging version of "Home on the Range." Her supporting cast includes the Ben Pollack big band, Bob Crosby's Bob Cats and several orchestras; a special bonus are two vocal duets with Bing Crosby. This out-of-print collection is thus far the definitive Connee Boswell album. —*Scott Yanow*

Chris Botti

Trumpet / Crossover Jazz

Though best known as a contemporary jazz performer, trumpeter Chris Botti made his initial splash on the pop music scene. A native of Oregon, he started playing at the age of ten, and while still in high school began performing professionally. After studying in the prestigious Indiana University music program under the noted jazz educator David Baker, Botti relocated to New York, where he served with saxophonist George Coleman and trumpet great Woody Shaw; under the guidance of producers including Hugh Padgham and Arif Mardin, he swiftly emerged as a highly regarded pop session player, lending his trumpet to recordings from figures including Bob Dylan, Aretha Franklin and Thomas Dolby. In 1990, Botti was asked to join Paul Simon's band, where he remained for the next five years; finally, in 1995, he recorded his solo debut *First Wish*, a record combining the sounds of contemporary pop-jazz with the textures of art-rock. After scoring the 1996 film *Caught*, Botti resurfaced in 1997 with his second LP, *Midnight Without You*. —*Jason Ankeny*

First Wish / 1995 / Verve/Forecast ✦✦✦

● **Midnight Without You** / 1997 / Polygram ✦✦✦✦

In the mid-1990s, Chris Botti, along with his predecessor Rick Braun, became a top pop-jazz trumpeter whose mellow music was frequently played on "smooth jazz" radio stations. Botti's mellow tone and impressive technique helped make what were essentially pop CDs quite listenable. At times on this set, Botti recalls Chuck Mangione, early Miles Davis and Chet Baker, although his sound is fairly original within the limited genre. A couple of the songs have throwaway vocals, all have a faceless electronic rhythm section, and most of the overall performance could be considered mood music with long melody statements rather than creative jazz. Superior background music. —*Scott Yanow*

Lester Bowie

b. Oct. 11, 1941, Frederick, MD
Trumpet, Fluegelhorn / Avant-Garde, Free Jazz

From the 1970s on, Lester Bowie has been the preeminent trumpeter of the jazz avant-garde—one of the few trumpet players of his generation to successfully and completely adopt the techniques of free jazz. Indeed, Bowie has been the most successful in translating the expressive demands of the music—so well suited to the tonally pliant saxophone—to the more difficult-to-manipulate brass instrument. Like a saxophonist such as David Murray or Eric Dolphy, Bowie invests his sound with a variety of timbral effects; his work has a more vocal quality, compared with that of most contemporary trumpeters. In a sense, he's a throwback to the premodern jazz of Cootie Williams or Bubber Miley, though Bowie is by no means a revivalist. Though he's certainly not afraid to appropriate the growls, whinnies, slurs, and slides of the early jazzers, it's always in the service of a thoroughly modern sensibility. And Bowie has chops; his style is quirky, to be sure, but grounded in fundamental jazz concepts of melody, harmony, and rhythm.

Bowie grew up in St. Louis, playing in local jazz and rhythm & blues bands, including those led by Little Milton and Albert King. Bowie moved to Chicago in 1965, where he became musical director for singer Fontella Bass. There Bowie met most of the musicians with whom he would go on to make his name—saxophonists Joseph Jarman and Roscoe Mitchell and drummer Jack DeJohnette among them. He was a founding member of the Association for the Advancement of Creative Musicians and (in 1969) the Art Ensemble of Chicago. Bowie's various bands have included From the Root to the Source—a sort of gospel/jazz/rock fusion group—and Brass Fantasy, an all-brass, post-modern big band that's become his most popular vehicle. Bowie's catholic tastes are evidenced by the band's repertoire; on albums, they have covered a nutty assortment of tunes, ranging from Jimmy Lunceford's "Siesta for the Fiesta" to Michael Jackson's "Black and White." Besides his work as a leader and with the Art Ensemble, Bowie has recorded as a sideman with DeJohnette, percussionist Kahil El'zabar, composer Kip Hanrahan, and saxophonist David Murray. He was also a member of the mid-'80s all-star cooperative the Leaders. Bowie's music occasionally leans too heavily on parody and aural slapstick to be truly affecting, but at its best, a Bowie-led ensemble can open the mind and move the feet in equal measure. —*Chris Kelsey*

Numbers 1 & 2 / Aug. 11, 1967+Aug. 25, 1967 / Nessa ✦✦✦
The music on this LP has been reissued in Nessa's limited-edition multi-CD box set which traces the beginnings of the Art Ensemble of Chicago. Trumpeter Bowie meets up with bassist Malachi Favors and Roscoe Mitchell, who is heard on alto, soprano, flute, clarinet and miscellaneous instruments; Joseph Jarman joins the trio on the second selection, playing alto, soprano, clarinet, bassoon and bells. The spontaneous music often wanders and rambles a bit, reaching some surprising conclusions and showing expert use of space; very advanced for 1967. —*Scott Yanow*

Fast Last / Sep. 10, 1974 / Muse ✦✦✦✦
As is often true of a Lester Bowie record, this set has surpising moments and a liberal use of absurd humor, along with some fine playing. Certainly one would not expect any other avant-garde trumpeter to play such songs as "Hello Dolly" (in duet with pianist John Hicks) and "F Troop Rides Again." On a more serious note are three collaborations with altoist Julius Hemphill, including Ornette Coleman's "Lonely Woman" and the nearly 13-minute "Fast Last C." A fine introduction to Lester Bowie's diverse music, although this album has not yet been reissued on CD. —*Scott Yanow*

Rope-A-Dope / Jun. 17, 1975 / Muse ✦✦✦✦
Trumpeter Lester Bowie's second of two projects for Muse (both are worth searching for) matches the witty and adventurous player with two fellow members of the Art Ensemble of Chicago (bassist Malachi Favors and drummer Don Moye, the second drums of Charles Bobo Shaw, brother/trombonist Joseph Bowie and, on the opening "Tender Openings," violinist Raymund Cheng. While "Rope-A-Dope" is supposedly a musical re-enactment of a Muhammad Ali fight, "St. Louis Blues" has its humorous moments. Throughout, the highly expressive Lester Bowie is heard in prime form. —*Scott Yanow*

Duet / Jan. 1978 / IAI ✦✦✦

The 5th Power / Apr. 12, 1978+Apr. 17, 1978 / Black Saint ✦✦✦✦
1978 quintet with Arthur Blythe (as), Amina Myers (p). Creative jazz and a progressive gospel segment. Bowie at his eclectic best. Essential. —*Michael G. Nastos*

Works / 1980-1985 / ECM ✦✦✦✦✦
This 1980-1985 anthology includes Art Ensemble of Chicago, Brass Fantasy, Stanton Davis, Rasul Siddik, Vincent Chancey, Steve Turre, Frank Lacy, Phillip Wilson, and Bob Stewart. —*AMG*

● **The Great Pretender** / Jun. 1981 / ECM ✦✦✦✦✦
This is one of trumpeter Lester Bowie's most accessible albums; certainly his brief versions of "It's Howdy Doody Time" and "When the Moon Comes over the Mountain" are not difficult to understand. But actually the bulk of this album is taken up with the 16-minute title cut and a variety of Bowie's colorful originals. The highly expressive trumpeter is mostly heard with a quartet (although "The Great Pretender" also adds two vocalists and baritonist Hamiet Bluiett) and this set offers many fine examples of his original approach to making music, technically avant-garde but also borrowing aspects of earlier styles in unusual combinations. —*Scott Yanow*

All the Magic! / Jun. 1982 / ECM ✦✦✦
Two very different sessions are combined on this two-LP set. Trumpeter Lester Bowie and a quintet also including Ari Brown on tenor and soprano, pianist Art Matthews, bassist Fred Williams, and drummer Phillip Wilson, are often used to accompany the soulful and gospel-oriented vocals of Fontella Bass and David Peaston (in addition to taking colorful solos). The 12-minute "For Louie" and a suite that is dominated by an emotional version of "Everything Must Change" are highlights; also memorable is a brief version of Albert Ayler's "Ghosts." The second album is quite a bit different, a set of unaccompanied trumpet solos by Bowie that are often quite humorous. On "Miles Davis Meets Donald Duck," the meeting does seem to take place; "Thirsty?" is a funny joke, and some of the other pieces (including "Organic Echo," "Dunce Dance" and "Fraudulent Fanfare") are brief but effective wisecracks. All in all, this two-fer shows off both Lester Bowie's playing abilities and his sense of humor. —*Scott Yanow*

I Only Have Eyes for You / Feb. 1985 / ECM ✦✦✦
The debut by Lester Bowie's Brass Fantasy (an octet consisting of four trumpets, both Craig Harris and Steve Turre on trombones, the French horn of Vincent Chancey, Bob Stewart on tuba and drummer Phillip Wilson) is one of their best recordings. Rather than playing their interpretations of pop tunes (which would be the direction Brass Fantasy would head in the future), this album finds the musicians performing originals by Bowie (including "When the Spirit Returns"), Stewart, trumpeters Bruce Purse and Malachi Thompson and the standard title cut. The music is both whimsical and explorative, making for a colorful set. —*Scott Yanow*

Avant Pop / Mar. 1986 / ECM ✦✦
Pop? Yes. Avant? No. Perhaps this was the logical progression for Lester Bowie, who in times past, did his stint with various R&B aggregations... And maybe ECM wanted to document his sincere desire to get lightly down in a further attempt to rekindle the affair they had going with a "poppier" audience via ex-ECMer Pat Metheny... The piece of real interest for the discriminating listener was the almost avant opener, which featured some lovely syncopated phrasing in the supporting riffs along with some creative textural manipulations of the horns that gave the sound an electronic ambience. —*Milo Fine, Cadence*

Twilight Dreams / Apr. 1987 / Venture ✦✦✦
Lester Bowie's Brass Fantasy, which comprises four trumpets, two trombones, French horn, tuba and drums, has rarely lived up to its potential on records. Bowie has enjoyed having the band take pop tunes ("Personality" and "Night Time Is the Right Time" on this album) and distort (and sometimes satirize) them but one imagines that this approach works better in concert than on record. There are some strong moments on this hard-to-find LP (such as Bowie's trumpet-drums duet with the late Phillip Wilson on "Duke's Fantasy") but this is a hit-and-miss affair. —*Scott Yanow*

Serious Fun / Apr. 4, 1989-Apr. 6, 1989 / DIW ✦✦✦

My Way / Jan. 22, 1990-Jan. 30, 1990 / DIW ✦✦
A transitional album by Lester Bowie's Brass Fantasy, this Japanese CD finds the tentet (four trumpets, two trombones, French horn, tuba, drums and percussion) performing three jazz pieces by the group's former trumpeter Bruce Purse plus eccentric interpretations of "My Way," "Honky Tonk" and James Brown's "I Got You." With such top players as trombonists Steve Turre and Frank Lacy (who sings "I Got You" as best he can) and trumpeter E.J. Allen having solo space along with the distorted sounds of the leader/trumpeter, this set certainly has its interesting moments, although it is a bit erratic. —*Scott Yanow*

Funky T, Cool T / Jan. 14, 1991-Jan. 16, 1991 / DIW ✦✦✦

The Fire This Time / May 1, 1992 / In & Out ✦✦✦

Charles Brackeen

b. 1940, White's Chapel, OK
Tenor Saxophone, Soprano Saxophone / Free Jazz, Avant-Garde

An excellent avant-garde tenor who has always been a bit underrated, Charles Brackeen originally studied violin and piano. Settling on tenor, he worked in both New York and Los Angeles, meeting and marrying pianist Joanne Brackeen. In New York he was associated with "the new thing" and in 1968 recorded an interesting set for Strata East with three of the members of the Ornette Coleman Quartet (Don Cherry, Charlie Haden and Ed Blackwell). After a long period of obscurity he began playing with Paul Motian (with whom he recorded for ECM) and in 1987 he started making records for Silkheart. An explorative high-energy player, Charles Brackeen's performances are always stimulating. —*Scott Yanow*

Rhythm X / Jan. 1968 / Strata East ◆◆◆◆
Avant saxophonist on early date. Wild, uninhibited. —*Michael G. Nastos*

Attainment / 1987 / Silkheart ◆◆◆
Tenor saxophonist Charles Brackeen is in ways a throwback to the 1960s. He sometimes builds off of childlike folk themes (like Albert Ayler), and Ornette Coleman's method of constantly improvising new melodies is also an influence. However, Brackeen's intense sound has a soul of its own, and his playing on the four lengthy originals (with strong contributions by bassist Fred Hopkins, drummer Andrew Cyrille and the underrated cornetist Olu Dara) is quite original. Intense yet fulfilling music which was recorded the same day as its companion album, *Worshippers Come Nigh.* —*Scott Yanow*

Bannar / 1987 / Silkheart ◆◆◆◆
An adventurous saxophonist, Charles Brackeen has been greatly underrecorded throughout his career. He cut an obscure disc for Strata East in 1968 and was featured on a couple of Paul Motian ECM discs, but did not have another opportunity to lead his own sessions until he cut three records for Silkheart in 1987; fortunately all have been reissued on CD. On his Silkheart debut, Brackeen teams up with trumpeter Dennis Gonzalez, bassist Malachi Favors and drummer Alvin Fielder for the unusual "Three Monks Suite" (an 8-minute episodic work that was completely written out and has the tenorman switching to soprano), along with four additional originals. Intriguing and often intense music that effectively uses simple folk melodies as vehicles for improvising. —*Scott Yanow*

● Worshippers Nigh / Nov. 28, 1987 / Silkheart ◆◆◆◆
Tenorman Charles Brackeen's third of three Silkheart CDs (recorded at the same session as *Attainment*) matches his powerful playing with cornetist Olu Dara, bassist Fred Hopkins and drummer Andrew Cyrille. All of the Silkheart sets are worth picking up, but this one (due to its extra intensity and the five particularly strong Brackeen originals) gets a slight edge. Brackeen's passionate playing shows that free jazz was still very much alive (if underground) in the 1980s. —*Scott Yanow*

Joanne Brackeen

b. Jul. 26, 1938, Ventura, CA
Piano / Post-Bop
A brilliant pianist flexible enough to play free, modal music and standards, Joanne Brackeen has been a major player for 25 years. She taught herself to play jazz piano. During 1958-59 Brackeen worked in Los Angeles with Teddy Edwards, Harold Land, Dexter Gordon and Charles Lloyd. After marrying Charles Brackeen (they later divorced) she took time off to bring up their four children. Brackeen moved to New York in 1965, worked with Woody Shaw and David Liebman and became the first female member of Art Blakey's Jazz Messengers (1969-72). After working regularly with Joe Henderson (1972-75) and Stan Getz (1975-77), Brackeen (an original stylist) has mostly performed as a leader of her own trios, making numerous records for Choice, Timeless, Tappan Zee and Concord. —*Scott Yanow*

Six Ate / Mar. 16, 1975 / Candid ◆◆◆◆
Although this Candid CD (put out through Koch) may have an unfamiliar title, it is actually a reissue of pianist Joanne Brackeen's first album as a leader which was originally called *Snooze*. Assisted by bassist Cecil McBee and drummer Billy Hart, Brackeen (who was already 36) even in 1975 already had her own sound although she was more influenced by McCoy Tyner than she would be in later years. Brackeen interprets four of her own challenging originals plus Miles Davis' rarely performed "Circle," Wayne Shorter's "Nefertiti," the standard "Old Devil Moon" and a previously unreleased rendition of "I Didn't Know What Time It Was." This recording (cut between her stints with Joe Henderson and Stan Getz) was a strong step forward in Joanne Brackeen's brilliant career. —*Scott Yanow*

New True Illusion / Jul. 15, 1976 / Timeless ◆◆◆◆
Pianist Joanne Brackeen, already a powerful force by 1976, had her roots in McCoy Tyner but early on developed her own personal voice. This set of post-bop duets with bassist Clint Houston features obscurities by Tyner and Chick Corea, a pair of standards and two of Brackeen's quirky originals. The improvisations are quite advanced, yet often surprisingly melodic and rhythmic. An excellent early effort. —*Scott Yanow*

Tring-A-Ling / Mar. 20, 1977 / Choice ◆◆◆◆
Pianist Joanne Brackeen's fourth recording as a leader was her first to include a horn, but she made a strong choice. Tenor great Michael Brecker is on three of

Brackeen's challenging originals, along with alternating bassists Cecil McBee and Clint Houston, plus drummer Billy Hart. The pianist's music is complex and quite tricky, but more accessible than expected due to the close interplay between the superb musicians and the variety of rhythms utilized. Open-minded listeners are advised to check this one out. —*Scott Yanow*

Prism / Aug. 1978 / Choice ◆◆◆
The third of Joanne Brackeen's three Choice recordings is a set of piano-bass duets with Eddie Gomez. As usual for the era, all of the compositions are Brackeen's, and the music is both challenging and spontaneous, at least for musicians skilled enough to master the structures. Although underrated, Joanne Brackeen has long been one of the giants of modal post-bop piano, and this fine set serves as additional proof. —*Scott Yanow*

Trinkets and Things / Aug. 13, 1978 / Timeless ◆◆◆◆
Joane Brackeen has always been a powerful two-handed pianist. This program of duets with guitarist Ryo Kawasaki finds Brackeen utilizing her left hand in creative fashion, sometimes striding or playing basslines and occasionally implying rather than stating the time. Kawasaki also has plenty of stimulating solos on the set, which comprises his title cut plus six of Brackeen's originals. —*Scott Yanow*

Keyed In / May 11, 1979-May 12, 1979 / Columbia ◆◆◆◆
It seemed fairly odd in 1979 when the adventurous pianist Joanne Brackeen was signed to Bob James' Tappan Zee label, but fortunately Brackeen was not pressured to perform commercial music. In fact, her two releases for the label (this date would be followed by *Ancient Dynasty*) are in a similar style as earlier work for smaller labels. Teamed up with bassist Eddie Gomez and drummer Jack DeJohnette, Brackeen sounds quite distinctive on seven of her originals, hinting a little at McCoy Tyner but coming up with fresh and advanced improvisations. This rewarding LP (not yet reissued on CD) will most likely be difficult to locate. —*Scott Yanow*

Aft / Sep. 1979 / Timeless ◆◆◆
This is one of the more obscure Joanne Brackeen recordings. Although the pianist is heard in a trio with guitarist Ryo Kawasaki and bassist Clint Houston, the music sounds nothing like Nat King Cole or Oscar Peterson. Actually Brackeen long ago developed her own distinctive chord voicings, and, even when one hears touches of McCoy Tyner or Chick Corea in her solos, in reality she sounds like no one else. Her close interplay with Kawasaki and Houston on the six group originals (four by Brackeen) is consistently impressive and unpredictable. —*Scott Yanow*

Ancient Dynasty / 1980 / Columbia ◆◆◆
Bob James surprised many when he signed the adventurous pianist Joanne Brackeen to his Tappan Zee subsidiary of Columbia. As it turned out, James signed her for the simple reason that he was impressed by her music, and Brackeen's Columbia recordings fortunately ended up not being any "simpler" or more "accessible" than her earlier small-label dates. This now out-of-print album features Brackeen with an all-star quartet featuring her former boss, Joe Henderson, on tenor, bassist Eddie Gomez and drummer Jack DeJohnette. The four complex Brackeen originals are all at least nine minutes long and are quite challenging for both the musicians and the listener alike. —*Scott Yanow*

Special Identity / Dec. 8, 1981+Dec. 9, 1981 / Antilles ◆◆◆
For the third straight album, pianist Joanne Brackeen was joined in 1981 by bassist Eddie Gomez and drummer Jack DeJohnette. The potentially forbidding music (which has advanced modal-based solos) is often surprisingly accessible and full of subtle surprises and close interplay by the musicians. Although not her definitive release, this album (which is currently out of print) keeps Joanne Brackeen's record perfect; every one of her recordings stands up well over time. —*Scott Yanow*

Havin' Fun / Jun. 1985 / Concord Jazz ◆◆◆◆
After three year's off records, Joanne Brackeen returned by getting signed to Concord and cutting her first standards album. Joined by bassist Cecil McBee and drummer Al Foster, Brackeen explores such unlikely tunes as "I've Got the World on a String," "This Is Always" and "Day by Day," but that does not mean that she was suddenly sounding like Teddy Wilson. Brackeen's distinctive style is heard very much intact in this fairly accessible format, and she makes the ancient tunes sound fresh. Recommended. —*Scott Yanow*

● Fi-Fi Goes to Heaven / 1986 / Concord Jazz ◆◆◆◆◆
While her previous Concord release stuck to standards, this very well-rounded outing finds the adventurous pianist Joanne Brackeen splitting the program between four originals and three veteran tunes (including "Stardust"). In addition to bassist Cecil McBee and drummer Al Foster, the CD is quite special, for it matches Brackeen with trumpeter Terence Blanchard and Branford Marsalis (whom she insisted play mostly on his earlier specialty, alto). The Young Lions work well with Brackeen and her rhythm mates on this consistently stimulating and occasionally playful set. A perfect introduction to Joanne Brackeen's music. —*Scott Yanow*

Live at Maybeck Recital Hall / Jun. 1989 / Concord Jazz ✦✦✦✦✦

The first entry in the extensive series of piano solo recitals held at Maybeck Recital Hall features the great Joanne Brackeen. Although classified by some originally as an avant-gardist inspired by McCoy Tyner, Brackeen continued to grow in stature and by the late '80s had her own style. She is respectful but passionate on seven standards (keeping the melody in mind during her explorations) while her four originals are given more adventurous improvisations. "Dr. Chu Chow" is a good example of her power as is the quirky "Curved Space" with its catchy and delayed 6/4 rhythmic pattern. Although not a stride player, Brackeen is clearly a two-handed pianist and, as shown on her "African Aztec," able to play music that hints in an abstract way at earlier styles (in this case blues and boogie-woogie) while remaining quite advanced and original. Well worth checking out. —*Scott Yanow*

Breath of Brazil / Apr. 18, 1991-Apr. 19, 1991 / Concord Jazz ✦✦✦

For Joanne Brackeen, this was an unusual record. The brilliant post-bop pianist performs three originals, plus a variety of Brazilian songs (including some by Jobim, Ivan Lins, Gilberto Gil and Egberto Gismonti) with her longtime bassist Eddie Gomez and two Brazilian musicians, drummer Duduka Da Fonseca and percussionist Waltinho Anastacio. Although one would not think that Brackeen's percussive and adventurous style would sound comfortable playing softer Brazilian pieces, the pianist modified her style a bit and shows surprising flexibility. This is a delightful set, with the highlights including "Waters of March," "Velas" and "So Many Stars." —*Scott Yanow*

Where Legends Dwell / Sep. 3, 1991-Sep. 4, 1991 / Ken Music ✦✦✦✦

Extraordinary trio with Eddie Gomez on bass and Jack DeJohnette on drums, this is her best work of the past decade. Twelve tracks are all originals. Over 70 minutes of incredibly ingenious jazz included. This is easy to dig into. —*Michael G. Nastos*

Turnaround / Feb. 27, 1992-Feb. 28, 1992 / Evidence ✦✦✦✦

The talented and highly original pianist Joanne Brackeen leads an all-star quartet (with altoist Donald Harrison, bassist Cecil McBee and drummer Marvin "Smitty" Smith) at Sweet Basil for this 1992 live session. Brackeen is in top form digging into two standards, Ornette Coleman's "Turnaround" (which is taken as a conventional blues) and three of her originals including a 16-minute "Picasso." The explorative music holds one's interest throughout. —*Scott Yanow*

Take a Chance / June 15, 1993-June 16, 1993 / Concord Jazz ✦✦✦

Joanne Brackeen previously tackled Afro-Latin and Brazilian music with authority on *Breath of Brazil*. This sequel isn't quite as dynamic or energetic as its predecessor, but it doesn't miss by much. The main difference is that Brackeen is more light than assertive on several numbers, opting to showcase Brazil's romantic/sentimental side as much as its steamy, rhythmic element. But she doesn't spare any energy on "Recade Bossa Nova," "Ducka" or the title track. This isn't a CD for those who only want the classic Brazilian sound; Brackeen is interested in current affairs, although she can and does occasionally return to the glorious bossa nova and samba past. —*Ron Wynn*

Don Braden

b. Nov. 20, 1963, Cincinnati, OH
Tenor Saxophone / Hard Bop, Post-Bop

A talented, thick-toned tenor whose sound is inspired a bit by Joe Henderson and the hard-bop stylists, Don Braden has been a part of many sessions during the past 15 years. Born in Cincinnati but raised in Louisville, Braden began playing tenor when he was 13 and started performing professionally two years later. He played with the McDonald's All American High School Jazz Band, attended Harvard (1981-84), and studied for a short time with Bill Pierce and Jerry Bergonzi. After moving to New York in 1984, Braden gained recognition for his work with the Harper Brothers, Lonnie Smith and Betty Carter. He toured with Wynton Marsalis (1986-87) and had stints with Out of the Blue, Roy Haynes, Tony Williams, Freddie Hubbard, J.J. Johnson, Tom Harrell, Art Farmer, the Mingus Big Band and Winard Harper, in addition to leading his own band. Braden, who has recorded as a leader for Criss Cross, Landmark, Epicure and RCA (1996), has a potentially significant future. —*Scott Yanow*

● **The Time Is Now** / Jan. 2, 1991 / Criss Cross ✦✦✦✦

Don Braden's debut as a leader found the 27-year-old already a talented hard bop-based tenor saxophonist. Teamed up with other young all-stars (trumpeter Tom Harrell, pianist Bennie Green, bassist Christian McBride and drummer Carl Allen), Braden performs three originals, a trio of superior standards (including "Softly As in a Morning Sunrise" and "Will You Still Be Mine"), and an obscure Jackie McLean blues ("Condition Blue"), plus an acoustic version of Herbie Hancock's funky "Butterfly." The young tenor was on his way to shedding his influences and

developing a strong voice of his own, and this largely straightahead date is excellent. —*Scott Yanow*

Landing Zone / May 9, 1994-May 10, 1994 / Landmark ✦✦✦

Tenor saxophonist Don Braden is a highly competent young hard bopper with an attractively reedy tone, flexible technique, and a sure sense of time. This is a straightahead jazz album like dozens of others released in the mid-to-late '90s—better than many, no different from most. Pleasant, untroubling, and ultimately forgettable. Braden's a decent player who might have the potential to be something more. His is an agreeable musical personality, but he's got some stretching to do if he wants to make a lasting contribution. —*Chris Kelsey*

Organic / Aug. 29, 1995 / Columbia ✦✦✦

The Voice of the Saxophone / Feb. 15, 1997-Mar. 4, 1997 / RCA ✦✦✦

Bobby Bradford

b. Jul. 19, 1934, Cleveland, MS
Cornet, Trumpet / Avant-Garde, Post-Bop

One of the best trumpeters to emerge from the avant-garde, Bobby Bradford largely fulfilled the potential of Don Cherry (whose chops declined through the years due to the amount of time allocated to performing on flute and other instruments). Bradford grew up in Dallas, playing trumpet locally with such local players as Cedar Walton and David Newman. In 1953 he moved to Los Angeles where he met and played with Ornette Coleman and Eric Dolphy. Bradford spent time in the military and in school before becoming Don Cherry's replacement with the Ornette Coleman Quartet in 1961-63, a period when the group unfortunately rarely worked. After moving to Los Angeles, Bradford became a school teacher and also began a longtime association with clarinetist John Carter; his mellow trumpet blended in well with Carter's dissonant flights. He recorded with Ornette Coleman in 1971 but otherwise is best known for his playing and recordings with Carter. Since the clarinetist's death, Bradford has frequently led a quintet (the Mo'tet) featuring Vinny Golia and occasionally Marty Ehrlich. He has also performed since the early '90s with John Stevens's Freebop, the David Murray Octet and Charlie Haden's Liberation Music Orchestra. —*Scott Yanow*

With John Stevens and the Spontaneous Music Ensemble, Vol. 1 / Jul. 9, 1971 / Nessa ✦✦✦

In the first of two LPs, trumpeter Bobby Bradford fits right into drummer John Stevens' Spontaneous Music Ensemble, a quintet with leader-drummer Trevor Watts on alto and soprano, trombonist Bob Norden, bassist Ron Herman and (on two of the four selections) the haunting voice of Julie Tippetts. Tippetts' wordless vocals give an otherworldly quality to her appearances, while the two instrumentals (including a tribute to Louis Armstrong titled "His Majesty Louis") look more towards the free bop of Ornette Coleman. Stimulating and adventurous music. —*Scott Yanow*

With John Stevens, Vol. 2 / Jul. 9, 1971 / Nessa ✦✦✦

This album is worth picking up for the two lengthy jams (including the nearly 19-minute "Rhythm Piece") because a top freebop quintet comprising trumpeter Bobby Bradford, Trevor Watts on alto and soprano, trombonist Bob Norden, bassist Ron Herman and drummer John Stevens creates some colorful music. The two vocals by Julie Tippetts however are only for specialized tastes for many will find her abstract singing difficult to listen to. Fortunately it does not dominate. —*Scott Yanow*

Lost in L.A. / Jun. 8, 1983-Jun. 8, 1983 / Soul Note ✦✦✦✦

Cornetist Bobby Bradford has recorded far too infrequently throughout his career. A mellow-toned player with an adventurous style that is usually surprisingly accessible, Bradford is well featured on this excellent quintet date with altoist James Kousakis, both Roberto Miguel Miranda and Mark Dresser on bass and drummer Sherman Ferguson. Together they perform five of Bradford's originals, music that at its best (particularly on "Sho Nuff Blues" and "Dirty Rag") looks both backwards to earlier styles and extends the innovations of Ornette Coleman. Recommended. —*Scott Yanow*

● **One Night Stand** / Nov. 1986 / Soul Note ✦✦✦✦✦

A melodic player with a healthy sense of humor who has become more expressive through the years, Bobby Bradford really got a chance to stretch out on this fine session. Although pianist Frank Sullivan is essentially a bop player, he did a good job of keeping up during the more adventurous performances. Bassist Scott Walton (who has learned from the innovations of Charlie Haden) and drummer Billy Bowker were excellent in support. "Ashes" (a calypso version of "I Got Rhythm") and the mysterious "Woman" were the high points of this highly recommended disc. —*Scott Yanow, Cadence*

Comin' On / May 29, 1988 / Hat Art ✦✦✦

An uneven 1988 date that still contains some glorious moments, mostly when Bradford and his longtime cohort, clarinetist John Carter, play together. Bradford's solos aren't as universally sharp or focused as usual, but he doesn't totally falter. Drummer Andrew Cyrille and bassist Richard Davis dominate in the rhythm section. —*Ron Wynn*

Will Bradley

b. Jul. 12, 1912, Newton, NJ, **d.** Jul. 15, 1989, Flemington, NJ
Trombone / Swing

Will Bradley was a reluctant celebrity. His name became closely associated with boogie-woogie due to the commercial success of "Beat Me Daddy, Eight to the Bar" but he much preferred to play ballads. A technically skilled trombonist, Bradley was a busy studio musician throughout much of his career. He worked with Red Nichols (1931-32) and Ray Noble (1935-36) but was an unknown (except to his fellow musicians) when he formed a big band in 1939 with Ray McKinley. McKinley's drumming and vocals along with Freddie Slack's piano solos helped the group catch on. But by 1942 Bradley had tired of the project and he returned to the security and anonymity of studio work, only emerging to play Dixieland, ballads or boogie-woogie on an occasional basis. —*Scott Yanow*

● **Best of Big Bands** / Sep. 19, 1939-Jun. 23, 1941 / Columbia ◆◆◆◆
This 16-song sampler from the Will Bradley Orchestra should be a definitive collection but the crummy packaging (not bothering to list the recording dates or personnel) along with some odd choices among the songs makes this set a bit of a disappointment. Bradley's biggest hits ("Celery Stalks at Midnight," "Beat Me Daddy, Eight to the Bar" and "Down the Road A-piece") are here along with some lesser vocal pieces. Since the music is better than the packaging and there are not many Will Bradley recordings currently available on CD, this set is worth picking up anyway. —*Scott Yanow*

Rock-a-Bye the Boogie / Mar. 15, 1940-Jun. 23, 1941 / Bandstand ◆◆◆◆◆
The first of three Will Bradley LPs put out by the Bandstand label in the 1970s (some of the music has since been reissued on CD by Aero) has 15 of the trombonist's big band's finest recordings. This jazz-oriented set starts off with Bradley's biggest hit ("Beat Me Daddy, Eight to the Bar") and includes other boogie-woogie performances including the Dixielandish "Basin Street Boogie," "Rhumboogie," "Scrub Me Mama, With aBoogie Beat," "Boogie Woogie Conga," "Booglie Wooglie Piggy," "Rock-a-Bye the Boogie" and "I Boogied When I Should Have Woogied." Other high points include "In the Land of the Sky Blue Water," "Down the Road Apiece" and "Dark Eyes." With Ray McKinley driving the band on drums and taking some good-humored vocals and pianist Freddie Slack having many feature spots, this is a definitive set. —*Scott Yanow*

Let's Dance / Jan. 21, 1941-Jan. 8, 1942 / Bandstand ◆◆◆◆
The second of three Will Bradley LP samplers on Bandstand has some of the high points from the second half of the short-lived group's existence. After the success of "Beat Me Daddy, Eight to the Bar," the Bradley orchestra emphasized big band boogie-woogie arrangements against the wishes of the trombonist-bandleader who actually preferred to play ballads. This album includes several songs in that vein (including "Bounce Me Brother with a Solid Four" and "Fry Me a Cookie with a Can of Lard") plus some more conventional swing arrangements and small-group outings on "Tea for Two" and a broadcast version of "Basin St. Boogie." With drummer Ray McKinley contributing some good-natured vocals and the band's soloists including trumpeter Steve Lipkins, Peanuts Hucko on tenor and clarinet and either Freddie Slack or Billy Maxted on piano, this was one of the most swinging orchestras of the 1939-42 period. —*Scott Yanow*

Featuring Ray McKinley 1941 / Jan. 22, 1941+Sep. 7, 1941 / Circle ◆◆◆
This LP features the 1941 Will Bradley Orchestra on noncommercial performances made as radio transcriptions. Although famous for its big-band boogie-woogie hits, there is less boogie on these dozen numbers (other than "The Booglie Wooglie Piggy") than one would expect. Bradley's orchestra (which he co-led with drummer Ray McKinley) was also an excellent swing band. The obscure performances are quite brief (only one exceeds three minutes) but have their moments of interest (particularly the solos of pianist Freddie Slack) and are easily recommended to swing collectors. —*Scott Yanow*

In Disco Order, Vol. 8 / Oct. 16, 1941-1947 / Ajax ◆◆◆◆
By the end of 1941, trombonist Will Bradley was tired of playing boogie-woogie big-band charts despite his orchestra's commercial success. While Bradley preferred ballads, his unbilled co-leader drummer Ray McKinley loved boogie-woogie and was soon motivated to quit the group, leading to its eventual demise. On the eighth of nine Ajax LPs that document most of Bradley's career, the last two sessions by his big band (highlighted by "Fry Me Cookie with a Can of Lard" and "Request for a Rhumba") are included plus a Dixieland boogie-woogie date from 1944 (which also stars trumpeter Billy Butterfield and pianist Johnny Guarnieri) and four very obscure titles from postwar studio big-band sessions. This album

and *Vol. 9* in particular are highly recommended to swing collectors due to the rare material. —*Scott Yanow*

In Disco Order, Vol. 9 / 1947-1953 / Ajax ◆◆◆◆
The ninth and final LP volume from the collector's Ajax label contains some very rare recordings. Although trombonist Will Bradley led a successful big band during 1939-42, after the orchestra broke up he became a studio musician for the rest of his life. This album has five songs from a 1947 big-band date in which Bradley is at the head of a group of studio players; a remake of "Celery Stalks at Midnight" and the unusual "Bop 'n' Boogie" are most memorable. In addition, Bradley is part of a nonet backing the talented but obscure singer Dorothy Ann on two titles in 1950. Best are eight Dixieland performances from 1953 that feature Bradley in a group with either Yank Lawson or Rex Stewart on trumpet, clarinetist Bill Stegmeyer and tenor saxophonist Bud Freeman. None of this music has been reissued on CD and the Dixieland titles in particular are quite enjoyable. Well worth searching for by fans of prebop jazz. —*Scott Yanow*

Ruby Braff

b. Mar. 16, 1927, Boston, MA
Cornet, Trumpet / Swing, New Orleans Jazz

One of the great swing/Dixieland cornetists, Ruby Braff went through long periods of his career unable to find work because his music was considered out-of-fashion but his fortunes improved by the 1970s. A very expressive player who in later years liked to build his solos up to a low note, Braff's playing is instantly recognizable within seconds.

Braff mostly worked around Boston in the late '40s. He teamed up with Pee Wee Russell when the clarinetist was making a comeback (they recorded live for Savoy) and after moving to New York in 1953 he fit easily into a variety of Dixieland and mainstream settings. Braff recorded for Vanguard as a leader and with Vic Dickenson, Buck Clayton and Urbie Green. He was one of the stars of Buck Clayton's Columbia jam sessions and in the mid-'50s worked with Benny Goodman. But despite good reviews and occasional recordings, work was hard for Braff to come by at times. In the 1960s he was able to get jobs by being with George Wein's Newport All-Stars and at jazz festivals, but it was not until the cornetist formed a quartet with guitarist George Barnes in 1973 that he became more secure. Since that time Braff has been heard in many small-group settings including duets with Dick Hyman and Ellis Larkins (he had first met up with the latter in the 1950s), quintets with Scott Hamilton and matching wits with Howard Alden. He remains one of the greats of mainstream jazz. —*Scott Yanow*

Hustlin' and Bustlin' / 1951-Jun. 9, 1954 / Black Lion ◆◆◆◆◆
Trumpeter Ruby Braff puts so much passion into each note he plays that, even when performing familiar Dixieland and swing tunes, he is able to immediately uplift the material. On this CD reissue of a Black Lion LP, Braff is heard with three different groups. The bulk of the date features him in a quintet with tenor saxophonist Sam Margolis, pianist Ken Kersey, bassist Milt Hinton and drummer Bobby Donaldson; highlights include "Hustlin' and Bustlin' for Baby," "There's a Small Hotel" and "Shoe Shine Boy." In addition there are three numbers recorded live at Storyville with an all-star sextet that includes trombonist Vic Dickenson and clarinetist Edmond Hall and one number ("When It's Sleepy Time Down South") with an octet. This set offers listeners a good example of Ruby Braff's playing in his early days. —*Scott Yanow*

Adoration of the Melody / Mar. 17, 1955-Mar. 18, 1955 / Bethlehem ◆◆◆◆◆

Swing with Ruby Braff / Apr. 25, 1955 / Jazztone ◆◆◆
This out-of-print LP (part of which has been reissued on CD by the collector's label Jazz Connoisseur) features trumpeter Ruby Braff playing mainstream jazz. The music ranges from swing (with touches of Dixieland) to cool and is notable for showcasing the obscure but talented tenor Sam Margolis (who often recalls late-period Lester Young) and trombonist Billy Byers (who is better known as an arranger); the fine rhythm section consists of pianist Marty Napoleon, bassist Milt Hinton and drummer Jo Jones. Braff is not as forceful on the set as usual but he is in generally fine form on such numbers as the ad-lib "Only a Blues," "In the Shade of the Old Apple Tree," "I'm Shooting High" and "Love Me or Leave Me." —*Scott Yanow*

● **Two by Two: Ruby and Ellis Play Rodgers and Hart** / Oct. 14, 1955 / Vanguard ◆◆◆◆◆
In 1955 trumpeter Ruby Braff recorded two duet albums with the sensitive pianist Ellis Larkins and both projects were very well received. This CD reissue brings back the second session in which they perform a dozen songs written by Rodgers and Hart. The passionate Braff and Larkins (a masterful accompanist) work quite well together. Although the emphasis is on ballads, there are a few hotter pieces that find Braff pushing Larkins a bit. Highlights include "Mountain Greenery," "Blue Moon," "My Romance" and "You Took Advantage of Me." —*Scott Yanow*

Braff! / Jun. 26, 1956-Jul. 10, 1956 / Portrait ✦✦✦✦

This reissue LP from 1989 in CBS's short-lived *Portrait* series features the great trumpeter Ruby Braff playing with three very different but equally swinging groups. Four of the best performances, including "Stardust" and "It's Been So Long," showcase Braff with a rhythm section that includes pianist Dave McKenna. Braff also meets up with tenor saxophonist Coleman Hawkins, baritonist Ernie Caceres and trombonist Lawrence Brown in an all-star nonet and with vibraphonist Don Elliott in a sextet. The emphasis is on veteran swing standards (Braff does contribute the original "Here's Freddie") and jamming ensembles. This enjoyable program, which is worth searching for, will hopefully be reissued on CD. —*Scott Yanow*

This Is My Lucky Day / Aug. 19, 1957-Dec. 26, 1957 / Bluebird ✦✦✦

This Bluebird CD reissue brings back seven of the nine selections that trumpeter Ruby Braff recorded with an impressive octet that also included trombonist Benny Morton, clarinetist Pee Wee Russell, tenor saxophonist Dick Hafer and a rhythm section led by pianist Nat Pierce. The material, superior swing standards highlighted by "It's Been So Long," "I'm Comin' Virginia" and "Did I Remember," features several tributes to the great Bunny Berigan, putting the emphasis on Braff's passionate horn although Russell gets in some of his unique licks. The remainder of this CD reissues half of an earlier LP, the complete session of Aug. 19, 1957. Braff is matched with fellow trumpeter Roy Eldridge for an interesting but slightly inhibited affair; there are few of the expected fireworks between these normally fiery players. Despite the excess of mutual respect, there are quite a few strong moments, particularly on "Give My Regards to Broadway," "This Is My Lucky Day" and "The Song Is Ended." —*Scott Yanow*

Easy Now / Aug. 11, 1958+Aug. 19, 1958 / RCA ✦✦✦

This LP has two separate sessions featuring trumpeter Ruby Braff. Braff's encounter with fellow trumpeter Roy Eldridge in a sextet has been reissued on CD but is actually a slight disappointment with surprisingly few fireworks between the potentially combative players. The other session (which has not been reissued) is better, an all-star octet with Braff, trumpeter Emmett Berry, trombonist Vic Dickenson, clarinetist Bob Wilber (doubling on tenor) and a four-piece rhythm section. Throughout Braff is quite passionate in his playing; highlights include "When My Sugar Walks Down the Street," "Give My Regards to Broadway" and "Little Man, You've Had a Busy Day." —*Scott Yanow*

Ruby Braff with Buddy Tate & the Newport All Stars / Oct. 28, 1967 / Black Lion ✦✦✦✦✦

Cornetist Ruby Braff and tenor saxophonist Buddy Tate make for a very complementary team on this fine CD reissue which also includes pianist George Wein, bassist Jack Lesberg and drummer Don Lamond. Several alternate takes and a previously unreleased "Lullaby of the Leaves" expand this fine session which has among its highlights enjoyable versions of "Mean to Me," "My Monday Date," "Take the 'A' Train" and "The Sheik of Araby" among others. This is high-quality small-group swing by some of the best which was recorded at a time when the idiom was considered very much out-of-style by the modernists. —*Scott Yanow*

Hear Me Talkin' / Nov. 8, 1967 / Black Lion ✦✦✦✦✦

This is a fun Dixieland/swing date featuring cornetist Ruby Braff with an octet led by the fine English trumpeter Alex Welsh. In addition to the two leads, trombonist Roy Williams, tenor saxophonist Al Gay and baritonist Johnny Barnes get some solo space on the mixture of standards, 1920s obscurities (including Don Redman's "No One Else but You") and basic originals. Everyone sounds in a good mood and is heard swinging in prime form throughout this recommended CD reissue. —*Scott Yanow*

On Sunnie's Side of the Street / Feb. 27, 1968-Feb. 29, 1968 / Blue Angel Jazz Club ✦✦✦✦

Cornetist Ruby Braff teams up with the great stride pianist Ralph Sutton, bassist Milt Hinton and drummer Mousey Alexander for these informal live sessions recorded in 1968. The quartet plays predictably excellent and swinging versions of seven familiar standards with the high points including "Someday Sweetheart," "I Found a New Baby," "I'm Crazy 'Bout My Baby" and "St. Louis Blues." This collector's LP, recorded at a time when this style of music was being neglected, will be difficult to find but is worth the search. —*Scott Yanow*

Plays Louis Armstrong / Oct. 20, 1969 / BYG ✦✦✦✦

This obscure LP will be difficult to find but should be placed high on most Ruby Braff fans' want list. Accompanied by pianist George Wein, guitarist Barney Kessel, bassist Larry Ridley and drummer Don Lamond, Braff investigates eight songs that Louis Armstrong played, generally avoiding the obvious ones in favor of tunes such as "Cornet Chop Suey," "It's Wonderful" and "I'm Thankful." As usual Braff pours plenty of passion and sincere feeling into each note and, even though he never really sounds like Armstrong (he always had a distinctive sound of his

own), Braff recaptures Satch's spirit. Other highlights include "I've Got a Feeling I'm Falling," "Swing That Music" and "Someday You'll Be Sorry." —*Scott Yanow*

The Grand Reunion / Oct. 14, 1972 / Chiaroscuro ✦✦✦✦

In 1955 cornetist Ruby Braff and pianist Ellis Larkins recorded a well-received set of duets. In 1972 they had a reunion which has not yet been reissued on CD. Since Larkins is a superior ballad player and accompanist, the emphasis on this date is on slower numbers although Braff does provide some fiery moments. The ten duets include "Fine and Dandy," "Skylark," "If Dreams Come True," "Liza" and "Love Walked In." Twenty years later Braff and Larkins would get together again with equally successful results. —*Scott Yanow*

The Ruby Braff-George Barnes Quartet / Apr. 22, 1974 / Chiaroscuro ✦✦✦✦✦

Ruby Braff & the George Barnes Quartet Play Gershwin / Jul. 26, 1974 / Concord Jazz ✦✦✦✦

The Ruby Braff-George Barnes Quartet (comprising cornetist Braff, Barnes and Wayne Wright on guitars and bassist Michael Moore) recorded five albums within a two-year period and all are well worth getting. For this live set from the 1974 Concord Jazz Festival, the group explores 11 Gershwin songs with consistent success. The melodic swing group (a perfect setting for Braff) is heard at its best on "S'Wonderful," "I Got Rhythm," "But Not for Me," "Love Walked In" and "They Can't Take That Away from Me." —*Scott Yanow*

Plays Rodgers & Hart / Oct. 1974 / Concord Jazz ✦✦✦✦

For the fourth of five recordings made by the classic Ruby Braff-George Barnes Quartet, ten songs by Rodgers and Hart are given melodic, swinging, creative treatment. Cornetist Braff and guitarist Barnes fed off of each other and worked very well together, while rhythm guitarist Wayne Wright and bassist Michael Moore always gave them impeccable support. Highlights of this enjoyable set include "Isn't It Romantic," "Blue Room," "You Took Advantage of Me" and "The Lady Is a Tramp." —*Scott Yanow*

To Fred Astaire with Love / 1975 / RCA ✦✦✦✦

The final recorded collaboration between cornetist Ruby Braff and guitarist George Barnes (in a quartet with rhythm guitarist Wayne Wright and bassist Michael Moore) features concise versions of ten songs (all but one is under three minutes) introduced in the 1930s by Fred Astaire. Although this LP is not essential, the arrangements make the veteran standards (which include "Cheek to Cheek," "They Can't Take That Away from Me," "A Shine on Your Shoes" and "They All Laughed") sound fresh and lively. Astaire himself approved of the project. —*Scott Yanow*

With the Ed Bickert Trio / Jun. 14, 1979 / Sackville ✦✦✦✦✦

With the breakup of his quartet with guitarist George Barnes (which had become less spontaneous and more arranged during its final period), cornetist Ruby Braff was again touring as a single and free to play as he liked. On this sparse quartet record with three fine Canadian musicians (the cool-toned guitarist Ed Bickert, bassist Don Thompson and drummer Terry Clarke), Braff stretches out on ten superior standards including Cole Porter's "True Love," "The World Is Waiting for the Sunrise," the obscure "After Awhile," "What Is There to Say" and "The Song Is Ended." A fine example of Braff's passionate style. —*Scott Yanow*

Fireworks / 1983 / Inner City ✦✦✦✦✦

Any time that cornet Ruby Braff and pianist Dick Hyman meet up, the results tend to be memorable. For this duet concert they perform a wide range of swing-oriented material including "Somebody Loves Me," the Dixieland standard "High Society," "Sugar" and even Tchaikovsky's "Swan Lake." Hyman, who takes "Liza" as a piano solo, is brilliant as usual and inspires Braff to some of his hottest playing. —*Scott Yanow*

Mr. Braff to You: The Ruby Braff Quintet / Dec. 15, 1983 / Phontastic ✦✦✦

This is a very enjoyable set. The veteran cornetist Ruby Braff is teamed with the hot, young, swing tenor player Scott Hamilton in a quintet for a set of nine songs associated with Benny Goodman. Braff and Hamilton are both in top form, playing off of each other and sounding mutually inspired. Backed by a supportive drumless rhythm section led by pianist John Bunch, the two classic horn players are subtle and often a bit restrained but bring out some fresh insights to these familiar standards. This is a fine release from the Swedish Phontastic label. —*Scott Yanow*

America the Beautiful / 1984 / George Wein Collection ✦✦✦✦✦

For this unusual set (available through Concord Jazz), cornetist Ruby Braff and Dick Hyman have one of their infrequent and always-rewarding collaborations. What is different on this date is that pianist Hyman exclusively plays pipe organ. Somehow Hyman is able to swing the lumbering instrument and the duo is heard at its best on such numbers as "When My Sugar Walks Down the Street," "As Long As I Live," "Louisiana" and even "America, the Beautiful." —*Scott Yanow*

A First / Feb. 1985 / Concord Jazz ✦✦✦✦

Although it is implied with its title that this was the first collaboration between cornetist Ruby Braff and tenor saxophonist Scott Hamilton, they had recorded a date back in December 1983 for the Swedish Phontastic label. Accompanied by Hamilton's regular quartet of the period (pianist John Bunch, guitarist Chris Flory, bassist Phil Flanigan and drummer Chuck Riggs), Braff and Hamilton inspire each other and play some explosive and consistently passionate solos. Highlights include a surprisingly hard-swinging "Rockin' Chair," "Dinah," "All My Life" and "Bugle Blues." Recommended. —*Scott Yanow*

● **A Sailboat in the Moonlight** / Feb. 1985 / Concord Jazz ✦✦✦✦✦

Taken from the same sessions as *A First*, this collaboration between veteran cornetist Ruby Braff and the relatively young tenor great Scott Hamilton lives up to its potential. With strong assistance from pianist John Bunch, guitarist Chris Flory, bassist Phil Flanigan and drummer Chuck Riggs, Braff and Hamilton are a perfect team on such joyful swing tunes as "A Sailboat in the Moonlight," "'Deed I Do," "Jeepers Creepers" and "Sweethearts on Parade." All eight selections (even the obscure "Milkman's Matinee") are well worth hearing, making this a highly recommended set. —*Scott Yanow*

Bravura Eloquence / Jun. 1988 / Concord Jazz ✦✦✦✦

From the same sessions that resulted in *Me, Myself and I*, the great cornetist Ruby Braff, who has always had a distinctive sound of his own, once again teams up with guitarist Howard Alden and bassist Jack Lesberg in a trio. Alden's versatility serves him well on a program that includes "Ol' Man River," medleys of tunes associated with Charlie Chaplin and Judy Garland, "I've Grown Accustomed to Her Face," and "Royal Garden Blues." Braff is heard at the top of his game throughout this enjoyable outing. —*Scott Yanow*

Me, Myself & I / Jun. 1988 / Concord Jazz ✦✦✦✦

Although often overlooked in popularity polls, cornetist Ruby Braff during the 1980s and '90s recorded many classics and near-classics. For this trio set with guitarist Howard Alden and bassist Jack Lesberg, Braff's repertoire ranges from the Dixieland tunes "Muskrat Ramble" and "When You're Smiling" to superior popular numbers such as "You've Changed," "When I Fall in Love" and "You're a Lucky Guy." As usual he brings an individual sound, swing, melodic creativity and passion to each of his improvisations. —*Scott Yanow*

Music from My Fair Lady / Jul. 1989 / Concord Jazz ✦✦✦✦✦

The many Lerner and Loewe songs written for the play *My Fair Lady* have long been rightfully acclaimed. Even with several decades of fine recordings, this duet set by cornetist Ruby Braff and pianist Dick Hyman is one of the finest interpretations of the famous album. Braff and Hyman come up with new ideas during melodic versions of such songs as "Wouldn't It Be Lovely," "I Could Have Danced All Night," "On the Street Where You Live" and "Get Me to the Church on Time" among others. Every Braff-Hyman collaboration is well worth getting and this set is no exception. —*Scott Yanow*

● **Music from "South Pacific"** / Jun. 12, 1990-Jun. 13, 1990 / Concord Jazz ✦✦✦✦✦

This CD is much better than it looks. Cornetist Ruby Braff and pianist Dick Hyman can always be relied upon to create exciting music but the songs from *South Pacific* (best known are "Some Enchanted Evening" and "Younger than Springtime") would not seem to have much potential. However, through witty frameworks and creativity, Braff and Hyman greatly uplift the music, particularly their two versions of "Bali Ha'i." This consistently surprising CD is well worth checking out. —*Scott Yanow*

Cornet Chop Suey / Mar. 27, 1991-Mar. 28, 1991 / Concord Jazz ✦✦✦✦

For this Concord CD, the great veteran cornetist Ruby Braff is joined by guitarist Howard Alden, bassist Frank Tate and (on five of the twelve numbers) clarinetist Ken Peplowski and drummer Ronald Zito. Braff has never recorded a dull album and his highly expressive playing is the main reason to acquire this disc although Alden is also in particularly good form. Highlights include a rapid rendition of "Cornet Chop Suey," "Do It Again," an unusual instrumental version of "It's the Same Old South," an emotional "It Had to Be You" and a medley of songs from the film *High Society*. —*Scott Yanow*

Ruby Braff & His New England Songhounds, Vol. 1 / Apr. 29, 1991 / Concord Jazz ✦✦✦✦✦

Cornetist Ruby Braff and tenor saxophonist Scott Hamilton have teamed up on several memorable occasions. On the first of two CD volumes Braff and Hamilton are joined by a fine quartet ("The New England Songhounds") which comprises guitarist Howard Alden, pianist Dave McKenna, bassist Frank Tate and drummer Alan Dawson. Alternating stomps with warm ballads, the horns sound at their best on such numbers as "I'm Crazy 'Bout My Baby," "This Can't Be Love," "My Shining Hour," "Down in Honky Tonk Town" and "More Than You Know." Highly recommended to mainstream and straightahead jazz fans. —*Scott Yanow*

Ruby Braff & His New England Songhounds, Vol. 2 / Apr. 30, 1991 / Concord Jazz ✦✦✦✦

Recorded a day after the first volume of cornetist Ruby Braff with his "New England Songhounds" (a sextet featuring tenor saxophonist Scott Hamilton, guitarist Howard Alden, pianist Dave McKenna, bassist Frank Tate and drummer Alan Dawson), this CD is almost up to the same level; Braff and Hamilton usually bring out the best in each other. High points of the melodic and swinging date include "Indian Summer," "Cabin in the Sky," a slow rendition of "Lullaby of Birdland" (which is taken as a ballad) and "Keepin' Out of Mischief Now." —*Scott Yanow*

As Time Goes By / May 16, 1991 / Candid ✦✦✦✦

Live at the Regattabar / Nov. 22, 1993 / Arbors ✦✦✦✦✦

The Ruby Braff Quartet heard on this fine session is reminiscent of the 1970s version with George Barnes. The instrumentation is the same (with guitarists Gray Sargent and Jon Wheatley and bassist Marshall Wood), but in this case, both guitarists get a chance to solo. Braff had recorded nearly all of the selections previously; however, he comes up with plenty of fresh statements on such songs as "It's Wonderful," "Louisiana," "Crazy Rhythm" and "Give My Regards to Broadway," among others. Throughout this enjoyable date, Braff often displays his ability to build up his solos to a low note. —*Scott Yanow*

Controlled Nonchalance, Vol. 1 / Nov. 26, 1993-Nov. 27, 1993 / Arbors ✦✦✦✦

Cornetist Ruby Braff has teamed up with tenor saxophonist Scott Hamilton on several occasions and the combination always proves to be exciting. This live sextet session, which also features the great swing pianist Dave McKenna and guitarist Gray Sargent, finds the classic players bringing new life to eight veteran standards including "Rosetta," "Struttin' with Some Barbecue" and "The Lady Is a Tramp." Braff in particular is full of subtle surprises and sly humor, spontaneously concluding a slower-than-usual version of "Sunday" with a quick tribute to Louis Armstrong. Dixieland and swing fans should go out of their way to get this one. —*Scott Yanow*

Calling Berlin, Vol. 1 / Jun. 28, 1994-Jul. 1, 1994 / Arbors ✦✦✦✦

Cornetist Ruby Braff and pianist Ellis Larkins recorded a classic album of duets in 1955 and had a reunion in 1972. They waited another 22 years before cutting their third set but, despite the passing of time, the magic heard on their earlier recordings is still very much present on their Arbors release. Both Braff and Larkins love melodies and rarely leave the themes behind in their improvisations. They perform 15 Irving Berlin tunes, ranging from the famous ("Alexander's Ragtime Band," "Easter Parade" and "How Deep Is the Ocean") to the more obscure ("My Walking Stick," "You're Laughing at Me" and "Steppin' Out with My Baby"). In all cases the interpretations are loving, personal and uplifting. Guitarist Bucky Pizzarelli makes the group a trio on two numbers and his mellow playing fits right in to the intimate setting. Because Braff (who has always had his own sound) has long been a jazz giant and Larkins is rightfully considered an extraordinary accompanist and perfect on melodic ballads, their most recent matchup is quite successful and delightful. —*Scott Yanow*

Calling Berlin, Vol. 2 / Jun. 28, 1994-Jul. 1, 1994 / Arbors ✦✦✦✦

Cornetist Ruby Braff and pianist Ellis Larkins have recorded quite a few lyrical duet albums since the 1950s. Their two Arbors CDs of Irving Berlin tunes, both dedicated to Ella Fitzgerald, find the pair still in top form. While the very subtle Larkins takes some melodic solos and serves as a sparse orchestra behind Braff, the cornetist displays his typically wide range of emotions, making every highly expressive note count. The repertoire mixes together familiar tunes (such as "Cheek to Cheek," "Always" and "The Song Is Ended") with some real Berlin obscurities ("Remember the Night," "Better Luck Next Time" and "How About Me"). Charming music. —*Scott Yanow*

Play Nice Tunes / Jul. 2, 1994 / Arbors ✦✦✦✦

All of cornetist Ruby Braff's duet collaborations with pianist Dick Hyman are something special. The success of this set was a bit unlikely because the great cornetist was very ill just a few months earlier. Luckily he recovered and does not show any weakness, hesitancy or diminishing abilities on his duet date. The emphasis is on slower renditions of superior standards, but there is also plenty of fire and subtle invention displayed during the thoughtful interpretations. Hyman is typically imaginative in his accompaniment and virtuosic solos, while Braff makes the most out of every note. Highlights include Fats Waller's "Sweet Savannah Sue," "Why Was I Born," "Thanks a Million" and "You're Lucky to Me." —*Scott Yanow*

Inside & Out / Feb. 27, 1996 / Concord Jazz ✦✦✦

Kellaway's next sparring partner was an old hand at stripped-down duets, cornetist Ruby Braff—he of the Ellis Larkins and Dick Hyman connection—and Braff seems to encourage Kellaway's out-there side more frequently on this all-standards CD. Terse and to the point, almost offhand in his penchant for placing odd notes in the strangest places, Braff's cornet opens holes in the texture for Kellaway to explore his freely eclectic muse. A highly unorthodox "I Got Rhythm" gives vent to a spectacular near-Tatumesque outburst from Roger, and there are streaks of Romantic, Impressionistic and contemporary classical pianism, boogie-woogie, and of course, stride. Yet Braff has his sweet moments too, as on "Memories of You," where he sets Kellaway off in his nostalgic *All in the Family* mode. The cover photo speaks volumes about the music within this package—a pensive, dour, laconic Braff and a jaunty-hatted, inviting, perhaps slightly mischievous Kellaway. —*Richard S. Ginell*

● **Ruby Braff Remembers Louis Armstrong: Being with You** / Apr. 15, 1996-Apr. 16, 1996 / Arbors ✦✦✦✦

Braff Plays Wimbledon—The First Set / Sep. 10, 1996+Sep. 23, 1996 / Zephyr ✦✦✦

Cornetist Ruby Braff sound fine on this set for the British label Zephyr. Most of the selections find him taking passionate and typically lyrical solos on swing standards in a quintet with pianist Brian Lemon, guitarist Howard Alden, bassist Dave Green and drummer Allan Ganley. A few numbers add Warren Vache on fluegelhorn and trombonist Roy Williams, but perhaps due to too much mutual respect, few fireworks fly. One would hope that Braff and Vache would match wits against each other, but this is largely Braff's show. Still, the music overall (which is highlighted by "Someday Sweetheart," "I've Got a Feeling I'm Falling" and "China Boy") should please trad jazz and mainstream collectors. —*Scott Yanow*

George Braith

b. Jun. 27, 1939, New York, NY
Soprano Saxophone, Tenor Saxophone, Stritch / Soul Jazz, Post-Bop
George Braith, like Roland Kirk before him, is best known for playing multiple reed instruments, simultaneously. His Braithophone consists of two soprano saxes, welded together. However, Braith's music is more understated and conventional than is Kirk's more avant-garde style.

George Braith (Braithwaite) was born on June 27, 1939, in New York City, the youngest of nine children. His parents (originally from the West Indies) and siblings were all musical and Braith was encouraged to play music from an early age. He learned piano from his father and played music with his mother (who sang) in church. Braith became interested in reed instruments and by the age of 11 was playing in a calypso band, appearing on a TV show and in theaters in the neighborhood area.

He learned the clarinet and sax (baritone and alto) in junior high, where he earned extra money playing in small bands. At 15, he led a quintet for a summer job in the Catskills. In 1956, he was first discovered by jazz writer Nat Hentoff. Subsequently he studied music theory, flute, and bassoon in high school. His main early influences were Charlie Parker, Art Tatum, Ernie Henry, and Gerry Mulligan, but also Miles Davis, Sonny Rollins, John Coltrane, and Gil Evans.

In 1957, after graduating from high school, Braith toured Europe that summer with his group, the American Jazz Quintet. During that trip, he met and heard Lucky Thompson and was so impressed that he took up the tenor sax. He enrolled in the Manhattan School of Music that fall and remained there for something less than two years. His night gigs finally led to Braith dropping out of school and traveling up and down the East Coast and to Bermuda.

Braith, who was aware of the work of Roland Kirk, began playing multiple horns himself sometime in 1961. He started with a custom alto stritch, playing it simultaneously with a special soprano saxophone. The horns were configured so that he could play all the notes on each horn with a single hand. In time, Braith settled on a special pair of horns (two soprano saxes, welded together), which he called the "Braithophone." He would play the two instruments in rhythmic unison, but using different kinds of intervals between the horns, very conscious of space.

George Braith went on to do several albums on Blue Note and Prestige, and was a sideman on others, including Big John Patton's *Blue John*. Although some of his material is available in Japan, his major work has yet to be released on CD in the US. His song "Braith-a-Way" on the album *Two Souls in One* was quite popular.

George Braith is still in the New York area, where he still does gigs and has been quite successful working as a street musician, using drummer Mark Johnson. —*Michael Erlewine*

Two Souls in One / Sep. 4, 1963 / Blue Note ✦✦✦

In some ways, it's hard to view George Braith's playing a soprano and alto saxophone simultaneously as anything other than a gimmick, especially since it's nearly presented that way on his debut album, *Two Souls in One*. Braith plays the two horns on the folk calypso "Mary Ann" and the nursery rhyme "Mary Had a Little Lamb," limiting himself to the melody and bridges, probably because it's hard to finger anything else but simple lines when you're playing two instruments at once. Furthermore, the tone of the double sax is jarring—thin, reedy and layered with harmonic overtones, it sounds inhuman and utterly bizarre. Rahsaan Roland

Kirk, who pioneered double reeds, explored the harmonic possibilites inherent with the dueling instruments, but Braith saves his explorations for solo alto excursions. He's quite good at these alto solos, as the elegant "Poinciana" and the hot solos of "Mary Had a Little Lamb" prove, but he sounds restrained, not freed, by the double horn. Nevertheless, *Two Souls in One* remains an enjoyable, occasionally rewarding, collection of soul-jazz and cautiously adventurous hard bop. Guitarist Grant Green and organist Billy Gardner both shine during their time in the spotlight, particularly in the infectious rhythms of "Mary Ann." And Braith himself does leave a large impression, especially in the 14-minute tour de force "Braith-Away," which reveals the full strength of his talent instead of simply hinting at it. —*Stephen Thomas Erlewine*

Soul Stream / Dec. 16, 1963 / Blue Note ✦✦✦✦

Picking up where "Braith-Away," the final and most successful song on *Two Souls in One*, left off, *Soul Stream* finds George Braith coming into his own. Where his debut felt hampered by uneven material and unsure execution of Braith's trademark double-sax attack, *Soul Stream* is confident and assured. *Soul Stream* concentrates on mildly adventurous hard bop with soul-jazz overtones, which usually come from organist Billy Gardner and guitarist Grant Green. Braith doesn't rely on the double horn nearly as much as before, using it for harmonic coloring and musical texture. Only on "Billy Told," a languid reworking of "The William Tell Overture," does the technique fall flat—on the other songs, the double sax sounds bizarre, but it accentuates the way Braith wants to push boundaries. Unfortunately, Braith never truly cuts loose, but there's enough provocative material and cerebral grooves on *Soul Stream* to make it a worthwhile listen. —*Stephen Thomas Erlewine*

● **Extension** / Mar. 24, 1965-Mar. 27, 1965 / Blue Note ✦✦✦✦✦

Pushing to the side the double sax that became his trademark, George Braith turned in his strongest record with *Extension*. Largely freed from the restraints of the dueling horns, Braith is able to explore the outer reaches of his music. He still remains grounded in soul-jazz—any guitar-organ combo is bound to have soul-jazz roots—but he pushes the music toward adventurous hard bop, often with rewarding results. His compositions are fully realized, with interesting melodic statements and plenty of opportunities for him and mainstays Grant Green on guitar and Billy Gardner on organ to stretch out. And when Braith does reach back for the double-sax technique, such as on the title track, it works because its otherwordly tone is better suited to this searching, adventurous music, than on the more basic fare that dominated *Two Souls in One*. The double horns do make Cole Porter's "Ev'ry Time We Say Goodbye" sound a little awkward, but even that song is redeemed by excellent solos. Nevertheless, it's the originals, and the way the quartet of Braith, Green, Gardner and drummer Clarence Johnston executes them, that make *Extension* the definitive Braith album. —*Stephen Thomas Erlewine*

Laughing Soul / Mar. 1, 1966 / Prestige ✦✦✦

Musart / Nov. 21, 1966-Jan. 3, 1967 / Prestige ✦✦

Wellman Braud

b. Jan. 25, 1891, St. James Parish, LA, d. Oct. 27, 1966, Los Angeles, CA
Bass / Swing
One of the top string bassists of the 1920s, Wellman Braud was the first of the great Duke Ellington bass players, a tradition that would later include Jimmy Blanton, Oscar Pettiford and even Charles Mingus. Braud grew up playing music in New Orleans occasionally switching to guitar or drums. By the time he moved to Chicago in 1917, Braud was strictly a bassist. He was with Charlie Elgar (1920-22) and toured Europe with Will Vodery's Plantation Revue before freelancing to New York. Braud became a key member of Duke Ellington's Orchestra (1927-35) and his well-recorded bass (his only close competitor on his instrument during the period was Pops Foster) really drove the band during their many records. After leaving Ellington, Braud played with the Spirits of Rhythm (1935-37) before forming his own trio. He recorded with Jelly Roll Morton (1939-40) and Sidney Bechet (1940-41) but opened a poolroom in New York in 1940 and thereafter became a part-time player. Among his later musical experiences were reunions with Duke Ellington (1944 and 1961) and stints with Bunk Johnson (1947) and Kid Ory's Creole Jazz Band (1956). —*Scott Yanow*

Anthony Braxton

b. Jun. 4, 1945, Chicago, IL
Alto Saxophone, Clarinet, Reeds, Piano, Flute / Avant-Garde, Free Jazz
Of all the current leaders of the avant-garde, Anthony Braxton's music has possibly the least chance of ever being accepted by the bebop establishment. His complex lines, staccato attack and enormous quantity of compositions have a logic all their own. Some detractors (like Wynton Marsalis) may deny that Braxton's music

is even jazz but, because it does contain a large amount of improvisation and the feeling of the blues, it is unquestionably jazz. And for what it is worth, this writer regards him as an obvious genius although the huge quantity of his work can be rather daunting.

Braxton began studying music when he was 17 and after serving in the military he became involved in Chicago's AACM in 1966. He made his recording debut in 1968 and from the start Braxton's approach was unusual; he used diagrams as song titles and wrote difficult-to-understand liner notes. Although alto has always been his main ax (and his second recording as a leader was an unprecedented double LP of unaccompanied alto explorations), Braxton eventually mastered virtually every reed instrument from the clarinet and sopranino to the contrabass clarinet and bass sax. He went to France for a period in 1969 and the following year teamed up with Chick Corea, Dave Holland and Barry Altschul in the mostly free-form unit Circle. When Corea decided to quit the group so as to play more accessible music, Braxton kept Holland and Altschul and added trumpeter Kenny Wheeler to his quartet; in 1976 trombonist George Lewis took his place. From this point forward Braxton's chronology is difficult to follow because each of his recordings seemed to use a different combination of musicians and a large number of his projects were documented. Luckily Braxton had a good relationship with Arista in the 1970s; since that time he has recorded extensively for many European labels (including Hat Art and Black Saint) and recently the American company Music and Arts. Braxton has cut duet albums with Joseph Jarman, Muhal Richard Abrams, Evan Parker, Derek Bailey and Max Roach, utilized a big band (the Creative Music Orchestra), performed standards with a trio headed by Tete Montoliu (with very advanced improvisations from the altoist), come out with a three-LP set of wholly written-out orchestral works, paid tribute (in an abstract way) to the music of Charlie Parker, Thelonious Monk and Warne Marsh, and recorded more unaccompanied alto solos. Since 1984 Braxton has often toured with a quartet comprising the brilliant pianist Marilyn Crispell, either John Lindberg or Mark Dresser on bass and drummer Gerry Hemingway. In addition, Braxton has been a teacher at Mills College and Wesleyan University.

Anthony Braxton's accomplishments and contributions to jazz will take decades to fully assess. —*Scott Yanow*

Three Compositions of New Jazz / Mar. 27, 1968+Apr. 10, 1968 / Delmark ✦✦✦✦✦

Anthony Braxton's first record as a leader (which has been reissued on this CD) features the innovative saxophonist coming up with an alternative to the dense high-energy freedom music of the era. Utilizing space, dynamics, "little instruments" and ideas gained from associations with the AACM, Braxton teams up with violinist Leroy Jenkins, trumpeter Leo Smith and (on one selection) pianist Muhal Richard Abrams for three lengthy originals. The music frequently takes a while to get going but rewards repeated listenings and eventually builds up to some furious interplay. —*Scott Yanow*

For Alto Saxophone / Oct. 1968 / Delmark ✦✦✦✦

Anthony Braxton's second recording as a leader is a stunning and somewhat unprecedented two-LP set, eight unaccompanied alto solos. Braxton's sound and innovative style were already quite distinctive and his very advanced playing, which combines together emotional intensity with logic and a dramatic use of space, is memorable if sometimes startling. This two-fer was not as influential as some of his later recordings but it does show that Braxton was a somewhat forbidding master musician from virtually the start of his very productive career. —*Scott Yanow*

Anthony Braxton / Oct. 10, 1969 / Affinity ✦✦✦

Anthony Braxton's first recording during his three-year stay in Europe is in some ways a continuation of his initial release, utilizing a similar personnel. The music performed by altoist Anthony Braxton (who also plays soprano, clarinet, contrabass clarinet, flute, "sound machine" and chimes), trumpeter Leo Smith, violinist Leroy Jenkins and drummer Steve McCall is very freely improvised, includes "little instruments" for their variety in sound, and contrasts high-energy playing with space. This Affinity LP will be difficult to find and the music (one composition apiece from Braxton, Smith and Jenkins) is far from accessible but is generally worth the struggle. —*Scott Yanow*

The Complete Braxton / Feb. 4, 1971+Feb. 5, 1971 / Arista ✦✦✦✦

This two-LP set features the innovative multireedist in a variety of settings. Recorded while he was a member of the group Circle, Braxton is heard in two duets with pianist Chick Corea, three fairly exciting quartet tracks with trumpeter Kenny Wheeler, bassist Dave Holland and drummer Barry Altschul, an unaccompanied solo on contrabass clarinet, a piece (which Braxton wrote but does not play on) for five tubas, and a selection in which he overdubbed four sopranino saxes. Lots of very interesting performances come from a master of the avant-garde who has always followed his own musical path. —*Scott Yanow*

Saxophone Improvisations, Series F / Feb. 25, 1972 / America ✦✦✦

This set runs the gamut from furious to tortured and back. Braxton's solo albums require intense scrutiny from the listener; he seldom plays sentimental or light material, and will go into segments featuring long minutes filled with a host of squalls, squeaks, screams, and honks. It's well played, but very intense and probably only essential to Braxton fans and collectors. —*Ron Wynn*

Town Hall (1972) / May 22, 1972 / Pausa ✦✦✦

After three years in Europe, altoist Anthony Braxton returned to the US in 1972, performing a concert at Town Hall that was first released on this 1992 CD. Braxton stretches out on alto during two performances with a trio also including bassist Dave Holland and drummer Philip Wilson: a medley of a pair of Braxton's tunes and an abstract but hard-swinging version of "All the Things You Are." The second half of this rewarding and typically adventurous set finds Braxton (switching between six different reeds) in a quintet with tenor saxophonist John Stubblefield, singer Jeanne Lee, bassist Holland and percussionist Barry Altschul. The music is quite invigorating and colorful, worthy of several listens. —*Scott Yanow*

Live at Wigmor / 1974 / Inner City ✦✦✦

This rather forbidding two-LP set (originally released by Emanen) has four lengthy improvisations (plus two briefer "Rehearsal Extracts") by multireedist Anthony Braxton (who plays alto, flute, clarinet, contrabass clarinet and sopranino) and the very adventurous guitarist Derek Bailey. They worked out a compromise beforehand in which the plot of some of the "areas" of the pieces were predetermined (such as playing staccato in one segment, using repetition or long sections) but in general the music is freely improvised. An exception is a segment on which Braxton plays contrabass clarinet. This out-of-print two-fer is primarily for listeners with a very open mind who do not dismiss such free-form playing as "noise." —*Scott Yanow*

In the Tradition, Vol. 1 / May 29, 1974 / Steeple Chase ✦✦

The great avant-gardist Anthony Braxton threw the jazz world a curve with this album (and its second volume). Braxton, filling in for an ill Dexter Gordon, was joined by pianist Tete Montoliu, bassist Niels Pedersen and drummer Tootie Heath for a set of five jazz standards. After playing the melodies fairly straight, Braxton tears into Warne Marsh's "Marshmallow," "Just Friends" and "Lush Life" with very complex and abstract improvisations that are generally ignored by the rhythm section who go about playing in their usual bop-oriented style. An exception is a duet with bassist Pedersen on a very spooky "Goodbye Pork Pie Hat," one of two songs on which Braxton plays contrabass clarinet. His solo on "Ornithology" on that instrument is a bit silly, for the contrabass clarinet is so low that one has difficulty telling some of its notes apart from each other. A historical curiosity, this set is not as essential as Braxton's explorations of his own music. —*Scott Yanow*

In the Tradition, Vol. 2 / May 29, 1974 / Steeple Chase ✦✦

The second of two Anthony Braxton albums that team the avant-garde altoist with a conventional rhythm section (pianist Tete Montoliu, bassist Niels Pedersen and drummer Albert "Tootie" Heath) features Braxton exploring five standards ("What's New," "Body and Soul," "Donna Lee," "My Funny Valentine" and "Half Nelson"). Braxton pays tribute to each song's melody before making his abstract improvisations; the rhythm section mostly ignores what he plays. A short "Duet" (which teams the leader with Pedersen) is a change of pace and much freer. These two records are historical curiosities but feature much less interaction between the trio and Anthony Braxton than one would hope. —*Scott Yanow*

Trio and Duet / Sep. 15, 1974 / Sackville ✦✦✦✦

This is a well-rounded album that features the remarkable Anthony Braxton in two separate settings. Braxton (on clarinet, contrabass clarinet and percussion) interacts with trumpeter Leo Smith and Richard Teitelbaum's synthesizer on an abstract original for 19 minutes. The remainder of the program has Braxton (on alto) performing three standards ("The Song Is You," "Embraceable You" and "You Go to My Head") in duets with bassist Dave Holland; those successful interactions are superior to Braxton's earlier "In the Tradition" projects. Recommended. —*Scott Yanow*

New York (Fall 1974) / Sep. 27, 1974 / Arista ✦✦✦✦

Anthony Braxton, who switches here between alto, flute, clarinet, sopranino and contrabass clarinet, is heard interpreting six of his originals in a wide variety of settings. Most accessible are his three performances with a quartet also including trumpeter Kenny Wheeler, bassist Dave Holland and drummer Jerome Cooper. Braxton also adds violinist Leroy Jenkins to the group on one piece and has a duet with Richard Teitelbaum's moog synthesizer. However, the most historic performance is by an unaccompanied saxophone quartet consisting of Braxton, Julius Hemphill, Oliver Lake and Hamiet Bluiett; this band (with David Murray in Braxton's place) would soon emerge as the World Saxophone Quartet. The wide amount of variety on this set makes this album a perfect introduction to Anthony Braxton's potentially forbidding but logical music. —*Scott Yanow*

Five Pieces (1975) / Jul. 1, 1975-Jul. 2, 1975 / Arista ✦✦✦
This out-of-print album features one of Anthony Braxton's great combos, a quartet with trumpeter Kenny Wheeler, bassist Dave Holland and drummer Barry Alstchul. Braxton (who switches between alto, clarinet, sopranino, flutes and contrabass clarinet) explores four of his diverse originals plus the standard "You Stepped Out of a Dream." The tightness of his very alert and versatile group and the strength of the compositions make this one of Anthony Braxton's most rewarding records of the mid-1970s. —*Scott Yanow*

★ **Anthony Braxton Live** / Jul. 20, 1975+Nov. 4, 1976 / Bluebird ✦✦✦✦✦
With the exception of a 23-minute classical piece that was left out, this single CD has all of the music from Anthony Braxton's two-LP set *The Montreux/Berlin Concerts*. There are three Braxton originals apiece taken from two concerts and featuring either trumpeter Kenny Wheeler or trombonist George Lewis, bassist Dave Holland and drummer Barry Atschul; the leader switches between alto, soprano, contrabass sax, flute and clarinet. The six compositions (all of which have diagrams for titles) are among Braxton's strongest and the improvisations (particularly the interplay between Braxton and Lewis) is continually fascinating. Those listeners who claim that Anthony Braxton does not have a strong sense of humor and is incapable of swinging are particularly recommended to acquire this colorful disc. A gem. —*Scott Yanow*

Creative Orchestra Music (1976) / Feb. 1976 / Arista ✦✦✦✦
This is one of Braxton's most interesting recordings. Six of his compositions are performed by groups ranging from 15-20 pieces and featuring such soloists as trumpeters Cecil Bridgewater, Leo Smith, Kenny Wheeler and Jon Faddis, baritonist Bruce Johnstone, trombonist George Lewis, reed player Roscoe Mitchell, bassist Dave Holland, pianist Muhal Richard Abrams and Braxton himself. There is a lot of variety on this set. One of the pieces finds Braxton combining free elements with a Sousa-type march while another one looks towards Ellington. There are quite a few memorable moments on this program. —*Scott Yanow*

Elements of Surprise: Braxton/Lewis Duo / Jun. 7, 1976 / Moers ✦✦✦

Duets (1976) / Aug. 1, 1976-Aug. 2, 1976 / Arista ✦✦

Donaueschingen (Duo) 1976 / Oct. 23, 1976 / Hat Art ✦✦✦✦✦
A live set featuring duets by trombonist George Lewis and the reeds of Anthony Braxton might seem as if it would be a bit tedious but the instant communication between the two keep the music continually fascinating. Braxton (who is heard on alto, sopranino, clarinet, contrabass clarinet, flutes and contrabass saxophone) and Lewis engage in some colorful sound explorations on their compositions on a continuous basis for 41 minutes, showing off not only their technique but their very sharp imagination. As an encore they surprised everyone by playing an effective 3-minute version of Charlie Parker's "Donna Lee." Listeners with open ears will enjoy this colorful set. —*Scott Yanow*

★ **Dortmund (Quartet-1976)** / Oct. 31, 1976 / Hat Art ✦✦✦✦✦
This is the perfect Anthony Braxton recording for listeners to start with. The innovative multireedist (heard here on alto, clarinet, soprano, flute and the remarkable contrabass sax) led a particularly strong group during part of 1976, a quartet with trombonist George Lewis, bassist Dave Holland and drummer Barry Altschul. This CD releases for the first time the often-stunning music they performed at their final concert. Braxton's complex but exciting compositions are among his most accessible (one of them is based on a circus march and another is a hard-swinging original dedicated to Lou Donaldson), both Braxton and Lewis take consistently emotional solos, Holland really drives the group, Altschul contributes his colorful percussion and the ensembles are very spirited. Give this recording to a bebopper who claims that what Anthony Braxton plays is not jazz. —*Scott Yanow*

Creative Orchestra (Koln) 1978 / May 12, 1978 / Hat Art ✦✦✦✦✦
Although Anthony Braxton does not play on this double CD (whose contents were released for the first time in 1995), his presence is certainly felt. He conducts the band through a fairly free improvisation and five of his compositions. Braxton showed a great deal of insight in originally picking the personnel, for nearly every one of the 21 musicians has had an important career in advanced jazz, particularly Marty Ehrlich, Vinny Golia, Michael Mossman, Leo Smith, Kenny Wheeler, Ray Anderson, George Lewis, Marilyn Crispell and John Lindberg. The music is often dense and atonal but never dull and the closing composition is a superb piece that displays Braxton's love of marching band music! Although one wishes that Anthony Braxton himself had played, there is a set easily recommended to his fans. —*Scott Yanow*

Alto Saxophone Improvisations (1979) / Nov. 28, 1978-Jun. 21, 1979 / Arista ✦✦✦
This double LP features Anthony Braxton playing his strongest horn (alto sax) unaccompanied on ten of his diverse originals plus a trio of standards ("Red Top," "Along Came Betty" and "Giant Steps"). The thoughtful yet emotional improvisations contain enough variety to hold one's interest throughout despite the sparse

setting; this two-fer (as with many of Braxton's Arista recordings) is long overdue to be reissued on CD. —*Scott Yanow*

Performance (9-1-1979) / Sep. 1, 1979 / Hat Hut ✦✦✦
This two-LP set has a continuous 71-minute performance by Anthony Braxton's 1979 quartet, a unit that features the leader on alto, clarinets and contrabass clarinet along with the masterful (and sometimes hilarious) trombonist Ray Anderson, bassist John Lindberg and percussionist Thurman Barker. The group interprets seven of Braxton's compositions (which he outlines in extensive and generally readable liner notes) including a closing and somewhat humorous march. Since the Braxton-Anderson musical partnership did not last all that long and resulted in some real fireworks, this two-fer is one that Braxton's fans will want to search for. —*Scott Yanow*

Six Compositions: Quartet / Oct. 21, 1981-Oct. 22, 1981 / Antilles ✦✦✦
Anthony Braxton (who on this album switches between alto, tenor, clarinets and contrabass clarinet) heads an all-star avant-garde quartet for a set also including pianist Anthony Davis, bassist Mark Helias and veteran drummer Ed Blackwell. There is plenty of diversity in Braxton's six originals and it is quite interesting to hear him perform with this unique one-time group. —*Scott Yanow*

Open Aspects (1982) / Mar. 18, 1982 / Hat Art ✦✦✦
Anthony Braxton's (alto sax, sopranino) work as a free improviser can be quite stimulating. Here, he returned for a second vinyl dialogue (the first being *Time Zones*) with Richard Teitelbaum (synthesizer, microcomputer). It provided less intense stimulation and more comfortable friendly dialogue than their earlier record. Using the free context, they utilized a number of strategies from ballad to sparse to melodic variations to dense passages bordering on blowouts. The most precious was "No. 2," which centered around a major pentatonic scale figure (a nod to "the tradition?"). The only interesting aspect of this cut also used elsewhere was Teitelbaum's seeming recording of Braxton as the reed man played, and then the re-feeding of the material into the ongoing improvisation, having the effect of a "mirage" Braxton playing in the background. Highlights for this listener included the opener (the only cut featuring the sopranino) which shifted dynamics and textures a number of times and had some strong, rough lines and slurred bending tones from the reed man hitting an early stride; "No. 4," a rousing flurried piece complete with machine gun-like rhythm box textures; and the haunting textures accompanying the balladlike "No. 5." A word also about Teitelbaum's multilayered sound production: he not only produced obvious textures, but also sounds, lines, and clusters appearing in various distances from the immediate sound, which made for a continuously engaging listening experience. —*Milo Fine, Cadence*

Four Compositions (Quartet-1984) / Oct. 10, 1984-Oct. 11, 1984 / Black Saint ✦✦✦
Anthony Braxton (who on this set plays alto, soprano, C-melody sax, clarinet and flute) met up with his longtime pianist Marilyn Crispell for the first time on this Black Saint release. With bassist John Lindberg and drummer Gerry Hemingway forming what would be (with Mark Dresser in Lindberg's place) a regular group for nearly a decade, his quartet was off to a strong start. Braxton seems quite comfortable playing this complex music, and his diagrams (which serve as song titles) are actually fairly humorous. But why is this album called *Four Compositions* when it actually contains six? —*Scott Yanow*

Seven Standards (1985), Vol. 1 / Jan. 30, 1985-Jan. 31, 1985 / Magenta ✦✦✦
On the first of two LPs released by Windham Hill's mid-'80s jazz subsidiary Magenta, the great avant-garde altoist Anthony Braxton teams up with a modern bop trio (consisting of pianist Hank Jones, bassist Rufus Reid and drummer Victor Lewis) to explore seven jazz standards. Included along with a few familiar pieces are such obscurities as Clifford Jordan's "Toy" and Warne Marsh's "Background Music." Braxton generally plays the melodies fairly straight before taking off into abstract improvisations; unfortunately his sidemen seem to mostly operate independently of the altoist. —*Scott Yanow*

Seven Standards 1985, Vol. 2 / Jan. 30, 1985-Jan. 31, 1985 / Magenta ✦✦✦
The second of two LPs featuring the advanced altoist Anthony Braxton interpreting jazz standards once again matches him with pianist Hank Jones, bassist Rufus Reid and drummer Victor Lewis. Braxton's flights on such tunes as "Moment's Notice," "Groovin' High" and Thelonious Monk's "Trinkle, Tinkle" are far beyond the bop-oriented accompaniment of his sidemen but this spirited outing does have its memorable moments. —*Scott Yanow*

London (Quartet-1985) / Nov. 13, 1985 / Leo ✦✦✦

Five Compositions (1986) / Jul. 2, 1986-Jul. 3, 1986 / Black Saint ✦✦✦
Anthony Braxton's 1986 quartet, although fairly strong, is not quite on the level of the longtime group he would have with pianist Marilyn Crispell. Pianist David Rosenboom, bassist Mark Dresser and drummer Gerry Hemingway do an expert job of interpreting Braxton's five difficult compositions (all of which are identified by numbers and humorous pictures). The leader (switching between alto, tenor,

sopranino, C-melody sax, clarinet and flute) is in top form, as usual, and is the dominant voice throughout this complex music. —*Scott Yanow*

Six Monk's Compositions (1987) / Jun. 30, 1987+Jul. 1, 1987 / Black Saint ✦✦✦
Altoist Anthony Braxton and drummer Bill Osborne are joined on this quartet outing by two musicians with a strong affinity for the music of Thelonious Monk: pianist Mal Waldron and bassist Buell Neidlinger. Together they perform hard-driving renditions of four of Monk's more difficult compositions ("Brilliant Corners," "Played Twice," "Four in One" and "Skippy") plus two of Thelonious' more enduring ballads: "Reflections" and the wistful "Ask Me Now." Braxton's improvisations are sometimes quite fiery and abstract but he clearly studied this music and keeps the melodies of Monk's tunes in mind. Worth checking out. —*Scott Yanow*

19 (Solo) Compositions (1988) / Apr. 1988 / New Albion ✦✦✦✦
These live concerts feature Anthony Braxton on 19 selections (16 originals plus "You Go to My Head," "'Round Midnight" and "Half Nelson"), each of which explore a different idea or mood. Some of the one or two-word descriptions are "ballade," "relationship," "triplet diatonic," "multiphonic," and "quarter." Although free in spots, Braxton's performances also have their own logic and are quite concise with the longest piece ("Half Nelson") clocking in at just 5:06. —*Scott Yanow*

2 Compositions (Jarvenpaa) 1988, Ensemble Braxtonia / Nov. 7, 1988 / Leo ✦✦✦✦
How will Anthony Braxton be regarded 50 years from now, after the polemicists of today are dead and/or no longer interested, when something like an objective and knowledgeable evaluation of his work becomes possible? For all his undeniable brilliance as a composer, Braxton's seeming indifference toward the craft of composition will undermine his reputation to a significant degree. Which might not be fair, actually. Perhaps Braxton's problem is that he suffers from a condition virtually unprecedented in the history of Western art music—he writes music for a type of musician that does not exist. Braxton writes the most technically demanding music of any composer working in a jazz-related idiom. His written lines are often incredibly difficult to play; their serial-like contours do not fall naturally under the fingers. His rhythms are irregular in the extreme and presumably very elaborately notated. Braxton's music calls for players who can read and interpret the written note in a manner of the very finest classical players, yet who can also improvise in a free jazz vernacular on a very high level. Such players are very rare, to say the least; improvisers rarely read especially well, and good readers rarely improvise, so Braxton is inevitably required to strike a balance. For obvious reasons, he almost always leans toward the improvisers when forming his large groups. Occasionally, he catches lightning in a bottle, and manages to harness a team of good free improvisers who can also read down his difficult written passages. This album is a fairly good example of that. Recorded with a septet of Finnish musicians that manifests a pronounced affinity for his music, Braxton's *Compositions No. 144* and *145* are given a vigorous, warm, and reasonably tight rendering, of a sort made difficult by the usual lack of rehearsal time and scarcity of appropriate collaborators. The soloists, including and especially the leader, are uniformly excellent, but most importantly, the written parts are realized in a way that does justice to the concept. That said, Braxton's command over large forms is uncertain. One might not always be convinced of the necessity for so many extended group improvisations, for example. Yet this is a work of striking and substantive originality that should not be underestimated. —*Chris Kelsey*

Eugene (1989) / Jan. 31, 1989 / Black Saint ✦✦✦
The innovative alto saxophonist and composer Anthony Braxton leads the Northwest Creative Orchestra (a 16-piece big band) through eight of his compositions on this CD. Few of the sidemen have yet gained more than a local reputation (trumpeter Rob Blakeslee is the biggest "name"), but they perform the complex music quite well, although it would have been nice if the liner notes had identified the soloists and listed what reeds the saxophonists play. A stimulating set of avant-garde music. —*Scott Yanow*

Seven Compositions (Trio) 1989 / Mar. 21, 1989 / Hat Art ✦✦✦✦
The great avant-garde reed player Anthony Braxton (who on this set switches between alto, C-melody sax, clarinet, flute, soprano and sopranino), bassist Adelhard Roidinger and drummer Tony Oxley play five of Braxton's complex originals, Oxley's "The Angular Apron" and the standard "All the Things You Are." As usual Braxton's improvising is quite advanced and original but is colorful and fiery enough to always hold on to open-eared listeners' attention. This is one of literally dozens of stimulating Anthony Braxton sessions currently available. —*Scott Yanow*

Vancouver Duets (1989) / Jun. 30, 1989 / Music & Arts ✦✦✦
For this duet set with pianist Marilyn Crispell from the 1989 Vancouver Jazz Festival, Anthony Braxton (who plays alto and flute) performs six of his complex originals. The music is a mixture of composition and improvisation (it is often difficult to know which is which). Although it will not win any new converts who are put

off by the complexity of Braxton's music, repeated listenings to these dynamic performances will result in listeners gaining better understanding and appreciating these masterful musicians. —*Scott Yanow*

Tristano Compositions (1989) / Dec. 10, 1989-Dec. 11, 1989 / Hat Art ✦✦✦✦✦
This is a particularly interesting and somewhat accessible Anthony Braxton set. The avant-garde reed master (who sticks here to alto, sopranino and flute) performs eight Lennie Tristano compositions (including two versions of "Victory Ball") plus a pair of standards and Warne Marsh's "Sax of a Kind." With baritonist John Raskin, pianist Dred Scott, bassist Cecil McBee and drummer Andrew Cyrille swinging in an advanced way, Braxton pays close attention to performing the complex melody lines correctly before going off on his free flights. This music might cause some beboppers to reassess their opinion of Anthony Braxton. —*Scott Yanow*

Willisau (Quartet) / 1991 / Hat Art ✦✦✦✦✦
This four-CD set features Anthony Braxton's longtime quartet (with pianist Marilyn Crispell, bassist Marc Dresser and drummer Gerry Hemingway) performing the leader's complex compositions both live and in the studio (two CDs apiece). On this occasion Braxton switches between alto (his main ax), clarinet, contrabass clarinet, flute and sopranino. Since Braxton sometimes had his players perform two or three of his compositions simultaneously and the music was difficult to begin with, it may take a few listens to appreciate the performances but the results are of a consistently high caliber. This release will not convert any detractors but should be of great interest to Braxton's followers for he plays at the top of his form. —*Scott Yanow*

Eight Compositions / Feb. 21, 1991-Feb. 23, 1991 / Music & Arts ✦✦✦✦
To followers of Anthony Braxton, every recording that the multireedist makes (and there are now scores) has its value. To his detractors, the opposite is true, but those listeners with open minds and the ability to appreciate jazz that is far beyond bop will come closer to adopting the former view. His live duet set with bassist Peter Naklas Wilson (which features Braxton on two songs apiece playing contrabass clarinet, soprano, flute, and alto) is quite adventurous but each piece seems to have its point, demonstrating a specific idea or concept. Wilson is never a mere accompanist to Braxton but an equal partner in creating this innovative music. —*Scott Yanow*

9 Standards (Quartet) 1993 / Feb. 25, 1993 / Leo ✦✦✦✦✦
Anthony Braxton opens this one with a blues on alto. And does he play the blues. Not the neat, buttoned-down, arrogantly self-possessed kind of blues that epitomized jazz in the '90s, but the dirty, lowdown, heavily expressionistic blues that hearkens back to the music's beginning—a blues that communicates something more than just an attitude. It's not slick, it's not pretty, but it's eminently real. This double-disc set, recorded live at Wesleyan University with the quite capable straightahead pianist Fred Simmons' trio, is full of such moments. Braxton shows one and all that he's a jazz musician, first and last—if there's any doubt, listen to his incredible work on "Cherokee." Taken at an extremely burning tempo, Braxton tears the heart out of the tune and serves it up on a platter to his doubters. Amazingly, he's managed to find a fresh approach to the old warhorse, one that doesn't ignore its basics. He makes the changes, he plays time, but not as anyone else ever has. There's not a derivative bone in the body of his improvisation, a solo characterized by great linear invention, and some of the most unusual articulations ever played by a saxophonist—a tour de force that has to be heard to be believed. Braxton plays this entire live set as if he's got something to prove, and the result is very possibly the most inspired mainstream playing he's ever put on record. —*Chris Kelsey*

Twelve Compositions / Jul. 13, 1993-Jul. 16, 1993 / Music & Arts ✦✦✦✦
Of all of the avant-garde players of the past 30 years, Anthony Braxton has been perhaps the most diligent at documenting his work. The brilliant multireedist has been very fortunate to have a stable quartet for the past nine years with the frequently astounding pianist Marilyn Crispell, bassist Mark Dresser and drummer Gerry Hemingway doing justice to his very complex originals. This double-CD set features Braxton and his group on two continuous and complete live performances. Not only do the musicians tackle a dozen of Braxton's complicated originals, but during part of four of them individual members are assigned the task of playing a different composition than the rest of the group. Obviously this is not music to be taken lightly or merely played in the background. However listeners with the time and interest will find much to enjoy in the very lively explorations from these masterful musicians. —*Scott Yanow*

Quartet (Santa Cruz) 1993 / Jul. 19, 1993 / Hat Art ✦✦✦✦
This double CD features multireedist Anthony Braxton's longtime quartet (with the remarkable pianist Marilyn Crispell, bassist Mark Dresser and drummer Gerry Hemingway) performing a continuous program comprising 11 Braxton originals. The music covers a wide range of moods; Braxton switches between

many of his reeds, and the performance never loses one's interest. The quartet had been together eight years at the time, but a few months later, Braxton felt that they had run their course, making this valuable two-fer of both historic and musical interest. Recommended to open-eared listeners. —*Scott Yanow*

Charlie Parker Project 1993 / Oct. 21, 1993-Oct. 23, 1993 / Hat Art ◆◆◆◆
On this double CD the innovative altoist Anthony Braxton (who also plays a bit of his sopranino and the remarkable contrabass clarinet) interprets 13 bebop songs (two taken twice), 11 of which were composed by Charlie Parker. However, do not mistake these performances (which comprise both a studio session and a club set) with the type of music often played by the Young Lions. In fact, those listeners who consider themselves bop purists are advised to look elsewhere. Performing with an adventurous sextet that also includes Ari Brown on tenor and soprano, trumpeter Paul Smoker, pianist Misha Mengelberg (the most consistently impressive of the supporting cast), bassist Joe Fonda and either Han Bennink or Pheeroan AkLaff on drums, Braxton uses the melodies and some of the original structures of such tunes as "Hot House," "Night in Tunisia," "Bebop" and "Ko Ko" as the basis for colorful and often-stunning improvisations. He does not feel restricted to the old boundaries of the 1940s and '50s, preferring to pay tribute to the spirit and chance-taking of Charlie Parker rather than to merely recreate the past. The passionate and unpredictable results are quite stimulating and full of surprises, fresh ideas and wit. It's highly recommended to those jazz followers who have very open ears. —*Scott Yanow*

Duo (Wesleyan) 1994 / 1994 / Leo ◆◆◆◆◆
Another chapter in Leo Records' exhaustive documentation of Anthony Braxton's many-sided art, this two-disc set omprises improvised duos with the percussionist Abraham Adzinyah. Braxton is never better than when he allows himself the most freedom. Here, though he is reined in a bit by the regular beat of Adzinyah's Middle-Eastern drumming, the saxophonist is relatively unencumbered by formal concerns; this is the best possible framework in which to hear Braxton's improvising. He and Adzinyah concoct some very intense vamps. The percussionist is a subtle accompanist. His time isn't great, by jazz standards; the pulse wanders a bit, though in this context, it's hardly relevant. Adzinyah has a nice feel for changing timbres, within the limitations of his apparently minimal drum set-up. In contexts like this, Braxton is the most focused and intense of improvisors. It's evident, when listening to him play what is essentially "free" music, how little he really needs in the way of external organization. Braxton's greatest strength (his always intriguing and sometimes brilliant compositions notwithstanding) is as a creator of his own spontaneous structures. This set is a prime example of how transcendent an artist he can be, when left to his own devices. —*Chris Kelsey*

Knitting Factory (Piano/Quartet) 1994 Vol. 1 / 1995 / Leo ◆◆◆◆
Braxton debuted as a small-group pianist during a week-long engagement at the Knitting Factory in late 1994. This gargantuan two-disc set documents that semi-auspicious occasion. The band is made up of solid downtown-NYC professionals—Marty Ehrlich on saxes and clarinet, Joe Fonda on bass, and Pheeroan AkLaff on drums; the repertoire comprising several not-too-familiar standards by Charles Mingus, Lennie Tristano, and Thelonious Monk, among others. Braxton's pianistic style is much like his alto style. His rhythms are not even subdivisions of the beat. Braxton treats the pulse as a fence on which to hang the rhythms when he feels the urge, though he's just as likely to run alongside it, or ignore its existence altogether; he treats the harmonies with a similar bashful regard. His technique is that of an ingenious autodidact; he can definitely play, in his own way, but the way he treats the music is almost too personal. There's not much here that relates to tradition, and this vein of jazz is inextricably bound to tradition. This album is interesting in its way, but better to hear Braxton perform his own compositions in his native tongue than someone else's tunes in a borrowed language, even if he speaks that language in such a colorful and discerning dialect. —*Chris Kelsey*

Seven Standards 1995 / 1995 / Knitting Factory ◆◆◆
With the exception of alto saxophonist Thomas Chapin (who, in the tradition of his model, Rahsaan Roland Kirk, epitomizes what a post-modern mainstream jazz saxophonist should be) none of the players on this album are doing what they do best, hence the relatively low rating. As a pianist, Braxton's solo versions of standards bear repeated listening, but here—when faced with the much stricter necessities of chordal improv within a traditional small-group setting—the results are less successful. Braxton's strategy of ignoring the specific harmony and concentrating instead on a composition's overall contour is fine when he's playing alone. However, the piano being such a domineering harmonic presence, the clash between his extremely unfettered style and the demands placed upon the music by the conventional rhythm section of Mario Pavone and drummer Pheeroan AkLaff is nearly fatal. Perhaps if the rest of the band went as far out as Braxton, the music would thrive, but they do not. Trumpeter Dave Douglas is a fine outjazz composer and player; however, his concept does not translate particularly well into a more straightahead language—though his innate quirkiness does bring

about some occasionally revelatory insights. Bassist and co-leader Pavone is a solid mainstream player, as is drummer AkLaff, yet even they are heard to better advantage in more loosely structured settings. Braxton has every right to put his own inimitable spin on the classics; it's interesting and entertaining in a way, yet hardly on a level with his own, very personally idiomatic work as a composer and saxophonist. —*Chris Kelsey*

10 Compositions (Duet) 1995 / Aug. 11, 1995 / Konnex ◆◆◆◆◆
This is Anthony Braxton doing what he does best—playing and improvising on his own idiosyncratic small-group compositions, this time in duet with bassist Joe Fonda. The two also have a go at a pair of standards, which come off as well as one might expect—you either love or hate the way Braxton interprets traditional material—but they are heard to best advantage on the several originals written by each. Fonda's tunes are very much in a similar vein as Braxton's—unstable or non-existent tonalities, odd-time or out-of-time rhythms, and lots of angular melodies. Braxton's control over his instruments seems a bit less certain than usual; consequently, the air of emotional vulnerability that's always characterized his playing seems more pronounced. Fonda is a fine free bassist, nicely responsive to Braxton's twists and turns. He also manages to play the saxophonist's difficult written lines reasonably well—no small feat in itself. The pieces are intensely conversational and very focused. This album is a small, rough-cut gem from the mine of available Braxton recordings. —*Chris Kelsey*

Solo Piano (Standards) 1995 / Dec. 27, 1995 / No More ◆◆◆◆
This is Braxton's first solo piano album, finally recorded after years of woodshedding on the traditional jazz repertoire. That it doesn't sound like any other pianist as much as it sounds like Braxton the saxophonist should not surprise anyone. Braxton approaches standards on piano in much the same way he does on alto. He doesn't just go "out" on the structure; he uses the chords, but he doesn't play patterns or contrived licks over them in the way a bebop player would. Every time he approaches a piece, it's as if he's playing it for the first time, using his accumulated knowledge to decipher just that specific composition's secrets. Braxton doesn't use the tune as a whole. Rather, he dissects the component parts, using the separate elements as material for his improvisation as he makes his way through the piece. It's as if he's telling you about a trip that he's just taken, only instead of saying "I went to San Francisco," he tells you every detail of the trip just as it occurred. You don't know for certain his final destination until story's end; when it's revealed, it's a wonderful surprise made even more interesting by Braxton's discursive narrative. —*Chris Kelsey*

Joshua Breakstone

b. Jul. 22, 1955, Elizabeth, NJ
Guitar / Cool
A fine bop-based guitarist, Joshua Breakstone discovered jazz when he was 14. He studied for several years with Sal Salvador yet at the time was gigging regularly with a rock group. He attended Berklee and in 1977 toured Canada with the reed player Glen Hall, making his recording debut on Hall's Sonora release. During and after teaching guitar at the Rhode Island Conservatory of Music (1979-81), Breakstone worked in New York with Warne Marsh, Emily Remler, Dave Schnitter and Vic Juris. In 1983 he recorded his first album (*Wonderful!*) for Sonora. While that date had Barry Harris on piano, his follow-up featured Kenny Barron. Breakstone has since recorded for Contemporary (including a quartet date featuring Pepper Adams), Capri and Evidence, helping keep the legacy of quiet bop guitar alive. —*Scott Yanow*

Wonderful / May 24, 1983 / Sonora ◆◆◆
This studio date for the guitarist with the Barry Harris Trio features two Breakstone tunes and five standards from Tristano, Dameron, Gershwin, and Django. This was a good portent of things to come. —*Michael G. Nastos*

4/4 = 1 / Jun. 1984 / Mobile Fidelity ◆◆◆◆
An audiophile CD reissue of guitarist Joshua Breakstone's second recording as a leader (originally out on Sonora), this was Breakstone's first opportunity to record with pianist Kenny Barron. With bassist Earl Sauls and drummer Victor Jones completing the quartet, the guitarist is heard not only on the seven selections that formed the earlier LP, but also on six previously unreleased selections (only two of which are alternate takes). Breakstone's boppish single-note style was already recognizable, and he sounds in fine form during such numbers as "You Say You Care," "Cherokee," "I Could Write a Book" and even two versions of "When the Red, Red Robin Comes Bob, Bob, Bobbin' Along." —*Scott Yanow*

Echoes / Feb. 19, 1986 / Contemporary ◆◆◆◆
Guitarist Joshua Breakstone gained some initial recognition for this recording, his first for a medium-size label (following two sets for the tiny Sonora company). Breakstone welcomes two major players (baritonist Pepper Adams and pianist Kenny Barron) to a bop-oriented program also including bassist Dennis Irwin and

drummer Keith Copeland. The repertoire is quite interesting, for in addition to a pair of Rodgers & Hart tunes, Breakstone's quintet performs Thad Jones' "Bird Song," Bud Powell's "Oblivion" and two obscure but swinging Barry Harris songs. There are fine solos all around, particularly from Pepper Adams, who only had eight months left to live. Worth searching for. —*Scott Yanow*

Self-Portrait in Swing / Jan. 18, 1989 / Contemporary ✦✦✦✦
Throughout his series of recordings for Contemporary, Joshua Breakstone consistently showed that he was one of the top bop-based guitarists to emerge in the 1980s, playing in the tradition of Charlie Christian, Tal Farlow, Barney Kessel, Herb Ellis and Kenny Burrell. On this set he is matched with pianist Kenny Barron, bassist Dennis Irwin and drummer Kenny Washington. "Self-Portrait in Swing" (a line based on "Just One of Those Things"), "Will You Still Be Mine" and "Some Enchanted Evening" cook at very fast tempos, "Count Your Blessings" is a ballad feature for the guitarist and the last two songs ("If Ever I Would Leave You" and "Don't Take Your Love from Me") are somewhere in between. Breakstone (who tosses in the oddest song quotes at times) sounds relaxed at each of the tempos, the rhythm section is beyond criticism and the release overall is a flawless bop date. —*Scott Yanow*

9 by 3 / Oct. 30, 1990 / Contemporary ✦✦✦
Guitarist Joshua Breakstone's fourth and final recording in a string of dates for Contemporary finds him avoiding using the big names of the past and instead improvising in a pianoless trio with bassist Dennis Irwin and drummer Kenny Washington. Breakstone, whose musical path has been consistent since his early days, sticks to bop on a program including two originals, a few standards, and songs by Bud Powell and Thelonious Monk (he takes "Monk's Mood" unaccompanied). All of Joshua Breakstone's recordings thus far are worth getting by straightahead jazz fans. —*Scott Yanow*

Walk Don't Run / Aug. 1991 / Evidence ✦✦✦
Although it is not noted anywhere except in the liner notes, this 1991 session could be subtitled "tribute to the Ventures." Guitarist Joshua Breakstone covers ten tunes originally recorded by the surf guitar legends, but does not rip through them or make any concession to a more rock or pop approach. Instead, he takes them as he does any composition, playing in a gentle, relaxed pace, investigating the melody, slowly interpreting and revising via his solos. Breakstone's sound and approach are reminiscent of Jim Hall's, although his voicings are not as full, and his comping and tone are his own. Breakstone and company give Ventures fans and jazz audiences something to ponder with their explorations of these ten tunes. —*Ron Wynn*

● **Evening Star** / Jan. 14, 1992 / Contemporary ✦✦✦✦
As with his initial Contemporary date, guitarist Joshua Breakstone utilizes two well-respected veterans (trombonist Jimmy Knepper and pianist Tommy Flanagan) on a quintet set, along with two younger players (bassist Dave Shapiro and the returning drummer Keith Copeland). In addition to a pair of standards, Breakstone performs his own "Childsplay," Benny Carter's "Evening Star" and obscurities by Wes Montgomery and Barry Harris. The guitarist's single-note solos often make him seem like a horn player, so he never clashes with the pianist. It is a special treat getting to hear the under-recorded Jimmy Knepper stretching out on this CD. —*Scott Yanow*

Sittin' on the Thing with Ming / Jan. 29, 1993 / Capri ✦✦✦✦
Joshua Breakstone's guitar solos are almost entirely single-note runs (without any chording) and are quite hornlike. His outing for Capri puts the emphasis on his originals and finds Breakstone heading a top quartet comprising pianist Kenny Barron, bassist Ray Drummond and drummer Keith Copeland. The guitarist is heard in typically swinging form on these straightahead pieces, playing in a smooth-toned boppish style that has a few surprising twists and turns. —*Scott Yanow*

Remembering Grant Green / Jan. 29, 1993+Mar. 5, 1993 / Evidence ✦✦✦✦

Let's Call This Monk / Dec. 11, 1996 / Double-Time ✦✦✦✦

Lenny Breau

b. Aug. 5, 1941, Auburn, ME, **d**. Aug. 12, 1984, Los Angeles, CA
Guitar / Post-Bop
An outstanding jazz improviser who performed on both acoustic and electric guitars. Breau's right hand drew on classical, flamenco, and country (Travis/Atkins) finger-picking techniques. He was among the first guitarists to digest the impressionistic, post-bop chord voicings of pianist Bill Evans. Breau developed the ability to simultaneously comp chords and improvise single-string melodies, creating the illusion of two guitarists playing together. His facility with artificial harmonics remains the envy of many guitarists. Late in his career, Breau began using a seven-string guitar that extended the instrument's range in the upper register.

Breau's early RCA recordings are eclectic and technically dazzling. His later work is less flashy, but communicates on a deeper level.

Born to Canadian country music singers, Lenny Breau started out playing country in a sophisticated manner. Chet Atkins himself helped Breau get an RCA recording contract in 1968. However Breau's jazz-oriented style and remarkable tehnicque caused him to quickly be uncategorizable. Problems with drugs made his career erratic and he is now considered an underground guitar legend. A new label (Guitarchives) was formed in 1995 specifically to release private tapes of his performances. —*Richard Lieberson and Scott Yanow*

Guitar Sounds of Lenny Breau / Apr. 2, 1968 / RCA ✦✦✦
The debut album from the amazing guitarist Lenny Breau features several pop tunes as well as jazz-flavored melodies. Difficult to find on LP, it's well worth looking for. —*Paul Kohler*

Velvet Touch of Lenny Breau / Apr. 28, 1969 / One Way ✦✦✦
Recorded live, this album features a trio setting of bass, guitar, and drums. Musically the record spans the gamut from jazz, pop, blues, to Indian music. His ability to play chords, melody, and a bass line simultaneously has to be heard to be believed. —*Paul Kohler*

Five O'Clock Bells / Oct. 1977 / Genes ✦✦✦✦✦
1977 & 1978. Solo guitar and vocals. This includes five Breau originals, two standards, and McCoy Tyner's "Visions." Guitar students, this is your homework—find this album. —*Michael G. Nastos*

Mo' Breau / 1977 / Adelphi ✦✦✦✦✦
1977 & 1978. The companion to *5 O'Clock Bells* features solo versions of four of Breau's originals, one melded to McCoy Tyner's "Ebony Queen" and three nice standards, including "Emily." —*Michael G. Nastos*

The Livingroom Tapes, Vol. 1 / Oct. 1978 / MHS ✦✦✦✦
The privately recorded performances heard on this CD were not issued until after guitarist Lenny Breau's death. Breau is featured solo and on some duets with the fine (if obscure) clarinetist Brad Terry; the spontaneous jams give Breau a real opportunity to stretch out. The majority of the seven selections are standards and they feature Breau and the unknown Terry in top form. Highlights include "How High the Moon," "The Claw" and "My Foolish Heart." A second volume from the same dates has also been released. —*Scott Yanow*

The Livingroom Tapes, Vol. 2 / Oct. 1978 / MHS ✦✦✦✦
The follow up to *Volume 1* features both Brad Terry on clarinet and Breau on guitar. At least 80 percent of this CD is Breau playing solo guitar. —*Paul Kohler*

The Legendary Lenny Breau . . . Now!! / 1979 / Soundhole ✦✦✦
Recorded with the help of guitar master Chet Atkins, this record showcases Breau in the solo guitar spotlight. A few tunes feature him soloing against a separate rhythm guitar track that he also played. Breau's version of McCoy Tyner's "Visions" is astounding!! —*Paul Kohler*

Lenny Breau Trio / 1979 / Direct Disk ✦✦✦
Guitarist Lenny Breau, who did not gain the recognition he deserved during his relatively brief lifetime, is heard in fine form on this obscure Adelphi LP. Breau performs five numbers (two originals, songs by Bob Dylan and John Coltrane, and "You Needed Me") in a trio with a pair of talented Canadians: bassist-pianist Don Thompson and drummer Claude Ranger. Breau mixed together elements from country music and jazz to develop an original sound and style. This album gives listeners a strong example of his legendary artistry. —*Scott Yanow*

● **Live at Bourbon St.** / Jun. 14, 1983 / Guitarchives ✦✦✦✦✦
The late Lenny Breau, an underground hero, is considered such a masterful guitarist by his admirers that it somehow does not seem surprising that the Guitarchives label was started specifically to release his music. This two-CD set (which was put out in 1995) contains a previously unreleased duet concert from 1983 featuring Breau and bassist Dave Young. The music (full of close musical communication) is subtle and quiet yet consistently inventive. It is obvious after a few minutes of listening that Breau had complete control of his guitar and an original voice of his own. Although most of the repertoire is standards (with just two fairly basic originals), there is little predictable about the playing. Highlights include Breau's interpretations of "There Is No Greater Love," "All Blues," McCoy Tyner's "Vision," "Beautiful Love" and a cooking "There Will Never Be Another You" but all 17 performances have their rewarding moments. Overall this two-fer gives one a definitive portrait of the nearly forgotten legend. —*Scott Yanow*

Quietude / Jun. 14, 1983 / Electric Muse ✦✦✦
These were recordings in Toronto with bassist Dave Young. The album includes four standards, one Breau piece, and a reprise (11 minutes plus) on "Visions." Features pristine playing by two virtuosos. —*Michael G. Nastos*

Legacy / 1984 / Relaxed Rabbit ◆◆◆◆

Released shortly after Breau passed away, this album was recorded live at a small club in Toronto, Canada. Assisted by David Young (b), this album once again demonstrates Breau's musical beauty. —*Paul Kohler*

Brecker Brothers

f. 1974, New York, NY, **db.** 1980

Group / Funk, Crossover Jazz, Fusion

In the '70s, brothers Michael and Randy co-led a band of New York session big shots that included, at various times, David Sanborn, Don Grolnick, Will Lee, and George Duke, among others. When they chose, the Brecker Brothers Band could be one of the most intelligent and creative fusion outfits. Chief composer/trumpeter Randy's best tunes were structurally unpredictable, melodically intricate, and harmonically complex—inside/out bop heads played in an impossibly precise manner over a bed of funk rhythms. Unlike the bulk of jazz-funk (then and now), the Breckers—on their first record, at least—kept the pandering to a minimum. Though it had a certain commercial appeal, 1975's *Back to Back* was an artistic success as well. The Brothers' music was a smart combination of extended pop forms, top-notch jazz improvisation, and sophisticated compositional techniques. On later albums, the temptation to sell lots of records apparently became too great to resist. Even the otherwise excellent first record bore some marks of disco, and with each subsequent album, the band's creative IQ shrank by several points. Still, virtually every record had something of substance to recommend it. In the early '90s, RCA issued a pair of compilation CDs that combined the best of the band's purely instrumental, jazz-based work. By 1982, the brothers had ceased working together. They reunited for touring and recording in the early '90s. —*Chris Kelsey*

● **The Brecker Brothers** / Jan. 1975 / One Way ◆◆◆◆◆

First date for brothers from 1975. Side one is solid jazz/funk/fusion. They called it "skunk-funk." With David Sanborn (as) and Don Grolnick (k). —*Michael G. Nastos*

The Brecker Brothers Collection, Vol. 1 / Jan. 1975-1981 / Novus ◆◆◆◆◆

During 1975-82, Michael Brecker and his brother Randy regularly teamed together as the Brecker Brothers, generally playing R&B funk with Randy's trumpet often electrified (à la Miles of a few years earlier) while Michael stuck to hot licks on his John Coltrane-influenced tenor. Sometimes originality slipped through and certainly the musicianship of their various bands (which often included David Sanborn on alto) was quite high, but the grooves and vamps were much closer to R&B than to jazz and they could get numbingly repetitive. This CD reissues music from at least five of the Brecker Brothers' albums and the electronics (so up-to-date at the time) sound quite dated today. There are some strong moments on the "best of" disc, particularly the ballad "Dream Theme," but the co-leaders' individual output since 1980 is far superior to the old funk. The true Brecker Brothers fans will prefer to get the complete sessions on the original LPs anyway. —*Scott Yanow*

Back to Back / 1975-1976 / One Way ◆◆◆

Blue Montreux: 1978 Montreux Jazz Festival / Jul. 21, 1978-Jul. 22, 1978 / Bluebird ◆◆◆◆

At the 1978 Montreux Jazz Festival, a variety of artists (including keyboardist Warren Bernhardt, tenor saxophonist Michael Brecker, guitarists Steve Khan and Larry Coryell, trumpeter Randy Brecker and vibraphonist Mike Mainieri) recorded a dozen funky selections which were originally released on two Arista LPs. This single CD has the eight top performances from these important fusion stylists; Michael Brecker in particular is in good form. The results are not essential but offer listeners a time capsule of where R&B-oriented fusion was in 1978. —*Scott Yanow*

Heavy Metal Be-Bop / 1978 / One Way ◆◆◆

Recorded live in New York, this explosive set of jazz, funk, and rock material was without question ahead of its time. Michael and Randy's use of electronically altered saxophone and trumpet sounds is amazing. —*Paul Kohler*

Detente / 1980 / One Way ◆◆◆

Don't Stop the Music / 1980 / One Way ◆◆

This features the Breckers with a large band. —*AMG*

Straphangin' / 1980 / One Way ◆◆◆

Straphangin' was to be the final release of the Brecker Brothers early to mid-'80s period. This superb album is perhaps without doubt their strongest recording from all of their early period releases. —*Paul Kohler*

Return of the Brecker Brothers / Apr. 1992-Aug. 1992 / GRP ◆◆◆◆◆

A good one. Michael Brecker reflects some of his experience with African music while on tour with Paul Simon. —*Michael Erlewine*

Out of the Loop / 1994 / GRP ◆◆◆

Michael Brecker

b. Mar. 29, 1949, Philadelphia, PA

Tenor Saxophone / Post-Bop, Crossover Jazz, Fusion

A remarkable technician and a highly influential tenor saxophonist (the biggest influence on other tenors since Wayne Shorter), Michael Brecker took a long time before getting around to recording his first solo album. He has spent much of his career as a top-notch studio player who often appeared backing pop singers, leading some jazz listeners to overlook his very strong improvising skills.

Michael Brecker originally started on clarinet and alto before switching to tenor in high school. Early on he played with rock and R&B-oriented bands. In 1969 he moved to New York and soon joined Dreams, an early fusion group. Brecker was with Horace Silver during 1973-74, gigged with Billy Cobham and then co-led the Brecker Brothers (a commercially successful funk group) with his brother-trumpeter Randy Brecker for most of the 1970s. He was with Steps (later Steps Ahead) in the early '80s, doubled on an EWI (electronic wind instrument) and made a countless number of studio sessions during the 1970s and '80s, popping up practically everywhere (including with James Taylor, Yoko Ono and Paul Simon). With the release of his first album as a leader in 1987 (when he was already 38), Brecker started appearing more often in challenging jazz settings. He recorded additional sets as a leader (in 1988 and 1990), teamed up with McCoy Tyner on one of 1995's most rewarding jazz recordings and toured with a reunited Brecker Brothers band. —*Scott Yanow*

Cityscape / 1983 / Warner Brothers ◆◆◆

● **Michael Brecker** / Dec. 1986-1987 / Impulse! ◆◆◆◆◆

Although he had been a major tenor saxophonist in the studios for nearly 20 years and was quite popular for his work with the Brecker Brothers, this MCA/Impulse set was Michael Brecker's first as a leader. Playing in a quintet with guitarist Pat Metheny, keyboardist Kenny Kirkland, bassist Charlie Haden and drummer Jack DeJohnette, Brecker performs three of his originals, two by producer Don Grolnick and Mike Stern's "Choices." The music in general is straightahead but far from predictable; the tricky material really challenges the musicians and Michael Brecker is in consistently brilliant form, constantly stretching himself. Highly recommended. —*Scott Yanow*

Don't Try This at Home / 1988 / Impulse! ◆◆◆◆

Michael Brecker's second album as a leader is almost the equal of his first. Surprisingly, only one song ("Suspone") uses his working quintet of the period (which consists of guitarist Mike Stern, pianist Joey Calderazzo, bassist Jeff Andrews and drummer Adam Nussbaum) although those musicians also pop up on other selections with the likes of pianists Don Grolnick and Herbie Hancock, bassist Charlie Haden, drummer Jack DeJohnette and violinist Mark O'Connor. Brecker (on tenor and the EWI) is in superb form, really ripping into the eight pieces (mostly group originals). Recommended. —*Scott Yanow*

Now You See It . . . Now You Don't / 1990 / Impulse! ◆◆◆

For *Now You See It*, Michael Brecker's third recording as a leader, the tenor great uses different personnel on most of the selections but plays consistently well. Jim Beard's synthesizers are utilized for atmosphere to set up a funky groove or to provide a backdrop for the leader. Some of the music sounds like updated John Coltrane (Joey Calderazzo's McCoy Tyner-influenced piano helps) while other pieces could almost pass for Weather Report, if Wayne Shorter rather than Joe Zawinul had been the lead voice. Most of the originals (either by Brecker, Jim Beard or producer Don Grolnick) project moods rather than feature strong melodies, but Michael Brecker's often-raging tenor makes the most of each opportunity. —*Scott Yanow*

Tales from the Hudson / 1996 / GRP ◆◆◆◆

Michael Brecker, a major influence on today's young saxophonists, shows off his own influences a bit throughout this fine modern straightahead set. Brecker sounds surprisingly like Stanley Turrentine on parts of "Midnight Voyage" and otherwise displays his roots in Ernie Watts and John Coltrane. With the exception of Don Grolnick's "Willie T," the music on the CD comprises group originals (five by the leader) and falls into the 1990s mainstream of jazz. While the tenor saxophonist has plenty of blowing space (really letting loose on the exciting closer "Cabin Fever"), Pat Metheny is mostly fairly restrained (in a Jim Hall bag) except for his wild solo on guitar synth during "Song for Bilbao." Pianist Joey Calderazzo starts out sounding a bit like McCoy Tyner on "Slings and Arrows" before his own musical personality is revealed. When Tyner himself plays on "Song for Bilbao" (one of two guest appearances), one can certainly tell the difference between master and pupil. All of Michael Brecker's recordings as a leader (as opposed to his cameos as a sideman on pop records) are easily recommended and show why he is considered a giant by many listeners. —*Scott Yanow*

Randy Brecker

b. Nov. 29, 1945, Philadelphia, PA

Trumpet, Fluegelhorn / Bop, Crossover Jazz, Fusion

Randy Brecker is essentially a fine hard-bop trumpet soloist but one versatile enough to fit into nearly any setting including in the pop world, funk bands and electronic fusion. He studied classical trumpet and attended Indiana University. Brecker was with Blood, Sweat & Tears in 1967 and spent 1968-69 playing with Horace Silver's Quintet. He also appeared with the big bands of Clark Terry, Duke Pearson, Frank Foster and the Thad Jones/Mel Lewis Orchestra. After playing with the early fusion group Dreams in 1969, he worked with Larry Coryell's Eleventh House and Billy Cobham in addition to keeping very busy with studiowork. He teamed up with Michael Brecker in the popular funk-oriented Brecker Brothers (1974-79), in the 1980s often collaborated with his wife, pianist/vocalist Eliane Elias, and in the '90s toured with the reunited Brecker Brothers. But Randy Brecker still sounds best when in a freewheeling bebop combo and fortunately he occasionally records in that type of spontaneous setting. —*Scott Yanow*

Score / Jan. 24, 1969+Feb. 3, 1969 / Blue Note ✦✦✦✦
Considering the emphasis on group originals on this set and his work around the period with Dreams (not to mention the upcoming Brecker Brothers), trumpeter Randy Brecker's debut as a leader is often surprisingly straightahead and has some worthwhile solos along with period trappings. This CD reissue of a Solid State album features Brecker with two overlapping groups, utilizing his brother Michael on tenor, guitarist Larry Coryell, keyboardist Hal Galper, either Eddie Gomez or Chuck Rainey on bass, Mickey Roker or Bernard Purdie on drums and alto flutist Jerry Dodgion. Overall this is an effective (if somewhat obscure) set. —*Scott Yanow*

Amanda / Feb. 1985-Mar. 1985 / Passport ✦✦
Considering the talents of trumpeter Randy Brecker and his wife, pianist Eliane Elias, one would expect their 1985 collaboration to be quite worthwhile. However this out-of-print LP is a disappointment for they perform generally weak material, emphasize electronics and utilize rather dull rhythms. Brecker's tone is distorted on many of the numbers and even the presence of altoist Sadao Watanabe, tenor saxophonist Michael Brecker, bassist Mark Egan and drummer Danny Gottlieb on some selections does not save this effort. —*Scott Yanow*

In the Idiom / Oct. 19, 1986-Oct. 25, 1986 / Denon ✦✦✦✦
This Denon CD has one of trumpeter Randy Brecker's infrequent straightahead dates and is one of his strongest recordings. Teamed up with tenor saxophonist Joe Henderson, pianist David Kikoski, bassist Ron Carter and drummer Al Foster, Brecker performs eight of his own compositions. These range from the early-'60s funk of "No Scratch" and the tricky "Hit or Miss" to the ballad "You're in My Heart" and the fairly free "Little Miss P"; the best title is "There's a Mingus a Monk Us!" This Japanese import is worth searching for. —*Scott Yanow*

● **Live at Sweet Basil: Randy Brecker Quintet** / Nov. 18, 1988+Nov. 20, 1988 / GNP ✦✦✦✦

Toe to Toe / Aug. 1989 / MCA ✦✦

Into the Sun / Dec. 1995 / Concord Jazz ✦✦✦

Willem Breuker

b. Nov. 4, 1944, Amsterdam, Netherlands

Clarinet, Soprano Saxophone, Tenor Saxophone / Avant-Garde

A leader in the European avant-garde and free music community, Dutch saxophonist, clarinetist, composer and bandleader Willem Breuker has worked to ensure recording and performance opportunities for many performers. His compositions incorporate several influences; free jazz, contemporary and avant-garde classical and new music, plus film themes, dance and European folk sounds. Breuker also includes a large dose of humor and even absurdist lyrics and sentiments into his works. That same humor carries over into his playing, which blends screams, shrieks and various effects with honking bleats and also moments of almost straight, bebop-inspired soloing. He helped form the Instant Composers Pool, a nonprofit organization that sponsors performances and recordings of music by European free players. Breuker has played and recorded with the Globe Unity Orchestra, Peter Brotzmann, Misha Mengelberg, Han Bennink, Alexander Schlippenbach, Gunther Hampel and many others. He formed the Kollektief in the mid-'70s, and toured Europe. It visited America and Canada in the '80s. Breuker was awarded the Dutch National Jazz Prize in 1970 and the Jazz Prize of the West German Music Critics in 1976. As a leader he has recorded for MPS, Marge and About Time but most notably for his own BVHaast label. —*Ron Wynn*

Live in Berlin / Nov. 1975 / FMP ✦✦✦✦
This was one of reedman Willem Breuker's works for larger group and while there were an obvious set of structures within these, it was quite open. —*Bob Rusch, Cadence*

On Tour / Mar. 3, 1977 / BVHaast ✦✦✦
It was recorded live at Rouen University in France. —*AMG*

Summer Music / Feb. 4, 1978 / Marge ✦✦✦

. . . Superstars / Mar. 1978 / FMP ✦✦✦

In Holland / Apr. 21, 1981-May 6, 1981 / BVHaast ✦✦✦

Driebergen-Zeist / Sep. 12, 1983-Sep. 13, 1983 / BVHaast ✦✦✦

● **Willem Breuker Kollektief** / Oct. 31, 1983 / About Time ✦✦✦✦

De Klap / 1985 / BVHaast ✦✦✦

Metropolis / Jan. 1989-Apr. 1989 / BVHaast ✦✦

To Remain / Jan. 1989-Apr. 1989 / BVHaast ✦✦✦

Parade / 1990-1991 / BVHaast ✦✦✦

Teresa Brewer

b. May 7, 1931, Toledo, OH

Vocals / Pop, Swing, Traditional Pop

Teresa Brewer started out as a spunky novelty vocalist in the 1950s and weathered the rise of rock to emerge as an exuberant jazz singer in the 1970s. Though some find it disconcerting to hear her cutesy, slightly nasal, *Your Hit Parade*-style delivery in a jazz context, at her best she can swing with a loose and easy fervor, aided greatly by the distinguished company she often keeps on her records. Brewer started singing on *Major Bowes' Amateur Hour* at the age of five and scored her first big hit as a teenager in 1950 with the diabolically catchy "Music! Music! Music!" That ditty found its way onto almost every jukebox in the land and launched a series of hit singles on Coral stretching all the way to 1961. Her marriage to record producer Bob Thiele in 1972 led to her re-emergence via a long string of albums for Thiele's labels (Doctor Jazz, Signature, Red Baron), often in tandem with such luminaries as Count Basie, Benny Carter, Duke and Mercer Ellington, Stephane Grappelli, Earl Hines and Clark Terry. —*Richard S. Ginell*

● **The Best of Teresa Brewer: Music! Music! Music!** / 1951-1959 / Varese ✦✦✦✦✦
The highlights from Teresa Brewer's time on Coral Records are included on *Best of Teresa Brewer: Music! Music! Music!*, as well as her hit version of the title song, recorded for London. —*Stephen Thomas Erlewine*

Songs of Bessie Smith / Feb. 1973-Apr. 1973 / Signature ✦✦✦✦

Live at Carnegie Hall & Montreux, Switzerland / Apr. 5, 1978-Jul. 22, 1983 / Doctor Jazz ✦✦✦
Brewer has good technique, but little soul or earthiness. —*Ron Wynn*

A Sophisticated Lady / 1981 / Columbia ✦✦
There are those who love her. I do not, though her albums are well produced and tasteful, and she sings with energy and style. —*Ron Wynn*

In London / 1982 / Signature ✦✦

Midnight Cafe (A Few More for the Road) / 1982 / Doctor Jazz ✦✦✦

I Dig Big Band Singers / 1983 / Doctor Jazz ✦
Brewer has good technique, but little soul or earthiness. —*Ron Wynn*

We Love You Fats / 1983 / Doctor Jazz ✦✦✦

American Music Box, Vol. 1 (Songs of Irving Berlin) / Jul. 7, 1983-Jul. 8, 1983 / Doctor Jazz ✦✦
This contains some wonderful selections. —*Ron Wynn*

On the Road Again / 1984 / Doctor Jazz ✦✦✦

What a Wonderful World / 1989 / Signature ✦✦✦
A 1989 release of Brewer singing and being backed by Stephane Grappelli and Ruby Braff. I'd rather hear them. —*Ron Wynn*

Cotton Connection / 1990 / Doctor Jazz ✦✦✦
A fine 1990 session. Here Mercer Ellington is in charge. —*Ron Wynn*

Memories of Louis / Jan. 15, 1991-Mar. 12, 1991 / Red Baron ✦✦✦
The singing of Teresa Brewer was always producer Bob Thiele's blind spot. Although equipped with a voice quite suitable for pop and country music, Brewer always sounded overly cute and out of place when performing jazz, despite her husband's successful attempts to team her with the who's who of jazz. This CD is quite remarkable, for there are few singers who sound less like Louis Armstrong than Brewer, yet here she is singing a dozen of Satch's standards. What's more, she is joined by a different trumpeter on each track: Clark Terry, Nicholas Payton, Ruby Braff, Freddie Hubbard, Wynton Marsalis, Roy Hargrove, Harry "Sweets" Edison, Lew Soloff, Terence Blanchard, Yank Lawson, Red Rodney and Dizzy

Gillespie. (Where was Miles Davis?) Fortunately, each of the brassmen gets a worthwhile amount of solo space, only two songs are under four-and-a-half minutes, and Brewer generally takes just two choruses. None of the boppish renditions sound at all close to New Orleans jazz, nor do any of the trumpeters show off much of a Louis Armstrong influence. A strange but very intriguing record. —*Scott Yanow*

Softly I Swing / Mar. 21, 1991-Mar. 22, 1991 / Red Baron ♦♦

American Music Box, Vol. 2 / Sep. 7, 1993-Sep. 8, 1993 / Red Baron ♦♦
Teresa Brewer albums are generally frustrating affairs. She is usually joined by great musicians (in this case cornetist Ruby Braff, pianist John Bunch, guitarist Bucky Pizzarelli, bassist Jay Leonhart and drummer Grady Tate) and is generous enough to allocate a liberal amount of solo space to her sidemen. But Brewer's wide vibrato and overly cute phrasing ruin most of her recordings; even after all these years she has not learned how to sing jazz. This CD (which has ten fine Harry Warren songs) is therefore only recommended to Ruby Braff completists. —*Scott Yanow*

Cecil Bridgewater

b. Oct. 10, 1942, Urbana, IL
Trumpet, Fluegelhorn / Hard Bop
An excellent hard-bop trumpeter, Cecil Bridgewater has been the longtime trumpeter with the Max Roach quartet. After studying music at the University of Illinois, he teamed up with tenorman Ron Bridgewater in the Bridgewater Brothers Band (1969). He was married to singer Denise Garrett (aka Dee Dee Bridgewater) for part of the 1970s. In 1970 the trumpeter was with Horace Silver and then he worked with the Thad Jones/Mel Lewis Orchestra (1970-76). Bridgewater started playing with Max Roach in the early '70s and has been a key part of his groups ever since. He recorded his long overdue debut as a leader on a Blue Moon disc in 1993. —*Scott Yanow*

● **I Love Your Smile** / Dec. 4, 1992 / Blue Moon ♦♦♦♦
For one of trumpeter Cecil Bridgewater's few sessions as a leader, the longtime Max Roach sideman welcomes Roach to a few of these selections along with altoist Antonio Hart, trombonist Steve Turre, pianist Roland Hanna, singer Vanessa Rubin (on "Never Too Young to Dream") and others. A high point of this modern hard bop set is Bridgewater's duet with Hanna on "Sophisticated Lady." —*Scott Yanow*

Dee Dee Bridgewater (Dee Dee Garrett)

b. May 27, 1950, Memphis, TN
Vocals / Standards
One of the best jazz singers of her generation, Dee Dee Bridgewater (who was married to trumpeter Cecil Bridgewater in the early '70s) had to move to France to find herself. She performed in Michigan during the 1960s and toured the Soviet Union in 1969 with the University of Illinois big band. She sang with the Thad Jones/Mel Lewis Orchestra (1972-74) and appeared in the Broadway musical *The Wiz* (1974-76). Due to erratic records and a lack of direction, Dee Dee Bridgewater was largely overlooked in the jazz world by the time she moved to France in the 1980s. She appeared in the show *Lady Day* and at European jazz festivals, and eventually formed her own backup group. By the late '80s Bridgewater's Verve recordings were starting to alert American listeners as to her singing talents. Her 1995 Horace Silver tribute disc (*Love and Peace*) is a gem and resulted in the singer extensively touring the US. —*Scott Yanow*

Dee Dee Bridgewater / 1976 / Atlantic ♦♦

Just Family / 1977 / Elektra ♦♦

Live in Paris / Nov. 24, 1986-Nov. 25, 1986 / MCA ♦♦♦
After showing early potential, Dee Dee Bridgewater wandered into commercialism and then moved to France. This 1986 recording started her artistic "comeback" and showed that she had developed and matured during her years in Europe. Backed by her regular French rhythm section, Bridgewater is in spirited and creative form on such numbers as "All Blues," "There Is No Greater Love" and "Cherokee," among others. Her arrival as a major singer during the decade since this set has been a welcome event. Recommended. —*Scott Yanow*

In Montreux / Jul. 18, 1990 / Verve ♦♦♦♦
Dee Dee Bridgewater's move to France awhile back has resulted in her having a relatively low profile in jazz. This excellent live set should help restore her reputation. Whether it be a three-song Horace Silver medley, the warhorse "All of Me," Jobim's "How Insensitive," "Night in Tunisia" or the rarely performed "Strange Fruit," Bridgewater (who is backed by a French rhythm section) is in top form, singing with swing and sensitivity. —*Scott Yanow*

Keeping Tradition / Dec. 8, 1992-Dec. 10, 1992 / Verve ♦♦♦♦

● **Love and Peace: A Tribute to Horace Silver** / Oct. 1995 / Verve ♦♦♦♦♦
Dee Dee Bridgewater performs 13 of Horace Silver's songs on her very well-conceived release. On most selections she is accompanied by her French quintet but there are also two guest appearances apiece for organist Jimmy Smith and pianist Silver ("Nice's Dream" and "Song for My Father"). Bridgewater uplifts Silver's lyrics, proves to be in prime form and swings up a storm. Other high points include "Filthy McNasty," "Doodlin'" and "Blowin' the Blues Away." A gem. —*Scott Yanow*

Nick Brignola

b. Jul. 17, 1936, Troy, NY
Baritone Saxophone, Soprano Saxophone / Hard Bop
A strong baritone soloist in the tradition of Pepper Adams, Nick Brignola has long been overshadowed by Adams and Gerry Mulligan but actually ranks near the top. He occasionally doubles on other instruments (soprano, alto and flute). After studying at Ithaca College and Berklee he played and recorded with Reese Markewich in the late '50s, Herb Pomeroy, Cal Tjader and the Mastersounds. Brignola worked with Woody Herman's Orchestra (1963), Sal Salvador and Ted Curson (1967) but has generally been a leader of his own small groups. For a time he played fusion in the early '70s but since then has mostly performed hard bop. Among the many labels Nick Brignola has recorded for are Priam (his own company), Beehive, Interplay, Sea Breeze, Discovery and Reservoir. —*Scott Yanow*

Baritone Madness / Dec. 22, 1977 / Bee Hive ♦♦♦♦
This album lives up to its title. Nick Brignola is matched up with fellow baritone great Pepper Adams in a sextet also including trumpeter Ted Curson, pianist Derek Smith, bassist Dave Holland and drummer Roy Haynes. The personnel differs throughout the program, with the full group being heard on "Billie's Bounce" and "Marmaduke," Curson sitting out on "Donna Lee," "Body and Soul" being a feature for Brignola, and "Alone Together" showcasing the rhythm section. It is obvious from the song titles that this is very much a bebop jam session date, and quite a few sparks do fly. —*Scott Yanow*

New York Bound / Oct. 30, 1978 / Interplay ♦♦♦

Burn Brigade / Jun. 19, 1979 / Bee Hive ♦♦♦
Three of the greatest baritone saxophonists of the post-1970 period teamed up for this jam-session date: Nick Brignola, Ronnie Cuber and Cecil Payne. With the assistance of pianist Walter Davis, Jr., bassist Walter Booker and drummer Jimmy Cobb, the trio of baritonists romp on a pair of Brignola originals (the basic "Nick Who's Blues" and the more complex "Busy B's"), "I'm Getting Sentimental over You" and two jazz standards. The music is often quite exciting (the horns battle each other to a draw) and is easily recommended to fans of the bebop baritone sax. —*Scott Yanow*

L.A. Bound / Oct. 17, 1979 / Sea Breeze ♦♦♦♦
Baritonist Nick Brignola (who doubles on soprano) meets up with trombonist Bill Watrous in a quintet also including pianist Dwight Dickerson, bassist John Heard and drummer Dick Berk for boppish music that is often explosive. On a superior repertoire including Horace Silver's "Quicksilver," Billy Strayhorn's "Smada" and Kenny Dorham's "Blue Bossa," the individual solos and the interplay between Brignola and Watrous give one plenty of reasons to search for this swinging release. —*Scott Yanow*

Signals . . . In from Somewhere / Jun. 21, 1983 / Discovery ♦♦♦
Nick Brignola (switching between baritone and soprano) is in fine form on this out-of-print LP, leading a quartet also including pianist Bill Dobbins, bassist John Lockwood and drummer David Calarco. The group interprets three Brignola compositions, two by Dobbins and one apiece from Lockwood and Calarco in addition to the Tadd Dameron classic "Tadd's Delight." The music is harmonically advanced hard bop and among the more memorable selections is a Brignola-Calarco duet on "Fun." A fine showcase for the baritonist. —*Scott Yanow*

Northern Lights / Jul. 3, 1984 / Discovery ♦♦♦

Raincheck / Sep. 12, 1988+Sep. 13, 1988 / Reservoir ♦♦♦♦
The fine baritonist Nick Brignola (who here also plays a bit of soprano, tenor and clarinet) is well featured on a wide range of superior standards and obscurities. With the strong assistance of pianist Kenny Barron, bassist George Mraz and drummer Billy Hart, Brignola is heard at his best playing everything from bop and swing to Ralph Towner's ballad "North Star." —*Scott Yanow*

On a Different Level / Sep. 25, 1989 / Reservoir ♦♦♦

What It Takes / Oct. 9, 1990 / Reservoir ♦♦♦
Brignola is matched with playing equals, and he comes out burning. He also plays alto sax and clarinet in addition to his customary baritone and soprano. Pianist Kenny Barron and bassist Rufus Reid lift any session, while drummer Dick Berk defers to them, but doesn't lose the reins while doing so. Randy Brecker takes a

welcome break from fusion and studio work to show that his trumpet chops can handle hard bop and mainstream fare. —*Ron Wynn*

It's Time / Dec. 2, 1991 / Reservoir ✦✦✦

Live at Sweet Basil—First Set / Aug. 28, 1992 / Reservoir ✦✦✦

● **Like Old Times** / May 19, 1994 / Reservoir ✦✦✦✦

Some jazz recordings take pages to explain and analyze. Such is not the case with Nick Brignola's Reservoir release, for the great baritonist (who ranks up with Gerry Mulligan, Hamiet Bluiett and Ronnie Cuber as pacesetters on the instrument in the mid-'90s) jams four standards and three straightahead originals with an all-star quintet featuring trumpeter Claudio Roditi and pianist John Hicks. In addition to his many robust baritone solos, Brignola has excellent outings on clarinet ("More Than You Know") and soprano. With bassist George Mraz and drummer Dick Berk ably supporting the group and both Roditi and Hicks heard at the peak of their powers, Brignola's album is a strong set of bop-oriented music. —*Scott Yanow*

Flight of the Eagle / Jun. 17, 1996 / Reservoir ✦✦✦✦

Alan Broadbent

b. Apr. 23, 1947, Auckland, New Zealand
Piano / Post-Bop
An unsung hero of the acoustic piano, Alan Broadbent is a highly lyrical and melodic bebopper/post-bopper who has cited Bill Evans, Wynton Kelly, Tommy Flanagan, Nat King Cole and Red Garland as some of his favorite pianists. Raised in New Zealand, he moved to Boston in 1966 to study at the prestigious Berklee College of Music. After staying on the road with Woody Herman (for whom he was a writer, arranger and soloist) from 1969-72, he settled in Los Angeles and has lived there ever since. Broadbent went on to work as a sideman for Chet Baker, tenor saxmen Warne Marsh and Gary Foster and the late singer Irene Kral in the '70s and with Bud Shank and arranger Nelson Riddle in the '80s.

The '90s have found him writing arrangements for Natalie Cole, Marian McPartland, Scott Hamilton, and others, and playing alongside bassist Charlie Haden, tenor saxman Ernie Watts and drummer Larance Marable in Haden's Quartet West—a unique and conceptual L.A.-based group that is known for including bits of dialogue from film-noir movies between bop performances. Broadbent's excellent trio albums for Discovery in the '80s and Concord in the '90s make it clear that he deserves to be much better known as a soloist. —*Alex Henderson*

Palette / 1979 / Granite ✦✦✦✦

Good 1979 session that lets Broadbent show his arranging and playing skills in his favorite setting, the big band. These are also his compositions, and he's done a fine job whipping the band into shape. The top soloists include Don Menza, Pete Christlieb, and Bill Perkins. —*Ron Wynn*

Everything I Love / Apr. 1, 1986+Apr. 2, 1986 / Discover ✦✦✦

Another Time / Jul. 2, 1987+Jul. 3, 1987 / Trend ✦✦✦

Away from You / Jan. 16, 1989-Jan. 17, 1989 / Trend ✦✦✦

● **Live at Maybeck Recital Hall, Vol. 14** / Apr. 21, 1991 / Concord Jazz ✦✦✦✦✦

Best known as an arranger, Alan Broadbent takes the solo stage in another release from Concord's fine Maybeck series. He plays charming, sometimes compelling melodies and demonstrates good technique, but Broadbent is nowhere near the rhythmic stylist or harmonic creator of some others who have come before him. It's still a fine album, just not in the upper echelon of those in this line. —*Ron Wynn*

Concord Duo Series, Vol. 4 / Mar. 1993 / Concord Jazz ✦✦✦

Pacific Standard Time / Jan. 23, 1995-Jan. 24, 1995 / Concord Jazz ✦✦✦✦

Personal Standards / Oct. 7, 1996-Oct. 8, 1996 / Concord Jazz ✦✦✦✦

Brian Bromberg

b. 1960
Bass / Post-Bop, Fusion, Hard Bop
A very versatile acoustic and electric bassist capable of playing straightahead jazz, funk and fusion, Brian Bromberg is also one of the few bassists to master the tapping technique made famous by Stanley Jordan, sometimes sounding like three bassists at once during his often-thunderous solos. Although he was a drummer at the age of 13, the following year Bromberg started classical lessons on bass. He developed quickly and by the time he was 19, he was part of Stan Getz's group. Bromberg has been a valuable sideman with many bands since, including those led by Horace Silver, Monty Alexander, Dizzy Gillespie, Richie Cole, Lee Ritenour, Dave Grusin and Freddie Hubbard. He recorded his first album as a leader in 1986 (*A New Day* for the Black Hawk label) and has since led sessions for Intima

and Nova; unfortunately all of those record companies have since gone out of business! Brian Bromberg in the late 1990s remains one of the most underrated bassists in jazz. —*Scott Yanow*

Basically Speaking / Oct. 1985-Jun. 1986 / Nova ✦✦✦

New Day / Oct. 1985-Jun. 1986 / Black Hawk ✦✦✦✦

Bassist Brian Bromberg's debut as a leader finds him alternating between acoustic and electric and welcoming such guests as tenorman Ernie Watts, Joe Farrell (on his final recording date) and, during "Take a Walk in the Park with Me," fluegelhornist Freddie Hubbard. This diverse LP (which has not yet been reissued on CD) ranges from fairly straightahead to some funk and fusion; Bromberg performs six originals, plus "Summertime" and "My Funny Valentine." An enjoyable set, although not essential. —*Scott Yanow*

Basses Loaded / 1988 / Intermedia ✦✦✦

The versatile Brian Bromberg plays fretted bass, piccolo bass and a piccolo bass guitar synthesizer on this electric set. Heading a septet that also includes Ernie Watts on tenor and soprano and the rhythm guitar of Russ Freeman, Bromberg performs seven originals and an obscurity. The music is generally funky and touched by R&B, but it has its creative moments and certainly shows off Bromberg's impressive technique. —*Scott Yanow*

Magic Rain / 1989 / Intima ✦✦✦✦

This CD is an example of high-quality fusion. Not only are the electronics state-of-the-art for 1989 and the musicianship impeccable but several of the original melodies are memorable, there are lots of funky grooves and the solos are fiery. Bromberg, a virtuoso player on both electric and acoustic basses (including the piccolo bass) often sounds a bit like a guitarist; few can match his technique as he shows on his two unaccompanied solos "Just the Bass" and "Interlude." Keyboardist Jeff Lorber sounds more creative during his three guest spots here than he does on his own dates and there are also some worthwhile solos from tenor saxophonist Ernie Watts. This CD from the defunct Intima label will be hard to find but fans of electric jazz will consider it worth the search. —*Scott Yanow*

● **It's About Time: The Acoustic Project** / May 21, 1991-May 22, 1991 / Nova ✦✦✦✦✦

After a few electric projects, bassist Brian Bromberg decided to record a purely acoustic project. With such sidemen as pianists Mike Garson and Mitch Forman, brother Dave Bromberg on drums, trumpeter Freddie Hubbard (on three songs), and tenors Ernie Watts (on five) and Doug Webb (on two), Bromberg holds his own with the fast company. Some of the selections on this CD are quite memorable, particularly Hubbard's "Dear John," Watts' interpretation of Wayne Shorter's "Yes or No" and the trumpeter's feature on "If I Should Lose You." Although the Nova label has since gone belly-up, this excellent CD might still be found and is certainly worth a search. —*Scott Yanow*

Brian Bromberg / 1993 / Nova ✦✦✦✦

You Know That Feeling / 1997 / Zebra ✦✦✦✦

Bob Brookmeyer

b. Dec. 19, 1929, Kansas City, MO
Valve Trombone, Arranger, Piano / Cool, Post-Bop
Bob Brookmeyer has long been the top valve trombonist in jazz and a very advanced arranger whose writing is influenced by modern classical music. He started out as a pianist in dance bands but was on valve trombone with Stan Getz (1953). He gained fame as a member of the Gerry Mulligan quartet (1954-57), was part of the unusual Jimmy Giuffre Three of 1957-58 (which consisted of Giuffre's reeds, Brookmeyer's valve trombone and Jim Hall's guitar) and then rejoined Mulligan as arranger and occasional player with his Concert Jazz Band. Brookmeyer, who was a strong enough pianist to hold his own on a two-piano date with Bill Evans, occasionally switched to piano with Mulligan. He co-led a part-time quintet with Clark Terry (1961-66), was an original member of the Thad Jones/Mel Lewis Orchestra (1965-67) and became a busy studio musician. Brookmeyer was fairly inactive during much of the 1970s but made a comeback in the late '70s with some very advanced arrangements for the Mel Lewis band (of which he became musical director for a time). Brookmeyer has since moved to Europe where he continually writes and occasionally records on his distinctive valve trombone. —*Scott Yanow*

The Dual Role of Bob Brookmeyer / Jan. 6, 1954+Jun. 30, 1955 / Original Jazz Classics ✦✦✦

This CD reissue has four selections apiece from two different bands, both of which feature subtle interplay and cool tones. Bob Brookmeyer plays valve trombone and piano on two songs apiece with his 1955 quartet, a group also including guitarist Jimmy Raney, bassist Teddy Kotick and drummer Mel Lewis. The other half of this disc is actually led by vibraphonist Teddy Charles who features Brookmeyer on both of his instruments along with bassist Teddy Kotick and drummer Ed Shaughnessy; Nancy Overton takes a vocal on "Nobody's Heart." Although the overall set is not all that essential, the music is pleasing and reasonably creative. —*Scott Yanow*

Traditionalism Revisited / Jul. 13, 1957+Jul. 16, 1957 / World Pacific ✦✦✦
This out-of-print Pacific Jazz album (which was last reissued by the English Affinity label as a 1984 LP) is a bit unusual. Bob Brookmeyer (on valve trombone and piano), Jimmy Giuffre (switching between clarinet, baritone and tenor), guitarist Jim Hall, either Joe Benjamin or Ralph Pena on bass and drummer Dave Bailey perform eight songs from the 1920s and '30s including some obscurities. While these selections have occasionally been revived by Dixieland and swing bands, Brookmeyer and his group use harmonies that were modern for the 1950s to update such tunes as "Louisiana," "Truckin'," "Honeysuckle Rose" and even "Santa Claus Blues." Because the musicians have a respect for the older styles, they extend rather than break the tradition; the results are quite enjoyable. —*Scott Yanow*

Kansas City Revisited / Oct. 23, 1958 / United Artists ✦✦✦
Cool jazz meets swing on this valuable but long out-of-print LP. Valve trombonist Bob Brookmeyer, tenors Al Cohn and Paul Quinichette, guitarist Jim Hall, bassist Addison Farmer and drummer Osie Johnson perform four songs associated with the late-'30s Count Basie Orchestra plus a couple of numbers ("A Blues" and "Travlin' Light") that are sung by the underrated vocalist Big Miller who was making his recording debut at the time. This memorable set is long overdue to be reissued on CD. —*Scott Yanow*

The Ivory Hunters / May 12, 1959 / United Artists ✦✦✦✦
This is a rather surprising session, since Bob Brookmeyer, normally a valve trombonist, switched to piano and is heard playing in a quartet with pianist Bill Evans, bassist Percy Heath and drummer Connie Kay. The two-piano experiment was supposed to be for just a couple of songs, but the interplay between Brookmeyer and Evans was so delightful that they decided to make a full album out of it. Brookmeyer brought out the playful side of Evans on the six standards, making this straight CD reissue of the original LP a swinging success. —*Scott Yanow*

Brookmeyer and Guitars / June 29, 1961 / Kimberly ✦✦

Gloomy Sunday and Other Bright Moments / Nov. 6, 1961-Nov. 8, 1961 / Verve ✦✦✦✦

And Friends / May 25, 1964-May 27, 1964 / Columbia ✦✦✦
This somewhat obscure session was reissued on LP by Columbia in 1980. Valve trombonist Bob Brookmeyer and tenor-great Stan Getz (who had played together regularly a decade ago) had a reunion for this date, performing five standards and three Brookmeyer originals. The young rhythm section (pianist Herbie Hancock, vibraphonist Gary Burton, bassist Ron Carter and drummer Elvin Jones) uplifts what would have been a fairly conventional (although high-quality) bop date. —*Scott Yanow*

Back Again / 1978 / Sonet ✦✦✦✦
This session was valve trombonist Bob Brookmeyer's first jazz date in 13 years after a period writing for the studios and then away from music altogether. Brookmeyer, who is featured in a quintet with cornetist Thad Jones, pianist Jimmy Rowles, bassist George Mraz and drummer Mel Lewis, proves to still be in prime form playing in an unchanged style. Other than the leader's uptempo blues "In a Rotten Mood" and a Latin piece ("Carib"), the quintet sticks to veteran standards. Highlights include "Sweet and Lovely," "Caravan" and "You'd Be So Nice to Come Home To." —*Scott Yanow*

Live at Sandy's Jazz Revival / Jul. 28, 1978-Jul. 29, 1978 / Gryphon ✦✦✦
Live at Sandy's in Beverly, MA, in 1978. With Michael Moore (b), Jack Wilkins (g), Joe La Barbera (d). Mostly standards, some music of Andy LaVerne. Two Brookmeyer originals. All arrangements by Brookmeyer. Fine group effort. —*Michael G. Nastos*

Bob Brookmeyer Live at the Village Vanguard / Feb. 1980 / Gryphon ✦✦✦✦
A year after Thad Jones' decision to end his musical partnership with drummer Mel Lewis, Lewis' jazz orchestra was changing its sound. Valve trombonist Bob Brookmeyer became the big band's chief arranger for a time, and his charts show the influence of modern classical music while usually still swinging. This hard-to-find LP features the orchestra playing live at their homebase (the Village Vanguard), and such soloists as pianist Jim McNeely and Dick Oatts on alto and soprano, fluegelhornist Clark Terry, and Brookmeyer himself are featured on the nearly 16-minute "El Co" and "The Fan Club." Worthwhile if not essential music. —*Scott Yanow*

Through a Looking Glass / Jan. 1982 / Finesse ✦✦✦✦
Valve trombonist Bob Brookmeyer was one of the key arranger-composers for the Mel Lewis Orchestra when he recorded this LP for the now-defunct Finesse label. Brookmeyer used drummer Lewis plus the young trumpeter Tom Harrell and sev-

eral of Lewis' top sidemen (soprano saxophonist Dick Oatts, pianist Jim McNeely and bassist Marc Johnson) for a set comprising seven of his complex originals. The high musicianship keeps up with the material and the result is consistently stimulating and thoughtful music. —*Scott Yanow*

Oslo / Sep. 1986 / Concord Jazz ✦✦✦✦
Bob Brookmeyer has been so busy as a writer since the mid-'60s that his valve trombone playing has been somewhat underrecorded. This quartet set with pianist Alan Broadbent (who also plays a bit of synthesizer), bassist Eric Von Essen and drummer Michael Stephans finds Brookmeyer in top form on four standards and a quartet of his originals (including "Later Blues," "Tootsie Samba" and "Who Could Care"). His valve trombone playing had grown and evolved through the years and, although he still had the cool tone, Brookmeyer's solos are often quite complex while not completely abandoning chordal improvisation. This Concord release is well worth picking up. —*Scott Yanow*

Dreams / Aug. 1988 / Dragon ✦✦

Electricity / Mar. 1991 / Blue Jackel ✦✦✦

● **Paris Suite** / Oct. 15, 1993-Jan. 5, 1994 / Challenge ✦✦✦✦
Veteran valve-trombonist/composer Bob Brookmeyer has not recorded many small-group dates during the 1980s and '90s, making this Challenge CD with a young European rhythm section (pianist Kris Goessens, bassist Riccardo Del Fra and drummer Dre Pallemaerts) a bit special. Brookmeyer plays eight obscurities (four by him and three by his pianist) that are complex, harmonically advanced and yet still able to be swung. Well worth searching for. —*Scott Yanow*

Roy Brooks

b. Sep. 3, 1938, Detroit, MI
Drums / Hard Bop
Roy Brooks is a flexible drummer able to play anything from bop to the avant-garde. He gained early experience gigging with Yusef Lateef and became known for his period with the Horace Silver Quintet (1959-64). During the next few years he played with a wide variety of top musicians including Pharoah Sanders, Wes Montgomery, Sonny Stitt, Jackie McLean, Dexter Gordon, Abdullah Ibrahim, Randy Weston, Charles Mingus, Milt Jackson and Lateef. In 1970 he became a founding member of Max Roach's M'Boom, an all-percussion group that allows him to play some musical saw. In 1976 Roy Brooks moved to Detroit where he became very involved in teaching jazz. He has continued performing to the present time and recorded a set of stimulating duets on Enja. —*Scott Yanow*

● **The Free Slave** / Apr. 26, 1970 / Muse ✦✦✦✦
Recorded at Left Bank Jazz Society in Baltimore, MD, this all star quintet features George Coleman (ts), Woody Shaw (tpt), Hugh Lawson (p), Cecil McBee (b), and Brooks (d/per). There are four originals, all extended, with room to stretch for musicians. Wild club date. —*Michael G. Nastos*

Live at Town Hall / May 26, 1974 / Baystate ✦✦✦
NYC. With Marcus Belgrave (tpt), Sonny Fortune (as), Sonny Red (as), and Eddie Jefferson (v). There are three standards and Brooks' famous "Prophet" and "Blues for the Carpenter's Saw." —*Michael G. Nastos*

Duet in Detroit / Aug. 26, 1983-Feb. 25, 1989 / Enja ✦✦✦✦
This CD features drummer Roy Brooks (who also plays musical saw on one piece) on two duets apiece (recorded live over a period of six years) with trumpeter Woody Shaw and pianists Randy Weston, Don Pullen and Geri Allen. The music is full of surprises and generally holds one's interest with the trumpet-drums duets being the most unusual. —*Scott Yanow*

Tina Brooks (Harold Floyd Brooks)

b. Jun. 7, 1932, Fayetteville, NC, d. Aug. 13, 1974, New York, NY
Tenor Saxophone / Hard Bop
A fine hard-bop tenor player who after a burst of activity largely faded out of jazz in 1962 (due to continual drug problems), Tina Brooks never reached his potential but did record some rewarding music. He made his recording debut in 1951 on four titles with Sonny Thompson's R&B band. After time spent touring with Amos Milburn and Lionel Hampton and freelancing in New York, Brooks began to record for Blue Note in 1958. In addition to four sessions as a leader cut between 1958-61, he appeared on Blue Note dates as a sideman with Jimmy Smith, Kenny Burrell, Freddie Hubbard, Freddie Redd, Jackie McLean and with Howard McGhee on Felsted. But his last session was on June 17, 1961, and, although he continued playing (mostly Latin and R&B jobs in New York), Brooks let his drug habit ruin his life. He died of kidney failure when he was 42. Ironically Tina Brooks is probably better known now (due to the release of a definitive Mosaic four-LP box set) than he was in his lifetime. —*Scott Yanow*

Minor Move / Mar. 16, 1958 / Blue Note ✦✦✦✦

Tina Brooks' first session for Blue Note was recorded in March of 1958, a month after he appeared on Jimmy Smith's sessions for *The Sermon* and *House Party,* but the music wasn't released at the time. The sessions remained unreleased for years, eventually appearing as *Minor Move,* it's hard to see why the record was shelved. Not only does it feature Brooks in robust form, but he's supported by pianist Sonny Clark, trumpeter Lee Morgan, bassist Doug Watkins and drummer Art Blakey—a first-rate lineup if there ever was one. Stylistically, the music here is no great surprise—it's straightahead, driving hard-bop—but the performances are exceptional. Brooks has no problem keeping up with Morgan and Clark, who both have more than their fair share of fine moments here. He has a rich, full-bodied tone and clever phrasing, keeping the music fresh on standards like "The Way You Look Tonight" and "Everything Happens to Me." His original compositions "Nutville" and "Minor Move" are equally impressive, offering the entire band opportunities to stretch out and improvise vigorously. It is true that *Minor Move* is right within the hard-bop tradition, but fans of that style will find much to treasure here. —*Stephen Thomas Erlewine*

The Complete Blue Note Recordings / Mar. 16, 1958-Mar. 2, 1961 / Mosaic ✦✦✦✦✦

Tenor saxophonist Tina Brooks, although he lived until turning 42 in 1974, made his last recordings in 1961 and was soon forgotten. Brooks, who recorded with Jimmy Smith, Kenny Burrell, Freddie Hubbard, Freddie Redd, Jackie McLean and Howard McGhee during 1958-61, was a fine player whose smooth tone sometimes stood out from the crowd. Mosaic's four-LP set has all four of Brooks' Blue Note albums as a leader, two of which had not previously been released while one had initially come out in Japan years after his death; only *True Blue* was released during his lifetime. Brooks holds his own with his impressive sidemen (trumpeters Lee Morgan, Freddie Hubbard, Blue Mitchell and Johnny Coles, pianists Sonny Clark, Duke Jordan and Kenny Drew, bassists Doug Watkins, Sam Jones, Paul Chambers and Wilbur Ware, drummers Art Blakey, Art Taylor and Philly Joe Jones and, on one cut, altoist Jackie McLean). It is ironic that all of those players are better known than Brooks and that Tina is more famous now (thanks to the release of this definitive box set) than he ever was when he was alive. Although now out-of-print, the music on this release is essential for hard-bop collectors. —*Scott Yanow*

● **True Blue** / Jun. 25, 1960 / Blue Note ✦✦✦✦✦

Although a four-LP Mosaic box set purportedly includes every recording led by the obscure but talented tenor saxophonist Tina Brooks, this 1994 CD has previously unreleased alternate takes of "True Blue" and "Good Old Soul" that Mosaic overlooked. Brooks is teamed with the young trumpeter Freddie Hubbard (on one of his earliest sessions), pianist Duke Jordan, bassist Sam Jones and drummer Art Taylor for a set dominated by Brooks' originals. None of the themes may be all that memorable ("Nothing Ever Changes My Love for You" comes the closest) but the hard-bop solos are consistently excellent. —*Scott Yanow*

Back to the Tracks / Sep. 1, 1960+Oct. 20, 1960 / Blue Note ✦✦✦✦✦

The music that comprises *Back to the Tracks* was recorded in September 1960, months after the sessions for *True Blue,* but it sat on the shelves until Mosaic reissued it as part of their *Complete Blue Note Recordings* box, even though it was penciled in for release. Like *Minor Move,* Brooks' first session that stayed unreleased for over 20 years, *Back to the Tracks* is an excellent hard-bop set, and it's hard to understand why it wasn't released at the time. Brooks leads a fantastic band featuring alto saxophonist Jackie McLean, trumpeter Blue Mitchell, pianist Kenny Drew, bassist Paul Cambers and drummer Art Taylor through three originals and two standards. Each musician has opportunity to shine, but Brooks remains the center of attention. His style is remarkably fluid, capable of graceful, elegant turns on the ballads and clean, speedy improvisations on the uptempo bop. Each of the five songs have breathtaking moments, confirming Brooks' talents as a saxophonist, composer and leader. Listening to *Back to the Tracks,* it's impossible to figure out why the record wasn't released at the time, but it's a hard-bop gem from the early '60s to cherish. —*Stephen Thomas Erlewine*

Peter Brötzmann

b. Mar. 6, 1941, Remscheid, Germany

Tenor Saxophone, Bass Saxophone / Free Jazz, Avant-Garde

Peter Brötzmann is a longtime champion of Europe's avant-garde, and a self-taught saxophonist famous for animated, swirling solos and lengthy, twisting dialogues. Brötzmann played initially in local Dixieland bands in Germany, then was an early member of the Fluxus movement and began playing free jazz by 1964. A year later, Brötzmann, Peter Kowald and Sven-Ake Johannsson formed a group. Brötzmann toured Europe in 1966 with a quintet that included Mike Mantler and Carla Bley. He also began working with the Globe Unity Orchestra, and continued

with them until 1981. Brötzmann was a founder of the co-operative FMP in 1969, an organization that sponsors and issues free jazz releases. He also founded a trio with Han Bennink and Fred Van Hove that became extremely influential through its blend of European theater and folk music and African rhythms. Van Hove left the group in 1976, but continued playing with Bennink until 1979. During the '80s his associations included Harry Miller, Louis Moholo, Willie Kellers, Andrew Cyrille, the Alarm Orchestra, Cecil Taylor and Last Exit. Among the most ferocious of the free jazz players, Peter Brötzmann has also recorded on baritone, bass sax, clarinet, alto, soprano and bass clarinet. —*Ron Wynn*

● **For Adolphe Sax** / Jun. 1967 / FMP ✦✦✦✦✦

Machine Gun / May 1968 / FMP ✦✦✦

Balls / Aug. 1970 / FMP ✦✦✦

Outspan No. 1 / Apr. 1974 / FMP ✦✦✦

Outspan No. 2 / May 1974 / FMP ✦✦✦

Solo / May 1976 / FMP ✦✦✦

Three Points and a Mountain / Feb. 1979 / FMP ✦✦✦

The Nearer the Bone, The Sweeter the Meat / Aug. 1979 / FMP ✦✦✦✦

Opened, But Hardly Touched / Nov. 1980 / FMP ✦✦✦

Pica Pica / Sep. 1982 / FMP ✦✦✦

14 Love Poems / Aug. 1984 / FMP ✦✦✦

Berlin Djungle / Nov. 1984 / FMP ✦✦✦

Low Life / Jan. 1987 / Celluloid ✦✦✦

Reserve / Nov. 1988 / FMP ✦✦✦

No Nothing / Aug. 1990 / FMP ✦✦✦

Last Home / 1990 / Pathological ✦✦✦✦

It is a cliché to say that new age is the perfect music to wash dishes by. In contrast, *Last Home* could serve as the soundtrack of a war. The violent interplay between Caspar Brötzmann's acid rock guitar feedback (which often sounds like three guitars) and Peter Brötzmann's bass sax, tenor, clarinet and tarogato on this duo encounter at first is quite jarring. However frequent playing of the CD (if it does not drive one nuts) reveals a logic to the free improvisations. It may not thrill one's neighbors at 3 a.m. but the performances are certainly quite stimulating and creative. Intense sound explorations. —*Scott Yanow*

Dare Devil / Oct. 1991 / DIW ✦✦✦

Clifford Brown

b. Oct. 30, 1930, Wilmington, DE, **d.** Jun. 26, 1956, Pennsylvania

Trumpet / Hard Bop

Clifford Brown's death in a car accident at the age of 25 was one of the great tragedies in jazz history. Already ranking with Dizzy Gillespie and Miles Davis as one of the top trumpeters in jazz, Brownie was still improving in 1956. Plus he was a clean liver and was not even driving; the up-and-coming pianist Richie Powell and his wife (who was driving) also perished in the crash.

Clifford Brown accomplished a great deal in the short time he had. He started on trumpet when he was 15 and by 1948 was playing regularly in Philadelphia. Fats Navarro, who was his main influence, encouraged Brown as did Charlie Parker and Dizzy Gillespie. After a year at Maryland State University he was in a serious car accident in June 1950 that put him out of action for a year. In 1952 Brown made his recording debut with Chris Powell's Blue Flames (an R&B group). The following year he spent some time with Tadd Dameron and from August to December was with Lionel Hampton's band, touring Europe and leading some recording sessions. In early 1954 he recorded some brilliant solos at Birdland with Art Blakey's quintet (a band that directly preceded the Jazz Messengers) and by mid-year had formed a quintet with Max Roach. Considered one of the premiere hard-bop bands, the group lasted until Brown's death, featuring Harold Land (and later Sonny Rollins) on tenor and recording several superb sets for EmArcy. Just hours before his death, Brownie appeared at a Philadelphia jam session that was miraculously recorded and played some of the finest music of his short life.

Clifford Brown had a fat warm tone, a boppish style quite reminiscent of the equally ill-fated Fats Navarro and a mature improvising approach; he was as inventive on melodic ballads as he was on rapid jams. Amazingly enough, a filmed appearance of him playing two songs in 1955 on a Soupy Sales variety show has recently turned up after being lost for 40 years, the only known footage of the great trumpeter. Fortunately, virtually all of his recordings are currently available including his Prestige dates (in the OJC series), his work for Blue Note and Pacific Jazz (on a four-CD set) and his many EmArcy sessions (reissued on a magnificent ten-disc set). But the one to pick up first is Columbia's *The Beginning and the End* which has Brown's first and last recordings. —*Scott Yanow*

★ **The Beginning and the End** / Mar. 21, 1952+Jun. 25, 1956 / Columbia ✦✦✦✦✦
This CD, a straight reissue of the original LP, has some incredible music. Trumpeter Clifford Brown is heard at the beginning of his tragically brief career, taking solos on a pair of R&B sides by Chris Powell's Blue Flames. The remainder of the package features Brown on the last night of his life, just a few hours before his death in a car accident. Performing in his hometown of Philadelphia before a loving crowd, the 25-year-old is heard playing at his absolute peak. He performs "Walkin" with a local sextet that includes Billy Root on tenor and pianist Sam Dockery (a future member of Art Blakey's Jazz Messengers), "A Night in Tunisia" with a quintet and concludes both his night and his career with a quartet rendition of "Donna Lee" that is simply brilliant. Brownie's death was one of the great tragedies of jazz history and his "goodbyes" to the audience are ironic and in retrospect quite sad; don't listen to it twice. But Clifford Brown's playing on this date is so memorable that the CD is essential for all jazz collections. —*Scott Yanow*

● **Clifford Brown Quartet in Paris** / 1953 / Original Jazz Classics ✦✦✦✦✦
This straight CD reissue of a Clifford Brown LP features the great trumpeter with a quiet rhythm section consisting of pianist Henri Renaud, bassist Pierre Michelot and drummer Benny Bennett. There are six songs and six alternate takes (including three versions apiece of "I Can Dream, Can't I" and "You're a Lucky Guy") but each of Brownie's solos are different and his tone is so warm that every performance is well worth hearing. Ironically the finest solo, a classic version of "It Might as Well Be Spring," was improvised in one take. Highly recommended. —*Scott Yanow*

Brownie Eyes / Jun. 9, 1953-Aug. 28, 1953 / Blue Note ✦✦✦✦✦
The great trumpeter Clifford Brown is heard in several settings on this LP, all of whose titles have since been reissued in a box set by Mosaic. The songs find Brown with a quintet featuring altoist Lou Donaldson and pianist Elmo Hope ("De-Dah" and "Brownie Speaks" are the most memorable). There is an alternate take of "Get Happy" with a sextet headed by trombonist J.J. Johnson, and the remaining five titles have Brown teamed in a sextet with altoist Gigi Gryce and tenor saxophonist Charlie Rouse. Of the latter, "Easy Living" and "Cherokee" are classics. Although superseded by later reissues, this set has more than its share of superb music. —*Scott Yanow*

Complete Blue Note-Pacific Jazz / Jun. 9, 1953-Aug. 13, 1954 / Pacific Jazz ✦✦✦✦✦
This four-CD set has the exact same music as an earlier Mosaic five-LP box, but is highly recommended to those listeners not already possessing the limited-edition set. Trumpeter Clifford Brown is heard on the most significant recordings from the first half of his tragically brief career. Whether co-leading a date with altoist Lou Donaldson, playing as a sideman with trombonist J.J. Johnson, interacting with an all-star group of West Coast players, or jamming with the first (although unofficial) edition of Art Blakey's Jazz Messengers (a two-disc live performance with a quintet that also includes the drummer/leader, Donaldson and pianist Horace Silver), Brown is the main star. Highlights are many, including versions of "Brownie Speaks," Elmo Hope's "De-Dah," "Cherokee," "Get Happy," "Daahoud" and "Joy Spring." The attractive packaging, with its 40 pages of text and many rare pictures, is an added bonus. —*Scott Yanow*

Memorial / Jun. 11, 1953+Sep. 15, 1953 / Original Jazz Classics ✦✦✦✦✦
This CD reissues a Prestige LP plus a "new" alternate take of "Choose Now." Trumpeter Clifford Brown is heard in two unusual and unrelated sessions. On four selections, Brown is featured with arranger/pianist Tadd Dameron's Orchestra; other soloists include Benny Golson on tenor and altoist Gigi Gryce. The other date was recorded in Sweden while Brown was touring with Lionel Hampton's Orchestra. Clifford Brown and fellow trumpeter Art Farmer play four Quincy Jones arrangements with a Swedish group that includes altoist Arne Domnérus, baritonist Lars Gullin and pianist Bengt Hallberg. "Lover Come Back to Me" really cooks and Brownie and Farmer get to trade off in exciting fashion during "'Scuse These Blues." —*Scott Yanow*

Memorial [Blue Note] / Aug. 28, 1953+Jun. 9, 1953 / Blue Note ✦✦✦
This was a grab bag of sessions Clifford Brown cut for Blue Note in the '50s with many great players, among them Lou Donaldson, Art Blakey, Gigi Gryce, Charlie Rouse, and Elmo Hope. This has been reissued on a double CD, although there was some material from this date also released on the vinyl album *Alternate Takes* that has not yet been reissued on disc. —*Ron Wynn*

The Paris Collection, Vol. 1 / Sep. 28, 1953-Sep. 29, 1953 / Inner City ✦✦✦
This out-of-print Inner City LP mostly duplicates material available on two Original Jazz Classics CDs although it does include one song ("Deltitnu") not included because trumpeter Clifford Brown does not solo. Three of the songs (plus two alternate takes) feature a big band headed by altoist Gigi Gryce and have both Americans from the 1953 Lionel Hampton Orchestra (including Brown, trumpeter Art Farmer, trombonist Jimmy Cleveland and tenorman Clifford Solomon) and

French players (such as pianist Henri Renaud and bassist Pierre Michelot). "Brown Skins" and the trade-offs by Brown and Farmer on "Keeping Up with Jonesy" (which was arranged and composed by the young Quincy Jones) are noteworthy. The second side showcases Brown and Gryce in a sextet with four songs plus two alternates; "I Cover the Waterfront" and the two versions of "All the Things You Are" are among the high points. But since the material is available elsewhere, this hard-to-find LP can be skipped by. —*Scott Yanow*

Clifford Brown Big Band in Paris / Sep. 28, 1953-Oct. 11, 1953 / Original Jazz Classics ✦✦✦✦
Although Lionel Hampton forbid his sidemen from recording during their trip to France in 1953, many of the musicians fortunately ignored his orders; the band broke up soon anyway. Trumpeter Clifford Brown is heard on this LP mostly with a big band actually put together by Gigi Gryce. A few of these tracks are excerpts but the two takes of "Brownskins" and "Keeping up with Jonesy" are fairly long as is a nearly eight-minute "Chez Moi." The music is not essential but Brownie did not live long enough to record anything less than excellent. —*Scott Yanow*

The Clifford Brown Sextet in Paris / Sep. 29, 1953-Oct. 8, 1953 / Original Jazz Classics ✦✦✦✦✦
While in Paris with Lionel Hampton's Orchestra, trumpeter Clifford Brown teamed up with altoist Gigi Gryce and a top-notch rhythm section (which includes pianist Henri Renaud, guitarist Jimmy Gourley, bassist Pierre Michelot and drummer Jean-Louis Viale) for two fine sessions that are reissued in full (other than a couple of rare alternate takes) on this enjoyable CD. Although Gryce was not a major soloist, he held his own with the trumpeter and was a talented composer. Most of the songs on this date are his including "Minority" (Gryce's most famous original). But it is for Brownie's brilliant playing on such tunes as "All the Things You Are," "I Cover the Waterfront" and "Minority" that this CD is most significant. —*Scott Yanow*

Clifford Brown / Oct. 8, 1953 / Inner City ✦✦✦
This out-of-print LP from the defunct Inner City label has the complete contents of a sextet session co-led by trumpeter Clifford Brown and altoist Gigi Gryce; the rhythm section consists of pianist Henri Renaud, guitarist Jimmy Gourley, bassist Pierre Michelot and drummer Jean-Louis Viale. Of the eight performances, six are available on a CD in the Original Jazz Classics series but there are also two previously unissued alternate takes: one apiece of "Minority" and "Baby." Every performance by the ill-fated trumpeter is valuable and Brownie is in good form on these Gigi Gryce originals (which include three versions of "Minority"). However due to the scarcity of this LP and the many alternate takes (eight performances of just four songs), this album is not essential except for Clifford Brown completists. —*Scott Yanow*

The Best of Max Roach and Clifford Brown in Concert / Apr. 1954-Aug. 30, 1954 / GNP ✦✦✦✦✦
This set has the earliest documented performances of the Clifford Brown/Max Roach Quintet. Trumpeter Brown and drummer Roach, along with tenor saxophonist Teddy Edwards, pianist Carl Perkins and bassist George Bledsoe, perform four numbers including hot versions of "All God's Chillun Got Rhythm" and Edwards' "Sunset Eyes." In addition there is a later set with the permanent lineup of the Quintet: Brown, Roach, tenorman Harold Land, pianist Richie Powell and bassist George Morrow. Together they play "Jordu," Brown's feature on "I Can't Get Started" and versions of "I Get a Kick Out of You" and "Parisian Thoroughfare" that are both heated and colorful. This is a very rewarding and somewhat historic release of high-quality straightahead jazz from one of the great hard-bop bands. —*Scott Yanow*

Brown and Roach, Inc. / Aug. 2, 1954-Aug. 6, 1954 / EmArcy ✦✦✦✦
The first of the EmArcy recordings of the Clifford Brown/Max Roach Quintet (which has been reissued in several ways on CD), this LP features trumpeter Brown, drummer Max Roach, tenor saxophonist Harold Land, pianist Richie Powell and bassist George Morrow in fine form. High points include "Stompin' at the Savoy," "I Get a Kick Out of You" and Brownie's ballad feature on "Ghost of a Chance." Near-classic music from a legendary group. —*Scott Yanow*

Jordu / Aug. 2, 1954-Feb. 25, 1955 / Trip ✦✦✦✦✦
The second EmArcy album by the quintet co-led by trumpeter Clifford Brown and drummer Max Roach (music that has been reissued in full on a massive ten-CD set), this Trip LP has quite a few memorable performances, particularly a colorful rendition of "Parisian Thoroughfare," definitive versions of Brownie's compositions "Joy Spring" and "Daahoud" and a heated "Blues Walk." This set (which is essential in one form or another) is a classic. —*Scott Yanow*

More Study in Brown / Aug. 3, 1954-Feb. 16, 1956 / Trip✦✦
This LP is less valuable now that it has been succeeded by EmArcy's massive ten-CD set *Brownie.* Comprised mostly of alternate takes with a few previously unissued items, these tracks feature the classic Clifford Brown-Max Roach Quintet of

1954-56. Best is a "new" version of "I'll Remember April" that also features tenor saxophonist Sonny Rollins and a fully restored "Jordu." But get the EmArcy "complete" set instead. —*Scott Yanow*

☆ **Brownie: The Complete EmArcy Recordings of Clifford Brown** / Aug. 3, 1954-Feb. 25, 1956 / EmArcy ♦♦♦♦♦
Although undoubtedly an expensive acquisition, this ten-CD set is perfectly done and contains dozens of gems. The remarkable but short-lived trumpeter Clifford Brown has the second half of his career fully documented (other than his final performance) and he is showcased in a wide variety of settings. The bulk of the numbers are of Brownie's Quintet with co-leader and drummer Max Roach, either Harold Land or Sonny Rollins on tenor, pianist Richie Powell and bassist George Morrow (including some previously unheard alternate takes) but there is also much more. Brown stars at several jam sessions (including a meeting with fellow trumpeters Clark Terry and Maynard Ferguson), accompanies such singers as Dinah Washington, Helen Merrill and Sarah Vaughan and is backed by strings on one date. Everything is here including classic versions of "Parisian Thoroughfare," "Joy Spring," "Daahoud," "Coronado," a ridiculously fast "Move," "Portrait of Jenny," "Cherokee," "Sandu," "I'll Remember April" and "What Is This Thing Called Love." Get this set while it stays in print. —*Scott Yanow*

Best Coast Jazz / Aug. 11, 1954 / Trip ♦♦♦♦♦
The music on this out-of-print Trip LP has been reissued on CD, most notably in a ten-CD set of Clifford Brown's EmArcy recordings. This particular album features an all-star group with trumpeter Brown, the altos of Herb Geller and Joe Maini, Walter Benton on tenor, pianist Kenny Drew, bassist Curtis Counce and drummer Max Roach. They perform two lengthy numbers, a medium-tempo blues "Coronado" and the ballad "You Go to My Head." "Coronado" is climaxed by an exciting trade-off by the four horns that gets down to two beats apiece! "You Go to My Head" has fine solos all around but Brownie's closing statement cuts everyone. —*Scott Yanow*

Jazz Immortal / Aug. 13, 1954 / Pacific Jazz ♦♦♦
Sextet. This album includes some takes and Brown material unavailable elsewhere. —*Ron Wynn*

Jam Session / Aug. 14, 1954 / EmArcy ♦♦♦♦♦
The lineup of this jam session is quite remarkable: trumpeters Clifford Brown, Clark Terry and Maynard Ferguson, altoist Herb Geller, tenor saxophonist Harold Land, Richie Powell or Junior Mance on piano, Keter Betts or George Morrow on bass and drummer Max Roach. A nearly 15-minute "What Is This Thing Called Love" gives one the opportunity to compare the three very different trumpeters, "Darn That Dream" is a ballad feature for singer Dinah Washington, "Move" is taken at an incredible tempo which holds up for 14 minutes and this set concludes with a four-song ballad medley; Brownie's playing on "It Might as Well Be Spring" is classic. A brilliant set that is highly recommended (and included in full on Clifford Brown's ten-CD EmArcy box). —*Scott Yanow*

Clifford Brown with Strings / Jan. 18, 1955-Jan. 20, 1955 / EmArcy ♦♦♦
There are two schools of thought regarding this Clifford Brown with strings session (which has been reissued on CD). Brownie plays quite beautifully and shows off his warm tone on such numbers as "Portrait of Jenny," "Memories of You," "Embraceable You" and "Stardust." But on the other hand the string arrangements by Neal Hefti border on Muzak and Brown never really departs from the melody. So the trumpeter's tone is the only reason to acquire this disc which to this listener is a slight disappointment, not living up to its potential. —*Scott Yanow*

A Study in Brown / Feb. 23, 1955-Feb. 25, 1955 / EmArcy♦♦♦♦
This CD reissue features the 1955 version of the Clifford Brown/Max Roach Quintet, a group also including tenor saxophonist Harold Land, pianist Richie Powell and bassist George Morrow. One of the premiere early hard-bop units, this band had unlimited potential. Highlights of this set are "Cherokee" (during which trumpeter Brownie is brilliant), "Swingin'" and "Sandu." All of the group's recordings (which have been included in the Clifford Brown ten-CD box set) are well worth acquiring. —*Scott Yanow*

At Basin Street / Jan. 4, 1956-Feb. 17, 1956 / EmArcy ♦♦♦♦♦
The last official album by the Clifford Brown/Max Roach Quintet is the only one that featured the great Sonny Rollins on tenor. With pianist Richie Powell and bassist George Morrow completing the group, this CD reissue is a hard-bop classic. Brownie and Rollins fit together perfectly on memorable versions of "What Is This Thing Called Love," "I'll Remember April" and a witty arrangement of "Love Is a Many Splendored Thing." Highly recommended. —*Scott Yanow*

Pure Genius / 1956 / Elektra ♦♦♦♦
The release of this LP in 1982 doubled the total recorded output by this classic group. Trumpeter Clifford Brown and drummer Max Roach had been co-leading a hard-bop quintet since 1954 but tenor saxophonist Sonny Rollins had just joined up and together they recorded just one studio album (not counting a date under

Rollins' leadership) before Brownie's death along with pianist Richie Powell in a tragic car accident. The live performances on this album, put out for the first time in 1982, add to this group's legacy and are reasonably well recorded. In addition to a remake of "I'll Remember April," the date includes lyrical and often-exciting versions of "What's New," "Daahoud," "Lover Man" and "52nd Street Theme." This important music is long overdue to be reissued on CD. —*Scott Yanow*

Donald Brown

b. Mar. 28, 1954, Hernando, MI
Piano / Hard Bop
A fine pianist and an educator, Donald Brown has also been a prolific composer. He grew up in Memphis and actually started out on drums and trumpet. By the time he attended Memphis State University (1972-75) he was playing jazz piano. After years of local work Brown replaced James Williams with the Jazz Messengers (1981-82) before arthritis forced him to leave. He has since taught at Berklee (1983-85) and the University of Tennessee (starting in 1988), recorded albums as a leader for Sunnyside and Muse, and had his compositions performed and recorded by a wide variety of top modern jazz players. —*Scott Yanow*

Early Bird / Jun. 4, 1987-Jun. 5, 1987 / Sunnyside ♦♦♦♦
Pianist Donald Brown, who has been often overshadowed by his contemporaries, is a talented modern mainstream pianist with a sound of his own. This CD, his debut as a leader, features Brown in a sextet that also stars altoist Donald Harrison (quite exploratory), trumpeter Bill Mobley, vibraphonist Steve Nelson and Wynton Marsalis' rhythm section of the time (bassist Bob Hurst and drummer Jeff "Tain" Watts). Together they perform six of Brown's diverse and generally colorful originals, plus "Speak Low" and the pianist's solo showcase "If You Could See Me Now." It's an impressive and enjoyable outing. —*Scott Yanow*

The Sweetest Sounds / Jun. 1988 / Jazz City ♦♦♦
With the exception of "Embraceable You" (one of two songs on this CD that are "bonus" cuts not on the LP version), pianist Donald Brown wrote all of the material. The strong quintet (which also features Eddie Henderson and altoist Gary Bartz) really digs into the diverse originals which are often reminiscent of a Blue Note date circa 1967. —*Scott Yanow*

Sources of Inspiration / Aug. 11, 1989 / Muse ♦♦♦
People Music / Mar. 19, 1990-Mar. 21, 1990 / Muse ♦♦♦
Fine 1990 date by a Memphis pianist. He plays nice bluesy chords and gospel-influenced phrases, but is also an effective straightahead and hard-bop improviser. He's backed by a large group that features an interesting configuration with a trumpet/alto sax/vibes front line, and also uses vocals at times. Vincent Herring plays with fire on alto, while Steve Nelson adds a different dimension on vibes. —*Ron Wynn*

Cause & Effect / Aug. 16, 1991-Aug. 18, 1991 / Muse ♦♦♦
Send One Your Love / 1992 / Muse ♦♦♦♦
Pianist Donald Brown continues to play with authority, bluesy edge and gusto, and his writing remains intriguing, even though only three of the nine numbers on this disc are originals. Instead, he displays his ability to interpret and lead his group through quality versions of classics by Benny Golson ("Whisper Not") and Barry Harris ("Crazeology"), plus a contemporary number from Mulgrew Miller ("The Sequel"). Brown's playing on Stevie Wonder's title track and the standards "The Second Time Around" and "The Sweetest Sounds" caresses the melody, then takes off and presents his impressive variations and statements. —*Ron Wynn*

● **Cartunes** / Sep. 2, 1993 / Muse ♦♦♦♦

Jeri Brown

b. 1952, Mississippi
Vocals / Standards, Bop
One of the top up-and-coming jazz singers of the 1990s, the Montreal-based Jeri Brown came from a musical family (her grandfather played sax and her uncle was a trumpeter). After growing up in St. Louis and graduating college, she toured Europe singing light opera and spirituals before switching to jazz. An excellent scat singer and an expressive interpreter of lyrics, Jeri Brown has recorded several excellent sets for Justin Time. —*Scott Yanow*

Mirage / 1991 / Justin Time ♦♦♦
● **Unfolding the Peacocks** / Feb. 1992 / Justin Time ♦♦♦♦♦
A talented improviser blessed with a lovely voice and a wide range, Jeri Brown's expressive powers are heard at their best on this set during her lengthy wordless interplay with Michel Dubeau's flute on "The Peacocks" and on the two bop-era standards "If You Could See Me Now" and "Woody 'n You." Backed by pianist Kirk Lightsey, guitarist Peter Leitch, bassist Rufus Reid and drummer Wali Muhammad,

Music Map

Big Bands

First Important Jazz Big Bands
Fletcher Henderson
Paul Whiteman

1920s

Jean Goldkette	McKinney's Cotton
King Oliver	Pickers
Ben Pollack	Bennie Moten

Beyond Category
Duke Ellington

Early Swing Bands

Earl Hines	Luis Russell
Cab Calloway	Casa Loma Orchestra
Benny Carter	Jimmy Lunceford
Don Redman	

Swing Era

Benny Goodman	Tommy Dorsey
Jimmy Dorsey	Chick Webb
Louis Armstrong	Artie Shaw
Count Basie	Glenn Miller
Charlie Barnet	Andy Kirk
Bob Crosby	Harry James
Erskine Hawkins	Jay McShann
Gene Krupa	Lionel Hampton
Buddy Johnson	

Bop-Era Big Bands
Billy Eckstine
Dizzy Gillespie
Woody Herman (First and Second Herds)
Claude Thornhill
Boyd Raeburn
Machito

Uncategorizable
Stan Kenton

1950s
Count Basie • Dizzy Gillespie • Maynard Ferguson

1960s
Gerry Mulligan Concert Jazz Band
Gerald Wilson
Buddy Rich
Don Ellis
Thad Jones-Mel Lewis Orchestra
Kenny Clarke-Francy Boland

Avant-Garde Orchestras
Sun Ra Arkestra
Jazz Composers Orchestra
Charlie Haden's Liberation Music Orchestra
Globe Unity Orchestra
Anthony Braxton's Creative Music Orchestra
Vienna Art Orchestra
George Gruntz Concert Jazz Band
Pierre Dorge's New Jungle Orchestra
David Murray Big Band
Maria Schneider
London Jazz Composers Orchestra

1970s
Toshiko Akyoshi/Lew Tabackin
Gil Evans
Bill Watrous
Louie Bellson
Bill Berry

1980s
Capp-Pierce Juggernaut
Rob McConnell's Boss Brass
Jaco Pastorius' Word Of Mouth Orchestra
Illinois Jacquet
Irakere
Mel Lewis

1990s
Mingus Big Band
McCoy Tyner
Carla Bley's Rather Large Orchestra
Bob Florence's Limited Edition
Clayton-Hamilton Jazz Orchestra
Bill Holman
Either/Orchestra

Brown does overwhelm "Orange Colored Sky" a bit to humorous effect but otherwise is in superlative form throughout the impressive date. —*Scott Yanow*

Fresh Start / May 1995-Dec. 1995 / Justin Time ◆◆◆
Jeri Brown is a talented singer with an original scatting style and a wide range. The problem with this particular record is that the material (half of which was co-written by Brown herself) is often not worthy of her. "Come, Come and Play with Me" is an off-the-mark attempt to play the role of a sex symbol, the irony in Tadd Dameron's obscure "You're a Joy" is greatly lessened by the repetition and most of the other selections are forgettable. Brown fares best on the two most familiar

tunes (Artie Shaw's "Moonray" and a wordless "Bohemia After Dark") while a few of the funkier pieces (with Cyrus Chestnut on electric keyboards) are rather dull. Some listeners may enjoy this set but in general I recommend checking out Jeri Brown's earlier releases first. —*Scott Yanow*

April in Paris / Apr. 28, 1996-Apr. 29, 1996 / Justin Time ◆◆◆◆
Jeri Brown, who has emerged to become one of the top jazz singers of the 1990s, pays tribute to the passion of Paris on this CD without performing the title cut. Sticking to ballads (other than a medium-tempo "Summertime"), Brown's sensuous voice (particularly her low notes) are well suited to the complex material,

which includes a song co-written with Kenny Wheeler ("Gentle Piece"), a pair of Michel Legrand numbers that add the effective accordion of Roberto De Brashov, a brief poem, a couple of standards and mostly high-quality obscurities. The music is atmospheric and sometimes haunting, swinging lightly and filled with subtle invention by the talented singer and her supportive trio. —*Scott Yanow*

Lawrence Brown

b. Aug. 3, 1907, Lawrence, KS, d. Sep. 5, 1988, New York City, NY
Trombone / Swing

One of the great swing trombonists, Lawrence Brown tends to be underrated because he spent so much of his career with Duke Ellington's Orchestra. Actually Brown's initial solos with Ellington upset some of Duke's fans because it was feared that his virtuosity did not fit into a band where primitive effects and mutes were liberally utilized. But over time Brown carved out his own place in the Ellington legacy.

Lawrence Brown learned piano, violin and tuba before deciding to stick to the trombone. He recorded with Paul Howard's Quality Serenaders (1929-30) and Louis Armstrong (with Les Hite's Orchestra in 1930) in Los Angeles before joining Ellington in 1932, staying until 1951 when he left to join Johnny Hodges' new small group. After 1955 Brown became a studio musician in New York but then spent 1960-70 back with Ellington (where he reluctantly had to play some solos with a plunger mute) before retiring. Although he only led two albums of his own (a 1955-56 outing for Clef and 1965's *Inspired Abandon* for Impulse), Brown was well featured on many recordings with Ellington through the years; "The Sheik of Araby" (1932) and "Rose of the Rio Grande" (1938) were favorites. —*Scott Yanow*

Inspired Abandon / Mar. 8, 1965 / Impulse! ◆◆◆◆

Les Brown (Lester Raymond Brown)

b. Mar. 14, 1912, Reinerton, PA
Leader / Swing

The leader of a first-class jazz-oriented dance band for nearly 60 years, Les Brown's music was never innovative but was generally quite pleasing. While attending Duke University in 1935 he put together his first big band, the Duke Blue Devils. After the group broke up in 1936, Brown worked as an arranger before forming a permanent orchestra in 1938. Influenced by the swing of Benny Goodman but gradually forging its own sound, the Les Brown Orchestra had major hits in "Sentimental Journey" (featuring Doris Day in 1944) and a catchy arrangement of "I've Got My Love to Keep Me Warm." Several excellent soloists spent time with the band (including Abe Most and Ted Nash). In 1947 Brown started working with Bob Hope and the association, although putting the band in a subsidiary role, made it possible for the orchestra to stay together for so many decades. The Dave Pell Octet, which was quite popular in the mid-'50s, comprised some of Brown's sidemen. —*Scott Yanow*

The Early Years / Nov. 25, 1936-Sep. 1937 / Golden Era ◆◆◆

Les Brown's first traveling band, the Blue Devils, are showcased on this out-of-print LP. These radio transcriptions feature Brown's no-name crew on 14 jazz-oriented selections including such numbers as "The Big Apple," "Let 'Er Go," "52nd Street Fever," "House Hop," "Dancing with a Debutante" and "Rigamarole." Although not flawless, these performances will certainly be enjoyed by swing collectors. Brown would soon break up his orchestra before trying again a year later. —*Scott Yanow*

Doris Day with Les Brown / Nov. 28, 1940-Sep. 14, 1946 / Columbia ◆◆◆◆

This CD gives listeners a sampling of Doris Day's recordings when she was the band vocalist with Les Brown's Orchestra during 1940-41 and 1945-46. Unfortunately the breezy liner notes do not bother to list the orchestra's personnel or even give recording dates but the music is generally worth hearing. Doris Day's big hit ("Sentimental Journey") is not on this disc but there are fine versions of "Aren't You Glad You're You," "Come to Baby, Do," "We'll Be Together Again" and "It Could Happen to You" among the 16 songs. Fine music, lousy packaging. —*Scott Yanow*

Les Brown and His Greatest Vocalists / May 22, 1941-Nov. 14, 1950 / Columbia/Legacy ◆◆

This okay sampler features the Les Brown Orchestra (a superior dance band that sometimes played jazz) in a supporting role behind some of their vocalists of the 1940s. Easily the best known is Doris Day whose "Sentimental Journey" is a classic. She is also featured on two other songs while Lucy Ann Polk ("Rock Me to Sleep") nails down second place. The other singers (who vary in quality and relevance) include the mildly humorous Butch Stone, Betty Bonney, Ralph Young, Gordon Drake, Jack Haskell, Eileen Wilson and Ray Kellogg. For collectors only. —*Scott Yanow*

● **Best of the Big Bands** / Sep. 17, 1941-Mar. 14, 1961 / Columbia ◆◆◆◆

As is often true of Columbia's early-'90s CD series titled *Best of the Big Bands*, the music is more rewarding than the packaging, illogical programming or vacuous liner notes. The recording dates and personnel of the 16 Les Brown recordings on this disc are inexcusably left off. However most of Brown's biggest hits are here (including his theme "Leap Frog," "Sentimental Journey," "Bizet Has His Day," "I've Got My Love to Keep Me Warm" and "My Dreams Are Getting Better All the Time") and the program (although not in chronological order) is consistently satisfying. This is the Les Brown CD to get, at least until a better reissue series comes along. —*Scott Yanow*

The Uncollected Les Brown & His Orchestra, Vol. 1 (1944-1946) / 1944-1946 / Hindsight ◆◆◆

The first of three Les Brown Hindsight LPs has radio transcriptions from 1944-46 when Brown's big band was at the height of its popularity. Doris Day takes five vocals (including "Sentimental Journey") and the orchestra plays a dozen jazz-oriented numbers (highlighted by "Flip Lid," "Lover's Leap," "I Can't Believe That You're in Love with Me" and "I've Got My Love to Keep Me Warm") plus their theme song "Leap Frog." These alternate renditions (which differ a bit from the band's famous records) should delight Les Brown and swing fans, if they can find the LP. —*Scott Yanow*

The Uncollected Les Brown & His Orchestra, Vol. 2 (1949) / 1949 / Hindsight ◆◆◆

The second of three Les Brown Hindsight LPs, like the third, features the Band of Renown during the height of the bebop era. These radio transcriptions are more modern than one would expect (although "Bopple Sauce" is the only overtly bop tune) and there are solos from such fine players as clarinetist Abe Most, trombonist Ray Sims, tenorman Dave Pell and trumpeter Frank Beach. Lucy Ann Polk takes six lightly swinging vocals and the band is well showcased on the concise (mostly under three-minute) instrumentals. All three of these Hindsight albums are easily recommended to swing collectors. —*Scott Yanow*

The Uncollected Les Brown & His Orchestra, Vol. 3 (1949) / 1949 / Hindsight ◆◆◆

By 1949 most of the surviving swing bands were incorporating some boppish ideas into their arrangements, even Les Brown's. This set of radio transcriptions (the third of three Hindsight Les Brown LPs) finds the Band of Renown playing such modern numbers as "Boptized," "Teasey Toe" and "Ah-Boo Ah-Boo." Lucy Ann Polk takes two vocals and there is one apiece from Butch Stone and Stumpy Brown but the instrumentals are the most memorable selections, often featuring trumpeters Wes Hensel and Frank Beach, trombonist Ray Sims, clarinetist Abe Most and tenorman Dave Pell. Bop fans who do not think of Les Brown as having a "modern" orchestra will find this music particularly interesting. —*Scott Yanow*

Lullaby in Rhythm / Dec. 1954-Jan. 1955 / Drive Archives ◆◆◆

Les Brown had one of his finest big bands during the mid-'50s but the previously unissued live performances heard on this CD are more notable for being among the first stereo recordings than for their musical content. The 14 selections (mostly veteran swing standards) are given overly concise interpretations and the danceable arrangements allocate relatively little space for solos. Trumpeter Don Fagerquist's three choruses on "Our Love Is Here to Stay" are a highlight while Jo Ann Greer does a good job on her three straightforward vocals. —*Scott Yanow*

Les Brown All-Stars / Jun. 15, 1955-Jun. 27, 1955 / Capitol ◆◆◆◆

22 Original Big Band Recordings (1957) / 1957 / Hindsight ◆◆◆

The 1957 Les Brown Orchestra is featured on this Hindsight CD which comprises concise (all but one of the 22 numbers are under three minutes) radio transcriptions. Brown always had a first-class dance band but none of the soloists are particularly distinctive. Best is singer Jo Ann Greer who always had a pleasing style, but this set is not too essential. —*Scott Yanow*

Les Brown and His Band of Renown / 1957 / Hindsight ◆◆

Although Les Brown gets top billing on this set of 1957 radio airchecks, his big band actually functions as a backup orchestra for singers Julie London, Jo Ann Greer, June Christy and (on "Oh Baby") band member Stumpy Brown; only "My Baby Just Cares for Me" is an instrumental. Each of the vocalists are in fine form with Greer holding her own with the better-known Christy and London. Since most of these selections are only about two minutes long, the band has little to do other than read its parts so this CD is recommended mostly to fans of the singers. —*Scott Yanow*

Digital Swing / Nov. 21, 1986+Dec. 8, 1986 / Fantasy ◆◆◆

To celebrate his 50th anniversary as a bandleader, Les Brown recorded what would be his only American record of the 1980s. This CD, which has 16 selections, mostly sticks to veteran standards although fortunately there are no remakes of earlier hits or any attempts at outright nostalgia. Among the main soloists during the instrumental set are trumpeter Don Rader, trombonist Andy Martin and guitarist Mundell Lowe. Jack Sperling drives the band on drums and two of Brown's earliest players (bass trombonist Stumpy Brown and baritonist Butch Stone) were still playing their parts although neither gets to solo or sing. This is a decent set that makes one wish that Les Brown had recorded more jazz during the past 30 years. —*Scott Yanow*

Anything Goes / 1990 / USA ✦✦
Smooth. Good sound quality. —*Ron Wynn*

Marion Brown

b. Sep. 8, 1935, Atlanta, GA
Alto Saxophone, Flute / Free Jazz, Avant-Garde
One of the brightest and most lyrical voices of the 1960s avant-garde, Marion Brown participated in many stimulating recordings during the '60s and '70s while never really becoming an influential force. He played alto in high school and in Army bands and attended Clark College. In 1965 Brown moved to New York and recorded the monumental *Ascension* with John Coltrane and *Fire Music* with Archie Shepp. Soon Brown was leading his own dates for ESP and Impulse. He worked with Sun Ra, lived in Europe during 1968-70 and in the early '70s in the US played with Leo Smith. Since recording with Gunter Hampel in 1983 and making an unaccompanied solo date in 1985, ill health has limited Marion Brown's musical activities. —*Scott Yanow*

Marion Brown Quartet / Nov. 1965 / ESP ✦✦✦✦✦
Altoist Marion Brown's debut as a leader is a typical ESP free-form blowout. He performs three numbers (two are quite lengthy) with either trumpeter Alan Shorter or tenor saxophonist Bennie Maupin (who was at the beginning of his career), both Ronnie Boykins and Reggie Johnson on basses and drummer Rashied Ali. The fiery performances feature the musicians stretching themselves and playing with great intensity; at this early point Marion Brown was already recognizable. —*Scott Yanow*

Why Not? / Oct. 23, 1966 / ESP ✦✦✦✦
Marion Brown's second of two ESP discs is an excellent showcase for his advanced alto in a quartet with pianist Stanley Cowell, bassist Norris Jones and drummer Rashied Ali. None of the four Brown compositions caught on elsewhere but they serve as fine vehicles for his adventurous flights. —*Scott Yanow*

Juba-Lee / Nov. 1966 / Fontana ✦✦✦

● **Three for Shepp** / Dec. 1, 1966 / Impulse! ✦✦✦✦✦
As a sort-of answer to Archie Shepp's album *Four for Trane*, altoist Marion Brown recorded *Three for Shepp*, a set split evenly between Brown and Shepp compositions. This LP (which is long overdue to be reissued on CD) features Brown interacting with either Dave Burrell or Stanley Cowell on piano, bassist Norris Jones and drummers Bobby Capp or Beaver Harris on drums. Although none of the selections (including the Shepp songs) ever became well known, Marion Brown is heard in prime form throughout the colorful performances. It seems strange that he would not get a chance to record for Impulse again until 1973. —*Scott Yanow*

Porto Nova / Dec. 13, 1967 / Arista ✦✦✦✦
This was one of altoist Marion Brown's best recordings. Although a very adventurous improviser, Brown usually brought lyricism and a thoughtful (if unpredictable) approach to his music. Accompanied by bassist Maarten van Regteben Altena and drummer Han Bennink for this stimulating session (recorded in Holland), Brown stretches out on five of his compositions and is heard at the peak of his creative powers. —*Scott Yanow*

Afternoon of a Georgia Faun / Aug. 10, 1970 / ECM ✦✦✦

Vista / Feb. 18, 1975-Feb. 19, 1975 / Impulse! ✦✦
Altoist Marion Brown, one of the potentially great high-energy saxophonists to emerge in the mid-'60s (he was on John Coltrane's famous *Ascension* record), has had somewhat of a directionless career. This out-of-print LP certainly boasts an impressive backup crew (including both Anthony Davis and Stanley Cowell on keyboards along with bassist Reggie Workman and some appearances by drummer Ed Blackwell) but does not seem to know what it wants to be. The solos are relatively short, there is a poppish vocal by Allen Murphy on a Stevie Wonder tune and little that is all that memorable actually occurs. Better to acquire Marion Brown's earlier recordings. —*Scott Yanow*

La Placita / Live in Willisau / Mar. 26, 1977 / Timeless ✦✦✦
For a time this European session by the underrated avant-garde altoist Marion Brown was available through Muse. Brown, who had never before recorded standards, is heard performing adventurous (and somewhat eccentric) renditions of "Sonnymoon for Two" and "Soft Winds" along with three diverse originals (including the somber "Fortunato") and one song by guitarist Brandon Ross. Brown, Ross, bassist Jack Gregg and drummer Steve McCraven recorded this music in Switzerland in 1977 as Brown, after making some notable recordings, was starting to drift

into obscurity. The overlooked set is one of Brown's better albums of the 1970s. —*Scott Yanow*

Solo Saxophone / Jul. 2, 1977 / Sweet Earth ✦✦✦✦✦
This obscure effort features altoist Marion Brown playing six unaccompanied solos during a 1977 concert. His renditions of "Hurry Sundown," "Angel Eyes" and his melodic original "And Then They Danced" are particularly memorable. Brown, whose lyrical approach to improvising contrasted with his adventurous flights, would soon fade away from the major jazz scene; in fact his solo recording was for a tiny label. This late-period LP is worth searching for by open-minded collectors. —*Scott Yanow*

Reed 'n Vibes / Jan. 1978 / IAI ✦✦✦
This 1978 session reunited vibist and flutist Gunther Hampel with alto saxophonist, flutist and percussionist Marion Brown, who previously recorded together in Europe in the late '60s. The two men acted/reacted with lines of notes which, because of their sensitivity, caused concepts like "tonality," "polytonality," "atonality" to become meaningless and give way to the overall term of "music." Hampel created rich full backdrops for his own ideas (his solo "And Then They Embraced") and for those of Brown. He literally ebbed and flowed on the vibes unlike any other practitioner of that instrument. His flute work showcased during the first section of "Flute Song" was also strong. Brown's alto playing, featured on his "Solo" and throughout the duets, was ever growing. "Solo" was a call-to-arms-like piece that Brown used as a vehicle for his explorations through the various ranges of the horn, always slying, bending and twisting, constantly stimulating. —*Milo Fine, Cadence*

Back to Paris / Feb. 14, 1980 / Freelance ✦✦✦
At La Dreher in Paris. Quartet with pianist Hilton Ruiz. Excellent, moving music. —*Michael G. Nastos*

Gemini / Jun. 1983 / Birth ✦✦✦

Recollections: Ballads and Blues for Saxophone / 1985 / Creative Works ✦✦✦

Native Land / Mar. 9, 1990-Mar. 10, 1990 / ITM ✦✦

Norman Brown

b. , Kansas City, MO
Guitar / R&B, Soul Jazz
A talented guitarist who plays in a style similar to George Benson's in the 1970s, Norman Brown has recorded several bestselling sets for the MoJazz label. He started playing guitar when he was eight and was already gigging while in high school. Signed to MoJazz in 1990, Brown has become a popular attraction, performing R&B-ish jazz, but has yet to develop his own sound. —*Scott Yanow*

Just Between Us / 1992 / MoJazz ✦✦✦

● **After the Storm** / 1994 / MoJazz ✦✦✦✦✦

Better Days Ahead / 1996 / Motown ✦✦✦
Although it isn't as focused or direct as *After the Storm*, *Better Days Ahead* showcases Norman Brown's growth as a musician. Brown seamlessly fuses jazz, R&B, pop and soul together, creating a distinctive hybrid that has the technique of an accomplished jazz musician and the accessibility of pop. The songs on *Better Days Ahead* aren't quite as memorable as those on *After the Storm*, but Brown's dazzling ability on the guitar makes it worthwhile listening. —*Stephen Thomas Erlewine*

Oscar Brown, Jr.

b. Oct. 10, 1926, Chicago, IL
Vocals / Standards
The multitalented Oscar Brown, Jr., has written several classic pieces including the lyrics to "Dat Dere," "Work Song," "Watermelon Man" and "The Entertainer" (the latter a bittersweet biography of Scott Joplin) and the compositions "Signifyin' Monkey" and "But I Was Cool." An important social commentator and playwright, Oscar Brown, Jr., acted on a regular network radio soap opera while in high school. After a wide variety of careers (including public relations, real estate, ad copy and running unsuccessfully for political office), he became a professional songwriter, starting with "Brown Baby" (which was recorded by Mahalia Jackson) and collaborating with Max Roach on the "Freedom Now Suite." A dramatic singer, Brown was signed to Columbia in 1960 where he recorded several classic albums. In 1962 he was the M.C. on the legendary *Jazz Scene USA* television series (some episodes of which have been made available on video). Brown has performed and written many shows through the years and served as artist-in-residence at several colleges. After recording steadily, he was off records altogether during 1975-94 until returning with *Then & Now* for the Weasel Disc label in 1995, a disc full of both fresh remakes and new material. —*Scott Yanow*

● **Sin & Soul & Then Some** / Jun. 20, 1960-Oct. 23, 1960 / Columbia/Legacy ✦✦✦✦✦

Oscar Brown, Jr.'s debut recording, which was finally reissued on CD in 1996, is a true classic. A brilliant lyricist, a dramatic singer, and a highly individual genius in his own way, Brown performed a dozen memorable selections for this album. His lyrics to "Work Song," "Watermelon Man," "Afro-Blue" and particularly "Dat Dere" are famous, "But I Was Cool" and "Signifyin' Money" are humorous, "Bid 'Em In" is a chilling depiction of a slave auction, and "Rags and Old Iron" is quite touching. In addition to the original program, five previously unreleased selections from the same sessions (most of which were later remade) were added to this reissue, including four from the Brown musical *Kicks and Company*. Decades later, Oscar Brown, Jr., still performs many of these pieces. Essential music from an underrated great. —*Scott Yanow*

Then and Now / 1995 / Weasel ✦✦✦✦

Singer/lyricist/social commentator Oscar Brown, Jr., had been off records for 20 years when he finally had a chance to return to the studios. Brown recorded eight remakes of songs from his first two albums (*Sin & Soul* and *Between Heaven and Hell*), plus eight newer pieces. His lyrics are as relevant as ever, his voice was still very much in its prime, and the backup (a rhythm section with a few guests) gives him suitable accompaniment. Among the many highlights of this superb set are "Dat Dere," "Afro Blue," "Rags and Old Iron," "The Entertainer" and "Old Man." —*Scott Yanow*

Pete Brown (James Ostend Brown)

b. Nov. 9, 1906, Baltimore, MD, **d.** Sep. 20, 1963, New York, NY
Alto Saxophone / Swing

Pete Brown had an unusual and distinctive swing-based style that sometimes used staccato phrases which could be speechlike. Starting originally on piano and also for a time doubling on trumpet, Pete Brown's main ax was the alto by the time he came to New York in 1927 with Bernie Robinson's band. Brown worked many short-time engagements with obscure bandleaders in New York but, starting in the mid-'30s, he often teamed up on excellent records with the underrated trumpeter Frankie Newton. They were both members of the early version of John Kirby's small group in 1937 before departing. Brown worked steadily throughout the late '30s and '40s, often on 52nd Street and sometimes as a bandleader. However, the rise of bop in the mid-'40s resulted in him being neglected and ill health led to him being only semiactive in the 1950s. Brown's recorded appearance at the 1957 Newport Jazz Festival found him past his prime and being completely overshadowed by Coleman Hawkins and Roy Eldridge. It is best to search out Pete Brown's many sideman appearances on records from the late '30s, particularly a Newton session from 1939 with James P. Johnson. —*Scott Yanow*

1944 / Jan. 16, 1944 / Progressive ✦✦✦✦

On January 16, 1944, altoist Pete Brown recorded some transcriptions for radio airplay. Brown, who was at the peak of his powers during that year, and the spectacular trumpeter Jonah Jones fronted a lesser-known rhythm section comprising pianist Zed Jackson, bassist Dallas Bartley and drummer Edward Nicholson. Every note they played that day was released for the first time on this 1997 CD. In addition to the eight accepted versions of tunes, including such likable riff originals as "Said Zed" and "That's the Lick," plus "Rosetta" and "Lowdown Blues," which has a rare Brown vocal, the CD also has four false starts, five incomplete performances and eight full-length alternate takes. Due to the many truncated versions, it is recommended that one eventually program their CD player to play only the accepted (and very enjoyable) versions. Brown and Jones made for a very potent team on these hot swing numbers. —*Scott Yanow*

● **Harlem Jump and Swing** / Nov. 16, 1954-Dec. 1954 / Affinity ✦✦✦✦

Other than the 1942-45 period, altoist Pete Brown only led three record sessions in his career, and his last one (from 1961) was actually originally put out under guitarist Bernard Addison's name. This particular LP (imported from England) finds Brown and his sextet (which includes the lyrical trumpeter Joe Wilder and pianist Wade Legge) sharing the album with a couple of sessions headed by trumpeter Jonah Jones from the same period. Brown's half of the record consists of five swing standards and a couple of blues, and although there are touches of bop, the music is essentially mainstream. Actually, the Jonah Jones tracks (three of the seven of which also feature clarinetist Edmond Hall and trombonist Vic Dickenson) are more extroverted and memorable, with plenty of spectacular trumpet playing on such tunes as "Beale Street Blues," "Down by the Riverside" and "J.J. Special." —*Scott Yanow*

Pete's Last Date / Oct. 21, 1961 / 77 ✦✦✦✦

Originally put out under guitarist Bernard Addison's leadership, this LP (which overlaps with but only partly duplicates the mono 77 album of the same name) features the veteran swing altoist Pete Brown. Still in good form this late in his career (even if his jump style was out of date), Brown is showcased in a quintet

with trumpeter Johnny Letman, guitarist Addison (getting one of his rare opportunities to stretch out in later years), bassist Hayes Alvis and drummer Sonny Greer. Sticking to standards and fairly basic material, Brown and company sound quite upbeat during this spirited jam session. Easily recommended for mainstream collectors. —*Scott Yanow*

Ray Brown

b. Oct. 13, 1926, Pittsburgh, PA
Bass / Bop

The huge and comfortable sound of Ray Brown's bass has been a welcome feature on bop-oriented sessions for a half-century. He played locally in his native Pittsburgh in his early days.

Arriving in New York in 1945, on his first day in town Brown met and played with Dizzy Gillespie, Charlie Parker and Bud Powell! He was hired by Gillespie for his small groups and his big band; "One Bass Hit" and "Two Bass Hit" were early features and he can be seen with Dizzy in the 1947 film *Jiving in Bebop*. Although not a soloist on the level of an Oscar Pettiford, Brown's quick reflexes and ability to accompany soloists in a swinging fashion put him near the top of his field. After playing with Jazz at the Philharmonic, he married Ella Fitzgerald (their marriage only lasted during 1948-52) and for a time led his own trio to back the singer. Brown recorded with an early version of the Modern Jazz Quartet (under Milt Jackson's leadership) and then became a permanent member of the Oscar Peterson Trio (1951-66).

With Peterson the bassist travelled the world, guested with other top jazz artists, was featured on JATP tours, became famous and recorded constantly. He began playing cello in the late '50s and used it on a few of his own dates. After leaving Peterson, Brown settled in Los Angeles, worked in the studios, continued recording jazz and worked as a manager of several artists (including the Modern Jazz Quartet and Quincy Jones). He played with the L.A. 4 starting in 1974, did a great deal to revive the careers of Ernestine Anderson and Gene Harris and recorded extensively for Pablo and Concord. The Ray Brown Trio of the 1990s has featured pianists Gene Harris, Bennie Green and Geoff Keezer along with drummers Jeff Hamilton and Greg Hutchison, recorded for Concord and Telarc. —*Scott Yanow*

Much in Common/All Star Band / Jan. 22, 1962-Jan. 5, 1965 / Verve ✦✦✦

Bassist Ray Brown and vibraphonist Milt Jackson have been good friends for decades, collaborating on an occasional basis through the years. Three of their former LPs are reissued in full on this double CD. The first two sets (originally titled *Ray Brown with the All-Star Big Band* and *Ray Brown-Milt Jackson*) are big-band dates with most of the music arranged by either Ernie Wilkins or Oliver Nelson. Although Brown and Bags are generally well featured (the bassist switches to cello on three songs), other musicians also get their spots, most notably altoist Cannonball Adderley and his brother, cornetist Nat, who plays one of the earliest versions of the hit "Work Song." The second date finds Milt Jackson more as a co-equal with Brown; both contributed two songs to the eight-tune program. While those two sessions are strictly middle-of-the-road jazz, swinging but with no real surprises, the remaining set is a bit more unusual. The small-group date, which also features organist Wild Bill Davis or pianist Hank Jones, has an added bonus, the gospel vocals of Marion Williams on a few of the numbers. This was Williams' first recorded encounter with jazz musicians, and although she goes over the top in places, she emerges as the wild card (and most memorable aspect) of an otherwise well-played but unremarkable two-fer. —*Scott Yanow*

This One's for Blanton / Dec. 5, 1972 / Original Jazz Classics ✦✦✦✦

One of Duke Ellington's last small-group sessions (mistakenly dated on this album as Dec. 5, 1973), this is a set of duets between the pianist and bassist Ray Brown. Performed in tribute to bassist Jimmy Blanton, the duo plays "See See Rider," four of Ellington's standards (including "Pitter Panther Patter," which was originally recorded as an Ellington-Blanton duet) and the four movements of "Fragmented Suite for Piano and Bass." Brown's solid swing and large tone bring out the best in Ellington's playing, making this an enjoyable and consistently swinging date. —*Scott Yanow*

Brown's Bag / Dec. 1975 / Concord Jazz ✦✦✦

Bassist Ray Brown's debut for Concord (and his first recording as a leader in six years) features him with two separate groups: a quintet also including trumpeter Blue Mitchell, tenor saxophonist Richie Kamuca, pianist Art Hillery and drummer John Guerin and (on three of the seven songs) a quartet with keyboardist Dave Grusin, guitarist John Collins and drummer Jimmie Smith. While the former group has some hot moments (particularly on "Blues for Eddie Lee" and "Surrey with the Fringe on Top"), the latter band sticks to dreamy ballads. The fact that this CD reissue has less than 35 minutes is a minus; plus none of the selections are really all that memorable despite the strong playing. Not one of the more significant Ray Brown albums. —*Scott Yanow*

As Good As It Gets / Dec. 22, 1977 / Concord Jazz ✦✦✦
Although the title of this CD reissue has a bit of bragging, this is an excellent duet set which features bassist Ray Brown and pianist Jimmy Rowles. There are many subtle surprises on the set including Rowles' striding on "Like Someone in Love" and Brown's melodic lead on "Honey." Other highlights include "Sophisticated Lady," Rowles' "Looking Back," a playful version of "Love" and "Rosalie." Delightful music. —*Scott Yanow*

Something for Lester / Jun. 22, 1979-Jun. 24, 1979 / Original Jazz Classics ✦✦✦
This excellent trio session forms a sort of transition between bassist Ray Brown's work with the Oscar Peterson Trio and his own small-group sessions of the '80s and '90s. With pianist Cedar Walton and drummer Elvin Jones, Brown explores seven strong melodies (four standards, two by Walton and the bassist's "Slippery") in typically swinging and bluish fashion. —*Scott Yanow*

Live at the Concord Jazz Festival / Aug. 1979 / Concord Jazz ✦✦✦✦

Tasty / Oct. 22, 1979 / Concord Jazz ✦✦✦
The second of two duet albums by bassist Ray Brown and pianist Jimmy Rowles, this subtle and delightful CD reissue is the equal of the first. Rowles, who plays some surprising stride on "I'm Gonna Sit Right Down and Write Myself a Letter," shows his sly wit in several spots along with harmonic sophistication. Brown's huge tone is well displayed in the sparse setting. Highlights include "A Sleepin' Bee," "My Ideal" and "Nancy (With the Laughing Face)." —*Scott Yanow*

Ray Brown Three / Feb. 1982 / Concord Jazz ✦✦✦
Brown took a fresh approach for this 1982 date, retaining the trio format but substituting flute for drums and using Monty Alexander instead of regular pianist Gene Harris. The results were intriguing; Most provided colors and sounds that haven't been on a Brown date since, while Alexander added some Caribbean flavor and a bit more adventurous sound. —*Ron Wynn*

Soular Energy / Aug. 1984 / Concord Jazz ✦✦✦✦
This album is important as an early milestone in pianist Gene Harris' second career. Harris, who had led the popular Three Sounds in the 1960s, had been living in obscurity in Boise, Idaho, for several years before he was urged by bassist Ray Brown to come to the West Coast for some recording sessions. Harris became a permanent member of Brown's regular trio for quite a few years before launching his own quartet. He had lost none of his technique, soul or swing in the interim as he shows throughout this fine release. Seven of the eight numbers (highlighted by "Exactly Like You," "Teach Me Tonight" and "Sweet Georgia Brown") feature Brown, Harris and drummer Gerryck King playing soulful bop while "Mistreated But Undefeated Blues" adds guitarist Emily Remler and the tenor of Red Holloway. An excellent effort. —*Scott Yanow*

Bye Bye Blackbird / Apr. 1985 / Paddle Wheel ✦✦✦✦

Don't Forget the Blues / May 1985 / Concord Jazz ✦✦✦
Bassist Ray Brown heads an all-star quintet on this 1985 Concord release consisting of trombonist Al Grey, guitarist Ron Eschete, pianist Gene Harris and drummer Grady Tate. The majority of selections on the set are blues (including "Night Train," "Rocks in My Bed," "Jumpin' the Blues" and a pair of Brown originals) with "If I Could Be with You One Hour Tonight" being a temporary departure. Grey, Eschete, Harris and Brown have plenty of concise solos, Tate is typically excellent in support and the results should please straightahead jazz fans. —*Scott Yanow*

The Red Hot Ray Brown Trio / Nov. 1985-Dec. 1985 / Concord Jazz ✦✦✦
Bassist Ray Brown's 1985 trio (featuring pianist Gene Harris and drummer Mickey Roker) is heard in fine form throughout this swinging set. In addition to five standards and Brown's own blues "Captain Bill," there are a couple of unlikely but successful selections: Tyree Glenn's "How Could You Do a Thing Like This to Me" and "Love Me Tender." Although there is actually only one blues among the eight numbers, Gene Harris infuses all of the selections with the feeling of the blues and consistently steals the show. —*Scott Yanow*

Summer Wind: Live at the Loa / Jul. 1988 / Concord Jazz ✦✦✦✦
Brown's trio with Gene Harris (k) and Jeff Hamilton (d). Perhaps Brown's very best. —*Michael G. Nastos*

Bam Bam Bam / Dec. 1988 / Concord Jazz ✦✦✦
The Ray Brown Trio is caught on this CD live at a Tokyo concert and sounds obviously inspired by the enthusiastic crowd. The group (which also stars pianist Gene Harris and drummer Jeff Hamilton) stretches out on four standards, "Put Your Little Right Out," Victor Feldman's "Rio" and two Brown originals: "F.S.R. (For Sonny Rollins)" and the title cut. This release is a perfect introduction to the many fine Ray Brown-Gene Harris Concord recordings; it consistently swings with soul. —*Scott Yanow*

Black Orpheus / 1989 / Evidence ✦✦✦✦
Whether accompanying or leading a band, bassist Ray Brown has long been among jazz's greatest players. These cuts, mostly from 1989 except for two num-

bers done in 1991, feature Brown backing soulful pianist Gene Harris and steady drummer Jeff Hamilton on a program combining Afro-Latin material with standards from Johnny Mercer, Fats Waller and others, as well as an excellent rendition of Percy Mayfield's blues/R&B standard "Please Send Me Someone to Love." The songs are long enough to display each musician's skills, but not so lengthy that they become repetitious. It's a well-played, delightful example of the kind of high-powered material that's been Ray Brown's stock in trade. —*Ron Wynn*

Super Bass / 1989 / Capri ✦✦✦✦
This live Boston summit meeting between Ray Brown, Christian McBride and John Clayton was the logical outcome of several joint appearances, as well as an extension of a one-off bass troika track that McBride included on his first solo album. The idea of a bass trio on records probably would have been unthinkable in the primitive days of recording when Brown was coming up, but Telarc's fabulously deep yet clear engineering makes it seem like a natural thing to do. Whether pizzicato or bowed, whether taking the melodic solo or plunking down the 4/4 bottom line, all three perform with amazing panache, taste, humor, lack of ego, and the sheer joy of talking to and against each other beneath the musical staff. But if one has to pick out a single star, the choice has to be McBride, whose unshakeable time, solid tone and amazing ability to play his cumbersome bull fiddle like a horn stands out in astonishing fashion on the right speaker. On two tracks, the fleet-fingered Bennie Green and drummer Gregory Hutchinson join Brown to form a conventional trio that serves as an effective change of pace. It's a fun set without a doubt, but these guys are also clearly making coherent music, and that is what will hold our interest over the long haul. —*Richard S. Ginell*

Moore Makes 4 / May 22, 1990 / Concord Jazz ✦✦✦
The members of the Ray Brown Trio (the bassist-leader, pianist Gene Harris and drummer Jeff Hamilton) all grew to love the playing of tenor saxophonist Ralph Moore when the four were traveling as members of Gene Harris' big band. On this Ray Brown CD, the veteran bassist virtually turned over the entire session to Moore. The quartet performs a variety of veteran standards (including some from the bop era such as Charlie Parker's "Quasimodo" and Dizzy Gillespie's "The Champ") plus Wes Montgomery's "SOS" and Brown's "Ralph's Boogie." Ralph Moore rises to the occasion and shows that, even though his sound is inspired by John Coltrane, he was fully capable of playing tunes from the swing and bop era; Moore sounds delighted to have the Ray Brown Trio as his backup group. This is a fine collaboration that works quite well. —*Scott Yanow*

New Two Bass Hits / Apr. 29, 1991 / Capri ✦✦✦

Three Dimensional / Aug. 4, 1991 / Concord Jazz ✦✦✦
Excellent trio date with Brown's formidable bass interaction with drummer Jeff Hamilton and pianist Gene Harris. Harris plays with his usual bluesy punch and delicate touch, while Hamilton fits like a glove with Brown. This is heady, solidly professional material. —*Ron Wynn*

Bass Face / Apr. 1993 / Telarc ✦✦✦✦
For this Telarc CD, bassist Ray Brown and pianist Bennie Green split the solo chores almost evenly with drummer Jeff Hamilton, giving them stellar and creative support. Green has his best improvisations on "Phineas Can Be" and "Taking a Chance on Love" and the trio plays very close attention to dynamics (often swinging very quietly) and quickly reacting to each other's ideas. Rather than merely jamming the songs (the majority of which are standards), the bop-oriented group gives each melody a colorful framework filled with plenty of subtle surprises. —*Scott Yanow*

● **Don't Get Sassy** / Apr. 21, 1994-Apr. 22, 1994 / Telarc ✦✦✦✦
Bassist Ray Brown, pianist Bennie Green and drummer Jeff Hamilton make for a perfect team on their Telarc CD. The tight yet swinging arrangements are full of subtle surprises and serve as a perfect format for the players, particularly Green. Highlights include Thad Jones' "Don't Get Sassy," Oscar Peterson's "Kelly's Blues," "Tanga," "Brown's New Blues" and a three-song Duke Ellington medley. Recommended. —*Scott Yanow*

Some of My Best Friends Are...The Piano Players / Nov. 18, 1994+Nov. 21, 1994 / Telarc ✦✦✦
On his Telarc disc Ray Brown teams up with five different piano players but, rather than this being a tribute to the veteran bassist (who has solo space on every selection), the CD ends up being a celebration of the great Oscar Peterson because Bennie Green, Dado Moroni and Geoff Keezer have to, various degrees, based their styles on O.P. The individual standout is actually Ahmad Jamal who had never previously recorded with Brown. Together with Lewis Nash they perform two blues and "Love Walked In," all renditions that make a liberal use of space and pay close attention to dynamics. Bennie Green, who plays his "Ray of Light" along with two standards, had performed regularly with Brown in recent years and his selections offer few surprises. Dodo Moroni is fine on "My Romance" and inserts a bit of Erroll Garner on "Giant Steps" while Geoff Keezer (who had also

never played with Brown) swings well on "Close Your Eyes." The CD concludes with a reunion between Oscar Peterson (who had recently recovered from a stroke) and Brown on "St. Tropez" and the upbeat "How Come You Do Me Like You Do?" The results overall are pleasing and swinging (serving as a sampler of the pianists' styles) but not all that innovative. — *Scott Yanow*

Seven Steps to Heaven / May 22, 1995-May 23, 1995 / Telarc ✦✦✦✦✦
The Ray Brown Trio in 1995 featured pianist Bennie Green and drummer Gregory Hutchinson along with the leader/bassist. In the tradition of the mid-'50s Oscar Peterson Trio, the group featured tight arrangements with concise but consistently brilliant solos. For this Telarc session, guitairst Ulf Wakenius (a little reminiscent of Herb Ellis) fits in perfectly. Highlights include "Seven Steps to Heaven" and "Cottontail." — *Scott Yanow*

Some of My Best Friends Are . . . The Sax Players / Nov. 20, 1995-Feb. 13, 1996 / Telarc ✦✦✦✦
As a follow-up to bassist Ray Brown's previous record in which he collaborated with several of his favorite pianists, for this set he features six major saxophonists (tenors Joe Lovano, Ralph Moore, Joshua Redman and Stanley Turrentine plus altoists Benny Carter and Jesse Davis) on two songs apiece with his regular trio. Although more than 60 years separate the ageless Carter from Redman, each of the saxes originally developed their own voice in the straightahead jazz tradition. Highlights of the colorful set include Benny Carter's playful rendition of "Love Walked In," Moore's cooking solo on "Crazeology" (a Benny Harris bop classic which the record mistakenly lists as written by Bud Freeman), Davis ripping through "Moose the Mooche" and Turrentine's romp on the blues "Port of Rico." Pianist Bennie Green and drummer Gregory Hutchinson provide suitable accompaniment (Green's solos are consistently excellent) and all dozen of the songs are successful and swinging. As an extra bonus, on the latter part of the CD each of the saxophonists has a brief chat (between 26 seconds and a minute apiece) with Brown about their early influences. There is so much good feeling and obvious mutual respect shown that one wishes these talks were at least twice as long; the Benny Carter segment is most memorable. This well-conceived project is easily recommended. — *Scott Yanow*

Live at Scullers Jazz Club / 1996 / Telarc ✦✦✦
Staying young by working with the young, Ray Brown and cohorts Bennie Green (piano) and Greg Hutchinson (drums) lay down a set of jazz and pop standards at a club in a Boston DoubleTree Hotel. Though Brown is the leader and anchor of the date, quite obviously the pianist is going to dominate the act—and Green definitely puts on a show, wiping everyone out with the pyrotechnics of "You're My Everything," engaging in a gentle stride opening to "But Not for Me" and coming logically to a bombastic climax. Hutchinson is capable, swinging, and occasionally volatile, and Brown mostly steps back and gives these guys a firm underpinning, with a sly solo now and then ("Bye, Bye Blackbird." There are few surprises or deviations from the mainstream here, but a good time will be had by anyone who gives this a spin. — *Richard S. Ginell*

Ruth Brown

b. Jan. 30, 1928, Portsmouth, VA
Vocals / R&B, Jump Blues
They called Atlantic Records "the house that Ruth built" during the 1950s, and they weren't referring to the Sultan of Swat. Ruth Brown's regal hitmaking reign from 1949 to the close of the '50s helped tremendously to establish the New York label's predominance in the R&B field. Later, the business all but forgot her—she was forced to toil as domestic help for a time—but she's back on top now, her status as a postwar R&B pioneer (and tireless advocate for the rights and royalties of her peers) recognized worldwide.

Young Ruth Weston was inspired initially by jazz chanteuses Sarah Vaughan, Billie Holiday, and Dinah Washington. She ran away from her Portsmouth home in 1945 to hit the road with trumpeter Jimmy Brown, whom she soon married. A month with bandleader Lucky Millinder's orchestra in 1947 ended abruptly in Washington, D.C., when she was canned for delivering a round of drinks to members of the band. Cab Calloway's sister Blanche gave Ruth a gig at her Crystal Caverns nightclub and assumed a managerial role in the young singer's life. DJ Willis Conover dug Brown's act and recommended her to Ahmet Ertegun and Herb Abramson, bosses of a fledgling imprint named Atlantic.

Unfortunately, Brown's debut session for the firm was delayed by a nine-month hospital stay caused by a serious auto accident en route to New York that badly injured her leg. When she finally made it to her first date in May of 1949, she made up for lost time by waxing the torch ballad "So Long" (backed by guitarist Eddie Condon's band), which proved to be her first hit.

Brown's seductive vocal delivery shone incandescently on her Atlantic smashes "Teardrops in My Eyes" (an R&B chart-topper for 11 weeks in 1950), "I'll Wait for You" and "I Know" in 1951, 1952's "5-10-15 Hours" (another No. 1 rocker), the sem-

inal "(Mama) He Treats Your Daughter Mean" in 1953, and a tender Chuck Willis-penned "Oh What a Dream" and the timely "Mambo Baby" the next year. Along the way, Frankie Laine tagged her "Miss Rhythm" during an engagement in Philly. Brown belted a series of her hits on the groundbreaking TV program "Showtime at the Apollo" in 1955, exhibiting delicious comic timing while trading sly one-liners with emcee Willie Bryant (ironically, ex-husband Jimmy Brown was a member of the show's house band!).

After an even two dozen R&B chart appearances for Atlantic that ended in 1960 with "Don't Deceive Me" (many of them featuring hell-raising tenor sax solos by then-hubby Willis "Gator" Jackson), Brown faded from view. After raising her two sons and working a nine-to-five job, Brown began to rebuild her musical career in the mid-'70s. That comedic sense served her well during a TV sitcom stint co-starring with McLean Stevenson in *Hello, Larry;* in a meaty role in director John Waters' 1985 sock-hop satire film *Hairspray,* and during her 1989 Broadway starring turn in *Black and Blue* (which won her a Tony Award).

There have been more records for Fantasy in recent years (notably 1991's jumping *Fine and Mellow*), and a lengthy tenure as host of National Public Radio's "Harlem Hit Parade" and "BluesStage." Brown's nine-year ordeal to recoup her share of royalties from all those Atlantic platters led to the formation of the nonprofit Rhythm & Blues Foundation, an organization dedicated to helping others in the same frustrating situation.

Factor in all those time-consuming activities, and it's a wonder Ruth Brown has time to sing anymore. But she does (quite royally, too), her pipes mellowed but not frayed by the ensuing decades that have seen her rise to stardom not once, but twice. — *Bill Dahl*

Sweet Baby of Mine (1949-1956) / Apr. 6, 1949-Mar. 2, 1956 / Route 66 ✦✦✦✦✦
Excellent collection covering blues and R&B songs Brown did prior to becoming a huge hit artist for Atlantic in the late '50s. These were R&B gems, but such artists as Patti Page and Georgia Gibbs were covering them for the white market and Brown was locked out until 1957. But she enjoyed 11 Top Ten R&B hits, which are contained on this anthology. — *Ron Wynn*

★ **The Best of Ruth Brown [Rhino]** / May 25, 1949-Mar. 7, 1959 / Rhino ✦✦✦✦✦
For those who want a cheaper and more concise collection of her best Atlantic cuts than the two-CD *Miss Rhythm,* this superb 23-track CD has the cream of her '50s work, including no less than 19 Top Ten R&B singles. Charting her evolution from her jazzy debut, "So Long," through jump blues and early rock 'n' roll, it also adds a bonus of two previously unissued live cuts from 1959. — *Richie Unterberger*

★ **Miss Rhythm (Greatest Hits and More)** / May 25, 1949-Aug. 30, 1960 / Rhino ✦✦✦✦✦
They used to refer to Atlantic Records in its early years as "the house that Ruth built," and the 40 tracks inhabiting these two discs offer unassailable insight as to why. As one of the premier R&B divas of the early '50s, Brown's seductive, earthy style found her belting the rockers (the R&B chart-toppers "Teardrops From My Eyes," "Mama He Treats Your Daughter Mean," "5-10-15 Hours") and caressing the ballads ("So Long," "Have a Good Time," "Oh What a Dream"), backed by some of New York's finest session players (including then-hubby Willis "Gator" Jackson on scorching tenor sax). Covers 1949-1960 and takes Brown from the beginnings of R&B to the heyday of rock ("Wild Wild Young Men" is positively frantic, while the Bobby Darin-penned "This Little Girl's Gone Rockin'" is lightweight yet utterly charming). Essential stuff! — *Bill Dahl*

Late Date with Ruth Brown / Jan. 27, 1959-Feb. 5, 1959 / Atlantic ✦✦✦✦
Good after-hours, smoky blues and R&B session featuring Ruth Brown in prime form. Nobody, male or female, sang with more spirit, sass, and vigor than Brown during the '50s, and this session reminded those who had forgotten that Brown could also hold her own with sophisticated material as well as sexy stuff. — *Ron Wynn*

Have a Good Time / Jun. 10, 1988-Jun. 11, 1988 / Fantasy ✦✦✦✦
Ruth Brown, a top-selling artist in the 1950s, endured over two decades of relative obscurity before she began to be noticed again in 1988. Recorded live at the Cinegrill in Hollywood, Brown is assisted by a fine quintet (which includes tenor great Red Holloway, altoist Charles Williams and organist Bobby Forrester) for fresh remakes of some of her hits, along with some newer material. All of Brown's Fantasy CDs feature a mature singer still in her prime. Highlights of this particular release (her debut for the label) include "Gee Baby, Ain't I Good to You," "Teardrops from My Eyes," "When I Fall in Love" and "Mama He Treats Your Daughter Mean." — *Scott Yanow*

Blues on Broadway / Jun. 12, 1989-Jun. 13, 1989 / Fantasy ✦✦✦✦✦
Ruth Brown was starring on Broadway in *Black and Blue* when she recorded her second Fantasy set. The emphasis is on ancient standards (mostly from the 1920s) that predated Brown's rise as an R&B star in the 1950s. Assisted by trumpeter Spanky Davis, tenorman Red Holloway, trombonist Britt Woodman, a rhythm sec-

tion led by pianist/organist Bobby Forrester and (on three numbers) altoist Hank Crawford, Brown makes such songs as "Nobody Knows You When You're Down and Out," "If I Can't Sell It, I'll Keep Sittin' on It" and "Am I Blue" sound as if they were written for her. —*Scott Yanow*

Fine and Mellow / Apr. 1, 1991-Aug. 13, 1991 / Fantasy ✦✦✦✦
Nice contemporary effort with a strongly swinging R&B flavor running throughout. Ruth Brown goes back to the '40s (Louis Jordan's "Knock Me a Kiss," Dinah Washington's "Salty Papa Blues") and '50s (Brook Benton's "It's Just a Matter of Time," Jackie Wilson's "I'll Be Satisfied," the Lula Reed/Ray Charles dirge "Drown in My Own Tears") for much of the disc, paying loving tribute to her main lady Billie Holiday with the tasty title cut and delivering a pair of Duke Ellington numbers along the way. —*Bill Dahl*

Songs of My Life / Mar. 1993 / Fantasy ✦✦✦
Before Ruth Brown became an R&B and rock legend in the '50s, she was a jazz, blues, and gospel stylist. She shows that aspect of her talent on *The Songs of My Life*, a fine set produced by guitarist Rodney Jones, who also did the arrangements and conducted the backing band. While she displays her timing, interpretative skills, and still-impressive delivery and enunciation throughout, Brown also demonstrates on her rendition of Eric Clapton's "Tears in Heaven" that she retains an interest and awareness of contemporary songs that fit her style. Ruth Brown proves that it's not the song or the lyric but the singer who makes a tune work. —*Ron Wynn*

R&B = Ruth Brown / Jan. 20, 1997-Feb. 28, 1997 / Bullseye Blues ✦✦✦✦
This is laidback New Orleans rhythm & blues that packs more into what it doesn't do than most discs are able to capture on tape. Ruth Brown has a voice that has been honed to the sharpness of a microfine edge, as well as the timing and phrasing most singers only wish they could have. Listen to what she does with the Doc Pomus-George Fishhoff tune "Destination Heartbreak," a lesson in timing, phrasing, and intimation that would benefit most R&B singers. Then listen to the control and latent power of her voice on "Too Little Too Late." It's not just her voice and presence which shine here; it's also the musicianship of the stellar cast of New Orleans musicians backing her. The arrangers deserve special mention here—six songs are arranged and conducted by Wardell Quezegue, Victor Goines arranged four tunes, and Bobby Forrester did one. It may take a couple of listenings to get used to Ruth Brown's power in this laidback New Orleans style, but one is able to see all the subtle nuances under the pure power she normally sings with. —*Bob Gottlieb*

Tom Browne

b. 1954, New York, NY
Trumpet / Crossover Jazz, Hard Bop
Tom Browne was a familiar figure on the R&B charts during the 1979-89 period when he was recording pop-oriented material for GRP and Arista. Browne studied piano for a year when he was 11 and then switched to trumpet, attending New York City's High School of Music and Art. Originally interested in classical music, Browne discovered jazz while in college in the mid-'70s. He worked with Sonny Fortune, recorded with Lonnie Smith and then signed with GRP. Although influenced by Freddie Hubbard and occasionally recording a hard-bop number, most of Browne's output during that era was clearly geared towards the marketplace. A commercial pilot, Browne largely dropped out of music by the late '80s but came back in 1994, recording for Hip Bop in several settings including the credible jazz date *Another Shade of Browne*, which made one wonder, "What took so long?" —*Scott Yanow*

Browne Sugar / 1979 / GRP ✦✦✦✦
Straight fusion set by trumpeter Tom Browne, replete with double-tracked vocals and songs heavy on backbeats and light on solos. Everything is nicely played, and the album did do moderately well on charts and with Adult Contemporary audiences. —*Ron Wynn*

Love Approach / 1979 / GRP ✦✦✦

Magic / 1981 / Arista ✦✦

Yours Truly / 1981 / GRP ✦✦✦
During the early '80s, Tom Browne sold a lot of records playing R&B-ish dance music. Occasionally, he would display his Freddie Hubbard-inspired trumpet and hint at potential that he has yet to realize. This particular album was better than most, for in addition to throwaway tunes (five of the seven commercial numbers have forgettable vocals), Browne plays two John Coltrane songs (a swinging "Lazy Bird" and "Naima") with a sextet and fares fairly well. It is a pity that the remainder of the album is not on the same level. —*Scott Yanow*

Rockin' Radio / 1983 / Arista ✦

Tommy Gun / 1984 / Arista ✦

Mo' Jamaica Funk / 1994 / Hip Bop ✦✦

● **Another Shade of Browne** / Apr. 1996 / Hip Bop ✦✦✦✦
Tom Browne gained some fame for his R&Bish/funk recordings cut for Arista and GRP during 1979-86. In those days he would often record an occasional straightahead number in the middle of his crossover sets; 1981's *Yours Truly* has a fine version of "Lazy Bird." In 1986 Browne was dropped by GRP and since then he has become a commercial pilot. On the liner notes of his "comeback" album, he disavows his earlier recordings, saying that at heart he was a hard-bop player all along. During this 1996 set Browne, who is most influenced by Freddie Hubbard and Lee Morgan, occasionally has inventive ideas that his chops cannot quite play; it can be tough being a part-time player. The music is strictly straightahead in the Blue Note vein with plenty of solo space for Javon Jackson's tenor and pianist Larry Goldings and fine support offered by bassist Ron Carter and drummer Idris Muhammad. With the exception of "In a Sentimental Mood," all of the numbers were either composed by or associated with a trumpeter and, even with an occasional misstep, Tom Browne's playing in this setting is well worth hearing. —*Scott Yanow*

Dave Brubeck

b. Dec. 6, 1920, Concord, CA
Piano / Cool
Dave Brubeck has long served as proof that creative jazz and popular success can go together. Although critics who had championed him when he was unknown seemed to scorn him when the Dave Brubeck Quartet became a surprise success, in reality Brubeck never watered down or altered his music in order to gain a wide audience. Creative booking (being one of the first groups to play regularly on college campuses) and a bit of luck resulted in great popularity and Dave Brubeck today remains as one of the few household names in jazz.

From nearly the start Brubeck enjoyed utilizing polyrhythms and polytonality (playing in two keys at once). He had classical training from his mother but fooled her for a long period by memorizing his lessons and not learning to read music. He studied music at the College of the Pacific during 1938-42. Brubeck led a service band in General Patton's Army during World War II and then in 1946 he started studying at Mills College with the classical composer Darius Milhaud who encouraged his students to play jazz. During 1946-49 Brubeck led a group mostly consisting of fellow classmates and they recorded as the Dave Brubeck Octet; their music (released on Fantasy in 1951) still sounds advanced today with complex time signatures and some polytonality. The octet was too radical to get much work so Brubeck formed a trio with drummer Cal Tjader (who doubled on vibes) and bassist Ron Crotty. The trio's Fantasy recordings of 1949-51 were quite popular in the Bay Area but the group came to an end when Brubeck hurt his back during a serious swimming accident and was put out of action for months.

Upon his return in 1951, Brubeck was persuaded by altoist Paul Desmond to make the group a quartet. Within two years the band had become surprisingly popular. Desmond's cool-toned alto and quick wit fit in well with Brubeck's often heavy chording and experimental playing; both Brubeck and Desmond had original sounds and styles that owed little to their predecessors. Joe Dodge was the band's early drummer but after he tired of the road the virtuosic Joe Morello took his place in 1956 while the revolving bass chair finally settled on Eugene Wright in 1958. By then Brubeck had followed his popular series of Fantasy recordings with some big sellers on Columbia and had appeared on the cover of *Time* (1954). The huge success of Paul Desmond's "Take Five" (1960) was followed by many songs played in "odd" time signatures such as 7/4 and 9/8; the high-quality soloing of the musicians kept these experiments from sounding like gimmicks. Dave and Iola Brubeck (his wife and lyricist) put together an anti-racism show featuring Louis Armstrong (*The Real Ambassadors*) which was recorded but its only public appearance was at the Monterey Jazz Festival in the early '60s.

The Dave Brubeck Quartet constantly travelled around the world until its breakup in 1967. After some time off during which he wrote religious works, Brubeck came back the following year with a new quartet featuring Gerry Mulligan, although he would have several reunions with Desmond before the altoist's death in 1977. Brubeck joined with his sons Darius (keyboards), Chris (electric bass and bass trombone) and Danny (drums) in Two Generations of Brubeck in the 1970s. In the early '80s tenor saxophonist Jerry Bergonzi was in the Brubeck Quartet and since the mid-'80s clarinetist Bill Smith (who was in the original Octet) has alternated with altoist Bobby Militello.

There is no shortage of Dave Brubeck records currently available, practically everything he has cut for Fantasy, Columbia, Concord and Telarc (his most recent label) are easy to locate. Brubeck, whose compositions "In Your Own Sweet Way," "The Duke" and "Blue Rondo a La Turk" have become standards, has remained very busy (despite some bouts of bad health) into the late-'90s. —*Scott Yanow*

The Dave Brubeck Octet / 1946-Jul. 1950 / Original Jazz Classics ✦✦✦✦
On infrequent occasions during 1946-50, pianist Dave Brubeck led an octet that was dominated by students of the composer Darius Milhaud. This pioneering West Coast outfit combined bop with modern classical music to form an interesting new blend of styles but, since they only recorded one LP's worth of material (which has remained obscure through the decades), the octet's life and general influence were limited. With such players as trumpeter Dick Collins, altoist Paul Desmond, Bill Smith on clarinet and baritone, tenor saxophonist Dave Van Kreidt and a rhythm section comprising Brubeck, bassist Ron Crotty and Cal Tjader on drums, this fascinating group performs highly original music throughout this CD reissue. —*Scott Yanow*

● **Time Signatures: A Career Retrospective** / 1946-May 7, 1991 / Columbia ✦✦✦✦
This four-CD box set does a near-perfect job of summing up Dave Brubeck's extensive recorded legacy. Drawing its recordings from not only Columbia but Fantasy, Atlantic and Music Masters, the attractive package also includes an extensive booklet written by Doug Ramsey that can serve as a mini-biography. The focus is naturally on Brubeck's quartet with altoist Paul Desmond but there is also music from before and after their association, even including one otherwise unissued performance, a remarkable polytonal polyrhythmic version of "Tritonis." Although completists will prefer to acquire Dave Brubeck's individual releases, this set is perfect for those just beginning to explore the magic of his music. —*Scott Yanow*

24 Classic Original Recordings / Sep. 1949-Nov. 1950 / Fantasy ✦✦✦✦✦
During 1949-51 pianist Dave Brubeck led a San Francisco-based trio with bassist Ron Crotty and Cal Tjader doubling on drums and vibes. This CD has all 24 of this group's recordings, interpretations of standards that are full of surprising moments. Even at this early stage, Brubeck had his own style and sounds nothing at all like Bud Powell, the dominant influence of the era. —*Scott Yanow*

Greatest Hits from the Fantasy Years (1949-1954) / 1949-1954 / Fantasy ✦✦✦✦
A nice overview of his material in the years before he crossed over and became a celebrity. —*Ron Wynn*

Stardust / Aug. 1951-Jun. 1955 / Fantasy ✦✦✦✦
This CD features the Dave Brubeck Quartet in its early days. Although the dates are unaccountably left off of this two-fer, most of the music is from 1951-52 and features such short-term sidemen as bassists Norm Bates, Fred Dutton (who doubled on bassoon) and Wyatt "Bull" Reuther and drummers Herb Barman and Lloyd Davis in addition to pianist Brubeck and altoist Paul Desmond. Highlights include "Crazy Chris," "Lyons Busy," "Look for the Silver Lining" and "Alice in Wonderland." Two later selections ("Stardust" and a fourteen-and-a-half-minute version of "At a Perfume Counter") are from 1954-55 when the personnel stabilized with bassist Bob Bates and drummer Joe Dodge. —*Scott Yanow*

Dave Brubeck/Paul Desmond / Sep. 1952-Mar. 30, 1954 / Fantasy ✦✦✦✦
This CD reissues two earlier Fantasy LPs titled *Jazz at the Black Hawk* and *Jazz at Storyville*. Pianist Dave Brubeck and altoist Paul Desmond are the two main constants while bassists Ron Crotty and Wyatt Ruther and drummers Lloyd Davis, Herb Barman and Joe Dodge are heard on some tracks. There are many high points to this interesting set including Brubeck-Desmond duets on "Over the Rainbow" and "You Go to My Head," an unaccompanied piano solo on "My Heart Stood Still" and quartet versions of "Jeepers Creepers," "Trolley Song" and "Crazy Chris." —*Scott Yanow*

Jazz at Oberlin / Mar. 2, 1953 / Original Jazz Classics ✦✦✦✦
Although a touch underrated, this is one of the early Dave Brubeck classic recordings. The interplay between the pianist-leader and altoist Paul Desmond on "Perdido" borders on the miraculous and their renditions of "The Way You Look Tonight," "How High the Moon" and "Stardust" are quite memorable. Brubeck's piano playing on "These Foolish Things" in one spot is so percussive and atonal as to sound like Cecil Taylor, who would not emerge for another two years. With bassist Ron Crotty and drummer Lloyd Davis giving the Quartet quiet and steady support, Brubeck and Desmond were free to play at their most adventurous. Highly recommended. —*Scott Yanow*

Featuring Paul Desmond in Concert / Mar. 2, 1953-Dec. 14, 1953 / Fantasy ✦✦✦
This odd CD has four of the five selections from *Jazz at Oberlin* and five of the six from *Jazz at College of the Pacific*, both of which are available in more complete form on two CDs. The music (which features pianist Dave Brubeck and altoist Paul Desmond in top form while being supported by bassist Ron Crotty and either Lloyd Davis or Joe Dodge on drums) is excellent, but the logic behind this fragmented release is questionable. —*Scott Yanow*

Brubeck & Desmond at Wilshire-Ebell / Jun. 20, 1953 / Fantasy ✦✦✦✦
One of the rarest of all early Dave Brubeck recordings, this Fantasy LP features pianist Brubeck, altoist Paul Desmond, bassist Ron Crotty and drummer Lloyd Davis in top form on six standards. Although Brubeck would record most of this

material again (including "Let's Fall in Love," "Stardust" and "All the Things You Are"), these versions are often quite a bit different than the more familiar recordings. There was plenty of magical interplay to be heard during that era between Brubeck and Desmond, making this set worth an extensive search. —*Scott Yanow*

Jazz at the College of the Pacific / Dec. 14, 1953 / Original Jazz Classics ✦✦✦✦✦
This CD brings back a near-classic (one of many from this period) by the Dave Brubeck Quartet. Drummer Joe Dodge had just joined the group and he joins with bassist Ron Crotty in laying down a solid and subtle foundation. However the real action takes place up front with pianist Dave Brubeck and altoist Paul Desmond. Their individual solos are full of creative ideas on six standards (most memorable are "All the Things You Are," "Laura" and "I'll Never Smile Again") and their interaction and trade-offs are timeless. Recommended. —*Scott Yanow*

Brubeck & Desmond: Jazz at Storyville (1954) / Dec. 1953-Jul. 22, 1954 / Columbia ✦✦✦
Taken from three separate occasions, this LP features the Dave Brubeck Quartet (with altoist Paul Desmond, drummer Joe Dodge and either Ron Crotty or Bob Bates on bass) romping through five standards and "Back Bay Blues." The beautiful cool tone of Desmond, although criticized by writers who felt that everyone should sound like Charlie Parker, was always a major asset to the Quartet, contrasting with the complex chord voicings of Brubeck; they made a perfect team. This long out-of-print LP is long overdue to be reissued on CD. —*Scott Yanow*

Jazz Collection / Mar. 9, 1954-1970 / Columbia ✦✦✦
This two-CD set gives one a fine overview of the Dave Brubeck Quartet during their years on Columbia. All of the 28 selections are available elsewhere so longtime collectors will want to skip this reissue, but those listeners just beginning to discover Brubeck's special music may want to acquire this set for a start. The main "hits" ("Take Five," "Blue Rondo à la Turk," etc.) are here but, even with guest appearances by Carmen McRae, Louis Armstrong, Charles Mingus and Jimmy Rushing (along with two later selections that have baritonist Gerry Mulligan in altoist Paul Desmond's place), the emphasis is very much on the classic Quartet. —*Scott Yanow*

☆ **Jazz Goes to College** / Mar. 1954 / Columbia ✦✦✦✦✦
A true classic, this CD reissues the original LP. Altoist Paul Desmond's lengthy solo on the blues "Balcony Rock" was one of the greatest of his career with one fresh idea leading (through repetition and gradual development) logically into another; pianist Brubeck's improvisation on this piece almost reaches the heights of Desmond's. Bassist Bob Bates and drummer Joe Dodge give a solid and quiet accompaniment to Desmond and the unpredictable pianist/leader with other highlights including "Out of Nowhere," "The Song Is You" and "Don't Worry 'Bout Me." This is the Brubeck Quartet at its best. —*Scott Yanow*

Jazz: Red, Hot and Cool / Oct. 12, 1954-Aug. 8, 1955 / Columbia ✦✦✦✦
Recorded live at the Basin Street Club in New York, this LP is most notable for introducing Dave Brubeck's composition "The Duke." The pianist/leader, altoist Paul Desmond, bassist Bob Bates and drummer Joe Dodge are also in fine form on a variety of standards including "Little Girl Blue," "Sometimes I'm Happy" and "Love Walked In." Half of the contents have since been reissued on the CD *Interchanges '54*. —*Scott Yanow*

Brubeck Time / Oct. 1954-Nov. 1954 / Columbia ✦✦✦✦
This LP (which has been reissued on CD as part of *Interchanges '54*) introduced Paul Desmond's beautiful ballad "Audrey" and found the early Dave Brubeck Quartet (with pianist Brubeck, altoist Desmond, bassist Bob Bates and drummer Joe Dodge) making a rare studio recording; up to this point all of their most popular records were club performances. With fresh versions of such songs as "Jeepers Creepers," "Pennies from Heaven" and "A Fine Romance," this music is certainly worth acquiring. —*Scott Yanow*

Interchanges '54: Featuring Paul Desmond / Oct. 1954-Nov. 1954 / Columbia ✦✦✦✦
This excellent CD reissues the LP *Brubeck Time* plus half of *Red Hot and Cool*. One of the few early studio (as opposed to club) recordings by the early Dave Brubeck Quartet (this version has bassist Bob Bates and drummer Joe Dodge in addition to pianist Brubeck and altoist Paul Desmond), the fine unit performs nine standards plus three new compositions: "Stompin' for Mili," "Audrey" (dedicated to Audrey Hepburn) and Brubeck's classic, "The Duke." —*Scott Yanow*

Greatest Hits / 1954-1971 / Sony ✦✦✦
While *Greatest Hits* albums from jazz artists are sometimes dubious propositions, Dave Brubeck is the rare exception to the rule. Brubeck concentrated on the song as much as the performance, which is one of the reasons why he appealed to such a wide audience and it's also the reason why *Greatest Hits* is such an entertaining and effective sampler. Featuring such familiar items as "Take Five," "In Your Own Sweet Way," "The Duke," "Trolley Song," "Unsquare Dance" and "Blue Rondo à la Turk," the collection provides a fine introduction to Brubeck's collegiate jazz for

the uninitiated. *Time Out* remains the best place to start a Brubeck appreciation, but this is an excellent single-disc sampler. —*Stephen Thomas Erlewine*

Brubeck Plays Brubeck / Mar. 1956-Apr. 1956 / Columbia ✦✦✦

Dave Brubeck has had a strikingly original style ever since he appeared on records, avoiding the usual Bud Powell runs and instead expressing his training in classical music and his interest in polyrhythms and polytonality while never forgetting to swing. On his first solo piano record, Brubeck not only plays quite well but introduces such new compositions as "In Your Own Sweet Way" and "One Moment Worth Years" in addition to performing a remake of "The Duke." Long out-of-print, it's still worth searching for. —*Scott Yanow*

Dave Brubeck and Jay & Kai at Newport / Jul. 6, 1956 / Columbia ✦✦✦

This historic LP finds the Dave Brubeck Quartet performing two standards ("Take the 'A' Train" and "I'm in a Dancing Mood") along with the pianist/leader's "In Your Own Sweet Way" and "Two-Part Contention." Altoist Paul Desmond is in fine form as is the supportive drummer Joe Dodge who would soon leave the Quartet; Joe Morello was his eventual replacement. The second part of this LP is the final performance by the two-trombone J.J. Johnson-Kai Winding Quintet before they broke up after two years of steady work. Overall, this album gives one a good look at two of the most popular jazz groups of 1956. —*Scott Yanow*

Jazz Impressions of the U.S.A. / Nov. 16, 1956-Nov. 26, 1956 / Columbia ✦✦✦

For this new musical adventure, pianist Dave Brubeck wrote eight diverse songs, of which "Summer Song" would be the best known. This out-of-print LP was the debut of drummer Joe Morello with Brubeck's Quartet which at the time also featured altoist Joe Morello and bassist Norman Bates. Excellent music, although it's not quite as essential as their live performances of the era. —*Scott Yanow*

Live (1956-1957) / 1956-1957 / Jazz Band ✦✦✦✦

Considering how popular the Dave Brubeck Quartet was during the 1950s (even before recording "Take Five"), it is surprising that there are not more semi-authorized live sessions available. This CD from the small Jazz Band label features the pianist/leader, altoist Paul Desmond, bassist Norman Bates and drummer Joe Dodge on a pair of well-recorded 1956 radio broadcasts live from Basin Street in New York; in addition there are three cuts from a March 1957 appearance at Chicago's Blue Note (with Joe Morello on drums). Although the songs are from Brubeck's usual repertoire of the era, the solos are much different and the group sounds consistently inspired. Highlights of the cool jazz collection include "Stardust," "Stompin' for Willie," "The Song Is You," "In Your Own Sweet Way" and "The Duke." Easily recommended to Dave Brubeck fans. —*Scott Yanow*

Plays and Plays And . . . / Feb. 8, 1957 / Original Jazz Classics ✦✦✦

Dave Brubeck's second solo piano album differs from the first in that only two of the nine songs he performs are his originals. However Brubeck's versions of such standards as "Imagination," "Our Love Is Here to Stay" and "You'd Be So Nice to Come Home To" sound quite fresh and contain more than their share of surprises. Fortunately the formerly rare music is now available on this CD. —*Scott Yanow*

Reunion / Feb. 1957 / Original Jazz Classics ✦✦

Tenor saxophonist Dave Van Kreidt, a former member of Dave Brubeck's octet in the late '40s, had a reunion with the pianist, altoist Paul Desmond and bassist Bob Bates for this unusual session; Brubeck's new drummer Joe Morello made the group a quintet. Van Kreidt supplied all of the compositions (some of which are fairly complex), giving this set a sound very much different than the usual Brubeck Quartet outing. Interesting if not essential classical-influenced music that predates the Third Stream movement. —*Scott Yanow*

Jazz Goes to Junior College / May 1, 1957-May 2, 1957 / Columbia ✦✦✦✦

As a sort-of follow-up to *Jazz Goes to College* (which was actually recorded three years earlier) and the final album in his "college" series, pianist Dave Brubeck and his Quartet (with altoist Paul Desmond, bassist Norman Bates and drummer Joe Morello) recorded at Fullerton Junior College in 1957. The musicians were clearly inspired by the enthusiastic audience and they perform the definitive version of Brubeck's "One Moment Worth Years," dig into the lengthy "Bru's Blues" and play fresh versions of three standards that were in their repertoire throughout the 1950s: "These Foolish Things," "St. Louis Blues" and "The Masquerade Is Over." Most Dave Brubeck records are well worth acquiring, particularly concert albums, so it seems odd that this frequently superb outing has not yet been reissued in full on CD. —*Scott Yanow*

Dave Digs Disney / Jun. 29, 1957-Aug. 3, 1957 / Columbia/Legacy ✦✦✦✦

This CD contains the original LP of the same name plus two previously unissued songs ("Very Good Advice" and "So This Is Love"). Inspired by a trip with his family to Disneyland, Dave Brubeck recorded eight songs taken from four Disney movies (*Alice in Wonderland, Pinocchio, Snow White* and *Cinderella*), including such melodies as "Give a Little Whistle," "Heigh Ho," "When You Wish upon a Star" and "Someday My Prince Will Come." The funny part is that all of these

songs were already in the Brubeck Quartet's repertoire. The results are pleasing although, due to a misprint, the CD booklet only contains half of the original liner notes. —*Scott Yanow*

The Dave Brubeck Quartet in Europe / Mar. 3, 1958 / Columbia ✦✦✦

Although many people associate the Dave Brubeck Quartet's great popularity with their recording of "Take Five," the band was actually a major attraction several years before cutting that hit record. This LP, recorded in concert in Copenhagen, finds the Quartet (which for the first time featured bassist Eugene Wright and drummer Joe Morello along with altoist Paul Desmond) performing such numbers as "Tangerine," "Like Someone in Love" and "Wonderful Copenhagen." —*Scott Yanow*

Jazz Impressions of Eurasia / Jul. 28, 1958-Aug. 23, 1958 / Columbia ✦✦✦✦

In 1958 Dave Brubeck's Quartet, one of the most popular jazz groups in the world, played 80 concerts in 14 countries during a three-month period. To salute the marathon road trip, the pianist/leader composed six songs for a new recording (which is now out on this CD). "Nomad" and "Brandenburg Gate" are the best-known originals but all of the other selections are equally enjoyable, featuring fine solos from Brubeck and altoist Paul Desmond. —*Scott Yanow*

Newport (1958) / Jul. 1958 / Columbia ✦✦✦

For their appearance at the 1958 Newport Jazz Festival, the Dave Brubeck Quartet performed a set of tunes associated with Duke Ellington including "Things Ain't What They Used to Be," "Perdido," an excerpt from the "Liberian Suite" and "C Jam Blues." Rounding off this excellent LP (which features pianist Brubeck, altoist Paul Desmond, bassist Eugene Wright and drummer Joe Morello) is Brubeck's original, "The Duke." It is well deserving of being reissued on CD. —*Scott Yanow*

Gone with the Wind / Apr. 22, 1959 / Columbia ✦✦

For this LP, Dave Brubeck and his Quartet (featuring altoist Paul Desmond) interpret eight songs (including two versions of "Camptown Races") associated with the South such as "Swanee River," "Georgia on My Mind" and "Ol' Man River." Although not one of their most significant recordings, the Brubeck Quartet is still in good form for these interesting performances. —*Scott Yanow*

★ Time Out / Jun. 25, 1959-Aug. 18, 1959 / Columbia ✦✦✦✦✦

This is one of the most popular jazz recordings of all time. Altoist Paul Desmond's memorable "Take Five" became a huge hit, showing that it is possible for creative jazz to sell. In addition to "Take Five" (which is still a standard), other high points of this classic album include "Blue Rondo à la Turk" and "Three to Get Ready." Bassist Eugene Wright and drummer Joe Morello (whose talents made it possible for Brubeck's Quartet to play in different time signatures) are superb in support of the two lead voices. This classic set (which has been reissued many times including on a 1997 CD) is essential for all jazz collections. —*Scott Yanow*

The Riddle / Aug. 12, 1959 / Columbia ✦✦

Clarinetist Bill Smith, a member of Dave Brubeck's octet in the late '40s and a future soloist with Brubeck's Quartet starting in the '80s, recorded three albums with the pianist in the interim. *The Riddle* finds him temporarily taking altoist Paul Desmond's place with the Quartet and contributing all eight compositions which utilize folkish melodies that are related to the English song "Heigh, Ho, Nobody Home." Although not too essential, this little-known set gives Dave Brubeck a chance to play some unusual material. —*Scott Yanow*

Southern Scene / Aug. 1959-Oct. 1959 / Columbia ✦✦

For some reason Dave Brubeck was motivated to record a second album of songs associated with the South (as a follow-up to *Gone with the Wind*) and the results form this LP, a trio set without altoist Paul Desmond. The eight standards range from "Oh Susanna" and "Little Rock Getaway" to "Darktown Strutters Ball" and "Darling Nellie Gray"; in addition two originals in the style round out the well-played but somewhat forgettable program. —*Scott Yanow*

Dave Brubeck and Jimmy Rushing / Jan. 29, 1960-Aug. 4, 1960 / Columbia ✦✦✦

Although associated with the more modern styles of jazz, Brubeck always had a great respect (if not reverence) for the masters of the past. On ten standards Brubeck, altoist Paul Desmond and the Quartet fit in perfectly behind the great swing/blues singer Jimmy Rushing who sounds rejuvenated by the fresh setting. This LP, a surprising success, is well worth searching for. —*Scott Yanow*

Brubeck Plays Bernstein / Jan. 30, 1960-Feb. 14, 1960 / Columbia ✦✦✦✦

For this historic LP, the Dave Brubeck Quartet met with the New York Philharmonic under the direction of Leonard Bernstein for a program subtitled "Bernstein Plays Brubeck Plays Bernstein." Together they perform Howard Brubeck's side-long "Dialogues for Jazz Combo and Orchestra" along with five Bernstein songs (including four from *West Side Story*). This is one of the more successful "Jazz Meets the Symphony" ventures and deserves to be reissued on CD. —*Scott Yanow*

Brubeck à la Mode / May 1960 / Original Jazz Classics ✦✦
One of Brubeck's three recordings of the 1959-61 period that featured clarinetist Bill Smith in the place of altoist Paul Desmond with the Quartet, this one finds Smith contributing ten originals that use various modes and unusual scales. The music generally swings and there are some fine solos but none of the individual pieces are all that memorable. —*Scott Yanow*

Tonight Only! [With Carmen McRae] / Sep. 9, 1960 / Columbia ✦✦
One of the more obscure Dave Brubeck albums is really a showcase for the young singer Carmen McRae who performs nine numbers: six composed by the pianist/leader, one song apiece by altoist Paul Desmond and bassist Eugene Wright and the lesser-known standard "Paradiddle Joe." McRae is in fine voice but strangely enough all of the songs (except for "Strange Meadowlark") have been long forgotten. Stronger material would have resulted in a more memorable session. —*Scott Yanow*

Summit Sessions / 1960-1973 / Columbia ✦✦✦✦
It would not be an understatement to say that these 13 performances, mostly dating from the 1960s, cover quite a bit of ground. Brubeck is heard with such performers as Tony Bennett, Indian percussionist Palghat Raghu, the folk team of Addiss & Crofut, in a remarkable piano duet with Thelonious Monk on "C Jam Blues," with son Darius Brubeck on second piano, on "Blues in the Dark" with singer Jimmy Rushing, in separate recordings with Peter, Paul & Mary, Charles Mingus, Carmen McRae, Gerry Mulligan, Leonard Bernstein and the New York Philharmonic and Louis Armstrong. There's quite a lot of contrast on this largely successful LP. —*Scott Yanow*

Countdown Time in Outer Space / May 3, 1961-Jun. 28, 1961 / Columbia ✦✦✦✦
One of Dave Brubeck's more adventurous albums, this LP (not yet available on CD) finds his Quartet exploring originals in a variety of potentially difficult time signatures including 11/4 and a polyrhythmic version of the dates' one standard "Someday My Prince Will Come." Other highlights include "Countdown," "Castilian Drums" and "Three's a Crowd." It's highly recommended along with Brubeck's other *Time* recordings. —*Scott Yanow*

Time Further Out / May 3, 1961-1963 / Columbia ✦✦✦✦✦
Unlike most sequels, *Time Further Out* is a worthy successor to *Time Out*. Among the numbers introduced on this impressive set are "It's a Raggy Waltz" and "Unsquare Dance" (the latter an ancestor of Don Ellis' "Pussy Wiggle Stomp"). The selections, which range in time signatures from 5/4 to 9/8, are handled with apparent ease (or at least not too much difficulty) by pianist Brubeck, altoist Paul Desmond, bassist Eugene Wright and drummer Joe Morello on this near-classic. The 1996 CD reissue adds a previously unissued "Slow and Easy" and a version of "It's a Raggy Waltz" from the Quartet's 1963 Carnegie Hall concert to the original program. —*Scott Yanow*

Brandenburg Gate Revisited / Aug. 21, 1961-Aug. 22, 1961 / Columbia ✦✦✦
Dave Brubeck's Quartet is joined by a symphony orchestra for the nearly 20-minute "Brandenburg Gate" and four shorter pieces on this LP. The solos of the pianist/leader and altoist Paul Desmond add a great deal of spontaneity to what could have been a weighed-down Third Stream effort. —*Scott Yanow*

Near-Myth with Bill Smith / Aug. 1961 / Original Jazz Classics ✦✦✦
The third and final of the Dave Brubeck albums from 1959-61 that feature clarinetist/composer Bill Smith in Paul Desmond's place with the Quartet has some unusual moments as when Smith utilizes multiphonics or actually has a mute on his horn. As usual Smith provided all of the music which displays his interest in classical music and academia. —*Scott Yanow*

Real Ambassadors / Sep. 1961-Dec. 1961 / Columbia ✦✦✦✦
In 1961 Dave Brubeck put together a remarkable musical show. Using the talents of Louis Armstrong and his All-Stars, Carmen McRae, the innovative bop vocal group Lambert, Hendricks and Ross and his own rhythm section, Brubeck and his wife, lyricist Iola, wrote a largely upbeat play full of anti-racism songs and tunes that celebrated human understanding. Although it had only one live performance (at the 1962 Monterey Jazz Festival), *The Real Ambassadors* was recorded for posterity and now, with its reissue on CD, the original 15 selections have been augmented by five more. It is important to listen to this music without prior expectations because Paul Desmond is nowhere to be found, Louis Armstrong does not play that much trumpet here and Lambert, Hendricks and Ross essentially function as background singers. However Satch and Carmen McRae make for a very potent team and there are many touching and surprising moments. —*Scott Yanow*

Bossa Nova Usa / Jan. 3, 1962 / Columbia ✦✦✦
With the popularization of bossa nova in the early '60s, practically every recording artist had to have at least one bossa nova album. This effort by the Dave Brubeck Quartet is better than most due to the high quality of the compositions, of which the title cut is best known. The date's two standards ("This Can't Be Love" and "Trolley Song") also fare well on this upbeat session. —*Scott Yanow*

My Favorite Things / Jun. 11, 1962-Sep. 22, 1965 / Columbia ✦✦✦
Although recorded in sessions in 1962 and 1965, this set of Richard Rodgers tunes by the Dave Brubeck Quartet has a strong unity about it due to the consistent performances of the veteran group. With altoist Paul Desmond and the pianist-leader contributing some fine solos (and bassist Eugene Wright and drummer Joe Morello excellent in support), the Rodgers songs are treated with respect and swing. This comparatively gentle version of "My Favorite Things" would never be mistaken for John Coltrane's. —*Scott Yanow*

Angel Eyes / Jul. 2, 1962 / Columbia ✦✦✦
As with Dave Brubeck's Richard Rodgers set (*My Favorite Things*), his tribute to composer Matt Dennis was recorded partly in 1962 with the remainder three years later. Each of these seven standards (which include "Let's Get Away from It All," "Violets for Your Furs" and "Will You Still Be Mine?") are given superior and swinging treatments with fine solos from Brubeck and altoist Paul Desmond. —*Scott Yanow*

Brubeck in Amsterdam / Dec. 3, 1962 / Columbia ✦✦✦✦
One of the Dave Brubeck Quartet's lesser-known albums, this LP features the group performing six instrumental versions of songs from *The Real Ambassadors* plus "Dizzy Ditty" and a 12-minute rendition of "Brandenburg Gate." Brubeck, altoist Paul Desmond, bassist Eugene Wright and drummer Joe Morello seem inspired during this concert by the fresh material, making this hard-to-find album a bit of a collector's item. —*Scott Yanow*

At Carnegie Hall / Feb. 22, 1963 / Columbia ✦✦✦✦✦
The Dave Brubeck Quartet's Carnegie Hall concert found the popular band at the height of its powers. This two-LP set is highlighted by definitive versions of "St. Louis Blues," "Bossa Nova USA," "Pennies from Heaven," "Three to Get Ready," "Eleven-Four," "It's a Raggy Waltz" and especially "Blue Rondo à la Turk." Only an overly rapid "Take Five" (which was apparently the only time that drummer Joe Morello counted off the tempo for the Quartet) misses the mark. This essential music should be reissued in full on CD. —*Scott Yanow*

Time Changes / Dec. 1963-Jan. 1964 / Columbia ✦✦✦
For this entry in Dave Brubeck's series of *Time* albums, his Quartet with altoist Paul Desmond performs "Elementals" with an orchestra and plays five briefer originals including four that have unusual time signatures; "World's Fair" is in 13/4 time. It's not an essential purchase but a good example of Dave Brubeck's music. —*Scott Yanow*

Jazz Impressions of Japan / Jun. 16, 1964-Jun. 17, 1964 / Columbia ✦✦✦✦
Inspired by a tour of Japan in the Spring of 1964, Brubeck composed eight songs that pay tribute to the Quartet's visit. "Koto Song" is the best-known of these originals but all of the melodies are enjoyable. Even after being together 13 years, the Quartet was able to consistently perform new music with enthusiasm and creativity. —*Scott Yanow*

Jazz Impressions of New York / Jun. 16, 1964-Aug. 21, 1964 / Columbia ✦✦
This CD, a straight reissue of the original LP, contains 11 songs written for the soundtrack of the long-forgotten television series *Mr. Broadway*. It pays tribute to New York in a more abstract way than *Jazz Impressions of Japan* celebrated Japan, for Brubeck had to concern himself with having the music fit in with the show. In general these themes and the melodic improvisations of Brubeck and altoist Paul Desmond hold their own without the show although none of the songs became standards. —*Scott Yanow*

The Canadian Concert of Dave Brubeck / Aug. 22, 1965 / Can-Am ✦✦✦
The Dave Brubeck Quartet (with altoist Paul Desmond, bassist Eugene Wright and drummer Joe Morello) is in excellent form for this typical program from the mid-'60s. In addition to standards such as "St. Louis Blues," "Tangerine" and "These Foolish Things," they perform Brubeck's originals "Cultural Exchange" and "Koto Song" along with a brief version of "Take Five." This LP is worth searching for. —*Scott Yanow*

Time In / Sep. 20, 1965-Oct. 13, 1965 / Columbia ✦✦✦✦
The last of the Dave Brubeck *Time* albums introduced eight new Brubeck originals, including "40 Days," "Travellin' Blues" and "He Done Her Wrong" (the latter based on "Frankie and Johnny"). The consistently swinging, if occasionally complex music is enjoyable and adds evidence to the belief that there are no unworthy Dave Brubeck albums. —*Scott Yanow*

Anything Goes: The Music of Cole Porter / Dec. 8, 1965-Feb. 17, 1966 / Columbia ✦✦✦
The Quartet performs eight of Cole Porter's most famous songs on this enjoyable outing. Few surprises occur but the music often swings hard, pianist Brubeck and altoist Paul Desmond take several excellent solos and bassist Eugene Wright and drummer Joe Morello really push the group. —*Scott Yanow*

Jackpot / Jun. 14, 1966-Jun. 15, 1966 / Columbia ✦✦

One of the lesser Dave Brubeck albums, this LP features eight songs built around the theme of gambling towns such as "Ace in the Hole," "Chicago" and the title cut. The music is certainly upbeat but the out-of-tune piano and crowd noises (this date was recorded live in Las Vegas) are a bit distracting. It's strictly for Brubeck completists. —*Scott Yanow*

Bravo! Brubeck! / May 12, 1967-May 14, 1967 / Columbia ✦✦✦✦

One of the better Dave Brubeck LPs from the later period of the Quartet with altoist Paul Desmond, this set is unusual in that it only contains one Brubeck original. On such tunes as "Cielito Lindo," the beautiful "La Paloma," "Besame Mucho" and "Estrellita," the Quartet is augmented by guitarist Chamin Correa and percussionist Rabito Agueros. The results are melodic but swinging treatments of a variety of famous themes. —*Scott Yanow*

The Last Time We Saw Paris / Nov. 13, 1967 / Columbia ✦✦✦✦✦

Taken from the final tour of the Quartet before their breakup, this LP is full of timeless performances. All six selections are worth mentioning: "Swanee River," a 12-minute version of "These Foolish Things," "Forty Days," "One Moment Worth Years," "La Paloma Azul" and "Three to Get Ready." Throughout these extended renditions, Brubeck and altoist Paul Desmond rekindle some of the magic from their concerts of the early '50s while also simultaneously showing just how far they had grown as musicians. This LP is long overdue to be reissued on CD. —*Scott Yanow*

The Light in the Wilderness / Mar. 19, 1968-Mar. 20, 1968 / MCA ✦✦✦

Dave Brubeck broke up his famous quartet in 1967 in order to start fulfilling his ambitions as a composer of religious concert works, and this fascinating, highly eclectic oratorio was the first result. Sprawling over two LPs, it remains Brubeck's longest work to date, and it lays down a general blueprint for much of what was to follow—uninhibited thrusts into idioms that Brubeck had never explored in a jazz combo format, some interludes for his jazz trio, distinctively Brubeckian polytonal writing, and tricky meters and rhythms for the chorus and orchestra to follow. At one point, Brubeck's piano goes into an Indian raga, with tablas instead of a drum kit for backing (this was, after all, conceived in the flower-power era). At other times, he can be heard in strong, affirmative form with the trio in segments that dovetail neatly in and out of the classical writing. In one memorable stretch in Part I, the jazz rhythm section and classical forces meet, and the fusion is amazingly tight and right. No doubt it helped to have an open-minded conductor like the young Erich Kunzel (of later "pops" concert fame) who could get the elephantine Cincinnati Symphony to swing and wail like a big band when needed. Above all, there is a guileless sincerity about this piece that communicates even if you don't share Brubeck's religious convictions. The set is currently available on CD by mail order on a Musical Heritage Society reissue. —*Richard S. Ginell*

Compadres / May 23, 1968-May 25, 1968 / Columbia ✦✦✦✦✦

This fine LP was the debut of Brubeck's new Quartet, a group featuring baritonist Gerry Mulligan, bassist Jack Six and drummer Alan Dawson. Recorded live in Mexico, the album (unlike the previous *Bravo! Brubeck* which mostly stuck to traditional folk melodies) has three originals apiece from Brubeck and Mulligan, although the most memorable pieces are the two standards "Adios, Mariquita Linda" and "Amapola." This enjoyable set showed that for Brubeck there was life after Paul Desmond. —*Scott Yanow*

Blues Roots / Oct. 4, 1968 / Columbia ✦✦✦

Although this is a blues-oriented set, there is plenty of variety in tempos and grooves. The 1968 Quartet featured the leader/pianist, baritonist Gerry Mulligan, bassist Jack Six and drummer Alan Dawson. The repertoire on this LP ranges from "Limehouse Blues" (which is not really a blues) to "Things Ain't What They Used to Be" and several originals. —*Scott Yanow*

The Gates of Justice / Oct. 1969 / Decca ✦✦✦

Written in the wake of Dr. Martin Luther King, Jr.'s assassination, Dave Brubeck's second religious concert work—actually a cantata—finds his outlook darkening as he contemplates the historic struggles of Jews and Blacks. Yet he remains optimistic about his overarching theme, the brotherhood of man. This is a more violent piece than *The Light in the Wilderness*, the music at first anchored in abrasive Hebraic modes, then somber Negro spirituals, and gradually, everything but the kitchen sink gets tossed into the mix in the wild "The Lord Is Good" segment. The then-current Brubeck Trio with Jack Six (bass) and Alan Dawson (drums) is on hand, though even Dave's fervent aficionados may be jarred by his polytonal playing of an out-of-tune rock combo organ, and Erich Kunzel ably conducts a brass ensemble from Cincinnati and the New York-based Westminster Choir. While the music of *Gates* isn't quite as consistent as that of *Wilderness*, the vitality of Brubeck's writing sees the work through. This LP awaits a CD reissue, even though Brubeck still performs the work frequently in concert. —*Richard S. Ginell*

Elementals for Jazzcombo, Orchestra and Baritone-Solo / May 1970 / Decca ✦✦✦

The Dave Brubeck Quartet (featuring baritonist Gerry Mulligan) collaborated with the Cincinnati Symphony Orchestra for this version of "Elementals" and four more concise Brubeck originals, including "The Duke." This is one of the more successful "jazz meets the symphony" recordings, with the orchestra being logically integrated into Brubeck's music. —*Scott Yanow*

Live at the Berlin Philharmonie / Nov. 7, 1970 / Columbia/Legacy ✦✦✦✦

Out of the 13 selections included on this double CD, six were originally released just in Europe, two ("Out of Nowhere" and "Mexican Jumping Bean") were never out before and only five songs were on the American LP. Considering how inspired the Dave Brubeck Quartet sounds, it is surprising that the music has been so obscure for so long. Baritonist Gerry Mulligan is particularly heated on the opening two numbers (the unreleased tracks), pianist Dave Brubeck really stretches himself (check him out on "Things Ain't What They Used to Be" where he progresses from stride to free) and bassist Jack Six and drummer Alan Dawson, in addition to their solo space, are quite alert and constantly pushing the lead voices. Not only are the musicians in top form but the audience is very enthusiastic, demanding three encores. The extensive liner notes by Geoffrey Smith are also a major plus. Highly recommended. —*Scott Yanow*

Last Set at Newport / Jul. 3, 1971 / Atlantic ✦✦✦✦

The Dave Brubeck-Gerry Mulligan Quartet is heard in a very inspired performance at the Newport Jazz Festival on this LP, just a short time before a riot by the audience closed the festival. These versions of "Take Five" and "Open the Gates" are memorable but it is the extended "Blues for Newport" that is truly classic. Mulligan and Brubeck (backed by bassist Jack Six and drummer Alan Dawson) constantly challenge each other during this exciting performance, making this set well worth searching for. —*Scott Yanow*

We're All Together Again (For the First Time) / Oct. 26, 1972-Nov. 4, 1972 / Atlantic ✦✦✦✦

During 1968-72, Brubeck's Quartet usually featured baritonist Gerry Mulligan, bassist Jack Six and drummer Alan Dawson. For this very logical record, altoist Paul Desmond (who was with Brubeck from 1951-67) makes the group a quintet and his interplay with Mulligan is consistently delightful. Together they are heard live in Europe on "Truth," Mulligan's "Unfinished Woman," "Rotterdam Blues" and a definitive 16-minute rendition of "Take Five." In addition, Desmond is showcased on "Koto Song" and as an encore Brubeck plays a lighthearted if brief "Sweet Georgia Brown." —*Scott Yanow*

All the Things We Are / Jul. 17, 1973 / Atlantic ✦✦✦✦

This album is a bit unusual in the Dave Brubeck discography. The pianist is heard in a quartet with altoist Lee Konitz on "Like Someone in Love" and a brief "Don't Get Around Much Anymore," avant-garde giant Anthony Braxton (also on alto) is featured on "In Your Own Sweet Way" and both Konitz and Braxton team up for "All the Things You Are." In addition, the Brubeck Trio (with bassist Jack Six and drummer Alan Dawson) plays an exquisite and frequently exciting 21-minute fivesong "Jimmy Van Heusen Medley." A total success, this "experimental" Brubeck set is highly recommended. —*Scott Yanow*

Two Generations of Brubeck / Aug. 1973 / Atlantic ✦✦✦

This very interesting set features the pianist with three of his sons (Darius on keyboards, Chris doubling on trombone and bass and Danny on drums), and a wide variety of musicians including tenor saxophonist Jerry Bergonzi, clarinetist Perry Robinson and Peter "Madcat" Ruth on harmonica. To hear such numbers as "Three to Get Ready," "Blue Rondo à la Turk" and "Unsquare Dance" (along with some newer pieces) performed by these younger players casts new light on the durability and flexibility of these classic Brubeck songs. This fine LP (along with its follow-up) is not yet available on CD. —*Scott Yanow*

Brother, the Great Spirit Made Us All / Jun. 1974 / Atlantic ✦✦✦

Pianist Dave Brubeck and three of his sons (keyboardist Darius, drummer Danny and Chris on trombone and bass), with the assistance of such players as Jerry Bergonzi (on tenor and soprano), clarinetist Perry Robinson and Madcat Ruth on harmonica, perform colorful treatments of a wide variety of swinging pieces. Highlights include "It's a Raggy Waltz," "Temptation Boogie" and "Christopher Columbus"; Dave Brubeck takes "The Duke" solo. This fine music was last available on LP. —*Scott Yanow*

Brubeck & Desmond: Duets (1975) / Jun. 10, 1975-Sep. 16, 1975 / A&M ✦✦✦✦✦

Pianist Dave Brubeck and altoist Paul Desmond had a reunion for this set of lyrical duets. They had performed "You Go to My Head" onboard a jazz cruise and that duet was so enjoyable that this full LP resulted. In addition to four standards, the duo plays three Brubeck originals (including "Koto Song" and "Summer Song") and the blues "Balcony Song." This near-classic set was reissued on CD in 1987. —*Scott Yanow*

La Fiesta de la Posada [Festival of the Inn] / 1976 / Columbia ✦✦✦

This is a problematic release, for it is a so-so realization of a wonderful piece of music, Brubeck's most frequently performed choral concert work. An evocation of a Mexican Christmas festival, the piece works for several reasons—a tight structural game plan, marvelous tunes injected with Mexican folk material, catchy off-kilter rhythms and a youthful naive exuberance that masks the rigors of counterpoint and all the other technical stuff that went into its writing. The problem here is that the performance on this CD is rather flat; reported nonmusical tensions at the recording session were supposedly responsible. Conductor Dennis Russell Davies hurries through the piece with the St. Paul Chamber Orchestra and Dale Warland Singers, and even Brubeck, in three brief appearances with his trio, seems to go through the motions. Moreover, this was one of the earliest experimental digital productions—issued on an audiophile LP in its time—and the sound is wiry and dim, mastered at a very low level on the CD (you really have to crank up the volume). *La Fiesta* can really shine—Brubeck's exultant live performances of the work prove that—yet this recording only conveys the outlines of a terrifically uplifting experience. Alas, this is the only recording we have, so buy it and pray that Telarc or someone else records a new one someday. —*Richard S. Ginell*

25th Anniversary Reunion / Mar. 10, 1976-Mar. 12, 1976 / A&M ✦✦✦✦

This classic LP was the last time that pianist Dave Brubeck recorded with the late altoist Paul Desmond. The reunion of the most famous version of Brubeck's Quartet (which also included bassist Eugene Wright and drummer Joe Morello) found all of the players enthusiastic and still in their prime (although Morello's eyesight was failing). "St. Louis Blues," the tender "Don't Worry 'Bout Me," "Three to Get Ready" and yet another version of "Take Five" are among the high points of this historic final session. —*Scott Yanow*

Live at Montreux / Jul. 17, 1977 / Tomato ✦✦

For a period in 1977-78 (after the death of altoist Paul Desmond), pianist Dave Brubeck had a quartet with his sons, keyboardist Darius, drummer Dan and Chris on bass and trombone. This Montreux concert features five of Dave Brubeck's originals (including "It's a Raggy Waltz" and "In Your Own Sweet Way") along with the standard "It Could Happen to You" and finds father Dave in fine form even if Desmond is clearly missed. —*Scott Yanow*

A Cut Above / Feb. 27, 1978-Feb. 28, 1978 / Direct Disk ✦✦

This direct-to-disk double LP is "a cut below" the usual Dave Brubeck recordings. Pianist Brubeck is in good form and his rhythm section (with bassist Chris Brubeck and drummer Dan Brubeck) is fine but keyboardist Darius Brubeck's electronic effects get tiring quickly. Also, some of the performances are much too long and these renditions of "Blue Rondo à la Turk" and "Take Five" are not in the same league with most of the other versions. —*Scott Yanow*

Back Home / Aug. 1979 / Concord Jazz ✦✦✦✦

The first of three Concord LPs by this particular edition of the Quartet (with Jerry Bergonzi on tenor, Chris Brubeck doubling on electric bass and trombone, and drummer Butch Miles, whose successor would soon be Randy Jones) found Brubeck enthusiastically playing three of his originals along with the standards "Yesterdays," "Caravan" and "The Masquerade Is Over." Bergonzi's Coltrane-influenced tenor gave this unit a different sound than the earlier Quartets and meshes surprisingly well with the pianist/leader. —*Scott Yanow*

Tritonis / Mar. 10, 1980-Mar. 11, 1980 / Concord Jazz ✦✦✦✦

This underrated but talented version of the Dave Brubeck Quartet (featuring tenor saxophonist Jerry Bergonzi, drummer Randy Jones and Chris Brubeck on electric bass and bass trombone) performs "Brother, Can You Spare a Dime?," a sparkling version of "Like Someone in Love," Howard Brubeck's "Theme for June" and three fairly recent Dave Brubeck compositions. Bergonzi's Coltranish tenor acts as a perfect foil for Brubeck's unpredictable piano, making this LP worth searching for. —*Scott Yanow*

Paper Moon / Sep. 1981 / Concord Jazz ✦✦✦✦✦

The third of three Concord albums by this version of the Quartet (with Jerry Bergonzi on tenor, Chris Brubeck on bass and bass trombone and drummer Randy Jones) is the most rewarding of the trio although each one is recommended. Brubeck and the Coltrane-influenced tenor Bergonzi take consistently exciting solos on seven standards which are highlighted by "Music, Maestro, Please," "I Hear a Rhapsody" and "It's Only a Paper Moon"; Brubeck's solo version of "St. Louis Blues" is also noteworthy. —*Scott Yanow*

Concord on a Summer Night / Aug. 1982 / Concord Jazz ✦✦✦

In 1982 pianist Dave Brubeck welcomed clarinetist Bill Smith (who he had played with back in his octet days in the late '40s) as a permanent member of his Quartet along with drummer Randy Jones and Chris Brubeck on electric bass and occasional bass trombone. This album features the new Quartet at the Concord Jazz Festival playing what would become their typical mixture of songs: three Brubeck compositions ("Benjamin," "Koto Song" and "Softly, William, Softly"), a standard

("Black and Blue") and yet another remake of "Take Five." These are fine performances. —*Scott Yanow*

For Iola / Aug. 1984 / Concord Jazz ✦✦✦

In addition to the standard "I Hear a Rhapsody" and Dave Brubeck's "Summer Song," this enjoyable CD has five of his lesser-known originals including one called "Big Bad Basie." This particular Quartet (with clarinetist Bill Smith, drummer Randy Jones and Chris Brubeck on electric bass and bass trombone) has been together for quite awhile and all of their releases have their memorable moments. —*Scott Yanow*

Reflections / Dec. 1985 / Concord Jazz ✦✦✦

This is one of Dave Brubeck's more obscure recordings but not because of its quality. Somewhat lost in the shuffle, this excellent quartet session with clarinetist Bill Smith, Chris Brubeck (on electric bass and bass trombone) and drummer Randy Jones finds the pianist/leader performing eight of his compositions; only "Blues for Newport" caught on a little. The emphasis is on slower tempos and wistful solos (particularly on the Paul Desmond tribute "We Will All Remember Paul") but the music is stimulating enough to hold one's interest throughout. Dave Brubeck has never allowed himself to become predictable. —*Scott Yanow*

Blue Rondo / Nov. 1986 / Concord Jazz ✦✦✦✦

The 1987 edition of the Brubeck Quartet featured pianist Brubeck, his son Chris on electric bass and bass trombone, clarinetist Bill Smith and drummer Randy Jones. In addition to remakes of "Blue Rondo à la Turk," "Strange Meadowlark" and "Swing Bells," the leader contributed six new originals including "I See, Satie" and a tribute to Dizzy Gillespie and Stan Getz called "Dizzy's Dream." Bill Smith, who uses electronics with taste on his clarinet during a few songs, has long been a major asset to the later Brubeck Quartets. This is one of their better Concord CDs. —*Scott Yanow*

Moscow Nights / Mar. 1987 / Concord Jazz ✦✦✦✦

In 1987 Brubeck, after decades of trying, finally had an opportunity to perform with his Quartet in the Soviet Union. The enthusiastic crowd (many of whom had grown up on Brubeck's music) clearly inspired the musicians which included clarinetist Bill Smith, electric bassist Chris Brubeck and drummer Randy Jones. Together they perform exciting versions of a variety of the leader's tunes plus Howard Brubeck's "Theme for June," "St. Louis Blues" and of course "Take Five." —*Scott Yanow*

New Wine / Jul. 3, 1987 / Music Masters ✦✦✦

The Quartet (which for the past five years had included clarinetist Bill Smith, electric bassist Chris Brubeck and drummer Randy Jones in addition to the pianist/leader) teamed up with the Montreal International Jazz Festival Orchestra for this live recording. Featured are six Brubeck compositions (including "Blue Rondo à la Turk" and "Koto Song") along with "Take the 'A' Train," all of which was in the Quartet's repertoire. In general the orchestra (which has some members of the Montreal Symphony) does not weigh down the proceedings and the music, although not all that "new," is enjoyable. —*Scott Yanow*

Quiet as the Moon / Sep. 20, 1988-May 8, 1991 / Music Masters ✦✦✦

Brubeck is heard at three separate recording sessions on this CD playing music that was used in the *Peanuts* cartoon series. The music ranges from such standards as "Bicycle Built for Two" and "When You Wish upon a Star" and Vince Guaraldi classics (including "Cast Your Fate to the Wind") to Brubeck originals. The varying personnel includes Bobby Militello (sitting in for Bill Smith) on flute, alto and tenor, either Chris Brubeck or Jack Six on bass, Dan Brubeck or Randy Jones on drums and cellist Matthew Brubeck. This well-paced set stands by itself apart from the *Peanuts* series. —*Scott Yanow*

Once When I Was Young / May 6, 1991-May 7, 1991 / Music Masters ✦✦✦

On this nostalgic and often wistful set, Dave Brubeck and his 1991 Quartet (clarinetist Bill Smith, bassist Jack Six and drummer Randy Jones) play eight songs from the pianist's childhood, such numbers as "Shine on Harvest Moon," "Stardust" and "Among My Souvenirs." In addition Brubeck (who is in top form) contributed "Dancin' in Rhythm" and the title cut which in its second version is performed by a choral group. —*Scott Yanow*

Trio Brubeck / Jun. 8, 1993 / Music Masters ✦✦✦

Pianist Dave Brubeck and two of his sons (Chris Brubeck on electric bass and bass trombone and drummer Dan Brubeck) are in high spirits on this rather spontaneous trio set. Highlights include "I Cried for You," "Broadway Bossa Nova," "One Moment Worth Years" and "Over the Rainbow." —*Scott Yanow*

Late Night Brubeck / Oct. 5, 1993-Oct. 7, 1993 / Telarc ✦✦✦✦

Dave Brubeck teams up with Bobby Militello (heard here on alto, tenor and flute), bassist Jack Six and drummer Randy Jones for a set that emphasizes ballads and slower tempos. Militello brings back the spirit of Paul Desmond while Brubeck's own playing continues to be full of surprises. On "Theme for June" he breaks out into stride, a Duke Ellington medley seems to develop quite spontaneously and

"Mean to Me" really works well. With bassist Jack Six and drummer Randy Jones fine in support, this CD is a strong effort from Dave Brubeck, who has nearly 100 worthwhile recordings currently in print. —*Scott Yanow*

Nightshift / Oct. 5, 1993-Oct. 10, 1993 / Telarc ✦✦✦✦
This is a particularly well-balanced set with pianist Dave Brubeck (then 73) in typically creative form. Although Brubeck (who is accompanied throughout by bassist Jack Six and drummer Randy Jones) is actually the real star of every selection (coming up with continually inventive ideas whether in ensembles, behind soloists or during his own solos), he is joined by three of his favorite horn players on some of the numbers. Bobby Militello shows a great deal of versatility with some blazing alto on "Yesterdays," melodic playing in a Paul Desmond vein on "I Can't Give You Anything But Love," soulful tenor on "Travelin' Blues" and plenty of intensity on "Knives." Clarinetist Bill Smith is well featured on "You Go to My Head" and the boisterous bass trombone of Chris Burbeck makes several welcome appearances. This recommended set has more than its share of variety and surprising moments. —*Scott Yanow*

Just You Just Me / 1994 / Telarc ✦✦✦
It had been nearly 40 years since Dave Brubeck's last solo piano recording when he recorded this relaxed set. Brubeck sounds typically creative yet often wistful on the seven standards, four originals and a "Tribute to Stephen Foster." This is a fine addition to Brubeck's extensive yet consistently satisfying discography. —*Scott Yanow*

In Their Own Sweet Way / Jan. 3, 1994-Sep. 8, 1995 / Telarc ✦✦✦✦
A rare reunion of the far-flung Brubeck family, this attractive CD came about by sheer accident. A massive New York snowstorm caused the cancellation of a classical two-piano recording session and the Brubeck clan, then celebrating the holiday season at Dave's home in Wilton, CT, happened to be available on short notice. Here the quartet—Dave, Darius, Chris and Dan—becomes a quintet for the first time with the addition of cellist Matthew, whose straight classical technique adds a brooding dimension to the group in certain optimum settings, though he remains somewhat of an outsider. As do most of Dave's Telarc albums, this one has an autumnal tone as the mellowing septuagenarian pianist plays the wise old master, playing in a more lyrical, reflective manner, revisiting past work and contributing a few new tunes. When Dave and Darius play together, Dave still remains the more immediately striking personality while Darius leans more toward mainstream jazz styles. On the relaxed two-piano blues duet "Dave 'n' Darius," the two blend well together without overloading the sound; Darius even adroitly picks up the ball where his dad's ideas leave off. Chris contributes most of the humorous touches, whether on bass or bass trombone, and Dan's drums offer mostly subtle support and cooking New Orleans funk (in 7/4 time!) on the sole non-Brubeck tune, "Sweet Georgia Brown." Dave Brubeck's Indian summer continues to be an unusually fruitful one. —*Richard S. Ginell*

Young Lions & Old Tigers / Jun. 29, 1994-Jun. 27, 1995 / Telarc ✦✦✦
To celebrate his 75th birthday, Dave Brubeck recorded one number apiece with quite a variety of top jazz stars, both young and old. Some of the performances (which alternate duets with quartets) work better than others (eight are recent Brubeck compositions) but all of the musicians display mutual respect and it is obvious that the guests are all fans of the still-masterful pianist. Trumpeter Roy Hargrove plays beautifully on his lyrical feature but Jon Hendricks, who sings "How High the Moon" as a ballad, takes it at such a slow tempo as to be dreary. Tenor saxophonist Michael Brecker is fine on "Michael Brecker Waltz" although he sounds a bit restrained, the wittily titled "Here Comes McBride" is a good-humored romp with bassist Christian McBride, Joe Lovano (on tenor) works well with Brubeck, and particularly memorable is the first meeting on record between Brubeck and fellow pianist George Shearing, a chance-taking interpretation of "In Your Own Sweet Way." Joshua Redman performs fine hard bop on one song, "Together" is a well-conceived duet for baritonist Gerry Mulligan and Brubeck, James Moody plays tenor, sings and yodels on the minor blues "Moody," Mulligan returns for the contrapuntal "Gerry-Go-Round," and, although the obscure fluegelhornist Ronnie Buttacavoli sounds very out of place on his boring feature, the set closes with one of the strongest performances, a solo piano showcase for Brubeck on "Deep in a Dream." Overall this is quite a mixed bag but, even with its occasional misses, the CD is a must for Dave Brubeck fans because the pianist is consistently inventive throughout the unusual set. —*Scott Yanow*

Clora Bryant

b. , Dennison, TX
Trumpet / Bop
It seems very strange that Clora Bryant has thus far only led one record session, a 1957 date that has been reissued by V.S.O.P. A fine trumpeter who ranges from bop to Dixieland, Bryant has mostly lived in Los Angeles throughout her career. She made some headlines when she played in the Soviet Union during the Gor-

bachev years and she was a member of the Cheathams for a time but otherwise has been greatly underrated. —*Scott Yanow*

● **Gal with a Horn** : Clora Bryant / 4 / Jun. 1957 / V.S.O.P. ✦✦✦✦
It seems strange that trumpeter Clora Bryant, who has been active in jazz for over 40 years, has thus far only had one opportunity to lead her own record date. This V.S.O.P. CD (which reissues a Mode LP from 1957) features Bryant heading a quartet (comprising pianist Roger Fleming, bassist Ben Tucker and drummer Bruz Freeman) that is sometimes augmented by Walter Benton on tenor and trumpeter Normie Faye (who sticks to section work). Bryant, who also sings, does a fine job of interpreting eight standards with the highlights including "Sweet Georgia Brown," "Tea for Two" and "This Can't Be Love." —*Scott Yanow*

Ray Bryant (Raphael Bryant)

b. Dec. 24, 1931, Philadelphia, PA
Piano / Bop, Swing, Soul Jazz, Groove
Although he could always play bop, Ray Bryant's playing combines together older elements (including blues, boogie-woogie, gospel and even stride) into a distinctive, soulful and swinging style; no one plays "After Hours" quite like him.

The younger brother of bassist Tommy Bryant and the uncle of Kevin and Robin Eubanks (his sister is their mother), Bryant started his career playing with Tiny Grimes in the late '40s. He became the house pianist at the Blue Note in Philadelphia in 1953 where he backed classic jazz greats (including Charlie Parker, Miles Davis and Lester Young) and made important contacts. He accompanied Carmen McRae (1956-57), recorded with Coleman Hawkins and Roy Eldridge at the 1957 Newport Jazz Festival (taking a brilliant solo on an exciting version of "I Can't Believe That You're in Love with Me") and played with Jo Jones' trio (1958). Bryant settled in New York in 1959, played with Sonny Rollins, Charlie Shavers and Curtis Fuller and soon had his own trio. He had a few funky commercial hits (including "Little Susie" and Cubano Chant) which kept him working for decades. Bryant has recorded often throughout his career (most notably for Epic, Prestige, Columbia, Sue, Cadet, Atlantic, Pablo and EmArcy) and even his dates on electric piano in the '70s are generally rewarding. However Ray Bryant is heard at his best when playing the blues on unaccompanied acoustic piano. —*Scott Yanow*

Ray Bryant Trio / Apr. 5, 1957 / Original Jazz Classics ✦✦✦✦
This CD reissues Ray Bryant's Prestige debut and his fourth album as a leader. Bryant has been notable from the start for being a versatile pianist, well-versed in bop, expert in the blues and able to comfortably play swing. He leans more towards the modern idiom on this trio set with bassist Ike Isaacs and drummer Specs Wright, coming up with colorful interpretations of such songs as "Django," "The Thrill Is Gone," Clifford Brown's "Daahoud," "Golden Earrings" and two of his originals. —*Scott Yanow*

Alone with the Blues / Dec. 19, 1958 / Original Jazz Classics ✦✦✦
Ray Bryant's first solo piano album is rightfully considered a classic. Bryant, at the time thought of as a young modern traditionalist, has always felt perfectly at home playing the blues. He performs five original and diverse blues on this set along with "Lover Man" and "Rockin' Chair," showing that he really never needed a bassist or a drummer to sound like a complete band. This Prestige album was reissued in the Original Jazz Classics but thus far only as an LP; highly recommended in any case. —*Scott Yanow*

Now's the Time / Oct. 29, 1959-Nov. 6, 1959 / Doctor Jazz ✦✦✦
This 1986 reissue LP of a program originally made for Bob Thiele's Signature label features pianist Ray Bryant and his trio (which also includes bassist Tom Bryant and drummer Oliver Jackson, Jr.) in a tribute to modern jazz composers and jazz standards. Bryant swings his way through a program that includes such numbers as John Lewis' "Delauney's Dilemma," "Misty," Horace Silver's "Doodlin'," "Walkin'" and the obscure Duke Ellington piece "A Hundred Dreams from Now." This album gives listeners a strong sampling of Ray Bryant's accessible playing during his early period. —*Scott Yanow*

Ray Bryant Plays / Oct. 29, 1959-Nov. 6, 1959 / Signature ✦✦✦

Little Susie / Dec. 10, 1959+Jan. 19, 1960 / Columbia ✦✦✦
Pianist Ray Bryant's debut for Columbia was named after "Little Susie," a hit single he had a short time earlier recorded for Signature. The trio LP with bassist Tommy Bryant and either Gus Johnson or Eddie Locke on drums (reissued by Columbia Special Products in the early 1970s) has a remake of "Little Susie," a few other originals that did not catch on as hits and Bryant's interpretations of such songs as "By Myself," "Willow Weep for Me" and Cole Porter's "So in Love." —*Scott Yanow*

Con Alma / Nov. 25, 1960-Jan. 26, 1961 / Columbia ✦✦✦✦
This 1988 reissue brought back one of pianist Ray Bryant's favorite trio records. Supported by either Bill Lee or Arthur Harper on bass and drummer Mickey Roker, Bryant is typically soulful, swinging and reasonably explorative on nine

songs (including a previously unreleased version of "Django") that are highlighted by "Con Alma," "Milestones," his popular "Cubano Chant" and "Autumn Leaves." —*Scott Yanow*

MCMLXX / Mar. 4, 1970 / Atlantic ✦✦✦
Despite some commercial tendencies, this 1970 LP (not yet reissued on CD) is better than it looks. Pianist Ray Bryant uplifts such pop material as "Let It Be," "Bridge over Troubled Waters," "Hey Jude" and "Spinning Wheel." Four selections find Bryant's trio (with electric bassist Chuck Rainey and drummer Jimmy Johnson) augmented by either horns (on "Let It Be") or by strings effectively arranged by Eumir Deodata. The colorful results are not essential but are less dated than one might think. —*Scott Yanow*

Alone at Montreux / Jul. 1972 / Atlantic ✦✦✦✦
Ray Bryant has long been a well-rounded and versatile yet distinctive pianist. His style, modern compared to the swing and stride players but traditional when matched against the boppers, is flexible enough to fit into many settings. This solo outing finds Bryant playing swing standards, blues, soulful versions of a couple of current pop tunes and even a bit of boogie. This LP's only fault is that it is out of print. —*Scott Yanow*

Hot Turkey / 1975 / Classic Jazz ✦✦✦
This fine LP (Ray Bryant's last session before signing with the Pablo label) has three selections (two swing standards plus the pianist's "Hot Turkey") played in a trio with bassist Major Holley and drummer Panama Francis. However the main reason to search for this out-of-print album is to hear Bryant uplift three familiar standards ("St. Louis Blues," "Take the 'A' Train" and "Sophisticated Lady") and a blues with his soulful and swinging solo piano interpretations. Virtually every Ray Bryant album is well worth picking up for his accessible and flexible style should appeal to fans of most jazz styles. —*Scott Yanow*

Here's Ray Bryant / Jan. 10, 1976-Jan. 12, 1976 / Original Jazz Classics ✦✦✦
Pianist Ray Bryant teams up with bassist George Duvivier and drummer Grady Tate for a set of soulful and bluesy interpretations of five standards and three originals. Oddly enough there are no 12-bar blues on this date (a Pablo session reissued on CD in the OJC series) but Bryant infuses such songs as "Girl Talk," "Good Morning Heartache" and "Li'l Darlin'" with plenty of blues feeling anyway. A relaxed outing, not essential but enjoyable. —*Scott Yanow*

Solo Flight / Dec. 21, 1976 / Original Jazz Classics ✦✦✦
Ray Bryant, although he has made many fine trio albums through the years, is at his best when playing unaccompanied solos. For this album (surprisingly not yet reissued on CD), Bryant introduces such original old-timey blues as "In de Back Room" and "Blues in de Big Brass Bed," pours soul into Bobby Timmons' "Moanin'," has no difficulty with the sophisticated ballad "What Are You Doing the Rest of Your Life" and romps through "St. Louis Blues" and "Take the 'A' Train." This is an excellent recording that deserves to be much more widely available. —*Scott Yanow*

● **Montreux '77** / Jul. 13, 1977 / Original Jazz Classics ✦✦✦✦
Ray Bryant's fourth recorded solo piano recital (and second in less than a year) was performed at the 1977 Montreux Jazz Festival and is a particularly well-rounded set. Bryant plays spirituals, blues, swing standards, John Lewis' "Django" and the obscure "Jungle Town Jubilee." His distinctive and soulful style fits well into every setting, making this an easily recommended set that will satisfy most musical tastes. —*Scott Yanow*

All Blues / Apr. 10, 1978 / Original Jazz Classics ✦✦✦
Ray Bryant (piano), Sam Jones (bass), and Grady Tate (drums)—a classic trio of jazz greats playing bluesy jazz. Mostly at slower tempos, this is very listenable. Most important, the groove is maintained throughout, so you know what you are getting. —*Michael Erlewine*

Potpourri / May 13, 1980+May 14, 1980 / Original Jazz Classics ✦✦✦
Ray Bryant's fifth and final album for Pablo (all are quite worthwhile) features his 1980 trio which also includes bassist Jimmy Rowser and drummer Mickey Roker. It is a pity that this excellent session is not yet available on CD for it is a delight for both bebop and small-group swing fans. Bryant stretches out on eight superior jazz standards with the highlights including Lester Young's "D.B. Blues," "One O'Clock Jump," "In Walked Bud" and "My One and Only Love." Actually all eight numbers are quite enjoyable, making this one of Ray Bryant's best trio records. —*Scott Yanow*

Ray Bryant Trio Today / Feb. 13, 1987-Feb. 14, 1987 / EmArcy ✦✦✦✦
"Today" is of course a relative term but this EmArcy release (the first in a series) does feature pianist Ray Bryant's 1987 trio (which includes bassist Rufus Reid and drummer Freddie Waits). Bryant revives his near-classic "Slow Freight," performs his original "Tonk" and plays songs by Nat Adderley ("The Old Country"), Miles Davis, Thelonious Monk, Billy Strayhorn, Benny Carter and John Lewis ("Afternoon in Paris"). No matter the source of the material, Bryant gives most of the

songs bluish interpretations, often providing a fresh slant on some of the more familiar tunes. Nearly all of Ray Bryant's recordings from the past four decades are well worth picking up and this one is no exception. —*Scott Yanow*

Blue Moods / Feb. 15, 1987 / EmArcy ✦✦✦✦
Outstanding trio date with Bryant offering teeming phrases, sweeping statements, and some wonderful ballads, backed by bassist Rufus Reid and drummer Freddie Waits. Not only great playing all around, but an excellent recording as well. —*Ron Wynn*

Plays Basie and Ellington / Feb. 15, 1987-Feb. 16, 1987 / EmArcy ✦✦✦
This was the first new music of Ray Bryant to be released in seven years although his EmArcy album *Ray Bryant Trio Today* was actually recorded two days earlier. Pianist Bryant (along with bassist Rufus Reid and drummer Freddie Waits) performs four songs associated with Count Basie (including Neal Hefti's obscure "Teddy the Toad"), his own "Blues for Basie," five Duke Ellington tunes (including a three-song ballad medley) and Mercer Ellington's "Things Ain't What They Used to Be." Although it is a shame that ("Teddy" excepted) Bryant stuck to fairly obvious material (particularly on the Ellington half of the program), his typically swinging and soulful renditions are always fun to hear. —*Scott Yanow*

Golden Earrings / Jan. 23, 1988-Jan. 26, 1988 / EmArcy ✦✦✦
Pianist Ray Bryant's records of the 1980s are consistently enjoyable but sometimes the repertoire could be fresher. Virtually every song on this EmArcy release was recorded earlier by Bryant except possibly "I'm a Fool to Want You." Bryant, bassist Rufus Reid and drummer Freddie Waits explore such numbers as "'Round Midnight," "Misty," Duke Ellington's "What Am I Here For" and Bryant's "Lullabye," but the lack of surprises makes this a rather predictable effort. —*Scott Yanow*

All Mine . . . And Yours / Oct. 19, 1989-Oct. 20, 1989 / EmArcy ✦✦✦

Ray's Tribute to His Jazz Piano Friends / Jun. 26, 1997-Jun. 27, 1997 / JVC ✦✦✦✦
Ray Bryant (who is joined for this set by bassist Ray Drummond and drummer Winard Harper) pays tribute to 11 of his favorite pianists by playing a song apiece associated with Duke Ellington, Ramsey Lewis, Dave Brubeck, Horace Silver, Vince Guaraldi, Count Basie, Thelonious Monk, Bobby Timmons, Kenny Barron, Randy Weston and Joe Zawinul. Bryant's timeless style lends itself well to such songs as "The Duke," "Doodlin'," "Moanin'," and even "The 'In' Crowd" and "Birdland." —*Scott Yanow*

Rusty Bryant

b. Nov. 25, 1929, Huntington, WV, d. Mar. 25, 1991, Columbus, OH
Tenor Saxophone / Post-Bop, Soul Jazz, Groove, Hard Bop
Among the finest funky and soul-jazz tenors of the '70s, Bryant is noted for his thick tone, robust sound, and jam-session-style albums. Rusty Bryant is one of the original bar-walking sax players.

Royal G. "Rusty" Bryant was born on November 25, 1929, in Huntington, WV, but was raised in Columbus, OH. He credits Gene Ammons and Sonny Stitt as his main influences. He played with and learned from Tiny Grimes and Stomp Gordon, and was leading his own groups by 1951. Bryant toured with Hammond organist Mike Marr during the 1960s. He settled in Columbus, OH. —*Michael Erlewine & Ron Wynn*

Rusty Bryant Returns / Feb. 17, 1969 / Original Jazz Classics ✦✦✦✦
Rusty Bryant, a veteran R&B tenor player, was somewhat forgotten at the time of his debut Prestige album, but due to the commercial success of this former LP (reissued on CD in the OJC series), Bryant would record seven more sessions for Prestige during the next five years. Actually, this date is a bit surprising, with Bryant sticking exclusively to alto and sometimes using an electrified model similar to what Lou Donaldson was playing at the time. The music (mostly blues-oriented originals) is enjoyable, with plenty of boogaloos and soulful vamps. In addition to Bryant, the main soloists are guitarist Grant Green, in excellent form, and organist Sonny Phillips. —*Scott Yanow*

Night Train Now! / Oct. 6, 1969 / Prestige ✦✦✦
An effort very much consistent with producer Bob Porter's Prestige "house" soul-jazz sound, utilizing players who would contribute to many other similar efforts in the late '60s and early '70s, particularly guitarist Boogaloo Joe Jones and drummer Bernard Purdie. These beefy, straightforward grooves include a remake of Bryant's arrangement of "Night Train" (one of his most popular recordings in the version he cut for Dot). The writing credit for "Funky Rabbits" is given as "unknown," but it sure sounds a lot to these ears like a retitled version of Ray Charles' "Hallelujah, I Love Her So." The *Legends of Acid Jazz* CD reissue combines this and the 1970 session *Soul Liberation* onto one disc. —*Richie Unterberger*

● **Legends of Acid Jazz** / Oct. 6, 1969+Jun. 15, 1970 / Prestige ✦✦✦✦✦
Presenting both the 1969 album *Night Train Now!* and the 1970 follow-up *Soul Liberation* in their entirety, this 73-minute disc is the best document of Bryant at his soul-jazz peak. —*Richie Unterberger*

Soul Liberation / Jun. 15, 1970 / Prestige ✦✦✦✦✦

This has a bluesier, harder R&B feel than his previous effort (*Night Train Now*), courtesy of a revamped lineup featuring Charles Earland on organ, Melvin Sparks on guitar, and Idris Muhammad on drums. The title track is Bryant's most famous composition. The *Legends of Acid Jazz* CD reissue combines this and the 1970 session *Soul Liberation* onto one disc. —*Richie Unterberger*

Jeanie Bryson

b. 1959
Vocals / Standards

Jeanie Bryson is a subtle and somewhat sensuous singer with a small and appealing voice. Dizzy Gillespie's illegitimate daughter (a fact hidden from the general public during his lifetime), her mother is the songwriter Connie Bryson. She graduated from Livingston College in 1981 and freelanced for a decade, visiting Europe several times. Bryson recorded several fine albums for Telarc starting in 1992 including a Peggy Lee tribute; she also sang on Terence Blanchard's recorded set of Billie Holiday-associated songs. —*Scott Yanow*

● **I Love Being Here with You** / Jan. 24, 1993-Jan. 26, 1993 / Telarc ✦✦✦✦

Jeanie Bryson, Dizzy Gillespie's daughter, made her recording debut on this CD. Her voice is highly appealing and often sensuous, hinting at Peggy Lee and Susannah McCorkle. A fine middle-of-the-road song stylist (rather than a jazz singer), Bryson does an excellent job on a set dominated by standards. She mostly concentrates on melody statements with subtle improvising and is at her best on ballads. Steve Nelson's vibes fit in well during his appearances and trumpeter Wallace Roney (as usual sounding like Miles Davis) also takes some good solos. This is a promising beginning for Jeanie Bryson. —*Scott Yanow*

Tonight I Need You So / Jan. 25, 1994-Feb. 20, 1994 / Telarc ✦✦✦

Bryson's soft warm voice at times recalls Maxine Sullivan and on "Solamente Tu" she comes very close to the fragility of Astrud Gilberto. There are a few memorable selections on her second Telarc disc, most notably the exuberant "Simple Song" (which has some jubilant playing from altoist Paquito D'Rivera), a sensuous "Honeysuckle Rose" and a fine version of "Skydive." Unfortunately the set also has an excess of forgettable poppish material that weighs down the content somewhat. However Bryson mostly overcomes the material and her likable and easygoing style compensates. This release is not essential but is enjoyable. —*Scott Yanow*

Milt Buckner

b. Jul. 10, 1915, St. Louis, MO, d. Jul. 27, 1977, Chicago, IL
Organ, Piano / Swing, Groove

Milt Buckner had a dual career. As a pianist he largely invented the "locked hands" style (parallel chords) that was adopted by many other players including George Shearing and Oscar Peterson. And as an organist he was one of the top pre-Jimmy Smith stylists, helping to popularize the instrument.

The younger brother of altoist Ted Buckner (who played with Jimmie Lunceford), Milt Buckner grew up in Detroit and gigged locally in addition to arranging for McKinney's Cotton Pickers in 1934. He came to fame as pianist and arranger with Lionel Hampton (1941-48, 1950-52 and occasionally in later years) where he was a crowd pleaser. During 1948-50 Buckner led his own bands and after 1952 he generally played organ with trios or quartets. In later years he sometimes teamed up with Illinois Jacquet or Jo Jones. Buckner recorded many dates as a leader, particularly for Black & Blue in the 1970s. —*Scott Yanow*

● **Rockin' Hammond** / Feb. 22, 1956-Mar. 15, 1956 / Capitol ✦✦✦✦✦

Classic organ combo with a master. A fine representation of Buckner's brilliance. —*Michael G. Nastos*

Milt Buckner [Black & Blue] / Dec. 7, 1967 / Black & Blue ✦✦✦

Crazy Rhythm / Dec. 7, 1967-Sep. 1968 / Black & Blue ✦✦✦

Green Onions / Feb. 21, 1975 / Inner City ✦✦✦✦

From 1966-77, organist Milt Buckner recorded often for European labels. This particular set (originally cut for the Black & Blue label) was one of the very few to be made available domestically. It came out on Inner City's Classic Jazz subsidiary, and it is a bit of an oddity. Buckner, through overdubbing, performs on organ, piano and vibes (which he rarely played), and even takes an eccentric vocal on "Green Onions." To confuse matters, pianist Andre Persiany is also heard on some numbers, along with blues guitarist Roy Gaines, bassist Roland Lobligeois and drummer Panama Francis. The music itself is much less complicated, swing standards plus Buckner's "Pour Toutes Mes Soeurs" and "Milt's Boogie." Fun good-time music that will be difficult to find. —*Scott Yanow*

Teddy Buckner

b. Jul. 16, 1909, Sherman, TX, d. Sep. 22, 1994, Los Angeles, CA
Trumpet / Dixieland

A strong Dixieland player, Teddy Buckner spent most of his career emulating his idol Louis Armstrong, not really developing a sound of his own despite having impressive technique. He worked on the West Coast in the 1930s and was with Buck Clayton's orchestra in Shanghai, China (1934). Louis Armstrong's stand-in on the 1936 film *Pennies from Heaven*, Buckner never attempted to advance with the times. He worked with Benny Carter (1945-48), Lionel Hampton (1947-1948) and most notably with Kid Ory's Creole Jazz Band (1949-54). Starting in 1955 Buckner led his own Dixieland group and he held his own with the fiery Sidney Bechet at a few French concerts in 1958. Buckner worked regularly for a long period with his band at Disneyland (1965-81) and through the years recorded several albums for GNP/Crescendo and its subsidiary Dixieland Jubilee. —*Scott Yanow*

Teddy Buckner / Feb. 6, 1955 / GNP ✦✦✦

Teddy Buckner in Concert at the Dixieland Jubilee / Oct. 15, 1955 / Dixieland Jubilee ✦✦✦

A Salute to Louis Armstrong / 1957-1958 / GNP ✦✦✦✦

Teddy Buckner, a fine technical player who spent his life emulating Louis Armstrong in Dixieland settings, logically pays tribute to Satch on this enjoyable set. Using a sextet that also features trombonist John "Streamling" Ewing and clarinetist Joe Darensbourg, Buckner jams through ten songs that Louis Armstrong recorded in the 1920s and '30s. Avoiding Armstrong's later hits, Buckner does a fine job of interpreting such tunes as "My Monday Date," "Potato Head Blues," "High Society" and "I Want a Big Butter and Egg Man." This hard-to-find LP will satisfy Dixieland fans. —*Scott Yanow*

Teddy Buckner and the All Stars / Apr. 1958 / GNP ✦✦✦

Session modeled along the lines of Louis Armstrong small combo-dates, with Buckner operating in Armstrong's role as leader and trumpet soloist, and band members including frequent Armstrong collaborators Trummy Young and Billy Kyle. There are some cliched moments and other numbers where Buckner and company mesh, particularly on "Mahogany Hall Romp." —*Ron Wynn*

● **On the Sunset Strip** / 1960 / Dixieland Jubilee ✦✦✦✦

The extroverted Dixieland trumpeter Teddy Buckner recorded a series of fun albums for Dixieland Jubilee (a subsidiary of GNP/Crescendo) during the mid- to late 1950s, most of which have not yet been reissued on CD. This particular LP was one of his last before he started working regularly at Disneyland. Joined by a spirited group that includes trombonist John "Streamline" Ewing and Count Basie veteran Caughey Roberts on clarinet, Buckner mostly sticks to Dixieland standards such as "Original Dixieland One Step," "China Boy," "Mack the Knife" and a lengthy "Down in Jungletown." Teddy Buckner was never a great original but he believed in his music and had impressive range and power. —*Scott Yanow*

Midnight in Moscow / 1962 / GNP ✦✦✦

Buckshot LeFonque

Group / Fusion, Hip Hop

When Branford Marsalis decided to stir up a little trouble in 1994 by juxtaposing and fusing mainstream jazz with hip-hop rhythms, rap, R&B, rock, reggae and half a dozen other idioms, he chose to present his new music under the group name Buckshot LeFonque. This fanciful moniker is actually a resurrection of a pseudonym Cannonball Adderley used in the 1950s when moonlighting on a record label other than his own. The group's eponymous first album, a brilliant, playful, musically rich realization of this anything-goes fusion, unfortunately drew a lot of fire from critics in every genre, a situation that Marsalis lamented on the group's equally eclectic yet less striking second album, *Music Evolution*. Nevertheless, Marsalis was so enthused by his new group that he left his high-profile job as bandleader of the *Tonight Show* in part so that he could tour with Buckshot LeFonque in 1994-95. The 1997 edition of Buckshot, as heard on *Music Evolution*, contains a nucleus of Marsalis (saxophones, keyboard and drum programming), DJ Apollo ("wheels o' steel"), Frank McComb (vocals, keyboards), Carl Burnett (guitar), Russell Gunn (trumpet), Reginald Veal (bass), Rocky Bryant (drums) and 50 Styles: The Unknown Soldier (rap vocals). Of all of Marsalis' diverse pursuits, none project his unique combination of virtuosity and irreverence as completely as does Buckshot LeFonque. —*Richard S. Ginell*

Buckshot LeFonque / 1994 / Columbia ✦✦✦

Lots of records are touted as breakthroughs by the hype machines and spinmasters, but this one really is—a marvelously playful and, above all, musical fusion of the old jazz verities and newer currents swirling around the 1990s. "Buckshot LeFonque" was a pseudonym for Cannonball Adderley in the 1950s, and you'll squint long and hard trying to find Branford's name on the jacket and cover except for the tiny note, "Produced by B. Marsalis." Maybe he was hedging his bets against the expected (and received) flak from the jazz purists, but the reality is that he has found a brilliant way to fuse hip-hop rhythms with mainstream jazz licks without compromising either idiom. The best number is a lovely setting of Maya Angelou's poem "I Know Why the Caged Bird Sings," with absolutely gorgeous soprano by Marsalis, some great Miles-tinged muted trumpet from Roy Hargrove, and Angelou reciting her words against the big electronic backbeat. The free-thinking Branford also injects real funk into Elton John's "Mona Lisas (and Mad Hatters)"; throws in a little reggae, rap and lots of sampling; gets down and dirty with Kevin Eubanks' slide guitar on the truckin' cut "Some Cow Fonque"; and unifies most of the package with a couple of recurring, catchy riffs and touches of horseplay. The only misfire is a totally incongruous, totally dull soul ballad called "Ain't It Funny" (sung by Tammy Townsend) that sounds as if someone suddenly switched CDs on your changer. Nevertheless, regardless of what the neo-boppers might say, this is a more imaginative record than any of Branford's estimable straight jazz projects—and a lot more fun. —*Richard S. Ginell*

● **Music Evolution** / Apr. 1, 1997 / Columbia ✦✦✦✦

Despite the occasional lapse into aimless fusion, Buckshot LeFonque's second album, *Music Evolution*, is a stronger, more confident record than its eponymous debut, capturing Branford Marsalis and his band—including cameos by David Sanborn, Guru and Laurence Fishburne—finding a vibrant, exciting common ground between hard bop and hip-hop. —*Leo Stanley*

John Bunch

b. Dec. 1, 1921, Tipton, IN
Piano / Swing, Mainstream Jazz

John Bunch has had a long and distinguished career even if his abilities as an accompanist and supportive player have long led to him often being taken for granted. He started on piano when he was 11 and within a year was playing in local clubs. Bunch, a flexible pianist who was most inspired by Teddy Wilson, generally played locally until working with the big bands of Woody Herman (1956-57), Benny Goodman and Maynard Ferguson (1958) when he was already in his mid-30s. Bunch worked in the small groups of Buddy Rich, Al Cohn-Zoot Sims and Gene Krupa (1961-64), was a member of Rich's 1966 big band and accompanied Tony Bennett during 1966-72. Off and on with Benny Goodman during the '60s and '70s, Bunch also recorded five albums as a leader during 1975-77 for Famous Door, Chiaroscuro (an exquisite solo piano set of Kurt Weill compositions later reissued on CD) and Progressive. In the 1980s and '90s John Bunch has often been employed by the young mainstream stars such as Scott Hamilton and Warren Vache and has recorded for Concord and Arbors. —*Scott Yanow*

John's Bunch / 1975 / Famous Door ✦✦✦

● **John Bunch Plays Kurt Weill** / May 1975-Jan. 31, 1991 / Chiaroscuro ✦✦✦✦✦

John Bunch, an excellent mainstream pianist, is heard on this reissue CD at the peak of his form. The original LP consisted of a dozen Kurt Weill compositions interpreted solo by Bunch; highlights include "The Alabama Song," "My Ship," "This Is New" and "Speak Low." To fill out the CD, Bunch recorded five additional Weill songs in 1991. Mixing together standards and complete obscurities (and surprisingly not including "Moritat," the famous "Mack the Knife" theme), Bunch also varied the moods and tempos. The results are quite memorable, with plenty of subtle creativity, one of John Bunch's finest recordings from a long career. —*Scott Yanow*

John's Other Bunch / 1977 / Famous Door ✦✦✦✦

Slick Funk / 1977 / Famous Door ✦✦✦

Jubilee / Mar. 1, 1977 / Audiophile ✦✦✦✦

Pianist John Bunch, who did not get an opportunity to record as a leader until he was already 53 in 1975, is heard on this set in fine form leading a drumless trio that also includes guitarist Cal Collins and bassist George Mraz. Although Collins and Mraz had not actually met before the session, the interplay between the three musicians is quite impressive. Bunch performs numbers by Hoagy Carmichael (the title cut), Johnny Mandel, Ahmad Jamal, Cole Porter, Bud Powell (the classic "Celia"), Lil Harden (a swinging "Struttin' with Some Barbecue") and his own "It's Love in the Spring" and "Cincinnati Slick." This fine mainstream set should satisfy fans of swing piano. —*Scott Yanow*

● **The Best Thing for You** / Jun. 1987 / Concord Jazz ✦✦✦✦✦

A fairly lyrical set with an occasional stomp (most notably "'Deed I Do" and "Au Privave") for variety, this Concord date features the excellent mainstream pianist John Bunch, bassist Phil Flanigan and drummer Chuck Riggs. Although few surprises occur, the ten standards all benefit from the treatments given by the excellent musicians. —*Scott Yanow*

NY Swing / 1992 / LRC ✦✦✦

Struttin' / Nov. 7, 1995-Nov. 8, 1995 / Arbors ✦✦✦✦

John Bunch has long been a very flexible pianist able to play Dixieland, swing, bop and more modern material with equal skill. His set of duets with bassist Phil Flanigan on his Arbors CD may have an intimate and quiet sound, but there is plenty of diversity in tempos and some heat generated. Whether it be Benny Harris' "Crazeology," a jazz interpretation of Chopin's "Prelude in C Minor," the always-welcome "As Long As I Live" or a Dixielandish "Struttin' with Some Barbecue," the music always swings, the interplay between the two musicians is strong, and the performances hold one's attention at all times. An excellent effort. —*Scott Yanow*

Solo, Vol. 1 / Nov. 4, 1996-Nov. 5, 1996 / Arbors ✦✦✦✦

Teddy Bunn

b. 1909, Freeport, NY, d. Jul. 20, 1978, Lancaster, CA
Guitar / Swing, Classic Jazz

A fine single-note acoustic guitar soloist, Teddy Bunn was one of the top jazz guitarists of the 1930s. Largely self-taught, Bunn first gained recognition when he recorded with Duke Ellington in 1929 and played with the Washboard Rhythm Kings in the late-'20s/early-'30s period. A few years later he was one of the stars with the Spirits of Rhythm (which played regularly at the Onyx Club). During 1938-40 Bunn recorded with Jimmie Noone, Johnny Dodds, Trixie Smith, J.C. Higginbotham, Sidney Bechet, Lionel Hampton and was on the famous Mezz Mezzrow-Tommy Ladnier sessions; in addition he made four unaccompanied solos for Blue Note. Switching to electric guitar Bunn led his own groups in the 1940s and rejoined the Spirits of Rhythm; in the '50s he played R&B with a variety of groups (including Jack McVea, Edgar Hayes and Louis Jordan). Although fairly obscure after the early '40s, Bunn worked regularly until the late '60s when health problems forced his retirement. —*Scott Yanow*

● **Teddy Bunn (1929-1940)** / Sep. 16, 1929-Mar. 28, 1940 / RST ✦✦✦✦

Teddy Bunn was one of the finest acoustic jazz guitarists of the 1930s, although he had relatively few opportunities to be showcased on record. This CD (from the Austrian RST label) features Bunn on a series of hokum vocal duets with Spencer Williams (Clarence Profit or James P. Johnson provide the piano accompaniment), backing singers Buck Franklin, Fat Hayden and Walter Pichon, jamming with clarinetist Mezz Mezzrow and trumpeter Tommy Ladnier (six alternate takes from the famous Panassie sessions) and leading a session of his own. The latter (which is also included on a Mosaic box set) features Bunn on two memorable unaccompanied guitar solos and on three occasions (including an alternate take of "Blues Without Words") backing his own vocals. It is strange that Bunn recorded so rarely after 1940 for he lived until 1978. This is his definitive set. —*Scott Yanow*

Jane Bunnett

b. Oct. 22, 1956, Toronto, Canada
Flute, Soprano Saxophone / Post-Bop, Latin Jazz, Afro-Cuban Jazz

One of the finest soprano saxophonists in jazz of the 1990s, Jane Bunnett originally studied classical piano but tendonitis cut short that career. After seeing the Charles Mingus group in San Francisco, Bunnett was inspired to play advanced jazz. On soprano she recalls Steve Lacy a bit (who she has studied with) while her flute playing is quite distinctive. Bunnett has always had major players on her records; in addition to her husband trumpeter Larry Cramer, the late pianist Don Pullen had been a fixture on her records, her 1988 debut for Dark Light also featured Dewey Redman and she has utilized Sheila Jordan and Jeanne Lee.

Bunnett has recorded for Dark Light, Music & Arts (a series of duets with Pullen) and Denon. Her most adventurous work thus far is 1991's *Spirits of Havana* which matches her playing with many of Cuba's top jazz musicians in Cuba. In recent years Jane Bunnett has been living in Paris. —*Scott Yanow*

In Dew Time / Feb. 25, 1988-Feb. 26, 1988 / Dark Light ✦✦✦✦

Jane Bunnett's debut album uses different personnel on every selection. She starts out quite strong (playing flute in a duet with pianist Don Pullen on his catchy "Big Alice") and continues the momentum throughout a set that includes two of her originals, an obscure Carla Bley song, the title cut (written by her husband-trumpeter Larry Cramer) and a medley of her "Five" and the standard "As Long As There Is Music." At that point in her career, Bunnett was a little more original on flute than on soprano but already quite talented on both. In addition to members of her Canadian group (Cramer, pianist Brian Dickenson, bassist Scott Alexander and drummer Claude Ranger), Bunnett welcomes Don Pullen, tenor great Dewey Redman and the French horn of Vincent Chancey on some of the selections. The inside/outside music is quite colorful, unpredictable and ultimately logical. A very impressive debut. —*Scott Yanow*

New York Duets / 1989 / Music & Arts ✦✦✦✦

This strong outing matches together Jane Bunnett on soprano and flute and the great pianist Don Pullen. The adventurous music holds onto the tradition of chordal improvisation yet is also quite free in spots. Pullen's rhythmic playing makes his solos seem more accessible and traditional than they really were and it is to Bunnett's great credit that she keeps up with him. In addition to six of their originals, the duo performs a pair of complex Thelonious Monk songs ("Bye-Ya" and "Little Rootie Tootie") and a Cuban theme "For Merceditas." Thought-provoking and unpredictable music. —*Scott Yanow*

Live at Sweet Basil / 1990 / Denon ✦✦✦

Jane Bunnett's first live album finds the talented reedist (who doubles on soprano and flute) leading a quintet comprising trumpeter Larry Cramer, pianist Don Pullen, bassist Kieran Overs and drummer Billy Hart. The group stretches out on three Bunnett compositions, one apiece by Cramer (a remake of "In Dew Time") and Pullen (a nearly 16-minute "Double Arc Jake") and the standard "You Don't Know What Love Is." The solos are consistently stimulating and the music (which ranges from advanced hard bop to free sections) always holds onto one's attention. —*Scott Yanow*

● **Spirits of Havana** / Sep. 27, 1991-Oct. 4, 1991 / Denon ✦✦✦✦✦

On this remarkable CD, Jane Bunnett (doubling on flute and soprano) performs Cuban music on its own terms quite successfully. Bunnett and a pair of fellow Canadians (trumpeter Larry Cramer and bassist Kieran Overs) recorded in Havana with some of the top Cuban musicians including Guillermo Barreto (who supervised the sessions, played some timbales and was an inspiration to Bunnett), singer Merceditas Valdes, pianists Hilario Duran, Gonzalo Rubalcaba and Frank Emilio, several top percussionists and others. The very original music (including a fresh rendition of Thelonious Monk's "Epistrophy") is well worth several listens and is a classic of its kind. —*Scott Yanow*

Water Is Wide / Aug. 18, 1993-Aug. 19, 1993 / Evidence ✦✦✦✦

This intriguing set has more than its share of variety. Jane Bunnett pays tribute to Rahsaan Roland Kirk with some speechlike flute on "Serenade to a Cuckoo," recalls Steve Lacy a bit with her soprano on two Thelonious Monk pieces ("Pannonica" and "Brake's Sake") and her originals (along with those of trumpeter Larry Cramer) range from advanced bop to fairly free improvising. Vocalists Sheila Jordan (wonderful on "You Must Believe in Spring") and Jeanne Lee have individual features and are both major parts of the ancient hymn "The Water Is Wide" while the rhythm section (pianist Don Pullen, bassist Kieran Overs and drummer Billy Hart) consistently displays flexibility and creative reactions to the directions of the lead voices. —*Scott Yanow*

Jane Bunnett and the Cuban Piano Masters / Sep. 15, 1993+Sep. 16, 1993 / Blue Note ✦✦✦✦✦

Jane Bunnett, a talented flutist and soprano saxophonist from Canada, has consistently cut through red tape and bureaucracy in order to perform with Cuban musicians. For this project, Bunnett puts the focus on a pair of talented Cuban pianists (Jose Maria Vitier and Frank Emilio Flynn), performing in a variety of settings that also sometimes include bassist Carlitos del Puerto. The leader actually sits out on three of the ten songs. As strong as the playing is (and the interplay between Bunnett and the pianists is consistently delightful), the rich melodies (five by Vitier, one from Flynn and four obscurities) are most memorable. Influenced by classical music and the pianist's Cuban heritage, the highly appealing themes stick in one's mind long after the CD is finished. Several of the tunes could very well catch on as standards in the future, if enough musicians hear this CD. Recommended, as are all of Jane Bunnett's recordings to date. —*Scott Yanow*

Rendez-Vous / May 20, 1995-May 21, 1995 / Justin Time ✦✦✦✦

Dave Burrell (Herman Davis Burrell)

b. Sep. 10, 1940, Middletown, OH
Piano / Avant-Garde, Free Jazz, Post-Bop

Since the mid-'60s, Dave Burrell has been a quality sideman on a number of freejazz recordings led by the likes of Archie Shepp, Pharoah Sanders, and Marion Brown. Burrell's voice combines the entire history of jazz from Dixieland to free, though it is as an inside/outside player that he most excels. His is a percussive, syncopated style, well suited to the heavily rhythmic concept favored by one of Burrell's steadiest employers, tenorist David Murray.

Burrell was born in Connecticut, but grew up in Hawaii. Both of his parents sang. According to W. Royal Stokes, his mother was once asked to join the Delta Rhythm Boys; it was a visit to the family home by singer Herb Jeffries that first interested Burrell in jazz. As a teenager, Burrell played in the requisite rock 'n' roll band. He attended the University of Hawaii from 1958-60 before eventually getting his degree in 1965 from Boston's Berklee School of Music. While at Berklee, he played with Tony Williams and Sam Rivers. After graduation, Burrell moved to

New York, where he formed a group with saxophonist Byard Lancaster, bassist Sirone, and drummer Bobby Kapp, called the Untraditional Jazz Improvisational Team. Burrell also fell in with Marion Brown and Grachan Moncur, recording with the former in 1966 and the latter in 1969. In 1968, Burrell co-founded the 360 Degree Music Experience with Moncur and drummer Beaver Harris. In 1969, he traveled to Algiers, where he participated in a Pan-African Festival. That year, he also taught in Harlem for the Community Thing Organization. Burrell recorded with Sanders, Shepp, Alan Silva, and Sunny Murray at various times in the late '60s and early '70s. In the late '70s, Burrell wrote that rarest of musical works, a jazz opera. Entitled *Windward Passages*, Burrell recorded portions of the work as a soloist in 1979. In the '80s and '90s, Burrell formed a fruitful association with Murray, with whose octet and quartet he would record on a number of occasions. The two recorded in duo, as well, notably including the 1997 Black Saint release *Windward Passages*, which featured Burrell's wife, singer Monika Larsson, on some tracks. —*Chris Kelsey*

High One High Two / Feb. 6, 1968+Sep. 9, 1968 / Arista ✦✦✦✦

Dave Burrell has long had a highly original style on piano, not quite outside but far from conventional. This CD reissues a trio set with bassist Sirone and either Bobby Kapp or Sonny Murray on drums. Most intriguing is a 19-minute "West Side Story Medley" that features Burrell playing many of the songs from Leonard Bernstein's work in abstract fashion. There is also the lengthy "East Side Colors," five brief (around three minutes apiece) versions of five of Burrell's originals and the "Theme Stream Medley" which has reprises of the five songs plus a sixth piece ("Inside Ouch"). This interesting set rewards repeated listenings. —*Scott Yanow*

Daybreak / Mar. 30, 1989 / Gazell ✦✦✦

Jelly Roll Joys / 1991 / Gazell ✦✦

In Concert / Oct. 1991 / Victor ✦✦✦

Brother to Brother / 1993 / Gazell ✦✦✦

● **Windward Passages** / Dec. 8, 1993 / Black Saint ✦✦✦✦

Kenny Burrell (Kenneth Earl Burrell)

b. Jul. 31, 1931, Detroit, MI
Guitar / Bop, Groove

Kenny Burrell has been a very consistent guitarist throughout his career. Cooltoned and playing in an unchanging style based in bop, Burrell has always been the epitome of good taste and solid swing. Duke Ellington's favorite guitarist (though he never actually recorded with him), Burrell started playing guitar when he was 12 and he debuted on records with Dizzy Gillespie in 1951. Part of the fertile Detroit jazz scene of the early '50s, Burrell moved to New York in 1956. Highly in demand from the start, Burrell has appeared on a countless number of records during the past 40 years as a leader and as a sideman. Among his more notable associations have been dates with Stan Getz, Billie Holiday, Milt Jackson, John Coltrane, Gil Evans, Sonny Rollins, Quincy Jones, Stanley Turrentine and Jimmy Smith. Starting in the early '70s Burrell began leading seminars and teaching, often focusing on Duke Ellington's music. He toured with the Phillip Morris Superband during 1985-86 and has led three-guitar quintets but generally Kenny Burrell plays at the head of a trio/quartet. —*Scott Yanow*

Introducing Kenny Burrell / May 29, 1956 / Blue Note ✦✦✦✦

Despite its title, this LP was actually guitarist Kenny Burrell's second Blue Note album, although the first to be released. Teamed with pianist Tommy Flanagan, bassist Paul Chambers, drummer Kenny Clarke and the conga of Candido, Burrell displays what was already an immediately recognizable tone. At 24, Burrell had quickly emerged to become one of the top bop guitarists of the era, and he is in particularly excellent form on "This Time the Dreams on Me," "Weaver of Dreams" and "Delilah." A bonus of this set is a percussion duo by Clarke and Candido on "Rhythmorama." Enjoyable music. —*Scott Yanow*

Monday Stroll / Dec. 17, 1956+Jan. 5, 1957 / Savoy ✦✦✦

Although this LP was reissued under guitarist Kenny Burrell's name, it was originally led by Frank Wess, who is heard doubling on flute and tenor. With the assistance of Burrell, rhythm guitarist Freddie Green, bassist Eddie Jones and either Kenny Clarke or Gus Johnson on drums, Wess is in excellent form on a set very reminiscent (not too surprisingly considering the personnel) of the Count Basie band. Wess contributed four of the songs, Burrell brought in "Southern Exposure" and the quintet also plays "Over the Rainbow" and the obscure "Woolafunt's Lament." This out-of-print LP (put out by Arista in 1978) is a fine straightahead date, with Wess' flute taking solo honors. —*Scott Yanow*

All Night Long / Dec. 28, 1956 / Original Jazz Classics ✦✦✦✦

Two of guitarist Kenny Burrell's best sessions from the 1950s were this release (reissued on CD in the OJC series) and its companion *All Day Long*. Burrell is teamed with an impressive group of young all-stars, including trumpeter Donald

Byrd, tenor saxophonist Hank Mobley, Jerome Richardson on flute and tenor, pianist Mal Waldron, bassist Doug Watkins and drummer Art Taylor. In addition to the lengthy "All Night Long" and three group originals (two by Mobley and one from Waldron), the LP program has been augmented by a medley of "Body and Soul" and "Tune Up" from the same session. Jam sessions such as this one are only as good as the solos; fortunately, all of the musicians sound quite inspired, making this an easily recommended set. —*Scott Yanow*

All Day Long / Jan. 4, 1957 / Prestige ✦✦✦
For this CD reissue, "C.P.W." has been added to the original LP program. Guitarist Kenny Burrell and the young all-stars (trumpeter Donald Byrd, Frank Foster on tenor, pianist Tommy Flanagan, bassist Doug Watkins and drummer Art Taylor) sound fine on the four group compositions, but the 18-minute blues "All Day Long" is easily the most memorable selection. Well worth picking up, as is *All Night Long*, which was recorded a week earlier. —*Scott Yanow*

Blue Moods / Feb. 1, 1957 / Prestige ✦✦✦✦✦
Smooth, cool, yet musically impressive late-'50s date that has both blowing session fervor and soulful undergirding. Burrell's fluid guitar voicings and Cecil Payne's robust baritone make nice partners, while Tommy Flanagan adds his usual sparkling piano riffs and solos, and bassist Doug Watkins teams with Elvin Jones, who shows he can drive a date without dominating things on drums. —*Ron Wynn*

Kenny Burrell, Vol. 2 / Feb. 1, 1957 / Original Jazz Classics ✦✦✦
Guitarist Kenny Burrell, 25 at the time, is heard during one of his earlier sessions playing in his already recognizable straightahead style with a quintet that also features the underrated baritonist Cecil Payne, pianist Tommy Flanagan, bassist Doug Watkins and drummer Elvin Jones. This CD reissue of the original LP is a bit brief in time (just over 36 minutes) but contains plenty of fine swinging on tunes such as "Don't Cry Baby," "Drum Boogie," "All of You" and Bud Powell's "Strictly Confidential." It's enjoyable music. —*Scott Yanow*

K.B. Blues / Feb. 10, 1957 / Blue Note ✦✦✦
Worth searching for. Burrell with funky pianist Horace Silver and Hank Mobley on tenor sax. As you might guess, the tunes are mostly blues. —*Michael Erlewine*

Two Guitars / Mar. 5, 1957 / Original Jazz Classics ✦✦✦
For this 1957 studio session (which has been reissued on CD in the OJC series), the two distinctive but complementary guitarists Kenny Burrell and Jimmy Raney are teamed together in a septet with trumpeter Donald Byrd, altoist Jackie McLean, pianist Mal Waldron, bassist Doug Watkins and drummer Art Taylor. The full group gets to stretch out on originals by Watkins, McLean ("Little Melonae"), and three from Waldron, while the two standards ("Close Your Eyes" and "Out of Nowhere") are individual features for Burrell and Raney. This is a well-rounded set that may not contain any real surprises but will be enjoyed by collectors of hard bop. —*Scott Yanow*

Kenny Burrell & John Coltrane / Mar. 7, 1958 / Original Jazz Classics ✦✦✦✦
John Coltrane recorded many interesting jam session-type dates in the 1950s. This matchup with guitarist Kenny Burrell (in a quintet with pianist Tommy Flanagan, bassist Paul Chambers and drummer Jimmy Cobb) finds the group stretching out on two Flanagan compositions, Burrell's "Lyresto," and the standard "I Never Knew." In addition, Coltrane and Burrell play a short duet on "Why Was I Born." Overall, the music is excellent for the time period, with Coltrane displaying some of his sheets of sound and Burrell sounding inspired by 'Trane's presence. It was formerly available as the first half of a two-LP set, *Kenny Burrell/John Coltrane*. —*Scott Yanow*

● **Blue Lights, Vols. 1-2** / May 14, 1958 / Blue Note ✦✦✦✦✦
The music on this 1997 two-CD set was originally on two LPs and already previously reissued as a pair of CDs. Guitarist Kenny Burrell leads a very coherent jam session in the studio with a particularly strong cast that also includes trumpeter Louis Smith, both Junior Cook and Tina Brooks on tenors, either Duke Jordan or Bobby Timmons on piano, bassist Sam Jones and drummer Art Blakey. The material consists of basic originals and standards and has excellent playing all around; six of the nine tunes are over nine minutes long. At that point in time, Cook and Brooks had similar sounds, but fortunately, the soloists are identified in the liner notes for each song. The solo star is often trumpeter Louis Smith, who fell into obscurity after a few notable appearances on Blue Note during the period (including his own brilliant date, *Here Comes Louis Smith*). He was one of the finest of the Clifford Brown-influenced players of the period and deserves much greater recognition. This is a recommended reissue for hard-bop collectors who do not already have the two individual CDs. —*Scott Yanow*

Moonglow / Nov. 7, 1958-Sep. 14, 1962 / Prestige ✦✦
It seems strange that the music on this double LP was reissued in the early '80s under guitarist Kenny Burrell's name for two of the three sessions were originally headed by tenor saxophonist Coleman Hawkins. Reissued is the complete album

The Hawk Relaxes plus half of *Bluesy Burrell* and *Soul*. The emphasis is on ballads (particularly during the first two dates which were cut for the Moodsville label) and, although everyone plays well, it would have been preferable to hear Hawkins and Burrell roaring on some uptempo material too. The supporting cast includes pianists Ronnell Bright, Tommy Flanagan and Ray Bryant. Enjoyable but not essential. —*Scott Yanow*

On View at the Five Spot Cafe / Aug. 25, 1959-Aug. 26, 1959 / Blue Note ✦✦✦✦
This likable live set from guitarist Kenny Burrell has a strong supporting cast (Tina Brooks on tenor, either Bobby Timmons or Roland Hanna on piano, bassist Ben Tucker and drummer Art Blakey) and the original five-song program has been expanded on this CD to eight tunes. The swinging music, highlighted by "Lady Be Good," "Birks Works," the blues "36-23-36" and Burrell's feature on "Lover Man," is quite mainstream for the period and predictably excellent. —*Scott Yanow*

A Night at the Vanguard / Sep. 16, 1959-Sep. 17, 1959 / Chess ✦✦✦
For this CD reissue (which adds versions of "I Can't See for Lookin'" and "Cheek to Cheek" to the original Chess LP), guitarist Kenny Burrell is heard in a sparse trio setting with bassist Richard Davis and drummer Roy Haynes. The focus is almost exclusively on Burrell, who is tasteful, swinging and melodically creative on such numbers as "Will You Still Be Mine," Erroll Garner's "Trio," "Broadway" and Thelonious Monk's "Well You Needn't." —*Scott Yanow*

Bluesin' Around / Nov. 21, 1961-Apr. 30, 1962 / Columbia ✦✦✦
Released for the first time on this 1983 LP, the music on the set features guitarist Kenny Burrell in quartet/quintets with either tenor great Illinois Jacquet, trombonist Eddie Bert or altoist Leo Wright and either pianist Hank Jones or organist Jack McDuff. It is odd that Columbia did not issue any of the straightahead music at the time, considering McDuff's popularity, for the results, even with a few slanted numbers such as "Mambo Twist," are excellent. After a short while, this LP went out of print and the music has yet to resurface on CD. —*Scott Yanow*

Bluesy Burrell / Sep. 14, 1962 / Original Jazz Classics ✦✦✦
Another great team. With Coleman Hawkins (sax). —*Michael G. Nastos*

★ **Midnight Blue** / Jan. 6, 1963 / Blue Note ✦✦✦✦✦
This album was one of guitarist Kenny Burrell's best-known sessions for the Blue Note label, although it has yet to be reissued on CD. Burrell is matched with tenor saxophonist Stanley Turrentine, bassist Major Holley, drummer Bill English and Ray Barretto on conga for a blues-oriented date highlighted by "Chitlins con Carne," "Midnight Blue," "Saturday Night Blues" and the lone standard "Gee Baby Ain't I Good to You." —*Scott Yanow*

Crash! / Jan. 8, 1963-Jan. 26, 1963 / Prestige ✦✦✦

Freedom / Mar. 27, 1963-Apr. 2, 1963 / Blue Note ✦✦✦✦
A date with the Kenny Burrell Sextet that includes Stanley Turrentine (sax), Herbie Hancock (p), Ben Tucker (b), Bill English (d), and Ray Barrett (cga). A funky blues set. —*Michael Erlewine*

Blue Bash / Jul. 16, 1963-Jul. 16, 1963 / Verve ✦✦✦
Groove great Kenny Burrell and Jimmy Smith (Hammond organ) together on the same album. Includes a rendition of "Fever." —*Michael Erlewine*

Soul Call / Apr. 7, 1964 / Original Jazz Classics ✦✦✦
Guitarist Kenny Burrell alternates blues and ballads on this swinging quintet set with pianist Will Davis, bassist Martin Rivera, drummer Bill English and Ray Barretto on congas. The music is melodic and boppish, although no real surprises occur. By this time, Burrell was a very respectful player, upholding the tradition rather than offering any real innovations. This CD reissue will still be enjoyed by his fans. —*Scott Yanow*

Guitar Forms / Dec. 4, 1964-Apr. 12, 1965 / Verve ✦✦✦✦
Though this ranks as one of arranger Gil Evans' minor achievements in the grand scheme of things, for Kenny Burrell it was a career-defining moment, one of his most individual, most multifaceted, most emotionally affecting recordings. Whether playing straightahead and countrified blues on electric guitar, dipping into the bossa nova and brooding post-*Sketches of Spain* backgrounds on acoustic guitar, or interpreting classical music, Burrell quietly lets the world know that he can be as versatile as he is tasteful. Evans collectors should know that Evans' charts only appear on five of the selections. On three others, Burrell is featured with a swinging conga-accented combo that includes pianist Roger Kellaway, and Burrell goes solo on a transcribed excerpt from George Gershwin's "Prelude No. 2" for piano. What is special about this release is not so much the improved sound as the inclusion of a truckload of outtakes from the small-group sessions, which have the effect of doubling the length of the original album. All of them—four takes each of the bluesy "Downstairs" and "Breadwinner" and three of "Terrace Theme"—are worth hearing, for Burrell's invention rarely flags, and what fluffs there are do not upset the group's swinging rapport. The outtakes, though, are

grouped by title at the end of the CD in a way that might induce fatigue; you could shuffle the order with your programming controls and get a more listenable lineup that way. —*Richard S. Ginell*

Soulero / Apr. 4, 1966-Sep. 1967 / GRP/Chess ✦✦✦
This CD reissues the ten selections on guitarist Kenny Burrell's Cadet LP *The Tender Gender,* a version of "My Favorite Things" from a Christmas album and five selections from his 1967 date *Ode to 52nd Street.* The former set showcases Burrell with a quartet also including pianist Richard Wyands, bassist Marty Rivera and drummer Oliver Jackson while the other numbers feature him accompanied by orchestras arranged by Richard Evans. Burrell plays typically tasteful throughout the performances, displaying a clear tone and a solid mastery of the bebop vocabulary. No real surprises occur except perhaps for the repertoire which includes such unlikely numbers as "People," "Girl Talk" (which works quite well) and "Wild Is the Wind." —*Scott Yanow*

A Generation Ago Today / Dec. 15, 1966-Mar. 28, 1967 / Verve ✦✦✦
Guitarist Kenny Burrell interprets eight swing standards associated with the Benny Goodman Sextet and Charlie Christian on this Verve album. Burrell is joined by bassist Ron Carter, drummer Grady Tate and either altoist Phil Woods or (on "Wholly Cats") pianist Richard Wyands; vibraphonist Mike Mainieri guests on "As Long As I Live." Unfortunately the playing time of this LP is brief (a touch under 32 minutes) and the now-obscure set has been out-of-print for quite awhile but the music is excellent. Highlights include "Poor Butterfly," "Stompin' at the Savoy," "Rose Room" and "A Smooth One." —*Scott Yanow*

Ode to 52nd Street / Sep. 1967 / Cadet ✦✦✦
Despite the title of this out-of-print LP, the music has nothing to do with 52nd Street. Richard Evans arranged and conducted an unidentified string orchestra behind guitarist Kenny Burrell on the four-part "Suite for Guitar and Orchestra" and five briefer pieces (three Evans originals plus Dizzy Gillespie's "Con Alma" and "Wild Is the Wind"). Burrell plays quite well, as usual (he is among the most consistent of jazz improvisers), and, even if the music is not all that memorable, the results are pleasing. —*Scott Yanow*

God Bless the Child / May 1971 / CTI ✦✦✦
Guitarist Kenny Burrell's one CTI album is a decent but not essential affair, featuring three of his originals plus lengthy versions of the ballads "A Child Is Born" and "God Bless the Child." Trumpeter Freddie Hubbard helps out and flutist Hubert Laws is on one track, while the arrangements for a cello section are provided by Don Sebesky. This generally lyrical LP has been long out-of-print. —*Scott Yanow*

★ **Ellington Is Forever, Vol. 1** / Feb. 4, 1975-Feb. 5, 1975 / Fantasy ✦✦✦✦✦
This two-CD set is a splendid and well-conceived tribute to Duke Ellington by guitarist Kenny Burrell. In a variety of settings, he utilizes such special players as trumpeters Thad Jones, Snooky Young and Jon Faddis, tenors Joe Henderson and Jerome Richardson, organist Jimmy Smith and a fine rhythm section headed by pianist Jimmy Jones. Ernie Andrews has two vocals, all of the horn players get their chances to solo and 15 Ellington and Strayhorn songs receive tasteful yet inventive treatments. It's recommended along with the second volume. —*Scott Yanow*

Ellington Is Forever, Vol. 2 / 1977 / Fantasy ✦✦✦✦
The second two-CD set to result from guitarist Kenny Burrell's marathon tribute to Duke Ellington is even wider ranging than the first. In addition to such stars as guitarist Burrell, trumpeters Snooky Young and Thad Jones, tenors Joe Henderson and Jerome Richardson, organist Jimmy Smith, pianist Jimmy Jones, and singer Ernie Andrews, this release has solo space for cornetist Nat Adderley, trombonist Quentin Jackson, altoist Gary Bartz and pianist Roland Hanna. By varying the personnel and instrumentation from track to track, Kenny Burrell pays homage in a memorable fashion to 15 classic songs by Ellington and Strayhorn. It comes recommended, as does the first volume. —*Scott Yanow*

Tin Tin Deo / Mar. 23, 1977 / Concord Jazz ✦✦✦
This CD reissue brings back a typically tasteful set by guitarist Kenny Burrell. Performing in a sparse trio with bassist Reggie Johnson and drummer Carl Burnette, Burrell plays boppish and swinging versions of his own blues "The Common Ground," Erroll Garner's playful "La Petite Mambo" and six jazz standards. Nothing particularly surprising occurs but Burrell is heard throughout in above-average form and this release should please his fans. —*Scott Yanow*

Handcrafted / Feb. 27, 1978-Mar. 1, 1978 / Muse ✦✦✦
Steady, consistently swinging trio date with Burrell's fine guitar playing as the focus, and bassist Reggie Johnson and drummer Sherman Ferguson effective but subdued in a supporting mode. There's nothing exceptional here, but the breezy pace and bluesy feel are nice. —*Ron Wynn*

When Lights Are Low / Sep. 1978 / Concord Jazz ✦✦✦
This session (which has been reissued on CD) is so relaxed and tasteful as to be rather dull. Guitarist Kenny Burrell (featured on five standards and a pair of basic

originals in a trio with bassist Larry Gales and drummer Carl Burnette) seems so intent on every note being appropriate that the results are overly safe and predictable. —*Scott Yanow*

Live at the Village Vanguard / Dec. 15, 1978 / Muse ✦✦✦
Trio date at the famed Village Vanguard, with Burrell backed by bassist Larry Gales and drummer Sherman Ferguson. The location and live context combine to make this a more exuberant session than many Burrell cuts in the '70s. His playing has more fire, and he takes longer solos and puts more fervor behind them. —*Ron Wynn*

Moon and Sand / Dec. 1979 / Concord Jazz ✦✦✦✦
This is a surprising release from Kenny Burrell, for the veteran guitarist plays half of the selections on acoustic guitar and does a very effective job giving a bossa nova rhythm (à la Laurindo Almeida and Charlie Byrd) to some of the tunes. The CD reissue, which also features bassist John Heard, drummer Roy McCurdy and percussionist Kenneth Nash, is mostly laidback, although the renditions of Billy Strayhorn's "U.M.M.G." and "Stolen Moments" swing. Best are the more lyrical pieces (such as "My Ship" and an unaccompanied "Lost in the Stars"), which allow Burrell to show off his pretty tone. —*Scott Yanow*

Heritage / May 27, 1980-May 28, 1980 / AudioSource ✦✦
By 1980 it seemed as if guitarist Kenny Burrell was spending at least as much time looking backwards (paying tribute to the past greats) as he was creating new music. This out-of-print LP from the obscure AudioSource label features Burrell performing nine jazz standards ranging from "Night in Tunisia" and "A Child Is Born" to "Struttin' with Some Bar-B-Que" and even "When the Saints Go Marching In." The personnel varies but often includes trumpeter Oscar Brashear, Patrice Rushen or Pete Jolly on piano and occasionally the reeds of Marshall Royal, Jerome Richardson, Don Menza and Matt Catingub. A worthwhile if not particularly innovative set. —*Scott Yanow*

Listen to the Dawn / Dec. 9, 1980-Dec. 12, 1980 / Muse ✦✦✦
Sharp trio set. Burrell is backed by excellent bass/drums duo of Rufus Reid and Ben Riley, both of whom are Burrell's playing equals. The results are uniformly solid, sometimes more emphatic than others. Burrell is still playing in a relaxed, easy groove, but occasionally increases the energy level. —*Ron Wynn*

Ellington à la Carte / Aug. 19, 1983-Aug. 20, 1983 / Muse ✦✦✦
This quiet live set features duets from guitarist Kenny Burrell and bassist Rufus Reid. The emphasis (as is often the case on Burrell's recordings) is on material from the Duke Ellington songbook. In fact, except for "Don't Worry 'Bout Me" and Burrell's "Blues for Duke," all of the music (including a four-song 11 1/2-minute medley) are from Ellington's repertoire. The playing is excellent and the interplay creative in a subtle way, but nothing out of the ordinary or particularly memorable occurs. However Kenny Burrell fans will enjoy this. —*Scott Yanow*

Togethering / Apr. 5, 1984-Apr. 23, 1984 / Blue Note ✦✦✦
This CD matches together guitarist Kenny Burrell with the popular saxophonist Grover Washington, Jr., in a quintet also including bassist Ron Carter, drummer Jack DeJohnette and percussionist Ralph Macdonald. The setting gives Washington a rare chance to play strictly straightahead jazz but unfortunately he mostly sticks to his comparatively lightweight soprano instead of playing his gutsier tenor. The music is therefore merely pleasing rather than really being all that historic. High points include "A Beautiful Friendship" and "What Am I Here For." —*Scott Yanow*

Generation / Oct. 24, 1986-Oct. 25, 1986 / Blue Note ✦✦✦
On this set, Kenny Burrell teams up with a couple of younger players in what he calls his "Jazz Guitar Band." The only trouble is that it is next to impossible to tell Burrell apart from Rodney Jones or Bobby Broom; they all sound nearly alike. With bassist Dave Jackson and drummer Kenny Washington giving the three guitarists fine support, the result is some fine bop-oriented music (on such songs as "High Fly," "Jumpin' the Blues" and "Fungii Mama"), but little that is very memorable. —*Scott Yanow*

Pieces of Blue and the Blues / Oct. 24, 1986-Oct. 25, 1986 / Blue Note ✦✦✦
Taken from the same "Live at the Village Vanguard" gig that resulted in *Generation,* Kenny Burrell is teamed up with two younger guitarists (Rodney Jones and Bobby Broom), both of whom have styles and sounds very similar to the older player; it is fortunate that the liners tell who is playing what. Bassist Dave Jackson and drummer Kenny Washington are fine in support of the three guitarists on a variety of blues and bop standards including "Raincheck," "Jeannine" and "'Round Midnight." Nothing all that unexpected or surprising occurs but this is a fine straightahead set. —*Scott Yanow*

Guiding Spirit / Aug. 4, 1989-Aug. 5, 1989 / Contemporary ✦✦✦✦
This "live at the Village Vanguard" CD has a combination that works: guitarist Kenny Burrell, vibist Jay Hoggard, bassist Marcus McLaurine and drummer Yoron Israel. Burrell and Hoggard blend together quite well, and the superior tunes they picked for this date (including two from Duke Ellington, Mal Waldron's "Soul

Eyes," John Coltrane's "Moment's Notice" and Hoggard's title cut) challenge the soloists. This strong straightahead outing is one of Kenny Burrell's better sets from the past decade. —*Scott Yanow*

Sunup to Sundown / Jun. 10, 1991-Jun. 12, 1991 / Contemporary ✦✦✦✦
Guitarist Kenny Burrell has a strong all-around showcase on this release from Contemporary. Assisted by pianist Cedar Walton, bassist Rufus Reid, drummer Lewis Nash and percussionist Ray Mantilla, Burrell swings harder than he usually does when paying tribute to the past, coming up with fresh statements on the varied material. Although there are a few standards in the program (such as "I'm Old Fashioned," "Autumn Leaves" and "Speak Low"), there are also such obscurities as "Out There" (a medium-uptempo blues), "Sunup to Sundown" and "Love Dance." This set serves as an excellent introduction to Kenny Burrell's enjoyable brand of straightahead playing. —*Scott Yanow*

Lotus Blossom / Oct. 1995 / Concord Jazz ✦✦✦

Midnight at the Village Vanguard / Oct. 1995 / Evidence ✦✦✦

Live at the Blue Note / Jul. 17, 1996+Jul. 18, 1996 / Concord Jazz ✦✦✦

Buddy Burton

b. Feb. 1890, Louisville, KY, **d.** Jul. 6, 1977, Louisville, KY
Piano / Classic Jazz
A talented if generally overlooked pianist, Buddy Burton also played organ, drums and percussion as well as kazoo. After freelancing both in and out of music, Burton moved from Louisville to Chicago in 1923. He recorded on drums (1923) and kazoo (1925) with Jelly Roll Morton and in 1928 did the bulk of his recordings including as a soloist (both singing and playing piano), in piano duets with Jimmy Blythe, backing blues singers Tillie Johnson and Mae Mathews and playing with the Dixie Four and the Harlem Trio. Other than two numbers in 1929, duets with pianist Bob Hudson in 1932 and accompanying singer Irene Sanders in 1936, little is known of Burton's later life except that he probably remained active (although off records) in Chicago for decades until returning to Louisville in 1965. —*Scott Yanow*

● **W.E. "Buddy" Burton & Ed "Fats" Hudson** / Feb. 1928-Apr. 2, 1936 / RST ✦✦✦✦
Buddy Burton (also known as W.E. Burton), a minor figure in jazz history, was a fine pianist and a spirited vocalist. His recordings as a soloist—dates backing singers Tillie Johnson, Mae Matthews, and Irene Sanders, duets with fellow pianist Jimmy Blythe (their "Dustin' the Keys" is a near-classic) and performances with the Dixie Four, the Harlem Trio and drummer Marcus Norman (the latter under the title "Alabama Jim and George")—are all on this definitive CD. In addition, the only four recordings by the even more obscure pianist Bob Hudson (heard dueting with Burton, backing trombonist Roy Palmer and playing banjo with pianist Jimmy Blythe) round out this generous 25-cut set. The good-time music may not be essential but 1920s collectors will love this very complete reissue. —*Scott Yanow*

Gary Burton

b. Jan. 23, 1943, Anderson, IN
Vibes / Post-Bop, Early Fusion
One of the two great vibraphonists to emerge in the 1960s (along with Bobby Hutcherson), Gary Burton's remarkable four-mallet technique (best displayed on an unaccompanied version of "No More Blues" from 1971) can make him sound like two or three players at once. He has recorded in a wide variety of settings and always sounds distinctive. Self-taught on vibes, Burton made his recording debut with country guitarist Hank Garland when he was 17, started recording regularly for RCA in 1961 and toured with George Shearing's Quintet in 1963. He gained some fame while with Stan Getz's pianoless quartet during 1964-66 and then put together his own groups. In 1967 with guitarist Larry Coryell, he led one of the early "fusion" bands; Coryell would later be succeeded by Sam Brown, Mick Goodrick, John Scofield, Jerry Hahn and Pat Metheny. Burton recorded duet sets with Chick Corea (they also toured extensively), Ralph Towner, Steve Swallow and Paul Bley and collaborated on an album apiece with Stephane Grappelli and Keith Jarrett. Among his sidemen in the late '70s/'80s were Makoto Ozone, Tiger Okoshi and Tommy Smith. Very active as an educator at Berklee since joining its faculty in 1971, Burton (who teamed up with Eddie Daniels in the early '90s for an interesting Benny Goodman/Lionel Hampton tribute tour and recording) has remained a prominent stylist up until the present time. He has recorded during different periods of his career extensively for RCA, Atlantic, ECM, GRP and Concord. —*Scott Yanow*

New Vibe Man in Town / Jul. 6, 1961-Jul. 7, 1961 / RCA ✦✦✦✦
Vibraphonist Gary Burton's debut as a leader shows that he was a brilliant player from the start of his career. Utilizing a sparse trio that also includes bassist Gene Cherico and drummer Joe Morello, Burton even at this early stage sounds quite

original and unlike his predecessors (Lionel Hampton, Red Norvo and Milt Jackson). Highlights of the CD (a straight reissue of the original LP) include "Joy Spring," "You Stepped Out of a Dream" and Burton's original "Our Waltz." This boppish set is easily recommended. —*Scott Yanow*

3 in Jazz / Feb. 14, 1963 / RCA ✦✦✦✦
This CD, a straight reissue of an RCA LP, has three unrelated but consistently interesting sessions that were recorded in 1963. Three selections with tenor saxophonist Sonny Rollins (the only performances currently available elsewhere) are rather free (and fascinating) versions of standards and also feature cornetist Don Cherry, bassist Henry Grimes and drummer Billy Higgins. Vibraphonist Gary Burton's quartet (with trumpeter Jack Sheldon, bassist Monty Budwig and drummer Vernell Fournier) is fine if not overly memorable on their four numbers but fluegelhornist Clark Terry (with pianist Hank Jones, bassist Milt Hinton, drummer Osie Johnson and Willie Rodriguez on Latin percussion) is in superior form, playing with great exuberance on "When My Dream Boat Comes Home" and "Cielito Lindo." Well worth picking up. —*Scott Yanow*

Something's Coming / Aug. 4, 1963 / RCA ✦✦✦
Gary Burton's third full-length album as a leader finds him rapidly developing into a fresh new voice on the vibes. Engaged in close interplay with guitarist Jim Hall, bassist Chuck Israels and drummer Larry Bunker, Burton performs four lyrical standards, including "Little Girl Blue" and "Summertime," Hall's "Careful" and a couple of numbers from his new friend Michael Gibbs. Excellent music, but this long-out-of-print LP will be difficult to find. —*Scott Yanow*

● **Artist's Choice** / Aug. 15, 1963-Aug. 16, 1967 / Bluebird ✦✦✦✦✦
This session traces vibist Gary Burton's musical evolution during 1963-1968 with selections taken from eight of Burton's 13 RCA LPs. Burton was among the very first to incorporate elements of rock, pop and freer forms of jazz into his own music without trivializing any of the styles. *Artist's Choice* is a fine retrospective of the early Gary Burton, although one wishes these sessions were available in full rather than piecemeal. —*Scott Yanow*

The Time Machine / Apr. 5, 1966+Apr. 6, 1966 / RCA ✦✦✦✦
This Gary Burton LP was a bit unusual in that he overdubbed piano and marimbas in addition to his distinctive vibes. There is still plenty of interaction with bassist Steve Swallow and drummer Larry Bunker, and the material (which includes Swallow's "Falling Grace," "Norwegian Wood" and "My Funny Valentine") is strong. Also unusual is that Burton (normally never a composer) contributed several pieces, including "The Sunset Bell," "Six-Nix, Quix, Flix" and a few short "Interims." A highlight is the vibraphonist's earliest recording of Jobim's "No More Blues," although it is not on the same level as his classic unaccompanied version of a few years later. Interesting music overall, but this set has not yet been reissued on CD by RCA. —*Scott Yanow*

Tennessee Firebird / Sep. 19, 1966-Sep. 21, 1966 / RCA ✦✦✦
While the concept of "jazz-rock" was in its embryonic stages, Burton was experimenting with a style combining jazz improvisation with rock energy and rhythms. This 1967 session added another ingredient to the musical mix: country and bluegrass sensibility. Burton used Nashville session players like bassist/harmonica player Charlie McCoy, the great Chet Atkins, fiddler Buddy Spicher, and pedal steel guitarist Buddy Emmons. The results were impressive and artistically intriguing; the country players provided a loose, loping feel, while Burton's solos were smooth and delicate but forceful enough to hold the distinct styles together. While it is a short disc at less than 38 minutes, it includes one unissued take and is worth the steep import price. —*Ron Wynn*

Duster / Apr. 18, 1967-Apr. 20, 1967 / RCA ✦✦✦✦✦
This LP is quite important and in some ways can be considered one of the first fusion records. Vibraphonist Gary Burton had just added the young rock/blues guitarist Larry Coryell to his quartet (which also included bassist Steve Swallow and drummer Roy Haynes), and Coryell's influence can be felt throughout the performances. Highlights include Michael Gibbs' "Sweet Rain," Swallow's "General Mojo's Well Laid Plan," Coryell's exploratory and speedy "One, Two, 1-2-3-4" and Carla Bley's "Sing Me Softly of the Blues." Although Burton's basic sound had not changed from the previous year, his openness towards other styles made his quartet one of the most significant jazz groups of the period. This was the first of the four Burton-Coryell recordings. —*Scott Yanow*

Lofty Fake Anagram / Aug. 15, 1967-Aug. 17, 1967 / One Way ✦✦✦✦✦
The second recording of guitarist Larry Coryell as part of the Gary Burton Quartet (which included the vibraphonist/leader, bassist Steve Swallow and drummer Bobby Moses) is more memorable for the sound of the group than for any of the eight originals by Burton, Swallow, Carla Bley or Michael Gibbs. In fact, the closest piece to a "standard," Duke Ellington's then-recent "Fleurette Africaine," has the catchiest melody. But it is the interplay between Burton and the rockish Coryell in

this early fusion group (predating Miles Davis' *Bitches Brew* by two years) that makes this out-of-print LP most notable. —*Scott Yanow*

A Genuine Tong Funeral / Nov. 20, 1967 / One Way ♦♦♦♦
One of vibraphonist Gary Burton's most intriguing recordings, *A Genuine Tong Funeral* (Carla Bley's suite which musically depicts attitudes towards death) was called by its composer a "Dark Opera Without Words." Burton's classic quartet (which also includes guitarist Larry Coryell, bassist Steve Swallow and drummer Bob Moses) is augmented by six notable all-stars: soprano saxophonist Steve Lacy, trumpeter Mike Mantler, Gato Barbieri on tenor, trombonist Jimmy Knepper, Howard Johnson on tuba and baritone and Bley herself on piano and organ. The music is dramatic, occasionally a little humorous, and a superb showcase for Gary Burton's vibes. —*Scott Yanow*

Gary Burton Quartet in Concert / Feb. 23, 1968 / RCA ♦♦♦♦
The final recording by Gary Burton's classic quartet (how about a reunion someday?) features the vibraphonist/leader, guitarist Larry Coryell, bassist Steve Swallow and drummer Bob Moses mixing together aspects of rock, country and folk music in their advanced improvisations. The material (by Mike Gibbs, Burton, Coryell and Bob Dylan) is quite strong, and there are some hints of the avant-garde (including "One, Two, 1-2-3-4" and Burton's freely improvised solo piece "Dreams"). All of the influential Burton-Coryell recordings (among the earliest fusion records) are currently difficult to find and are deserving reissue as a box set. —*Scott Yanow*

Country Roads and Other Places / Sep. 24, 1968-Sep. 27, 1968 / RCA ♦♦♦♦
With longtime bassist Steve Swallow, the return of drummer Roy Haynes and the debut of guitarist Jerry Hahn, Gary Burton's second quartet continued his open-minded policy towards other styles of music. In addition to both melodic and advanced jazz, Burton incorporates elements of country, rock, pop and even classical music on this fairly rare LP. Whether it be a "Ravel Prelude," "Wichita Breakdown" or "My Foolish Heart," the music is full of logical surprises that foreshadow the eclectic nature of much of 1980s and '90s jazz. —*Scott Yanow*

★ **Gary Burton & Keith Jarrett/Throb** / Jun. 2, 1969-Jul. 23, 1970 / Rhino ♦♦♦♦♦
Two of vibraphonist Gary Burton's albums from 1969-70 and reissued in full on this single CD. Burton teams up with pianist Keith Jarrett for five numbers (including four of Jarrett's originals) in 1970, using a quintet that also features guitarist Sam Brown, bassist Steve Swallow and drummer Bill Goodwin. The other session has more of an avant-country flavor with Burton, Swallow and Goodwin joined by guitarist Jerry Hahn and violinist Richard Greene; Michael Gibbs and Steve Swallow contributed most of the obscurities. Burton was at his most explorative during this period which is why he can be considered one of the pioneers of fusion (although his music never really fit into a tight category). This is excellent music that mostly still sounds fresh. —*Scott Yanow*

Good Vibes / Sep. 2, 1969-Sep. 4, 1969 / Atlantic ♦♦♦

Paris Encounter / Nov. 4, 1969 / Atlantic ♦♦♦♦♦
Atlantic has thus far been very slow to reissue its six valuable Gary Burton records. This particular set is the most accessible of the group, for it matches the advanced vibraphonist with the classic violinist Stephane Grappelli in a quartet also including electric bassist Steve Swallow and drummer Bill Goodwin. The music alternates between standards and originals (including Swallow's famous "Eiderdown"), and both Grappelli and Burton prove to be flexible enough to have much common ground despite a 35-year difference in age. A frequently delightful set. —*Scott Yanow*

☆ **Alone at Last** / Jun. 19, 1971-Sep. 7, 1971 / Atlantic ♦♦♦♦♦
Because Gary Burton uses four mallets simultaneously, he has long been able to sound like two or three players at once. This remarkable solo set has three selections in which Burton overdubs vibes with piano, electric piano and organ, but those are far overshadowed by three unaccompanied vibes showcases from the 1971 Montreux Jazz Festival and a slightly later (and very memorable) studio rendition of "Chega de Saudade (No More Blues)." The latter is one of the high points of Gary Burton's career. Wondrous music. —*Scott Yanow*

The New Quartet / Mar. 5, 1973+Mar. 6, 1973 / ECM ♦♦♦♦
Not only does this CD feature a "new quartet," but it was the beginning of Gary Burton's longtime association with ECM. In general, Burton's ECM dates were more introverted and laidback than his more diverse Atlantics, but they always had their moments of interest. On this set, the vibraphonist, guitarist Mick (then known as Michael) Goodrick, bassist Abraham Laboriel and drummer Harry Blazer perform numbers by Chick Corea ("Open Your Eyes, You Can Fly"), Keith Jarrett ("Coral"), Gordon Beck, Carla Bley and Mike Gibbs, in addition to Burton's "Brownout." Intriguing if not essential music. —*Scott Yanow*

Hotel Hello / May 13, 1974+May 14, 1974 / Polygram ♦♦♦
Vibraphonist Gary Burton and bassist Steve Swallow had played together on a regular basis since 1967. This duet outing finds Burton switching between vibes, organ and marimba while Swallow doubles on occasional piano. As expected, the music is introverted, quiet, and occasionally swinging, but mostly floating. Burton and Swallow perform group originals (generally by Swallow), plus Carla Bley's "Vashkar" and Mike Gibbs' "Inside In." Thoughtful background music with no real surprises or excitement. —*Scott Yanow*

Ring / Jul. 23, 1974+Jul. 24, 1974 / ECM ♦♦♦♦
W/ Eberhard Weber. These nice arrangements are a bit more energetic than standard ECM. —*Ron Wynn*

Matchbook / Jul. 26, 1974+Jul. 27, 1974 / ECM ♦♦♦
This set of duets by vibraphonist Gary Burton and guitarist Ralph Towner features a logical matchup, since both musicians are open to folk melodies and are generally quiet improvisers. In addition to six Towner originals and Burton's "Brotherhood," the set has thoughtful versions of "Some Other Time" and "Goodbye Pork Pie Hat." More tempo and mood variation would have uplifted the otherwise fine music. —*Scott Yanow*

Dreams So Real / Dec. 1975 / ECM ♦♦♦♦♦
This recording (reissued on CD) is most notable for documenting the young guitarist Pat Metheny's short but important stint as a member of vibraphonist Gary Burton's group. Actually Metheny at the time was the least known of the five players (which also include guitarist Mick Goodrick, bassist Steve Swallow and drummer Bob Moses) and his contributions are not as significant as those of Burton and composer Carla Bley who contributed all six of the originals. The moody music, which still sounds quite fresh, is highlighted by the title cut, "Ictus/Syndrome" and "Intermission Music." —*Scott Yanow*

Passengers / Nov. 1976 / ECM ♦♦♦♦
Guitarist Pat Metheny was a member of vibraphonist Gary Burton's group from 1974-76, but although he had recorded with Burton twice previously, both of those dates also included guitarist Mick Goodrick. This particular set puts more of a focus on Metheny in a quintet that also includes drummer Danny Gottlieb and both Steve Swallow and Eberhard Weber on basses. Metheny contributed three of the six selections, which are joined by a song apiece from Swallow, Weber and Chick Corea ("Sea Journey"). Although none of the individual songs caught on, the attractive sound of the post-bop unit and an opportunity to hear Pat Metheny in his formative period make this a CD reissue worth exploring. —*Scott Yanow*

Times Square / Jan. 1978 / ECM ♦♦♦♦
After a decade of leading quartets that matched his vibes with a variety of top young guitarists, Gary Burton decided that it was time for a change. While he is joined by a pair of longtime associates (bassist Steve Swallow and drummer Roy Haynes), the fourth member of the group on this set is the young trumpeter Tiger Okoshi. Since Burton has never been a major composer, the CD reissue finds the group playing five Swallow originals, two by Keith Jarrett, and Jim Hall's "Careful." Okoshi's presence adds more fire to this session than was typical of most of Burton's previous records. A fine outing. —*Scott Yanow*

Duet / Oct. 23, 1978+Oct. 25, 1978 / ECM ♦♦♦♦
Vibraphonist Gary Burton and pianist Chick Corea had first recorded together in 1972 for Crystal Silence (released under Corea's name). Six years later, they teamed up for renditions of two Steve Swallow tunes, plus Corea's lengthy "Duet Suite," four of his sketchy "Children's Songs," "Song to Gayle" and his classic "La Fiesta." This subtle set finds Burton and Corea consistently inspiring each other through melodic and very spontaneous improvising. Well worth a close listen. —*Scott Yanow*

Easy As Pie / Jun. 1980 / ECM ♦♦♦
Although best known for leading quartets that feature top young guitarists (his alumni include Larry Coryell, Pat Metheny and John Scofield), vibraphonist Gary Burton has actually headed different types of combos since at least 1978. On this ECM CD reissue, Burton is joined by altoist Jim Odgren, longtime bassist Steve Swallow and drummer Mike Hyman. The repertoire is stronger and less introverted than usual, featuring songs by Chick Corea, Mick Goodrick, Carla Bley ("Reactionary Tango"), Billy Strayhorn ("Isfahan") and Oscar Levant ("Blame It on My Youth"). Swinging sections alternate with more thoughtful pieces, resulting in a particularly well-rounded set. —*Scott Yanow*

Picture This / Jan. 1982 / ECM ♦♦♦
One of vibraphonist Gary Burton's lesser-known units was his early-'80s quartet with altoist Jim Odgren, electric bassist Steve Swallow and drummer Mike Hyman. Burton always had the ability to blend in with nearly anyone, and the alto/vibes front line is attractive. In addition to two obscurities by Odgren, this CD reissue has numbers by three of Burton's favorite composers (Michael Gibbs, Chick Corea and Carla Bley), plus Charles Mingus' "Duke Ellington's Sound of Love." Well-played, if not overly memorable music. —*Scott Yanow*

Real Life Hits / Nov. 1984 / ECM ✦✦✦✦
Gary Burton has always been notable for his ability to recognize talent in young players. The first time he regularly featured a pianist with his quartet was in the mid-'80s, when he helped bring pianist Makoto Ozone to prominence. With electric bassist Steve Swallow and drummer Mike Hyman completing the group, Burton and Ozone explore originals by Carla Bley (including the title cut), John Scofield ("The Beatles"), Swallow, Ozone, and an obscurity, plus Duke Ellington's "Fleurette Africaine." The appealing group sound and the spontaneous yet tight ensembles and solos make this a worthwhile acquisition. —*Scott Yanow*

Gary Burton and the Berklee All Stars / Jul. 28, 1985 / JVC ✦✦✦✦
This set (reissued in 1995 on CD) was a change of pace for vibraphonist Gary Burton after so many relatively introspective sets for ECM. Burton is featured with a octet that also includes Bill Pierce on tenor, altoist Larry Monroe and trumpeter Jeff Stout. The music is generally modern hard bop with some real cookers (such as Cedar Walton's "Firm Roots") alternating with solid ballads. Among the highlights are James Williams' jazz waltz "Soulful Bill," John Scofield's playful "Why'd You Do It" and Burton's unaccompanied workout on the thoughtful "Crystal Silence." This mostly straightahead set is not all that essential but does add to the strong musical legacy of Gary Burton. —*Scott Yanow*

Whiz Kids / Jun. 1986 / ECM ✦✦✦✦
In addition to his longtime bassist Steve Swallow and drummer Martin Richards, vibraphonist Gary Burton features a couple of young players on this date who he would classify as "whiz kids": pianist Makoto Ozone and the Coltrane-inspired tenorman Tommy Smith. The repertoire (all obscurities) and post-bop solos have more fire than one would normally expect on a Gary Burton record, and there are plenty of colorful moments on this subtle but adventurous set, Burton's final date for ECM after 14 years. —*Scott Yanow*

Times Like These / 1988 / GRP ✦✦✦✦✦
For his GRP debut, vibraphonist Gary Burton reunited with his alumnus, guitarist John Scofield, interacted with bassist Marc Johnson and drummer Peter Erskine, and welcomed guest tenor Michael Brecker to two of the eight selections. Performing originals by Makoto Ozone, Vince Mendoza, Jay Leonhart ("Robert Frost"), Chick Corea and Scofield, plus his own "Was It So Long Ago," Burton sounds fine on the diverse material. Since John Scofield had not had an opportunity to record with the vibraphonist during his year with Burton's Quartet more than a decade earlier, this fine set made up for lost time. —*Scott Yanow*

Reunion [With Pat Metheny] / May 6, 1989-May 10, 1989 / GRP ✦✦✦✦✦
The leader reunites with his prize student. —*Ron Wynn*

Collection / May 6, 1989-Nov. 1, 1994 / GRP ✦✦✦✦

Right Time, Right Place / Mar. 29, 1990 / GNP ✦✦✦
Although they have utilized the talents of some of the same musicians through the years (most notably Steve Swallow) and both recorded for ECM, vibraphonist Gary Burton and pianist Paul Bley had not recorded before this 1990 Copenhagen session. The combination generally works, with some of Burton's romanticism and melodic approach rubbing off on Bley during the date (the usually somber pianist actually sounds a little lighthearted during "Isn't It Romantic") while the vibist sometimes emulates Bley's emphasis on space. On their six duets, Burton and Bley do not take turns soloing per se as much as alternate being the lead voice. Their unaccompanied features (three apiece) are generally in the same introspective but exploratory mood, making this a quiet program of thought-provoking if occasionally sleepy music. —*Scott Yanow*

Cool Nights / 1991 / GRP ✦✦✦

Six Pack / Oct. 10, 1991-Apr. 25, 1992 / GRP ✦✦✦✦

It's Another Day / May 1993 / GRP ✦✦
Although vibraphonist Gary Burton gets top billing, this CD is actually a showcase for vocalist Rebecca Paris. The material is dominated by newer "contemporary" songs and pop tunes; every song except the closing voice-vibes duet is given a routine funk rhythm. Paris' voice is somewhat dull, her delivery is generally overpowering and her phrasing usually outside of jazz. Burton's atmospheric vibes are just not enough to save this forgettable set. —*Scott Yanow*

Face to Face / Oct. 31, 1994-Nov. 1, 1994 / GRP ✦✦✦✦✦
This set of duets between vibraphonist Gary Burton and pianist Makoto Ozone is a bit of a surprise, not the quiet and introverted date one might expect but a consistently exciting outing. The duo (who first started working together back in 1982) clearly inspire each other and a lot of sparks fly. The music ranges from three of Ozone's diverse originals and Astor Piazzola's "Laura's Romance" to a pair of Thelonious Monk tunes, a few standards and a romping version of the Benny Goodman-associated "Opus Half"; on the latter Ozone plays some creditable stride piano. More than half of the selections are taken at medium-to-fast tempos and, whether it be "Blue Monk," a memorable version of Jobim's "O Grande Amor" or

a heated rendition of Steve Swallow's "Eiderdown," this is a highly enjoyable outing, one of Burton's finest of the past decade. —*Scott Yanow*

Astor Piazzolla Reunion: A Tango Excursion / Dec. 2, 1996-Dec. 5, 1996 / Concord Jazz ✦✦✦
Gary Burton's *Astor Piazzolla Reunion—A Tango Excursion* is a fine, sensitive tribute to the master of tango, highlighted by "Mi Refugio," a solo performance by Piazzolla that now features Burton's electronically overdubbed vibes. —*Stephen Thomas Erlewine*

Departure / Mar. 4, 1997 / Concord Jazz ✦✦✦✦
For his first album for the Concord jazz imprint, vibraphonist Gary Burton goes back: back to some of the most enduring compositions in the jazz lexicon, constructing the program on *Departure* completely from jazz standards except for "Tossed Salads and Scrambled Eggs" (the theme from the television show *Frasier*). Along with guitarist John Scofield, drummer Peter Erskine, pianist Fred Hersch, and bassist John Patitucci, Burton also returns here to the quicksilver, porcelain sound of the George Shearing Quintet, Burton's first job after graduating from the Berklee College of Music. For the uninitiated, *Departure* is a worthwhile introduction to Burton's style on vibes, with his strong sense of swing swaddled in a sound that's most often elegant yet sometimes surprisingly funky. Scofield really shines here, too. *Departure* is also a great way to discover less known compositions by some of the best-known composers and performers in the history of jazz, including Duke Ellington ("Depk," from his "Far East Suite"), Chick Corea ("Japanese Waltz") and Horace Silver ("Ecaroh"—"Horace" spelled backwards), as well as Mel Tormé ("Born to Be Blue") and "If I Were a Bell," a staple which rang throughout in the 1950s repertoire of Miles Davis and whose title chimes harmoniously with the sonorities of Burton's vibes. —*Chris Slawecki*

Joe Bushkin (Joseph Bushkin)

b. Nov. 7, 1916, New York, NY
Piano / Swing, Traditional Pop
One of the last survivors of the Eddie Condon gang (he recorded with Condon back in 1938), Bushkin has long been a fine swing pianist who shifted easily into middle-of-the-road pop/cabaret by the 1950s. He first played professionally with Frank LaMarr in 1932, worked on 52nd Street from 1935 on, recorded with Billie Holiday in 1936 and was with Bunny Berigan's Orchestra during 1937-38. In addition to jam sessions with Condon, Bushkin was with Louis Prima and Muggsy Spanier in 1939 and during 1940-42 was a member of Tommy Dorsey's Orchestra. A period in the military was followed by a stint with Benny Goodman, an acting role on Broadway in *The Rat Race*, tours with Louis Armstrong in 1953 and a long engagement at the Embers. Bushkin led his own groups throughout the 1950s and '60s, retired for a period, came back to tour with Bing Crosby (1976-77) and has been semi-retired ever since. His two best-known compositions are "Oh Look at Me Now" and "A Hot Time in the Town of Berlin." —*Scott Yanow*

The Road to Oslo & Play It Again Joe / Oct. 4, 1977-1985 / DRG ✦✦✦
Although Joe Bushkin started his career in swing bands and recordings with Eddie Condon, this CD (which reissues his sessions from 1978 and 1985) has little spontaneity and no real surprises. Bushkin's piano here plays closer to cocktail music than to jazz and his vocals, although charming enough, are not worth hearing twice. Bing Crosby sings on two short numbers from what must have been among his final recordings and a few excellent swing players (including cornetist Warren Vache and clarinetist Phil Bodner) pop up on the later date, but no real excitement occurs. Most of these performances are in the "and then I wrote" vein, Joe Bushkin seemed to have either forgotten his jazz roots or not considered it worth revisiting, making this pleasant set a disappointment from the jazz standpoint. —*Scott Yanow*

Henry Butler

Piano, Vocals / Blues, R&B, Post-Bop
Influenced by McCoy Tyner but a distinctive player himself, Henry Butler is a post-bop pianist who dabbles in R&B and blues. Butler, who is blind, worked in New Orleans clubs as a teenager before studying voice at Southern University under clarinetist Alvin Batiste. In 1980, he moved to L.A., where he attracted attention sitting in with Charlie Haden, Billy Higgins, and others. Butler was among those recording for Impulse! Records when MCA reactivated the label in 1986. He showed considerable promise on his debut album of 1986, *Fivin' Around*, and lived up to it with his sophomore effort, 1987's *The Village*. In 1990, Butler devoted an entire album to Crescent City-style R&B and blues on the vocal-oriented *Orleans Inspiration* on Windham Hill. Unfortunately, he hasn't been in the studio often enough—it wasn't until 1995's *For All Seasons* on Atlantic that Butler recorded another jazz project. —*Alex Henderson*

Fivin' Around / 1985-1986 / MCA ✦✦✦

Pianist Henry Butler's recording debut as a leader was also the first record released by the "new" Impulse label. Cut in the mid-'80s when MCA was directly involved with Impulse, the program features Butler with some rather notable musicians—bassist Charlie Haden, drummer Billy Higgins, trumpeter Freddie Hubbard and tenorman Azar Lawrence plus occasional color provided by flutist Steve Kujala and the oboe of Jeff Clayton. Two selections (including "Giant Steps") add a string quartet, and Butler sings "I Want Jesus to Walk with Me." The wide-ranging repertoire (which also has seven diverse originals and the standard "Old Folks") and the inventive frameworks make this a memorable and very successful set. —*Scott Yanow*

The Village / Feb. 1987-Mar. 1987 / MCA ✦✦✦✦

Henry Butler's second Impulse recording is a two-LP set (not yet reissued on CD) that is essentially a post-bop performance. The influence of the pianist's New Orleans heritage (which is partly felt on his version of Scott Joplin's "The Entertainer") and gospel music would be explored more fully in the future. Butler is joined by bassist Ron Carter, drummer Jack DeJohnette and occasionally by clarinetist Alvin Batiste, John Purcell (on soprano, flute, oboe and English horn) and (for "The Entertainer") Bob Stewart on tuba. Butler sings "Music Came," but essentially this is an advanced trio set that shows how fine a pianist he is. —*Scott Yanow*

● **Orleans Inspiration** / Jul. 27, 1989-Jul. 28, 1989 / Windham Hill ✦✦✦✦

Henry Butler, who had recorded a pair of post-bop sets for MCA/Impulse, switches to New Orleans R&B on this spirited program, cut live at Tipitina's in New Orleans. Assisted by guitarist Leo Nocentelli, bassist Chris Severin, drummer Herman Jackson and the synthesizer of Michael Goods, Butler puts on a fine show. He plays and sings (in a gospelish baritone voice) a variety of originals, plus Leonard Bernstein's "Somewhere," "Goin' Down Slow" and Professor Longhair's "Tipitina's" and "Mardi Gras in New Orleans." —*Scott Yanow*

Blues & More, Vol. 1 / 1992 / Windham Hill ✦✦✦

A versatile pianist with a passionate voice, Henry Butler emphasizes the bluesy side of his musical personality throughout this CD of unaccompanied solos. Most of the selections on the date (other than "Down by the Riverside," "That Lucky Old Sun" and "Jamaica Farewell") are his own, and Butler puts plenty of feeling and soulful swing into the music. An accessible and generally creative outing. —*Scott Yanow*

For All Seasons / Jun. 14, 1995-Jun. 16, 1995 / Atlantic ✦✦✦

On some of his recordings, Henry Butler has performed gospel music and/or New Orleans funk, taken soulful vocals, and played some electric keyboard. This trio outing, however, is purely acoustic and mostly in the straightahead vein. With assistance from bassist Dave Holland and drummer Herman Jackson (trombonist Steve Turre dropped by to play the romantic melody on "Souvenir d'un Amour"), Butler explores such numbers as "St. Louis Blues," "How Insensitive," "Without a Song," and several of his originals. This is one of Butler's strongest jazz dates and finds him displaying his individuality on basic but viable chord structures. —*Scott Yanow*

Billy Butterfield (Charles William Butterfield)

b. Jan. 14, 1917, Middletown, OH, d. Mar. 18, 1988, North Palm Beach, FL
Trumpet / Dixieland, Swing, Traditional Pop

A versatile pre-bop trumpeter with a beautiful tone, Billy Butterfield could play pretty ballads and heated Dixieland with equal skill. After early experience in the mid-'30s with the bands of Austin Wylie and Andy Anderson, Butterfield became famous while playing with Bob Crosby's Orchestra (1937-40), taking the main solo on the original version of "What's New" and making numerous records with both the big band and the Bobcats. In 1940 he was with Artie Shaw, participating in the famed Gramercy Five sessions and taking a classic solo on Shaw's rendition of "Stardust"; in addition Butterfield can be seen and heard playing "Concerto for Clarinet" with Shaw in the film *Second Chorus*. After stints with Benny Goodman (1941) and Les Brown, Butterfield spent time in the military and then led a lyrical (but commercially unsuccessful) big band (1945-47). He worked mostly in the studios during the 1950s and '60s, occasionally emerging for Dixieland dates with Eddie Condon, and was a key member of the World's Greatest Jazz Band (1968-72). In later years he continued popping up in Dixieland settings both for records and concerts. —*Scott Yanow*

● **The Uncollected Billy Butterfield & His Orchestra (1946)** / 1946 / Hindsight ✦✦✦✦✦

Billy Butterfield, a trumpet star with the Bob Crosby and Artie Shaw big bands during the swing era, put together his own orchestra a bit too late. By the time his big band hit its stride in 1946, it was nearly impossible for most leaders to keep their heads above water by touring with a jazz orchestra; the public's musical

tastes had gradually changed. This Hindsight LP has 14 performances by Butterfield's now-forgotten big band that were recorded as radio transcriptions. In addition to the leader's trumpet, other key soloists include pianist Mickey Crane, altoist Sam Marowitz and tenor saxophonist Bob Levine. The band essentially plays swing standards, ignoring the innovations of bebop. Butterfield was not all that proud of his three vocals (he never had a desire to sing) but they are quite listenable. Since the band's regular studio recordings for Capitol are long out-of-print, this album is the best collection that has been put out of the Billy Butterfield Orchestra. —*Scott Yanow*

With Ted Easton's Jazzband / Jun. 28, 1975 / Circle ✦✦✦✦

Trumpeter Billy Butterfield recorded fairly frequently in Dixieland settings during 1975-82. On this set Butterfield is heard jamming in Holland with drummer Ted Easton's excellent quintet on five Dixieland and swing standards including "Rosetta," "Stardust" and "Blue Lou." The climax of the date is a 14-minute version of "How Come You Do Me Like You Do" which features tenor saxophonist Bud Freeman, soprano saxophonist Bob Wilber, trombonist Roy Williams and pianist Brian Lemon "sitting in." Fun music. —*Scott Yanow*

Watch What Happens / Nov. 7, 1977 / Jazzology ✦✦✦✦✦

Trumpeter Billy Butterfield ended a five-week tour of Europe by joining tenor saxophonist Benny Simkins' octet for a lively recording session. Butterfield's warm horn is featured with the rhythm section on the ballads "Don't Blame Me," "Watch What Happens" and "A Hundred Years from Today," and jams with the full group on seven more heated pieces. Among the highlights of the latter songs are "Since My Best Gal Turned Me Down," "Spain" and "Oh Baby." Of the supporting cast, clarinetist Randy Colville gets honors. This set is easily recommended to Dixieland fans and to listeners who want a late-period example of Billy Butterfield's beautiful sound. —*Scott Yanow*

Swinging at the Elks / Dec. 1, 1978-Dec. 2, 1978 / Fat Cat Jazz ✦✦✦

Due to the looseness of the setting, the all-star band on this out-of-print Fat Cat LP does not live up to its potential. The lineup is certainly impressive (trumpeter Billy Butterfield, clarinetist Kenny Davern, trombonist Spiegel Wilcox, bass saxophonist Spencer Clark, pianist Dick Wellstood, guitarist Marty Grosz, bassist Van Perry and drummer Tony DiNicola) except on "Carolina in the Morning" which matches Butterfield with some lesser-known players. The band plays seven warhorses from Dixieland and swing and there are some good individual moments (particularly Butterfield on his feature "I Can't Get Started") but nothing all that special occurs despite some heated ensembles. —*Scott Yanow*

You Can Depend on Me / Dec. 4, 1980-Dec. 5, 1980 / Fat Cat Jazz ✦✦✦

The series of Manassas Jazz Festivals always featured Dixieland jam sessions, some of which were more under control than others. The music on this out-of-print LP has its moments even if Johnson McRee (head of the label) takes three spirited but unnecessary vocals. Trumpeter Billy Butterfield is easily the most consistent soloist, pianist Dill Jones gets in a few spots and McKinney's Cotton Pickers' veteran Dave Wilborn sings "Am I Blue." Highlights include "Keeping Out of Mischief Now" and "Sunday" but this music was better seen live than heard years later on record. —*Scott Yanow*

Just Friends / May 8, 1982 / Jazzology ✦✦✦✦

Trumpeter Billy Butterfield's final record (he died in 1988) features him performing eight veteran standards (mostly from the swing era) with a talented but no-name sextet. Butterfield shows on these songs (which include "Dear Old Southland," "Just Friends" and the lone stomp of the date "I Found a New Baby") that at age 65 he was still capable of playing stirring music. Worth picking up. —*Scott Yanow*

Jaki Byard (John A. Byard, Jr.)

b. Jun. 15, 1922, Worcester, MA
Piano / Bop, Stride, Free Jazz, Post-Bop

Possessor of a very eclectic style, Jaki Byard has long been able to play stride, swing, bop, completely free and funky in addition to being able to imitate closely both Erroll Garner and Dave Brubeck. His playing fit perfectly with Charles Mingus' band in 1964 during their famous European tour with Eric Dolphy but otherwise he has never been given the recognition he deserved.

As a youth he played piano and trumpet, switched to trombone while in the army and then (back on piano) gigged with Earl Bostic (1949-50). Byard (also a fine tenor saxophonist) played with the big bands of Herb Pomeroy and Maynard Ferguson (1959-61) and then gigged and recorded with Dolphy, Don Ellis, Booker Ervin, Charlie Mariano and Mingus (1962-65 and 1970); he also recorded as a leader frequently in the 1960s and collaborated with Rahsaan Roland Kirk. Although he has recorded fairly often through the years (including duet albums with Earl Hines and Ran Blake) and headed a big band (the Apollo Stompers), Byard has been mostly active as an educator since the late '60s. —*Scott Yanow*

● **Blues for Smoke** / Dec. 16, 1960 / Candid ✦✦✦✦✦
Pianist Jaki Byard's first recording as a leader was not released domestically until this 1988 CD. That fact seems strange for Byard is absolutely brilliant on the solo piano set. Many of his selections (all nine tunes are his originals) look both backwards to pre-bop styles and ahead to the avant-garde including such numbers as "Pete and Thomas (Tribute to the Ticklers)," "Spanish Tinge No. 1" and "One, Two, Five." The most remarkable selection is "Jaki's Blues Next" which has Byard alternating between James P. Johnson-type stride and free form à la Cecil Taylor; at its conclusion he plays both styles at the same time. A highly recommended outing from a very underrated pianist. —*Scott Yanow*

Here's Jaki / Mar. 14, 1961 / Original Jazz Classics ✦✦✦

Out Front! / Mar. 14, 1961-May 28, 1964 / Original Jazz Classics ✦✦✦
Although Jaki Byard is a very eclectic pianist, this is a surprisingly conventional set. On most selections he is joined by bassist Bob Cranshaw and drummer Walter Perkins (in 1964) for fairly straightahead renditions of standards and obscurities. A few of the numbers add Booker Ervin on tenor and trumpeter Richard Williams, and of these by far the most original performance is the episodic "European Episode." Rounding off the set is a 1961 performance (with Byard on both alto and piano) playing "When Sunny Gets Blue." It's fine music but one has to lower their expectations a bit. —*Scott Yanow*

Hi-Fly / Jan. 30, 1962 / Original Jazz Classics ✦✦✦✦

Live! / Apr. 15, 1965 / Prestige ✦✦✦✦
Except for a ballad medley, this CD reissues all of the music from two earlier LPs featuring pianist Jaki Byard, Joe Farrell (who plays tenor, soprano, flute and even some drums), bassist George Tucker and drummer Alan Dawson (doubling on vibes). The set, recorded live at Lennie's-on-the-Turnpike in Massachussets, is a superior outing for all of the players. Farrell shows just how strong a player he was while Byard's versatility (and full knowledge of all jazz piano styles) keeps the proceedings continually unpredictable. Recommended. —*Scott Yanow*

On the Spot / Apr. 15, 1965+Feb. 16, 1967 / Prestige ✦✦✦✦
This out-of-print LP mostly features pianist Jaki Byard (who plays alto on "A-Toodle-oo, Toodle-oo") with a quartet comprising trumpeter Jimmy Owens, bassist Paul Chambers and drummer Billy Higgins in 1967. With a repertoire stretching from "I Fall in Love Too Easily" and the boppish "Second Balcony Jump" to "GEB Piano Roll" and even "Alexander's Ragtime Band," the music serves as a perfect outlet for Jaki Byard's eclectic talents; a highlight is the Byard-Chambers duet "P.C. Blues." This album is rounded off by a leftover track ("Spanish Tinge") from a 1965 live session featuring Byard, bassist George Tucker and drummer Alan Dawson. —*Scott Yanow*

Freedom Together / Jan. 11, 1966 / Original Jazz Classics ✦✦✦✦

Sunshine of My Soul / Oct. 31, 1967 / Prestige ✦✦✦

With Strings / Apr. 2, 1968 / Prestige ✦✦✦✦
This out-of-print album is quite unusual. Although pianist Jaki Byard is technically featured "with strings," the strings consist of violinist Ray Nance (who sings "Ray's Blues"), guitarist George Benson, cellist Ron Carter and bassist Richard Davis (along with drummer Alan Dawson). The repertoire includes a jammed version of "How High the Moon," a couple of tricky Byard originals and the then-current pop tune "Music to Watch Girls By." But more significant than the songs is the playing by the distinctive musicians who almost make the band sound like a regular group rather than a one-time get-together. Hopefully Fantasy will get around to reissuing this valuable music on CD eventually. —*Scott Yanow*

The Jaki Byard Experience / Sep. 17, 1968 / Prestige ✦✦✦✦✦
Pianist Jaki Byard and the wondrous Roland Kirk (here switching between tenor, clarinet and manzello) were two of the few jazz musicians who could play in literally every jazz style, from New Orleans to bop and free form. If only they had recorded a history-of-jazz album. Fortunately, they did meet up on a few occasions, including this brilliant quartet session with bassist Richard Davis and drummer Alan Dawson. They romp on Bud Powell's "Parisian Thoroughfare," Thelonious Monk's "Evidence," "Shine on Me" and "Teach Me Tonight." Byard duets with Davis on his own "Hazy Eve" but best of all is the pianist's duet with Kirk on "Memories of You." This set was also reissued as half of the Roland Kirk two-LP set *Pre-Rahsaan.* —*Scott Yanow*

Solo Piano / Jul. 31, 1969 / Prestige ✦✦✦

There'll Be Some Changes Made / Dec. 27, 1972 / Muse ✦✦✦✦
Jaki Byard's solo piano set for Muse ranges in styles from ragtime and stride to bop and the avant-garde. In addition to some off-the-wall choices (including "There'll Be Some Changes Made," "Besame Mucho" and Leonard Bernstein's "Lonely Town"), Byard performs some of his better originals and displays his mastery of virtually every jazz style. This is one of his best all-round albums. —*Scott Yanow*

Family Man / Apr. 28, 1978+May 1, 1978 / Muse ✦✦✦
Pianist Jaki Byard (who also plays a bit of tenor and alto) uses a trio/quartet on this Muse album consisting of bassist Major Holley (switching to tuba on one tune), drummer J.R. Mitchell (on the 17-minute five-part "Family Suite") and drummer-percussionist Warren Smith. In addition to a two-song medley of Duke Ellington and Billy Strayhorn, Byard performs the episodic "Family Suite," his early theme "Just Rollin' Along," the eccentric "L.H. Gatewalk Rag" and the thoughtful "Ballad for Louise." A typically stimulating and eclectic program of music by Jaki Byard. —*Scott Yanow*

To Them—To Us / May 27, 1981 / Soul Note ✦✦✦

Phantasies, Vol. 1 / Sep. 25, 1984-Sep. 26, 1984 / Soul Note ✦✦
This outing by Jaki Byard's big band the Apollo Stompers does not quite live up to its potential. The 17-piece orchestra has few distinctive soloists (other than the pianist/leader) and all of the performances (which include three medleys) are quite brief; also the two vocals by Byard's daughters are just so-so. The real reason to acquire this admittedly spirited set is for the occasional (and always notable) piano solos. —*Scott Yanow*

Phantasies, Vol. 2 / Aug. 23, 1988+Aug. 24, 1988 / Soul Note ✦✦✦
The second CD featuring Jaki Byard's Apollo Stompers (a young big band) is actually superior to the first one. Although most of the soloists (other than guitarist Peter Leitch and trumpeter Graham Haynes) remain obscure, the material is more stimulating than on the debut set. In addition to a few standards, Byard penned tributes to B.B. King and Count Basie along with a two-part "Concerto Grosso." His very versatile piano has its share of short solos, hinting at many earlier jazz styles. —*Scott Yanow*

Foolin' Myself / Aug. 25, 1988 / Soul Note ✦✦✦

Live at Maybeck Recital Hall, Vol. 17 / Sep. 8, 1991 / Concord Jazz ✦✦✦✦
Jaki Byard has to be considered one of the most underrated jazz pianists of all time. Very few other keyboardists have mastered as many styles as he has and yet Byard generally sounds like himself. This solo-piano CD finds Byard revisiting his lengthy "Family Suite," doing a three-song Thelonious Monk medley, showing respect for the early stride pianists on "Tribute to the Ticklers" and uplifting a pair of standards. An excellent outing, one of Byard's few recordings in the 1990s. —*Scott Yanow*

Empirical / Jan. 24, 1992 / Muse ✦✦✦

Don Byas

b. Oct. 21, 1912, Muskogee, OK, **d.** Aug. 24, 1972, Amsterdam, Netherlands
Tenor Saxophone / Bop, Swing
One of the greatest of all tenor players, Don Byas' decision to move permanently to Europe in 1946 has resulted in him being vastly underrated in jazz history books. His knowledge of chords rivalled Coleman Hawkins and, due to their similarity in tones, Byas can be considered an extension of the elder tenor. He played with many top swing bands including those of Lionel Hampton (1935), Buck Clayton (1936), Don Redman, Lucky Millinder, Andy Kirk (1939-40) and most importantly Count Basie (1941-43). An advanced swing stylist, Byas' playing looked towards bop. He jammed at Minton's Playhouse in the early 1940s, appeared on 52nd Street with Dizzy Gillespie and performed a pair of stunning duets with bassist Slam Stewart at a 1944 Town Hall concert. After recording extensively during 1945-46 (often as a leader), Byas went to Europe with Don Redman's band and (with the exception of a 1970 appearance at the Newport Jazz Festival) never came back to the US. He lived in France, the Netherlands and Denmark, often appeared at festivals and worked steadily. Whenever American players were touring, they would ask for Byas who had opportunities to perform with Duke Ellington, Bud Powell, Kenny Clarke, Dizzy Gillespie, Jazz at the Philharmonic (including a recorded tenor battle with Hawkins and Stan Getz), Art Blakey and (on a 1968 recording) Ben Webster. Byas also recorded often in the 1950s but was largely forgotten in the US by the time of his death. —*Scott Yanow*

● **1944-1945** / Jul. 28, 1944-Mar. 1945 / Classics ✦✦✦✦✦
Don Byas was one of the great tenor saxophonists of the 1940s, a Coleman Hawkins-influenced improviser who developed a complex style of his own. His permanent move to Europe in 1946 cut short any chance he had of fame but Byas recorded many worthy performances during the two years before his departure. On Classics' first Don Byas CD (which contains his first 21 numbers as a leader), Byas matches wits and power with trumpeter Charlie Shavers on two heated sessions with pianist Clyde Hart and bassist Slam Stewart, plays swing with trumpeter Joe Thomas and pianist Johnny Guarnieri in a 1945 quintet and leads a quartet that on four of its eight numbers welcomes the great blues guitarist-singer Big Bill Broonzy. Highlights include "Riffin' and Jivin'," "Don's Idea," the two-part "Savoy Jam Party," "1944 Stomp" (which has been adopted by 1990s saxophonist James Carter), "Pennies from Heaven," "Jamboree Jump" and "Just a Dream." This

music was originally put out by Savoy, Jamboree and Hub. Highly recommended. —*Scott Yanow*

Savoy Jam Party: The Savoy Sessions / Jul. 28, 1944-Aug. 21, 1946 / Savoy ✦✦✦✦

What a lazy way to reissue music: a former two-LP set with 32 tracks becomes a single CD consisting of the first 25 numbers. The packaging was shrunk to the point where the liner notes (which refer to all 32 songs) is so microscopic as to be completely unreadable. But at least it is "an exact reproduction." Although this reissue from the Japanese Denon label is utterly ridiculous, the music is excellent. Don Byas, one of the great tenors of the 1940s, is featured with groups ranging from a quartet to a sextet; the sidemen include trumpeters Charlie Shavers, Emmett Berry and Benny Harris, altoist Rudy Williams, pianists Clyde Hart, Dave Rivera, Jimmy Jones, Teddy Brannon and Sanford Gold, bassists Slam Stewart and Milt Hinton and drummers J.C. Heard and Max Roach. Byas is in superior form on these late-period swing performances but the packaging is so dumb that I advise collectors who have the original two-LP set (put out by Arista in the 1970s) to keep it. —*Scott Yanow*

Don Byas in Paris / Oct. 18, 1946-Jan. 5, 1949 / Prestige ✦✦✦✦✦

The valuable music on this out-of-print LP features the great tenor saxophonist Don Byas on three sessions cut shortly after he moved permanently to Europe. Byas is heard on five numbers with a quartet also including pianist Billy Taylor, jamming with a septet that co-stars Taylor, trumpeter Peanuts Holland and trombonist Tyree Glenn, and in 1949 leading a quintet with trumpeter Bill Coleman and pianist Bernard Peiffer. The music throughout is advanced swing with slight touches of bop. Despite some fine playing by Coleman and Taylor in particular, Byas is the star throughout, particularly on such numbers as "Blue and Sentimental," "Gloria," "Yesterdays" and "Liza." —*Scott Yanow*

On Blue Star / Jan. 13, 1947 / EmArcy ✦✦✦✦✦

The material on this CD is gracious and generally mellow and fans of the mainstream tenor of Byas will have good reason to acquire the material. —*Bob Rusch, Cadence*

Don Byas [Inner City] / Dec. 2, 1953-May 19, 1955 / Inner City ✦✦✦✦✦

The music on this 1980 Inner City LP has been reissued in different forms several times but not recently. The masterful tenorman Don Byas, whose current obscurity is due to him having moved permanently to Europe in 1946, is in excellent form with three separate rhythm sections. Six selections match Byas with the great pianist Mary Lou Williams (who contributed four originals) in a quartet, he fronts the Beryl Booker Trio on three numbers and the final three tunes (two of which were previously unissued at the time) showcase Byas with a French rhythm section that includes vibraphonist Fats Sadi. Byas, who updated the style of Coleman Hawkins, deserved much more recognition than he received and this now obscure release (the music was originally put out by the French Vogue label) is well worth searching for. —*Scott Yanow*

A Tribute to Cannonball / Dec. 17, 1961 / Columbia ✦✦✦✦

The title of this LP is misleading for, although Cannonball Adderley produced the session, no "tribute" takes place. Adderley could always recognize talent and he was wise to get the veteran tenor Don Byas (who had not recorded since 1955) back on record. Teamed in Paris with trumpeter Idrees Sulieman, pianist Bud Powell, bassist Pierre Michelot and drummer Kenny Clarke, Byas proved to be in prime form on a variety of jazz standards including "Just One of Those Things," "Cherokee" and "Jeannine." This set has since been reissued on CD under Bud Powell's name. —*Scott Yanow*

A Night in Tunisia / Jan. 13, 1963-Jan. 14, 1963 / Black Lion ✦✦✦✦

The first of two CDs documenting two nights at the Montmartre in Copenhagen, this release features the great tenor Don Byas in a quartet with pianist Bent Axen, bassist Niels Pederson (still a teenager) and drummer William Schiopffe. Alternating romps with ballads, Byas tears into such songs as "I'll Remember april," "Anthropology" and "A Night in Tunisia." He shows that, despite being overseas since 1946, he had lost nothing of his power and inventiveness. This release (along with *Walkin*) is easily recommended, among the best recordings from Byas' European years. —*Scott Yanow*

Walkin' / Jan. 13, 1963-Jan. 14, 1963 / Black Lion ✦✦✦✦

The second of two CDs taken from the same appearances at the Montmartre in Copenhagen as *A Night in Tunisia*, this release showcases the masterful (if underrated) tenor Don Byas in a quartet with pianist Ben Axen, bassist Niels Pedersen and drummer William Schiopffe. Byas was always a powerful player and he digs into such songs as "There'll Never Be Another You," "Billie's Bounce" and "All the Things You Are," coming up with exciting and consistently inventive ideas. All jazz collections should have at least a couple of Don Byas albums. —*Scott Yanow*

Charlie Byrd

b. Sep. 16, 1925, Chuckatuck, VA

Guitar / Bop, Brazilian Jazz, Bossa Nova, Latin Jazz

Charlie Byrd has two notable accomplishments to his credit—applying acoustic classical guitar techniques to jazz and popular music and helping to introduce Brazilian music to mass North American audiences. Tasteful, low-key, and ingratiatingly melodic, Byrd is always a pleasure to listen to in concert. Born into a musical family, Byrd experienced his first brush with greatness while a teenager in France during World War II, playing with his idol Django Reinhardt. After some postwar gigs with Sol Yaged, Joe Marsala and Freddie Slack, Byrd temporarily abandoned jazz to study classical guitar with Sophocles Papas in 1950 and Andrés Segovia in 1954. However he re-emerged later in the decade gigging around the Washington D.C. area in jazz settings, often splitting his sets into distinct jazz and classical segments. He started recording for Savoy as a leader in 1957, and also recorded with the Woody Herman band in 1958-59. A tour of South America under the aegis of the US State Department in 1961 proved to be a revelation, for it was in Brazil that Byrd discovered the emerging bossa nova movement. Once back in D.C., he played some bossa nova tapes to Stan Getz, who then convinced Verve's Creed Taylor to record an album of Brazilian music with himself and Byrd. That album *Jazz Samba* became a pop hit in 1962 on the strength of the single "Desafinado" and launched the bossa nova wave in North America. Thanks to the bossa nova, several albums for Riverside followed, including the defining *Bossa Nova Pelos Passaros,* and he was able to land a major contract with Columbia, though the records from that association often consisted of watered-down easy-listening pop. In 1973, he formed the group Great Guitars with Herb Ellis and Barney Kessel, and also that year, wrote an instruction manual for the guitar that has become widely used. From 1974 onward, Byrd recorded for the Concord Jazz label in a variety of settings, including sessions with Laurindo Almeida and Bud Shank. —*Richard S. Ginell*

First Flight / Feb. 4, 1957 / Savoy ✦✦✦✦

Guitarist Charlie Byrd's first record features him at age 31 playing his Spanish guitar in a style that was already recognizable. Most of the selections on this out-of-print LP showcase Byrd with bassist Al Lucas, drummer Bobby Donaldson and flutist Tommy Newsom performing lyrical versions of ballads. However "Chuck-a-Tuck" (which has Newsom on tenor) and "Homage to Charlie Christian" are major departures. On those two songs, Byrd switches to electric guitar and shows that he could play bebop with the best of his contemporaries. Other highlights include "My Funny Valentine," "My Heart Stood Still" and "Spring Is Here." —*Scott Yanow*

Midnight Guitar / Aug. 4, 1957 / Savoy ✦✦✦

Charlie Byrd's second album as a leader (not yet reissued on CD) features the acoustic guitarist in a trio with bassist Keter Betts and drummer Gus Johnson. One side of this LP finds the trio interpreting four swing-era standards (including "Blues My Naughty Sweetie Gave to Me" and "Jive at Five") while the flip side consists of the three-part suite "Blues for Night People." Listeners only familiar with Byrd's bossa nova performances may find this early recording (which predates the emergence of Jobim) a bit of a surprise although the lyrical guitarist is easily recognizable. —*Scott Yanow*

Classical Byrd / 1958-1960 / Milestone ✦✦✦✦✦

Single-disc, 77-minute compilation of two long-unavailable classical LPs that Byrd recorded in 1958-60 for the Washington label, *An Anthology of Music for the Guitar—The Sixteenth Century* and *Lodovico Roncalli Suites.* (Unfortunately, one of the tracks from *An Anthology of Music for the Guitar—The Sixteenth Century,* "Tres Fantasies (Three Fantasies)," was deleted for space reasons). Byrd interprets courtly dances and folk songs of Spanish composers of the 16th century on *Anthology,* and presents four longer (average track length: ten minutes) suites from the 17th century by the little-known Italian composer Lodovico Roncalli on *Lodovico Roncalli Suites.* It's a fine compendium of Byrd's talents as a virtuoso classical interpreter, and one would guess that works such as this were an influence on guitarist Sandy Bull in the 1960s. —*Richie Unterberger*

The Guitar Artistry of Charlie Byrd / 1960 / Original Jazz Classics ✦✦✦✦

Before he toured South America and discovered bossa nova, guitarist Charlie Byrd already had his recognizable sound formed. A master on the acoustic guitar who was well trained in classical music, Byrd performed regularly in Washington D.C. from 1958-60, recording for the tiny Offbeat label. This CD reissue of a set originally on Offbeat and then put out by Riverside features Byrd and his regular trio (with bassist Keter Betts and drummer Buddy Deppenschmidt) performing concise versions of eight jazz standards, including two songs under two minutes, and longer versions of three obscurities, plus "The House of the Rising Sun." The melodic music is pleasing (if not too substantial), predictable and reasonably enjoyable, with the highlights including "Moonlight in Vermont," "Nuages," "Django" and the lengthy "Taboo." —*Scott Yanow*

Charlie Byrd at the Village Vanguard / Jan. 15, 1961 / Original Jazz Classics ✦✦✦

Shortly before departing on his epochal 1961 State Department tour of South America, the one that ignited his love affair with bossa nova—and subsequently, ours—Charlie Byrd played this trio gig at New York City's Village Vanguard. At first, "Just Squeeze Me" goes at an easygoing stroll as Byrd adheres swingingly to the beat, and "Why Was I Born" isn't terribly eventful. But then, there are definitely hints of things to come in the fluid samba-like rhythm that the trio kicks up on "You Stepped Out of a Dream." The 20-minute fantasia on the old union rouser "Which Side Are You On?" also has a Brazilian-tinged groove, and the combination of that and Byrd's low-key classical savvy keeps you as mesmerized as the quiet audience must have been. It is also significant that both of Byrd's cohorts on the date, bassist Keter Betts and drummer Buddy Deppenschmidt, would play on Byrd's historic *Jazz Samba* album with Stan Getz a year later. The direction is clear; Byrd was about to open the door to bossa nova, and you can hear him inching up to the starting gate here. —*Richard S. Ginell*

● **Latin Byrd** / 1961-1963 / Milestone ✦✦✦✦✦

This single CD reissues two complete Charlie Byrd LPs (*Latin Impressions* and *Charlie Byrd's Bossa Nova*), some of which had been available previously on a 1970s two-fer. Byrd, the master of the acoustic guitar whose gentle and lyrical style perfectly fit bossa nova, is heard in prime form on 23 rather pretty numbers. There are six unaccompanied solos and many workouts with his quartet which is sometimes augmented by four cellos, a French horn, trumpeter Hal Posey, vibraphonist Tommy Gwaltney and/or extra percussionists. Surprisingly there are only two Antonio Carlos Jobim songs among the ones performed but the other selections (which include five Byrd originals) are very much in the idiom. This CD shows that pretty music does not have to be Muzak or new age. Highly recommended. —*Scott Yanow*

Bossa Nova Pelos Passaros / Sep. 28, 1962-Apr. 4, 1963 / Original Jazz Classics ✦✦✦

Having been a major part of Stan Getz's very popular *Jazz Samba* album, it was only fitting that guitarist Charlie Byrd would start recording his own bossa nova records. This CD reissue brings back the 12 songs originally on the Riverside LP *Bossa Nova Pelos Passaros* plus six of the 11 tunes from *Once More/Charlie Byrd's Bossa Nova*. Byrd and his trio (which included bassist Keter Betts and drummer Bill Reichenbach) are augmented on some selections by strings, extra percussion plus horns. In reality the background musicians are not needed since Byrd was at the top of his form in those days. Unlike some of his earlier sets, these pretty and melodic recordings are very concise (lacking a sense of adventure), clocking in between 1:48 and 3:26 and looking towards the guitarist's later Columbia dates. Highlights include "Meditation," "O Barquinho," "Desafinado," "Bim Bom," "O Passaro" and "Limehouse Blues." —*Scott Yanow*

Once More! Bossa Nova / Feb. 21, 1963+Apr. 4, 1963 / Riverside ✦✦

Byrd at the Gate / May 9, 1963-May 10, 1963 / Original Jazz Classics ✦✦✦✦✦

This CD reissue has a rare straightahead set by guitarist Charlie Byrd, whose trio with bassist Keter Betts and drummer Bill Reichenbach welcomes trumpeter Clark Terry and tenor saxophonist Selden Powell to a few numbers. The emphasis is on swing and a repertoire mostly filled with standards (including "Shiny Stockings," "Butter and Egg Man," "I Left My Heart in San Francisco" and "Broadway"). The CD adds two unissued selections to the original program: "Let's Do It" and "Jive at Five." Recommended. —*Scott Yanow*

Brazilian Byrd / Dec. 21, 1964-Feb. 8, 1965 / Columbia ✦✦✦✦

The arrangements by Tommy Newsome for strings, brass and woodwinds may be a bit sweet and the 13 performances (which on the CD reissue includes a previously unreleased take of "Engano") may be overly concise (often under three minutes), but the resulting music is strangely pleasing. Acoustic guitarist Charlie Byrd always had a strong affinity for Brazilian jazz and he sticks exclusively to Antonio Carlos Jobim songs (including "So Danco Samba," "Corcovado," "Dindi" and "The Girl from Ipanema") during this tasteful and melodic effort. Truly beautiful music. —*Scott Yanow*

Travelin' Man / Mar. 16, 1965 / Columbia ✦✦✦

Byrdland / Aug. 25, 1966-Aug. 27, 1966 / Columbia ✦✦✦

Most of Charlie Byrd's Columbia albums of 1965-71 feature the acoustic guitarist (usually accompanied by a string section) playing brief versions of inferior pop tunes. This LP is better than most of Byrd's Columbias for the tunes (with a couple of exceptions) are more timeless and the trio (which also includes bassist Joe Byrd and drummer Bill Reichenbach) are just joined by trumpeter Hal Posey and Teo Macero on tenor. There are several fine bossa nova tunes on the date plus such selections as a pair of Alec Wilder ballads ("I'll Be Around" and "It's So Peaceful in the Country") and "Work Song." —*Scott Yanow*

Byrd by the Sea / Mar. 1, 1974-Mar. 3, 1974 / Fantasy ✦✦

Mild, smooth trio date with Byrd playing light jazz, occasional Afro-Latin, and even a mock classical number, backed by bassist Joe Byrd and drummer Bertill Knox. This sometimes comes close to, but never becomes, mood music. —*Ron Wynn*

Great Guitars / Jul. 28, 1974 / Concord Jazz ✦✦✦✦

Charlie Byrd was teamed up with Barney Kessel and Herb Ellis (along with bassist Joe Byrd and drummer John Rae) for this rather exciting concert. While Ellis and Kessel have three unaccompanied duets, the inclusion of Byrd (thought of as a Brazilian specialist rather than a bopper) is the wild card that makes this set a major success. While Byrd is excellent on his features "Charlie's Blues" and "O Barquinho," it is the three stomps featuring all the guitarists ("Undecided," "Topsy" and "Benny's Bugle") that are most memorable. —*Scott Yanow*

Top Hat / Feb. 6, 1975-Feb. 7, 1975 / Fantasy ✦✦✦

This out-of-print Fantasy LP features the highly appealing Brazilian-styled guitarist Charlie Byrd with Joe Byrd (on electric bass), drummer Johnny Rae, and for two songs apiece, percussionist Depo Indetto and cornetist Nat Adderley. Nothing all that unusual occurs. Byrd, on tunes ranging from Chick Corea's "Sometime Ago" and Irving Berlin's "Top Hat, White Tie and Tails" to "Feel Like Making Love" and Jobim's "Agua de Beber," performs melodic improvisations backed by a lightly swinging rhythm section. Pleasing if not overly memorable music. —*Scott Yanow*

Charlie Byrd Swings Downtown / Jun. 1976 / Improv ✦✦✦

This is one of the more obscure Charlie Byrd LPs, a live set recorded for Tony Bennett's short-lived Improv label. The distinctive acoustic guitarist performs a wide variety of tunes with his trio (which also includes bassist Joe Byrd and drummer Wayne Phillips) including such unlikely material as "Hey Jude," "Feelings" and "I Write the Songs." Much better are Byrd's interpretations of Scott Joplin's "Solace," "Limehouse Blues" and his own "Swing 59." No matter what the source, the music is tasteful, concise and lightly swinging. —*Scott Yanow*

Blue Byrd / Aug. 1978 / Concord Jazz ✦✦✦✦✦

This delightful album (reissued on CD) is one of Charlie Byrd's finest for Concord. Teamed up with bassist Joe Byrd and drummer Wayne Phillips, the acoustic guitarist had a real chance to show off his versatility on a wide-ranging repertoire. Highlights include "It Don't Mean a Thing" (which really cooks), "Jitterbug Waltz," the memorable "Carinhoso" and "Isn't It a Lovely Day." Byrd made his vocal debut on spirited versions of "I Ain't Got Nothin' but the Blues" and an uptempo "Saturday Night Fish Fry," sounding like a cross between Bob Dorough and Mose Allison. This set is particularly recommended to listeners who think that Charlie Byrd could only play Brazilian music. —*Scott Yanow*

Sugarloaf Suite / Aug. 1979 / Concord Jazz ✦✦✦

For this trio album with bassist Joe Byrd and drummer Wayne Phillips, Charlie Byrd (who long ago became an innovator by bringing the classical guitar into jazz) performs a bossa nova-oriented program which, in addition to a pair of Antonio Carlos Jobim tunes, Luiz Bonfa's "The Gentle Rain" and Dori Caymmi's "Saudade Da Bihia," includes four of Byrd's own compositions in the style. The music is typically exquisite, pretty and subtle and the performances grow in interest with each listen. —*Scott Yanow*

Brazilville / May 1981 / Concord Jazz ✦✦✦

This Concord release has a logical combination, teaming together guitarist Charlie Byrd's trio (which also includes bassist Joe Byrd and drummer Charles Redd) with the alto of Bud Shank. Shank had recorded an early version of bossa nova with guitarist Laurindo Almeida in the mid-'50s while Byrd helped to popularize the attractive idiom in the early '60s. Shank and Byrd mix together very well, performing a few standards and some obscurities, mostly with samba rhythms. This music is both accessible and creative; recommended. —*Scott Yanow*

Isn't It Romantic / Mar. 1984 / Concord Jazz ✦✦✦✦

On this enjoyable set, Charlie Byrd's trio performs five classics by Rodgers & Hart, and numbers by Ray Noble, Irving Berlin, Hoagy Carmichael, George Gershwin and Jimmy Van Heusen. All of the songs are quite familiar but Byrd (along with his brother Joe on bass and drummer Chuck Riggs) makes such potential warhorses as "Cheek to Cheek," "Thou Swell" and "I Thought About You" sound fresh and alive. Charlie Byrd's solo guitar interpretation of "Someone to Watch over Me" is a highlight. —*Scott Yanow*

Byrd and Brass / Apr. 1986 / Concord Jazz ✦✦✦

This Concord album is a change of pace for acoustic guitarist Charlie Byrd. His trio (which also includes bassist Joe Byrd and drummer Chuck Redd) is joined by the Annapolis Brass Quintet, a nonimprovising chamber group. The arrangements (mostly by Tommy Newsom) nicely blend the two groups together. In addition to six swing-era standards, the musicians perform the three movements of "Byrd & Brass" along with David Amram's "En Memoria de Chano Pozo." This project successfully mixes together swinging jazz, classical music and bossa nova; worth checking out. —*Scott Yanow*

It's a Wonderful World / Aug. 1988 / Concord Jazz ✦✦✦✦
Some of acoustic guitarist Charlie Byrd's albums can get a bit sleepy while tenor saxophonist Scott Hamilton has recorded so much throughout his career that there is always a danger of a certain sameness pervading. Hamilton sits in with Byrd's trio (which also includes bassist John Goldsby and drummer Chuck Redd) on this CD and the combination is somewhat magical. The bossa nova rhythms give Hamilton a new setting while Byrd is clearly inspired by the tenor's presence. They perform 11 mostly well-known standards, coming up with fresh ideas on such songs as "Between the Devil and the Deep Blue Sea," "My Shining Hour," "Street of Dreams" and "Let's Fall in Love." Easily recommended to fans of both Charlie Byrd and Scott Hamilton. —*Scott Yanow*

The Bossa Nova Years / Apr. 16, 1991-Apr. 17, 1991 / Concord Jazz ✦✦✦✦

The Washington Guitar Quartet / 1992 / Concord Jazz ✦✦✦
Romanticism, Afro-Latin voicings and classical stylings are the three primary components of Charlie Byrd's most recent release. It blends his playing with that of Carlos Barbosa-Lima, Jeffrey Meyerriecks, Myrna Sislen and Larry Snitzler, and the quintet members expertly complement and contrast each other on a program of American popular standards, compositions by Vivaldi, Mozart, Antonio Carlos Jobim and three superb interpretations of the Bix Beiderbecke masterpieces "In a Mist," "Candlelights" and "In the Dark." It's more structured than improvisatory, but the playing is so compelling and exquisite that it should appeal to both guitar lovers and music fans generally. —*Ron Wynn*

Aquarelle / Aug. 10, 1993 / Concord Concerto ✦✦✦

Moments Like This / 1994 / Concord Jazz ✦✦✦

I've Got the World on a String / Jul. 4, 1994-Jul. 5, 1994 / Timeless ✦✦✦
This Timeless CD is a bit unusual in that guitarist Charlie Byrd sings the first six numbers; it is only the second time in his career he has taken vocals on record. His singing is simple and generally effective if not too memorable. The final 11 numbers are instrumentals (odd programming) and also surprising in that the emphasis is on standards, often from the swing era; there is only one Brazilian song (Antonio Carlos Jobim's "So Danca Samba"). Byrd (in a trio with bassist Joe Byrd and drummer Chuck Redd) is in generally fine form overall although it is doubtful that he will get too many requests to feature his singing in the future! —*Scott Yanow*

Au Courant / 1997 / Concord Jazz ✦✦✦✦
That old Django Reinhardt buff Charlie Byrd actually gets something resembling the drive of the Hot Club Quintette on this CD at times, but with unusual means. With Charlie on acoustic guitar and brother Joe Byrd on bass, Charlie's longtime drummer Chuck Redd shifts over to the vibraphone, and the three independent voices tumble intricately all around each other in a collection of standards. While not absolutely impeccable in technique, Byrd continues to get around his instrument in a swinging manner, and Redd proves to be a more-than-serviceable performer on the vibes. Inevitably (for Byrd), the Brazilian influence surfaces on tracks like "On a Clear Day," Jobim's "If You Never Came to Me" and Rodgers/Hart's "There's a Small Hotel," all of which bring us gently back to 1962. A modest yet pleasing experiment for the Charlie Byrd collector. —*Richard S. Ginell*

Donald Byrd (Donaldson Toussaint L'Ouverture Byrd II)

b. Dec. 9, 1932, Detroit, MI
Trumpet / Hard Bop, Crossover Jazz, Funk, R&B
In the late '50s and early '60s, Donald Byrd carved out a niche for himself as one of the most adept hard boppers of his generation. Never a wildly original player, Byrd nevertheless captured the tenor of his times as a solid, clean-toned, lyrical improviser in the manner of contemporaries like Clifford Brown and Freddie Hubbard. Byrd studied music at Wayne State University, from which he received his bachelor's degree in 1954. He went on to receive a master's degree from the Manhattan School of Music in the mid-'50s. At the same time, he recorded for the Prestige, Riverside, Blue Note, and Savoy labels (among others), both as a leader and as a sideman. Following stints with the likes of Max Roach, Art Blakey, and Sonny Rollins, Byrd co-led a band with the baritone saxophonist Pepper Adams from 1958-61. Byrd studied composition in Europe from 1962-63, then returned to the US, where he established himself as an academician, teaching at Rutgers, Howard University, and the Hampton Institute. Byrd received his law degree in 1976; he subsequently taught at North Carolina Central University. In 1982, he received his doctorate from Columbia Teachers College. Byrd continued to perform and record, releasing a number of fine straightahead Blue Note albums throughout the '60s. In the '70s, his music took a decidedly commercial turn. Byrd recorded a number of heavily produced, pop-oriented albums on which his horn was subjugated by disco-fied vocals and string sections. In the '80s and '90s Byrd returned to his jazz

roots, recording with peers such as Joe Henderson and Bobby Hutcherson, and with younger musicians like Kenny Garrett and Mulgrew Miller. —*Chris Kelsey*

First Flight / Aug. 23, 1955 / Delmark ✦✦✦
This CD reissue contains trumpeter Donald Byrd's debut on records. Recorded in his native Detroit with such local players as tenor saxophonist Yusef Lateef, pianist Berry Harris and Bernard McKinney on euphonium, Byrd is heard at the age of 22 when he was very much influenced by Clifford Brown. Unlike Byrd, Lateef already had his own style at this early stage. The sextet mostly performs bop originals plus a blues, "Yusef" and "Torsion Level"; all of the music is straightahead and swinging. A fine beginning for the very interesting career of Donald Byrd. —*Scott Yanow*

Long Green / Sep. 29, 1955 / Savoy ✦✦✦
This was trumpeter Donald Byrd's second session as a leader, following his lesser-known debut for Transition by a little over a month. Just 22 years old at the time, Byrd did not have his own style yet but already was a promising soloist. Heard in a quintet with tenor saxophonist Frank Foster, pianist Hank Jones, bassist Paul Chambers and drummer Kenny Clarke, Byrd jams on three group originals and a trio of standards. Nothing all that unusual occurs, but there are some strong moments on this enjoyable blowing. —*Scott Yanow*

House of Byrd / Aug. 3, 1956+Nov. 2, 1956 / Prestige ✦✦✦✦
This two-LP set combines together the music from *Two Trumpets* and *The Young Bloods*. The former session has both Donald Byrd and Art Farmer on trumpets in a sextet with altoist Jackie McLean and pianist Barry Harris while the latter is actually stronger, featuring Byrd, altoist Phil Woods and pianist Al Haig in a quintet. These blowing sessions (typical of Prestige's albums of the 1950s) have their enjoyable moments with Farmer and Woods taking overall solo honors. —*Scott Yanow*

Early Byrd / Feb. 5, 1957-Sep. 5, 1957 / Columbia ✦✦✦✦✦
For a period trumpeter Donald Byrd and altoist Gigi Gryce led a group that they called the Jazz Lab Quintet. This fine double LP contains two of their Columbia albums (*Jazz Lab* and *Modern Jazz Perspective*), neither of which have been reissued to date on CD. The first set, which adds five horns on some of the selections, is most notable for emphasizing such then-recent jazz compositions as "Speculation," "Nice's Tempo," Randy Weston's "Little Niles" and "I Remember Clifford." The melody line of Gryce's "Blue Concept" is particularly memorable. The second session has three extra horns on some tunes, a few vocals by Jackie Paris and such numbers as Benny Golson's "Stablemates" and the Gryce originals "An Evening in Casablanca" and "Social Call." It is a pity that this group did not last longer and that this valuable double LP from 1973 is difficult to find these days. —*Scott Yanow*

Young Byrd / Feb. 7, 1957-Apr. 15, 1958 / Milestone ✦✦✦
This double LP from 1977 tried to capitalize a bit on trumpeter Donald Byrd's fame. Although reissued under Byrd's name, the two sessions were originally led by baritonist Pepper Adams and altoist Gigi Gryce; both dates have since been reissued under the correct leader's names on CD. The straightahead music is consistently excellent. Byrd and Adams frequently teamed together in the late '50s and in this instance they were fortunate to have pianist Bobby Timmons, bassist Doug Watkins and the young drummer Elvin Jones in their band. The 1957 quintet with Gryce was a regularly working (if short-lived) group that also included pianist Wade Legge, bassist Wendell Marshall and drummer Art Taylor. The emphasis throughout is on obscurities and originals (with "You're My Thrill," "Love for Sale" and "Zing! Went the Strings of My Heart!" being the exceptions) and uncomplicated swinging. —*Scott Yanow*

Star Eyes / Sep. 10, 1957 / Savoy ✦✦✦
This LP has the feel of a jam session. Trumpeter Donald Byrd co-led the date with the Charlie Parker-influenced altoist John Jenkins; their sidemen were trombonist Curtis Fuller, pianist Tommy Flanagan, bassist Doug Watkins and drummer Art Taylor. Although the other musicians play well, it is for Jenkins' playing that this date is most highly recommended for he did not make that many sessions before dropping out of music. Jenkins contributed three originals to this date (highlighted by the long blues "Rockaway") which alternate with fine versions of the standards "Star Eyes" and "Darn That Dream." This is an excellent album that deserves to be reissued on CD. —*Scott Yanow*

Byrd in Paris, Vols. 1 & 2 / Oct. 22, 1958 / Polydor ✦✦✦✦
Trumpeter Donald Byrd spent a few months in France during 1958. A Paris concert resulted in two LPs' worth of material which were reissued on this Polydor CD in 1988. Byrd's quintet at the time included Bobby Jaspar (on tenor and flute), pianist Walter Davis, Jr., bassist Doug Watkins and drummer Art Taylor. Byrd was just beginning to find his own sound in the late '50s and he is in excellent form on "Dear Old Stockholm," Sonny Rollins' "Paul's Pal," Jaspar's "Flute Blues," "Ray's

Idea" and "The Blues Walk." This is a fine all-around har- bop session that is equaled by the second CD. —*Scott Yanow*

Off to the Races / Dec. 2, 1958 / Blue Note ◆◆◆◆
From the crackling opening notes of "Lover Come Back to Me," it's clear that *Off to the Races* is one of Donald Byrd's most invigorating sessions of the late '50s. Working with a stellar supporting band—Jackie McLean (alto sax), Wynton Kelly (piano), Pepper Adams (bari sax), Sam Jones (bass), Art Taylor (drums)—Byrd turns in one of his strongest recordings of the era. Throughout the album, Byrd switches between hard bop, ballads, laidback blues and soul-jazz. Two of the numbers are standards, one is a cover and three are Byrd originals, but what matters is the playing. Over the course of the album, Byrd proves he has matured greatly as a soloist, capable of sweet, melodic solos on the slower numbers and blistering runs of notes on the faster songs. McLean is just as vigorous and lyrical, contributing some fine moments to the record, as do Adams and Kelly. There's nothing surprising about *Off to the Races;* it's simply a set of well-performed, enjoyable hard bop, but sometimes that's enough. —*Stephen Thomas Erlewine*

Byrd in Hand / May 31, 1959 / Blue Note ◆◆◆◆◆
For this excellent album, trumpeter Donald Byrd teams up with tenor saxophonist Charlie Rouse, baritonist Pepper Adams, pianist Walter Davis, Jr., bassist Sam Jones and drummer Art Taylor. Together the sextet performs three Byrd originals, two Davis songs and the standard "Witchcraft." Although none of the new tunes caught on, the group (which includes two distinctive saxophonists and the rapidly maturing trumpet of Donald Byrd) plays consistently creative and spirited solos in the hard bop idiom. —*Scott Yanow*

Fuego / Oct. 4, 1959 / Blue Note ◆◆◆◆
This CD reissue brings back a typically excellent Donald Byrd Blue Note session; virtually all of the trumpeter's most rewarding dates were for that label. Teamed with altoist Jackie McLean, pianist Duke Pearson, bassist Doug Watkins and drummer Lex Humphries, Byrd plays six of his originals with the most memorable ones being "Fuego," "Funky Mama" and "Amen." An above-average hard-bop set that still sounds fresh nearly 40 years later. —*Scott Yanow*

Stardust / 1960 / Bethlehem ◆◆◆◆
Trumpeter Donald Byrd and baritonist Pepper Adams always made for a potent team. With guitarist Kenny Burrell, pianist Tommy Flanagan, bassist Paul Chambers and drummer Louis Hayes (using the pseudonym of "Hey Lewis") completing the sextet, this was a particularly strong group. For the Bethlehem LP (not yet reissued on CD), Byrd and Adams play two of Pepper's originals, Errol Garner's rarely performed "Trio," Thad Jones' "Bitty Ditty" and a lengthy and memorable rendition of "Stardust." Well worth searching for. —*Scott Yanow*

Byrd in Flight / Jan. 17, 1960-Jul. 10, 1960 / Blue Note ◆◆◆◆◆
Two separate dates are combined on this Blue Note album. Trumpeter Donald Byrd, pianist Duke Pearson and Lex Humphries are heard in both quintets with either tenorman Hank Mobley or altoist Jackie McLean and Doug Watkins or Reggie Workman on bass. The consistently strong originals by Pearson and Byrd ("Little Boy Blue" is the lone standard) give this set its own personality and purpose. An excellent example of early '60s hard bop. —*Scott Yanow*

● **Donald Byrd at the Half Note Cafe, Vols. 1-2** / Nov. 11, 1960 / Blue Note ◆◆◆◆◆
This 1997 two-CD set was last available as a pair of single CDs. Trumpeter Donald Byrd and huge-toned baritonist Pepper Adams always made for a potent combination, and fortunately, they recorded together quite a bit from 1960-61. The live set has four originals apiece by Byrd and pianist Duke Pearson, plus four standards. The material is consistently rewarding (including the definitive jazz version of Henry Mancini's "Mr. Lucky"), and the quintet (which also includes pianist Duke Pearson, bassist Laymon Jackson and drummer Lex Humphries) sounds quite inspired, and the often joyful music is quite inventive within the hard-bop genre. Highlights include "My Girl Shirl," "Chant," "A Portrait of Jennie" and "Jeannine." Highly recommended to straightahead fans not already owning the previous CDs. —*Scott Yanow*

Chant / Apr. 17, 1961 / Blue Note ◆◆◆◆◆
Not released until 1979, this excellent quintet session features the always formidable team of trumpeter Donald Byrd and baritonist Pepper Adams. The accompanying rhythm section includes pianist Herbie Hancock shortly before he joined Miles Davis. The repertoire consists of six likable tunes including an uptempo "I'm an Old Cowhand," "That's All," "Sophisticated Lady," two Byrd originals and Duke Pearson's "Chant." This is superior hard bop from the early '60s. —*Scott Yanow*

The Cat Walk / May 2, 1961 / Blue Note ◆◆◆◆
Of the many albums shared by trumpeter Donald Byrd and baritonist Pepper Adams, this Blue Note LP is one of the most rewarding. The compositions (three by pianist Duke Pearson, Byrd's "The Cat Walk" and a collaboration by the pair on "Each Time I Think of You," along with Neal Hefti's "Cute") are superior, and the musicians (which also include Pearson, bassist Laymon Jackson and drummer

Philly Joe Jones) sound consistently inspired. High points of this enjoyable hard-bop date include Pearson's "Duke's Mixture," "Hello Bright Sunflower," and the complex title cut. —*Scott Yanow*

Hip-Interainment, Vol. 1 / Jun. 24, 1961 / VGM ◆◆◆
This collector's LP from the VGM label is valuable in that it features pianist Herbie Hancock in one of his earliest recordings, as a member of the bop quintet co-led by Donald Byrd and baritonist Pepper Adams; bassist Cleveland Eaton and drummer Teddy Robinson complete the group. The recording quality on this live project is decent if not flawless and the band really stretches out during 9- to 14-minute versions of four of Byrd's originals. As is often the case with ambitious projects, there was never a second volume. —*Scott Yanow*

Royal Flush / Sep. 21, 1961 / Blue Note ◆◆◆◆
Donald Byrd was at his peak as a straightahead hard-bop bandleader in the early '60s, turning a series of remarkably solid, enjoyable sessions for Blue Note. *Royal Flush* is no exception to the rule. Recorded in the fall of 1961, *Royal Flush* finds Byrd once again working with baritonist Pepper Adams, but adding bassist Butch Warren, drummer Billy Higgins and, most importantly, a young pianist named Herbie Hancock. For the most part, the quintet plays a set of vital hard bop, swinging hard on the bluesy groove "Hush" and laying back on the pop standard "I'm a Fool to Want You." But what's really interesting is when they begin pushing the boundaries of bop. All three of Byrd's original pieces—"Jorgie's," "Shangri-La," "6M's"—are harmonically complex and have subtly shifting rhythms; all three are successful, but "Shangri-La" is particularly noteworthy. Similarly, Hancock's graceful "Requiem" calls attention to its fluid melodic lines and rhythm. Throughout the date, Byrd and Adams are typically impressive, alternating between punchy, hard-hitting and graceful solos, but Hancock is just as good, signalling early on in his career his deep, unique talent. —*Stephen Thomas Erlewine*

Free Form / Dec. 11, 1961 / Blue Note ◆◆◆◆
Trumpeter Donald Byrd was in his prime during the 1960s and this CD reissue (which adds "Three Wishes" to the original five-song program) finds him stretching the limits of hard bop. With the assistance of four other young forward-thinking musicians (tenor saxophonist Wayne Shorter, pianist Herbie Hancock, bassist Butch Warren and drummer Billy Higgins), Byrd plays some of his more adventurous originals. High points include "Pentecostal Feeling," Hancock's ballad "Night Flower" and the unpredictable "Free Form." Highly recommended. —*Scott Yanow*

Groovin' for Nat / Jan. 12, 1962 / Black Lion ◆◆◆◆
On this somewhat obscure Black Lion release (which has been reissued on CD), Donald Byrd teams up with fellow trumpeter Johnny Coles, pianist Duke Pearson, bassist Bob Cranshaw and drummer Walter Perkins for a set of music dominated by hard-bop originals; "Angel Eyes" and "Out of This World" are the only standards. Augmented by three previously unreleased alternate takes, this straightahead session finds Cole's brittle tone sounding more distinctive than Byrd's (who is in more of a Lee Morgan vein) but everyone plays well. Recommended. —*Scott Yanow*

A New Perspective / Jan. 12, 1963 / Blue Note ◆◆◆◆◆
This unusual set (reissued on CD by Blue Note) was one of the most successful uses of a gospel choir in a jazz context. Trumpeter Donald Byrd and a septet that also includes tenor saxophonist Hank Mobley, guitarist Kenny Burrell and pianist Herbie Hancock are joined by an eight-voice choir directed by Coleridge Perkinson. The arrangements by Duke Pearson are masterful and one song, "Cristo Redentor," became a bit of a hit. This is a memorable effort that is innovative in its own way, a milestone in Donald Byrd's career. —*Scott Yanow*

Up with Donald Byrd / Nov. 3, 1964-Nov. 4, 1964 / Verve ◆◆
Trumpeter Donald Byrd took a brief vacation from Blue Note to record this one album for Verve; it has since been reissued on CD as part of a two-fer put out under guitarist Grant Green's name. The music is mostly forgettable despite such top sidemen as tenors Stanley Turrentine and Jimmy Heath, pianist Herbie Hancock and guitarist Kenny Burrell. Byrd mostly sticks to current pop tunes and most of the songs utilize a rather average vocal group listed as "The Donald Byrd Singers." The arrangements by Claus Ogerman, Byrd and Hancock are unimaginative and these renditions of "House of the Rising Sun," "My Babe" and a few of Hancock's originals are quite forgettable. A lesser effort. —*Scott Yanow*

I'm Tryin' to Get Home / Dec. 17, 1964-Dec. 18, 1964 / Blue Note ◆◆◆
A follow-up to trumpeter Donald Byrd's hit *A New Perspective*, this LP (not yet reissued on CD) also features an eight-voice choir conducted by Coleridge Perkinson and arrangements by Duke Pearson and the leader. The vocalists have a larger role than in the earlier date and Byrd's quintet (with tenor saxophonist Stanley Turrentine and pianist Herbie Hancock) is augmented by organist Freddie Roach, guitarist Grant Green and a dozen brass players. But despite some strong moments, the date (which resulted in no real hits) does not quite reach the heights

of *A New Perspective* although it has plenty of interesting moments. —*Scott Yanow*

Mustang! / Jun. 24, 1966 / Blue Note ◆◆◆◆
Donald Byrd, a talented hard-bop trumpeter during his prime (although rarely reaching the technical heights of Lee Morgan and Freddie Hubbard), performs a varied repertoire on this CD reissue. "Dixie Lee" has dated rhythms, and "Mustang" was an attempt to achieve a hit on the level of Morgan's "The Sidewinder." However, Byrd sounds fine on those numbers; he digs into the complex chord changes of "Fly Little Bird Fly," is sensitive on "I Got It Bad," swings on his "I'm So Excited by You" and performs his memorable countermelody to "On the Trail," which had been recorded earlier by several other musicians. Teamed with a typically impressive Blue Note crew (altoist Sonny Red, tenor saxophonist Hank Mobley, pianist McCoy Tyner, bassist Walter Booker and drummer Freddie Waits), Byrd performs high-quality straightahead jazz that fits the modern mainstream of the era. Also on this CD are a pair of selections ("Gingerbread Boy" and "I'm So Excited by You") from an earlier quintet date (with tenorman Jimmy Heath, Tyner, bassist Walter Booker, and drummer Joe Chambers) that, despite being excellent, went unissued until this 1997 CD. —*Scott Yanow*

Blackjack / Jan. 9, 1967 / Blue Note ◆◆◆
One of three Donald Byrd albums from 1967 (the end of his hard-bop period), this LP features the trumpeter/leader with altoist Sonny Red, tenor saxophonist Hank Mobley, pianist Cedar Walton, bassist Walter Booker and drummer Billy Higgins. The six tunes (five of which are originals by Byrd or Red) are all quite obscure and to one extent or another quite explorative. One can sense that Byrd wanted to break through the boundaries and rules of hard bop but had not yet decided on his future directions. The music does swing and highlights include "West of the Pecos" and "Beale Street"; Byrd and Red in particular are in excellent form throughout the date. —*Scott Yanow*

Slow Drag / May 12, 1967 / Blue Note ◆◆◆
This LP was one of trumpeter Donald Byrd's final hard-bop dates. Teamed with altoist Sonny Red, pianist Cedar Walton, bassist Walter Booker and drummer Billy Higgins (who takes a surprise vocal on the title cut), this quintet outing features originals by Byrd, Walton and Red along with the standards "Secret Love" and "My Ideal." The music in general finds Byrd looking both backwards towards the blues and forwards towards modal music and hints of the avant-garde. A fine effort. —*Scott Yanow*

The Creeper / Oct. 5, 1967 / Blue Note ◆◆◆
This LP was trumpeter Donald Byrd's final album in the hard-bop idiom and it went unissued until 1981. For the last time, Byrd was heard in prime form in an acoustic format. His notable sextet also included altoist Sonny Red, baritonist Pepper Adams, pianist Chick Corea, bassist Miroslav Vitous and drummer Mickey Roker. With the exception of Michel Legrand's "I Will Wait for You," all of the songs were composed by either Byrd, Red or Corea and, although none of the originals caught on as standards (or have been performed since), together as a whole they give one a lot of variety in the then-modern hard-bop field. Pity that this album has been out of print since the mid-'80s. —*Scott Yanow*

Fancy Free / May 9, 1969-Jun. 6, 1969 / Blue Note ◆◆◆◆
This CD reissue brings back one of trumpeter Donald Byrd's final jazz recording before going completely commercial with his R&B group the Blackbyrds; he would not return to jazz until the 1980s and by then the many years of not playing his horn would clearly show. *Fancy Free* was Byrd's first to use electric keyboards and on it the trumpeter found a highly satisfying balance between jazz improvisation and funky rhythms, the acoustic and the electric; pity that he did not continue in that direction. The melody of "Fancy Free" is memorable, a few of the songs are danceable without being simplistic and Byrd and tenor saxophonist Frank Foster have lyrical solos on the ballad "I Love the Girl." —*Scott Yanow*

Kofi / 1969-1970 / Blue Note ◆◆◆
This previously unreleased material (taken from two sessions in 1969-70) contains some of trumpeter Donald Byrd's final jazz recordings before he shifted completely to R&B-funk. On "Kofi" Lew Tabackin's flute solo easily takes honors while "Fufu" (which is also from the earlier date) has some fine Byrd trumpet in a Miles Davis vein. The other three performances from a year later feature Byrd and Foster in excellent form on moody material which merges together hard bop with early fusion; it is remarkable how much Byrd sounds like Miles Davis of the period on some of these numbers. Unfortunately he would not be pursuing this path in the future, making this transitional CD a historic and somewhat unique venture that is well worth investigating. —*Scott Yanow*

Early Byrd: The Best of the Jazz Soul Years / Jun. 24, 1966- 1969 / Blue Note ◆◆◆
Early Byrd: The Best of the Jazz Soul Years contains a selection of nine tracks from Donald Byrd's mid-'60s recordings, bypassing his funkier fusions of the late '60s

and early '70s. These songs—including such numbers as "Slow Drag," "Jellyroll," "Mustang," "Blackjack" and "The Dude"—feature the trumpeter at his grittiest and funkiest. Fans of his early hard-bop years will still find enough improvisation here to make it interesting, while latter-day fans will find enough grooves. It's a solid introduction to one of Byrd's most prolific periods. —*Stephen Thomas Erlewine*

Electric Byrd / May 15, 1970 / Blue Note ◆◆◆
This CD brings back trumpeter Donald Byrd's last worthwhile jazz recording before his descent into commercial success (and artistic oblivion) in the R&B/funk world. Byrd contributed three of the four originals (the fourth is from percussionist Airto) and he explores music that combines together the vestiges of hard bop, Miles Davis-style fusion, modern Brazilian music and touches of R&B. There are some worthwhile solos by the leader along with such saxophonists as Frank Foster and Lew Tabackin on tenors and his old friend baritonist Pepper Adams. The funky rhythm section (which includes the electric piano of producer Duke Pearson, guitarist Wally Richardson, bassist Ron Carter and drummer Mickey Roker in addition to Airto) keeps the proceedings interesting and this set is far superior to Byrd's work throughout the rest of the 1970s. —*Scott Yanow*

Ethiopian Knights / Aug. 25, 1971-Aug. 26, 1971 / Blue Note ◆◆
Interesting jam-session feel. Top jazz players manage to retain credibility in essentially R&B setting. Album cited by many as reflective of label's trend away from its roots in the '70s. Concept was brainchild of George Butler. —*Ron Wynn*

Black Byrd / Apr. 3, 1972-Apr. 4, 1972 / Blue Note ◆◆◆
Starting in 1969 with some transition projects, trumpeter Donald Byrd gradually moved away from hard bop into funk and R&B. This particular set (which has been reissued on CD) is completely outside of jazz and was a major seller when it was released in 1972. The only problem is that the very dated R&B-pop music (which earned Byrd the reputation of being a sellout) sounds even worse now than it did at the time. Under the direction of producer Larry Mizell, who contributed all of the arrangements and compositions, the music is even weak and derivative from the R&B standpoint, unless one thinks of Donald Byrd as being a great vocalist. It would take the label's death and subsequent rebirth before Blue Note recovered its earlier credibility. —*Scott Yanow*

Street Lady / Jun. 13, 1973-Jun. 15, 1973 / Blue Note ◆◆◆
Not so much a fusion album as an attempt at mainstream soul and R&B, *Street Lady* plays like the soundtrack to a forgotten blaxploitation film. Producer/ arranger/composer Larry Mizell conceived *Street Lady* as a concept album to a spirited, independent prostitute, and while the hooker with a heart of gold concept is a little trite, the music uncannily evokes an urban landscape, circa the early '70s. Borrowing heavily from Curtis Mayfield, Isaac Hayes and Sly Stone, Donald Byrd and Mizell have created an album that is overflowing with wah-wah guitars, stuttering electric pianos, percolating percussion, soaring flutes, and charmingly anemic, tuneless vocals. It's certainly not jazz, or even fusion, but it isn't really funk or R&B, either—the rhythms aren't elastic enough, and each of the six songs are simply jazzy vamps without clear hooks. But the appeal of *Street Lady* is how its polished neo-funk and pseudo-fusion sounds uncannily like a jive movie or television soundtrack from the early '70s—you can picture the Street Lady, decked out in polyester, cruising the streets surrounding by pimps with wide-brimmed hats and platform shoes. And while that may not be ideal for jazz purists, it's perfect for kitsch and funk fanatics. —*Stephen Thomas Erlewine*

Places and Spaces / Aug. 1975-Sep. 1975 / Blue Note ◆◆
Reuniting with Larry Mizell, the man behind *Street Lady,* Donald Byrd continues to explore contemporary soul, funk and R&B with *Places and Spaces.* In fact the record sounds more urban than its predecessor, which often played like a Hollywood version of the Inner City. Keeping the Isaac Hayes, Curtis Mayfield, and Sly Stone influences of *Street Lady, Places and Spaces* adds elements of Marvin Gaye, Earth Wind & Fire, and Stevie Wonder, which immediately makes the album funkier and more soulful. Boasting sweeping string arrangements, sultry rhythm guitars, rubbery bass, murmuring fluegelhorns and punchy horn charts, the music falls halfway between the cinematic neo-funk of *Street Lady* and the proto-disco soul of Earth Wind & Fire. Also, the title *Places and Spaces* does mean something—there are more open spaces within the music, which automatically makes it funkier. Of course, it also means that there isn't much of interest on *Places and Spaces* for jazz purists, but the album would appeal to most fans of Philly soul, lite funk and proto-disco. —*Stephen Thomas Erlewine*

Caricatures / Apr. 1976-May 1976 / Blue Note ◆◆◆
Donald Byrd, a respected hard-bop trumpeter during 1955-71, became an R&B star of sorts with the release of *Black Byrd* in 1972. He followed that pop/R&B set (which sounds awfully dated today) with other similar efforts that were even worse. The money-making purpose behind *Caricatures* is all too obvious. Under the direction of producer Larry Mizell, Byrd de-emphasized (and eventually totally neglected) his trumpet playing in favor of singing and letting his oversized rhythm

section vamp excessively. This particular LP was one of the artistic lowpoints of Donald Byrd's career and has fortunately not yet been reissued on CD. —*Scott Yanow*

Thank You . . . For F.U.M.L. (Funking Up My Life) / Jul. 1978 / Elektra ✦

Love Byrd: Donald Byrd and 125th St, N.Y.C. / 1981 / Elektra ✦✦

Harlem Blues / Sep. 22, 1987+Sep. 24, 1987 / Landmark ✦✦✦
This Landmark release was trumpeter Donald Byrd's first jazz album in over 15 years after a long (and commercially if not artistically successful) detour into poppish R&B/funk. In the 1980s Byrd had neglected his trumpet playing in order to direct the Blackbyrds and teach. The period away from his instrument shows in spots on this well-intentioned set. Byrd gathered together four excellent players (altoist Kenny Garrett, pianist Mulgrew Miller, bassist Rufus Reid and drummer Marvin "Smitty" Smith) to play four group originals, W.C. Handy's "Harlem Blues" and "Blue Monk." Ironically Byrd's own playing was not at this point up to the level of his sidemen although his chops would improve during the next couple of years. —*Scott Yanow*

Getting Down to Business / Oct. 10, 1989-Oct. 12, 1989 / Landmark ✦✦✦✦
Trumpeter Donald Byrd's second jazz album during his comeback after years of playing R&B/funk and then totally neglecting his horn finds him starting to regain his former form. The strong supporting cast (altoist Kenny Garrett, tenor saxophonist Joe Henderson, pianist Donald Brown, bassist Peter Washington and drummer Al Foster) sometimes overshadows the leader on this CD but the music overall (modern hard bop) is rewarding. The sextet performs originals by Byrd, Henderson, Donald Brown, Bobby Hutcherson, James Williams and Duke Ellington ("I Got It Bad"). —*Scott Yanow*

A City Called Heaven / Jan. 17, 1991-Jan. 19, 1991 / Landmark ✦✦✦

Don Byron

b. Nov. 8, 1958, New York, NY
Clarinet, Bass Clarinet / Avant-Garde, Post-Bop, Klezmer
The most intriguing new jazz clarinetist to emerge since Eddie Daniels, Don Byron has eclectic musical interests that are reflected in his playing. He studied classical clarinet but switched to jazz at the New England Conservatory of Music. His 1992 album *Tuskegee Experiments* gave him recognition and since that time, in addition to guesting with such players as Bill Frisell, Ralph Peterson and Bobby Previte, Byron has recorded both advanced (and unpredictable) jazz and klezmer. —*Scott Yanow*

● **Tuskegee Experiments** / Nov. 1990-Jul. 1991 / Elektra/Nonesuch ✦✦✦✦
Clarinetist Don Byron immediately became famous in the jazz world after the release of his debut CD as a leader. The strong themes (all but a melody apiece from Robert Schumann and Duke Ellington are originals), the advanced yet logical improvising, and the often-dramatic music make this a particularly memorable set. Byron, doubling on clarinet and bass clarinet, is heard in settings ranging from an unaccompanied solo and duets with bassist Reggie Workman and pianist Joe Berkovitz to medium-size groups with such sidemen as guitarist Bill Frisell, bassist Lonnie Plaxico, drummer Ralph Peterson, Jr., pianist Edsel Gomez and others. Although several songs involve justifiable social protest (including the title cut

which has a poem by Sadiq), the music also stands alone outside of the issues. Highly recommended. —*Scott Yanow*

Plays the Music of Mickey Katz / Sep. 1992 / Elektra/Nonesuch ✦✦✦
No one recognized the manic possibilities of klezmer more than clarinetist Mickey Katz, whose 1945-47 tenure with Spike Jones spawned a comedy band that launched such funny travesties as the Yiddish cowpoke ditty "Haim Afen Range" or the Jewish-Hawaiian "Mechaye War Chant." Katz used humor to expand the musical boundaries of klezmer, thrusting it into the laps of World War II mainstream American at a time when Yiddish was identified as a victim's language and most Jewish music looked backward in time because the post-Holocaust present was intolerable. Playing Katz's songs demands prodigious chops, hence the attraction of Katz to molecule-splitting clarinetist Don Byron, who demonstrates nerve presenting Katz the monologist as the equal of Katz the composer. In sum, convoluted, kaleidoscopic silliness topped with Byron's usual dazzling self. —*Bob Tarte*

No-Vibe Zone: Live at Knitting Factory / Jan. 7, 1996 / Knitting Factory ✦✦✦✦
Don Byron is the quintessential clarinetist of the modern mainstream, and this is a tolerably good example of his work as an improvisor, composer, and bandleader. Byron swings and grooves well in a conventional sense, yet his slippery phrasing runs clear of rhythmic cliché. His tone is clear and pure, as well, but what's even more important than his considerable instrumental skill is the manifest originality and inspiration that drives his art. Byron's tendency to quote other musics and musicians is a bit off-putting, but such appropriation is an aspect of the jazz tradition that Byron embraces convincingly and creatively. His bandmates operate on a similarly high level. Guitarist David Gilmore is an intelligent and very exciting player, possessing an inherently lyrical approach that's compromised a bit by forays into heavy metal timbres. Drummer Marvin "Smitty" Smith has a comprehensive technique, and sets incredible grooves, but tends to overplay in the ensemble. Pianist Uri Caine is a versatile, resourceful accompanist and soloist, as is bassist Kenny Davis. A strong, loose, exciting performance by one of straightahead jazz's most able exponents. —*Chris Kelsey*

Bug Music / May 1996 / Nonesuch ✦✦✦✦✦
This CD is a tribute to the music of Raymond Scott's Quintette, John Kirby's Sextet and Duke Ellington headed by the remarkably versatile clarinetist Don Byron. Raymond Scott's legendary compositions feature eccentric song titles (including on this set "Siberian Sleighride," "Tobacco Auctioneer" and "War Dance For Wooden Indians"), complex and thoroughly-composed arrangements (all of which were originally memorized rather than being written out) and unique melodies. Kirby's brand of swing, which is quite complementary to Scott's novelties, often utilized themes from classical music and had solos, but were also tightly arranged (even "St. Louis Blues" and "Royal Garden Blues"). The CD begins and ends with four Ellington/Strayhorn pieces that fit well into the idiom (particularly "The Dicty Glide" and "Cotton Club Stomp"). In addition to Byron, the key players on the project include altoist Steve Wilson (one of the best of the younger swing stylists), trombonist Craig Harris and pianist Uri Caine, in addition to four other horns and several rhythm sections. Other than a silly rendition of Ellington's "Blue Bubbles" and an adventurous interpretation of "Snibor," the selections are played with respect and great understanding of the somewhat forgotten style. None of the modern musicians sound as if swing were only their second language, making the continually surprising set a major success. —*Scott Yanow*

George Cables

b. Nov. 14, 1944, New York, NY
Piano, Keyboards / Post-Bop, Hard Bop

Equally skilled as a leader or as a sideman, George Cables has helped to define modern mainstream jazz piano of the 1980s and '90s. When he was 18 and at Mannes College he formed the Jazz Samaritans with Steve Grossman and Billy Cobham. Cables gained recognition during his stints with Art Blakey's Jazz Messengers, Sonny Rollins (both in 1969), Joe Henderson (1969-71) and Freddie Hubbard (1971-76). He was with Dexter Gordon (1976-78) during the tenor's successful return to the US and became known as Art Pepper's favorite pianist (1979-82). In addition to his occasional work with Bebop and Beyond (starting in 1984), Cables has appeared in a countless number of situations through the years and has recorded frequently as a leader, most notably for Contemporary (including the 1979 classic *Cables Vision*), Concord and Steeple Chase. —*Scott Yanow*

Circles / Mar. 27, 1979-Mar. 28, 1979 / Contemporary ✦✦✦
Aggressive date with robust solos from Joe Farrell (ts), decisive playing by Cables. —*Ron Wynn*

● **Cables' Vision** / Dec. 17, 1979-Dec. 19, 1979 / Original Jazz Classics ✦✦✦✦✦
One of the most satisfying recordings to be released in 1980 (and since reissued on CD in the OJC series), this date by pianist George Cables (who contributed four of the six group originals) features trumpeter Freddie Hubbard (who brought in "Byrdlike") and tenor saxophonist Ernie Watts in fiery form; the two horn players took time off from their much more commercial efforts for other labels. Vibraphonist Bobby Hutcherson is also in the sextet/septet with bassist Tony Dumas, drummer Peter Erskine and sometimes percussionist Vince Charles; the one departure is "The Stroll," which is an adventurous piano-vibes duet by Cables and Hutcherson. The solos overall are concise and make expert use of each note. Cables' tunes (including "Morning Song," "I Told You So" and "Inner Glow") are generally catchy and memorable while "Byrdlike" gives the virtuosos an uptempo blues to romp through. This logically conceived and well-paced set is a gem that is highly recommended. —*Scott Yanow*

Phantom of the City / May 14, 1985-May 15, 1985 / Contemporary ✦✦✦✦
For this trio set with bassist John Heard and drummer Tony Williams, pianist George Cables is in excellent form on two standards, four of his originals and the little-known "Waltz for Monday." Cables has long been a talented player in what could be called the "modern mainstream": not breaking down any new boundaries but developing his own style in the flexible boundaries of hard bop. This album is an excellent example of his talents. —*Scott Yanow*

By George / Feb. 27, 1987 / Contemporary ✦✦✦
Assisted by bassist John Heard and drummer Ralph Penland on four of the six tracks, pianist George Cables explores six very familiar George Gershwin compositions. The fact that he was able to come up with fresh statements on these warhorses (and still stay melodic) says a great deal about Cables' inventiveness. —*Scott Yanow*

I Mean You / Apr. 1993 / Steeple Chase ✦✦✦✦

Live at Maybeck Recital Hall, Vol. 35 / Jan. 9, 1994 / Concord Jazz ✦✦✦

Joey Calderazzo

b. Feb. 27, 1965, New Rochelle, NY
Piano / Post-Bop

A potentially significant pianist playing in the modern mainstream, Joey Calderazzo's career has gotten off to a strong start with a series of fine Blue Note albums. He studied classical piano from age eight, discovered jazz a few years later and hit the big time when he joined Michael Brecker's band in 1987. He has since recorded with Brecker, Bob Belden, Jerry Bergonzi, Rick Margitza and Bob Mintzer in addition to his own projects. —*Scott Yanow*

● **In the Door** / 1991 / Blue Note ✦✦✦✦
A wonderful debut album with a cast of great sidemen, it included Michael Brecker (sax), Branford Marsalis (tpt), and Jerry Bergonzi (ts). Very modern chord changes. —*Paul Kohler*

To Know One / 1991 / Blue Note ✦✦✦
A potentially significant pianist, Joey Calderazzo is somewhat overshadowed by his notable sidemen on this modern mainstream set. Many selections feature bassist Dave Holland and drummer Jack DeJohnette while Branford Marsalis (on tenor and soprano) and tenor saxophonist Jerry Bergonzi are heard on respectively three and five numbers apiece although never together. Calderazzo contributed the majority of the songs (all of which are originals by group members except Richie Beirach's "See Saw") and plays quite well although at this point he was not yet a distinctive improviser. —*Scott Yanow*

The Traveler / 1993 / Blue Note ✦✦✦✦
At the time of this CD, Joey Calderazzo was an excellent interpreter of the Herbie Hancock acoustic piano style who, although showing touches of originality here and there, had not yet developed his own voice. However, this is a fine trio recording featuring Calderazzo with either John Patitucci or Jay Anderson on bass and Peter Erskine or Jeff Hirshfield on drums. Together they perform five standards, three of the pianist's originals and one song apiece by pianist Larry Willis and Patitucci. Calderazzo does show a great deal of maturity in his playing, sounding just as comfortable on uptempo versions of "Yesterdays" and his "Lunacy" as he does on the ballads. He is a superior middle-of-the-road jazz pianist whose most significant work is most likely in the future. —*Scott Yanow*

Secrets / Oct. 1995 / Audio Quest ✦✦✦

California Ramblers

f. 1921, **db.** 1931
Group / Classic Jazz, Traditional Jazz

Two major myths surround the California Ramblers band that recorded for the Edison record company in the mid-1920s. First, despite the fact that both Tommy and Jimmy Dorsey served tenures with the group, this was *not* the Dorsey Brothers' college band immortalized in their Hollywood biopic. Secondly, the group was not from California (by all reports they never even played in that state), but was formed in Ohio by banjoist Ray Kitchenman in 1921.

The California Ramblers were one of the very first big bands on record that aimed for dance music with strong jazz overtones. Although Paul Whiteman and Jean Goldkette (both of whom employed Bix Beiderbecke at various junctures) were mining this turf around the same period, their recordings sound almost quaint in comparison to the Ramblers. The band had a drumming dynamo in Stan King, an early playing partner of Benny Goodman's, whose rock-solid beat induced dancing. On bass saxophone was Adrian Rollini, a musical genius who could shine on multiple instruments. Add to this the aforementioned Dorsey brothers, Red Nichols, the straightahead rhythm of banjoist Kitchenman and clarinetist Fud Livingston (comedian Jerry Colonna served a brief tenure with the band on trombone before finding his true leather-lunged calling) and you have a society dance band with real bite and verve. They also hold a parenthetical place in jazz history, hiring trumpet man Bill Moore, the first African-American jazz musician to work with a White band. Although their time in the limelight was brief, with several of their members going on to bigger and better things by decade's end, the California Ramblers stand as the quintessential White dance band of the 1920s. —*Cub Koda*

● **Hallelujah, Vol. 2** / Jan. 19, 1925-Aug. 1, 1929 / Biograph ✦✦✦✦
The second of two Biograph LPs that feature superior jazz-influenced dance music by the California Ramblers has a dozen titles originally recorded for the Edison label, five of which are over four minutes long (which was quite extended for the 1920s). Some of the soloists include bass saxophonist Adrian Rollini, altoist Bobby Davis, clarinetist Jimmy Dorsey, trumpeter Red Nichols and trombonist Tommy Dorsey; the latter two just appear on a memorable version of "Everything Is

Hotsy-Totsy Now." Despite the general lack of big names, the high musicianship of the group (which comprised top studio musicians), the catchy arrangements and functional solos combine to create music that perfectly fits the era. —*Scott Yanow*

Volume One / Apr. 1, 1925-Nov. 18, 1927 / The Old Masters ✦✦✦✦
The California Ramblers was one of the finest dance bands of the 1920s, recording nearly a ton of selections, most of which are quite listenable (at least for fans of the era) and danceable. This collector's LP (which looks like a bootleg and fails to give much personnel or date information) has 16 fairly rare performances from the 1925-27 era. Cornetist Red Nichols, trombonist Tommy Dorsey and clarinetist Jimmy Dorsey are on a few of the earlier titles while most of the other selections have bass saxophonist Adrian Rollini and Bobby Davis (on clarinet and alto) as the most significant soloists. Until a more comprehensive reissue series comes along, this rare album is worth picking up (as is *Vol. 2*). —*Scott Yanow*

● **Miss Annabelle Lee, Vol. 1** / Apr. 2, 1925-Jun. 20, 1927 / Biograph ✦✦✦✦
The first of two LPs released by Biograph that give listeners a sampling of the music of the California Ramblers, this set has many examples of high-quality hot dance music from the 1920s. There is one number ("State and Madison") from the obscure Joe Herlihy Orchestra and 11 by the 1925-27 versions of the California Ramblers. Such soloists are heard from as bass saxophonist Adrian Rollini, cornetist Red Nichols, Jimmy Dorsey (on alto and clarinet), altoist Bobby Davis, trombonist Jimmy Dorsey and a variety of lesser-known players. Originally recorded for Edison, the performances mostly clock in between 3 and 4 minute s which are more extended than the usual 2- to 3-minute recording s of the 78 era. Few bands better symbolized the white jazz-influenced dance music of the mid- to late-'20s than the California Ramblers; the period vocals are delightful in their own way and highlights include "Charleston," "Five Foot Two," "Crazy Words, Crazy Tune," "Manhattan" and "Clap Hands Here Comes Charlie." —*Scott Yanow*

Volume Two / Mar. 29, 1927-Jul. 23, 1928 / The Old Masters ✦✦✦✦
Although this out-of-print LP (the second of two) looks like a bootleg and gives virtually no information about the personnel or recording dates, the 16 performances on the set (14 by the California Ramblers and two by a small group from the orchestra called the Little Ramblers) are well worth hearing by fans of 1920s hot dance music. None have been reissued yet on CD and there are plenty of spirited solos (along with period vocals) from the likes of bass saxophonist Adrian Rollini, the Dorsey Brothers and lesser-known but talented players. Highlights include such remarkable titles as "Yes She Do," "Vo-Do-Do-De-O Blues," "Nothin' Does Does Like It Used to Do Do Do," and "Make My Cot Where the Cot-Cot-Cot-ton Grows." —*Scott Yanow*

Edison Laterals 2 / Nov. 5, 1928-Oct. 9, 1929 / Diamond Cut ✦✦✦
This CD contains 20 performances by the California Ramblers during a one-year period of time, rare selections that were originally released by the Edison label. During the era there weren't any big names in the group as there had been earlier, but such soloists as trumpeter Fred Van Eps, Jr., (who was influenced by Bix Beiderbecke) and Pete Pumiglio (on alto and clarinet) uplifted the hot dance arrangements of this fine group. Trombonist Miff Mole and bass saxophonist Adrian Rollini have guest appearances but basically this was a no-name unit by 1929. Fans of 1920s jazz will want the attractively packaged set. —*Scott Yanow*

Red Callender (George Sylvester Callender)

b. Mar. 8, 1916, Haynesville, VA, d. Mar. 8, 1992, Saugus, CA
Bass, Tuba / Bop, Cool, Swing
A busy studio musician who appeared on a countless number of recordings during his productive (and generally lucrative) career, Red Callender is the only player to turn down offers to join both Duke Ellington's Orchestra and the Louis Armstrong All-Stars! After briefly freelancing in New York, Callender settled in Los Angeles in 1936, debuting on record the next year with Louis Armstrong. In the early '40s he was in the Lester and Lee Young band and then formed his own trio. Callender in the 1940s recorded with Nat King Cole, Erroll Garner, Charlie Parker, Wardell Gray and Dexter Gordon among many others and can be seen and heard taking a bebop break on bass in the 1946 film *New Orleans* (which was supposed to depict the city's music scene of 1915!). After a period spent leading a trio in Hawaii, Callender returned to Los Angeles, becoming one of the first Black musicians to work regularly in the commercial studios. On his 1954 Crown LP *Speaks Low*, Callender was one of the earliest modern jazz tuba soloists and he would occasionally double on that instrument in future years. His composition "Primrose Lane" became a Top Ten hit in 1959 when recorded by Billy Wallace. Some of the highlights of the bassist's later career include recording with Art Tatum (1955-56), playing with Charles Mingus at the 1964 Monterey Jazz Festival, working with James Newton's avant-garde woodwind quintet (on tuba), and performing as a regular member of the Cheatham's Sweet Baby Blues Band. Callender's mid-'80s autobiography *Unfinished Dream* is quite informative and colorful. —*Scott Yanow*

Red Callender Speaks Low / 1954 / Crown ✦✦✦
Swingin' Suite / 1956 / Modern ✦✦✦✦
This obscure LP features bassist Red Callender in one of his very infrequent occasions as a leader, heading an octet featuring a variety of talented Los Angeles players (including trumpeter Parr Jones, Buddy Collette on tenor and flute, altoist Bill Green and pianist Eddie Beal) on a dozen of his melodic originals. The music swings lightly, has attractive chord changes suitable for jamming, and fits into the cool-toned West Coast jazz genre. This session will hopefully be reissued on CD (along with many other obscure sets cut for Crown) someday. —*Scott Yanow*

The Lowest / Apr. 30, 1958+May 1, 1958 / Metrojazz ✦✦✦
● **Night Mist Blues** / 1984 / Hemisphere ✦✦✦✦
Red Callender's first date as a leader in 11 years (and only second in 26) is a relaxed trio set with pianist Gerry Wiggins and drummer Sherman Ferguson. The veteran bassist (also heard on tuba on a couple numbers including "Lush Life") does an effective job of singing "Baby, I'm Gone." With Wiggins providing some sly wit and swinging solos influenced at times by Erroll Garner and Art Tatum, and Ferguson fine in support, this is a highly enjoyable trio outing. —*Scott Yanow*

Cab Calloway (Cabell Calloway)

b. Dec. 25, 1907, Rochester, NY, d. Nov. 18, 1994, Delaware
Vocals, Leader / Swing
One of the great entertainers, Cab Calloway was a household name by 1932 and never really declined in fame. A talented jazz singer and a superior scatter, Calloway's gyrations and showmanship on stage at the Cotton Club sometimes overshadowed the quality of his always-excellent bands. The younger brother of singer Blanche Calloway (who made some fine records before retiring in the mid-'30s), Cab grew up in Baltimore, attended law school briefly and then quit to try to make it as a singer and a dancer. For a time he headed the Alabamians but the band was not strong enough to make it in New York. The Missourians, an excellent group that had previously recorded heated instrumentals but had fallen upon hard times, worked out much better. Calloway worked in the 1929 revue "Hot Chocolates," started recording in 1930, and in 1931 hit it big with both "Minnie the Moocher" and his regular engagement at the Cotton Club. Calloway was soon (along with Bill Robinson, Ethel Waters, Louis Armstrong and Duke Ellington) the best-known Black entertainer of the era. He appeared in quite a few movies (including 1943's *Stormy Weather*) and "Minnie the Moocher" was followed by such recordings as "Kicking the Gong Around," "Reefer Man," "Minnie the Moocher's Wedding Day," "You Gotta Hi-De-Ho," "The Hi-De-Ho Miracle Man" and even "Mister Paganini, Swing for Minnie." Among Calloway's sidemen through the years (who received among the highest salaries in the business) were Walter "Foots" Thomas, Bennie Payne, Doc Cheatham, Eddie Barefield, Shad Collins, Cozy Cole, Danny Barker, Milt Hinton, Mario Bauza, Chu Berry, Dizzy Gillespie, Jonah Jones, Tyree Glenn, Panama Francis and Ike Quebec. His 1942 recording of "Blues in the Night" was a big hit.

With the end of the big-band era, Calloway had to reluctantly break up his orchestra in 1948 although he continued to perform with his Cab Jivers. Since George Gershwin had originally modelled the character "Sportin' Life" in *Porgy and Bess* after Calloway, it was fitting that Cab got to play him in a 1950s version. Throughout the rest of his career Calloway made special appearances for fans who never tired of hearing him sing "Minnie the Moocher." —*Scott Yanow*

Cab Calloway and the Missourians (1929-1930) / Jun. 3, 1929-Dec. 23, 1930 / JSP ✦✦✦✦
This English import starts off with the dozen selections recorded by the Missourians (plus two alternate takes) during 1929-30. The excellent group is heard playing a variety of instrumentals, many of which are based on "Tiger Rag." The heated soloing by trumpeters R.Q. Dickerson and Lammar Wright, trombonist De Priest Wheeler and the reeds of Andrew Brown and Walter Thomas makes one surprised that this group was commercially unsuccessful. Cab Calloway permanently took over the Missourians in 1930 and his earliest ten recordings form the second half of this CD. The Calloway performances (which directly precede his hit "Minnie the Moocher") are highlighted by "St. Louis Blues," "Nobody's Sweetheart" and a classic rendition of "St. James Infirmary" and make clear from the start why he was considered one of the most popular and exciting performers of the 1930s. —*Scott Yanow*

● **1930-1931** / Jul. 24, 1930-Jun. 17, 1931 / Classics ✦✦✦✦✦
Cab Calloway is long overdue for a reappraisal. Long put down by some writers as a mere entertainer, he was actually a superior jazz-influenced singer whose vocal abilities were often overshadowed by his showmanship. The ideal way to acquire his best recordings are to get the 11 CDs in Classics' *Complete* series. Not only do these reissues include his hits, but also some jazz instrumentals and enjoyable obscurities that give one a more well-rounded picture of the "Hi-De-Ho Man." This

particular Classics CD has his first 24 recordings; from the start, his colorful style was already fully formed. It is particularly interesting to hear Calloway performing some material associated with others, especially "Happy Feet" (Paul Whiteman), "The Viper's Drag" and "I'm Crazy 'Bout My Baby" (the latter two with Fats Waller), and several Duke Ellington hits. One of the better Harlem orchestras, Calloway's early band had formerly been known as the Missourians and included several fine soloists, particularly trumpeter Lammar Wright and Walter Thomas on tenor and baritone. Highlights include "St. Louis Blues," "Some of These Days," a classic rendition of "St. James Infirmary," "Nobody's Sweetheart" and the original version of "Minnie the Moocher." —*Scott Yanow*

Jazz Heritage: Mr. Hi-De-Ho (1930-1931) / Jul. 24, 1930-Oct. 21, 1931 / MCA ✦✦✦

This LP from MCA's *Jazz Heritage* series of the early '80s gives listeners a sampling of Cab Calloway's early recordings. Sixteen of his best performances from 1930-31 are here, including "St. Louis Blues," "Nobody's Sweetheart," a classic version of "St. James Infirmary," "Bugle Call Rag," "Kickin' the Gong Around" and the original recording of "Minnie the Moocher." Although superceded by the much more complete Classics CD series, this is a fine set of early material. —*Scott Yanow*

Kicking the Gong Around / 1931-1938 / ASV/Living Era ✦✦✦✦

Cab's naughtier side, with the virtues of substance use imbuing the lyrical text of several tunes included here. If you thought drug songs didn't start until the late '60s in rock music, be prepared for a shock. —*Cub Koda*

Cab Calloway and Company / Mar. 2, 1931-Nov. 29, 1949 / RCA ✦✦✦

This is a very appealing double LP from French RCA's *Jazz Tribune* series. The first 22 of the 34 selections (including four rare alternate takes) feature the Cab Calloway Orchestra of 1933-34, a vastly underrated early swing band which, in addition to its colorful leader/singer, features good soloists in trumpeter Lammar Wright, clarinetist Eddie Barefield and tenor saxophonist Walter "Foots" Thomas. Highlights include "Harlem Hospitality," "The Lady with the Fan," "Harlem Camp Meeting," "Kickin' the Gong Around," "Margie" and two remakes of "Minnie the Moocher." In addition this two-fer (which has all of Calloway's recordings for Victor) contains four long-forgotten items from 1949 including a hilarious version of "I Beeped When I Shoulda Bopped" (in which Calloway satirizes not only bebop but his own style), six numbers from his older sister Blanche Calloway in 1931 (highlighted by "I Need Lovin'") and two obscure items from singer Billy Banks in 1932. Until it is reissued on CD, this two-fer (which contains over 100 minutes of high-quality and entertaining music) is well worth searching for. —*Scott Yanow*

1931-1932 / Jul. 9, 1931-Jun. 7, 1932 / Classics ✦✦✦✦

The second of 11 Classics CDs that reissue all of Cab Calloway's recordings from 1930-42 has 23 performances that trace the singer's success during an 11-month period. He shows what he learned from his older sister Blanche on some of the songs, but on "You Rascal You," "Aw You Dawg" and "Kickin' the Gong Around," the singer could be mistaken for no one else but himself. There is a bit of surface noise on some of the tracks (sometimes sounding like a light rain) and even a skip on "Without Rhythm" but the wonderful music far outvalues the minor technical faults. Due to the solos of trumpeter Lammar Wright, clarinetist Arville Harris and the tenor of Walter Thomas, the tight ensembles and Calloway's exuberant (in the case of "Basin Street Blues," rather silly) singing, there are many memorable selections on this set. Highlights include "Bugle Call Rag," "Stardust," "Trickeration," "Kickin' the Gong Around," "Corrine Corinna," "The Scat Song" and "Dinah." This is very enjoyable and often-classic music that lets one know immediately why Cab Calloway was so popular during the 1930s. —*Scott Yanow*

1932 / Jun. 7, 1932-Dec. 7, 1932 / Classics ✦✦✦

The third of 11 Cab Calloway CDs put out by Classics (which on a whole reissues the master takes of all of the popular singer's recordings from 1930-42) covers a busy six-month period. His big band (which tended to be greatly overshadowed) was actually quite excellent with good soloists in trumpeter Lammar Wright, clarinetist Eddie Barefield, Walter Thomas on tenor and pianist Bennie Payne, but of course Calloway was the main star. Highlights of this very enjoyable set include "Old Yazoo," "Reefer Man," "Old Man of the Mountain," "You Gotta Ho-De-Ho," "I've Got the World on a String," the bizarre "Dixie Doorway," "Beale Street Mama" and "The Man from Harlem." Many of the titles on this rewarding release had never been reissued before, making the Classics series a collection worth picking up in a hurry before it disappears. —*Scott Yanow*

1932-1934 / Dec. 7, 1932-Sep. 4, 1934 / Classics ✦✦✦

The Depression may have been at its height during the two years covered by this Classics CD (the fourth in their series of 11 complete Cab Calloway sets), but there was nothing depressed about Calloway's often-jubilant vocals, the playing of his vastly underrated orchestra or the infectious (and sometimes) crazy lyrics. Trumpeter Lammar Wright, clarinetist Eddie Barefield and Walter Thomas on tenor

contribute some fine solos, but the focus is very much on the leader's vocals and he is in peak form on such songs as "The Lady with the Fan," "Harlem Camp Meeting," "Kickin' the Gong Around," "'Long About Midnight" and "Margie" (even if "Chinese Rhythm" is rather absurd). This easily recommended set also has a remake of "Minnie the Moocher" and an all-star recording of "Doin' the New Lowdown" with the Mills Brothers and Don Redman's Orchestra. —*Scott Yanow*

1934-1937 / Sep. 4, 1934-Mar. 3, 1937 / Classics ✦✦✦✦

Cab Calloway, who first became popular in 1930, retained his popularity (despite a lot of competition) throughout the swing era. On this excellent CD (the fifth of 11 in the European label Classics' *Complete* Calloway series), highlights include "Keep That Hi-De-Hi in Your Soul," "Nagasaki," "Copper Colored Gal," "Frisco Flo" and a crazy "That Man Is Here Again." With fine soloists in trumpeters Lammar Wright and Shad Collins, trombonist Claude Jones and (by 1936) the great tenor Ben Webster (along with a top-notch rhythm section that includes bassist Milt Hinton), this was a much better swing orchestra than it is generally rated in jazz history books. —*Scott Yanow*

★ **Are You Hep to the Jive?** / 1935-1945 / Sony ✦✦✦✦✦

The Hi-De-Ho Man / Jul. 2, 1935-Dec. 11, 1947 / RCA ✦✦✦

This double LP from 1974 is a bit brief, only including 20 performances by Cab Calloway and his orchestra (around an hour of music). Several periods are covered with titles from 1935 ("Nagasaki"), the 1938-42 period and nine fairly rare selections from 1945-47. High points include "Jumpin' Jive," "Fifteen Minute Intermission," a 1941 version of "St. James Infirmary," "Hi De Ho Man" and a 1942 rendition of "Minnie the Moocher." On the later tracks Calloway tries to adapt his sound to rhythm & blues but, despite his best efforts, his orchestra would not survive the 1940s. The earlier titles have been reissued on CD by the Classics label and hopefully Columbia will get around to compiling a more generous Cab Calloway package in the future. The music on this two-fer is generally not classic but will be found enjoyable by his fans. —*Scott Yanow*

1937-1938 / Mar. 3, 1937-Mar. 23, 1938 / Classics ✦✦✦✦

The swing era may have been at its height during the time covered by this CD (the sixth of 11 put out by the Classics label that reissue all of Cab Calloway's 1930-42 recordings) but the colorful vocalist held onto his audience and remained a household name. With such soloists as Ben Webster or Chu Berry on tenor, trumpeters Shad Collins and Lammar Wright and a rhythm section including guitarist Danny Barker and bassist Milt Hinton, Calloway had a particularly strong (if generally overlooked) orchestra. Among the more memorable selections of the 24 included on this CD are "Swing, Swing, Swing," "She's Tall, She's Tan, She's Terrific," "Bugle Blues" and "Hi-De-Ho Romeo." —*Scott Yanow*

Penguin Swing / Dec. 10, 1937-Mar. 5, 1941 / Jazz Archives ✦✦✦

The music on this Dutch import CD was previously available as a collectors' LP put out by Jazz Archives. The 16 studio recordings by Cab Calloway's Orchestra from the 1937-41 period put the focus on the tenor solos of Chu Berry with eight of the numbers being unissued performances, usually alternate takes. In addition to Berry and of course the leader's exuberant vocals, trumpeters Lammar Wright, Dizzy Gillespie and Jonah Jones also have solo space. Highlights include "Penguin Swing," "Bugle Blues," "Calling All Bars," "Bye Bye Blues" and "Jonah Joins the Cab." This CD is worth picking up (due to the rarer tracks) even by collectors who have been wise enough to get the many Cab Calloway CDs put out by the Classics label. —*Scott Yanow*

1938-1939 / Mar. 23, 1938-Feb. 20, 1939 / Classics ✦✦✦✦

The seventh of the Classics label's 11 Cab Calloway CDs traces his progress during an 11-month period through 24 recordings. The band's main soloists at the time included trumpeters Shad Collins and Irving Randolph, trombonists Claude Jones and Keg Johnson and especially tenor great Chu Berry (the band gets four instrumentals on this set). Singer June Richmond has a couple of vocals, but obviously Cab Calloway is the main reason that the orchestra was working so steadily. With such songs as "Shout, Shout, Shout," "Do You Wanna Jump Children" and "F.D.R. Jones" among the more memorable tracks, this CD (along with the others in the valuable series) is well worth picking up. —*Scott Yanow*

1939-1940 / Mar. 28, 1939-Mar. 8, 1940 / Classics ✦✦✦✦

Cab Calloway had one of his strongest orchestras during the period covered by this CD, the eighth of 11 put out by the European Classics label that reissued all of his studio recordings from 1930-42. Trumpeter Dizzy Gillespie joined the band by the time of its Aug. 30, 1939 session and he has several short solos on these tracks in addition to being well-featured on the adventurous "Pickin' the Cabbage." In addition, the great tenor Chu Berry gets plenty of solo space, the impressive rhythm section (with guitarist Danny Barker, bassist Milt Hinton and drummer Cozy Cole) really propels the ensembles and Cab Calloway is in typically exuberant voice. Among the highlights are "The Ghost of Smoky Joe," "Crescendo in

Drums" (a feature for Cole), "Pluckin' the Bass" (Hinton's showcase) and even "Jiveformation Please." —*Scott Yanow*

1940 / Mar. 8, 1940-Aug. 28, 1940 / Classics ✦✦✦✦
With such soloists as trumpeter Dizzy Gillespie, Chu Berry on tenor and trombonist Tyree Glenn, along with a rhythm section that includes bassist Milt Hinton and drummer Cozy Cole, this was a particularly strong edition of the Cab Calloway Orchestra. There are six instrumentals among the 22 selections on this Classics CD (the ninth of 11 Calloway *Complete* sets) including Berry's famous version of "Ghost of a Chance" and a spot for Gillespie on "Bye Bye Blues," but nearly every performance has its interesting solos; most of the ones with short spots for Gillespie have rarely been reissued. Cab Calloway, who as usual is the main star, is in spirited form. The other highlights include "Hi-De-Ho Serenade," "Fifteen Minute Intermission," "Papa's in Bed with His Britches On" and "Are You Hep to the Jive?" It's recommended, as are all of the CD's in this important series. —*Scott Yanow*

1940-1941 / Aug. 28, 1940-Jul. 24, 1941 / Classics ✦✦✦✦
Cab Calloway is in superior form throughout this CD (the tenth of 11 Calloway releases from the European Classics label), but it is often the short solos by his sidemen that hold onto one's interest, particularly those of trumpeter Dizzy Gillespie and tenor Chu Berry. By the last ten numbers (including his feature "Jonah Joins the Cab"), trumpeter Jonah Jones had become a member of this powerful band, which could rank at the top echelon of swing orchestras. Calloway is also heard near the peak of his powers and the highlights of this fine set include Benny Carter's "Lonesome Nights" (one of six instrumentals among the 22 numbers), "A Chicken Ain't Nothin' but a Bird," "Ebony Silhouette," "Hep Cat's Love Song" and two versions of "St. James Infirmary." —*Scott Yanow*

1941-1942 / Jul. 24, 1941-Jul. 27, 1942 / Classics ✦✦✦✦
The final of the European Classics label's 11 *Complete* Cab Calloway CDs (reissuing all of his studio recordings of 1930-42) has the last recordings of trumpeter Dizzy Gillespie and tenor Chu Berry with Cab; other soloists include trumpeter Jonah Jones and trombonist Tyree Glenn. Calloway retained his popularity throughout the World War II years and was still in prime form during these 22 recordings. Highlights include a memorable "Blues in the Night," "A Smo-o-o-oth One," "Virginia, Georgia and Caroline" and a new version of "Minnie the Moocher." All of the 11 Classics CDs are highly recommended to Cab Calloway and swing fans; they are perfectly done. —*Scott Yanow*

Jazz off the Air, Vol. 4 / 1943-1946 / Spotlite ✦✦✦
Cab Calloway and his orchestra are heard on selections taken from four radio broadcasts dating from the 1943-46 era, a period when they were not recording that frequently. Although there are a few spots for Cab Calloway's vocals, the emphasis on this collectors' LP from the English Spotlite label is on such fine soloists as tenors Illinois Jacquet and Ike Quebec, trombonist Tyree Glenn and trumpeter Jonah Jones. Although not essential, swing collectors will enjoy this set. —*Scott Yanow*

Michel Camilo

b. Apr. 4, 1954, Santo Domingo, Dominican Republic
Piano / Hard Bop, Latin Jazz
An exciting and high-powered virtuoso pianist, Michel Camilo came from a very musical family (with all nine of his uncles being musicians). Originally playing accordion, he switched to piano when he was 16. After moving to New York in 1979, his song "Why Not?" became a hit for the Manhattan Transfer and caught on as a standard and "Caribe" entered the repertoire of Dizzy Gillespie. Camilo, who worked with Paquito D'Rivera's band for three years (cutting an album with "Why Not" as the title cut), has recorded for Electric Bird (sessions reissued by Evidence) and Columbia and worked as a leader for the past decade. —*Scott Yanow*

Why Not / Feb. 25, 1985-Feb. 27, 1985 / Evidence ✦✦✦
Pianist Michel Camilo made his recording debut as a leader with this session for the Japanese King label. Camilo was anxious to show everything, and did so on such cuts as "Thinking of You" and the title track. He ripped through phrases, added powerhouse chords and rippling lines, switched tempos and meters, and moved from a hard-bop feel to an Afro-Latin groove in the middle of a piece. His intensity and energy were impressive, but at times he tried too much and stumbled getting back to the melody. It wasn't an unflawed debut, but Camilo showed that he would be a pianist to be reckoned with down the line. —*Ron Wynn*

Suntan / Jun. 29, 1986-Jun. 30, 1986 / Evidence ✦✦✦
Pianist Michel Camilo did some intensive recording for the Japanese Suntan label over a two-day period in 1986. These five selections were in a trio format with Dave Weckl and Joel Rosenblatt alternating on drums and Anthony Jackson on bass throughout. Camilo displayed the Afro-Latin and Latin jazz side of his key-

board personality with slashing, attacking rhythms and phrases. He sacrificed some of his celebrated speed and thought more about ideas, pace, melodies, and harmonic creativity. Camilo's playing emerged as dominant as Jackson was content to work off his leads, and both drummers were equally willing to interact rather than try to influence the music's direction. As a result, Camilo got the chance to demonstrate his full range and did so in a workmanlike, effective manner. —*Ron Wynn*

Michel Camilo / Jan. 30, 1988-Feb. 1, 1988 / Portrait ✦✦✦✦
Michel Camilo was one of the most stimulating jazz pianists to emerge in the mid-to-late '80s. His powerful two-handed attack (full of impressive technical skills), his knowledge of both jazz and Afro-Cuban music, and his willingness to constantly take chances make each of his solos into an adventure. This now out-of-print Portrait set, his first date as a leader to be made available domestically, features Camilo in a pair of trios with either Marc Johnson or Lincoln Goines on bass and Dave Weckl or Joel Rosenblatt on drums; Mongo Santamaria makes some guest appearances on congas. On the spirited outing, Michel Camilo sticks to originals, with the exception of "Blue Bossa." —*Scott Yanow*

● **On Fire** / Jun. 20, 1989-Jun. 25, 1989 / Epic ✦✦✦✦✦
A particularly strong outing by pianist Michel Camilo, this CD showcases him in trios with either Michael Bowie or Marc Johnson on bass, and Dave Weckl, Marvin "Smitty" Smith or Joel Rosenblatt on drums; percussionist Sammy Figueroa dropped by for a song titled "… And Sammy Walked In." An exception from the trio format is "Hands & Feet," a duet with the flamenco dancer Raul. As with Michel Camilo's earlier Portrait release, all of the songs save one (in this case "Softly as in a Morning Sunrise") are his originals. Exciting and powerful music. —*Scott Yanow*

On the Other Hand / Apr. 1990 / Epic ✦✦✦
When it comes to pure rhythmic excitement, few can compete with pianist Michel Camilo and his frequently polyrhythmic attack. Although his powerful style is evident throughout the calypso-oriented title cut, this CD is actually a fairly laidback album. With "City of the Angels" used as a ballad feature for Chris Hunter's soprano, the two versions of "Silent Talk" being quite tender, "Forbidden Fruit" mostly an R&Bish vocal by D.K. Dyson and Kacey Cysik, and some of the other cuts finding Camilo in a supportive role, this is a very different album than the pianist's first two. Overall this set is a slight disappointment considering what Camilo is capable of. —*Scott Yanow*

Rendezvous / Jan. 18, 1993-Jan. 20, 1993 / Columbia ✦✦✦

One More Once / May 20, 1994-May 26, 1994 / Columbia ✦✦✦✦

Thru My Eyes / Oct. 30, 1996-Nov. 3, 1996 / RMM ✦✦✦

John Campbell

b. Jul. 7, 1955, Bloomington, IL
Piano / Hard Bop
Pianist John Campbell, a powerful player who is creative within the tradition, is best known for his associations with Mel Tormé and the Terry Gibbs-Buddy DeFranco Quintet. He started piano lessons at seven and in 1977 moved to Chicago. His trio/quartet (known originally as Campbell's Group) was soon in demand to accompany touring artists (including Eddie Jefferson/Richie Cole, Eddie Harris and James Moody) and in 1981 he toured Europe with Clark Terry. In 1984 Campbell moved to New York and he subbed for Jim McNeely with Stan Getz's group. In 1986 he joined Mel Tormé and soon afterward hooked up with Terry Gibbs. In 1993 Campbell recorded a solo disc for Concord (*Live at Maybeck Recital Hall, Vol. 29*). —*Scott Yanow*

After Hours / Aug. 23, 1988 / Contemporary ✦✦✦✦
This CD reissue adds "O Grande Amor" to the original nine-song program. The frequently hard-charging pianist John Campbell is in top form in a trio with bassist Todd Coolman and drummer Gerry Gibbs. Other than Terry Gibbs' "Lonely Days," the music comprises standards, many (including "Donna Lee," "Relaxin' at Camarillo" and Bud Powell's "Hallucinations") dating from the bebop era. Campbell, whose influences at the time included Oscar Peterson, takes consistently exhilarating and unpredictable solos on the straightahead repertoire, showing that he has long been an underrated talent. Recommended. —*Scott Yanow*

Turning Point / Jun. 18, 1990-Jun. 19, 1990 / Contemporary ✦✦✦✦
A good second album for pianist Campbell on the Contemporary label, this one had an added bonus of excellent contributions from jazz immortal Clark Terry. His spry solos and presence elevated both the session and the other participants, particularly Campbell, who played with much more edge and energy than on his previous release. He used different rhythm section personnel as well, this time recruiting Jay Anderson and Joel Spencer. —*Ron Wynn*

● **Live at Maybeck Recital Hall, Vol. 29 [John Campbell at Maybeck]** / May 1993 / Concord Jazz ✦✦✦✦

Pianist John Campbell stretches out during the eight standards he performs during his Maybeck Recital Hall solo set. An exuberant player, Campbell often switches back and forth between two keys during a song (sometimes during every chorus), a device he sometimes overuses. An uptempo version of "Emily" is a particular surprise and his explorations of "Just Friends," "You and the Night and the Music" and "Easy to Love" are particularly memorable. — *Scott Yanow*

Candido (Candido Camero)

b. Apr. 22, 1921, Havana, Cuba

Percussion / Bop, Afro-Cuban Jazz, Latin Jazz

Candido was *the* Latin percussionist of the 1950s, the first person that jazz people would call when they wanted a conga or bongo player. Early on he had recorded in his native Cuba with Machito and he worked regularly with the house band at the Tropicana Club in Havana for six years. Dizzy Gillespie heard him and encouraged him to move to New York in 1952. Soon Candido was performing and recording with Gillespie. During 1953-54 he was in the Billy Taylor quartet and in 1954 he performed and recorded with Stan Kenton. Since that time Candido has recorded with the who's who of jazz including Erroll Garner, Gene Ammons, Art Blakey, Sonny Rollins, Wes Montgomery, Elvin Jones and Lionel Hampton among many others. — *Scott Yanow*

● **Candido Featuring Al Cohn** / Apr. 9, 1956-Apr. 10, 1956 / ABC/Paramount ✦✦✦✦

The Volcanic Candido / Feb. 20, 1957-Feb. 25, 1957 / ABC/Paramount ✦✦✦

In Indigo / Apr. 28, 1958-Mar. 4, 1959 / ABC/Paramount ✦✦✦

Latin Fire / Feb. 20, 1959-Mar. 4, 1959 / ABC/Paramount ✦✦✦

Conga Soul / 1961-1962 / Roulette ✦✦✦

Thousand Finger Man / Sep. 4, 1969+Sep. 9, 1969 / Solid State ✦✦

Beautiful / Oct. 20, 1970-Oct. 27, 1970 / RCA ✦✦✦

Drum Fever / 1973 / Polydor ✦✦✦

Conte Candoli

b. Jul. 12, 1927, Mishawaka, IN

Trumpet / Bop, Cool

Conte Candoli is a solid player in the cool bop vein, the younger brother of Pete. Besides the band with his brother, Conte played in the '40s with Woody Herman, Chubby Jackson, Stan Kenton and Charlie Ventura. He worked in the '50s with Charlie Barnet and Kenton again, before moving to Chicago to head his own group. But he came back to California later in 1954, and played with both his brother's band and Howard Rumsey's Lighthouse All Stars through the end of the '50s. Candoli recorded and played with Terry Gibbs from 1959 to 1962, and recorded with Gerry Mulligan and Sonny Criss during the '60s. He played with Woody Herman at the Monterey Festival and with Kenton's Los Angeles Neophonic Orchestra. Candoli also played regularly with Shelly Manne, worked in the studios on film and television projects, and was in "The Tonight Show" band. During the '70s, he recorded with Frank Strazzeri and Teddy Edwards. Candoli was a member of Supersax in the '70s. The brothers have worked together into the '90s, and have recorded for Dot, Mercury, Crown and Somerset, among others, as a joint band. Conte Candoli has recorded solo sessions for Bethlehem, Atlantic and Andex. — *Ron Wynn and Michael Erlewine*

● **Conte Candoli Quartet** / Jun. 1957 / V.S.O.P. ✦✦✦✦✦

Reissued by the V.S.O.P. label, this session features the excellent bop trumpeter Conte Candoli in a quartet with pianist Vince Guaraldi, bassist Monty Budwig and drummer Stan Levey. In addition to the joy of hearing Candoli so well-showcased, this set is recommended because of the interesting repertoire. In addition to "Flamingo," "Diane" and "No Moon at All," one gets to hear rare selections penned by the likes of Al Cohn, Osie Johnson, Conte's brother Pete Candoli and the leader himself. — *Scott Yanow*

Mucho Calor / Oct. 1957 / Andex ✦✦✦✦

Little Band, Big Jazz / Feb. 3, 1960 / Crown ✦✦✦

Opportunities to lead his own record date have been surprisingly rare through the years for the talented bop trumpeter Conte Candoli. This obscure LP is one of only two albums Candoli headed during 1958-84! Candoli teams up with other West Coast players of the era (tenor saxophonist Buddy Collette, pianist Vince Guaraldi, bassist Leroy Vinnegar and drummer Stan Levey) for six of his fairly basic originals including such numbers as "Muggin' the Minor," "Mambo Diane" and "Countin' the Blues." There are no real surprises in the music but the performances swing nicely. — *Scott Yanow*

Conversation / May 25, 1973 / RCA ✦✦✦✦

Considering that this session was cut for RCA and features trumpeter Conte Candoli and trombonist Frank Rosolino, one would think that the music would have gotten more recognition and a follow-up date would have been made. As it is, the 1976 LP went quickly out-of-print and Candoli would not lead another session until 1985. Accompanied by a fine Italian rhythm section, Candoli and Rosolino perform a ballad apiece, the trombonist scats on "Conversation" and there are two other Rosolino originals plus the lone standard of the session, "Star Eyes." The boppish music is lively and fresh, making this an underrated and generally overlooked album that is easily recommended to straightahead jazz fans. — *Scott Yanow*

Old Acquaintance / Sep. 30, 1985-Oct. 1, 1985 / Pausa ✦✦✦✦✦

Trumpeter Conte Candoli and altoist Phil Woods make for a perfect team on this set, which has unfortunately only been released on LP by the now-defunct Pausa label. In addition to the principals, the sextet includes vibraphonist Charlie Shoemake, pianist Terry Trotter, bassist Monty Budwig and drummer Bill Goodwin; singer Sandi Shoemake makes a cameo appearance for a chorus of "Don't Worry About Me." The music is essentially modern bebop with such tunes as Bud Powell's "Wail," Fats Navarro's "Nostalgia" and "Just You, Just Me" alternating with a few recent obscurities. Everyone plays up-to-par during what was one of Candoli's very few opportunities to lead a record session. Unfortunately this LP will be difficult to find. — *Scott Yanow*

Pete Candoli (Walter Joseph Candoli)

b. Jun. 28, 1923, Mishawaka, IN

Trumpet / Swing, Bop, Big Band

The elder of the trumpet-playing Candoli brothers, Pete initially made the greater impact of the two in Woody Herman's First Herd at the tail end of the Swing Era. A powerful, flamboyant soloist, his big moment came toward the end of "Apple Honey," where he would appear in a Superman costume and cut loose scorching, dissonant flurries of high notes. Pete started with the Sonny Dunham band in his 17th year (1940-41) and passed through the bands of Will Bradley, Benny Goodman, Ray McKinley, Tommy Dorsey, Freddie Slack and Charlie Barnet before settling into the Herman band from 1944 to 1946. He worked for Tex Beneke (1947-49) and Jerry Gray (1950-51) before moving to Los Angeles where he became immersed in studio work, with side trips into the Les Brown (1952) and Stan Kenton (1954-56) bands. From 1957 to 1962, he co-led a group with Conte and later fronted his own band, while recording on his own for Columbia, Warner Bros, Kapp and Somerset. He has been married to singers Betty Hutton and Edie Adams; with the latter, he formed a nightclub act in 1972 in which he sang, danced, led the orchestra and played. He would continue to perform with Conte off and on into the 1990s. Although Pete's profile had been low and his trumpet technique slipped in later years, he could still burn in a swing-grounded manner in the '90s. — *Richard S. Ginell*

The Brothers Candoli / Dec. 5, 1958-Dec. 6, 1958 / MCA/Impulse! ✦✦✦

Originally titled *Bell, Book and Candoli*, this former Dot LP was reissued by the revived Impulse label in the early '80s. Trumpeters Pete and Conte Candoli have collaborated on an occasional basis over the past half-century, and their album was one of four that they recorded during 1957-59. Joined by pianist John Williams, guitarist Barney Kessel, either Joe Mondragon or Red Mitchell on bass and drummer Alvin Stoller, the brothers play concise versions of ten songs that include four standards (including "Boulevard of Broken Dreams" and "What Is This Thing Called Love"), Morton Gould's "Pavanne," and five Pete Candoli originals. The music is enjoyable if not substantial, swinging but not essential. — *Scott Yanow*

For Pete's Sake / Oct. 25, 1960-Dec. 10, 1960 / Kapp ✦✦✦

● **Blues, When Your Lover Has Gone** / 1961 / Somerset ✦✦✦✦

Considering his long career, trumpeter Pete Candoli has led relatively few sessions. He did cut four albums from 1959-61, but has only headed one set since then. This out-of-print but worthy LP features Candoli with fellow L.A.-based studio players (trombonist Milt Bernhart, tenor saxophonist Ted Nash, pianist Jimmy Rowles, guitarist Al Hendrickson, bassist Red Mitchell and drummer Shelly Manne). Although ostensibly a program of blues, half of the songs are merely bluesy, rather than actual blues. Candoli sounds fine and is heard in prime form throughout the relaxed set. — *Scott Yanow*

Valerie Capers

b. , New York, NY

Piano / Hard Bop

Although her 1995 Columbia recording *Come on Home* was released in a *Legendary Pioneers of Jazz* series, Valerie Capers is much too obscure and under-recorded to be a legend, and not old enough to be a pioneer! She picked out songs on the piano as a child before losing her sight at the age of six. Her blindness did not stop her from learning to read music in Braille and becoming the first blind graduate from the Julliard School of Music. Although a classical player at the time, she was attracted to jazz and was soon working with Mongo Santamaria. In 1965 Capers recorded for Atlantic; 17 years later she would finally cut her second date (a self-produced effort for the tiny KM Arts label) and it would be another 13 years before her Columbia set. Capers did work with Ray Brown, Slide Hampton, James Moody, Max Roach and Dizzy Gillespie in the interim but was mostly employed as a high-level educator. Hopefully she will have more opportunities to record in the future. —*Scott Yanow*

Portrait in Soul / 1965 / Atlantic ✦✦✦
Rare septet, all Capers originals. Worth searching for. —*Michael G. Nastos*

Affirmation / Jun. 29, 1982 / K-M-Arts ✦✦✦
All standards, and well played. A good one to find. —*Michael G. Nastos*

● **Come on Home** / 1995 / Columbia ✦✦✦✦
Valerie Capers has managed to stay somewhat obscure despite a busy schedule and her obvious talents. When Columbia gave her a rare opportunity to record, she made the most of it. Capers sings several of the songs (most winningly Horace Silver's "Come on Home") but especially notable is her strong bop-based piano playing; her trio also includes drummer Terry Clarke and either John Robinson III or Bob Cranshaw on bass. Trumpeter Wynton Marsalis helps out on two numbers ("Odyssey" and "It's All Right with Me") and altoist Paquito D'Rivera is an asset on four (including "A Night in Tunisia"), but the main significance of this long overdue CD is that it gives Valerie Capers her chance to shine. —*Scott Yanow*

Frank Capp (Frank Cappuccio)

b. Aug. 20, 1931, Worchester, MA
Drums, Leader / Bop, Swing
Frank Capp, a flexible and consistently swinging drummer, loves to drive a big band. As leader of the Juggernaut (a group he co-led with Nat Pierce starting in 1975 until the pianist's death in 1992), he gets to push and inspire some of Los Angeles' best. Capp found his initial fame playing with Stan Kenton's Orchestra (1951). Two years later he settled in Los Angeles, became a busy studio musician and played with everyone from Ella Fitzgerald, Harry James and Charlie Barnet to Stan Getz, Art Pepper and Dave Pell. He recorded often with Andre Previn's Trio (1957-64) and also made records with Benny Goodman (1958), Terry Gibbs and Turk Murphy. Capp worked steadily on television shows and in the film studios in the 1960s and (starting in the 1970s) has recorded extensively in a variety of settings for Concord. The Capp-Pierce Juggernaut (now known simply as the Juggernaut) sometimes sounds identical to the 1970s Count Basie Orchestra and serves as a perfect format for the drummer's colorful playing. —*Scott Yanow*

Juggernaut / Aug. 8, 1976 / Concord Jazz ✦✦✦✦
The debut recording by the Frankie Capp-Nat Pierce Juggernaut features a big band full of all-stars playing swing standards in the style of Count Basie; the CD reissue adds two selections to the original set. With such soloists as trombonist Buster Cooper, tenors Richie Kamuca and Plas Johnson, trumpeter Blue Mitchell, altoist Marshal Royal and pianist Pierce (who consistently sounds like Basie), the renditions of such songs as "Avenue 'C,'" "Moten Swing" and "Dickie's Dream" are quite enjoyable. Ernie Andrews sings the final three numbers, not slowing down the momentum on this spirited live session one bit. Recommended. —*Scott Yanow*

● **The Live at the Century Plaza** / Jul. 21, 1978 / Concord Jazz ✦✦✦✦✦
The packaging for this reissue CD could be better (it leaves out the personnel listing and even the recording date) but the Capp/Pierce Juggernaut is heard throughout the live session in fine form. The main soloists in the 1978 version of the 17-piece orchestra are pianist co-leader Nat Pierce, trumpeter Al Aarons, trombonist Buster Cooper, tenors Bob Cooper and Herman Riley and altoist Marshall Royal; co-leader Frank Capp has a drum feature on "Capp This." The Count Basie soundalike band (which sounds surprisingly like Duke Ellington's on "Fiesta in Brass") performs Pierce's arrangements with swing and spirit. An added plus is that Joe Williams sits in for "Joe's Blues" (during which he sings some of his favorite blues stanzas) along with a throwaway version of "What the World Needs Now Is Love." —*Scott Yanow*

Juggernaut Strikes Again / Oct. 1981-Nov. 1981 / Concord Jazz ✦✦✦✦
The 1981 edition of the Frank Capp/Nat Pierce Juggernaut sticks to its vision of being a Count Basie soundalike big band. The repertoire is a bit farther reaching than on its previous releases including Pierce's "One for Marshal" (featuring altoist Marshall Royal), "I Remember Clifford," Buck Clayton's then-recent "Chops, Fingers and Sticks" and a medley of Charlie Parker tunes. Among the key soloists are Royal, pianist Pierce, tenors Pete Christlieb and Bob Cooper, trombonist Buster

Cooper and fluegelhornist Al Aarons. Ernie Andrews helps out with two vocals. A typically swinging Juggernaut album; all are recommended. —*Scott Yanow*

Live at the Alley Cat / Jun. 1987 / Concord Jazz ✦✦✦
This was the fourth and final album by the Juggernaut before its co-leader pianist Nat Pierce's death. The five instrumentals (other than "Queer Street") find the band getting a bit away from their trademark Count Basie sound; the main soloists are Pierce, trumpeters Bill Berry and Conte Candoli, tenors Red Holloway and Bob Cooper and altoist Joe Romano. The final four numbers feature vocals by guest singer Ernestine Anderson, most notably on a lengthy and definitive rendition of "Never Make Your Move Too Soon." A fine effort overall even if the orchestra is not featured much on the second half of the program. —*Scott Yanow*

Presents Rickey Woodard / 1991 / Concord Jazz ✦✦✦✦
This CD was the first small-group date to feature the swinging tenor of Rickey Woodard. Drummer Frank Capp, along with pianist Tom Ranier and bassist Chuck Berghofer, jam with Woodard on a set of jazz standards including "Oleo," "Au Privave" and "Polka Dots and Moonbeams." For a change of pace Berghofer sings Bobby Troup's humorous "Three Bears" and the date concludes with Woodard switching to alto for his own "You Tell Me." A fine bop set. —*Scott Yanow*

In a Hefti Bag / Nov. 3, 1994-Mar. 21, 1995 / Concord Jazz ✦✦✦✦
The Frank Capp Juggernaut's interpretations of 16 Neal Hefti compositions (which were originally written and arranged for the 1950s-era Count Basie Orchestra) brings new life to the highly appealing music without directly copying the earlier recordings. Capp and his 16-piece orchestra are in typically swinging form on obvious classics such as "Cute," "Whirly Bird" and "Li'l Darlin'," several songs whose ensembles are more familiar than their titles (such as "Flight of the Foo Birds," "Scoot" and "Bag-A-Bones") and some high-quality obscurities. Many soloists are featured including the late altoist Marshall Royal (who takes his last recorded solo on "It's Awf'lly Nice to Be with You"); tenors Rickey Woodard and Pete Christlieb; altoist Lanny Morgan; trumpeters Conte Candoli, Bob Summers and Snooky Young; and trombonists Thurman Green, Alan Kaplan and Andy Martin. Special mention should be made of the work of Gerry Wiggins, who is former co-leader Nat Pierce's permanent replacement and fits right into the Count Basie chair with enthusiasm and obvious skill. As for Frank Capp, he gets his share of drum breaks (including on "Cute" and "Whirly Bird") while thoroughly enjoying himself driving the ensembles. Fans of swinging big bands cannot do much better than picking up this highly recommended release. —*Scott Yanow*

Quality Time / 1995 / Concord Jazz ✦✦✦✦
Drummer Frank Capp heads a quartet/quintet that features the fine tenor Rickey Woodard on a variety of straightahead material. With pianist Tom Ranier, bassist Chuck Berghofer and (on two of the nine numbers) trumpeter Nolan Smith, Capp and Woodard (who switches to alto on two songs) play six standards and three group originals. Highlights of this swinging mainstream session (which was released by Concord in 1995) include Woodard's "Dip Stick," Clifford Brown's "Daahoud," "Tadd's Delight" and "Things Ain't What They Used to Be." —*Scott Yanow*

Play It Again Sam / Sep. 24, 1996-Oct. 8, 1996 / Concord Jazz ✦✦✦✦

Mutt Carey

b. 1891, Hahnville, LA, d. Sep. 3, 1948
Trumpet / New Orleans Jazz
An important New Orleans trumpeter whose best work was generally not captured on record, Mutt Carey became an inspiration for revivalists. Born to a musical family and able in his early days to play drums, guitar and alto, Carey switched permanently to cornet (and later trumpet) in 1912. He played in the Crescent Orchestra before joining Kid Ory's band for the first time in 1914. Carey visited Chicago for the first time in 1917 with Lawrence Duhe's band and, after returning to New Orleans, he went to Los Angeles with Ory in 1919. They recorded two numbers as Spikes' Seven Pods of Pepper Orchestra in 1922 and accompanied a few singers. When Ory left for Chicago in 1925, Carey took over the group, which appeared in a few silent films and provided background music for a few Hollywood studios in the '20s. Carey often had a day job during the Depression, but in 1944, he rejoined Kid Ory's band and finally had further opportunities to record, both with the trombonist and (after leaving Ory in 1947) as a leader shortly before his death. —*Scott Yanow*

● **Mutt Carey & Lee Collins** / 1947 / American Music ✦✦✦✦

Caribbean Jazz Project

f. 1993
Group / Latin Jazz
For a special concert at the Central Park Zoo in 1993, vibraphonist Dave Samuels (who doubles on marimba) put together the Caribbean Jazz Project for the first

time. Teaming Samuels with the brilliant (and pioneer) jazz steel drummer Andy Narell and saxophonist Paquito D'Rivera (who alternates between alto, clarinet and soprano), and eventually joined by pianist Dario Eskenazi, bassist Oscar Stagnaro and drummer Mark Walker, the group quickly developed a unique and highly appealing sound. Describing their goal as "a musical tour of the Caribbean," the band also ventures musically to several South American countries and Dizzy Gillespie-era New York. The Caribbean Jazz Project has toured on a part-time basis (recording a couple of fine sets for Heads Up) ever since. —*Scott Yanow*

Larry Carlton (Larry Eugene Carlton)

b. Mar. 2, 1948, Torrance, CA
Guitar / Crossover Jazz, Fusion

Like so many other Los Angeles studio musicians, guitarist and composer Larry Carlton was faced with a choice a number of years back: whether to go solo and develop a name for himself or to continue the less risky, more lucrative existence as a session guitarist, making good money and recording with prominent musicians. Fortunately for fans of this eclectic guitarist, he chose the former, and has recorded under his own name for Warner Bros., MCA Records and GRP Records since 1978.

Carlton's studio credits from the 1970s and early '80s include musicians and groups like Steely Dan, Joni Mitchell, Michael Jackson, Sammy Davis, Jr., Herb Alpert, Quincy Jones, Bobby Bland, Dolly Parton, Linda Ronstadt and literally dozens of others. Among his more notable projects as a session guitarist were Joni Mitchell's critically acclaimed *Court and Spark* album and Donald Fagen's *Nightfly* album. For much of the 1970s, Carlton was active as a session guitarist, recording on up to 500 albums a year. Although he recorded a number of LPs under his own name as early as 1968's *With a Little Help from My Friends* (Uni), and 1973's *Singing/Playing*, he didn't land a major-label contract until 1978, when he signed with Warner Bros.

Carlton began taking guitar lessons when he was six. His first professional gig was at a supper club in 1962. After hearing Joe Pass on the radio, he was inspired to play jazz and blues. Wes Montgomery and Barney Kessel became important influences soon after he discovered the jazz guitar stylings of Pass. B.B. King and other blues guitarists had an impact on Carlton's style as well. He honed his guitar-playing skills in the clubs and studios of greater Los Angeles. He attended a local junior college and Long Beach State College for a year until the Vietnam War ended. Carlton toured with the Fifth Dimension in 1968 and began doing studio sessions in 1970. His early session work included studio dates with pop musicians like Vicki Carr, Andy Williams and the Partridge Family. In 1971, he was asked to join the Crusaders shortly after they'd decided to drop the word "Jazz" from their name, and he remained with the group until 1976. In between tours with the Crusaders, he also did studio session work for hundreds of recordings in every genre. But it was while he was with the Crusaders that he developed the highly rhythmic, often bluesy style he has now. His credits include performing on more than 100 gold albums. His theme music credits for TV and films include *Against All Odds*, *Who's the Boss*, and the theme for *Hill Street Blues*. The latter won a Grammy award in 1981 for Best Pop Instrumental Performance.

Carlton delivered his self-titled debut for Warner Bros. in 1978, shortly after he was recognized for his groundbreaking guitar playing on Steely Dan's *Royal Scam* album. (Carlton contributed the memorable guitar solo on "Kid Charlemagne.") He released four more albums for Warner Bros., *Strikes Twice* (1980), *Sleepwalk* (1981), *Eight Times Up* (1982), and the Grammy-nominated *Friends* (1983), before being dropped from the label.

He continued studio session work and touring, emerging again in 1986 on MCA Records with an all-acoustic album, *Discovery*, which contained an instrumental remake of Michael McDonald's hit "Minute by Minute." The single won a Grammy Award for Best Pop Instrumental Performance in 1987. Carlton's live album, *Last Nite*, released in 1987, got him a Grammy nomination for Best Jazz Instrumental Performance.

While working on his next album for MCA, *On Solid Ground*, Carlton was the victim of random gun violence. He was shot in the throat by gun-wielding juveniles outside Room 335, his private studio near Burbank, California. The bullet shattered his vocal cord and caused significant nerve trauma, but after intensive therapy and keeping a positive frame of mind, Carlton completed work on *On Solid Ground* in 1989. Carlton formed Helping Innocent People (HIP), a non-profit group to aid victims of random gun violence.

Carlton's most recent albums include two releases in 1996 for GRP Records, *Gift* and *With a Little Help from My Friends*. His other recordings include 1990s *Collection* and 1992's *Kid Gloves* for the same label, *Playing/Singing* (1995, Edsel), and *Renegade Gentleman*, a 1993 release for GRP.

Despite the tragedy that was foisted on him in the late '80s after he was shot, dragging him through a long and dark period of hospitalization and rehabilitation, Carlton's output over the years has been steady through the 1980s and 1990s.

Carlton seems to have slowed down his touring schedule a bit, but certainly not his recording schedule. Always happy to meet with the press, Carlton has a sweet, peaceful personality, and one can hear it in his unique, rhythmic, warm guitar chords and ringing guitar tones. —*Richard Skelly*

● **Larry Carlton** / 1978 / Warner Brothers ♦♦♦♦♦
His best. —*Michael G. Nastos*

Strikes Twice / 1980 / MCA ♦♦♦

Sleepwalk / 1981 / MCA ♦♦

Friends / 1983 / MCA ♦♦♦

Last Nite / Feb. 17, 1986 / MCA ♦♦♦♦
This live set is one of Larry Carlton's best recordings because the guitarist stretches himself. Joined by keyboardist Terry Trotter, bassist Abraham Laboriel, drummer John Robinson and percussionist Alex Acuna (and an occasional three-piece horn section), Carlton plays five- to eight-minute versions of four originals (including "The B.P. Blues"), plus Miles Davis' "So What" and "All Blues." Recorded at the Baked Potato in North Hollywood in California, Carlton is heard throughout at his very best, making one wonder why he has recorded so few albums of a similar spontaneous nature in his career. —*Scott Yanow*

Alone/But Never Alone / 1986 / MCA ♦♦♦

Discovery / 1986 / MCA ♦♦♦

On Solid Ground / 1989 / MCA ♦♦♦
This is a fairly typical Larry Carlton date, with a mixture of music (funky jazz, R&B, some rock influences and a bit of pop) and some distinctive if unadventurous guitar playing. Carlton, who is joined by an electric rhythm section (including keyboardists Terry Trotter and Alan Pasqua) and occasionally saxophonist Kirk Whalum, sounds fine, but the music appears to have been geared towards potential radio airplay. The biggest surprise is a version of Eric Clapton's "Layla." —*Scott Yanow*

The Larry Carlton Collection, Vol. 2 / 1987-1992 / GRP ♦♦♦♦♦
The Larry Carlton Collection, Vol. 2 is an excellent, 11-track collection that rounds up highlights from his late-'80s and '90s albums *On Solid Ground*, *Larry & Lee*, *Kid Gloves*, *Discovery* and *The Gift*. For casual fans of Carlton's smooth, eclectic style, this is an excellent summary and introduction to one of the most popular periods of the guitarist's career. —*Stephen Thomas Erlewine*

Renegade Gentleman / Mar. 1991-Apr. 1993 / GRP ♦♦

Playing/Singing / Nov. 21, 1995 / Edsel ♦♦♦♦

Gift / Sep. 24, 1996 / GRP ♦♦♦

Hoagy Carmichael (Howard Hoagland Carmichael)

b. Nov. 11, 1899, Bloomington, IN, **d.** Dec. 27, 1981, Palm Springs, CA
Piano, Vocals / Standards, Classic Jazz, Show Tunes, Traditional Pop

One of the great composers of the American popular song, Hoagy Carmichael differed from most of the others (with the obvious exception of Duke Ellington) in that he was also a fine performer. Such Carmichael songs as "Stardust," "Georgia on My Mind," "Up the Lazy River," "Rockin' Chair," "The Nearness of You," "Heart and Soul," "In the Cool, Cool, Cool of the Evening," "Skylark" and "New Orleans" have long been standards, each flexible enough to receive definitive treatment numerous times. Carmichael, who was supposed to become a lawyer, loved jazz almost from the start, and particularly the cornet playing of Bix Beiderbecke. His first composition, "Riverboat Shuffle," was recorded by Bix and the Wolverines in 1924 and became a Dixieland standard. Hoagy, as a pianist, vocalist and occasional trumpeter, eventually abandoned law to concentrate on jazz, particularly after recording "Washboard Blues" with Paul Whiteman in 1927. He led a few jazz sessions of his own in the late '20s (including one that interpreted "Stardust" as an uptempo stomp!) but became more popular as a skilled songwriter. By 1935 he was working in Hollywood and he became an occasional character actor, appearing in 14 films including "To Have and Have Not" and "The Best Years of Our Lives," generally playing a philosophical and world-weary pianist/vocalist. In the 1940s Carmichael recorded some trio versions of his hits and in 1956 he cut a full set of vocals while backed by a modern jazz group that included Art Pepper. After that he drifted into semi-retirement, dissatisfied with how the music business had changed. His two autobiographies (1946's *The Stardust Road* and 1965's *Sometimes I Wonder*) are worth picking up. —*Scott Yanow*

Curtis Hitch and Hoagy Carmichael / Sep. 19, 1923-May 5, 1928 / Fountain ♦♦♦♦
This generous LP from the English Fountain label has 19 selections featuring bands from 1920s Indiana. There are nine obscure numbers by Hitch's Happy Harmonists dating from 1923 and 1925. The most significant performances are the final two, for they feature Hoagy Carmichael on piano introducing his composi-

tions "Boneyard Shuffle" and "Washboard Blues." The flip side starts with the three songs cut at Carmichael's first dates as a leader. Two of his tunes are long forgotten ("Friday Night" is notable for featuring Hoagy's primitive cornet playing), but most memorable is the original version of "Stardust." Taken as a medium-tempo instrumental (Mitchell Parish had not yet written the lyrics), Carmichael's piano playing shows the impact that Bix Beiderbecke had already had on his music. In addition, this hard-to-find LP has five selections by pianist Emil Seidel's Orchestra in 1927 and two songs by Carmichael's Collegians: the rambunctious "March of the Hoodlums" and "Walkin' the Dog." Collectors of 1920s music should consider the well-conceived collection to be essential, if now scarce. —*Scott Yanow*

Classic Hoagy Carmichael / May 9, 1927-Dec. 15, 1987 / Smithsonian ✦✦✦✦✦

The talented Hoagy Carmichael gained fame in his lifetime for his singing, acting and to a lesser extent his skills at the piano, but his most important contributions to music were made as a composer. This handsome three-LP box set (which includes a classy 64-page booklet) has recordings of Carmichael's songs from a 60-year period and a wide variety of performers. Programmed more or less in chronological order, the box includes no less than six versions of "Stardust" along with fairly definitive versions of his bigger hits along with some obscurities. The music is not strictly jazz although one gets Bix Beiderbecke, Louis Armstrong, the Boswell Sisters, Mildred Bailey, Benny Goodman, Artie Shaw, Billie Holiday, Ella, Mel Tormé, Art Pepper and even Wynton Marsalis. In addition, there are selections featuring Bob Hope, Kate Smith, Frank Sinatra, Betty Hutton, Bing Crosby, Jane Wyman, Ray Charles (guess which song) and Margaret Whiting along with ten appearances by Carmichael himself. There are many more than its share of classics in this admirable package which is highly recommended to all. —*Scott Yanow*

Stardust (1927-1932) / Oct. 31, 1927-Sep. 1, 1932 / Historical ✦✦✦✦

Hoagy Carmichael is best remembered today as a skilled composer and a personality in Hollywood films. During the period covered by this Historical LP (all but one number is from 1927-30), Carmichael was a struggling singer-pianist who enjoyed playing jazz when he was not involved in plugging his songs. On the album Hoagy is heard on piano and singing in a variety of jazz-oriented settings. Highlights include the earliest recorded version of "Stardust," a couple of rare opportunities to scat sing, a few hot numbers with Carmichael's Collegians and previously unreleased test pressing versions of "Rockin' Chair" and "March of the Hoodlums." —*Scott Yanow*

● **Stardust & Much More** / Nov. 18, 1927-Mar. 1, 1960 / RCA/Bluebird ✦✦✦✦✦

This is the definitive Hoagy Carmichael CD, documenting his most significant recordings of the 1927-34 period when he evolved from a little-known jazz pianist-vocalist to being widely recognized as a major composer. The 21-song CD starts and ends with previously unreleased solo versions of "Stardust" featuring Carmichael in 1960. Also on the release is Hoagy's recording of his "Washboard Blues" with Paul Whiteman's Orchestra, "So Tired" with Jean Goldkette, dates led by Carmichael (including four songs in 1930 that have solos from cornetist Bix Beiderbecke), a guest spot singing "Come Easy, Go Easy Love" with Sunny Clapp's Band O'Sunshine and five solo piano/vocal numbrs from 1933-34 (including "Stardust"). Highly recommended. —*Scott Yanow*

Hoagy Carmichael Sings Hoagy Carmichael / Feb. 25, 1939-Mar. 1, 1951 / MCA ✦✦✦✦

Not to be confused with the Pacific Jazz album *Hoagy Sings Carmichael,* this LP from English MCA is much better than American MCA's *The Stardust Road,* which covers the same timespan. Sixteen of Hoagy Carmichael's most rewarding recordings of the 1939-51 period (mostly 1942-47) are here and all of the songs are his compositions. Although the exclusion of a personnel listing and even the recording dates is inexcusable, the music overcomes the major oversight. Carmichael, who sometimes leads a trio on these performances when he is not accompanied by an orchestra (including two 1939 numbers with the Casa Loma Orchestra), is heard in prime form on such songs as "The Old Music Master," "Memphis in June," "Riverboat Shuffle," "Georgia on My Mind," "Stardust," "Baltimore Oriole" and "In the Cool, Cool, Cool of the Evening." This album is worth searching for since the material is not yet readily available on CD. —*Scott Yanow*

The Stardust Road / Feb. 25, 1939-Mar. 1, 1951 / MCA ✦✦✦

The performances are excellent on this long out-of-print MCA LP but there is less than half an hour of music and no personnel listing. Composer-singer-pianist Hoagy Carmichael is mostly featured with trios from his Decca years although there are also a few orchestral tracks. With the exception of 1951's "My Resistance Is Low" (which was a hit at the time) the music dates from 1939, 1942 and 1946-47. Hoagy performs ten of his songs including "Stardust," "Rockin' Chair," "Riverboat Shuffle," "The Old Music Master" and "Ole Buttermilk Sky." Hopefully this delightful music will someday resurface on CD in more complete fashion. —*Scott Yanow*

Hoagy Sings Carmichael / Sep. 10, 1956-Sep. 13, 1956 / Pacific Jazz ✦✦✦✦✦

Hoagy Carmichael's last significant recording is a project whose format should have been repeated in later years. Sticking to vocals, Carmichael performs ten of his compositions including "Georgia on My Mind," "New Orleans," "Skylark," "Baltimore Oriole," "Rockin' Chair" and "Lazy River." What is unusual is that he is accompanied by an 11-piece all-star jazz group and that his voice takes its turn with trumpeters Harry "Sweets" Edison and Don Fagerquist, altoist Art Pepper and pianist Jimmy Rowles. The matchup works quite well because Hoagy's songs have long been viable devices for jazz improvising. The CD reissue of this unique set adds a previously unreleased instrumental rendition of "Georgia on My Mind" to the already impressive program. —*Scott Yanow*

Judy Carmichael

b. 1952, Lynwood, CA

Piano / Stride, Swing

Judy Carmichael is a real rarity, a pianist that came up since 1950 who specializes in the pre-World War II piano style called stride. Carmichael, who was not even born in 1950, started on piano when her grandfather offered $50 to the first grandchild who could play "Maple Leaf Rag." She played music for the first time professionally when she was 19 and was a ragtime pianist at Disneyland when she discovered stride piano. In 1980 she made her recording debut on Progressive, utilizing four veteran players (including Marshall Royal and Freddie Greene). The following year Carmichael moved to New York and has worked steadily ever since. She recorded more sets for Progressive/Statiras and most recently for her own C&D label. Judy Carmichael plays at the same level as the classic masters. —*Scott Yanow*

Two Handed Stride / Apr. 4, 1980+Apr. 29, 1980 / Statiras ✦✦✦✦

The recording debut of pianist Judy Carmichael was a major if somewhat unheralded event. The first important stride pianist to emerge in nearly 30 years, Carmichael has proved to be a consistently creative and exciting performer (rather than imitative) within the genre of classic jazz and swing during the years since her debut. For this set (originally out on Progressive and not yet reissued on CD), Carmichael is joined by altoist Marshall Royal, guitarist Freddie Green, bassist Red Callender and drummer Harold Jones, which gives some of the music a Count Basie feel. However Carmichael's own musical personality was already nearly fully formed by the date. Highlights of the joyous music include "Christopher Columbus," "Honeysuckle Rose," "A Handful of Keys" and "I Would Do Anything for You." —*Scott Yanow*

Jazz Piano / Jun. 11, 1983 / Statiras ✦✦✦✦

Judy Carmichael's second recording was her first full set of unaccompanied solos. Already a masterful stride pianist (one of the very few in her generation), Carmichael performs a variety of standards from the 1920s and '30s on this 1983 LP, all but two of which were composed by pianists: Earl Hines, Fats Waller, Duke Ellington, James P. Johnson, George Gershwin and Clarence Williams. Carmichael is in typically swinging form on such numbers as "Rosetta," "Alligator Crawl," "Lady Be Good," "Carolina Shout" and "Nagasaki." Classic jazz fans should be interested in all of Judy Carmichael's recordings, even this hard-to-find album (which was also released by Progressive). —*Scott Yanow*

Old Friends / Jun. 11, 1983+Nov. 11, 1985 / C&D ✦✦✦✦

Released on CD by her own label, this highly enjoyable effort matches the brilliant stride pianist Judy Carmichael with cornetist Warren Vache and guitarist Howard Alden. Such numbers as "Oh Baby," "Love Is Just Around the Corner" and "Everybody Loves My Baby" are enthusiastically performed as heated, swinging jams. Vache sits out on Fats Waller's "Fractious Fingering," while Jelly Roll Morton's "Grandpa's Spells" is taken as a piano solo. Although three of the songs were recorded nearly two year s before the remainder of the program, the playing of Carmichael, Vache and Alden is quite consistent. Recommended to pre-bop jazz collectors. —*Scott Yanow*

Pearls / Sep. 11, 1985-Sep. 12, 1985 / Statiras ✦✦✦✦✦

The CD reissue of what was originally a Statiras set by pianist Judy Carmichael expands the original ten song program to 18. Carmichael teams up with cornetist Warren Vache, guitarist Howard Alden and bassist Red Callender for a spirited set of classic jazz and swing standards. Seven of the eight "new" selections are actually alternate takes, so this CD is really two records in one. However when the songs played are of the caliber of "Lulu's Back in town," "I'm Gonna Sit Right Down and Write Myself a Letter," "Between the Devil and the Deep Blue Sea" and "Everybody Loves My Baby," one does not really mind hearing two versions. —*Scott Yanow*

Trio / Jan. 6, 1989-Jan. 7, 1989 / C&D ✦✦✦✦

Stride piano master Judy Carmichael stars throughout this CD from her JC label. Featured in an unusual trio with guitarist Chris Flory and Michael Hashim (who doubles on alto and soprano), Carmichael excels on a variety of swing era standards including "The Joint Is Jumpin'," "Them There Eyes," "Swing 42," "I Got Rhythm" and "Honeysuckle Rose." All of Judy Carmichael's recordings are well worth picking up for no other stride pianist who has emerged since Ralph Sutton, Dick Wellstood and Dick Hyman in the early '50s is in her class. —*Scott Yanow*

Basie Called Her Stride / Jul. 11, 1994 / C&D ♦♦♦

● **Judy** / Sep. 18, 1994-Sep. 19, 1994 / C&D ♦♦♦♦♦
Although she could certainly recreate the recordings of James P. Johnson and Fats Waller if she wanted to, talented pianist Judy Carmichael plays stride not as a precious museum piece but rather as a natural part of her musical vocabulary. On this excellent release, she is teamed successfully with electric guitarist Chris Flory whose solos greatly recall Charlie Christian. Carmichael is in particularly wonderful form on the slower pieces (such as "Gee Baby, Ain't I Good to You?" and "Lazy River"),but she also includes several stomps for variety, making this an easily recommended CD. —*Scott Yanow*

Chops / Oct. 8, 1994 / C&D ♦♦♦♦♦
Stride piano has been a nearly extinct art form for the past half-century, although kept alive for a time by its originators (who are now all gone) and a few successors and revivalists. Before Bud Powell made the presence of a bassist necessary by shifting the function of the left hand to playing irregularly stated chords, the jazz pianist was an orchestra by him or herself. One's left hand not only hit chords, but strode back and forth in order to generate a steady and frequently exciting rhythm. Many of today's stride pianists are amateurs with stiff, metronomic rhythms, or converted ragtime players with impressive technique who barely improvise. Judy Carmichael has long had the technique, but also the rare ability of bringing life to veteran standards, even while playing at rapid tempos. On her latest release from C&D, Carmichael revives 13 pre-bop tunes ranging from "Dill Pickles" and "Lady Be Good" to "Christopher Columbus" and Jelly Roll Morton's "Grandpa's Spells." Her solo disc is a bit unusual in that, like Dick Hyman, Carmichael performed the music a year before it was actually recorded, using a modern player piano (in this case a PianoDisc). Fortunately, player pianos have advanced quite a bit since their pre-1920 heyday, and are now able to pick up the complex rhythms and subtleties of masterful players. This enjoyable set, which has many joyous stomps and plenty of spontaneity, is highly recommended to fans of swing, classic jazz and solo piano. —*Scott Yanow*

Harry Carney

b. Apr. 1, 1910, Boston, MA, **d.** Oct. 8, 1974, New York, NY
Baritone Saxophone / Swing
Although he was not the first jazz baritone-saxophonist, Harry Carney achieved his goal of making the instrument "necessary" in a big band. His tone was huge and definitive, and his style mixed together Coleman Hawkins and Adrian Rollini; he was also one of the first jazz musicians to master circular breathing (which he generally used to hold an endless long note). Early on he played piano, clarinet and alto before deciding on baritone. Carney joined Duke Ellington's Orchestra when he was 17 in 1927 and remained for over 46 years, passing away in 1974 a few months after Ellington. Although he originally doubled on alto for Duke, added bass clarinet in later years and traditionally took the clarinet solo on "Rockin' in Rhythm," he otherwise stuck exclusively to baritone. Other than two obscure record dates as a leader, Harry Carney can only be heard on Duke Ellington-associated recordings but he has many short solos and his presence was always felt in the ensembles. —*Scott Yanow*

Moods for Girl and Boy / Dec. 14, 1954 / Verve ♦♦♦♦

James Carney

Piano / Post-Bop
An excellent Los Angeles-based pianist with an advanced style that builds upon the innovations of the past, James Carney was originally an orchestral brass player and a pop keyboardist from New York. He began playing jazz in 1986, studied at the California Institute of the Arts (where he graduated in 1990), and since then has recorded a couple of stimulating sessions for the Jacaranda label. —*Scott Yanow*

● **Fables from the Aqueduct** / Aug. 7, 1993-Aug. 8, 1993 / Jacaranda ♦♦♦♦♦
During an era when many up-and-coming players emulate their predecessors a bit too closely, pianist James Carney performs music that, although linked to the tradition, pushes ahead into uncharted territory. A talented composer and an original voice on piano, Carney leads a group of young players (with the alternating horns including trumpeter Ralph Alessi, tenors Ravi Coltrane and Chuck Manning, altoist Scott Mayo and Peter Epstein on soprano, tenor or alto) through ten of his challenging originals. With alert playing from bassist Darek Oles and drummer Dan Morris, Carney's thoroughly unpredictable and tricky arrangements

(which leave plenty of room for spontaneity both from soloists and the entire group) are consistently intriguing. Highly recommended. —*Scott Yanow*

Offset Rhapsody / May 27, 1997 / Jacaranda ♦♦♦♦

Ian Carr

b. Apr. 21, 1933, Dumfries, Scotland
Trumpet, Fluegelhorn / Fusion, Post-Bop
Scottish trumpeter and fluegelhorn player Ian Carr has achieved fame as a player, composer and author. A self-taught trumpeter, Carr has made effective contributions to many bands in the '60s, '70s and '80s. He's played with taste and spark in jazz and jazz-rock bands. He's also composed several pieces and written critically acclaimed books. Carr studied English literature in college before serving in the army during the late '50s. He played in his brother Mike Carr's band the Emcee Five in the early '60s. Carr co-led a group with Don Rendell from 1962 to 1969; he also played with Joe Harriott, Don Byas and John McLaughlin during this period. He founded Nucleus in 1969, a band that became among the most popular and influential jazz-rock groups of all time. They played at the Montreux and Newport Jazz Festivals during the '70s, did several international tours and recorded 13 albums. They also appeared on many radio and television broadcasts. Carr also recorded with Neil Ardley's New Jazz Orchestra, the Spontaneous Music Ensemble and Keith Tippets' Centipede, and worked with Michael Garrick. He helped form the United Jazz and Rock Ensemble, which performed into the '80s. Carr composed a piece for the 1974 celebration of William Shakespeare's birthday at the Globe Theater in London. His writings on music include *Miles Davis: A Critical Biography,* published in the mid-'70s. He became an associate professor of music at the Guildhall School of Music and Drama in London in 1982. Carr also became a member of The Royal Society of Musicians of Great Britain and won the Calabria Award in 1982. He's recorded for Columbia, Argo and Capitol, as well as English companies Vertigo and Gull, but currently has no sessions available on CD in America. —*Ron Wynn*

Belladonna / Jul. 1972 / Core ♦♦♦

● **Old Heartland** / Apr. 1988-May 1988 / MMC ♦♦♦♦

Terri Lyne Carrington

b. 1962, Medford, MA
Drums / Instrumental Pop, Hard Bop
An in-demand sideperson who contributes her funky drum style to many different settings, Terri Lyne Carrington still has plenty of potential in her mid-30s. Carrington was a bit of a prodigy, impressing many veteran jazz players while still a child, and was one of the first significant female drummers in jazz. She was seen by millions on a nightly basis as a member of the band on the Arsenio Hall show and worked well with Wayne Shorter's late-1980s band. But her debut recording as a leader (for Verve Forecast in 1989) was disappointingly lightweight and has thus far not been followed by an encore. Into the late 1990s, Carrington has continued working steadily and is heard best in funk settings, but thus far she has not yet lived up to her great potential in the jazz world. —*Scott Yanow*

Real Life Story / 1989 / Verve/Forecast ♦♦

Baikida Carroll

b. Jan. 15, 1947, St. Louis, MO
Trumpet, Fluegelhorn / Avant-Garde
One of the better accompanists and section musicians, Baikida Carroll has added textures, colors and bright solos to various free jazz ensembles and groups, among them the Black Artists Group (BAG) in St. Louis. He's been an active composer, having written film soundtracks and scores and displayed a striking, full sound and solo approach. Carroll attended Southern Illinois University and the Armed Forces School of Music before directing the BAG's free jazz band. He went to Europe with other group members in the mid-'70s, and recorded in Paris in 1974. Carroll has recorded with Oliver Lake, Michael Gregory Jackson, Muhal Richard Abrams, Jack DeJohnette and David Murray in the '70s and '80s, as well as cutting a solo album in the late '70s and heading a combo in the early '80s. A 1994 session on Soul Note features Carroll in fine form with a quintet. —*Ron Wynn*

● **Shadows and Reflections** / Jan. 12, 1982-Jan. 20, 1982 / Soul Note ♦♦♦♦
Trumpeter Baikida Carroll was once again in the company of alto saxophonist Julius Hemphill for a Jan. 1982 recording with pianist Anthony Davis, bassist Dave Holland and drummer Pheeroan Ak Laff for Soul Note called *Shadows & Reflections.* The material here sounded like it could have been a late Blue Note recording; in fact, there were times when the horns brought flashbacks of the Jackie McLean-Charles Tolliver front line of the '60s. And for all their avant-garde credentials, this group sounded very comfortable and at home with the squirrelly free bop displayed here. —*Bob Rusch, Cadence*

Door of the Cage / May 2, 1995 / Soul Note ✦✦✦

Ernie Carson

b. Dec. 4, 1937, Portland, OR
Cornet / Dixieland

With the passing of Wild Bill Davison in 1989, Ernie Carson has come the closest of anyone to filling the gap left by the colorful and highly expressive cornetist. Carson began playing trumpet while in grammar school and was working in theatre bands by the time he was a junior in high school. A member of the Castle Jazz Band during 1954-56 before spending two years (1956-58) in the Marines, Carson played with such groups in the Los Angeles area as those led by banjoist Dave Wierbach, Jig Adams and Ray Bauduc before joining Turk Murphy (1961-62). Since then, Ernie Carson has appeared in countless settings (including with singer Pat Yankee) and has often led his own groups, including (since 1972) the Capital City Jazz Band and (starting in 1992) his own Castle Jazz band. Carson, who doubles effectively on piano and is also an exuberant and humorous singer, lived in Atlanta during 1972-95 and has since been based out of Oregon. He has recorded as a leader for Pearl (1964), Jazzology, GHB, Fat Cat Jazz and Stomp Off, and is considered one of the top classic jazz cornetists of the 1990s. — *Scott Yanow*

Ernie Carson and His Capital City Jazz Band / 1968 / Jazzology ✦✦✦✦

One of the finest Dixieland-oriented cornetists of the past few decades, Ernie Carson is in excellent form leading his regular group of the period. On what was only his second album as a leader, Carson has many hot solos on a good-time set that mixes together a few standard jams with such rarely played tunes as "Storybook Ball," "Mammy O'Mine" and "Moving Picture Ball." The sidemen include the great stride pianist Don Ewell, trombonist Skip Diringer, clarinetist Herman Foretich and banjoist Bill Rutan, who takes a few vocals. This somewhat obscure set is easily recommended for Dixieland fans. — *Scott Yanow*

Ernie Carson and Rhythm / 1975 / Jazzology ✦✦✦✦✦

Most of cornetist Ernie Carson's recordings have been made with Dixieland bands, making this quintet outing, on which he is the only horn, a particular delight. The colorful brassman (whose tone and expressive emotions sometimes recall Wild Bill Davison) is joined by a four-piece piano-banjo-tuba-drums rhythm section on 11 diverse songs that perfectly fit his lyrical yet extroverted style. Highlights include "I Double Dare You," "If Dreams Come True," "Flat Foot" and his own "My Cross-Eyed Cutie." Carson and banjoist Bill Rutan take two harmless and spirited vocals apiece, but it is for the leader's cornet that this set is most memorable. — *Scott Yanow*

Old Bones / Oct. 25, 1993-Mar. 21, 1994 / Stomp Off ✦✦✦✦

Cornetist Ernie Carson is a fiery Dixieland player who also takes a few good-humored vocals on this Stomp Off CD. Kim Cusack (doubling on clarinet and alto), trombonist Tom Bartlett and pianist Pete Clute are also fine soloists, but clarinetist Bob Helm (who is consistently out of tune) was clearly past his prime at this point. The generally cheerful set revives quite a few long-forgotten ditties, including "Onion Bender's Lament," "Could You Be True to Eyes of Blue," "My Castle in Spain Is a Shack in the Lane" and "All Birds Look Like Chickens to Me." — *Scott Yanow*

● **Wher'm I Gonna Live?** / Mar. 20, 1994-Mar. 21, 1994 / Stomp Off ✦✦✦✦✦

Veteran cornetist Ernie Carson, one of the better Dixieland players of the 1980s and '90s, leads a spirited septet on this enjoyable set. Carson has a few humorous vocals (most memorably on "Say It with Liquor" and "Gonna Get a Girl"), is assisted in the front line by clarinetist Kim Cusack and trombonist Tom Bartlett and plays quite well throughout the set of obscurities. Other highlights include "Lila," "Whose Honey Are You," "If the Rest of the World Don't Want You" and "It's the Girl." Fun music. — *Scott Yanow*

Benny Carter (Bennett Lester Carter)

b. Aug. 8, 1907, New York, NY
Alto Saxophone, Trumpet, Arranger, Composer/ Swing

To say that Benny Carter has had a remarkable and productive career would be an extreme understatement. As an altoist, arranger, composer, bandleader and occasional trumpeter, Carter has been at the top of his field since at least 1928, and in 1996 Carter was as strong an altoist at the age of 88 as he was in 1936 (when he was merely 28)! His gradually evolving style has not changed much through the decades but neither has it become at all stale or predictable except in its excellence. Benny Carter has been a major figure in every decade since the 1920s and his consistency and longevity are unprecedented.

Essentially self-taught, Benny Carter started on the trumpet and, after a period on C-melody sax, switched to alto. In 1927 he made his recording debut with Charlie Johnson's Paradise Ten. The following year he had his first big band (working at New York's Arcadia Ballroom) and was contributing arrangements to Fletcher

Henderson and even Duke Ellington. Carter was with Henderson during 1930-31, briefly took over McKinney's Cotton Pickers and then went back to leading his own big band (1932-34). Already at this stage he was considered one of the two top altoists in jazz (along with Johnny Hodges), a skilled arranger and composer ("Blues in My Heart" was an early hit and would be followed by "When Lights Are Low") and his trumpet playing was excellent; Carter would also record on tenor, clarinet (an instrument he should have played more) and piano although his rare vocals show that even he was human!

In 1935 Benny Carter moved to Europe where in London he was a staff arranger for the BBC dance orchestra (1936-38); he also recorded in several European countries. Carter's "Waltzing the Blues" was one of the very first jazz waltzes. He returned to the US in 1938, led a classy but commercially unsuccessful big band (1939-41) and then headed a sextet. In 1943 he relocated permanently to Los Angeles, appearing in the film *Stormy Weather* (as a trumpeter with Fats Waller) and getting lucrative work writing for the movie studios. He would lead a big band off and on during the next three years (among his sidemen were J.J. Johnson, Miles Davis and Max Roach) before giving up on that effort. Carter has written for the studios for over 50 years but he continued recording as an altoist (and all-too-rare trumpeter) during the 1940s and '50s, making a few tours with Jazz at the Philharmonic and participating on some of Norman Granz's jam session albums. By the mid-'60s his writing chores led him to hardly playing alto at all, but he made a full "comeback" by the mid-'70s and has maintained a very busy playing and writing schedule even at his advanced age. Even after the rise of such stylists as Charlie Parker, Cannonball Adderley, Eric Dolphy, Ornette Coleman and David Sanborn (in addition to their many followers), Benny Carter still ranks near the top of active altoists! — *Scott Yanow*

Benny Carter (1928-1952) / Jan. 24, 1928-Oct. 2, 1952 / RCA ✦✦✦✦

This French RCA double LP features the great altoist Benny Carter in a variety of settings, including selections with Charlie Johnson's Paradise Ten in 1928 and with pickup bands led by Mezz Mezzrow, Lionel Hampton, Ethel Waters and Una Mae Carlisle, in addition to his own orchestra on four complete sessions from 1940-41 and seven odd commercial sides cut in 1952. Altogether this package contains Carter's complete output for Victor. The later titles nonwithstanding, there are many swing classics scattered throughout this very enjoyable but out-of-print set. — *Scott Yanow*

1929-1933 / Sep. 18, 1929-May 19, 1933 / Classics ✦✦✦✦✦

The European Classics series has been reissuing on CD the complete output of many top jazz artists of the '20s and '30s. Benny Carter's music at last receives the treatment it deserves in this program. His first volume features the great altoist with a pickup group (the Chocolate Dandies) from 1929-30 that showcases sidemen from Fletcher Henderson's Orchestra, with his own orchestra in 1932-33 (three of the five numbers have rare vocals from Carter) and on 11 sides with Spikes Hughes' all-star band, an orchestra that also features trumpeter Red Allen, trombonist Dicky Wells, Wayman Carver on flute and the tenors of Coleman Hawkins and Chu Berry. This is wonderful and, in many cases, formerly rare music. — *Scott Yanow*

Skyline Drive and More / Nov. 6, 1929-Sep. 15, 1982 / Phontastic ✦✦✦✦✦

The bulk of this CD reissues a brilliant 1982 session featuring altoist Benny Carter with the tenors of Plas Johnson and Jerome Richardson, plus a variety of top European mainstream players including altoist Arne Domnérus, clarinetist Putte Wickman, trumpeter Jan Allen and pianist Bengt Hallberg. Some of the music is reminiscent of Carter's famous European four-saxophone session of 1937, and these renditions of "Doozy" and "Easy Money" are quite definitive and exciting. In addition to the eight original selections on the LP, eight other numbers from the 1929-39 period have been added to the set to double its length. These include examples of Carter's work on both alto and trumpet with McKinney's Cotton Pickers, the Chocolate Dandies, Lionel Hampton, in Europe in the 1930s, and with Teddy Wilson/Billie Holiday ("Sugar"). All in all, this CD acts both as a reminder of how strong Carter's 1982 date was, when he was a mere 75, and as a retrospective of his musical legacy. — *Scott Yanow*

1933-1936 / May 19, 1933-Apr. 1936 / Classics ✦✦✦✦✦

The second volume of the complete early Benny Carter from the European Classics label features Carter on alto, trumpet, clarinet and as arranger (in addition to contributing a bit of piano and even a vocal) on three numbers with Spike Hughes' all-star orchestra, as part of the 1933 edition of the Chocolate Dandies (an interracial outfit put together by Mezz Mezzrow) and with his own big band in 1933-34 and in England two years later. Highlights include "Symphony in Riffs," "Blue Lou" and "Everybody Shuffle." — *Scott Yanow*

● **All of Me** / May 7, 1934-Mar. 1959 / Bluebird ✦✦✦✦

A strong sampling of Benny Carter's music is heard in this hodgepodge CD reissue. Twelve of the altoist's 16 Bluebird big-band recordings of 1940-41 (including a previously unissued version of "Ill Wind") precede nine titles gathered from a wide variety of sessions with one song apiece taken from dates led by Mezz Mezzrow, Willie Bryant, Ethel Waters, Artie Shaw and Lucky Thompson, and four performances reissued from Carter's soundtrack album of his score for the *M Squad* in 1959. Obviously not a set recommended to completists (the European Classics series is much preferred), the high quality of the music ("All of Me" has a classic Carter arrangement) makes this a worthwhile purchase for more casual collectors. —*Scott Yanow*

1936 / Jun. 1936-Oct. 19, 1936 / Classics ✦✦✦✦
The third volume in Classics complete chronological reissue of Benny Carter's recordings of the 1930s covers a four-month period during Carter's long period in Europe. Many of these recordings (cut in London, Copenhagen and Stockholm) were formerly quite rare. Carter (on alto, clarinet, tenor, trumpet and even piano and two vocals) is typically flawless, sophisticated and swinging, whether jamming with a quartet behind singer Elizabeth Welch, matching talents with trumpeter Tommy McQuater in a quintet, heading an English orchestra or guesting with an obscure Danish big band. All of the CDs in this very worthy series are highly recommended. —*Scott Yanow*

1937-1939 / Jan. 11, 1937-Jun. 29, 1939 / Classics ✦✦✦✦
The fourth CD in Classics' complete chronological reissue of Benny Carter's early recordings as a leader finds Carter (on alto, trumpet, clarinet, tenor and even one vocal) leading orchestras in London, Laren, the Hague, Paris and (for the final three selections) New York. High points include "Nagasaki," "I'm in the Mood for Swing," "Blues in My Heart," "I'm Coming Virginia" (from a three-song session that also features Django Reinhardt) and "Melancholy Lullaby." In addition, the great tenor Coleman Hawkins plays a prominent role on four of the performances. Carter is in top form throughout these often formerly rare but very vital swing recordings. His fans should quickly acquire all of these invaluable Classics releases. —*Scott Yanow*

Melancholy Benny / May 20, 1939-Jan. 30, 1940 / Tax ✦✦✦
The Benny Carter big band of 1939-41 was not a huge commercial success but musically this outfit could compete with practically anyone else. Carter (doubling on alto and trumpet) contributed the many colorful arrangements, and quite a few compositions as can be heard in this reissue LP that contains three complete studio sessions and a radio broadcast from 1939-40. Other soloists include trumpeter Joe Thomas, trombonist Vic Dickenson, pianist Eddie Heywood and, on one session, the great tenor Coleman Hawkins. Recommended to those Benny Carter collectors who do not have this excellent music yet on CD, the broadcast is particularly rare. —*Scott Yanow*

1939-1940 / Jun. 29, 1939-May 20, 1940 / Classics ✦✦✦✦
This CD, the fifth in Classics' complete chronological reissue of Benny Carter's early recordings as a leader, features his 1939-40 big band, an orchestra that never did catch on commercially. Most selections have trumpeter Joe Thomas, trombonist Vic Dickenson and pianist Eddie Heywood as the main soloists other than the leader (who plays alto and trumpet), although the last date on this disc has a reorganized band with trumpeter Bill Coleman and trombonist Sandy Williams among the principal players. Among the high points from this enjoyable but underrated big band are "Savoy Stampede," "Scandal in a Flat," "Shufflebug Shuffle," "Night Hop" and "When Lights Are Low." —*Scott Yanow*

1940-1941 / May 25, 1940-Oct. 16, 1941 / Classics ✦✦✦✦
Most of the selections on the sixth and final Classics' CD to reissue all of Benny Carter's pre-war recordings as a leader feature the altoist's commercially unsuccessful big band. With such major soloists as the leader, trumpeter Jonah Jones and Sidney DeParis, trombonists Benny Morton and Jimmy Archey and pianist Sonny White, it is surprising that this orchestra did not make it. The October 23, 1940 recording session (which has three vocals by Roy Felton, including one in which he is joined by the Mills Brothers) is quite rare, while the opening set from eight days earlier is a small group date with Bill Coleman and Benny Morton that features a pair of W.C. Handy blues sung by Big Joe Turner. Excellent swing music overall. —*Scott Yanow*

The Uncollected Benny Carter / 1944 / Hindsight ✦✦✦
Benny Carter's wartime big band only made a handful of studio recordings but seems to have broadcast fairly regularly, particularly from California. This Hindsight LP gives a fine all-around look at Carter's 1944 band although the complete personnel is not known. Clarinetist Barney Bigard guests on "Tea for Two," the young trombone master J.J. Johnson is heard throughout "J.J. Jump" and Carter himself has three features on trumpet in addition to many alto solos. Although not essential, this swinging music is quite enjoyable. —*Scott Yanow*

In Hollywood 1944-46 / 1944-Oct. 1946 / Jazz Society ✦✦✦
Altoist Benny Carter took his big band to the West Coast in 1944 and soon permanently relocated in L.A. This LP from the Swedish Jazz Society label has 14 selec-

tions taken from radio broadcasts dating from 1944-46. Although Carter had many talented sidemen during this era (including trumpeters Emmett Berry, Gerald Wilson and Walter Williams, trombonists J.J. Johnson and Al Grey, tenorman Bumps Myers, pianists Gerald Wiggins and Sonny White and drummer Max Roach), the leader is the most impressive soloist throughout, not only on alto but also occasionally on trumpet. These airchecks are not duplicated on other Benny Carter albums currently available and have among its highlights "Jump Call," "Sunday," "Rose Room," "Sleep" and "La Rosita." —*Scott Yanow*

Jazz Off the Air, Vol. 3 / 1944-1948 / Spotlite ✦✦✦
Benny Carter's mid-'40s big band is relatively forgotten today because it only made a few studio recordings but, on evidence of the broadcasts heard on this LP, it was a rather significant transition orchestra between swing and bop. Consider that these airchecks, in addition to solos by Carter on alto and trumpet, feature concise statements from such young modernists as trombonists J.J. Johnson and Al Grey, trumpeter Miles Davis and the tenors of Dexter Gordon and Lucky Thompson. In addition, there are guest appearances by pianist Mary Lou Williams, clarinetist Barney Bigard and cornetist Rex Stewart. The recording quality is sometimes just so-so, but obviously the importance of this frequently exciting music overrides other factors. —*Scott Yanow*

Deluxe Recordings, Vol. 1 / Jan. 5, 1946-Aug. 1946 / Contact ✦✦✦
During 1946, Benny Carter led his final regular big band before giving up the struggle and deciding to get involved in studio work and performing in much smaller groups, leading big bands only for special projects. This LP, imported from Denmark, contains Carter's dozen orchestral recordings of 1946, 12 sides that were originally on the rare Deluxe label. Most of these performances feature all-star bands rather than Carter's regular group, allowing the great altoist/arranger to use such musicians as trumpeters Shorty Rogers, Joe Newman and Emmett Berry, trombonists Trummy Young and Dickie Wells, clarinetist Tony Scott, and Dexter Gordon, tenormen Flip Phillips and Don Byas; in addition, Maxine Sullivan has a pair of fine vocals. The music, an interesting mixture of swing and bop, is well worth hearing, if quite obscure. —*Scott Yanow*

The Complete Benny Carter on Keynote / Apr. 22, 1946 / Verve ✦✦✦✦
Here's a fine representative sampling of prime Carter '40s cuts. With Arnold Ross Quintet, his own L.A. group at the time. —*Ron Wynn*

Swing 1946 / Aug. 23, 1946-Sep. 6, 1946 / Prestige ✦✦✦
The swing era was quickly being supplanted by bop in 1946, but many of the top swing stylists were still recording and playing at their creative peak. Frenchman Charles Delaunay visited the US and recorded these three unrelated sessions for his Swing label. Altoist Benny Carter leads a sextet with trumpeter Buck Clayton and tenor saxophonist Ben Webster; Gene Sedric (on tenor and clarinet) jams with some Fats Waller alumni and trumpeter Lincoln Mills; and Jonah Jones is heard with a fine group of Cab Calloway sidemen, including tenorman Ike Quebec. There are many excellent examples of heated swing on this enjoyable and rather historic LP, showing that—contrary to what is written in the more simplistic jazz history books—the best swing players had not run out of gas by the mid-'40s. —*Scott Yanow*

Late Forties / Aug. 1946-May 1949 / Official ✦✦
Imported from Denmark, this LP contains a variety of mostly obscure and overlooked Benny Carter recordings from the 1946-49 era. Carter is heard on two performances with a big band, backing a few decent—but not particularly special—singers and jamming with two hot small groups that also feature trumpeter Buck Clayton, Al Grey or Vic Dickenson on trombone and the great tenor Ben Webster. It is for the latter sessions that this LP is of greatest interest, capturing Carter and Webster during a time when they were being overshadowed by the bebop generation. —*Scott Yanow*

Cosmopolite: The Oscar Peterson Verve Sessions / Sep. 18, 1952-Nov. 12, 1954 / Verve ✦✦✦✦
These timeless Benny Carter performances match the great altoist with pianist Oscar Peterson, bassist Ray Brown, either Barney Kessel or Herb Ellis on guitar, Buddy Rich, J.C. Heard or Bobby White on drums, and, on four numbers, trombonist Bill Harris. The 17 standards (four of which are also heard in alternate versions) are treated with respect, taste and swing. Carter always sounds flawless and is in excellent form throughout this enjoyable set. —*Scott Yanow*

New Jazz Sounds: Urbane Sessions / Sep. 18, 1952-Mar. 23, 1955 / Polygram ✦✦✦✦
The remarkable Benny Carter, who had first recorded 25 years earlier, was not even halfway through with his career when he started making sessions for Verve. This double CD wraps up the complete reissuance of all of his Verve albums. The distinctive and lyrical altoist is backed by strings throughout the first disc (16 songs plus ten alternate takes), but there is nothing sleepy about the music. The string arrangements (half by Joe Glover and half by Carter himself) are tasteful

and provide a cushion for Carter's melodic but unpredictable horn; this is far from mere mood music. Most of the second disc matches the ageless altoist with trumpeter Roy Eldridge and a rhythm section. Some heat is generated, and most unusual are four unique numbers on which Eldridge duets with drummer Alvin Stoller (one has Roy overdubbing some basic piano), although Roy mostly follows the chord changes. In addition, there is a leftover alternate take from a Carter session with the Oscar Peterson quartet and two exciting selections in a sextet with trumpeter Dizzy Gillespie and trombonist Bill Harris. Easily recommended, this is a perfectly conceived series. —*Scott Yanow*

3, 4, 5: The Verve Small Group Sessions / Mar. 1955 / Verve ◆◆◆◆
Has there ever been a more consistent performer in jazz history over a longer period of time than Benny Carter? The classic altoist, who had fully formed his sound by the early '30s (he first recorded in 1927), has not altered his style very much in the past 65 (and counting) years. The music on this Verve reissue CD features Carter in three settings: in a trio with pianist Teddy Wilson and drummer Jo Jones (those performances were only previously released in Japan); heading a quartet with pianist Don Abney, bassist George Duvivier and drummer Louis Bellson; and showcased with three previously unissued tracks with the Oscar Peterson trio plus drummer Bobby White. Carter knew most of these standards extremely well and he glides effortlessly over the chord changes, infusing the music with swing and subtle creativity. —*Scott Yanow*

Jazz Giant / Jul. 22, 1957-Apr. 21, 1958 / Original Jazz Classics ◆◆◆◆
Benny Carter had already been a major jazz musician for nearly 30 years when he recorded this particularly strong septet session for Contemporary. With notable contributions from tenor saxophonist Ben Webster, trombonist Frank Rosolino and guitarist Barney Kessel, Carter (who plays a bit of trumpet on "How Can You Lose") is in superb form on a set of five standards and two of his originals. This timeless music is beyond the simple categories of "swing" or "bop" and should just be called "classic." —*Scott Yanow*

Aspects / 1958 / United Artists ◆◆◆◆
This CD reissues an enjoyable obscurity. Although originally associated with big bands, the set has what was Benny Carter's only big-band recording as a playing leader during 1947-86. While the song titles are a bit gimmicky, saluting the 12 months of the year (including "June in January," "I'll Remember April," "June Is Busting Out All Over," etc.), the music (which includes four alternate takes) is solid, mainstream big-band swing. The less familiar titles include four Carter originals written for the date, plus Hal Schaefer's "February Fiesta." The leader/altoist solos on every selection, and among the other top West Coast studio players featured are trumpeters Shorty Sherock, Pete Candoli and Joe Gordon, trombonists Frank Rosolino and Herbie Harper, vibraphonist Larry Bunker, pianists Arnold Ross and Gerry Wiggins, and guitarist Barney Kessel. Two overlapping big bands were utilized, and the music alternates between being forceful and lyrical. —*Scott Yanow*

Swingin' the Twenties / Nov. 2, 1958 / Original Jazz Classics ◆◆◆
Combining altoist Benny Carter with pianist Earl Hines in a quartet is an idea with plenty of potential, but the results of this 1958 session are relaxed rather than explosive. Carter and Hines explore a dozen tunes (standards as well as forgotten songs such as "All Alone" and "Mary Lou") with respect and light swing, but one wishes that there were a bit more competitiveness to replace some of the mutual respect. —*Scott Yanow*

☆ **Further Definitions** / Nov. 13, 1961-Nov. 15, 1961 / GRP/Impulse! ◆◆◆◆◆
This essential single-CD combines altoist/arranger Benny Carter's classic *Further Definitions* with the related *Additions to Further Definitions*. The former set was a revisit, instrumentation-wise, to the famous 1937 session that Carter and tenor saxophonist Coleman Hawkins made in France with two top European saxophonists (Andre Ekyan and Alix Combelle) and guitarist Django Reinhardt. The all-star group (which also includes Hawkins, altoist Phil Woods, Charlie Rouse on second tenor, pianist Dick Kats, guitarist John Collins, bassist Jimmy Garrison and drummer Jo Jones) performs a particularly inspired repertoire. Carter's charts, which allow Hawkins to stretch out on "Body and Soul," give everyone a chance to shine. "Honeysuckle Rose" and "Crazy Rhythm" hold their own with the 1937 versions, and "Blue Star" and "Doozy" prove to be two of Benny's finest originals. The second date does not quite reach the same heights, but is enjoyable in its own right. This time, Carter contributed six of the eight selections (including a remake of "Doozy"), and the band was gathered from jazzmen then working in the L.A. studios, including Carter and Bud Shank on altos, and tenors Teddy Edwards and either Buddy Collette or Bill Perkins. Although Benny Carter was not actively playing much at the time (this was his only small-group recording during 1963-75), he is heard in typically prime form. Very highly recommended. —*Scott Yanow*

B.B.B. & Co. / 1962 / Original Jazz Classics ◆◆◆
One of Benny Carter's last jazz recordings before he became totally immersed in writing for the studios, this set matches his alto and trumpet with tenor great Ben Webster, clarinetist Barney Bigard and trumpeter Shorty Sherock on a pair of lengthy blues and Carter's "Lula" and "When Lights Are Low." All of the swing all-stars are in fine form, making one wish that they were not being so neglected by critics and fans alike during this era; Webster soon left the US permanently for Europe. Although not essential, this set is fun. —*Scott Yanow*

Additions to Further Definitions / Mar. 2, 1966 / Impulse! ◆◆◆
This LP is a reprise of Benny Carter's brilliant *Further Definitions* session of 1961 and, like most sequels, it is not quite on the same level as the original. Utilizing five saxes (Bud Shank and his own altos, tenors Buddy Collette and Teddy Edwards and baritonist Bill Hood), Carter's arrangements for six of his originals, "Fantastic, That's You" and "If Dreams Come True" are colorful, although the solos are less memorable than on the earlier session; who could replace Coleman Hawkins? But, evaluated by itself, this date (Carter's only small-group album from 1963-75) has enough enjoyable moments to be recommended. —*Scott Yanow*

The King / Feb. 11, 1976 / Original Jazz Classics ◆◆◆◆
The great Benny Carter was so much in demand as an arranger/composer in the studios that for 15 years, starting in the early '60s, he rarely recorded or performed in jazz settings, instead choosing to concentrate on writing movie scores. The drought ended when Carter, then in his late 60s, started recording for Pablo. As *The King* (his first small-group session since 1966) proves, the masterful altoist had not lost a thing through the years. In a sextet with vibraphonist Milt Jackson, guitarist Joe Pass and pianist Tommy Flanagan, Benny Carter is in masterful form, stretching out on eight of his own compositions and showing that his name always has to be ranked near the top of jazz improvisers, whether one is considering the 1930s or the 1990s. —*Scott Yanow*

Carter, Gillespie, Inc. / Apr. 27, 1976 / Original Jazz Classics ◆◆◆
Although they were from different musical generations (Benny Carter was born ten years before Dizzy Gillespie), it is little wonder that the swing altoist and the bop trumpeter could match up so well on this sextet session; they were quite compatible. Surprisingly, the material they chose to perform could have been better (there is only one Carter composition among the six songs), but on "Broadway" and "A Night in Tunisia," the two veteran hornmen (along with pianist Tommy Flanagan and guitarist Joe Pass) sound at their best. —*Scott Yanow*

Wonderland / Nov. 1976 / Original Jazz Classics ◆◆◆◆
For this 1976 LP, the veteran altoist Benny Carter (who was then nearing age 70) was teamed with tenor saxophonist Eddie "Lockjaw" Davis, trumpeter Harry "Sweets" Edison and a strong rhythm section headed by Ray Bryant on a vintage Pablo session. Although it often has the feeling of a jam session, the fact that, in addition to two standards, there are five obscure Carter compositions makes one realize that more planning than usual went into this date, and it shows. —*Scott Yanow*

Live and Well in Japan / Apr. 29, 1977 / Original Jazz Classics ◆◆◆◆
Benny Carter headed a talent-filled tentet for this frequently exciting concert. With trumpeters Cat Anderson and Joe Newman, trombonist Britt Woodman, Cecil Payne on baritone and Budd Johnson doubling on tenor and soprano, it is not at all surprising that the results would be memorable, but this date actually exceeds one's expectations. In addition to fine jam versions of "Squatty Roo," "Them There Eyes" and "It Don't Mean a Thing," there is a remarkable Louis Armstrong medley on which Carter (on trumpet) plays "When It's Sleepy Time Down South," Cat Anderson follows with a high note solo on "Confessin'" and then Joe Newman (who rarely recorded vocals) does a near-perfect imitation of Louis Armstrong singing on "When You're Smiling." —*Scott Yanow*

Benny Carter 4: Montreux 1977 / Jul. 13, 1977 / Pablo ◆◆◆◆
For this concert at the 1977 Montreux Jazz Festival, Benny Carter was in his musical prime, a condition he has thus far stayed at for over 65 years. Joined by the Ray Bryant Trio, the altoist romps through seven standards and plays some tasteful trumpet on "Body and Soul," proving once again that he really is ageless; Carter was nearly 70 years old at the time. —*Scott Yanow*

Summer Serenade / Aug. 17, 1980 / Storyville ◆◆◆
Benny Carter has recorded so many excellent swing sessions throughout his lengthy career that it is very difficult to pick out the best ones; there's too much competition. This quartet date for the Danish Storyville label matches his alto with pianist Kenny Drew, bassist Jesper Lundgaard and drummer Ed Thigpen for four of Carter's originals and three standards. As a bonus, Richard Boone sings the good-humored "All That Jazz." —*Scott Yanow*

Skyline Drive / Sep. 15, 1982 / Phontastic ◆◆◆

All Stars, Featuring Nat Adderley & Red Norvo / Jul. 8, 1985-Jul. 9, 1985 / Gazell ✦✦✦

After recording very few jazz sessions during 1963-75, Benny Carter has returned to the scene with a vengeance, but no one is complaining. Virtually all of Carter's recordings are worth acquiring and this Gazell LP, although not essential, is no exception. Vibraphonist Red Norvo (on one of his last recordings before his retirement) is featured on "Here's That Rainy Day," cornetist Nat Adderley gets to perform yet another version of his "Work Song" (taking a rare vocal) and Carter joins the sextet for "Memories of You" and three of his own compositions. This nice session offers few surprises but satisfying music. —*Steve Yanow*

A Gentleman and His Music / Aug. 1985 / Concord Jazz ✦✦✦

For this 1985 session, altoist Benny Carter (then a week short of turning 78 years old) is teamed with the lyrical trumpeter Joe Wilder and the Concord All-Stars, a contingent that also features tenor saxophonist Scott Hamilton, guitarist Ed Bickert and pianist Gene Harris. The results are predictably excellent with the septet swinging with spirit and creativity on four standards, a blues and Carter's original "A Kiss from You." —*Scott Yanow*

My Kind of Trouble / Aug. 20, 1986 / Pablo ✦✦✦

With the exception of one song, Benny Carter had never previously recorded with an organist during his first 60 years on record. This Pablo set teams the classic Carter alto with organist Art Hillery and guitarist Joe Pass in a fine quintet. Actually, other than the instrumentation, there is little unusual about this date. On four Carter compositions and two standards, Benny Carter (who was nearing age 81) is in typical flawless form, swinging effortlessly. —*Scott Yanow*

Meets Oscar Peterson / Nov. 14, 1986 / Original Jazz Classics ✦✦✦✦

Altoist Benny Carter had recorded with pianist Oscar Peterson back in the early '50s for Norman Granz's Verve label. More than 30 years later he teamed up with Peterson again, this time for Granz's Pablo company. There was no sign of decline or disillusionment in either of the co-leaders' playing; in fact, if anything, they had improved with age. Joined by guitarist Joe Pass, bassist Dave Young and drummer Martin Drew, Carter and Peterson are both in a joyous mood and in typically swinging form on six standards and a blues. —*Scott Yanow*

Central City Sketches / 1987 / Music Masters ✦✦✦✦

One of the many Benny Carter recordings cut after he returned to jazz on a full-time basis in the mid-'70s, this double-LP set is the jewel among the seemingly countless number of gems. Eight of Carter's compositions are performed by the all-star American Jazz Orchestra ("Doozy" gets two versions) along with his old theme song "Sleep" and his recently written six-part "Central City Sketches." Virtually every player in this big band was a potential star soloist; among the more notable musicians are trombonist Jimmy Knepper, tenors Lew Tabackin and Loren Schoenberg and either John Lewis or Dick Katz on piano. But, as is often the case, Benny Carter frequently steals solo honors and his brief trumpet spot on "Central City Blues" is memorable. —*Scott Yanow*

The Best of Benny Carter [Music Masters] / Feb. 27, 1987-May 19, 1994 / Music Masters ✦✦✦

In the Mood for Swing / Nov. 9, 1987-Nov. 12, 1987 / Music Masters ✦✦✦

All 11 of the songs are somewhat obscure and therefore fresh Carter compositions ("Summer Serenade" is perhaps the best known) and Dizzy Gillespie sits in with the group for three songs. But even with Gillespie, guitarist Howard Alden and pianist Roland Hanna, the solo star throughout is the ageless Benny Carter, who at the age of 80 still seemed to be improving. —*Scott Yanow*

Cookin' at Carlos, Vol. 1 / Oct. 5, 1988-Oct. 9, 1988 / Music Masters ✦✦✦✦

During the late '80s up to the present, Benny Carter (now an octogenarian) has recorded a string of consistently excellent and frequently superb CDs for Music Masters. This particular effort is a rare live recording for Carter with his regular group, which in 1988 consisted of pianist Richard Wyands, bassist Lisle Atkinson and drummer Al Harewood. The repertoire is typical of his club performances: five standards, a blues and just one of Carter's compositions, "Key Largo." A special treat is Carter's trumpet solo on "Time for the Blues"; otherwise his wonderful alto dominates this fine set. —*Scott Yanow*

Over the Rainbow / Oct. 18, 1988-Oct. 19, 1988 / Music Masters ✦✦✦✦

Benny Carter has recorded so frequently since the mid-'70s that it must be a constant challenge to come up with new settings for his alto. This particular Music Masters CD finds Carter taking his place in a saxophone section with fellow altoist Herb Geller, the tenors of Jimmy Heath and Frank Wess and baritonist Joe Temperley. The program is split evenly between standards and Carter compositions with the altoist also writing all of the colorful arrangements. This swinging and tasteful Benny Carter recording is a credit to his superb series of Music Masters dates. —*Scott Yanow*

My Man Benny, My Man Phil / Nov. 21, 1989-Nov. 22, 1989 / Music Masters ✦✦✦✦

It is extremely difficult to believe that Benny Carter was 82 years old at the time of this recording, for his strong sound (nothing feeble about his playing) and fertile ideas on alto make him sound as if he were a contemporary of Phil Woods, who was born 24 years later. Together Carter and Woods form a mutual-admiration society, which can be heard on "My Man Phil." The repertoire on this CD is particularly inspired (highlighted by "Sultry Serenade," "I'm Just Wild About Harry" and two versions of the atmospheric "Just a Mood"). Carter takes two trumpet solos while, on "We Were in Love," Woods contributes some tasteful clarinet. A special and relaxed but occasionally hard-swinging date, this Music Masters CD is quite enjoyable. —*Scott Yanow*

All That Jazz: Live at Princeton / Nov. 11, 1990 / Music Masters ✦✦✦

For this 1990 concert, altoist Benny Carter teams up with the great fluegelhornist Clark Terry on a set of standards. Vocalist Billy Hill joins the quintet for four numbers (including a humorous collaboration with Clark Terry on Carter's "All That Jazz"), but it is the octogenarian altoist who often takes honors. —*Scott Yanow*

Harlem Renaissance / Feb. 7, 1992-Feb. 9, 1992 / Music Masters ✦✦✦✦

Benny Carter is a true marvel. At the time of this recording (a double CD), the classic altoist was already age 84, yet showed no signs of slowing down either his playing or his writing schedule. For his specially assembled big band and the Rutgers University Orchestra (which includes a full string section), Carter wrote entirely new arrangements that demonstrate that his talents have not diminished with age. While the first disc mostly sticks to older material, the second disc comprises two new suites "Tales of the Rising Sun" and "Harlem Renaissance." In addition, Carter's alto is often the solo star although he does not hog the spotlight; it just naturally drifts back to him. —*Scott Yanow*

Legends / Jun. 16, 1992-Jun. 17, 1992 / Music Masters ✦✦✦✦

For once, the term "legend" is not being misused. The great altoist Benny Carter is in typically remarkable form at age 85 with a quartet, on five duets with pianist Hank Jones, and on three selections with the truly remarkable trumpeter Doc Cheatham (87 years old at the time). Whether on the spirited jams of "Honeysuckle Rose" and "There Is No Greater Love" or original ballads, there is not a weak track on this classic disc. This set would be recommended even if Carter were 55 rather than 85; the music is timeless and often glorious. —*Scott Yanow*

Elegy in Blue / 1994 / Music Masters ✦✦

Benny Carter, 87 at the time of this recording, could pass musically for 57. His alto playing is as flawless as ever but 79-year-old trumpeter Harry "Sweets" Edison very much sounds his age and falters constantly throughout the date. Pianist Cedar Walton (who sounds, probably the only time in his career, like Oscar Peterson), guitarist Mundell Lowe, bassist Ray Brown and drummer Jeff Hamilton make up a strong rhythm section, but Edison and the so-so material cause this session to fall far short of its potential. —*Scott Yanow*

New York Nights / Jun. 22, 1995+Jun. 24, 1995 / Music Masters ✦✦✦✦

To say that Benny Carter is a marvel is to make an obvious understatement. Eighty-seven at the time of this live quartet set (which also includes pianist Chris Neville, bassist Steve LaSpina and drummer Sherman Ferguson), Carter could easily pass for 47, playing without any hesitant or faltering moments in a timeless swing style that he largely invented. There are no surprises to the repertoire other than the fact that Carter's perennial set opener "On Green Dolphin Street" (which is to him what "Indiana" was to Louis Armstrong in the 1950s) is programmed sixth. Two of the songs ("Easy Money" and "When Lights Are Low") are Carter's, while the other pieces have been performed by him hundreds of times through the years. No matter; Benny Carter comes up with fresh variations during his enthusiastic solos, including a classic statement on "Secret Love." His logical and thoughtful improvisations manage to be unpredictable, except in their consistent excellence. An easily recommended set from an apparently ageless master. —*Scott Yanow*

Songbook, Vol. 2 / Jun. 26, 1995-Jul. 28, 1995 / Music Masters ✦✦✦

Songbook / Jun. 26, 1995-Aug. 26, 1995 / Music Masters ✦✦✦✦✦

Due to his being such a talented altoist, arranger and occasional trumpeter for seven decades, it is often forgotten that Benny Carter wrote some worthy songs along the way. "When Lights Are Low" and "Blues in My Heart" are standards while "Only Trust Your Heart," "Key Largo" and the novelty hit "Cow-Cow Boogie" are close. For this unusual set, 14 different singers had opportunities to interpret one or two Carter compositions while joined by a fine quintet consisting of cornetist Warren Vache, pianist Chris Neville, bassist Steve LaSpina, drummer Sherman Ferguson and Carter himself (88 at the time!) on alto. The ambitious program includes five Carter songs that were receiving their world premiere; in addition, Carter also wrote or co-wrote the lyrics to nine of the pieces. The singers all show respect for the melody and words, with Jon Hendricks being playful on "Cow-Cow

Boogie," Joe Williams quite touching on "I Was Wrong" and a weakened Peggy Lee making a memorable cameo on "I See You." The vocalists consistently seem quite inspired by the unique project. There are many short Carter and Warren Vache solos and, even with the emphasis on ballads, there is more variety than one might expect. The well-conceived tribute (which also has fine appearances by Dianne Reeves, Carmen Bradford, Kenny Rankin, Marlena Shaw, Diana Krall, Billy Stritch, Shirley Horn, Bobby Short, Ruth Brown, Weslia Whitfield and Nancy Marano) is easily recommended.—*Scott Yanow*

Betty Carter (Lorraine Carter)

b. May 16, 1930, Flint, MI
Vocals / Avant-Garde, Bop

A long period of struggling and near-complete obscurity preceded Betty Carter's surprising rise to fame; through it all she never compromised her musical vision. Although she has never cared much for avant-garde jazz, her own interpretations of standards and originals are still so radical (with tonal distortions, a very wide range of tempos and many unexpected changes of direction) that there is simply no other term to describe her unique music. Carter studied piano and worked as a singer in Detroit in 1946. During 1948-51 she toured with Lionel Hampton (where she was nicknamed Betty "Bebop" Carter). After that association ended she settled in New York, gradually developed her style and recorded with Gigi Gryce in 1956. Although she recorded a 1961 duet album with Ray Charles that received some attention, it would be quite awhile before she gained much recognition. After doing some records for Roulette, Carter retired for a few years to raise a family. In 1969 she formed a trio and in 1971 organized her own record label Bet-Car. Gradually Betty Carter's innovative singing began to be recognized, and after she signed with Verve in the early '80s she finally became a household name (and a consistent pollwinner) in the jazz world. Carter's singing is not to everyone's taste but her willingness to take chances is quite admirable and her ability as a talent scout (her pianists have included John Hicks, Mulgrew Miller, Bennie Green, Stephen Scott and Cyrus Chestnut) is beyond criticism. —*Scott Yanow*

Meet Betty Carter and Ray Bryant / May 13, 1955-Apr. 25, 1956 / Columbia/Legacy ++++

This CD features singer Betty Carter and pianist Ray Bryant at the beginning of their careers, reissuing their very first recordings as leaders. The 25-year-old Carter's voice was already quite recognizable, although the improvising style on her 11 titles here is much more conservative than it would be from the 1970s on. However, Carter's scatting on "Frenesi" (which sounds like a wigged-out Carmen McRae) shows individuality, and her renditions of "Social Call," "I Could Write a Book" and "Moonlight in Vermont" are memorable. In addition, this CD has eight selections by Ray Bryant's trio with bassist Wendell Marshall and drummer Philly Joe Jones, a unit that also served as Carter's backup group on seven of her performances. A well-rounded and unclassifiable player who even at the beginning of his career mixed the drive and joy of swing with more advanced harmonies, Bryant was already long on his way towards developing his own sound in the mid-'50s. This version of "Get Happy" was previously unreleased, while "Bryant's Folly" (a rollicking blues) and "Threesome" are high points. A historic and enjoyable set. —*Scott Yanow*

● **I Can't Help It** / Feb. 1958 / GRP +++++

This single-CD reissues the second batch of Betty Carter recordings, her Peacock and ABC-Paramount dates that followed her Epic/Columbia titles by two years. Formerly available as a two-LP set (*What a Little Moonlight Can Do*), the 24 selections find the already-distinctive vocalist carving out her own sound from the bebop tradition; her more innovative work was in the future. Quite a few of the renditions are memorable, including "I Can't Help It" (which is somewhat autobiographical), "You're Driving Me Crazy," "What a Little Moonlight Can Do," "Jazz (Ain't Nothin' but Soul)" and "Don't Weep for the Lady." While the second half of the CD has Carter accompanied by an orchestra arranged by Richard Wess, the first 12 numbers feature such top players as trumpeters Ray Copeland and Kenny Dorham, either Jerome Richardson or Benny Golson on tenor and pianist Wynton Kelly. Highly recommended. —*Scott Yanow*

The Modern Sound of Betty Carter / Aug. 18, 1960-Aug. 30, 1960 / ABC +++++
Some spectacular cuts. Find it in used record shops.—*Ron Wynn*

Round Midnight / Aug. 10, 1962-Jan. 15, 1963 / Roulette ++++
Betty Carter recorded only two albums during the 1961-68 period. Her chance-taking style and unusual voice were mostly ignored and it would not be until the late '70s that she was finally "discovered." This Atlantic CD finds Carter backed by orchestras arranged by Claus Ogerman and Oliver Nelson. Her style was a lot freer than it had been in her earlier records but was still more accessible than it would be. Her repertoire, which includes the title cut, "Theme from Dr. Kildare," "Two Cigarettes in the Dark" and her own "Who What Why Where When," was already becoming eclectic. This is an interesting historic release.—*Scott Yanow*

Inside Betty Carter / Apr. 1964-May 26, 1965 / Roulette ++++
These recordings can be considered the final ones of Betty Carter's early period; by the time she next appeared on record (in 1969), the singer was much more adventurous in her improvisations. This CD reissues eight selections from Carter's rather brief 1964 Roulette LP (under 26 minutes) plus it adds seven previously unissued numbers from 1965. On the former date Carter (who is quite memorable on "This Is Always," "Some Other Time" and "Spring Can Really Hang You Up the Most") is accompanied by pianist Harold Mabern, bassist Bob Cranshaw and drummer Roy McCurdy, while the "new" session ("There Is No Greater Love" and "You're a Sweetheart" are the standouts) features guitarist Kenny Burrell plus an unknown rhythm section in the backup band. Highly recommended to Betty Carter fans and to those listeners who find her later work somewhat forbidding. —*Scott Yanow*

Finally / Dec. 6, 1969 / Roulette ++++
The title of this CD reissue probably refers to the fact that this was singer Betty Carter's first released recording in five years; a second CD (*Round Midnight*) also originated from the same concert. The mature Betty Carter is heard for the first time on this record, which finds her taking wild chances on a set mostly dominated by standards. With the alert accompaniment of pianist Norman Simmons, bassist Lisle Atkinson and drummer Al Harewood, Carter sings some ballads very slow while other tunes are taken at rapid tempos; the music is consistently unpredictable and often fascinating. —*Scott Yanow*

At the Village Vanguard / May 16, 1970 / Verve ++++
Betty Carter's remarkable early-'70s LPs were initially available only on her own poorly distributed label. This live date captured Carter when her voice was its most pliable, her delivery in full bloom and her range and power at their peak. She could scat with a fury and rhythmic intensity that were almost magical, then turn a slow tune like "The Sun Died" or "Body and Soul" into a showcase by emphasizing key lyrics, subtly changing each stanza, or increasing the pace at an unexpected moment. This deserves full attention, as it represents Betty Carter still evolving and perfecting her matchless technique. —*Ron Wynn*

The Betty Carter Album / 1972 / Verve +++
Originally put out by singer Betty Carter on her Bet-Car label, this set from her struggling years has since been reissued on CD by Verve. Joined by either Daniel Mixon or Onaje Alan Gumbs on piano, bassist Buster Wiliams and Louis Hayes or Chip Lyles on drums, Betty Carter really digs into the material (the majority of which are her originals), using unusual tempos (and sometimes quick changes) and coming up with rather spontaneous and sometimes abstract interpretations; "You're a Sweetheart" (which has remained in Carter's repertoire for years) is a highlight. —*Scott Yanow*

Now It's My Turn / Mar. 9, 1976-Jun. 22, 1976 / Roulette ++++
The title of this out-of-print Roulette album was a bit premature because it would not be until the late '80s before Betty Carter was finally "discovered." An adventurous jazz singer whose musical integrity is almost as impressive as her talents at improvising, Carter is heard in top form throughout her obscure album. Assisted by pianist John Hicks, bassist Walter Booker and an unidentified drummer, Carter performs memorable renditions of such unlikely material as "Wagon Wheels," "Most Gentlemen Don't Like Love" and medleys of "Music Maestro Please/Swing Brother Swing" and "Just Friends/Star Eyes." Worth searching for. —*Scott Yanow*

The Audience with Betty Carter / Dec. 6, 1979-Dec. 8, 1979 / Verve ++++
Definitive two-fer live set with John Hicks Trio. A must-buy. —*Michael G. Nastos*

Whatever Happened to Love / 1982 / Verve +++
Rangy, adventurous, appealing vocals. —*Ron Wynn*

Look What I Got / 1988 / Verve +++++
This well-rounded set gives listeners a good look at the adventurous music of Betty Carter. For this CD, she is joined by one of two rhythm sections (with either Bennie Green or Stephen Scott on piano) and, on four of the nine songs, tenor saxophonist Don Braden. Carter twists and turns some familiar songs (such as "The Man I Love," "Imagination" and "The Good Life") along with a variety of lesser-known material including two songs of her own. Consistently unpredictable (whether scatting or stretching out ballads), Betty Carter's recordings are always quite stimulating. —*Scott Yanow*

Droppin' Things / May 25, 1990-May 26, 1990 / Verve ++++
Betty Carter's second Verve album solidified her credentials as one of jazz's top singers. Her trio of the period (pianist Marc Cary, bassist Tarus Mateen and drummer Gregory Hutchinson) are joined by trumpeter Freddie Hubbard (shortly before his decline) and tenor saxophonist Craig Handy on four of the seven selections, while a medley of "Stardust" and "Memories of You" finds Carter accompanied by pianist Geri Allen. Other highlights include "I Love Music," "What's the Use of Wond'rin'" and "Droppin' Things." With the exception of the Geri Allen medley, this consistently stimulating music was recorded live at the Bottom Line in New York. —*Scott Yanow*

It's Not About the Melody / 1992 / Verve ✦✦✦✦
A song's melody is simply a reference point and a beginning for Carter; she takes words and inverts, probes and extends them, embellishes themes, changes moods and alters rhythms. She's a vocal improviser in a manner few have equaled, and if her voice lacks the clarity and timbre of the all-time greats, she's more than compensated with incredible timing, flexibility and power. Throughout this 11-track effort, Carter's vocals direct and steer the responses of pianist Cyrus Chestnut, bassist Ariel J. Roland and drummer Lewis Nash. It was yet another memorable outing for Betty Carter, an all-time great. —*Ron Wynn*

Feed the Fire / Oct. 30, 1993 / Verve ✦✦✦✦

I'm Yours, You're Mine / Jan. 14, 1996-Jan. 25, 1996 / Verve ✦✦✦✦

James Carter

b. Jan. 3, 1969, Detroit, MI
Tenor Saxophone, Bass Clarinet, Alto Saxophone, Baritone Saxophone, Soprano Saxophone / Avant-Garde, Swing, Post-Bop
James Carter caused a sensation in the mid-'90s with his DIW and Atlantic recordings. Similar in some ways to Rahsaan Roland Kirk (although he only plays one instrument at a time!), Carter has the ability to play in any jazz style from the slap-tongue staccato of early-'20s tenors and Dixieland to swing, bop, 1950s R&B, free form and funk while still sounding like himself. A high-powered player skilled on most reeds (with tenor being his main instrument), Carter often switches quickly and unexpectedly between styles and the effect can be exhilarating or numbing. Carter started played sax when he was 11, performed in the Blue Lake Monster Ensemble with Marcus Belgrave, and before he graduated high school in 1986 he gigged with Wynton Marsalis. In 1988 Carter played with Lester Bowie in New York and he soon appeared on two Bowie DIW recordings with the New York Organ Ensemble. He has since worked with the Charles Mingus Big Band, the Lincoln Center Jazz Orchestra, Julius Hemphill, recorded with the Tough Young Tenors and led his own highly versatile group. James Carter has unlimited potential and he seems destined to be one of the giants of jazz. —*Scott Yanow*

JC on the Set / Apr. 14, 1993-Apr. 15, 1993 / DIW/Columbia ✦✦✦✦✦
Twenty-five at the time of this CD, James Carter had already absorbed much of the tradition. His debut as a leader includes compositions by the classic tenors Don Byas and John Hardee, Duke Ellington's "Sophisticated Lady" and even a Sun Ra ballad. He also shows that he has the courage to play completely outside whenever it seems logical to him; in fact, on the title cut Carter moves from Gene Ammons and Illinois Jacquet to outbursts à la David Murray in the stratosphere. But most importantly, at this early stage James Carter already had his own sound. He switches between the tenor (his main ax) to alto and baritone, shows self-restraint on the ballads and fills his improvisations with continual surprises. Joined by the supportive pianist Craig Taborn, bassist Jaribu Shahid and drummer Tani Tabbal, James Carter puts on quite a tour de force throughout this very impressive set. —*Scott Yanow*

● **Jurassic Classics** / Apr. 16, 1994-Apr. 17, 1994 / DIW/Columbia ✦✦✦✦✦
The young but already great saxophonist James Carter explores seven jazz standards with pianist Craig Taborn (himself a young master capable of playing in several styles), bassist Jaribu Shahid and drummer Tani Tabbal. Among the most versatile and knowledgeable of today's saxophonists, Carter draws on many top stylists during these lengthy solos yet always sounds quite individual. His violent depiction of a train whistle on "Take the 'A' Train" perfectly launches that romp and he also really stretches out on "Epistrophy," plays the blues on John Coltrane's "Equinox" and shows quite a bit of fire on "Oleo." A very stimulating session. —*Scott Yanow*

Real Quiet Storm / Oct. 6, 1994-Nov. 20, 1994 / Atlantic ✦✦✦
Despite this CD's title and a slight emphasis on ballads, this is not an easy-listening record. James Carter, one of the great new discoveries of the 1990s (and whose versatility on a variety of reed instruments and seeming encyclopedic knowledge of jazz styles makes him a possible successor to Rahsaan Roland Kirk), is heard playing tenor, alto, soprano, baritone, bass clarinet and bass flute on the nine selections with the impressive pianist Craig Taborn, either Dave Holland or Jaribu Shahid on bass and Leon Parker or Tani Tabbal on drums. Although some of the ballad statements (such as his statements on baritone on "'Round Midnight" and "Eventide") are fairly straightforward, Carter also has some explosive moments. His rendition (on soprano) of Don Byas' "1944 Stomp" is memorable as is his interpretations of "Born to Be Blue" and two originals. The results are a bit restrained compared to his live performances, but this is an enjoyable and unpredictable outing, music that will not be played on the "Quiet Storm." —*Scott Yanow*

Conversin' with the Elders / Oct. 2, 1995-Feb. 5, 1996 / Atlantic ✦✦✦✦
The brilliant saxophonist James Carter and his quartet (which also includes pianist Craig Taborn, bassist Jaribu Shahid and drummer Tani Tabbal) welcome some of

Carter's musical heroes as guests throughout this CD. Carter matches wits with the eccentric trumpeter Lester Bowie on "Freereggaehibop" and the often-hilarious "Atitled Valse"; he also features the legendary (but rarely recorded) Detroit altoist Larry Smith on "Parker's Mood," showcases Count Basie veterans Harry "Sweets" Edison and Buddy Tate on two swing standards apiece (Tate's work on clarinet during "Blue Creek" is memorable), and interacts with baritonist Hamiet Bluiett on "Naima" and an Anthony Braxton march. Switching between tenor, alto, baritone and bass clarinet, Carter makes each of his guests feel at home while pushing them to stretch themselves. A consistently colorful and generally swing-oriented set. —*Scott Yanow*

Joe Carter

b. 1956
Guitar / Cool
An excellent cool-toned guitarist, Joe Carter started playing music when he was around ten. He considers Jim Hall, Bill Evans, Paul Desmond and Ed Bickert his main influences and has stuck to playing straightahead jazz throughout his career. Carter, who has recorded several recommended sets for his own Empathy label, has also taught guitar extensively. —*Scott Yanow*

Too Marvellous for Words / Mar. 27, 1981 / Empathy ✦✦✦✦
Guitarist Joe Carter's recording debut was for his own Empathy label, the first of several that he cut during the first half of the 1980s. A cool-toned player with a fine bop-based style, Carter performs seven duets with bassist Rufus Reid, five standards (with the highlights including "Valse Hot," "Too Marvelous for Words" and "You Stepped Out of a Dream") and two originals ("Like Jim" is a tribute to Jim Hall). The interplay between the two players is tasteful and often intuitive, resulting in quiet but, in its own way, passionate set of music. —*Scott Yanow*

Chestnut / Aug. 4, 1983+Aug. 11, 1983 / Empathy ✦✦✦
For his second recording, lyrical guitarist Joe Carter performs four duets with bassist Harvie Swartz and two numbers ("A Minor Blues in F" and "She's as Wild as Springtime") in a trio that also includes altoist Lee Konitz. The combination of subtle but exploratory musicians works quite well on this continually interesting post-bop date. —*Scott Yanow*

● **My Foolish Heart** / Oct. 25, 1984-Oct. 26, 1984 / Empathy ✦✦✦✦
The third Joe Carter LP for his Empathy label has the quiet guitarist performing three jazz standards, two of his originals and Chick Corea's "Day Waves" in a quartet with fluegelhornist Art Farmer, bassist Harvie Swartz and drummer Akira Tana. Hopefully, all of the early Empathy sets will be reissued on CD someday, for each one serves as a fine example of subtle improvisation, based in but not held captive by the bop tradition. —*Scott Yanow*

Um Abraco No Rio / Aug. 24, 1992-Aug. 25, 1992 / Empathy ✦✦✦
Recorded in 1992 but released in 1996 for the first time, this set featured the cool-toned guitarist Joe Carter in a pleasing bossa nova date. Carter teams up with three Brazilian musicians (Mauricio Einhorn on harmonica, bassist Luis Alves and drummer Joao Cortez) for a set that includes five Antonio Carlos Jobim songs, Luis Bonfa's "Samba de Orfeu" and two originals by Einhorn among the ten tunes. Of Carter's sidemen, Einhorn's harmonica playing immediately reminds one of Toots Thieleman's although his technique is not on the same level (whose is?), while Alves and Cortez play the gentle rhythms with taste and sensitivity. Most of the set can easily fall into the genre of easy listening because Carter's playing is quite soothing and peaceful. Little excitement occurs but the music is so well played that one rarely minds. —*Scott Yanow*

Samba Rio Trio / Nov. 6, 1993-Nov. 7, 1993 / Empathy ✦✦✦✦

Duets / Mar. 15, 1994 / Stash ✦✦✦

John Carter

b. Sep. 24, 1929, Fort Worth, TX, **d.** Mar. 31, 1991, Inglewood, CA
Clarinet / Avant-Garde
John Carter was a major clarinet innovator, turning the swing-associated instrument into a device for very advanced explorations. His upper-register screeches could be grating, but his solos had a logic all their own, and his five-part suite depicting the history of Blacks in America (released on Black Saint and Gramavision) displayed his compositional talents. Carter taught in the Fort Worth public school system during 1949-61 before switching to Los Angeles (1961-82). He played with Ornette Coleman and Charles Moffett as early as the late '40s and in L.A. of the 1960s he became one of the leaders of the local scene's avant-garde, originally doubling on clarinet and alto. In 1964 he formed the New Art Jazz Ensemble with cornetist Bobby Bradford, who would be his longtime musical partner. Carter (who by 1974 was playing clarinet exclusively) played with Bradford on a fairly regular basis during the remainder of his life in settings ranging from duets to a larger orchestra. By the 1980s with his suite, participation in Clar-

inet Summit and formation of the Wind College with James Newton, Red Callender and Charles Owens, John Carter finally received some long overdue recognition. —*Scott Yanow*

West Coast Hot / 1969 / Novus ✦✦✦✦✦
This very valuable release documents two important but underrated avant-garde units that were based in Los Angeles. Clarinetist John Carter (here also heard on tenor and alto) and trumpeter Bobby Bradford co-led bands for many years in virtual obscurity. With bassist Tom Williamson and drummer Buzz Freeman, they are both abstract and logical on four originals with Carter's passionate sounds contrasting, as usual, with Bradford's lyricism. The second half of this disc features L.A.'s great undiscovered legend, pianist Horace Tapscott. He is heard in superlative form on four tracks (including the 17-minute "The Giant Is Awakened") in a two bass quintet also co-starring the young altoist Arthur Blythe. Tapscott is still quite active in L.A. When will an enterprising label finally record his working band? —*Scott Yanow*

Seeking / Jan. 16, 1969 / Hat Art ✦✦✦✦
This CD reissue brings back clarinetist John Carter's first recording and the earliest example of his mutually beneficial teaming with trumpeter Bobby Bradford. Formerly out on Revelation, this Hat Art reissue is most surprising in that Carter mostly plays alto and tenor, with a rare appearance on flute and only one selection ("Sticks and Stones") on clarinet, the instrument that he would soon give up the others for. Less surprising is that the music is most influenced by Ornette Coleman although Carter's style was already showing individuality and the lyrical Bradford always had more technique than Don Cherry. Bassist Tom Williamson is excellent in support and drummer Bruz Freeman comes across as the most conventional player on the date. These freebop performances hold one's interest, vary moods and manage to be both free and melodic. —*Scott Yanow*

Flight for Four / Apr. 3, 1969 / Flying Dutchman ✦✦✦✦

Self-Determination Music / 1969-1970 / Flying Dutchman ✦✦✦

Secrets / Apr. 4, 1972 / Revelation ✦✦✦

Variations on Selected Themes for Jazz Quintet / Aug. 15, 1979 / Moers ✦✦✦

● **Dauwhe** / Feb. 25, 1982-Mar. 8, 1982 / Black Saint ✦✦✦✦✦
The first of clarinetist John Carter's five-part series in which he musically depicts the history of Black Americans is one of the strongest. For the only set on Black Saint (the following chapters were released by Gramavision), Carter utilizes a notable octet that also includes cornetist Bobby Bradford, flutist James Newton, Charles Owens on soprano, oboe and clarinet, bassist Roberto Miranda, the veteran Red Callender on tuba, drummer William Jeffrey and Luis Peralta on percussion. The five originals pay tribute to life in Africa a few centuries ago, mixing together folk melodies with very advanced improvising; Newton and Callender in particular really excel in this setting. Highly recommended for open-eared listeners. —*Scott Yanow*

Castles of Ghana / Feb. 1985 / Gramavision ✦✦✦✦
The second of clarinetist John Carter's five-part depiction of the history of African Americans deals with the capture of many Africans for shipment as slaves to the New World. Carter's octet on this date features such fine players as bass clarinetist Marty Ehrlich, cornetist Bobby Bradford, trombonist Benny Powell and trumpeter Baikida Carroll, and the music is as dramatic as the episodes it portrays. —*Scott Yanow*

Suite of Early American Folk Pieces for Solo Clarinet / Aug. 16, 1979 / Moers ✦✦✦

Dance of the Love Ghosts / Nov. 1986 / Gramavision ✦✦✦
The third of five chapters in John Carter's important work depicting the history of Black Americans has some of the most emotional music, as it covers the voyage across the Atlantic Ocean in slave ships. Clarinetist Carter features many top musicians on this set: Marty Ehrlich on bass clarinet and flute, cornetist Bobby Bradford, trombonist Benny Powell, Don Preston on synthesizer, bassist Fred Hopkins, drummer Andrew Cyrille, a few percussionists and violinist Terry Jenoure, who sings on "The Captain's Dilemma." Intense and often scary music, quite successful in telling the tragic story. —*Scott Yanow*

Fields / Mar. 1988 / Gramavision ✦✦✦
Clarinetist John Carter, a few years before his death, musically told the story of Black Americans in five albums. The first set concentrates on the years of slavery, which were filled with both despair and hope for the future. The octet (Carter; his longtime cornetist Bobby Bradford; violinist Terry Jenoure, who also sings; Marty Ehrlich on bass clarinet and flute; trombonist Benny Powell; keyboardist Don Preston; bassist Fred Hopkins; and drummer Andrew Cyrille) covers a wide range of moods in the seven Carter originals, and the voice of John Carter's late uncle reminiscing about the early days is also heard in spots. Memorable. —*Scott Yanow*

Shadows on a Wall / Apr. 1989 / Gramavision ✦✦
The fifth and final chapter of John Carter's project to musically portray the history of African Americans deals with the past hundred years. Because the music (despite titles such as "Sippi Strut" and "52nd Street Stomp") does not refer to earlier styles and instead stays unremittingly avant-garde, this set is a bit of a disappointment. Some of the playing by the octet (particularly trumpeter Bobby Bradford and trombonist Benny Powell) is quite excellent, but the singing of Terry Jenoure gets jarring within a short time. This music is easier to respect than to love. —*Scott Yanow*

Regina Carter

Violin / Post-Bop

A talented player with a beautiful tone, Regina Carter has the potential to become the most significant new violinist in jazz since Jean-Luc Ponty in the late 1960s. Carter began playing violin when she was four and, after graduating from Cass Technical High School, the New England Conservatory and Michigan's Oakland University, she became a member of Straight Ahead. In 1994, she left the band (which had recorded for Atlantic) to move to New York. Carter has since worked with the Uptown String Quartet, the String Trio of New York, Oliver Lake and Max Roach. Her debut set as a leader for Atlantic was a bit R&B- and pop-oriented, but her appearance near the end of Wynton Marsalis' Pulitzer Prize-winning *Blood on the Fields* during 1996-97 nearly always stole the show. —*Scott Yanow*

● **Something for Grace** / Apr. 1, 1997 / Atlantic ✦✦✦
Regina Carter (who has a beautiful tone and a swinging style) is one of the top new jazz violinists of the 1990s, and the more memorable selections on this CD are so strong that they almost allow one to overlook the three throwaway pop/R&B songs. Unfortunately, the opening "Downtown Underground" is one of the losers, and the Nicki Richards vocal piece "Late Night Mood" (which recording executive talked Carter into recording that turkey?) is so lightweight that it should have been released on another album. In contrast are near-classic renditions of Eddie Harris' "Listen Here" and Mal Waldron's "Soul Eyes"; Carter's haunting ballad "Reflections" deserves to become a standard. A mixed bag, but overall this CD is recommended, with reservations. —*Scott Yanow*

Ron Carter

b. May 4, 1937, Ferndale, MI

Bass, Cello, Piccolo Bass / Post-Bop, Hard Bop

The epitome of class and elegance, though not stuffy, Ron Carter has been a world-class bassist and cellist since the '60s. He's among the greatest accompanists of all time, but has also done many albums exhibiting his prodigious technique. He's a brilliant rhythmic and melodic player, who uses everything in the bass and cello arsenal: walking lines; thick, full, prominent notes and tones; drones and strumming effects; and melody snippets. His bowed solos are almost as impressive as those done with his fingers. Carter has been featured in clothing, instrument and pipe advertisments; he's close to being the bass equivalent of a Duke Ellington in his mix of musical and extra-musical interests. Carter is nearly as accomplished in classical music as jazz, and has performed with symphony orchestras all over the world. He's almost exclusively an acoustic player; he did play electric for a short time in the late '60s and early '70s, but hasn't used it in many, many years. Carter began playing cello at ten. But when his family moved from Ferndale, Michigan to Detroit, Carter ran into problems with racial stereotypes regarding the cello and switched to bass. He played in the Eastman School's Philharmonic Orchestra, and gained his degree in 1959. He moved to New York and played in Chico Hamilton's quintet with Eric Dolphy, while also enrolling at the Manhattan School of Music. Carter earned his master's degree in 1961. After Hamilton returned to the West Coast in 1960, Carter stayed in New York and played with Dolphy and Don Ellis, cutting his first records with them. He worked with Randy Weston and Thelonious Monk, while playing and recording with Jaki Byard in the early '60s. Carter also toured and recorded with Bobby Timmons' trio, and played with Cannonball Adderley. He joined Art Farmer's group for a short time in 1963, before he was tapped to become a member of Miles Davis' band. Carter remained with Davis until 1968, appearing on every crucial mid-'60s recording and teaming with Herbie Hancock and Tony Williams to craft a new, freer rhythm section sound. The high-profile job led to the reputation that's seen Carter become possibly the most recorded bassist in jazz history. He's been heard on an unprecedented number of recordings; some sources claim 500, others have estimated it to be as many as 1,000. The list of people he's played with is simply too great to be accurately and completely cited. Carter's been a member of the New York Jazz Sextet and New York Jazz Quartet, V.S.O.P. tour, Milestone Jazzstars and was in one of the groups featured in the film *Round Midnight* in 1986. He's led his own bands at various intervals since 1972, using a second bassist to keep time and establish harmony so he's free to provide solos. Carter even invented his own instrument, a piccolo bass.

Carter's also contributed many arrangements and compositions to both his groups and other bands. He's done duo recordings with either Cedar Walton or Jim Hall. Carter's recorded for Embryo/Atlantic, CTI, Milestone, Timeless, EmArcy, Galaxy, Elektra and Concord. —*Ron Wynn*

● **Where?** / Jun. 20, 1961 / Original Jazz Classics ♦♦♦♦♦
Essential session with Carter on both bass and cello. Awesome solos by Eric Dolphy (sax)—stunning pieces. w/ Mal Waldron. —*Ron Wynn*

Uptown Conversation / Oct. 6, 1969 / Atlantic ♦♦♦♦
A 1989 reissue of Embryo album that featured some rangy, vibrant Carter solos. —*Ron Wynn*

Blues Farm / Jan. 10, 1973 / Columbia ♦♦♦
One of his best dates as a leader. A good set with Bob James (k), Richard Tee (k), and Hubert Laws (fl)—revealing jazz chops they've seldom shown otherwise. —*Ron Wynn*

All Blues / Oct. 24, 1973 / CTI ♦♦♦♦♦
One of bassist Ron Carter's better albums as a leader, this CTI LP features a very compact quartet comprising tenor saxophonist Joe Henderson, pianist Roland Hanna (keyboardist Richard Tee sits in on one number), drummer Billy Cobham and Carter. All of the music (even the ballad "Will You Still Be Mine?") has a blues feeling although several are not really blues. However, the quality of the solos is high, and this date lives up to one's expectations. —*Scott Yanow*

Spanish Blue / Nov. 1974 / Columbia ♦♦♦
Interesting concept with good solos by Carter and Hubert Laws (fl). —*Ron Wynn*

Anything Goes / Jun. 1975-Jul. 1975 / Kudu ♦♦

Yellow and Green / May 1976 / Columbia ♦♦♦
With Billy Cobham (d) and Don Grolnick (k). A sleeper. —*Michael G. Nastos*

Pastels / Oct. 18, 1976+Oct. 19, 1976 / Original Jazz Classics ♦♦♦
Some tremendous playing by Carter, Kenny Barron (p), and Hugh McCracken (g), though the strings get intrusive. —*Ron Wynn*

Piccolo / Mar. 25, 1977-Mar. 26, 1977 / Milestone ♦♦♦♦
This double LP is mostly recommended to lovers of bass solos. With Ron Carter functioning as the main soloist on piccolo bass, only the solos of pianist Kenny Barron offer a bit of contrast. Bassist Buster Williams and drummer Ben Riley, who complete the quartet, are mostly featured in support. These performances, which are well played, are almost all quite long, so listeners who prefer more variety in their music are advised to look elsewhere. —*Scott Yanow*

Third Plane / Jul. 13, 1977 / Original Jazz Classics ♦♦♦
This reunion of Miles Davis' mid-'60s rhythm section (bassist Ron Carter, pianist Herbie Hancock and drummer Tony Williams) has its moments but is not particularly memorable. Performing three of Carter's songs, one apiece from Hancock and Williams and the standard "Stella by Starlight," the solos are fine but on the whole, little special occurs. The magic is missing. —*Scott Yanow*

Peg Leg / Nov. 18, 1977-Nov. 22, 1977 / Original Jazz Classics ♦♦
A 1991 reissue of a decent, though over-arranged, 1977 session. —*Ron Wynn*

A Song for You / Jun. 1978 / Milestone ♦♦♦
A change of pace session for Carter. He pairs his formidable bass lines and playing against a backdrop of four cellists, outstanding drummer Jack DeJohnette, and at various times pianists Kenny Barron or Leon Pendarvis, guitarist Jay Berliner, and percussionist Ralph McDonald. Things generally work, although sometimes the low energy level and lack of tension threaten to turn this into easy-listening material. —*Ron Wynn*

1 + 3 / Jul. 29, 1978 / Milestone ♦♦♦
Exactly the kind of impressive, high-level playing and interaction you'd expect from this trio. Pianist Herbie Hancock, bassist Ron Carter, and drummer Tony Williams comprised the rhythm section on many '60s Miles Davis classics; nearly three decades later, they're still in sync with each other. While it's Carter's session, there's really no leader or followers, just three wonderful musicians fully attuned to each other. —*Ron Wynn*

Standard Bearers / 03 / Original Jazz Classics ♦♦♦
Carter with some first-rate players including Red Garland (p), McCoy Tyner (p), Herbie Hancock (k), and many others, work their way through a program of jazz classics. CD has a bonus cut. —*Ron Wynn*

Parade / Mar. 1979 / Milestone ♦♦♦♦
Bassist Carter heads a sterling mid-sized band with three trumpeters and saxophonists and two trombones, but no bass or drums. He handles the job of being both the primary and secondary rhythm support, while guests Joe Henderson, Jon Faddis, and Frank Wess, among others, provide some standout solos. The ensemble interaction clicks as well. —*Ron Wynn*

New York Slick / Dec. 1979 / Original Jazz Classics ♦♦♦

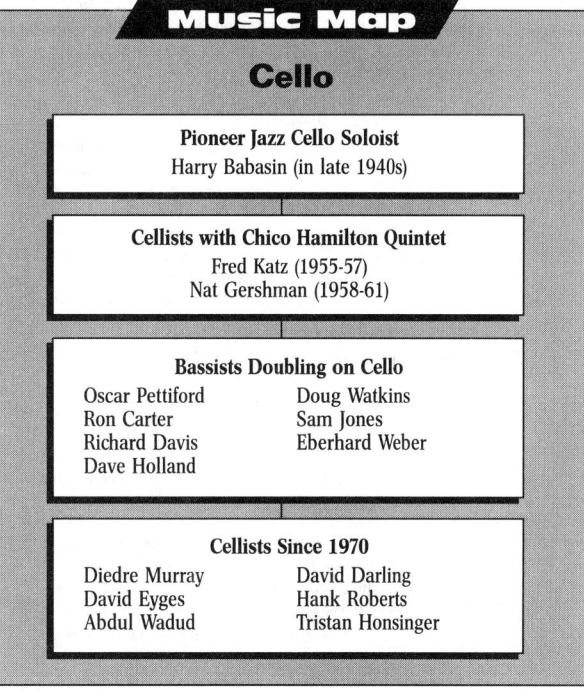

Music Map

Cello

Pioneer Jazz Cello Soloist
Harry Babasin (in late 1940s)

Cellists with Chico Hamilton Quintet
Fred Katz (1955-57)
Nat Gershman (1958-61)

Bassists Doubling on Cello

Oscar Pettiford	Doug Watkins
Ron Carter	Sam Jones
Richard Davis	Eberhard Weber
Dave Holland	

Cellists Since 1970

Diedre Murray	David Darling
David Eyges	Hank Roberts
Abdul Wadud	Tristan Honsinger

Patrao / May 19, 1980-May 20, 1980 / Original Jazz Classics ♦♦♦♦

Parfait / Sep. 29, 1980 / Milestone ♦♦

Heart and Soul / Dec. 1981 / Timeless ♦♦♦

Etudes / Sep. 1982 / Elektra ♦♦♦
Sophisticated, elegant quartet date from '82, with Art Farmer's serene trumpet and fluegelhorn playing setting the tone, backed by tenor and soprano saxophonist Bill Evans, who's more restrained than usual. Carter's bass and Tony Williams' drums are both understated and definitive in their support and backing rhythms. —*Ron Wynn*

Live at Village West / Nov. 1982 / Concord Jazz ♦♦♦♦
The CD reissue of these duets by bassist Ron Carter and guitarist Jim Hall adds two new selections (one original apiece) to the LP program (which comprised eight standards). Hall's harmonically advanced style always brings out the best in Carter and their quiet but passionate interplay is full of subtle surprises. —*Scott Yanow*

☆ **Telephone** / Aug. 1984 / Concord Jazz ♦♦♦♦♦
A live performance—a concert. Lots of space, and a slow pace. Music to listen to, perhaps a tad too intellectual. Still . . . lovely. —*Michael Erlewine*

All Alone / Mar. 29, 1988 / EmArcy ♦♦♦
Nice showcase for Carter's impeccable bass skills. —*Ron Wynn*

Panmanhattan / Jul. 23, 1990 / Evidence ♦♦♦
A series of duets with Ron Carter and French accordionist Richard Galliano. Not a common jazz instrument, the free-reed sound of the accordion on this recording is both subtle and lovely. Tempos range from ballads to medium, but tend to be on the slow side. Not breakthrough jazz, these duets (recorded live, in concert) are refreshing and what all good music should be, just good listening. —*Michael Erlewine*

Meets Bach / Dec. 15, 1991-Dec. 16, 1991 / Blue Note ♦♦♦

Friends / Dec. 27, 1992-Dec. 29, 1992 / Blue Note ♦♦♦♦

Jazz, My Romance / Jan. 4, 1994-Jan. 5, 1994 / Blue Note ♦♦
As with virtually all of Ron Carter's recordings as a leader, this CD is primarily a showcase for his bass solos. The unusual combination of musicians (a trio with guitarist Herb Ellis and pianist Kenny Barron) really does not live up to its potential. There are some short spots for Ellis and Barron but their roles are mostly in support of the bassist. Some of the selections (particularly "Sweet Lorraine" and the bassist's original "For Toddlers Only") do have their memorable moments but none of the songs are taken at faster than a medium tempo. Since bass solos (as

with most drum showcases) often lose a lot when transferred to record (as opposed to being seen live), this CD is recommended mostly to Ron Carter completists. —*Scott Yanow*

Mr. Bow Tie / 1995 / Blue Note ✦✦✦✦
Bassist Ron Carter varies the personnel often enough to keep one's interest throughout this CD. Carter, who contributed six of the ten compositions (which alternate with four familiar standards), takes his share of bass solos but also showcases pianist Gonzalo Rubalcaba (who is fairly restrained throughout) on the opening "Mr. Bow-Tie" and allocates a generous amount of solo space on some selections to trumpeter Edwin Russell (inspired by Miles Davis but possessing his own fire) and Javon Jackson, who often sounds like a close relative of Joe Henderson. Rubalcaba sits out on four of Carter's originals, making the group occasionally a pianoless quartet/quintet (depending on whether percussionist Steve Kroon is present). All of the music is straightahead and the playing is consistently colorful. This is an impressive effort that is easily recommended. —*Scott Yanow*

Brandenburg Concerto / Dec. 27, 1995 / Blue Note ✦✦✦

Wayman Carver

b. Dec. 25, 1905, Portsmouth, VA, **d.** May 6, 1967, Atlanta, GA
Flute, Multiple Reeds / Swing

Although not the first jazz flute soloist (Albert Soccarras preceded him by five years), Wayman Carver was virtually the only flutist to be featured on swing records in the 1930s. He picked up early experience playing with J. Neal Montgomery's band. In 1931 he settled in New York where he recorded with Dave Nelson. After a stint with Elmer Snowden (1931-32), he joined Benny Carter and recorded with Spike Hughes in 1933, taking some of his best solos. Carver was with Chick Webb's band during 1934-39 (mostly playing in the sax section) but was well featured on four 1937 titles by Chick Webb and his Little Chicks, a quintet matching his flute with Chauncey Haughton's clarinet. Carver remained with the orchestra as it continued under Ella Fitzgerald's leadership after Webb's death (1939-41) and then eventually settled in Atlanta as a professor of music at Clark College; among his students were George Adams and Marion Brown. —*Scott Yanow*

Dick Cary

b. Jul. 10, 1916, Hartford, CT, **d.** Apr. 6, 1994, Glendale, CA
Piano, Trumpet, Alto Horn / Dixieland, Swing

Dick Cary, best known for his stint with Louis Armstrong's All-Stars (1947-48), was most significant as a behind-the-scenes arranger and freelance musician in the trad jazz movement. He made his recording debut with Joe Marsala (1942), worked as a soloist at Nick's (1942-43) and played for short periods with the Casa Loma Orchestra and Brad Gowans. While in the army (1944-46) he was able to keep on recording including with Muggsy Spanier and Wild Bill Davison. After playing with Billy Butterfield and Louis Armstrong, Cary was with Jimmy Dorsey's big band (1949-50), wrote arrangements and played alto horn on Eddie Condon's television shows, and throughout the 1950s played and wrote for the Condon gang, recording with Condon, Pee Wee Russell, Max Kaminsky, Bud Freeman, Jimmy McPartland, Bobby Hackett and others. In 1959 he settled in Los Angeles, working as a freelance musician up until his death. In later years Cary led his Tuesday Night Band and performed often at Dixieland jazz festivals. —*Scott Yanow*

The Amazing Dick Cary / Oct. 27, 1975-Oct. 30, 1975 / Riff ✦✦✦
The versatile but underrated Dick Cary had his first opportunity to lead a record session in 16 years when he cut this fun album for the Dutch Riff label; it was later released domestically by Circle. Since the great stride pianist Ralph Sutton was also a guest on the date with drummer Ted Easton's excellent band, Cary only plays piano on two of the eight selections but he is well featured on trumpet, alto trumpet and alto horn. Other than Jimmy Van Heusen's "Sleighride in July," all of the selections are fairly familiar. Bob Wilber on soprano sits in on "What's New." Fine swing/Dixieland-oriented music with the highlights including "Mandy Make up Your Mind," "Sunday" and "Somebody Stole My Gal." —*Scott Yanow*

● **California Doings** / Jun. 1981 / Famous Door ✦✦✦✦
Although he is best remembered as a pianist, Dick Cary does not play piano on his Famous Door LP, leaving the piano bench for Ross Tompkins to fill. Instead, Cary doubles on trumpet and alto horn, provides all of the arrangements and was responsible for one original, "What's That You're Playing?" Cary blends in well with trombonist Bob Havens, both Dick Hafer and Tommy Newsom on tenors, Tompkins, bassist John Heard and drummer Nick Fatool during this excellent set, which shows the similarity between small-group swing and 1950s cool jazz. —*Scott Yanow*

And His Tuesday Night Friends / May 4, 1993-Aug. 10, 1993 / Arbors ✦✦✦✦
Dick Cary, best known for being an original member of the Louis Armstrong All-Stars in 1947 and for his work as a major force on the 1950s Los Angeles Dixieland scene, led a rehearsal band on a regular basis every Tuesday night for over a decade. A prolific composer and arranger, Cary reportedly wrote over 1,500 originals for his group even though the ensemble (generally around 12 pieces) rarely appeared in public. This 1996 CD, recorded less than a year before Cary's death, has 14 of his pieces, which range from modern swing to "Fugue" and a couple of classical-oriented works. Most of the horns get some opportunities to solo (particularly clarinetist Abe Most) and there are some swinging pieces in the set. However the arrangements are surprisingly modern (particularly considering Cary's background) and quite original. It is as if bebop never existed and jazz, from a swing base, continued evolving steadily after 1940. Although "The Tueday Night Band" has continued rehearsing on a regular basis after its leader's death, it is fortunate that they did record these sessions while Dick Cary was still around to supervise. Recommended. —*Scott Yanow*

Casa Loma Orchestra

f. 1927, **db.** 1963
Group / Big Band, Swing

When originally formed by saxophonist Glen Gray, the Casa Loma Orchestra was a cooperative orchestra. They made their recording debut in 1929 and during the next six years would be one of the top swing-oriented big bands in jazz (even though the term "swing" would not come into general usage until 1935). Although their ensembles were later criticized as sounding mechanical (thanks in part to the complexity of Gene Gifford's arrangements), the band did swing and had several fine soloists including clarinetist Clarence Hutchenrider, the high note trumpeter Sonny Dunham (whose display on "Memories of You" is still impressive) and trombonist/singer Pee Wee Hunt; Kenny Sargent offered smooth ballad vocals. After Benny Goodman's success in 1935 resulted in many new big bands being formed, the Casa Loma Orchestra was never again a pacesetter but it continued into the 1940s with such players as Red Nichols, Bobby Hackett and Herb Ellis. Glen Gray had top billing from the late '30s on, and after he stopped touring (around 1950) he started a commercially successful (if very predictable) series of recordings for Capitol that found the Casa Loma Orchestra (by then mostly studio players) constantly revisiting (and often recreating) the hits of the swing era. But its early original recordings of tunes such as "San Sue Strut," "Case Loma Stomp," "No Name Jive" and "Smoke Rings" are well worth acquiring. —*Scott Yanow*

Casa Loma Stomp / Oct. 29, 1929-Dec. 6, 1930 / Hep ✦✦✦✦✦
Although the later versions of the Casa Loma Orchestra were better known, the big band was an early pacesetter during the late '20s/early '30s when (particularly among white orchestra) there were few competitors. This LP from the Scottish Hep label has the orchestra's 14 best recordings out of the 21 that they cut during their first six sessions. The main soloists at the time were trumpeters Dub Shoffner and Frankie Martinez, trombonist Pee Wee Hunt and Les Arquette on tenor and clarinet, but the main star is Gene Gifford, who contributed the bulk of the arrangements and was thereby largely responsible for the group's musical personality. Most memorable are "China Girl," "San Sue Strut," "Casa Loma Stomp" and "Put on Your Old Grey Bonnet" but even the obscurities are quite rewarding. This set is recommended (at least until a more complete series finally comes along on CD) to classic jazz and early swing fans. —*Scott Yanow*

Casa Loma Orchestra: 1929/1932 / Oct. 29, 1929-Sep. 19, 1932 / Harrison ✦✦✦
On the first of two Casa Loma LPs from the collector's Harrison label, 15 of the pioneering swing big band's early recordings are reissued; many have not reappeared since. After the original version of "Smoke Rings," there are a variety of titles from 1929-32. Kenny Sargent takes four vocals, and there are spots for the singing of Pee Wee Hunt, Jack Richmond and Ray Eberle (eight years before he joined Glenn Miller's Orchestra), but it is the instrumentals that are of greatest interest, especially "Happy Days Are Here Again," "Clarinet Marmalade" and a rare version of "Casa Loma Stomp" that was originally released as a publicity record. —*Scott Yanow*

1930-1937, Vol. 2 / Apr. 18, 1930-Jul. 23, 1937 / Harrison ✦✦✦✦
The second (and overall better) of two Casa Loma LPs put out by the Harrison label in the 1970s starts off with the best-known version of their theme song "Smoke Rings" (the 1937 rendition) and has a couple of vocal numbers from 1930 but otherwise dates from 1933-35. Other than three Pee Wee Hunt vocals, the emphasis is on instrumentals, as the Casa Loma Orchestra shows what swing was like before the rise of Benny Goodman. Highlights include a three-song medley, "Old Man River," "Panama," "Avalon" and "Who's Sorry Now." —*Scott Yanow*

● **Best of the Big Bands** / Dec. 18, 1931-Dec. 24, 1934 / Columbia ✦✦✦✦
Despite indifferent packaging (which does not bother to include a personnel listing or the exact recording dates), this 16-song CD is recommended to general col-

lectors since no other major label has yet released a Casa Loma CD. Some of the orchestra's best early numbers are here (including its theme "Smoke Rings," "Black Jazz," "Maniac's Ball," "Casa Loma Stomp" and "Limehouse Blues"), clarinetist Clarence Hutcherider is well featured as the band's star soloist and these tricky Gene Gifford arrangements helped set the standard for the upcoming swing era. —*Scott Yanow*

And the Casa Loma Orchestra (1939) / 1939 / Circle ♦♦
The first of two Circle LPs featuring the Casa Loma Orchestra on radio transcriptions has six ballad vocals by Kenny Sargent, three more light-hearted ones from Pee Wee Hunt and just three instrumentals, none of which are all that exciting. Although the musicianship of the group is obviously high, the lack of any jazz-oriented material makes this release of lesser interest. —*Scott Yanow*

The Uncollected Glen Gray & the Casa Loma Orchestra, Vol. 1 (1939-1940) / 1939-1940 / Hindsight ♦♦♦
This Hindsight LP, which consists of radio transcriptions from 1939-40, puts the emphasis on the jazz side of the Casa Loma Orchestra; the 16 numbers only contain two Kenny Sargent vocals and just one from Pee Wee Hunt. Among the most interesting selections are a "new" rendition of the band's theme song "Smoke Rings," "Hindustan," "No-Name Jive," trumpeter Sonny Dunham's high-note feature on "Memories of You" and the Casa Loma's versions of three songs made famous by Glenn Miller: "Little Brown Jug," "In the Mood" and "Tuxedo Junction." This album is well worth picking up by swing collectors. —*Scott Yanow*

And the Casa Loma Orchestra (1940) / 1940 / Circle ♦♦
The second LP of radio transcriptions made by the Casa Loma Orchestra and released by Circle is, like the first, a bit of a disappointment. Of the dozen selections, only two ("Git Away Day" and "Jimtown Blues") are instrumentals and one has to sit through six of Kenny Sargent's "dreamy" ballad vocals plus three novelties featuring Pee Wee Hunt. The Casa Loma Orchestra was much more of a well-rounded outfit than is displayed on these performances, making this an album strictly for Glen Gray completists. —*Scott Yanow*

The Uncollected Glen Gray & the Casa Loma Orchestra, Vol. 2 (1943-46) / 1943-1946 / Hindsight ♦♦♦
The Casa Loma Orchestra made very few recordings after 1942, so this set of rare radio transcriptions are both historical and essential for swing collectors. Cornetist Red Nichols is featured on three numbers including a couple of very memorable Bill Challis arrangements: "Don't Take Your Love from Me" and "Dancing on the Ceiling." Cornetist Bobby Hackett is heard on five of the later selections, other soloists include the young guitarist Herb Ellis and pianist Lou Carter, and the arrangements of Challis, Carter and Ray Conniff gave the Casa Loma Orchestra a fresh new sound during the last years of the swing era. This LP is highly recommended. —*Scott Yanow*

Casa Loma in Hi-Fi! / Jun. 18, 1956-Jun. 21, 1956 / Capitol ♦♦♦
Glen Gray broke up his Casa Loma Orchestra in 1950. Six years later he was persuaded by Capitol to gather together alumni along with some studio musicians to recreate some of his more famous recordings for an LP. This album was a surprise hit, leading to Gray recording a series of records recreating the "sounds of the big bands." In reality these performances are quite predictable and are more nostalgic than creative. With trumpeters Manny Klein and Shorty Sherock, Murray McEachern on trombone and alto, tenor saxophonist Babe Russin, clarinetist Gus Bivona and pianist Ray Sherman contributing solos, the renditions of such songs as "No Name Jive," "Memories of You," "Maniac's Ball," "Casa Loma Stomp" and "Smoke Rings" are not without interest, but are generally not quite as exciting as the original versions. —*Scott Yanow*

Sounds of the Great Bands! / 1958 / Capitol ♦♦
One of the first of Glen Gray's series of albums that revisit the hits of the swing era in hi-fi, this set features a 17-piece band filled with top studio players, many of whom had come to maturity during the swing era. They perform hits by 12 different bandleaders, generally coming as close as possible to note-for-note recreations. Although such musicians as trumpeters Pete Candoli, Manny Klein and Shorty Sherock, clarinetist Gus Bivona, tenors Babe Russin and Plas Johnson and pianist Ray Sherman have their spots, their renditions of such songs as "Begin the Beguine," "Take the 'A' Train," "Flying Home," "Song of India" and "String of Pearls" add nothing to the originals and lack some of the original excitement and spontaneity. With the "real" versions readily available, decades later this nostalgic exercise seems quite pointless. —*Scott Yanow*

Al Casey

b. Sep. 15, 1915, Louisville, KY
Guitar / Swing
Although it has been over half a century since Fats Waller's death and Al Casey has been active during most of that time, he is still closely linked with Waller. He

started working with the pianist's group in the early '30s and was his main guitarist (with time off) up until Fats' demise in 1943, recording literally hundreds of performances. Sticking to acoustic guitar during that period, Casey was a very valuable rhythm player who also contibuted some excellent single-note solos. Casey, who had worked with Teddy Wilson's big band during part of 1939-40 and recorded with Billie Holiday, Frankie Newton and Chu Berry, briefly led a trio of his own and in 1944 worked with Clarence Profit's group. By that time he had switched to electric guitar and, inspired by Charlie Christian, he himself became influential for a time. Casey has spent the decades since freelancing in swing and blues settings. During 1957-61 he played R&B with King Curtis, in the 1980s he was often featured with the Harlem Blues and Jazz Band and in 1994 Al Casey recorded as a leader for Jazzpoint, a set not surprisingly titled *A Tribute to Fats*. —*Scott Yanow*

● Buck Jumpin' / Mar. 7, 1960 / Original Jazz Classics ♦♦♦♦
Al Casey, who will always be best known as Fats Waller's guitarist, makes one of his few appearances as a bandleader on the CD reissue of his Swingville album. Casey, in a quintet with Rudy Powell (who doubles on alto and clarinet) and pianist Herman Foster, sticks to blues and standards with several of the latter taken from Waller's songbook. The music consistently swings and it is a rare pleasure to hear Casey getting the opportunity to stretch out on acoustic guitar. Two previously unreleased numbers ("Gut Soul" and "I'm Gonna Sit Right Down and Write Myself a Letter") augment the original program. —*Scott Yanow*

Al Casey Quartet / Nov. 10, 1960 / Moodsville ♦♦♦
Companion to *Buck Jumpin'.* —*Michael G. Nastos*

Genius of Jazz Guitar / Jul. 1981 / JSP ♦♦♦
Side one with pianist Gene Rogers Trio, side two with Jay McShann or Mike Carr's Trio. Swing, blues, and gospel standards. —*Michael G. Nastos*

Best of Friends / 1981 / JSP ♦♦♦

Al Casey Remembers King Curtis / Jul. 21, 1985 / JSP ♦♦♦

A Tribute to "Fats" / May 22, 1994 / Jazzpoint ♦♦♦♦
Guitarist Al Casey is still best known for playing with pianist/composer Fats Waller on and off during 1934-42. Over a half-century later he recorded this CD, which mixes together standards and original riff tunes with a couple of Waller compositions ("Squeeze Me" and "Honeysuckle Rose"). The 79-year-old guitarist is assisted by pianist Red Richards (himself 82), bassist Jan Jankeje and drummer Imre Koszegi for this 1994 CD put out by the German Jazzpoint label. In addition to the Waller songs, highlights include "It Don't Mean a Thing," "After You've Gone" and "Cheek to Cheek." —*Scott Yanow*

Dick Cathcart

b. Nov. 6, 1924, Michigan City, IN, **d.** Nov. 8, 1993
Trumpet / Dixieland
A fine Dixieland trumpeter, Dick Cathcart became best known for his role of ghosting the playing of Pete Kelly (as played by Jack Webb) in a radio series, film and television show all titled *Pete Kelly's Blues*. Early on Cathcart played trumpet in the US Army Air Force Band. After stints with Alvino Rey, Ray McKinley and Bob Crosby, he worked in the MGM studios (1946-49), and with the bands of Ben Pollack and Ray Noble. In the 1950s he began recording albums with his own group (which was titled Pete Kelly's Big Seven). Cathcart remained active on the Dixieland circuit (including festivals) off and on until his death. —*Scott Yanow*

Bix MCMLIX / Dec. 12, 1958-Dec. 22, 1958 / Warner Brothers ♦♦♦♦

Philip Catherine

b. Oct. 27, 1942, London, England
Guitar / Post-Bop
Philip Catherine has been called the "Young Django" by none other than Charles Mingus—and upon hearing his elliptical, rapid-fire, expressively melodic acoustic guitar, there can be no doubt as to whose records he was absorbing as a youth. Born to a Belgian father and English mother living in London during World War II, Catherine went back with his family to Brussels after the war, where he learned guitar and turned professional at 17. The examples of Larry Coryell and John McLaughlin led Catherine into jazz-rock; he played with Jean-Luc Ponty's Experience from 1970 to 1972 before taking a year off to study at Boston's Berklee School. Back in Europe in 1973, he founded the band Pork Pie, which recorded into the mid- and late '70s; he also formed a duo with Niels-Henning Orsted Pedersen and worked with such musicians as Mingus and Stephane Grappelli. If anything, Catherine is best known in America for his duets with Coryell, which began spontaneously in Berlin in 1976, triggered some lovely duo albums for Elektra, and helped steer Coryell back to the acoustic guitar. —*Richard S. Ginell*

Nairam / Nov. 1976 / Warner Brothers ♦♦♦

Catherine/Escoude/Lockwood Trio / Sep. 1983-Oct. 1983 / Gramavision ◆◆◆◆
This is an interesting set featuring both Philip Catherine and the lesser-known Christian Escoude on guitars, plus violinist Didier Lockwood—not a typical trio record. The music often swings à la Django Reinhardt and Stephane Grappelli, but the repertoire (three songs apiece by each of the musicians) is more advanced, actually falling into the post-bop genre. Lockwood in particular excels in this setting, making one regret that this Gramavision LP has yet to be reissued on CD. —*Scott Yanow*

Transparence / Nov. 1986 / Triloka ◆◆◆

September Sky / Sep. 1988 / September ◆◆◆

Spanish Nights / May 11, 1989-May 13, 1989 / Enja ◆◆◆

● **I Remember You** / Oct. 19, 1990 / Criss Cross ◆◆◆◆

Moods, Vol. 1 / May 19, 1992-May 20, 1992 / Criss Cross ◆◆◆◆

Moods, Vol. 2 / May 19, 1992-May 20, 1992 / Criss Cross ◆◆◆◆

Live / Mar. 28, 1996 / Dreyfus ◆◆◆◆

Sidney "Big Sid" Catlett

b. Jan. 17, 1910, Evansville, IN, **d.** Mar. 25, 1951, Chicago, IL
Drums / Swing
"Big Sid" Catlett was one of the most flexible drummers in the history of jazz. On the one hand, Catlett was skilled enough in the pre-modern styles to be Louis Armstrong's favorite percussionist; on the other, Catlett's powerful swing and generous adaptability allowed him to play commendably on the early Parker/Gillespie bop sides. Catlett excelled particularly as a combo drummer in the swing era. A sensitive player possessed of great drive and spirit, he was every bit the equal of such better-known contemporaries as Jo Jones or Gene Krupa.

As a child in Chicago, Catlett played the piano and learned the rudiments of drumming. His first professional gig was with Darnell Howard in 1928. Catlett played with other undistinguished Chicago bands before moving to New York in 1930. There he became a hired gun, working and recording with such as Benny Carter (1932), McKinney's Cotton Pickers (1934-5), Fletcher Henderson (1936), and Don Redman (1936-8). Catlett became Louis Armstrong's drummer of choice; from 1938-42 he was featured with Pops' big band. In 1941, he played with a particularly excellent Benny Goodman big band that also included trumpeters Billy Butterfield and Cootie Williams. He also joined Duke Ellington briefly in 1945. Catlett led his own bands throughout the '40s, and played with pianist Teddy Wilson for a time around 1948. He played Dixieland with Armstrong's All-Stars from 1947-49. Though Catlett was not a bebop drummer per se, he made an effort to accommodate the new music. He played on one of the first bop recording dates in 1945, a session that produced the classic early Gillespie/Parker sides. Catlett was forced to quit touring in 1949 due to ill health, but he continued to play, becoming the house drummer at a Chicago club, Jazz, Ltd. He also worked with Eddie Condon and John Kirby in New York in his final years. In early 1951, Catlett suffered from a bout of pneumonia; in March he collapsed and died of a heart attack. —*Chris Kelsey*

Dave Catney

b. 1961, Fairmont, WV, **d.** Aug. 11, 1994, Houston, TX
Piano / Post-Bop
Dave Catney began playing piano by ear at the age of five. In school he studied clarinet, tuba, electric bass and piano. After graduating from high school, he majored in music at the University of North Texas; he later studied piano privately in New York with Richie Beirach, JoAnne Brackeen and Hal Galper. Catney also wrote music, and several of his originals made their way to such films as *And the Band Played On*, as well as television. He also ran a popular jazz nightclub in Houston called Cezanne. Signing with Justice Records in Houston in 1990, he recorded three CDs before dying from AIDS in 1994. He also contributed an original track with vocalist Sandra Dudley to *Last Night When We Were Young: The Ballad Album*, an AIDS education benefit CD produced by pianist Fred Hersch. —*Ken Dryden*

First Flight / 1990 / Justice ◆◆◆

● **Jade Visions** / 1991 / Justice ◆◆◆◆◆
The late pianist Dave Catney's second release for Justice was one of his finest recordings. One can hear touches of McCoy Tyner, Bill Evans and Herbie Hancock in his style but Catney had already largely gained a sound of his own. He interprets with great sensitivity (and with close attention to mood variations) a set of music dominated by obscurities, including Jerome Kern's "Up with the Lark" and Scott LaFaro's "Jade Visions." Working closely in the trio with bassist Marc Johnson and drummer Peter Erskine, Dave Catney (who takes a surprise vocal on "Lost in

the Stars") shows himself to have been a strong and underrated improviser. —*Scott Yanow*

Reality Road / 1994 / Justice ◆◆◆◆

Page Cavanaugh

b. Jan. 26, 1922, Cherokee, KS
Piano, Vocals / Swing
A talented veteran pianist/vocalist, Page Cavanaugh and his trio (with guitarist Al Viola and bassist Lloyd Pratt) was quite popular during the latter half of the 1940s. Cavanaugh started taking piano lessons when he was nine. He picked up early experience playing with the Ernie Williamson band (1938-39). While in the military he first met up with Viola and Pratt. After their discharge, the trio's swinging playing (inspired by the Nat King Cole Trio) plus their whispered vocals made them a hit during the mid- to late-'40s; among their bestsellers were "The Three Bears," "Walkin' My Baby Back Home" and "All of Me." The group appeared in several movies including *A Song Is Born* and *Romance on the High Seas*. Cavanaugh has worked steadily in the Los Angeles area for the past five decades, heading a septet (the Page 7) in the early '60s and performing regularly with his trio (which once again includes Al Viola) since the late '80s. His earlier RCA dates are difficult to find but he has recorded in recent times for Star Line. —*Scott Yanow*

An Explosion in Pop Music / Dec. 1963 / RCA ◆◆◆
After years of leading trios, pianist-vocalist Page Cavanaugh decided to try a change of pace. He formed a septet (the Page 7) consisting of trombonists Lew McCreary and Dave Wells, Bob Jung on baritone and alto and a four-piece rhythm section with guitarist John Pisano, bassist Don Bagley and drummer Jack Sperling. For awhile in the early to mid-'60s the group did a lot of business in the L.A. area, recording two LPs of which this was their first. They performed jazz-oriented pop music, renditions of melodic standards and originals that clocked in at less than three minutes apiece. The enjoyable if lightweight instrumental program on this out-of-print album is highlighted by "Putt It," "The Swingin' Saints," "Sweet and Sassy" and "The Preacher." —*Scott Yanow*

Impact at Basin Street East / 1964 / RCA ◆◆◆
The second of two LPs recorded by the Page Seven (a group led by pianist Page Cavanaugh that consists of trombonists Lew McCreary and Dave Wells, Bob Jung on baritone and alto, guitarist John Pisano, bassist Don Bagley and drummer Jack Sperling) has catchy arrangements of standards and originals, very concise playing (nothing clocks in over 3:02) and spirited if lightweight music. This album, which will be difficult to locate, has music that is in a similar vein of a group the Page 7 preceded, the Tijuana Brass. —*Scott Yanow*

Page Three / 1967 / Star Line ◆◆◆
This 1997 CD released for the first time some well-recorded tapes of Page Cavanaugh from 1967, a relatively low-profile period for the pianist/singer. Assisted by bassist Jerry Pulera and drummer Warren Nelson, Cavanaugh sticks mostly to standards and is in fine form. Highlights include an unusual version of "I Got Rhythm" (which was purposely given three extra beats during the melody choruses), "Summer Wind," "Sweet Georgia Brown" and "Samba De Orfeo." —*Scott Yanow*

● **The Digital Page: Page One** / Jan. 12, 1989 / Star Line ◆◆◆◆◆
Pianist-vocalist Page Cavanaugh's first recording in a decade (and his first CD) is a real gem. Still very much in his prime, Cavanaugh reunited with Al Viola (who was his regular guitarist in the 1940s) and used the fine supportive bassist Allen Jackson to complete the trio. The interplay between Cavanaugh and Viola is consistently impressive, Page's vocals on four of the 11 songs are charming and the tunes that are performed (which mix together swing standards with superior obscurities including Artie Shaw's "Love of My Life" and Bobby Troup's "There's No Spring") are all quite enjoyable. This set is one of the recorded high points of Page Cavanaugh's career, as is a second record (*Page Two*) culled from the same session. —*Scott Yanow*

● **The Digital Page: Page Two** / Jan. 12, 1989 / Star Line ◆◆◆◆◆
Page Cavanaugh first made history in the mid- to late '40s, leading a popular trio that included guitarist Al Viola. Four decades later Cavanaugh and Viola started teaming up again on a regular basis with bassist Allen Jackson in a highly enjoyable trio. Cavanaugh's piano playing had (if anything) grown in power and creativity through the years while exploring the same modern swing style that he had earlier helped to popularize. For this CD (taken from the same session that had resulted in the equally satisfying *Page One*), the trio stretches out on nine memorable standards plus Cavanaugh's "An Old Acquaintance"; the leader's vocals on three songs are quite personable. Highlights include "Too Marvelous for Words," "What Can I Say After I Say I'm Sorry," "As Long As I Live" and "Baby, Baby All the Time." Both Starline CDs are highly recommended. —*Scott Yanow*

Oscar Celestin

b. Jan. 1, 1884, Napoleonville, LA, **d.** Dec. 15, 1954, New Orleans, LA

Trumpet / New Orleans Jazz

Oscar Celestin's legendary career can easily be split into two different parts. A pioneer who moved to New Orleans in 1906, Celestin played with the Algiers Brass Band and the Olympia Band before heading the Tuxedo Brass Band and his original Tuxedo Orchestra (1917-early '30s). Although not a major trumpeter, Celestin's band was excellent and recorded some enjoyable performances in the 1920s. After the Depression hit, Celestin retired from music, but in 1946 he made a comeback with a new version of the Tuxedo Jazz Orchestra. This group, playing Dixieland standards and hymns, became a major tourist attraction in New Orleans, appearing on TV and radio, making some records and even playing a special concert at Dwight Eisenhower's White House in 1953. — *Scott Yanow*

Celestin's Original Tuxedo Jazz Orchestra / Apr. 13, 1926-Dec. 13, 1928 / VJM ✦✦✦✦✦

Except for his very first session (which resulted in three numbers in 1925), this British LP has all of cornetist Oscar "Papa" Celestin's recordings of the 1920s. The New Orleans bandleader's Tuxedo Jazz Orchestra could be a touch primitive but their performances (with the exception of a poor Charles Gillis vocal on "My Josephine") are near-classics, rare examples of a regularly working New Orleans jazz band in the early days. Of the sidemen, the most significant players are second cornetist Ricard Alexis (a fine soloist who worked with Celestin), altoist Paul Barnes and trombonist Bill Matthews. This set is a must for early New Orleans jazz collectors. — *Scott Yanow*

The Battle of the Bands / 1950 / Fairmont ✦✦✦✦

This collector's LP alternates performances by Oscar "Papa" Celestin's band (which featured the ancient clarinetist Alphonse Picou and trombonist Bill Matthews) and Sharkey Bonano's sextet (with clarinetist Lester Bouchon and drummer Monk Hazel among others). The two groups form a strong contrast with Celestin's being both primitive and spirited while Bonano's is hard-driving and smooth; essentially it gives one a chance to compare New Orleans jazz and Dixieland, two overlapping genres. This album will be difficult to find but the music makes the search worthwhile. — *Scott Yanow*

1950s Radio Broadcasts / Feb. 15, 1950-May 13, 1951 / Arhoolie ✦✦✦

Oscar "Papa" Celestin was at the height of his popularity during the last few years of his life. Although never a major trumpeter, Celestin was an important bandleader in New Orleans, and during the early 1950s his group included the legendary clarinetist Alphonse Picou, who here can be heard playing his famous solo on "High Society." Celestin's set of radio broadcasts, which had been available only in piecemeal fashion previously, is fully reissued on the well-conceived Arhoolie CD. Although the M.C.'s announcements are a bit condescending, the spirited music (which also features trombonist Bill Mathews, pianist Octave Crosby, bassist Ricard Alexis and drummer Christopher Goldston, plus vocals from several of the band members) is filled with the joy of classic New Orleans jazz. — *Scott Yanow*

Oscar "Papa" Celestin/George Lewis: the Radio Broadcasts: 1950-1951 / Feb. 15, 1950-May 13, 1951 / Folklyric ✦✦✦✦

Two of the most popular New Orleans jazz bands of 1950-51 are featured on this LP. Oscar Celestin's group (a sextet with the legendary clarinetist Alphonse Picou and trombonist Bill Mathews) run through a set of such crowd pleasers as "Oh Didn't He Ramble," "Lil' Liza Jane," "Eh, La Bas" and "When the Saints Go Marching In"; "High Society" has Picou playing his famous clarinet solo (which he had worked out on piccolo a half-century earlier). Although Celestin was never a major trumpeter, his solos were thoughtful, sincere and appealing, and his vocals were full of spirit. The flip side of the album features clarinetist George Lewis' group at a time when they were getting ready to emerge from New Orleans. With the exception of the trumpet slot (which is split between Elmer Talbert and Percy Humphrey), Lewis' personnel was set with trombonist Jim Robinson and pianist Alton Purnell being key soloists. "Bugle Boy March," "Running Wild" and "Sheik of Araby" are highlights of Lewis' portion. This set is easily recommended to fans of New Orleans revivalist jazz. — *Scott Yanow*

● **Marie Laveau** / 1950-Apr. 24, 1954 / GHB ✦✦✦✦✦

Papa Celestin's New Orleans Band was one of the most popular jazz groups for a short while in the early '50s. The veteran trumpeter (who was in his mid-60s but seemed older) performed spirited versions of New Orleans standards, even getting to play once at the White House in the Eisenhower years (a rare event during that era for a jazz band). This CD from GHB combines together two former LPs. Celestin is heard mostly singing on four numbers from 1954 (his final recordings and highlighted by the atmospheric title cut and an emotional "Down by the Riverside") and jamming with his sextet (a group including the ancient, but still viable, clarinetist Alphonse Picou) on ten Dixieland standards in 1950-51. The liner notes

may be a bit irrelevant (not even giving the recording dates), pianist Octave Crosby gets lost now and then and the ensembles sometimes slip out of tune, but the spirit and the joy of the music make this definitive Oscar Celestin CD a must for New Orleans jazz fans. — *Scott Yanow*

Bill Challis

b. Jul. 8, 1904, Wilkes Barre, PA, **d.** Oct. 4, 1994

Swing, Classic Jazz

As staff arranger for Jean Goldkette (1926) and Paul Whiteman (1927-30), Bill Challis was largely responsible for majority of the two big bands' most jazz-oriented charts including "Sunday," "My Pretty Girl," "Changes," "Dardanella" and most notably "San." Challis also wrote for Frankie Trumbauer's small-group dates with Bix Beiderbecke and assisted Bix in documenting piano pieces (including "In a Mist"). After leaving, he contributed arrangements to quite a few big bands including Fletcher Henderson, the Dorsey Brothers, the Casa Loma Orchestra, Artie Shaw ("Blues in the Night"), many radio orchestras and pop sessions. Challis was active into the 1960s and in 1986 many of his best arrangements were recorded by Vince Giordano's Nighthawks and Tom Pletcher (*The Goldkette Project*). — *Scott Yanow*

1936 / 1936 / Circle ✦✦✦

Bill Challis' claim to fame was as the most significant jazz arranger for the Jean Goldkette and Paul Whiteman Orchestras in the 1920s. By 1936, he was a freelance writer who often worked in the studios. On this LP and the follow-up set (both of which consist of radio transcriptions), Challis heads a large orchestra featuring such notable names as trumpeter Manny Klein, trombonists Jack Jenney and Will Bradley and clarinetist Artie Shaw, along with strings and a vocal quartet (going under the name of Bea and the Bachelors) that includes Bea Wain and Al Rinker. The performances (which include possibly the earliest version of "Let Yourself Go") are essentially dance music rather than jazz. There are few solos, and the emphasis is on the ensembles during such songs as "Temptation," "New Orleans" and "Broadway Rhythm," although "Clarinet Marmalade" has its moments. Decent music, but nothing too essential. — *Scott Yanow*

And His Orchestra—More 1936 / 1936 / Circle ✦✦✦

The second of two LPs taken from 1936 radio transcriptions by a large orchestra headed by arranger Bill Challis has its moments. Challis' old chart of "Dardanella" (written for Paul Whiteman in the 1920s) is revived, and among the better numbers are "Riverboat Shuffle," "More Than You Know" and an early rendition of "Let's Face the Music and Dance." However, the top-notch orchestra mostly sticks to ensembles, and the focus is on dance music rather than jazz. Bea and the Bachelors (a vocal quartet with Bea Wain and Al Rinker) pop up on four of the twelve numbers. It seems strange that Bill Challis recorded so little as a leader through the decades, making this set of at least historic interest. — *Scott Yanow*

● **The Goldkette Project** / 1988 / Circle ✦✦✦✦✦

Bill Challis contributed most of the best arrangements for the Jean Goldkette Orchestra from 1926-27. Sixty years later, he conducted Vince Giordano's Nighthawks in their versions of 16 of his charts (including a pair of three-song medleys). With cornetist Tom Pletcher taking Bix Beiderbecke's place and such top players as trumpeter Peter Ecklund, trombonist Dan Barrett, clarinetist Bob Wilber, pianist Dick Wellstood and Goldkette alumnus Spiegel Wilcox on trombone guesting with the Nighthawks, the results are outstanding and very enjoyable. Not only are such songs as "Proud of a Baby Like You," "My Pretty Girl" and "Clementine" brought back, but also some charts that Jean Goldkette's band played but never recorded (such as "The Blue Room," "I've Found a New Baby" and "Tiger Rag"). Highly recommended for 1920s and classic jazz collectors. — *Scott Yanow*

Serge Chaloff

b. Nov. 24, 1923, Boston, MA, **d.** Jul. 16, 1957, Boston, MA

Baritone Saxophone / Bop

One of the great baritone-saxophonists and the first major soloist on that instrument to emerge since Harry Carney (he preceded Gerry Mulligan), Serge Chaloff was a drug addict during his prime years, resulting in broken friendships and lost opportunities. After playing with the orchestras of Boyd Raeburn (1944-45), Georgie Auld (1945-46) and Jimmy Dorsey (1946-47), he found fame as one of the "Four Brothers" with Woody Herman's Second Herd (1947-49). After a stint with Count Basie's octet (1950), Chaloff returned to his native Boston where he eventually worked on kicking his dangerous habit. Ironically when he finally got off drugs, Chaloff contracted spinal paralysis and he played his final recording session (a reunion of the Four Brothers in 1957) seated in a wheelchair. Mosaic's 1993 limited-edition four-CD Serge Chaloff box set has all of his sessions as a leader and his exciting solos still put him near the top of his field. — *Scott Yanow*

● **The Complete Serge Chaloff Sessions** / Sep. 21, 1946-Mar. 14, 1956 / Mosaic
◆◆◆◆◆
This is the type of project the Mosaic label does best: releasing the complete output as a leader of a classic jazz musician including obscurities and a couple of fairly well-known sessions. Serge Chaloff, one of the top baritone-saxophonists in jazz history, is featured as the leader of bop-based small groups on sessions originally out on Dial, Savoy, Futurama, Motif, Storyville and Capitol. Such sidemen as trumpeters Red Rodney and Herb Pomeroy, tenorman Al Cohn, altoist Charlie Mariano and Boots Mussuli, vibraphonist Terry Gibbs and pianists Ralph Burns, George Wallington, Dick Twardzik, Russ Freeman, Barbara Carroll and Sonny Clark have solo space but it is the somewhat forgotten Chaloff who rightfully is the main focus. A definitive booklet rounds out this essential package. —*Scott Yanow*

Boston 1950 / 1946-1950 / Uptown ◆◆◆◆
The previously unreleased material included on this 1994 CD features the great baritonist Serge Chaloff performing on radio broadcasts from Boston. Most intriguing are four concise duets from 1946 (before Chaloff became famous) with pianist Rollins Griffith. Otherwise Chaloff is heard in 1950 with quartets and quintets, which often include pianist Nat Pierce and sometimes trombonists Sonny Truitt or Milt Gold. The recording quality is decent for the period and Chaloff (who at one point is briefly interviewed by a disc jockey) is in excellent form on the boppish material. Highlights include "The Goof and I," "Four Brothers," "Body and Soul," two versions of "Pennies from Heaven" and "Keen and Peachy." —*Scott Yanow*

The Fable of Mable / Jun. 9, 1954+Sep. 3, 1954 / Black Lion ◆◆◆◆
The great bebop baritonist Serge Chaloff is featured in two different Boston sessions on this excellent CD. Six selections showcase him in a quintet actually led by altoist Boots Mussulli and also including Russ Freeman on piano; "You Brought a New Kind of Love," "Oh Baby" and "All I Do Is Dream of You" are among the better tunes. The remainder of this release has six titles (and five previously unreleased alternate takes) from a Chaloff nonet date that also includes trumpeter Herb Pomeroy, altoist Charlie Mariano and pianist Dick Twardzik. The three versions of "The Fable of Mable" are each rewarding. This CD is easily recommended to fans of cool-toned bop who do not already own Serge Chaloff's very complete Mosaic box set. —*Scott Yanow*

Boston Blow-Up / Apr. 4, 1955+Apr. 5, 1955 / Capitol ◆◆◆◆
Baritonist Serge Chaloff was making a comeback in the mid-'50s after years of drug abuse. Having kicked the habit in his native Boston, he recorded *The Fable of Mable* in 1954 and this excellent session the following year. Chaloff is heard on a variety of obscure originals plus a couple of standards (including a near-classic "Body and Soul") in a sextet with trumpeter Herb Pomeroy and altoist Boots Mussulli. The ironic part is that, once Chaloff cleaned up his act, he contracted spinal paralysis and died in 1957. However the baritonist is very much in prime form on this out-of-print set, which has been made available on CD as part of Mosaic's Serge Chaloff limited-edition box. —*Scott Yanow*

Blue Serge / Mar. 4, 1956 / Capitol ◆◆◆◆◆
Baritonist Serge Chaloff's final recording as a leader was his best, this quartet outing with pianist Sonny Clark, bassist Leroy Vinnegar and drummer Philly Joe Jones. Chaloff had already contracted the spinal paralysis that would kill him a year later but there is no hint of any weakness on the date. Whether it be "The Goof and I," "I've Got the World on a String" or a beautiful rendition of "Stairway to the Stars," this recording features Serge Chaloff at his best. Unfortunately it is currently out-of-print although available as part of a limited-edition Mosaic CD box set dedicated to the great baritonist. —*Scott Yanow*

Joe Chambers

b. Jun. 25, 1942, Stoneacre, VA
Drums, Piano / Avant-Garde, Post-Bop
Joe Chambers is an extremely versatile, tasteful, master of all post-bop idioms. Chambers drives an ensemble with a light hand; his time is excellent, and his grasp of dynamics superb. He's not a flashy drummer by any means, but he's a generous collaborator who makes any group of which he's a part as good as it can possibly be. Chambers worked around Washington, D.C., in his late teens. After moving to New York in 1963, he played with Eric Dolphy, Freddie Hubbard, Jimmy Giuffre, and Andrew Hill. In the mid-'60s, Chambers played with a number of the more progressively inclined musicians associated with the Blue Note Label, such as vibist Bobby Hutcherson and saxophonists Joe Henderson, Wayne Shorter, and Sam Rivers. In 1970, Chambers joined Max Roach's percussion ensemble, M'Boom, as an original member. During the '70s, Chambers played with a great many of jazz's most prominent elder statesmen, including Sonny Rollins, Tommy Flanagan, Charles Mingus, and Art Farmer. With Flanagan and bassist Reggie Workman, Chambers formed the Super Jazz Trio. In the late '70s, he co-led a band

with organist Larry Young. Chambers recorded with bands led by trumpeter Chet Baker and percussionist Ray Mantilla in the early '80s. He's maintained his association with Roach into the '90s. Chambers has recorded infrequently as a leader; his output as a sideman, however, continues to be sizable. —*Chris Kelsey*

Double Exposure / Nov. 16, 1977 / Muse ◆◆◆
This is an unusual date. Joe Chambers, best known as a drummer, is heard on piano on four of these six tracks (including a fine effort on an unaccompanied version of "After the Rain"). The other selections are duets with the great organist Larry Young who would pass away four and a half months later. The music is somewhat adventurous with Chambers as the lead voice on the numbers on which he plays piano; the final two performances are organ-drum duets that put more of an emphasis on Young's unique sound. This interesting session has some surprising music. —*Scott Yanow*

● **Phantom of the City** / Mar. 8, 1991-Mar. 9, 1991 / Candid ◆◆◆◆
Drummer Joe Chambers works with an intriguing lineup on this 1991 quintet set. Young lion trumpeter Phillip Harper teams with journeyman Bob Berg, who holds his own with the lyrical, energetic Harper. Chambers never hurries or crowds the soloists, and he interacts easily and fully with pianist George Cables and bassist Santi Debriano. —*Ron Wynn*

Paul Chambers

b. Apr. 22, 1935, Pittsburgh, PA, d. Jan. 4, 1969, New York, NY
Bass / Hard Bop
One of the top bassists of 1955-65, Paul Chambers was among the first in jazz to take creative bowed solos (other than Slam Stewart who hummed along with his bowing). He grew up in Detroit where he was part of the fertile local jazz scene. After touring with Paul Quinichette, Chambers went to New York where he played with the J.J. Johnson-Kai Winding quintet and George Wallington. He spent the bulk of his prime years (1955-63) as a member of the Miles Davis Quintet, participating in virtually all of Davis's classic recordings of the era. When he left, "Mr. P.C." (as John Coltrane called him in one of his originals) worked with the Wynton Kelly Trio (1963-66) and freelanced until his death. Chambers, a consistently inspired accompanist who was an excellent soloist, made many recordings during his brief life including some with Sonny Rollins, Coltrane, Cannonball Adderley, Donald Byrd, Bud Powell and Freddie Hubbard in addition to a few as a leader —*Scott Yanow*

Chambers' Music / Mar. 1956-Apr. 20, 1956 / Blue Note ◆◆◆
This CD reissues bassist Paul Chambers' first sessions as a leader, recorded while he was a member of the Miles Davis Quintet. The first six selections feature Chambers with pianist Kenny Drew, drummer Philly Joe Jones and (on four numbers) the immortal tenor saxophonist John Coltrane. This somewhat obscure date includes such jazz standards as "Dexterity" and "Stablemates" along with "Easy to Love" and three straightahead group originals. Coltrane dominates the numbers he is on although his sound was not quite mature yet. The final three numbers (not on the original LP) are listed on the CD as being from April 20, 1955, but logic says that it must be exactly a year later. Chambers, Jones and Coltrane welcome two young musicians recently transplanted from Detroit: baritonist Pepper Adams and trombonist Curtis Fuller. In addition, pianist Roland Alexander is on the lengthy "Trane's Strain." Although none of this music (even the oddly titled "Nixon, Dixon and Yates Blues") is classic, it does give listeners a valuable early look at these important jazzmen. —*Scott Yanow*

Whims of Chambers / Sep. 21, 1956 / Blue Note ◆◆◆◆
Of the seven songs on this Blue Note CD reissue, four are more common than the other three because they contain solos by tenor saxophonist John Coltrane and have therefore been reissued more often. Actually there are quite a few solos in the all-star sextet (which includes the bassist-leader, Coltrane, trumpeter Donald Byrd, guitarist Kenny Burrell, pianist Horace Silver and drummer Philly Joe Jones) and all of the players get their chances to shine on this fairly spontaneous hard-bop set. Coltrane's two obscure compositions ("Nita" and "Just for the Love") are among the more memorable tunes and both are worth reviving. "Tale of the Fingers" features the quintet without Coltrane, the rhythm section stretches out on "Whims of Chambers" and "Tale of the Fingers" is a showcase for Chambers bowed bass. This is a fine effort and would be worth picking up by straightahead jazz fans even if John Coltrane had not participated. —*Scott Yanow*

Paul Chambers Quintet / May 19, 1957 / Blue Note ◆◆◆◆
This Blue Note CD reissues one of bassist Paul Chambers' rare outings as a leader. Chambers heads a group of up-and-coming all-stars (including trumpeter Donald Byrd, tenor saxophonist Clifford Jordan, pianist Tommy Flanagan and drummer Elvin Jones) on a program consisting of four originals by either the leader or Benny Golson plus a pair of standards; an alternate version of "Four Strings" was previously unissued. Chambers (who has "Softly as in a Morning Sunrise" as his

feature) and Byrd are the most impressive soloists while Jordan (who here mostly recalls Sonny Rollins with touches of John Coltrane) consistently swings although he had not yet found his own sound. The uncomplicated straightahead music falls securely into the modern mainstream of the period. —*Scott Yanow*

● **Bass on Top** / Jul. 14, 1957 / Blue Note ✦✦✦✦✦
Bass on Top is another thoroughly engaging set of straightahead, mainstream jazz from Paul Chambers. The bassist leads a quartet comprising guitarist Kenny Burrell, pianist Hank Jones and drummer Art Taylor through a selection of standards, including "Yesterdays," "You'd Be So Nice to Come Home To" and "Dear Old Stockholm," as well as a handful of contemporary jazz numbers and originals. There's a relaxed, friendly atmosphere to the music, both in its tone and in the fact that Chambers lets Jones and Burrell have some time in the spotlight. The result is a warm, entertaining collection of mainstream jazz that nevertheless rewards close listening. —*Stephen Thomas Erlewine*

Go / Feb. 2, 1959-Feb. 3, 1959 / Vee-Jay ✦✦✦
This interesting but out-of-print Vee-Jay LP is headed by bassist Paul Chambers and features four all-stars as sidemen: altoist Cannonball Adderley, pianist Wynton Kelly, drummer Jimmy Cobb and (on four of the six numbers) the young trumpeter Freddie Hubbard, who was at the beginning of his career. Other than Hubbard, all of the musicians were currently members of the Miles Davis Sextet, but the fiery and sometimes funky music sounds much more extroverted than much of Davis' output at the time. Cannonball and Kelly are the solo stars on three standards and a trio of Chambers originals while Hubbard sounds promising. Hopefully Vee-Jay will reissue this set (along with its follow-up *1st Bassman*) on CD eventually; the unavailable Japanese reissue has added quite a few alternate takes. —*Scott Yanow*

1st Bassman / May 12, 1960 / Vee-Jay ✦✦✦✦
Paul Chambers was one of the top bassists of the 1955-65 period, so it is somewhat surprising to realize that this out-of-print Vee-Jay LP was his final one as a leader. Actually tenor saxophonist Yusef Lateef, who contributed all five selections, is the most prominent musician on the album although trumpeter Tommy Turrentine, trombonist Curtis Fuller, pianist Wynton Kelly, drummer Lex Humprhies and Chambers are all strong assets. The music is straightahead without being overly predictable, falling into the hard-bop idiom and containing many fine moments. —*Scott Yanow*

Thomas Chapin

Alto Saxophone, Flute / Avant-Garde
A versatile reed player, Thomas Chapin had a wide variety of musical experience, including over five years (1981-86) as musical director and lead altoist for Lionel Hampton's big band, a lengthy stint with Chico Hamilton, and recordings with Ray Drummond and Mario Pavone, in addition to associations with NYC's avant-garde players. Chapin was a member of Machine Gun (a free jazz band that recorded for MuWorks), played duets with pianist Borah Bergman, headed the Radius Quartet and led sessions for Arabesque and Knitting Factory Works. Thomas Chapin passed away in early 1998. —*Scott Yanow*

Inversions / Mar. 30, 1992 / Muworks ✦✦✦✦✦

Insomnia / Dec. 1992 / Knitting Factory ✦✦✦✦✦
Thomas Chapin, who had fairly distinctive tones on alto and flute, was a versatile improviser capable of playing anything from swing to free jazz. His regular trio (with bassist Mario Pavone and drummer Michael Sarin) is joined by a brass quintet (two trumpets, two trombones and the tuba of Marcus Rojas) for a set of adventurous and unpredictable but generally very logical improvisations, often building off of simple ideas. Well worth a few close listens. —*Scott Yanow*

I've Got Your Number / Jan. 11, 1993 / Arabesque ✦✦✦✦
Although this is essentially a modern bop session, it is obvious that altoist Thomas Chapin was open to more explorative music. Chapin and his quintet (with pianist Ronnie Mathews) interpret three lesser-known standards and five of his own diverse originals. Chapin's tone at times recall aspects of Phil Woods and Jackie McLean but is largely original, and his style is a bit unpredictable. He also takes inventive flute solos on two pieces (including Bud Powell's "Time Waits"). The overall results are quite pleasing and often exciting within the modern mainstream of jazz. —*Scott Yanow*

Menagerie Dreams / Jul. 1994 / Knitting Factory ✦✦✦
Chapin's first Trio recordings in four years feature Mario Pavone on bass and Michael Sarin on drums. John Zorn and poet Vernon Frazier also make guest appearances. —*Jason Ankeny*

● **You Don't Know Me** / Aug. 23, 1994-Aug. 24, 1994 / Arabesque ✦✦✦✦✦
Throughout this well-rounded CD, Thomas Chapin (who switches between alto, soprano and flute) is in superb form, whether doing a humorous impression of Eric Dolphy on "Izzit," featuring his flute on "Namibian Sunset," jamming on the

chord changes of "Goodbye" (which is usually taken much slower) or putting plenty of feeling into the blues ballad "You Don't Know Me." Trumpeter Tom Harrell helps out on a few selections and pianist Peter Madsen has some outstanding solos but the album is recommended primarily for the exuberant and consistently creative playing of Chapin. —*Scott Yanow*

Haywire / Jan. 24, 1996+Jan. 27, 1996 / Knitting Factory ✦✦✦

Sky Piece / 1997 / Knitting Factory ✦✦✦✦

Dennis Charles

b. Dec. 4, 1933, St. Croix, Virgin Islands
Drums / Avant-Garde, Free Jazz
Dennis Charles is best known as the drummer with Cecil Taylor's earliest groups (1955-61). Although a steady timekeeper, he was flexible enough to fit in well with Taylor during his formative years. He moved to New York in the mid-'40s and played calypso and mambos before switching to jazz. In addition to his work with Taylor, Charles recorded with Steve Lacy (1957), Gil Evans (1959) and Sonny Rollins (1962) and performed with Lacy's 1963-64 group, Archie Shepp (1967) and Billy Bang (1981-82). Out of music for long periods, Dennis Charles has been more active since the 1980s. —*Scott Yanow*

● **Queen Mary** / Apr. 26, 1989-Apr. 27, 1989 / Silkheart ✦✦✦✦

Ray Charles (Ray Charles Robinson)

b. Sep. 23, 1930, Albany, GA
Piano, Vocals / Soul, R&B, Soul Jazz
Ray Charles was the musician most responsible for developing soul music. Singers like Sam Cooke and Jackie Wilson also did a great deal to pioneer the form, but Charles did even more to devise a new form of Black pop by merging '50s R&B with gospel-powered vocals, adding plenty of flavor from contemporary jazz, blues, and (in the '60s) country. Then there is his singing—his style is among the most emotional and easily identifiable of any 20th-century performer, up there with the likes of Elvis and Billie Holiday. He's also a superb keyboard player, arranger, and bandleader. The brilliance of his 1950s and 1960s work, however, can't obscure the fact that he's made few classic tracks since the mid-'60s, though he's recorded often and tours to this day.

Blind since the age of six (from glaucoma), Charles studied composition and learned many instruments at the St. Augustine School for the Deaf and the Blind. His parents had died by his early teens, and he worked as a musician in Florida for a while before using his savings to move to Seattle in 1947. By the late '40s, he was recording in a smooth pop/R&B style derivative of Nat King Cole and Charles Brown. He got his first Top Ten R&B hit with "Baby, Let Me Hold Your Hand" in 1951. Charles' first recordings have come in for their fair share of criticism, as they are much milder and less original than the classics that would follow, although they're actually fairly enjoyable, showing strong hints of the skills that were to flower in a few years.

In the early '50s, Charles' sound started to toughen as he toured with Lowell Fulson, went to New Orleans to work with Guitar Slim (playing piano on and arranging Slim's huge R&B hit, "The Things That I Used to Do"), and got a band together for R&B star Ruth Brown. It was at Atlantic Records that Ray truly found his voice, consolidating the gains of recent years and then some with "I Got a Woman," a No. 2 R&B hit in 1955. This is the song most frequently singled out as his pivotal performance, on which Charles first truly let go with his unmistakable gospelish moan, backed by a tight, bouncy horn-driven arrangement.

Throughout the '50s, Charles ran off a series of R&B hits that, although they weren't called "soul" at the time, did a lot to pave the way for soul by presenting a form of R&B that was sophisticated without sacrificing any emotional grit. "This Little Girl of Mine," "Drown in My Own Tears," "Hallelujah I Love Her So," "Lonely Avenue," and "The Right Time" were all big hits. But Charles didn't really capture the pop audience until "What'd I Say," which caught the fervor of the church with its pleading vocals, as well as the spirit of rock 'n' roll with its classic electric piano line. It was his first Top Ten pop hit, and one of his final Atlantic singles, as he left the label at the end of the '50s for ABC.

One of the chief attractions of the ABC deal for Charles was a much greater degree of artistic control of his recordings. He put it to good use on early-'60s hits such as "Unchain My Heart" and "Hit the Road Jack," which solidified his pop stardom with only a modicum of polish attached to the R&B he had perfected at Atlantic. In 1962, he surprised the pop world by turning his attention to country and western music, topping the charts with the "I Can't Stop Loving You" single, and making a hugely popular album (in an era in which R&B/soul LPs rarely scored high on the charts) with *Modern Sounds in Country and Western Music*. Perhaps it shouldn't have been so surprising; Charles had always been eclectic, recording quite a bit of straight jazz at Atlantic, with noted jazz musicians like David "Fathead" Newman and Milt Jackson.

Charles remained extremely popular through the mid-'60s, scoring big hits like "Busted," You Are My Sunshine," "Take These Chains from My Heart," and "Crying Time," although his momentum was slowed by a 1965 bust for heroin. This led to a year-long absence from performing, but he picked up where he left off with "Let's Go Get Stoned" in 1966. Yet by this time Charles was focusing increasingly less on rock and soul, in favor of pop tunes, often with string arrangements, that seemed aimed more at the easy-listening audience than anyone else. Charles' influence on the rock mainstream was as apparent as ever; Joe Cocker and Steve Winwood in particular owe a great deal of their style to him, and echoes of his phrasing can be heard more subtly in the work of greats like Van Morrison.

One approaches sweeping criticism of Charles with hesitation; he's an American institution, after all, and his vocal powers have barely diminished over the years. The fact remains, though, that his work since the late '60s on record has been very disappointing. Millions of listeners yearned for a return to the all-out soul of his 1955-1965 classics, but Charles had actually never been committed to soul above all else. Like Aretha Franklin and Elvis Presley, his focus is more upon all-around pop than many realize; his love of jazz, country, and pop standards is evident, even if his more earthy offerings are the ones that truly broke ground and will stand the test of time. He's dented the charts (sometimes the country ones) occasionally, and can command devoted international concert audiences whenever he feels like it. For good or ill, he's ensured his imprint upon the American mass consciousness in the 1990s by singing several ads for Diet Pepsi. The CD era has seen several excellent packages that focus on various chronological/thematic phases of the legend's career. —*Richie Unterberger*

The Birth of a Legend / 1949-1952 / Ebony ✦✦✦✦✦
Of all the countless compilations that have been stitched together of Ray Charles' early sides for Jack Lauderdale's Swing Time Records, this two-disc box is the only CD package that treats these enormously important works with the reverent respect that they deserve (meaning decent mono sound quality instead of murky electronic reprocessed stereo dubbed from vinyl, cogent liner notes, and full discographical annotation). This is where the Genius began, imitating Charles Brown at the very start (1949) and sounding like nobody but Brother Ray by 1952 (when he defected to Atlantic and hit the real big time). Forty-one tracks in all. —*Bill Dahl*

The Early Years [Tomato] / 1949-1952 / Tomato ✦✦✦
In the late '40s and early '50s, Charles recorded several dozen sides for the Swing-time/Downbeat label, 30 of which are presented here. As has been noted many times by critics, these usually found Charles in a Nat King Cole swing-blues groove that was much smoother than the gritty R&B/soul he'd record for Atlantic in the later '50s; the influence of urban blues balladeer Charles Brown is also evident. Some critical essays, in fact, may lead you to believe that this work is trivial, but while it's undeniably derivative, it's enjoyable on its own terms, and not without strong hints of the searing soulfulness that was to come. Some of the selections are delivered with such refined polish that it doesn't even sound like Charles. But on the more anguished and fast-tempoed cuts in particular, you can hear him starting to arrive at the phrasing and emotion that would flower in the mid-'50s. Unfortunately, like most Tomato reissues, the sound is substandard; even assuming that the master tapes can't be located, a better job was probably possible, and a couple of cuts even duplicate skips from the vinyl. Exact dates and songwriting credits are also missing, although Pete Welding's essay does at least discuss the material on the discs in some detail, unlike many of Tomato's liner notes. —*Richie Unterberger*

Genius & Soul: The 50th Anniversary Collection / Feb. 1949-1993 / Rhino ✦✦✦✦✦
As the first comprehensive, multi-label box set assembled on Ray Charles, the five-disc, 101-song *Genius & Soul: The 50th Anniversary Collection* is an extensive overview of one of the greatest musicians of the 20th century. Charles produced a body of work so rich and diverse that even five CDs only scratch the surface of his accomplishments. None of his instrumentals are on *Genius & Soul*, nor are his jazz and traditional pop efforts spotlighted. Instead, the box traces the evolution of his career, as he moves from an R&B pioneer to a mainstream pop crooner to a country-pop vocalist to a contemporary soul singer. Charles was a gripping, captivating vocalist, capable of making even bland music sound vital, but the fact is, his '70s and '80s recordings pale in comparison to his seminal '50s and '60s sides. Which means that the set becomes less compelling as it reaches the fifth disc, but the first three and a half discs are filled with timeless music that remains exciting, vital and altogether wondrous. —*Stephen Thomas Erlewine*

Complete Swing Time & Down Beat Recordings 1949-52 / 1949-1952 / Night Train ✦✦✦

Blues & Jazz / May 26, 1950-Jun. 26, 1959 / Rhino/Atlantic ✦✦✦✦✦
Another easy access point for Charles' seminal Atlantic catalog. This two-disc set is evenly split between his bluesiest sides on the first disc and a selection of his

greatest jazz sides on disc two (gorgeously showcasing the sax work of David "Fathead" Newman on several pieces). Charles was a masterful blues purveyor; his "I Believe to My Soul" is simultaneously invested with heartbreak and humor, while the earlier "Sinner's Prayer," "The Sun's Gonna Shine Again," and the gospel-based "A Fool for You" emanate both hope and deep pain. —*Bill Dahl*

☆ **The Birth of Soul** / 1951-1959 / Rhino ✦✦✦✦✦
The title isn't just hype—this absolutely essential three-disc box is where soul music first took shape and soared, courtesy of Ray Charles' church-soaked pipes and bedrock piano work. Brother Ray's formula for inventing the genre was disarmingly simple: he brought gospel intensity to the R&B world with his seminal "I Got a Woman," "Hallelujah I Love Her So," "Leave My Woman Alone," "You Be My Baby," and the primal 1959 call-and-response classic "What'd I Say." There's plenty of brilliant blues content within these 53 historic sides: Charles' mournful "Losing Hand," "Feelin' Sad," "Hard Times," and "Blackjack" ooze after-hours desperation. No blues collection should be without this boxed set, which comes with well-researched notes by Robert Palmer, a nicely illustrated accompanying booklet, and discographical info aplenty. —*Bill Dahl*

★ **The Best of Atlantic** / 1951-1961 / Rhino ✦✦✦✦✦
The 20-track compilation (only 12 tracks on cassette) *The Best of Atlantic* compiles all of Ray Charles' Top Ten R&B hits for Atlantic Records, from "I've Got a Woman" and "This Little Girl of Mine" to "Drown in My Own Tears," "Hallelujah I Love Her So," "Lonely Avenue," "(Night Time Is) The Right Time," and "What'd I Say (Part 1)." In addition to the big hits, there are minor hits that nevertheless showcase Charles at his peak, like "Swanee River Rock" and "Just for a Thrill." For fans that only want the hits and don't want to invest in the splendid three-disc set *The Birth of Soul*, *The Best of Atlantic* is an essential purchase. —*Stephen Thomas Erlewine*

The Great Ray Charles / 1956 / Atlantic ✦✦✦✦
This set is rather unusual, for it is strictly instrumental, allowing Ray Charles a rare opportunity to be a jazz-oriented pianist. Two selections are with a trio (bassist Oscar Pettiford joins Charles on "Black Coffee"), while the other six are with a septet taken from his big band of the period. Key among the sidemen are David Newman (soloing on both tenor and alto) and trumpeter Joseph Bridgewater; highlights include Quincy Jones' "The Ray," "My Melancholy Baby," "Doodlin'," and "Undecided." Ray Charles should have recorded in this setting more often in his later years. —*Scott Yanow*

The Genius After Hours / 1956 / Rhino ✦✦✦✦✦
Taken from the same three sessions as *The Great Ray Charles* but not duplicating any of the performances, this set casts Charles as a jazz-oriented pianist in an instrumental setting. Brother Ray has five numbers with a trio (three songs have Oscar Pettiford on bass) and jams three other tunes ("Hornful Soul," "Ain't Misbehavin'," and "Joy Ride") with a septet arranged by Quincy Jones; solo space is given to David "Fathead" Newman on tenor and alto and trumpeter Joseph Bridgewater. Fine music, definitely a change of pace for Ray Charles. —*Scott Yanow*

The Genius Hits the Road / 1956-1972 / Rhino ✦✦✦✦
In keeping with his jazz-pop crossover ambitions, Charles decided to record a concept album of sorts with a dozen songs devoted to various parts of the US—"Alabamy Bound," "Georgia on My Mind," "Moonlight in Vermont," "California, Here I Come," "Blue Hawaii," etc. The crossover vibe is further heightened by the brassy big-band arrangements, and material from the likes of Al Jolson and Hoagy Carmichael. It sounds a bit corny now, with an in-your-face gung-ho cheer. But it did what Charles wanted it to do, reaching the Top Ten of the album charts, and spinning off a big hit with "Georgia on My Mind." The 1997 CD reissue on Rhino adds seven bonus tracks from 1956-1972 that also had a travel/geographic theme, and the best of these are actually the highlights of the record, most notably "Hit the Road Jack," "Lonely Avenue," and his cover of Hank Snow's "I'm Movin' On." —*Richie Unterberger*

Soul Brothers/Soul Meeting / Sep. 12, 1957-Apr. 10, 1958 / Atlantic ✦✦✦✦
A great two-disc package that combined the pivotal Ray Charles sessions with Milt Jackson. The special release even had some bonus tracks, while the remastering and annotation were marvelous. There was no question about the quality of the tracks; Charles and Jackson were instantly compatible, with Jackson getting to display blues elements he normally suppressed when playing with the Modern Jazz Quartet, and Charles getting space to present his jazz and improvising skills. —*Ron Wynn*

Ray Charles at Newport / Jul. 5, 1958 / Atlantic ✦✦✦✦✦
For his appearance at the Newport Jazz Festival on July 5, 1958, Charles pulled out all the stops, performing raucous versions of "The Right Time," "I Got a Woman," and "Talkin' 'bout You." (This album was reissued in 1973 as a two-record set, packaged with *Ray Charles in Person* under the title *Ray Charles Live* [Atlantic SD 2-503].) —*William Ruhlmann*

The Genius of Ray Charles / 1959 / Atlantic ✦✦✦✦
Some players from Ray Charles' big band are joined by many ringers from the Count Basie and Duke Ellington bands for the first half of this program, featuring Charles belting out six songs arranged by Quincy Jones. "Let the Good Times Roll" and "Deed I Do" are highlights, and there are solos by tenorman David "Fathead" Newman, trumpeter Marcus Belgrave and (on "Two Years of Torture") tenor Paul Gonsalves. The remaining six numbers are ballads, with Charles backed by a string orchestra arranged by Ralph Burns (including "Come Rain or Come Shine" and "Don't Let the Sun Catch You Cryin'"). Ray Charles' voice is heard throughout in peak form, giving soul to even the veteran standards. —*Scott Yanow*

What'd I Say / May 28, 1959 / Atlantic ✦✦✦
At a concert held at Herndon Stadium in Atlanta on May 28, 1959, Ray Charles turns in a blistering version of "What'd I Say" and takes on the big band era with versions of Tommy Dorsey's "Yes Indeed!" and Artie Shaw's "Frenesi," not to mention performances of "The Right Time" and "Tell the Truth." (This album was reissued in 1960 under the title *Ray Charles in Person* and again in 1973 as a part of a two-record set, packaged with *Ray Charles at Newport* under the title *Ray Charles Live* (Atlantic 503). —*William Ruhlmann*

Standards / 1959-1977 / Rhino ✦✦✦✦
Standards is a 17-track collection of Ray Charles' versions of classic pop songs, culled recordings he made for Atlantic, ABC/Paramount, ABC/TRC and Crossover/Atlantic between 1959 and 1977. There are a handful of hits—"Georgia on My Mind," "Ruby," "That Lucky Old Sun," "Without Love (There Is Nothing)," "Makin' Whoopee"—but the collection concentrates on little-known album tracks and live cuts. Although the steady stream of repackages from Rhino can be a little overwhelming, the idea behind *Standards* is attractive, and it's executed well—it's nice to have all these songs on one collection, even if the live cuts can be a little distracting. Certainly, anyone looking for a collection of mellow ballads from Charles will not be disappointed by this set. —*Stephen Thomas Erlewine*

Genius + Soul Equals Jazz/My Kind of Jazz / Dec. 26, 1960-1970 / Rhino ✦✦✦✦
To launch Ray Charles' extensive Rhino reissue program, Rhino combined two of his jazz albums, *Genius + Soul Equals Jazz* and *My Kind of Jazz*. Although both records have "jazz" in their title, they are drastically different stylistically. *Genius + Soul* finds Charles playing Hammond organ with the Count Basie band, running through some Quincy Jones arrangements of standards such as "One Mint Julep." *My Kind of Jazz* is a totally different experience, functioning as his stab at funky soul-jazz. *Genius + Soul* is a better, more consistent record than *My Kind of Jazz*, but the latter is quite entertaining in its own right, and by presenting the two albums together this disc illustrates the depth and breadth of Charles' talent. —*Stephen Thomas Erlewine*

Genius + Soul Equals Jazz / 1960 / DCC ✦✦✦
This ABC/Paramount session (reissued on CD by the Audiophile DCC label) should have been a classic. Charles is joined by an all-star big band full of Count Basie sidemen, there are a few instrumentals (among the soloists are trumpeters Phillip Guilbeau and Clark Terry), and Brother Ray sings such standbys as "I'm Gonna Move to the Outskirts of Town," "I've Got News for You" and "Birth of the Blues." But for no logical reason, Charles plays organ instead of piano, and his lazy style causes this set to be much less interesting than it should have been, weighing down the music. The original LP program is augmented by three okay numbers from the 1960 album *Genius Hits the Road*. —*Scott Yanow*

Greatest Hits, Vol. 1 / 1961-1965 / DCC ✦✦✦✦✦
The first of two DCC compilations to collect the best of Brother Ray's 1960s stint at ABC-Paramount Records, when he flew off in a dozen different stylistic directions. Included on this 20-track disc are Charles' immortal rendering of "Georgia on My Mind," the sinuously bluesy "Unchain My Heart," the Latin-beat instrumental "One Mint Julep," personalized remakes of the country standards "Born to Lose," "Your Cheating Heart," and "Crying Time," and his exultant rendition of the soulful "Let's Go Get Stoned." —*Bill Dahl*

Greatest Hits, Vol. 2 / 1961-1965 / DCC ✦✦✦✦✦
More seminal performances from the '60s ABC catalog of the Genius (DCC split the classics evenly between the two discs, making both of them indispensable). His beloved "Hit the Road Jack" (one of several Percy Mayfield copyrights dotting Charles' repertoire), the daring country crossover "I Can't Stop Loving You," an electric-piano-powered "Sticks and Stones," a wise "Them That Got," and a wonderfully mellow "At the Club" rank with the 20-song disc's standouts (though versions of the Beatles' "Yesterday" and the corny "Look What They Done to My Song, Ma" end the set on a bummer note). —*Bill Dahl*

Ray Charles & Betty Carter / Jun. 13, 1961-1966 / ABC/Paramount ✦✦✦✦
This pairing of two totally idiosyncratic vocalists acquired legendary status over the decades in which it had been out of print. But the proof is in the listening, and frankly it doesn't represent either artist's best work. There is certainly a powerful,

often sexy rapport between the two—Charles in his sweet balladeering mode, Carter with her uniquely keening, drifting high register—and they definitely create sparks in the justly famous rendition of "Baby, It's Cold Outside." The main problem is in Marty Paich's string/choir arrangements, which too often cross over the line into treacle, whereas his charts for big band are far more listenable. Moreover, Charles' sweetness can get a bit cloying too, although some of the old grit emerges on "Takes Two to Tango." On the CD reissue—remixed by Charles himself—Dunhill adds the great, rare B-side to the "Unchain My Heart" single, "But on the Other Hand Baby," and two excellent if unrelated album cuts, "I Never See Maggie Alone" (1964) and "I Like to Hear It Sometime" (1966). —*Richard S. Ginell*

☆ **Modern Sounds in Country & Western Music** / 1961-1962 / Rhino ✦✦✦✦✦
Modern Sounds in Country & Western Music is historically important, and considered by most critics to be a classic, but some have mixed feelings about it. Charles' interpretations of songs previously recorded by Hank Williams, Eddy Arnold, Floyd Tillman, and Don Gibson are superb, but so often the arrangements by Marty Paich, Gerald Wilson, and Gil Fuller threaten to drown him in a sea of lachrymose bric-a-brac. "I Can't Stop Loving You" and "You Don't Know Me" were Top Ten pop and R&B. —*Rob Bowman*

☆ **Modern Sounds in Country & Western, Vol. 2** / 1962 / Rhino ✦✦✦✦✦
Charles' second installment of *Modern Sounds in Country and Western Music* is every bit as essential as the first, containing stellar interpretations of "Your Cheatin' Heart" and "You Are My Sunshine." —*Stephen Thomas Erlewine*

Ingredients in a Recipe for Soul / Jul. 1963 / DCC ✦✦✦
Although it was a big commercial success, reaching No. 2 on the LP charts, this record would typify the erratic nature of much of Charles' '60s output. It's too eclectic for its own good, really, encompassing pop standards, lowdown blues, Mel Tormé songs, and after-hours ballads. The high points are very high—"Busted," his hit reworking of a composition by country songwriter Harlan Howard, is jazzy and tough, and one of his best early-'60s singles. And the low points are very low, especially when he adds the snow-white backup vocals of the Jack Halloran Singers to "Over the Rainbow" and "Ol' Man River." A number of the remaining cuts are fairly respectable, such as the tight big-band arrangement of "Ol' Man Time" and the ominously urbane "Where Can I Go?" In 1997, it was paired with the 1964 LP *Have a Smile with Me* on a two-for-one CD reissue on Rhino, with the addition of historical liner notes. —*Richie Unterberger*

Ingredients in a Recipe for Soul/Have a Smile with Me / 1963-1964 / Rhino ✦✦✦
A two-for-one pairing of albums from 1963 (*Recipe for Soul*) and 1964 (*Have a Smile with Me*), with the addition of historical liner notes. Neither rate among his better albums—both are inconsistent mixtures of hard-edged jazz/pop/soul and mainstream pop standards. Each, though, has some fine cuts, notably the Top Ten hit "Busted" (on *Recipe*) and a jazzy cover of Hank Williams' "Move It On Over" (on *Smile*). The CD also adds two bonus tracks: both parts of the orchestral pop "Without a Song" single from 1965. —*Richie Unterberger*

Sweet & Sour Tears / 1964 / Rhino ✦✦✦
One of a series of ultra-loose concept albums Charles cut in the '60s, this one dedicated entirely to songs with titles or lyrical references to crying and tears. It's an excuse for Ray to choose his usual varied menu of upbeat jumpers, slow countrified weepers, and proudly saccharine pop standards. The production, as one might fear, also tends to the lachrymose side on the slow tunes, with the thick strings and backup vocals straight out of TV variety shows. One is almost tempted to think that Charles was toying with audience expectations by mixing unabashedly sentimental slow tunes with the far more bluesy, satisfying, and upbeat numbers, such as "Don't Cry, Baby" and "Baby, Don't You Cry," as well as his surprisingly brassy, punchy treatment of "Cry Me a River." These outings have always played much better with critics than the gloppy pop tunes, and for good reason—they are much better. The Rhino CD reissue adds seven bonus tracks from throughout his early career (1956-71) that also tapped into the "crying" motif. These threaten to steal the show from the *Sweet & Sour Tears* album it's supposedly embellishing, including the Bacharach-David penned 1964 single "I Wake Up Crying," the smoldering 1966 album track "No Use Crying," and the 1956 R&B chart-topper "Drown in My Own Tears," next to which much of the rest of the program sounds positively hokey. —*Richie Unterberger*

Have a Smile with Me / 1964 / ABC/Paramount ✦✦
The idea behind this LP was to offer a lighthearted sequel to its quasi-concept predecessor, *Sweet and Sour Tears*. There's nothing wrong with the idea of letting Ray just kick back and have fun, but "The Thing" and "The Man with the Weird Beard" transcend the boundaries of humor into silliness and, worse, stupidity. On the other hand, he also turns out a good jazzy version of Hank Williams' "Move It on Over" (the record's highlight), and manages to swing through fairly superficial fare such as "Ma (She's Making Eyes at Me)" and "Two Ton Tessie" with solid flair.

It was another inconsistent '60s set, the shortage of top-notch tunes disguised by a flimsy concept, though he elevates the material with soulful vocals and good arrangements, particularly when the Raeletts back him up (as they do on half the tracks). In 1997, it was paired with the 1963 LP *Ingredients in a Recipe for Soul* on a two-for-one CD reissue on Rhino, with the addition of historical liner notes. —*Richie Unterberger*

My Kind of Jazz / Apr. 1970 / Tangerine ✦✦✦✦

This LP came seemingly out of the blue as a showcase for the Ray Charles big band, spawning two little-known sequels later on in the '70s. It's a roaring, solid band, too, playing jazz standards like "This Here," "The Sidewinder," "Bluesette" and "Senor Blues," comfortable at slow loping tempos as well as in the rousers, with excellent mainstream soloists (none of whom are identified) and good conventional charts (also uncredited). The sole exception to the pattern—and a hit single in its own right—is a catchy, funky, Charles gospel/blues called "Booty Butt," where Ray adds multi-tracked gospel moans for his sole vocal contribution and the band chimes in only on the very last chord. Clearly the title and the appalling lack of credits say volumes about Charles' reputation as a control freak; this is his kind of jazz and nobody else's. —*Richard S. Ginell*

Ain't It So / Sep. 1979 / Atlantic ✦✦✦

One of the better albums from Charles' second sojourn at Atlantic in the '70s. Here, he gives us an uptempo version of Irving Berlin's "What'll I Do," and similarly revamps such standards as "Some Enchanted Evening" and "Blues in the Night." —*William Ruhlmann*

Teddy Charles (Theodore Charles Cohen)

b. Apr. 13, 1928, Chicopee Falls, MA

Vibes / Cool

Teddy Charles is a true rarity: a jazz musician who largely retired from the business. A skillful if not overly distinctive vibraphonist and (early in his career) quite capable on piano and drums, Charles was as important for his open-minded approach in the 1950s towards more advanced sounds as he was for his playing. He moved to New York to study percussion at Juilliard in 1946, but instead became involved in the jazz world. He had short stints with the big bands of Randy Brooks, Benny Goodman, Artie Shaw, Buddy DeFranco and Chubby Jackson from 1948-51 and then played with combos headed by Anita O'Day, Oscar Pettiford, Roy Eldridge and Slim Gaillard. He also became a member of the Jazz Composers' Workshop (1953-55) along with Charles Mingus and Teo Macero, opening his style up to the influences of classical music and freer improvising. Charles, who recorded with Mingus, Miles Davis and Wardell Gray, among many others, began leading his own stimulating record dates in 1951, and by 1953 he was also working as a record producer, a field that took much more of his time from 1956 on. He led his own sessions for Prestige, Atlantic, Savoy, Jubilee, Bethlehem (where he produced around 40 records, mostly for other artists) and Warwick from 1951-60, but was hardly heard from in the 1960s, other than a 1963 set for United Artists. Charles relocated to the Caribbean, where he opened a sailing business. After participating in a 1980 jam session, Teddy Charles eventually moved back to New York, making a "comeback" record for Soul Note in 1988, but still remaining semi-retired from music. —*Scott Yanow*

Collaboration: West / Dec. 23, 1952-Aug. 31, 1953 / Original Jazz Classics ✦✦✦

Vibraphonist Teddy Charles heads three West Coast-style sessions on this CD reissue that look a bit towards Third Stream and the avant-garde experiments of the early '60s. Although there are some swinging sections, much of the music is quite complex with difficult arrangements and some polytonality. One session has Charles (who doubles on piano) in a quartet with guitarist Jimmy Raney (those four numbers were not on the original LP) while the other originals feature trumpeter Shorty Rogers, bassist Curtis Counce, drummer Shelly Manne and sometimes Jimmy Giuffre on tenor and baritone. The music is thought-provoking if a bit cold and clinical, easier to respect than to love. —*Scott Yanow*

Evolution / Aug. 31, 1953+Jan. 6, 1955 / Original Jazz Classics ✦✦✦✦

Although somewhat overlooked in the jazz history books, vibraphonist Teddy Charles was for a period an important participant in the early Third Stream movement, using aspects of classical music to revitalize West Coast-style jazz. This CD reissue features trumpeter Shorty Rogers, tenor saxophonist Jimmy Giuffre, bassist Curtis Counce and drummer Shelly Manne on a couple of advanced originals (one apiece by Giuffre and Rogers) from 1953. After moving to New York, Charles teamed up for a short time with bassist Charles Mingus, performing six other numbers in a quartet with tenor saxophonist J.R. Monterose and drummer Gerry Segal. This session alternates cookers with sensitive ballads and is one of the better recorded showcases for Charles' vibes. Recommended. —*Scott Yanow*

● **Tentet [Jazzlore 48]** / Jan. 6, 1956-Nov. 12, 1956 / Atlantic ✦✦✦✦✦

Most of this CD features vibraphonist Teddy Charles heading an advanced tentet in 1956, a unit including the likes of trumpeter Art Farmer, altoist Gigi Gryce, tenor saxophonist J.R. Monterose, pianist Mal Waldron and guitarist Jimmy Raney. The arrangements of George Russell ("Lydian M-1"), Gil Evans (a year before *Miles Ahead*), Jimmy Giuffre, Mal Waldron and Charles are quite advanced but often leave room for some swinging spots. The final three selections on the CD are actually taken from a slightly later album. Of these, "Blue Greens" is a change of pace, a quartet outing for Charles, pianist Hall Overton, bassist Charles Mingus and drummer Ed Shaughnessy. All in all, this CD is fairly definitive of Teddy Charles' more adventurous music of the 1950s and it grows in interest with each listening. —*Scott Yanow*

Coolin' / Apr. 14, 1957 / Original Jazz Classics ✦✦✦✦

Although this sextet session was officially a co-op, vibraphonist Teddy Charles and pianist Mal Waldron were really the main organizers. The group plays five originals by band members that often have complex melodies but familiar chord changes. Trumpeter Idrees Sulieman excels on the one standard ("Everything Happens to Me"), altoist John Jenkins (making his recording debut) has some worthy solos and both bassist Addison Farmer and drummer Jerry Segal are fine in support. This obscure session (reissued on CD in the OJC series) is an excellent outing. —*Scott Yanow*

The Vibraphone Players of Bethlehem, Vol. 1 / Feb. 10, 1959 / Bethlehem ✦✦✦

Subtitled "Salute to Hamp," this CD reissue (available through Evidence) is a tribute to Lionel Hampton by his fellow vibraphonist Teddy Charles. Originally nine numbers, the new set adds six additional selections. Charles is the main soloist although there is some space for his notable sidemen (including pianist Hank Jones, valve trombonist Bob Brookmeyer, Zoot Sims on tenor and trumpeter Art Farmer) but few fireworks occur. The end results, even with occasional uptempo tunes, are a bit too relaxed and tasteful to recreate the excitement of a typical Lionel Hampton performance. —*Scott Yanow*

On Campus! / Nov. 21, 1959 / Fresh Sound ✦✦✦

This CD brings back a Bethlehem session, a rather unusual Teddy Charles set in that it is very much a jam session. Oddly enough Charles (despite being designated leader) is only on four of the nine numbers. With pianist Dave McKenna, bassist Bill Crow and drummer Ed Shaughnessy forming a swinging rhythm section, Charles is showcased on three numbers ("Yale Blue," "Whiffenpoof song" and "Nigerian Walk"), flutist Sam Most jams "That Old Black Magic," Zoot Sims is featured on two standards, Dave McKenna romps through "Struttin' with Some Barbecue," guitarist Jimmy Raney drops by for "Yesterdays" and the whole group comes together on "Rifftide." Few surprises occur but the obscure straightahead music is enjoyable enough. —*Scott Yanow*

Live at the Verona Jazz Festival (1988) / Jun. 25, 1988 / Soul Note ✦✦✦✦

Concert date with Harold Danko trio. Highlight is the Mingus composition "Nostalgia in Times Square." —*Michael G. Nastos*

The Charleston Chasers

Group / Big Band, Classic Jazz

The Charleston Chasers was a name used for a series of recording groups during the 1925-31 period; the jazz-oriented dance bands did not exist outside of the studios. The 1925 edition (which recorded two numbers) matched cornetist Leo McConville with trombonist Miff Mole and pianist Arthur Schutt. By their second session two years later, the Charleston Chasers was a group similar to Red Nichols' Five Pennies with Nichols on cornet, trombonist Mole, Jimmy Dorsey on clarinet and alto (he was later replaced by clarinetist Pee Wee Russell) and usually pianist Schutt, Dick McDonough on banjo or guitar, Joe Tarto on tuba and the inventive drummer Vic Berton. Other than two songs by a similar band (plus singer Scrappy Lambert) in 1928, the Charleston Chasers was inactive until mid-1929, when trumpeter Phil Napoleon became its lead voice. At first using Mole, Dorsey and Schutt, the group at various times included clarinetist Benny Goodman and trombonist Tommy Dorsey, along with Roy Evans and Eva Taylor on vocals. Probably the best-known session under the Charleston Chasers name was the final one, four songs cut on Feb. 9, 1931, by an 11-piece group that included trumpeter Charlie Teagarden, both Jack Teagarden and Glenn Miller on trombones, Benny Goodman and drummer Gene Krupa. While two songs had pop vocals by Paul Small, the renditions of "Basin Street Blues" and "Beale Street Blues" (featuring famous Jack Teagarden vocals) were arguably the high point of the group's existence and alone would have guaranteed the band's immortality. —*Scott Yanow*

Doc Cheatham (Adolphus Anthony Cheatham)

b. Jun. 13, 1905, Nashville, TN, **d.** Jun. 2, 1997, Washington D.C.
Trumpet, Vocals / Dixieland, Swing, Traditional Jazz

Doc Cheatham was without question the greatest 90-year-old trumpeter of all time; in fact no brass player over the age of 80 had ever played with his power, range, confidence and melodic creativity. Most trumpeters fade while in their 60s due to the physical difficulty of their instrument, but Cheatham did not truly find himself as a soloist until he was nearly 70!

Doc Cheatham's career reaches back to the early '20s when he played in vaudeville theatres backing such travelling singers as Bessie Smith and Clara Smith. He moved to Chicago, recorded with Ma Rainey (on soprano sax!), played with Albert Wynn, subbed for Louis Armstrong (his main idol) and had his own group in 1926. After stints with Wilbur DeParis and Chick Webb, he toured Europe with Sam Wooding. Due to his wide range and pretty tone, Cheatham worked as a non-soloing first trumpeter with McKinney's Cotton Pickers and Cab Calloway throughout the 1930s. He spent time with Teddy Wilson's big band and was with the commercially successful Eddie Heywood Sextet (backing Billie Holiday on some recordings). In the 1950s Cheatham alternated between Dixieland (Wilbur DeParis, guest spots with Eddie Condon) and Latin (Perez Prado, Herbie Mann) bands. He was with Benny Goodman during 1966-67 but it was not until the mid-'70s that Cheatham felt truly comfortable as a soloist. After pianist Sammy Price launched his new career and until his death in 1997 he recorded fairly prolifically including dates for Sackville, New York Jazz, Parkwood, Stash, GHB, Columbia and several European labels. Cheatham was also a charming singer whose half-spoken, half-sung vocals took nothing away from his chance-taking trumpet flights. *—Scott Yanow*

Hey Doc! / May 2, 1975 / Black & Blue ✦✦✦

Duets & Solos / Nov. 17, 1976-Nov. 1, 1979 / Sackville ✦✦✦✦
The music of three Sackville LPs is reissued on full in this double-CD set, a 1979 solo session by pianist Sammy Price and a pair of duet albums with trumpeter Doc Cheatham from 1976 and 1979. Cheatham, who was 71 at the time of the earlier date, was just beginning to emerge as a major soloist and in fact is in much more confident form on the later set where he makes many dramatic statements than on the first session. Price, who was three years younger than Doc, shows throughout the two-fer that he was much more than a blues and boogie-woogie specialist. The music mostly consists of veteran standards from the 1920s and '30s and even the most familiar songs sound fresh in this sparse setting. *—Scott Yanow*

Good for What Ails Ya / May 2, 1977 / Classic Jazz ✦✦✦✦
This Dixielandish session features the ageless trumpeter Doc Cheatham (who was then 71 and still improving) in a sextet with trombonist Gene "Mighty Flea" Conners, altoist Ted Buckner, pianist Sammy Price, bassist Carl Pruitt and drummer J.C. Heard on eight veteran standards. It is great fun to hear these classic players jam on this kind of tunes as "Rosetta," "What Can I Say Dear After I Say I'm Sorry?" and "Rose Room." *—Scott Yanow*

I've Got a Crush on You / Oct. 25, 1982-Oct. 26, 1982 / New York Jazz ✦✦✦
The playing time on this LP is brief (under 32 minutes) but this is a particularly strong showcase for trumpeter Doc Cheatham (who was then 77). Cheatham is heard on four duets with guitarist Howard Alden, taking the vocals and playing some heated but relaxed trumpet. The other four selections feature him with an octet that also allocates a generous amount of solo space to bassist Milt Hinton. *—Scott Yanow*

Too Marvelous for Words / Oct. 25, 1982-Oct. 26, 1982 / New York Jazz ✦✦✦
Veteran trumpeter Doc Cheatham is in fine form on this session with the Hot Jazz Orchestra of New York, an octet that also includes trombonist Dan Barrett, Joe Muranyi's reeds, guitarist Howard Alden and a fine rhythm section; there is one vocal apiece by Cynthia Sayer, Lew Micallef and Eddy Davis. The playing time is a bit brief even for an LP (just over a half-hour) and few surprises occur but this set is still quite enjoyable. *—Scott Yanow*

It's a Good Life / Dec. 6, 1982-Dec. 7, 1982 / Parkwood ✦✦✦✦
The 77-year-old trumpeter proves to be very much in his prime during this excellent session. In fact Cheatham, who is backed by a fine rhythm section led by pianist Chuck Folds, dominates this set, taking melodic but passionate trumpet solos and contributing charming vocals. His versions of "Struttin' with Some Barbecue" and "You're Lucky to Me" are particularly memorable. *—Scott Yanow*

At the Bern Jazz Festival / Apr. 30, 1983-Jan. 5, 1985 / Sackville ✦✦✦✦
Veteran trumpeter Doc Cheatham and soprano saxophonist Jim Galloway co-lead these three separate live sessions. The sextet (which also includes trombonist Roy Williams) explores a variety of standards including "Cherry," "Love Is Just Around the Corner," "Swing That Music" and a ballad medley. Everyone is in fine form on this small-group swing CD. *—Scott Yanow*

● **The Fabulous** / Nov. 16, 1983-Nov. 17, 1983 / Parkwood ✦✦✦✦✦
The ageless trumpeter Doc Cheatham (who was 78 years old at the time of this studio session) is remarkable. Most trumpeters fade when they hit their 60s, but he continues to gain in strength, hitting reasonably high notes with confidence and power; his melodic invention also continues to develop. This quartet session with the late pianist Dick Wellstood is one of his finest recordings. Cheatham is in particularly top form on "Deed I Do," "Swing That Music" and "I Double Dare You," but all nine selections (which also feature his charming whispered vocals) are quite enjoyable. *—Scott Yanow*

Highlights in Jazz / Dec. 12, 1985 / Stash ✦✦
This overly loose LP teams together the great veteran trumpeter Doc Cheatham with tenor saxophonist George Kelly and Joey Cavaseno (doubling on clarinet and alto) for six standards. Although Cheatham sounds fine, the performances tend to be overly long and they ramble a bit. This live swing-oriented music has its moments but is not too essential. *—Scott Yanow*

Tribute to Billie Holiday / May 13, 1987-May 14, 1987 / Kenneth ✦✦✦✦
Doc Cheatham (a month short of turning age 82) is in excellent form on this set of eight songs associated with Billie Holiday. Fortunately, the octet avoids the obvious tunes like "God Bless the Child" and "Lover Man" and instead plays songs such as "I Cried for You" and "On the Sunny Side of the Street" that are more adaptable as jazz instrumentals (although Cheatham does take a couple of vocals). Joined by a band filled with top Swedish players, he is in excellent form for this heartfelt and successful tribute. *—Scott Yanow*

Tribute to Louis Armstrong / May 6, 1988-May 7, 1988 / Kenneth ✦✦✦✦
Listening to Doc Cheatham play trumpet on this Louis Armstrong tribute, it is impossible to believe that he was nearly 83 years old. Cheatham's solos are played with confidence and power and they display a still impressive range; there is nothing feeble about his sound. Cheatham performs ten songs associated with Louis Armstrong assisted by a group of Swedish all-stars and Armstrong's former pianist Dick Cary. He comes up with fresh interpretations on such songs as "Swing That Music," "Our Monday Date," and "Jeepers Creepers" on this easily recommended LP. *—Scott Yanow*

Dear Doc / Aug. 30, 1988-Aug. 31, 1988 / Orange Blue ✦✦✦✦
An excellent outing, this little-known French CD features the ageless Doc Cheatham when he was a mere 83. Assisted by pianist Kenny Drew, bassist Jimmy Woode and drummer Idris Muhammad, Cheatham is the main star throughout, displaying a strong range, plenty of power and ideas that are both creative and melodic in addition to taking some charming vocals. Highlights include "I Only Have Eyes for You," "Dinah," "I Double Dare You," "Rump Steak Serenade" and "New Orleans." Worth searching for. *—Scott Yanow*

You're a Sweetheart / Mar. 29, 1992+Nov. 15, 1992 / Sackville ✦✦✦
Trumpeter Doc Cheatham (87 at the time) gets top billing and is well featured on six of this CD's 11 selections, but the release from the Canadian label Sackville is more significant for helping to introduce Rosemary Galloway's Swing Sisters. This fine quintet (originally all women but now just three out of five) features the excellent trumpeter Sarah McElcheran and the local legend Jane Fair on tenor and clarinet. The repertoire mostly consists of swing obscurities and Cheatham is delightful during his two vocals (sharing "Baby It's Cold Outside" with the bassist/leader). The performances without Cheatham sound quite a bit more modern, leaning more towards early-'60s hard bop. This well-rounded set has some fine individual moments. *—Scott Yanow*

Echoes of New Orleans / Apr. 18, 1992 / Big Easy ✦✦✦✦
The remarkable Doc Cheatham, two months shy of 87 at the time, leads a fine sextet through a variety of Dixieland and swing numbers on this live set. Clarinetist Sammy Rimington has some good solos; trombonist Jerry Zigmont, pianist Jon Marks and drummer John Russell are competent without leaving much of an impression; and bassist Arvell Shaw is in top form, taking a couple of spirited vocals. However, it is Cheatham who dominates the upbeat performances, which range from "Clarinet Marmalade" and "Pennies from Heaven" to "Ain't Misbehavin'" and "Struttin' with Some Barbecue." *—Scott Yanow*

The Eighty-Seven Years of Doc Cheatham / Sep. 17, 1992+Sep. 18, 1992 / Columbia ✦✦✦✦✦
There has never been a trumpeter in recorded history over the age of 80 on Doc Cheatham's level. Age 87 at the time of this CD, he plays with power, creativity and confidence on this quartet set of swing standards. He dominates the music with his trumpet solos and quiet but charming vocals and, even with the participation of a strong rhythm section led by pianist Chuck Folds, Cheatham is the obvious star. This historic set is a real gem on several levels and is highly recommended. *—Scott Yanow*

Doc Cheatham & Nicholas Payton / Oct. 9, 1994 / Verve ◆◆◆◆◆

This matchup between trumpeters Doc Cheatham (91 at the time) and Nicholas Payton (just 23) is quite logical and delightful. Cheatham, one of the few survivors of the 1920s, was still in remarkably fine form, while Payton (a flexible New Orleans player capable of ranging from Dixieland to Freddie Hubbard) is both respectful and inspiring. With Doc contributing occasional vocals and the settings ranging from a quartet to an octet with clarinetist Jack Maheu and pianist Butch Thompson, the brassmen explore a variety of 1920s and '30s standards, including a couple of obscurities ("Do You Believe in Love at Sight?" and "Maybe"). The interplay between the co-leaders, the many subtle tributes to Louis Armstrong, and the consistent enthusiasm of this swinging set make this a historic success and a very enjoyable outing. —*Scott Yanow*

Jeannie and Jimmy Cheatham

Vocals, Piano / Swing, Kansas City Blues

The husband and wife duo of Jimmy & Jeannie Cheatham have been working together since the mid-'50s and married since the late '50s. Her energetic, joyful vocals and his good-natured trombone riffs and accompaniment have been featured on a succession of fine Concord albums in the '80s and '90s. But their professional affiliation began after they met on stage in Buffalo during the '50s. Jeannie Cheatham had performed in clubs, while Jimmy Cheatham had played in Broadway bands and on television, as well as with Bill Dixon, Duke Ellington, Lionel Hampton, Thad Jones and Ornette Coleman. He'd even been Chico Hamilton's music director. Jeannie Cheatham studied piano as a child, later accompanied Dinah Washington, Al Hibbler and Jimmy Witherspoon among others. They attended the University of Wisconsin in the '70s and taught in the jazz program, then moved to San Diego in the late '70s. While Jimmy Cheatham taught at the University of California, Jeannie was president of the Lower California Jazz Society. The duo worked in clubs and organized weekly jam sessions. Jeannie Cheatham appeared on a public television special with Sippie Wallace and Big Mama Thornton that was shown in 1983. Concord signed the duo in the mid-'80s, and they've been recording ever since, working with both their regular band and such special guests as Charles McPherson, Eddie "Lockjaw" Davis, Eddie "Cleanhead" Vinson and Red Callendar. —*Ron Wynn*

Sweet Baby Blues / Sep. 1984 / Concord Jazz ◆◆◆◆◆

The debut release by Jeannie and Jimmy Cheatham's Sweet Baby Blues Band is the first of their many very enjoyable recordings. Jeannie's powerful piano playing and strong voice are major assets, but the octet also has five major horn soloists (trumpeter Snooky Young, both Curtis Peagler and Charles McPherson on altos, bass trombonist Jimmy Cheatham, and making his debut, Jimmie Noone, Jr., on soprano and clarinet), plus veteran Red Callender (on bass and tuba) and drummer John "Ironman" Harris. The spirited ensemble plays five Kansas City blues standards and three originals, including their hit "Meet Me with Your Black Drawers On." Wonderful and swinging music. —*Scott Yanow*

Midnight Mama / Nov. 1985 / Concord Jazz ◆◆◆◆

For their second release, the Cheathams not only featured five top horn soloists (trumpeter Snooky Young, altoist Curtis Peagler, both Dinky Morris and Jimmie Noone, Jr., on tenor, and bass trombonist Jimmy Cheatham), but also guest tenor Eddie "Lockjaw" Davis. (Noone and Davis alternate.) Pianist/singer Jeannie Cheatham is the lead voice, but there is plenty of solo space, while the rhythm section (bassist Red Callender and drummer John "Ironman" Harris) drives the ensembles. The program is split between older blues and more recent originals in a similar style, all of it swinging. A special highlight is the trio feature on "Midnight Mama." Spirited music that crosses many boundaries. —*Scott Yanow*

Homeward Bound / Jan. 1987 / Concord Jazz ◆◆◆◆

This time around, the Cheathams' guest is altoist/singer Eddie "Cleanhead" Vinson—a perfect choice, since his ability to play both blues and Kansas City swing/bop is similar to the style of the Sweet Baby Blues Band. Although the emphasis is on swinging blues, there are a few departures, including Jeannie Cheatham's wistful vocal on "Detour Ahead," and a hot instrumental "Homeward Bound." In addition to Vinson and Jeannie (a splendid pianist), soloists include the tenors of Jimmie Noone, Jr. (doubling on clarinet), and Dinky Morris, altoist Curtis Peagler, trumpeter Snooky Young and bass trombonist Jimmy Cheatham. Not to be overlooked are bassist Red Callender and drummer John "Ironman" Harris. But it is the heated and riffing ensembles, along with the pure joy this band generates, that make all of their Concord recordings easily recommended. —*Scott Yanow*

Back to the Neighborhood / Nov. 1988 / Concord Jazz ◆◆◆◆

The Sweet Baby Blues Band not only expanded from an octet to a nonet by this time, but welcomed guest violinist Papa John Creech to three of the nine selections. The music is full of Jeannie Cheatham's catchy and soulful vocals, riffing ensembles and hot soloists. Four bluesy standards are joined by five Cheathams-penned originals, including "Big Bubba's Back Rub Boogie Blues," "Rock Me in

Your Arms Tonight" and "Take the Wrinkles out Your Birthday Suit." In addition to Jeannie and Creech, soloists include both Snooky Young and Clora Bryant on trumpets; bass trombonist Jimmy Cheatham; altoist Curtis Peagler; Jimmie Noone, Jr., on tenor, soprano and clarinet; and baritonist Dinky Morris; as usual, bassist Red Callender and drummer John "Ironman" Harris are quite supportive. Because Noone was ailing, Herman Riley replaces him on half of the selections. The performances bridge the gap between swing and blues, bop and early R&B. Fun and very enjoyable music. —*Scott Yanow*

Luv in the Afternoon / May 1990 / Concord Jazz ◆◆◆◆

The Sweet Baby Blues Band is a perfect mixture of big band swing (with colorful arrangements by Jimmy Cheatham), jazz soloing and the blues. Unlike most blues bands that utilize a horn section, there is a generous amount of solo space for nearly all of the sidemen but, unlike most jazz groups, a blues star such as Clarence "Gatemouth" Brown can also feel at home sitting in on three numbers as he does on this release. Jeannie Cheatham's vocals are both properly emotional and easy to understand while her piano playing is a credit to the Kansas City blues tradition. The tunes on this CD range from Muddy Waters' "Baby Please Don't Go," Buddy Johnson's "You Won't Let Me Go" and Danny Barker's famous "Don't You Feel My Leg" (done here as an instrumental featuring trumpeter Snooky Young) to a variety of original blues and the bluish ballad "Trav'lin Light." With the other soloists including altoist Curtis Peagler, clarinetist Jimmy Noone, Jr., and trumpeter Nolan Smith, *Luv in the Afternoon* is very enjoyable and highly recommended. —*Scott Yanow*

Basket Full of Blues / Nov. 6, 1991-Nov. 8, 1991 / Concord Jazz ◆◆◆◆◆

For their sixth Concord recording, there was a major change in the personnel of the Cheathams' Sweet Baby Blues Band. Jimmie Noone, Jr., had passed away, and his replacement was the popular tenor Rickey Woodard, who on this set also plays some effective alto and clarinet (the latter on "Buddy Bolden's Blues"). But Woodard is only one of a bunch of colorful soloists, which include pianist/singer Jeannie Cheatham, Jimmy Cheatham on bass trombone, altoist Curtis Peagler, Snooky Young and Nolan Smith on trumpets, baritonist Dinky Morris and guest Frank Wess on tenor and flute. With bassist Red Callender and drummer John "Ironman" Harris keeping the ensembles swinging and driving, this is a particularly memorable set. Three standards are joined by nine originals by the Cheathams, including "Blues Like Jay McShann," "Baby, Where Have You Been," "Ballad of the Wannabes" and "Don't Cha Boogie with Your Black Drawers Off." —*Scott Yanow*

● **Blues & The Boogie Masters** / Jul. 1993 / Concord Jazz ◆◆◆◆◆

The Kansas City swing blues of the Sweet Baby Blues Band is very difficult not to enjoy. Jeannie Cheatham's exuberant vocals (propelled by her forcefully swinging piano) inspire the many soloists on the blues-oriented material, and there is plenty of variety in tempo and feeling to keep this set continually interesting. Among the main soloists are the ageless trumpeter Snooky Young, tenorman Rickey Woodard (making his debut on clarinet on two cuts) and guest altoist Hank Crawford who sits in on four songs. —*Scott Yanow*

Gud Nuz Bluz / Sep. 27, 1995-Sep. 28, 1995 / Concord Jazz ◆◆◆◆

The Cheathams' Sweet Baby Blues Band, a five-horn octet that emphasizes Kansas City-style blues with occasional room for a ballad or a standard, is such fun to hear that it is surprising that it has not been more influential. Other than Roomful of Blues, it is difficult to think of a similar ensemble that, even with a strong vocalist (Jeannie Cheatham), leaves plenty of space for the horns to romp individually and as an ensemble. Too often in blues and R&B, the saxes and brass are confined to repetitive riffing. Such is not the case with this group. On their eighth release for Concord, the Cheathams feature fine solos from Rickey Woodard (on tenor, clarinet and soprano), altoist Louis Taylor, Charles Owens (baritone and bass clarinet), trumpeter Nolan Smith and co-leader Jimmy Cheatham on bass trombone in addition to the pianist-singer. As if that were not enough, trumpeter Snooky Young joins in on three numbers and guest tenor Plas Johnson gets to jam on four others. Highlights include a tenor battle by Plas and Woodard on a tribute to Curtis Peagler ("Mr. C.P."), the interplay between Woodard's clarinet and Owens' bass clarinet during "Low Line Blues" and the high-note outbursts of Snooky Young. Jeannie Cheatham is in good voice throughout and this group sounds as spirited and rambunctious as ever. A perfect jazz party band. —*Scott Yanow*

Chelsea Bridge

f. 1992

Group / Post-Bop

An excellent Canadian jazz quartet comprising Rob Frayne on tenor and soprano, bassist John Geggie, drummer Jean Martin and singer Tena Palmer (whose voice is effectively integrated as part of the group's ensemble), the group (which has recorded several CDs for Unity) mostly plays originals by Frayne, Geggie and Palmer. Their spontaneous performances are adventurous but also often melodic and accessible. —*Scott Yanow*

Blues in a Sharp Sea / Oct. 11, 1992-Oct. 13, 1992 / Unity ✦✦✦✦

Ranging from advanced straightahead to freer explorations, the Canadian group Chelsea Bridge is a quartet notable for including singer Tena Palmer's voice as part of the ensembles. With Rob Frayne (tenor, soprano and flute), bassist John Geggie and drummer Jean Martin all proving to be alert team players and fine soloists, and Palmer displaying an appealing voice, Chelsea Bridge is an excellent post-bop group. Their debut release, on which ten of the eleven selections are originals by group members, was a strong start for this very interesting unit. —*Scott Yanow*

Tatamagouche—Next Left / Dec. 4, 1993-Dec. 7, 1993 / Unity ✦✦✦✦

● **Double Feature** / Mar. 16, 1995-Mar. 17, 1995 / Unity ✦✦✦✦

Chelsea Bridge is an intriguing Canadian quartet that stars Rob Frayne on tenor and flute along with singer Tena Palmer. On this mostly live set, the postbop unit is joined by six other musicians including two trumpeters, two woodwinds, baritonist David Mott and guitarist Roddy Ellias. They perform nine originals that contain plenty of memorable moments and moods ranging from eccentric to haunting. Palmer's voice is a major asset in the ensembles and on "Real Estate" she proves to be a strong interpreter of lyrics. Baritonist Mott's unaccompanied display on the dramatic "A Lament for the Clear-Cut Atlantic" and Ellias' emotional guitar make strong impressions. This otherwise rewarding set however would have benefitted from liner notes that identified the soloists and told the stories behind some of the stranger song titles. —*Scott Yanow*

Don Cherry

b. Nov. 18, 1936, Oaklahoma City, OK, **d.** Oct. 19, 1995, Malaga, Spain

Cornet, Flute / Free Jazz, Avant-Garde, World Fusion

The second track from *Tomorrow Is the Question*—Ornette Coleman's 1959 wake-up call to the fusty hard bop movement—is a medium tempo blues, "Tears Inside." After the statement of the tune's two-beat, countrified-bebop theme, trumpeter Don Cherry plays a solo that—for all its frail beauty and general adherence to modern jazz's harmonic conventions—sounds as if it might have been played by Miles Davis or Chet Baker. Coleman and Cherry were vanguardists, to be sure, and they were received as such by critics, musicians, and audiences alike. Even so, today, in listening to these early free jazz sides, one wonders what all the fuss was about, for it's clear that both musicians—especially Cherry—played in a style derived from the mainstream of jazz's development.

Naturally, the passing of four decades provides us a perspective denied listeners at the time; changes that seem slight to us today were magnified then. Coleman and Cherry's elastic relationship to pitch and swing-time were certainly a liberation from the tyranny of equal temperament and literal pulse. Despite the music's revolutionary characteristics, however, no one would now deny that the work of these men is an extension or interpretation of the jazz tradition. This is particularly obvious in Cherry's case; abstracted from his contexts, Don Cherry's style was in a real sense grounded in bebop. He wasn't an especially strong bebop player by classic standards—his range and facility were somewhat limited, for one thing—but externally, his style bore the marks of modern jazz in terms of melody, harmony, rhythm, and phrasing.

Evaluating Cherry in classic terms is a mistake, for like Miles Davis—and Coleman, for that matter—concepts of Western musical objectivity were nearly irrelevant to his work. Cherry was not gifted with extraordinary chops, but those are classicist concerns, and his was a wholly romantic art. Cherry's greatest strength was less easily quantified, less tangible: an ability to convey emotional depth via a subtle manipulation of musical elements. An improvised Don Cherry line might bear all the typical contours of bebop, but Cherry micro-managed every aspect of his playing, rhythmically, harmonically, melodically, timbrally, and dynamically. Like Coleman, Cherry's sound came as close to the expressive qualities of the human voice as was instrumentally possible. And his playing was utterly spontaneous; Cherry was among the most unpredictable of improvisers. His frequent stutters in mid-solo may have stemmed from a limited vocabulary of canned phrases, but his resultant recoveries were the stuff of which great jazz is made.

Cherry first attained prominence with Coleman, with whom he began playing around 1957. At that time Cherry's instrument of choice was a pocket trumpet (or cornet)—a miniature version of the full-sized model. The smaller instrument—in Cherry's hands, at least—got a smaller, slightly more nasal sound than is typical of the larger horn. Though he would play a regular cornet off and on throughout his career, Cherry remained most closely identified with the pocket instrument. Cherry stayed with Coleman through the early '60s, playing on the first seven (and most influential) of the saxophonist's albums. In 1960, he recorded *The Avant-Garde* with John Coltrane. After leaving Coleman's band, Cherry played with Steve Lacy, Sonny Rollins, Archie Shepp, and Albert Ayler. In 1963-4, Cherry co-led the New York Contemporary Five with Shepp and John Tchicai. With Gato Barbieri,

Cherry led a band in Europe from 1964-6, recording two of his most highly regarded albums, *Complete Communion* and *Symphony for Improvisers*. Cherry taught at Dartmouth College in 1970, and recorded with the Jazz Composer's Orchestra in 1973. He lived in Sweden for four years; he used the country as a base for his travels around Europe and the Middle East. Cherry became increasingly interested in other, mostly non-Western styles of music. In the late '70s and early '80s, he performed and recorded with Codona, a cooperative group with percussionist Nana Vasconcelos and multi-instrumentalist Collin Walcott. Codona's music was a pastiche of African, Asian, and other indigenous musics. Concurrently, Cherry joined with ex-Coleman associates Charlie Haden, Ed Blackwell, and Dewey Redman to form Old and New Dreams, a band dedicated to playing the compositions of their former employer. After the dissolution of Codona, Cherry formed Nu with Vasconcelos and saxophonist Carlos Ward. In 1988, he made *Art Deco*, a more traditional album of acoustic jazz, with Haden, Billy Higgins, and saxophonist James Clay. Until his death in 1995, Cherry would continue to combine disparate musical genres; his interest in world music never abated. Cherry learned to play and compose for wood flutes, tambura, gamelan, and various other non-Western instruments. Elements of these musics inevitably found their way into his later compositions and performances, as on 1990s *Multi Kulti*, a characteristic celebration of musical diversity. As a live performer, Cherry was notoriously uneven. It was not unheard of for him to arrive very late for gigs, and his technique—never great to begin with—showed on occasion a considerable, perhaps inexcusable decline. In his last years, especially, Cherry seemed less self-possessed as a musician. Yet, his musical legacy is one of such influence that his personal failings fade in relative significance. —*Chris Kelsey*

Complete Communion / Dec. 24, 1965 / Blue Note ✦✦✦

Trumpeter Don Cherry, best known for his association with altoist Ornette Coleman, matched his innovative—but relatively mellow—horn with ferocious tenors on his three Blue Note albums (all of which have since been reissued in a Mosaic box set). This LP, which finds Cherry, bassist Henry Grimes and drummer Ed Blackwell joined by the passionate tenor of the young Gato Barbieri, consists of two four-song suites that were all composed by Cherry. The unexpected twists and turns of the music and Gato's high-register screams will excite some listeners and turn off others. This is chance-taking and intense music. —*Scott Yanow*

The Complete Blue Note Recordings of Don Cherry / Dec. 24, 1965-Nov. 11, 1966 / Mosaic ✦✦✦✦

This limited-edition two-CD set reissues trumpeter Don Cherry's three Blue Note albums: *Complete Communion, Symphony for Improvisers* and *Where Is Brooklyn*. The avant-garde cornetist is teamed with the tenors of Gato Barbieri and Pharoah Sanders on one album apiece and with both of them on the explosive *Symphony*. All of the music (much of which is performed as continuous medleys) is quite fiery and free and displays Cherry's musical direction during his post-Ornette Coleman and pre-world music phase. These sessions are not essential but they make for stimulating listening. —*Scott Yanow*

● **Symphony for Improvisers** / Sep. 19, 1966 / Blue Note ✦✦✦✦

Don Cherry's second of three Blue Note albums (all have been included in a Mosaic box set) is quite a heated affair. That fact is not too surprising when one considers that the lyrical cornetist is joined by the tenors of the young Gato Barbieri and Pharoah Sanders in addition to a four-piece rhythm section that includes two bassists. This stirring music (eight of Cherry's originals) is performed continuously and has plenty of heated moments full of classic avant-garde fire. —*Scott Yanow*

Where Is Brooklyn / Nov. 11, 1966 / Blue Note ✦✦✦

Don Cherry's third Blue Note album (each has been reissued in full on a Mosaic box set) features the cornetist in a quartet with bassist Henry Grimes, drummer Ed Blackwell and the fiery tenor of Pharoah Sanders. Although the instrumentation is not that much different than it had been with the Ornette Coleman Quartet, the presence of Sanders keeps the music quite passionate and stirring. This group plays the lengthy "Unite" and four shorter pieces, all composed by Cherry and full of the passion of the mid-'60s avant-garde fire. —*Scott Yanow*

Eternal Rhythm / Nov. 11, 1968-Nov. 12, 1968 / Saba ✦✦✦

Beginning of expansion beyond jazz. Cherry is sparkling on cornet, and switches to a variety of flutes and other instruments. Albert Mangelsdorff (tb) and Sonny Sharrock (g) join the party. —*Ron Wynn*

Mu, First Part & Second Part / Aug. 22, 1969 / Actuel ✦✦✦✦

Electrifying duets with Ed Blackwell (d). This music has been released both as one set and as two separate albums. —*Ron Wynn*

Don Cherry [BYG] / Apr. 22, 1971 / BYG ✦✦✦✦✦

Cherry is accessible and full of surprises. Percussive, slightly electric, and always potent. Easy to recommend. —*Michael G. Nastos*

Relativity Suite / Feb. 14, 1973 / JCOA ✦✦✦
With Jazz Composers Orchestra. Cutting-edge music. Features many of Cherry's familiar themes. —*Michael G. Nastos*

Brown Rice / 1975 / A&M ✦✦
This CD (a reissue of Horizon 717) has always been a bit of a disappointment. Don Cherry's trumpet playing is only heard sparingly (he only plays piano on the title cut) and little memorable occurs. "Brown Rice" is closer to R&B than jazz and Cherry's verbal recitation on "Degi-Degi" is not something one needs to hear twice. He also "vocalizes" a bit on "Chenrezig," and, although bassist Charlie Haden is a strong asset and the leader's trumpet is fine on "Malakauns," this release can be safely passed by. —*Scott Yanow*

Hear and Now / Dec. 1976 / Atlantic ✦✦

El Corazon with Ed Blackwell / Feb. 1982 / ECM ✦✦✦✦
Trumpet and drum duets are not exactly commonplace, making this collaboration between Don Cherry and Ed Blackwell something special. The music is often quite sparse (Cherry also plays a little bit of piano, melodica and organ) and the colorful Blackwell often steals the show (although the trumpeter's unaccompanied "Voice of the Silence" is a high point). The use of space is consistently impressive and those listeners with open ears will find this thoughtful date quite interesting. —*Scott Yanow*

Art Deco / Aug. 27, 1988-Aug. 30, 1988 / A&M ✦✦✦✦
Although it is not mentioned anywhere on the outside of this CD, this session is very much a reunion. Trumpeter Don Cherry is reunited with bassist Charlie Haden and drummer Billy Higgins from the early Ornette Coleman Quartet and, most importantly, tenor saxophonist James Clay. Clay, who after playing with Cherry in Los Angeles in the 1950s and doing a few recordings moved back to Texas, had been in obscurity for decades. Fortunately, his playing is quite strong on what turns out to be a surprising bop-oriented session. Comprising superior standards, a few group originals and three Ornette Coleman tunes (including the classic "The Blessing"), this set is quite accessible and finds all of the musicians in top form. —*Scott Yanow*

Multi Kulti / Dec. 27, 1988-Feb. 23, 1990 / A&M ✦✦
This is a rather erratic although often-interesting Don Cherry release. Cherry, on pocket trumpet, melodica, piano, flute and the doussn' gouni, plays five solo pieces (four of which are just short sketches), interacts with tenor saxophonist Peter Apfelbaum on four other songs (two featuring Apfelbaum's Hieroglyphics Ensemble) and uses a synthesizer player on two small-group numbers. Best is "Pettiford Bridge," which features Cherry in a freebop quartet with altoist Carlos Ward, Bob Stewart on tuba and drummer Ed Blackwell. However this CD overall is recommended only to listeners with open ears towards folk and world music; Cherry does not play all that much trumpet throughout the set. —*Scott Yanow*

Dona Nostra / Mar. 1993 / ECM ✦✦✦
Don Cherry (sticking to trumpet) teams up with five European musicians (including pianist Bob Stenson and multi-reedist Lennart Aberg) for a cool and introspective ECM CD. Other than a pair of Ornette Coleman songs ("Race Face" and "What Reason Could I Give"), the music consists of group originals. Although there is not much variety in mood, it is a pleasure to hear Cherry stretching out a bit on trumpet (leaving his flute at home) this late in his career. —*Scott Yanow*

Cyrus Chestnut

b. Jan. 17, 1963, Baltimore, MD
Piano / Hard Bop, Post-Bop
Cyrus Chestnut first studied piano with his father at the age of five, with official lessons beginning two years later. By the age of nine, he was enrolled in the prep program at the Peabody Institute. He graduated from Berklee with a degree in jazz composition and arranging. Chestnut took his time, working with a number of top-notch musicians (Jon Hendricks, Betty Carter, Terence Blanchard and Donald Harrison) before finally recording his first solo CD at the age of 30. Chestnut enjoys mixing styles and resists being typecast in any one niche, though his gospel sound is apparent on a number of his recordings. His initial dates as a leader were recorded for the Japanese label Alfa (reissued on Evidence), and he became an Atlantic artist in 1994. —*Ken Dryden*

Nut / Jan. 18, 1992 / Evidence/Alfa Jazz ✦✦✦✦
Nut is a two-CD set that marked Cyrus Chestnut's 1992 debut as a leader, though it was originally recorded in the US for release in Japan as two separate CDs. Joined by two equally talented Young Lions, bassist Christian McBride and drummer Carl Allen, he covers a wide mix of standards, including a light, swinging version of Massenet's "Elegie," a tense "Caravan," and a sparkling miniature of "Duke's Place" (the instrumental version is properly called "C Jam Blues"). His originals "Sweet Potato Pie and Kool Aid" and "Jazzmine's Island" should stand the test of time, too. —*Ken Dryden*

Another Direction / Apr. 7, 1993 / Evidence ✦✦✦✦
This single CD features a trio with fellow Young Lions Christian McBride and Carl Allen. "Revol" is a racehorse opener. The timeless ballad "My Funny Valentine" has a well-disguised introduction that adds to its melancholy mood. "Blue Skies" is driven by a funky vamp and highlights McBride's skills as a soloist. —*Ken Dryden*

Revelation / Jun. 7, 1993-Jun. 8, 1993 / Atlantic ✦✦✦

Dark Before the Dawn / Aug. 23, 1994-Aug. 25, 1994 / Atlantic ✦✦✦

● **Earth Stories** / Nov. 28, 1995-Nov. 30, 1995 / Atlantic ✦✦✦✦✦
Cyrus Chestnut's third Atlantic CD continues to showcase his tremendous growth as a thought-provoking pianist and composer. "In the Garden" is an inspirational solo indicating his gospel roots. "East of the Sun (And West of the Moon)" proves his ability to create a novel trio arrangement of a standard tune covered by numerous musicians. The remaining tracks include a number of outstanding originals, especially the reflective "My Song in the Night" and the playful "Maria's Folly." —*Ken Dryden*

Blessed Quietness: Collection of Hymns, Spirituals, Carols / Apr. 15, 1996-Apr. 16, 1996 / Atlantic ✦✦✦
Cyrus Chestnut covers a wide range of hymns, carols and spirituals on this outstanding solo piano CD. A very dramatic "Holy, Holy, Holy" would inspire any congregation, while the rich voicings in "We Three Kings" are subtle yet moving. "Sometimes I Feel Like a Motherless Child" is the most compelling track, with a thought-provoking arrangement that makes great use of space. —*Ken Dryden*

Warren Chiasson

b. Apr. 17, 1934, Cheticamp, Canada
Vibes / Bop
Master vibraphonist Warren Chiasson was born and raised in Nova Scotia, and made his move to New York in 1959. A pioneer of the four-mallet technique, his mastery of the instrument wasn't widely known—except by fellow jazz musicians—until a 1988 concert with Benny Goodman at Carnegie Hall.

After moving to New York, he joined pianist George Shearing's quintet and worked with Shearing until 1961 to lead his own group. Others Chiasson has performed with include the Chet Baker Quartet and the Tal Farlow Trio. Throughout the rest of the 1960s, he played vibes at the New York World's Fair and was a percussionist for four years in the Broadway hit musical *Hair*. He teamed up with Shearing again in 1972, and later recorded his first album as a leader, *Quartessence*, for Van Los Records. After touring and recording with Roberta Flack, he was back to pursuing a solo career again, and recorded *Good Vibes for Kurt Weill* in 1977 for Monmouth/Evergreen Records. A third album, Point/Counterpoint, for the Empathy label, was released in 1988.

As a youngster, Chiasson's influences included Charlie Parker as well as pianists Paul Bley, Bud Powell and Shearing. Touches of their styles can be heard in his original compositions. Chiasson can be heard on B.B. King's album *Blues 'n' Jazz*, on MCA Records, which won a Grammy Award in 1984. His other session credits include Roberta Flack's self-titled debut for Atlantic, Hank Crawford's *Centerpiece* album for Buddha/Arista, Les McCann's *Les Plays the Hits* for Mercury, Helen Ward's *Songbook, Vol. 1* for Mercury, and Chuck Wayne's *Travelling* for Progressive. —*Richard Skelly*

● **Point Counterpoint** / Jul. 30, 1986+Mar. 12, 1987 / Empathy ✦✦✦✦

Good Vibes for Kurt Weill / Sep. 13, 1977+Sep. 15, 1977/ Audiophile ✦✦✦

Billy Childs

b. Mar. 8, 1957, Los Angeles, CA
Piano / Post-Bop
One of the most promising of the pianist-composers of the 1990s, Billy Childs is a superb player and an underrated writer. He toured with J.J. Johnson (with whom he made his recording debut), graduated from USC, had an important association with Freddie Hubbard (1978-84) and led Night Flight (a group with Dianne Reeves). Childs recorded four albums as a leader for Windham Hill Jazz (starting in 1988) and one for Stretch, started writing commissioned works in 1992 (including a 1994 concerto for the Monterey Jazz Festival) and has worked with Allan Holdsworth, Eddie Daniels, Bobby Hutcherson and Branford Marsalis among others in addition to leading his own regular quartet. —*Scott Yanow*

Take for Example This . . . / 1988 / Windham Hill Jazz ✦✦✦✦
This brilliant debut album has exceptional playing and compositions. —*Paul Kohler*

Twilight Is upon Us / 1989 / Windham Hill ✦✦✦✦
Billy Childs' second CD as a leader puts as much emphasis on his composing and arranging talents as his skills as a pianist. There is a lot of variety in Childs' eight originals ,which manage to be both adventurous and sometimes fairly accessible.

Childs, who utilizes a synthesizer on three of the numbers, varies the instrumentation on each cut, often featuring the underrated talent Bob Sheppard (on tenor, soprano and flute). It was clear even at this fairly early stage that Billy Childs was on his way to developing an original voice. —*Scott Yanow*

His April Touch / 1991 / Windham Hill ✦✦✦✦
Billy Childs focuses on his piano playing during his third Windham Hill Jazz CD (although he contributed seven of the eight numbers), and he demonstrates that he was quickly rising to the top of his field. Childs uses either acoustic bassist Tony Dumas or electric bassist Jimmy Johnson, drummer Mike Baker, Bob Sheppard (on tenor, soprano, alto and flute) and, for section work (on respectively one or two cuts), trombonist Bruce Fowler and trumpeter Walt Fowler. A highlight is Childs' trio exploration of McCoy Tyner's "Four by Five." The pianist's music is complex and quite original, not fitting securely into any preconceived category except as "modern jazz." This is one of Billy Childs' best all-round sessions to date. —*Scott Yanow*

● **Portrait of a Player** / 1993 / Windham Hill ✦✦✦✦✦
Although relatively underpublicized, Billy Childs is gradually becoming one of the giants of jazz, both as a writer and as a pianist. Two of his compositions (including "Flanagan" a tribute for Tommy Flanagan) are included in this set's repertoire but the emphasis on this trio date is very much on Childs' skills as a pianist. With bassist Tony Dumas and drummer Billy Kilson, Childs explores a variety of high-quality material including John Coltrane's "Satellite," Ivan Lins' "The Island," Cedar Walton's "Bolivia" and Bill Evans' "34 Skidoo." Most impressive is the fact that Billy Childs does not sound like anyone else. —*Scott Yanow*

I've Known Rivers / 1994 / Stretch ✦✦✦

Child Within / Jan. 29, 1996-Jan. 31, 1996 / Shanachie ✦✦✦✦

Herman Chittison (Herman "Ivory" Chittison)

b. Oct. 15, 1908, Flemingsburg, KY, d. Mar. 8, 1967, Cleveland, OH
Piano / Stride
A very talented stride pianist whose great technique in his early days sometimes dominated his style (it was more in balance by the later '30s), Herman Chittison started out with Zack Whyte's Chocolate Beau Brummels (1928-31), a superior territory band. He recorded with Clarence Williams and in 1934 travelled to Europe with Willie Lewis' band. Chittison was featured on Louis Armstrong's European tour that year (he can be seen on film playing three numbers with Satch in Scandinavia) and recorded a series of piano solos. When he left Lewis in 1938, Chittison took some of the other sidemen to Egypt where they played for two years before returning to the US in 1941. After working with Mildred Bailey in 1941, Chittison led his trio in New York for most of the remainder of his life, appearing regularly on a radio series for nine years, recording on an irregular basis for Musicraft, Columbia and a variety of tiny labels, and ending up playing in Akron, Columbus and Cleveland, OH. —*Scott Yanow*

Master of the Stride Piano / Jul. 17, 1933-Sep. 17, 1941 / Meritt ✦✦✦✦✦
It is a pity that this valuable music has thus far only been made available in complete form on this obscure (and difficult to find) collector's LP. Herman Chittison, a brilliant if not particularly influential stride pianist, is heard on two numbers backing guitarist-singer Ikey Robinson and on 17 piano solos, all but the final two recorded in Paris during 1934 or 1938. On his earlier performances (which show a strong Art Tatum influence and are highlighted by a stunning version of "Honeysuckle Rose"), Chittison sounds a bit mechanical (although his technique was quite impressive) but by 1938 he was putting more feeling into his solos. These historic records will certainly interest prebop collectors and fans of the stride piano, if they can find this LP. —*Scott Yanow*

The Melody Lingers On / Jan. 3, 1944 / Audiophile ✦✦✦
This LP would receive a higher rating if its programming were more logical. On January 3, 1944, the talented stride pianist Herman Chittison and his trio (which also included guitarist James Shirley and bassist Cedric Wallace) recorded some radio transcriptions for the World Broadcasting Systems. Every note of music (nine issued songs plus 11 alternate takes, four incomplete performances and six false starts) is included on this album and there are some fine examples of Chittison's playing along with some good interplay by the trio. Unfortunately not all of the issued takes are programmed together; nor is the music in strictly chronological order. Some of the songs appear on both sides of the LP, making this a confusing set to study or enjoy. However, for listeners willing to put up with this inconvenience, there are some fine performances, particularly "How High the Moon," "The Song Is Ended," "Just One of Those Things" and "Persian Rug." —*Scott Yanow*

Piano Genius / Dec. 8, 1944-May 1, 1945 / Musicraft ✦✦✦✦
Considering his talent, pianist Herman Chittison recorded relatively little throughout his career. Fortunately during a five-month period in 1944-45, he documented

16 selections for Musicraft; 15 (all but an alternate take of "I Should Care") are on this excellent LP. Chittison plays four songs (including "Schubert's Serenade" and "How High the Moon") with guitarist Jimmy Shirley and bassist Carlton Powell in a trio, seven numbers feature Chittison, Powell and guitarist Carl Lynch (including three with Thelma Carpenter vocals) and, best of all, Chittison takes four unaccompanied piano solos including jazz interpretations of Chopin's "Triste" and "To a Wild Rose." Although not generally as hyper as his 1930s solos, these performances (compiled on an LP in 1980) feature Chittison in top form. Recommended. —*Scott Yanow*

● **P.S. with Love** / Jun. 5, 1964-1967 / IAJRC ✦✦✦✦
Herman Chittison was one of the top jazz pianists to emerge during the 1930s but, since he spent some of his most important years in Europe and generally recorded for obscure labels, he never achieved much recognition. These previously unreleased piano solos from two separate occasions were made available for the first time on this collector's CD with the second half of the set dating from just two months before the pianist passed away. Overall Chittison sounds fine, relatively modern in spots without losing his melodic style. There are some weak show tunes from the era (such as "Getting to Know You," "The Sound of Music" and "People") but in general Chittison overcomes the material and comes up with some inventive solos. —*Scott Yanow*

Charlie Christian

b. Jul. 29, 1916, Dallas, TX, d. Mar. 2, 1942, New York, NY
Guitar / Swing, Bop
It can be said without exaggeration that virtually every jazz guitarist that emerged during 1940-65 sounded like a relative of Charlie Christian. The first important electric guitarist, Christian played his instrument with the fluidity, confidence and swing of a saxophonist. Although technically a swing stylist, his musical vocabulary was studied and emulated by the bop players and when one listens to players ranging from Tiny Grimes, Barney Kessel and Herb Ellis to Wes Montgomery and George Benson, the dominant influence of Christian is obvious.

Charlie Christian's time in the spotlight was terribly brief. He played piano locally in Oklahoma and began to utilize an amplified guitar in 1937, after becoming a student of Eddie Durham, a jazz guitarist who invented the amplified guitar. John Hammond, the masterful talent scout and producer, heard about Christian (possibly from Mary Lou Williams), was impressed by what he saw and arranged for the guitarist to travel to Los Angeles in August 1939 and try out with Benny Goodman. Although the clarinetist was initally put off by Christian's primitive wardrobe, as soon as they started jamming on "Rose Room," Christian's talents were obvious. For the next two years he would be well featured with Benny Goodman's Sextet, there were two solos (including the showcase "Solo Flight") with the full orchestra and the guitarist had the opportunity to jam at Minton's Playhouse with such up-and-coming players as Thelonious Monk, Kenny Clarke and Dizzy Gillespie. All of the guitarist's recordings (including guest spots and radio broadcasts) are currently available on CD. Tragically he contracted tuberculosis in 1941 and died at the age of 25 on March 2, 1942. It would be 25 years before jazz guitarists finally moved beyond Charlie Christian. —*Scott Yanow*

Charlie Christian with Benny Goodman and the Sextet / Aug. 10, 1939-Jun. 1941 / Jazz Archives ✦✦✦✦
The collector's label Jazz Archives unearthed these radio broadcast performances in the mid-'70s. The pioneering electric guitarist Charlie Christian is featured throughout with Benny Goodman's Sextet and, on "Solo Flight" (here titled "Chonk, Charlie, Chonk") with Benny Goodman's big band. All of these titles (except for one of the versions of "Wholly Cats") have since been reissued on CD by Vintage Jazz Classics. —*Scott Yanow*

Solo Flight (1939-1941) / Aug. 19, 1939-Jun. 1941 / Vintage Jazz ✦✦✦✦✦
Charlie Christian, who died in 1942 at the age of 25, was the first important electric guitarist and his solos would be the basis of jazz guitar for the next 25 years. This CD is filled with live performances (mostly from radio shows) of the Benny Goodman Sextet featuring Christian solos on every track. With such sidemen as vibraphonist Lionel Hampton and later tenor saxophonist Georgie Auld and trumpeter Cootie Williams, this unit was a perfect outlet for both Christian and Benny Goodman. And, in addition to a big band performance of "Solo Flight" (virtually a tour-de-force for the guitarist), there are five selections from a remarkable all-star group comprising Goodman, Christian, trumpeter Buck Clayton, Lester Young on tenor and Count Basie along with his rhythm section. This CD is highly recommended as an example of some of the very best in small-group swing and as a tribute to Charlie Christian's highly influential style. —*Scott Yanow*

★ **The Genius of the Electric Guitar** / Oct. 2, 1939-Mar. 13, 1941 / Columbia ✦✦✦✦✦
This set contains some of guitarist Charlie Christian's greatest recordings (although he did not live long enough to record any bad ones). Christian is heard

with the Benny Goodman Sextet on famous versions of "Seven Come Eleven," "Benny's Bugle" and "Air Mail Special"; is showcased with Goodman's orchestra on "Solo Flight"; and jams with the members of the Sextet (minus their leader) on "Blues in B" and a fascinating ad-lib, "Waitin' for Benny." This important release belongs in every jazz collection and contains a great deal of essential music. —*Scott Yanow*

Solo Flight the Genius of Charlie Christian / Oct. 2, 1939-Mar. 13, 1941 / Columbia ✦✦✦✦

Prior to the advent of the CD, this two-LP set was the definitive Charlie Christian release and it is still quite impressive. The great electric guitarist is heard on most of his more famous recordings with the Benny Goodman Sextet (including "Seven Come Eleven," "Air Mail Special," "Royal Garden Blues" and "Breakfast Feud"), on his two features with the Goodman Orchestra ("Honeysuckle Rose" and "Air Mail Special"), with the Metronome All-Stars, leading a jam session that also features Jerry Jerome on tenor (the only selections not yet reissued on CD) and at a practice with the other members of BG's Sextet in which they came up with some hot riffs on the ad-lib "Waitin' for Benny." It's a well-conceived two-fer. —*Scott Yanow*

☆ **Live 1939-1941** / 1939-1941 / Jazz Archives ✦✦✦✦✦

The 140 minutes of music here should speak for itself to any fan of Charlie Christian, or of great guitar playing. That's just about as much of his music as there is everywhere else combined—these concert, broadcast, and amateur recordings are an indispensable addition to his output. The sound quality varies, in keeping with the low level of available technology at the time, but it's all priceless stuff, as Christian breaks new ground with practically every note of each guitar solo here. Beginning with a 1939 live performance of "Flying Home" with Benny Goodman and company, where Christian gives a brief but striking improvisation on the break, the territory on this double-CD set lengthens and broadens along with the solos. The value of the radio transcriptions and amateur recordings can be appreciated on numbers such as "I Got Rhythm" and "Stardust" as performed by the Jerry Jerome Quartet at the Harlem Breakfast Club in Minneapolis in Sept. 1939, jams running nearly six minutes each, giving Christian more than enough room to bend some strings and the notes with them. Some songs run close to 10 minutes, offering the longest Charlie Christian-featured numbers available anywhere, and it's all overpowering (his work on "Tea for Two" alone is a humbling experience). The Benny Goodman Sextet (with Lionel Hampton and Fletcher Henderson), the Jerry Jerome Quartet, and a series of jams with the Count Basie Orchestra, featuring Buck Clayton, Lester Young, and Jo Jones (captured at the 1939 "From Spirituals to Swing" Carnegie Hall show) make up the groups included here. —*Bruce Eder*

Charlie Christian/Lester Young: Together 1940 / Oct. 28, 1940-Jan. 15, 1941 / Jazz Archives ✦✦✦✦

This Jazz Archives LP, which was withdrawn shortly after its release, is a real collector's item. It starts out with the five selections Benny Goodman and Count Basie recorded privately at a period of time when the clarinetist was toying with breaking up his big band and forming this septet (which also included the great electric guitarist Charlie Christian, tenor saxophonist Lester Young and trumpeter Buck Clayton). That material has since been reissued on CD but the other 11 performances are taken from rehearsals of the Benny Goodman Sextet and were apparently not supposed to be released. These alternate versions of their recordings feature one of Goodman's strongest units with creative solos from Christian, trumpeter Cootie Williams, tenorman Georgie Auld and either pianist Count Basie or Ken Kersey. —*Scott Yanow*

Jazz Immortal / May 8, 1941+May 12, 1941 / Everest ✦✦✦✦

The recording quality is streaky on this budget release and the personnel listing and recording date are omitted, but the music (which has been reissued several times) is quite historic. Cut live at Minton's Playhouse and Monroe's Uptown House, these jam sessions feature the great pioneering electric guitarist Charlie Christian on the longest solos of his that still exist, really stretching out during the Eddie Durham composition "Swing to Bop" (really it's "Topsy"), "Up on Teddy's Hill" and "Stompin' at the Savoy"; his improvisation on the latter was one of the finest of his short life. The trumpeter on those selections is the erratic Joe Guy but Thelonious Monk can be heard taking some swing-oriented solos, his earliest appearance on records. Some of the other jams (two versions of "Stardust" and "Kerouac") feature Dizzy Gillespie, who at age 24 was still searching for his style. This is very significant music from sessions that led to the birth of bebop. —*Scott Yanow*

Christie Brothers Stompers

f. 1951, db. 1953

Group / Trad Jazz, Dixieland

Although now somewhat obscure, the Christie Brothers Stompers was one of the most influential British New Orleans-style jazz bands of the early 1950s, recording

several years before England's trad boom. In 1951, a group of musicians from the Crane River and Humphrey Lyttelton Bands recorded under the Christie Brothers name for Esquire, and the popularity of the records led to trombonist Keith Christie and clarinetist Ian Christie deciding to launch a regular group of their own with at first Ken Colyer on cornet (in 1952 trumpeter Dick Hawdon took his place) and a rhythm section that included pianist Pat Hawes. Their recordings for Melodisc (dating from Aug. 1951-Aug. 1953) have been reissued on a British Cadillac CD and display the enthusiasm and power of the fine band. Influenced the most by the Kid Ory and Bunk Johnson groups, but also open to aspects of King Oliver, Jelly Roll Morton and Louis Armstrong, the Christie Brothers Stompers managed to develop their own exuberant sound without directly copying their predecessors. After the band broke up in 1953, Keith Christie eventually modernized his style and, other than a four-song partial reunion session in 1958, the group was soon forgotten. —*Scott Yanow*

Christie Brothers Stompers / Jun. 18, 1951-Sep. 26, 1952 / Cadillac ✦✦✦✦

In the early 1950s, the English trombonist Keith Christie and his brother, clarinetist Ian Christie, teamed up to co-lead a fine New Orleans-style septet. Other than some slightly earlier recordings for Esquire and a more modern 1958 session, this CD has all of the group's records. With Ken Colyer (who is on the first nine of the 23 cuts) or Dickie Hawdon on trumpet and Pat Hawes or Charlie Smith on piano, this was a spirited group with plenty of fine soloists who improvised in the older style. Although the first three numbers are not very well recorded, the technical quality greatly improves with the second session. Among the highlights are "Heebie Jeebies," "Salutation Stomp" (one of several originals), "Hiawatha Rag," "Farewell to Storyville" and "Them There Eyes." Easily recommended to New Orleans jazz and Dixieland fans. —*Scott Yanow*

Pete Christlieb

b. Feb. 16, 1945, Los Angeles, CA

Tenor Saxophone / Bop

Pete Christlieb is probably one the world's most famous anonymous tenor saxophonists. For years, he played jazz tenor in Doc Severinsen's "Tonight Show" big band. His big, beefy sound and aggressive solos were heard mostly in brief snippets as the show came out of commercials, unfortunately denying the American public a chance to hear a very fine saxophonist improvise at length. Though he's done good work elsewhere, Christlieb's biggest claim to fame away from Severinsen and Carson is a Warner Brothers album he recorded in 1978 with fellow tenorist Warne Marsh. *Apogee* is one of the most compelling straightahead jazz albums of the '70s. Christlieb's cocky, rhythmically assured style contrasts effectively with Marsh's looser, more querulous manner. The record's overall air of curious abandon foretold (somewhat wrongly, as it turned out) a bright future for mainstream acoustic jazz in the coming decade.

Christlieb was born into a musical family. He began playing the violin at seven, and tenor sax at 13. After playing with a variety of L.A.-based bands in the early '60s, including those led by Chet Baker, Woody Herman, and Sy Zentner, Christlieb joined drummer Louis Bellson's band in 1967, with which he would continue to play into the '80s. His first record as leader was the deleted *Jazz City*, an LP released in 1971. The tenorist started his own label, Bosco Records, in 1981; Bosco would issue small-group albums by Christlieb, as well records by Bellson and Bob Florence. Christlieb has long been in demand as a studio player; he's played innumerable sessions of every type. Other prominent jazz figures with whom he's played include Count Basie, Benny Goodman, Quincy Jones, and Sarah Vaughan. —*Chris Kelsey*

Apogee / 1978 / Warner Brothers ✦✦✦✦

Because this set was produced by the leaders of Steely Dan (Walter Becker and Donald Fagen) for Warner Brothers during a period when that label rarely recorded jazz, this LP received more publicity than expected. The two distinctive tenors of Pete Christlieb and Warne Marsh (backed by pianist Lou Levy, bassist Jim Hughart and drummer Nick Ceroli) are in combative form for the enjoyable blowing session. Joe Roccisano contributed charts for four of the six songs but the main points of interest are the strong tenor solos. It's worth searching for and long overdue for reissue. —*Scott Yanow*

● **Conversations with Warne, Vol. 1** / Sep. 15, 1978 / Criss Cross ✦✦✦✦✦

Pete Christlieb had a special opportunity to record with one of his idols, fellow tenor Warne Marsh, on this quartet session with bassist Jim Hughart and drummer Nick Ceroli. Christlieb, a powerful player himself, blends in well with Marsh and the results are both complementary and competitive. Two CDs worth of material resulted from the one night's work. As was usual with Marsh and his teacher Lennie Tristano, the "originals" were all based on the chord changes of standard songs and most of the songtitles (such as "Weeping Willow," "India No Place" and "Woody and You") give away the original sources. This stimulating music is easily recommended to fans of straightahead jazz and the Tristano school; Christlieb not only held his own with Marsh but clearly inspired him. — *Scott Yanow*

Conversations with Warne, Vol. 2 / Sep. 15, 1978 / Criss Cross ✦✦✦✦

This matchup works quite well. With alert contributions made by bassist Jim Hughart and drummer Nick Ceroli, tenors Pete Christlieb and Warne Marsh match wits, swing and ideas throughout nine run-throughs on "originals" based on common chord changes. This second of two CDs has four alternate takes of songs included on the earlier CD plus five other numbers. With titles such as "Woody and You," "Bess You Is My Man" and "So What's Old," experts should have little difficulty in most cases figuring out which standards the "new" pieces are based on. Because Marsh and Christlieb had very different sounds but competitive natures, plenty of sparks flew during this date. — *Scott Yanow*

Self Portrait / 1981 / Bosco ✦✦✦✦

On the debut LP of his own label, tenor saxophonist Pete Christlieb welcomed some of his musical friends to play two standards and a variety of originals. Christlieb used different personnel on each selection including tenor great Warne Marsh (one of his idols), altoist Joe Roccisano, fluegelhornist Steve Huffsteter, guitarist John Morell, pianist Lou Levy, organist Mike Melvoin, bassist Jim Hughart and Dick Berk or Nick Ceroli on drums. A special moment occurs on "Vu-Ja-Day" for Pete's father, Don Christlieb, contributes some bassoon. Overall this is a fine showcase for the underrated Pete Christlieb although the album (along with the other Bosco releases) will be difficult to find. — *Scott Yanow*

Going My Way / 1982 / Bosco ✦✦✦

Most of the selections on this obscure but enjoyable LP feature tenor saxophonist Pete Christlieb's 1982 quartet, a unit also including pianist Alan Broadbent, bassist Jim Hughart and drummer Michael Whited. Mike Melvoin (on organ) and drummer Donald Bailey (doubling on harmonica) make colorful guest appearances. Christlieb and company perform three standards ("Gone with the Wind," "Detour Ahead" and Gigi Gryce's "Minority") along with a trio of his complex originals. The music is largely straightahead and Christlieb constantly shows just how powerful a player he is despite his lack of fame. — *Scott Yanow*

The Dino's '83 / 1983 / Bosco ✦✦✦

Mosaic / Feb. 16, 1983 / Capri ✦✦✦✦

Pete Christlieb shares the spotlight on this CD with fellow tenor Bob Cooper. Accompanied by pianist Mike Wofford, bassist Chuck Berghofer and drummer Donald Bailey, the two tenors stretch out on such songs as "The Touch of Your Lips," Dizzy Gillespie's "Shaw 'Nuff," "Limehouse Blues" and Cooper's "Bit O' Sweets." Christlieb's hard tone contrasts well with Cooper's cool sound. Cooper is showcased on "Come Sunday," while the rhythm trio has "The Late, Late Show" as their feature. An enthusiastic and consistently swinging session. — *Scott Yanow*

June Christy

b. Nov. 20, 1925, Springfield, Il, **d.** Jun. 21, 1990, Los Angeles, CA
Vocals / Cool, Show Tunes, Traditional Pop

Although she originally sounded heavily influenced by Anita O'Day, June Christy's cool-toned yet cheerful style grew to be quite individual and popular, being both sensual and nonthreatening. She sang locally in Chicago and then received her big break, replacing O'Day with Stan Kenton's Orchestra in 1945. She had hits with "Tampico," "Shoo-Fly Pie" and "How High the Moon" and her renditions of ballads and novelties helped to keep the Kenton Orchestra going, contrasting with their more experimental and "progressive" works. Christy married tenor saxophonist Bob Cooper, cut her first solo recordings in 1947 and, after Kenton broke up his band in 1948, she had a very successful career. Her series of Capitol records in the 1950s (particularly *Something Cool* and *The Misty Miss Christy*) defined the "cool jazz" singing style and sold quite well. Christy had occasional reunions with Kenton and, even after she drifted into retirement after 1965, she appeared with the bandleader at the 1972 Newport Jazz Festival. Though she came back for one final record in 1977, June Christy will always be associated with the 1950s. — *Scott Yanow*

The Uncollected June Christy with the Kentones (1946) / 1946 / Hindsight ✦✦✦✦✦

The well-recorded radio transcriptions on this collector's LP predate all of singer June Christy's regular solo recordings; she had only been with Stan Kenton's Orchestra for about a year at the time. The identification of the backup personnel has been lost to history (despite the anonymous title of "the Kentones"), but Christy is the star of the 14 concise performances anyway. June Christy had the ability to swing in any song she was given, and in this case, all of the selections (except for "June's Blues") are superior standards. The young singer is heard in her early prime on such numbers as "Don't Worry 'Bout Me," "The One I Love," "September in the Rain," "Wrap Your Troubles in Dreams" and "Get Happy." — *Scott Yanow*

Day Dream / Feb. 24, 1947-Sep. 11, 1950 / Capitol ✦✦✦✦

This CD includes all of singer June Christy's Capitol recordings from 1947-50 outside of the Stan Kenton Orchestra, including four previously unreleased titles. Christy, a subtle and cheerful improviser, was always willing to take chances, and her repertoire here ranges from novelties and jazz standards to a version of "Everything Happens to Me" on which she is backed by a typically radical arrangement by Bob Graettinger. In addition to the performances with orchestras led by Frank DeVol, Bob Cooper, Pete Rugolo and Shorty Rogers (highlighted by "Get Happy"), there are also two songs from her 1955 duet date with pianist Stan Kenton that were released on this CD for the first time. June Christy is in superior form throughout this highly enjoyable and somewhat historical set. — *Scott Yanow*

The Best of June Christy: Jazz Sessions / Sep. 29, 1949-Jun. 27, 1968 / Capitol ✦✦✦✦

Along with "Something Cool," Christy's biggest hit, this collection of her Capitol work from the 1950s includes "Baby All the Time," her duet with bandleader Stan Kenton, as well as "How High the Moon," a reunion date with the Kenton Orchestra. — *Jason Ankeny*

★ Something Cool / 1953 / Capitol ✦✦✦✦✦

June Christy's classic *Something Cool* has been expanded from 11 songs to 24 on this essential CD with two unreleased cuts and six songs only previously out as singles. Christy's attractive "cool" tone was a trademark of jazz in the 1950s, her version of "Something Cool" remains a classic and many of the other numbers are nearly as memorable. Accompanied by Pete Rugolo's Orchestra, Christy is heard at her best on such numbers as "Whee Baby," "You're Making Me Crazy," "Midnight Sun," "A Stranger Called the Blues," "Softly as in a Morning Sunrise," "This Time the Dream's on Me" and "The Night We Called It a Day." — *Scott Yanow*

Duet / May 5, 1955-May 9, 1955 / Capitol ✦✦✦✦

This set of duets between singer June Christy and pianist Stan Kenton is often quite emotional. Christy's cool sound and careful diction hint at darker feelings than appear on the surface during these ballads while Kenton provides sparse but effective piano. Emotions and melody are much more significant in this setting than mere chord changes and this haunting music is surprisingly memorable. — *Scott Yanow*

The Misty Miss Christy / Jul. 26, 1955-May 23, 1956 / Capitol ✦✦✦✦✦

Singer June Christy is heard in prime form on this set. The reissue CD adds two numbers ("You Took Advantage of Me" and "Intrigue") to the original LP program. Backed by orchestras filled with West Coast jazz all-stars and arranged by Pete Rugolo, Christy is particularly memorable on "I Didn't Know About You," "Day Dream," "Dearly Beloved" and "There's No You." This is one of her finest all-round recordings. — *Scott Yanow*

A Lovely Way to Spend a Evening / 1957 / Jasmine ✦✦✦

Taken from radio transcriptions, this CD features singer June Christy in 1957 in brief (generally under three minute) performances. She is assisted by either the Jerry Gray Orchestra, drummer Shelly Manne's Trio (with pianist Russ Freeman and bassist Monty Budwig) and on "Rock Me to Sleep" the Manne Quintet (which has altoist Herb Geller and trumpeter Stu Williamson added). June Christy's voice is in fine form (she was in her prime throughout the 1950s) and highlights include "From This Moment On," "How High the Moon," "Midnight Sun" and "That's All." But due to the lack of stretching out, this set is primarily of interest to June Christy completists. — *Scott Yanow*

June Fair and Warmer / Jan. 3, 1957-Jan. 21, 1957 / Capitol ✦✦✦✦

This out-of-print Capitol LP, one of many that June Christy cut during the 1950s, features her soft but swinging vocals accompanied by a 12-piece group arranged by Pete Rugolo. While the backup musicians include trumpeter Don Fagerquist, trombonist Frank Rosolino, altoist Bud Shank and tenor saxophonist Bob Cooper (all of whom are unidentified in the very brief liner notes), the cool-toned singer is the main star. Highlights include a definitive "I Want to Be Happy," "Imagination," "When Sunny Gets Blue" and "It's Always You." All of June Christy's Capitol dates are well worth picking up. — *Scott Yanow*

Gone for the Day / Jun. 18, 1957-Jul. 15, 1957 / Capitol ✦✦✦✦

The dozen songs on this June Christy LP mostly have to do with having a peaceful life, taking time off and enjoying the weather; highlights include "It's So Peaceful in the Country," "When the Sun Comes Out," "Love Turns Winter to Spring," "Lazy Afternoon," "Give Me the Simple Life" and Eddie Miller's "Lazy Mood." Pete Rugolo contributed the arrangements and used three separate groups on four songs apiece. Christy is accompanied either by a sextet with strings that includes flutist Bud Shank and John Cave's Frech horn, a tentet with five trombones or a septet with flutist Bud Shank and Bob Cooper's tenor plus strings. The results in all cases are quite enjoyable, making one wish that this rare gem (and all of June Christy's other Capitol dates) were available on CD. — *Scott Yanow*

Music Map

Clarinet

Pioneers on Record
Larry Shields
(1917, with Original Dixieland Jazz Band)
Leon Rappolo (1922, with New Orleans Rhythm Kings)

New Orleans Early Classic Greats
Sidney Bechet • Johnny Dodds • Jimmy Noone

Other Top Clarinetists of the 1920s
Buster Bailey	Jimmy Dorsey
Frankie Teschemacher	Albert Nicholas
Barney Bigard	Omer Simeon

Commercial Vaudeville Players
Wilbur Sweatman	Ted Lewis
Wilton Crawley	Boyd Senter
Fess Williams	

Clarinet Giants of the Swing Era
Benny Goodman • Artie Shaw

Other Top Pre-Bop Clarinetists
Pee Wee Russell	Joe Marsala
Edmond Hall	Peanuts Hucko
Johnny Mince	Woody Herman
Irving Fazola	Dick Johnson
Abe Most	Bob Wilber
Kenny Davern	Ken Peplowski

New Orleans Revival
Alphonse Picou	George Lewis
Bob Helm	Pete Fountain
Dr. Michael White	

Bop
Stan Hasselgard	Tony Scott
Jimmy Hamilton	Putte Wickman
Eiji Kitamura	

Two Virtuoso Clarinet Innovators
Buddy DeFranco • Eddie Daniels

Saxophonists Who Occasionally Played Clarinet
Lester Young	Eddie Miller
Buddy Collette	Rahsaan Roland Kirk
Art Pepper	Phil Woods
Paquito D'Rivera	

Avant-Garde
John LaPorta	Jimmy Giuffre
Bill Smith	Anthony Braxton
Perry Robinson	Alvin Batiste
John Carter	Marty Ehrlich
Michael Moore	Louis Sclavis
Don Byron	

June's Got Rhythm / Jun. 1958-Jul. 14, 1958 / Capitol ✦✦✦✦
Many of singer June Christy's popular Capitol albums feature her cool-toned vocals backed by an orchestra. This out-of-print LP is an exception. Christy excels on a jazz-oriented set with a nonet that includes trumpeter Ed Leddy, trombonist Frank Rosolino and her husband Bob Cooper (who arranged the set) on tenor and oboe. Christy accurately called this music "intimate swing." Her versions of such songs as "I'm Glad There Is You," "My One and Only Love," "When Lights Are Low" and "Blue Moon" are tasteful, sincere and often quite memorable. —*Scott Yanow*

June Christy Recalls Those Kenton Days / 1959 / Capitol ✦✦✦
On various selections during this Capitol LP (which was last made available by Pausa in the mid-'80s), June Christy is accompanied by an orchestra, a big band or a tentet, all arranged by Pete Rugolo. She performs ten selections that she recorded a decade or so earlier while with Stan Kenton's big band although the charts had been updated somewhat. The light-hearted "Tampico" is missing but "Just A-Sittin' and A-Rockin'," "The Lonesome Road," "Easy Street" and "Across the Alley from the Alamo" are all here. This album will hopefully be reissued on CD in the future. —*Scott Yanow*

The Song Is June! / 1959 / Capitol ✦✦✦✦
This single-CD reissue from 1997 has the complete contents of two formerly hard-to-find June Christy records (*The Song Is June* and *Off Beat*), both of which feature the singer backed by Pete Rugolo's generally creative and unpredictable arrangements for an unidentified orchestra. Christy had a cool sound and a subtle style that made her performances quite accessible no matter how complex the music. She sang with confidence, sincere feeling for the lyrics and swing at any tempo.

Although the majority of these selections are ballads, there is enough variety and suspense throughout the often-haunting renditions to continually hold one's interest. The many highlights of this two-fer include "Spring Can Really Hang You Up the Most," "Night Time Was My Mother," "Out of This World" and "A Sleepin' Bee." —*Scott Yanow*

Impromptu / Jun. 7, 1977-Jun. 9, 1977 / Discovery ✦✦
After a long series of recordings for Capitol during 1952-65, June Christy gradually retired from singing. She only returned to the studios once, for this Discovery LP. Assisted by the Lou Levy sextet (which consisted of the leader-pianist, trumpeter Jack Sheldon, trombonist Frank Rosolino, tenorman Bob Cooper, bassist Bob Daugherty and drummer Shelly Manne), Christy avoided revisiting her hits and instead mixed in some newer material (such as "Once Upon a Summertime," "Everything Must Change" and "Sometime Ago") with a few older standards. A little rusty during this final effort, June Christy's sincerity and swing will win over listeners. —*Scott Yanow*

Clarinet Summit

f. 1984, db. 1987
Group / Avant-Garde

In 1984 for a concert at the Public Theatre in New York, John Carter organized a unique group consisting of David Murray on bass clarinet and the clarinets of Alvin Batiste, Jimmy Hamilton and himself. Hamilton (who was with Duke Ellington's Orchestra for 26 years) and the flexible Batiste played some spontaneous swing, Carter and Murray went outside during their features and all four had opportunities to inspire each other. The results of the concert were released on two

India Navigation LPs (and one reissue CD). In 1987 the unique group came together for a reunion and made a studio record for Black Saint. —*Scott Yanow*

● **Clarinet Summit** / 1984 / India Navigation ✦✦✦✦
Clarinet Summit comprised four diverse clarinetists: Duke Ellington alumnus Jimmy Hamilton, the adventurous Alvin Batiste, leading avant-gardist John Carter, and David Murray (normally a tenor), who kept the bottom strong with his bass clarinet. In 1984, the quartet performed at the Public Theater without a rhythm section, and the result was two LPs released by India Navigation. In 1991 the label combined all of the selections (except for a brief "Satin Doll") on a single 73-minute CD. The music ranges from brief swing numbers for Hamilton and a Murray showcase on "Sweet Lovely" to some wild group improvisations, including "Solo and Ballad for Four Clarinets" and the 17-minute "Clariflavors." This very interesting, if sometimes abrasive music was extended four years later with a reunion of the group for a studio date (released on Black Saint). —*Scott Yanow*

Southern Bells / Mar. 29, 1987 / Black Saint ✦✦✦
In 1984, clarinetists John Carter, Alvin Batiste, Jimmy Hamilton and David Murray (on bass clarinet) performed a concert that was recorded and released by India Navigation. Three years later, they regrouped for a studio session. Three selections are slightly "traditional" ("I Want to Talk About You," a Hamilton-Carter duet on "Perdido" and a brief "Don't Get Around Much Anymore"), but the bulk of this set is taken up with more advanced improvising, including Batiste's lengthy "Fluffy's Blues" and Murray's free improv "Mbizo." Intriguing music (Jimmy Hamilton really stretches himself); recommended to avant-garde listeners rather than Duke Ellington fans. —*Scott Yanow*

Sonny Clark (Conrad Yeatis Clark)

b. Jul. 21, 1931, Herminie, PA, **d.** Jan. 13, 1963, New York, NY
Piano / Bop, Hard Bop
Before drugs drastically shortened his life, Sonny Clark was one of the top Bud Powell-inspired bop pianists. He worked in San Francisco with Vido Musso and Oscar Pettiford in the early '50s, settled in Los Angeles, made his first recordings with Teddy Charles and then worked with Buddy DeFranco's quartet (1953-56); all of his records with DeFranco have been reissued by Mosaic on a deluxe limited-edition box set. During the same period he worked with Sonny Criss, Frank Rosolino and the Lighthouse All-Stars. Moving to New York in 1957, Clark became a fixture on Blue Note, recording several classics as a leader (*Dial S for Sonny, Cool Struttin'* and *Sonny's Crib* to name three from 1957 alone) and appearing as a sideman with Sonny Rollins, Hank Mobley and Curtis Fuller among many others. Sonny Clark's premature death (at age 31) was a major loss to jazz. —*Scott Yanow*

The Sonny Clark Memorial Album / Jan. 15, 1954 / Xanadu ✦✦✦
Sonny Clark was only 22 at the time of this private recording but he already had his Bud Powell-based piano style together. Clark is heard unaccompanied and, for two lengthy songs, in a trio with bassist Simon Brehm and drummer Bobby White. The solo tracks in particular are quite interesting for they are very spontaneous with some rambling resulting in ad-lib medleys. The music gives one a rare chance to hear Sonny Clark in a relaxed setting, thinking aloud musically. This valuable document (which is reasonably well recorded for a live date of the era) was first released in 1975 as a Xanadu LP. —*Scott Yanow*

Oakland, 1955 / Jan. 13, 1955 / Uptown ✦✦✦
This live concert (which was released for the first time on this 1995 CD) features the great pianist Sonny Clark in prime form in a trio with bassist Jerry Good and drummer Al Randall. The recording quality is a bit primitive (lowering the music's value) but since there are not an excess of Sonny Clark records available and the pianist's interpretations of the dozen selections (mostly jazz standards) is consistently swinging and inventive, this boppish CD is worth picking up anyway. —*Scott Yanow*

Dial "S" for Sonny / Jul. 21, 1957 / Blue Note ✦✦✦✦
Dial "S" for Sonny, Sonny Clark's first session for Blue Note Records and his first session as a leader, is a terrific set of laidback bop, highlighted by Clark's liquid, swinging solos. Clark leads a first-rate group—Art Farmer (trumpet), Curtis Fuller (trombone), Hank Mobley (tenor sax), Wilbur Ware (bass), Louis Hayes (drums)—through four originals and two standards, balancing the selections between swinging bop and reflective ballads. There are traces of Bud Powell in Clark's style, but he's beginning to come into his own, developing a style that's alternately edgy and charmingly relaxed. Mobley, Farmer and Fuller have their moments, but Clark steals the show in this set of fine, straightahead bop. —*Stephen Thomas Erlewine*

● **Sonny's Crib** / Oct. 9, 1957 / Blue Note ✦✦✦✦✦
One of the great Sonny Clark albums, this is the one that is best known for featuring John Coltrane. Actually 'Trane's tenor is only one of six distinctive voices in a

---

Music Map

Bass Clarinet

Early Days
Harry Carney
(doubles with Duke Ellington's Orchestra)

Clarinetists Playing Bass Clarinet
Omer Simeon (1926, reluctantly takes solo on Jelly Roll Morton's "Someday Sweetheart")
Benny Goodman (1931, two songs with Red Norvo)
Buddy DeFranco (1964, "Blues Bag" with Art Blakey)

No real bass clarinet specialists until the 1960s

Bass Clarinet Innovator
Eric Dolphy

Other Bass Clarinetists
Herbie Mann (switched from flute in 1957 and 1959)
Bennie Maupin
Gunter Hampel
David Murray
Howard Johnson
Roscoe Mitchell
John Surman
John Purcell
Marty Ehrlich
Hamiett Bluiett (alto clarinet)
Doug Ewart
Don Byron

---

sextet also including trumpeter Donald Byrd, trombonist Curtis Fuller, the pianist-leader, bassist Paul Chambers and drummer Art Taylor. The CD reissue adds alternate takes to three of the five performances ("With a Song in My Heart," "Speak Low" and "Sonny's Crib"); every song but "Come Rain or Come Shine" and "News for Lulu." The now-legendary musicians are a joy to hear on this classic Blue Note set. —*Scott Yanow*

Sonny Clark Trio / Nov. 13, 1957 / Bainbridge ✦✦✦✦
Pianist Sonny Clark sounds very much at home on this trio set with bassist Paul Chambers and drummer Philly Joe Jones. Sticking to bop standards, Sonny Clark essentially plays his version of Bud Powell, carving out his own approach to the influential style. The CD reissue adds three alternates to the six selections and includes such gems as "Two Bass Hit," "Be-Bop" and "Tadd's Delight." —*Scott Yanow*

Sonny Clark Quintets / Dec. 8, 1957-Jan. 5, 1958 / Blue Note ✦✦✦
Of interest to fans of the superb hard-bop pianist, this recording combines material from two separate dates. "Royal Flush" and "Lover" are from the January 1958 *Cool Struttin'* session and are available domestically on the CD release of the same name. The remaining tunes, "Minor Meeting," "Eastern Incident" and "Little Sonny," were never released during Clark's tragically short life—they are special for fans of Sonny, as they include guitarist Kenny Burrell. Clark rarely worked with a guitarist, although he recorded some wonderful material with Grant Green, Tal Farlow, and Jimmy Raney, three masterful players. His playing here never clashes harmonically or rhythmically with the guitar, a challenging feat for any jazz pianist. These three original tunes are also welcome additions to the consistently excellent body of work that Sonny Clark composed. —*Lee Bloom*

Cool Struttin' / Jan. 5, 1958 / Blue Note ✦✦✦✦
Pianist Sonny Clark leads a quintet comprising young hard-bop all-stars on this

1958 session, which has been reissued on CD. Trumpeter Art Farmer, altoist Jackie McLean, bassist Paul Chambers, drummer Philly Joe Jones and the leader stretch out on seven numbers (originals and standards) including three performances that were previously only out in Japan. Clark's title cut is a high point. —*Scott Yanow*

Standards / Nov. 16, 1958-Dec. 7, 1958 / Blue Note ✦✦✦✦
The sessions that comprise the 14-track *Standards* were recorded by Sonny Clark at the end of 1958, with the intention that his interpretations would be issued as 45-rpm singles. His takes on these 12 standards (two of the tracks are alternate takes) are exceptional. Supported by drummer Wes Landers and, on varying dates, either Paul Chambers or Jymie Merritt on bass, Clark turns in lyrical, sensitive renditions of "Dancing in the Dark," "All of You," "I Cover the Waterfront," "I Can't Give You Anything but Love," "Black Velvet" and "I'm Just a Lucky So and So," among others. Although some of the performances are a little brief, limiting his opportunity to solo, *Standards* is a lovely collection of beautiful music that's a welcome addition to Clark's catalog. —*Stephen Thomas Erlewine*

High Fidelity / Mar. 23, 1960 / Bainbridge ✦✦✦✦

Sonny Clark Trio / Mar. 23, 1960 / Time ✦✦✦✦
This lesser-known Sonny Clark session (his only studio album not made for Blue Note) is sometimes issued under drummer Max Roach's name too. They are joined by bassist George Duvivier for a set of generally obscure Clark originals including "Minor Meeting," "Blues Mambo" and "My Conception" (which is taken as an unaccompanied piano solo). Although not obvious while listening to his recording, Sonny Clark's life was on the decline and this would be his second-to-last date as a leader. —*Scott Yanow*

Leapin' and Lopin' / Nov. 13, 1961 / Blue Note ✦✦✦✦✦
Sonny Clark's final recording as a leader gives no hint as to his increasingly erratic lifestyle (he passed away in January 1963). Heading a quintet with trumpeter Tommy Turrentine, tenor saxophonist Charlie Rouse, bassist Butch Warren and drummer Billy Higgins, Clark introduces such originals as the modestly titled "Somethin' Special," "Melody for C" and "Voodoo"; "Deep in a Dream" was the date's only standard. The CD reissue adds Clark's formerly unknown "Zellmar's Delight" and the alternate of "Melody for C" to the original six-song program. The music is high-quality hard bop and keeps Sonny Clark's record perfect. During his shortened life, every one of the albums that Clark led was excellent. —*Scott Yanow*

Kenny Clarke

b. Jan. 9, 1914, Pittsburgh, PA, **d.** Jan. 26, 1985, Paris, France
Drums / Bop
Kenny Clarke was a highly influential if subtle drummer who helped to define bebop drumming. He was the first to shift the time-keeping rhythm from the bass drum to the ride cymbal, an innovation that has been copied and utilized by a countless number of drummers since the early '40s.

Clarke played vibes, piano and trombone in addition to drums while in school. After stints with Roy Eldridge (1935) and the Jeter-Pillars band, Clarke joined Edgar Hayes' Big Band (1937-38). He made his recording debut with Hayes (which is available on a Classics CD) and showed that he was one of the most swinging drummers of the era. A European tour with Hayes gave Clarke an opportunity to lead his own session, but doubling on vibes was a definite mistake! Stints with the orchestras of Claude Hopkins (1939) and Teddy Hill (1940-41) followed and then Clarke led the house band at Minton's Playhouse (which also included Thelonious Monk). The legendary after-hours sessions led to the formation of bop and it was during this time that Clarke modernized his style and received the nickname "Klook-Mop" (later shortened to "Klook") due to the irregular "bombs" he would play behind soloists. A flexible drummer, Clarke was still able to uplift the more traditional orchestras of Louis Armstrong and Ella Fitzgerald (1941) and the combos of Benny Carter (1941-42), Red Allen and Coleman Hawkins; he also recorded with Sidney Bechet. However, after spending time in the military, Clarke stayed in the bop field, working with Dizzy Gillespie's big band and leading his own modern sessions; he co-wrote "Epistrophy" with Monk and "Salt Peanuts" with Gillespie. Clarke spent the late '40s in Europe, was with Billy Eckstine in the US in 1951 and became an original member of the Modern Jazz Quartet (1951-55). However he felt confined by the music and quit the MJQ to freelance, performing on an enormous amount of records during 1955-56.

In 1956 Clarke moved to France where he did studio work, was hired by touring American all-stars and played with Bud Powell and Oscar Pettiford in a trio called the Three Bosses (1959-60). Clarke was co-leader with Francy Boland of a legendary all-star big band (1961-72), one that had Kenny Clarke playing second drums! Other than a few short visits home, Kenny Clarke worked in France for the remainder of his life and was a major figure on the European jazz scene. —*Scott Yanow*

The Paris Bebop Sessions / Mar. 2, 1948-Oct. 9, 1950 / Prestige ✦✦✦✦
This LP, which has not yet been reissued on CD by Fantasy, has three separate sessions led by drummer Kenny Clarke during his first two visits to Paris (which led to him eventually becoming an expatriate). The pair of 1948 sessions mostly feature notable young American boppers including trumpeters Howard McGhee and Benny Bailey, altoist Jimmy Heath, baritonist Cecil Payne and pianist John Lewis. The 1950 date showcases tenor saxophonist James Moody in a quartet with bassist Pierre Michelot and pianist Ralph Schecroun, who would later rename himself Errol Parker. These fairly rare titles are valuable for the exciting playing of McGhee, Moody, Bailey and the forgotten altoist John Brown along with the modern and supportive drumming of Clarke. —*Scott Yanow*

Kenny Clarke All-Stars / Nov. 1, 1954+Feb. 7, 1955 / Savoy ✦✦✦
Recorded with Frank Morgan (sax) and Milt Jackson (vib). —*David Szatmary*

Septet / Mar. 30, 1955 / Savoy ✦✦✦

Bohemia After Dark / Jun. 26, 1955-Jul. 26, 1955 / Savoy ✦✦✦✦
The June 26, 1955, session is most notable for being the recorded debut of the recently discovered altoist Cannonball Adderley and his brother, cornetist Nat (who is also featured on the lone number from July 26, a quartet version of "We'll Be Together Again"). Although drummer Kenny Clarke is the nominal leader and the other sidemen include trumpeter Donald Byrd, Jerome Richardson on tenor and flute, pianist Horace Silver and bassist Paul Chambers, the impressive performance by the young Adderleys makes this a historic session that has often been reissued under Cannonball's name. —*Scott Yanow*

Klook's Clique / Feb. 6, 1956 / Savoy ✦✦✦
An indispensable session by the bop pioneer, with John LaPorta (sax) and Donald Byrd (tpt). —*David Szatmary*

Kenny Clarke Meets the Detroit Jazzmen / Apr. 30, 1956+May 9, 1956 / Savoy ✦✦✦✦
Drummer Kenny Clarke, who was the first to record with Cannonball Adderley, was an underrated talent scout. On this album, Clarke utilizes bassist Paul Chambers and three relative unknowns who had recently arrived in New York from Detroit: baritonist Pepper Adams, pianist Tommy Flanagan and guitarist Kenny Burrell. During what would be the drummer's last date as a leader before permanently moving to Europe, the quintet performs one original apiece by each of the Detroiters plus four jazz standards. This high-quality hard bop set in 1956 showed that the latest NY imports were already major leaguers. —*Scott Yanow*

Kenny Clarke in Paris, Vol. 1 / Sep. 23, 1957-Sep. 26, 1957 / Disques Swing ✦✦✦
In 1956 trumpeter Kenny Clarke emigrated permanently to Europe, robbing the US of an innovative drummer and helping to keep the European jazz scene quite vital. Four complete sessions that were originally released in France as EPs (extended-play 45 rpm albums) were made available domestically for the first time on this 1986 LP. Clarke is heard in a quartet with tenor saxophonist Lucky Thompson, pianist Martial Solal and bassist Pierre Michelot (quite a group), performing Michelot's arrangements with a tentet that includes Thompson, playing in a group with tenor great Don Byas and pianist Francy Boland, and performing Christian Chevalier originals with talented French musicians. The advanced and swinging music heard throughout this wonderful LP should greatly interest bop collectors. —*Scott Yanow*

● **Clarke-Boland Big Band** / Oct. 29, 1969 / RTE ✦✦✦✦✦
One of the great jazz orchestras of the 1960s and '70s and one rarely heard (either live or on record) in the US was the Kenny Clarke-Francy Boland Big Band. This overseas group (which was equally filled with Americans and Europeans) was a hard-swinging modern mainstream ensemble, analogous in ways to Rob McConnell's Boss Brass of the 1980s and '90s. Its double-CD (which was put out in 1992 but not made available in the US until 1995) has a particularly exciting live concert performance by the big band. Overflowing with soloists (including trumpeters Benny Bailey, Art Farmer and Idrees Sulieman, trombonist Ake Persson and a sax section comprising Derek Humble, Johnny Griffin, Sahib Shihab, Tony Coe and Ronnie Scott), the band is quite powerful throughout the set with Griffin generally taking solo honors. Easily recommended. —*Scott Yanow*

Pieces of Time / Sep. 16, 1983-Sep. 17, 1983 / Soul Note ✦✦✦
Standout session late in his career, with fellow drummers Andrew Cyrille, Milford Graves, and Don Moye. —*Ron Wynn*

Stanley Clarke

b. Jun. 30, 1951, Philadelphia, PA
Bass / Post-Bop, R&B, Fusion, Funk
A brilliant player on both acoustic and electric basses, Stanley Clarke has spent much of his career outside of jazz although he has the ability to play jazz with the very best. He played accordion as a youth, switching to violin and cello before settling on bass. He worked with R&B and rock bands in high school, but after mov-

ing to New York he worked with Pharoah Sanders in the early '70s. Other early gigs were with Gil Evans, Mel Lewis, Horace Silver, Stan Getz, Dexter Gordon and Art Blakey; everyone was impressed by his talents. However, Clarke really hit the big time when he started teaming up with Chick Corea in Return to Forever. When the group became a rock-oriented fusion quartet, Clarke mostly emphasized electric bass and became an influential force, preceding Jaco Pastorius. But starting with his *School Days* album (1976) and continuing through his funk group with George Duke (the Clarke/Duke Project) up to his current projects writing movie scores, Stanley Clarke has largely moved beyond the jazz world into commercial music; his 1988 Portrait album *If This Bass Could Only Talk* and his 1995 collaboration with Jean Luc Ponty and Al DiMeola on the acoustic *The Rite of Strings* are two of his few jazz recordings of the past decade. —*Scott Yanow*

Children of Forever / Dec. 26, 1972+Dec. 27, 1972 / One Way ◆◆◆
Early, instructive fusion set from super bassist Stanley Clarke, then establishing his identity as a leader. Clarke had made many mainstream jazz dates in the '60s, and was also part of Chick Corea's Return to Forever. His bass playing, as always, was remarkable, and while the songs and production were predictable, there were enough electric moments to indicate that Clarke had a future in the fusion and pop world. —*Ron Wynn*

Stanley Clarke / 1974 / Epic ◆◆◆◆
Definitive early-period funk/fusion. Clarke's finger-pop bass is up front. —*Michael G. Nastos*

Journey to Love / 1975 / Epic ◆◆◆
Prolific bassist Stanley Clarke's second jazz-rock album in the early '70s marked the beginning of what proved to be an extremely profitable collaboration with keyboardist George Duke. The album includes guest appearances from Chick Corea, John McLaughlin, Lenny White, and rocker Jeff Beck. —*Ron Wynn*

School Days / 1976 / Epic ◆◆◆
Crossover appeal. —*Ron Wynn*

Live (1976-1977) / 1976-1977 / Epic ◆◆
This CD features what was probably Stanley Clarke's favorite group of the many he led, the "School Days" band. One can understand Clarke's joy at playing this music, for his basslines are very prominent and danceable, but from a jazz standpoint there is much less of interest here than there was in Return to Forever; Chick Corea's compositional talents are a key missing ingredient. The music is mostly bombastic rock that is dominated by the funky rhythm section (which includes guitarist Raymond Gomez, keyboardist Peter Robinson and drummer Gerry Brown) with assists from an R&B-ish horn section. Other than an overly long duet with pianist David Sancious on "Bass Folk Song No. 3" and an uneventful acoustic trio exploration with guitarist John McLaughlin and percussionist Darryl Munyunga Jackson, this is essentially a set of dated rock music. —*Scott Yanow*

Modern Man / 1978 / Nemperor ◆◆
I Wanna Play for You / Nov. 1979 / Epic ◆◆◆
A late-'70s two-album (now two-disc) set that blends studio and live sessions. Those who only knew Clarke from his heavily produced, sometimes silly Urban Contemporary dates should check out the frequently amazing bass work. He was a top acoustic jazz player before switching to electric, and those qualities sometimes can be heard even in his plugged-in solos. The live tracks are more ambitious and impressive than the studio cuts. —*Ron Wynn*

Rocks, Pebbles and Sand / 1980 / Epic ◆◆
Amazing technique but little jazz content or reference. —*Ron Wynn*

The Clarke/Duke Project, Vol. 1 / 1981 / Epic ◆◆
A big hit among The Fusion/Quiet Storm crowd. —*Ron Wynn*

Let Me Know You / 1982 / Columbia ◆◆
More pop and rock than jazz. —*Ron Wynn*

The Clarke/Duke Project, Vol. 2 / 1983 / Columbia ◆◆
Time Exposure / 1984 / Epic ◆◆◆
More fusion/rock. —*Ron Wynn*

Find Out / 1985 / Epic ◆◆
Hideaway / 1986 / Epic ◆◆
● **If This Bass Could Only Talk** / 1988 / Portrait ◆◆◆◆
This was bassist Stanley Clarke's twelfth solo set, and one of his very few that would be recommended to jazz (as opposed to funk and R&B) listeners. On the instrumental set, Clarke's bass is featured in a wide variety of settings, including duets with tap dancer Gregory Hines and drummer John Robinson, a quartet with Wayne Shorter ("Goodbye Pork Pie Hat"), in a power trio with guitarist Allan Holdsworth and drummer Stewart Copeland, a piece with George Duke (on acoustic piano for a change) and soprano saxophonist George Howard, a quartet with the synthesizers of Steve Hunt, and "Funny How Time Flies," which has a colorful

Freddie Hubbard trumpet solo. Throughout, Clarke's bass has plenty of solo space, and he shows how strong a player he can be when given decent material. —*Scott Yanow*

3 / 1990 / Epic ◆◆
Both an accomplished acoustic player and a pioneering electric bassist, Stanley Clarke found new success in two other areas during the '80s and '90s. One was scoring films; the other was cutting Urban Contemporary hits with George Duke. This was their third venture, and it continued in the path of its predecessors: short songs, little solo space, double-tracked background vocals, and lots of wah-wah and synthesizer effects. —*Ron Wynn*

Passenger 157 / 1992 / Epic ◆◆
Live at the Greek / 1993 / Epic ◆◆◆
Bassist Stanley Clarke heads a quintet consisting of guitarist Larry Carlton, saxophonist Najee, keyboardist Deron Johnson and drummer Billy Cobham on this rock-oriented live set. There are some worthwhile solos with Najee being in fine form (his flute on "All Blues" and Ernie Watts-influenced tenor are enjoyable) and Larry Carlton's passionate solos keep the music from getting too mundane. Their version of "School Days" is way too long and the music does get a bit bombastic at times but listeners with an open mind towards fusion will want to acquire this all-star CD. —*Scott Yanow*

Benn Clatworthy

b. 1956, London, England
Tenor Saxophone / Hard Bop
A fixture in Los Angeles area clubs since 1980, Benn Clatworthy was originally heavily influenced by late-'50s John Coltrane but in recent years has softened his tone and sometimes sounds a little like Warne Marsh with touches of Sonny Rollins. He debuted on record in 1990 with his Discovery release *Thanks Horace* (which also features pianist Cecilia Coleman) and in 1995 released *While My Lady Sleeps* on his own label (featuring Cedar Walton as a guest). —*Scott Yanow*

Thanks Horace / Dec. 16, 1989+Mar. 15, 1990 / Discovery ◆◆◆
Benn Clatworthy's debut recording as a leader helped to introduce not only his Coltrane-inspired tenor but the talented young pianist Cecilia Coleman. Performing in a quartet with bassist Dave Carpenter and drummer Kendall Kay, Clatworthy is well showcased on five of his originals, two by Coleman and three standards (including "My Shining Hour"). This Discovery reissue CD features not only potential but fine advanced hard-bop music from these fresh voices. —*Scott Yanow*

● **While My Lady Sleeps** / Feb. 11, 1995+Mar. 11, 1995 / BCM ◆◆◆◆
A fixture in Los Angeles jazz clubs throughout the 1980s and '90s, tenor saxophonist Benn Clatworthy has recorded surprisingly little. This CD from his own private label gives one a strong sampling of his talents; the supporting cast includes pianist Cedar Walton (on three of the nine tunes), guitarist Rick Zunigar, either Larry Gales or Darek Oles on bass and drummer Albert "Tootie" Heath. Clatworthy's style is influenced by John Coltrane (circa 1959) but his tone has gradually become softer and more original. Highlights include a duet version of "My Ship" with Walton, "Blue Room," a rare revival of "While My Lady Sleeps" and several of the tenor's originals. —*Scott Yanow*

James Clay

b. Sep. 8, 1935, Dallas, TX, d. 1994, Dallas, TX
Tenor Saxophone / Hard Bop
A fine tenor saxophonist with an appealing tone and a boppish style, James Clay was an early associate of Ornette Coleman's back in Texas of the 1950s. He came up North, made a few records (including a 1956 date with Lawrence Marable and two Riverside albums in 1960 as a leader) and then went back to Texas. Nearly three decades later he appeared on Don Cherry's *Art Deco* album playing in a style unchanged from the past and just as strong. James Clay recorded a pair of excellent straightahead albums for Antilles before his death. —*Scott Yanow*

The Sound of the Wide Open Spaces / Apr. 26, 1960 / Original Jazz Classics ◆◆◆◆
James Clay's debut album as a leader (and one of only two that he cut before moving back to Dallas for nearly 30 years) matches him with fellow Texas tenor David "Fathead" Newman, pianist Wynton Kelly, bassist Sam Jones and drummer Art Taylor. Cannonball Adderley supervised the session, putting the spotlight on the competitive horns who really battle it out on the Babs Gonzales blues "Wide Open Spaces." Clay, who plays flute on the date's lone standard "What's New," holds his own with Newman and plenty of sparks fly. This Riverside album was reissued in the Original Jazz Classics series as an LP in the 1980s. —*Scott Yanow*

● **A Double Dose of Soul** / Oct. 11, 1960 / Original Jazz Classics ◆◆◆◆
James Clay only led two record sessions before settling in obscurity in Texas where he would not be rediscovered until the late '80s. Cannonball Adderley

helped present him on Riverside in 1960, so it seemed fair that Clay utilized several of Adderley's sidemen on this session (cornetist Nat Adderley or vibraphonist Victor Feldman, bassist Sam Jones and drummer Louis Hayes) along with a young Gene Harris on piano. Clay splits his time between his lyrical flute and tough tenor, proving to be an excellent bop-based improviser. This CD reissue adds two alternate takes to the original LP program and is highlighted by Feldman's "New Delhi," "Come Rain or Come Shine" and Nat's blues "Pockets." —*Scott Yanow*

I Let a Song Go out of My Heart / Jan. 20, 1989 / Antilles ◆◆◆◆
His first album in years. Excellent collection of standards, most in ballad mode. With Cedar Walton Trio. —*Michael G. Nastos*

Cookin' at the Continental / Jun. 18, 1991-Jun. 19, 1991 / Antilles ◆◆◆◆
With Fathead Newman (sax), Roy Hargrove (tpt). Three old standards, six more from Horace Silver, Bobby Timmons, Charlie Parker, and Babs Gonzalez. An up mode. —*Michael G. Nastos*

Buck Clayton (Wilbur Dorsey Clayton)
b. Nov. 12, 1911, Parsons, KS, d. Dec. 8, 1991, New York, NY
Trumpet / Swing, Mainstream Jazz
An excellent bandleader and accompanist for many vocalists including Billie Holiday, Buck Clayton was a valued soloist with the Count Basie orchestra during the '30s and '40s, and later was a celebrated studio and jam session player, writer and arranger. His tart, striking tone and melodic dexterity were his trademark, and Clayton provided several charts for Basie's orchestra and many other groups. Clayton began his career in California, where he organized a big band that had a residency in China in 1934. When he returned, Clayton led a group and played with other local bands. During a 1936 visit to Kansas City, he was invited to join Basie's orchestra as a replacement for Hot Lips Page. Clayton was also featured on sessions with Lester Young, Teddy Wilson and Holiday in the late '30s. He remained in the Basie band until 1943, when he left for army service. After leaving the army, Clayton did arrangements for Basie, Benny Goodman, and Harry James before forming a sextet in the late '40s. He toured Europe with this group in 1949 and 1950. Clayton continued heading a combo during the '50s, and worked with Joe Bushkin, Tony Parenti and Jimmy Rushing among others. He organized a series of outstanding recordings for Columbia in the mid-'50s under the title Jam Session (compiled and reissued by Mosaic in 1993). There were sessions with Rushing, Ruby Braff, and Nat Pierce. Clayton led a combo with Coleman Hawkins and J.J. Johnson at the 1956 Newport Jazz Festival, then reunited with Goodman in 1957 at the Waldorf Astoria. There was another European tour, this time with Mezz Mezzrow. He appeared in the 1956 film *The Benny Goodman Story* and played the 1958 Brussels World Fair with Sidney Bechet. Clayton later made another European visit with a Newport Jazz Festival tour. He joined Eddie Condon's band in 1959, a year after appearing in the film *Jazz on a Summer's Day*. Clayton toured Japan and Australia with Condon's group in 1964, and continued to revisit Europe throughout the '60s, often with Humphrey Lyttelton's band, while playing festivals across the country. But lip and health problems virtually ended his playing career in the late '60s. After a period outside of music, Clayton once again became active in music, this time as a nonplaying arranger, touring Africa as part of a State Department series in 1977. He provided arrangements and compositions for a 1974 Lyttelton and Buddy Tate album, and did more jam session albums for Chiaroscuro in 1974 and 1975. He also became an educator, teaching at Hunter College in the early '80s. Clayton led a group of Basie sidemen on a European tour in 1983, then headed his own big band in 1987 that played almost exclusively his compositions and arrangements. That same year Clayton's extensive autobiography *Buck Clayton's Jazz World* with Nancy Miller-Elliot was published. —*Ron Wynn*

Buck Clayton Rarities, Vol. 1 / Mar. 16, 1945-1953 / Swingtime ◆◆◆
This LP lives up to its name. The fine swing trumpeter Buck Clayton is heard with three different groups (14 selections in all) on consistently obscure but enjoyable performances. Clayton is the solo star with an octet headed by pianist Horace Henderson on two songs, fits right in with trombonist Trummy Young's Lucky Seven (a septet with tenorman Ike Quebec and pianist Ken Kersey) and there are eight songs from a date headed by singer/trumpeter Taps Miller in 1953. Buck solos on five of the tunes and his playing offers a good contrast with Miller's Louis Armstrong-inspired trumpet. This European LP is worth searching for by swing collectors. —*Scott Yanow*

The Classic Swing of Buck Clayton / 1946 / Original Jazz Classics ◆◆◆◆
This limited-edition CD features small-group swing originally issued on the H.R.S. label from three different sessions in 1946. On one date, the great trumpeter Buck Clayton heads an octet with both Trummy Young and Dicky Wells on trombones; on another occasion he leads an unusual pianoless quartet that also includes clarinetist Scoville Brown, guitarist Tiny Grimes and bassist Sid Weiss. In addition, Clayton is heard as a sideman with Trummy Young's septet, which also features

clarinetist Buster Bailey. Swing was going very much out of style at the time, and these somewhat obscure dates can be considered among the final small-group swing sessions of the classic era. More importantly, all of the principals sound creative and full of spirit. —*Scott Yanow*

Buck Clayton in Paris / Oct. 10, 1949-Oct. 21, 1953 / Vogue ◆◆◆◆
There are lots of rare and swinging performances on this valuable reissue CD from Vogue. The great swing trumpeter Buck Clayton (for whom critic Stanley Dance coined the phrase "mainstream") is heard in a sextet that co-stars tenor saxophonist Don Byas, heading a nonet that also features fellow trumpeter Bill Coleman (who gets almost as much solo space as Buck) and tenor saxophonist Alix Combelle, and guesting with Combelle's 14-piece orchestra in 1953; the latter group performs eight of its leader's originals, all arranged in swinging fashion by Clayton. This disc is easily recommended to straightahead jazz fans. —*Scott Yanow*

Dr. Jazz Series, Vol. 3 / Dec. 13, 1951-Jan. 24, 1952 / Storyville ◆◆◆◆
Storyville has released a series of CDs taken from the legendary *Dr. Jazz* radio series of 1951-52, a program which each week featured some of the top Dixieland bands then currently playing in New York clubs. Trumpeter Buck Clayton was a swing rather than a Dixieland player but during this era he decided to increase his versatility (and potential for getting jobs) by learning the basic Dixieland repertoire. He fares fairly well in a sextet that also has plenty of solo space for trombonist Herb Flemming, clarinetist Buster Bailey and drummer Kenny Kersey. Highlights of these fairly well-recorded jams include "There'll Be Some Changes Made," "Struttin' with Some Barbecue," "'Deed I Do" and "Crazy Rhythm." —*Scott Yanow*

How Hi the Fi / Dec. 14, 1953+Mar. 31, 1954 / Columbia ◆◆◆◆
The first of the famous Buck Clayton jam sessions, the exciting music on this long out-of-print LP has been reissued as part of a Mosaic box set. Two songs ("Sentimental Journey" and "Moten Swing") are from a December 1953 session in which the trumpeter/leader is teamed with trumpeter Joe Newman, trombonists Urbie Green and Benny Powell, altoist Lem Davis, Julian Dash on tenor, baritonist Charlie Fowlkes, pianist Sir Charles Thompson, guitarist Freddie Green, bassist Walter Page and drummer Jo Jones. However it is "How Hi the Fi" (cut along with "Blue Moon" on March 31, 1954) that is most memorable. Buck and fellow trumpeter Joe Thomas, trombonists Urbie Green and Trummy Young, clarinetist Woody Herman, Davis and Dash, Al Cohn on second tenor, pianist Jimmy Jones, guitarist Steve Jordan, bassist Walter Page and drummer Jo Jones are all in inspired form. The most memorable soloists are the rambunctious Trummy Young, the harmonically advanced chordings of Jimmy Jones and an exuberant Woody Herman, who was rarely heard in this type of jam session setting. With Clayton having worked out some ensemble riffs for the horns beforehand and plenty of space left for spontaneity, this music has plenty of magic. —*Scott Yanow*

☆ **Complete CBS Buck Clayton Jam Sessions / Dec. 14, 1953-Mar. 5, 1956 / Mosaic ◆◆◆◆◆**
Trumpeter Buck Clayton led a series of exciting studio jam sessions during the mid-'50s. All of the performances are on this superlative three-CD box set including a few "new" alternate takes and several that have been restored to their full length. Among the many soloists (most of them swing-oriented stylists) are Clayton, Joe Newman, Joe Thomas, Billy Butterfield and Ruby Braff on trumpets, trombonists Urbie Green, Benny Powell, Henderson Chambers, Trummy Young, Bennie Green, Dickie Harris, J.C. Higginbotham and Tyree Glenn, altoist Lem Davis, tenors Coleman Hawkins, Al Cohn and Buddy Tate, Julian Dash doubling on tenor and alto, baritonist Charlie Fowlkes, several rhythm sections with pianists Sir Charles Thompson, Jimmy Jones, Billy Kyle, Ken Kersey and the forgotten Al Waslohn and a guest appearance by Woody Herman on clarinet. These generally lengthy performances contain plenty of spontaneous riffing behind soloists and lots of special moments; "How Hi the Fi" is quite memorable. —*Scott Yanow*

The Essential Buck Clayton / 1953-1957 / Vanguard ◆◆◆◆
This excellent CD contains over 80 minutes of music and reissues 14 of the 16 selections included on a two-LP set from 1977. There are three (rather than five) numbers from a date led by pianist Mel Powell that features trumpeter Buck Clayton and clarinetist Edmond Hall, eight songs from the 1957 Buck Clayton septet (with trombonist Vic Dickenson and altoist Earle Warren) and three tunes from a matchup between the trumpets of Buck Clayton and Ruby Braff (along with the tenor of Buddy Tate and trombonist Benny Morton). The consistently swinging music includes some Count Basie-associated tunes plus seven Clayton originals with fine solos from all of the principals. Mainstream may not have been the dominant form of jazz during this period but many of its exponents (including those heard on this CD) were very much in their prime. —*Scott Yanow*

Copenhagen Concert / Sep. 17, 1959 / Steeple Chase ◆◆◆◆
This double-CD documents a concert by a group of swing all-stars dominated by Count Basie alumni: trumpeters Buck Clayton and Emmett Berry, altoist Earle

Warren, Buddy Tate on tenor, trombonist Dicky Wells, pianist Al Williams, bassist Gene Ramey and drummer Herbie Lovelle. While the group is fine on the first disc playing five instrumentals (including three of Clayton's lesser-known songs), they really come alive on the second CD when they are joined by the great swing/blues singer Jimmy Rushing. Mr. Five by Five not only is in strong voice on three standards and three famous blues but he inspired the other musicians to play some hard-swinging and colorful solos. It is for Rushing's performance that this set is chiefly recommended. —*Scott Yanow*

Tenderly / Nov. 16, 1959-Nov. 17, 1959 / Inner City ◆◆◆
This out-of-print Inner City LP has tasteful playing by Buck Clayton with a French quintet comprising Jean-Claude Pelletier on piano and organ, guitarist Jean Bonal, bassist Roland Lobligeois and expatriate drummer Kansas Fields. The emphasis is on ballads and standards (although there are a pair of obscure Sidney Bechet tunes) but Clayton's appealing sound, naturally melodic style and swinging solos make all of the concise performances of interest to mainstream jazz fans. —*Scott Yanow*

Jammin' at Eddie Condon's, Vol. 1 / 1960 / Jazz Up ◆◆◆
The great swing trumpeter Buck Clayton had many Dixieland gigs in the 1950s, including this decent effort from 1960. Teamed with either Bennie Morton or Cutty Cutshall on trombones, clarinetist Peanuts Hucko, pianist Dave McKenna, bassist Bob Haggart and drummer Buzzy Drootin, Clayton sounds fine on such warhorses as "Lulu's Back in Town," "At the Jazz Band Ball" and "Wolverine Blues." Although he was capable of playing more advanced music, Clayton gives a generous amount of spirit to these Dixieland tunes and the results should satisfy trad fans. This CD is the first of two volumes. —*Scott Yanow*

Jammin' at Eddie Condon's, Vol. 2 / 1960 / Jazz Up ◆◆◆
The second of two CD volumes continues the documentation of a Dixieland session featuring trumpeter Buck Clayton (who was normally a swing player), either Benny Morton or Cutty Cutshall on trombones, clarinetist Peanuts Hucko, pianist Dave McKenna, bassist Bob Haggart and drummer Buzzy Drootin. The repertoire (other than a ballad medley) is a bit stale (including "The Saints," "Ballin' the Jack," "Indiana" and "Bye Bye Blackbird") but the music has plenty of spirit and drive. Clayton generally comes up with something fresh to say in his solos and the ensembles have fire. —*Scott Yanow*

Goin' to Kansas City / Oct. 5, 1960-Oct. 6, 1960 / Original Jazz Classics ◆◆◆◆
Although trumpeter Buck Clayton gets top billing, this CD reissue actually features Tommy Gwaltney's *Kansas City Nine*, an unusual group sporting arrangements by Gwaltney and tenor saxophonist Tommy Newsom (who decades later became famous for his work on "The Tonight Show"). The group has an unusual combination of major names (Clayton, trombonist Dickie Wells, guitarist Charlie Byrd, pianist John Bunch, bassist Whitey Mitchell and drummer Buddy Schutz) along with Gwaltney (who doubles on reeds and vibes), Newsom and Bobby Zottola (playing second trumpet and peck horn). Although the nonet performs a variety of songs associated with Kansas City Jazz of the swing era, the arrangements are modern and unpredictable. —*Scott Yanow*

Buck and Buddy / Dec. 20, 1960 / Original Jazz Classics ◆◆◆
Count Basie veterans Buck Clayton and tenorman Buddy Tate teamed up during 1960-61 for a pair of Swingville recordings. This CD reissues the first one, a quintet outing with pianist Sir Charles Thompson, bassist Gene Ramey and drummer Mousie Alexander. The repertoire is split between three standards (including "When a Woman Loves a Man") and three Clayton originals. The melodic music consistently swings and practically defines "mainstream" jazz. Worth picking up. —*Scott Yanow*

★ **Olympia Concert (22 April 61)** / Apr. 22, 1961 / Vogue ◆◆◆◆◆
A splendid set with vintage sensibility and a jam session atmosphere. Buddy Tate (ts) and Sir Charles Thompson (p) are on the money. —*Ron Wynn*

Buck Clayton All-Stars, 1961 / Apr. 1961 / Storyville ◆◆◆◆

Swiss Radio Days, Vol. 7: Basel 1961 / May 2, 1961 / TCB ◆◆◆◆

Passport to Paradise / May 15, 1961 / Inner City ◆◆◆
Trumpeter Buck Clayton was in Paris at the time of this tasteful and typically melodic quintet date. Joined by a four-piece rhythm section that features pianist Sir Charles Thompson and guitarist Jean Bonal, Clayton (who generally states the opening melody muted and then closes the piece with an open horn) never really cuts loose but is quite pleasing to hear on these standards. —*Scott Yanow*

Buck & Buddy Blow the Blues / Sep. 15, 1961 / Original Jazz Classics ◆◆◆
Trumpeter Buck Clayton and tenor saxophonist Buddy Tate, both Count Basie veterans, teamed up with the Basieish pianist Sir Charles Thompson, bassist Gene Ramey and drummer Mousie Alexander in 1960 for a set of three standards and a trio of Clayton originals. Although the musicians all play well on this mainstream

set, few surprises or exciting moments occur and the performances are not as memorable as one would expect. —*Scott Yanow*

With Humphrey Lyttelton and His Band / Nov. 1964 / Harlequin ◆◆◆
For this LP (plus one in 1966), trumpeter Buck Clayton sits in with British trumpeter Humphrey Lyttelton's excellent sextet, and together, they perform high-quality small-group swing. The fresh repertoire (three underplayed standards, two blues and five originals by either Clayton or Lyttelton), the excellent solos (including some from Tony Coe on tenor and baritonist Joe Temperley) and the high spirits overcome any minor technical deficiencies. Recommended to all straightahead jazz fans. —*Scott Yanow*

Meets Joe Turner / Jun. 2, 1965 / Black Lion ◆◆◆
Despite its title, trumpeter Buck Clayton and blues singer Big Joe Turner actually perform on three separate songs apiece, only coming together on the concluding "Too Late, Too Late." Recorded in Yugoslavia, these performances also utilize a four-piece Yugoslavian quartet, with vibraphonist Bosko Petrovic the only player to receive much fame through the years. Turner sounds fine on a pair of his blues and "I Want a Little Girl," while Buck jams enthusiastically on "Honeysuckle Rose," "I Can't Get Started" and "Perdido." Nothing all that surprising occurs, but the music is quite satisfying. —*Scott Yanow*

Baden, Switzerland 1966 / Feb. 6, 1966 / Sackville ◆◆◆◆◆
For this Swiss concert, the great swing trumpeter Buck Clayton is joined by three Swiss players (Michel Pilet on tenor, pianist Henri Chaix and bassist Isla Eckinger) in addition to the veteran swing drummer Wallace Bishop. Clayton is in particularly inspired form even though he had played the songs in this repertoire (seven swing standards plus a blues) a countless number of times. His range was at its peak during this period and Clayton comes up with consistently creative ideas on such warhorses as "All of Me," "Stompin' at the Savoy," "You Can Depend on Me" and "One O' Clock Jump." Highly recommended to swing collectors. —*Scott Yanow*

Le Vrai Buck Clayton, Vol. 2 / May 25, 1966 / 77 ◆◆◆

A Swingin' Dream / Oct. 23, 1988 / Stash ◆◆◆◆
The premise for this CD is so logical that it is surprising (and disappointing) that only one recording resulted. Trumpeter Buck Clayton was forced to retire due to lip problems in the late '60s, but he had always been a talented arranger. Finally, in the mid-'80s, he put together a big band to play some new charts he had written. This 13-piece unit has such fine players as trumpeters Spanky Davis and Johnny Letman, trombonist Dan Barrett, altoist Chuck Wilson, baritonist Joe Temperley, guitarist Chris Flory and drummer Mel Lewis, among others. "Avenue C" is the only older tune included on this swinging date; Clayton's big band should have recorded many more sessions. —*Scott Yanow*

Jeff Clayton

b. 1954, Venice, CA
Alto Saxophone / Hard Bop, Soul Jazz, Swing

A talented altoist whose sound sometimes comes quite close to that of Cannonball Adderley, Jeff Clayton has played in a wide variety of settings, mostly in the Los Angeles area (although in the late-1990s he relocated to the East Coast). He teamed up with his brother, bassist John Clayton, as the Clayton Brothers (off and on since 1977) and as co-leaders (along with drummer Jeff Hamilton) of the Clayton-Hamilton Jazz Orchestra. Clayton also played for a short period with the Count Basie Orchestra when it was led by Thad Jones. Jeff Clayton is quite talented on tenor, flute and various woodwinds, but his main voice is on alto. —*Scott Yanow*

John Clayton

b. 1952, Venice, CA
Bass, Arranger, Leader / Swing, Hard Bop

A multi-talented musician, John Clayton deserves much more recognition. A brilliant bassist whose bowed solos are exquisite, Clayton is also a top-notch arranger and composer. A protege of Ray Brown (whom he recorded with on a couple of occasions, including a late-'90s collaboration with fellow bassist Christian McBride), Clayton picked up important early experience playing with Count Basie's Orchestra for two years. He has co-led the Clayton Brothers with his younger brother, altoist Jeff, off and on since 1977, and in 1985 put together the Clayton-Hamilton Jazz Orchestra, along with Jeff Clayton and drummer Jeff Hamilton. Clayton's charts for the big band, which are sometimes a little reminiscent of Thad Jones, give it its own muscial personality. John Clayton has also worked extensively as a freelance bassist and arranger. —*Scott Yanow*

Clayton-Hamilton Jazz Orchestra

f. 1985

Group / Bop, Swing

The Clayton-Hamilton Jazz Orchestra is unusual in that it has three leaders: drummer Jeff Hamilton, altoist Jeff Clayton and bassist John Clayton. While Hamilton (who has played regularly with Oscar Peterson, Ray Brown, Monty Alexander, Gene Harris and the L.A. Four) really drives the band and Jeff Clayton (whose sound is inspired by Cannonball Adderley) is one of the orchestra's top soloists, it is John Clayton's colorful and unpredictable arrangements that really give this big band its own personality. In addition, Clayton (who was formerly with Count Basie) is a very talented soloist, particularly when bowing. The swinging orchestra, filled with top Los Angeles players (including such soloists as Rickey Woodard, Charlie Owens, Bobby Bryant, Snooky Young, Oscar Brashear, George Bohanon, Thurman Green and Bill Cunliffe), can hold its own with any other big band of the 1990s as shown on its two Capri sets (*Groove Shop* and *Heart and Soul*) and its Lake Street release *Absolutely*. —*Scott Yanow*

● **Groove Shop** / Apr. 18, 1989-Apr. 19, 1989 / Capri ◆◆◆◆◆

This Capri CD was the debut of the Clayton-Hamilton Jazz Orchestra, a notable L.A.-based big band co-led by bassist John Clayton, altoist Jeff Clayton and drummer Jeff Hamilton. The 18-piece group has many top soloists, most notably the three co-leaders, tenor saxophonist Rickey Woodard, trumpeters Snooky Young, Clay Jenkins and Oscar Brashear and trombonist George Bohanon. However it is the arrangements of John Clayton that give the orchestra its own sound. Highlights include "Raincheck," Snooky's vocal and trumpet feature on "T'Aint What You Do," Hamilton's showcase on "Brush This," Oscar Brashear's "Sashay" (which has a Clayton chart that recalls Thad Jones) and "Night Train." Highly recommended. —*Scott Yanow*

Heart and Soul / Feb. 1991 / Capri ◆◆◆◆

The second Capri CD from the Clayton-Hamilton Jazz Orchestra is the equal of their first. This hard-swinging L.A. big band plays a full set of bassist John Clayton's colorful arrangements including Benny Carter's "Easy Money," a slower-than-usual "Heart and Soul," "I Be Serious 'Bout Dem Blues" and "Blues Blower's Blues"; the latter features all five of the group's saxophonists (Jeff Clayton, Bill Green, Rickey Woodard, Charlie Owens and Lee Callet) jamming on tenor. Other key soloists include pianist Bill Cunliffe, trombonist George Bohanon and trumpeters Clay Jenkins, Snooky Young and Oscar Brashear. This greatly underrated big band has been one of the finest of the 1990s. —*Scott Yanow*

Absolutely! / Apr. 16, 1995 / Lake Street ◆◆◆◆

Featuring some of Los Angeles' finest jazz musicians, the Clayton-Hamilton Jazz Orchestra (which has drummer Jeff Hamilton and altoist Jeff Clayton among its three leaders) performs the arrangements of the other co-leader, bassist John Clayton. There are several classic charts on this CD, including "Blues for Stephanie," "For All We Know" and "Reverence"; all ten selections are well worth hearing. The swinging music has its share of subtle surprises and many fine solos, including some by tenors Rickey Woodard and Charles Owens, pianist Bill Cunliffe, altoist Clayton and trumpeters Oscar Brashear, Snooky Young and Clay Jenkins. Highly recommended for big band fans. —*Scott Yanow*

Jimmy Cleveland

b. May 3, 1926, Wartrace, TN

Trombone / Bop, Hard Bop

One of the finest trombonists to emerge during the 1950s, Jimmy Cleveland has been overlooked since moving to Los Angeles in the late '60s. He started on trombone when he was 16 and his first important job was with Lionel Hampton (1950-53). After Hampton's European tour of 1953, Cleveland became a busy freelance musician in New York, making many recording sessions (including with Dizzy Gillespie, Gil Evans, Oliver Nelson, Oscar Pettiford, Lucky Thompson, James Moody and Gerry Mulligan). He toured Europe with Quincy Jones in 1959-60 and played with Thelonious Monk's 1967 octet but otherwise stayed in New York until going to the West Coast to play with "The Merv Griffin Show's" band and to continue recording for Quincy Jones. Jimmy Cleveland remains one of the most technically skilled of the bop-based trombonists and still appears on an irregular basis in Los Angeles clubs. —*Scott Yanow*

● **Introducing Jimmy Cleveland and His All Stars** / Aug. 4, 1955-Nov. 19, 1955 / EmArcy ◆◆◆◆

The first of five albums headed by trombonist Jimmy Cleveland during 1955-59 (he has not led any since), this out-of-print LP (which was reissued by Trip in the 1970s) features Cleveland in medium-size groups with trumpeter Ernie Royal, either Lucky Thompson or Jerome Richardson on tenor, baritonist Cecil Payne, Hank Jones, John Williams or Wade Legge on piano, Barry Galbraith, Paul Chambers or Oscar Pettiford on bass and either Max Roach, Osie Johnson or Joe Harris

on drums. The all-star cast interprets a variety of Quincy Jones arrangements, alternating standards with lesser-known originals and, although many of his sidemen get fine spots, Cleveland generally wins solo honors. —*Scott Yanow*

Cleveland Style / Dec. 12, 1957+Dec. 13, 1957 / EmArcy ◆◆◆

Although trombonist Jimmy Cleveland is the main star of this album, arranger Ernie Wilkins comes in a close second. Wilkins' charts for the septet make inventive use of either Jay McAllister or Don Butterfield on tuba and he also brought in two excellent originals (including one called "Goodbye Ebbets Field"). With trumpeter Art Farmer, tenor saxophonist Benny Golson, pianist Wynton Kelly, bassist Eddie Jones and drummer Charlie Persip also featured with the septet, it is not surprising that the result is high-quality straightahead jazz. Worth searching for. —*Scott Yanow*

Rosemary Clooney

b. May 23, 1928, Maysville, KY

Vocals / Standards, Swing

Vocalist Rosemary Clooney's rise to fame in the '50s came on the strength of songs that in many instances were without question novelty tunes; she's not a vocal improviser like Carmen McRae, Betty Carter or Sarah Vaughan. She is an excellent lyric interpreter, has fine timing, phrases skillfully and intelligently, and performs with the dramatic quality evident among all great singers. Her background and foundation are jazz, even if her technique doesn't always adhere to rigid jazz scrutiny. Clooney entered amateur events with her sister Betty in Cincinnati, and they sang on radio stations. The duo worked in Tony Pastor's band during the late '40s, then Clooney started as a soloist. She joined the Columbia roster in 1950, and made several hits for them, among them "You're Just in Love," "Beautiful Brown Eyes," "Half as Much," "Hey There," "This Ole House," the No. 1 hit "Come On-A My House" co-written by Ross Bagdasarian of Chipmunks fame and "If Teardrops Were Pennies." Clooney had 13 Top 40 hits in the early '50s, among them duets with Guy Mitchell and Marlene Dietrich. She also appeared in such films as *The Stars Are Singing, Here Come the Girls, White Christmas* and *Red Garters* in 1953 and 1954. Clooney recorded with the Benny Goodman sextet, the Hi-Lo's and Duke Ellington in the '50s. She moved to RCA in the '60s, and recorded with Bing Crosby. There were also dates for Coral, Reprise, and Capitol, among them another session with Crosby. The rock revolution and a decision to spend more time with her family resulted in Clooney going into semi-retirement. She returned in the late '70s, singing with renewed power and confidence while making swing-influenced dates and combo sessions for Concord. She's maintained that relationship through the '80s and '90s, doing standards, repetory albums and demonstrating a resiliency and energy that validates her position among the fine jazz-based vocalists in American music. —*Ron Wynn and Bill Dahl*

Blue Rose / Jan. 23, 1956+Jan. 27, 1956 / Columbia ◆◆◆◆

This record must have surprised many listeners when it came out in the mid-'50s. Rosemary Clooney, who was not thought of at the time as a jazz singer, does an excellent job singing 11 Duke Ellington/Billy Strayhorn tunes with the Ellington Orchestra. Strayhorn contributed most of the arrangements and, although Clooney's parts are actually overdubbed, her collaboration with Duke's men seems quite natural and spontaneous. Clooney swings her way through such numbers as "Hey Baby," "I Let a Song Go out of My Heart," "It Don't Mean a Thing," the recent "Blue Rose" (which features her wordless vocalizing) and "I'm Checkin' out Goodbye." Among the main soloists are baritonist Harry Carney, trumpeter Ray Nance, altoist Johnny Hodges and clarinetist Jimmy Hamilton. The recommended music (one of Rosemary Clooney's top sessions of the 1950s) has been reissued several times through the years. —*Scott Yanow*

Rosie Solves the Swingin' Riddle / May 25, 1960-Jun. 2, 1960 / Koch ◆◆◆◆

● **Everything's Coming up Rosie** / July 7, 1977 / Concord Jazz ◆◆◆◆

Rosemary Clooney's first album for the Concord label set the standard for her work of the next 20 years. Long associated with middle-of-the-road pop music, Clooney really excelled in the jazz-oriented settings with the Concord All-Stars. Although she does not really improvise, her very pleasing voice and subtle phrasing should appeal to most jazz followers. On her Concord debut, Clooney is joined by trumpeter Bill Berry, tenor saxophonist Scott Hamilton, pianist Nat Pierce, bassist Monty Budwig and drummer Jake Hanna. She lets the band run loose on two instrumentals and then really digs into her eight vocals, finding fresh things to say on eight familiar standards. —*Scott Yanow*

Rosie Sings Bing / Jan. 6, 1978 / Concord Jazz ◆◆◆◆

Shortly after Bing Crosby's death, his good friend Rosemary Clooney recorded ten songs associated with Bing. Since she had such a wide range of repertoire to choose from, Clooney was able to easily come up with a variety of tunes (mostly dating from the 1930s) that fit her easy-swinging style. With fine support from tenor saxophonist Scott Hamilton, guitarist Cal Collins, pianist Nat Pierce, bassist

Monty Budwig and drummer Jake Hanna, the singer is in particularly fine form on such numbers as "Pennies from Heaven," "I Surrender Dear," "It's Easy to Remember" and "Just One More Chance." —*Scott Yanow*

Here's to My Lady / Sep. 1978 / Concord Jazz ✦✦✦✦✦

This CD reissue of Rosemary Clooney's third Concord album (which was originally titled *Here's to My Lady*) is one of her best. Clooney sings ten songs associated with Billie Holiday and she is in prime form on such numbers as "I Cover the Waterfront," "Mean to Me," "Comes Love" and a swinging "Them There Eyes." The backup group is quite noteworthy too: tenor saxophonist Scott Hamilton, cornetist Warren Vache, guitarist Cal Collins, pianist Nat Pierce, bassist Monty Budwig and drummer Jake Hanna. Recommended. —*Scott Yanow*

Rosemary Clooney Sings the Lyrics of Ira Gershwin / Oct. 1979 / Concord Jazz ✦✦✦✦

Ira Gershwin himself approved this record. Rosemary Clooney sings ten of his classic sets of lyrics, including eight songs written in collaboration with his brother George; the exceptions are "Long Ago and Far Away" (music by Jerome Kern) and "The Man That Got Away" (a later Harold Arlen song). Although not an improviser herself, Clooney excels in this swinging setting and includes occasional solos by cornetist Warren Vache, tenor saxophonist Scott Hamilton, flutist Roger Glenn, pianist Nat Pierce and guitarist Cal Collins. All of Clooney's Concord albums are well worth acquiring. —*Scott Yanow*

With Love / Nov. 1980 / Concord Jazz ✦✦✦

Rosemary Clooney sings both old and new songs on this 1980 Concord album. With the emphasis on ballads (including "Just the Way You are," "The Way We Were," "Hello Young Lovers" and "Tenderly"), there is less variety on this set than usual although a swinging rendition of "Will You Still Be Mine" is a fine closer. Clooney is heard in prime voice as usual and there are some fine concise solos by tenor saxophonist Scott Hamilton, cornetist Warren Vache, guitarist Cal Collins, pianist Nat Pierce and guest vibraphonist Cal Tjader. —*Scott Yanow*

Sings the Music of Cole Porter / Jan. 1982 / Concord Jazz ✦✦✦

All of Rosemary Clooney's Concord albums are easily recommended to jazz listeners, although she is not an improviser herself (preferring to state melodies fairly straight but with sincere feeling and a light swing), Clooney has featured top mainstream soloists on each of her records. This album (which features tenor saxophonist Scott Hamilton, cornetist Warren Vache, guitarist Cal Collins, pianist Nat Pierce and vibraphonist Cal Tjader) is fortunately no exception. Clooney's straightforward but enthusiastic and understanding interpretations of Cole Porter's sophisticated lyrics uplift even the most familiar of the tunes. Highlights include "I Get a Kick out of You," "Get out of Town," "Just One of Those Things," "I've Got You Under My Skin" and "You're the Top." —*Scott Yanow*

Sings the Music of Harold Arlen / 1983 / Concord Jazz ✦✦✦

Rosemary Clooney's eighth album for Concord once again gives her the opportunity to interpret the music of a composer, this time Harold Arlen. With a superior sextet that features cornetist Warren Vache, tenor saxophonist Scott Hamilton, pianist Dave McKenna and guitarist Ed Bickert, Clooney sounds very enthusiastic and swings lightly on such songs as "Hurray for Love," "Ding Dong the Witch Is Dead," "My Shining Hour" and "Stormy Weather." —*Scott Yanow*

My Buddy / Aug. 1983 / Concord Jazz ✦✦✦

Considering how consistent Rosemary Clooney's CDs are for Concord, the failure of this collaboration with the Woody Herman Orchestra is a surprise. The problem is that the material is erratic, and Clooney just sounds silly interpreting such fairly recent material as "I Believe in Love" (a really terrible opener), James Taylor's "Don't Let Me Be Lonely Tonight" and "You've Made Me So Very Happy." She sounds much more comfortable on "You're Gonna Hear from Me" and a touching version of "My Buddy," but those do not fully compensate for the misfires. Also, the Herman Orchestra is largely wasted, sounding like a stage band and mostly heard in a supportive role with only a few short solos. Herman himself only emerges three times and does not make much of an impression. Skip this one. —*Scott Yanow*

Sings the Music of Irving Berlin / Jun. 1984 / Concord Jazz ✦✦✦

Ever since hooking up with the Concord label in 1977, Rosemary Clooney has had a renaissance. On this enjoyable set, she interprets ten of Irving Berlin's songs (including a couple of obscurities) with fine backup from a swinging septet that includes tenorman Scott Hamilton, cornetist Warren Vache, both Chris Flory and Ed Bickert on guitars and pianist John Oddo. Highlights include "Be Careful, It's My Heart," "Cheek to Cheek," "The Best Thing for You Would Be Me" and "What'll I Do." —*Scott Yanow*

Sings Ballads / Apr. 1985 / Concord Jazz ✦✦✦

Rosemary Clooney continued her string of jazz sets for Concord in 1985 with this lyrical program. Clooney interprets ten ballads with the assistance of tenor saxophonist Scott Hamilton, cornetist Warren Vache, guitarist Ed Bickert, pianist John

Oddo (her musical director), bassist Chuck Israels and drummer Jake Hanna. Clooney's versions of such songs as "The Shadow of Your Smile," "A Nightingale Sang in Berkeley Square," "Easy Living" and "It Never Entered My Mind" are filled with sincere feeling and rank with the best versions ever. However a general sameness of tempo keeps this album from being quite as highly recommended as most of Rosie's other Concord records although it is well worth picking up. —*Scott Yanow*

Sings the Music of Jimmy Van Heusen / Aug. 1986 / Concord Jazz ✦✦✦

A special treat of this tribute to composer Jimmy Van Heusen is that Rosemary Clooney sings two songs ("The Second Time Around" and "Call Me Irresponsible") while accompanied only by guitarist Ed Bickert; she excels in the intimate setting. Other selections feature tenor saxophonist Scott Hamilton (a fixture on Clooney's Concord recordings), cornetist Warren Vache, guitarist Emily Remler (on six of the ten songs), pianist John Oddo, bassist Michael Moore and drummer Joe Cocuzzo. In addition to some famous numbers ("I Thought About You," "It Could Happen to You" and "Like Someone in Love"), a few lesser-known Jimmy Van Heusen compositions are included, such as "My Heart Is a Hobo" and "Walking Happy." An easily recommended, well-rounded set that finds Rosemary Clooney in prime voice. —*Scott Yanow*

Sings Lyrics of Johnny Mercer / Aug. 1987 / Concord Jazz ✦✦✦

After a long period of indifferent recordings in the 1960s and early '70s, Rosemary Clooney underwent a renaissance after she began recording regularly for Concord in 1977. Backed by swinging ensembles and encouraged to record songbooks and special projects involving superior songs, Clooney blossomed and her career regained its momentum, continuing into the late '90s. This album finds Rosie singing 11 songs that have Johnny Mercer lyrics including "Something's Got to Give," "Laura," "I Remember You," "Skylark" and even "Hooray for Hollywood." Joined by such fine soloists as tenor saxophonist Scott Hamilton, cornetist Warren Vache, trombonist Dan Barrett, guitarist Ed Bickert and her musical director pianist John Oddo, Rosemary Clooney is heard in excellent form throughout the colorful program. —*Scott Yanow*

Show Tunes / Aug. 1988-Nov. 1988 / Concord Jazz ✦✦✦

This Rosemary Clooney project (part of an extensive series she has made for Concord) has a more open topic than her songbooks. The show tunes on the set range from older songs such as "Manhattan" and "Taking a Chance on Love" to "I Stayed Too Long at the Fair" and the Bergman's "Where Do You Start." With a few exceptions, Clooney avoids the more familiar tunes in favor of underrated obscurities and she is assisted by a fine quintet that includes tenor saxophonist Scott Hamilton, cornetist Warren Vache and pianist-arranger John Oddo. All of Clooney's Concord recordings are well worth getting by listeners who enjoy swinging middle-of-the-road vocalists, and this one is no exception. —*Scott Yanow*

Sings Rodgers, Hart & Hammerstein / Oct. 1989 / Concord Jazz ✦✦✦

This Rosemary Clooney recording differs from all of her previous Concord albums in that she is joined by the L.A. Jazz Choir (a 12-voice group) on half of the dozen selections. The choral backing is a bit of an acquired taste for jazz listeners but Clooney's backup sextet does consist of tenor saxophonist Scott Hamilton, trumpeter Jack Sheldon (who helps out Clooney with his vocal on "People Will Say We're in Love"), trombonist Chauncey Welsch, pianist John Oddo (who is responsible for both the choral and instrumental arrangements), bassist John Clayton and drummer Joe La Barbera. Clooney interprets the music of Richard Rodgers and lyrics that are split almost evenly between Lorenz Hart and Oscar Hammerstein. Most of the tunes are fairly well-known (including "It Might as Well Be Spring," "I Could Write a Book," "You Took Advantage of Me" and "My Romance") but Rosemary Clooney makes them sound fresh and alive. —*Scott Yanow*

For the Duration / Oct. 15, 1990-Oct. 17, 1990 / Concord Jazz ✦✦✦

For this CD, Rosemary Clooney sings 14 selections that had their greatest meaning during World War II but have since become recognized as timeless. She is joined by her usual sidemen (including tenor saxophonist Scott Hamilton, cornetist Warren Vache and her musical director/pianist John Oddo) plus (on six of the selections) a string section. Whether it be "Don't Fence Me In," "Ev'ry Time We Say Goodbye," "September Song", "The White Cliffs of Dover" or a touching "I'll Be Seeing You," Clooney is heard in prime form, giving each song just the right amount of emotion and sensitivity. —*Scott Yanow*

Girl Singer / Nov. 1991-Dec. 1991 / Concord Jazz ✦✦✦

This CD differs a bit from Rosemary Clooney's previous Concord albums. For the first time, tenor saxophonist Scott Hamilton is not in the supporting cast and Clooney is joined by a big band. She celebrates the legacy of the "girl singers" of the swing era in style although some of the selections (such as Dave Frishberg's "Sweet Kentucky Ham," "Let There Be Love" and "Wave") were certainly not around during the big-band era. With such soloists as trumpeter Warren Luening, trombonist Chauncey Welsch, flutist Gary Foster and tenors Bob Cooper and Pete

Christlieb having short spots, Clooney performs a fine program which alternates light swingers with ballads. —*Scott Yanow*

Do You Miss New York? / Sep. 14, 1992-Sep. 17, 1992 / Concord Jazz ✦✦✦✦
As is usual for Rosemary Clooney's very consistent string of Concord albums, this is a jazz-oriented set with the highly appealing singer interpreting veteran standards from the 1930s and '40s plus a couple of newer songs (Dave Frishberg's "Do You Miss New York" and "I Wish You Love"). Using a fine sextet with her favorite horn players (tenorman Scott Hamilton and cornetist Warren Vache) plus her musical director-pianist John Oddo and guitarist Buck Pizzarelli, Clooney is heard in top form. John Pizzarelli makes a guest appearance, sharing the vocal and playing guitar on "It's Only a Paper Moon"; other highlights include "As Long as I Live," "I Ain't Got Nothin' but the Blues" and "We'll Be Together Again." Recommended. —*Scott Yanow*

Still on The Road / 1993 / Concord Jazz ✦✦✦
Rosemary Clooney was in the midst of a major career revival, doing credible jazz tunes and mixing pre-rock pop, standards, and even some pop and country. Clooney didn't falter on Willie Nelson's "On the Road Again" or Paul Simon's "Still Crazy After All These Years," but she seemed more at home on more conventional fare like Cole Porter's "Take Me Back to Manhattan" or Irving Berlin's "How Deep Is the Ocean." Clooney's voice remains clear and confident, her timing and pacing solid, and her range good, if diminished a bit. While some of this isn't jazz, most of it does meet the requirements, and none of it is poorly performed. —*Ron Wynn*

Dedicated to Nelson / Sep. 27, 1995-Sep. 30, 1995 / Concord Jazz ✦✦✦✦
During 1956-57, the Rosemary Clooney television show featured the singer with arrangements provided by Nelson Riddle. Nearly four decades later, pianist/arranger John Oddo and Clooney listened to many hours of audio tapes from the show and picked 16 of Riddle's charts to revive. Since the music was no longer available on paper, it had to be transcribed off of the tapes and in many cases extended beyond the one or two original choruses; writers Eddie Karam and David Berger also assisted on the project. A 17-piece big band was utilized plus (on six of the 16 tunes) seven strings and a harp. Although liner note writer Gary Giddins raves about the music and claims that this project was unprecedented, bands reviving 1920s music transcribe off of records all of the time. Despite some short solos by trumpeter Warren Luening, Tommy Newsom on tenor, altoist Gary Foster and trombonist Chauncey Welsh, the presence of a swinging rhythm section and the high-quality repertoire, most of the music (which sticks to the melodies) is closer to middle-of-the-road pop than to jazz. Clooney sings in near-peak form throughout this labor of love and the music is pleasing but the results are rather predictable. —*Scott Yanow*

White Christmas [Concord] / Apr. 1, 1996-Apr. 4, 1996 / Concord Jazz ✦✦✦
Although Rosemary Clooney had a major part in the famous film *White Christmas* back in 1954, this was her first full Christmas album and it was a big seller when it was released late in 1996. From the jazz standpoint, there is not much here, as Clooney is accompanied by a huge orchestra conducted and mostly arranged by Peter Matz. Although there are a few brief solos from altoist Gary Foster, tenor saxophonist Dan Higgins, trombonist Chauncey Welsch and trumpeter Warren Luening, the music is essentially nostalgic middle-of-the-road pop with Clooney joined on several numbers by the Earl Brown Singers (who also take brief a cappella versions of some veteran Christmas tunes); one tune apiece features appearances by Michael Feinstein and Rosemary's brother Nick Clooney. But jazz content aside, Rosemary Clooney is in good voice, and the heartfelt emotions that she expresses on these Yuletide favorites communicate quite well. —*Scott Yanow*

Mothers & Daughters / Jun. 23, 1996-Oct. 24, 1996 / Concord Jazz ✦✦
Although a strong seller, this CD is actually among Rosemary Clooney's weakest of her productive Concord period. Tenor saxophonist Scott Hamilton is missing, the selections (some of which deal with children) are often overly sentimental and the jazz content (despite some brief spots for the reeds of Gary Foster) is nearly nonexistent; the occasional string section does not help. Clooney is in reasonably good voice (she was 68 at the time) and it is good to have the classic "Sisters" (from *Holiday Inn*) on record, but some of the numbers (particularly a vocal duet with Keith Carradine on "Turn Around") are so sticky as to be difficult to sit through and it is strange to have the meaning of "Thank Heaven for Little Girls" (which is associated with Maurice Chevalier) totally changed. Pass on this one! —*Scott Yanow*

Clusone Trio

f. 1988
Group / Avant-Garde
One of the most humorous and consistently inventive of the avant-garde groups, the Clusone Trio (comprising Michael Moore on clarinet and alto, cellist Ernst

Reijseger and drummer Han Bennink) came together briefly in 1980 but, although all three musicians had extensive experience and overlapping engagements in various situations in the 1980s, the group did not become official until 1988. They have since recorded several sets for Gramavision, including an often-hilarious "tribute" to Irving Berlin, *Soft Lights and Sweet Music.* —*Scott Yanow*

● **Soft Lights & Sweet Music**/ Nov. 2, 1993-Nov. 3, 1993 / Hat Art ✦✦✦✦✦
The Clusone Trio (which comprises Michael Moore on clarinet, bass clarinet and alto, cellist Ernst Reijseger and percussionist Han Bennink) performs avant-garde music that even haters of free jazz will enjoy due to their crazy (yet accessible) humor. For this highly recommended CD, the trio interprets 19 Irving Berlin songs, turning them inside out yet usually showing respect for the original melodies. Their versions of such songs as "There's No Business like Show Business," "What'll I Do," "A Pretty Girl Is like a Melody" and "White Christmas" are quite unique. This is a CD worth taking a chance on. —*Scott Yanow*

I Am An Indian / Oct. 1995 / Gramavision ✦✦✦✦✦
The trio of Michael Moore (on clarinet, alto and bass clarinet), cellist Ernst Reijseger and percussionist Han Bennink mixes together very explorative playing with a full knowledge of the tradition and a wacky sense of humor. For the often-eccentric series of live performances, the trio alternates group originals with works from Duke Ellington, Irving Berlin, Herbie Nichols, Dewey Redman, Bud Powell and Misha Mingelberg. This is one of the most accessible of all avant-garde groups due to the humor and there are many highlights to the enjoyable (if nutty) program. —*Scott Yanow*

Love Henry / Jul. 13, 1996 / Gramavision ✦✦✦✦
The Clusone Trio (comprising Michael Moore on alto, clarinet and flute, cellist Ernst Reijseger and drummer/percussionist Han Bennink) is so humorous and accessible that they could be considered avant-garde jazz for listeners who do not like the avant-garde. This live set finds the group playing spontaneous medleys with eccentric sound explorations leading to off-the-wall standards, including several Irving Berlin songs, Lee Konitz's "It's You" and Johnny Mercer's "Cuckoo in the Clock." One of the most colorful and satisfying regular groups in the more exploratory side of jazz (each of its members has his own sound and the ability to switch between several styles), the Clusone Trio's recordings are all worth experiencing several times. This nutty but generally logical performance is no exception and is better heard than described. —*Scott Yanow*

John Coates, Jr.

b. Feb. 17, 1938, Trenton, NJ
Piano / Cool
A fixture at the Deer Head Inn in Pennsylvania's Delaware Water Gap for over 25 years, John Coates (an early inspiration for Keith Jarrett) has been creating worthy music (a bit in the Bill Evans vein) for several decades in general obscurity. He started playing piano quite young, studied at Mannes College of Music and the Dalcroze School of Music, and thought seriously of becoming a concert pianist. But after he discovered jazz, he changed his direction. In 1955, at the age of 17, Coates recorded a set for Savoy (*Portrait*), and toured with Charlie Ventura. He toured with Ventura's band for another three years, leaving in 1958. After graduating from Rutgers in 1962, he worked for a music publisher in Delaware Water Gap as a composer/arranger and started performing regularly at the Deer Head Inn. John Coates recorded a set for Omnisound in 1974 and made quite a few records for the tiny label from 1977-80 before going back to his low profile. After a bout with bad health, he recorded a couple of CDs for Pacific St. in 1996-97. —*Scott Yanow*

● **Portrait** / Nov. 17, 1955-Jun. 21, 1956 / Savoy ✦✦✦✦
Pianist Johnny Coates recorded so many records for his Omnisound label during 1974-80 that it is surprising to realize that he had only led one album during the 20 previous years. This CD reissue brings back Coates' 1955-56 trio performances with bassist Wendell Marshall and drummer Kenny Clarke. The liner notes are dated and the playing time is only the length of an LP but the music (mostly standards with two Coates originals) should appeal to fans of Dave Brubeck, who at this early point was a prime influence on the young pianist. —*Scott Yanow*

The Jazz Piano of John Coates, Jr. / Feb. 3, 1974 / Omnisound ✦✦✦✦

Alone and Live at the Deer Head / Jun. 24, 1977-Jul. 1, 1977 / Omnisound ✦✦✦✦

After the Before / Mar. 5, 1978 / Omnisound ✦✦✦

Tokyo Concert / Nov. 28, 1979 / Omnisound ✦✦✦

The Trio Session / 1996 / Pacific St. ✦✦✦✦

Arnett Cobb

b. Aug. 10, 1918, Houston, TX, **d.** Mar. 24, 1989, Houston, TX
Tenor Saxophone / Swing, Early R&B Jazz, Groove, Soul Jazz

A stomping Texas tenor player in the tradition of Illinois Jacquet, Arnett Cobb's accessible playing was between swing and early rhythm & blues. After playing in Texas with Chester Boone (1934-36) and Milt Larkin (1936-42), Cobb emerged in the big leagues by succeeding Illinois Jacquet with Lionel Hampton's Orchestra (1942-47). His version of "Flying Home No. 2" became a hit and he was a very popular soloist with Hampton. After leaving the band, Cobb formed his own group, but his initial success was interrupted in 1948 when he had to undergo an operation on his spine. After recovering he resumed touring. But a major car accident in 1956 crushed Cobb's legs and he had to use crutches for the rest of his life. However, by 1959 he returned to active playing and recording. Cobb spent most of the 1960s leading bands back in Texas but starting in 1973 he toured and recorded more extensively, including a tenor summit with Jimmy Heath and Joe Henderson in Europe as late as 1988. Arnett Cobb made many fine records through the years for such labels as Apollo, Columbia/OKeh, Prestige (many of the latter are available on the OJC series), Black & Blue, Progressive, Muse and Bee Hive. —*Scott Yanow*

● **Blows for 1300** / May 1947-Aug. 1947 / Delmark ✦✦✦✦✦
This Delmark CD reissues all 15 of Arnett Cobb's recordings for Apollo. The spirited tenor (who straddled the boundaries between swing and early R&B) is in prime early form with his sextet on a variety of basic material, much of it blues-oriented. Milt Larkin takes vocals on three of the tracks and there are short solos by either Booty Wood or Al King on trombone, but otherwise the main focus is on Cobb's tough tenor. This very accessible music is both danceable and full of exciting performances that were formerly rare. —*Scott Yanow*

Blow, Arnett, Blow / Jan. 9, 1959 / Original Jazz Classics ✦✦✦✦
Arnett Cobb's debut for Prestige and his first recording as a leader in three years (due to a serious car accident in 1956) is an explosive affair. Cobb is matched up with fellow tough tenor Eddie "Lockjaw" Davis and there are plenty of sparks set off by their encounter. With organist Wild Bill Davis, bassist George Duvivier and drummer Arthur Edgehill keeping the proceedings heated, Cobb and Davis tangle on a variety of basic material, alternating uptempo romps such as "Go Power" and "Go Red Go" with slightly more sober pieces highlighted by "When I Grow Too Old to Dream." This is a great matchup (reissued on CD in the OJC series) that lives up to its potential. —*Scott Yanow*

Smooth Sailing / Feb. 27, 1959 / Original Jazz Classics ✦✦✦✦
This CD reissue brings back a typically swinging date by tenor saxophonist Arnett Cobb. The colorful trombonist Buster Cooper (who was not featured in enough small group sessions through the years) seems to inspire Cobb; the rhythm section (organist Austin Mitchell, bassist George Duvivier and drummer Osie Johnson) is also a strong asset for this music. Four standards (three from the swing era plus Cobb's "Smooth Sailing") alternate with a blues and a couple of uptempo riff numbers. Arnett Cobb's solos are typically emotional and generally exciting during the fine set. —*Scott Yanow*

Party Time / May 14, 1959 / Original Jazz Classics ✦✦✦✦
Tenor saxophonist Arnett Cobb, who was inactive inactive between 1957 and 1958 due to a serious auto accident, recorded three strong albums for Prestige during the first half of 1959. This CD reissue is the only one of the trio that features Cobb as the only horn and backed by a pianist (Ray Bryant) instead of an organ player. With bassist Wendell Marshall, drummer Art Taylor and Ray Barretto on conga completing the group, most of the focus is on Cobb's tough yet flexible tenor. Such songs as "When My Dreamboat Comes Home," "Blues in the Closet" and a remake of "Flying Home" make this the definitive Arnett Cobb album from the era. Highly recommended. —*Scott Yanow*

Blue and Sentimental / Oct. 31, 1960-Nov. 13, 1960 / Prestige ✦✦✦
This CD reissue combines together tenor saxophonist Arnett Cobb's two LPs, *Sizzlin'* and *Ballads by Cobb*. The former session has a good mixture of stomps and ballads with highlights including "Black Velvet," "Georgia on My Mind" and "The Way You Look Tonight." The latter date (originally cut for the Moodsville label) is all slow ballads and, despite the warmth in Cobb's tone, a certain sameness pervades the performances. Pianist Red Garland and drummer J.C. Heard are on both sessions with either George Tucker or George Duvivier on bass. Good music but not quite essential. —*Scott Yanow*

Wild Man from Texas / May 6, 1976-May 30, 1976 / Classic Jazz✦✦✦
This Black & Blue session, made available domestically on a Classic Jazz LP in the late '70s, has some typically rambunctious playing by tenor saxophonist Arnett Cobb. The tough tenor is featured in a larger group than usual (a nonet also including trumpeter Wallace Davenport, trombonist Buster Cooper, fellow tenor Eddie Chamblee and organist Milt Buckner) with side one consisting of three

romps (including "Smooth Sailing" and "Flying Home") and the second half made up of three ballads (highlighted by "The Nearness of You"). Cobb, who had emerged a couple years earlier after a decade spent sticking close to Texas, was still in prime form, making this hard-to-find set worth the search. —*Scott Yanow*

Arnett Cobb Is Back / Jun. 27, 1978 / Progressive ✦✦✦✦
One of the great tough Texas tenors, Arnett Cobb roars and stomps throughout this excellent LP. Joined by pianist Derek Smith, bassist George Mraz and drummer Billy Hart, Cobb sounds quite comfortable on the basic material which comprises blues, ballads, standards and "Flying Home." —*Scott Yanow*

Live at Sandy's/ Aug. 25, 1978-Aug. 26, 1978 / Muse ✦✦✦✦
This CD reissues eight of the nine selections originally put out on two Muse LPs from the same two-day engagement at Sandy's Jazz Revival in Beverly, Massachusetts. Oddly enough the original liner notes from the first album (which mentions the missing selection "Broadway") are reproduced (along with three more recent paragraphs) and no explanation is given as to why the one selection (which would have fit) was left off the CD. In any case, the music is quite enjoyable and spirited. Muse Records fully documented two nights of music featuring the tenors of Arnett Cobb and Buddy Tate, altoist Eddie "Cleanhead" Vinson, pianist Ray Bryant, bassist George Duvivier and drummer Alan Dawson. Six LPs originally resulted (two apiece led by the three saxophonists). Cobb's portion of the show has five quartet features (including a passionate version of "On the Sunny Side of the Street"), a couple of collaborations with Tate ("Go Red Go" and "Flyin' Home") and one selection ("Blues for Lester") with all three saxophonists. Fun music. —*Scott Yanow*

Funky Butt / Jan. 22, 1980 / Progressive ✦✦✦✦
Arnett Cobb, a tenor from the 1940s who (like Illinois Jacquet) fused together some of the most exciting aspects of swing and early R&B, is in typically exuberant form on this quartet set with pianist Derek Smith, bassist Ray Drummond and drummer Ronnie Bedford. Cobb is warm on the ballads but the stomps (particularly "Jumpin' at the Woodside" and "I Got Rhythm") are what make this record most memorable. —*Scott Yanow*

Keep on Pushin' / Jun. 27, 1984 / Bee Hive ✦✦✦
Arnett Cobb, at 66, still had plenty of energy as he demonstrates on this Bee Hive LP. The thick-toned tenor (who is joined by pianist Junior Mance, bassist George Duvivier and drummer Panama Francis) sounds warm on "Stardust," reverent on a brief "Deep River" (which is a duet with Duvivier) and quite spirited on "Cheatin' on Me" and his "Blues for Lisette." Trumpeter Joe Newman and trombonist Al Grey join Cobb to swing their way through a blues ("Keep on Pushin'") and "Indiana." This is an excellent mainstream set that deserves to be reissued on CD. —*Scott Yanow*

Showtime / Aug. 10, 1987 / Fantasy ✦✦✦
Tenor saxophonist Arnett Cobb's next-to-last recording was cut at a concert in Houston that was held to celebrate his 69th birthday. Cobb is in typically fine form. He plays three numbers with a rhythm section comprising four local players; best is "Just a Closer Walk with Thee" although the lack of any romps is disappointing. His friend trumpeter Dizzy Gillespie helps out on two songs, an okay version of "Night in Tunisia" (Dizzy was past his prime) and "Sweet Mama," which contains some of Gillespie's humorous vocalizing. Jewel Brown, best known for singing with Louis Armstrong in the 1960s, made her first public appearance in 17 years for this date, resulting in two so-so numbers. Closing the album is veteran pianist Sammy Price jamming a blues in a trio. This CD is a mixed bag, not essential but generally quite interesting. —*Scott Yanow*

Tenor Tribute, Vol. 1 / Apr. 30, 1988 / Soul Note ✦✦✦✦
This blowing session (comprising Charlie Parker's "Steeple Chase," Arnett Cobb's "Smooth Sailing," "Lester Leaps In," a four-song ballad medley and "I Got Rhythm") is of greatest interest for featuring the contrasting styles of tenors Arnett Cobb, Joe Henderson and Jimmy Heath; the latter also plays a bit of soprano and flute. This being one of Cobb's final recordings (he died less than a year later), he holds his own against the younger tenors during this German concert, taking "Smooth Sailing" as his feature. One should have little trouble telling the three tenor masters apart. —*Scott Yanow*

Tenor Tribute, Vol. 2 / Apr. 30, 1988 / Soul Note ✦✦✦

Billy Cobham (William C. Cobham)

b. May 16, 1946, Panama
Drums / Fusion, Post-Bop

Considered the definitive fusion drummer in the 1970s, Billy Cobham's fame has subsided a bit since then but he remains a very capable player who is more flexible than one might think. His family moved to New York from Panama when he was three. After spending time performing with a military band in the Army, Cobham spent eight months with Horace Silver (1968). He then became a busy session musician, played with the jazz-rock band Dreams (1969-70), appeared on some very important Miles Davis records (*Bitches Brew, Live-Evil* and *Jack Johnson*) and joined John McLaughlin in the Mahavishnu Orchestra (1971-73) where he became an influential force. Cobham led his own band (Spectrum) from 1973 on, making a strong initial impact but by the late '70s he was mostly freelancing. Since that time he has led electric bands on an occasional basis, been involved in teaching and remains a busy studio player. — *Scott Yanow*

● **Spectrum** / May 14, 1973-May 16, 1973 / Atlantic ✦✦✦✦
Drummer Billy Cobham was fresh from his success with the Mahavishnu Orchestra when he recorded his debut album, which is still his best. Most of the selections showcase Cobham in a quartet with keyboardist Jan Hammer, guitarist Tommy Bolin and electric bassist Lee Sklar. Two other numbers include Joe Farrell on flute and soprano and trumpeter Jimmy Owens with guitarist John Tropea, Hammer, bassist Ron Carter and Ray Barretto on congas. The generally high-quality compositions (which include "Red Baron") make this fusion set a standout, a strong mixture of rockish rhythms and jazz improvising. — *Scott Yanow*

Shabazz / Jul. 4, 1974-Jul. 13, 1974 / Atlantic ✦✦✦

Crosswinds / 1974 / Atlantic ✦✦✦✦
Billy Cobham's second date as a leader was one of his better sessions, although, as with most of his Atlantic recordings, it has gone out of print. Four songs (all originals by the leader-drummer) comprise "Spanish Moss—A Sound Portrait," and, in addition, Cobham contributed three other pieces. The selections team him with guitarist John Abercrombie, both of the Brecker Brothers, trombonist Garnett Brown, keyboardist George Duke, bassist John Williams and Latin percussionist Lee Pastora. In general, the melodies and the vamps are reasonably memorable. Cobham also takes an unaccompanied drum solo on "Storm." Worth searching for by fusion collectors. — *Scott Yanow*

Total Eclipse / 1974 / Atlantic ✦✦✦

A Funky Thide of Sings / 1975 / Atlantic ✦✦

Alivemutherforya / Nov. 1977-Dec. 1977 / Columbia ✦✦✦✦
Drummer Billy Cobham is heard on this live set heading an all-star quintet also including Tom Scott on tenor, soprano and lyricon; keyboardist Mark Soskin; guitarist Steve Khan; and electric bassist Alphonso Johnson. Although the music is mostly funky and uses plenty of electronics (Scott sounds quite faceless on lyricon), there are some strong solos, particularly from Khan and Scott (when he is on tenor). The six group originals are highlighted by "Bahama Mama," "Some Punk Funk" and "On a Magic Carpet Ride." Due to the amount of variety and spontaneity, *Alivemutherforya* is superior to most of these musicians' individual projects of the era. — *Scott Yanow*

Magic / 1977 / Columbia ✦✦✦
Billy Cobham tends to make more significant records as a sideman than as a leader. On this out-of-print Columbia LP, Cobham is joined by some intriguing players (including both Joachim Kuhn and Mark Soskin on keyboards, guitarist Pete Naunu and clarinetist Alvin Batiste), but none of the funky originals are memorable or particularly catchy. The results are decent fusion, but not all that special. — *Scott Yanow*

Flight Time / Jun. 1980 / Inakustik ✦✦✦

Stratus / Mar. 18, 1981 / Inakustik ✦✦✦

Smokin' / Jul. 1982 / Elektra ✦✦✦
This live LP features Billy Cobham's Glass Menagerie quartet of 1982, a group consisting of the drummer/leader, guitarist Dean Brown, keyboardist Gil Goldstein and electric bassist Tim Landers. Although their playing is fairly spontaneous, the rockish group never really carved out a niche for itself or developed its own individual sound. Of the five band originals, the best is Cobham's "Red Baron," though this version is not on the same level as the original recording. Overall, the out-of-print release is spirited, but really just a so-so effort. — *Scott Yanow*

Power Play / 1986 / GRP ✦✦

Picture This / 1987 / GRP ✦✦✦
Most of drummer Billy Cobham's recordings have featured his groups of the period, but this set for GRP matches him with a variety of all-stars. Three songs feature Grover Washington, Jr., on soprano or tenor; Randy Brecker takes a fluegelhorn solo on "Taurian Matador"; and other guests include Tom Scott (on his anonymous-sounding lyricon), keyboardist George Duke and bassist Ron Carter. Nothing all that surprising or memorable occurs on the melodic but routine set. — *Scott Yanow*

Traveler / Nov. 1993 / Evidence ✦✦✦

Tony Coe (Anthony George Coe)

b. Nov. 29, 1934, Canterbury, England
Tenor Saxophone, Clarinet, Alto Saxophone/ Post-Bop, Bop
An adventurous and flexible improviser, Tony Coe has long been one of England's top jazzmen. He has performed in settings ranging from straightahead bop and borderline Dixieland to post-bop and free, keeping his own strong musical personality intact throughout his career. Coe started on clarinet and was self-taught on tenor. He performed in an army band during 1953-56 and played with Humphrey Lyttelton's mainstream group during 1957-62. After heading his own band (1962-64), Coe was offered a spot with Count Basie's Orchestra, but difficulties with immigration foiled that opportunity.

Coe's versatility was clearly in evidence by the late 1960s. In addition to playing with John Dankworth's big band (1966-69) and the Kenny Clarke-Francy Boland Orchestra (1967-73), he also worked with Derek Bailey's very avant-garde Company, Stan Tracey, and several of his own groups. Associations with the United Jazz and Rock Ensemble and with the Mike Gibbs big band were also beneficial. Coe, whose tenor is well featured during Henry Mancini's *Pink Panther* films, has also written advanced works for orchestras. In 1995, he won the Danish Jazzpar Prize. Influenced most by Paul Gonsalves on tenor, in addition to being a very fluent clarinetist, Coe has led sessions for a variety of European labels including Nixa, Phillips, Columbia, 77, Nato, Hat Art and Hot House. — *Scott Yanow*

Some Other Spring / 1964-1965 / Hep ✦✦✦✦✦
The music on this live session was released for the first time on this 1993 CD from the Scottish Hep label. The versatile Tony Coe, who would play in freer settings later in his career, heads a quartet also including pianist Brian Lemon, bassist Dave Green and drummer Phil Seaman. Coe, switching between tenor (where he sometimes recalls Paul Gonsalves) and clarinet, comes across as a fairly distinctive and fresh bop-based player on these mid-'60s performances, introducing his "Aristotle Blues" and "Some Other Autumn" and coming up with inventive statements on such tunes as "Body and Soul," "Perdido" and "In a Mellow Tone." This CD offers listeners a strong example of Tony Coe's early playing. — *Scott Yanow*

Some Other Autumn / Jan. 25, 1971-Jan. 26, 1971 / Hep ✦✦✦✦

Nutty (On) Willisau / Apr. 1985 / Hat Art ✦✦✦✦

Canterbury Song / 1988 / Hot House ✦✦✦
A fine English tenor saxophonist and clarinetist who has been flexible through the years (able to sound comfortable in both bop and free settings), Tony Coe is in excellent form on this quintet LP from the British Hot House label. Joined by three American expatriates (trumpeter Benny Bailey, pianist Horace Parlan and bassist Jimmy Woode) and drummer Idris Muhammad, Coe performs two of his originals and six less-played standards (highlighted by Thelonious Monk's "Light Blue," Bill Evans' "Re: Person I Knew" and "I Guess I'll Hang My Tears out to Dry"). The music is fine if not innovative or all that memorable, and it should satisfy modern mainstream jazz collectors. — *Scott Yanow*

● **Jazzpar 95** / Mar. 6, 1995-Mar. 19, 1995 / Storyville ✦✦✦✦✦
The winner of the prestigious Jazzpar award in 1995, Tony Coe is featured on this adventurous and diverse CD with the Danish Radio Jazz Orchestra (arranged by Bob Brookmeyer, who is also heard on valve trombone) and, on three of the eight selections, with Brookmeyer in a quintet/sextet. Coe, playing very effectively on tenor (where he is influenced by Paul Gonsalves), clarinet, and soprano, is a bop-based improviser who evolved through the years to become an advanced player. In addition to several of his own originals and two by drummer Steve Arguelles, Coe performs works by Brookmeyer, Maria Schneider, and a pair of standards ("How Long Has This Been Going On" and "Fools Rush In"). This is an exciting release that rewards repeated listenings, one of Tony Coe's finest recordings to date. — *Scott Yanow*

Porky Cohen

b. Jun. 2, 1924, Springfield, MA
Trombone / R&B, Swing
Best known for his years as trombonist with Roomful of Blues, Porky Cohen finally had his recording debut as a leader in 1996, a highly enjoyable outing for Bullseye Blues with many of the members of the group. He started playing trombone at 13 and considers Jack Teagarden his most important early influence. Cohen worked local engagements from age 15 and took lessons from Miff Mole after graduating high school in 1941. After a tryout with Benny Goodman, Cohen played with Tony Pastor's band, Charlie Barnet (off and on during 1943-48), the Casa Loma Orchestra, Lucky Millinder, Tommy Dorsey, Boyd Raeburn, Artie Shaw (1949-50), with a variety of Dixieland bands in the 1950s, Bob Wilber and the Six, and the Jewels of Dixie (from the late 1950s to the late '70s). Porky Cohen was a strong asset to Roomful of Blues from 1979-86 before choosing to semi-retire. — *Scott Yanow*

● **Rhythm & Bones** / 1996 / Bullseye ◆◆◆◆◆

Although trombonist Porky Cohen has played in the jazz major leagues since the early 1940s (including periods with Tony Pastor, Charlie Barnet, the Casa Loma Orchestra, Lucky Millinder, Boyd Raeburn, Tommy Dorsey, Artie Shaw, Bobby Hackett, the Six with Bob Wilber and various Dixieland bands) and toured regularly with Roomful of Blues during 1979-87, this CD was his first opportunity to lead his own date. Seventy at the time, Cohen is heard in prime form leading a romping session featuring some of the members of Roomful of Blues along with his successor trombonist Carl Querfurth. The joyous music, which only has two vocals among the 13 numbers (updates of Jimmy Rushing and Bessie Smith songs featuring Sugar Ray Norcia and Michelle Willson), mixes together heated swing and 1950s style R&B blues to exhilarating effect; Illinois Jacquet would feel quite comfortable in this setting. There are plenty of opportunities for not only Cohen to solo but all of the other horn players. An added plus are the lengthy and definitive liner notes, which fully relate (along with many photos) the Porky Cohen story. Highly recommended. —*Scott Yanow*

Al Cohn

b. Nov. 24, 1925, New York, NY, **d.** Feb. 15, 1988, Stroudsburg, PA
Tenor Saxophone, Arranger / Bop, Cool

An excellent tenor saxophonist and a superior arranger/composer, Al Cohn was greatly admired by his fellow musicians. Early gigs included associations with Joe Marsala (1943), Georgie Auld, Boyd Raeburn (1946), Alvino Rey and Buddy Rich (1947). But it was when he replaced Herbie Steward as one of the "Four Brothers" with Woody Herman's Second Herd (1948-49) that Cohn began to make a strong impression. He was actually overshadowed by Stan Getz and Zoot Sims during this period but, unlike the other two tenors, he also contributed arrangements including "The Goof and I." He was with Artie Shaw's short-lived bop orchestra (1949), and then spent the 1950s quite busy as a recording artist (making his first dates as a leader in 1950), arranger for both jazz and nonjazz settings and a performer. Starting in 1956 and continuing on an irregular basis for decades, Cohn co-led a quintet with Zoot Sims. The two tenors were so complementary that it was often difficult to tell them apart! Al Cohn continued in this fashion in the 1960s (although playing less); in the 1970s he recorded many gems for Xanadu. During his last few years when his tone became darker and more distinctive, Cohn largely gave up writing to concentrate on playing. He made many excellent bop-based records throughout his career for such labels as Prestige, Victor, Xanadu and Concord; his son Joe Cohn is a talented cool-toned guitarist. —*Scott Yanow*

The Progressive Al Cohn / Jul. 29, 1950+Jun. 23, 1953 / Savoy ◆◆◆

This out-of-print Savoy LP (released by Arista in 1979) has tenor saxophonist Al Cohn's first two sessions as a leader. Cohn, who was very influenced during the era by Lester Young, is in fine early form with a 1950 quartet that also includes pianist George Wallington, bassist Tommy Potter and drummer Tiny Kahn, and with a 1953 quintet that has trumpeter Nick Travis, pianist Horace Silver, bassist Curley Russell and drummer Max Roach. All but two numbers ("How Long Has This Been Going On" and an excellent version of "Let's Get Away from It All") are Cohn's inventive originals; best are "Infinity," "That's What You Think" (heard in two versions) and "Ah-Moore." —*Scott Yanow*

The New York Sessions, Vol. 2 / Feb. 28, 1954-Mar. 7, 1954 / Inner City ◆◆◆◆

Although tenor saxophonist Al Cohn and trombonist J.J. Johnson get co-billing on this LP of material originally cut for the Vogue label, the real leader is French pianist Henri Renaud, who was in New York to record with top American players. Four selections (three of which are Al Cohn originals) find Renaud leading a septet that includes Cohn, trumpeter Jerry Hurwitz, J.J. Johnson and Gigi Gryce on baritone. Cohn is showcased with a quartet on "The Things We Did Last Summer" and "Once in Awhile" while a ten-minute version of "If I Had You" has J.J. and Cohn joined in a sextet by vibraphonist Milt Jackson, who wins solo honors. Overall this is a typically excellent straightahead set of 1950s jazz, cool but swinging. —*Scott Yanow*

Broadway (1954) / Jul. 29, 1954 / Original Jazz Classics ◆◆◆

This long-lost session was originally cut for the Progressive label in 1954 and was not released until Prestige put it out in 1970. Now available on CD, one can hear tenor saxophonist Al Cohn and bassist Red Mitchell in fine form in a quintet with three lesser-known players: altoist Hal Stein, pianist Harvey Leonard and drummer Christy Febbo. The music (Mitchell's "Help Keep Your City Clean Blues," a four-song ballad medley and two versions apiece of "Broadway" and "Suddenly It's Spring") is fine although there are no surprises. The most interesting aspect to this obscure session is how similar the light-toned Cohn and altoist Stein (who tended to emphasize lower notes) sounded to each other. —*Scott Yanow*

The Natural Seven / Feb. 5, 1955 / Victor ◆◆◆

Some but not all of the material on this out-of-print LP has since been reissued on CD on a Bluebird set shared by Freddie Green and Al Cohn. Although originally associated with Woody Herman and cool jazz, Cohn always felt equally comfortable playing with swing-styled players. His "Natural Seven" looks towards the Kansas City Seven and includes two members of Count Basie's band (trumpeter Joe Newman and guitarist Freddie Green) among the personnel (which also has trombonist Frank Rehak, Basie soundalike pianist Nat Pierce, bassist Milt Hinton and drummer Osie Johnson). Although the music includes a few Basie-associated songs, Cohn also contributed several of his own swinging originals; Osie Johnson's vocal on "Osie's Blues" is surprisingly effective. —*Scott Yanow*

The Brothers! / Jun. 24, 1955 / Victor ◆◆◆

Lester Young's influence on younger tenor players was at its height in the early to mid-'50s. This enjoyable if out-of-print LP matches together the three tenors of Al Cohn, Bill Perkins and Richie Kamuca, but good luck telling them apart! Backed by pianist Hank Jones, either Barry Galbraith or Jimmy Raney (who used the pseudonym on this date of Sam Beethoven) on guitar, bassist John Beal and drummer Chuck Flores, the tenors play concise versions of originals by Cohn, Perkins, Nat Pierce, Bill Potts and Bob Brookmeyer in addition to the lone standard "Blue Skies." The music is fun and swinging if not all that original or distinctive. —*Scott Yanow*

From A to Z / Jan. 23, 1956-Jan. 24, 1956 / Bluebird ◆◆◆◆

The very complementary tenors Al Cohn and Zoot Sims (whose similar styles often made them seem to sound identical) teamed up many times through the years; this CD reissue brings back their first joint recording. Joined by either Dave McKenna or Hank Jones on piano, bassist Milt Hinton, drummer Osie Johnson and (on some selections) the forgotten trumpeter Dick Sherman, Al and Zoot avoid obvious material ("Somebody Loves Me" and "East of the Sun" are the only standards) in favor of swinging "modern" originals by Cohn, Sherman, Osie Johnson, Ralph Burns, Manny Albam, Ernie Wilkins and Milty Gold. Zoot contributed "Tenor for Two Please, Jack," his answer to the song "Dinner for One Please, James." The CD adds four alternate takes to the original 12-song program and gives one a good example of the occasional Cohn-Sims musical partnership. —*Scott Yanow*

Be Loose / Sep. 29, 1956 / Biograph ◆◆◆

Al Cohn's repertoire on his Biograph LP (a reissue of material originally cut for the Dawn label) is a major plus with some superior but lesser-known originals alternating with mostly 1920s and '30s era songs (including "Singing the Blues" and "When Day Is Done"). Cohn blends in well with trombonist Frank Rehak, the rhythm section (pianist Hank Jones, bassist Milt Hinton and drummer Osie Johnson) was state-of-the-art for the period and the music is both spontaneous and organized enough to make the results coherent and with enough diversity to challenge the musicians. —*Scott Yanow*

Al and Zoot / Mar. 26, 1957-Mar. 27, 1957 / MCA/Decca ◆◆◆◆

Tenors Al Cohn and Zoot Sims led a regular two-tenor quintet for a few years in the late '50s and then had an occasional musical partnership during the next couple of decades. Accompanied by pianist Mose Allison (who was then unknown), bassist Teddy Kotick and drummer Nick Stabulas, the two very complementary tenors play five of Cohn's swinging originals (including "Halley's Comet," named after John Haley "Zoot" Sims!) plus five standards; "Gone with the Wind" originally was on a sampler and has been added to the CD reissue. The mid- to late '50s was a period of intense recording activity and this album was one of the underrated gems that was somewhat overlooked during the time. —*Scott Yanow*

You 'n Me / Jun. 1, 1960+Jun. 3, 1960 / Mercury ◆◆◆◆

The most unusual selection on this Al Cohn-Zoot Sims set from 1960 is "Improvisation for Unaccompanied Saxophones," a short but effective two-tenor workout that through a clever arrangement by Cohn gives one the impression that both saxophonists are using circular breathing. Another departure is "Angel Eyes," which has both Cohn and Sims switching to clarinet and showcases Major Holley's singing and bowed bass. Otherwise, the co-leaders stick to their main instruments and enjoy swinging together with the assistance of Holley, pianist Mose Allison (who would soon be starting his own successful solo career), and drummer Osie Johnson. Reissued on Trip in the 1970s, this out-of-print LP is worth the search. —*Scott Yanow*

Jazz Mission to Moscow / Jul. 12, 1962 / Colpix ◆◆◆

In 1962 Benny Goodman had a historic visit to the Soviet Union, touring with a big band full of young all-stars. After the orchestra returned to the US, tenor saxophonist Al Cohn (who had not made the trip but did write some of Goodman's charts) put together an album (also released by Colpix) using many of the sidemen and paying tribute to the event. Strangely none of the six numbers are Cohn originals and he does not play on the record although he arranged all of the music. Of the six songs, "Mission to Moscow," "Let's Dance" and "Russian Lullaby" were part of Goodman's repertoire. Altoist Phil Woods effectively doubles on clarinet and other soloists include tenor saxophonist Zoot Sims, trumpeter Marky

Markowitz and trombonist Willie Dennis. An interesting set of modern swing but this LP has been unfortunately long out-of-print. —*Scott Yanow*

Body and Soul / Mar. 23, 1973 / Muse ✦✦✦✦
Other than a couple of albums for tiny collector's labels, this Muse album was Al Cohn's first album as a leader since 1962. Cohn had spent much of the interim as a fulltime writer for studios and was finally returning to active playing. He renewed his musical partnership with Zoot Sims on this quintet date for Muse, which also includes pianist Jaki Byard, bassist George Duvivier and drummer Mel Lewis. Cohn and Sims still had very complementary sounds and personalities so their collaboration holds its own against their earlier dates. Zoot switches to soprano on "Jean," Cohn is in top form on "Body and Soul" and a three-song "Brazilian Medley" works quite well. This is pleasing and frequently lyrical music. —*Scott Yanow*

Motoring Along / Nov. 25, 1974 / Gazell ✦✦✦
Al Cohn and Zoot Sims were lifelong friends who were frequent collaborators both in the studios and in clubs. Cohn only led four recording sessions (two for tiny labels) during 1963-74; all featured Sims. For their Sonet date, Al and Zoot are joined by pianist Horace Parlan, bassist Hugo Rasmussen and drummer Sven Erik Norregaard, and they perform three standards, two Cohn songs and Jimmy McGriff's "Motoring Along." Zoot plays some effective soprano on "Yardbird Suite." As usual the two saxophonists mutually inspire each other on the cool-toned but frequently heated bop date. —*Scott Yanow*

Play It Now / Jun. 19, 1975 / Xanadu ✦✦✦✦
Tenor saxophonist Al Cohn did some of his finest playing during his period (1975-80) with Xanadu. For this quartet set, Cohn is ably backed by the great bop pianist Barry Harris, bassist Larry Ridley and drummer Alan Dawson. Cohn, who has spent much of his career as a successful arranger/composer, contributed only one of the six numbers ("Play It Now") on the album and was content to jam spiritedly on such tunes as "Lover," "Irresistible You" and "It's Sand, Man." —*Scott Yanow*

True Blue / Oct. 22, 1976 / Xanadu ✦✦✦✦
The first of two LPs taken from an all-star jam session, this album features Al Cohn and Dexter Gordon on tenors, trumpeters Blue Mitchell and Sam Noto, pianist Barry Harris, bassist Sam Jones and drummer Louis Hayes. Together they perform "Lady Bird" (the two trumpets play Miles Davis' "Half Nelson," which has the same chord changes, at the same time), the ballad "How Deep Is the Ocean" and a 17-minute blues "True Blue." All of the musicians play up to their usual standard. This album was soon joined by *Silver Blue* from the same date. —*Scott Yanow*

Silver Blue / Oct. 22, 1976 / Xanadu ✦✦✦✦
Recorded at the same session as *True Blue*, this Xanadu LP gets the edge due to a remarkable version of "On the Trail" that is a fascinating unaccompanied duet by tenors Al Cohn and Dexter Gordon. Cohn and Gordon are joined by pianist Barry Harris, bassist Sam Jones and drummer Louis Hayes for a heated and competitive version of "Allen's Alley" and then the group becomes a septet with the addition of trumpeters Blue Mitchell and Sam Noto for a side-long 19-minute "Silver Blue," a slow blues. Highly recommended for bop fans. —*Scott Yanow*

America / Dec. 6, 1976 / Xanadu ✦✦✦✦✦
Al Cohn's series of albums for Xanadu were among the happiest and most exciting of his career. Freed of his usual writing duties, Cohn sounds exuberant jamming through seven songs with pianist Barry Harris, bassist Sam Jones and drummer Leroy Williams. In addition to some superior standards (including "My Shining Hour," "Night and Day" and "Skylark"), Cohn performs a memorable bossa nova version of "America the Beautiful." This LP is recommended although, as is true with most of Xanadu releases, this music has not yet reappeared on CD. —*Scott Yanow*

Heavy Love / Mar. 15, 1977 / Xanadu ✦✦✦✦
This duet set by tenor saxophonist Al Cohn and pianist Jimmy Rowles is a classic and has fortunately been reissued on CD. From the start (with Cohn ripping through an unaccompanied chorus on "Them There Eyes") through the six standards (including a previously unissued version of "For All We Know") and the ad-lib blues "Bar Talk," the momentum and excitement of this encounter never slows down. Cohn and Rowles' swing-oriented styles, wit and ability to come up with fresh ideas on older songs are quite complementary; they continually bring out the best in each other. This highly recommended set is a real gem, a high point in both of the musicians' long careers. —*Scott Yanow*

No Problem / Dec. 18, 1979 / Xanadu ✦✦✦✦✦
Tenor saxophonist's Al Cohn's Xanadu albums of 1975-80 found him at the peak of his powers. On this record, his third quartet date with pianist Barry Harris (bassist Steve Gilmore and drummer Walter Bolden complete the group), Cohn performs three originals (including "Zoot Case"), two Duke Ellington songs and a pair of swing standards. Two of the highlights are a cooking "All the Things You Are" and

a version of "Mood Indigo" that is taken as a jazz waltz. Recommended, as are all of Cohn's swinging and boppish Xanadu dates. —*Scott Yanow*

Night Flight to Dakar / Mar. 14, 1980-Mar. 19, 1980 / Xanadu ✦✦✦✦
Although tenor saxophonist Al Cohn gets first billing on this Xanadu album, it is very much a co-op date with fellow tenor Billy Mitchell, pianist Dolo Coker (who is featured with the trio on "Don't Let the Sun Catch You Crying"), bassist Leroy Vinnegar and drummer Frank Butler making strong contributions. The performances may have been recorded during an African tour but the music is very much American bop with heated versions of "Blues Up and Down," "Sweet Senegalese Brown" and "The King" featuring the tenors in competitive form. —*Scott Yanow*

Nonpareil / Apr. 1981 / Concord Jazz ✦✦✦✦
Al Cohn's debut for Concord continues where his Xanadu albums left off. On this quartet set with pianist Lou Levy, bassist Monty Budwig and drummer Jake Hanna, Cohn performs two originals and numbers by Johnny Mandel (including "El Cajon," which was named after him), Billy Strayhorn, Antonio Carlos Jobim ("The Girl from Ipanema"), Kurt Weill and Gary McFarland; the CD reissue adds the previously unissued "Expense Account." The tasteful and swinging music is quite enjoyable, and virtually all of Al Cohn's many sessions through the years are recommended to collectors of straightahead jazz. —*Scott Yanow*

Tour de Force / Aug. 11, 1981 / Concord Jazz ✦✦✦✦
Al Cohn gets top billing on this CD (formerly a double-LP) but that was because among the three tenors his name comes first alphabetically. This is a jam session set featuring the tenors of Cohn, Scott Hamilton and Buddy Tate. They battle it out to a draw, mostly jamming on fairly basic material such as "Blues Up and Down," "Tickle Toe," "Soft Winds," "Broadway" and "Jumpin' at the Woodside." With guitarist Cal Collins, pianist Dave McKenna, bassist Bob Maize and drummer Jake Hanna offering swinging support, this set is easily recommended to fans of Jazz at the Philharmonic and mainstream jazz. —*Scott Yanow*

Overtones / Apr. 1982 / Concord Jazz ✦✦✦✦
As can be heard on this quintet set, tenor saxophonist Al Cohn's former "cool school" tone deepend during his later years and had become much more distinctive than it had been earlier. This set is special in that Cohn's backup group includes his son, the cool-toned guitarist Joe Cohn. Also providing fine support are pianist Hank Jones, bassist George Duvivier and drummer Akiri Tana. The quintet performs four of Cohn's originals (including "High on You" and the catchy "P-Town") plus Hank Jones' "Vignette," a couple of obscurities and Cole Porter's "I Love You." A typically excellent Al Cohn set. —*Scott Yanow*

● **Standards of Excellence** / Nov. 1983 / Concord Jazz ✦✦✦✦
This was tenor saxophonist Al Cohn's last Concord recording, and despite how well he was playing during this era, he would not record as a leader again until three final efforts in 1987. Joined by a pianoless trio comprising guitarist Herb Ellis, bassist Monty Budwig and drummer Jimmie Smith, Cohn performs eight standards with his usual creative invention and driving swing. The biggest surprise about the repertoire is the absence of any Cohn originals or obscurities. Highlights include "Russian Lullaby," "I Want to Be Happy" and "When Day Is Done." —*Scott Yanow*

Al Cohn Meets Al Porcino / Mar. 30, 1987 / Red Baron ✦✦✦
This was one of Al Cohn's last recordings, a live session with trumpeter Al Porcino's European big band. Cohn's Lester Young-influenced tone had darkened quite a bit through the years and his tough tone was now closer to Illinois Jacquet than to Young. However he still swung in a boppish style and is the main soloist throughout this excellent outing, playing eight of his arrangements plus older charts from Gerry Mulligan and Bill Holman among others. Surprisingly Al Porcino does not take a single solo, being content to play in the ensembles and listen to his old friend perform in prime form. —*Scott Yanow*

Keeper of the Flame / May 28, 1987 / Frog ✦✦✦✦
Although a recording with Al Porcino's big band was titled *The Final Performance*, tenor saxophonist Al Cohn made two later recordings before his death in 1988. *Keeper of the Flame*, his next-to-last album, is a somewhat obscure set recorded in London with "the Jazz Seven." Although none of the sidemen would qualify as household names, they are quite professional and fine bop players. Cohn, who is the main soloist, stretches out on four group originals, "Mood Indigo" and his own "High on You." His tone had deepened through the years and Al Cohn is actually more distinctive on this recording than he had been in the 1950s. This little-known British LP is worth searching for. —*Scott Yanow*

Rifftide / Jun. 1987 / Timeless ✦✦✦✦
This was tenor saxophonist Al Cohn's final recording. His tone had deepened quite a bit during his last few years (he no longer sounded like Zoot Sims) but Cohn showed no signs of decline on this fine quartet date. Joined by pianist Rein de Graaff, bassist Koos Serierse and drummer Eric Ineke, Cohn plays a riff tune

called "The Thing" and seven jazz standards including two ("Secret Love" and "Do Nothing till You're True," which is really "Do Nothing till You Hear from Me") that mistakenly list him as composer. This is fine bop-based music that features Al Cohn exiting on top. —*Scott Yanow*

Dolo Coker (Charles Mitchell Coker)

b. Nov. 16, 1927, Hartford, CT, **d.** Apr. 13, 1983, Los Angeles, CA
Piano / Bop

A fine bop pianist who never became all that famous, Dolo Coker's most high-profile period was when he recorded regularly for Xanadu in the late '70s. Back in the 1950s he had worked and recorded with Sonny Stitt (1955-57), Gene Ammons, Lou Donaldson, Art Pepper (appearing on his Contemporary recording *Intensity*), Philly Joe Jones and Dexter Gordon (1960-61). He settled in Los Angeles in 1961, leading his own trio. In the 1970s Coker worked with Stitt again in addition to Herb Ellis, Blue Mitchell, Red Rodney, Lee Konitz, Sonny Criss and Supersax in addition to many artists associated with the Xanadu label. —*Scott Yanow*

● **Dolo!** / Dec. 26, 1976 / Xanadu ✦✦✦✦

Although by 1976 pianist Dolo Coker had already had a lengthy career, this quintet session was his first opportunity to record as a leader. Four of the six songs are his (three of those were written in 1959), and along with Harold Land's "Smack Up," they are performed in swinging fashion by Coker, trumpeter Blue Mitchell, Land on tenor, bassist Leroy Vinnegar and drummer Frank Butler. The remaining track, "Never Let Me Go," gives the trio a chance to be featured. The music is as hard-swinging as one would expect from this personnel; fortunately, Coker would lead three more Xanadu albums within the next two years. —*Scott Yanow*

California Hard / Dec. 27, 1976 / Xanadu ✦✦✦✦

Pianist Dolo Coker had just four opportunities to lead his own record dates during his career, all for the Xanadu label during 1976-79. The title of this LP refers to the fact that the music is not California "cool jazz" but intense hard bop from the Golden State. In addition to bassist Leroy Vinnegar and drummer Frank Butler (who appear on Coker's first three Xanadu albums) and trumpeter Blue Mitchell (who was on the preceding LP *Dolo*), the great altoist Art Pepper (doubling on tenor) makes one of his very rare appearances as a sideman. The well-rounded set has originals by Coker, Pepper ("Mr Yohe") and Mitchell (a drum feature for Butler on "Roots 4FB") along with a showcase for the trio ("Gone Again") and a vintage standard ("Gone with the Wind"). A strong effort. —*Scott Yanow*

Third Down / Nov. 18, 1977 / Xanadu ✦✦✦✦

With the exception of two guest appearances by trumpeters Harry "Sweets" Edison (on the blues "Sweet Coke" and "Out of Nowhere"), this is a trio session featuring pianist Dolo Coker, bassist Leroy Vinnegar and drummer Frank Butler. The boppish pianist, who spent many of his key years in Los Angeles and was therefore always underrated, shows throughout this set that he was a creative player within the hard-bop idiom. The LP gives one a fine example of Dolo Coker's talents and is highlighted by two of the pianist's originals, both of which are worth reviving: "Third Down" and "There Is No Other Way." —*Scott Yanow*

All Alone / Nov. 28, 1979 / Xanadu ✦✦✦

Dolo Coker's fourth and final album as a leader is a set of unaccompanied piano solos with the emphasis on reflective ballads (although there are also a couple of swinging tunes). Coker performs six of his little-known (but generally rewarding) originals plus "Cabin in the Sky" and "Try a Little Tenderness." All of Dolo Coker's Xanadu dates are worth picking up but they may be hard to find. —*Scott Yanow*

Cozy Cole

b. Oct. 17, 1909, East Orange, NJ, **d.** Jan. 29, 1981, Columbus, OH
Drums / Swing

A popular performer throughout much of his career, Cozy Cole was one of the top drummers to emerge during the 1930s. He recorded with Jelly Roll Morton in 1930 (including a song titled "Load of Cole") and played with the big bands of Blanche Calloway (1931-33), Benny Carter (1933-34) and Willie Bryant (1935-36). His stint with Stuff Smith at the Onyx Club (1936-38) gave him some recognition. Cole was well featured with Cab Calloway's Orchestra (1938-42), playing in a strong rhythm section with Bennie Payne, Danny Barker and Milt Hinton; his showcases included "Crescendo in Drums" and "Paradiddle." Cole popped up in many different types of jazz and studio settings throughout the 1940s and headed several record sessions with swing all-stars. He was with Louis Armstrong's All-Stars (1949-53), opened a drum school with Gene Krupa and in 1957 toured Europe with Jack Teagarden and Earl Hines. A 1958 recording of "Topsy" became a surprise hit, allowing Cole to lead his own band throughout much of the 1960s; he also played with Jonah Jones' quintet later in the decade. —*Scott Yanow*

1944 / Feb. 22, 1944-Sep. 18, 1944 / Classics ✦✦✦✦

● **1944-1945** / Nov. 14, 1944-Apr. 1945 / Classics ✦✦✦✦✦

This Classics CD reissues drummer Cozy Cole's sessions for Continental, Keynote and Guild, most of which have been out-of-print for years. The two Continental dates feature overlapping all-star groups (with trumpeter Charlie Shavers; clarinetist Hank D'Amico; Coleman Hawkins, Walter "Foots" Thomas, and/or Don Byas on tenors; Clyde Hart or Johnny Guarnieri on piano; guitarist Tiny Grimes; bassist Slam Stewart and the drummer/leader) but are sometimes a bit frustrating. Since every player is a potential soloist and the performances are limited to around three minutes apiece, the solos are almost cameos, generally eight or 16 bars apiece. The most memorable spot, Hawkins' exploration of "When Day Is Done," finds the great tenor doing what he can with his half-chorus. The Keynote session is most notable for Don Byas' solos and for the recording debut of 20-year-old trumpeter Shorty Rogers. The Guild sides have Don Byas well showcased in a quintet, two extensive drum features ("Stompin" and "Strictly Drums") and three dramatic vocals from June Hawkins. Overall this is an interesting and enjoyable CD, swing music with slight touches of bop. —*Scott Yanow*

Topsy / 1957 / Love ✦✦✦

Cozy's Caravan / Earl's Backroom / Feb. 7, 1958 / Felsted ✦✦✦

French Festival: Nice All Stars / Jul. 19, 1974 / Classic Jazz ✦✦✦✦

This session for the French Black & Blue label (which was released domestically on an LP by Classic Jazz) features an all-star swing sextet comprising trumpeter Wallace Davenport, trombonist Vic Dickenson, tenor saxophonist Buddy Tate, pianist Claude Hopkins, bassist Arvell Shaw and drummer Cozy Cole. They perform swing and Dixieland standards along with a feature for Cole and Shaw on the more recent "Eva." Other highlights include "I Never Knew I Could Love Anybody," "Linger Awhile" and "Farewell Blues." Nothing too surprising occurs but these highly expressive players come up with consistently colorful ideas that should please mainstream fans. —*Scott Yanow*

Lionel Hampton Presents Louis Armstrong Alumni / Oct. 5, 1977 / Who's Who In Jazz ✦✦✦

Although drummer Cozy Cole is listed as leader (which makes this LP the last recording session that he headed), in reality it is a co-op set supervised by vibraphonist Lionel Hampton. Five alumni from Louis Armstrong's All-Stars (Cole and bassist Arvell Shaw from the late '40s and pianist Marty Napoleon, clarinetist Joe Muranyi and trombonist Big Chief Russell Moore from the 1960s) team up with Hamp and trumpeter Johnny Letman to pay tribute to Satch. Two of the songs ("Louis' Dream" and "Short Ribs") have nothing to do with Armstrong but the band forms a cohesive group sound on those tunes plus six standbys from the All-Star days (including "Someday You'll Be Sorry," "Mack the Knife" and "Indiana"). Nothing all that remarkable occurs but this LP gives the fine trumpeter Johnny Letman a rare opportunity to stretch out. —*Scott Yanow*

Freddy Cole

b. Oct. 15, 1931, Chicago, IL
Vocals, Piano / Swing, Bop

The younger brother of Nat King Cole and uncle of Natalie Cole, singer/pianist Freddy Cole sounds a great deal like his celebrated sibling, yet has a personality of his own. Cole, whose vocals tends to be a bit darker and slightly rougher, began playing piano at five or six. He was interested in playing football professionally, but decided to pursue a career in music after a hand injury ended his career as an athlete. Cole debuted on vinyl in 1952, when he recorded the single "The Joke's on Me" for the obscure Chicago-based Topper Records. His next single, "Whispering Grass" on Columbia's OKeh label, was a moderate hit in 1953. In the '60s and '70s he developed a small following recording for various small labels. Cole founded his First Shot label in the '80s and went on to record for Sunnyside and LaserLight in the early '90s. A few years later, he signed with Fantasy and enjoyed his greatest visibility so far. —*Alex Henderson*

● **I'm Not My Brother, I'm Me** / Dec. 4, 1990 / Sunnyside ✦✦✦✦✦

One can sympathize with Freddie Cole's plight. The younger brother of Nat King Cole, Freddie has spent most of his life in his brother's shadow, even though Nat died in 1965. The problem is that Freddie is also a pianist/vocalist and sometimes performs similar material. In fact, the title of this CD is absurd, since Cole is heard playing in the same type of group that Nat made famous (a trio with guitarist Ed Zad and bassist Eddie Edwards) and his repertoire includes such songs as "Home Fried Potatoes," "To Whom It May Concern," "The Best Man" and a ten-minute, six-song "Nat Cole Medley." Add to that such originals as "He Was the King" and "I'm Not My Brother, I'm Me," and one is not allowed to forget for a moment that Freddie was Nat's brother. Actually, Freddie has an older and raspier voice (which is natural, since he has outlived Nat), and his piano style is more tied to 1950s jazz (such as Red Garland) than to swing. This fairly definitive CD from Freddie Cole does give one a strong sampling of his talents. —*Scott Yanow*

Live at Birdland West / Apr. 18, 1992 / LaserLight ✦✦✦

This release from the budget LaserLight label mostly finds Freddie Cole singing a repertoire similar to his brother's, including such tunes as "Walkin' My Baby Back Home," "Send for Me" and "Ballerina," plus two originals ("He Was the King" and "I'm Not My Brother, I'm Me") that he had recorded just two years earlier for Sunnyside. What makes the set different is that Cole is joined by the great Red Holloway (on tenor and alto), guitarist Jerry Byrd, bassist Delbert Felix and drummer Harold Mason, plus the fact that this is a live set. Everyone sounds in fine form, making the CD a worthy acquisition for fans of both Freddie and Nat King Cole. —*Scott Yanow*

This Is the Life / Jan. 13, 1993 / Muse ✦✦✦

A Circle of Love / Sep. 26, 1993-Dec. 5, 1995 / Fantasy ✦✦✦✦

Always / Dec. 1994 / Fantasy ✦✦✦

It's Crazy, But I'm in Love / 1996 / After 9 ✦✦✦

Live at Vartan Jazz / Oct. 1, 1996 / Vartan Jazz ✦✦✦✦

Freddy Cole's smoky, silky voice automatically invites comparison to his famous brother Nat, but as a pianist he shows a host of influences. Joined by guitarist Jerry Byrd and bassist Tom Hubbard, Cole's live session gently swings through a collection of standards, including an understated "You'd Be So Nice to Come Home To." His humorous version of "You've Let Yourself Go" is side-splitting, but it is his reserved piano style on tracks like "I Remember You" that helps make him worth remembering. —*Ken Dryden*

To the Ends of the Earth / Jan. 6, 1997-Jan. 7, 1997 / Fantasy ✦✦✦✦

Holly Cole

b. 1963, Halifax, Nova Scotia, Canada

Vocals / Cabaret, Standards, Traditional Pop

Holly Cole's music is difficult to classify. She takes familiar standards and casts them in a new ironic light that is sometimes sinister and occasionally humorous. She also performs sets of diverse music that have more variety than one would think could possibly be successful; somehow it works. Both of her parents are classical musicians and she studied classical piano for a time. But after discovering Sarah Vaughan when she was 15, she switched to jazz. Cole sang with a big band in Toronto and in 1985 she formed a permanent trio with pianist Aaron Davis and bassist David Piltch. Their first album *Girl Talk* (released only in Canada) was a success and led to three records (thus far) for Manhattan: *Blame It on My Youth*, *Don't Smoke in Bed* and a nonjazz set of Tom Waits' music. —*Scott Yanow*

Blame It on My Youth / Jun. 1991-Jul. 1991 / Manhattan ✦✦✦✦

Holly Cole's debut recording is a delight. Although she infuses a variety of standards with sensuality (including "If I Were a Bell," "On the Street Where You Live," "Honeysuckle Rose" and "I'll Be Seeing You"), she is also clearly laughing at her image at the same time. Joined by pianist Aaron Davis and bassist David Piltch with guest appearances by violinist Johnny Frigo (on two songs) and bass clarinetist Robert Stevenson (for one), Cole's interpretations of the mostly veteran material are both haunting and ironic, making this a memorable and surprisingly original outing. —*Scott Yanow*

● **Don't Smoke in Bed** / Feb. 1993-Mar. 1993 / Manhattan ✦✦✦✦

Holly Cole explores a number of styles on her second album, *Don't Smoke in Bed*, without overreaching her grasp. Adding pop, blues, country, and a French ballad to her standard, low-key jazz, Cole demonstrates that not only does she have impeccable taste, but she has the talent to make all of the material sound convincing. —*Stephen Thomas Erlewine*

Temptation / 1995 / Metro Blue ✦✦

Holly Cole is one of the most intriguing jazz singers on the scene today, able to turn a standard inside out, pouring on an equal dosage of sensuality and sly wit while often laughing at herself. This CD finds her interpreting 16 Tom Waits compositions but, rather than try to uplift or distort the material, she lets the lyrics mostly speak for themselves and unfortunately few of the surprisingly mundane words would qualify as poetry. Even with the heat that she gives some of the songs (most notably "Take Me Home" and "Temptation"), this set is mostly a bore from the jazz standpoint with relatively little improvisation taking place. —*Scott Yanow*

It Happened One Night / Jun. 28, 1995 / Metro Blue ✦✦✦✦

Dark Dear Heart / 1997 / Metro Blue ✦✦✦

Although a few songs on *Dark Dear Heart* are ill-suited for Holly Cole's style—nothing Sheryl Crow has written could translate to a cocktail jazz setting—the album remains another solid entry in her catalog, illustrating that she is one of the best interpretative singers of the '90s. —*Leo Stanley*

Nat King Cole (Nathaniel Adams Cole)

b. Mar. 17, 1917, Montgomery, AL, d. Feb. 15, 1965, Santa Monica, CA

Piano, Vocals / Swing, Pop

Nat King Cole had two overlapping careers. He was one of the truly great swing pianists, inspired by Earl Hines and a big influence on Oscar Peterson. And he was a superb pop ballad singer whose great commercial success in that field unfortunately resulted in him greatly de-emphasizing his piano after 1949. Perhaps if his talents had been divided between two different people!

Nat Cole grew up in Chicago and by the time he was 12 he was playing organ and singing in church; his three brothers (Eddie, Fred and Isaac) would become jazz musicians. After making his recording debut with Eddie Cole's Solid Swingers in 1936, he left Chicago to lead the band for the revival of the revue *Shuffle Along*, and settled in Los Angeles when the show ended. Cole struggled a bit, put together a trio with guitarist Oscar Moore and bassist Wesley Prince and eventually settled in for a long residency in Hollywood. In the early days (documented on radio transcriptions), most of the group's repertoire comprised instrumentals although the Trio often sang jivey novelty vocals together. However, by the time the Trio had its first opportunity to record for Decca in December 1940, Nat Cole had gained more confidence in his own singing. "Sweet Lorraine" resulted from that session and the Trio soon became quite popular. In future years Art Tatum, Oscar Peterson and Ahmad Jamal would all form piano/guitar/bass combos inspired by Cole's group.

Nat Cole recorded a great deal of exciting jazz during the 1940s, including dates featuring Lester Young and Illinois Jacquet, the first Jazz at the Philharmonic concert (1944) and a countless number of selections for Capitol with his trio; all of the latter are included on a gigantic Mosaic limited-edition box set. Although his singing began to become quite popular by the mid-'40s (and particularly after "The Christmas Song" and "Nature Boy"), Cole mostly performed with his Trio during this era; Johnny Miller took over on bass and in 1947 Irving Ashby became the guitarist. Nat King Cole was open to the influence of bop and in 1949 started utilizing Jack Costanzo on bongo and conga for some songs. However his career changed permanently in early 1950 with the recording of "Mona Lisa," which became a No. 1 hit. Suddenly Nat King Cole became famous to the nonjazz public as a singer, and many new fans never realized that he also played piano! During the 1950s and '60s he mostly recorded pop ballads although there were a few exceptions (including 1956's *After Midnight* album) and he never lost his ability to play stimulating jazz. Cole had a regular television show during 1956-57 (some of which has been released on video), but due to the racism of the period he could never find a sponsor. However, the popularity of his records and public appearances remained at a remarkable level and the world mourned Nat King Cole's death from lung cancer in early 1965 at age 47. —*Scott Yanow*

From the Very Beginning / Jul. 28, 1936-Oct. 23, 1941 / MCA ✦✦✦✦

This double LP only contains 20 selections (an hour of music) but it perfectly sums up his early period. Cole's first recording date (as a sideman in his brother Eddie Cole's Solid Swingers) is included along with his four sessions for Decca with his trio, which at the time featured guitarist Oscar Moore and bassist Wesley Prince. Although there are plenty of early radio transcriptions currently available, this set has all of his most significant studio recordings up until late 1942. Highlights include his first hit "Sweet Lorraine," "Honeysuckle Rose" and "Hit That Jive Jack." —*Scott Yanow*

☆ **Complete Early Transcriptions** / Oct. 1938-Feb. 1941 / Vintage Jazz ✦✦✦✦✦

This four-CD set contains 112 performances by the Trio from 1938-41, radio transcriptions made especially to be played on the air. The early trio is instantly recognizable and, although there is a greater reliance on group vocals and guest singers (including Bonnie Lake, Juanelda Carter, Pauline and Her Perils and the Dreamers) rather than on Cole's solo vocals, the music is not all that different from what the King Cole Trio would be playing a few years later when they became much better known. —*Scott Yanow*

Nat King Cole & the King Cole Trio 1938-39 / Jan. 14, 1939-Jul. 23, 1940 / Savoy ✦✦✦✦

This LP, which does not duplicate the Vintage Jazz Classics set called *The Complete Early Transcriptions*, contains the Nat King Cole Trio's earliest studio recordings, four selections apiece from Jan. 14 and Dec. 1939 that were originally released on the tiny Ammor and Davis & Schwegler labels. In addition, there are 12 radio transcriptions, four of which have vocals by Maxine Johnson. Fans of the Trio will enjoy these swinging obscurities. —*Scott Yanow*

● **Hit That Jive Jack: The Earliest Recordings** / Dec. 6, 1940-Oct. 22, 1941 / Decca ✦✦✦✦✦

Nat King Cole's 16 trio recordings for Decca have been reissued many times (including on this CD) and rightfully so. Cole was already one of the top swing pianists by 1940, his vocal style (best displayed on his first hit "Sweet Lorraine") was quite recognizable and his trio with guitarist Oscar Moore and bassist Wesley

Prince had a memorable sound. Cole's Decca records (his first for a major label) were a breakthrough for Nat although his Capitol recordings (which started in 1943) really paved the way towards major success. In addition to "Sweet Lorraine," highlights of this fine CD include "Honeysuckle Rose," "I Like to Riff" and "Hit That Jive Jack" (which has the Trio's most famous group vocal). —*Scott Yanow*

Great Beginnings / Dec. 6, 1940-1945 / Avid ◆◆◆
This English reissue CD has ten of the Nat King Cole Trio's 16 Decca recordings, plus 16 selections taken from their early days with Capitol. A single-disc sampler that can be most enjoyed by casual listeners rather than completists, the Avid set contains quite a few classic moments, including two of Cole's first hits ("Straighten Up and Fly Right" and the remake of "Sweet Lorraine"), many fine solos (the versions of "What Is This Thing Called Love," "Body and Soul" and "Easy Listenin' Blues" are particularly memorable), and strong interplay between pianist Cole, guitarist Oscar Moore and either Wesley Prince or Johnny Miller on bass. Although Nat does a bit of singing, there are almost as many group vocals and a healthy dose of instrumentals. All of the material is available elsewhere. —*Scott Yanow*

The Nat King Cole Trio Recordings / 1940-1956 / LaserLight ◆◆◆◆◆
This five-CD set, despite the lack of definitive liner notes, is highly recommended. The bulk of this package (most of four discs) features the Trio on radio transcriptions during 1944-45 and these renditions are easily the equal of their more famous studio recordings. The fifth disc is a hodgepodge that reaches back to 1940 for six numbers and forward to 1956 for a few songs performed on the Dorsey Brothers TV Show and on Nat Cole's own program. Although the music could actually have fit on three discs (averaging around 40 minutes apiece), this set is usually available at a budget price and contains many exciting performances. —*Scott Yanow*

The MacGregor Years, 1941-45 / Feb. 25, 1941-May 25, 1994 / Music & Arts ◆◆◆◆◆
On this four-CD set are included the bulk of Nat King Cole's radio transcriptions of 1941 and 1944-45. Although the programming could be a little better (the complete sessions are not compiled strictly in chronological order), the music has a strong unity and is consistently enjoyable. Pianist-vocalist Cole and his trio (which also includes important contributions by guitarist Oscar Moore and either Johnny Miller or Wesley Prince on bass) are featured extensively both as a unit and as an accompanying group to singers Anita Boyer, Ida James, Anita O'Day and the Barrie Sisters on 33, 15, five and five songs respectively. There are 120 selections altogether (some are quite brief) including two six-song instrumental medleys that put the emphasis on Cole's piano playing. Some of the music had already been reissued by LaserLight but this compilation is more complete. Highly recommended to all fans of the King Cole Trio. —*Scott Yanow*

WWII Transcriptions / 1941-1944 / Music & Arts ◆◆◆◆◆
With the exception of a couple of Anita Boyer vocals from 1941, this CD (which contains 30 broadcast transcriptions by Nat King Cole's Trio) dates from 1944. Two numbers apiece feature vocals from a young Anita O'Day and Ida James, but otherwise, Cole and his Trio usually sing four other songs. The emphasis is on instrumentals (including two interesting medleys) and the leader's talents as a great swing pianist. Most of this material does not duplicate the LaserLight CDs, making this a recommended set for Nat King Cole's jazz fans. —*Scott Yanow*

☆ **Nat King Cole Meets the Master Saxes** / Jul. 15, 1942-1943 / Spotlite ◆◆◆◆◆
This very interesting LP finds Cole during 1942-43 recording outside of his trio. All of these selections originally came out on obscure 78s from tiny labels, but the personnel is anything but unknown. His piano is heard in a trio with the great tenor Lester Young and bassist Red Callender, with a quintet featuring tenorman Illinois Jacquet and trumpeter Shad Collins, and in a combo with 20-year-old Dexter Gordon on tenor and trumpeter Harry "Sweets" Edison. The late-period swing music is consistently wonderful, historical and formerly quite rare. —*Scott Yanow*

☆ **The Complete Capitol Trio Recordings** / Oct. 11, 1942-Mar. 2, 1961 / Mosaic ◆◆◆◆◆
This 18-CD box set lives up to its title, containing not only all of the Nat King Cole Trio's recordings for Capitol during 1943-49 but a remarkable amount of previously unavailable radio transcriptions owned by Capitol. Also, all of Cole's post-1949 recordings that at least have the presence of the trio are here, including the entire *After Midnight* sessions of 1956 and various odds and ends that feature Cole's piano—349 selections in all with a countless number of formerly unissued tracks. Since this is a limited-edition set that will sell out, get this remarkable box as soon as possible. —*Scott Yanow*

Straighten Up and Fly Right / Dec. 1942-Jan. 28, 1948 / Vintage Jazz ◆◆◆◆
This CD consists of some of the Nat King Cole Trio's radio appearances, including guest shots on shows hosted by Bing Crosby, Perry Como and Frank Sinatra; Ol' Blue Eyes sits in with the trio on "I've Found a New Baby" and "Exactly like You."

Considering that 12 of these 25 songs were never recorded commercially by the Trio, this set is quite valuable for fans of swing and Nat Cole's piano. The colorful music is easily recommended. —*Scott Yanow*

The Best of Nat King Cole Trio: Vocal Classics, Vol. 1 (1942-46) / 1942 / Capitol ◆◆◆◆◆

Jumpin' at Capitol / Nov. 30, 1943-Jan. 5, 1950 / Rhino ◆◆◆◆◆
For those who cannot afford or get a hold of the magnificent Mosaic 18-CD box set, this single CD offers a fine sampling of Nat King Cole's talents as a pianist and jazz singer with his popular trio in the 1940s. These 16 selections (highlighted by "Straighten up and Fly Right," "Sweet Lorraine" and "Route 66") are still quite enjoyable a half-century later. —*Scott Yanow*

The Capitol Collector's Series / Nov. 30, 1943-Jun. 3, 1964 / Capitol ◆◆◆◆◆
This 20-song single CD gives one an excellent introduction to the very popular singing of Nat King Cole. Concentrating on his hits, it contains virtually all of the biggest, including "Route 66," "The Christmas Song," "Nature Boy," "Mona Lisa" and even "Those Lazy-Hazy-Crazy Days of Summer." It has since been succeeded by the more ambitious four-CD box set *Nat King Cole* but is recommended to those with a tight budget. —*Scott Yanow*

★ **Nat King Cole [Capitol]** / Nov. 30, 1943-Jun. 3, 1964 / Capitol ◆◆◆◆
For an overview of Nat King Cole's years as a remarkably popular singer, this four-CD box would be difficult to top. Containing 100 songs spanning a 20-year period, this box has virtually all of Cole's hits, some of his best jazz sides and more than its share of variety including a humorous previously unreleased version of "Mr. Cole Won't Rock & Roll." Recommended to beginners and veteran collectors alike, its attractive booklet is also a major asset. —*Scott Yanow*

Best Of: The Instrumental Classics / 1943-1949 / Capitol ◆◆◆◆
Eighteen instrumental classics, long unavailable, were assembled into one package—the first of three CDs to be released on Capitol to document Nat King Cole's great trio of 1943-49. This collection will be in great demand by Cole fans and jazz fans as well. Titles include "Jumpin' at Capitol," "The Man I Love," "Body and Soul," "Smoke Gets in Your Eyes," "Bop Kick," and "Peaches." —*Roundup Newsletter*

● **The Greatest Hits** / 1944-1963 / Capitol ◆◆◆◆◆
For all the resurgence in interest in Nat King Cole since 1991, when his daughter Natalie recorded a duet patching her new vocal with his from 40 years earlier and scored a gold-selling hit, Capitol Records lacked a single-disc hits collection that covered Cole's most successful singles for the label. This 22-track, 62-plus-minute CD/cassette collection does the trick. Cole scored 21 Top Ten hits between 1944 and 1963, and 19 of them are here, from "Straighten Up and Fly Right" to "Those Lazy-Hazy-Crazy Days of Summer." The only ones missing are seasonal hits, "The Christmas Song" and "Frosty The Snow Man." In their places, you get the original and later versions of "Unforgettable" (neither of which, as it happens, quite made the Top 10). You also get Cole's four No.1 songs, "Mona Lisa," "Nature Boy," "(I Love You) For Sentimental Reasons," and "Too Young," along with such memorable tunes as "Walkin' My Baby Back Home," "Smile," and "(Get Your Kicks On) Route 66." The non-chronological sequencing emphasizes the stylistic and qualitative consistency of Cole's work; it doesn't much matter if you juxtapose a song recorded in the '40s ("Nature Boy") against one recorded in the '60s ("Ramblin' Rose"), you still get the same warmth and assurance in Cole's singing, the same tastefulness in the arrangements. One might have hoped for more in the way of packaging (there are no liner notes), but this is the single album to buy to hear Nat King Cole's best-known vocal performances. —*William Ruhlmann*

Spotlight on Nat King Cole / 1944-1960 / Capitol ◆◆◆◆◆
Part of a Capitol reissue series called "Great Ladies and Gentlemen of Song," *Spotlight on . . . Nat King Cole* is a 18-track compilation that, for once, eschews the over-familiar Cole hits in favor of pop standards originally strewn across several of his late-'50s and early-'60s albums, plus a couple of previously unreleased Cole Trio recordings. Here, Cole sings Rodgers and Hart, Gershwin, Berlin, Mercer, and Ellington, among others, with arrangements by Nelson Riddle, among others, and backed in some cases by the Count Basie Band. It's classy stuff, and Cole handles it all effortlessly. Longtime fans may find this set largely redundant, but it makes a good introduction to the breadth of the singer's work for those who know him only for "Nature Boy," "Mona Lisa," and "Unforgettable." —*William Ruhlmann*

★ **Jazz Encounters** / Mar. 30, 1945-Jan. 5, 1950 / Blue Note ◆◆◆◆◆
This CD has many of Cole's most interesting Capitol dates away from his trio. The great jazz pianist is heard with the 1947 Metronome All-Stars, jamming with the all-star Capitol International Jazzmen, backing the straight vocals of Jo Stafford and collaborating with Nellie Lutcher, Woody Herman (on a remarkable version of "Mule Train") and Johnny Mercer (highlighted by the joyful "Save the Bones for Henry Jones"). This colorful set is highly recommended. —*Scott Yanow*

Anatomy of a Jam Session / Jun. 9, 1945 / Black Lion ✦✦✦✦

Cole is heard on this quintet session purely as a pianist, co-starring with trumpeter Charlie Shavers and tenor saxophonist Herbie Haymer; bassist John Simmons and drummer Buddy Rich play mainly in support. The quintet only actually performs five songs but seven alternate takes fill in the program and it is very interesting hearing the musicians gradually form the shape of their solos. —*Scott Yanow*

The King Cole Trios Live: 1947-1948 / Mar. 1, 1947-Mar. 13, 1948 / Vintage Jazz ✦✦✦✦

This excellent CD contains five of the Trio's radio shows for NBC during 1947-48. There are some guests (singer Clark Dennis, the Dinning Sisters, Pearl Bailey, Woody Herman and Duke Ellington) for a song apiece, but the focus is on the Trio with occasional vocals from Cole. This historical music is enjoyable although the performances (many around the two-minute mark) are sometimes frustratingly brief. It's still worth acquiring. —*Scott Yanow*

The Best of Nat King Cole: Vocal Classics, Vol. 2 (1947-50) / 1947-1950 / Capitol ✦✦✦✦

Lush Life / Mar. 29, 1949-Jan. 11, 1952 / Capitol ✦✦✦✦✦

This is a very interesting transitional collection featuring Nat King Cole when he was gradually emphasizing his vocals over his jazz piano playing and phasing out his Trio. All 25 of the selections on this generous set feature the arrangements of Pete Rugolo; highlights include "Lush Life," "Time Out for Tears," "That's My Girl," "Red Sails in the Sunset," "It's Crazy" and "You Stepped out of a Dream." There is enough jazz content and popular appeal on this CD to satisfy both of Cole's audiences. —*Scott Yanow*

The Unforgettable Nat King Cole / 1950-1958 / Capitol ✦✦✦

A '92 reissue designed to take advantage of the success Cole's daughter Natalie had with a reworked version of "Unforgettable" that featured her doing duets with her father via digital technology. The album offered Cole doing the original and other selected songs in the same vein. —*Ron Wynn*

Big Band Cole / Aug. 16, 1950-Sep. 6, 1961 / Capitol ✦✦✦✦✦

Cole's collaborations with the Count Basie and Stan Kenton Orchestras (all of which are included on this CD) found him mostly sticking to singing but enjoying the jazz-oriented backgrounds. He first met up with Kenton in 1950, recording the memorable "Orange Colored Sky" and starring on piano during the instrumental "Jam-Bo." They had a reunion in 1960-61, cutting a remake of "Orange Colored Sky" and two more poppish songs. The matchup with Basie showcased Cole purely as a singer in 1958; Gerald Wiggins took Basie's place at the keyboards. One of Cole's better vocal sessions, he is in top form on a variety of standards (particularly on "The Late Late Show" and "Welcome to the Club"); pity he did not sit in with the band on piano. This CD is recommended for its rare examples of Nat King Cole as a big-band singer. —*Scott Yanow*

The Billy May Sessions / Sep. 4, 1951-Nov. 22, 1961 / Capitol ✦✦✦✦

Nat King Cole recorded with arranger/bandleader Billy May on several occasions and all of their collaborations are on this excellent double CD. Dating from 1951, 1953, 1954, 1957 and 1961, some of the more memorable numbers include "Walkin' My Baby Back Home," "Angel Eyes," "Papa Loves Mambo," "Send for Me," "Who's Sorry Now," "The Party's Over" and "When My Sugar Walks Down the Street." Cole also takes organ solos on three of the selections from 1961 (the only time he ever recorded on that instrument;), though he plays no piano on this set. It's recommended for his superior middle-of-the-road singing. —*Scott Yanow*

Sings for Two in Love / 1954 / Capitol ✦✦✦✦✦

Nat King Cole Sings for Two in Love was Nat King Cole's first album to be specifically for the new 12-inch LP format. Like Frank Sinatra, with whom he shared a record company and a conductor, Cole made a thematic album, in this case a set of 12 romantic ballads. But they aren't actually all for "two in love." There are songs for two who think "This Can't Be Love" or that it's "Almost like Being in Love" or who tell each other "Let's Fall in Love." And then there are post-love songs—"Autumn Leaves," "Dinner for One Please, James." If Cole really wants to sing for two in love, he's telling them good news and bad. Of course, his plaintive, undisturbed singing makes the happy and sad sentiments seem equally content, and Nelson Riddle's orchestrations consistently support the singer without challenging him or getting in his way. (The CD reissue contained three bonus tracks culled from the 1959 album *To Whom It May Concern*.) —*William Ruhlmann*

Piano Stylings / Jun. 7, 1955-Aug. 27, 1955 / Capitol ✦✦✦✦

One of Cole's most obscure albums, these 16 selections from 1955 feature his piano backed by an orchestra arranged by Nelson Riddle; no vocals. Different in style than the earlier recordings by the Trio, these performances put the focus purely on his lyrical and swinging playing and his improvisations are often quite inspired. This CD deserves to be much better known. —*Scott Yanow*

Complete After Midnight Sessions / Aug. 15, 1956-Sep. 2, 1956 / Capitol ✦✦✦✦

After several years of hearing criticism from the jazz press about his decision to break up his Trio and become a pop singer, Nat King Cole was persuaded to record this jazz set. Joined by a strong rhythm section (including guitarist John Collins), Cole welcomed four guests for several selections apiece: altoist Willie Smith, trumpeter Harry "Sweets" Edison, violinist Stuff Smith and valve trombonist Juan Tizol. The performances on this CD (which include five selections released for the first time) are quite enjoyable, highlighted by "Just You, Just Me," "Sweet Lorraine," "It's Only a Paper Moon" and "Route 66." Cole did hedge his bet a bit by not recording any instrumentals or having any performances feature his trio without a guest. Despite that, this is a great set, and the last time that Nat King Cole would perform an album's worth of jazz material. —*Scott Yanow*

Love Is the Thing / 1957 / Capitol ✦✦✦

This 1996 gold audiophile CD reissue of a 1956 Nat King Cole vocal set is augmented by three numbers taken from his similar 1963 album *Where Did Everyone Go?* By the mid-'50s, Cole was primarily known to the general public as a superb ballad vocalist, and he sticks exclusively to that role on these 15 selections, which include "When I Fall in Love," "Stardust," "Love Letters" and "When Sunny Gets Blue." On both dates, he is accompanied by a string orchestra arranged and conducted by Gordon Jenkins, so the jazz content is quite low. However, listeners who want to hear why Nat King Cole was so popular during the era (and those who love the sound of his voice) will enjoy this fine reissue. —*Scott Yanow*

Just One of Those Things / May 14, 1957-Nov. 22, 1961 / Capitol ✦✦✦

Just One of Those Things is a theme album comparable to one of Frank Sinatra's uptempo swing albums of the same period (*Come Fly with Me*, etc.), and employing the same arranger/conductor, Billy May. Cole is a bit less effective than Sinatra at uptempo material; he tends to undersing these sprightly standards, and May saves his dramatic horn charts and percussion shots for moments when Cole is away from the microphone. Even so, by the fifth track, "These Foolish Things Remind Me of You," May has retreated to ballad time, and though his embellishments threaten to break out behind the singer, Cole gives an assured, unhurried performance. And that's the point: That Cole has tamed the rambunctious May does not mean he doesn't give wonderful interpretations to some wonderful songs—"Don't Get Around Much Anymore," "Just One of Those Things," "The Song Is Ended (But the Melody Lingers On)." And the light-handed swing supports those efforts well. Originally released in November 1957, *Just One of Those Things* was reissued on CD in March 1987 under the title *Just One of Those Things (And More)*. The reissue contained three bonus tracks previously released on the 1964 album *Let's Face the Music!*, an album on which Billy May took a more aggressive posture and, notably on "I'm Gonna Sit Right Down (and Write Myself a Letter)," included here, Cole matched him note for note. —*William Ruhlmann*

St. Louis Blues / Jan. 29, 1958-Jan. 31, 1958 / Capitol ✦✦✦

The filmed version of W.C. Handy's life, *St. Louis Blues*, is a fictional abomination full of every bad cliché that Hollywood could come up with. Its one saving grace was the dignified performance given by Nat King Cole in the lead role (even if Handy was never a singing pianist). This LP, in addition to featuring Nelson Riddle's "Overture" from the film, finds Cole singing ten of Handy's finest compositions (including "Beale Street Blues," "Careless Love" and the title song) while backed by an orchestra playing Riddle's arrangements. —*Scott Yanow*

To Whom It May Concern / 1958 / Capitol ✦✦✦

The albums that Nat King Cole, Frank Sinatra, and other classic pop singers made in the 1950s usually consisted of standards from the golden era of pop songwriting in the 1920s, '30s, and '40s. For this album, Cole had the idea of putting together a set of newly written songs in the classic style, with typically sympathetic arrangements by Nelson Riddle. "Personally, I hear the magic in all these selections," Cole wrote in the liner notes. "It will be interesting to see whether I'm right." The magic we hear today is in Cole's voice, not in the songs, all of which are as forgotten as most of the songwriters. (There are a couple of ringers, such as Johnny Burke, Sammy Cahn, and Paul Weston, but they're not at their best.) —*William Ruhlmann*

Nat King Cole at the Sands / Jan. 14, 1960 / Capitol ✦✦✦✦

Nat King Cole's only live recording from his later years, this posthumously released LP features him singing before his fans in Las Vegas while backed by an orchestra directed by David Cavanaugh and conducted by Antonio Morelli. Cole always sounded comfortable in front of a big band and he interprets a variety of jazz-oriented material (including "The Continental," "Thou Swell," "Surrey with the Fringe on Top" and "Miss Otis Regrets") along with some ballads and remakes of "Ballerina" and "Funny." A special treat is a swinging instrumental rendition of "Where or When," which finds Cole having a rare outing on piano. But despite the loud applause and cries for "more," his spot on piano is just a cameo. Nevertheless, this is an excellent outing from his final years that documents what a Nat King Cole show sounded like. —Scott Yanow

Nat King Cole Story / Mar. 22, 1961-Jul. 30, 1961 / Capitol ✦✦✦✦

This double CD finds him revisiting his earlier hits with new versions. The 36 selections mostly focus on his pop successes of the 1950s, although there are a few wistful looks back at his trio days. Not as essential as the original renditions of these popular recordings, these remakes nevertheless find Cole in peak form and present a highly enjoyable retrospective of his vocal career. —Scott Yanow

Nat King Cole Sings, George Shearing Plays / Dec. 19, 1961-Dec. 22, 1961 / Capitol ✦✦✦✦

Although it would have been interesting to hear Nat Cole play some piano and perhaps accompany a vocal by George Shearing instead of exclusively the other way around, this session was a big success. Cole is in prime form on such songs as "September Song," "Pick Yourself Up," and "Serenata." Shearing's accompaniment is tasteful and lightly swinging, and the string arrangements help to accentuate the romantic moods. This CD adds three "new" selections from the same sessions to the original program. —Scott Yanow

Ramblin' Rose / 1962 / Capitol ✦✦

The title track was among Cole's biggest '60s pop hits, while the other tracks are wonderfully sung, but many are insubstantial and reflect Cole's dilemma: the bigger he got, the more overproduced his songs became and he was taken further away stylistically from his jazz roots. Still, there's plenty of lush, romantic and beautiful singing here. Originally released in August 1962, *Ramblin' Rose* [Capitol 1793] was reissued in 1980 [Capitol 16032]. It was reissued on CD in 1991 [Capitol 46651]. —Ron Wynn

Richie Cole

b. Feb. 29, 1948, Trenton, NJ

Alto Saxophone / Bop

Back in the mid-'70s when bebop was being greatly overshadowed by fusion, Richie Cole showed that not only was bop not old-fashioned but it could be quite fun. His "Alto Madness" was essentially the idea that any tune, no matter how unlikely its source, could be turned into exuberant bop. Through the years he has successfully recorded such songs as "The *I Love Lucy* Theme," "Holiday for Strings," "Horray for Hollywood," "The White Cliffs of Dover," "Come Fly with Me," "The *Star Trek* Theme," and even "La Bamba!" Influenced by Phil Woods and Charlie Parker, Richie Cole heard jazz from an early age because his father owned a jazz club in New Jersey. He started on alto when he was ten, attended Berklee for two years and joined Buddy Rich's big band in 1969. After a stint with Lionel Hampton Cole formed his own group, doing a great deal to popularize bebop in the 1970s. Some of his finest recordings were his early ones for Muse during a period when he often teamed up with singer Eddie Jefferson. His humor sometimes left critics cold but Cole was one of the top bop-oriented players of the 1980s, and his Heads Up releases of the '90s (after a few years off the scene) are excellent. —Scott Yanow

Battle of Saxes, Vol. 1 / May 26, 1976-May 27, 1976 / Muse ✦✦✦✦

Except for one obscure release from the year before, this Muse LP has the earliest recording of Richie Cole as a leader (actually a co-leader with fellow altoist Eric Kloss). Cole and Kloss battle it out on four lengthy songs with "Harold's House of Jazz" (which is actually based on "Cherokee") being the high point. Actually the set does not quite live up to its potential due to the electric rhythm section (Mickey Tucker on electric piano, Rick Laird partly on electric bass and drummer Eddie Gladden) and the obscure material, but there are enough sparks to make this LP (and its second volume) worth searching for. —Scott Yanow

New York Afternoon: Alto Madness / Oct. 13, 1976 / Muse ✦✦✦✦

This Muse album features the group that altoist Richie Cole and the late singer Eddie Jefferson co-led in the mid-'70s. They had a mutually beneficial relationship, with Cole learning from the older vocalist and Jefferson gaining extra exposure from associating with the popular young saxophonist. Their spirited set, which has two Jefferson vocals, is highlighted by "Waltz for a Rainy Be-Bop Evening," "New York Afternoon," "Stormy Weather" and "Alto Madness." —Scott Yanow

Alto Madness / Dec. 1977 / Muse ✦✦✦✦✦

Some of altoist Richie Cole's finest records were made for the Muse label during 1976-81 when he did a great deal to help revive bebop. Cole has long had the ability to turn almost anything into jazz and on this out-of-print LP he manages to swing both the theme from "The Price Is Right" and the main melody from *Last Tango in Paris*. In addition to solo space for pianist Harold Mabern and guitarist Vic Juris, singer Eddie Jefferson is featured on two numbers: "The Common Touch" and "Moody's Mood '78." Muse should reissue all of their Richie Cole albums. —Scott Yanow

Keeper of the Flame / Sep. 6, 1978 / Muse ✦✦✦✦

This is one of altoist Richie Cole's best-ever albums. He rips through surprisingly effective medium-to-uptempo versions of "As Time Goes By" and "Holiday for Strings," welcomes the great vocalese singer Eddie Jefferson to "Harold's House of Jazz" and "New York Afternoon," has a humorous dig at free jazz on "Strange Groove," introduces his "Keeper of the Flame" and comes up with a near-classic solo on "I Can't Get Started." This LP is long overdue to be reissued by Muse on CD. —Scott Yanow

Live / Oct. 1, 1978 / Just Jazz ✦✦✦✦

Altoist Richie Cole is heard in prime form on a live session recorded at the Douglas Beach House in Half Moon Bay in northern California. The music, released for the first time on this 1995 Just Jazz CD, features the fiery Cole bebopping his way in spirited fashion with the assistance of pianist Smith Dobson, bassist Bob Maize and drummer Jeep Duquesne on three selections including his own "Tokyo Rose Sings the Blues" and a surprisingly cooking version of "As Time Goes By." Cole welcomes felow altoist Bishop Norman Williams to an explosive "Donna Lee" and a less successful "Big Bo's Paradise"; singer Eddie Jefferson guests on brief versions of "Summertime" and "Lester Leaps In." Overall this CD gives one a good example of Richie Cole's exciting "Alto Madness" playing of the late '70s, showing that bebop could be accessible and quite fun. —Scott Yanow

● Hollywood Madness / Apr. 25, 1979 / Muse ✦✦✦✦✦

This is one of Richie Cole's most successful LPs and Muse should be persuaded to reissue it on CD. Four songs utilize the Manhattan Transfer, the great vocalese singer Eddie Jefferson (heard two weeks before his tragic death) makes his final appearance on records, there are some good solos by pianist Dick Hindman and guitarist Bruce Forman, and Tom Waits makes an eccentric guest appearance. But it is altoist Cole who stars throughout on an unlikely program highlighted by boppish versions of such tunes as "Hooray for Hollywood," "Hi-Fly," "Relaxin' at Camarillo," "I Love Lucy" and his original "Tokyo Rose Sings the Hollywood Blues." A gem. —Scott Yanow

Side by Side / Jul. 25, 1980+Jul. 26, 1980 / Muse ✦✦✦✦

This set features a very logical matchup. Richie Cole's main influence has long been Phil Woods, so these concert performances pitting the two altoists together have plenty of fire and extroverted improvisations. With pianist John Hicks, bassist Walter Booker and drummer Jimmy Cobb backing the soloists, Woods and Cole really push each other on "Scrapple from the Apple," "Donna Lee" and "Side by Side." Tenor-great Eddie "Lockjaw" Davis sits in on "Save Your Love for Me," the younger altoist has "Polka Dots and Moonbeams" to himself and Cole and Woods have fun on a brief free-form "Naugahyde Reality." It's a generally high-powered and enjoyable set. —Scott Yanow

Some Things Speak for Themselves / Feb. 1, 1981 / Muse ✦✦✦✦✦

There is less joking around than usual on this live quintet session by altoist Richie Cole. Recorded at a Japanese concert, Cole (along with guitarist Bruce Forman, pianist Smith Dobson, bassist Marshall Hawkins and drummer Scott Morris) performs versions of his "Tokyo Rose Sings the Hollywood Blues" along with three bop standards ("Lady Bird," "I Can't Get Started" and "Cherokee") and the lengthy "Irish Folk Song" (which is a disguised original based on "I Got Rhythm" that finds him switching to tenor). This out-of-print LP is an excellent example of Richie Cole's talents at playing colorful bebop. —Scott Yanow

Cool "C" / Feb. 7, 1981-Feb. 8, 1981 / Muse ✦✦✦✦

Recorded during his first visit to Japan, this out-of-print LP features altoist Richie Cole playing five bop standards, his own "Cool 'C'" and pianist Himiko Kikuchi's "Back to Bop." Cole is joined by eight brass players, a rhythm section and two percussionists, all of whom are fine Japanese musicians. The results are generally hard-swinging bop with enough humor and color to hold one's interest. The focus is on Cole throughout and he makes a rare appearance on tenor during "On Green Dolphin Street." —Scott Yanow

Alive! at the Village Vanguard / Jun. 24, 1981 / Muse ✦✦✦✦✦

Richie Cole is in top form on this Muse LP as he is on virtually all of his recordings for that label. Cole had a strong quintet at the time (with guitarist Bruce Forman, the "Wildman" Bobby Enriquez on piano, bassist Marshall Hawkins and drummer Scott Morris) and together they play some wild bebop on such songs as "Punishment Blues," "Samba De Orfeu" (an Enriquez feature), "Yardbird Suite" and "Alto Acres" (which ironically finds Cole switching to tenor). Cole also comes up with some fresh ideas on "Body and Soul," making this an album well worth searching for. —Scott Yanow

Return to Alto Acres / Feb. 16, 1982 / Palo Alto ✦✦✦✦

On his first LP for Palo Alto, Richie Cole got to meet up for the only time on record with altoist Art Pepper. Together with pianist Roger Kellaway, bassist Bob Magnusson and drummer Billy Higgins, Cole and Pepper play four basic originals, "Things We Did Last Summer" (Cole's feature) and "Broadway." What is particularly unusual about this date is that Cole not only plays alto but tenor and baritone while Pepper also gives listeners a taste of his clarinet. The historic bebop encounter has unfortunately been long out-of-print since Palo Alto is long defunct. —*Scott Yanow*

Alto Annie's Theme / Jul. 31, 1982 / Palo Alto ✦✦✦✦
Bop altoist Richie Cole features his regular quartet of the early '80s on this hard-to-find album. With pianist Dick Hindman, bassist Brian Bromberg and drummer Victor Jones, Cole (who also plays some tenor and baritone on the extroverted set) is heard at his best on a near-classic rendition of "Jeannine," "Boplicity," "Tangerine" and "Easy to Love." —*Scott Yanow*

Yakety Madness! / Aug. 25, 1982-Nov. 15, 1982 / Palo Alto ✦✦✦
This is a somewhat unlikely album that largely succeeds. Bebop altoist Richie Cole and cornball tenorman Boots Randolph meet up somewhere between jazz and country. Actually Randolph sounds quite comfortable on such songs as "Body and Soul," "Good Morning Heartache" and even "Barnyard Be-Bop" while Cole makes tunes such as "Yakety Sax" and "Wabash Cannonball" completely crazy. The two sessions allow Randolph and Cole to guest with each other's groups and, with the exception of the dumb seven-song, four-minute medley that ends the LP, this encounter is better than expected. —*Scott Yanow*

Bossa Nova Eyes / 1985 / Palo Alto ✦✦✦
Altoist Richie Cole's first album in three years is typically hard-swinging but adds little to his legacy. Best are "I Remember Sonny Stitt," "Makin' Whoopee" and "Serenata" although "Seems like Old Times" was not too necessary. Cole plays a bit of his rarely heard baritone, pianist Dick Hindman has some good solos and singer Janis Siegel guests on the title track but few surprises occur. —*Scott Yanow*

Pure Imagination / Nov. 1986 / Concord Jazz ✦✦✦✦✦
This 1986 set is altoist Richie Cole's best recording for Concord. Cole, whose exuberant brand of bebop is difficult to resist, turns such songs as "There'll Be Bluebirds over the White Cliffs of Dover," "Come Fly with Me" and "Flying Down to Rio" into heated jazz. With the help of the fine guitarist Vic Juris, bassist Ed Howard and drummer Victor Jones, Cole is in excellent form, contributing three originals and really ripping into "Blue Room." Recommended. —*Scott Yanow*

Popbop / Jun. 4, 1987-Jun. 6, 1987 / Milestone ✦✦✦✦
Altoist Richie Cole has long felt that he could turn any music into bebop. On this set he really stretches that concept, tackling such numbers as "La Bamba," "Spanish Harlem," the "Theme from Star Trek" and Rudy Wiedoeft's early-'20s feature "Saxophobia." Cole is joined by a basic quintet featuring guitarist Vic Juris and pianist Dick Hindman, plus, on some selections, "The Violins of Madness"; in addition, "La Bamba" utilizes a Latin group. This is enjoyable, often humorous and somewhat eccentric music. —*Scott Yanow*

Bossa Nova International / Jul. 16, 1987 / Milestone ✦✦✦✦
Richie Cole meets up with fellow altoist Hank Crawford on a spirited concert set. With guitarist Emily Remler, bassist Marshall Hawkins and drummer Victor Jones, Cole and Crawford romp on such numbers as "Confirmation," "Fantasy Blues," "Samba De Orpheus" and "Cherokee." This jam session date has its exciting moments and is easily recommended to bebop fans. —*Scott Yanow*

Signature / Jul. 1988 / Milestone ✦✦✦✦
There is a lot of variety on this Richie Cole set with such musicians as pianists Tee Carson, Ben Sidran and Dick Hindman, guitarist Vic Juris and steel drum wizard Andy Narell getting plenty of solo space. With the exception of a duet version of "America the Beautiful" with Hindman, the altoist/leader's repertoire is less off-the-wall than usual but he is in good form on such tunes as "Sunday in New York," Charles Mingus' "Peggy's Blue Skylight" and his own "Take the Cole Train." On two songs Cole overdubbed himself on six additional saxes, calling it the "Mega-Universal Saxophone Orchestra." —*Scott Yanow*

Profile / Apr. 5, 1993-Apr. 7, 1993 / Heads Up ✦✦✦
Profile was Cole's first recording in four years, and it found the altoist's sound and style virtually unchanged from the earlier days. Joined by a superior rhythm section that includes pianist Dick Hindman and guitarist Henry Johnson, Cole is in top form on diverse material ranging from his original "Presidential Sax" and the lyrical "Street of Dreams" to three Carroll Coates originals and the pop tune "Volare." It's a particularly uplifting bop session. —*Scott Yanow*

The Kush: Music of Dizzy Gillespie / Dec. 9, 1994 / Heads Up ✦✦✦✦
Altoist Richie Cole makes a full-fledged comeback on this fairly inspired release. He performs nine Dizzy Gillespie compositions (plus "You Go to My Head," which was actually co-written by Haven Gillespie) while joined by groups ranging from a two-guitar trio to a 13-piece band, all arranged in colorful fashion by Bob Belden. In addition to Cole, fellow altoist Paquito D'Rivera battles it out on "Kush" and plays some excellent clarinet on "Salt Peanuts" while trumpeter Jack Walrath has a few spots. Other highlights include "Be-Bop," "Birk's Works," "A Night in Tunisia" and "Manteca." —*Scott Yanow*

West Side Story / Mar. 28, 1996-Mar. 29, 1996 / Music Masters ✦✦✦✦
On this enjoyable CD, bebop altoist Richie Cole performs seven of the main themes from *West Side Story,* plus his own complex "West Side Blues." Cole teams up with his longtime guitarist Vic Juris, pianist Lou Forestieri, bassist Ed Howard, drummer Tommy Campbell and veteran percussionist Ray Mantilla to give the familiar melodies his "alto madness" treatment, being respectful of the themes while stretching out. Highlights include "America," "Maria" and "Tonight." —*Scott Yanow*

Bill Coleman (William Johnson Coleman)

b. Aug. 4, 1904, Paris, KY, d. Aug. 24, 1981, Toulouse, France
Trumpet / Dixieland, Swing
A mellow-toned swing trumpeter with a distinctive sound and a lyrical style, Bill Coleman was a consistent if never particularly famous musician. In 1927 he went to New York with Cecil and Lloyd Scott's band with whom he made his recording debut. He worked with Luis Russell (1929-32) and Charlie Johnson and then in 1933 travelled to France with Lucky Millinder. Coleman recorded with Fats Waller (1934) and played with Teddy Hill's Orchestra (1934-35) but then moved to France for the first time in 1935. While overseas he recorded frequently as a leader (really coming into his own) with Willie Lewis' Orchestra and on dates with Django Reinhardt. He ventured as far as Bombay and spent 1938-40 in Egypt with Herman Chittison. Returning to New York, Coleman played with Benny Carter, Teddy Wilson, Andy Kirk, Mary Lou Williams and John Kirby during 1940-45, and recorded with Lester Young and Coleman Hawkins (both in 1943). However he preferred life in Europe and, after period with groups led by Sy Oliver and Billy Kyle, in 1948 Coleman moved permanently back to France, staying active and recording fairly regularly up until his death in 1981. —*Scott Yanow*

● **Bill Coleman in Paris 1936-1938** / Jan. 31, 1936-Sep. 28, 1938 / Swing ✦✦✦✦✦
With the exception of two obscure titles from early 1936, this generous LP (which has an hour's worth of music) contains trumpeter Bill Coleman's first 16 selections as a leader plus two songs apiece in which he is featured with the bands of Alix Combelle and Eddie Brunner. Coleman, a top American swing trumpeter who spent most of the 1930s in Europe (he expatriated permanently to France in the late '40s), is well featured with some of the top European musicians of the era. Among his sidemen are American pianist Herman Chittison, guitarists Django Reinhardt ("Bill Coleman Blues" is a trumpet-guitar duet) and Oscar Aleman, violinist Stephane Grappelli and tenor saxophonist Big Boy Goudie. Bill Coleman is heard at the peak of his powers throughout this exciting swing set with the many highlights including "Joe Louis Stomp," "Coquette," "Indiana," "Swing Guitars," "In a Little Spanish Town" and two versions of "After You've Gone." Some of this valuable music has been reissued on CD. —*Scott Yanow*

Bill Coleman 1936-1938 / Jan. 24, 1936-Sep. 28, 1938 / Classics ✦✦✦✦

The Great Parisian Session / Jan. 21, 1960-Jan. 22, 1960 / Polydor ✦✦✦✦
The talented swing trumpeter Bill Coleman spent much of his career living in Europe which has resulted in him being underrated in jazz history books. He recorded fairly frequently as a leader in the 1950s for Phillips and Columbia. This Brunswick set (originally titled *From Boogie to Funk*) has been reissued as a French Polydor CD. Coleman used several American musicians who were touring Europe with Quincy Jones' Orchestra at the time: trombonist Quentin Jackson, tenor saxophonist Budd Johnson, pianist Patti Bown, bassist Buddy Catlett, drummer Joe Harris and (on two of the five numbers) guitarist Les Spann. The band performed five of Coleman's blues-oriented originals including the 16-minute "From Boogie to Funk," "Afromotive in Blue" and "Have Blues, Will Play 'Em." This is an excellent set, making one wish that the trumpeter's other recordings from the 1950s and '60s were also readily available.w—*Scott Yanow*

Bill Coleman Meets Guy Lafitte / Jul. 4, 1973 / Black Lion ✦✦✦✦
This CD reissues trumpeter Bill Coleman's complete set at the 1973 Montreux Jazz Festival, expanding the original LP from six to eight songs. Coleman matches well with the thick-toned tenor of Guy Lafitte and both seem to inspire each other. On swing standards, blues and basic originals, the two horns are assisted by pianist Marc Hemmeler, bassist Jack Sewing and drummer Daniel Humair. There are not many Bill Coleman CD's available domestically (he owed his near-anonymity to the fact that he spent so many decades living in Europe), making this one well worth picking up. Coleman excels in the small-group setting, performing such numbers as "Blue Lou," "Idaho" and "I Want a Little Girl" (singing the latter). Recommended. —*Scott Yanow*

Blowing for the Cats / Nov. 15, 1973-Nov. 16, 1973 / DRG ✦✦✦
Although this LP is subtitled "The Final Big Band Sessions," trumpeter Bill Coleman would still be recording for another seven years. The veteran swing trumpeter performs a dozen of his original ballads while backed by a big band that also contains a string section. Coleman plays well enough although the lack of

variety in mood and tempo keeps this album (which is out-of-print) from being essential. —*Scott Yanow*

Really I Do / May 15, 1980 / Black & Blue ✦✦✦
This was one of trumpeter Bill Coleman's final recordings (he passed away in Aug. 1981), but there is no hint of his decline on these joyful swing performances. Coleman is teamed up with tenor saxophonist Guy Lafitte (they had recorded together many times previously), pianist Red Richards, bassist Bill Pemberton and drummer Panama Francis for run-throughs of familiar standards such as a heated "Crazy Rhythm," "You've Changed" and "I've Got My Love to Keep Me Warm," the lesser-known Dickie Wells line "Hello Babe," and two of Coleman's basic originals. The result is an upbeat set of swinging music featuring Bill Coleman in surprisingly good form. —*Scott Yanow*

Cecilia Coleman

b. 1962, Long Beach, CA
Piano / Post-Bop
Leader of a stimulating quintet and a talented pianist/composer whose music is becoming more original with each year, Cecilia Coleman performs regularly in Los Angeles clubs. She began on piano when she was six. After graduating from college in 1986, she played in the L.A. area with Charlie Shoemake, Phil Upchurch and Shelley Moore among others and was a member of the Benn Clatworthy Quartet (with whom she recorded for Discovery) during 1987-91. She made her debut as a leader for the L.A.P. label and then, after forming her quintet (which also includes trumpeter Steve Huffsteter, tenor Andy Suzuki on reeds, bassist Dean Taba and drummer Kendall Kay), recorded two CDs for Resurgent that not only feature her piano playing but her inventive writing. —*Scott Yanow*

● **Young and Foolish** / Dec. 1993 / Resurgent ✦✦✦✦
This CD not only features Cecilia Coleman's increasingly distinctive piano improvisations and seven of her diverse and complex originals but it is the recording debut of her excellent quintet. The soft-toned trumpeter Steve Huffsteter and the harder-edged tenor saxophonist Andy Suzuki offer contrasting solo styles, while bassist Dean Taba and drummer Kendall Kay do not just accompany the lead voices but push them to come up with forceful statements. Although she is generous in allocating solo space, the main star throughout is Coleman. Her tricky yet melodic originals cover a variety of moods and force Huffsteter and Suzuki to play at their most creative level. Whether it be the somber "Somalia," the vintage Blue Note sound of "The Real Thing" or an uptempo version of Bud Powell's "Celia," virtually every track on this impressive release by the talented Cecilia Coleman is memorable. —*Scott Yanow*

Home / Jul. 25, 1995-Jul. 26, 1995 / Resurgent ✦✦✦✦✦

Earl Coleman

b. Aug. 12, 1925, Port Huron, MI, **d.** Jul. 14, 1995, New York, NY
Vocals / Standards
A fine ballad singer with a deep baritone voice influenced by Billy Eckstine, Earl Coleman made his place in history by recording "This Is Always" and "Dark Shadows" in 1947 while being accompanied by Charlie Parker. He had sung previously with Jay McShann (1943) and Earl Hines (1944). Despite the success of "This Is Always" (which was a minor hit), Coleman never really caught on and was fairly obscure throughout much of his career. He did record now and then with the likes of Fats Navarro (1948), Art Farmer, Sonny Rollins (both in 1956), and on his own dates including two sets for Xanadu (1977 and 1979) and one for Stash (1984). —*Scott Yanow*

● **Earl Coleman Returns** / Mar. 2, 1956-Jun. 8, 1956 / Original Jazz Classics ✦✦✦✦
Singer Earl Coleman, who had an early hit with "This Is Always" (cut with Charlie Parker in 1947), had a rather sporadic recording career. The music reissued on this CD (which adds four "bonus cuts" to the original Prestige LP) was, with the exception of a couple selections on Sonny Rollins and Elmo Hope albums, the singer's only recordings during 1949-66 and (other than an obscure Atlantic album) his only sessions from 1949-76. Coleman, who had a deep baritone voice influenced by Billy Eckstine, clearly deserved better. Although not an improviser, Coleman could swing as he shows on these performances with the assistance of such fine players as trumpeter Art Farmer, altoist Gigi Gryce and pianist Hank Jones; highlights include "It's You or No One," "Social Call" and a remake of "This Is Always." —*Scott Yanow*

A Song for You / Sep. 9, 1977 / Xanadu ✦✦✦✦
Earl Coleman's first recording in a decade and only second as a leader in 21 years finds the baritonist in prime form. He tackles a couple of newer ballads ("A Song for You" and "All in Love Is Fair"), revisits "Dark Shadows" (which he recorded with Charlie Parker in 1947) and sings some veteran standards. Coleman's rich voice is accompanied by pianist Hank Jones, bassist George Duvivier and drum-

mer Leroy Williams; four songs are uplifted by the playing of guest tenor Al Cohn. This LP, the better of Coleman's two Xanadu albums, unfortunately did not result in the commercial success that Earl Coleman deserved. —*Scott Yanow*

Stardust / Sep. 1984 / Stash ✦✦✦✦
Earl Coleman's final recording (although he would live another decade) features the baritonist still in his musical prime. As usual he mostly sticks to ballads during the obscure Stash set. Pianist Michael Abene contributed the arrangements for the quintet (which also includes bassist George Duvivier, drummer Walter Bolden, Jerry Dodgion on reeds and trumpeter Tom Harrell). Among the high points are "I Hear a Rhapsody," "Star Eyes" and "This Time the Dream's on Me." It seems strange that Earl Coleman's deep and appealing voice never resulted in him becoming a popular attraction like Billy Eckstine and Johnny Hartman. —*Scott Yanow*

George Coleman

b. Mar. 8, 1935, Memphis, TN
Tenor Saxophone / Hard Bop
George Coleman's highest visibility occurred when he was a member of the Miles Davis Quintet (1963-64), playing alongside Miles, Herbie Hancock, Ron Carter and Tony Williams. His decision to leave the group after several notable recordings cut short his potential fame (his eventual replacement was Wayne Shorter) but Coleman has created a great deal of rewarding music since. Part of the rich Memphis jazz scene of the early '50s, he started playing in blues bands in South (including with B.B. King in 1952 and 1955-56). He moved to Chicago in 1957 (where he played with the MJT+3) and to New York the following year. Coleman was with the Max Roach Quintet (1958-59), Slide Hampton's Octet (1959-61) and Wild Bill Davis (1962) before joining Davis. Following that association he was with Lionel Hampton, Elvin Jones and Charles McPherson. Since the mid-'70s George Coleman has mostly led his own groups and has recorded both as a leader (for Timeless, Theresa and Verve) and as a sideman quite frequently; one of his more notable appearances from earlier years was on Herbie Hancock's 1964 classic *Maiden Voyage*. —*Scott Yanow*

Meditation / Feb. 20, 1977 / Timeless ✦✦✦

Amsterdam After Dark / Nov. 2, 1977-Nov. 3, 1977 / Timeless ✦✦✦✦
Legendary tenor saxophonist blows up a storm with the Hilton Ruiz Trio. This has been reissued on CD. Best cut is "New Arrival." —*Michael G. Nastos*

Big George / Nov. 2, 1977-Nov. 3, 1977/ Charly ✦✦✦

Playing Changes / Apr. 1979 / Jazz House ✦✦✦✦

Manhattan Panorama / 1985 / Evidence ✦✦✦✦
Why George Coleman is not immediately mentioned when the discussion turns to great tenor sax veterans baffles me, because there are not many better mainstream/blues stylists. Other than a good-natured but ultimately empty vocal, Coleman was routinely brilliant on every number during this live Village Vanguard set originally issued on Theresa vinyl. Pianist Harold Mabern's bluesy, vibrant phrases and bassist Jami Nasser's supple licks and accompaniment are ably punctuated by Idris Muhammad's capable drumming. There is a no-nonsense (the opener aside), no-frills attitude exemplified by the quartet. —*Ron Wynn*

● **At Yoshi's** / Aug. 1987 / Evidence ✦✦✦✦✦
A CD reissue of a George Coleman Theresa LP, this set features the great tenor in prime form heading a quartet also including pianist Harold Mabern, bassist Ray Drummond and drummer Alvin Queen. The seven selections (two added for the CD) give Coleman an opportunity to stretch out, and he really digs into such tunes as "They Say It's Wonderful," "Good Morning Heartache," and a 14-minute version of "Up Jumped Spring." A definitive release from a major tenor saxophonist. —*Scott Yanow*

My Horns of Plenty / Mar. 4, 1991-Mar. 5, 1991 / Verve ✦✦✦✦
On this excellent set, George Coleman plays his usual tenor on four tunes, alto on "Old Folks," and soprano on "Conrad." With the assistance of pianist Harold Mabern, bassist Ray Drummond and drummer Billy Higgins, Coleman is heard at the top of his game, coming up with interesting variations on lengthy version of "Lush Life," "My Romance" and "Old Folks." Recommended for hard-bop and post-bop collectors. —*Scott Yanow*

Ornette Coleman

b. Mar. 9, 1930, Fort Worth, TX
Alto Saxophone, Composer, Violin, Trumpet / Free Jazz, Avant-Garde, Free Funk
One of the most important (and controversial) innovators of the jazz avant-garde, Ornette Coleman gained both loyal followers and lifelong detractors when he seemed to burst on the scene in 1959 fully formed. Although he and Don Cherry in his original quartet played opening and closing melodies together, their solos

dispensed altogether with chordal improvisation and harmony, instead playing quite freely off of the mood of the theme. Coleman's tone (which purposely wavered in pitch) rattled some listeners and his solos were emotional and followed their own logic. In time his approach would be quite influential and the quartet's early records still sound advanced over 35 years later.

Unfortunately Ornette Coleman's early development was not documented. Originally inspired by Charlie Parker, he started playing alto at 14 and tenor two years later. His early experiences were in R&B bands in Texas, including those of Red Connors and Pee Wee Crayton, but his attempts to play in an original style were consistently met with hostility both by audiences and fellow musicians. Coleman moved to Los Angeles in the early '50s where he worked as an elevator operator while studying music books. He met kindred spirits along the way in Don Cherry, Charlie Haden, Ed Blackwell, Bobby Bradford, Charles Moffett and Billy Higgins, but it was not until 1958 (after many unsuccessful attempts to sit in with top L.A. musicians) that Coleman had a nucleus of musicians who could play his music. He appeared as part of Paul Bley's Quintet for a short time at the Hillcrest Club (which is documented on live records) and recorded two very interesting albums for Contemporary. With the assistance of John Lewis, Coleman and Cherry attended the Lenox School of Jazz in 1959 and had an extended stay at the Five Spot in New York. This engagement alerted the jazz world towards the radical new music and each night the audience was filled with curious musicians who alternately labelled Coleman a genius or a fraud.

During 1959-61 Ornette Coleman recorded a series of classic and somewhat startling quartet albums for Atlantic (all of which have been reissued on a six-CD set by Rhino). With Don Cherry, Charlie Haden, Scott LaFaro or Jimmy Garrison on bass and Billy Higgins or Ed Blackwell on drums, Coleman created music that would greatly affect most of the other advanced improvisers of the 1960s including John Coltrane, Eric Dolphy and the free jazz players of the mid-60s. One set, a nearly 40-minute jam called *Free Jazz* (which other than a few brief themes was basically a pulse-driven group free improvisation) had Coleman, Cherry, Haden, LaFaro, Higgins, Blackwell, Dolphy and Freddie Hubbard forming a double quartet.

In 1962 Ornette Coleman, feeling that he was worth much more money than the clubs and his label were paying him, surprised the jazz world by retiring for a period. He took up trumpet and violin (playing the latter as if it were a drum!) and in 1965 he recorded a few brilliant sets on all his instruments with a particularly strong trio featuring bassist David Izenzon and drummer Charles Moffett. Later in the decade Coleman had a quartet with the very complementary tenor Dewey Redman, Haden and either Blackwell or his young son Denardo Coleman on drums. In addition Coleman wrote some atonal and wholly-composed classical works for chamber groups and had a few reunions with Don Cherry.

In the early '70s Ornette Coleman entered the second half of his career. He formed a "double quartet" comprising two guitars, two electric bassists, two drummers and his own alto. The group, called "Prime Time," featured dense, noisy and often-witty ensembles in which all of the musicians are supposed to have an equal role but the leader's alto always ended up standing out. He now calls his music "Harmolodics" (symbolizing the equal importance of harmony, melody and rhythm) although "free funk" (combining together loose funk rhythms and free improvising) probably fits better; among his sidemen in Prime Time have been drummer Ronald Shannon Jackson and bassist Jamaaladeen Tacuma in addition to his son Denardo.

Prime Time was a major (if somewhat unacknowledged) influence on the M-Base music of Steve Coleman and Greg Osby. Pat Metheny (a lifelong Ornette admirer) collaborated with Coleman on the intense *Song X*, Jerry Garcia played third guitar on one recording and Ornette had irregular reunions with his original quartet members in the 1980s.

Ornette Coleman, who currently records for Verve, has remained true to his highly original vision throughout his career and, although not technically a virtuoso and still considered controversial, is an obvious giant of jazz. —*Scott Yanow*

The Music of Ornette Coleman: Something Else!!! / Feb. 10, 1958-Mar. 24, 1958 / Original Jazz Classics ✦✦✦✦

This important CD reissue brings back altoist Ornette Coleman's first recording. His radical free jazz style was already nearly fully developed, even though his quartet had not been formed yet. Coleman is joined by two future quartet members (trumpeter Don Cherry and drummer Billy Higgins), plus pianist Walter Norris (who is out of place) and bassist Don Payne (much more closely tied to the chord structure than Charlie Haden would be). Highlights of this significant recording include two of Coleman's best compositions, "The Blessing" and "When Will the Blues Leave?" —*Scott Yanow*

Coleman Classics, Vol. 1 / Oct. 1958 / Improvising Artists ✦✦✦✦✦

These fascinating live performances from the Hillcrest Club in Los Angeles feature the original Ornette Coleman Quartet (with Coleman on alto, trumpeter Don

Cherry, bassist Charlie Haden and drummer Billy Higgins) all as sidemen with pianist Paul Bley's Quintet. Recorded between Coleman's first and second Contemporary albums, these numbers (extended versions of "When Will the Blues Leave" and "Ramblin" along with briefer renditions of "Crossroads" and "How Deep Is the Ocean") show that Coleman already had his very original style pretty much together at this early stage. Paul Bley was wise enough to mostly stay out of the way and he clearly benefited from this encounter with some of the pioneers of free jazz. —*Scott Yanow*

Tomorrow Is the Question! / Jan. 16, 1959-Mar. 10, 1959 / Original Jazz Classics ✦✦✦

Ornette Coleman's second of two studio albums for Contemporary, which has been reissued on CD in the OJC series, finds him dropping the piano and interacting closely with trumpeter Don Cherry. The rhythm section (Percy Heath or Red Mitchell on bass and drummer Shelly Manne) is still not loose enough for the music (nine Coleman originals, of which "Turnaround" and "Tears Inside" are the best known), but the freedom heard in the playing of the two horns is quite notable, particularly for 1959. A very interesting session. —*Scott Yanow*

The Shape of Jazz to Come / May 22, 1959 / Atlantic ✦✦✦✦✦

Altoist Ornette Coleman's first Atlantic recording was his first with his somewhat revolutionary quartet, which included cornetist Don Cherry, bassist Charlie Haden and drummer Billy Higgins. Because the solos did not follow any set chord pattern, this music became known as "free jazz." This CD reissue, which has also been included in Rhino's six-CD Ornette Coleman box set, is highlighted by the original version of Coleman's most famous composition, "Lonely Woman," plus "Peace" and "Congeniality." This music would greatly influence jazz of the mid-'60s and still sounds quite advanced. —*Scott Yanow*

Twins / May 22, 1959 / Atlantic ✦✦✦✦

The five performances on this LP were not released until 1981. Of greatest interest is a shorter version of the nearly 40-minute "Free Jazz," which at 17 minutes was simply titled "First Take." In addition, the innovative altoist is heard on four quartet numbers with cornetist Don Cherry, either Charlie Haden or Scott LaFaro on bass and Ed Blackwell or Billy Higgins on drums; "First Take" has all of these musicians plus bass clarinetist Eric Dolphy and trumpeter Freddie Hubbard. All of this valuable music, which also includes "Little Symphony" and "Monk and the Nun," has been reissued on Rhino's *Complete Ornette on Atlantic* CD box set. —*Scott Yanow*

The Art of the Improvisers / May 22, 1959-Mar. 27, 1961 / Atlantic ✦✦✦✦

The seven selections on this valuable LP are performances by various versions of the Ornette Coleman Quartet that were not released until this 1988 album came out; all of the contents were reissued in Rhino's large Coleman CD box set. The very original altoist is in excellent form and joined by cornetist Don Cherry, either Charlie Haden, Scott LaFaro or Jimmy Garrison on bass and Billy Higgins or Ed Blackwell on drums. The lyrical ballad "Just for You" is one of the highlights, and some of the song titles ("The Legend of Bebop" and "The Fifth of Beethoven") allude both to Coleman's often overlooked wit and his roots. The music is quite advanced, unpredictable and stimulating. —*Scott Yanow*

☆ **Beauty Is a Rare Thing: The Complete Atlantic Recordings** / May 22, 1959-Mar. 27, 1961 / Rhino/Atlantic ✦✦✦✦✦

This six-CD box set (which includes a very informative and colorful 70-page booklet) has all of altoist Ornette Coleman's recordings for the Atlantic label. These performances, considered quite revolutionary at the time since Coleman did not use any chord changes, still sound futuristic today. Not only is all the music included from the albums *The Shape of Jazz to Come*, *This Is Our Music*, *Free Jazz*, *Ornette* and *Ornette on Tenor* along with the two later sets of unissued material (*The Art of the Improvisers* and *Twins*) but a record only previously out in Japan (*To Whom Who Keeps a Record*), two songs that feature Coleman on a Gunther Schuller album and six cuts never out before. Although more general listeners may be content with one or two of Ornette's albums, serious collectors will want to get this very valuable set while it is still around for it contains some of the most important jazz recordings of the early '60s. —*Scott Yanow*

● **Change of the Century** / Oct. 8, 1959-Oct. 9, 1959 / Atlantic ✦✦✦✦✦

Altoist Ornette Coleman originally recorded six albums for Atlantic (not counting later releases of temporarily discarded tracks), and this particular one was his second. With Don Cherry (on pocket trumpet), bassist Charlie Haden and drummer Billy Higgins, Coleman introduces such interesting and unpredictable "free" pieces as the rhythmic "Una Muy Bonita," "Ramblin'" and "Bird Food." This important (and still advanced) music deserves to be heard either in this set or as part of the comprehensive Rhino six-CD box of Coleman's Atlantic recordings. —*Scott Yanow*

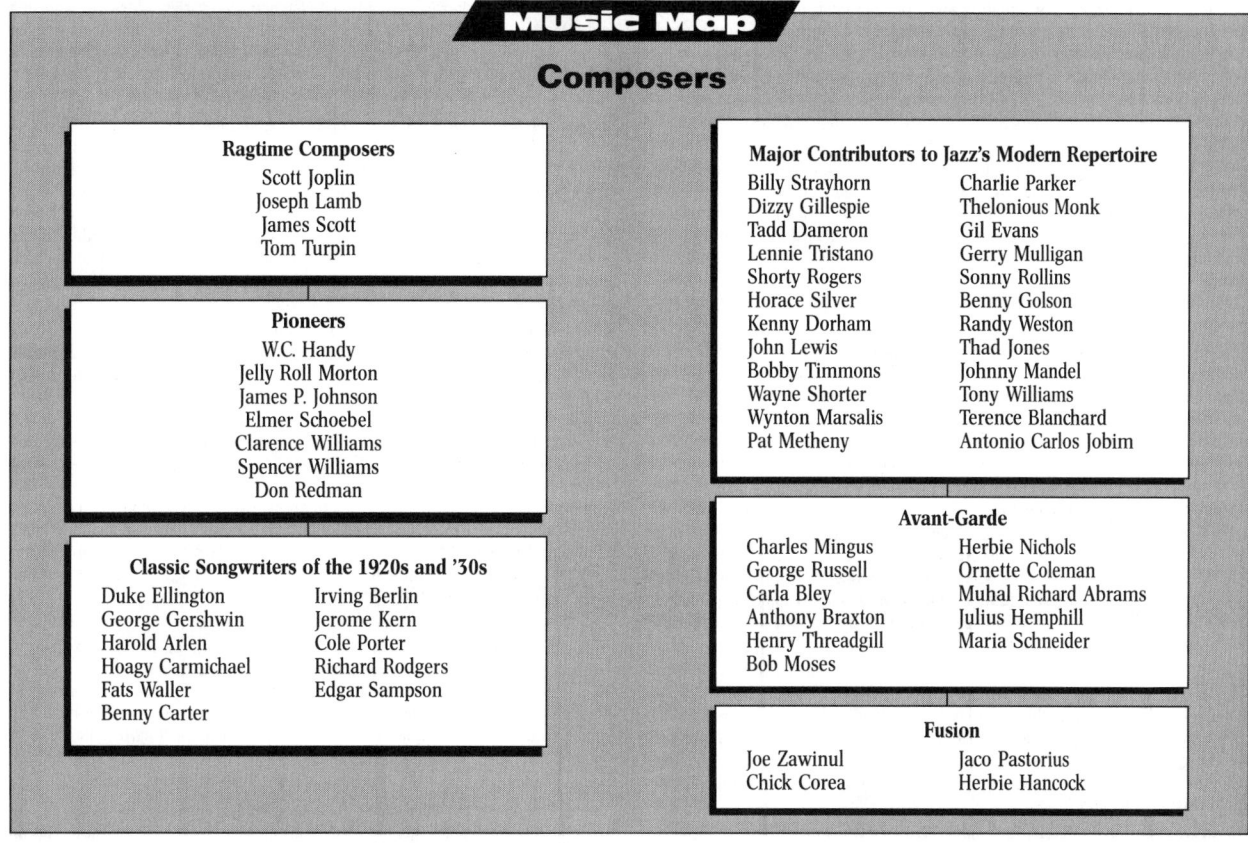

Music Map

Composers

Ragtime Composers
Scott Joplin
Joseph Lamb
James Scott
Tom Turpin

Pioneers
W.C. Handy
Jelly Roll Morton
James P. Johnson
Elmer Schoebel
Clarence Williams
Spencer Williams
Don Redman

Classic Songwriters of the 1920s and '30s
Duke Ellington	Irving Berlin
George Gershwin	Jerome Kern
Harold Arlen	Cole Porter
Hoagy Carmichael	Richard Rodgers
Fats Waller	Edgar Sampson
Benny Carter	

Major Contributors to Jazz's Modern Repertoire
Billy Strayhorn	Charlie Parker
Dizzy Gillespie	Thelonious Monk
Tadd Dameron	Gil Evans
Lennie Tristano	Gerry Mulligan
Shorty Rogers	Sonny Rollins
Horace Silver	Benny Golson
Kenny Dorham	Randy Weston
John Lewis	Thad Jones
Bobby Timmons	Johnny Mandel
Wayne Shorter	Tony Williams
Wynton Marsalis	Terence Blanchard
Pat Metheny	Antonio Carlos Jobim

Avant-Garde
Charles Mingus	Herbie Nichols
George Russell	Ornette Coleman
Carla Bley	Muhal Richard Abrams
Anthony Braxton	Julius Hemphill
Henry Threadgill	Maria Schneider
Bob Moses	

Fusion
Joe Zawinul	Jaco Pastorius
Chick Corea	Herbie Hancock

This Is Our Music / Jul. 19, 1960-Aug. 2, 1960 / Atlantic ✦✦✦✦
The third of altoist Ornette Coleman's six Atlantic albums (not counting later compilations of unreleased material) is most notable for his lyrical and childlike interpretation of the only non-original recorded during this era, "Embraceable You," and for the memorable "Blues Connotation." The other five numbers are lesser known, but "Beauty Is a Rare Thing" and "Humpty Dumpty" also stick in one's mind. Ornette, trumpeter Don Cherry, bassist Charlie Haden and drummer Ed Blackwell, the latter making his recording debut with the group, formed a classic unit in which each musician was somehow able to quickly figure out in what direction the others were heading. Their brand of "free jazz" or "avant-garde jazz" caused quite a stir during this era and indirectly influenced many groups later in the 1960s. —*Scott Yanow*

Free Jazz (A Collective Improvisation) / Dec. 21, 1960 / Atlantic ✦✦✦✦✦
This was one of the most controversial jazz recordings of the period, although when compared to John Coltrane's *Ascension* of five years later, *Free Jazz* sounds quite melodic and even slightly conservative. Altoist Ornette Coleman gathered together a "double quartet" comprising bass clarinetist Eric Dolphy, Don Cherry and Freddie Hubbard on trumpets, Scott LaFaro and Charlie Haden on basses and both Billy Higgins and Ed Blackwell on drums. Although there is an opening melody, a steady pulse and loose but organized parts between the solos, otherwise this music (which is continuous for around thirty-six-and-a-half-minutes) is completely free. While one player improvises, the other musicians are free to "comment" behind the solo. The ten-minute stretch when Ornette Coleman is the lead voice and the other three horns come up with free "riffs" is the high point of this very interesting recording (which has also been reissued in Rhino's six-CD Coleman box set). —*Scott Yanow*

Jazzlore: Ornette Coleman, Vol. 29 / Jan. 31, 1961 / Atlantic ✦✦✦✦
This Atlantic session by the Ornette Coleman Quartet is most notable for featuring the ill-fated Scott LaFaro on bass. With the leader's alto, trumpeter Don Cherry and drummer Ed Blackwell all contributing their unpredictable ideas and surprisingly close musical communication, the group is in near-peak form on Coleman's four originals, which are given abbreviated names (such as "W.R.U. and "R.P.D.D."). It would take "free jazz" another four years before it became a dominant force, but

it would be recordings such as this one that would influence jazz of the mid-'60s. —*Scott Yanow*

Ornette on Tenor / Mar. 22, 1961+Mar. 27, 1961 / Atlantic ✦✦✦✦
Altoist Ornette Coleman's final album in a series of classic and highly influential Atlantic recordings (which have been reissued in Rhino's *Complete Ornette* six-CD box set) is most unusual because Coleman sticks exclusively to tenor. His gutbucket sound makes his music even more passionate and inaccessible than usual, although listeners who study this record closely will be able to grasp its logic. The "free jazz" improvising by Coleman, trumpeter Don Cherry, bassist Jimmy Garrison (shortly before he joined the John Coltrane Quartet) and drummer Ed Blackwell is quite original and impressive; the often-startling "Cross Breeding" is a high point. —*Scott Yanow*

Town Hall Concert 1962 / Dec. 21, 1962 / ESP ✦✦✦
Ornette Coleman's decision to temporarily retire from music (this ESP disc was his only recording from a four-year period) was unfortunate. His alto playing was getting stronger and, on evidence of this CD, he had plenty of original ideas that should have been documented. For this Town Hall concert, Coleman debuts with his new trio (a unit that would return in 1965) featuring the remarkable bassist David Izenson and drummer Charles Moffett. Together they perform "Doughnut," "Sadness" and an extensive twenty-three-and-a-half-minute version of "The Ark." In addition a string quartet performs Colemans' "Dedication to Poets and Writers." Although Ornette's string writing (which leaves no room for improvising) is pretty well outside of jazz, his playing on the other tracks holds one's interest throughout. —*Scott Yanow*

The Great London Concert / Aug. 29, 1965 / Freedom ✦✦✦✦
Ornette Coleman emerged from three years of retirement in 1965 to bring back the trio he had utilized briefly in 1962, a group also featuring the very impressive bassist David Izenson and drummer Charles Moffett. Coleman's alto playing had become a lot stronger by this time and although his improvising on violin (which he played like a drum) and trumpet were at a much lower level, they were utilized fairly sparingly. This double-LP has the side-long "Forms and Sounds for Wind Quintet," a wholly written out atonal work for flute, oboe, clarinet, bassoon and French horn that is rather boring. However the trio's perforances of the other

seven selections are quite stimulating and Coleman (who only plays violin and trumpet on "Falling Stars") is consistently brilliant and explorative. Worth searching for by listeners with open ears. —*Scott Yanow*

At the "Golden Circle" in Stockholm, Vol. 1 / Dec. 3, 1965-Dec. 4, 1965 / Blue Note ✦✦✦✦✦

Ornette Coleman was at the peak of his powers by 1965. His alto playing had become quite a bit stronger than in his early days, and Coleman's trio with bassist David Izenson and drummer Charles Moffett was as exciting as his earlier quartet. On this CD reissue of a Blue Note LP, he stretches out on four of his originals ("Faces and Places," "European Echoes," "Dee Dee" and "Dawn") and plays consistently innovative and surprising solos that probably confused the majority of his audience while delighting others. This set is recommended, as is the second volume. —*Scott Yanow*

At the "Golden Circle" in Stockholm, Vol. 2 / Dec. 3, 1965-Dec. 4, 1965 / Blue Note ✦✦✦✦✦

The second of two volumes (reissued on CD) documenting a series of concerts in Stockholm, Sweden, by the 1965 Ornette Coleman Trio is almost the equal of the first. Coleman plays his primitive violin and trumpet on "Snowflakes and Sunshine" but sticks to alto (at its prime during this period) during his other three originals ("Morning Song," "The Riddle" and "Antiques"). The interplay between brilliant bassist David Izenson and drummer Charles Moffett is also quite impressive on this recommended set of free jazz. —*Scott Yanow*

Who's Crazy / 1966 / Affinity ✦✦✦✦

This two-LP set contains the soundtrack Ornette Coleman and his trio contributed for the obscure Belgian film of the same name. Coleman (switching between alto, trumpet and violin), bassist Dave Izenson and drummer Charles Moffett did not merely provide filler music but full-blown improvisations that stand very much on their own. Fans of Coleman's very explorative music are advised to search for this valuable two-fer. —*Scott Yanow*

Empty Foxhole / Sep. 9, 1966 / Blue Note ✦✦✦

The music on this LP is better than expected. Ornette Coleman uses his son Denardo (who was ten at the time) on drums along with bassist Charlie Haden and plays either trumpet or violin (instead of his customary alto) on half of the six selections. Although the results are not essential, there are plenty of exciting moments to be heard in this adventurous music and Denardo surprisingly mostly holds his own. —*Scott Yanow*

Forms and Sounds / Mar. 17, 1967+Mar. 31, 1967 / Bluebird ✦✦

Legendary as the performer/composer who freed jazz from the harmony and songforms of Tin Pan Alley ballads, these pieces show more of Coleman's path since his densely chromatic orchestral piece "Skies of America" (some movements are entitled "Holiday for Heroes," "Place in Space," "Foreigner in a Free Land," "Sunday in America"). This CD includes "Forms and Sounds" played by The Philadelphia Woodwind Quartet, and "Space Flight" performed by the Chamber Symphony of Philadelphia String Quartet. —*Blue Gene Tyranny*

Live in Milano, 1968 / Feb. 1968 / Jazz Up ✦✦✦

Love Call / Apr. 29, 1968+May 7, 1968 / Blue Note ✦✦✦✦✦

Ornette Coleman's 1968 Quartet featured the explorative tenor of Dewey Redman (who blended in very well with Coleman's alto), bassist Jimmy Garrison and drummer Elvin Jones. For this CD reissue, which was recorded at the same sessions that resulted in *New York Is Now*, the original four songs are augmented by two "new" alternate takes and "Just for You," which was previously available only in Japan. The interplay between Coleman and Redman on these free jazz jams and the similarity of their approaches, even though they had different sounds, make this unit a particularly strong group. This CD is about as accessible as Ornette Coleman ever became. —*Scott Yanow*

New York Is Now / Apr. 29, 1968+May 7, 1968 / Blue Note ✦✦✦✦✦

Altoist Ornette Coleman had a particularly strong group at the time of his 1968 Blue Note recordings, which resulted in the music heard on this CD and its companion, *Love Call*. Dewey Redman was the equivalent of Coleman on tenor, while bassist Jimmy Garrison and drummer Elvin Jones were alumni of John Coltrane's Quartet. For the CD reissue, a "new" alternate take of "Broad Way Blues" was added to the original program and, although none of the melodies caught on, the complementary playing by Coleman and Redman in particular is quite impressive, making this free jazz set highly recommended. —*Scott Yanow*

Crisis / Mar. 22, 1969 / Impulse! ✦✦

Ornette at 12 / Jun. 16, 1969 / Impulse! ✦✦✦

Friends and Neighbors / Feb. 14, 1970 / Flying Dutchman ✦✦✦

This out-of-print LP contains one of Ornette Coleman's lesser-known sessions. In addition to his own alto (and occasional trumpet and violin), Coleman is joined by Dewey Redman on tenor, bassist Charlie Haden, drummer Ed Blackwell, and (on

one of the two versions of "Friends and Neighbors") a variety of friends who sing along as best they can. Actually, the most notable tracks are the two extended pieces "Long Time No See" and "Tomorrow." The music is typically adventurous, melodic in its own way, yet still fairly futuristic, even if (compared with his other releases) the set as a whole is not all that essential. —*Scott Yanow*

Science Fiction / Sep. 9, 1971-Sep. 13, 1971 / Columbia ✦✦✦

This LP has quite a bit of variety and finds altoist Ornette Coleman joined by most of his alumni. Three pieces feature a reunion of his original quartet with trumpeter Don Cherry, bassist Charlie Haden and drummer Billy Higgins; three others match Coleman with trumpeter Bobby Bradford, Dewey Redman on tenor, Haden and drummer Ed Blackwell; and the remaining three pieces utilize either Indian vocalist Asha Puthli or poet David Henderson. The generally dissonant and still radical music will take several listens to absorb, but it is worth the effort. —*Scott Yanow*

Broken Shadows / Sep. 1971-Sep. 1972 / Columbia ✦✦✦

This LP contains eight selections taken from Ornette Coleman's three-year period with Columbia that were previously unreleased. Cut prior to Coleman's formation of Prime Time, these performances serve as an unintentional retrospective of his career up to that point. Not that any of the original compositions (all by Coleman) had ever been recorded before but such alumni as trumpeters Don Cherry and Bobby Bradford, tenor saxophonist Dewey Redman, bassist Charlie Haden, and drummers Ed Blackwell and Billy Higgins appear on most of the selections in one combination or another (and all of them are on two septet selections). In addition, a pair of numbers ("Good Girl Blues" and "Is It Forever") have Coleman, Redman, Haden and Blackwell joined by guitarist Jim Hall, pianist Cedar Walton, a singer and a woodwind section; these look back a bit at Ornette's guest appearances on a John Lewis/Gunther Schuller album. —*Scott Yanow*

The Belgrade Concert / Nov. 2, 1971 / Jazz Door ✦✦✦

This valuable live import CD features Ornette Coleman (on alto with a touch of trumpet and violin) and his 1971 Quartet (which also includes tenor saxophonist Dewey Redman, bassist Charlie Haden and drummer Ed Blackwell) performing Haden's "Song for Che" and four obscure Coleman compositions. The recording quality is decent and Redman proves to be a perfect musical partner for Ornette. Superior and often exciting freebop music. —*Scott Yanow*

Skies of America / May 1972 / Columbia ✦✦

At the time it was unveiled, *Skies of America* was a watershed for Ornette Coleman, for not only was it his first important orchestral work, it was here that he introduced the word harmolodics as a concept. Alas, the so-far sole recording of the piece is a travesty that does not represent Coleman's intentions. At the recording sessions in London, he was prohibited from using his quartet by arcane British union rules, the piece was heavily cut by over a third in order to fit a single LP, the London Symphony Orchestra (led by David Measham) is clearly lost at sea, and the results are poorly recorded. From what one can make out here, Coleman's writing for a symphony orchestra is uncompromisingly dissonant, pitched deliberately in the high register, often in unrelieved homophonic unison. Occasionally, a rhythm section breaks through the acid texture and Coleman's harshly pitched alto flies in the face of angry strings and thundering tympani. Some familiar strands of material turn up in later Coleman pieces, such as a repeated riff that later became "Theme from a Symphony." In light of a revelatory live performance by Coleman and the New York Philharmonic that opened the 1997 Lincoln Center Festival, one cannot gain any idea of the work's structure from this LP, although repeated hearings soften the initial shock and reveal the uneasy serenity of the Charles Ives-like conclusion. As a piece of music, *Skies of America* is a problem child and probably always will be, but this fascinating clash between American and European elements does make sense when heard in its entirety, and this LP (as yet unissued on CD) does the piece a disservice. —*Richard S. Ginell*

Dancing in Your Head / Jan. 1973+Dec. 1976 / A&M ✦✦

This CD reissue of an A&M album finds altoist Ornette Coleman interacting with musicians from Joujouka, Morocco on the four-and-a-half-minute "Midnight Sunrise" in 1973 and introducing his innovative group Prime Time in 1976 on the nearly 27-minute "Theme from a Symphony." While the playing time would be brief for an LP (and doesn't even fill up half of the CD's capacity), this disc's main fault is that the melody for "Theme from a Symphony" is very repetitive and ultimately annoying. Coleman stretches himself and his group (with Bern Nix and Charlie Ellerbee on guitars, bassist Rudy MacDaniel and drummer Roland Shannon Jackson) shows potential, but much of the music is simply unlistenable. There are many more significant and enjoyable Ornette Coleman sets currently available. —*Scott Yanow*

Body Meta / Dec. 19, 1976 / Artists House ✦✦✦✦

The short-lived but classy Artists House label debuted with this early Prime Time album by Ornette Coleman. At that point Coleman was utilizing guitarists Bern

Nix and Charlie Ellerbee, bassist Jamaaladeen Tacuma and drummer Roland Shannon Jackson. The music (five Coleman originals) features dense ensembles with free funk rhythms. Although the musicians were supposed to be given an equal status, Ornette Coleman's alto always stands out above the complex and overlapping rhythms. Fortunately this formerly rare LP was reissued in 1996 by Verve. —*Scott Yanow*

Soapsuds, Soapsuds / Jan. 30, 1977 / Verve ◆◆◆◆
This unusual album found Coleman taking time off from his electric free funk group, Prime Time, to record acoustic duets with his longtime associate, bassist Charlie Haden. Coleman switches to tenor and trumpet for the challenging music, which includes three of his originals, Haden's "Human Being" and oddly enough, the theme from the TV show *Mary Hartman, Mary Hartman*. Haden, who had proved to be the perfect bassist for the original Ornette Coleman Quartet (who else could have filled his shoes in 1959?), is the equal of Coleman on this 1996 reissue CD, inspiring the saxophonist to play near his peak. —*Scott Yanow*

Of Human Feelings / Apr. 25, 1979 / Antilles ◆◆◆◆
When one thinks of Ornette Coleman's innovative Prime Time band, it is of crowded ensembles played by the altoist/leader, two guitars, two electric bassists and two drummers. Actually, Jamaaladeen Tacuma, who plays enough for two musicians, is the only bassist on this date, but guitarists Charlie Ellerbee and Bern Nix, along with drummers Denardo Coleman and Calvin Weston, keep the ensembles quite exciting. None of the eight Coleman originals (which includes a tune titled "What Is the Name of That Song?") would catch on, but in this context they serve as a fine platform for Coleman's distinctive horn and often witty and free (but oddly melodic) style. Hopefully, Antilles will eventually reissue this set on CD. —*Scott Yanow*

Opening the Caravan of Dreams / 1985 / Caravan of Dreams ◆◆◆◆
Ornette Coleman's innovative Prime Time band is heard at the peak of its powers on this LP from the small Caravan of Dream label. The altoist/leader is the main voice throughout the otherwise very democratic ensembles, which feature guitarists Bern Nix and Charles Ellerbee, bassists Jamaaladeen Tacuma and Albert Mac-Dowell, and drummers Denardo Coleman and Sabir Kamal. The six originals, which include such titles as "To Know What to Know," "Harmolodic Bebop" and "Sex Spy," feature dense ensembles, equal doses of dissonance and wit, and more than their share of high energy. This was the leading "free funk" band of the 1980s, and this LP, which is worth a search by open-eared listeners, gives one a definitive look into the group's unusual music. —*Scott Yanow*

Prime Design Time Design / 1985 / Caravan of Dreams ◆◆

In All Languages / Feb. 1987 / Caravan of Dreams ◆◆◆◆
This is an unusual and very stimulating double CD that was originally put out on LP by the tiny Caravan of Dreams label. On the first CD, Ornette Coleman, on alto and tenor, has a reunion with his original quartet, which comprises trumpeter Don Cherry, bassist Charlie Haden and drummer Billy Higgins. The second CD features Coleman's then-current edition of his "double quartet" Prime Time with guitarists Charlie Ellerbe and Bern Nix, electric bassists Jamaaladeen Tacuma and Al MacDowell, and drummers Denardo Coleman and Calvin Weston. Five of the ten songs the quartet plays are also heard in versions by Prime Time, and the latter electric group almost makes the acoustic unit sound conservative in comparison. While the quartet displays subtle use of space and interplay between the musicians, Prime Time comes across as overcrowded and loud, but no less stimulating. Highly recommended to fans of Ornette Coleman. —*Scott Yanow*

Virgin Beauty / 1988 / Portrait ◆◆◆
This CD is often quite exciting, if a bit messy. Ornette Coleman (on alto, trumpet and violin) is heard with his "double quartet" Prime Time, which at the time comprised guitarists Bern Nix and Charlie Ellerbee, electric bassists Al MacDowell and Chris Walker, and drummers Denardo Coleman (who also plays some keyboards) and Calvin Weston. As if the ensembles are not dense and overcrowded enough, Jerry Garcia sits in on third guitar on three of the 11 Coleman originals. The music is frequently exciting, but will take several listens to absorb. Worth investigating. —*Scott Yanow*

Tone Dialing / Oct. 1995 / Harmolodic/Verve ◆◆◆◆
Ornette Coleman's first album in several years and first recording for a major label in quite some time features his 1995 version of Prime Time with two guitars, two bassists, son Denardo Coleman on drums and Badal Roy on tables and percussion. In addition the band includes Dave Bryant, Coleman's first keyboardist in decades (although his part is actually fairly minor). The ensembles are funky and quite dense, Coleman really wails on alto (also playing a bit of violin and trumpet) and, despite the inclusion of one obnoxious rap, this free funk set is well worth picking up by open-minded listeners. —*Scott Yanow*

Hidden Man / 1996 / Harmolodic/Verve ◆◆◆◆
For this project, altoist Ornette Coleman made one of his very few recordings with a pianist. On a vacation from his electrified Prime Time group, the innovative saxophonist (who also plays a bit of trumpet and his percussive violin) teams up with a purely acoustic trio (pianist Geri Allen, bassist Charnett Moffett and drummer Denardo Coleman) to perform 13 of his originals, plus the traditional "What a Friend We Have in Jesus." Most unusual is that another CD released at the same time (*Three Women*) has different versions of the exact same Coleman originals (plus one other song). Ornette Coleman shows throughout that he had not mellowed with age, and his concise yet adventurous improvisations (which are full of pure melody) are quite intriguing. —*Scott Yanow*

Three Women / 1996 / Harmolodic/Verve ◆◆◆◆
In 1996, altoist Ornette Coleman simultaneously released a pair of 14-song CDs; 13 of his pieces are heard in different versions on both releases. Joined by a particularly stimulating rhythm section (pianist Geri Allen, bassist Charnett Moffett and drummer Denardo Coleman), Coleman (who also contributes some trumpet and violin) is in superior form throughout the performances. On "Don't You Know by Now" (the one tune that is only heard on this CD), Lauren Kinhan and Chris Walker take passionate vocals. Otherwise, this is an excellent showcase for Ornette's searching and emotional (yet melodic) improvisations, one of the very few occasions since 1958 when he can be heard using a conventional three-piece rhythm section. —*Scott Yanow*

Colors: Live from Leipzig / Aug. 31, 1996 / Harmolodic/Verve ◆◆◆◆
Ornette Coleman is certainly full of surprises in his 60s, recording a duo album with—believe it or not—a pianist. For this project, he chose the German pianist Joachim Kühn, who gratefully claims that it was Ornette's example that originally led him down the road to free jazz, and they recorded eight Coleman compositions live in the opera house of Kühn's hometown, Leipzig. Yet their collaboration is not really a radical departure from Ornette's sound worlds in his acoustic groups or in the electric Prime Time. The two seem to exist on parallel planes, not interacting or reacting rhythmically or harmonically, but carving out their occasionally entwined melodic lines separately. Nor does Ornette change his own alto sax manner; at times, he performs in the same rhetorical fashion as he does with Prime Time, while venturing on the outside far more often and scraping away on the violin or burbling on his trumpet when the odd impulse strikes. The music ranges from the relatively funky "Faxing"—no doubt a spinoff from *Tone Dialing*—to the atonal complexity of "Three Ways to One," and the technically formidable Kühn gets an ovation for his extremely intricate solo passage in the latter. Here is an example of the artist having it both ways, reintroducing an instrument that he became famous for banishing, yet without compromising the artistic conception that led to its banishment in the first place. Thus, *Colors* is a fascinating addition to the Ornette Coleman catalogue. —*Richard S. Ginell*

Steve Coleman

b. Sep. 20, 1956, Chicago, IL
Alto Saxophone / Free Funk, Post-Bop
The leader of what he termed "M-Base" (short for macro-basic array of structured extemporization), Steve Coleman has a strikingly original alto style (very different from bebop) and his groups through the years have utilized funk rhythms and some nonjazz elements in an unpredictable and creative fashion. Coleman started on alto when he was 15 and played R&B in his early days. After moving to New York in 1978, Coleman played with the Thad Jones-Mel Lewis Orchestra, Cecil Taylor and Sam Rivers. After the mid-'80s he has usually been heard either with his group Five Elements or with such M-Base players as Greg Osby, Gary Thomas, Graham Haynes, Robin Eubanks, Geri Allen and Cassandra Wilson. Coleman has recorded sessions as a leader for JMT and Novus and been a sideman with David Murray, Dave Holland and Branford Marsalis. He is one of the most potentially significant saxophonists of the 1990s. —*Scott Yanow*

Motherland Pulse / Mar. 1985 / JMT ◆◆◆
Steve Coleman's debut recording as a leader was the beginning of the documentation of his M-Base music on record. Coleman teams up with some of his top associates of the era, including pianist Geri Allen, bassist Lonnie Plaxico, and drummer Marvin "Smitty" Smith; plus, there are guest appearances by Cassandra Wilson (who sings on "No Good Time Fairies") and trumpeter Graham Haynes. The funky yet creative music has less crowded ensembles than Coleman's upcoming records would, and serves as a fine showcase for the talented and strikingly original altoist who contributed six of the eight numbers. —*Scott Yanow*

On the Edge of Tomorrow / Jan. 1986+Feb. 1986 / JMT ◆◆◆◆
Steve Coleman's second recording as a leader introduces his M-Base music in its prime. Essentially creative and avant-garde funk, the performances feature dense but coherent ensembles and crowded grooves. The altoist is teamed up with trumpeter Graham Haynes, Geri Allen (on synthesizer), guitarist Kelvyn Bell, electric

bassist Kevin Bruce Harris, both Marvin "Smitty" Smith and Mark Johnson on drums and percussion, and the up and coming singer Cassandra Wilson. Not for everyone's taste, this frequently exciting set hints at a future that has not yet come. —*Scott Yanow*

World Expansion / Nov. 1986 / JMT ✦✦✦
With Geri Allen (k) and Robin Eubanks (tb). Not his jazziest release, but a lot of good clean funk. —*Michael Erlewine*

Strata Institute Cipher Syntax / 1986 / JMT ✦✦✦

Sine Die / Dec. 1987-Jan. 1988 / Pangaea ✦✦✦
This obscure set for the short-lived Panagea label features altoist Steve Coleman and what could be called the "M-Base All-Stars": trumpeter Graham Haynes, trombonist Robin Eubanks, a crowded rhythm section, singer Cassandra Wilson and such guests (on one or two songs apiece) as keyboardist Geri Allen and saxophonists Branford Marsalis, Gary Thomas and Greg Osby. Although the grooves and funk rhythms are creative and unpredictable, Cassandra Wilson consistently sounds out of place; this crowded jungle was no place for a singer. The music is erratic, but never boring. —*Scott Yanow*

Rhythm People (The Resurrection of Creative Black Civilization) / 1990 / Novus ✦✦✦
The music on this "M-Base" recording, despite the difference in instrumentation, does not sound radically different than Ornette Coleman's harmelodic music of the 1980s. Altoist Steve Coleman is the lead voice throughout most of his originals and his solo style (often relying heavily on whole-tone runs and unexpected interval jumps) is intriguing, but it would be surprising if his rhythm section did not get bored playing the funky (although eccentric) rhythms after awhile. Two tunes include angry raps that lower the quality of the record. Steve Coleman's CD is obviously not "The Resurrection of Creative Black Civilization" (its immodest subtitle) for how can one resurrect something that has never died? However it does contain plenty of creative (if disturbing) improvisations. —*Scott Yanow*

● **Black Science** / 1991 /Novus ✦✦✦✦
The mixture of complex funk rhythms and inside/outside soloing performed by the "M-Base" stylists, although similar to Ornette Coleman's "free funk," is quite different from any other earlier idiom. Altoist Steve Coleman's CD is recommended as a good example of his music. The improvisations are dynamic, unpredictable and quite original and the ensemble (which includes pianist James Weidman, guitarist David Gilmore and three guest vocals by Cassandra Wilson) is tight. Coleman, who wrote all but one of the originals, is the dominant force behind this often-disturbing but generally stimulating music. —*Scott Yanow*

Rhythm in Mind (The Carnegie Project) / Apr. 29, 1991 / Novus ✦✦✦
This is an interesting set, teaming the adventurous altoist Steve Coleman with a group of veteran all-stars including tenor saxophonist Von Freeman, one of his inspirations. Also in the band are Dave Holland and the other members of the bassist's group at the time (trumpeter Kenny Wheeler and drummer Marvin "Smitty" Smith in addition to Coleman), plus guitarist Kevin Eubanks, second drummer Ed Blackwell and (in a bit of a surprise) pianist Tommy Flanagan. The music is essentially a quirky version of straightahead jazz with generally strong solos from the diverse players, hints of Coleman's M-Base music, and some blues. Intriguing but not essential. —*Scott Yanow*

Drop Kick / 1992 / Novus ✦✦

The Tao of Mad Phat / May 6, 1993-May 23, 1993 / Novus ✦✦✦

Def Trance Beat (Modalities of Rhythm) / Jun. 14, 1994-Jun. 17, 1994 / Novus ✦✦✦

Myths, Modes & Means: Live at Hot Brass [March '95] / Mar. 24, 1995+Mar. 25, 1995 / RCA ✦✦
One of a trio of RCA CDs taken from altoist Steve Coleman's week at Paris' Hot Brass Club, three of the six performances on this set ("Finger of God," "Song of the Beginnings" and "Transits") are over 19 minutes long, and, with the exception of a rap on "The Initiate" and one during the last part of "Song of the Beginnings," this is a jazz set. On "Finger of God," Yassir Chadly's spiritual chant is followed by some intense Coleman alto over a drone by the keyboards. Other selections feature passionate free funk with plenty of Coleman alto and Ralph Alessi trumpet solos; Vijay Iyer's spooky keyboards and Miya Masaoka's koto are assets in the ensembles. Not everything works, but one cannot fault Steve Coleman for stretching himself and taking chances. —*Scott Yanow*

Way of the Cipher: Live at Hot Brass [March '95] / Mar. 26, 1995+Mar. 28, 1996 / RCA ✦
Steve Coleman deserves a great deal of respect and credit for developing a strikingly original way of improvising that has a different logic than bebop. However, purists should be warned that this CD allows the contributions of three rappers to dominate the focus. Listeners whose ears are attuned to jazz/rap fusion may find

this live set (one of three CDs taken from a week-long engagement by Coleman at Paris' Hot Brass Club) enjoyable, but for purists, it is extremely difficult to sit through, especially since the three rappers (Kokayi, Sub-Zero and Black Indian) are featured on all but one brief extract, and the contributions of altoist Coleman and his band are in a purely supportive role. —*Scott Yanow*

Curves of Life / Mar. 29, 1995 / RCA ✦✦✦✦
The innovative altoist Steve Coleman and his Five Elements constantly prove that it is possible to play creative funk. When one thinks of modern funk (as opposed to the Horace Silver variety), it is of repetitious basslines and drum machines but Coleman's music is actually quite spontaneous. The bass and drum parts are danceable but unpredictable and Coleman's improvising is fresh and distinctive. On this live session, Coleman and his quartet jam through a mostly continuous set with one song flowing into another. David Murray (on tenor) sits in on two pieces and for a change of pace Coleman duets with pianist Andy Milne on a rhapsodic and respectful version of "The Gypsy." The one flaw to the set is the final selection, a 13-minute "I'm Burnin' Up" which is dominated by three annoying rappers. —*Scott Yanow*

The Sign & the Seal: Transmissions of Metaphysics Culture / Jan. 14, 1997 / RCA ✦✦✦
Steve Coleman's Mystic Rhythm Society traveled to Cuba in 1996 and met up with the AfroCuba de Matanzas, a group of percussionists and singers who keep ancient African rituals and rhythms alive. Their joint recording (which followed a concert at the Havana Jazz Festival) is an interesting mixture of musics, although the seemingly endless chanting/vocalizing (sometimes joined by Kokayi's rapping) is certainly an acquired taste. Altoist Coleman, tenor saxophonist Ravi Coltrane and trumpeter Ralph Alessi play important parts in the often-dense ensembles and have some solos, but jazz listeners will prefer Steve Coleman's earlier instrumental sets instead. —*Scott Yanow*

Johnny Coles

b. Jul. 3, 1926, Trenton, NJ, d. Dec. 20, 1996
Trumpet, Fluegelhorn / Hard Bop
A fine trumpeter with a distinctive cry, Johnny Coles long had the ability to say alot with a few notes. He played with a few top R&B bands including Eddie "Cleanhead" Vinson (1948-51), Bull Moose Jackson (1952) and Earl Bostic (1955-56), was with James Moody's group (1956-58) and appeared on several Gil Evans records between 1958-64. Probably his most significant association was with the 1964 Charles Mingus Sextet that toured Europe. Also in the group were Eric Dolphy, Clifford Jordan, Jaki Byard and Dannie Richmond! Coles can be seen holding his own against those giants on a European television show (available on a Shanachie video), but he had to leave the tour halfway through due to a sudden illness. He also played with Herbie Hancock's Sextet (1968-69), Ray Charles (1969-71), Duke Ellington (1971-74), Art Blakey's Jazz Messengers (briefly in 1976), Dameronia, Mingus Dynasty and the Count Basie band when it was under Thad Jones' leadership (1985-86), but fame has managed to elude him. Coles led sessions through the years for Epic, Blue Note, Mainstream and finally for Criss Cross before passing away from cancer. —*Scott Yanow*

The Warm Sound / Apr. 10, 1961+Apr. 13, 1961 / Koch ✦✦✦✦
Trumpeter Johnny Coles, best known for his association with Charles Mingus in 1964, made his recording debut as a leader on this Epic session, which was reissued on CD in 1995 by Koch. A bop-based trumpeter with a lyrical sound of his own, Coles is showcased here with an excellent quartet (Kenny Drew or Randy Weston on piano, bassist Peck Morrison and drummer Charlie Persip). He is in top form on a pair of standards (including "If I Should Lose You"), his own blues "Room 3" and four Weston originals; the reissue adds an alternate take of "Hi-Fly" to the original program. A fine outing. —*Scott Yanow*

● **Little Johnny C** / Jul. 18, 1963+Aug. 9, 1963 / Blue Note ✦✦✦✦✦
Although this Blue Note session (reissued on CD in 1996) is led by trumpeter Johnny Coles, pianist Duke Pearson (who contributed the arrangements and five of the six compositions) really functioned as leader. The typically impressive Blue Note lineup (which includes Leo Wright on alto and flute, tenor saxophonist Joe Henderson, bassist Bob Cranshaw and either Walter Perkins or Pete La Roca on drums in addition to Coles and Pearson) handles the obscure material with creative invention. Most memorable are the catchy title cut and the somber ballad "So Sweet My Little Girl." Cole's brittle trumpet is the lead voice throughout although the young Joe Henderson was already instantly recognizable. —*Scott Yanow*

New Morning / Dec. 19, 1982 / Criss Cross ✦✦✦✦
Other than an obscure 1971 Mainstream date, this Criss Cross album was trumpeter Johnny Coles' first as a leader since 1963. Best remembered for being part of Charles Mingus' 1964 Sextet, Coles had continued growing as a trumpeter

through the years while keeping his brittle sound and advanced hard-bop style. His quartet set with pianist Horace Parlan, bassist Reggie Johnson and drummer Billy Hart finds Coles sticking exclusively to fluegelhorn and performing three of his originals along with one apiece by Charles Mingus ("Duke Ellington's Sound of Love"), Wayne Shorter and Charles Davis. The fresh material and Coles' enthusiastic solos make this an album worth picking up. —*Scott Yanow*

Buddy Collette (William Marcell Collette)

b. Aug. 6, 1921, Los Angeles, CA
Flute, Tenor Saxophone, Alto Saxophone, Clarinet / Cool, West Coast Blues
An important force in the Los Angeles jazz community, Buddy Collette was an early pioneer at playing jazz on the flute. Collette started on piano as a child and then gradually learned all of the woodwinds. He played with Les Hite in 1942, led a dance band while in the Navy during World War II and then freelanced in the L.A. area with such bands as the Stars of Swing (1946), Edgar Hayes, Louis Jordan, Benny Carter and Gerald Wilson (1949-50). An early teacher of Charles Mingus, Collette became the first Black musician to get a permanent spot in a West Coast studio band (1951-55). He gained his greatest recognition as an important member of the Chico Hamilton Quintet (1955-56) and he recorded several albums as a leader in the mid- to late '50s for Contemporary. Otherwise he mostly stuck to the L.A. area, freelancing, working in the studios, playing in clubs, teaching and inspiring younger musicians. Although a fine tenor player and a good clarinetist, Collette's most distinctive voice is on flute; he recorded an album with one of his former students, the great James Newton (1989). In addition Collette participated in a reunion of the Chico Hamilton Quintet and recorded a two-disc "talking record" for the Issues label in 1994 in which he discussed some of what he had seen and experienced through the years. —*Scott Yanow*

Tanganyika / 1954 / V.S.O.P. ♦♦♦
This set, presented by disc jockey Sleepy Stein but actually led by multireedist Buddy Collette, slightly predates the Chico Hamilton Quintet and hints strongly at that chamber jazz group. Comprising Collette, drummer Chico Hamilton, trumpeter John Anderson, pianist Gerald Wiggins, guitarist Jimmy Hall and bassist Curtis Counce—if one substitutes cellist Fred Katz for Anderson and Wiggins and changes the bassist, the result is the Chico Hamilton Quintet of 1955. The music is mostly group originals (five by Collette) and is an excellent example of cool jazz. V.S.O.P. has reissued this worthy recording from the obscure DIG label on CD. —*Scott Yanow*

● **Man of Many Parts** / Feb. 13, 1956-Apr. 17, 1956 / Original Jazz Classics ♦♦♦♦♦
This CD reissue of a Contemporary session shows off the many parts of multireedist Buddy Collette. Collette is showcased on tenor, alto, clarinet and his strongest ax, flute; he also contributed nine of the dozen selections. The cool jazz set (which sometimes uses advanced harmonies) also features among the sidemen trumpeter Gerald Wilson, guitarist Barney Kessel and pianist Gerald Wiggins, ranking with Buddy Collette's best work of the 1950s. —*Scott Yanow*

Nice Day with Buddy Collette / Nov. 6, 1956-Feb. 18, 1957 / Original Jazz Classics ♦♦♦♦
Nice Day with Buddy Collette is a nice recording for multireedist Buddy Collette who plays alto, clarinet, flute and tenor during the three sessions heard on the CD reissue. Five of the ten selection's are Collette's originals and, although the title cut and "Fall Winds" (which was renamed "Desert Sands") are both better-known for the versions he recorded with the Chico Hamilton Quintet than for these renditions, the original runthroughs are also excellent. Collette is the main voice throughout this set of lightly swinging music although he gets support from the fine rhythm sections (which include either Don Friedman, Dick Shreve or Calvin Jackson on piano). Overall this set serves as a good all-around showcase for Buddy Collette's playing and writing talents. —*Scott Yanow*

Porgy & Bess / 1957 / Interlude ♦♦
This is one of the odder interpretations of the music from George Gershwin's folk opera *Porgy & Bess* that has yet been recorded. The music on the out-of-print LP pays respect to eight of Gershwin's melodies, utilizing an instrumentation consisting of flute/bass clarinet (Buddy Collette), accordion (Pete Jolly), organ (Gerald Wiggins), guitar (Jim Hall), bass (Red Callender) and drums (a very restrained Louie Bellson). But, other than the unusual colors, little all that surprising happens during the obscure cool jazz effort. —*Scott Yanow*

Jazz Loves Paris / Jan. 24, 1958 / Original Jazz Classics ♦♦♦
Buddy Collette (switching between alto, tenor, flute and clarinet) performs ten songs associated with Paris on this 1958 session originally cut for Specialty. The CD reissue adds four alternate takes to what is still a brief program. Collette utilizes the tuba of Red Callender in some of the ensembles quite colorfully and there is solo space for trombonist Frank Rosolino, guitarist Howard Roberts and bassist Red Mitchell; Bill Douglass or Bill Richmond contribute tasteful support on

drums. Such melodies as "I Love Paris," "La Vie En Rose," "C'est Si Bon" and the "Song from 'Moulin Rouge'" are given concise but swinging treatment on this likable date. —*Scott Yanow*

Buddy Collette and His Swinging Shepherds / Mar. 1959 / Mercury ♦♦♦
With the success of Moe Koffman's "Swinging Shepherds Blues" in 1957, suddenly the flute became popular. Buddy Collette, who in the early '50s was one of the pioneer jazz flutists, heads this out-of-print Mercury LP that features his playing along with three other flutists (Paul Horn, Harry Klee and Bud Shank). Assisted by a fine West Coast rhythm section, Collette and his fellow flutists perform concise versions of 11 songs that were used in the movies. The repertoire ranges from standards such as "Laura," "I Can't Believe That You're in Love with Me" and "Invitation" to a few lesser-known numbers. The treatments are quite respectful but of interest to jazz listeners. —*Scott Yanow*

The Buddy Collette Quintet / 1962 / Studio West ♦♦♦♦
The fourth of four CDs released by Studio West, a subsidiary of V.S.O.P. Records, that is taken from previously unissued transcriptions made for the radio show "The Navy Swings" features the Buddy Collette Quintet, which in 1962 comprised the leader on flute, clarinet, tenor and alto, guitarist Al Viola, pianist Jack Wilson, bassist Jimmy Bond and drummer Bill Goodwin. As good as Collette (who contributed four melodic originals) plays on these very concise performances (all clocking in around three minutes or less), it is the six often-touching vocals of Irene Kral that particularly make this a recommended disc. Kral's versions of "The Meaning of the Blues," "Nobody Else but Me" and especially "Spring Can Really Hang You Up the Most" are quite definitive and memorable. —*Scott Yanow*

Flute Talk / Jul. 4, 1988-Jul. 5, 1988 / Soul Note ♦♦♦♦
Other than a couple of releases for tiny labels in 1973, this Soul Note CD was Buddy Collette's first session as a leader since 1964. Collette and his former pupil, the great flutist James Newton, team up with pianist Geri Allen, bassist Jaribu Shahid and drummer Gianpiero Prina for six of Collette's melodic originals (including "Blues in Torrance"), one of Newton's, and a free improvisation created by the two flutists. Collette, who also plays some alto and clarinet on the date, sounds quite happy to be reunited with Newton and to finally be recording again. Although the music is primarily straightahead, there are some adventurous moments. —*Scott Yanow*

A Jazz Audio Biography / 1993-1994 / Issues ♦♦♦♦
This is an unusual double CD; a talking record. Throughout the 132 minutes, veteran reed player Buddy Collette, who has been part of the Los Angeles jazz scene since the mid-'40s, tells a bit about what he has seen and experienced through the years. Collette actually talks very little about himself, preferring to reminisce about his associates including Charles Mingus (highlighted by the complete story behind Mingus' infamous Town Hall Concert and a touching interlude about the last time Collette visited the bassist), Charlie Parker (including Bird's explanation of the origin of his nickname), Paul Robeson, Josephine Baker, Eric Dolphy, the Central Avenue scene of the '40s and the long struggle to integrate the Los Angeles Musicians' Union and the studios in the 1950s. The only music heard are brief interludes by Collette on his horns between the spoken sections. The often-fascinating storytelling could have been twice as long. —*Scott Yanow*

Cal Collins

b. May 5, 1933, Medora, IN
Guitar / Bop, Swing
During his period on the Concord label, Cal Collins made a strong impression although his decision to return to Cincinnati has given him a much lower profile during the past decade. After serving in the Army, he settled in Cincinnati in the 1950s, working in the studios and appearing in clubs locally. Collins was with Benny Goodman for three years in the early '70s at the same time as Scott Hamilton and Warren Vaché. The guitarist signed with Concord and recorded often as a leader (six albums during 1978-81) and with Hamilton and Vaché. Since returning to Cincinnati, Collins has recorded for Mopro and in 1990 was heard on a quartet date for Concord but has been somewhat forgotten considering his talent. —*Scott Yanow*

Milestones / Apr. 28, 1974 / Pausa ♦♦♦
Cal Collins' recording debut (performed over three years before he started making records for Concord) was actually not released until 1984. This live set (cut in Cincinnati) features Collins in a trio with Kenny Poole on "Epiphone Guitar" (which sounds like a bass) and drummer Terry Moore. The musicians stretch out on five selections on this LP including a couple of swing-era standards ("I'm Through with Love" and "Hand Me Down My Walking Cane"), "My Favorite Things" and "Milestones." Collins already had his style down at this early stage, making this out-of-print album of interest to straightahead jazz guitar collectors. —*Scott Yanow*

Cincinnati to L.A. / Jan. 5, 1978 / Concord Jazz ✦✦✦✦
Good swing-tinged trio session, the second featuring guitarist Cal Collins as a leader, playing with pianist Monte Budwig and drummer Jake Hanna. The selections were mostly familiar standards, like "Willow Weep For Me" and "Easy Living." All were executed with a modicum of energy and showed the trio's harmonic expertise. —*Ron Wynn*

In San Francisco / Jul. 25, 1978 / Concord Jazz ✦✦✦✦
Guitarist Cal Collins made such a strong impression with his Concord recordings that it is surprising to realize he was only with the label from 1978-81; during that era he seemed to be everywhere. This trio set with bassist Monty Budwig and drummer Jeff Hamilton is a strong example of his talents. A talented straightahead bop player with roots in the swing era, Collins is heard in top form throughout the excellent program. Highlights include Miles Davis' "Blue Haze," "Sometimes I'm Happy," "Miles' Theme" and "So What." —*Scott Yanow*

Blues on My Mind / Apr. 1979 / Concord Jazz ✦✦✦✦
Restrained, nicely played swing-tinged late-'70s quartet date led by guitarist Cal Collins. He's a fluid, tasteful stylist, not given to excess and leaning more toward light, sentimental solos than energetic or blues-oriented phrasing. He's backed by pianist Larry Vuckovich, bassist Bob Maize, and drummer Jeff Hamilton, who all approach the music the same way. —*Ron Wynn*

By Myself / Dec. 1979 / Concord Jazz ✦✦✦✦

Interplay / Aug. 1980 / Concord Jazz ✦✦✦
Cal Collins teams up with fellow guitarist Herb Ellis on this generally relaxed set recorded live at the 1980 Concord Jazz Festival. With bassist Ray Brown and drummer Jake Hanna completing the quartet, Collins and Ellis prove to be quite complementary on such tunes as "Besame Mucho," "People Will Say We're in Love" and "Limehouse Blues." The two guitarists have similar but distinctive sounds and blend together quite well even if few sparks actually occur. —*Scott Yanow*

Cross Country / Apr. 1981 / Concord Jazz ✦✦✦
Cal Collins' second of two unaccompanied guitar sets was also his final Concord album as a leader before he decided to return to his native Cincinnati. Because his style was based in the swing era, Collins' style is quite melodic and self-sufficient; one does not miss the other rhythm section players. He performs concise interpretations of nine standards plus his own "Suzie Q." The highlights include "On the Atchison, Topeka and the Santa Fe," "But Beautiful," "Autumn in New York" and Hank Williams' "I Can't Help It." —*Scott Yanow*

● **Crack'd Rib** / Nov. 1983-Mar. 1984 / Mo Pro ✦✦✦✦✦
Guitarist Cal Collins had the highest visibility of his career when he was recording regularly for Concord during 1978-81. Since he returned permanently to Cincinnati in the early '80s, Collins has had a lower profile in the jazz world although his talent has not declined. On the first of two recordings for Mopro, the swing-based guitarist teams up with pianist Steve Schmidt, bassist Lynn Seaton and drummer John Van Ohlen for five veteran standards (including "Castle Rock," "Wabash Blues" and "I'm Getting Sentimental over You") plus his own "Crack'd Rib Blues." This hard-to-find LP contains excellent straightahead music that features Cal Collins in top form. —*Scott Yanow*

Ohio Style / Nov. 1990 / Concord Jazz ✦✦✦✦
Guitarist Cal Collins' first album as a leader in four years was also his first for Concord in nine years. Collins' reputation as a swinging and appealing improviser was formed during his Concord years (1978-81) before he moved to Cincinnati. This "comeback" CD was recorded in Cincinnati with some fine local musicians: fluegelhornist Jerry Van Blair, bassist Lou Lausche and drummer Tony Sweet. With the exception of the off-the-wall choice of "Tumbling Tumbleweeds" (Collins was always open to the influence of country music), all of the selections are veteran jazz standards. The guitarist manages to give such tunes as "East of the Sun," "Skylark," "Ghost of a Chance" and "Sweet Sue" fresh interpretations that swing and are creative within the genre of mainstream jazz. Recommended. —*Scott Yanow*

Joyce Collins

Piano, Vocals / Bop, Hard Bop
A fine pianist/vocalist based in the Los Angeles area who has also been a popular jazz educator, Joyce Collins was with the Frankie Carle band (1954) and with Oscar Pettiford (1955) before settling in Los Angeles. She worked regularly with Bob Cooper at the Lighthouse in the late '50s and recorded a trio album for Riverside in 1960. Collins toured Europe and Mexico with her trio, gigged with Benny Carter, recorded with the Gene Estes Big Band (1969) and toured with Paul Horn in 1969 but has mostly worked locally including in the studios. She played and recorded with Bill Henderson and led record sessions for Discovery (1981) and Audiophile (1990). —*Scott Yanow*

Moment to Moment / Jan. 16, 1981 / Discovery ✦✦✦✦
Pianist-vocalist Joyce Collins, who has spent much of her career as an educator in the Los Angeles area, has recorded remarkably few albums as a leader. In fact this Discovery date was only her second opportunity to lead a session, following her Jazzland debut by 21 years. Joined by trumpeter Jack Sheldon (for half of the selections), bassist Chuck Domanico and drummer Jim Plank on the out-of-print LP, Collins shows that she is a fine pianist and (on a few of the numbers) an equally expressive singer. Highlights include "Alone Together," "Don't Ever Leave Me," "I Get Along Without You Very Well" (which has a second theme composed by singer Jeri Southern) and a piano rendition of "Some Other Time." This album is worth searching for. —*Scott Yanow*

● **Sweet Madness** / Apr. 9, 1990-Apr. 27, 1990 / Audiophile ✦✦✦✦✦
Joyce Collins, who is joined here by either Andy Simpkins or Octavio Bailey on bass and Ralph Penland or Claudio Slon on drums, had a rare opportunity to record as a leader on this Audiophile CD but she made the most of it. Collins takes two vocals (including one on a rather depressing if insightful "The Job Application") but the emphasis is mostly on her skillful piano playing. Joyce Collins is in top form on such numbers as "Thinking of You," "You and the Night and the Music," Ornette Coleman's "Turn Around" and McCoy Tyner's "Inception." Recommended. —*Scott Yanow*

Lee Collins

b. Oct. 17, 1901, New Orleans, LA, **d.** Jul. 3, 1960, Chicago, IL
Trumpet / New Orleans Jazz
A talented early New Orleans trumpeter, Collins started out his career playing as a teenager in various brass bands including the Young Eagles, the Columbia Band and the Young Tuxedo Band. In 1924 Collins went to Chicago where he was Louis Armstrong's replacement with King Oliver; he also recorded with Jelly Roll Morton. He returned to New Orleans and cut four brilliant sides with the Jones-Collins Astoria Hot Eight in 1929, played briefly in 1930 with Luis Russell in New York and then went back to Chicago. Throughout the 1930s and '40s Collins often accompanied blues singers and was a regular fixture in Chicago clubs. After touring Europe with Mezz Mezzrow in 1951 and 1954, he became ill and had to retire. His autobiography (*Oh Didn't He Ramble*) is filled with priceless stories about the early days of New Orleans jazz. —*Scott Yanow*

Lee Collins-Ralph Sutton's Jazzola Six, Vol. 1 / Aug. 1, 1953+Aug. 8, 1953 / Rarities ✦✦✦✦
Although Lee Collins was one of the more talented New Orleans trumpeters and he spent much time in Chicago, he had very few opportunities to record as a leader. In fact his three albums consist of a very obscure effort for the tiny New Orleans Rec. label plus two live records for Rarities; all are difficult to find. The first of his two Rarities volumes has a pair of radio broadcasts from San Francisco's Hangover Club in 1953. The trumpeter heads a sextet also including Pud Brown on clarinet, soprano and tenor, trombonist Burt Johnson, the great stride pianist Ralph Sutton, bassist Dale Jones and drummer Smokey Stover. The band uses "Do You Know What It Means to Miss New Orleans" as its theme and performs a total of nine Dixieland and swing standards with spirit and some excitement. Both broadcasts are highlighted by a solo performance from its "intermission pianist" Joe Sullivan. This LP (along with *Vol. 2*) is recommended to New Orleans jazz collectors who are lucky enough to find it. —*Scott Yanow*

Alice Coltrane

b. Aug. 27, 1937, Detroit, MI
Piano, Harp, Organ / Avant-Garde, Free Jazz
Music obviously ran in Alice Coltrane's family; her older brother was bassist Ernie Farrow, who in the '50s and '60s played in the bands of Barry Harris, Stan Getz, Terry Gibbs and especially, Yusef Lateef. Alice McLeod began studying classical music at the age of seven. She attended Detroit's Cass Technical High School with pianist Hugh Lawson and drummer Earl Williams. As a young woman she played in church, and in the bands of such local musicians as Lateef and Kenny Burrell. McLeod traveled to Paris in 1959 to study with Bud Powell. She met John Coltrane while touring and recording with Gibbs around 1962-63; she married the saxophonist in 1965, and joined his band—replacing McCoy Tyner—a year later. Alice stayed with John's band until his death in 1967. Subsequently, she formed her own bands with players such as Pharoah Sanders, Joe Henderson, Frank Lowe, Carlos Ward, Rashied Ali and Jimmy Garrison. Coltrane moved to California in 1972. She became increasingly concerned with spiritual matters, founding a center for the study of Eastern religions in 1975. Since the mid-'70s, Coltrane has performed with decreasing frequency. She did record *Transfiguration* with Roy Haynes and Reggie Workman in 1978, and in 1987 led a quartet that included her sons in a John Coltrane tribute concert at the Cathedral of St. John the Divine in New York City. By most accounts, Alice Coltrane was a fine bebop pianist in her early years. With

John Coltrane, on albums such as *Live at the Village Vanguard Again* or *Concert in Japan*, her playing is characterized by rhythmically ambiguous arpeggios and a pulsing thickness of texture. —*Chris Kelsey*

Monastic Trio / Jan. 29, 1968 / Impulse! ♦♦♦

Reflection on Creation and Space / 1968-1972 / Impulse! ♦♦♦♦♦
This album is worth acquiring in its original vinyl form, just for the quadraphonic remixes—this alone makes it far more than just the average compilation. Selections are drawn from all of Alice Coltrane's Impulse releases (with *Ptah, The El-Daoud* receiving the least attention) and arranged into a musically functional running order, rather than a strict chronological order. —*Steven McDonald*

● **Ptah the El Daoud** / Jan. 26, 1970 / Impulse! ♦♦♦♦♦
After John Coltrane's death in 1967, his widow Alice Coltrane recorded a few albums and then dropped out of the jazz scene to raise a family and become much more involved in her religious life. This album was arguably her finest post-1967 recording. Playing piano and harp in a quintet with the tenors of Pharoah Sanders and Joe Henderson, bassist Ron Carter and drummer Ben Riley, Coltrane stretches out on four of that composers. She had grown as a pianist during the past three years and it is a pity that she did not continue after this session on a full-time basis. —*Scott Yanow*

Journey in Satchidananda / Jul. 4, 1970+Nov. 8, 1970 / MCA ♦♦♦
Harp and strings with jazz and Indian influences. Extraordinarily beautiful. —*Michael G. Nastos*

Transfiguration / Apr. 16, 1978 / Warner Brothers ♦♦♦
Eleven years after her husband John Coltrane's death, Alice Coltrane was no longer playing on a fulltime basis although she sounds in relatively good form on this obscure double-LP, her last major recording. Stretching out on organ and some piano, Coltrane (along with bassist Reggie Workman, drummer Roy Haynes and eight strings) performs a 37-minute version of John Coltrane's "Leo" along with a few of her more concise originals. The spiritual music sometimes drones on too long (Alice was always better at setting moods than developing ideas) but generally holds one's interest. —*Scott Yanow*

John Coltrane

b. Sep. 23, 1926, Hamlet, NC, d. Jul. 17, 1967, New York, NY
Tenor Saxophone, Soprano Saxophone, Leader, Composer / Hard Bop, Avant-Garde, Free Jazz, Groove
The most influential jazz musician of the past 40 years (only Miles Davis comes close), one of the greatest saxophonists of all time and a remarkable innovator, John Coltrane certainly made his impact on jazz!

Unlike most musicians, Coltrane's style changed gradually but steadily over time. His career can be divided into at least five periods: early days (1947-54), searching stylist (1955-56), sheets of sound (1957-59), the classic quartet (1960-64) and avant-garde (1965-67). Originally an altoist, he played in a Navy band during his period in the military, recording four privately issued songs in 1946. He settled in Philadelphia and then toured with King Kolax (1946-47), switched to tenor when he played with Eddie "Cleanhead" Vinson (1947-48), joined the Dizzy Gillespie big band (1948-49) and was with Dizzy's sextet (1950-51). Radio broadcasts from the latter association find Coltrane sounding heavily influenced by Dexter Gordon and hinting slightly at his future sound. He followed that gig with periods spent with the groups of Gay Crosse (1952), Earl Bostic (1952), Johnny Hodges (1953-54) and in Philadelphia for a few weeks with Jimmy Smith (1955).

The John Coltrane story really starts with his joining the Miles Davis Quintet in 1955. At first some observers wondered what Miles saw in the 28-year-old tenor who had an unusual sound and whose ideas sometimes stretched beyond his technique. However Davis was a masterful talent scout who could always hear potential greatness. Coltrane improved month by month and by 1956 was competing with Sonny Rollins as the top young tenor; he even battled him to a draw on their recording of "Tenor Madness." Coltrane (along with Red Garland, Paul Chambers and Philly Joe Jones) formed an important part of the classic Miles Davis Quintet, recording with Miles for Prestige and Columbia during 1955-56. In addition Coltrane was starting to be featured on many of Prestige's jam-session-oriented albums.

The key year in John Coltrane's career was 1957. Fired by Miles Davis due to his heroin addiction, Coltrane permanently kicked the habit. He spent several months playing with Thelonious Monk's Quartet, a mutually beneficial association that gave Monk long-overdue acclaim and greatly accelerated the tenor's growth. His playing became even more adventurous than it had been, he recorded *Blue Train* (his first great album as a leader) and, when he rejoined Miles Davis in early 1958, Coltrane was unquestionably the most important tenor in jazz. During his next two years with Davis, "Trane" (whose style had been accurately dubbed "sheets of sound" by critic Ira Gitler) really took the chordal improvisation of bop to the

breaking point, playing groups of notes with extreme speed and really tearing into the music. In addition to being one of the stars of Davis' recordings (including *Milestones* and *Kind of Blue*), Coltrane signed a contract with Atlantic and began to record classics of his own; "Giant Steps" (with its very complex chord structure) and "Naima" were among the many highlights.

By 1960 John Coltrane was long overdue to be a leader and Miles Davis reluctantly let him go. 'Trane's direction was changing from utilizing as many chords as possible (it would be difficult to get any more extreme in that direction) to playing passionately over one or two-chord vamps. He hired pianist McCoy Tyner, drummer Elvin Jones and went through several bassists (Steve Davis, Art Davis, Reggie Workman) before settling on Jimmy Garrison in late 1961. The first artist signed to the new Impulse label, Coltrane was given complete freedom to record what he wanted. He had recently begun doubling on soprano, bringing an entirely new sound and approach to an instrument previously associated with the Dixieland of Sidney Bechet (although Steve Lacy had already started specializing on it) and Coltrane's 1960 Atlantic recording of "My Favorite Things" became a sort of theme song that he revisited on a nightly basis.

John Coltrane continued to evolve during 1961-64. He added Eric Dolphy as part of his group for a period and recorded extensively at the Village Vanguard in late 1961; the lengthy explorations were branded by conservative critics as "anti-jazz." Partly to counter their stereotyping (and short memories), 'Trane recorded with Duke Ellington in a quartet, a ballad program and a collaboration with singer Johnny Hartman; his playing throughout was quite beautiful. But live in concert his solos (which could be 45 minutes in length) were always intense and continually searching. He utilized such songs as "Impressions" (which used the same two-chord framework as Miles Davis' "So What") and "Afro Blue" for long workouts and took stunning cadenzas on the ballad "I Want to Talk About You." In addition to the Impulse recordings, European radio broadcasts have since been released that show Coltrane's progress and consistency. And in December 1964 he displayed his vast interest in Eastern religion by recording the very popular *A Love Supreme*.

In 1965 it all began to change. Influenced and inspired by the intense and atonal flights of Albert Ayler, Archie Shepp and Pharoah Sanders, Coltrane's music dropped most of the melodies and essentially became passionate sound explorations. *Ascension* from mid-year featured six additional horns (plus a second bassist) added to the quartet for almost totally free improvisations. Fast themes (such as "One Down, One Up" and "Sun Ship") were quickly disposed of on the way to waves of sound. Coltrane began to use Pharoah Sanders in his group to raise the intensity level even more and when he hired Rashied Ali as second drummer, it eventually caused McCoy Tyner (who said he could no longer hear himself) and Elvin Jones to depart.

In 1966 Coltrane had a quintet consisting of his wife Alice on piano, Sanders, Ali and the lone holdover Jimmy Garrison. After a triumphant visit to Japan, Coltrane's health began to fail. Although the cause of his death on July 17, 1967, was listed as liver cancer, in reality it was probably overwork. Coltrane used to practice ten to 12 hours a day and when he had a job (which featured marathon solos), he would often spend his breaks practicing in his dressing room! It was only through such singlemindedness that he could reach such a phenomenal technical level, but the net result was his premature death.

Virtually every recording that John Coltrane made throughout his career is currently available on CD, quite a few books about him have been written and a video (*The Coltrane Legacy*) gives today's jazz followers an opportunity to see him performing on a pair of half-hour television shows. Since Coltrane's passing no other giant has dominated jazz on the same level. In fact many other saxophonists have built their entire careers on exploring music from just one of John Coltrane's periods! —*Scott Yanow*

The Last Giant: Anthology / 1946-1967 / Rhino ♦♦
This deluxe two-CD set is a major disappointment. It contains a few revelations (a brief 1946 recording of "Hot House" featuring a 20-year-old Coltrane, an aircheck with Dizzy Gillespie and a rare side by Gay Crosse's Good Humor Six in 1952) but mostly repackages familiar material and includes nothing from Coltrane's very important years with Impulse. Why weren't all four of the 1946 sides included and why are only the first 90 seconds heard from Coltrane's final performance before it fades out? The accompanying booklet is quite attractive, but this set (which will greatly frustrate completists) only gives an incomplete picture of the great saxophonist. —*Scott Yanow*

Coltrane 1951 / Jan. 13, 1951 / Oberon ♦♦♦♦
It is unusual to give such a high rating to what is essentially a bootleg LP of radio broadcasts but much of the music on this set is extraordinary. John Coltrane is heard as a featured solost with Dizzy Gillespie's Sextet (which also includes vibraphonist Milt Jackson, pianist Jimmy Foreman, bassist Percy Heath and drummer Art Blakey) four years before he joined Miles Davis. Gillespie has several brilliant

trumpet solos ("Good Bait" is quite memorable) and this LP allows one to hear the early influence that Dexter Gordon had on the young Coltrane. It's difficult to find but is well worth searching for. —*Scott Yanow*

First Broadcasts, Vol. 2 / Jan. 13, 1951 / Oberon ✦✦✦✦
The second LP of Dizzy Gillespie broadcasts from early 1951 once again liberally features John Coltrane at the age of 24, four years before he first started recording with Miles Davis. Although Gillespie is clearly the star (he is often in brilliant form), it is fascinating to hear Coltrane this early in his development, sounding like a mixture of Dexter Gordon and Lester Young. This bootlegish set will be hard to find and deserves to be reissued with its counterpart on CD. —*Scot Yanow*

High Step / Apr. 20, 1955 / Blue Note ✦✦✦
Bassist Paul Chambers gets co-billing on this two-LP set, but the main reason to acquire these three sessions is to hear Coltrane during a period when he was just beginning to develop his unique sound. 'Trane is well featured on six selections in a quartet with Chambers, pianist Kenny Drew and drummer Philly Joe Jones, heard during four numbers with a sextet that includes trumpeter Donald Byrd and on three cuts (two of which were previously unknown until the release of this two-fer) from April 1955 in a group with trombonist Curtis Fuller and baritonist Pepper Adams. Overall the music is not essential but is consistently excellent, fine examples of early hard bop from some of its top young players. —*Scott Yanow*

☆ **John Coltrane: The Prestige Recordings** / May 7, 1956-Dec. 26, 1958 / Prestige ✦✦✦✦✦
During 1956-58 Coltrane participated in 27 recording sessions for the Prestige label (not counting his three dates with the Miles Davis Quintet), both as a leader and as a sideman. Although these recordings are not as significant on a whole as Coltrane's later Impulse albums, there are many gems among the jam sessions and all of the music (except the Davis sessions) have been released in its entirety on this somewhat remarkable 16-CD set. Coltrane and a constantly changing all-star cast perform such classics as "Tenor Madness" (his one-time meeting on records with Sonny Rollins), "On a Misty Night," "While My Lady Sleeps," "Like Someone in Love," "Black Pearls" and "Stardust" among many others. This expensive box may not be for all jazz collections, but any true fan of John Coltrane will have to acquire it. —*Scott Yanow*

On a Misty Night / Sep. 7, 1956-Oct. 26, 1956 / Prestige ✦✦✦✦
This two-LP set combines together two very different sessions. John Coltrane is just one of four tenor saxophonists (along with Hank Mobley, Zoot Sims and Al Cohn) heard on the first of two lengthy jam session selections that comprise the first date while the other one showcases 'Trane in a quartet with pianist/composer Tadd Dameron (who wrote all six of the songs they perform), bassist John Simmons and drummer Philly Joe Jones. The latter date, with such high points as "On a Misty Night," "Mating Call" and "Soultrane," was one of Coltrane's very best early records. —*Scott Yanow*

Tenor Conclave / Sep. 7, 1956 / Original Jazz Classics ✦✦✦
Although this CD is not actually a John Coltrane session (preceding his first album as a leader by seven months), this fine jam session set has often been released under Coltrane's name. 'Trane is teamed with three other tenors (Al Cohn, Zoot Sims and Hank Mobley), all of whom get to stretch out on four numbers. While Cohn and Sims had similar cool-toned sounds at the time, Mobley and especially Coltrane are quite distinctive. With fine support from pianist Red Garland, bassist Paul Chambers and drummer Art Taylor, the four horns are in excellent (and occasionally competitive) form on "Tenor Conclave," "Just You, Just Me," "Bob's Boys" and "How Deep Is the Ocean." —*Scott Yanow*

Interplay for 2 Trumpets and 2 Tenors / Mar. 22, 1957 / Original Jazz Classics ✦✦✦✦
Although generally reissued under John Coltrane's name, the most significant musician on this CD is pianist Mal Waldron who contributed four of the five complex compositions including the original version of "Soul Eyes"; Jimmy Heath's "C.T.A." is also performed. Coltrane teams up with fellow tenor Bobby Jaspar, trumpeters Idrees Sulieman and Webster Young, guitarist Kenny Burrell, bassist Paul Chambers, drummer Art Taylor and either Waldron or Red Garland on piano. With so many soloists present on this advanced hard bop date, Coltrane is only one star among many although he does emerge as the standout. —*Scott Yanow*

Dakar / Mar. 22, 1957-Apr. 20, 1957 / Original Jazz Classics ✦✦✦
On this two-LP set, a pair of his lesser-known Prestige sessions are combined. The great tenor, whose sound was developing month-by-month during 1957, is heard in an unusual sextet with the baritones of Cecil Payne and Pepper Adams and also in an octet with fellow-tenor Bobby Jaspar and the trumpets of Idrees Sulieman and Webster Young. What these sessions have in common is the emphasis on new compositions including five from pianist Mal Waldron (highlighted by the original version of "Soul Eyes"), three by Teddy Charles and two from Pepper Adams in addition to Jimmy Heath's "C.T.A." —*Scott Yanow*

John Coltrane with Kenny Burrell / Apr. 18, 1957-Mar. 7, 1958 / Prestige ✦✦✦
Tenor saxophonist John Coltrane and guitarist Kenny Burrell are the alleged co-leaders of the two sessions included on this two-LP set but actually the second date (originally titled *The Cats*) was really under pianist Tommy Flanagan's direction; in fact Flanagan contributed four of the five compositions. Throughout, though, Coltrane is really the most significant soloist, whether on a brief duet with Burrell ("Why Was I Born"), in a quintet or (with the addition of trumpeter Idrees Sulieman) a sextet. —*Scott Yanow*

Wheelin' / Apr. 19, 1957-Sep. 20, 1957 / Original Jazz Classics ✦✦✦
This two-fer from the excellent Prestige series of two-LP sets features Coltrane at a pair of jam-session-type settings in 1957. He is heard along with fellow tenor Paul Quinichette and Frank Wess on flute and tenor on two long versions apiece of "Wheelin'" and "Dealin" in addition to a fine rendition of "Things Ain't What They Used to Be" and a 15-minute version of "Robbins Nest." In addition, there are two numbers from a sextet session with trumpeter Bill Hardman and altoist Jackie McLean. Overall the music is not all that essential (since there are so many other Coltrane recordings available) but is quite enjoyable on its own terms and worth picking up. —*Scott Yanow*

Bahia / May 17, 1957-Dec. 26, 1958 / Original Jazz Classics ✦✦✦
This two-LP set matches together the very different sounding tenors of John Coltrane and Paul Quinichette in a jam-session type setting from 1957 (although three of the five songs were actually composed by pianist Mal Waldron) in addition to Coltrane's final Prestige date, which also has appearances by the trumpeters Freddie Hubbard (on "Then I'll Be Tired of You") and an uncredited Wilbur Harden ("Something I Dreamed Last Night"). This is nice if not overly memorable music. —*Scott Yanow*

Coltrane [OJC] / May 31, 1957 / Original Jazz Classics ✦✦✦✦
This CD reissue brings back the music originally released as *First Trane*. The classic of the set is the emotional and eerie "While My Lady Sleeps," but all six selections (including "Violets for Your Furs") are notable for tenor saxophonist John Coltrane's passionate solos. This was his first full session as a leader (as opposed to heading jam-session dates) and it also features either Mal Waldron or Red Garland on piano, bassist Paul Chambers, drummer Al "Tootie" Heath and on some numbers trumpeter Johnny Splawn and baritonist Sahib Shihab. As with 'Trane's other Prestige sessions, this valuable music is also available in his huge box set; recommended in one form or another. —*Scott Yanow*

First Trane / May 31, 1957 / Prestige ✦✦✦✦

More Lasting Than Bronze / May 31, 1957 / Prestige ✦✦✦✦
Of the ten double LPs of John Coltrane's recordings reissued by Prestige, this is the one to get. All but one selection dates from 1957 and nearly every number is a gem, including three performances ("Like Someone in Love," "I Love You" and "Trane's Slo Blues") on which the great tenor is backed by just bass and drums, a lengthy version of "Lush Life" with trumpeter Donald Byrd, three tunes with a trio led by pianist Red Garland and four other songs (including the very memorable "While My Lady Sleeps") with a sextet. Coltrane is in inspired form on virtually every track. This music has since been reissued on CD in the massive box *The Prestige Recordings* but for those with a tight budget and the good luck to find this two-fer, the set is highly recommended. —*Scott Yanow*

Lush Life / May 31, 1957-Jan. 10, 1958 / Original Jazz Classics ✦✦✦✦
The music on this CD reissue is taken from three separate sessions led by John Coltrane. Most rewarding are memorable versions of "Like Someone in Love," "I Love You" and "'Trane's Slo Blues" that feature the masterful tenor accompanied by just bassist Earl May and drummer Art Taylor; "Like Someone in Love" in particular is given definitive treatment. Of the two other songs, "I Hear a Rhapsody" finds Coltrane accompanied by pianist Red Garland, bassist Paul Chambers and drummer Al "Tootie" Heath, while "Lush Life" is played with a quintet also featuring trumpeter Donald Byrd, Garland, Chambers and drummer Louis Hayes. —*Scott Yanow*

Rain or Shine / Aug. 16, 1957 / Prestige ✦✦✦
This particular two-fer (mostly from 1958) contains two alternate takes of "Trane's Slo Blues," two numbers with trumpeter Donald Byrd that emphasize Coltrane's "sheets of sound" approach and five selections that feature Coltrane's tenor with pianist Red Garland in a quartet. Excellent music from 'Trane's hard bop years will fill some gaps among Coltrane collectors. —*Scott Yanow*

The Last Trane / Aug. 16, 1957-Mar. 26, 1958 / Original Jazz Classics ✦✦✦
Despite its title (which was due to the original LP containing the last of Prestige's John Coltrane material to be released for the first time), this CD reissue does not have Coltrane's final recordings either of his career or for Prestige. These "leftovers" are generally rewarding with an alternate take of "Trane's Slo Blues" (called "Slotrane") being joined by three slightly later numbers ("Lover," "By the Numbers" and "Come Rain or Come Shine") taken from quintet sessions with

trumpeter Donald Byrd, pianist Red Garland, bassist Paul Chambers and either Louis Hayes or Art Taylor on drums. Enjoyable if not essential hard bop from John Coltrane's productive Prestige period. —*Scott Yanow*

Traning In / Aug. 23, 1957 / Original Jazz Classics ✦✦✦

This CD brings back a good session but one that does not quite live up to its great potential. Tenor saxophonist John Coltrane, halfway through his one-year hiatus from Miles Davis' group, performs five songs with the assistance of pianist Red Garland, bassist Paul Chambers and drummer Art Taylor. Although "Traneing In" and "You Leave Me Breathless" have their moments, in general this set is less memorable than one might expect; inspiration was lacking that day. —*Scott Yanow*

John Coltrane / Aug. 23, 1957+Feb. 7, 1958 / Prestige ✦✦✦

This two-LP set reissues the full contents of the earlier albums *Traneing In* and *Soultrane*. In both cases tenor saxophonist John Coltrane was joined by pianist Red Garland, bassist Paul Chambers and drummer Art Taylor. High points include "Traneing In," "You Leave Me Breathless," Coltrane's first version of "I Want to Talk About You" and a lengthy "Good Bait." It's excellent advanced hard bop music, although 'Trane's most significant work was still in the future. —*Scott Yanow*

★ Blue Train / Sep. 15, 1957 / Blue Note ✦✦✦✦✦

A landmark album—stunning. This is Coltrane's only Blue Note recording as a leader, and he never made a better album in this particular hard-bop style. A must-hear for all jazz fans, Blue Train includes Coltrane's most impressive early composition, "Moment's Notice." With outstanding performances from sidemen Lee Morgan (tpt), Curtis Fuller (tb), and Kenny Drew (p). [*Blue Train* was reissued in 1997 with early takes of "Blue Train" and "Lazy Bird" added.] —*Michael Erlewine*

Wheelin' and Dealin' / Sep. 20, 1957 / Original Jazz Classics ✦✦✦

A decent but not memorable session (brought back in expanded form on CD), this set teams together John Coltrane with his fellow tenors Paul Quinichette and Frank Wess (who doubles on flute), pianist Mal Waldron, bassist Doug Watkins and drummer Art Taylor. Very much a jam session, the performances of a couple of Mal Waldron blues ("Wheelin'" and "Dealin'," both of which are heard in two versions), "Things Ain't What They Used to Be" and "Robbins Nest" are notable mostly for contrasting the cool tones of Quinichette (a Lester Young soundalike) and Wess with the more explorative and explosive Coltrane. The music is fun (everyone plays well), just not essential. —*Scott Yanow*

The John Coltrane/Ray Draper Quintet / Dec. 20, 1957 / Prestige ✦✦✦

When one thinks of modern jazz instruments, the tuba does not come immediately to mind, but Ray Draper performs well on this quintet session with John Coltrane and a standard rhythm section. Draper's three compositions (along with three jazz standards) comprise this interesting if not essential hard bop session; Coltrane is in fine form throughout. —*Scott Yanow*

Black Pearls / Jan. 10, 1958-May 23, 1958 / JVC ✦✦✦✦

Four of the six performances on this two-LP set are over ten minutes long, giving tenor saxophonist John Coltrane (heard at the peak of his "sheets of sound" period), trumpeter Donald Byrd, pianist Red Garland, bassist Paul Chambers and drummer Art Taylor plenty of space in which to stretch out. 'Trane takes some miraculous solos (by 1958 he was the leading tenor saxophonist in jazz and already long on his way to becoming a giant), sounding ten years ahead of his sidemen. The young trumpeter Freddie Hubbard makes an appearance on "Do I Love You Because You're Beautiful?" and this two-fer also finds Coltrane for the first time playing a McCoy Tyner composition ("The Believer"), two years before Tyner joined his Quartet. —*Scott Yanow*

The Believer / Jan. 10, 1958-Dec. 26, 1958 / Original Jazz Classics ✦✦✦

This LP (whose music is currently only available on CD as part of John Coltrane's huge Prestige box set) only contains a half-hour of music. The masterful tenor saxophonist John Coltrane is joined by pianist Red Garland, bassist Paul Chambers, drummer Louis Hayes and either Donald Byrd or a young Freddie Hubbard on trumpet. An interesting aspect to the set is that it is the first example of Coltrane being associated with pianist McCoy Tyner. Tyner is not on the date but he contributed "The Believer," which Coltrane performs along with Calvin Massey's "Nakatini Serenade" and the Rodgers & Hammerstein ballad "Do I Love You Because You're Beautiful?" —*Scott Yanow*

Soultrane / Feb. 7, 1958 / Original Jazz Classics ✦✦✦✦

Tenor saxophonist John Coltrane, who had recently rejoined Miles Davis' group, teams up with pianist Red Garland, bassist Paul Chambers and drummer Art Taylor for a fine set which has been reissued on CD. Coltrane performs his earliest rendition of "I Want to Talk About You" (although without a closing cadenza), "Good Bait," "You Say You Care," "Theme for Ernie" and "Russian Lullaby." This is

excellent music that falls short of being classic, but Coltrane and Garland always made for a complementary team. —*Scott Yanow*

Jazzlore: Countdown, Vol. 24 / Mar. 13, 1958 / Savoy ✦✦

This two-LP set is strictly for collectors for, in addition to six competent but not overly original compositions by the obscure fluegelhornist Wilbur Harden, there are three lengthy alternate takes. The previously unreleased title cut (which is heard in two versions) has no relation to John Coltrane's "Countdown" from his *Giant Steps* album. The music, featuring John Coltrane on tenor, Harden and a fine rhythm section (pianist Tommy Flanagan, bassist Doug Watkins and drummer Louis Hayes), is reasonably enjoyable but not all that memorable; just another hard-bop jam session from the 1950s. —*Scott Yanow*

Dial Africa / May 13, 1958-Jun. 24, 1958 / Savoy ✦✦✦

For this sextet date with fluegelhornist Wilbur Harden and trombonist Curtis Fuller (which is taken from the same sessions as *Gold Coast*), Coltrane performs four Harden originals (including two versions of "B.J.") and the standard "Once in a While." The music is excellent but much more conservative than most of 'Trane's recordings from this era. This LP is worth picking up but is not essential. —*Scott Yanow*

Gold Coast / May 13, 1958-Jun. 24, 1958 / Savoy ✦✦✦

John Coltrane's Savoy recordings with fluegelhornist Wilbur Harden are enjoyable but not particularly innovative. This LP contains "Tanganyika Strut," "Gold Coast" and alternate takes of "Dial Africa" and "B.J." Despite all of the emphasis on Africa in the song titles, the music is essentially American bebop featuring Coltrane, Harden and trombonist Curtis Fuller; Harden and Fuller contributed two originals apiece. This album is a companion of *Dial Africa*. —*Scott Yanow*

Settin' the Pace / May 26, 1958 / Original Jazz Classics ✦✦✦✦✦

Tenor saxophonist John Coltrane recorded quite a few records with the rhythm section of pianist Red Garland, bassist Paul Chambers and drummer Art Taylor during 1957-58. On this particular CD reissue, Coltrane performs "Rise and Shine," "I See Your Face Before Me," "If There Is Someone Lovelier than You" and "Little Melonae." But more significant than the material are Coltrane's searching and passionate improvisations, which were pointing the way towards the future. This music (along with 'Trane's other Prestige recordings) is also available as part of his huge *Complete on Prestige* box set. —*Scott Yanow*

Standard Coltrane / Jul. 11, 1958 / Original Jazz Classics ✦✦

Although the music on this CD reissue is quite worthwhile, the four songs are available along with four others from the same day on *The Stardust Session*, making this a rather pointless set. But if found at a budget price, the release might be worth picking up for tenor saxophonist John Coltrane is in excellent form on some standards (including "Invitation") played with a quintet also featuring fluegelhornist Wilbur Harden, pianist Red Garland, bassist Paul Chambers and drummer Jimmy Cobb. —*Scott Yanow*

The Stardust Sessions / Jul. 11, 1958 / Prestige ✦✦✦✦

This CD reissue consolidates a very good session by tenor saxophonist John Coltrane. Originally these eight standards (which include the title cut, "Invitation," "My Ideal" and "I'll Get By") were scattered on three separate LP's even though they all took place on the same day. With strong support from the rhythm section (pianist Red Garland, bassist Paul Chambers and drummer Jimmy Cobb) and good solos from fluegelhornist Wilbur Harden, Coltrane is heard near the end of his "sheets of sound" period, perfecting his distinctive sound and taking colorful and aggressive solos. —*Scott Yanow*

Coltrane Time / Oct. 13, 1958 / Blue Note ✦✦✦✦

This is a most unusual CD due to the inclusion of Cecil Taylor on piano. Although Taylor and John Coltrane got along well, trumpeter Kenny Dorham (who is also on this quintet date) hated the avant-garde pianist's playing and was clearly bothered by Taylor's dissonant comping behind his solos. With bassist Chuck Israels and drummer Louis Hayes doing their best to ignore the discord, the group manages to perform two blues and two standards with Dorham playing strictly bop, Taylor coming up with fairly free abstractions and Coltrane sounding somewhere in between. The results are unintentionally fascinating. —*Scott Yanow*

Like Sonny / Nov. 1958 / Roulette ✦✦✦

This Roulette CD combines two unrelated sessions. Coltrane is heard in a quintet with the tuba player Ray Draper (their second album together) playing five standards (including "Doxy" and "Oleo") and Draper's "Essii's Dance." The 1960 performances are more significant for they are the earliest recorded collaborations by Coltrane and pianist McCoy Tyner. Together with bassist Steve Davis and drummer Billy Higgins they perform "One and Four," "Like Sonny" and two takes of "Exotica," music that barely predates 'Trane's classic quartet and succeeds on its own terms. —*Scott Yanow*

The Coltrane Legacy / Jan. 15, 1959-May 25, 1961 / Atlantic ✦✦✦
When this LP was released in 1970, it debuted some valuable Coltrane recordings covering a two-year period. Three of the selections are alternates taken from his Atlantic album with vibraphonist Milt Jackson, "Original Untitled Ballad" (later titled "To Her Ladyship") is from the session that resulted in Coltrane's *Ole* album with Eric Dolphy and Freddie Hubbard, and the remaining two numbers ("26-2" and "Exotica") find 'Trane meeting up with both pianist McCoy Tyner and drummer Elvin Jones (along with bassist Steve Davis) on records for the first time. Historically significant music, it's generally quite enjoyable. —*Scott Yanow*

☆ **Heavyweight Champion: The Complete Atlantic Recordings** / Jan. 15, 1959-May 25, 1961 / Rhino/Atlantic ✦✦✦✦✦
John Coltrane's two years with Atlantic can be thought of as his "middle period" during which he evolved from his sheets of sound approach to intense explorations over two-chord vamps. It is difficult to see how Rhino could have done a better job with this reissue—they have come out with every scrap that could be found from Coltrane's Atlantic period. On the seven-CD box set is reissued the complete contents of the albums *Bags & Trane*, *Giant Steps*, *Coltrane Jazz*, *My Favorite Things*, *Coltrane Plays the Blues*, *Olé Coltrane*, *The Avant-Garde* and *Coltrane's Sound*, the selections originally issued on *Alternate Takes* and three "new" alternate takes, plus (for the final CD) many previously unheard versions of five numbers including nine takes of "Giant Steps!" With such supporting players as vibraphonist Milt Jackson (who was actually the co-leader of *Bags and Trane*); pianists Hank Jones, Cedar Walton, Tommy Flanagan, Wynton Kelly, and McCoy Tyner; bassists Paul Chambers, Charlie Haden, Percy Heath, Steve Davis, Art Davis and Reggie Workman; drummers Connie Kay, Lex Humphries, Art Taylor, Jimmy Cobb, Ed Blackwell and Elvin Jones; trumpeters Don Cherry and Freddie Hubbard and Eric Dolphy on alto and flute, it is not too surprising that the music is both innovative and classic. This box (which also has a fine booklet) is essential for all serious jazz collections. —*Scott Yanow*

Alternate Takes / Apr. 1, 1959 / Atlantic ✦✦✦✦
This LP, released in the mid-'70s, gave listeners their first opportunity to hear alternate versions of eight John Coltrane recordings from 1959-60. The original versions of five of these songs (including "Giant Steps," "Naima" and "Countdown") were from the *Giant Steps* sessions, "Body and Soul" was from *Coltrane's Sound* and the other two selections were from *Coltrane Jazz*. It is always interesting to hear "new" versions of classic recordings. All of this music has since been reissued on CD (as is true of most Coltrane LPs). —*Scott Yanow*

★ **Giant Steps** / Apr. 1, 1959 / Atlantic ✦✦✦✦✦
This is one of John Coltrane's classic sets; in fact, this CD reissue (which adds alternate takes to five of the seven original recordings) almost doubles one's pleasure. In "Giant Steps" Coltrane built a tongue-twister of chord changes (stretching bop to its logical breaking point), which he would soon abandon in favor of long drones on simpler patterns. Not only does this CD give one the two earliest versions of "Giant Steps" but also "Naima," "Cousin Mary," "Spiral," "Syeeda's Song Flute," the underrated but remarkable "Countdown" and "Mr. P.C." Recorded while Coltrane was still with Miles Davis' group, this CD (which mostly features pianist Tommy Flanagan, bassist Paul Chambers and drummer Art Taylor) made it obvious that Coltrane had something very important of his own to say and that he would need his own band in the future to fully express himself. —*Scott Yanow*

Coltrane Jazz / Nov. 24, 1959-Dec. 2, 1959 / Atlantic ✦✦✦✦
This CD contains the original LP program plus alternate takes of "Like Sonny" and "I'll Wait and Pray." With the exception of "Village Blues" (which features Coltrane's 1960 Quartet) and the earlier alternate of "Like Sonny," this set features Coltrane in 1959 with the Miles Davis rhythm section of the time: pianist Wynton Kelly, bassist Paul Chambers and drummer Jimmy Cobb. "My Shining Hour" and "Harmonique" are among the highlights of this excellent release. —*Scott Yanow*

The Avant Garde / Jun. 20, 1960-Jul. 8, 1960 / Atlantic ✦✦✦✦
This CD is a straight reissue of the original LP. Despite the title, it is actually a fairly relaxed and somewhat conservative session for these players. Tenor saxophonist John Coltrane (who on "The Blessing" makes his debut on soprano) works well with the sidemen of the Ornette Coleman Quartet (trumpeter Don Cherry, bassist Charlie Haden or Percy Heath and drummer Ed Blackwell) on three Coleman compositions (this version of "The Blessing" is a classic), Don Cherry's "Cherryco" and Thelonious Monk's "Bemsha Swing." It's an enjoyable set of early free-bop. —*Scott Yanow*

Coltrane Plays the Blues / Oct. 24, 1960 / Atlantic ✦✦✦✦
Recorded during the same week as his original version of "My Favorite Things," this LP by John Coltrane features six blues-oriented originals (five by 'Trane) including "Blues to Bechet" and "Mr. Syms." The music is more melodic than usual with Coltrane playing soprano on two of the six tracks; "Blues to You" is the best showcase for his intense tenor. —*Scott Yanow*

Coltrane's Sound / Oct. 24, 1960 / Atlantic ✦✦✦✦
Although one may not think of *Coltrane's Sound* as being one of John Coltrane's most famous recordings, when one looks at its contents it quickly becomes obvious that this set ranks near the top. This CD reissue contains such classic material as "Central Park West," "Equinox," a reharmonized (and influential) version of "Body and Soul," the underrated "Satellite," "Liberia" and an intense rendition of "The Night Has a Thousand Eyes." Also included on this reissue is an alternate version of "Body and Soul" and the lesser-known "262." Co-starring pianist McCoy Tyner, bassist Steve Davis and drummer Elvin Jones, this set is highly recommended. —*Scott Yanow*

★ **My Favorite Things** / Oct. 24, 1960-Oct. 26, 1960 / Atlantic ✦✦✦✦✦
This LP was very influential when it came out and remains a classic. The first full album by the classic John Coltrane Quartet (with pianist McCoy Tyner, drummer Elvin Jones and their bassist of the time Steve Davis) consists of a fiery "Summertime," the lyrical "But Not for Me," a nice ballad for 'Trane's soprano on "Everytime We Say Goodbye" and most importantly, the lengthy "My Favorite Things." On the latter, Coltrane, who had used a seemingly endless number of chords on the prior year's "Giant Steps," reduces the chords to a minimum and plays passionately over a repetitious vamp, creating startlingly new music. This set has since been reissued on CD and in one form or another is essential. —*Scott Yanow*

Live at the Village Vanguard: The Master Takes / 1961 / GRP ✦✦✦✦
Released several months after the historic box set *The Complete Live at the Village Vanguard*, *The Master Takes* in many ways supplants the original *Live at the Village Vanguard*, containing many of the same tracks. For anyone wanting a sampler of these sublime performance and reluctant to spend the money for a four-disc box set, this is a perfect summary of a few nights of great music. —*Stephen Thomas Erlewine*

Complete Africa/Brass Sessions / May 23, 1961+Jun. 4, 1961 / Impulse! ✦✦✦✦✦
John Coltrane's first recordings for Impulse are different than any of his later ones for they feature the saxophonist accompanied by large brass-heavy 14-17 piece groups. This two-CD set has all of the music that was originally released on *Africa/Brass*, the later *Africa/Brass Sessions, Vol. 2* and *Trane's Modes*. In general the arrangements are essentially an expansion of the style and sound of the John Coltrane Quartet with much of the improvising ("Blues Minor" excepted) taking place over two-chord vamps. Eric Dolphy wrote all but a pair of the charts (there are one apiece from McCoy Tyner and Calvin Massey) and he based his orchestrations on the piano voicings of Tyner. The only soloists are Coltrane (on both tenor and soprano) and his regular quartet members; it is disappointing that Dolphy, Freddie Hubbard and Booker Little are not really heard from. While Massey's "The Damned Don't Cry" falters and sounds under-rehearsed, the three renditions of "Africa" are quite colorful. But since over half of the performance time is taken up by "Africa," this two-CD set is not for everyone. —*Scott Yanow*

From the Original Master Tapes / May 23, 1961-1962 / MCA ✦✦✦
This early CD sampler of John Coltrane's Impulse years gives the personnel listing but leaves off the recording dates. All of the music ("Soul Eyes," "Song of the Underground Railroad," "Dear Lord," "Vilia," "India," "Spiritual" and "Big Nick") has been reissued again on CD, making this set of greatest interest to those listeners just beginning to explore the music of the great saxophonist; the emphasis here is the more melodic and conservative performances, although several classics are included. "Vilia" (which was originally released on an LP sampler) was formerly the rarest selection. —*Scott Yanow*

Ole Coltrane / May 25, 1961 / Atlantic ✦✦✦✦
One of John Coltrane's most interesting sessions for Atlantic was also his last before exclusively switching to Impulse. This CD, which contains the original three selections from the LP ("Ole," "Dahomey Dance" and "Aisha") in addition to one item from the same date that was not released until decades later ("To Her Ladyship"), features the great saxophonist leading an all-star group (Eric Dolphy on alto and flute, trumpeter Freddie Hubbard, pianist McCoy Tyner, bassists Reggie Workman and Art Davis and drummer Elvin Jones) on a variety of very interesting material. "Ole" is quite haunting and "Dahomey Dance" became a minor standard. The solos are more concise than is usual on a Coltrane session and this set is quite accessible even to listeners who prefer his earlier "sheets of sound" recordings. —*Scott Yanow*

Newport '63 / Nov. 2, 1961-Jul. 7, 1963 / Impulse! ✦✦✦✦
Three of the four lengthy performances on this CD are taken from one of the John Coltrane Quartet's greatest performances: the 1963 Newport Jazz Festival. With pianist McCoy Tyner, bassist Jimmy Garrison and drummer Roy Haynes (filling in for an absent Elvin Jones), Coltrane performs what is arguably his greatest version of "My Favorite Things" along with memorable renditions of "Impressions" and "I Want to Talk About You." Two of those selections originally appeared on the LP *Selflessness* while "Impression" was included in a later collection. This set is

rounded out by "Chasin' Another Trane," the only recording from 'Trane's famous Nov. 1961 engagement at the Village Vanguard that had Roy Haynes sitting in for Elvin Jones; altoist Eric Dolphy is also heard from on that heated selection. —*Scott Yanow*

Complete 1961 Village Vanguard Recordings / Nov. 1, 1961-Nov. 5, 1961 / Impulse! ✦✦✦✦✦
All of the music that survives from John Coltrane's famous 1961 five-day engagement at the Village Vanguard has been released on this 1997 four-CD box set. The original *Live at the Village Vanguard* album just had three selections; 16 others came out on various releases through the years, and this attractive box has all 19 of those cuts, plus three previously unreleased performances. During the period, the great tenor and soprano saxophonist was joined by pianist McCoy Tyner, both Reggie Workman and Jimmy Garrison on bass, drummer Elvin Jones, and usually Eric Dolphy on alto and bass clarinet; "India" usually adds Ahmed Abdul-Malik on oud and Garvin Bushell on oboe and contrabassoon, while Bushell also appears on "Spiritual," and Roy Haynes sits in for Jones on "Chasin' Another Trane." Although the band was considered controversial and branded as "anti-jazz" by critic John Tynan, the music is not as "far out" as was once thought with the benefit of decades of hindsight. Coltrane and Dolphy do take plenty of extended and adventurous solos, often over one or two-chord vamps, but the improvising seems quite logical and properly emotional. There are multiple versions of most of the songs, with all of the treatments holding one's interest. Included are "Brasilia," "Chasin' Another Trane," "Softly as in a Morning Sunrise," two versions of "Chasin' the Trane," "Greensleeves," a thinly disguised "Naima" and "Miles' Mode," three of "Impressions," and four of "India" and "Spiritual." All true John Coltrane fans have to own this set. —*Scott Yanow*

Other Village Vanguard Tapes / Nov. 1, 1961-Nov. 5, 1961 / Impulse! ✦✦✦
This double LP augments the original *Live at the Village Vanguard* album with six more performances taken from John Coltrane's famous Nov. 1961 engagement. In addition to Coltrane on soprano and tenor, pianist McCoy Tyner and drummer Elvin Jones, the participants include both bassist Reggie Workman and his eventual replacement, Jimmy Garrison, and (for atmosphere) veteran Garvin Bushell on oboe and contrabassoon on two numbers and Ahmed Abdul-Malik added on oud for one. The music comprises "India," "Greensleeves," "Chasin' the Trane," two versions of "Spiritual" and a lengthy "Untitled Original." Throughout this two-fer the music is passionate, often intense and innovative with Coltrane reducing the number of chords down to a minimum in favor of drones and vamps. —*Scott Yanow*

Live at the Village Vanguard / Nov. 2, 1961-Nov. 3, 1961 / Impulse! ✦✦✦✦
This CD reissue only includes the original LP program. However, the music is consistently excellent, with the moody "Spiritual" (which features Coltrane's soprano and Eric Dolphy's bass clarinet) living up to its title. 'Trane jams spiritedly on a beboppish "Softly as in a Morning Sunrise" and roars on a marathon tenor solo during "Chasin' the Trane." —*Scott Yanow*

Impressions / Nov. 5, 1961-Apr. 29, 1963 / Impulse! ✦✦✦
This LP is a hodgepodge of memorable John Coltrane performances from the 1961-63 period. "India" and "Impressions" are taken from 'Trane's famous Nov. 1961 engagement at the Village Vanguard; bass clarinetist Eric Dolphy is heard on the former while the latter features a marathon solo from Coltrane on tenor. Also included on this set are 1962's "Up 'Gainst the Wall" and the classic of the album, 1963's "After the Rain." —*Scott Yanow*

The Complete Paris Concerts / Nov. 18, 1961 / Magnetic ✦✦✦✦
John Coltrane collectors will want this double CD. Coltrane's 1961 quintet (with Eric Dolphy on alto, bass clarinet and flute; pianist McCoy Tyner; bassist Reggie Workman and drummer Elvin Jones) is heard during two different concerts recorded the same night. This set gives us "Impressions" and two versions apiece of "I Want to Talk About You," "Blue Train" and "My Favorite Things"; none of the music was previously issued. The recording quality is good and the solos are quite passionate. —*Scott Yanow*

Live Trane / Nov. 22, 1961-Jul. 28, 1965 / BYG ✦✦✦✦
This Japanese three-LP box set from the German company BYG captures Coltrane at four separate European concerts from a four-year period. At a Stockholm concert from Nov. 22, 1961, Coltrane and his quintet (with Eric Dolphy on alto, flute and bass clarinet; pianist McCoy Tyner; bassist Reggie Workman and drummer Elvin Jones) perform a 20-minute "My Favorite Things" and much more concise versions of "Naima," "Blue Train" and "Impressions." The classic quartet (with Tyner, bassist Jimmy Garrison and Jones) interprets "I Want to Talk About You," "Traneing In," "Spiritual" and "Mr. P.C." at a Stockholm concert from Oct. 22, 1963, and the same group at concerts in Antibes and Paris on July 27 and 28, 1965, really tears into "Blue Valse," "Afro Blue," "Naima" and two versions of "Impressions." This hard-to-find set, even if the liner notes are in Japan, is highly recom-

mended to true John Coltrane fans, for these live recordings are often quite intense and dazzling, particularly the later performances. —*Scott Yanow*

Ballads / Dec. 21, 1961 / Impulse! ✦✦✦
Stung by criticism from conservative jazz critics, Coltrane decided to show his detractors that he had not forgotten how to embrace a melody; the problem is that on this brief set (reissued on CD by GRP in an attractive fold-out package) he never really gets away from the themes. While Trane (who sticks to tenor) plays quite pretty, pianist McCoy Tyner actually has the more interesting solos. Coltrane shows the tunes an excess of respect, making this outing with his classic quartet enjoyable as background music but lacking much passion. —*Scott Yanow*

The Gentle Side of John Coltrane / 1961-1964 / GRP ✦✦✦
Excellent two-fer that was recently reissued on CD. —*Michael G. Nastos*

Bye Bye Blackbird / 1962 / Original Jazz Classics ✦✦✦✦
A straight reissue of the Pablo LP, this CD only contains 36 minutes of music but the quality is quite high. John Coltrane and his quartet (pianist McCoy Tyner, bassist Jimmy Garrison and drummer Elvin Jones) perform extended versions of "Bye Bye Blackbird" and "Traneing In" that gradually build up to great intensity. Well recorded, this European concert (of uncertain origin) is worth hearing, particularly by Coltrane collectors who already have his more essential recordings, although it does not quite live up to the label that producer Norman Granz gave it: "His Greatest Concert Performance!" —*Scott Yanow*

Coltrane [Impulse] / Apr. 11, 1962-Jun. 29, 1962 / Impulse! ✦✦✦✦
John Coltrane and his classic quartet (pianist McCoy Tyner, bassist Jimmy Garrison and drummer Elvin Jones) are in fine form for this 1962 studio LP. High points include a passionate "Out of This World" (what did Johnny Mercer think of this version?) and a classic version of Mal Waldron's "Soul Eyes." The remainder of the program includes "The Inch Worm" and the two Coltrane compositions "Tunji" and "Miles' Mode." Not as intense as many of 'Trane's other albums, this is still a recommended, enjoyable set. —*Scott Yanow*

The Paris Concert / Nov. 17, 1962 / Original Jazz Classics ✦✦✦
This excellent CD by the classic John Coltrane Quartet (with pianist McCoy Tyner, bassist Jimmy Garrison and drummer Elvin Jones) is highlighted by a 26-minute version of "Mr. P.C." Also included on the album are "The Inch Worm" and the ballad "Every Time We Say Goodbye." Although the sound and passion of the group on this date will not surprise veteran listeners, it is always interesting to hear new variations of songs already definitively recorded in the studios. It's recommended to all true Coltrane fanatics. —*Scott Yanow*

Visit to Scandinavia / Nov. 19, 1962+Nov. 22, 1962 / Jazz Door ✦✦✦✦
John Coltrane's performances were often broadcast on the radio during his European tours, resulting in many live sets being saved for posterity. This double CD has seven selections from a Stockholm, Sweden, concert and two songs that were performed in Copenhagen, Denmark. Coltrane is heard with his classic quartet (pianist McCoy Tyner, bassist Jimmy Garrison and drummer Elvin Jones) playing his repertoire of the period including "Naima," "Impressions," a 21-minute version of "My Favorite Things," "Bye Bye Blackbird" and "I Want to Talk About You." The recording quality is good and, even if few surprises occur, the music is quite passionate and often exciting. —*Scott Yanow*

Ev'rytime We Say Goodbye / Nov. 28, 1962 / Natasha ✦✦✦
Taken from a concert in Graz, Austria, this well-recorded outing by the classic John Coltrane Quartet features fresh versions of "The Inch Worm," "Everytime We Say Goodbye" and "Impressions." Although only containing 38 minutes of music, this CD has more than its share of passion and the quartet really digs into the familiar material. —*Scott Yanow*

John Coltrane Quartet Live at the Half Note / Feb. 23, 1963-May 7, 1965 / Audio Fidelity ✦✦✦
Despite the inaccurate information given on this three-LP box set (which states that all of the music was recorded at the Half Note in 1963; none of it actually was), these rare performances are quite fascinating. "I Want to Talk About You" and "One Up, One Down" actually originated from Birdland on Feb. 23, 1963, and, although the other six performances are from Half Note, they date from March 19 ("Impressions" and "Chim Chim Cheree"), April 12 ("Untitled Original") and May 7 ("Brazilia," "Song of Praise" and "My Favorite Things") of 1965. Coltrane is in particularly fiery form on the later tracks and with four of the eight selections being over 19 minutes long, there is plenty of room for him to stretch out. It's recommended despite the erratic packaging but sure to be hard to find. —*Scott Yanow*

☆ **John Coltrane and Johnny Hartman** / Mar. 7, 1963 / Impulse! ✦✦✦✦✦
John Coltrane's matchup with singer Johnny Hartman, although quite unexpected, works extremely well. Hartman, who had not recorded since 1956, was in prime form on the six ballads and his versions of "Lush Life" and "My One and Only Love" have never been topped. Coltrane's playing throughout the session is beautiful, sympathetic and still explorative; he sticks exclusively to tenor on the date. At

only a half-hour one wishes there were twice as much music but what is here is classic, essential for all jazz collections. —*Scott Yanow*

Dear Old Stockholm / Apr. 29, 1963+May 26, 1965 / Impulse! ✦✦✦✦
This CD contains five excellent performances by the John Coltrane Quartet from two occasions when drummer Roy Haynes filled in for Elvin Jones. A definitive "Dear Old Stockholm" and Coltrane's mournful ballad "After the Rain" are from Apr. 29, 1963, while the beautiful "Dear Lord" and two long and raging performances ("One Down, One Up" and "After the Crescent") date from May 26, 1965. Although Haynes had a different approach on the drums than Jones, he fit in perfectly with the group, stimulating Coltrane to play brilliantly throughout these two sessions. —*Scott Yanow*

Selflessness / Jul. 7, 1963-Oct. 1965/ Impulse! ✦✦✦
In the current CD reissue program run by GRP, this particular LP has been taken apart with its contents put on either *Newport '63* ("I Want to Know About You" and what is arguably the best version of "My Favorite Things") or *The Major Works of John Coltrane* (the atmospheric "Selflessnes," from Oct. 1965). The realignment is logical but if one sees this LP at a reasonable price, it is still well worth acquiring, particularly for the passionate "My Favorite Things." —*Scott Yanow*

★ **Live at Birdland** / Oct. 8, 1963 / Impulse! ✦✦✦✦✦
Arguably John Coltrane's finest all-around album, this LP (which has since been reissued on CD) has brilliant versions of "AfroBlue" and "I Want to Talk About You"; the second half of the latter features Coltrane on unaccompanied tenor tearing into the piece but never losing sight of the fact that it is a beautiful ballad. The remainder of this album ("Alabama," "The Promise" and "Your Lady") is almost at the same high level. It is highly recommended, either on LP or CD. —*Scott Yanow*

Afro Blue Impressions / 1963 / Pablo ✦✦✦✦
Taken from several European concerts (producer Norman Granz is vague about the exact dates but those listed are educated guesses), this double CD finds John Coltrane and his classic quartet playing their standard repertoire of the period. The nine songs include "Chasin' the Trane," "My Favorite Things," "Afro Blue," "I Want to Talk About You," "Impressions" and "Naima." No new revelations occur but this is a strong all-around set of 'Trane near his peak. —*Scott Yanow*

The European Tour / Oct. 22, 1963 / Pablo ✦✦✦✦✦
Norman Granz produced a couple of the John Coltrane Quartet's European tours, releasing some of their live performances years later. Although this LP states that these performances of "The Promise," "I Want to Talk About You," "Naima" and "Mr. P.C." are from Nov. 1962, they are actually taken from their Stockholm concert of Oct. 22, 1963. Coltrane fans will find these new variations to be of great interest (even if they are not the definitive versions of any of these songs) since the solos vary greatly from the orignal recordings. —*Scott Yanow*

Crescent / Apr. 27, 1964+Jun. 1, 1964 / Impulse! ✦✦✦
One of only two studio albums cut by the John Coltrane Quartet during 1964, *Crescent* is most notable for including five Coltrane compositions including the title cut, "Lonnie's Lament" and the swinging "Bessie's Blues." The music is excellent although not as fiery as the quartet's live performances of the period. —*Scott Yanow*

★ **A Love Supreme** / Dec. 9, 1964 / Impulse! ✦✦✦✦
John Coltrane recorded more exciting albums than this one (which has been reissued on CD but GRP), but the highly influential *A Love Supreme* is the project that meant the most to him, his gift to God. In addition to the famous chanting of the title, Coltrane performs a couple of particularly memorable themes (it is surprising that "Resolution" did not become a standard) and the soloing is on a consistently high level. This recording (which also features pianist McCoy Tyner, bassist Jimmy Garrison and drummer Elvin Jones) closed the book on what could be considered 'Trane's most significant period; he would begin to more fully explore atonality with the coming of 1965. —*Scott Yanow*

Feelin' Good / Feb. 18, 1965-Sep. 22, 1965 / Impulse! ✦✦✦
This interesting double LP contains a variety of previously unissued performances by the classic John Coltrane Quartet in 1965, their most controversial (and final) year. Two of these selections ("Living Space" and "Joy") were originally issued posthumously by Alice Coltrane with strings and percussion overdubbed, but here they are heard as they were originally played. In addition to those tracks, "Feelin' Good," "an alternate version of "Nature Boy" and "My Favorite Things" (the latter recorded at the 1965 Newport Jazz Festival), this two-fer includes three unknown Coltrane compositions, only one of which ("Dusk-Dawn") actually has a title. It is most highly recommended to Coltrane collectors. —*Scott Yanow*

John Coltrane Quartet Plays Chim Chim Cheree, Song of Praise, Nature Boy, Brazilia / Feb. 18, 1965 / Impulse! ✦✦✦✦
The year 1965 was one of the turning points in the career of John Coltrane. The great saxophonist, whose playing was always very explorative and searching,

crossed the line into atonality during 1965, playing very free improvisations (after stating quick throwaway themes) that were full of passion and fury. This particular studio album (the CD is a straight reissue of the original LP) has two standards (a stirring "Chim Chim Cheree" and "Nature Boy") along with two recent Coltrane originals ("Brazilia" and "Song of Praise"). Art Davis plays the second bass on "Nature Boy," but otherwise this set (a perfect introduction for listeners to Coltrane's last period) features the classic quartet comprising the leader, pianist McCoy Tyner, bassist Jimmy Garrison and drummer Elvin Jones. —*Scott Yanow*

Transition / May 26, 1965-Jun. 10, 1965 / Impulse! ✦✦✦✦
The title of this CD (a straight reissue of the LP) fits perfectly for Coltrane was certainly at an important transitional point in his career at the time. Although he was still utilizing the same Quartet that he had had for over three years (pianist McCoy Tyner, bassist Jimmy Garrison and drummer Elvin Jones) and his music had always been explorative, now he was taking his solos one step beyond into passionate atonality, usually over simple but explosive vamps. Other than the tender ballad "Welcome," most of this set is uncompromisingly intense; in fact, the closing 9-minute "Vigil" is a fiery tenor-drums duet. The 21-minute "Suite," even with sections titled "Prayer and Meditiation: Day" and "Affirmation," is not overly peaceful. It must have seemed clear, even at this early point, that McCoy Tyner and perhaps Elvin Jones would not be with the band much longer. —*Scott Yanow*

Kulu Se Mama / Jun. 16, 1965-Oct. 14, 1965 / Impulse! ✦✦
This LP, whose contents have been reissued in different sets on CD, features John Coltrane in four different settings. "Vigil" and the spiritual ballad "Welcome" showcase tenor saxophonist Coltrane with his classic quartet (pianist McCoy Tyner, bassist Jimmy Garrison and drummer Elvin Jones) in June 1965. The main piece, "Kulu Se Mama," has been reissued on the two-CD set *The Major Works of John Coltrane*. Dating from October 14, 1965, it adds tenor saxophonist Pharoah Sanders, Donald Garrett on bass clarinet and second bass, second drummer Frank Butler and percussionist-vocalist Juno Lewis to the quartet and is a bit of an oddity. Lewis' chanting and colorful percussion make this a unique if not essential entry in Coltrane's discography. —*Scott Yanow*

Ascension / Jun. 28, 1965 / Impulse! ✦✦✦✦
This historic outing can be looked at as John Coltrane's answer to Ornette Coleman's *Free Jazz* of four years earlier. Coltrane, who progressed steadily throughout 1965 until he was largely specializing in atonality, is heard leading a large ensemble through a 40-minute piece that, except for some brief passages, is freely improvised. While the rhythm section (pianist McCoy Tyner, both Jimmy Garrison and Art Davis on basses and drummer Elvin Jones) kept the music moving, seven adventurous horn players performed emotional and sometimes violent solos and fiery ensembles. With Coltrane, Archie Shepp and Pharoah Sanders on tenors, John Tchicai and Marion Brown on altos and trumpeters Freddie Hubbard and Dewey Johnson, the results are very ferocious and a bit scary. This performance (plus a rarer alternate take and some other long pieces) has been reissued on the two-CD set *The Major Works of John Coltrane*. —*Scott Yanow*

☆ **The Major Works of John Coltrane** / Jun. 28, 1965-Oct. 14, 1965 / Impulse! ✦✦✦✦✦
Some of John Coltrane's more adventurous and eccentric works from 1965 have been reissued on this important two-CD set. The two versions of the 38-40 minute "Ascension" (one of which was formerly quite rare) dominate the program. The innovative tenor saxophonist, other than on a few short transitions, allowed his expanded group to play very freely on the rather violent work. Such musicians as tenors Pharoah Sanders and Archie Shepp, altoists John Tchicai and Marion Brown, trumpeters Freddie Hubbard and Dewey Johnson, pianist McCoy Tyner, bassists Jimmy Garrison and Art Davis and drummer Elvin Jones were turned loose for solos and furious ensembles. Also on the stimulating two-fer are "Om," "Kulu Se Mama" and "Selflessness." Among the musicians added to Coltrane's classic quartet for these pieces are tenor saxophonist Pharoah Sanders, Donald Garrett on bass clarinet and second bass, flutist Joe Brazil (on "Om") and the oddly memorable vocalizing and percussion of Juno Lewis (on "Kulu Se Mama"). Far from Coltrane's most accessible recordings, the groundbreaking and influential explorations are all worthy of several listens by openminded listeners. —*Scott Yanow*

New Thing at Newport / Jul. 2, 1965 / Impulse! ✦✦✦✦
This CD reissue (recorded at the 1965 Newport Jazz Festival) is an expanded version of the original LP. The first two selections are the main reason to acquire the set for they find the classic John Coltrane Quartet (with pianist McCoy Tyner, bassist Jimmy Garrison and drummer Elvin Jones) breaking new ground with the explosive "One Down, One Up" and updating past triumphs with "My Favorite Things." The second half of the program features tenorman Archie Shepp's fiery quartet (with vibraphonist Bobby Hutcherson, bassist Barre Phillips and drummer Joe Chambers). Shepp's recitation on "Skag" is a bit hard to take but his passionate

playing on the other numbers (particularly "Gingerbread, Gingerbread Boy") is well worth hearing. —Scott Yanow

Sun Ship / Aug. 26, 1965 / Impulse! ✦✦✦✦
Other than *First Meditations*, which was not released at the time, *Sun Ship* (reissued on CD by Impulse) was the final studio album by John Coltrane's classic quartet (with pianist McCoy Tyner, bassist Jimmy Garrison and drummer Elvin Jones) before Pharoah Sanders joined the band on second tenor. At this point in time, Coltrane was using very short repetitive themes as jumping off points for explosive improvisations, often centered around one chord and a very specific spiritual mood. Tyner sounds a bit conservative in comparison, but Jones keeps up with 'Trane's fire (especially on "Amen"). Even in the most intense sections (and much of this music is atonal), there is a logic and thoughtfulness about Coltrane's playing. —Scott Yanow

First Meditations / Sep. 2, 1965 / Impulse ✦✦✦✦
Not released initially until 1977, the music on this 1992 CD was the last recording made by the classic John Coltrane Quartet; other slightly later records found the group augmented by additional musicians. Four of the five movements on this release (which are augmented by a lengthier second version of "Joy") would become part of the better-known *Meditations* album (along with another movement) two months later when tenor saxophonist Pharoah Sanders and drummer Rashied Ali temporarily made the group a sextet. Coltrane (sticking here exclusively to tenor) plays passionately, alternating ferocious explorations with more lyrical sections. —Scott Yanow

Live in Seattle / Sep. 30, 1965 / Impulse ✦✦✦✦
This double CD features John Coltrane at a concert in Sept. 1965 with his expanded sextet (which included pianist McCoy Tyner, bassist Jimmy Garrison, drummer Elvin Jones, Pharoah Sanders on tenor and Donald Garrett doubling on bass clarinet and bass). Coltrane experts know that 1965 was the year that his music became quite atonal and, with the addition of Sanders, often very violent. This music, therefore, is not for fans of Coltrane's earlier sheets of sound period or for those who prefer jazz as melodic background music. The program from the original double LP (the nearly free "Cosmos," an intense workout on "Out of This World," a bass feature and the truly wild "Evolution") is augmented by previously unissued versions of "Body and Soul" and a 34-minute "Afro Blue" that is incomplete because the tape ran out. Throughout much of this set Coltrane plays some miraculous solos, Sanders consistently turns on the heat, Garrett makes the passionate ensembles a bit overcrowded, Tyner is barely audible, Garrison drones in the background and Jones struggles to make sense of it all. This is innovative and difficult music that makes today's Young Lions (not to mention the pop saxophonists) sound very old-fashioned in comparison. —Scott Yanow

Om / Oct. 1, 1965 / Impulse! ✦✦✦
The music on this LP (which totals less than 29 minutes) was performed continuously, making its reissue as part of the two-CD set *The Major Works of John Coltrane* the best way to acquire the performance. A spiritual and at times eccentric work, *Om* finds tenor saxophonist John Coltrane, pianist McCoy Tyner, bassist Jimmy Garrison and drummer Elvin Jones joined by second tenor Pharoah Sanders, Donald Garrett on bass clarinet and bass, and flutist Joe Brazil. The recitation, Brazil's flute and the intense playing makes this a unique if not essential work; worth hearing by Coltrane collectors but not the first Trane recording to recommend. —Scott Yanow

Meditations / Nov. 23, 1965 / Impulse! ✦✦✦✦
This CD reissues what was arguably the finest of the John Coltrane-Pharoah Sanders collaborations. On five diverse but almost consistently intense movements ("The Father and the Son and the Holy Ghost," "Compassion," "Love," "Consequences" and "Serenity"), the two tenor saxophonists, pianist McCoy Tyner, bassist Jimmy Garrison and both Elvin Jones and Rashied Ali on drums create some powerful, dense and emotional music. Unlike some of the live jams of 1966, the passionate performances never ramble on too long and the screams and screeches fit logically into the spiritual themes. This would be the last recording of Coltrane with Tyner and Jones. —Scott Yanow

Live in Antibes (1965) / 1965 / France's Concert ✦✦✦✦
Vital, transitional John Coltrane with the quartet near its end; this 1965 Antibes concert may have featured familiar material ("Naima," "My Favorite Things," "Afro Blue" and "Impressions" among the five selections), but that was the only thing that linked it with the ensemble's past offerings. Coltrane's tenor was frenetic, as he turned song structure inside out, honked, soared and explored, seeking fresh directions and alternative statements within each blistering solo. Likewise, this version of "My Favorite Things" had an edgy, unfulfilled quality, while even "Naima" was more inquisitive than satisfying. While it's still incredible, pivotal music, there was also the realization that change was near and inevitable. —Ron Wynn

Live at the Village Vanguard Again! / May 28, 1966 / Impulse! ✦✦✦
This LP was always a bit of a disappointment. John Coltrane plays passionately on "My Favorite Things" and with great beauty on "Naima," but Pharoah Sanders' ferocious screeching on the latter piece largely ruins the almost-sacred ballad. Pianist Alice Coltrane, bassist Jimmy Garrison and drummer Rashied Ali mostly vamp behind the saxophonists. This album is worth getting for Coltrane's passionate but coherent playing, but one wishes that Sanders (who comes across as a much more limited player) had sat the night out. —Scott Yanow

Live in Japan / Jul. 11, 1966–Jul. 22, 1966 / Impulse! ✦✦✦
This very interesting four-CD set contains two sets of music by the 1966 John Coltrane Quintet, recorded in Tokyo, Japan. Most of the music had not been released in the US until 1991. Coltrane (heard on tenor, soprano and alto) engages in some ferocious interplay with Pharoah Sanders (on tenor, alto and bass clarinet), pianist Alice Coltrane, bassist Jimmy Garrison and drummer Rashied Ali; fans of Trane's earlier records may not like these atonal flights. However, listeners who enjoy avant-garde jazz will find many stirring moments among the very lengthy performances. The shortest piece is the 25-minute version of "Peace on Earth" and "My Favorite Things" goes on for over 57 minutes. —Scott Yanow

Stellar Regions / Feb. 15, 1967 / Impulse! ✦✦✦✦
This is a major set, "new" music from John Coltrane that was recorded February 15, 1967 (five months before his death), but not released for the first time until 1995. One of several "lost" sessions that were stored by Alice Coltrane for decades, only one selection ("Offering," which was on *Expression*) among the eight numbers and three alternates was ever out before. The music, although well worth releasing, offers no real hints as to what Coltrane might have been playing had he lived into the 1970s. The performances by the quartet (with pianist Alice Coltrane, bassist Jimmy Garrison and drummer Rashied Ali) are briefer (2:48-8:54) than Coltrane's recordings of the previous year, but that might have been due to the fact that this music was played in the studio (as opposed to the marathon live blowouts with Pharoah Sanders) or to Coltrane's worsening health. Actually 'Trane (who sticks here exclusively to tenor) is as powerful as usual, showing no compromise in his intense flights and indulging in sound explorations that are as free (but with purpose) as any he had ever done. Coltrane's true fans will want to go out of their way to acquire this intriguing CD. —Scott Yanow

Expression / Feb. 15, 1967-Mar. 7, 1967 / Impulse! ✦✦✦✦
This CD reissue has John Coltrane's final recordings, some of which were recorded just four months before his death. Three selections ("Ogunde," "Expression" and "Offering") feature Trane on tenor playing quite passionately while accompanied by pianist Alice Coltrane, bassist Jimmy Garrison and drummer Rashied Ali. The overlong 16-minute "To Be" is a true oddity, with Coltrane's flute "battling" Pharoah Sanders' flute and piccolo, while "Number One" is a Coltrane-Ali tenor-drums duet from the session that resulted in *Interstellar Space*. This stimulating and largely atonal music does not hint at Trane's imminent demise or give any real clues as to what he might have been playing in future years had he lived for several more years. —Scott Yanow

Interstellar Space / Feb. 22, 1967 / Impulse! ✦✦✦✦
Not released for the first time until 1974 but now available in expanded form as a CD, this set of duets by tenor saxophonist John Coltrane and drummer Rashied Ali are full of fire, emotion and constant abstract invention. The original four pieces ("Mars," "Venus," "Jupiter" and "Saturn") are joined by "Leo" and "Jupiter Variation." Coltrane alternates quiet moments with sections of great intensity, showing off his phenomenal technique and ability to improvise without the need for chordal instruments. Rousing if somewhat inaccessible music. —Scott Yanow

The Bethlehem Years / Oct. 1957-Dec. 1957 / Evidence ✦✦✦✦
The title of this double-CD is rather humorous because John Coltrane only recorded two albums for Bethlehem and both as a sideman within a two-month period. Coltrane was part of *The Winner's Circle* (an all-star octet) and also recorded with drummer Art Blakey in a big band and a quintet. Among the other key sidemen were trumpeter Donald Byrd, tenorman Al Cohn, trombonist Jimmy Cleveland and pianist Walter Bishop, Jr. The double CD greatly expands upon the original sessions, adding 15 alternate takes to the 12 songs. Obviously this two-fer is not for general collectors but John Coltrane completists will have to get it. —Scott Yanow

Ravi Coltrane

b. Aug. 6, 1965, Huntington, NY
Soprano Saxophone, Tenor Saxophone / Post-Bop
The son of John and Alice Coltrane, Ravi was not even two years old when his father died. He was in his early 20s when he seriously started playing jazz and, although his father's music was a slight influence, Ravi Coltrane actually sounds closer to Branford Marsalis and Joe Henderson. He picked up valuable experience

playing with Elvin Jones' band during 1991-93 and has since performed as a sideman with many top musicians including Geri Allen, Kenny Barron and Cindy Blackman. —*Scott Yanow*

Ken Colyer (Kenneth Colyer)

b. Apr. 18, 1928, Great Yarmouth, Norfolk, England, **d.** Mar. 8, 1988, France
Cornet / New Orleans Jazz, Skiffle

As one of England's leading trad jazz exponents, Ken Colyer's influence would have been confined to his own country were it not for a spinoff that would inadvertently lead to great changes in the music world at large. Self-taught on trumpet and guitar, Colyer was a founding member of the Crane River Jazz Band (1949-53), a New Orleans-styled band that he left in late 1951 in order to join the Merchant Marines with the intention of shipping out to New Orleans itself and jamming with local legends. Upon his return to England in March 1953, Colyer joined a group founded by Monty Sunshine and Chris Barber that soon became Ken Colyer's Jazzmen. As in the Crane River group, Colyer's shows included a "band within a band" segment that purported to educate audiences about the roots of jazz, playing a guitar-based, highly rhythmic mutation of American folk music that became known as skiffle. When Colyer left the Jazzmen in 1954, the group coalesced around Barber and its banjo player, Lonnie Donegan, who went on to have a hit skiffle record "Rock Island Line" that caught the imagination of a Liverpool youngster named John Lennon . . . and you know the rest of that story. Beginning in 1954, Colyer split his time between leading trad jazz groups as a trumpeter and skiffle groups as a guitarist, recording frequently for English Decca. Colyer's melodic Bunk Johnson-influenced lead trumpet gave his jazz bands a distinctive flavor of their own while his skiffle groups had a "blacker" sound than those of most English skifflers, grounded in the Leadbelly 78s that Colyer brought back from New York when he was 19. Colyer's jazz band of the mid-'50s rivaled Barber's group as the leading British trad band of the day, featuring such sidemen as Acker Bilk, Ian Wheeler and Mac Duncan. Colyer would lead bands in the '60s and '70s with time out for bouts with illness, running his own KC record label, appearing at his own club Studio 11, and returning in the early '80s at the helm of the All-Star Jazzmen. —*Richard S. Ginell*

The Complete 1953 Recordings / Feb. 23, 1953-Feb. 24, 1953 / 504 Records ◆◆
British cornetist Ken Colyer spent parts of 1952-53 in New Orleans, and the opportunity to play with some black jazz pioneers inspired him for years to come. This CD has all of the recordings that took place during a two-day period when Colyer teamed up with trombonist Harrison Brazlee, clarinetist Emile Barnes, banjoist Bill Huntington, either Albert Glenny (who had been a member of Buddy Bolden's band) or George Fortier on bass, and drummer Albert Jiles. Unfortunately, the music (14 songs plus ten alternate takes) was primitively recorded, and the 44-year-old tape was not in the best of shape when it was transferred to this CD. The sincerity of the music on such tunes as "New Orleans Hop Scop Blues," "Climax Rag," "Gravier Street Blues" and "That's a Plenty" comes through, but plenty of erratic moments, plus the frequently weak technical quality, makes this release of primarily historic interest. —*Scott Yanow*

In the Beginning / Nov. 1953-Sep. 1954 / Lake ◆◆◆◆
This excellent CD features trumpeter Ken Colyer at the beginning of his career. Eight songs feature him with a potentially significant, if short-lived, group that includes a couple of future trad stars: trombonist Chris Barber and clarinetist Monty Sunshine. Their collaborations are the main reason for New Orleans jazz fans to acquire this release. The second half of the set has Colyer's 1954 band, but it finds clarinetist Acker Bilk (who would be a big name in the 1960s) sounding quite erratic. Despite that fault, the music, which often emphasizes ensembles in the tradition of George Lewis, is enjoyable and full of spirit. —*Scott Yanow*

The Decca Skiffle Sessions (1954-1957) / Jun. 1954-Nov. 1957 / Lake ◆◆◆◆
This music from Ken Colyer is much different from what one would expect. Rather than playing New Orleans-style cornet, Colyer is heard as a folk singer and guitarist, reviving older songs such as "Casey Jones," "Go Down, Old Hannah," "Stack-O-Lee Blues" and "This Train." Joined by various rhythm sections (including guitarist Alexis Korner), Colyer performs what would be called "skiffle," a mixture of blues, jug band tunes, country, gospel and folk music, predating the folk revival by over five years. The music is enjoyable, if not as significant as Colyer's jazz records. —*Scott Yanow*

● **The Decca Years 1955-1959** / Apr. 19, 1955-May 1958 / Lake ◆◆◆◆◆
New Orleans-styled trumpeter Ken Colyer is heard at the peak of his powers throughout this highly recommended CD reissue. During this period of time, his sextet included trombonist Mac Duncan, clarinetist Ian Wheeler, banjoist Johnny Bastable, either Dick Smith or Ron Ward on bass and Stan Grieg or Colin Bowden on drums; pianist Ray Foxley joined the group in 1958. The 14 selections on the set all feature strong musicianship, the influence of the George Lewis and Kid Ory bands, plenty of ensembles and colorful solos. In addition to New Orleans stan-

dards, a special treat are several versions of rags including "Heliotrope Bouquet," "The Entertainer" and "Sensation." One of the best Ken Colyer collections currently available. —*Scott Yanow*

Serenading Auntie / Jun. 14, 1955-Aug. 4, 1960 / Upbeat ◆◆◆◆
Trumpeter Ken Colyer's influential New Orleans-style bands of the 1950s are featured on this British CD. The 21 performances are taken from five live performances taped for the BBC. While the first six numbers (from 1960) match Colyer with trombonist Graham Stewart and clarinetist Sammy Rimington, the other numbers feature trombonist Mac Duncan and clarinetist Ian Wheeler in Colyer's sextet/septet. The recording quality varies from date to date, as do the musicians' intonations (they are usually in tune). The repertoire is highlighted by jazz versions of some ragtime tunes (including "Thriller Rag," "Hilarity Rag" and "Heliotrope Bouquet"), as well as obscurities from the 1920s and a few standards. Trad fans will enjoy this formerly rare music. —*Scott Yanow*

● **When I Leave the World Behind** / Mar. 1963 / Lake ◆◆◆◆
CDs featuring trad jazz trumpeter Ken Colyer are not that common, so the issue of this previously unreleased concert in 1996 was a welcome event. Colyer is heard at the head of a 1963 sextet also including clarinetist Sammy Rimington, trombonist Geoff Cole, banjoist Johnny Bastable, bassist Ron Ward and drummer Pete Ridge. The trumpeter's clipped phrases were quite distinctive (a little like Kid Thomas Valentine), while Rimington's clarinet solos are strongly reminiscent of George Lewis. On tunes such as "Dr. Jazz," "Down Home Rag," "After You've Gone," and J.C. Higginbotham's "Give Me Your Telephone Number," the emphasis is on heated ensembles and melodic solos. Highly recommended to New Orleans jazz fans. —*Scott Yanow*

● **Painting the Clouds with Sunshine** / Jan. 1972 / Black Lion ◆◆◆◆

Colyer in Stockholm / Jun. 28, 1986 / Jazz Crusade ◆◆◆
This was Ken Colyer's final recording. By 1986 he no longer had his own regular group and his health was gradually declining (he would pass away less than two years later) but, when he was invited to play a jazz festival in Stockholm, the English trad trumpeter got along well musically and personally with the members of the Classic Jazz Band. A few months later he returned to Stockholm and privately taped one of their joint concerts. The balance of the instruments is a bit off with the horns generally low in the mix but the music is quite listenable. Ken Colyer's sparse lead (mostly short notes) leaves a lot of space in the ensembles and, although clarinetist Goran Erikson and trombonist Jens Lindgren are fine, the most impressive voice is actually drummer Cacka Ekhe, whose colorful percussive sounds recall Baby Dodds. The pianoless sextet performs a variety of old standards and even if the music is not flawless and is occasionally rather aimless, New Orleans jazz fans should appreciate this historically significant music. —*Scott Yanow*

Ken Colyer Trust New Orleans Band / Mar. 26, 1996 / Jazz Crusade ◆◆◆◆
Although cornetist Ken Colyer passed away in 1988, his music has not been forgotten, particularly in his native England, as shown on this CD. Partly a reunion of Colyer alumni, partly a tribute to his Original Crane River Jazz Band, the music would have pleased the cornetist. The emphasis on this New Orleans jazz set is on ensembles; there are some fine short solos, and the musicianship of this New Orleans-style group is excellent. The front line (trumpeters Norman Thatcher and Sonny Morris, clarinetist Norman Field and trombonist Dave Vickers) is both exciting and coherent, while the four-piece rhythm section keeps the momentum flowing. Highlights include "Down in Jungle Town," "Wolverine Blues," "Walk Through the Streets of the City," and "Sister Kate." —*Scott Yanow*

Alix Combelle

b. Jun. 15, 1912, Paris, France, **d.** Mar. 2, 1978, Mantes, France
Tenor Saxophone, Clarinet / Swing

Alix Combelle was France's best-known tenor saxophonist of the 1930s and '40s, an excellent player influenced by Coleman Hawkins but able to hold his own on a few famous performances with Hawkins, Benny Carter and Django Reinhardt. He started on drums, switching permanently to tenor (and occasional clarinet) in 1932. Combelle played with Gregor et ses Gregoriens (1932-33), Arthur Briggs, Michel Warlop, and Ray Ventura, and often led his own groups. He visited the US twice in the 1930s and was offered a job with Tommy Dorsey, but preferred to stay in Paris. Somehow, during the World War II occupation of France by the Nazis, Combelle was able to continue recording swinging jazz. He drifted into obscurity by the late 1940s, although getting the opportunity to play with such visiting Americans as Buck Clayton, Jonah Jones and expatriate Bill Coleman, and made his last full record as a leader in 1960. Fortunately, three CDs have been released by Classics that contain all of Alix Combelle's sessions as a leader during 1935-43 with the whos-who of French jazz. —*Scott Yanow*

● **1935-1940** / Sep. 1, 1935-Oct. 21, 1940 / Classics ◆◆◆◆

1940-41 / Oct. 21, 1940-Mar. 12, 1941 / Classics ✦✦✦✦
1942-1943 / Jun. 1942-Sep. 9, 1943 / Classics ✦✦✦

Eddie Condon (Albert Edwin Condon)

b. Nov. 16, 1905, Goodland, IN, **d.** Aug. 4, 1973, New York, NY
Guitar, Leader / Dixieland

A major propagandist for freewheeling Chicago jazz, an underrated rhythm guitarist and a talented wisecracker, Eddie Condon's main importance to jazz was not so much through his own playing as in his ability to gather together large groups of all-stars and produce exciting, spontaneous and very coherent music.

Condon started out playing banjo with Hollis Peavey's Jazz Bandits when he was 17, and worked with members of the famed Austin High School Gang in the 1920s. In 1927 he co-led (with Red McKenzie) the McKenzie-Condon Chicagoans on a record date that helped define Chicago jazz (and featured Jimmy McPartland, Jimmy Teschemacher, Joe Sullivan and Gene Krupa). After organizing some other record sessions, Condon switched to guitar, moved to New York in 1929, worked with Red Nichols' Five Pennies and Red McKenzie's Blue Blowers, and recorded in several settings including with Louis Armstrong (1929) and the Rhythm Makers (1932). During 1936-37 he co-led a band with Joe Marsala.

Although Condon had to an extent laid low since the beginning of the Depression, in 1938 with the opportunity to lead some sessions for the new Commodore label, he became a major name. Playing nightly at Nick's (1937-44), Condon utilized top musicians in racially mixed groups. He started a long series of exciting recordings (which really continued on several labels up until his death) and his Town Hall concerts of 1944-45 (which were broadcast weekly on the radio) were consistently brilliant and gave him an opportunity to show his verbal acid wit; the GHB label has been at last reissuing them complete and in chronological order. Condon opened his own club in 1945, recorded for Columbia in the 1950s (all of those records have been made available by Mosaic on a limited-edition box set) and wrote three colorful books including his 1948 memoirs *We Called It Music*. A partial list of the classic musicians who performed and recorded often with Condon include trumpeters/cornetists Wild Bill Davison, Max Kaminsky, Billy Butterfield, Bobby Hackett, Rex Stewart and Hot Lips Page; trombonists Jack Teagarden, Lou McGarity, Cutty Cutshall, George Brunis and Vic Dickenson; clarinetists Pee Wee Russell, Edmond Hall, Joe Marsala, Peanuts Hucko and Bob Wilbur; Bud Freeman on tenor; baritonist Ernie Caceres, pianists Gene Schroeder, Joe Sullivan, Jess Stacy and Ralph Sutton; drummers George Wettling, Dave Tough, and Gene Krupa; a string of bassists and singer Lee Wiley. Many Eddie Condon records are currently available and no jazz collection is complete without at least a healthy sampling. —*Scott Yanow*

Eddie Condon's World of Jazz / Sep. 28, 1927-Jun. 24, 1954 / Columbia ✦✦✦
This double LP is not strictly an Eddie Condon record (although the rhythm guitarist and bandleader is on a few of the recordings) but a collection of performances that he enjoyed by some of his friends. The 27 recordings feature a who's who of classic jazz, programmed in alphabetical order from Red Allen to Lee Wiley. Although most of the recordings have since been reissued in more complete fashion on CD, this two-fer is a good introduction to the freewheeling musical personalities that inhabited Condon's world. —*Scott Yanow*

The Commodore Years / Jan. 17, 1938-Nov. 30, 1938 / Atlantic ✦✦✦✦✦
The contents of this two-LP set have fortunately been reissued in various forms on CD, for the music is quite classic. The first album contains three sessions that define the Eddie Condon "Nicksieland" sound and set the standard for Dixieland. Such distinctive players as cornetist Bobby Hackett, trombonists Jack Teagarden and George Brunis, clarinetist Pee Wee Russell, tenorman Bud Freeman and pianists Jess Stacy and Joe Bushkin are in consistently inspired form. Among the many high points of this album are Russell's solo on "Love Is Just Around the Corner," Hackett's lyrical lead on "Embraceable You" (a later favorite of Miles Davis), Teagarden's melody statement on "Diane," and versions of "California Here I Come" and "Sunday" that are filled with joyous ensembles and the enthusiastic drumming of Lionel Hampton. The second set, a marvelous trio outing by Bud Freeman, Jess Stacy and drummer George Wettling, is no less exciting. It's essential music in one form or another. —*Scott Yanow*

Jammin' at Commodore / Jan. 17, 1938-Nov. 30, 1938 / Commodore ✦✦✦✦
Featured on these 1938-44 recordings is The Windy City Seven date that launched the Commodore label, plus a Bud Freeman-led combo. Musicians include Pee Wee Russell, Bobby Hackett, George Brunis, Dave Tough, Jess Stacy, and others. —*Bruce Raeburn*

Dixieland All Stars / Aug. 11, 1939-Mar. 27, 1946 / GRP/Decca ✦✦✦✦✦
Some but not all of Eddie Condon's studio recordings for Decca are included on this single CD. Since five of the 20 selections are actually previously unissued alternate takes and several songs are bypassed altogether, this release will proba-

bly drive some collectors mad, but the music is consistently enjoyable. The rhythm guitarist heads an impresssive outfit (with trumpeter Max Kaminsky, valve trombonist Brad Gowans, clarinetist Pee Wee Russell, Bud Freeman on tenor and pianist Joe Sullivan) on four titles from 1939 along with a variety of groups from 1944-46 that feature other top stylists including trumpeters Billy Butterfield, Bobby Hackett, Yank Lawson, Max Kaminsky and Wild Bill Davison; trombonists Jack Teagarden and Lou McGarity; baritonist Ernie Caceres; clarinetists Edmond Hall, Tony Parenti and Joe Dixon; the latter bands perform a variety of standards including eight George Gershwin songs. Dixieland and small-group swing fans will enjoy this set, which serves as a strong example of Eddie Condon's music, at least until a more complete reissue of the valuable recordings takes place. —*Scott Yanow*

Gershwin Program / Mar. 1941-Mar. 16, 1951 / Decca ✦✦✦
Some of the music on this long out-of-print LP has been reissued on CD but not all of it has reappeared yet. There is a song apiece featuring pianists Joe Sullivan and Jess Stacy along with two numbers ("Embraceable You" and "But Not for Me") from a group headed by cornetist Bobby Hackett, but the bulk of the performances of George Gershwin compositions are by Eddie Condon's all-star groups of 1944-45. Trombonist/vocalist Jack Teagarden is showcased on "Somebody Loves Me" and there are two vocals by Lee Wiley; other stars include trumpeters Billy Butterfield, Max Kaminsky and Yank Lawson; trombonist Lou McGarity; clarinetists Pee Wee Russell, Joe Dixon and Edmond Hall; and the vastly underrated baritonist Ernie Caceres. This is classic music that deserves to be reissued on CD complete and in chronological order. —*Scott Yanow*

Live at Town Hall (1944) / Mar. 11, 1944 / Jass ✦✦✦✦✦
This consistently exciting CD predates all of the Eddie Condon Town Hall concerts released by Jazzology by a couple of months. Rhythm guitarist Condon, as usual, put together a spontaneous but logical show featuring quite a few top Dixieland all-stars. Trumpeter/vocalist Hot Lips Page takes honors with his "Uncle Sam Blues," but there are also two well-received features apiece for pianists Cliff Jackson and Joe Bushkin and plenty of solo space for trumpeters Billy Butterfield and Max Kaminsky, cornetist Bobby Hackett (whose chops are just a little off), trombonist Miff Mole and clarinetists Edmond Hall and Pee Wee Russell; bassists Bob Casey and Pops Foster and drummers Kansas Fields and George Wettling also make notable contributions. With Condon as the wisecracking M.C. and such highlights as "Muskrat Ramble," "Ja Da" and the lengthy "Impromptu Ensemble," this CD is highly recommended to Eddie Condon and Dixieland fans. —*Scott Yanow*

Jam Sessions (1944) / Mar. 30, 1944+Dec. 14, 1944 / Jazzology ✦✦✦
A pair of sessions cut as radio transcriptions during 1944 are released in full on this two-LP set. Unfortunately the programming does not always make sense with alternate takes and false starts often separated from the "real" versions, but in general the performances are quite enjoyable, as one would expect from the two all-star groups. The players perform up-to-par and the lineup tells the story: trumpeters Max Kaminsky, Billy Butterfield and Bobby Hackett; trombonists Jack Teagarden and Wilbur DeParis; clarinetist Pee Wee Russell; baritonist Ernie Caceres; pianists Joe Bushkin and Gene Schroeder; bassists Bob Casey and Bob Haggart; drummer George Wettling; and vocalists Red McKenzie, Lee Wiley and Teagarden. —*Scott Yanow*

Town Hall Concerts, Vol. 1 / May 20, 1944-Jun. 10, 1944 / Jazzology ✦✦✦✦✦
Eddie Condon's *Town Hall Concerts* were historic in several ways. These weekly half-hour radio shows were very uncommercial (in fact, they could not attract a sponsor), featured interracial bands and gave Condon an opportunity to put together well-paced programs. He would gather together a core band of Condonites who would have ensemble jams and individual features, and there were always a couple of numbers set aside for guest artists who would also join in on the show's concluding jam (titled "Impromptu Ensemble") with the regulars. Plus Condon, despite making a few too many jokes at the expense of Pee Wee Russell, proved to be a perfect host. After decades of only being available as incomplete excerpts, these programs have finally been issued complete and in chronological order on a series of two-CD sets by George Buck of Jazzology. The first volume, which has four complete shows, features such classic players as trumpeters Billy Butterfield, Bobby Hackett, Max Kaminsky, Hot Lips Page and Rex Stewart; clarinetists Pee Wee Russell and Edmond Hall; trombonists Bill Harris, Miff Mole and Benny Morton; the greatly underrated baritonist Ernie Caceres; and pianists James P. Johnson and Gene Schroeder. Although the recording quality of the very first show is subpar (the only one in the series that is less than flawless technically), all of the volumes in this wonderful series (which find the participants at the peak of their powers) are highly recommended. —*Scott Yanow*

Definitive, Vol. 1 / Jun. 8, 1944-Oct. 24, 1944 / Stash ✦✦✦✦
The year 1944 was busy for Eddie Condon with the start of his legendary Town Hall concerts and the growing popularity of Chicago jazz. Among his projects at

that time were recording selections for radio transcriptions, music made specifically to be played over the air (as opposed to being sold to the general public). Two sessions (complete with alternate takes and breakdowns) are released on this CD and it finds the all-stars in spirited form. As many as 11 musicians play together at a time and Condon drew his talent from this lineup: cornetist Bobby Hackett and Muggsy Spanier; trumpeters Billy Butterfield, Max Kaminsky, and Hot Lips Page; trombonists Benny Morton and Lou McGarity; clarinetists Pee Wee Russell and Edmond Hall; Ernie Caceres on baritone or clarinet; pianists Gene Schroeder and Jess Stacy; bassist Bob Haggart; drummers George Wettling and Joe Grauso and vocals from Lee Wiley, Liza Morrow and Hot Lips Page. This hot music is easily recommended to Dixieland and small-group swing fans. —*Scott Yanow*

● **Town Hall Concerts, Vol. 2** / Jun. 17, 1944-Jul. 8, 1944 / Jazzology ✦✦✦✦
This two-CD set has four complete radio shows featuring Eddie Condon's all-star groups during their legendary series of Town Hall concerts. Despite having large ensembles of classic players, Condon was able to feature virtually everyone on every show, still leaving room for ensemble pieces and interplay between the unique musicians. In addition, the verbal commentary of Condon and announcer Fred Robbins is informative and witty (even if they picked on Pee Wee Russell a bit too much). Among the musicians heard on the well-recorded set (which like the other volumes in this extensive series is highly recommended to fans of Chicago jazz) include trumpeters Bobby Hackett, Hot Lips Page, Max Kaminsky, Jonah Jones and Billy Butterfield; trombonists Bill Harris and Benny Morton; clarinetists Pee Wee Russell, Joe Marsala and Edmond Hall; baritonist Ernie Caceres and pianists James P. Johnson, Willie "The Lion" Smith and Gene Schroeder. —*Scott Yanow*

Town Hall Concerts, Vol. 3 / Jul. 15, 1944-Aug. 5, 1944 / Jazzology ✦✦✦✦
The third volume in this very valuable series of two-CD sets contains four half-hour weekly radio shows featuring Eddie Condon's all-star ensembles at Town Hall concerts. Condon (who supplies verbal commentary along with announcer Fred Robbins) programmed each show quite skillfully, featuring the large groups of all-stars in logical fashion. This set (which is highly recommended along with the other volumes in the series to followers of traditional jazz) features quite a roster: trumpeters Bobby Hackett, Jonah Jones, Max Kaminsky and Sterling Bose; trombonist Benny Morton; baritonist Ernie Caceres (who is really in peak form throughout the Condon programs); clarinetists Edmond Hall and Pee Wee Russell; guitarists Carl Kress and Tony Mottola; pianist Harry "The Hipster" Gibson (taking a couple of rare solos), Willie "The Lion" Smith, Jess Stacy and Gene Schroeder; bassist Bob Haggart; drummers Gene Krupa, Joe Grauso and George Wettling and singer Lee Wiley. —*Scott Yanow*

Town Hall Concerts, Vol. 4 / Aug. 12, 1944-Sep. 2, 1944 / Jazzology ✦✦✦✦
Although they were never able to get a paying sponsor, the *Eddie Condon Town Hall Concerts* (a weekly half-hour radio show) was quite popular at the time and became legendary. For *Volume 4* of this colorful series of well-recorded two-CD sets (which is highly recommended to all followers of Chicago jazz), there are four complete programs featuring a remarkable ensemble of top musicians (virtually all of whom are showcased individually and collectively in logical fashion): trumpeters Billy Butterfield, Bobby Hackett, Jonah Jones, Max Kaminsky and Muggsy Spanier; trombonists Bill Harris, Miff Mole and Benny Morton; baritonist Ernie Caceres; clarinetists Edmond Hall, Joe Marsala and Pee Wee Russell and pianists James P. Johnson, Willie "The Lion Smith, and Gene Schroeder, in addition to guest drummer Gene Krupa and singer Lee Wiley. —*Scott Yanow*

Town Hall Concerts, Vol. 5 / Sep. 9, 1944-Sep. 30, 1944 / Jazzology ✦✦✦✦
This two-CD set, as is true of the other very valuable releases in the Eddie Condon Town Hall series (which had never before been reissued complete and in chronological order), features four well-recorded radio shows that logically showcase the individual members of Condon's remarkable all-star groups. These Dixielandish (but never corny or overly predictable) performances are generally exciting and the verbal commentary of Eddie Condon adds to the flavor and wit of the music. And check out this lineup of musicians: trumpeters Billy Butterfield, Bobby Hackett, Max Kaminsky and Muggsy Spanier; trombonist Miff Mole; baritonist Ernie Caceres; clarinetists Edmond Hall and Pee Wee Russell; pianists James P. Johnson, Jess Stacy and Gene Schroeder; bassists Bob Haggart, Sid Weiss and Jack Lesberg; drummers Cozy Cole, Joe Grauso and Gene Krupa and singers Red McKenzie and Lee Wiley. The spontaneous yet well-planned performances find the classic players in peak form and the results are quite memorable. —*Scott Yanow*

The Town Hall Concerts, Vol. 6 / Oct. 7, 1944-Oct. 28, 1944 / Jazzology ✦✦✦✦
Volume 6 of this very valuable series of two-CD sets has four complete (and well-recorded) half-hour radio shows taken from a legendary program billed as *Eddie Condon's Town Hall Concerts* (even though by late 1944 the performances were actually being held at the Ritz Theatre). Every week Condon gathered together a large ensemble of his favorite players and featured them individually and collec-

tively in exciting fashion, finishing each Dixieland-oriented show with an "Impromptu Ensemble." All of the volumes in this series (which contain shows that had never been coherently reissued before) have more than their share of memorable moments. This particular two-fer features such classic players as trumpeters Billy Butterfield, Max Kaminsky and Muggsy Spanier; trombonists Lou McGarity, Bennie Morton, and Miff Mole; baritonist Ernie Caceres; clarinetists Edmond Hall and Pee Wee Russell; pianists Jess Stacy and Gene Schroeder and singers Lee Wiley and Red McKenzie. Condon somehow manages to feature each of the highly individual musicians and still save some space for his witty and acerbic comments. This is timeless music from an era that can never be quite duplicated. —*Scott Yanow*

The Town Hall Concerts, Vol. 7 / Nov. 4, 1944-Dec. 2, 1944 / Jazzology ✦✦✦✦
The *Eddie Condon Town Hall Concerts* were a series of half-hour radio programs during 1944-45 that gave the guitarist-bandleader an opportunity to present many classic jazz greats in spontaneous settings. The seventh volume of this very significant Jazzology reissue series of double CDs differs from the previous ones in that, due to scheduling conflicts, a couple of the shows were shorter than usual so there are five (rather than four) included on the set. Condon features quite an impressive lineup: trumpeters Billy Butterfield, Bobby Hackett, Max Kaminsky, Wingy Manone, Hot Lips Page and Muggsy Spanier; trombonists Lou McGarity and Jack Teagarden; clarinetists Jimmy Dorsey and Pee Wee Russell; baritonist Ernie Caceres; pianists Dick Cary, Cliff Jackson, Gene Schroeder, Jess Stacy and Norma Teagarden; bassists Bob Casey and Jack Lesberg; drummers Johnny Blowers and George Wettling and singers Red McKenzie and Lee Wiley. The Teagarden show is particularly inspired but all of the volumes in this series are highly recommended to fans of the era; the well-recorded performances allowed the many stars not only to be featured individually but to interact with each other in "Impromptu Ensembles." —*Scott Yanow*

A Night at Eddie Condon's / Dec. 12, 1944-Aug. 6, 1947 / Decca ✦✦✦
This hard-to-find LP has a dozen performances by Eddie Condon's all-star Chicago jazz bands of 1944-47. Five of the songs feature vocals by the great trombonist Jack Teagarden (including "The Sheik of Araby" and "Aunt Hagar's Blues"), pianist James P. Johnson is showcased on "Just You, Just Me" and the music (much of which has not been reissued on CD) also stars trumpeters Bobby Hackett, Billy Butterfield, Max Kaminsky and Wild Bill Davison; valve trombonist Brad Gowan; clarinetists Pee Wee Russell, Joe Dixon, Peanuts Hucko and Tony Parenti; tenorman Bud Freeman and baritonist Ernie Caceres. The spirited playing is consistently delightful and hard-swinging but unfortunately many of these recordings have not yet appeared on CD. —*Scott Yanow*

The Town Hall Concerts, Vol. 8 / Dec. 16, 1944-Jan. 6, 1945 / Jazzology ✦✦✦✦
The eighth double CD in this essential series has four more half-hour shows that were billed as *The Eddie Condon Town Hall Concerts*. Condon, who was always more important as an instigator than as a guitarist, was a perfect host for the program, not only offering witty and sometimes sarcastic commentary but designing the shows so all of the all-stars were properly featured, both individually and collectively. The eighth volume has the usual incredible roster: trumpeters Billy Butterfield, Bobby Hackett, Max Kaminsky and Wingy Manone; trombonists Tommy Dorsey, Benny Morton and Jack Teagarden; Sidney Bechet on soprano; baritonist Ernie Caceres; clarinetist Pee Wee Russell; pianists Dick Cary, Gene Schroeder and Jess Stacy; bassists Bob Casey, Jack Lesberg and Sid Weiss; drummers Johnny Blowers and George Wettling and vocalist Lee Wiley. As usual there are dozens of highlights from these spontaneous yet logical jam sessions, easily recommended to Dixieland and Chicago jazz fans. —*Scott Yanow*

The Town Hall Concerts, Vol. 9 / Jan. 13, 1945-Feb. 3, 1945 / Jazzology ✦✦✦✦
Eddie Condon certainly had good taste in musicians. On his legendary *Town Hall Concert* series (a regular weekly half-hour radio program reissued by Jazzology on double CDs), he showcased some of the very best New Orleans and Chicago-style players, musicians who in some cases were quite happy to get away from their regular gigs within the confines of a big band and get a rare chance to stretch out. *Volume 9* has four half-hour shows and the usual remarkable lineup of players: trumpeters Billy Butterfield, Wild Bill Davison (the latter making his debut on the show), Max Kaminsky and Muggsy Spanier; trombonists Tommy Dorsey and Lou McGarity; Sidney Bechet on soprano; baritonist Ernie Caceres; clarinetists Pee Wee Russell, Edmond Hall, Joe Marsala and Woody Herman; pianists Earl Hines, Dick Cary, Gene Schroeder and Jess Stacy; bassist Sid Weiss; drummer George Wettling and singers Red McKenzie and Lee Wiley. The music lives up to its potential. —*Scott Yanow*

● **The Town Hall Concerts, Vol. 10** / Feb. 10, 1945-Mar. 3, 1945 / Jazzology ✦✦✦✦
The tenth double-CD of 11 put out by Jazzology that completely document the Eddie Condon Town Hall Concerts that were broadcast over the radio during 1944-45 as usual has more than its share of exciting performances. Condon, a fre-

quently sarcastic M.C., was an expert at gathering together overloaded all-star groups and somehow featuring everyone adequately. The main guests on the four shows included in this set are soprano saxophonist Sidney Bechet, Jimmy Dorsey (on clarinet and alto) and trombonist Tommy Dorsey who join the remarkable Condon crew (trumpeters Billy Butterfield, Max Kaminsky, Yank Lawson and Muggsy Spanier; trombonist Lou McGarity; baritonist Ernie Caceres; clarinetists Hank D'Amico and Pee Wee Russel;, pianist Jess Stacy, bassists Bob Casey, Jack Lesberg and Sid Weiss; drummers George Wettling and Johnny Blowers and singers Red McKenie and Lee Wiley) for some freewheeling performances. All of the volumes in this essential series are highly recommended to fans of Dixieland and Chicago jazz. —*Scott Yanow*

The Town Hall Concerts, Vol. 11 / Mar. 10, 1945-Apr. 7, 1945 / Jazzology ✦✦✦✦✦
The 11th and final Jazzology set that documents all of Eddie Condon's legendary Town Hall concerts of 1944-45 is a three-CD release. In addition to having five complete shows, there are a couple of briefer demo programs that were never aired before. Although not containing as many heights (or guest artists) as previous programs, there is plenty of exciting "Americondon" music to be heard on the final few of his 46 Town Hall concerts. Among the many top players are trumpeters Max Kaminsky, Billy Butterfield and Muggsy Spanier; trombonists Lou McGarity, Miff Mole and Vernon Brown; clarinetists Pee Wee Russell and Edmond Hall; baritonist Ernie Caceres; pianists Jess Stacy, Joe Bushkin and Gene Scroeder; drummers George Wettling and Big Sid Catlett and singers Red McKenzie and Lee Wiley. Trad jazz fans are well advised to pick up this entire series (which numbers 23 CDs). —*Scott Yanow*

Dr. Jazz Series, Vol. 11 / Dec. 10, 1951-Apr. 7, 1952 / Storyville ✦✦✦
This CD contains performances taken from broadcasts of the Dr. Jazz radio show. Although the band is led by rhythm guitarist Eddie Condon (who is mostly inaudible), the star throughout is cornetist Wild Bill Davison, who receives co-billing on the set. Teamed up with trombonist Cutty Cutshall, the distinctive clarinetist Edmond Hall, pianist Gene Schroeder, Bob Casey or Bill Goodall on bass and Buzzy Drootin, George Wettling or Cliff Leeman on drums, Davison is typically explosive and highly expressive on a variety of Dixieland warhorses. Few surprises occur during tunes such as "Dippermouth Blues," "At the Jazz Band Ball," "I Want to Be Happy" and "Fidgety Feet," but Dixieland fans will enjoy the spirit and drive of the music. —*Scott Yanow*

Dr. Jazz Series, Vol. 5 / Dec. 24, 1951-Mar. 31, 1952 / Storyville ✦✦✦
The *Dr. Jazz* radio series (which was on from Dec. 1950 to June 1952) presented for a half-hour each week some of the finest Dixieland then being performed regularly in New York City. This particular CD features Eddie Condon's freewheeling band with consistently heated solos taken by cornetist Wild Bill Davison, trombonist Cutty Cutshall, clarinetist Edmond Hall and either Gene Schroeder or Ralph Sutton on piano. Together they romp through a variety of veteran standards and a ballad medley. The excellent programming on this Storville disc (which actually draws its material from eight different broadcasts) makes the results sound like a complete show. Chicago jazz and Eddie Condon fans are advised not only to acquire this CD but to investigate the entire series from this Danish import label. —*Scott Yanow*

Dr. Jazz Series, Vol. 1 / Jan. 21, 1952-Jun. 2, 1952 / Storyville ✦✦✦
Part of a Storyville CD series that has released rare performances taken from the *Dr. Jazz* radio shows of 1952, these 17 selections by Eddie Condon's band are most valuable for featuring the talented but largely forgotten trumpeter Johnny Windhurst. The Dixieland standards also have spots for the highly expressive clarinetist Edmond Hall, trombonist Cutty Cutshall, pianist Gene Scroeder, either Bob Casey or Bill Goodall on bass and Buzzy Drootin, Cliff Leeman or Mort Herbert on drums but it is Windhurst's solos that generally take honors. Easily recommended (along with the entire series) to Dixieland fans. —*Scott Yanow*

Dr. Jazz Series, Vol. 8 / Jan. 21, 1952-Jun. 2, 1952 / Storyville ✦✦✦✦
This CD, which takes its material from the Dr. Jazz radio show, features rhythm guitarist Eddie Condon's regular 1952 band live from his club. It gives listeners a valuable look at the ill-fated trumpeter Johnny Windhurst (who is in excellent form), some typically passionate solos from clarinetist Edmond Hall, and some of the best playing on record by trombonist Cutty Cutshall. With pianist Gene Schroeder, bassist Bob Casey and either Buzzy Drootin or Cliff Leeman on drums, the music is essentially straightforward Dixieland with a three-song ballad medley being the only departure. Although no real surprises occur, the performances are spirited, with the highlights including "Struttin' with Some Barbecue," a medium-tempo "Sentimental Journey," "It All Depends on You" and "Easter Parade." —*Scott Yanow*

Music Map

Cornet

The cornet was the main brass instrument in jazz until it was succeeded by the trumpet in the mid-1920s.

New Orleans Pioneers
Buddy Bolden
(his 1895 band is considered the first jazz group)
Freddie Keppard
Manuel Perez

Important Cornetists of the 1920s
Nick LaRocca (with the Original Dixieland Jazz Band)
Paul Mares (with the New Orleans Rhythm Kings)
King Oliver
Oscar Celestin
Lee Collins
Punch Miller
Tommy Ladnier
George Mitchell (with Jelly Roll Morton)
Red Nichols

The Two Most Significant Cornetists
Louis Armstrong (switched to trumpet during 1926-27)
Bix Beiderbecke

Other Important Pre-Bop Players
Bunk Johnson   Rex Stewart
Ray Nance   Bobby Hackett
Jimmy McPartland   Wild Bill Davison
Muggsy Spanier   Ruby Braff
Warren Vache

Bop
Nat Adderley
Thad Jones

Avant-Garde
Don Cherry
Bobby Bradford
Butch Morris
Olu Dara
Joe McPhee

☆ **The Complete CBS Eddie Condon All Stars** / Nov. 24, 1953-Sep. 4, 1962 / Mosaic ✦✦✦✦✦
Chicago jazz and Dixieland fans should go out of their way to pick up this limited-edition five-CD boxed set. The first four discs date from 1953-57 and feature freewheeling performances (originally out on seven LPs) with such classic soloists as cornetists Wild Bill Davison and Bobby Hackett; trumpeter Billy Butterfield; trombonists Cutty Cutshall, Lou McGarity and Vic Dickenson; clarinetists Edmond Hall, Peanuts Hucko, Bob Wilber and Pee Wee Russell and tenorman Bud Freeman among others. Eddie Condon's comments during his band's waterlogged perfor-

mance at the 1957 Newport Jazz Festival alone are worth the price. The final disc of material (all from 1962) is somewhat commercial but still has its moments of interest. —*Scott Yanow*

Condon Concert / 1956-1957 / Jazzology ♦♦♦

This somewhat obscure LP from the collector's Jazzology label features the 1956 version of Eddie Condon's band, a septet starring the great cornetist Wild Bill Davison, trombonist Cutty Cutshall and clarinetist Bob Wilber. Nothing all that surprising occurs, other than a four-song ballad medley, but these freewheeling performances (the best are "At the Jazz Band Ball," "High Society" and Wild Bill's feature on "I Can't Give You Anything but Love") will be enjoyed by Dixieland fans. —*Scott Yanow*

Dixieland Jam / Aug. 19, 1957-Sep. 25, 1957 / Columbia ♦♦♦

If you like traditional jazz, you'll love any and all Eddie Condon. —*Ron Wynn*

Tiger Rag and All That Jazz / 1958 / World Pacific ♦♦♦♦

One of the lesser-known Eddie Condon groups is the one he led in 1958 that featured cornetist Rex Stewart. Of their three albums, this rare World Pacific LP is the most rewarding, featuring the group on eight mostly heated stomps including seven tunes recorded decades earlier by the original Dixieland Jazz Band. With the exception of some animal imitations on "Livery Stable Blues," there is no attempt to recreate the past and the songs are used as a good excuse for some colorful jamming. In addition to Stewart, trombonist Cutty Cutshall, Bud Freeman on tenor, clarinetist Herb Hall, pianist Gene Schroeder, bassist Leonard Gaskin, drummer George Wettling and the guitarist/leader are heard from but the fiery cornetist generally takes solo honors. —*Scott Yanow*

That Toddlin' Town / Feb. 26, 1959-Feb. 27, 1959 / Warner Brothers ♦♦♦♦

To celebrate the 20th anniversary of the first jazz album (meaning a specially released series of 78s that came out in 1939), a variety of Chicago jazz veterans under the leadership of rhythm guitarist Eddie Condon (all of whom gigged regularly with Condon anyway) jammed through ten Dixieland standards. Trumpeter Max Kaminsky, trombonist Cutty Cutshall, tenor saxophonist Bud Freeman and clarinetist Pee Wee Russell formed a particularly potent front line and their LP (which has yet to be reissued on CD) has such highlights as spirited versions of "Chicago," "I've Found a New Baby," "Love Is Just Around the Corner," "Oh Baby" and "Nobody's Sweetheart Now." —*Scott Yanow*

In Japan / Mar. 1964-Apr. 1964 / Chiaroscuro ♦♦♦♦

By 1964, Eddie Condon was not recording all that regularly; in fact, this CD has his only recording from the 1963-67 period. Condon, who does some announcing and contributes some barely audible rhythm guitar, is joined by a particularly strong group consisting of trumpeter Buck Clayton, trombonist Vic Dickenson, tenor saxophonist Bud Freeman, clarinetist Pee Wee Russell, pianist Dick Cary (doubling on alto horn), bassist Jack Lesberg and drummer Cliff Leeman. The band plays Dixieland and swing standards with spirit and enthusiasm while singer Jimmy Rushing takes four vocals including a previously unissued "Blues Medley." The CD reissue also adds "new" versions of "Caravan" and "Basin Street Blues"; other highlights include "I Can't Believe That You're in Love with Me," "Pee Wee's Blues," "Royal Garden Blues" and Dickenson's charming feature on "Manhattan." Recommended. —*Scott Yanow*

Jazz As It Should Be Played / Dec. 1, 1968 / Jazzology ♦♦♦

This little-known LP would be worth picking up if only for the occasionally hilarious wisecracking of Eddie Condon, trumpeter Wild Bill Davison and trombonist George Brunis. However, there is also a fair sampling of fine Chicago Dixieland from these unique veterans along with clarinetist Tommy Gwaltney, pianist Don Ewell, bassist Bill Goodall and drummer Frank Marshall. Particularly enjoyable are "At the Jazz Band Ball," Brunis' vocal on "Sister Kate," "That's a Plenty" and "I've Found a New Baby." —*Scott Yanow*

And His Strolling Reunion Commodores / Dec. 7, 1969 / Fat Cat Jazz ♦♦

By 1969 veteran bandleader and rhythm guitarist Eddie Condon was only performing on a sporadic basis. This LP features his band of the era (cornetist Wild Bill Davison, trombonist George Brunis, clarinetist Tommy Gwaltney, pianist John Eaton, bassist Bill Goodall and drummer Cliff Leeman) playing a variety of Dixieland standards and a four-song ballad medley. The spontaneous concert performances are a bit loose at times (particularly by the later cuts) and there is a lot of joking around, but Condon collectors will want this spirited release. —*Scott Yanow*

Eddie Condon Jam Session / 1970 / Jazzology ♦♦♦♦

For one of Eddie Condon's final recordings (and what was possibly his last studio session), he largely let cornetist Wild Bill Davison run the show. Two of the five songs ("Time After Time" and "Crazy Rhythm") have arrangements for the septet, which includes Davison, trombonist Ed Hubble, clarinetist Johnny Mince and pianist Dill Jones, while the other three pieces ("How Come You Do Me like You Do,"

"Them There Eyes" and "Eddie's Blues") are looser and more freewheeling. This LP contains enjoyable and somewhat historic music. —*Scott Yanow*

The Spirit of Condon / Dec. 5, 1971+May 6, 1973 / Jazzology ♦♦♦

This posthumously released LP has five selections from one of bandleader Eddie Condon's final concerts, an appearance at the 1971 Manassas Jazz Festival. "Washboard Blues" features pianist Art Hodes and the other four standards use a couple of overlapping groups with such fine players as cornetist Wild Bill Davison, trumpeter Wallace Davenport, trombonist Herb Gardner, clarinetist Joe Muranyi and Deane Kincaide on tenor and baritone. In addition there is a short parody (titled "Condon") by trombonist George Brunis (who sings and plays piano) that was taped for the ailing rhythm guitarist in 1973 but did not reach him before he passed away. Overall this out-of-print LP is not essential but it does have its strong moments and will be savored by Eddie Condon's many fans. —*Scott Yanow*

● **Live at the New School 1972** / Apr. 1972 / Chiaroscuro ♦♦♦♦♦

This CD reissue (which adds two previously unreleased and rather loose selections to the original program) is historic because it has the final recordings of both rhythm guitarist Eddie Condon and drummer Gene Krupa (who ironically back in 1927 made their recording debut together). More importantly the spirited music made by this quintet (which also features cornetist Wild Bill Davison, Kenny Davern on soprano and pianist Dick Wellstood) is quite enjoyable and creative within the boundaries of Dixieland and swing. Wellstood in particular is in excellent form, making up for the absence of a bass, and it is very rewarding to hear Krupa in such a spontaneous setting on what may have been the best recording of his final decade. —*Scott Yanow*

Harry Connick, Jr.

b. Sep. 11, 1967, New Orleans, LA
Piano, Vocals / Swing, Traditional Pop

With very few exceptions, the career of Harry Connick, Jr., can be divided in half—his first two albums encompassed straightahead New Orleans jazz and stride piano while his later career (which paralleled his rising celebrity status) alternated between more contemporary New Orleans music and pop vocals with a debt to Frank Sinatra. Born in New Orleans on September 11, 1967, Connick grew up the son of two lawyers who owned a record store. After beginning on keyboards at the age of three, he first performed publicly at six, and recorded with a local jazz band at ten. Connick attended the New Orleans Center for the Creative Arts and studied with Ellis Marsalis and James Booker. A move to New York to study at Hunter College and the Manhattan School of Music gave him the opportunity to look up a Columbia Records executive who had asked to see him, and Connick's self-titled album debut—a set of mostly unaccompanied standards—appeared in 1987. Jazz critics praised Connick's maturity and engaging style as well as his extended stays at New York hot spots during the year. His second album, named for his age in 1988, was the first to feature him on vocals.

Already well known within jazz circles, Harry Connick, Jr., entered the American consciousness with the soundtrack to 1989's popular film *When Harry Met Sally.* Director Rob Reiner had asked Connick to compose a soundtrack, and he recorded several warm standards ("It Had to Be You," "Let's Call the Whole Thing Off," "Don't Get Around Much Anymore") with a big-band backing. A world tour followed, and *When Harry Met Sally* eventually made double-platinum status. With Connick a major celebrity, he diverged into an acting career, playing a tail gunner in 1990s *Memphis Belle.* That same year, he released two albums simultaneously: one, *We Are in Love,* was another vocal outing with similar standards as had appeared on *When Harry Met Sally,* while *Lofty's Roach Souffle* was all-instrumental. (Of course, the vocal album performed much better on the pop charts, hitting double-platinum, while the instrumentals worked better with jazz audiences.) Connick toured again, this time with a big band, and recorded the group on 1991's *Blue Light, Red Light.* Though his celebrity decreased slightly during the mid-'90s, Connick's albums continued to reach platinum status, including 1992's *25,* a 1993 Christmas album, and 1994's *She.* Connick continued his acting work with a starring role in 1995's *Copycat* (where he played a serial killer) and married actress Jill Goodacre. In 1996, he had a brief role in the year's biggest blockbuster, *Independence Day,* but his album *Star Turtle* failed to connect with pop audiences. —*John Bush*

11 / Nov. 4, 1978+Nov. 11, 1978 / Columbia ♦♦

The music on this spirited but amateurish Dixieland record would never have been released by Columbia if not for the presence of an 11-year-old pianist named Harry Connick, Jr. His solos are quite basic (not on the level of Sergio Salvatore) while his vocal on "Doctor Jazz" is only cute the first time around. The loose group jams through nine familiar Dixieland standards. The erratic trumpeter Teddy Riley leads the ensembles while Walter Payton (Nicholas' father) drives the group effectively on bass. This CD is only really of historical interest. —*Scott Yanow*

Harry Connick, Jr. / 1987 / Columbia ✦✦✦

Harry Connick's first Columbia album features him mostly playing stride piano solos in a style heavily influenced by Thelonious Monk. Bassist Ron Carter drops by for a duet on his own "Little Waltz" while "E" finds Connick welcoming bassist Reginald Veal and drummer Herman Riley. The instrumental set is generally colorful even if Connick's time was not too steady at this point. Standards alternate with forgotten originals with the highlights being "On the Sunny Side of the Street," "I Mean You" and "On Green Dolphin Street." —*Scott Yanow*

20 / May 4, 1988-Jun. 29, 1988 / Columbia ✦✦✦✦

On a set of mostly unaccompanied piano solos and vocals, Harry Connick, Jr., shows a great deal of potential. His renditions of eleven standards are highlighted by collaborations with singer-organist Dr. John on "Do You Know What It Means to Miss New Orleans" and especially a memorable vocal duet with Carmen McRae on "Please Don't Talk About Me When I'm Gone." In addition, bassist Bob Hurst helps out on "Do Nothin' till You Hear from Me." Years later, this still remains one of Harry Connick, Jr's finest recordings. —*Scott Yanow*

● **When Harry Met Sally** / Jun. 1989 / Columbia ✦✦✦✦✦

Harry Connick, Jr's vocals perfectly fit the moods throughout the 1989 Billy Crystal film *When Harry Met Sally*. This soundtrack album (which stands apart from the movie) was a big hit and a major step forward for the young pianist-vocalist although, from the vantage point of the late '90s, it appears to have been the high point of his career. Connick warmly sings such numbers as "It Had to Be You," "Our Love Is Here to Stay," "But Not for Me" and "Let's Call the Whole Thing Off" while usually accompanied by bassist Benjamin Wolfe, drummer Jeff "Tain" Watts and a big band; Frank Wess' warm tenor makes a brief appearance on "Our Love Is Here to Stay." In addition, there are a few melodic instrumentals including some solo Connick piano on "Winter Wonderland" and "Autumn in New York." Highly recommended. —*Scott Yanow*

We Are in Love / 1990 / Columbia ✦✦✦

At one point in 1990, two Harry Connick, Jr. albums were released almost simultaneously, an instrumental outing with his trio (*Lofty's Roach Souffle*) and this vocal-oriented album. Oddly enough, *We Are in Love* is the more successful of the two. Connick's vocals, while limited, are personable, guitarist Russell Malone gets in some short solos and Branford Marsalis has two strong guest appearances (one apiece on tenor and soprano). Most selections utilize an orchestra and, although Connick is heard on piano, the emphasis is on his voice. He contributed most of the tunes but the high points are the two standards ""A Nightingale Sang in Berkeley Square" and "It's Alright with Me." —*Scott Yanow*

Lofty's Roach Souffle / Apr. 4, 1990-Apr. 22, 1990 / Columbia ✦✦✦

At virtually the same time, Harry Connick, Jr. in 1990 released two CDs; one a vocal date and the other an instrumental album with his trio. *Lofty's Roach Souffle* is the latter, an outing with bassist Benjamin Wolfe and drummer Shannon Powell. Connick performs 11 of his originals on this set and, although he shows some growth from his earlier days as a sort-of Thelonious Monk imitator, he did not yet have a piano style of his own and none of his compositions are all that memorable. However, Connick's time had improved (helped a lot by the presence of a steady drummer) and the program finds him playing about as advanced as he ever has. —*Scott Yanow*

Blue Light, Red Light / Jun. 27, 1991-Jul. 14, 1991 / Columbia ✦✦

In 1991 Harry Connick, Jr. toured with a big band. Unfortunately the presence of the orchestra seemed to result in an inflated ego for Connick, who rarely allowed his sidemen an opportunity to be featured. On this forgettable CD he wrote all 12 selections (none of which caught on) and mostly uses the big band as a prop behind his Frank Sinatra-inspired vocals. Connick's piano playing is greatly de-emphasized and, although there are some names among the backup players (particularly guitarist Russell Malone and, buried in the trumpet section, Leroy Jones), the show is for better or worse (mostly the latter) a showcase for Harry Connick; what was the purpose of hiring 14 horns? —*Scott Yanow*

25 / Oct. 2, 1992-Oct. 9, 1992 / Columbia ✦✦✦✦

This 1992 CD is a throwback to Harry Connick's earlier sets for it mostly features the pianist-vocalist on a solo set of standards. Ellis Marsalis drops by to back Connick's vocal on "Stardust," Connick accompanies Johnny Adams' singing on "Lazybones" and "On the Atchison, Topeka and the Santa Fe" is a trio outing with tenor saxophonist Ned Gold and bassist Ray Brown. Otherwise it is all Connick and he sounds in good form on such tunes as "Music, Maestro, Please," "On the Street Where You Live," "After You've Gone" and "Muskrat Ramble." It is a pity that Connick has not continued in this direction. —*Scott Yanow*

She / 1994 / Columbia ✦✦

Star Turtle / Dec. 1995 / Columbia ✦✦

When Harry Connick first emerged as a teenager, he was hailed as a pianist-singer with great potential in the jazz world who might possibly keep swing and older

standards alive. Unfortunately the ensuing years have not seen any significant improvement or development in his musical skills and Connick has veered towards routine pop. In fact, *Star Turtle* is strictly a pop-rock set with no real piano solos. The emphasis is put on Connick's forgettable originals and his rather limited voice, with the derivative results failing not only as jazz but also as pop music. —*Scott Yanow*

To See You / 1997 / Columbia ✦✦✦✦

Harry Connick is heard in three roles on this CD. As a jazz pianist, he makes some cameo appearances and shows that his playing had evolved a bit from his earlier years. Connick had matured as a vocalist, and he sounds fine backed by a string orchestra and his quartet, never stretching himself. All ten selections (ballads dealing with love) are his originals, and Connick displays some talent as a composer/lyricist/arranger, although it is doubtful that any of these numbers will become standards in the future. A more interesting set overall than his preceding pop date, this CD was a step in the right direction for Harry Connick, Jr., also featuring brief, warm tenor solos from Charles Goold. —*Scott Yanow*

Chris Connor

b. Nov. 8, 1927, Kansas City, MO
Vocals / Cool, Traditional Pop

Along with June Christy, Helen O'Connell and Julie London, Chris Connor epitomized "cool" jazz singing in the 1950s. Influenced by Anita O'Day, the torchy, smoky singer wasn't one for aggression. Like Chet Baker on the trumpet or Paul Desmond and Lee Konitz on alto sax, she used subtlety and restraint to maximum advantage. At the University of Missouri, Connor (who had studied clarinet at an early age) sang with a Stan Kenton-ish big band led by trombonist Bob Brookmeyer before leaving her native Kansas City for New York in 1947. Quite appropriately, she was featured in the lyrical pianist Claude Thornhill's orchestra in the early 1950s. After leaving Thornhill, Connor was hired by Kenton at Christy's recommendation, and her ten-month association with him in 1952-53 resulted in the hit "All About Ronnie." Connor debuted as a solo artist in 1953, recording three albums for Bethlehem before moving to Atlantic in 1955 and recording 12. Connor reached the height of her popularity in the 1950s, when she delivered her celebrated versions of Billy Strayhorn's "Lush Life" and George Shearing's "Lullaby of Broadway" and recorded such excellent albums as *The Rich Sound of Chris Connor* and *Lullabies ofBirdland* for Bethlehem and *Chris Craft* and *Ballads of the Sad Cafe* for Atlantic. Connor made a poor career move in 1962, the year she left Atlantic and signed with a label her manager was starting, FM Records—Connor had recorded only two albums for FM when it folded. Connor's recording career was rejuvenated in the 1970s, and she went on to record for Progressive, Stash and Contemporary in the '70s and/or '80s. Connor maintained a devoted following in the 1990s and continued to tour internationally. —*Alex Henderson*

Lullabies of Birdland / Dec. 17, 1953-Aug. 21, 1954 / Evidence ✦✦✦✦✦

This CD reissue draws its music from singer Chris Connor's first three sessions as a leader. The set comprises three of the four songs that Connor recorded with Sy Oliver's Orchestra, five of the eight tunes (plus a "new" alternate take of "Why Shouldn't I") from a meeting with pianist Ellis Larkins' trio and six of the eight selections from a date with the Vinnie Burke quintet, a group featuring clarinetist Ronnie Oldrich and the accordion of Don Burns. Connor, who was 26 during this period, is in top form in all of the different settings and displays a wider range than one might expect. Highlights include "Lullaby of Birdland," "Spring Is Here," "Ask Me," "A Cottage for Sale" and a rare vocal version of "Goodbye." Recommended. —*Scott Yanow*

Chris / Aug. 9, 1954-Apr. 1955 / Bethlehem ✦✦✦

The music on this CD reissue by Evidence is excellent, but the packaging, which has breezy and inaccurate liner notes and no real personnel or date listings, is inexcusable. Chris Connor, whose deep voice sometimes sounds eerily close to Chet Baker's, is featured on four sessions from the 1954-55 period with backing by the Ellis Larkins trio, a quintet led by bassist Vinnie Burke (and including Ronnie Oldrich on flute and clarinet), a different quintet with flutist Herbie Mann and guitarist Joe Puma, and a unit that has some prominent trombone playing from J.J. Johnson and Kai Winding. In addition to the dozen selections (which include "All About Ronnie"), this CD also issues for the first time an alternate take apiece of each of the songs, so it is really two records in one. But why such poor packaging? —*Scott Yanow*

☆ **Cocktails and Dusk** / Apr. 1955 / Bethlehem ✦✦✦✦✦

During 1953-55, singer Chris Connor recorded regularly for Bethlehem. This reissue LP has her final recordings for the label (before moving up to Atlantic) with such fine sidemen as Herbie Mann (doubling on flute and tenor), pianist Ralph Sharon, guitarist Joe Puma, bassist Milt Hinton and drummer Osie Johnson. The two-trombone team of J.J. Johnson and Kai Winding (which had recently become very popular) is prominent on four of the ten selections. Connor's cool tone, subtle, emotional delivery and haunting voice were perfect for the music of the 1950s. Highlights of this superior set include "The Thrill Is Gone," "Blame It on My Youth" and "I Concentrate on You," but all ten numbers are rewarding. —*Scott Yanow*

Chris Connor / Jan. 23, 1956+Feb. 8, 1956 / Atlantic ✦✦✦
First date for Atlantic upon leaving Bethlehem in a huff. Nice arrangements; Zoot Sims (ts) has good solos. —*Ron Wynn*

● **Sings the George Gershwin Almanac of Song** / Jun. 5, 1956-Jan. 23, 1961 / Atlantic ✦✦✦✦✦
Most of this highly recommended two-CD set is taken from a series of 1957 sessions in which singer Chris Connor exclusively interprets songs of George Gershwin. To fill out the CDs, additional Gershwin cuts from other, otherwise unrelated dates by the vocalist have been added. Connor's cool delivery gives many of the largely familiar songs new life. She is assisted by such fine musicians as trumpeter Joe Newman, tenorman Al Cohn, flutist Herbie Mann, vibraphonist Milt Jackson and pianist Ralph Sharon, who add tasteful and concise solos. Many of the selections were quite rare before this well-conceived and appealing reissue was put together. —*Scott Yanow*

● **A Jazz Date with Chris Connor** / Nov. 16, 1956-Mar. 23, 1958 / Rhino ✦✦✦✦✦
Two of singer Chris Connor's finest Atlantic albums are reissued in full on this single CD. The laidback yet coolly emotional jazz singer is heard backed by top-notch rhythm sections (with either Ralph Sharon or Stan Free being the pianist/arranger) and occasional horns (trumpeter Joe Wilder and tenors Al Cohn and Lucky Thompson, flutist Bobby Jaspar and Al Epstein on English horn and bass clarinet) adding some short solos. Connor (then around 30) was in her prime, and her renditions of such songs as "Poor Little Rich Girl," "Lonely Town," "I'm Shooting High," "Moonlight in Vermont" and even "Johnny One Note" are memorable and sometimes haunting. —*Scott Yanow*

Chris Craft / Apr. 8, 1958+May 23, 1958 / Atlantic ✦✦✦✦✦
More upbeat, daring. —*Ron Wynn*

A Portrait of Chris / Dec. 5, 1960-Jan. 23, 1961 / Atlantic ✦✦✦✦

Double Exposure: Jazzlore, Vol. 21 / Dec. 5, 1960-Jan. 23, 1961 / Atlantic ✦✦✦✦
Singer Chris Connor was nearing the end of her Atlantic years (which were really her prime) when she recorded this interesting, if not quite classic set with the Maynard Ferguson Orchestra, last reissued on a 1984 LP. With the exception of trumpeter Ferguson, there are few significant solos, and the big band mostly acts as an ensemble. Both Connor and MF were Kenton alumni, and there are moments where the orchestra reminds one of that band, but the focus is mostly on the singer. She is in particularly fine form on "I Only Have Eyes for You," "It Never Entered My Mind," "Spring Can Really Hang You Up the Most" and "The Lonesome Road," although one wishes there was more interplay with the orchestra. —*Scott Yanow*

Free Spirits / Dec. 11, 1961-Apr. 30, 1962 / Atlantic ✦✦✦
Looser, more feeling. —*Ron Wynn*

Sings Gentle Bossa Nova / 1965 / ABC/Paramount ✦✦✦
Her turn at the bossa nova craze. —*Ron Wynn*

Sweet and Swinging / Feb. 3, 1978+Feb. 28, 1978 / Progressive ✦✦✦✦
Not all that much was heard from Chris Connor after her last Atlantic record in 1962 until this date. Her recordings for FM, ABC-Paramount (quite commercial), Bainbridge and Japanese Sony in the interim were all quite obscure. But at the age of 50, she began to make a comeback and showed that her voice was still strong and her cool style intact. Accompanied by pianist Michael Abene, bassist Michael Moore, drummer Ronnie Bedford and Jerry Dodgion on alto and flute, Connor performs 11 diverse tunes, including remakes of a few earlier numbers. Highlights include "Out of This World," "Where Flamingos Fly" and "When Sunny Gets Blue." —*Scott Yanow*

Lover Come Back to Me / Sep. 25, 1981 / Evidence ✦✦✦

Love Being Here with You / Sep. 12, 1983+Sep. 19, 1983 / Stash ✦✦✦
At the age of 55, Chris Connor's style had become rather conservative, and her voice was starting to age a bit, but she still sounds fine on this little-known set. With tasteful backup by pianist Russ Kassoff, guitarist Bucky Pizzarelli, bassist Dick Sarpolo and drummer Tony Tedesco, Connor revisits "The Thrill Is Gone," "Like Someone in Love" and "Come Rain or Come Shine." She also sings some tunes that were added to her repertoire in later years, including Baia and Richard Rodney Bennett's "Anyone Home." Jazz vocalist and cabaret collectors may want to search for this set. —*Scott Yanow*

Classic / Aug. 5, 1986-Aug. 6, 1986 / Contemporary ✦✦✦
Chris Connor, even as she got older, mostly retained her strong voice and cool style. This date finds her assisted by either Michael Abene or Richard Rodney Ben-

nett on piano, bassist Rufus Reid, drummer Akira Tana and the very welcome team of altoist Paquito D'Rivera and trumpeter Claudio Roditi. D'Rivera and Roditi boost the jazz content of the set while being sympathetic to Connor's singing. The emphasis is on love songs, and Connor, while feeling free to swing the tunes and improvise with subtlety, often sticks close to the lyrics and the melody. Highlights include "Let's Face the Music and Dance," "In Love in Vain," "Blame It on My Youth" and "Brazil." —*Scott Yanow*

New Again / Aug. 1987 / Contemporary ✦✦✦✦
The follow-up album to Chris Connor's *Classic* is similar in the moods it covers, the style of music and the instrumentation. Michael Abene and Richard Rodney Bennett split the keyboard duties, trumpeter Claudio Roditi and Bill Kirchner (on various reeds) have some short solos, and flutist Dave Valentin makes a couple of guest appearances. Connor, at 59, still had a powerful and haunting voice, as she shows on "Dearly Beloved," "My Foolish Heart," and even on a couple of medleys (one of Fred Astaire tunes and the other a "Jukebox Medley"). Listeners should acquire a good sampling of Chris Connor's 1950s recordings first, but her two Contemporary CDs have their value too. —*Scott Yanow*

As Time Goes By / Mar. 30, 1991-Apr. 2, 1991 / Enja ✦✦✦
Sixty-three at the time, Chris Connor's voice was still quite husky and recognizable when she recorded this 1991 session with pianist Hank Jones, bassist George Mraz and drummer Keith Copeland. As usual, she performs superior standards, sounding best on such songs as "September in the Rain," "Gone with the Wind," "A Lovely Way to Spend an Evening" and "A Foggy Day." Connor's timeless cool style (which was always full of inner heat and fire) did not decline with age, and this CD (although not as classic as her 1950s recordings) should greatly interest her fans. —*Scott Yanow*

Bill Connors

b. Sep. 24, 1949, Los Angeles, CA
Guitar / Fusion, Post-Bop
Bill Connors' great moment of fame occurred when he was with Chick Corea's Return to Forever during 1973-74, recording the influential *Hymn of the Seventh Galaxy*. His decision to leave RTF to concentrate more on acoustic guitar may have been satisfying artistically but it cut short any chance he had at commercial success. Previously he had played electric guitar with Mike Nock and Steve Swallow in San Francisco but his post-1974 work has been primarily acoustic, particularly in the 1970s when he recorded a series of atmospheric albums for ECM (including with Jan Garbarek). In the mid-'80s for Pathfinder, Connors' music became more rock-oriented but those releases did not make much of an impact despite his talent. —*Scott Yanow*

Theme to the Guardian / Nov. 1974 / ECM ✦✦✦✦
This is an album of terrific solo acoustic guitar from a former member of Return to Forever. —*Paul Kohler*

Of Mist and Melting / Dec. 1977 / ECM ✦✦✦
An atmospheric jazz album, it includes Jack DeJohnette (d), Gary Peacock (b), and Jan Garbarek (ts). —*Paul Kohler*

● **Swimming with a Hole in My Body** / Aug. 1979 / ECM ✦✦✦✦
Brilliant solo acoustic guitar with some overdubs. Required listening. —*Paul Kohler*

Step It! / Jun. 12, 1984-Oct. 15, 1984 / Evidence ✦✦
This session accented the funk/R&B and rock elements of Connors' arsenal; the eight selections were dominated both by drummer Dave Weckl's prominent backbeats and Connors' riffs and dashing licks, as well as catchy hooks, progressions, and patterns from bassist Tom Kennedy. Such songs as "A Pedal," "Brody," and the title cut weren't melodically sophisticated, but had a bass-heavy structure and quick, animated solos. Although the date is a bit old, its qualities prove a perfect fit on several new adult contemporary and lite-jazz outlets. —*Ron Wynn*

Double-Up / 1986 / Evidence ✦✦✦
Guitarist Bill Connors has forged a successful career by mixing light, pop-oriented fusion cuts with more ambitious works that showcase his considerable solo abilities and compositional skills. This was a trio date with Connors (who doubled as producer) playing in an introspective vein, showing his funk and rock side, and then playing with more imagination and style. The playing time was quite short (35 minutes-plus), but there was enough of Connors' guitar work presented to satisfy his fans and fusion/pop/light jazz followers. —*Ron Wynn*

Assembler / Jun. 1987 / Evidence ✦✦✦✦
His third electric release is in an Alan Holdsworth style. All his electric albums are highly recommended. —*Paul Kohler*

Contemporary Piano Ensemble

f. 1991
Group / Post-Bop
In 1990, James Williams and three fellow pianists (Harold Mabern, Mulgrew Miller and Geoff Keezer) paid tribute to Phineas Newborn on a CD on which they recorded two trio numbers apiece, plus a version of "It Don't Mean a Thing," where the four players took turns on one piano. At the 1991 Montreal Jazz Festival, the same pianists performed together, this time on four pianos. With the addition of Donald Brown as their fifth pianist (although they continued taking turns on four pianos, with one player sitting out), bassist Christian McBride and drummer Tony Reedus, the Contemporary Piano Ensemble was born. They recorded a set for DIW/Columbia in 1993 and the following year played concerts in 20 cities. Although necessarily a part-time venture, the group also appeared at the Monterey Jazz Festival and toured in 1996 for a couple of weeks, showing that it is possible to create swinging, coherent and surprisingly uncrowded music with four pianos. —*Scott Yanow*

Four Pianos for Phineas / Jun. 30, 1989 / Evidence ✦✦✦✦
Although the Contemporary Piano Ensemble consisted of the four pianists heard on this CD (James Williams, Harold Mabern, Mulgrew Miller and Geoff Keezer), plus Donald Brown, the group had actually not formed at the time of this recording. And, unlike the group's later performances, which typically featured four of the pianists at one time, this set actually has two numbers apiece showcasing each of the players in a trio with bassist Bob Cranshaw and drummer Billy Higgins. Only on the concluding "It Don't Mean a Thing," on which the four pianists take turns soloing on one piano, is there any interaction between the keyboardists. However, despite the use of the future group's name, this is an excellent set. All four of the pianists (who in their different ways were paying tribute to Phineas Newborn on this CD) are in superior form, whether playing originals, Newborn's "Back Home," or standards performed by the late, great pianist. In fact, since everyone is in top form, it is impossible to say that one particular player takes honors. A consistently strong set easily recommended to fans of the modern mainstream piano. —*Scott Yanow*

● **The Key Players** / Aug. 12, 1993-Aug. 13, 1993 / DIW/Columbia ✦✦✦✦✦
The Contemporary Piano Ensemble consists of five pianists (James Williams, Donald Brown, Harold Mabern, Mulgrew Miller and Geoff Keezer), bassist Christian McBride and drummer Tony Reedus. Since there were only four pianos in the studio, not every pianist plays on every selection. A tribute of sorts to both Phineas Newborn and Art Blakey, this set includes two medleys and such numbers as "Moanin'" and "Just Squeeze Me," in addition to some group originals. Somehow, the ensembles do not get overcrowded, despite the excess of keyboards, and the music contains more than its share of surprises. —*Scott Yanow*

Junior Cook (Herman Cook)

b. Jul. 22, 1934, Pensacola, FL, **d.** Feb. 3, 1992, New York, NY
Tenor Saxophone / Hard Bop
An expert hard bop tenor who tended to be overshadowed by more innovative contemporaries, Junior Cook was always a solid improviser. After playing with Dizzy Gillespie in 1958, Cook gained some fame for his longtime membership in the Horace Silver Quintet (1958-64); when he and Blue Mitchell left the popular band, Cook played in Mitchell's quintet (1964-69). Later associations included Freddie Hubbard, Elvin Jones, George Coleman, Louis Hayes (1975-76), Bill Hardman (1979-81) and the McCoy Tyner big band. In addition to many appearances as a sideman, Junior Cook recorded as a leader for Jazzland (1961), Catalyst (1977), Muse and Steeple Chase. —*Scott Yanow*

Junior's Cookin' / Apr. 10, 1961 / Jazzland ✦✦✦
This is a hard-driving first session as a leader. —*David Szatmary*

Good Cookin / Jun. 7, 1979 / Muse ✦✦✦✦
This all-star hard-bop cast includes Bill Hardman (tpt) and Slide Hampton (tb). —*David Szatmary*

Pressure Cooker / Nov. 1, 1977-Nov. 2, 1977 / Affinity ✦✦✦

● **Somethin's Cookin'** / Jun. 12, 1981 / Muse ✦✦✦✦✦
Junior Cook, who was best known for playing tenor with the Horace Silver Quintet during the period that Blue Mitchell was the group's trumpeter, recorded relatively few sessions as a leader during his career. The muscular but smooth saxophonist is heard at his best on this Muse quartet release which really showcases his playing (with fine support from pianist Cedar Walton, bassist Buster Williams and drummer Billy Higgins. The original program (which includes originals by Walton and Larry Willis) is augmented by four alternate takes for the CD reissue. —*Scott Yanow*

The Place to Be / Nov. 23, 1988 / Steeple Chase ✦✦✦

On a Misty Night / Jun. 1989 / Steeple Chase ✦✦✦✦

● **You Leave Me Breathless** / Dec. 1991 / Steeple Chase ✦✦✦✦✦
Tenor saxophonist Junior Cook's final recording, cut less than two months before his death, finds the veteran hard bop stylist in surprisingly prime form, taking upbeat solos and swinging hard. On this CD, one can really hear the mutual influence that Cook had on Joe Henderson. Trumpeter Valery Ponomarev is also in particularly fine form, and the rhythm section (pianist Mickey Tucker, bassist John Webber and drummer Joe Farnsworth) is somewhat obscure but excellent. Three group originals, Cedar Walton's "Fiesta Espanol" and four standards (including a warm tenor feature on "Warm Valley" and a hard-swinging "Mr. P.C.") comprise what was one of Junior Cook's finest sessions as a leader; he definitely exited on top. —*Scott Yanow*

Jackie Coon

b. Nebraska
Fluegelhorn / Dixieland
A middle-register, cool-toned fluegelhornist who also contributes occasional vocals, Jackie Coon has been an asset to many informal mainstream sessions. Coon, who grew up in Southern California, was inspired to play trumpet after hearing Louis Armstrong's "West End Blues." He spent a few months with Jack Teagarden's band (some of the music from radio broadcasts has been released by Arbors) and had gigs with Charlie Barnet, Louis Prima and Earl Hines, making his recording debut with Barney Bigard in 1957 and playing mellophone on Red Nichols' greatest version of "Battle Hymn of the Republic." Due to his decision to stay in California, fame has eluded Jackie Coon, but he worked for nine years at Disneyland, played regularly in local clubs, and appeared at jazz festivals. The popular fluegelhornist led his first record session for Sea Breeze in 1986 and since 1991 has recorded fairly often for Arbors. —*Scott Yanow*

● **Jazzin' Around** / Feb. 3, 1986-Feb. 4, 1986 / Sea Breeze ✦✦✦✦
After 30 years of playing in the Dixieland and mainstream field, fluegelhornist Jackie Coon finally made his recording debut as a leader on this 1986 set. Coon is heard in several different settings, including three quartet numbers with pianist Johnny Varro; two tunes in which he meets with up Varro and clarinetist Bill Wood in a quintet; four numbers with an octet also including trombonist Bob Havens, Dick Hafer on tenor and clarinet, and arranger Dick Cary (who switches between trumpet, the obscure alto trumpet and alto horn); and in a lyrical duo version of "My Romance" with guitarist Dave Koonse. Coon, who also takes four likable vocals, sounds relaxed and calm throughout, swinging softly but with inner passion. Highlights include "Riverboat Shuffle," "Struttin' with Some Barbecue," "Singin' the Blues" and "Willie the Weeper." —*Scott Yanow*

Back in His Own Backyard / Feb. 24, 1992-Feb. 25, 1992 / Arbors ✦✦✦✦
Although a part of the Dixieland/mainstream scene since the 1950s, Jackie Coon did not get a chance to record regularly as a leader until hooking up with Arbors in the early '90s. Teamed up with his old friend Rick Fay (who switches between tenor, clarinet and soprano), Eddie Erickson on banjo and guitar, pianist Johnny Varro, bassist David Stone and drummer Gene Estes, Coon plays cool-toned but upbeat solos on ten standards and an ad-lib blues. This is a particularly enjoyable CD for fans of straightahead jazz, Dixieland and swinging music. Included are fine versions of "Back in Your Own Backyard," "Down by the Riverside" (which features both Coon and Erickson singing), "Louisiana," and "Stumbling." —*Scott Yanow*

Jazzin' with Jackie / Feb. 24, 1992-Feb. 27, 1992 / Arbors ✦✦✦✦
The mellow-toned Jackie Coon had a rare opportunity to lead a record session for this Arbors CD. Coon's fluegelhorn and occasional vocals are well featured in a sextet with his old friend Rick Fay (tripling on clarinet, tenor and soprano), pianist Johnny Varro, bassist David Stone and drummer Gene Estes. Highlights of the Dixie/swing date include "Lady Be Good," "When My Dreamboat Comes Home," "When I Grow Too Old to Dream" and "Pick Yourself Up"; even "Me and My Shadow" works well. —*Scott Yanow*

The Coon-Sanders Nighthawks

f. 1918, **db.** 1932
Group / Classic Jazz
Although today largely forgotten, the Coon-Sanders Nighthawks were one of the top big bands of the 1920s. Drummer Carleton Coon (b. Feb. 5, 1894, Rochester, MN) and pianist/arranger Joe Sanders (b. Oct. 15, 1894, Thayer, KS) met in December 1918 in a Kansas City music store. The two soon formed the Coon-Sanders Novelty Orchestra. They recorded four numbers in 1921, only one of which was released, and then more importantly, on Dec. 5, 1922, they made their first radio broadcast. Soon they caught on big; the orchestra was renamed the Nighhawks (since their show was on late, from midnight until 2 a.m.) and became very popu-

lar in the Midwest. The Coon-Sanders Nighthawks recorded regularly from 1924 on, cutting around 75 selections during the next eight years; they relocated to Chicago later in 1924 and prospered on both road trips and the radio. Although none of the sidemen became individually famous, the band featured lots of brief solos, while Sanders' arrangements were full of surprises, and the two co-leaders' vocals were consistently heated whether performing stomps, novelties or rare ballads. Only Coon's sudden death on May 5, 1932, after an operation on a septic tooth, halted the magic. Joe Sanders lived until May 1965 and led a band on and off through 1959, but it never recorded again. The Old Masters label has recently started a CD reissue series slated to include all of the very enjoyable Coon-Sanders Nighthawks recordings, which still sound fun more than seven decades later. —*Scott Yanow*

● **Coon-Sanders Nighthawks, Vol. 1** / Mar. 24, 1921-Dec. 21, 1925 / Old Masters ✦✦✦✦✦

The Coon-Sanders Nighthawks, one of the most popular bands of the 1920s, was also one of the finest of the decade. Co-led by pianist Joe Sanders and drummer Carleton Coon, the orchestra became famous through their radio programs and were a household name until Coon's death in the early 1930s. Sanders' arrangements were consistently exciting and full of surprises; the co-leaders were both hot singers (no dull ballad features); and the musicianship of the group (which grew during the time covered by this CD from eight to ten pieces) was impeccable. The first volume of their records has the orchestra's initial 23 recordings: one selection from 1921 ("Some Little Bird") and 22 from the 1924-25 period. During the era, few regular outfits were on the same level as the Nighthawks (other than those led by Fletcher Henderson and Paul Whiteman). With short solos from a variety of obscure horn players, many memorable numbers (including "Red Hot Mama," "Some of These Days," "Everything Is Hotsy-Totsy Now" and "Flamin' Mamie"), and Sanders' inventive charts, the jazz-oriented band always put on a great show. Although their most significant recordings will be included in later volumes, this particular CD is highly recommended to 1920s collectors. —*Scott Yanow*

Bob Cooper

b. Dec. 6, 1925, Pittsburgh, PA, d. Aug. 5, 1993, Hollywood, CA
Tenor Saxophone, Oboe / Cool, Hard Bop

One of the great West Coast tenors, Bob Cooper made even the most complex solos sound swinging and accessible. "Coop" joined Stan Kenton's big band in 1945 and he was a fixture with several of the editions (including the Innovations Orchestra) through 1951; in 1947 he married Kenton's singer, June Christy. After leaving Kenton, Cooper settled in Los Angeles where he was a busy studio musician for the next four decades. He was a regular member of the Lighthouse All-Stars from 1952-62, sometimes playing oboe and English horn (being the first strong jazz soloist on both of those instruments). The cool-toned tenor (whose sound fit into the "Four Brothers" style) was on many records in the 1950s (including those of Shorty Rogers, Pete Rugolo and June Christy) and continued working steadily in Los Angeles-area clubs up until his death. He appears on records with the big bands of Frank Capp/Nat Pierce, Bob Florence and the 1980s version of the Lighthouse All-Stars and participated in the 1991 Stan Kenton 50th-anniversary celebration. As a leader Cooper recorded for Capitol in the 1950s, Contemporary, Trend, Discovery and Fresh Sound. —*Scott Yanow*

Group Activity / May 5, 1954-Aug. 2, 1954 / Affinity ✦✦✦✦✦

This generous English import LP has five Capitol sessions from 1954 (18 selections in all) that are led by either Bob Cooper or Bill Holman. The cool-toned but hard-driving tenor Coop is heard on his first two dates as a leader, jamming through standards and swinging originals with Bud Shank (who surprisingly sticks here exclusively to baritone), pianist Claude Williamson, guitarist Howard Roberts, either Joe Mondragon or Curtis Counce on bass and Shelly Manne or Stan Levey on drums. The remainder of this album features ten compositions by Bill Holman who not only wrote for the octet but takes some fine tenor solos. His sidemen include Don Fagerquist or Nick Travis and Stu Williamson on trumpets, valve trombonist Bob Enevoldsen, altoist Herb Geller, baritonist Bob Gordon, Curtis Counce or Max Bennett on bass and drummer Stan Levey. The generally exciting music shows that the stereotype of most West Coast jazz as bloodless was quite inaccurate. Well worth searching for. —*Scott Yanow*

Shifting Winds / Apr. 26, 1955-Jun. 14, 1955 / Capitol ✦✦✦✦

Worthy reissue of an intriguing session with Cooper on unusual instruments (oboe and English horn), plus tenor. —*Ron Wynn*

● **Coop! the Music of Bob Cooper** / Aug. 26, 1958-Aug. 27, 1958 / Original Jazz Classics ✦✦✦✦✦

Tenor saxophonist Bob Cooper's only Contemporary album (reissued on CD in the Original Jazz Classics series) is a near-classic and one of his finest recordings. Coop, along with trombonist Frank Rosolino, vibraphonist Victor Feldman, pianist

Lou Levy, bassist Max Bennett and drummer Mel Lewis, performs colorful versions of five standards (best are "Confirmation," "Easy Living" and "Somebody Loves Me") that show off his attractive tone and ability to swing at any tempo. Half of the release consists of his "Jazz Theme and Four Variations," a very interesting work that holds together quite well throughout 23-minutes and five movements; three trumpeters (including Conte Candoli) and one trombone are added to make the ensembles richer. This set is an underrated gem. —*Scott Yanow*

Tenor Sax Jazz Impressions / May 6, 1979 / Discovery ✦✦✦
Well-done material from late 70s. —*Ron Wynn*

The Music of Michel Legrand, Vol. 1 / Jul. 31, 1980 / Discovery ✦✦✦
Other than a few titles in 1961, the great tenor saxophonist Bob Cooper did not lead any recording sessions during 1958-78. For his second Discovery album, Cooper performs eight Michel Legrand compositions of which "Watch What Happens" and "What Are You Doing the Rest of Your Life" are easily the best known. The emphasis throughout is on ballads although a couple of the pieces are taken at quicker tempos. Cooper plays well (as does pianist Mike Wofford, bassist Tom Azarello and drummer Jim Plank) but there is not much mood or tempo variation on this out-of-print LP. —*Scott Yanow*

In a Mellotone / Oct. 27, 1985 / Contemporary ✦✦✦✦
Tenor saxophonist Bob Cooper teams up with a group of hard-swinging mainstreamers (trumpeter Snooky Young, pianist Ross Tompkins, guitarist Doug MacDonald, bassist Monty Budwig and Jeff Hamilton) on this LP to play a program filled with veteran standards and a few newer pieces. The emphasis is on no-nonsense swinging, particularly during such numbers as "In a Mellotone" and "Jumpin' at the Woodside." The underrated vocalist Ernie Andrews is featured on four numbers (a blues, "Satin Doll" and two ballads) that add some variety to the upbeat proceedings. —*Scott Yanow*

For All We Know / Aug. 15, 1990-Aug. 16, 1990 / Fresh Sound ✦✦✦✦

Bob Cooper/Conde Candoli Quintet / Jun. 25, 1995 / V.S.O.P. ✦✦✦✦
It is difficult to believe, listening to this enthusiastic bop date, that tenor saxophonist Bob Cooper would pass away only 41 days after the recorded concert. Cooper never declined, and he certainly sounds right in his prime, jamming eight standards with trumpeter Conte Candoli (long an underrated great), pianist Ross Tompkins, bassist John Leitham and drummer Paul Kreibich. Whether it be a romping "Confirmation," "Airegin," "Hackensack" or a medium-tempo "Come Sunday," this is a highly enjoyable straightahead set with everyone in excellent form. Bob Cooper certainly went out on top. —*Scott Yanow*

Buster Cooper

b. Apr. 4, 1929, St. Petersburg, FL
Trombone

An extroverted trombone stylist best known for his association with Duke Ellington, Buster Cooper has a witty style (which sometimes involves hitting repeated, humorous high notes at the conclusion of a song) and is always a joy to hear. Early on, he played with Nat Towles' territory band in Texas. Cooper worked with Lionel Hampton in 1953, was in the Apollo Theatre's house band for two years, played with Benny Goodman and formed the Cooper Brothers Band with his brother Steve on bass. The trombonist had plenty of solo space with Duke Ellington's Orchestra from 1962-69, spent time in Florida and moved to Los Angeles in 1973, where for the next couple of decades he played with many local jazz orchestras, including the Juggernaut and Bill Berry's L.A. Band. Oddly enough, the colorful Buster Cooper has not yet had the opportunity to lead his own record date. —*Scott Yanow*

Marc Copland

Piano / Post-Bop

Marc Copland actually began his musical career as a saxophonist, playing alto with Chico Hamilton in the early 1970s shortly after arriving in New York. However, he soon took time off, changed direction, and re-emerged as a pianist whose lyricism sometimes recalls Bill Evans and Keith Jarrett. Copland has recorded as a leader for Sunnyside, Savoy and Jazzline and has also been a talented sidemen for a variety of modern mainstream all-stars. —*Scott Yanow*

Chick Corea (Armando Anthony Corea)

b. Jun. 12, 1941, Chelsea, MA
Piano, Keyboards / Fusion, Post-Bop, Free Jazz

Chick Corea has been one of the most significant jazzmen of the past 30 years. Not content at any time to rest on his laurels, Corea has been involved in quite a few important musical projects and his musical curiosity has never dimmed. A masterful pianist who along with Herbie Hancock and Keith Jarrett was one of the top stylists to emerge after Bill Evans and McCoy Tyner, Corea is also one of the few electric keyboardists to be quite individual and recognizable on synthesizers. In addition he has composed several jazz standards including "Spain," "La Fiesta" and "Windows."

Corea began playing piano when he was four and early on Horace Silver and Bud Powell were influences. He picked up important experience playing with the bands of Mongo Santamaria and Willie Bobo (1962-63), Blue Mitchell (1964-66), Herbie Mann and Stan Getz. He made his recording debut as a leader with 1966's *Tones for Joan's Bones,* and his 1968 trio set (with Miroslav Vitous and Roy Haynes) *Now He Sings, Now He Sobs* is considered a classic. After a short stint with Sarah Vaughan, Corea joined Miles Davis as Herbie Hancock's gradual replacement, staying with Miles during a very important transitional period (1968-70). He was persuaded by the trumpeter to start playing electric piano and was on such significant albums as *Filles de Kilimanjaro, In a Silent Way, Bitches Brew* and *Miles Davis at the Fillmore.* When he left Davis, Corea at first chose to play avant-garde acoustic jazz in Circle, a quartet with Anthony Braxton, Dave Holland and Barry Altschul. But at the end of 1971 he changed directions again.

Leaving Circle, Corea played briefly with Stan Getz and then formed Return to Forever, which started out as a melodic Brazilian group with Stanley Clarke, Joe Farrell, Airto and Flora Purim. Within a year Corea (with Clarke, Bill Connors and Lenny White) had changed Return to Forever into a pacesetting and high-powered fusion band; Al DiMeola took Connors' place in 1974. While the music was rock-oriented, it still retained the improvisations of jazz and Corea remained quite recognizable, even under the barrage of electronics. When RTF broke up in the late '70s, Corea retained the name for some big-band dates with Clarke. During the next few years he generally emphasized his acoustic playing and appeared in a wide variety of contexts including separate duet tours with Gary Burton and Herbie Hancock, a quartet with Michael Brecker, trios with Miroslav Vitous and Roy Haynes, tributes to Thelonious Monk and even some classical music.

In 1985 Chick Corea formed a new fusion group, the Elektric Band, which eventually featured bassist John Patitucci, guitarist Frank Gambale, saxophonist Eric Marienthal and drummer Dave Weckl. To balance out his music, a few years later he formed his Akoustic Trio with Patitucci and Weckl. When Patitucci went out on his own in the early '90s the personnel changed but Corea has continued leading stimulating groups (including a recent quartet with Patitucci and Bob Berg) up until the present time. During 1996-97 Corea toured with an all-star quintet (including Kenny Garrett and Wallace Roney) that played modern versions of Bud Powell and Thelonious Monk compositions. He remains an important force in modern jazz and every phase of his development has been well documented on records. —*Scott Yanow*

Music Forever and Beyond: the Selected Works of Chick Corea / 1949-1996 / GRP ♦♦♦♦♦

This very attractive five-CD set does an excellent job of summing up the rather productive career of pianist-keyboardist Chick Corea. The first two discs have highlights from the 1964-82 period including a few sideman appearances, a previously unissued version of "Windows" played with Stan Getz, the original version of "Spain," four pieces from the Return to Forever days and numbers from his freelance projects of the late '70s (highlighted by the exciting "Central Park"). The third disc concentrates on Corea's GRP projects (1986-94), particularly his Elektric and Akoustic Bands (two selections were previously unissued) while the fourth CD is quite a grab bag that includes collaborations with Herbie Hancock (a version of "Liza" that progresses from stride to free), Gayle Moran, John McLaughlin, Paco DeLucia, Gary Burton, Bobby McFerrin and Miles Davis (a new duet version of "I Fall in Love So Easily" from 1969). In addition Corea is heard as an eight-year-old in 1949 on a privately recorded 78 playing a short piano solo and on a version of "'Round Midnight" with strings that was recorded for this 1996 box. In fact the fifth disc consists exclusively of new recordings of standards (plus one original) by Corea in an acoustic quartet with tenor saxophonist Bob Berg (who has rarely sounded more exciting). This well-conceived set is highly recommended even to Chick Corea fans who might have some of his earlier records. A gem. —*Scott Yanow*

Inner Space / 1966 / Atlantic ♦♦♦♦

This double LP reissues Chick Corea's first album as a leader, *Tones for Joan's Bones,* adding two previously unissued tracks from the same session plus a pair of performances from a Hubert Laws date of the period that feature Corea's piano and writing. With such players as Joe Farrell on tenor and flute, trumpeter Woody Shaw, bassist Steve Swallow and drummer Joe Chambers on this Corea date, the pianist performs five of his originals plus "This Is New" while the Laws cuts include Corea's "Windows." Throughout, this advanced hard bop music, which keeps an open attitude towards the avant-garde innovations of the period, is consistently stimulating. Even at this early stage, Chick Corea's playing is quite recognizable. —*Scott Yanow*

Now He Sings, Now He Sobs / Mar. 14, 1968-Mar. 27, 1968 / Blue Note ♦♦♦♦♦

The original LP (using the same title) only had five selections, but this CD contains 13, with the added eight (from the same sessions) having first been released on the double-LP *Circling In.* Age 26 at the time, and on the brink of gaining major recognition in the jazz world, pianist Chick Corea is featured with a very strong trio that also includes bassist Miroslav Vitous and drummer Roy Haynes. The music includes 11 of Corea's originals including "Matrix," "Windows" and "Samba Yantra," Thelonious Monk's "Pannonica" and the standard "My One and Only Love" and is essentially advanced hard bop with an open-minded attitude towards free jazz. Listen to how part of "Steps-What Was" has hints of Corea's future composition "Spain." —*Scott Yanow*

Is / Jun. 30, 1969 / Solid State ♦♦

Listeners most familiar with Chick Corea through his work with Return to Forever and the Elektric Band will be very surprised if they stumble across this LP. The music on the sextet date (which includes trumpeter Woody Shaw and Hubert Laws on flute) is often quite free and explorative, exploring a variety of moods (some of them rather violent). Rambling and uneven (particularly during the 29-minute "Is"), this set is not essential but has its interesting moments. —*Scott Yanow*

Sundance / 1969 / Groove Merchant ♦♦

Recorded during the same period as *Is, Sundance* has four very advanced (if forgettable) Chick Corea compositions interpreted by a septet that includes trumpeter Woody Shaw, Hubert Laws on flute and Bennie Maupin on reeds. Actually, this is a lesser Corea item with plenty of rambling moments (although it is generally not as free as *Is*) and is recommended mostly to completists of the pianist who are interested in his early development. —*Scott Yanow*

Early Circle / Apr. 8, 1970-Oct. 18, 1970 / Blue Note ♦♦♦♦

Chick Corea's most esoteric music of his career was performed when he was a member of Circle, an avant-garde quartet that during 1970-71 featured pianist Corea, the reeds of Anthony Braxton, bassist Dave Holland and drummer Barry Altschul. This CD contains some of their briefer performances including bass/piano and clarinet/piano duets, two versions of "Chimes," "Percussion Piece," a free ballad and Braxton's "73 Degrees—A Kelvin." These free explorations are worth listening to closely, but one has to put away any preconceptions that they have about Corea. The title of this CD is a bit silly though, for Circle broke up only a few months after these recordings. —*Scott Yanow*

Song of Singing / Apr. 7, 1970-Apr. 8, 1970 / Blue Note ♦♦♦♦

This LP features the rhythm section of Circle (pianist Chick Corea, bassist Dave Holland and drummer Barry Altschul) playing rather advanced improvisations on group originals (highlighted by Holland's "Toy Room") and "Nefertiti." Influenced by the early Art Ensemble of Chicago, this music is rather free and avant-garde but rewards close listenings. —*Scott Yanow*

Circulus / Aug. 21, 1970 / Blue Note ♦♦♦

Chick Corea has had a very diverse career and has consistently been among the most popular of all jazzmen, but his avant-garde music of 1970-71 certainly will not appeal to fans of his fusion band, Return to Forever. His group, Circle, is well showcased on this two-LP set, which finds Corea, reed master Anthony Braxton, bassist Dave Holland and drummer Barry Altschul performing three lengthy group improvisations. In addition, Altschul is showcased on "Percussion Piece" and Braxton sits out on the trio selection "Drone." The music is generally quite difficult with sound explorations emphasized over melodic development, and is much closer to the direction that Braxton would explore than what Corea would be playing two years later. But open-eared listeners who enjoy avant-garde jazz will find much to savor during these fascinating performances from one of the new music's top (if short-lived) regular groups. —*Scott Yanow*

A.R.C. / Jan. 1971 / ECM ♦♦♦♦

This LP features pianist Chick Corea, bassist Dave Holland and drummer Barry Altschul during the brief period that, along with Anthony Braxton, they were members of the fine avant-garde quartet Circle. The music heard on this set is not quite as free as Circle's but often very explorative. Four of the six songs are Corea originals that, in addition to Holland's "Vedana" and Wayne Shorter's "Nefertiti," form a very viable set of adventurous jazz, recorded just a few months before Corea changed direction. —*Scott Yanow*

Circle/Paris-Concert / Feb. 21, 1971 / ECM ♦♦♦♦♦

Of all of the recordings from the short-lived avant-garde quartet Circle, this double-LP is the most rewarding. Cut live in Paris, this set features pianist Chick Corea, the reeds of Anthony Braxton, bassist Dave Holland and drummer Barry Altschul playing a wide variety of fairly free explorations. Highlights include their reinterpretation of the standard "There Is No Greater Love," the playful "Toy Room—Q & A," Braxton's "73 Degrees Kelvin" and "Nefertiti." The music is often quite abstract but generally colorful and innovative; Chick Corea would soon break up the band for other musical adventures, but this set remains one of the high points of his productive career. —*Scott Yanow*

Piano Improvisations, Vol. 1 / Apr. 21, 1971-Apr. 22, 1971 / ECM ✦✦✦

After spending a year with the avant-garde quartet Circle, Chick Corea's desire to communicate to a wider audience led to him deciding to break up the unit. His first post-Circle recordings were two LPs of piano solos. *Vol. 1* features six of his originals including the eight sketches of "Where Are You Now?," and the debut of the future standard "Sometime Ago." These performances are sometimes a bit precious, but they succeed in being acccessible and serve as a transition between Circle and Return to Forever. —*Scott Yanow*

Piano Improvisations, Vol. 2 / Apr. 21, 1971-Apr. 22, 1971 / ECM ✦✦✦

This is the second of two LPs recorded by Chick Corea shortly after he broke up the avant-garde quartet Circle, saying that he wanted to communicate to a larger audience. As with the first set, these brief sketches are melodic and a bit precious but contain some strong moments. In addition to seven Corea originals, he interprets Thelonious Monk's "Trinkle Tinkle" and Wayne Shorter's "Masquellero." Not essential but worth acquiring. —*Scott Yanow*

★ **Light as a Feather** / Sep. 1972 / Polydor ✦✦✦✦✦

Of the three versions of Return to Forever, the initial version is of the greatest interest from the jazz standpoint. With Joe Farrell on reeds, bassist Stanley Clarke, Airto on drums and percussion and Flora Purim contributing vocals, this contingent was one of the finest groups of the 1972-73 period even if they only actually cut two records. This particular set includes the original version of Chick Corea's greatest composition ("Spain") along with versions of "500 Miles High" and "Captain Marvel." This music crosses many boundaries and still sounds fresh two decades later. —*Scott Yanow*

Return to Forever / Feb. 2, 1972-Feb. 3, 1972 / ECM ✦✦✦✦

Chick Corea's original version of Return to Forever (featuring Joe Farrell on flute and soprano, bassist Stanley Clarke, Airto on drums and percussion and singer Flora Purim along with the pianist/leader) was only in existence long enough to record two albums. This self-titled set is highlighted by a side-long medley of "Sometime Ago" and "La Fiesta" and demonstrates that it is possible to create music that is both strong jazz and popular. —*Scott Yanow*

Crystal Silence / Nov. 6, 1972 / ECM ✦✦✦✦

Chick Corea and Gary Burton teamed up for a series of piano/vibraphone duets on November 6, 1972, playing originals by Corea and Steve Swallow along with Mike Gibbs' "Feeling and Things." The most memorable performances on this introspective but fairly joyful set are "Senor Mouse" and "What Game Shall We Play Today." —*Scott Yanow*

● **Hymn of the Seventh Galaxy** / Aug. 1973 / Polydor ✦✦✦✦✦

The second (and most popular) version of Return to Forever debuted with this strong fusion effort. This was guitarist Bill Connors' only recording with the group, and he is particularly fiery on "Captain Senor Mouse" and "Hymn of the Seventh Galaxy." With Chick Corea on keyboards, Stanley Clarke on electric bass and drummer Lenny White, this was one of the top fusion bands, mixing together the power and sound of rock with the sophisticated improvisations of jazz. Fans of late-'60s rock were able to enter the world of jazz through albums such as this near-classic. —*Scott Yanow*

Where Have I Known You Before / Jul. 1974-Aug. 1974 / Polydor ✦✦✦✦

This historic set was Chick Corea's first recording with the fiery young guitarist Al DiMeola (who had replaced Bill Connors) and the first Return to Forever set with DiMeola, bassist Stanley Clarke and drummer Lenny White. Although none of the originals (six by Corea and one apiece by Clarke and White) became major hits, the power and colorful sound of the talented band's passionate playing made RTF one of the most popular of all the fusion groups of the 1970s. This set (which is not recommended to acoustic jazz purists) is a fusion classic. —*Scott Yanow*

The Leprechaun / 1975 / Polydor ✦✦

Chick Corea took a break from his fusion group, Return to Forever, to record this slightly more jazz-oriented effort. Such players as saxophonist Joe Farrell, trombonist Bill Watrous and bassist Eddie Gomez are on the date (as is vocalist Gayle Moran) but few of the tracks are all that memorable. A somewhat forgettable effort. —*Scott Yanow*

Romantic Warrior / Feb. 1976 / Columbia ✦✦✦

Return to Forever still had plenty of power left by the time of this later recording. Keyboardist Chick Corea, guitarist Al DiMeola, electric bassist Stanley Clarke and drummer Lenny White brought rock to a high creative level while leaving many jazz listeners behind with efforts such as this high-energy fusion set. —*Scott Yanow*

★ **My Spanish Heart** / Oct. 1976 / Polydor ✦✦✦✦✦

Chick Corea has long been one of the most distinctive of all electric keyboardists, being able to transfer his mastery of the acoustic piano successfully to synthesizers. This double-LP, a classic of its genre, is full of delightful new melodies (particularly the last section of "El Bozo") and masterful keyboard playing along with a few guest appearances by a string quartet, a small brass section, singer Gayle Moran, bassist Stanley Clarke and drummer Steve Gadd. —*Scott Yanow*

Music Magic / Jan. 1977-Feb. 1977 / Columbia ✦✦

The third and final edition of Return to Forever gave Chick Corea an excuse to write for a four-piece brass section and to tour with bassist Stanley Clarke, his old friend saxophonist Joe Farrell, drummer Gerry Brown and his future wife, vocalist Gayle Moran. Unfortunately, the compositions are not too memorable on this set and the lyrics are a bit lightweight. Better to acquire this group's live recording if possible. —*Scott Yanow*

R.T.F. Live / May 20, 1977-May 21, 1977 / Columbia ✦✦✦✦

The final Return to Forever album, by Chick Corea's third group to use that name, is a massive four-LP box set that documents a complete concert. This band, in addition to the keyboards of Chick Corea, featured electric bassist Stanley Clarke and singer Gayle Moran plus the reeds of Joe Farrell, drummer Gerry Brown and a five-piece brass section. The music is generally jazz-oriented with extended versions of such songs as "The Musician," "So Long Mickey Mouse," "Musicmagic" and "Spanish Fantasy" along with a piano/bass duet encore version of "On Green Dolphin Street." Worth searching for. —*Scott Yanow*

Live at Midem / Jan. 22, 1978-Feb. 1978 / Who's Who ✦✦✦

With the breakup of the final Return to Forever, Chick Corea began a long period of freelancing, resulting in some unlikely collaborations. For much of this concert performance, the pianist teams up with veteran vibraphonist Lionel Hampton for some swinging music. Corea is heard without Hamp on "Fiesta" and on singer Gayle Moran's feature on "Come Rain or Come Shine" and joins in with the ageless vibist for "Moments Notice" and the spirited blues "I Ain't Mad at You." Not essential music, but this LP is fun. —*Scott Yanow*

Homecoming: Corea and Hancock / Feb. 1978 / Polydor ✦✦✦

In 1978, Chick Corea and Herbie Hancock surprised the jazz world by temporarily putting aside their electric keyboards and touring as an acoustic piano duet. Two double LPs resulted (Columbia's *An Evening With . . .* was released under Hancock's name), and both feature lengthy improvisations. This particular two-fer has three Corea compositions (including "La Fiesta"), Hancock's "Maiden Voyage," a brief classical piece by Bartok, and a collaboration on "The Hook." Since Hancock and Corea have overlapping styles and an obvious mutual affection, their playing on this set is quite complementary, although enjoyably competitive in spots, and they leave plenty of room for each other in the ensembles. —*Scott Yanow*

Delphi I: Solo Piano Improvisations / Oct. 26, 1978+Oct. 27, 1978 / Polydor ✦✦

This set of acoustic piano improvisations by Chick Corea (the eight-part Delphi series, "Children's Song No. 20" and the seven-part "Stride Time") is surprisingly dull. In the liner notes, Corea states that whatever the message is that he is trying to get across with this music is not complete without the next two volumes. To date they have never been released. This disappointing LP can be safely passed by. —*Scott Yanow*

Friends / 1978 / Polydor ✦✦✦✦

Although this set contains eight lesser-known Chick Corea compositions, it is in reality a fine blowing date. Corea, on both acoustic and electric pianos, is joined by his old friend Joe Farrell on reeds, bassist Eddie Gomez and drummer Steve Gadd for some fine straightahead jazz. —*Scott Yanow*

The Mad Hatter / 1978 / Polydor ✦✦✦

This post-Return to Forever Chick Corea LP is a bit of a mixed bag. Corea is heard on his many keyboards during an atmospheric "The Woods," interacts with a string section on "Tweedle Dee," features a larger band plus singer Gayle Moran on a few other songs and even welcomes fellow keyboardist Herbie Hancock for the "Mad Hatter Rhapsody." The most interesting selection, a quartet rendition of "Humpty Dumpty" with tenorman Joe Farrell set the stage for his next project, *Friends*. Overall, this is an interesting and generally enjoyable release. —*Scott Yanow*

Secret Agent / 1978 / Polydor ✦✦✦

This orchestral project finds Chick Corea using colleagues from the final version of Return to Forever and singer Gayle Moran along with occasional strings and some newer associates such as trumpeter Al Vizzutti, electric bassist Bunny Brunel and drummer Tom Brechtlein. A bit of a mixed bag, most of the music is quite satisfying, particularly the exciting "Central Park." —*Scott Yanow*

Chick Corea and Gary Burton in Concert / Oct. 23, 1978+Oct. 25, 1978 / ECM ✦✦✦

During Chick Corea's freelance period after Return to Forever broke up and before he formed his Elektric Band, the pianist collaborated with many of his favorite musicians. This two-LP set contains eight duets with vibraphonist Gary Burton (highlighted by "Senor Mouse," "Bud Powell" and a remake of "Crystal Silence") along with one solo performance apiece by the two masterful musicians. The music is often introspective, but there are some exciting moments. —*Scott Yanow*

Live in Montreux / 1981 / Stretch ✦✦✦✦

Three Quartets / Jan. 1981-Feb. 1981 / Stretch ✦✦✦✦✦

This encounter between Chick Corea (sticking to acoustic piano), tenor saxophonist Michael Brecker, bassist Eddie Gomez and drummer Steve Gadd lives up to one's expectations. The original program featured three lengthy "Quartet" pieces including sections dedicated to Duke Ellington and John Coltrane. The CD reissue adds four briefer pieces that were previously unissued including an unaccompanied Brecker workout on "Confirmation" that would be perfect for "blindfold" tests. This blowing date is highly recommended for all true jazz fans. —*Scott Yanow*

Trio Music / Nov. 1981 / ECM ✦✦✦✦

Pianist Chick Corea had a reunion with bassist Miroslav Vitous and drummer Roy Haynes for this double LP, 13 years after they had recorded *Now He Sings, Now He Sobs*. The first half of this two-fer consists of duet and trio-free improvisations and is sometimes a touch lightweight even with moments of interest; playing free was not as natural to Corea by this time as it had been in the 1960s. However, the second album, seven Thelonious Monk compositions, comes across quite well as Corea does justice to the spirit of Monk without losing his own strong musical personality. —*Scott Yanow*

Tap Step / Dec. 1978-Jan. 1980 / Warner Brothers ✦✦✦

This interesting collection finds Chick Corea playing seven then-new originals with a variety of musicians including flutist Hubert Laws, tenor saxophonist Joe Farrell, trumpeter Al Vizzutti, bassist Stanley Clarke and, on "Flamenco," tenor saxophonist Joe Henderson. The music is pleasing and spirited if not all that memorable; an average release from a hugely talented jazzman. —*Scott Yanow*

Touchstone / 1982 / Stretch ✦✦✦

Chick Corea was involved in a wide variety of projects during the early 1980s, some acoustic, others electric, and everything from solos and duets to orchestral projects. Touchstone really displays quite a bit of diversity with features for flamenco guitarist Paco DeLucia, a one-song ("Compadres") reunion of Return to Forever (with guitarist Al DiMeola, bassist Stanley Clarke and drummer Lenny White), a spot for alto-great Lee Konitz ("Duende") and a conventional sextet outing on "Dance of Chance." A bit uneven but with its interesting moments, *Touchstone* is worth checking out. —*Scott Yanow*

Again and Again / Mar. 23, 1982 / Elektra ✦✦✦

Chick Corea's regularly working band of 1982, a quintet with Steve Kujala on flute, soprano and tenor, took time off from a tour of South Africa to record six of the keyboardist's originals. The music, although sometimes electric, is generally modern mainstream with some adventurous moments. None of the newer songs (such as "Diddle Diddle" and "Twang") caught on and they were all more or less forgotten when this band broke up. However the music is still enjoyable, capturing Corea at a transitional point in his career. —*Scott Yanow*

The Meeting / Jun. 27, 1982 / Philips ✦✦✦

Chick Corea spent the years between the breakup of Return to Forever and the formation of his Elektric Band indulging in many one-time collaborations with musicians he admired. This LP finds Corea teaming up with fellow pianist Friedrich Gulda for lengthy improvisations that mix together jazz (including "Someday My Prince Will Come") and classical themes. There are some surprising moments during these long performances, with Corea and Gulda inspiring each other to come up with creative ideas. —*Scott Yanow*

Lyric Suite for Sextet / Sep. 1982 / ECM ✦✦✦

For this meeting between pianist Chick Corea and vibraphonist Gary Burton, their duets are augmented by a string quartet. The seven sections of the "Lyrics Suite for Sextet" (which includes a "Sketch" for Thelonious Monk) contain more variety than one might expect and this set rewards repeated listenings. —*Scott Yanow*

Children's Songs / Jul. 1983 / ECM ✦✦

This solo LP finds pianist Chick Corea playing his 20 *Children's Songs*, brief (under three minute) sketches that quickly set a mood and then end; none are fully developed or memorable by themselves. It's one of Corea's less significant efforts. —*Scott Yanow*

Voyage / Jul. 1984 / ECM ✦✦

For this somewhat obscure Chick Corea LP, the pianist teams up with flutist Steve Kujala for a set of duets. Together they perform three of Corea's lesser-known originals along with two melodic free improvisations. It's pleasant music but not particularly memorable compared to Corea's group projects. —*Scott Yanow*

Septet / Jul. 1984-Oct. 1984 / ECM ✦✦

Trio Music: Live in Europe / Sep. 1984 / ECM ✦✦✦✦

Pianist Chick Corea had a reunion with bassist Miroslav Vitous and drummer Roy Haynes for this well-rounded set of trio performances. In addition to three standards (including "I Hear a Rhapsody" and "Night and Day"), the group performs a touch of classical music and four originals. —*Scott Yanow*

The Elektrik Band / 1986 / GRP ✦✦✦✦

Nine years after the breakup of the final version of Return to Forever, Chick Corea ended a long period of freelance projects by forming his Elektrik Band. This set, the group's initial release, finds Corea meeting up for the first time with the great bassist John Patitucci and drummer Dave Weckl; half of the selections also have either Carlos Rios or Scott Henderson on guitar. Due to the high musicianship, the personalities of the players and Corea's colorful compositions, the Elektrik Band quickly became one of the top fusion groups of the late '80s. -*Scott Yanow*

Priceless Jazz Collection / 1986-1993 / GRP ✦✦✦

Priceless Jazz Collection is a budget-priced compilation that intends to give neophytes an affordable introduction to Chick Corea's GRP recordings. Although purists and collectors will find this sampler incomplete and inconsequential, it nevertheless gives new listeners a good idea of Corea's work during this era by featuring such necessary items as "Make a Wish, Pts. I & II," "Spain," "Blue Miles" and "Light Years." —*Stephen Thomas Erlewine*

Light Years / 1987 / GRP ✦✦✦✦

The second recording by Chick Corea's Elektric Band was the first to feature altoist Eric Marienthal and guitarist Frank Gambale in addition to bassist John Patitucci, drummer Dave Weckl and the leader/keyboardist. Unlike most other fusion groups, these musicians displayed original musical personalitites and Corea's compositions tended to be memorable. This is one of the Elektric Band's better releases. —*Scott Yanow*

Eye of the Beholder / 1988 / GRP ✦✦✦✦✦

During an era when the word "fusion" was applied to any mixture of jazz with pop or funk, Chick Corea's Elektric Band reinforced the word's original meaning: a combination of jazz improvisations with the power, rhythms and sound of rock. *Eye of the Beholder,* which found guitarist Frank Gambale, saxophonist Eric Marienthal and bassist John Patitucci displaying increasingly original solo voices, is one of this group's finest recordings and ranks with the best fusion of the latter half of the 1980s. —*Scott Yanow*

Akoustic Band / 1989 / GRP ✦✦✦✦

As a contrast to his Elektric Band, Chick Corea formed the Akoustic Band with bassist John Patitucci and drummer Dave Weckl. This trio gave him a chance to stretch out acoustically in a straightahead setting on a variety of standards and originals. Their debut release is highlighted by "Bessie's Blues," "My One and Only Love," "Someday My Prince Will Come" and Corea's "Spain." —*Scott Yanow*

Inside Out / 1990 / GRP ✦✦✦✦

Chick Corea's Elektric Band was always a well-intergrated unit, featuring passionate solos from the rockish guitarist Frank Gambale and the R&Bish saxophonist Eric Marienthal in addition to major statements from the distinctive leader who utilized a battery of keyboards yet remained quite recognizable. With John Patitucci (arguably jazz's top electric bassist) and drummer Dave Weckl pushing the ensemble, this pacesetting fusion unit is heard at its peak on these Corea originals. —*Scott Yanow*

Alive / 1991 / GRP ✦✦✦✦

The second effort by Chick Corea's Akoustic Band (a trio with bassist John Patitucci and drummer Dave Weckl) is an enjoyable set of straightahead jazz with such standards explored as "On Green Dolphin Street," "Sophisticated Lady" and Thelonious Monk's "Hackensack," along with two Corea originals. —*Scott Yanow*

Beneath the Mask / Aug. 22, 1991 / GRP ✦✦✦

The fifth and final recording by the original version of Chick Corea's Elektric Band is not quite up to the level of the past few sets due to some forgettable compositions. The keyboardist/leader, guitarist Frank Gambale and saxophonist Eric Marienthal create some fine solos and the ensembles (with bassist John Patitucci and drummer Dave Weckl) are tight, making this a worthwhile but not essential release from the top fusion group. —*Scott Yanow*

Expressions / 1993 / GRP ✦✦✦✦

Although Chick Corea has recorded quite a few releases throughout his career, solo albums are rare, particularly ones in which he explores standards. This acoustic set (which he dedicated to Art Tatum) finds Corea performing such songs as "Lush Life," "My Ship," Bud Powell's "Oblivion" and even the veteran warhorse "I Want to Be Happy" with individuality, respect and creativity. —*Scott Yanow*

Paint the World / 1993 / GRP ◆◆◆◆

Chick Corea's Elektric Band II found bassist John Patitucci, drummer Dave Weckl and guitarist Frank Gambale going out on their own and being replaced by Jimmy Earl, Gary Novak and Mike Miller. Saxophonist Eric Marienthal was the only sideman from the first Elektric Band to stick with Corea. Although the new members are not as distinctive as their predecessors, the high-quality material played on this release (which includes Jimmy Heath's "CTA," "Blue Miles" and a variety of Corea originals) is very jazz-oriented and occasionally there are straightahead sections. This set is recommended even to listeners who have not yet acquired a taste for fusion. —*Scott Yanow*

Time Warp / 1995 / GRP ◆◆◆

Chick Corea features an acoustic quartet on this CD, performing a full set of original material. Although the music is tied to a lengthy, complicated and philosophical fictional piece outlined in great length in the liner notes (which are not really worth bothering with), the performances by the group (which comprises Corea on piano, Bob Berg on tenor and soprano, bassist John Patitucci and drummer Gary Novak) are excellent. Berg continues to grow and show individuality beyond the Michael Brecker influence (especially on soprano), the interplay between Corea and Patitucci is as impressive as ever and Novak is alert to the constantly changing musical events. Although none of these songs are destined to become standards, the almost-continuous music holds on to one's attention. —*Scott Yanow*

Return to the Seventh Galaxy / Sep. 1972-1975 / Polygram ◆◆◆◆

This two-CD set is a bit of a mixed bag. It serves as a retrospective of the first two versions of Chick Corea's Return to Forever, with three selections from *Light as a Feather* (featuring saxophonist Joe Farrell and singer Flora Purim), three from *Hymn of the Seventh Galaxy* (which has guitarist Bill Connors), five selections from *Where Have I Known You Before* and four taken from *No Mystery;* the latter two dates match keyboardist Corea with guitarist Al DiMeola, electric bassist Stanley Clarke and drummer Lenny White. However, the real reason for serious collectors to acquire this double-CD set is for the four previously unreleased selections (totaling 39 minutes), including three taken from 1973 and matching Corea and Clarke with guitarist Connors, drummer Steve Gadd and percussionist Mingo Lewis (highlighted by a 14-minute rendition of "Spain"). Whether RTF fans will want to duplicate the other performances to get these four is a bit debatable, making one wish that the "new" material had been released separately. —*Scott Yanow*

Remembering Bud Powell / 1997 / Stretch ◆◆◆◆◆

Pianist Chick Corea in 1996 gathered together some notable young all-stars (tenor saxophonist Joshua Redman, trumpeter Wallace Roney, altoist Kenny Garrett, bassist Christian McBride, plus veteran drummer Roy Haynes) for explorations of tunes by the innovative pianist Bud Powell. Although "Bouncin' with Bud," "Tempus Fugit" and "Celia" have been occasionally recorded by others, most of the complex songs (including "Mediocre," "Dusk in Sandi," "Oblivion" and "Glass Enclosure") have rarely been played in recent decades. Rather than play revivalist bebop, Corea and his associates (after authentically stating the melody) perform modern post bop improvisations in their own styles, so much of the music is way beyond bop. In addition to nine Powell songs, Corea contributed a song rightfully titled "Bud Powell." All of the talented musicians have a fair amount of solo space and sound consistently inspired, making this a very successful and easily recommended project. —*Scott Yanow*

Native Sense: The New Duets / 1997 / Stretch ◆◆◆◆

The Chick Corea/Gary Burton series resumed in the late '90s after a long hiatus with this beautiful CD of acoustic duets on piano, vibes and occasionally marimba. These collaborations sound remarkably fresh and spontaneous, with an inevitable sense of sweep and flow like a river rushing through rapidly changing terrain. Chick contributes the lion's share of compositions here; most are uniformly strong pieces of work. Some, like ""No Mystery" and the Spanish-tinged "Love Castle," are from the past; others, like the title track, with its attractively revolving ostinato base, the brooding "Post Script," and "Rhumbata," were composed for the sessions. The exceptions to the Corea monopoly are Bartok's Bagatelle No. 6, which serves as a prelude for Corea's brooding "Post Script," Bartok's exuberantly dissonant Bagatelle No. 2, and a madly rippling rendition of Monk's "Four on One" as the sole bop-style workout of the session. This is the product of two mature masters in their mid-50s from the jazz/rock era who know precisely what they want from their instruments and reject stylistic boundaries. —*Richard S. Ginell*

Larry Coryell

b. Apr. 2, 1943, Galveston, TX
Guitar / Fusion, Post-Bop

As one of the pioneers of jazz-rock—perhaps *the* pioneer in the ears of some—Larry Coryell deserves a special place in the history books. He brought what amounted to a nearly alien sensibility to jazz electric guitar playing in the 1960s, a hard-edged, cutting tone, phrasing and note-bending that owed as much to blues, rock and even country as it did to earlier, smoother bop influences. Yet as a true eclectic, armed with a brilliant technique, he is comfortable in almost every style, covering almost every base from the most decibel-heavy, distortion-laden electric work to the most delicate, soothing, intricate lines on acoustic guitar. Unfortunately, a lot of his most crucial electric work from the '60s and '70s is missing on CD, tied up by the erratic reissue schemes of Vanguard, RCA and other labels and by jazz-rock's myopically low level of status in the CD era (although that mindset is slowly changing).

According to Coryell, his interest in jazz took hold at the age of four, and after his family moved from Galveston to the state of Washington three years later, he began to learn the guitar, studying records by Tal Farlow, Barney Kessel and Johnny Smith. As a teenager, he played in a band led by pianist Mike Mandel, and by 1965 he gave up his journalism studies at the University of Washington in order to try his luck in New York as a musician. Before the year was out, he attracted much attention jamming in Greenwich Village and replaced Gabor Szabo in Chico Hamilton's band. In 1966, he made a startling recorded debut on Hamilton's *The Dealer* album, where his blues and rock ideas came to the fore, and that year he also played with a proto-jazz-rock band, the Free Spirits. Coryell's name spread even further in 1967-68 when he played with Gary Burton's combo, and he was one of the most prominent solo voices on Herbie Mann's popular *Memphis Underground* album (recorded in 1968). He, Mandel and Steve Marcus formed a group called Foreplay in 1969 (no relation to today's Fourplay), and by 1973, this became the core of the jazz-rock band Eleventh House, which after a promising start ran aground with a string of albums of variable quality.

In 1975, Coryell pulled the plug, concentrating on acoustic guitar and turning in a prolific series of duo and trio sessions with the likes of Philip Catherine, Emily Remler, John Scofield, Joe Beck, Steve Khan and John McLaughlin. In the mid-'80s, Coryell toured with McLaughlin and Paco DeLucia, and in 1986 participated in a five-way guitar session with his old idol Farlow, Scofield, Larry Carlton and John Abercrombie for the Jazzvisions series. Coryell has also recorded with Stephane Grappelli, Charles Mingus, Sonny Rollins and Kenny Barron, and has taped Brazilian music with Dori Caymmi for CTI, mainstream jazz for Muse, solo guitar for Shanachie, and (for Nippon Phonogram in Japan) an album of classical transcriptions of music by Stravinsky and Rimsky-Korsakov. In other words, Coryell will probably remain as eclectic as ever throughout his career, which will no doubt make life difficult for musicologists with a yen for pigeonholing. —*Richard S. Ginell*

Basics (1968-1969) / 1968-1969 / Vanguard ◆◆

This album of leftovers from Vanguard sessions is better than it appears but far from essential. The personnel listing is confusing (and inexcusably leaves off the name of tenor saxophonist Jim Pepper). The music, which ranges from basic blues to early fusion and only clocks in at around 31 minutes, also features organist Mike Mandel and several rhythm sections. Fans of guitarist Larry Coryell (a fusion pioneer) may find some moments of interest here. —*Scott Yanow*

The Essential Larry Coryell / 1968-1975 / Vanguard ◆◆◆◆◆

When Larry Coryell recorded the sides gathered on this 70-minute CD, fusion was still a new and radical idea—and the guitarist was one of the adventurers who did more than his part to get the ball rolling. Coryell's diehard followers will be familiar with most of this material, but for novices, *The Essential Larry Coryell* can serve as a splendid introduction to his Vanguard output. This diverse compilation ranges from 1968's landmark "Stiffneck" (a duet with drummer Elvin Jones that is among the earliest examples of fusion) to the abrasive, Jimi Hendrix-influenced "The Jam with Albert" to the haunting "Spaces (Infinite)," which unites Coryell with another very influential fusion guitarist: John McLaughlin. It's hard to miss Miles Davis' influence on "Yin," a gem underscoring the initial excellence of Coryell's *Eleventh House.* But even so, there's no mistaking the fact that Coryell was very much a visionary in his own right. —*Alex Henderson*

Spaces / Jul. 1970 / Vanguard ◆◆◆

This album (not yet reissued on CD) features the pioneer fusion guitarist Larry Coryell with quite an all-star group. Two selections match Coryell with fellow guitarist John McLaughlin, bassist Miroslav Vitous (doubling on cello) and drummer Billy Cobham, all important fusion players at the time. "Rene's Theme" is a guitar duet with McLaughlin, while "Gloria's Steps" (a Scott LaFaro composition) has Coryell, Vitous and Cobham jamming as a trio. Chick Corea sits in on electric keyboard for "Chris," and the 20-second closer ("New Year's Day in Los Angeles—1968") finds Coryell playing alone. Overall, the music has its energetic moments, but also contains some lyricism often lacking in fusion of the mid-'70s. In addition, all of the musicians already had their own original voices, making this a stimulating LP worth searching for. —*Scott Yanow*

Barefoot Boy / 1971 / Flying Dutchman ✦✦✦✦✦
Tremendous interaction between Steve Marcus (tenors/soprano sax) and Coryell. Roy Haynes stars on drums. —*Ron Wynn*

The Eleventh House [With Larry Coryell] / 1972 / Vanguard ✦✦✦✦
The Eleventh House during 1972-75 was one of the stronger working groups in fusion, led by one of the unsung heroes of the idiom, guitarist Larry Coryell. This CD reissue brings back the Eleventh House's first recording and, in addition to Coryell's guitar, most heavily featured are trumpeter Randy Brecker (who would later be replaced by Mike Lawrence) and keyboardist Mike Mandel; bassist Danny Trifan and drummer Alphonse Mouzon are strong in backup roles. The influence of Miles Davis, Weather Report and Herbie Hancock is apparent but the Eleventh House also offered a sound of its own. Brecker's solos are often both fiery and lyrical (although his use of an occasional electric wa-wa device is less interesting), Coryell and Mandel blend together quite well and the original grooves on this set often have distinctive personalities. Pity that the reissue does not have any liner notes. Otherwise, it is easily recommended to fans of early fusion. —*Scott Yanow*

Offering / Jan. 17, 1972-Jan. 20, 1972 / Vanguard ✦✦✦
This album directly preceded the formation of Larry Coryell's Eleventh House. In fact, the influential guitarist is joined by a future member, keyboardist Mike Mandel, and the style of fusion is similar to what would develop. Steve Marcus contributes some fiery soprano solos, while bassist Mervin Bronson and drummer Harry Wilkinson push the soloists. None of the six originals were destined to catch on, and this LP has yet to be reissued on CD, but it does have its moments of interest for listeners who enjoy hearing rock-oriented jazz. —*Scott Yanow*

At Montreux (1974) / Jul. 4, 1974 / Vanguard ✦✦✦
Guitarist Larry Coryell's Eleventh House was a particularly interesting fusion group of the mid-1970s. In addition to the leader, keyboardist Mike Mandel, bassist Danny Trifan and the dynamic drummer Alphonse Mouzon, the unit featured trumpeter Michael Lawrence. Their appearance at the 1974 Montreux Jazz Festival makes for a rather brief CD (under 34 minutes) but has its moments of interest. Coryell starts the proceedings by playing his unaccompanied acoustic guitar on a classical piece, that number is followed by four passionate group originals full of fire and dated electronics, and the set finishes with the strongest piece, "The Eleventh House Blues." Although the music is not essential nor particularly innovative, the mixture of straightahead elements with prime period fusion is often stimulating. —*Scott Yanow*

Planet End / 1975 / Vanguard ✦✦✦
During 1968-75, guitarist Larry Coryell recorded a wide variety of interesting material for Vanguard. This album, a CD reissue of the original LP, was Coryell's final one for the label. The five selections, although originals, have the feel of a jam session. Coryell's Eleventh House (which includes trumpeter Mike Lawrence, keyboardist Mike Mandel, bassist Danny Trifan and drummer Alphonse Mouzon) is featured on two tracks (their final recordings), Coryell plays all of the instruments on the brief "The Eyes of Love" and on two lengthy jams he is matched with fellow guitarist John McLaughlin, bassist Miroslav Vitous, drummer Billy Cobham and (on Larry Young's "Tyrone") keyboardist Chick Corea. The lively music is very much of the period and this CD is a bit brief (at 34 minutes) but the high quality of the solos makes this one worth picking up by listeners interested in Larry Coryell's early period. —*Scott Yanow*

Twin House / 1976 / Atlantic ✦✦✦

Standing Ovation / Mar. 8, 1978+Mar. 11, 1978 / Mood ✦✦
A mixed bag with classical, traditional Indian songs, originals, and even modified funk played by Coryell and L. Subramaniam on violin and tampura. Coryell also plays a little piano and proves an effective partner, although sometimes the stylistic leaping around can be jarring. —*Ron Wynn*

Tributaries / Aug. 17, 1978-Sep. 1979 / Novus ✦✦✦
This CD reissue brings back material that guitarist Larry Coryell recorded for the Novus subsidiary when it was run by Arita. Most of the set matches Coryell with fellow guitarists John Scofield and Joe Beck in acoustic trios, two duets and one overdubbed solo performance. The variation of moods and the jazz-oriented material make this summit meeting a success even if the guitarists tend to sound more distinctive on their electric counterparts; after about 20 minutes of similar sounding acoustic guitars, it is difficult not to doze off. Expanding the original program are four Coryell solo acoustic performances that were originally included in the

Artista Novus LP *European Impressions*. Once again, they are well played but primarily of interest to guitarists. —*Scott Yanow*

Return / Jun. 4, 1979+Jun. 6, 1979 / Vanguard ✦✦✦
Larry Coryell made his earliest recordings as a leader for Vanguard and most of his sessions from 1968-75. After working for a variety of other labels, he came back for this lone effort in 1979. Coryell's basic sound was still the same as in his early fusion days, but the setting had changed. Joined by three of the Brubeck brothers (keyboardist Darius, electric bassist Chris and drummer Dan), along with percussionist Ray Mantilla, the guitarist performs three of his originals (including "Cisco at the Disco"), two Darius Brubeck numbers, and a selection co-written by Al DiMeola and Paco DeLucia. Although not one of his most significant dates, Larry Coryell sounds in fine form throughout this modern mainstream LP, stretching himself a bit. —*Scott Yanow*

Bolero / Apr. 18, 1981-Nov. 1983 / Evidence ✦✦✦
Among the most flexible of jazz guitarists, Larry Coryell performs ten unaccompanied and largely acoustic solos and plays four duets with fellow guitarist Brian Keane (who has "A Piece for Larry" to himself). The intimate selections often come across as improvised classical music (although all but a couple of Ravel themes were composed by one of the two guitarists), with Coryell emphasizing the beauty of his tone and the melodic side of his style. This CD reissue was originally issued by the German String label. —*Scott Yanow*

A Quiet Day in Spring / Nov. 11, 1983 / Steeple Chase ✦✦✦✦
Although originally associated with fusion and then acoustic explorations, Larry Coryell has often shown that he can play practically any style. This little-known set finds him jamming with violinist Michel Urbaniak and bassist Jesper Lundgaard in a trio. Although the music is generally straightahead, all seven of the selections were composed by either Coryell or Urbaniak, and the music is never all that predictable. Worth exploring. —*Scott Yanow*

Comin' Home / Feb. 7, 1984 / Muse ✦✦✦✦
This is one of guitarist Larry Coryell's most straightahead sets, a bop-flavored session recorded in one day with a fine quartet that had just played a week at the Village Vanguard. With pianist Albert Dailey, bassist George Mraz and drummer Billy Hart clearly inspiring him, Coryell performs three largely swinging originals (including "No More Booze, Minor Blues" and "Good Citizen Swallow," which was dedicated to bassist Steve Swallow), Jimmy Webb's "Glorielle," and a pair of bop standards ("Confirmation" and "It Never Entered My Mind"). The latter piece has an effective vocal from the guitarist's wife, Julie Coryell. Throughout, Larry Coryell shows that he could have been a top bop stylist if he had wanted to pursue that direction, instead of his more innovative and eclectic path. —*Scott Yanow*

● **Together** / Aug. 1985 / Concord Jazz ✦✦✦✦✦
This interesting and one-time matchup features Larry Coryell and Emily Remler on a set of guitar duets. It is easy to tell the two players apart, yet their styles are quite complementary. Highlights of the date (which has four standards, Pat Martino's "Gerri's Blues," and two Coryell originals) include "Joy Spring," "How My Heart Sings" and "How Insensitive." —*Scott Yanow*

Toku Do / Sep. 1987 / Muse ✦✦✦
Despite the exotic title, this is one of three fairly straightahead sets that guitarist Larry Coryell recorded for Muse from 1985-89. Assisted by pianist Stanley Cowell, bassist Buster Williams and drummer Beaver Harris, Coryell performs five veteran jazz standards (including "Moment's Notice," "'Round Midnight" and "My Funny Valentine"), plus the title cut, which is actually a boppish blues by Williams. Excellent playing all around. —*Scott Yanow*

Shining Hour / Oct. 20, 1989 / Muse ✦✦✦
Coryell shows he can work in traditional jazz bands. Marvelous musical assistants available, among them Kenny Barron on piano. —*Ron Wynn*

Dragon Gate / 1990 / Shanachie ✦✦✦✦
This is a strong jazz-oriented date that features Larry Coryell exclusively on acoustic guitar, playing two standard blues unaccompanied, using one or two overdubs on six other tracks and performing a pair of duets with fellow guitarist Stefan Grossman. The music covers a bit of ground from a superior version of "Giant Steps" and tributes to Wes Montgomery and Duke Ellington to some introspective originals, one of which hints at Bob Dylan. The original LP issue also includes a 16-page pamphlet with transcriptions (for guitar) of each of the melodies except "Giant Steps." Recommended, especially to guitarists and those who primarily associate Larry Coryell with fusion. —*Scott Yanow*

Twelve Frets to One Octave / 1991 / Shanachie ✦✦✦
A guitar showcase for Coryell, who has always been among the more accomplished players on either electric or acoustic. He goes through old blues, jazz standards, and everything in between. There's absolutely nothing else to support him, enabling Coryell to display his complete technical arsenal. —*Ron Wynn*

Live from Bahia / 1992 / Rhino ✦✦✦

Nice Afro-Latin set with Coryell on acoustic guitar, recorded in Bahia. The assembled cast includes drummer Billy Cobham, alto saxophonist Donald Harrison, and several Brazilian musicians, notably vocalist Dori Caymmi. —*Ron Wynn*

Fallen Angel / 1993 / CTI ✦✦

Sketches of Coryell / 1996 / Shanachie ✦✦✦

Spaces Revisited / Feb. 25, 1997+Feb. 26, 1997 / Shanachie ✦✦✦✦

What started as a project to reunite Coryell with Billy Cobham on drums in order to take a second look at the sound and style of the Chick Corea album *Spaces* ended up creating a whole new chapter instead. With Richard Bona on bass and Bireli Lagrene on guitar, these nine songs capture the spirit of that 30-year-old session with new, adventuresome playing and vigor. Coryell takes great pride in the spontaneity of this project—one day rehearsal, two days recording—and well he should, since it contains musicians interacting with each other in a loose yet totally on-top-of-their-game manner. Bireli shines on the 9/8 section "Variations on Goodbye Pork Pie Hat," while Bona solos beautifully on "Blues for Django and Stephane." Yet it's ultimately Coryell's and Cobham's show, and their playing throughout is sublime with the on-the-spot recording of "Hong Kong Breeze"—an off-the-cuff head arrangement done in one take—showcasing their two players/one mind interplay. Maybe you can't go home again, but this album clearly proves you can always take your luggage with you and build a whole new house. —*Cub Koda*

Eddie Costa

b. Aug. 14, 1930, Atlas, PA, **d.** Jul. 28, 1962, New York, NY
Piano, Vibes / Bop

Eddie Costa emerged from an unlikely background into a heralded, if too brief career in jazz. Born in a rural coal mining town, Costa studied piano with his brother Bill and developed a taste for the swing greats; later, exposure to Bud Powell turned him to bop. Self-taught on vibes, Costa became known as an excellent sight reader, which produced a lot of studio work. On piano, his trademark sound was the emphasis of the middle and lower registers while nearly ignoring the top two octaves. In addition to recording as a sideman with Tal Farlow, Woody Herman, Johnny Smith, the Bob Brookmeyer-Clark Terry Quintet, and Bill Evans, Costa led his own trio and quintet dates. Sadly, most of Costa's recorded output remains unavailable on CD, with the notable exception of the V.S.O.P. reissue of his Quintet LP. Costa died when his car careened off of a busy New York parkway in 1962. —*Ken Dryden*

Eddie Costa with the Vinnie Burke Trio / Feb. 1956 / Jubilee ✦✦✦

This solid session was recorded with Vinnie Burke (b.). —*David Szatmary*

● **Eddie Costa Quintet** / Jul. 13, 1957 / V.S.O.P. ✦✦✦✦✦

(Originally released as Mode 118.) Eddie Costa's outing on Mode features him both on piano and vibes, in the company of Phil Woods and Art Farmer.

The House of Blue Lights / Jan. 29, 1959+Feb. 2, 1959 / Dot ✦✦✦

This adventurous date (with Paul Motian [d]) borders on the avant-garde. —*David Szatmary*

Johnny Costa

b. Jan. 18, 1922, Arnold, PA, **d.** Oct. 11, 1996
Piano / Swing

Johnny Costa made a number of fine recordings over his long musical career, but he will probably be better remembered for his musical contributions to television. After initially studying accordion in childhood, he took up the piano, studying with a teacher who had also taught Oscar Levant. Costa discovered he had perfect pitch and earned two college degrees in music education, though teaching was only a backup plan to his real goal of performing. He spent 15 years as music director for KDK-TV in Pittsburgh and recorded LPs for Savoy Coral and Dot in the 1950s. He achieved his greatest fame as the music director for the long-running public TV series "Mister Rogers Neighborhood," where he insisted on playing jazz, reasoning that children will gravitate to good music. He was correct, as he remained with the program for the final three decades of his life. He did several sessions for Chiaroscuro in the 1990s, with *Dream* being released around the time of his death from leukemia in 1996. —*Ken Dryden*

In My Own Quiet Way / Jul. 9, 1959 / Dot ✦✦✦✦✦

● **Classic Costa** / Apr. 18, 1990-Feb. 1991 / Chiaroscuro ✦✦✦✦✦

Johnny Costa's obscurity is due to his decision to spend his career playing background piano for many years on the children's show "Mr. Rogers' Neighborhood." This CD was his first unaccompanied solo session, and it makes one wonder what took so long. Nearly 70 at the time, Costa proves to be a virtuoso whose florid technique could be mistaken for cocktail piano if his mood variations and impro-

vising skills did not elevate the music. Sticking primarily to swing standards, Costa is best on the uptempo pieces (particularly "Get Happy"), where he strongly resembles his idol Art Tatum, but also hints at times at Oscar Peterson, Dave McKenna and George Shearing, in addition to showing off his interest in classical music. This CD, which is wrapped up by an effective eight-minute "Jazzspeak" during which Costa essentially gives his life story, is quite impressive and is his most rewarding jazz recording. —*Scott Yanow*

Flying Fingers / Apr. 8, 1990-Mar. 18, 1992 / Chiaroscuro ✦✦✦✦✦

Good piano session from an underrated and undervalued player who dropped out of the jazz scene and became famous playing on the "Mister Rogers' Neighborhood" television program. These solo cuts were done in 1990 and 1992 and show that Costa is still a charming, enjoyable interpreter of standards. He doesn't really do anything new or different, but it's enchanting nonetheless. —*Ron Wynn*

A Portrait of George Gershwin / Oct. 2, 1993-Oct. 3, 1993 / Chiaroscuro ✦✦✦✦

Best known as the longtime musical director of "Mister Rogers' Neighborhood," the late pianist turns in another enjoyable set of solo piano. He covers many of George Gershwin's best-loved songs with flair and imagination, especially in his creative medleys such as the one combining "Concerto in F" with "Rhapsody in Blue." Also worth noting is his warm rendition of the timeless "Some One to Watch over Me" and the snappy "Clap Yo' Hands." Although most of this music has been covered extensively by other jazz musicians, Costa's fresh approaches merit comparison to the best of them. —*Ken Dryden*

Dream: Johnny Costa Plays Johnny Mercer / Mar. 1995-May 1995 / Chiaroscuro ✦✦✦✦

Tom Coster

b. Aug. 21, 1941, Detroit, MI
Piano, Keyboards / Fusion, Crossover Jazz

A fine keyboardist, Tom Coster originally studied accordion for ten years. He performed music while in the Air Force and in 1969 he played electric piano in a jazz/rock group called the Loading Zone. After a stint with Gabor Szabo in 1971, Coster spent 1972-78 with Santana. He played at the 1978 Montreux Jazz Festival with Billy Cobham, spent a couple of years outside of music and since then has primarily led his own fusion-oriented bands, other than an association with Vital Information. He has since recorded as a leader for Fantasy, Headfirst and JVC, and his son Tom Coster, Jr., is also an excellent keyboardist. —*Scott Yanow*

Ivory Expedition / 1982 / Fantasy ✦✦✦

This interesting jazz-rock album features Joaquin Lievano on guitar. —*Paul Kohler*

Did Jah Miss Me?!? / 1989 / Headfirst ✦✦✦

An album by ex-Santana keyboardist, it features Frank Gambale and D. Chambers. —*Paul Kohler*

From Me to You / 1990 / Headfirst ✦✦

Brief moments of glory sandwiched between long stretches of tedium. —*Ron Wynn*

Gotcha!! / 1992 / JVC ✦✦✦✦

Keyboardist Tom Coster has shown in his JVC recordings (of which this is the first) that fusion was not only alive in the 1990s (if somewhat underground) but still had potential for creativity. With assistance from altoist Marc Russo (formerly with the Yellowjackets), guitarist Chris Camozzi, electric bassist Alfonso Johnson, drummer Dennis Chambers and two guest spots for saxophonist Norbert Stachel, Coster performs spirited versions of 11 of his originals. —*Scott Yanow*

● **Let's Set the Record Straight** / Sep. 14, 1993 / JVC ✦✦✦✦

Keyboardist Tom Coster looks to the 1970s for inspiration on this set, particularly towards Chick Corea's Return to Forever and Miles Davis. The music mixes together funk and jazz with liberal doses of R&B and Latin, and the passionate rhythms add to the power of the improvisations. Coster, Bob Berg on tenor and guitarist Frank Gambale take strong solos that give the CD plenty of stimulating moments. Acoustic purists are advised to look elsewhere but fusion fans will enjoy this fine set. —*Scott Yanow*

Forbidden Zone / 1994 / JVC ✦✦✦

For this excellent outing (his third project for JVC), keyboardist Tom Coster performs 11 originals plus "Lover Man." Although his fusion-oriented music is full of funky ensembles, there is more variety than expected. Coster shares the solo space with tenor saxophonist Bob Berg and the fiery guitarist Scott Henderson, creating a colorful and sometimes unpredictable program of music. —*Scott Yanow*

From the Street / 1995 / JVC ✦✦✦✦✦

Tom Coster's more commercial albums (such as *Gotcha!!*) were far from bad, and certainly had more soul and integrity than so much of the homogenized drivel labeled smooth jazz. But even so, they failed to adequately demonstrate just how adventurous and commanding a soloist and composer he can be. Like *Let's Set the*

Record Straight and *Forbidden Zone, From the Street* is a gutsy, hard-edged and uncompromising fusion date defined by its passion, complexity and spontaneity. Instead of avoiding the cerebral, Coster thrives on it. The Santana graduate has plenty of room to let loose and blow, as do such inspired sidemen as tenorist Michael Brecker and his disciple Bob Malach. And Dennis Chambers' intense drumming is superb throughout this fine and often abstract jazz/rock/funk CD. —*Alex Henderson*

Curtis Counce

b. Jan. 23, 1926, Kansas City, MO, **d.** Jul. 31, 1963, Los Angeles, CA
Bass / Hard Bop
Curtis Counce was an in-demand session bassist and one of the first African-Americans to get heavily involved in the West Coast jazz movement in the 1940s. He studied violin and tuba in addition to bass before leaving his native city for employment with the Nat Towles Band in Omaha at the age of 16. He moved to L.A. in 1945, taking a job with Johnny Otis at the Club Alabam and made his recording debut with Lester Young the following year. He recorded prolifically as a sideman (Shelly Manne, Lyle Murphy, Teddy Charles, Clifford Brown) before starting his famous quintet in 1956. His premature death from a heart attack was a tragic loss to jazz. All of Counce's Contemporary dates as a leader have been reissued, as has the once rare *Exploring the Future*. An added bonus was the appearance of previously unreleased Contemporary masters on the 1989 CD *Sonority*. —*Ken Dryden*

● **Landslide** / Oct. 8, 1956+Oct. 15, 1956 / Original Jazz Classics ◆◆◆◆◆
During 1956-57 bassist Curtis Counce led an excellent Los Angeles-based hard bop quintet comprising trumpeter Jack Sheldon, tenor saxophonist Harold Land, pianist Carl Perkins, bassist Curtis Counce and drummer Frank Butler. They recorded four albums worth of material for Contemporary, all of which have been reissued on CD (three as part of the Original Jazz Classics series). For their debut album, the group performs selections by Land ("Landslide"), Perkins, Sheldon and two by Gerald Wiggins (including "Sonar") plus the lone standard "Time After Time." All of Counce's recordings (which include a slightly later album for Dootone) are well worth getting by collectors interested in 1950s straightahead jazz; this disc is an excellent place to start. —*Scott Yanow*

Counceltation / Oct. 8, 1956-Sep. 3, 1957 / Contemporary ◆◆◆◆◆
Bassist Curtis Counce led one of the finer West Coast-based groups of the 1950s, a quintet that was greatly underrated. With trumpeter Jack Sheldon, tenor saxophonist Harold Land, pianist Carl Perkins and drummer Frank Butler completing the group, this was a band with plenty of solo strength. Their second Contemporary recording features five standards (including "Stranger in Paradise") and two numbers by the leader. This excellent music falls somewhere between hard bop and cool jazz. —*Scott Yanow*

You Get More Bounce with Curtis Counce / Oct. 8, 1956-Sep. 3, 1957 / Original Jazz Classics ◆◆◆◆
Although the title and even the cover photo have been changed, this CD reissue has the same music as was earlier issued as *Counceltation;* the "bonus cut" "Woody 'n You " has also been reissued on *Sonority*. In any case, the program features the underrated but talented Curtis Counce Quintet of 1956-57, a group consisting of the bassist-leader, trumpeter Jack Sheldon, tenor saxophonist Harold Land, pianist Carl Perkins and drummer Frank Butler. Counce contributed two originals but otherwise the band sticks to jazz standards with some of the best moments being on "Too Close for Comfort," "Mean to Me" and Charlie Parker's "Big Foot." —*Scott Yanow*

Sonority / Oct. 15, 1956-Jan. 6, 1958 / Contemporary ◆◆◆
This CD, which adds "Drum Conversation" (a Frank Butler feature) to the earlier LP, contains material taken from bassist Curtis Counce's Contemporary sessions that resulted in three other albums, but these particular performances were not released until 1989. Half of the program features Counce's 1956 quintet (which includes trumpeter Jack Sheldon, tenor saxophonist Harold Land, pianist Carl Perkins and drummer Frank Butler) while the remaining selections are from 1958 when the group had Gerald Wilson on trumpet and pianist Elmo Hope (who contributed three originals). "Sonor" and "Landslide" are heard in alternate versions and "Woody 'n You " has also been since reissued as a "bonus" cut on the CD *You Get More Bounce with Curtis Counce.* The playing is quite rewarding, and all four of the Counce reissues are easily recommended to hard bop collectors. —*Scott Yanow*

Carl's Blues / Aug. 29, 1957-Jan. 6, 1958 / Original Jazz Classics ◆◆◆◆
Although the Curtis Counce Quintet was not a commercial success, their four Contemporary albums (which have been reissued on CD) were all timeless in their own way, undated examples of high-quality hard bop from the late '50s. This set features the bassist-leader, either Jack Sheldon or Gerald Wilson on trumpet, tenor

saxophonist Harold Land, pianist Carl Perkins and drummer Frank Butler interpreting both jazz standards (including "Love Walked In" and Clifford Brown's "Larue") and originals (such as the drummer's "The Butler Did It"). Excellent music that still sounds fresh four decades later. —*Scott Yanow*

Exploring the Future / Apr. 1958 / Boplicity ◆◆◆

Stanley Cowell

b. May 5, 1941, Toledo, OH
Piano / Post-Bop, Hard Bop
An excellent modern mainstream pianist who is adaptable to many acoustic jazz settings, Stanley Cowell has long been underrated except among musicians. He studied the piano from the time he was four and Art Tatum made an early impact. After attending Oberlin College Conservatory and the University of Michigan, Cowell (who had played with Rahsaan Roland Kirk while at Oberlin) moved to New York in 1966. He played regularly with Marion Brown (1966-67), Max Roach (1967-70) and the Bobby Hutcherson-Harold Land Quintet (1968-71). In the early '70s Cowell worked in Music Inc. with Charles Tolliver and they co-founded the label Strata East. He played regularly with the Heath Brothers during 1974-83 and since 1981 has been a busy jazz educator. Cowell has recorded as a leader for Arista-Freedom (1969), ECM (1972), Strata East, Galaxy, Unisson, DIW, Concord and Steeple Chase. —*Scott Yanow*

Blues for the Viet Cong / Jun. 5, 1969-Jun. 6, 1969 / Freedom ◆◆◆◆
Stanley Cowell's debut as a leader features his piano (and on two selections rare outings on electric keyboards) with a trio also including bassist Steve Novosel and drummer Jimmy Hopps. Cowell's style at the time was often modal and already quite powerful. After hearing seven of his often-somber pieces, Cowell's stride version of "You Took Advantage of Me" (inspired by Art Tatum) is a welcome change of pace. —*Scott Yanow*

Brilliant Circles / Sep. 25, 1969 / Arista ◆◆◆◆
Pianist Stanley Cowell's second recording as a leader finds him leading a powerful all-star sextet that includes trumpeter Woody Shaw, Tyrone Washington on tenor, flute and clarinet, vibraphonist Bobby Hutcherson, bassist Reggie Workman and drummer Joe Chambers. The challenging repertoire (an original apiece by Cowell, Washington, Shaw and Hutcherson) falls between advanced hard bop and the avant-garde, consistently inspiring the talented players to play at their most creative. Recommended. —*Scott Yanow*

Illusion Suite / Nov. 29, 1972 / ECM ◆◆◆
Trio with Stanley Clarke (b). —*Michael G. Nastos*

Regeneration / Apr. 27, 1975 / Strata East ◆◆◆
Larger ensemble. Afro-American stance. Excellent. —*Michael G. Nastos*

Waiting for the Moment / Jul. 6, 1977-Jul. 8, 1977 / Galaxy ◆◆◆
This out-of-print LP is a solo set by Stanley Cowell. The first side has five acoustic numbers which range from the "Ragtime" and "Boogie Woogie" sections of Jimmy Heath's "Afro-American Suite of Evolution" to "'Round Midnight" and Bud Powell's "Parisian Thoroughfare." The flip side finds Cowell utilizing both electronics and overdubbing to perform four of his more modern originals. An interesting if not quite essential program. —*Scott Yanow*

Talkin' 'bout Love / 1978 / Galaxy ◆◆

Equipoise / Nov. 28, 1978-Nov. 30, 1978 / Galaxy ◆◆◆◆
Pianist Stanley Cowell introduced his most famous composition "Equipoise" on this trio set with bassist Cecil McBee and drummer Roy Haynes. Actually the entire LP (which is unfortunately out of print) is a fine all-round showcase for Cowell who also plays three of his other lesser-known originals, McBee's "Lady Blue" and Jackie McLean's "Dr. Jackle." Cowell has long had an original style within the modern mainstream and his interplay with his notable sidemen on this program always holds one's interest. —*Scott Yanow*

● **Live at Cafe Des Copains** / Jun. 26, 1985 / Unisson ◆◆◆◆◆
In 1985 Stanley Cowell performed solo at the Toronto club Cafe des Copains and fortunately one night's music was recorded. On what was only his second album of unaccompanied solos (and his first had used overdubbing and electronics), Cowell performs six bop standards (including "Waltz for Debbie," "Joy Spring" and "My One and Only Love"), his own "Equipoise" and a surprising stride version of "You Took Advantage of Me," which was inspired by seeing Art Tatum play when he was a child. This set offers listeners a highly enjoyable all-round overview of Stanley Cowell's talents as a pianist. —*Scott Yanow*

We Three / Dec. 5, 1987 / DIW ◆◆◆

Back to the Beautiful / Jul. 1989 / Concord Jazz ◆◆◆◆
Pianist Stanley Cowell displays some of his versatility on this Concord CD, performing pieces that range from "It Don't Mean a Thing" and Bud Powell's boppish "Wail" to four of his own inventive originals. Most of the tunes are performed in a

trio with bassist Santi Debriano and drummer Joe Chambers while guest Steve Coleman (on alto and soprano) helps out on three songs, sounding quite effective on "Sylvia's Place" and "Come Sunday." —*Scott Yanow*

Sienna / Jul. 1989 / Steeple Chase ✦✦✦✦

Live at Maybeck Recital Hall, Vol. 5 / Jun. 1990 / Concord Jazz ✦✦✦✦✦
Playing at Maybeck Recital Hall before a small but attentive crowd seems to bring out the best in many pianists. Stanley Cowell performs a well-planned program of 14 selections on this 1990 CD. On a two-minute "Softly as in a Morning Sunrise," Cowell runs through all 12 keys. He pays tribute to the stride-piano tradition on "Stompin'" at the Savoy," explores some bop, Latin-jazz (a transformed "Autumn Leaves") and post bop music, plays "Jitterbug Waltz" in the style of Art Tatum, inteprets "Stella by Starlight" in 5/4 time and performs J.J. Johnson's "Lament" with just his left hand. A very interesting recital. —*Scott Yanow*

Close to You Alone / Aug. 2, 1990 / DIW ✦✦✦
Released on a CD by the Japanese label DIW (and briefly made available in the US through Columbia), this trio outing with bassist Cecil McBee and drummer Ronnie Burrage finds Cowell in typically creative form. Other than "Stella by Starlight" and the leader's "Equipoise," the repertoire (originals by each of the three musicians) is unfamiliar but Cowell's appealing post-bop style makes the music both unpredictable and fairly accessible. The performances are stimulating but this Japanese import will be difficult to find. —*Scott Yanow*

Mandara Blossoms / Dec. 1995 / Steeple Chase ✦✦
Although pianist Stanley Cowell is the leader of this CD, the music is dominated by the vocals of Karen Francis, who interprets six of Cowell's originals (including his best-known tune "Equipoise"), Billy Strayhorn's "Daydream" and the obscure "A Whole New World." Francis has a pleasant voice but is not an improviser and the lyrics fail to hold one's interest for long. There are some good spots for Cowell and tenor saxophonist Bill Pierce to stretch out (bassist Jeff Halsey and drummer Ralph Peterson are fine in support) but overall the solos are more interesting than the compositions, which are more interesting than the vocals, which are better than the lyrics. —*Scott Yanow*

Ida Cox

b. Feb. 25, 1896, Toccoa, GA, **d.** Nov. 10, 1967, Knoxville, TN
Vocals / Blues, Classic Jazz, Classic Female Blues
One of the finest classic blues singers of the 1920s, Ida Cox was singing in theaters by the time she was 14. She recorded regularly during 1923-29 (her "Wild Woman Don't Have the Blues" and "Death Letter Blues" are her best-known songs). Although she was off record during much of the 1930s, Cox was able to continue working and in 1939 she sang at Cafe Society, appeared at John Hammond's "Spirituals to Swing" concert and made some new records. Ida Cox toured with shows until a 1944 stroke forced her into retirement; she came back for an impressive final recording in 1961.

Cox left her hometown of Toccoa, Georgia, as a teenager, travelling the south in vaudeville and tent shows, performing both as a singer and a comedienne. In the early '20s, she performed with Jelly Roll Morton, but she had severed her ties with the pianist by the time she signed her first record contract with Paramount in 1923. Cox stayed with Paramount for six years, recording 78 songs, which usually featured accompaniment by Love Austin and trumpeter Tommy Ladnier. During that time, she also cut tracks for a variety of labels, including Silvertone, using several different pseudonyms, including Velma Bradley, Kate Lewis, and Julia Powers.

During the '30s, Cox didn't record often, but she continued to perform frequently, highlighted by an appearance at John Hammond's 1939 Spirituals to Swing concert at Carnegie Hall. The concert increased her visibility, particularly in jazz circles—following the concert, she recorded with a number of jazz artists, including Charlie Christian, Lionel Hampton, Fletcher Henderson, and Hot Lips Page. She toured with a number of different shows in the early '40s until she suffered a stroke in 1944. Cox was retired for most of the '50s, but she was coaxed out of retirement in 1961 to record a final session with Coleman Hawkins. In 1967, Ida Cox died of cancer. —*Scott Yanow & Stephen Thomas Erlewine*

● **The Uncrowned Queen of the Blues** / Jun. 1923-Aug. 1924 / Black Swan ✦✦✦✦✦
Ida Cox was one of the most talented of the classic blues singers of the 1920s. This Black Swan CD has 20 of her first 32 recordings, and although one regrets that it is not a "complete" series (hopefully the dozen other titles will be reissued by Black Swan eventually), the music is consistently enjoyable and timeless. In fact, quite a few of the lyrics (many of which were written by Cox) were later permanently "borrowed" by Jimmy Rushing and Joe Williams; the first stanza of "Goin' to Chicago" was taken from "Chicago Monkey Man Blues" and "Bear-Mash Blues" has a couple of Williams' best lines. When one considers that the music on this CD is taken from 1923-24, it can certainly be considered ahead of its time! Most of the musicians backing Ida Cox are excellent, particularly pianist Lovie Austin and (on

five numbers) cornetist Tommy Ladnier and clarinetist Jimmy O'Bryant. The recording quality (even with some surface noise) has been greatly cleaned up for this reissue and Cox's singing is very easy to understand. Although uncrowned, Ida Cox (who after retiring in 1945 came back for a final recording in 1961) can still communicate to today's listeners, something that can be said about very few other singers from 1923. —*Scott Yanow*

★ **Blues for Rampart Street** / Apr. 11, 1961-Apr. 12, 1961 / Original Jazz Classics ✦✦✦✦✦
Classic blues singer Ida Cox had not recorded since 1940 nor performed regularly since the mid-'40s when she was coaxed out of retirement to record a date for Riverside in 1961. At 65 years old (some books list her as being 72), Cox's voice was a bit rusty and past its prime but she still had the feeling, phrasing and enough tricks to perform a strong program. With assistance from trumpeter Roy Eldridge, tenor saxophonist Coleman Hawkins, pianist Sammy Price, bassist Milt Hinton and drummer Jo Jones (swing-era veterans who came up after Cox was already a major name), the singer does her best on such numbers as "Wild Women Don't Have the Blues," "Blues for Rampart Street," "St. Louis Blues" and "Death Letter Blues." Since she passed away in 1967, this final effort (reissued on CD) was made just in time and is well worth acquiring by 1920s jazz and blues collectors. —*Scott Yanow*

Lol Coxhill (Lowen Coxhill)

b. Sep. 19, 1932, Portsmouth, Hampshire, England
Soprano Saxophone / Avant-Garde
Famous for his unaccompanied, unorthodox concerts and albums, Lol Coxhill has an immediately identifiable soprano and sopranino style. He's perhaps Steve Lacy's prime rival in getting odd sounds out of the soprano with his wrenching, twisting, quirky solos. While Coxhill is an accomplished saxophonist and can play conventional bebop, it's his winding, flailing soprano and sopranino lines that make him stand out. Coxhill actually started playing more conservatively; Coxhill backed visiting American soul and blues vocalists in the '60s, playing behind Rufus Thomas, Lowell Fulson and Champon Jack Dupree. He worked with Steve Miller's group Delivery in 1969 and 1970, and played with them at the Berlin Music Festival. But his debut album *Ear of the Beholder* established a new direction for Coxhill. Since then, he's worked with both bebop and free musicians, among them Chris McGregor, Trevor Watts, Bobby Wellins and Company. Coxhill's also played with such groups as the Recedents, Standard Conversions and the Melody Four. He currently has no releases available on CD in America. —*Ron Wynn*

Ear of the Beholder / Jul. 12, 1970-Jul. 18, 1970 / Ampex ✦✦✦✦

The Story So Far . . . Oh Really [1 Side] / 1974 / Caroline ✦✦✦

Fleas in the Custard / 1975 / Caroline ✦✦✦

Lid / Jul. 1978 / Ictus ✦✦✦

Slow Music / Apr. 19, 1980-May 1980 / Pipe ✦✦✦

Digwell Duets / May 11, 1978-Jul. 1978 / Random Radar ✦✦✦

Johnny Rondo Duo Plus Mike Cooper / May 3, 1980 / FMP ✦✦✦

Dunois Solos / Nov. 6, 1981 / Nato ✦✦✦

● **Instant Replay** / Nov. 3, 1981-Sep. 4, 1982 / Nato ✦✦✦✦

10:02 / Mar. 25, 1985-Mar. 26, 1985 / Nato ✦✦✦

Toverbal Sweet / 1997 / See For Miles ✦✦✦✦

Bob Cranshaw

b. Dec. 10, 1932, Evanston, IL
Bass / Hard Bop
The bass equivalent of a seasoned saxophone veteran who's never been a giant, but is well respected for consistent excellence, Bob Cranshaw has worked steadily with several top jazz musicians. Despite having a light tone, Cranshaw's timing, musical knowledge and versatility have been featured in an impressive array of recording sessions and tours since the late '50s. Cranshaw played piano and drums before switching to bass and tuba in high school. He was a founding member of Walter Perkins' MJT + 3 band in 1957. Cranshaw went to New York with the group in 1960 and joined Sonny Rollins when they disbanded in 1962. He also worked with Duke Pearson's small groups and big band. Cranshaw started a parallel career in television, being known for his years on "Sesame Street." He's also worked in theater orchestras. But jazz dates have been plentiful; Cranshaw's played with Lee Morgan, Wes Montgomery, Coleman Hawkins, Johnny Hodges, Horace Silver, McCoy Tyner, Thelonious Monk, Jimmy Heath, James Moody and Buddy Rich, as well as toured with George Shearing, Joe Williams, Ella Fitzgerald and Oscar Peterson. Cranshaw expanded his repertoire and added electric bass in the '70s. He's frequently worked with Rollins in the '80s and '90s. Cranshaw has no

albums as a leader available on CD, but can be heard on numerous current and reissued dates by Rollins, McCoy Tyner, and the MJT + 3 among others. —*Ron Wynn*

Hank Crawford (Bennie Ross Crawford, Jr.)

b. Dec. 21, 1934, Memphis, TN
Alto Saxophone / R&B, Soul Jazz, Hard Bop, Groove
Hank Crawford's greatest contribution to music has been his soulful sound, one that is immediately idenitifiable and flexible enough to fit into several types of settings. Early on he played with B.B. King, Bobby Bland and Ike Turner in Memphis before moving to Nashville to study at Tennessee State College. He gained fame with Ray Charles (1958-63), at first playing baritone before switching to alto and becoming the music director. During 1959-69 Crawford recorded a popular series of soul jazz albums for Atlantic that made his reputation. His 1970s sets for Kudu were more commercial and streakier but in 1982 Crawford started recording regularly for Milestone, often matched up with organist Jimmy McGriff or pianist Dr. John. An influence on David Sanborn, Crawford's very appealing sound can still be heard in prime form in the mid-'90s. —*Scott Yanow*

Heart and Soul / Jul. 5, 1958-Sep. 9, 1992 / Rhino/Atlantic ◆◆◆◆
This is one of the better of Rhino's two-CD samplers of Atlantic jazz artists. Altoist Hank Crawford, one of the most soulful stylists to emerge during the 1960s, is heard on 31 of his best recordings, 27 as a leader plus sideman appearances with Ray Charles, David "Fathead" Newman, B.B. King and Etta James. Crawford's sound and style were virtually the same in the 1990s as they were in the '60s although the settings changed a bit. Highlights of this well-conceived introduction include "Please Send Me Someone to Love," "Two Years of Torture," "Don't Get Around Much Anymore," "The Very Thought of You," "Trouble in Mind" and "Hank's Groove." Recommended to listeners not familiar with the beauty of Hank Crawford's playing. —*Scott Yanow*

More Soul / Oct. 7, 1960 / Atlantic ◆◆◆
Memphis Ray/Touch of Moody / Oct. 7, 1960-Feb. 11, 1965 / 32 Jazz ◆◆◆◆◆
Soul of the Ballad / Feb. 16, 1963-Feb. 20, 1963 / Atlantic ◆◆
This Atlantic LP has been repackaged in a classy audiophile reissue LP by Mobile Fidelity. The soulful altoist Hank Crawford plays a dozen ballads while backed by the Marty Paich Orchestra and the sound reproduction is flawless. Unfortunately the quality of the music itself is not high at all. The repertoire includes more than its share of losers (including "I Left My Heart in San Francisco," "Whispering Grass" and "Time Out for Tears"), the arrangements are quite dull and Crawford does little more than caress the melodies. Definitely a lesser effort. —*Scott Yanow*

True Blues / Jun. 7, 1963-Mar. 19, 1964 / Atlantic ◆◆◆
This lesser-known Hank Crawford set has plenty of enjoyable numbers that fit into the R&Bish soul-jazz idiom. Crawford, who plays piano on two of the ten songs but otherwise sticks to his distinctive alto, is the main soloist other than three short spots for either John Hunt or Phil Guilbeau on trumpet. Most of the selections on this out-of-print LP are quite catchy with the highlights including "Shake A-Plenty," a passionate "Merry Christmas Baby," "Save Your Love for Me" and "Two Years of Torture." —*Scott Yanow*

After Hours / Oct. 19, 1965-Jan. 19, 1966 / Atlantic ◆◆◆◆
The most unusual aspect to this straight CD reissue of a Hank Crawford Atlantic LP is that the altoist plays some very effective piano on two numbers including a lengthy feature on "After Hours." Fortunately his alto playing is not neglected and he really shows off his appealing tone on "Who Can I Turn To," "Makin' Whoopee" and "When Did You Leave Heaven." A fine soulful crossover set that is quite accessible and melodic. —*Scott Yanow*

It's a Funky Thing to Do / Dec. 10, 1970 / Cotillion ◆◆◆
This was altoist Hank Crawford's final recording for Atlantic after a commercially successful ten-year run. The soulful altoist is backed by a funky rhythm section (either Eric Gale or Cornell Dupree on guitar, keyboardist Richard Tee, Chuck Rainey or Ron Carter on electric bass and drummer Bernard Purdie) that often sounds as if it is just going through the motions. Crawford plays well as usual but, other than "Parker's Mood," none of the seven selections are particularly memorable nor stand out from the crowd. One can almost feel Atlantic's executives looking at the potential dollar signs. —*Scott Yanow*

We Got a Good Thing Going / Sep. 1972-Oct. 1972 / Columbia ◆◆◆◆
Of Hank Crawford's somewhat erratic output for Kudu during 1971-78, this is the album to get. The Don Sebesky arrangements for strings and an oversized rhythm section fit Crawford's soulful style well and the altoist performs consistently strong material that was also commercially successful. Of the nine numbers, Crawford is heard at his best on "Imagination," "The Christmas Song," "Alone Again (Naturally)" (the definitive version of that pop standard), "I'm Just a Lucky So and So" and "Winter Wonderland." A minor gem. —*Scott Yanow*

Wildflower / Jun. 1973 / Columbia ◆◆
Tico Rico / Nov. 1976 / Kudu ◆◆
With a couple of exceptions, altoist Hank Crawford's Kudu recordings of the 1970s did not reach the levels of his best Atlantic dates from the 1960s or his later Milestone albums. This LP has generally weak material ("Teach Me Tonight" is the only standard), the arrangements by David Matthews are routine and Crawford's soulful alto sounds obviously overdubbed over the string section; the "background" vocals on "Lullaby of Love" also do not help. The only reason to acquire this album is to hear Crawford's always appealing sound, but there are many more rewarding Hank Crawford recordings currently available. —*Scott Yanow*

Centerpiece / Oct. 1978-Nov. 1978 / Buddah ◆◆◆
This little-known Hank Crawford LP was a transitional record between his long associations with Kudu and Milestone. More straightahead than his Kudu dates, the program is highlighted by the Harry "Sweets" Edison blues "Centerpiece," "Gee Baby Ain't I Good to You" and Slide Hampton's "Frame for the Blues." In addition to Crawford (who splits his time between his soulful alto and a Fender Rhodes electric piano), guitarist Calvin Newborne (the brother of pianist Phineas) has plenty of solo space. Crawford provided the arrangements for a five-piece horn section and the results are soulful and pleasing. —*Scott Yanow*

Midnight Ramble / Nov. 4, 1982-Nov. 10, 1982 / Milestone ◆◆◆◆
After a four-year absence from records, Hank Crawford started an extensive series of recordings for Milestone that were consistently soulful but also largely straightahead, the perfect setting for his alto. Crawford's Milestone debut also features Dr. John on piano and organ, guitarist Calvin Newborne and background work from a five-piece horn section playing the leader's arrangements. Highlights of the CD include "Midnight Ramble," Phineas Newborn's "Theme for Basie," Ray Charles' "Mr. C" and "Street of Dreams." —*Scott Yanow*

Indigo Blue / Aug. 22, 1983-Aug. 23, 1983 / Milestone ◆◆◆◆
All of altoist Hank Crawford's many Milestone recordings of the 1980s and '90s are fine examples of his soulful approach to playing straightahead jazz. This CD, which ranges in repertoire from "The Very Thought of You" and "Things Ain't What They Used to Be" to Willie Nelson's "Funny," showcases Crawford's immediately distinctive alto in a quintet with pianist-organist Dr. John and guitarist Melvin Sparks that is augmented by a four-piece horn section arranged by the leader. Accessible and reasonably creative music. —*Scott Yanow*

Down on the Deuce / Jun. 18, 1984-Jun. 19, 1984 / Original Jazz Classics ◆◆◆
This Hank Crawford LP (which has not yet been reissued on CD) was his third for Milestone and follows his appealing soul jazz formula. Crawford's alto is the main voice throughout although there is some solo space for keyboardist Cedar Walton, guitarists Jimmy Ponder and Melvin Sparks, and David Newman on tenor and flute. Crawford is joined by a funky four-piece rhythm section plus four horns and, although the material is not as strong as usual, there are some good performances, particularly on "Down Home Blues" and "When a Man Loves a Woman." —*Scott Yanow*

Roadhouse Symphony / Aug. 5, 1985-Aug. 12, 1985 / Milestone ◆◆◆
All of Hank Crawford's many recordings for Milestone in the 1980s and '90s are worth picking up by his fans although this reasonably enjoyable outing (not yet reissued on CD) is not one of the more essential ones. The soulful altoist is joined by Dr. John on piano and organ, guitarist Melvin Sparks, bassist Wilbur Bascomb, Jr., drummer Bernard Purdie and a five-piece horn section (Houston Person and David "Fathead" Newman get a tenor solo apiece) for a set mostly comprising group originals plus the old ballad "Say It Isn't So" and Thomas A. Dorsey's spiritual standard "Precious Lord"; Dr. John takes a vocal on his "Tragick Magick." —*Scott Yanow*

Soul Survivors / Jan. 29, 1986-Jan. 30, 1986 / Milestone ◆◆◆◆
Hank Crawford's fifth in his long string of Milestone recordings was the first of several to team the soulful altoist with organist Jimmy McGriff. Guitarists George Benson and the lesser-known Jim Pittsburgh are on three songs apice while Bernard Purdie is on drums except on "Frim Fram Sauce" where Mel Lewis takes his spot. The superior material and the infectious swing supplied by McGriff and his rhythm mates inspire Hank Crawford to some of his best playing of the era. Recommended. —*Scott Yanow*

Mr. Chips / Nov. 1986 / Milestone ◆◆◆
A decent but not overly memorable outing by Hank Crawford, this CD (other than "Robbins Nest") features the distinctive altoist mostly playing R&Bish material while accompanied by a funky rhythm section that includes guitarist Cornell Dupree and keyboardist Richard Tee plus a four-horn rhythm section; Leon Thomas takes a vocal on "You Send Me." —*Scott Yanow*

Steppin' Up / Jun. 15, 1987-Jun. 16, 1987 / Milestone ◆◆◆◆
Altoist Hank Crawford and organist Jimmy McGriff met up for a second time on this 1987 CD, and the results are predictably soulful and pleasing. With guitarist

Jimmy Ponder and drummer Vance James completing the quartet and pianist Billy Preston (rarely heard in this type of setting) sitting in successfully on three of the seven numbers, this is a highly enjoyable outing, easily recommended for soul-jazz fans. Among the highlights are "River's Invitation," "Tippin' In" and "McGriff's Steppin' Up." —*Scott Yanow*

Night Beat / Sep. 1988-Oct. 1988 / Milestone ✦✦✦
Altoist Hank Crawford teams up with pianist/organist Dr. John on this accessible and enjoyable soul-jazz outing. Crawford made quite a few CDs in this format for Milestone during the 1980s, using a funky four-piece rhythm section and a small horn section to play recent originals and a few vintage classics. Highlights of the above-average effort include "For the Love of You," "K.C. Blues" and "Trouble in Mind." —*Scott Yanow*

● **On the Blue Side** / Apr. 4, 1989+Aug. 9, 1989 / Milestone ✦✦✦✦✦
With Jimmy McGriff on Hammond organ and Jimmy Ponder on guitar. Funky, mellow, and gritty. —*Ron Wynn*

Groove Master / Jan. 1990-Mar. 1990 / Milestone ✦✦✦

Portrait / Mar. 19, 1991-Mar. 20, 1991 / Milestone ✦✦✦
With David "Fathead" Newman on tenor sax, Jimmy Ponder on guitar, and Johnny Hammond on the organ. —*Ron Wynn*

South Central / Aug. 11, 1992+Aug. 27, 1992 / Milestone ✦✦✦

Tight / Apr. 8, 1996-May 13, 1996 / Milestone ✦✦✦
Altoist Hank Crawford is in typically soulful form on this set of standards, blues and ballads. Joined by a crack eight-piece band (with some notable playing from guitarist Melvin Sparks), Crawford sounds particularly fine on "I Had a Dream," "Mona Lisa," Freddie Hubbard's "Little Sunflower" and "Everything I Have Is Yours." The music, however, is quite safe and some of pianist Danny Mixon's song quotes are a touch corny. Good music that is easily recommended to Crawford's fans, but no real surprises occur. —*Scott Yanow*

Road Tested / Jun. 30, 1997-Jul. 1, 1997 / Milestone ✦✦✦✦
Jimmy McGriff continued on a high roll on his second tour with Milestone, taping another dual-billed soul-jazz album with the redoubtable Hank Crawford. You know what to expect by now—hardass, down-home, blues-drenched organ trio-plus-sax grooving—but this is a really potent gusher of that genre, rising to the level of McGriff's idiom-defining *The Dream Team* from 1996. Throughout, Crawford produces some sterling roadhouse tenor work and guitarist Wayne Boyd stays resolutely in the pocket. Drummer Bernard Purdie stokes the engines from the opening crack of the funky "Peanuts," contributes to a refreshingly kicking trans-formation of "I Only Have Eyes for You," and lays on a devastating backbeat whenever asked. John Coltrane's minor blues "Mr. P.C." also responds well to the soul-jazz treatment. Recorded the old-fashioned Prestige way—in two sessions, with Bob Porter producing in Rudy Van Gelder's studio—it's amazing and gratify-ing that bluesicians are still allowed to make records this way. —*Richard S. Ginell*

Ray Crawford

b. Feb. 7, 1924, Pittsburgh, PA
Guitar / Hard Bop, Soul Jazz
Ray Crawford played tenor and clarinet with Fletcher Henderson during 1941-43 but tuberculosis forced him to give them up. He switched to guitar and was an important part of Ahmad Jamal's early groups (1949-55); his ability to make his guitar sound like bongos by hitting it was soon adopted by Herb Ellis. Crawford also recorded with Gil Evans (1959-60), played off and on with Jimmy Smith from 1958 into the 1980s and in the '60s settled in Los Angeles. He led fairly obscure records for Candid (1961, but not released until the '80s), Dobre (1977) and United National (1978). —*Scott Yanow*

● **Smooth Groove** / Feb. 10, 1961 / Candid ✦✦✦✦
Guitarist Ray Crawford, best known for his associations with pianist Ahmad Jamal and organist Jimmy Smith, only led one session in his early years. Because the Candid label soon went bankrupt, the set went unreleased altogether until this 1988 CD. Comprising five Crawford originals, the session finds the guitarist play-ing fairly advanced hard bop with trumpeter Johnny Coles, baritonist Cecil Payne (in top form), pianist Junior Mance, bassist Ben Tucker and drummer Frankie Dunlop. Everyone sounds fine, making one regret that this set fell between the cracks for so many years. —*Scott Yanow*

Marilyn Crispell

b. Mar. 30, 1947, Philadelphia, PA
Piano / Avant-Garde
One of the finest pianists of the avant-garde, Marilyn Crispell has been greatly inspired by Cecil Taylor and can be nearly as powerful but also is not shy to use space or occasionally play a spiritual standard. She studied piano at the Peabody

Music School in Baltimore from age seven and later went to the New England Conservatory. Crispell was outside of music during 1969-75 but then became very interested in advanced jazz. She met Anthony Braxton, toured Europe with his Creative Music Orchestra in 1978 and has been in his regular quartet since the early '80s. Marilyn Crispell has also led her own groups (both live and on records) since then, recording several notable sets for Leo, Cadence and Music & Arts. She is near the top of her field. —*Scott Yanow*

● **Spirit Music** / May 15, 1981+Jan. 13, 1982 / Cadence ✦✦✦✦✦
Marilyn Crispell is one of the most significant piano voices of the avant-garde. A powerful player influenced by Cecil Taylor but who has her own way of using space, Crispell has been closely associated with Anthony Braxton's group during the past decade. This Cadence release, however, finds her leading her own trio, an unusual group that also includes violinist Billy Bang and drummer John Betsch. On one of the four lengthy improvisations heard on this set, guitarist Wes Brown makes the band a quartet. These stirring performances serve as a fine introduction to the passionate music of Marilyn Crispell. —*Scott Yanow*

Live in Berlin / Nov. 4, 1982 / Black Saint ✦✦✦✦
One of the major avant-garde pianists to emerge during the 1980s, Marilyn Crispell shows a great deal of passion on three of her originals, including the 23-minute "ABC" (which was dedicated to Anthony Braxton) and the free ballad "Chant." Violinist Billy Bang (who has some strong solos of his own), bassist Peter Kowald and drummer John Betsch complete the quartet on this intense concert performance. —*Scott Yanow*

Rhythms Hung in Undrawn Sky / May 7, 1983 / Leo ✦✦✦✦
As strong as she sounds in groups, pianist Marilyn Crispell is consistently heard at her best when playing unaccompanied solos. She explores five originals (includ-ing the two part "Archaic Visions") on this fairly rare Leo album, ranging from tunes titled "Love" and "Sadness" to "Song for Abdullah (Ibrahim)." The music is quite intense, if occasionally lyrical, with Crispell displaying both the influence of Cecil Taylor and her own musical personality. —*Scott Yanow*

A Concert in Berlin / Jul. 2, 1983 / FMP ✦✦✦✦

And Your Ivory Voice Sings / Mar. 1985 / Leo ✦✦✦
The explosive pianist Marilyn Crispell is joined by drummer Doug James for a set of passionate duets. On six originals (including tributes to Jeanne Lee and Cecil Taylor) and a spiritual version of John Coltrane's "After the Rain," Crispell plays with impressive power and more emotional variety than one might expect. Open-eared listeners will enjoy this somewhat obscure Leo release. —*Scott Yanow*

Gaia / Mar. 15, 1987 / Leo ✦✦✦

Labyrinths / Oct. 2, 1987 / Les Disques ✦✦✦

The Kitchen Concerts / Feb. 2, 1989-Feb. 4, 1989 / Leo ✦✦✦

Live in Zurich / Apr. 12, 1989 / Leo ✦✦✦✦
Crispell keeps cranking out furious, aggressive free dates for the European mar-ket. They're devoid of any devices now in vogue on the jazz circuit: no standards, no electronics, no hard bop, Adult Contemporary, strings, or fusion. If you enjoy hearing spirited dialogues between Crispell, bassist Reggie Workman, and drum-mer Paul Motian, this one's for you. —*Ron Wynn*

● **Live in San Francisco** / Oct. 20, 1989 / Music & Arts ✦✦✦✦✦
This is the Marilyn Crispell CD to start out with. The avant-garde pianist, most influenced by Cecil Taylor but increasingly original through the years, explores eight selections during a dynamic live set. In addition to five originals, Crispell plays very fresh (and unpredictable) versions of "When I Fall in Love," Thelonious Monk's "Ruby, My Dear" and John Coltrane's spiritual "Dear Lord." In addition, the 55 minutes of solo piano are joined by two numbers featuring Crispell that were also released on other Music & Arts releases: a duet with Anthony Braxton and "Wha's Nine" from a very adventurous Reggie Workman set with vocalist Jeanne Lee and clarinetist Don Byron. Invigorating music. —*Scott Yanow*

Circles / 1990 / Victor ✦✦✦✦

Overlapping Hands: Eight Segments / 1990 / FMP ✦✦✦

Images / Aug. 1991 / Music & Arts ✦✦✦✦✦
The current piano favorite among the new generation of outside players, Crispell doesn't tone down the intensity until she concludes the session. Her approach, attack, tone, and phrasing have often been compared to her mentor Cecil Taylor, but she's not quite as percussive (no one is). However, this is as close as any living being can get to duplicating his energy and power. —*Ron Wynn*

Crispell & Hemingway Duo / 1992 / Knitting Factory ✦✦✦✦

Marilyn Crispell Trio: Highlights from the Summer of 1992 American Tour / 1992 / Music & Arts ✦✦✦✦

Stellar Pulsations / Feb. 2, 1992-Jul. 13, 1992 / Leo ✦✦✦

Hyperion / Jun. 25, 1992 / Music & Arts ✦✦✦
Hyperion documents the second-ever meeting of pianist Marilyn Crispell, saxophonist Peter Brotzmann and percussionist Hamid Drake, recorded live at the 1992 Toronto Jazz Festival. *—Jason Ankeny*

Inference / Jun. 25, 1992 / Music & Arts ✦✦✦
An avant-gardist whose playing (even at its most intense) is lyrical, the remarkable pianist Marilyn Crispell was originally influenced by Cecil Taylor but has since carved out her own musical personality. For this particular CD she is teamed with altoist Tim Berne, who also has a fresh and lively style. Their six duets (three originals apiece) often have arranged sections that sound like improvisations and vice-versa. Berne's "Inference" is the most memorable track, with sections divided by the main theme and several emotions explored, but all of the performances are well worth hearing. "Bass Voodoo" finds Berne sounding a little like Anthony Braxton, "Sorrow" is quite emotional without being downbeat and "For Alto and Piano II" contrasts the different approaches of the two musicians. This set has plenty of stimulating and unpredictable interplay by the two giants (both of whom sound as if they have large ears). Music & Arts deserves thanks from the jazz world for making these noncommercial sounds available. *— Scott Yanow*

Cascades / Jun. 26, 1993 / Music & Arts ✦✦✦
Crispell and occasional collaborator Gerry Hemingway are joined by bassist Barry Guy on the 1996 improv session *Cascades*. *—Jason Ankeny*

Band on the Wall / May 26, 1994 / Matchless ✦✦✦✦
Pianist Marilyn Crispell and drummer Eddie Prevost match together very well on this avant-garde duet concert that was recorded live in Manchester, England. Although 13 songs are listed (all but Denny Zeitlin's "Quiet Now" are originals by one or both musicians), this is actually a continuous performance. Crispell, a very talented pianist who can play with tremendous power and freedom, is also not afraid to occasionally wring out sincere emotions on straightforward melodies. Her performance covers several different moods and, although often very free form and percussive, she leaves space and can be quite lyrical. Prevost follows her musical directions closely and has four solo interludes of his own. The results are a stimulating set of adventurous music that is sometimes surprisingly accessible. *—Scott Yanow*

Live at Mills College 1995 / Jan. 27, 1995 / Music & Arts ✦✦✦
On this rare solo piano outing, Crispell plays a number of her own compositions along with songs by Thelonius Monk and Weisman, Garrett & Wayne. *—Jason Ankeny*

Nothing Ever Was, Anyway: The Music of Annette Peacock / 1997 / ECM ✦✦✦✦
Marilyn Crispell's double-disc *Nothing Ever Was, Anyway: The Music of Annette Peacock* is an enchanting, ambitious tribute to Peacock. Crispell is backed by Gary Peacock (double bass) and Paul Motian (drums), two musicians who have worked with and interpreted Annette Peacock's music since the '60s, and the trio created a wonderful, complex salute to her music that emphasizes the strength of the compositions, as well as Crispell's complex, intricate playing. Peacock herself sings on "Dreams (I Time Weren't)." *—Leo Stanley*

Sonny Criss (William Criss)

b. Oct. 23, 1927, Memphis, TN, d. Nov. 19, 1977, Los Angeles, CA
Alto Saxophone / Hard Bop
A talented bop altoist, Sonny Criss was influenced by Charlie Parker but had his own heavier sound. He spent most of his life in the Los Angeles area starting in 1942. In 1946 he worked in Howard McGhee's band with Charlie Parker and Teddy Edwards and can be heard on several jam sessions on Savoy in 1947. Criss spent periods playing with Johnny Otis, Gerald Wilson, and Billy Eckstine (1950-51) and was with Stan Kenton in 1955. He also worked with Howard Rumsey's Lighthouse All-Stars and Buddy Rich's quartet (1958) in addition to leading his own groups, recording three albums for Imperial in 1956. Criss lived in Europe during 1962-65, recorded some excellent sets for Prestige during 1966-69 and in the 1970s headed sessions for Fresh Sound, Xanadu, Muse and a couple of commercial efforts for Impulse. After European tours in 1973 and 1974, Sonny Criss' career seemed on an upswing. But due to the pain of cancer, he chose to commit suicide in 1977. *—Scott Yanow*

Memorial Album / Oct. 17, 1947-Jun. 15, 1965 / Xanadu ✦✦✦✦
This out-of-print LP contains several formerly rare sessions featuring the talented bop altoist Sonny Criss. The first five numbers (which were only previously available on the collector's label Jazz Showcase) were privately recorded and feature a sextet that Billy Eckstine was using for his backup band at the time. Criss teams up with the high-note trumpeter Al Killian and tenor saxophonist Wardell Gray and already sounds quite distinctive on the transitional swing-to-bop performances. Also on this LP is a 1950 vocal by Damita Jo on "I Can't Give You Anything but Love" that has some prominent Criss, a 1952 quartet rendition of "Strike

Up the Band" and five songs that comprised a previously unheard demonstration record of Criss' quartet (with pianist Hampton Hawes) in 1965. This album is quite a collector's item and recommended to bop collectors lucky enough to run across it. *—Scott Yanow*

Intermission Riff / Oct. 12, 1951 / Original Jazz Classics ✦✦✦
Released for the first time in 1988, the music on this set is taken from a 1951 Jazz at the Philharmonic concert held at the Shrine Auditorium in Los Angeles. The septet is very different from the usual Norman Granz gang, consisting of trumpeter Joe Newman, trombonist Bennie Green, Eddie Lockjaw Davis on tenor, pianist Bobby Tucker, bassist Tommy Potter, drummer Kenny Clarke and the main solo star, altoist Sonny Criss. The five songs (four standards and a jump tune) are fairly typical for JATP (highlighted by lengthy versions of "How High the Moon" and "Perdido") and the recording quality is listenable but not pristine. However Criss' passionate playing (and that of the other musicians) makes this release of interest to collectors of historic straightahead jazz. *—Scott Yanow*

Sonny Criss and Kenny Dorham, Vol. 1: The Bopmasters / Apr. 4, 1956-1959 / ABC/Impulse! ✦✦✦✦
Released as the first volume in Impulse's short-lived reissue program titled *The Dedication Series*, this two-LP set combines together a pair of unrelated sessions. Trumpeter Kenny Dorham leads his Jazz Prophets, a quintet in 1956 that also stars tenor saxophonist J.R. Monterose and pianist Dick Katz. They ably perform four of Dorham's originals plus the ballad "Don't Explain." The Sonny Criss session from 1959 has trombonist Ole Hansen and pianist Wynton Kelly among the other soloists but Criss' alto dominates the set. The music by both groups is high-quality hard bop and these rare sides are worth getting. Pity that this valuable series quickly went out of print. *—Scott Yanow*

Go Man! / Nov. 28, 1956 / Imperial ✦✦✦
By the mid-'50s, William "Sonny" Criss was maturing as a significant voice on the alto saxophone. Heavily influenced by Charlie Parker, much of Criss' earlier output was plagued by a hurried time feel, awkward phrasing and an uncomfortably tense vibrato. *Go Man!*, one of three dates he did for the Imperial label, showcases a confident, energetic Criss on ten standard tunes and two original lines. This hard-to-find collection is a must-have for fans of pianist Sonny Clark, heard in fine form (a bit more aggressive and "on top of the beat" than usual) along with the very coherent team of bassist Leroy Vinnegar and drummer Lawrence Marable. Only 24 years old at the time of recording, Clark had recently settled in California and was establishing himself as an inspired accompanist and soloist with the groups of Buddy DeFranco and Howard Rumsey. Clark's piano introduces nearly every cut on this recording, and his crisp, inventive soloing is a perfect compliment for Criss' brightly expressive, lightening quick lines. Overall, a lively assortment of concisely rendered, boppish treatments. *—Lee Bloom*

This Is Criss! / Oct. 21, 1966 / Original Jazz Classics ✦✦✦✦
The first of seven Prestige albums that altoist Sonny Criss made during 1966-69 (all are excellent in their own way) was Criss' first record for an American label since 1959. Joined by pianist Walter Davis, bassist Paul Chambers and drummer Alan Dawson, Criss is in fine form on eight selections; the CD reissue adds a previously unissued "Love for Sale." He displays his usual distinctive tone and shows that the years of critical neglect had not lessened his creativity within the bop idiom. *—Scott Yanow*

Portrait of Sonny Criss / Mar. 12, 1967 / Original Jazz Classics ✦✦✦✦
Sonny Criss' second of seven Prestige albums (which has been reissued on CD in the OJC series) finds the passionate altoist using the same rhythm section as on the earlier date: pianist Walter Davis, bassist Paul Chambers and drummer Alan Dawson. Criss is in fine form on five jazz standards (including a heated "Wee" and an emotional version of "Smile") plus Davis' gospelish "A Million or More Times." An excellent outing. *—Scott Yanow*

Sonny's Dream / May 8, 1968 / Original Jazz Classics ✦✦✦✦
For Sonny Criss this was an unusual date. The altoist is backed for the set by a nonet arranged by the great Los Angeles-legend Horace Tapscott. The arrangements are challenging but complementary to Criss' style and he is top form on the six Tapscott originals. The CD reissue includes two additional alternate takes and is highly recommended for both Criss' playing and Tapscott's writing. *—Scott Yanow*

I'll Catch the Sun / Jan. 20, 1969 / Original Jazz Classics ✦✦✦✦
Altoist Sonny Criss made some of his finest recordings for Prestige during the mid- to late '60s; *I'll Catch the Sun* was the seventh and final. Since this CD reissue is only 35 minutes long, it is overly brief but the straightahead music (featuring Criss with pianist Hampton Hawes, bassist Monty Budwig and drummer Shelly Manne) is often excellent as the altoist performs two blues, two standards (including a passionate "Cry Me a River") and two forgotten pop tunes from the era. *—Scott Yanow*

★ **Crisscraft** / Feb. 24, 1975+Oct. 20, 1975 / Muse ✦✦✦✦
This is one of the very best Sonny Criss albums. The distinctive altoist, who is here joined by guitarist Ray Crawford, pianist Dolo Coker, bassist Larry Gales and drummer Jimmy Smith, is in prime form on a lengthy "The Isle of Celia," Benny Carter's "Blues in My Heart," the boppish blues "Crisscraft" and two shorter pieces. Criss, who had not recorded as a leader in six years, was really ready for this session, making this his definitive set to get. The CD reissue adds an alternate version of "Blues in My Heart" plus a slightly later version of "Out of Nowhere" to the original (and memorable) program. —*Scott Yanow*

Saturday Morning / Mar. 1, 1975 / Xanadu ✦✦✦✦
Just a week after recording the classic *Crisscraft* for Muse, altoist Sonny Criss made the nearly equal *Saturday Morning* for Xanadu. Assisted by the great bop pianist Barry Harris, bassist Leroy Vinnegar and drummer Lenny McBrowne, Criss performs four superior if often-overlooked standards ("Angel Eyes," "Tin Tin Deo," "My Heart Stood Still" and "Until the Real Thing Comes Along"), his blues "Jeannie's Knees" and one of his better originals, "Saturday Morning." Criss, an underrated altoist who was instantly recognizable within three notes, was neglected during long portions of his career but he did leave behind several memorable recordings, such as this one. Recommended. —*Scott Yanow*

Out of Nowhere / Oct. 20, 1975 / Muse ✦✦✦✦
Sonny Criss never became a major name or a pollwinner, but he was one of the great altoists. His recordings for Muse in the 1970s were often classics, including this superb effort. Assisted by pianist Dolo Coker, bassist Larry Gales and drummer Jimmie Smith, Criss comes up with one inventive chorus after another on two of his originals, a song by Coker, and four standards including "All the Things You Are," "My Ideal" and "Out of Nowhere." Criss' distinctive sound, mastery of bop and consistently swinging ideas are three strong reasons to acquire this CD reissue. —*Scott Yanow*

Warm & Sonny / 1976 / Impulse! ✦✦
Altoist Sonny Criss' next-to-last recording (as with his final effort, *The Joy of Sax*) is a commercial date in which he is accompanied by a funky rhythm section, strings and horns. Even on his own "Blues for Willie" (and definitely on "The Way We Were," "Bumpin'" and "Memories"), Sonny Criss sounded like he was going out of his way to record a hit; at that he failed. The music on this out-of-print LP is pleasant but badly dated. —*Scott Yanow*

The Joy of Sax / 1976 / ABC/Impulse! ✦✦
Altoist Sonny Criss' final album (he passed away in 1977) is disappointingly commercial. Not only is most of the material (which includes songs by Phil Spector, Stevie Wonder and Billy Preston among others) rather inferior but the electric rhythm section, strings and unnecessary horns inhibit much spontaneity. Criss, who sounds best on "Stolen Moments" (which also includes trumpeter Blue Mitchell) and his own "Midnight Mellow," was still in his musical prime, so it is a pity that his career ended with this rather dated outing. —*Scott Yanow*

Bing Crosby (Harry Lillis Crosby)

b. May 3, 1903, Tacoma, WA, d. Oct. 14, 1977, Madrid, Spain
Vocals / Swing, Standards, Traditional Pop
Bing Crosby was, without doubt, the most popular and influential media star of the first half of the 20th century. The undisputed best-selling artist until well into the rock era (with over half a billion records in circulation), the most popular radio star of all time, and the biggest box-office draw of the 1940s, Crosby dominated the entertainment world from the Depression until the mid-'50s, and proved just as influential as he was popular. Unlike the many vocal artists before him, Crosby grew up with radio, and his intimate bedside manner was a style perfectly suited to emphasize the strengths of a medium transmitted directly into the home. He was also helped by the emerging microphone technology: scientists had perfected the electrically amplified recording process scant months before Crosby debuted on record, and in contrast to earlier vocalists, who were forced to strain their voices into upper registers to make an impression onto mechanically recorded tracks, Crosby's warm, manly baritone crooned to its heart's content without a thought of excess.

Not to be forgotten in charting Bing Crosby's influence is the music itself. His song knowledge and sense of laidback swing was learned from early jazz music, far less formal than the European-influenced classical and popular music used for inspiration by the vocalists of the 1910s and '20s. Jazz was by no means his main concentration, though, especially after the 1930s; Crosby instead blended contemporary pop hits with the best songs from a wide range of material (occasionally recording theme-oriented songs written by non-specialists as well, such as Cole Porter's notoriously un-Western "Home on the Range"). His wide repertoire covered showtunes, film music, country & western songs, patriotic standards, religious hymns, holiday favorites, and ethnic ballads (most notably Irish and Hawaiian). The breadth of material wasn't threatening to audiences because Crosby put

his own indelible stamp on each song he recorded, appealing to many different audiences while still not endangering his own fan base. Bing Crosby was among the first to actually read songs, making them his own by interpreting the lyrics and emphasizing words or phrases to emphasize what he thought best.

His influence and importance in terms of vocal ability and knowledge of American popular music is immense, but what made Bing Crosby more than anything else was his persona—whether it was an artificial creation or something utterly natural to his own personality. Crosby represented the American everyman—strong and stern to a point yet easygoing and affable, tolerant of other viewpoints but quick to defend God and the American way—during the hard times of the Depression and World War II, when Americans most needed a symbol of what their country was all about.

Bing Crosby was born Harry Lillis Crosby in Tacoma, Washington, on May 3, 1903. (Bingo was a childhood nickname from one of his favorite comic strips.) The fourth of seven children in a poor family that loved to sing, he was briefly sent to vocal lessons early on by his mother, until he grew tired of classical training. An early admirer of Al Jolson, Crosby met his hero after his family moved to Spokane; Jolson appeared there in a touring production named *Bombo*. Crosby sang in a high-school jazz band, and when he began attending nearby Gonzaga College (to become a lawyer), he ordered a drum set through the mail and practiced on the set. Introduced to a local bandleader named Al Rinker, he was invited to join Rinker's group, the Musicaladers, singing and playing drums with the group throughout college.

Though the Musicaladers broke up soon after his graduation in 1925, Crosby was ready to stick with the music business. He had made quite a bit of money during the band's career, and with the help of Rinker—who was the brother of Mildred Bailey—the duo were confident they could make it in California. They packed up their belongings and headed out for Los Angeles, finding good money working in vaudeville until they were hired by Paul Whiteman, leader of the most popular jazz band in the country (and known as the "King of Jazz" in an era when black pioneers like Louis Armstrong were mostly ignored since they were unmarketable). For a few songs during Whiteman's shows, Rinker and Crosby sang as the Rhythm Boys with Harry Barris (a pianist, arranger, vocal effects artist and songwriter later renowned for "I Surrender Dear" and "Wrap Your Troubles in Dreams"). With their clever songwriting and stage routines, the trio soon became one of the orchestra's most popular attractions, and Crosby and Rinker took vocals on two of Whiteman's biggest hits of 1927-28, "My Blue Heaven" and "Ol' Man River." Besides appearing on vinyl with Whiteman's Orchestra, the Rhythm Boys also recorded on their own—though an opportunity to enlarge their parts in the 1930 film *The King of Jazz* with a solo song went unrealized, as Crosby sat in the clink for a drunk-driving altercation.

At that point, however, the Rhythm Boys—Crosby least of all—hardly needed Whiteman; the group was gaining valuable airtime from a Los Angeles radio show under the leadership of Gus Arnheim's Orchestra, and Crosby himself had already recorded several obscure sides for Columbia on his own, even before the end of the 1920s. When Paul Whiteman's Orchestra again hit the road in 1930, the Rhythm Boys stayed behind on the West Coast. Just as the trio had outpaced Whiteman to the point of leaving him behind, though, Crosby began sprinting ahead of Rinker and Harris by 1931, the year of his big breakout into mainstream success. After hiring big brother Everett as his manager, he began recording with Brunswick Records in early 1931, and by year's end had chalked up some of the year's biggest hits, including "Out of Nowhere," "Just One More Chance," "I Found a Million-Dollar Baby" and "At Your Command." He appeared in three films that year, and in September began a popular CBS radio series. Its success was similarly unprecedented; in less than a year, the show was among the nation's most popular and earned Crosby a starring role in 1932's *The Big Broadcast*, which brought radio stars like Burns & Allen to the screen. By the midpoint of the decade, Crosby was among the top ten most popular film stars. His musical success had, if anything, gained momentum during the same time, producing some of the biggest hits of 1932-34: "Please," "Brother, Can You Spare a Dime?," "You're Getting to Be a Habit with Me," "Little Dutch Mill," "Love in Bloom" and "June in January."

"June in January," itself the biggest hit at that point in Crosby's young career, signalled a turn in his career. Brunswick executive Jack Kapp had just struck out on his own with an American subsidiary of the British Decca Records, and Crosby was lured over with the promise of higher royalty rates. Though his initial releases on Decca were recordings from his films of the year—"June in January" was taken from *Here Is My Heart*—Crosby began stretching out with religious material (such as "Silent Night, Holy Night," which became one of his biggest sellers, estimated at up to ten million). Late in 1935, he signed a contract for a radio show with NBC called *Kraft Music Hall*, an association that lasted into the mid-'40s. Because Kraft encouraged more classical music on the program, Crosby was later forced to fire musical director Jimmy Dorsey. Songwriter friend Johnny Burke recommended

John Scott Trotter (previously with the Hal Kemp Orchestra) as a replacement, and Trotter quickly cinched the job when his arrangements for the 1936 film *Pennies from Heaven* produced the biggest hit of the year in its title song. Trotter would continue as Bing's orchestra arranger and bandleader into the mid-'50s.

After the biggest hit of 1936, Bing Crosby followed up with—what else?—the biggest of 1937, just months later. "Sweet Leilani," from the similarly Hawaiian film *Waikiki Wedding*, showed Bing the direction his career could take over the course of the 1940s and '50s. Though he had recorded several cowboy songs earlier in the 1930s as well as the occasional song of inspiration, Crosby began covering everything under the sun, the popular hits of every genre of contemporary music. These weren't cast-offs either; many of his 1940s country & western covers were hits, such as "New San Antonio Rose," "Chattanoogie Shoe Shine Boy," "You Are My Sunshine," "Deep in the Heart of Texas," "Pistol-Packin' Mama" and "San Fernando Valley."

With the advent of American involvement in World War II, Bing Crosby entered the peak of his career. Three of the biggest hits of 1940 ("Sierra Sue," "Trade Winds," "Only Forever,") were followed later in the year by the first of his popular *Road* movies with old friend Bob Hope and Dorothy Lamour. Crosby and Hope had first met in 1932, when the two both performed at the Capitol Theater in New York. They reunited later in the '30s to open a racetrack, and after reprising some old vaudeville routines, a Paramount Pictures producer decided to find a vehicle for the pair and came up with *The Road to Singapore*.

More popular success followed in 1941 with the introduction of the biggest hit of Papa Bing's career, "White Christmas." Written by Irving Berlin for 1942's *Holiday Inn* (a film that featured a Berlin song for each major holiday of the year), the single was debuted on Bing's radio show on Christmas Day, 1941. Recorded the following May and released in October, "White Christmas" stayed at No. 1 for the rest of 1942. Reissued near Christmas for each of the next 20 years, it became the best-selling single of all time, with totals of over 30 million copies. It was a favorite for soldiers on the various USO tours Crosby attended during the war years, as was another holiday song, "I'll Be Home for Christmas." Crosby's popular success continued after the end of the war, and he remained the top box-office draw until 1948 (his fifth consecutive year at No. 1).

As with all the jazz-oriented stars of the first half of the 20th century, Crosby's chart popularity was obviously affected by the rise of rock 'n' roll in the mid-'50s. Though 1948's "Now Is the Hour" proved to be his last major hit, the lack of chart success proved to be a boon: Crosby now had the time to concentrate on album-oriented projects and collaborations with other vocalists and name bands, definitely a more enjoyable venture than singing pop hits of the day on his radio show, *ad nauseam*. Inspired by the '50s adult-oriented album concepts of Frank Sinatra (who had no doubt been inspired by Bing in no small way), Crosby began to record his most well-received records in ages, as *Bing Sings Whilst Bregman Swings* (1956) and *Bing with a Beat* (1957) returned him to the hot jazz he had loved and performed back in the 1930s. His recording and film schedule began to slow in the 1960s, and though he made several movies during the '70s (plus a collaboration LP with Count Basie), Crosby rested on his considerable laurels. He was golfing in Spain on October 14, 1977, when he collapsed and died of a heart attack. —*John Bush*

1926-1932 / Dec. 22, 1926-Feb. 11, 1932 / Timeless ✦✦✦✦✦
Some of Bing Crosby's finest early recordings are on this single CD. The first track, 1926's "Pretty Lips," was allegedly previously unissued, but in reality it had come out before, and Bing is not even on it. Otherwise, this is a strong release, with Crosby featured with Paul Whiteman's Orchestra (cornetist Bix Beiderbecke has a few spots), as part of the Rhythm Boys, and on dates with Sam Lanin, the Dorsey Brothers Orchestra, Duke Ellington ("Three Little Words" and "St. Louis Blues") and Gus Arnheim ("One More Time"). Although not a "complete" set, there are many high points to be heard, including "Mississippi Mud," "Changes," "From Monday On," "You Took Advantage of Me," "Let's Do It," "and "Dinah" (co-starring the Mills Brothers). Recommended as an excellent sampler of Bing Crosby's years as a jazz singer. —*Scott Yanow*

The Classic Years in Digital Stereo: 1927 to 1934 / 1927-1934 / BBC ✦✦✦✦
One of the first Bing Crosby CD compilations released, this BBC production has some of the best sound quality and remastering ever realized on Crosby recordings of this vintage. The 16-track collection works well, featuring "I Surrender Dear," "Where the Blue of the Night Meets the Gold of the Day," "Beautiful Girl," "St. Louis Blues," "Someday Sweetheart" and "Love in Bloom." Unfortunately, the disc went out of print by the mid-'90s. —*John Bush*

Bing Crosby the Crooner: The Columbia Years 1928-34 / 1928-1934 / Columbia ✦✦✦✦
The first box set covering Bing Crosby, this three-disc CBS release appeared in 1988 with good remastering across its 65 tracks, numerous alternate takes, and a fabulous job on the liner notes, with anecdotes about each of the offerings.

Although the material is all pre-Decca and a bit inferior to much of his later output, CBS put together a good package for collectors and aficionados. Unfortunately, the box became out of print by the mid-'90s. —*John Bush*

★ **Bing! His Legendary Years, 1931 to 1957** / Nov. 23, 1931-Dec. 27, 1957 / MCA ✦✦✦✦
This four-CD set does a superb job of summing up Bing Crosby's years with Decca. After nine titles from 1931 (which were acquired by Decca later on), the program concentrates on the 1934-57 period and, in addition to the expected hits, all aspects of his career are covered. Despite a few Dixieland-flavored selections, Crosby had largely abandoned jazz by the late '30s but his phrasing (which was influenced by Louis Armstrong) and appealing voice should be of interest to jazz listeners. In later years his ballads grew in stature while the uptempo performances tended to be less memorable novelties. Although it should be augmented by collections that focus on his recordings of the 1920s and early '30s, this is the definitive Bing Crosby set. —*Scott Yanow*

Bing Crosby Sings Irving Berlin and Rodgers & Hart / Mar. 8, 1932-Jun. 1, 1942 / Conifer ✦✦✦✦✦
The most surprising thing about this 22-track, 65-minute compilation is that during the early period of his solo recording career, 1932-42, covered by this disc, Bing Crosby, the most successful singer of the time, recorded so few of the songs of Irving Berlin, the most successful songwriter of the time. So few, in fact, that in order to fill up the album, the compilers have included the only four songs written by Richard Rodgers and Lorenz Hart that Crosby recorded during the same period. Annotator Geoff Mine suggests that a feud between Crosby and Rodgers & Hart after the use of three of their songs in the 1935 film *Mississippi* led to the omission of the rest of their work until Crosby deigned to cut the patriotic "The Bombadier Song" seven years later. But all the major Broadway composers, including Cole Porter, George Gershwin, and Jerome Kern, are under-represented in the Crosby catalog for the period, probably for the simple reason that they spent their time writing for the New York stage while the singer was singing mostly newly written songs for his Hollywood movies. Still, Crosby did manage to make a No. 1 hit out of Rodgers & Hart's "Soon" and "Easy to Remember" from *Mississippi* and to reach the charts with a duet with Connee Boswell on Berlin's "Alexander's Ragtime Band." He also charted with "God Bless America." But the real turning point came with 1942's *Holiday Inn*, for which Berlin wrote all the songs. And all ten of them are here, including "Easter Parade," "Be Careful, It's My Heart" and, of course, "White Christmas." (Note that these are not actual soundtrack recordings, but studio recordings made shortly before the film's release.) Fred Astaire and Margaret Lenhart join Crosby on "I'll Capture Your Heart." Mastered from 78s, the tracks are sometimes scratchy, especially early on. But the compilation has a consistency that makes you wish there were more Crosby/Berlin recordings from the period (and that you didn't have to search out British imports of vintage Crosby). —*William Ruhlmann*

And Some Jazz Friends / Aug. 8, 1934-May 27, 1942 / GRP ✦✦✦✦
On an occasional basis through the years, Bing Crosby recorded in Dixieland and swing-oriented settings. This fine CD collects 20 selections on which he is heard teaming up with various jazz all-stars. Among his musical partners are Louis Jordan, Connie Boswell, Louis Armstrong ("Pennies from Heaven" and "Gone Fishin'"), Lionel Hampton, Lee Wiley, Woody Herman, brother Bob Crosby and the Eddie Condon gang. Particularly delightful is "The Waiter and the Porter and the Upstairs Maid," a Johnny Mercer number from the film *Birth of the Blues* that co-stars Jack Teagarden and Mary Martin. Overall, a particularly enjoyable release. —*Scott Yanow*

Bing Crosby & the Andrews Sisters: Their Complete Recordings Together / Sep. 20, 1939-Feb. 21, 1952 / MCA ✦✦✦✦✦
Just what the title says: a double-CD of 53 tracks from 1939-52 that includes all their official releases (many of which were substantial hits), as well as rarities that have only been available on bootlegs and some outtakes. There are also Christmas songs and a couple of tunes that also feature vocalist Dick Haymes, letting you know that this package is firmly targeted toward the serious '40s vocals fan. It's not the first (or second) preferred purchase for fans of either Crosby or the Andrews Sisters. On the other hand, if your interest in either Crosby or the Andrews is serious enough to warrant more than a greatest-hits CD, you'll likely enjoy this reissue. —*Richie Unterberger*

Bing Sings Whilst Bregman Swings / Jun. 11, 1956-Jun. 12, 1956 / Mobile Fidelity ✦✦✦✦
This audiophile CD reissue (originally on Verve) brings back one of Bing Crosby's better albums from the 1950s. Joined by a big band arranged and conducted by Buddy Bregman, Crosby is in prime voice on a dozen standards that (according to the breezy liner notes) he had never recorded before. The concise performances (all between two-to-four minutes) are straightforward and generally swinging.

Highlights include "'Deed I Do," "Heat Wave," "The Blue Room" and "Jeepers Creepers." —*Scott Yanow*

The Complete United Artists Sessions / 1974-1977 / EMI ✦✦✦

Released to commemorate the 20th anniversary of Bing Crosby's death, *The Complete United Artists Sessions* compiles onto three discs all of his material for UA, recorded for the most part during 1974-77, the last three years of his life. Included are his album with Fred Astaire, a couple of live songs from a 1976 show at the London Palladium previously unreleased, plus several duets with Johnny Mercer and Bob Hope. Of course, the recordings made at the end of his life pale in comparison to those from his prime, but Crosby seemed happy and in good spirits, and this set can be enjoyed by any Crosby fan, not just the collectors. —*John Bush*

Bob Crosby (George Robert Crosby)

b. Aug. 25, 1913, Spokane, WA, **d.** Mar. 9, 1993, La Jolla, CA
Vocals, Bandleader / Dixieland, Swing, Jazz, Big Band, Traditional Jazz

Bob Crosby, Bing's younger brother, often found himself in the odd position of being the least important member of his own orchestra! An ok singer, Crosby was much more important as the leader of a memorable swing band that found its own style by looking backwards at the 1920s. To Crosby's credit, he seemed aware of his predicament and not uncomfortable at allocating most of the solo space to his talented sidemen, featuring them with his big band and his Bobcats, the latter a hot Dixieland band taken out of his orchestra. After stints with Anson Weeks in 1932 and the Dorsey Brothers' orchestra during 1934-5, Crosby was voted the frontman of a new big band that was formed out of the remains of Ben Pollack's orchestra. The period 1935-42 was Crosby's heyday with his band featuring such classic soloists as Yank Lawson, Billy Butterfield, Eddie Miller, Matty Matlock, Irving Fazola, Joe Sullivan, Bob Zurke, Jess Stacy and Muggsy Spanier. During an era when swing was the thing and New Orleans jazz was considered by many to be ancient history, Crosby's crew led the way to the eventual New Orleans revival. Such classic recordings as "South Rampart Street Parade" and "What's New" (both composed by bassist Bob Haggart) along with the many Dixieland stomps kept the band quite popular. The orchestra broke up in late 1942, Crosby served in the Marines during 1944-45 and then spent the rest of his life in a variety of activities, often bringing back versions of the Bobcats for special concerts and recordings, taking an occasional vocal but mostly letting his sidemen play. Some of Crosby's many Decca recordings are currently available. —*Scott Yanow*

★ South Rampart Street Parade / Apr. 13, 1936-Feb. 17, 1942 / GRP ✦✦✦✦✦

Bob Crosby led one of the hottest big bands of the 1930s, a unit that although filled with swing stylists could play Dixieland with the joy and spontaneity of a small group. In time, Bob Crosby's Bobcats would overshadow the big band, but this definitive CD shows how enjoyable the orchestra could be. With such soloists as trumpeters Yank Lawson and Billy Butterfield, clarinetists Matty Matlock and Irving Fazola, Eddie Miller (on tenor and clarinet) and pianists Bob Zurke, Joe Sullivan and Jess Stacy among others, the Crosby aggregation could hold its own with any other band of the time. On their CD, 20 of Bob Crosby's finest performances (17 of which are from 1936-39) are included, with the high points being "Little Rock Getaway" (Zurke's classic interpretation of Sullivan's most famous song), "South Rampart Street Parade," "Big Noise from Winnetka," the original version of "What's New" (known at the time as "I'm Free"), "My Inspiration," "Jimtown Blues," and several heated Dixieland standards. Essential music for any serious jazz collection. —*Scott Yanow*

1937-1938 / Feb. 8, 1937-Oct. 19, 1938 / DRG ✦✦✦

Part of engineer Robert Parker's series of pre-bop reissues (all of which feature recordings that are made to sound surprisingly close to stereo), this CD has some of the highlights of the Bob Crosby Orchestra and Bobcats output of 1937-38. The 18 numbers (a dozen by the Bobcats) definitely emphasize jazz, with many Dixieland standards being prominent. The solo stars include trumpeter Yank Lawson, trombonist Warren Smith, clarinetist Matty Matlock, tenorman Eddie Miller and pianist Bob Zurke. Among the many classic recordings are "South Rampart Street Parade," "March of the Bobcats," "The Big Noise from Winnetka" (the famous duet by bassist/whistler Bob Haggart and drummer Ray Bauduc), and "Honky Tonk Train Blues," but there is not a throwaway in the entire set. Particularly recommended to Dixieland fans. —*Scott Yanow*

Bob Crosby & His Orchestra (1938) / 1938 / Circle ✦✦

I Remember You / Sep. 1941-Jul. 1942 / Vintage Jazz ✦✦✦

The Bob Crosby Orchestra was going through a personality crisis in the early '40s. Although the big band gained its fame a few years later as one of the top Dixieland bands, it was leaning towards more routine swing and commercialism by the early war years in an attempt to increase its audience; the move had the opposite effect. This CD contains radio transcriptions of some of the tunes hint a bit at Dixieland

(particularly the ones featuring trumpet solos from Yank Lawson and spots for Eddie Miller's tenor) but there are also many forgettable vocals. So, although there are some good moments, this music is a bit erratic and overall not up to the level of Bob Crosby's more famous recordings. —*Scott Yanow*

The Uncollected Bob Crosby & His Orchestra (1941-1942) / 1941-1942 / Hindsight ✦✦✦

☆ 22 Original Big Band Records / 1952-1953 / Vanguard ✦✦✦✦

Recent 1988 reissue of early-50s cuts. —*Ron Wynn*

Bob Crosby & His Orchestra (1952-1953) / 1952-1953 / Hindsight ✦✦✦

Off to a New Start / Feb. 22, 1990-Jun. 12, 1992 / BCBC ✦✦✦

Although Bob Crosby passed away in 1993, his Bobcats still live on. The musicians heard on this recording were originally members of Crosby's last backup group, Swing 'n' Dixie. On February 22, 1990, with Crosby's approval, they recorded a full CD, *Play It the Bob Cat Way*, that had 15 songs associated with the Bobcats. Now under the name of Bob Crosby's Bob Cats, 11 of the 15 selections from the original CD have been joined by two unissued numbers from the same date, plus four tunes recorded in 1992 (although nowhere on the back cover does it say that most of this music is being reissued). The musicians (trumpeter Werner Lutz, trombonist Parke Frankenfield, tenorman Bobby "Lips" Levine, clarinetist Paul Hubbell, and pianist Ed Metz, Sr., plus a rhythm section) were quite familiar with both the music and the style and emulate their predecessors without copying them too closely. Few surprises occur (the tenor tradeoff by Levine and Hubbell on "Washington and Lee Swing" is a highlight), but fans of the 1930s group will certainly enjoy this spirited later extension of the original Dixieland-oriented concept. —*Scott Yanow*

Israel Crosby

b. Jan. 19, 1919, Chicago, IL, **d.** Aug. 11, 1962, Chicago, IL
Bass / Swing, Cool

One of the finest bassists to emerge during the 1930s, Israel Crosby was young and flexible enough to still sound quite modern in the early '60s. He started on trumpet when he was five and then played trombone and tuba before settling on bass. In 1935, when he was 16, Crosby took one of the first full-length bass solos on record ("Blues for Israel") during a pickup date led by Gene Krupa. He played with Albert Ammons (1935-36), Fletcher Henderson (1936-38), the Three Sharps and a Flat, Horace Henderson (1940), Teddy Wilson (1940-42) and then in the studios. He was with Ahmad Jamal during most of 1954-62, propelling some of the pianist's finest trios. He toured with Benny Goodman during part of 1955-56 and in 1962 joined the George Shearing Quintet but died of a heart attack two months after recording with Shearing. —*Scott Yanow*

Connie Crothers

b. Jun. 2, 1941, Palo Alto, CA
Piano / Post-Bop, Avant-Garde, Free Jazz

Connie Crothers is a member of that unfortunately not-so-exclusive club of first-rate jazz improvisers who (for reasons unfair) have been relegated to the fringes of the jazz public's consciousness. Why she's not more well known and/or critically acclaimed has nothing to do with any lack of skill or originality, because Crothers has both to spare. Perhaps the determining non-musical factor in her neglect is the fact that she's an unrepentant disciple of that most neglected of jazz geniuses, the late Lennie Tristano. The knotty intricacies of Crothers' hyper-linear style are indeed frequently invested with her mentor's measured reserve, yet her manifestly intellectual approach to the demands of jazz improvisation does not preclude the expression of emotion. Crothers' playing is very intense; for all her self-possession, she can be quite extroverted. The defining aspect of her style is the freedom she conveys and exploits within the circumscribed boundaries of jazz's standard small-group format.

Crothers began taking piano lessons and composing at the age of nine. As a youngster she frequently played recitals and concerts, sometimes performing her own compositions. She attended the University of California at Berkeley, where she majored in music with an emphasis on composition. Crothers could find little with which to relate in contemporary approaches to composition, so she turned to jazz as a creative outlet. She became enamored of Tristano's music, and in 1962 she moved to New York in order to study with him. Formal and informal lessons continued with Tristano for ten years. In 1972, Crothers began performing privately for small audiences in Tristano's home. After a year of these, Tristano produced her first "gig"—a solo concert in Carnegie Recital Hall. In 1974, Crothers recorded her first album, *Perception*, on the Steeple Chase label. The next year, she returned to Carnegie Recital Hall in a performance with tenor saxophonist Warne Marsh, drummer Roger Mancuso, and bassist Joe Solomon. In 1979, Crothers co-produced (with saxophonist Lenny Popkin) the Lennie Tristano Memorial Concert at Town Hall in New York; that same year she also co-founded the Lennie Jazz Foundation. Crothers recorded *Swish*, a duo album with drummer Max Roach, in 1982. In the '80s and '90s, the pianist worked as a soloist and in groups that at various times included Popkin, alto saxophonist Richard Tabnik, tenor saxophonist Charlie Krachy, bassist Cameron Brown, and drummer Carol Tristano, among others. Crothers remains at or near the center of a group that perpetuates the Tristano ideal, though her own music retains a personal identity. —*Chris Kelsey*

Perception / Jun. 21, 1974-Sep. 24, 1974 / Steeple Chase ✦✦✦✦
Connie Crothers' debut as a leader finds her playing four fairly free piano solos and performing six tunes in a trio with bassist Joe Solomon and drummer Roger Mancuso. It is ironic that Lennie Tristano is quoted in the liner notes as calling Crothers the most original musician he has worked with, because at this early point Crothers sounded like a close relative of Tristano's. She does show some of her own musical personality in spots, and the music (eight of her originals, plus "My Old Flame" and "All the Things You Are") holds one's interest. —*Scott Yanow*

Solo / 1980 / Jazz ✦✦✦
Pianist Connie Crothers plays fairly well throughout this double LP, alternating rather precious ballads with heated basslines reminiscent of her teacher, Lennie Tristano. The audience reaction (which often has one or two women literally screaming in spots) is a bit annoying, and Crothers at this early point in her development did not show much individuality. A "Love Suite" with sections titled "Roy Eldridge," "Sheila Jordan" and "Max Roach" does not particularly sound like any of the performers' styles, but some of Crothers' more heated explorations are successful. Still, her most significant work was in the future. —*Scott Yanow*

Swish / Feb. 26, 1982 / New Artists ✦✦✦✦
Pianist Connie Crothers and drummer Max Roach are heard on the initial release by the New Artists label performing six duets. The music is generally free, and Crothers shows that she had shed much of her original Lennie Tristano influence while remaining true to his musical principles. As for Roach, he sounds quite enthusiastic in this adventurous setting. —*Scott Yanow*

Concert at Cooper Union / Jan. 27, 1984 / New Artists ✦✦✦

Duo Dimension / Mar. 21, 1987 / New Artists ✦✦✦

Love Energy / Apr. 14, 1988+Apr. 21, 1988 / New Artists ✦✦✦✦
On one of pianist Connie Crothers' better recordings, she shares the lead with the cool-toned and generally adventurous tenor Lenny Popkin. Bassist Cameron Brown and drummer Carol Tristano (Lennie's daughter) fulfill their timekeeping roles well and often push the soloists. Crothers and Popkin consistently inspire each other on three group improvs, an original apiece, "How Deep Is the Ocean" and Lennie Tristano's "It's You." Thought-provoking, fairly melodic and spontaneous music. —*Scott Yanow*

In Motion / Nov. 23, 1989-Nov. 25, 1989 / New Artists ✦✦✦

New York Night / Dec. 4, 1989 / New Artists ✦✦✦

● **Jazz Spring** / Mar. 26, 1993 / New Artists ✦✦✦✦✦

Music From Everyday Life / 1993-1996 / New Artists ✦✦✦✦

The Crusaders

f. 1960, db. 1988
Group / Soul Jazz, Hard Bop, Crossover Jazz, Fusion
Back in 1954, Houston pianist Joe Sample teamed up with high-school friends tenor saxophonist Wilton Felder and drummer Stix Hooper to form the Swingsters. Within a short time they were joined by trombonist Wayne Henderson, flutist Hubert Laws and bassist Henry Wilson, and the group became the Modern Jazz Sextet. With the move of Sample, Felder, Hooper and Henderson to Los Angeles in 1960, the band (a quintet with the bass spot constantly changing) took on the name of the Jazz Crusaders. The following year they made their first recordings for Pacific Jazz and throughout the 1960s the group was a popular attraction, mixing together R&B and Memphis soul elements with hard bop; its trombone/tenor front line became a trademark. By 1971 when all of the musicians were also busy with their own projects, it was decided to call the group simply the Crusaders so it would not be restricted to only playing jazz. After a few excellent albums during the early part of the decade (with guitarist Larry Carlton a strong asset), the group began to decline in quality. In 1975 the band's sound radically changed when Henderson departed to become a full-time producer. "Street Life" (1979) was a hit but also a last hurrah. With Hooper's decision to leave in 1983, the group no longer sounded like the Crusaders and gradually disbanded. In the mid-'90s Henderson and Felder had a reunion as the Crusaders but in reality only Joe Sample has had a true solo career. —*Scott Yanow*

Freedom Sounds / May 1961 / Pacific Jazz ✦✦✦✦
The first album by the Jazz Crusaders (which started an extensive series for Pacific Jazz) introduced the colorful quintet. With trombonist Wayne Henderson and tenor

saxophonist Wilton Felder giving the ensembles a unique sound, the group (also featuring regular members pianist Joe Sample and drummer Stix Hooper along with guests Jimmy Bond on bass and guitarist Roy Gaines) managed to strike a balance between creative hard bop and accessible soul jazz. In addition to their version of "Theme from Exodus" (hoping to jump on the bandwagon created by Eddie Harris' hit rendition), the Jazz Crusaders perform originals by Felder, Henderson and Sample ("Freedom Sound"). This LP (as with so much of their enjoyable Pacific Jazz material) is out of print. —*Scott Yanow*

Looking Ahead / 1961 / Pacific Jazz ✦✦✦✦
The Jazz Crusaders' second recording is most notable for the introduction of Wayne Henderson's "The Young Rabbits," the best known of the seven group originals that are performed on this LP along with "Song of India" and Leonard Bernstein's "Tonight." The tenor-trombone front line created by Wilton Felder and Henderson, along with the funky yet swinging playing of pianist Joe Sample, drummer Stix Hooper and bassist Jimmy Bond on this hard-to-find set made the group instantly recognizable and surprisingly popular from the start. —*Scott Yanow*

Way Back Home / 1961-Mar. 26, 1996 / GRP ✦✦✦
The music on this four-CD box set is mostly excellent, and this is not a bad sampler of the recordings of the (Jazz) Crusaders, but there are some problems. The 1961-70 group is covered much too quickly in the first disc, and the last two discs jump around chronologically throughout the '70s. The lack of recording dates is rather inexcusable, and the odd programming makes it difficult to trace the popular band's evolution. On the other hand, the extensive liner notes by Quincy Troupe are refreshingly honest, and many of the high points of the group's existence (including "The Young Rabbits," "Freedom Sound," "Eleanor Rigby," "Put It Where You Want It," their classic rendition of "So Far Away," and "Street Life") are included. Worth picking up by beginners, although veteran collectors will prefer to get the more complete original sets instead. —*Scott Yanow*

At the Lighthouse / Aug. 5, 1962+Aug. 6, 1962 / Pacific Jazz ✦✦✦

Heat Wave / 1963 / Pacific Jazz ✦✦✦
With all 11 songs on this LP clocking in under four minute s (eight are less than three minutes), the performances by the Jazz Crusaders (tenor saxophonist Wilton Felder, trombonist Wayne Henderson, pianist Joe Sample, drummer Stix Hooper and bassist Bobby Haynes) are concise and melodic. Some of the material is rather unlikely for the popular hard bop group (particularly "Mr. Sandman," Hoyt Axton's "Green Back Dollar" and "On Broadway"), but the band performs those tunes plus a few originals with their usual ingenuity and soulful approach. —*Scott Yanow*

Tough Talk / Feb. 1963 / Pacific Jazz ✦✦✦✦
With bassist Bobby Haynes joining the four Jazz Crusaders (trombonist Wayne Henderson, tenor saxophonist Wilton Felder, pianist Joe Sample and drummer Stix Hooper), this hard-to-find LP features the group performing eight group originals (none of which caught on) plus a soulful version of "Brahms Lullaby." In the 1960s the Jazz Crusaders managed to be both accessible and creative, funky and swinging, traditional (with the influence of R&B and gospel) yet modern; no wonder the group was so popular in the jazz world. —*Scott Yanow*

Talk That Talk / 1966 / Pacific Jazz ✦✦✦
For a change of pace, the Jazz Crusaders on this 1966 LP (which, as with most of its Pacific Jazz albums, is long out of print) are joined by an unidentified big band. The solos (particularly by tenor saxophonist Wilton Felder and trombonist Wayne Henderson) are fine but the material (a few group originals plus pop tunes such as "Walk on By" and "Hey Girl") is uniformly lightweight and rather forgettable. —*Scott Yanow*

Live at the Lighthouse '66 / Jan. 14, 1966-Jan. 16, 1966 / Pacific Jazz ✦✦✦✦
Because the Jazz Crusaders in the early '70s dropped the "Jazz" from their name and later in the decade veered much closer to R&B and pop music than they had earlier, it is easy to forget just how strong a jazz group they were in the 1960s. This CD reissues one of their rarer sessions, augmenting the original seven-song LP program (highlighted by "Blues Up Tight," "Doin' That Thing" and "Milestones") with previously unissued versions of "'Round Midnight" and John Coltrane's "Some Other Blues." The Jazz Crusaders (comprising tenor saxophonist Wilton Felder, trombonist Wayne Henderson, pianist Joe Sample, drummer Stix Hooper and during his classic period bassist Leroy Vinnegar) are heard in prime form. Felder shows the strong influence of Coltrane, Henderson recalls J.J. Johnson, Sample displays the most originality and the quintet on a whole (with its tenor-trombone front line) sounds quite distinctive. An excellent set of primarily straightahead (but soulful) jazz. —*Scott Yanow*

Uh Huh / May 15, 1967 / Pacific Jazz ✦✦✦✦
One of the best of the Jazz Crusader LPs, this outing features fairly lengthy investigations of six group originals including "Uh Huh" and "Watts Happening." Tenor saxophonist Wilton Felder, trombonist Wayne Henderson, pianist Joe Sample,

drummer Stix Hooper and guest bassist Buster Williams all sound as if they are pushing each other. Their brand of soulful hard bop (utilizing their distinctive tenor-trombone front line) is heard throughout at its prime. —*Scott Yanow*

Lighthouse 69 / 1969 / Pacific Jazz ♦♦♦♦
This LP was the fourth and final *Live at the Lighthouse* recording by the Jazz Crusaders, following equally successful sets from 1962, 1966 and 1968. Although the repertoire (four pop and R&B tunes including the Beatles' "Get Back" and four originals) would not seem to be too promising, as usual the group transforms the music into their own brand of soulful and funky hard bop. Pianist Joe Sample is heard for one of the first times doubling on electric piano and there are fine solos by tenor saxophonist Wilton Felder and trombonist Wayne Henderson. —*Scott Yanow*

Give Peace a Chance / 1969 / Liberty ♦♦♦
On what was one of the Jazz Crusaders' final recordings before they dropped the "jazz" from their name, tenor saxophonist Wilton Felder, trombonist Wayne Henderson, pianist Joe Sample, drummer Stix Hooper and bassist Buster Williams play throwaway versions of "Give Peace a Chance," "Black Bird" and "The Thrill Is Gone" but are heard in more inventive form on five of their originals including the 11-minute "Space Settlement" and Sample's "Another Blues." Although the group was changing, they still retained their original sound as long as Henderson was a part of the band. —*Scott Yanow*

● **Crusaders, Vol. 1** / 1971 / MCA ♦♦♦♦♦
The Jazz Crusaders dropped the "jazz" from their name in 1971 but fortunately jazz remained a significant part of their music throughout the remainder of their existence. This double-LP stands as one of the high points of the (Jazz) Crusaders' productive career. In addition to the founding members (Wilton Felder on tenor and electric bass, trombonist Wayne Henderson, keyboardist Joe Sample and drummer Stix Hooper), the band is joined by three guitarists (most notably Larry Carlton) and electric bassist Chuck Rainey. "Put It Where You Want It" was a minor hit at the time and the other compositions are excellent but best is a colorfully reworked (and nearly 12-minute) exploration of Carole King's "So Far Away," the only non-original among the dozen songs. When will this highly enjoyable music be reissued in full on CD? —*Scott Yanow*

Pass the Plate / May 1971 / Chisa ♦♦♦
The Jazz Crusaders dropped the "jazz" from their name after over a decade of popular recordings for the Pacific Jazz label, and they switched record companies for the first time. Although a little funkier than previously, there was no major change (at least immediately) in the group's sound. This somewhat obscure LP comprises tunes by trombonist Wayne Henderson (including the five-part 15-minute "Pass the Plate"), keyboardist Joe Sample and drummer Stix Hooper. Original member Wilton Felder (on tenor and electric bass) completes the basic quartet which is joined by guitarist Arthur Adams. Good music although nothing all that memorable occurs. —*Scott Yanow*

Second Crusade / 1972 / Chisa ♦♦♦
The second straight double-LP by the Crusaders for Blue Thumb does not reach the heights of *Crusaders, Vol. 1* although it has its strong moments. Once again the four original members of the Crusaders (drummer Stix Hooper, keyboardist Joe Sample, Wilton Felder on tenor and electric bass and trombonist Wayne Henderson) are joined by a trio of guitarists of whom Larry Carlton takes quite a few worthy solos. None of the 13 originals caught on ("Tough Talk" came the closest), but the musicians do a typically fine job of developing their own sound out of the mixture of hard bop, soul jazz, R&B and funk. —*Scott Yanow*

Unsung Heroes / Aug. 1973 / MCA ♦♦♦
The music on this later Crusaders set is quite pleasant but unfortunately none of the original melodies are all that catchy or unique; a remake of "Hard Times" (which was recorded by David Newman back in 1960) is easily the most memorable cut and a revisit to Joe Sample's "Freedom Sound" from the early days of the Jazz Crusaders is under two minutes long. There are some good solos from the soulful tenor saxophonist Wilton Felder, trombonist Wayne Henderson, electric keyboardist Joe Sample and guitarist Larry Carlton, but this CD reissue does not reach the heights (or have the strong material) of *Crusaders, Vol. 1*. —*Scott Yanow*

Chain Reaction / 1975 / MCA ♦♦♦

Scratch / 1975 / MCA ♦♦♦♦
One of their best. This is a prime example of the Crusaders doing the soul-jazz they invented and perfected. —*Ron Wynn*

Those Southern Knights / 1975 / MCA ♦♦
This has an upbeat title track but is otherwise fairly timid. —*Ron Wynn*

Southern Comfort / 1976 / Blue Thumb ♦♦♦
This has good jam-session touches. Gold album. —*Ron Wynn*

Free as the Wind / Dec. 1976 / MCA ♦♦

Images / 1978 / MCA ♦♦♦
The Crusaders' sound had changed by 1978 due to the decision of trombonist Wayne Henderson to become a fulltime producer, and the gradual dominance of funky R&B rhythms. Although the band (which consisted of keyboardist Joe Sample, Wilton Felder on tenor and soprano, drummer Stix Hooper and for this LP guitarist Billy Rogers and bassist Pops Popwell) now had a more conventional instrumentation, its music remained infectious and at least to an extent influenced by jazz. However none of the seven group originals on this little-known date are all that memorable. —*Scott Yanow*

Street Life / 1979 / MCA ♦♦♦♦
Although the Crusaders could not have known it at the time, their recording of "Street Life" (which features a memorable vocal by Randy Crawford) was a last hurrah for the 20-year-old group. Their recordings of the next few years would decline in interest until the band gradually faded away in the 1980s. However this particular set is well worth picking up for the 11-minute title cut and there is good playing by the three original members (Wilton Felder on tenor, soprano and electric bass, keyboardist Joe Sample and drummer Stix Hooper) along with guitarist Barry Finnerty; horn and string sections plus additional guitarists are utilized on Sample's commercial but listenable arrangements —*Scott Yanow*

Rhapsody & Blues / Mar. 1980 / MCA ♦♦
The Crusaders' follow-up to *Street Life* did not result in any additional hits (does anyone remember Bill Withers' vocal on "Soul Shadows?") and found the group's R&Bish music sounding closer to a formula. Each of the three remaining original Crusaders (Wilton Felder on tenor, soprano, alto and electric bass, keyboardist Joe Sample and drummer Stix Hooper), who are joined by an expanded rhythm section, contribute at least one original apiece but the group's concept was starting to sound a bit tired. —*Scott Yanow*

Standing Tall / 1980 / MCA ♦♦

Live in Japan / Jan. 1981 / GRP ♦♦♦♦
This CD consists of a complete concert recorded shortly before drummer Stix Hooper left the Crusaders. Far superior to most of the Crusader's later studio recordings, the funky date (which is an excellent summation of the group's previous five years) was one of the band's last worthwhile recordings. The passionate solos of tenorman Wilton Felder and keyboardist Joe Sample take chances within the genre and make this a particularly spirited date. —*Scott Yanow*

Royal Jam / Sep. 1981 / MCA ♦♦

The Good and the Bad Times / 1986 / MCA ♦♦

Life in the Modern World / 1988 / MCA ♦

Healing the Wounds / 1991 / GRP ♦♦
The Crusaders became a part-time group after the early '80s and by 1986 drummer Stix Hooper had departed. This final set by what was left of the group finds the two original members (keyboardist Joe Sample and saxophonist Wilton Felder) sharing the spotlight with bassist-producer Marcus Miller and an oversized rhythm section. The funky music (which includes originals by Sample and Miller in addition to "Mercy, Mercy, Mercy" and a Stevie Wonder piece) is pleasant but not too memorable. Considering the upcoming infighting that found Felder and the group's former trombonist Wayne Henderson forming a "New Crusade" over Sample's objections, the title of this CD is rather ironic. —*Scott Yanow*

Ronnie Cuber

b. Dec. 25, 1941, New York, NY
Baritone Saxophone / Hard Bop

A powerful baritonist in the tradition of Pepper Adams, Ronnie Cuber has been making excellent records for over 20 years. He was in Marshall Brown's Newport Youth Band at the 1959 Newport Jazz Festival and was featured with the groups of Slide Hampton (1962), Maynard Ferguson (1963-65) and George Benson (1966-67). After stints with Lionel Hampton (1968), Woody Herman's Orchestra (1969) and as a freelancer, he recorded a series of fine albums (both as a leader and as a sideman) for Xanadu and performed with Lee Konitz's nonet (1977-79). In the mid-'80s Cuber recorded for Projazz (in both straightahead and R&Bish settings), in the early '90s he headed dates for Fresh Sound and Steeple Chase and Cuber performed regularly with the Mingus Big Band. —*Scott Yanow*

● **Cuber Libre** / Aug. 20, 1976 / Xanadu ♦♦♦♦♦
This quartet session was a perfect setting for baritonist Ronnie Cuber, who was 34 years old at the time. Joined by the impeccable pianist Barry Harris, bassist Sam Jones and drummer Albert "Tootie" Heath, Cuber gets to swing hard on such standards as "Star Eyes," "Rifftide" and "Tin Tin Deo." Throughout this bop-oriented date, Cuber shows why he has been considered one of the top masters of the baritone during the past 20 years. —*Scott Yanow*

The Eleventh Day of Aquarius / Jan. 31, 1978 / Xanadu ✦✦✦✦
Baritonist Ronnie Cuber performs six fairly recent compositions (including his own "Klepto") on this quintet set with trumpeter Tom Harrell, pianist Mickey Tucker, bassist Dennis Irwin and drummer Eddie Gladden. The music is essentially advanced hard bop performed by underrated but talented jazz improvisers. A fine workmanlike date, most notable for featuring Cuber's deep-toned baritone. —*Scott Yanow*

Passion Fruit / Feb. 29, 1985 / Projazz ✦✦✦
George Benson (g) makes a guest appearance on this well-engineered recording. —*Ron Wynn*

Two Brothers / Nov. 21, 1985+Dec. 9, 1985 / Projazz ✦✦✦
The accent is on R&Bish rhythms during this CD. Baritonist Ronnie Cuber teams up with altoist David Sanborn and a five-piece rhythm section (which includes bassist Will Lee and drummer Steve Gadd) for a variety of rhythmic originals plus "On Green Dolphin Street." Pleasing music but not too memorable. —*Scott Yanow*

Live at the Blue Note / Nov. 3, 1986 / Projazz ✦✦✦✦
This is the most rewarding of baritonist Ronnie Cuber's three Projazz CDs which were originaly made for the Japanese King label and released domestically through Intersound. Cuber romps with trumpeter Randy Brecker, organist Lonnie Smith and drummer Ronnie Burrage on two of his originals ("Trane's Waltz" and "Philly's Blues") and a variety of jazz standards. In some ways this band was a throwback to Cuber's early recordings with George Benson and Lonnie Smith despite the lack of a guitar. Enjoyable and often-heated hard bop. —*Scott Yanow*

The Scene is Clean / Dec. 1993 / Milestone ✦✦✦

Jim Cullum, Jr.

b. Sep. 20, 1941, San Antonio, TX
Cornet, Leader / Dixieland, Classic Jazz
A powerful cornetist inspired by Louis Armstrong, Jim Cullum has led an exciting jazz band in San Antonio since his father's death in the 1970s. A clarinetist, Jim Sr. led the Happy Jazz Band with Jim Jr. on cornet, recording for their own Audiophile and Happy Jazz labels. The younger Cullum, who has recorded a *Porgy and Bess* jazz set for Sony and tributes to Louis Armstrong and Hoagy Carmichael, has made quite a few rewarding albums for Stomp Off and Audiophile, plus a Christmas record for World Jazz. Since the late 1980s, Cullum's band has been featured on a highly enjoyable radio series *Riverwalk, Live from the Landing*, whose special shows have given the group the opportunity to show its versatility. Among Cullum's most notable sidemen of the 1980s and '90s have been clarinetists Allan Vache (brother of cornetist Warren) and Brian Oglivie, trombonist Mike Pittsley and pianist John Sheridan. —*Scott Yanow*

Look Over Here / Sep. 19, 1976-Sep. 20, 1976 / Audiophile ✦✦✦✦
After clarinetist Jim Cullum, Sr.'s death in the early '70s, his Happy Jazz Band was taken over by his son, cornetist Jim Cullum, Jr. There was quite a bit of turnover at first before the personnel stabilized, but the quality and basic style of the Dixieland-based group remained consistently high. On this 1976 LP, Cullum and pianist Cliff Gillette were the only holdovers from the 1973 band. Starring along with Cullum and Gillette are two musicians who would be with the group for quite awhile: trombonist Randy Reinhart and clarinetist Allan Vache. In addition to a few warhorses, such fresh tunes as Wilbur DeParis' "Wrought Iron Rag," Dick Cary's "The Albatross," Matty Matlock's "Dixieland Shuffle" and Lu Watters' "Sage Hen Strut" are among the highlights. —*Scott Yanow*

Live and Swinging / 1979 / American Jazz ✦✦✦✦
The 1979 edition of Jim Cullum, Jr.'s Happy Jazz Band was one of the finest Dixieland bands around. The cornetist/leader, trombonist Mike Pittsley and clarinetist Allen Vache made for a potent front line, while pianist John Sheridan, banjoist Howard Elkins, bassist Jack Wyatt and drummer Kevin Hess kept the proceedings continually swinging. For this LP, Cullum's band performs songs associated with Bix Beiderbecke and Louis Armstrong, along with "I've Got a Crush on You" and "Bienville Blues." The music should please trad-jazz fans. —*Scott Yanow*

Jim Cullum's Happy Jazz Band / 1979+1990 / Jazzology ✦✦✦✦
This CD reissues one of cornetist Jim Cullum's American Jazz releases from 1979, augmenting the eight selections with four songs recorded in 1990 but not previously out. Cullum's band (with the exception of a change in drummers) had the same personnel on both dates (including trombonist Mike Pittsley, clarinetist Allen Vache, pianist John Sheridan, banjoist Howard Elkins, bassist Jack Wyatt and either Kevin Hess or Ed Torres on drums) and its appealing brand of extroverted yet thoughtful Dixieland stayed the same. Hot jazz fans will certainly enjoy this music, which is highlighted by "Big Boy," "Irish Black Bottom," "Ole Miss," "Tank Town Bump" and "Swing That Music." —*Scott Yanow*

Live at the Memphis Jazz Festival / Jun. 1982 / Jazzology ✦✦✦✦
The first recording by the Happy Jazz Band (founded by Jim Cullum, Sr., in 1962) to be on a label other than ones owned by the Cullums (American Jazz, Happy Jazz and Audiophile), this enjoyable LP finds the septet (which features cornetist Jim Cullum, Jr., trombonist Mike Pittsley, clarinetist Allan Vache and pianist John Sheridan) stretching out on six selections associated with Jelly Roll Morton, Sidney Bechet ("Egyptian Fantasy"), King Oliver and Louis Armstrong; nearly all of the numbers date from the 1920s. Decently recorded, these live performances have plenty of exciting moments, particularly from Cullum's cornet. —*Scott Yanow*

'Tis the Season . . . To Be Jammin' / Jun. 3, 1984 / World Jazz ✦✦✦✦✦
One of the finest of all the Christmas jazz albums, this well-planned LP features Jim Cullum's Jazz Band, a septet comprising the leader-cornetist, trombonist Randy Reinhart, clarinetist Allan Vache, pianist John Sheridan, Howard Elkins on banjo, guitar and vocals, bassist Jimmy Johnston and drummer Ed Torres. Their rendition of Schubert's "Ave Maria" is beautiful, Sheridan is showcased on "Nutcracker Rag" and other highlights include heated versions of "Sleigh Ride," "Home for the Holidays" and "Santa Claus Is Comin' to Town." Highly recommended yet now difficult to find. —*Scott Yanow*

Porgy & Bess / Dec. 1985+Jan. 1987 / Columbia ✦✦✦✦
Unlike most adaptations of *Porgy & Bess* that stick to the "greatest hits" from George Gershwin's folk opera, this extensive rendition by Jim Cullum's Jazz Band (a septet featuring the cornetist-leader, either Randy Reinhart or Ed Hubble on trombone, clarinetist Allan Vache and pianist John Sheridan) has nearly every bit of music that appears in the play, 22 themes in all. Such obscure numbers as "They Pass by Singin'," "It Take a Long Pull to Get There" and "Oh, Dere's Somebody Knockin' At De Do'" are interpreted in the same order as they originally were sung in the show along with "Summertime," "I Got Plenty of Nuttin'," "It Ain't Necessarily So" and "I Loves You Porgy." Jim Cullum (and his main arranger Sheridan) strike a balance on this CD between paying respect to Gershwin's melodies and allowing the musicians to come up with fresh variations. A very successful effort that is most highly recommended to fans of the folk opera. —*Scott Yanow*

Super Satch / Oct. 21, 1986-Oct. 22, 1986 / Stomp Off ✦✦✦✦✦
On this tribute to Louis Armstrong, Jim Cullum's Jazz Band at times expands from being a septet to an octet with the addition of trombonist Ed Hubble and (on some selections) the switching of Randy Reinhart from trombone to second cornet behind the leader. Cullum is a spectacular player who was influenced by (but does not copy) Armstrong. The band performs a dozen selections from the 1920s and '30s that were associated with Satch. Cullum showed a lot of courage in remaking such classics as "Potato Head Blues," "West End Blues" and "Weather Bird," but his versions are different enough from the originals so as to avoid close comparison. Other highlights include "Fireworks," the underrated "Hustlin' and Bustlin' for Baby," "Beau Koo Jack" and "Chicago Breakdown." Highly recommended to prebop jazz collectors. —*Scott Yanow*

Fireworks! Red Hot & Blues / Jul. 1, 1989-Apr. 19, 1995 / Riverwalk ✦✦✦✦
"Riverwalk, Live from the Landing" has since its debut in 1988 been one of the finest of all jazz radio series. Featuring cornetist Jim Cullum's excellent septet with a variety of guests, each show is well scripted, educational and entertaining, generally based around a specific theme. This particular set is an excellent sampler of the series. The Jim Cullum Jazz band (featuring trombonist Mike Pittsley, either Brian Oglivie or Allan Vache on clarinet and pianist John Sheridan) has three numbers to themselves (including a brilliant version of "Fireworks") and is joined by such notable guests as pianist Dick Hyman, bassist Bob Haggart, singer Vernel Bagneris (heard on "Dr. Jazz"), tap dancer Savion Glover (who follows an excerpt from a 1932 recording of Bill Bojangles Robinson on "Doin' the New Lowdown"), cornetist Leon Oakley, Linda Hopkins (who sings "St. Louis Blues") and the great Clark Terry (on "It Don't Mean a Thing" and "Mumbles"). In addition, Hyman and Sheridan engage in a heated piano duet on "Grandpa's Spells," Lionel Hampton jams "7 Come 11," clarinetist Ken Peplowski romps through "Ring Dem Bells" and Joe Wiliams sings a tender version of Eubie Blake's "A Dollar for a Dime" in a duet with pianist Sheridan. All 15 selections are quite enjoyable, the radio audience is rightfully enthusiastic and this CD has more than its share of high points. Highly recommended to classic jazz fans. —*Scott Yanow*

● **Hooray for Hoagy!** / Jan. 1990 / Audiophile ✦✦✦✦✦
Cornetist Jim Cullum leads one of the finest classic jazz/Dixieland bands of the 1990s. For this Audiophile CD his septet (which also includes trombonist Mike Pittsley, clarinetist Allan Vache and pianist John Sheridan) plays 14 Hoagy Carmichael songs including such rarely performed numbers as "Kinda Lonesome," "I Walk with Music" and "Snowball" and a few of the "hits" (including "Stardust" and "Skylark"). A special high point is the multi-tempoed treatment given "Washboard Blues" during its nearly nine-and-a-half minutes. Easily recommended both for

the melodic ensembles (many of which are arranged) and the strong solo work. —*Scott Yanow*

American Love Songs, Vol. 7 / May 31, 1990-Sep. 10, 1996 / Riverwalk ✦✦✦✦✦

Shootin' the Agate / Aug. 9, 1992-Aug. 10, 1992 / Stomp Off ✦✦✦✦

On this very enjoyable Stomp Off CD, the Jim Cullum Jazz band performs 14 Jelly Roll Morton compositions plus one song ("The Chant") associated with the innovative pianist-composer-bandleader. Cullum, a hot cornetist with a frequently exciting style, is heard in top form jamming through the classic numbers with his regular septet, a group also starring clarinetist Allan Vache, trombonist Mike Pittsley and pianist John Sheridan. Highlights of the release (which is a good place to begin exploring Cullum's playing) include "Kansas City Stomp," "The Pearls," "Black Bottom Stomp" and "Tank Town Bump." —*Scott Yanow*

Battle of the Bands: San Antonio Vs. New Orleans / 1992-1993 / Riverwalk ✦✦✦✦

One of the finest regular jazz radio series of the 1990s has been "Riverwalk, Live from the Landing," which features cornetist Jim Cullum's Jazz Band and guests performing music in tribute to the 1920s and '30s. The well-planned shows always have some special highlights; several CDs of radio performances have been made available. Jim Cullum and singer Banu Gibson have led two of the finest classic jazz bands in the world during the 1980s and '90s, so it was logical that they would meet up someday. For the "Battle of the Bands" program, the "combat" is good-humored, and the contest reaches a predictable conclusion (with the audience being the true winner). Both bands have opportunities to stretch out, and each pulls out a few surprises. William Warfield (who does some narration about New Orleans) sings W.C. Handy's "Long Gone"; pianists John Sheridan and David Boeddinghaus jam together on "Honky Tonk Train Blues"; and young Savion Glover tap-dances in the tradition of Bojangles on "Doin' the New Low Down." While the first half of the program clearly finds Cullum's band (featured on "New Orleans Stomp" and "Dippermouth Blues") ahead on points, Banu Gibson's tapping with Glover on "Wrap Your Cares in Rhythm and Dance" (which she also sings) and her five other vocals (including "She's Crying for Me" and "Dinah") eventually take honors. Despite the lack of liner notes or exact recording dates, this entire series is quite fun and well worth investigating by trad jazz fans. —*Scott Yanow*

New Year's All Star Jam / 1993 / Riverwalk ✦✦✦✦

"Riverwalk, Live From the Landing" is one of the finest jazz radio series of the past few decades, featuring lively and creative classic jazz with the emphasis on songs from the 1920s and '30s. Cornetist Jim Cullum's regular group is utilized as the show's house band, with intelligent narration provided by David Holt (centered around whatever the program's topic is that week) and plenty of guest stars. On this CD, Cullum and his septet (which includes clarinetist Brian Oglivie, trombonist Mike Pittsley and pianist John Sheridan) perform Sidney Bechet's "Sweetie Dear" and a lengthy rendition of Hoagy Carmichael's "Washboard Stomp." Various selections find the band welcoming trombonist Dan Barrett (emulating Jack Teagarden on "Wherever There's Love"), pianist Dick Hyman, bassist Bob Haggart, singer Carol Woods, singer/guitarist Marty Grosz ("You Hit the Spot") and trumpeter Doc Cheatham (showcased on "I've Got the World on a String"). Since the show is supposed to have taken place (or at least been broadcast) on New Year's Eve, the joyous studio audience is in a party mood, and the program concludes with a Dixielandish "Auld Lang Syne." An enjoyable release easily recommended to fans of trad jazz. —*Scott Yanow*

Honky Tonk Train: The Boogie Woogie Craze / 1994 / Riverwalk ✦✦✦✦

This entry in the valuable series of Jim Cullum radio broadcasts ("Riverwalk, Live from the Landing") focuses on the history of boogie-woogie. There is some narration, with excerpts from some historical recordings and lots of exciting piano from Dick Hyman and John Sheridan. Cullum's hot jazz band (a septet with the cornetist/leader, Sheridan, clarinetist Allan Vache and trombonist Mike Pittsley) has several romps, including "Jammin' the Boogie," "Roll 'Em" and "Beat Me Daddy Eight to the Bar." Most intriguing is "Celestial Express," in which Hyman switches to celeste and is joined in a quartet by Vache, guitarist Howard Elkins and bassist Don Mopsick. Fun music that is easily recommended. —*Scott Yanow*

Bessie & The Blues: Riverwalk Live, Vol. 3 / Dec. 7, 1995 / Riverwalk ✦✦✦✦

This particular radio program from the notable "Riverwalk, Live from the Landing" series features the Jim Cullum Jazz band (a septet that at the time featured cornetist Cullum, clarinetist Brian Oglivie, trombonist Mike Pittsley and pianist John Sheridan) paying tribute to the empress of the blues, Bessie Smith. David Holt's narration is intelligent and concise, but most notable is the singing of guest Topsy Chapman. Chapman emulates Bessie on such numbers as "Down Hearted Blues," "You've Been a Good Old Wagon but You Done Broke Down," "Gimme a Pigfoot" and "St. Louis Blues." There are also a couple of instrumentals for the

band ("At a Georgia Camp Meeting" and the out-of-place but enjoyable "West End Blues"). Recommended for trad jazz and early blues fans. —*Scott Yanow*

Bill Cunliffe

b. Jun. 26, 1956, Lawrence, MA
Piano / Post-Bop, Hard Bop

One of the more promising pianists currently based in the L.A. area, Bill Cunliffe has been careful to have each of his recordings display its own personality. He won the 1989 Thelonious Monk jazz piano award, for a time led the fusion band Porcupine, works with Natalie Cole and in the studios, and is a regular member of both the Clayton-Hamilton Jazz Orchestra and the Clayton Brothers Quartet. Cunliffe's recordings for Discovery have included *A Paul Simon Songbook* (on which he turned a dozen of Simon's pop tunes into jazz), *A Rare Connection* (a post-bop set filled with new originals) and *Bill in Brazil* (a bossa nova and Latin-jazz program). —*Scott Yanow*

● **Rare Connection** / Jun. 19, 1993 / Discovery ✦✦✦✦✦

Los Angeles-based keyboardist Bill Cunliffe is in excellent form on his Discovery CD, performing two standards, Wayne Shorter's "Miyako" and seven of his originals. Cunliffe utilizes some of L.A.'s top players (Bob Sheppard on tenor and bass clarinet, trumpeter Clay Jenkins, trombonist Bruce Paulson, bassist Dave Carpenter, drummer Peter Erskine and percussionist Kurt Rasmussen) for a set of modern mainstream, jazz that is straightahead but not without some surprising twists and turns. "Jamaican Lounge Lizards," which Cunliffe describes as going "from having a Jamaican reggae feel to a barroom brawl," is a highlight of this enjoyable disc. —*Scott Yanow*

A Paul Simon Songbook / Jul. 1993-Aug. 1993 / Discovery ✦✦✦

Pianist Bill Cunliffe tries to expand jazz's repertoire on this CD by performing creative versions of a dozen Paul Simon songs. Although not much can be done with most of the more famous pieces (such as "Scarborough Fair," "Mrs. Robinson" and "Bridge over Troubled Waters"), some of the other numbers (such as "You Can Call Me Al," "Still Crazy After All These Years" and "Feelin' Groovy") are more flexible. Gerald Albright's sax helps out on two songs, guitarist Thom Rotella is an asset and Cunliffe comes up with some surprisingly fresh interpretations even on the warhorses. Although not every rendition is classic, at least this CD did not feature yet another Cole Porter program. —*Scott Yanow*

Bill in Brazil / Jul. 25, 1994-Nov. 18, 1994 / Discovery ✦✦✦✦

Pianist Bill Cunliffe performs Brailizan-flavored music throughout this CD, part of which was actually recorded in Brazil. Cunliffe's regular trio with bassist Dave Carpenter and drummer Joe La Barbera is also heard from along with a variety of guests. Although the accessible program puts an accent on the strong melodies, Cunliffe (occasionally sounding a little like Herbie Hancock and Chick Corea) digs in and comes up with some consistently rewarding improvisations. —*Scott Yanow*

Bob Curnow

Arranger, Leader / Post-Bop

Bob Curnow toured with Stan Kenton's Orchestra for a time in the mid-'60s, worked as general manager and producer for Kenton's Creative World label in the 1970s and has extensive experience as a jazz educator. In 1994 Curnow wrote arrangements of a dozen pieces by Pat Metheny and/or Lyle Mays for his 20-piece big band and the successful (and unusual) results were released on a MAMA Foundation CD. —*Scott Yanow*

● **Music of Pat Metheny & Lyle Mays** / 1994 / MAMA ✦✦✦✦✦

Arranger Bob Curnow transcribed a dozen compositions by Pat Metheny and/or Lyle Mays (originally recorded by the Pat Metheny Group) and adapted them for his Stan Kenton-influenced big band. The instrumentation differs drastically from Metheny's quartet and some of the pieces were originally very electric, but somehow these new renditions make the songs sound as if they were originally designed for this orchestra. The 20-piece big band is full of some of the cream of L.A.'s jazz scene and includes such soloists as trombonists Andy Martin and Rick Culver, saxophonists Bob Sheppard, Rob Lockart and Danny House, pianist Bill Cunliffe and a mighty trumpet section. This is an unusual concept that somehow works perfectly and with surprising logic. —*Scott Yanow*

Ted Curson

b. Jun. 3, 1935, Philadelphia, PA
Trumpet / Avant-Garde, Post-Bop, Hard Bop

An excellent and flexible trumpeter, Ted Curson will always be best known for his work with Charles Mingus' 1960 quartet (which also included Eric Dolphy and Dannie Richmond). He studied at Granoff Musical Conservatory, moved to New York in 1956 and played in New York with Mal Waldron, Red Garland and Philly Joe Jones, and recorded with Cecil Taylor (1961). After the 1959-60 Mingus association (which resulted in some classic recordings), Curson co-led a quintet with Bill Barron (1960-65), played with Max Roach and led his own groups. He spent time from the late '60s on in Europe (particularly Denmark) but has had a lower profile than one would expect since his return to the US in 1976. Ted Curson has led sessions for Old Town (1961), Prestige, Fontana, Atlantic, Arista, Inner City, Interplay, Chiaroscuro and several European labels but has been barely on records at all since 1980. —*Scott Yanow*

The Canadian Concert of Ted Curson / Sep. 15, 1962 / Can-Am ✦✦✦✦
Other than an obscure release for the tiny Old Town label, this radio broadcast (released on an LP but not yet on CD) was trumpeter Ted Curson's recording debut as a leader. Teamed up with local players (altoist Al Doctor, pianist Maury Kaye, bassist Charles Biddles and drummer Charles Duncan) for the advanced hard-bop date, Curson sounds in fine form on five of his originals; best-known is "Quicksand." —*Scott Yanow*

● **Fire Down Below** / Dec. 10, 1962 / Original Jazz Classics ✦✦✦✦✦
The main fault to this otherwise superior CD reissue is that there is only 31 minutes of music. Trumpeter Ted Curson, who by the early '60s had his own distinctive sound and an advanced yet accessible style, performs two standards ("Show Me" and "Falling in Love with Love") and four obscurities with pianist Gildo Mahones, bassist George Tucker, drummer Roy Haynes and (on four numbers) Montego Joe on conga. Curson, 27 at the time, is heard in top form on one of the very few of his sessions to be reissued on CD. —*Scott Yanow*

Flip Top / Aug. 1, 1964 / Freedom ✦✦✦✦
The first half of this release is from the same session that resulted in Ted Curson's *Tears for Dolphy*. The three selections (performed by the trumpeter in a pianoless quartet with tenor saxophonist Bill Barron, bassist Herb Bushler and drummer Dick Berk) are of the same high quality as the other cuts, highlighted by Curson's "Searchin' for the Blues." The second half of the program features Curson with the Zagreb Radio Orchestra at the 1966 Yugoslavian Jazz Festival. Zita Carno provided the arrangements to three of the trumpeter's originals (including "Quicksand" and "Flip Top") and Curson plays (in his own words) with "one foot in avant-garde, one foot in mainstream." A recommended and consistently stimulating release. —*Scott Yanow*

● **Tears for Dolphy** / Aug. 1, 1964 / Black Lion ✦✦✦✦✦
Although the term "avant-garde" is used several times in the liner notes, this quartet outing by trumpeter Ted Curson, tenor saxophonist Bill Barron, bassist Herb Bushler and drummer Dick Berk actually falls between hard bop and free bop. Curson and Barron in particular made for a potent team and their interplay on nine originals (five by Curson, four by Barron) is quite impressive, swinging and occasionally witty. This CD reissue brings back the entire *Tears for Dolphy* album plus three of the six songs from the *Flip Top* LP, all recorded the same day. Although the title cut does not live up to its potential, such tunes as "Kassim," "7/4 Funny Time," "Quicksand" and "Searchin' for the Blues" manage to be both explorative and surprisingly accessible. —*Scott Yanow*

Ted Curson and Co. / Jul. 1, 1976 / India Navigation ✦✦✦
The distinctive trumpeter Ted Curson is well showcased on this LP, a workout with a particularly strong quartet comprising pianist Jim McNeely, bassist Cecil McBee and drummer Steve McCall. Curson stretches out on four of his originals (including the 12-minute "Blue Piccolo") and "All the Things You Are." As usual his solos are both adventurous and (due to his appealing tone and roots in earlier styles of jazz) fairly accessible. Worth searching for. —*Scott Yanow*

Jubilant Power / Oct. 16, 1976+Oct. 17, 1976 / Inner City ✦✦✦✦
Slashing, dynamite exchanges, and an intense approach make this the Curson to grab. —*Ron Wynn*

Snake Johnson / 1979 / Chiaroscuro ✦✦✦
Trumpeter Ted Curson plays his own interpretations of advanced hard bop on this somewhat obscure LP. He utilizes a larger group than usual (an octet with baritonist Nick Brignola, tenor–saxophonist Bill Barron, altoist Charlie Williams, pianist Jim McNeely, bassist David Friesen, drummer Steve McCall and percussionist Lawrence Killian) to perform six of his quirky but often-swinging originals including "Snake Johnson," "Searching for the Blues" and "LSD, Take a Holiday." —*Scott Yanow*

Traveling On / Jun. 23, 1996 / Evidence ✦✦✦✦✦
Some people may never get past referring to Ted Curson as "the other soloist" in the great Charles Mingus bands with Eric Dolphy, but that hasn't deterred the trumpet player from pursuing his own, albeit less commercially and critically acclaimed, path. He just keeps *Traveling On*, the title of his twentieth album and his first release in 17 years. Even though Curson is *Traveling On*, he looks back long enough to pay tribute to several of the magnificent musicians with whom he's been partnered in the past with "Tears for Dolphy," "Reava's Waltz (More Mingus)" and the set-ending "Song of the Lonely One (Ode to Booker Ervin)" (another

Mingus-Curson connection). This set also includes well-executed covers of Herbie Hancock's venerated "Watermelon Man," the traditional "When the Saints Go Marching In" and "Flip Flop and Fly." Curson's playing is confident, taut and swinging throughout, and, on four of these nine selections, it benefits greatly from the addition of four percussionists to the traditional bass/drum/piano backing. *Traveling On* proves worth the 17-year wait. —*Chris Slawecki*

Andrew Cyrille

b. Nov. 10, 1939, New York, NY
Drums / Avant-Garde, Free Jazz, Post-Bop
Andrew Cyrille is perhaps the preeminent free-jazz percussionist of the 1980s and '90s. Few free-jazz drummers play with a tenth of Cyrille's grace and authority. His energy is unflagging, his power absolute, tempered only by an ever-present sense of propriety. Cyrille is at his best in an utterly free context, as on his encounters with the ambidextrous pianist Borah Bergman, where his serrated rhythms and variable textures are given maximum latitude. Cyrille began playing drums in a drum and bugle corps at the age of 11. At 15, he played in a trio with guitarist Eric Gale. For a period in his teens, Cyrille studied chemistry before enrolling in Juilliard School of Music in 1958. In the late '50s and early '60s, he worked with such mainstream jazzers as Mary Lou Williams, Roland Hanna, Roland Kirk, Coleman Hawkins, and Junior Mance. He recorded with Hawkins, as well as tenor saxophonist Bill Barron, for the Savoy label. Cyrille succeeded Sunny Murray as Cecil Taylor's drummer in 1964. He stayed with the pianist until 1975, during which time he played on many of Taylor's classic albums. During that period he played with a good many other top players, including Marion Brown, Grachan Moncur III and Jimmy Giuffre. He also served for a time as artist in residence at Antioch College and recorded a solo percussion album, 1969's *What About?*, on BYG. Cyrille, Rashied Ali, and Milford Graves collaborated on a series of mid-'70s concerts entitled "Dialogue of the Drums." Beginning in 1975 and lasting into the '80s, Cyrille led his own group, called Maono, which included the tenor saxophonist David S. Ware, trumpeter Ted Daniel, pianist Sonelius Smith, and at various times bassists Lisle Atkinson and Nick DiGeronimo. During this time Cyrille also played with the Group, a band that included the violinist Billy Bang, bassist Sirone, altoist Brown, and trumpeter Ahmed Abdullah. With Graves, Don Moye, and Kenny Clarke, Cyrille recorded the all-percussion album *Pieces of Time* for Soul Note in 1983. When not leading his own bands, he also worked ubiquitously as a sideman with, among others, John Carter, Muhal Richard Abrams, and Jimmy Lyons. Cyrille continued as a leading player into the late '90s, recording fairly prolifically for Black Saint/Soul Note, FMP, and DIW. —*Chris Kelsey*

Dialogue of the Drums / 1974 / Institute Percussive ✦✦✦

● **Metamusicians' Stomp** / Sep. 1978 / Black Saint ✦✦✦✦✦

Nuba / 1979 / Black Saint ✦✦✦✦
Drummer Andrew Cyrille and alto saxophonist Jimmy Lyons developed an impressive chemistry during their years with Cecil Taylor. Cyrille's array of percussion instruments and mastery of multiple styles, from hard bop to Afro-Latin, enabled him to play rippling rhythms or light, tinkling lines, attack or lay back. Lyons' alto solos were alternately driving and soft, sometimes searing in their intensity, sometimes more laidback and introspective. Those seeking a standard trio or straight jazz date are advised to look elsewhere; there was nothing conventional or predictable about this one. —*Ron Wynn*

Special People / Oct. 21, 1980+Oct. 22, 1980 / Soul Note ✦✦✦

Double Clutch / 1981 / Silkheart ✦
During a two-day period in 1981, drummer Andrew Cyrille played a pair of duo concerts, one with altoist Jimmy Lyons and the one contained on this CD, with the synthesizers of Richard Teitelbaum. A set of free-form improvisations that emphasize sound explorations, the latter collaboration comes across essentially as a long Cyrille drum solo joined by Teitelbaum's bizarre electronic sounds. Although some of the textures are colorful, much of the playing seems rather random, aimless and ultimately pointless. One can understand getting into this music live in concert, where one can see the musicians creating the sounds, but there is no real reason to put on this rather dull CD a second time. Pass. —*Scott Yanow*

Andrew Cyrille Meets Peter Brotzmann in Berlin / Mar. 19, 1982-Mar. 21, 1982 / FMP ✦✦✦✦
One sensed that this encounter could literally just be the tip of the iceberg in terms of what these two could get into. "Wolf Whistle" lasted all of side one. Essentially, Brotzmann began on tenor with some melodic material and in jumped Cyrille (drums), cooking and driving. Brotzmann, interestingly enough, played off melodic angles a great deal of the time, though still building to those almost patented multiphonic wails from time to time. There was a break in the dialogue about half way through as Cyrille took a tasteful solo. Upon Brotzmann's re-entry, a horn was sounded (most likely by Cyrille). This appeared to startle Brotzmann

for a moment, as he stopped, listened, matched the sound, and then the two were off and running again with occasional drops in intensity and volume. The cut suffered slightly from their constant parallel interaction and the almost monophonic energy level, but it was still fun. Side two featured a three-part piece entitled "Quilt." "A" began with Cyrille's ratchet and a brief, VERY quiet drum solo, which ended with a bit more volume on bicycle horn and shakers. Over this entered Brotzmann (on alto?) in the overtone register, creating variations around the bicycle horn. This was simple and convincing, perhaps the LP's highlight. "B" also started with a drum solo which quickly moved into a dialogue with Brotzmann on baritone. It was a succinct hard blower into "A Night in Tunisia." "C" closed the album with another understated and very musical drum solo. —*Milo Fine, Cadence*

The Navigator / Sep. 21, 1982+Sep. 22, 1982 / Soul Note ✦✦✦✦
Cyrille displayed his facility at sympathetically and smartly guiding other players throughout this date, interacting with bassist Nick Di Geronimo to design a framework that allowed trumpeter Ted Daniel maximum space and room for his piercing solos, and spurred pianist Sonelius Smith. When necessary, Cyrille soloed with a rigorous discipline and percussive vitality, but was more concerned with overall group dynamics and sound. Daniel was particularly impressive on longer cuts, where his lines, phrases and solos were crisp, expertly articulated and surging. The sound was bright and full, and this is an example of thoughtful, nicely played group improvisation. —*Ron Wynn*

Galaxies / Jun. 1990 / Music & Arts ✦✦✦

My Friend Louis / Nov. 18, 1991-Nov. 19, 1991 / DIW/Columbia ✦✦✦✦
Fiery, rampaging session with drummer Andrew Cyrille anchoring a stirring set featuring the dynamic tenor saxophonist David S. Ware. This is uncompromising, exciting material, far from sedate standards or derivative hard-bop recitations. —*Ron Wynn*

X Man / May 8, 1993-May 9, 1993 / Black Saint ✦✦✦

Good to Go: A Tribute To Bu / Oct. 17, 1995-Oct. 18, 1995 / Soul Note ✦✦✦✦
This is an intriguing set, featuring the combination of drummer Andrew Cyrille, flutist James Newton and bassist Lisle Atkinson, a different kind of power trio. The music ranges from fairly free flights to "Inch Worm" (arranged by Sheila Jordan) and two versions of "A Tribute to Bu" (for Art Blakey). Due to the variety of the material (mostly originals) and the consistent brilliance of Newton, this CD is recommended to fans of advanced jazz. —*Scott Yanow*

Les Czimber

Piano / Post-Bop
An excellent advanced pianist able to bring his own conception to straightahead jazz, Les Czimber considers it a miracle that he ever made it to the US. He discovered jazz in Communist Hungary by listening to the Voice of America broadcasts, and as a teenager he led a band in Budapest. Serving in the Hungarian Army during their 1956 revolution, his patrol was captured by the Russians. When a Russian officer discovered that he was a musician, they had a lengthy conversation about music, and the lives of the soldiers (unlike many others) were spared. After the revolution failed, Czimber escaped from Hungary by walking all night through the snow to Yugoslavia. A few months later, he moved to Milwaukee.

Czimber received some recognition when he set a world record by playing music for over 78 hours (with only a ten-minute break each 60 minutes) in a department store window, a record he later broke by topping 79. In Milwaukee, Czimber met the young singer Al Jarreau, and they worked together for several years, including five months in San Francisco. Czimber spent the latter half of the 1960s leading a show band, and then in 1971 moved to Southern California. Since then, he has generally played with a trio (using bassist John Patitucci for a long period) in the Orange County area, displaying a style influenced by, but not derivative of, Bill Evans. —*Scott Yanow*

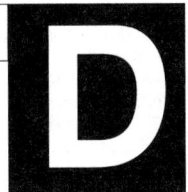

Paulinho Da Costa

b. May 31, 1948, Rio de Janeiro, Brazil
Percussion / World Fusion, Brazilian Jazz, Latin Jazz
The Brazilian-born Paulinho Da Costa, an endlessly adaptable percussionist with a knack for hitting precisely the right isolated beat at the right time, became one of the most in-demand sidemen in Los Angeles' busy recording studios in the late 1970s and early 1980s. He started playing his instruments at age seven, eventually accumulating over 200 drums, bells, whistles and other percussion instruments. Prior to leaving Brazil, he toured the world with various Brazilian ensembles and even danced with samba groups. Upon settling in the US in 1973, he joined Sergio Mendes and Brasil '77 for four years (1973-1977), and in his spare time, recorded with the likes of Dizzy Gillespie (including the notorious disco album *Dizzy's Party*), Milt Jackson, Joe Pass and Freddie Hubbard. Soon the recording studios beckoned full-time, and Da Costa was in demand for all kinds of recording gigs, playing on albums by Herbie Hancock, Ahmad Jamal, Nancy Wilson and Ella Fitzgerald, among many others. Da Costa has also recorded sporadically as a leader for the Pablo label. —*Richard S. Ginell*

Agora / Aug. 6, 1976-Aug. 16, 1976 / Original Jazz Classics ✦✦✦

● **Happy People** / 1979 / Original Jazz Classics ✦✦✦✦
Whomever the real Paulinho Da Costa is, there isn't any doubt that he was heavily plugged into the American R&B hitmaking mode when this, one of his few albums as a leader, was made. With a whole warehouse full of his L.A. studio colleagues on hand (Larry Carlton, Greg Phillinganes, Nathan Watts, et al.), Da Costa leads an extremely slick, flashy, energy-driven R&B session that could have been mistaken for an Earth, Wind and Fire album. Amidst the formulaic horn charts, period rhythm guitars, and commercial sound-alike soul lead vocalists, though, you can hear Da Costa give these tracks extra zip by weaving in some extremely funky congas, rattling a few exotic percussion instruments, and blowing his whistles. The best, most original-sounding track, oddly enough, is a tune with the Freudian-slip title "Put Your Mind On Vacation." The surprise is that this came out on Norman Granz's supposedly conservative Pablo label, but hey, Pablo had to pay its own way now and then in 1979, too—and in any case, this was conservative music in its own way, for it followed established trends. —*Richard S. Ginell*

Tudo Bem! / 1982 / Pablo ✦✦

Sunrise / 1984 / Pablo ✦✦

Breakdown / 1987 / A&M ✦✦
Exacting, demanding rhythms are obscured by generic arrangements and playing. —*Ron Wynn*

Albert Dailey

b. Jun. 16, 1939, Baltimore, MD, **d.** Jun. 26, 1984, Denver, CO
Piano / Post-Bop, Hard Bop
A sorely-neglected and underrated pianist during his lifetime, Albert Dailey's skill and verve as a soloist was greatly appreciated and eulogized following his death. An often hypnotic stylist, his shimmering harmonies and phrases were particularly admired by Stan Getz, with whom he worked in the mid-'70s. Daily began piano studies at an early age, then played in the Baltimore Royal Theater's house band in the early and mid-'50s. He attended Morgan State and Peabody Conservatory in the late '50s. Dailey toured with vocalist Damita Jo from 1960 to 1963, then led a trio at the Bohemia Caverns in Washington, DC before moving to New York in 1964. Dailey played with Dexter Gordon, Roy Haynes, Sarah Vaughan and Charles Mingus, while recording with Freddie Hubbard. He performed and recorded with Woody Herman at the 1967 Monterey Jazz Festival, and was in Art Blakey's Jazz Messengers during the late '60s and again in the mid-'70s. Dailey played periodically with Sonny Rollins, toured and recorded with Stan Getz, and also cut sessions with Elvin Jones and Archie Shepp in the '70s. He performed at Carnegie Hall and in the Mobil Summerpier Concerts series in the '80s, while also playing in The Upper Manhattan Jazz Society with Charlie Rouse, Benny Bailey and Buster Williams. He recorded for Columbia, Steeple Chase, Muse and Elektra, with his '72 debut, *The Day After The Dawn*, getting widespread critical praises

but not enough sales to keep Columbia from dropping him after that one date. He has only one session currently available on CD. —*Ron Wynn*

That Old Feeling / Jul. 13, 1978 / Steeple Chase ✦✦✦

Textures / Jun. 4, 1981 / Muse ✦✦✦✦
This 1981 session has Dailey working with a pianoless trio keyed by saxophonist Arthur Rhames, plus bassist Rufus Reid and drummer Eddie Gladden. Dailey was a particular favorite of Stan Getz, and was especially strong doing uptempo material. —*Ron Wynn*

● **Poetry** / 1983 / Elektra ✦✦✦✦✦

Meredith D'Ambrosio

b. 1941, Boston, MA
Piano, Vocals / Cool
A soft-toned singer whose intelligent interpretation of lyrics is always thoughtful, Meredith D'Ambrosio is also an effective accompanist as a pianist. Her father sang with big bands, while her mother played piano in nightclubs. At age six, D'Ambrosio began to study piano and sing. After graduating from high school and attending the Boston Museum School (1958-59), she was a professional musician in addition to being a painter. In 1966, she was invited by John Coltrane to be part of his Japanese tour, but, feeling she was not ready, D'Ambrosio turned him down. More than a decade later, her confidence was higher and she began to record, often with her husband, pianist Eddie Higgins. An introverted but accessible performer for those who listen closely, Meredith D'Ambrosio has recorded rewarding sets for Spring Inc. (1978), Shiah (1981), Palo Alto (an 1982 album later reissued on CD by Sunnyside) and quite a few dates for Sunnyside (starting in 1985). —*Scott Yanow*

Lost in His Arms / Jul. 1978-Oct. 1978 / Spring ✦✦✦✦✦

Another Time / Feb. 6, 1981 / Sunnyside ✦✦✦

Little Jazz Bird / Mar. 2, 1982 / Palo Alto ✦✦✦
Fine '82 combo session in which D'Ambrosio shows her ability to handle a variety of songs supplied by composers as diverse as harpist Deborah Henson-Conant and vocalist David Frishberg. Phil Woods heads a capable backing band and supplies his customary heated alto sax solos, while Hank Jones lends some flair on piano. —*Ron Wynn*

It's Your Dance / Mar. 27, 1985+Mar. 28, 1985 / Sunnyside ✦✦✦✦
A first-rate trio date, possibly D'Ambrosio's finest in that format. Her singing has punch, variety, and dimension, and her phrasing is creative and expertly constructed. Kevin Eubanks' guitar contributions are concise, thoughtful, and without any gimmicks or wasted riffs. D'Ambrosio and Harold Danko interact smoothly, and his piano backing is delicate and supportive. —*Ron Wynn*

The Cove / Oct. 27, 1987-Oct. 28, 1987 / Sunnyside ✦✦✦✦

South to a Warmer Place / Feb. 1989 / Sunnyside ✦✦✦
Eddie Higgins Trio joined by trumpeter Lou Columbo. Two lyrics by singer. Sweetness and light. —*Michael G. Nastos*

● **Love Is Not a Game** / Dec. 19, 1990-Dec. 20, 1990 / Sunnyside ✦✦✦✦✦
With husband Eddie Higgins Trio. Dreamy, soft-voiced D'Ambrosio makes a definitive emotional statement. Fifteen tracks, nine standards (three adapted or modified by D'Ambrosio). Five written by her. Nice twisting on "I Love You/You I Love," "Oh, Look at Me Now/But Now Look at Me," and "Lament/This Lament." —*Michael G. Nastos*

Sleep Warm / Feb. 23, 1991 / Sunnyside ✦✦✦

Silent Passion / Jan. 15, 1996-Jan. 16, 1996 / Sunnyside ✦✦✦✦

Tadd Dameron

b. Feb. 21, 1917, Cleveland, OH, **d.** Mar. 8, 1965, New York, NY
Piano, Arranger, Composer / Bop
The definitive arranger/composer of the bop era, Tadd Dameron wrote such standards as "Good Bait," "Our Delight," "Hot House," "Lady Bird," and "If You Could

See Me Now." Not only did he write melody lines but full arrangements, and he was an influential force from the mid-'40s on even though he never financially prospered. Dameron started out in the swing era touring with the Zack Whyte and Blanche Calloway bands, he wrote for Vido Musso in New York, and most importantly contributed arrangements for Harlan Leonard's Kansas City Orchestra, some of which were recorded. Soon Dameron was writing charts for such bands as Jimmie Lunceford, Count Basie, Billy Eckstine and Dizzy Gillespie (1945-47), in addition to Sarah Vaughan. Dameron was always very modest about his own piano playing but he did gig with Babs Gonzales' Three Bips and a Bop in 1947, and led a sextet featuring Fats Navarro (and later Miles Davis) at the Royal Roost during 1948-49. Dameron co-led a group with Davis at the 1949 Paris Jazz Festival, stayed in Europe for a few months (writing for Ted Heath) and then returned to New York. He wrote for Artie Shaw's last orchestra that year, played and arranged R&B for Bull Moose Jackson (1951-52), and in 1953 led a nonet featuring Clifford Brown and Philly Joe Jones. However, drug problems started to get in the way of his music. After recording a couple of albums (including 1958's *Mating Call* with John Coltrane), he spent much of 1959-61 in jail. After he was released, Dameron wrote for Sonny Stitt, Blue Mitchell, Milt Jackson and Benny Goodman, but was less active in the years before his death from cancer. Tadd Dameron's classic Blue Note recordings of 1947-48, his 1949 Capitol sides and Prestige/Riverside sets of 1953, 1956, 1958 and 1962 are all currently in print on CD. *—Scott Yanow*

Anthropology / 1949 / Spotlite ✦✦✦✦

Fontainebleau / Mar. 9, 1956 / Original Jazz Classics ✦✦✦✦
Pianist-composer-arranger Tadd Dameron led relatively few sessions in his career, making the half-hour of music on this CD reissue quite valuable. Dameron performs five of his originals (best-known are the complex "Fontainebleau" and "The Scene Is Clean") with an octet comprising trumpeter Kenny Dorham, trombonist Henry Coker, altoist Sahib Shihab, tenor saxophonist Joe Alexander, baritonist Cecil Payne, bassist John Simmons, drummer Shadow Wilson and the leader's sparse piano. As is usual with most Dameron dates, the emphasis is on his inventive arrangements although there is space (most notably on the 11-minute blues "Bula-Beige") for individual solos. Recommended. *—Scott Yanow*

Mating Call / Nov. 30, 1956 / Original Jazz Classics ✦✦✦✦✦
Sometimes issued under John Coltrane's name, this excellent quartet session features pianist Tadd Dameron (who contributed all six compositions) with the great tenor, bassist John Simmons and drummer Philly Joe Jones. Dameron (who was a fairly basic pianist) has a rare opportunity to stretch out, and his originals (best-known are "Soultrane" and "On a Misty Night") clearly inspire Coltrane. Available on CD, this set is a gem. *—Scott Yanow*

● The Magic Touch of Tadd Dameron / Feb. 27, 1962 / Original Jazz Classics ✦✦✦✦✦
Tadd Dameron's final session as a leader (he died in 1965) is a definitive set that sums up much of his career. Some of Dameron's best-known originals are here (including "On a Misty Night," "Fontainebleau," "If You Could See Me Now" and "Our Delight"), and this CD reissue has three previously unreleased alternate takes. For once, Dameron had a large group of all-stars at his exposure (up to 14 pieces) and could concentrate on providing the arrangements, while Bill Evans took care of the piano playing. Among the sidemen are tenor saxophonist Johnny Griffin, trumpeters Charlie Shavers, Joe Wilder and Clark Terry, trombonist Jimmy Cleveland, Julius Watkins on French horn and drummer Philly Joe Jones; Barbara Winfield takes two fine vocals. Highly recommended to all bop collectors. *—Scott Yanow*

Dameronia

f. 1982, **db.** 1985
Group / Bop
In the early '80s, drummer Philly Joe Jones, with the strong assistance of trumpeter Donald Sickler (who transcribed the arrangements), revived the music of Tadd Dameron in a nonet called Dameronia. Two Uptown records resulted (with such sidemen as Walter Davis, Jr., Britt Woodman, Frank Wess and Cecil Payne) before Jones' 1985 death. In 1989 Sickler gathered together the alumni (with Kenny Washington on drums) for a special Paris concert that was documented on Soul Note. *—Scott Yanow*

● To Tadd with Love / Jun. 28, 1982 / Uptown ✦✦✦✦✦
Drummer Philly Joe Jones during his last years led the group Dameronia, a band dedicated to performing the music of the great composer Tadd Dameron. Their debut disc for Uptown features Donald Sickler's transcriptions of six Dameron originals (including "Philly J.J.," "Soultrane" and "On a Misty Night"). The nonet comprises many fine veteran players: trumpeters Sickler and Johnny Coles, trombonist Britt Woodman, altoist Frank Wess, Charles Davis on tenor, baritonist Cecil Payne, pianist Walter Davis, Jr., bassist Larry Ridley and Jones himself. This loving tribute

(which perfectly balances the arrangements with concise solo space) is highly recommended. *—Scott Yanow*

● Look Stop and Listen / Jul. 11, 1983 / Uptown ✦✦✦✦✦
Tadd Dameron was arguably the top composer/arranger of the early bebop years. Drummer Philly Joe Jones put together the group Dameronia specifically to perform Dameron's music, and this was their second and final album before Jones' death. The lineup of this band was very impressive (trumpeters Don Sickler and Virgil Jones, trombonist Benny Powell, altoist Frank Wess, Charles Davis on tenor, baritonist Cecil Payne, pianist Walter Davis Jr., bassist Larry Ridley and Jones on drums) and, when one adds in guest soloist Johnny Griffin on tenor and Sickler's accurate transcriptions of the seven Dameron compositions (plus Benny Golson's "Killer Joe"), the result is an album that is significant both historically and musically. In other words, get this one. *—Scott Yanow*

Live at the Theatre Boulogne / May 30, 1989 / Soul Note ✦✦✦✦
Dameronia, a group organized by drummer Philly Joe Jones to perform the great bop-era arrangements of Tadd Dameron, came back together four years after Jones' death for a concert in France. Fortunately, it was recorded and released on this Soul Note CD, for since that time, tenor saxophonist Clifford Jordan and pianist Walter Davis, Jr., have also passed away. In addition to those two masters, the 1989 version of Dameronia included trumpeters Don Sickler (whose transcriptions made this group possible) and Virgil Jones, trombonist Benny Powell, Frank Wess on alto and flute, baritonist Cecil Payne, bassist Larry Ridley and drummer Kenny Washington. The ensembles are very much in Dameron's classic style, but all of the musicians also have plenty of solo space. Tadd Dameron's legacy was very well served by Dameronia, and this set is a fine tribute. *—Scott Yanow*

Eddie Daniels

b. Oct. 19, 1941, New York, NY
Clarinet, Tenor Saxophone / Hard Bop, Post-Bop
One of the truly great jazz clarinetists (ranking at the top with Benny Goodman, Artie Shaw and Buddy DeFranco), Daniels makes the impossible look effortless. On his first GRP release *Breakthrough* in 1984, Daniels switched back and forth on a second's notice between jazz and classical and he has since explored Charlie Parker, Roger Kellaway tunes, crossover and even swing with consistent brilliance. He is also a dazzling tenor player. Daniels appeared at the 1957 Newport Jazz Festival in Marshall Brown's Youth band (playing alto) an,d after graduating from Juilliard in 1966, he played tenor with the Thad Jones/Mel Lewis Orchestra for six years. Daniels recorded *First Prize* as a leader (1966) and made albums with Freddie Hubbard (1969), Richard Davis, Don Patterson, and duets with Bucky Pizzarelli (1973). Although he recorded as a leader for Muse and Columbia during 1977-78, Eddie Daniels did not make it big until he started specializing on clarinet and recording regularly for GRP in 1984. In 1992 he started doubling on tenor again since his reputation on clarinet was secure. *—Scott Yanow*

First Prize / Sep. 8, 1966+Sep. 12, 1966 / Original Jazz Classics ✦✦✦✦✦
When one hears this early Eddie Daniels CD (a straight reissue of the original LP), it is surprising to realize that he would remain in relative obscurity for almost another 20 years. As shown on three of the eight selections on which he plays clarinet, Daniels (even at this early stage) ranked near the top while his tenor playing on the remaining numbers was already personal and virtuosic. With the assistance of the Thad Jones/Mel Lewis rhythm section of the time (pianist Roland Hanna, bassist Richard Davis and drummer Mel Lewis), Daniels is in top form on three standards, four originals and the pop tune "Spanish Flea." *—Scott Yanow*

Flower for All Seasons / Feb. 1973 / Choice ✦✦✦
For this intimate jazz set, Eddie Daniels not only plays clarinet on three pieces and bass clarinet on one but flute on seven others, all on duets with guitarist Bucky Pizzarelli. Daniels, who has long since given up the flute, proves to be effective on that instrument but it his clarinet workouts (particularly on "As Long as I Live" and a ridiculously fast "Shine") that are most memorable. Pizzarelli, who takes a brief "Two for the Road" as a solo piece, sounds quite comfortable on the diverse material which ranges from swing standards and a bit of classical music to selections by Roland Hanna, Pat Williams and Les McCann. Worth searching for. *—Scott Yanow*

Brief Encounter / Jul. 11, 1977 / Muse ✦✦✦✦
Eddie Daniels splits his time almost equally on this underrated LP between tenor, flute and clarinet. Joined by keyboardist Andy LaVerne, bassist Rick Laird and drummer Billy Mintz, Daniels is in consistently creative form on the six selections with highlights that include his clarinet on the uptempo "There Is No Greater Love" and his work on four overdubbed flutes (one of which is a bass flute) for a haunting rendition of "A Child Is Born." It seems strange that it would still be another eight years before Eddie Daniels gained recognition as a masterful improviser and technician because in 1977 he was already pretty much there. Recommended. *—Scott Yanow*

Morning Thunder / 1978 / Columbia ✦✦✦
This is an odd and interesting record. Eddie Daniels, who at the time was largely unknown, plays clarinet and occasional alto in commercial settings while backed by a large rhythm section, reeds, strings and even some voices; typical for an over-produced Columbia album of the period. The material is largely forgettabl, but Daniels' clarinet playing is so brilliant that he completely overcomes the surroundings and drastically uplifts the music. Although not on the level of his upcoming GRP projects, this out-of-print LP is surprisingly rewarding. —*Scott Yanow*

★ **Breakthrough** / 1986 / GRP ✦✦✦✦✦
This classic recording is a breakthrough in several ways. One of the most successful of all "Third Stream" efforts, the arrangements by Jorge Calandrelli, Torrie Zito and Nan Schwartz for the London Philharmonia Orchestra are a superior blend of aspects of jazz and classical music. This album (reissued on CD) was also a major breakthrough for clarinetist Eddie Daniels, who finally became a major name. Daniels proved that (with the possible exception of Buddy DeFranco) he was on a higher level than any other clarinetist of the post-swing era. He effortlessly switches back and forth between rapid classical music passages and inventive jazz on "Solfeggietto/ Metamorphosis" and easily holds one's interest throuout Calandrelli's 22-minute three-part "Concerto for Jazz Clarinet and Orchestra." To call Eddie Daniels' playing "brilliant" on this release would be an understatement. Essential music. —*Scott Yanow*

Eddie Daniels Collection / 1986-1993 / GRP ✦✦✦
This 10-track collection presents the songs and styles that have elevated Daniels from the ranks of steady, untouted musician to top-selling, acclaimed star. He's done light classical, pop/fusion, retro jazz and quasi-new age material during his GRP tenure, and there are samples of each on the disc. Daniels is backed by acoustic trios and quartets, symphony orchestras, and even drum machines and DX7 synthesizers. While Daniels displays great facility and versatility, his solos have minimal intensity and excitement, even on longer pieces. As a result, the listener is never hooked by these songs, and they become impressive examples of technical acumen rather than tunes you'll remember. —*Ron Wynn*

To Bird with Love / 1987 / GRP ✦✦✦✦✦
Following his remarkable classical/jazz recording *Breakthrough*, clarinetist Eddie Daniels performed a set of Charlie Parker tunes with pianist Fred Hersch, bassist John Patitucci and drummer Al Foster; "This Is the Time" (an abstract rendition of "Now's the Time") has pianist Roger Kellaway sitting in. Daniels' playing is often remarkable throughout the program, and the highlights include "East of the Sun" (which finds Hersch using a synthesizer to simulate strings), "Just Friends," "Passport" and a Bird medley of three of his blues lines. Recommended. —*Scott Yanow*

Memos from Paradise / Dec. 16, 1987-Jan. 4, 1988 / GRP ✦✦✦
Clarinetist Eddie Daniels mostly plays the music of keyboardist Roger Kellaway on this colorful set, including the four-part "Memos from Paradise." Kellaway, who also arranged all of the music (including Daniels' "Dreaming"), utilized a string quartet, a fine rhythm section (with bassist Eddie Gomez and either Terry Clarke or Al Foster on drums), plus (on "Eight Pointed Star") marimba and harp. Daniels' clarinet is the main voice throughout (with some spots for Kellaway's piano) and shows off both his virtuosity and his improvising talents. Stimulating music. —*Scott Yanow*

Blackwood / 1989 / GRP ✦✦✦
Eddie Daniels is such a monster on the clarinet that all of his GRP recordings are worth acquiring. This one, however, due to the somewhat commercial nature of some of the tunes (and the lightly funky rhythm sections), is of lesser interest compared to the classics such as *Breakthrough*. Daniels sounds fine but he is far better than much of the material (generally written by either the clarinetist, Rob Mounsey or Dave Grusin). —*Scott Yanow*

Nepenthe / Dec. 6, 1989-Dec. 9, 1989 / GRP ✦✦✦

This Is Now / 1991 / GRP ✦✦✦✦
Most of clarinetist Eddie Daniels' projects for GRP had a central theme. This CD was an exception in that the material is quite wide-ranging, from Duke Ellington ("In a Sentimental Mood" and "Body and Soul") to Thad Jones and Bill Evans songs. Pianist Billy Childs, who contributed three originals (Daniels brought in four), is a key player in the music, clearly inspiring the clarinetist to come up with consistently challenging statements. With either Tony Dumas or Jimmy Johnson on bass, and Ralph Penland or Vinnie Colaiuta on drums, these quartet performances feature Eddie Daniels and Billy Childs at their best. —*Scott Yanow*

Benny Rides Again / Jan. 14, 1992-Jan. 15, 1992 / GRP ✦✦✦
During 1991-92, clarinetist Eddie Daniels and vibraphonist Gary Burton teamed up on a tour, performing a tribute to Benny Goodman and Lionel Hampton. Never mind that they sound nothing at all like their predecessors. On the CD that resulted from the collaboration, the duo use pianist Mulgrew Miller (who sounds much more like McCoy Tyner than Teddy Wilson), bassist Marc Johnson and drummer Peter Erskine for 11 songs associated with the King of Swing plus Bix Beider-

becke's "In a Mist." Actually, the most memorable selection is "Knockin' on Wood," which has nothing to do with Goodman or Hampton (it was a feature for Red Norvo) and features Burton romping on a xylophone. Other highlights include a surprisingly brief "Sing, Sing, Sing," "Airmail Special," "Slipped Disc" and "Avalon." —*Scott Yanow*

Under the Influence / 1993 / GRP ✦✦✦✦✦
After a decade of exclusively playing clarinet (and establishing himself as one of the greats), Eddie Daniels began doubling on tenor again on this recording. Switching between his two axes, Daniels sounds in top form on some diverse but consistently rewarding originals and a few standards ("I Hear a Rhapsody," "Weaver of Dreams," "I Fall in Love Too Easily" and an exciting version of Bill Evans' "Five"). Joined by pianist Alan Pasqua, bassist Mike Formanek and drummer Peter Erskine, Eddie Daniels really digs into these tunes, and both his virtuosity and his inventive improvisations are quite impressive. —*Scott Yanow*

Real Time / Mar. 26, 1994-Mar. 27, 1994 / Chesky ✦✦✦✦

Five Seasons / Aug. 1995 / Shanachie ✦✦✦

Beautiful Love / Oct. 24, 1996-Oct. 28, 1996 / Shanachie ✦✦
This outing from Eddie Daniels is a definite disappointment. A remarkable clarinetist who ranks at the top of his field, Daniels sounds quite restrained throughout the easy-listening set, just throwing in a few complex runs on "Beautiful Love" as if to remind listeners who he is. With a tasteful but rather anonymous-sounding rhythm section (including guitarist Chuck Loeb and pianist Bob James), Daniels mostly sticks to melodic interpretations during a theme apiece by Bach, Erik Satie and Rachmaninoff, four of his own originals, two by Loeb and the title cut. The music, subtitled "Intimate Jazz Portraits," is supposed to be quiet, but that is no excuse for it being uniformly dull. The clarinetist is obviously capable of much more significant work. —*Scott Yanow*

Palle Danielsson

b. Oct. 15, 1946, Stockholm, Sweden
Bass / Post-Bop
Palle Danielsson is best-known for his work as a sidemen with a variety of top leaders. He studied violin for five years starting when he was eight. Danielsson then switched to bass and was playing professionally when he was 15. After studying at the Stockholm Royal Academy of Music (1962-66), he began to play with some of the top Scandinavian musicians including Jan Garbarek and Bobo Stenson. When American jazzmen passed through his country, they often asked for Danielsson; he worked with Bill Evans, George Russell, Ben Webster and Charlie Shavers. He gained fame for being part of Keith Jarrett's European quartet (1974-79), a group that also included Jan Garbarek. Danielsson has also toured and recorded with Charles Lloyd (early '80s), Michel Petrucciani and Kenny Wheeler. —*Scott Yanow*

Contra Post / Dec. 12, 1995 / Caprice ✦✦✦

Harold Danko

b. Jun. 13, 1947, Ohio
Piano / Hard Bop, Post-Bop
An underrated but consistently creative modern jazz pianist, Harold Danko has been an asset to many sessions through the years. He graduated from Youngstown State University and played in big bands led by Chet Baker, Woody Herman and Thad Jones/Mel Lewis, plus the combos of Gerry Mulligan and Lee Konitz and with his own groups. Danko, who has been on the faculty of the Manhattan School of Music and the New School, often teamed up with tenor saxophonist Rich Perry in the 1990s. He has recorded as a leader for Inner City, Dreamstreet, Sunnyside and Steeple Chase. —*Scott Yanow*

Harold Danko Quartet (Featuring Gregory Herbert) / Apr. 5, 1975 / Inner City ✦✦✦✦
Pianist Harold Danko's debut as a leader was made for the soon-defunct Inner City label. The most significant aspect of this excellent modern mainstream date (which has four Danko originals, plus "You Made Me Love You" and "Sweet Georgia Brown") is that it is one of the few examples of the late tenor saxophonist Gregory Herbert really stretching out. Herbert, who also plays some alto, soprano and piccolo, passed away less than three years later and is the main star of these performances. Also on the date are bassist Dave Shapiro, drummer Jimmy Madison and, on one song, flutist Lawrence Feldman. Worth searching for, this now-obscure LP will hopefully be reissued on CD someday. —*Scott Yanow*

Chasin' the Bad Guys / 1979 / Inner City ✦✦✦

Coincidence / Apr. 1979 / Dreamstreet ✦✦✦✦
For his second set as a leader, pianist Harold Danko is heard at the head of an impressive group of young all-stars comprising tenor saxophonist Frank Tiberi

(doubling quite effectively on his atmospheric bassoon), trumpeter Tom Harrell, bassist Rufus Reid and drummer Joe La Barbera. The repertoire is wide-ranging, including a selection apiece by Danko and Tiberi, Hugh Masekela's "Coincidence," Horace Silver's "Cape Verdean Blues" (a feature for the trio), and four standards. High-quality and advanced hard bop, but this album will be difficult to find. —*Scott Yanow*

● **Mirth Song** / Apr. 6, 1982+Apr. 8, 1982 / Sunnyside ✦✦✦✦✦
The debut release by Sunnyside resulted in one of pianist Harold Danko's finest recordings to date. The set of duets with bassist Rufus Reid allows Danko to stretch out and display his advanced hard bop style. Highlights include "In Walked Bud," Jackie McLean's "Omega," "Red Cross" and Danko's title cut. Recommended. —*Scott Yanow*

Ink and Water / Sep. 20, 1983 / Sunnyside ✦✦✦✦
For this date, pianist Harold Danko performed 16 spontaneously composed originals. Although the sketches were later given titles such as "Sunrise Watch," "Icicles in the Cave," "Snow Blossoms" and "Leaves in the Rock Garden," the music is far from new age. Even at its most impressionistic, Danko's solos have blues feeling, some guts and plenty of sincerity. An intriguing if obscure set. —*Scott Yanow*

Alone But Not Forgotten / Nov. 26, 1985-May 12, 1986 / Sunnyside ✦✦✦

The First Love Song / Mar. 1988 / Jazz City ✦✦✦

Next Age / Oct. 1993 / Steeple Chase ✦✦✦

After the Rain / 1994 / Steeple Chase ✦✦✦✦✦

New Autumn / Apr. 1995 / Steeple Chase ✦✦✦✦✦
By 1995, pianist Harold Danko had led the same quartet for several years and his musicians had really mastered and grown into Danko's complex originals. Danko and tenor saxophonist Rich Perry (both of whom had developed fairly original voices) often sound as if they are thinking alike during this CD. Their mutual intuitiveness is a vital element in interpreting the tricky and constantly surprising music; bassist Scott Colley and drummerer Jeff Hirshfield are quite alert in support. The dividing line between composition and improvisation on some of the less conventional songs is sometimes difficult to find and there are many occasions where the lead voices (and sometimes all four musicians) are soloing together or at least freely commenting on each other's flights. Some performances swing while others float. *New Autumn* is a subtle yet explorative recording that will grow on most listeners over time. —*Scott Yanow*

Feeling of Jazz / Mar. 1996 / Steeple Chase ✦✦✦✦✦
This is an unusual CD. Pianist Harold Danko, tenor saxophonist Rich Perry, bassist Scott Colley and drummer Jeff Hirshfield perform the same seven songs (in the same order) as Duke Ellington and John Coltrane did during the famous recorded meeting in 1962. These renditions are lengthier than the originals, and there is no attempt to imitate Duke and 'Trane, although their interpretations are purposely hinted at in places. In addition to "In a Sentimental Mood" and "Take the Coltrane," there are revivals of several songs that deserve to become standards: "Big Nick," "Stevie" and the catchy "Angelica." A very enjoyable outing. —*Scott Yanow*

Tidal Breeze / 1997 / Steeple Chase ✦✦✦

James Dapogny

b. Sep. 3, 1940, Berwyn, IL
Piano, Leader / Swing, Classic Jazz
An excellent stride and swing pianist and an important musicologist, James Dapogny's recordings (particularly his recent ones for Discovery) have helped to keep classic jazz alive. An educator who has taught jazz theory and history at the University of Michigan since 1966, Dapogny has written a complete book of transcriptions of the work of Jelly Roll Morton. As a pianist/bandleader, he has generally been based in Chicago, giving veteran blues singer Sippie Wallace exciting support in her 1982 Atlantic release and recording an excellent series of CDs with his combo for Discovery; the two recent sets focus on the music of Morton and small-group swing, respectively. —*Scott Yanow*

The Piano Music of J.R. Morton / 1976 / Smithsonian ✦✦✦
Pianist James Dapogny, in his recording debut as a leader, does a good job of interpreting a dozen of Jelly Roll Morton's compositions. Dapogny's improvisations are fairly subtle, mostly sticking close to Morton's written-out music and giving listeners a good introduction to the jazz pioneer's style. This deluxe LP also has extensive and definitive liner notes. —*Scott Yanow*

Chicago Jazz Band / Jun. 17, 1982 / Jazzology ✦✦✦✦
The debut recording by pianist James Dapogny's (other than a set backing blues singer Sippie Wallace) features plenty of hot playing by the octet. From classic jazz and Dixieland to more arranged renditions of vintage tunes, Dapogny and his group (which includes cornetist Paul Klinger, the reeds of Peter Ferran and Russ Whitman and the excellent drummer Hal Smith) revitalize 1920s jazz throughout

their performance, displaying both high musicianship and creative ideas within the idiom. Highlights include "At the Jazz Band Ball," "Oh Peter, You're So Nice," "Copenhangen," "I Never Knew What a Gal Could Do" and a Fats Waller composition that Waller never recorded ("Caught"). Recommended. —*Scott Yanow*

Back Home in Illinois / Jun. 17, 1982 / Jazzology ✦✦✦✦
During the 1980s and '90s, pianist James Dapogny has led one of the top trad bands around. For his second Jazzology album with his octet (which features cornetist Paul Klinger, trombonist Bob Smith, Kim Cusack on clarinet, and alto and tenor saxophonist Russ Whitman on reeds, in addition to the talented leader), Dapogny performs warhorses (such as "Chicago" and "Charleston"), 1920s and '30s obscurities ("'Tain't No Sin," "Junk Man" and "Back Home in Illinois," his own "For No Reason at All in E-Flat" and even the theme from *The Muppet Show*. Highly recommended to fans of hot pre-swing jazz. —*Scott Yanow*

How Could We Be Blue? / Feb. 20, 1988-Feb. 21, 1988 / Stomp Off ✦✦✦✦
James Dapogny and Butch Thompson, two of the top classic jazz pianists, play a very appealing set of duets on this Stomp Off LP. Eight of the performances (including a three-song Fats Waller medley) are piano duets; Thompson switches to clarinet for two songs; and the pianists take a solo feature apiece. Although piano duets can be overcrowded, Dapogny and Thompson leave plenty of room for each other. Since they are both experts in Jelly Roll Morton's music, he is represented along with Duke Ellington, Waller, W.C. Handy and Sidney Bechet, among others. Highlights of the enjoyable and sometimes stomping collaboration include "How Could I Be Blue," "Panama," "Honeysuckle Rose" and the ad-lib "Today's Blues." —*Scott Yanow*

The Way We Feel Today / Aug. 11, 1988-Oct. 20, 1991 / Stomp Off ✦✦✦✦
The talented pianist James Dapogny teams up with clarinetist Kim Cusack and drummer Wayne Jones from his regular band to perform a set of 1920s style trios on this Stomp Off CD. Their role models were the various Jelly Roll Morton trios, although there are also some pop tunes of the era included along with their original "Odostomp." Among the more enjoyable numbers are "Lucky Day," "Turtle Twist," "Shreveport Stomp," "Baby," "Little Girl" and "Mandy, Make Up Your Mind." —*Scott Yanow*

● **Laughing at Life** / 1992 / Discovery ✦✦✦✦✦
The first of three Discovery CDs by James Dapogny's Chicago Jazz Band features the eight-piece group (which includes the pianist-leader, trumpeter Jon-Erik Kellso, trombonist Bob Smith, Kim Cusack on clarinet and alto, and Russ Whitman doubling on tenor and baritone) playing a variety of Dixieland and classic jazz selections. There are plenty of hot soloists in this group and such numbers as "That Da-Da Strain," "Lulu's Back in Town," "Swing Mr. Charlie," "California, Here I Come" and "Grandpa's Spells" receive frequently exciting treatment. This CD serves as a strong example to James Dapogny's music. —*Scott Yanow*

Original Jelly Roll Blues [Music of Jelly Roll Morton] / Jul. 9, 1993-Jul. 12, 1993 / Discovery ✦✦✦✦✦
Pianist James Dapogny and his octet (plus a few guests) pay tribute to the immortal pianist/composer/arranger Jelly Roll Morton on this enjoyable set. They perform 17 of Morton's compositions, often with a twist. Six of the songs were never recorded by Jelly Roll's groups (such as "Frog-I-More Rag," "Milenberg Joys" and "King Porter Stomp"), and most of those that were are given fresh arrangements in the style of Morton's Red Hot Peppers. Dapogny's regular octet (with trumpeter Jon-Erik Kellso and the reeds of Kim Cusack and Russ Whitman) is joined on some numbers by Peter Ferran's reeds, cornetist Paul Klinger and Mike Walbridge's tuba. This is classic music that, due to the new arrangements, sounds intriguingly unpredictable. —*Scott Yanow*

Hot Club Stomp: Small Band Swing / Jun. 17, 1994-Jun. 19, 1994 / Discovery ✦✦✦✦✦
Stride pianist James Dapogny, who had previously recorded a tribute to Jelly Roll Morton, moves his band's style up ten years for this exciting tribute to the small groups of the swing era. Most of the 14 selections are obscure but enjoyable, and the arranged ensembles allow plenty of room for hot solos. The four-horn octet is full of talent with trumpeter Jon-Erik Kellso a standout. Classic pre-bop music is played by some of the best. —*Scott Yanow*

On the Road / Dec. 1, 1995 / Schoolkids ✦✦✦
Pianist James Dapogny's Chicago Jazz Band celebrated its 20th anniversary with this release. With a few exceptions (such as "Beale Street Blues," "Flying Home" and "The Washington Post March"), the emphasis is on lesser-known material from the 1920s and '30s. The octet (which also features clarinetist Kim Cusack, Russ Whitman on reeds, cornetist Jon-Erik Kellso and trombonist Christopher Smith) sounds fine on such forgotten numbers as Fats Waller's "Sittin' Up Waitin' for You," "It Was a Sad Night In Harlem," "Moody Hollywood" and "Hobo's Prayer," but there are less inspiring and memorable moments than in Dapogny's previous Discovery

CDs. Worth picking up by trad and mainstream jazz fans, even if the music falls short of essential. —*Scott Yanow*

David Darling

b. Mar. 4, 1941, Elkhart, IN
Cello / Post-Bop, Classical, Avant-Garde

A classically trained cellist who is a fine improviser, David Darling has long been a fixture on the ECM label, adding his strong sound to many atmospheric sessions. He began on piano when he was four, switching to cello six years later and playing string bass and alto in school bands. He graduated from Indiana State College in 1965 after studying classical cello and worked as an educator from 1966-70. However, Darling switched to full-time performing when he was a member of Paul Winter's Consort (1970-78). He recorded with Ralph Towner the following year, led the chamber jazz group Gallery in the early 1980s, and has since then recorded fairly regularly for ECM as both a sideman and a leader, including his solo set *Cello* (1991-92). —*Scott Yanow*

● **Journal October** / Oct. 1979 / ECM ✦✦✦✦
Although not strictly a jazz album, David Darling's 1979 solo release *Journal October* deserves attention. His technique is amazing, even if a lot of times he's more interested in colors and textures than in rhythms. He's certainly influenced by contemporary classical music, and at times things get so introspective he almost seems detached. But it's worth investigating, for Darling is capable of exciting statements. This has been reissued on CD. —*Ron Wynn*

Cycles / Nov. 1981 / ECM ✦✦✦✦
Cellist David Darling, best known at the time for his long stint with Paul Winter's Consort, mostly performs spacy ballads on this ECM release. Teamed up in different combinations (three unaccompanied solos, a duet, two trios and a quintet number) with Collin Walcott (who doubles on sitar and tabla), pianist Steve Kuhn, Jan Garbarek (on tenor and soprano), acoustic guitarist Oscar Castro-Neves and bassist Arild Andersen, Darling and his sidemen give the music a wide variety of sounds. However, the sleepy mood is very much in the stereotypical ECM mold, making this set mostly of interest for selected tastes. —*Scott Yanow*

Cello / Nov. 1991-Jan. 1992 / ECM ✦✦
Superior cello playing by David Darling, a brilliant stylist who's not strictly, or even mainly, a jazz player. But he's an improviser, and his bowed and plucked solos are often astonishing in their clarity, depth, speed, and construction. He's also benefited by ECM's always-excellent production and mastering. —*Ron Wynn*

Dark Wood / Jul. 1993 / ECM ✦✦✦
David Darling's *Dark Wood*, an album of experimental chamber music, comprises four suites. —*John Bush*

Kenny Davern (John Kenneth Davern)

b. Jan. 7, 1935, Huntington, NY
Clarinet, Soprano Saxophone / Dixieland, Swing

One of the finest clarinetists in traditional jazz of the past 30 years (and able to hit notes far above the normal register), Davern has been an excellent player since the 1950s. He started playing professionally when he was 16, and in 1954 made his recording debut with Jack Teagarden. He picked up experience playing with Phil Napoleon's Memphis Five (1955), Pee Wee Erwin, Wild Bill Davison, Red Allen, Buck Clayton and Jo Jones. Davern led a band at Nick's in the early '60s and was with the Dukes of Dixieland during 1962-63. After associations with Eddie Condon, Herman Autrey and Ruby Braff, Davern co-led Soprano Summit during 1974-79 with Bob Wilber. Up until that point, Davern had doubled on clarinet and soprano but after the group's breakup he decided to specialize exclusively on clarinet. He formed the Blue Three (with Dick Wellstood and Bobby Rosengarden) in the early '80s, recorded several fine sets for Music Masters in the 1980s and '90s, and in recent times has had several matchups with Bob Wilber in a new Soprano Summit retitled Soprano Reunion. —*Scott Yanow*

John and Joe / Oct. 23, 1977 / Chiaroscuro ✦✦✦✦✦
Although already 42 at the time of this LP and widely respected as a talented swing/Dixieland clarinetist and soprano saxophonist for 20 years, this was only Kenny Davern's second album as a leader (and the first was a very obscure effort for Elektra in 1958). Actually, Davern (switching between soprano, clarinet and C-melody sax) shares the spotlight with the hot swing tenor Flip Phillips (who also contributes some bass clarinet and soprano) in a quintet with pianist Dave McKenna, bassist George Duvivier and drummer Bobby Rosengarden. The quintet performs six veteran standards (and the more recent "Elsa's Dream") in spirited fashion with plenty of interplay between the two horns. This version of "Mood Indigo" (with its clarinet and bass clarinet front line) is a near-classic, Flip takes "Candy" as his feature and "Cottontail" really cooks. —*Scott Yanow*

Unexpected / May 30, 1978 / Kharma ✦✦✦✦
This obscure effort is definitely a surprise. The two sopranos, Kenny Davern (known for playing in trad settings) and Steve Lacy (the leading avant-gardist), meet up in a quartet also including electric bassist Steve Swallow and drummer Paul Motian. Although Lacy had originally started out in Dixieland, the two horns here exclusively play adventurous free jazz pieces. Davern not only holds his own in the unfamiliar setting, but contributed two of the eight group originals. Although Davern's usual fans may not care for this free music, Lacy's followers will find the unique effort to be of strong interest. Oddly enough, this would be one of Davern's last recordings on soprano before deciding to stick exclusively to the clarinet. —*Scott Yanow*

The Free-Swinging Trio in the Jazz Tradition / Dec. 2, 1979 / Fat Cat Jazz ✦✦✦✦
One of three trio albums that clarinetist Kenny Davern led that featured pianist Dick Wellstood and drummer Chuck Riggs, this is a somewhat rare LP put out by the defunct Fat Cat Jazz label. With the exception of "Eccentric Rag," all seven of the songs that the trio performs are warhorses (including "Maple Leaf Rag," "Fidgety Feet" and "That's a Plenty") but their enthusiastic interpretations and wit keep the music from being overly predictable. This is one for classic jazz collectors to search for. —*Scott Yanow*

● **The Hot Three** / Jul. 1, 1979 / Monmouth ✦✦✦✦✦

El Rado Schuffle / Jun. 7, 1980 / Kenneth ✦✦✦
A tribute to Jimmy Noone. With Swedish sextet. —*Michael G. Nastos*

Live Hot Jazz / Dec. 18, 1983 / Statiras ✦✦✦✦
Clarinetist Kenny Davern and the great stride pianist Dick Wellstood always made for an exciting combination. With drummer Chuck Riggs completing the trio, Davern and Wellstood perform fresh versions of eight standards, all quite well known except for "Then You've Never Been Blue." However, the musicians come up with fresh and sometimes-surprising variations on the songs including "Rose Room," "Lady Be Good," "Rosetta" and "Beale Street Blues." The music (more classic jazz than Dixieland) is quite accessible, spontaneous and enjoyable; Jazzology's *Stretchin' Out* album was recorded the same day by these fine musicians. —*Scott Yanow*

Stretchin' Out / Dec. 1983 / Jazzology ✦✦✦✦
This CD reissue is as successful as one would expect from a trio date matching clarinetist Kenny Davern, pianist Dick Wellstood (less than four years before his premature death), and drummer Chuck Riggs. Rather than playing tunes from the 1920s or Dixieland standards, the trio jams on five superior standards from the 1930s (including "The Man I Love," "Lover Come Back to Me" and "There Is No Greater Love"), plus the hot 1929 number "Chicago Rhythm." Wellstood's stride piano and Davern's clarinet always worked well together. —*Scott Yanow*

The Very Thought of You / 1983 / Milton Keynes Music ✦✦✦

Kenny Davern and Dick Wellstood / Jan. 15, 1984 / Challenge ✦✦✦✦✦
Clarinetist Kenny Davern and pianist Dick Wellstood make for a potent duo on this live session. Two of the top trad jazz musicians to emerge during the 1940s (thereby making them a bit out-of-place in their generation), both Davern and Wellstood developed their own individual voices. Their strong performance of stomps and ballads also has a bit of storytelling as Wellstood talks about how he got started and the challenges of playing stride piano while Davern recalls his reaction when he first heard fellow clarinetist Pee Wee Russell. But more important, the music is very enjoyable and often surprisingly wistful. This CD release from the Dutch label Challenge is fortunately readily available in the US. —*Scott Yanow*

Kenny Davern Big Three / Nov. 25, 1985 / Jazzology ✦✦✦✦✦

I'll See You in My Dreams / Jan. 1988 / Music Masters ✦✦✦✦
Recorded at the same two sessions as *One Hour Tonight*, this CD gets the edge due to more tempo variation. Clarinetist Kenny Davern, guitarist Howard Alden, bassist Phil Flanigan and drummer Giampaolo Biagi are all heard in excellent form, coming up with fresh ideas on "Blue Lou," "Riverboat Shuffle," "My Melancholy Baby," "Royal Garden Blues" and six other veteran standards. Easily recommended to mainstream and Dixieland collectors. —*Scott Yanow*

One Hour Tonight / Jan. 1988 / Music Masters ✦✦✦✦
The emphasis is on relaxed tempos (although not exclusively) on this fine small-group swing date. Clarinetist Kenny Davern teams up with guitarist Howard Alden, bassist Phil Flanigan and drummer Giampaolo Biagi for some intimate renditions of such tunes as "Pretty Baby," "Comes Love," "Pee Wee's Blues" and "Oh, Baby." Although this CD is not quite essential, Davern has yet to record an uninspired record and his fans will enjoy the music. —*Scott Yanow*

My Inspiration / Sep. 11, 1991 / Music Masters ✦✦✦
Traditional jazz and light swing by distinguished clarinetist Kenny Davern, working with a sympathetic rhythm section and symphony orchestra. His wavery, floating solos aren't subsumed or obscured by the strings, while guitarist Howard

Alden, drummer Bobby Rosengarden, and bassist Bob Haggart fall in perfectly in the middle. —*Ron Wynn*

East Side, West Side / Jun. 24, 1994 / Arbors ✦✦✦✦

The most unusual aspect to this trad jazz sextet session led by clarinetist Kenny Davern is that it features trombonist Dan Barrett playing cornet on all but one selection. Although Barrett is not as distinctive as on his normal ax, his solos are quite enjoyable and hold their own with Davern, trombonist Joel Helleny and guitarist Buck Pizzarelli; bassist Bob Haggart and drummer Tony DeNicola complete the fine group. The repertoire mostly comprises underplayed standards with the highlights including "There'll Be Some Changes Made," "Delta Bound," "Sidewalks of New York," "There's Yes! Yes! in Your Eyes" and "Please Be Kind," It's recommended to swing and classic jazz fans. —*Scott Yanow*

Kenny Davern & the Rhythm Men / Jun. 15, 1995 / Arbors ✦✦✦✦

Never in a Million Years / Oct. 1, 1995 / Challenge ✦✦✦

Breezin' Along / Jun. 13, 1996 / Arbors ✦✦✦✦✦

By the time of this 1996 CD, Kenny Davern already had a full career of accomplishments, and for years, he had had his own sound and a technique that allowed him to hit very high notes with ease. For this set, he is joined by two masterful guitarists (Howard Alden and Bucky Pizzarelli) in a pianoless rhythm section that also includes bassist Greg Cohen and drummer Tony DeNicola. The strong repertoire (mostly Dixieland and swing standards, plus the leader's minor-tinged song "My Mama Socks Me") , the quiet but heated backup group and Davern's own enthusiasm results in this being one of his finest showcases. Highlights include "Jazz Me Blues," "My Honey's Lovin' Arms" and "Breeezin' Along with the Breeze." Highly recommended to fans of the pre-bop clarinet. —*Scott Yanow*

Anthony Davis

b. Feb. 20, 1951, Paterson, NJ
Piano / Avant-Garde, Post-Bop

Anthony Davis, a major composer of the late twentieth century, stretches beyond jazz into modern classical music, although he has recorded quite a few rewarding jazz sessions. He studied classical music as a child and in 1975 graduated from Yale. A member of the New Delta Ahkri during 1974-77 (which was led by Leo Smith) , Davis moved to New York in 1977, played with Oliver Lake, Anthony Braxton, Chico Freeman, George Lewis and Leroy Jenkins' trio (1977-79) , and worked often with James Newton and Abdul Wadud. Davis formed an octet (Episteme) in 1981, which played both improvised and wholly-composed music. Anthony Davis composed the opera *X* (based on the life of Malcolm X) in the early '80s and he taught at Yale. Davis has recorded for India Navigation, Red, Sackville and Gramavision. —*Scott Yanow*

Past Lives / Jun. 7, 1978 / Red ✦✦✦

Engaging and appealing; it could be his best "jazz" piano playing. —*Ron Wynn*

Of Blues and Dreams / Jul. 30, 1978-Jul. 31, 1978 / Sackville ✦✦✦

On the cutting edge of avant-garde. With violinist Leroy Jenkins and cellist Abdul Wadud. —*Michael G. Nastos*

Song for the Old World / Jul. 1978 / India Navigation ✦✦✦✦

Pianist/composer Anthony Davis has long been one of the most interesting musicians of his generation. His music is difficult to categorize, ranging from explorative jazz to classical with many stops in between. This early album (with a quartet also featuring vibraphonist Jay Hoggard, bassist Mark Helias and drummer Ed Blackwell) finds Davis performing six of his wide-ranging compositions. In addition to a feature for Hoggard and tributes to the bebop generation and Andrew Hill, the most impressive piece is the title cut which has fragments of melodies from Africa and Asia. This subtle album rewards repeated listenings. —*Scott Yanow*

Hidden Voices / 1979 / India Navigation ✦✦✦✦

Pianist Anthony Davis, flutist James Newton, trombonist George Lewis, bassist Rick Rozie and drummer Pheeroan AkLaff make for a potent and very exploratory team on a set of originals by Davis and Newton. The music is quite unpredictable and free in spots, yet does not neglect the use of melody and space. Thought-provoking performances. —*Scott Yanow*

Under the Double Moon / Sep. 1, 1980-Sep. 2, 1980 / Pausa ✦✦✦

This is an interesting set of duets by pianist Anthony Davis and vibraphonist Jay Hoggard. With the exception of Duke Ellington's advanced "The Clothed Woman," the duo sticks to originals, some of which are quite complex. However, the mellow sound of their instruments make the improvisations more accessible than they really are. Unfortunately, this LP (originally put out by the German MPS label and made available domestically by the now-defunct Pausa company) will probably be quite difficult to locate. —*Scott Yanow*

Lady of the Mirrors / 1980 / India Navigation ✦✦✦✦✦

New reissue of a stunning late-70s set has one bonus cut. —*Ron Wynn*

Episteme / 1981 / Gramavision ✦✦✦

Masterful compositions and arrangements. —*Ron Wynn*

● ### I've Known Rivers / Apr. 1982 / Gramavision ✦✦✦✦✦

This combination of musicians works very well. The trio of pianist Anthony Davis, flutist James Newton and cellist Abdul Wadud are all grounded in the jazz tradition, yet are very adventurous players who are quite versatile. Although the four originals are often complex (and sometimes tightly structured) , the players sound quite spontaneous and inspired. Recommended. —*Scott Yanow*

Variations in Dreamtime / 1982 / India Navigation ✦✦✦

Hemispheres / Jul. 1983 / Gramavision ✦✦✦

A 1990 reissue of one of Davis' more advanced works. —*Ron Wynn*

Middle Passage / 1984 / Gramavision ✦✦

Anthony Davis, a brilliant pianist/composer, performs four of his compositions as solo piano pieces, utilizing electronics on the lengthy "Particle W." Even if none of the individual compositions are all that memorable by themselves, Davis' combination of avant-garde jazz and hints of the tradition with contemporary classical music is quite intriguing and full of surprises. —*Scott Yanow*

Undine / Jun. 1986 / Gramavision ✦✦✦

Pianist Anthony Davis and his Episteme ensemble perform two lengthy and complex pieces ("Still Waters" and "Undine") that mix together aspects of avant-garde jazz and contemporary classical music. Davis' group includes J.D. Parran on flute, clarinet and contrabass clarinet; Marty Ehrlich on clarinet, bass clarinet and flute; cellist Abdul Wadud and percussionist Gerry Hemingway, plus bassoon and violin. Unusual music (reissued on CD) that takes a few listens to fully absorb. —*Scott Yanow*

Ghost Factory / 1987 / Gramavision ✦✦✦

The gifted pianist/composer demonstrates his facility with contemporary classical and jazz pieces, playing sometimes in duos, other times trios, and also interacting with The Kansas City Symphony Orchestra. Percussionists Pheeroan Ak Laff or Gerry Hemingway and violinist Shem Guibbory are his partners, while all the compositions are Davis'. —*Ron Wynn*

Trio, Vol. 2 / 1989 / Gramavision ✦✦✦✦✦

One of the most rewarding settings for Anthony Davis' music and piano solos is when he performs in a trio with flutist James Newton and cellist Abdul Wadud, as on *I've Known Rivers* and this CD. The all-star group performs pieces by Davis and Newton, Roland Hanna ("Thursday's Child") , Charles Mingus ("Eclipse") and the exciting collective improvisation "Flat Out." Highly recommended. —*Scott Yanow*

Art Davis

b. Dec. 5, 1934, Harrisburg, PA
Bass / Post-Bop, Hard Bop

A top-rate player, Art Davis has attained as much acclaim within the jazz community for his work as an educator and teacher as he has for his talents as a bassist. Davis came to the bass late; he studied piano and tuba first, winning a national competition as a tub player before starting on bass in 1951. He played with Max Roach in 1958 and 1959, then toured Europe with Dizzy Gillespie in 1959 and 1960. David was extremely busy in the early '60s; he recorded and played with John Coltrane in 1961 and in 1965, and was featured in the bands of Gigi Gryce, Lena Horne, Booker Little, Quincy Jones, Rahsaan Roland Kirk, Oliver Nelson, Freddie Hubbard, Clark Terry and Art Blakey at various times. In addition, Davis was a member of the NBC, CBS and Westinghouse television orchestras between 1962 and 1970. His teaching career began to expand in the '70s. Davis taught at Manhattan Community College from 1971-1973. He earned a BA from Hunter College in 1972, MA degrees from SUNY and New York University in music and psychology in 1976 and a doctorate in psychology in 1981. Davis has since combined being a psychologist with playing music, doing sessions, playing in a duo with Hilton Ruiz in 1985 and 1986, and recording as a leader in 1980 (for Interplay) and 1985 (Soul Note) . His 1975 book *The Arthur Davis Method for Double Bass* is one of the finest instructional works for the instrument. —*Ron Wynn*

Reemergence / Jan. 3, 1980 / Interplay ✦✦✦✦

Bassist Art Davis was 45 when he finally had his first opportunity to lead his own record session. This superior trio set with pianist Hilton Ruiz and drummer Greg Bandy serves as a fine feature for the adventurous bassist who contributed three of the five selections including the 20-minute "Add." Although the young Ruiz is naturally the main voice in the ensembles, Davis takes plenty of solo space, displaying his huge tone and consistently creative ideas. —*Scott Yanow*

● **Life** / Oct. 5, 1985 / Soul Note ✦✦✦✦✦

Bassist Art Davis, who occasionally played with John Coltrane in the early '60s, has led relatively few sessions throughout his career. A very talented player with complete control over his instrument, Davis contributed all four selections to this impressive outing, which is highlighted by "Duo" (matching his bass with tenor saxophonist Pharoah Sanders) and the nineteen-and-a-half-minute four-part "Add." Davis' all-star quartet also includes pianist John Hicks and drummer Idris Muhammad. —Scott Yanow

Time Remembered / Jan. 14, 1995-Jan. 15, 1995 / Jazz Planet ✦✦✦✦✦

Charles Davis

b. May 20, 1933, Goodman, MI
Baritone Saxophone / Hard Bop
Although he has performed previously on tenor and alto, Charles Davis is best-known for his fine baritone playing, both as a soloist and for his dependable work in sax sections. Early on he gigged with Sun Ra (off and on from 1954 into the 1980s), Brother Jack McDuff, Ben Webster, Billie Holiday and Dinah Washington (1957-58). Davis gained some attention when he was with Kenny Dorham's band (1959-62). He also played with Illinois Jacquet, Lionel Hampton, the Jazz Composers' Orchestra (1966-76), Louis Hayes' Sextet (1972-74), Clark Terry's big band and the Thad Jones/Mel Lewis Orchestra. In the 1980s he was with Damerdonia (1981-84), Philly Joe Jones, Barry Harris and Abdullah Ibrahim. Charles Davis has led sessions for Strata East, West 54, Nilva, Red and L&R. —Scott Yanow

Dedicated to Tadd / Mar. 1, 1979-Mar. 2, 1979 / West 54 ✦✦✦

Super 80 / Jan. 12, 1982 / Nilva ✦✦✦

● **Reflections** / Feb. 19, 1990 / Red ✦✦✦✦✦

Eddie "Lockjaw" Davis

b. Mar. 2, 1922, New York, NY, **d.** Nov. 3, 1986, Culver City, CA
Tenor Saxophone / Bop, Hard Bop, Swing, Groove, Soul-Jazz
Possessor of a cutting and immediately identifiable tough tenor tone, Eddie "Lockjaw" Davis could hold his own in a saxophone battle with anyone. Early on he picked up experience playing with the bands of Cootie Williams (1942-44), Lucky Millinder, Andy Kirk (1945-46) and Louis Armstrong. He began heading his own groups from 1946, and Davis' earliest recordings as a leader tended to be explosive R&B affairs with plenty of screaming from his horn; he matched wits successfully with Fats Navarro on one session. Davis was with Count Basie's Orchestra on several occasions (including 1952-53, 1957 and 1964-73) and teamed up with Shirley Scott's trio during 1955-60. During 1960-62 he collaborated in some exciting performances and recordings with Johnny Griffin, a fellow tenor who was just as combative as Davis. After temporarily retiring to become a booking agent (1963-64), Davis rejoined Basie. In his later years, Lockjaw often recorded with Harry "Sweets" Edison and he remained a busy soloist up until his death. Through the decades he recorded as a leader for many labels including Savoy, Apollo, Roost, King, Roulette, Prestige/Jazzland/Moodsville, RCA, Storyville, MPS, Black & Blue, Spotlite, Steeple Chase, Pablo, Muse and Enja. —Scott Yanow

Rarest Sessions of the '40s / May 1946-1948 / Pinnacle ✦✦✦✦

Most of tenor saxophonist Eddie "Lockjaw" Davis' earliest recordings as a leader (the majority of the ones not cut for Savoy) are on this collector's LP. Davis' fiery tone was already quite distinctive, although he was more R&B-oriented at the time than he would become. These explosive performances mostly feature Lockjaw in combos where he was the only horn and accompanied by such fine pianists as Argonne Thornton, Al Haig and John Acea. The last four titles are with a swinging octet also including trumpeter Shad Collins, trombonist Milt Larkin and two other tenors. Fun music but this LP will be difficult to find. —Scott Yanow

Jaws N' Stitt at Birdland / 1954 / Roulette ✦✦✦

Sonny Stitt (sticking to tenor on this set) sat in with fellow tenor Eddie "Lockjaw" Davis' trio (which also includes organist Doc Bagby and drummer Charlie Rice) for a spirited and typically competitive jam session. Since Davis and Stitt had different sounds (one has little difficulty telling them apart) and were equally skilled, their collaboration is a draw. In addition to three standards, this CD has five basic originals. The original LP's four numbers are joined by four equally heated selections from the same date that were previously put out by the Phoenix label. Easily recommended to bebop collectors. —Scott Yanow

Eddie's Function / Feb. 2, 1956-Jun. 14, 1957 / Affinity ✦✦✦✦

For this Bethlehem reissue LP, tenor saxophonist Eddie "Lockjaw" Davis teams up with either Doc Bagby or Shirley Scott on organ, sometimes Carl Pruitt or Bill Pemberton on bass, drummers Charlie Rice or Arthur Edgehill and the congas or Ray Baretto. The concise renditions of a dozen songs (three group originals and nine standards) all clock in around three minutes apiece and were made primarily for the jukebox audience, so there is an emphasis on the melodies and in maintaining a solid rhythm for a dancing audience. However, the music (which is overdue to be reissued on CD) still communicates fairly well and should be of interest to jazz listeners. —Scott Yanow

Countin' with Basie / Dec. 17, 1957-Dec. 19, 1957 / Vogue ✦✦✦

After recording extensively for the R&B King label during 1955-57, tenor saxophonist Eddie Lockjaw Davis made a jazz-oriented set for Roulette that was presented by Count Basie. Last put out by the French Vogue label on a 1984 LP, this set features the tough-toned tenor with organist Shirley Scott, bassist George Duvivier, drummer Butch Ballard and (on the majority of the tracks) trumpeter Joe Newman and pianist Count Basie himself. Not too surprisingly, the music swings and the mixture of swing standards (such as "Broadway" and "Street of Dreams") and basic originals bring out the best in these fine players. —Scott Yanow

The Eddie Lockjaw Davis Cookbook / Jun. 20, 1958 / Prestige ✦✦✦✦

This CD reissue adds a slightly later version of "Avalon" to the original LP program. Tenor saxophonist Eddie "Lockjaw" Davis and his regular organist of the period, Shirley Scott, are joined by bassist George Duvivier, drummer Arthur Edgehill and flutist Jerome Richardson for the first of three entries in their *Cookbook* series; two of the originals on the set are "The Chef" and "In the Kitchen." In addition to three blues at various tempos, Davis is quite warm on the ballad "But Beautiful" while the boppish "Three Deuces" finds Richardson switching to tenor and holding his own with Lockjaw. —Scott Yanow

Jaws / Sep. 12, 1958 / Original Jazz Classics ✦✦✦

Tenorman Eddie "Lockjaw" Davis and organist Shirley Scott co-led a popular combo during 1956-60, recording many albums and helping to popularize the idiom. This particular CD reissue of an LP (which at 37 minutes is a bit brief) finds the quartet (with bassist George Duvivier and drummer Arthur Edgehill) interpreting eight swing standards, alternating ballads with romps. It's a fine all-around showcase for the accessible group. —Scott Yanow

Smokin' / Sep. 12, 1958+Dec. 5, 1958 / Original Jazz Classics ✦✦✦✦

Tenor saxophonist Eddie "Lockjaw" Davis cut enough material during these two sessions to fill up four records. The seven selections included on this brief 36-minute CD (a straight reissue of an LP recorded during the same period as Davis' better-known *Cookbook* albums) also include Jerome Richardson (switching between flute, tenor and baritone) on three of the numbers, bassist George Duvivier and drummer Arthur Edgehill. Together the group swings hard on basic originals, blues and an occasional ballad, showing why this type of accessible band was so popular during the era. —Scott Yanow

The Eddie Lockjaw Davis Cookbook, Vol. 2 / Dec. 1958 / Original Jazz Classics ✦✦✦✦

Eddie "Lockjaw" Davis' *Cookbook* series helped make the group that the tenorman had in the late '50s with organist Shirley Scott famous. The quintet (which also includes flutist Jerome Richardson, bassist George Duvivier and drummer Arthur Edgehill) is heard on this CD reissue performing three Davis-Scott originals, "Stardust," "I Surrender Dear" and a version of "Willow Weep for Me" that was originally part of a sampler. The straightahead music is interpreted quite colorfully by Davis and his group, one of the first popular organ combos. —Scott Yanow

The Eddie Lockjaw Davis Cookbook, Vol. 3 / Dec. 15, 1958 / Prestige ✦✦✦✦

Tenorman Eddie "Lockjaw" Davis made quite a few records with organist Shirley Scott during the late '50s. The basic originals in their *Cookbook* series tended to have titles that dealt with cooking; in this case "Heat 'n' Serve," "The Goose Hangs High" and "Simmerin'" apply as does the standard "My Old Flame." Jerome Richardson's flute, baritone and tenor gives this CD reissue some variety, bassist George Duvivier and drummer Arthur Edgehill are fine in support, and Shirley Scott shows that she was one of the top organists to emerge after the rise of Jimmy Smith. But Davis is the main star and his instantly recognizable sound is the most memorable aspect to this swinging session. —Scott Yanow

Very Saxy / Apr. 29, 1959 / Prestige ✦✦✦✦

Tenor saxophonist Eddie "Lockjaw" Davis and his quartet (which includes organist Shirley Scott, bassist George Duvivier and drummer Arthur Edgehill) welcome three immortal tenors (Coleman Hawkins, Arnett Cobb and Buddy Tate) to what became a historic and hard-swinging jam session. On three blues, an original based on the chord changes of "Sweet Georgia Brown" and "Lester Leaps In," the four tenors battle it out, and the results are quite exciting. The spirited music on this memorable LP will hopefully be reissued on CD eventually for the performances live up to their great potential. —Scott Yanow

Jaws in Orbit / May 1, 1959 / Original Jazz Classics ✦✦✦✦

The group that Eddie "Lockjaw" Davis led with organist Shirley Scott during the latter half of the 1950s was quite accessible and did a great deal to popularize the organ band in jazz. This CD reissue features the duo joined by bassist George Duvivier, drummer Arthur Edgehill and the obscure trombonist Steve Pulliam for a typically swinging set of basic originals and standards. Highlights include a hard-swinging "Intermission Riff" and "Our Delight." —*Scott Yanow*

Gentle Jaws / Dec. 11, 1959+Jan. 31, 1960 / Prestige ◆◆◆
The Moodsville label was a subsidiary of Prestige in the late '50s/early '60s that sought to document jazz artists exclusively playing ballads so as to win over the mood music audience of the time. This 75-minute reissue CD combines together two sessions featuring the warm tenor of Eddie "Lockjaw" Davis. On the first half he "sits in" with the Red Garland Trio (that date was originally issued under Garland's name), while on the latter half he is backed by the Shirley Scott Trio with organist Scott switching to piano. The standard-dominated program is tasteful but uneventful and the similarity of the tempos succeed in making the results more successful as background music than as creative jazz. —*Scott Yanow*

Trane Whistle / Sep. 20, 1960 / Original Jazz Classics ◆◆◆◆◆
This CD reissue brings back an Eddie "Lockjaw" Davis session in which the distinctive tenor saxophonist is joined by a 13-piece big band arranged by Oliver Nelson. Most significant is the inclusion of the original version of "Stolen Moments" (here called "The Stolen Moment" and predating the more famous Oliver Nelson recording by several months). Eric Dolphy is in the backup group but is not heard from in a solo capacity. There are some spots for trumpeters Richard Williams, Clark Terry and Bobby Bryant along with Nelson on alto, but this is primarily Davis' showcase. On a set comprising four Oliver Nelson originals, the ballad "You Are Too Beautiful" and the leader's "Jaws," Lockjaw as usual shows plenty of emotion during his driving solos. —*Scott Yanow*

The Tenor Scene / Jan. 6, 1961 / Original Jazz Classics ◆◆◆◆◆
Formerly knows as *The Breakfast Show*, the music on this CD reissue was one of four albums cut by the Eddie "Lockjaw" Davis-Johnny Griffin quintet during a single evening. With swinging support by pianist Junior Mance, bassist Larry Gales and drummer Ben Riley, the two combative but complementary tenors stretch out on lengthy versions of Lockjaw's "Light and Lovely," "Straight, No Chaser" and "I'll Remember April," plus more concise renditions of "Woody 'n You" and Davis' "Bingo Domingo." The straightahead music contains plenty of sparks; this was a classic group. —*Scott Yanow*

Afro Jaws / May 4, 1961+May 12, 1961 / Original Jazz Classics ◆◆◆◆
This set was a change of pace for tenor saxophonist Eddie "Lockjaw" Davis. Backed by three trumpeters (Clark Terry gets some solos), a rhythm section (pianist Lloyd Mayers, bassist Larry Gales and drummer Ben Riley) and a percussion section led by Ray Barretto, Lockjaw performs four compositions by Gil Lopez (who arranged all of the selections) plus "Tin Tin Deo," "Star Eyes" and his own "Afro Jaws." The Afro-Cuban setting is perfect for the tough-toned tenor, who romps through the infectious tunes. —*Scott Yanow*

Streetlights / Nov. 15, 1962 / Prestige ◆◆◆◆◆
This CD combines together the music from two complete LPs (*I Only Have Eyes for You* and *Trackin'*) that were recorded the same day with the identical personnel. Eddie "Lockjaw" Davis' tough tenor is well featured with his regular group of the time, a combo consisting of the powerful organist Don Patterson (who dominates many of the ensembles), guitarist Paul Weeden (talented but quite obscure), drummer Billy James and guest bassist George Duvivier. The emphasis is on standards and intense blowing (even on the ballads) with the set being a good example of a strong tenor organ band. —*Scott Yanow*

Save Your Love for Me / Jun. 20, 1966-Aug. 3, 1967 / Bluebird ◆◆◆
This "best of" collection draws its 14 selections from three Victor albums by tenor saxophonist Eddie "Lockjaw" Davis: *Lock the Fox*, *The Fox and the Hounds* and *Love Calls*. Although it would be preferable to acquire all three out-of-print albums (which represent the bulk of Davis' 1963-69 recordings), there are some strong performances included on this sampler. Lockjaw is heard as the only horn in a sextet with pianist Ross Tompkins and percussionist Ray Barretto, accompanied by a 17-piece big band arranged by Bobby Plater and on a combo date highlighted by two numbers ("The Man with the Horn" and "A Weaver of Dreams") in which he interacts with fellow tenor Paul Gonsalves. —*Scott Yanow*

Tough Tenors Again 'n Again / Apr. 24, 1970 / Pausa ◆◆◆◆
Tenors Eddie "Lockjaw" Davis and Johnny Griffin, who co-led a popular group in the early '60s, had a reunion for this European session originally put out by the MPS label. Assisted by pianist Francy Boland, bassist Jimmy Woode and drummer Kenny Clarke, the two tenors battle it out on a few uptempo pieces and show off their warm tones on Griffin's ballad "When We Were One" and "If I Had You." This album, which contains plenty of colorful music, is currently difficult to find. —*Scott Yanow*

Sweet and Lovely / Jul. 26, 1975 / Classic Jazz ◆◆◆
Also put out on the French Black & Blue label, this is one of the more obscure LPs to team together tenor saxophonist Eddie "Lockjaw" Davis and trumpeter Harry "Sweets" Edison. Lockjaw and Sweets always made for an exciting combination,

constantly challenging each other to play with fire. Highlights of this particular encounter include "Jim Dawg," "Intermission Riff" and "Light and Lovely"; the two distinctive horn stylists are even able to uplift "The Good Life." —*Scott Yanow*

Swingin' Till the Girls Come Home / Mar. 8, 1976 / Steeple Chase ◆◆◆◆◆
Tenor saxophonist Eddie "Lockjaw" Davis is in top form during this European quartet set (put out domestically at one time by Inner City) with pianist Thomas Clausen, bassist Bo Stief and drummer Alex Riel. Lockjaw romps through such numbers as "Swingin' Till the Girls Come Home," a rapid rendition of "Love for Sale," his original "Locks" and "Indiana." Fun, accessible and mostly hard-swinging straightahead music. —*Scott Yanow*

Straight Ahead / May 3, 1976 / Original Jazz Classics ◆◆◆◆
A perfect example of Eddie "Lockjaw" Davis' playing, this superior quartet set (a Pablo date that has been reissued on CD) features the tough-toned tenor swinging hard on standards, showing his warmth on ballads and coming up with inventive ideas within the swing/bop tradition. With sterling support by pianist Tommy Flanagan, bassist Keter Betts and drummer Bobby Durham (Ella Fitzgerald's trio at the time), Lockjaw sounds at his best on such numbers as "Lover," "On a Clear Day" and even "The Good Life." —*Scott Yanow*

Montreux '77 / Jul. 15, 1977 / Original Jazz Classics ◆◆◆◆
Part of Norman Granz's extensive documentation of the 1977 Montreux Jazz Festival, this excellent outing for tenor saxophonist Eddie "Lockjaw" Davis teams him with pianist Oscar Peterson, bassist Ray Brown and drummer Jimmie Smith. Lockjaw plays six of his favorite standards (including a rapid "This Can't Be Love," "Angel Eyes" and "Blue Lou"), plus his own "Telegraph." A typically swinging and highly expressive recording by the unique tenorman. —*Scott Yanow*

The Heavy Hitter / Jan. 18, 1979 / Muse ◆◆◆◆
Eddie "Lockjaw" Davis recorded many albums during the 15 years before his death in 1986; virtually all are recommended. This album is a little-known quartet set with pianist Albert Dailey, bassist George Duvivier and drummer Victor Lewis, Davis' only recording for Muse. Lockjaw had never worked with Dailey or Lewis before but they have little difficulty interpreting the tough-toned tenor's usual repertoire. Highlights of the fine straighahead set include "Just One of Those Things," "Secret Love" and "You Stepped Out of a Dream." —*Scott Yanow*

Jaw's Blues / Feb. 11, 1981 / Enja ◆◆◆◆
Hard-to-find session is now generally available on CD. Horace Parlan makes an all-too-infrequent guest spot as pianist. —*Ron Wynn*

● **All of Me** / Aug. 23, 1983 / Steeple Chase ◆◆◆◆◆
Tenorman Eddie "Lockjaw" Davis had already been a potent force in jazz for 35 years when he recorded this set, but as it turned out his Steeple Chase date (his next-to-last session) was one of the strongest of his career. Accompanied by a trio led by pianist Kenny Drew, Lockjaw really tears into these standards, which are highlighted by "I Only Have Eyes for You," two versions of "There Is No Greater Love" (the alternate version was released for the first time on this CD reissue), "Four" and the title cut. Davis was at the peak of his powers during this recording, making his lone Steeple Chase outing one of his very best. —*Scott Yanow*

Emery Davis

Violin / Avant-Garde
A talented and advanced jazz violinist, Emery Davis has received some recognition for his Accurate recordings. His grandfather was the society bandleader Meyer Davis, and his father plays clarinet. Emery Davis began on violin when he was four and learned classical music at the Manhattan School of Music. In Boston, he studied with Jerry Bergonzi. After recording his debut album, *Dante's Blues*, Emery Davis moved to Paris, although he returned to the US in 1993 in order to record *Sauce*. —*Scott Yanow*

● **Dante's Blues** / Dec. 5, 1989-Dec. 6, 1989 / Accurate Jazz ◆◆◆◆
Sauce / Feb. 9, 1993-Feb. 10, 1993 / Accurate Jazz ◆◆◆◆

Jackie Davis

b. Dec. 13, 1920, Jacksonville, FL
Organ / Groove, Soul-Jazz
Organist Jackie Davis laying around town since he was nine years old and became part of an orchestra at ten. At the age of eleven, Davis had saved and bought his own piano for $45. He played for dances, one nighters, and wherever he could find a gig. He studied with Earl Hines. Davis graduated from Florida A&M in 1942 with a degree in music. He was listening to players like Milt Herth and George Wright, but it was "Wild" Bill Davis who opened his eyes to the power of the organ. He was a student of Louis Jordan and spent some 14 months in his band. He recorded with Capitol Records for sixteen years. Davis made several albums in the '50s and '60s for Pacific Jazz, Vic, Trend, Capitol and Warner Bros. in the '50s

and '60s, most of them done in a soul jazz vein, though he switched to gospel for his last recordings. These were mostly small trio or combo dates, though there was also one with a trombone group, another with a vocal choir. —*Michael Erlewine & Ron Wynn*

Jumpin' Jackie / Oct. 1957 / Capitol ✦✦✦

Jackie Davis Meets the Trombones / 1959 / Capitol ✦✦✦

● **Easy Does It** / Jan. 15, 1963 / Warner Brothers ✦✦✦✦

Jackie Davis / 1980 / EMI ✦✦✦

Jesse Davis

b. Nov. 9, 1965, New Orleans, LA
Alto Saxophone / Hard Bop
A fine altoist whose style comes out of the Cannonball Adderley tradition, Jesse Davis made a strong impression with his Concord recordings. He started on alto when he was 11, attended the New Orleans Center for Creative Arts, and learned from Ellis Marsalis. Davis studied at Northeastern Illinois University (1983-86), played locally in Chicago, was in the Illinois Jacquet big band (1987-90), and worked with Chico Hamilton. After recording with Tana Reid in 1990, he was signed to Concord and today is one of the most promising of the young hard bop stylists. —*Scott Yanow*

Horn of Passion / Jan. 24, 1991-Jan. 25, 1991 / Concord Jazz ✦✦✦✦
Altoist Jesse Davis' debut as a leader finds the talented altoist very much influenced by Cannonball Adderley's sound at this early stage. He holds his own with the top-notch rhythm section (comprising pianist Mulgrew Miller, bassist Rufus Reid and drummer Jimmy Cobb) on five standards and his own "C.P. Time," and performs four originals with a different quartet that includes tenor saxophonist Antoine Roney (brother of Wallace), bassist Tyler Mitchell and drummer Eric McPherson (son of Charles). Davis (25 at the time) showed a great deal of potential at this point and also displayed surprising maturity on the ballads. An impressive start to his career. —*Scott Yanow*

● **As We Speak** / Feb. 13, 1992 / Concord Jazz ✦✦✦✦✦
Good straightahead session that comprises the second album by alto saxophonist Jesse Davis, who hasn't gotten as much ink as many other young lion players. The menu features pre-rock and bop anthems, plus hard bop originals, keyed by Davis' aggressive, often soothing solos and fine assistance from trombonist Robin Trowers, pianist Jacky Terrasson, guitarist Peter Bernstein, bassist Dwayne Burno, and drummer Leon Parker. —*Ron Wynn*

Young at Art / Aug. 24, 1993-Aug. 25, 1993 / Concord Jazz ✦✦✦✦
Jesse Davis comes close to capturing the sound and exuberant spirit of Cannonball Adderley on this release, while also hinting strongly at Charlie Parker, Phil Woods and Richie Cole. Davis utilizes a strong backup crew that includes guitarist Peter Bernstein and pianist Brad Mehldau to perform a set of superior tunes. The music is not particularly innovative, but is a fine example of high-quality bebop played by some promising young players. —*Scott Yanow*

High Standards / Jun. 13, 1994-Jun. 14, 1994 / Concord Jazz ✦✦✦✦

From Within / Apr. 24, 1996-Apr. 25, 1996 / Concord Jazz ✦✦✦✦

Miles Davis

b. May 25, 1926, Alton, IL, d. Sep. 28, 1991, Santa Monica, CA
Trumpet / Bop, Cool, Hard Bop, Avant-Garde, Fusion, Groove, Jazz-Fusion
Miles Davis had quite a career, one with so many innovations that his name is one of the few that can be spoken in the same sentence with Duke Ellington. As a trumpeter, Davis was never a virtuoso on the level of his idol Dizzy Gillespie but by 1947 he possessed a distinctive cool-toned sound of his own. His ballad renditions (utilizing a Harmon mute) were exquisite yet never predictable, he mastered and then stripped down the bebop vocabulary to its essentials and he generally made every note count; as with Thelonious Monk, less was more in Miles' music.

But Miles Davis was much more than just a trumpeter. As a bandleader he was a brilliant talent scout, able to recognize potential in its formative stage and bring out the best in his sidemen. Among the musicians who greatly benefitted from their association with Davis were Gerry Mulligan (virtually unknown when he played with Miles' Birth of the Cool Nonet), Gil Evans, John Coltrane, Red Garland, Paul Chambers, Philly Joe Jones, Cannonball Adderley, Bill Evans, Jimmy Cobb, Wynton Kelly, George Coleman, Wayne Shorter, Herbie Hancock, Ron Carter, Tony Williams, Chick Corea, Jack DeJohnette, Dave Holland, John McLaughlin, Joe Zawinul, Keith Jarrett, Steve Grossman, Gary Bartz, Dave Liebman, Al Foster, Sonny Fortune, Bill Evans (the saxophonist), Kenny Garrett, Marcus Miller, Mike Stern and John Scofield. This partial list forms a who's who of modern jazz.

In addition to his playing and nurturing of young talent, Miles Davis was quite remarkable in his rare ability to continually evolve. Most jazz musicians (with the

exceptions of John Coltrane and Duke Ellington) generally form their style early on and spend the rest of their careers refining their sound. In contrast, Miles Davis every five years or so would forge ahead, and due to his restless nature he not only played bop but helped found cool jazz, hard bop, modal music, his own unusual brand of the avant-garde and fusion. Jazz history would be much different if Davis had not existed.

Born in Alton, IL, Miles Davis grew up in a middle-class family in East St. Louis. He started on trumpet when he was nine or ten, played in his high-school band, and picked up early experience gigging with Eddie Randall's Blue Devils. Miles Davis has said that the greatest musical experience of his life was hearing the Billy Eckstine Orchestra (with Dizzy Gillespie and Charlie Parker) when it passed through St. Louis.

In September 1944, Davis went to New York to study at Juilliard but spent much more time hanging out on 52nd Street and eventually dropped out of school. He played with Coleman Hawkins, made his recording debut in early 1945 (a rather nervous session with singer Rubberlegs Williams) and by late 1945 was playing regularly with Charlie Parker. Davis made an impression with his playing on Bird's recordings of "Now's the Time" and "Billie's Bounce." Although influenced by Dizzy Gillespie, even at this early stage the 19 year old had something of his own to contribute.

When Charlie Parker went with Gillespie out to California, Miles followed him a few months later by travelling cross-country with Benny Carter's Orchestra. He recorded with Parker in California and when Bird formed a quintet in New York the following year, Davis was a key member. By late 1948 when he went out on his own, Miles Davis had formed a nonet that, with arrangements by Gerry Mulligan, Gil Evans and John Lewis, helped usher in "cool jazz." Although the group only had one paying job (two weeks in September 1948 as an intermission band for Count Basie at the Royal Roost), its dozen recordings for Capitol were highly influential in the West Coast jazz movement.

Typically, by the time his nonet dates were renamed "Birth of the Cool," Miles Davis had moved on. He played at the Paris Jazz Festival in 1949 with Tadd Dameron and during 1951-54 was recording music with such sidemen as J.J. Johnson, Jimmy Heath, Horace Silver, Art Blakey and Sonny Rollins that directly led to hard bop. However, this was very much an off period for Miles because he was a heroin addict who was only working on an irregular basis. In 1954 he used all of his will power to permanently kick heroin and his recording that year of "Walkin'," although overlooked at the time, is a classic.

1955 was Miles Davis' breakthrough year. His performance of "'Round Midnight" at the Newport Jazz Festival alerted the critics that he was "back." Davis formed his classic quintet with John Coltrane, Red Garland, Paul Chambers and Philly Joe Jones, and during 1955-56 they recorded four well-received albums for Prestige and *'Round Midnight* for Columbia. Davis' muted ballads were very popular and he became a celebrity. Even the breakup of the quintet in early 1957 did not slow up the momentum. Miles recorded the first of his full-length collaborations with arranger Gil Evans (*Miles Ahead*), which would be followed by *Porgy and Bess* (1958) and *Sketches of Spain* (1960); on these recordings Davis became one of the first trumpeters to stretch out on fluegelhorn. In 1957, he went to France to record the soundtrack for *Lift to the Scaffold*, and then in 1958 he formed his greatest band, a super sextet with Coltrane, Cannonball Adderley, Bill Evans, Paul Chambers and Philly Joe Jones. Although Evans and Jones were eventually succeeded by Wynton Kelly and Jimmy Cobb, all of the recordings by this remarkable group somehow live up to their potential with *Milestones* and *Kind of Blue* being all-time classics that helped to introduce modal (or scalar) improvising to jazz.

If Miles Davis had retired in 1960, he would still be famous in jazz history, but he had many accomplishments still to come. The sextet gradually changed with Adderley departing and Coltrane's spot being taken first by Sonny Stitt then Hank Mobley. Although 1960-63 is thought of as a sort of resting period for Davis, his trumpet chops were in prime form and he was playing at the peak of his powers. With the departure of the rhythm section in 1963, it was time for Miles to form another group. By 1964 he had a brilliant young rhythm section (Herbie Hancock, Ron Carter and Tony Williams) who were open to the innovations of Ornette Coleman in addition to funky soul-jazz. With George Coleman on tenor, the sidemen really inspired Davis and, although he was sticking to his standard repertoire, the renditions were full of surprises and adventurous playing. By late 1964, Coleman had departed and, after Sam Rivers filled in for a European tour, Wayne Shorter was the new tenor. During 1965-68, Miles Davis' second classic quintet bridged the gap between hard bop and free jazz, playing inside/outside music that was quite unique. Although at the time the quintet was overshadowed by the avant-garde players, in the 1980s the music of this group would finally become very influential, particularly on Wynton and Branford Marsalis.

During 1968-69, Miles Davis' music continued to change. He persuaded Hancock to use electric keyboards, Shorter started doubling on soprano, the influence of rock began to be felt and, after the rhythm section changed (to Chick Corea,

Dave Holland and Jack DeJohnette), Davis headed one of the earliest fusion bands. Rock and funk rhythms combined with jazz improvisations to form a new hybrid music and Miles' recordings of *In a Silent Way* and *Bitches Brew* (both of which used additional instruments) essentially launched the fusion era.

Many of Miles Davis' fans essentially write off his post-1968 music, not realizing that not all of the recordings sound the same and that some were more successful than others. If Miles Davis had sold out so as to gain a larger audience, than why did he record so many 20-minute jams that could not possibly be played on the radio? During 1970-75, the ensembles of his group (which sometimes utilized two or three guitars and a couple of keyboardists) became quite dense, the rhythms were often intense, and Davis unfortunately often used electronics that distorted the sound of his horn. Actually the only album from this era that is a complete failure is *On the Corner* (which is largely absent from that fiasco) and *Live/Evil, Jack Johnson* and 1975's *Panagea* all have memorable sections.

And then suddenly, in 1975, Miles Davis retired. He was in bad health and, as he frankly discusses in his autobiography *Miles*, very much into recreational drugs. The jazz world speculated about what would happen if and when he returned. In 1981 Davis came back with a new band that was similar to his '70s group except that the ensembles were quite a bit sparser. The rock influence was soon replaced by funk and pop elements and, as he became stronger, Miles Davis' trumpet playing proved to still be in excellent form. He toured constantly during his last decade and his personality seemed to have mellowed a bit. Where once he had been quite forbidding and reluctant to be friendly to nonmusicians, Davis was at times eager to grant interviews and talk about his past. Although he had never looked back musically, in the summer of 1991 he shocked everyone by letting Quincy Jones talk him into performing Gil Evans arrangements from the past at the Montreux Jazz Festival. Even if he had Wallace Roney and Kenny Garrett take some of the solos, Davis was in stronger-than-expected form playing the old classics. And then two months later he passed away at the age of 65.

There are currently over 120 valuable Miles Davis recordings in print including many live sets issued on European labels. Taken as a whole, these form quite a legacy. —*Scott Yanow*

First Miles / Apr. 24, 1945+Aug. 14, 1947 / Savoy ✦✦
This unusual set includes Davis' first recording session and his initial date as a leader. The former is more historical than musical: four blues featuring singer Rubberlegs Williams, Herbie Fields' tenor and the noticeably nervous 18-year-old trumpeter who is actually only heard in ensembles. The latter recording finds him much more confident in 1947, heading the Charlie Parker Quintet (with Bird switching to tenor) on "Milestones," "Little Willie Leaps," "Half Nelson" and "Sippin' at Bells"; All of the alternate takes (both complete and partial) are included from both sessions. Since the later date has also been reissued on various Charlie Parker collections, this set is more for completists than for general listeners. —*Scott Yanow*

Bopping the Blues / Oct. 18, 1946 / Black Lion ✦✦✦
When this CD was initially released, it had quite a few jazz collectors scratching their heads wondering why they had never heard of it. Previously unissued, these formerly unknown performances (just four songs with eight alternate takes) feature the vocals of Earl Coleman and Ann Baker in 1946 but the backup group is of great interest for it includes trumpeter Miles Davis and tenor saxophonist Gene Ammons. It's not essential music but bop collectors will still want to pick it up. —*Scott Yanow*

Pre Birth of the Cool '49 / Sep. 4, 1948 / Jazz Live ✦✦✦✦
This Italian LP featured the first release of these two important broadcasts, although this music has since been reissued on CD. Miles Davis' *Birth of the Cool* nonet recorded a dozen influential performances during 1949-50 but only actually appeared in public for one gig: a two-week stint in 1948 as the intermission band at the Royal Roost for Count Basie's Orchestra. This set features nine performances taken from radio broadcasts and are near-classic. This version of the nonet features Davis, baritonist Gerry Mulligan, altoist Lee Konitz, pianist John Lewis and drummer Max Roach, in addition to French horn, tuba, trombone and bass. Other than getting to hear "new" and extended versions of some of the Nonet's studio sides, this set offers otherwise unrecorded arrangements of "Why Do I Love You?" and "S'il Vous Plait." —*Scott Yanow*

Quintet With Lee Konitz; Sextet With Jackie McLean / Sep. 25, 1948-May 3, 1952 / Fresh Sound ✦✦✦
This imported CD from Spain features Miles Davis during a 1948 broadcast from the Royal Roost and on a pair of 1952 radio airchecks from Birdland. The former set matches the trumpeter with altoist Lee Konitz, pianist John Lewis, bassist Curly Russell and drummer Max Roach. A week earlier, the five had been joined by four other musicians during the only live broadcast by Davis' *Birth of the Cool* Nonet. Their quintet outing is a bit more conventional, although Konitz's tone (which blends perfectly with Miles') is unique; Poncho Hagood takes the vocal on "You Go to My Head." The remainder of the disc features Davis, altoist Jackie McLean, pia-

nist Gil Coggins, bassist Connie Henry, drummer Connie Kay and Don Elliot on vibes and mellophone in a more jam session-flavored program. The sound quality is listenable if not state-of-the-art but Miles Davis collectors will want this rare material. —*Scott Yanow*

★ **Birth of the Cool** / Jan. 21, 1949-Mar. 9, 1950 / Capitol ✦✦✦✦✦
This CD contains all 12 of the recordings by Miles Davis' highly influential *Birth of the Cool* nonet. Emphasizing arrangements and softer tones than bebop, this music led the way for West Coast jazz of the 1950s. With arrangements by Gil Evans, Gerry Mulligan, John Lewis, Johnny Carisi and Davis, and concise solos from Davis, altoist Lee Konitz, baritonist Mulligan and either J.J. Johnson or Kai Winding on trombones, this music still sounds fresh and exciting today. —*Scott Yanow*

☆ **The Blue Note and Capitol Recordings** / Jan. 21, 1949-Mar. 9, 1958 / Capitol ✦✦✦✦✦
This four-CD set is actually just a repackaging of four CDs that are available separately: the classic *Birth of the Cool* sessions, Cannonball Adderley's 1958 date with Miles Davis as a sideman (*Somethin' Else,*) *Volume One* and *Volume Two.* The latter two sets feature three often-overlooked sessions from 1952-54 that actually are among the earliest hard bop recordings, starring Davis, trombonist J.J. Johnson, tenorman Jimmy Heath, altoist Jackie McLean, pianist Horace Silver and drummer Art Blakey, among others. All of this music was quite influential and is essential (in one form or another) to all jazz libraries. —*Scott Yanow*

The Paris Festival International / May 8, 1949-May 11, 1949 / Columbia ✦✦✦✦✦
Miles Davis was best-known during the late '40s for offering an alternative approach to trumpeters Dizzy Gillespie and Fats Navarro, emphasizing his middle register, a softer tone and a more thoughtful approach. This concert performance, which was not released until nearly three decades later, shows that Davis was just as capable of playing hard-driving bebop as most of his contemporaries. In a quintet with tenor saxophonist James Moody and pianist-composer Tadd Dameron, Davis confounded the French audience by playing very impressive high notes and displaying an extroverted personality. Never content to merely satisfy the expectations of his fans, he was already moving in surprising directions. This LP also gives one a very rare opportunity to hear Miles Davis verbally introducing songs in a voice not yet scarred. —*Scott Yanow*

Birdland Days / Feb. 18, 1950-Sep. 29, 1951 / Fresh Sound ✦✦✦
This CD from the Spanish Fresh Sound label consists of three broadcasts originating from Birdland during 1950-51 that feature the early Miles Davis with such notable players as trombonist J.J. Johnson, tenors Stan Getz, Sonny Rollins, Eddie "Lockjaw" Davis and Big Nick Nicholas, pianists Tadd Dameron, Kenny Drew and Billy Taylor; bassists Gene Ramey, Tommy Potter and Charlie Mingus; and drummer Art Blakey. The repertoire is filled with bop classics and, although the recording quality is sometimes a little erratic, the enthusiastic solos from these young players (most of whom were still in their 20s) makes this set both historic and enjoyable. —*Scott Yanow*

Ballads and Blues / Mar. 9, 1950-Mar. 9, 1958 / Blue Note ✦✦✦✦
What a treat! An incredible compilation for those Davis fans who love his cooler bluesy/modal material. The brilliant producer Michael Cuscuna has combed through the early Davis "Birth of the Cool" sessions (1950), several Blue Note sessions in 1952 and 1954, plus one cut from the classic Adderley/Davis album *Somethin' Else* to create a cool blues compilation of Davis' stuff stripped of all the bop up-tempo elements. The result is a precursor to *Kind of Blue*, an album that shows all of the bluesy cool Miles Davis that many of us are so very fond of. Don't miss it. —*Michael Erlewine*

And Horns / Jan. 17, 1951+Feb. 19, 1953 / Original Jazz Classics ✦✦✦
The music from two of Miles Davis' lesser-known Prestige sessions is reissued on this CD. There are four titles from a 1953 date that finds the great trumpeter playing arrangements by Al Cohn in a sextet with tenors Cohn and Zoot Sims; trombonist Sonny Truitt joins the group on "Floppy." Those obscure performances (which include "Tasty Pudding" and "For Adults Only") are joined by four songs plus an alternate take from a 1951 date featuring Miles with tenor saxophonist Sonny Rollins (their first recordings together) and trombonist Bennie Green. Davis is a bit subpar on such tunes as "Whispering" and "Blue Room" but his emotional playing is still worth hearing. —*Scott Yanow*

☆ **Chronicle: The Complete Prestige Recordings (1951-1956)** / Jan. 17, 1951-Oct. 26, 1956 / Prestige ✦✦✦✦✦
This eight-CD set does indeed have all 17 of trumpeter Miles Davis' Prestige sessions. The music is also available in separate CDs in the Original Jazz Classics series. Most significant are the many performances by Davis' classic quintet of 1955-56 with tenor saxophonist John Coltrane, pianist Red Garland, bassist Paul Chambers and drummer Philly Joe Jones but there are also dates featuring Sonny Rollins, Charlie Parker (on tenor), Thelonious Monk, Milt Jackson, Jackie McLean, Lee Konitz, Lucky Thompson and J.J. Johnson among others. Much of this music is

classic and dates from the period when Miles Davis was really beginning to emerge as an innovator. —*Scott Yanow*

Dig / Oct. 5, 1951 / Original Jazz Classics ✦✦✦
Although his lifestyle was erratic during this period, trumpeter Miles Davis is in fine form for a sextet outing with two of the top young saxophonists of the early '50s: Sonny Rollins and Jackie McLean. Pianist Walter Bishop, bassist Tommy Potter (Charles Mingus takes his place on "Conception") and drummer Art Blakey complete the impressive group that is heard on the OJC CD reissue. In addition to two standards ("My Old Flame" and "It's Only a Paper Moon"), there are four obscure originals and McLean's "Dig" (based on "Sweet Georgia Brown"). Excellent early hard bop. —*Scott Yanow*

Collector's Items / Oct. 5, 1951-Mar. 16, 1956 / Original Jazz Classics ✦✦✦✦✦
This two-LP set lives up to its title by including such interesting sessions as the 1953 date on which Miles Davis welcomed the two tenors of Sonny Rollins and Charlie Parker other meetings with Rollins in 1951 and 1956 and a moody 1955 date with bassist Charles Mingus, trombone, vibes and drums (a young Elvin Jones). Highlights include "No Line," "Vierd Blues," "In Your Own Sweet Way," "Nature Boy" and "There's No You." It's classic if often overlooked music from a variety of immortal jazzmen. —*Scott Yanow*

Miles Davis, Vol. 1 / May 9, 1952-Mar. 6, 1954 / Blue Note ✦✦✦✦
Miles Davis' recordings of 1951-54 tend to be overlooked because of his erratic lifestyle of the period and because they predated his first classic quintet. Although he rarely recorded during this era, what he did document was often quite classic. The two sessions included on this CD (which includes three alternate takes) are among the earliest hard bop recordings and would indirectly influence the modern mainstream music of the 1960s. The first session features Davis in a sextet with trombonist J.J. Johnson, altoist Jackie McLean, pianist Gil Coggins, bassist Oscar Pettiford and drummer Kenny Clarke; highlights include "Dear Old Stockholm," "Woody 'n You " and interpretations of "Yesterdays" and "How Deep Is the Ocean." The remaining six numbers showcase Davis in a quartet with pianist Horace Silver, bassist Percy Heath and drummer Art Blakey, really stretching out on such numbers as "Take Off" and "Well You Needn't." However, on "It Never Entered My Mind," Davis' muted statement (his only one on this set) looks towards his treatments of ballads later in the decade. —*Scott Yanow*

Live at the Barrel / 1952 / Prestige ✦✦
In 1952 during his "off period," Miles Davis sat in with tenor saxophonist Jimmy Forrest's quintet at a club in his hometown of St. Louis. Because the recording quality is not the best and Davis recorded many more significant sessions through the years, this CD only gets an "OK" rating, but collectors may want to acquire it anyway. Included are performances of bop standards including Dizzy Gillespie's "A Night in Tunisia." —*Scott Yanow*

Live at the Barrel, Vol. 2 / 1952 / Prestige ✦✦
Davis' scuffling lifestyle in the early '50s resulted in many low-profile gigs in lowly nightclubs. In 1952 he passed through his hometown St. Louis and sat in with the popular tenor Jimmy Forrest. Three decades later, Prestige released two LPs from this forgotten engagement. The recording quality is low-fi and the performances are competent but hardly memorable. Still, completists will probably want to get this second volume, which has performances of five standards, two of them Tadd Dameron compositions. —*Scott Yanow*

Miles Davis, Vol. 2 / Apr. 20, 1953 / Blue Note ✦✦✦✦
This CD contains all of the music recorded by a particularly strong sextet in 1953, six selections and five alternate takes. With trumpeter Miles Davis, trombonist J.J. Johnson, tenor saxophonist Jimmy Heath, pianist Gil Coggins, bassist Percy Heath and drummer Art Blakey all in fine form, "Tempus Fugit" and "C.T.A." receive definitive treatment along with two Johnson compositions. —*Scott Yanow*

Miles Tones / May 16, 1953-May 17, 1958 / Jazz Tones ✦✦✦
Quite a few albums have been released of Miles Davis live performances from the 1950s, many of them in the bootleg category. This particular LP is of strong interest for, in addition to a forgettable 1953 version of "I Got Rhythm" that is dominated by the scatting of Joe Carroll, there are three tracks with Davis' otherwise undocumented quintet of 1957 (featuring the great tenor of Sonny Rollins) and three numbers by the 1958 quintet with John Coltrane, Bill Evans, Paul Chambers and Philly Joe Jones. Not as essential as his studio albums, this LP still has more than its share of strong moments. —*Scott Yanow*

Blue Haze / May 19, 1953-Apr. 3, 1954 / Original Jazz Classics ✦✦✦✦
This CD reissue features trumpeter Miles Davis with three different pick-up recording groups that are full of fellow all-stars. "Tune Up," "Miles Ahead," "When Lights Are Low" (which uses slightly different chord changes than its composer Benny Carter originally intended) and "Smooch" find Davis joined by pianist John Lewis (Charles Mingus plays piano on "Smooch"), bassist Percy Heath and drummer Max

Roach. With pianist Horace Silver, bassist Heath and drummer Art Blakey offering solid accompaniment, Davis introduces "Four" and performs "Old Devil Moon" and "Blue Haze." Finally, with altoist Dave Schildkraut, Silver, Heath and drummer Kenny Clarke, Miles jams through "I'll Remember April." Although not as essential as the trumpeter's classic quintet records of 1955-56, several of the performances (most notably "Tune Up" and "Four") are quite memorable and the straightahead playing is of consistently high quality. —*Scott Yanow*

At Last / Sep. 13, 1953 / Original Jazz Classics ✦✦
This set has odds and ends recorded at the Lighthouse on a Sunday when Miles Davis was in town. He jams with the regular sextet (which included trumpeter Rolf Ericson, altoist Bud Shank, Bob Cooper on tenor and drummer Max Roach) on two numbers and has "'Round Midnight" as his feature. Max Roach takes "Drum Conversation" unaccompanied and trumpeter Chet Baker plays "At Last" with pianist Russ Freeman. The recording quality is merely decent but the viable and occasionally exciting historical music makes this a set worth picking up. —*Scott Yanow*

☆ **Bags Groove** / 1954 / Original Jazz Classics ✦✦✦✦✦
Sterling sessions with Miles and Monk (p), Milt Jackson (vib), Sonny Rollins (ts), and Horace Silver (p). —*Ron Wynn*

Walkin' / 1954 / Original Jazz Classics ✦✦✦✦✦
In 1954 Miles Davis was on the verge of making a comeback. Somewhat obscure during 1951-53 due to his erratic lifestyle and low-profile gigs, Davis at 28 was entering his creative prime. On April 3 of that year he recorded three fine numbers (including his "Solar") in a quintet with the forgotten altoist Dave Schildkraut and pianist Horace Silver, but the real reasons to acquire this set are for the exciting versions of "Walkin'" and "Blue 'n' Boogie" performed by Davis, Silver, trombonist J.J. Johnson and tenor saxophonist Lucky Thompson. —*Scott Yanow*

☆ **Miles Davis & the Modern Jazz Giants** / Dec. 24, 1954 / Original Jazz Classics ✦✦✦✦✦
This CD (which contains almost 58 minutes of music) has the complete session of Dec. 24, 1954, the classic date that matched together trumpeter Miles Davis, vibraphonist Milt Jackson, pianist Thelonious Monk, bassist Percy Heath and drummer Kenny Clarke. Davis and Monk actually did not get along all that well and the trumpeter did not want Monk playing behind his solos, but a great deal of brilliant music occurred on the day of their encounter. There are two very different versions apiece of "Bags' Groove" (Monk's solo on the first take was one of his best) and "The Man I Love" along with single performances of "Bemsha Swing" and "Swing Spring"; the shortest selection is eight minutes long. Timeless music that defies easy classification, this set belongs in every jazz collection. —*Scott Yanow*

The Musings of Miles / Jun. 7, 1955 / Original Jazz Classics ✦✦✦
Miles Davis was in the process of forming his first classic quintet when he recorded this date, a Prestige set reissued by the audiophile label DCC Compact Classics. The trumpeter is featured on a quartet outing with pianist Red Garland, bassist Oscar Pettiford and drummer Philly Joe Jones, playing four standards plus a blues ("Green Haze") and "I Didn't," his answer to Thelonious Monk's "Well You Needn't." Garland and Jones would soon be in Miles' group, although the fiery Pettiford proved too difficult for the trumpeter to handle and was quickly succeeded by Paul Chambers. The interpretations are generally lyrical and melodic; even "A Night in Tunisia" sounds a bit mellow. Likable if not essential music. —*Scott Yanow*

Odyssey / Aug. 5, 1955 / Prestige ✦✦✦
One of the most obscure of his Prestige recordings, this CD only contains a half-hour of music but the quality is fairly high. Davis is heard outside of his regular group, playing with vibraphonist Milt Jackson, pianist Ray Bryant (who was left out of the personnel listing), bassist Percy Heath, drummer Art Taylor and, on two of the four numbers, altoist Jackie McLean. This set (formerly known as *Miles Davis and Milt Jackson*) is highlighted by "Dr. Jackle" and "Minor March." —*Scott Yanow*

☆ **Miscellaneous Miles Davis 1955-1957** / Jul. 17, 1955-Dec. 18, 1957 / Jazz Unlimited ✦✦✦✦✦
One of the great legendary moments took place during the 1955 Newport Jazz Festival (the very first) when Miles Davis unexpectedly sat in on a jam session and (with Thelonious Monk playing behind him) constructed a brilliant solo on "'Round Midnight." Davis had been in danger of being forgotten but that moment, which took place before many of the top jazz critics, was a minor sensation and gave momentum to his career. Now for the first time the performance (which also includes versions of "Hackensack" and "Now's the Time" with a sextet featuring baritonist Gerry Mulligan and Zoot Sims on tenor) has been made available, and it lives up to its legendary status. Also on this essential CD are three numbers on which Miles plays with the Rene Urtreger Trio (the great Lester Young sits in on "Lady Be Good"), two songs with his 1957 quintet with Bobby Jaspar on tenor and three tunes in which Davis is backed by a European orchestra. This Danish import is highly recommended. —*Scott Yanow*

★ **Round About Midnight** / Oct. 27, 1955-Sep. 10, 1956 / Columbia ✦✦✦✦✦

Davis' first Columbia album is a classic. His quintet (with tenor saxophonist John Coltrane, pianist Red Garland, bassist Paul Chambers and drummer Philly Joe Jones) was quickly becoming one of the pacesetters in jazz, and each of these six performances are memorable. In addition to the definitive non-Monk rendition of "'Round Midnight," one hears the quintet making such diverse songs as "Ah-Leu-Cha," Cole Porter's "All of You," "Tadd's Delight" and "Dear Old Stockholm" sound as if they were all written for the group. Their version of "Bye Bye Blackbird" is the ultimate in cool sophistication. —*Scott Yanow*

☆ **Miles & Coltrane** / Oct. 27, 1955-Jul. 4, 1958 / Columbia ✦✦✦✦✦

In addition to two selections ("Little Melonae" and "Budo") from his first session for Columbia, this CD contains his complete performance at the 1958 Newport Jazz Festival. When one considers that Davis' sextet at the time included such giants as tenor saxophonist John Coltrane, altoist Cannonball Adderley, pianist Bill Evans, bassist Paul Chambers and drummer Jimmy Cobb, it is not surprising that fireworks resulted. Still, the power and drive of this intense version of "Ah-Leu-Cha" is a revelation and the band really swings and stretches out on "Straight, No Chaser," "Fran Dance," "Two Bass Hit" and "Bye Bye Blackbird." —*Scott Yanow*

Facets / Oct. 27, 1955-Aug. 23, 1962 / Columbia ✦✦✦

This LP is an interesting hodgepodge of Miles Davis recordings. Davis is heard with his classic 1955-56 quintet playing "Sweet Sue" and "Budo," with large orchestras performing "Jazz Suite for Brass" and "Three Little Feelings" (early third-stream works that put the spotlight totally on Davis' fluegelhorn), on a couple of odd tracks from 1962 with vocalist Bob Dorough ("Devil May Care" and "Blue Xmas") and, most significantly, on four numbers arranged by Michel Legrand for an 11-piece group in 1958 that also feature altoist Phil Woods, John Coltrane and pianist Bill Evans. Worth searching for, this set will fill gaps in many collections. —*Scott Yanow*

Circle in the Round / Oct. 27, 1955-Jan. 27, 1970 / Columbia ✦✦✦

This two-CD set is highly recommended to collectors for it contains many interesting performances, all but one of which were previously unissued at the time of this two-fer's release. Spanning 15 years, this program includes a 1955 version of "Two Bass Hit" from Davis' first classic quintet, an extended version of "Love for Sale" by his 1958 sextet, a reunion between Miles and drummer Philly Joe Jones in 1961, the side long "Circle in the Round" from Davis' 1967 quintet (with guest guitarist Joe Beck), a few unfinished works from his transitional 1968 band and a lengthy workout by Davis' fusion group in early 1970. There are lots of unusual performances on this worthy collection. —*Scott Yanow*

☆ **Cookin'** / Nov. 16, 1955-Oct. 26, 1956 / Original Jazz Classics ✦✦✦✦✦

Trumpeter Miles Davis (along with tenor saxophonist John Coltrane, pianist Red Garland, bassist Paul Chambers and drummer Philly Joe Jones) are heard on this CD reissue performing such tunes as "My Funnny Valentine" (Davis' earliest version of this standard), "Blues by Five," "Airegin" and a medley of "Tune Up" and "When Lights Are Low." Both the quintet and the music qualify as classic; all four of their Prestige albums are easily recommended. —*Scott Yanow*

☆ **Workin'** / May 11, 1956-Oct. 26, 1956 / Original Jazz Classics ✦✦✦✦✦

Miles Davis' 1956 Quintet was one of his classic groups, featuring tenor saxophonist John Coltrane, pianist Red Garland, bassist Paul Chambers and drummer Philly Joe Jones. They recorded four albums for Prestige in two marathon sessions. Among the highlights are "It Never Entered My Mind," "Four," "In Your Own Sweet Way" and two versions of "The Theme." The music is essential in one form or another. —*Scott Yanow*

☆ **Relaxin'** / May 11, 1956-Oct. 26, 1956 / Original Jazz Classics ✦✦✦✦✦

One of the strongest of Miles Davis' recordings with his first classic quintet (a group also including the young tenor saxophonist John Coltrane, pianist Red Garland, bassist Paul Chambers and drummer Philly Joe Jones), this CD reissue is highlighted by "If I Were a Bell," "I Could Write a Book" and Sonny Rollins' "Oleo." Actually all six selections are quite rewarding and helped set the standard for bands of the era. —*Scott Yanow*

☆ **Steamin'** / May 11, 1956-Oct. 26, 1956 / Original Jazz Classics ✦✦✦✦✦

This classic Prestige session (one of four cut for the label by Davis' first permanent group) has been reissued many times. Davis is heard with his classic quintet of 1956 (which featured tenor saxophonist John Coltrane, pianist Red Garland, bassist Paul Chambers and drummer Philly Joe Jones) performing six numbers, all of which are somewhat memorable. High points are "Surrey with the Fringe on Top," "Diane" and "When I Fall in Love;" Davis' muted tone rarely sounded more beautiful. —*Scott Yanow*

Miles Davis / May 11, 1956-Oct. 26, 1956 / Prestige ✦✦✦✦

This two-LP set (which launched Prestige's very valuable reissue series of two-fers) features the two albums originally known as *Cookin'* and *Relaxin'.* With John Coltrane on tenor, pianist Red Garland, bassist Paul Chambers and drummer Philly

Joe Jones, Davis was in fine form for these runthroughs on the Quintet's usual club repertoire. Most of the music is medium-tempo with the high points including "My Funny Valentine," "If I Were a Bell," "I Could Write a Book" and "Oleo." —*Scott Yanow*

The Miles Davis: The Columbia Years 1955-1985 / Jun. 5, 1956-Feb. 27, 1985 / Columbia ✦✦✦

This was the first real attempt by Columbia to make any comprehensive sense of Miles Davis' colossal output for the label. And it was a tall order; to summarize everything that Miles achieved over the three-decade span on four CDs or five LPs is virtually impossible. This set, then, was bound to be controversial no matter how it turned out, but even so, Columbia could have done better with a strictly chronological approach. Instead, producer/compiler Jeff Rosen had the cockeyed notion of organizing each of the original five LPs around a single theme. Disc 1 was called *Blues,* disc 2 was devoted to *Standards,* disc 3 had Miles *Originals,* disc 4 was something vaguely entitled *Moods* and all of the electric recordings were segregated on disc 5 (the CDs naturally screw up the "logic" with overlaps). Thus, the first four sections jam together all kinds of unrelated sessions from different eras and the listener never gets any idea of how Miles' music evolved and changed over the years. Also, Rosen made dishearteningly little use of Columbia's vast trunk of unreleased Miles. There are only four outtakes, three of which are gratuitous alternate takes of "Someday My Prince Will Come," "Pinocchio," and "Flamenco Sketches" and the fourth is a live "I Thought About You" from Antibes. But now that Columbia/Legacy's impressive emerging series of Miles boxed sets is setting things right, *The Columbia Years* remains useful as a casual collage—the only way, actually, to acquire a bop-to-rock, fairly representative selection of Miles from those decades in one package. Also, one must admit that the electric section, despite the chronological chaos, is put together very cleverly, opening with precisely the hottest stretch of music from *Live-Evil* (the opening three minutes of "Sivad") and closing with the long, swaggering "Miles Runs the Voodoo Down" from *Bitches Brew.* Nat Hentoff's biographical essay makes good reading—and of course, along the way you'll hear some of the greatest music of the twentieth century. —*Richard S. Ginell*

Miles Davis/Stan Getz: Tune Up / Nov. 12, 1956-Jul. 1961 / Natasha ✦✦✦

Miles Davis and Stan Getz do not actually play together on this CD but Davis does perform with Lester Young and the Modern Jazz Quartet on two songs recorded in Germany in 1956; a big band "sits in" one of those numbers. Prez sounds a bit weak but blends well. Davis also plays two short songs with a fine French rhythm section. Stan Getz's three performances are taken from the 1961 Newport Jazz Festival and find him stretching out with his fine trio (pianist Steve Kuhn, bassist Scott LaFaro and drummer Roy Haynes). Overall, this historical music, although not essential, is enjoyable. —*Scott Yanow*

★ **Miles Ahead** / May 6, 1957-May 27, 1957 / Columbia ✦✦✦✦✦

Miles Davis' first collaboration with arranger Gil Evans since *The Birth of the Cool* recordings of 1949-50 resulted in this classic album. Reissued three times on CD (the first one, which substituted alternate takes in places, was a disaster), the third version (which came out in 1997) augments the original ten selections with four excellent and complete alternates. An advantage that this CD reissue has over the LP is that, since the music was recorded as a continuous suite, there is no break between the fifth and sixth songs. Davis' trumpet (backed by Evans' 19-piece orchestra) is heard at its best on such classics as "The Duke," "My Ship," "Miles Ahead," "Blues for Pablo" and "I Don't Wanna Be Kissed." Highly recommended for all collections. —*Scott Yanow*

☆ **Miles Davis & Gil Evans: The Complete Columbia Studio Recordings** / May 6, 1957-Feb. 16, 1968 / Sony ✦✦✦✦✦

Over the course of six compact discs, *Miles Davis & Gil Evans: The Complete Columbia Studio Recordings* collects every bit of music the legendary duo recorded together between the years 1957 and 1968. Each of the original albums—*Miles Ahead, Porgy and Bess, Sketches of Spain,* and *Quiet Nights*—are presented in their original running order on separate discs; each individual disc is augmented with revealing alternate takes and rarities, like the duo's long-unavailable music for "The Time of the Barracudas" at the end of the *Quiet Nights* disc. The remaining two discs are filled with alternate takes, rehearsals, overdubbed solos, studio chatter, and outtakes. All of the music sounds splendid and often revelatory—for instance, in addition to being released in stereo for the first time ever, *Miles Ahead* is presented in its original version for the first time on compact disc. Each disc is enclosed in a sleeve that replicates the original album release (both covers of *Miles Ahead* are included within the set) and housed in the immense, detailed, gold-bound 197-page book. In fact, if there is any fault with the set it is this—the sleeves are bound within the set itself, making it very hard to admire the artwork, see the individual track listings, or read the liner notes. Since the notes and discs are bound together within one thick book, *Miles Davis & Gil Evans: The Complete Columbia Studio Recordings* feels like a library piece instead of a functional, listenable retrospective—it takes effort to listen to individual discs, and the more that you listen to it, the weaker the binding on the book gets. This is vital music that will be accessed often by anyone willing to invest in the set, so the box set should have been designed with that in mind. Nevertheless, *Miles Davis & Gil Evans: The Complete Columbia Studio Recordings* is filled with so much visionary and beautiful music, it makes the slight flaws in packaging forgivable. —*Stephen Thomas Erlewine*

Ascenseur Pour L'Echafaud / Dec. 4, 1957 / Fontana ◆◆◆
In 1957, Miles Davis went to France for a short tour and while there he recorded the soundtrack for the film *Ascenseur Pour L'Echafaud*. This CD contains the original LP of material plus 19 minutes of unreleased alternate versions. Better than many soundtracks, this music (which also features the tenor of Barney Wilen and pianist Rene Urtreger) does not really stand on its own without the film, so it's of mostly historical interest. —*Scott Yanow*

The Complete Amsterdam Concert / Dec. 8, 1957 / Celluloid ◆◆◆
This two-LP set is a real rarity, a performance by trumpeter Miles Davis while he was in Europe in late 1957. Joined by drummer Kenny Clarke and three excellent French players (tenor saxophonist Barney Wilen, pianist Rene Urtreger and bassist Pierre Michelot), the same unit with which Davis recorded a French soundtrack during this period, the quintet jams through ten songs from Davis' repertoire. Although all of this music (around 56 minutes worth) could have been put on one rather than two LPs, this hard-to-find set is recommended for the rare opportunity to hear Miles Davis stretching out with these musicians. —*Scott Yanow*

☆ **Milestones** / Apr. 2, 1958-Apr. 3, 1958 / Columbia ◆◆◆◆◆
Kind of Blue might have received most of the acclaim but *Milestones*, the recorded debut of the Miles Davis Sextet, is in the same league. This remarkable super group (featuring Davis' trumpet, tenor saxophonist John Coltrane, altoist Cannonball Adderley, pianist Red Garland, bassist Paul Chambers and drummer Philly Joe Jones) was arguably the greatest one Miles Davis ever led. "Two Bass Hit" features the two saxes trading off with fire and "Billy Boy" showcases the Red Garland trio (showing what they learned from Ahmad Jamal), but "Straight, No Chaser" really demonstrates what a powerhouse band this was. —*Scott Yanow*

58 Sessions Feat. Stella by Starlight / May 26, 1958-Jul. 28, 1958 / Columbia ◆◆◆◆
Miles Davis had quite an all-star group in 1958: Tenor saxophonist John Coltrane, altoist Cannonball Adderley, pianist Bill Evans, bassist Paul Chambers and drummer Jimmy Cobb (who had recently replaced Philly Joe Jones). This frequently exciting CD has three of the four performances originally on an LP titled *Jazz at the Plaza* ("Straight, No Chaser," "My Funny Valentine," and "Oleo"), a lengthy "Love for Sale" that was unreleased until the 1970s and three other songs ("On Green Dolphin Street," "Fran Dance" and "Stella by Starlight") most notable for the lyricism of Davis and Evans. —*Scott Yanow*

At Newport / May 26, 1958-Apr. 15, 1961 / Columbia ◆◆◆◆
This French Columbia LP features the Sextet (with John Coltrane and Cannonball Adderley) at the 1958 Newport Jazz Festival; their rapid version of "Ah Leu Cha" is thunderous and "Straight, No Chaser" swings like mad. This set also includes three laidback selections ("On Green Dolphin Street," "Fran Dance" and "Stella by Starlight") from a slightly earlier studio date along with a different version of "On Green Dolphin Street" from 1961. This classic music has since been reissued on CD. —*Scott Yanow*

★ **Porgy & Bess** / Jul. 22, 1958-Aug. 18, 1958 / Columbia ◆◆◆◆◆
The second of the three great Miles Davis-Gil Evans collaborations features the trumpeter backed by Evans' 18-piece orchestra on 13 selections from George Gershwin's *Porgy and Bess*. This version of "Summertime" (with Evans' countermelody) is definitive and the entire suite should be savored in one sitting. Other highlights include "Bess, You Is My Woman Now," "My Man's Gone Now" and "I Loves You Porgy." In 1997, this classic was reissued on CD and augmented by alternate versions of "I Loves You Porgy" and "Gone." A more expanded documentation is currently available on Columbia's complete Miles Davis/Gil Evans box. —*Scott Yanow*

Jazz at the Plaza, Vol. 1 / Jul. 28, 1958 / Columbia ◆◆◆◆
Recorded at a Columbia press party in 1958, this spontaneous LP features the Miles Davis Sextet that had the giant talents of John Coltrane, Cannonball Adderley and Bill Evans. Their performances of "Straight, No Chaser" (mistitled here "Jazz at the Plaza"), "My Funny Valentine" (Davis' feature), "If I Were a Bell" and "Oleo" are consistently exciting. Three of these selections (all but "If I Were a Bell") have since been reissued on CD. —*Scott Yanow*

All Stars / Jan. 3, 1959-Feb. 1959 / Jazz Band ◆◆◆
This LP contains two valuable radio broadcasts of the Miles Davis Sextet of early 1959, a unit that also featured John Coltrane, Cannonball Adderley and (if the personnel listing can be believed) pianist Red Garland. There are only five selections on this set ("All of Me" is actually "All of You") but any surviving recording by this

classic group (arguably the greatest band Miles Davis ever led) is well worth getting. —*Scott Yanow*

★ **Kind of Blue** / Mar. 2, 1959-Apr. 22, 1959 / Columbia ◆◆◆◆◆
Miles Davis' most famous recording remains his most influential. It is not just that this album helped popularize modal jazz (improvising based on modes or scales rather than running chord changes) or that it introduced two future standards ("So What" and "All Blues") and three other gems ("Freddie Freeloader," "Blue in Green" and "Flamenco Sketches"). Most impressive is how the solos of Miles Davis, John Coltrane and Cannonball Adderley (what a lineup), despite their differing styles, fit the songs perfectly. Bill Evans returned to the sextet for this date (Wynton Kelly plays piano on "Freddie Freeloader") while bassist Paul Chambers and drummer Jimmy Cobb are superb in support. The 1997 reissue has the music at last at the correct pitch and added an alternate take of "Flamenco Sketches" to the classic program. —*Scott Yanow*

☆ **Sketches of Spain** / Nov. 15, 1959-Mar. 10, 1960 / Columbia ◆◆◆◆◆
The third and final of the great Miles Davis-Gil Evans collaborations of 1957-59 was also their most ambitious. This set finds Davis in the forefront improvising on two numbers associated with Spanish music and three Evans compositions in that idiom. Much of the music is quite dramatic and emotional (notably "Saeta") and Davis plays at his best throughout, really stretching the boundaries of jazz. The 1997 CD reissue adds the brief "Song of Our Country" plus an alternate take of "Concierto De Aranjuez" to the original program. —*Scott Yanow*

Directions / Mar. 11, 1960-Feb. 27, 1970 / Columbia ◆◆◆
This double LP of leftover items not previously issued features Davis over a ten-year period. "Song of Our Country" is from the sessions that led to *Sketches of Spain* and there is a "new" version of "'Round Midnight" from 1961 along with "So Near, So Far" dating from 1963. Otherwise, the remainder of this two-fer is from the transitional 1967-70 period when Davis was experimenting with combining jazz and rock. Some of the selections ramble on a bit too long but the music is mostly quite fascinating, featuring such players as Wayne Shorter, Herbie Hancock, Joe Zawinul, Chick Corea and John McLaughlin. It's most highly recommended to collectors with an open ear towards fusion. —*Scott Yanow*

Live in Stockholm 1960 / Mar. 22, 1960 / Royal Jazz ◆◆◆◆
This remarkable two-CD set features John Coltrane with the Miles Davis Quintet just a short time before 'Trane went out on his own. Davis sounds inspired by his star tenor, and although Coltrane was reportedly bored with the repertoire ("On Green Dolphin Street," "All Blues," "Fran Dance," "Walkin'" and two versions of "So What"), he is at his most explorative throughout this often-stunning music. In addition, the rhythm section (pianist Wynton Kelly, bassist Paul Chambers and drummer Jimmy Cobb) had been together for two years and is really tight. This highly recommended set also includes a brief interview with Coltrane from this period. —*Scott Yanow*

Miles & Coltrane Quintet / Apr. 9, 1960 / Unique ◆◆◆
This LP from a collector's label features the last documented appearance of John Coltrane with the Miles Davis Quintet before he departed to lead his own group. The repertoire ("On Green Dolphin Street," "Walkin'," "Theme," "So What" and "'Round Midnight") offers no surprises but the soloing of Davis, Coltrane and pianist Wynton Kelly is consistently excellent and sometimes quite exciting. —*Scott Yanow*

Live in Europe / Oct. 6, 1960-Nov. 4, 1967 / Jazz ◆◆◆◆
This very interesting CD has two unusual live performances. Miles Davis' short-lived quintet with Sonny Stitt as John Coltrane's replacement (and the strong rhythm section of pianist Wynton Kelly, bassist Paul Chambers and drummer Jimmy Cobb) plays "All of You," but the bulk of this disc features his 1967 band (with Wayne Shorter, Herbie Hancock, Ron Carter and Tony Williams) performing a wandering but coherent 45-minute medley that hints at a variety of older tunes from Davis' repertoire. —*Scott Yanow*

Miles Davis & Sonny Stitt / Oct. 13, 1960 / Dragon ◆◆◆◆
When John Coltrane departed from the Miles Davis Quintet, it left a major gap that would not be fully filled for several years. Veteran Sonny Stitt was with the band for six months in 1960 but the association was totally unrecorded until this two-LP set came out. Stitt (who plays alto on nine of the 12 numbers and tenor on the remainder) sounded much more conventional than Coltrane did at the time, turning these standards into a bebop jam session. Davis and the great trio (pianist Wynton Kelly, bassist Paul Chambers and drummer Jimmy Cobb) along with Stitt are in fine form on the seven lengthy performances, all but one being over 11 minutes. —*Scott Yanow*

Someday My Prince Will Come / 1961 / Columbia ◆◆◆◆
Miles Davis' 1961 quintet was more relaxed and less adventurous than his earlier groups with John Coltrane. The trumpeter was at the peak of his powers in the early '60s and comfortable with his own playing. This CD, a straight reissue of the

earlier LP, features Davis, tenor saxophonist Hank Mobley, pianist Wynton Kelly, bassist Paul Chambers, either Jimmy Cobb or Philly Joe Jones on drums and, as a special bonus, guest appearances by John Coltrane (the last time he would record with Miles) on "Teo" and the title cut. —*Scott Yanow*

In Person: Friday Night at the Blackhawk / Apr. 21, 1961 / Columbia ✦✦✦✦
The first of two sets recorded during a weekend in 1961 features the Miles Davis Quintet at a period of time when Hank Mobley was on tenor and the rhythm section comprised pianist Wynton Kelly, bassist Paul Chambers and drummer Jimmy Cobb. Davis is in particularly strong form on "Walkin'," "Bye Bye Blackbird" and "No Blues" and Kelly proved to be the perfect pianist for this hard-driving and swinging set. —*Scott Yanow*

In Person: Saturday Night at the Blackhawk / Apr. 22, 1961 / Columbia ✦✦✦
The second of two sets documenting the Miles Davis Quintet in 1961 finds tenor saxophonist Hank Mobley being a minor character (although two of his solos are fully restored from the edited original issue) but the trumpeter/leader and pianist Wynton Kelly play many memorable solos on standards such as "Well You Needn't," "So What," "Oleo" and "If I Were a Bell." Both of these sets, although not innovative, are recommended as strong examples of Miles Davis' trumpet playing. —*Scott Yanow*

At Carnegie Hall / May 19, 1961 / Columbia ✦✦✦✦
For this concert, the Quintet (with tenor saxophonist Hank Mobley and pianist Wynton Kelly) are featured along with the Gil Evans Orchestra. The small group plays "So What," "Spring Is Here," "No Blues," "Oleo" and "Someday My Prince Will Come" before the 21-piece big band backs the trumpeter on three numbers originally recorded for the *Miles Ahead* album. Although nothing all that new occurs in these remakes, this retrospective of Davis' previous four years has fresh solos and enthusiastic performances. —*Scott Yanow*

Live Miles: More Music from the Legendary Carnegie Hall Concert / May 19, 1961 / Columbia ✦✦✦
This additional music from his Carnegie Hall concert of 1961 once again features the great trumpeter with the Gil Evans Orchestra (for a 16-minute version of "Concierto De Aranguez") and with his quintet of the period (with tenor saxophonist Hank Mobley and pianist Wynton Kelly) for three shorter numbers (the modal "Teo," "Walkin'" and "I Thought About You"). It's not essential but Miles Davis fans will enjoy these performances. —*Scott Yanow*

Miles in St. Louis / Jun. 24, 1961-Jun. ??, 1963 / VGM ✦✦✦
This collector's LP mostly features the 1963 Miles Davis Quintet (which included tenor saxophonist George Coleman, pianist Herbie Hancock, bassist Ron Carter and drummer Tony Williams) during a live appearance in St. Louis. The previously unissued music is reasonably well-recorded and gives listeners additional versions of such standards as "I Thought About You," "All Blues" and "Seven Steps to Heaven." This LP is rounded out by a rendition of "Like Someone to Love" from 1961 that showcases the young Herbie Hancock with a trio, two years before he first joined Davis' group. —*Scott Yanow*

Transition / 1961-1963 / Magnetic ✦✦✦
This is the type of CD that should greatly interest Miles Davis collectors, although those listeners just getting into his music of the 1960s are advised to acquire his Columbia studio discs first. This CD features Davis with two very different quintets in 1961 (a group with tenor saxophonist Hank Mobley, pianist Wynton Kelly, bassist Paul Chambers and drummer Jimmy Cobb) and 1963 (which included George Coleman on tenor, pianist Herbie Hancock, bassist Ron Carter and drummer Tony Williams). The earlier session is more relaxed and less adventurous, while the latter (which is highlighted by lengthy versions of "All Blues" and "Seven Steps to Heaven") finds Miles Davis challenged by his younger sidemen. —*Scott Yanow*

Quiet Nights / Jul. 27, 1962-Nov. 6, 1962 / Columbia ✦✦✦
Miles Davis' final official collaboration with arranger Gil Evans resulted in their weakest project. There were only 27 minutes of music on the original *Quiet Nights* LP, and six minutes were taken up by a quintet performance of "Summer Night." The six remaining tracks are enjoyable enough (highlighted by "Once Upon a Summertime" and "Corcovado"), but rather brief, making one wonder why Evans could not have been persuaded to write more material. The 1997 CD reissue adds "The Time of the Barracudas" (which clocks in at 12:45), which was not released until the 1996 *Complete Miles Davis/Gil Evans* box set. The latter is an interesting but not too substantial mini-suite written for a stage play that features the late-1963 Miles Davis Quintet joined by four brass, three woodwinds and a harp. Overall, this CD has its moments of interest, but it has an incomplete feel and is not too essential. —*Scott Yanow*

Sorcerer / Aug. 23, 1962-May 24, 1967 / Columbia ✦✦✦✦
This 1993 CD was a straight reissue of the original Miles Davis LP although with new liner notes. Davis' second classic quintet (which also includes tenor saxophonist Wayne Shorter, pianist Herbie Hancock, bassist Ron Carter and drummer Tony

Williams) performs four originals by Shorter, Hancock's title cut and Williams' "Pee Wee." The music is quite moody, takes unusual turns, and stands apart from both the jazz mainstream and the avant-garde of the period—intriguing performances by a unique band. This release is rounded off by a brief, out-of-place Bob Dorough vocal piece ("Nothing Like You") from 1962. —*Scott Yanow*

Seven Steps to Heaven / Apr. 16, 1963-May 14, 1963 / Columbia ✦✦✦✦✦
In 1963, Miles Davis was at a transitional point in his career, without a regular group and wondering what his future musical direction would be. At the time he recorded the music heard on this CD (a straight reissue of the earlier LP given new liner notes), he was in the process of forming a new band, as can be seen from the personnel: Tenor saxophonist George Coleman, Victor Feldman (who turned down the job) and Herbie Hancock on pianos, bassist Ron Carter, and Frank Butler and Tony Williams on drums. Recorded at two separate sessions, this set is highlighted by the classic "Seven Steps to Heaven," "Joshua" and slow passionate versions of "Basin Street Blues" and "Baby Won't You Please Come Home." —*Scott Yanow*

Cote Blues / Jul. 26, 1963 / Jazz Music Yesterday ✦✦✦✦
These five live versions of Davis classics ("All Blues," "Stella by Starlight," "Seven Steps to Heaven," "If I Were a Bell" and "So What") find Davis and his new quintet (with tenor saxophonist George Coleman, pianist Herbie Hancock, bassist Ron Carter and drummer Tony Williams) in superior form, stretching out with creative solos, particularly on the twenty-one-and-a-half-minute "Seven Steps." —*Scott Yanow*

Miles Davis in Europe / Jul. 27, 1963 / Columbia ✦✦✦✦
The official debut of his new Quintet features the brilliant trio of pianist Herbie Hancock, bassist Ron Carter and drummer Tony Williams along with the fine tenor saxophonist George Coleman and the 47-year-old trumpeter/leader. These lengthy versions of "Autumn Leaves," "Milestones," "Joshua," All of You" and a 16-minute "Walkin'" on this hour-long LP really show what this powerful band could do, even in their early days. —*Scott Yanow*

☆ **The Complete Concert: 1964 (My Funny Valentine & "Four More")** / Feb. 12, 1964 / Columbia ✦✦✦✦✦
This two-CD set, which completely reissues the two lengthy LPs *My Funny Valentine* (a set of lyrical ballads) and *Four & More* (which is filled with very rapid versions of Davis' standard repertoire), features the 1963-64 Quintet at its best. This particular unit consisted of the greatly underrated tenor saxophonist George Coleman and the young rhythm section of pianist Herbie Hancock, bassist Ron Carter and drummer Tony Williams. Since Davis' future studio albums with this group (after Wayne Shorter replaced Coleman) would be sticking exclusively to group originals, this exciting set gives one the opportunity to hear this band really stretching out on older tunes, showing off the influence of the avant-garde along with the players' own individual styles. It's highly recommended transitional music. —*Scott Yanow*

Miles in Tokyo / Jul. 14, 1964 / Columbia ✦✦✦✦
After George Coleman left the Miles Davis Quintet, tenor saxophonist Sam Rivers took his place for a short period including a tour of Japan. Davis did not care for Rivers' avant-garde style (they failed to develop any chemistry) and soon replaced him, but this live LP (originally only issued in Japan) survived to document this brief association. The music (five lengthy versions of standards) is actually of high quality with both Davis and Rivers in fine form and the young rhythm section (pianist Herbie Hancock, bassist Ron Carter and drummer Tony Williams) pushing the trumpeter/leader to open up his style. —*Scott Yanow*

Miles in Berlin / Sep. 25, 1964 / CBS/Sony ✦✦✦
Originally released only in Japan, this LP contains the earliest documentation of tenor saxophonist Wayne Shorter performing as a regular member of the Quintet. Unlike the band's upcoming studio albums, this set features lengthy versions of four standards ("Milestones," "Autumn Leaves," "So What" and "Walkin'") that had been in Davis' repertoire for at least five years, making for an interesting comparison between this group's treatments of the songs and their predecessors. The rhythm section in particular (pianist Herbie Hancock, bassist Ron Carter and drummer Tony Williams) really opens up this music, exploring fresh avenues in their improvisations. —*Scott Yanow*

Paris, France / Oct. 1, 1964 / Moon ✦✦✦
Wayne Shorter was still a new member of the Davis Quintet at the time of this concert recording. Although the group (which also includes pianist Herbie Hancock, bassist Ron Carter and drummer Tony Williams) would soon begin recording exclusively originals in the studios, their live performances would feature standards for several years to come. In addition to an unidentified "Miles Impro," the group performs such standbys as "Stella by Starlight," "Walkin'," "Autumn Leaves" and "So What" on this date. Recording quality is decent if not great but the improvisations by the fiery young group are excellent, extending the boundaries of bop.

This valuable music was released for the first time on this European CD. —*Scott Yanow*

Davisiana / Oct. 8, 1964 / Moon ✦✦✦

Recorded in Germany, this early document from his second classic quintet features Davis, Wayne Shorter, Herbie Hancock, Ron Carter and Tony Williams stretching the trumpeter's standard repertoire, playing four of his veteran songs ("Autumn Leaves," "Joshua," "So What" and "Milestones") as a pair of adventurous two-song medleys. His young sidemen were really pushing Davis and the result was very stimulating and unpredictable music. —*Scott Yanow*

Anthology / 1964 / Suisa ✦✦✦✦

A three-CD collection of live recordings drawn from 1964, 1967, 1969 and 1989 European shows. There are high points from start to finish, though the last disc, drawn from a 1989 show in Perugia, leaves one wishing that the producers had seen fit to add two or three more cuts to fill up the disc. Davis and his various bands are in fine form throughout, and the mastering, with the aid of the CEDAR system, is solid. —*Steven McDonald*

☆ **The Complete Live at the Plugged Nickel** / Dec. 22, 1965-Dec. 23, 1965 / Columbia ✦✦✦✦✦

All of the music that trumpeter Miles Davis and his second classic quintet (with tenor saxophonist Wayne Shorter, pianist Herbie Hancock, bassist Ron Carter and drummer Tony Williams) played at the Plugged Nickel in Chicago on two nights in 1965 have been released on this eight-CD box. The packaging is a bit confusing because Davis' group actually performed seven full sets, but, since their second one on the 22nd ran over, it has been issued on two CDs but placed inside the same package. In any case, the music during these two nights, primarily explorative versions of standards (as opposed to Miles' all-original studio albums of the period), is continually fascinating. A few titles are repeated, but the interpretations differ greatly from each other. The trumpeter's chops are actually not quite in peak form (although his creativity is) but Wayne Shorter (who often takes solo honors) is consistently brilliant and the rhythm section (propelled by Tony Williams) was one of the best of the period. Although some of this music had been issued earlier on three LPs, most of it had been out previously only in Japan. This was a very significant group (even if it were somewhat overshadowed by John Coltrane's Quartet at the time) and their advanced versions of such Miles Davis standards as "Walkin,'" "My Funny Valentine," "I Fall in Love Too Easily," "If I Were a Bell," "Stella by Starlight" and "So What" are among the many highlights. One of the top releases of 1995. —*Scott Yanow*

Highlights from the Plugged Nickel / Dec. 22, 1965-Dec. 23, 1965 / Columbia ✦✦✦

Replacing the previous records *Cookin' at the Plugged Nickel* and *Live at the Plugged Nickel*, *Highlights from the Plugged Nickel* collects a handful of tracks from the mammoth eight-CD set *The Complete Live at the Plugged Nickel 1965*. Two of the tracks on *Highlights* are songs that were issued in their complete versions on the box, but that isn't what makes the album preferable to *Cookin'* and *Live*. On *Highlights*, the fidelity is stunning and the selection is first-rate—the disc flows like one of the original concerts captured on the box. For listeners that don't want to invest in the box, *Highlights* is a worthwhile purchase. —*Stephen Thomas Erlewine*

E.S.P. / Jan. 20, 1965-Jan. 22, 1965 / Columbia ✦✦✦✦✦

The first of six studio albums by Miles Davis' second classic quintet features seven originals by band members including "Eighty-One," "Agitation," "Iris" and "E.S.P." This music was quite original although somewhat overshadowed at the time by John Coltrane and some of the avant-garde players. Influenced by Ornette Coleman, the soloing by Davis, Wayne Shorter and Herbie Hancock was quite advanced by this time and this band's music would later be a major influence on Wynton and Branford Marsalis. —*Scott Yanow*

★ **Miles Smiles** / Oct. 24, 1966-Oct. 25, 1966 / Columbia ✦✦✦✦✦

Of the six studio albums recorded by Miles Davis' second classic quintet, *Miles Smiles* is their definitive set. This CD reissue of the original LP (which has been given new liner notes) features the trumpeter/leader, tenor saxophonist Wayne Shorter, pianist Herbie Hancock, bassist Ron Carter and drummer Tony Williams in superb form on adventurous versions of "Freedom Jazz Dance," "Gingerbread Boy," Wayne Shorter's "Footprints" and three lesser-known pieces ("Orbits," "Circle" and "Dolores"). The music is challenging but quite rewarding. —*Scott Yanow*

Nefertiti / Jun. 7, 1967-Jul. 19, 1967 / Columbia ✦✦✦✦

The fourth of the six studio albums by the Miles Davis Quintet of the 1960s was their last all-acoustic session. Wayne Shorter, Herbie Hancock and Tony Williams contributed all of the music to this adventurous set including such classics as "Nefertiti," "Riot" and "Pinocchio." This CD reissue of the original LP (which has new liner notes) is brief at under 40 minutes, but the music is consistently stimulat-

ing and unpredictable. It's funny that this group's playing had little influence on the music of 1967 for by 1987 it was becoming the mainstream of jazz. —*Scott Yanow*

Water Babies / Jun. 1967-Nov. 1968 / Columbia ✦✦✦

This studio LP was first released almost a decade after it was recorded. The first half features the 1967 Quintet (with Wayne Shorter on tenor and soprano, pianist Herbie Hancock, bassist Ron Carter and drummer Tony Williams) performing three otherwise unknown Shorter compositions. The flip side finds Davis in 1968 leading the same group (with possibly Chick Corea and Dave Holland replacing Hancock and Carter) on two early fusion jams that look a bit towards *Bitches Brew*. Although not an essential set, this album fills in some gaps during Davis' transitional period from adventurous acoustic playing to early electric performances. —*Scott Yanow*

☆ **Miles Davis Quintet, 1965-'68: The Complete Columbia Studio Recordings/** Jan. 20, 1965-Jun. 21, 1968 / Columbia/Legacy ✦✦✦✦✦

There's little argument that the quintet Miles Davis led between 1965 and 1968 was one of the classic combos in the history of jazz. By teaming with the adventurous young musicians Wayne Shorter (tenor sax), Herbie Hancock (piano), Ron Carter (bass) and Tony Williams (drums), Davis pushed mainstream jazz toward the avant-garde, expanding on the modal jazz he inaugurated with *Kind of Blue* and laid the groundwork for fusion. Four of their five studio albums—*ESP, Miles Smiles, Sorcerer, Nefertiti*—were essential, and even when they were slightly off the mark, as on *Miles in the Sky*, they were still filled with provocative sounds and ideas. That's the reason why *The Miles Davis Quintet 1965-'68: The Complete Columbia Studio Recordings* is an essential release. It contains all the music from each of the five studio records, plus half of the material released on *Filles De Kilimanjaro* and *Water Babies*, as well as several alternate takes and 13 previously unreleased selections. There's no question that this material is necessary for any jazz collection, but this may not necessarily be the best way to acquire it. The strict chronological sequencing is according to session order, which means the sequencing of the original albums—which was quite effective in conveying the combo's ideas—is thrown out of line, and the long stretches where alternates and master takes are back to back may be tedious to some listeners. Also, packaging all the discs within cardboard mock-record sleeves in a bound booklet may look attractive, but it's impractical and not designed for heavy listening. It is true that the remastered sound is spectacular, but some fans may want to wait for the previously unreleased selections—all of which are interesting, but ultimately not terribly revealing— to be reissued as bonus tracks on the remastered individual discs that are bound to follow. After all, that's what happened with the six-disc Gil Evans box. In other words, this music is essential, and this set will appeal to most serious jazz fans and historians, but some listeners may be more satisfied by the original albums than by the box. —*Stephen Thomas Erlewine*

No Blues / Nov. 6, 1967 / Jazz Music Yesterday ✦✦✦✦✦

The Miles Davis Quintet only recorded new material during 1965-68 but in their live performances they still played some of the trumpeter's older standards. Until recent times, few of the live sessions by the Quintet made it onto record, but this very valuable CD features the group in late 1967 playing such songs (for nearly the final time) as "'Round Midnight," "No Blues," "I Fall in Love Too Easily," "Walkin'" and "Green Dolphin Street" in addition to the newer songs "Mascalero" and "Riot." It is utterly fascinating to hear the Quintet at that late date stretching out on these veteran songs and coming up with fresh new ideas one more time. This Italian import is well worth searching for; it fills an important gap in jazz history. —*Scott Yanow*

Miles in the Sky / Jan. 16, 1968-May 17, 1968 / Columbia ✦✦✦✦

The fifth of the six studio albums by the second classic Quintet found Davis continuing to move ahead. For the first time Herbie Hancock is heard a bit on electric piano, guitarist George Benson guests on "Paraphernalia" and the extended performances were just beginning to open themselves to the influences of pop and rock music. This CD reissues the original LP but has new liner notes. This important set of music can be seen as either early fusion, the beginning of the end of the Miles Davis Quintet, or both. —*Scott Yanow*

Filles de Kilimanjaro / Jun. 19, 1968-Sep. 24, 1968 / Columbia ✦✦✦✦✦

The sixth and final studio album by Miles Davis' second classic Quintet finds the group looking towards early fusion. Herbie Hancock (who doubles on electric piano) and bassist Ron Carter are replaced by Chick Corea and Dave Holland on the two selections from Sept. 24, 1968, although Wayne Shorter and drummer Tony Williams are still key members of Davis' band. The music is more esoteric than his music of a year or two earlier, with funky rhythms and hints at pop and rock music becoming more prevalent although not dominant yet. To many of the jazz purists, this was Miles Davis' final jazz album, but to those with open ears towards electronics and danceable rhythms, this set was the predecessor of his next great innovation. This CD reissue of the original LP is well worth checking out. —*Scott Yanow*

☆ **In a Silent Way** / Feb. 18, 1969 / Columbia ✦✦✦✦✦
The beginning of fusion (although other groups such as Gary Burton's Quartet with Larry Coryell had hinted strongly at it), this set found Miles Davis for the first time really combining jazz improvising with the rhythms and power of rock. On this LP, Davis jams with an octet (which includes the magical names of tenor saxophonist Wayne Shorter, keyboardists Herbie Hancock, Chick Corea and Joe Zawinul, guitarist John McLaughlin, bassist Dave Holland and drummer Tony Williams; all future bandleaders) on two lengthy side-long medleys. Those jazz purists with their minds closed towards electronics of any kind are advised to check out this fairly accessible date before tackling *Bitches Brew*. The strong solos on this early fusion classic might very well win them over. —*Scott Yanow*

It's About That Time / Jul. 1969 / Jazz Door ✦✦✦✦✦
This exciting live set (released for the first time on this European CD in the mid-'90s) finds Miles Davis at a particularly intriguing point in his evolution. He had finished recording *In a Silent Way* five months earlier and was just a few weeks before starting *Bitches Brew*. His working quintet (captured during a seven-song continuous set at the Montreux Jazz Festival) at that time comprised Wayne Shorter on tenor and soprano, keyboardist Chick Corea, Dave Holland on electric bass and drummer Jack DeJohnette. In addition to performing versions of "Miles Runs the Voodoo Down" and "Sanctuary" that predate *Bitches Brew,* they also play the last versions thus far released of Davis performing two of his standards: "Milestones" and 'Round About Midnight." The recording quality is excellent, and Miles Davis was in fine form for this very interesting transitional date, which captures the trumpeter just before he permanently turned his music completely into fusion. —*Scott Yanow*

★ **Bitches Brew** / Aug. 19, 1969-Aug. 21, 1969 / Columbia ✦✦✦✦✦
No jazz collection is complete without this double CD. This very influential set was one of the first successful attempts to form a new music (soon termed fusion) by combining jazz solos with rock rhythms. "Miles Runs the Voodoo Down" is the most memorable of the six lengthy selections, featuring a fascinating ensemble with Davis' trumpet, Wayne Shorter's soprano, Bennie Maupin's bass clarinet, guitarist John McLaughlin, the keyboards of Chick Corea and Larry Young (Joe Zawinul is on some of the other selections), Dave Holland and Harvey Brooks on basses, drummers Jack DeJohnette, Charles Alias and Lenny White and percussionist Jim Riley. Not for the close-minded, this music brought many rock listeners into jazz and gave jazz musicians new possibilities to explore. —*Scott Yanow*

Big Fun / Nov. 19, 1969-Jun. 12, 1972 / Columbia ✦✦
This double LP features Davis on four side-long jams taken from different sessions during 1969-72. "Great Expectations" features most of the players from *Bitches Brew* along with two sitarists and "Ife" has the trumpeter's 1972 band (with saxophonists Carlos Garnett and Sonny Fortune) but the two best tracks ("Lonely Fire" and "Go Ahead John") are from 1970; the latter features the quintet of Davis, Steve Grossman on soprano, guitarist John McLaughlin, bassist Dave Holland and drummer Jack DeJohnette. Very interesting if erratic music, it's not essential but fans of Davis' fusion years will enjoy much of it. —*Scott Yanow*

Live-Evil / Feb. 6, 1970-Dec. 19, 1970 / Columbia ✦✦✦✦
Forget the inexcusably ugly (and somewhat racist) artwork and a few of the weaker tracks. At its best, this double CD reissue has some of Davis' finest playing of the 1970s, and the solos by altoist Gary Bartz, guitarist John McLaughlin and keyboardist Keith Jarrett are not that far behind on such lengthy pieces as "What I Say" and "Funky Tonk." This is fusion at its most adventurous (and sometimes most riotous), before the record labels and radio stations turned it into meaningless "smooth jazz." —*Scott Yanow*

A Tribute to Jack Johnson / Apr. 7, 1970 / Columbia ✦✦✦✦✦
Davis' odd soundtrack for a documentary on the boxer Jack Johnson did not really fit the movie (it was far too modern) but stands alone very well as a strong piece of music. On this straight reissue of the original LP, the two lengthy jams (25-minute-plus versions of "Right Off" and "Yesternow") feature fine playing by a sextet comprising Davis' trumpet, Steve Grossman's soprano sax, keyboardist Herbie Hancock, guitarist John McLaughlin, electric bassist Michael Henderson and drummer Billy Cobham. Even listeners who write off the fusion years will find moments of interest on this set. —*Scott Yanow*

Miles Davis at Fillmore: Live at the Fillmore East / Jun. 17, 1970-Jun. 20, 1970 / Columbia/Legacy ✦✦✦
The four set-long excursions on this double CD reissue (which for the first time lists the titles of the songs) are full of self-indulgent moments, particularly when Chick Corea and Keith Jarrett almost literally battle each other on their arsenal of electric keyboards but there are also hot solos from Miles Davis and occasionally saxophonist Steve Grossman. This occasionally out-of-control set (which also

includes electric bassist Dave Holland, drummer Jack DeJohnette and percussionist Airto) will not win any converts to Davis' fusion years but it does have its humorous (check out the way each night ends with a spaced-out "The Theme") and grooving moments. —*Scott Yanow*

Black Beauty: Miles Davis at Fillmore West / Apr. 10, 1970 / Columbia ✦✦✦✦
Prior to 1997, when the music was finally released domestically on a double CD, this particular Miles Davis concert was only available in Japan. The trumpeter used what was essentially a stripped-down *Bitches Brew* sextet (with Steve Grossman on soprano, Chick Corea on Fender Rhodes, electric bassist Dave Holland, drummer Jack DeJohnette and percussionist Airto) to play a continuous 80-minute set. Grossman's soprano playing gets a bit limited at times, and Corea's banging of the electric piano is sometimes a little monotonous, but Miles is heard in superior form, and the rhythm section (with Airto adding many colorful sounds) is excellent. The jam (which includes "Directions," a very brief "I Fall in Love Too Easily," Wayne Shorter's "Sanctuary" and "Bitches Brew," among others) is quite intriguing, high-quality fusion with plenty of surprising turns. —*Scott Yanow*

Hooray for Miles Davis, Vol. 3 / Nov. 26, 1971 / Session ✦✦✦
The sound quality of this bootleg LP is just okay but the two medleys played by Davis' 1971 quintet (with altoist Gary Bartz, keyboardist Keith Jarrett, electric bassist Mike Henderson and drummer Jack DeJohnette) combines some of his better groove tunes of the era (including "What I Say," "Miles Runs the Voodoo Down" and "Yesternow"). It's a spirited session of creative fusion. —*Scott Yanow*

On the Corner / Jun. 1, 1972-Jun. 6, 1972 / Columbia ✦✦✦
On the Corner is Miles Davis' most controversial album. Jazz purists detest the album, dismissing it out of hand for the very reason that its fans celebrate it—there are no fully formed songs on the record, just funky rhythmic vamps. Davis assembled a large group of musicians, who aren't credited on the record, and had them play one groove, which demonstrated a heavy debt to Sly Stone. Miles rarely plays trumpet on the record and when he does, it is distorted and processed. Instead, he plays organ, blending into the dense, electric funk. None of the players take extended solos and all of the songs are brief, but improvisation isn't the point of the record. *On the Corner* is about funk and rhythm, not about jazz. With this record, Davis laid the foundation of the genre-blurring hip-hop and acid-jazz revolutions in popular music in the '80s and '90s. —*Stephen Thomas Erlewine*

Get Up with It / Sep. 6, 1972-Oct. 7, 1974 / Columbia ✦✦✦
This double LP, featuring a variety of Miles Davis' electric ensembles of 1974, has plenty of variety, ranging from a side-long dirge for Duke Ellington ("He Loved Him Madly") and a dumb but interesting "Red China Blues," to heated jams on "Honky Tonk," "Calypso Frelimo" and "Mtume." Although Davis plays organ rather than trumpet half the time, the dense ensembles and passionate improvisations are creative rather than predictable. —*Scott Yanow*

In Concert / Sep. 29, 1972 / Columbia ✦✦
This 1997 double-CD reissues one of Miles Davis' few duds (which was originally available as a two-LP set). *In Concert* (which is in a similar vein as *In the Corner*) has two continuous performances featuring throwaway vamps, lots of repetition, and (worst of all) an endless use of the wah-wah pedal. Davis' trumpet sound is distorted and almost unrecognizable throughout (sounding like a keyboard); Carlos Garnett (heard on tenor and soprano) is mostly buried; and the rhythm section (keyboardist Cedric Lawson, guitarist Reggie Lucas, Khalil Balakrishna on sitar, electric bassist Michael Henderson, drummer Al Foster, Badal Roy on tabla, and percussionist Mtume) sounds unimaginative and instantly dated. The long jams do not progress much and get rather tedious after a period, although the reissue (which for the first time identifies the songs and the personnel) does have much better sound than the earlier LPs. —*Scott Yanow*

Dark Magus / Mar. 3, 1974 / Columbia ✦✦✦
The music on this double CD, released domestically for the first time in 1997, was only previously out in Japan and was formerly among the rarest of Miles Davis recordings. Featured is one of the trumpeter's most controversial bands, a noisy ensemble with three guitarists (Reggie Lucas, Pete Cosey and Dominique Gaumont), electric bassist Michael Henderson, drummer Al Foster, percussionist Mtume, Dave Liebman on tenor, soprano and flute, and guest tenorman Azar Lawrence. The spontaneous music has plenty of repetitive funk sounds from the guitars and bits of aimless rambling, along with some strong moments from Davis and Liebman. If drastically edited, the double CD would have made a killer single disc, for there are some very interesting stretches when magic occurs, but these are often succeeded by overlong vamps. Worth checking out, but not essential. —*Scott Yanow*

Agharta / Feb. 1, 1975 / Columbia ✦✦✦
Recorded the same day as *Pangaea* but not up to its level, this two-LP set features Davis just prior to his six-year retirement. He actually sounds a bit weak on this set (although he takes a rare straightahead solo on "Interlude") but altoist Sonny For-

tune has his moments. The dense and rockish ensembles (with the guitars of Pete Cosey and Reggie Lucas) will scare most jazz listeners away. —*Scott Yanow*

Pangaea / Feb. 1, 1975 / Columbia ✦✦✦✦
Although Davis' health was shaky at the time of this two-CD set (recorded the same day as the weaker *Agharta*), he has a few strong trumpet solos on these two very lengthy pieces ("Zimbabwe" and "Gondwana"); Davis would drift into retirement for six years shortly after this concert. The music is actually quite rewarding (at least it will be for listeners with open ears) with the dense ensembles and heated solos (Sonny Fortune on soprano, alto and flute and the guitars of Pete Cosey and Reggie Lucas being quite dangerous, as opposed to the safe fusion of the 1990s. *Pangaea* is the finest recording from the least-understood period of Davis' career (1971-75). —*Scott Yanow*

The Man with the Horn / 1981 / Columbia ✦✦✦
Miles Davis' first comeback period finds the trumpeter a bit shaky (he would improve, album-by-album, during the next few years) and has a few poppish throwaway tracks; it is doubtful if anyone really remembers the title cut or "Shout." But with Bill Evans on soprano and electric bassist Marcus Miller, the other four selections are more rewarding with Davis forming the nucleus of his new band. —*Scott Yanow*

We Want Miles / Jun. 27, 1981-Oct. 4, 1981 / Columbia ✦✦✦✦
Davis' second recording since ending his six-year retirement was one of his best of the 1980s. Unlike his bands from the 1970s, this particular unit leaves plenty of space and plays much more melodically. Guitarist Mike Stern lets loose some fury but electric bassist Marcus Miller is not reluctant to walk now and then in a straightahead fashion, drummer Al Foster and percussionist Mino Cinelu are tasteful, and Bill Evans gets in a few good spots on soprano. As for Davis, he was gradually regaining his earlier form. This double LP is highlighted by "Back Seat Betty," a side-long investigation of "My Man's Gone Now" and two versions of Davis' childlike "Jean Pierre." —*Scott Yanow*

Star People / Sep. 1, 1982-Jan. 5, 1983 / Columbia ✦✦✦✦
On this 1983 release, Miles Davis rediscovers the blues. He really stretches out on "Star People," making dramatic use of silence and placing each note carefully. "Come Get It" is also memorable although "U 'N' I" (which had the potential to catch on) is only heard in a truncated version. In general Davis is in fine form on this set and, although saxophonist Bill Evans is barely heard from (many of his solos were edited out), the contrasting guitars of Mike Stern and John Scofield hold one's interest. —*Scott Yanow*

Decoy / Jun. 30, 1983-Sep. 11, 1983 / Columbia ✦✦
This rather streaky set of music features Davis with keyboardist Robert Irving III (who has since slipped into obscurity) and guitarist John Scofield contributing most of the compositions and the other solos. There are some moments of interest (Branford Marsalis is heard on some cuts on soprano) but it is doubtful if anyone will be reviving "Robot 415," "Freaky Deaky" or "Code M.D." anytime soon. —*Scott Yanow*

You're Under Arrest / Jan. 26, 1984-Jan. 1985 / Columbia ✦✦
Miles Davis' final Columbia recording (other than *Aura*, which was released several years later) includes his straightforward ballad interpretations of Cyndi Lauper's "Time After Time" and the Michael Jackson-associated "Human Nature," two songs he would play in most of his concerts for the remainder of his life. Other tunes (including "You're Under Arrest," "One Phone Call" and "Ms. Morrisine") were quickly discarded. In addition to Davis (who had regained his earlier chops), tenor saxophonist Bob Berg, guitarist John Scofield and guest John McLaughlin join in a few decent solos on this competent but not overly memorable effort. —*Scott Yanow*

Aura / Jan. 31, 1985-Feb. 4, 1985 / Columbia ✦✦✦
Miles Davis' final Columbia release was this two-LP set, an unusual effort from his fusion years. Palle Mikkelborg composed a challenging nine-part suite that finds the trumpeter in fairly inspired form, joined by a colorful big band. Guitarist John McLaughlin and bassists Niels Pedersen and Bo Stief have some solos, but otherwise the spotlight is entirely on Davis, who mostly rises to the occasion. —*Scott Yanow*

Tutu / Jan. 6, 1986-Mar. 25, 1986 / Warner Brothers ✦✦✦
This controversial but memorable recording is mostly a duet between Miles Davis and the many overdubbed instruments of producer Marcus Miller (although violinist Michel Urbaniak, percussionist Paulinho da Costa and keyboardist George Duke are among the other musicians making brief appearances). Certainly the results are not all that spontaneous, but Davis is in top form and some of the selections (most notably the title cut) are quite memorable. —*Scott Yanow*

Music from Siesta / Jan. 19 1987-Mar. 1987 / Warner Brothers ✦✦✦
This collaboration between Davis and producer Marcus Miller (who, except for some cameos, plays all of the other instruments) is quite successful and a bit of a surprise since it is essentially a soundtrack to an obscure film. Dedicated to arranger Gil Evans, the music is greatly influenced by his style, with Miller creating

an electrified but very warm orchestra to accompany Davis' melodic solos. This was the first of several instances in which Miles Davis, in the twilight of his life, returned to his roots. It's worth searching for. —*Scott Yanow*

Live Around the World / Aug. 7, 1988-Sep. 1991 / Warner Brothers ✦✦✦✦✦
This single CD gives one a definitive look at Miles Davis' live show from his last three years. Using funky but unpredictable rhythm sections and leaving space for plenty of solos, Davis created a unique brand of fusion that has yet to be satisfactorily duplicated. Among his more notable sidemen during this era are altoist Kenny Garrett, Foley on lead bass (which he used as a lower-toned guitar), one or two keyboardists chosen from Joey De Francesco, Adam Holzman, Robert Irving III, Kei Akagi and John Beasley, various bassists, drummers and percussionists and on "Amandla" the tenor of Rick Margitza. Davis is in consistently strong form throughout the numbers, which include "In a Silent Way," "New Blues," "Human Nature," "Tutu" and "Time After Time." Quite often the live versions of these songs are more creative and exciting than the ones previously issued. This highly recommended CD (released in 1996) concludes with one number ("Hannibal") from Davis' final performance; it is not given a date but is most likely from just a few weeks before his death at age 65. No Miles Davis collection is complete without this important set. —*Scott Yanow*

Amandla / 1989 / Warner Brothers ✦✦✦✦
A particularly strong set by late-period Miles Davis, this set is highlighted by a surprisingly straightahead performance titled "Mr. Pastorius." In addition to Davis and his new altoist Kenny Garrett, various guests (including Marcus Miller, guitarist Jean Paul Boureiiy, Joey De Francesco on keyboards, Rick Margitza on tenor, pianist Joe Sample and bassist Foley) get their chances to play next to the great legend who is in top form. An excellent effort, it was really his last studio recording with his regular band. —*Scott Yanow*

Hot Spot / May 5, 1990-May 10, 1990 / Antilles ✦✦✦
This unusual blues-oriented soundtrack extensively features trumpeter Miles Davis and guitarist/vocalist John Lee Hooker (along with Taj Majal and slide guitarist Roy Rogers). More of a historical curiosity than an essential CD, the music has its strong moments, and it is particularly interesting to hear Davis in this setting. —*Scott Yanow*

Dingo / Mar. 1990 / Warner Brothers ✦✦
In 1990, Miles Davis starred in a movie about a veteran trumpeter (talk about typecasting) and had a rare opportunity to play part of the time in a straightahead setting. Fellow trumpeter Chuck Findley performs the solos for a younger musician who befriends Davis, and Michel Legrand arranged and composed the music. There are some good moments on these selections (Findley actually overshadows Davis in some places) but since this is a soundtrack, the music does not often stand up that well by itself. It's a worthy effort but is sure to become an obscurity. —*Scott Yanow*

Doo-Bop / Jan. 19, 1991-Feb. 1991 / Warner Brothers ✦✦
If *On the Corner* suggested hip-hop beats as far back as two decades ago, then consider *Doo-Bop* as offspring. Miles' teaming with producer Easy Mo Bee is a natural—more in league with England's acid jazz scene than anything in the trumpeter's recent canon. Those who've howled over the post-*Bitches' Brew* work will find no solace here; instead, chalk this up as one of Miles' most entertaining efforts. —*Steve Aldrich*

Miles & Quincy Live at Montreux / Jul. 8, 1991 / Warner Brothers ✦✦✦✦
This historically significant set found Miles Davis, just months before his death, doing what he always said he wouldn't: revisiting his past. Backed by a large orchestra (mostly George Gruntz's concert band) conducted by Quincy Jones, Davis plays music from his four collaborations with Gil Evans including "Boplicity" (from the *Birth of the Cool* days) and medleys from *Miles Ahead, Porgy and Bess* and *Sketches of Spain*. Unfortunately, Davis chose to be muted most of the time, leaving the more difficult (and generally exciting) sections to trumpeter Wallace Roney and delegating some solo space to altoist Kenny Garrett. The results are generally quite emotional and served as a suitable last hurrah for the innovative Miles Davis. —*Scott Yanow*

Nathan Davis

b. Feb. 15, 1937, Kansas City, KS

Tenor Saxophone, Soprano Saxophone / Hard Bop

Nathan Davis has split his career between being a fine tenor saxophonist and a jazz educator. He played briefly with Jay McShann in 1955, attended the University of Kansas, spent time in the Army in Berlin (1960-63), and stayed in Paris where he worked with Kenny Clarke (1963-69), Eric Dolphy (1964) and Art Taylor. He also toured Europe with Art Blakey (1965) and Ray Charles. Since 1969, Davis has been a professor of jazz at the University of Pittsburgh and Moorhead State University. His two most important musical associations have been heading the

Paris Reunion Band (1985-89) and leading Roots (which he formed in 1991). —*Scott Yanow*

● **The Hip Walk** / Sep. 1, 1965 / Saba ✦✦✦✦

London by Night / Aug. 1987 / Hot House ✦✦✦✦

Richard Davis

b. Apr. 15, 1930, Chicago, IL
Bass / Post-Bop, Hard Bop
One of the most technically skilled of all acoustic bassists, Richard Davis has played in symphony orchestras but fortunately has spent much of his career in the jazz world. His early jazz jobs included stints with Ahmad Jamal (1953-54), Don Shirley (1954-55) and Sarah Vaughan (1957-60). In addition to his symphony work in the 1960s (including for Stravinsky), Davis was a major asset on recordings by Eric Dolphy, Booker Ervin, Rahsaan Roland Kirk, Andrew Hill, Ben Webster, Stan Getz, Earl Hines, Hank Jones and Billy Cobham; in addition he was a regular member of the Thad Jones/Mel Lewis Orchestra during 1966-72. In 1977 he became an educator at the University of Wisconsin. Richard Davis' infrequent albums as a leader include dates for MPS, Muse, Flying Dutchman, Galaxy, Hep and Sweet Basil (1990). —*Scott Yanow*

Muses for Richard Davis / Dec. 3, 1969 / Pausa ✦✦✦

With Understanding / Jan. 1971 / Muse ✦✦✦
Chick Corea (k) center stage with fine Davis support. —*Ron Wynn*

Epistrophy / Now's the Time / Sep. 7, 1972 / Muse ✦✦✦✦
Originally two side-long avant-garde jams on bebop standards ("Now's the Time" and "Epistrophy" which both clock in at over 22 minutes apiece), this live session was expanded upon its CD reissue with the inclusion of a version of Clifford Jordan's "Highest Mountain." Although tenor saxophonist Jordan, pianist Joe Bonner, drummer Freddie Waits and bassist Richard Davis were on the date, trumpeter Marvin "Hannibal" Peterson is the most dominant force, both as a player and in his conception of opening up the music. These very unpredictable renditions reward repeated listenings. —*Scott Yanow*

Dealin' / Sep. 14, 1972 / Muse ✦✦✦

As One / Oct. 19, 1975+Oct. 25, 1975 / Muse ✦✦✦

Harvest / May 3, 1977 / Muse ✦✦✦
Premier bassist with groups of varying size. Most interesting listening for the adventurous jazz lover. —*Michael G. Nastos*

Fancy Free / Jun. 30, 1977+Jul. 1, 1977 / Galaxy ✦✦✦
It seems odd that this Galaxy LP was recorded at the same time as *Way Out West* for the rival Muse label. Bassist Richard Davis teams up with trumpeter Eddie Henderson, tenor saxophonist Joe Henderson, keyboardist Stanley Cowell and drummer Billy Cobham for five selections that are highlighted by "Silver's Serenade," "Nardis" and a rare cover version of Donald Byrd's "Fancy Free"; singer Dolly Hirota is featured on "I Still Love You, Baby." Overall, this is the stronger of the sets recorded during the two-day period in 1977, an advanced and mostly straightahead effort. —*Scott Yanow*

Way Out West / Jun. 30, 1977+Jul. 1, 1977 / Muse ✦✦✦
Recorded with the same musicians and during the same two days as the Galaxy release *Fancy Free*, this LP covers a wide area. Bassist Richard Davis is heard in an unaccompanied solo on the brief "A Peace for Richard," on a duet with tenor saxophonist Joe Henderson for "On the Trail" (one of the session's high points), heading a trio with pianist Stanley Cowell and drummer Billy Cobham on "I'm Old Fashioned" and otherwise playing with a quintet that also includes Henderson, Cowell (who doubles on a dated sounding electric piano), Cobham and trumpeter Eddie Henderson; three songs have vocals by the obscure Dolly Hirota. Ranging from straightahead to some funky pop, this is an interesting if not essential release from the masterful bassist. —*Scott Yanow*

Cauldron / Jan. 13, 1979 / Corvo ✦✦✦✦

One for Frederick / Jul. 6, 1989-Jul. 7, 1989 / Hep ✦✦✦

● **Live at Sweet Basil** / Aug. 8, 1990+May 21, 1991 / Evidence ✦✦✦✦✦

Walter Davis, Jr.

b. Sep. 2, 1932, Richmond, VA, **d.** Jun. 2, 1990, New York, NY
Piano / Bop, Hard Bop
In 1959, Walter Davis, Jr. led one of the great Blue Note sessions, a quintet set with Donald Byrd and Jackie McLean called *Davis Cup*. It seems strange that not only did he not have an opportunity for an encore but his next session as a leader was for Denon, in 1977! An excellent bop-based pianist, Walter Davis picked up early experience in the late '40s working with Babs Gonzales' Three Bips and a Bop before playing and recording with Charlie Parker in 1952. Following were associa-

tions with Max Roach (1952-53), Dizzy Gillespie's big band (1956), Donald Byrd (1959) and Art Blakey's Jazz Messengers (1959). After a long period outside of music, Davis came back to play with Sonny Rollins (1973-74), the Jazz Messengers (1975-77) and then as leader of his own group. He was on the soundtrack of the film *Bird* and recorded extensively as a leader during 1977-79 (for Denon, Bee Hive, Red and Owl) and in 1987-89 (for Jazz Heritage, Jazz City, Mapleshade and Steeple Chase). —*Scott Yanow*

● **Davis Cup** / Aug. 2, 1959 / Blue Note ✦✦✦✦✦
Walter Davis, Jr.'s debut record as a leader for Blue Note is a terrific hard bop session, a driving collection of six original tunes that emphasize the strengths not only of the pianist himself, but also his supporting band: trumpeter Donald Byrd, alto saxophonist Jackie McLean, bassist Sam Jones and drummer Art Taylor. Apart from the lovely ballad "Sweetness," *Davis Cup* moves along at a brisk pace, with the rhythm section urging the soloists to new heights. Byrd has rarely sounded better, and on this date, McLean provides ample evidence that he was moving beyond the conventions of hard bop and developing his own unique style. Davis, of course, does more than acquit himself—he contributes an engaging, energetic performance that keeps the music grounded. His compositions are just as captivating, whether it's the swinging "Rhumba Nhumba" or the darkly invigorating "Minor Mind." It all adds up to a wonderful straightahead hard bop date, one that's so good it's a wonder that Davis didn't receive another chance to lead a session until 1977. —*Stephen Thomas Erlewine*

Illumination / Feb. 19, 1977-Dec. 1, 1977 / Denon ✦✦✦✦

Blues Walk / Nov. 23, 1979 / Red ✦✦✦✦
This imaginative pianist recorded a solid effort. —*David Szatmary*

400 Years Ago, Tomorrow / Dec. 1979 / Owl ✦✦✦

In Walked Thelonious / Apr. 19, 1987 / Mapleshade ✦✦✦✦✦
Pianist Walter Davis, Jr. led relatively few recording sessions throughout his career despite his obvious talent. In fact this CD was his first opportunity to head a date for an American label since his lone Blue Note set back in 1959! Davis performs 14 Thelonious Monk songs (including two versions of "'Round Midnight") unaccompanied. To his credit he does not avoid the more difficult and obscure works (including "Gallop's Gallop," "Trinkle Twinkle" and "Criss Cross") and he consistently plays with creativity and a dose of the famous Monk wit. Walter Davis, Jr. knew Thelonious Monk both personally and musically, and his familiarity really shows on this easily recommended release. —*Scott Yanow*

Scorpio Rising / Aug. 1, 1994 / Steeple Chase ✦✦✦

Wild Bill Davis

b. Nov. 24, 1918, Glasgow, MO, **d.** Aug. 17, 1995, Moorestown, NJ
Organ / Swing, Groove
Prior to the rise of Jimmy Smith in 1956, Wild Bill Davis was the pacesetters among organists. He actually played guitar and wrote arrangements for Milt Larkin's legendary band during 1939-42. Davis played piano with Louis Jordan's Tympany Five (1945-49) before switching to organ in 1950 and heading his own influential organ/guitar/drums trios. Davis was originally supposed to record "April in Paris" with Count Basie's Orchestra in 1955 but when he could not make the session, Basie used his arrangement for the full band and had a major hit. In addition to working with his own groups in the 1960s, Davis made several albums with his friend Johnny Hodges, leading to tours during 1969-71 with Duke Ellington. In the '70s he recorded for *Black & Blue* with a variety of swing all-stars and played with Lionel Hampton, appearing at festivals through the early '90s. —*Scott Yanow*

The Music from Milk and Honey / Feb. 1962 / Prestige ✦✦

Con Soul and Sax / Jan. 7, 1965 / RCA ✦✦✦✦✦

Free, Frantic and Funky / Jul. 1965 / RCA ✦✦✦

● **In Atlantic City** / Aug. 10, 1966+Aug. 11, 1966 / RCA ✦✦✦✦✦

Doin' His Thing / Nov. 13, 1967-Nov. 15, 1967 / RCA ✦✦✦

Impulsions / May 9, 1972+May 10, 1972 / Black & Blue ✦✦✦

Wild Bill Davison

b. Jan. 5, 1906, Defiance, OH, **d.** Nov. 14, 1989, Santa Barbara, CA
Cornet / Dixieland
One of the great Dixieland trumpeters, Wild Bill Davison had a colorful and emotional style that ranged from sarcasm to sentimentality with plenty of growls and shakes. His unexpected placement of high notes was a highlight of his solos and his strong personality put him far ahead of the competition. In the 1920s he played with the Ohio Lucky Seven, the Chubb-Steinberg Orchestra (with whom he made his recording debut), the Seattle Harmony Kings and Benny Meroff. After he was involved in a fatal car accident that ended the life of Frankie Teschemacher in

1932 (his auto was blindsided by a taxi), Davison spent the remainder of the 1930s in exile in Milwaukee. By 1941 he was in New York and in 1943 made some brilliant recordings for Commodore (including a classic version of "That's a Plenty") that solidified his reputation. After a period in the Army, Davison became a fixture with Eddie Condon's bands starting in 1945, playing nightly at Condon's. In the 1950s he was quite effective on a pair of albums with string orchestras, but most of his career was spent fronting Dixieland bands either as a leader or with Condon. Wild Bill toured Europe often from the 1960s, recorded constantly, had a colorful life filled with remarkable episodes, and was active up until his death. A very detailed 1996 biography (*The Wildest One* by Hal Willard) has many hilarious anecdotes and shows just how unique a life Wild Bill Davison had. —*Scott Yanow*

● **Commodore Master Takes** / Nov. 27, 1943-Jan. 4, 1946 / GRP ♦♦♦♦♦
This 1997 CD contains some of the most rewarding Dixieland ever recorded. On November 27, 1943, cornetist Wild Bill Davison, trombonist George Brunis (in peak form), clarinetist Pee Wee Russell, pianist Gene Schroeder, rhythm guitarist Eddie Condon, bassist Bob Casey and drummer George Wettling cut a classic version of "That's a Plenty," along with three other songs that show just how exciting the style can be. Also on this CD are Davison's other Commodore sessions as a leader, 24 titles in all that include such outstanding players as clarinetists Edmond Hall, Joe Marsala and Albert Nicholas, trombonist Lou McGarity, pianists Dick Cary and Joe Sullivan, and drummers Danny Alvin and Dave Tough. With definitive versions of such tunes as "Muskrat Ramble," "At the Jazz Band Ball," "Jazz Me Blues," "Sensation" and "I'm Coming Virginia," this is an essential acquisition for anyone even remotely interested in freewheeling Chicago Dixieland jazz. —*Scott Yanow*

And His Jazz Band, 1943 / Dec. 3, 1944+Oct. 13, 1955 / Jazzology ♦♦♦♦
This CD contains the complete Wild Bill Davison session of December 3, 1944 (which was originally made as radio transcriptions) and part of a date led by the cornetist in 1955. The former set has five songs, plus five alternate takes, from a particularly mighty outfit also including trombonist George Brunis, clarinetist Pee Wee Russell, pianist Gene Schroeder, Eddie Condon on rhythm guitar, bassist Bob Casey and drummer George Wettling. Highlights include "That's a Plenty," the many different versions of "Royal Garden Blues" and "Muskrat Ramble." Only three songs are included from the later session, which matches Davison with trombonist Lou McGarity, clarinetist Tony Parenti, pianist Hank Duncan, bassist Pops Foster and drummer Zutty Singleton, but there are also 12 false starts and 11 alternate takes, eight of which are incomplete. Obviously this CD is mostly for true Dixieland completists and fanatics, but fans of Wild Bill Davison will find his many consistently colorful variations worth hearing. —*Scott Yanow*

This Is Jazz, Vol. 1 / May 3, 1947-Aug. 23, 1947 / Storyville ♦♦♦
This LP has 11 performances taken from Rudi Blesh's legendary *This Is Jazz* radio series of 1947. Although all of the music will be reissued on CD in more complete form by Jazzology, fans of the fiery cornetist Wild Bill Davison will find much of interest here. Davison's supporting cast includes trombonists George Brunis and Jimmy Archey, clarinetists Albert Nicholas and Edmond Hall, Joe Sullivan, James P. Johnson or Ralph Sutton on piano, guitarist Danny Barker, Pops Foster or Sid Weiss on bass and Baby Dodds, Johnny Blowers, Morey Feld or Freddy Moore on drums. The Dixieland music (which includes "Panama," "Sensation," "China Boy" and "California, Here I Come") is quite enjoyable. —*Scott Yanow*

★ **Showcase** / Dec. 27, 1947-Oct. 19, 1976 / Jazzology ♦♦♦♦♦
Two unrelated but rewarding sessions by the great Dixieland cornetist Wild Bill Davison are combined on this delightful CD. The first session, a six-song, ballad-oriented date that also includes trombonist Jimmy Archey, Garvin Bushell on clarinet and (on "Yesterdays") bassoon, pianist Ralph Sutton, bassist Sid Weiss and drummer Morey Feld, has some particularly ferocious playing from Davison (who takes his first recorded vocal on "Ghost of a Chance"). The remaining dozen tunes come from a very successful matchup in 1976 between Davison and the Classic Jazz Collegium Orchestra, a talented ten-member Czechoslovakian group. Some of the numbers (most notably a classic rendition of "Sunday") have inventive arrangements that make the band sound like a unit from the 1920s. Wild Bill is quite inspired throughout, making this one of his most rewarding sets of the 1970s. Highly recommended. —*Scott Yanow*

Individualism Of... / Nov. 6, 1951-Nov. 10, 1951 / Savoy ♦♦♦♦
The recording quality of the two sessions on this two-LP set is not exactly state-of-the-art, but the fire and excitement of cornetist Wild Bill Davison definitely shines through. Wild Bill is teamed with trombonist Eddie Hubble, clarinetist Frank Chase (who sounds a bit like Pee Wee Russell), pianist George Wein, bassist John Field and John Vine on the earlier set (recorded at the Storyville club in Boston), and with Eddie Condon's usual group (with trombonist Cutty Cutshall, clarinetist Edmond Hall, pianist Gene Schroeder, bassist Bob Casey and either Cliff Leeman or Buzzy Drootin on drums) in 1955. The emphasis is on hard-driving Dixieland with such songs as "Dippermouth Blues," "Mandy Make Up Your Mind," "At the

Jazz Band Ball" and "Struttin' with Some Barbecue" receiving spirited treatment. Few surprises occur but the music (which includes a three-song ballad medley), some of which has been reissued on CD, should please trad jazz fans. —*Scott Yanow*

Live! Miami Beach (1955) / Nov. 27, 1955+Nov. 29, 1955 / Pumpkin ♦♦♦
Cornetist Wild Bill Davison is heard as the lead voice in the 1955 version of Eddie Condon's All-Stars on this collector's LP. With clarinetist Pee Wee Russell getting in some typically unusual solos and fine work from trombonist Lou McGarity, pianist Gene Schroeder, bassist Walter Page and drummer George Wetting, the Condon Gang runs through seven Dixieland warhorses plus a ballad medley that peaks with Davison's chorus on "Rockin' Chair"; other highlights include "Beale St. Blues," "Singin' the Blues" and "I Want to Be Happy." —*Scott Yanow*

Pretty Wild / Feb. 22, 1956-Feb. 23, 1956 / Columbia ♦♦♦
This now out-of-print LP was a surprise big seller when it came out in 1956. The highly expressive cornetist Wild Bill Davison is backed by a string section led by Percy Faith and arranged by Marty Manning. The music is dominated by ballads and, although the charts are not at all challenging (making the style fall between jazz and mood music), Davison's melodic variations on such tunes as "Mandy Make Up Your Mind," "When Your Lover Has Gone" and "She's Funny That Way" hold one's interest. —*Scott Yanow*

With Eddie Condon's All-Stars / 1961-1964 / Storyville ♦♦♦♦
Cornetist Wild Bill Davison is featured with two similar Dixieland-oriented bands on this LP from the Storyville label. The first six songs (highlighted by "Royal Garden Blues" and "Blue and Broken Hearted") feature Davison, trombonist Cutty Cutshall, clarinetist Peanuts Hucko (showcased on "Stealin' Apples"), pianist Johnny Varrin and a rhythm section. The other four numbers, from 1964, are listed as being by Davison but with unknown personnel; the septet actually includes Wild Bill, Cutshall, clarinetist Edmond Hall and pianist Dick Wellstood. Davison's playing on "Wild Bill Blues" is most memorable. Easily recommended to Dixieland collectors. —*Scott Yanow*

S'Wonderful / Jun. 1, 1962+Nov. 1972 / Jazzology ♦♦♦
Originally put out as the only release by the Davison record label, this CD reissue has 11 selections featuring the fiery cornetist Wild Bill Davison, trombonist Vic Dickenson, clarinetist Buster Bailey, pianist Dick Wellstood, bassist Willie Wayman and drummer Cliff Leeman in 1962. Heard in prime form, Wild Bill as usual tosses in high notes in unexpected spots, mixes together sarcasm with sentimentality, and shows on tunes such as "Eccentric" and "Riverside Shuffle" that few could drive an ensemble like he could. A pair of numbers ("Memories of You" and "Who's Sorry Now") from the 1972 Manassas Jazz Festival (with clarinetist Tom Gwaltney and trombonist Slide Harris) were added to the reissue, which is recommended to Wild Bill Davison fans. —*Scott Yanow*

Rompin' 'n' Stompin' / Oct. 30, 1964 / Jazzology ♦♦♦
Cornetist Wild Bill Davison was teamed with the spirited amateur group the Tailgate Ramblers in 1964 for a Jazzology recording session. They romp and stomp their way through 11 Dixieland standards including "Pagan Love Song," "Hello Dolly," "Angry" and "My Monday Date." Davison took a rare vocal on "Save It Pretty Mama" and although none of his sidemen in the banjo-tuba group are standouts, their ensemble sound fits in well with the cornetist. This fun set has been reissued on CD by Jazzology. —*Scott Yanow*

Blowin' Wild / Feb. 14, 1965 / Jazzology ♦♦♦

With Freddy Randall and His Band / Feb. 1965 / Jazzology ♦♦♦♦
Originally put out by Black Lion, this Dixieland set matches the great cornetist Wild Bill Davison with British trumpeter Freddy Randall's septet. In addition to the two brassmen, the session includes trombonist George Chisholm, Bruce Turner (on clarinet and alto), pianist Lennie Felix and vibraphonist Ronnie Gleaves. But despite the fine supporting cast, it is for Wild Bill's emotional solos on such numbers as "Memories of You," "Ghost of a Chance," "Struttin' with Some Barbecue" and "Sunday" that this album is most highly recommended. —*Scott Yanow*

Surfside Jazz / Aug. 19, 1965 / Jazzology ♦♦♦
Reissued on CD with three extra selections, this set matched together for the first time Wild Bill Davison and one of his top followers, fellow cornetist Tom Saunders. With Saunders' regular no-name, Detroit-based group of the period giving Davison support during the 1965 set, Wild Bill blasts out some of his typically heated solos. A few of the numbers are a bit off-the-wall ("Coney Island Washboard," "Old Cape Cod," "Long Gone John" and "Holy Roller") but the music is pure Dixieland. —*Scott Yanow*

After Hours / Apr. 6, 1966-Apr. 10, 1966 / Jazzology ♦♦♦♦
The fiery cornetist Wild Bill Davison is heard in a rather sparse setting on this CD reissue, jamming 13 standards in a quartet with clarinetist Kenny Davern, pianist Charlie Queener and drummer George Wettling. Actually, the live set finds Davison sitting in with the Wettling Trio, and the results are generally quite exciting. High-

lights include "I Never Knew," "Big Butter and Egg Man," "Song of the Wanderer," "Wolverine Blues" and "You're Lucky to Me." Enjoyable and spirited Dixieland. —*Scott Yanow*

Wild Bill at Bull Run / Sep. 1966 / Jazzology ✦✦✦

I'll Be a Friend with Pleasure / Feb. 11, 1968 / Fat Cat Jazz ✦✦✦
This loose set features cornetist Wild Bill Davison jamming through some numbers with a pickup group comprising trombonist Herb Gardner, clarinetist Tommy Gwaltney, pianist John Eaton, rhythm guitarist Steve Jordan, bassist Bill Goodall and drummer Jack Connor; Fat Cat McRee contributes a few spirited vocals. Because little was planned in advance and the musicians stay within the boundaries of Dixieland, there are no real surprises, but Davison's occasional blasts into his upper register are always fun to hear. This LP from the defunct Fat Cat Jazz label will be a difficult one to find. —*Scott Yanow*

Lady of the Evening / Feb. 11, 1968+Apr. 1971 / Jazzology ✦✦✦
The emphasis on this ballad-oriented set (which was originally released on the Fat Cat Jazz label) is on cornetist Wild Bill Davison's melodic variations. His highly expressive playing during a quintet outing with pianist John Eaton, rhythm guitarist Steve Jordan, bassist Jack Lesberg and drummer Cliff Leeman is full of emotion, with each note and growl standing out; "My Honey's Lovin' Arms" is about the only stomp. "Duet" is a leftover track from a 1968 album with trombonist Herb Gardner and clarinetist Tommy Gwaltney. —*Scott Yanow*

The Jazz Giants / Mar. 27, 1968+Mar. 29, 1968 / Sackville ✦✦✦✦
This was one of the first releases from the Canadian Sackville label. Cornetist Wild Bill Davison leads the sextet but most significant is the playing of the underrated clarinetist Herb Hall in one of his best recordings. Filling out the fine swing-based group are trombonist Benny Morton, pianist Claude Hopkins, bassist Arvell Shaw and drummer Buzzy Drootin. Highlights include "Struttin' with Some Barbecue," "I Would Do Anything for You" and "I Found a New Baby." —*Scott Yanow*

Jazz on a Saturday Afternoon, Vol. 1 / Jun. 13, 1970 / Jazzology ✦✦✦✦
In 1970, the Atlanta Jazz Society imported cornetist Wild Bill Davison for one of their monthly concerts; all of the music has been released on two CDs. Davison was not familiar with any of the musicians, except for possibly Ernie Carson (who here sticks to piano except when switching to his usual cornet on a spirited "Royal Garden Blues"), but it is obvious that he was pleasantly surprised by their playing. In fact, by the third song on this nine-selection CD, Wild Bill sounds somewhat jubilant. Trombonist Wray Thomas and clarinetist Herman Foretich were playing above their heads, and the music (highlighted by "Avalon," "Struttin' with Some Barbecue," "You Took Advantage of Me" and the two-cornet "Royal Garden Blues") is quite exciting. The second volume is even better, and both are recommended to Dixieland collectors. —*Scott Yanow*

Jazz on a Saturday Afternoon, Vol. 2 / Jun. 13, 1970 / Jazzology ✦✦✦✦
The second of two CDs recorded at a concert held by the Atlanta Jazz Society in 1970 has the second half of a performance featuring the great cornetist Wild Bill Davison with a sextet of fine local musicians. Best-known among the latter is Ernie Carson, who during this half plays second cornet on seven of the nine numbers, switching to piano for a pair of ballads. The interplay between Wild Bill and Carson (for whom Davison was always a strong influence) is generally quite exciting, resulting in plenty of heated playing. Trombonist Wray Thomas and clarinetist Herman Foretich also get in some fine solos. Highlights of this recommended Dixieland date include "Jazz Me Blues," "I Found a New Baby," "Fidgety Feet" and "That's a Plenty." —*Scott Yanow*

In a Mellow Tone / Aug. 1971 / Jazzology ✦✦✦✦
Although he turned 65 in 1971, cornetist Wild Bill Davison was only at about the halfway point (quantity-wise) of his recording career; the 1970s would be quite busy. Davison teams up with fellow cornetist Tommy Saunders (a sort-of protégé) and his Detroit-based group (which also features trombonist Guy Roth and Earl Stuart on clarinet and tenor) for a typically spirited Dixieland set. The repertoire has a couple of offbeat selections ("Jasper, the Swinging Ghost" and "Surfside Samba"), along with the usual warhorses and a few swing/mainstream standards. But the songs are secondary to the colorful solos, and Wild Bill is heard in excellent form throughout the date. —*Scott Yanow*

Big Horn Jazz Fest '72 / May 29, 1972 / Big Horn ✦✦✦✦
This LP is a real obscurity, probably the only release from the Big Horn label. Recorded at the 1972 Big Horn Jazzfest in Ivanhoe, Illinois, this jam session is very much Wild Bill Davison's date. He heads a sextet also including veteran trombonist George Brunis, Bob Wilber (on clarinet and soprano), pianist Art Hodes (Bobby Wright takes his place on two of the six numbers), bassist Rail Wilson and drummer Barrett Deems. The music is loose and quite lively, with "Tin Roof Blues" the closest any of the songs gets to being a ballad. Highlights include "Avalon," "What Can I Say Dear After I Say I'm Sorry" and "Running Wild." Dixieland fans will want to search for this rarity. —*Scott Yanow*

Live at the Rainbow Room / Jul. 7, 1973-Jul. 8, 1973 / Chiaroscuro ✦✦✦
One of five albums that cornetist Wild Bill Davison led during his 67th year, this live set features eight veteran standards being performed in spirited fashion by Davison, trombonist Ed Hubble, clarinetist Jerry Fuller, pianist Claude Hopkins, bassist George Duvivier and either Cliff Leeman or Dorothy Dodgion on drums. Wild Bill was in great form during the era as can be heard on such numbers as "I Never Knew," "Memories of You," "Wolverine Blues" and "Runnin' Wild." This LP is long overdue to be reissued on CD. —*Scott Yanow*

Tie a Yellow Ribbon 'Round the Old Oak Tree / Sep. 1, 1973 / Fat Cat Jazz ✦✦✦✦
One of cornetist Wild Bill Davison's better outings for Fat Cat Jazz, this studio session teams him with the fine clarinetist Jack Maheu and Maheu's regular Rochester-based group. Best-known among the sidemen is drummer Danny D'Imperio (who would later gain some recognition for his hard bop recordings); his father Bob D'Imperio contributes some fine piano playing. With trombonist Will Alger and bassist Barney Mallon completing the sextet, the band jams through seven standards (all dating from the early '30s or before), "Blues for Eddie Condon" (who had recently passed away) and the then-current pop tune "Tie a Yellow Ribbon 'Round the Old Oak Tree." Unfortunately this LP (as is true of most of the releases from the obsolete Fat Cat Jazz) will be difficult to find. —*Scott Yanow*

Just a Gig / Nov. 1973 / Jazzology ✦✦✦
Just another Wild Bill Davison recording. The fiery cornetist is in good form on this loose jam session date recorded at the 1973 Manassas Jazz Festival. Concert producer "Fat Cat" Johnson McRee has fun taking a couple of goodtime vocals, and trombonist Slide Harris also has one on "I Ain't Gonna Give Nobody None of My Jelly Roll." More significant are the solos of Davison and clarinetist Tom Gwaltney on the Dixieland warhorses. This CD's music (which is highlighted by "I Want to Be Happy," "Jazz Me Blues" and "Indiana") is enjoyable, if not essential. —*Scott Yanow*

But Beautiful / Feb. 6, 1974-May 27, 1975 / Storyville ✦✦✦
Cornetist Wild Bill Davison recorded often in 1974-77 during his annual visits to Copenhagen and virtually all of those albums (usually released by Storyville) are recommended to Dixieland fans. For this set, Wild Bill is heard either backed by a rhythm section or by a medium-sized group with a sax section. The repertoire is full of ballads, although there is plenty of tempo and mood variation. Davison was in his late prime during the era as can be heard on superior versions of "You Took Advantage of Me," "But Beautiful," "I'm Confessin'" and "Blue Turning Gray over You." —*Scott Yanow*

Wild Bill Davison & Papa Bue / Feb. 10, 1974 / Storyville ✦✦✦✦
Veteran cornetist Wild Bill Davison (who was 68 in 1974) recorded several worthy albums with trombonist Papa Bue Jensen's Viking Jazz Band in Copenhagen. This Storyville set has a rare Davison vocal on "Save It Pretty Mama" and spirited jams on such numbers as "Christopher Columbus," "Runnin' Wild" and "China Boy." Nearly all Wild Bill Davison records are easily recommended to Dixieland fans, and this fine outing is no exception. —*Scott Yanow*

Wild Bill Davison/Papa Bue's Viking Jazz Band / Feb. 10, 1974-Jan. 26, 1977 / Storyville ✦✦✦✦
This release draws its material from five sessions that cornetist Wild Bill Davison recorded in Copenhagen with trombonist Papa Bue Jensen's Viking Jazz Band, not duplicating any music released elsewhere. Davison, who sings "A Cottage for Sale," clearly enjoyed playing with Jensen and his band (which also featured clarinetist Jorgen Svarre and occasionally tenor saxophonist Bent Jaedig) and he sounds quite inspired. High points include "I'm Confessin'," "I Never Knew," "Blues My Naughty Sweetie Gives to Me" and "You're Lucky to Me." —*Scott Yanow*

Wild Bill in Denmark, Vol. 1 / Feb. 10, 1974-Jan. 26, 1977 / Storyville ✦✦✦✦
This CD, the first of two taken from the great Dixieland cornetist Wild Bill Davison's collaborations with Papa Bue Jensen's Viking Jazzband in Copenhagen, features Wild Bill in a perfect setting. He is joined by a supportive but stimulating four-piece rhythm section, clarinetist Joren Svare, trombonist Jensen (who sometimes recalls Kid Ory), and on one song, the Budd Johnson-inspired tenor Bent Jaedig. The music is primarily swing and Dixieland standards (along with a couple of blues), and the performances find Davison in prime form. The first nine selections (from Feb. 10, 1974) were out on LP before, but the final four numbers were previously unreleased. Highlights include a lengthy "Christopher Columbus," "Runnin' Wild," Davison's vocal on "Save It Pretty Mama," "China Boy," a dramatic "When It's Sleepy Time Down South" and an emotional version of "Memories of You." This set is highly recommended, as is Vol. 2. —*Scott Yanow*

Beautifully Wild / Mar. 11, 1974 / Audiophile ✦✦✦✦
Cornetist Wild Bill Davison was mostly heard in Dixieland bands throughout his long career but occasionally he would record in more intimate settings for a change of pace. On this Audiophile release, Davison is backed by a four-piece rhythm section that includes vibraphonist Kenny Mason and pianist Don Reitan. The ten standards lean towards ballads and the swing era, and the interpretations

are more mainstream than Dixie. One of the most expressive of all brass players (Davison's growls and shakes allowed him to express both sarcasm and sentimentality, sometimes at the same time), Wild Bill is in fine form on melodic versions of such songs as "She's Funny That Way," "Mean to Me," "What's the Use" and "Everything Happens to Me." —*Scott Yanow*

Wild Bill in Denmark, Vol. 2 / Feb. 6, 1974-1975 / Storyville ◆◆◆◆
Cornetist Wild Bill Davison is heard in typically exuberant form on this second 1996 CD of performances made with trombonist Papa Bue's Viking Jazz Band in the mid-'70s. While Jensen (who can emulate Kid Ory whenever he wants to), the fluid clarinetist Jorgen Svare and guest tenor Ben Jaedig have their spots, Davison is the dominant force; every note that he plays is full of intense emotion. Best is a lengthy and riffing rendition of "Christopher Columbus" (which has Jaedig's only appearance), but other highlights include Wild Bill's repeated stabbing high notes on "Creole Love Call" and the hot playing on "Our Monday Date," "Fidgety Feet" and "White Cliffs of Dover"; even Davison's vocal on "All of Me" is full of spirit. Highly recommended to Dixieland and Chicago jazz collectors, as is the first volume. —*Scott Yanow*

Driftin' Down the River / Jan. 27, 1975-May 27, 1975 / Storyville ◆◆◆◆
Cornetist Wild Bill Davison visited Copenhagen on an annual basis during 1974 and 1977. He is in fine form on this album and, although 69, was still in his musical prime. Joined by trombonist Papa Bue's Viking Jazzband, Davison plays beautifully and with his usual drive and extroverted personality on a variety of standards including "Original Dixieland One Step," "Our Monday Date," "Fidgety Feet" and "White Cliffs of Dover." Easily recommended to Dixieland fans. —*Scott Yanow*

Wild Bill in New Orleans / Apr. 1975 / Jazzology ◆◆◆◆
During his 69th year, Wild Bill Davison led seven albums. The definitive Dixieland cornetist, Wild Bill was still in prime form in the mid-'70s, as he shows on this spirited pickup date in New Orleans. Best-known among his sidemen in the sextet are trombonist George Masso and the ancient bassist Ed Garland, while soprano saxophonist Noel Kalet and pianist David Paquette have remained unknowns. Eight veteran standards (mostly from the 1930s) are interpreted in typically spirited fashion by Davison; "Undecided," "Love Is Just Around the Corner," "You Took Advantage of Me" and "Rosetta" are most memorable. Recommended. —*Scott Yanow*

Wild Bill Meets the Colonial Boys / Aug. 20, 1975 / Fat Cat Jazz ◆◆◆◆
Cornetist Wild Bill Davison collaborated with a fine group of Australian trad players for this obscure but worthy LP. Best-known among the supporting cast is trumpeter Bob Barnard (who is featured on the one number that Davison sat out on, "Mahogany Hall Stomp"). Fat Cat McRee does an okay job on three vocals (he did own the record label) and Wild Bill sounds fine on the usual Dixieland and swing standards, including "September in the Rain," "Chicago," "Sweethearts on Parade" and "Dinah." —*Scott Yanow*

Sweet and Lovely / Aug. 6, 1976-Aug. 8, 1976 / Storyville ◆◆◆◆
The arrangements for the 12-piece string section on this Storyville set may not be all that inspiring (functioning primarily as background music), but cornetist Wild Bill Davison's solos are thoughtful, very expressive and consistently inspired. Wild Bill performs a dozen of his favorite ballads and, although violinist Finn Ziegler has a few solos and there are guest spots for clarinetist Jesper Thilo and trombonist Ole "Fessor" Lindgreen, Davison is largely the entire show. His warm playing on such numbers as "Sugar," "Serenade in Blue," "She's Funny That Way" and "If I Had You" is sometimes both haunting and memorable. —*Scott Yanow*

Together Again / May 23, 1977-May 24, 1977 / Storyville ◆◆◆◆
Cornetist Wild Bill Davison and the masterful stride pianist Ralph Sutton team up on this Copenhagen session with five fine Danish musicians, including Jesper Thilo (who switches between tenor, clarinet and soprano) and trombonist Ole "Fessor" Lindgreen. The program emphasizes swing standards and finds Davison (71 at the time) still in exciting form. Among the memorable selections on the exuberant set are "Everybody Loves My Baby," "Shine," "Running Wild" and Davison's vocal on "After I Say I'm Sorry." The superior playing of Wild Bill and Sutton make this one of the better Storyville trad sets of the past few decades. —*Scott Yanow*

At the King of France Tavern / Aug. 20, 1978 / Fat Cat Jazz ◆◆◆◆
The 1970s were a golden era for Wild Bill Davison, whose cornet playing seemed to defy the passing of time. Although 72 when this somewhat obscure live LP was recorded, Davison's sarcastic tone, his variety of growls and shakes, and his melodic and sentimental style were unchanged from 20 years earlier. He heads a quintet with Kenny Davern (who doubles on clarinet and soprano), pianist Larry Eanet, bassist Carlos Laguana and drummer Eddie Phyfe, jamming through eight familiar standards. Even though Davison had played such tunes as "Our Love Is Here to Stay," "My Monday Date" and "Rosetta" a countless number of times by 1978, his enthusiasm and hard-charging style make the songs sound new. Worth searching for, although this LP from the extinct Fat Cat Jazz label will not be found too easily. —*Scott Yanow*

Wild Bill Davison in London / Jun. 27, 1980 / Jazzology ◆◆◆◆
After many recordings throughout the 1970s, cornetist Wild Bill Davison was finally starting to show his age when he made this album in 1980. At 74, Davison's sound was still very much intact, although he was not aiming for as many high notes as earlier. Teamed up with five top British musicians (including trombonist Roy Williams and the reeds of Johnny Barnes), Davison clearly enjoyed himself during the session. He takes a vocal on "Is It True What They Say About Dixie" and jams such numbers as "From Monday On," "You Can Depend on Me" and "I Never Knew" with sincere feeling and colorful melodic variations. Worth picking up by Dixieland and Wild Bill fans. —*Scott Yanow*

Wild Bill Davison's 75th Anniversary Jazz Band / Jan. 4, 1981 / Jazzology ◆◆◆◆
At age 75, cornetist Wild Bill Davison continued his nearly nonstop touring, performing and recording; 1981 would be Davison's last major year on record, leading five albums for as many different labels. Wild Bill's range had shrunk but his distinctive sound was still intact, as he shows on this spirited workout with trombonist Bill Allred, clarinetist Chuck Hedges, pianist Fred Hunt, bassist Jack Lesberg and drummer Barrett Deems. Davison, who stuck to his musical vision throughout his career, plays his usual repertoire (how many times in his career did he record "Mandy, Make Up Your Mind?") with enthusiasm, while the underrated clarinetist Hedges in particular fares quite well during the live recording. —*Scott Yanow*

Wild Bill Davison and Eddie Miller Play Hoagy Carmichael / Mar. 12, 1981-Mar. 13, 1981 / Real Time ◆◆◆
This direct-to-disc effort has always been a bit of a disappointment. Although two great veterans (the 75-year old cornetist Wild Bill Davison and tenor saxophonist Eddie Miller) comprise the front line and the rhythm section (guitarist Howard Alden, pianist Nat Pierce, bassist Bob Maize and drummer Frank Capp) is swinging, the music lacks any real excitement. The sextet performs ten fine numbers by Hoagy Carmichael but no real sparks occur; Davison in particular really plays it safe. So what should have been a near-classic is pleasant but surprisingly forgettable. —*Scott Yanow*

Solo Flight / Oct. 1981 / Jazzology ◆◆◆◆
Although cornetist Wild Bill Davison sticks mostly to his typical repertoire during this spirited CD, the setting is a bit unusual. Davison is joined by both Denny Wright and Paul Sealey on guitars and bassist Harvey Weston, a similar instrumentation as Ruby Braff's popular group with George Barnes. Although the guitarists get their solos, it is the 75-year-old cornetist who is clearly the leader, showing that in 1981 he still had plenty of fire and emotion left. Highlights include "Blue Room," "I Never Knew," "You Took Advantage of Me," "I Want to Be Happy" and two versions of "I Surrender Dear." —*Scott Yanow*

Live at the Memphis Jazz Festival / Jun. 23, 1982-Jun. 27, 1982 / Jazzology ◆◆◆
Cornetist Wild Bill Davison's next-to-last recording (he was 76 at the time) is a loose jam-session date recorded at the 1982 Memphis Jazz Festival. Five numbers are instrumentals with a fine sextet that also includes trombonist Jim Beebe, clarinetist Chuck Hedges, pianist Joe Johnson, bassist Milt Hinton and drummer Barrett Deems ("Someday You'll Be Sorry" and "Monday Date" are most impressive). The three other songs feature vocalist Sheri Connor and have Doc Ryan on second cornet. The music is fun and recommended to Dixieland fans, but nothing too essential or unusual occurs. —*Scott Yanow*

All-Stars / Oct. 19, 1986 / Timeless ◆◆◆
Cornetist Wild Bill Davison's final recording (made when he was 80, three years before his death) is a typically upbeat affair recorded in West Germany. Davison's tone had shrunk quite a bit, but still had plenty of fire; he is on six of the dozen numbers including a vocal on "Save It Pretty Mama" and a memorable showcase during "I Surrender Dear." There are also features for cornetist Tom Saunders (who sings "Old Folks"), the great vocalist Banu Gibson (heard on "Dr. Jazz" and "Lover Man"), pianist Johnny Varro ("You Stepped Out of a Dream"), tenor saxophonist Danny Moss ("Sweet and Lovely"), trombonist Bill Allred ("Sweet Sue") and clarinetist Chuck Hedges ("When You're Smiling"). Although not essential, this release from the Dutch Timeless label is historic and has its enjoyable moments. —*Scott Yanow*

Alan Dawson

b. Jul. 14, 1929, Marietta, PA, **d.** Feb. 23, 1996, Boston, MA
Drums / Hard Bop

A musician's musician if ever there was one, drummer Alan Dawson was one of those solid, highly professional mainstream jazz musicians who seemingly played with everyone, yet never attained widespread notoriety among the jazz public at large. In the early '50s, Dawson freelanced around Boston and worked steadily with the band of drummer Sabby Lewis. He toured with Lionel Hampton in 1953, then returned to Lewis' group, with which he remained from 1953-56. Around 1954, the father of young drummer Clifford Jarvis approached Dawson about teaching his son; thus began a long and illustrious career as an educator. Dawson would go on to teach many players who would have a significant impact, including most notably Tony Williams. In 1957 he joined the faculty of the Berklee School of Music, where he would teach for the next 18 years. Dawson spent the greater part of his professional life in Boston, playing with a variety of big-name players when they passed through town. One of his longest-lived collaborations was with pianist Jaki Byard and tenor saxophonist Booker Ervin, with whom he recorded for Prestige in the '60s. Dawson also spent the years from 1968-74 with pianist Dave Brubeck's quartet, succeeding Joe Morello in the drum chair. After leaving Berklee in 1975, Dawson continued to teach privately, earning a reputation as one who encouraged young drummers to develop a comprehensive musicality. Among other prominent leaders with whom the versatile Dawson recorded are Lee Konitz, Tal Farlow, Al Cohn, Ruby Braff, Sonny Criss, and Dexter Gordon. Dawson's 1972 date under Sonny Stitt—*Tune Up*—is considered by many to be the saxophonist's finest recording. *—Chris Kelsey*

Bill DeArango (William [Buddy] DeArango)

b. Sep. 20, 1921, Cleveland, OH
Guitar / Bop, Free Jazz, Hard Bop
Bill DeArango's 1993 GM recording was a major revelation, for not only was DeArango (who had been little heard from in jazz since the mid-1950s) still in top form, but he had continued to advance through the years and was now engaging in very advanced improvising. DeArango had played Dixieland locally while growing up, but in 1939 began to play more advanced music. After getting out of the Army in 1944, he moved to New York and was soon an important fixture on 52nd Street. DeArango was a regular member of Ben Webster's group, and during 1945-47, he recorded with Sarah Vaughan (a session that included Dizzy Gillespie and Charlie Parker), Slam Stewart and Red Norvo, Charlie Kennedy, Ike Quebec, Ben Webster, Eddie "Lockjaw" Davis, Charlie Ventura, Dizzy Gillespie (four numbers in 1946, including "A Night In Tunisia" and "Anthropology") and two sessions of his own with Webster as a sideman. Some of DeArango's solos were so advanced (particularly with Gillespie) that it almost sounded as if he were playing backwards. After 1947, Bill DeArango returned to Cleveland, where he led a session in 1954 and then largely dropped out of sight. However, he owned a music store and continued playing on a part-time basis, keeping up with the latest developments, as shown on the impressive 1993 CD. *—Scott Yanow*

● **Anything Went** / Apr. 1, 1993-Apr. 2, 1993 / GM ✦✦✦✦
Guitarist Bill DeArango is best-known for participating on a classic Dizzy Gillespie combo date back in 1946, taking such advanced solos that it almost seemed as if he was playing his guitar backwards. Remarkably little has been heard from DeArango since, with only four obscure recordings made since 1954 before this 1993 CD (which was released in 1996). DeArango, who has spent the past 50 years living in his hometown of Cleveland, making local gigs, teaching and running a music store, was never a revivalist. As this CD shows, he kept up with current trends and was quite familiar with up-to-date electronic devices. Tenor saxophonist Joe Lovano, bassist Ed Schuller and drummer George Schuller are strong assets on this set, which has four brief guitar-tenor duets, four hornless trio pieces and three numbers featuring the full quartet. With the exception of three standards and Ed Schuller's lyrical "Song For D," the performances are all free-form improvisations with DeArango often distorting his sound (à la Bill Frisell). While not everything works (the duets are generally too brief and some songs end inconclusively), there are plenty of fireworks and heated moments. It is rewarding not only to have Bill DeArango back on records again but to hear a veteran of the bop era playing such adventurous music a half-century later. *—Scott Yanow*

Blossom Dearie

b. Apr. 28, 1926, East Durham, NY
Piano, Vocals / Bop, Standards
Blossom Dearie has one of the most unusual styles to be heard in jazz and cabaret music. A fine bop-based pianist, Dearie has a little girl's voice that is definitely an acquired taste but charming in its own way. Early on she sang with the Blue Flames (a vocal group featured with the Woody Herman Orchestra), the Blue Reys (part of Alvino Rey's band) and, in 1952, she recorded the original version of "Moody's Mood for Love" with King Pleasure. That year she went to Paris where she performed with Annie Ross and formed her own vocal group, the Blue Stars. In 1956, Dearie returned to the US and led her own trio, having a successful solo career highlighted by her versions of Dave Frishberg's "Peel Me a Grape" and her original "Hey John." In 1974, she started recording exclusively for her own Daffodil label. *—Scott Yanow*

● **Blossom Dearie** / Sep. 11, 1956-Apr. 9, 1959 / Verve ✦✦✦✦✦
Other than a pair of sessions for the French Barclay label during 1955-56, this set (which has been reissued on CD) has pianist-vocalist Blossom Dearie's first record-

ings as a leader. Teamed up with bassist Ray Brown and drummer Jo Jones, Dearie is heard in her early prime. Although her voice has always been an acquired taste, its sincerity and sense of swing wins one over after a few songs and Dearie's piano playing is first class. In addition to the 14 original selections (mostly swing-era standards plus a couple of French songs), there are three previously unreleased numbers including "Blossom's Blues" which dates from 1959. This CD is the perfect introduction for listeners to the unique sound of Blossom Dearie. *—Scott Yanow*

Verve Jazz Masters 51 / Sep. 12, 1957-Feb. 19, 1960 / Verve ✦✦✦✦✦
Blossom Dearie's music is an acquired taste. While her piano playing is quite sophisticated, her singing utilizes a voice that sounds like a little girl and can get annoying at times. This sampler CD does an expert job of reissuing many of her best early recordings and skipping over the more dated ones. Dearie is heard with three different trio/quartets (which include such sidemen as bassist Ray Brown, Jo Jones or Ed Thigpen on drums and sometimes guitarist Mundell Lowe) and on one song ("Rhode Island Is Famous for You") with Russ Garcia's orchestra. This is as good a Blossom Dearie record to start with as any. Highlights include "Once Upon a Summertime," "Little Jazz Bird," "Tea for Two," a slower-than-usual "The Surrey with the Fringe on Top" and "Manhattan." *—Scott Yanow*

May I Come In? / Feb. 13, 1964-Feb. 15, 1964 / Daffodil ✦✦✦
Pianist-vocalist Blossom Dearie's lone Capitol session is probably her best-known album. Backed by an unidentified orchestra, Dearie sings concise versions of a dozen songs, all of which clock in under three minutes. Her small and cutesy voice will not appeal to all listeners but she has long had a cult following. Highlights include "I'm in Love Again," "Quiet Nights," "May I Come In" and "I'm Old Fashioned." *—Scott Yanow*

Summertime / Sep. 12, 1958-Sep. 13, 1958 / Verve ✦✦✦
Vocalist Blossom Dearie's *Summetime* is a low-key collection of chamber-jazz arranged for a small trio. Working with guitarist Mundell Lowe, bassist Ray Brown, and drummer Ed Thigpen, Dearie sings the material with a gentle conviction; she may never sound passionate, but she never sounds like she doesn't care. The result is a pleasant record that might never be a compelling listen, but it's never a bad one. *—Thom Owens*

John D'earth

b. Mar. 30, 1950, Holliston, MS
Trumpet / Post-Bop, Hard Bop
An excellent straightahead trumpter who is sometimes adventurous, John D'Earth worked with the big bands of Buddy Rich, Thad Jones-Mel Lewis and Lionel Hampton before recording with Bob Moses, Harvie Swartz and Emily Remler. He led his first session in 1989 for Enja. *—Scott Yanow*

One Bright Glance / Apr. 11, 1989 / Enja ✦✦✦✦

Barrett Deems

b. Mar. 1, 1914, Springfield, IL
Drums / Swing
It is ironic that Barrett Deems' highest profile gig, touring with the Louis Armstrong All-Stars, found him very much out-of-place, reduced to playing cliches in a Dixieland setting. In reality, Deems has had a lengthy career with other lesser-known high points. He was with Paul Ash's group when he was just 15 and had his own groups during much of the 1930s. Deems was with the Joe Venuti big band (1937-44), Red Norvo (1948), Charlie Barnet (1951) and Muggsy Spanier (1951-54); during that era he was billed almost accurately as "the world's fastest drummer." Deems was with Louis Armstrong during 1954-58, a period when he was criticized by many jazz writers despite giving the music his best effort. After playing with Jack Teagarden (1960-63), he settled in Chicago where he played locally with many top swing stars. Deems toured Eastern Europe with Benny Goodman's sextet in 1976 and visited South America with Wild Bill Davison. Barrett Deems has, for the past few years, led a fairly modern big band in Chicago and he recorded a strong set with the orchestra for Delmark after he turned 80; his playing now sounds modelled after Buddy Rich. *—Scott Yanow*

Deemus / Apr. 22, 1978 / Delmark ✦✦✦✦

● **Barrett Deems Big Band** / Mar. 6, 1994-Mar. 7, 1994 / Delmark ✦✦✦✦
Barrett Deems, 81 at the time of this recording, will always be best known for his stint with the Louis Armstrong All-Stars in the 1950s. After settling in Chicago, the drummer became the leader of a top-notch jazz orchestra that made its recording debut on this Delmark release. Deems, whose musical role model is Buddy Rich, is in top form throughout the set, which is a bit surprising considering his shaky health at the time. The performances (mostly veteran standards) are usually hard-driving and always swing. The many concise solos are unfortunately unidentified; trumpeter Brad Goode is the only one of the sidemen really known outside of Chi-

cago, although vibraphonist Duane Thamm is clearly a strong asset to the 18-piece band. Few surprises occur during this conventional date, but the music is very enjoyable and makes one aware of some of the many musical talents that reside in Chicago. —*Scott Yanow*

Joey De Francesco

b. Apr. 10, 1971, Springfield, PA

Organ, Trumpet / Bop, Soul Jazz, Hard Bop, Groove

The comeback of the organ in jazz during the late '80s was partly due to the rise of Joey De Francesco, a brilliant and energetic player whose style is heavily influenced by Jimmy Smith. Joey De Francesco was raised in the Philadelphia area. The son of Papa John DeFrancisco, a fierce Hammond organ player himself, Joey got an early start on piano when he was five, and within a year had switched to his father's instrument, the organ. He won all kinds of major awards in high school including the Philadelphia Jazz Society's McCoy Tyner Scholarship. In the first Thelonious Monk International Jazz Piano Competition in 1987, he was a finalist at the age of 16. He is a decent piano player too. He had a record contract with Columbia, was playing with Miles Davis (1988) by the time he left high school and has led his own groups ever since. De Francesco is the most important new organist to emerge during the past decade. He has recorded for Columbia, Muse and Big Mo. —*Scott Yanow & Michael Erlewine*

All of Me / 1989 / Columbia ✦✦✦✦✦

Organist Joey De Francesco's debut as a leader would be impressive even if he had not been 17 at the time! De Francesco, whose sound has always been strongly influenced by Jimmy Smith (sounding like an exact duplicate on "All of Me"), is backed by an eight-piece horn section on two songs and a 16-piece string section on three others but more important to the music is the playing of guitarist Lou Volpe, drummer Buddy Williams and the electric bass of Alex Blake. Houston Person's tenor is also a strong asset on two of the eight numbers in a program that ranges from swing to more modern funk. A strong start to a colorful career. —*Scott Yanow*

● **Where Were You?** / Jun. 1990 / Columbia ✦✦✦✦✦

On his second recording, organist Joey De Francesco is heard in settings ranging from a quartet to a large orchestra. Although he is generally the main star, De Francesco welcomes such guests as tenors Illinois Jacquet and Kirk Whalum (heard on two songs apiece including both jamming on "Red Top") and guitarist John Scofield. De Francesco holds his own and is in top form on such selections as "Teach Me Tonight," "Where Were You," "But Not for Me" and "Love Attack." —*Scott Yanow*

Part III / 1991 / Columbia ✦✦✦

Substantial fluctuation in material quality and performances. De Francesco has a good flair for soul-jazz and hard bop but gets bogged down at times in pop-tinged pablum. —*Ron Wynn*

Reboppin' / 1992 / Columbia ✦✦✦✦

Organist Joey De Francesco had an opportunity on his fourth Columbia project to mostly perform with his own group, a trio consisting of guitarist Paul Bollenback and drummer Byron Landham. Among the guests on a few selections are trumpeter Jim Henry, tenor saxophonist Tony Malaby and, on "Family Jam," guitarist Johnny De Francesco (Joey's brother) and organist John De Francesco (their father). Special treats are Joey De Francesco's effective trumpet solos on four of the 14 selections; highlights overall include "Sister Sadie," "Big Bad Jim," "Evidence" and "Bye Bye Blackbird." —*Scott Yanow*

Live at the 5 Spot / 1993 / Columbia ✦✦✦

Organist Joey De Francesco clearly had a good time during this jam session. His fine quintet (which has strong soloists in altoist Robert Landham, trumpeter Jim Henry and especially guitarist Paul Bollenback) starts things off with a runthrough of "rhythm changes" during "The Eternal One" and the hornless trio cuts loose on a swinging "I'll Remember April," but otherwise all of the other selections feature guests. Tenors Illinois Jacquet, Grover Washington, Jr., Houston Person and Kirk Whalum all fare well on separate numbers (Jacquet steals the show on "All of Me") and on the closing blues De Francesco interacts with fellow organist Captain Jack McDuff. Few surprises occur overall (the tenors should have all played together) but the music is quite pleasing and easily recommended to De Francesco's fans. —*Scott Yanow*

All About My Girl / 1994 / Muse ✦✦✦✦

The Street of Dreams / 1995 / Big Mo ✦✦✦

Buddy DeFranco (Boniface Ferdinand Leonardo DeFranco)

b. Feb. 17, 1923, Camden, NJ

Clarinet / Bop

Buddy DeFranco is one of the great clarinetists of all time and, until the rise of Eddie Daniels, he was indisputably the top clarinetist to emerge since 1940. It was DeFranco's misfortune to be the best on an instrument that after the swing era dropped drastically in popularity and, unlike Benny Goodman and Artie Shaw, he has never been a household name for the general public.

When he was 14, DeFranco won an amateur swing contest sponsored by Tommy Dorsey. After working with the big bands of Gene Krupa (1941-42) and Charlie Barnet (1943-44), he was with TD on and off during 1944-48. DeFranco, other than spending part of 1950 with Count Basie's septet, was mostly a bandleader from then on. Among the few clarinetists to transfer the language of Charlie Parker onto his instrument, DeFranco has won a countless number of polls and appeared with the Metronome All-Stars in the late '40s. He recorded frequently in the 1950s (among his sidemen were Art Blakey, Kenny Drew and Sonny Clark) and participated in some of Norman Granz's Verve jam session. During 1960-63, DeFranco led a quartet that also featured the accordion of Tommy Gumina and he recorded an album with Art Blakey's Jazz Messengers on which he played bass clarinet. However, work was difficult to find in the 1960s, leading DeFranco to accept the assignment of leading the Glenn Miller ghost band (1966-74). He has found more artistic success co-leading a quintet with Terry Gibbs off and on since the early '80s and has recorded through the decades for many labels. —*Scott Yanow*

★ **Complete Verve Recordings of Buddy DeFranco with Sonny Clark** / Apr. 7, 1954-Aug. 26, 1955 / Mosaic ✦✦✦✦✦

Clarinetist Buddy DeFranco recorded extensively for Norgran and Verve during 1953-58. For a little over a year, Sonny Clark was his regular pianist and all of their small-group recordings have been reissued on this limited-edition five-LP set. With bassist Eugene Wright (a couple years before he joined the Dave Brubeck Quartet) and drummer Bobby White completing the quartet and guitarist Tal Farlow making the group a quintet on its final 11 numbers, DeFranco had one of his strongest bands. The majority of the 39 selections on the typically attractive Mosaic box are standards or based on a familiar tune's chord changes. Buddy DeFranco had no real competitors (other than Benny Goodman) during the era, while Sonny Clark was one of the most talented of the Bud Powell-influenced pianists; they made for a mutually inspiring team. —*Scott Yanow*

Closed Session / Oct. 30, 1957-Nov. 1, 1957 / Verve ✦✦✦✦

This 1979 LP contains select selections taken from sessions that found clarinetist Buddy DeFranco paying tribute to the music of Benny Goodman and Artie Shaw. DeFranco, who actually sounds nothing like the earlier swing pacesetters, is heard in an octet with trumpeter Don Fagerquist and tenor saxophonist Georgie Auld and in a sextet with trumpeter Ray Linn. The music (which has not yet been reissued on CD) swings but is generally fairly boppish, while occasionally hinting at the earlier recordings. Highlights include "After You've Gone," "Softly as In a Morning Sunrise" and "S'Wonderful." —*Scott Yanow*

Cross-Country Suite / Jun. 27, 1959-Jul. 3, 1959 / Dot ✦✦✦

Nelson Riddle's 11 originals and arrangements for an orchestra on this obscure LP are a bit lightweight and not overly memorable but clarinetist Buddy DeFranco's playing is typically fluid, swinging and explorative within the bop tradition. There are some short spots for trumpeter Don Fagerquist and altoist Herb Geller but DeFranco is the main star and the real reason to search for this long out-of-print rarity. —*Scott Yanow*

The Girl from Ipanema / 1964 / Mercury ✦✦✦✦

During 1960-64, clarinetist Buddy DeFranco co-led a quartet/quintet with accordionist Tommy Gumina. They recorded five albums that have been long out-of-print, including this session for Mercury, which was their last before the group broke up. Actually, DeFranco plays a fairly minor role on the date. In the ensembles, he blends in with the accordion so closely as to be almost inaudible. Gumina takes the lion's share of the solo space on the standards and ballads and is well showcased on the rapid and somewhat bizarre "Lunar Lunacy." Other highlights include the title tune, "Satin Doll" and "It Could Happen to You." This LP will be difficult to find but it is better than it looks. —*Scott Yanow*

Free Fall / Jul. 29, 1974 / Choice ✦✦✦

Other than as leader of the ghost Glenn Miller Orchestra, clarinetist Buddy DeFranco had not recorded as a leader for a decade before cutting this adventurous set for Choice. With keyboardist Victor Feldman, guitarist John Chiodini, bassist Victor Sproles and drummer Joe Cocuzzo, DeFranco avoids bop standards and instead performs his lengthy "Threat of Freedom," Feldman's "Free Fall," a couple of standards and guitarist Jim Gillis' "Free Sail." Although DeFranco's boppish clarinet style had not changed much through the years, his ears were open to more modern ideas and he stretches himself throughout the generally challenging material. —*Scott Yanow*

Borinquin / 1975 / Sonet ✦✦✦✦

Clarinetist Buddy DeFranco's young group in 1975 was fairly modern, consisting of pianist Ran Santisi, guitarist John Chiodini, bassist Mike Richmond and drummer Randy Jones. However, the virtuosic clarinetist had no trouble keeping up with his sidemen and he really cooks on the rapid renditions of "But Not for Me" and "The Song Is You" while also faring well on the group's harmonically advanced originals. This European import gives listeners a good example of how DeFranco was advancing with the times without watering down his talents. —*Scott Yanow*

Buddy DeFranco / 1977 / Classic Jazz ✦✦✦

This is a rather unusual record. The duo of clarinetist Buddy DeFranco and guitarist Jim Gillis perform ten "Etudes" that had been commissioned as an educational project for jazz clarinet students. Since the music contains some strong (if not particularly memorable) melodies, DeFranco and Gillis decided to record the pieces and improvise off of them. The results are pleasing, making this somewhat rare LP a bit of a collector's item. —*Scott Yanow*

Waterbed / Jan. 1977-May 1977 / Choice ✦✦

Back in the early '60s, clarinetist Buddy DeFranco teamed up regularly with the fine jazz accordion player Tommy Gumina. For this 1977 recording, DeFranco meets up with the accordion of Canadian Gordie Fleming in a quartet (along with bassist Michel Donato and drummer Peter Magadini). On four obscure songs by the songwriting team of Rob Adams and Al Baculis and a couple of ballads ("Lush Life" and "Here's That Rainy Day"), DeFranco and Fleming make for a compatible team. The results are not overly memorable (there are many hotter recordings available by the great clarinetist) but are pleasing and grow in interest with each listen. —*Scott Yanow*

☆ Like Someone in Love / Mar. 11, 1977 / Progressive ✦✦✦✦

An all-star quintet comprising clarinetist Buddy DeFranco, guitarist Tal Farlow, pianist Derek Smith, bassist George Duvivier and drummer Ronnie Bedford performs two obscure DeFranco originals, Jim Gillis' "Coasting at the Palisades," a couple of Gershwin classics and the title cut. DeFranco and Farlow made for an appealing team in the mid-'50s when they briefly played together regularly and the old magic (fueled by Derek Smith's fine swing solos) was still present for this excellent 1977 session. —*Scott Yanow*

Mood Indigo / Nov. 27, 1980 / Hep ✦✦✦✦✦

The musicians who are heard on this LP with clarinetist Buddy DeFranco (pianist Jorge Navarro, guitarist Richard Lew, bassist Jorge Lopez-Ruiz and drummer Osvaldo Lopez) from a concert in Buenos Aires, Argentina, may not be known in the US, but their fine playing inspires the clarinetist to come up with lengthy and frequently exciting improvisations. DeFranco really stretches out on "Mood Indigo," "Street of Dreams," "The Song Is You" and an 11-minute "Scrapple from the Apple," making this set well worth acquiring by fans of straightahead jazz and DeFranco's boppish clarinet. —*Scott Yanow*

Mr. Lucky / Jan. 5, 1981+Jan. 6, 1981 / Original Jazz Classics ✦✦✦

Considering that he recorded extensively for Norman Granz's Norgran and Verve labels in the 1950s, it is surprising that it took until 1984 before clarinetist Buddy DeFranco finally led a session for Granz's Pablo Records. On the first of his two Pablo dates, DeFranco is joined by the cool-toned guitarist Joe Cohn, pianist Albert Dailey, bassist George Duvivier and drummer Ronnie Bedford for some standards along with obscurities by Victor Feldman ("Your Smile"), Al Cohn, Bernie Senensky and Eddie Higgins; he also greatly uplifts Henry Mancini's "Mr. Lucky." To his credit, DeFranco (who, at that point, had ranked near the top for 40 years) had not given up his search for fresh material in which to test himself. —*Scott Yanow*

On Tour: UK / Sep. 28, 1983 / Hep ✦✦✦

Hark / Apr. 30, 1985 / Original Jazz Classics ✦✦✦✦✦

This CD reissue of a Pablo date by clarinetist Buddy DeFranco teams him with pianist Oscar Peterson, guitarist Joe Pass, bassist Niels Pedersen and drummer Martin Drew. They perform a few obscure originals plus Duke Ellington's "All Too Soon," "By Myself" and Clifford Brown's "Joy Spring." DeFranco has been very consistent throughout his long recording career, but the presence of Peterson and Pass clearly inspired him to play even better than usual. Recommended. —*Scott Yanow*

Born to Swing! / 1988 / Hindsight ✦✦✦

For this obscure session, the great clarinetist Buddy DeFranco is accompanied by the swing band of Al Raymond. DeFranco is the main star on six of the eight selections but there is also solo space for trombonist Al Grey and pianist Pete Jackson among others. The repertoire includes some swing tunes and originals by DeFranco and Denis DiBlasio; the latter along with George Rabbai contributes a scat vocal to "Buy It and Fry It." The music is pleasing and swinging if somewhat predictable. —*Scott Yanow*

Holiday for Swing / Aug. 22, 1988-Aug. 23, 1988 / Contemporary ✦✦✦✦✦

The two virtuosos clarinetist Buddy DeFranco and vibraphonist Terry Gibbs always inspire each other. Gibbs is such a hyper player and DeFranco can play very fast with no difficulty, so they make for a perfectly compatible team. Most of their joint projects have been released under Gibbs' name but on this occasion, DeFranco received first billing. With pianist John Campbell, bassist Todd Coolman and drummer Gerry Gibbs forming a powerhouse rhythm section, DeFranco and Gibbs romp on such material as "Holiday for Strings," "Seven Come Eleven," "Carioca," Bud Powell's "Parisian Thoroughfare" and Gibbs' "Fickle Fingers." Joyous music. —*Scott Yanow*

Chip off the Old Bop / Jul. 28, 1992-Jul. 29, 1992 / Concord Jazz ✦✦✦

Pianist Larry Novak, guitarist Joe Cohn, bassist Ketter Betts and drummer Jimmy Cobb form a stimulating and supportive rhythm section behind the advanced flights of the still-remarkable clarinetist Buddy DeFranco. This bop-oriented set mixes together standards with some lesser-known material (such as Flip Phillips' "Hashimoto's Blues," guitarist Jim Gillis' "Chip Off the Old Bop" and DeFranco's "Out to Lunch") and will consistently satisfy and sometimes excite straightahead jazz collectors. —*Scott Yanow*

Jack DeJohnette

b. Aug. 9, 1942, Chicago, IL
Drums, Keyboards / Avant-Garde, Post-Bop, Fusion

At his best, Jack DeJohnette one of the most consistently inventive jazz percussionists extant. DeJohnette's style is wide-ranging, yet, while capable of playing convincingly in any modern idiom, he always maintains a well-defined voice. DeJohnette has a remarkably fluid relationship to pulse. His time is excellent; even as he pushes, pulls and generally obscures the beat beyond recognition, a powerful sense of swing is ever-present. His tonal palette is huge as well; no drummer pays closer attention to the sounds that come out of his kit than DeJohnette. He possesses a comprehensive musicality rare among jazz drummers.

That's perhaps explained by the fact that, before he played the drums, DeJohnette was a pianist. From the age of four, he studied classical piano. As a teenager, he became interested in blues, popular music, and jazz; Ahmad Jamal was an early influence. In his late teens, DeJohnette began playing drums, which soon became his primary instrument. In the early '60s occurred the most significant event of his young professional life—an opportunity to play with John Coltrane. In the mid-'60s, DeJohnette became involved with the Chicago-based Association for the Advancement of Creative Musicians. He moved to New York in 1966, where he played again with Coltrane, and also with Jackie McLean. His big break came as a member of the very popular Charles Lloyd Quartet from 1966-68. The drummer's first record as a leader was 1968's *The DeJohnette Complex*. In 1969, DeJohnette replaced Tony Williams in Miles Davis' band; later that year, he played on the trumpeter's seminal jazz-rock recording *Bitches Brew*. DeJohnette left Davis in 1972, and began working more frequently as a leader. In the '70s and '80s, DeJohnette became something like a house drummer for ECM, recording both as leader and sideman with such label mainstays as Jan Garbarek, Kenny Wheeler, and Pat Metheny.

DeJohnette's first band was Compost; his later, more successful bands were Directions and Special Edition. The eclectic, avant-fusion Directions was originally comprising the bassist Mike Richmond, guitarist John Abercrombie, and saxophonist Alex Foster. In a subsequent incarnation—called, appropriately, New Directions—bassist Eddie Gomez replaced Richmond and trumpeter Lester Bowie replaced Foster. From the mid-'70s, Directions recorded several albums in its twin guises for ECM. Beginning in 1979, DeJohnette also led Special Edition, a more straightforwardly swinging unit that featured saxophonists David Murray and Arthur Blythe. For a time, both groups existed simultaneously; Special Edition would eventually become the drummer's performance medium of choice. The band began life as an acoustic free-jazz ensemble, featuring the drummer's esoteric takes on the mainstream. It evolved into something quite different, as DeJohnette's conception changed into something considerably more commercial; with the addition of electric guitars and keyboards, DeJohnette began playing what is essentially a very loud, backbeat-oriented—though sophisticated—instrumental pop music. To be fair, DeJohnette's fusion efforts are miles ahead of most others'. His abilities as a groove-centered drummer are considerable, but one misses the subtle colorations of his acoustic work. That side of DeJohnette is shown to good effect in his work with Keith Jarrett's Standards trio, and in his occasional meetings with Abercrombie and Dave Holland in the Gateway trio. —*Chris Kelsey*

The DeJohnette Complex / Dec. 26, 1968-Dec. 27, 1968 / Original Jazz Classics ✦✦✦✦

Drummer Jack DeJohnette's debut as a leader (which has been reissued on CD) has quite a bit of variety. The music ranges from advanced swinging to brief free improvisations and some avant-funk. DeJohnette (who doubles on melodica) is joined by Bennie Maupin (on tenor and flute), keyboardist Stanley Cowell, bassists Miroslav Vitous and Eddie Gomez, and drummer Roy Haynes. He uses six different combinations of musicians on the eight songs (five of his originals, John Coltrane's "Miles' Mode," Cowell's "Equipoise" and Vitous' "Mirror Image"). Intriguing and generally successful music. —*Scott Yanow*

Have You Heard? / Jul. 4, 1970 / Epic ♦♦♦
A high-level Japanese session. —*Ron Wynn*

Sorcery / Mar. 1974 / Original Jazz Classics ♦♦
A lot of rambling takes place on this interesting but erratic CD reissue. Drummer Jack DeJohnette (doubling on keyboards) performs three songs with a group featuring bass clarinetist Bennie Maupin and the guitars of John Abercrombie and Mick Goodrick, music that shows the influence of fusion (most obviously on "The Rock Thing") and has its strong moments (much of the nearly 14-minute "Sorcery No. 1"); however the attempt at humor on "The Right Time" is self-indulgent. The second half of this release, trios by DeJohnette, bassist Dave Holland and Michael Fellerman on metaphone (whatever that is), are less memorable. While one admires DeJohnette's willingness to take chances, this music has not dated well. —*Scott Yanow*

Cosmic Chicken / Apr. 24, 1975+Apr. 26, 1975 / Prestige ♦♦♦
Funk suggestiveness, improvisatory energy. —*Ron Wynn*

Directions / Feb. 1976 / ECM ♦♦♦

Pictures / Feb. 1976 / ECM ♦♦♦

New Rags / May 1977 / ECM ♦♦♦
Drummer Jack DeJohnette's "Directions" was a rather unusual quartet. With the leader doubling on piano and matching his creativity with guitarist John Abercrombie, Alex Foster (on tenor and soprano) and bassist Mike Richmond, this was obviously a talented all-star group. The compositions on *New Rags* (all by DeJohnette or Foster) are difficult, rather dry and unpredictable, and the ensemble is not shy to utilize electronics and the subtle influence of rock. It is easy to see why this unit did not catch on, but its music is still fresh. —*Scott Yanow*

New Directions / Jun. 1978 / ECM ♦♦
New Directions (a quartet with Jack DeJohnette on drums and piano, guitarist John Abercrombie, trumpeter Lester Bowie and bassist Eddie Gomez) is a group that never seemed to live up to its potential. On this set of three DeJohnette compositions (including the wittily titled "Where or Wayne") and two group improvisations, the music is a bit dull, making too much use of space and featuring less of Bowie's trumpet and wit than one would hope. There are some strong moments (particularly from Abercrombie and DeJohnette) but this band (to use a cliché) was less than the sum of its parts. —*Scott Yanow*

★ Special Edition / Mar. 1979 / ECM ♦♦♦♦
The debut recording by Jack DeJohnette's Special Edition is a classic. The drummer (who also plays some piano and melodica) is joined for three of his stimulating originals (including "Zoot Suite") and a pair of John Coltrane songs ("Central Park West" and "India") by tenor saxophonist David Murray (doubling on bass clarinet), altoist Arthur Blythe and bassist Peter Warren (who also plays some cello). The challenging frameworks are full of color, variety and highly expressive moods that push the musicians (both collectively and individually) to play at their very best and most explorative. This was one of the great groups of the late '70s and the finest version of DeJohnette's Special Edition; highly recommended. —*Scott Yanow*

New Directions in Europe / Jun. 1979 / ECM ♦♦♦
Drummer Jack DeJohnette's New Directions tended to promise much more than it delivered. The quartet (comprising the leader on drums and piano, trumpeter Lester Bowie, guitarist John Abercrombie and bassist Eddie Gomez) was certainly full of talent, but their performances often rambled excessively before finding its purpose. This live set has four lengthy pieces, three of which are DeJohnette originals (including "Where or Wayne") and a free improvisation by the band. There are some colorful moments but overall the music is not all that memorable. —*Scott Yanow*

Tin Can Alley / Sep. 1980 / ECM ♦♦♦♦
Special Edition has long been the best vehicle for Jack DeJohnette's drumming, occasional keyboard work and writing. The 1980 version of this quartet featured Chico Freeman on tenor and bass clarinet, John Purcell's work on baritone and alto, and bassist Peter Warren. The wide-ranging music on this fine set ranges from African rhythms and colors reminiscent of Duke Ellington to some boppish moments and a bit of light funk. Although not the most powerful version of Special Edition, this set is recommended. —*Scott Yanow*

Inflation Blues / Sep. 1982 / ECM ♦♦♦
The only recording by Jack DeJohnette's Special Edition to use a trumpeter (guest Baikida Carroll), this is a particularly strong outing by the 1982 edition of the group. With Chico Freeman (on tenor, bass clarinet and soprano), John Purcell (alto, flutes and baritone), bassist Rufus Reid and the leader-drummer (who also contributes some piano), it is not surprising that the music is adventurous yet quite coherent, with the solo and group statements being both spontaneous and logical. Recommended. —*Scott Yanow*

Album, Album / Jun. 1984 / ECM ♦♦♦♦♦
Most of Special Edition's recordings are quite rewarding and this set is no exception. Drummer/keyboardist Jack DeJohnette contributed five of the six compositions (all but "Monk's Mood") and they cover a wide range of styles and moods, from "New Orleans Suite" and "Festival" to the ambitious "Third World Anthem" and a revisit to his "Zoot Suite." This was one of the most stimulating jazz groups of the 1980s and this particular lineup (with John Purcell on alto and soprano, tenor saxophonist David Murray, Howard Johnson doubling on tuba and baritone, and bassist Rufus Reid) was one of DeJohnette's strongest. —*Scott Yanow*

The Jack DeJohnette Piano Album / Jan. 14, 1985-Jan. 15, 1985 / Landmark ♦♦♦
This album was a surprise when it was released for it features drummer Jack DeJohnette exclusively on piano and synthesizer in a trio with bassist Eddie Gomez and drummer Freddie Waits. On a couple of the tunes, DeJohnette was among the very first pianists to really capture the sound of Thelonious Monk. Other selections are more in his own style and he displays a strong technique that does not sound like the work of a drummer who is moonlighting. In addition to three of his originals, there are selections by Gigi Gryce ("Minority"), John Coltrane, Denny Zeitlin and Cyndi Lauper ("Time After Time"). Worth checking out. —*Scott Yanow*

Zebra / May 8, 1985-May 10, 1985 / MCA ♦♦
The music on this obscure LP was used as the soundtrack for a video program. Jack DeJohnette is heard on synthesizers and is usually joined by trumpeter Lester Bowie. The performances are moody and it has its colorful moments although most of it does not stand alone all that well without the film. Superior background music, recommended mostly to Jack DeJohnette completists. —*Scott Yanow*

Irresistible Force / Jan. 1987 / MCA ♦♦♦
Jack DeJohnette's first Special Edition recording in five years finds him using completely different personnel than earlier. Greg Osby (on alto and soprano) and Gary Thomas (doubling on tenor and flute) bring M-Base influences to the band (their improvisations have a fresh new logic) while guitarist Mick Goodrick, bassist Lonnie Plaxico, percussionist Nana Vasconcelos (who doubles on keyboards) all make strong contributions. Other than Osby's "Osthetics," the repertoire comprises DeJohnette's originals, and the somewhat unique music gives all of the musicians opportunities to express themselves and inspire each other. —*Scott Yanow*

Audio-Visualscapes / Feb. 1, 1988-Feb. 3, 1988 / MCA ♦♦♦
This single CD (formerly a double LP) from Jack DeJohnette's Special Edition contains music that mixes together advanced hard bop, fusion, M-Base funk and avant-garde jazz. Greg Osby (alto and soprano), Gary Thomas (tenor, flute and bass clarinet), guitarist Mick Goodrick, bassist Lonnie Plaxico and drummer DeJohnette (who also plays some keyboards) are all highly original voices and they have plenty of opportunities to interact with each other on songs written by DeJohnette, Osby and Ornette Coleman ("The Sphinx"). The results are sometimes unsettling but rarely dull, well worth several listens. —*Scott Yanow*

Parallel Realities / 1990 / MCA ♦♦♦
An overlooked session with Pat Metheny (g) in definite jazz phase. Herbie Hancock shows his steadfast piano form. —*Ron Wynn*

Earthwalk / Jun. 1991 / Blue Note ♦♦♦♦
Jack DeJohnette's Special Edition in its infrequent recordings has produced consistently stimulating music. The 1991 version of the group is most significant in adding keyboardist Michael Cain to the band (in place of guitarist Mick Goodrick) and having DeJohnette stick exclusively to drums. The holdovers from 1988 are altoist Greg Osby (doubling on soprano), Gary Thomas (on tenor and flute) and bassist Lonnie Plaxico. The group performs ten of its leader's compositions including "It's Time to Wake Up and Dream," "Where or Wayne" and "Monk's Plumb." Unpredictable and always-stimulating music by the highly original unit. —*Scott Yanow*

Music for the Fifth World / Feb. 1992 / Manhattan ♦♦♦♦
Jack DeJohnette has long been more than "just" a drummer; he is also a fine keyboardist and a very talented composer. This CD finds him exploring music ranging from American Indian melodies to rockish fusion and his tribute "Miles." His group includes powerhouse guitarists Vernon Reid and John Scofield along with a chanting vocal choir. The music is stimulating if not as essential as DeJohnette's earlier work with Special Edition. —*Scott Yanow*

Extra Special Edition / 1994 / Blue Note ♦♦
The inclusion of Bobby McFerrin to drummer Jack DeJohnette's group should have been a definite plus since the singer can do so much with his voice (from substitut-

ing for a string bass to using his falsetto like a horn) but the mostly original program not only lacks more than one or two strong melodies but any real development as well, particularly on the selections that have McFerrin. Performances often start in what could just as well be the middle and end inconclusively with many of the pieces being little more than funky riffs for the rhythm section. Despite a few strong moments (mostly from pianist Michael Cain), only "Seventh D" and "Summertime" (both instrumentals) are worth hearing a second time. —*Scott Yanow*

Dancing with Nature Spirits / May 1995 / ECM ◆◆◆◆
For Jack DeJohnette's 1995 ECM release, the drummer teams up in an unusual trio with pianist Michael Cain (who has his own sound) and the atmospheric reeds of Steve Gorn (who is heard on soprano, clarinet and bansuri flute). The five group originals (two of which are over 20 minutes long) build gradually to a high level of intensity. Although there is no bass, the music swings in its own way and DeJohnnete's drums and percussion are consistently stimulating. This thoughtful but often-fiery music is worth a close listen. —*Scott Yanow*

Oneness / 1996 / ECM ◆◆◆
Oneness finds Jack DeJohnette in a subtle reflective mood, working with a minimal backing group highlighted by pianist Michael Cain. DeJohnette and Cain turn in a series of dialogues that finds the piano highlighting the statements and improvisations of the percussion. Things are at their noisiest on "Welcome Blessing," a duet with percussionist Don Alias, but *Oneness* stands as a welcome, minimalist and challenging effort from DeJohnette. —*Stephen Thomas Erlewine*

Barbara Dennerlein

b. Sep. 25, 1964, Munich, Germany
Organ / Post-Bop, Hard Bop
Barbara Dennerlein differs from most organists by not sounding all that much like Jimmy Smith. She utilizes MIDI with her organ in order to get a different sound and her baselines (which she operates through her foot pedals) really do sound like a bass. Dennerlein began playing organ at 11 and four years later was already gigging in local clubs. She recorded on her own Bebab label and since 1988 has also made albums for Enja that have created a bit of a stir in the US, using such sidemen as Ray Anderson and Mitch Watkins. —*Scott Yanow*

Orgelspiele / May 4, 1984-May 6, 1984 / Bebab ◆◆◆
Organist Barbara Dennerlein performs a wide variety of material on this little-known quartet session from her private German Bebab label. The repertoire ranges from "Blue Rondo a La Turk" and "This Masquerade" (the latter's authorship is mistakenly assigned to George Benson) to Stevie Wonder's "All in Love Is Fair," Chick Corea's "Spain" and pieces by Bach and Chopin. Dennerlein is one of the few original voices on the organ to emerge after Larry Young, and she is fine form on the swinging set. —*Scott Yanow*

Bebab / Jul. 27, 1985 / Bebab ◆◆◆◆
Even at this early stage, German organist Barbara Dennerlein had a fairly original conception on her instrument, escaping almost completely from the dominant Jimmy Smith influence. Dennerlein performs a bop-oriented set (comprising seven originals and "Au Privave") with her two-horn quintet and, although the brief liner notes are in German, the swinging music definitely communicates. —*Scott Yanow*

● **Straight Ahead** / Jul. 18, 1988-Jul. 20, 1988 / Enja ◆◆◆◆◆
After several recordings on her own Bebab label and for a few tiny German companies, organist Barbara Dennerlein came to the attention of a larger public with the release of this superior effort for Enja. Teamed up with the eccentric trombonist Ray Anderson, the fiery guitarist Mitch Watkins and drummer Ronnie Burrage, Dennerlein performs six of her swinging originals, one apiece by Anderson and Burrage plus "Opus de Funk" and "A Night in Tunisia." The colorful voices of these musicians constantly inspire each other and Dennerlein (whose sound with the use of MIDI had become quite original) quickly emerged as one of the brightest new stars of the organ in the late '80s. —*Scott Yanow*

Plays Classics / Nov. 28, 1988-Nov. 29, 1988 / Redken ◆◆◆◆
Barbara Dennerlein was (with Joey De Francesco) the most interesting jazz organist to emerge during the 1980s. She recorded several early albums for her German Bebab label before hooking up with Enja and later on Verve, and the hard-to-find recordings are all worth acquiring. This particular LP is one of her better ones, featuring the organist in a trio on seven standards and two of her originals. The liner notes are in German but the music certainly communicates, as Dennerlein swings hard on such tunes as "How High the Moon," "Take the 'A' Train" and even the Beatles' "Yesterday." —*Scott Yanow*

Hot Stuff / Jun. 6, 1990-Jun. 8, 1990 / Enja ◆◆◆◆
Organist Barbara Dennerlein's second Enja CD matches her distinctive organ and synthesizers with guitarist Mitch Watkins, drummer Mark Mondesir and (on five of the nine numbers) tenor saxophonist Andy Sheppard. Dennerlein contributed seven of the nine selections (the others are "Killer Joe" and "Seven Steps to

Heaven") and her music ranges from blues to advanced hard bop, offering organ fans an alternative to the Jimmy Smith/Joey De Francesco style. —*Scott Yanow*

That's Me / Mar. 3, 1992-Mar. 10, 1992 / Enja ◆◆◆◆◆
This CD reissues German organist Barbara Dennerlein's initial Enja release, which was her first to make a strong impression in the US. By adding synthesizers and MIDI to her sound, Dennerlein has largely escaped from the dominant Jimmy Smith influence that buries most organists' potential musical personalities. With the exception of the somewhat overblown "Love Affair—the Ballad," she excels on the swinging set, holding her own with such extroverted soloists as trombonist Ray Anderson, tenor saxophonist Bob Berg and guitarist Mitch Watkins; drummer Dennis Chambers completes the quintet. Dennerlein's expert foot pedal work often makes it sound as if there is an independent bassist on the colorful date. She contributed all of the originals except Anderson's "One for Miss D.," and the mixture of blues, ballads, a jazz waltz and more complex pieces works quite well. This set is a very good example of Barbara Dennerlein's appealing talents. —*Scott Yanow*

Take Off! / Mar. 1995 / Verve ◆◆◆◆◆

Junkanoo / 1996 / Verve ◆◆◆

Sidney DeParis

b. May 30, 1905, Crawfordsville, IN, **d.** Sep. 13, 1967, New York, NY
Trumpet / Dixieland
A distinctive trumpeter who fit into both New Orleans jazz and swing settings, Sidney DeParis was particularly expert with mutes. He worked with Charlie Johnson's Paradise Ten (1926-31), Don Redman (1932-36 and 1939), Zutty Singleton (1939-41), Benny Carter (1940-41) and Art Hodes (1941) and recorded on the famed Panassie sessions (1938) and with Jelly Roll Morton (1939) and Sidney Bechet (1940). DeParis recorded some highly enjoyable and freewheeling sessions as a leader in 1944 (for Commodore and Blue Note) and for Blue Note in 1951. He played with his brother Wilbur DeParis' New New Orleans Jazz Band throughout the 1950s before ill health forced his retirement in the 1960s. —*Scott Yanow*

● **Story 1928-1944** / 1928-1944 / Epm Musique ◆◆◆◆◆

Dixieland Hits Country & Western / 1962 / Swingville ◆◆◆◆
Trumpeter Sidney DeParis' only recordings as a leader were for Blue Note in 1944 and 1951 (those selections have been reissued in full on a Mosaic box set along with other sessions) and this obscure LP. For what would be possibly his final recordings, DeParis and a top-notch group (comprising trombonist Bennie Morton, clarinetist Kenny Davern, banjoist Lee Blair, pianist Charlie Queener, bassist Leonard Gaskin and drummer Herb Lovelle) perform Dixiefied versions of eight country songs. "Pistol Packin' Mama," "You Always Hurt the One You Love" and "Yellow Rose of Texas" fit easily into the format, and even the other five numbers (such as "You Call Everybody Darling" and "Ghost Riders in the Sky") are unlikely successes. Hopefully Fantasy will get around to reissuing this little-known date on CD someday. —*Scott Yanow*

Wilbur DeParis

b. Jan. 11, 1900, Crawfordsville, IN, **d.** Jan. 3, 1973, New York, NY
Trombone, Leader / Dixieland
Wilbur DeParis, an adequate soloist, was an excellent ensemble player and an important bandleader who helped keep New Orleans jazz alive in the 1950s. He started out on alto horn and in 1922 played C-melody sax while working with A.J. Piron before switching permanently to trombone. In 1925, DeParis led a band in Philadelphia and then had stints in the orchestras of Leroy Smith (1928), Dave Nelson, Noble Sissle, Edgar Hayes, Teddy Hill (1936-37), the Mills Blue Rhythm Band and Louis Armstrong (1937-40). Not as well-known as his brother, the talented trumpet soloist Sidney DeParis, Wilbur was with Roy Eldridge's big band and Duke Ellington (1945-47) and recorded with Sidney Bechet during 1949-50. However, it was in 1951 when he put together a band to play at Ryan's that included his brother and clarinetist Omer Simeon that he found his niche. Wilbur DeParis' New New Orleans Jazz Band did not just play Dixieland standards but marches, pop tunes and hymns, all turned into swinging and spirited jazz. Throughout the 1950s the group recorded consistently exciting sets for Atlantic (all of which are unfortunately long out-of-print) and they were the resident band at Ryan's during 1951-62, touring Africa in 1957. DeParis continued leading bands up until his death but his last recordings were in 1961. —*Scott Yanow*

● **Dr. Jazz Series, Vol. 7** / Dec. 12, 1951-Jun. 5, 1952 / Storyville ◆◆◆◆◆
Trombonist Wilbur DeParis and his brother trumpeter Sidney led one of the most exciting Dixieland bands of the 1950s. Unfortunately, virtually every one of their valuable Atlantic recordings are long out of print (all are worth searching for), making this set of broadcasts from the short-lived Dr. Jazz radio series a major release. With the great clarinetist Omer Simeon completing the front line, the sextet (no bass at this point) adds a lot of heat to such standards as "Bill Bailey," "Milenberg

Joys" and "Alexander's Ragtime Band" but also performs such underplayed tunes as "Too Much Mustard," "Russian Rag" and "Blame It on the Blues." A very colorful band heard in excellent form. —*Scott Yanow*

An Evening at Jimmy Ryan's / 1951-1958 / Jazz Crusade ✦✦✦
Trombonist Wilbur DeParis led one of the most exciting Dixieland bands in the 1950s, a unit that he said specialized in "New New Orleans Jazz." This CD from the Jazz Crusade label features music taken from broadcasts dating from 1951-52 along with the soundtrack of a television show from either 1955 or 1958. The recording quality is decent if not state-of-the-art, but the excitement of this unit (which also features cornetist Sidney DeParis and clarinetist Omer Simeon) definitely can be felt on such numbers as "Down in Honky Tonk Town," "Original Dixieland One Step," "Under the Double Eagle" and even "The Marine's Hymn." —*Scott Yanow*

Marchin' and Swingin' / Sep. 11, 1952 / Atlantic ✦✦✦✦✦
The first recording by trombonist Wilbur DeParis' "New New Orleans Jazz Band" (although it was actually released after their 1955 session) is full of fresh and lively Dixieland. DeParis and his all-stars (cornetist Sidney DeParis, clarinetist Omer Simeon, pianist Don Kirkpatrick, banjoist Eddie Gibbs, bassist Harold Jackson and drummer Freddie Moore) play a wide variety of material which includes the leader's colorful "Martinique," "Under the Double Eagle," Rachmaninoff's "Prelude in C Sharp Minor," a couple of Jelly Roll Morton tunes and "When the Saints Go Marching In"; the second part of the latter is taken at a blistering tempo. The DeParis band was one of the most consistently inventive Dixieland-oriented groups of the 1950s, so it is very unfortunate that its valuable Atlantic LPs are all long out-of-print. —*Scott Yanow*

That's a Plenty / Dec. 8, 1958+Apr. 20, 1959 / Atlantic ✦✦✦✦
One of a colorful string of Wilbur DeParis Atlantic recordings (all of which are quite difficult to find), this set contains more Dixieland warhorses than usual (only the leader's "Malta" and "Change O' Key Boogie" are lesser-known) but the frameworks and colorful solos uplift the music. While "That's a Plenty" and "Waiting for the Robert E. Lee" are taken at racehorse tempos, "Mack the Knife" and "In a Persian Market" are more relaxed. The trombonist-leader is joined by his brother Sidney (who due to ill health is only on four of the nine selections) and Doc Cheatham on trumpets, clarinetist Omer Simeon, pianist Sonny White, guitarist John Smith, bassist Hayes Alvis and drummer Wilbert Kirk for the well-varied and highly enjoyable program. —*Scott Yanow*

The Wild Jazz Age / May 9, 1960-May 10, 1960 / Atlantic ✦✦✦✦
All of trombonist Wilbur DeParis' Atlantic recordings with his "New New Orleans Jazz Band" are well worth searching for by classic jazz and Dixieland fans but none of the long out-of-print LPs will be easy to find. This set has ten songs from the 1920s (mixing together standards with such obscurities as "That Thing Called Love," "Railroad Man" and "Tell 'Em About Me") plus two of DeParis' originals. This particular group always had its own colorful sound, uplifting the idiom of trad jazz. In addition to the leader, the personnel includes both Sidney DeParis and Doc Cheatham on trumpets, clarinetist Garvin Bushell (who also has features on piccolo and bassoon), pianist Sonny White, guitarist John Smith, bassist Hayes Alvis, drummer Wilbert Kirk (who doubles on harmonica) and two vocals by Louis Bacon. Highlights include the aforementioned songs plus "Runnin' Wild," "Twelfth Street Rag," "When My Sugar Walks Down the Street" and "Minorca." —*Scott Yanow*

On the Riviera / Jul. 9, 1960 / Atlantic ✦✦✦
The next-to-last Atlantic album by Wilbur DeParis' band features his octet performing at the 1960 Antibes Jazz Festival. With the exception of "Tres Moutarde," all of the selections are Dixieland warhorses (including fairly lengthy versions of "Fidgety Feet" and "St. Louis Blues"), but the colorful frameworks and enthusiastic solos make the music sound both lively and fresh. At this late stage, the band consisted of the leader-trombonist, Sidney DeParis and Doc Cheatham on trumpets, clarinetist Garvin Bushell (who also plays a bit of bassoon), pianist Sonny White, guitarist John Smith, bassist Hayes Alvis and drummer Wilbert Kirk. It is a pity that all of this group's valuable Atlantic recordings have been out of print for decades. —*Scott Yanow*

Paul Desmond

b. Nov. 25, 1924, New York, NY, **d.** May 30, 1977, New York, NY
Alto Saxophone / Cool
The definitive "cool" alto saxophonist, Paul Desmond (who had a beautiful floating tone that owed little to Charlie Parker) took his time in his solos (rarely double-timing) but his melody ideas were full of surprising twists and turns. He played his first and his last gigs with Dave Brubeck and spent his prime years (1951-67) with Brubeck's popular quartet. Early on he studied clarinet in school and then, during 1948-50, recorded and gigged on alto with the Dave Brubeck

octet. During the years with the quartet, Desmond was a key part of the sound, indulging in counterpoint with the pianist-leader, writing "Take Five" (in his will he left the huge royalties of this hit to the Red Cross) and taking witty and logical solos that inspired Brubeck. Away from the group, Desmond occasionally recorded as a leader (usually in pianoless settings) including a couple of encounters with Gerry Mulligan and a series of records with Jim Hall. After the quartet broke up, Desmond was mostly semiretired, although a concert with the Modern Jazz Quartet (1971) was recorded and he teamed up with guitarist Ed Bickert on a few live albums. The altoist also had reunions with Brubeck during 1972-75 before his death from cancer. His Jim Hall sets have been reissued in a Mosaic box set, most of the Brubeck albums are currently in print, and Desmond also recorded as a leader for Fantasy, A&M, Finesse, CTI, Telarc and Artists House. —*Scott Yanow*

Sweet Paul, Vol. 1 / Jan. 19, 1950-Feb. 1958 / Philology ✦✦✦✦
Although this Italian CD has been issued under altoist Paul Desmond's name, six lengthy titles (clocking in between 8:15 and an 18:14 version of "Take the 'A' Train") feature Desmond with the Dave Brubeck Quartet during a pair of Feb. 1958 concerts. Although the recording quality is merely average, the previously unreleased music finds the group (which also includes bassist Eugene Wright and drummer Joe Morello) in superior form; the lengthy solos of Desmond and Brubeck are quite inventive and often brilliant. However, it is the final two titles that are most unusual, for Desmond is heard in January 1950 on a couple of brief tracks with drummer Jack Sheedy's hot combo. While "The Man I Love" has a little bit of Desmond alto (along with vibraphonist Cuz Cousineau), "Down in Honky Tonk Town" (which has some prominent trumpet from Jack Minger) is pure Dixieland and finds Desmond taking a half-chorus on clarinet. These are his earliest solos on record. So overall, although the release is obscure, this CD is a real must for Paul Desmond and Dave Brubeck fans. —*Scott Yanow*

Quintet/Quartet / Feb. 14, 1956 / Original Jazz Classics ✦✦✦✦

East of the Sun / Sep. 5, 1959-Sep. 7, 1959 / Discovery ✦✦✦✦
Quartet. First-rate quartet session. Jim Hall (g), Percy Heath (b), and Connie Kay (d) are super. —*Ron Wynn*

☆ **Paul Desmond: Jim Hall Recordings** / Sep. 5, 1959-Jun. 1, 1965 / Mosaic ✦✦✦✦✦
Incredible music! A six-disc boxed set of recordings from 1959-1965 featuring Desmond with Jim Hall. Desmond plays flawless sax, and Jim Hall likewise on guitar. In brief, these are classic cuts; the best. Whether a beginning listener or a jazz expert, this is satisfying music. Mosaic does it again. —*Michael Erlewine*

The Complete RCA Victor Recordings / Jun. 19, 1961-Jun. 1, 1965 / RCA ✦✦✦✦✦
This set is similar to but not exactly the same as a limited-edition Mosaic six-LP box from the early 1990s. The latter included a Warner Bros. LP that is replaced here by a Paul Desmond date with strings, plus one song formerly bypassed. Desmond recorded fairly regularly from 1961-65 for RCA while on brief hiatuses from Dave Brubeck's constantly traveling quartet. Included on this five-CD set are the complete contents of *Desmond Blue* (the string session with suitable arrangements by Bob Prince), *Take Ten*, *Glad to Be Happy*, *Bossa Antigua* and *Easy Living*; there are no previously unreleased selections. Most of the songs feature the cool-toned altoist in a pianoless quartet with the very complementary guitarist Jim Hall. The interplay between the two stylists is so subtle and logical that it takes several listens to fully appreciate their magic. Frequently exquisite music, mixing together standards with some melodic originals. —*Scott Yanow*

Late Lament / Sep. 14, 1961-Mar. 15, 1962 / Bluebird ✦✦✦
Good early material on an 1987 reissue. —*Ron Wynn*

● **Two of a Mind** / Jun. 26, 1962-Aug. 13, 1962 / RCA ✦✦✦✦✦
Altoist Paul Desmond and baritonist Gerry Mulligan always made for a perfect team during their infrequent collaborations. Both of the saxophonists had immediately distinctive light tones, strong wits and the ability to improvise melodically. For this RCA CD (a series that reissued some of the earlier Bluebirds under the RCA banner), the two masterful reed players are featured in pianoless quartets that also include Wendell Marshall, Joe Benjamin or John Beal on bass and Connie Kay or Mel Lewis on drums. The songs all utilize common chord changes including the two "originals" ("Two of a Kind" and "Blight of the Fumble Bee") and the interplay between Desmond and Mulligan is consistently delightful. Highly recommended. —*Scott Yanow*

Take Ten / Jun. 5, 1963-Jun. 25, 1963 / RCA/Bluebird ✦✦✦
Early '60s sessions reissued on a recent Bluebird CD. The title refers not to a song but the number of cuts that Desmond, guitarist Jim Hall, and others recorded. Bassist Percy Heath and drummer Connie Kay also participated. These sessions were partially reissued on CD before; this is the full date. —*Ron Wynn*

Easy Living / Sep. 9, 1964-Jun. 1, 1965 / Bluebird ✦✦✦
A wonderful reissue of a timeless, captivating set with Jim Hall (g), Percy Heath (b), and Connie Kay (d). —*Ron Wynn*

Summertime / Oct. 10, 1968-Dec. 20, 1968 / A&M ✦✦✦
Some beautiful playing by Paul Desmond, coupled with several lovely melodies, help overcome some heavily orchestrated and arranged songs on this 1968 set. Desmond's alto sax solos were pungent and enticing on such cuts as the title song, "Emily," and "Autumn Leaves." The assembled band had many West Coast and session pros, most of whom didn't get any individual space. —*Ron Wynn*

From the Hot Afternoon / Jun. 24, 1969-Aug. 14, 1969 / A&M ✦✦
A 1989 reissue of a satisfying, if unsubstantial, Desmond release. —*Ron Wynn*

Bridge over Troubled Water / 1969 / A&M ✦✦
Beautiful Desmond with fine Herbie Hancock on electric piano, but occasionally annoying orchestrations. —*Ron Wynn*

In Concert at Town Hall / Dec. 25, 1971 / Sony ✦✦✦✦
This delightful collaboration with MJQ has been reissued several times. —*Ron Wynn*

The Best of Paul Desmond / Jun. 7, 1972-Apr. 23, 1975 / Columbia ✦✦✦✦
Since Paul Desmond only recorded two albums for CTI, this best-of accumulation from that label stretches the definition a bit by including Desmond appearances on other CTI albums by Jim Hall, Chet Baker, Don Sebesky, and Jackie & Roy, along with extensive samplings from the solo albums. Of course, a more sweeping idea would have been to raid Columbia's vast Dave Brubeck archives for more prime Desmond, but the archivists presumably wanted a more musically unified package. In any case, during this period Desmond was working at a very relaxed pace, recording now and then, fitting into the carefully produced small-group CTI format and a handful of orchestral sessions. He plays beautifully at all times, with Creed Taylor's production inflating the famous dry-martini alto sax tone into something fuller and lusher. Yet he didn't have too much that was new and striking to say at this stage; the earlier Creed Taylor A&Ms are more eloquent and Desmond's true Indian summer would come in his later Horizon recordings with and without Brubeck. The lopsidedly swinging remake of "Take Ten" with Gabor Szabo on guitar, two tracks from *Pure Desmond* with guitarist Ed Bickert as Paul's subdued, inspired new sidekick ("Squeeze Me," "I'm Old Fashioned") and an absolutely gorgeous, "Song to a Seagull" from Sebesky's *Giant Box* stand out. As a summation of a particular period of Desmond's career, there is plenty to enjoy here. —*Richard S. Ginell*

Skylark / Nov. 7, 1973-Dec. 4, 1973 / Columbia ✦✦✦✦
Very glossy, with some beautiful moments. The 1997 reissue of this excellent set adds "new" alternate takes of "Skylark" (which finds guitarist Gabor Szabo losing interest near the end of his solo) and "Indian Summer" to the original program. —*Ron Wynn*

Pure Desmond / Sep. 24, 1974-Sep. 26, 1974 / Columbia ✦✦✦✦
Undemanding but nicely played set (1987 reissue). —*Ron Wynn*

Like Someone in Love / Mar. 29, 1975 / Telarc ✦✦✦✦

The Paul Desmond Quartet Live / Oct. 25, 1975-Nov. 1, 1975 / A&M ✦✦✦✦
During his post-Brubeck years, altoist Paul Desmond was semiretired, only playing in public on an occasional basis. When he did perform, it was often with the tasteful Canadian guitarist Ed Bickert in a quiet pianoless quartet. This double LP, put out by John Snyder's Horizon subsidiary for A&M, is melodic, subtle and consistently swinging. Desmond and Bickert (along with bassist Don Thompson and drummer Jerry Fuller) clearly enjoyed themselves matching wits and wisdom on the altoist's "Wendy" and the seven superior standards (which include Desmond's "Take Five"). —*Scott Yanow*

Trudy Desmond

Vocals / Cabaret, Standards
A fine jazz-influenced singer, Trudy Desmond has had several careers. She operated a successful interior design business, worked as an actress, produced cabaret and theater shows and ran a club for vocalists. As a singer, the Toronto-based singer has recorded for Unisson (her 1988 debut), Jazz Alliance and Koch. —*Scott Yanow*

RSVP / Nov. 24, 1988-Nov. 25, 1988 / Concord Jazz ✦✦✦✦
Trudy Desmond's debut as a jazz-influenced vocalist was originally out on the Canadian Unisson label before being reissued on CD by Jazz Alliance. Accompanied by keyboardist Don Thompson, either Ed Bickert or Rob Piltch on guitar, bassist Neil Swainson and drummer Terry Clarke, Desmond's appealing voice is well featured on 13 veteran standards. Highlights include "I've Got the World on a String," "If I Were a Bell," "I Concentrate on You," "Just for a Thrill" and "It's All Right with Me." Desmond is particularly effective on ballads. —*Scott Yanow*

● **Tailor Made** / Nov. 1991 / Jazz Alliance ✦✦✦✦
Trudy Desmond is a fine interpreter of lyrics who swings lightly while not departing much from the original melody. Joined by pianist Roger Kellaway, bassist Bob

Cranshaw, drummer Terry Clarke and a few guests (trumpeter Randy Brecker, trombonist Jim Pugh, cellist Carol Buck and guitarist Gene Bertoncini), Desmond mostly sticks to well-known standards on this enjoyable CD. Her tasteful interpretations fall between jazz and cabaret, uplifting such songs as "Day by Day," "Lucky to Be Me," "I Thought About You" and "People Will Say We're in Love." —*Scott Yanow*

Garry Dial

b. Jul. 2, 1954
Piano / Fusion, Hard Bop, Post-Bop, Mainstream Jazz
Garry Dial, co-leader of Dial & Oatts, first came to fame as an important modernizing force with the Red Rodney-Ira Sullivan Quintet. He began playing piano early in life and had important lessons with Mary Lou Williams. After attending Berklee, he played music in Bermuda during 1975-78. Moving to New York, Dial worked for Duke Ellington's sister, Ruth Ellington Boatwright, going through the entire Ellington archive and putting it on tape. Soon afterward, he met Red Rodney, and a group was formed with Ira Sullivan that avoided playing bebop standards in favor of new music. After Sullivan departed and was replaced by saxophonist Dick Oatts, Dial eventually formed a group with him that recorded for DMP. Garry Dial has also recorded his own trio for Continuum and has taught at the Manhattan School of Music and the New School. —*Scott Yanow*

Never Is Now / Dec. 3, 1984-Aug. 11, 1986 / Continuum ✦✦✦✦
Recorded when Garry Dial was the pianist with the Red Rodney-Ira Sullivan Quintet, but not released until this 1991 CD, this trio set gives one a strong sampling of the adventurous player. Assisted by bassist Jay Anderson and drummer Joey Baron, Dial performs 12 of his originals plus Anderson's "Around the Block with Willy." The music swings, but is fairly unpredictable and has its surprising moments. A fine early effort, recorded a few years before the formation of Dial & Oatts. —*Scott Yanow*

● **Dial & Oates** / Sep. 9, 1988-Oct. 18, 1988 / DMP ✦✦✦✦✦
Saxophonist Gary Dial and keyboardist Dick Oats co-lead a group backed by a huge string orchestra through a program of 15 originals. There are some nice solos, and it's well mastered, but sometimes the strings can be overwhelming. —*Ron Wynn*

Robert Dick

b. Jan. 4, 1950
Flute / Avant-Garde, Free Jazz, Contemporary Jazz
A brilliant and very adventurous flutist pushing the limits of his instrument, Robert Dick's New World CD *Third Stone From the Sun* (in which he interprets tunes by Jimi Hendrix) is a classic of its kind; imagine a flute imitating an electric guitar. Dick, who graduated from the Yale School of Music, has played with a who's who of "new music," including Steve Lacy, Evan Parker, George Lewis, John Zorn, Marty Ehrlich, New Winds and Tambastics. Robert Dick's recordings as a leader have been on the Attacca Babel, O.O. Discs, GM and New World labels, and he has the potential to be one of the more important flute players in improvised music. —*Scott Yanow*

● **Third Stone from the Sun** / Feb. 14, 1993-Feb. 15, 1993 / New World ✦✦✦✦✦
This is a most unusual CD with flutist Robert Dick paying tribute to rock guitar-great Jimi Hendrix. Dick creates a wide variety of sounds throughout this release that seem electronically altered but are actually totally acoustic. He plays chords, sings through his flute, and uses circular breathing and overdubbing to cast new light on four of Jimi Hendrix's compositions (along with three of his own). The "power trio" also features bassist Jerome Harris and drummer Jim Black, while The Soldier String Quartet makes a memorable appearance on "Tycho." Robert Dick not only manages to recapture the spirit of Jimi Hendrix in ingenuous ways but also creates some startling new music; this version of "It's Still Like It Wouldn't Be Yesterday" with six flutes and piccolos is absolutely spooky. —*Scott Yanow*

Worlds of If / Feb. 5, 1994-Feb. 27, 1995 / Leo ✦✦✦

Aurealis / 1995 / Victo ✦✦✦
Flutist Robert Dick, pianist John Wolf Brennan and contrabass player Daniele Patumi team on *Aurealis*, an intriguing and abstract fusion of opposing international styles. —*Jason Ankeny*

Jazz Standards on Mars / 1996 / Enja ✦✦✦
Flutist Robert Dick decided to do a CD with several of the spacier jazz standards, and with the Soldier String Quartet, he succeeds in bringing life to John Coltrane's "India" and Jimi Hendrix's "Machine Gun," among others. His highly expressive playing harks back to Eric Dolphy, and though this disc might not be a good choice for purists, the playing is highly enjoyable. —*John Bush*

Vic Dickenson

b. Aug. 6, 1906, Xenia, OH, **d.** Nov. 16, 1984, New York, NY
Trombone / Dixieland, Swing

A distinctive trombonist with a sly wit and the ability to sound as if he were playing underwater (!), Vic Dickenson was an asset to any session in which he appeared. He stated out in the 1920s and '30s playing in the Midwest. Associations with Blanche Calloway (1933-36), Claude Hopkins (1936-39), Benny Carter (1939), Count Basie (1940), Carter again (1941) and Frankie Newton (1941-43) preceded a high-profile gig with Eddie Heywood's popular sextet (1943-46); Dickenson also played and recorded with Sidney Bechet. From then on he was a freelancing soloist who spent time on the West Coast, Boston and New York, appearing on many recordings (including some notable dates for Vanguard) and on the legendary *Sound of Jazz* telecast (1957). In the 1960s, Dickenson co-led the Saints and Sinners, toured with George Wein's Newport All-Stars and worked regularly with Wild Bill Davison and Eddie Condon. During 1968-70, he was in a quintet with Bobby Hackett, in the 1970s he sometimes played with the World's Greatest Jazz Band and Vic Dickenson was active up until his death. —*Scott Yanow*

★ **The Essential Vic Dickenson** / Dec. 29, 1953-Nov. 29, 1954 / Vanguard ✦✦✦✦✦
This single CD reissues ten of the dozen songs originally on a double LP of the same name. Trombonist Vic Dickenson did not get to lead that many sessions, and he is generous in allocating solo space on these mainstream sessions. Trumpeters Ruby Braff and/or Shad Collins, along with the distinctive clarinetist Edmond Hall and pianist Sir Charles Thompson (who often sounds here like Count Basie), are well featured, and the music is enjoyable; highlights include "Russian Lullaby," a 12-minute rendition of "Jeepers Creepers," "Old Fashioned Love" and "Everybody Loves My Baby." —*Scott Yanow*

In Holland / Aug. 16, 1974 / Riff ✦✦✦✦
Trombonist Vic Dickenson was passing through Holland when he was persuaded to record with drummer Ted Easton's fine group. With trumpeter Klaas Wit, Dim Kesber on clarinet and soprano, banjoist Pim Hogervorst and bassist Jacques Kingma getting their spots, this is an exuberant session, available as an LP from the Dutch Riff label. Dickenson has an opportunity to stretch out on six standards (including "Sunday," "I'm Coming Virginia" and "Ole Miss"), plus Easton's "Chops Gone." At 68, the trombonist shows that he was still in his musical prime during the fine mainstream date. —*Scott Yanow*

Gentleman of the Trombone / Jul. 25, 1975 / Storyville ✦✦✦✦

Plays Bessie Smith: "Trombone Cholly" / Mar. 21, 1976 / Gazell ✦✦✦✦✦
This set is unusual for, although it is a tribute to Bessie Smith, there are no vocals. Trombonist Vic Dickenson takes the place of Smith's favorite trombonist Charlie Green, and his witty sound and expressive slides are well-showcased in a sextet with trumpeter Joe Newman and tenor saxophonist Frank Wess; Milt Hinton was the natural choice for the bass spot. Bessie Smith, though known as the "Empress of the Blues," actually recorded a lot of other material throughout her career so there is more variety on this enjoyable set (which is not recommended to 1920s purists) than one might expect. —*Scott Yanow*

Vic Dickenson Quintet / Apr. 13, 1976 / Storyville ✦✦✦
Trombonist Vic Dickenson, a sideman during most of his career, had several long overdue opportunities to record as a leader during 1974-76 when he was finally being recognized as a major mainstream stylist. Dickenson, tenor saxophonist Buddy Tate, pianist Red Richards, bassist George Duvivier and drummer Oliver Jackson perform seven standards (including such off-the-wall vehicles as "Isle of Golden Dreams," "Black Bottom" and "Five O'Clock Whistle") plus the trombonist's "Ding Dong." The trombonist's sly wit is very much in evidence on this strong set; he blends in well with Tate, and Dickenson plays throughout in prime form. Easily recommended to small group swing collectors. —*Scott Yanow*

Just Friends / Oct. 6, 1981-Mar. 16, 1985 / Sackville ✦✦✦✦
Trombonist Vic Dickenson's next-to-last recording (he did an obscure duet date with pianist Ralph Sutton in 1982), this outing features the distinctive stylist in a trio with pianist Red Richards and bassist John Williams. Dickenson and Richards have two vocals apiece and although the trombonist (who was 75) shows his age a bit, he had not lost his enthusiasm or creative abilities. Highlights include "If I Could Be with You," "Taking a Chance on Love" and "Me and My Shadow." Two songs ("Runnin' Wild" and "Sweet Sue") were recorded in 1985 by Richards and Williams as a tribute to Vic (who had died in 1984). —*Scott Yanow*

Walt Dickerson

b. 1931, Philadelphia, PA
Vibes / Post-Bop

Walt Dickerson made an impact when he first emerged in the early '60s—he won the *Down Beat* Critic's Poll as "New Star" in 1962—but as the years have passed,

he's become much less visible. Dickerson graduated from Morgan State College in 1953. After serving in the Army from 1953-1955, he settled in California, where he led a band that included Andrew Cyrille and Andrew Hill. In his early-'60s heyday, Dickerson played the clubs on the New York scene. He worked with Sun Ra, recording *Impressions of a Patch of Blue* in 1965. Shortly thereafter, Dickerson retired from performing for nearly a decade, returning in 1975. In the years 1977-78, he made the bulk of his recordings for the Steeple Chase label, which included duos with Sun Ra, guitarist Pierre Dorge, and bassist Richard Davis. Also in '78, Dickerson recorded in a quartet with pianist Albert Dailey. Dickerson has been one of the few vibists to exhibit an awareness of free-jazz techniques, though he's manifestly conversant in the language of post-bop. Dickerson reportedly still performs around his native Philadelphia, though his recording career is—for now, at least—at a standstill. —*Chris Kelsey*

● **A Sense of Direction** / May 5, 1961 / Original Jazz Classics ✦✦✦✦✦
Vibraphonist Walt Dickerson's second recording as a leader (reissued on CD in the OJC series) utilizes talented if obscure sidemen (pianist Austin Crowe, bassist Edgar Bateman and drummer Eustis Guillemet, Jr.) on a variety of challenging originals and three standards ("What's New," "You Go to My Head" and "If I Should Lose You"). Although Dickerson would not become an influential force himself, he was one of the first vibraphonists of the era to develop his voice away from Milt Jackson's influence, predating Bobby Hutcherson by a few years. —*Scott Yanow*

This Is Walt Dickerson! / Mar. 7, 1961 / Original Jazz Classics ✦✦✦✦
This CD reissue of vibraphonist Walt Dickerson's debut as a leader finds Dickerson (in a quartet with pianist Austin Crowe, bassist Bob Lewis and drummer Andrew Cyrille) performing six of his moody and generally advanced originals. One can hear the influence of Ornette Coleman in the soloin,g which does not stick exclusively to standard bebop chordal improvisation. The purposely monotonous backup on "Death and Taxes" and such songs as "The Cry" and "Infinite You" show that Dickerson was trying to get beyond the dominant Milt Jackson influence that affected most of the other vibists at the time. It's an interesting outing. —*Scott Yanow*

Relativity / Jan. 16, 1962 / Original Jazz Classics ✦✦✦✦
Vibraphonist Walt Dickerson always had a fairly unique sound, predating Bobby Hutcherson with his ability to straddle the boundaries between hard bop and the emerging avant-garde. On this quartet date with pianist Austin Crowe, bassist Ahmed Abdul-Malik and drummer Andrew Cyrille, Dickerson plays a fairly accessible program (three standards and four diverse originals) that serve as a strong introduction to his talents for the uninitiated. —*Scott Yanow*

To My Queen / Sep. 21, 1962 / Original Jazz Classics ✦✦✦
The somewhat introspective but adventurous vibraphonist Walt Dickerson is heard in prime form on this CD reissue. The personnel is unusually interesting, for it includes pianist Andrew Hill (just before he started recording for Blue Note), bassist George Tucker and drummer Andrew Cyrille (prior to his joining Cecil Taylor). The LP-length program (just thirty-two-and-a-half minutes) is unfortunately brief, but the interpretations of Dickerson's intriguing "To My Queen," "How Deep Is the Ocean" and a brief "God Bless the Child" (a vibes-bass duet) are continually thought-provoking. —*Scott Yanow*

Jazz Impressions of "Lawrence of Arabia" / 1963 / Dauntless ✦✦✦✦✦
This effort from the vibraphonist stretches the parameters of Maurice Jarre's themes. Rare, but great to have. —*Michael G. Nastos*

Dialogue / Feb. 9, 1977 / Steeple Chase ✦✦✦✦

Tenderness / Feb. 9, 1977 / Steeple Chase ✦✦✦✦
Recorded at the same session that resulted in *Divine Gemini*, this set of duets by vibraphonist Walt Dickerson and bassist Richard Davis features five Dickerson originals. Although the music is often complex and a touch esoteric, the attractive sound of the intimate duo makes the performances much more accessible than they would normally be. Both Walt Dickerson (who had recently come back from a long absence from the jazz scene) and Richard Davis have long been underrated greats and their interplay throughout the program is of a consistently high quality. —*Scott Yanow*

Divine Gemini / Feb. 9, 1977 / Steeple Chase ✦✦✦✦

Shades of Love / Nov. 6, 1977 / Steeple Chase ✦✦✦

Life Rays / Feb. 4, 1982-Feb. 5, 1982 / Soul Note ✦✦✦

Neville Dickie

b. Jan. 1, 1937, Durham, England
Piano / Stride

A brilliant pianist playing in the stride style of James P. Johnson and Fats Waller (but with a musical personality of his own), Neville Dickie has helped keep traditional jazz alive and healthy. He worked in London during 1958-68 playing in a trio, made his recording debut in 1966, cut four albums in the 1970s and '80s for the Stomp Off label and has led the Rhythmakers since 1985, occasionally appearing in the US. —*Scott Yanow*

Eye Opener / Nov. 6, 1982-Nov. 13, 1982 / Stomp Off ✦✦✦✦
Although Neville Dickie had recorded seven previous albums (five of them solo) since the late '60s, this was the first one to get some attention in the US. The talented British stride pianist performs 14 superior numbers from the likes of Fats Waller, Joe Sullivan, Bob Zurke, Willie "The Lion" Smith, Jelly Roll Morton and James P. Johnson, plus some early pop tunes. Highlights include "Beautiful Love," "My Little Pride and Joy," "Keep Your Temper," "Wolverine Blues" and Zurke's "Eye Opener." This LP gives listeners a strong introduction to the playing of Neville Dickie. —*Scott Yanow*

Taken in Stride / Apr. 21, 1983 / Stomp Off ✦✦✦✦
Pianist Neville Dickie's second solo set for Stomp Off has another strong program of standards and obscurities, all challenging workouts for Dickie's stride style. Among the highlights are his interpretations of "Carolina Shout," "Kansas City Stomp," Willie "The Lion" Smith's "Finger Buster," an adventurous reworking of "Maple Leaf Rag," "I'm Just Wild About Harry" and "Charleston." All classic jazz fans should be aware of Neville Dickie's playing and are advised to get his highly enjoyable Stomp Off releases. —*Scott Yanow*

● **Neville Dickie Meets Fats, the Lion, and the Lamb** / Feb. 7, 1988+Mar. 6, 1988 / Stomp Off ✦✦✦✦✦
Although pianist Neville Dickie, in his two previous solo Stomp Off dates, had performed a great deal of classic material, many of the songs were fairly well-known. That is not the case on this often-wondrous set. With the exception of "Nagasaki" and "Liza," the 15 selections are dominated by obscurities as Dickie pays tribute to Fats Waller, Willie "The Lion" Smith and Dave Lambert's classic styles. Certainly few listeners would have heard of the six Smith originals or even the four Waller numbers (of which "Alligator Crawl" and "How Can You Face Me" are easily the most famous); when was the last time anyone recorded "Conversation on Park Avenue," "Keep Fingering" and "Take It from Me"? The fresh material really seems to have challenged Neville Dickie, who is heard at the top of his form throughout the recommended Stomp Off set. —*Scott Yanow*

The Piano Has It / Apr. 14, 1993-Sep. 30, 1993 / Stomp Off ✦✦✦✦✦
On this excellent set of solos, duets and trios (with bassist Micky Ashman and drummer John Petters), the English pianist Neville Dickie interprets classic compositions by the likes of James P. Johnson, James Scott, Joseph Lamb, Spencer Williams and Don Ewell among others. Dickie's enthusiastic playing keeps these ancient works from sounding like museum pieces, infusing them with life and relevance. —*Scott Yanow*

Harlem Strut / Jun. 4, 1996 / Stomp Off ✦✦✦✦

Al DiMeola

b. Jul. 22, 1954, Jersey City, NJ
Guitar / Fusion, World Fusion, Jazz-Rock
Al DiMeola has had a dual career as a blazing fusion electric guitarist and as an acoustic player eager to explore music from other cultures. DiMeola burst upon the scene by replacing Bill Connors with Return to Forever in 1974 before he turned 20. He had been attending Berklee but essentially started out on top, immediately becoming an influential fusion guitarist. Criticized for playing an excess of notes and not showing enough feeling in his playing (faults he has since overcome), DiMeola has matured through the years. After Return to Forever broke up, he went on several tours with John McLaughlin and Paco DeLucia in an acoustic guitar trio, (1980-83). Since that time, DiMeola has led his own groups, alternating between electric and acoustic guitars and changing musical direction a few times. DiMeola, who toured with the Rite of Strings in 1995 (a trio with Jean Luc Ponty and Stanley Clarke), has recorded sets as a leader since 1976 including dates for Columbia, Manhattan and Tomato. —*Scott Yanow*

Land of the Midnight Sun / 1976 / Columbia ✦✦✦✦✦
One of the guitar heroes of fusion, Al DiMeola was just 22 years old at the time of his debut as a leader but already a veteran of Chick Corea's *Return to Forever*. The complex pieces (which include the three-part "Suite-Golden Dawn," an acoustic duet with Corea on "Short Tales of the Black Forest" and a brief Bach violin sonata) show DiMeola's range even at this early stage. With assistance from such top players as bassists Jaco Pastorius and Stanley Clarke, keyboardist Barry Miles and drummers Lenny White and Steve Gadd, this was a very impressive beginning to DiMeola's solo career. —*Scott Yanow*

Elegant Gypsy / 1976 / Columbia ✦✦✦✦
Guitarist Al DiMeola's second record as a leader is generally an explosive affair, although it does have a fair amount of variety. With Jan Hammer or Barry Miles on keyboards, electric bassist Anthony Jackson, drummer Lenny White (Steve Gadd

takes his place on the "Elegant Gypsy Suite"), and percussionist Mingo Lewis on most of the selections, DiMeola shows off his speedy and rockish fusion style. He was still a member of Return to Forever at the time and was a stronger guitarist than composer, but DiMeola did put a lot of thought into this music. The brief "Lady of Rome, Sister of Brazil" (an acoustic guitar solo) and "Mediterranean Sundance" (an acoustic duet with fellow guitarist Paco DeLucia) hints at DiMeola's future directions. A near-classic in the fusion vein. —*Scott Yanow*

Casino / 1977 / Columbia ✦✦✦✦✦
Guitarist Al DiMeola's third album as a leader (which has been reissued on CD) is still one of his finest recordings. The compositions (which include "Fantasia Suite for Two Guitars" and Chick Corea's "Senor Mouse") are strong and diverse, DiMeola is joined by a sympathetic backup group (which includes keyboardist Barry Miles, bassist Anthony Jackson and drummer Steve Gadd) and his own playing shows impressive growth since his period with Return to Forever (which had ended two years before). Some of the music is no-nonsense fusion/rock but the set also displays DiMeola's growing love for flamenco and the hot "Fantasia Suite" is purely acoustic. Recommended. —*Scott Yanow*

★ **Splendido Hotel** / 1979 / Columbia ✦✦✦✦✦
Talk about ambitious, this two-LP set finds guitarist Al DiMeola performing with his quintet of the time (featuring keyboardist Philippe Saisse), with studio musicians, solo, in a reunion with pianist Chick Corea, singing a love song and welcoming veteran Les Paul for a version of "Spanish Eyes." Most of the music works quite well and it shows that DiMeola (best-known for his speedy rock-oriented solos) is a surprisingly well-rounded and versatile musician. —*Scott Yanow*

Electric Rendezvous / 1981 / Columbia ✦✦✦
Al DiMeola's fifth of seven fusion albums as a leader for Columbia is a typically fiery effort, with DiMeola joined by keyboardist Jan Hammer, electric bassist Anthony Jackson, drummer Steve Gadd, percussionist Mingo Lewis and guest spots for flamenco guitarist Paco DeLucia ("Passion, Grace & Fire") and keyboardist Philippe Saisse. This lesser-known effort is easily recommended to fans of rockish jazz guitar. —*Scott Yanow*

Tour De Force: Live / Feb. 4, 1982 / Columbia ✦✦✦
Recorded shortly before Al DiMeola decided to de-emphasize his electric guitar in favor of his acoustic counterpart, this live set does a fine job of summing up his first six years of recordings. Four of the six numbers (all but "Nena" and "Advantage") were previously recorded by the pacesetting fusion guitarist. With strong and stimulating contributions made by keyboardist Jan Hammer, electric bassist Anthony Jackson, drummer Steve Gadd, percussionist Mingo Lewis and second keyboardist Victor Godsey (some additional keyboards and percussion were overdubbed later in the studio), DiMeola is typically stunning on such originals as "Elegant Gypsy Suite" and "Race with Devil on Spanish Highway." Unfortunately (as with most of his Columbia recordings), the music on this LP has gone out of print. —*Scott Yanow*

Scenario / 1983 / Columbia ✦✦✦

Cielo E Terra / 1985 / One Way ✦✦✦
Having grown a bit weary of playing loud fusion, Al DiMeola recorded a largely acoustic set on his debut for Manhattan. DiMeola, who augments his acoustic guitar with the orchestral Synclavier guitar, plays five unaccompanied solos and is joined on the other four numbers by percussionist Airto Moreira. Other than Keith Jarrett's "Coral," all of the moody selections are by the guitarist. An interesting, if not overly memorable, atmospheric set. —*Scott Yanow*

Soaring Through a Dream / 1985 / EMI ✦✦
This recently reissued 1985 date has plenty of electric bombast, along with ample examples of DiMeola's piercing acoustic style. What it lacks is the energy and creative integrity that underscores DiMeola's World Sinfonia sessions and his classic *Splendido Hotel*. There are some pretty melodies, an entrancing moment or two, and too many interludes where it seems that something is about to happen, but things cool down or degenerate into blandness. The longer compositions drone on without establishing anything substantial, while the short pieces fade in and out, offering bits and pieces of fine playing, but nothing thematically distinguished. When the CD ends, you realize that DiMeola is an excellent technician, but nothing left any lasting impression. —*Ron Wynn*

Kiss My Axe / Sep. 24, 1988-May 1991 / Tomato ✦✦✦✦✦
Despite the aggression its title implies, *Kiss My Axe* is the work of a softer, more reflective Al DiMeola, who had become greatly influenced by Pat Metheny's subtle lyricism, but still had a very recognizable and distinctive sound. DiMeola's new approach was perfectly summarized when, in 1991, he told *JazzTimes* he wanted to be "enchanted" by the music instead of dazzling listeners with his considerable chops. DiMeola still has fine technique, but avoids overwhelming us with it, and shows more restraint than before. One thing that remains is the guitarist's strong

Music Map

Drums

Pioneer
James I. Lent
(recorded "The Ragtime Drummer" in 1904!)

Top 1920s Drummers
Tony Sbarbaro
Baby Dodds
Chauncey Morehouse
Paul Barbarin

Ben Pollack
Vic Berton
Zutty Singleton

Swing Era
Jo Jones (with Count Basie)
Sonny Greer (with Duke Ellington)
Gene Krupa
Chick Webb
Dave Tough
Big Sid Catlett
Cozy Cole
Ray McKinley

Dixieland
George Wettling
Ray Bauduc
Nick Fatool

Unbeatable Virtuoso
Buddy Rich

Founders of Bebop Drums
Kenny Clarke
Max Roach
Art Blakey

1950s
Roy Haynes
Philly Joe Jones
Chico Hamilton
Connie Kay (with Modern Jazz Quartet)
Shelly Manne
Joe Morello (with Dave Brubeck)
Art Taylor
Jimmy Cobb
Ed Thigpen (with Oscar Peterson)
Stan Levey

Avant-Garde
Ed Blackwell (with Ornette Coleman)
Danny Richmond (with Charles Mingus)
Don Moye (with Art Ensemble of Chicago)
Gerry Hemingway (with Anthony Braxton)

Elvin Jones	Rashied Ali	Milford
Graves	Charles Moffett	
Dennis Charles	Andrew Cyrille	
Sunny Murray	Philip Wilson	
J.C. Moses	Clifford Jarvis	
Joe Chambers	Beaver Harris	
Pheeroan Ak Laff	Bob Moses	
Barry Altschul	Steve McCall	
Paul Motian	Joey Baron	
Han Bennink	Tony Oxley	
Paul Lovens	Bobby Previte	

Fusion
Billy Cobham
Lenny White (with Return To Forever)
Alphonse Mouzon
Steve Gadd
Peter Erskine (with Weather Report)
Ronald Shannon Jackson (free funk)
Dave Weckl (with Chick Corea's Elektric Band)
Bill Bruford

Big Band Drummers
Louie Bellson
Sonny Payne
Frank Capp
Sam Woodyard (with Duke Ellington)

Mel Lewis
Rufus Jones
Jeff Hamilton

1980s-1990s
T.S. Monk	Tony Williams
Jack DeJohnette	Billy Higgins
Jake Hanna	Louis Hayes
Roy McCurdy	Grady Tate
Roy Brooks	Mickey Roker
Alan Dawson	Joe LaBarbera
Al Foster	Billy Hart
Danny Gottlieb	Dennis Chambers
Victor Lewis	Jeff Watts
Herlin Riley	Ralph Penland
Adam Nussbaum	Ralph Peterson
Cyndi Blackman	Leon Parker
Terri Lyne Carrington	Marvin "Smitty" Smith
Kenny Washington	Carl Allen
Lewis Nash	Winard Harper

interest in world music—this imaginative session liberally incorporates Latin influences (Brazilian, Spanish, Peruvian and Afro-Cuban) as well as Middle Eastern and African elements. In that *JazzTimes* interview, DiMeola explained that this CD's title resulted in part from his frustration over the fact that many labels and commercial radio stations were choosing bloodless "elevator muzak" over more adven-

turous fusion. Consistently rewarding, *Axe* makes it clear that DiMeola did the right thing by refusing to compromise. —*Alex Henderson*

World Sinfonia / Oct. 1990 / Tomato ♦♦♦♦♦
Comparing early Al DiMeola dates like *Land of the Midnight Sun* and *Casino* to his albums of the 1990s, it's clear how much his playing has softened. The excep-

tional *World Sinfonia*, an entirely acoustic CD, makes it clear that what hasn't changed is his unpredictable, spontaneous nature. DiMeola's right-hand man throughout this highly introspective date is the soulful bandonean player Dino Saluzzi, with whom he enjoys an undeniably strong rapport. A long-time lover of world music, DiMeola incorporates South American, Spanish and Middle Eastern elements, and makes Argentinean tango a very high priority. The improvisor's reverence for Argentina's musical heritage is especially evident on Astor Piazzola's haunting "Tango Suite" and DiMeola's soulbearing ode to the tango legend "Last Tango for Astor." But *World Sinfonia's* standout track and most pleasant surprise of all is a 12-minute interpretation of Chick Corea's 1975 Return to Forever classic "No Mystery," which works quite well in an acoustic setting. —*Alex Henderson*

Plays Piazzolla / Sep. 1990-Oct. 1990 / Atlantic ✦✦✦✦
Latin music has been a strong influence on Al DiMeola since his early years, and in the '90s, he paid especially close attention to the music of Argentina. A welcome addition to his already impressive catalogue, *DiMeola Plays Piazzolla* pays homage to the late Argentinean tango master Astor Piazzolla (whose distinctive and very poetic brand of romanticism was considered quite daring and radical in Argentina). It would have been easy for an artist to allow his own personality to become obscured when saluting Piazzolla's legacy, but the charismatic DiMeola is too great an improvisor to let that happen. Though his reverence for Piazzola comes through loud and clear on these haunting classics, there's no mistaking the fact that this is very much an Al DiMeola project. —*Alex Henderson*

Tirami Su / Apr. 1987 / One Way ✦✦✦✦
Al DiMeola, who in his early days sometimes sacrificed feeling for speed (he always had remarkable technique), grew and developed through the years. His final of three Manhattan releases is his finest, a sextet outing with keyboardist Kei Akagi, electric bassist Anthony Jackson, acoustic bassist Harvie Swartz, drummer Tommy Brechtlein and his longtime percussionist Mino Cinelu. Having grown out of his fusion roots, DiMeola's interest in world music and folk music from other countries is displayed throughout this colorful set, particularly on such numbers as "Beijing Demons," "Song to the Pharoah Kings" and the exciting "Rhapsody of Fire." —*Scott Yanow*

Heart of the Immigrants / 1993 / Mesa ✦✦✦✦
Guitarist Al DiMeola has been alternating electric and acoustic projects for the past few years. For this acoustic affair, he teams up with Dino Saluzzi on bandoneon to pay tribute to the tango master Astor Piazzola. The music (even a duet version of "Someday My Prince Will Come") has the flavor of Argentina and uses a wide variety of instrumentations, including an occasional string section and the voice of Hernan Romero. It's recommended to lovers of world music, the modern tango and those who think of DiMeola's guitar playing as being one-dimensional and purely based on speed. —*Scott Yanow*

Orange & Blue / 1994 / Mesa ✦✦✦

Danny D'Imperio

b. 1945, Sydney, New York
Drums / Hard Bop
A fine drummer, Danny D'Imperio is best-known for his leadership and recordings with the Metropolitan Bopera House and his own groups. He picked up early experience playing with the Glenn Miller ghost band (1970-72) and two years apiece with the orchestras of Maynard Ferguson and Woody Herman. He subbed for Buddy Rich when Rich was ill in 1983, was the house drummer at Condon's and has freelanced quite a bit, but it is his V.S.O.P. recordings (which often feature obscure bop and hard bop songs being revived with enthusiasm) that have given D'Imperio a certain amount of fame. —*Scott Yanow*

Still Comin' on Up / 1986 / V.S.O.P. ✦✦✦✦
The debut by drummer Danny D'Imperio's quintet features a fine group of little-known players (Gary Pribek on alto, trumpeter John Marshall, pianist Steve Ash, bassist Dave Shapiro and the leader) performing bop and hard bop tunes. In addition to Vernon Duke's "Autumn in New York," there are selections by Tadd Dameron, Gil Fuller, Don Menza, Dizzy Gillespie, Sal Nistico and Joe Zawinul, giving one a good idea as to this band's style. To D'Imperio and his sidemen's credit, their performances on this LP do not sound like copies of the past but are creative within the older boundaries. It seems fitting that this was the first new recording made by the V.S.O.P. label, which had up to this point stuck exclusively to reissues from the 1950s. Easily recommended to hard bop fans. —*Scott Yanow*

Formidable / 1987 / V.S.O.P. ✦✦✦✦✦
The second album by The Metropolitan Bopera House, which would later evolve into the Danny D'Imperio sextet, features eight obscure hard bop compositions by Hank Mobley, George Shearing, J.R. Monterose, Duke Pearson, Walter Davis, Jr., Tommy Flanagan, Kenny Drew and Donald Byrd. The quintet—drummer D'Imperio, trumpeter John Marshall, altoist Gary Pribek, pianist Tardo Hammer and bass-

ist Dave Shapiro—all play quite creatively in the hard bop idiom, and there are many exciting moments on this spontaneous yet well-planned straightahead session. —*Scott Yanow*

Danny D'Imperio Sextet / May 19, 1988+May 20, 1988 / V.S.O.P. ✦✦✦✦
Danny D'Imperio has been committed to the revival and revitalization of bebop as it was played in the late '40s and '50s. His groups and recordings are masterful interpretations or recreations of memorable and lesser known works by the giants of bebop and hard bop. Many selections are extended and the total time on this compact disc is over 72 minutes. —*AMG*

● **Blues for Philly Joe** / Sep. 5, 1991+Sep. 6, 1991 / V.S.O.P. ✦✦✦✦✦
Danny D'Imperio has assembled another group revitalizing and updating bebop tunes and standards. An outstanding program featuring great musicianship. —*AMG*

Hip to It / Mar. 27, 1995 / V.S.O.P. ✦✦✦

Glass Enclosure / Mar. 12, 1996 / V.S.O.P. ✦✦✦✦✦
In his series of releases for V.S.O.P., drummer Danny D'Imperio has successfully kept hard bop not only alive, but creative and fresh. This CD has one of his finest recordings. The arrangements are quite inventive; the 11 rarely recorded songs are superior (including Quincy Jones' "Jessica's Day," Freddie Redd's "Thespian" and Lee Morgan's "Need I"), and the musicians (in settings up to a ten-piece) sound quite inspired. Their rendition of Bud Powell's complex "Glass Enclosure" is quite definitive. Among the star soloists are trumpeter Greg Gisbert, altoist Gary Pribek, Ralph Lalama on tenor and pianist Hod O'Brien. A high-quality and frequently exciting CD that rewards repeated listenings. —*Scott Yanow*

Joe Diorio (Joseph Louis Diorio)

b. Aug. 6, 1936, Waterbury, CT
Guitar / Post-Bop
A brilliant if generally overlooked guitarist with an adventurous spirit and a boppish style of his own, Joe Diorio has for quite a while made his main living as a teacher at the Guitar Institute in Hollywood. In the 1960s he was based in Chicago, playing with the likes of Sonny Stitt, Eddie Harris and Bennie Green. After moving to Miami (1968-77), Diorio often gigged with Ira Sullivan, Stan Getz, Stanley Turrentine and Freddie Hubbard among others; he also recorded as a leader for the Spitball label starting in 1975. His relocation to Los Angeles has not resulted in higher visibility but Diorio has recorded in recent times in several settings for RAM and has gained influence as an educator. —*Scott Yanow*

Straight Ahead to the Light / May 23, 1976 / Spitball ✦✦✦

Bonita / 1980 / Zdenek ✦✦✦✦
The talented guitarist Joe Diorio has mostly recorded for obscure record companies throughout his career including this set for the completely forgotten Zdenek label. The early-'80s LP features Diorio (who has always had his own sound) in a trio/quartet with other Los Angeles-based musicians: keyboardist Carl Schroeder, bassist Bob Magnusson and drummer Jim Plank. Diorio stretches out on five standards (including Jobim's "Bonita") plus one of his originals, playing some fine post-bop guitar that is often strikingly original. —*Scott Yanow*

Double Take / Apr. 1992 / RAM ✦✦✦

We Will Meet Again / May 1992 / RAM ✦✦✦

● **Breeze and I** / Jun. 9, 1993 / RAM ✦✦✦✦
This duet encounter between Joe Diorio and Ira Sullivan defies one's expectations. Diorio is normally thought of as a firebreathing guitarist and Sullivan as a versatile multi-instrumentalist at his best on both tenor and trumpet. However, this set comprises lyrical ballads with Sullivan sticking to flutes, soprano and alto. The music is quite atmospheric, haunting and beautiful, far superior to most one-mood new age performances. These introverted yet friendly duets, in addition to being superior background music, reward close scrutiny. —*Scott Yanow*

Narayani / Feb. 28, 1994+Mar. 1, 1994 / RAM ✦✦✦

To Jobim with Love / Sep. 2, 1995-Sep. 6, 1995 / RAM ✦✦✦✦✦
Long a Los Angeles legend and famous as a guitar teacher, Joe Diorio has recorded much less throughout his career than one with his great talent should. Fortunately, he partly rectified that situation by making several sessions for the Italian RAM label. This lyrical set features Diorio playing a program of unaccompanied solos consisting of his original ballad "To Jobim with Love" plus 16 of Antonio Carlos Jobim's most classic compositions. Highlights include "Corcovado," "Desafinado," "One Note Samba," "Triste," "Wave," "The Girl from Ipanema" and "No More Blues." Diorio wisely emphasizes each of the song's melodies and brings out the beauty of the themes. Although a relaxed affair, the music is never sleepy. It is best to play this music loud in order to hear all of the subtleties in Joe Diorio's memorable interpretations. —*Scott Yanow*

The Dirty Dozen Brass Band

f. 1975

Group / New Orleans R&B, New Orleans Brass Band

The Dirty Dozen Brass Band in its prime successfully mixed together R&B with the instrumentation of a New Orleans brass band. Featuring Kirk Joseph on sousaphone playing with the agility of an electric bassist, the group revitalized the brass band tradition, opening up the repertoire and inspiring some younger groups to imitate their boldness. Generally featuring five horns (two trumpets, one trombone and two saxes) along with the sousaphone, a snare drummer and a bass drummer, the DDBB was innovative in its own way, making fine recordings for Rounder, Columbia and the George Wein Collection (the latter released through Concord); guest artists have included Dr. John, Dizzy Gillespie and Danny Barker. Unfortunately, in recent years the group has become much more conventional, still using R&B riffs but now with a standard (and less distinctive) rhythm section. —*Scott Yanow*

● **My Feet Can't Fail Me Now** / 1984 / Concord Jazz ✦✦✦✦✦

Lots of rock and R&B influence, big name guests, and striving, robust cuts. —*Ron Wynn*

Live: Mardi Gras in Montreux / Jul. 1985 / Rounder ✦✦✦

Not at the same level as their debut (*My Feet Can't Fail Me Now*), this second outing by the Dirty Dozen Brass Band (taken from a couple sets performed at the 1985 Montreux Jazz Festival) is overly loose in spots and has some lightweight material that was better heard live than on record. The party music does have its strong moments, the mightly sousaphone playing of Kirk Joseph (who simulates an electric bass) pushes the group and the joy of the band is not to be denied, but "The Flintstones Meets the President" is only worth hearing once. —*Scott Yanow*

Voodoo / Aug. 1987-Sep. 1987 / Columbia ✦✦✦✦

The Dirty Dozen Brass Band certainly knew how to have a good time while playing their music. Their spirited blending of New Orleans jazz parade rhythms with R&Bish horn riffs made them flexible enough to welcome guests Dr. John (who sings and play piano on "It's All Over Now"), Dizzy Gillespie ("Oop Pop aDah") and Branford Marsalis ("Moose the Mooche") to their Columbia debut without altering their music at all. With Gregory Davis and Efrem Towns playing strong trumpet in the ensembles and occasional solos, and with sousaphonist Kirk Joseph not letting up for a moment, this is a typically spirited set by the unique DDBB. —*Scott Yanow*

New Orleans Album / Aug. 1989-Dec. 1989 / Columbia ✦✦✦

A bit of a hodge-podge, this CD features the Dirty Dozen Brass Band (comprising two trumpets, two saxes, sometimes one trombone, the sousaphone of Kirk Joseph, snare drum and bass drum) welcoming such guests as singer Eddie Bo, guitarist-vocalist Danny Barker (showcased on "Don't You Feel My Leg"), trumpeter Dave Bartholomew (heard on "The Monkey") and rock singer Elvis Costello. However, it is the R&Bish parade band that is the main star, romping through group originals plus Cannonball Adderley's "Inside Straight" and "Kidd Jordan's Second Line." —*Scott Yanow*

Open Up: Whatcha Gonna Do for the Rest of Your Life? / Jan. 1991-Apr. 1991 / Columbia ✦✦✦✦

The Dirty Dozen Brass Band sticks to originals (except for Johnny Dyanis' "Eyomzi") on this fairly adventurous set. The octet (which consists of two trumpets, two saxes, one trombone, sousaphone, snare drum and bass drum) still had a unique sound in 1991, but three songs on the date only used part of the unit and the DDBB seemed to be trying to escape the sound of the brass band tradition (they had long had a more modern repertoire). Not all of the pieces work although the music in general is fairly colorful and somewhat unpredictable, even if it falls short of essential. —*Scott Yanow*

Jelly / Aug. 1992-Jan. 1993 / Columbia ✦✦✦

The Dirty Dozen Brass Band, an innovative group that combines R&B with New Orleans parade rhythms, pays tribute to the great Jelly Roll Morton on this CD. Actually, the DDBB mostly ignores Morton's original recordings (and leaves out some of his themes) in an unusual set that does not find them neglecting their own individuality. A few Danny Barker monologues add to the authenticity of this music, which takes great liberties with Morton's compositions. Trumpeter Gregory Davis (who duets with guest pianist Eddie Bo on "Dead Man Blues") is the most impressive soloist, though it is the sound of the rollicking ensembles (propelled by the sousaphone of Keith Anderson) that gives this set its sense of purpose. Purists, however, should avoid this one. —*Scott Yanow*

Diva

f. 1995

Group / Big Band, Bop

DIVA is a 15-piece all-female big band that made its debut on records on the Perfect Sound label. Founded by Stanley Kay and headed by drummer Sherri Maricle, the group includes among its personnel altoist Carol Chaikin, Virginia Mayhew on tenor and trumpeter Ingrid Jensen. —*Scott Yanow*

● **Something Is Coming** / 1994 / Perfect Sound ✦✦✦✦

The all-female jazz orchestra Diva (which has the subtitle of "No Man's Band") makes their recording debut on this CD from Perfect Sound. Headed by drummer Sherri Maricle (whose Buddy Rich-inspired style had been previously featured on Stash), the 15-piece big band has arrangements by Maricle, Michael Abene, John La Barbera and Tommy Newsom. The charts are generally fairly conventional (with "Caravan," "Ding Dong the Witch Is Dead" and "Something's Coming" being the most colorful) but the clean ensembles, hard-swinging rhythm section and many talented soloists make Diva stand out from the crowd. Trumpeter Ingrid Jensen and tenor saxophonist Virginia Mayhew are best-known among the players and they have their spots but the main stars of this disc are the altoists Sue Terry and Carol Chaikin. Chaikin's soulful rendition of "If I Should Lose You" and Terry's intense interpretation of "My Favorite Things" are among the high points. Also notable are a driving "You Stepped out of a Dream," "Three Sisters and a Cousin" (which has Terry, Chiakin and Mayhew all soloing on alto) and a tasteful version of "Stardust." It's recommended for big-band fans. —*Scott Yanow*

Bill Dixon

b. Oct. 5, 1925, Nantucket, MA

Trumpet / Free Jazz, Avant-Garde

Bill Dixon is an unusual trumpeter, one who emphasizes low notes and space. A pioneer in the avant-garde, Dixon has spent much of his career as an educator but has recorded on an occasional basis during the past 30 years. He played with Cecil Taylor in 1958, in 1962-63 he led an advanced jazz group with Archie Shepp, and he played with the New York Contemporary Five. In 1964 Dixon presented six concerts (called "The October Revolution in Jazz") which helped to introduce free jazz to New York audiences. Dixon recorded with Cecil Taylor (*Conquistador*) and had his own session for RCA. He also organized the short-lived Jazz Composers Guild. Dixon started teaching at Bennington College in 1968 and has recorded on an occasional basis since for Cadence and Soul Note. —*Scott Yanow*

The Jazz Artistry of Bill Dixon / Oct. 10, 1966-Feb. 21, 1967 / RCA ✦✦✦

Collection / 1970-1976 / Cadence ✦✦✦

● **In Italy, Vol. 1** / Jul. 11, 1980-Jul. 13, 1980 / Soul Note ✦✦✦✦

This set, one of two Dixon issued on vinyl in 1980, was a rare release that showed why he is so admired by musicians, and has such a tough time getting recorded. The four songs contain no prominent beats or riffs, catchy hooks, sentimental melodies, or enticing devices. One is nearly 20 minutes long, with multiple movements ("For Cecil Taylor"); another is almost 13 minutes, with stretches of blistering exchanges between Dixon and fellow trumpeters Arthur Brooks and Stephen Haynes. Even the shorter pieces have exacting unison statements and prickly solos. An unfolding, unpredictable musical dialogue. —*Ron Wynn*

In Italy, Vol. 2 / Jul. 11, 1980-Jul. 13, 1980 / Soul Note ✦✦✦✦

A rare date from a distinctive trumpeter whose approach, clarity of tone, and directness set him apart in the '60s. The set included a fine three-part song dedicated to Cecil Taylor. The band mixed avant-garde types like bassist Alan Silva with mainstream figures like drummer Freddie Waits. It also had an unusual lineup, with two, sometimes three trumpeters and a saxophonist, bassist, and drummer. Dixon occasionally played piano. —*Ron Wynn*

November 1981 / Nov. 8, 1981 / Soul Note ✦✦✦

The music on this two-record set was typical of trumpeter Bill Dixon's hue and perhaps the most *in command* set of his so far released (1983). The first five tracks on sides one and two, (11/16 and 17/81), struck me as rather unresolved and tedious on first listening. The last four tracks on sides three and four, (11/8/81), grabbed me with both their immediacy and daring. Both sides impressed me with the dedication to purity which has always marked all of Dixon's music. Repeated listenings to record one brought out greater dimensions to the music, displaying an azure mellowness which ran deep with revolving panoramas. Record two opened with "Webern," a bold, biting piece which set the tone and segued into "Winterset." The record ended with "Velvet," returning to the solace which marked so much of record one, and "Latino Suite," a developing piece of trumpet hues over washes of free rhythm which, by the time it evolved mid-way into a bowed bass solo, was quite effective. It was interesting how some of this music, "Velvet" in particular, when played at 45 rpm maintained its pacing. It played faster but the pulse remained the same. —*Bob Rusch, Cadence*

Thoughts / May 16, 1985 / Soul Note ◆◆◆

The unusual trumpeter Bill Dixon (who often emphasizes silence over sound and feelings over phrases) has always had a strong liking for lower-toned instruments. On this set, Dixon (doubling on piano) is joined by altoist Marco Eneidi, John Buckingham on tuba, drummer Lawrence Cook and three bassists (Peter Kowald, William Parker, and Mario Pavone). The music (six originals, including the four-part suite "For Nelson and Winnie") is quite adventurous, yet thoughtful, disturbing without being forbidding. —*Scott Yanow*

Sons of Sisyphus / Jun. 1988 / Soul Note ◆◆◆◆

Bill Dixon's Soul Note exploration is typically thougtful, introverted and often downbeat. Two duets on piano with bassist Mario Pavone ("Silences for Jack Moore" and "Sumi-E") both put as much emphasis on space as on the sounds. The other pieces find Dixon's tonal distortions on the trumpet often joined by moaning long tones from the tuba of John Buckingham, the competing ideas of Pavone and the often-fiery drums of Laurence Cook. "Schema V1-88" uses a single sound as the basis for the group improvisation, while other pieces feature the musicians reacting quite freely to each other. These lyrical explorations move forward without a pulse and, once one gets used to the "style" (or lack of), they reward repeated listenings. —*Scott Yanow*

Vade Mecum, Vol. 2 / Aug. 2, 1993-Aug. 4, 1993 / Soul Note ◆◆◆

Baby Dodds

b. Dec. 24, 1898, New Orleans, LA, **d.** Feb. 14, 1959, Chicago, IL
Drums / Classic New Orleans Jazz

Arguably the first important jazz drummer, Baby Dodds was one of the earliest to vary his patterns during a performance; a strong example of his adventurous style can be heard on a trio performance (with Jelly Roll Morton and Baby's brother, Johnny) of "Wolverine Blues" in 1927. A major influence on Gene Krupa, Dodds worked in New Orleans with Willie Hightower, Bunk Johnson, Oscar Celestin and others, and played with Fate Marable's riverboat band in 1918. He joined King Oliver in San Francisco in 1922 and settled in Chicago the following year. In addition to recording with Oliver's classic Creole Jazz Band, Dodds was an important part of sessions led by Jelly Roll Morton and Louis Armstrong's Hot Seven. He remained in Chicago for decades, performing and recording regularly with his brother, Johnny Dodds, until the clarinetist's death in 1940. During the traditional jazz revival, Baby played with Jimmie Noone, Sidney Bechet, Bunk Johnson and Art Hodes, appeared on the *This Is Jazz* radio broadcasts of 1947 and visited Europe with Mezz Mezzrow the following year. During 1945-46, he recorded the first unaccompanied drum solos. Despite ill health in the 1950s, Baby Dodds kept playing until two years before his death; his memoirs are well worth reading. —*Scott Yanow*

Baby Dodds Trio / Jan. 6, 1946-May 1951 / GHB ◆◆◆◆

Although he receives first billing on this LP, drummer Baby Dodds is only on five of the 11 selections. However t,hese titles (three of which have Dodds in a trio with clarinetist Albert Nicholas and pianist Don Ewell while "Manhattan Stomp" is a feature for Ewell's fine stride piano) are historic. The two "Drum Improvisations" from 1946 are among the very first unaccompanied jazz drum solos ever recorded, and they really display Baby Dodds' colorful technique at its best. Four other songs on the album are from 1947 and feature Nicholas' clarinet in a quartet with pianist James P. Johnson, banjoist Danny Barker and bassist Pops Foster (with vocals in Creole by Barker and Nicholas), while the remaining number, "Danny's Banjo Blues," showcases Barker's solo playing in 1951. These unusual recordings, originally made for Rudi Blesh's Circle label, are highly recommended to New Orleans jazz collectors. —*Scott Yanow*

Johnny Dodds

b. Apr. 12, 1892, New Orleans, LA, **d.** Aug. 8, 1940, Chicago, IL
Clarinet / Classic New Orleans Jazz

One of the all-time great clarinetists and arguably the most significant of the 1920s, Johnny Dodds (whose younger brother, Baby Dodds, was among the first important drummers) had a memorable tone in both the lower and upper registers, was a superb blues player and held his own with Louis Armstrong (no mean feat) on his classic Hot Five and Hot Seven recordings. He did not start on clarinet until he was 17 but caught on fast, being mostly self-taught. Dodds was with Kid Ory's band during most of 1912-19, played on riverboats with Fate Marable in 1917, and joined King Oliver in Chicago in 1921. During the next decade, he recorded with Oliver's Creole Jazz Band, Jelly Roll Morton, Louis Armstrong and on his own heated sessions, often utilizing trumpeter Natty Dominique. He worked regularly at Kelly's Stables during 1924-30. Although Dodds continued

playing in Chicago during the 1930s, part of the time was spent running a cab company. The clarinetist led recording sessions in 1938 and 1940, but died just before the New Orleans revival movement began. —*Scott Yanow*

Jazz Heritage: Spirit of New Orleans (1926-1927) / May 29, 1926-Oct. 5, 1927 / MCA ◆◆◆◆

This 1980 LP from MCA's Jazz Heritage series is actually superior to the label's 1990 Johnny Dodds CD. The great New Orleans clarinetist is featured on two numbers with Jimmy Bertrand's Washboard Wizards (a trio with pianist Jimmy Blythe), with his own 1927 trio on five numbers (featuring pianist Lil Armstrong and guitarist Bud Scott), on alternate takes of two numbers from a session he led that featured Louis Armstrong and pianist Earl Hines, "Weary Way Blues" with Jimmy Blythe's Owls, and (best of all) four songs and an alternate with his Black Bottom Stompers on October 8, 1927. The latter date has a classic version of "Come On and Stomp, Stomp, Stomp" and other highlights of the album include "San," "The New St. Louis Blues," "When Erastus Plays His Old Kazoo" and two versions of "Oh Lizzie." This is wonderful and classic music that deserves to be reissued in full domestically on CD. —*Scott Yanow*

Chicago Mess Around / May 1926-Feb. 1929 / Milestone ◆◆◆

This out-of-print Milestone LP has excellent performances featuring clarinetist Johnny Dodds with Jimmy Blythe's Washboard Ragamuffins, Blind Blake, Tiny Parham, Lovie Austin's Blues Serenaders, the Dixieland Thumpers and the Paramount Pickers. The music has since been reissued on CD but these selections are generally among the great clarinetist's lesser-known recordings of the 1920s. In the supporting cast on some numbers are pianists Blythe, Parham and Austin, the washboard of W.E. Burton, trumpeter Tommy Ladnier, cornetist Natty Dominique and brother Baby Dodds on drums. The extensive liner notes by Johnny Dodds II in 1969 are particularly interesting. —*Scott Yanow*

★ **1926** / May 19, 192626 12 / Classics ◆◆◆◆◆

Dodds was one of the very finest New Orleans clarinetists, and the only noncreole among them. The peak experiences here, and some of the finest small-group recordings ever made, are The New Orleans Wanderers sessions—Armstrong's Hot Five with George Mitchell instead of Armstrong. Also present are a bunch of marginally lesser cuts that Dodds transmutes into gold. —*John Storm Roberts, Original Music*

Johnny Dodds and Kid Ory / Jul. 13, 1926-Jul. 3, 1928 / Columbia ◆◆◆◆

The music on this LP (which has been reissued on CD by the Classics label) features clarinetist Johnny Dodds in prime form. Not all of the personnel listings are accurate; Joe Clark is on alto with the New Orleans Wanderers and Bootblacks, while trombonist Honore Dutrey and drummer Baby Dodds are with the Chicago Footwarmers and the Dixieland Thumpers rather than Kid Ory and Jimmy Bertrand. However, most of the music is beyond criticism. The eight titles from the New Orleans Wanderers and the New Orleans Bootblacks feature what was Louis Armstrong's Hot Five with altoist Joe Clark added and cornetist George Mitchell in Armstrong's place. Best known is "Perdido Street Blues" but the other selections (especially "Gate Mouth" and "Papa Dip") are also superb examples of classic New Orleans jazz. In addition, there are four songs from other pickup groups matching Dodds with trumpeter Natty Dominique and pianist Jimmy Blythe; "Oriental Man" is most memorable. Highly recommended music in one form or another. —*Scott Yanow*

● **Blue Clarinet Stomp** / Dec. 11, 1926-Feb. 7, 1929 / Bluebird ◆◆◆◆◆

A French RCA double-LP from the late '70s had the complete Johnny Dodds on Victor, 30 selections in all. This single CD has just 21 of the performances, leaving out most alternates and a few other numbers. A good introductory set to the recordings of the great New Orleans clarinetist (but sure to frustrate veteran collectors and completists), this set features the masterful Dodds with a couple of trios, heading his own sextets and as a sideman with Jelly Roll Morton ("Wolverine Blues" and "Mr. Jelly Lord") and the Dixieland Jug Blowers. Classic New Orleans jazz by arguably the finest jazz clarinetist of the 1920s, this CD is recommended until something better comes along. —*Scott Yanow*

The Complete Johnny Dodds / Dec. 11, 1926-Feb. 7, 1929 / RCA ◆◆◆◆◆

This double-LP from French RCA cannot be improved upon for it has all of clarinetist Johnny Dodds' recordings for Victor, including alternate takes; if only its domestic counterpart cared enough to release these sessions complete on CD. The classic clarinetist is featured as a sideman with the spirited Dixieland Jug Blowers, Jelly Roll Morton's Trio (famous versions of "Wolverine Blues" and "Mr. Jelly Lord" that also include drummer Baby Dodds) and on blues singer Sippie Wallace's famous "I'm a Mighty Tight Woman." In addition, Dodds is featured as the leader of various small groups ranging from trios to sextet with cornetist Natty Dominique and trombonist Honore Dutrey. Highlights include "Blue Clarinet Stomp," "Bull Fiddle Blues" and "Too Tight." Essential music for 1920s collectors, although this two-fer will be difficult to locate. —*Scott Yanow*

1927 / Jan. 19, 1927-Aug. 10, 1927/ Classics ✦✦✦✦✦

South Side Chicago Jazz / Apr. 21, 1927-Jul. 24, 1929 / MCA ✦✦✦

Most of the music on this CD reissue is quite wonderful but unfortunately it has been reissued domestically as a sampler rather than giving listeners a complete look at clarinetist Johnny Dodds' MCA-owned recordings. The great clarinetist is heard with several small groups including four titles with his Black Bottom Stompers that feature Louis Armstrong (who tried to hide his identity with some restrained playing), a jubilant version of "Come on and Stomp, Stomp, Stomp" by a septet, a quartet rendition of "Forty and Tight" and a few trios. In addition, Dodds is heard as a star soloist with Jimmy Bertrand's Washboard Wizards and Jimmy Blythe's Owls. Collectors of 1920s jazz will want this CD if they do not have the complete sessions elsewhere for they showcase Dodds' distinctive style in prime form. —*Scott Yanow*

Bill Doggett

b. Feb. 16, 1916, Philadelphia, PA, **d.** Nov. 13, 1996, New York, NY

Organ, Piano / R&B, Swing, Soul Jazz, Blues

Although he was known as a fine swing-based pianist early on, Bill Doggett found his greatest fame in the 1950s as an R&Bish organist, particularly after recording his big hit "Honky Tonk" in 1956. He led his own big band in 1938, which accompanied Lucky Millinder for a year. After stints with Jimmy Mundy's short-lived orchestra (1939) and back with Millinder (1940-42), Doggett arranged for the Ink Spots (1942-44) and recorded with Johnny Otis and Illinois Jacquet (1945-47). He replaced Wild Bill Davis with Louis Jordan's Tympany Five (1948-51) and, following Davis' example, took up the organ. After recording with Eddie "Lockjaw" Davis and Ella Fitzgerald, Doggett led his own groups, recording frequently for King throughout the 1950s. He was heard in more jazz-oriented settings in the 1970s on sessions for the Black & Blue label and recorded for After Hours as recently as 1991. —*Scott Yanow*

● **Leaps N' Bounds** / Jan. 19, 1952-Apr. 11, 1959 / Charly ✦✦✦✦✦

Nineteen tracks from the 1950s, including both parts of the massive hit "Honky Tonk." The packaging could be a little more coherent, and the grooves may sometimes get a little too similar for some. But it's solid instrumental organ-sax-guitar jump blues on the verge of turning into rock 'n' roll, with occasional standouts like "Big Boy" supplying evidence that Doggett wasn't solely a one-song wonder. —*Richie Unterberger*

As You Desire Me / 1958 / Deluxe ✦✦✦

Dance Awhile / 1958 / Deluxe ✦✦✦✦✦

The emphasis on this release is on R&B-inflected combo jazz ranging from the soft (but not sappy) sound of Doggett's ethereal organ on "Misty Moon" and "Autumn Dreams" to the straightahead swing of "Bone Tones" and "The Song Is Ended." Of course, this wouldn't be a complete smorgasbord without a touch of the exotic, supplied on "Passion Flower" and "Chelsea Bridge." As always, there's plenty of grits 'n' gravy saxophone ("Tailor Made," "Smooche"), great guitar (isn't that Bill Jennings?) showcased on "The Kid from Franklin St.," and even some real soulful flute playing on "Flying Home" and "How Could You." —*Myles Boisen*

The Right Choice / May 14, 1991-May 15, 1991 / After Hours ✦✦✦✦

Considering his popularity and influence, it is surprising how few Bill Doggett albums have been reissued on CD. This late-period effort, which features the organist with several medium-sized groups, is quite jazz-oriented while not wandering far from Doggett's early R&B roots. Among the key sidemen are trumpeter Eddie Preston, Bubba Brooks and Howard Kimbo on tenors, altoists Bill Easley and Jimmy Cozier, and guitarists Gregory Townson and George Naha. In addition to the inevitable "Honky Tonk," Doggett plays "Things Ain't What They Used to Be" and a variety of basic originals. Fun music. —*Scott Yanow*

Doky Brothers

f. 1995

Group / Hard Bop, Post-Bop, Crossover Jazz, Contemporary Jazz

The Doky Brothers were a straightahead mainstream jazz duo that emerged in the mid-'90s with a pair of albums for Blue Note. The group's music was straight out of the hard bop traditions of the '60s, balanced by flourishes of contemporary production and fusion.

Natives of Copenhagen, Denmark, pianist Niels Lan Doky (b. October 3, 1963) and bassist Chris Minh Doky (b. February 7, 1969) are the product of a musical family; their father was a physician who played classical guitar, and their mother was a Danish pop singer. After spending a couple of years playing guitar, Niels switched to piano at the age 11, inspired by the Scott Joplin music that was featured in the hit Paul Newman/Robert Redford film *The Sting*. He gradually became acquainted with the major pianists in jazz history, and began playing professionally at the age of 13. Two years later, he played with trumpeter Thad Jones,

who was in Denmark leading a big band on radio. Jones was impressed with Niels' skill and encouraged him to move to America. The trumpeter wrote a recommendation for the young pianist, which led to a scholarship to the Berklee College of Music in Boston for Doky. Between 1981 and 1984, Niels Lan Doky attended Berklee, graduating magna cum laude with a degree in professional music. During his time in Boston, he performed with Terri Lyne Carrington, Cyrus Chestnut and Branford Marsalis, among many others. Following graduation, he moved to New York, where he began playing gigs and sessions. After playing with Joe Henderson and Woody Shaw, he recorded his debut album, *Here or There*, for Storyville Records. It was the first of a series of solo records from Doky, who recorded for Storyville, Milestone, DAM/Maracatu, Soul Note and Columbia.

In 1989, Nils began touring as a co-leader with his brother Chris Minh Doky. Like his brother, Chris began playing music as a child, starting on piano before switching to bass at the age of 15. He initially played electric, moving to acoustic two years later when he discovered jazz. After spending some time studying with Orsted Pedersen, he moved to New York in 1988, intending to attend the Berklee College of Music. While in New York, he met and performed with a number of musicians, including Randy Brecker and John Scofield. One of his acquaintences, Jimmy Cobb—a drummer who had formerly played with Miles Davis and Wes Montgomery—convinced Chris to stay in New York and receive his education by playing in clubs. In 1989, Chris Doky recorded his first album, *Appreciation*, for Storyville Records and began touring with his brother as a co-leader.

During the early '90s, the Doky Brothers continued to lead their own sessions as solo artists and touring as a team. Eventually, the pair decided to record together as the Doky Brothers. Their eponymous debut for Blue Note was produced by Niels and featured guest appearances by trumpeter Randy Brecker, saxophonist Michael Brecker, drummer Terri Lyne Carrington, guitarist Ulf Wakenius and singer Curtis Stigers. It was released in 1996 to good reviews and strong sales. Their second album was also produced by Niels and featured guest performances by guitarist John Scofield, harmonica player Toots Thielemans, saxophonist David Sanborn, saxophonist Bill Evans and trumpeter Randy Brecker. —*Stephen Thomas Erlewine*

● **Doky Brothers** / Aug. 1995-Sep. 1995 / Blue Note ✦✦✦✦

This release sounds "contemporary" in spots due to the prominence and virtuosity of bassist Chris Minh Doky (who sometimes shares in the melody statements), two appearances by Michael and Randy Brecker, the fact that the flavor of Chick Corea and Herbie Hancock (along with Oscar Peterson and Vince Guaraldi) can be heard in pianist Niels Lan Doky's spirited solos, and the inclusion of a song apiece by Jaco Pastorius and Carole King. However, the music should mostly be of interest to modern mainstream collectors due to the strong playing of the co-leaders. The vocals of Curtis Stigers (a straightforward "My One and Only Love") and Deborah Brown (a swinging "I Feel Pretty") give the set some variety as does the changing instrumentation, and even the occasional melodic poppish numbers are generally enjoyable. Although he does not yet have a distinctive sound, pianist Niels Lan Doky is an obvious up-and-coming talent, making this diverse CD recommended overall. —*Scott Yanow*

Doky Brothers, Vol. 2 / Sep. 1996-Jan. 1997 / Blue Note ✦✦✦

The Doky Brothers, Vol. 2 pales slightly in comparison to the duo's first release, but the album remains a fine example of contemporary mainstream jazz due to the exceptional playing of pianist Niels Lan Doky and bassist Chris Minh Doky. The pop numbers are occasionally a little sappy or silly, but the originals are melodic and memorable, providing the duo an excellent framework for their exciting solos. —*Leo Stanley*

Niels Lan Doky

b. Oct. 3, 1963, Copenhagen, Denmark

Piano / Post-Bop, Neo Bop, Contemporary Jazz

Although still not that well-known in the US, Niels Lan Doky is an impressive pianist who has recorded extensively, 14 albums as a leader by 1996. Born to a Danish mother who sang and had hit records and a Vietnamese father who was both a doctor and a classical guitarist, Niels first played guitar when he was seven, switching to piano when he was 12. Three years later, he played with Thad Jones, who wrote a letter recommending him to the Berklee School of Music. Doky lived in Boston while attending Berklee from 1981-84, spent a long period in New York, and eventually settled in Paris. He has worked with Joe Henderson, Woody Shaw, Jack DeJohnette, Bob Berg, Clark Terry, Tom Harrell and many others, and had such players as Niels-Henning Orsted Pedersen, Bob Berg, Terri Lyne Carrington and John Scofield as sidemen on his records. Niels Lan Doky has recorded as a leader for Storyville, Milestone and Soul Note, and occasionally co-leads the Doky Brothers with his younger sibling Chris, who plays bass; they have recorded for Blue Note. —*Scott Yanow*

Here or There / Jan. 17, 1986 / Storyville ◆◆◆◆
This set shows that pianist Niels Lan Doky was an impressive player from the start. Matched with fellow Scandinavian Niels-Henning Orsted Pedersen on bass and drummer Alvin Queen, Lan Doky performs five fairly straightahead (and inventive) originals, plus "Alone Together." Even at that early point in his career, the pianist was playing in his own modern mainstream voice. Nice music. —*Scott Yanow*

Target / Nov. 17, 1986-Nov. 18, 1986 / Storyville ◆◆◆◆
Pianist Niels Lan Doky's second date as a leader (he was 23 at the time) is as worthy as the first one. With bassist Niels Pedersen and drummer Jack DeJohnette, once again Lan Doky performs five hard bop-based originals, plus a lone standard, "Autumn in New York." Sometimes showing the slight influence of Oscar Peterson, Lan Doky more than holds his own with his illustrious sidemen. It seems strange that Niels Lan Doky (born in Denmark) has not become better known to American jazz audiences, for he is quite talented. —*Scott Yanow*

The Truth / Jun. 1987 / Storyville ◆◆◆◆◆
Pianist Niels Lan Doky developed quickly in his career to become a leading European jazz pianist. For this third album, he utilizes a quartet with tenor saxophonist Bob Berg, bassist Bo Stief and drummer Terri Lyne Carrington to perform three of his originals, Stief's "Ten Hours Later," and the standard "I Thought About You." By this time, Lan Doky (still just 23) was advancing beyond hard bop to play in a more adventurous (but still swinging) post-bop style. Recommended, as are Lan Doky's two earlier Storyville releases. —*Scott Yanow*

Daybreak / Sep. 18, 1988-Sep. 19, 1988 / Storyville ◆◆◆◆
For this project, pianist Niels Lan Doky enlisted a particularly strong group (guitarist John Scofield, bassist Niels Pederson and drummer Terri Lyne Carrington) to perform five of his originals and the standard "All Or Nothing at All." Twenty-five at the time, Doky was most influenced by McCoy Tyner but he manages to find his own niche within that style although Scofield usually takes solo honors. Excellent post bop music. —*Scott Yanow*

Close Encounter, Vol. 1 / Jul. 12, 1989 / Storyville ◆◆◆

Close Encounter, Vol. 2 / Jul. 13, 1989 / Storyville ◆◆◆

● **Dreams** / Aug. 22-23, 1989 / Milestone ◆◆◆◆
This fine effort features pianist Niels Lan Doky and his brother, bassist Christian Minh Doky, being joined by drummer Adam Nussbaum for three trio numbers and, on three other tracks, playing with larger groups including trumpeter Randy Brecker, tenor saxophonist Bob Berg and guitarist John Scofield. Almost as impressive as Lan Doky's piano playing are his compositional and arranging talents; all of the songs except "This is All I Ask" are his. A strong post-bop effort that finds the Doky brothers not being overshadowed by their famous sidemen, a major feat in itself. —*Ron Wynn*

Friendship / Aug. 18, 1990-Sep. 9, 1990 / Milestone ◆◆◆
This CD comprises two sessions, one in New York and the other in Copenhagen. Personnel include B. Evans, R. Brecker, R. Margitza, C. Minh Doky, A. Nussbaum, and more. It is an excellent followup to his *Dreams* CD. —*Paul Kohler*

Paris By Night / Apr. 2, 1992 / Soul Note ◆◆◆
While this is ostensibly a shared session, with pianist Niels Lan Doky, drummer Daniel Humair, bassist Chris Minh Doky and trumpeter Randy Brecker equal participants, it's Brecker's mix of mellow solos, bent notes, slurs and superb statements that dominate the date. While the others play nicely, Brecker's melodic and harmonic inventiveness dominates such songs as "Invitation," "Lover Man" and "Sonnymoon for Two." It's been many years since he's demonstrated such facility and command in a straight jazz setting, and those times he lays out the energy level dips considerably. The results are outstanding when Brecker's featured, and otherwise interesting, but subdued. —*Ron Wynn*

Klaus Doldinger

b. May 12, 1936, Berlin, Germany
Tenor Saxophone, Soprano Saxophone, Leader, Keyboards / Fusion, Post-Bop
Klaus Doldinger, best known for leading the excellent fusion group Passport in the 1970s and '80s, has had a diverse and episodic career. He started out studying piano in 1947 and clarinet five years later, playing in Dixieland bands in the 1950s. By 1961 he had become a modern tenor saxophonist, working with such top visiting and expatriate Americans as Don Ellis, Johnny Griffin, Benny Bailey, Idrees Sulieman, Donald Byrd and Kenny Clarke, recording as a leader for Philips, World Pacific and Liberty. However, in 1970 he initiated a long series of fusion-oriented sessions for Atlantic which featured his tenor, soprano, flute and occasional keyboards with an electric rhythm section. In addition to writing music for films (including *Das Boat*) and television in Europe, Doldinger has remained active as a player who occasionally explores his roots in hard bop into the late 1990s, but because he has always lived in Europe, he remains underrated in the US. —*Scott Yanow*

Constellation / 1983 / WEA ◆◆◆

Balance of Happiness / 1990 / Atlantic ◆◆◆◆
Since 1971, saxophonist Klaus Doldinger has mostly recorded creative fusion under the group name of Passport. This Atlantic CD features his soprano and occasional tenor backed by a five-piece rhythm section comprising some top German musicians. The music, all composed by Doldinger, effectively mixes together R&B, rock, pop and even some straightahead jazz into an impressive brew with Doldinger often extending himself with challenging solos. Several of the melodies are memorable, there are a wide variety of moods and grooves covered and the CD is proof that fusion can be played with imagination. —*Scott Yanow*

● **Doldinger in New York: Street of Dreams** / May 16, 1994-May 19, 1994 / Blue Moon ◆◆◆◆◆

Eric Dolphy

b. Jun. 20, 1928, Los Angeles, CA, d. Jun. 29, 1964, Berlin, Germany
Alto Saxophone, Bass Clarinet, Flute / Avant-Garde, Post-Bop, Free Jazz
Eric Dolphy was a true original with his own distinctive styles on alto, flute and bass clarinet. His music fell into the "avant-garde" category yet he did not discard chordal improvisation altogether (although the relationship of his notes to the chords were often fairly abstract). While most of the other "free jazz" players sounded very serious in their playing, Dolphy's solos often came across as ecstatic and exuberant. His improvisations utilized very wide intervals, a variety of nonmusical speechlike sounds and its own logic. Although alto was his main ax, Dolphy was the first flutist to move beyond bop (influencing James Newton) and he largely introduced the bass clarinet to jazz as a solo instrument. He was also one of the first (after Coleman Hawkins) to record unaccompanied horn solos, preceding Anthony Braxton by five years.

Eric Dolphy first recorded while with Roy Porter's Orchestra (1948-50) in Los Angeles, he was in the Army for two years and then played in obscurity in L.A. until he joined Chico Hamilton's Quintet in 1958. In 1959 he settled in New York and was soon a member of Charles Mingus' Quartet. By 1960, Dolphy was recording regularly as a leader for Prestige and gaining attention for his work with Mingus but throughout his short career he had difficulty gaining steady work due to his very advanced style. Dolphy recorded quite a bit during 1960-61 including three albums cut at the Five Spot while with trumpeter Booker Little, *Free Jazz* with Ornette Coleman, sessions with Max Roach and some European dates. Late in 1961 Dolphy was part of the John Coltrane Quintet; their engagement at the Village Vanguard caused conservative critics to try to smear them as playing "antijazz" due to the lengthy and very free solos. During 1962-63, Dolphy played Third Stream music with Gunther Schuller and Orchestra USA, and gigged all-too-rarely with his own group. In 1964 he recorded his classic *Out to Lunch* for Blue Note and travelled to Europe with Charles Mingus' Sextet (which was arguably the bassist's most exciting band as shown on *The Great Concert of Charles Mingus*). After he chose to stay in Europe, Dolphy had a few gigs but then died suddenly from a diabetic coma at the age of 36, a major loss.

Virtually all of Eric Dolphy's recordings are in print including a nine-CD box set of all of his Prestige sessions. In addition, Dolphy can be seen on film with John Coltrane (included on *The Coltrane Legacy*) and with Mingus from 1964 on a video released by Shanachie. —*Scott Yanow*

Outward Bound / Apr. 1, 1960 / Original Jazz Classics ◆◆◆◆◆
This very likable set, Eric Dolphy's first as a leader, has been reissued as a single CD and (along with some alternate takes) on Dolphy's huge Prestige box set. Teamed up with the young trumpeter Freddie Hubbard, pianist Jaki Byard, bassist George Tucker and drummer Roy Haynes, Dolphy introduces his tribute to Gerald Wilson, "G.W.," rips into "On Green Dolphin Street," stretches out on flute on "Glad to Be Unhappy," and takes a memorable bass clarinet solo on the delightful "Miss Toni." Hubbard and Byard are also both in good form. A perfect introduction to Eric Dolphy's versatile talents, this boppish set is more accessible than many of Dolphy's more innovative recordings. Recommended. —*Scott Yanow*

Here and There / Apr. 1, 1960-Sep. 6, 1961 / Original Jazz Classics ◆◆◆◆
This CD reissue has rarities from three different Eric Dolphy sessions. "April Fool" and the alternate take of "G.W." are drawn from Dolphy's initial date as a leader, a quintet outing with trumpeter Freddie Hubbard and pianist Jaki Byard. "Don't Blame Me" is taken from a Copenhagen concert but it is the two remaining numbers ("Status Seeking" and an unaccompanied rendition on bass clarinet of "God Bless the Child") that are of greatest interest. The latter cuts are taken from Dolphy's legendary gig at the Five Spot Cafe with trumpeter Booker Little, pianist Mal Waldron, bassist Richard Davis and drummer Ed Blackwell, not duplicating the seven more famous performances that are often thought of as the group's entire output. Although it is easy to think of this set on a whole as containing "leftovers," Dolphy's strong playing on alto, flute and bass clarinet makes the music of strong interest to his fans. —*Scott Yanow*

☆ **The Complete Prestige Recordings** / Apr. 1, 1960-Sep. 8, 1961 / Prestige ♦♦♦♦♦
During his 19 months with Prestige, Eric Dolphy recorded 13 sessions as a leader and sideman. All are included in this massive nine-CD set and, even when absorbed in two or three sittings, there is enough variety to hold on to any true jazz fan's attention. Dolphy, whether on alto, bass clarinet, flute and even on a couple of occasions clarinet, was a true original with distinctive sounds of his own and very unique (but ultimately logical) styles. Included in this box (which has no previously unissued material) are the complete contents of the albums *Outward Bound, Here & There, Dash One*, Oliver Nelson's *Screamin' the Blues*, Ken McIntyre's *Looking Ahead, Out There, Caribe* (with the Latin Jazz Quintet), Eddie Lockjaw Davis' *Trane Whistle* (during which Dolphy is an anonymous section player), *Far Cry*, Oliver Nelson's *Straight Ahead*, Ron Carter's *Where*, Mal Waldron's *The Quest, At the Five Spot* and *Eric Dolphy in Europe*. Even with the many impressive sidemen (which include trumpeters Freddie Hubbard, Richard Williams, and Booker Little, saxophonists Oliver Nelson, Ken McIntyre, Booker Ervin and Eddie Lockjaw Davis, pianists Jaki Byard, Richard Wyands, Walter Bishop, Jr. and Mal Waldron, bassists George Tucker, George Duvivier, Sam Jones, Ron Carter (who doubles on cello), Joe Benjamin and Richard Davis and drummers Roy Haynes, Art Taylor, Charlie Persip and Ed Blackwell), Eric Dolphy consistently emerges as the solo star. This often-remarkable music stands apart from the other styles prevalent during the era. —*Scott Yanow*

Other Aspects / Jul. 8, 1960-1962 / Blue Note ♦♦♦♦
This CD contains some unusual music by Eric Dolphy that was released for the first time more than two decades after his death. The lengthy "Jim Crow" matches the multi-instrumentalist with a classical singer and a rhythm section for a stirring performance while "Improvisations and Tukras" finds Dolphy on flute backed by two Indian percussionists. These two selections are unlike anything else in Dolphy's discography. In addition, this album has a duet with bassist Ron Carter and two brief unaccompanied flute solos. Consistently fascinating music. —*Scott Yanow*

☆ **Out There** / Aug. 15, 1960 / Original Jazz Classics ♦♦♦♦♦
Eric Dolphy's second session as a leader is one of his most intriguing. On this CD reissue, Dolphy is heard performing two songs apiece on alto, bass clarinet and flute, along with a rare appearance ("Eclipse") on clarinet. Joined by Ron Carter on cello, bassist George Duvivier and drummer Roy Haynes, Dolphy's playing is quite explorative and the hypnotic and somewhat spooky "Out There" finds both Dolphy's bass clarinet and Carter's cello sounding as if they are talking. —*Scott Yanow*

Caribe with the Latin Jazz Quintet / Aug. 19, 1960 / Prestige ♦♦♦
This record is the equivalent of throwing a stick of dynamite into a sedate, well-ordered dinner party, having the dynamite go off with a bang, and somehow leaving everything in its place. Such is the volatile Eric Dolphy, a serious wailer on the alto sax and even more idiosyncratic and radical on the bass clarinet, who barges into the lair of Juan Amalbert's Latin Jazz Quintet and doesn't perturb them in the least. The title track is sheer schizophrenia; the LJQ ambling along in a conga-accented blues walk while Dolphy fires all over the place on alto sax. Even the more animated "Mambo Ricci" has the same kind of group dynamic; Dolphy on fire, Gene Casey calm and deliberate on piano. Only on "Spring Is Here," where Dolphy switches to a contemplative-toned flute, do we find a balanced meeting ground, though his flute solo on "Sunday Go Meetin'" goes back out on a limb. Not an ideal match, then, but fascinating without a doubt. —*Richard S. Ginell*

Candid Dolphy / Oct. 20, 1960-Apr. 4, 1961 / Candid ♦♦♦♦
The great Eric Dolphy recorded several albums for the Candid label as a sideman including dates with bassist Charles Mingus, trumpeter Booker Little, singer Abbey Lincoln and the Newport Rebels. This CD features eight alternate takes from these sessions, six of which were previously unissued. "Reincarnation of a Love Bird" and "Stormy Weather" are with Mingus in a group also featuring trumpeter Ted Curson, two numbers have vocals by Abbey Lincoln (Coleman Hawkins is heard from on "African Lady"), Dolphy is matched with trombonist Jimmy Knepper and the veteran trumpeter Roy Eldridge on "Body and Soul," and he proves to be a perfect partner of Booker Little in a sextet. Even the "complete" box sets that have been issued of these sessions do not include all of this music, which in general is up to the level of the originally issued versions. —*Scott Yanow*

Far Cry / Dec. 21, 1960 / Original Jazz Classics ♦♦♦♦♦
Seven months before their famous matchup at the Five Spot, multireedist Eric Dolphy and trumpeter Booker Little teamed up for this quintet set with pianist Jaki Byard, bassist Ron Carter and drummer Roy Haynes. One of Dolphy's many Prestige recordings (all of which are also available on a massive box set), this CD reissue features Eric splitting his time between alto, bass clarinet and flute, taking "Tenderly" as an unaccompanied alto solo and showing a lot of feeling on "It's

Magic." Other highlights of the advanced hard bop session include "Ode to Charlie Parker," "Serene" and "Miss Ann." —*Scott Yanow*

Quartet 1961 / 1961 / Jazz Anthology ♦♦♦
Taken from Eric Dolphy's much-recorded European tour of 1961, this set matches the remarkable multi-instrumentalist with pianist Lalo Schifrin, bassist Bob Cunningham and drummer Mel Lewis, performing long versions of "On Green Dolphin Street" (over 23 minutes), "Softly as in a Morning Sunrise" and "The Way You Look Tonight." Although the rhythm section is conventional, Dolphy really tears into these standards, making this imported LP worth searching for. —*Scott Yanow*

Live! at the Five Spot, Vol. 1 / Jul. 16, 1961 / Original Jazz Classics ♦♦♦♦
On July 16, 1961, multi-instrumentalist Eric Dolphy and trumpeter Booker Little were extensively documented during the finish of a two-week engagement at the Five Spot in New York. Pianist Mal Waldron (overcoming an out-of-tune piano), bassist Richard Davis and drummer Ed Blackwell completed the quintet which, on the first of three CD reissues from this gig, performs Waldron's "Fire Waltz," Dolphy's "The Prophet" (which lasts 21 minutes) and two versions of Little's "Bee Vamp." During their short partnership, Dolphy and Little always inspired each other and their playing on the challenging tunes is quite stimulating. —*Scott Yanow*

Live! at the Five Spot, Vol. 2 / Jul. 16, 1961 / Original Jazz Classics ♦♦♦♦
The second of three CDs that document the Eric Dolphy/Booker Little Quintet's playing at the Five Spot (the third volume is titled *Memorial Album*) features the group (with pianist Mal Waldron, bassist Richard Davis and drummer Ed Blackwell) really stretching out during long versions of Little's "Aggression" and the standard "Like Someone in Love." Dolphy's playing (whether on alto, bass clarinet or flute) always defied categorization while Little (who passed away less than three months later) was the first new voice on the trumpet to emerge after Clifford Brown's death in 1956. An excellent set although, at just 36 minutes, one wishes that it had been combined with one of the other two volumes. —*Scott Yanow*

Memorial Album / Jul. 16, 1961 / Original Jazz Classics ♦♦♦
Despite its generic name, this is really the third volume of music that dates from one night in the short-lived and legendary Eric Dolphy/Booker Little Quintet. Recorded live at the Five Spot with pianist Mal Waldron, bassist Richard Davis and drummer Ed Blackwell, this CD reissue consists of two fairly lengthy renditions of Eric Dolphy compositions: "Number Eight" and "Booker's Waltz." Since there is only around a half-hour of music on the set, it is unfortunate that the advanced performances (which are also available as part of Eric Dolphy's nine-CD box set) were not combined with one of the two previous volumes. —*Scott Yanow*

The Great Concert of Eric Dolphy / Jul. 16, 1961 / Prestige ♦♦♦♦♦
For two weeks, the multi-instrumentalist (alto, flute and bass clarinet) Eric Dolphy appeared at the Five Spot in New York with a quintet comprising trumpeter Booker Little (who would pass away before the year ended), pianist Mal Waldron, bassist Richard Davis and drummer Ed Blackwell. One night, July 16, 1961, was fully recorded and the results released on three LPs. This three-LP box set contains all of the music, and, despite an out-of-tune piano, the results are consistently brilliant. The seven selections (all over 12 minutes long with "The Prophet" going on for over 21) give the principles plenty of space in which to stretch out, and the long improvisations consistently hold one's interest. All of the material (except the standard "Like Someone in Love") was composed by Dolphy, Little or Waldron. Classic and adventurous music. —*Scott Yanow*

Berlin Concerts / Aug. 30, 1961 / Enja ♦♦♦♦
This two-LP set features the great multi-instrumentalist Eric Dolphy mostly stretching out on standards, coming up with very original statements on such songs as "Hot House," "When Lights Are Low," "Hi Fly," "I'll Remember April" and "God Bless the Child" (the latter taken as an unaccompanied bass clarinet solo), in addition to two brief originals. With trumpeter Benny Bailey helping out on half of the selections along with a strong rhythm section, the two-fer would be a perfect introduction for listeners not familiar with Eric Dolphy's innovative style, but this set is very difficult to find. —*Scott Yanow*

The Complete Uppsala Concert / Sep. 4, 1961 / Jazz Door ♦♦♦
This two-CD set features the remarkable Eric Dolphy (tripling on alto, bass clarinet and flute) during a concert in Sweden. Accompanied by an obscure but talented rhythm section (pianist Rony Johansson, bassist Kurt Lindgren and drummer Rune Carlsson), Dolphy really stretches out on five of the seven numbers, particularly during a twenty-and-a-half-minute version of his blues "245." Other highlights include "Laura" (featuring Dolphy unaccompanied on alto), "Bag's Groove" (his only recording of that piece) and "I'll Remember April." With the exception of "245," all of the songs are bop standards but Eric Dolphy's improvisations are typically unpredictable and adventurous. The recording quality is decent, making this a good set to get after acquiring Dolphy's better-known sessions. —*Scott Yanow*

Eric Dolphy in Europe, Vol. 1 / Sep. 6, 1961+Sep. 8, 1961 / Original Jazz Classics ✦✦✦

The first of three CDs recorded in Copenhagen during Sept. 1961 by the unique Eric Dolphy, this date has the strongest program of the trio. Dolphy is heard on a definitive "God Bless the Child" playing unaccompanied bass clarinet, switches to flute for "Glad to Be Unhappy," romps on the bass clarinet on "Oleo," and plays alto for a duet with bassist Chuck Israel on Randy Weston's "Hi-Fly." Joined by a supportive Danish rhythm section (pianist Bent Axen, bassist Erik Moseholm and drummer Jorn Elniff) on the two quartet tracks, Dolphy is in excellent form throughout the well-rounded release. —*Scott Yanow*

Eric Dolphy in Europe, Vol. 2 / Sep. 6, 1961+Sep. 8, 1961 / Original Jazz Classics ✦✦✦

The second of three CDs that reissue a couple of concerts featuring multi-instrumentalist Eric Dolphy with a Danish rhythm section (pianist Bent Axen, bassist Erik Moseholm and drummer Jorn Elniff) in Copenhagen has its share of fine music. While the structures are generally boppish, Dolphy typically improvises in his own advanced vocabulary. He plays flute on two versions of "Don't Blame Me" and switches to alto for "The Way You Look Tonight," "Les" (which is mistitled "Miss Ann") and an emotional version of "Laura." Fine music that is also available as part of Dolphy's nine-CD "complete on Prestige" box set. —*Scott Yanow*

Eric Dolphy in Europe, Vol. 3 / Sep. 6, 1961+Sep. 8, 1961 / Original Jazz Classics ✦✦✦

This is the weakest of Eric Dolphy's three CDs that were recorded at a Copenhagen concert with a Danish rhythm section (pianist Bent Axen, bassist Erik Moseholm and drummer Jorn Elniff). The problem is that there are three straight versions of the rather dull "In the Blues" and none are all that interesting. Much better is Dolphy's exploration (on bass clarinet) of "When Lights Are Low" and his alto feature during "Woody 'n You ," but overall this is one of the less essential Eric Dolphy releases. —*Scott Yanow*

Stockholm Sessions / Sep. 25, 1961-Nov. 1, 1961 / Enja ✦✦✦✦

The music on this CD (the original LP program plus a second version of "Sorino") is taken from a radio aircheck and a TV special, both originating from Stockholm. The remarkable Eric Dolphy (switching between alto, bass clarinet and flute) performed two of his originals plus "Don't Blame Me" with a sympathetic quartet on the aircheck while the television show (does this film still exist?) features him in a quintet with trumpeter Idrees Sulieman playing three more originals, Mal Waldron's "Alone" and his unaccompanied bass clarinet feature "God Bless the Child." This innovative music can serve as a strong introduction of Eric Dolphy's talents to bebop fans who have not yet grasped the avant-garde. —*Scott Yanow*

Softly, As in a Morning Sunrise / Dec. 2, 1961 / Natasha ✦✦

This CD has a very interesting lineup of musicians: Eric Dolphy (sticking to bass clarinet throughout), pianist McCoy Tyner, bassist Reggie Workman and drummer Mel Lewis. Dolphy was actually touring with the John Coltrane Quintet (of which Tyner and Workman were a part) at the time and apparently Elvin Jones had passport problems so Lewis subbed for him. The playing on these four lengthy standards, including a twenty-three-and-a-half-minute "On Green Dolphin Street," is fine, but unfortunately, the recording quality from this Munich, Germany, concert is fairly bad, making much of this historic music fairly unlistenable. For Dolphy completists only. —*Scott Yanow*

Vintage Dolphy / Mar. 10, 1962-Apr. 18, 1963 / GM ✦✦✦✦

This posthumous collection features the remarkable Eric Dolphy in prime form. On three songs, Dolphy (switching between alto, bass clarinet and flute) performs two originals and Jaki Byard's "Ode to Charlie Parker" with a quartet that includes trumpeter Edward Armour, bassist Richard Davis and J.C. Moses. In addition, Dolphy is heard on three Third Stream avant-garde classical pieces by Gunther Schuller (taking a rare clarinet solo on "Densities") and jamming on a wild version of "Donna Lee" with an all-star group including players such as trumpeter Don Ellis, trombonist Jimmy Knepper, Benny Golson on tenor and guitarist Jim Hall that gets completely lost during its last two choruses! Highly recommended. —*Scott Yanow*

☆ **Jitterbug Waltz** / 1963 / Casablanca ✦✦✦✦✦

In 1963, Eric Dolphy recorded two of his most rewarding sessions which were originally released on two LPs: *Conversations* and *Iron Man*. This music has been reissued numerous times through the years, including in total on this two-LP set; it deserves to come out on CD. These dates are among Dolphy's finest with the challenging material interpreted by a constantly shifting personnel. Three numbers ("Jitterbug Waltz," "Iron Man" and "Mandrake") find the multi-instrumentalist (alto, flute and bass clarinet) playing unconventional music with a quintet that includes two masterful musicians at the beginning of their careers: vibraphonist Bobby Hutcherson and trumpeter Woody Shaw. Two other pieces ("Burning Spear" and "Music Matador") have Dolphy interacting with a variety of top young avant-gard-

ists including Shaw, Hutcherson, Clifford Jordan on soprano, altoist Sonny Simmons and Prince Lasha on flute. In addition, there are three duets with bassist Richard Davis ("Come Sunday," "Alone Together" and "Ode to Charlie Parker") and an unaccompanied alto piece (an intense "Love Me"). Quite a varied set, essential music for any jazz collection. —*Scott Yanow*

★ **Out to Lunch** / Feb. 25, 1964 / Blue Note ✦✦✦✦✦

Eric Dolphy's debut as a leader on Blue Note was also his last American recording before his unexpected death four months later. On this brilliant set, Dolphy performs five of his colorful originals with quite an all-star group (even though at the time none of these young players were all that well-known): trumpeter Freddie Hubbard, vibraphonist Bobby Hutcherson, bassist Richard Davis and drummer Tony Williams. Whether playing alto, flute or bass clarinet, Dolphy had a highly original style, and this set remains one of his finest statements. —*Scott Yanow*

☆ **Last Date** / Jun. 2, 1964 / Verve ✦✦✦✦✦

Although one slighty later session has since been discovered, *Last Date* remains a near-classic with the great Eric Dolphy (heard on alto, flute and bass clarinet) backed by a top European rhythm section—pianist Misha Mengelberg, bassist Jacques Schols and drummer Han Bennink—performing exciting versions of "Epistrophy," "You Don't Know What Love Is" and four of his originals. The innovative music points out what a giant loss Dolphy's premature death was; he passed away just 27 days after this memorable performance. —*Scott Yanow*

Naima / Jun. 11, 1964 / West Wind ✦✦✦✦

Recorded nine days after Eric Dolphy's *Last Date* album and at the same sessions that resulted in the other West Wind release *Unrealized Tapes*, this CD finds the great Eric Dolphy (just 18 days before his death) in excellent form. He plays flute on "Ode to Charlie Parker" and stretches out on alto and bass clarinet during lengthy versions of "Naima" and "Springtime." Although joined by a fine French rhythm section, trumpeter Donald Byrd and Nathan Davis on tenor, Dolphy is easily the dominant voice throughout the spirited set, showing listeners that he still had a great deal to say even though his time had run out. This European import is worth searching for. —*Scott Yanow*

Unreleased Tapes / Jun. 11, 1964 / West Wind ✦✦✦✦

For years, *Last Date* was thought of as Eric Dolphy's final recording until *Unrealized Tapes* (from nine days later) was released; Dolphy passed away only 18 days after performing this music. This LP from the European West Wind label features the great Dolphy on alto and bass clarinet with a sextet that includes trumpeter Donald Byrd, tenor saxophonist Nathan Davis and a French rhythm section performing four of his compositions including the otherwise unknown "Springtime." Eric Dolphy collectors will have to get this gem. —*Scott Yanow*

Natty Dominique (Anatie Dominique)

b. Aug. 2, 1896, New Orleans, LA, **d.** Aug. 30, 1982, Chicago, IL
Trumpet / New Orleans Jazz

An erratic trumpeter, Natty Dominique at his best in the 1920s (such as on "Brush Stomp" and "Oriental Man") played in an appealing rhythmic style with plenty of force. However, there were also times ("Tack 'Em Down") when his enthusiasm got the best of him! He played in brass bands as a teenager in New Orleans, left town in 1913 and freelanced in Chicago and the Midwest. Dominique recorded with Jelly Roll Morton in 1923 and played with Carroll Dickerson and Jimmie Noone but he is best remembered for his association with Johnny Dodds; they recorded together frequently. After appearing on Dodds' final records in 1940, Dominique's heart condition forced him to retire and he worked as an airport porter, but in the early '50s he started playing again on a part-time basis, often using Baby Dodds. —*Scott Yanow*

Natty Dominique's Creole Dance Band / Sep. 28, 1953 / American Music ✦✦✦

Natty Dominique is best-known for his erratic but sometimes quite rewarding playing with the great clarinetist Johnny Dodds in the 1920s. He made no recordings after 1940 except for the material on this CD; only two of the songs had been issued before 1993. Dominique is typically streaky in a septet that also includes clarinetist Darnell Howard, trombonist Preston Jackson and drummer Baby Dodds, sounding fine on a few of the ensembles where he plays in a style reminiscent of Freddie Keppard. Most interesting are two excerpts from interviews where Natty talks about playing with Dodds and remembers a lesson that he had from Louis Armstrong about the importance of being original. This is a historically significant if not really essential release. —*Scott Yanow*

Arne Domnérus

b. Dec. 20, 1924, Stockholm, Sweden
Alto Saxophone ,Clarinet / Bop, Swing

One of Sweden's top jazz musicians, Arne Domnérus led his first group in 1942, made his earliest recordings in 1945 and led his first record sessions in 1949. An altoist who combines together Johnny Hodges and Lee Konitz and an excellent swing clarinetist, Domnérus has led combos for over 45 years and worked steadily with the Swedish Radio Band and its successors. He has made many recordings for Swedish labels including Phontastic. — *Scott Yanow*

● **Portrait of Arne Domnérus** / Jun. 20, 1946-Jul. 20, 1993 / Phontastic ✦✦✦✦✦
This Phontastic CD gives listeners a fine cross-section of Arne Domnérus' career. Domnérus, an altoist inspired by Johnny Hodges and a Benny Goodman-influenced clarinetist whose style was very open to the influences of bebop and cool jazz, has long been one of Sweden's top jazzmen. On this CD there are eight selections from the 1946-60 period and ten dating from 1978-93; among the sidemen are Rolf Ericson, Putte Wickman, Bengt Hallberg, Rene Gustafsson and Jan Lundgren among others and, on "Stockholm Sweetnin'," Domnérus is heard with an all-star group that includes Clifford Brown, Art Farmer and arranger Quincy Jones. Considering Arne Domnérus' talent, it is not too surprising that he holds his own. An excellent overview of his career. — *Scott Yanow*

Arne Domnérus and His Favourite Groups / Aug. 1949-Mar. 1950 / Dragon ✦✦✦✦

Jazz at the Pawnshop, Vol. 4 / Dec. 6, 1976-Dec. 7, 1976 / Proprius ✦✦✦
The fourth of four CDs that document a two-day engagement by the Arne Domnérus Quintet at the Pawnshop club, this limited-edition set was put out as a souvenir to collectors of the other three volumes. It just has the first selection ("Mood Indigo") and the last ("Jeep's Blues") that was performed during this gig, just 19 minutes of music. The playing by altoist Arne Domnérus, pianist Bengt Hallberg, bassist Georg Riedel, drummer Egil Johansen and vibraphonist Lars Erstrand is typically swinging, making this hard-to-find disc a must for completists. — *Scott Yanow*

Duets for Duke / Jul. 27, 1978-Jul. 28, 1978 / Sonet ✦✦✦

Rapturous Reeds / Aug. 9, 1978-Feb. 27, 1979 / Phontastic ✦✦✦✦
It is not surprising that altoist Arne Domnérus (who doubles on clarinet) and Bob Wilber (heard here on alto, soprano and clarinet) make for a mutually inspiring team, for both of the musicians are flexible and swing-based. Although Wilber contributed a few originals and there are a couple of obscurities, the bulk of this sextet set with pianist Bengt Hallberg, guitarist Rune Gustafsson, bassist Sture Nordin and drummer Rune Carlsson consists of spirited versions of swing standards including "Jumpin' at the Woodside," "Stompin' at the Savoy" and "I Double Dare You." The CD reissue adds two Benny Goodman-associated numbers ("Seven Come Eleven" and "Rachel's Dream") from a slightly later session with a different rhythm section and the clarinets of Ove Lind and Anders Ohman. — *Scott Yanow*

Downtown Meetings / Sep. 5, 1978-Sep. 6, 1978 / Phontastic ✦✦✦✦
Swedish altoist/clarinetist Arne Domnérus and pianist Bengt Hallberg travelled to New York to record this Phontastic set with fluegelhornist Clark Terry (who is on half of the songs), bassist George Mraz and drummer Oliver Jackson. The program on this CD reissue, which has two more numbers than the original LP, boasts plenty of high spirits and swinging solos. The group performs three Swedish songs (including Hallberg's "Mulen") and a variety of swing standards that are highlighted by "Gone with the Wind," C.T.'s feature on "Come Sunday," "In a Mellotone" and "C Jam Blues." — *Scott Yanow*

Fragment / Jun. 4, 1982-Jun. 6, 1982 / Phontastic ✦✦✦✦✦
Arne Domnérus, best-known as an altoist, sticks to clarinet on this set and often pays tribute to Benny Goodman without directly copying the King of Swing excessively. Joined by pianist Bengt Hallberg, bassist Georg Riedel and drummer Egil Johansen, Domnérus performs his "Fragment" (which is based on excerpts from a variety of Benny Goodman recordings) and nine standards including "Avalon," "Symphony" and "Sweet Georgia Brown." High-quality swing from one of the Swedish giants of jazz. — *Scott Yanow*

Happy Together! / Dec. 13, 1995+Dec. 15, 1995 / Ladybird ✦✦✦
A pair of major Swedish veterans (clarinetist Putte Wickman and altoist Arne Domnérus) join forces with the talented young pianist Jan Lundgren, guitarist Rune Gustafsson, bassist Jesper Lundgaard and drummer Aage Tanggaard to perform two CDs full of straightahead music. Although Wickman and Domnérus (who switches to clarinet on "Barney Goin' Easy") sound fine during these live performances (which have announcements in Swedish), the emphasis is generally on slower tempos, and the interpretations are not as fiery or competitive as one might hope. Pleasing but not essential music, with some of the brighter moments occurring on "Fine and Dandy," "Moanin'," "Broadway" and "Move." — *Scott Yanow*

Barbara Donald

b. Feb. 9, 1942, Minneapolis, MN
Trumpet / Free Jazz, Avant-Garde
One of the top female trumpeters of all time, Barbara Donald has a powerful and explorative style that has been showcased on records far too little. She is best-

known for playing with altoist Sonny Simmons (her husband at the time) during 1963-72. She recorded a couple of impressive efforts for Cadence in the early '80s but little has been heard from her since. — *Scott Yanow*

● **Olympia Live** / Mar. 30, 1981 / Cadence ✦✦✦✦✦
Best-known for her collaboration with her then-husband altoist Sonny Simmons, the powerful trumpeter Barbara Donald recorded two excellent albums for Cadence in the early '80s. This particular set, cut live in Olympia, WA, features Donald with Carter Jefferson (who doubles on tenor and soprano) with a septet. Surprisingly, the music is mostly in a hard bop rather than free vein, with such songs as Cedar Walton's "Bolivia," Thelonious Monk's "Well You Needn't" and Donald's "Blues for You" receiving relatively straightahead but passionate treatment. It's worth searching for. — *Scott Yanow*

The Past and Tomorrows / Apr. 16, 1982+Apr. 17, 1982 / Cadence ✦✦✦✦
The powerful trumpeter Barbara Donald leads a strong sextet that also features the tenors of Carter Jefferson and Gary Hammon on Monk's "Pannonica" and several group originals. The music is advanced hard bop with plenty of room for stirring improvisations, particularly by the leader. In view of the fact that the talented Barbara Donald has rarely recorded since this album, someone should give her a recording contract. — *Scott Yanow*

Lou Donaldson

b. Nov. 1, 1926, Badin, NC
Alto Saxophone / Bop, Soul-Jazz, Hard Bop
Lou Donaldson has long been an excellent bop altoist influenced by Charlie Parker, but with a more blues-based style of his own. His distinctive tone has been heard in a variety of small-group settings, and he has recorded dozens of worthy and spirited (if somewhat predictable) sets through the years.

Donaldson started playing clarinet when he was 15, soon switching to the alto. He attended college and performed in a Navy band while in the military. Donaldson first gained attention when he moved to New York and in 1952 started recording for Blue Note as a leader. At the age of 25, his style was fully formed, and although it would continue growing in depth through the years, Donaldson had already found his sound. In 1954, he participated in a notable gig with Art Blakey, Clifford Brown, Horace Silver and Tommy Potter that was extensively documented by Blue Note and that directly predated the Jazz Messengers. However, Donaldson was never a member of the Messengers, and although he recorded as a sideman in the 1950s and occasionally afterwards with Thelonious Monk, Milt Jackson and Jimmy Smith, among others, he has been a bandleader from the mid-1950s up until the present.

Donaldson's early Blue Note recordings were pure bop. In 1958, he began often utilizing a conga player, and starting in 1961 his bands often had an organist rather than a pianist. Donaldson's bluesy style was easily transferable to soul-jazz, and he sounded most original in that context. His association with Blue Note (1952-63) was succeeded by some excellent (if now-scarce) sets for Cadet and Argo (1963-66). The altoist returned to Blue Note in 1967 and soon became caught up in the increasingly commercial leanings of the label. For a time, he utilized an electronic Varitone sax, which completely watered down his sound. The success of "Alligator Boogaloo" in 1967 led to a series of less interesting funk recordings that were instantly dated and not worthy of his talent.

However, after a few years off records, Lou Donaldson's artistic return in 1981 and subsequent soul-jazz and hard bop dates for Muse, Timeless and Milestone have found the altoist back in prime form, interacting with organists and pianists alike and showing that his style is quite timeless. — *Scott Yanow*

The Lou Donaldson Quartet/Quintet/Sextet / Jun. 10, 1952-Aug. 22, 1954 / Blue Note ✦✦✦✦✦
Since *Quartet/Quintet/Sextet* is Lou Donaldson's first full-length album, it's not surprising that it captures the alto saxophonist at the height of his Charlie Parker influence. Throughout the album on CD, the collection features all the music on the 12-inch LP, music from its 10-inch incarnation, and three alternate takes—Donaldson plays in a straight bop vein, whether on uptempo swingers or ballads. Most of the songs on the collection are standards, with a couple of fine originals from Donaldson and pianist Horace Silver spicing the mix; in particular, Silver's rollicking, Latin-tinged "Roccus" is a standout. While Donaldson's tone isn't quite as full as it would be within just five years, he impresses with his bold, speedy technique and fine phrasing. He doesn't play anything out of the ordinary, but he plays it very, very well, and his playing is enhanced by the three stellar bands that support him on these sessions. Among his fellow musicians on *Quartet/Quintet/Sextet* are Silver, bassist Gene Ramey, drummer Art Taylor, trumpeter Blue Mitchell, pianist Elmo Hope and trumpeter Kenny Dorham. Everyone plays in a straight bop and hard bop tradition, contributing fine performances to a strong debut effort by Donaldson. — *Stephen Thomas Erlewine*

Wailing with Lou / Jan. 27, 1957 / Blue Note ✦✦✦✦
Wailing with Lou is an appropriate title for this enjoyable set of straightahead bop. Whether he's riding the propulsive rhythms of "Caravan" or settling down into a ballad, Donaldson takes the center stage with his surprisingly full alto tone. He still displays a clear Charlie Parker influence, but he is beginning to break free and develop his own style. In particular, he relies on bluesy runs more than Bird, which give his music a soulful edge. But what makes *Wailing with Lou* so enjoyable is the hot interplay between Donaldson, trumpeter Donald Byrd, pianist Herman Foster, bassist Peck Morrison and drummer Art Taylor. All five musicians give enthusiastic, infectious performances. There's nothing out of the ordinary here—just hard-driving bop and sensitive ballads, which are sure to please fans of the style. —*Stephen Thomas Erlewine*

Lou Takes Off / Dec. 15, 1957 / Blue Note ✦✦✦✦✦
The influence of Charlie Parker can be heard in virtually every modern jazz musician, particularly players of the alto saxophone. Although considered to be one of "Bird's children," Lou Donaldson absorbed and synthesized other pre-Parker influences, such as Johnny Hodges and Benny Carter. This recording marks a period in his development prior to a stylistic shift away from bop and towards a stronger rhythm and blues emphasis. Three uptempo tunes are pure bebop; the remaining number is a medium blues, quite characteristic of the hard bop period. The front line on this set includes Donald Byrd and Curtis Fuller; the rhythm section is Sonny Clark, George Joyner and Art Taylor. Overall, *Lou Takes Off* breaks no new musical ground, but it is a solid, swinging session of high-caliber playing. —*Lee Bloom*

★ **Blues Walk** / Jul. 28, 1958 / Blue Note ✦✦✦✦✦
This early session from Lou Donaldson is pure bebop with the altoist romping on such pieces as "Blues Walk," "Move," "Play Ray" and "Callin' All Cats." The rhythm section (pianist Herman Foster, bassist Peck Morrison, drummer Dave Bailey) is supportive if not particularly distinctive, although the congas of Ray Barretto add some color to the accompaniment. No matter; Lou Donaldson is the main star of this swinging and enjoyable set. —*Scott Yanow*

Light Foot / Dec. 14, 1958 / Blue Note ✦✦✦
In many ways, *Blues Walk* marked the culmination of Lou Donaldson's prime period as a hard-driving, straightahead bop saxophonist. Until that point, he had been turning out intense, furious bop workouts—afterward, as its successor *Light Foot* shows, he began to slow down a bit. With *Light Foot*, Donaldson still was firmly grounded in bop, but the tempos began to slow down, and his blues influence came to the forefront; furthermore, the bop tracks are hard bop, not straight bop, which tended to dominate his previous recordings. That diversity makes *Light Foot* an interesting listen, but the record suffers from slightly uneven material and performances. His quintet—featuring pianist Herman Foster, bassist Peck Morrison, drummer Jimmy Wormsworth and conga player Ray Barretto—are usually up to the task at hand, but they tend to play conventionally. And, ultimately, that's what *Light Foot* is—an entertaining but conventional release from an alto saxophonist capable of greatness. —*Stephen Thomas Erlewine*

LD + 3: Lou Donaldson with the Three Sounds / Feb. 18, 1959 / Blue Note ✦✦✦✦✦
Lou Donaldson and the Three Sounds both had a tendency to slip into low-key grooves, which is what makes the hard-driving bop of the opener "Three Little Words" a little startling. Donaldson is at a fiery peak, spinning out Bird-influenced licks that nevertheless illustrate that he's developed a more rounded, individual style of his own. The Three Sounds are equally as impressive, working bop rhythms with a dexterity that their first albums only hinted at. That high standard is maintained throughout the album, one of the finest in either of their catalogs. Albums like this and *Blues Walk* established Donaldson's reputation as a first-rate alto saxophonist, since he flaunts a full, robust tone, a fondness for melody, and nimble solos over the course of the record. *LD + 3* is basically straight bop and hard bop, with little of the soul-jazz the two artists would later explore, but this collection of swinging standards, bop staples and a pair of Donaldson originals ranks as one of Lou's finest straight bop sessions. —*Stephen Thomas Erlewine*

Sunny Side Up / Feb. 5, 1960+Feb. 29, 1960 / Blue Note ✦✦✦
Sunny Side Up is closer to hard bop than the straightahead bop that characterized Lou Donaldson's '50s Blue Note records. There's a bit more soul to the songs here, which pianist Horace Parlan helps emphasize with his lightly swinging grooves. The pair help lead the group—which also features trumpeter Bill Hardman, drummer Al Harewood and bassist Sam Jones (Laymon Jackson plays bass on two of the eight songs)—through a mellow set of standards and bluesy originals from Donaldson and Parlan. Even the uptempo numbers sound relaxed, never fiery. Despite the general smoothness of the session, Donaldson stumbles a little—the quotation of "Flight of the Bumblebee" on "Blues for J.P." is awkward, as is the snippet of "Pop Goes the Weasel" on "Politely," and "Way Down Upon the Swanee River" sounds

lazy—but there's enough solid material to make *Sunny Side Up* a worthwhile listen for fans of Donaldson and early-'60s hard bop. —*Stephen Thomas Erlewine*

Midnight Sun / Jul. 22, 1960 / Blue Note ✦✦✦
Recorded in July of 1960, *Midnight Sun* sat unissued in Blue Note's vaults until the early '80s, when it was issued as part of their LT series. Like many of the previously unreleased albums in the series, it's clear that the only reason that this remained in the vaults was because the label was releasing too many records, not because the session itself was second-rate. Granted, there are a couple of awkward moments on the date, but for the most part, *Midnight Sun* is as strong as any of the hard bop records Donaldson released in the early '60s. Part of the reason the quality is so high is the fact his supporting quartet is so strong. Pianist Horace Parlan has a number of fine moments on the record, and Lou's longtime rhythm section of bassist Ben Tucker, drummer Al Harewood and conga player Ray Barretto is as reliable as effort. Any dedicated Donaldson fan should search for this record; even if it doesn't reach the heights of *Blues Walk* and *Here 'Tis*, it still has plenty of fine music. —*Stephen Thomas Erlewine*

Here 'Tis / Jan. 23, 1961 / Blue Note ✦✦✦✦
Here 'Tis is in the front rank of Lou Donaldson records, an exceptionally funky soul-jazz session that finds the saxophonist swinging harder than usual. As he moves from hard bop to soul-jazz, Donaldson reveals a bluesy streak to his playing while keeping the vigorous attack that defined his best bop. Donaldson's playing is among his finest in the soul-jazz vein, but what makes *Here 'Tis* such an enjoyable session is his interaction with his supporting trio of guitarist Grant Green, organist Baby Face Willette and drummer Dave Bailey. As support, all three know how to keep a groove gritty and flexible, following Lou's lead and working a swinging beat that keeps flowing, never growing static. Green and Willette also have their time in the spotlight, and both musicians are frequently stunning. Green's single-note leads are clean and inventive; Willette is rhythmic and forceful, but also capable of soulful, mellow leads on the slow blues. Their talent, combined with Donaldson at a peak, results in a terrific record. —*Stephen Thomas Erlewine*

Gravy Train / Apr. 27, 1961 / Blue Note ✦✦✦
This CD reissue is a fairly typical Lou Donaldson date, featuring the altoist on basic originals, standards, blues and ballads. Donaldson, who is supported by pianist Herman Foster (whose solos emphasize block chordings), bassist Ben Tucker, drummer Dave Bailey and Alec Dorsey on congas, is in fine form on this pleasing but rather predictable effort, playing his renditions of soulful and bluish bop. Highlights include "South of the Border," "Polka Dots and Moonbeams" and a medium-tempo rendition of "Candy." —*Scott Yanow*

The Natural Soul / May 9, 1962 / Blue Note ✦✦✦✦
The Natural Soul finds Lou Donaldson delving deeply into soul-jazz, recording a set of funky, greasy instrumentals with only a few references to hard bop. Donaldson occasionally sounds a little awkward with the relaxed groove of *The Natural Soul*, as does trumpeter Tommy Turrentine, but the trio of guitarist Grant Green, organist John Patton and drummer Ben Dixon keep things cooking. Green and Patton's solos often burn and are always invigorating, and Lou frequently matches their heights. The original compositions—which form the bulk of the album—aren't much more than blues and soul vamps, but they provide an excellent foundation for the combo to work hot grooves. And, in the end, that's what *The Natural Soul* is about—groove. It maintains the high standards Donaldson established with his first soul-jazz foray, *Here 'Tis*, and remains one of his best records in that genre. —*Stephen Thomas Erlewine*

Good Gracious / Jan. 24, 1963 / Blue Note ✦✦✦
Good Gracious may be Lou Donaldson's record, but guitarist Grant Green and organist John Patton steal the show. Working with a tight, soulful groove laid down by drummer Ben Dixon, the guitarist and organist trade hot lines that often steal the thunder from Donaldson, who nevertheless turns in a robust, tuneful performance. Donaldson's tone is richer and fuller than it is on many of his early '60s records, and he really connects with the laid-back R&B grooves and soul-jazz vamps on *Good Gracious*, turning in melodic, memorable solos. However, Grant and Patton take the songs even further with their intense solos and fills; Patton, in particular, sounds on fire even when the tempo is mellow. *Good Gracious* still falls prey to some of the lazy tempos that pop up on most Lou Donaldson records, but it remains one of his finest soul-jazz sessions. —*Stephen Thomas Erlewine*

At His Best / Aug. 30, 1966 / Cadet ✦✦✦

Lush Life / Jan. 20, 1967 / Blue Note ✦✦✦✦✦
After brief sojourns at Argo and Cadet, Lou Donaldson marked his 1967 return by recording *Lush Life*, the grandest project he ever attempted. With its plush arrangements and unabashedly pretty melodies, *Lush Life* stands in stark contrast to everything else he cut in the '60s. There are no blues, no stabs at soul-jazz grooves, no hard bop—only sweet, sensitive renditions of romantic standards. Donaldson shone on ballads before, but it's nevertheless surprising how successful he is on

this set of slow love songs. His tone is full and elegant—it's easy to get lost in his rich readings of these familiar melodies, as well as his slyly seductive improvisations. Of course, it helps that his instrumental backdrops are as lovely as those his nine-piece backing band provide. Nonets are unwieldy, to be certain, but Duke Pearson's arrangements are clean, sparkling and attractive, and the superstar band—Wayne Shorter (tenor sax), Jerry Dodgion (alto sax, flute), Pepper Adams (bari sax), Freddie Hubbard (trumpet), Garnett Brown (trombone), McCoy Tyner (piano), Ron Carter (bass), Al Harewood (drums)—knows enough to provide sympathetic support and not steal the show. When they do take solos, it enhances Donaldson's original statements, and helps make *Lush Life* the singularly enchanting record it is. —*Stephen Thomas Erlewine*

Alligator Bogaloo / Apr. 17, 1967 / Blue Note ✦✦✦✦
Altoist Lou Donaldson had a big hit at the time with the catchy title cut. This CD reissue (a straight reproduction of the original LP) features Donaldson in a quintet with cornetist Melvin Lastie, Sr., guitarist George Benson, organist Lonnie Smith and drummer Leo Morris. The material (originals by Donaldson, Smith and Freddie McCoy along with the standard "I Want a Little Girl") is fairly basic (generally bluesy and funky) but there are fine solos on this session from Donaldson, Benson and Smith. —*Scott Yanow*

Mr. Shing-A-Ling / Oct. 27, 1967 / Blue Note ✦✦✦
Lou Donaldson does attempt to loosen up a bit with *Mr. Shing-A-Ling*, but the whole affair is a bit stilted and misconceived. Not quite the full-fledged electric funk workout that was becoming commonplace for old-guard soul-jazz musicians in the late '60s, but not quite the bop-inflected soul-jazz of the early '60s either, *Mr. Shing-A-Ling* falls into a netherworld that won't connect either with jazz purists or fans of grooving jazz-funk. When the group does try to get funky on the record, the results just sound lazy—there's no spark to the rhythms, or to Donaldson's melody lines, especially on the embarrassing cover of the pop hit "Ode to Billie Joe." When the quintet settles into a mid-tempo vamp, Donaldson, trumpeter Blue Mitchell and organist Lonnie Smith do spin out some good solos, but the lack of energy and enthusiasm the group has for the material makes *Mr. Shing-A-Ling* a bit of a tiring listen. —*Stephen Thomas Erlewine*

The Best of Lou Donaldson, Vol. 2 / Oct. 27, 1967-Jan. 1970 / Blue Note ✦✦✦✦
Lou Donaldson's late '60s albums have usually been disdained by jazz purists, yet the loose-limbed, soulful funk of those records (*Say it Loud, Midnight Creeper, Mr. Shing-A-Ling, Hot Dog*) gained an audience in the '80s and '90s. Instead of jazz fans, dance and hip-hop fans latched on to these records because they consisted of long, funky vamps—the very thing that jazz purists criticized about the records. Truth be told, many of Donaldson's late-'60s records were wildly uneven, which is why *The Best of Lou Donaldson, Vol. 2* is so useful. Drawing from the best tracks from each of the albums, the compilation features the best funky grooves that Donaldson conjured during this era. The music still won't convert any purist, but fans of acid-jazz, jazzy hip-hop and soulful funk will find *The Best of Lou Donaldson, Vol. 2* wildly entertaining. —*Stephen Thomas Erlewine*

Midnight Creeper / Mar. 15, 1968 / Blue Note ✦✦✦✦
As he delved deeper into commercial soul-jazz and jazz-funk, Lou Donaldson became better at it. While lacking the bite of his hard-bop improvisations or the hard-swinging funk of *Alligator Bogaloo, Midnight Creeper* succeeds where its predecessor, *Mr. Shing-A-Ling*, failed—it offers a thoroughly enjoyable set of grooving, funky soul-jazz. The five songs—including two originals by Lou and one each by Lonnie Smith (who also plays organ on the record), Teddy Vann and Harold Ousley—aren't particularly distinguished, but the vibe is important, not the material. And the band—Donaldson, Smith, trumpeter Blue Mitchell, guitarist George Benson and drummer Leo Morris—strike the right note, turning in a fluid, friendly collection of bluesy funk vamps. Donaldson could frequently sound stilted on his commercial soul-jazz dates, but that's not the case with *Midnight Creeper*. He rarely is quite as loose on his late '60s/early '70s records as he is here, and that's what makes *Midnight Creeper* a keeper. —*Stephen Thomas Erlewine*

Say It Loud! / Nov. 8, 1968 / Blue Note ✦✦
The title of *Say It Loud!* is taken from James Brown's anthem "Say It Loud, I'm Black and I'm Proud," the R&B/funk classic that Lou Donaldson covers on this album. Instead of providing a thematic and musical touchstone for the rest of the record, the song is an attempt to prove that Lou is still on top of musical trends, but the lazy groove he and his band—trumpeter Blue Mitchell, guitarist Jimmy Ponder, organist Charles Earland, drummer Leo Morris—work up shows they're not quite comfortable with this contemporary funk. They sound much more at ease with standards like "Summertime" and "Caravan," which give them a chance to stretch out, even if they are arranged like commercially oriented soul-jazz. Nevertheless, their simple presence on the album puts the stiffness of Donaldson's groove-oriented soul-jazz in sharper relief. *Midnight Creeper* was a successful soul-jazz record because the group managed to hit the right tone and groove, but here his group

sounds awkward and uneasy. There are a few good moments scattered throughout the album, particularly by Mitchell, but overall, *Say It Loud!* is one of the weakest records in Donaldson's catalog. —*Stephen Thomas Erlewine*

Hot Dog / Apr. 25, 1969 / Blue Note ✦✦
This CD reissues one of altoist Lou Donaldson's weakest recordings. Dating from the declining years of Blue Note, Donaldson plays decent enough (although when he utilizes a baritone sax it greatly dilutes his sound) but the very weak material features R&B rhythms, endless vamping and automatic pilot riffing from organist Charles Earland. The "glee club" vocal on "Who's Making Love" is incredibly bad, laughably so. Guitarist Melvin Sparks and trumpeter Ed Williams do their best during their solos but the material sinks the date. —*Scott Yanow*

Everything I Play Is Funky / Aug. 22, 1969+Jan. 9, 1970 / Blue Note ✦✦
It is always a bit painful to hear creative jazz musicians play well below their potential and it would not be an overstatement to say that altoist Lou Donaldson is capable of much better than the music heard on this CD. His calypso "West Indian Daddy" is okay (if not at all memorable), he jams reasonably well on the driving blues "Minor Bash" and plays honestly (if overly straight) on "Over the Rainbow." But the three other tracks are throwaways, trumpeter Blue Mitchell shows so little personality that the unknown Eddie Williams (who replaces Mitchell on two cuts) proves to be his equal, and the rhythm section (with either Lonnie Smith or Charles Earland on organ) does little except chug away. This set is a major disappointment. —*Scott Yanow*

Pretty Things / Jan. 9, 1970-Jun. 12, 1970 / Blue Note ✦✦
Lou Donaldson has recorded many strong sessions throughout his career, but this CD reissue brings back one of the less-significant ones. Organist Leon Spencer dominates the ensembles, the material is a bit trivial, and the altoist/leader uses a baritone sax on some of the selections, which makes him sound much less individual than usual. Trumpeter Blue Mitchell's solos and a fine closing jam on "Love" help upgrade the music a bit but there are many better Donaldson recordings to acquire first. —*Scott Yanow*

The Scorpion: Live at the Cadillac Club / Nov. 7, 1970 / Blue Note ✦✦
This previously unreleased live set, which has been issued on Blue Note's *Rare Groove Series*, will bore anyone who listens closely. The repertoire is dominated by lengthy funk grooves that are quite danceable but never develop beyond the obvious. Altoist Lou Donaldson was using a baritone horn at the time that gave him a generic and unappealing tone, the obscure trumpeter Fred Ballard does his best to no avail, and the enthusiastic rhythm section (guitarist Melvin Sparks, organist Leon Spencer, Jr., and drummer Idris Muhammad) keeps the grooves repetitious. Bob Porter's liner notes (which colorfully gives readers the history of Newark jazz of the past 30 years) are superlative but, even with the inclusion of a fast blues, musically nothing much happens. —*Scott Yanow*

Sophisticated Lou / Dec. 8, 1972-Dec. 18, 1972 / Blue Note ✦✦✦
For the most part, *Sophisticated Lou* found Lou Donaldson returning to standards after spending several years cranking out commercially oriented soul-jazz. Supported by a lush string section, Donaldson plays sensitive, pretty versions of such familiar items as "Stella By Starlight," "What Are You Doing the Rest of Your Life," "Autumn in New York" and "Time After Time," plus a new reading of his "Blues Walk" and a cover of Stevie Wonder's "You Are the Sunshine of My Life." *Sophisticated Lou* pales when compared to the great *Lush Life*, but it remains a fairly successful effort, and it's a nice change of pace after several albums of funky soul-jazz. —*Stephen Thomas Erlewine*

Sweet Poppa Lou / Jan. 7, 1981 / Muse ✦✦✦✦

Forgotten Man / Jul. 2, 1981 / Timeless ✦✦✦
Altoist Lou Donaldson was never exactly a "forgotten man," but his boppish style had been largely overlooked since his commercial electric funk sessions for Blue Note in the early to mid-'70s. This is a straightahead acoustic quartet date with pianist Herman Foster (whose block chord solos on a couple of numbers are quite exciting), bassist Geoff Fuller and drummer Victor Jones. Donaldson romps through some bop standards, Tadd Dameron's lesser-known "This Is Happiness" and his own "Tracy," and takes a humorous vocal on "Whiskey Drinkin' Woman." Although not essential, this album should easily please Lou Donaldson's fans, for it finds him in exuberant form. —*Scott Yanow*

Back Street / 1982 / Muse ✦✦✦
Stately, yet still funky. —*Ron Wynn*

Live in Bologna / Jan. 1984 / Timeless ✦✦✦✦

Play the Right Thing / Dec. 19, 1990-Dec. 20, 1990 / Milestone ✦✦✦✦
This is the latest in a long line of sumptuous soul/jazz/funky workouts. —*Ron Wynn*

Birdseed / Apr. 28, 1992-Apr. 29, 1992 / Milestone ✦✦✦✦
Recent album with Donaldson and small organ group. Nice music. Nothing exceptional. Bop and ballads, with one blues (Donaldson sings on this one) and a bossa nova. —*Michael Erlewine*

Caracas / Jul. 1993 / Milestone ✦✦✦

Sentimental Journey / Aug. 14, 1994-Aug. 15, 1994 / Columbia ✦✦✦✦
This Lou Donaldson Quintet set (which also features organist Lonnie Smith, guitarist Peter Bernstein, drummer Fukushi Tainaka and the percussion of Ray Mantilla) offers few surprises but no real disappointments either. Altoist Donaldson plays his usual mixture of blues, ballads and standards with a fine organ trio and the results are predictably swinging. The music could have been performed in 1965 but strangely enough the familiar style heard on this CD has not dated and still communicates. The enthusiasm of the musicians (who sound perfectly at home) has kept this popular idiom alive and sounding reasonably fresh. —*Scott Yanow*

Dorothy Donegan

b. Apr. 6, 1924, Chicago, IL, d. May 19, 1998, Los Angeles, CA
Piano / Bop, Swing, Stride, Boogie-Woogie
A brilliant virtuoso, Dorothy Donegan constantly switched between boogie-woogie, bop, stride, Art Tatum-style swing and classical music, sometimes in the same chorus! In concerts, she often put together spontaneous medleys of unrelated songs and was never shy to dance while she played. She studied at the Chicago Conservatory and Chicago Music College and made her recording debut in 1942. Donegan made a sensational appearance in the film *Sensations* of 1945 but never caught on that big despite her remarkable technique. She recorded a lot less than one would expect (six obscure albums during 1954-63 and nothing during 1964-74) and was not really that well-known in the jazz world until the mid-'80s. A couple of live Chiaroscuro CDs from 1990-91 found her in peak form. —*Scott Yanow*

● **Dorothy Romps: A Piano Retrospective (1953-1979)** / 1953-Mar. 16, 1979 / Rosetta ✦✦✦✦✦
Dorothy Donegan, one of the great jazz pianists, was only sporadically documented prior to the mid-'70s. She cut two songs for Bluebird back in 1942, a few scattered numbers for Continental and a few obscure labels, five long out-of-print albums in the 1950s for Jubilee, Capitol and Roulette, and just one LP during 1962-74. This retrospective put out on CD by Rosetta is therefore quite valuable. Six of the 15 selections (which skip back and forth between 1953, 1957-58, 1960-63 and 1979) were originally released on obscure albums, while the other nine performances were never out before. Despite the constant jumping of decades, there is a uniformity to the music with Donegan often sounding in exuberant form. She explores stride, boogie-woogie, bop, blues and classical music, sometimes during the same piece. This CD (which has lengthy and informative liner notes) is a perfect introduction to Dorothy Donegan's often-overlooked artistry. —*Scott Yanow*

Dorothy Donegan at the Embers / Mar. 23, 1957 / Roulette ✦✦✦
One of Dorothy Donegan's few early albums, this obscure LP (which finds her joined by Bill Pemberton or Oscar Pettiford on bass and drummer Charlie Smith, all of whom are unidentified) may look like a budget record but it features some exciting music. Donegan, whose piano technique was on the level of Art Tatum, rips through two originals and ten standards including "That Old Black Magic," "My Funny Valentine," "Humoresque" and "Lullaby of Birdland." The performances are all brief (clocking in around three minutes apiece) but there is no shortage of notes from the hyper pianist, who puts on a typically colorful show. This album (along with Dorothy Donegan's other early sets) is long overdue to be reissued on CD. —*Scott Yanow*

Dorothy Donegan Live! / Mar. 23, 1957' / Roulette ✦✦✦
One of several Dorothy Donegan LPs that may be found in used record stores but have yet to be reissued on CD, this exuberant trio set (which finds the pianist accompanied by an unidentified bassist and drummer) was recorded at the Embers in New York in 1958. As usual, Donegan, after usually stating a swing-based melody, rips into the music and comes up with lots of surprising ideas, often switching styles and showing off her virtuosity and flexibility. It is strange that she did not become a major box-office sensation during the era. —*Scott Yanow*

Explosive Dorothy Donegan / Mar. 31, 1980 / Progressive ✦✦✦✦✦
After a long period of neglect, the great pianist Dorothy Donegan made this Progressive album, her first American recording in 17 years. Joined by bassist Jerome Hunter (who had to be very alert to follow Donegan's wild flights) and drummer Ray Mosca, Donegan performs nine songs (seven veteran standards plus two of her originals) in unpredictable fashion, displaying technique that is on the level of a masterful classical pianist; highlights include "Lover," "Love for Sale," "Donegan's Blues" and a very explorative "St. Louis Blues." Although this LP helped give her some recognition, Dorothy Donegan's next set for an American label would not take place until 1990. —*Scott Yanow*

Live in Copenhagen 1980 / May 12, 1980 / Storyville ✦✦✦
This live performance, released for the initial time on a 1996 CD, features virtuoso pianist Dorothy Donegan with the very alert bassist Mads Vinding and drummer Ed Thigpen. The very spontaneous concert features Donegan, as usual, playing whatever comes into her mind; "Out of Nowhere" segues smoothly into "Sweet Lorraine" before a gospelish "Send in the Clowns" is tacked in at the end. Full-length versions of "Rosetta," "The Best Things In Life Are Free" and "Take the 'A' Train" are highlights, although there are also four medleys with some wandering moments and a few quick fadeouts. An intriguing and sometimes eccentric set. —*Scott Yanow*

Live at the Widder Bar / Dec. 1986 / Timeless ✦✦✦✦
After years of obscurity, pianist Dorothy Donegan finally started to gain some recognition in the mid-1980s. A brilliant pianist whose playing often takes unusual and unexpected turns (she always keeps her bassist guessing), Donegan is fond of not only putting together unlikely medleys, but suddenly switching styles altogether. For this live session with bassist Jimmy Woode and drummer Norman Fearrington, Donegan mostly sticks to a modern mainstream style, but her song quotes are very surprising and she somehow makes a medley out of "Like Someone in Love," "Here's That Rainy Day," "For Once In My Life" (à la Erroll Garner) and "In the Mood." —*Scott Yanow*

Live at the 1990 Floating Jazz Festival / Oct. 29, 1990-Nov. 2, 1990 / Chiaroscuro ✦✦✦✦✦
The remarkable pianist Dorothy Donegan, who has been overlooked by many jazz fans and critics for decades, is heard in a typically exciting and occasionally riotous live session recorded on the SS Norway. Followed by bassist Jon Burr (who has to work hard to keep up with Donegan's many spontaneous changes of direction) and drummer Ray Mosca, Donegan performs a varied set that includes a few eccentric medleys (including one of "Someday My Prince Will Come" and "Tiger Rag," and another that combines together "Misty" and "Caravan"), an odd tribute to "Lena, Eartha, Pearl & Billie" and her "Blackbird Boogie." Switching between bop, boogie-woogie, stride and classical music, Dorothy Donegan puts on a colorful show. —*Scott Yanow*

The Incredible Dorothy Donegan Trio / 1991 / Chiaroscuro ✦✦✦✦

Live at the 1991 Floating Jazz Festival / Oct. 23+Oct. 30, 1991 / Chiaroscuro ✦✦✦✦

Dorothy Donegan Trio with Clark Terry / Oct. 25, 1992+Oct. 29, 1992 / Chiaroscuro ✦✦✦✦

I Just Want / Dec. 2, 1995 / Audiophile ✦✦✦

Pierre Dorge

b. Feb. 28, 1946, Copenhagen, Denmark
Guitar, Leader/ Avant-Garde, Post-Bop
Pierre Dorge has gained some fame for his work with his New Jungle Orchestra, a band that plays fresh interpretations of some classics (particularly by Duke Ellington and Thelonious Monk) along with its leader's originals. Dorge led his first band in 1960, was a member of John Tchicai's big band (1969-71), in 1978 headed a quartet called Thermaenius and in 1980 put together the New Jungle Orchestra. Dorge has recorded several very interesting sessions (including a duo with Tchicai) for the Steeple Chase label. —*Scott Yanow*

New Jungle Orchestra / Mar. 7, 1982-Mar. 8, 1982 / Steeple Chase ✦✦✦✦

● **Even the Moon Is Dancing** / Jul. 30, 1985 / Steeple Chase ✦✦✦✦✦

Johnny Lives / Apr. 1987 / Steeple Chase ✦✦✦✦

Live in Denmark / Sep. 11, 1987 / Olufsen ✦✦✦

Different Places, Different Bananas / Nov. 1988 / Olufsen ✦✦✦

Live in Chicago / Jul. 6, 1990 / Olufsen ✦✦✦

Music from the Danish Jungle / Nov. 1995-Dec. 1995 / Dacapo ✦✦✦✦✦
Guitarist Pierre Dorge's New Jungle Orchestra has a very fitting title, for although they do not perform any Duke Ellington songs on their varied CD (the moody "Fullmoon for a Rhino" comes the closest style-wise), the adventure of Duke's music (along with an inventive use of wah-wah mutes and tone colors) is certainly present. A major surprise occurs halfway through the program when one realizes that this "big band" has no regular trumpeters and utilizes just two trombones and two reeds. Performing 13 originals from band members (including ten by either the leader or pianist Irene Becker) plus Carl Nielsen's early church hymn, the New Jungle Orchestra mixes together advanced improvising, celebratory melodies ("Ritus Huju No. 1" sounds as if it could have come from Abdullah Ibrahim), and some tightly arranged pieces with infectious and inventive rhythms and constant surprises in their highly appealing program. The music often sounds as if it is part of a wondrous and unusual jungle, and even at its spaciest, the performances gen-

erally border on being jubilant. This continually intriguing set is a gem. —*Scott Yanow*

China Jungle / Aug. 5, 1997 / Dacapo ✦✦✦

Kenny Dorham

b. Aug. 30, 1924, Fairfield, TX, **d.** Dec. 5, 1972, New York, NY
Trumpet / Hard Bop

Throughout his career, Kenny Dorham was almost famous for being underrated since he was consistently overshadowed by Dizzy Gillespie, Fats Navarro, Miles Davis, Clifford Brown and Lee Morgan. Dorham was never an influential force himself but a talented bop-oriented trumpeter and an excellent composer who played in some very significant bands. In 1945, he was in the orchestras of Dizzy Gillespie and Billy Eckstine, he recorded with the Be Bop Boys in 1946 and spent short periods with Lionel Hampton and Mercer Ellington. During 1948-49, Dorham was the trumpeter in the Charlie Parker Quintet. After some freelancing in New York in 1954, he became a member of the first version of Art Blakey's Jazz Messengers and for a short time led a group called the Jazz Prophets, which recorded on Blue Note. After Clifford Brown's death, Dorham became his replacement in the Max Roach Quintet (1956-58) and then he led several groups of his own. He recorded several fine dates for Riverside (including a vocal album in 1958), New Jazz and Time, but it is his Blue Note sessions of 1961-64 that are among his finest. Dorham was an early booster of Joe Henderson (who played with his group in 1963-64). After the mid-'60s, Kenny Dorham (who wrote some interesting reviews for *Down Beat*) began to fade and he died in 1972 of kidney disease. Among his many originals is one that became a standard, "Blue Bossa." —*Scott Yanow*

Kenny Dorham Quintet / Dec. 15, 1953 / Original Jazz Classics ✦✦✦✦

Kenny Dorham's debut as a leader found the 29-year-old trumpeter more than ready to take control; unfortunately, he spent virtually his entire career in the shadows of other trumpeters (such as Dizzy Gillespie, Miles Davis, Clifford Brown and Lee Morgan). This set was originally released by the Debut label as a six-song, ten-inch LP and then reissued with two alternate takes as a regular album. Now available on CD with two additional blues and another alternate, the fine playing by the quintet (with Jimmy Heath on tenor and baritone, pianist Walter Bishop, bassist Percy Heath and drummer Kenny Clarke) is not watered down by the extra material. A special bonus is the fine arranging of Dorham for the ensemble, a much overlooked talent of a continually underrated musician. —*Scott Yanow*

★ **Afro-Cuban** / Jan. 30, 1955+Mar. 29, 1955 / Blue Note ✦✦✦✦✦

This is a particularly strong set from trumpeter Kenny Dorham, for it has the debut versions of "Lotus Flower," "Minor Holiday" and "La Villa," three of his most rewarding compositions. The first half of the set is Afro-Cuban in nature due to the inclusion of Carlos "Potato" Valdes' conga; also on the four songs (plus a previously unreleased alternate take of "Minor's Holiday") are trombonist J.J. Johnson, Hank Mobley on tenor, baritonist Cecil Payne, pianist Horace Silver, bassist Oscar Pettiford and drummer Art Blakey. The final four numbers (including a "new" song added to the CD reissue, "K.D.'s Cab Ride") are more straightahead in nature and drop out Valdes and Johnson while substituting Percy Heath for Pettiford. In both cases, Dorham has an all-star group of young hard boppers eager to play his challenging and memorable originals. —*Scott Yanow*

The Best of Kenny Dorham: Blue Note Years / Mar. 29, 1955-Sep. 4, 1964 / Capitol ✦✦✦✦

Dorham's 1955 to 1964 tenure as a bandleader under the Blue Note aegis is the focus of this set, which features "Una Mas" and "Blue Bossa" along with recordings with Joe Henderson, Herbie Hancock, McCoy Tyner, Art Blakey, Tony Williams, Elvin Jones, Hank Mobley and Philly Joe Jones. —*Jason Ankeny*

'Round About Midnight at the Cafe Bohemia, Vol. 1 & 2 / May 31, 1956 / Blue Note ✦✦✦✦

This is a double-CD reissue of two prior single CD reissues, which expand the original Kenny Dorham LP from 42 minutes to over two hours. Although not necessarily trumpeter Dorham's finest hour, this surprisingly consistent set features the trumpeter and his sextet (with J.R. Monterose on tenor, guitarist Kenny Burrell, pianist Bobby Timmons, bassist Sam Jones and drummer Arthur Edgehill) performing 17 selections, ten (counting alternate takes) are the trumpeter's hard bop originals, although one also gets fine versions of such standards as "'Round Midnight," "A Night in Tunisia" and "My Heart Stood Still." Considering how extensive this recording is (virtually the whole evening's performance), it is fortunate that Kenny Dorham's group (which was a short-lived venture called The Jazz Prophets) was in top form that night. —*Scott Yanow*

Jazz Contrasts / May 21, 1957+May 27, 1957 / Original Jazz Classics ✦✦✦✦✦

Some of trumpeter Kenny Dorham's finest recordings were his sessions as a leader for Riverside in the 1950s and fortunately all of that music has been reissued on

CD. This straight reissue of an original LP is a bit brief in time (41 minutes) but contains many memorable selections. Three of the songs ("Falling in Love with Love," a 12-minute version of "I'll Remember April" and the trumpeter's "La Villa") match Dorham in an all-star quintet with the great tenor Sonny Rollins, pianist Hank Jones, bassist Oscar Pettiford and drummer Max Roach. The other three numbers (of which only "My Old Flame" includes Rollins) adds a fine harp player (Betty Glamman) and focuses on Dorham's lyricism. —*Scott Yanow*

2 Horns, 2 Rhythms / Nov. 13, 1957+Dec. 1957 / Original Jazz Classics ✦✦✦✦

Trumpeter Kenny Dorham was one of the most underrated talents of the bop and hard bop eras. Although he did not hit high notes or influence a lot of players, Dorham's appealing sound and consistently creative ideas should have made him a star in the jazz world instead of just a journeyman. On this CD reissue (which adds an alternate take of "'Sposin'" to the original eight-song LP program), Dorham and altoist Ernie Henry (on his final session) are heard in a pianoless quartet (with either Eddie Mathias or Wilbur Ware on bass, and drummer G.T. Hogan) playing three of the trumpeter's originals (including "Lotus Blossom") and four standards. Highlights include "I'll Be Seeing You" and a rare revival of "Is It True What They Say About Dixie?" The sparse setting (unusual for a Dorham session) works quite well. —*Scott Yanow*

This Is the Moment / Jul. 1958-Aug. 1958 / Original Jazz Classics ✦✦

The release of this recording must have surprised most jazz listeners at the time for trumpeter Kenny Dorham sings on all ten selections. He had never hinted at any desire to sing previously (although he had sung blues regularly with Dizzy Gillespie's Orchestra in the 1940s) and, as it turned out, this was his one and only vocal album; the sales were probably quite a bit less than Chet Baker's records of the period. Dorham had an okay voice, musical if not memorable, but the arrangements for these selections (which utilize his trumpet and Curtis Fuller's trombone, both of which are muted all the time) are inventive and pleasing. The supportive rhythm section is also an asset; pianist Cedar Walton made his recording debut on this album, which is now available on CD, a historical curiosity. —*Scott Yanow*

Blue Spring / Feb. 18, 1959 / Original Jazz Classics ✦✦✦✦

This is one of trumpeter Kenny Dorham's most intriguing sessions. His arrangements of five songs that have "Spring" in their title plus the tune "Poetic" are colorful, making use of altoist Cannonball Adderley, baritonist Cecil Payne, the French horn of Dave Amram and a fine rhythm section. Plus, Dorham's melodic solos (he was never just a bop stylist) are often memorable. —*Scott Yanow*

Quiet Kenny / Nov. 13, 1959 / Original Jazz Classics ✦✦✦

This CD is a reissue of a Kenny Dorham quartet session that was also previously released as *1959*. Not everything on the set is necessarily "quiet" but the emphasis is on ballads and the beauty of the trumpeter's tone. Accompanied by pianist Tommy Flanagan, bassist Paul Chambers and drummer Art Taylor, Dorham is heard in fine form throughout, particularly on "Lotus Blossom," "My Ideal," "Alone Together," "Old Folks" and a brief rendition of "Mack the Knife." —*Scott Yanow*

Memorial Album / Jan. 10, 1960 / Xanadu ✦✦✦

This somewhat-obscure Kenny Dorham LP features the excellent hard bop trumpeter in a quintet with baritonist Charles Davis, pianist Tommy Flanagan, bassist Butch Warren and drummer Buddy Enlow. The straightahead music includes features for Davis ("When Sunny Gets Blue") and Warren, but Dorham consistently takes honors, particularly on his "Stage West," "I'm an Old Cowhand," "Stella by Starlight" and "Lazy Afternoon." —*Scott Yanow*

Jazz Contemporary / Feb. 11, 1960 / Bainbridge ✦✦✦

Originally on the Time label, this LP features the excellent (but always underrated) trumpeter Kenny Dorham heading a quintet that also includes baritonist Charles Davis, pianist Steve Kuhn, either Jimmy Garrison or Butch Warren on bass and drummer Buddy Enlow. The results are not quite essential but everyone plays up to par, performing three of Dorham's originals plus "In Your Own Sweet Way," "Monk's Mood" and "This Love of Mine." It's fine hard bop, the modern mainstream music of the period. —*Scott Yanow*

Showboat / Dec. 9, 1960 / Bainbridge ✦✦✦✦

This CD reissue of a Kenny Dorham session that was originally on the Time label features the talented trumpeter and an all-star quintet (with Jimmy Heath on tenor, pianist Kenny Drew, bassist Jimmy Garrison and drummer Art Taylor) playing six famous themes from the Jerome Kern play *Showboat*. All of the melodies ("Why Do I Love You?," "Nobody Else but Me," "Can't Help Lovin' Dat Man," "Make Believe," "Ol' Man River" and "Bill") are heard in likable and swinging versions. This is one of Dorham's better sessions from the era and is easily recommended to his fans and collectors of hard bop. —*Scott Yanow*

Whistle Stop / Jan. 15, 1961 / Blue Note ✦✦✦✦✦

Kenny Dorham was always underrated throughout his career, not only as a trumpeter but as a composer. This CD reissue features seven of his compositions, none of which have been picked up by any of the "Young Lions" of the 1990s despite their high quality and the many fresh melodies. Dorham teams up with tenor saxophonist Hank Mobley (who he had recorded with previously with Art Blakey and Max Roach), pianist Kenny Drew, bassist Paul Chambers and drummer Philly Joe Jones for a set of lively, fresh and consistently swinging music. This is a generally overlooked near-classic set. —*Scott Yanow*

West 42nd Street / Mar. 13, 1961 / Black Lion ✦✦✦

The date included on this CD reissue was originally led by the obscure tenor Rocky Boyd but has come back under trumpeter Kenny Dorham's name with the six songs augmented by four alternate takes. Boyd (whose style mixes together the influences of Hank Mobley and John Coltrane) blends in well with Dorham, the rhythm section (pianist Walter Bishop, Jr., bassist Ron Carter and drummer Pete La Roca) is excellent, and the repertoire (group originals plus "Samba De Orpheus" and two slow versions of "Stella by Starlight") generally inspires the players. It's funny how La Roca's original "Why Not" has exactly the same melody and chord structure as Coltrane's "Impressions." This CD is worth picking up by straightahead jazz collectors. —*Scott Yanow*

Osmosis / Oct. 4, 1961 / Black Lion ✦✦✦

Originally released under drummer Dave Bailey's name and given the accurate title *Modern Mainstream*, this Black Lion CD reissue has excellent straightahead jazz from Bailey, trumpeter Kenny Dorham, trombonist Curtis Fuller, the obscure but talented tenor Frank Haynes, pianist Tommy Flanagan and bassist Ben Tucker. The CD reissue not only has the original seven selections but four previously unreleased alternate takes. Dorham and Haynes are in fine form but it is pianist Flanagan (well-showcased on "Just Friends" and two versions of "Like Someone in Love") who often takes solo honors. —*Scott Yanow*

Matador / Inta Somethin' / Nov. 1961-Apr. 15, 1962 / Blue Note ✦✦✦✦

Two full LPs are combined on this single CD. Both dates feature trumpeter Kenny Dorham and altoist Jackie McLean (two very compatible players), although the rhythm sections (pianist Bobby Timmons or Walter Bishop, bassist Teddy Smith or Leroy Vinnegar and drummer J.C. Moses or Art Taylor) differ between the two sessions. McLean was beginning to look forward and be influenced by the avant-garde; the passion he puts into his tone on such tunes as "Smile," "Beautiful Love," "It Could Happen to You" and "Lover Man" is memorable. Dorham was able to keep up with the times during this era, and his three compositions (particularly "El Matador" and "Una Mas") add a lot to the music. This generous CD is worth picking up as an example of veteran players stretching the boundaries of hard bop. —*Scott Yanow*

Una Mas / Apr. 1, 1963 / Blue Note ✦✦✦✦

When one thinks of great talent scouts in jazz, the name of Kenny Dorham is often overlooked. However, many top young players benefitted from playing in his groups, and for proof one need look no further than the lineup on this 1963 CD reissue: tenor saxophonist Joe Henderson, bassist Butch Warren and (before either player joined Miles Davis) pianist Herbie Hancock and drummer Tony Williams. Together the quintet performs three of the trumpeter's originals ("Una Mas" is the most famous) along with the standard ballad "If Ever I Would Leave You." Even if the playing time (under 37 minutes) is a bit brief, the explorative yet swinging music lives up to its potential. —*Scott Yanow*

Scandia Skies / Dec. 5, 1963 / Steeple Chase ✦✦

This live performance from the Montmartre in Copenhagen is a disappointment considering the lineup. Both Kenny Dorham and Rolf Ericson are on trumpets and joined by a brilliant rhythm section (pianist Tete Montoliu, a teenaged Niels Pedersen on bass and drummer Alex Riel) but, instead of fireworks, the two trumpeters are overly relaxed and play in similar dull styles on the four standards (plus Dorham's title cut). Montoliu is easily the most impressive soloist. It was an off night, making this CD of limited interest. —*Scott Yanow*

Short Story / Dec. 19, 1963 / Steeple Chase ✦✦✦

This Steeple Chase CD, taken from a live concert from the Montmartre Jazzhus in Copenhagen, features trumpeter Kenny Dorham, fluegelhornist Allan Botschinsky, pianist Tete Montoliu, bassist Niels Pedersen (then only 17) and drummer Alex Riel stretching out on four standards and Dorham's "Short Story." Dorham (featured on "Manha de Carnival") and Botschinsky (who is showcased on "The Touch of Your Lips") display complementary styles but are not shy to occasionally play fiery phrases. However, Montoliu (in exciting form) often steals the show during the relaxed set. —*Scott Yanow*

Trompeta Tocatta / Sep. 4, 1964 / Blue Note ✦✦✦✦

It seems strange and somewhat tragic that this was trumpeter Kenny Dorham's last full album as a leader for he was only 40 at the time and still in his prime. Dorham contributed three of the four selections to the session (Joe Henderson's catchy "Mamacita" also receives its debut) and his very underrated abilities as a writer, trumpeter and talent scout are very much in evidence. This modern hard bop quintet set with Henderson on tenor, pianist Tommy Flanagan, bassist Richard Davis

and drummer Albert "Tootie" Heath served as a strong (if premature) ending to Dorham's impressive career as a solo artist. —*Scott Yanow*

Bob Dorough

b. Dec. 12, 1923, Cherry Hill, AR
Piano, Vocals / Bop, Cool

Although neglected and underexposed most of his life, Bob Dorough is an adventurous, risk-taking master of vocalese (the process of writing and singing lyrics to instrumental jazz solos) and scat singing who has directly or indirectly influenced Mark Murphy, Michael Franks, Mose Allison and most recently, Kurt Elling. The Arkansas native started out on piano in the 1940s, then took up singing in the early 1950s (when he played for boxer Sugar Ray Robinson, an entertainer at the time). From 1954-55, Dorough lived in Paris, where he recorded with singer Blossom Dearie. The improviser launched his own recording career when he signed with Bethlehem in 1955 and recorded the excellent *Devil May Care*, which introduced the defiant title song and lyrics to Charlie Parker's "Yardbird Suite." But sadly, he recorded only sporadically after that. In 1962, Dorough cowrote "Comin' Home Baby" (a hit for Mel Tormé) with Ben Tucker, and in 1966, he recorded his second album, *Just About Everything*, for Focus. In the early 1970s, he began writing and directing the series of educational children's TV programs, *Schoolhouse Rock*. Though instructional material became his bread and butter, Dorough recorded obscure jazz dates for 52 Rue East, Orange Blue, Pinnacle, Boomdido, Laissez-Faire and other tiny labels in the 1970s and 1980s. In 1997, a 73-year-old Dorough received some long-overdue attention from a major label when the Capitol-distributed Blue Note released *Right on My Way Home*. —*Alex Henderson*

Devil May Care / Oct. 1956 / Bethlehem ✦✦✦✦✦

Vocalist-pianist-lyricist Bob Dorough's first record as a leader is a fairly definitive set that has been reissued on CD through Evidence. Assisted by his longtime bassist Bill Takas, drummer Jerry Segal and sometimes trumpeter Warren Fitzgerald and vibraphonist Jack Hitchcock, Dorough performs near-classic renditions of such songs as "Old Devil Moon," "Yardbird Suite," "Baltimore Oriole," "Devil May Care" and "Johnny One Note." Recommended. —*Scott Yanow*

Oliver (Songs from the Hit Show) / 1963 / Classic Jazz ✦✦

● **Just About Everything** / Mar. 17, 1966+Mar. 21, 1966 / Evidence ✦✦✦✦

This CD reissue brings back Bob Dorough's definitive album. The vocalist-pianist, who is joined by guitarist Al Schackman, bassist Ben Tucker and drummer Percy Brice, was in top creative form for the set. His renditions of "Baltimore Oriole" and "Lazy Afternoon" are haunting, while his versions of "I've Got Just About Everything," "Better Than Anything" and "'Tis Autumn" are quite memorable. Dorough even manages to do a credible job on Bob Dylan's "Don't Think Twice," and in 1966 must have been one of the few jazzmen to cover a current rock tune. Dorough's unusual voice and swinging piano are heard at their best throughout the highly recommended release. —*Scott Yanow*

Beginning to See the Light / Apr. 1976 / Laissez-Faire ✦✦✦✦

This CD reissue from Bob Dorough's label Laissez-Faire reissues a 1976 appearance at Concerts by the Sea. The pianist-vocalist performs duets with bassist Bill Takas that range from a couple of children's songs ("Simon Smith and the Dancing Bear" and Dr. Seuss' "Because We're Kids") to remakes of such "hits" as "Better than Anything," "I'm Hip" and "I've Got Just About Everything." In general this concert gives one a good all-round picture of Dorough's singing and piano talents; an acquired taste that is worth developing. —*Scott Yanow*

Skabadabba / 1987 / Pinnacle ✦✦✦✦

An obscure but worthy effort, this rare Bob Dorough album features the vocalist/pianist with old friend Lee Katzman on trumpet, electric bassist Bill Takas, drummer Peter Grant and percussionist Luther Rix. Dorough revisits such songs as "Au Privave" and "Everything But You," revives "Bijou," and introduces some newer material including "I Want to Prove I Love You" and Takas' "Bon Cover." Bob Dorough always had a unique, small voice and a witty style; both are on display on this excellent set. —*Scott Yanow*

Right on My Way Home / Apr. 30, 1997-May 6, 1997 / Blue Note ✦✦✦✦

As one of the key voices of *Schoolhouse Rock*, Bob Dorough acquired many fans, but no one ever knew his name. Even after the series ended, he was reluctant to pursue a full-fledged recording career, which made 1997's *Right on My Way Home*—an album he recorded when he was 73—something of an event. It was one of the rare occasions that Dorough was able to demonstrate the depth and range of his talent. Like Mose Allison, he has a friendly, idiosyncratic variation on bluesy scat and bop that sounds equally at home on standards ("Moon River," "Spring Can Really Hang You Up the Most") or originals ("I Get the Neck of the Chicken," "Something for Sidney," "Up Jumped a Bird"). Some tastes might Dorough find a bit too cutesy, yet there's no denying that he can make a song his own, and *Right on My Way Home* is one of the best proofs of that statement. —*Stephen Thomas Erlewine*

The Dorsey Brothers

f. 1928, **db.** 1935
Swing

Tommy and Jimmy Dorsey first teamed up together on records as the Dorsey Brothers in 1928 but the groups they led through 1933 were strictly studio affairs, featuring classic jazz and hot dance music along with some ballads. In 1934, they decided to put together a regular orchestra and by 1935, with Bob Crosby (and later Bob Eberle) taking the vocals and Glenn Miller providing many of the arrangements, the group was on the brink of success in the early swing era. However, a well-publicized argument at a ballroom over the tempo of "I'll Never Say Never Again" led to Tommy Dorsey immediately leaving and starting his own separate orchestra.

By 1953, both brothers had had major success with their bands and had long since patched up their differences. Because their orchestras were struggling, it was decided that Jimmy would break up his band and co-lead Tommy's. For nearly four years the Dorsey Brothers Orchestra featured first-class dance music with occasional solos from trumpeter Charlie Shavers and the two brothers; they also had their own television show. With Tommy's sudden death in November 1956 (Jimmy followed seven months later), the partnership came to an end. —*Scott Yanow*

The Dorsey Brothers, Vol. 1 / Feb. 14, 1928-Nov. 2, 1928 / TOM ✦✦✦✦
This LP (the first of two volumes) has the first 16 recordings led by The Dorsey Brothers. There are no personnel or date listings but this set is well worth acquiring, for it includes many fine examples of hot dance music, featuring Tommy's trombone, Jimmy's clarinet and alto, and appearances by trumpeters Leo McConville and Phil Napoleon along with a variety of dated singers. Their version of "My Melancholy Baby" is a classic with TD playing some fine trumpet and bass saxophonist Adrian Rollini heard in a prominent role. —*Scott Yanow*

The Dorsey Brothers, Vol. 2 / Oct. 1928-Nov. 7, 1930 / TOM ✦✦✦
The second of two LP volumes from the collector's label TOM has 16 more examples of Tommy and Jimmy Dorsey in their early days. The music strikes a balance between hot jazz and commercial dance music with the leaders, tenorman Bud Freeman and guitarist Eddie Lang having many fine spots, even if the varying singers also get plenty of space. It's well worth acquiring since most of this material has not been reissued on CD yet. —*Scott Yanow*

● **Best of the Big Bands** / Sep. 14, 1932-Apr. 23, 1934 / Columbia ✦✦✦✦✦
The Dorsey Brothers Orchestra was actually just a series of studio groups until Jimmy and Tommy decided to hit the road in 1934. This strong jazz-oriented CD covering the 1932-34 period actually finds the exciting trumpeter Bunny Berigan consistently stealing solo honors. Highlights include Bill Challis' torrid arrangement of "Someone Stole Gabriel's Horn," "The Blue Room," the novelty tune "Annie's Cousin Fanny" and the original version of what would later become Tommy Dorsey's theme song, "I'm Getting Sentimental over You." —*Scott Yanow*

Mood Hollywood / Sep. 24, 1932-Oct. 17, 1933 / Hep ✦✦✦✦
This excellent LP features 16 performances (including four alternate takes) by The Dorsey Brothers during 1932-33. Bunny Berigan's trumpet solos are the most memorable aspect of these early swing recordings, many of which feature an octet rather than a big band. Highlights include "Someone Stole Gabriel's Horn," two takes of "I'm Getting Sentimental over You" and the brothers' many fine solos. —*Scott Yanow*

Harlem Lullaby / Feb. 1933-Jul. 1933 / Hep ✦✦✦

The Decca Sessions (1934-1935) / Aug. 15, 1934-Feb. 6, 1935 / MCA ✦✦
This budget LP from MCA includes only ten recordings by The Dorsey Brothers Orchestra (less than a half-hour of music) and has a barely readable personnel listing. The only thing that saves this set is the generally strong jazz-oriented music performed by this first-class dance band (heard only a short time before its breakup) including fine versions of "Dippermouth Blues," "Milenberg Joys" and "Honeysuckle Rose." —*Scott Yanow*

The Dorsey Brothers' Orchestra 1935 / Jan. 17, 1935 / Circle ✦✦✦
This LP contains music recorded for radio transcriptions by The Dorsey Brothers Orchestra, one of the most interesting new bands heard during this era. The music by this dance band is generally jazz-oriented (although Bob Crosby's three vocals are quite straight) with fine solos from Tommy's trombone and Jimmy's alto and clarinet; the lead trumpet of Charlie Spivak is also heard from. —*Scott Yanow*

1955 / Jun. 3, 1955-Jun. 4, 1955 / Jazz Unlimited ✦✦✦
In 1955, Tommy and Jimmy Dorsey's Orchestra was doing well, as the swing-era survivors satisfied a dancing audience with nostalgic remakes of hits and some

newer charts in the swing idiom. This set of very well recorded live performances (released for the first time on this 1995 CD) alternates jazz-oriented tracks (with concise but worthy contributions from trumpeter Charlie Shavers and drummer Louie Bellson), spots for both trombonist Tommy and altoist Jimmy, and some vocal cuts featuring Lynn Roberts, Bill Raymond and Bruce Snyder. Nothing surprising occurs, and the music sounds conservative (even for the period), but swing fans will find the performances to be enjoyable. —*Scott Yanow*

Dorsey-Itis / Mar. 1956-May 1956 / Drive Archive ✦✦✦✦
This budget CD reissue is much better than it looks. As usual, the Dorsey Brothers Orchestra of the 1950s can be counted on to provide first-class dance music, but the jazz content of these radio broadcasts is much higher than expected. Even with a few throwaway vocals, there is strong solo space for the Dorseys (particularly Jimmy on clarinet), trumpeter Charlie Shavers and tenorman Buzzy Brauner, while drummer Louie Bellson really pushes the band. A special high point is a wild Dixielandish version of "Panama." —*Scott Yanow*

Jimmy Dorsey

b. Feb. 29, 1904, Shenandoah, PA, **d.** Jun. 12, 1957, New York, NY
Alto Saxophone , Clarinet, Leader / Swing, Big Band

The older of the two Dorsey Brothers, Jimmy was the superior jazz player. An excellent clarinetist and one of the finest altoists to emerge during the 1920s, JD's jazz playing was overshadowed during the swing era by the commercial hits of his orchestra. Trumpet was actually his first instrument and Jimmy recorded on it a couple of times in the 1920s, but by the time he was a teenager he was specializing on reeds. He started out playing with his brother Tommy in Dorsey's Novelty Six, the Scranton Sirens and the California Ramblers, and his solos with Red Nichols' Five Pennies made a strong impression. Dorsey recorded with Frankie Trumbauer (including Bix Beiderbecke's "Singin' the Blues"), Jean Goldkette and Paul Whiteman, and became a busy studio musician during the Depression. In addition, starting in 1928 he co-led the Dorsey Brothers Orchestra with Tommy. Strictly a studio group at first, the Dorseys put together a full-time big band in 1934, only to break up in late 1935. Jimmy took over the nucleus of the band and, after a period of struggle, the orchestra hit it big in the early '40s with a series of vocal records featuring Bob Eberle and Helen O'Connell. By late in the decade, Dorsey was alternating between some boppish big band performances (Maynard Ferguson was among his sidemen) and Dixieland jams with his Dorseyland Band. In 1953, he broke up the band to join Tommy in a new Dorsey Brothers Orchestra that emphasized dance music. After Tommy's sudden death in late 1956, Jimmy took over the orchestra and had a surprise hit in "So Rare" before passing away from cancer. —*Scott Yanow*

★ **Contrasts** / Jul. 7, 1936-Oct. 7, 1943 / GRP ✦✦✦✦✦
This CD, virtually the only example of Jimmy Dorsey's orchestra currently available on CD, puts the emphasis on his jazz sides rather than the vocal bestsellers. Popular singer Helen O'Connell does make three appearances (including the hit, "Tangerine"), but most of these selections are instrumentals with Dorsey's alto and clarinet in outstanding form (it was easy to forget how talented an instrumentalist he was during these commercial years). Most of the other fine soloists are lesser names, although they include future-bandleaders Ray McKinley (on drums) and pianist Freddie Slack. Highlights are "Parade of the Milk Bottle Caps," "I Got Rhythm," "John Silver," "Ducks in Upper Sandusky," Dorsey's theme "Contrasts," and "King Porter Stomp," although there isn't a weak track on this release. Recommended, this is Dorsey's definitive set. —*Scott Yanow*

The Uncollected Jimmy Dorsey & His Orchestra, Vol. 1 (1939-1940) / 1939-1940 / Hindsight ✦✦✦
The first of five Hindsight LPs to document Dorsey's radio transcriptions, this set gives a good all-around picture of his orchestra shortly before it became a major commercial success. There are four vocals apiece by Helen O'Connell and Bob Eberly, along with eight fine instrumentals and, although Dorsey (on alto and clarinet) is the only distinctive soloist, the music overall is first-class swing and dance music. —*Scott Yanow*

The Uncollected Jimmy Dorsey & His Orchestra, Vol. 2 (1942-1944) / 1942-1944 / Hindsight ✦✦✦✦
The second of five LPs released by Hindsight that contain performances cut for radio airplay by the Jimmy Dorsey Orchestra is more jazz-oriented than his usual recordings. Helen O'Connell has a pair of vocals but there are also hot versions of "Just You, Just Me," "I Got Rhythm," "I Would Do Anything for You" and the boppish "Grand Central Getaway," which was composed and arranged by Dizzy Gillespie himself. Such players as pianist Johnny Guarnieri, trumpeter Ray Linn and tenorman Babe Russin are heard from during this fine overview of Dorsey's wartime orchestra. —*Scott Yanow*

Wartime V-Disc Sessions / Oct. 1943-1945 / Sandy Hook ✦✦✦✦✦
On this excellent LP, one gets to hear the overlooked and under-recorded Jimmy Dorsey Orchestra of 1943-44 on some strong jazz-oriented performances (with only one vocal) originally recorded for V-Discs and not released commercially. A special bonus are three selections from 1945 that find the Jimmy and Tommy Dorsey Orchestras playing together noisily but with coherence. It was the Dorsey brothers' first musical reunion since their breakup a decade earlier. Overall this is a fine LP of late-period swing. —*Scott Yanow*

Featuring Maynard Ferguson / Mar. 1949-May 1949 / Big Band Archives ✦✦✦✦✦
The 1949 Jimmy Dorsey Orchestra was one of the most interesting (if overlooked) big bands of the era. Although Dorsey had mostly played commercial music earlier in the decade, he had never lost his love for jazz. By 1949 he had hired some bebop musicians and was playing some modern charts, but at the same time was also performing Dixieland with a small group from his orchestra. This LP of radio broadcasts not only features Dorsey's alto and clarinet and the Dixielandish trumpet of Charlie Teagarden but the outstanding high-note trumpet of Maynard Ferguson, heard a year before he became famous playing with Stan Kenton. Since Ferguson was not with Dorsey long enough to record with him commercially, these radio aircbecks are particularly valuable historically in addition to being musically enjoyable. —*Scott Yanow*

The Uncollected Jimmy Dorsey & His Orchestra, Vol. 3 (1949-1951) / 1949+1951 / Hindsight ✦✦✦
The third of five Hindsight LPs featuring Dorsey's orchestra is particularly interesting because it features his big bands of 1949 and 1951, a period of time when he no longer had hits or prospered financially; in fact, in 1952 he disbanded and joined brother Tommy's orchestra. Other than one Claire Hogan vocal, these two sessions comprise instrumentals, featuring both Dorsey and many members of his talented but no-name crew. —*Scott Yanow*

Muscat Ramble / 1950 / Swing House ✦✦✦✦
During 1949-50, Dorsey enjoyed leading a small group taken out of his big band to play Dixieland. This English LP finds the hot band (which featured Charlie Teagarden's trumpet and sometimes Cutty Cutshall's trombone) jamming on a set of Dixieland standards. Jimmy Dorsey, who mostly sticks to clarinet, clearly enjoyed playing this music; perhaps he should have spent the 1950s in similar small combos instead of permanently joining his brother's orchestra in 1952. —*Scott Yanow*

The Uncollected Jimmy Dorsey & His Orchestra, Vol. 4 (1950) / 1950 / Hindsight ✦✦✦✦
The fourth of five LPs issued by Hindsight that feature rare aircbecks of Jimmy Dorsey's orchestra showcases his band in its declining days. However, despite the three commercial vocals heard on this set, Dorsey's band in 1950 was potentially a strong jazz outfit, featuring Charlie Teagarden and Shorty Sherock on trumpets along with the leader's alto and clarinet. JD's workout on "Fingerbustin'" and the renditions of "Lover" and "King Porter Stomp" are high points of this swinging set. —*Scott Yanow*

The Uncollected Jimmy Dorsey & His Orchestra, Vol. 5: Dorseyland Band (1950) / 1950 / Hindsight ✦✦✦✦
Although he still struggled to keep his orchestra together, during 1949-50 Dorsey often returned to his roots, leading a small contingent out of his big band that he termed "the Original Dorseyland Band." The seven-piece group, featuring Charlie Teagarden's trumpet, trombonist Frank Rehak, Artie Lyons on tenor and Dorsey mostly on clarinet but also on alto, is heard on these transcriptions playing a variety of Dixieland tunes in spirited fashion. —*Scott Yanow*

The Fabulous Jimmy Dorsey / Nov. 11, 1956-Jan. 1958 / Fraternity ✦✦
After Tommy Dorsey's death in 1956, Jimmy Dorsey took over his orchestra, although it turned out that he himself was dying from cancer. Ironically, JD's final recording date resulted in his first hit in over a decade, "So Rare." Dorsey's alto is actually only heard on four of the 13 selections on this LP; after he passed away, trumpeter Lee Castle took over the band and altoist Dick Stabile filled in on the remaining selections. Despite its historic value, this mostly forgettable dance and pop music from 1956-57 conclusively proves that by then the big-band era was long dead. —*Scott Yanow*

Leon Lee Dorsey

b. Mar. 12, 1958, Pittsburgh, PA
Bass / Post-Bop
Leon Lee Dorsey made a strong impression with his 1995 debut disc as a leader, *The Watcher* (on Landmark). A graduate from Oberlin College, the University of Wisconsin and the Manhattan School of Music, he has played as a sideman with a wide variety of top players inlcuding Benny Carter, Max Roach, Freddie Hubbard, Horace Silver and Cassandra Wilson. —*Scott Yanow*

● **The Watcher** / Feb. 5, 1994 / Landmark ✦✦✦✦
This is an intriguing debut as a leader for bassist Leon Lee Dorsey. Dorsey, who has played with everyone from Benny Carter and Freddie Hubbard to Oliver Lake and Don Pullen, has really put together two CDs in one. The first six selections are very modern originals which feature his quintet (starring an inspired Vincent Herring on alto and soprano and the hard-toned tenor of Don Braden along with pianist Lafayette Harris, Jr., and drummer Cecil Brooks) in top form. While "Miles," which has plenty of simultaneous fiery improvising by the two saxes, does not really remind one of Miles Davis' music, it is quite memorable as is the haunting ballad "I Am with You Always," which features Herring's soprano as the lead voice. The second half of the program (a blues "Centre Avenue Shuffle," three standards and Ron Carter's "United") are more straightahead and give the principals an opportunity to really swing hard within an older format. Dorsey, who only takes a couple of long solos (most notably on "Misty"), is generous in allocating the spotlight but is clearly responsible for this colorful session's success. —*Scott Yanow*

Tommy Dorsey

b. Nov. 19, 1905, Shenandoah, PA, **d.** Nov. 26, 1956, Greenwich, CT
Trombone , Leader / Swing, Big Band
Tommy Dorsey was the definitive ballad player of the swing era possessing a beautiful tone and very impressive breath control. A better jazz player than he thought, Dorsey enjoyed playing Dixieland now and then but preferred later in life to stick to ballads. In his early days, he played with older brother Jimmy in Dorsey's Novelty Six and the Scranton Sirens before moving to New York and appearing on records with Jean Goldkette, Paul Whiteman and Red Nichols. TD occasionally doubled on trumpet in the 1920s, playing in a style as rough and primitive as his trombone was smooth. He was a busy studio player during the Depression until agreeing to co-lead the Dorsey Brothers Orchestra in 1934. Late in 1935, a blowup on stage led to Tommy leaving and forming his own big band, taking over the Joe Haymes Orchestra. After a short struggle, major hits in 1937 ("Marie" and "Song of India," both highlighted by classic Bunny Berigan trumpet solos) made the Tommy Dorsey Orchestra into a major attraction. TD, who learned from Paul Whiteman how to mix together a diverse repertoire, alternated swing romps, ballads (often featuring the vocals of his girlfriend Edythe Wright), novelties and Dixieland from his Clambake Seven (which at times included Yank Lawson and Bud Freeman). In the early '40s with the hiring of Sy Oliver as chief arranger, drummer Buddy Rich and a vocal group featuring Frank Sinatra and Jo Stafford, the orchestra evolved and continued to have hits including "I'll Never Smile Again" and "Opus One." In 1942, Dorsey was able to hire the string section of the Artie Shaw Orchestra, greatly expanding his band. By the end of World War II and the collapse of the swing era, TD had to drop the strings and cut back a bit, even breaking up his band for a period after 1946. He appeared in the unfortunate fictional movie *The Fabulous Dorseys* with Jimmy in 1947, reformed his orchestra and did his best to ignore bop (which he detested). Charlie Shavers was the key soloist in Tommy Dorsey's band from the mid-'40s on. In 1953, Jimmy Dorsey agreed to join forces with his brother. Tommy Dorsey's band was renamed the Dorsey Brothers Orchestra, emphasizing dance music. The nostalgia formula worked well until Tommy's sudden death in November 1956. —*Scott Yanow*

Trumpets and Trombones, Vol. 1 / Aug. 16, 1927-Nov. 18, 1929 / Broadway Intermission ✦✦✦✦✦
This superb LP contains 20 early selections featuring Tommy Dorsey on both trombone and trumpet; he rarely played the latter after 1930. Most of these performances were quite rare (six were issued on this LP for the first time) and they find him featured with Paul Whiteman, Hoagy Carmichael, Seger Ellis, Arthur Schutt and, on most selections, The Dorsey Brothers Orchestra. This hot dance music contains many fine jazz solos from some of the top New York studio players of the late '20s and gives one a valuable look at Tommy Dorsey years before he became "the Sentimental Gentleman of Swing." —*Scott Yanow*

Trumpets and Trombones, Vol. 2 / Apr. 21, 1930-Feb. 1946 / Broadway Intermission ✦✦✦✦
This second LP of Tommy Dorsey rarities features him both in his early studio days with The Dorsey Brothers' Orchestra and with his successful big band. These 14 selections include soundtracks from films, unissued V-Discs, radio broadcasts and early obscure sides from the early '30s. All of the music is quite interesting with "Three Moods" and "Dust" being dance-band classics. Both volumes from this collectors series are highly recommended to all true swing collectors. —*Scott Yanow*

The Complete Tommy Dorsey, Vol. 1 (1935) / Sep. 26, 1935-Dec. 21, 1935 / Bluebird ✦✦✦✦
The most complete series of Tommy Dorsey reissues was a two-fer LP program that succeeded in issuing, in chronological order, all of his recordings from the beginnings of his big band in September 1935 up to March 1939 (eight volumes in all), before corporate indifference brought the program to a halt at its halfway

mark. Since Dorsey led a dance band that performed novelties and commercial vocal features in addition to jazz, not all of his recordings were classics. General collectors might be more satisfied with samplers rather than getting everything. *Volume I* in this series has as its high points "Weary Blues," Dorsey's theme "I'm Getting Sentimental over You" and the first sides by his Clambake Seven, including "The Music Goes Round and Round." —*Scott Yanow*

Seventeen Number Ones / Oct. 14, 1935-Jul. 1, 1942 / RCA ✦✦✦

Good 1990 overview of their biggest-selling popular music standards. —*Ron Wynn*

● **Big Bands** / Oct. 18, 1935-1945 / Time-Life ✦✦✦✦✦

Culled from the vaults of RCA Victor, Time-Life's survey of Tommy Dorsey's career is not a greatest-hits collection, including only four of his 17 chart-topping records ("Marie," "The Dipsy Doodle," "Music, Maestro, Please," and "I'll Never Smile Again") among its 21 selections. But it is a tastefully chosen compilation, balancing hits with Dorsey signature material, such as his theme song, "I'm Getting Sentimental Over You," and his memorable jazz showcases "Yes, Indeed!" and "Opus No. 1." The Dorsey band was among the most versatile of the swing era, able to play effectively in both the sweet and hot styles, and though no single disc can capture its range, this one hits the high points, from the mock classical style of "Song of India" to the novelty of "You've Gotta Eat Your Spinach, Baby" (written for a Shirley Temple film). And unlike many Dorsey compilations, this one is not top-heavy with Frank Sinatra vocals, including only five and also finding room for such important Dorsey singers as Edythe Wright and Jack Leonard. —*William Ruhlmann*

Having a Wonderful Time / Dec. 9, 1935-Mar. 2, 1946 / RCA ✦✦✦✦

The Clambake Seven was a small Dixieland-oriented group taken out of Tommy Dorsey's big band. Its main period was during 1935-39, although the leader-trombonist occasionally revived the concept in later years. This CD is an exact reissue of an original 16-song LP and has many of the group's finest recordings, all but 1946's "Don't Be a Baby, Baby" dating from 1935-40. With such hot soloists as trumpeters Sterling Bose, Max Kaminsky, Pee Wee Erwin and Yank Lawson, clarinetists Joe Dixon and Johnny Mince, tenor saxophonist Bud Freeman and TD plus many vocals by Edythe Wright, the Clambake Seven can be heard at their best on this program which is highlighted by "The Music Goes 'Round and 'Round" "At the Codfish Ball," "When the Midnight Choo-Choo Leaves for Alabam'," "Chinatown, My Chinatown," "You Must Have Been a Beautiful Baby" and "Rancho Grande." Recommended. —*Scott Yanow*

Music Goes Round and Round / Dec. 9, 1935-Feb. 25, 1947 / Bluebird ✦✦✦✦✦

In 1935, Tommy Dorsey first jammed with musicians from his big band in a Dixieland format, calling the little band The Clambake Seven. He recorded frequently with the unit up until 1939 and then on a rare basis up until 1950. This particular CD has 21 of The Clambake's better performances and, although it would have been preferable to reissue all of the group's recordings, this serves as a strong introduction to their music. With such soloists as trumpeters Yank Lawson, Max Kaminsky and Pee Wee Erwin, clarinetists Johnny Mince and Joe Dixon, tenorman Bud Freeman and TD himself, this music was quite joyous and spirited. Edythe Wright ably sings on many of the songs, which are highlighted by the title cut, "At the Codfish Ball," two versions of "The Sheik of Araby" and "When the Midnight Choo-Choo Leaves for Alabam'." These are Dixieland recordings that predated the New Orleans revival of 1940. —*Scott Yanow*

The Complete Tommy Dorsey, Vol. 2 (1936) / Feb. 3, 1936-Oct. 18, 1936 / RCA ✦✦✦✦✦

The second of eight two-fer LPs that trace complete and in chronological order all of Dorsey's recordings from 1935 up to March 1939, this set (like the others) includes gems and duds. During 1936, his band was popular enough to keep going but had not broken through to the bigtime yet. With trumpeter Max Kaminsky, clarinetist Joe Dixon and the great tenor Bud Freeman contributing solos, and Edythe Wright and the commercial singer Jack Leonard heard on vocals, the music ranges from pop schlock to some big-band swing (such as "Royal Garden Blues," "That's a Plenty" and "After You've Gone") and two songs by Dorsey's Clambake Seven. —*Scott Yanow*

The Complete Tommy Dorsey, Vol. 3 (1936-1937) / Nov. 18, 1936-Mar. 20, 1937 / Bluebird ✦✦✦✦

The third LP two-fer in this *Complete* series (which died after the eighth volume when Bluebird lost interest), this set is the most essential of the bunch because it includes the 18 selections that the great trumpeter Bunny Berigan cut with Dorsey. Not only do these include the major hits "Marie" and "Song of India" (which made Tommy Dorsey into a household name) but memorable solos on "Mr. Ghost Goes to Town," "Melody in F," "Liebestraum" and "Mendelssohn's Spring Song." Not all of the other songs cut directly before and after Berigan's stint were classics, but there are superior versions of "Keepin' out of Mischief Now," "Black Eyes" and "Jammin'." —*Scott Yanow*

Radio Days, Vol. 1 / Nov. 30, 1936-Jan. 4, 1937 / Star Line ✦✦✦

Solid swing music comes from Dorsey's orchestra just before he hit it big with "Marie." Although Bunny Berigan is on a few of these songs, the main soloists on this CD are tenorman Bud Freeman, trumpeter Max Kaminsky and clarinetist Joe Dixon along with Dorsey's trombone. Swinging instrumentals and vocals by Edythe Wright and the Three Esquires are heard in an enjoyable program of Dorsey radio appearances. —*Scott Yanow*

The Complete Tommy Dorsey, Vol. 4 (1937) / Apr. 15, 1937-Jul. 10, 1937 / RCA ✦✦✦✦

The post-Berigan era found Dorsey heading one of the most popular of all big bands, rivaling Benny Goodman's. This fourth of eight LP two-fers has all of his recordings cut during a three-month period, including 15 selections by Dorsey's Clambake Seven (which was now featuring Pee Wee Erwin, Bud Freeman's tenor and clarinetist Johnny Mince in addition to singer Edythe Wright) and a variety of big-band titles, most memorably "Satan Takes a Holiday," "Beale Street Blues" and a truly bizarre version of "Am I Dreaming?" —*Scott Yanow*

The Complete Tommy Dorsey, Vol. 5 (1937) / Jul. 10, 1937-Oct. 14, 1937 / Bluebird ✦✦✦✦

The fifth in Bluebird's superb series of LP two-fers that trace *The Complete Tommy Dorsey* up until 1939 is highlighted by 11 performances by his Dixielandish Clambake Seven along with "Night and Day" and "Once in a While" from his big band. As with the others in this admirable series, there are also plenty of novelties and forgettable vocals included, but Dorsey fanatics should go out of their way to get all of these highly appealing sets. —*Scott Yanow*

The Complete Tommy Dorsey, Vol. 6 (1937-1938) / Dec. 6, 1937-Mar. 10, 1938 / Bluebird ✦✦✦✦

The sixth out of the eight volumes in *The Complete Tommy Dorsey* series of two-fer LPs has only two Clambake Seven performances and no major hits but, even with the large amount of so-so Jack Leonard vocals, there are also many examples of first-class dance music and swing from the very versatile orchestra. It's worth picking up by those Dorsey fans who are wise enough to search for all eight volumes. —*Scott Yanow*

The Complete Tommy Dorsey, Vol. 7 (1938) / Apr. 11, 1938-Sep. 22, 1938 / Bluebird ✦✦✦✦

The seventh in this series of eight LP two-fers contains all of the recordings made by his orchestra during a five-month period in 1938. Seven commercial Jack Leonard vocals are compensated for by seven performances from Dorsey's Clambake Seven, a Dixieland outfit taken out of his big band. With such tunes as "Music, Maestro Please," "Panama," "Chinatown, My Chinatown," "The Sheik of Araby" and the big hit "Boogie Woogie," this set (along with all the others in this valuable series) is recommended to all true Tommy Dorsey fans. —*Scott Yanow*

The Complete Tommy Dorsey, Vol. 8 (1938-1939) / Sep. 29, 1938-Mar. 8, 1939 / Bluebird ✦✦✦✦

The eighth and unfortunately the final volume in this superb LP two-fer series closed the program of Tommy Dorsey recordings partway through the session of March 8, 1939, thanks to the indifference of RCA Records. This very worthy series reissued all of his studio recordings during the four years since he formed his own band, and, although it necessarily included both gems and duds, the former generally outnumbered the latter. *Volume VIII* is highlighted by "Tin Roof Blues," "Hawaiian War Chant," the two-part "Milenberg Joys" and The Clambake Seven's "You Must Have Been a Beautiful Baby." All of the volumes in this increasingly hard-to-find series are recommended to serious swing fans. —*Scott Yanow*

★ **Yes, Indeed!** / Jun. 15, 1939-Sep. 20, 1945 / Bluebird ✦✦✦✦✦

This CD includes many of Tommy Dorsey's very best recordings from 1939-42 along with four selections dating from 1944-45. During this period, the sound of his orchestra had changed from the earlier days, thanks in large part to Sy Oliver's arrangements and the hard-driving drums of Buddy Rich. With such soloists as trumpeter Ziggy Elman, tenor saxophonist Don Lodice and clarinetist Johnny Mince (in addition to Dorsey's trombone), this orchestra could play jazz with the best of their contemporaries, although many of their other recordings (not included here) actually showcased vocals and dance music. Highlights of this recommended disc include "Well, All Right," "Stomp It Off," "Quiet Please," "Swing High," "Swanee River," "Deep River" and "Well, Git It!," while the later tracks include "Opus No. 1," the Charlie Shavers feature "At the Fat Man's" and a guest appearance by Duke Ellington on "The Minor Goes Muggin'." —*Scott Yanow*

All-Time Greatest Dorsey/Sinatra Hits, Vol. 1-4 / 1940-1942 / RCA ✦✦✦✦

When RCA decided to issue its early-'40s Tommy Dorsey recordings containing Frank Sinatra vocals on compact disc, it abandoned the chronological sequencing found on the Grammy-winning album series *The Dorsey/Sinatra Sessions* and instead jumped back and forth through the catalog. This first volume of four contains some of the biggest hits, notably "I'll Never Smile Again" and "I'll Be Seeing

You," and thus is the best selection for beginners. But be sure to move on to Vol. 2 and Vol. 3 and, especially, Vol. 4, which contains Sinatra's first solo session. —*William Ruhlmann*

Well Git It! / Sep. 30, 1943-Jan. 4, 1946 / Vintage Jazz ✦✦✦
Tommy Dorsey's wartime orchestra is well featured on these radio airchecks. With such stars as drummer Buddy Rich (and on three songs, Gene Krupa), clarinetist Buddy DeFranco and trumpeter Charlie Shavers, Dorsey kept up his musical standards despite the change in both the public's taste and the continuing evolution of jazz. With the Sentimentalists, Bonnie Lou Williams and Stuart Foster contributing vocals, the mixture of jazz and dance music heard on this CD is typical of Dorsey's mid-'40s music. —*Scott Yanow*

The Post-War Era / Jan. 31, 1946-Jun. 13, 1950 / Bluebird ✦✦✦
The funny part about this CD is that there is relatively little Dorsey on it. His trombone is mostly heard in a cameo role with the exception of "Trombonology." The real stars of this fine CD are arranger Bill Finegan (who wrote the charts for the majority of these 22 performances) and the fiery trumpeter Charlie Shavers, although drummer Louis Bellson also gets featured on "Drumology." After 1946, Tommy Dorsey's music was definitely behind the times (he always had a strong resistance to bebop) and some of these later tracks sound like tired dance music, but this CD does an excellent job of summing up his better recordings of the 1946-50 period, leaving out the real dog tunes and bad vocalists he sometimes utilized. —*Scott Yanow*

At the Fat Man's / May 29, 1946-Nov. 8, 1948 / Hep ✦✦✦
This English LP features three different versions of The Tommy Dorsey Orchestra heard in radio performances: his mid-'40s unit, the new big band he reorganized in 1947, and the unit he led the following year that never recorded commercially due to the recording strike. With trumpeter Charlie Shavers, tenorman Don Lodice and drummer Louis Bellson among the stars, these are good examplesv of Dorsey's postwar music, a period of time when the swing he continued to play with enthusiasm was slipping permanently behind the times. —*Scott Yanow*

Tommy Dorsey (1950-1952) / 1950-1952 / First Time ✦✦✦
In the early '50s, Tommy Dorsey mostly recorded commercial (and long out-of-print) music for Decca, so these live performances are quite welcome. Emphasizing Dorsey's jazz side, one not only hears Dorsey's trombone but Charlie Shavers' trumpet and Sam Donahue's tenor featured throughout this LP as well. Bill Finegan contributed some of the arrangements to what would be Tommy Dorsey's last big band before rejoining forces with his brother Jimmy Dorsey for a final nostalgia-based orchestra. —*Scott Yanow*

Dave Douglas

Trumpet / Klezmer, Free Jazz, Avant-Garde, Post-Bop
Dave Douglas has arguably become the most original trumpeter/composer of his generation. Douglas' stylistic range is broad, yet unaffected; his music is not a pastiche, but, rather, a personal aesthetic that reflects an wide variety of interests—he explicitly cites such diverse influences as Igor Stravinsky, Stevie Wonder, and John Coltrane. As a composer, Douglas adapts and synthesizes unusual forms and creates his own out of disparate elements. As a trumpeter, Douglas possesses a comprehensive jazz technique; certainly, one hears the ghost of Lester Bowie in Douglas' expressive manipulations of timbre and pitch, but more pronounced is the integration of distinctive compositional and improvisational conceptions that ultimately defines his work.

Douglas grew up in the New York City area. He started playing piano at the age of five, then trombone at seven before discovering the trumpet at nine. He learned jazz harmony in high school, and began playing improvised music as an exchange student in Barcelona, Spain. From 1981-83, he studied in Boston, first at Berklee School of Music, then the New England Conservatory. He moved to New York City in 1984, where he attended New York University and studied with Carmine Caruso. In 1987, he toured Europe with Horace Silver. The early '90s saw Douglas begin to record in earnest; he led or co-led dates for the Hat Art, Soul Note, New World, and Arabesque labels. His various bands include the Tiny Bell Trio, a self-described "jazz-Balkan-improv" group with drummer Jim Black and guitarist Brad Schoeppach; his String Group, which includes violinist Mark Feldman, cellist Erik Friedlander, and bassist Mark Dresser; and his Quartet and Sextet, which includes notably drummer Joey Baron. Douglas has also recorded as a sideman with Myra Melford, John Zorn, and Anthony Braxton, among others. —*Chris Kelsey*

Parallel Worlds / Mar. 17, 1993+Mar. 18, 1993 / Soul Note ✦✦✦✦
Trumpeter Dave Douglas is attracting attention among fans and critics on the underground and avant-garde/free music trail. He shows what the hype is all about on this session with some surging solos, high-note explosiveness and impressive playing. But Douglas doesn't merely spew unconnected lines or flashy solos; his playing is a vital part of several originals that feature an intriguing violin/cello/

bass backing section. The compositions range from loose, spacy tunes to animated, fierce ones. This isn't another hard bop outing or a completely freewheeling session; instead, it's got elements of both, and a departure as well. It requires close scrutiny and a completely open mind, because Dave Douglas is following no direction except his own. —*Ron Wynn*

The Tiny Bell Trio / 1994 / Songlines ✦✦✦

● **In Our Lifetime** / Dec. 7, 1994-Dec. 8, 1994 / New World ✦✦✦✦✦
Trumpeter Dave Douglas' New World CD is consistently intriguing, the type of music that gains in interest with each listening. Douglas is quick to acknowledge the influence of Booker Little (the early-'60s trumpeter who was among the first to emerge from Clifford Brown's shadow) and on this set he performs three of Little's tunes plus his own "Four Miniatures after Booker Little." However, it is the two lengthier pieces, "In Our Lifetime" and "Bridges" (the latter over 17 minutes long), that are of greatest interest. Douglas' originals, which are episodic and avant-garde (but not afraid to swing) while expertly mixing together improvisation with composition, are consistently colorful. His flexible band (Chris Speed on tenor and clarinet, trombonist Josh Roseman, pianist Uri Caine, bassist James Genus, drummer Joey Baron and guest bass clarinetist Marty Ehrlich on the title cut) is able to switch grooves quickly and interpret the frequently dramatic music with sensitivity and wit. —*Scott Yanow*

Constellations / Aug. 25, 1995 / Hat Hut ✦✦✦✦

Five / Aug. 28, 1995 / Soul Note ✦✦✦✦✦
Trumpeter Dave Douglas' unusual string group (which also includes violinist Mark Feldman, cellist Erik Friedlander, bassist Drew Gross and drummer Michael Sarin) is reminiscent in some ways of Ornette Coleman's free-jazz quartet despite not playing any of Ornette's originals and having a very different instrumentation. All of the musicians function as equals, the interaction is often intuitive, and the improvising on eight Douglas originals (including tunes dedicated to Steve Lacy, Wayne Shorter, Mark Dresser, Woody Shaw, John Cage and John Zorn), Thelonious Monk's "Who Knows," and Rahsaan Roland Kirk's "The Inflated Tear" is on a high level. Well worth exploring. —*Scott Yanow*

Sanctuary / Aug. 6, 1996+Aug. 27, 1996 / Avant ✦✦✦

Stargazer / 1997 / Arabesque ✦✦✦

Ray Draper (Raymond Allen Draper)

b. Aug. 3, 1940, New York, NY, **d.** Nov. 1, 1982, New York, NY
Tuba / Hard Bop
Ray Draper was an excellent tuba soloist, one of the few in the 1950s to utilize the instrument for bop improvisations. After attending the Manhattan School of Music, he played and recorded with Jackie McLean (1956-57), worked with Donald Byrd and recorded with John Coltrane (1958). Draper was with Max Roach's band (1958-59) and worked with Don Cherry in the early '60s. However, from that point on drugs played havoc with his life. He did play later in the 1960s with Horace Tapscott, Archie Shepp, Brother Jack McDuff (recording with him in 1971) and Howard Johnson's group Gravity but had largely dropped out of music by the time he was killed during a robbery. Draper led sessions during 1957-60 for Prestige, New Jazz, Jubilee and Epic. —*Scott Yanow*

Tuba Sounds / Mar. 15, 1957 / Prestige ✦✦✦

● **Ray Draper Quintet Featuring John Coltrane** / Dec. 20, 1957 / Prestige ✦✦✦✦

A Tuba Jazz / 1958 / Jubilee ✦✦✦

Kenny Drew

b. Aug. 28, 1928, New York, NY, **d.** Aug. 4, 1993, Copenhagen, Denmark
Piano / Hard Bop
A talented bop-based pianist (whose son has been one of the brightest pianists of the 1990s), Kenny Drew was somewhat underrated due to his decision to move permanently to Copenhagen in 1964. He made his recording debut in 1949 with Howard McGhee and in the 1950s was featured on sessions with the who's who of jazz including Charlie Parker, Coleman Hawkins, Lester Young, Milt Jackson, Buddy DeFranco's quartet, Dinah Washington and Buddy Rich (1958). Drew led sessions for Blue Note, Norgran, Pacific Jazz, Riverside and the obscure Judson label during 1953-60; most of the sessions are currently available on CD. He moved to Paris in 1961 and relocated to Copenhagen in 1964 where he was co-owner of the Matrix label. He formed a duo with Niels-Henning Orsted Pederson and worked regularly at the Montmartre. Drew recorded many dates for Steeple Chase in the 1970s and remained active up until his death. —*Scott Yanow*

Talkin' and Walkin' / Nov. 18, 1955+Dec. 1955 / Blue Note ✦✦✦✦
Kenny Drew, one of the top young bop-oriented pianists to emerge in the 1950s, would not make his one official Blue Note recording as a leader until 1960, but this set (originally released by Pacific Jazz) has been reissued on CD under the Blue

Note name. Drew's regular group of the period (a quartet with altoist Joe Maini, bassist Leroy Vinnegar and drummer Lawrence Marable) is featured on nine pieces (including six Drew originals) that swing but are not overly predictable. Maini, who died prematurely, has a rare opportunity to stretch out and all of the musicians are in fine form. In addition, this CD has three selections with the same group under trumpeter Jack Sheldon's leadership (two Drew songs plus "It's Only a Paper Moon"), which were originally released on samplers. Excellent modern mainstream music of the mid-'50s. —*Scott Yanow*

The Kenny Drew Trio / Sep. 20, 1956+Sep. 26, 1956 / Original Jazz Classics ✦✦✦✦

Kenny Drew, with the assistance of bassist Paul Chambers (whose bowed solos are always welcome) and drummer Philly Joe Jones, explores six standards and two of his originals. Although Drew would have to move to Europe in the early '60s in order to get the recognition he deserved, it is obvious (in hindsight) from this enjoyable date that he was already a major improviser. —*Scott Yanow*

Trio-Quartet-Quintet / Sep. 20, 1956-Oct. 15, 1957 / Original Jazz Classics ✦✦✦
A wonderful collection of first-rate pianist in varied contexts, w/ Donald Byrd (tpt), Paul Chambers (b), and Philly Joe Jones (d) on the job. —*Ron Wynn*

Plays the Music of Harry Warren and Harold Arlen / Feb. 1957 / Milestone ✦✦✦✦

This CD reissue combines together the complete contents of two similar sessions by pianist Kenny Drew. With the assistance of bassist Wilbur Ware, Drew performs a dozen songs apiece from the Harry Warren and Harold Arlen songbooks. The interpretations, originally released on the Judson label, are quite melodic, tasteful and lightly swinging. Drew does not come out with any new revelations while playing songs such as "Lullaby of Broadway," "I Only Have Eyes for You," "That Old Black Magic" and "It's Only a Paper Moon," but these versions do not sound overly nostalgic or tired either. This is a nice set if not all that essential. —*Scott Yanow*

This Is New / Apr. 3, 1957 / Original Jazz Classics ✦✦✦
Pianist Kenny Drew teams up with other young hard bop players on this CD reissue. Trumpeter Donald Byrd, tenor saxophonist Hank Mobley (who is on half of the program which is subtitled "Quintet/Quartet"), bassist Wilbur Ware and drummer G.T. Hogan perform four standards (including "It's You or No One" and "Why Do I Love You") and selections by Drew, Byrd and Sonny Rollins ("Paul's Pal"). Kenny Drew's recording career was quite consistent (none of his releases were throwaways) and this session should appeal to straightahead bop collectors. —*Scott Yanow*

★ **Pal Joey** / Oct. 15, 1957 / Original Jazz Classics ✦✦✦✦✦
It seems strange that (with the exception of a 1960 session for Blue Note) this would be pianist Kenny Drew's last session as a leader until 1973. With bassist Wilbur Ware and drummer Philly Joe Jones, Drew interprets eight Rodgers and Hart tunes, five written for the play *Pal Joey* and three of their earlier hits that were included in the film version. Drew contributes swing and subtle bop-based improvising to these superior melodies (which are highlighted by "Bewitched, Bothered, and Bewildered," "I Could Write a Book" and "The Lady Is a Tramp") and the results are quite memorable. —*Scott Yanow*

Undercurrent / Dec. 11, 1960 / Blue Note ✦✦✦✦✦
Kenny Drew recorded fairly frequently in the 1950s but after his Blue Note album (reissued on this CD), he moved to Europe and did not appear as a leader on records until 1973. Still just 32 in 1960, Drew was teamed with the young trumpeter Freddie Hubbard (who already showed great potential), tenor saxophonist Hank Mobley, bassist Sam Jones and drummer Louis Hayes on six of his originals (including "Undercurrent," "The Pot's On" and "Groovin' the Blues"). A fine hard bop set. —*Scott Yanow*

Duo, Vol. 1 / Apr. 2, 1973 / Steeple Chase ✦✦✦✦

Everything I Love / Oct. 1973-Dec. 1973 / Steeple Chase ✦✦✦

Duo, Vol. 2 / Feb. 11, 1974-Feb. 12, 1974 / Steeple Chase ✦✦✦✦
After a long period off of records (at least as a leader), pianist Kenny Drew emerged in 1973 for a duo session with bassist Niels Pedersen. For their rematch in 1974, Drew and Pedersen performed one original apiece, five standards (including "A Child Is Born" and "My Shining Hour") and jazz interpretations of a couple of Scandinavian folk songs. The pianist's style was largely unchanged from the 1950s except that he had grown a bit as a player and was open to some more modern chord voicings. The music on this encounter with the virtuosic bassist Niels Pedersen should easily appeal to Kenny Drew's fans. —*Scott Yanow*

If You Could See Me Now / May 21, 1974-May 22, 1974 / Steeple Chase ✦✦✦✦

Morning / Sep. 8, 1975 / Steeple Chase ✦✦✦

In Concert / Feb. 3, 1977 / Steeple Chase ✦✦✦
By the late 1970s, Kenny Drew had migrated to Europe, where he recorded extensively. This live trio date with the superb bassist Niels Pedersen and guitarist Phillip Catherine is worth looking for. "Django" opens with a lyrical Catherine acoustic solo before Drew and Pedersen take a bluesy detour. "Here's That Rainy Day" is given a lengthy workout, while the leader's "Sunset" opens with a meandering theme before evolving into a gentle ballad. The romping interplay within "Blues In the Closet" and "On Green Dolphin Street" close the performance with a flourish. —*Ken Dryden*

Lite Flite / Feb. 6, 1977 / Steeple Chase ✦✦✦✦

Ruby My Dear / Aug. 23, 1977 / Steeple Chase ✦✦✦

Home Is Where the Soul Is / Oct. 15, 1978 / Xanadu ✦✦✦
The fine bop-based pianist Kenny Drew permanently left the US in 1961 to live in Europe and eventually Copenhagen. He only recorded back in his homeland during a 1978 visit that resulted in a pair of Xanadu LPs. For this date, Drew teamed up with bassist Leroy Vinnegar and drummer Frank Butler for three familiar standards, an obscurity and three of his recent straightahead originals. The years overseas had not hurt the pianist in the least and he had clearly grown as an improviser. Worth searching for. —*Scott Yanow*

For Sure / Oct. 16, 1978 / Xanadu ✦✦✦✦
Kenny Drew recorded two Xanadu albums in two days during one of his very rare visits to the US after he moved to Europe in 1961. This rare quintet outing (with altoist Charles McPherson, trumpeter Sam Noto, bassist Leroy Vinnegar and drummer Frank Butler) features Drew playing at the peak of his powers. The material (four originals by the pianist plus two obscurities) is strong, is sometimes quite boppish and contains plenty of variety. This out-of-print LP was underrated at the time and is worth searching for. —*Scott Yanow*

It Might as Well Be Spring / Nov. 23, 1981 / Soul Note ✦✦✦

Your Soft Eyes / Nov. 25, 1981-Nov. 26, 1981 / Soul Note ✦✦✦

And Far Away / Feb. 21, 1983 / Soul Note ✦✦✦
He can still drive a group and play with class, elegance and beauty. —*Ron Wynn*

Recollections / May 14, 1989-May 15, 1989 / Timeless ✦✦✦

Kenny Drew, Jr.

b. 1958, New York, NY
Piano / Hard Bop, Post-Bop
Despite sharing his father's name, Kenny Drew, Jr. was raised by his aunt and grandparents and does not consider Kenny Drew, Sr. to be an influence. He was taught classical music by his mother and grandmother and gigged in clubs as a teenager. He made his recording debut with Charnett Moffett and worked with Stanley Jordan and OTB and recorded with Eddie Gomez, Sadao Watanabe, and the Mingus Big Band. In 1990 Drew won the Great American Jazz Piano competition at the Jacksonville Jazz Festival. He first led sessions for the Japanese label Jazz City and has since had record dates for Antilles, Concord (a solo Maybeck Recital Hall concert) and Claves. —*Scott Yanow*

The Flame Within / Nov. 1987 / Jazz City ✦✦✦

Third Phase / Jun. 1989 / Jazz City ✦✦✦

Kenny Drew, Jr. / Jun. 6, 1991-Jun. 7, 1991 / Antilles ✦✦✦✦✦
Debut album by the gifted son of a jazz legend. Kenny Drew, Jr. demonstrated that genetics do sometimes play a role in jazz. He doesn't yet have the total command or timing of his famous father, but Kenny Drew, Jr. showed he was well on his way to developing those skills. —*Ron Wynn*

Look Inside / Jun. 22, 1992-June 24, 1992 / Verve ✦✦✦✦

Portraits of Mingus & Monk / Jun. 21, 1994-Jun. 23, 1994 / Claves Jazz ✦✦✦

● **Maybeck Recital Hall Series, Vol. 39** / Aug. 7, 1994 / Concord Jazz ✦✦✦✦✦

Paquito D'Rivera

b. Jun. 4, 1948, Havana, Cuba
Alto Saxophone, Clarinet, Soprano Saxophone / Bop, Afro-Cuban Jazz, Latin Jazz
One of Cuba's finest exports, Paquito D'Rivera is a distinctive altoist with an impressive upper register and a skilled clarinetist. He studied at the Havana Conservatory from 1960 and played professionally starting when he was 14. After playing in an army band, D'Rivera joined the Orquesta Cubana de Musica Moderna and Irakere (1973-80); the latter was Cuba's top band. After defecting to the US in 1980, D'Rivera moved to New York and worked with Dizzy Gillespie and McCoy Tyner before starting his own band. He has directed Dizzy Gillespie's last group, the United Nation Orchestra, since Dizzy's death. D'Rivera has recorded an impressive string of albums for Columbia, Chesky, Messidor and Candid and has toured as part of the Caribbean Jazz Project. —*Scott Yanow*

Blowin' / 1981 / CBS ✦✦✦✦

Altoist Paquito D'Rivera's first American recording after defecting from Cuba is an often-jubilant affair. D'Rivera, who also plays some soprano and flute on this album, is heard in groups ranging from a duet with pianist Jorge Dalto to a septet. The impressive lineup also includes pianist Hilton Ruiz, bassist Eddie Gomez and drummer Ignacio Berroa, among others. The music is high-quality modern bebop with a strong dose of Latin rhythms—a fine example of D'Rivera's talents. —*Scott Yanow*

● **Taste of Paquito** / 1981-1987 / Columbia ✦✦✦✦

Not a "greatest hits" album (like he was shooting for "hits"), nor a thoroughgoing anthology of Paquito D'Rivera's Columbia period (only the first five of his seven albums are covered), the word "taste" is an intriguing choice, though at 74 minutes the CD is a bit more than just a taste. But then, since Sony has done a real number on his catalog by not reissuing those first five albums, *A Taste* is all that CD buyers can sample from Paquito's first American recordings. Up to a point, we receive a fairly good idea as to what the commotion was initially about, starting from the time two years after D'Rivera's defection from Cuba when he was primarily a joyous, shouting Latin bopper with a hot hand on the alto sax. The CD concentrates upon smaller group sessions, leaving off at the point where Paquito was starting to incorporate larger groups and more eclectic wanderings into his music. Two of the more memorable tracks are the poignant "Song to My Son" (recorded when Paquito's wife and son were still left behind in Cuba) and the robust Dizzy-inspired humor of "Just Kidding." Watch out for some booboos in the track credits, such as the listing of Hilton Ruiz on acoustic bass instead of piano on "Miami" and omitting mention of Toots Thielemans on "Brussels in the Rain," which was merely written for the Belgian harmonica virtuoso in the first place. —*Richard S. Ginell*

Mariel / 1982 / Columbia ✦✦✦✦✦

Paquito D'Rivera's string of Columbia albums (his first in the US after defecting from Cuba) are consistently enjoyable. This LP features D'Rivera (mostly on alto but also playing a bit of soprano) performing four originals, two obscurities and John Coltrane's "Moment's Notice." The Afro-Cuban jazz set (which has some more commercial sections) features among Paquito's sidemen trumpeter Randy Brecker, keyboardist Hilton Ruiz, drummer Ignacio Berroa and percussionist Daniel Ponce among others; Brenda Feliciano has a guest vocal on "New York Is You." —*Scott Yanow*

Live at Keystone Korner / Jun. 17, 1983-Jun. 18, 1983 / Columbia ✦✦✦✦

Altoist Paquito D'Rivera teams up with trumpeter Claudio Roditi on a live sextet date also featuring keyboardist Carlos Franzetti, bassist Steve Bailey, drummer Ignacio Berroa and percussionist Daniel Ponce. The material (mostly group originals) is fairly obscure but the pieces serve as fine vehicles for the very complementary horns of the explorative D'Rivera and the comparatively mellow Roditi. This is high-quality Afro-Cuban jazz that makes one regret that Columbia has yet to reissue their Paquito D'Rivera LPs on CD. —*Scott Yanow*

Why Not / Jun. 19, 1984-Jun. 21, 1984 / Columbia ✦✦✦✦✦

Paquito D'Rivera's fourth album since his defection from Cuba is a refreshingly eclectic project, roaming all over Latin America, North America and even Belgium for players, sources and inspiration. The leadoff track, "Gdansk," is a tough, bumping electric jazz rallying cry for Lech Walesa and his Polish labor union. "Waltz for Sonny" has a Venezuelan flavor in the rhythm; "Manteca" is another homage to his Afro-Cuban jazz forebears. "Samba for Carmen," an often wild Brazilian salvo, has D'Rivera shining on clarinet and Claudio Roditi contributing some fine trumpet licks. The record is graced by the inimitable harmonica, guitar and whistling of Toots Thielemans; D'Rivera's tune "Brussels in the Rain" is a most comfortable vehicle for the Belgian. Paquito negotiates all of the journey's zigzags with technical ease, humor, eloquence, and more than a little flamboyance. —*Richard S. Ginell*

Explosion / Jul. 1985 / Columbia ✦✦✦✦

Paquito D'Rivera heads out in two directions on *Explosion*, continuing his invigorating explorations of Latin American music and trying his hand at arranging for a small string section. On three tracks, Paquito makes his strings seem more lush than their numbers indicate, while never overloading the texture with schmaltz; a good effort all around. The big attractions of this album, though, are the Latin workouts, at once more stimulating and swinging than before, with marvelous trombone from Claudio Roditi and impressive piano from Michel Camilo. In homage to his island roots, Paquito plays marvelously on a jiggling rendition of Mario Bauza's "Mambo Inn," all the alto registers perfectly integrated from top to bottom. Among the other high points, Camilo's "Just Kidding" is a humorous metamorphosis of Dizzy Gillespie's "Salt Peanuts," and Roditi's "The Monster and the Flower" has a great Brazilian guitar groove. —*Richard S. Ginell*

Manhattan Burn / Sep. 1986-Oct. 1986 / Columbia ✦✦✦

Even for Paquito D'Rivera, *Manhattan Burn* is diversity run riot as he spreads his stylistic net even further afield. At first, perhaps in an effort to stir up some

sales—or more kindly, in the spirit of adventure—Paquito turns to an easier-listening direction on the opening tracks, with Daniel Freiberg laying down the usual bland synth textures and Paquito limiting his playing to sweet muzak licks. But "Guataca City" reignites the raucous Latin flame, and in a more or less straight-ahead jazz vein, Paquito teams up with tenor sax bopper George Coleman on the Chick Corea-penned "Paquito" and "A Lo Tristano." There is a requisite samba, with Claudio Roditi back on fluegelhorn and Paquito dazzling as usual on clarinet, and there is even a graceful composition for classical guitar and clarinet, "Two Venezuelan Waltzes." Another solid album, though a bit short of the satisfying standards of *Why Not?* and *Explosion*. —*Richard S. Ginell*

Celebration / Sep. 1987-Oct. 1987 / Columbia ✦✦✦✦

The "celebration" in question refers to Paquito becoming a US citizen seven years after defecting from Cuba—and without question, he lives it up here by lavishing string arrangements on the majority of the tracks. Again, Paquito chooses to roam freely around the Latin and jazz spectrums, yet there is an appealing, newfound elegance in these tracks, even when the going gets raucous. "Wapango" has a stark, neoclassical string chart by Paquito, and Roger Kellaway contributes the fascinating, dreamlike arrangement on "Heart of the Kingdom." Both of these tracks, which feature superb Paquito clarinet work, are along the lines of what Eddie Daniels was recording around this time. Claudio Roditi is back on bebop trumpet and Makoto Ozone, Daniel Freiberg and the always unpredictable Kellaway alternate in the piano chair. Paquito also repaid Chick Corea for his "Paquito" track on *Manhattan Burn* with a jazz/funk piece of his own called "Chick." Columbia unfortunately put a damper on the celebration by dropping Paquito after this album was released, despite the fact that it is clearly one of the ex-Cuban musician's finest projects. Blame the accountants, not the music. —*Richard S. Ginell*

Return to Ipanema / Mar. 1, 1989-Mar. 2, 1989 / Town Crier ✦✦✦✦

Return to Ipanema resurrects the spirit of classic samba on the engaging *Brazilian Jazz*, a set encompassing both original material as well as wild covers, including a show-stopping rendition of Gershwin's "Summertime." —*Jason Ankeny*

Tico! Tico! / Jun. 28, 1989-Aug. 16, 1989 / Chesky ✦✦✦✦

Paquito D'Rivera's alto and clarinet skills were ably displayed on this session, which featured him working in Afro-Latin, salsa, funk, swing and hard bop. Compositions ranged from intense, jam-flavored numbers with torrid solos, like "Recife's Blue" and the title tune, to introspective ballads, group pieces with rhythmically explosive sections and numbers displaying classical influences. The unifying force was D'Rivera, who also played tenor but was most prominent on clarinet, doing both swing-oriented and looser, freer solos. While not as strict a jazz vehicle as his Columbia dates, this session presented a more eclectic, versatile Paquito D'Rivera. —*Ron Wynn*

Reunion / 1990 / Messidor ✦✦✦✦

Excellent session done for German label, distributed domestically by Rounder. D'Rivera is at the top of his game. —*Ron Wynn*

★ **Who's Smoking?!** / May 21, 1991-May 22, 1991 / Candid ✦✦✦✦✦

Hot, surging Afro-Latin set by alto saxophonist Paquito D'Rivera, matching him with both celebrated veterans and established session stars. D'Rivera doesn't falter through any of these pieces and gets strong assistance from special guest James Moody and super trumpet solos by Claudio Roditi. The percussive backgrounds supplied by Danilo Perez and Al Foster are varied and constantly shifting and changing. —*Ron Wynn*

Havana Cafe / Aug. 28, 1991-Aug. 29, 1991 / Chesky ✦✦✦✦

This excellent all-round session features Paquito D'Rivera on alto, clarinet and soprano with his sextet, which comprises either Fareed Haque or Ed Cherry on guitar, the great pianist Danilo Perez, bassist David Finck, drummer Jorge Rossy and percussionist Sammy Figueroa. The program has some strong group originals (such as "Havana Cafe," "Jean Pauline," "Who's Smoking" and "Bossa Do Brooklyn") and the result is an often-fiery set of modern Afro-Cuban jazz. —*Scott Yanow*

40 Years of Cuban Jam Sessions / 1993 / Messidor ✦✦✦✦

Despite its title, this CD does not offer one a sampler of Cuban jams of the past 40 years but it does contain a recent session featuring 25 of the top Cuban expatriates. Organized to a large extent by altoist Paquito D'Rivera (who is only actually on six of the 11 selections), these performances utilize a wide variety of instrumentations. Carlos Gomez has a vocal, there is a laidback feature for Jose Silva's tenor, Juan Pablo Torres takes a couple of impressive trombone solos and, on "Descarga Para Banda Y Combo," there is a humorous blending of circus music, Dixieland and a boppish blues. With D'Rivera in fine form on alto and clarinet during his appearances, this is a continually interesting and stimulating set. —*Scott Yanow*

A Night in Englewood / Jul. 1993 / Messidor ✦✦✦✦✦

After Dizzy Gillespie's death in 1991, his colorful Afro-Cuban United Nation Orchestra (which was formed in 1988) was headed by altoist-clarinetist Paquito D'Rivera. With the better-known sidemen on this 1993 CD including first trumpeter Byron Stripling, trombonist Conrad Herwig and tenor saxophonist Mario Rivera, additional solo space allocated to some of the other talented players and guest spots for trumpeter Claudio Roditi, trombonist Slide Hampton and vibraphonist Dave Samuels, this is an easily recommended set. The music is very Latin-oriented and shows that the orchestra had moved away from Gillespie's usual repertoire to exclusively featuring originals by band members (including D'Rivera's "I Remember Diz"). Definitely worth investigating. —*Scott Yanow*

Portraits of Cuba / Feb. 6, 1996-Feb. 7, 1996 / Chesky ◆◆◆◆

Ray Drummond

b. Nov. 23, 1946, Brookline, MA
Bass / Hard Bop
Early on, Ray Drummond played with Michael White and Bobby Hutcherson in San Francisco. After attending Stanford Business School (1974-77) he has had countless jobs as a supportive bassist with everyone from David Murray and Pharoah Sanders to the New York Quartet, Mingus Dynasty and Kenny Barron. Drummond has also led sessions for Nilva, Criss Cross, DMP and Arabesque. —*Scott Yanow*

Susanita / Jul. 17, 1984-July 19, 1984 / Nilva ◆◆◆

Camera in a Bag / Dec. 28, 1989 / Criss Cross ◆◆◆◆◆

The Essence / Oct. 8, 1990-Oct. 9, 1990 / DMP ◆◆◆◆
Although bassist Ray Drummond is the leader of this trio set, he shares the spotlight quite evenly with pianist Hank Jones and drummer Billy Higgins. Drummond contributed two originals (including a tribute piece to Higgins) but otherwise the repertoire comprises jazz standards including "Things Ain't What They Used to Be," "Whisper Not," "Love Walked In" and "Imagination." Jones in particular is in excellent form on the fine modern mainstream set. —*Scott Yanow*

Excursion / 1993 / Arabesque ◆◆◆

● **Continuum** / Jan. 16, 1994 / Arabesque ◆◆◆◆◆
Bassist Ray Drummond and an all-star group that includes trumpeter Randy Brecker, flutist Thomas Chapin, guitarist John Scofield, pianist Kenny Barron, vibraphonist Steve Nelson and drummer Marvin "Smitty" Smith perform a variety of challenging compositions including a few veteran pieces (such as "Sophisticated Lady" and "The Intimacy of the Blues"), obscurities (Scott LaFaro's "Gloria's Step" and Tom Harrell's "Sail Away") and a couple of Drummond's originals. Alternating some blues-oriented numbers with more complex pieces, Drummond put together a varied program that brings out the best in his illustrious sidemen. —*Scott Yanow*

Vignettes / Aug. 23, 1995-Aug. 24, 1995 / Arabesque ◆◆◆◆
For this date, bassist Ray Drummond heads an all-star quintet which includes altoist Gary Bartz, Chris Potter on tenor, pianist Renee Rosnes and drummer Billy Hart. They perform five of Drummond's tunes, John Handy's near-classic jazz waltz "Dance to the Lady" and a pair of standards. On what is generally an extroverted session, the bassist's two "Ballade Poetiques" serve as a change of pace, fairly free flights for the trio that are quite introspective. Otherwise the underrated giant Bartz emerges as the main star, taking "Poor Butterfly" as his showcase, showing off his John Coltrane roots on "Eleanor Rigby" and making a powerful statement on "Dance to the Lady." A fine post bop session. —*Scott Yanow*

Urszula Dudziak

b. Oct. 22, 1943, Straconka, Poland
Vocals / Fusion, Post-Bop
Urszula Dudziak, wife of violinist Michal Urbaniak, made a big impression in the mid-'70s with three innovative albums for Arista and Inner City but has maintained a low profile ever since. Dudziak had piano lessons and took up singing in her native Poland in the late '50s. She met Urbaniak in 1962, performed in Scandinavia (1965-69) and in 1974 settled in New York. Dudziak employed electronics to accentuate her wide range and explorative style, recording both with and without Urbaniak and working in the 1980s with Archie Shepp, Lester Bowie and Bobby McFerrin. —*Scott Yanow*

● **Urszula** / 1976 / Arista ◆◆◆◆◆
Singer Urszula Dudziak's second recording as a leader and first American record introduced to the jazz world a somewhat bizarre stylist. By sometimes using electronics to distort her voice and displaying a very wide range along with the ability to improvise freely, Dudziak was quite unique. All ten selections on this out-of-print Arista LP (including "Zavinul," "Mosquito Dream" and a "Just the Way You Are" which is no relation to the later Billy Joel hit) are originals by the singer, with the emphasis on "original." The backup group includes guitarists Reggie Lucas and Joe Caro, keyboardist Harold Ivory Williams and a guest appearance on one song by Dudziak's husband Michal Urbaniak on lyricon. —*Scott Yanow*

Midnight Train / 1977 / Arista ◆◆◆◆
Urszula Dudziak is such an odd and unique improviser (who uses electronics on her voice, displays a huge range and is able to come up with a wide variety of other-worldly sounds) that this standards-oriented release is the best introduction to her singing. Not that Dudziak's interpretations of "Lover," "Misty," "Night in Tunisia" and "Bluesette" (along with three originals) is even close to conventional but at least one can recognize the melodies. This valuable but hard-to-find LP features Dudziak backed by an electronic rhythm section plus her husband Michal Urbaniak on violin, tenor, lyricon and keyboards. Recommended to adventurous listeners. —*Scott Yanow*

Future Talk / Feb. 1979 / Inner City ◆◆◆◆
The unusual singer Urszula Dudziak is heard on this set performing four unaccompanied solos, a duet with Michal Urbaniak's lyricon and six group pieces with such players as altoist Zbigniew Namyslovski, guitarist John Abercrombie, keyboardist Kenny Kirkland and bassist Marcus Miller. Although her backup crew is strong, Dudziak is the dominant force for few other singers could create with the sounds that she can. The eccentric avant-garde music (last out on this out-of-print LP) takes several listens to absorb. —*Scott Yanow*

Sorrow Is Not Forever . . . But Love Is / 1983 / Keytone ◆◆◆

George Duke

b. Jan. 12, 1946, San Rafael, CA
Keyboards, Piano / Funk, Instrumental Pop, Crossover Jazz
George Duke showed a great deal of promise early in his career as a jazz pianist and keyboardist, but has forsaken creative music to be a pop producer. Inspired early on by Les McCann, he worked with a trio in San Francisco during the mid-'60s. In 1969, Duke accompanied Jean-Luc Ponty, recording with the violinist. After eight months with Don Ellis' Orchestra, he joined Frank Zappa for much of 1970. Duke spent 1971-72 with Cannonball Adderley and then returned to Zappa for 1973-75. In 1975 he worked with Sonny Rollins, co-led a group with Billy Cobham, then formed a funk band (the Clarke-Duke Project) with Stanley Clarke. By the late '70s he was completely outside of jazz, playing R&B and producing projects for pop artists. Although he has since expressed interest in returning to active playing, little of George Duke's post-1976 work is relevant to jazz. —*Scott Yanow*

Presented by the Jazz Workshop of San Francisco / Jan. 1966 / Saba ◆◆◆◆
This LP is a real collector's item. Just barely 20 at the time, pianist George Duke made his recording debut with a straightahead quartet also including the obscure bass trumpeter David Simmons, bassist John Heard and drummer George Walker. This was one of Duke's very few all-standards sets, and he proved to be a fine hard bop/soul-jazz pianist; unfortunately, that phase would not last long. Highlights include "The Night Has a Thousand Eyes," "Jeannine" and "Secret Love." But by the time the pianist recorded his second date as a leader three years later, this particular George Duke would be history. —*Scott Yanow*

I Love the Blues: She Heard My Cry / 1975 / Polydor ◆◆◆

● **Solo Keyboard Album (1976)** / 1976 / Epic ◆◆◆◆
Not very many of George Duke's recordings are of interest to jazz listeners, since he has spent much of his career as either a funk keyboardist or a pop producer. Despite the title, this album is not a very spontaneous set, for Duke is heard playing piano, various keyboards, guitar, drums and organ, most of it overdubbed. The seven selections (which include "Mr. McFreeze," "Spock Gets Funky" and "Vulcan Mind Probe") do have their moments of interest, with some good grooves and melodies, and George Duke has long been proud of this particular effort. —*Scott Yanow*

Reach for It / 1977 / Epic ◆◆◆
By 1977, the jazz content of George Duke's albums had decreased considerably, and soul and funk had become his main priorities. *Reach for It* has more to offer from an R&B standpoint than a jazz standpoint, though the fusion it does contain is first rate—including the Latin-influenced "Hot Fire" and "Lemme at It" (an aggressive gem that's in a class with some of the keyboardist/pianist's best work with the Cobham/Duke Band). *Reach*'s heavy R&B content resulted in Duke facing the same accusation as George Benson, Patrice Rushen and other improvisors who moved away from jazz in the 1970s—that he was a sellout. But none of this CD's R&B content comes across as contrived or formulaic—and in fact, Duke is downright inspired on the haunting "Just for You" and the Parliament-influenced title song. Even so, it's always regrettable when a gifted improvisor pretty much abandons jazz—and Duke is a prime example. It should be stressed that the high rating this writer awarded this CD is primarily from an R&B standpoint—and that those strictly interested in hearing Duke playing jazz would be better off investing in earlier efforts like *Faces in Reflection*. —*Alex Henderson*

Brazilian Love Affair / 1979 / Epic ◆◆◆◆

George Duke had been fairly visible in the R&B world thanks to funk gems like "Reach for It" and "Dukey Stick" when he ventured to Rio to record *Brazilian Love Affair*, a superb date employing such greats as singers Flora Purim (vocals) and Milton Nascimento and percussionist Airto Moreira. Although not the return to instrumental jazz some hoped it would be, this heartfelt effort does contain its share of jazz-influenced material. From a jazz standpoint, the CD's most noteworthy songs include Nascimento's "Cravo E Canela," the charming "Brazilian Sugar," "Love Reborn" and the exuberant "Up from the Sea It Arose and Ate Rio in One Swift Bite." Meanwhile, listeners who like Duke's smooth stylings, or want to become acquainted with his work, will find *Best of George Duke: The Elektra Years* a strong collection, containing such early career staples as "Good Friend" and "African Violet." For die-hard fans, there's the added attraction of two previously unreleased tracks—"Come to Me" and "Baby Love," the latter of which features Jody Watley on vocals. —*Stephen Thomas Erlewine*

Best of George Duke: The Elektra Years / 1981-1986 / Elektra ◆◆◆◆

Best of George Duke: The Elektra Years culls the highlights from Duke's three mid-'80s albums for Elektra—*Thief in the Night, George Duke* and *Night After Night*. During these years, Duke completed his shift from jazz to smooth jazz, fusion and urban R&B, which means there is very little here of interest to serious jazz fans. However, listeners who like Duke's smooth stylings, or want to become acquainted with his work, will find *Best of George Duke: The Elektra Years* a strong collection, containing such early career staples as "Good Friend" and "African Violet." For die-hard fans, there's the added attraction of two previously unreleased tracks—"Come to Me" and "Baby Love," the latter of which features Jody Watley on vocals. —*Stephen Thomas Erlewine*

Secret Rendezvous / 1983 / Epic ◆◆

Muir Woods Suite / Jul. 12, 1993 / Warner Brothers ◆◆◆

Recorded live at the Montreux Jazz Festival on July 12, 1993, but not released for two-and-a-half years, George Duke's *Muir Woods Suite* is a musical work for orchestra (L'orchestre National de Lille, conducted by Ettore Strata) and jazz group (himself on piano, Stanley Clarke on bass, Chester Thompson on drums, Paulinho Dacosta on percussion). As that combination suggests, it's eclectic. Some sections make full use of the orchestra in passages reminiscent of 19th century classical music, but then a bass or drum solo leads into a jazz section. Consistently engaging, but disparate, the suite has the air of a movie soundtrack. —*William Ruhlmann*

Is Love Enough / 1997 / Warner Brothers ◆◆◆

Although George Duke planned to make this recording half R&B and half jazz, the former dominates. In fact, other than brief moments from the keyboardist/leader and short contributions by the likes of Dianne Reeves, Everette Harp, George Howard, Norman Brown and Jonathan Butler, this is essentially a highly produced R&B set (even if it rose high on *Billboard*'s contemporary jazz chart). The rating is for its danceable qualities, some catchy melodies and the high musicianship. Those listeners not enamored with Duke's vocal talents are advised to look elsewhere. —*Scott Yanow*

Dukes of Dixieland

f. 1948, db. 1974
Group / Dixieland

Trumpeter Frank Assunto (who was also a fine singer) and his brother/trombonist Fred Assunto formed the Dukes of Dixieland in 1948 and won a Horace Heidt talent contest. In 1950 they started a long engagement at the Famous Door in New Orleans. An early member of the group was clarinetist Pete Fountain, and the Assuntos' father Papa Jac joined the band in 1955 on banjo and second trombone. The group's first recordings were for Band Wagon in 1951 and Fountain appeared on their 1955 VIK date, but the Dukes really caught on with a dozen albums cut for Audio Fidelity during 1956-60. During this period, the Dukes also recorded twice with Louis Armstrong. The band hit its peak with their Columbia records of 1961-64 (featuring clarinetist Jerry Fuller), particularly an exciting set recorded at Disneyland. Their Decca and Coral dates of 1965-66, although of some interest, are a step down in quality. Both Fred (1966) and Frank (1974) died of cancer. In the late '70s a new Dukes of Dixieland was formed, but this group is somewhat corny and inferior in quality, having no real connection to the original band. —*Scott Yanow*

Satchmo and the Dukes of Dixieland / 1959 / Happy Hour ◆◆◆◆

During his latter years, many criticized Louis Armstrong for falling into set patterns and putting more emphasis on entertaining than playing. His critics have since re-evaluated much of his final output and found that there was more substance in his solos and vocals than they had assumed. That's the case on this 1959 date with his favorite New Orleans band, The Dukes of Dixieland. While there's certainly nothing new from a song standpoint, Armstrong and the group made hot, frequently dazzling, traditional jazz. The date was digitally remastered for this 1988 CD, and Armstrong's singing and playing sound even more vivid. —*Ron Wynn*

Breakin' It Up on Broadway / Aug. 29, 1961 / Columbia ◆◆◆◆

The original Dukes of Dixieland's recording career can be easily divided into three parts by record label: Audio Fidelity (1956-60), Columbia (1961-64) and Decca (1965-66). While the popular group was well recorded in each of these phases (and there were a few earlier dates that preceded their signing with Audio Fidelity), the Columbia albums (few of which have been reissued on CD yet unfortunately) are the most rewarding. During that period, the group utilized a more modern rhythm section than most Dixieland bands, including on this set pianist Gene Schroeder, bassist Jim Atlas (formerly with Jimmy Giuffre), drummer Charlie Lodice and (in the biggest surprise) guitarist Jim Hall. However, the main reason to search for these Dukes of Dixieland sets is for the front line (which includes both Fred Assunto and Jac Assunto on trombones), particularly for clarinetist Jerry Fuller and the great trumpeter Frank Assunto (who also took occasional vocals). Highlights of this particular album by the Dukes include "Runnin' Wild," "Lady Be Good," If I Were a Bell" and "I Can't Give You Anything But Love." —*Scott Yanow*

Now Hear This / Jan. 15, 1962 / Columbia ◆◆◆◆◆

One of the Dukes of Dixieland's most exciting records (but unfortunately not yet available on CD), this album has many highlights. Trumpeter Frank Assunto is heard in prime form, clarinetist Jerry Fuller was always a major asset, and the hard-swinging rhythm section includes pianist Gene Schroeder and guitarist Herb Ellis. All 11 selections are quite rewarding, particularly "When You're Smiling," "After You've Gone," "At the Jazz Band Ball," and "Honeysuckle Rose." —*Scott Yanow*

● **The Dukes of Dixieland at Disneyland** / Sep. 29, 1962 / Columbia ◆◆◆◆◆

This is not only the finest of all the Dukes of Dixieland records (the alternate title "The Best of the Dukes of Dixieland" is accurate), but one of the hottest of all Dixieland albums. The only one of the Dukes' sets thus far reissued on CD (although it was little noticed and dropped out of print again), this album features trumpeter Frank Assunto (an underrated great), trombonist Fred Assunto, the talented clarinetist Jerry Fuller, pianist Gene Schroeder, either Herb Ellis or Al Hendrickson on guitar, Jac Assunto on banjo and second trombone, bassist Bob Casey and drummer Charles Lodice. They perform fairly lengthy versions of "Original Dixieland One Step" (which has some great clarinet), "Wolverine Blues," "Royal Garden Blues," "The Saints," "Canal Street Blues" and the usual New Orleans funeral routine (with "Oh Didn't He Ramble"). Classic music. —*Scott Yanow*

Dixieland Hootnanny / Dec. 1962 / Columbia ◆◆◆

This is a most unusual record. Since 1962 was near the height of the folk music fad, the Dukes of Dixieland are heard performing 12 traditional folk songs, including such unlikely material as "My Darling Nellie Gray," "House of the Rising Sun," "Black Is the Color of My True Love's Hair" and "Wreck of the Old '97." Oddly enough, the titles were slightly altered, but the melodies are quite familiar. As usual, trumpeter Frank Assunto is the star, although guest clarinetist Edmond Hall sits in on a few of the numbers, and guitarist Herb Ellis is in the rhythm section. —*Scott Yanow*

Struttin' at the World's Fair / Feb. 17, 1964+Mar. 23, 1964 / Columbia ◆◆◆◆

The final Dukes of Dixieland Columbia album features the group in excellent form on a variety of material, some of which is unlikely. With trumpeter/vocalist Frank Assunto, trombonist Fred Assunto and clarinetist Jerry Fuller forming a very impressive front line, and pianist Gene Schroeder, banjoist Jac Assunto, bassist Red Brown and either Barrett Deems or Nick Fatool on drums, the music consistently swings in a joyful fashion. Highlights include "Colonel Bogey March," "Swingin' Sousa," "The Dukes Come Marching Home" and "Paducah Parade." Unfortunately, this album has yet to be reissued on CD. —*Scott Yanow*

Candy Dulfer

b. Sep. 19, 1969, Amsterdam, Netherlands
Alto Saxophone / Pop, Crossover Jazz, Instrumental Pop

Alto saxophonist Candy Dulfer was brought into the limelight by the artist formerly known as Prince, who introduced her to the world via his video, for "Party Man." Raised in a family heavily involved in the Dutch jazz scene, Dulfer is the daughter of Hans Dulfer, a respected jazz tenor saxophonist. Thanks to him, she listened to and studied the recordings of Sonny Rollins, Coleman Hawkins and Dexter Gordon. He also introduced her to the stage early in life. When she was 12 she began playing in a band with Rosa King, an American expatriate who lived in Holland. Her career began by playing with brass bands but soon she was fronting her own band, Funky Stuff, who were invited to back up Madonna for part of her European tour. She began leading the band at age 15, and by 1987 they were sufficiently experienced to back Madonna on parts of her European tour. Her appearances with Prince led to session work with Eurythmics guitarist/producer Dave Stewart, who gave Dulfer a credit on "Lily Was Here," which reached No. 6 in the UK and No. 1 on the Dutch radio charts in 1990. Recording sessions for her debut album were followed by more guest star dates with Van Morrison, Aretha Franklin and Pink Floyd.

Her debut, *Saxuality*, released later in 1990 for RCA Records, was very successful in Europe and the US. While it was by no means a straightahead jazz album, her funky alto sax stylings caught on with fans of contemporary jazz at several recently launched "smooth jazz" radio stations around the US. *Saxuality* was nominated for a Grammy and certified gold for sales in excess of a half-million units worldwide. Her 1991 album, *Sax-a-Go-Go*, includes "Sunday Afternoon," a song by Prince, and also teams her up with some of her musical mentors, the JB's and the Tower of Power horns. Her other influences include Sonny Rollins and David Sanborn, and while Dulfer hasn't carved the niche for herself that Sanborn has in the jazz world, she does have a great career ahead of her as she continues to synthesize classic R&B, blues, pop and jazz to in her own unique, creative ways. —*Richard Skelly*

● **Saxuality** / 1991 / Arista ✦✦✦✦
In the early '90s, Arista Records marketed Candy Dulfer in the much same way it would market a pop or rock singer and did everything it could to exploit the Dutch saxophonist's great looks. Unfortunately, the sexy publicity shots Arista sent out with her debut effort, *Saxuality*, were more impressive than the album itself—a forgettable R&B/pop/jazz recording that's smothered by excessive production. Though the R&B-ish compositions (many written by producer Unco Bed) aren't bad, the highly predictable Dulfer consistently comes across as a poor man's David Sanborn and does very little improvising. A funk-influenced version of Miles Davis' "So What" might have been worthwhile, but is destroyed by its stiff production and Dulfer's refusal to improvise. —*Alex Henderson*

Sax-a-Go-Go / 1993 / RCA ✦✦✦

Candy-a-Go-Go / 1994 / Arista Japan ✦✦✦

Big Girl / 1996 / RCA ✦✦✦

For the Love of You / Oct. 21, 1997 / N2K ✦✦✦
It is somewhat remarkable how bad this CD is. Many of the selections are dominated by loud funk rhythms and vocals that have juvenile lyrics, annoying samples, an endless supply of cliches about partying and forgettable themes. When Candy Dulfer does play her alto, she does little other than come up with poor imitations of David Sanborn. One would think when playing poppish R&B music that originality would be of some importance in maintaining a career, but thus far Dulfer's model looks are much more significant than anything she can create musically. In fact, the only reason to acquire this dud is for the 14 color pictures of Dulfer, who looks better posing next to a saxophone than she sounds trying to play it. —*Scott Yanow*

Johnny Dunn

b. Feb. 19, 1897, Memphis, TN, **d.** Aug. 20, 1937, Paris, France
Cornet / Classic Jazz
Before Louis Armstrong arrived in New York in 1924, Johnny Dunn was considered the top cornetist in the city. His staccato style, double-time effects and utilization of wah-wah mutes gave him notoriety for a time. Dunn had attended Fisk University in Nashville and had a solo act in Memphis before being discovered by W.C. Handy. He joined Handy's band in 1917 and during the next three years became known for his feature on "Sergeant Dunn's Bugle Call Blues" (which later became the basis for "Bugle Call Rag"). A pioneer with plunger mutes, Dunn's double-time breaks, with their inflexible and jerky rhythms, had a direct link to military bands. He recorded with Mamie Smith in 1920-21, leaving in the latter year to lead his own Original Jazz Hounds. From 1921-23, the cornetist recorded frequently, both with his own group and backing singer Edith Wilson. He joined Will Vodery's Plantation Orchestra in 1922, visiting Europe with the revue "Dover to Dixie" the following year. However, the Chicago musicians were much farther advanced than Dunn, and once Louis Armstrong began influencing brassmen with his swinging, legato solos for Fletcher Henderson, Dunn was instantly out of date. After visiting Europe again (this time with the "Blackbirds of 1926" show), Dunn briefly led his own big band and then in 1928 made his finest recordings, four numbers with Jelly Roll Morton and two with both James P. Johnson and Fats Waller on pianos. Strangely enough, he never recorded again, moving permanently to Europe, where he played with Noble Sissle in Paris, worked with his own group (the New Yorkers) mostly in Holland, and was largely forgotten before his early death. All of Johnny Dunn's recordings, other than his Mamie Smith sides, are on two RST CDs. —*Scott Yanow*

Johnny Dunn & Edith Wilson, Vol. 1 / Sep. 13, 1921-Sep. 29, 1922 / RST ✦✦✦✦
This CD from the Austrian RST label (the first of two) has 16 selections from the early classic blues singer Edith Wilson, one of the best vocalists on record during the 1921-22 period. Her backup is by cornetist Johnny Dunn's Original Jazz Hounds and it is particularly interesting to hear such an early version of "He May Be Your Man (But He Comes to See Me Sometimes)." Also included are the first six selections led by Dunn who was considered to be one of the best cornetists in New

York before the arrival of Louis Armstrong in 1924. Actually, his first session ("Bugle Blues" and "Birmingham Blues") sounds as if the band were recorded in a wind tunnel, and Dunn is probably not present on the second. Overall, the second CD is preferable to the first but the "complete" programming is quite definitive. —*Scott Yanow*

● **Johnny Dunn, Vol. 2** / Dec. 1922-Mar. 26, 1928 / RST ✦✦✦✦
Johnny Dunn, whose staccato phrasing, use of the wah-wah mute and fondness for bugle calls were part of a distinctive if dated style in the early '20s, is heard on his finest recordings on this Austrian RST CD, the second of two reissues. Edith Wilson has vocals on the first two numbers, and there are eight pieces from Johnny Dunn's Original Jazz Hounds (including early renditions of "Sugar Blues" and "Jazzin' Babies Blues"), a pair of atmospheric duets with pianist Leroy Tibbs and four titles by the Plantation Orchestra from 1926. Best are four selections with Jelly Roll Morton in 1928 and Dunn's final two recordings (the classic "What's the Use of Being Alone?" and "Original Bugle Blues"), which feature both James P. Johnson and Fats Waller romping on piano. Recommended for vintage jazz collectors. —*Scott Yanow*

Cornell Dupree

b. Dec. 1942, Fort Worth, TX
Guitar / Soul-Jazz, Groove, Blues
Long a top R&B session player, Cornell Dupree led excellent jazz-oriented sets for Amazing and Kokopelli in the early '90s, showing that he was capable of also playing swinging jazz. Dupree was with King Curtis in 1962 before becoming a studio musician. He has recorded with artists like Harry Belafonte, Joe Cocker, Michael Bolton, Lou Rawls, Roberta Flack, Robert Palmer, Lena Horne, and Mariah Carey—over 2500 albums as a sideman! He toured with Aretha Franklin (1967-76) and a variety of top pop and R&B acts, and in the early '70s worked with the group Stuff. Dupree's blues-oriented guitar style continues to be in demand. —*Michael Erlewine & Scott Yanow*

Shadow Dancing / Aug. 14-Aug. 25, 1978 / Versatile ✦✦✦
Dupree on guitar with Hank Crawford on alto sax and organist Jimmy Smith playing the electric piano. Includes a rendition of "The Creeper." —*Michael Erlewine*

Can't Get Through / Jun. 1991 / Amazing ✦✦✦✦
Cornell Dupree's classic guitar sound has been pervasive in popular music for the past four decades, having graced more than 2,500 albums by a dazzling array of artists. His work with the superstar session band Stuff was highly praised. More recently, he played on *Return to the Wide Open Spaces* with saxophonist James Clay and others, drawing uniformly rave reviews. *Can't Get Through*, recorded in New York City last year, contains nine tracks, most of them instrumental, done with his regular working band in a soul-jazz/funk vein. Titles include "Double Clutch," "Sweet Thing," and "Duck Soup." —*Roundup Newsletter*

Child's Play / May 26, 1993 / Amazing ✦✦✦

● **Bop 'n' Blues** / Nov. 15, 1994-Feb. 13, 1995 / Kokopelli ✦✦✦✦
Guitarist Cornell Dupree has long been famous for his blues and R&B solos, so even he was surprised (and a bit apprehensive) when label-head Herbie Mann suggested he record a variety of bop-oriented standards. As it turned out, several of the tunes were blues anyway (such as "Bags' Groove," "Now's the Time" and "Walkin'") and Dupree was free to adapt the other songs to his own style. "Freedom Jazz Dance" became a funky vamp while "My Little Suede Shoes" was drastically slowed down and stretched out. With backing from a versatile rhythm section and occasional contributions from altoist Bobby Watson, trumpeter Terell Stafford and baritonist Ronnie Cuber, Dupree sounds perfectly at home throughout this fine CD, even on "Manteca" and "'Round Midnight." —*Scott Yanow*

Eddie Duran (Edward Lozano Duran)

b. Sep. 6, 1925, San Francisco, CA
Guitar / Cool
Eddie Duran had been long identified with the San Francisco jazz scene, backing many local and visiting stars with his tasty bop and classical-inspired lead and rhythm guitar work. He started on piano at age seven, but switched to guitar at 12, which he began teaching to himself after about seven months of lessons. He began playing professionally at 15, and from the mid-'40s played with such visiting musicians as Stan Getz, Charlie Parker, George Shearing, Red Norvo and Earl Hines. He would be best known, however, for his work on Fantasy recordings by Bay Area musicians like childhood friend Vince Guaraldi, with whom he played on trio sessions in 1956, a Cal Tjader/Getz sextet in 1958, and again in a Latin-tinged quintet and sextet in 1963-64. Duran led his own trio from 1960 to 1967, became a member of Benny Goodman's orchestras from 1976 to 1981, and made recordings with Tania Maria in 1980-82. Finally, in the late 1980s, Duran moved to New York City and organized a quartet there. Interestingly, Duran was also a licensed barber at one time. —*Richard S. Ginell*

Jazz Guitarist / 1957 / Fantasy ✦✦✦✦

The San Francisco-based Eddie Duran has only led two recording sessions to date, and this was his first. Teamed up with the obscure Howard Dundune (on clarinet and tenor), bassist Dean Reilly and drummer Johnny Markham, Duran performs a likable brand of melodic cool jazz, swinging hard in spots but also emphasizing his pretty tone and thoughtful ideas. He takes "My Shining Hour" as an unaccompanied guitar solo, and other highlights include "Soon," Neal Hefti's "Why Not" and "It Could Happen to You." —*Scott Yanow*

● **Ginza** / Mar. 1979 / Concord Jazz ✦✦✦✦✦

Although a steady fixture in the San Francisco jazz scene, guitarist Eddie Duran has rarely recorded through the decades, and his second set as a leader follows his first by 22 years. Bassist Dean Reilly (who was on the first outing) and drummer Benny Barth complete the tasteful trio, which performs a pair of Billy Strayhorn ballads, a Latin-jazz original by Duran, and a variety of swinging if obscure material (highlighted by a hot rendition of "Breakfast Feud"). Well worth picking up by fans of the jazz guitar. —*Scott Yanow*

Eddie Durham

b. Aug. 19, 1906, San Marcos, TX, **d.** Mar. 6, 1987, New York, NY
Guitar, Trombone, Arranger / Swing

Eddie Durham, a somewhat forgotten name in jazz history, was the first important jazz soloist to be featured on electric guitar (in 1938 with the Kansas City Five), predating Charlie Christian by a year. He also played trombone throughout most of his career and was significant as a swing-era arranger too. He started playing guitar and trombone with six siblings in the Durham Brothers band. Durham toured in territory bands in the Midwest, was with Walter Page's Blue Devils and worked with Bennie Moten (1929-33) with whom he made his recording debut. After moving to New York in 1934, Durham worked as an arranger with Willie Bryant and then played with Jimmie Lunceford (1935-37) and Count Basie (1937-38). He contributed arrangements to Artie Shaw and Glenn Miller, in 1940 led a short-lived big band and during 1941-43 was the musical director for the International Sweethearts of Rhythm. Durham later led an otherwise all-female group and freelanced mostly as an arranger. In 1969 he returned to active playing with Buddy Tate and in later years played with the Countsmen (with whom he recorded) and the Harlem Blues and Jazz Band. Among Durham's most famous arrangements through the years were "Moten Swing" for Bennie Moten, Jimmy Lunceford's "Lunceford Special," several notable charts for Count Basie ("Topsy," "Swinging the Blues" and "Jumpin' at the Woodside") and Glenn Miller's "In the Mood." —*Scott Yanow*

Dutch Swing College Band

f. 1945
Group / Dixieland

Formed in May 1945 by clarinetist Peter Schilperoort, the Dutch Swing College Band has long been considered one of Europe's top Dixieland and swing bands. In addition to many albums on their own, the group welcomed such guests as Sidney Bechet (1951), Hot Lips Page, Albert Nicholas, Jimmy Witherspoon, Billy Butterfield, Joe Venuti and Teddy Wilson, recording with all but Page and Nicholas. The band has continued to tour despite the death of Schilperoort in 1990, although its peak years were the 1970s. —*Scott Yanow*

Swinging Studio Sessions / Dec. 24, 1959-Jun. 11, 1969 / Philips ✦✦✦✦

Although the Dutch Swing College Band made many recordings during its long existence, not that many have been made available domestically. This fine CD gives listeners highlights from seven of the popular Dixieland group's sessions. Though the music spans a decade, the band's sound was unchanged during the era. The pianoless sextet/septet (with leader Peter Schilperoort usually on baritone) is heard in fine form on such rousing numbers as "At the Jazz Band Ball," "Fidgety Feet," "Tiger Rag," "Cornet Chop Suey" and "Dippermouth Blues." —*Scott Yanow*

The Dutch Swing College Band Meets Teddy Wilson / Feb. 1, 1964-Oct. 12, 1973 / Timeless ✦✦✦✦

Throughout its four decades of activity, the Dutch Swing College Band (a Dixieland sextet/septet) often featured guest soloists. On this Timeless album, the veteran swing pianist Teddy Wilson sits in on six selections from the 1972-73 period, including "Riverboat Shuffle," "Rhythm King" and "China Boy"; Wilson easily fits right in with the spirited group. The remaining five selections are from 1964-67 and are of the same high quality. In addition to the leader Peter Schilperoort (heard on baritone, tenor and clarinet), the album features Bert De Kort or Ray Kaart on trumpet, trombonist Dick Kaart and clarinetist Bob Kaper. This is enjoyable music that is recommended to pre-bop jazz collectors. —*Scott Yanow*

Dutch Swing College Band Meets Joe Venuti / Nov. 15, 1971+Jan. 25, 1972 / Everest ✦✦✦

Violinist Joe Venuti is actually only on half of this LP, playing three songs from his

earlier days, two standards and a blues with the Dutch septet. The remaining five selections are between Dixieland and swing and feature fine playing by leader Peter Schilperoort and Bob Kaper on reeds, cornetist Bert De Kort and trombonist Dick Kaart. Last available as a budget LP from Everest. —*Scott Yanow*

Live 1974 / 1974 / Challenge ✦✦✦

Digital Dixie / Jul. 12, 1981 / Philips ✦✦✦✦✦

Digital Dutch / Jul. 18, 1982 / Philips ✦✦✦✦

Digital Anniversary / Jul. 12, 1985 / Philips ✦✦✦✦

Johnny Dyani

b. Nov. 30, 1945, East London, South Africa, **d.** July 11, 1986, Berlin, Germany
Bass / Avant-Garde

One of the top South African expatriates, Johnny Dyani had a lyrical style and an authoritative tone on bass. He was with Chris McGregor's Blue Notes during 1962-65, leaving South Africa with them. He settled in London for five years, working with the top local players, and recorded in South America with Steve Lacy and Enrico Rava in 1968. Dyani was also with the Spontaneous Music Ensemble (1969). In the early '70s he moved to Denmark where he worked with John Tchicai, Don Cherry, Abdullah Ibrahim, David Murray and Joseph Jarman. Dyani can be heard on many Steeple Chase recordings. —*Scott Yanow*

Witchdoctor's Son / Mar. 15, 1978 / Steeple Chase ✦✦✦

● **Song for Biko** / Jul. 18, 1978 / Steeple Chase ✦✦✦✦✦

Bassist Johnny Dyani had a large tone and a relaxed yet authoritative style. On this classic Steeple Chase release he teams up with two other South African expatriates (altoist Dudu Pukwana and drummer Makay Ntshoko) plus cornetist Don Cherry for music that is haunting, emotional, somewhat adventurous, yet also melodic. While "Song for Biko" is the most memorable piece, all five of Dyani's originals (including the 16 -minute "Jo'burg-New York") are special. The music combines together Dyani's South African folk heritage with Ornette Coleman's free bop and elements of the jazz avant-garde. Highly recommended. —*Scott Yanow*

African Bass / Nov. 14, 1979 / Red ✦✦✦

Mbizo / Feb. 24, 1981 / Steeple Chase ✦✦✦

Grandmother's Teaching / Mar. 1983 / JAM ✦✦✦

Afrika / Oct. 1, 1983 / Steeple Chase ✦✦✦✦✦

The South African bassist/pianist/composer with septet. Well-respected as a musician worldwide. A unique amalgam of styles. —*Michael G. Nastos*

Born under the Heat / Nov. 18, 1983 / Dragon ✦✦✦

Angolian Cry / Jul. 23, 1985 / Steeple Chase ✦✦✦✦

Bassist Johnny Dyani's final recording as a leader (he died a year later at the age of 40) matches his warm sound with trumpeter Harry Beckett, John Tchicai (doubling on tenor and bass clarinet) and drummer Billy Hart on six of his melodic yet explorative originals. Dyani's atmospheric and colorful music was long underrated but, like that of Abdullah Ibrahim (a fellow expatriate from South Africa), Johnny Dyani was a major composer whose flights were tempered by a strong emphasis on fresh melodies. Stimulating music. —*Scott Yanow*

Ann Dyer

Vocals / Avant-Garde

An impressive chance-taking singer, Ann Dyer was one of the hits of the 1994 Monterey Jazz Festival, stretching out standards and really pouring a lot of emotion into Ornette Coleman's "Lonely Woman." She graduated from Mills College in 1979 with a modern dance degree and had plans to be a dancer but her singing gained better reviews. Dyer recorded her debut for the Mr. Brown label in 1993. —*Scott Yanow*

● **Ann Dyer & The No Good Time Fairies** / Aug. 30, 1993-Sep. 1, 1993 / Mr. Brown ✦✦✦✦✦

One of the most exciting new singers of the mid-'90s, Ann Dyer is a true improviser who is not afraid to really cut loose and show her emotions. Blessed with a wide range and a very appealing voice, Dyer takes all kinds of wild chances throughout her debut. Among the highlights are a spaced-out "I'll Remember April," an intense version of Ornette Coleman's "Lonely Woman," a nutty rendition of Wayne Shorter's "Pinnochio" and a slightly demented yet swinging interpretation of Gigi Gryce's "Social Call." The singer is greatly assisted by the rockish but versatile guitar of Jeff Buenz, bassist John Shifflett, drummer Jason Lewis and Hafez Modirzadeh on tenor and bass clarinet. Ann Dyer has the same adventurous spirit as the most creative jazz musicians, making this a highly recommended disc. —*Scott Yano*

Dominique Eade

b. 1958, London, England
Vocals / Post-Bop
One of the top up-and-coming jazz singers of the late '90s, Dominique Eade had quite a bit of experience before she ever recorded. The daughter of an American Air Force officer, she spent much of her childhood moving around, living in different places in Europe. Eade had piano lessons as a child and decided that she was going to be a singer when she was in the second grade; she also played guitar as a teenager while living mostly in Germany. An English major at Vassar, Eade for a time sang in a band called Naima that also included Joe McPhee. She soon transferred to Berklee College and also attended the New England Conservatory of Music; Ran Blake was one of her more significant teachers. She has taught at the New England Conservatory since 1984 while working as a singer. Dominique Eade, who is also a talented composer, recorded two CDs for Accurate (1991 and 1994) that gained some attention, and in 1997 recorded her debut for RCA, a tribute to June Christy and Chris Connor. —*Scott Yanow*

The Ruby and the Pearl / Sep. 8, 1992 / Accurate ♦♦♦

My Resistance is Low / Jan. 11, 1994-Jan. 12, 1994 / Accurate ♦♦♦♦

● **When the Wind Was Cool** / Mar. 17, 1997-Mar. 21, 1997 / RCA ♦♦♦♦
Dominique Eade interprets 13 songs from the 1950s on this CD, most of which had been recorded previously by Chris Connor and June Christy. Eade's voice captures the essence of those cool-toned singers, yet she also sounds fairly distinctive. The instrumentation varies from cut to cut with such players as tenor saxophonist Benny Golson, bass clarinetist Bruce Williamson, vibraphonist Steve Nelson, pianist Fred Hersch, guitarist Peter Leitch and bassist James Genus (featured on "Tea for Two" in a duet with Eade), among others, making strong contributions. Among the highlights are Eade's timeless yet fresh renditions of "Moonray," "Something Cool," "All About Ronnie," "The Wind" and "Lullaby of Birdland"; the appealing singer herself wrote half of the arrangements. Recommended. —*Scott Yanow*

Allen Eager

b. Jan. 10, 1927, New York, NY
Tenor Saxophone / Bop, Cool
At one point in the early '50s, Allen Eager sounded nearly identical to Stan Getz, Zoot Sims, Al Cohn and Brew Moore; in fact, all five tenors (from the Lester Young-influenced "Four Brothers" school) recorded together. But of the five, Eager has had the least impressive career, lacking the desire to really work on jazz full-time. He had played during World War II as a teenager with the bands of Bobby Sherwood, Sonny Dunham, Shorty Sherock, Hal McIntyre, Woody Herman (1943-44), Tommy Dorsey and Johnny Bothwell. By 1945 he was appearing regularly on 52nd Street and during 1946-48 he recorded as a leader. Eager did well with Tadd Dameron's band in 1948 but by the early '50s he seemed to be losing interest in jazz. He recorded with Gerry Mulligan (1951), Terry Gibbs (1952), played with Buddy Rich and led his own band during 1953-55. After living in Paris during 1956-57 and recording with Mulligan in 1957, he largely dropped out of music. Eager did make a comeback album for Uptown in 1982 but has been little-heard of since, apparently much more interested in racing cars! —*Scott Yanow*

Renaissance / Mar. 25, 1982 / Uptown ♦♦♦
Allen Eager, a talented cool-toned tenor saxophonist who was at his prime in the late '40s, largely dropped out of music after 1957. Twenty-five years later he returned for this recording before disappearing again. Eager sounds a bit rusty on the quartet set with pianist Hod O'Brien, bassist Teddy Kotick and drummer Jimmy Wormworth but also has some fiery moments and shows that he was familiar with later musical developments (including John Coltrane whose "Equinox" he plays). Performing jazz standards plus his own "Room Service Blues," Eager displays some fire in spots on this straightahead date and makes one wish that he had decided to return to jazz fulltime. —*Scott Yanow*

Jon Eardley

b. Sep. 30, 1928, Altoona, PA, **d.** Apr. 4, 1997, France
Trumpet / Bop, Cool
Somewhat forgotten in the US, Jon Eardley was long active in Europe. He began playing trumpet when he was 11. After working in an Air Force band (1946-49), he played locally (1950-53) and then worked in New York with Phil Woods (1954). Eardley gained some visibility playing on and off with Gerry Mulligan's quartet and sextet (1954-57) and is still best-known for that association today. After working back in Pennsylvania for several years, the cool-toned bopper moved to Belgium in 1963 and in 1969 relocated to Germany to play in a radio orchestra. Eardley can be heard at his best on three Spotlite albums, all from 1977. —*Scott Yanow*

● **From Hollywood to New York** / Dec. 25, 1954+Mar. 14, 1955 / Original Jazz Classics ♦♦♦♦♦
Trumpeter Jon Eardley's first two sessions as a leader (he would only lead two others during the next 20 years) are combined on this reissue CD. A fine boppish player who mostly stuck to the middle register of his horn, Eardley would soon be joining Gerry Mulligan's group. He is heard on four selections heading a quartet with pianist Pete Jolly (who was just starting his career), bassist Red Mitchell and drummer Larry Bunker, and on four other numbers with tenor saxophonist J.R. Monterose, pianist George Syran, bassist Teddy Kotick and drummer Nick Stabulas. The music (five originals and three standards) is essentially cool-toned bop and was quite modern for the period. —*Scott Yanow*

The Jon Eardley Seven / Jan. 13, 1956 / Original Jazz Classics ♦♦♦♦
The soft-toned trumpeter Jon Eardley (who was playing with Gerry Mulligan's Sextet at the time) holds his own with tenor saxophonist Zoot Sims and altoist Phil Woods on this excellent straightahead septet set; also in the group are trombonist Milt Gold, pianist George Syran, bassist Teddy Kotick and drummer Nick Stabulas. The CD reissue (Eardley's third and final American session as a leader) features the excellent group on three of the trumpeter's originals, one apiece by Syran and Woods plus the standard "There's No You." —*Scott Yanow*

Namely Me / Aug. 12, 1977-Aug. 13, 1977 / Spotlite ♦♦♦♦
Although trumpeter Jon Eardley had been active in Europe since moving abroad in 1963, this album (other than two dates for obscure Dutch labels during 1969-70) was Eardley's first session as a leader since 1956. He contributed six of the seven selections (all but the standard "Namely Me") and shows throughout the date that his cool sound and boppish style were largely unchanged from the early days. Eardley teams up with altoist Pete King, pianist John Taylor, bassist Ron Mathewson and drummer Mickey Roker on some fine straightahead music. —*Scott Yanow*

Stablemates / Sep. 16, 1977 / Spotlite ♦♦♦
Veteran trumpeter Jon Eardley and the early bop pianist Al Haig teamed up for the first time on this Spotlite session. Performing with a quintet also including tenor saxophonist Art Themen, bassist Daryl Runswick and drummer Alan Ganley, Eardley and Haig are heard in creative form on six jazz standards including "'Round Midnight," "Tangerine" and "Love Walked In." A historic and rewarding one-time encounter. —*Scott Yanow*

Charles Earland

b. May 24, 1941, Philadelphia, PA
Organ, Synthesizer / Soul Jazz, Hard Bop, Groove
Charles Earland came into his own at the tail end of the great 1960s wave of soul-jazz organists, gaining a large following and much airplay with a series of albums for the Prestige label. While heavily indebted to Jimmy Smith and Jimmy McGriff, Earland comes armed with his own swinging, technically agile, light-textured sound on the keyboard and one of the best walking-bass pedal techniques in the business. Though not an innovative player in his field, Earland can burn with the best of them when he is on. Earland actually started his musical experiences surreptitiously on his father's alto sax as a kid, and when he was in high school, he played baritone in a band that also featured fellow Philadelphians Pat Martino on guitar, Lew Tabackin on tenor, and yes, Frankie Avalon on trumpet. After playing in the Temple University band, he toured as a tenor player with McGriff for three

years, became infatuated with McGriff's organ playing, and started learning the Hammond B-3 at intermission breaks. When McGriff let him go, Earland switched to the organ permanently, forming a trio with Martino and drummer Bobby Durham. He made his first recordings for Choice in 1966, then joined Lou Donaldson for two years (1968-69) and two albums before being signed as a solo artist to Prestige. Earland's first album for Prestige, *Black Talk!*, became a best-selling classic of the soul-jazz genre; a surprisingly effective cover of the Spiral Starecase's pop-rock hit "More Today Than Yesterday" from that LP received saturation airplay on jazz radio in 1969. He recorded eight more albums for Prestige, one of which featured a young unknown Philadelphian named Grover Washington, Jr., then switched to Muse before landing contracts with Mercury and Columbia. By this time, the organ trio genre had gone into eclipse, and in the spirit of the times, Earland acquired some synthesizers and converted to pop/disco in collaboration with his wife, singer-songwriter Sheryl Kendrick. Kendrick's death from sickle-cell anemia in 1985 left Earland desolate, and he stopped playing for awhile, but a gig at the Chickrick House on Chicago's South Side in the late '80s brought him out of his grief and back to the Hammond B-3. Two excellent albums in the old soul-jazz groove for Milestone followed, and the '90s found him returning to the Muse label. —*Richard S. Ginell*

★ **Black Talk** / Dec. 15, 1969 / Original Jazz Classics ✦✦✦✦✦

This CD reissue of a Prestige date is one of the few successful examples of jazz musicians from the late '60s taking a few rock and pop songs and turning them into creative jazz. Organist Charles Earland and his sextet, which includes trumpeter Virgil Jones, Houston Person on tenor and guitarist Melvin Sparks, perform a variation of "Eleanor Rigby" titled "Black Talk," two originals, a surprisingly effective rendition of "Aquarius" and a classic rendition of "More Today Than Yesterday." Fans of organ combos are advised to pick up this interesting set. —*Scott Yanow*

Soul Crib / 1969 / Choice ✦✦✦

Earland with George Coleman on tenor sax, Jimmy Ponder on guitar, and Walter Perkins on drums. —*Michael Erlewine*

Black Drops / Jun. 1, 1970 / Prestige ✦✦✦

Early soul-jazz, occasional R&B and pop cuts from organist Charles Earland, just cutting his third album as a leader at that time. His organ solos were sometimes churning and impressive, but at other times bogged down in clichés and repetitive phrases. But the potential Earland showed on most cuts has since materialized. —*Ron Wynn*

Living Black / Sep. 17, 1970 / Prestige ✦✦✦✦✦

Although a few of his recordings on the obscure Rare Bird and Choice labels precede them, organist Charles Earland came to his original fame with his Prestige albums. This is a lesser-known effort, but no less worthy than the more famous dates. Recorded live at a Newark club, this obscure LP (not yet reissued on CD) is most valuable for giving listeners some of Grover Washington, Jr.'s earliest solos; he had been called in from Philadelphia when Earland's regular tenor could not make the date. Completing the group are trumpeter Gary Chandler, guitarist Maynard Parker, drummer Jesse Kilpatrick and Buddy Caldwell on conga. The band performs two basic Earland pieces ("Key Club Cookout" and "Westbound No. 9"), plus "Milestones" and a fourteen-and-a-half-minute "Killer Joe," with soul and swing on this near-classic set. —*Scott Yanow*

Charles 3 / Feb. 16, 1972+Feb. 17, 1972 / Prestige ✦✦✦

Sparkling vocals by Joe Lee Wilson. —*Ron Wynn*

Leaving This Planet / Dec. 11, 1973-Dec. 13, 1973 / Prestige ✦✦✦✦✦

A definite departure from the type of earthy, groove-oriented soul-jazz he usually embraced, *Leaving This Planet* is perhaps Charles Earland's most ambitous album—not necessarily his best, but certainly his most surprising. Responding to the fusion revolution, Earland plays keyboards and various synthesizers in addition to his usual Hammond B-3 organ and thrives in a very electric setting. The album (reissued on a 79-minute CD in 1993) isn't fusion in the same sense as Miles Davis, Larry Coryell or Weather Report—rather, it incorporates funk and rock elements in a manner not unlike the early-'70s experiments of tenor saxophonist Joe Henderson and trumpeter Freddie Hubbard. And in fact, those greats (as well as trumpeter Eddie Henderson) are among the superb soloists featured. Whether the Philadelphian is embracing Hub's "Red Clay" or Henderson's "Recorda-Me" or fine compositions of his own (which range from the congenial, pleasant "Brown Eyes" to the abstract "Warp Factor 8"), he leaves no doubt just how much he's enjoying this surprising change of pace. —*Alex Henderson*

Smokin' / 1977 / Muse ✦✦✦

Fine mid-'70s sextet set featuring Earland's customary soul-jazz, blues, and funk, with uptempo and ballad originals. Tenor saxophonists David Schnitter and George Coleman excel, as does guitarist Jimmy Ponder. —*Ron Wynn*

Pleasant Afternoon / Apr. 19, 1978 / Muse ✦✦✦

With Houston Person on tenor sax, Bill Hardman on trumpet, and Melvin Sparks on guitar. It was recorded at Englewood Cliffs, NJ. —*AMG*

Infant Eyes / 1978 / Muse ✦✦✦

Coming to You Live / 1979 / Columbia ✦✦

In the Pocket / 1982 / Muse ✦✦✦

The final in a long string of Muse albums stretching back to 1977, this is a fairly typical Charles Earland set. The organist, who is joined by tenorman Houston Person, guitarist Melvin Sparks and drummer Idris Muhammad, performs five group originals, and the music swings and grooves predictably but with spirit. —*Scott Yanow*

Front Burner / Jun. 27, 1988-Jun. 28, 1988 / Milestone ✦✦✦✦

Charles Earland is among the most consistent of organists, with nearly every one of his recordings on that instrument (as opposed to his interlude on synthesizers) being easily recommended to soul-jazz and hard bop collectors. For this CD, Earland heads a sextet also including trumpeter Virgil Jones (long an underrated player), Bill Easley on tenor, guitarist Bobby Broom, drummer Buddy Williams and occasionally Frank Colon on conga. Other than a throwaway version of the theme from *Moonlighting*, the mostly basic music on this set is rewarding, with Earland infusing the tunes with plenty of grease and funk. —*Scott Yanow*

Third Degree Burn / May 15, 1989-May 16, 1989 / Milestone ✦✦✦✦

This excellent CD features organist Charles Earland, guitarist Bobby Broom, drummer Buddy Williams and percussionist Ralph Dorsey being joined by trumpeter Lew Soloff and either Grover Washington (on two songs) or David Newman (appearing on the other four) on tenor or soprano. The material may be unfamiliar (other than a Michael Jackson song), but the music is prime soul-jazz, with Earland's cooking organ keeping the proceedings quite heated. One of Charles Earland's best recordings of the 1980s. —*Scott Yanow*

Whip Appeal / May 23, 1990 / Muse ✦✦✦✦✦

A jazz version of Babyface's "Whip Appeal?" It's hard to believe, but then Charles Earland has always had an impressive ability to recontextualize pop and R&B songs that seem most unlikely vehicles for jazz improvisation. On this fine CD, which marked the beginning of his association with Muse Records, Earland transforms that "urban contemporary" number into hard-swingin' soul-jazz, successfully revisits the Spiral Staircase's "More Today Than Yesterday" and adds a lot of grit and spice to something not exactly known for those things: Kenny G's "Songbird." The latter does have a pretty melody, and it becomes quite soulful in the imaginative hands of Earland—whose excellent support includes fellow Philadelphian Johnny Coles (fluegelhorn) and longtime ally Houston Person (tenor sax). —*Alex Henderson*

Unforgettable / Dec. 6, 1991 / Muse ✦✦✦✦

Charles Earland is definitely a survivor. The Hammond hero had lost his first wife to cancer when he made a triumphant return to soul-jazz in the late '80s, and he had recovered from a major heart attack when he recorded the appropriately titled *Unforgettable*. Earland was in the Intensive Care Unit in August 1991, and by December 1991, was back in the studio to record this superb and varied CD. The Philadelphian stressed that he was lucky to be alive, and he celebrates his survival with imaginative interpretations of everything from Joe Henderson's "The Kicker" to Nat King Cole's "Unforgettable" (which he takes at a medium speed instead of its usual ballad tempo) to Santana's "Europa." Earland has consistently demonstrated that commercial appeal and accessibility can go hand-in-hand with musical integrity, and *Unforgettable* is one of many fine examples. —*Alex Henderson*

I Ain't Jivin', I'm Jammin' / Dec. 11, 1992 / Muse ✦✦✦

The easygoing and the laidback dominate *I Ain't Jivin', I'm Jammin',* an album that isn't quite in a class with *Black Talk!, Whip Appeal* or *Unforgettable,* but is nonetheless a welcome addition to Charles Earland's catalogue. The improviser swings hard and passionately on Wayne Shorter's "Tell It Like It Is," but his mellow side wins out on such congenial, groove-oriented jazz/R&B fare as pianist Neal Creque's "Cease the Bombing" and the originals "Sweety Pie," "World of Competition" and "Thinking of You." Even at his most relaxed, though, Earland's music is undeniably gritty. Among the noteworthy soloists employed this time are trombonist Clifford Adams, guitarist Oliver Nevels and the promising young tenor & soprano saxman Eric Alexander. —*Alex Henderson*

Ready 'n' Able / Jan. 1, 1995 / Muse ✦✦✦✦

Blowing the Blues Away / 1997 / High Note ✦✦✦✦✦

Bill Easley

Tenor Saxophone, Clarinet, Flute, Alto Saxophone / Hard Bop
An extremely versatile and gifted reed player, Bill Easley's displayed a polished, forceful sound on alto, tenor and baritone saxophones, flute and clarinet. He

attended Memphis State University during the '60s, and later worked with Isaac Hayes and did sessions at Stax. Easley moved back to New York, and has recorded sessions for Sunnyside and Milestone. He's played with Sir Roland Hanna, James Williams, Bill Mobley, Mulgrew Miller, Grady Tate, George Caldwell, Victor Gaskin and Billy Higgins among others. His sessions are available on CD. —*Ron Wynn*

● **Wind Inventions** / Sep. 1, 1986-Sep. 2, 1986 / Sunnyside ◆◆◆◆◆
Premier clarinetist in a neo-contemporary setting. Very attractive music. —*Michael G. Nastos*

First Call / Oct. 22, 1990-Oct. 29, 1990 / Milestone ◆◆◆
Blues and bop from versatile saxophonist. Includes notable appearances by old and new Memphis jazz stars from George Caldwell to Bill Mobley. —*Ron Wynn*

Easley Said / 1997 / Evidence ◆◆◆◆

Eastern Rebellion

f. 1974
Group / Hard Bop, Post-Bop
First formed in 1974 and continuing on an irregular basis ever since, Eastern Rebellion is a cooperative group with pianist Cedar Walton the first among equals. The band's original lineup was Walton, bassist Sam Jones, drummer Billy Higgins and tenor saxophonist Clifford Jordan. By 1975 and their first official recording, George Coleman was on tenor. In future years, trombonist Curtis Fuller would sometimes make the band a quintet; David Williams became the bassist and Bob Berg (succeeded in the 1990s by Ralph Moore) took over the tenor spot; trumpeter Alfredo "Chocolate" Armenteros sat in on a 1983 recording. Eastern Rebellion has recorded for Timeless and (in 1990) Music Masters. Their debut recording from 1975 is definitive and has the classic version of Walton's "Bolivia." —*Scott Yanow*

Eastern Rebellion, Vol. 1 / Dec. 10, 1975 / Timeless ◆◆◆◆◆
This CD reissue brings back a classic set featuring four giants of the modern mainstream: pianist/leader Cedar Walton, tenor saxophonist George Coleman, bassist Sam Jones and drummer Billy Higgins. All five performances are noteworthy, particularly a definitive version of Walton's most famous composition "Bolivia," Coleman's tricky "5/4 Thing" and Jones' boppish "Bittersweet." The veteran musicians all sound quite inspired on this advanced straightahead set. A gem. —*Scott Yanow*

Eastern Rebellion, Vol. 4 / May 25, 1983 / Timeless ◆◆◆
The fourth Cedar Walton release under the name "Eastern Rebellion" is not quite on the same level as his previous ones. Veteran trumpeter Alfredo "Chocolate" Armenteros (who does his best) sounds a bit past his prime. There are some good spots for trombonist Curtis Fuller and tenor saxophonist Bob Berg, while pianist Walton is in his usual consistent form and works well with bassist David Williams and drummer Billy Higgins. The sextet performs four standards and a pair of Walton originals, but not much magic occurs during this workmanlike performance. —*Scott Yanow*

Cedar's Blues / Mar. 1985 / Red ◆◆◆◆
Although the Eastern Rebellion name is not used on this release, the personnel of the quintet (pianist Cedar Walton, tenor saxophonist Bob Berg, trombonist Curtis Fuller, bassist David Williams and drummer Billy Higgins) is the same as the mid-'80s version of that hard bop group. Their live set (recorded in Bologna, Italy) features the band performing four Walton originals (including "Cedar's Blues" and "Ugestu") plus "Over the Rainbow." The results may not be unique, but the solos of Walton, Berg and Fuller are consistently satisfying, making this date easily recommended to hard bop collectors. —*Scott Yanow*

Mosaic / Dec. 14, 1990+Dec. 16, 1990 / Music Masters ◆◆◆◆

Simple Pleasure / Jun. 6, 1992-Jun. 7, 1992 / Music Masters ◆◆◆◆

● **Just One of Those Nights: At the Village Vanguard** / 1994 / Music Masters ◆◆◆◆

Eastern Rebellion / Dec. 20, 1975 / Muse ◆◆◆◆◆

Madeline Eastman

b. San Francisco, CA
Vocals / Bop, Standards
A fine singer who takes chances during her solos, Madeline Eastman recorded three excellent albums for the Madkat label during 1990-94. She has been a fixture in the San Francisco area since the late '70s. —*Scott Yanow*

Point of Departure / 1990 / Madkat ◆◆◆◆
Jazz vocalist Madeline Eastman's debut is quite impressive. With strong assistance from trumpeter Tom Harrell, pianist Mike Wofford (Paul Potyen fills in on one song), bassist Rufus Reid and drummer Vince Lateano, Eastman performs a wide-ranging set. Highlights include such unlikely singing material as "Wild Is the Wind," a minor-toned "You Are My Sunshine" (inspired by Mose Allison's version), Joe Henderson's "Inner Urge," and Bobby Hutcherson's "Little B's Poem" along with

"Little Boat," "Nobody Else but Me" and "I Only Have Eyes for You." Lots of chances are taken on this enjoyable CD, and Madeline Eastman shows that she has a flexible enough voice to handle all of the creative challenges. Highly recommended. —*Scott Yanow*

● **Mad About Madeline!** / Jan. 1991 / Madkat ◆◆◆◆◆
Madeline Eastman's second recording would be recommended if only for the "backup" group (altoist Phil Woods, pianist Cedar Walton, bassist Tony Dumas and Vince Lateano plus a guest vocal by Mark Murphy on Bob Dorough's "You're the Dangerous Type"), but even if the musicians were anonymous, this set would be worth checking out. Madeline Eastman is a creative singer with an appealing voice. Most of the tunes are standards but they also include such offbeat choices as "Freedom Jazz Dance," "Four" and "Never Never Land." Other highlights include renditions of "Cheek to Cheek," "Turn Out the Stars" and "All of You." —*Scott Yanow*

Art Attack / Jun. 1994 / Madkat ◆◆◆
Singer Madeline Eastman's third release for the Madkat label shoots out in a lot of different directions, some more successful than others. Eastman is at her best on explorative workouts (such as a wordless version of "Nefertiti" in which she is joined by The Turtle Island String Quartet), uptempo pieces where she can scat and swing and on sensuous ballads such as "The Thrill Is Gone." In contrast, her treatment of "Gypsy in My Soul" comes across as overly pushy, the lyrics of Blossom Dearie's "I Like You, You're Nice/I Like You" are not too inspired, and Eastman's decision to sing in Portuguese (as heard on Ivan Lins' "Sonhos") is a mistake. An energetic version of Thelonious Monk's "Evidence" and a hard-swinging "My Heart Stood Still" are much better. The supporting cast includes a trio with pianist Kenny Barron and drummer Tony Williams on half of the program; Bay Area musicians were enlisted for most of the other tracks. To Madeline Eastman's credit, she consistently stretches herself and is not afraid to take chances. The hits far outnumber the misses on this very interesting release. —*Scott Yanow*

Peter Ecklund

b. 1945, Woodbridge, CT
Cornet / Classic Jazz
Best known as the cornetist with Marty Grosz's Orphan Newsboys, Ecklund has always been attracted to pre-swing-era jazz. A superior ensemble player whose crisp solos are a delight, Ecklund graduated from Yale in 1967 and worked with a wide variety of musicians, including Gregg Allman, Maria Muldaur, Leon Redbone and Paul Butterfield. He helped form the Galvanized Jazz Band shortly after graduating from Yale and toured with singer Paul Lockheart, but also played with rock bands and did a lot of freelancing in the 1970s and early '80s. Most importantly, Ecklund began subbing in Vince Giordano's Nighthawks and became a permanent member and co-leader of the Orphan Newsboys (a perfect outlet for his talents) when it was formed in 1988. Also a fine whistler, Ecklund has played with the who's-who of trad jazz and mainstream at jazz parties and festivals, leading recording dates for Stomp Off and Arbors. —*Scott Yanow*

● **And the Melody Makers** / Jun. 17, 1987-Mar. 30, 1988 / Stomp Off ◆◆◆◆◆
Cornetist Peter Ecklund's debut as a leader is a gem. On five superior songs (including Jabbo Smith's "Jazz Battle" and "I Double Dare You"), he is showcased in a quartet with clarinetist Joe Muranyi, banjoist Eddie Davis and Barbara Dreiwitz on tuba. Four other tunes have Ecklund teaming up with clarinetist Ken Peplowski, bassist Bill Conway and acoustic guitarist Marty Grosz (who sings "The Lady's in Love with You" and "If I Had a Talking Picture of You" with his usual wit). The remaining five numbers feature Ecklund, Muranyi and Grosz along with trombonist Dan Barrett, bass saxophonist Vince Giordano and guitarist Frank Vignola. Overall, this is particularly for fans who think that Louis Armstrong invented scat singing. —*Scott Yanow*

Strings Attached / Apr. 22, 1992-Mar. 3, 1995 / Arbors ◆◆◆◆

Ecklund in Elkhart / Aug. 10, 1994 / Jazzology ◆◆◆◆

Billy Eckstine

b. Jul. 8, 1914, Pittsburgh, PA, d. Mar. 8, 1993, Pittsburgh, PA
Vocals / Bop, Standards, Pop, Traditional Pop
An influential ballad singer with a very appealing baritone voice, Billy Eckstine made a very important contribution to jazz early on, leading one of the first bebop big bands and keeping it together (while turning down lucrative offers to work as a single) as long as possible. He worked in Chicago starting in 1937 and was with the Earl Hines Orchestra during 1939-43, having a few hit records including the blues "Jelly Jelly." Near the end of his stay with Hines, the big band had become bop-oriented with such sidemen as Dizzy Gillespie, Charlie Parker and the young Sarah Vaughan. After leaving Hines, Eckstine hired more than a part of his very modern orchestra, and other members of his band during parts of 1944-47 included Gene Ammons, Dexter Gordon, Frank Wess, Miles Davis, Kenny

Dorham, Fats Navarro, Sonny Stitt, Leo Parker and Art Blakey; virtually all of the musicians were fairly unknown at the time. Unfortunately they did not make many recordings in 1944 (and by then Charlie Parker was gone) but they did have a minor hit with "Blowin' the Blues Away" and recorded more frequently during 1945-47; the latter performances have been reissued by Savoy. Eckstine, who occasionally took decent solos on valve trombone and trumpet, alternated ballads with bop instrumentals and made a short film in 1945 but by 1947 was forced financially to give up the band. Switching to middle-of-the-road pop ballads, Mr. B. became a very popular attraction (in a later era he would have been a romantic movie star), recording many string-filled arrangements for MGM that were bestsellers. But he never lost his feeling for jazz, and a 1959 collaboration with Count Basie finds Eckstine swinging with the best. —*Scott Yanow*

● **I Want to Talk About You** / Feb. 13, 1940-Mar. 4, 1945 / Xanadu ✦✦✦✦✦
The warm baritone voice of Billy Eckstine made him one of the most popular vocalists of the '40s and '50s. Although not a jazz singer himself, Eckstine always had a strong sympathy for the music, and his championing of a bebop big band during 1944-47 (when he could have made a lucrative living as a single) was quite heroic. This Xanadu LP features Eckstine's earliest recordings, 13 selections taken from his 1940-41 Victor sides with Earl Hines' Orchestra. Ballads naturally dominate but "Jelly Jelly" (Eckstine's first hit), "The Jitney Man" and "Stormy Monday Blues" are among the more memorable performances. This set is rounded out by three ballads taken from a 1945 broadcast with his own big band. Bop collectors will prefer to get a full set of orchestral sides by Eckstine's pioneering big band, but fans of his warm vocals should pick up this appealing album. —*Scott Yanow*

Mr. B / Apr. 13, 1944-Sep. 5, 1944 / Audio Lab ✦✦✦✦✦

Blowing the Blues Away / Apr. 13, 1944-Jul. 9, 1953 / Swingtime ✦✦✦✦
All of the 1944 Billy Eckstine Orchestra's recordings are on this imported Danish LP. Although Charlie Parker had already departed, otherwise the somewhat revolutionary Eckstine bebop big band was very much intact, including such sidemen as trumpeters Dizzy Gillespie, Freddie Webster and Shorty McConnell, trombonist Trummy Young, altoist Budd Johnson, tenors Wardell Gray (on the first date), Dexter Gordon and Gene Ammons, baritonist Leo Parker, Clyde Hart or John Malachi on piano, bassist Oscar Pettiford and Shadow Wilson or Art Blakey on drums. Because the two 1944 sessions were made for the tiny Deluxe label, these important recordings have been scarce through the years (hopefully they will show up on CD eventually) and there is sometimes some surface noise. Most of the tunes feature Eckstine's ballad vocals; however the music is often quite special, particularly "Blowing the Blues Away" (heard in two versions and featuring a famous tradeoff by Ammons and Dexter) and "Opus X." This LP is rounded off by Eckstine's two guest appearances (on "How High the Moon" and "St. Louis Blues") with the 1953 Metronome All-Stars, exciting jazz-oriented performances which have since been reissued by Verve. —*Scott Yanow*

Airmail Special / Feb. 1945-Mar. 1945 / Drive Archive ✦✦✦✦
This Drive Archive budget CD reissues an Alamac LP, material that has also appeared on the English Spotlite label. Singer Billy Eckstine led one of the first bebop big bands, and this set of 1945 broadcasts features such important modernists as trumpeter Fats Navarro, the tenors of Gene Ammons and Budd Johnson, drummer Art Blakey and singer Sarah Vaughan. The arrangements of the instrumentals (particularly "Airmail Special" and "Opus X") are a bit futuristic; Eckstine takes four fine vocals, and Sarah Vaughan's two features ("Mean to Me" and "Don't Blame Me") are among her earliest appearances on record. The recording quality overall is just decent but the fire of the music makes these performances worth acquiring (in one form or another) by bop collectors. —*Scott Yanow*

The Legendary Big Band of Billy Eckstine Together! / Feb. 1945-Mar. 1945 / Spotlite ✦✦✦✦

★ **Mister B and the Band** / May 2, 1945-Oct. 6, 1946 / Savoy ✦✦✦✦✦
This double-LP (put out by Arista when they were handling the Savoy catalogue in 1976) has 32 of singer Billy Eckstine's best Savoy recordings. Taken from the period when he was leading a notable big band full of modernists (including at times trumpeters Fats Navarro, Kenny Dorham and Miles Davis, altoists Budd Johnson and Sonny Stitt, tenors Gene Ammons and Dexter Gordon, baritonist Leo Parker and drummer Art Blakey), Eckstine alternates ballad vocals with hotter jazz numbers. Highlights include "A Cottage for Sale," "I Love the Rhythm in a Riff," "The Jitney Man," "Second Balcony Jump," "Cool Breeze," two versions of "Oo Bop Sh'Bam" and "Jelly Jelly"; the last eight selections find the influential baritone singer backed by strings. Overall this two-fer gives listeners an excellent sampling of Billy Eckstine's early recordings. —*Scott Yanow*

☆ **Everything I Have Is Yours** / May 20, 1947-Apr. 26, 1957 / Verve ✦✦✦✦✦
This two-CD set improves upon the original two-LP package by adding 14 more songs. The pop side of Billy Eckstine was emphasized during his period with MGM and many of these selections (including hit versions of "Everything I Have Is

Yours," "Blue Moon," "Caravan," "My Foolish Heart" and "I Apologize") feature his warm baritone backed by string sections. There are some exceptions including "Mr. B's Blues" (which gives Eckstine a chance to solo on valve trombone), dates with Woody Herman and George Shearing, eight numbers on which the singer is accompanied by the Bobby Tucker Quartet and a pair of wonderful performances with the Metronome All-Stars in 1953 (a group that includes trumpeter Roy Eldridge, both Lester Young and Warne Marsh on tenors and vibraphonist Terry Gibbs). Although not as essential from the jazz standpoint as Billy Eckstine's earlier big-band dates, this two-fer features the singer at the peak of his powers; five ballad duets with Sarah Vaughan are a highlight. —*Scott Yanow*

The MGM Years / May 20, 1947-Apr. 26, 1957 / Verve ✦✦✦✦
Two-fer with a ton of great songs and great singing. —*Michael G. Nastos*

No Cover, No Minimum / Aug. 30, 1960 / Roulette ✦✦✦✦
This CD has an unusual cover picture showing Billy Eckstine singing while holding a trumpet. He does indeed take a few short trumpet solos on the well-rounded program, 24 songs (13 previously unissued) performed during one night in Las Vegas. Eckstine, who is backed by an orchestra arranged by his pianist Bobby Tucker, is heard in prime form on a variety of standards. His baritone voice (which was quite influential) straddles the boundary between middle-of-the-road pop and jazz on such numbers as "I've Grown Accustomed to Her Face," "Without a Song," "Prisoner of Love," "I Apologize," "Alright, Okay, You Win" and "'Deed I Do." A good example of his talents. —*Scott Yanow*

Billy Eckstine Sings with Benny Carter / Nov. 17, 1986-Nov. 18, 1986 / Verve ✦✦✦
Billy Eckstine's final recording (although he would live until 1993) finds the 72-year-old singer showing his age. Mr. B's famous baritone voice at this late date only hints at his earlier greatness, although his phrasing and enthusiasm uplift what could have been a depressing affair. Ironically altoist Benny Carter (who was 79) still sounds in his prime on alto and he takes an effective trumpet solo on "September Song." Singer Helen Merrill opens and closes the set by interacting vocally with Eckstine on "You'd Be So Nice to Come Home To" and "Didn't We." Eckstine, backed by a trio headed by his longtime pianist Bobby Tucker, does his best on such songs as "My Funny Valentine," "Memories of You" and "Autumn Leaves," but his earlier recordings are the ones to get. —*Scott Yanow*

Harry "Sweets" Edison

b. Oct. 10, 1915, Columbus, OH
Trumpet / Swing

Harry "Sweets" Edison gets the most mileage out of a single note, like his former boss Count Basie. Edison, who is immediately recognizable within a note or two, has long used repetition and simplicity to his advantage while always swinging. He played in local bands in Columbus and then in 1933 joined the Jeter-Pillars Orchestra. After a couple years in St. Louis, Edison moved to New York where he joined Lucky Millinder, and then in June 1938 Count Basie, remaining with that classic orchestra until it broke up in 1950. During that period he was featured on many records, appeared in the 1944 short *Jammin' the Blues* and gained his nickname "Sweets" (due to his tone) from Lester Young. In the 1950s Edison toured with Jazz at the Philharmonic, settled in Los Angeles and was well-featured both as a studio musician (most noticeably on Frank Sinatra records) and on jazz dates. He had several reunions with Count Basie in the 1960s, and by the '70s was often teamed with Eddie "Lockjaw" Davis; Edison also recorded an excellent duet album for Pablo with Oscar Peterson. One of the few swing trumpeters to be influenced by Dizzy Gillespie, Sweets has led sessions through the years for Pacific Jazz, Verve, Roulette, Riverside, Vee-Jay, Liberty, Sue, Black & Blue, Pablo, Storyville and Candid among others. Although his playing faded during the 1980s and '90s, Edison can still say more with one note than nearly anyone. —*Scott Yanow*

Jawbreakers / Apr. 18, 1962 / Original Jazz Classics ✦✦✦✦✦
Harry "Sweets" Edison and Eddie "Lockjaw" Davis always made for a logical combination, for both had immediately recognizable sounds and could say an awful lot with one note. This early collaboration (reissued on CD), their first joint recording, finds the pair joined by pianist Hugh Lawson, bassist Ike Isaacs and drummer Clarence Johnston. The repertoire (three basic Edison originals plus five jazz standards) serves as a strong vehicle for swinging solos with highlights including "Broadway," "Four" and "A Gal in Calico." Easily recommended to straightahead jazz fans, as are the later Sweets-Lockjaw recordings. —*Scott Yanow*

Home with Sweets / Aug. 1964 / Vee-Jay ✦✦

Just Friends / Jul. 26, 1975 / Black & Blue ✦✦✦✦
Trumpeter Harry "Sweets" Edison's first recording as a leader in a decade was this obscure LP from the French Black and Blue label, preceding his first Pablo album by a year. Teamed up with tenor saxophonist Eddie "Lockjaw" Davis (all of their joint recordings are easily recommended), pianist Gerry Wiggins, bassist Major

Holley and drummer Oliver Jackson, Sweets performs five veteran standards (including "Sunday" and "There Is No Greater Love") and a couple of basic originals based on other tunes. The English "translation" of the French liner notes is fairly erratic but the playing by the quintet is consistently enjoyable. —*Scott Yanow*

Harry "Sweets" Edison—Eddie "Lockjaw" Davis & Richard Boone / Feb. 27, 1976-Dec. 19, 1976 / Storyville ✦✦✦

Although trumpeter Harry "Sweets" Edison gets top billing on this Storyville LP, he is only on half of the selections and none of the ones that feature tenor saxophonist Eddie "Lockjaw" Davis and vocalist Richard Boone (who mostly sings his three features straight). Leonardo Pedersen's Jazzkapel (a Danish 11-piece group) is a small big band that sometimes bows in the direction of Count Basie and backs the three guests. Actually nothing all that essential occurs, but Edison and Davis completists and fans of mainstream jazz may want to get this set. —*Scott Yanow*

★ **Edison's Lights** / May 5, 1976 / Original Jazz Classics ✦✦✦✦✦

Although trumpeter Harry "Sweets" Edison and tenor saxophonist Eddie "Lockjaw" Davis recorded several albums together in the 1970s, this CD reissue was their only Pablo date as a team. Edison is the nominal leader and he contributed four of the eight selections (which alternate with four veteran standards), but the competitive Lockjaw gets in his fiery licks too. While bassist John Heard and drummer Jimmie Smith are part of the quintet and pianist Dolo Coker is on half of the program, Count Basie himself drops by for four songs to cheer on his former sidemen. All of the musicians sound quite inspired and are heard throughout playing at their best and most colorful. —*Scott Yanow*

Harry Sweets Edison and Eddie Lockjaw Davis, Vol. 1 / Jul. 6, 1976 / Storyville ✦✦✦✦✦

Plenty of fireworks occur on this typically exciting encounter between trumpeter Harry "Sweets" Edison and tenor saxophonist Eddie "Lockjaw" Davis. In Denmark they recorded enough material in one day with pianist Kenny Drew, bassist Hugo Rasmussen and drummer Svend Erik Norregaard (with guest spots for trombonist John Darville) to result in two Storyville albums. While Davis is showcased on "Angel Eyes" and Sweets gets "September Song" as his ballad feature, it is the four medium-tempo jams (Edison's "Lullaby for Dancers," "Lester Leaps In," "Spotlite" and "Blues Walk"), two of which add Darville to the group, that are most memorable. Recommended, as is the follow-up album *Opus Funk*. —*Scott Yanow*

Harry Sweets Edison and Eddie Lockjaw Davis, Vol. 2 / Jul. 6, 1976 / Storyville ✦✦✦✦✦

The second of two albums cut in one day in 1976 is the equal of the first. Trumpeter Harry "Sweets" Edison and tenor saxophonist Eddie "Lockjaw" Davis, although having different approaches, always seemed to bring out the best in each other. With pianist Kenny Drew, bassist Hugo Rasmussen and drummer Svend Erik Norregaard forming a supportive trio and trombonist John Darville guesting on two of the six numbers, this is a well-rounded set. Sweets has a duet with bassist Rasmussen on "There Is No Greater Love," Lockjaw takes "You Are Too Beautiful" as his ballad feature and there are four jams of which this version of "Candy" is a near-classic. Recommended. —*Scott Yanow*

Opus Funk / Jul. 6, 1976 / Storyville ✦✦✦✦
Nice straightahead date. —*Ron Wynn*

Simply Sweets / Sep. 22, 1977 / Original Jazz Classics ✦✦✦

Trumpeter Harry "Sweets" Edison and tenor saxophonist Eddie "Lockjaw" Davis always made a potent pair. They both possessed immediately identifiable sounds, were veterans of Count Basie's Orchestra and never had any difficulty swinging. The repertoire of this Edison album is not too creative, with five blues among its eight songs and one of the others, "Feelings," being quite forgettable. However, the playing of the principals (along with pianist Dolo Coker, who also makes a couple of surprising appearances on electric keyboard) holds one's interest throughout. —*Scott Yanow*

'S Wonderful / Oct. 19, 1982 / Pablo ✦✦✦

This out-of-print Pablo LP (which will certainly be reissued on CD in the future) is from the later days of the label. Trumpeter Harry "Sweets" Edison was just beginning to fade around this period but he still sounds in fine form, teamed up with Zoot Sims (who plays tenor on three and soprano on one of the six selections), pianist Mike Wofford, bassist Monty Budwig and drummer Shelly Manne. They perform the leader's "Elegante" plus five standards, with the highlights including "Centerpiece" (Sweets' famous blues line) and "Sunday." Fine swinging mainstream jazz. —*Scott Yanow*

For My Pals / Apr. 18, 1988-Apr. 19, 1988 / Pablo ✦✦

Harry "Sweets" Edison, 72 at the time, sounds past his prime throughout this Pablo CD. His trumpet solos are weak and his decision to sing "Good Night" was a mistake. There are some good moments contributed by the colorful trombonist Buster Cooper, Curtis Peagler on tenor and alto, and the veteran rhythm section (pianist Art Hillery, bassist Andy Simpkins and drummer Albert "Tootie" Heath), but these

well-intentioned tributes to Edison's friends (including a forgettable version of "It's a Wonderful World") are generally a misfire. —*Scott Yanow*

Can't Get out of This Mood / Oct. 1988-Nov. 1988 / Orange Blue ✦✦✦

Swing Summit / Apr. 27, 1990-Apr. 28, 1990 / Candid ✦✦✦

Live at the Iridium / Apr. 10, 1997-Apr. 11, 1997 / Telarc ✦✦✦

Even for a label that likes to catch veteran jazz stars very late in their careers, Telarc nearly outdoes itself by rounding up Harry "Sweets" Edison (81), Clark Terry (76), Frank Wess (75) and Junior Mance (68) and recording them in a West Side New York nightclub a stone's throw from Lincoln Center. Though the flesh is a little weak at times in the trumpeters, the spirit is fortunately more than willing, and plenty of their inimitable trademarks—Edison's terse repeated notes and Terry's slippery phrases—come through in this swinging, blues-dominated mainstream session. Wess is in fine shape on flute and tenor, and pianist Mance contributes a lot of sparkling, stirring, two-fisted blues and a lovely, searching interpretation of "Emily." Edison wrote half of the eight songs on the disc—three blues (including his standard "Centerpiece") and a pleasing token bossa nova ("Sweets' Bossa"). If this gig often has the joyous ambience (and occasional signatures) of a Basie jam, why not?: all three horns are Basie alums. —*Richard S. Ginell*

Cliff Edwards (Ukulele Ike)

b. Jun. 14, 1895, Montreal, Quebec, Canada, **d.** Jul. 18, 1972, Hollywood, CA
Vocals, Ukulele / Pop, Classic Jazz

Cliff Edwards, best known as "Ukulele Ike," gained his greatest fame in 1939 as the voice of Jiminy Cricket in *Pinocchio* (singing "When You Wish upon a Star"), but spent much of his life as an alcoholic B-movie actor (appearing in over 50 films) who was used for weak comedy relief. Few probably realize that Cliff Edwards was one of the first jazz singers on record, predating Louis Armstrong with swinging phrases and heated scatting. Edwards left home as a teenager to work in show business, starting in bars in St. Louis. He played successfully in vaudeville and in Broadway shows. In 1924, Edwards introduced "Fascinatin' Rhythm" in the Gershwin show *Lady Be Good*, was in the Ziegfeld Follies in 1927, and made "Singin' in the Rain" famous in the film *Hollywood Revue of 1929*. Edwards' recordings of 1922-28 found him not only performing solo (featuring his vocals, scatting, ukulele and some colorful kazoo playing), but interacting quite successfully with such players as bass saxophonist Adrian Rollini, cornetist Red Nichols, trombonist Miff Mole, clarinetist Jimmy Dorsey and guitarist Eddie Lang. Edwards' sweet voice worked quite well on tunes such as "I'll See You in My Dreams," contrasting with his wicked sense of humor and scatting. After 1928, Edwards' recordings declined in jazz quality, but he made occasional sessions, recording a Dixieland record as late as 1956 and somehow living until 1972, despite a self-destructive life full of drinking, gambling, problems with the IRS and decades of obscurity. —*Scott Yanow*

● **Cliff Edwards and His Hot Combination (1925-1926)** / Feb. 1925-Oct. 1926 / Retrieval ✦✦✦✦✦

The Vintage Recordings of Cliff Edwards (Ukulele Ike) / Jul. 1928-1944 / Totem ✦✦✦✦

The early jazz singer, ukulele player and movie personality Cliff Edwards (best known as "Ukulele Ike") is featured on 14 selections on this LP, 11 of which date from 1928-33. The backup personnel is unfortunately not given (sometimes it includes either Eddie Lang or Dick McDonough on guitar), but the music generally swings, and Edwards is heard throughout in prime voice. Highlights include his hit "Singin' in the Rain," "That's My Weakness Now," "I'll See You in My Dreams" and "It's Only a Paper Moon." This collector's album is rounded by two numbers ("A Love Like Ours" and "It Had to Be You") taken from unissued test pressings cut in 1944. Well worth searching for, at least until Ukulele Ike's many enjoyable recordings are properly reissued on CD. —*Scott Yanow*

Live Radio Transcriptions / 1944-1947 / Collectors Choice Music ✦✦✦

Despite his popularity in vaudeville, on Broadway, on records, and in the movies from the 1920s to the '40s, Cliff Edwards, the ukulele player with the warm manner and the conversational tenor, lapsed into obscurity long before he died destitute in 1972. 1997 saw the release of two Edwards albums, however—Sony Music Special Products' ten-track *Ukulele Ike*, and this album of radio performances. Despite its title, more than half of the album comes from June 1947. The 1947 material finds Edwards in a friendly, bantering mood, while the 1930s performances are isolated tracks. Edwards sings some of the songs most closely associated with him, including his biggest hit, "I Can't Give You Anything but Love," and "Fascinating Rhythm," which he sang in the Gershwin musical *Lady Be Good*. There are also '20s hits such as "Ain't He Got Fun?" and "If You Knew Susie," while Edwards' rendition of "Sweet Leilani" demonstrates his influence on Bing Crosby, who had the hit with it. If Edwards' music was more generally available, this release would be nonessential, though enjoyable. Under the circumstances, it's a vital portrait of an unjustly forgotten singer. —*William Ruhlmann*

I Want a Little Girl / 1944 / Totem ✦✦✦
Due to his alcoholism, Cliff Edwards ("Ukulele Ike") had an up and down career, ending his life in complete obscurity. At the peak of his fame in the late 1920s, but off records after 1935 (except for a final effort in 1956), Edwards did make a series of radio transcriptions in 1944 that were released on four Totem LPs. This one has Edwards (who also plays occasional kazoo) backed by an unidentified small band and mostly singing nostalgic songs from the 1920s. Edwards' voice was still in decent form, and he sounds fine on such tunes as ""When My Sugar Walks Down the Street," "Somebody Stole My Gal," "If You Knew Susie" and "Sleepy Time Gal." —*Scott Yanow*

Teddy Edwards

b. Apr. 26, 1924, Jackson, MS
Tenor Saxophone / Bop, Hard Bop
Teddy Edwards was, with Dexter Gordon and Wardell Gray, the top young tenor of the late '40s. Unlike the other two, he chose to remain in Los Angeles and has been underrated through the years but, even in his early 70s, Edwards remains in prime form. Early on he toured with Ernie Fields' Orchestra, moving to L.A. in 1945 to work with Roy Milton as an altoist. Edwards switched to tenor when he joined Howard McGhee's band and was featured in many jam sessions during the era, recording "The Duel" with Dexter Gordon in 1947. A natural-born leader, Edwards did work briefly with Max Roach and Clifford Brown (1954), Benny Carter (1955) and Benny Goodman (1964), and he recorded in the 1960s with Milt Jackson and Jimmy Smith. But it is his own records for Onyx (1947-48), Pacific Jazz, Contemporary (1960-62), Prestige, Xanadu, Muse, Steeple Chase, Timeless and Antilles that best show off his playing and writing; "Sunset Eyes" is Edwards' best-known original. —*Scott Yanow*

★ **Teddy's Ready** / Aug. 17, 1960 / Original Jazz Classics ✦✦✦✦✦
Tenor saxophonist Teddy Edwards' debut for Contemporary (which has been reissued on CD in the OJC series) gives listeners a strong sampling of the underrated tenor's talents. Edwards, a contemporary of Dexter Gordon and Wardell Gray but sometimes overlooked due to his decision to spend most of his life living in Los Angeles, is showcased on a quartet set with the obscure but talented pianist Joe Castro, bassist Leroy Vinnegar and drummer Billy Higgins. Performing three standards, three originals (of which "Higgins' Hideaway" is most memorable) and Hampton Hawes' "The Sermon," Edwards has a chance to stretch out, and he makes the most of the opportunity, creating some excellent straightahead music. —*Scott Yanow*

Back to Avalon / Dec. 7, 1960-Dec. 13, 1960 / Contemporary ✦✦✦
Although rejected at the time it was recorded, this octet session by tenor saxophonist Teddy Edwards sounded fairly good when it was finally released in 1995. There are some minor slip-ups in some of the ensembles and Edwards is the only significant soloist (although altoist Jimmy Woods and baritonist Modesto Brisenio were talented players), but the leader is in fine form and his arrangements manage to be both complicated and swinging. Five of the nine songs (all but "You Don't Know What Love Is," "Sweet Georgia Brown" and two versions of "Avalon") are Edwards', highlighted by "Our Last Goodbye" and "Good Gravy." A worthwhile if not essential release. —*Scott Yanow*

Together Again! / May 15, 1961+May 17, 1961 / Contemporary ✦✦✦✦✦
Tenor saxophonist Teddy Edwards and trumpeter Howard McGhee had played together regularly during 1945-47. For their recorded reunion, they are assisted by the masterful pianist Phineas Newborn, bassist Ray Brown and drummer Ed Thigpen. Edwards, McGhee and Brown contributed one new song apiece, which alternates with a trio of standards ("You Stepped Out of a Dream," "Misty" and Charlie Parker's "Perhaps"). The trumpeter was having a short-lived comeback at the time and he had largely regained his earlier form. Edwards sounds as strong as ever and Newborn was an up-and-coming talent. Their collaboration for this boppish date (reissued on CD) is generally quite memorable. —*Scott Yanow*

Good Gravy! / Aug. 23, 1961-Aug. 25, 1961 / Original Jazz Classics ✦✦✦✦
Teddy Edwards has long been one of the most underrated of the bop tenors, due in large part to his decision to settle in Los Angeles. Edwards is in typically swinging form on this quartet date with either Phineas Newborn, Jr., or Danny Horton on piano, bassist Leroy Vinnegar and drummer Milt Turner. The tenor contributed four originals and also performs the obscure "A Little Later" and four standards with warmth and creativity within the hard bop genre. —*Scott Yanow*

Heart and Soul / Apr. 24, 1962 / Original Jazz Classics ✦✦✦
With pianist Gerry Wiggins exclusively playing organ, this is a slightly unusual date for tenor saxophonist Teddy Edwards; bassist Leroy Vinnegar and drummer Milt Turner complete the quartet. Edwards is in typically fine form on four diverse

blues, his "No Regrets" and the standard "Secret Love." Even if Wiggins was not the most inspiring organist around (although he was quite competent), Teddy's playing makes this CD reissue worthwhile. —*Scott Yanow*

Nothin' but the Truth! / Dec. 13, 1966 / Original Jazz Classics ✦✦✦✦
This CD reissue is quite brief (just 32 minutes) but it does give one a fairly definitive look into the style of tenor saxophonist Teddy Edwards. Accompanied by pianist Walter Davis, Jr., guitarist Phil Orlando, bassist Paul Chambers, drummer Billy Higgins and percussionist Montego Joe, Edwards plays three of his originals plus a trio of standards. His warm tenor (alternately boppish and soulful) is heard at its best during "On the Street Where You Live" and "But Beautiful." —*Scott Yanow*

It's All Right / May 24, 1967+May 27, 1967 / Original Jazz Classics ✦✦✦✦
This is an interesting transitional set by tenor saxophonist Teddy Edwards, originally cut for Prestige and now available as a CD in the OJC series. Although the music (mostly Edwards originals) is essentially hard bop, there are hints of the avant-garde here and there in the harmonies and solos. Edwards plays as well as usual, and his supporting cast (trumpeter Jimmy Owens, trombonist Garnett Brown, pianist Cedar Walton, bassist Ben Tucker and drummer Lenny McBrowne) is impressive. None of the tunes caught on as standards, and Edwards would not have an opportunity to record as a leader for another seven years, but the largely straightahead music has dated fairly well. —*Scott Yanow*

Feelin's / Mar. 25, 1974 / Muse ✦✦✦✦
This session finds Edwards in good swinging company. All originals (except "Georgia on My Mind"). Forthright and well done. —*Ron Wynn*

Inimitable / Jun. 25, 1976 / Xanadu ✦✦✦✦✦
The underrated tenor great Teddy Edwards had only recorded one album as a leader during the previous nine years when he made this Xanadu date, and he would have to wait around four before his next session. The neglect had much more to do with geography (he spent his career living in Los Angeles) than it did with talent. Edwards, backed by pianist Duke Jordan, bassist Larry Ridley and drummer Freddie Waits, is in top form throughout these five standards (including his most famous original "Sunset Eyes") plus Edwards' newer piece "One on One." Whether it be "Stella by Starlight" (which has an opening tenor cadenza), a relaxed "Mean to Me" or a cooking rendition of "That Old Black Magic," this LP contains a superior outing. —*Scott Yanow*

Out of This World / Dec. 5, 1980 / Steeple Chase ✦✦✦✦
A typically excellent set by the underrated tenor saxophonist Teddy Edwards (one of the top tenors to emerge during the mid-'40s), this quartet date with pianist Kenny Drew, bassist Jesper Lundgaard and drummer Billy Hart features the distinctive Edwards on two originals ("No Name No. 1" and "April Love") and four standards. The CD reissue adds a second version of "Summertime" to the original program. Teddy Edwards has yet to record an unworthy set, and his swinging session (one of only two that he made as a leader during 1977-90) will be enjoyed by bop collectors. —*Scott Yanow*

Good Gravy / Dec. 26, 1981 / Timeless ✦✦✦✦
This obscure live CD features the underrated tenor saxophonist Teddy Edwards in top form stretching out on three standards ("Lady Be Good," "Oleo" and "Georgia on My Mind") and his own "Good Gravy." Joined by a Dutch rhythm section (pianist Rein De Graaff, bassist Henk Haverhoek and drummer John Engels), Edwards builds up his solos expertly and plenty of sparks fly. Recommended. —*Scott Yanow*

Mississippi Lad / Mar. 13, 1991-Mar. 14, 1991 / Antilles ✦✦✦
☆ **Blue Saxophone** / Jun. 8, 1992-Jun. 10, 1992 / Antilles ✦✦✦✦✦
One of the major tenor saxophonists in jazz since his emergence in the mid-'40s, Teddy Edwards has not led enough sessions throughout his career considering his great talent. In the 1990s, he has been making up for lost time by putting a great deal of planning into his releases. For this ambitious effort he is joined by five brass, five strings, a harp, a four-piece rhythm section, and on three songs the fine young singer Lisa Nobumoto. As if that were not enough, Edwards wrote ten of the 12 songs, arranged all of them, takes "Prelude" unaccompanied and plays a bit of clarinet on "Serenade in Blue." It's an impressive effort. —*Scott Yanow*

Horn to Horn / Dec. 27, 1994 / Muse ✦✦✦✦✦
This is a logical and very successful collaboration featuring the East Coast tenor Houston Person and L.A.'s legendary Teddy Edwards. Although one can generally tell the two veterans apart (Person has a heavier sound than the comparatively light-toned Edwards), the co-leaders are quite complementary and work together well in the tradition of Sonny Stitt and Gene Ammons. With fine backup from pianist Richard Wyands, bassist Peter Washington and drummer Kenny Washington, Edwards and Person pay tribute to eight great tenors of the past (John Coltrane, Ben Webster, Lester Young, Stan Getz, Coleman Hawkins, Gene Ammons, Dexter Gordon and Eddie "Lockjaw" Davis) through their renditions of eight standards. Highlights include a romp on "Lester Leaps In," a surprisingly successful version of "The Girl from Ipanema" and a spirited "Red Top." Recommended. —*Scott Yanow*

Midnight Creeper / Mar. 7, 1997 / High Note ✦✦✦✦✦

This CD is really two recordings in one. It starts off with three fine originals by tenor saxophonist Teddy Edwards, who is featured with a quintet also consisting of the underrated trumpeter Virgil Jones, pianist Richard Wyands, bassist Buster Williams and drummer Chip White. However the music really becomes memorable when Edwards performs a slower than usual, 10 -minute version of "Lady Be Good." He also has melodic and swinging renditions of "Don't Blame Me," "Tenderly" and "Almost Like Being in Love" as warm quartet features and jams "Sunday" with Jones. 52 years after his recording debut, Teddy Edwards proved to still be in his musical prime. —*Scott Yanow*

Mark Egan

b. Jan. 14, 1951, Brockton, MA
Bass / Post-Bop, Crossover Jazz, Fusion
Mark Egan, who has a floating sound, is best known for his leadership of Elements with drummer Danny Gottlieb. His first instrument was the trumpet, switching to bass at 16. Egan played with Ira Sullivan's group in Miami during 1974-76 and then moved to New York, where he toured with the Pointer Sisters and David Sanborn. Egan's big break was when he became a member of the Pat Metheny Group (1977-80), recording and touring extensively. Since leaving Metheny he has worked in many situations, including with Stan Getz, Jim Hall, the Gil Evans Orchestra (1983-85) and John McLaughlin. Elements, which usually also features Bill Evans on reeds and keyboardist Clifford Carter, was formed in 1982 and has existed on a part-time basis ever since, recording for Philo, Antilles, Novus and Blue Moon. —*Scott Yanow*

Mosaic / 1985 / Hip Pocket ✦✦

Touch of Light / 1988 / GRP ✦✦✦

● **Beyond Words** / 1990-1991 / Blue Moon ✦✦✦✦

From spacy mood music to some funkier sounds, this is a fine outing for the distinctive electric bassist Mark Egan. Teamed up in various combinations with guitarist Toninho Horta, and Steve Khan, saxophonist Bill Evans, keyboardist Clifford Carter, drummer Danny Gottlieb and the percussion of Don Alias, Manolo Badrena and Gordon Gottlieb, Egan is often in the spotlight during a set dominated by originals (plus John Coltrane's spiritual "After the Rain"). Fans of the group Elements should enjoy this CD, too. —*Scott Yanow*

Marty Ehrlich

b. 1955, St. Louis, MO
Clarinet, Flute, Bass Clarinet, Alto Saxophone, Tenor Saxophone, Soprano Saxophone / Avant-Garde
A versatile player, Marty Ehrlich has led stimulating sessions and been a valuable sideman in several different situations. First recording with the Human Arts Ensemble in 1972, Ehrlich studied at the New England Conservatory of Music and in 1978 he moved to New York. Since then he has worked with many top musicians including Muhal Richard Abrams, Anthony Braxton, Julius Hemphill and Bobby Bradford (where he fills in for the late John Carter). Ehrlich has also duetted with Anthony Cox, led his Dark Woods Ensemble and recorded as a leader for Cecma, Sound Aspects, Muse, New World and most often Enja. —*Scott Yanow*

The Welcome / Mar. 21, 1984 / Sound Aspects ✦✦✦

Pliant Plaint / Apr. 1987 / Enja ✦✦✦✦

The first of two Enja sets matching Marty Ehrlich (on clarinet, bass clarinet, alto, flute and alto flute) with Stan Strickland (tenor, soprano and flute), this inside/outside music also features bassist Anthony Cox and drummer Bobby Previte. The complex yet consistently colorful repertoire has plenty of variety, including one piece ("After After All") that is totally composed and has Ehrlich as the only musician, overdubbing on several of his horns. The many tone colors provided by the two horn players and the strong originals make this a set worth searching for by listeners into the more adventurous side of jazz. —*Scott Yanow*

The Traveller's Tale / May 30, 1989-Jun. 1, 1989 / Enja ✦✦✦✦

Solid, energized solos by Marty Ehrlich on a variety of saxophones and flute, plus equally animated playing from co-saxophonist Stan Strickland on tenor, soprano, and flute. The two-sax front line, plus tasteful, probing bass/drum help from Lindsey Horner and Robert Previte, not only fills the spaces open due to the absence of a pianist, but periodically shifts the mood, focus, and tempo. —*Ron Wynn*

Falling Man / Oct. 3, 1989-Nov. 3, 1989 / Muse ✦✦✦

An intriguing, but sometimes disjointed, duo outing between multi-instrumentalist Marty Erhlich and bassist Anthony Cox. They venture into free, fusion, funk, and rock territory, and while all their duets are exceptionally played, the compositions aren't uniformly interesting. The best cut is their emphatic duet "You Don't Know What Love Is," which was a signature song for Eric Dolphy. —*Ron Wynn*

Emergency Peace / Dec. 14, 1990-Dec. 16, 1990 / New World ✦✦✦

This is a fascinating blend of improvisation and original structures. —*Myles Boisen*

Side by Side / Jan. 1991 / Enja ✦✦✦✦

● **Can You Hear a Motion?** / Sep. 22, 1993-Sep. 23, 1993 / Enja ✦✦✦✦✦

This quartet release matches the cool-toned reeds of Marty Ehrlich (heard on clarinet, alto and soprano) and Stan Strickland (doubling on flute and tenor) with bassist Michael Formanek (who operates as an active partner) and the quietly supportive drummer Bobby Previte. Their unpredictable music ranges from free bop à la Ornette Coleman (including a tenor-alto duet rendition of Coleman's "Comme Il Faut") and a pair of John Carter tributes to Jaki Byard's "Ode to Charlie Parker" (which includes transcriptions of part of trumpeter Booker Little's solo from its original recording) and the modern classical harmonies of "Pictures in a Glass House." Throughout the improvisations are a logical outgrowth of the written sections and vice versa. The musicians constantly react to each other, making this stimulating and passionate but quiet music well worth acquiring. —*Scott Yanow*

New York Child / Feb. 24, 1995+Feb. 25, 1995 / Enja ✦✦✦✦

Marty Ehrlich's music tends to be both melodic and exploratory, comfortable yet full of unexpected twists and turns. Switching between four reeds on his quintet set (which co-stars the complementary tenor of Stan Strickland in the front line), Ehrlich emphasizes lyricism and strong themes, expertly setting up improvisations with well-conceived arrangements. The leader's nine originals flow together quite well, so one does not remember individual pieces as much as the friendly atmosphere and attractive colors on a whole. An underrated clarinetist who certainly ranks in the top ten of the 1990s, Ehrlich also displays a fresh musical personality on alto, soprano and bass clarinet, while his notable rhythm section (pianist Michael Cain, bassist Michael Formanek and drummer Bill Stewart) is both tight and spontaneous. Together with the fine tenor of Strickland, they create an unclassifiable set of surprisingly accessible modern jazz. —*Scott Yanow*

Just Before the Dawn / Apr. 10, 1995-Apr. 11, 1995 / New World ✦✦✦✦

Light at the Crossroads / Jan. 20, 1996-Jan. 21, 1996 / Songlines ✦✦✦✦

Live Wood / Mar. 2, 1996-Apr. 4, 1996 / Music & Arts ✦✦✦✦

Either/Orchestra

f. 1985
Group / Big Band, Post-Bop, Avant-Garde
The Either/Orchestra was founded in 1985 by tenor saxophonist Russ Gershon. An adventurous medium-sized seven-horn ten-piece group based in Massachusetts, the ensemble often has the sound of a big band but the looseness of a combo and, although occasionally reminiscent of some of Charles Mingus' groups, it has developed its own sound over time. Gershon in 1987 founded Accurate Records and the Either/Orchestra, recording four memorable albums for the label during 1987-90. —*Scott Yanow*

Dial E / Jul. 8, 1986-Jul. 9, 1986 / Accurate Jazz ✦✦✦✦

The 11-piece seven-horn Either/Orchestra is a notable medium-sized group that has the power of a big band and the inventiveness of a combo. Their debut recording sometimes shows the influence of Charles Mingus and features the group on two originals by leader/tenor Russ Gershon, along with pieces by Sonny Rollins ("Doxy"), Thelonious Monk ("Brilliant Corners") and Rahsaan Roland Kirk ("Lady's Blues"). The colorful ensembles and advanced solos give the Either/Orchestra its own sound. Virtually all of their recordings (including this one) are easily recommended. —*Scott Yanow*

Across the Omniverse / Jul. 8, 1986-Sep. 7, 1995 / Accurate Jazz ✦✦✦✦

Radium / Aug. 2, 1987-Jan. 31, 1988 / Accurate Jazz ✦✦✦✦

Includes three standards and five originals. Trombonist Curtis Hasselbring and baritone saxophonist Charles Kohlhase stand out as soloists. "Born in a Suitcase" and Roscoe Mitchell's "Odwallah" are the best tracks. —*Michael G. Nastos*

The Half-Life of Desire / 1989 / Accurate Jazz ✦✦✦✦✦

Led by saxophonist/composer Russ Gershon, this shows progressive sensibilities with jazz aesthetics. Recorded at Van Gelder's, this album features great originals and interesting twists on "Temptation," "Circle in the Round/I Got It Bad and That Ain't Good," and King Crimson's "Red." —*Michael G. Nastos*

The Calculus of Pleasure / Apr. 25, 1990-Jun. 27, 1990 / Accurate Jazz ✦✦✦✦

● **Brunt** / Apr. 22, 1993-May 11, 1993 / Accurate Jazz ✦✦✦✦✦

At the time of its formation the Either/Orchestra asked "why should a seven-horn band only limit themselves in ensembles to playing three basic parts (for trumpets, trombones and reeds) when having seven parts would be much more exciting?" Gradual tempo changes within a song, the use of emotional outbursts, humor and group improvising, and the ability to look both backwards and forwards stylistically at the same time are qualities that make the Either/Orchestra a logical outgrowth of Charles Mingus' innovations. This CD is full of extroverted solos, wild group interplay, hard-swinging and unpredictable performances and quite a bit of variety. Even with the many strong solos, it is the occasionally overcrowded ensembles of the stimulating group that stick in one's mind. —*Scott Yanow*

Roy Eldridge (David Roy Eldridge)

b. Jan. 30, 1911, Pittsburgh, PA, d. Feb. 26, 1989, Valley Stream, NY
Trumpet / Swing

One of the most exciting trumpeters to emerge during the swing era, Roy Eldridge's combative approach, chance-taking style and strong musicianship were an inspiration (and an influence) to the next musical generation, most notably Dizzy Gillespie. Although he sometimes pushed himself farther than he could go, Eldridge never played a dull solo! Roy Eldridge started out playing trumpet and drums in carnival and circus bands. With the Nighthawk Syncopators he received a bit of attention by playing a note-for-note recreation of Coleman Hawkins' tenor solo on "The Stampede." Inspired by the dynamic playing of Jabbo Smith (Eldridge would not discover Louis Armstrong for a few years), Eldridge played with some territory bands including Zack Whyte and Speed Webb, and in New York (where he arrived in 1931) he worked with Elmer Snowden (who nicknamed him "Little Jazz"), McKinney's Cotton Pickers and most importantly Teddy Hill (1935). Eldridge's recorded solos with Hill, backing Billie Holiday and with Fletcher Henderson (including his 1936 hit "Christopher Columbus"), gained a great deal of attention. In 1937 he appeared with his octet (which included brother Joe on alto) at the Three Deuces Club in Chicago and recorded some outstanding selections as a leader including "Heckler's Hop" and "Wabash Stomp." By 1939 Roy had a larger group playing at the Arcadia Ballroom in New York. With the decline of Bunny Berigan and the increasing predictability of Louis Armstrong, Eldridge was arguably the top trumpeter in jazz during this era.

During 1941-42 Eldridge sparked Gene Krupa's Orchestra, recording classic versions of "Rockin' Chair" and "After You've Gone" and interacting with Anita O'Day on "Let Me Off Uptown." The difficulties of travelling with a White band during a racist period hurt him, as did some of the incidents that occurred during his stay with Artie Shaw (1944-45), but the music during both stints was quite memorable. Eldridge had a short-lived big band of his own, toured with Jazz at the Philharmonic and then had a bit of an identity crisis when he realized that his playing was not as modern as the beboppers. A successful stay in France during 1950-51 restored his confidence when he realized that being original was more important than being up-to-date. Eldridge recorded steadily for Norman Granz in the 1950s, was one of the stars of JATP (where he battled Charlie Shavers and Dizzy Gillespie), and by 1956 was often teamed with Coleman Hawkins in a quintet; their 1957 appearance at Newport was quite memorable. The 1960s were tougher as recording opportunities and work became rarer. Eldridge had brief and unhappy stints with Count Basie's Orchestra and Ella Fitzgerald (feeling unnecessary in both contexts) but was leading his own group by the end of the decade. He spent much of the 1970s playing regularly at Ryan's and recording for Pablo and, although his range had shrunk a bit, Eldridge's competitive spirit was still very much intact. Only a serious stroke in 1980 was able to halt his horn. Roy Eldridge recorded throughout his career for virtually every label. —*Scott Yanow*

★ **Little Jazz [1954]** / Feb. 26, 1935-Apr. 2, 1940 / Columbia ✦✦✦✦✦
This CD contains the best recordings from the early years of the fiery trumpeter Roy Eldridge. Eldridge, one of the great swing trumpeters and a powerful player into the 1970s, is heard with Teddy Hill's Orchestra, backing singer Putney Dandridge, on four titles with Fletcher Henderson (including the hit "Christopher Columbus"), starring on a four-song session with Teddy Wilson, joining Billie Holiday on "Falling in Love Again," soloing on two numbers with Mildred Bailey (his "I'm Nobody's Baby" solo is years ahead of its time) and, best of all, leading a small group through six songs (plus an alternate) from his own explosive sessions of Jan. 1937. This brilliant music is essential for all serious jazz collections. —*Scott Yanow*

The Early Years / Feb. 26, 1935-May 9, 1949 / Columbia ✦✦✦✦
Next to Louis Armstrong and Bunny Berigan, Roy Eldridge was one of the big three of jazz trumpeters who were active in the second half of the '30s. His stirring outbursts were consistently exciting and became a major influence on the playing of his contemporaries. This two-LP set has many of the high points of Eldridge's early years, particularly on the first album. He is heard in 1935 with Teddy Hill's Orchestra, guesting with Teddy Wilson in 1939 and on three titles with Mildred Bailey the following year (taking a futuristic solo on "I'm Nobody's Baby"), but it is the six numbers that he recorded with his own small group in 1937 that are most outstanding, particularly "Wabash Stomp," "Heckler's Hop," "That Thing" and his first version of "After You've Gone." The second album is more unusual, for it includes alternate takes of ten numbers that Eldridge recorded with Gene Krupa's Orchestra during 1941-42 including "new" versions of such hits as "Green Eyes," "Let Me Off Uptown," "After You've Gone" and "Rockin' Chair." This two-fer con-

cludes with a pair of numbers from 1949, when Eldridge briefly returned to Krupa's band. —*Scott Yanow*

After You've Gone / Feb. 5, 1936-Sep. 24, 1946 / GRP ✦✦✦✦
This excellent CD features the great swing trumpeter Roy Eldridge shortly after the breakup of the Gene Krupa Orchestra. Eldridge is heard leading his own recording groups (mostly big bands) and, although his own orchestra never really caught on, the trumpet solos are always quite exciting. This CD skips over five of Eldridge's Decca sides (it should have been a "complete" set) but does include three previously unissued performances plus a recently discovered jam on "Christopher Columbus" from 1936. —*Scott Yanow*

Live at the Three Duces / Feb. 1937 / Jazz Archives ✦✦✦
Trumpeter Roy Eldridge's octet, which recorded six songs in Jan. 1937, is heard on this LP stretching out during a couple of radio broadcasts from later that year. Actually, despite the fine playing of altoists Joe Eldridge and Scoops Carey, tenor Dave Young and the four-piece rhythm section, the focus is generally on the exciting trumpeter/leader. The recording quality is erratic but the performances are often quite heated, with Eldridge showing what he learned from listening to Louis Armstrong, most notably how to build a solo gradually up to a high note. Highlights include "Little Jazz," "Basin Street Blues," "Heckler's Hop" and "Chinatown, My Chinatown." —*Scott Yanow*

Arcadia Shuffle / Aug. 5, 1939-Sep. 9, 1939 / Jazz Archives ✦✦✦
On this LP the great swing trumpeter Roy Eldridge is heard leading his ten-piece group at New York's Arcadia Ballroom. These radio broadcasts were somewhat primitively recorded, but the excitement of Eldridge's playing shines through. Although this particular band did record eight titles later in the year, most of the music on this set (including "Little Jazz," "Mahogany Hall Stomp," "Shine," "Woodchopper's Ball" and "Lady Be Good") was not recorded by the trumpeter during the era. This album is worth searching for by swing collectors. —*Scott Yanow*

At Jerry Newman's / Nov. 19, 1940 / Xanadu ✦✦
This LP is strictly for collectors. The music at this jam session is loose with multiple versions of some titles, the musicians (which include altoist Willie Smith, Herbie Fields on tenor, guitarist Mike Bryan and various pianists and drummers) never really come together as a unified band, and the recording quality is erratic. But then again, trumpeter Roy Eldridge (who was not documented very well during this period) is in consistently intense and creative form, uplifting the performances and making this a worthwhile (and somewhat historic) album, which his fans should enjoy despite its faults. —*Scott Yanow*

Little Jazz: Big Band / Nov. 16, 1943-Sep. 24, 1946 / Sounds of Swing ✦✦✦✦✦
This collectors' LP contains 16 of the 28 Decca recordings made by the somewhat forgotten Roy Eldridge big band of the mid-'40s. The trumpeter was in peak form during the era, yet this exciting series of performances has yet to be reissued complete and in chronological order. Many of the selections have since appeared on CD, but not all of them. Eldridge is generally the whole show and his versions of "Rockin' Chair," "Body and Soul," "Twilight Time," "After You've Gone" and "The Gasser" are among the many memorable highlights of this fine LP. —*Scott Yanow*

Roy Eldridge in Paris / Jun. 9, 1950+Jun. 14, 1950 / Vogue ✦✦✦✦✦
In 1950, trumpeter Roy Eldridge was having a bit of an identity crisis. Once considered one of the pacesetters, the emergence of Dizzy Gillespie and the bop stylists left Eldridge unsure what to do. But that year, when he travelled to France with Benny Goodman, the future seemed clearer. The Parisian audiences demanded that Eldridge play himself rather than try to copy the modernists, and he took their advice. This CD reissue features the complete output (including seven alternate takes) from two exciting recording sessions. Eldridge heads a quintet with tenor saxophonist Zoot Sims; two songs have vocals from Anita Love, and Roy does a good job of singing on the good-humored "Ain't No Flies on Me." While "Wrap Your Troubles in Dreams" (heard in two versions) is the classic of that session, the later date features Roy with a quartet, and he is in top form on "If I Had You" and "Someone to Watch Over Me." —*Scott Yanow*

I Remember Harlem / Oct. 28, 1950-Mar. 29, 1951 / Inner City ✦✦✦✦
This out-of-print LP features Roy Eldridge in generally superb form. Recorded during his visit to Paris with the Benny Goodman Sextet, the well-rounded set finds him a dominant force on seven selections (six of which are his compositions) with a French septet. In addition, Eldridge is heard in an exciting quintet with tenor saxophonist Don Byas (the trumpeter's "Oh Shut Up" is based on the chords of "Please Don't Talk About Me When I'm Gone"), Eldridge and Claude Bolling perform "Wild Man Blues" and "Fireworks" as duets reminiscent of the interplay of Louis Armstrong and Earl Hines, and Eldridge even takes three loose but fun piano solos. This music is recommended but will probably be difficult to find. —*Scott Yanow*

Roy's Got Rhythm / Jan. 1951 / EmArcy ✦✦✦✦
Between his Paris sessions of 1950 and 1951 for Vogue, trumpeter Roy Eldridge traveled to Sweden and recorded nine spirited selections for Metronome, which

were reissued on this EmArcy LP. None of Eldridge's sidemen (except for clarinetist Ove Lind, who is on just two songs) gained much of a reputation outside of Sweden, but they fare well during these fairly basic performances which are based in swing but also influenced a little by early rhythm & blues. Highlights include "The Heat's On," the two-part "Saturday Nite Fish Fry," "School Days," "Echoes of Harlem" and a pair of numbers that feature Charles Norman on harpsichord. A bit of a collector's item, this LP will be difficult to find. —*Scott Yanow*

Dale's Wail / Dec. 13, 1952-Sep. 1954 / Verve ✦✦✦✦✦
This two-LP set features the great swing trumpeter at the peak of his powers. Eldridge is virtually the whole show on these four sessions for, although he is backed by the Oscar Peterson Trio plus either J.C. Heard, Jo Jones, Alvin Stoller or Buddy Rich on drums, Peterson (who is on organ for half of the selections) does not have much solo space. High points include "Little Jazz," "Wrap Your Troubles in Dreams," "Rockin' Chair," "Somebody Loves Me," "Sweethearts on Parade," "The Song Is Ended" and the title cut. —*Scott Yanow*

Little Jazz Live in 1957 / 1957 / Jazz Band ✦✦✦
Rare live performances (all from 1957) featuring trumpeter Roy Eldridge in four different settings are heard on this collectors' LP. He excels with a no-name quintet and a quartet, leads an all-star group (taken from a television show) that includes Bud Freeman on tenor, clarinetist Buddy DeFranco, trombonist J.J. Johnson and Art Van Damme on accordion for two numbers, and jams a blues with Freeman and an otherwise-unidentified band. The recording quality is decent and, although the results are not essential, this English import album will be greatly enjoyed by Roy Eldridge's fans, for the fiery trumpeter is heard in his prime. —*Scott Yanow*

● **Just You Just Me, Live in 1959** / 1959 / Stash ✦✦✦✦✦
In the late '50s trumpeter Roy Eldridge and tenor saxophonist Coleman Hawkins teamed up on a fairly regular basis. Since they always brought out the best in each other (their solos could be quite competitive and fiery), all of their joint recordings are recommended. Two LPs from their gig at Washington, DC's Bayou Club in 1959 were previously released on the Honeysuckle Rose label. Five of those selections plus four previously unissued cuts are included on this Stash CD. Most of the tunes are medium-tempo jams such as "Just You, Just Me," "Rifftide," and "How High the Moon," but there is also an excellent ballad medley. Backed by a local rhythm section, Eldridge and Hawk are both in superior form, making this a highly recommended disc even for listeners who already have the earlier LPs. —*Scott Yanow*

Comin' Home Baby / Aug. 25, 1965-Mar. 25, 1966 / Pumpkin ✦✦
With the exception of a European date in 1962, it had been five years since trumpeter Roy Eldridge led a record session when he performed the music on this LP, and these two sessions were not initially released until 1978. Teamed with the cool-toned but hard-swinging tenor Richie Kamuca and a rhythm section headed by pianist Dick Katz, the trumpeter is in fine form on five standards plus "Comin' Home Baby." Nothing that surprising occurs, but there is enough intensity and passion to make this an album recommended to straightahead jazz collectors. —*Scott Yanow*

The Nifty Cat Strikes West / Jul. 1966 / Master Jazz ✦✦✦
Trumpeter Roy Eldridge's first studio album as a leader in six years and only one of two from a 15-year period (his swing-based style was out of vogue) matches his fiery and competitive playing with trombonist Grover Mitchell, the tenor of Eric Dixon, pianist Bill Bell, bassist Norman Keenan and drummer Louis Bellson on five standards and two group originals. At the time Eldridge was a member of Count Basie's Orchestra (an association that only lasted a brief time) and all of the players on this LP (except of course pianist Bell) were also Basie-ites. It is therefore not too surprising that the music swings, the solos are quite melodic, and that no real surprises occur. The results are pleasing if conservative. —*Scott Yanow*

Nifty Cat / Nov. 24, 1970 / New World ✦✦✦✦
One of only two Eldridge-led studio sessions from the 1961-74 period, this CD reissue of a set originally recorded for Master Jazz matches the great swing trumpeter with Budd Johnson (who doubles on tenor and soprano), trombonist Benny Morton, pianist Nat Pierce, bassist Tommy Bryant and drummer Oliver Jackson. All six of the jump tunes are by Eldridge, with "5400 North" and "Ball of Fire" being best-known. For this album the veteran trumpeter had a very rare opportunity to call his own shots on a recording date, and the generally inspired playing makes this CD a fine example of small-group swing from the early '70s. —*Scott Yanow*

Little Jazz & The Jimmy Ryan All-Stars / Apr. 7, 1975 / Pablo ✦✦✦✦
During the 1970s, Roy Eldridge had a regular gig at Jimmy Ryan's in New York, playing music that fell between swing and Dixieland. For this Pablo LP, he sought to play a program with his regular group (Joe Muranyi on clarinet and soprano, trombonist Bobby Pratt, pianist Dick Katz, bassist Major Holley and drummer Eddie Locke) that, although recorded in the studio, would sound like one of the Jimmy Ryan sets. So, in addition to such standards as "Between the Devil and the Deep Blue Sea" and "All of Me," Eldridge also performs (and takes occasional vocals on) some older tunes like "St. James Infirmary," "Beale Street Blues" and

"Bourbon Street Parade." The music is quite joyful and spirited, with Eldridge in exuberant form. This LP is recommended and well-deserving of being reissued on CD. —*Scott Yanow*

Jazz Maturity. . . .Where It's Coming From / Jun. 3, 1975 / Original Jazz Classics ✦✦
Teaming together Dizzy Gillespie and Roy Eldridge should result in some classic music, but by 1975, Eldridge (although still a fierce competitor) was past his prime and Gillespie was starting to fade. The material performed for this CD reissue is just not all that inspiring—a few overly played standards and blues. Despite some good efforts by Gillespie and Eldridge, pianist Oscar Peterson easily emerges as the most impressive soloist; better to acquire the magnificent collaborations of the 1950s instead. —*Scott Yanow*

Happy Time / Jun. 4, 1975 / Original Jazz Classics ✦✦✦
Eldridge actually spends as much time singing as playing during the ten standards here, but the solos he takes (although concise) have their explosive moments. With pianists Oscar Peterson, guitarist Joe Pass, bassist Ray Brown and drummer Eddie Locke providing the support, the music always swings in an exuberant fashion. This CD reissue, although not essential, is worth acquiring. —*Scott Yanow*

What It's All About / Jan. 16, 1976 / Original Jazz Classics ✦✦✦✦
What It's All About is swinging, building up solos to potentially ferocious levels and going for broke. That was always the philosophy that Roy Eldridge followed and, even though it was rather late in his career by the time he recorded this Pablo CD reissue, he was still pushing himself. His septet on the album is full of talented veterans, including altoist Norris Turney, Budd Johnson on tenor, pianist Norman Simmons and (on half of the set) vibraphonist Milt Jackson. The music (three Eldridge originals and two obscurities) features plenty of lengthy and spirited soloing. —*Scott Yanow*

★ **Montreux 1977** / Jul. 13, 1977 / Original Jazz Classics ✦✦✦✦✦
Eldridge's final recording as a leader is a real gem. Although his chops were no longer in prime form, he was still pushing himself to the limit. With a brilliant rhythm section egging him on (pianist Oscar Peterson, bassist Niels Pedersen and drummer Bobby Durham), Eldridge still went for the high notes (and generally hit them) during this exciting set from the 1977 Montreux Jazz Festival. Although the musicians did not know it at the time, the last two songs ("Perdido" and "Bye Bye Blackbird") were a perfect ending to a brilliant career. This dramatic CD reissue is highly recommended. —*Scott Yanow*

Roy Eldridge & Vic Dickenson / May 20, 1978 / Storyville ✦✦✦✦
Roy Eldridge is in better-than-expected form for what would be his final recording before a heart attack forced him to give up the trumpet. Teamed up with trombonist Vic Dickenson, tenorman Budd Johnson, pianist Tommy Flanagan, bassist Major Holley and drummer Eddie Locke (who was actually the organizer of the date), Eldridge and his friends play a lengthy ad-lib blues and eight familiar standards. This Storyville CD is well worth picking up by straightahead, swing and mainstream jazz fans. —*Scott Yanow*

Elements

Group / Crossover Jazz, Post-Bop
Bassist Mark Egan and drummer Danny Gottlieb have been longtime friends, starting with their days at the University of Miami in the early 1970s and continuing during their period with Pat Metheny (Egan was in the guitarist's group from 1978-80, while Gottlieb stayed until 1983). They formed Elements in 1982, which, from its start, also included Bill Evans on soprano and tenor and keyboardist Clifford Carter, guitarist Steve Khan, keyboardist Gil Goldstein, several percussionists, saxophonist David Mann and other players as guests. Their music (documented on Philo, Antilles, Hip Pocket, Novus, GRP, Blue Moon and Wavetone) is a quiet and thoughtful form of fusion, filled with subtle creativity. —*Scott Yanow*

Forward Motion / Jul. 5, 1985-Jul. 7, 1985 / Antilles ✦✦✦
Another from fusion ensemble Elements, this one more introspective and heavily produced than some earlier releases. It was reissued on CD in 1991. Mark Egan and Danny Gottlieb were the central performers and group's compositional backbone. —*Ron Wynn*

● **Illumination** / Aug. 1987 / Novus ✦✦✦✦✦
Interesting group; Bill Evans on sax is the best improviser. —*Ron Wynn*

Liberal Arts / 1989 / Novus ✦✦✦

Spirit River / Feb. 19, 1990 / Novus ✦✦✦✦
Quiet clearly, Mark Egan's years with Pat Metheny had a lasting impact on his composing and playing. When *Spirit River* was recorded in 1990, a decade had passed since the electric bassist's departure from the Metheny Group; but Metheny's influence remained. Nonetheless, the album makes it clear that Egan and drummer Danny Gottlieb (Elements' other leader) have a collective vision of their

own. This charming jazz-pop date isn't about intense or aggressive swinging, and tends to have an introspective, floating quality. Saxman Bill Evans (not to be confused with the late piano legend) is characteristically expressive and soulful on soprano, and Brazilian greats Flora Purim (vocals) and Airto Moreira (percussion) make some valuable, heartfelt contributions to the engaging CD. —*Alex Henderson*

Far East, Vol. 1 / Jul. 1992 / Wavetone ✦✦✦

Untold Stories / 1996 / Wavetone ✦✦✦

Mark Elf

b. Dec. 13, 1949, Queens, NY
Guitar / Bop

An excellent bop-based guitarist, Mark Elf has created a stir with his own small-group recordings. He attended Berklee (1969-71), picked up experience playing with a who's who of modern mainstream jazz (including Wynton Marsalis, Clark Terry, Dizzy Gillespie, Lionel Hampton, Benny Golson, Al Grey, Branford Marsalis and Slide Hampton) and has recorded as a sideman with Lou Donaldson, Freddie Hubbard, Joe Henderson, Wynton Marsalis, Jon Hendricks and others. Elf spent time with Jimmy Heath's group, but has achieved his greatest recognition thus far with his recordings for the Jen Bay Jazz label and a set recorded in Chile (Alerce) made available in the US. —*Scott Yanow*

Mark Elf Trio, Vol. 1 / Jun. 1986-Jul. 1987 / Half Note ✦✦✦✦

Guitarist Mark Elf's debut as a leader is a swinging trio set with bassist Paul Brown and either Leroy Williams or Al Harewood on drums. The repertoire includes a blues, a tune based on the chords of "You Stepped Out of a Dream," five jazz standards (including "Joy Spring" and "Limehouse Blues"), and an unaccompanied guitar solo on "People" that works well. Of the cool-toned Elf's consistently rewarding output, this LP will be the most difficult to locate, but is up to the level of the others. —*Scott Yanow*

The Eternal Triangle / Dec. 22, 1988 / Jen Bay ✦✦✦✦

Mark Elf, a quiet guitarist who is quite capable of taking burning bop-based solos, debuted on his own Jen Bay label in 1996 with the initial release of an older session from 1988. Elf is matched with four veterans (pianist Hank Jones, tenorman Jimmy Heath, bassist Ray Drummond and drummer Ben Riley), and together they perform tunes by Sonny Stitt, Freddie Redd (the attractive "So Samba"), Tadd Dameron ("Hot House"), Benny Golson, Kenny Dorham, Duke Ellington, Jerome Kern and Gordon Jenkins, along with a pair by the leader. It is a major achievement that Elf holds his own solo-wise with the notable supporting cast, for Hank Jones in particular is in inspired form. Easily recommended to fans of the prefusion jazz guitar. —*Scott Yanow*

Mark Elf Trio / Feb. 1993 / Alerce ✦✦✦✦

A soft-toned guitarist whose fresh musical personality includes hints of Jimmy Raney and Jim Hall, Mark Elf toured Europe with Dizzy Gillespie back in 1987 and has had a strong reputation in musician circles for quite some time. His set for the Alerce label is unusual in that it was recorded in Santiago, Chile, with South American musicians. Fortunately the CD is readily available domestically, for Elf is in particularly creative form. Most selections feature the guitarist with a trio that also includes bassist Ramon Romero and drummer Alejandro Espinosa. "Body and Soul" adds Claudia Acuna for a warm vocal while "Sweet and Lovely" utilizes four local horn players. Otherwise the focus is on Elf and his interplay with his sidemen. Most impressive is the guitarist's clarity on a speedy "Giant Steps" (every note rings out clearly), his quiet unhurried playing on a rapid "Straw Nuff" and his ability to sing along with his instrument on "It's You or No One." —*Scott Yanow*

● **Minor Scramble** / Nov. 27, 1996-Dec. 17, 1996 / Jen Bay ✦✦✦✦✦

Mark Elf's third self-produced CD is another gem. The guitarist's trio selections, with bassist Peter Washington and drummer Louis Nash, include a snappy miniature arrangement of "After You've Gone," a rarely heard ballad by Harold Arlen, "It Is Written in the Stars," and his bluesy original title track. Elf's guests include the young trumpet star Nicholas Payton on a conversational "Come Rain or Come Shine" and the delightful pianist Bennie Green on a lively cover of "Nobody Else but Me." Mark Elf's taste and consistency have helped him break the seeming stranglehold that larger labels have on jazz radio charts; if you haven't yet heard him, start with this highly recommended CD. —*Ken Dryden*

Trickynometry / Nov. 24, 1997+Nov. 26, 1997 / Jen Bay ✦✦✦✦

This is a particularly interesting program by boppish guitarist Mark Elf. The date starts out strong (with "Trickynometry" and "Dot Com Blues"), featuring a quintet that includes trumpeter Nicholas Payton, and one regrets that Payton is only on one of the remaining ten numbers. In addition to Elf (who is in top form), the musicians include Bobby LaVell on tenor (for the same three songs as Payton), either Christian McBride or Neal Miner on bass and drummer Yoron Israel. Grady Tate and Miles Griffith take a vocal apiece, but most tunes feature Elf in a trio. The music is consistently excellent with other highlights including "Just in Time,"

"Milestones" and "Monk Like"; if only Payton (who sounds very fiery in spots) had been persuaded to stick around for the other songs too. —*Scott Yanow*

Eliane Elias

b. Mar. 19, 1960, Sao Paulo, Brazil
Piano, Vocals / Post-Bop, Brazilian Jazz

A versatile pianist, Eliane Elias has played straightahead jazz, fusion and Brazilian jazz with equal skill. After working in her native Brazil she moved to New York on Eddie Gomez's advice in 1981, became a member of Steps Ahead and married Randy Brecker in 1983. She debuted as a leader in 1986, signed with Blue Note in 1989 and toured with her trio. Elias has also sung on some of her records, but her piano playing is really her most significant musical talent; she held her own with Herbie Hancock on her 1995 release *Solos and Duets*. —*Scott Yanow*

Illusions / Oct. 22, 1986-Oct. 24, 1986 / Denon ✦✦✦✦

Eliane Elias' debut as a leader (she had been a member of Steps Ahead) finds her abandoning the electric keyboards in favor of acoustic piano. On seven songs she is joined by bassist Eddie Gomez and either Al Foster or Steve Gadd on drums; the remaining two selections feature her accompanied by bassist Stanley Clarke and drummer Lenny White. With harmonica great Toots Thielemans making guest appearances on two numbers, Elias was at the time easily the least-known of the players on her own CD. However the pianist was already far along toward developing her own sound as she shows on four originals, two obscurities, Herbie Hancock's "Chan's Song," Blossom Dearie's "Sweet Georgia Fame" and the standard "Falling in Love with Love." A fine start to a significant solo career. —*Scott Yanow*

Cross Currents / Mar. 16, 1987-Mar. 21, 1987 / Denon ✦✦✦✦

Pianist Eliane Elias' second of two Denon CDs recorded before she hooked up with Blue Note is a lesser-known but worthy session. Elias is mostly featured in a trio with bassist Eddie Gomez and drummer Jack DeJohnette performing originals, a pair of Charles Mingus compositions ("Peggy's Blue Skylight" and "East Coastin' "), "Beautiful Love," "When You Wish upon a Star" and Bud Powell's "Hallucinations." Elias was quickly developing into a strong modern mainstream pianist. The concluding number ("Coming and Going") was written by her grandmother in 1927 at age 12, and features Elias with Gomez, drummer Peter Erskine, guitarist Barry Finnerty , percussionist Cafe and nine singers (including a few family members). Well worth searching for. —*Scott Yanow*

So Far So Close / 1988 / Blue Note ✦✦✦

Eliane Elias' debut for Blue Note is a bit of a disappointment. Having established her credentials as a fine acoustic pianist, she switched back to her less personal synthesizer work and contributed some wordless vocals that are rather mundane. The music (which includes some solos from tenor saxophonist Michael Brecker and Randy Brecker on fluegelhorn) is not terrible but it lacks a sense of adventure and sounds as if potential radio airplay was its main goal. —*Scott Yanow*

Eliane Elias Plays Jobim / Dec. 1989 / Blue Note ✦✦✦✦✦

This CD has some surprising music. Although it was not unexpected that the Brazil-born pianist Eliane Elias would eventually explore the music of Antonio Carlos Jobim, these interpretations of his melodies (performed with bassist Eddie Gomez, drummer Jack DeJohnette and percussionist Nana Vasconcelos) largely strip the music of its bossa nova rhythms and instead recasts the songs as creative jazz. The versions of such familiar tunes as "Sabia," "Desafinado," "Dindi" and "One Note Samba" cast new light on the songs and make them sound quite different than they had previously. —*Scott Yanow*

A Long Story / 1991 / Blue Note ✦✦✦✦

Fantasia / Mar. 1992 / Blue Note ✦✦✦✦✦

Eliane Elias continues exploring Brazilian music on this latest release, doing both classics such as "The Girl from Ipanema" and a Milton Nasciemento medley, plus several Ivan Lins tunes. She uses alternating bassists and drummers, with Eddie Gomez, Marc Johnson, Jack DeJohnette, and Peter Erskine dividing time, plus Nana Vasconcelos on percussion, with Lins helping out on vocals. —*Ron Wynn*

Paulistana / Oct. 5, 1993 / Blue Note ✦✦✦

Eliane Elias continues to revist and update her Brazilian heritage on this Blue Note CD. The music ranges from South American folk songs and such standards as "Brazil" and "Black Orpheus" to newer originals. Elias mostly sticks to acoustic piano and is primarily heard in a trio format with occasional percussion added. She hints strongly at Keith Jarrett and Bill Evans in spots but by this time has largely formed her own personal style out of her earlier influences. A few vocals (including a collaboration with Ivan Lins) weaken some of the tracks, for Elias' singing is on a much lower level than her more individual playing. Still, even with its minor flaws, *Paulistana* is recommended. —*Scott Yanow*

● **Solos & Duets** / Nov. 18, 1994+Dec. 1994 / Blue Note ✦✦✦✦✦

This release is a change of pace for Eliane Elias. Instead of interpreting Brazilian songs, fusion or modern bop, Elias shows off her classical technique on a set of acoustic solos plus six duets with Herbie Hancock. She really digs into the standards (sometimes sounding a little like Keith Jarrett) and creates some fairly free and unexpected ideas while putting the accent on lyricism. Some of the music is introspective and there are wandering sections, but the net results are logical and enjoyable. As for the duets, Elias and Hancock mostly stay out of each other's way, which is an accomplishment when one considers that the four-part "Messages" is a series of free improvisations. There are playful spots (particularly on the adventurous ten-minute rendition of "The Way You Look Tonight") and, since Elias knows Hancock's style well (and was clearly thrilled to have him on the date), their collaborations work quite well. A successful outing. —*Scott Yanow*

Three Americas / 1996 / Blue Note ♦♦♦♦
Two sides of Eliane Elias are on display on this CD. She is heard as an effective soft-toned singer of bossa nova and (particularly on the last few numbers) as a strong post-bop jazz pianist. The bossas (which often feature guitarist Oscar Castro-Neves and flutist Dave Valentin) are enjoyable, if a bit lightweight, and "Chorango" (which has Gil Goldstein on accordion and violinist Mark Feldman) is a modern tango. But it is as a pianist that Elias is most significant, and fortunately, there are enough instrumentals on this release to make it worth picking up by jazz listeners. —*Scott Yanow*

Kurt Elling

b. Nov. 2, 1967, Chicago, IL
Vocals / Post-Bop
During an era when the number of significant male jazz singers under the age of 60 can be counted on one hand, Kurt Elling's arrival is very welcome. Influenced by Mark Murphy, Elling combines poetry with jazz and is a chance-taking improviser who often makes up lyrics as he goes along. He discovered jazz while attending college and, although he had planned to become a professor in the philosophy of religion, he eventually became a professional singer instead. After a period of struggle Elling recorded a demo tape that was accepted by Blue Note, resulting in the impressive 1995 release *Close Your Eyes*. —*Scott Yanow*

● **Close Your Eyes** / 1995 / Blue Note ♦♦♦♦♦

Messenger / Apr. 8, 1997 / Blue Note ♦♦♦♦♦
This is one of the most interesting jazz vocal sets to be released in 1997. Kurt Elling covers a wide range of music, continually taking chances and coming up with fresh approaches. He is assisted by his longtime pianist Laurence Hopgood, different bassists and drummers, and on various tracks trumpeter Orbert Davis and the tenors of Edward Petersen and Eddie Johnson. Among the more memorable selections are Elling's vocalese version of Dexter Gordon's solo on the lengthy "Tanya Jean," his spontaneous storytelling on "It's Just a Thing" (a classic of its kind), some wild scatting on "Gingerbread Boy," the fairly free improvising of "Endless," and his mostly straightforward renditions of "Nature Boy," "April in Paris" and "Prelude to a Kiss." Cassandra Wilson drops by for "Time of the Season," but does not make much of an impression. This rewarding and continually intriguing set is particularly recommended to listeners who feel that jazz singing has not progressed much beyond bop. —*Scott Yanow*

Duke Ellington (Edward Kennedy Ellington)

b. Apr. 29, 1899, Washington, DC, **d.** May 24, 1974, New York, NY
Piano, Composer, Arranger, Leader / Swing, Big Band, Traditional Jazz
Duke Ellington's contributions to jazz and American music were simply enormous. As a bandleader, his orchestra during 1926-74 was always among the top five, whether it be 1929 or 1969. As a composer, Ellington ranked with George Gershwin, Cole Porter, Irving Berlin and their contemporaries. He wrote literally thousands of songs (the exact number is not known) of which hundreds became standards. As an arranger Ellington was particularly innovative, writing for his very individual players rather than for an anonymous horn section and, not being content to play his songs the same way every time, he constantly rearranged them; "Mood Indigo" sounded different in 1933 than it did in 1953 or 1973. As a pianist Duke Ellington was originally an excellent stride player who gained the respect of such giants as James P. Johnson, Fats Waller and his main influence Willie "The Lion" Smith. Unlike virtually all of his contemporaries (other than Mary Lou Williams), Duke was able to modernize his style through the years, keeping the percussive approach of the stride players but leaving more space and using more complex chords; his playing was an influence on Thelonious Monk and (in a more abstract fashion) Cecil Taylor. Duke Ellington always considered his orchestra to be his main instrument and with it he recorded constantly from 1926 on. In the early days he recorded for many labels, sometimes under pseudonyms, and by the 1950s he often seemed to live in the studios when not performing before audiences, trying out new material and fresh versions of older songs. The result is that there are currently a countless number of Ellington albums available (way over 200) with "new" (previously unissued) ones coming out nearly every month as if

he were still alive. What is more remarkable than the quantity is the consistently high quality; there are few if any throwaways in Ellington's entire discography!

There is simply no explanation for Edward Kennedy Ellington's musical genius. Although he started studying piano when he was seven, for a time it seemed that Duke (who picked up his lifelong nickname early) was going to be an artist. However he so enjoyed hearing the ragtime and barrelhouse piano players of the era that he soon chose music. Ellington started playing music in Washington, DC, in 1917 and, after wisely taking out the biggest ad in the telephone yellow pages, was soon leading several bands despite the fact that his repertoire was very limited. Ellington, whose first composition "Soda Fountain Rag" was written during this era, worked on building up his technique by slowing down James P. Johnson piano rolls and analyzing the fingering. A brief visit to New York in 1922 (playing with Wilbur Sweatman) was unsuccessful, but Ellington returned the following year and was such hometown friends as Sonny Greer, Otto Hardwicke and Arthur Whetsol worked for a period under banjoist Elmer Snowden's leadership and then, after an argument over missing money, Ellington became the leader. His early group was called the Washingtonians.

Duke Ellington soon gained a job at the Hollywood Club (later renamed the Kentucky Club) for his band. For a brief time Sidney Bechet starred on soprano, but more important to Duke's development was the playing of trumpeter Bubber Miley, a brilliant plunger specialist who largely founded the "jungle sound" that made Ellington's group sound different than anyone else. Duke recorded two titles with his group in November 1924 ("Choo Choo" and "Rainy Nights") that found his band already sounding recognizable despite only having three horns (with altoist Otto Hardwicke and trombonist Charles Irvis). Oddly enough, the eight other selections that he recorded during 1925-26 are quite primitive and disappointing; Miley is absent and the band sounds as if it were struggling. However, with the debut of Ellington's early theme song "East St. Louis Toodle-oo" along with "Birmingham Breakdown" on the session of November 29, 1926, the Duke Ellington Orchestra was essentially born. The band was up to 11 pieces including the wonderful wa-wa trombonist Tricky Sam Nanton, who made for a perfect team with Miley. 1927 was the breakthrough year for Duke Ellington. In addition to recording more versions of "East St. Louis Toodle-oo," he debuted "Black and Tan Fantasy" and "Creole Love Call"; the latter used Adelaide Hall's voice as an instrument. Baritonist Harry Carney (who would remain with Duke nonstop through 1974!) became a key member of the ensemble. And Ellington's band (through the help of manager Irving Mills) gained a permanent spot at the Cotton Club. Not only would its radio broadcasts soon make Ellington famous throughout the country, but he had the opportunity to write for the floor shows and the experience led to him growing rapidly as a composer/arranger.

Duke Ellington's life would never be a good topic for a Hollywood movie, because from 1927 on it was success after another. In 1928 clarinetist Barney Bigard and altoist Johnny Hodges became longtime members and Arthur Whetsol (whose lyrical trumpet offered a contrast to the speech-like playing of Miley) gained a more prominent role. In early 1929 Bubber Miley, whose alcoholism led to him becoming increasingly unreliable, was reluctantly let go, but his replacement, Cootie Williams, would eventually be a more flexible soloist. Ellington appeared in his first film (*Black and Tan*) that year, and unlike most other Black celebrities of the 1920s and '30s, his performance did not find him acting as a clown or inferior to White people. Ellington always appeared as a classy and charming genius (just as he did in real life) and, despite the "inconvenience" of being Black in a racist society, Duke Ellington was able to survive (and eventually prosper) due to his brilliance without compromising himself.

While most big bands might have three or four notable soloists, Ellington's Orchestra in the 1930s featured eight: trumpeters Cootie Williams and Rex Stewart (the latter joined on cornet in 1935), trombonists Tricky Sam Nanton and Lawrence Brown, clarinetist Barney Bigard, altoist Hodges, baritonist Carney and the leader on piano; in addition Ivie Anderson was their fine singer. After leaving the Cotton Club in 1931 (although he would return on an occasional basis throughout the rest of the decade), the Ellington Orchestra became a road band, touring Europe and Sweden in 1933 and 1939 and becoming a major attraction in every key city in the US. Ellington, who had recorded a two-sided six-minute version of "Tiger Rag" in 1929, began to compose longer works including "Creole Rhapsody" (1931), and "Reminiscing in Tempo" (1935), and his three-minute masterpiece "Daybreak Express" found the orchestra doing an uncanny imitation of a train's journey. Although there was a lot more competition from big bands with the rise of the swing era in 1935, Ellington remained a major name. Such compositions as "Mood Indigo," "Rockin' in Rhythm," "It Don't Mean a Thing If It Ain't Got That Swing," "Sophisticated Lady," "Drop Me Off at Harlem," "In a Sentimental Mood," "Caravan" (written by valve trombonist Juan Tizol), "I Let a Song Go Out of My Heart," "Prelude to a Kiss," "Solitude" and "Boy Meets Horn" became standards. By 1940 Duke Ellington's Orchestra had become, if anything, even stronger. Ben Webster joined as their first major voice on tenor, the innovative bassist Jimmy Blanton became the first important soloist on his instrument in jazz history, and Billy Strayhorn, as arranger and composer, became Ellington's musical partner up until his death in 1967. When Cootie Williams departed in late 1940, Ray Nance (a fine trumpeter, violinist and vocalist) easily fit into the spot. Many critics consider Duke's 1940-42 big band to be his greatest. Certainly there was an explosion of activity, with such new pieces as "Concerto for Cootie," "Cottontail," "Harlem Air Shaft," "All Too Soon," "Warm Valley," "Take the 'A' Train," "Just A-Settin' and A-Rockin'," "I Got It Bad," "Jump for Joy," "Chelsea Bridge," "Perdido," "The 'C' Jam Blues," "Johnny Come Lately" forming only a partial list of the orchestra's accomplishments.

In 1943 Duke Ellington gave his first Carnegie Hall concert (it would be an annual series lasting until 1950) and debuted his 50-minute work "Black, Brown and Beige" which, although it received mixed reviews, can now be heard and evaluated as a major success. The turnover in his orchestra increased during the latter half of the 1940s, but the quality remained consistently high and, despite the collapse of the big-band era and the rise of bebop (a music that Ellington accepted and borrowed from), Duke's orchestra never did break up; his royalty payments from his hits helped keep the big band together. Such new players as trumpeters Taft Jordan, Shorty Baker and the remarkable high-note player Cat Anderson (who had several long stints with Duke), Tyree Glenn (on trombone and vibes), Al Sears on tenor and bassist Oscar Pettiford passed through the band, and clarinetist Jimmy Hamilton stayed into the late '60s. "Don't Get Around Much Anymore" was a hit and Ellington also wrote such lengthy works as "The Perfume Suite," "The Deep South Suite" and "The Liberia Suite"; the last theme of "Happy Go Lucky Local" was "borrowed" by Jimmy Forrest and retitled "Night Train."

By the early '50s, Duke Ellington was in the only slump of his career, but it was more a commercial slip than an artistic one. Johnny Hodges, Lawrence Brown and Sonny Greer suddenly left to form a small group under Hodges' leadership. In what was called "The Great James Robbery," Duke persuaded three members of Harry James' Orchestra to join him: drummer Louie Bellson, altoist Willie Smith and Juan Tizol (who had left Ellington in the 1940s). But by 1953-54 the orchestra was struggling a bit during an era when few big bands survived. However, in 1955 Hodges returned to the fold, and at the 1956 Newport Jazz Festival tenor saxophonist Paul Gonsalves took an exciting marathon solo on "Diminuendo and Crescendo in Blue" that caused a sensation. Ellington was big again and the momentum would continue through the remainder of his life.

With such fine soloists as trumpeters Clark Terry, Ray Nance, Cat Anderson and Willie Cook, trombonists Buster Cooper and Britt Woodman and a reed section that was together for over a decade (Hodges, Carney, Hamilton, Gonsalves and Russell Procope on clarinet and alto), Ellington's late-'50s orchestra could hold its own with any of his groups. Although "Satin Doll" in the early '50s was his last pop hit, Duke continued working major works with Strayhorn. In the 1960s he turned toward religion, writing music for three sacred concerts and also composing "The Far East Suite," a very impressive and modern work. Duke also recorded albums on which he played piano in a trio with Charles Mingus and Max Roach, sat in with both the Louis Armstrong All-Stars and the John Coltrane Quartet and he had a double big-band date with Count Basie and a combo session with Coleman Hawkins. Constantly travelling the world and receiving long overdue honors (although not a Pulitzer Prize), Duke Ellington was finally recognized as a remarkable national treasure. By the latter half of the '60s, Ellington's associates were starting to die off. Billy Strayhorn's loss in 1967 was major, as was Johnny Hodges' passing in 1970. There were important new members in Harold Ashby on tenor, altoist Norris Turney and (in 1973) trumpeter Barry Lee Hall. But in 1974 Duke Ellington was stricken with cancer and spent his 75th birthday in a hospital. His death four weeks later has left a huge hole that will never be filled. — *Scott Yanow*

The Birth of a Band, Vol. 1 / Nov. 1924-Dec. 1926 / EPM ◆◆◆
This CD contains virtually all of Duke Ellington's recordings before he had developed his own musical identity. Starting off with a piano roll from 1924 and including obscure vocals by Alberta Hunter, Florence Bristol, Alberta Jones and Jo Trent, the valuable set also has all of Ellington's earliest instrumentals, cut during the years that his Washingtonians successfully struggled and landed an important association with the Kentucky Club. Highly recommended to collectors but certainly too primitive for most of Ellington's fans. — *Scott Yanow*

Complete, Vol. 1: 1925-1928 / Sep. 1925-Oct. 1928 / Columbia ◆◆◆◆
French Columbia, in the mid- to late '70s, put out a perfectly conceived Duke Ellington series that eventually totalled 15 double LPs. As with the French RCA program, Columbia reissued every Ellington recording they owned, including all of the alternate takes, but unfortunately both of these definitive series are very difficult to acquire, and current CD programs are less complete. All of the Columbia two-fers are worth tracking down if possible. *Volume 1* has four early sides from 1925-26 that find Ellington struggling to find his own musical personality. Then suddenly, with "East St. Louis Toodle-oo" from March 22, 1927, he emerges as a

major force. The contrasting trumpets of Bubber Miley and Arthur Whetsol, along with trombonist Tricky Sam Nanton and a variety of emerging soloists, star throughout this wonderful set, which is mostly from 1928. — *Scott Yanow*

☆ **Early Ellington (1926-1931)** / Nov. 29, 1926-Jan. 20, 1931 / Decca ◆◆◆◆◆
This three-CD set, which has all of Duke Ellington's recordings for the Brunswick and Vocalion labels, dwarfs all of the earlier reissues that Decca and MCA have put out of this important material. Starting with the first session in which the Ellington Orchestra sounds distinctive ("East St. Louis Toodle-oo" and "Birmingham Breakdown" from Nov. 29, 1926) and progressing through the Cotton Club years, this essential release (which contains 67 performances) adds a few "new" alternate takes and rare items ("Soliloquy" and a few titles by the "Six Jolly Jesters") to make this collection truly complete, at least for MCA's holdings (since Ellington also recorded for Columbia and Victor-owned labels during the same period). With such major soloists as trumpeters Bubber Miley (and his replacement Cootie Williams), Freddy Jenkins and Arthur Whetsol, trombonist Tricky Sam Nanton, clarinetist Barney Bigard, altoist Johnny Hodges, baritonist Harry Carney and the pianist/leader, along with the classic arrangements/compositions, this set is essential for all serious jazz collections. — *Scott Yanow*

The Brunswick Recordings, Vol. 1 (1926-1929) / Dec. 29, 1926-Jan. 8, 1929 / MCA ◆◆◆◆
The first of two CDs featuring high points from the Ellington recordings owned by MCA, this set features music from the Bubber Miley era including "Immigration Blues" (from the first session when Duke Ellington's band established its identity) to early versions of "East St. Louis Toodle-oo" and "Black and Tan Fantasy," an alternate take of "Black Beauty" and the exciting two-part version of "Tiger Rag." Trumpeters Bubber Miley and Arthur Whetsol and trombonist Tricky Sam Nanton star throughout. — *Scott Yanow*

☆ **The Works of Duke, Vols. 1-5** / Jan. 10, 1927-Nov. 21, 1930 / RCA ◆◆◆◆◆
In the '70s, French RCA did a perfect job of reissuing Duke Ellington's priceless recordings for its associated labels, releasing everything cut through 1952 (including all of the alternate takes) on 24 LPs also available in five box sets. No other reissue program conducted by RCA (whether on LP or on CD) comes close, although these sets are unfortunately out of print. The five volumes trace Ellington's legacy from 1927-30 and, along with a few period vocals and novelties, is overflowing with classics. Get it if you can. — *Scott Yanow*

OKeh Ellington / Mar. 22, 1927-Nov. 8, 1930 / Columbia ◆◆◆◆◆
Although generally not as celebrated as his Victor recordings of the same period, Duke Ellington's performances for OKeh (later acquired by Columbia) are among the best of the period, featuring distinctive solos by the likes of trumpeter Bubber Miley (and later his replacement Cootie Williams), trombonist Tricky Sam Nanton (who, like Miley, was an expert with wa-wa mutes), clarinetist Barney Bigard and altoist Johnny Hodges among others. These 50 performances (which bypass Ellington's alternate takes) contain many classics, including his original theme "East St. Louis Toodle-oo," "Black and Tan Fantasy," "The Mooche," "Mood Indigo" and his two earliest solo piano sides. This is one of the best sets of early Ellington currently available. — *Scott Yanow*

Flaming Youth / Oct. 26, 1927-Jan. 6, 1929 / RCA ◆◆◆
Of all of the single LPs released of early Duke Ellington in the '60s and '70s, *Flaming Youth* was the definitive one, for it seemed to include the most exciting versions of each of Ellington's classics of the era. These versions of "Black and Tan Fantasy," "Jubilee Stomp," "The Mooche" and especially "East St. Louis Toodle-oo" have never been topped and, if only for the contributions of the unique trumpeter Bubber Miley, this set was a perfect introduction to early Ellington during the LP era. — *Scott Yanow*

Early Ellington (1927-1934) / Oct. 26, 1927-Jan. 10, 1934 / Bluebird ◆◆◆◆
Thus far RCA, in its Bluebird series, has released three CDs of early Duke Ellington. Although not comparable in quantity to its earlier "complete" series on French RCA LPs, this first disc is well worth acquiring and is a perfect place for collectors to start in exploring Duke Ellington's music of the '20s and early '30s. High points include "Black and Tan Fantasy," "Creole Love Call," "East St. Louis Toodle-oo," the lyrical "Black Beauty," "Mood Indigo" and the remarkable "Daybreak Express," on which Ellington has his unique orchestra colorfully depicting a train ride. Some of his music still sounds futuristic today. — *Scott Yanow*

Jungle Nights in Harlem / Dec. 19, 1927-Jan. 9, 1932 / Bluebird ◆◆◆◆
This second of three CDs of early Ellington released by Bluebird has the loose theme of his Cotton Club days as an excuse to release a variety of recordings from a five-year period. Highlights include the two-part "A Night at the Cotton Club" (essentially a medley), some of the hotter songs from the Broadway musical *Blackbirds of 1928* ("Bandanna Babies," in addition to an odd vocal, has one of trumpeter Bubber Miley's greatest solos), some mood pieces and two lengthy medleys from 1932. Although the music deserves to be reissued as complete sessions, this

sampler is consistently delightful and shows that, when it came to swing, Ellington (along with Fletcher Henderson) predated everyone. —*Scott Yanow*

Jubilee Stomp / Mar. 26, 1928-May 9, 1934 / Bluebird ✦✦✦
The third of three CDs of early Ellington put out by Bluebird, this set has mostly lesser-known recordings, including a few pop tunes and mood pieces. Collectors will want to acquire the complete sessions (hopefully RCA will get around to reissuing this timeless music in a more definitive fashion in the future), but this CD has plenty of fine moments, including memorable versions of "Bugle Call Rag" and the hot title tune. —*Scott Yanow*

Greatest Hits [RCA] / Oct. 30, 1928-Sep. 1, 1967 / RCA Victor ✦✦✦
Unlike some of the entries in RCA Victor's beginners' introduction to jazz CD series, this collection does contain quite a few "hits." Other than 1928's "I Can't Give You Anything but Love" and a 1967 rendition of "Lotus Blossom," the music on the set dates from 1941-46. The performances (available in more coherent and complete form elsewhere) are all worth hearing, although the packaging (which does not bother to list the personnel other than a few soloists) is poor. But novices who can find this set at a reasonable price may want to pick it up; highlights include the original version of "Take the 'A' Train," "I Got It Bad" and remakes of "Mood Indigo," "Caravan" and a spirited version of "It Don't Mean a Thing." —*Scott Yanow*

Complete, Vol. 2: 1928-1930 / Oct. 1928-Nov. 20, 1929 / Columbia ✦✦✦✦
The second volume of this regrettably unavailable series of two-fers contains all of CBS' Ellington recordings from October 1928 up to January 29, 1930, a period when trumpeter Cootie Williams replaced Bubber Miley and altoist Johnny Hodges quickly developed into one of the major soloists in jazz. There are lots of valuable rarities on this highly enjoyable two-fer. —*Scott Yanow*

The Brunswick Era, Vol. 2 (1929-1931) / Jan. 8, 1929-Jan. 20, 1931 / Decca ✦✦✦✦
The second of two CDs featuring highlights from MCA's collection of early Duke Ellington (but not as complete as the three CD *Early Ellington* set put out by Decca), this enjoyable set is filled with performances from the early Depression years including the jubilant "Wall Street Wail" (recorded only a short while after the crash of 1929), "Mood Indigo," "Rockin' in Rhythm" and his two-part "Creole Rhapsody." During this period, altoist Johnny Hodges emerged as a major soloist and Cootie Williams became more comfortable as the replacement for the great Bubber Miley. —*Scott Yanow*

Cotton Club Stomp / 1929-1935 / Biograph ✦✦✦
For the true Ellington fanatic who needs every one of his recordings, this LP contains the soundtracks from three of his earliest film appearances. One gets the soundtrack of 1929's *Black and Tan* (which featured trumpeter Arthur Whetsol in a prominent role), 1933's *A Bundle of Blues* (including Ivie Anderson singing "Stormy Weather") and 1935's *Symphony in Black;* the latter has one blues chorus by Billie Holiday. A well-done package but not essential. —*Scott Yanow*

The Complete, Vol. 3: 1930-1932 / Jan. 29, 1930-Feb. 4, 1932 / Columbia ✦✦✦✦✦
The third of 15 volumes that document every Duke Ellington recording for CBS and its related labels up to 1940, this hard-to-find double LP has many alternate takes and even more gems from 1930-32, including rare remakes of "The Mooche" and "Black and Tan Fantasy" and the original "It Don't Mean a Thing If It Ain't Got That Swing." —*Scott Yanow*

Works of Duke, Vols. 6-10 / Nov. 26, 1930-Jul. 22, 1940 / RCA ✦✦✦✦✦
The second of five priceless box sets put out by French RCA in the '70s, these five LPs cover Ellington from 1930-34 and also when he returned to Victor in 1940. Loads of brilliant music; even the weaker items have their great moments. —*Scott Yanow*

Reflections in Ellington / Feb. 3, 1932-Sep. 26, 1940 / Everybodys'✦✦✦
For this LP there are previously unissued broadcast performances from 1940 (most of them quite rewarding) that feature one of Duke Ellington's greatest orchestras, along with two medleys from 1932 that are heard for the first time in stereo. Apparently the latter items were originally recorded using two sets of microphones and, although the notes are unchanged from the more conventional release, one can hear a bit of separation between the two channels. This LP is well worth searching for. —*Scott Yanow*

Complete, Vol. 4: 1932 / Feb. 4, 1932-Dec. 21, 1932 / Columbia ✦✦✦✦✦
From the French CBS series of two-fer LPs that reissued all of Duke Ellington's output (including alternate takes) for his associated labels, this set finds his orchestra still flourishing musically at the height of the Depression. Most of these titles generally miss getting reissued by "best-of" series but are all worth hearing. Best known are the two versions of "St. Louis Blues" with guest Bing Crosby and Ellington's famous recording of "The Sheik of Araby" that is highlighted by a famous chorus by trombonist Lawrence Brown. —*Scott Yanow*

Solos, Duets and Trios / Feb. 9, 1932-Aug. 30, 1967 / Bluebird ✦✦✦✦
This CD puts the focus on Duke Ellington the piano player, featuring the genius in several different settings. He is heard playing two duets with Billy Strayhorn, taking rare piano solos in 1932, 1941 and 1967, meeting up with Earl Hines in 1965 and leading a trio in 1945. However the real reason to acquire this set are the four duets (plus five alternate takes) with Jimmy Blanton, the first important bass soloist in jazz history. From 1940, those recordings find Blanton sounding like the Charles Mingus of 20 years later and Ellington unselfishly but masterfully playing the role of an accompanist. —*Scott Yanow*

Complete, Vol. 5: 1932-1933 / Dec. 21, 1932-May 16, 1933 / Columbia ✦✦✦✦✦
The fifth of 15 double LPs from French CBS that document Ellington's long period in the '30s on Columbia's labels has many fine recordings that often elude reissue. Among the high points are collaborations with guest vocalists like the Mills Brothers, Ethel Waters and Adelaide Hall, a couple versions apiece of two medleys from The Blackbirds of 1928 and the original recordings of "Sophisticated Lady" and "Drop Me Off at Harlem." —*Scott Yanow*

Complete, Vol. 6: 1933-1936 / Aug. 15, 1933-Jan. 20, 1936 / Columbia ✦✦✦✦✦
It would be difficult to improve upon this French CBS reissue series; if only it were made available on CD. *Volume Six* covers a session apiece from 1933 and 1934 and then most of 1935. Among the classics are a spirited version of "In the Shade of the Old Apple Tree," "In a Sentimental Mood," "Truckin'" and the four-part "Reminiscing in Tempo." Recommended if it can be found. —*Scott Yanow*

★ **The Duke's Men: Small Groups, Vol. 1** / Dec. 12, 1934-Jan. 19, 1938 / Columbia ✦✦✦✦✦
In the '30s Ellington started recording prolifically with small groups taken from his big band. It gave him an opportunity to both debut new works and to let his sidemen stretch out and act as leaders once in awhile (under his direction). This two-disc set contains 45 recordings, almost all of them brilliant, including sessions ostensibly under the leadership of cornetist Rex Stewart (including two selections cut before he joined Ellington), clarinetist Barney Bigard, trumpeter Cootie Williams and altoist Johnny Hodges. In addition to early versions of such future standards as "Caravan," "Stompy Jones" and "Echoes of Harlem," there are many hot stomps performed that feature strong solos from these very distinctive stylists. Brilliant music, highly recommended. —*Scott Yanow*

Complete, Vol. 7: 1936-1937 / Feb. 27, 1936-Mar. 5, 1937 / Columbia ✦✦✦✦✦
From the definitive French CBS reissue program of two-LP sets, this volume covers 1936 and a bit of 1937 with small-group sessions led by Rex Stewart and Barney Bigard (the latter includes the original version of "Caravan") and many lesser-known big-band sides including a pair of rare solo piano performances by Ellington and Rex Stewart's feature "Trumpet in Spades." —*Scott Yanow*

Complete, Vol. 8: 1937 / Mar. 5, 1937-May 20, 1937 / Columbia ✦✦✦✦✦
A continuing French CBS definitive reissue series of Duke Ellington's '30s recordings for its labels, this two-LP set sticks to the first half of 1937. Highlighted by small-group sessions from Cootie Williams and his Rug Cutters, Barney Bigard's Jazzopators and the first part of Johnny Hodges initial session as a leader, there are many gems among even the obscurities. —*Scott Yanow*

Complete, Vol. 9: 1937 / May 20, 1937-Sep. 20, 1937 / Columbia ✦✦✦✦✦
Continuing French CBS' comprehensive mid-'70s reissue of all of Duke Ellington's recordings during the '30s for its labels, this very enjoyable two-fer has small-group sessions led by Johnny Hodges, Barney Bigard and Rex Stewart and such titles by the big band as "Diminuendo in Blue," "Crescendo in Blue" and the exciting "Harmony in Harlem." Other bands during this era may have been better known to the general public, but in reality Duke Ellington's orchestra had no close competitors. —*Scott Yanow*

Complete, Vol. 10: 1937-1938 / Oct. 26, 1937-Mar. 28, 1938 / Columbia ✦✦✦✦✦
The majority of this volume from French CBS' complete reissue of Duke Ellington's '30s recordings focuses on the many rewarding small-group sessions led by his sidemen (and actually directed by Ellington). Cootie Williams, Barney Bigard and Johnny Hodges all get their chances to act as leaders while the big band is heard on such selections as "The New Black and Tan Fantasy" and "I Let a Song Go out of My Heart." —*Scott Yanow*

Complete, Vol. 11: 1938 / Mar. 28, 1938-Aug. 4, 1938 / Columbia ✦✦✦✦✦
This 11th of 15 volumes from French CBS continues the complete reissue of all Duke Ellington's recordings during the '30s for Columbia's associated labels. With small-group sessions led by Cootie Williams and Johnny Hodges and many fine big-band sessions, this set proves that Duke Ellington had a brilliant orchestra before the 1939-42 edition made history. Included are two versions of Lawrence Brown's famous solo on "Rose of the Rio Grande." —*Scott Yanow*

The Duke's Men: Small Groups, Vol. 2 / Mar. 28, 1938-Mar. 20, 1939 / Columbia/ Legacy ◆◆◆◆◆

This second two-disc set, like the first, includes all of the master takes (no alternates) from the small-group sessions led by Duke Ellington's sidemen. During the year covered on this volume, Johnny Hodges, Cootie Williams and Rex Stewart all had opportunities to head sessions and the results included early versions of "Jeep's Blues," "Pyramid," "Prelude to a Kiss," "The Jeep's Jumping" and "Hodge Podge" along with many hot obscurities. There are few duds and many memorable performances during these 43 recordings. —*Scott Yanow*

Complete, Vol. 12: 1938 / Aug. 4, 1938-Dec. 22, 1938 / Columbia ◆◆◆◆◆

This two-LP set from French CBS' superb reissue series of the mid- to late '70s covers a five-month period with small-group sessions by Johnny Hodges (including "Prelude to a Kiss" and "The Jeep Is Jumpin'") and Cootie Williams, along with such big-band selections as "Battle of Swing" and Rex Stewart's famous "Boy Meets Horn." —*Scott Yanow*

Complete, Vol. 13: 1938-1939 / Dec. 22, 1938-Jun. 2, 1939 / Columbia ◆◆◆◆

Taken from the period just prior to bassist Jimmy Blanton joining his orchestra, this two-LP set finds Duke Ellington playing in several formats, including small groups drawn from his orchestra led by altoist Johnny Hodges, trumpeter Cootie Williams and cornetist Rex Stewart, on a pair of rare piano solos (originally unissued) and some big-band classics. High points include "Dooji Wooji," "Pussy Willow," "Finesse" and two versions of "Portrait of the Lion." —*Scott Yanow*

Complete, Vol. 14: 1939 / Jun. 2, 1939-Oct. 14, 1939 / Columbia ◆◆◆◆◆

The next-to-last volume in French CBS' definitive (but now out-of-print) LP series, this two-fer has combo sides led by altoist Johnny Hodges, clarinetist Barney Bigard and trumpeter Cootie Williams, a pair of numbers with a vocal group called The Quintones and bassist Jimmy Blanton's first recordings with Ellington's full orchestra. Whether it be "I'm Checkin' out Go'om Bye," "The Sergeant Was Shy," "Tootin' Through the Roof" or some of the lesser-known tracks, this music is consistently enjoyable and timeless. —*Scott Yanow*

In Boston 1939-1940 / Jul. 26, 1939+Jan. 9, 1940 / Jazz Unlimited ◆◆◆◆

This CD has two formerly rare broadcasts featuring the Duke Ellington Orchestra near the peak of its powers. The earlier session is highlighted by "Jazz Potpourri," "Rose of the Rio Grande" and "Pussy Willow" while the later date (which finds Jimmy Blanton on bass) has fine versions of "Little Posey," "Tootin' Through the Roof" and "Merry-Go-Round" among others. With trumpeters Cootie Williams and Rex Stewart, trombonists Tricky Sam Nanton and Lawrence Brown, clarinetist Barney Bigard, altoist Johnny Hodges, baritonist Harry Carney and Ellington himself among the main soloists, and Ivie Anderson and Herb Jeffries contributing vocals, it would be surprising if this CD were not on the want lists of many Ellington collectors. —*Scott Yanow*

Complete, Vol. 15: 1939-1940 / Oct. 14, 1939-Feb. 15, 1940 / Columbia ◆◆◆◆◆

The final two-LP set in French CBS' definitive reissue of Duke Ellington's recordings for their associated labels, this package finds the orchestra poised for greatness, just prior to switching to RCA. Bassist Jimmy Blanton was now in the band, tenor saxophonist Ben Webster was aboard by the second half of this set, and such longtime stars as trumpeter Cootie Williams, cornetist Rex Stewart, trombonists Tricky Sam Nanton and Lawrence Brown, clarinetist Barney Bigard and altoist Johnny Hodges were very much in their prime. Hodges, Bigard and Cootie get to lead some small-group sessions, Ellington is heard solo on "Blues," there are two Ellington-Blanton piano-bass duets (which were unprecedented for the time), and the full orchestra backs singer Ivie Anderson on one of her finest sessions. Overall, this series is a brilliant effort that should be duplicated on CD. —*Scott Yanow*

The Blanton-Webster Years / 1939-1942 / Bluebird ◆◆◆◆◆

This attractive three-CD set contains the master takes of all 66 selections recorded by Duke Ellington's Orchestra during what many historians consider its peak period. Left out are the many alternate takes, last released by European labels, and the Duke Ellington-Jimmy Blanton duets, which are available on a different CD. Included are dozens of classics, including "Ko-Ko," "Concerto for Cootie," "Cottontail," "Harlem Air Shaft," "All Too Soon," "In a Mellotone," "Warm Valley," "Take the 'A' Train," "Jumpin' Punkins," "I Got It Bad," "Jump for Joy," "Rocks in My Bed," "Chelsea Bridge," "Perdido," "The C Jam Blues" and "Johnny Come Lately," among many others. The arrangements and originals of Ellington and Billy Strayhorn are full of surprises, and even the lesser-known pieces are generally gems. With such soloists as trumpeter Cootie Williams, cornetists Rex Stewart and Ray Nance, trombonists Tricky Sam Nanton and Lawrence Brown, clarinetist Barney Bigard, altoist Johnny Hodges, tenor saxophonist Ben Webster, baritonist Harry Carney, bassist Jimmy Blanton and the leader/pianist (plus singers Ivie Anderson and Herb Jeffries), Ellington led quite a remarkable unit. This music is essential for all jazz collections. —*Scott Yanow*

The Indispensable Duke Ellington, Vols. 5 & 6 / Mar. 6, 1940-Dec. 28, 1940 / RCA ◆◆◆◆◆

This two-CD set from French RCA duplicates material already available on other CDs. Duke Ellington was very productive during 1940, and this reissue has most of his best recordings for Victor (leaving out almost all of the vocals) including "Jack the Bear," two versions of "Ko-Ko," "Concerto for Cootie," "Cottontail," "All Too Soon" and "In a Mellotone." The two-fer concludes with two takes apiece of Ellington's duets with bassist Jimmy Blanton. This is essential music even if this particular release is not necessarily a must. —*Scott Yanow*

Sophisticated Lady [RCA] / Mar. 15, 1940-Sep. 3, 1946 / RCA ◆◆◆◆

This RCA CD reissue contains 19 Duke Ellington recordings from 1940-42 and 1945-46, and serves as a good introduction to Ellington's music of that era, although veteran collectors will already have the material. Among the gems are the original version of "Take the 'A' Train," "I Got It Bad," "Perdido," "Caravan," a rendition of "It Don't Mean a Thing" that uses the voices of Joya Sherrill, Kay Davis and Marie Ellington, and "St. Louis Blues." —*Scott Yanow*

In a Mellotone / May 28, 1940-Jun. 26, 1942 / RCA ◆◆◆

This CD is a straight reissue of an RCA album from the early '60s. Comprising 16 performances by Duke Ellington's Orchestra during what many consider to be his peak period, the program is highlighted by such classics as the original version of "Take the 'A' Train," "Just A-Settin' and A-Rockin'," "I Got It Bad," "Perdido," "Cottontail" and "All Too Soon." With such soloists as trumpeter Cootie Williams (who was replaced by Ray Nance) and Rex Stewart, trombonists Tricky Sam Nanton and Lawrence Brown, altoist Johnny Hodges, clarinetist Barney Bigard, Ben Webster on tenor, baritonist Harry Carney and the innovative bassist Jimmy Blanton (in addition to the leader/pianist), this was one of the all-time great orchestras. Ellington's recordings are available in more complete form elsewhere, but this is a strong sampling. —*Scott Yanow*

Jimmy Blanton Years / Jun. 1940-Oct. 9, 1941 / Queen ◆◆◆◆

Longtime Ellington collectors should love this LP, for it includes rare radio broadcasts of the Duke Ellington Orchestra during 1940-41 and four selections that find Ellington and bassist Jimmy Blanton making guest appearances with John Scott Trotter's studio orchestra. A perfect LP for those Ellington fanatics who think they have everything. —*Scott Yanow*

☆ **Works of Duke, Vols. 11-15** / Jul. 24, 1940-Jul. 2, 1941 / RCA ◆◆◆◆◆

The third of three brilliant box sets put out by French RCA in the '70s, this five-LP package covers a year in the life of Duke Ellington, one of his very best. Complete with all of the alternate takes, this music has more than its share of classic performances. Unfortunately, it is long out of print, but worth bidding for on auction lists. —*Scott Yanow*

The Great Ellington Units / Nov. 2, 1940-Sep. 29, 1941 / RCA ◆◆◆◆

Beginning in the '30s, Duke Ellington started recording with small groups taken out of his orchestra under the leadership of his sidemen. These highly enjoyable recordings offered the musicians some variety and the chance to debut some new material. All but two of the small-group recordings cut for Victor during 1940-41 are included on this very enjoyable CD, including such future Ellington-associated standards as "Day Dream," "Things Ain't What They Used to Be," "Passion Flower" and "C Jam Blues." With altoist Johnny Hodges, cornetist Rex Stewart and clarinetist Barney Bigard acting as leaders (and bassist Jimmy Blanton inspiring the soloists), the music is consistently brilliant. —*Scott Yanow*

☆ **Fargo, ND, November 7, 1940** / Nov. 7, 1940 / Vintage Jazz ◆◆◆◆◆

One winter night in late 1940, Jack Towers (then a young Ellington fan) received permission to record the orchestra on his portable disc cutter at a dance in Fargo, ND. Little did he know that it was a historic night (as trumpeter Ray Nance made his debut with the band) and that the band would be in inspired form. Decades later the music came out on LP, and now this double CD includes every scrap of music that has survived. The Duke Ellington Orchestra was at one of its peaks during this period, overflowing with distinctive and unique soloists, and propelled by the top bassist in jazz (Jimmy Blanton). With the accelerated writing activity of Ellington and his new musical partner Billy Strayhorn, there was no better orchestra at the time, and rarely since. Tenor saxophonist Ben Webster is heard in top form on "Stardust," cornetist Rex Stewart, trombonists Tricky Sam Nanton and Lawrence Brown, clarinetist Barney Bigard and altoist Johnny Hodges also have some very strong moments, and Ray Nance does his best to fit in; many in the band were hearing him for the first time. It is indeed fortunate that Jack Towers was present for what would have been a forgotten one-night stand. —*Scott Yanow*

Take the 'A' Train: The Legendary Blanton-Webster / Jan. 15, 1941-Dec. 3, 1941 / Vintage Jazz ◆◆◆◆

During 1941, one of Ellington's peak years, not only did he record frequently in the studios, but made this CD's worth of transcriptions for radio. Of the 26 selections on this generous set, eight of the songs were never recorded commercially and six others are heard here in their earliest versions, including his theme "Take the 'A' Train" and "Perdido." The all-star orchestra is propelled by the great bassist Jimmy Blanton. Highly recommended. —*Scott Yanow*

☆ **The Works of Duke, Vols. 16-20** / Jul. 2, 1941-May 15, 1945 / RCA ◆◆◆◆◆
The fourth of five mammoth box sets documenting Duke Ellington's Victor recordings (including all alternate takes), this one has five LPs. Small group sessions by Rex Stewart, Johnny Hodges and Barney Bigard alternate with full-band classics (including two versions of "Chelsea Bridge" and the original renditions of "Perdido" and "C Jam Blues") during the first half of this set. The remainder traces Ellington's activity in the war years (including his four-part studio version of "Black, Brown and Beige") up to 1945 when he remade many of his hits from the previous decade, most successfully a hot vocal version of "It Don't Mean a Thing." —*Scott Yanow*

★ **The Carnegie Hall Concerts (January 1943)** / Jan. 23, 1943-Jan. 28, 1943 / Prestige ◆◆◆◆◆
This two-CD set captures one of the milestones in Duke Ellington's long and extremely productive career, highlighted by his monumental suite "Black, Brown and Beige" in the only full-length version ever recorded by his orchestra; soon it was only performed as excerpts. In addition, Ellington's all-star orchestra (including such stylists as trumpeters Rex Stewart, Ray Nance and Shorty Baker, trombonists Tricky Sam Nanton and Lawrence Brown and a saxophone section boasting Johnny Hodges, Ben Webster and Harry Carney) excels on the shorter pieces, a mixture of older and recent compositions. Every serious jazz library should contain this set. —*Scott Yanow*

At Carnegie Hall / Dec. 11, 1943 / Everest ◆◆◆◆
Prestige has up to this point released the performances from four of Duke Ellington's Carnegie Hall concerts, but they have not acquired this one, his second recital of 1943. This budget LP only has some highlights, but they include exuberant versions of standards and two excerpts from "Black, Brown and Beige." Unless it is released in a more complete form elsewhere, this LP version is worth searching for. —*Scott Yanow*

1944-1945 / Dec. 1, 1944-Apr. 7, 1945 / Classics ◆◆◆◆◆
The 29th in Classics' reissuance of Duke Ellington's recordings as a leader (which unfortunately skips most alternate takes) features his orchestra shortly after the recording ban of 1942-44 had finally ended. In addition to several vocal numbers for Joya Sherrill (including the hit "I'm Beginning to See the Light"), Al Hibbler and Kay Davis, there are features for trombonist Lawrence Brown ("Blue Cellophane") and altoist Johnny Hodges ("Mood to Be Wooed"), the original four-part studio version of "Black, Brown and Beige" (which totals 18 minutes), a four-song session headed by drummer Sonny Greer that features altoist Otto Hardwicke, trumpeter Taft Jordan and clarinetist Barney Bigard (despite what it says in the liner notes, the pianist is the obscure Duke Brooks and not Duke Ellington) and the early V-disc version of "The Perfume Suite." Excellent music from an underrated edition of the Duke Ellington Orchestra. —*Scott Yanow*

The Carnegie Hall Concerts (December 1944) / Dec. 19, 1944 / Prestige ◆◆◆◆
The Ellington orchestra was undergoing personnel (and personality) changes during this era, none of it unexciting. This Carnegie Hall concert (available on two CDs) introduced Ellington's "Perfume Suite," and includes a half-hour series of selections from "Black, Brown and Beige," but also in the shorter pieces shows the impact of tenorman Al Sears and high-note wizard Cat Anderson on the band's sound, making it a more potentially boisterous and extroverted ensemble. Lots of great moments from this brilliant orchestra occurred during this concert. —*Scott Yanow*

Black, Brown and Beige / 1944-1946 / Bluebird ◆◆◆◆

☆ **The Works of Duke, Vols. 21-24** / May 16, 1945-Apr. 25, 1953 / RCA ◆◆◆◆◆
The final box set (four LPs this time) put out by French RCA (why doesn't the American counterpart make all of Ellington's recordings available?) finishes off this program with his studio performances from 1945-46 and a live concert dating from 1952. There is plenty of surprising material (such as "Indiana," "Lover Man" and three W.C. Handy tunes), two trio performances, the original version of "The Perfume Suite," Ellington's appearances with several all-star groups and many other high points. The concert also has a fine version of "Harlem." A strong ending to an exciting but sadly out-of-print series. —*Scott Yanow*

The Carnegie Hall Concerts (January 1946) / Jan. 4, 1946 / Prestige ◆◆◆
This two-CD set contains another of Duke Ellington's exciting Carnegie Hall concerts of the '40s; all are recommended. The 1946 concert is not as memorable as the others (the only work premiered was the three-part "Tonal Group" and "Black, Brown and Beige" was now down to 19 minutes) but the many major soloists (including alto-great Johnny Hodges and the robust tenor of Al Sears) still make this lesser item an enjoyable listening experience. —*Scott Yanow*

The Great Chicago Concerts / Jan. 20, 1946+Nov. 10, 1946 / Music Masters ◆◆◆◆
The 1946 Duke Ellington Orchestra is heard in superior form throughout this highly recommended set. Split between a pair of separate concerts that took place in Chicago, this two-CD release of mostly previously unissued material features such top soloists as trumpeters Taft Jordan, Cat Anderson, Harold "Shorty" Baker and Ray Nance, trombonist Lawrence Brown, altoist Johnny Hodges, clarinetist Jimmy Hamilton, Al Sears on tenor, baritonist Harry Carney and the pianist/leader. Four selections from the later concert have the great guitarist Django Reinhardt as a special guest but, although he plays well, there is virtually no interaction with the band. In addition to fresh versions of many of Ellington's standards and then-current arrangements, this two-fer has a lengthy excerpt from "Black, Brown & Beige," Ellington's three-part "Tonal Group" and the rarely heard "Deep South Suite." —*Scott Yanow*

The Uncollected Duke Ellington & His Orchestra, Vol. 1 (1946) / Mar. 28, 1946 / Hindsight ◆◆◆◆
Hindsight has released five excellent LPs of radio transcriptions by Duke Ellington from 1946-47, one of his most underrated periods. With the trumpet section now starring Taft Jordan and the phenomenal high-note virtuoso Cat Anderson, Tricky Sam Nanton still in the trombone section, and veterans Harry Carney and Johnny Hodges joined in the saxophone section by clarinetist Jimmy Hamilton and tenorman Al Sears (not to mention the presence of bassist Oscar Pettiford), Ellington's orchestra was far from in decline. There are lots of colorful moments provided throughout this series by all of the above, and *Volume One* gets it off to a solid start. —*Scott Yanow*

The Uncollected Duke Ellington & His Orchestra, Vol. 2 (1946) / Mar. 28, 1946-Nov. 16, 1946 / Hindsight ◆◆◆◆
The second of five Hindsight LPs containing Duke Ellington's radio transcriptions from 1946-47 has lots of strong moments including "Perdido," the rousing "Suddenly It Jumped," a version of "One O'Clock Jump" and the only performance of a feature for bassist Oscar Pettiford, "Tip Toe Topic." —*Scott Yanow*

The Uncollected Duke Ellington & His Orchestra, Vol. 3 (1946) / Jul. 16, 1946-Jul. 17, 1946 / Hindsight ◆◆◆◆
The third of five volumes in this LP series of Duke Ellington radio transcriptions finds Ellington's orchestra in spirited form on a set of standards and obscurities. Al Sears' tenor is powerful on "The Suburbanite," and "Just You, Just Me" and "Indiana" are quite enjoyable but it is the great Tricky Sam Nonton's solo on "The Mooche" (recorded four days before his death) that takes honors. —*Scott Yanow*

The Uncollected Duke Ellington & His Orchestra, Vol. 4 (1947) / Jan. 7, 1947-Jun. 9, 1947 / Hindsight ◆◆◆◆
On this fourth volume of the five-LP series of radio transcriptions from Duke Ellington's underrated orchestra of 1946-47, all of the sets are enjoyable, often surpassing the level of Ellington's studio recordings of the period. Now with a six-member trumpet section and relatively new soloists in Al Sears, Jimmy Hamilton and Taft Jordan, Ellington continued his reign as one of the top bandleaders with swinging versions of "Happy Go Lucky Local," three W.C. Handy tunes and "Jam-A-Ditty." —*Scott Yanow*

The Uncollected Duke Ellington & His Orchestra, Vol. 5 (1947) / Mar. 28, 1946-Jun. 10, 1947 / Hindsight ◆◆◆◆
The final volume in this very worthy five-LP series of radio transcriptions, this set features the 1947 Duke Ellington Orchestra on plenty of material not generally associated with Ellington, including "How High the Moon," "Royal Garden Blues" and "Embraceable You." The whole series casts a new light on this often neglected period in his career and there are more highlights than one can list. For two, try these versions of "Jumpin' Punkins" and "Jump for Joy." —*Scott Yanow*

Sir Duke / Oct. 23, 1946-Dec. 25, 1946 / Drive Archive ◆◆◆
Although many critics think of Duke Ellington's 1946 orchestra as a bit less significant than his band of five years earlier, it still ranked with the very best of the period. Eleven of Ellington's studio recordings of the period (including the two-part renditions of "Overture to a Jam Session" and "Happy Go Lucky Local") are included on this budget CD reissue. Highlights include the exciting "Jam-A-Ditty," a trumpet battle on "Blue Skies" (which was renamed "Trumpets No End" by its arranger Mary Lou Williams), Johnny Hodges' lyrical alto on "Sultry Sunset" and "Magenta Haze," and the theme from the last part of "Happy Go Lucky Local," which would later be "borrowed" note-for-note by Jimmy Forrest to create "Night Train." —*Scott Yanow*

The Golden Duke / Oct. 23, 1946-Nov. 1950 / Prestige ◆◆◆
This double LP contains some very valuable Duke Ellington studio recordings that have since been reissued as separate sessions. The 13 titles from late 1946 include the hot "Jam-A-Ditty," a classic trumpet battle on "Blue Skies," Ray Nance's colorful vocal on "Tulip or Turnip" and the original version of "Happy-Go-Lucky Local,"

which Jimmy Forrest would "borrow" a few years later and rename "Night Train." The second half of this two-fer features duets by Duke Ellington and Billy Strayhorn (the radical-sounding "Tonk" is memorable) and four showcases for Oscar Pettiford's cello. This music is recommended in one form or another. —*Scott Yanow*

The Complete Duke Ellington (1947-1952) / Aug. 14, 1947-Dec. 22, 1952 / CBS ✦✦✦✦✦

French CBS did a perfect job on this six-LP set of covering a somewhat forgotten period in the career of Duke Ellington. Big bands were breaking up, rhythm & blues and pop vocalists were taking away the audiences (as was television), yet somehow Ellington kept his orchestra together. This wonderful box set has its share of forgettable vocals and attempts at pop hits, but also contains the "Liberian Suite," "Controversial Suite" and many three-minute classics. The personnel underwent a lot of turnover during these five years, giving one the opportunity to hear such new solo stars as Tyree Glenn (on trombone and vibes), high-note trumpeter Al Killian and tenor saxophonist Jimmy Forrest (and eventually Paul Gonsalves), along with the usual Ellington greats. This set also finds Ellington surviving the defection of altoist Johnny Hodges in 1951, proving that he never had an off period. —*Scott Yanow*

The Carnegie Hall Concerts (December 1947) / Dec. 27, 1947 / Prestige ✦✦✦✦✦
One of Duke Ellington's most enjoyable Carnegie Hall concerts, this two-CD set contains among its high points a superior live version of the "Liberian Suite," a Johnny Hodges medley, the beautiful "On a Turquoise Cloud," a roaring version of "Cottontail" (featuring Al Sears' tenor), the nearly atonal "Clothed Woman" and a trumpet battle on "Blue Skies." Well worth acquiring. —*Scott Yanow*

The Carnegie Hall Concerts (November 1948) / Nov. 13, 1948 / Vintage Jazz ✦✦✦✦✦

The sixth and final of Duke Ellington's acclaimed Carnegie Hall concerts, this two-CD set allows one to hear the largely undocumented 1948 orchestra, which was kept off record because of a musicians union strike. With Ben Webster temporarily back in the band and such solo stylists as altoist Johnny Hodges, Al Sears on tenor, clarinetist Jimmy Hamilton and trumpeters Ray Nance and Shorty Baker, the Ellington orchestra performs both newer material (such as "The Tattooed Bride" and several obscurities) and some surprising older compositions, including a revival of "Reminiscence in Tempo") and a "hits medley." An oddity is one of the few Ellington performances of Billy Strayhorn's classic "Lush Life." —*Scott Yanow*

Cornell University Concert / Dec. 10, 1948 / Music Masters ✦✦✦✦
Due to the second recording ban, Duke Ellington made no studio recordings in 1948, which makes the concert tapes from that year especially interesting. The Cornell University concert in December is especially interesting in contrast to Ellington's sixth annual Carnegie Hall appearance, which had occurred four weeks earlier and which had premiered such works as "Lady of the Lavender Mist" and "The Tattooed Bride," which were repeated here. In the course of a difficult roadtrip, the band got a good reception at Cornell, and they played well. (Note that the group included tenor saxophonist Ben Webster, on his second and final sojourn with the band, which would last only until the spring of 1949.) The Music Masters CD, the fourth in its Travelog series, released in January 1996, contains 15 tracks and runs 75 minutes. It is an adequate mono recording with occasional rough spots. —*William Ruhlmann*

The 1949 Band Salutes Ellington '90 / Feb. 1, 1949-Feb. 20, 1949 / Marlor Productions ✦✦✦
The 1949 Duke Ellington big band made few worthwhile studio recordings, which makes this LP (consisting of material from radio broadcasts) of great interest to Ellington collectors. Recorded when Al Killian was leading the trumpet section and both Ben Webster and Al Sears were on tenor, this nearly one-hour set contains an extended version of "The Tattooed Bride," superior versions of "How High the Moon," "St. Louis Blues" (and even "Singin' in the Rain") and many fine solos from a somewhat forgotten version of Duke Ellington's orchestra. —*Scott Yanow*

Great Times! Piano Duets with Billy Strayhorn / Sep. 13, 1950-Nov. 1950 / Original Jazz Classics ✦✦✦✦
This CD reissues three unusual combo dates by Duke Ellington. Two of the sessions feature Ellington and his longtime musical partner Billy Strayhorn both playing piano (while assisted by either Wendell Marshall or Joe Shulman on bass and sometimes an unidentified drummer). The futuristic "Tonk" is the best-known performance, but all eight numbers (which include "Cottontail" and "Johnny Come Lately") are quite fascinating. The remaining date has four songs that primarily serve as features for the cello of Oscar Pettiford who is accompanied by Ellington, bassist Lloyd Trotman, drummer Jo Jones and (on two tunes) the celeste of Strayhorn; "Perdido" and "Take the 'A' Train" are most memorable. Intriguing music. —*Scott Yanow*

Masterpieces by Ellington / Dec. 18, 1950 / Columbia ✦✦✦
For this record, Duke Ellington for the first time took advantage of the extra time that the LP offered (as opposed to the three-minute 78). Ellington and his orchestra perform stretched-out versions of three of his best-known songs ("Mood Indigo," "Sophisticated Lady" and "Solitude") and the more recently composed "The Tattooed Bride." Superior pacing, careful attention to dynamics and variety, and the strong material itself make this a recommended set. —*Scott Yanow*

☆ **Uptown** / Dec. 7, 1951-Dec. 8, 1952 / Columbia ✦✦✦✦✦
Although some historians have characterized the early '50s as Duke Ellington's "off period" (due to the defection of alto-star Johnny Hodges), in reality his 1951-52 orchestra could hold its own against his best. This set has many classic moments, including Betty Roche's famous bebop vocal on "Take the 'A' Train," a version of "The Mooche" that contrasts the different clarinet styles of Russell Procope and Jimmy Hamilton, a hot "Perdido" that is highlighted by some great Clark Terry trumpet, Louie Bellson's drum solo on "Skin Deep," a definitive version of "The Harlem Suite" and the two-part "Controversial Suite" which contrasts New Orleans jazz with futuristic music worthy of Stan Kenton. One of the great Duke Ellington sets. —*Scott Yanow*

1952 Seattle Concert / Mar. 28, 1952 / Bluebird ✦✦✦
The early '50s have often been written about as if they were an off-period for Duke Ellington but in reality his concert performances were very much up to par. This fine CD features drummer Louie Bellson on "Skin Deep" and "The Hawk Talks," showcases trombonist Britt Woodman on "Sultry Serenade," altoist Willie Smith on "Sophisticated Lady," trumpeter Clark Terry throughout an impressive version of "Perdido" and the lead of valve trombonist Juan Tizol on his "Caravan." In addition to a brief hits medley and a typically heated "Jam with Sam," one of the best versions ever of "Harlem Suite" highlights this enjoyable if not quite essential release. —*Scott Yanow*

The Duke Is on the Air at the Blue Note / Jul. 30, 1952+Aug. 13, 1952 / Aircheck ✦✦✦
This LP contains two complete broadcasts of Duke Ellington's 1952 Orchestra from the Blue Note in Chicago. The underrated band (which had such fine soloists as trombonist Quentin Jackson, clarinetist Jimmy Hamilton, tenorman Paul Gonsalves, baritonist Harry Carney, the pianist/leader, drummer Louie Bellson and four trumpet stylists: Clark Terry, Willie Cook, Ray Nance and Cat Anderson) plays their usual program of the period. Jimmy Grissom, Ray Nance and Betty Roche ("Take the 'A' Train" and "All of Me") have vocals and the overall album is pleasing but nothing all that surprising occurs and there are many more significant Ellington releases currently available. Still, Duke Ellington fanatics will want this LP anyway. —*Scott Yanow*

At Birdland 1952 / Nov. 20, 1952+Nov. 24, 1952 / Jazz Unlimited ✦✦✦
In 1952, Duke Ellington celebrated the 25th anniversary of his entrance into the big leagues (his gig at the Cotton Club in 1927). This CD features Ellington and his orchestra during two well-recorded radio broadcasts that emanated from Birdland. Duke mostly plays his usual repertoire of the era; there are brief verbal salutes from a variety of celebrities, and such top soloists as trumpeters Clark Terry and Ray Nance, trombonist Quentin Jackson and tenorman Paul Gonsalves (along with vocalist Betty Roche on two versions of "Take the 'A' Train") are heard in fine form. Although this CD offers no new revelations, it will be savored by Duke Ellington fans. —*Scott Yanow*

The Pasadena Concert (1953) / Mar. 30, 1953 / GNP ✦✦✦
Gene Norman often recorded jazz bands live when they appeared in Southern California, including a couple of Duke Ellington concerts. This particular one has its fine moments (particularly a good early version of "Diminuendo and Crescendo in Blue" and a feature on "Perdido" for guest Oscar Pettiford on cello) but three Jimmy Grissom vocals and a long medley of Ellington's hits weigh the music down a bit. —*Scott Yanow*

The Complete Capitol Recordings of Duke Ellington / Apr. 6, 1953-May 19, 1955 / Mosaic ✦✦✦✦✦
This five-CD box set from Mosaic documents Duke Ellington's least-known period, his two years on Capitol. Although thought of by some as his off-years due to the absence of Johnny Hodges, the set serves as evidence that a great deal of viable music was created. During this period the orchestra had 11 distinctive soloists including four very different trumpeters (Clark Terry, Cat Anderson, Willie Cook and Ray Nance). In addition to a well-known trio set that showcases Ellington's underrated piano playing, there are quite a few unissued selections highlighted by four numbers from 1955 that find Ellington playing electric piano. Even vocalist Jimmy Grissom (best on "Balling the Blues") sounds better than usual and one should not miss Ray Nance's humorous singing and playing on "Basin Street Blues." Toss in the original version of "Satin Doll," the unusual *Ellington '55* album (which found the band playing their versions of swing hits associated with other

orchestras) and an oddity such as "Twelfth Street Rag Mambo" and one has a highly enjoyable reissue that Duke Ellington fans should pick up immediately. —*Scott Yanow*

Jazz Profile / Apr. 6, 1953-Oct. 22, 1971 / Capitol ✦✦
Duke Ellington never recorded for Blue Note, but his sessions for Capitol, United Artists and Solid State are all owned (along with Blue Note) by EMI, making this single-CD sampler possible. On this hodgepodge (and almost random) collection, Duke's orchestra is heard during 1953-54 and at his 70th birthday concert in 1969. In addition, Ellington appears on two trio numbers with bassist Charles Mingus and drummer Max Roach, and plays "Happy Reunion" in 1971 with tenorman Paul Gonsalves in a quartet. Although there are some good performances included (1969's "Take the 'A' Train" is superb), there is a great deal missing, most notably 1954's "Flying Home" and Cat Anderson's miraculous solo on 1969's "Satin Doll"; instead one gets the 1953 hit version, which is remarkably dull. Otherwise, the music on this odd set is fine, but far from essential. —*Scott Yanow*

Piano Reflections / Apr. 13, 1953-Dec. 3, 1953 / Capitol ✦✦✦✦✦
At the time of its release this was a true rarity, a full album of Duke Ellington featured with a trio sans his orchestra. Although his talents at the piano sometimes have been overshadowed by his many accomplishments as a composer, arranger and bandleader, Ellington was actually one of the very few stride pianists (along with Mary Lou Williams) to effectively make the transition into more modern styles of jazz without losing his own musical personality; in fact Duke was an early influence on both Thelonious Monk and Cecil Taylor. Throughout this CD (which contains one previously unissued track), Ellington sounds modern (especially rhythmically and in his chord voicings) and shows that he could have made a viable career out of just being a pianist. —*Scott Yanow*

Happy Birthday, Duke! The Birthday Sessions, Vols. 1-5 / Apr. 29, 1953-Apr. 29, 1954 / LaserLight ✦✦✦
Quite by coincidence, Duke Ellington celebrated his birthday in both 1953 and 1954 by performing with his orchestra at McElroy's Ballroom in Portland, OR. LaserLight has released the results (recorded by engineer Wally Heider) on a five-CD box set which is also available as five separate CDs. The 1953-54 period has never been considered the peak years for Ellington; in fact his orchestra's popularity was low and he was struggling to keep his group together. However, as these performance show, he still had one of the most exciting big bands in the world and its commercial difficulties had little to do with the music. There are not many surprises on these dance dates but it is always fun to hear new solos on Ellington's standards played by his illustrious sidemen. Although only containing around three hours of music (fairly brief for five CDs), the budget price of LaserLight's releases makes this an excellent buy. —*Scott Yanow*

In Hamilton / Feb. 8, 1954 / Radiex ✦✦✦✦
The collector's label Radiex issued a two-CD set that brings back a Duke Ellington concert performed in Ontario, Canada. The 1954 Ellington band tends to be underrated but it certainly had many strong soloists including four very different trumpet stylists (Clark Terry, Willie Cook, Cat Anderson and Ray Nance), trombonists Quentin Jackson and Britt Woodman, clarinetists Jimmy Hamilton and Russell Procope, Paul Gonsalves on tenor and baritonist Harry Carney in addition to the pianist/leader. No lengthy works were performed at this particular concert but there are spirited versions of such pieces as "The Mooche," "How High the Moon," "Theme for Trambean" (featuring Britt Woodman), "Perdido," and even "The Bunny Hop Mambo." Ellington fans will definitiely want to search for this rare set. —*Scott Yanow*

Los Angeles Concert (1954) / Apr. 13, 1954 / GNP ✦✦✦
This LP has an excellent performance by the Duke Ellington Orchestra at a time when its commercial fortunes were near the bottom. The struggles however are not reflected in the music, which is full of enthusiasm and creative invention with trumpeter Clark Terry, tenorman Paul Gonsalves and trombonist Britt Woodman (on "Theme for Trambean") standing out among the many stars during a well-paced program. —*Scott Yanow*

Duke (1956-1962), Vol. 3 / Jan. 1, 1956-Mar. 3, 1961 / Columbia ✦✦
Unlike the first two volumes of this series of alternate takes and unissued performances that Duke Ellington recorded for Columbia during 1956-62, this is a single (rather than double) LP that finds the orchestra accompanying a wide variety of vocalists including Rosemary Clooney, Ozzie Bailey, Margaret Tynes, Jimmy Grissom, Lil Greenwood, Milt Grayson and even Johnnie Ray. A well-designed series although this album is not too essential. —*Scott Yanow*

The Bethlehem Years, Vol. 1 / Feb. 7, 1956-Feb. 8, 1956 / Bethlehem ✦✦✦✦
In this two-volume series, Duke Ellington mostly revisited some of his songs from the '30s but, as was his custom, the standards were rearranged and came out sounding nearly brand new. With Johnny Hodges back in the orchestra, the all-star

ensemble once again had no weak points and, other than an overly rapid "Ko-Ko," this set is a gem. —*Scott Yanow*

Duke Ellington Presents / Feb. 1956 / Evidence ✦✦✦
This unusual set (reissued on CD through Evidence) only has four Duke Ellington compositions among the 11 songs. He features a different soloist on most of the songs (which include seven standards not associated with Ellington's music). There are showcases for trumpeter Cat Anderson, Ray Nance (who sings and plays violin on "I Can't Get Started"), singer Jimmy Grissom, baritonist Harry Carney, the altos of Johnny Hodges and Russell Procope on alto, and two apiece for clarinetist Jimmy Hamilton and tenor saxophonist Paul Gonsalves. The closing "Blues" gives many of the players an additional opportunity to be heard. Although this set is not essential, the music is enjoyable and it is interesting to hear Duke Ellington playing "Laura," "My Funny Valentine" and "Indian Summer." —*Scott Yanow*

The Private Collection, Vol. 1: Studio Sessions, Chicago 1956 / Mar. 17, 1956-Dec. 16, 1956 / Saja ✦✦✦
The first of ten CDs of previously unreleased material recorded privately by Ellington between engagements, all of which was eventually reissued first on LMR and then Saja/Atlantic. Each of the sets has its interesting moments, offering previously unknown compositions and performances. *Volume One,* recorded in Chicago during March and December 1956, has plenty of spots for Clark Terry, Ray Nance, Johnny Hodges and Paul Gonsalves among the orchestra's many great soloists. —*Scott Yanow*

Ellington at Newport / Jul. 7, 1956 / Columbia ✦✦✦✦✦
After several years of struggle, Duke Ellington made a spectacular commercial comeback, launched by this memorable appearance at the Newport Jazz Festival. Following an inventive but overlooked "Newport Jazz Festival Suite" and a routine version of Johnny Hodges' feature "Jeep's Blues," the orchestra launched into "Diminuendo and Crescendo in Blue" with great intensity. The passion really grew during a marathon 27-chorus blues solo by tenor saxophonist Paul Gonsalves that inspired some wild dancing and a near-riot in the audience; the crowd's reaction can easily be heard on this recording. Following Gonsalves, the full ensemble built to a tremendous climax with trumpeter Cat Anderson screaming on top. This performance made headlines all around the world and Ellington's "off period" was finally over. It can all be heard on this classic recording. —*Scott Yanow*

A Drum Is a Woman / Sep. 1956-Dec. 1956 / Columbia ✦✦
Duke Ellington's fanciful tale of Carribee Joe and his drum, which evolved into a woman known as Madam Zajj (and a very abstract telling of the evolution of jazz) became a television special in the late '50s but does not translate all that well to record. Dominated by vocals and narration, the music often plays a backseat to the story, which is worth hearing twice at the most. —*Scott Yanow*

The Private Collection, Vol. 7: Studio Sessions, 1957 & 1962 / Jan. 1957-Jun. 6, 1962 / Saja ✦✦✦
One of ten CDs of previously unreleased and even unknown studio and concert performances by Duke Ellington's orchestra, these sets allow one to hear him experimenting with his ensemble. Some selections were essentially works-in-progress that would develop within the next few years, others were quickly discarded originals or rearrangements of older tunes. This seventh volume is split between big-band sessions from 1957 and 1962 and a get-together from an octet that included Ellington's former drummer Sonny Greer in the latter year. Ellington fans will want all ten in this valuable series. —*Scott Yanow*

The Private Collection, Vol. 8: Studio Sessions, 1957, 1965-67, San Francisco, Chicago, New York / Jan. 1957-Jul. 11, 1967 / Saja ✦✦✦
The eighth of ten CDs in this valuable series of previously unknown Duke Ellington recordings is mostly taken from the 1965-67 period (with one selection from 1957) and features particularly strong moments from trumpeter Cat Anderson, altoist Johnny Hodges and tenorman Paul Gonsalves on many little-played Ellington compositions (along with versions of "Cottontail" and "Moon Mist"). Drummer Louie Bellson guests on a few selections. All ten volumes in this series are recommended. —*Scott Yanow*

Such Sweet Thunder / Apr. 1957-May 1957 / Sony Special Products ✦✦✦
Duke Ellington's tribute to Shakespeare is witty, full of fresh melodies and gives his famed sidemen many opporunities to solo in unusual settings. Trombonist Britt Woodman stars on "Sonnet to Hank Cinq," trumpeter Cat Anderson gets to go nuts on "Madness in Great Ones" and there are notable features for Johnny Hodges, Paul Gonsalves and Quentin Jackson. —*Scott Yanow*

Ella Fitzgerald/The Duke Ellington Songbook / Jun. 25, 1957-Sep. 57, 1957 / Verve ✦✦✦✦
The first lady of song meets the genius of jazz on this delightful two-LP set. Unlike many other albums in which a singer is backed by a big band, there are many spots for Ellington's sidemen to shine; in fact the four-part "Portrait of Ella Fitzgerald" is purely instrumental until the final movement. It is wonderful to hear her

sing such songs as "Drop Me Off in Harlem," "Rockin' in Rhythm" and "Perdido" along with the ballads. Recommended. —*Scott Yanow*

All Star Road Band, Vol. 2 / Jun. 1957 / Doctor Jazz ◆◆◆

This double LP was recorded at a typical dance date, a one-night stand in Carrolltown, PA, by the Duke Ellington Orchestra. Although Ellington's band could be erratic on gigs like this, playing for a partying dancing crowd, the music is consistently enjoyable, occasionally a bit loose and always full of the spontaneity of jazz. With a few exceptions, most of the songs are standards (including "Take the 'A' Train," "Mood Indigo," "Sophisticated Lady" and "I Got It Bad") but they sound fresh and through Ellington's rearrangements, almost new as played by his all-star orchestra. —*Scott Yanow*

Live at the 1957 Stratford Festival / Jul. 1957 / Music & Arts ◆◆◆◆

Now that Duke Ellington had regained his former commercial success with his performance at the 1956 Newport Jazz Festival, he was free for the remainder of his career to essentially play what he pleased. This live performance from 1957 ranges from old favorites like "I Got It Bad" and "Sophisticated Lady" to the spectacular Britt Woodman trombone feature on "Theme Trambene," the whimsical "Pretty and the Wolf," a fresh rendition of "Harlem Air Shaft" featuring trumpeter Clark Terry and the extended "Harlem Suite." Baritonist Harry Carney, high-note trumpet wizard Cat Anderson and altoist Johnny Hodges all have their great moments on this enjoyable set. —*Scott Yanow*

Indigos / Sep. 9, 1957-Oct. 10, 1957 / Columbia ◆◆

An easy-listening set of ballads (only three of the ten songs were associated with Ellington), this is a relaxing if unexciting program. On this reissue, two "new" performances ("Night and Day" and a trio version of "All the Things You Are") were added to the original LP, but one song ("The Sky Fell Down") was dropped and an alternate version of "Autumn Leaves" was substituted for the original; all 12 performances could have easily fit. Nice subtle music, but not essential. —*Scott Yanow*

The Girl's Suite and the Perfume Suite / Dec. 2, 1957-Aug. 20, 1961 / Columbia ◆◆

This Columbia LP collects together Duke Ellington's ten-song *Girl's Suite* plus a remake of his more famous four-part *Perfume Suite*. The former work, even with the inclusion of reworkings of some older tunes (including "Peg O' My Heart," "Sweet Adeline," "Clementine" and "Diane") plus tributes to Mahalia Jackson and Lena Horne, is surprisingly forgettable despite some good solos from Duke's star sidemen. As is usual with *The Perfume Suite*, the "Dancers in Love" movement (which showcases Duke's piano) is the high point. Overall this set mostly comprises lesser Ellington but it is certainly not without its interesting moments. —*Scott Yanow*

Black, Brown & Beige / Feb. 5, 1958-Feb. 12, 1958 / Tristar ◆◆◆

This album, Duke Ellington's revised version of his formerly 50-minute long "Black, Brown and Beige," has always been a bit of a disappointment. Stung by criticism from 15 years before, Ellington divided the suite into six much shorter sections, leaving in "Come Sunday" (which is hurt by Johnny Hodges' absence due to a brief illness) and "Work Song" and featuring gospel singer Mahalia Jackson during two of the parts. Despite some good moments, this rendition has little of the power of the original arrangement. —*Scott Yanow*

Blues in Orbit / Feb. 5, 1958-Dec. 3, 1959 / Columbia ◆◆◆◆

This LP features the Duke Ellington Orchestra in late 1959 on a variety of his shorter originals. At the time, the band's instrumentation was unusual, with Ray Nance temporarily the only trumpet, but the saxophone section was very much intact. The emphasis is on blues-oriented tunes and there are many fine spots for Nance, baritonist Harry Carney, altoist Johnny Hodges, clarinetist Jimmy Hamilton and Ellington himself. Excellent music by a timeless orchestra. —*Scott Yanow*

The Private Collection, Vol. 2: Dance Concerts, California, 1958 / Mar. 4, 1958 / Saja ◆◆◆

The second of ten CDs of previously unissued recordings of Duke Ellington, this set differs from the others by being from a single live session, a dance concert from 1958. The orchestra at the time boasted such stars as trumpeters Shorty Baker, Clark Terry and Ray Nance, trombonists Quentin Jackson and Britt Woodman and a superb saxophone section (although Johnny Hodges is temporarily absent). The music on this CD sticks to standards (some of which were not usually associated with Ellington) and can be thought of as a live version of *Ellington Indigos* although the inclusion of some uptempo material (including a totally ad-lib "Lady Be Good") adds more variety. A typically excellent example of 1958 Duke Ellington. —*Scott Yanow*

The Private Collection, Vol. 6: Dance Dates, California, 1958 / Mar. 4, 1958-Mar. 5, 1958 / Saja ◆◆◆

The sixth of ten CDs in this series of previously unknown private recordings is actually related to *Volume 2*. Some of these performances are from the same con-

cert at Travis Air Force Base while the remainder were recorded the next day at Mather Air Force Base. Although altoist Johnny Hodges and high-note trumpeter Cat Anderson were absent, the music did not suffer in the slightest for Ellington still had ten other distinctive soloists. Quite informal and sometimes a bit loose, these spirited performances (mostly of standards) gives such players as trumpeters Shorty Baker, Clark Terry and Ray Nance along with the many other stars plenty of opportunities to stretch out. Recordings like this give one a chance to hear how Ellington re-arranged tunes to make them sound fresh year after year (sometimes decade after decade). —*Scott Yanow*

Duke Ellington at the Bal Masque / Mar. 1958 / Columbia ◆◆◆

One of Duke Ellington's more unusual albums of the '50s, this live session finds the orchestra performing such songs as "Got a Date with an Angel," "The Peanut Vendor," "Indian Love Call" and even "Who's Afraid of the Big Bad Wolf." Amazingly enough the music works quite well for Ellington and his all-star orchestra manage to transform what could be a set of tired revival swing into superior dance music and swinging jazz. While certainly not the most essential Ellington record, *At the Bal Masque* is a surprising success. —*Scott Yanow*

Cosmic Scene: Duke Ellington's Spacemen / Apr. 12, 1958 / Columbia ◆◆◆◆

This is the original LP version of a fine session featuring a small group from Duke Ellington's orchestra which, due to the time period, he dubbed his "Spacemen." For this nonet Duke chose three of his most modern soloists (trumpeter Clark Terry, clarinetist Jimmy Hamilton and tenor saxophonist Paul Gonsalves), along with his trombone section and the rhythm section. In general the tunes are standards that give each of the three main horns plenty of space in which to display their distinctive sounds. —*Scott Yanow*

Blues Summit / Aug. 14, 1958-Feb. 20, 1959 / Verve ◆◆◆◆

Reissued as the two CD's *Back to Back* and *Side to Side*, this very enjoyable double LP includes two related sessions. The main one is both unusual and delightful for it features altoist Johnny Hodges and trumpeter Harry "Sweets" Edison leading a sextet that found Duke Ellington on piano. The repertoire is inspired, a variety of jam tunes including several by W.C. Handy, and both Sweets and Hodges are heard at their most expressive. The remainder of this two-fer teams Hodges and trombonist Lawrence Brown with tenor-great Ben Webster and the exciting trumpeter Roy Eldridge; this time Billy Strayhorn is on piano and the music is almost as memorable. Highly recommended in one form or another. —*Scott Yanow*

Jazz at the Plaza, Vol. 2 / Sep. 9, 1958 / Columbia ◆◆◆◆

In 1958 Columbia Records hosted a jazz party that resulted in two records, one by the Miles Davis Sextet and the other featuring Duke Ellington's orchestra during a prime period. In addition to features for Johnny Hodges, Clark Terry and Paul Gonsalves (along with the "Jazz Festival Suite"), Ellington welcomes Count Basie's former vocalist, Jimmy Rushing, for three numbers, and Billie Holiday (in okay form for this late in her life) stops by for two numbers with a small group that includes trumpeter Buck Clayton. Excellent music. —*Scott Yanow*

At the Blue Note in Chicago / Dec. 28, 1958 / Vogue ◆◆◆

A typically excellent club appearance by Duke Ellington's orchestra near the end of 1958, it exists on CD because CBS happened to broadcast this date. Nearly all of the selections were composed by Ellington and his associates. Johnny Hodges stars throughout while trumpeter Clark Terry is tops among the supporting players. Not essential but well worth owning. —*Scott Yanow*

Jazz Party / Feb. 19, 1959-Feb. 25, 1959 / Columbia ◆◆◆

A most unusual Duke Ellington record, two selections feature nine symphonic percussionists on tymmpani, vibes, marimbas and xylophones. Dizzy Gillespie makes a historic appearance with Ellington's orchestra on "U.M.M.G." (a meeting that should have been repeated often, but sadly never was), Jimmy Rushing (Count Basie's former vocalist) sings "Hello Little Girl," and both Johnny Hodges ("All of Me") and Paul Gonsalves ("Ready Go!") have chances to blow. —*Scott Yanow*

The Ellington Suites / Feb. 25, 1959-Dec. 5, 1972 / Original Jazz Classics ◆◆◆

It took until 1976 before these three extended works ("The Queen's Suite," "The Goutelas Suite" and "The Uwis Suite") were released and their obscurity is somewhat deserved. Although there are some good moments from Ellington's orchestras of 1959 and 1971-72, few of the themes (outside of "The Single Petal of a Rose" from "The Queen's Suite") are all that memorable. But even lesser Ellington is of great interest and veteran collectors may want to pick this up. —*Scott Yanow*

Anatomy of a Murder / May 29, 1959-Jun. 2, 1959 / Rykodisc ◆◆◆

Duke Ellington's music was used surprisingly little in movies. *Anatomy of a Murder* was a landmark film and his writing fit in perfectly. Like all good soundtracks, the music's role was to accompany and enhance the story, so to hear the soundtrack on CD does leave one with a somewhat incomplete feeling. However, Ellington's writing was colorful enough to largely stand on its own even in this setting so this set, although not essential, does not disappoint. —*Scott Yanow*

Newport Jazz Festival (1959) / Jul. 4, 1959 / EmArcy ✦✦✦
Duke Ellington's concert at the 1959 Newport Jazz Festival lacked the excitement and adventure of his appearances in 1956 and 1958. Ellington and his orchestra played their usual program of standards and features with the 14-and-a-half-minute "Idiom '59" being introduced (and then quickly forgotten). Fine music but nothing that historic or essential occurred this time around. — *Scott Yanow*

Live at the Blue Note (1959) / Aug. 9, 1959 / Roulette ✦✦✦✦
This two-CD set gives one a good example of how Duke Ellington's Orchestra sounded in 1959. Greatly expanded from the original single LP, the release essentially brings back a full night by the Ellington band, three nearly complete sets. The music ranges from old favorites to some newer material and highlights include Billy Strayhorn sitting in on his "Take the 'A' Train," several selections from the recent *Anatomy of a Murder* soundtrack, versions of "Drawing Room Blues" and "Tonk" that have both Ellington and Strayhorn on piano, an 11-minute rendition of "Mood Indigo" and quite a few features for altoist Johnny Hodges. — *Scott Yanow*

Festival Session / Sep. 8, 1959 / Columbia ✦✦✦
This LP included Ellington's new works for 1959 along with a superior version of "Perdido"(featuring Clark Terry) and a Johnny Hodges workout on "Things Ain't What They Used to Be." None of the newer pieces ("Duael Fuel," "Copout Extension," "Idiom '59" and "Launching Pad") caught on but all are enjoyable and show that Ellington's creativity at age 60 had not slowed down. — *Scott Yanow*

Duke (1956-1962), Vol. 2 / Dec. 2, 1959-Jun. 21, 1962 / Columbia ✦✦✦✦
The second of three volumes, this two-LP set from French Columbia includes unissued alternate takes and rarities recorded by Duke Ellington for Columbia during 1959-62. Of primary interest to veteran collectors, there is much to enjoy here, including new renditions of the "Asphalt Jungle Suite," "Tulip or Turnip," "Paris Blues," two versions of "Jingle Bells" and a pair of selections from the one-time meeting on record between the Ellington and Count Basie Orchestras that were not included on the original set. — *Scott Yanow*

Three Suites / Mar. 3, 1960-Oct. 10, 1960 / Columbia ✦✦✦✦✦
One of Duke Ellington's most delightful adaptations of another composer's material is his reworking of Tchaikovsky's "Nutcracker Suite" into jazz; this version is a classic and well worth treasuring. Ellington's reworking of Grieg's "Peer Gynt Suites" (including "In the Hall of the Mountain King") and his tribute to John Steinbeck ("Suite Thursday") are also among his better extended works, really utilizing the unique tones of his distinctive sidemen. Highly recommended. — *Scott Yanow*

Piano in the Background / May 1960-Jun. 1960 / Columbia ✦✦✦✦
One of Ellington's rarer studio sessions and last out on this French CD, the main plot behind this runthrough of his standards is that the leader's piano is featured at some point in every song. His sidemen are also heard from and everyone is in fine form. Ellington's solo abilities were always a bit underrated due to his brilliance in other areas, but this set shows just how modern he remained through the years as a player. — *Scott Yanow*

Unknown Session / Jul. 14, 1960 / Columbia ✦✦✦✦
Discovered in Columbia's vaults 19 years after it was performed, this recording features a septet from Duke Ellington's orchestra keeping busy in the studios mostly playing standards and blues. With altoist Johnny Hodges, baritonist Harry Carney, trombonist Lawrence Brown and cornetist Ray Nance all having ample solo space, these renditions are quite enjoyable, swing hard and sound fresh. Ellington fans should pick this one up. — *Scott Yanow*

Hot Summer Dance / Jul. 22, 1960 / Red Baron ✦✦✦
There have been so many releases of live concert performances by Duke Ellington's orchestra that it is easy to become blasé about them. It is true that one does not really need all of these CDs but, on the other hand, virtually all of the releases contain excellent music. When one considers the consistent high quality of Ellington's material and the many distinctive soloists that he employed, the result is that practically everything released of his orchestra is quite worthwhile. *Hot Summer Dance* features the 1960 Duke Ellington Orchestra performing their usual repertoire from that era including excerpts from "The Nutcracker Suite" and "Such Sweet Thunder," a three-song medley of jungle pieces from the '20s, several Johnny Hodges features and a new version of "Diminuendo and Crescendo in Blue." It may not be essential, but Ellington collectors will enjoy this CD. — *Scott Yanow*

Paris Blues / Dec. 14, 1960-1961 / United Artists ✦✦
The soundtrack to the flawed but intriguing jazz movie *Paris Blues* has a few strong melodies (including "Guitar Amour," the title track and a new version of "Mood Indigo") along with an appearance by Louis Armstrong on "Battle Royal," but there is actually less than a half-hour of music on this LP. Even with the prominence of Paul Gonsalves' tenor, this is of lesser interest. — *Scott Yanow*

Piano in the Foreground / Mar. 1, 1961 / Columbia ✦✦✦
This rare trio session by Duke Ellington (on which he is joined by bassist Aaron Bell and drummer Sam Woodyard) was the first of several in the early '60s that fea-

tured his piano in a variety of settings. It is particularly interesting hearing Ellington, along with three standards and a blues, performing some of his rarer compositions such as "Cong-go, Fontainbleau Forest," "It's Bad to Be Forgotten" and "A Hundred Dreams Ago." One wishes that today's revivalists when playing "the Duke Ellington Songbook" would bring back some of his true obscurities, such as the ones on this somewhat forgotten session. — *Scott Yanow*

The Duke Ellington: Louis Armstrong Years / Apr. 3, 1961-Apr. 4, 1961 / Roulette ✦✦✦✦✦
Although Duke Ellington and Louis Armstrong were jazz music's most famous and acclaimed musicians, their only meeting on record (other than a couple of isolated selections in the '40s) is the music contained on this two-CD set. Rather than have Armstrong sit in with the orchestra, Ellington temporarily became a member of Satch's All-Stars. For this all-Ellington program, Armstrong is inspired by the fresh repertoire and his vocals are often jubilant. With strong assistance from trombonist Trummy Young and clarinetist Barney Bigard (a former Ellington band member then travelling with Armstrong), Pops and Ellington created a very memorable and quite unique program of classic music. — *Scott Yanow*

☆ **First Time! The Count Meets Duke** / Jul. 6, 1961 / Columbia ✦✦✦✦✦
At first glance this collaboration should not have worked. The Duke Ellington and Count Basie Orchestras had already been competitors for 25 years but the leaders' mutual admiration (Ellington was one of Basie's main idols) and some brilliant planning made this a very successful and surprisingly uncrowded encounter. On most selections Ellington and Basie both play piano (their interaction with each other is wonderful) and the arrangements allowed the stars from both bands to take turns soloing. "Segue in C" is the high point but versions of "Until I Met You," "Battle Royal" and "Jumpin' at the Woodside" are not far behind. — *Scott Yanow*

Duke Ellington/Johnny Hodges / Jan. 9, 1962-Aug. 27, 1964 / Storyville ✦✦✦
This LP contains the soundtrack of a half-hour TV special featuring the 1962 Duke Ellington Orchestra along with four selections from a Johnny Hodges-led small group drawn from the band in 1964. Few surprises occur, but the soloing is at a high level. — *Scott Yanow*

Masters of Jazz, Vol. 6 / Jan. 9, 1962-Feb. 25, 1966 / Storyville ✦✦✦
This LP largely duplicates *Duke Ellington/Johnny Hodges* (Storyville), featuring six of the seven selections performed by the Duke Ellington Orchestra for a half-hour television special. However it is the additional material that is of greatest interest, for Duke Ellington is also heard solo in 1966 playing a lengthy medley of his popular numbers and a version of "New World A-Comin'." For that reason this LP is preferred over the other Storyville set. — *Scott Yanow*

All American / Jan. 1962 / Columbia ✦✦
Throughout this LP, the Duke Ellington Orchestra is largely wasted playing ten selections from the now-forgotten play *All American*. None of the melodies caught on, but Ellington does the best he can with them, featuring his many all-stars on concise and respectful performances. The music is harmless enough, but there are at least 100 other more worthy Ellington releases available. — *Scott Yanow*

Midnight in Paris / Jan. 1962-Jun. 1962 / Columbia ✦✦
One of the odder Duke Ellington collections, only three of the 13 numbers were written by Ellington or Strayhorn (including a remake of "Paris Blues" and "Guitar Amour") and the music (some of it associated with Paris) sticks pretty much to melodic ballads like "I Wish You Love" and "Comme Ci, Comme Ca." Pretty music, but far from essential. — *Scott Yanow*

The Feeling of Jazz / Feb. 13, 1962-Jul. 3, 1962 / Black Lion ✦✦✦✦
This is a nice all-around set by the 1962 Duke Ellington Orchestra. Whether it be the lightweight but fun "Taffy Twist," "I'm Gonna Go Fishin'" (the theme from *Anatomy of a Murder*) or the many songs revived from decades earlier (such as "What Am I Here For?," "Black and Tan Fantasy" and "Jump for Joy"), this CD is filled with consistently swinging music. — *Scott Yanow*

New Mood Indigo / Jul. 3, 1962-Mar. 29, 1966 / Doctor Jazz ✦✦✦✦
A very interesting collection of Duke Ellington studio material from 1962-66, it was first issued in 1985. The title cut finds Ellington giving a rare double-time treatment to his classic "Mood Indigo"; three selections put the focus on the cornet and vocals of Ray Nance; and a special treat are the four selections from the Mercer Ellington Septet, a combo consisting of six of Ellington's sidemen plus a then-unknown 24-year old pianist named Chick Corea. It gives one a rare chance to hear Corea playing with the likes of Johnny Hodges, Paul Gonsalves and Harry Carney. — *Scott Yanow*

The Private Collection, Vol. 3: Studio Sessions, New York, 1962 / Jul. 25, 1962-Sep. 13, 1962 / Saja ✦✦✦✦
This is the third of ten volumes of previously unknown Duke Ellington sessions made available in this valuable CD series. One of the strongest in *The Private Collection*, these rarities from 1962 include early versions of several selections that would later be included in Duke's Sacred Concerts, two otherwise unknown but

fun Paul Gonsalves originals titled "Major" and "Minor," Thelonious Monk's composition "Monk's Dream" (here mistitled "Blue Monk") and "September 12th Blues," which welcomed trumpeter Cootie Williams back into the band after a 22-year absence. Recommended. —*Scott Yanow*

Duke Ellington Meets Coleman Hawkins / Aug. 18, 1962 / Impulse ✦✦✦✦
Reissued on CD by GRP in 1995, this classic set is made even more attractive than usual by the inclusion of fresh pictures from the session along with the original colorful liner notes. In 1962 Coleman Hawkins, after nearly four decades at the top, finally had an opportunity to record with Duke Ellington. The great tenor does not actually play with Duke's full orchestra but jams with an all-star octet that includes Ellington on piano, Ray Nance (doubling on cornet and violin), trombonist Lawrence Brown, altoist Johnny Hodges, baritonist Harry Carney, bassist Aaron Bell and drummer Sam Woodyard. Hawkins fits right in and the highlights include "Mood Indigo," "Self Portrait of the Bean," "Solitude" (a bonus track from the date that was not on the original LP) and a memorable version of "The Jeep Is Jumpin." —*Scott Yanow*

Money Jungle / Sep. 17, 1962 / Blue Note ✦✦✦✦✦
In 1962 Duke Ellington was teamed on record with a trio consisting of bassist Charles Mingus and drummer Max Roach. The setting may have seemed "modern" for a pianist from his generation, but one should realize that he was a major influence on both Thelonious Monk and Cecil Taylor. Ellington, one of the few veterans of the '20s to make a smooth transition to the relatively modern era, is in superlative form on this date, even when challenged on "Money Jungle" by the potentially combative Mingus. This LP version includes four selections not on the original release; the later CD also added a couple of "new" alternate takes. Well worth acquiring. —*Scott Yanow*

☆ **Duke Ellington and John Coltrane** / Sep. 26, 1962 / Impulse ✦✦✦✦✦
For this classic encounter, Duke Ellington "sat in" with the John Coltrane Quartet for a set dominated by Ellington's songs; some performances have his usual sidemen (bassist Aaron Bell and drummer Sam Woodyard) replacing Jimmy Garrison and Elvin Jones in the group. Although it would have been preferable to hear Coltrane play in the Duke Ellington Orchestra instead of the other way around, the results are quite rewarding. Their version of "In a Sentimental Mood" is a high point, and such numbers as "Take the Coltrane," "Big Nick" and "My Little Brown Book" are quite memorable. Ellington always recognized talent, and Coltrane seemed quite happy to be recording with a fellow genius. —*Scott Yanow*

Will Big Bands Ever Come Back? / Nov. 29, 1962-Jan. 4, 1963 / Reprise ✦✦
In general the '60s were not a good period for big bands and many veteran jazz artists. The labels often pressured musicians to play the more faddish tunes of the day or to come up with gimmicks that would increase their record sales. In Duke Ellington's case, he largely avoided the traps that were set for so many others of his era, with the exception of four albums. This one found him playing 11 tunes from the swing era and, although not that painful (at least there were no note-for-note recreations), the results are also not all that stimulating. It's interesting to hear Ellington play such material as "Smoke Rings," "Artistry in Rhythm" and "Sentimental Journey," once. —*Scott Yanow*

Afro-Bossa / Nov. 29, 1962-Jan. 5, 1963 / Musicraft ✦✦✦✦
Inspired by their world travels, Duke Ellington and Billy Strayhorn composed 11 new compositions (along with performing the standard "Pyramid") that paid tribute to the rhythms and cultures of many countries. "Purple Gazelle" and "Eighth Veil" became part of the Ellington orchestra's regular repertoire, but each of these dozen selections have their memorable moments. It's one of his better sessions of the '60s. —*Scott Yanow*

The Great London Concerts / Jan. 22, 1963+Feb. 20, 1964 / Music Masters ✦✦✦✦
This previously issued material (released on a single CD by Music Masters) features the Duke Ellington Orchestra during a very busy era. The veteran musicians were getting older, but their very individual voices were still powerful, and Ellington was far from running out of gas. The five standards taken from the earlier performance date from the brief period when both Cootie Williams and Ray Nance were in the trumpet section, while the later pieces are highlighted by "Caravan" (featuring the mighty Williams), an early version of "Isfahan," a rare Ernie Shephard vocal on "Take the 'A' Train," and a fine rendition of "Harlem." —*Scott Yanow*

The Symphonic Ellington / Jan. 31, 1963-Feb. 21, 1963 / Musicraft ✦✦✦
In 1963 Duke Ellington realized his longtime goal: to record some of his extended works using both a symphony orchestra and his regular big band. Included on this fine CD are the three movements of "Night Creature," the relatively brief "Non-Violent Integration," "La Scala" and an adaptation of Ellington's "Harlem Air Shaft." With most of his all-star soloists heard in this program, and a complete avoidance of trying to sound "respectable" or self-consciously third-stream, Ellington's arrangements keep the strings from weighing down the proceedings, and the music is actually quite successful. —*Scott Yanow*

The Great Paris Concert / Feb. 1, 1963-Feb. 23, 1963 / Atlantic ✦✦✦✦✦
A definitive look at the early-'60s edition of the Duke Ellington Orchestra, this live two-LP set contains many highlights: fresh versions of "Rockin' in Rhythm," "Concerto for Cootie" (featuring Cootie Williams) and "Jam with Sam," extended renditions of "Suite Thursday" and the "Harlem Suite," and a few newer selections. Eleven soloists (without counting the pianist/leader) are heard from in memorable settings, including both Cootie Williams and Ray Nance. Highly recommended music, either as a two-fer or on CD. —*Scott Yanow*

Jazz Violin Session / Feb. 22, 1963 / Atlantic ✦✦✦✦
This is a unique entry in Duke Ellington's massive discography. During half of this LP, Ellington and his rhythm section are joined by violinists Stephane Grappelli and Ray Nance, and Svend Asmussen on viola; the remainder of the set adds three horns for background work. On both ancient standards and a few newer pieces put together specifically for this date, the contrasting yet complementary styles of the three string players and the general infectious enthusiasm makes this a memorable encounter. —*Scott Yanow*

Duke Ellington's Greatest Hits / Feb. 23, 1963 / Reprise ✦✦✦
Despite the brief playing time, this is a worthwhile LP featuring Ellington's orchestra during a typical gig. At this live concert, he ran through his usual repertoire: ten compositions composed between the late '20s and early '50s. The high point is an emotional medley of "Black and Tan Fantasy," "Creole Love Call" and "The Mooche." —*Scott Yanow*

The Private Collection, Vol. 4: Studio Sessions, New York, 1963 / Apr. 17, 1963-Jul. 18, 1963 / Atlantic ✦✦✦✦
The fourth of ten CDs released in this valuable series, these studio sessions from 1963, in addition to rare revivals of "Harmony in Harlem" and "Blue Rose," are filled with previously unknown Ellington compositions, a stockpile of fresh material well worth a full investigation by contemporary musicians. Throughout all but the four full-band tracks, the focus is on cornetist Ray Nance, who is the only brass player present on most of this set. Johnny Hodges, Jimmy Hamilton and Paul Gonsalves also receive a good sampling of solo space on this strong entry in *The Private Collection* program. —*Scott Yanow*

My People / Aug. 20, 1963-Aug. 28, 1963 / Red Baron ✦✦✦
In 1963 Duke Ellington wrote the music for a short-lived show titled *My People*, which was a sort of combination of his early-'40s *Jump for Joy* play, along with some of the music from his "Black, Brown and Beige" suite. Using an orchestra comprising Ellingtonians past, present and future, along with a few compatible outsiders, and featuring a variety of vocalists that include Joya Sherrill, Jimmy Grissom and Lil Greenwood, Ellington created music whose message of racial harmony remains timeless. Due to the high quality of the "Black, Brown and Beige" suite and the shorter originals, this interesting set is more enjoyable than one might expect. —*Scott Yanow*

Harlem / Mar. 9, 1964 / Pablo ✦✦✦
Taken from a concert in Stockholm, Sweden, this well-recorded CD mostly features trumpeters Cootie Williams and Cat Anderson, tenor saxophonist Paul Gonsalves and altoist Johnny Hodges as the main soloists in a set with Duke Ellington's orchestra. "The Opener," "Blow by Blow" and "The Prowling Cat" have rarely been recorded, and even the more familiar pieces are given new life, highlighted by a definitive rendition of "Harlem." —*Scott Yanow*

New York Concert: In Performance at Columbia University / May 20, 1964 / Music Masters ✦✦✦✦
Duke Ellington was so brilliant as a bandleader, arranger and composer that sometimes his piano playing was taken for granted. He gave few solo concerts in his career which makes this particular Music Masters disc something special. At a 1964 appearance before the New York chapter of the Duke Ellington Society, the pianist played several trio numbers ("Take the 'A' Train," "Satin Doll," "Caravan," a drum showcase and a "Blues Medley") with his bassist Peck Morrison and drummer Sam Woodyard. There is also a joyous feature for Willie "The Lion" Smith (Duke's biggest influence) on "Carolina Shout," a remake of the Ellington-Billy Strayhorn piano duet "Tonk" and (best of all) four unaccompanied Ellington solos which are generally thoughtful and moody. This set is a must for Duke Ellington collectors. —*Scott Yanow*

All Star Road Band, Vols. 1 & 2 / May 31, 1964 / Doctor Jazz ✦✦✦✦
This two-LP set finds Duke Ellington's orchestra in surprisingly inspired form playing at a dance in Chicago. With solo highlights provided by trumpeters Cootie Williams and Cat Anderson, trombonists Lawrence Brown and Buster Cooper and the very stable saxophone section (Johnny Hodges, Russell Procope, Jimmy Hamilton, Paul Gonsalves and Harry Carney), the all-star ensemble brings new life to the potentially tired repertoire, introduces some relatively new arrangements and seems to have a good time playing for an enthusiastic audience. Excellent music. —*Scott Yanow*

Mary Poppins / Sep. 4, 1964-Sep. 9, 1964 / Reprise ✦✦✦✦

This rare LP (a real collector's item) is a surprise success. Duke Ellington was somehow persuaded into revising and recording a dozen songs from the score of Walt Disney's *Mary Poppins*, and the results are actually quite memorable. With such soloists as altoist Johnny Hodges, baritonist Harry Carney, trumpeter Cootie Williams, tenor saxophonist Paul Gonsalves, clarinetist Jimmy Hamilton and trombonist Lawrence Brown getting their spots, the Ellington orchestra turns such songs as "A Spoonful of Sugar," "Chim Chim Cheree" (a much happier version than John Coltrane's), "The Life I Lead" and even "Supercalifragilisticexpialidocious" into swinging jazz. —*Scott Yanow*

Live at Carnegie Hall (1964), Vol. 1 / 1964 / New Sound Planet ✦✦✦

Duke Ellington's 1964 Carnegie Hall concert did not find him debuting any major works but it gave his famed orchestra an opportunity to run through some lesser-known new material plus a variety of Ducal standards. The first of two CDs documenting their performance has among its highlights a medley of Ellington songs from the 1920s ("Black and Tan Fantasy," "Creole Love Call" and "The Mooche"), a version of "Perdido" featuring trumpeter Rolf Ericson and an excellent version of "Harlem." Not essential but Ellington collectors will enjoy this set. —*Scott Yanow*

Live at Carnegie Hall (1964), Vol. 2 / 1964 / New Sound Planet ✦✦✦

The second of two CDs taken from Duke Ellington's 1964 Carnegie Hall concert finds trumpeter Cootie Williams in emotional form on "Caravan" and "Tutti for Cootie" and altoist Johnny Hodges typically soulful and bluish on "Isfahan," "Things Ain't What They Used to Be" and the obscure "Banquet." The rest of the set is more routine but still worth hearing, as are all of the recordings in Duke Ellington's massive discography. —*Scott Yanow*

Berlin '65, Paris '67 / Feb. 3, 1965-Mar. 10, 1967 / Pablo ✦✦✦

The previously unreleased performances on this 1997 CD feature Duke Ellington's Orchestra on four songs from a Berlin concert in 1965 and six from a Paris engagement two years later. As usual, the music is quite enjoyable, with all ten selections being worthwhile. "Midriff" and "Chelsea Bridge" (the latter a feature for tenor saxophonist Paul Gonsalves) are revived; the lengthy "Ad Lib on Nippon" is the most recent piece; there are four features for altoist Johnny Hodges (including the 1937 piece "Harmony in Harlem"); the versions of "Happy-Go-Lucky Local" and "Rockin' in Rhythm" are up to par, and Ellington shows off his still viable stride style on "The Second Portait of the Lion." Although not definitive or essential, this excellent CD should please Duke Ellington fans and is a worthy addition to his vast discography. —*Scott Yanow*

The Private Collection, Vol. 10: Studio Sessions, New York & Chicago, 1965, 1966 & 1971 / Mar. 4, 1965-May 6, 1971 / Saja ✦✦✦✦

The tenth and final volume of this valuable series of previously unknown Duke Ellington recordings, this CD contains excerpts from his monumental "Black, Brown & Beige" suite recorded in 1965 (with this version of "The Blues" dating from 1971), a lengthy version of "Ad Lib on Nippon" (which was taken from Ellington's "The Far East Suite") and a 1966 rendition of "Harlem." Each of these extended works is rich enough to deserve several interpretations and it is always fascinating to hear how Duke altered his arrangements through the decades. —*Scott Yanow*

Concert in the Virgin Islands / Apr. 14, 1965 / Discovery ✦✦✦✦

Although in his mid-sixties, Duke Ellington proves on this program of mostly new music that he never declined nor lost his creativity. Four of the pieces comprise "The Virgin Islands Suite," and there are new versions of "Things Ain't What They Used to Be" and "Chelsea Bridge," and also a variety of miniature classics. In 1965 the Ellington orchestra had 11 very distinctive soloists; eight are heard from during this memorable set. —*Scott Yanow*

The Duke at Tanglewood / Jul. 28, 1965 / RCA ✦

In 1965 Duke Ellington appeared at a concert with Arthur Fiedler's Boston Pops Orchestra and a recording resulted. Ellington's piano is fine throughout this LP, but unfortunately the arrangements were written by Richard Hayman and are hilariously overblown and pompous; "Caravan" is an unintentional scream. Those Ellington collectors without a strong sense of humor are obliged to skip this odd greatest-hits performance. —*Scott Yanow*

Duke Ellington (1965-1972) / 1965-Aug. 2, 1972 / Music Masters ✦✦✦

This is the type of CD that Duke Ellington collectors should love, for it contains a variety of unusual and fascinating performances. Highlights include Jimmy Hamilton's stomping tenor on "The Old Circus Train," the colorful "Trombone Buster," early versions of songs later included in "The New Orleans Suite" and three selections featuring organist Wild Bill Davis. —*Scott Yanow*

Duke Ellington (1966) / Jan. 19, 1966-Jan. 2, 1965 / Reprise ✦✦

A follow-up to *Ellington '65*, this out-of-print LP finds him playing a wide variety of mostly unsuitable pop tunes from the mid-'60s, including "Red Roses for a Blue

Lady," "People," "Days of Wine and Roses," "Moon River" and even "I Want to Hold Your Hand." A true historical curiosity, but often downright weird. —*Scott Yanow*

Orchestral Works / Apr. 10, 1966 / MCA ✦✦

Duke Ellington's collaboration with Erich Kunzel and the Cincinnatti Symphony Orchestra gives one an opportunity to hear Ellington's "The Golden Broom & the Green Apple" and "New World A'Coming" in rare performances along with a symphonic version of "Harlem." Ellington, who is featured throughout on piano, adds verbal "poetic commentary" between sections and the arrangements (which may have been by Luther Henderson) are fine but one misses his illustrious orchestra. Interesting but not essential music. —*Scott Yanow*

The Pianist / Jul. 18, 1966-Jan. 7, 1970 / Original Jazz Classics ✦✦✦

Duke Ellington had so many talents (composer, arranger, bandleader, personality) that his skills as a pianist could easily be overlooked. Fortunately he did record a fair amount of trio albums through the years so there is plenty of evidence as to his unique style which was both modern and traditional at the same time. *The Pianist* has trio performances from 1966 and 1970, and finds Ellington shifting smoothly between styles and moods while always remaining himself. —*Scott Yanow*

Ella and Duke at the Cote d'Azur / Jul. 28, 1966 / Verve ✦✦✦

Ella Fitzgerald and Duke Ellington did not team up in concerts until relatively late in their careers (although she did record her *Ellington Songbook* with him in the '50s). This live double LP actually finds Fitzgerald singing six numbers with the Jimmy Jones Trio and only "Mack the Knife" and a scat-filled "It Don't Mean a Thing" with the orchestra. Ellington has eight numbers for his band, mostly remakes of older tunes (including a guest appearance by former associate Ben Webster on "All Too Soon," a remarkable Buster Cooper trombone feature and a rowdy version of "The Old Circus Train Turn-Around Blues"). This is a spirited set of music that with better planning could have been great. [The 1997 CD reissue of *At the Cote d'Azur* was expanded to a double disc set with the addition of several bonus tracks. The double-CD was released as a teaser for the 1998 release of the eight-disc *The Complete Ella & Duke at Cote d'Azur*.] —*Scott Yanow*

Soul Call / Jul. 28, 1966 / Verve ✦✦

The centerpiece of this live album is Ellington's "La Plus Belle Africaine," one of his better late-period works. Otherwise an overly fast "Jam with Sam," two short Paul Gonsalves features and a lengthy drum solo comprise the remainder of the program, making this a lesser Ellington item. —*Scott Yanow*

The Far East Suite (Special Mix) / Dec. 19, 1966-Dec. 21, 1966 / Bluebird ✦✦✦✦✦

This CD differs from the previous release of "The Far East Suite" by the inclusion of four "new" alternate takes. This particular nine-part suite was arguably Duke Ellington's finest major work of the 1960s. The haunting ballad "Isfahan" (a showcase for altoist Johnny Hodges) is the best-known section but several of the other pieces (particularly "Bluebird of Delhi," "Mount Harissa" and "Ad Lib on Nippon") are also quite memorable. Clarinetist Jimmy Hamilton and tenor saxophonist Paul Gonsalves co-star with Hodges, but it is the creative writing of Ellington and Billy Strayhorn that makes this CD quite essential. —*Scott Yanow*

The Far East Suite / Dec. 20, 1966-Dec. 21, 1966 / Bluebird ✦✦✦✦

Duke Ellington could have been forgiven if, by the time he was 67, he had gradually lost his creative desire not to mention his writing skills. But his genius never dimmed as witness the new music ("The Far East Suite" and "Ad Lib on Nippon") on this superb set. "The Far East Suite" is in reality eight separate compositions of which the beautiful "Isfahan" (a memorable Johnny Hodges feature) became the best-known melody; Paul Gonsalves and Jimmy Hamilton are also among the main stars with the clarinetist being showcased throughout "Ad Lib on Nippon." But it is the writing of Ellington and Strayhorn in their late prime that makes this one of his more memorable recordings. —*Scott Yanow*

Live in Italy, Vol. 1 / Feb. 22, 1967 / Jazz Up ✦✦✦

The first of two volumes, this CD captures Duke Ellington's orchestra during a European tour late in his career, but when he still retained virtually all of his star sidemen. The inclusion of some lesser-known compositions increase the value of this set as do the excellent solos of tenor saxophonist Paul Gonsalves, trombonist Lawrence Brown, Johnny Hodges and, on "Salome" and "Wild Onions," the phenomenal high-note trumpeter Cat Anderson. Typically brilliant music from Duke Ellington. —*Scott Yanow*

Live in Italy, Vol. 2 / 1967 / Jazz Up ✦✦✦

Intimacy of the Blues / Mar. 15, 1967-Jun. 15, 1970 / Original Jazz Classics ✦✦✦

Lots of rare music was uncovered when these recordings were first released. Duke Ellington did a remarkable number of private recordings with small groups taken from his orchestra and the selections included on this CD reissue are some of the best. A "Combo Suite" from 1967 introduces Billy Strayhorn's "Intimacy of the Blues" along with five forgotten but worthy originals, while the music on the second half of the program (some of which features organist Wild Bill Davis) dates from 1970; "All Too Soon" showcases Ellington's new tenor Harold Ashby. Excellent music. —*Scott Yanow*

Live at the Rainbow Grill / Aug. 1967 / Moon ✦✦✦
This concert date (released for the first time on this 1993 CD) features Duke Ellington with an octet taken from his big band. Trumpeter Cat Anderson (the most surprising choice) jams on Ellington standards with trombonist Lawrence Brown, altoist Johnny Hodges, tenorman Paul Gonsalves, bassist John Lamb, drummer Steve Little and the pianist/leader. First Ellington summons the other musicians to the stand by playing piano on "Heaven" and "Le Sucrier Velours." After a few other informal numbers, a radio broadcast begins and Duke sticks to familiar (although enthusiastically) played material such as "Take the 'A' Train," "Perdido" and "Things Ain't What They Used to Be." A good if not essential outing. —*Scott Yanow*

☆ **And His Mother Called Him Bill** / Aug. 28, 1967-Sep. 1, 1967 / RCA ✦✦✦✦✦
Shortly after Billy Strayhorn's early death in 1967, the Duke Ellington Orchestra recorded a dozen of his compositions during a series of emotional and passionate sessions. The results are consistently inspired with such selections as "Blood Count" (Strayhorn's final composition), "Rain Check," "Lotus Blossom" and "The Intimacy of the Blues" receiving definitive versions. In addition, this CD reissue also contains an alternate take of "Lotus Blossom" and remakes of three more Strayhorn classics that were previously unissued. This was one of Duke Ellington's finest sessions and, considering his huge recorded legacy, that is saying a lot. —*Scott Yanow*

Second Sacred Concert / 1968 / Prestige ✦✦✦
Duke Ellington's second (of three) sacred concerts, originally out as a two-LP set, has been reissued as a single CD while leaving out two of the weaker tracks. As is usual with these elaborate and very sincere affairs, some of the music is weighed down by heavy-handed sermonizing but there are a few strong moments. Best is "Praise God," which features Harry Carney's baritone, "The Shepherd (Who Watches over the Night Flock)" which is a wonderful showcase for trumpeter Cootie Williams and the memorable "Heaven," which puts the focus on the beautiful voice of Alice Babs along with altoist Johnny Hodges. Most of the other selections feature choirs with Ellington and his band taking a supportive role. Interesting music but not essential. —*Scott Yanow*

Yale Concert / Jan. 26, 1968 / Original Jazz Classics ✦✦✦
The great Duke Ellington Orchestra was still intact and in its late prime at the time of this performance from 1968. With the death of Billy Strayhorn the year before, Ellington (perhaps sensing his own mortality) accelerated his writing activities, proving that even as he neared seventy, he was still at his peak. Other than a Johnny Hodges medley and the theme ("Take the 'A' Train"), all of the music on this set was fairly new. Included are showcases for Cootie Williams, Harry Carney, Paul Gonsalves and Cat Anderson, an 11-minute "The Little Purple Flower," "Swamp Goo" (which gives Russell Procope a chance to play some New orleans-style clarinet) and a jazz version of Yale's famous "Boola, Boola." —*Scott Yanow*

Latin American Suite / Oct. 1968 / Original Jazz Classics ✦✦✦
Written after his orchestra's successful debut in South America, Duke Ellington's seven-part suite celebrates the atmosphere and rhythms of the many south-of-the-border countries that he visited. The usual horn stars have their moments, but the pianist himself is the main voice throughout this enjoyable set of fresh music. —*Scott Yanow*

The Private Collection, Vol. 5: The Suites, New York, 1968 & 1970 / Nov. 6, 1968-Jun. 15, 1970 / Saja ✦✦✦✦
One of the most interesting of the ten volumes released in *The Private Collection* series, this CD contains "The Degas Suite" (music for a soundtrack of an art film that was never produced) and a ballet score titled "The River." Ellington is mostly the lead voice but his star sidemen are heard from on these formerly very rare and somewhat unusual performances. Clearly his genius was strong enough to fill three lifetimes full of new music and this CD contains some melodies that might have been more significant if he had lived long enough to find a place for them. —*Scott Yanow*

The Private Collection, Vol. 9: Studio Sessions, New York, 1968 / Nov. 23, 1968-Dec. 3, 1968 / Saja ✦✦✦
The ninth of ten volumes of music from Duke Ellington's *Private Collection* of unknown tapes, this CD captures him in 1968 shortly after clarinetist Jimmy Hamilton left the band and tenor saxophonist Harold Ashby joined up. Even after 30 years of playing some of these standards, Ellington found new ways to re-arrange such songs as "Sophisticated Lady," "Mood Indigo" and "Just Squeeze Me." In addition, there are a few new obscurities such as "Knuf" (which finds Jeff Castleman switching to electric bass), "Reva" and the somewhat dated Trish Turner vocal on "Cool and Groovy." Lots of surprises on this fine CD. —*Scott Yanow*

April in Paris / 1969 / West Wind ✦✦
Recorded in the same period of time as Duke Ellington's acclaimed Seventieth Birthday Concert, this single CD has its moments. Although subtitled "Feat. Wild

Bill Davis," the organist is only on a few of the selections, including a version of "Satin Doll" that unfortunately has Cat Anderson's miraculous high-note trumpet solo way off mike. However there are good versions of "Rockin' in Rhythm," "Take the 'A' Train" (starring trumpeter Cootie Williams), a hits medley and Paul Gonsalves' tenor feature on "Diminuendo and Crescendo in Blue." This disc is not essential but Ellington collectors will find it an interesting addition to their collections. —*Scott Yanow*

The Intimate Ellington / Apr. 25, 1969-Jun. 29, 1971 / Original Jazz Classics ✦✦
This Pablo set has odds and ends taken from nine different recording/rehearsal sessions that find Ellington experimenting with instrumentation and personnel, even taking a vocal on the tongue-in-cheek "Moon Maiden." Performances range from a couple of vigorous trio workouts and spots for Wild Bill Davis' organ to a few big-band performances. Even this late in his life, Duke Ellington had a great deal to say musically and his band continued to rank near the top. —*Scott Yanow*

Up in Duke's Workshop / Apr. 25, 1969-Dec. 1972 / Original Jazz Classics ✦✦
This CD reissue is primarily for Duke Ellington completists and scholars. Some of the performances are runthroughs of works that would soon be discarded or rewritten, while others are true obscurities. Best is trumpeter Cootie Williams' feature on "Love Is Just Around the Corner" and a jam on "Blem." There are also several spots for organist Wild Bill Davis and such underfeatured Ellingtonians as trumpeter Money Johnson, Geezil Minerve (on piccolo), trombonist Malcolm Taylor and trumpeter Fred Stone. But nothing all that essential or historic occurs and there are over 100 currently available Duke Ellington recordings that one would recommend first. —*Scott Yanow*

Seventieth Birthday Concert / Nov. 25, 1969-Nov. 26, 1969 / Blue Note ✦✦✦✦✦
This double CD reissues a Solid State double-LP that ranked as one of Duke Ellington's finest recordings of this last decade. The live performance gives listeners a good idea as to just how Duke's ensemble sounded in concert, and it serves as both a retrospective and a display of the strengths of Ellington's mighty band. Among the many highlights are definitive renditions of "Rockin' in Rhythm" and "Take the 'A' Train" (the latter has some wonderful Cootie Williams trumpet), some features for altoist Johnny Hodges, a tenor battle on "In Triplicate," a few guest spots for organist Wild Bill Davis and a sixteen-and-a-half-minute nine-song medley that works really well. The most memorable chorus of all is an incredible high-note display by Cat Anderson on "Satin Doll" that is arguably his most miraculous solo ever; each note he hits is virtually impossilbe to play on the trumpet! This gem is essential for all serious jazz collections. —*Scott Yanow*

New Orleans Suite / Apr. 27, 1970+May 13, 1970 / Atlantic ✦✦✦
This late-period Duke Ellington album is perhaps most notable for including altoist Johnny Hodges' final recordings. In fact Hodges was supposed to record his first soprano solo in nearly 30 years on "Portrait of Sidney Bechet," but he passed away before the second session. The set consists of the five-song "New Orleans Suite" plus tributes to Wellman Braud, Bechet (tenor saxophonist Paul Gonsalves took Hodges' place as its soloist), Louis Armstrong (a feature for trumpeter Cootie Williams) and Mahalia Jackson. Interesting if not essential music with a few memorable themes being the main reason to acquire this release. —*Scott Yanow*

The Afro-Eurasian Eclipse / Feb. 11, 1971-Feb. 17, 1971 / Original Jazz Classics ✦✦✦✦
This CD reissue brings back one of Duke Ellington's most intriguing works from his later years. "Acht O'Clock Rock" actually shows the influence of rock while some of the other selections hint at both African folk music and more advanced areas of jazz. However the familiar Ellington sound was still very much intact in 1971. The main soloists include Harold Ashby and Paul Gonsalves on tenors, baritonist Harry Carney (featured on "Didjeridoo") and altoist Norris Turney; the versatility of drummer Rufus Jones really helps the colorful music. —*Scott Yanow*

Toga Brava Suite / Oct. 22, 1971+Oct. 24, 1971 / Blue Note ✦✦✦✦
This single CD reissues all of the contents of the original United Artists double LP. By the time of these concerts from England, the Duke Ellington Orchestra had suffered quite a few losses of veteran personnel with Johnny Hodges having passed away and such greats as Cat Anderson, Ray Nance, Lawrence Brown and Jimmy Hamilton having departed. However the band was still a major force and this set has plenty of high points. Ellington's four-part "Togo Brava Suite" contains some memorable themes, there are spirited remakes of "C Jam Blues," "Cottontail," "In a Mellotone" and "I Got It Bad" (the latter featuring vocalist Nell Brookshire) and among the solo stars are the ancient-sounding trumpeter Cootie Williams, trombonist Booty Wood, Norris Turney on alto and flute (his "Checkered Hat" is a fine tribute to Hodges), the tenors of Paul Gonsalves and Harold Ashby and pianist Ellington himself. —*Scott Yanow*

Live at the Whitney / Apr. 10, 1972 / Impulse! ✦✦✦
Late in his career, Duke Ellington was persuaded on three occasions to take a brief hiatus from his big band and give trio recitals that focused on his piano playing.

The final occasion is included on this CD, which was released for the first time in 1995. Although Duke apparently planned very little in advance, his program is a well-rounded set of old standards and newer (and more obscure) works. A week short of his 73rd birthday, Ellington's fingers sound rusty in spots, but he clearly gets stronger as the concert progresses. He romps through the beginning parts of his very first composition (the James P. Johnson-inspired "Soda Fountain Rag") and then abruptly stops, making a few jokes about how "Things Ain't What They Used to Be." Considering that he never commercially recorded this piece, the excerpt is quite valuable. Also among the highlights is his delightful "A Mural from Two Perspectives," a nine-minute exploration of "New World A-Coming," and an emotional "Lotus Blossom." Many of the performances (half are solo and the remainder use bassist Joe Benjamin and drummer Rufus Jones) are brief—under three or even two minutes long—but there is a great deal of music on this previously unissued program, and some of the moments are quite precious. The audience is enthusiastic and loving, singing along on "I'm Beginning to See the Light" and snapping their fingers on Duke's cues during "Dancers in Love." —*Scott Yanow*

This One's for Blanton / Dec. 5, 1972 / Original Jazz Classics ✦✦✦✦
For this set of duets, pianist Duke Ellington is teamed with bassist Ray Brown in performances reminiscent of Duke's with Jimmy Blanton three decades before. In addition to the four-part "Fragmented Suite for Piano and Bass," the duo plays five standards (including "Pitter Panther Patter" from the Blanton days and three other Ellington-associated tunes). Delightful and often-playful music. —*Scott Yanow*

The Duke's Big Four / Jan. 8, 1973 / Pablo ✦✦✦✦✦
One of Duke Ellington's finest small group sessions from his final decade was this frequently exciting quartet date with guitarist Joe Pass, bassist Ray Brown and drummer Louie Bellson. Ellington's percussive style always sounded modern and he comes up with consistently strong solos on such numbers as "Love You Madly," "The Hawk Talks" and especially "Cottontail," easily keeping up with his younger sidemen. Highly recommended. —*Scott Yanow*

Eastbourne Performance / Dec. 1, 1973 / RCA ✦✦✦
Duke Ellington's final recording (made 49 years after his first) was made during a concert in Eastbourne, England. The Ellington Orchestra was a bit weaker than it had been (many of the veterans had either died or retired) but it was still a mighty outfit with such new members as tenor saxophonist Percy Marion and trumpeters Barry Lee Hall, Johnny Coles (featured on "How High the Moon") and Money Johnson (who sings "Basin Street Blues"). Also featured on the date are clarinetist Russell Procope, altoist Harold Minerve, tenor saxophonist Harold Ashby and vocalist Anita Moore (who does what she can with "New York, New York"); other highlights include "Tiger Rag" and a tenor battle on "Woods". Actually the most impressive soloist on the album (which has yet to be reissued on CD) is Ellington himself, who plays both "The Piano Player" and a touching version of "Meditation" (the closer on this final album) as unaccompanied solos. A fitting ending to a truly remarkable career. —*Scott Yanow*

Mercer Ellington

b. Mar. 11, 1919, Washington, DC, **d.** Feb. 8, 1996, Copenhagen, Denmark
Leader / Swing

Mercer Ellington had the impossible task of trying to escape from his father Duke Ellington's shadow and he never really succeeded, perhaps not trying hard enough. He studied music early on and made several attempts to lead his own band (1939, 1946-49 and 1959) that were all ultimately unsuccessful. During the ASCAP strike of the early '40s when Duke was desperate for new material, Mercer wrote several notable songs including "Things Ain't What They Used to Be," "Jumpin' Punkins," "Moon Mist" and "Blue Serge," but nothing he composed since then approached their stature. Among his many other jobs were working as road manager for Cootie Williams' Orchestra, musical director for Della Reese, and as a salesman, a record-company executive and a disc jockey. Finally in 1965 he gave up trying to be independent and became Duke Ellington's road manager and a nonsoloing section trumpeter. After Duke's death in 1974, Mercer took over the band, but within a couple years it had greatly declined. Mercer wrote a biography in 1978, *Duke Ellington in Person*, directed the so-so musical *Sophisticated Ladies* (1981-83), supervised the release of many previously unavailable Ellington recordings and led the inaccurately titled "Duke Ellington Orchestra" on an occasional basis, recording a few dates that often had all-stars as ringers. —*Scott Yanow*

Black and Tan Fantasy / Jul. 14, 1958-Mar. 16, 1959 / MCA ✦✦✦✦
Throughout his erratic life in music, Mercer Ellington made several attempts to put together bands but none caught on. During 1958-59 he borrowed most of the Duke Ellington Orchestra (using either Billy Strayhorn or Jimmy Jones on piano) for a pair of albums made for the Coral label. This 1973 MCA LP has 14 of the 24 selections and contains quite a bit of fine swinging music. There are seven songs apiece by Mercer and his father Duke Ellington but, although Mercer did some of the arranging (along with Luther Henderson and Andy Gibson), this sounds very

much like a Duke Ellington album. Among the main soloists are trumpeters Harold Baker and Clark Terry, clarinetist Jimmy Hamilton, altoist Johnny Hodges and tenor saxophonist Ben Webster. —*Scott Yanow*

Continuum / Jul. 14, 1974-May 12, 1975 / Fantasy ✦✦✦✦
Although Duke Ellington passed away on May 24, 1974, this posthumous effort can be thought of as his orchestra's final record. Duke's son Mercer took over the big band and at least for a short time still had some surviving veterans in which to form a nucleus. Baritonist Harry Carney is heard on two numbers (taking a solo on "Drop Me Off in Harlem") from the LP's first session before he too passed away. Also quite prominent is trumpeter Cootie Williams along with such new (and temporary) band members as tenor saxophonist Ricky Ford, trumpeter Barry Lee Hall, trombonist Art Baron and altoist Geezil Minerve. The music (which includes the tribute "Carney," a fine feature for the band's new baritonist Joe Temperley) is very much in the Ellington style and mostly consists of updated remakes of Ducal standards. This out-of-print LP served as a fine finish for the classic jazz institution. —*Scott Yanow*

Take the Holiday Train / Jul. 28, 1980-Jul. 29, 1980 / Special Music ✦✦
This is the type of record that Duke Ellington would never have done. Mercer Ellington, as leader of what was left of Duke's Orchestra, has his ensemble play nine Christmas songs, four of which have vocals by Anita Moore. Although the group has such fine players as bassist Ron Carter, altoist Kenny Garrett (before he joined Miles Davis), trumpeters Barrie Lee Hall and Joe Wilder and trombonist Britt Woodman, little significant occurs. The Christmas songs are given melodic and lightly swinging but rather routine treatment not worthy of the Ellington name. —*Scott Yanow*

Hot and Bothered / June 22, 1984 / Doctor Jazz ✦✦✦✦
Probably the best example of the Mercer Ellington Orchestra of the 1980s, this LP has new and revised versions of nine vintage Duke Ellington compositions/arrangements, all dating before 1935. Whether it be 1927's "Hot and Bothered," the great train re-creation "Daybreak Express," "East St. Louis Toodle-oo" (Ellington's theme before "Take the 'A' Train") or "Ring Dem Bells," this is a spirited set. There were few of Duke's alumni in Mercer's band (other than trumpeter Barrie Lee Hall, trombonists Art Baron and Chuck Connors and altoist Geezil Minerve), but the many soloists bring back the spirit of Duke's music, particularly Barry Lee Hall (a fine successor to Bubber Miley, Cootie Williams and Ray Nance). Unfortunately this worthy LP has yet to be reissued on CD. —*Scott Yanow*

Digital Duke / 1987 / GRP ✦✦✦✦
The Duke Ellington Orchestra pretty much fell apart after its leader's death in 1974, but his son, Mercer, on an occasional basis has put together pickup bands to perform Duke's music. This particular CD uses quite an all-star group, mixing together such Ellington alumni as fluegelhornist Clark Terry, trumpeter Barry Lee Hall, altoist Norris Turney, trombonist Britt Woodman and on four cuts, drummer Louie Bellson with such other major players as trumpeter Lew Soloff, clarinetist Eddie Daniels, tenorman Branford Marsalis (on two songs), trombonist Al Grey and pianist Roland Hanna. The big band does a fine job of performing a dozen songs associated with Duke, making this one of the best of Mercer Ellington's efforts. —*Scott Yanow*

● **Music Is My Mistress** / 1988 / Music Masters ✦✦✦✦✦
By the late '80s, Mercer Ellington was leading a part-time Duke Ellington Orchestra (he should have used his own name to avoid confusion with the classic band) and doing his best to preserve Duke's legacy. In addition to fresh versions of some vintage tunes (including "C Jam Blues," "Black and Tan Fantasy," "Jack the Bear" and Billy Strayhorn's "A Flower Is a Lovesome Thing"), this CD contains Duke's obscure "Queenie Pie Reggae" (which features a steel drummer) and a couple of Mercer's originals including the five-movement (but generally uneventful) "Music Is My Mistress." Among the better-known soloists are trumpeter Barrie Lee Hall (the last significant player to emerge from Duke Ellington's Orchestra), guest pianist Roland Hanna (Mulgrew Miller was the regular pianist at the time), clarinetist Bill Easley and (on "The Duke's Suite") altoist Kenny Garrett. An interesting if not essential set. —*Scott Yanow*

Only God Can Make a Tree / 1996 / Music Masters ✦✦✦✦
This was the final project of Mercer Ellington who, even this late in his life (within a year of his death), was unable (or unwilling) to escape from the shadow of his father; he should at least have renamed his big band after himself. Actually, this is one of Mercer's finest individual recordings, for although the majority of the selections were composed by Duke (including "Caravan" and "Ballet of the Flying Saucers"), the arrangements (two by the leader) are fresh, the orchestra hints at Duke's without sounding much like it, and the colorful music is an effective tour of the world. Other than just a couple of alumni (trumpeter Barrie Lee Hall and trombonist Art Baron), the band members are fairly young, and among the guests are drummer Max Roach (for one number) and Professor Ken Philmore on steel

drums. If only Mercer Ellington had had the confidence to carve out his own musical path many years earlier. —*Scott Yanow*

Richard Elliot

Tenor Saxophone, Soprano Saxophone / R&B, Crossover Jazz, Instrumental Pop, Fusion

Although he's called a "smooth jazz artist," saxophonist Richard Elliot is equally at home with most rock 'n' roll and the kind of classic R&B performed by the group Tower of Power. For five years in the 1980s, he was a big part of the classic R&B band's horn-based sound. The Scottish-born Elliot was raised in Los Angeles, where he quickly became a fan of West Coast classic R&B. Elliot landed his first job while still a teenager with Natalie Cole and the Pointer Sisters. A few years later, he was tapped to record with some of his idols from Motown Records, which had relocated from Detroit to Los Angeles. In the 1970s, he had the chance to record with Smokey Robinson, the Four Tops and the Temptations. Elliot was later tapped to record with the Yellowjackets on their second album. After touring with Melissa Manchester for a time, he was asked to become a full-fledged member of the Tower of Power horns in 1982. He stayed with the group until 1987, and looks back fondly on those years, for they shaped the style he has today. When he's not playing he over 100 dates a year, Elliot pilots a small aircraft and is partner in PacifNet, an Internet multimedia company that develops websites for the music and entertainment industries. Although Elliot has a smooth jazz sound that could be compared with Kenny G.'s, his take on contemporary jazz is more firmly rooted in tradition. —*Richard Skelly*

What's Inside / 1976 / Blue Note ♦♦
New reissue of prolific fusion-pop player. —*Ron Wynn*

Trolltown / 1986 / Blue Note ♦♦
Not as consistently boring as many of Richard Elliot's subsequent albums, *Trolltown* contains a few decent tracks. "Ducks From Mars" and "Stankfoot" are gritty jazz/R&B numbers that have a lot more bite than one generally expects from the tenor, alto and soprano saxman, and the edgy "Come to My Apartment" is surprisingly rock-influenced. But those selections are the exception instead of the rule; the CD is dominated by the type of unlistenable and painfully dull "elevator music" Elliot is best known for. Especially embarrassing is his note-for-note cover of Stevie Wonder's "Until You Come Back to Me (That's What I'm Going to Do)"—what was a memorable R&B-pop hit in the hands of Wonder and Aretha Franklin sounds like pure schlock when Elliot gets ahold of it. Elliot has butchered his share of R&B classics, and this is one of the worst examples. *Trolltown* may not be as bad as some of the albums Elliot would record in the 1990s, but is nonetheless the work of someone who was always willing to throw artistic integrity to the wind. —*Alex Henderson*

On the Town / Dec. 4, 1991 / Blue Note ♦♦
Richard Elliot is the Michael Bolton of the saxophone—an instrumentalist whose knee-jerk pop/R&B solos are, like Bolton's singing, consistently formulaic, contrived and vacuous. Even by the low standards of NAC and so-called "smooth jazz" radio, *On the Town* is dreadful. Such homogenized, cliché-ridden "muzak" as "By My Side" and "Into the Light" is bloodless and devoid of soul, and on funk-influenced tracks like "Stiletto Heels" and the title song, the robotic Elliot fails to express any honest emotion. But the CD's worst embarrassment of all is a saccharine and downright insulting cover of "Over the Rainbow" (Howard Arlen's classic from the Wizard of Oz). For jazz, pop and R&B fans alike, *On the Town* is among the many Elliot albums to avoid. —*Alex Henderson*

Soul Embrace / 1992 / Manhattan ♦♦
Richard Elliot's Manhattan CD from 1992 is a blatant attempt to win over the Kenny G. audience. As usual the tenor saxophonist emphasizes long tones that any high-school musician could hit and plays with great emotion no matter what notes he is hitting. As instrumental pop this music is tolerable but its lack of originality and honest soul is troubling. —*Scott Yanow*

After Dark / 1994 / Blue Note ♦♦
Richard Elliot seems to have as his main desire the goal to be the next Kenny G. One wishes him well although his recordings thus far have little or nothing to do with jazz since he does not improvise. On this pop CD Elliot mostly sticks to long tones, emphasizing every note with equal intensity and playing the rather mundane melodies with such sincerity and force that one would think they were special. —*Scott Yanow*

● **City Speak** / 1996 / Blue Note ♦♦♦♦

Jumpin' Off / 1997 / Metro Blue ♦♦♦
For his tenth album, *Jumpin' Off*, Richard Elliot decided to leave the producer's chair for only the second time in his career, letting Paul Brown—the producer behind hit albums by Rick Braun, Peter White and Boney James—take the helm. Working with Brown has given Elliot a bit of a contemporary edge, which is neces-

sary, considering that his records were beginning to sound a little formulaic. The music remains predictable—it's smooth jazz, with the ballads outweighing the midtempo, vaguely soulful workouts—but it sounds relatively fresh. There's no mistaking Elliot's professional instrumental with improvisatory jazz—even his solos sound as if they were written prior to recording—but it's the kind of album that will please his large contingent of fans. —*Stephen Thomas Erlewine*

Don Ellis

b. Jul. 25, 1934, Los Angeles, CA, **d.** Dec. 17, 1978, Hollywood, CA
Trumpet, Leader / Post-Bop, Avant-Garde

A talented trumpeter with a vivid musical imagination and the willingness to try new things, Don Ellis led some of the most colorful big bands of the 1965-75 period. After graduating from Boston Unversity, Ellis played in the big bands of Ray McKinley, Charlie Barnet and Maynard Ferguson (he was featured with the latter on "Three More Foxes"), recorded with Charles Mingus and played with George Russell's sextet (at the same time as Eric Dolphy). Ellis led four quartet and trio sessions during 1960-62 for Candid, New Jazz and Pacific Jazz, mixing together bop, free jazz and his interest in modern classical music. However it was in 1965 when he put together his first orchestra that he really started to make an impression in jazz. Ellis' big bands were distinguished by their unusual instrumentation (which in its early days had up to three bassists and three drummers including Ellis himself), the leader's desire to investigate unusual time changes (including 7/8, 9/8 and even 15/16), its occasionally wacky humor (highlighted by an excess of false endings) and an openness towards using rock rhythms and (in later years) electronics. Ellis invented the four-valve trumpet and utilized a ring modulator and all types of wild electronic devices by the late '60s. By 1971 his band consisted of an eight-piece brass section (including French horn and tuba), a four-piece woodwind section, a string quartet and a two-drum rhythm section. A later unrecorded edition even added a vocal quartet. Among Don Ellis' sidemen were Glenn Ferris, Tom Scott, John Rlemmer, Sam Falzone, Frank Strozier, Dave MacKay and the brilliant pianist (straight from Bulgaria) Milcho Leviev. The orchestra's most memorable recordings (none are out on CD yet) were *Autumn*, *Live at the Fillmore* and *Tears of Joy* (all for Columbia). After suffering a mid-'70s heart attack, Ellis returned to live performing, playing the "superbone" and a later edition of his big band featured Art Pepper. Ellis' last recording was at the 1977 Montreux Jazz Fesival, a year before his heart finally gave out. —*Scott Yanow*

How Time Passes / Oct. 4, 1960-Oct. 5, 1960 / Candid ♦♦♦♦♦
Trumpeter Don Ellis' initial recording as a leader (and first of four small-group dates from the 1960-62 period) found him stretching the boundaries of bop-based jazz and experimenting a bit with time and tempo. Teamed up with Jaki Byard (who doubles on piano and alto), bassist Ron Carter and drummer Charlie Persip, Ellis (whose sound was already fairly distinctive) performs four of his unusual originals (including the 22-minute "Improvisational Suite No. 1") plus Byard's "Waste." Although these musical experiments failed to be influential (Ellis himself went in a different direction a few years later), the unpredictable music is still quite interesting to hear. —*Scott Yanow*

Out of Nowhere / Apr. 21, 1961 / Candid ♦♦♦♦
This formerly unknown date was released for the first time on this 1988 CD; chances are that the short-lived Candid label died before the music could be put out. Don Ellis, one of the most original trumpeters to emerge in the early 1960s, performs ten standards on a trio session with pianist Paul Bley and bassist Steve Swallow (who was making his recording debut) but the music is far from routine or predictable. Ellis takes an unaccompanied trumpet solo on "Just One of Those Things," "All the Things You Are" is a trumpet-bass duet and Ellis interacts with Bley on a moody "My Funny Valentine." The players constantly take chances with time but there are few slip-ups or hesitant moments. A fascinating and long-lost session. —*Scott Yanow*

New Ideas / May 11, 1961 / Original Jazz Classics ♦♦♦♦
It seems strange that three out of four of Don Ellis' obscure small group sessions from the early 1960s are currently available on CD while all of his famous big band albums for Pacific Jazz, Columbia and Atlantic are out-of-print. On this 1961 quintet set for Prestige (with vibraphonist Al Francis, pianist Jaki Byard, bassist Ron Carter and drummer Charlie Persip), Ellis experiments with time, new chord structures and free improvising; a highlight is his brief unaccompanied workout on the free form "Solo." Don Ellis, who switches to piano during part of "Tragedy," already had a sound of his own although he would change the direction of his music within a few years. Even over 35 years later, his thoughtful musical experiments of the early 1960s are often quite fascinating to hear. —*Scott Yanow*

Essence / Jul. 15, 1962-Jul. 17, 1962 / Pacific Jazz ♦♦♦♦
The rarest of all Don Ellis sessions (this LP has not been reissued since 1962), the album matches the trumpeter with pianist Paul Bley, bassist Gary Peacock and either Nick Martinis or Gene Stone on drums. Ellis, who sought during this period

to transfer ideas and concepts from modern classical music into adventurous jazz, often experimented with time, tempos and the use of space while still swinging. His renditions of Billy Strayhorn's "Johnny Come Lately," "Angel Eyes" and "Lover" are quite fresh, he contributes four interesting originals and introduces Carla Bley's "Wrong Key Donkey" (here simply called "Donkey"). This is thought-provoking music that is certainly way overdue to be reissued. —*Scott Yanow*

Don Ellis at Monterey / Sep. 17, 1966-Sep. 18, 1966 / Pacific Jazz ♦♦♦♦♦
The first effort by the Don Ellis big band, as with all of his other orchestral projects, has yet to be reissued on CD. One of the most exciting new jazz big bands of the period, Ellis' ensemble became notorious for its ability to play coherently in odd time signatures. One of the four originals heard on this acclaimed outing from the 1966 Monterey Jazz Festival is titled "33 222 1 222" to show how the band manages to perform in 19/4 time. The other selections are Hank Levy's "Passacaglia and Fugue," "Concerto for Trumpet" (in 5/4) and "New Nine." In addition to the time signatures, Ellis enjoyed utilizing unusual combinations of instruments; the instrumentation on this date consists of five trumpets, three trombones, five saxes, piano, three bassists, two drummers and a percussionist. Among the more notable sidemen are a young Tom Scott (who solos on alto) and tenor saxophonist Ira Schulman. Highly recommended but unfortunately this album will be difficult to find. —*Scott Yanow*

Live in 3/4 Time / Oct. 1966 / Pacific ♦♦♦♦♦
One of the most fun jazz bands of the late 1960s, Don Ellis' orchestra (which at the time consisted of five trumpets, three trombones, five reeds, piano, three basses, two drummers and three percussionists!) mastered the impossible art of playing logical solos in unusual time signatures. On "Barnum's Revenge," they perform some satirical Dixieland in 5/4 time, "Orientation" alternates between 7/8 and 9/8 and "Upstart" is in 11/8 (or 3 2/3 beats to the measure). More importantly, Ellis' music was not gimmicky; his band managed to swing and there were some strong soloists (particularly the trumpet-leader, Ira Schulman on tenor and clarinet, pianist Dave Mackay and Tom Scott on saxello). Their second album (not yet out on CD) is taken from appearances in 1966 at Shelly's Manne Hole and the Pacific Jazz Festival and is quite enjoyable and innovative in its own way. —*Scott Yanow*

Electric Bath / Sep. 17, 1967-Sep. 20, 1967 / Columbia ♦♦♦♦♦
For his first studio recording with his colorful big band, Don Ellis utilized five trumpets, three trombones, five reeds, Mike Lang on keyboards, three bassists, drummer Steve Bohannon and three percussionists to perform some remarkable new music. The most memorable selection is "Indian Lady" (accurately described as a "hoedown in 5/4"), which with its false endings is often quite humorous. The other four originals (the trumpet-leader's feature on "Alone," "Turkish Bath," "Open Beauty" and the 17/4 "New Horizons"), while lesser-known, are also quite spirited. For the first time Ellis opened his band to the influence of rock (making liberal use of electronics) and the results lend themselves to some hilarity. Well worth searching for. —*Scott Yanow*

Shock Treatment / Feb. 14, 1968-Feb. 15, 1968 / Columbia ♦♦♦
Trumpeter Don Ellis' big bands of 1966-77 always performed stimulating music full of riotous humor, innovative ideas and odd time signatures, particularly in its early years. This studio album is decent but not quite up to the level of the preceding *Electric Bath* set. The orchestra (which differed from other big bands at the time by using three bassists, a drummer and three percussionists) is in fine form on such numbers as "The Tihai" (which is influenced by Indian music), "Beat Me Daddy, Seven to the Bar" and the soulful "Homecoming" but in general there are less memorable moments on this album than on Ellis' more essential sessions. —*Scott Yanow*

★ **Autumn** / Aug. 1968 / Columbia ♦♦♦♦♦
Don Ellis' Orchestra is heard at the peak of its powers on this out-of-print Columbia LP. "Pussy Wiggle Stomp," a variation on "My dad's better than your dad" but performed in 7/4 time, became the band's theme song and it has its riotous moments. The nineteen-and-a-half-minute six-part "Variations for Trumpet" is a major showcase for Ellis, "Scratt and Fluggs" is a brief bit of silliness and the relatively straightforward "K.C. Blues" features altoist Frank Strozier, John Klemmer on tenor and keyboardist Pete Robinson. However it is the seventeen-and-a-half-minute "Indian Lady" (a live remake) that really finds the band going crazy. Ellis, trombonist Glen Ferris and keyboardist Robinson play humorous solos before tenors John Klemmer and Sam Falzone engage in a long and nutty trade-off that is often quite hilarious. The many false endings at the end of this performance add to the general atmosphere. This is a classic release; why hasn't Columbia reissued it on CD yet? —*Scott Yanow*

New Don Ellis Band Goes Underground / Jan. 1969 / Columbia ♦♦
Coming as it did between two of Don Ellis' greatest records (*Autumn* and *Don Ellis at Fillmore*), this LP was always a disappointment. The dozen concise perfor-

mances are generally overarranged, the solos are too brief and the melodies (with two exceptions) are not memorable. The ridiculously complex "Bulgarian Bulge" and "Eli's Coming" (which would soon join the repertoire of Maynard Ferguson) are the standouts but the other R&B-oriented material, which often has so-so vocals by Patti Allen, is quite forgettable. One of trumpeter Don Ellis' lesser efforts. —*Scott Yanow*

Don Ellis at Fillmore / 1970 / Columbia ♦♦♦♦♦
This is a crazy and consistently riotous two-LP set that features the Don Ellis Orchestra at its height. The 20-piece orchestra (which finds trumpeter Ellis doubling on drums and also utilizes a regular drummer and two percussionists) often used electronic devices (such as ring modulators) at the time to really distort their sound. When coupled with odd time signatures and such exuberant soloists as Ellis, trombonist Glen Ferris, tenor saxophonist John Klemmer (showcased on the remarkable "Excursion II"), guitarist Jay Graydon, altoists Fred Selden and Lonnie Shetter and tenor Sam Falzone, the results are quite memorable. Highlights of the date include "Final Analysis" (which contains a countless number of false endings), a bizarre rendition of "Hey Jude" and an often-hilarious remake of "Pussy Wiggle Stomp." This set is well worth a search but Columbia should be chided for not yet reissuing it on CD. —*Scott Yanow*

Tears of Joy / May 20, 1971-May 23, 1971 / Columbia ♦♦♦♦
By 1971, the Don Ellis Orchestra had calmed down a bit but was still utilizing unusual time signatures. The trumpeter-leader never stopped experimenting and for this double-LP (not available yet on CD) his band consists of four trumpets, French horn, trombone, bass trombone, tuba, four woodwinds, a string quartet, pianist Milcho Leviev (an important new addition), bass, two drummers and a percussionist. Ellis (who later added an unrecorded vocal quartet) was able to group his big band into a brass octet, a woodwind quartet, a small string section and a rhythm section in addition to using the full ensemble. The potential was enormous (the seventeen-and-a-half-minute "Strawberry Soup" really shows what the band could do) but this particular orchestra did not last that long. Other highlights of the memorable two-fer include "5/4 Getaway" (a cheerful adaptation of "Little Rock Getaway"), a remake of "Bulgarian Bulge" (featuring Milcho Leviev) and "Blues in Elf," the latter a blues for Leviev and the string section, in 11/4. This was Don Ellis' last essential recording. —*Scott Yanow*

Connection / 1972 / Columbia ♦♦♦
Trumpeter-bandleader Don Ellis had success with his film score to the movie *The French Connection* so the popular theme is included on this Columbia LP. There are some worthwhile tracks on the set (including "Put It Where You Want It," "Alone Again (Naturally)" and Hank Levy's "Chain Reaction") but the emphasis on recent pop material (from the likes of Yes, Carole King, Procol Harum and Bill Withers) and the brevity of the performances (only "Chain Reaction" is over five minutes long) keeps this rather commercial effort from being recommended to anyone but Don Ellis completists. —*Scott Yanow*

Haiku / 1973 / MPS ♦♦♦
This album is a very different Don Ellis record. Rather than using a big band, the trumpeter is well showcased while backed by a large string section on ten moody originals. Although the rhythm section includes keyboardist Milcho Leviev and bassist Ray Brown, the focus throughout this set is almost entirely on Ellis, who plays beautifully on his ten picturesque pieces. In some ways this out-of-print LP is an ancestor of new age, for much of the music is quite mellow. A definite change of pace for Don Ellis. —*Scott Yanow*

Soaring / 1974 / MPS ♦♦♦♦
The last album by Don Ellis' big band before the trumpeter suffered a heart attack that would ultimately cut short both his career and his life, this underrated set finds Ellis' orchestra consisting of seven brass (including tuba), four strong woodwind players, a string quartet, and an enlarged six-piece rhythm section that includes guitarist Jay Graydon and keyboardist Milcho Leviev. A special highlight is "Invincible" which is an outstanding feature for altoist Vince Denham; whatever happened to him? Ellis composed four of the eight originals including one titled "The Devil Made Me Write This Piece!" This out-of-print LP is well worth searching for. —*Scott Yanow*

Music from Other Galaxies and Planets / 1977 / Atlantic ♦
This LP is the only complete misfire of Don Ellis' career. The trumpeter-bandleader had the distinction of being the first jazz musician to record the theme from *Star Wars*, but his forgettable version was soon greatly overshadowed by Maynard Ferguson's hit record. In addition to "Star Wars" and "Princess Leia's Theme" (also from the film), Ellis performs eight rather lightweight originals, all of which were given outer space names to try to capitalize on the movie's success. Ellis' big band has little to do other than play mundane ensembles and take occasional short solos. This is the one Don Ellis record that should be skipped. —*Scott Yanow*

Live at Montreux / Jul. 1977 / Atlantic ♦♦♦

Don Ellis' final record as a leader (he passed away from a bad heart in Dec. 1978) is a worthwhile effort. Ellis' large orchestra (four reeds, eight brass, one keyboard, two bassists, two drummers, two percussionists and a string quartet) performs six of the leader's originals and, although none of the songs are all that memorable, there are many fine solos. The main players are trumpeter Ellis, Ted Nash on tenor, alto and clarient and trombonist Alan Kaplan. —*Scott Yanow*

Herb Ellis (Mitchel Herbert Ellis)

b. Aug. 4, 1921, Farmersville, TX
Guitar / Bop, Swing

An excellent bop-based guitarist with a slight country twang to his sound, Herb Ellis became famous playing with the Oscar Peterson Trio during 1953-58. Prior to that he had attended North Texas State Unversity and played with the Casa Loma Orchestra, Jimmy Dorsey (1945-47) and the sadly under-recorded trio Soft Winds. While with Peterson, Ellis was on some Jazz at the Philharmonic tours and had a few opportunities to lead his own dates for Verve, including his personal favorite, *Nothing but the Blues* (1957). After leaving Peterson, Ellis toured a bit with Ella Fitzgerald, became a studio musician on the West Coast, made sessions with the Dukes of Dixieland, Stuff Smith and Charlie Byrd, and in the 1970s became much more active in the jazz world. He is on the first three Concord releases (interacting with Joe Pass on the initial two), and toured with the Great Guitars (along with Byrd and Barney Kessel) through much of the 1970s into the '80s. After a long series of Concord albums, Herb Ellis cut a couple of excellent sessions in the 1990s for Justice. —*Scott Yanow*

☆ **Nothing but the Blues** / Oct. 11, 1957-May 1, 1958 / Verve ♦♦♦♦♦

Guitarist Herb Ellis considers this his favorite personal album and it is easy to see why. With trumpeter Roy Eldridge and tenor saxophonist Stan Getz contributing contrasting but equally rewarding solos and lots of inspired riffing, while bassist Ray Brown and drummer Stan Levey join Ellis in the pianoless rhythm section, these performances have plenty of color and drive. Ellis does indeed stick to the blues during the original eight selections yet there is also a surprising amount of variety. This CD reissue has been augmented by four numbers from 1958 originally recorded for a European soundtrack. Getz, Eldridge and Coleman Hawkins all have their features but Dizzy Gillespie fares best. —*Scott Yanow*

★ **Herb Ellis Meets Jimmy Giuffre** / Mar. 26, 1959 / Verve ♦♦♦♦♦

Unusual team; Giuffre (sax) fits in effectively. —*Ron Wynn*

Softly . . . But with That Feeling / Oct. 12, 1961-Oct. 13, 1961 / Verve ♦♦♦♦

This somewhat obscure Herb Ellis LP (the fifth and final one that the guitarist led for Verve) is a relaxed affair. Joined by vibraphonist Victor Feldman, bassist Leroy Vinnegar and drummer Ronnie Zito, Ellis swings lightly and easily on such songs as "One Note Samba" (which had not become a bossa nova standard yet), "Like Someone in Love," "John Brown's Body" and Ray Brown's "Gravy Waltz." —*Scott Yanow*

Together / Jan. 8, 1963 / Koch ♦♦♦♦♦

This Koch CD reissues an interesting and very successful matchup between guitarist Herb Ellis and the great swing violinist Stuff Smith. Pianist Lou Levy and Bob Enevoldsen (doubling on his cool-toned tenor and valve trombone) contribute some solos and drummer Shelly Manne adds fine support. The reissue (which has three alternate takes in addition to the original six-song program) features plenty of cooking and strong interplay between Stuff and Ellis on some blues, the ancient standard "How Come You Do Me Like You Do" (which has one of the violinist's two personable vocals) and Smith's two originals "Hillcrest" and "Skip It." This is one of Ellis' personal favorite records and one of the best recordings from Stuff Smith's later years. —*Scott Yanow*

Guitar/Guitar / Aug. 30, 1963-Aug. 31, 1963 / Columbia ♦♦♦

Herb Ellis and Charlie Byrd (along with Barney Kessel) would team up as Great Guitars in the mid-'70s. However, a decade before, Ellis and Byrd shared this record date, a quartet outing with bassist Keter Betts and drummer Buddy Deppenschmidt. The 11 selections are all quite concise (only "Things Ain't What They Used to Be" exceeds four minutes) and fall into the easy-listening category; even "Lady Be Good" is taken fairly slow. A few sparks do occur between the distinctive guitar stylists (highlights include "Carolina in the Morning," "Three Quarter Blues" and "So Danco Samba") and this out-of-print LP is worth searching for, but there are more significant Herb Ellis and Charlie Byrd recordings readily available. —*Scott Yanow*

Jazz at Concord / Jul. 29, 1973 / Concord Jazz ♦♦♦♦

The very first release by the Concord label (recorded at the 1973 Concord Jazz Festival and now available on CD) was a quartet set featuring guitarists Herb Ellis and Joe Pass, bassist Ray Brown and drummer Jake Hanna. Ellis and Pass (the latter was just beginning to be discovered) always made for a perfectly complementary

team, constantly challenging each other. The boppish music (which mixes together standards with "originals" based on the blues and a standard) is enjoyable with the more memorable tunes including "Look for the Silver Lining," "Honeysuckle Rose," "Georgia," "Good News Blues" and "Bad News Blues." This was a strong start for what would become the definitive mainstream jazz label. —*Scott Yanow*

Seven, Come Eleven / Jul. 29, 1973 / Concord Jazz ♦♦♦♦

The second Concord album was recorded the day after the first with the same lineup: guitarists Herb Ellis and Joe Pass, bassist Ray Brown and drummer Jake Hanna. Pass would sign with Pablo but Ellis would be a fixture on the Concord label throughout the 1970s. If anything, the guitarists' rematch was a bit stronger than their first due to material better suited for jamming including "In a Mellotone," a speedy "Seven Come Eleven," "Perdido" and "Concord Blues." Although Pass would soon be recognized as a giant, Ellis battles him to a draw on this frequently exciting bop-oriented date, which has been reissued on CD. —*Scott Yanow*

Two for the Road / Jan. 30, 1974-Feb. 20, 1974 / Original Jazz Classics ♦♦♦♦♦

This recording was the third and final matchup between guitarists Herb Ellis and Joe Pass and, unlike the first two (which were both made for Concord), this is a duo date rather than a quartet session. Pass was just beginning to gain recognition for his remarkable unaccompanied solos, but Ellis had not recorded in this sparse a setting before. They complement each other quite well on such tunes as "Love for Sale," "Seven Come Eleven," "Lady Be Good," "I've Found a New Baby" and two versions of "Cherokee." Highly recommended. —*Scott Yanow*

After You've Gone / Aug. 1974 / Concord Jazz ♦♦♦♦

This set from the 1974 Concord Jazz Festival (reissued on CD) is a follow-up to the studio record *Soft Shoe* and uses similar personnel: guitarist Herb Ellis, bassist Ray Brown, drummer Jake Hanna, trumpeter Harry "Sweets" Edison, tenor saxophonist Plas Johnson and, in a rare straightahead outing, pianist George Duke. Each of the musicians has their chance to be featured; Ellis and Brown play a duet version of "Detour Ahead," and Edison is quite lyrical on "Mood Indigo." This is a bright, swinging set that helped to launch the Concord label. —*Scott Yanow*

● **Soft Shoe** / Aug. 1974 / Concord Jazz ♦♦♦♦♦

This early Concord recording (which is available on CD) is unusual in a couple of ways. Guitarist Herb Ellis and bassist Ray Brown (who are the co-leaders) are joined not only by trumpeter Harry "Sweets" Edison (who is in colorful form) and drummer Jake Hanna but pianist George Duke in one of his very few mainstream records. Their repertoire includes jazz versions of such unlikely tunes as "Inka-Dinka-Doo," "Easter Parade" and "The Flintstones Theme"; the latter version (which is based on the familiar "I Got Rhythm" chord changes) was the first of many to turn that cartoon melody into jazz. In addition Brown ("Soft Shoe"), Edison and Ellis contribute a song apiece plus there is a brief rendition of "Green Dolphin Street" that is taken as a Brown-Ellis duet. Recommended. —*Scott Yanow*

Hot Tracks / 1975 / Concord Jazz ♦♦♦♦

Guitarist Herb Ellis was the leader of six of the first dozen Concord releases. This lesser-known set has some fine playing from Ellis, trumpeter Harry "Sweets" Edison, tenor saxophonist Plas Johnson, bassist Ray Brown, drummer Jake Hanna and keyboardist Mike Melvoin, although Melvoin's electric piano sounds a bit dated today. As usual the music is uncomplicated, straightahead, swinging and tasteful. Six of the songs are originals by group members which are performed along with Johnny Hodges' "Squatty Roo" and the ballad "But Beautiful." —*Scott Yanow*

Rhythm Willie / 1975 / Concord Jazz ♦♦♦

Guitarist Herb Ellis is joined by rhythm guitarist Freddie Green, pianist Ross Tompkins, bassist Ray Brown and drummer Jake Hanna for this lightly swinging but uneventful program which has been reissued on CD. Since Green as usual does not solo, his contribution is purely as a background player. Ellis, Tompkins and Brown are the lead voices on a variety of swing tunes; best are "It Had to Be You," "A Smooth One" and "When My Dream Boat Comes Home." —*Scott Yanow*

Pair to Draw / 1976 / Concord Jazz ♦♦

Guitarist Herb Ellis and pianist Ross Tompkins perform nine standards on this duet set with the emphasis on light tasteful swinging and ballads. The melodic results are pleasant but sometimes a touch dull and generally lacking in excitement or any real surprises. None of the songs (which include "Someday My Prince Will Come," "You Stepped Out of a Dream," "A Child Is Born" and "The More I See You") have exactly been underplayed through the years. —*Scott Yanow*

Wildflower / Oct. 1977 / Concord Jazz ♦♦♦♦

This album is most significant for being the first jazz recording in a few decades by guitarist Remo Palmier (who was also known early on as Palmieri). Fellow guitarist Herb Ellis is the leader but he gives his guest just as much solo space as he takes and, with the tasteful accompaniment of bassist George Duvivier and drummer Ron Traxler, the two old friends challenge each other on a variety of appealing chord changes, including "The Night Has a Thousand Eyes," "Close Your Eyes,"

"Walkin'" and Jobim's "Triste." The success of this boppish set led to Palmieri getting his own Concord album the following year. —*Scott Yanow*

Soft & Mellow / Aug. 1978 / Concord Jazz ✦✦✦✦
Despite the title of this record by guitarist Herb Ellis, the songs are not all sleepy ballads. In fact, the opening number played by the quartet (which also includes pianist Ross Tompkins, bassist Monty Budwig and drummer Jake Hanna) is a rapid version of "Shine," and there is also an uptempo rendition of "Rosetta" to close the date. In between, Ellis and his group perform five standards (including a few ballads) plus his original "Jeff's Bad Blues," dedicated to Concord head Carl Jefferson. An excellent all-round set of swinging music. —*Scott Yanow*

Herb Ellis at Montreux / Jul. 1979 / Concord Jazz ✦✦✦
Guitarist Herb Ellis was featured with two different rhythm sections at the 1979 Montreux Jazz Festival for three songs apiece: a quartet with pianist Ross Tompkins, bassist Ray Brown and drummer Jake Hanna and a trio with bassist Michael Moore and drummer Jeff Hamilton. Due to the brief playing time (under 32 minutes) and predictable nature of the straightahead music, this release is not essential but there are some fine versions of six standards, particularly "Love Walked In" and "There Will Never Be Another You." —*Scott Yanow*

Herb Mix / Jun. 1981 / Concord Jazz ✦✦
This Herb Ellis trio session with bassist Bob Maize and drummer Jimmie Smith is a bit sleepy with such offbeat songs as "It's a Small World," "The Girl from Ipanema," "Give My Regards to Broadway" and "The Way We Were" receiving unnecessary revivals. Only the guitarist's blues "Deep" and "The Preacher" have much fire, making this pleasant but rather routine date one of Herb Ellis' less significant efforts. —*Scott Yanow*

Doggin' Around / Mar. 1988 / Concord Jazz ✦✦✦✦
After recording many albums for Concord (including the majority of the label's first releases), Herb Ellis did not lead any sessions for seven years until this duet date with bassist Red Mitchell. Other than three originals (including Mitchell's "Big 'N' and the Bear" which features the bassist's vocal), the repertoire is taken from the swing era. The interplay by the two greats on tunes such as "Sweethearts on Parade," a medium-tempo "Over the Rainbow," "Lady Be Good" and Mitchell's "Life's a Take" plus the classic cover drawing by cartoonist Gary Larson (depicting a jazz club run by and for dogs called "The Stuffed Cat") are good reasons to acquire this high-quality straightahead session. —*Scott Yanow*

☆ Roll Call / 1991 / Justice ✦✦✦✦✦
Herb Ellis' first full set as a leader since leaving the Concord label (where he had been during 1973-88) finds him in inspired form. The veteran guitarist is heard in a trio with the recently rediscovered organist Mel Rhyne and drummer Jake Hanna plus guest violinist Johnny Frigo and Jay Thomas on tenor and fluegelhorn. A fire seemed to have been lit under Ellis for he plays on the well-rounded program with much more passion than he had on most of his later Concord albums. This CD is highlighted by "Just Blue," "Limehouse Blues," "Sugar Hill Stomp," and "Detour Ahead" but all 11 selections are worth hearing. Recommended. —*Scott Yanow*

Down-Home / Sep. 13, 1991 / Justice ✦✦✦✦

Texas Swings / 1992 / Justice ✦✦✦✦
Texas-born guitarist Herb Ellis teams up with a variety of country musicians on this Justice CD for a set of Western swing-oriented jazz. Essentially an instrumental country date with Ellis as one of the lead voices, the enjoyable set also has Willie Nelson's guitar added on some of the tracks along with steel guitar, two violinists and a standard rhythm section. The twangy sound of the steel guitar may not appeal to everyone but the fairly basic music (mostly swing standards) is played with plenty of spirit. This recording gives Ellis a fresh setting after years in trios and quartets. —*Scott Yanow*

Ziggy Elman (Harry Finkelman)

b. May 26, 1914, Philadelphia, PA, **d.** Jun. 26, 1968, Los Angeles, CA
Trumpet / Swing
In a word-association game, the name Ziggy Elman will always be followed by "And the Angels Sing," his one hit. He started out playing trombone with Alex Bartha's band, making his recording debut in 1932. In 1936 he hit the big time by joining Benny Goodman's Orchestra but the hiring of Harry James (who had a similar style) within a year greatly cut Elman's solo opportunities and potential for fame. However he had his moments, as on "Bed Mir Bist Du Schon" in 1937 which had a section similar to "And the Angels Sing." Elman, who was part of BG's famous trumpet section with James and Chris Griffin, had opportunities in 1938-39 to record 20 songs as a leader. One of them, "Fralich in Swing," was soon given a Martha Tilton vocal and recorded as "And the Angels Sing."

In what could be considered a mistake, Ziggy Elman left Goodman in 1940, not to lead his own orchestra but to join Tommy Dorsey. He was well-featured during his long stay (1940-47), but by the time he decided to form his own big band (off

and on during 1947-52), the swing era was over. He became a studio musician and gradually faded out of the jazz world without becoming a star or fulfilling his potential. —*Scott Yanow*

● And the Angels Sing / Dec. 28, 1938-Dec. 26, 1939 / Sunbeam ✦✦✦✦✦
During a 12-month period of time while still a regular member of Benny Goodman's Orchestra, trumpeter Ziggy Elman had an opportunity to lead five recording sessions, resulting in 20 songs. Sixteen of the performances were reissued on this out-of-print Sunbeam LP from 1973; all have since been collected in a Classics CD. Elman, who had a similar style to Harry James (who overshadowed him with Goodman), is mostly accompanied by Goodman's reed and rhythm sections, appearing as the only brass instrument on the swing-oriented selections. The first song, "Fralich in Swing," would a year later (with a Martha Tilton vocal) become Elman's big hit "And the Angels Sing." Other highlights include "Sugar," "Zaggin' with Zig," "Deep Night" and "Tootin' My Baby Back Home"; among the other soloists are pianists Jess Stacy and Johnny Guarnieri. —*Scott Yanow*

1947 / Mar. 6, 1947+Apr. 11, 1947 / Circle ✦✦✦
When Tommy Dorsey temporarily broke up his big band at the end of 1946, his star trumpeter Ziggy Elman decided to take the plunge and start his own orchestra; the only problem was that the big band era was not easy to survive. Elman struggled on and off for five years but his swing band never did catch on. In 1947 his orchestra recorded radio transcriptions and this release (a CD reissue) has all of the titles, around 38 minutes of music. There are only four instrumentals among the 11 full-length numbers with many vocals by the somewhat forgettable Virginia Maxey and Bob Manning. The complete personnel is not given although there are short spots for tenor saxophonist Johnny Hayes and clarinetist Clint Garvin on "Hub-Je-De-Bee." However, other than the leader's trumpet (best heard on "Zaggin' with Zig"), this is a rather routine set of dance music that was already quickly going out of style in 1947. —*Scott Yanow*

Zaggin' with Zig / 1947-1952 / Swing Era ✦✦✦✦
This collectors LP has some of trumpeter Ziggy Elman's best jazz recordings with his short-lived big band of 1947-52. The personnel is not given (other than the band's occasional vocalist Virginia Maxey) but Elman is generally the main star anyway. "Boppin' with Zig" (a successor to "Zaggin' with Zig" and "Samba with Zig") is quite interesting as Elman tries to adapt to a boppish arrangement worthy of Dizzy Gillespie's big band. Otherwise the music (which includes "I Found a New Baby," "Birth of the Blues," "Hup-Je-De-Bee" and "I'll Get By") is solid swing. Worth searching for by big-band fans. —*Scott Yanow*

Bob Enevoldsen (Robert Martine Enevoldsen)

b. Jan. 11, 1920, Billings, MT
Valve Trombone, Tenor Saxophone / Cool
Bob Enevoldsen has long been the perfect utility jazz player. Although best known as a valve trombonist, Enevoldsen is also a talented tenorman and has filled in on string bass too. He had mostly been a music teacher when he moved to Los Angeles in 1951 and became a busy studio musician, appearing on West Coast jazz dates headed by Gerry Mulligan, Shorty Rogers, Shelly Manne and Marty Paich among many others. During 1954-55 he was the bassist in Bobby Troup's trio and during 1962-64 he worked on Steve Allen's television series. He remains active up to the present day, generally playing valve trombone in L.A.-based big bands. Enevoldsen recorded as a leader during 1954-55 for Nocturne, Tampa (reissued on V.S.O.P.) and Liberty. —*Scott Yanow*

● Bob Enevoldsen Quintet / 1955 / V.S.O.P. ✦✦✦✦
This CD reissue brings back an unusual, but consistently swinging, release from the 1950s Tampa label. Bob Enevoldsen, in one of only three albums that he had as a leader, alternates between valve trombone and tenor and is joined by Marty Paich (tripling on piano, organ and accordion), vibraphonist Larry Bunker (who switches to drums on a lengthy "Blues"), bassist Red Mitchell and drummer Don Heath. The music (three basic originals, "Topsy" and "Don't Be That Way") is more conventional than the instrumentation but is a fine outing for all concerned with plenty of swinging solos. —*Scott Yanow*

Bobby Enriquez

b. 1943, Philippines, **d.** Aug. 6, 1996
Piano / Bop, Afro-Cuban Jazz
Bobby Enriquez had the nickname of "The Madman," and it is a title he had earned through his very hyper piano playing. A virtuoso who was largely self-taught from the age of four, Enriquez was a professional by the time he was 14. In the 1960s he played in Manila, Hong Kong and Honolulu, becoming Don Ho's musical director for a time. He arrived on the mainland in the early '70s, toured with Richie Cole during 1980-81 and made his debut on record in 1981. Enriquez cut eight albums for GNP/Crescendo during 1981-85 which made his reputation.

Due to putting an excess of song quotes in his solos (some of them very silly), Enriquez was not known for his exquisite taste, but his technique and ability to think very fast were quite impressive. He also recorded for Portrait (1987) and a 1990 date for the Japanese Paddle Wheel label has been issued domestically on Evidence. —Scott Yanow

Wild Man / 1981 / GNP ✦✦✦✦

Although not as explosive as the title suggests, some strong piano work by Bobby Enriquez in an early '80s quartet session. The material is divided between originals and standards like "Sweet Georgia Brown" and bop anthems like "Confirmation." Drummer Alex Acuna and Pancho Sanchez on congas provide solid Afro-Latin backgrounds and interact smoothly with star fusion bassist Abe Laboriel. —Ron Wynn

Wildman Meets the Madman / 1981 / GNP ✦✦✦

The second recording by pianist Bobby Enriquez is a crazy affair. Enriquez, who had the tendency to throw in an excess of silly song quotes, meets up with the equally crazy Richie Cole, and they bring out the worst in each other. With guitarist Bruce Forman, bassist Bob Magnusson and drummer Shelly Manne keeping the proceedings swinging, Enriquez and Cole generally start out their solos well before getting bogged down in topping each other's absurdity. This set is not without interest, and some of the humor (such as Cole's "vocal" on "Wild Man Blues") works, but much of it is tiresome by the second or third listen. —Scott Yanow

Espana / 1982 / GNP ✦✦✦✦

A tremendous pianist whose lack of restraint was his only musical fault, Bobby Enriquez is in splendid form for this collaboration with Japanese arranger Bingo Miki. Enriquez's piano is in the forefront throughout the six-song "Andalucia Suite" (written by Cuban composer Ernesto Lecuona in 1928), plus four shorter numbers. The orchestral backing clearly inspired Enriquez, making this a recommended set. —Scott Yanow

Live! in Tokyo / Aug. 7, 1982 / GNP ✦✦✦✦✦

The first of two sets taken from Bobby Enriquez's Japanese tour of 1982 features the powerful pianist in a trio with bassist Isoo Fukui and drummer Shinji Mori. Enriquez often seems unable to control himself musically, really ripping into the nine selections. He takes "Airegin" and "Donna Lee" at ridiculously fast tempos, doubletimes "Misty," jams Jobim's "Meditation" as a bop tune, and rips into "Holiday for Strings." Spectacular playing, not for the faint-hearted. —Scott Yanow

Live in Tokyo, Vol. 2 / Aug. 6, 1982-Aug. 7, 1982 / GNP ✦✦✦

The second of two albums taken from a 1982 Japanese tour features pianist Bobby Enriquez (who is joined by bassist Isoo Fukui and drummer Shinji Mori) attacking seven jazz standards and even Barry Manilow's "Could It Be Magic." Enriquez always played with passion and aggression, and his high-powered versions of "Jeannine," "Confirmation" and "Scrapple from the Apple" are among this exciting set's highlights. —Scott Yanow

The Prodigious Piano / 1983 / GNP ✦✦✦

Bobby Enriquez was a technically gifted pianist who could play very explosive versions of standards. On this excellent set with bassist Abraham Laboriel, drummer Alex Acuna and percussionist Poncho Sanchez, Enriquez brings a lot of personality and witty ideas to such tunes as "This Masquerade," "Billie's Bounce," "Senor Blues" and "Cherokee." An excellent example of Enriquez's talents. —Scott Yanow

Live at Concerts by the Sea, Vol. 2 / 1985 / GNP Crescendo ✦✦✦✦

With alert backing by bassist John Pena and drummer Alex Acuna, pianist Bobby Enriquez is typically hyper and passionate during six extended live performances. Particularly colorful are his treatments of Chick Corea's "Spain," "Boplicity" and a ten-and-a-half-minute medley of "A Night In Tunisia" and "Tonga." All of Enriquez's recordings (most of which were made during 1981-85 for GNP/Crescendo) are exciting, if bordering on out of control. —Scott Yanow

● **Wild Piano** / Dec. 22, 1987 / Portrait ✦✦✦✦✦

Bobby "The Wild Man" Enriquez's lone effort for the Portrait label continues in the same exciting vein as his GNP/Crescendo sets. With bassist Eddie Gomez and drummer Al Foster successfully holding on, the exuberant pianist turns eight jazz standards inside out, and takes "Classical Gas" as an unaccompanied solo. Highlights of the typically high-powered Enriquez date include "All Blues," "Bye Bye Blackbird," Thelonious Monk's "Four In One" and "Cherokee." —Scott Yanow

The Wildman Returns / Apr. 19, 1990 / Evidence ✦✦✦✦✦

Despite his nickname and the disc's title, pianist Bobby Enriquez starts things off laid-back and mellow on the opening numbers. He smartly intersperses parts of the James Bond theme with the *Pink Panther* theme and is smooth and beguiling on "Our Love Is Here to Stay." But he kicks it into gear on "Groovin' High," and for the remainder of the date justifies his reputation with some furious phrases, spinning licks, percussive right-hand lines, booming two-handed riffs, and plenty of bluesy block chords. —Ron Wynn

Rolf Ericson

b. Aug. 29, 1922, Stockholm, Sweden, d. Jun. 16, 1997, Stockholm, Sweden
Trumpet, Fluegelhorn / Bop, Swing

One of Sweden's finest trumpeters, Rolf Ericson played in the US often enough to gain a strong reputation. He started on trumpet when he was eight and, after hearing Louis Armstrong play in Stockholm in 1933, he switched to jazz. Ericson recorded in Sweden with Alice Babs and others starting in 1945, moved to New York in 1947 and played with Charlie Barnet (1949) and Woody Herman (1950). After returning to Sweden in 1950, he recorded as a leader and with Arne Domnérus and Leonard Feather's Swinging Swedes. He also toured and recorded with Charlie Parker. Back in the US during 1953-56, Ericson played with the big bands of Charlie Spivak, Harry James, the Dorsey Brothers and Les Brown and was with the Lighthouse All-Stars. In 1956 he toured Sweden and played with Ernestine Anderson and Lars Gullin. During 1956-65 in the US, Ericson was with Dexter Gordon, Harold Land, Stan Kenton, Woody Herman, Maynard Ferguson (1960-61), Buddy Rich, Benny Goodman, Gerry Mulligan, and Charles Mingus among others. There were also occasional tours with Duke Ellington during 1963-71 and plenty of freelance jobs. In 1971 he settled in Germany as a studio musician but Ericson returned to the US several times over the next couple of decades. His warm tone and creative yet melodic style were always considered an asset. —Scott Yanow

Rolf Ericson and His American All Stars / Jun. 21, 1956+Jul. 30, 1956 / Dragon ✦✦✦✦

In 1956 Swedish trumpeter Rolf Ericson headed an American group for a tour of his native land. Unfortunately the group (also consisting of baritonist Cecil Payne, pianist Duke Jordan, bassist John Simmons and drummer Art Taylor) included several drug addicts and, after two of the musicians got in trouble, all four Americans were sent home. Their only recording session (which resulted in four songs including a vocal for the young Ernestine Anderson) opens up this Dragon CD. To fill out the remainder of the tour, Ericson was able to quickly get baritonist Lars Gullin, pianist Freddie Redd, bassist Tommy Potter and drummer Joe Harris along with Anderson. The only existing live broadcast of the band takes up the majority of this first-time release. Anderson is featured on five straight songs in a mini-set, and among the instrumentals "Dig," Lady Be Good" and "Night in Tunisia" are the hotter cuts; there are also brief features for bassist Potter and baritonist Gullin. The recording quality is decent if not up to the level of the studio date and overall this is a worthwhile if not quite essential set. —Scott Yanow

● **Stockhom Sweetnin'** / Aug. 21, 1984-Aug. 22, 1984 / Dragon ✦✦✦✦✦

Trumpeter Rolf Ericson was 62 when he made this recording (only his second as a leader in 13 years and third in 28 years) but he was still in his prime. Teamed up with drummer Mel Lewis and three fellow Swedes (tenor saxophonist Nils Sandstrom, pianist Goran Lindberg and bassist Sture Nordin), Ericson's cool bop style is well featured on five standards, Nordin's "Mel's Bells" (based on "If I Were a Bell"), Thad Jones' catchy "Bird Song" and Ericson's jazz waltz "Evelyn." A fairly definitive sampling of Ericson in his later years with plenty of fine straightahead swinging. —Scott Yanow

Peter Erskine

b. Jun. 5, 1954, Somers Point, NJ
Drums / Fusion, Post-Bop

A very versatile drummer, Peter Erskine has excelled in several types of jazz settings. He was with Stan Kenton's Orchestra (1972-75) and Maynard Ferguson's big band (1976-78) before gaining fame with Weather Report (1978-82) where he made a perfect team with Jaco Pastorius. Since that time he has been a member of Steps Ahead (which he had originally joined when they were Steps in 1979), John Abercrombie's band, Bass Desires, and groups headed by Kenny Wheeler in addition to leading his own units. Peter Erskine has led sessions for Contemporary (1982), Denon, Ah-Um, Novus and most recently ECM. —Scott Yanow

● **Peter Erskine** / Jun. 22, 1982+Jun. 23, 1982 / Original Jazz Classics ✦✦✦✦✦

Drummer Peter Erskine's debut as a leader (originally made for Contemporary and reissued on CD in the OJC series) finds him using top players (most of whom had played with Steps Ahead) in various combinations. Erskine performs a few of his own originals (including an 11-minute "All's Well That Ends") and a short drum solo) plus "My Ship," Wayne Shorter's "E.S.P." and Bob Mintzer's "Change of Mind." With such musicians as trumpeter Randy Brecker, tenors Michael Brecker and Mintzer, pianist Kenny Kirkland and vibraphonist Mike Mainieri getting some solo space, this post bop music (from an often-overlooked set) is of consistent high quality. —Scott Yanow

Transition / Oct. 16, 1986-Oct. 17, 1986 / Denon ✦✦

The music on Peter Erskine's second recording as a leader (all but two songs are by either the drummer-leader or Vince Mendoza) is disappointingly forgettable, including Erskine's five-part 22-minute "Suite: Music from Shakespeare's 'King

Richard II." With such fine players as Joe Lovano and Bob Mintzer on tenors, guitarist John Abercrombie, keyboardists Kenny Werner and Don Grolnick, bassist Marc Johnson and Peter Gordon on French horn, the solos are generally quite good but the lack of any memorable melodies and the dated-sounded synthesizers largely sink the effort. —*Scott Yanow*

Big Theatre / 1986-1989 / Ah Um ✦✦✦

Motion Poet / Apr. 25, 1988-May 1, 1988 / Denon ✦✦
An excellent percussionist makes an uneven, but ambitious statement. —*Ron Wynn*

Aurora / Nov. 14, 1988-Nov. 15, 1988 / Denon ✦✦✦✦✦

Sweet Soul / Mar. 4, 1991-Mar. 5, 1991 / Novus ✦✦✦✦
Six of the 11 selections on this CD (most of which were written by drummer Peter Erskine, Vince Mendoza or Kenny Werner) feature Joe Lovano on tenor (and in one instance soprano) in a quartet with pianist Werner, bassist Marc Johnson and Erskine; Lovano (who would soon hit it big) already sounds mature and creative. Three of the other numbers have slightly larger groups (with guitarist John Scofield, tenor saxophonist Bob Mintzer and trumpeter Randy Brecker appearing on some of the cuts), Dave Brubeck's "In Your Own Sweet Way" is taken by the Werner-Johnson-Erskine trio and the brief "But Is It Art?" is a drum solo. Throughout the date, the solos uplift the material and make this CD a worthy purchase for listeners who enjoy challenging but sometimes accessible postbop music. —*Scott Yanow*

You Never Know / Jul. 1992 / ECM ✦✦✦

Time Being / Nov. 1993 / ECM ✦✦✦
Although it is easy to stereotype Peter Erskine as a fusion drummer due to his notable work with Weather Report, in reality he is a very flexible percussionist. On his trio session for ECM, Erskine is mostly content to back his sidemen (pianist John Taylor and bassist Palle Danielsson). This CD is actually most interesting for the playing of Taylor who contributes three of the originals and plays in a style not that far from Keith Jarrett. In general the music starts out fairly quiet but builds its intensity and holds one's interest. —*Scott Yanow*

From Kenton to Now / Apr. 30, 1995 / Fuzzy Music ✦✦✦✦
Drummer Peter Erskine mostly plays in support during this high-quality bop-oriented quartet date. The lead voice, tenor saxophonist Richard Torres (who had been with Stan Kenton during the period Erskine was there), displays an original tone sometimes slightly reminiscent of Ernie Watts, a swinging style, and the ability to improvise logical yet unpredictable solos. With strong assistance provided by pianist Alan Pasqua and bassist Dave Carpenter (both of whom make excellent use of their solo space), along with the drummer, Torres explores six of his basic originals, plus the ancient standard "Sweetheart of All My Dreams," Erskine's "Modern Drummer Blues" and (from the Kenton book) a wistful version of "Artistry in Rhythm" and a straightahead "Intermission Riff." Easy music to enjoy, this CD will make one want to see the underrated Richard Torres play in person. —*Scott Yanow*

History of the Drum / 1995 / Interworld ✦✦✦

As It Is / Sep. 1995 / ECM ✦✦✦
Although led by a drummer, this trio session mostly showcases English pianist John Taylor who is heavily influenced by Keith Jarrett. His interplay with bassist Palle Danielsson and drummer Peter Erskine on the group originals is impressive, leaving plenty of space and developing quite slowly, but also holding on to one's attention. —*Scott Yanow*

Booker Ervin

b. Oct. 31, 1930, Denson, TX, d. Jul. 31, 1970, New York, NY
Tenor Saxophone / Hard Bop, Post-Bop, Avant-Garde
A very distinctive tenor with a hard passionate tone and an emotional style that was still tied to chordal improvisation, Booker Ervin was a true original. He was originally a trombonist but taught himself tenor while in the Air Force (1950-53). After studying music in Boston for two years, he made his recording debut with Ernie Fields' R&B band (1956). Ervin gained fame while playing with Charles Mingus (off and on during 1956-62), holding his own with the volatile bassist and Eric Dolphy. He also led his own quartet, worked with Randy Weston on a few occasions in the '60s and spent much of 1964-66 in Europe before dying much too young from kidney disease. Ervin, who is on several notable Charles Mingus records, made dates of his own for Bethlehem, Savoy and Candid during 1960-61, along with later sets for Pacific Jazz and Blue Note, but it his nine Prestige sessions of 1963-66 (including *The Freedom Book*, *The Song Book*, *The Blues Book* and *The Space Book*) that are among the high points of his career. —*Scott Yanow*

The Book Cooks / Jun. 1960 / Bethlehem ✦✦✦✦
Booker Ervin's debut as a leader teamed the intense tenor saxophonist with fellow tenor Zoot Sims (one will have little difficulty telling the cool-toned Zoot apart

from Booker), trumpeter Tommy Turrentine, pianist Tommy Flanagan, bassist George Tucker and drummer Dannie Richmond. Ervin (who has his ballad "Largo" as a feature) performs five originals and "Poor Butterfly"; best are the slow blues "The Blue Book" and the rapid blues "The Book Cooks." The music on this LP has not yet been reissued domestically on CD. —*Scott Yanow*

Down in the Dumps / Nov. 26, 1960+Jan. 5, 1961 / Savoy ✦✦✦
This LP from 1978 reissues tenor saxophonist Booker Ervin's second session as a leader (with a quintet also including trumpeter Richard Williams, pianist Horace Parlan, bassist George Tucker and drummer Dannie Richmond) plus two songs ("When You're Smilin'" and "The Trolley Song") from an obscure set by singer Barbara Long that contain Ervin solos. The main session has four Ervin originals plus two standards. The intense tenor, whose sound had roots in early R&B but was open to the influence of the avant-garde, was instantly recognizable by 1960 and this music, although not essential (it has not yet been reissued in complete form on CD domestically), has strong solos by Ervin, Williams and Parlan. —*Scott Yanow*

That's It / Jan. 6, 1961 / Candid ✦✦✦✦✦
Booker Ervin, who always had a very unique sound on the tenor, is heard in prime form on his quartet set with pianist Horace Parlan, bassist George Tucker and drummer Al Harewood. In virtually all cases, the jazz and blues musicians who recorded for Candid in 1960-61 (during its original brief existence) were inspired and played more creatively than they did for other labels. That fact is true for Ervin, even if he never made an indifferent record. In addition to "Poinciana" and "Speak Low," Ervin's quartet (which was a regular if short-lived group) performs four of the leader's originals; best known is "Booker's Blues." —*Scott Yanow*

Back from the Gig / Feb. 15, 1963+Jun. 24, 1968 / Blue Note ✦✦✦✦✦
This two-LP set consists of a pair of classic Blue Note sets that were not originally released until 1976. The great tenor Booker Ervin (whose hard passionate sound was always immediately recognizable) is well-showcased with the Horace Parlan Sextet in 1963 (a group also featuring pianist Parlan, trumpeter Johnny Coles and guitarist Grant Green) and with his own all-star quintet from 1968 (which also stars trumpeter Woody Shaw and pianist Kenny Barron). The stimulating group originals and advanced solos (which fall somewhere between hard bop and the avant-garde) still sound fresh and frequently exciting. —*Scott Yanow*

Exultation! / Jun. 19, 1963 / Original Jazz Classics ✦✦✦✦
Booker Ervin's debut for Prestige (which has been reissued on CD with two shorter alternate takes added) matches the intense tenor with altoist Frank Strozier, pianist Horace Parlan, bassist Butch Warren and drummer Walter Perkins for some bop-based music that is actually quite adventurous. Highlights include "Mour" (based on "Four"), "Black and Blue" and Ervin's "Mooche Mooche." Ervin and Strozier made a mutually inspiring team; pity that this was their only recording together. —*Scott Yanow*

The Freedom Book / Dec. 3, 1963 / Original Jazz Classics ✦✦✦✦✦
One of the finest groups that tenor saxophonist Booker Ervin ever led was the quartet that recorded *The Freedom Book* and ten months later *The Space Book*. The trio of pianist Jaki Byard, bassist Richard Davis and drummer Alan Dawson really could not be improved upon but unfortunately this band only existed in the recording studios on an irregular basis. For this CD reissue, Ervin performs four of his obscure but worthy originals plus Randy Weston's "Cry Me Not." Although the music is not as "free" as the title might hint, the music does take advantage of the recent innovations and is a couple steps beyond hard bop. These stimulating performances, as with the other entries in the *Book* series that were to come (*The Song Book*, *The Blues Book* and *The Space Book*), are heartily recommended. —*Scott Yanow*

Groovin' High / Dec. 3, 1963-Oct. 2, 1964 / Original Jazz Classics ✦✦✦✦✦
This CD reissue features four selections from the same sessions (but not released on the original sets) that resulted in *The Freedom Book*, *The Blues Book* and *The Space Book*. "Groovin' High" features the intense tenor of Booker Ervin playing comparatively lighthearted bebop in a quintet with trumpeter Carmell Jones, pianist Gildo Mahones, bassist Richard Davis and drummer Alan Dawson. The other numbers ("The Second No. 2," "Bass-IX" and a brief "Stella by Starlight") match Ervin with the trio of pianist Jaki Byard, Davis and Dawson. Although these performances are not quite classic, Booker Ervin fans will want this CD to round out their collection, for Ervin was at the peak of his powers during this era. —*Scott Yanow*

The Song Book / Feb. 27, 1964 / Original Jazz Classics ✦✦✦✦
The second in tenor saxophonist Booker Ervin's *Book* series, this CD reissue may seem a bit more conservative than the others due to the inclusion of six standards (including "Come Sunday," "All the Things You Are" and "Just Friends"), but Ervin and his quartet (with pianist Tommy Flanagan, bassist Richard Davis and drummer Alan Dawson) come up with fresh interpretations of the warhorses. Booker Ervin never sounded like anyone else. —*Scott Yanow*

● **The Blues Book** / Jun. 30, 1964 / Original Jazz Classics ✦✦✦✦
For this CD reissue in his series of *Books*, Ervin and his quintet (with trumpeter Carmell Jones, pianist Gildo Mahones, bassist Richard Davis and drummer Alan Dawson) perform four very different blues: the speedy "One for Mort," a lowdown "No Booze Blooze," the modal "True Blue" and the minor-toned "Eerie Dearie." The consistently passionate Ervin makes each of the fairly basic originals sound fresh and the performances are frequently exciting inside/outside music. —*Scott Yanow*

The Space Book / Oct. 2, 1964 / Original Jazz Classics ✦✦✦✦✦
Tenor saxophonist Booker Ervin's quartet with pianist Jaki Byard, bassist Richard Davis and drummer Alan Dawson was so strong and dynamic that it is surprising that it only existed in the recording studio, and only for two sessions. For the fourth and final of Ervin's series of *Books*, the music is indeed somewhat spacey. The group explores two standards ("I Can't Get Started" and "There Is No Greater Love") along with a pair of Ervin originals (the intense "Number Two" and "Mojo"), stretching the boundaries of hard bop without totally abandoning the chord changes. This CD is a straight reissue of the original LP and a fine example of Booker Ervin's unique style. —*Scott Yanow*

Settin' the Pace / Oct. 27, 1965 / Prestige ✦✦✦✦
This CD reissue has the complete contents of two former LPs, both recorded at the same session. With very stimulating playing by pianist Jaki Byard, bassist Reggie Workman and drummer Alan Dawson, tenors Booker Ervin and Dexter Gordon battle it out on marathon (nineteen- and twenty-two-and-a-half-minute) versions of "Setting the Pace" and "Dexter's Deck." Although Gordon is in good form, Ervin (who sometimes takes the music outside) wins honors. The other two selections ("The Trance" and "Speak Low") are by the same group without Dexter, and these long (nineteen-and-a-half- and fifteen-minute) showcases also find Booker in top form, sounding quite distinctive and completely original playing inside/outside music. An exciting set. —*Scott Yanow*

The Trance / Oct. 27, 1965 / Original Jazz Classics ✦✦✦
The immediately recognizable tenor saxophonist Booker Ervin recorded a string of very rewarding albums for Prestige in the 1960s. This worthy effort (reissued on CD in 1997) matches Ervin with pianist Jaki Byard, bassist Reggie Workman and drummer Alan Dawson on his blues "Grovin' at the Jamboree" and long versions of Ervin's "The Trance" (19 minute s) and the standard "Speak Low." The tunes themselves are less memorable than the tenor's long, passionate flights, which manage to be both adventurous and full of soul. —*Scott Yanow*

Lament for Booker Ervin / Oct. 29, 1965 / Enja ✦✦✦✦
At an overbooked all-star saxophone concert held in 1965 Berlin, the musicians were supposed to only play for 15 minutes. Tenor saxophonist Booker Ervin protested against the restrictive situation by performing the intense and stirring "Blues for You" for 27 minutes, tearing down the house. A decade later (after Ervin's 1970 death) the performance (with pianist Kenny Drew, bassist Neils Pedersen and drummer Alan Dawson) was released for the first time and its passion was worth waiting for. Also on this historic album is pianist Horace Parlan's somber solo tribute to Ervin ("Lament for Booker"), recorded in 1975. —*Scott Yanow*

Heavy! / Sep. 9, 1966 / Prestige ✦✦✦✦
For a change of pace, on this somewhat obscure LP (which has not yet been reissued on CD) the immediately recognizable tenor saxophonist Booker Ervin heads a sextet (rather than his usual quartet) that also includes trumpeter Jimmy Owens, trombonist Garnett Brown and the great rhythm section of pianist Jaki Byard, bassist Richard Davis and drummer Alan Dawson. Brown and Byard contributed originals and Ervin is showcased on a quartet rendition of "You Don't Know What Love Is," but the most memorable performance is a rapid, intense and hard-swinging version of "Bei Mir Bist Du Schon." —*Scott Yanow*

Structurally Sound / Dec. 1966 / Pacific Jazz ✦✦✦✦
Tenor saxophonist Booker Ervin and the young trumpeter Charles Tolliver make for a logical combination on this quintet set with pianist John Hicks, bassist Red Mitchell and drummer Lennie McBrowne. Both Tolliver and Ervin are grounded in the tradition but had their own sounds and styles that looked towards the future. Ironically, five of the eight selections that they perform on the out-of-print LP are standards (although they modernize and come up with fresh interpretations of the tunes); in addition the quintet plays Randy Weston's "Berkshire Blues" and an original apiece by the two horns. Ervin (who is showcased on "Dancing in the Dark") is in typically intense form throughout the rewarding if somewhat forgotten set. —*Scott Yanow*

Booker 'n' Brass / 1967 / Pacific Jam ✦✦✦
Stirring Ervin tenor in a big-band setting. —*Ron Wynn*

The In Between / Jan. 12, 1968 / Blue Note ✦✦✦✦
Booker Ervin headed to Blue Note in 1968 for *The In Between*, a record that found him continuing in the vein of his later Prestige sessions. Supported by trumpeter Richard Williams, pianist Bobby Few, bassist Cevera Jeffries and drummer Lennie

McBrowne, Ervin created an album that pushed the boundaries of hard bop. Every song on *The In Between* is an Ervin original designed to challenge the musicians. The music rarely reaches avant-garde territory—instead, it's edgy, volatile hard bop that comes from the mind as much as the soul. Appropriately, Ervin balances his full-bodied tone with a forceful, aggressive attack that even sounds restless on the slower numbers. The result is a satisfying, cerebral set of adventurous hard bop that finds Booker Ervin at a creative peak. —*Stephen Thomas Erlewine*

Pee Wee Erwin (Geroge Erwin)

b. May 30, 1913, Falls City, NE, **d.** Jun. 20, 1981, Teaneck, NJ
Trumpet / Dixieland, Swing
An excellent trumpeter who spent most of his career on the fringe of fame, Pee Wee Erwin made many fine records during his career. He began playing trumpet when he was four. Stints with territory bands were followed by gigs with Joe Haymes (1931-33) and Isham Jones (1933-34). Erwin then moved to New York and became a busy studio musician, working often on radio including with Benny Goodman during 1934-35. After playing with Ray Noble in 1935 he succeeded Bunny Berigan in both the Benny Goodman (1936) and Tommy Dorsey (1937-39) orchestras. Erwin put together an unsuccessful big band in 1941-42 and tried again with little luck in 1946. He worked steadily playing Dixieland at Nick's during the 1950s, ran a trumpet school with Chris Griffin in the 1960s (Warren Vache was one of his students) and played steadily until the end of his life. Pee Wee Erwin led sessions on an occasional basis in the 1950s (including a couple for United Artists) and made six albums during 1980-81 including three for Qualtro and one for Jazzology, still sounding good that late in his career. —*Scott Yanow*

And His Dixieland Band / 1951-May 15, 1965 / Broadway Intermission ✦✦✦✦
Trumpeter Pee Wee Erwin, an excellent Dixieland-based player who never really became all that famous, led the regular house band at Nick's for most of the 1950s. The first half of this collector's album features Erwin in a sextet live from Nick's that also includes trombonist Andy Russo, clarinetist Phil Alivella, pianist Billy Maxted, bassist Jack Fay and drummer Cliff Leeman. The latter section of the album is from a 1965 concert with trombonist Lou McGarity, Bob Wilber (on clarinet and soprano), pianist Dave McKenna, bassist Roland Evans and drummer Sonny Igoe. The music on both sets is fairly similar, spirited Dixieland with some fine solos by the key players. Highlights include "Darktown Strutters Ball," "Panama" and "Indiana." —*Scott Yanow*

Oh, Play That Thing! / Oct. 1958 / United Artists ✦✦✦✦

● **Pee Wee in New York** / Jan. 21, 1980 / Qualtro ✦✦✦✦

Swingin' That Music / Mar. 24, 1980 / Jazzology ✦✦✦✦
Pee Wee Erwin only led recording sessions throughout his career on a very irregular basis. Although recorded just a year before his death, this album (which has Dixieland-oriented versions of ten standards) finds the 66-year old trumpeter still in prime form. Trombonist Harry Hagan and clarinetist Herman Foretich complete the front line, while the rhythm section comprises pianist Freddie DeLand, bassist Ike Isaacs and the up and coming drummer Hal Smith. Among the songs receiving favorable and spirited treatment are "Swing That Music," "Rosetta," "I Want to Be Happy" and "Oh Baby." Recommended to Dixieland collectors. —*Scott Yanow*

Pee Wee in Hollywood / May 26, 1980-May 27, 1980 / Qualtro ✦✦✦

Pee Wee Erwin Memorial / May 28, 1981-May 29, 1981 / Jazz Crooner ✦✦✦

Bruce Eskovitz

b. California
Tenor Saxophone / Hard Bop
After a couple of crossover records, Bruce Eskovitz really stretched out on his Koch Jazz release (*One for Newk*) as he paid tribute to Sonny Rollins. One selection ("Tenor Madness") features him holding his own with the great Ernie Watts. Eskovitz started playing tenor when he was 11 and at age 20 was composing music for the Merv Griffin television show. He has mostly worked as a studio musician and a jazz educator but appears regularly in Los Angeles area clubs. —*Scott Yanow*

Bruce Eskovitz / May 6, 1992 / Cexton ✦✦✦

● **One for Newk** / Nov. 18, 1993-Nov. 19, 1993 / Koch ✦✦✦✦✦
This is a record that all lovers of bebop have to get. Tenor saxophonist Bruce Eskovitz has a fat tone and a hard-driving style that is most reminiscent of Don Menza and Lew Tabackin, making him a perfect person to record a tribute to Sonny Rollins. If he sounded exactly like Newk this set would not be all that effective since there is no reason to hear an imitation when the original is also quite prominent on records. But by paying homage to Rollins without directly copying him, Eskovitz has put together a very enjoyable set. With the exception of "Poor Butterfly" and "Count Your Blessings," all ten numbers are Rollins compositions. Eskovitz is greatly assisted by pianist Bill Mays, vibraphonist Charlie Shoemake, bassist Ray

Drummond and drummer Larance Marable on such numbers as "No Moe," "Aire-gin," "Valse Hot," "Strode Rode" and "Pent-Up House." As intense as some of the jam session-style performances are, it is the final number that is the most passion-ate, for "Tenor Madness" is a ten-minute blowout with guest Ernie Watts challeng-ing (but not overwhelming) Eskovitz. Highly recommended. — *Scott Yanow*

Ruth Etting

b. Nov. 23, 1897, David City, NE, **d.** Sep. 24, 1978
Vocals / Pop, Classic Jazz
One of the most popular singers of the late-'20s/early-'30s period, Ruth Etting was not really a jazz singer (unlike her contemporary Annette Hanshaw) but a supe-rior middle-of-the-road pop singer who was often accompanied by top jazz musi-cians. She recorded over 200 songs between 1926-37, appeared on stage, was in 35 film shorts and three full-length movies and was a fixture on radio before her bad marriage cut short her career. She made a minor comeback in the late '40s and was still singing on an occasional basis in the mid-'50s when a semifictional Holly-wood movie on her life (*Love Me or Leave Me*) was released. A superb torch singer with a cry in her voice even when she smiled, Etting recorded the definitive ver-sions of "Ten Cents a Dance" and "Love Me or Leave Me." — *Scott Yanow*

★ **Ten Cents a Dance** / Apr. 14, 1926-Sep. 29, 1930 / Living Era ✦✦✦✦✦
This English import has 20 recordings featuring the early jazz-influenced pop singer Ruth Etting. Although the music is not programmed in chronological order (and there is no personnel listing given), many of Etting's greatest performances are here: the emotional "Ten Cents a Dance," "Button Up Your Overcoat," "Mean to Me," "Sam, the Old Accordion Man," "You're the Cream in My Coffee" and "Love Me or Leave Me." This CD gives one a definitive look into Ruth Etting's talents dur-ing her prime period and is easily recommended as a fine example of superior pop singing of the 1920s. — *Scott Yanow*

Queen of the Torch Singers / Feb. 1, 1927-1947 / Broadway Intermission ✦✦✦✦
This LP from the collector's label Broadway Intermission has a variety of odds and ends featuring the superior 1920s pop singer Ruth Etting. She is heard on eight of her lesser-known studio recordings of 1927-33 (including "Don't Tell Her What Happened to Me," "My Man" and "All of Me"), five songs taken from soundtracks of her film shorts dating from the early '30s, six tunes from appearances on radio shows in London in 1936 and a 1947 broadcast version of "Shine on Harvest Moon" performed during her short-lived comeback. Although not essential, this hard-to-find LP should greatly interest Ruth Etting's fans since most of the perfor-mances have not yet been reissued on CD. — *Scott Yanow*

Goodnight My Love / 1930-1937 / Take Two ✦✦✦

Kevin Eubanks

b. Nov. 15, 1957, Philadelphia, PA
Guitar / Post-Bop
During the past couple of years Kevin Eubanks has been seen by millions of view-ers nightly due to being the leader of Jay Leno's Tonight Show Band where his main purpose is to assist the comedian/host rather than play creative jazz. Eubanks comes from a musical family that included Ray and Tommy Bryant as uncles and older brother/trombonist Robin Eubanks. After studying at Berklee, Eubanks was with the Art Blakey big band (1980-81), had stints with Roy Haynes, Slide Hampton and Sam Rivers and then in 1983 started leading his own groups. After debuting on Elektra, starting in 1985 Eubanks began recording regularly for GRP. Some of the sets were a bit commercial while others were fairly explorative. Switching to Blue Note in the 1990s, Eubanks has been emphasizing acoustic gui-tar in more recent years. — *Scott Yanow*

Guitarist / May 1982-Aug. 1982 / Elektra ✦✦✦
Acoustic guitar solos and group works, with Ralph Moore (ts), Roy Haynes (d), Charles David (p), and Robin Eubanks (tb). This is a fine debut album. — *Michael G. Nastos*

Sundance / Dec. 1984 / GRP ✦✦✦
Simplistic and dreamy. — *Ron Wynn*

The Best of Kevin Eubanks / 1984-1989 / GRP ✦✦✦
The Best of Kevin Eubanks contains ten highlights from the seven albums he recorded for GRP Records. It's a good portrait of Eubanks' friendly, mainstream hard bop, featuring performances with Branford Marsalis, Ron Carter, Dave Grusin and Marcus Miller, among many others. — *Stephen Thomas Erlewine*

Opening Night / 1985 / GRP ✦✦✦✦
By far his best. Accept no substitute. — *Michael G. Nastos*

Face to Face / 1986 / GRP ✦✦✦

The Heat of Heat / 1987 / GRP ✦✦

Shadow Prophets / Jan. 1988 / GRP ✦✦✦

The Searcher / Nov. 1988 / GRP ✦✦✦

Promise of Tomorrow / Nov. 13, 1989-Nov. 19, 1989 / GRP ✦✦✦
Good, has real jazz content. — *Ron Wynn*

● **Turning Point** / Dec. 16, 1991-Jan. 9, 1992 / Blue Note ✦✦✦✦✦
Turning Point is a highly appropriate title for this album. After recording his share of commercial fluff for GRP, Kevin Eubanks switched to Blue Note with this heart-felt CD and strived for excellence instead of going out of his way to avoid it. Cre-ativity, improvisation and spontaneity are main ingredients of the album, which unites the talented electric and acoustic guitarist with bass explorer Dave Holland and drummer Marvin "Smitty" Smith, among others. Like so much intellectual jazz, *Turning Point* requires several listenings in order to be fully appreciated. — *Alex Henderson*

Spiritalk / Apr. 19, 1993-Apr. 23, 1993 / Blue Note ✦✦✦✦
Kevin Eubanks plays acoustic guitar on this Blue Note release as much as he does electric. His nine originals set moods and/or grooves much more than they state memorable melodies, but they do provide a stimulating framework for solos from Eubanks, his brother trombonist Robin Eubanks and Kent Jordan on alto flute; the quintet is completed by bassist Dave Holland and either Marvin "Smitty" Smith or Mark Mondesir on drums. Some songs are mildly funky, others are melancholy ballads or straightahead, but no matter what the rhythm, none of the music is pre-dictable. This CD, which has the feel of a logical suite, is well worth checking out. — *Scott Yanow*

Live at Bradley's / May 21, 1994 / Blue Note ✦✦✦✦

Spiritalk 2 / Jun. 25, 1994-Jun. 28, 1994 / Blue Note ✦✦✦
The most notable aspect to this CD from Kevin Eubanks is the instrumental blend between his acoustic guitar, trombonist Robin Eubanks and the alto flute of Kent Jordan; bassist Dave Holland and either Marvin "Smitty" Smith or Gene Jackson on drums completes the quintet. Eubanks' originals are moody and thoughtful (even in the more heated moments), but do little more than set introspective moods; none of the themes are particularly memorable. The playing is of a consis-tent high quality on this set but the music is much easier to respect than to love. — *Scott Yanow*

Robin Eubanks

b. Oct. 25, 1955, Philadelphia, PA
Trombone / Post-Bop
The older brother of guitarist Kevin Eubanks, Robin Eubanks has made his mark playing in his brother's groups, on his own JMT releases and interacting with many of the top M-Base players, such as Steve Coleman and Greg Osby. Capable of playing anything from bop to free, Eubanks came to New York in 1980, played with Slide Hampton and Sun Ra, toured with Stevie Wonder and then spent time with Art Blakey's Jazz Messengers. A versatile player, Eubanks has freelanced in many contexts including with the McCoy Tyner big band. — *Scott Yanow*

● **Different Perspectives** / 1988 / JMT ✦✦✦✦✦
Exceptional first album from this trombonist. A great listening album with many components, mostly in a progressive vein. — *Michael G. Nastos*

Dedications / Apr. 1989 / JMT ✦✦✦✦
This CD teams together two of the brightest young trombonists of the period, Robin Eubanks and Steve Turre. The music covers a wide area with "The New Breed" placing the horns over a complex 7/4 funk rhythm (with pianist Mulgrew Miller making his recording debut on synthesizer), "V.O." being a modern Latin original, "Red, Black & Green Blues" featuring the band jamming on a blues remi-niscent of the Jazz Messengers and "Trance Dance" evolving from a free form introduction to a nearly impossible-to-play solo section (with 45 beats every four bars). The funky "Perpetual Groove" is succeeded by a ballad dedicated to Woody Shaw, the straightahead "Koncepts" (similar to "Giant Steps") and the uptempo "Victory." Eubanks and Turre had worked together on and off for nearly four yaers at this point and their familiarity with each other's playing shows. Add to the two trombones a strong and flexible rhythm section and the result is a stimulating and varied set of modern jazz. — *Scott Yanow*

Karma / May 1990 / JMT ✦✦✦
Trombonist Robin Eubanks' *Karma* begins with a throwaway rap piece and then moves up to a higher level. Eubanks' versatility is displayed on a World Music per-formance with percussion and a choir ("Mino"), a ballad with sampled strings ("Maybe Next Time"), a Monkish piece based on Thelonious' "Evidence" ("Evi-dently"), Latin funk ("Send One Your Love"), more commercial funk ("Never Give Up"), a jazz original for sextet ("The Yearning"), the rhythmically monotonous "Pentacourse," a vocal feature for Cassandra Wilson ("Resolution of Love") and a hard bop original dedicated to Art Blakey ("Remember When"). This CD, which has contributions from altoist Greg Osby, Branford Marsalis on tenor and guitarist Kevin Eubanks, is quite a mixed bag. — *Scott Yanow*

Mental Images / Jul. 1994 / JMT ✦✦✦

Jim Europe

b. Feb. 22, 1881, Mobile, AL, **d.** May 10, 1919, Boston, MA
Ragtime, Dance Bands

An early Black music pioneer, Jim Europe did not live long enough to play jazz but his large orchestra utilized jazz instruments (including a full banjo section) and performed ragtime, marches and dance music of the 1912-19 period. His pre-World War I group often accompanied the legendary dancers Vernon and Irene Castle. During the war he toured Europe with his huge military band and seemed poised to repeat his success in the US in 1919 when he was stabbed to death by an irate musician. Europe recorded as early as 1912 but, except for isolated tracks, none of his recordings have been reissued yet on CD. —*Scott Yanow*

Bill Evans

b. Aug. 16, 1929, Plainfield, NJ, **d.** Sep. 15, 1980, New York, NY
Piano, Leader / Post-Bop, Cool

Bill Evans was (along with McCoy Tyner) the most influential pianist in jazz during the 1960s and '70s, and since his death in 1980 his influence has exceeded Tyner's. Evans, who was the next step beyond Bud Powell, had a sophisticated way of voicing chords that has been adopted by a countless number of pianists. Very popular even among nonjazz audiences to his sensitive interpretations of ballads, Evans could always swing as hard as anyone when he was inspired.

After attending Southewestern Louisiana University, working with Mundell Lowe and Red Mitchell and serving in the Army, Evans first emerged on the New York scene playing with Tony Scott in 1956 and that year he made his first trio album, *New Jazz Conceptions*. After working with George Russell and recording with Charles Mingus, Evans was part of the 1958 Miles Davis Sextet with John Coltrane and Cannonball Adderley. Other than a few live dates and "So What" from the 1959 classic *Kind of Blue*, Evans did not record all that much during his months with Davis but he made a strong impact and contributed one future standard, "Blue in Green," which ranks with "Waltz for Debby" as his most famous original. By 1959 Bill Evans was leading his own trio which soon used the great bassist Scott LaFaro and drummer Paul Motian. The interplay among the three musicians (with an almost equal role by each of the players) was influential and nearly telepathic. Tragically, shortly after they recorded at the Village Vanguard in June 1961, LaFaro was killed in a car accident. Evans went into isolation for the remainder of the year. In 1962 he re-emerged with Chuck Israels as his new bassist and recorded the first of two classic albums in duet with guitarist Jim Hall. In future Evans would continue touring and recording with his trio which utilized such sideman as bassists Israels (1962-65), Gary Peacock (1963), Eddie Gomez (1966-77) and Marc Johnson (1978-80) and drummers Motian (1959-62), Larry Bunker (1963-65), Philly Joe Jones (1967), Jack DeJohnette (1968), Marty Morell (1969-75), Eliot Zigmund (1975-78) and Joe La Barbera (1979-80). Drug addiction cut short Bill Evans' life prematurely but he fortunately recorded extensively from 1956 on, most notably for Riverside, Verve, Fantasy and Warner Bros. Several videos are also available of this major force in modern jazz whose innovations helped form the styles of Herbie Hancock and Keith Jarrett. —*Scott Yanow*

New Jazz Conceptions / Sep. 18, 1956-Sep. 27, 1956 / Original Jazz Classics ✦✦✦✦

Bill Evans' debut as a leader found the 27-year old pianist already sounding much different than the usual Bud Powell-influenced keyboardists of the time. Even in 1956 (more than a year before he joined Miles Davis' Sextet), Evans had his own chord voicings and a lyrical yet swinging style. Three selections (including the original version of his classic "Waltz for Debby") on this CD version are taken solo while the other nine (including his future theme "Five," "Speak Low" and two versions of "No Cover, No Minimum") are performed in a trio with bassist Teddy Kotick and drummer Paul Motian. A strong start to a significant career. —*Scott Yanow*

☆ **The Complete Riverside Recordings** / Sep. 27, 1956-May 31, 1963 / Riverside ✦✦✦✦✦

This magnificent 12-CD set contains all of Bill Evans' Riverside recordings as a leader, an extremely important period in the influential pianist's development. The first session predates Evans' period with the Miles Davis Sextet. Other significant sessions include his sets with bassist Scott LaFaro and drummer Paul Motian (highlighted by the marathon Village Vanguard session of June 25, 1961), Evans' return nearly a year after LaFaro's death in a car accident with a new trio (consisting of Motian and bassist Chuck Israels), a sideman set with altoist Cannonball Adderley, the *Interplay* sessions with either trumpeter Freddie Hubbard or tenor saxophonist Zoot Sims, an extensive and rather somber solo set and a 1963 appearance at Shelly's Manne Hole with bassist Israels and drummer Larry Bunker. Twenty sessions are released in full, 151 selections in all including 24 performances that had been previously unissued at the time. Fortunately for listeners with a budget,

nearly all of this material has since been reissued on single CDs (mostly as part of the Original Jazz Classics series) but true Bill Evans fanatics will have to get this remarkable box. —*Scott Yanow*

The Complete Bill Evans on Verve / Jul. 6, 1957-May 27, 1970 / Verve ✦✦✦✦✦

First of all, it must be stated that the packaging of this 18-CD set is somewhat atrocious. The valuable music is housed inside a rusty steel box, and one can easily be cut trying to remove a disc too fast. The 158-page booklet has lots of valuable information, but it could have been twice as large since some of the writing borders on the microscopic. However, the music itself is on a much higher level. Bill Evans, one of the most influential jazz pianists of all time, is heard in Don Elliott's band on three titles from 1957 and then quite extensively during the 1962-70 period. There are six superb titles in which he guests with the Gary McFarland Orchestra (featuring some of McFarland's most inventive writing). Also featured are Evans' two overdubbed piano solo sets (*Conversations With Myself* and *Further Conversations With Myself* which both still sound fresh), a set of duets with guitarist Jim Hall, and a date in which his trio backs singer Monica Zetterlund. Although an orchestral date with Claus Ogerman is rather dull, the last 2 discs (which mostly deal with his *From Left to Right* set, during which he doubles on electric piano) is quite interesting, despite the many alternate takes. Most of the rest of this huge reissue (which does have every Bill Evans Verve recording) features the pianist in his trio, including the teams of Monty Budwig and Shelly Manne, Gary Peacock and Paul Motian, Chuck Israels and Larry Bunker and Eddie Gomez with either Manne, Philly Joe Jones, Jack DeJohnette or Marty Morell. There is also a humorous vocal version of "Santa Claus Is Coming to Town" (Evans' only singing on record, for obvious reasons) and a meeting with tenor saxophonist Stan Getz that has some moments, although it did not really come off. The latter date is actually highlighted by an excerpt in which Getz, Evans (playing stride), Richard Davis and Elvin Jones play a funny version of "Dark Eyes": Jones does an expert imitation of Gene Krupa. Throughout this continually interesting (if gigantic) reissue, there are dozens of classic performances. Highly recommended to Bill Evans fans, despite the ghastly packaging. —*Scott Yanow*

Everybody Digs Bill Evans / Dec. 15, 1958 / Original Jazz Classics ✦✦✦✦

Bill Evans' second album as a leader was made shortly after he left Miles Davis' group. Evans, whose style was already fully formed, performs seven songs in a trio with bassist Paul Chambers and drummer Philly Joe Jones, really digging in for most of the songs and playing with a stronger aggression than usual; highlights include "Minority," "Night and Day" and "Oleo." However, it is his three piano solos, particularly the brilliant "Peace Piece," that are most memorable. —*Scott Yanow*

On Green Dolphin Street / Jan. 19, 1959+Jun. 25, 1961 / Milestone ✦✦✦

This obscure Bill Evans trio set (with bassist Paul Chambers and drummer Philly Joe Jones) went unissued until the mid-'70s when the pianist decided that it was worth releasing as a fine example of bassist Chambers' work. Very much a spontaneous set (recorded after the rhythm section made part of a record accompanying trumpeter Chet Baker), the group runs through a few standards such as "You and the Night and the Music," "Green Dolphin Street" and two versions of "Woody 'n You ." Although lacking the magic of Evans' regular bands, this CD reissue has its strong moments and the pianist's fans will be interested in getting the early sampling of his work. A special bonus is the rare first take of "All of You" from the legendary Village Vanguard engagement by the 1961 Evans Trio (with bassist Scott LaFaro and drummer Paul Motian). —*Scott Yanow*

Portrait in Jazz / Dec. 28, 1959 / Original Jazz Classics ✦✦✦✦✦

The first of two studio albums by the Bill Evans-Scott LaFaro-Paul Motian trio (both of which preceded their famous engagement at the Village Vanguard), this CD reissue contains some wondrous interplay, particularly between pianist Evans and bassist LaFaro on the two versions of "Autumn Leaves." Other than introducing Evans' "Peri's Scope," the music comprises standards, but the influential interpretations were far from routine or predictable at the time. LaFaro and Motian were nearly equal partners with the pianist in the ensembles and their versions of such tunes as "Come Rain or Come Shine," "When I Fall in Love" and "Someday My Prince Will Come" (which preceded Miles Davis' famous recording by a couple years) are full of subtle and surprising creativity. A gem. —*Scott Yanow*

Explorations / Feb. 2, 1961 / Original Jazz Classics ✦✦✦✦✦

The second and final studio recording by pianist Bill Evans with bassist Scott LaFaro and drummer Paul Motian is nearly the equal of the earlier *Portrait in Jazz*. LaFaro was borrowing a bass for the date while his regular instrument was being repaired and, since it apparently sounded better in its lower register than its higher one, he tends to emphasize lower notes than usual. No matter, the interplay between the musicians once again is consistently magical, uplifting such tunes as Miles Davis' "Nardis," "Israel," "How Deep Is the Ocean" and two versions of "Beautiful Love." —*Scott Yanow*

★ **Sunday at the Village Vanguard** / Jun. 25, 1961 / Original Jazz Classics ✦✦✦✦✦

Ten days before bassist Scott LaFaro's tragic death in a car accident, he was extensively documented at the Village Vanguard during one night with the Bill Evans Trio (which also featured drummer Paul Motian). LaFaro's innovative playing (which often emphasized high notes, speedy runs and close interplay with Evans) was ahead of its time and would be quite influential on bassists of the next 20 years. This CD reissue plus *Waltz for Debby* together have 20 of the 21 existing performances from the night at the Vanguard (only a third version of "All of You" is absent) and they feature one of Evans' finest groups. Although four of the six selections on this particular CD are heard in two versions, the interpretations often differ quite a bit from each other and each number has its own subtle surprises. Essential music. —*Scott Yanow*

☆ **Waltz for Debby** / Jun. 25, 1961 / Original Jazz Classics ✦✦✦✦✦

The companion to *Sunday at the Village Vanguard* (the two CD reissues bring back nearly the entire night's music), this set features pianist Bill Evans, bassist Scott LaFaro (only ten days before his death in a car accident) and drummer Paul Motian stretching the boundaries of piano trio playing. Each of the musicians have a nearly equal role (although Evans is generally the lead voice among equals) and they consistently inspire each other. There are seven selections on this disc plus three alternate takes and the highlights include the two versions of Evans' most famous original "Waltz for Debby," a touching interpretation of "My Foolish Heart," "Some Other Time" and "Milestones." Highly recommended. —*Scott Yanow*

Undercurrent / Apr. 24, 1962+May 14, 1962 / Blue Note ✦✦✦✦✦

Other than four piano solos from April 4, 1962, this set was pianist Bill Evans' first recordings after a hiatus caused by bassist Scott LaFaro's tragic death in a car accident. The first of two meetings on record in a duo format with guitarist Jim Hall, the collaborations are often exquisite. Both Evans and Hall had introspective and harmonically advanced styles along with roots in hard-swinging bebop. The six selections on the original LP have been expanded to ten for this CD reissue with the inclusion of two alternate takes and previously unheard versions of "Stairway to the Stars" and "I'm Getting Sentimental over You." There is more variety than expected on the fine set with some cookers, ballads, waltzes and even some hints at classical music. Recommended. —*Scott Yanow*

How My Heart Sings! / May 17, 1962-Jun. 5, 1962 / Original Jazz Classics ✦✦✦✦

When pianist Bill Evans returned to the active jazz scene in 1962 after taking time off due to bassist Scott LaFaro's death in a car accident, he was persuaded by producer Orrin Keepnews to record two projects: a ballad album and a set of more uptempo tunes. This CD reissue contains the latter. Evans has a reunion with drummer Paul Motian and, with the fine bassist Chuck Israels in LaFaro's place, performs such numbers as "How My Heart Sings," "34 Skidoo," "Show-Type Tune" and two versions of "In Your Own Sweet Way." —*Scott Yanow*

Moonbeams / May 17, 1962-Jun. 5, 1962 / Original Jazz Classics ✦✦✦

This all-ballads album (reissued on CD) was recorded at the same sessions as *How My Heart Sings!*, a program of more uptempo tunes. Evans, his new bassist Chuck Israels and drummer Paul Motian are in typically sensitive and lyrical form on such numbers as the original version of "Re: Person I Knew" (an anagram of producer Orrin Keepnews' name), "Very Early," "I Fall in Love Too Easily," "If You Could See Me Now" and four others. —*Scott Yanow*

Interplay / Jul. 16, 1962 / Original Jazz Classics ✦✦✦✦

This is a CD reissue of a particularly strong Bill Evans set. The pianist, in one of his first sessions after returning to active playing a year after bassist Scott LaFaro's tragic death, is teamed with bassist Percy Heath, drummer Philly Joe Jones, guitarist Jim Hall and trumpeter Freddie Hubbard for a rare all-star jam session. Other than the title cut, the musicians perform five veteran standards (highlighted by "You and the Night and the Music," "You Go to My Head" and "Wrap Your Troubles in Dreams"). This reissue also adds a second take of "I'll Never Smile Again." Excellent music. —*Scott Yanow*

Interplay Sessions / Jul. 16, 1962+Aug. 22, 1962 / Milestone ✦✦✦✦

Although pianist Bill Evans had been recording as a leader steadily since 1959 (with one date in 1956), the two albums included in this two-LP set were his first to use horns. The earlier date features Evans with trumpeter Freddie Hubbard, guitarist Jim Hall, bassist Percy Heath and drummer Philly Joe Jones performing five veteran standards plus the pianist's blues "Interplay." While that session (highlighted by "You and the Night and the Music" and "Wrap Your Troubles in Dreams") came together fairly smoothly, the follow-up album, an outing with tenor saxophonist Zoot Sims, Hall, bassist Ron Carter and Jones, had so many problems that it was not released at the time. Evans had had the underrehearsed group play seven of his recent originals but the date was soon forgotten and lost in the vaults. When this 1982 two-fer was prepared, the "Loose Bloose" set was rediscovered and found to be better than expected; in fact, because four of the songs were never again

recorded by Evans, its historic value is also quite strong. Both of these "Evans with Horn Quintets" have fortunately been reissued on CD. —*Scott Yanow*

Empathy/A Simple Matter of Conviction / Aug. 14, 1962+Oct. 11, 1966 / Verve ✦✦✦✦

Two of pianist Bill Evans' better Verve recordings are combined on this single CD. Although separated by over four years time, in both cases the lyrical pianist is joined by drummer Shelly Manne; the bass spot is taken by either Monty Budwig or Eddie Gomez (the latter was making his recorded debut with Evans). The earlier session (the pianist's first project for Verve) has some unusual material including a pair of Irving Berlin obscurities ("The Washington Twist" and "Let's Go Back to the Waltz"), "Danny Boy" and "I Believe in You." The later date is most notable for including four obscure Evans tunes (including "Only Child" and "These Things Called Changes") plus his interpretation of "My Melancholy Baby" and some more conventional material. In any case, fans of the influential pianist will want to pick up this set which contains nearly 73 minutes of intriguing music. —*Scott Yanow*

Loose Blues / Aug. 21, 1962+Aug. 22, 1962 / Milestone ✦✦✦✦

This long-lost session, not released initially until 1982, features pianist Bill Evans, tenor saxophonist Zoot Sims, guitarist Jim Hall, bassist Ron Carter and drummer Philly Joe Jones interpreting seven of the pianist's recent originals. Due to some difficulties during the recording process (none of the sidemen were familiar with the often-complex numbers), the results were originally shelved and lost for a couple of decades. This CD reissue shows that the music was actually much better than originally thought. While "Time Remembered," "Funkallero" and "My Bells" would become Evans standards, it is quite interesting to hear such forgotten obscurities as "Loose Bloose" (heard in two versions), "There Came You," "Fun Ride" and "Fudgesickle Built for Four"; a couple of the songs could stand to be revived. It is a pity that Evans and Zoot (a logical combination) never did record together again. —*Scott Yanow*

V.I.P.S Theme Plus Others / 1963 / MGM ✦✦

The Solo Sessions, Vol. 1 / Jan. 10, 1963 / Milestone ✦✦✦

In need of money and wanting to quickly fulfill his contractual obligations to Riverside, Bill Evans recorded two albums worth of solos in one day. The emotional and rather stark music was not initially released until the late '80s although it is now available on a pair of CDs. Due to the lack of much mood or tempo variation, this particular set is recommended mostly for Evans completists and longtime fans. There are two medleys (the pianist was playing one tune after another and a few songs overlapped) and every number would be recorded by Evans (generally in trio formats) at other times. Interesting but not essential music. —*Scott Yanow*

The Solo Sessions, Vol. 2 / Jan. 10, 1963 / Milestone ✦✦✦

Apparently pianist Bill Evans was in bad shape at the time of this recording, both due to his heroin addiction and his grief over the premature death of his bassist Scott LaFaro in 1961. Evans' playing is a bit hesitant at times but the solo set (released for the first time in the late 1980s) actually has its strong moments. Although his interpretations of standards are mostly somewhat somber, Evans sounds quite cheerful on "Santa Claus Is Coming to Town" and fairly inventive on thoughtful versions of such songs as "All the Things You Are," "What Kind of Fool Am I" and "Ornithology." —*Scott Yanow*

Conversations with Myself / Jan. 1963-Feb. 1963 / Verve ✦✦✦✦✦

A classic of its kind, for this Verve project Bill Evans recorded three piano parts via overdubbing. Accurately-titled, the music on the CD reissue has a surprising amount of spontaneity with Evans constantly reacting to what he had just recorded, and the results are sometimes haunting. The highlights include "How About You," "The Love Theme from 'Spartacus,'" "Blue Monk" and "Just You Just Me." —*Scott Yanow*

Bill Evans Trio at Shelly's Manne-Hole / May 30, 1963+May 31, 1963 / Original Jazz Classics ✦✦✦✦

Pianist Bill Evans' final Riverside album, a live set with bassist Chuck Israels and drummer Larry Bunker, is reissued on this CD which also contains a previously unreleased version of "All the Things You Are." An earlier two-LP set (*Time Remembered*) actually has 16 tunes from the engagement (as opposed to nine on the CD) but will be hard to locate. After a year of steady work, the underrated Evans-Israels-Bunker Trio was in top form for an enjoyable, swinging and sensitive outing with highlights including "Isn't It Romantic," "The Boy Next Door," "'Round Midnight" and "Blues in F." —*Scott Yanow*

Trio '64 / Dec. 18, 1963 / Verve ✦✦✦✦

For this Bill Evans session (reissued on CD), bassist Gary Peacock was temporarily in Chuck Israels' place and drummer Paul Motian had returned, filling in for Larry Bunker. The pianist's playing is typically excellent and he sounds inspired by Peacock's presence; the bassist was normally associated around the period with Paul Bley. In addition to a cartoon theme ("Little Lulu"), the group sticks to standards although there are a couple of unusual choices: Noel Coward's "I'll See You Again" and an effective interpretation of "Santa Claus Is Coming to Town." Although not a major release overall, this fine outing is certainly not without interest and should please Bill Evans' fans. —*Scott Yanow*

Trio Live / May 14, 1964-May 19, 1964 / Verve ◆◆◆◆

The Best of Bill Evans Live on Verve / Jul. 7, 1964-Jun. 15, 1968 / Polygram ◆◆◆◆

While on the surface it may seem like a quixotic task to choose a single disc as a sampler for something like Verve's elephantine 18-disc *The Complete Bill Evans on Verve* box, in this specialized case of *The Best of Bill Evans Live on Verve*, the concept does work. Evans' primary live vehicle was the piano trio, with the post-bop approach and format rarely varied, and this collection of mid-'60s tracks drawn from four live albums catches an intelligent cross-section of his usual palette of standards with a handful of originals thrown in. Among the best choices are a particularly well-structured "Turn Out the Stars" from the Village Vanguard from 1967 (drummer Philly Joe Jones could light an especially hot fire underneath Evans) and a lovely solo "I Loves You Porgy" from Montreux. There is also a good balance between introspection and the lesser-known yet undeniably swinging side of Evans. The catholic-minded among us, though, can do without the outlandish lead sentence of the booklet notes—"Bill Evans played piano better than anyone"—which, despite the disclaimer further down the page, is all too typical of a lot of uncritical writing about Evans these days. —*Richard S. Ginell*

Trio '65 / Jan. 1965 / Verve ◆◆◆◆

Although all eight of the selections heard on this Verve release have been recorded on other occasions by pianist Bill Evans, these renditions hold their own. Teamed up with bassist Chuck Israels and drummer Larry Bunker (his regular trio of 1963-65), Evans plays definitive versions of such songs as Johnny Carisi's "Israel," "How My Heart Sings," "Who Can I Turn To" and "If You Could See Me Now." Thus far this fine LP has not yet been reissued as an individual CD. —*Scott Yanow*

Paris (1965) / Feb. 1965 / Royal Jazz ◆◆◆◆◆

Time to Remember (Live in Europe 1965-1972) / Feb. 1965-Feb. 1972 / Natasha ◆◆◆

Pianist Bill Evans and his trio are featured at three European concerts (either in France or Italy) on this CD. The recording quality is just decent and the overall results are not really all that essential. Evans (with bassist Chuck Israels and drummer Larry Bunker) performs four songs associated with Miles Davis in 1965, plays his famous "Waltz for Debby" in 1969 with bassist Eddie Gomez and drummer Marty Morell, and explores three of his other originals with the same group in 1972. Recommended primarily for Bill Evans completists. —*Scott Yanow*

Bill Evans Trio with Symphony Orchestra / Sep. 29, 1965-Dec. 16, 1965 / Verve ◆◆

This collaboration (reissued on CD) is predictably dull. Bill Evans and his 1965 trio (which also includes bassist Chuck Israels and drummer Larry Bunker) meet a symphony orchestra conducted and arranged by Claus Ogerman. They perform adaptations of six classical themes plus a pair of Evans compositions ("Time Remembered" and "My Bells") but, as one might expect, the strings weigh down the music and Evans' improvisations are somewhat buried beneath the unimaginative arrangements. This is one of Bill Evans' least significant recordings, a weak Third Stream effort. —*Scott Yanow*

Bill Evans at Town Hall / Feb. 21, 1966 / Verve ◆◆◆◆

This CD (which adds three songs including a previously unreleased version of "One for Helen" to the original LP program) is a superior effort by Bill Evans and his trio in early 1966. The last recording by longtime bassist Chuck Israels (who had joined the Trio in 1962) with Evans (the tastefully supportive drummer Arnold Wise completes the group), this live set features the group mostly performing lyrical and thoughtful standards; highlights include "I Should Care," "Who Can I Turn To" and "My Foolish Heart." However the most memorable piece is the 13 -minute "Solo—In Memory of His Father," an extensive unaccompanied exploration by Evans that partly uses a theme that became "Turn Out the Stars." —*Scott Yanow*

The Secret Sessions / Mar. 1966-Jan. 26, 1975 / Milestone ◆◆◆◆

During an 18-year period, fan Mike Harris went to the Village Vanguard whenever pianist Bill Evans appeared and privately taped his performances. More than a decade after Evans' death, Harris made all the proper legal arrangements and producer Orrin Keepnews released music from 26 different occasions on this eight-CD box set, 104 selections in all. With the exception of the first date (and to a lesser extent the last one), the recording quality is surprisingly good, making this a real bonanza for Bill Evans' other fans. The pianist is joined by bassist Eddie Gomez on all of the numbers (except for the first date, which have Teddy Kotick) along with drummers Arnie Wise, Joe Hunt, Philly Joe Jones, Jack DeJohnette (clearly the most modern of the drummers), John Dentz, Marty Morell and Eliot Zigmund. Since Evans' style did not evolve much during the period, Eddie Gomez's growth as a soloist and the way that the various drummers adapt their styles to Evans' are

probably the two main reasons to acquire the set. But Bill Evans fanatics do not have to be told twice about this attractive package's existence. —*Scott Yanow*

Intermodulation / Apr. 7, 1966-May 10, 1966 / Verve ◆◆◆

The second of two recorded duets by pianist Bill Evans and guitarist Jim Hall has been reissued as a 31-minute CD; its brevity is responsible for the lower-than-expected rating. Actually the quality generally makes up for the lack of quantity for Evans and Hall often thought alike musically and these six lyrical performances (only "The Jazz Samba" is taken at a medium tempo) are quite haunting. Most memorable is "My Man's Gone Now" and "Turn Out the Stars." —*Scott Yanow*

Further Conversations with Myself / Aug. 9, 1967 / Verve ◆◆◆

At the Montreux Jazz Festival / Jun. 15, 1968 / Verve ◆◆◆◆

Bill Evans, with bassist Eddie Gomez and his drummer of the period Jack DeJohnette (just prior to him joining Miles Davis), is in excellent form on this well-rounded CD reissue. Evans performs two of his originals (including "One for Helen" which was dedicated to his longtime manager Helen Keane), Denny Zeitlin's "Quiet Now," Earl Zindars' "Mother of Earl" and a few of his favorite standards, tunes that are generally ballads and harmonically rich. The interplay between Evans and Gomez was growing month-by-month (the bassist had been with him for almost two years at this point) and is the main reason to acquire this disc although DeJohnette does offer some stimulating support. —*Scott Yanow*

What's New / Jan. 30, 1969-Mar. 11, 1969 / Verve ◆◆◆◆

This CD reissue has the debut of drummer Marty Morell with Bill Evans and bassist Eddie Gomez; that particular trio would keep the same personnel for six productive years. Actually this is a quartet set with guest flutist Jeremy Steig, whose playing recalls Herbie Mann's recording (*Nirvana*) with Evans back in the early '60s. Both flutists were always open to the influences of pop and rock although in both of their collaborations with Bill Evans, the music is very much on the pianist's turf. With the exception of Evans' "Time Out for Chris" and the "Spartacus Love Theme," the songs performed on this date would fit securely in the Miles Davis repertoire of the late '50s. Steig is in particularly fine form on the program which includes tunes such as "Straight, No Chaser," "Autumn Leaves" and "So What." —*Scott Yanow*

Jazzhouse / Nov. 24, 1969 / Milestone ◆◆◆◆

This set is one of two albums (both reissued on CD) recorded by the Bill Evans Trio (with bassist Eddie Gomez and drummer Marty Morell) at Copenhagen's Montmartre on one night in 1969 but not released initially until the late '80s. Evans sounds relaxed and swinging playing his usual repertoire. All of the songs (mostly standards) have been recorded by Evans at other times but the pianist's many fans certainly will not mind hearing these "alternate" versions of such tunes as "How Deep Is the Ocean," "How My Heart Sings," "Sleepin' Bee" and a light-hearted "California Here I Come." —*Scott Yanow*

You're Gonna Hear from Me / Nov. 24, 1969 / Milestone ◆◆◆◆

This CD reissue is the companion to *Jazzhouse*, for both were recorded on the same night at the Montmartre in Copenhagen. Evans' regular trio of the time (which included bassist Eddie Gomez and drummer Marty Morell) is in exuberant form performing before an enthusiastic crowd. In addition to versions of "Waltz for Debby" and "Time Remembered," Evans plays seven of his favorite standards, including "You're Gonna Hear from Me," "Nardis" and "Emily." An excellent all-around set that was not originally released until 1988. —*Scott Yanow*

Alone / Dec. 12, 1969 / Verve ◆◆

The recording date of this solo outing by pianist Bill Evans has been listed as both September 1968 and December 1969; the latter seems the more logical entry. In any case, Evans' final Verve album is one of his weaker dates. He plays five often-rambling solos (including a 14 -minute exploration of "Never Let Me Go") and one senses that he misses the usual interplay that he had with his sidemen. In addition, the repertoire (which also includes "Here's That Rainy Day," "A Time for Love," "Midnight Mood" and "On a Clear Day") is not too inspiring and lacks much variety. This set is therefore only recommended to Bill Evans completists who already have 50 of his other recordings. —*Scott Yanow*

Montreux, Vol. 2 / Jun. 19, 1970 / CTI ◆◆◆
Return to where he did several unforgettable releases. —*Ron Wynn*

From Left to Right / 1970 / MGM ◆◆

Bill Evans Album / May 11, 1971-Jun. 9, 1971 / Columbia ◆◆◆◆
On this CD reissue (which adds three "new" alternate takes to the original seven song program), Bill Evans made his debut on electric piano, usually playing it in conjunction with his acoustic piano. Joined by bassist Eddie Gomez and drummer Marty Morell, Evans performs seven of his stronger originals including "Funkallero," "The Two Lonely People," "Re: Person I Knew," "T.T.T." and "Waltz for Debby." Although not as distinctive on the electric keyboard as he was on the acoustic

counterpart, Evans sounds inspired by its possibilities and is heard in top creative form throughout the date. — Scott Yanow

Living Time / May 12, 1972-May 14, 1972 / Columbia ♦♦

Pianist Bill Evans' second and final Columbia album was a rematch of sorts with composer-arranger George Russell; Evans had been on a couple of Russell's more significant albums of the late '50s. The music on this set unfortunately is not all that interesting. Russell's lengthy and episodic work "Living Time" (which has eight "events") features crowded ensembles as played by Evans' trio plus 19 musicians (including two additional keyboardists). Despite the major names in the "backup group" (including the reeds of Jimmy Giuffre, Sam Rivers and Joe Henderson), the focus throughout is on Evans' acoustic and electric keyboards. The problem is that the music is rather dull and surprisingly forgettable. — Scott Yanow

The Tokyo Concert / Jan. 20, 1973 / Original Jazz Classics ♦♦♦

From the Seventies / Nov. 1973-May 1977 / Fantasy ♦♦♦

When this LP was put out in 1983, all seven selections (taken from four separate sessions) were being released for the first time. With the emergence of CDs, these numbers are being used as "bonus tracks" to fill in the original programs that they came from, so this particular set went out-of-print. Bill Evans collectors who happen to run across the album may want to pick it up anyway for there are six fine trio numbers with bassist Eddie Gomez and either Marty Morell or Eliot Zigmund on drums. In addition one of the two versions of "Nobody Else but Me" is taken from the quintet date that Evans had with tenor saxophonist Harold Land and guitarist Kenny Burrell. — Scott Yanow

Eloquence / Nov. 19, 1973-Dec. 18, 1975 / Original Jazz Classics ♦♦♦

This interesting album was originally released posthumously in 1982. Pianist Bill Evans is featured on four duets with his longtime bassist Eddie Gomez in 1974-75, exploring a quartet of superior standards. The second half of the program (which dates from 1973 and 1975) is not on the same level. Evans is heard playing two songs he was not all that familiar with late at night at a club, and he performs two other songs and a wandering medley while rehearsing in a recording studio. Being a musical perfectionist, it is a bit doubtful if he would have wanted this music to be released although longtime Bill Evans collectors will find the explorations to be intriguing. — Scott Yanow

☆ **The Complete Fantasy Recordings** / Nov. 1973-May 13, 1979 / Fantasy ♦♦♦♦♦

Bill Evans' Fantasy recordings of 1973-79 have often been underrated in favor of his earlier work but, as this remarkable nine-CD set continually shows, the influential pianist continued to grow as a musician through the years while holding on to his original conception and distinctive sound. The collection has all of the 98 selections recorded at Evans' 11 Fantasy sessions including nine numbers from a previously unreleased 1976 concert with his trio. In addition, Evans' appearance on Marian McPartland's *Piano Jazz* radio program is tacked on as a bonus and it is actually among McPartland's finest shows; a fascinating hour of discussion and music with Evans. Nearly all of the performances on this box (which includes duets with bassist Eddie Gomez and singer Tony Bennett, trio outings with Gomez and either Marty Morell or Eliot Zigmund on drums, and a couple of quintet sets with the likes of tenors Harold Land and Warne Marsh, altoist Lee Konitz, guitarist Kenny Burrell, bassist Ray Brown and drummer Philly Joe Jones) are available individually on CD, but Bill Evans' more passionate collectors will certainly want this definitive box. The only minus is Gene Lees' typically self-serving liner notes; he always seems to love to write about himself. — Scott Yanow

Re: Person I Knew / Jan. 11, 1974-Jan. 12, 1974 / Original Jazz Classics ♦♦♦

Recorded at the same Village Vanguard sessions that resulted in *Since We Met*, this posthumous collection (first put out in 1981 and later reissued on CD) features Bill Evans, bassist Eddie Gomez and drummer Marty Morell playing material that was passed over for release at the time; some of the songs were considered overly familiar while others were early works-in-progress. But even though the results fall short of classic, they should interest Bill Evans collectors; highlights include remakes of "Re: Person I Knew," "Alfie," "T.T.T." and "34 Skidoo." — Scott Yanow

Since We Met / Jan. 11, 1974-Jan. 12, 1974 / Original Jazz Classics ♦♦♦

Thirteen years after his legendary Village Vanguard recordings, Bill Evans recorded at the famous New York establishment again. Using his trio of the era (which includes bassist Eddie Gomez and drummer Marty Morell), Evans explores both familiar ("Time Remembered," "Turn Out the Stars" and "But Beautiful") and new (Joe Zawinul's "Midnight Mood," "See-Saw" and "Sareen Jurer") material. This CD reissue gives listeners a good example of Bill Evans' early-'70s trio as it typically sounded in clubs. — Scott Yanow

The Canadian Concert of Bill Evans / Jul. 1974 / Can-Am ♦♦♦♦

Pianist Bill Evans had had the same musicians in his trio (bassist Eddie Gomez and drummer Marty Morell) for over five years when he was caught at a Quebec concert that was broadcast over Canadian radio. This LP finds the trio in its typically explorative, occasionally introspective and generally swinging form. The repertoire,

other than "Morning Glory," sticks to material that Evans had previously recorded including several of his own compositions, but these renditions are both fresh and spirited. — Scott Yanow

But Beautiful / Aug. 9, 1974+Aug. 16, 1974 / Milestone ♦♦♦♦♦

Pianist Bill Evans and tenor saxophonist Stan Getz only recorded in the studio together on one occasion, making these previously unreleased concert performances (issued for the first time in 1996) quite valuable. Evans (due to a misunderstanding) sits out on much of "Stan's Blues" and there are two trio features without the tenor but otherwise the other seven numbers match Getz with Evans, bassist Eddie Gomez and drummer Marty Morell. Although released under the pianist's name, this CD is very much Stan Getz's show and his beautiful tone sounds quite exquisite on "But Beautiful," "Emily," "The Peacocks" and the swinging "You and the Night and the Music." This historic and somewhat unique release has many enjoyable moments. — Scott Yanow

Blue in Green / Aug. 1974 / Milestone ♦♦♦♦♦

This CD reissue contains a Canadian concert by the Bill Evans Trio. Pianist Evans, bassist Eddie Gomez and drummer Marty Morell had been playing regularly together since 1969 (Gomez had joined the group back in 1966). The tight and almost telepathic musical communication between the musicians, the strong repertoire (six Evans originals, a pair of ballads and "So What") and the appreciative audience make this a fairly definitive recording by this classic unit. — Scott Yanow

Intuition / Nov. 7, 1974-Nov. 8, 1974 / Original Jazz Classics ♦♦♦♦

After having played together on a regular basis for eight years, it is not surprising that this set of duets by pianist Bill Evans and bassist Eddie Gomez are intuitive and bordering on the telepathic. The material is quite fresh. Evans might have recorded "Invitation" and "Show-Type Tune" previously but the other six songs were getting their debut in his hands. Whether it be "Hi Lili, Hi Lo," Claus Ogerman's "A Face Without a Name," Steve Swallow's "Falling Grace" or "Blue Serge," the sensitive and generally introspective playing on this CD reissue definitely holds one's interest. — Scott Yanow

Live in Europe, Vol. 1 / 1974 / EPM ♦♦♦

There are many bootleg CDs available of Bill Evans, particularly from his final decade. This French release, the first of two, features Evans, bassist Eddie Gomez and drummer Marty Morell playing at a concert presumably in Europe sometime in 1974. The repertoire (split between familiar originals and standards) offers no real surprises and, although the playing is fine, the recording quality is a bit erratic, making this one strictly for the more fanatical collectors. — Scott Yanow

Live in Europe, Vol. 2 / 1974 / EPM ♦♦♦

The second of two French EPM Bill Evans CDs of questionable origin (both are probably bootlegs) also features the influential pianist, bassist Eddie Gomez and drummer Marty Morell sometime in 1974 playing at a European concert. The renditions of tunes such as "Up with the Lark," "Quiet Now," "The Two Lonely People" and "Waltz for Debby" find the trio playing at their usual high level but the recording quality is not always the best and there are many more worthy (and legitimate) Bill Evans sets currently available. — Scott Yanow

The Tony Bennett/Bill Evans Album / Jun. 10, 1975-Jun. 13, 1975 / Original Jazz Classics ♦♦♦♦

Exquisite collaboration between a great romantic vocalist and a tremendous melodic interpreter. Bennett and Evans mesh as though they had been working together for years, never having any problems with tempo, pacing, or mood. This has been reissued on CD. — Ron Wynn

Montreux, Vol. 3 / Jul. 20, 1975 / Original Jazz Classics ♦♦♦♦

For this duet set from the 1975 Montreux Jazz Festival (a Fantasy date that has been reissued on CD in the OJC series), Bill Evans alternates between acoustic and electric pianos while Eddie Gomez offers alert support and some near-miraculous bass solos. The audience is attentive and appreciative as they should be for the communication between the two masterful players (on such songs as "Milano," "Django," "I Love You" and their encore "The Summer Knows") is quite special. — Scott Yanow

Alone (Again) / Dec. 16, 1975 / Original Jazz Classics ♦♦♦

Bill Evans plays well enough on this set of unaccompanied solos (reissued on CD), but the material is generally not worth the intense explorations that it receives. Other than Dave Brubeck's "In Your Own Sweet Way" and perhaps Ray Noble's "The Touch of Your Lips," the songs are not deserving of this type of treatment: "Make Someone Happy," "What Kind of Fool Am I" and a nearly 13-minute version of "People." — Scott Yanow

Quintessence / May 1976 / Original Jazz Classics ♦♦♦

Most of pianist Bill Evans' recordings were in a trio format, making this quintet date a nice change of pace. Evans' all-star group consists of tenor saxophonist Harold Land, guitarist Kenny Burrell, bassist Ray Brown and drummer Philly Joe

Jones and the results are quite tasteful and explorative in a subtle way. This version of Thad Jones' "A Child Is Born" is most memorable. —*Scott Yanow*

Cross-Currents / Feb. 28, 1977-Mar. 2, 1977 / Original Jazz Classics ✦✦✦✦✦
This superior set was a logical idea. One of pianist Bill Evans' earlier influences was Lennie Tristano, so on the date Evans' trio (with bassist Eddie Gomez and drummer Eliot Zigmund) was teamed with Tristano's two top "students": altoist Lee Konitz and tenor saxophonist Warne Marsh. The quintet performs four standards (all of which fit easily into Evans' repertoire) plus "Pensativa" and Steve Swallow's "Eiderdown." Konitz and Marsh always worked very well together and their cool-toned improvising makes this outing by Bill Evans special. The CD reissue adds three alternate takes to the original program. Recommended. —*Scott Yanow*

I Will Say Goodbye / May 11, 1977-May 13, 1977 / Original Jazz Classics ✦✦✦✦
The title refers to the Michel Legrand piece performed twice on the date, and to the fact that pianist Bill Evans was on the verge of switching labels from Fantasy to Warner Bros. For his final Fantasy album, Evans, bassist Eddie Gomez and drummer Eliot Zigmund perform memorable renditions of such songs as Herbie Hancock's "Dolphin Dance," Johnny Mandel's "Seascape" and Burt Bacharach's underrated "A House Is Not a Home." The CD reissue adds two additional selections ("Nobody Else but Me" and "Orson's Theme") from this excellent series of sessions. Fine postbop music from an influential piano giant. —*Scott Yanow*

You Must Believe in Spring / Aug. 23, 1977-Aug. 25, 1977 / Warner Brothers ✦✦✦✦
This well-rounded set (released posthumously) features the highly influential pianist Bill Evans in a set of typically sensitive trio performances. With his longtime bassist Eddie Gomez and his drummer of the period, Eliot Zigmund, Evans explores such songs as "We Will Meet Again," Jimmy Rowles' classic "The Peacocks" and the "Theme from M*A*S*H*." It's a solid example of the great pianist's artistry. —*Scott Yanow*

New Conversations / Jan. 26, 1978-Feb. 16, 1978 / Warner Brothers ✦✦✦✦
Bill Evans' third and final recording of overdubbed solos differs from the previous two in that he utilizes an electric piano in addition to his acoustic playing. Evans plays quite well on this LP (which includes four of his later originals, obscurities by Cy Coleman, Cole Porter and Duke Ellington, and "Nobody Else but Me") but the results are less memorable than one might expect as Bill Evans seemed to be at his best in trio settings. —*Scott Yanow*

Affinity / Oct. 30, 1978-Nov. 2, 1978 / Warner Brothers ✦✦✦
Pianist Bill Evans (who doubles on electric piano on this LP for the final time in the recording studio) welcomes guest harmonica player Toots Thielemans and Larry Schneider (on tenor, soprano and alto flute) to an outing with bassist Marc Johnson (making his recording debut with Evans) and drummer Eliot Zigmund. The material contains some surprises (including Paul Simon's "I Do It for Your Love" and Michel Legrand's "The Other Side of Tonight") and only two jazz standards ("Body & Soul" and "Blue and Green") with the latter being the only Evans composition. Excellent if not essential music that Evans generally uplifts. —*Scott Yanow*

We Will Meet Again / Aug. 6, 1979-Aug. 9, 1979 / Warner Brothers ✦✦✦✦
This was pianist Bill Evans' final studio session, a rare outing with a quintet (starring trumpeter Tom Harrell and Larry Schneideron tenor and soprano) and his first recording with the members of his final regular trio (bassist Marc Johnson and drummer Joe La Barbera). Although a straight CD reissue of the original LP, the playing time is over 61 minutes. The group interprets "For All We Know" and seven Evans originals including "Peri's Scope" and "Five." The thoughtful session is full of lyrical melodies and strong solos; even Evans' electric keyboard work on a few tunes is distinctive. —*Scott Yanow*

Paris Concert, Edition One / Nov. 26, 1979 / Elektra ✦✦✦✦✦
The two LPs recorded at this Paris concert are the last examples of Bill Evans' playing that have been released to date although there are other concert performances from 1980 that are expected to come out eventually. With bassist Marc Johnson and drummer Joe La Barbera, Evans has one of the strongest trios of his career, as can be heard on such pieces as "My Romance," "I Loves You Porgy" and "Beautiful Love." The close communication between the players is reminiscent of Evans' 1961 unit with Scott LaFaro and Paul Motian. —*Scott Yanow*

Paris Concert, Edition Two / Nov. 26, 1979 / Elektra ✦✦✦✦
Bill Evans' death in 1980 ended the career of the most influential (along with McCoy Tyner) acoustic pianist in jazz of the past 20 years. This second of two LPs features Evans, bassist Marc Johnson and drummer Paul Motian closely interacting on four of the pianist's originals, Gary McFarland's "Gary's Theme" and Miles Davis' "Nardis." The music is sensitive and subtly exciting. Until some later live sessions from 1980 are released, this can be considered Bill Evans' final recording and serves as evidence that, rather than declining, he was showing a renewed vitality and enthusiasm in his last year. —*Scott Yanow*

Turn Out the Stars: Final Village Vanguard Recordings / Jun. 4, 1980-Jun. 8, 1980 / Warner Brothers ✦✦✦✦
Just three months before his death, pianist Bill Evans was extensively recorded at the Village Vanguard. Originally, one or two LPs were to be released featuring his brilliant new trio (with bassist Marc Johnson and drummer Joe La Barbera), but after the innovative pianist's death, the project was stalled for over 15 years. Finally, when Warner Brothers got around to it, a definitive six-CD box set was released (although unfortunately in limited-edition form). Evans sounded quite energized during his last year, Johnson was developing quickly as both an accompanist and a soloist, and the interplay by the trio members (with subtle support from La Barbera) sometimes bordered on the telepathic. The playing throughout these consistently inventive performances ranks up there with the Evans-Scott LaFaro-Paul Motian trio of 20 years earlier. —*Scott Yanow*

Artist's Choice: Highlights from Turn Out the Stars / Jun. 4, 1980-Jun. 8, 1980 / Warner Brothers ✦✦✦✦
In 1996, Warner Bros. came out with a limited-edition six-CD set featuring pianist Bill Evans and his trio (with bassist Marc Johnson and drummer Joe La Barbera) playing at the Village Vanguard just a few months before Evans' death. This single CD is taken from the expensive collection and reportedly includes Evans' favorite performances from what was originally planned to be a two-LP set. Although Bill Evans completists and collectors will prefer the larger box, this superior CD should satisfy more general listeners. It does feature the highly influential pianist in top form on nine selections, including the ironically titled "Bill's Hit Tune," "My Foolish Heart," "Like Someone in Love," the title cut and a five-and-a-half-minute excerpt from a much lengthier "Nardis." —*Scott Yanow*

Letter to Evan / Jul. 21, 1980 / Dreyfus ✦✦✦✦
Recorded during pianist Bill Evans' last visit to England (less than two months before his death), Evans is heard with one of his finest trios on this CD, the unit with bassist Marc Johnson and drummer Joe La Barbera. The recording quality of the live set (recorded at Ronnie Scott's) is excellent, and Evans is in surprisingly enthusiastic and creative form; there is no hint that the end is near. Highlights of the very worthwhile release include "Days of Wine and Roses" (which alternates back and forth between two keys), "Knit for Mary," and "Stella by Starlight." Easily recommended for true Bill Evans fans. —*Scott Yanow*

Turn Out the Stars / Aug. 2, 1980 / Dreyfus ✦✦✦
On one of Bill Evans' final recordings (a live set from England made just six weeks before his death), the innovative and highly influential pianist is in fine form, emphasizing more introspective material. Evans and his last trio (which also includes bassist Marc Johnson and drummer Joe La Barbera) formed a brilliant and intuitive unit, as can be heard on such numbers as "Turn Out the Stars," "My Romance" and "Two Lonely People." Although it does not reach the emotional heights of his slightly earlier Dreyfus set *Letter to Evan* and the Warner Brothers box, this music should be of great interest to Bill Evans collectors. —*Scott Yanow*

The Brilliant / Aug. 31, 1980-Sep. 7, 1980 / Timeless ✦✦✦✦
The music on this live CD is much better played than expected, for pianist Bill Evans would pass away on the following September 15. Recorded at San Francisco's Keystone Korner during his last engagement, Evans (along with bassist Marc Johnson and drummer Joe La Barbera) still seems in surprisingly prime form on four originals (including "Letter to Evan" and "Bill's Hit Tune"), three obscurities, and the "Theme from M*A*S*H*." Hopefully, the music from this well-documented gig will eventually be released completely and in chronological order, for the influential pianist shows no obvious sign of decline during the highly intuitive post-bop performance. —*Scott Yanow*

Bill Evans

b. Feb. 9, 1958, Clarendon Hills, IL
Tenor Saxophone, Soprano Saxophone / Post-Bop, Crossover Jazz
No relation to the other Bill Evans, this saxophonist has an adventurous spirit and strong improvising skills despite his utilization of a rapper on some recent records. Evans started on piano before switching to tenor. He moved to New York in 1978 and was with Miles Davis during most of 1981-84. He also played with John McLaughlin's short-lived reformed Mahavishnu Orchestra in the mid-'80s, was with Elements from 1982 on and has recorded as a leader for Lipstick including with his 1990s group Petite Blonde. —*Scott Yanow*

Moods Unlimited / Oct. 28, 1982+Oct. 30, 1982 / Evidence ✦✦✦
This was one of the more unconventional jazz trios assembled in recent years, including veteran bebop and hard-bop pianist Hank Jones, equally venerable bassist Red Mitchell, and relative youngster Bill Evans, best known from Miles Davis' band of the '80s. They came together for a 1982 session that has been reissued by Evidence, and the results are mostly good, despite occasional flubs and meandering by Evans, who did not always sound confident. But it is easy to understand why

when listening to the fluid, smooth, routinely brilliant playing of Jones. The absence of a drummer made the instrumental mix and contrast even more vivid; Evans' tenor and soprano stood almost naked at times without covering rhythms. But he mostly met the challenge well, showing some subtlety and depth on soprano. —*Ron Wynn*

Living in the Crest of a Wave / Nov. 1983 / Elektra ✦✦✦

Although this is thought of as saxophonist Bill Evans' debut as a leader, a 1982 Japanese session (later reissued on Evidence) actually precedes it by a year. Evans (on tenor, soprano, flute and synth) teams up with keyboardist Mitch Forman, bassist Mark Egan, drummer Adam Nussbaum (Danny Gottlieb takes his place on one song) and percussionist Manolo Badrena for a set of his funky originals, excellent crossover music for 1983 although it sounds a touch dated today. The performances on this out-of-print LP have yet to be reissued on CD. —*Scott Yanow*

Alternative Man / Jan. 1985-May 1985 / Blue Note ✦✦✦

The fact that Bill Evans' years as a Miles Davis sideman had so positive an effect on him is evident on *Alternative Man*—an unpredictable fusion date that, although overproduced at times, is full of spirited blowing and adventurous composing. Ranging from the reggae-influenced "The Path of Resistance" to the addictive "Let the Juice Loose!" to the angular "Jojo," Evans' material is consistently impressive. A Michael Brecker disciple but definitely his own man, Evans tends to be robust and aggressive on tenor and more reflective on soprano. Guest John McLaughlin (electric guitar) is characteristically persuasive on the poetic "Flight of the Falcon." —*Alex Henderson*

● Petite Blonde / Oct. 1992 / Lipstick ✦✦✦✦✦

A live recording with cuts from two concerts in Germany, it was recorded live to 24-track and later remixed for an amazing sound quality for a live album. Evans expands on the style of the late Miles Davis and the album is sometimes reminiscent stylistically of *We Want Miles*, but has an individual touch due to the contributions from the different band members. It's one of the rare live albums that is really enjoyable even if you were not at one of the shows. This album was voted Best Album of the Month by several large German publications. —*Joanna Curzon*

Push / 1993 / Lipstick ✦✦✦

Live in Europe / Nov. 24, 1994 / Lipstick ✦✦

If it were possible to give this live CD a split rating, it would get both "Best" and "Poor." Saxophonist Bill Evans (switching between tenor and soprano) plays creative jazz-funk on five selections with plenty of heated solos and strong support from a rhythm section including guitarist Gary Poulson and keyboardist Charles Blenzig. If the whole recording were of that quality, this set would be close to essential. Unfortunately Evans then "welcomes" rapper KC Flight to four other numbers and his monotonous talking and shouting are annoying in the extreme, essentially ruining those performances. So this CD is recommended only if it is sold at half price. —*Scott Yanow*

Escape / Dec. 1995-Jan. 1996 / Escapade ✦✦✦✦

From Miles Davis' *Doo-Bop* to albums by Greg Osby and Steve Coleman, much of the "jazz/rap fusion" released has been more hip-hop than jazz—essentially, hip-hop with jazz overtones. Bill Evans, however, has featured rappers in much the way a hard bopper would feature a singer—on "Reality" and the poignant, reggae-influenced "La Di Da," rapper Ahmed Best successfully interacts with an actual, spontaneous, improvisatory band instead of merely pre-recorded tracks. Best's rapping style—a cerebral approach akin to De La Soul and A Tribe Called Quest instead of more hardcore rappers like Tupac Shakur and Ice-T—is well-suited to this challenging and complex jazz-fusion setting. On the instrumental side, *Escape*'s triumphs range from the hard-edged jazz-funk pieces "Undercover" and "Rattletrap" to the sensuous, Brazilian-influenced "Coravillas." Though capable of tenderness and vulnerability, Evans has the good sense to avoid bloodless "smooth jazz" altogether. —*Alex Henderson*

Music of Cole Porter / Nov. 23, 1996 / Double-Time ✦✦✦✦

Starfish and the Moon / 1997 / Escapade ✦✦✦✦

After providing an abundance of hard-edged, aggressive jazz-funk and jazz-rap on *Live* and *Escape*, Bill Evans surprised his followers by being so relaxed on *Starfish and the Moon*. This excellent, highly melodic CD was hailed as "Bill Evans' acoustic album," which was misleading because *Starfish* has its share of keyboards and synthesizers as well as electric bass and electric guitar. But it is accurate to say that the rap-free *Starfish* uses more acoustic instruments and less amplification than one had come to expect from the soprano and tenor saxophonist, who favors subtlety on such introspective, lyrical jazz-pop as "The Last Goodbye," "Something in the Rose" and "I'll Miss You." Even when he gets into a funk-minded groove on "Whiskey Talk" and "Shady Lady," Evans is moody and evocative rather than intense. Though the Chicago native has often played lyrically in the past, he was never as consistently restrained as he is on *Starfish*, a curve ball that was the last thing one would have expected to follow *Escape*. —*Alex Henderson*

Doc Evans (Paul Wesley Evans)

b. Jun. 20, 1907, Spring Valley, MN, d. Jan. 10, 1977, Minneapolis, MN
Cornet / Dixieland

A fine Dixieland cornetist, Doc Evans freelanced in the Midwest before leading his own bands in Chicago starting in the 1940s. He recorded extensively for Audiophile during 1949-59. Evans settled in Minneapolis later in life, playing music up until near his death; his last recordings were in 1975. —*Scott Yanow*

● Doc Evans and His Dixieland Jazz Band / Apr. 25, 1947-Apr. 26, 1947 / Folkways ✦✦✦✦✦

Cornetist Doc Evans was 39 when he recorded the dozen selections made available on this Folkways LP, his recording debut. The fine Dixieland player is teamed with four all-stars (trombonist Ed Hubble, clarinetist Tony Parenti, pianist Joe Sullivan and drummer George Wettling) for six songs apiece taken from the repertoire of the Original Dixieland Jazz Band and the New Orleans Rhythm Kings. Highlights include spirited versions of "Original Dixieland One-Step," "Fidgety Feet," "Bugle Call Rag" and "Panama." Easily recommended to Dixieland fans. —*Scott Yanow*

Down in Jungle Town / May 1953 / Audiophile ✦✦✦

Dixieland cornetist Doc Evans made many records for Audiophile in the 1950s and this 1987 LP (from the revived Audiophile label) has his first recording for the company. Unfortunately there is only 31 minutes of music but the Minnesota-based cornetist (heard in a sextet full of obscure local players) is in generally fine form on such tunes as "Riverside Blues," "Mama's Gone Goodbye," "Diga Diga Doo" and "Maryland, My Maryland." —*Scott Yanow*

Muskrat Ramble / 1959 / Audiophile ✦✦✦✦

This Dixieland LP is more creative than usual. Cornetist Doc Evans and his septet/octet (which also includes pianist Knocky Parker) perform fresh versions of three songs by Jelly Roll Morton, two by Clarence Williams, the standard "Fidgety Feet" and Evans' original "King Bolden on Parade." A special bonus is "Fantasy on Muskrat Ramble" which takes the warhorse through a variety of surprising changes. This LP has been out-of-print for several years but is well worth picking up; Doc Evans was always an excellent player. —*Scott Yanow*

Rx for the Blues / Aug. 1959 / Audiophile ✦✦✦

Eight of the nine selections on this out-of-print Audiophile LP (all but "Four or Five Times") has fortunately been reissued along with a similar session on a Jazzology CD titled *Stomps and Blues*. Cornetist Doc Evans is teamed with clarinetist Albert Nicholas, pianist Knocky Parker, bassist Earl Murphy and drummer Gene Juckem for a fun Dixieland-oriented set that does contain slight departures in "Sweet Lorraine" and "Willow Weep for Me." Highlights include a spirited "Ole Miss" and "I'm Drifting Back to Dreamland." —*Scott Yanow*

At the Gas Light / Apr. 12, 1967 / Audiophile ✦✦✦✦

Cornetist Doc Evans, who spent most of his life living in Minneapolis (which is why he is not better known) was an excellent if limited Dixieland cornetist. This release (which was reissued on a 1988 LP) features Evans in a typical septet (trombonist Alan Frederickson from the Queen City Jazz Band is the best known sidemen) playing "Bienville Blues" and seven standards including "Panama," "Creole Belles" and "Two Deuces." A fine all-round trad session. —*Scott Yanow*

The Golden Horn Speaks Jazz / Dec. 1, 1973-Dec. 6, 1975 / Fat Cat Jazz ✦✦✦✦

This out-of-print LP has five jams from December 1973 plus a version of "Save It Pretty Mama" from December 1975 that was cornetist Doc Evans' final recording; he passed away at age 69 in 1977. Evans is heard in fine form on six fairly lengthy selections ("Louisiana" is nearly 11 minutes long) and his sidemen contain both obscure and famous jazzmen including clarinetist Tommy Gwaltney, soprano saxophonist Kenny Davern, bass saxophonist Spencer Clark, pianists Dick Wellstood and Art Hodes, and drummer Cliff Leeman. Highlights include "Wolverine Blues," "When My Sugar Walks Down the Street" and "Hesitatin' Blues." It is a pity that this excellent album from the defunct Fat Cat Jazz label will be difficult to find. —*Scott Yanow*

Gil Evans (Ian Ernest Gilmore Green)

b. May 13, 1912, Toronto, Canada, d. Mar. 20, 1988, Cuernavaca, Mexico
Piano, Arranger, Leader, Composer / Cool, Fusion, Post-Bop

One of the most significant arrangers in jazz history, Gil Evans' three album-length collaborations with Miles Davis (*Miles Ahead*, *Porgy and Bess* and *Sketches of Spain*) are all considered classics. Evans had a lengthy and wide-ranging career that sometimes ran parallel to the trumpeter. Like Davis, Gil became involved in utilizing electronics in the 1970s and preferred not to look back and recreate the past. He led his own band in California (1933-38) which eventually became the backup group for Skinnay Ennis; Evans stayed on for a time as arranger. He gained recognition for his somewhat futuristic charts for Claude Thornhill's Orchestra (1941-42 and 1946-48) which took advantage of the ensemble's cool tones, utilized French horns and a tuba as front line instruments and by 1946 incorporated the influence of bop. He met Miles Davis (who admired his work with Thornhill) during this time and contributed arrangements of "Moon Dreams" and "Boplicity" to Davis' "Birth of the Cool" nonet.

After a period in obscurity, Evans wrote for a Helen Merrill session and then collaborated with Davis on *Miles Ahead*. In addition to his work with Miles (which also included a 1961 recorded Carnegie Hall concert and the half-album *Quiet Nights*), Evans recorded several superb and highly original sets as a leader (including *Gil Evans and Ten*, *New Bottle Old Wine* and *Great Jazz Standards*) during the era. In the 1960s among the albums he worked on for other artists were notable efforts with Kenny Burrell and Astrud Gilberto. After his own sessions for Verve during 1963-64, Evans waited until 1969 until recording again as a leader. That year's *Blues in Orbit* was his first successful effort at combining acoustic and electric instruments; it would be followed by dates for Artists House, Atlantic (*Svengali*) and a notable tribute to Jimi Hendrix in 1974. After 1975's *There Comes a Time* (which features among its sidemen David Sanborn), most of Evans' recordings were taken from live performances. Starting in 1970 he began playing with his large ensemble on a weekly basis in New York clubs. Filled with such all-star players as George Adams, Lew Soloff, Marvin "Hannibal" Peterson, Chris Hunter, Howard Johnson, Pete Levin, Hiram Bullock, Hamiet Bluiett and Arthur Blythe among others, Evans' later bands were top-heavy in talent but tended to ramble on too long. Gil Evans, other than sketching out a framework and contributing his keyboard, seemed to let the orchestra largely run itself, inspiring rather than closely directing the music. There were some worthwhile recordings from the 1980s (when the band had a long string of Monday night gigs at Sweet Basil in New York) but in general they do not often live up to their potential. Prior to his death, Gil Evans recorded with his "arranger's piano" on duets with Lee Konitz and Steve Lacy and his body of work on a whole ranks with the top jazz arrangers. —*Scott Yanow*

★ **Gil Evans and Ten** / Sep. 6, 1957-Oct. 10, 1957 / Original Jazz Classics ◆◆◆◆◆

Although arranger Gil Evans had been active in the major leagues of jazz ever since the mid-'40s and had participated in Miles Davis' famous *Birth of the Cool* recordings, this set was his first opportunity to record as a leader. The CD reissue features a typically unusual 11-piece unit consisting of two trumpets, trombonist Jimmy Cleveland, Bert Varsalona on bass trombone, French horn player Willie Ruff, Steve Lacy on soprano, altoist Lee Konitz, Dave Kurtzer on bassoon, bassist Paul Chambers and either Nick Stabulas or Jo Jones on drums, plus the leader's sparse piano. As good an introduction to his work as any, this program includes diverse works ranging from Leadbelly to Leonard Bernstein, plus Evans' own "Jambangle." The arranger's inventive use of the voices of his rather unique sidemen make this a memorable set. —*Scott Yanow*

New Bottle, Old Wine / Apr. 9, 1958-May 26, 1958 / Blue Note ◆◆◆◆◆

Gil Evans' second album as a leader (a World Pacific set that has been reissued by Blue Note) features his reworking of eight jazz classics including "St. Louis Blues," "Lester Leaps In" and "Struttin' with Some Barbecue." Evans' charts utilize three trumpets, three trombones, a French horn, a prominent tuba, one reed player, altoist Cannonball Adderley and a four-piece rhythm section. Most memorable is a classic rendition of "King Porter Stomp" featuring the exuberant altoist Cannonball Adderley, who is the main soloist on most of the selections. Other key voices include Evans' piano, guitarist Chuck Wayne and trumpeter Johnny Coles. This is near-classic music that showed that Gil Evans did not need Miles Davis as a soloist to inspire him to greatness. —*Scott Yanow*

Great Jazz Standards / 1959 / Blue Note ◆◆◆◆◆

A follow-up to *New Bottle, Old Wine*, this Gil Evans set has colorful arrangements of five jazz standards plus "Ballad of the Sad Young Men" and Evans' "Theme." Using a band consisting of three trumpets, three trombones, a French horn, Bill Barber's tuba, soprano saxophonist Steve Lacy (the first important post-swing player on his instrument), tenor saxophonist Budd Johnson (on half of the program) and a four-piece rhythm section (including the leader's piano), Evans contributes some very memorable written ensemble passages, most notably on "Straight, No Chaser." In addition to Lacy and Johnson, the main soloists are trumpeter Johnny Coles, trombonists Curtis Fuller and Jimmy Cleveland, and guitarist Ray Crawford. Highly recommended. —*Scott Yanow*

Out of the Cool / Nov. 18, 1960-Dec. 15, 1960 / MCA ◆◆◆◆

Gil Evans recordings (particularly those without Miles Davis) were not a common occurrence in the pre-1970 era, making this set a special treat. Evans' 14-piece band (which includes trumpeter Johnny Coles, trombonist Jimmy Knepper, Budd Johnson on tenor and soprano and guitarist Ray Crawford among others) investigates a wide variety of complex material including the leader's "La Nevada" and "Sunken Treasure," John Benson Brooks' obscure "Where Flamingos Fly," George Russell's "Stratusphunk" and Kurt Weill's "Biobao"; some reissues of this album

also add Horace Silver's "Sister Sadie." The orchestrations are both thoughtful and colorful, the main reason to acquire this music. —*Scott Yanow*

Into the Hot / Oct. 10, 1961 / MCA/Impulse! ◆◆◆

Although this album (reissued on CD) proudly states that it is by the Gil Evans Orchestra and has Evans' picture on the cover, the arranger actually had nothing to do with the music. Three songs have the nucleus of his big band performing numbers composed, arranged and conducted by John Carisi (who also plays one of the trumpets). Those selections by the composer of "Israel" are disappointingly forgettable. The other three performances are even further away from Evans for they are actually selections by avant-garde pianist Cecil Taylor's septet! Taylor's music features trumpeter Ted Curson, trombonist Roswell Rudd, altoist Jimmy Lyons, tenor saxophonist Archie Shepp, bassist Henry Grimes and drummer Sunny Murray and is quite adventurous and exciting, the main reason to acquire this somewhat misleading set. —*Scott Yanow*

The Individualism of Gil Evans / Sep. 1963-Oct. 29, 1964 / Verve ◆◆◆◆

Although Gil Evans had gained a lot of acclaim for his three collaborations with Miles Davis in the 1950s and his own albums, this CD contains (with the exception of two tracks purposely left off), Evans' only dates as a leader during 1961-68. The personnel varies on the six sessions that comprise the CD (which adds five numbers including two previously unreleased to the original LP) with such major soloists featured as tenorman Wayne Shorter, trombonist Jimmy Cleveland, trumpeter Johnny Coles and guitarist Kenny Burrell. Highlights include "Time of the Barracudas," "The Barbara Song," "Las Vegas Tango" and "Spoonful." Highly recommended to Gil Evans fans; it is a pity he did not record more during this era. —*Scott Yanow*

Blues in Orbit / 1969 / Enja ◆◆◆◆◆

Arranger Gil Evans' first recording as a leader in five years found him leading an orchestra that could be considered a transition between his 1950s groups and his somewhat electric band of the 1970s. Several of these charts, particularly his reworking of George Russell's "Blues in Orbit," are quite memorable, and Evans utilizes his many interesting sidemen, including the distinctive voices of trombonist Jimmy Cleveland, Howard Johnson on tuba and baritone, tenor saxophonist Billy Harper and guitarist Joe Beck, in unexpected and unpredictable ways. A near-classic release which has been available on CD by Enja. —*Scott Yanow*

Where Flamingos Fly / 1971 / Artists House ◆◆◆

This transitional LP (which has been long out-of-print) features arranger Gil Evans shortly after he decided to put together a permanent big band. Although the music didn't come out until a decade later, it is actually quite worthwhile. Evans is heard at the head of two different (but overlapping) units ranging from ten to fifteen pieces, and he utilizes synthesizers for the first time. The key soloists are tenor saxophonist Billy Harper and Howard Johnson, mostly on baritone, but the emphasis is on Evans' writing, unlike his later live recordings. Most memorable is "Zee Zee," "Hotel Me," "Where Flamingos Fly" and a seventeen-and-a-half-minute version of "El Matador." —*Scott Yanow*

Svengali / May 30, 1973+Jun. 30, 1973 / Atlantic ◆◆◆◆◆

This is one of Gil Evans' finest recordings of the 1970s. He expertly blended together acoustic and electronic instruments, particularly on an exciting rendition of "Blues in Orbit" (which includes among its soloists a young altoist named David Sanborn). All six selections have their memorable moments (even a one-and-a-half-minute version of "Eleven"); colorful solos are contributed by guitarist Ted Dunbar, Howard Johnson on tuba and fluegelhorn, the passionate tenor of Billy Harper and bassist Herb Bushler, among others; and Evans' arrangements are quite inventive and innovative. Rarely would he be so successful in balancing written and improvised sections in his later years. This LP is highly recommended but may be difficult to find. —*Scott Yanow*

Gil Evans' Orchestra Plays the Music of Jimi Hendrix / Jun. 11, 1974-Jun. 13, 1974 / Bluebird ◆◆◆◆◆

This CD reissue (which adds additional material to the original LP program) is much more successful than one might have expected. Jimi Hendrix was scheduled to record with Gil Evans' Orchestra but died before the session could take place. A few years later, Evans explored ten of Hendrix's compositions with his unique 19-piece unit, an orchestra that included two French horns, the tuba of Howard Johnson, three guitars, two basses, two percussionists and such soloists as altoist David Sanborn, trumpeter Hannibal Marvin Peterson, Billy Harper on tenor and guitarists Ryo Kawasaki and John Abercrombie. Evans' arrangements uplift many of Hendrix's more blues-oriented compositions and create a memorable set that is rock-oriented but retains the improvisation and personality of jazz. Recommended. —*Scott Yanow*

There Comes a Time / Mar. 6, 1975-Jun. 12, 1975 / Bluebird ◆◆◆◆◆

This CD reissue differs greatly from the original LP of the same name. Not only are there three previously unreleased performances ("Joy Spring," "So Long" and "Buzzard Variation") but "The Meaning of the Blues" has been expanded from six minutes to 20, two numbers ("Little Wing" and "Aftermath the Fourth Movement Children of the Fire") have been dropped (the former was reissued on Evans' Jimi Hendrix tribute) and the remaining four tracks were re-edited and remixed under Evans' direction. So in reality, this 1987 CD was really a "new" record when it came out. The remake of "King Porter Stomp" (with altoist David Sanborn in Cannonball Adderley's spot) is a classic, the "new" version of "The Meaning of the Blues" is memorable and overall the music (which also has solos by Billy Harper and George Adams on tenors along with trumpeter Lew Soloff) is quite rewarding, creative big band fusion that expertly mixes together acoustic and electric instruments. This was one of Gil Evans' last truly great sets. —*Scott Yanow*

Priestess / May 13, 1977 / Antilles ✦✦✦✦

After the success of his studio sessions of the early to mid-'70s, Gil Evans primarily recorded live in concert during the remainder of his career. This is one of the better sets, for although two of the four selections are over 12 minutes long ("Priestess" exceeds nineteen-and-a-half minutes), the music is generally under control. Evans' eccentric 16-piece group consists of three trumpets, trombone, French horn, two tubas, three saxes and a five-piece rhythm section including Pete Levin on synthesizer. With such soloists as altoists David Sanborn and Arthur Blyte, trumpeter Lew Soloff and George Adams on tenor, the music is quite stimulating and exciting. —*Scott Yanow*

Little Wing / Oct. 1978 / Inner City ✦✦✦

For a 1978 European tour, Gil Evans used a nonet, a much smaller-than-usual band. However, all of the ingredients (good and bad) from his later groups are very much present on the German concert preserved on this LP (which was originally put out by Circle). The three performances ("Dr. Jekyll," "The Meaning of the Blues" and Jimi Hendrix's "Little Wing") are generally much too long, with "Little Wing" only two seconds short of twenty-six-and-a-half minutes. While Evans is on electric piano, his contributions are rather minor, as his sidemen take overly long solos which alternate exciting and somewhat aimless sections. Prominently featured are altoist Gerry Niewood, trumpeter Terumasa Hino, George Adams on tenor, trumpeter Lew Soloff and the synthesizer of Peter Levin. An interesting set but, as is usually true with Gil Evans' later recordings, not too essential. —*Scott Yanow*

Live at the Public Theater in New York, Vol. 1 / Feb. 8, 1980-Feb. 9, 1980 / Black Hawk ✦✦✦

One of arranger Gil Evans' main talents was his ability to fuse diverse, unique performers into a unified ensemble. He accomplishes that on the first of two LPs taken from a pair of 1980 concerts, even if his presence is felt more than heard. Although Evans is on electric piano, he also employed two other synthesizer players (Masabumi Kikuchi and Pete Levin) in his eclectic band, which at the time included such notables as Lew Soloff, Jon Faddis and Hannibal Marvin Peterson on trumpets, altoist Arthur Blythe, trombonist George Lewis, baritone saxophonist Hamiet Bluiett and drummer Billy Cobham, among others. A lengthy "Anita's Dance" and a remake of "Gone, Gone, Gone" are the more memorable selections. —*Scott Yanow*

Live at the Public Theatre in New York, Vol. 2 / Feb. 8, 1980-Feb. 9, 1980 / Black Hawk ✦✦✦

The second of two Gil Evans LPs originally recorded for the Japanese Trio label and put out in the US on the now-defunct Black Hawk company features the veteran arranger leading a 14-piece group at a pair of 1980 concerts. The five selections (which include Jimi Hendrix's "Stone Free," Charles Mingus' "Orange Was the Color of Her Dress" and Evans' "Zee Zee") are given colorful treatment by the unique band, which consists of three keyboardists, a rhythm section propelled by drummer Billy Cobham, three trumpets (Lew Soloff, Jon Faddis and Hannibal Marvin Peterson), two trombones (including George Lewis), John Clark on French horn, baritone saxophonist Hamiet Bluiett and altoist Arthur Blythe. Although the end results do not quite live up to the potential of this unique ensemble, there are plenty of colorful moments. —*Scott Yanow*

British Orchestra / 1983 / Mole ✦✦✦

Although the 13-piece ensemble heard on this CD comprises mostly English players, somehow it still sounds like the Gil Evans Orchestra. Evans travelled to England to lead the all-star group in 1983 and altoist Chris Hunter would eventually join Evans' US outfit. Other impressive soloists include John Surman on baritone and soprano and Stan Sulzmann on tenor and soprano while guitarist Ray Russell is showcased on Jimi Hendrix's "Little Wing." The four selections (which also include "Hotel Me," "London" and Thelonious Monk's "Friday the 13th") tend to be a bit overlong but the spirit and enthusiasm of the players (who sound thrilled to be working with Evans) make this a worthy set. —*Scott Yanow*

Live at Sweet Basil, Vol. 1 / Aug. 20, 1984+Aug. 27, 1984 / Evidence ✦✦

Despite some exciting moments, this CD (which was originally a Gramavision two-LP set) has always been a bit of a disappointment. By 1984, arranger/keyboardist

Gil Evans, who exercised such tight control over his earlier groups, had become very much a laissez-faire leader in that he let his sidemen ramble on and on as long as they felt inspired. During an eighteen-and-a-half-minute "Parabola" and the over twenty-four-and-a-half-minute "Blues in 'C,'" it's as if Evans was not even on the bandstand. His sidemen were obviously quite talented, since they include Lew Soloff and Hannibal Marvin Peterson on trumpets, tenorman George Adams, altoist Chris Hunter, Howard Johnson on tuba, baritone and bass clarinet, guitarist Hiram Bullock and Pete Levin on synthesizer, but the lack of direction by Evans on the eclectic repertoire (which also includes two tunes apiece by Charles Mingus and Jimi Hendrix, in addition to Herbie Hancock's "Prince of Darkness") does not live up to its potential. —*Scott Yanow*

Live at Sweet Basil, Vol. 2 / Aug. 27, 1984 / Evidence ✦✦

This volume (available originally on Gramavision as a two-LP set and reissued on CD by Evidence) has the same faults as the first. Although arranger/keyboardist Gil Evans is the leader of the 14-piece band, he has a very minor presence on the set, letting his talented sidemen get self-indulgent and take seemingly endless solos. Because the supporting cast includes such fine players as trumpeter Lew Soloff, George Adams on tenor, altoist Chris Hunter, guitarist Hiram Bullock and Pete Levin on synthesizer, the music is not without interest. However these endless jams (which range from 11 to almost 23 minutes) on such songs as "Jelly Roll," Thelonious Monk's "Friday the 13th," "Gone" and Jimi Hendrix's "Stone Free" must have been more interesting live than on record. This is a lesser effort that should have been a memorable one. —*Scott Yanow*

Farewell—Live at Sweet Basil / Dec. 1, 1986+Dec. 22, 1986 / Evidence ✦✦✦

This CD (plus *In Memoriam*, another Projazz set taken from the same sessions) contains the last recordings of arranger/pianist Gil Evans with his regular orchestra, other than a set backing rock singer Sting. As was typical for Evans' later-period work, he is content to play quietly while letting his ensemble run somewhat wild. The four pieces, which include the umpteenth remake of Jimi Hendrix's "Little Wing," are all overly long but not without interest. Sidemen include trumpeter Lew Soloff, trombonist Dave Bargeron, John Clark on French horn, altoist Chris Hunter, Bill Evans on tenor and soprano, baritone saxophonist Hamiet Bluiett, guitarist Hiram Bullock and both Peter Levin and Gil Goldstein on synthesizers; fluegelhornist Johnny Coles is a welcome guest. Fans of Gil Evans' 1950s work may not much care for his 1980s electronic band, but this set is fairly coherent and has its exciting moments. —*Scott Yanow*

In Memoriam: Bud and Bird / Dec. 1, 1986+Dec. 22, 1986 / Projazz ✦✦✦

Released posthumously, this CD features the 1986 version of Gil Evans' Monday Night Orchestra. As usual in his later years, Evans' presence is felt rather than heard and he lets his 15-piece ensemble stretch out; in fact four of the five numbers (all but Gil's "Bud and Bird") are group originals. In general the players in Evans' band were fairly young at the time although many of them have had fairly substantial careers since. Among the soloists are altoist Chris Hunter (who sounds fairly close tonewise to David Sanborn), veteran baritonist Hamiet Bluiett, guest trumpeter Johnny Coles, Bill Evans on tenor and soprano, trumpeter Lew Soloff, trombonist Dave Bargeron, John Clark on French horn and Gil Goldstein on synthesizer. Still, there are times during this music when it would have been beneficial for Gil Evans to have played a bigger part; "Groove from the Louvre" certainly did not need to be nearly 22 minutes long. —*Scott Yanow*

Rhythm-A-Ning / Nov. 2, 1987-Nov. 26, 1987 / EmArcy ✦✦✦

This is a very interesting recording. Aging arranger/pianist Gil Evans agreed after much persuasion to come to Paris and play his music at a few concerts with Laurent Cugny's Orchestra. After only one rehearsal, the first event took place, and it gratified Evans to realize that the young French musicians were not only excellent players but big Gil Evans fans. Their interpretations of Thelonious Monk's "Rhythm-A-Ning," "London" and "La Nevada" rank with the best versions of Evans' regular Monday Night Band, and Cugny's "Charlie Mingus' Sound of Love" (an answer to Mingus' "Duke Ellington's Sound of Love") is also excellent. Few of the sidemen, other than tenor saxophonist Andy Sheppard and percussionist Marilyn Mazur, are known in the US, but they did an excellent job of bringing Gil Evans' music to life. —*Scott Yanow*

Paris Blues / Nov. 30, 1987-Dec. 1, 1987 / Owl ✦✦

Recorded just three months before arranger/pianist Gil Evans' death, this duet album teams Evans with the great soprano saxophonist Steve Lacy. In truth, Evans' playing here is generally little more than melody statements and comping behind Lacy and, although the soprano is in top form, little of significance occurs. The duo performs lengthy versions of three Charles Mingus tunes, Duke Ellington's "Paris Blues" and Lacy's "Esteem." Evans was never a masterful keyboardist and clearly was not in Lacy's league as a player, so this CD is of greater interest from a historical standpoint than musical. —*Scott Yanow*

A Tribute to Gil / Jul. 8, 1988-Jul. 24, 1988 / Soul Note ✦✦✦

Four months after arranger/pianist Gil Evans' death, his Monday Night Band fulfilled their engagements playing at Italian jazz festivals. With several alumni and guests added on, the 16-piece ensemble stretches out on two marathon performances ("Orgone" and "London"), makes very concise (under two-minute) statements on "Moonstruck One" and "Eleven," and features the eccentric singer Urszula Dudziak on "Duet." The results are colorful if not all that memorable; among the soloists are trumpeters Lew Soloff and Miles Evans, altoist Chris Hunter, Alex Foster on tenor, guitarist Bireli Legrene (who is quite rockish on "Prelude to Orgone"), violinist Michal Urbaniak and Pete Levin on synthesizer. Gil Evans would have enjoyed this set. —*Scott Yanow*

Herschel Evans

b. Mar. 9, 1909, Denton, TX, **d.** Feb. 9, 1939, New York, NY
Tenor Saxophone / Swing

One of the earliest "tough Texas tenors," Herschel Evans' hard sound was a perfect contrast to that of the cool-toned Lester Young in the Count Basie Orchestra. He started out playing in territory bands including Troy Floyd (1929-31) with whom he made his recording debut and Benny Moten (1933-35). In 1936 Evans had stints with Lionel Hampton and Buck Clayton in Los Angeles and then joined Count Basie just in time to enjoy the band's success and to participate on many recordings; his most famous solo was on a ballad feature "Blue and Sentimental" from 1938. Sadly Herschel Evans died of a heart ailment before his 30th birthday. —*Scott Yanow*

Don Ewell (Donald Tyson Ewell)

b. Nov. 14, 1916, Baltimore, MD, **d.** Aug. 9, 1983, Pompano Beach, FL
Piano / Stride

A major if underrated stride pianist, Don Ewell was inspired by Jelly Roll Morton and Earl Hines but could stride like Fats Waller too. He started leading his own trios in Baltimore in the mid-'30s, played during the New Orleans jazz revival (starting in the mid-'40s) with Bunk Johnson, Muggsy Spanier, Sidney Bechet and Kid Ory (1953) and was with Jack Teagarden during 1957-64. Ewell sometimes played duets with the weakening Willie "The Lion" Smith in the late '60s before moving to New Orleans where he worked regularly during his last years. He recorded for Good Time Jazz (three 1956-57 dates are available on CD), GHB/Audiophile/Jazzology, Delmark, Fat Cat Jazz and Chiaroscuro; previously unreleased sets were issued posthumously by Stomp Off and Pumpkin. —*Scott Yanow*

Music to Listen to Don Ewell By / Mar. 13, 1956-Mar. 14, 1956 / Good Time Jazz ✦✦✦✦✦

Stride pianist Don Ewell made three albums for Good Time Jazz during 1956-57 and all are quite enjoyable. This CD reissues the first of his LPs (great title!) and features Ewell on five solos and seven pieces with a trio that also includes clarinetist Darnell Howard and drummer Minor Hall. Ewell is in top form and the many highlights include "I Can't Believe That You're in Love with Me," Howard's "Bush Street Scramble," "You Took Advantage of Me" and "My Honey's Lovin' Arms." —*Scott Yanow*

Chicago '57 / 1957 / Stomp Off ✦✦✦✦

This valuable program of piano solos by the underrated classic jazz pianist Don Ewell (who was 40 in 1957) was first released in 1984 as a Stomp Off LP. Privately recorded for fans who wanted examples of his playing, Ewell explored tunes associated with Fats Waller and Jelly Roll Morton plus a few favorite standards and his own "Frisco Rider." Although the sound quality is not perfect, the music (highlighted by "Everybody Loves My Baby," "Handful of Keys," "Sunday," "Just You, Just Me" and "The Pearls") is quite wonderful and easily compensates for the minor imperfections. —*Scott Yanow*

Free 'n Easy / Jun. 21, 1957-Jun. 22, 1957 / Good Time Jazz ✦✦✦✦

This out-of-print LP, recorded the same two days as *Man Here Plays Fine Piano* (which is more easily available on CD), is the equal of its companion. Five pieces are taken as piano solos by Don Ewell (including Jelly Roll Morton's "Chicago Breakdown" and "Just You, Just Me"), "Blue Turning Grey over You" has Ewell joined by drummer Minor Hall and the remaining five numbers are quartet explorations by Ewell, Hall, bassist Pops Foster and the fine New Orleans-style clarinetist Darnell Howard; of the latter tunes "Wolverine Blues" and "Blues My Naughty Sweetie Gives to Me" are most memorable. Well worth searching for, hopefully Fantasy will reissue this excellent set on CD someday. —*Scott Yanow*

● **Man Here Plays Fine Piano** / Jun. 21, 1957-Jun. 22, 1957 / Good Time Jazz ✦✦✦✦✦

During a two-day period in 1957, pianist Don Ewell teamed up with clarinetist Darnell Howard, bassist Pops Foster and drummer Minor Hall to record enough music for two albums. While this set has been reissued on CD, *Free 'n' Easy* remains out-

of-print. In addition to six fine quartet pieces (including "Everybody Loves My Baby" and "Keepin' Out of Mischeif Now"), there are four solo performances that fully showcase the underrated but talented New Orleans piano of Don Ewell. Easily recommended to fans of classic jazz. —*Scott Yanow*

Don Ewell and His All-Stars / 1965 / Jazzology ✦✦✦✦

One of the top pianists to emerge from the New Orleans revival of the 1940s (he would have been a major name in jazz history books if he had been born 20 years earlier), Don Ewell always sounded good no matter what the setting. On this spirited LP he is joined by four obscure players (trumpeter Larry Conger, trombonist Charlie Bornemann, bassist Johny Haines and drummer Don "Pops" Campbell) plus pianist Butch Thompson who on the date exclusively plays clarinet. The high-quality compositions (including "Rose of Washington Square," Johnny Dodds' "Oriental Man," "Home" and "Take Me to the Land of Jazz"), the spirited playing and the excellent pacing make this an album that New Orleans and classic jazz fans will want to search for. —*Scott Yanow*

Don Ewell in New Orleans / Apr. 22, 1965 / GHB ✦✦

Pianist Don Ewell teams up with the Jazzology poll winners of 1964 for a somewhat primitive if sincere effort. Ewell, a superior improviser able to play both stride and Jelly Roll Morton's music with creativity, is a bit out-of-place in this group which also includes the emotional and erratic trumpeter Kid Thomas Valentine, the fine trombonist Jim Robinson, veteran clarinetist George Lewis, banjoist George Guesnon, bassist Alcide Pavageau and drummer Cie Frazier. Although Ewell is supposedly the leader, he is not that well-featured and the repertoire (which includes rough versions of "Sentimental Journey," "The Sheik of Araby," "Ciribiribin" and "'Lil Liza Jane") and the loose ensembles are not up to his usual standards. —*Scott Yanow*

Don Ewell's Hot 4 / Jun. 5, 1966 / Biograph ✦✦✦

This LP is a charming if not essential session in which pianist Don Ewell is teamed up with clarinetist George Lewis and drummer Cie Frazier for five trios and (with the addition of trombonist Jim Robinson) five quartet numbers. The music generally features strong melodies with an emphasis on group improvising although Ewell does get in a few piano solos. Highlights include "When My Dreamboat Comes Home," "Stumblin'," "Baby Face" and two versions of "Georgia Camp Meeting." —*Scott Yanow*

Denver Concert / Dec. 14, 1966 / Pumpkin ✦✦✦✦

This collector's LP is one of the better Don Ewell records. Captured in concert in 1966, Ewell performs duets with bassist Charles Burrell (including Jelly Roll Morton, Earl Hines and Fats Waller medleys), plays a couple of other Morton numbers ("The Pearls" and "Sweet Substitute") and backs singer Barbara Dane on four trad jazz favorites. A well-rounded effort that finds Ewell paying tribute to his main influences, this frequently joyous album is becoming increasingly difficult to find. —*Scott Yanow*

Jazz on a Sunday Afternoon / Jan. 19, 1969+May 9, 1969 / Fat Cat Jazz ✦✦✦✦

Don Ewell's first full-length set of piano solos since 1957 finds the 52-year old stride pianist in top form. He emphasizes songs that he had not recorded in this setting before in three medleys (two of which feature tunes associated with Earl Hines and McKinney's Cotton Pickers), plays obscurities by Jelly Roll Morton and Fats Waller (his two main influences) and, in addition to a few standards, performs a pair of originals. Ewell, one of the underrated greats, is sometimes left out of jazz history books because he matured in the 1950s rather than the 1920s. This fine LP (originally put out by Fat Cat Jazz and then reissued by Storyville) is worth searching for. —*Scott Yanow*

Don Ewell Quintet / Feb. 1971 / Jazzology ✦✦✦

For this Dixieland date, pianist Don Ewell travelled to England and recorded with four fine British players: trumpeter Pat Halcox (best-known for his long association with Chris Barber's band), clarinetist John Defferray (a protege of Albert Nicholas), bassist Jackie Flavelle and drummer Barry Martyn. Ten veteran songs (mostly well-known standards) were performed and, although no real surprises occur, Ewell and his sidemen take consistently satisfying and swinging solos. Easily recommended to Dixieland fans although Ewell's solo and trio recordings are generally more essential. —*Scott Yanow*

Don Ewell / Sep. 25, 1973-1974 / Chiaroscuro ✦✦✦✦

This out-of-print Chiaroscuro LP features the superb stride pianist Don Ewell with two different small groups. Four songs (swing era standards) are performed with tenor saxophonist Buddy Tate, bassist George Duvivier and drummer Cliff Leeman while the other five tunes (which date back to the 1920s) are played in a trio with Leeman and clarinetist Herb Hall. Ewell is heard throughout in prime form, whether soloing in a style influenced by Jelly Roll Morton, Earl Hines and Fats Waller or accompanying the horns. The enjoyable set is long overdue to be reissued on CD. —*Scott Yanow*

Jon Faddis

b. Jul. 24, 1953, Oakland, CA
Trumpet / Bop

When Jon Faddis burst onto the jazz scene as a teenager, observers were amazed by his technique and his ability to sound like an identical twin of Dizzy Gillespie (whose complex style had never been successfully duplicated before). After a period he was typecast as a Dizzy imitator, but Faddis' remarkable range (hitting higher notes than Gillespie ever could) and the gradual development of his individual sound have helped him to overcome the early fault. In fact Faddis can now also imitate Roy Eldridge and Louis Armstrong quite well too. Dizzy was always Jon Faddis' idol, from the time he started playing trumpet at age eight. After moving to New York in the early '70s, Faddis played with Lionel Hampton and Charles Mingus (guesting on a recorded concert with the bassist when Roy Eldridge became ill) and then recorded two notable albums for Pablo including a duet session with Oscar Peterson. After playing a bit with Dizzy Gillespie (their best encounters in the mid-'70s were unfortunately not recorded), Faddis seemed to disappear, sticking to studio work and playing first trumpet with the Thad Jones/Mel Lewis Orchestra. After re-emerging in the mid-'80s, Jon Faddis recorded for Concord and Epic and in 1993 became the musical director of the Carnegie Hall Jazz Orchestra. —*Scott Yanow*

Jon & Billy / Mar. 13, 1974 / Evidence ♦♦♦
Just 20 at the time, trumpeter Jon Faddis meets up with the intense tenor Billy Harper on this quintet set with pianist Roland Hanna (who doubles on electric keyboard), bassist George Mraz and drummer Motohiko Hino. Recorded in Tokyo, the music is actually a bit disturbing, since Faddis and Harper do not blend together that well, and the advanced pieces (by Hanna, Harper and Ron Bridgewater) do not fit the boppish style of Faddis. There are some fireworks (mostly by Harper), but this obscure session (the first to be issued under Jon Faddis' name) is only a limited success. —*Scott Yanow*

Youngblood / Jan. 8, 1976-Jan. 9, 1976 / Pablo ♦♦♦♦♦
Jon Faddis burst onto the jazz scene at an early age, recording a brilliant duo album with pianist Oscar Peterson and this quartet date before disappearing into the studios for a few years. 22 at the time, Faddis (heavily influenced by Dizzy Gillespie but possessing a superior high-note technique) holds his own with pianist Kenny Barron, bassist George Mraz and drummer Mickey Roker. The repertoire has two Dizzy tunes, "'Round Midnight," "Samba De Orpheus," and an effective and emotional rendition of the "Gershwin Prelude No. 2." —*Scott Yanow*

Good and Plenty / Aug. 1978-Sep. 1978 / Buddah ♦♦

● **Legacy** / Aug. 1985 / Concord Jazz ♦♦♦♦♦
After too long a period in the studios, the talented trumpeter Jon Faddis returned to jazz with this brilliant effort. Best known for his ability to closely emulate his idol Dizzy Gillespie (far from an easy feat), Faddis pays tribute to Dizzy with "Night in Tunisia" and "Things to Come." However, he also does a close imitation of Roy Eldridge on "Little Jazz," pays homage to Louis Armstrong on "West End Blues," shows sensitivity on Thad Jones' "A Child Is Born" and performs three other numbers. With the assistance of tenor saxophonist Harold Land, pianist Kenny Barron, bassist Ray Brown and drummer Mel Lewis, Jon Faddis is in superb form throughout this outstanding release, his definitive recording to date. —*Scott Yanow*

Into the Faddisphere / May 2, 1989-May 8, 1989 / Epic ♦♦
At the age of 36, after many years in the shadow of his idol Dizzy Gillespie, trumpeter Jon Faddis was consciously going after developing his own voice. His rhythm section, led by pianist Renee Rosnes (who displays a style influenced by McCoy Tyner), is modern and Faddis plays six of his own compositions (in addition to Donald Brown's "The Early Bird" and "Ciribiribin"). But the trumpeter's seeming inability during this era to stay out of his upper register for more than a minute straight is often quite annoying, completely ruining the modal arrangement of "Ciribiribin." The title cut, a showcase for Faddis' high-note heroics, is also difficult to sit through. A disappointing mixed bag. —*Scott Yanow*

Hornucopia / 1991 / Epic ♦♦♦
This CD finds trumpeter Jon Faddis shooting in all directions with uneven but sometimes colorful results. Faddis performs an orchestra piece ("High Fire") that has his high notes contrasting with the five lower brass. He wa-waas behind Vivian Cherry's blues singing on "Reckless Blues," performs a rather silly "Ahbeedunseedja," plays a faceless ballad ("Forevermore"), raps about Dizzy Gillespie on "Rapartee," and then the two muted trumpeters jam on a brief "Cherokee." "Dewey's Dance" is a dull and overlong tribute of sort to Miles Davis, "Squeezin'" is a relaxed original, "March That Thang" sounds like a funky marching band, "Dizzy Atmosphere" is a fast but brief bop and "I Surrender All" closes the CD with a gospelish duet also including pianist James Williams. There are some good moments on the set but it is too erratic to be recommended very highly. —*Scott Yanow*

The Carnegie Hall Jazz Band / 1995 / Blue Note ♦♦♦
Although the repertoire on this CD includes "In the Mood," "Sing, Sing, Sing" and "I'm Getting Sentimental Over You," this is not a swing revival set. All eight of the standards performed by the all-star Carnegie Hall Jazz Band were rearranged and to an extent reinvented, particularly the more vintage material. Jim McNeely's complex charts for the older songs, while retaining the melody and hints of the famous versions in spots, generally sound like new music. "Shiny Stockings" is given a new chart by Slide Hampton that is not half as memorable as the original and it somehow seems unfair that the more recent "Giant Steps" and "Frame for the Blues" were allowed to keep their original flavor while the swing tunes were drained of their more joyful harmonies. Randy Sandke's arrangement of "South Rampart Street Parade" uses the original framework but has dissonant ensembles and exaggerated parade rhythms that on the whole sound rather dumb. In the program there are some fine solos from trumpeter Jon Faddis (who is also a major force in the ensembles), saxophonists Ted Nash, Jerry Dodgion and Dick Oatts (the latter's Coltranish soprano on "Sing, Sing, Sing" is a high point), trombonists Slide Hampton, Dennis Wilson and Steve Turre, trumpeter Ryan Kisor, pianist Renee Rosnes and drummer Lewis Nash, in addition to guest tenors Lew Tabackin and Frank Wess. But the overall results seem rather pointless, tearing down the past in favor of a concert stage band sound. —*Scott Yanow*

Don Fagerquist (Donald A. Fagerquist)

b. Feb. 6, 1927, Worcester, MA, **d.** Jan. 24, 1974, Los Angeles, CA
Trumpet / Bop, Cool

An excellent trumpeter of the bop and cool eras who largely faded out in the 1960s, Don Fagerquist only had two sessions as a leader, a half-date for Capitol in 1955 and an excellent outing for Mode (reissued on V.S.O.P.) in 1957. Fagerquist was a key soloist with Gene Krupa (off and on during 1944-50), Artie Shaw's Orchestra and Gramercy Five (1949-50), and Woody Herman's Third Herd (1951-52). He was with Les Brown in 1953 and a major soloist with Dave Pell's Octet (1953-59). From 1956 on, Fagerquist worked as a staff musician for Paramount films, although he still recorded jazz now and then with Pete Rugolo, Mel Tormé and Art Pepper among others. —*Scott Yanow*

● **Eight by Eight** / Sep. 14, 1957 / V.S.O.P. ♦♦♦♦♦
With the exception of three selections from 1955, this was the only session that trumpeter Don Fagerquist ever led. Performing in a nonet arranged by Marty Paich (who also plays piano), Faqerquist's attractive and mellow tone is well showcased on this CD reissue, as is his fine boppish style. The supporting cast, which includes altoist Herb Geller and valve trombonist Bob Enevoldsen, also gets chances to shine during the eight standards. Easily recommended to bop fans. —*Scott Yanow*

Charles Fambrough

b. Aug. 25, 1950, Philadelphia, PA
Bass / Post-Bop, Hard Bop

Best known for his stint with Art Blakey's Jazz Messengers, bassist Charles Fambrough has led three very effective all-star dates for CTI that were filled with his stimulating originals. He originally studied classical piano but switched to bass when he was 13. In 1968 Fambrough began playing with local pit bands for musicals and after some freelancing in 1970 he joined Grover Washington, Jr.'s band, staying with the popular saxophonist up until 1974. Fambrough was with Airto (1975-77), McCoy Tyner (1978-80) and then Art Blakey (1980-82). Since that time he has freelanced in many different situations. Fambrough's sidemen on his CTI recordings have thus far included Wynton and Branford Marsalis, Roy Hargrove, Kenny Kirkland, Jerry Gonzalez, Steve Turre, Donald Harrison, Kenny Garrett, Abdullah Ibrahim and Grover Washington, Jr.! —*Scott Yanow*

● **The Proper Angle** / May 29, 1991-May 31, 1991 / CTI ✦✦✦✦

Bassist Charles Fambrough gathered together a rather impressive lineup of young greats (including on various cuts trumpeters Wynton Marsalis and Roy Hargrove, saxophonists Branford Marsalis and Joe Ford, keyboardist Kenny Kirkland, drummer Jeff Watts and three percussionists) for a set of tricky hard bop originals. The interplay between the two Marsalises on the rapid "Broksi" is a high point, but the solos throughout the date are uniformly strong. Fambrough (who contributed seven of the pieces) stated accurately that the music reflects his periods with McCoy Tyner, Art Blakey, Grover Washington, Jr., and Airto. His well-conceived set is highly recommended. —*Scott Yanow*

The Charmer / Oct. 22, 1991-Sep. 24, 1992 / CTI ✦✦✦✦

As usual, bassist Charles Fambrough assembled an impressive all-star group for this CD. Such players as altoist Kenny Garrett, Grover Washington, Jr. (on soprano), trumpeter Roy Hargrove, pianist Kenny Kirkland and even pianist Abdullah Ibrahim (making a rare appearance as a sideman for his own "Beautiful Love") are heard from, along with a few overlapping rhythm sections. The music ranges from light swing and some funky moments to Ibrahim's spiritual piece. Fambrough is generous in allocating solo space, allowing his illustrious guests to make strong impressions. —*Scott Yanow*

Blues at Bradley's / Feb. 25, 1993-Feb. 26, 1993 / CTI ✦✦✦✦

Charles Fambrough, who first gained recognition as a bassist with Art Blakey's Jazz Messengers, has proven with his releases thus far that he is also a talented composer and bandleader. Four of the five diverse pieces on this CD are his, and Fambrough's octet (which includes altoist Donald Harrison, trombonist Steve Turre and Joe Ford on soprano) does a splendid job of interpreting the often-challenging but swinging repertoire. This is high-quality modern mainstream music. —*Scott Yanow*

City Tribes / Apr. 10, 1995-Apr. 12, 1995 / Evidence ✦✦✦✦

Upright Citizen / 1997 / Nu Groove ✦✦✦

Tal Farlow (Talmadge Farlow)

b. Jun. 7, 1921, Greensboro, NC
Guitar / Bop, Cool

Nearly as famous for his reluctance to play as for his outstanding abilities, guitarist Tal Farlow has been semi-retired since 1958, although whenever he gets around to playing, he sounds in peak form. He did not take up the guitar until he was already 21 but within a year was playing professionally and in 1948 was with Marjorie Hyams' band. While with the Red Norvo Trio (which originally included Charles Mingus) from 1949-53, Farlow became famous in the jazz world. His huge hands and ability to play rapid yet light lines made him one of the top guitarists of the era. After six months with Artie Shaw's Gramercy Five in 1953, Farlow put together his own group, which for a time included pianist Eddie Costa. Late in 1958 Farlow settled in New England, became a sign painter and just played locally. He only made one record as a leader during 1960-75 but emerged a bit more often during 1976-84, recording for Concord fairly regularly before largely disappearing again. Profiled in the definitive documentary *Talmage Farlow*, the guitarist can be heard on his own records for Blue Note (1954), Verve, Prestige (1969) and Concord. —*Scott Yanow*

The Tal Farlow Album / Apr. 11, 1954-Jul. 5, 1955 / Verve ✦✦✦✦✦

Guitarist Tal Farlow's second album as a leader (following a very obscure effort for Blue Note), as is true of his other valuable Verve releases, has not yet been reissued on CD. Joined by rhythm guitarist Barry Galbraith, bassist Oscar Pettiford and drummer Joe Morello on eight numbers, and pianist Claude Williamson and bassist Red Mitchell for the remaining four, Farlow is heard in his early prime. thirty-two at the time, Farlow was a brilliant technician who could play extremely fast yet clean and with a light touch. His solos on the 11 standards (which include Pettiford's "Blues in the Closet," "Stompin' at the Savoy" and "You and the Night and the Music"), plus his own "Gibson Boy," are hard-swinging and creative, yet thoughtful. —*Scott Yanow*

Autumn in New York / Nov. 15, 1954 / Verve ✦✦✦✦

A generally relaxed date (only "Cherokee" is uptempo), Tal Farlow's pretty tone and tasteful improvising style are the main reasons to search for this rare LP. Pianist Gerry Wiggins, bassist Ray Brown and drummer Chico Hamilton offer quiet and swinging support of the great guitarist, who performs two originals ("And She Remembers Me" and "Tal's Blues"), plus six superior standards. All of Farlow's difficult-to-find Verve releases of the 1950s are recommended. —*Scott Yanow*

Tal / Jun. 1956 / Verve ✦✦✦✦✦

The perfect setting for the brilliant guitarist Tal Farlow is the format heard on this classic LP, a drumless trio. Farlow, pianist Eddie Costa and bassist Vinnie Burke made for an exciting team, really romping on the uptempo pieces. Highlights of the often-heated set include "There Is No Greater Love," "Anything Goes," "Yesterdays" and "Broadway," but all eight numbers are quite enjoyable. —*Scott Yanow*

Fuerst Set / Dec. 18, 1956 / Xanadu ✦✦✦✦

The "Fuerst" in the title refers to Ed Fuerst, who had frequent jazz parties in his apartment and recorded this set and its follow-up. Featured is one of guitarist Tal Farlow's finest groups, a trio with pianist Eddie Costa (whose lower-register solos were distinctive) and bassist Vinnie Burke. The group stretches out on four lengthy numbers: "Jordu," "Have You Met Miss Jones?," a nearly fifteen-and-a-half-minute rendition of "Out of Nowhere" (which has a vocal by Gene Williams) and "Opus De Funk." There are many hot sections on the album, and the recording quality is quite listenable. —*Scott Yanow*

Second Set / Dec. 18, 1956 / Xanadu ✦✦✦✦

Tal Farlow was one of the finest guitarists to emerge during the 1950s. The exciting trio he performs with during this record (which was recorded in a friend's apartment) also features pianist Eddie Costa and bassist Vinnie Burke. The recording quality is generally quite good and the lengthy performances of the four standards never lose their momentum, except when the tape ran out during "Let's Do It." These boppish performances (with plenty of impressive interplay by the musicians) will certainly please straightahead jazz fans. —*Scott Yanow*

The Return of Tal Farlow: 1969 / Sep. 23, 1969 / Original Jazz Classics ✦✦✦✦✦

After recording a series of rewarding albums in the 1950s, guitarist Tal Farlow largely dropped out of the jazz scene, being quite content to be a sign painter in New England. This Prestige set (reissued on CD) was his first in a decade and would be followed by another seven years of silence. Fortunately, Farlow had continued playing on a low-profile basis in the interim, and he was still very much in top form. Joined by pianist John Scully, bassist Jack Six and drummer Alan Dawson, Farlow performs swinging versions of seven standards, including "Straight, No Chaser," "I'll Remember April" and "Crazy, She Calls Me." Recommended. —*Scott Yanow*

A Sign of the Times / Aug. 2, 1976 / Concord Jazz ✦✦✦

Guitarist Tal Farlow's debut for the Concord label was only his second album as a leader since 1959. Farlow, who had given up the hectic lifestyle of a full-time jazz musician to become a sign painter who played guitar on the side, had not lost any of his power or creative swing through the years. Teamed up in a drumless trio with pianist Hank Jones and bassist Ray Brown, Farlow is in typically brilliant form on such numbers as a rapid "Fascinating Rhythm," a slower-than-usual "Stompin' at the Savoy," Dave Brubeck's "In Your Own Sweet Way" and even "Put on a Happy Face." This CD is a fine example of Tal Farlow's talents. —*Scott Yanow*

On Stage / Aug. 1976 / Concord Jazz ✦✦✦✦

Other than a Prestige date in 1969, this was guitarist Tal Farlow's first recording in nearly 17 years. He is heard at a reunion with vibraphonist Red Norvo and matching wits with pianist Hank Jones, bassist Ray Brown and drummer Jake Hanna. Recorded at the 1976 Concord Jazz Festival, this was Farlow's first of six Concord albums, and it led to a slightly higher profile for him than during the previous decade. Highlights of the joyous occasion include Norvo's feature on "The One I Love Belongs to Somebody Else," a heated "Lullaby of Birdland" and a colorful rendition of "My Shining Hour." Highly recommended to straightahead jazz fans. —*Scott Yanow*

Trilogy / Sep. 14, 1976+Sep. 21, 1976 / Inner City ✦✦✦

This lesser-known LP was originally released by Japanese Columbia, was made available domestically by Inner City in 1981, and then went out of print when the label folded. The music is typically excellent (Tal Farlow has yet to record an unworthy date), with the very fluent bop guitarist jamming on seven standards and two originals with pianist Mike Nock, bassist Lynn Christie and (on just one song) drummer Bob Jaspe. Pick this one up if you see it. —*Scott Yanow*

Tal Farlow 1978 / Sep. 15, 1977 / Concord Jazz ✦✦✦

Farlow tends to dominate this good trio date. —*Ron Wynn*

Chromatic Palette / Jan. 1981 / Concord Jazz ✦✦✦✦

This album is most notable for the interplay between veteran guitarist Tal Farlow and pianist Tommy Flanagan. With bassist Gary Mazzaroppi completing the trio, the musicians perform Tal's "Blue Art, Too" (based on a blues), plus seven superior standards including "Nuages," "If I Were a Bell" and "St. Thomas." In general, the music is on the relaxed side but there is plenty of inner heat to be felt on the fine set. —*Scott Yanow*

● **Cookin' on All Burners** / Aug. 1982 / Concord Jazz ✦✦✦✦✦
On the fifth of six Concord albums (a surprising amount of activity considering that he only played locally in the New England area during most of 1957-75, the brilliant bop-based guitarist Tal Farlow performs concise renditions (none over six-and-a-half minutes) of nine standards with pianist James Williams, bassist Gary Mazzaroppi and drummer Vinnie Johnson. Highlights of the excellent straightahead date include "You'd Be So Nice to Come Home To," "I've Got the World on a String," "Love Letters" and "Just Friends." —*Scott Yanow*

The Legendary / Sep. 1984 / Concord Jazz ✦✦✦✦
Strange as it seems, this was only the third Tal Farlow album (and first since 1959) to have a horn player. Sam Most (a classic flutist who is also a fine cool-toned tenor saxophonist) is on five of the eight standards, and he blends quite well with Farlow. With pianist Frank Strazzeri, bassist Bob Maize and drummer Al "Tootie" Heath completing the quintet, Farlow (63 at the time) sounds quite inspired. "You Stepped out of a Dream," "When Lights Are Low" and "Who Cares?" are most memorable. —*Scott Yanow*

Art Farmer

b. Aug. 21, 1928, Council Bluffs, IA
Fluegelhorn, Trumpet / Cool, Hard Bop, Bop
Largely overlooked during his formative years, Art Farmer's consistently inventive playing has been more greatly appreciated as he continues to develop. Along with Clark Terry, Farmer helped to popularize the fluegelhorn among brass players. His lyricism gives his bop-oriented style its own personality. Farmer studied piano, violin and tuba before settling on trumpet. He worked in Los Angeles from 1945 on, performing regularly on Central Avenue and spending time in the bands of Johnny Otis, Jay McShann, Roy Porter, Benny Carter and Gerald Wilson among others; some of the groups also included his twin brother bassist Addison Farmer (1928-63). After playing with Wardell Gray (1951-52) and touring Europe with Lionel Hampton's big band (1953), Farmer moved to New York and worked with Gigi Gryce (1954-56), Horace Silver's Quintet (1956-58) and the Gerry Mulligan Quartet (1958-9). Farmer, who made many recordings in the latter half of the 1950s (including with Quincy Jones and George Russell and on some jam-session dates for Prestige), co-led the Jazztet with Benny Golson (1959-62) and then had a group with Jim Hall (1962-64). He moved to Vienna in 1968, where he joined the Austrian Radio Orchestra, worked with the Kenny Clarke-Francy Boland Big Band and toured with his own units. Since the 1980s Farmer has visited the US more often and has remained greatly in demand up to the present day. Art Farmer has recorded many sessions as a leader through the years, for labels including Prestige, Contemporary, United Artists, Argo, Mercury, Atlantic, Columbia, CTI, Soul Note, Optimism, Concord, Enja and Sweet Basil. —*Scott Yanow*

The Art Farmer Septet Plays Arrangents / Jul. 2, 1953-Jun. 7, 1954 / Original Jazz Classics ✦✦✦✦
This CD reissue features the mellow-toned but hard-swinging trumpeter Art Farmer on a pair of four-song sessions from 1953 and 1954. Among Farmer's sidemen are trombonist Jimmy Cleveland, either Clifford Solomon or Charlie Rouse on tenor and Horace Silver or Quincy Jones on piano. In addition, Farmer is showcased on a version of "When Your Lover Has Gone" that is taken from a 1956 album titled *Two Trumpets*. Highlights overall include "Mau Mau," "Up in Quincy's Room," "Evening in Paris" and "Elephant Walk." An excellent early hard bop set. —*Scott Yanow*

Early Art / Jan. 20, 1954+Nov. 9, 1954 / Original Jazz Classics ✦✦✦✦
Two of trumpeter Art Farmer's earlier sessions as a leader are reissued on this CD in the OJC series. Farmer teams up with an all-star quintet (which includes tenor saxophonist Sonny Rollins, pianist Horace Silver, bassist Percy Heath and drummer Kenny Clarke) for four songs and dominates a quartet (with pianist Wynton Kelly, bassist Addison Farmer and drummer Herbie Lovelle) on six other tunes. Farmer's sound is lyrical even on the uptempo pieces and he is heard throughout in his early prime. Highlights include "Soft Shoe," "I'll Take Romance," "Autumn Nocturne" and an uptempo "Gone with the Wind." One should note that the programming differs from what is listed, with "Soft Shoe" (which should have been the opener) actually appearing fifth and the songs listed as appearing second through fifth moving up to first through fourth. Despite that flaw, the music is quite enjoyable and a must for 1950s bop collectors. —*Scott Yanow*

When Farmer Met Gryce / May 19, 1954+May 26, 1955 / Original Jazz Classics ✦✦✦✦
This CD reissue brings back a former LP featuring trumpeter Art Farmer, altoist Gigi Gryce and two rhythm sections with either Horace Silver or Freddie Redd on piano, Percy Heath or Addison Farmer on bass and Kenny Clarke or Art Taylor on drums. The early hard bop music is highlighted by "Social Call" (one of Gryce's best-known compositions), "Capri," "A Night at Tony's" and "Blue Concept," but all eight numbers will easily be enjoyed by straightahead jazz fans. —*Scott Yanow*

The Art Farmer Quintet / Oct. 21, 1955 / Original Jazz Classics ✦✦✦✦✦
During 1955 trumpeter Art Farmer had a short-lived quintet with altoist Gigi Gryce but, because neither of the co-leaders was a big name at the time, the band did not last long. Fortunately they did record two records of material, of which this CD reissue (originally known as *Evening in Casablanca*) was the second. In addition to Farmer and Gryce, the unit includes pianist Duke Jordan, bassist Addison Farmer and drummer Philly Joe Jones. With the exception of Duke Jordan's "Forecast," the cool-toned hard bop date consists entirely of Gigi Gryce compositions of which "Evening in Casablanca" and "Nice's Tempo" are best known. Excellent music, well deserving a close listen. —*Scott Yanow*

Last Night When We Were Young / Mar. 28, 1957-Apr. 29, 1957 / ABC/Paramount ✦✦✦✦
The beauty of Art Farmer's tone is well featured on this out-of-print ABC/Paramount album. Farmer is backed by a string orchestra arranged by Quincy Jones as he plays lyrical solos on eight standards and Dizzy Gillespie's "Tangorine." Farmer mostly sticks close to the melodies but he makes such tunes as "Two Sleepy People," "Ill Wind" and "When I Fall in Love" sound fresh and pretty. Although worth searching for, this obscure session will probably not be reissued on CD anytime soon. —*Scott Yanow*

Portrait of Art Farmer / Apr. 19, 1958+May 1, 1958 / Original Jazz Classics ✦✦✦✦✦
This CD reissue (which adds a version of "The Folks Who Live on the Hill" to the original LP program) is an excellent showcase for trumpeter Art Farmer in the 1950s. Farmer is showcased with a quartet that also includes pianist Hank Jones, bassist Addison Farmer and drummer Roy Haynes. The repertoire alternates veteran standards with lesser-known material including three of Farmer's originals and George Russell's "Nita," along with a particularly strong version of Benny Golson's "Stablemates." An excellent outing. —*Scott Yanow*

Modern Art / Sep. 10, 1958-Sep. 14, 1958 / Blue Note ✦✦✦✦
For this CD reissue from over a year before the Jazztet was formed, trumpeter Art Farmer teams up with his future co-leader, tenor saxophonist Benny Golson. With a strong rhythm section consisting of pianist Bill Evans, bassist Addison Farmer and drummer Dave Bailey, Farmer and Golson perform two of their originals and such songs as "Darn That Dream," "Like Someone in Love" and "Cool Breeze." The straightahead hard bop music (originally out on United Artists) is as successful as one would expect; Farmer and Golson always brought out the best in each other. —*Scott Yanow*

★ **Meet the Jazztet** / Feb. 6, 1960-Feb. 10, 1960 / MCA/Chess ✦✦✦✦✦
Although this CD has the same program as the original LP, it gets the highest rating because it is a hard bop classic. Not only does it include superior solos from trumpeter Art Farmer, trombonist Curtis Fuller, tenor saxophonist Benny Golson and pianist McCoy Tyner (who was making his recording debut), along with fine backup from bassist Addison Farmer and drummer Lex Humphries, it features the writing of Golson. Highlights include the original version of "Killer Joe" along with early renditions of "I Remember Clifford" and "Blues March." This was Fuller and Tyner's only recording with the original Jazztet and all ten selections (which also include "Serenata," "It Ain't Necessarily So," "It's All Right with Me" and "Easy Living") are quite memorable. —*Scott Yanow*

Blues on Down / Sep. 16, 1960-May 15, 1961 / Chess ✦✦✦✦
Musically this set finds the Jazztet in top form, but the CD reissue is faulty and incomplete, only including seven of the nine selections from the studio date *Big City Sounds* and four of the six numbers from the concert *The Jazztet at Birdhouse*. Why the "sampler" approach to such valuable and historical material? The Jazztet recorded six albums during 1960-62 before breaking up and this single CD has "highlights" from the second and fourth dates; a two-CD set would have allowed GRP/Chess to reissue the complete contents of the group's second, fourth and long out-of-print third dates. In any case, the music is excellent, featuring trumpeter Art Farmer, tenor saxophonist Benny Golson and trombonist Tom McIntosh along with pianist Cedar Walton, bassist Tommy Williams and drummer Albert "Tootie" Heath. Golson's writing (four of his compositions are here) and arranging gave this group its own sound. High points include "Hi-Fly," the atmospheric "Five Spot After Dark," "Con Alma," "Farmer's Market" and a lengthy

"'Round Midnight." This CD is worth picking up until GRP (or its European equivalent) gets around to reissuing the material properly. —*Scott Yanow*

Perception / Oct. 25, 1961-Oct. 27, 1961 / Argo ✦✦✦✦
The mellow-toned Art Farmer, who during this period switched from trumpet to playing exclusively fluegelhorn, is well showcased on what is unfortunately a long-unavailable LP. Accompanied by pianist Harold Mabern, bassist Tommy Williams and drummer Roy McCurdy (all members with Farmer of the Jazztet at the time), Art sounds quite thoughtful and relaxed, even on the hotter tunes. Among the highlights are Tom McIntosh's "The Day After," "Lullaby of the Leaves," "Blue Room" and "Change Partners." —*Scott Yanow*

Here and Now / Feb. 28, 1962+Mar. 2, 1962 / Mercury ✦✦✦✦
The Jazztet had been in existence for two years when they recorded what would be their final LPs, this date plus *Another Git Together.* The personnel (other than the two co-leaders, fluegelhornist Art Farmer and tenor saxophonist Benny Golson) had completely changed since 1960 but the group sound was the same. The 1962 version of the Jazztet included trombonist Grachan Moncur III, pianist Harold Mabern, bassist Herbie Lewis and drummer Roy McCurdy and it is remarkable to think that this talent-filled group could not find enough jobs to stay together. Highlights of their excellent out-of-print LP include Ray Bryant's "Tonk," "Whisper Not," "Just in Time" and Thelonious Monk's "Ruby My Dear." A classic if short-lived hard bop group. —*Scott Yanow*

Another Git Together / May 28, 1962+Jun. 21, 1962 / Mercury ✦✦✦✦
Recorded at the same sessions that resulted in *Here and Now,* this Mercury LP was the sixth and final one that documented the Jazztet before their breakup. The group lasted less than three years, which is surprising considering the talent. The 1962 edition of the Jazztet consisted of fluegelhornist Art Farmer, tenor saxophonist Benny Golson, trombonist Grachan Moncur III, pianist Harold Mabern, bassist Herbie Lewis and drummer Albert "Tootie" Heath. This spirited and swinging set has six strong selections, with the most memorable including Moncur's "Space Station," Golson's "Along Came Betty" and the standard "This Nearly Was Mine." Along with the other Jazztet dates, this LP is long overdue to be reissued in full on CD. —*Scott Yanow*

Live at the Half Note / Dec. 5, 1963-Dec. 7, 1963 / Atlantic ✦✦✦✦✦
After the Jazztet that he co-led with tenor saxophonist Benny Golson broke up, fluegelhornist Art Farmer led a pianoless quartet during 1963-64 with guitarist Jim Hall. For this reissue in the Atlantic *Jazzlore* series, Farmer and Hall are joined by bassist Steve Swallow and drummer Walter Perkins. Their repertoire is a bit surprising since four of the five songs were veteran swing standards; all but Miles Davis' obscure "Swing Spring." Hall (who has "I'm Gettin' Sentimental over You" as his feature) was a perfect musical partner for Farmer since both musicians have mellow sounds and thoughtful improvising styles that are more complex than expected. This 1987 reissue is well worth picking up. The group only lasted long enough to make three records, all of which are out of print. —*Scott Yanow*

The Time and the Place / Feb. 8, 1967 / Columbia ✦✦✦✦
Recorded shortly before he moved to Europe, this spirited hard bop set features Art Farmer leading an all-star quintet with tenor saxophonist Jimmy Heath, pianist Cedar Walton, bassist Walter Booker and drummer Mickey Roker. Ten of the twelve numbers were recorded at a live concert (the other two were cut slightly later in the studios), and this two-LP set increases the original release from seven to twelve cuts. Farmer is particularly inspired on the ballads, including "The Shadow of Your Smile," and the highlights also include "Make Someone Happy," "On the Trail" and "Blue Bossa." Hopefully, the music on this 1982 two-fer will appear on CD. —*Scott Yanow*

Art Farmer Quintet Plays the Great Jazz Hits / May 16, 1967-Jun. 7, 1967 / Columbia ✦✦✦
The title of this reissue LP is a bit ironic for jazz was really struggling commercially in 1967 and the "hits" were few and far between. In fact, fluegelhornist Art Farmer, who leads the notable hard bop quintet (with Jimmy Heath on tenor, pianist Cedar Walton, bassist Walter Booker and drummer Mickey Roker), would be moving to Europe the following year, where he would work much more often than he had in the US. The ten numbers on this LP were fairly popular, particularly such tunes as "Song for My Father," "The Sidewinder," "Watermelon Man" and "Take Five." The quintet's concise interpretations (no performance is over six minutes) are melodic without being overly predictable. As usual, Farmer's lyricism by itself is a good reason to search for this underrated album. —*Scott Yanow*

From Vienna with Art / Sep. 7, 1970 / MPS ✦✦✦
This album features a standard quintet with fluegelhornist Art Farmer, Jimmy Heath (on tenor, soprano and flute) and pianist Fritz Pauer taking the solos. What makes this out-of-print LP (last available on Pausa) more special than normal are the six rarely performed compositions, none of which became standards but all of

which hold one's interest. Tom McIntosh's "The Day After," the Farmer-Heath collaboration "Con-Fab" and Fritz Pauer's "Whole Tone Stomp" are good vehicles for these musicians' talents. —*Scott Yanow*

Gentle Eyes / 1972 / Mainstream ✦✦
Fluegelhornist Art Farmer has recorded very few albums through the years that are not worth getting, but this sleepy affair with a European string section is unremittingly dull. Farmer sticks to ballads including "Didn't We?," "We've Only Just Begun" and "God Bless the Child," and the arrangements for the 15 strings, five horns and rhythm section are quite boring. There are many rewarding Art Farmer dates currently available, so skip this misfire. —*Scott Yanow*

To Duke with Love / Mar. 5, 1975 / Inner City ✦✦✦✦✦
Recorded less than a year after Duke Ellington's death, this Inner City LP (originally cut for the Japanese East Wind label) features fluegelhornist Art Farmer performing five Ellington pieces along with Billy Strayhorn's "Lush Life." With impeccable support by pianist Cedar Walton, bassist Sam Jones and drummer Billy Higgins, Farmer sounds melodic, lyrical, swinging and typically inventive on such numbers as "In a Sentimental Mood," "It Don't Mean a Thing," "The Brown Skin Gal" and "Love You Madly." This tasteful set (which is long out of print) features Art Farmer at his best. —*Scott Yanow*

Summer Knows / May 12, 1976-May 13, 1976 / Inner City ✦✦✦
This relaxed session features fluegelhornist Art Farmer in a quartet with pianist Cedar Walton, bassist Sam Jones and drummer Billy Higgins. The material (which includes such tunes as "Alfie," "When I Fall in Love" and "I Should Care") is given lyrical treatment by these masterful players on this ballad-dominated date. —*Scott Yanow*

Art Farmer Quintet at Boomer's / May 14, 1976-May 15, 1976 / Inner City ✦✦✦✦
Although fluegelhornist Art Farmer permanently moved to Europe in 1968, he has returned many times to the US to play. For this live LP (recorded for East Wind and released domestically by the defunct Inner City label), Farmer joins up with tenor saxophonist Clifford Jordan, pianist Cedar Walton, bassist Sam Jones and drummer Billy Higgins for lengthy versions of Charlie Parker's blues "Barbados," "I Remember Clifford," "'Round Midnight" and "Will You Still Be Mine?" The group had not rehearsed beforehand, but rehearsals were not really needed for these hard bop veterans and even an uptempo version of the ballad "Will You Still Be Mine" comes off quite well. —*Scott Yanow*

On the Road / Jul. 26, 1976-Aug. 16, 1976 / Original Jazz Classics ✦✦✦✦
This CD reissue of a Contemporary set from 1976 features a logical but only one-time collaboration between fluegelhornist Art Farmer and altoist Art Pepper. With pianist Hampton Hawes, bassist Ray Brown and either Steve Ellington or Shelly Manne on drums completing the quintet, the five standards and Hawes' original "Downwind" were certainly in good hands. A special highlight is a duet version of "My Funny Valentine" featuring Farmer and Hawes. Everyone plays up to par on this spirited straightahead set. —*Scott Yanow*

Crawl Space / Jan. 1977 / CTI ✦✦✦✦
Some of the finer CTI recordings of the late '70s were those led by fluegelhornist Art Farmer. Although the emphasis was generally on obscure material (in this case Farmer plays one original, two songs by Dave Grusin and one piece by pianist Fritz Pauer) and often featured musicians who did not normally play together, the results were generally quite rewarding. For this CTI LP (long out of print), the focus is almost entirely on Farmer who is joined by keyboardist Grusin, guitarist Eric Gale, flutist Jeremy Steig, either Will Lee or George Mraz on bass and drummer Steve Gadd. The moody music holds one's interest throughout. —*Scott Yanow*

Something You Got / Jul. 1977 / CTI ✦✦✦✦✦
Of Art Farmer's four CTI albums, this is the most rewarding set. The fluegelhornist is teamed with tenor saxophonist Yusef Lateef and a big band arranged by David Matthews, and the results are quite memorable. The catchy "Something You Got," Clifford Brown's "Sandu" and Chick Corea's "Spain" are three of the high points but the other three selections are also strong. Farmer and Lateef worked very well together; it is a pity that this was their only meeting on records, and that this LP has not yet been reissued on CD. —*Scott Yanow*

Big Blues / Feb. 2, 1978-Feb. 3, 1978 / CTI ✦✦✦✦
Fluegelhornist Art Farmer and guitarist Jim Hall had had a regular group for a time in the mid-'60s but (except for one occasion) had not played together since, until this 1978 LP. This is an unusual effort for CTI in that it is a quintet set without added horns, strings or keyboards. Farmer and Hall are joined by vibraphonist Mike Mainieri, bassist Michael Moore and drummer Steve Gadd for two standards, the title cut and a jazz adaptation of a piece by Ravel. Since Farmer and Hall have long had very complementary styles (both being lyrical, harmonically advanced and thoughtful in their improvisations), it is little surprise that this set is

a complete success. Pity that all of Farmer's CTI dates are out of print. —*Scott Yanow*

Yama / Apr. 1979 / CTI ♦♦♦

Fluegelhornist Art Farmer's fourth and final LP for CTI also features tenor saxophonist Joe Henderson. The material (which includes originals by Clare Fischer, Joe Zawinul, Don Grolnick and Mike Mainieri) is not the most memorable and the funky rhythm section (which is greatly expanded) does not really blend all that well with the styles of Farmer and Henderson, so this set is not as exciting as one might hope. A decent but largely forgettable effort. —*Scott Yanow*

Foolish Memories / Aug. 6, 1981-Aug. 7, 1981 / Optimism ♦♦♦

Fluegelhornist Art Farmer has lived in Europe (mostly Austria) since 1968 but not many of his European sessions have been available domestically. This Optimism CD contains music originally released by the Bellaphon label. Farmer heads a European quintet that features the tenor of Harry Sokal and his longtime pianist Fritz Pauer. Pauer contributed two of the six selections, which include Duke Ellington's "In a Sentimental Mood," "Ah-Leu-Cha" (which is mistakenly attributed to Charlie Parker) and the umpteenth remake of "Farmer's Market. The swinging bop-oriented music on this fairly obscure release is enjoyable enough although not particularly unique. —*Scott Yanow*

Work of Art / Sep. 1981 / Concord Jazz ♦♦♦♦♦

Fluegelhornist Art Farmer is in top form on this quartet set with pianist Fred Hersch, bassist Bob Bodley and drummer Billy Hart. Farmer had, if anything, grown through the years and although he had lived in Europe for 13 years at the time of this album, he was still getting better. Farmer is heard in peak form on such numbers as Charlie Parker's "Red Cross," "She's Funny That Way," "Change Partners" and "Love Walked In." A fine example of his artistry. —*Scott Yanow*

Manhattan / Nov. 29, 1981-Nov. 30, 1981 / Soul Note ♦♦♦♦

Mirage / Sep. 18, 1982-Sept. 19, 1982 / Soul Note ♦♦♦

Warm Valley / Sep. 1982 / Concord Jazz ♦♦♦♦♦

The second of fluegelhornist Art Farmer's two Concord albums is the equal of his first. For this Concord outing, the mellow-toned brassman performs four standards (including "Moose the Mooche," "Three Little Words" and the title cut) along with selections from Fred Hersch (who plays piano on this quartet outing), Tommy Flanagan and Benny Golson. With fine support from bassist Ray Drummond and drummer Akira Tana, Art Farmer is heard in prime form, playing in his appealing lyrical bop style. —*Scott Yanow*

The Jazztet: Moment to Moment / May 1983 / Soul Note ♦♦♦♦

In Concert / Aug. 15, 1984 / Enja ♦♦♦♦

This informal and swinging set has the feel of a jam session. Fluegelhornist Art Farmer teams up with trombonist Slide Hampton, pianist Jim McNeely, bassist Ron McClure and drummer Adam Nussbaum on four bop standards. Farmer takes "Darn That Dream" as a feature and the quintet sounds quite at home stretching out on long versions of "Half Nelson," Charlie Parker's "Barbados" and "I'll Remember April." Nothing all that unusual occurs but each of the veterans plays up to par and the results are pleasing. —*Scott Yanow*

You Make Me Smile / Dec. 13, 1984+Dec. 15, 1984 / Soul Note ♦♦♦♦

Among the most consistent of jazzmen, fluegelhornist Art Farmer sounds in fine form on this quintet outing with tenor saxophonist Clifford Jordan, pianist Fred Hersch, bassist Rufus Reid and drummer Akira Tana. The material, other than the standards "Nostalgia" and "Have You Met Miss Jones?" is more obscure than usual, with an adaptation of a Scriabin classical prelude and numbers by Rufus Reid, Farmer ("Flashback") and Benny Carter ("Souvenir"). Creative bop-based music, with Farmer's usual subtlety clearly in evidence. —*Scott Yanow*

Back to the City / Feb. 21, 1986-Feb. 22, 1986 / Original Jazz Classics ♦♦♦♦

Recorded at the same sessions as *Real Time*, this set features a reunion by the Jazztet, a classic sextet that originally broke up in 1963 due to lack of work. Twenty-three years later, fluegelhornist Art Farmer and trombonist Curtis Fuller are heard playing in their unchanged styles, while tenor saxophonist Benny Golson (who had evolved from a Don Byas-type approach to a sound influenced by Archie Shepp) is in fine form. With pianist Mickey Tucker, bassist Ray Drummond and drummer Marvin "Smitty" Smith completing the group, the band plays four lesser-known Golson compositions, Farmer's "Write Soon" and the standard "Speak Low." Timeless hard bop music. —*Scott Yanow*

Real Time / Feb. 21, 1986-Feb. 22, 1986 / Contemporary ♦♦♦♦♦

This CD features the reunited Jazztet with fine playing from fluegelhornist Art Farmer, tenor saxophonist Benny Golson and trombonist Curtis Fuller (who was actually only on the very first Jazztet record); all three veterans are heard in prime form. With the assistance of a supportive rhythm section (pianist Mickey Tucker, bassist Ray Drummond and drummer Marvin "Smitty" Smith), the group per-

forms "Autumn Leaves" and four Golson compositions, including "Whisper Not" and "Along Came Benny." This highly recommended disc is a near-classic that was recorded at the same sessions that resulted in *Back to the City*. —*Scott Yanow*

☆ **Something to Live for: The Music of Billy Strayhorn** / Jan. 14, 1987-Jan. 15, 1987 / Contemporary ♦♦♦♦♦

This very logical set is a real gem. The lyrical fluegelhornist Art Farmer and his quintet (which consists of tenor saxophonist Clifford Jordan, pianist James Williams, bassist Rufus Reid and drummer Marvin "Smitty" Smith) interpret seven of Billy Strayhorn's compositions. Highlights include "Isfahan," "Johnny Come Lately," "Raincheck" and the title cut. Farmer brings the right combination of sensitivity, swing, respect for the melody and creativity to these renditions, and the results are quite memorable. —*Scott Yanow*

Azure / Jun. 25, 1987-Sep. 10, 1987 / Soul Note ♦♦♦

Although the personnel listing mistakenly lists pianist Fritz Pauer as playing bass, this mellow release features his duets with fluegelhornist Art Farmer. Pauer has been Farmer's regular pianist overseas since the fluegelhornist moved to Europe in 1968. Together they perform three of Pauer's moody originals, an Austrian folk song and tunes by Al Cohn, Mal Waldron ("Soul Eyes"), Duke Ellington, Benny Golson and Tadd Dameron ("If You Could See Me Now") with the emphasis on ballads. A peaceful and mostly introspective release. —*Scott Yanow*

Blame It on My Youth / Feb. 4, 1988-Feb. 8, 1988 / Contemporary ♦♦♦♦♦

This is one of the better Art Farmer recordings of the 1980s, which is saying a great deal, for the fluegelhornist is among the most consistent of all jazz musicians. The two ballads that open and close this set ("Blame It on My Youth" and "I'll Be Around") give Farmer an opportunity to display his warm and attractive sound (with fine support from pianist James Williams, bassist Rufus Reid and drummer Victor Lewis), while the other five pieces (Benny Carter's "Summer Serenade" and more obscure material) add the great tenor saxophonist (and so-so soprano player) Clifford Jordan to the group. It's an enjoyable and very successful outing. —*Scott Yanow*

Ph.D. / Apr. 3, 1989-Apr. 4, 1989 / Contemporary ♦♦♦♦

Fluegelhornist Art Farmer recorded quite a few records with tenor saxophonist Clifford Jordan during the late '80s/early '90s. This sextet outing (which also includes guitarist Kenny Burrell, pianist James Williams, bassist Rufus Reid and drummer Marvin "Smitty" Smith) was one of their better efforts. With the exception of "Like Someone in Love," all of the material is obscure. James Williams contributes three tunes that alternate with songs by Donald Brown, Thad Jones, Kenny Drew and Clifford Jordan. The advanced hard bop music has enough unpredictable moments to hold one's interest. —*Scott Yanow*

Central Avenue Reunion / May 26, 1989-May 27, 1989 / Contemporary ♦♦♦♦♦

Three of the five musicians on this quintet date (fluegelhornist Art Farmer, altoist Frank Morgan and pianist Lou Levy) had played on Central Avenue in Los Angeles of the late '40s. Not all of the eight songs that they perform with bassist Eric Von Essen and drummer Albert "Tootle" Heath are from the era ("Blue Minor" and "Cool Struttin'" were written by Sonny Clark several years later), but the outing is very much in the bop style of the period. Their live set is highlighted by spirited versions of "Star Eyes," "Farmer's Market," "I Remember You" and "Donna Lee." This CD is filled with high quality bebop that is easily recommended to straightahead jazz fans. —*Scott Yanow*

Soul Eyes / May 1991 / Enja ♦♦♦

Live at Sweet Basil / Mar. 28, 1992 / Evidence ♦♦♦

Art Farmer (who at this time was playing the newly devised flumpet, a combination fluegelhorn/trumpet) teams up with pianist Geoff Keezer, bassist Kenny Davis, drummer Yoron Israel and Clifford Jordan on this interesting set. Unfortunately Jordan, who was a very distinctive tenor, plays his more anonymous soprano on nearly half of the tracks, so this CD is not as essential as one might expect. The material includes two Thelonious Monk standards, "Yesterdays," Jimmy Heath's "Ellington's Stray Horn," a tune by Jordan and two complex works from Farmer's European pianist Fritz Pauer. This is swinging and often thought-provoking music, but Jordan should have stuck to tenor. —*Scott Yanow*

Company I Keep / 1994 / Arabesque ♦♦♦♦

Fluegelhornists Art Farmer and Tom Harrell meet up on this 1994 Arabesque CD, and although few fireworks occur (the two brassmen mostly sound fairly complementary and mellow), the music is tasteful, enjoyable advanced hard bop. With Ron Blake (doubling on tenor and soprano), pianist Geoff Keezer, bassist Kenny Davis and drummer Carl Allen completing the group, Farmer and Harrell explore group originals, a song by Fritz Pauer, Duke Ellington's "TGTT" and Bill Evans' "Turn Out the Stars." —*Scott Yanow*

Silk Road / Jun. 11, 1996-Jun. 12, 1996 / Arabesque ♦♦♦♦

Joe Farrell (Joseph Carl Firrantello)

b. Dec. 16, 1937, Chicago Heights, IL, **d.** Jan. 10, 1986, Los Angeles, CA
Tenor Saxophone, Soprano Saxophone, Flute / Hard Bop, Crossover Jazz

Joe Farrell's CTI albums of 1970-76, which combined his hard bop style with some pop and fusion elements, made him briefly popular among listeners not familiar with his earlier work. He began playing clarinet when he was 11 and, after graduating from the University of Illinois in 1959, Farrell moved to New York where he worked with the Maynard Ferguson Big Band (1960-61) and Slide Hampton (1962), and recorded with Charles Mingus, Dizzy Reece and a notable series with Jaki Byard (1965). A member of both the Thad Jones/Mel Lewis Orchestra (1966-69) and Elvin Jones' combo (1967-70), Farrell's distinctive sound on tenor and general versatility were assets. A member of the original version of Return to Forever (1971-72), Farrell was fairly prosperous during the 1970s when his solo CTI records sold well, but a drug problem gradually caught up with him. After performing with Mingus Dynasty in the late '70s and recording with Louis Hayes in 1983, he moved to Los Angeles where he scuffled during his last couple of years. In addition to CTI, Farrell recorded as a leader for Warner Bros, Xanadu, Contemporary, Realtime, Timeless and (with Airto and Flora Purim) for Reference. —*Scott Yanow*

● **Joe Farrell Quartet** / Jul. 1, 1970+Jul. 2, 1970 / CTI ◆◆◆◆◆
Joe Farrell, known in the 1960s as a solid hard bop tenor saxophonist, branched out in the 1970s. On this near-classic album, Farrell switches among tenor, soprano, flute and even oboe while being joined by a rather notable backup crew: keyboardist Chick Corea, guitarist John McLaughlin, bassist Dave Holland and drummer Jack DeJohnette. In addition to a famous version of McLaughlin's "Follow Your Heart," the material includes originals by Farrell and Corea, and the leader makes a strong impression on each of his horns. —*Scott Yanow*

Outback / Nov. 1971 / CTI ◆◆◆◆
Joe Farrell's series of six CTI albums have been a bit underrated through the years. Featuring major names, interesting melodies and plenty of versatility from Farrell, even the weaker ones are well worth picking up. Farrell, heard on this second set on tenor, soprano, flute, alto flute and piccolo, is joined by keyboardist Chick Corea, bassist Buster Williams, drummer Elvin Jones and percussionist Airto Moreira for four obscure but worthy pieces—originals by Farrell and Corea, plus the theme song from the movie *Outback*. —*Scott Yanow*

Moon Germs / Nov. 21, 1972 / Columbia ◆◆◆
For his third CTI set as a leader, Joe Farrell left his tenor at home and stuck to soprano and flute. Joined by keyboardist Herbie Hancock, bassist Stanley Clarke (listed as "Stan Clarke") and drummer Jack DeJohnette, Farrell plays a memorable version of Chick Corea's "Times Lie," plus two of his originals and Clarke's "Bass Folk Song." Excellent music which (as with all of his CTI recordings) deserves to be reissued on CD. —*Scott Yanow*

Penny Arcade / Oct. 1973 / CTI ◆◆◆
Joe Farrell gained his greatest fame with his popular string of CTI recordings. For this set, he performs three of his originals (none of which caught on), guitarist Joe Beck's "Penny Arcade," and a 13-minute version of Stevie Wonder's "Too High." Farrell (heard on tenor, soprano, flute and piccolo) is in excellent form, as are keyboardist Herbie Hancock, Beck, bassist Herb Bushler, drummer Steve Gadd and Don Alias on conga. As is true of his other CTI sets, this Joe Farrell effort expertly mixes together some slightly commercial elements and superior recording quality with strong solos. —*Scott Yanow*

Upon This Rock / Mar. 1974 / CTI ◆◆◆
As one might guess from the album's title, this Joe Farrell date is a bit rock-oriented in places. Guitarist Joe Beck is the co-star, and Farrell (who switches between tenor, soprano and flute) is also joined by bassist Herb Bushler and drummer Jim Madison; "I Won't Be Back" has Farrell, Beck and Bushler joined by keyboardist Herbie Hancock, drummer Steve Gadd and the conga of Don Alias. Good music, but not as essential as Farrell's first three CTI dates. —*Scott Yanow*

Canned Funk / Nov. 1974-Dec. 1974 / CTI ◆◆◆
Joe Farrell's final of six CTI dates has fairly lengthy versions of four of his originals. Farrell, who adds baritone to his usual trio of instruments (tenor, soprano and flute), once again welcomes guitarist Joe Beck as his co-star, along with bassist Herb Bushler, drummer Jim Madison and percussionist Ray Mantilla. The music is melodic, sometimes funky, and enjoyable if not essential, but all of Joe Farrell's CTI sets are worth acquiring. —*Scott Yanow*

La Cathedral y El Toro / Apr. 1978 / Warner Brothers ◆

Night Dancing / 1978 / Warner Brothers ◆◆
After his association with CTI ended, Joe Farrell made two weak and rather commercial sets for Warner Bros., of which this LP is the second. Although Farrell gets in a few good spots on tenor, soprano and flute, the strictly for-the-money

arrangements of Trevor Lawrence and the excess of musicians sink this effort. The version of Stevie Wonder's "Another Star" is dominated by dull "background" vocalists; most songs have instantly dated funk played by the rhythm section, and the talents of keyboardists Herbie Hancock and Victor Feldman are wasted. Only a three-and-a-half minute unaccompanied tenor solo on "Come Rain or Come Shine" by Farrell still sounds good 20 years later. —*Scott Yanow*

Skateboard Park / Jan. 29, 1979 / Xanadu ◆◆◆◆
This is one of Joe Farrell's strongest sessions, an advanced straightahead outing in which he sticks exclusively to tenor. With a quartet comprising keyboardist Chick Corea, bassist Bob Magnusson and drummer Larance Marable, Farrell stretches out on three of his interesting originals, Corea's "High Wire—The Aerialist," and the standards "Speak Low" and "You Go to My Head." This valuable and very musical outing is long overdue to be reissued on CD. —*Scott Yanow*

Sonic Text / Nov. 27, 1979-Nov. 28, 1979 / Original Jazz Classics ◆◆◆◆
This is an excellent straightahead outing matching Joe Farrell (who takes four songs on tenor and one apiece on soprano and flute) with trumpeter Freddie Hubbard, keyboardist George Cables, bassist Tony Dumas and drummer Peter Erskine. Originally cut for the Contemporary label, the set has six group originals (by Farrell, Hubbard and Cables) that are performed at the perfect length, mostly between six and eight-and-a-half minutes (other than the 12-minute "Malibu"). The concise solos make expert use of every note, and the results are both fresh and swinging. —*Scott Yanow*

Darn That Dream / May 23, 1982 / Drive Archive ◆◆◆
Tenor saxophonist Joe Farrell recorded two albums' worth of material for Real Time in March 1982. This CD reissue by Drive Archive has most of the best material, including three selections featuring altoist Art Pepper in one of his final recordings; Pepper is best on his showcase "Darn That Dream." Farrell (who is joined by pianist George Cables, bassist Tony Dumas and drummer John Dentz) is in consistently fine form throughout the other selections, sounding particularly adventurous on "Mode for Joe" and coming up with some fresh statements on such standards as "Blue & Boogie," "You Stepped out of a Dream" and "Someday My Prince Will Come." —*Scott Yanow*

Vim 'n' Vigor / Nov. 6, 1983 / Timeless ◆◆◆◆
One should ignore the frivolous cover photos (which show a bikini-clad "Miss Holland" posing with a bass and flexing her muscles) in evaluating this music. Actually, the performances are quite good on what would be Joe Farrell's next-to-last album as a leader. Accompanied by drummer Louis Hayes and a pair of fine Dutch musicians (pianist Rob Van Den Broeck and bassist Harry Emmery), Farrell (who alternates between tenor, soprano and flute) is in surprisingly strong form this late in his life. He stretches out on John Coltrane's "Miles' Mode," two standards (including an abstract version of "Three Little Words") and a pair of his originals. The music ranges from hard bop to post-bop, and throughout, Joe Farrell takes consistently inventive solos. Worth searching for. —*Scott Yanow*

Fattburger

Group / Fusion, Crossover Jazz

Fattburger was a smooth fusion group that had a number of successful records in the late '80s and early '90s. While the group never received much attention from jazz critics, they were quite popular. Despite frequent personnel changes, the group's light, polished fusion of jazz, funk and R&B remained the same. By the late '90s, Fattburger featured bassist Mark Hunter, keyboardist Carl Evans, Jr., drummer Kevin Koch, percussionist Tommy Aros and guitarist Evan Marks. —*Stephen Thomas Erlewine*

One of a Kind / Jan. 1985-Feb. 1985 / Sindrome ◆◆◆◆

● **The Best of Fattburger** / 1985-1988 / Manhattan ◆◆◆◆
The Best of Fattburger is a fine 12-track collection that contains highlights from the fusion group's '80s recordings. The disc distills the essence of the group's polished, pop-oriented fusion and provides a strong introduction to the first part of their career. —*Stephen Thomas Erlewine*

Good News / Jun. 1986-Apr. 1987 / Intima ◆◆◆

Living in Paradise / Apr. 1988-Jun. 1988 / Intima ◆◆◆

Come and Get It / Feb. 26, 1991 / Enigma ◆◆◆

On a Roll / 1992 / Sindrome ◆◆◆

● **Livin' Large** / Jan. 1994-Jun. 1994 / Shanachie ◆◆◆◆
Fattburger, which is essentially a five-piece rhythm section, would benefit from the inclusion of a lead voice. Saxophonist Hollis Gentry helps out on three of the ten selections on this CD but his presence is missed on the other selections despite some good solos from guitarist Evan Marks and keyboardist Carl Evans, Jr. The result is a high-quality set of rhythmic background music, good for dancing but not for close listening. —*Scott Yanow*

All Natural / 1996 / Shanachie ✦✦✦

Malachi Favors

b. Aug. 22, 1937, Chicago, IL

Bass / Early Free, Avant-Garde, Free Jazz, Modern Creative

The long-time bassist with the Art Ensemble of Chicago has also played a variety of miscellaneous instruments (including banjo, zither, bells, gong, harmonica, melodica and percussion) on their many records. In his early days he played bop in Chicago with Andrew Hill (mid-'50s) and other local musicians. Favors was in the AACM from the start, being a member of Muhal Richard Abrams' Experimental Band as early as 1961. In 1966 he joined Roscoe Mitchell's quartet, which soon became the Art Ensemble. In addition to his work with that important group, Favors has recorded with Archie Shepp, Sunny Murray, Dewey Redman, Abrams and Lester Bowie. —*Scott Yanow*

Rick Fay

b. Chicago, IL

Clarinet, Tenor Saxophone, Soprano Saxophone / Dixieland

Unrecorded until 1989, Rick Fay has made up for lost time with many fine records for the Arbors label. He had worked for the Disney Music Department for 24 years (in California and later in Florida) and played regularly at Disney World and in freelance jobs with Wild Bill Davison, Pete Dailey, the Firehouse Five Plus Two and others. On the many Arbors releases, Rick Fay has had the opportunity to record frequently as both a leader and a sideman with such players as Jackie Coon, Dan Barrett and Johnny Varro and he has held his own. —*Scott Yanow*

Hello Horn! / Apr. 23, 1990 / Arbors ✦✦✦

The second release from the Arbors label once again features multi-reedist Rick Fay on clarinet, tenor and soprano. The most notable aspect of this CD is that the colorful cornetist Ernie Carson is well showcased, featured with the septet that also includes trombonist Charlie Bornemann and a four-piece rhythm section. All three of the horn players sing in spots as best they can, but it is the instrumentals (most notably "Shine," "Japanese Sandman," "Spain" and "Cake Walkin' Babies from Home") that make this a recommended set for Dixieland fans. —*Scott Yanow*

Memories of You / Jan. 21, 1991-Jan. 22, 1991 / Arbors ✦✦✦✦

Rick Fay, whose tenor recalls Eddie Miller a little, gathered together an impressive front line of top-notch players for this CD: cornetist Ernie Carson, veteran swing-era clarinetist Johnny Mince and trombonist Dan Barrett. The rhythm section swings lightly, the four musician vocals (two apiece by Fay and guitarist Bob Leary) are painless enough, and even the more familiar tunes on the Dixieland set sound fresh and enthusiastic. Two songs, "Up a Lazy River" and "Ice Cream," feature Fay with a cornet/guitar/bass quartet and put more of a focus on his fine Bechet-ish soprano. An enjoyable set for Dixieland fans. —*Scott Yanow*

Glendena Forever / May 13, 1991-May 14, 1991 / Arbors ✦✦✦

Saxophonist Rick Fay (originally from Pasadena) and fluegelhornist Jackie Coon (at one time a Glendale resident) played together back in the late '40s, so their reunion CD merges their two former homes in its title! The good-time Dixieland date has an awful lot of vocals (only three of the fourteen performances are instrumental) which, although harmless enough, take time away from the solos. Coon has always been a very relaxed and soft-toned player in the manner of Bobby Hackett, while Fay is best on clarinet and soprano; Charlie Bornemann's trombone is also a strong asset and pianist Bob Phillips takes "Cherry" as an unaccompanied feature. The constant and unimaginative banjotuba rhythm gets a bit tiring after awhile and there are few surprises on the date but the music (consisting of Dixieland standards) is cheerful, swinging and full of good feelings. —*Scott Yanow*

Sax-O-Poem Poetry and Jazz / Sept. 2, 1992-Sep. 3. 1992 / Arbors ✦✦✦

● Rick Fay's Endangered Species / Mar. 2, 1993-Mar. 3, 1993 / Arbors ✦✦✦✦

This nine-piece unit boasts quite a few strong talents. While leader Rick Fay is fine on tenor and soprano, he is matched by fluegelhornist Jackie Coon, trombonist Dan Barrett, Betty O'Hara (who plays bass trumpet, double-bell euphonium, cornet and fluegelhorn), clarinetist Bobby Grodon and a four-piece rhythm section led by pianist Johnny Varro. With Fay, Coon, O'Hara and banjoist Eddie Erickson all contributing one or two vocals apiece, there is plenty of variety on this program of swing and Dixieland standards. It's enjoyable and generally hard-swinging music. —*Scott Yanow*

Live at the State / Oct. 7, 1996 / Arbors ✦✦✦✦

This CD, which documents a live concert from St. Petersburg, Florida, is also available as a video. Rick Fay (doubling on tenor and soprano) welcomes an impressive band including the up and coming trumpeter Jon-Erik Kellso, trombonist Dan Barrett, clarinetist Chuck Hedges, pianist Chuck Folds, bassist Bob

Haggart and drummer Eddie Graham. The music consists of 11 Dixieland and swing standards filled with Chicago-type ensembles and heated solos. Among the high points are "Way Down Yonder in New Orleans," "Beale Street Blues," "I Would Do Anything for You" and "South Rampart Street Parade." —*Scott Yanow*

Leonard Feather

b. Sep. 13, 1914, London, England, d. Sep. 22, 1994, Sherman Oaks, CA

Piano, Composer / Bop, Swing

Leonard Feather was best known as easily the most famous jazz critic in the world, writing at least ten jazz books (including the famed *Encyclopedia of Jazz* series) and thousands of liner notes along with articles and reviews for all of the jazz magazines and most of the daily newspapers. Feather, who was very modest about his piano playing, produced many important sessions from the late '30s on but his inclusion in this book is due to his skills as a lyricist/composer. He was responsible for such songs as "Evil Gal Blues" (a hit for Dinah Washington), "Blowtop Blues," the memorable "Mighty like the Blues," "I Remember Bird," "Signing Off," "Twelve Tone Blues" and "How Blue Can You Get?" Feather also led record dates on an irregular basis starting from 1937 (some of which he played on), most notably two 1971 sets for Mainstream with his Night Blooming Jazzmen, a group including Blue Mitchell and Ernie Watts. —*Scott Yanow*

● 1937-1945 / May 4, 1937-Jan. 1, 1945 / Classics ✦✦✦✦

This very interesting CD reissues six diverse sessions organized and led by jazz critic Leonard Feather, who plays piano or celeste on 11 of the 22 selections (including all of the music during the final two dates). On their two dates, Feather's British "Olde English Swynge Band" performs swing versions of English folk songs in 1937 and 1938, including "There's a Tavern in the Town," "Colonel Bogey March" and "Drink to Me Only with Thine Eyes"; the tenor of Buddy Featherstonehaugh (on the earlier session) and trumpeter Dave Wilkins are the solo stars of the rare performances. Better known are Feather's two "All Star Jam Bands," which feature such notables as cornetist Bobby Hackett, altoist Pete Brown, Benny Carter (doubling on alto and trumpet) and clarinetist Joe Marsala on some unusual material, including "Jammin' the Waltz." Eccentric singer Leo Watson's spots on "For He's a Jolly Good Feather" and "Let's Get Happy" (based on "Happy Birthday") are memorable. A 1944 all-star group finds Feather comping decently behind trumpeter Buck Clayton (featured on "Scram!"), clarinetist Edmond Hall and tenor saxophonist Coleman Hawkins, while the final set has four basic chord changes (mostly blues) explored by both Feather and fellow writer Dan Burley on pianos; guitarist Tiny Grimes easily takes honors. —*Scott Yanow*

52nd Street / Jul. 1957-Sep. 1957 / V.S.O.P. ✦✦✦

Leonard Feather organized this tribute to the bebop era, utilizing altoist Phil Woods (the date's real leader), either Idrees Sulieman or Thad Jones on trumpet, pianist George Wallington, bassist Curley Russell and either Denzil Best or Art Taylor on drums. Although allegedly a salute to 52nd Street, the music ignores the diversity of the Street and sticks exclusively to bebop standards, including "Lemon Drop," "Anthropology," "Shaw 'Nuff" and "Billie's Bounce." The biggest surprise is that Baird Parker (the five-year old son of the late Charlie Parker) takes the "vocal" on "Salt Peanuts." Otherwise, the music (reissued on CD by V.S.O.P.) is uneventful, although swinging. —*Scott Yanow*

Oh, Captain! / 1958 / MGM ✦✦

This long-out-of-print album is a true obscurity, a jazz treatment of the long-forgotten score of the Broadway show "Oh Captain." The jazz-oriented vocals (by Marilyn Moore and Jackie Paris, plus one by drummer Osie Johnson) are fine, and the musicians are quite notable, including trumpeter Harry "Sweets" Edison, tenor saxophonist Coleman Hawkins, trumpeter Art Farmer, Tony Scott on a variety of reeds, and the date's musical director, pianist Dick Hyman. Definitely a historical curiosity, this was billed as the first jazz showtune album with vocals. —*Scott Yanow*

Jazz from Two Sides / Jun. 1959 / Concept ✦✦✦✦

This English LP from 1987 features a pair of previously unreleased 1959 sessions presented by Leonard Feather that were recorded in England and the US. The British contingent was headed by Vic Lewis and includes trombonist George Chisholm and tenor saxophonist Ronnie Scott among the main names, while the US group (both bands are nonets) has such West Coast all-stars as trumpeter Pete Candoli, altoist Bud Shank, guitarist Barney Kessel and drummer Shelly Manne and was put together by Jack Marshall. In both cases, the music swings and has its enjoyable moments, sounding as if it could have been arranged by Shorty Rogers. Worth searching for by cool jazz collectors. —*Scott Yanow*

Encyclopedia of Jazz in the Sixties, Vol. 1: The Blues / 1966 / Verve ✦✦✦

This diverse LP, which was released in conjunction with Leonard Feather's *Encyclopedia of Jazz in the Sixties*, is most significant for including three songs by a group led by arranger Oliver Nelson that was called "Leonard Feather's Encyclopedia of Jazz All-Stars." A high point is "I Remember Bird," which features altoist Phil Woods. The flip side of the LP has material available elsewhere: organist Jimmy Smith and guitarist Wes Montgomery playing "OGD," Count Basie's Orchestra jamming "Blues for Eileen" and a rendition of "C Jam Blues" by a quintet co-led by pianist Earl Hines and altoist Johnny Hodges. Although this LP was allegedly supposed to focus on the blues, only three of the six songs are actually blues. —*Scott Yanow*

Night Blooming Jazzmen / Aug. 23, 1971-Aug. 24, 1971 / Mainstream ✦✦✦✦✦

In 1971, critic Leonard Feather, who only recorded on a very infrequent basis through the decades, led two albums by a group that he called the Night Blooming Jazzmen. The two Mainstream LPs were briefly reissued on CD in the early '90s. Feather, who plays background piano throughout the date, performs eight of his originals with trumpeter Blue Mitchell, Ernie Watts (on tenor, alto and flute), guitarist Fred Robinson, organist Charles Kynard, Al McKibbon on acoustic or Max Bennett on electric bass, drummer Paul Humphrey and percussionist Chino Valdes; Kitty Doswell takes the vocal on "Evil Gal Blues." In addition to "Evil Gal," Feather's best-known numbers on the set are "I Remember Bird" (an excellent showcase for Watts' alto) and "Signing Off," while "Nam M'Yoho Ren'ge Kyo" is a particularly catchy number. Worth searching for. —*Scott Yanow*

Freedom Jazz Dance / Aug. 1971-Sept. 1971 / Mainstream ✦✦✦

For the second and final album by Leonard Feather's Night Blooming Jazzmen, he performs "Freedom Jazz Dance" and two of his originals with the same group that was on the first set (including trumpeter Blue Mitchell, the reeds of Ernie Watts, organist Charles Kynard, and Kitty Doswell, who sings "Counting My Tears"). The latter half of the date retains Mitchell but this time has Lew Tabackin on tenor and flute, guitarist Joe Pass, bassist Andy Simpkins, drummer Stix Hooper, Willie Bob on conga and, masquerading as "Phil Johnson," Leonard Feather himself on piano. Their three numbers (all Feather tunes) include the complex "Twelve Tone Blues." This worthwhile set (along with the first recording) was briefly available on CD in the early '90s. —*Scott Yanow*

Wilton Felder (Wilton Lewis Felder)

b. Aug. 31, 1940, Houston, TX
Tenor Saxophone , Bass / Soul Jazz, Crossover Jazz
Wilton Felder spent over 30 years with the group known as the Jazz Crusaders (and later the Crusaders). In the mid-'50s, while in high school in Houston, Felder, Joe Sample and Stix Hooper became the founding members of the group, which soon picked up Wayne Henderson as an additional member. Felder moved to Los Angeles with the other musicians in the late '50s and by 1961 they were recording for Pacific Jazz as the Jazz Crusaders. Felder's soulful blues-based tone and hard bop style fit well in the popular band. Around 1968 he started doubling on electric bass and has backed many top players outside of the group on that instrument. However, his own solo albums (for World Pacific in 1969, MCA and Par) have generally found him cast as a third-rate Grover Washington, Jr., and have not caught on. Felder remained with the Crusaders until its end in the late '80s and had a reunion with Wayne Henderson in the '90s in a new version of the group. —*Scott Yanow*

Secrets / 1983 / MCA ✦✦✦

Nocturnal Moods / 1991 / Par ✦✦

It is strange that none of tenor saxophonist Wilton Felder's solo releases are very significant, for he was an important part of the Jazz Crusaders' (and later Crusaders') sound. On his derivative and poppish date, Felder emulates Grover Washington, Jr. (but without the sincerity and drive), the electronic background is propelled by a drum machine, and there are many simple rhythmic vamps disguised as "originals." Ironically, Felder is the least important element to the dance date; the drum machine rules. —*Scott Yanow*

● Forever Always / 1992 / Par ✦✦✦✦

Throughout this routine R&B-oriented jazz date, Wilton Felder comes across as a second-rate Grover Washington, Jr., playing predictable solos over a variety of unimaginative funky vamps in a tired style very similar to his previous albums. Felder has a nice sound (particularly on tenor) but he should stick to being a hired sideman, or at least come up with some original ideas. At best this is a pleasant dance date. —*Scott Yanow*

Victor Feldman

b. Apr. 7, 1934, London, England, d. May 12, 1987, Los Angeles, CA
Piano, Vibes, Drums, Keyboards / Cool, Post-Bop, Crossover Jazz
Victor Feldman was a child prodigy who was a professional from the age of seven and sat in on drums with Glenn Miller's Army Air Force Band in 1944 when he was ten. He was active in his native England through the bebop years (mostly on

drums), debuting as a leader in 1948. By 1952 Feldman was getting better known for his vibes playing and he recorded extensively during the 1950s. After touring with Woody Herman (1956-57), he decided to move to the US in 1957 where he worked at the Lighthouse with Howard Rumsey. Feldman recorded (on vibes and piano) for Mode, Contemporary and Riverside during 1957-61, a period in which he became a busy studio musician. Feldman was with Cannonball Adderley's Quintet (mostly as a pianist) for six months in 1960-61 and recorded his original "Seven Steps to Heaven" with Miles Davis in 1963. Although Davis offered him a job with his new quintet, Feldman remained in L.A. and the studios. He cut jazz dates for Choice, Concord, Palo Alto and TBA, and in the 1980s up until his death he led a soulful crossover group (The Generation Band) that often featured his son Trevor Feldman on drums. —*Scott Yanow*

★ Suite Sixteen / Aug. 19, 1955-Sep. 21, 1955 / Original Jazz Classics ✦✦✦✦✦

This interesting set (a CD reissue of the original LP) features Victor Feldman shortly before he left England for the US. Feldman, mostly heard on vibes but also making strong appearances on piano and drums, heads several groups filled with English All-Stars including such notable musicians as trumpeters Jimmy Deuchar and Dizzy Reece, tenors Ronnie Scott and Tubby Hayes and pianist Tommy Pollard. The music is boppish, with some surprises in the consistently swinging arrangements, giving one a definitive look at Victor Feldman near the beginning of his career. —*Scott Yanow*

With Mallets a Fore Thought / Sep. 1957 / V.S.O.P. ✦✦✦

This CD reissue of a set from the long-defunct Interlude label brings back an outing by vibraphonist Vic Feldman. Feldman is showcased in a quartet with pianist Carl Perkins, bassist Leroy Vinnegar and drummer Stan Levey on half of the selections, while the remaining tracks add trombonist Frank Rosolino and tenor saxophonist Harold Land. An obscurity ("Chart of My Heart"), two standards, and four Feldman originals comprise this enjoyable and relaxed bop date. —*Scott Yanow*

The Arrival of Victor Feldman / Jan. 21, 1958-Jan. 22, 1958 / Contemporary ✦✦✦✦

Victor Feldman had first recorded as a leader when he was 13 and a swing-based drummer. In 1957, he moved from his native London to the US, and by early 1958 (when he was 23) was in great demand as a pianist and vibraphonist. For his second American release and debut for the Contemporary label (which was last reissued as an LP in the Original Jazz Classics series), Feldman is completely in the spotlight. Joined by the brilliant bassist Scott La Faro (whose playing is a strong reason to acquire the album) and drummer Stan Levey, Feldman performs a mostly boppish set including "Serpent's Tooth," "There Is No Greater Love," Dizzy Gillespie's "Bebop," a Chopin waltz and three of his diverse originals. An excellent showcase for the still-developing Victor Feldman. —*Scott Yanow*

Latinsville / Mar. 2, 1959-May 4, 1959 / Contemporary ✦✦✦

This is an intriguing ten-piece band date with an Afro-Latin flavor. —*Ron Wynn*

Merry Olde Soul / Dec. 16, 1960-Jan. 11, 1961 / Original Jazz Classics ✦✦✦

Victor Feldman's one Riverside date as a leader (which has been reissued on CD) features him playing piano on five songs and vibes on four others (three of which add Hank Jones on piano). Joined by bassist Sam Jones and drummer Louis Hayes (both of whom were at the time, with Feldman, the rhythm section of the Cannonball Adderley Quintet), Feldman is in excellent form on a straightahead set. The trio/quartet performs five mostly underplayed standards, plus four of the leader's originals. Tasteful and swinging music. —*Scott Yanow*

Your Smile / 1973 / Choice ✦✦✦

Victor Feldman's first record as a leader in six years (which has been reissued on CD in Japan) matches the versatile player (who switches between piano, vibes and percussion) with bassist Chuck Domanico, drummer John Guerin and the young Tom Scott (who is heard on tenor, alto and flute). The music ranges from Brazilian jazz and the humorous "Crazy Chicken" to a rapid rendition of the theme from "I Love Lucy" and a remake of Feldman's most famous composition, "Seven Steps to Heaven." The leader plays well, and this is one of Tom Scott's best jazz dates. —*Scott Yanow*

The Artful Dodger / Jan. 24, 1977-Jan. 26, 1977 / Concord Jazz ✦✦✦

On what was only Victor Feldman's second album as a leader in six years, the multi-instrumentalist stuck to piano and electric keyboards to perform a mostly straightahead jazz set. Assisted by either Chuck Domanico or Monty Budwig on bass, drummer Colin Bailey and a guest appearance by trumpeter-vocalist Jack Sheldon (on the second of two versions of the memorable "Haunted Ballroom"), Feldman is quite creative on four of his originals and particularly on fresh versions of four standards: "Limehouse Blues," Stevie Wonder's "Isn't She Lovely?" "Smoke Gets in Your Eyes" and "St. Thomas." This CD reissue is well worth picking up. —*Scott Yanow*

Rio Nights / Dec. 4, 1977-May 10, 1987 / TBA ✦✦

If one is to believe the dates given on this LP, three of the selections were recorded by keyboardist Victor Feldman just two days before his death. More likely is that those straightahead acoustic numbers with bassist John Patitucci and drummer Trevor Feldman were previously unreleased tunes from their 1983 date. The later tracks ("Don't Ask Oscar," "You Gave Me the Runaround" and "Basin Street Blues") are actually the high point of this album, for the other seven numbers (originally released as *In My Pocket* by the Coherent Sound label in 1988) are electronic, funky and rather lightweight. In the latter case, Feldman is joined by several studio musicians plus flutist Hubert Laws, and although the grooves are nice, the material is forgettable. Overall, this posthumous set is a mixed bag. —*Scott Yanow*

In My Pocket / Dec. 4, 1977/ Coherant ✦✦✦

Soft Shoulder / 1981 / TBA ✦✦✦✦

During the last period of his life, multi-instrumentalist Victor Feldman recorded often with his somewhat commercial and often funky Generation Band. This set (originally on Nautilus and reissued on CD by TBA) was one of the best recordings by the group, due to some particularly catchy melodies (especially the witty "Leroy," "Locomotive" and "Soft Shoulder") and some fiery solos from Tom Scott (mostly on alto). Feldman, who switches among piano, electric keyboards, marimba, xylophone, vibes and congas, sounds as if he was having a fun time. Other musicians include guitarists Robben Ford and Dan Sawyer, electric bassist Nathan East and Victor's son Trevor Feldman (then around 17) on drums. —*Scott Yanow*

To Chopin with Love / May 7, 1983-May 8, 1983 / Palo Alto ✦✦✦

Victor Feldman's final trio set (recorded four years before his death) features Feldman strictly on acoustic piano, along with bassist John Patitucci and his son Trevor Feldman on drums. The music on this difficult-to-find LP is a bit unusual, for it finds the pianist turning seven Frederic Chopin melodies into jazz. The interpretations are fine but not all that adventurous in spite of Victor Feldman's talents, making this a set of limited interest. —*Scott Yanow*

Call of the Wild / Jan. 19, 1984 / TBA ✦✦

One in a series of records made by keyboardist-vibraphonist-percussionist Victor Feldman with his Generation Band, this obscure album finds him utilizing some of the musicians from the L.A. Express (including Tom Scott on tenor, alto, soprano and lyricon, guitarist Robben Ford and bassist Max Bennett) along with other studio musicians, plus his son Trevor Feldman on drums. Most memorable is "Chasin' Sanborn" (which finds Scott hinting at altoist David Sanborn) and Tom Scott's playing in general. Not all of the numbers are equally rewarding (a drum synthesizer feature is frivolous, and Scott's lyricon playing on two songs is quite faceless) and the music does seem a bit dated, although the record as a whole does have its interesting moments. —*Scott Yanow*

Fiesta / Jun. 8, 1984-Aug. 1984 / TBA ✦✦

Good arrangements. Feldman plays with some vigor, though not as strongly as on his more jazz-oriented releases. —*Ron Wynn*

Secrets of the Andes / 1985 / Palo Alto ✦✦✦

This out-of-print Palo Alto label was one of Victor Feldman's more commercial releases. Feldman sticks to keyboards this time around and is joined by flutist Hubert Laws (who gets in the best solos), guitarist Lee Ritenour, electric bassist Abraham Laboriel, drummer Harvey Mason, and Alex Acuna and Milt Holland on percussion. Little significant occurs, and the overall results, although pleasant enough, sound a bit dated. —*Scott Yanow*

High Visibility / Feb. 19, 1985-Apr. 1985 / TBA ✦✦

Maynard Ferguson

b. May 4, 1928, Verdun, Quebec, Canada
Trumpet, Leader / Bop, Hard Bop, Crossover Jazz

When he debuted with Stan Kenton's Orchestra in 1950, Maynard Ferguson could play higher than any other trumpeter up to that point in jazz history, and he was accurate. Somehow he has kept most of that range through the decades and since the 1970s has been one of the most famous musicians in jazz. Never known for his exquisite taste (some of his more commercial efforts are unlistenable), Maynard Ferguson has nevertheless led some important bands and definitely made an impact with his trumpet playing.

After heading his own big band in Montreal, Ferguson came to the US in 1949 with hopes of joining Kenton's orchestra, but that ensemble had just recently broke up. So instead, MF gained experience playing with the big bands of Boyd Raeburn, Jimmy Dorsey and Charlie Garnet. In 1950 with the formation of Kenton's Innovations Orchestra, Ferguson became a star, playing ridiculous high notes with ease. In 1953 he left Kenton to work in the studios of Los Angeles and three years later led the all-star "Birdland Dreamband." In 1957 he put together a regu-

lar big band that lasted until 1965, recorded regularly for Roulette (all of its recordings with that label are on a massive Mosaic box set) and performed some of the finest music of his career. Such players as Slide Hampton, Don Ellis, Don Sebesky, Willie Maiden, John Bunch, Joe Zawinul, Joe Farrell, Jaki Byard, Lanny Morgan, Rufus Jones, Bill Berry and Don Menza were among the more notable sidemen.

After economics forced him to give up the impressive band, Ferguson had a few years in which he was only semiactive in music, spending time in India and eventually forming a new band in England. After moving back to the US, Ferguson in 1974 drifted quickly into commercialism. Young trumpeters in high school and colleges were amazed by his high notes but jazz fans were dismayed by the tasteless recordings, which resulted in hit versions of such songs as the themes from *Star Wars* and *Rocky*, and much worse. After cutting back on his huge orchestra in the early '80s, Ferguson recorded some bop in a 1983 session, led a funk band called High Voltage during 1987-88, and then returned to jazz with his "Big Bop Nouveau Band," a medium-sized outfit with which he still tours the world. Although MF's range finally started to shrink a little in the 1990s, he is still an enthusiastic and exciting player —*Scott Yanow*

Verve Jazz Masters, Vol. 52 / Dec. 21, 1951-Aug. 2, 1957 / Verve ✦✦✦

As part of Verve's extensive *Jazz Masters* reissue series, this CD has some highlights from trumpeter Maynard Ferguson's recordings for EmArcy and Mercury. There is one selection ("King's Riff") from a date with tenorman Ben Webster and altoist Benny Carter, five songs from an album with West Coast all-stars (*Dimensions*), a version of "Can't We Talk It Over?" that features MF with arranger Pete Rugolo, and selections from Ferguson's early big band LPs *Around the Horn* and *Boy with Lots of Brass*. Best known as a high-note trumpeter, Maynard Ferguson did his best on these performances to show off his other abilities, including taking solos on valve trombone and playing jazz in the trumpet's lower register. The bop-based music is enjoyable, there are many other prominent soloists (including altoists Bud Shank, Herb Geller and Anthony Ortega), and Irene Kral sings an effective rendition of "Moonlight in Vermont." But more serious collectors are advised to search for the complete original records. —*Scott Yanow*

Jam Session Featuring Maynard Ferguson / Feb. 23, 1953 / EmArcy ✦✦✦

This out-of-print EmArcy LP consists of lengthy versions of "Our Love Is Here to Stay" and an original blues, "Air Conditioning." Trumpeter Maynard Ferguson is heard jamming with an all-star group of West Coast players consisting of altoist Herb Geller, Bob Cooper on tenor, baritonist Bob Gordon, trombonist Milt Bernhart, pianist Claude Williamson, bassist John Simmons and drummer Max Roach. Although the music contains no real surprises, this album has its exciting moments and will be enjoyed by bebop fans. —*Scott Yanow*

Stratospheric / Feb. 19, 1954-May 12, 1956 / EmArcy ✦✦✦✦

This two-LP set from 1976 gives listeners a good overview of trumpeter Maynard Ferguson's four Mercury albums of 1954-56. M.F. is heard in several different settings ranging from octets to a big band, with arrangements by Bill Holman and Willie Maiden; among the many other soloists are altoists Bud Shank and Herb Geller, baritonist Bob Gordon, trombonists Herbie Harper and Milt Bernhart, and tenors Bob Cooper and Georgie Auld. Although it would be preferable to get all of the performances from the four albums since those remain out of print, this twofer is worth searching for in the meantime. This is excellent bop-based music with highlights including "The Way You Look Tonight," Ferguson's feature on "Over the Rainbow" and a variety of strong Holman originals. —*Scott Yanow*

Dimensions / Feb. 1954+Aug. 1955 / EmArcy ✦✦✦

This Trip LP is a reissue of an earlier EmArcy album that has not yet appeared on CD. The always-impressive trumpeter Maynard Ferguson is featured with a nonet arranged by Bill Holman in 1955 and a septet from 1954. The concise performances include both standards and originals, with all but two four-minute songs clocking in around three minutes; the soloists include Ferguson, trombonists Milt Bernhart and Herbie Harper, altoists Herb Geller and Bud Shank, baritonist Bob Gordon and Bob Cooper on tenor. Although not essential, the bop-oriented music is well-played and gives one a good taste of early Ferguson. —*Scott Yanow*

● **The Birdland Dream Band** / Sep. 7, 1956-Dec. 24, 1956 / Bluebird ✦✦✦✦✦

In 1956 Maynard Ferguson had the opportunity to put together a "dreamband." Fortunately (in addition to a tour) the orchestra cut a pair of albums, most of which is included on this single CD. With arrangements from Al Cohn, Bob Brookmeyer, Jimmy Giuffre, Ernie Wilkins, Bill Holman, Marty Paich, Willie Maiden, Johnny Mandel and Herb Geller, it is not too surprising that these charts sound both modern and quite exciting. In addition to Ferguson's high note trumpet work, the main soloists are trombonist Jimmy Cleveland, altoist Herb Geller and Al Cohn on tenor. Overall this music serves a particularly strong start to Maynard Ferguson's career as a major bandleader. —*Scott Yanow*

Maynard Ferguson and His Original Dreamband / Dec. 1956 / Artistry ✦✦✦✦

Ferguson's first significant orchestra was the "Dreamband" he had in 1956. This live set (put out on an LP in 1984 by the Artistry label) contains originals by Bill Holman, Al Cohn, Marty Paich, Manny Albam, Ernie Wilkins and Johnny Mandel; one would presume that the arrangements are also by the composers. The music generally jumps and is modern for the period. Such soloists as the leader-trumpeter, altoist Herb Geller and tenors Richie Kamuca and Nino Tempo are heard from and the rhythm section is driven by drummer Mel Lewis. Excellent music, it's also well-recorded. —*Scott Yanow*

Boy with Lots of Brass / Jul. 1957 / EmArcy ✦✦✦

After his specially assembled "Birdland Dreamband" broke up, trumpeter Maynard Ferguson put together a regular big band that would exist for the next decade. This Mercury LP features his 13-piece unit at a time when it featured trombonist Jimmy Cleveland, Willie Maiden on tenor, altoists Jimmy Ford and Anthony Ortega, pianist Bobby Timmons and singer Irene Kral; the latter is heard on four of the dozen standards that make up the album. The arrangements are by Maiden, Al Cohn, Bill Holman and Ernie Wilkins, and they show off the talented orchestra and its memorable leader quite well. —*Scott Yanow*

A Message from Newport/Newport Suite / May 6, 1958-Mar. 22, 1960 / Roulette ✦✦✦✦✦

Two of trumpeter Maynard Ferguson's best-ever albums are combined on this double LP; all of the music has since been reissued on Mosaic's massive *The Complete Roulette* CD box set. Slide Hampton, Willie Maiden and Don Sebesky contributed most of the colorful arrangements and there are strong solos from Ferguson (on trumpet, valve trombone and baritone horn), trombonist Hampton, altoist Jimmy Ford, Carmen Leggio, Maiden and Joe Farrell on tenors and pianist Jaki Byard among others. Highlights include "Tag Team," "Frame for the Blues," "Three Little Foxes," "Newport," "Got the Spirit," "Ol' Man River" and "Three More Foxes." —*Scott Yanow*

★ **The Complete Maynard Ferguson on Roulette** / May 6, 1958-Mar. 1962 / Mosaic ✦✦✦✦✦

Trumpeter Maynard Ferguson led his greatest big band during the years that he was signed to Roulette, and all of the music from his 13 Roulette LPs (plus 11 previously unissued selections) are included on this deluxe limited-edition ten-CD box set. Although three of the LPs were originally recorded as dance records (and stick close to the melodies), this box as a whole finds Maynard at his peak and with an orchestra that includes such talented soloists as trombonists Slide Hampton and Don Sebesky (both of whom contributed arrangements), altoist Lanny Morgan, the tenors of Carmen Leggio, Willie Maiden, Joe Farrell and Don Menza, pianists Jaki Byard and Joe Zawinul and drummer Rufus Jones in addition to the leader. The music is very jazz-oriented and contains more than its share of classic moments, particularly the sessions that resulted in *A Message from Newport* and *Newport Suite*. It's highly recommended. —*Scott Yanow*

Jazz for Dancing / Oct. 1959 / Roulette ✦✦✦

Although trumpeter Maynard Ferguson's Roulette recordings are generally considered among his best, a few of the dates (including the music on this LP) were recorded strictly as background music for dancers who were nostalgic for the swing era. Sticking mostly to veteran standards and emphasizing melodic statements (but not recreating the past), Ferguson and his excellent orchestra purposely play it safe, performing pleasing but unadventurous music that is not as exciting as their more jazz-oriented sessions of the era. —*Scott Yanow*

Maynard '61 / Oct. 14, 1960-Jan. 20, 1961 / Roulette ✦✦✦

Maynard Ferguson led his finest orchestra during his period with Roulette; all of the excellent recordings have since been reissued on a ten-CD box set by Mosaic. For those Maynard fans who do not have the box, this single CD gives one some examples of his orchestra, reissuing the original *Maynard '61* LP along with one selection ("Saturday Night") from *Maynard '64* and adding two previously unissued performances. In addition to the leader-trumpeter, the main soloists are trombonist Slide Hampton, altoist Lanny Morgan, Joe Farrell on tenor and pianist Jaki Byard; trumpeters Rolf Ericson and Bill Berry are also heard on "Blues for Kapp," one of the CD's many highlights. —*Scott Yanow*

Two's Company / Dec. 15, 1960-Jan. 30, 1961 / Roulette ✦✦✦

Singer Chris Connor and trumpeter Maynard Ferguson first met up as members of Stan Kenton's Orchestra in 1953. This CD reissue is a rather strange record because Connor performs very dramatic material that often sounds as if it were lifted directly from Broadway shows. Although Ferguson gets to throw in some high-register blasts now and then, his orchestra is mostly used as a prop behind Connor. The singer does her best (her voice was in prime form around this time), but the flamboyant and often-pompous arrangements (which are uncredited) take away from any real spontaneity or swing. An odd set. —*Scott Yanow*

"Straightaway" Jazz Themes / Jul. 21, 1961+Jul. 27, 1961 / Roulette ✦✦✦

In the early '60s trumpeter Maynard Ferguson composed a variety of jazz-oriented themes for a television show about race car drivers titled *Straightaway*. This LP (all of the music has since been reissued on a M.F. CD box set by Mosaic) features Ferguson's orchestra interpreting ten of the themes, with arrangements provided by Willie Maiden and Don Sebesky. Actually this is one of the lesser Maynard recordings from this busy era (none of the material is all that memorable) but fans of his big band should enjoy the somewhat obscure music anyway. —*Scott Yanow*

Maynard '63 / Mar. 1962 / Roulette ✦✦✦

Nearly all of Maynard Ferguson's Roulette recordings are well worth picking up. This LP (which has been reissued on CD by Roulette) features M.F.'s 14-piece band in 1962 and is not an exception to the rule. In addition to the exciting leader-trumpeter, the main soloists are altoist Lanny Morgan, Don Menza and Willie Maiden on tenors and pianist Mike Abene, all of whom excel on the bop-oriented music. This was one of the best big bands of the era. —*Scott Yanow*

Si! Si!/Maynard '64 / 1962 / Roulette ✦✦✦✦

This single CD reissues the contents of two former LPs by the Maynard Ferguson Orchestra: *Si! Si!* and *Maynard '64*. These 16 performances have been reissued by Mosaic in a ten-CD box set but those listeners who do not have that set should get this one. In addition to the high-note trumpet master, the boppish performances feature such soloists as altoist Lanny Morgan, the tenors of Willie Maiden and Don Menza and pianist Mike Abene. The arrangements (by Ernie Wilkins, Marty Paich, Don Sebesky, Don Rader, Maiden, Abene and Menza) took advantage of the band's many strengths and the result is a solid set (actually two) of swinging music. —*Scott Yanow*

Message from Maynard / Mar. 1962 / Roulette ✦✦✦

The 1962 Maynard Ferguson Orchestra performs five Don Menza arrangements/compositions, plus two by Don Rader and one apiece from Mike Abene and Don Sebesky, on this well-rounded LP. None of the originals caught on, but there are plenty of fine solos from the leader-trumpeter, Menza on tenor, altoist Lanny Morgan and pianist Abene; plus, the rhythm section is really pushed by drummer Rufus Jones. All of this enjoyable music has since been reissued in Mosaic's ten-CD *Maynard Ferguson on Roulette* box set. —*Scott Yanow*

The New Sound of Maynard Ferguson / 1964 / Cameo ✦✦✦

The sound was not all that new but the label was, as Maynard Ferguson and his orchestra, which had just concluded a long association with Roulette, switched briefly to Cameo. The big band was still in prime form, playing both swing standards and originals with power, swing and spirit. In addition to Ferguson's screaming trumpet, altoist Lanny Morgan, Willie Maiden and Frank Vicari on tenors, baritonist Ronnie Cuber and pianist Mike Abene are heard from prominently while Abene, Maiden and Don Sebesky contribute most of the arrangements. This rare LP (which has not yet been reissued on CD) is worth the search. —*Scott Yanow*

Color Him Wild / Sep. 15, 1964-Sep. 16, 1964 / Mainstream ✦✦✦

After eight years the Maynard Ferguson Orchestra was in its last period when it recorded a couple of LPs for Mainstream. The band's sound and winning spirit were still unchanged from its prime days and this excellent album (which features solos from the trumpeter-leader, valve trombonist Rob McConnell, altoist Lanny Morgan, Willie Maiden on tenor, baritonist Ronnie Cuber and pianist Mike Abene) is a fine example of the orchestra's music. Highlights include "Airegin," "Green Dolphin Street" and a remake of "Three More Foxes" (although their version of "People" can be safely skipped). —*Scott Yanow*

Blues Roar / Dec. 1, 1964-Dec. 11, 1964 / Mainstream ✦✦✦

This rather brief (under 36 minutes) CD is a straight reissue of a Mainstream LP by the Maynard Ferguson Orchestra. M.F. and his crew perform a variety of blues-oriented material including "Every Day I Have the Blues," "Night Train," "What'd I Say?" and "I've Got a Woman." Willie Maiden, Don Sebesky and Mike Abene were responsible for the arrangements and the main soloists are Ferguson (on trumpet and valve trombone), altoists Lanny Morgan and Charlie Mariano, Frank Vicari on tenor and pianist Mike Abene. A fine set, it's the last recording by this excellent orchestra. —*Scott Yanow*

Six by Six: Maynard Ferguson and Sextet / Sep. 13, 1965-Sep. 14, 1965 / Mainstream ✦✦✦✦

After trumpeter Maynard Ferguson reluctantly broke up his big band in late 1964 after eight years, he formed a more economical sextet with two of his top soloists (Willie Maiden on tenor and baritone and altoist Lanny Morgan) and his rhythm section (pianist Mike Abene, bassist Ron McClure and drummer Tony Inzalaco). Although this group did not last long, their mainstream recording has excellent performances and good solos from the somewhat forgotten band; highlights include Maiden's ballad "April Fool," the cooking "No More Wood" and "Summertime." —*Scott Yanow*

Sextet 1967 / May 19, 1967 / Just A Memory ✦✦
Recorded during trumpeter Maynard Ferguson's Montreal trip to 1967 (when he was between bands), this CD finds Ferguson in fine form but is only a mixed success. Altoist John Cristie and tenor saxophonist Brian Barley share the spotlight on some numbers and their tones sound rather uncomfortable while their ideas try to reconcile the avant-garde innovations of the period to hard bop. Barley (who on "Polecat" almost resembles Booker Ervin at one point) would develop beyond this point in the near future. The obscure rhythm section is fine in support without really standing out. But MF fans will probably want this one because the trumpeter is showcased on three ballads ("I Can't Get Started," "Who Can I Turn To?" and "Over the Rainbow"), takes a large portion of "Summertime 'Revisited'" as a duet with the bassist and makes his presence felt on the other selections. —*Scott Yanow*

Orchestra 1967 / Jun. 8, 1967 / Just A Memory ✦✦✦✦
In May 1967 when Maynard Ferguson was invited to appear at the Canadian Pavillion at Expo in Montreal, his Roulette period was behind him but his style and musical tastes had not really changed. Although he did not appear on record at all in 1966 (other than the soundtrack of a television show) and would not have a regular orchestra until 1970, the music on this CD sounds very much as if it were being played by an edition of the Maynard Ferguson big band. The obscure sidemen (all local players gathered together for the occasion) boast high musicianship and a few excellent (but unfortunately unidentified) soloists. MF is the main star throughout, showing off his remarkable technique and coming up with consistently exciting and generally creative solos in addition to enthusiastically leading the shouting ensembles. —*Scott Yanow*

Trumpet Rhapsody / Dec. 1967 / MPS ✦✦
This is one of the less significant Maynard Ferguson albums but the music is still fairly enjoyable. Accompanied by the German Rolf Hans Muller Orchestra in Dec. 1967, the great trumpeter sticks mostly to ballads, showcasing his tone and sometimes his range with restraint and an accent on lyricism. The music is enjoyable enough but not too essential. With the exception of one obscure record, Ferguson would not record again for over two years, until he started his commercial comeback with Columbia. —*Scott Yanow*

M.F. Horn, Vol. 1 / Feb. 1970 / Columbia ✦✦✦
Trumpeter Maynard Ferguson began his successful "comeback" (after several years of low-profile activity) with this well-received Columbia LP. Featuring his English orchestra (and such soloists as altoist Pete King and Danny Moss on tenor), Ferguson had a minor hit in "MacArthur Park," showcases some Indian musicians on "Chala Nata" and shows throughout that his mind was open to both newer forms of jazz and pop music. It's an interesting if not essential set. —*Scott Yanow*

M.F. Horn, Vol. 2 / Jan. 1972 / Columbia ✦✦
During his period on Columbia, Maynard Ferguson showed a willingness (and sometimes even an eagerness) to record pop material. His trumpet playing is frequently brilliant throughout this LP with his English orchestra but not too many jazz purists will be thrilled with his renditions of "Theme from *Shaft*," "Spinning Wheel" and "Hey Jude." The music is actually better than it seems, but do not look here for any bop. —*Scott Yanow*

M.F. Horn, Vol. 3 / Apr. 18, 1973 / Columbia ✦✦✦
Maynard Ferguson's *M.F. Horn* series for Columbia mixed together jazz versions of pop and rock music, hurting the trumpeter's reputation with the jazz collectors but helping him to become practically a household name. This set has some worthwhile pieces (notably "Awright, Awright," "'Round Midnight" and "Nice 'n' Juicy") and some spirited ensemble playing; the most notable among Ferguson's sidemen in this English big band are pianist Pete Jackson, drummer Randy Jones and baritonist Bruce Johnstone. The music on the LP is not essential but has its exciting moments. —*Scott Yanow*

Maynard Ferguson / Apr. 18, 1973-May 1979 / Columbia ✦✦✦
Most of trumpeter Maynard Ferguson's recordings for Columbia were rather erratic, alternating very commercial pop performances with occasional jazz selections. This sampler LP reissues eight of the latter, allowing jazz listeners to truly get the "best of" Ferguson from the 1970s. Certainly few but Maynard's greatest fans will want to get his album *Hot* just for this version of "Naima" or *New Vintage* for "Airegin." This consistent sampler lets one avoid his more dated material and sticks to the more rewarding jazz. —*Scott Yanow*

M.F. Vol. 4 & 5 / Jul. 10, 1973 / Columbia ✦✦✦✦
This double LP is easily Maynard Ferguson's best jazz-oriented recording for Columbia. With the exception of a remake of "MacArthur Park" (which isn't bad), the music sticks exclusively to jazz with the highlights including "I'm Gettin' Sen-

Music Map

Fluegelhorn

Early Uses of Fluegelhorn
Joe Bishop (1936 with Woody Herman's Orchestra)
Shorty Rogers (early 1950s)
Miles Davis (1957, on *Miles Ahead*)

By the mid-1960s nearly all trumpeters used the fluegelhorn as a double.

Most Important Fluegelhorn Specialists

Clark Terry	Art Farmer
Freddie Hubbard	Chuck Mangione
Thad Jones	Kenny Wheeler
Jackie Coon	

timental over You," "Two for Otis," "Stay Loose with Bruce," "The Fox Hunt" and "Got the Spirit." In addition to Ferguson's powerful trumpet, other musicians making strong impressions include first trumpeter Lin Biviano, altoist Andy MacIntosh, Ferdinand Povel on tenor, baritonist Bruce Johnstone and keyboardist Pete Jackson. This very enjoyable set is long overdue to be reissued on CD. —*Scott Yanow*

Chameleon / Apr. 1, 1974+Apr. 4, 1974 / Columbia ✦✦
This is a really streaky CD reissue from Maynard Ferguson's generally commercial Columbia period. The trumpeter's version of Herbie Hancock's hit "Chameleon" is enjoyable and he does a good job on Chick Corea's "La Fiesta," the standard "I Can't Get Started" and "Superbone Meets the Bad Man" (which co-features baritonist Bruce Johnstone). However, his renditions of such pieces as "The Way We Were," Paul McCartney's "Jet" and "Livin' for the City" are quite forgettable and lightweight, making this reissue an unnecessary frivolity. —*Scott Yanow*

Carnival / May 15, 1978 / Columbia ✦✦
Maynard Ferguson's version of "Birdland" from this LP was a bit of a hit and he fares fairly well on "Stella by Starlight" and "Over the Rainbow" but overall this typically commercial Columbia album is of lesser interest. MF, at the height of his popularity, was clearly looking for a hit, which is why he recorded the "Theme from *Battlestar Galactica*" and roughly half of the poppish material on this rather forgettable effort. The trumpeter-bandleader would record worse albums than this LP but this one is weak enough. —*Scott Yanow*

Storm / Jun. 23, 1982-Jun. 24, 1982 / Palo Alto ✦✦
Maynard Ferguson had led many big bands before recording this Palo Alto LP. This was not one of his more significant units (few of the sidemen have been heard from much since) and the music, although more jazz-oriented than his earlier Columbias (including versions of "Take the 'A' Train" and a vocal feature for MF on "As Time Goes By"), is not really that memorable. It's a lesser effort. —*Scott Yanow*

Hollywood / 1982 / Columbia ✦

Live from San Francisco / May 27, 1983 / Palo Alto ✦✦✦✦
This LP was Maynard Ferguson's strongest jazz album in quite a few years. Utilizing a small big band comprising 12 pieces, Ferguson is in consistently fiery form during a session recorded live from the Great American Music Hall in San Francisco. "Bebop Buffet" (which has quotes from many bop classics) is a high point and these versions of "Lush Life" and "On the Sunny Side of the Street" (along with four group originals) are quite enjoyable; baritonist Denis DiBlasio's arrangements are a major asset. This fine straightahead date deserves to be reissued on CD. —*Scott Yanow*

Body and Soul / Jan. 1986 / Black Hawk ✦✦
Trumpeter Maynard Ferguson cut back on his big band around this time, utilizing an 11-piece group with six horns and an expanded rhythm section; best known among his sidemen is tenor saxophonist Rick Margitza. MF uses electronics on some of the selections and swings a bit on "Body and Soul." In addition to Margitza, the other soloists include guitarist Michael Higgins, altoist Tim Ries and

keyboardist Todd Carlon. The music is pleasing but not all that memorable, although Ferguson's mastery of his upper register remains quite impressive. —*Scott Yanow*

High Voltage, Vol. 2 / Jul. 1988-Sep. 1988 / Intima ♦♦
For a period in the mid- to late '80s, trumpeter Maynard Ferguson broke up his usual little big band and had a funky combo, a septet with just two horns and a large rhythm section. For the second of his two *High Voltage* CDs, Ferguson primarily plays group originals (plus a slower-than-usual "Star Eyes") that come across as fairly routine and predictable. There is nothing particularly memorable about this pleasant but unadventurous set of music. —*Scott Yanow*

Big Bop Nouveau / 1988-1989 / Intima ♦♦♦
Maynard Ferguson broke up his funk combo High Voltage around this time and put together a 15-piece straightahead group that emphasized swinging and big band-oriented charts. Although there is a throwaway "Maynard Ferguson Hit Medley," such pieces as "Blue Birdland," "Cherokee" and "But Beautiful" better showcase the remarkable trumpeter. The sidemen include Christopher Hollyday on alto. This is an excellent all-round showcase for MF, but the CD from the now-defunct Intima label will be hard to find. —*Scott Yanow*

Live from London / 1993 / Avenue Jazz ♦♦♦♦
Utilizing a 13-piece band that includes ten horns, Maynard Ferguson performs bebop with his Big Bop Nouveau on this CD. All of the music is fairly basic, using common chord changes and charts that leave plenty of room for solos. Ferguson shows that at age 65 he still has most of his outstanding range and, assisted by a trumpet section full of screamers, the performances are boisterous and sometimes a bit bombastic. Chip McNeill takes a passionate soprano solo on "A Night in Tunisia," Matt Wallace has a couple of rewarding spots on tenor, and trumpeter Walter White fares well on "Fox Hunt," but it is the leader who gives this music its main personality. —*Scott Yanow*

These Cats Can Swing / 1994 / Concord Jazz ♦♦♦♦

One More Trip to Birdland / Jun. 3, 1996-Jun. 7, 1996 / Concord Jazz ♦♦♦♦
Even at the age of 67, Maynard Ferguson shows on this CD that he could still belt out the high notes. His "Big Bop Noveau" band consists of four trumpets, trombonist Tom Garling (who takes a rockish guitar solo on "Birdland"), Matt Wallace and Chris Farr on saxophones, and a rhythm section. With the exception of "Birdland," the music is strictly bebop, with plenty of screaming trumpet and heated playing; Wallace's alto outbursts often take honors. Highlights include "Manteca," "Cajun Cookin'," "Milestones" and a hyper "It Don't Mean a Thing." —*Scott Yanow*

Rachelle Ferrell

b. Philadelphia, Pennsylvania
Vocals / Adult Contemporary
Composer, lyricist, arranger, musician and vocalist Rachelle Ferrell is a recent arrival on the contemporary jazz scene, but her visibility on the pop/urban contemporary scene has boosted her audience's interest in her jazz recordings.

Born and raised in Philadelphia, Ferrell got started singing in the second grade at age six. This no doubt contributed to the eventual development of her startling six-and-change octave range. She decided early on, after classical training on violin, that she wanted to try to make her mark musically as an instrumentalist and songwriter. In her mid-teens, her father bought her a piano with the provision that she learn to play to a professional level. Within six months, Ferrell had secured her first professional gig as a pianist-singer. She began performing at 13 as a violinist, and in her mid-teens as a pianist and vocalist. At 18, she enrolled in the Berklee College of Music in Boston to study composition and arranging, where her classmates included Branford Marsalis, Kevin Eubanks, Donald Harrison and Jeff Watts. She graduated in a year and taught music for awhile with Dizzy Gillespie for the New Jersey State Council on the Arts. Through the 1980s and into the early '90s, she'd worked with some of the top names in jazz, including Gillespie, Quincy Jones, George Benson and George Duke.

Ferrell's debut, *First Instrument,* was released in 1990 in Japan only. In 1995, Blue Note/Capitol released her Japanese debut for US audiences, and the response was similarly positive. Her 1992 self-titled US debut, a more urban pop-contemporary album, was released on Capitol Records. Ferrell was signed to a unique two-label contract, recording pop and urban contemporary for Capitol Records and jazz music for Blue Note Records. For four consecutive years in the early '90s, Ferrell put in festival-stopping performances at the Montreux Jazz Festival.

Although Ferrell has captured the jazz public's attention as a vocalist, she continues to compose and write songs on piano and violin. Ferrell's work ethic has paid off, and Gillespie's predictions about her becoming a "major force" in the jazz industry came true. Her prolific songwriting abilities and ability to accompany herself on piano seem only to further her natural talent as a vocalist.

Ferrell has made her mark not as a straightahead jazz singer and pianist, but as a crossover artist who's equally at home with urban contemporary pop, gospel, classical music and jazz. Expect more great vocal albums, both jazz and pop, from this one-of-a-kind vocalist, arranger, songwriter and instrumentalist. —*Richard Skelly*

First Instrument / Dec. 16, 1989-Feb. 1990 / Blue Note ♦♦
Rachelle Ferrell made her name performing R&B but this strictly acoustic jazz CD is her earliest recording. Her voice is quite soulful (making her later shift to R&B less of a surprise in hindsight) but Ferrell seems quite unsure how to use her wide range and her improvisations are often quite eccentric. Her lack of warmth and subtlety (along with a tendency to scream and screech in unexpected spots without a buildup) makes several of the numbers on this standards-oriented set difficult to listen to. Trumpeter Terence Blanchard and Wayne Shorter on tenor make worthwhile cameo appearances but Rachelle Ferrell at that point in her career did not really sound ready for prime time despite her potential. —*Scott Yanow*

● **Rachelle Ferrell** / 1992 / Manhattan ♦♦♦

Manfredo Fest

b. Porto Alegre, Brazil
Piano / Brazilian Jazz, Latin Jazz, World Fusion, Fusion
Until recently one of the better-kept secrets among Brazil's bossa nova pioneers, Manfredo Fest's popularity and profile have risen dramatically in the 1990s. Legally blind since birth, Fest's greatest early influence was George Shearing, but he has since developed his own approach apart from Shearing and other Brazilian jazz pianists, unleashing relentlessly flowing streams of bop-flavored notes against a Brazilian pulse, occasionally letting his classical roots show.

Fest's father, an emigre from Germany, was a concert pianist who chaired the University of Porto Alegre's music department. Accordingly, Fest studied classical piano as a youth, learning to read music in Braille, but after graduating from the University of Rio Grande do Sul, his tastes turned toward jazz and samba. Fest was part of the gathering of Brazilian musicians of the late '50s who were developing the bossa nova movement, and he made a number of trio recordings in that vein from 1961 to 1966. After emigrating to Minneapolis in 1967, Fest moved to Los Angeles where he served as keyboardist and arranger for Bossa Rio and toured with Sergio Mendes. By 1973, Fest had moved to Chicago, playing there and on the Playboy Club circuit, and in 1988, he settled in Palm Harbor, Florida. After recording for a few independent labels, Fest finally achieved a breakthrough in the American market upon signing with Concord Picante in the early 1990s, producing a series of energetic, Brazilian-flavored, bop-grounded, small-group albums. —*Richard S. Ginell*

Manifestations / 1978 / Tabu ♦♦♦

Braziliana / Jul. 23, 1987-Jul. 26, 1987 / DMP ♦♦♦
Pianist Manfredo Fest alternates between Afro-Latin material and Latin jazz originals on this 1987 session. Fest is a decent, sometimes engaging accompanist and moderately accomplished soloist. Drummer Porthinho and percussionist Cyro Baptista add some tasty rhythms, while vocalist Roberta Davis and bassist Paul Socolow fill in competently. —*Ron Wynn*

● **Jungle Cat** / Jun. 15, 1989-Jun. 18, 1989 / DMP ♦♦♦♦
This CD has an energetic set of Brazilian-flavored jazz. Manfredo Fest mostly sticks to acoustic piano, occasionally switching to electric keyboards for color, and balancing the program almost evenly between standards and originals. To his credit, Fest (who uses a four-piece rhythm section) does not let the Brazilian aspects of the music detract from the jazz, which is quite boppish and harmonically sophisticated. Trumpeter Claudio Roditi's cameo appearances are also a plus on this enjoyable set. —*Scott Yanow*

Oferenda / Jul. 8, 1992-Jul. 10, 1992 / Concord Picante ♦♦♦♦

Comecar De Novo / Jan. 12, 1995-Jan. 13, 1995 / Concord Picante ♦♦♦

Fascinating Rhythm / Feb. 8, 1995-Feb. 9, 1995 / Concord Picante ♦♦♦

Amazonas / Mar. 4, 1997 / Concord Picante ♦♦♦♦

Dale Fielder

b. 1956, East Liverpool, OH
Tenor Saxophone / Post-Bop
Dale Fielder has emerged in the 1990s as one of the top up-and-coming saxophonists in the Los Angeles area. He started studying music (clarinet and then alto) at the age of nine and played R&B while in high school. Fielder attended the University of Pittsburgh and played regularly around town. In 1980 he moved to New York and gigged with the calypso band of the Mighty Sparrow. While in New York Fielder formed the Clarion label and recorded an LP, *Scene from a Dream,* that featured Geri Allen. In 1988 he relocated to Los Angeles and since then has

played regularly in town and up and down the Coast. Dale Fielder has recorded two CDs recently for his Clarion label including a strong tribute to Wayne Shorter. —*Scott Yanow*

Know Thyself / May 5, 1994-Sep. 20, 1994 / Clarion ✦✦✦✦
Dale Fielder, an advanced hard bop-based saxophonist, doubles on alto and tenor on this excellent set. Using his regular group of the period (trumpeter Dan Bagasoul, pianist Greg Kurstin, bassist Bill Markus and drummer Ocie Davis III, Fielder explores six of his originals, "Sometime Ago," "But Beautiful" and Tina Brooks' obscure "Theme for Doris." The music is grounded in the tradition yet adventurous in spots, an excellent showcase for the L.A.-based Fielder. —*Scott Yanow*

● **Dear Sir: Tribute to Wayne Shorter** / Mar. 5, 1995-Jul. 17, 1995 / Clarion ✦✦✦✦✦
The young tenor saxophonist Dale Fielder, in a quartet with pianist Jane Getz, bassist Bill Markus and drummer Thomas White, performs four Wayne Shorter compositions, Gil Evans' "Barracudas" (which featured Shorter) and six originals that sound a bit influenced by Shorter's conception. Trumpeter Dan Bagasoul makes the quartet a quintet on two songs. Fielder is a strong up-and-coming talent and although not a Wayne Shorter clone, he hints strongly at the older saxophonist on several of these well-conceived tributes. In fact, this music sounds like something Wayne Shorter might have come up with if he had not changed direction in the early '70s. Recommended. —*Scott Yanow*

Ocean of Love and Mercy / Dec. 22, 1996 / Cadence ✦✦✦

Brandon Fields

b. 1958, Indiana
Alto Saxophone, Soprano Saxophone, Tenor Saxophone / Post-Bop, Crossover Jazz
A talented altoist influenced by David Sanborn, Brandon Fields has the versatility to be able to play both R&B/crossover and hard bop. Fields grew up in Orange County, CA, and started playing alto when he was ten. A freelance musician since he was a teenager, Fields moved to Los Angeles in 1982 and has worked steadily ever since. He toured with George Benson in 1985, was a regular member of the Rippingtons, has long been a busy session player, and recorded four CDs as a leader for Nova and one recently for Positive music. —*Scott Yanow*

● **The Other Side of the Story** / Feb. 13, 1985-Feb. 14, 1985 / Nova ✦✦✦✦✦
An excellent, quite versatile altoist influenced a bit sound-wise by David Sanborn, Brandon Fields has mostly been buried as a session musician. His occasional solo projects tend to be quite rewarding, particularly to listeners who do not mind mixing in some funk with their jazz. For this out-of-print LP, put out by the defunct Nova label, Fields sounds fine on alto, tenor, soprano and flute and is joined by trumpeter Walt Fowler, keyboardist David Garfield, up-and-coming bassist John Patitucci and drummer Gregg Bissonette. In addition, tenorman Albert Wing sits in on two songs, and guitarist Robben Ford makes his presence felt on "Bullfunk." The nine songs are all Fields originals, and they cover a wide span of moods, from heated romps to lyrical ballads. —*Scott Yanow*

Other Places / Mar. 24, 1992 / Nova ✦✦
Brandon Fields, whose main influence is David Sanborn, has proved many times that he can play creative R&B-influenced jazz. This CD has a few such moments (particularly during a heated "The Face on Mars" and an all-too-brief "You Got It") but Phil Perry's Al Jarreau soundalike pop vocals on "Know How" and "Old San Juan" lower the jazz content of the disappointingly routine (and out-of-print) CD. —*Scott Yanow*

Everybody's Business / Jul. 6, 1992 / Nova ✦✦✦

Firehouse Five Plus Two

f. 1949, db. 1969
Group / Dixieland
The Firehouse Five Plus Two started out as an amateur Dixieland band mostly comprising cartoon animators from the Disney Studios. Their spontaneous sessions (led by trombonist Ward Kimball) were so successful that they started recording for Good Time Jazz in 1949 and soon became a poular attraction, while never giving up their day jobs! In addition to colorful Dixieland ensembles and solos, the band often let off a siren during their hotter choruses and was not shy to inject their music with a healthy dose of humor. They recorded regularly for Good Time Jazz during 1949-60, with additional albums cut in 1962, 1964 and 1969. In addition to Kimball, the band included trumpeter Johnny Lucas (for the first session), cornetist Danny Alguire, clarinetist Clarke Mallery and, from 1960 on, George Probert on soprano and clarinet. —*Scott Yanow*

● **The Firehouse Five Plus Two Story** / May 13, 1949-Mar. 31, 1954 / Good Time Jazz ✦✦✦✦✦
This double-CD reissues the first three LPs by the Firehouse Five Plus Two, a very popular Dixieland group in the 1950s. In addition to trombonist Ward Kimball

(who occasionally lets loose on a siren), the main soloists are generally trumpeter Danny Alguire and either Clarke Mallery, Tom Sharpsteen or George Probert on clarinet. The spirited jamming mixes together standards, a few obscurities and an occasional original (including "Firehouse Stomp," "Fireman's Lament" and "Firechief Rag"). Although not exactly innovative, the music is quite fun and easily recommended to Dixieland fans. —*Scott Yanow*

Firehouse Five Plus Two Goes South / Jan. 23, 1954-Oct. 10, 1956 / Good Time Jazz ✦✦✦✦
The Firehouse Five Plus Two's humor sometimes came dangerously close to corn although their musicianship was usually quite strong, with soprano saxophonist George Probert being a first-class soloist. Comprising mostly members of the creative staff of Walt Disney, these part-time musicians always seemed to enjoy themselves and had a wide audience during the 1950s. This CD reissue is straightforward Dixieland, featuring a crisp lead by cornetist Danny Alguire and even two siren breaks from trombonist/leader Ward Kimball. Fun music. —*Scott Yanow*

Firehouse Five Plus Two Plays for Lovers / Sep. 23, 1955+Dec. 19, 1955 / Good Time Jazz ✦✦✦✦
This CD is a straight reissue of the original LP. The Firehouse Five Plus Two, an upbeat Dixieland band, performs a dozen songs having to do with love, including ten that have "love" as part of their title ("Careless Love," "Love Is Just Around the Corner," "The Love Nest," "Love Songs of the Nile," etc.), but there is nothing sentimental or sticky about the music. The musicians, all employed at the time by Disney, romp through the tunes with their usual brand of good humor; the front line of cornetist Danny Alguire, trombonist Ward Kimball and clarinetist George Probert keeps the results stimulating. —*Scott Yanow*

Firehouse Five Plus Two Goes to Sea / Feb. 24, 1957-Nov. 18, 1957 / Good Time Jazz ✦✦✦
The Firehouse Five Plus Two, a spirited Dixieland group that often used humor in a good-natured way (such as having a siren go off during their hotter final choruses), recorded a few "concept" albums where a group of titles had a theme of sorts. For this CD reissue of a former LP, the band mostly plays songs having to do with the sea, such as "When My Dreamboat Comes Home," "A Sailboat in the Moonlight," "She Was Just a Sailor's Sweetheart" and "Asleep in the Deep"; however, "Peoria" is a bit of a stretch. The group at the time consisted of trombonist Ward Kimball, trumpeter Danny Alguire, George Probert on soprano sax, pianist Frank Thomas, banjoist Dick Roberts, Ralph Ball or George Bruns on tuba, and drummer Eddie Forrest. Fun music. —*Scott Yanow*

Firehouse Five Plus Two Crashes a Party / Sep. 29, 1958-Nov. 10, 1959 / Good Time Jazz ✦✦✦
One of the few Firehouse Five Plus Two records not to be reissued on CD yet, this album is one of their more humorous sets. Using friends and relatives to simulate a party, the Firehouse Five play exuberant Dixieland over the crowd noise of partyers, and between songs there are shouts for requests, along with other drunken-sounding remarks. The spirited Dixieland band performs such numbers as "Let's Have a Party," "At the Fireman's Ball," "Ballin' the Jack," "Bill Bailey" and "When the Saints Go Marching In" with swing and humor. It does sound very much like a party, and the humor has dated fairly well. Leader/trombonist Ward Kimball, trumpeter Danny Alguire and George Probert on soprano are all heard in prime form amidst the merriment. —*Scott Yanow*

16 Dixieland Favorites / Sep. 29, 1958-Mar. 14, 1969 / Good Time Jazz ✦✦✦✦
This CD reissues the complete set originally titled *Dixieland Favorites* plus adds five other selections from other dates. Most of the music dates from 1958-60 when the Firehouse Five Plus Two was at the peak of its popularity. Unlike most of their other releases, all of the selections on this CD are Dixieland standards including such songs as "Fidgety Feet," "Muskrat Ramble," "Royal Garden Blues" and even "When the Saints Go Marching In." An excellent second-level band, the Firehouse Five Plus Two made up in spirit for what they generally lacked in originality. A fun release. —*Scott Yanow*

Firehouse Five Plus Two Around the World / Nov. 18, 1958-Mar. 27, 1960 / Good Time Jazz ✦✦✦
For this CD reissue, the popular Firehouse Five Plus Two travels the world through such songs as "Japanese Sandman," "Panama," "When Irish Eyes Are Smiling," "It Happened in Monterey" and even "Lady of Spain." As was often the case with their records, the song titles are more exotic than the music, which is essentially straightforward Dixieland with a healthy dose of good humor. The strong front line (comprising trumpeter Danny Alguire, trombonist Ward Kimball and soprano saxophonist George Probert) and the driving rhythm section resulted in the group forming its own identifiable sound. All of the FFPT recordings are easily recommended to Dixieland fans. —*Scott Yanow*

At Disneyland / Jul. 27, 1962-Jul. 28, 1962 / Good Time Jazz ✦✦✦
It was only fitting that the Firehouse Five Plus Two would eventually record at Disneyland, for all of its members had important day jobs at Disney. This CD reissue (which has the same music as the earlier LP) was the popular group's only truly live record, and they play a variety of often-rambunctious crowd pleasers. Highlights include a humorous version of "Anvil Stomp," "Lassus Trombone," "Coney Island Washboard" and "Tiger Rag." —*Scott Yanow*

The Firehouse Five Plus Two Goes to a Fire / Apr. 1964-Jun. 1964 / Good Time Jazz ✦✦✦✦
The Firehouse Five Plus Two always played a joyous brand of Dixieland, and this LP, their next-to-last recording, finds their enthusiasm at a high level. The fine septet (which features solos from cornetist Danny Alguire, trombonist Ward Kimball and soprano saxophonist George Probert) performs a dozen songs with titles having something to do with fires, such as "Keep the Home Fires Burning," "Hot Lips," "Fireman, Save My Child," "A Hot Time in the Old Town," "I Don't Want to Set the World on Fire," etc. Fans of the group will not be disappointed with this spirited effort. —*Scott Yanow*

Twenty Years Later / Oct. 6, 1969-Oct. 8, 1969 / Good Time Jazz ✦✦✦
Five years after their previous recording, the Firehouse Five Plus Two came together for one last record date, celebrating their 20th anniversary as a group. This CD reissue has two numbers from 1966 ("Mame" and "Winchester Cathedral"), but is otherwise from 1969. Rather than emphasizing standards (only "High Society" qualifies as a true Dixieland warhorse), the group chose to play more offbeat material, including jazz pop hits such as "Mame," "Hello Dolly," "Midnight In Moscow" and "Stranger on the Shore." For the only time, the front line had two trumpets (Danny Alguire and Don Kinch) in addition to the group's leader, Ward Kimball, on trombone and George Probert on soprano, but the band's sound was unchanged. It was only fitting that since the Firehouse Five Plus Two's first record launched the Good Time Jazz label, its final set was the last release by the original label. —*Scott Yanow*

Clare Fischer

b. Oct. 22, 1928, Durand, MI
Piano, Keyboards, Arranger, Composer / Latin Jazz, Hard Bop
Clare Fischer has had a varied career as keyboardist, composer, arranger and bandleader. The composer of two standards, "Pensativa" and "Morning," Fischer has long had an interest in Latin rhythms. After graduating from Michigan State University he moved to Los Angeles in 1957, working as accompanist and arranger for the Hi-Lo's. He wrote for a 1960 Dizzy Gillespie album (*A Portrait of Duke Ellington*) and recorded bossa nova as early as 1962; that same year he recorded two trio sets and the following year he led his first big-band date. Fischer, who has alternated between the two formats through the years, has recorded in a wide variety of settings, from solo piano to heading a vocal-dominated Latin group Salsa Picante. Based in Los Angeles, Fischer (who is also an effective organist and a strong electric keyboardist) has recorded extensively through the years for such labels as Pacific Jazz/World Pacific, Revelation, Discovery, MPS, and Concord. —*Scott Yanow*

Extension / 1963 / Discovery ✦✦✦✦
This was arranger/pianist/organist Clare Fischer's first recording as a leader of an orchestra and was reissued on a 1984 Discovery LP. Fischer always had his own arranging style, and he contributed all eight originals. Despite the presence of many top West Coast players, the only soloists on the set are Fischer and the cool-toned tenor saxophonist Jerry Coker. Coker, who has made far too few recordings in his career, is in top form and is really the co-star of this fairly straightahead but somewhat unpredictable music. —*Scott Yanow*

'Twas Only Yesterday / Oct. 1968 / Discovery ✦✦✦✦
Clare Fischer's 18-piece big band recorded an obscure set for Atlantic in 1968 that quickly went out of print. Fortunately, the Discovery label brought it back in 1979, and even though Discovery's releases eventually disappeared too, there is at least a better chance of finding this highly enjoyable effort. Fischer had a particularly strong group at the time, featuring such major soloists as trumpeters Steve Huffsteter and Conte Candoli, Warne Marsh on tenor, baritonist Bill Perkins (showcased on "Calamus") and altoist Gary Foster, all of whom receive solo space. The leader contributed half of the selections (which also include Lennie Tristano's "Lennie's Pennies" and Billy Strayhorn's "Upper Manhattan Medical Group") and takes a very rare alto solo on the brief "In Memoriam" (dedicated to the slain Kennedys). One of Clare Fischer's finest recordings. —*Scott Yanow*

Duality / 1969 / Discovery ✦✦✦

Memento / Jul. 3, 1969 / Discovery ✦✦✦
Clare Fischer has inherited the crown from Cal Tjader as Latin music's leading non-Latin bandleader and figure. These 13 selections, pulled from three Fischer albums done in the late '60s and early and mid-'80s, show Fischer's straight jazz and big band work. It does include the title song and "Preludio," but this is mostly straightahead swing, bop, and cool fare, with nice reworkings of such anthems as "Giant Steps," "Jeru," and "Old Folks." His band contains many West Coast household names, like Bill Perkins, Gary Foster, and Bud Shank, plus bassist John Patitucci on board part-time. —*Ron Wynn*

Salsa Picante / Jan. 30, 1978 / Discovery ✦✦✦✦
Nice set with Fischer and company in a salsa groove. This is among his harder, more energetic dates, with plenty of strong solos, intense percussive dialogues, and extended jamming. —*Ron Wynn*

Machacha / May 16, 1979-May 17, 1979 / Discovery ✦✦✦✦
Salsa picante at its instrumental best. Latin jazz-hots with Rick Zunigar (g), Gary Foster on saxophone and flute, and Alex Acuna and Poncho Sanchez on percussion. —*Michael G. Nastos*

Whose Woods Are These? / 1982 / Discovery ✦✦✦
This colorful set features pianist/arranger Clare Fischer's writing for five woodwinds and a rhythm section (which also includes the young electric bassist John Patitucci and drummer Vinnie Colaiuta). Chief among the reeds is Gary Foster, who is heard on alto, flute and clarinet. The other musicians all play flute, clarinet and/or bass clarinet, and, in Jack Nimitz's case, contrabass clarinet. The high-quality material—highlighted by Fischer's three-part, 15-minute "Blues Trilogy" and a version of "Lennie's Pennies" that starts out as a "Free Interlude" for Fischer and Foster—makes this an LP well worth searching for; only two of the five selections have thus far been reissued on CD (on a sampler). —*Scott Yanow*

● **Starbright** / Nov. 23, 1982 / Discovery ✦✦✦✦✦
Since keyboardist/arranger Clare Fischer and altoist/flutist Gary Foster had recorded together in many settings since 1963, it was natural that they would eventually record a duet set. This LP (which has only been partly reissued on CD) finds the compatible pair exploring three Fischer originals and five jazz standards, including "Cherokee," "I Love You" and "Sippin' at Bells." The performances are quite spontaneous and often exciting, bringing out the best in both players. —*Scott Yanow*

Lembrancas / June 1989 / Concord Picante ✦✦
This '89 date takes Fischer's Latin sound into a lighter, more pop direction. The leader plays only synthesizer and the rhythms; although they adhere to Latin patterns, they aren't as explosive or varied as on earlier Fischer sessions. Dick Mitchell isn't as aggressive as other Fischer saxophonists, either. The results are certainly pleasant and competent, but not among his best. —*Ron Wynn*

Just Me: Solo Piano Excursions / Mar. 31, 1995+Apr. 7, 1995 / Concord Jazz ✦✦✦✦

Rockin' in Rhythm / 1997 / JMI ✦✦✦
Due to the inadequate packaging, it is impossible for anyone running across this CD in a store to have any idea what the music sounds like, or to realize that the performances are dominated by six vocalists. Essentially a Latin jazz date that looks toward both Cuba and Brazil, the set features arrangements and electric keyboard solos by Clare Fischer, spots on woodwinds for Don Shelton (who also sings tenor with the vocalists), four instrumentals among the 11 songs and plenty of spirited group singing. An interesting effort. —*Scott Yanow*

Ella Fitzgerald

b. Apr. 25, 1917, Newport News, VA, d. Jun. 15, 1996, Beverly Hills, CA
Vocals / Bop, Swing, Traditional Pop, Classic Female Blues
"The First Lady of Song," Ella Fitzgerald was arguably the finest female jazz singer of all time (although some may vote for Sarah Vaughan or Billie Holiday). Blessed with a beautiful voice and a wide range, Ella could outswing anyone, was a brilliant scat singer and had near-perfect elocution; one could always understand the words she sang. The one fault was that, since she always sounded so happy to be singing, Ella did not always dig below the surface of the lyrics she interpreted and she even made a downbeat song such as "Love for Sale" sound joyous. However, when one evaluates her career on a whole, there is simply no one else in her class.

One could never guess from her singing that Ella Fitzgerald's early days were as grim as Billie Holiday's. Growing up in poverty, Ella was literally homeless for the year before she got her big break. In 1934 she appeared at the Apollo Theater in Harlem, winning an amateur contest by singing "Judy" in the style of her idol, Connee Boswell. After a short stint with Tiny Bradshaw, Ella was brought to the attention of Chick Webb by Benny Carter (who was in the audience at the Apollo). Webb, who was not impressed by the 17-year-old's appearance, reluctantly persuaded to let her sing with his orchestra on a one-nighter. She went over well and soon the drummer recognized her commercial potential. Starting in 1935, Ella began recording with Webb's orchestra and by 1937 over half of the band's selections featured her voice. "A-Tisket, A-Tasket" became a huge hit in 1938 and "Undecided" soon followed. During this era Fitzgerald was essentially a pop-swing singer who was best on ballads, while her medium-tempo performances were generally juvenile novelties. She already had a beautiful voice but did not improvise or scat much; that would develop later.

On June 16, 1939 Chick Webb died. It was decided that Ella would front the orchestra even though she had little to do with the repertoire or hiring or firing the musicians. She retained her popularity and when she broke up the band in 1941 and went solo, it was not long before her Decca recordings contained more than their share of hits. She was teamed with the Ink Spots, Louis Jordan and the Delta Rhythm Boys for some bestsellers and in 1946 began working regularly for Norman Granz's Jazz at the Philharmonic. Granz became her manager although it would be nearly a decade before he could get her on his label. A major change occurred in Ella's singing around this period. She toured with Dizzy Gillespie's big band, adopted bop as part of her style and started including exciting scat-filled romps in her set. Her recordings of "Lady Be Good," "How High the Moon" and "Flying Home" during 1945-47 became popular and her stature as a major jazz singer rose as a result. For a time (1948-52) she was married to bassist Ray Brown and used his trio as a backup group. Ella's series of duets with pianist Ellis Larkins in 1950 (a 1954 encore with Larkins was a successful follow-up) found her interpreting George Gershwin songs, predating her upcoming *Songbook* series.

After appearing in the film *Pete Kelly's Blues* in 1955, Ella signed with Norman Granz's Verve label and over the next few years she would record extensive "Songbooks" of the music of Cole Porter, the Gershwins, Rodgers and Hart, Duke Ellington, Harold Arlen, Jerome Kern and Johnny Mercer. Although (with the exception of the Ellington sets) those were not her most jazz-oriented projects (Ella stuck mostly to the melody and was generally accompanied by string orchestras), the prestigious projects did a great deal to uplift her stature. At the peak of her powers around 1960, Ella's hilarious live version of "Mack the Knife" (in which she forgot the words and made up her own) from *Ella in Berlin* is a classic and virtually all of her Verve recordings are worth getting.

Ella's Capitol and Reprise recordings of 1967-70 are not on the same level, as she attempted to "update" her singing by including pop songs such as "Sunny" and "I Heard It Through the Grapevine," sounding quite silly in the process. But Ella's later years were saved by Norman Granz's decision to form a new label, Pablo. Starting with a Santa Monica Civic concert in 1972 that is climaxed by Ella's incredible live version of "C Jam Blues" (in which she trades off with and "battles" five classic jazzmen), Fitzgerald was showcased in jazz settings throughout the 1970s with the likes of Count Basie, Oscar Peterson and Joe Pass among others. Her voice began to fade during this era and by the 1980s her decline due to age was quite noticeable. Troubles with her eyes and heart knocked her out of action for periods of time, although her increasingly rare appearances found Ella still retaining her sense of swing and joyful style. By 1994, Ella was in retirement and she passed away two years later, but she remains a household name and scores of her recordings are easily available on CD. —*Scott Yanow*

1935-1937 / Jun. 12, 1935-Jan. 14, 1937 / Classics ✦✦✦✦
The first of six Ella Fitzgerald CDs in the European label Classics "complete" series has her earliest 25 recordings, with two numbers ("My Melancholy Baby" and "All My Life") from a session with Teddy Wilson, three songs (including "Goodnight My Love") cut with Benny Goodman's big band, four tunes from her initial session as a leader and the remainder with Chick Webb's orchestra, which mainly acted as a backup band for the young singer. Even at the age of 17, Ella Fitzgerald had a beautiful voice and a strong sense of swing (although she would not seriously scat for another decade). "I'll Chase the Blues Away," "When I Get Low I Get High," "Sing Me a Swing Song" and "You'll Have to Swing It" are among the high points of this fine set. —*Scott Yanow*

The Early Years, Pt. 1 / Jun. 12, 1935-Oct. 6, 1938 / GRP ✦✦✦✦
This two-CD set contains 43 of the best recordings that Ella Fitzgerald recorded during her apprentice period with Chick Webb's orchestra. Although only 16 years old at the time of her recording debut, she already had a strong and likable voice. She would not learn to really scat sing until the mid-'40s but, on the strength of "A-Tisket, A-Tasket," by 1938 Fitzgerald was one of the most popular of all the big-band singers. This set, which contains only a few examples of the Webb Orchestra's instrumental powers, is highlighted by "I'll Chase the Blues Away," "Sing Me a Swing Song," "You'll Have to Swing It," "Organ Grinder's Swing," "If Dreams Come True" and "You Can't Be Mine." —*Scott Yanow*

1937-1938 / Jan. 14, 1937-May 2, 1938 / Classics ✦✦✦✦
The second of six CDs in the Classics label's complete reissue of Ella Fitzgerald's early recordings features the singer as a teenager with the Chick Webb Orchestra, in addition to leading two sessions that use Webb's sidemen and performing a pair of songs ("Big Boy Blue" and "Dedicated to You") with the Mills Brothers. Highlights include "I Want to Be Happy," "If Dreams Come True" and her big hit,

"A-Tisket, A-Tasket." Although not yet the brilliant jazz singer she would become, Fitzgerald already had a highly appealing voice and the ability to swing on any song she was given. —*Scott Yanow*

1938-1939 / May 2, 1938-Feb. 17, 1939 / Classics ✦✦✦✦
After her giant hit of "A-Tisket, A-Tasket," the already-popular Ella Fitzgerald became the main attraction with the Chick Webb Orchestra and the majority of their recordings from 1938 feature the singer, who was then 20. She is particularly strong on the ballads (such as "You Can't Be Mine") and had a hit in "Undecided" (the lone 1939 selection on this CD) although her work on the novelties is less memorable. All of these Classics releases are worth picking up for a definitive (and very complete) look at early Fitzgerald. —*Scott Yanow*

☆ **75th Birthday Celebration** / May 2, 1938-Aug. 5, 1955 / GRP ✦✦✦✦✦
This attractive two-CD set, released to celebrate Fitzgerald's 75th birthday, is a perfect greatest-hits collection spanning the first half of her very productive career. All 39 songs are winners, highlighted by "A-Tisket, A-Tasket," "Undecided," "Flying Home," "Lady Be Good," "How High the Moon," "Smooth Sailing," "Airmail Special," "Lullaby of Birdland" and "Hard Hearted Hannah." During the period covered by this package, she developed from a fine big-band pop vocalist into the definitive jazz singer, one who could scat and swing with the best musicians. This set is a perfect introduction to her magic. —*Scott Yanow*

Ella: The Legendary Decca Recordings / May 2, 1938-Aug. 5, 1955 / GRP ✦✦✦✦
The four-CD, 80-track, four-hour boxed set retrospective *The Legendary Decca Recordings* represented both an attempt to present the essence of Ella Fitzgerald's two-decade tenure at Decca Records and to defend that period against the conventional wisdom that not until she moved to Verve Records in the mid-1950s was her talent given full rein. In accomplishing these tasks, reissue producers Orrin Keepnews and Joel Dorn divided Fitzgerald's Decca recordings into four sections, each occupying a CD of 20 tracks and roughly an hour's length. First was "The Very Best of Ella," culled from a list of favorites prepared by Milt Gabler, Fitzgerald's producer in her second decade at Decca. This was not exactly a greatest hits set, though it began with her first big hit, "A-Tisket, A-Tasket," and included such chart successes as "Undecided," "Five O' Clock Whistle," "Cow-Cow Boogie," "Stone Cold Dead in the Market," "My Happiness," and "Smooth Sailing." Also included were such classics of scat singing as "Oh, Lady Be Good" and "How High the Moon" and the signature song "You'll Have to Swing It (Mr. Paganini)." Thus, with only one disc Keepnews and Dorn had accomplished their goals of including Fitzgerald's most memorable work for Decca and demonstrating that that work was as good as any she ever did. The second disc, "Ella & Friends," featured duets with Louis Armstrong, the Ink Spots, Louis Jordan, the Delta Rhythm Boys, and the Mills Brothers, and again featured some of Fitzgerald's major hits: "Into Each Life Some Rain Must Fall," "I'm Making Believe," "The Frim Fram Sauce," "Petootie Pie," "Baby, It's Cold Outside," "I'll Never Be Free," and "Can Anyone Explain?" Having thoroughly explored Fitzgerald's popular and jazz successes on Decca, the producers went on to show how her Decca recordings anticipated the ones on Verve. The third disc, "Ella Sings Gershwin & Others," comprised two albums of standards on which Fitzgerald was accompanied only by pianist Ellis Larkins: *Ella Sings Gershwin*, recorded in 1950, and *Songs In A Mellow Mood*, recorded in 1954. Of course, the popular Verve songbooks featured not only song standards but also name arrangers, and the fourth disc, "Ella & the Arrangers," demonstrated that, again, Decca had gotten there first, pairing her with Sy Oliver, Gordon Jenkins, Andre Previn, Benny Carter, and Toots Camarata. Ella Fitzgerald recorded a great deal of material for Decca over the years, and some of it certainly justifies the criticisms made of the catalog in general. But *The Legendary Decca Recordings*, by being selective and coming up with a structured approach to her Decca work, presented it in the best possible light and included the most impressive sides from the period. —*William Ruhlmann*

1939 / Feb. 17, 1939-Jun. 29, 1939 / Classics ✦✦✦✦
Unlike GRP, which has merely reissued the "best" of early Ella Fitzgerald domestically, the European Classics label has released all of the great singer's early recordings (from the 1935-41 period) on six CDs. This, the fourth volume, has her final recordings with Chick Webb's orchestra (before the legendary drummer's premature death) and her first after she took control of his big band. Fitzgerald is best on "'Tain't What You Do" and the ballads (particularly "Don't Worry About Me," "Little White Lies," "Stairway to the Stars" and "Out of Nowhere") although she is less memorable on such uptempo novelties as "Chew-Chew-Chew Your Bubble Gum" and "I Want the Waiter with the Water." This CD is well worth acquiring along with the other entries in this definitive series. —*Scott Yanow*

The Early Years, Pt. 2 / Feb. 17, 1939-Jul. 31, 1941 / GRP ✦✦✦✦
On this two-CD set, GRP reissues 42 of the 69 recordings that Ella Fitzgerald cut during a two-and-one-half-year period. Not as valuable as the European Classics "complete" series, this set does give one a good introduction to the classic singer's

music during a time when she led Chick Webb's orchestra after the drummer's death. Highlights include "Undecided," "Don't Worry About Me," "Stairway to the Stars," "Taking a Chance on Love," "The One I Love" and "Can't Help Lovin' Dat Man"; the medium-tempo novelties are less significant. It is recommended to the more casual collector. —*Scott Yanow*

1939-1940 / Aug. 18, 1939-May 9, 1940 / Classics ✦✦✦✦
This fifth in the six-CD series by the European Classics label documents Fitzgerald's recordings during a nine-month period starting shortly after she took over the late Chick Webb's orchestra. During this era she was much better on the ballads than on the uptempo novelties, many of which (such as "My Wubba Dolly") were not worth saving. Fortunately this CD has a good sampling of ballads (such as "My Last Goodbye," "Moon Ray," "Sugar Blues" and "Imagination") along with two rare instrumentals by her big band. The music is not essential but fans will enjoy this look at her early days. —*Scott Yanow*

Ella Fitzgerald and Her Orchestra / Feb. 26, 1940+Mar. 4, 1940 / Sunbeam ✦✦✦
This LP looks stronger than it actually is. Ella Fitzgerald was put at the head of the former Chick Webb Orchestra after the drummer's premature death and her studio recordings rarely gave the big band a chance to stretch out instrumentally. This album contains two broadcasts (which are mixed together), and eight of the 14 numbers are instrumentals. During the band features, Fitzgerald often mutters the first name of the soloist but the personnel and exact dates are inexcusably missing. However, the real disappointment is the erratic sound quality, which occasionally makes the musicians sound distorted. Trumpeter Taft Jordan, trombonist Sandy Williams and tenorman Teddy McRae are the main soloists and Fitzgerald sounds at her best for the period on "Sugar Blues" and her worst on the dumb novelty "Chewin' Gum." But the technical deficiencies make this set of interest only to completists. —*Scott Yanow*

1940-1941 / Mar. 9, 1940-Jul. 31, 1941 / Classics ✦✦✦✦
The sixth in Classics' six-CD series that completely reissues all of Ella Fitzgerald's early recordings has her final 23 performances as the head of what was formerly the Chick Webb Orchestra. Just 22 during most of this period, she is generally in superb voice and the ballads (highlighted by "Shake Down the Stars," "Taking a Chance on Love," "The One I Love" and "Can't Help Lovin' Dat Man") are frequently exquisite; her expertise at scatting would come a few years later. It's recommended, as are all of the entries in this valuable series (which is superior to GRP's Decca program). —*Scott Yanow*

The War Years / Oct. 6, 1941-Dec. 20, 1947 / GRP/Decca ✦✦✦✦
Covering an important six-year period in Ella Fitzgerald's career, this two-CD set contains some of the highlights of the period as she develops from a top big-band singer into a masterful jazz improviser. Although one wishes that this survey were "complete," the 43 selections do feature Fitzgerald in a wide variety of settings, including with small groups, collaborating with the Ink Spots, the Delta Rhythm Boys, Louis Jordan, Louis Armstrong and fronting various studio groups. Most of her hits from the period are here along with previously unissued alternate takes of "It's Only a Paper Moon," "Flying Home" and two of "How High the Moon," making this a strong introduction to her early years. —*Scott Yanow*

1941-1944 / 1941 / Classics ✦✦✦✦
This Classics CD traces Ella Fitzgerald's recordings from the beginning of her solo career. Having finally broken up the Chick Webb ghost orchestra, Ella mostly recorded ballads during her first few years as a solo artist; her jazz and scat singing would develop much more quickly starting in 1945. On some selections she is joined by a mundane vocal group called the Four Keys, but her three collaborations with the Ink Spots (particularly "Cow Cow Boogie" and "Into Each Life Some Rain Must Fall") are quite delightful. Other high points from this release (which finds Ella at 24 to 27 years old) include "This Love of Mine," "My Heart and I Decided" and "I'm Confessin'." —*Scott Yanow*

The Ultimate Ella Fitzgerald / 1949-1961 / Verve ✦✦✦✦
In order to recycle its holdings yet again, Verve hit upon a fascinating gimmick: get celebrity guest "DJs" to select the tracks and provide the liner notes. So here, Joe Williams is the man on the spot, and he comes up with 16 of his favorite Ella tunes, a good connoisseur's mix of orchestrated ballads, pure jazz workouts, sessions with big bands, duets, and intimate pairings with pianists. Most of them are on their umpteenth trip onto CD—obvious basic library stuff like the live "A-Tisket, A-Tasket," "Mr. Paganini," "How High the Moon," "Bess, You Is My Woman Now" with Satchmo, and the famous Berlin "Mack the Knife"—but a few are comparatively unusual, like "Robbins Nest" with a trio at Carnegie Hall from 1949. There is also an apparent goof; the guys in the mastering lab used a Williams solo version of "Too Close for Comfort" instead of a promised duet with Ella. Williams' "notes"—actually a transcribed interview—emphasize the sheer fun that Ella had onstage, her innate sense of rhythm and storytelling ability, and even includes a bit of humor (when citing "Lush Life" as a textbook recording of the tune, he says

he's heard singers say "distant gay places" instead of "distingue places"). Ultimately—pardon the pun—it's about as good as one can expect a mere single-disc sampling of Verve's vast Ella holdings to be. —*Richard S. Ginell*

Ella Fitzgerald Set / Sep. 18, 1949-Sep. 17, 1954 / Verve ✦✦✦
This LP released for the first time selections from Ella Fitzgerald sets that were performed while touring with Jazz at the Philharmonic. Pianist Raymond Tunia, bassist Ray Brown and drummer Buddy Rich give effective support during six numbers from 1953-54 (highlighted by "The Man That Got Away" and "Hernando's Hideaway"), pianist Hank Jones along with Brown and Rich accompany the singer in 1949 on such songs as "Robbins Nest," "Black Coffee" and "Basin St. Blues" (during the latter she imitates Louis Armstrong) and, for a grand finale, five horn players back Fitzgerald on "Flying Home," which also features some hot tenor by Flip Phillips. —*Scott Yanow*

● **The First Lady of Song** / Sep. 18, 1949-Jul. 29, 1966 / Verve ✦✦✦✦
This attractive three-CD set gives listeners an overview of Ella Fitzgerald's Verve recordings, although the inclusion of seven previously unissued cuts (in addition to 44 that are mostly available in more complete form elsewhere) will frustrate some completists. However, the careful selection of representative performances along with the informative and lengthy text make this highly enjoyable reissue (which captures her in prime form) recommended even to collectors who have most of the singer's albums. —*Scott Yanow*

Pure Ella / Sep. 11, 1950-Mar. 30, 1954 / GRP/Decca ✦✦✦✦
In 1950, six years before her acclaimed *Songbook* series for Verve, Fitzgerald recorded eight George and Ira Gershwin classics in intimate duets with the sensitive and lightly swinging pianist Ellis Larkins. Four years later she recorded a dozen more songs (this time by a variety of composers) with Larkins and all 20 performances are included on this wonderful CD. Although the emphasis is on ballads and fairly straightforward treatment of the high-quality melodies, she does improvise with subtlety and gives great meaning to the lyrics. The exquisite and very memorable set is highlighted by "But Not for Me," "How Long Has This Been Going On?," "People Will Say We're in Love," "Stardust" and "My Heart Belongs to Daddy." It is highly recommended. —*Scott Yanow*

Bluella: Ella Fitzgerald Sings the Blues / Nov. 18, 1953-Jul. 12, 1979 / Pablo ✦✦✦
Part of a Fantasy sampler series that features musicians (and in this case a notable vocalist) performing the blues, this CD features Ella Fitzgerald on 11 performances taken from a variety of sessions. Although she never specialized in the blues, Ella had no difficulty swinging over blues changes and sometimes putting strong emotion into the lowdown variety. There is one song apiece from the 1950s and '60s, while the remainder of the program dates from 1971-79. Ella's rendition of "C-Jam Blues" at the Santa Monica Civic in 1972 is a true classic, and other highlights include "Duke's Place" (with Duke Ellington's Orchestra in 1966), "I'm Walkin'," and the lengthy "Basiella," with Count Basie's big band. But the material is easily available in more complete form elsewhere, making this reissue a bit unnecessary. —*Scott Yanow*

The Concert Years / Nov. 18, 1953-1983 / Pablo ✦✦✦✦
On this four-CD set are some of Ella Fitzgerald's finest live performances during the years when she was managed by Norman Granz. All of the material (which is taken from ten different performances in 1953, 1966, 1967, 1971, 1972, 1974, 1975, 1977, 1979 and 1983) was previously released on various Pablo albums. Since this is a "best of" collection and it was lovingly put together by the knowledgeable producer Eric Miller, the music is consistently rewarding and emphasizes the interpretive skills, scatting and jazz phrasing of the First Lady of Song. Although mostly backed by her trio/quartets of the period, Ella does get to jam "Perdido" with the 1953 JATP All-Stars, is backed by the Duke Ellington and Count Basie orchestras on some songs and revisits "Flying Home" with an all-star group in 1983. The most remarkable performance is 1972's "C Jam Blues," which features Ella trading off remarkable musical jokes with Al Grey, Stan Getz, Harry "Sweets" Edison, Eddie "Lockjaw" Davis and Roy Eldridge. —*Scott Yanow*

Love Songs: The Best of the Verve Songbooks / Feb. 7, 1956-Oct. 2, 1964 / Verve ✦✦✦
Love Songs: The Best of Verve Songbooks distills 16 songs from *The Complete Ella Fitzgerald Songbook on Verve* box set, picking songs from classic composers like Cole Porter and George Gershwin. The compilation doesn't have any unifying theme—the songs are pulled from different sessions and don't spotlight any particular composer or style of music—but it's an enjoyable listen nonetheless. —*Thom Owens*

The Best of the Songbooks: The Collection / Feb. 7, 1956-Oct. 20, 1964 / Verve ✦✦✦
Ella Fitzgerald recorded a series of "songbooks" during 1956-64, full sets of the music of various composers and (in the case of Johnny Mercer) a masterful lyricist. This three-CD box set is a reissue of three samplers that are available sepa-

rately and titled *The Best of the Songbooks, The Best of the Songbooks: The Ballads* and *Love Songs: The Best of the Verve Songbooks.* All eight of Ella's orchestral songbook projects are represented on the attractive box but her true fans will want the complete series rather than these "best of" collections which jump around quite a bit chronologically. —*Scott Yanow*

☆ **The Complete Ella Fitzgerald Songbooks** / Feb. 7, 1956-Oct. 21, 1964 / Verve ◆◆◆◆◆

With her signing to Verve in 1956, Ella Fitzgerald (under producer Norman Granz's guidance) began a series of *Songbook* projects in which the singer (backed by orchestras) performed the works of various major composers. Her *Cole Porter Songbook* was so well-received that it was followed by ones featuring the music of Rodgers and Hart, Duke Ellington (half of which featured his band), Irving Berlin, a massive salute to George and Ira Gershwin, Harold Arlen, Jerome Kern and Johnny Mercer. This 16-CD box set is not for everyone (due to its cost) and is not the most jazz-oriented of Ella Fitzgerald's recordings (she does not scat much and some of the string arrangements weigh the music down a little) but her voice is in peak form and this was a very classy (and extensive) project. The reissue (which uses miniature reproductions of the original LPs along with a definitive book, all placed in a red box) is a gem, perfectly done. —*Scott Yanow*

For the Love of Ella / Feb. 7, 1956-Jul. 20, 1966 / Verve ◆◆◆

This double CD gives listeners some of the highlights from Ella Fitzgerald's period with Verve, 32 performances divided into "Monuments of Swing" and "Ballads & Blues." Putting all of the uptempo works on one CD is an odd idea and the music is not placed in chronological order. There are many gems on this French import but the more serious collectors will prefer to get her other more complete reissues instead. —*Scott Yanow*

Ella & Louis / Aug. 16, 1956 / Verve ◆◆◆◆

Ella Fitzgerald and Louis Armstrong make for a charming team on this CD. Accompanied by pianist Oscar Peterson, guitarist Herb Ellis, bassist Ray Brown and drummer Buddy Rich, Fitzgerald and Armstrong perform 11 standards with joy and swing. There are touches of Satch's trumpet but this is primarily a vocal set with the emphasis on tasteful renditions of ballads. Its follow-up *Ella & Louis Again* is also worth getting. —*Scott Yanow*

The Complete Ella Fitzgerald & Louis Armstrong on Verve / Aug. 16, 1956-Oct. 14, 1957 / Verve ◆◆◆◆◆

Almost all of these summit meetings have been in print virtually since CDs first appeared in our lives, but never in one package. Here, you get all of *Ella and Louis,* the double LP sets *Ella and Louis Again* and *Porgy and Bess,* and two live tracks recorded at the Hollywood Bowl in 1956—all in an unusual 3-CD album that partially unfolds into an accordion-file (what will Verve's inventive packaging wizards think of next?). There are two booklets, one of which contains a rare recent interview with producer Norman Granz, and the other the notes from the original albums. Of the two wonderfully relaxed *Ella and Louis* albums, with their Oscar Peterson-driven rhythm quartets, the sequel strikes me as a more diverse, more involving collection, although Satch doesn't play as much trumpet on *Again* as he does on the first album. Also, the two go it alone on several tracks, but one is not at all inconvenienced by the inclusion of solo gems like Armstrong's sly catalog of intercouplings on "Let's Do It." The *Porgy* session is an entirely different creature, a big, formal presentation with Russ Garcia's lush yet atmospheric and even powerful orchestrations, reverberant sound (normally a Granz no-no), grandly moving vocal performances by the two, and a handful of tremendous trumpet solos from Pops. Alas, no unissued tracks turn up here, and of course, MCA still controls all of the earlier Decca duets (hence the disclaimer "Complete On Verve")—so veteran Ella/Louis collectors may opt to hang onto earlier issues. But for those who don't have everything, this is irresistible. —*Richard S. Ginell*

● **Sings the Rodgers & Hart Songbook** / Aug. 21, 1956-Aug. 31, 1956 / Verve ◆◆◆

The second of Ella Fitzgerald's famed *Songbook* series features her singing 34 of the best songs co-written by Richard Rodgers & Lorenz Hart. The arrangements by Buddy Bregman for the string orchestra and big band only border on jazz, but she manages to swing the medium-tempo numbers and give sensitivity to the ballads. With such songs as "You Took Advantage of Me," "The Lady Is a Tramp," "It Never Entered My Mind," "Where or When," "My Funny Valentine" and "Blue Moon," it is not too surprising that these recordings (originally released on a two-LP set) were so popular. This entire program is currently available in the massive box set *The Complete Ella Fitzgerald Songbooks.* —*Scott Yanow*

Sings the Duke Ellington Songbook / Sep. 4, 1956-Oct. 17, 1957 / Verve ◆◆◆◆◆

Volume 1 is with Ellington's orchestra, *Volume 2* is with smaller groups including Ben Webster, Stuff Smith, and Oscar Peterson. Outstanding recordings, worthwhile both as documents of a fertile period for her, and simply as the great music they are. —*Michael G. Nastos*

Like Someone in Love / 1957 / Verve ◆◆◆

Ella Fitzgerald was accompanied by an orchestra arranged by Frank DeVol for this fine studio session; the CD reissue has been augmented by four selections recorded a month later. Most of the songs are veteran standards, Stan Getz's warm tenor helps out on four tunes and, although this is not an essential release, her voice was so strong and appealing during this era that all of her recordings from the mid- to late '50s are enjoyable and easily recommended. —*Scott Yanow*

Ella Fitzgerald and Jazz at the Philharmonic, 1957 / Apr. 28, 1957-Apr. 29, 1957 / Tax ◆◆

Although billed as a Jazz at the Philharmonic tour, the music on this CD from the Swedish Tax label is not as spontaneous or as exciting as one would expect from JATP. Actually, the instrumentals feature a scaled-down group with trumpeter Roy Eldridge and violinist Stuff Smith joined by the Oscar Peterson Quartet (which includes guitarist Herb Ellis, bassist Ray Brown and drummer Jo Jones); best is Smith's showcase on "Bugle Call Rag." Otherwise this is strictly an Ella Fitzgerald date and, although she is in fine form on nine numbers, nothing too surprising occurs. —*Scott Yanow*

Ella and Louis Again / Jul. 23, 1957-Aug. 23, 1957 / Mobile Fidelity ◆◆◆◆

This double CD from the audiophile label Mobile Fidelity differs from the single Verve CD in that not only does it contain the duets by Ella Fitzgerald and Louis Armstrong from their second round of joint recordings but it has seven numbers featuring one of the two singers. All of the Ella-Satchmo collaborations are charming (they had obvious love for each other) and, although one wishes that there was more space set aside for Armstrong's trumpet, many of these performances are memorable; highlights include "They All Laughed," "I Won't Dance," "Let's Call the Whole Thing Off," "A Fine Romance" and an out-of-control "Stompin' at the Savoy." —*Scott Yanow*

Hello, Love / Jul. 24, 1957-Mar. 25, 1959 / Verve ◆◆◆

The three sessions that make up this somewhat obscure Ella Fitzgerald LP feature the immortal singer backed by an unidentified orchestra led by Frank DeVol; guitarist Herb Ellis is prominent in the accompaniment. Ella sounds typically enthusiastic on a dozen standards that did not fit into her many songbooks of the era, including "You Go to My Head," "Everything Happens to Me," "I've Grown Accustomed to His Face" and "Stairway to the Stars." The music is swinging, but only average for the great Ella. —*Scott Yanow*

Porgy & Bess / Aug. 18, 1957-Oct. 15, 1957 / Verve ◆◆◆

There have been many recordings of the music from the Gershwin opera *Porgy and Bess,* but this is one of the more rewarding ones. Louis Armstrong and Ella Fitzgerald sing all of the parts, performing 16 of the play's best melodies. Unfortunately, there is not much Armstrong trumpet to be heard, but the vocals are excellent and occasionally wonderful, making up for the unimaginative Russ Garcia arrangements assigned to the backup orchestra. —*Scott Yanow*

At the Opera House / Sep. 29, 1957+Oct. 7, 1957 / Verve ◆◆◆

Taken from a Jazz at the Philharmonic tour, Ella Fitzgerald is backed by pianist Oscar Peterson, guitarist Herb Ellis, bassist Ray Brown and drummer Jo Jones on two well-rounded sets. Actually the two dates are quite similar, with eight of the nine songs being repeated (although the second "Stompin' at the Savoy" and "Lady Be Good" find her backed by a riffing eight-horn all-star group) so this reissue CD is mostly recommended to her greatest fans. However, the music is wonderful, there are variations between the different versions and her voice was at its prime. —*Scott Yanow*

Sings the Irving Berlin Songbook, Vol. 1 / Mar. 13, 1958-Mar. 19, 1958 / Verve ◆◆◆

Brilliant and beautiful. Berlin never sounded so good! —*Ron Wynn*

Ella in Rome: The Birthday Concert / Apr. 25, 1958 / Verve ◆◆◆◆◆

This concert performance finds Ella Fitzgerald celebrating her 40th birthday. A top singer for 23 years at that point, she was at the peak of her powers. Backed by her regular rhythm section (with pianist Lou Levy, bassist Max Bennett and drummer Gus Johnson), she puts on her usual show of the period, uplifting the ballads and swinging the faster material. Highlights include "St. Louis Blues," "Caravan," "It's All Right with Me" and "I Can't Give You Anything but Love," during which she imitates both Louis Armstrong and Rose Murphy. This set concludes with a jam version of "Stompin' at the Savoy" with the Oscar Peterson Trio and drummer Gus Johnson. —*Scott Yanow*

Ella Swings Lightly / Nov. 22, 1958-Nov. 23, 1958 / Verve ◆◆◆

CD reissue featuring Ella Fitzgerald's flowing vocals and Marty Paich's Dek-tette band backing her. This was among several hit albums that Fitzgerald enjoyed in the '50s, when she was reaching the mass audience cutting pre-rock standards. —*Ron Wynn*

Ella Swings Brightly with Nelson / Jan. 5, 1959-Dec. 27, 1961 / Verve ✦✦✦✦
Nelson Riddle, whose arrangements were an asset on some of Ella Fitzgerald's *Songbook* projects, also made two albums with her during 1961: this one plus *Ella Swings Gently with Nelson*. The singer has rarely sounded better than during this period. For the *Swings Brightly* set (which gets a slight edge over the other one) Fitzgerald sticks mostly to familiar standards and is particularly memorable on "Don't Be That Way," "What Am I Here For?" "I'm Gonna Go Fishin'" and "I Won't Dance." Three slightly earlier "bonus" tracks round out this enjoyable big-band effort. —*Scott Yanow*

☆ **The Complete Ella in Berlin** / Feb. 13, 1960 / Verve ✦✦✦✦✦
Ella Fitzgerald was at the peak of her form during her 1960 tour of Europe. Her Berlin concert is most remembered for her hilariously inventive version of "Mack the Knife" during which she forgot the words and substituted ones of her own that somehow fit, amazing herself in the process. In addition to the original LP program, this CD has two previously unissued titles and a pair of others only briefly released on a very rare LP. With fine support from her quartet (pianist Paul Smith, guitarist Jim Hall, bassist Wilfred Middlebrooks and drummer Gus Johnson), Fitzgerald is brilliant throughout the well-rounded set, with highlights including "Misty" (a version very different from Sarah Vaughan's), "The Lady Is a Tramp," "Too Darn Hot" and a scat-filled "How High the Moon." This is essential music. —*Scott Yanow*

The Intimate Ella / Apr. 14, 1960-Apr. 19, 1960 / Verve ✦✦✦✦
This is a most unusual Ella Fitzgerald recording, reissued on CD by Verve. Recorded around the time when she performed some of these songs for the film *Let No Man Write My Epitaph*, the masterful singer is heard in duets with pianist Paul Smith interpreting 13 songs (even "I Cried for You," "I Can't Give You Anything but Love" and "Who's Sorry Now?") at slow expressive tempos. Listeners who feel that Ella Fitzgerald was mostly a scat singer who had trouble giving the proper emotional intensity to lyrics will be surprised by this sensitive and often-haunting set. —*Scott Yanow*

● **Sings the Harold Arlen Songbook** / Aug. 1, 1960-Jan. 16, 1961 / Verve ✦✦✦✦✦
Of all of her *Songbooks* (which are now available on the remarkable 16-CD set *The Complete Ella Fitzgerald Songbooks*), the Harold Arlen and Duke Ellington sets are the most jazz-oriented. With perfectly suitable arrangements by Billy May for the big band and occasional strings, she really digs into the 26 Arlen songs, giving her own sympathetic interpretations to such classics as "Blues in the Night," "Stormy Weather," "My Shining Hour," "That Old Black Magic," "Come Rain or Come Shine" "It's Only a Paper Moon" and even "Ding-Dong! The Witch Is Dead." —*Scott Yanow*

Ella Returns to Berlin / Feb. 11, 1961 / Verve ✦✦✦✦
Ella Fitzgerald's Berlin concert of Feb. 13, 1960, highlighted by her ad-lib version of "Mack the Knife," is considered a classic. The performance on this CD dates from the following year and is almost as rewarding. Accompanied by pianist Lou Levy, guitarist Herb Ellis, bassist Wilfred Middlebrooks and drummer Gus Johnson, she sings 18 songs in a varied and well-paced set. Highlights include "Take the 'A' Train," "Anything Goes," "If You Can't Sing It You'll Have to Swing It," "'Round Midnight," a new (but less humorous) version of "Mack the Knife" and an encore, "This Can't Be Love," that has the singer joined by the Oscar Peterson Trio. —*Scott Yanow*

Ella in Hollywood / May 11, 1961+May 21, 1961 / Verve ✦✦✦✦✦
It seems strange that this is a fairly obscure Ella Fitzgerald record because the classic singer rarely sounded better. In fact, on "Take The 'A' Train" she takes her longest (nearly nine minutes) recorded scat vocal of her career. For chorus after chorus Ella comes up with consistently creative and swinging ideas that are quite exciting. The rest of the program (which includes "I've Got the World on a String," "You're Driving Me Crazy," "Mr. Paganini" and "Air Mail Special") is not exactly anticlimactic and Ella (who is backed by pianist Lou Levy, guitarist Herb Ellis, bassist Wilfred Middlebrooks and drummer Gus Johnson) is heard throughout at the peak of her powers. This LP is begging to be reissued on CD. —*Scott Yanow*

Clap Hands, Here Comes Charlie! / Jun. 22, 1961-Jun. 23, 1961 / Verve ✦✦✦
Another typically wonderful CD reissue of Ella Fitzgerald in her prime, this set augments the original LP (which finds Ella joined by pianist Lou Levy, guitarist Herb Ellis, bassist Joe Mondragon and drummer Stan Levey) with three previously unreleased selections from the same era (with Levey, bassist Wilfred Middlebrooks and drummer Gus Johnson). Ella is in fine form on such numbers as "Night in Tunisia," an emotional "You're My Thrill," "Jersey Bounce," "Clap Hands, Here Comes Charlie!" and an unissued "The One I Love Belongs to Somebody Else." Although not reaching the heights of her live performances, this is an excellent (and somewhat underrated) set. —*Scott Yanow*

Ella Swings Gently with Nelson / Nov. 13, 1961-Apr. 10, 1962 / Verve ✦✦✦
In 1961 Ella Fitzgerald recorded two albums with Nelson Riddle's Orchestra. Her voice was in peak form and, even if the backup band was somewhat anonymous, Fitzgerald uplifted the 15 songs on this set; "All of Me" was from a different obscure sampler and "Call Me Darling" was previously unissued. Although the accent is on ballads, several of the songs are taken at medium tempos and she swings throughout. Highlights include "Georgia on My Mind," "The Very Thought of You," "It's a Pity to Say Goodnight," "Darn That Dream," "Body and Soul" and a cooking "All of Me." —*Scott Yanow*

Sings the Jerome Kern Songbook / Jan. 5, 1963-Jan. 7, 1963 / Verve ✦✦✦✦✦
By 1963, Ella Fitzgerald's *Songbook* series had almost run its course and was becoming much less ambitious in scope. Her Jerome Kern set features her interpretations of 14 songs while backed by an orchestra arranged by Nelson Riddle. Treatments of such classics as "A Fine Romance," "All the Things You Are" and "Yesterdays" are fairly straightforward and would have pleased the composer. All of her songbooks are now included in the massive 16-CD box set *The Complete Ella Fitzgerald Songbooks*. —*Scott Yanow*

Ella and Basie / Jul. 16, 1963+Jul. 17, 1963 / Verve ✦✦✦✦✦
Vocalist Ella Fitzgerald and bandleader/pianist Count Basie came together on a July (16 & 17) 1963 date arranged by Quincy Jones. It was originally issued as *Ella & Basie!* It was later reissued with slightly different cover art as *On the Sunny Side of the Street*. The music remained the same, a controlled, tough big band hiply backing the wonderful swinging of Fitzgerald. About the only way one could have improved with this combination would have been to turn them loose, extemporizing in front of a live audience. —*Bob Rusch, Cadence*

These Are the Blues / Oct. 28, 1963 / Verve ✦✦✦
Ella Fitzgerald was never thought of as a blues singer but she does a surprisingly effective job on the ten blues included on this CD reissue, including Bessie Smith's "Jailhouse Blues," "See See Rider," "Trouble in Mind" and "St. Louis Blues." She somehow sings more or less in the style of the classic blues vocalists of the 1920s and largely pulls it off. Trumpeter Roy Eldridge, who has few solos and is low in the mix, is largely wasted, as organist Wild Bill Davis (with assistance from guitarist Herb Ellis, bassist Ray Brown and drummer Gus Johnson) dominates the ensembles. It's an interesting set. —*Scott Yanow*

Sings the Johnny Mercer Songbook / Oct. 19, 1964-Oct. 21, 1964 / Verve ✦✦✦
Glittering. A landmark of popular song. —*Ron Wynn*

Ella at Duke's Place / Oct. 18, 1965-Oct. 20, 1965 / Verve ✦✦✦✦✦
This CD reissues Ella Fitzgerald's second studio session with Duke Ellington, following her first (the *Ellington Songbook*) by eight years. The underrated set begins quietly with four emotional ballads (who else could hold their own with Johnny Hodges on "Passion Flower"?) before Fitzgerald gets to scat a bit on the closing vamp of "Azure," comes up with fresh ideas on "Duke's Place" and closes the show by scatting up a storm on "Cottontail." The band makes its presence known in the ensembles, some solos by tenor saxophonist Paul Gonsalves, altoist Hodges and trumpeter Cootie Williams (whose opening spot on "Duke's Place" is quite jubilant), and the high-note trumpet of Cat Anderson is heard in peak form throughout this date. Recommended. —*Scott Yanow*

Stockholm Concert, 1966 / Feb. 7, 1966 / Pablo ✦✦✦
Ella Fitzgerald was teamed up with the Duke Ellington Orchestra for this spirited concert performance. Ellington himself only appears on a furious "Cottontail" (which features Fitzgerald scatting at her best) but there are some good solo spots for tenor saxophonist Paul Gonsalves, altoist Johnny Hodges and trumpeter Cootie Williams, and she is in good voice throughout this CD reissue. —*Scott Yanow*

Brighten the Corner / 1967 / Capitol ✦✦✦
Even though Ella Fitzgerald performs 14 religious hymns and the arrangements (which use the Ralph Carmichael Choir and Orchestra) are tasteful and reverent, she cannot help giving a little swing to a few of these songs. The music is taken quite straight and is outside of jazz yet, due to the beauty of her voice, this listenable set is still worth picking up. —*Scott Yanow*

Thirty by Ella / Jul. 1968-Aug. 1968 / Capitol ✦✦✦
This LP is a weird concept that mostly works. Fitzgerald participates in six medleys consisting of five of her vocals and an instrumental, with each song ranging from one to two minutes apiece. Most of the pieces are swing standards and obviously not much development takes place, but altoist Benny Carter, trumpeter Harry "Sweets" Edison, tenor saxophonist Georgie Auld and guitarist John Collins all have some solo space. It's a historical curiosity. —*Scott Yanow*

Sunshine of Your Love / Feb. 1969-Mar. 1969 / Verve ✦✦
During her long career, every once in awhile Ella Fitzgerald would attempt to "get with it" and record contemporary pop tunes. In 1968 for a live concert with a big band and the Tommy Flanagan Trio, the First Lady of the American Song did what she could with such unsuitable material as "Hey Jude," "Sunshine of Your

Love," "Watch What Happens" and "A House Is Not a Home." The results (despite her sincerity) sometime borders on the embarassing; there is no way anyone can swing "Hey Jude." A few of the other numbers (particularly "Give Me the Simple Life," "Old Devil Moon" and "Love You Madly") are of a higher quality but when Ella tries to turn "Alright, Okay, You Win" into funk, it is time to switch records. —*Scott Yanow*

Ella a Nice / Jul. 21, 1971 / Pablo ✦✦✦✦
With some spry Tommy Flanagan piano. —*Ron Wynn*

Dream Dancing / Jun. 12, 1972+Feb. 13, 1978 / Pablo ✦✦✦✦
Originally released on Atlantic as *Ella Loves Cole* and then reissued on Pablo with two extra cuts from 1978, this set features the great Ella Fitzgerald (still in excellent form) performing an extensive set of Cole Porter songs, backed by an orchestra arranged by Nelson Riddle. Fifteen years earlier Fitzgerald had had great success with her *Cole Porter Songbook* and this date, even with a few hokey arrangements, almost reaches the same level. Trumpeter Harry "Sweets" Edison and pianist Tommy Flanagan are among the supporting cast. Highlights include "I Get a Kick out of You," "I've Got You Under My Skin," "All o' You," "My Heart Belongs to Daddy" and "Just One of Those Things." —*Scott Yanow*

Newport Jazz Festival: Live at Carnegie Hall / Jul. 5, 1973 / Columbia ✦✦✦✦✦
This two-CD set (a reissue of an earlier two-LP set plus six previously unreleased numbers) brings back a memorable Carnegie Hall concert that both features and pays tribute to Ella Fitzgerald. The great singer is joined on a few numbers by a Chick Webb reunion band that has a few of the original members (plus an uncredited Panama Francis on drums). Although the musicians do not get much solo space (why wasn't trumpeter Taft Jordan featured?), the music is pleasing. Ella performs three exquisite duets with pianist Ellis Larkins and then sits out while the Jazz at the Philharmonic All-Stars romp on a few jams and a ballad medley. Trumpeter Roy Eldridge's emotional flights take honors although tenorman Eddie "Lockjaw" Davis and trombonist Al Grey are also in good form. Ella comes out for the second half of the show and sings 14 numbers with guitarist Joe Pass (including a pair of tender duets) and the Tommy Flanagan trio. Although her renditions of "I've Gotta Be Me" and "What's Going On?" are unnecessary, Ella sounds beautiful on "Good Morning Heartache," "Don't Worry About Me" and "These Foolish Things" and swings hard on the scat-filled "Lemon Drop." An excellent retrospective of Ella Fitzgerald's first 40 years in jazz. —*Scott Yanow*

Take Love Easy / 1973 / Pablo ✦✦✦
Ella Fitzgerald and guitarist Joe Pass teamed up in a set of duets for this album, which has been reissued on CD. Because the emphasis is on ballads and not all of the songs are that well suited to Fitzgerald's musical personality (particularly "Lush Life" and "I Want to Talk About You"), this set is only a mixed success. Much more successful are "Don't Be That Way" and "A Foggy Day" but this is not one of the more essential Ella Fitzgerald records. —*Scott Yanow*

Ella Fitzgerald Jams / Jan. 8, 1974 / Pablo ✦✦✦
Although Ella Fitzgerald was a little past her prime at this point, the all-star group (which includes trumpeters Harry "Sweets" Edison and Clark Terry, the tenors of Zoot Sims and Eddie "Lockjaw" Davis, pianist Tommy Flanagan, guitarist Joe Pass, bassist Ray Brown and drummer Louie Bellson) inspire her to sing at her best for this late period. High points include "I'm Just a Lucky So and So," "Rockin' in Rhythm," and "'Round Midnight." —*Scott Yanow*

☆ **Ella in London** / Apr. 11, 1974 / Pablo ✦✦✦✦✦
This is one of Fitzgerald's most enjoyable recordings from her later years. With pianist Tommy Flanagan, guitarist Joe Pass, bassist Keter Betts and drummer Bobby Durham serving as a backup group (not a bad band), she swings everything from "Sweet Georgia Brown" and "It Don't Mean a Thing" to "Lemon Drop" and even Carole King's "You've Got a Friend." Her ballad interpretations are only topped by her scatting talents. This set serves as a perfect introduction to the mature Ella Fitzgerald. —*Scott Yanow*

Ella and Oscar Peterson / May 19, 1974 / Pablo ✦✦✦✦
For this Pablo set (reissued on CD), Ella Fitzgerald is heard on half of the program in duets with pianist Oscar Peterson and for the remainder in trios with Peterson and bassist Ray Brown. In general the performances are memorable (particularly "How Long Has This Been Going On?," "More than You Know," "Midnight Sun" and "April in Paris") with the emphasis on ballads. Although her voice had slipped a little by this time, the results are still rewarding and swinging. —*Scott Yanow*

At the Montreux Festival / 1975 / Original Jazz Classics ✦✦✦✦
This CD from the 1975 Montreux Jazz Festival has a typical late-period set from Ella Fitzgerald. Backed by the Tommy Flanagan Trio (with bassist Keter Betts and drummer Bobby Durham), she is in fine form on such songs as "Teach Me Tonight," "It's All Right with Me," "How High the Moon" and even "The Girl from

Ipanema." This is a good example of Fitzgerald singing in the 1970s with some scatting, a few ballads and lots of swinging. —*Scott Yanow*

Fitzgerald and Pass . . . Again / Jan. 29, 1976-Feb. 8, 1976 / Pablo ✦✦✦
The second of three duet albums by Ella Fitzgerald and guitarist Joe Pass (which has been reissued on CD) finds the duo uplifting 14 superior standards with subtle improvising and gentle swing. High points include the wordless "Rain," "I Ain't Got Nothin' but the Blues," "That Old Feeling," "You Took Advantage of Me" and "The One I Love"; even "Tennessee Waltz" comes out sounding like classic swing. —*Scott Yanow*

Montreux '77 / Jul. 14, 1977 / Original Jazz Classics ✦✦✦
Ella Fitzgerald, 42 years after her recording debut, showed on this late concert recording that she still had the magic. Backed by pianist Tommy Flanagan, bassist Keter Betts and drummer Bobby Durham, she sounds fairly strong at times, mostly singing veteran ballads but also getting hot on "Billie's Bounce." It's not essential but worth checking out. —*Scott Yanow*

Lady Time / Jun. 19, 1978-Jun. 20, 1978 / Original Jazz Classics ✦✦✦
This CD places Ella Fitzgerald (then 60) in an unusual setting. Joined only by organist Jackie Davis and drummer Louie Bellson, she tackles a wide variety of material that ranges from "I'm Walkin'" and "I Cried for You" to "Mack the Knife" (which did not need to be remade) and "And the Angels Sing." Not one of her more essential releases, *Lady Time* does show that even at this fairly late stage in her career, Ella Fitzgerald could outswing just about anyone. —*Scott Yanow*

A Classy Pair / Feb. 15, 1979 / Pablo ✦✦✦
This studio album matches Ella Fitzgerald and the Count Basie Orchestra 16 years after they first recorded together. Basie's sidemen are unfortunately restricted to backup work in the Benny Carter arrangements but Basie has a few piano solos and Fitzgerald is in good voice and in typically swinging form. Highlights include "Just a Sittin' and a Rockin'," "Teach Me Tonight" and "Honeysuckle Rose." —*Scott Yanow*

Perfect Match / Jul. 12, 1979 / Pablo ✦✦✦
Although Count Basie gets co-billing with Ella Fitzgerald on this concert recording from the 1979 Montreux Jazz Festival, the veteran pianist is only on the final of the 11 songs. His big band, along with pianist Paul Smith, backs the veteran singer for a set of standards and, although Fitzgerald was beginning to fade, she could still hint strongly at her former greatness. Highlights include "Sweet Georgia Brown," "'Round Midnight" and "Honeysuckle Rose." —*Scott Yanow*

Ella Abraca Jobim / Sep. 17, 1980-Mar. 20, 1981 / Pablo ✦✦✦

The Best Is Yet to Come / Feb. 4, 1982-Feb. 5, 1982 / Original Jazz Classics ✦✦

Speak Love / Mar. 21, 1982+Mar. 22, 1982 / Pablo ✦✦
This set of duets with guitarist Joe Pass finds Ella Fitzgerald near the end of her career. Her voice mostly hinted at her former greatness and the setting was perhaps too intimate for what she had left. Fitzgerald's phrasing remained a joy despite the limited range, but there are many more significant records by the singer than this CD reissue, despite touching versions of "Comes Love," "There's No You" and "Gone with the Wind." —*Scott Yanow*

Nice Work If You Can Get It / May 23, 1983 / Pablo ✦✦✦
Ella Fitzgerald, who in the late '50s recorded the very extensive *George and Ira Gershwin Songbook*, revisits their music on this duet outing with pianist Andre Previn. Her voice was past her prime by this point but she was able to bring out a lot of the beauty in the ten songs, giving the classic melodies and lyrics tasteful and lightly swinging treatment. This is not an essential CD but is a reasonably enjoyable outing. —*Scott Yanow*

Easy Living / 1986 / Pablo ✦✦
For her third duo recording with guitarist Joe Pass, Ella Fitzgerald swings 15 mostly familiar standards that range from "My Ship" and "Don't Be That Way" to "Why Don't You Do Right?" and "Slow Boat to China." At 66, her voice was visibly fading although her charm and sense of swing were still very much present. But this CD is not one of her more significant recordings other than being one of the final chapters. —*Scott Yanow*

All That Jazz / Mar. 15, 1989-Mar. 22, 1989 / Pablo ✦
Ella Fitzgerald's final recording is a bit sad. At the age of 69, she no longer had much range or power and she could only hint at her former greatness. Her sidemen (who include such veterans as trumpeters Harry "Sweets" Edison and Clark Terry, trombonist Al Grey, pianists Kenny Barron and Mike Wofford, bassist Ray Brown, drummer Bobby Durham and the apparently ageless altoist Benny Carter) do their best but this noble effort is more important historically than musically. —*Scott Yanow*

Tommy Flanagan

b. Mar. 16, 1930, Detroit, MI

Piano / Bop, Hard Bop

Known for his flawless and tasteful playing, Tommy Flanagan received long-over-due recognition for his talents in the 1980s. He played clarinet when he was six and switched to piano five years later. Flanagan was an important part of the fertile Detroit jazz scene (other than 1951-53 when he was in the army) until he moved to New York in 1956. He was used for many recordings after his arrival during that era, cut sessions as a leader for New Jazz, Prestige, Savoy, and Moodsville and worked regularly with Oscar Pettiford, J.J. Johnson (1956-58), Harry "Sweets" Edison (1959-60) and Coleman Hawkins (1961). Flanagan was Ella Fitzgerald's regular accompanist during 1963-65 and 1968-78, which resulted in him being underrated as a soloist. However, starting in 1975 he began leading a series of superior record sessions and since leaving Ella, Flanagan has been in demand as the head of his own trio, consistently admired for his swinging and creative bop-based style. Among the many labels that he has recorded for since 1975 are Pablo, Enja, Denon, Galaxy, Progressive, Uptown, Timeless and several European and Japanese companies. —*Scott Yanow*

The Cats, with John Coltrane and Kenny Burrell / Apr. 18, 1957 / Original Jazz Classics ✦✦✦✦

Tenor saxophonist John Coltrane was part of a 4/18/57 blowing session along with Idrees Sulieman (trumpet), Kenny Burrell (guitar), Doug Watkins (bass), Louis Hayes (drums) and the obvious leader, though uncredited, Tommy Flanagan (piano). —*Bob Rusch, Cadence*

In Stockholm 1957 / Aug. 15, 1957 / Dragon ✦✦✦✦

Other than a co-op New Jazz jam session sometimes reissued under his name, this set of trio performances is the earliest example of pianist Tommy Flanagan as a leader. Recorded in Stockholm, Flanagan teams up with bassist Wilbur Little and drummer Elvin Jones at a time when the three formed the rhythm section for the J.J. Johnson Quintet. The nine selections (plus three alternate takes), which were originally put out by the Metronome label, have been reissued by the Swedish Dragon label and briefly by Prestige. Flanagan's bright, boppish style was already fairly recognizable (he was 27 at the time), and the swinging music can be enjoyed by bop collectors. —*Scott Yanow*

It's Magic / Sep. 5, 1957 / Savoy ✦✦✦

A fairly typical hard bop session from 1957 (the back cover says 1947), this set teams up-and-coming pianist Tommy Flanagan with altoist Sonny Red, trombonist Curtis Fuller, bassist George Tucker and drummer Louis Hayes. Although the four originals are not that memorable, they do give the musicians worthy chord changes to stretch out on. Best is a three-song ballad medley, on which Fuller takes honors. —*Scott Yanow*

Jazz ... Its Magic / Sep. 5, 1957 / Savoy ✦✦✦

A late '50s quintet date, one of the earliest that established pianist Tommy Flanagan as a tremendous soloist and leader. He headed a superior group, with alto saxophonist Sonny Red, bassist George Tucker, trombonist Curtis Fuller, and drummer Louis Hayes. It preceded by two years the sessions he cut with Coltrane that became the *Giant Steps* album, and was done the same year he and Coltrane had recorded for Prestige. Although he wasn't yet as accomplished on ballads, his harmonic brilliance was already evident. —*Ron Wynn*

Plays the Music of Rodgers & Hammerstein / Sep. 23, 1958-Sep. 30, 1958 / Savoy ✦✦✦✦

This CD reissue (put out in 1990) may be hard to find, now that Savoy has been sold to the Japanese Denon label. Originally issued under fluegelhornist Wilbur Harden's name, the 1958 quartet (which also includes pianist Tommy Flanagan, bassist George Duvivier and drummer Granville T. Hogan) performs nine Rodgers & Hammerstein songs mostly taken from *The King and I,* plus a reprise and an alternate take of "Hello Young Lovers." The interpretations are tasteful yet swinging, and include such familiar tunes as "Getting to Know You" and "We Kiss In a Shadow," along with some obscurities. Enjoyable music. —*Scott Yanow*

The Tommy Flanagan Trio / May 18, 1960 / Original Jazz Classics ✦✦✦

Since this set (reissued on CD) was originally recorded for the Prestige subsidiary Moodsville, most of the selections are taken at slow tempos. With bassist Tommy Potter and drummer Roy Haynes giving the pianist fine support, the trio cooks a bit on Flanagan's "Jes' Fine" but otherwise plays such songs as "You Go to My Head," "Come Sunday" (which is taken as a solo piano feature) and "Born to Be Blue" quietly and with taste. —*Scott Yanow*

The Tokyo Recital / Feb. 15, 1975 / Original Jazz Classics ✦✦✦✦

When this set was recorded, pianist Tommy Flanagan had spent so much time as Ella Fitzgerald's accompanist (the past seven years, plus two before that) that many jazz followers had forgotten how strong a soloist he was. In a trio with bass-

ist Keter Betts and drummer Bobby Durham on this straight CD reissue of a former LP, Flanagan is heard in superior form. He interprets a full set of Duke Ellington and Billy Strayhorn-associated songs. Highlights include "UMMG," "Mainstem," "Chelsea Bridge," and a particularly memorable rendition of "The Intimacy of the Blues." Highly recommended. —*Scott Yanow*

Trinity / Oct. 1975-Nov. 1975 / Inner City ✦✦✦

Only Tommy Flanagan's second album as a leader in 15 years, this little-known date (a trio session with bassist Ron Carter and drummer Roy Haynes) was recorded at a period when the pianist was suffering from the anonymity (if gaining financial security) of backing singer Ella Fitzgerald. All but four of the nine selections are quite obscure, but the music is accessible and consistently swinging. This out-of-print LP is worth picking up if it can be found. —*Scott Yanow*

Eclypso / Feb. 4, 1977 / Enja ✦✦✦

Exceptional late '70s trio date, with pianist Tommy Flanagan displaying the hard bop proficiency that's been taken for granted because he earned a reputation as a great accompanist backing Tony Bennett and Ella Fitzgerald. His lines, phrasing, and creative solos, plus his interaction with bassist George Mraz and drummer Elvin Jones, won the album rave reviews. —*Ron Wynn*

Montreux 1977 / Jul. 13, 1977 / Original Jazz Classics ✦✦✦✦

This Pablo recording was cut at a time when pianist Tommy Flanagan was almost forgotten due to his long stint with Ella Fitzgerald's backup band. This fine trio outing with bassist Keter Betts and drummer Bobby Durham has been reissued on CD in the Original Jazz Classics series with one track ("Heat Wave") added to the original program. The two ballad medleys are enjoyable, but it is on "Barbados," "Woody 'n You " and "Blue Bossa" that Flanagan shows how hard-swinging a pianist he can be. His solo career really started to take off a few years after this concert appearance. —*Scott Yanow*

Alone Too Long / Dec. 8, 1977 / Denon ✦✦✦✦

Wonderful solo piano. —*Ron Wynn*

More Delights with Hank Jones / Jan. 28, 1978 / Galaxy ✦✦✦✦

This set is a companion piece to the originally released *Our Delights.* Once again, Tommy Flanagan and Hank Jones, two highly compatible pianists, are heard on a set of duos. Six of these performances are actually alternate takes to the songs included on the first album. These "new" performances (plus duo versions of "'Round Midnight" and "If You Could See Me Now") are as tasteful and as enjoyable as the "older" ones. —*Scott Yanow*

Our Delights / Jan. 28, 1978 / Original Jazz Classics ✦✦✦✦

Piano duets have the potential danger of being overcrowded and a bit incoherent, but neither happens on this rather delightful set. Hank Jones and Tommy Flanagan, two of the four great jazz pianists (along with Barry Harris and Roland Hanna) to emerge from Detroit in the '40s and '50s, have similar styles and their mutual respect is obvious. Their renditions of seven superior bop standards (including "Jordu, " "Confirmation" and Thad Jones' "A Child Is Born") plus an alternate take of "Robbins Nest" on this CD reissue are tasteful, consistently swinging and inventive within the tradition. —*Scott Yanow*

Something Borrowed, Something Blue / Jan. 30, 1978 / Original Jazz Classics ✦✦✦

This is a typically flawless trio set from the tasteful and swinging bop-based pianist Tommy Flanagan. With the assistance of bassist Keter Betts and drummer Jimmie Smith on this CD reissue, Flanagan plays his original title cut and jazz originals by Thad Jones ("Bird Song"), Tadd Dameron, Horace Silver, Thelonious Monk ("Friday the 13th"), Wes Montgomery and Dizzy Gillespie. If Flanagan had not recorded so many equally rewarding sets during the past 20 years, this fine CD would have received a higher rating; virtually every one of his recordings is well worth picking up. —*Scott Yanow*

Plays the Music of Harold Arlen / Sep. 30, 1978-Oct. 2, 1978 / Inner City ✦✦✦

Originally released by the Japanese Trio label and reissued on a DIW CD in that country, this Tommy Flanagan session has only appeared in the US thus far on an Inner City LP. The very consistent pianist performs nine Harold Arlen tunes with bassist George Mraz and drummer Connie Kay. Highlights include "Between the Devil and the Deep Blue Sea," "Sleepin' Bee," "One for My Baby" and "My Shining Hour." Producer Helen Merrill takes a sensitive vocal on "Last Night When We Were Young." Excellent music, but this one will be difficult to locate. —*Scott Yanow*

Ballads and Blues / Nov. 15, 1978 / Enja ✦✦✦

For the CD reissue of this session, two selections were added to the original seven-song LP release. Pianist Tommy Flanagan and bassist George Mraz do not really stick to the plot of the title, playing a few bop standards that are neither blues nor ballads (such as "Scrapple From the Apple," "Star Eyes" and "How High the Moon") in addition to some blues and ballads (most notably Tom McIntosh's haunting "With Malice Toward None"). The intimate and mostly lightly swinging music is fine, but one does miss the momentum that would have been provided by a drummer. —*Scott Yanow*

Together with Kenny Barron / Dec. 6, 1978 / Denon ◆◆◆

A fine, well-produced album by two piano masters. —*Michael G. Nastos*

Super-Session / Feb. 4, 1980 / Enja ◆◆◆

This CD reissues a session that teams together three "super" players: pianist Tommy Flanagan, bassist Red Mitchell and drummer Elvin Jones. On two of Flanagan's better originals ("Minor Perhaps" and "Rachel's Rondo") and four jazz standards (including "Django" and "Things Ain't What They Used to Be"), the musicians communicate quite well (Flanagan and Jones had played together back in the mid-'50s in Detroit) and often think as one. Fine straightahead music. —*Scott Yanow*

You're Me / Feb. 24, 1980 / Phontastic ◆◆◆

A dose of blues and funk with bassist Red Mitchell. —*Ron Wynn*

The Magnificent Tommy Flanagan / Jul. 2, 1981+Jul. 3, 1981 / Progressive ◆◆◆◆

The title of this set is not an overstatement. Tommy Flanagan has long been one of the top bop-based jazz pianists and, although he was somewhat neglected during his stints with Ella Fitzgerald's group, he has been a steady poll-winner since finally going out on his own. This trio session with bassist George Mraz and drummer Al Foster (featuring seven standards and Thad Jones' "Blueish Grey") is as tasteful and consistently swinging as one would expect from players of this caliber. —*Scott Yanow*

Giant Steps / Feb. 17, 1982+Feb. 18, 1982 / Enja ◆◆◆◆◆

Pianist Tommy Flanagan's playing seems to be more direct, edited and stronger as he gets older; certainly his re-emergence in the mid-'70s as a solo artist produced his strongest work. *Giant Steps* was a Feb. '82 tribute to John Coltrane with super backing from bassist George Mraz and drummer Al Foster... This set was particularly inventive; it was Coltrane's music, but it drinks of its own spirit. You won't listen for the familiar Trane solos, but you will listen! —*Bob Rusch, Cadence*

● **Thelonica** / Nov. 30, 1982-Dec. 1, 1982 / Enja ◆◆◆◆◆

Recorded just ten months after Thelonious Monk's death, pianist Tommy Flanagan's tribute features eight of Monk's compositions plus Flanagan's own "Thelonica." Assisted by bassist George Mraz and drummer Art Taylor, Flanagan does not sound at all like Monk but he recaptures his spirit and hints strongly now and then at his style on this fine (and often introspective) outing. —*Scott Yanow*

Nights at the Vanguard / Oct. 18, 1986-Oct. 19, 1986 / Uptown ◆◆◆◆

Pianist Tommy Flanagan (in a trio with bassist George Mraz and drummer Al Foster) mostly sticks to lesser-known material (with a few exceptions such as "More than You Know" and "All God's Children") on this enjoyable live date. Flanagan was very much in his prime during the period, revitalizing the bop and hard bop traditions. Highlights include Phil Woods' "Goodbye Mr. Evans," Benny Golson's "Out of the Past," "A Biddy Ditty" and "I'll Keep Loving You." A good example of the fine pianist's talents —*Scott Yanow*

Jazz Poet / Jan. 17, 1989-Jan. 19, 1989 / Timeless ◆◆◆◆◆

● **Beyond the Blue Bird** / Apr. 29, 1990+Apr. 30, 1990 / Timeless ◆◆◆◆◆

Veteran pianist Tommy Flanagan, in a quartet with guitarist Kenny Burrell, bassist George Mraz and drummer Lewis Nash, performs blues, ballads and some obscurities during one of his most rewarding recordings. Flanagan has never recorded an indifferent album, but this set seems more inspired than most, making it a perfect introduction to this tasteful, swinging and creative (within the bop mainstream) pianist. —*Scott Yanow*

Let's Play the Music of Thad Jones / Apr. 4, 1993 / Enja ◆◆◆◆◆

This relatively little-known trio set by pianist Tommy Flanagan (with bassist Jesper Lundgaard and drummer Lewis Nash) is a minor classic. Flanagan performs 11 of cornetist Thad Jones' compositions, the majority of which had never been played by a piano trio before. Easily the best-known selection is "A Child Is Born" with "Mean What You Say," "Three in One" and "Quietude" being the closest of the other songs to being standards. But, despite their relative obscurity, this body of work is quite diverse and flexible enough to be covered by other jazz musicians. Congratulations are due Tommy Flanagan for putting together a consistently swinging and tasteful salute to Thad Jones, a very talented composer. —*Scott Yanow*

Lady Be Good ... For Ella / 1994 / Verve ◆◆◆◆◆

Sea Changes / Mar. 11, 1996-Mar. 12, 1996 / Evidence ◆◆◆◆

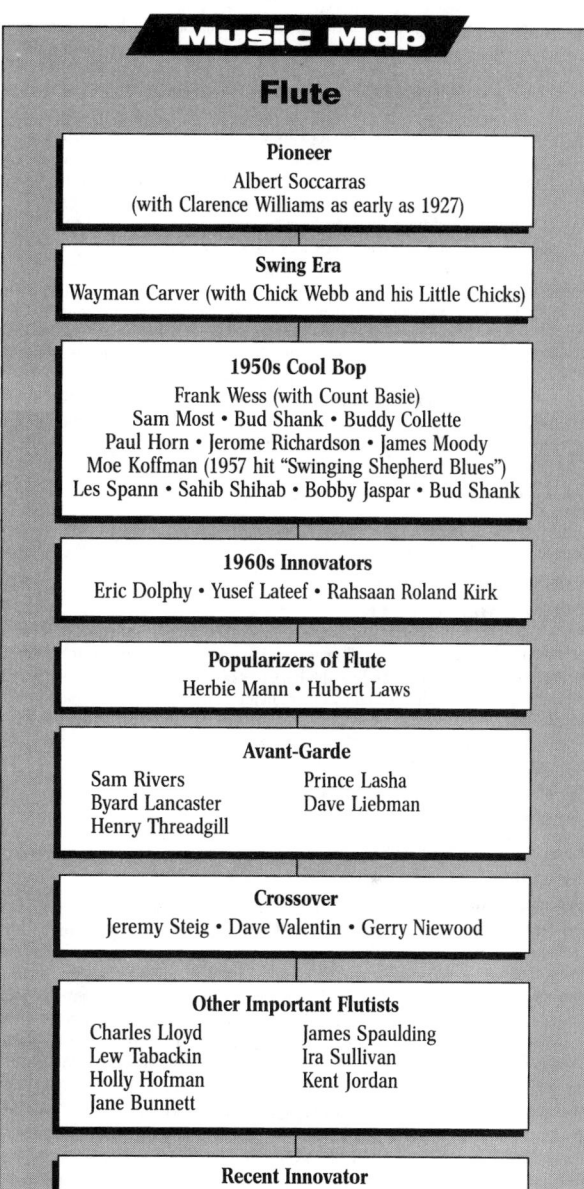

Music Map

Flute

Pioneer
Albert Soccarras
(with Clarence Williams as early as 1927)

Swing Era
Wayman Carver (with Chick Webb and his Little Chicks)

1950s Cool Bop
Frank Wess (with Count Basie)
Sam Most • Bud Shank • Buddy Collette
Paul Horn • Jerome Richardson • James Moody
Moe Koffman (1957 hit "Swinging Shepherd Blues")
Les Spann • Sahib Shihab • Bobby Jaspar • Bud Shank

1960s Innovators
Eric Dolphy • Yusef Lateef • Rahsaan Roland Kirk

Popularizers of Flute
Herbie Mann • Hubert Laws

Avant-Garde
Sam Rivers   Prince Lasha
Byard Lancaster   Dave Liebman
Henry Threadgill

Crossover
Jeremy Steig • Dave Valentin • Gerry Niewood

Other Important Flutists
Charles Lloyd   James Spaulding
Lew Tabackin   Ira Sullivan
Holly Hofman   Kent Jordan
Jane Bunnett

Recent Innovator
James Newton

Béla Fleck

b. 1958, New York, NY

Banjo / Fusion, Post-Bop, Progressive, Bluegrass

Premiere banjo player Béla Fleck is considered one of the most innovative pickers in the world and has done much to demonstrate the versatility of his instrument, which he uses to play everything from traditional bluegrass to progressive jazz. He was born in New York City and named after composer Béla Bartok. Around age 15, Fleck became fascinated with the banjo after hearing Flatt & Scruggs' "Ballad of Jed Clampett" and Weissberg & Mandell's "Dueling Banjos," and his grandfather soon gave him one. While attending the High School of Music and Art in New York, Fleck worked on adapting bebop music for the banjo. Fleck always had diverse musical interests, and his own style was influenced by Tony Trischka, Earl Scruggs, Chick Corea, Charlie Parker, John Coltrane, the Allman Brothers, Aretha Franklin, the Byrds and Little Feat. After graduation, he joined the Tasty Licks, a group from Boston. They recorded two albums and dissolved in 1979. Afterwards, Fleck joined the Kentucky band Spectrum. That year, only five years after he took up the instrument, he made his solo recording debut with *Crossing the Tracks*, which the Readers' Poll in *Frets* magazine named Best Overall Album. In 1982, he joined New Grass Revival and stayed with them until the end of the decade. During this time, his reputation continued to grow and in 1990, *Frets* magazine added his name to their Hall of Greats. In 1988, one of his compositions, "Drive" (from the album *New Grass Revival*), was nominated for a Grammy. Fleck, mandolin player Sam Bush, fiddler Mark O'Connor, bassist Edgar Meyer and dobro player Jerry Douglas teamed up in 1989 to form Strength in Numbers and record *The Telluride Sessions*. Late that year, Fleck was asked by PBS television to play on the upcoming *Lonesome Pine Special*; in response he gathered together a veritable "dream team" of musicians to form the Flecktones. The original members included Howard Levy, who played piano, harmonica and ocarina, among other instruments; bass guitarist Victor Wooten; and his brother Roy "Future Man" Wooten on the drumitar, an electronic drum shaped like a guitar. Though the special wasn't aired until 1992, the Flecktones recorded their eponymous debut album in 1990 and followed it up with *Flight of the Cosmic Hippo* (1991). In 1993 they released their third album, *UFO Tofu*, which featured music blending different genres ranging from bluegrass to R&B to worldbeat. In 1995, they released *Tales from an Acoustic Planet.* —*Sandra Brennan*

Crossing the Tracks / 1979 / Rounder ✦✦✦✦

Natural Bridge / 1982 / Rounder ✦✦✦

Double Time / Dec. 1982-1983 / Rounder ✦✦✦

Deviation / 1984 / Rounder ✦✦✦

Inroads / 1986 / Rounder ✦✦✦

Now available for the first time on compact disc, this 1986 release features banjoist Béla Fleck performing an all-instrumental group of original compositions. Fleck is well known for expanding the horizons of bluegrass, and he creates lots of new sounds here, ably assisted by other talented musicians such as mandolinist Sam Bush, dobroist Jerry Douglas, and violinist Mark O'Connor. Tracks include "Ireland," "Four Wheel Drive," "Perplexed," and "The Old Country." —*Roundup Newsletter*

60 Plus Series / 1987 / Rounder ✦✦✦

Daybreak / 1988 / Rounder ✦✦✦✦✦

Drive / 1988 / Rounder ✦✦✦

Places / 1988 / Rounder ✦✦✦

Béla Fleck & The Flecktones / 1990 / Warner Brothers ✦✦✦✦✦

After disbanding New Grass Revival, Béla Fleck began re-creating the role of the banjo in the same way Charlie Parker redefined the role of the saxophone. But Fleck may be the least-innovative member of this quartet: Howard Levy gets chromatics from his blues harp, Victor Wooten picks banjo rolls on his bass, and Roy "Future Man" Wooten plays a Frankenstein-monster drum-machine/guitar synthesizer. For all the flash, there's little pretense; the group's astonishing musicianship keeps an "aw-shucks" accessibility that lets everybody follow the melody while they marvel. —*Brian Mansfield*

● **Flight of the Cosmic Hippo** / 1991 / Warner Brothers ✦✦✦✦✦

The Flecktones owe more to bebop than bluegrass, and here the group finally names its style "blu-bop." That's why *Cosmic Hippo* topped the jazz, not the country, chart. The Flecktones continue to make it look easy, adding banjo power chords to "Turtle Rock" and reworking Lennon-McCartney's "Michelle." —*Brian Mansfield*

Live Art / 1991-1995 / Warner Brothers ✦✦✦

Live Art is a double-disc, 20-track anthology of live performances by Béla Fleck & the Flecktones, spanning four years in the mid-'90s. The song selections cover the group's entire career, ranging from new arrangements of several of classics to covers and seven previously unrecorded originals. There are a couple of vocals on the record, but the core of the album is Fleck and the Flecktones' dynamite instrumental improvisations, where they can demonstrate the true range of their eclecticism and talent. Of special note are the songs that feature jams with Branford Marsalis, Chick Corea and Bruce Hornsby, who help spur the Flecktones to new heights. —*Thom Owens*

UFO Tofu / 1992 / Warner Brothers ✦✦✦

Though the Flecktones didn't change their formula with their third album, *UFO Tofu*, they did manage to craft one of their more consistent and impressive efforts. The band's fusion of jazz, bluegrass and funk gels quite well on *UFO Tofu*—not only does Béla Fleck turn in a rich, eclectic performance, but pianist Howard Levy's deft lines and inventive phrasing dominates the album. Occasionally, the material is lightweight, functioning as mere vehicle for the group's solos. Then

again, the whole point of Fleck's music *is* the solos, so that shouldn't upset his fans too much. Of course, it doesn't help him win new ones, either. —*Thom Owens*

Three Flew over the Cuckoo's Nest / 1993 / Warner Brothers ✦✦✦

Tales from the Acoustic Planet / Jan. 1994-Mar. 1994 / Warner Brothers ✦✦✦✦

Bob Florence

b. May 20, 1932, Los Angeles, CA
Piano, Arranger, Composer, Leader / Post-Bop

A top arranger influenced by Bill Holman, Bob Florence regularly leads a big band in the Los Angeles area. He worked as a pianist and arranger for Si Zentner's band during 1959-64; his chart on "Up a Lazy River" was a hit in 1960. Florence has worked extensively in the studios and in commercial music (he is the long-time musical director for Julie Andrews) and played with the 1980s version of the Dave Pell Octet, but has also led his own orchestra off and on since 1958. That year he recorded an obscure trio date and a couple of big-band albums. His orchestra backed Big Miller in 1961 and there were recordings in 1965 and 1968 but Florence hit his stride in 1979 with a big-band set for Trend. Since then he has recorded fairly regularly for Trend/Discovery, Bosco, USA and most recently the MAMA Foundation. Florence's arrangements are among the most colorful (and challenging) in jazz. —*Scott Yanow*

Here and Now / 1965 / Liberty ✦✦✦

Except for an obscure and commercial effort for World Pacific in 1968, this album was arranger Bob Florence's only record as a leader from 1962-78. At 32, Florence already largely had his writing style together. He utilized top L.A. studio players for this set, including such soloists as altoist Bud Shank, the tenors of Bill Perkins and Bob Hardaway, and trombonist Herbie Harper, but it is the tricky charts on the four originals and four standards (including "The Song Is You" and "Straight, No Chaser") that make this an LP worth searching for. —*Scott Yanow.*

Live at Concerts by the Sea / Jun. 15, 1979-Jun. 18, 1979 / Trend ✦✦✦✦✦

The first of a consistently enjoyable string of big-band recordings by Bob Florence's L.A.-based orchestra (at least since 1965), this set has six originals by the leader, including "Be Bop Charlie" (dedicated to local disc jockey Chuck Niles), the pretty "Lonely Carousel" (which features trumpeter Warren Luening), "Wide Open Spaces," and "Party Hearty." Among the main soloists are the three tenors of Bob Hardaway, Pete Christlieb (showcased on "I'll Remember") and Bob Cooper. All of Bob Florence's big-band albums are recommended, although it is a pity that only a few selections from his valuable Discovery and Trend albums have thus far been reissued on CD. —*Scott Yanow*

Jewels / Jun. 15, 1979-Nov. 25, 1986 / Discovery ✦✦✦

CD reissue featuring sessions from 1979, 1981, 1983, and 1986 with bandleader Bob Florence and the Limited Edition orchestra. The lineup at various times included Rick Baptist, Buddy Childers, Charley Davis, and Gene Goe, and they performed stomping uptempo tunes, standards, and ballads. —*Ron Wynn*

Westlake / Mar. 3, 1981 / Discovery ✦✦✦✦

Bob Florence, one of the top jazz arrangers of the 1980s and '90s, has a writing style influenced by Bill Holman. On this sadly out-of-print Discovery LP, Florence features such talented sidemen as Pete Christlieb and Bob Cooper on tenors, trumpeters Steve Huffsteter and Warren Luening, trombonist Charlie Loper, and Ray Pizzi on soprano. The music (all Florence originals) includes a trio of waltzes titled "One, Two, Three," "Carmelo's by the Freeway" and "Westlake"; the leader's fluent piano is showcased on the latter. —*Scott Yanow*

Soaring / Oct. 1982 / Bosco ✦✦✦✦

Since tenor saxophonist Pete Christlieb had been a member of Bob Florence's Limited Edition for a long period, it seemed right that he would have Florence's orchestra record for his Bosco label at one point. The leader's six originals all have his typically distinctive and unpredictable arrangements, along with solo space for Kim Richmond on soprano, altoist Lanny Morgan, the tenors of Bob Cooper and Christlieb (who are both featured on "Jeff n' Jeff"), trumpeter Warren Luening, and baritonist Bob Efford. Worth searching for by fans of modern big bands. —*Scott Yanow*

Magic Time / Nov. 29, 1983+Nov. 30, 1983 / Trend ✦✦✦✦

The third of Bob Florence's four albums for the Trend and Discovery labels (which unfortunately have only been reissued on CD thus far in piecemeal fashion) has typically unpredictable arrangements from Florence on six of his originals. The first of Florence's recordings to bill his 18-piece band as the "Limited Edition" has fine solos by trumpeters Warren Luening and Steve Huffsteter, altoist Lanny Morgan (featured on "Rhythm and Blues"), baritonist Bob Efford, and Bob Cooper on tenor. Easily recommended. —*Scott Yanow*

Trash Can City / Nov. 24, 1986-Nov. 25, 1986 / Trend ✦✦✦✦

The fourth and final recording by Bob Florence's Limited Edition for the Trend and Discovery labels is on the same level as the previous releases. Most unusual about this date is that Julie Andrews (for whom Florence has long been piano accompanist) takes a rare vocal in this context during "Jewels." Other highlights include the quote-filled "Bebop Treasure Chest," "The Babbling Brook" (dedicated to Bob Brookmeyer), and a remake of "Here and Now." Among the main soloists are altoist Lanny Morgan, trombonists Rick Culver and Charlie Loper, trumpeters Warren Luening and Steve Huffsteter, Bob Cooper on tenor, and baritonist Bob Efford. —*Scott Yanow*

State of the Art / 1988 / USA ✦✦✦✦✦

The first of two sets by Bob Florence's Limited Edition Orchestra for the USA label breaks from his tradition in that only four of the nine selections are Florence originals. The arranger completely reworks such familiar tunes as "Just Friends," "Moonlight Serenade," "All the Things You Are" and even "Auld Lang Syne." Among the key players are altoist Lanny Morgan, trumpeter Steve Huffsteter, Bob Cooper on tenor, and Kim Richmond on alto and soprano. Modern, swinging and unpredictable music. —*Scott Yanow*

Treasure Chest / 1990 / USA ✦✦✦✦

Arranger Bob Florence's second of two USA CDs (cut before he signed with the MAMA label) finds his 19-piece orchestra exploring four standards and a quartet of originals. Florence's writing makes such tunes as "Body and Soul" and "Chicago" sound quite modern, while his somewhat humorous "Big Band Treasure Chest" contains 24 quotes from swing-era recordings. With such top players as altoists Lanny Morgan and Kim Richmond, tenorman Bob Militello, trumpeters Warren Luening and Steve Huffsteter, and even valve trombonist Rob McConnell (during his brief residence in Los Angeles) among the many heard from, this is a superlative effort from the Limited Edition big band and serves as a fine example of Bob Florence's inventive writing talents. —*Scott Yanow*

Funupsmanship / 1993 / MAMA ✦✦✦✦✦

Bob Florence has long been one of the most stimulating arrangers in jazz and this live set from his big band features some of his most interesting charts. With such soloists as trumpeters Steve Huffsteter and Warren Luening, trombonists Alex Iles, Charlie Loper and Rick Culver, altoist Lanny Morgan and the reeds of Kim Richmond, Don Shelton and Bob Efford (along with the pianist/leader), Florence's dense and often-witty ensembles alternate with fine improvisations. Highlights of this consistently exciting set include "Slimehouse" (based on "Limehouse Blues"), "Funupsmanship," "Lester Left Town" and "All Blues." —*Scott Yanow*

● **With All the Bells and Whistles** / Feb. 20, 1995-Feb. 21, 1995 / MAMA ✦✦✦✦

Arranger-pianist Bob Florence's release for the MAMA Foundation may very well be his finest; it certainly offers a strong sampling of his talents. Four of the ten songs are standards and "Oceanography" is based closely on "How Deep Is the Ocean?" but Florence's complex yet logical arrangements make each piece sound like it was written for the band. To name a few examples, "In a Mellow Tone" appears to be in two keys at once at times, "Laura" (normally an emotional ballad) really cooks and "Teach Me Tonight" is so intense as to be purposely humorous in spots. Among the other highlights of this well-conceived release are Don Shelton's clarinet feature on "Shimmer," the competitive interplay between Dick Mitchell and Terry Harrington throughout "Tenors, Anyone?" and the fluency of trombonist Bob McChesney on "In a Mellow Tone." The ensembles are consistently clean, exciting and remarkably relaxed considering how tricky some of the charts must be. This CD offers modern big-band jazz at its best. —*Scott Yanow*

Earth / Aug. 14, 1996-Aug. 15, 1996 / MAMA ✦✦✦✦

For this superior 1997 release, Bob Florence's Limited Edition performs five of the leader's originals plus "Emily," a heated and inventive version of "Straight, No Chaser" and Duke Ellington's "Black and Tan Fantasy." Florence has been very consistent with his output since the mid-1980s and this stimulating release (with its many surprises, crowded ensembles and consistent swing) is up to his usual level. Among the key soloists are trumpeters Steve Huffsteter and Carl Saunders, Dick Mitchell and Terry Harrington on tenors and altoist Kim Richmond. —*Scott Yanow*

Chris Flory

Guitar / Swing

An excellent swing-based guitarist, Chris Flory first worked professionally in Providence, Rhode Island in 1974. A long-time associate of Scott Hamilton (who he first played with in 1976), Flory has also worked with Benny Goodman (1979-85), Roy Eldridge, Illinois Jacquet, Bob Wilber, Buddy Tate and Ruby Braff among others and toured China in 1992 with Judy Carmichael. He has appeared on many Concord records, leading two sessions of his own and playing regularly with Hamilton. —*Scott Yanow*

For All We Know / Jan. 1988 / Concord Jazz ✦✦✦✦

Guitarist Chris Flory, bassist Phil Flanigan and drummer Chuck Riggs were all regular members of tenor saxophonist Scott Hamilton's Quintet at the time of this CD, while organist-pianist Mike Ledonne was often a substitute for John Bunch, so the quartet's renditions of standards are predictably tasteful and swinging. Flory's style, most influenced by Wes Montgomery (especially on "Tenderly") fits easily into the mainstream legacy established by Barney Kessel, Herb Ellis and Tal Farlow. LeDonne's 50s bop piano and Jimmy Smith-influenced organ keep the proceedings cooking, laying down a perfect groove for Flory's well-constructed and melodic solos. "Air Mail Special" is a particular joy. An excellent modern swing session. —*Scott Yanow*

● **City Life** / Mar. 18, 1993-Mar. 19, 1993 / Concord Jazz ✦✦✦✦✦

Chris Flory, a talented swing-based guitarist, tackles standards, Latin tunes and a few hot jam-session numbers on his second Concord CD with a solid quartet that also features pianist John Bunch, bassist John Webber and drummer Chuck Riggs. Highlights include an enjoyable "So Danco Samba," the uptempo blues "Drafting," "Besame Mucho," "S'Posin'" and a spirited rendition of "My Shining Hour." This swinging session is consistent with the high-quality music to be found throughout Concord's impressive catalog. —*Scott Yanow*

Word On the Street / Sep. 22, 1996 / Double-Time ✦✦✦

Carl Fontana (Charles Fontana)

b. Jul. 18, 1928, Monroe, LA

Trombone / Bop, Cool

A brilliant trombonist who has spent much of the past 40 years playing commercial music in Las Vegas, Carl Fontana occasionally emerges to remind listeners just how technically skilled he is. The son of a saxophonist, Fontana started out playing in his father's group during 1941-45 but did not gain prominence until he was with Woody Herman's Orchestra (1952-53). Fontana spent time in the big bands of Lionel Hampton (1954), Hal McIntyre (1954-55) and most importantly Stan Kenton (1955-56), being well featured with the latter. After playing in Kai Winding's four-trombone band (1956-57), Fontana moved to Las Vegas but he has emerged on an occasional basis, touring with Woody Herman in 1966, recording with Supersax (1973), co-leading a group with Jake Hanna (1975), playing with the World's Greatest Jazz Band and appearing at jazz parties. In 1995 Carl Fontana recorded a fine album with Bobby Shew. —*Scott Yanow*

● **The Great Fontana** / Sep. 5, 1985-Sep. 6, 1985 / Uptown ✦✦✦✦✦

Considering his ability and strong reputation, it is very surprising that this was trombonist Carl Fontana's first recording date as a leader at age 57. Fontana's fluent horn matches well with tenor saxophonist Al Cohn, pianist Richard Wyands, bassist Ray Drummond and drummer Akira Tana. The CD reissue of the Uptown release expands the original six-song program to ten. An excellent effort from an underrated but talented bop-based trombonist. —*Scott Yanow*

Ricky Ford

b. Mar. 4, 1954, Boston, MA

Tenor Saxophone / Hard Bop, Post-Bop

An excellent veteran tenor inspired by Dexter Gordon and Sonny Rollins, Ricky Ford was playing creative hard bop several years before Wynton Marsalis and his talent has been often overlooked. After studying at the New England Conservatory, he recorded in 1974 with Gunther Schuller. After touring with the Duke Ellington Orchestra (under Mercer Ellington's leadership during 1974-76), Ford was with Charles Mingus (1976-77), Dannie Richmond's Quintet (1978-81), Lionel Hampton and Mingus Dynasty (1982); he also played in 1985 with Abdullah Ibrahim. Ricky Ford has recorded as a leader for New World, an excellent string of dates for Muse (1978-89) and more recently for Candid. —*Scott Yanow*

Loxodonta Africana / Jun. 1977 / New World ✦✦✦

Tenor saxophonist Ricky Ford's first record as a leader preceded the beginning of his highly rated string of Muse albums by a year. 23 at the time, Ford already had a recognizable sound that was influenced by Dexter Gordon. For this ambitious effort (which displayed the impact of his stint with Charles Mingus), Ford performs five of his originals (including one called "Dexter"), plus John Coltrane's "One Up, One Down" and the standard "My Romance." Ford is well showcased in a sextet with both Oliver Beener and Charles Sullivan on trumpets and a nonet that adds altoist James Spaulding, trombonist Janice Robinson, and the tuba of Jonathan Dorn; the rhythm section in both cases comprises bassist Richard Davis and Mingus' pianist (Bob Neloms) and drummer (Dannie Richmond). This obscure and impressive Ricky Ford LP is well deserving of reissue on CD. —*Scott Yanow*

Manhattan Plaza / Aug. 1, 1978 / Muse ✦✦✦
Ricky Ford's first Muse album (and his second record as a leader) teams him with the obscure trumpeter Oliver Beener, the masterful pianist Jaki Byard, bassist David Friesen and drummer Dannie Richmond. Byard and Ford contributed three numbers apiece, which are joined by "If You Could See Me Now"; Byard's "Diane's Melody" serves as a memorable tenor-piano duet. The music, advanced hard bop, has dated quite well and makes one wonder why Ricky Ford never quite became a pollwinner in the jazz world. —*Scott Yanow*

Flying Colors / Apr. 24, 1980 / Muse ✦✦✦✦
Although often overlooked (his music is beyond bop but not really in the avant-garde and certainly not in the fusion genre), Ricky Ford was one of the top tenors to emerge during the '70s and early '80s. This Muse set finds him matched with a top-notch rhythm section (pianist John Hicks, bassist Walter Booker and drummer Jimmy Cobb) for "Take the Coltrane," Thelonious Monk's "ByeYa," Billy Strayhorn's "Chelsea Bridge" and four of Ford's originals including the mournful "Portrait of Mingus." It was a fine showcase for the up-and-coming tenor. —*Scott Yanow*

Tenor for the Times / Apr. 6, 1981+Jul. 1, 1981 / Muse ✦✦✦✦✦
Ricky Ford, a fine tenor saxophonist whose main influences have been Sonny Rollins and Dexter Gordon (although he has his own sound), is in excellent form throughout this quartet date. Accompanied and inspired by pianist Albert Dailey, bassist Rufus Reid, drummer Jimmy Cobb and, on one song, trumpeter Jack Walrath, Ford investigates seven of his diverse originals, really digging into the material. It's a good introduction to his talents. —*Scott Yanow*

Interpretations / Feb. 22, 1982 / Muse ✦✦✦✦
Other than Mercer Ellington's "Moon Mist" and a remake of his "Dexter," Ricky Ford performs five originals in his "Opus" series (none of which caught on) during this enjoyable advanced hard bop LP. The music is straightahead but unpredictable, with Ford joined by pianist John Hicks, bassist Walter Booker, drummer Jimmy Cobb and (on three of the seven numbers) trumpeter Wallace Roney and altoist Bobby Watson. —*Scott Yanow*

Future's Gold / Feb. 9, 1983 / Muse ✦✦✦✦
What makes this outing by tenor saxophonist Ricky Ford a bit different than his previous ones is that in addition to the fine trio (pianist Albert Dailey, bassist Ray Drummond and drummer Jimmy Cobb), Larry Coryell is an important voice on the record, playing electric guitar on the first four songs and acoustic 12-string guitar on the remaining four tunes. Ford, a vastly underrated but talented tenor-man, contributes six originals (including "Centenarian Waltz" for the 100-year-old Eubie Blake) and does a fine job of interpreting "Goodbye, Pork Pie Hat" by former boss Charles Mingus and the standard "You Don't Know What Love Is." An excellent record, it is recommended for both the contributions of Ford and the surprisingly versatile Coryell. —*Scott Yanow*

● **Shorter Ideas** / Aug. 28, 1984 / Muse ✦✦✦✦✦
Ford, who has usually recorded with small groups, here heads an all-star sextet with altoist James Spaulding and trombonist Jimmy Knepper—an inspired idea that works. They perform four Wayne Shorter numbers, a couple of Ford's originals and Duke Ellington's "Happy Reunion." Ford takes the lion's share of the solo space and is clearly up to the task, making these sometimes complex compositions seem accessible and logical. Ford has long been underrated (too old to be a young lion and too young to be an elder statesman), but, based on the evidence of this recording alone, he clearly deserves much greater acclaim. —*Scott Yanow*

Looking Ahead / Feb. 14, 1986-Oct. 9, 1986 / Muse ✦✦✦✦
An outstanding session, with a first-rate supporting cast. —*Ron Wynn*

Saxotic Stomp / Sep. 4, 1987 / Muse ✦✦✦✦
This is one of tenor saxophonist Ricky Ford's finer Muse recordings, although all nine are recommended. The talented tenor's six originals (including tributes to Mary Lou Williams, Art Blakey and Ben Webster) and Thelonious Monk's "Ba-Lue Bolivar Ba-Lues-Are" inspire the impressive sextet, which also includes altoist James Spaulding, baritonist Charles Davis, pianist Kirk Lightsey, bassist Ray Drummond and drummer Jimmy Cobb. Ford's arrangements, while giving everyone adequate solo space, keep the proceedings moving. Well worth several listens. —*Scott Yanow*

Hard Groovin' / Feb. 24, 1989 / Muse ✦✦✦✦
The consistent tenor saxophonist Ricky Ford, who was often the youngest player on the bandstand when he first emerged in the late '70s, is easily the oldest musician on this energetic modern bop album. Trumpeter Roy Hargrove, pianist Geoff Keezer, bassist Bob Hurst and drummer Jeff "Tain" Watts are among the main Young Lions of the late '80s and '90s, but Ford (heard on both alto and tenor) is easily the most impressive solo voice on this high-quality outing. Ford and his quintet perform five of his originals, a Geoff Keezer song and the standards "Jit-

terbug Waltz" and "Minority" with driving swing and personable creativity. —*Scott Yanow*

Manhattan Blues / Mar. 4, 1989 / Candid ✦✦✦✦✦
This CD is a particularly well-rounded program, with tenor saxophonist Ricky Ford digging into three jazz standards ("In Walked Bud," "Misty" and "Half Nelson"), plus six originals that include tributes to Charles Mingus and Billy Strayhorn. In addition to the versatile pianist Jaki Byard (an underrated great) and drummer Ben Riley, Ford is joined by veteran bassist Milt Hinton, who is quite effective on this modern material. Stimulating music. —*Scott Yanow*

Ebony Rhapsody / Jun. 2, 1990 / Candid ✦✦✦✦
A high-level date with Jaki Byard immense on piano. —*Ron Wynn*

Hot Brass / Apr. 30, 1991 / Candid ✦✦✦✦✦
Nice session matching tenor saxophone standout Ricky Ford with crew of fiery trumpet and trombone players, plus bassist Christian McBride, drummer Carl Allen, and percussionist Danilo Perez. Ford was a young lion back in the '70s, when there was no hype. He's now an experienced, skilled veteran, and teams superbly with trumpeters Lew Soloff and Claudio Roditi and trombonist Steve Turre. —*Ron Wynn*

American-African Blues / Sep. 1, 1991 / Candid ✦✦✦✦

Tenor Madness Too / Aug. 12, 1992 / Muse ✦✦✦

Robben Ford

b. Dec. 16, 1951, Ukiah, CA
Guitar / Modern Electric Blues, Fusion, Crossover Jazz
Robben Ford has had a diverse career. He taught himself guitar when he was 13 and considered his first influence to be Mike Bloomfield. At 18 he moved to San Francisco to form the Charles Ford Band (named after his father, who was also a guitarist) and was soon hired to play with Charles Musselwhite for nine months. In 1971 the Charles Ford Blues Band was re-formed and recorded for Arhoolie in early 1972. Ford played with Jimmy Witherspoon (1972-73), the L.A. Express with Tom Scott (1974), George Harrison and Joni Mitchell. In 1977 he was a founding member of the Yellowjackets which he stayed with until 1983, simultaneously having a solo career and working as a session guitarist. In 1986 Ford toured with Miles Davis and he had two separate periods (1985 and 1987) with Sadao Watanabe but he seemed to really find himself in 1992 when he returned to his roots, the blues. Robben Ford formed a new group, the Blue Line, and has since recorded a couple of blues-rock dates for Stretch that are among the finest of his career. —*Scott Yanow*

Discovering the Blues / 1972-1978 / Rhino ✦✦✦
Discovering the Blues is culled from a series of concerts Robben Ford gave in the early '70s at Huntington Beach's Golden Bear and Ash Grove in Hollywood. At the time, Ford was just beginning his career, and his style wasn't nearly as accomplished as it would later be. Instead, he simply burns, tearing through blues classics with a passion and vigor—there is a joy of discovery in his playing that makes the music nearly transcendent, even with its flaws. *Discovering the Blues* is rawer than most records in Ford's catalog, but any serious fan will find it a necessary addition to their collection. —*Thom Owens*

Talk to Your Daughter / 1988 / Warner Brothers ✦✦✦
Efficient, sometimes electrifying playing but detached, uneven material. —*Ron Wynn*

Robben Ford & the Blue Line / 1992 / Stretch ✦✦✦
The debut set by guitarist Robben Ford with his Blue Line trio (a blues band with bassist Roscoe Beck and drummer Tom Brechtlein) finds Ford returning to his roots and playing the music that best fits his style. He's an effective singer, but it is for Ford's powerful guitar playing that this CD (which has seven originals among the nine numbers) is most highly recommended to blues collectors. —*Scott Yanow*

Mystic Mile / 1993 / Stretch ✦✦✦✦

● **Handful of Blues** / Sep. 12, 1995 / Blue Thumb ✦✦✦✦
On *Handful of Blues*, Robben Ford strips his sound back to the basics, recording a set of blues with only a bassist and a drummer. The group runs through a handful of standards, including "Don't Let Me Be Misunderstood" and "I Just Want to Make Love to You," and a number of made-to-order originals. Throughout the album, the musicians play well, but Ford's voice is never commanding. However, this is a minor flaw, since his guitar speaks for itself. —*Stephen Thomas Erlewine*

Blues Connection / ITM ✦✦✦

Tiger Walk / 1997 / Blue Thumb ✦✦✦

Bruce Forman

b. 1956, Springfield, MA

Guitar / Bop

An exciting bop-oriented guitarist who is a fixture at the Monterey Jazz Festival, Bruce Forman moved to San Francisco in 1971. He has mostly headed his own groups in the Bay Area but played and toured with Richie Cole during 1978-82. Forman has led his own dates for Muse, Concord and Kamei. —*Scott Yanow*

Coast to Coast / Oct. 19, 1978 / Choice ♦♦♦

River Journey / Mar. 10, 1981 / Muse ♦♦♦

An upbeat album from the early '80s by guitarist Bruce Forman, playing with a group that includes torrid alto saxophonist Richie Cole. His fluid, bluesy solos on fast, mid-tempo, and slow numbers injects some spark into the date, and also make Forman extend himself. —*Ron Wynn*

20/20 / Sep. 1, 1981 / Muse ♦♦♦♦

Bruce Forman's third recording as a leader features the hard-swinging guitarist with pianist Albert Dailey, bassist Mike Richmond and drummer Billy Hart on five numbers, two of which also star trumpeter Tom Harrell. They perform three of Forman's originals (including "Trane's Idea," which is built from some Coltrane blues motives), an obscurity, and "Softly as in a Morning Sunrise." Fine straightahead jazz. —*Scott Yanow*

In Transit / Jun. 9, 1982 / Muse ♦♦♦♦

Bruce Forman, who has long been based in Northern California, teams up with organist Ed Kelly and drummer Eddie Marshall (both from San Francisco) on this fine trio set. On "Mood Indigo," Horace Silver's "Peace," "Waltzing Matilda" (which feels a bit like John Coltrane's version of "My Favorite Things"), and five mostly swinging Forman originals, the group sounds both exploratory and tied to the tradition. Although this album is not as memorable as his best dates, every Bruce Forman recording is well worth checking out for fans of the bop guitar. —*Scott Yanow*

The Bash / Nov. 2, 1982 / Muse ♦♦♦♦

Good mid-'80s date by guitarist Bruce Forman, with pianist Albert Dailey, bassist Buster Williams, and drummer Eddie Gladden. Forman, a mainstream stylist solidly in the Jim Hall/Herb Ellis/Joe Pass school, plays with a precise, delicate mastery. —*Ron Wynn*

Full Circle / May 1984 / Concord Jazz ♦♦♦♦♦

A good mid-80s date with a tremendous lineup that includes Bobby Hutcherson and George Cables. —*Ron Wynn*

Dynamics with George Cables / Feb. 1985 / Concord Jazz ♦♦♦

Although many guitarists have trouble playing with pianists (and vice versa), this guitar-piano duet set by Bruce Forman and George Cables works quite well. The players leave room for each other and sound clearly inspired by the other's presence. All of the performances are concise (clocking in between 3:36 and 6:22, with only "Doxy" over 5:13) and mix standards (such as "Be My Love" and Thelonious Monk's "I Mean You") with a pair of originals and a few obscurities. The volume of this duo may often be low, but the passion can be felt. —*Scott Yanow*

There Are Times / Aug. 1986 / Concord Jazz ♦♦♦♦

Because he has spent most of his life living in northern California, guitarist Bruce Forman tends to be underrated, if not completely overlooked, but he has always been an exciting bop-oriented player. This outing with pianist George Cables, bassist Jeff Carney, drummer Eddie Marshall and guest vibraphonist Bobby Hutcherson has an excellent assortment of songs (including "All the Things You Are," "Strike Up the Band" and Thelonious Monk's "Little Rootie Tootie"), inventive solos, and an upbeat feel throughout. Recommended. —*Scott Yanow*

Pardon Me! / Oct. 1988 / Concord Jazz ♦♦♦♦♦

This strong effort finds guitarist Bruce Forman exploring music that is sometimes adventurous (particularly John Coltrane's "Countdown" and Dave Liebman's "Once Again"), along with some more basic tunes (the ballad "I Thought About You" and his "Blues for Wes"). An added plus to the date is that the quartet (which also includes bassist Jim Carney and drummer Eddie Marshall) co-stars the superb pianist Bill Childs. —*Scott Yanow*

Still of the Night / 1991 / Kamei ♦♦♦♦♦

This CD serves as a perfect introduction to the appealing bop-based style of guitarist Bruce Forman. Accompanied by bassist John Clayton and drummer Albert "Tootie" Heath, Forman is heard in top form on such numbers as "In the Still of the Night," "Cherokee," "I've Grown Accustomed to Her Face" and "Lady Be Good"; in addition, he contributed three diverse originals. Recommended to fans of straightahead jazz guitar. —*Scott Yanow*

● **Forman on the Job** / 1992 / Kamei ♦♦♦♦♦

Guitarist Bruce Forman's second CD for the small San Francisco-based Kamei label features him with bassist John Clayton, drummer Vince Lateano and sometimes percussionist John Santos, plus guests. Pianist Mark Levine is on eight of the 11 tracks, tenor great Joe Henderson helps out on four, and steel drummer Andy Narell drops by for two. Although there are three Forman originals and one by Clayton ("Angels Just Are"), the emphasis is on bop-era tunes including Bud Powell's "Un Poco Loco," "A Night in Tunisia" and a swinging "I Concentrate on You." The beautiful "Autumn Nocturne" is a high point. —*Scott Yanow*

Mitchel Forman

b. Jan. 1956, New York, NY

Keyboards / Fusion, Post-Bop

Mitchel Forman has had a continually surprising career. After graduating from the Manhattan School of Music (1978), he recorded three solo acoustic piano albums for the Japanese New Wave and Soul Note labels and worked with Stan Getz, Gerry Mulligan, Carla Bley and Mel Tormé. However, he made his strongest impression on electric keyboards, playing with the reformed Mahavishnu Orchestra and Wayne Shorter and recording for Magenta (1985) and Novus (1991). Forman surprised many by performing a very effective Bill Evans tribute for Novus (1992) with an acoustic trio, and then went back to playing modern fusion on *Lipstick* (1993). Talented on both acoustic and electric keyboards, Mitchel Forman's future progress should be well worth watching! —*Scott Yanow*

Childhood Dreams / Feb. 1982 / Soul Note ♦♦♦

Only a Memory / Aug. 2, 1982-Aug. 3, 1982 / Soul Note ♦♦♦

This set, which predates his more electronic recordings, features Mitchel Forman on solo piano and a bit of organ. The six originals range from wistful explorations to a dedication to "The Police." Forman shows off the influences of Keith Jarrett, Chick Corea and Bill Evans a bit, but his musical voice was already on its way to becoming fairly original. —*Scott Yanow*

Train of Thought / 1985 / Magenta ♦♦♦♦

● **Now & Then: a Tribute to Bill Evans** / Dec. 8, 1992-Dec. 10, 1992 / Novus ♦♦♦♦♦

Mitchel Forman, who usually plays electric keyboards in more "contemporary" settings, sticks to acoustic piano during his heartfelt tribute to Bill Evans. Forman performs eight songs associated with the late pianist along with two of his originals. At times the pianist's style comes remarkably close to his idol's, and it helps that his trio has two of Evans' most famous sidemen (bassist Eddie Gomez and drummer Jack DeJohnette) helping out. The music is tasteful and swinging and Forman's title cut is strong enough to possibly become a standard itself in the future. —*Scott Yanow*

Hand Made / 1993 / Lipstick ♦♦♦

Michael Formanek

b. May 7, 1958, San Francisco, CA

Bass / Avant-Garde, Post-Bop

An excellent bassist who has emerged as a talented bandleader, Michael Formanek has had a versatile career. He started off playing professionally in 1974 with saxophonist Norman Williams in San Francisco and then during the next few years worked with Eddie Henderson, Joe Henderson, Tony Williams and Dave Liebman among others. After moving to New York in 1978, Formanek was a sideman with Tom Harrell, Herbie Mann and Chet Baker. During much of 1980 he performed with the Media Band in West Germany and then in 1982 he joined the quintet Gallery. Formanek has since led sessions for Enja and Soul Note that feature such stimulating sidemen as Greg Osby, Mark Feldman, Tim Berne, Dave Douglas and Marty Ehrlich. —*Scott Yanow*

● **Wide Open Spaces** / Jan. 25, 1990+Jan. 26, 1990 / Enja ♦♦♦♦♦

Bassist Michael Formanek, who contributed all 15 selections to this CD (some of which are quite brief), utilizes an adventurous quintet also including Greg Osby on alto and soprano, violinist Mark Feldman, guitarist Wayne Krantz, and drummer Jeff Hirshfield. The very distinctive voices of Osby and Feldman, the quirky melodies (some of which sound as if they could have been written by Ornette Coleman) and the consistent surprises make this memorable set highly recommended to open-eared listeners. —*Scott Yanow*

Extended Animation / Nov. 21, 1991-Nov. 23, 1991 / Enja ♦♦♦♦

Bassist Michael Formanek's second album continues the pattern established on his debut. He features mostly originals and keeps things moving with varied rhythms and arrangements that don't emphasize any particular style. He's assisted by guitarist Wayne Krantz, violinist Mark Feldman, and drummer Jeff Hirschfield. —*Ron Wynn*

Loose Cannon / Oct. 26, 1992-Oct. 28, 1992 / Soul Note ✦✦✦✦✦

Low Profile / Jun. 28, 1994 / Enja ✦✦✦✦
Bassist Michael Formanek, an underrated composer who wrote the ten pieces explored on this CD, welcomes an all-star group of adventurous improvisers. Marty Ehrlich (on clarinet, bass clarinet, alto and soprano), Tim Berne (doubling on alto and baritone), trumpeter Dave Douglas, trombonist Frank Lacy, pianist Salvatore Bonafede and drummer Marvin "Smitty" Smith all make strong contributions to the difficult but colorful music. Well worth checking out. —*Scott Yanow*

Nature of the Beast / Mar. 31, 1996-Apr. 1, 1996 / Enja ✦✦✦

Jimmy Forrest

b. Jan. 24, 1920, St. Louis, MO, d. Aug. 26, 1980, Grand Rapids, MI
Tenor Saxophone / Swing, Early R&B, Groove
A fine all-round tenor player, Jimmy Forrest is best-known for recording "Night Train," a song that he "borrowed" from the last part of Duke Ellington's "Happy Go Lucky Local." While in high school in St. Louis, Forrest worked with pianist Eddie Johnson, the legendary Fate Marable and the Jeter-Pillars Orchestra. In 1938 he went on the road with Don Albert and then was with Jay McShann's Orchestra (1940-42). In New York Forrest played with Andy Kirk (1942-48) and Duke Ellington (1949) before returning to St. Louis. After recording "Night Train," Forrest became a popular attraction and recorded a series of jazz-oriented R&B singles. Among his most important later associations were those with Harry "Sweets" Edison (1958-63), Count Basie's Orchestra (1972-77) and Al Grey, with whom he co-led a quintet until his death. Forrest recorded for United (reissued by Delmark), Prestige/New Jazz (1960-62) and Palo Alto (1978). —*Scott Yanow*

★ **Night Train** / Nov. 27, 1951-Sep. 7, 1953 / Delmark ✦✦✦✦✦
Jimmy Forrest had a tremendous hit in 1951 with "Night Train," a simple blues riff he lifted from Duke Ellington's "Happy Go Lucky Local." Although the tenorman was not able to duplicate that song's appeal with any other recording, he was a popular performer in the R&B circuit throughout the 1950s. Virtually all of his records from the era (originally made for the United label) are on this CD reissue, including five selections not previously released. The tough-toned Forrest was not really a screamer or a honker, and the 17 numbers on the set should be of interest to both early R&B and jazz collectors. Recorded in Chicago, Forrest fronts a rhythm section that includes either Charles Fox or Bunky Parker on piano, and sometimes trumpeter Chauncey Locke or trombonist Bert Dabney. The music is very enjoyable and highly recommended. —*Scott Yanow*

All the Gin Is Gone / Dec. 10, 1959-Dec. 12, 1959 / Delmark ✦✦✦✦
This was the first album that tenor saxophonist Jimmy Forrest made after his R&B phase ended. Particularly notable is that the set served as the recording debut of guitarist Grant Green; completing the band are pianist Harold Mabern, bassist Gene Ramey and drummer Elvin Jones. The top-notch group performs two ballads, "Caravan" and three basic Forrest originals, including the title cut. The music is essentially melodic and blues-based hard bop that looks toward souljazz. Everyone sounds in fine form. —*Scott Yanow*

Black Forrest / Dec. 10, 1959-Dec. 12, 1959 / Delmark ✦✦✦
This 1972 LP, a complement to *All the Gin Is Gone*, released the remainder of tenor saxophonist Jimmy Forrest's two Delmark sessions, including four alternate takes and five other songs. Forrest sounds fine, guitarist Grant Green was making his debut on record, and the rhythm section (pianist Harold Mabern, bassist Gene Ramey and drummer Elvin Jones) plays up to par. Get *All the Gin Is Gone* first, and then, if one wants to hear the rest of the story, this set. —*Scott Yanow*

Forrest Fire / Aug. 9, 1960 / Original Jazz Classics ✦✦✦✦
During 1961, Jimmy Forrest recorded four albums for Prestige and its subsidiary New Jazz, all of which have been reissued on CD in the Original Jazz Classics series. The appealing tenor is matched up with 20-year-old organist Larry Young, guitarist Thornel Schwartz and drummer Jimmie Smith. They perform two jump tunes ("Dexter's Deck" and Doug Watkins' "Help"), a pair of blues, a swinging version of Irving Berlin's "Remember," and a lone ballad ("When Your Lover Has Gone"). Excellent music that is also quite accessible. —*Scott Yanow*

Out of the Forrest / Apr. 18, 1961 / Original Jazz Classics ✦✦✦✦
This CD reissue is an excellent example of tenor saxophonist Jimmy Forrest in a soulful but fairly straightahead setting. Accompanied by pianist Joe Zawinul, bassist Tommy Potter and drummer Clarence Johnston, Forrest revives his "Bolo Blues," plays his basic "Crash Program," and otherwise sticks to melodic standards. His highly expressive powers and ability to say a lot with a few notes is very much in evidence on this excellent set. —*Scott Yanow*

Sit Down and Relax with Jimmy Forrest / Sep. 1, 1961 / Original Jazz Classics ✦✦✦✦
The large warm tone of Jimmy Forrest is well featured on this CD reissue of a Prestige LP. Joined by guitarist Calvin Newborn (pianist Phineas' brother has

rarely had such a good opportunity to stretch out), pianist Hugh Lawson, bassist Tommy Potter and drummer Clarence Johnston, Forrest plays melodically but with his own brand of soul. The group performs three swing-era standards, "Tin Tin Deo," Duke Ellington's "Rocks in My Bed," "The Moon Was Yellow" and a version of "That's All" that was recorded on the same date but originally issued on a different album. This CD gives one a good example of Jimmy Forrest's playing and fortunately his solos are not as relaxed and laidback as the album's title might imply. —*Scott Yanow*

Most Much / Oct. 19, 1961 / Original Jazz Classics ✦✦✦✦✦
Jimmy Forrest was a very consistent tenor, able to infuse bop and swing standards with soul and his distinctive tone. With the assistance of pianist Hugh Lawson, bassist Tommy Potter, drummer Clarendon Johnson and Ray Barretto on congas, Forrest explores mostly veteran tunes, such as a jumping "Annie Laurie," the calypso "Matilda," a sentimental "My Buddy," "Robbins Nest," and even "Sonny Boy." Enjoyable music from the warm tenor. —*Scott Yanow*

Heart of the Forrest / Dec. 28, 1978 / Palo Alto ✦✦✦
Despite his general popularity, tenor saxophonist Jimmy Forrest only led this one session after 1962. Recorded less than two years before his death, Forrest was at the time co-leading a group with trombonist Al Grey. This live club date (released on a 1982 Palo Alto LP and not reissued yet on CD) features Forrest in a trio with organist Shirley Scott and drummer Randy Marsh. Although nothing too unexpected occurs on the five veteran standards (which include "Annie Laurie," "Take the 'A' Train," and Forrest's big hit, "Night Train"), the swinging and soulful music is quite infectious. —*Scott Yanow*

Sonny Fortune (Cornelius Fortune)

b. May 19, 1939, Philadelphia, PA
Alto Saxophone, Flute, Tenor Saxophone / Post-Bop
Sonny Fortune has continued to grow with time and in the mid-'90s he is in prime form. Fortune started his career playing in R&B groups in Philadelphia. He moved to New York in 1967 where he worked with Elvin Jones, Mongo Santamaria (1967-70) and McCoy Tyner (1971-73 and occasionally since). After a stint with Buddy Rich, Fortune played quite effectively with Miles Davis (1974-75). His solo albums during the 1970s for Horizon and Atlantic were generally unsuccessful mixtures of advanced jazz with funk and pop elements. However he has cut excellent dates for Konnex (1984, 1991 and 1993), including a well-received Monk set, and Fortune has toured in recent times with Nat Adderley and (on tenor, an instrument he should play more often) with Elvin Jones' Jazz Machine. —*Scott Yanow*

Long Before Our Mothers Cried / Sep. 8, 1974+Sep. 15, 1974 / Strata East ✦✦✦
A large-ensemble recording. A fully realized creative album and very listenable as well. With Charles Sullivan (tpt) and Stanley Cowell (p). —*Michael G. Nastos*

Awakening / Aug. 28, 1975-Sep. 9, 1975 / Horizon ✦✦

Waves of Dreams / Mar. 22, 1976+Mar. 23, 1976 / Horizon ✦✦
Considering his talent, this was a rather weak and overly commercial effort by the great altoist Sonny Fortune. On several of the numbers, Fortune is joined by some dated electronics; his playing on flute and soprano (during two of the five songs) is not on the same level as his alto, and the songs (four of which are his originals) are forgettable. The tricky time signatures and some of the solos are worthwhile (in the supporting cast are trumpeter Charles Sullivan and keyboardist Michael Cochrane), but the set overall is not the least bit memorable. Sonny Fortune eventually showed that he was capable of much better. —*Scott Yanow*

Serengeti Minstrel / Apr. 6, 1977-Apr. 8, 1977 / Atlantic ✦✦✦
Studio date from this virile Philadelphia saxophonist/flutist, who tackles the Coltrane legacy in fine fashion with Woody Shaw (tpt) and Kenny Barron (p). —*Michael G. Nastos*

Infinity Is / 1978 / Atlantic ✦✦✦
Altoist Sonny Fortune (also heard here on soprano and flute) recorded three albums for Atlantic from 1976-78, but none are all that exciting. On this date, the emphasis is on funkier sounds during originals by either keyboardist Larry Willis or Fortune. Although there are a few decent solos (this was an early effort for trumpeter Tom Browne), it is doubtful that anyone will be calling Atlantic demanding that they reissue this commercial LP's music on CD. —*Scott Yanow*

It Ain't What It Was / Dec. 1991 / Konnex ✦✦✦✦

● **Four in One** / Jan. 25, 1993-Jan. 26, 1993 / Blue Note ✦✦✦✦✦
After years of erratic albums (other than two obscure efforts for the European Konnex label), altoist Sonny Fortune finally made a great recording with this release. Most selections feature Fortune (who plays flute on "Pannonica") joined by pianist Kirk Lightsey, bassist Buster Williams and drummer Billy Hart; "Reflections" is a duet with Lightsey. Fortune, who admitted that he had not been very familiar with Thelonious Monk's music until 1990, performs ten of Monk's more

complex compositions, including "Criss Cross," "Trinkle Tinkle" and the beautiful "Ask Me Now." Fortune plays quite passionately and really digs into the material, creating one of the finest recordings of his career. —*Scott Yanow*

A Better Understanding / Feb. 20, 1995-Feb. 21, 1995 / Blue Note ✦✦✦✦✦

Monk's Mood / Nov. 17, 1995 / Konnex ✦✦✦

From Now On / Mar. 11, 1996-Mar. 12, 1996 / Blue Note ✦✦✦
This release from altoist Sonny Fortune is a particularly strong session, a mostly high-powered modal modern mainstream date with Fortune playing at his best and contributing five of the eight compositions. Trumpeter Eddie Henderson (who is filling the gap left by the ailing Freddie Hubbard) and tenor saxophonist Joe Lovano are major assets on three songs (they both appear on "Glue Fingers" and the 17-minute "Thoughts" while playing one song apiece with Fortune in a quintet) but the focus is mostly on the leader and the rhythm section (which consists of pianist John Hicks, bassist Santi Debriano and drummer Jeff "Tain" Watts). For Sonny Fortune (who has been underrated throughout his career), this is a fairly definitive session. —*Scott Yanow*

Frank Foster

b. Sep. 23, 1928, Cincinnati, OH
Tenor Saxophone, Arranger / Swing, Hard Bop, Groove
A very talented tenor saxophonist and arranger, Frank Foster has been associated with the Count Basie Orchestra off and on since 1953. Early on he played in Detroit with the many talented local players and, after a period in the army (1951-53), he joined Basie's big band. Well-featured on tenor during his Basie years (1953-64), Foster also contributed plenty of arrangements and such originals as "Down for the Count," "Blues Backstage" and the standard "Shiny Stockings." In the latter half of the 1960s Foster was a freelance writer. In addition to playing with Elvin Jones (1970-72) and occasionally with the Thad Jones/Mel Lewis Orchestra, he led his Loud Minority big band. In 1983 Foster co-led a quintet with Frank Wess and he toured Europe with Jimmy Smith in 1985. Although influenced by John Coltrane in his playing, Foster was able to modify his style when he took over the Count Basie ghost band in 1986, revitalizing it and staying at the helm until 1995. Outside of his Basie dates, Foster has led sessions for Vogue, Blue Note (1954 and 1968), Savoy, Argo, Prestige, Mainstream, Denon, Catalyst, Bee Hive, Steeple Chase, Pablo and Concord. —*Scott Yanow*

Two Franks Please! / Mar. 5, 1956-Oct. 13, 0957 / Savoy ✦✦✦✦
Frank Foster and Frank Wess teamed up several times through the years. Both of the tenors came to prominence in the 1950s with Count Basie's orchestra. This double LP mostly features a 1956 septet that, in addition to the two Franks (Wess doubles on flute), also has trombonists Henry Coker and Benny Powell, guitarist Kenny Burrell, bassist Eddie Jones and drummer Kenny Clarke. The remaining three selections are more of a showcase for Foster, featured in a sextet with trumpeter Donald Byrd and Coker. With the exception of "Serenata" and "Dancing on the Ceiling," all of the selections are group originals (mostly by Foster and Wess) with the emphasis on viable chord changes for cool-toned swinging. Enjoyable straightahead music, which has partially been reissued on CD. —*Scott Yanow*

Fearless Frank Foster / Dec. 2, 1965 / Original Jazz Classics ✦✦✦
Shortly after leaving Count Basie's Orchestra, tenor saxophonist Frank Foster led this quintet set for Prestige, which in 1997 was reissued on CD in the Original Jazz Classics series. Foster shows off the influence of John Coltrane (as opposed to his earlier cool-toned style) and matches well with the occasionally fiery trumpet of Virgil Jones, pianist Albert Dailey, bassist Bob Cunningham and drummer Alan Dawson. In addition to Fats Waller's "Jitterbug Waltz," Foster performs five originals, some of which (like "Raunchy Rita") fall into the area of funky hard bop. Spirited music. —*Scott Yanow*

Manhattan Fever / Mar. 21, 1968 / Blue Note ✦✦✦
Excellent sextet with trumpeter Marvin Stamm. —*Michael G. Nastos*

Loud Minority / 1974 / Mainstream ✦✦✦
Progressive big-band music. Impressive. —*Michael G. Nastos*

Here and Now / Jun. 1976 / Catalyst ✦✦✦
This obscure LP is as notable for some late-period playing by trumpeter Richard Williams as it is for the solos of tenor saxophonist Frank Foster. With flutist Artie Webb, guitarist Roland Smith, pianist Harold Mabern, bassist David Lee, drummer Freddie Waits and percussionist Azzedin Weston completing the group, the music (four forgettable originals by Foster, Billy Mitchell and Hale Smith) has some good improvising and shows the influence that funk and, to a lesser extent, fusion had on the modern mainstream jazz of the 1970s. —*Scott Yanow*

Twelve Shades of Black / Jul. 1978 / Leo ✦✦✦
Topflight large-group sessions. —*Ron Wynn*

The House That Love Built / Sep. 1982 / Steeple Chase ✦✦✦✦

Two for the Blues / Oct. 11, 1983+Oct. 12, 1983 / Original Jazz Classics ✦✦✦✦
This CD reissue of a Pablo date features Frank Foster (on tenor and soprano) and Frank Wess (tenor, flute and alto) at their best. They perform three Wess originals, one by Foster, and a variety of mostly underplayed standards (including Neal Hefti's "Two for the Blues," plus "Spring Can Really Hang You up the Most") and a surprisingly uptempo "Send in the Clowns." With pianist Kenny Barron, bassist Rufus Reid and drummer Marvin "Smitty" Smith offering stimulating support, this is an excellent showcase for the two Franks. A follow-up Concord set (*Frankly Speaking*) used the same personnel. —*Scott Yanow*

Frankly Speaking / Dec. 1984 / Concord Jazz ✦✦✦✦✦
Using the same personnel as the previous year's *Two for the Blues* (Frank Foster on tenor and soprano, Frank Wess on tenor and flute, pianist Kenny Barron, bassist Rufus Reid and drummer Marvin "Smitty" Smith), this set gets the slight edge and is an excellent introduction to the playing of the two Count Basie saxophonists. Foster contributes two originals (including the classic "Blues Backstage"), Wess brought in "Up and Coming," and the quintet also performs five jazz standards including "When Did You Leave Heaven?," Hoagy Carmichael's "One Morning In May" and Neal Hefti's "Two Franks." Recommended. —*Scott Yanow*

● **Leo Rising** / Aug. 23, 1996-Aug. 24, 1996 / Arabesque ✦✦✦✦✦
Frank Foster, who in 1995 willingly gave up leadership of the Count Basie Orchestra after nine years of traveling the world (and playing "Jumpin' at the Woodside" and his own "Shiny Stockings" on a nightly basis), is heard here at the top of his form. Whether swinging on his blues "You're Only as Old as You Look," showing off the influence of John Coltrane during some modal material, playing some intense soprano on the title track, or jamming on rhythm changes with guest trumpeter Derrick Gardner during "Derricksterity," Foster (67 at the time) makes every note count. The all-star rhythm section sounds quite inspired by the veteran tenor's ideas and enthusiasm (Scott and McBride have many excellent short solos), while trumpeter Gardner contributes a pair of fiery statements. This is one of Frank Foster's finest small-group dates and is highly recommended. —*Scott Yanow*

Gary Foster (Gary N. Foster)

b. May 25, 1936, Leavensworth, KS
Alto Saxophone / Cool, Bop
An excellent cool-toned straightahead altoist influenced by Lee Konitz and Warne Marsh, Gary Foster's years in the studios have often been underrated despite his talents. He graduated from the University of Kansas in 1961 and soon settled in the Los Angeles area, where he has been active ever since in the studios, as a woodwind teacher, and in big bands, including those of Clare Fischer (since 1965), Louie Bellson, Toshiko Akiyoshi (in the 1970s) and the Marty Paich Dek-tette. Foster also played often with Warne Marsh, Laurindo Almeida and Jimmy Rowles, recorded with Cal Tjader, Poncho Sanchez and Mel Tormé, and led sessions of his own for Revelation (four records during 1968-85) and Concord. —*Scott Yanow*

Subconsciously / Apr. 2, 1967-Oct. 18, 1968 / Revelation ✦✦✦

Grand Cru Classe / Jan. 12, 1969-Mar. 9, 1969 / Revelation ✦✦✦

● **Make Your Own Fun** / Jan. 1991 / Concord Jazz ✦✦✦✦
This is an easy CD to recommend. Gary Foster's pleasing alto is two parts Phil Woods and one part Lee Konitz. Pianist Jimmy Rowles displays his distinctive and tasteful chord voicings, bassist John Heard and drummer Joe La Barbera use their talents in very supportive background work, and the quartet is tight but spontaneous. A strong point of the session is the repertoire, which includes Rowles' most popular composition (a typically haunting "The Peacocks"), a tribute to Warne Marsh, the pianist's raspy but effective vocal on "What a Life" and a catchy Sonny Red blues called "'Teef." This set will satisfy fans of bop-based jazz. —*Scott Yanow*

Pops Foster

b. May 18, 1892, McCall, LA, **d.** Oct. 30, 1969, San Francisco, CA
Bass / Classic Jazz, New Orleans Jazz
One of the first important bassists (along with Steve Brown, Bill Johnson and Wellman Braud), Pops Foster had the longest career and he kept the tradition of slap bass solos alive into the late '60s. Foster was playing in bands around New Orleans as early as 1906. He played tuba with Fate Marable's group on riverboats (1918-21) and was with Kid Ory's band in California. Foster was in St. Louis in the mid-'20s, working with Charlie Creath and Dewey Jackson. After he arrived in New York in 1928, Foster played with King Oliver and then joined the great Luis Russell Orchestra, where his thumping bass really propelled the ensembles. Pops stayed with Russell during the long period (1935-40) when the orchestra was really the backup group for Louis Armstrong. After that stint ended, Foster was in demand during the New Orleans revival period, freelancing with many bands including those of Art Hodes, Mezz Mezzrow, Sidney Bechet (1945) and Bob Wil-

ber. He toured Europe with Sammy Price during 1955-56, played with Earl Hines in San Francisco (1956-61) and then spent 1963-64 with Elmer Snowden's trio. He also wrote his autobiography, which was published posthumously in 1971. —Scott Yanow

Ronnie Foster

b. May 13, 1950, Buffalo, NY

Keyboards, Organ / Contemporary Funk, Soul Jazz, Groove, Instrumental Pop

Since his initial solo style favored funky vamps instead of risky improvisation, organist Ronnie Foster was frequently dismissed by jazz purists during the peak of his career in the first half of the '70s. However, he was a talented mainstream funk and soul-jazz keyboardist who managed to cultivate a successful career as a sideman (working frequently with George Benson, in particular) and producer during the late '70s, '80s and '90s. Furthermore, his '70s records for Blue Note became cult items among a new generation of listeners raised on acid jazz. Even if he rarely led a session after 1979, Foster wound up playing some sort of a role in mainstream and funk jazz during the '80s and '90s.

A native of Buffalo, New York, Foster learned to play piano as a child, being taught in the traditional classical style. However, jazz intrigued him more, and when he was a teenager he began to pursue that direction. Eventually, he attended a jam session where there was an organ in addition to a piano. After playing the organ, he decided to concentrate on the instrument. He listened to Jimmy Smith, gradually making his way to more adventurous players like Larry Young. A local Buffalo organist, Joe Madison, gave him advice, and Foster practiced regularly at a studio where he would rent a room with an organ for 60 cents an hour.

Eventually, Foster began playing local and New York clubs. He slowly built a following, playing with such musicians as Stanley Turrentine, Grant Green and George Benson. By the early '70s, he had formed a group called Energy II. Grant Green had Foster play on his *Alive* album, and the organist's performance impressed the label's Dr. George Butler, who offered Foster a contract.

Ronnie Foster recorded *The Two Headed Freap*, his first album for Blue Note, in January of 1972. A funky set of soul-jazz, the album didn't receive much attention or critical praise, and neither did its follow-up, *Sweet Revival*, which was recorded in December of that year. He cut *Live at Montreux* in July of 1973, which was followed in 1974 by *On the Avenue* and in 1975 by *Cheshire*, his final album for Blue Note. He then moved to Columbia, where he released *Love Satellite* in 1978 and *Delight* in 1979.

A session for ProJazz, entitled *The Racer*, followed a few years later, but Foster effectively retired from leading groups in the early '80s in order to concentrate on session work. During the '70s, he had played on numerous George Benson records, as well as records by Stevie Wonder, Roberta Flack, Earl Klugh, Jimmy Ponder, Stanley Clarke and Lalo Schifrin. Throughout the '70s, Foster continued to play on a wide variety of sessions and eventually moved into production. Among the musicians he worked with in the '80s were Jimmy Smith, Klugh, Flack, Harvey Mason, Stanley Turrentine, David Sanborn, Djavan and Grover Washington Jr. Foster continued the same path in the '90s, playing with many of the same musicians, as well as Lee Ritenour, Roland Vazquez and the Temptations, among others. His own records were rediscovered by a new generation of listeners in the '90s, as well, with several of his records used as source material for sample-heavy acid jazz and hip-hop records. —Stephen Thomas Erlewine

The The Two Headed Freap / Jan. 20, 1972-Jan. 21, 1972 / Blue Note ✦✦✦✦✦

Ronnie Foster's debut album *Two Headed Freap* is a set of contemporary funky soul-jazz from the early '70s, which means it sounds closer to the soundtrack of a lost blaxploitation flick than *Back at the Chicken Shack, Pt. 2*. Foster certainly does display a debt to Jimmy Smith, but his playing is busier than Smith's and a bit wilder. Ironic, then, that his playing is in service to the groove and blends into the mix of wah-wah guitars, funk rhythms, electric bass, harps and percolating percussion. Everything on *Two Headed Freap* is about glitzy groove—it sounds cinematic, colorful and funky. It's true that there is little real improvisation here and the songs all have a similar groove, but it's worked well, and the music is ultimately appealing to fans of this genre. Jazz purists—even soul-jazz purists—will likely find this music a little monotonous and commercial, but fans of early-'70s funk from Sly Stone to Herbie Hancock will find something of interest here. —Stephen Thomas Erlewine

Sweet Revival / Dec. 14, 1972-Dec. 15, 1972 / Blue Note ✦✦✦✦

"Let me begin by saying that this is not the greatest Jazz album you've ever heard." So states critic/DJ Harry Abraham in the liner notes on the back of *Sweet Revival*, Ronnie Foster's second album as a leader. Abraham was obviously trying to deflect criticism that this record is, in his words, "a commercial album that could just as easily been titled 'Ronnie Foster plays the Top 40 hits of the Seventies with Horns, Strings and Voices,'" but nothing he could write would make this album acceptable to jazz purists. Foster's fondness for funky soul-jazz

would be enough to earn the disdain of some critics, but he compounds his problems by piling on contemporary funk, soul and pop influences. Sweet, sweeping strings straight out of Philadelphia are all over *Sweet Revival*, as are wah-wah and fuzz guitars, slap bass, electric pianos, vocal choruses and electric sitars. Half of the album is devoted to pop covers ("Back Stabbers," "Me and Mrs. Jones," "Alone Again (Naturally)"), with a couple of fusion numbers and originals thrown in for good measure. Fans of that sound will find much of the album appealing, even if the vocals can sound eerie (check out the heavily echoed intro to "Where Is the Love?") and the sitars sound silly. Although the album sounds dated, the grooves are funky, and *Sweet Revival* remains one of the most engaging records of groovy, jazzy funk-soul of its era. —Stephen Thomas Erlewine

Live at Montreux / Jul. 5, 1973 / Blue Note ✦✦✦

● **On the Avenue** / Apr. 30, 1974+May 1, 1974 / Blue Note ✦✦✦✦✦
His most interesting jazz-influenced release. —Ron Wynn

Cheshire / Mar. 21, 1975+Mar. 24, 1975 / Blue Note ✦✦✦

Love Satellite / 1978 / Columbia ✦✦✦

Delight / 1979 / Columbia ✦✦✦

The Racer / 1986 / Projazz ✦✦

Pete Fountain

b. Jul. 3, 1930, New Orleans, LA

Clarinet / Dixieland

One of the most famous of all New Orleans jazz clarinetists, Pete Fountain has the ability to play songs that he has performed a countless number of times (such as "Basin Street Blues") with so much enthusiasm that one would swear he had just discovered them! His style and most of his repertoire have remained unchanged since the late '50s yet he never sounds bored. In 1948 Fountain (who is heavily influenced by Benny Goodman and Irving Fazola) was a member of the Junior Dixieland Band and this was followed by a stint with Phil Zito and an important association with the Basin Street Six (1950-54) with whom the clarinetist made his first recordings. In 1955 Fountain was a member of the Dukes of Dixieland, but his big breakthrough came when he was featured playing a featured Dixieland number or two on each episode of *The Lawrence Welk Show* during 1957-59. After he left, he moved back to New Orleans, opened his own club and has played there regularly since. Fountain's finest recordings were a lengthy string for Coral during 1959-65 (they turned commercial for a period after that) although he has made relatively few CDs considering his continuing popularity. —Scott Yanow

The Blues / 1959 / Coral ✦✦✦

Accompanied by an enthusiastic big band featuring some solos from tenor great Eddie Miller, trombonist Moe Schneider, Jackie Coon on mellophone and the trumpets of John Best and Conrad Gozzo, Pete Fountain is in excellent form on a dozen blues-oriented pieces. Since the swinging arrangements are uncluttered and attention was paid to varying tempos and moods, this LP is one of Fountain's better ones from his earlier days. As is true with all of his Coral recordings (which are generally his most inspired and best planned), none of these performances have yet to appear on CD. —Scott Yanow

Pete Fountain's New Orleans / Feb. 1959 / Coral ✦✦✦

This LP is an excellent showcase for Pete Fountain in his early days. The clarinetist (who is the only horn in a quartet with pianist Stan Wrightsman, bassist Morty Corb and drummer Jack Sperling) sounds typically enthusiastic on the Dixieland warhorses, turning "The Saints" into a march and coming up with fresh things to say on such songs as "Do You Know What It Means to Miss New Orleans?," "Basin Street Blues" and "Tin Roof Blues." —Scott Yanow

Pete Fountain Day / Oct. 29, 1959 / Coral ✦✦✦✦

This attractive LP gives one a definitive look at clarinetist Pete Fountain in his early days. With fine backup from vibraphonist Godfrey Hirsch, pianist Merle Koch, bassist Don Bagley and drummer Jack Sperling, Fountain enthusiastically and melodically swings his way through ten veteran standards. The music falls between swing and Dixieland and is consistently joyous; in other words, it's a typically enjoyable Pete Fountain set. —Scott Yanow

The Best of Pete Fountain / 1959 / GRP /Decca ✦✦

The title of this CD is quite inaccurate, for although it draws its 22 selections from clarinetist Pete Fountain's best period (his years on the Coral label), the selections picked are sometimes a bit eccentric. Fountain is heard playing Dixieland with some of his bands, but is also joined by inappropriate choral groups and occasional strings; worse yet, no personnel listing or even recording dates are included. There is some good music along the way (such as "While We Danced at the Mardi Gras," "China Boy," "High Society," "Over the Waves" and "Indiana"), but these otherwise out-of-print recordings (few of which are available elsewhere on CD) deserved much more knowledgeable treatment than this shoddy reissue. —*Scott Yanow*

At the Bateau Lounge / 1960 / Coral ✦✦✦

Pete Fountain's steady series of recordings for Coral were among the most rewarding of his career. This particular set found him playing live at Dan's Bateau Lounge, his home base in New Orleans prior to opening his own club. The repertoire for the quartet (which also includes pianist Merle Koch, bassist Don Bagley and drummer Jack Sperling) consists of a variety of standards along with a few folk songs (including "Londonderry Air" and "Deep River") and a rare Fountain original "Creole Gumbo." This is excellent music from one of Dixieland's most enduring stars. —*Scott Yanow*

Mr. New Orleans Meets Mr. Honky Tonk / 1960 / Coral ✦

This is a hilariously bad LP. Pete Fountain's Dixieland group alternates (often chorus by chorus) with pianist Big Tiny Little's very corny honky tonk band, really tearing apart (quite unintentionally) a dozen veteran standards. Add to the general bedlam quite a few sound effects and the results are remarkable: music to offend everyone. Also quite humorous are Leonard Feather's liner notes, which attempt to justify this nonsense. —*Scott Yanow*

Salutes the Great Clarinetists / 1960 / Coral ✦✦✦

Pete Fountain plays a dozen songs associated with seven different clarinetists ranging from Benny Goodman and Woody Herman to Irving Fazola and even Ted Lewis. Backed by a big band directed by Bud Dant on some of the selections, Fountain is in excellent form playing in his own swing-Dixieland style. Unfortunately this LP, as with all of his enjoyable Coral dates, is long out-of-print but might be found at secondhand record stores. —*Scott Yanow*

The New Orleans Scene / 1961 / Coral ✦✦✦

Trumpeter Al Hirt gets co-billing with Pete Fountain on this album but unfortunately only joins the clarinetist on four of the eight selections; best is "Panama." While those performances also include trombonist Jack Delaney and drummer Monk Hazel among the personnel, the other four numbers find Fountain utilizing his usual quartet of the time with pianist Stan Wrightman. Nothing too unexpected happens on these Dixieland warhorses (which are augmented by Leonard Feather's "Mighty like the Blues") but this LP should satisfy Dixieland fans; Fountain always sounds so enthusiastic. —*Scott Yanow*

On Tour / 1961 / Coral ✦✦✦✦

Pete Fountain (backed by pianist Stan Wrightsman, bassist Morty Corb and drummer Jack Sperling) is in his usual enthusiastic and swinging form on a dozen songs, all of which have a location in their title (such as "New Orleans," "San Antonio Rose," "Manhattan," "Indiana" and "Moonlight in Vermont"). The clarinetist is well-showcased and the frameworks have more variety than one might expect, making this out-of-print LP worth searching for. —*Scott Yanow*

Pete Fountain's French Quarter / 1961 / Coral ✦✦✦✦✦

In the early-to-mid '60s Pete Fountain recorded a series of rewarding albums for Coral, none of which have yet been reissued on CD. This album, a quintet set with vibraphonist Godfrey Hirsch, pianist Stan Wrightsman, bassist Morty Corb and drummer Jack Sperling, celebrated the opening of the clarinetist's New Orleans club, the French Quarter Inn. Fountain always sounds enthusiastic when he plays (as if he were discovering veteran Dixieland and swing standards for the first time) and he is heard in top form on such songs as "Dear Old Southland," "Someday Sweetheart," "Is It True What They Say About Dixie?," "That Da Da Strain" and even "The Birth of the Blues." —*Scott Yanow*

Music from Dixie / Mar. 20, 1961-Mar. 22, 1961 / Coral ✦✦✦✦✦

Clarinetist Pete Fountain's group expands from a sextet to a nonet on this enjoyable LP with the addition of trumpeter Charlie Teagarden, trombonist Moe Schneider and tenor great Eddie Miller. The music falls between Dixieland and swing, as Fountain leads the spirited crew through a dozen songs, including his own "Bye Bye Bill Bailey," "High Society," "Struttin' with Some Barbecue," "Milenberg Joys" and "When You're Smiling." Dixieland fans will want to search for this album, along with many of Fountain's other Coral LPs. —*Scott Yanow*

New Orleans at Midnight / Mar. 20, 1961-Mar. 25, 1963 / Coral ✦✦✦

The dozen selections on this excellent Pete Fountain LP are taken from several different sessions although the music had not been released previously. Fountain, who must have been starting to run out of songs to record by 1963 (since he cut so many albums for Coral during the early-to-middle '60s), swings such material as "Creole Love Call," "Brahms' Lullaby," Rod McKuen's "Midnight Pete" and "Battle Hymn of the Republic" along with a variety of swing and Dixieland standards. The music is enjoyable as is true of all of Pete Fountain's performances from this era, his prime period. Unfortunately none of Fountain's Coral recordings have surfaced on CD yet. —*Scott Yanow*

Plenty of Pete / Nov. 28, 1962 / Coral ✦✦✦

Coral certainly offered Dixieland fans plenty of Pete Fountain in the early '60s, for he recorded at least 16 albums for the label during 1959-63. Fortunately this was the clarinetist's prime period (although he always sounds good) but unfortunately none of the recordings have been reissued on CD yet. For *Plenty of Pete*, Fountain is heard showcased with an orchestra on five of the eight numbers (including an attempt to capitalize on the success of "Stranger on the Shore") and jams with his rhythm section on the remaining pieces plus a lengthy and rather odd medley. The latter somehow combines together "Stardust," "Is It True What They Say About Dixie?," "The Saints" and "Dixie," shifting back and forth between those unrelated songs. As with most of his output for Coral, this Pete Fountain LP is worth picking up if one is lucky enough to run across it. —*Scott Yanow*

South Rampart Street Parade / Mar. 23, 1963 / Coral ✦✦✦✦

This is an unusual Pete Fountain record, for the popular Dixieland-swing clarinetist's regular group (which at the time had trumpeter Jackie Coon and trombonist Moe Schneider) is joined by four drummers (Godfrey Hirsch, Jack Sperling, Nick Fatool and Paul Barbarin) and four trombones for a set of parade music. Actually, many of the songs (such as "South Rampart Street Parade," "Over the Waves" and "Farewell Blues") are also part of the usual Dixieland repertoire but plenty of space was left for the drummers to be heard. This is a surprisingly successful and fun outing. —*Scott Yanow*

Walking Through New Orleans / 1963-1968 / Coral ✦✦✦

For this LP, one of Pete Fountain's last ones for Coral, the clarinetist is heard in a variety of settings spanning a five-year period (although none of the performances was released on other albums). Fountain leads a marching band on some songs and otherwise is accompanied by his ten-piece combo of the time; in addition, a harmless vocal group also pops up on one song. The music ranges from swing standards to blues and some Dixieland. This record is not an essential acquisition but does have its strong moments. —*Scott Yanow*

● Standing Room Only / 1965 / Coral ✦✦✦✦✦

This is one of the best Pete Fountain records, for the clarinetist (who recorded so often with just a rhythm section or very subservient horns) is challenged by the presence of trumpeter Charlie Teagarden, trombonist Bob Havens and the great tenor Eddie Miller. With drummer Nick Fatool pushing the rhythm section, the band romps through eight standards (highlighted by "Muskrat Ramble," "Struttin' with Some Barbecue" and "You Are My Sunshine") and a memorable four-song "Ramblin'" Medley." This LP, as with all of Pete Fountain's valuable output for Coral, has yet to be reissued on CD. —*Scott Yanow*

Pete Fountain's Crescent City / 1973 / MCA ✦✦

Clarinetist Pete Fountain gives a melodic swing-Dixie approach to a wide variety of material on this obscure LP, ranging from "Muskrat Ramble" and "At the Jazz Band Ball" to "Dream" and even "Tie a Yellow Ribbon 'Round the Old Oak Tree." Although tenor saxophonist Eddie Miller and drummer Jack Sperling are in the accompanying group, they are very much confined to the background during this so-so set of unsurprising music. —*Scott Yanow*

Alive in New Orleans / 1977 / First American ✦✦

Few sparks occur during this melodic LP by clarinetist Pete Fountain. The tunes include some Dixieland ("Jazz Me Blues" and "Indiana"), a few ballads ("When Your Lover Has Gone" and "Georgia") and a revival of a pop hit ("Stranger on the Shore") but, despite a few solos from Eddie Miller on tenor, the emphasis is very much on Fountain's melodic solos. It's pleasant music, though totally lacking in surprises. —*Scott Yanow*

Jazz Reunion / 1981 / Jucu ✦✦✦

This set from the short-lived Jucu label features clarinetist Pete Fountain heading a quintet comprising Frank Flynn on marimbas, guitarist Bob Bain, bassist Ray Leatherwood and drummer Jack Sperling. Alternating standards (ranging from Dixieland to "Just Friends") with some lesser-known material, Fountain seems a bit inspired by the unusual instrumentation and he comes up with some fiery solos. This LP will be hard to find but it is one of Fountain's better efforts from the 1980s. —*Scott Yanow*

Swingin' Blues / 1990 / Ranwood ✦✦

Clarinetist Pete Fountain interacts with musicians from both the Dixieland and country music world on this okay effort. Most of the selections on the CD are the usual Dixieland standards but there is also "Walking the Floor over You," "Honky Tonk" and "Amazing Grace." This is fairly predictable but reasonably pleasing melodic music from the always-enthusiastic clarinetist. —*Scott Yanow*

Live at the Ryman / 1992 / Sacramento ✦✦✦

Pete Fountain plays warhorses with such enthusiasm and delight that it often sounds as if he is discovering songs such as "Basin Street Blues" and "Way Down Yonder in New Orleans" for the first time. On this typically excellent live performance Fountain, in a quintet that also features vibraphonist Godfrey Hirsch and pianist Merle Koch, really stretches out on lengthy versions of "Avalon" and "Up a Lazy River." Koch has well-played if somewhat slapdash features on "Little Rock Getaway" and "Kansas City Stomp" while Hirsch's vibes are well-displayed on "Stardust" (in the Lionel Hampton tradition). Even if "Stardust" gets a bit lost in a pointless detour into "Dixie," Fountain and company have a fine time throughout this very accessible swing-Dixie session (which would have benefited from some liner notes) that will probably be enjoyed by his fans. —*Scott Yanow*

Cheek to Cheek / May 1993 / Ranwood ♦♦

Clarinetist Pete Fountain designed this CD as a romantic and very danceable ballad album and even such songs as "Rose Room" and "I Can't Believe That You're in Love with Me" are taken at slow tempos. Accompanied by an inflexible rhythm section that probably regarded jazz as a second language and a dull trombone section, Fountain still sounds enthusiastic. His tone is the only reason to acquire this disappointing set. —*Scott Yanow*

New Orleans All Stars / Tradition ♦

The blurb on the back of this CD says that "this comprehensive collection of various sessions features inspired solos by Fountain, pianists, trombonists, trumpeters, and even the occasional tuba player." Pity that no tuba player ever appears. With all due respect to liner note writer Allen Lowe and the others involved in this reissue, one wonders if any of them actually heard the music. Although a personnel listing is given for the entire set, it only applies to the four live songs, and even then there is no second reed (despite the listing of Lester Bouchon). The unlisted Sam DeKemel is well showcased on "Bugle Call Rag"; the other main players are clarinetist Pete Fountain, trumpeter Tony Almerico and trombonist Jack Delaney. Two other songs match Fountain with a restrained Al Hirt on trumpet. The mistitled "In the Shade of the Old Apple Tree" (from another session altogether) is actually an unidentified ballad with a charming, if occasionally faltering, Bix Beiderbecke-oriented trumpeter, a conventional six-piece unit and no Fountain. For the punchline, "St. James Infirmary" and "When the Saints Go Marching In" have a personnel bearing no resemblance to what is listed (with trumpeter Buck Clayton, Bud Freeman on tenor, trombonist Vic Dickenson and clarinetist Pee Wee Russell). This is probably the first time that Pee Wee Russell has been identified as Pete Fountain! Everyone involved in this misfire should be embarrassed! —*Scott Yanow*

Fourplay

f. 1991

Group / Instrumental Pop, Crossover Jazz

This all-star group (comprising keyboardist Bob James, guitarist Lee Ritenour, bassist Nathan East and drummer Harvey Mason) was formed in 1991 after the quartet all came together on part of James' *Grand Piano Canyon* album. They have since recorded three CDs for Warner Bros. that have all been big sellers, not surprising considering the popularity of James and Ritenour. The group's music borders on jazz with some strong improvisations mixed in with large doses of pop and R&B, about what one would expect from these studio musicians. —*Scott Yanow*

Fourplay / 1991 / Warner Brothers ♦♦

A pleasant fusion effort, it never really lives up to potential possibilities. —*Steve Aldrich*

● **The Best of Fourplay** / 1991-1996 / Warner Brothers ♦♦♦♦

Considering that this CD draws eight of its selections from Fourplay's three former releases while adding four newer cuts, one would think that this would be a definitive release. However, from a jazz standpoint, this sampler is surprisingly weak. Fourplay (consisting of guitarist Lee Ritenour, keyboardist Bob James, bassist Nathan East and drummer Harvey Mason) often takes a back seat to pop vocals by El DeBarge, Chaka Khan and Phil Collins, and even the instrumentals barely rise above the level of pleasant, danceable background music. The musicians all sound as if they are on automatic pilot, and nearly every note seems to be planned in advance. Everyone sounds reluctant to take any chances, making for an instantly dated recording. —*Scott Yanow*

Between the Sheets / Aug. 17, 1993 / Warner Brothers ♦♦♦

It is not too surprising that Fourplay started out fairly popular, for the group, in addition to bassist Nathan East and drummer Harvey Mason, teams together keyboardist Bob James and guitarist Lee Ritenour. Their playing on this Warner Bros. release results in rather predictable background music, easy-listening crossover with touches of jazz heard in the melodic solos along with poppish R&B rhythms. Nathan East's vocals dominate a few selections. Nothing very substantial occurs. —*Scott Yanow*

Elixir / 1994 / Warner Brothers ♦♦♦♦

Panama Francis (David Albert Francis)

b. Dec. 21, 1918, Miami, FL

Drums, Leader / Early R&B Jazz, Swing, Jump Blues

Panama Francis has had a long and versatile career, equally at home in swing and R&B sessions. Church revival meetings were among his earliest gigs and he also gigged with George Kelly's group the Cavaliers in Florida (1934-38) before moving to New York. The following year he worked with Roy Eldridge (making his recording debut) and this was followed by a long period at the Savoy with the Lucky Millinder big band (1940-46) and an association with Cab Calloway (1947-52). Francis then became a busy studio drummer, performing anonymously on many pop and rock 'n' roll records. In 1979 when he was in danger of being forgotten, Francis formed the Savoy Sultans, a group based on the small unit that used to play opposite Millinder at the Savoy. The Sultans recorded a steady stream of exciting hot swing records for Black & Blue and Stash during 1979-83. Since that time Panama Francis has continued freelancing including recording and touring with the Statesmen of Jazz (1994-95). —*Scott Yanow*

Panama Francis & His Savoy Sultans / Jan. 31, 1979 / Black & Blue ♦♦♦

● **Savoy Sultans** / Jan. 31, 1979-Feb. 11, 1979 / Classic Jazz ♦♦♦♦♦

Although their recordings do not always show it, the Savoy Sultans in the late '30s were considered one of the hottest small swing groups in existence. Decades later, drummer Panama Francis decided to revive the group's concept by putting together a new Savoy Sultans, using occasional alumni but mostly utilizing other surviving veteran players. This Classic Jazz LP finds the group at its best, cooking on such numbers as "Song of the Islands," "Frenzy," "Little John Special" and "Clap Hands, Here Comes Charlie!" With George Kelly contributing the arrangements as well as his tenor, and such other fine soloists as trumpeters Francis Williams and Irv Stokes, altoists Norris Turney and Howard Johnson and pianist Red Richards, this is a hot band that could outswing the original group. This LP deserves to be reissued on CD. —*Scott Yanow*

Everything Swings / Oct. 3, 1983+Oct. 10, 1983 / Stash ♦♦♦♦

Panama Francis' Savoy Sultans was one of the top mainstream jazz combos of the late '70s and early '80s, reviving the joy of small-group swing with its riffing and concise but heated solos. This excellent effort, its fourth and thus far final recording, finds the group expanding to ten pieces and featuring hot solos from the likes of trumpeters Irv Stokes and Spanky Davis, veteran tenor George Kelly and (in a bit of a surprise) the modern but flexible altoist Bobby Watson. Sticking mostly to swing standards, the Savoy Sultans uplift and bring joy to such songs as "Air Mail Special," "Stompin' at the Savoy," "In the Mood" and "Just You, Just Me." —*Scott Yanow*

Free Flight

f. 1981

Group / Post-Bop, Classical, Fusion

Founded originally by the masterful classical flutist Jim Walker and the very versatile keyboardist Milcho Leviev (who after some internal dissension was replaced in 1984 by Mike Garson), Free Flight on their recordings for Arabesque, Palo Alto and CBS have successfully fused together classical passages, straightahead jazz and fusion, sometimes switching between all three idioms in the same chorus! Walker's long and complex unison choruses with Garson are a highlight of the latter-day group; neither virtuoso seems to ever make a mistake. Bassist Jim Lacefield and drummer Peter Erskine were also founding members of the group. Ralph Humphrey took Erskine's spot by 1982 and, with the death of Lacefield, the bass and drum chairs are filled with a variety of flexible players. Free Flight (now a collaboration between Walker and Garson) has continued on a part-time basis into the mid-'90s. —*Scott Yanow*

Free Flight / 1981 / Voss ♦♦♦♦

This obscure LP was the debut album for Free Flight, a remarkable group that was always capable of playing jazz, classical and crossover, often switching back and forth. Flutist Jim Walker and pianist Milcho Leviev were the co-founders (bassist Jimmy Lacefield and drummer Peter Erskine complete the quartet), and the emphasis on this album (unlike later ones) was on jazz interpretations of classical themes. Leviev adapted melodies by Bach, Samuel Barber, Henri Dutilleux, Debussy and Poncho Vladigerov. In addition, the group plays Leviev's "Pavane for a True Musical Prince" (dedicated to Don Ellis) and his classic "Bulgarian Boogie" (which is in 33/16 time!). Well worth searching for. —*Scott Yanow*

● **The Jazz/Classic Union** / Mar. 1982 / Palo Alto ♦♦♦♦♦

Free Flight's second recording is a true classic. The flexible classical flutist Jim Walker and pianist Milcho Leviev proved that they could play practically any style perfectly, and their long and complex unisons are flawless. The quartet (which also includes bassist Jim Lacefield and drummer Ralph Humphrey) lives up to the name of the album, turning classical melodies by Chopin, Paganini (the remarkable "Paganini Caprice"), Pachelbel and Bach into jazz, making Dave Brubeck's "Blue Rondo A La Turk" sound like a classical exercise and also performing four of Leviev's originals. There are many remarkable moments on this LP, making one wish that this gem would reappear soon. —*Scott Yanow*

Soaring / 1983 / Palo Alto ✦✦✦✦
The third Free Flight album was the last to feature keyboardist Milcho Leviev. The quartet (comprising Leviev, the very impressive flutist Jim Walker, bassist Jim Lacefield and drummer Ralph Humphrey) performs jazz adaptations of themes by Ravel, J. Rodrigo, and Bach, plus originals by Leviev, Walker and Roger Kellaway ("Spur of the Moment"). The mixture of jazz and classical music is once again quite successful. —*Scott Yanow*

Beyond the Clouds / 1984 / Palo Alto ✦✦✦✦
Free Flight's fourth recording (and third for the now-defunct Palo Alto label) was its first with Mike Garson on keyboards. Garson and flutist Jim Walker (whose roots are very much in classical music) blend together very well, and they constantly challenge each other on long, impeccably played unisons. With bassist Jim Lacefield and drummer Ralph Humphrey, the group performs works by Prokofiev (the remarkable "Tocatta"), Beethoven, Khachaturian and the Beatles ("Norwegian Wood"), plus one by Humphrey and four by Mike Garson (highlighted by "What Is This Thing Called Jazz?"). Highly recommended, but this album, as with all of Free Flight's recordings, will be difficult to find. —*Scott Yanow*

Illumination / 1986 / Columbia ✦✦✦
Free Flight's debut for Columbia is generally less interesting than its previous four releases, with a funkier emphasis in the rhythms. However, the interplay between flutist Jim Walker and keyboardist Mike Garson is still quite impressive, whether exploring a Beethoven piano sonata, "Take Five" or the many group originals (mostly by Garson). Guest appearances by bassist Stanley Clarke and altoist Gary Herbig are unnecessary and do not add much. Interesting music, but not all that essential. —*Scott Yanow*

Slice of Life / 1988 / Columbia ✦✦✦
Free Flight's sixth and thus far last recording has its brilliant moments, particularly "Mo's Art" (a virtuosic adaptation of a Mozart piano sonata) and some of Mike Garson's originals, even if their version of Carole King's "You've Got a Friend" is not too memorable. Flutist Jim Walker is as impressive as ever and works well with keyboardist Mike Garson, bassist Jim Lacefield, and drummer Ralph Humphrey (guitarist Mike Miller makes a guest appearance on one number), but the erratic material results in less magic than on the group's earlier Palo Alto releases. Worthwhile but not essential. —*Scott Yanow*

Free Flight 2000 / 1996 / CPP Media ✦✦✦✦
For Free Flight's first recording in several years, flutist Jim Walker and keyboardist Mike Garson are in typically wondrous form. With drummer Joe Taylor and either Dave Carpenter or Tom Warrington on bass, Walker and Garson interpret classical themes in a jazz setting and show off their remarkable virtuosity, particularly when playing endless unisons (where a simple mistake would stand out). Among the composers represented are Paganini, Rachmaninoff, Bach, Ravel, Rodgers & Hammerstein ("Climb Every Mountain") and Garson. This excellent CD is distributed by Warner Bros. —*Scott Yanow*

Nnenna Freelon

b. Cambridge, MA
Vocals / Standards
When Nnenna Freelon recorded her debut album for Columbia, a string-filled affair titled *Nnenna Freelon*, she was quickly labelled a Sarah Vaughan imitator. However her second date, *Heritage*, which featured her backed by just a trio and occasionally a couple of horns, was a major improvement and she displayed a much more adventurous and original style, showing that first impressions are not always correct. Freelon, after graduating from Simmons College, raised three children and had a career in health services in Durham, NC, before really starting her vocal career. She performed well at an Atlanta jam session with Ellis Marsalis and two years later, on the strength of that jam, she was signed to Columbia. In 1996 she switched to the Concord label and, despite her late start, Nnenna Freelon seems to have a productive career ahead of her. —*Scott Yanow*

Nnenna Freelon / Jul. 1, 1992 / Columbia ✦✦✦
Singer Nnenna Freelon's debut recording was a bit of a misstep that gave her a bad reputation among some in the jazz world. Although her voice is appealing throughout the set, she sounds too close to Sarah Vaughan for comfort and made some listeners wonder if she was going to spend her career as an imitator. As it turned out, Freelon's follow-up record (*Heritage*) would be a much more creative and highly original effort. The singer's debut (which finds her backed by a string orchestra arranged by Bob Freedman) is really not bad, and her interpretations of three originals and a variety of veteran standards (including "Close Your Eyes,"

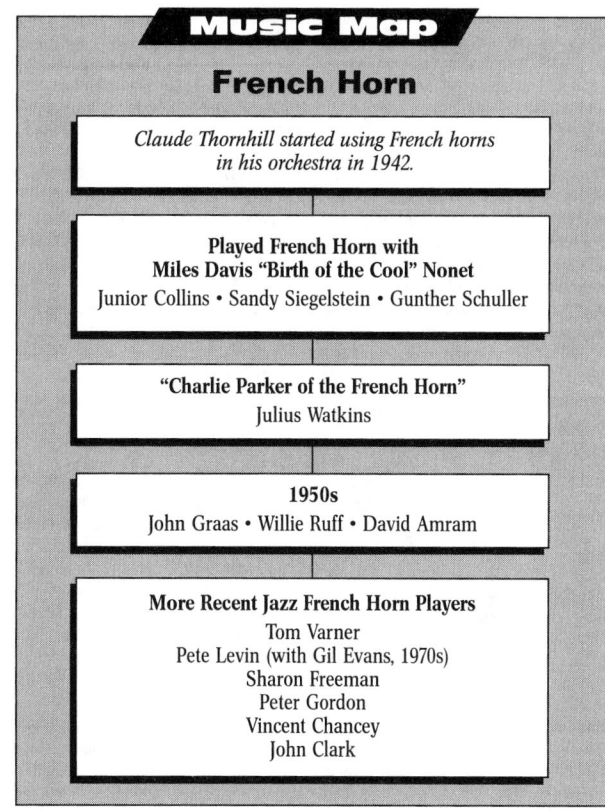

Music Map
French Horn

Claude Thornhill started using French horns in his orchestra in 1942.

Played French Horn with Miles Davis "Birth of the Cool" Nonet
Junior Collins • Sandy Siegelstein • Gunther Schuller

"Charlie Parker of the French Horn"
Julius Watkins

1950s
John Graas • Willie Ruff • David Amram

More Recent Jazz French Horn Players
Tom Varner
Pete Levin (with Gil Evans, 1970s)
Sharon Freeman
Peter Gordon
Vincent Chancey
John Clark

"Skylark," "Yesterdays" and "The Island") have their moments; Grady Tate joins her for a vocal duet on "I Fall In Love Too Easily." But the overall results pale next to Nnenna Freelon's second recording. —*Scott Yanow*

Heritage / 1993 / Columbia ✦✦✦✦✦
A major improvement on her debut (which found Nnenna Freelon overly influenced by Sarah Vaughan), the singer's second effort has many high points, including outstanding versions of "'Tis Autumn," Duke Ellington's "Heritage" (a challenging and very personal song), "Prelude to a Kiss" and "Comes Love." Backed by a superior rhythm seciton and occasional horns, Freelon (even if this set bogs down a bit near the end due to too many ballads) is quite expressive, relaxed and consistently creative. This is a very impressive effort from one of the most promising jazz vocalists of the 1990s. —*Scott Yanow*

Listen / 1994 / Columbia ✦✦✦✦

● **Shaking Free** / Feb. 26, 1996-Feb. 27, 1996 / Concord Jazz ✦✦✦✦✦
For this excellent effort, Nnenna Freelon solidifies her position as one of the better female jazz singers of the 1990s. Her appealing voice and versatility are well displayed throughout a set that includes a 5/4 version of "Out of This World," the folk song "Black Is the Color of My True Love's Hair," "Birk's Works," "I Thought About You," "Nature Boy" and three originals. Freelon is ably assisted by her regular rhythm section of the period (pianist Bill Anschell, bassist John Brown and drummer Woody Williams), and there are worthwhile guest spots for guitarist Scott Sawyer, Rickey Woodard on tenor and soprano, and Alex Acuna on conga. —*Scott Yanow*

Bud Freeman (Lawrence Freeman)

b. Apr. 13, 1906, Chicago, IL, **d.** Mar. 15, 1991, Chicago, IL
Tenor Saxophone / Dixieland, Swing, Traditional Jazz
When Bud Freeman first matured, his was the only strong alternative approach on the tenor to the harder-toned style of Coleman Hawkins and he was an inspiration for Lester Young. Freeman, one of the top tenors of the 1930s, was also one of the few saxophonists (along with the slightly later Eddie Miller) to be accepted in the Dixieland world and his oddly angular but consistently swinging solos were an asset to a countless number of hot sessions.

Freeman, excited (as were the other members of the Austin High School Gang in Chicago) by the music of the New Orleans Rhythm Kings, took up the C-melody sax in 1923, switching to tenor two years later. It took him time to develop his playing, which was still fairly primitive in 1927 when he made his recording debut with the McKenzie-Condon Chicagoans. Freeman moved to New York later that year and worked with Red Nichols' Five Pennies, Roger Wolfe Kahn, Ben Pollack, Joe Venuti, Gene Kardos and others. He was starred on Eddie Condon's memorable 1933 recording "The Eel." After stints with Joe Haymes and Ray Noble, Freeman was a star with Tommy Dorsey's Orchestra and Clambake Seven (1936-38) before having a short unhappy stint with Benny Goodman (1938). He led his short-lived but legendary Summe Cum Laude Orchestra (1939-40) which actually an octet, spent two years in the military and then from 1945 on alternated between being a bandleader and working with Eddie Condon's freewheeling Chicago jazz groups. Freeman travelled the world, made scores of fine recordings and stuck to the same basic style that he had developed by the mid-'30s (untouched by a brief period spent studying with Lennie Tristano). Bud Freeman was with the World's Greatest Jazz Band (1968-71), lived in London in the late '70s and ended up back where he started, in Chicago. He was active into his 80s and a strong sampling of his recordings are currently available on CD. —Scott Yanow

1928-1938 / Dec. 3, 1928-Nov. 30, 1938 / Classics ✦✦✦✦✦
Bud Freeman was virtually the only key tenor saxophonist of the 1928-35 period who did not sound heavily influenced by Coleman Hawkins. Freeman, whose style fell between Dixieland and swing and who has long had a distinctive sound, is heard on this Classics CD at the head of several studio groups. There are two titles from 1928 with an octet also including obscure trumpeter Johnny Mendel, pianist Dave North, drummer Gene Krupa and (on "Can't Help Lovin' That Man") singer Red McKenzie. While those performances have early examples of Freeman's style, the tenor's sound was very much formed by the time of the 1935 sextet date with the brilliant trumpeter Bunny Berigan; Bud and Bunny made for an exciting team. The bulk of this CD features Freeman in prime form jamming in a trio with pianist Jess Stacy and drummer George Wettling; these versions of "You Took Advantage of Me," "I Got Rhythm," "Keep Smiling at Trouble" and "My Honey's Loving Arms" are definitely classics. Also on this CD are five numbers on which Freeman leads an all-star octet also including cornetist Bobby Hackett, clarinetist Pee Wee Russell, Stacy and Eddie Condon. Although this music has been reissued in many different settings through the years, it is certainly essential (in one form or another) to all historical jazz collections. —Scott Yanow

Chicago Styled, Vol. 1 / Nov. 2, 1935-Apr. 4, 1940 / Swaggie ✦✦✦✦✦
Musically, this is a tremendous set, but the LP from the Australian Swaggie label may be difficult to find; fortunately, the Classics label has been reissuing this important music too. Bud Freeman, one of the few tenor saxophonists prior to Lester Young not to sound like Coleman Hawkins, is heard on four hot titles with his "Windy City Five" in 1935. Good as Bud is on tunes such as "Keep Smiling at Trouble" and "What Is There to Say?," solo honors generally go to the exciting trumpeter Bunny Berigan; the rhythm section (pianist Claude Thornhill, rhythm guitarist Eddie Condon, bassist Grachan Moncur and drummer Cozy Cole) is quite notable. The bulk of the album consists of three four-song sessions by Freeman's Summa Cum Laude Orchestra, a hot octet consisting of Bud, trumpeter Max Kaminsky, valve trombonist Brad Gowans, clarinetist Pee Wee Russell, pianist Dave Bowman, Condon, either Clyde Newcombe or Pete Peterson on bass, and Al Seidle or Morey Feld on drums. Although under Freeman's leadership and having some arrangements by Gowans, the group often sounds like an Eddie Condon "Nicksieland" band. Eight of their 12 numbers are taken from the songbook of the Wolverines in 1924 (which featured Bix Beiderbecke), but the solos and ensembles are quite fresh, rather than just re-creations. Spirited and historic music, easily recommended to Dixieland and small-group swing collectors. —Scott Yanow

Chicagoans in New York / Dec. 4, 1935-Jul. 23, 1940 / Dawn Club ✦✦✦✦
A complementary LP to Swaggie's *Chicago Styled, Vol. 1* (none of the titles are duplicated), much of this music has fortunately since been reissued on CD. There are alternate takes to two numbers by tenor saxophonist Bud Freeman's "Windy City Five" (a 1935 sextet with the great trumpeter Bunny Berigan), a four-song session plus an alternate take by Freeman's Summa Cum Laude Orchestra in 1939 (a short-lived but memorable octet also including trumpeter Max Kaminsky, valve trombonist Brad Gowans and clarinetist Pee Wee Russell), and the complete July 23, 1940 date by Freeman's "Famous Chicagoans"—eight numbers plus three alternate takes. The latter set not only features Freeman, Kaminsky and Russell, but the great trombonist Jack Teagarden (who also sings "Jack Hits the Road"). All in all, there are 18 selections on this generous LP, making it worth a search by Dixieland and Eddie Condon fans. —Scott Yanow

1939-1940 / Jul. 19, 1939-Jul. 23, 1940 / Classics ✦✦✦✦
The second Bud Freeman Classics CD has all of the studio sessions (the master takes, but not the alternates) by Freeman's short-lived all-star Summe Cum Laude Orchestra. The Dixieland octet sounds very much like a well-organized Eddie Condon band, and the rhythm guitarist is among the personnel. Teaming up with Freeman (one of the first early tenormen to form a distinctive sound of his own) are such notable players as trumpeter Max Kaminsky, valve trombonist Brad Gowans, clarinetist Pee Wee Russell, pianist Dave Bowman and a rhythm section; the final set has the great trombonist Jack Teagarden (who takes a notable vocal on "Jack Hits the Road") in Gowans' place. The music, which includes eight titles originally recorded by Bix Beiderbecke's Wolverines, has more than its share of high points, and this CD is highly recommended to Dixieland fans. All of the musicians (many of whom would be performing a similar repertoire for the next few decades) sound fresh, enthusiastic, young and at the peak of their powers. —Scott Yanow

See What the Boys in the Back Room Will Have / Mar. 26, 1940-Sep. 26, 1940 / IAJRC ✦✦
During 1939-40, tenor saxophonist Bud Freeman tried unsuccessfully to keep together his Summa Cum Laude Orchestra, an excellent Dixieland-ish octet that included trumpeter Max Kaminsky, clarinetist Pee Wee Russell and valve trombonist Brad Gowans (who provided many of the arrangements). In addition to four instrumental sessions, the band backed singers Teddy Grace, Buddy Clark and Doris Rhodes on dates that were reissued in full on this collector's set from IAJRC. Best are the four Grace titles, but these are also available with most of her other work on a highly recommended Timeless CD. The four Buddy Clark performances (plus an alternate take) have some nice moments from pianist Jess Stacy, but are otherwise fairly routine. The same can be said for the extensive Doris Rhodes date, four songs augmented by three alternate takes and three breakdowns. Collectors will want this well-conceived album, particularly for the contributions of Freeman and Russell, but it is far from essential for more general listeners, who are advised to get the Teddy Grace CD instead. —Scott Yanow

1945-1946 / Aug. 9, 1945-1946 / Classics ✦✦✦✦
The third Bud Freeman CD in Classics' reissues of all of his early sessions as a leader has some memorable performances. The classic tenor heads an all-star octet (with trumpeter Yank Lawson, trombonist Lou McGarity and clarinetist Edmond Hall) on four hot numbers; he creates a pair of hilarious verbal introductions to a couple of satirical V-Disc numbers ("The Latest Thing In Hot Jazz" and "For Musicians Only"); and on "The Atomic Era," Freeman performs an unusual duet with drummer Ray McKinley. However, this CD gets a lower rating than expected because 12 of the 21 performances showcase the Five De Marco Sisters, a pleasant but fairly mediocre swing vocal group. Although there are some good solos and ensembles on those selections, the recordings overall are only of interest to completists. —Scott Yanow

Test of Time / Jul. 1955 / Bethlehem ✦✦✦✦
This album features the warm and quirky tenor of Bud Freeman showcased on two different sessions from the same month. Six titles are quartet outings with pianist Dave Bowman, bassist Al Hall and drummer George Wettling, and these are highlighted by "You Took Advantage of Me" and "Perdido." The remaining five numbers have some typically passionate playing from trumpeter Ruby Braff, along with pianist Ken Kersey, Hall and Wettling; "At Sundown" and "Exactly Like You" are the standouts. This album, which will hopefully be reissued on CD someday, is closer to mainstream than to Dixieland and is a fine example of Bud Freeman's work at the halfway point of his productive career. —Scott Yanow

☆ **Chicago/Austin High School Jazz in Hi Fi** / Mar. 7, 1957-Jul. 8, 1957 / RCA Victor ✦✦✦✦✦
The music on this LP is so exciting that it seems remarkable that it has yet to be reissued in full on CD. Three overlapping groups are heard from and they revisit the repertoire of the McKenzie-Condon Chicagoans of 1927 (playing new versions of the four songs originally recorded) and Bud Freeman's 1939-40 Summa Cum Laude Orchestra. The two septets and the octet feature such immortal Condonites as tenor saxophonist Bud Freeman, Jimmy McPartland and Billy Butterfield on trumpets, trombonists Tyree Glenn and Jack Teagarden (who also takes some vocals), clarinetists Pee Wee Russell and Peanuts Hucko, pianists Gene Schroeder and Dick Cary, rhythm guitarist Al Casamenti (but surprisingly no Eddie Condon), bassists Milt Hinton, Al Hall and Leonard Gaskin, and drummer George Wettling. The veterans were all still in prime form at the time, and they sound quite inspired. Highlights include "Nobody's Sweetheart," "China Boy," "Chicago," "There'll Be Some Changes Made," and "Jack Hits the Road." Essential music, but it will be difficult to find until RCA is woken up about its existence. —Scott Yanow

Summer Concert 1960 / 1960 / Jazz Archives ✦✦✦
In 1960, tenor saxophonist Bud Freeman recorded an album for Swingville with a quintet that included the lyrical trumpeter Harold "Shorty" Baker. This concert LP from the Jazz Archives collectors' label has Freeman and Baker joined by trombonist Tyree Glenn (showcased on "The Lonesome Road"), pianist Gene Schroeder, bassist Bob Haggart and drummer George Wettling. In addition, three of the eight numbers add trumpeter Red Allen, who dominates the music. The performances are solid mainstream music that hints equally at both Dixieland and small-group swing. Nothing essential, but fans of the idiom will enjoy this rarity. —*Scott Yanow*

The All Stars with Shorty Baker / May 13, 1960 / Prestige ✦✦✦✦
Tenor sax great Bud Freeman, who is often associated with the Eddie Condon school of Nicksieland, is heard heading an excellent swing quintet for this 1960 studio session. Trumpeter Harold "Shorty" Baker (best known for his periods with Duke Ellington) made too few small-group recordings throughout his life so this is one of his best. With the often-overlooked but virtuosic stride pianist Claude Hopkins heard in the rhythm section along with bassist George Duvivier and drummer J.C. Heard, the group plays superior standards and a couple of originals on this fine swing date. —*Scott Yanow*

Something to Remember You By / Jan. 15, 1962 / Black Lion ✦✦✦✦✦
This CD reissue is a perfect place for listeners to start exploring the warm tenor sound of Bud Freeman. A distinctive player whose style straddles the boundary between swing and Dixieland, Freeman is heard here in a quartet also including pianist Dave Frishberg (years before he became famous as a composer/vocalist), bassist Bob Haggart and drummer Don Lamond. Freeman (55 at the time) is heard at the peak of his powers on a dozen standards (some of which are rarely played), plus five alternate takes. Highlights include "You're a Sweetheart," "Chicago," "It's Only a Paper Moon" and "Somebody Stole My Gal." —*Scott Yanow*

Chicago / Jan. 15, 1962-Feb. 2, 1962 / Black Lion ✦✦✦
Three of the selections on this LP are taken from a January 15, 1962 session reissued in full on a Black Lion CD. The great veteran tenor Bud Freeman is in fine form, fronting a quartet also including pianist Dave Frishberg, bassist Bob Haggart and drummer Don Lamond. The other five numbers are part of a lesser date actually led by guitarist Elmer Snowden and featuring trumpeter Roy Eldridge, who takes a couple of vocals. Freeman is actually a bit out of place on the spirited if erratic set, which also includes pianist Ray Bryant, bassist Tommy Bryant and drummer Jo Jones. Get the Black Lion CD instead. —*Scott Yanow*

The Compleat Bud Freeman / Dec. 10, 1969+Dec. 12, 1969 / Monmouth ✦✦✦✦
Bud Freeman's only recording as a leader from 1967-73 and first American release since 1963 is an excellent effort recorded while he was a member of the World's Greatest Jazz Band. Backed by the WGJB's rhythm section (pianist Ralph Sutton, bassist Bob Haggart and drummer Gus Johnson), Freeman is in top form on six wonderful quartet numbers (including "Dinah," "You Took Advantage of Me" and "What Is There to Say?"), plus six other numbers (highlighted by "Out of My Road, Mr. Toad," "That D Minor Thing" and "Just One of Those Things") on which Bob Wilber (on tenor and soprano) makes the group a quintet. This Monmouth LP, one of Bud Freeman's best later sets, is long overdue to be reissued on CD. —*Scott Yanow*

Superbud / 1974+Aug. 13, 1992 / Jazzology ✦✦✦✦
The bulk of this CD is a reissue of a 1974 LP put out by the British "77" label featuring tenor saxophonist Bud Freeman (in consistently exuberant form) with pianist Keith Ingham, bassist Pete Chapman and drummer Johnny Armitage; among the highlights are "Please," "'S Wonderful," "You Took Advantage of Me" and "Tea for Two." Although a piano solo by Ingham has been left off, in 1992 he recorded six additional solos of rarely performed Freeman compositions (including "After Awhile," "Craz-e-ology" and "Tillie's Downtown Now") to add to this set. High-quality mainstream jazz that should please pre-bop collectors. —*Scott Yanow*

Jazz Meeting in Holland / May 13, 1975 / Circle ✦✦✦

Song of the Tenor / Nov. 4, 1975-Nov. 5, 1975 / Philips ✦✦✦
A mid-'70s session with Roy Williams on trombone. —*Michael G. Nastos*

Two Beautiful / Mar. 31, 1976 / Circle ✦✦✦
The two distinctive swing-era tenors Bud Freeman and Buddy Tate team up with a Dutch rhythm section (pianist Chris Smildiger, bassist Koos van der Sluis and drummer Ted Easton) for a variety of veteran standards, plus a three-song ballad medley, on this live set from Scheveningen, Holland. Few surprises occur, other than the fact that the two tenors met up, but the music should satisfy mainstream jazz collectors. —*Scott Yanow*

● **California Session** / Jan. 9, 1982 / Jazzology ✦✦✦✦✦
By the time of this previously unreleased 1982 concert (put out on CD in 1997), tenor saxophonist Bud Freeman was 75 and had been playing at a major league

level for over 55 years, but there was nothing tired about his timeless style. Freeman, who happened to be in Los Angeles, was invited to a concert put on by the Poor Angel Hot Jazz Society and agreed to appear on a few numbers. However, he was so impressed by the band that during the first song he quickly put his horn together and played throughout the entire performance. Freeman was joined by trumpeter Dick Cathcart, trombonist Betty O'Hara (doubling on double-belled euphonium), clarinetist Bob Reitmeier, the great swing pianist Ray Sherman, guitarist Howard Alden (just 23 at the time), bassist Phil Stephens and drummer Nick Fatool. The repertoire on this CD consists of eight familiar standards, but the interpretations are full of inspiration and joy. On some tunes, Alden, already a masterful player, weaves lines around Freeman, and there are a few individual features for the tenorman (most notably a rollicking "Tea for Two" and a double-time rendition of "Body and Soul"). The group numbers are all enjoyable and full of high spirits, particularly "Struttin' with Some Barbecue" and "Just a Closer Walk with Thee." Highly recommended to Dixieland and straightahead fans. —*Scott Yanow*

The Real Bud Freeman (1984) / Dec. 2, 1983-Dec. 3, 1983 / Principally Jazz ✦✦✦
Bud Freeman's final record (originally a nine-song LP program that in its CD version expanded to 12 tunes) found the 77-year-old tenor great still in good form. Having recently returned to Chicago after an extended stay in England, Freeman is joined by a Chicago-based rhythm section (pianist Stuart Katz, guitarist Bob Roberts, bassist John Bany and drummer Barrett Deems) for two standards and five of his inventive and often witty originals. In addition, Freeman duets with Roberts on "I Cover the Waterfront" and with Katz on a lyrical "My Romance." Although not quite essential compared to his earlier work (and this set will be difficult to find), Bud Freeman's last recording was up to his usual standards and certainly has its enjoyable moments. —*Scott Yanow*

Chico Freeman (Earl Lavon Freeman, Jr.)

b. Jul. 17, 1949, Chicago, IL
Tenor Saxophone, Soprano Saxophone, Flute / Post-Bop
An excellent tenor saxophonist and the son of Von Freeman, Chico Freeman has had a busy and diverse career, with many recordings ranging from advanced hard bop to nearly free avant-garde jazz. He originally played trumpet, not taking up the tenor until he was a junior in college. Freeman graduated from Northwestern University in 1972, played with R&B groups and joined the AACM. In 1977 he moved to New York where he worked with Elvin Jones, Sun Ra, Sam Rivers' big band, Jack DeJohnette's Special Edition and Don Pullen in addition to leading his own groups. He recorded a dozen albums as a leader during 1975-82. Starting in 1984 Freeman has played on a part-time basis with the Leaders; he has recorded on a few occasions with his father and in 1989 he put together an electric band called Brainstorm. Chico Freeman has recorded through the years as a leader for Dharma, India Navigation, Contemporary, Black Saint, Elektra/Musician, Black Hawk, Palo Alto, Jazz House and In & Out. —*Scott Yanow*

Morning Prayer / Sep. 8, 1976 / India Navigation ✦✦✦
Tenor saxophonist Chico Freeman's second recording as a leader (the first was an obscurity for Dharma in 1975) was originally cut for the Japanese Trio label before being made available domestically by India Navigation. An impressive effort, the adventurous music (five compositions by Freeman) features the leader on tenor, soprano, flute and pan-pipe, Henry Threadgill (switching between alto, baritone and flute), pianist Muhal Richard Abrams, bassist Cecil McBee (in the first of his many collaborations with Freeman), flutist Douglas Ewart, and the percussion of Steve McCall and Ben Montgomery. The performances are unpredictable yet logical inside/outside music. This set has not yet reappeared on CD. —*Scott Yanow*

Chico / 1977 / India Navigation ✦✦✦✦
Tenor saxophonist Chico Freeman's third recording as a leader has been reissued on this CD. The 24-minute three-part "Moments" (which has been expanded a little for the reissue) and "And All the World Moved" are explorative duets by Freeman and bassist Cecil McBee, while the 16-minute "Merger" (the set's high point) finds the pair joined by pianist Muhal Richard Abrams (who is in excellent form), drummer Steve McCall and percussionist Tito Sampa. Freeman (who switches between tenor, bass clarinet and flute) shows why he was rated so high during this early productive period. —*Scott Yanow*

Beyond the Rain / Jun. 21, 1977-Jun. 23, 1977 / Original Jazz Classics ✦✦✦✦✦
This CD reissue has one of tenor saxophonist Chico Freeman's best early efforts. Freeman (who plays flute on his picturesque "Beyond the Rain") teams up with pianist Hilton Ruiz, bassist Junie Booth, percussionist Jumma Santos and the great drummer Elvin Jones for challenging but often melodic originals by Abrams and the leader, plus a warm version of "My One and Only Love." Fine music from the flexible tenorman. —*Scott Yanow*

Kings of Mali / Sep. 1977 / India Navigation ✦✦✦✦
Chico Freeman recorded frequently from 1977-84, documenting his inside/outside music during an era when fusion was somewhat dominant. Many of his more adventurous sets were made for the India Navigation label and are gradually being reissued on CD. This fine set with vibraphonist Jay Hoggard, pianist Anthony Davis, bassist Cecil McBee and drummer Don Moye has yet to reappear. Freeman, who also plays soprano and flute, stretches out on four of his colorful and complex originals, which are dedicated to the ancient kingdom of Mali. —*Scott Yanow*

● **The Outside Within** / 1978 / India Navigation ✦✦✦✦✦
Tenor saxophonist Chico Freeman (doubling here on bass clarinet) performs the nineteen-and-a-half-minute "Undercurrent" (an original by bassist Cecil McBee) and three shorter compositions with McBee, pianist John Hicks and drummer Jack DeJohnette on this enjoyable set, which has been reissued on CD. The music is often influenced by the scales of the Far East, yet also has the warmth and extroverted emotions of the West. All of the musicians have opportunities to make strong contributions, and the top-notch players (some of the finest of the past 30 years) are heard throughout in top form. —*Scott Yanow*

No Time Left / Jun. 8, 1979-Jun. 9, 1979 / Black Saint ✦✦✦
Chico Freeman (tripling on this album on tenor, soprano and bass clarinet) made many records from 1977-84, and all are worth picking up by fans of adventurous jazz. Freeman's warm tone and knowledge of more traditional areas of jazz make even his more abstract flights seem fairly accessible. Joined by vibraphonist Jay Hoggard, bassist Rick Rozie and drummer Don Moye on this somewhat obscure effort, Freeman stretches out on lengthy renditions of his originals "No Time Left," "Uhmla," and a briefer "Circle." —*Scott Yanow*

Spirit Sensitive / Sep. 1979 / India Navigation ✦✦✦✦
This set was a change of pace for Chico Freeman, for it features the usually adventurous tenor (who doubles on soprano) mostly playing warm versions of standards. The CD reissue adds four previously unissued selections (including a pair of Coltrane tunes, "Lonnie's Lament" and "Wise One") to the original program. With pianist John Hicks, bassist Cecil McBee and either Billy Hart or Don Moye on drums offering fine support (vibraphonist Jay Hoggard sits in on "Carnival"), Freeman pushes at but does not break the boundaries of hard bop. Highlights include "Autumn in New York" (a duet with McBee), Horace Silver's "Peace," "It Never Entered My Mind" and the bassist's "Close to You Alone." —*Scott Yanow*

Peaceful Heart, Gentle Spirit / Mar. 6, 1980-Mar. 7, 1980 / Contemporary ✦✦✦✦✦
Chico Freeman (a tenor saxophonist who on this date also plays soprano, flute, alto flute, clarinet and bass clarinet) recorded many sessions in the late '70s and early '80s but this is one of his very best. Utilizing an unusual instrumentation (flutist James Newton, pianist Kenny Kirkland, vibraphonist Jay Hoggard, cello, bass, drums and two percussionists), Freeman infuses his five challenging—but generally logical—compositions with rich tone colors and shades. This music is stimulating and represents one of the high points of Freeman's rather streaky career. —*Scott Yanow*

Freeman and Freeman / Apr. 1981 / India Navigation ✦✦✦
The two tenors Chico Freeman and father Von Freeman had an opportunity to team up on this CD. Recorded live in concert, the Freemans are assisted by pianist Kenny Barron (Muhal Richard Abrams takes his place on "Paying New York Dues"), bassist Cecil McBee and drummer Jack DeJohnette. Von actually sounds the more modern of the two (due to his unusual tone) on a set mostly comprising standards, plus McBee's "Undercurrents" and the lengthy jamming blues "Jug Ain't Gone," a tribute to Gene Ammons. The straightahead but sometimes eccentric music has its surprising moments, and the Freemans mostly battle to a tie. —*Scott Yanow*

Destiny's Dance / Oct. 29, 1981-Oct. 30, 1981 / Original Jazz Classics ✦✦✦✦
By 1981, after six years of steady recording, Chico Freeman had gained a strong reputation as a flexible reed player able to play both avant-garde and fairly straightahead jazz. For this straight CD reissue of a Contemporary LP, Freeman doubles on tenor and bass clarinet in settings ranging from a quartet to a sextet. Trumpeter Wynton Marsalis (then just barely 20) is in superior form during his four appearances, vibraphonist Bobby Hutcherson is on all six songs, and also in fine form are pianist Dennis Moorman, bassist Cecil McBee and drummer Ronnie Burrage; percussionist Paulinho da Costa guests on one tune. The music comprises originals by Freeman, Hutcherson and McBee that, although based in the foundations of the past (Freeman's "Embracing Oneness" is dedicated to Duke Ellington and Thelonious Monk), also looks forward. —*Scott Yanow*

Tradition in Transition / 1982 / Elektra ✦✦✦✦
This is another excellent effort by Chico Freeman, who is heard on tenor, flute and bass clarinet. The instrumentation varies on each selection during the LP, which also features trumpeter Wallace Roney, pianist Clyde Criner, bassist Cecil McBee,

drummer Billy Hart, and Jack DeJohnette on drums and piano. Other than Thelonious Monk's "Jackie-ing" (Monk had recently passed away), the repertoire comprises originals by Freeman, McBee and Criner. Even if none of the songs individually caught on, they help set an exploratory yet fairly accessible mood, as Chico Freeman does his best to move the mainstream of jazz forward a bit. This worthwhile LP will be difficult to locate. —*Scott Yanow*

The Search / 1982 / India Navigation ✦✦✦
The last of tenorman Chico Freeman's long string of India Navigation LPs (which started in 1976) is a solid effort comprising three of his originals, plus bassist Cecil McBee's "Close to You Alone." The vocals by Val Eley are not too memorable, but Freeman (doubling on flute), McBee, vibraphonist Jay Hoggard, pianist Kenny Barron, drummer Billy Hart, and percussionist Nana Vasconcelos are in typically fine form. The moody pieces on the album (which has not yet been reissued on CD) range from seven-and-a-half to over eleven-and-a-half minutes. —*Scott Yanow*

Pied Piper / Apr. 9, 1984 / Black Hawk ✦✦✦
The first of two Chico Freeman recordings for the soon-defunct Black Hawk label finds the leader switching between tenor, alto, sopranino, soprano, bass clarinet, bass flute and C flute. John Purcell "only" limits himself to five reeds (alto, baritone, oboe, alto flute and piccolo), and the horns are joined by either Kenny Kirkland or Mark Thompson on piano, bassist Cecil McBee and drummer Elvin Jones. The many combinations of reeds highlight this set, which has originals by Freeman, Mark Thompson ("Monk 2000"), John Stubblefield, Alex North and Cecil McBee ("Blues on the Bottom"), in addition to the standard "Softly as in a Morning Sunrise." The style ranges from straightahead to more exploratory sounds, and this colorful album is worth searching for. —*Scott Yanow*

Tales of Ellington / Apr. 9, 1984-Mar. 7, 1987 / Black Hawk ✦✦✦
One of the few Black Hawk LPs to be released on CD before the label went belly-up, this is a tribute to Duke Ellington featuring Chico Freeman on tenor, alto, soprano and baritone saxophones; and bass and alto clarinets; among other instruments. The music comes from several sessions and finds Freeman matched with fellow reedist John Purcell in a quintet, taking a medley of his "Sonnet" and Duke's "Sophisticated Lady" on unaccompanied tenor, interacting with the synthesizer of Larry Willis and drummer Fred Waits in a trio, and sharing quartet/quintets with pianists George Cables and Mark Thompson, bassists Herbie Lewis and Cecil McBee, and drummers Eddie Moore and Elvin Jones, plus (on "Dark Blue") trumpeter Johnny Coles. Freeman performs some Ellington obscurities (including "Lightning Bugs & Frogs" and "In the Beginning God"), some of Duke's ballads, and a few originals dedicated to Ellington. Heartfelt music. —*Scott Yanow*

Tangents / 1984 / Elektra ✦✦✦
An interesting if quite diverse set, this album is best remembered for featuring up-and-coming singer Bobby McFerrin on a few selections. McFerrin has his moments, as do tenor saxophonist Chico Freeman and such notable sidemen as altoist Steve Coleman, John Purcell on reeds, either Kenny Werner or Mark Thompson on piano, Freeman's longtime bassist Cecil McBee and drummer Billy Hart, among others. The material (by Freeman, Thompson and Werner) is actually not that significant, and the date on a whole is less memorable than many of Chico Freeman's earlier sets, but it has its enjoyable spots. —*Scott Yanow*

You'll Know When You Get There / Aug. 12, 1988-Aug. 31, 1988 / Black Saint ✦✦✦

The Mystical Dreamer / May 1989 / In & Out ✦✦

Up and Down / Jul. 26, 1989-Jul. 27, 1989 / Black Saint ✦✦✦

Sweet Explosion / Apr. 1990 / In & Out ✦✦

In the Moment / Oct. 15, 1992-Oct. 16, 1992 / Edgetone ✦✦✦
For these live performances tenor saxophonist Chico Freeman (who sounds better here than he has on record in at least five years) sits in with the San Francisco Bay Area-based group Jazz on the Line. The fiery music is often quite free although coherent and logical. Aaron Repke (on alto, soprano, baritone and flute) and trumpeter Jason Olaine co-star on this fine small-label release. —*Scott Yanow*

Threshold / Oct. 27, 1992-Oct. 28, 1992 / In & Out ✦✦

Focus / May 16, 1994 / Contemporary ✦✦✦

The Emissary / Nov. 29, 1995-Dec. 2, 1995 / Clarity ✦✦✦

Russ Freeman

b. May 28, 1926
Piano / Cool
Not to be confused with the leader of the Rippingtons, this Russ Freeman is best-known for his work in the West Coast scene of the 1950s, most noticeably with the first Chet Baker Quartet. He moved to Los Angeles in the mid-'40s and worked with Howard McGhee, sat in with Charlie Parker and recorded with Dexter Gor-

don (1947), Art Pepper, Wardell Gray, the Lighthouse All-Stars, Shorty Rogers and Baker (1954). Freeman was with Shelly Manne's Men for a long period (1955-66) and toured with Benny Goodman in 1959. After the mid-'60s he appeared less often in jazz settings (other than a 1978 recording with Art Pepper and a 1982 duet set for Atlas with Shelly Manne), mostly working in the studios; by the mid-'80s he was largely retired. Freeman made records as a leader for Pacific Jazz and Jazz West Coast during 1953-59. His song "The Wind" has been recorded by several other artists including Keith Jarrett. —*Scott Yanow*

● **Trio with Richard Twardzik** / Oct. 27, 1953-Aug. 12, 1957 / Pacific Jazz ✦✦✦✦✦
This single CD contains 12 performances by pianist Russ Freeman (with either Joe Mondragon or Monty Budwig on bass and drummer Shelly Manne) plus the one regular studio session (eight songs) that the ill-fated pianist Richard Twardzik led (in a trio with bassist Carson Smith and drummer Peter Littman). Due to its rarity, the Twardzik date is more important historically but actually Freeman generally takes solo honors. Fine straightahead music from two of the mid-'50s' more promising pianists. —*Scott Yanow*

Freeman/Baker Quartet / Nov. 6, 1956 / Pacific Jazz ✦✦✦

Von Freeman (Earl Lavon Freeman, Sr.)

b. Oct. 3, 1922, Chicago, IL
Tenor Saxophone / Post-Bop
Veteran tenor Von Freeman is essentially a bop-oriented improviser whose unusual tone (admired by some, disliked by others) is an acquired taste. The father of tenor Chico Freeman and the brother of guitarist George Freeman and drummer Bruz Freeman, Von worked early on with Horace Henderson's Orchestra (1940-41), with a navy band while in the military (1941-45) and with Sun Ra (1948-49). He was in the house band at the Pershing Hotel in Chicago (1946-50) with his brothers Bruz and George, accompanying the many top bop stars who passed through town. Freeman, who did not record as a leader until 1972 and only three times until 1989, became a local legend, playing with many types of groups in Chicago. He had a quartet with his brothers in the 1950s that used Ahmad Jamal and later Andrew Hill as their pianist. Freeman also worked with many AACM musicians (including Muhal Richard Abrams), played with blues bands in the 1960s and from the early '70s on has generally led his own groups. Von Freeman has recorded as a leader for Atlantic (1972), Nessa, Daybreak, Columbia (a set with his son Chico in 1981), Southport and Steeple Chase. —*Scott Yanow*

Doin' It Right Now / 1972 / Atlantic ✦✦✦✦
Already 50 at the time, tenor saxophonist Von Freeman made his recording debut with this notable album, produced by Rahsaan Roland Kirk. Freeman's obscurity was due to his spending most of his career in Chicago, plus his unusual and distinctive tone. Accompanied by pianist John Young, bassist Sam Jones and drummer Jimmy Cobb, Freeman sounds inspired on the obscurity "Lost in a Fog," "Sweet and Lovely," five of his originals, and a haunting rendition of "The First Time Ever I Saw Your Face." This historic LP is one of many Atlantics that are long overdue to be reissued on CD. —*Scott Yanow*

Have No Fear / Jun. 11, 1975 / Nessa ✦✦✦✦

● **Serenade and Blues** / Jun. 11, 1975 / Nessa ✦✦✦✦✦
It is surprising that Von Freeman's supporters never seem to grasp why the veteran tenor saxophonist has never become all that popular. Freeman has one of the odder tones of any saxophonist and it takes some getting used to. This Nessa release, which finds Freeman joined by pianist John Young, bassist Dave Shipp and drummer Wilbur Campbell, is as accessible as any of his recordings. Von Freeman performs lengthy versions of two ballads, an original blues and his theme song "After Dark." —*Scott Yanow*

Walkin' Tuff / 1989 / Southport ✦✦✦
The veteran Chicago tenor saxophonist, a blues, ballads, and standards master as well as an expert hard bop player, works with a relatively inexperienced band on this recent release. He does an admirable job of meshing with them, while also soaring during his solos. —*Ron Wynn*

Lester Leaps In / May 1992 / Steeple Chase ✦✦✦

Fire / Jun. 24, 1995 / Southport ✦✦✦✦

Don Friedman

b. May 4, 1935, San Francisco, CA
Piano / Post-Bop, Hard Bop
An excellent if underrated pianist, Don Friedman started off playing on the West Coast in 1956 with Dexter Gordon, Shorty Rogers, Buddy Collette, Buddy DeFranco and even the unknown altoist Ornette Coleman. After moving to New York in 1958, Friedman played in many settings including with his own trio, Pepper Adams, Booker Little (recording with him in 1961), the

Jimmy Giuffre Three (1964), a quartet with Attila Zoller, Chuck Wayne's trio (1966-67) and, by the end of the decade, Clark Terry's big band. He has continued working in New York as both a jazz educator and a pianist with wide musical interests and he was featured on Concord's Maybeck Recital Hall series (1993). Don Friedman, who also recorded for Riverside, Prestige, Progressive, Owl, Empathy and several Japanese labels, is not to be confused with vibraphonist David Friedman! —*Scott Yanow*

● **A Day in the City** / Jun. 12, 1961 / Original Jazz Classics ✦✦✦✦✦
For his debut as a leader, pianist Don Friedman (in a trio with bassist Chuck Israels and drummer Joe Hunt) performed six variations on a theme taken from an old folk song "The Minstrel Boy." Called "Dawn," "Midday," "Rush Hour," "Sunset," "Early Evening" and "Night," these "Six Jazz Variations on a Theme" are often quite abstract and not as picturesque as one would think considering their titles. However, Friedman's playing (which shows the strong influence of modern classical music, particularly in its chords) rewards repeated listenings. —*Scott Yanow*

Circle Waltz / May 14, 1962 / Original Jazz Classics ✦✦✦✦
Even ignoring bassist Chuck Israels' inclusion on this set and the similarity of some of the repertoire, it is difficult to overlook the fact that pianist Don Friedman sounds very similar to Bill Evans on this CD reissue. With drummer Pete La Roca completing the trio and such songs as "I Hear a Rhapsody," "In Your Own Sweet Way" and "So in Love" joining four of the leader's compositions, Friedman uses chord voicings similar to Evans' and engages in the same type of close interplay with his sidemen. However, since the music is of high quality and few other keyboardists sounded like Evans this early, the CD is worth picking up by post-bop collectors. —*Scott Yanow*

Flashback / 1963 / Original Jazz Classics ✦✦✦
Friedman, bassist Dick Kniss and drummer Dick Berk come together on this spartan hard bop set, which includes performances of "How Deep Is the Ocean?," "Ochre" and "Ballad in G-Sharp Minor." —*Jason Ankeny*

Hot Knepper and Pepper / Jun. 26, 1978 / Progressive ✦✦✦✦
This is a fine jam session-flavored set featuring pianist Don Friedman, baritonist Pepper Adams, trombonist Jimmy Knepper, bassist George Mraz and drummer Billy Hart. Knepper and Pepper match together musically as well as their names do on three standards, a four-song ballad medley and selections by Sonny Rollins ("Audobon") and Adams ("Hellure"). The emphasis is on extroverted bop during the enjoyable session, which, in its CD version, adds three alternate takes to the program. —*Scott Yanow*

I Hear a Rhapsody / Sep. 22, 1984 / Stash ✦✦✦
This obscure LP contains a lyrical and generally swinging solo set by pianist Don Friedman. Performing five standards (including "If I Should Lose You" and "Body and Soul"), plus a couple of diverse originals, Friedman's fairly original style, based in the hard bop tradition, is heard in excellent form; pity that the album has yet to be reissued on CD. —*Scott Yanow*

Don Friedman at Maybeck / Sep. 5, 1993 / Concord Jazz ✦✦✦✦

David Friesen

b. May 6, 1942, Tacoma, WA
Bass / Post-Bop
David Friesen's music ranges from hard bop to mood music that borders on spiritual new age but on a higher emotional level. While stationed in Germany with the army in 1961, he taught himself the bass. After short stints with John Handy and Marian McPartland, Friesen worked with Joe Henderson for two years. He toured Europe with Billy Harper (1975), made his recording debut as a leader that same year on Muse, started a longtime musical association with guitarist John Stowell (1976) and appeared with Ted Curson at the 1977 Monterey Jazz Festival. After working with Ricky Ford, Duke Jordan and Mal Waldron and touring the USSR with Paul Horn (1983), Friesen settled in the Pacific Northwest. He often plays the Oregon bass (an electrified acoustic bass) these days and has recorded as a leader for Muse, Inner City, Steeple Chase, Palo Alto, ITM (including an intriguing series of duets during 1992-93) and Global Pacific in addition to some smaller labels. —*Scott Yanow*

Color Pool / Oct. 1, 1975 / Muse ✦✦✦

● **Star Dance** / Nov. 8, 1976 / Inner City ✦✦✦✦
Bassist David Friesen's 1976 outing as a leader remains his finest straight jazz date; it also contains some extraordinary playing, particularly the cut "Duet and Dialogue," where he blends both plucked and bowed work in the same song while using both hands. —*Ron Wynn*

Waterfall Rainbow / Jun. 1977-Aug. 1977 / Inner City ✦✦✦✦
A moody and introspective set that would be very much at home on the ECM label, this out-of-print LP generally has David Friesen's bass in the forefront with

fine support from acoustic guitarist Ralph Towner, electric guitarist John Stowell, Nick Brignola (a fine baritonist here heard exclusively on flute), Paul McCandless (tripling on oboe, English horn and bass clarinet), drummer Bobby Moses, and percussionist Jim Saporito. With the exception of Jeff Lorber's "Song of Switzerland," all of the compositions are Friesen originals, and with such titles as "Spring Wind," "The Peace That Passes Understanding" and "Song of the Stars," it is not surprising that the music sometimes hints at new age. —*Scott Yanow*

Through the Listening Glass / Jul. 7, 1978 / Inner City ✦✦✦

This is a subtle and sometimes sleepy set by bassist David Friesen (also heard on shakuhachi flute) and acoustic guitarist John Stowell. Gary Campbell (on soprano and tenor) adds atmosphere to four of the dozen selections, and there is a fair amount of overdubbing of additional guitars, basses and percussion. But in general, the set (not yet reissued on CD) rarely rises above the level of colorful background music. —*Scott Yanow*

Other Mansions / Nov. 1979 / Inner City ✦✦✦

For this duet album, bassist David Friesen also plays bamboo flute, piano and percussion, while guitarist John Stowell adds some mandolin, thumb piano and percussion of his own; there is a liberal amount of overdubbing. As is true of the previous *Through the Listening Glass*, this obscure LP filled with Friesen's original religious-based themes offers background music with little incentive given to anyone to listen closely, although the musicianship is excellent. —*Scott Yanow*

Paths Beyond Tracing / Feb. 12, 1980 / Steeple Chase ✦✦

Heart to Heart / 1980 / Golden Flute ✦✦✦

Storyteller / Apr. 13, 1981 / Muse ✦✦✦

Amber Skies / Jan. 1983+Apr. 1983 / Palo Alto ✦✦✦✦

One of bassist David Friesen's better jazz sessions as a leader, this set (which has been reissued by other labels on CD) has some excellent playing by tenor saxophonist Joe Henderson on "Amber Skies" and "Underlying," a rare opportunity for flutist Paul Horn to take a solo in a straightahead setting ("Blue and Green"), and was the first opportunity that pianist Chick Corea and drummer Paul Motian had to work together; percussionist Airto completes the sextet. The diverse originals, all by Friesen, feature each of the players quite favorably, and the overall results are stimulating. —*Scott Yanow*

Encounters / Mar. 18, 1984 / Muse ✦✦✦

Solid date. Superb contributions from Mal Waldron (p). —*Ron Wynn*

Inner Voices / 1987 / Global Pacific ✦✦

Bassist Friesen moves into a more atmospheric, lighter, and expressionist mode with this session for Global Pacific. He's always been an excellent bassist, but stays in the background, mostly supporting others. There's minimal energy, and arrangements and production are the dominant factors. —*Ron Wynn*

Other Times, Other Places / 1989 / Global Pacific ✦✦✦

The main reason to acquire this Global Pacific release is for the fine playing of Canadian saxophonist Phil Dwyer, who is heard on tenor and soprano. Otherwise, the music has its moments, particularly the interplay between pianist Denny Zeitlin and bassist David Friesen, and there are two vocals by Flora Purim, but the overall results are not all that memorable. Many of Friesen's dates as a leader tend to be on the sleepy and introspective side, fitting into the genre usually championed by Global Pacific but making the music less interesting than hoped for by jazz fans. —*Scott Yanow*

Departure / Jul. 1990 / Global Pacific ✦✦✦

Good combination of Afro-Latin-jazz and chamber music with guests Airto (per) and Flora Purim (v). —*Ron Wynn*

Johnny Frigo

b. Dec. 27, 1916, Chicago, IL

Violin, Bass / Swing

Johnny Frigo has really had two careers. He started out playing violin in grammar school and after switching to tuba in order to play in his junior high school band he took up the bass. Frigo started playing professionally as a bassist in 1934 and had some low-profile jobs until joining Jimmy Dorsey in the mid-'40s. In 1947 he formed a trio with guitarist Herb Ellis and pianist Lou Carter called Soft Winds that was popular for a few years; they co-wrote "Detour Ahead" and "I Told Ya I Love Ya, Now Get Out." After the group disbanded in the early '50s, Frigo became a studio bassist in Chicago for decades, playing sessions, jingles and club dates. Although Frigo had an opportunity to record an album on violin in 1957 for Mercury, it was not until 1988 that he returned to his first instrument, guesting on a Herb Ellis Justice CD and leading two excellent and swinging dates of his own for Chesky that put him near the top of his field. —*Scott Yanow*

Live from Studio A in New York City / Nov. 16, 1988 / Chesky ✦✦✦✦

At the age of 71, Johnny Frigo finally had his debut as a leader on records, except for an obscure effort in 1957. Although he had spent much of his career as a studio bassist, Frigo successfully switched full-time to his first love, the violin, and was immediately considered one of the top swing-based violinists. Joined by both Bucky and John Pizzarelli on guitars, either Ron Carter or Michael Moore on bass, and drummer Butch Miles, Frigo is in wonderful form on 14 standards, including "Pick Yourself Up," "Detour Ahead" (which he had co-written while with the Soft Winds in the late 1940s), "Stompin' at the Savoy" and "The Song Is You." This recommended CD launched the Chesky label. —*Scott Yanow*

● **Debut of a Legend** / 1994 / Chesky ✦✦✦✦✦

Violinist Johnny Frigo's third album as a leader (he had previously made a forgotten date for Mercury in 1957 and a Chesky CD in 1988) is his definitive set, even though he was 77 at the time. With a good supporting cast (guitarist Gene Bertoncini, Bob Kindred on tenor and clarinet, pianist Joe Vito, bassist Michael Moore and drummer Bill Goodwin), Frigo mostly explores standards, plus two of his originals. The music, falling between swing and bop, is superior straightahead jazz; among the highlights are "Get Happy," "Bow Jest," "Jitterbug Waltz" and "Jeannine." Frigo's sudden prominence in his 70s (considering he spent most of his career as a bassist) was as unlikely and welcome an event as trumpeter Doc Cheatham's late-period triumphs. —*Scott Yanow*

Bill Frisell

b. Mar. 18, 1951, Baltimore, MD

Guitar / Modern Creative, Post-Bop, Avant-Garde, Fusion, Early Jazz-Rock

One of the most remarkable guitarists of the 1980s and '90s, Bill Frisell consistently creates bizarre (and sometimes humorous) sounds on his instrument that have not been heard before. Immediately recognizable, Frisell has the ability to sound like a Nashville country session guitarist, a heavy metal specialist, a Jim Hall devotee or an eccentric avant-gardist. After growing up in Denver, he went to Berklee in the mid-1970s, toured England with Mike Gibbs' orchestra (1978) and recorded with Eberhard Weber (1979). Frisell soon began appearing on many recordings for ECM including dates led by Jan Garbarek and Paul Motian. He had two ECM albums of his own during 1982-84 before forming a quartet with cellist Hank Roberts, bassist Kermit Driscoll and drummer Joey Baron. Frisell, who has recorded in several pianoless, bassless groups with Motian, with Marc Johnson's Bass Desires and as a guest on many other artists' albums, is heard at his best on his own sessions. 1992's *Have A Little Faith* (which ranges from Sousa to Madonna with stops for Aaron Copland, Stephen Foster and Muddy Waters) is a good place to start! —*Scott Yanow*

In Line / Aug. 1982 / ECM ✦✦✦

Intense, though erratic conceptually. —*Ron Wynn*

Works / 1982-1987 / ECM ✦✦✦

Good representations of creative impulses. Not definitive, but a good point of reference. —*Michael G. Nastos*

Rambler / Aug. 1984 / ECM ✦✦✦✦✦

This relatively early set from Bill Frisell is a fine showcase for the utterly unique guitarist. Frisell has the ability to play nearly any extroverted style of music and his humor (check out the date's "Music I Heard") is rarely far below the surface. This particular quintet (with trumpeter Kenny Wheeler, tuba player Bob Stewart, electric bassist Jerome Harris and drummer Paul Motian) is not exactly short of original personalities and their outing (featuring seven Frisell compositions) is one of the most lively of all the ones in the ECM catalog. —*Scott Yanow*

Smash & Scatteration / Dec. 1984 / Rykodisc ✦✦✦

The powerful guitarists Bill Frisell and Vernon Reid team up for this hectic and passionate set of duets. Frisell also plays guitar synthesizer, "prepared guitar" and dx drums while Reid brought along his own guitar synth, "revisionist dx drums" and banjo. Although this set has some quieter moments, the nine group originals are generally fairly intense and full of personality. —*Scott Yanow*

Lookout for Hope / Mar. 1987 / ECM ✦✦✦✦✦

Guitarist Bill Frisell had one of the most stimulating and eccentric regular bands of the mid- to late 1980s. The highly versatile Frisell, whose playing ranges from Jim Hall to rock and Nashville while including sounds never previously heard on guitar, found complementary spirits in cellist Hank Roberts, bassist Kermit Driscoll and drummer Joey Baron. Together, the quartet performs nine of Frisell's diverse and colorful originals on this wide-ranging set, plus Thelonious Monk's "Hackensack." Well worth several listens by open-eared (and tolerant) jazz fans. —*Scott Yanow*

Before We Were Born / Aug. 1988-Sep. 1988 / Elektra ✦✦✦✦

Bill Frisell has been one of the most unique jazz-based guitarists of the 1980s and '90s, a very eclectic player who can switch styles and sounds on a moment's notice, yet is always quite distinctive. On this atmospheric and picturesque set, Frisell uses his regular quartet of the time (cellist Hank Roberts, bassist Kermit Driscoll and drummer Joey Baron) on some selections, but also interacts with fellow guitarist Arto Lindsay, keyboardist Peter Scherer and, on "Some Song and Dance," baritonist Doug Wieselman and both Julius Hemphill and Billy Drewes on altos. A special highlight is the episodic "Hard Plains Drifter," which has this as a subtitle: "As I take my last breath and the noose grows tight, the incredible events of the past three days flash before my eyes." A very intriguing and colorful set of eccentric music. —*Scott Yanow*

Is That You? / Aug. 1989 / Elektra ♦♦♦

Where in the World? / Oct. 1990-Feb. 1991 / Elektra ♦♦♦

Live / Oct. 27, 1991 / Gramavision ♦♦♦

★ **Have a Little Faith** / Mar. 1992 / Elektra/Nonesuch ♦♦♦♦♦

Bill Frisell has long been one of the most unique guitarists around. Able to switch on a moment's notice from sounding like a Nashville studio player to heavy metal, several styles of jazz and just pure noise, Frisell can get a remarkable variety of sounds and tones out of his instrument. This set features Frisell in a quintet with Don Byron (on clarinet and bass clarinet), Guy Klucevsek on accordion, bassist Kermit Driscoll and drummer Joey Baron. To call the repertoire wide-ranging would be an understatement. In addition to eight melodies from Aaron Copland's *Billy the Kid*, Frisell and company explore (and often re-invent) pieces written by Charles Ives, Bob Dylan, Muddy Waters, Madonna, Sonny Rollins, Stephen Foster and John Phillip Sousa. This is one of the most inventive recordings of the 1990s and should delight most listeners from any genre. —*Scott Yanow*

This Land / Oct. 1992 / Elektra ♦♦♦

In the Same Breath / Mar. 1995 / CMP ♦♦♦

Nashville / Sep. 1995-Nov. 1996 / Elektra/Asylum ♦♦♦♦♦

The vague country elements long dwelling on the fringes of Bill Frisell's music rise to the forefront on *Nashville*, an exquisitely atmospheric collection recorded in Music City with the aid of dobro legend Jerry Douglas, Union Station members Adam Steffey and Ron Block, and Lyle Lovett's Large Band bassist Viktor Krauss. Produced by Wayne Horvitz, the record is both genuine and alien—while played with real affection for the country form and without any *avant* posturing, its sound is original and distinct, a cinematic variation on C&W tenets. While primarily instrumental and comprising largely Frisell originals, *Nashville* does welcome vocalist Robin Holcomb for a pair of more traditional numbers—Hazel Dickens' "Will Jesus Wash the Bloodstains From Your Hands?" and the Skeeter Davis hit "The End of the World"—as well as a cover of Neil Young's "One of These Days." —*Jason Ankeny*

Bill Frisell Quartet / 1996 / Nonesuch ♦♦♦♦

Guitarist Bill Frisell has become well known for his eccentric and highly versatile style. Able to sound like Jim Hall, a heavy metal player, or a Nashville studio guitarist at a moment's notice, Frisell has created sounds on the guitar that had never been heard before. This CD uses a rather unusual instrumentation, a quartet comprising Frisell, trumpeter Ron Miles, trombonist Curtis Fowlkes and Eyvind Kang, who doubles on violin and tuba. Ten of the 13 Frisell originals on the release were originally written for films (including Gary Larson's *Tales From the Far Side* and the Buster Keaton movie *Convict 13*), and the resulting music is tightly arranged yet spontaneous, episodic, and sometimes a bit nutty, but also strangely logical. Whether it be the oldtimey theme to "Dead Ranch," the blues "Convict 13," a few somber ballads, or hints at early Duke Ellington (particularly by Miles' wah-wah trumpet), this is a continually interesting, offbeat set. —*Scott Yanow*

Gone, Just Like a Train / 1997 / Nonesuch ♦♦♦♦

Drawing from all over the musical spectrum, Frisell selects drummer Jim Keltner (best known for his records with George Harrison, Eric Clapton and other rock stars) and bassist Viktor Krauss (a fixture in Lyle Lovett's country band), and comes up with an immensely likable, easy-grooving CD that defies one to put a label on it. If anything, Frisell leans toward a drawling country twang heavily indebted to Chet Atkins in his guitar work here, but there is a freewheeling jazz sensibility at work on every track. Keltner contributes the heavy rock element with his emphatic strokes, occasionally pushing Frisell in that direction. Yet Keltner is also capable of surprising subtlety, and Krauss provides firm, unflashy underpinning. Above all, this is thoughtful, free-thinking, ear-friendly jamming that was recorded in bustling Burbank, CA. but sounds as if it was laid down in a relaxed cabin in the hills. —*Richard S. Ginell*

Dave Frishberg

b. Mar. 23, 1933, St. Paul, MN

Piano, Vocals, Lyricist / Swing, Bop

Arguably the top living lyricist, Dave Frishberg has written more than his share of witty (yet insightful) classics including "I'm Hip," "Peel Me a Grape," "Dear Bix," "The Underdog," "Saratoga Hunch," "Slappin' the Cakes on Me," "Z's," "My Attorney Bernie," "Blizzard of Lies," "Another Song About Paris," "You Are There," "El Cajon," "Can't Take You Nowhere" and "Let's Eat Home." A fine swing pianist and a world-weary-sounding vocalist, the multi-talented Dave Frishberg moved to New York in 1957. He worked early on as a pianist with Carmen McRae, Kai Winding, Gene Krupa (1960-63), Wild Bill Davison, Bud Freeman, Ben Webster, the Al Cohn-Zoot Sims Quintet and Bobby Hackett, among others, and cut an album with Jimmy Rushing. He recorded a commercial record for CTI (1968) that generated a surprise hit in "Van Lingle Mungo." However, it was not until Frishberg moved to the West Coast (1971) and started recording for the Concord label (1977) as a vocalist-pianist that he began to make a big impression. Dave Frishberg has since cut albums for Omnisound, Fantasy, and Bloomdido and a purely instrumental duet set with Dixieland trumpeter Jim Goodwin (1992) for Arbors. Many of his originals have been recorded by other vocalists. —*Scott Yanow*

Oklahoma Toad / 1968 / CTI ♦♦

Solo and Trio / 1975 / Seeds ♦♦♦

Other than a commercial and surprisingly dull effort for CTI in 1968, this obscure LP was Dave Frishberg's debut as a leader. A purely instrumental set, Frishberg is featured on seven unaccompanied piano solos and three trio numbers with bassist Monty Budwig and drummer Donald Bailey. Although he performs two originals ("Saratoga Hunch" and "Cuttin' Some Hogs"), the emphasis is on such swing and classic jazz standards as "Drop Me off in Harlem," "Willie the Weeper," "The Crave" and Billy Strayhorn's "Johnny Come Lately." Well worth searching for, this album shows that Dave Frishberg is one of the very few vocalist-lyricists who can record credible instrumental albums. —*Scott Yanow*

Getting Some Fun out of Life / Jan. 25, 1977-Jan. 26, 1977 / Concord Jazz ♦♦♦♦♦

One of Dave Frishberg's finest albums (and a set that gained him a great deal of recognition), this album can be easily split into two. Frishberg performs six enjoyable unaccompanied piano solos (including "In a Mist," "King Porter Stomp" and the title cut) and sings ten other numbers with a quintet also including trumpeter Bob Findley, altoist Marshall Royal, bassist Larry Gales and drummer Steve Schaeffer. Of the latter, his "Dear Bix" (taken in duet with Findley) is a classic, while "Lotus Blossom" and "Old Man Harlem" are also quite memorable. Highly recommended. —*Scott Yanow*

You're a Lucky Guy / Jul. 10, 1978 / Concord Jazz ♦♦♦♦

There is plenty of diversity on this prime Dave Frishberg set. Four songs (including vocal versions of "Truckin'" and "The Underdog") match Frishberg's piano with trombonist Bob Brookmeyer, tenor saxophonist Al Cohn, bassist Jim Hughart and drummer Nick Ceroli. Frishberg takes "That Old Feeling," "You're a Lucky Guy" (which he sings), and "Cheerful Little Earful" as piano solos, and there are also three wonderful duets with Cohn. Only two of the ten songs were written by Frishberg, so the emphasis is on his talents as a pianist and singer rather than as a lyricist. Recommended. —*Scott Yanow*

Dave Frishberg Classics / Apr. 29, 1981-Dec. 1982 / Concord Jazz ♦♦♦♦♦

This is the essential Dave Frishberg CD. Comprising all ten selections originally issued as an Omnisound LP (*The Dave Frishberg Songbook, Vol. 1*) and seven of the ten songs from *Vol. 2*, the release features the composer-lyricist singing and playing piano on many of his best-known originals. Highlights include "I'm Hip," "Van Lingle Mungo," "Slappin' the Cakes on Me," "Z's," "Sweet Kentucky Ham," "My Attorney Bernie," "Blizzard of Lies" and "You Are There." Frishberg is one of the top lyricists of the past 20 years, and this release has plenty of convincing evidence. A gem. —*Scott Yanow*

★ **Live at Vine Street** / Oct. 1984 / Original Jazz Classics ♦♦♦♦♦

Arguably the greatest living lyricist, Dave Frishberg sings and plays piano on this very enjoyable solo disc. His nine originals include such memorable (and humorous) tunes as "El Cajon" (a Johnny Mandel melody), "The Dear Departed Past" and "Blizzard of Lies." In addition, Frishberg plays a lengthy medley of Johnny Hodges-associated songs. This witty set is easily recommended. —*Scott Yanow*

Can't Take You Nowhere / Sep. 21, 1986 / Fantasy ♦♦♦♦

Recorded live at the Great American Music Hall in San Francisco, this solo set by pianist-vocalist Dave Frishberg has the earliest versions of his humorous "Can't Take You Nowhere" and "Zoot Walks In," spirited remakes of "My Attorney Bernie" and "Sweet Kentucky Ham," and such enjoyable instrumentals as medleys of Frank Loesser and Irving Berlin tunes, in addition to "Drop Me off in Harlem." A well-rounded set, the CD version adds an Irving Berlin medley and a version of

"I'm Hip" to the original LP program and gives listeners a strong sampling of the talented Dave Frishberg. —*Scott Yanow*

Let's Eat Home / Aug. 1989 / Concord Jazz ✦✦✦✦
This CD is most significant for having the original versions of Dave Frishberg's "Let's Eat Home," "I Was Ready" and "Lookin' Good." The pianist, who also takes several instrumentals (Al Cohn and Billy Strayhorn medleys, plus "The Mooche"), is assisted by valve trombonist Rob McConnell, trumpeter Snooky Young, bassist Jim Hughart and drummer Jeff Hamilton on most selections. Although not quite essential, this is an enjoyable outing by the pianist-singer-lyricist and ranks in his top five recordings. —*Scott Yanow*

Where You At? / Mar. 4, 1991 / Bloomdido ✦✦✦✦
This is one of the more obscure Dave Frishberg CDs, made for the French label Bloomdido. On some of the selections the pianist-vocalist-lyricist is joined by baritonist Turk Mauro, trombonist Glenn Ferris and bassist Michel Guadry, but he is the main star throughout. Frishberg sounds excellent on a pair of solo instrumental medleys of songs associated with Ivie Anderson and Duke Ellington and introduces his memorable lyrics to "Another Song About Paris." In addition Frishberg is in fine vocal form on "Where You At?" (which was given new words), "I'm an Old Cowhand" and "Tulip or Turnip." An excellent outing. —*Scott Yanow*

Double Play / Oct. 3, 1992-Oct. 4, 1992 / Arbors ✦✦✦✦
Dave Frishberg, best known for his impressive abilities as a lyricist and vocalist, sticks exclusively to instrumentals on this enjoyable disc. Frishberg the pianist is teamed with cornetist Jim Goodwin on a duet set comprising 17 trad and swing classics that mostly date from the 1920s and '30s. To their credit, the duo constantly walk a musical tightrope, taking chances within the idiom and not being afraid to make mistakes; neither musician felt that the music should be edited afterward. The result is colorful classic jazz interpreted by two strong stylists who, while paying tribute to their predecessors, infuse the music with their own personalities. It is easily recommended to trad fans. —*Scott Yanow*

Quality Time / May 28, 1993-May 29, 1993 / Sterling ✦✦✦
This Dave Frishberg CD is a more specialized project than the lyricist-vocalist-pianist's more definitive Concord releases. Five of the songs were written for a musical about baseball history that was never produced and several of these are of much more limited interest than usual. The most memorable selections on this release are the title cut (which is a near-classic about a yuppie couple halfheartedly struggling to make time for each other), a bittersweet "The Dear Departed Past" and a remake of "Dear Bix." In addition, there are two fine piano solos and short spots for trumpeter Rich Cooper and tenor saxophonist Lee Wuthernow. But, although a sincere effort, this CD is primarily for Frishberg completists who already have his Concord sets. —*Scott Yanow*

Tony Fruscella

b. Feb. 4, 1927, Orangeburg, NY, d. Aug. 14, 1969, New York, NY
Trumpet / Cool
A promising trumpeter whose career never had a chance to flourish due to a drug problem, Tony Fruscella had a style close to that of Chet Baker's, though he developed it independently. He played in an army band in the '50s, then worked with Lester Young and Gerry Mulligan, and performed and recorded with Stan Getz in 1955. He did some recordings heading his own group that same year, then was basically finished as a prime musician due to his habit. Fruscella did occasional dates with fellow trumpeter Don Joseph but was dead in 1969 at the age of 42. His 1955 album *I'll Be Seeing You* on Atlantic was an example of his potential. There's a Fruscella session available on CD released by Cool N' Blue, *Tony's Blues*, issued in 1992. Fruscella's also featured on a Getz Verve anthology. —*Ron Wynn and Michael Erlewine*

Debut / Dec. 10, 1948-1953 / Spotlite ✦✦✦
Trumpeter Tony Fruscella, a fine cool-toned bop musician with a lot of potential, made relatively few recordings in his short career. Spotlite greatly expanded his discography by releasing two sets of live recordings. For their first Fruscella release, the trumpeter is featured in a previously unreleased 1948 studio session with a quintet also including altoist Chick Maurers (who otherwise did not record), pianist Bill Triglia, bassist Red Mitchell, and drummer Dave Troy. They perform five songs ("Out of Nowhere" and four originals), plus three alternate takes. The second half of this release is from 1953 and showcases Fruscella at a club date as the only horn in a quartet also including Triglia, bassist Teddy Kotick and drummer Art Mardigan. The rare and historic music is easily recommended to bop collectors, for the musicians play quite well and the recording quality is listenable. —*Scott Yanow*

Fru 'n Brew / 1953 / Spotlite ✦✦✦
Spotlite's second release featuring the ill-fated and barely documented trumpeter Tony Fruscella is taken from a gig at New York's Open Door in 1953. Fruscella is

matched with the soft-toned tenor Brew Moore, pianist Bill Triglia, bassist Teddy Kotick and drummer Art Mardigan, and they perform mostly lengthy versions of five jazz tunes (including renditions of "Blue Lester" and Thelonious Monk's "Hackensack" that exceed ten minutes apiece). The set is quite valuable, both for allowing one to hear Fruscella take fairly long solos and for the spirit of the somewhat freewheeling music. —*Scott Yanow*

● **Tony Fruscella [Jazzlore #25]** / Mar. 29, 1955+Apr. 1, 1955 / Atlantic ✦✦✦✦✦
Trumpeter Tony Fruscella had strong potential before essentially throwing his life away. This was his only full-length album (although a few other isolated dates have since been released); fortunately, it is a very good one. Teamed in a septet with tenor saxophonist Allen Eager, baritonist Danny Bank, trombonist Chauncey Welsch, pianist Bill Triglia, bassist Bill Anthony and drummer Junior Bradley, Fruscella performs a pair of standards ("I'll Be Seeing You" and "Blue Serenade"), plus seven swinging originals by Phil Sunkel. Fruscella, Eager and Triglia take many fine solos, but it is such a pity that this was essentially the high point of the trumpeter's career. —*Scott Yanow*

Curtis Fuller

b. Dec. 15, 1934, Detroit, MI
Trombone / Hard Bop
Curtis Fuller belongs in the select circle with J.J. Johnson, Kai Winding and a few others who make the trombone sound fluid and inviting rather than awkward. His ability to make wide octave leaps and play whiplash phrases in a relaxed, casual manner is a testament to his skill. Fuller's solos and phrases are often ambitious and creative, and he's worked in several fine bands and participated in numerous great sessions. Fuller studied music in high school, then began developing his skills in an army band, where he played with Cannonball Adderley. He worked in Detroit with Kenny Burrell and Yusef Lateef, then moved to New York. Fuller made his recording debut as a leader on Transition in 1955, and recorded in the late '50s for Blue Note, Prestige, United Artists and Savoy. He was a charter member of the Jazztet with Benny Golson and Art Farmer in 1959, then played in Art Blakey's Jazz Messengers from 1961 to 1965. There were additional recording dates for Warwick, Smash/Trip, Epic, and Impulse in the '60s. Fuller toured Europe with Dizzy Gillespie's big band in 1968, then did several sessions in New York. During the '70s, he experimented for a time playing hard bop arrangements in a band featuring electronic instruments, heading a group with guitarist Bill Washer and Stanley Clarke. He concluded that phase with the '73 album *Crankin'.* Fuller toured with the Count Basie band from 1975 to 1977, and did dates for Mainstream, Timeless, and Bee Hive. He co-led the quintet Giant Bones with Winding in 1979 and 1980, and played with Art Blakey, Cedar Walton and Benny Golson in the late '70s and early '80s. During the '80s, Fuller toured Europe regularly with the Timeless All-Stars, and performed and recorded with the revamped Jazztet in addtion to leading a fine session for Savoy in 1993. —*Ron Wynn*

New Trombone / May 11, 1957 / Original Jazz Classics ✦✦✦
Trombonist Curtis Fuller's debut as a leader was a fine start to the 22-year-old's career. Already a strong player in the J.J. Johnson mold, Fuller blends in well with altoist Sonny Red, pianist Hank Jones, bassist Doug Watkins and drummer Louis Hayes on the fine straightahead date. The CD reissue adds "Alicia" to the original five-song program. While four of the six tunes are originals, their chord changes are generally easy to recognize (two are blues, and "Vonce No. 5" borrows from "I Got Rhythm"), and all of the musicians fare quite well. —*Scott Yanow*

Curtis Fuller with Red Garland / May 14, 1957 / Original Jazz Classics ✦✦✦✦
This CD reissue features trombonist Curtis Fuller in a quintet with altoist Sonny Red, pianist Red Garland, bassist Paul Chambers and drummer Louis Hayes, performing a pair of originals, two blues and a couple of ballad features. Red is outstanding on "Moonlight Becomes You" (one of his finest recordings) while Fuller does a fine job on "Stormy Weather." Even with the new material, this set has a feel of a jam session; the blend between the trombone and the alto is particularly appealing. Despite the overly critical liner notes (written in 1962), this is an excellent hard bop-oriented date. —*Scott Yanow*

With Hampton Hawes / May 18, 1957 / Prestige ✦✦✦
This is an unorthodox, intriguing date, with Hawes excellent on piano, Julius Watkins and David Amram on French horns. It's hard to find. —*Ron Wynn*

The Opener / Jun. 16, 1957 / Blue Note ✦✦✦✦✦
The Opener is trombonist Curtis Fuller's first album for Blue Note and it is a thoroughly impressive affair. Working with a quintet featuring tenor saxophonist Hank Mobley, pianist Bobby Timmons, bassist Paul Chambers and drummer Art Taylor, Fuller runs through a set of three standards—"A Lovely Way to Spend an Evening," "Here's to My Lady," "Soon"—two originals and an Oscar Pettiford-penned calypso. The six songs give Fuller a chance to display his warm, fluid style in all of its variations. "A Lovely Way to Spend an Evening" illustrates that he can

be seductive and lyrical on ballads, while the brassy "Hugore" and hard-swinging "Lizzy's Bounce" shows that he can play hard without getting sloppy. His backing musicians are equally impressive; in particular, Mobley's robust playing steals the show. In all, *The Opener*, along with his three earlier sessions for Prestige and New Jazz, establishes Fuller as one of the most distinctive and original hard bop trombonists of the late '50s. —*Stephen Thomas Erlewine*

The Complete Blue Note/UA Curtis Fuller Sessions / Jun. 16, 1957-Mar. 9, 1959 / Mosaic ♦♦♦♦♦

Trombonist Curtis Fuller, who developed his sound out of the style of J.J. Johnson, recorded prolifically as a leader from 1957-62. After recording three dates for Prestige and New Jazz within a seven-day period in 1957, Fuller made four albums for Blue Note from 1957-58, and after three albums for Savoy, he cut a lone session for United Artists in 1959. All of the five Blue Note and United Artists records (plus an alternate take of "Down Home") are on this excellent three-CD limited box set, released in 1996. Fuller is heard with four different quintets that include either tenor saxophonist Hank Mobley, baritonist Tate Houston, trumpeter Art Farmer or (on a date only previously out in Japan) fellow trombonist Slide Hampton; the rhythm sections consist of either Bobby Timmons or Sonny Clark on piano, Paul Chambers or George Tucker on bass, and Art Taylor, Louis Hayes or Charlie Persip in the drum slot. In addition, there is a sextet session with Lee Morgan, Mobley, Tommy Flanagan, Chambers and Elvin Jones that has arrangements by Gigi Gryce and Benny Golson. Throughout, the music is high-quality hard bop with plenty of fine features for the underrated but talented Curtis Fuller. —*Scott Yanow*

Bone and Bari / Aug. 4, 1957 / Blue Note ♦♦♦♦

Curtis Fuller emerged during the 1950s as a leading hard bop trombonist. A native of Detroit, Fuller was initially inspired by hearing J.J. Johnson, who became a mentor for the young musician. This recording was completed only weeks before Fuller went into the studio to record John Coltrane's *Blue Trane*. The session is unique in its pairing of trombone with the baritone sax of Tate Houston. The resultant front line sound is thick and rotund. The rhythm section of Sonny Clark, Paul Chambers and Art Taylor had a lovely rapport; individually and collectively, these three made many important recordings in the late 1950s, especially for the Blue Note label. Highlights of *Bone and Bari* include the title tune, penned by Fuller, and the group's rendering of the standard "Heart and Soul." —*Lee Bloom*

Curtis Fuller, Vol. 3 / Dec. 1, 1957 / Blue Note ♦♦♦♦

Trombonist Curtis Fuller settled in New York in April of 1957, after working for several years in his native Detroit. *Vol. 3* pairs him with trumpeter Art Farmer, along with a buoyant rhythm section comprising Sonny Clark (who also relocated to N.Y.C. in April '57), George Tucker and Louis Hayes. This third solo recording for Fuller on the Blue Note label is stronger than its predecessors, especially in showcasing the trombonist's writing talents. The five original tunes and one standard feature some fine ensemble playing and cover a broad range from Afro-Cuban to medium swing to ballad. Fuller's composition "Carvon" is exceptional; the main theme is played on trombone accompanied only by bowed bass. This recording firmly established Curtis Fuller as a serious, mature voice on his instrument. —*Lee Bloom*

● Blues-ette / May 21, 1959 / Savoy ♦♦♦♦♦

A legendary set that became very popular in Japan (leading to 1993's *Blues-ette Part II*), this is one of several pre-Jazztet recordings that teamed together trombonist Curtis Fuller and tenor saxophonist Benny Golson. The strong rhythm section (pianist Tommy Flanagan, bassist Jimmy Garrison and drummer Al Harewood), excellent material (including two songs apiece by Golson and Fuller) and inspired solos make this a hard bop gem. —*Scott Yanow*

Arabia / Aug. 25, 1959 / Savoy ♦♦♦♦

Trombonist Curtis Fuller appeared on many sessions during the 1957-62 period, as both a leader and sideman. While his Blue Notes have been reissued in full on a Mosaic box set, many of his equally valuable Savoys have yet to reappear on CD. This particular date did get issued as part of a two-LP set (All Star Sextets) in 1979. Fuller, trumpeter Lee Morgan, tenor saxophonist Benny Golson, pianist Wynton Kelly, bassist Paul Chambers and drummer Charlie Persip perform three standards (including a 14-minute version of Dizzy Gillespie's "Weightleigh Hall")

and debut a pair of Fuller's originals. The title cut, which would later be recorded by Fuller with Art Blakey, is the trombonist's best-known song. High-quality hard bop, with the 21-year-old Morgan clearly inspiring the other players. —*Scott Yanow*

The Curtis Fuller Jazztet / Aug. 25, 1959 / Savoy ♦♦♦♦

Imagination / Dec. 17, 1959 / Savoy ♦♦♦♦

Prior to the official formation of the Jazztet with trumpeter Art Farmer, trombonist Curtis Fuller and tenorman Benny Golson made several albums together, usually with other trumpeters. This somewhat rare date has trumpeter Thad Jones, bassist Jimmy Garrison, drummer Dave Bailey and, most significantly, pianist McCoy Tyner in his recording debut completing the sextet. Fuller arranged all five of the songs, four of which were his originals. Although the material (other than the lone standard "Imagination") is unfamiliar, the chord changes inspire the players to create some fine solos. Easily recommended to hard bop fans lucky enough to find this album. —*Scott Yanow*

Jazz Conference Abroad / Mar. 1961 / Smash ♦♦♦

This album, last reissued as a Trip LP, is very much a jam session featuring trombonist Curtis Fuller with musicians taken from Quincy Jones' touring orchestra of the time. The ten-piece outfit performs a pair of boppish blues ("Billie's Bounce" and "Blue 'n' Boogie"), plus Oliver Nelson's "Stolen Moments" (less than a month after the famous version) and Charlie Parker's "Scrapple from the Apple." Considering the personnel (Curtis Fuller and Ake Persson on trombones, the young Freddie Hubbard and Benny Bailey on trumpets, altoist Phil Woods, tenor saxophonist Eric Dixon, baritonist Sahib Shihab, pianist Patti Bown, bassist Buddy Catlett and drummer Stu Martin), it is not surprising that there are some excellent solos, but little unexpected occurs on this out-of-print album. —*Scott Yanow*

Smokin' / 1972 / Mainstream ♦♦

Trombonist Curtis Fuller's second Mainstream album has some dated electronics and funk rhythms, although there are some worthwhile solos from the leader, trumpeter Bill Hardman, and Jimmy Heath on tenor and soprano. The rhythm section (guitarist Earl Dunbar, Cedar Walton on electric piano, electric bassist Mickey Bass and drummer Billy Higgins) weighs down the music a bit despite their obvious talents. The band stretches out on four Fuller originals (best is the 11-minute "Smokin'") and "Stella by Starlight," but the results are not too essential. —*Scott Yanow*

Four on the Outside / Sep. 18, 1978 / Timeless ♦♦♦♦

This well-rounded set, reissued on CD, was one of trombonist Curtis Fuller's strongest. He matches well with baritonist Pepper Adams and the fine rhythm section (pianist James Williams, bassist Dennis Irwin and drummer John Yarling) and contributed five particularly strong compositions ("Hello Young Lovers" is also performed), particularly the memorable, 13-minute "Suite Kathy." Fuller is heard in prime form throughout this superior hard bop release. —*Scott Yanow*

Fire and Filigree / Dec. 6, 1978 / Bee Hive ♦♦♦♦

For this excellent hard bop date, trombonist Curtis Fuller and the powerful tenor Sal Nistico make for a potent front line. With pianist Walter Bishop Jr., bassist Sam Jones and drummer Freddie Waits keeping the momentum flowing, the quintet performs two Fuller originals, Kenny Dorham's "Minor's Holiday," and three standards. Although the bop-oriented BeeHive label has since become inactive, one might be able to find this swinging and enjoyable album, one of Curtis Fuller's best sets of the era. —*Scott Yanow*

Blues-ette, Part 2 / Jan. 4, 1993-Jan. 6, 1993 / Savoy ♦♦♦♦♦

The original *Blues-ette* album was a quintet session from 1959 featuring trombonist Curtis Fuller, tenor saxophonist Benny Golson, pianist Tommy Flanagan, bassist Jimmy Garrison and drummer Al Harewood. Thirty-four years later the same musicians (with bassist Ray Drummond filling in for the deceased Garrison) had a reunion for this Savoy CD. Three of the songs from the original session are given new versions and there are also performances of several recent compositions by both Golson and Fuller in addition to four standards. Although Golson's sound on tenor has evolved since the earlier date, the appealing blend between the two horns remains unchanged as do the styles of Fuller and Flanagan, making this an excellent example of swinging hard bop. —*Scott Yanow*

Kenny G. (Kenneth Gorelick)

b. 1959, Seattle, WA
Soprano Saxophone / Instrumental Pop, Crossover Jazz

Kenny G. has long been the musician many jazz listeners love to hate. A phenomenally successful instrumentalist whose recordings make the pop charts, G's sound has been a staple on adult contemporary and "smooth jazz" radio stations since the mid-1980s, making him a household name. Kenny G. is a fine player with an attractive sound (influenced a bit by Grover Washington, Jr.) who often caresses melodies, putting a lot of emotion into his solos. Because he does not improvise much (sticking mostly to predictable melody statements), his music largely falls outside of jazz. However because he is listed at the top of "contemporary jazz" charts and is identified with jazz in the minds of the mass public, he belongs in this book.

Kenny Gorelick started playing professionally with Barry White's Love Unlimited Orchestra in 1976. He recorded with Cold, Bold & Together (a Seattle-based funk group) and freelanced locally. After graduating from the University of Washington, G worked with Jeff Lorber's Fusion, making two albums with the group. Soon he was signed to Arista, recording his debut as a leader in 1982. His fourth album, *Duotones* (which included the very popular "Songbird"), made him into a star. Soon he was in demand for guest appearances on recordings of such famous singers as Aretha Franklin, Whitney Houston and Natalie Cole. Kenny G's own records have sold remarkably well, particularly *Breathless*, which has easily topped eight million copies in the US. Like most pop stars, Kenny G. now takes a long time between records, going out on occasional tours and filling stadiums. Whether he will ever choose to play jazz in the future is open to question (certainly there is no financial incentive), but he has made the soprano sax sound appealing to millions of fans, while simultaneously annoying many jazz purists. —*Scott Yanow*

● **Greatest Hits** / 1982-1992 / Arista ♦♦♦♦♦

Kenny G. / Feb. 1, 1982-Jun. 14, 1982 / Arista ♦♦
Although he hadn't perfected his stylish amalgam of pop melodies and jazz improvisation, Kenny G's first album is worthwhile to his fans, simply as a document of his formative era. Parts of *Kenny G.* may be rough, but it is sporadically enjoyable. —*Stephen Thomas Erlewine*

G Force / 1983 / Arista ♦♦

Gravity / 1985 / Arista ♦♦♦

● **Duotones** / 1986 / Arista ♦♦♦♦♦
Kenny G's breakthrough effort featured the hit "Songbird," which is the definitive example of the saxophonist's smooth, lyrical playing; the rest of the album is nearly as good, highlighting his melodic jazzy pop. —*Stephen Thomas Erlewine*

Silhouette / 1988 / Arista ♦♦♦♦
Kenny G. was at the top of his form with *Silhouette*, the follow-up to his breakthrough *Duotones*, turning in a set of smooth, melodic music that cemented his position as America's favorite pop instrumentalist. —*Stephen Thomas Erlewine*

Kenny G. Live / Aug. 26, 1989-Aug. 27, 1989 / Arista ♦♦♦♦

Breathless / 1992 / Arista ♦♦♦♦♦
One among many huge hit albums featuring the shimmering, willowy soprano sax solos of Kenny G. He's the best-selling saxophonist of all time, and has never claimed to be a jazz musician, which is accurate. These are simple, sometimes enjoyable, pop tunes with forgettable melodies, and no harmonic tension or rhythmic excitement. —*Ron Wynn*

The Moment / 1996 / Arista ♦♦♦♦
Although *The Moment* followed four years after Kenny G's blockbuster *Breathless*, the saxophonist didn't change his approach at all during his time off. Kenny G. remains a sweet, melodic instrumentalist, who works entirely in lush, slick adult contemporary pop settings. His playing has improved somewhat in those four years—he soars and dives with effortless skill, and his vibrato remains fleet and

elegant—yet after *The Moment* is finished, you wish that he had tried some new musical territories. That said, it is true that *The Moment* ranks second to only *Breathless* in terms of sheer consistency in Kenny G's catalog, thanks to the sustained vision of producer Babyface. Of particular note are the two vocal collaborations (Babyface's "Everytime I Close My Eyes," Toni Braxton's "That Somebody Was You"), which are the best duets to yet appear on any of Kenny G's records. —*Thom Owens*

Steve Gadd

b. 1945, Rochester, NY
Drums / Funk, Post-Bop, Crossover Jazz, Fusion

A well-respected drummer who has appeared in many types of settings in many genres, Steve Gadd's impressive technique and flexibility have been influential during the past 20 years. He started playing drums at the age of three, sat in with Dizzy Gillespie when he was 11 and, after extensive study and a stint in the Army, Gadd became an important studio drummer beginning in 1972. Among his more significant jazz associations have been with Chick Corea (starting in 1975), Bob James, Al DiMeola, Tom Scott, Grover Washington, Jr., David Sanborn, the group Stuff, the Manhattan Jazz Quintet and his own impressive band (the Gadd Gang) which recorded for Columbia in 1986 and 1988. —*Scott Yanow*

Slim Gaillard

b. Jan. 1, 1916, Detroit, MI, **d.** Feb. 26, 1991, London, England
Guitar, Vocals, Piano / Swing, Jive

A cult hero, Slim Gaillard was a frequently hilarious personality whose comedy (inventing his own jive language with a liberal use of the words "vout" and "oreenee") generally overshadowed his music. In the mid-'30s he had a solo act during which he played guitar while tap dancing! In 1936 Gaillard began teaming with bassist Slam Stewart as Slim and Slam. Their very first recording became his biggest hit, "Flat Foot Floogie." Slim and Slam were a popular attraction up to 1942 with such other songs as "Tutti Frutti" and "Laughin' in Rhythm." By 1945 Gaillard had a new bassist, Bam Brown (whose frantic vocals matched well with Slim's cool if nonsensical voice), and "Cement Mixer" and "Poppity Pop" caught on. Gaillard, who played electric guitar influenced by Charlie Christian, fairly basic boogie-woogie piano and vibes, led an unusual date with guests Charlie Parker and Dizzy Gillespie (1945) that was highlighted by "Slim's Jam." Throughout the 1940s in Los Angeles, Gaillard had a strong following, using such sidemen as Zutty Singleton and Dodo Marmarosa, but the popularity of jive singers (which included Harry "The Hipster" Gibson and Leo Watson) ran its course and after 1953 Gaillard only led two other record sessions (in 1958 and 1982). In the 1960s he was largely outside of music, running a motel in San Diego, but by the late '70s Slim Gaillard was back on a part-time basis, still singing "Flat Foot Floogie" and making one wonder why this comic whiz was neglected for nearly three decades. Many of his key recordings can be found on Tax (a box set has the complete Slim and Slam from 1938-42), Hep and Verve. —*Scott Yanow*

Groove Juice Special / Jan. 19, 1938-Apr. 4, 1942 / Columbia ♦♦♦
Singer/guitarist Slim Gaillard and bassist Slam Stewart made for a frequently hilarious and outrageous team. Gaillard's jive talk and the basic but memorable originals (best known of which is "The Flat Foot Floogie") made Slim & Slam a popular group in the late '30s. All of their joint recordings were reissued in a perfectly done box set for Affinity a few years ago, so this single disc pales in comparison. And since eight of the 20 numbers that included here are alternate takes (including "Floogie"), this is not quite a definitive introductory or greatest-hits set either, although beginners should be delighted by the music. The performances (which sometimes includes such guests as trumpeter Al Killian, clarinetist Garvin Bushell, drummers Kenny Clarke and Chico Hamilton and tenor great Ben Webster) are quite fun, but a bit more planning should have gone into the programming. —*Scott Yanow*

★ **Slim & Slam** / Feb. 17, 1938-Apr. 4, 1942 / Affinity ✦✦✦✦

Starting with his initial recording "Flat Foot Floogie" (whose original name was actually "Flat Fleet Floogee"), guitarist/singer/jokester Slim Gaillard was a cult hero and a masterful (if somewhat limited) entertainer. Teamed with bassist Slam Stewart (who sang along with his bowed solos), Gaillard became quite popular during the latter part of the swing era. This very complete three-CD set contains all of Slim Gaillard's 82 performances (usually with Slam) including several taken from radio broadcasts and quite a few alternate takes. Among the other sidemen are the underrated tenorman Kenneth Hollon, trumpeter Al Killan, pianist Loumell Morgan, clarinetist Garvin Bushell and Ben Webster on tenor. A definitive and perfectly realized reissue from the English Affinity label. —*Scott Yanow*

1945 / Sep. 1945-Dec. 1945 / Classics ✦✦✦✦✦

Slim Gaillard was in his heyday in 1945, recording constantly and becoming a big hit in Los Angeles, particularly at Billy Berg's club. This Classics CD has Gaillard's first studio recordings since 1942, and they are full of his outrageous humor and some solid swing. The sessions from September 1945 have Gaillard's quartet (with pianist Fletcher Smith, bassist Bam Brown and drummer/singer Leo Watson) augmented by up to five horns (taken from trumpeters Howard McGhee and Karl George, trombonist Vic Dickenson and Lucky Thompson, Teddy Edwards and Wild Bill Moore on tenors) for such numbers as "Voot Orenee," "Central Avenue Boogie" and "Slim's Cement Boogie." In addition, there are some trio numbers with Smith and Brown, and the CD concludes with a pair of sessions by a quartet with Brown, pianist Dodo Marmarosa and drummer Zutty Singleton. Of the latter, "Laguna," "Dunkin' Bagel" and "Ya Ha Ha" are classics of their kind. Recommended to all but the most straitlaced jazz collectors. —*Scott Yanow*

Tutti-Frutti / Sep. 1945-Dec. 1945 / Swingtime ✦✦✦

A sampler of Slim Gaillard's 1945 recordings, most of the music on this Danish LP has since been reissued on a Classics CD, although there are three slightly later titles. The guitarist/singer/comedian, also heard in spots on piano and harpsichord, is in typically exuberant form, whether leading a trio/quartet (with Fletcher Smith or Dodo Marmarosa on piano, bassist Bam Brown and sometimes drummer Zutty Singleton) or on a few numbers with an all-star ten-piece (including trumpeter Howard McGhee, trombonist Vic Dickenson and tenors Lucky Thompson and Teddy Edwards). The music (highlighted by "Voot Boogie," "Tutti-Frutti," "Slim's Cement Boogie" and "Jumpin' at the Record Shop") is quite enjoyable and often a touch crazy. —*Scott Yanow*

Cement Mixer, Putti, Putti / Dec. 1, 1945-Sep. 1949 / Folklyric ✦✦✦✦

A fine cross-section of guitarist/vocalist/comedian Slim Gaillard's 1945-49 studio recordings (most of which have not yet appeared on CD), this Folklyric release has most of the best titles that Gaillard made with his musical partner of the time, bassist Tiny "Bam" Brown, whose high-pitched voice contrasted well with Slim's smooth but nutty delivery. With appearances by pianist Dodo Marmarosa, either Zutty Singleton or Scat Man Carruthers on drums, and (in the 1949 session) pianist Cyril Haynes, this album (which contains 16 selections) has such odd gems as "Cement Mixer" (a huge hit), "Drei Six Cents," "Laguna Oroonee," "Groove Juice Jive," "Arabian Boogie" and "When Banana Skins Are Falling." Unique and often humorous performances. —*Scott Yanow*

Slim's Jam / Dec. 26, 1945-Jan. 1946 / Drive Archive ✦✦✦✦

This budget CD only has around 36 minutes of music, but the three four-song sessions feature guitarist-singer-comedian Slim Gaillard in prime form. Four of the numbers ("Flat Foot Floogie," "Dizzy Boogie," "Poppity Pop" and the classic "Slim's Jam") are famous, for they teamed Gaillard, bassist Bam Brown, pianist Dodo Marmarosa and drummer Zutty Singleton with altoist Charlie Parker, trumpeter Dizzy Gillespie and Jack McVea's tenor. The other two dates are rarer and lesser known but also quite rewarding, mostly putting the focus on Slim and Bam; pianist Wini Beatty takes two vocals and there is solo space for trumpeter Howard McGhee, tenor saxophonist Lucky Thompson and (sticking to clarinet) Marshall Royal. "Chicken Rhythm" is certainly unique, while several of the other numbers have some hard-swinging playing. Easily recommended to Slim Gaillard fans. —*Scott Yanow*

McVouty Slim & Bam / Dec. 1945-Jan. 1946 / Hep ✦✦✦✦

One of four Hep sets taken from Slim Gaillard's live performances of the 1945-51 period, this album has some truly crazy ad-libbing and stretching out, plus some fine jazz. The "Avocado Seed Soup Symphony," "Yep Roc Heresay," "Matzoh Balls" and "Operatic Aria" feature guitarist/singer, bassist/vocalist Bam Brown, and drummer Leo Watson at their nuttiest; they are assisted on some songs by altoist Jack McVea, trumpeter Karl George, trombonist Vic Dickenson and pianist Fletcher Smith. Pianist/singer Harry "The Hipster" Gibson drops by to perform his classic "Hey Stop That Dancing Up There," and "September in the Rain" is a straightforward jam by Gaillard with the Jubilee All-Stars (including cornetist Bobby Hack-

ett, Dickenson and altoist Willie Smith). A well-rounded if eccentric set, recommended to listeners open to jive talk of the mid-'40s era. —*Scott Yanow*

The Best of Slim Gaillard: Laughin' in Rhythm / Apr. 22, 1946-Jan. 1954 / Verve ✦✦✦✦

This CD has highlights from Slim Gaillard's 1946-47 and 1951-54 recordings for the Verve label. A fine Charlie Christian-inspired guitarist, an adequate pianist and a unique jive singer, Gaillard was always in his own category. Some of the selections on this CD are hilarious and highlights include the four-part "Opera in Vout," "Serenade to a Poodle" (which of course has plenty of barking), "Laughing in Rhythm," "Chicken Rhythm," "Potato Chips" and the previously unreleased (and modestly titled) "Genius" which features Gaillard overdubbing himself on trumpet, trombone, tenor, vibes, piano, organ, bass, drums and tap dancing. Although Gaillard's heyday was really the mid-'40s, this CD is quite memorable. —*Scott Yanow*

The Voutiest / Jun. 1946 / Hep ✦✦✦✦✦

Slim Gaillard had a strong cult following in the mid-1940s for his brand of swing, jive and eccentric comedy, which involved his own language. This set from Hep mostly consists of a live performance at Billy Berg's in June 1946 with Slim on piano and guitar, bassist Bam Brown (who plays a comic foil for Gaillard) and drummer Leo Watson; in addition, there are the soundtracks from two soundies filmed around that era with Scat Man Carruthers on drums. This valuable set gives one a strong example of what it was like to see Slim Gaillard perform live at his prime. Highlights include "Yep Roc Heresy," "Poppity Pop" and "Cement Mixer," but just hearing Gaillard ad-lib makes it all worthwhile. —*Scott Yanow*

In Birdland 1951 / Feb. 24, 1951-Sep. 29, 1951 / Hep ✦✦✦✦

By 1951, Slim Gaillard's popularity had largely passed its peak, but he had a sudden burst of activity that year with recordings for Clef and some live appearances. On this particular album, the guitarist/singer is heard live heading several groups that include such notable sidemen as bassist Slam Stewart (reuniting with Gaillard on "Flat Foot Floogie" and "Cement Mixer"), pianist Billy Taylor, the tenors of Brew Moore and Eddie "Lockjaw" Davis, vibraphonist Terry Gibbs and drummer Art Blakey, among others. While there are plenty of fine solos, it is Gaillard's vocal commentary on such tunes as "Serenade in Sulfur" and "Serenade in Vout" that gives this album its fresh and eccentric personality. A must for Slim Gaillard fans. —*Scott Yanow*

Dot Sessions / Nov. 1958 / MCA ✦✦✦

This budget LP from 1982 has just ten of the 14 selections recorded at what would be guitarist/pianist/vocalist/comedian Slim Gaillard's next-to-last album; it would be 24 years before his final effort. Gaillard's backup rhythm section is unidentified, and although the set has its humorous moments (such as "Tall and Slim," "Slim's Cee," "Rooster Rock" and "Walkin' & Cookin' Blues"), it is not quite on the same level as Slim's earlier classics. Also, it is inexcusable to leave out four tracks when the remaining ten only contain half an hour of music. —*Scott Yanow*

Anytime, Anyplace, Anywhere / Oct. 30, 1982 / Hep ✦✦✦

Slim Gaillard was at the peak of his fame from the mid- to late '40s. After 1953 he only recorded two full-length albums, one for Dot in 1958 and this CD reissue which was cut in London in 1982. As Gaillard shows on the opening "How High the Moon," he had not lost anything in the vocal or humor department; in fact the weirdly picturesque opener is the high point of the date. Gaillard is teamed with a fine combination of musicians that include Buddy Tate on tenor and clarinet, Jay Thomas on tenor, alto and trumpet, trumpeter Digby Fairweather and pianist Jay McShann. Not everything works on this date, particularly "Slim's Jam No. 2" which lacks the crazy brilliance and spontaneity of the original "Slim's Jam," or the travelogue "Everything's O.K. in the UK." However there are some good Buddy Tate solos (including a spot on clarinet on "Honeysuckle Rose") and plenty of high spirits throughout the date. Slim Gaillard should have been recorded much more extensively during his last three decades but one is grateful for this souvenir from late in his career. —*Scott Yanow*

Eric Gale

b. Sep. 20, 1938, New York, NY, d. May 25, 1994, Baja, CA
Guitar / R&B, Instrumental Pop, Blues

A guitarist who was used for many R&B-oriented dates and occasionally played jazz, Eric Gale had an appealing sound and was best while performing lazy melodic blues. He was most significant to the jazz world in the early '70s when he recorded often as a sideman for CTI, later on with the group Stuff and on isolated tracks on his own sessions. Gale's fine 1987 EmArcy set *In a Jazz Tradition* shows what he could really do. —*Scott Yanow*

Ginseng Woman/Multiplication / 1976-1977 / Columbia ✦✦

When it comes to smothering a recording with overproduction or being much too slick for his own good, keyboardist Bob James is an expert. In the 1970s, James lent his "expertise" to Eric Gale's albums *Ginseng Woman* and *Multiplication* (which were united on a single CD in 1991). To be sure, James' arranging is excessive. But the damage isn't as severe as one might imagine, and the ubiquitous jazz/R&B-pop guitarist actually has enough room to stretch out at times—as does Grover Washington, Jr. (tenor sax). Far from exceptional but generally decent and enjoyable, these albums make it clear that Gale could be a very appealing and tasteful soloist when given room to breathe. —*Alex Henderson*

Touch of Silk / 1980 / Columbia ✦✦✦✦

This is a well-rounded set mostly consisting of R&B-ish instrumentals. Guitarist Eric Gale had a perfect bluesy sound for that genre, and his backup group on the New Orleans set includes keyboardist Allen Toussaint and drummer James Black; Grover Washington helps out on "With You I'm Born Again." However, jazz listeners will be most interested to hear a real change of pace, a version of Charlie Parker's "Au Privave" that features altoist Arthur Blythe, tenor saxophonist Harold Vick, and organist Charles Earland in addition to Gale. —*Scott Yanow*

Blue Horizon / Oct. 1981-Nov. 1981 / Elektra ✦✦

Nice, basically mainstream session from funk and R&B session star Eric Gale. Gale showed his jazz and blues roots on this one, with several tasty, thoughtfully played solos. —*Ron Wynn*

● **In a Jazz Tradition** / Nov. 29, 1987-Nov. 30, 1987 / EmArcy ✦✦✦✦✦

Guitarist Eric Gale, best known for his work in R&B, funk and commercial settings, was presented by bassist/producer Ron Carter on a strictly jazz date in 1987. With tenor saxophonist Houston Person, organist Lonnie Smith and drummer Grady Tate completing the quintet, the music is soul-jazz with a strong dose of bebop. Gale performs his original "Eric's Gale," a couple of basic tunes by Carter, and four standards including Charlie Parker's "Bloomdido" and "Jordu." Since Eric Gale rarely recorded in this type of freewheeling group, the swinging set was his definitive jazz recording. —*Scott Yanow*

Let's Stay Together / 1989 / Artful Balance ✦✦✦

Jim Galloway (James Braidie Galloway)

b. Jul. 28, 1936, Kilwinning, Scotland

Soprano Saxophone, Tenor Saxophone, Clarinet / Swing, Dixieland

An excellent swing soprano player with a lighter tone than Sidney Bechet, Jim Galloway has made many recordings with like-minded veterans. He played locally in Scotland on clarinet and alto before emigrating to Canada in 1965. He soon began specializing on soprano, led the Metro Stompers (1968), put together the Wee Big Band (1978) and hosted the weekly jazz radio program *Toronto Alive!* (1981-87). Galloway, who has appeared at many jazz festivals and jazz parties, has recorded for Sackville, Hep and Music & Arts along with several smaller Canadian labels with such pianists as Dick Wellstood, Art Hodes and most often Jay McShann. —*Scott Yanow*

Three Is Company / Sep. 22, 1973 / Sackville ✦✦✦✦

Jim Galloway's debut as a leader matches the soprano saxophonist with the masterful stride pianist Dick Wellstood and drummer Pete Magadini for a spirited live set. The repertoire is mostly classic jazz and swing standards, including "Lulu's Back in Town," "After You've Gone" and "Everything." Galloway is heard along with tenor saxophonist Fraser MacPherson (on his final studio date), four trumpets, three trombones and a four-piece rhythm section that includes pianist Jay McShann and drummer Jake Hanna. The music emphasizes Kansas City-style swing and has a few numbers from the book of McShann's early-'40s big band, including "Moten Swing," "Sepian Bounce" and "You Say Forward, I'll March." Quite a few of the Canadian sidemen have opportunities to solo, and the music, which has among its other highlights "Blue and Sentimental," a McShann vocal on "Goin' to Chicago," and "One O'Clock Jump," is quite accessible, swinging, and enjoyable—*Scott Yanow*

● **Thou Swell** / June 15, 1981-June 16, 1981 / Sackville ✦✦✦✦✦

Jim and Jay's Christmas / Nov. 8, 1992-Nov. 9, 1992 / Sackville ✦✦✦

Jim Galloway (on soprano, tenor and baritone), veteran pianist Jay McShann (who takes the vocal on "Hootie's Christmas Baby"), bassist Neil Swainson and drummer Archie Alleyne team up to play some spirited Christmas jazz on this CD. Some of the treatments are a bit surprising, including a very somber opening "Silent Night"; a few of the tunes are obscure, particularly "Christmas Night in Harlem" and "Christmas in New Orleans," and the band easily swings through such tunes as "It Came upon the Midnight Clear," "Rudolph the Red-Nosed Reindeer" and "Silver Bells." A fine, swing-oriented mainstream set. —*Scott Yanow*

Wee Big Band / Apr. 23, 1993-Apr. 24, 1993 / Sackville ✦✦✦✦

Hal Galper

b. Apr. 18, 1938, Salem, MA

Piano / Post-Bop

An excellent if generally overlooked advanced hard-bop pianist, Hal Galper studied at Berklee (1955-58) and then worked in many groups including with Chet Baker, Stan Getz, the Brecker Brothers, Bobby Hutcherson and with such singers as Joe Williams, Chris Connor and Anita O'Day. He played electric piano (an instrument he has since dropped) with the Cannonball Adderley Quintet during its last years (1973-75) and spent time playing with Lee Konitz and John Scofield. Galper, who has recorded as a leader for Mainstream, Steeple Chase, Enja, Concord (including a solo set at Maybeck Recital Hall) and Black Hawk, gained his greatest notoriety for being pianist with Phil Woods' quartet/quintet during 1981-90. —*Scott Yanow*

Now Hear This / Feb. 15, 1977 / Enja ✦✦✦✦

Redux 1978 / Feb. 1978 / Concord Jazz ✦✦✦✦✦

Pianist Hal Galper, who spent the 1980s with Phil Woods' Quintet, led a short-lived quintet of his own in the late '70s that gave the Brecker Brothers a chance to get away from the studios and really stretch out. This live session (which was released for the first time on Galper's 1991 CD) has plenty of hard-blowing with tenor saxophonist Michael Brecker showing his mastery of John Coltrane on the ballad "I'll Never Stop Loving You" while brother Randy plays expert bop during the hotter jams and the intense ballad "Shadow Waltz." The pianist-leader (who is accompanied by bassist Wayne Dockery and drummer Bob Moses) does not get overshadowed and is in fine form throughout, particularly during his feature "My Man's Gone Now." Although there are only two standards on the set, the feeling is of a jam session with Galper leading the strong rhythm section through a variety of attractive chord changes. Recommended. —*Scott Yanow*

Children of the Night / Feb. 1978 / Double-Time ✦✦✦

● **Speak with a Single Voice** / Feb. 1978 / Enja ✦✦✦✦✦

First quintet recording, with the Brecker Brothers, at Rosie's in New Orleans. Essential. —*Michael G. Nastos*

Ivory Forest / Oct. 31, 1979-Nov. 1, 1979 / Enja ✦✦✦

Although a quartet is listed on this set (pianist Hal Galper, guitarist John Scofield, bassist Wayne Dockery and drummer Adam Nussbaum), only three of the selections are performed by the full group. Galper's "Continuity" (one of four of his originals) is a piano-guitar duet; Galper also duets with Dockery on "Yellow Days," but sits out altogether on Scofield's solo rendition of "Monk's Mood." Well-played, if not overly memorable, modern mainstream music. —*Scott Yanow*

Naturally / Jan. 1982 / Black Hawk ✦✦✦

Hal Galper tends to be underrated, but he is a talented pianist in the modern mainstream/post-bop genre. For this live trio date with bassist Rufus Reid and drummer Victor Lewis, Galper performs five standards, Nat Adderley's "Naturally," and Ronnell Bright's "Sweet Pumpkin." The music is thoughtful, always swings, and has some surprising twists and turns. Although released on both CD and LP, the set (one of Hal Galper's better recordings) will probably be difficult to locate. —*Scott Yanow*

Dreamsville / Mar. 3, 1986 / Enja ✦✦✦

Portrait / Feb. 1989 / Concord Jazz ✦✦✦✦✦

Pianist Hal Galper's interpretations of eight familiar standards on this trio set with bassist Ray Drummond and drummer Billy Hart are consistently surprising and unpredictable. "Giant Steps" is treated as a sensitive out-of-tempo ballad, "What Is This Thing Called Love" begins with abstract chordings over a riff reminiscent of "Manteca" before the trio launches into a very fast tempo, "If I Didn't Care" is given a melancholy countermelody and "Azure" is made funky. In addition "I Should Care" and "I'll Be Seeing You" (which are usually dramatic ballads) swing hard. By using the past to create new music, Hal Galper has developed fresh angles to old tunes, and the music on his CD has more than its share of successful surprises. —*Scott Yanow*

Live at Maybeck Recital Hall, Vol. 6 / Jul. 1990 / Concord Jazz ✦✦✦✦

First-rate, stately solo piano. —*Ron Wynn*

Invitation to a Concert / Nov. 18, 1990 / Concord Jazz ✦✦✦✦✦

Recorded shortly after he left the security of Phil Woods' Quintet, pianist Hal Galper's Concord CD is a thoughtful and relaxed outing for his trio. "The Lamp Is Low" gets a groove by bassist Todd Coolman reminiscent of Ahmad Jamal's treatment of "Poinciana," with Galper not even hinting at its melody until five minutes into the performance. "It Never Was You" is quite somber, while "Bright Moments" is optimistic and the only uptempo piece, "Hey There," finds the pianist displaying a very light touch à la Wynton Kelly. The other selections emphasize close communication between Galper, Coolman and drummer Steve Ellington. This subtle session grows in interest the closer one listens. —*Scott Yanow*

Tippin' / Nov. 16, 1992 / Concord Jazz ✦✦✦

Just Us / Sep. 20, 1993 / Enja ✦✦✦

Rebop / 1995 / Enja ✦✦✦

Fugue State / Feb. 8, 1997 / Blue Chip Jazz ✦✦✦

Fugue State captures the Hal Galper Trio—pianist Galper, bassist Jeff Johnson, drummer Steve Ellington—performing live at the Manchester Craftsmens' Guild on February 8, 1997. The trio runs through a number of standards—"The End of a Love Affair," "If You Are But a Dream," "It's Magic"—but the approach is anything but standard, as the group improvises imaginatively, working around themes and turning them inside out. As the title suggests, the end result is like a fugue in its circular structure and repetition, and that's the main reason why *Fugue State* is another solid entry in Galper's catalog. —*Leo Stanley*

Frank Gambale

b. Dec. 22, 1958, Canberra, Australia

Guitar / Fusion

Frank Gambale is best known for his fiery work with Chick Corea's Elektric Band. He was a student at the Guitar Institute of Technology while in his early 20s, wrote instructional books and during 1983-86 was on the school's faculty. He joined Corea in 1986 and has also performed with Steve Smith's Vital Information and as a leader on his own rock-oriented dates for JVC. —*Scott Yanow*

Brave New Guitar / 1986 / Legato ✦✦✦

This debut album features brilliant playing. —*Paul Kohler*

Present for the Future / May 11, 1987-June 30, 1987 / Legato ✦✦✦

A follow-up album with an excellent cast of sidemen, it has one song dedicated to Chick Corea. —*Paul Kohler*

Thunder from Down under / Nov. 1989 / JVC ✦✦✦

As promising as Frank Gambale's work with Chick Corea's Elektric Band was, his first sessions on his own weren't remarkable—generally decent, but not remarkable. While *Thunder from Down Under* isn't in a class with Gambale's accomplishments under Corea's leadership, the jazz-rock-pop date has its strong points—which range from "Samba de Somewhere" (a confident piece featuring Corea on electric keyboards) to the insistent "Humid Beings" to the pensive "Mamojambo." The Brazilian-influenced numbers "Obrigado Fukuoka" and "The Land of Nowhere" are pleasant enough, but never really take off. Quite often, Gambale fails to go that extra mile as he did with the Elektric Band. Switching from fusion guitarist to pop-rock singer on such forgettable material as "Obsessed with Life" and "Faster than an Arrow," Gambale sounds like a poor man's Sting. —*Alex Henderson*

● **Live** / 1989 / Legato ✦✦✦✦✦

You can't live without this intense live guitar album with over 64 minutes of blazing guitar virtuosity. —*Paul Kohler*

The Great Explorers / 1990 / JVC ✦✦✦✦

Frank Gambale was still a vital part of Chick Corea's ElektricBand when he recorded *The Great Explorers,* a hard-hitting, aggressive effort that generally has more in common with the instrumental rock of Steve Vai and Joe Satriani than the more complex jazz-fusion he embraced with Corea and Steve Smith's Vital Information. JVC asked retailers to place *Explorers* in both their jazz and rock sections, but in fact, the CD's jazz content isn't very sizeable (exceptions include the Pat Metheny-influenced "Cruising Altitude" and the poetic "Dawn over the Nullarbor"). Be that as it may, *Explorers* is a solid effort—nothing remarkable, but enjoyable and honest. Vai and Satriani fans would do well to pay close attention to *Explorers,* while those who are only interested in hearing the guitarist play jazz-fusion will probably want to pass. —*Alex Henderson*

Note Worker / 1991 / JVC ✦✦

Frank Gambale, best known as the guitarist in Chick Corea's Elektric Band, alternates between pop vocals and heated but largely forgettable fusion jams on his JVC CD. Gambale in the early '90s was not a strong enough composer to contribute all of the music to his own sessions (as he does here) and, despite some fine guitarwork and plenty of flashy fire, this is a lesser effort. —*Scott Yanow*

Passages / 1994 / JVC ✦✦✦

Thinking out Loud / May 1995 / JVC ✦✦

On this JVC CD, guitarist Frank Gambale plays in a surprisingly clear tone, avoiding rock (except for the closing "My Little Viper") and at times sounding unexpectedly close to George Benson. Keyboardist Otmaro Ruiz also plays creatively on his three appearances but unfortunately the weak Gambale compositions (funky but without soul or any worthwhile melodies) and the remarkably dull automatic pilot drumming of Dave Weckl makes this into a fairly routine set. Next time Gambale should apply his fine guitar playing to much better material; he still has a lot of potential. —*Scott Yanow*

Ganelin Trio

f. 1971, **db.** 1990

Group / Avant-Garde, Free Jazz

Comprisingpianist Vyacheslav Ganelin (b. 1944), saxophonist Vladimir Chekasin (b. 1947) and drummer Vladimir Tarasov (b. 1947), the Ganelin Trio created quite a stir when they were discovered by the West. The group from the Soviet Union played very explorative avant-garde jazz, a rare example of freedom behind the Iron Curtain. They mixed in ethnic free music and earlier jazz styles in their lengthy, colorful and often-humorous improvisations. In addition to their work for the Russian Melodija company, most of their recordings were made for the enterprising Leo label. The group, which had a few opportunities to tour in the West, broke up when Ganelin emigrated to Israel. —*Scott Yanow*

Poco a Poco / /Feb. 1978 / Leo ✦✦✦

Strictly for Our Friends / Mar. 1978 / Leo ✦✦✦

Encores / Jun. 15, 1978-Nov. 15, 1981 / Leo ✦✦

● **Concerto Grosso** / 1978 / Melodiya ✦✦✦✦✦

Ganelin-Tarasov-Checkasin. Russian trio of wildly pure improvisers. A must-buy for the challengable listener. —*Michael G. Nastos*

Ancora Da Capo, Vol. 1 / Nov. 15-16, 1980 / Leo ✦✦✦✦

Ancora Da Capo, Vol. 2 / Nov. 15-16, 1980 / Leo ✦✦✦

Poi Segue / 1981 / Eastwind ✦✦✦✦

Ganelin-Tarasov-Checkasin. Seamless, no-holds-barred free music. —*Michael G. Nastos*

Baltic Triangle / Nov. 15, 1981 / Leo ✦✦✦

New Wine . . . / Jun. 26, 1982 / Leo ✦✦✦✦

Non Troppo / 1982 / Hat Art ✦✦✦

Con Affetto / Nov. 20, 1983 / Leo ✦✦✦✦

Jerusalem February Cantible / Feb. 1989 / Leo ✦✦✦✦✦

The avant-garde lives overseas, as demonstrated by this free-wheeling, non-stop Russian trio. This is music as unrelenting and animated as anything that came from the '50s and '60s pioneers, and simply isn't being made in America much anymore. —*Ron Wynn*

Opuses / Dec. 24, 1989 / Leo ✦✦✦✦

Jan Garbarek

b. Mar. 4, 1947, Mysen, Norway

Tenor Saxophone, Soprano Saxophone, Flute / Post-Bop

The Norwegian saxophonist Jan Garbarek's icy tone and liberal use of space and long tones has long been perfect for the ECM sound and as a result he is on many recordings for that label, both as a leader and as a sideman. He had won a competition for amateur jazz players back in 1962, leading to his first gigs. Garbarek worked steadily in Norway throughout the remainder of the 1960s, usually as a leader but also for four years with George Russell (who was in Scandinavia for a long stretch). Garbarek began recording for ECM in the early '70s and, although he had opportunities to play with Chick Corea and Don Cherry, his association with Keith Jarrett's European quartet in the mid-'70s made him famous, resulting in the classic recordings *My Song* and *Belonging.* In the 1980s Garbarek's groups included bassist Eberhard Weber and at various times guitarists Bill Frisell and David Torn. Garbarek, whose sound is virtually unchanged since the 1970s, collaborated with the Hilliard Ensemble in 1993 (a vocal quartet singing Renaissance music) and the result was a surprisingly popular recording. —*Scott Yanow*

The Esoteric Circle / 1969 / Freedom ✦✦✦✦

The '69 album that introduced the stark, careening soprano sax of Norway's Jan Garbarek to American audiences. Composer and theorist George Russell helped get Garbarek entry to American recording studios, and the rest is history. —*Ron Wynn*

Afric Pepperbird / Sep. 22, 1970-Sep. 23, 1970 / ECM ✦✦✦✦

Jan Garbarek Group. His best, most exciting date from 1970. —*Ron Wynn*

Sart / Apr. 14, 1971-Apr. 15, 1971 / ECM ✦✦✦

Triptykon / Nov. 8, 1972 / ECM ✦✦✦

The third album featuring Norwegian tenor saxophonist Jan Garbarek, issued in 1972. He was a bit less frenetic and more assured, and he began incorporating non-jazz elements into his work, also experimenting with electronics. —*Ron Wynn*

● **Witchi-Tai-To** / Nov. 27, 1973-Nov. 28, 1973 / ECM ✦✦✦✦✦

One of the albums that defined the ECM Records sound. —*Michael G. Nastos*

Red Lanta / Nov. 1973 / ECM ✦✦✦

Dansere / Nov. 1975 / ECM ✦✦✦

Dis / Dec. 1976 / ECM ✦✦

Photo with Blue Sky, White Cloud, Wires, Windows and a Red Roof / Dec. 1978 / ECM ✦✦✦

Jan Garbarek's icy and haunting tones on tenor and soprano are in the forefront during much of this set. He performs six originals (which have simple but picturesque titles such as "Blue Sky," "Windows" and "The Red Roof") with the assistance of guitarist Bill Connors, pianist John Taylor, bassist Eberhard Weber and drummer Jon Christensen. Nothing too exciting occurs, but this is high-quality background music. —*Scott Yanow*

Aftenland / Dec. 1979 / ECM ✦✦

Eventyr / Dec. 1980 / ECM ✦✦✦

Paths, Prints / Dec. 1981 / ECM ✦✦✦

One of the better, more exciting releases—thanks to Bill Frisell (g). —*Ron Wynn*

Wayfarer / Mar. 1983 / ECM ✦✦✦

Bill Frisell (g) enlivens things considerably. —*Ron Wynn*

It's OK to Listen to the Gray Voices / Dec. 1984 / ECM ✦✦✦

The most interesting aspect of this spacy ECM release is the contrast between the cool tones of Jan Garbarek on tenor and soprano and the sometimes-explosive playing of guitarist David Torn, who also plays the guitar synthesizer. Bassist Eberhard Weber and drummer Michael DiPasqua offer subtle support on seven Garbarek originals, all of which are named after quotes from poems. —*Scott Yanow*

To All Those Born with Wings / Aug. 15, 1986 / ECM ✦✦

Legend of the Seven Dreams / Jul. 1988 / ECM ✦✦

Standard mood music. —*Ron Wynn*

I Took Up the Runes / Aug. 1990 / ECM ✦✦✦

Star / Jan. 1991 / ECM ✦✦✦✦

Places / Feb. 4, 1991 / ECM ✦✦✦

A fairly sleepy ECM date, this outing matches Jan Garbarek on tenor, soprano and alto with guitarist Bill Connors, John Taylor (doubling on organ and piano) and drummer Jack DeJohnette for lengthy explorations of four of his originals. With such titles as "Reflections," "Entering" and "Passing," it is not surprising that the music has plenty of space, is introspective, and often emphasizes long tones. —*Scott Yanow*

Madar / Aug. 1992 / ECM ✦✦✦

On this CD Jan Garbarek (doubling on tenor and soprano) is accompanied only by Anouar Brahem on oud and Ustad Shaukat Hussain's tabla. Garbarek shows off his distinctive tones and lyricism on a set of gradually developing group originals, two of which are based on traditional Norwegian melodies. It may take some time for listeners to get into this music and notice the fire beneath the ice but the close communication between the players is apparent from the start. Jan Garbarek has succeeded in carving out his own unique niche in improvised music and *Madar* (which also has individual features for Brahem and Shaukat) is a good example of how he can create a great deal out of what seems like very little. —*Scott Yanow*

Twelve Moons / Sep. 1992 / ECM ✦✦

Officium / Sep. 1993 / ECM ✦✦

Visible World / Jun. 1995 / ECM ✦✦✦

Laszlo Gardony

b. 1956, Hungary
Piano / Post-Bop

Laszlo Gardony is a superior jazz improviser who infuses his post bop music with references to his Hungarian folk roots. He studied at the Bela Bartok Conservatory in Budapest, graduating in 1979. Gardony recorded five albums on European labels, toured throughout Europe and then in 1983 emigrated to the US to attend Berklee. He performed with the group Forward Motion, recording two albums for Hep. Since graduating from Berklee, Gardony joined their faculty on a part-time basis, played with John Abercrombie and recorded as a leader for Antilles, Sunnyside and Avenue Jazz. —*Scott Yanow*

The Secret / 1986 / Antilles ✦✦✦✦

Pianist Laszlo Gardony's American debut (he had recorded a record in his native Hungary two years earlier) finds him holding his own with bassist Miroslav Vitous and drummer Ian Froman. Gardony performs six of his originals, which are fairly advanced and straightahead but influenced a bit by his Hungarian heritage and, to a lesser extent, classical music. Well worth searching for. —*Scott Yanow*

Legend of Tsumi / Nov. 20, 1988+Dec. 1, 1988 / Antilles ✦✦✦✦

Laszlo Gardony, a classically trained pianist from Hungary, moved to the US in 1983. The most impressive aspect of this performance is how the pianist totally

integrates his playing with that of his sidemen (bassist Dave Holland and drummer Bill Moses) so they speak in one unified voice. Moses is quite subtle throughout while Holland and Gardony follow each other's moves very closely. The leader's seven originals are not easy to play (often using tricky time signatures) yet all of the selections are heard in their first takes and there are never any signs of hesitation. The one flaw to the music is that at that point in time Laszlo Gardony sounded a great deal like Keith Jarrett, especially in his use of repetition and the infusion of folk melodies into a jazz setting. But otherwise, this is an easily recommended set of stimulating music. —*Scott Yanow*

● **Changing Standards** / Aug. 15, 1990 / Sunnyside ✦✦✦✦✦

Pianist Laszlo Gardony lives up to the title of his CD, performing a variety of standards (including such classics as "Body and Soul," "Take the 'A' Train," "Naima," "Caravan," "Doxy" and two Thelonious Monk tunes) but he re-invents them, altering the harmonies and chord structures, inserting large doses of passion and putting the emphasis on his own spontaneity. These performances are full of surprises and unusual interpretations. One should expect the unexpected while listening to this stimulating and consistently inventive session. —*Scott Yanow*

Breakout / 1994 / Avenue Jazz ✦✦✦

Red Garland (William M. Garland)

b. May 13, 1923, Dallas, TX, **d.** Apr. 23, 1984, Dallas, TX
Piano / Hard Bop

Red Garland mixed together the usual influences of his generation (Nat Cole, Bud Powell and Ahmad Jamal) into his own distinctive approach; Garland's block chords themselves became influential on the players of the 1960s. He started out playing clarinet and alto, switching to piano when he was 18. During 1946-55 he worked steadily in New York and Philadelphia, backing such major players as Charlie Parker, Coleman Hawkins, Lester Young and Roy Eldridge but still remaining fairly obscure. That changed when he became a member of the classic Miles Davis Quintet (1955-58), heading a rhythm section that also included Paul Chambers and Philly Joe Jones. After leaving Miles, Garland had his own popular trio and recorded very frequently for Prestige, Jazzland and Moodsville during 1956-62 (the majority of which are currently available in the Original Jazz Classics series). The pianist eventually returned to Texas and was in semi-retirement but came back gradually in the 1970s, recording for MPS (1971) and Galaxy (1977-79) before retiring again. —*Scott Yanow*

P.C. Blues / May 11, 1956-Aug. 9, 1957 / Original Jazz Classics ✦✦✦✦

This CD reissues a trio album from 1957 that features pianist Red Garland with bassist Paul Chambers (the "P.C." in the title) and drummer Art Taylor. In addition to the four original titles (which are highlighted by a sensitive version of "Lost April" and the lengthy "Tweedle Dee Dee"), Garland's feature on a 1956 Miles Davis record, "Ahmad's Blues" (which features Red with Chambers and drummer Philly Joe Jones), adds to the value of this thoughtful but swinging release. —*Scott Yanow*

Garland of Red / Aug. 17, 1956 / Original Jazz Classics ✦✦✦✦✦

Thirty-three at the time of this, his first recording as a leader, pianist Red Garland already had his distinctive style fully formed and had been with the Miles Davis Quintet for a year. With the assistance of bassist Paul Chambers (also in Davis' group) and drummer Art Taylor, Garland is in superior form on six standards, Charlie Parker's "Constellation" (during which he shows that he could sound relaxed at the fastest tempos) and his own "Blue Red." Red Garland recorded frequently during the 1956-62 period and virtually all of his trio recordings are consistently enjoyable, this one being no exception. —*Scott Yanow*

High Pressure / Nov. 15, 1956+Dec. 13, 1957 / Original Jazz Classics ✦✦✦✦

The distinctive pianist Red Garland, tenor saxophonist John Coltrane (then 31 and already breaking away from the pack) and trumpeter Donald Byrd, along with the supportive bassist George Joyner and drummer Art Taylor, perform five jazz standards on this CD reissue. Highlights include "Soft Winds," "Undecided," and an explosive version of "Two Bass Hit" that foreshadowed the rendition that 'Trane would record with Miles Davis and Cannonball Adderley the following year. High-quality hard bop from some true "Young Lions." —*Scott Yanow*

Red Garland's Piano / Dec. 14, 1956+Mar. 22, 1957 / Original Jazz Classics ✦✦✦✦

Red Garland's third session as a leader finds the distinctive pianist investigating eight standards (including "Please Send Me Someone to Love," "Stompin' at the Savoy," "If I Were a Bell" and "Almost Like Being in Love") with his distinctive chord voicings, melodic but creative ideas and solid sense of swing. Joined by bassist Paul Chambers and drummer Art Taylor, Garland plays up to his usual consistent level, making this an easily recommended disc for straightahead fans. —*Scott Yanow*

Groovy / May 24, 1957 / Original Jazz Classics ✦✦✦✦

As the liner notes properly state, this CD (Red Garland's fourth as a leader for the Prestige label) has "jazz standards, ballad standards, blues ballads and just plain blues." The pianist's trio (with bassist Paul Chambers and drummer Art Taylor) swings such numbers as "C Jam Blues," "Will You Still Be Mine" (the latter from the Ahmad Jamal songbook) and "What Can I Say After I Say I'm Sorry" with spirit and subtle invention. All of Red Garland's Prestige recordings are worth getting. —*Scott Yanow*

Soul Junction / Nov. 15, 1957 / Original Jazz Classics ✦✦✦✦

Pianist Red Garland's very relaxed, marathon blues solo on the 16-minute "Soul Junction" is the most memorable aspect of this CD reissue. With such soloists as tenor saxophonist John Coltrane and trumpeter Donald Byrd, plus steady support provided by bassist George Joyner and drummer Art Taylor, Garland gets to stretch out on the title cut and four jazz originals, including "Birk's Works" and "Hallelujah." Coltrane is in excellent form, playing several stunning sheets of sound solos. —*Scott Yanow*

All Mornin' Long / Nov. 15, 1957 / Original Jazz Classics ✦✦✦✦

On November 15, 1957, a quintet headed by pianist Red Garland recorded enough material for two records. This CD reissue (whose companion is *Soul Junction*) has a 20-minute version of "All Morning Long," along with briefer renditions of "They Can't Take That Away from Me" (a mere ten minutes) and Tadd Dameron's "Our Delight." More important than the material is that, in addition to Garland, the main soloists are John Coltrane and trumpeter Donald Byrd. Byrd was on his way to getting his sound together, while 'Trane, very much in his sheets-of-sound period, was already blazing a new path for jazz to follow. An excellent and often quite colorful jam session-flavored hard-bop set. —*Scott Yanow*

Dig It! / Dec. 13, 1957-Feb. 7, 1958 / Original Jazz Classics ✦✦✦

1989 reissue contains more from the mammoth Garland late-50s output, with Donald Byrd (tpt), John Coltrane (ts), Paul Chambers (b), Art Taylor (d), and the underrated George Joyner (b). —*Ron Wynn*

Manteca / Apr. 11, 1958 / Original Jazz Classics ✦✦✦✦

This is a solid CD reissue that differs from most sets by pianist Red Garland in that, in addition to bassist Paul Chambers and drummer Art Taylor, he employs Ray Barretto on conga. The Latin flavor does not affect the music much (other than on the title cut), but Barretto does light a fire under the other musicians. In addition to the original five songs, a version of "Portrait of Jenny" from the same date is a bonus cut. A nice, swinging session. —*Scott Yanow*

Blues in the Night / Apr. 11, 1958-Jul. 15, 1960 / Prestige ✦✦✦✦

The emphasis is on the blues (although not exclusively) on this CD reissue. The original eight-song program has been joined by "A Portrait of Jennie" by the same trio (pianist Red Garland, bassist Sam Jones and drummer Art Taylor) from an earlier date. Most unusual about the set is that Garland makes a rare (and effective) appearance on organ during "Halleloo-Y'All." Otherwise, this is a conventional but enjoyable set of bluesy bop, highlighted by "Revelation Blues," "Everytime I Feel the Spirit" and "Rocks in My Bed." —*Scott Yanow*

Rediscovered Masters, Vol. 1 / Jun. 1958 / Original Jazz Classics ✦✦✦

Originally released for the first time on a 1977 double LP and later reissued on two separate CDs, these performances are up to pianist Red Garland's usual level. Since he was teamed with bassist Paul Chambers, drummer Art Taylor and Ray Barretto on conga, the same lineup used on the Manteca date of two months earlier, the date went unreleased for decades, but in reality, the music is excellent. Highlights include "Lover," "Blues in Mambo," "Estrellita" and "East of the Sun." —*Scott Yanow*

Can't See for Lookin' / Jun. 27, 1958 / Original Jazz Classics ✦✦✦✦

Pianist Red Garland recorded many sets in the late 1950s and early '60s, often (as in this case) with bassist Paul Chambers and drummer Art Taylor. Despite the LP length of this CD reissue (under 35 minutes), this is a particularly strong example of Garland's talents. His block chords are distinctive, as is his use of space, and the music always swings. The trio sounds in top form on "I Can't See for Looking," George Gershwin's "Soon," "Blackout" and a driving version of the classic blues "Castle Rock." Recommended. —*Scott Yanow*

Rojo / Aug. 22, 1958 / Original Jazz Classics ✦✦✦✦

Pianist Red Garland recorded frequently with trios for Prestige during the second half of the 1950s. For this set (reissued on CD), Garland, bassist George Joyner and drummer Charlie Persip are joined by Ray Barretto on congas and the emphasis is on forceful swinging. Garland takes such ballads as "We Kiss in a Shadow" and "You Better Go Now" at faster-than-expected tempos. "Ralph J. Gleason Blues" and the Latin feel of "Rojo" are among the highlights of this enjoyable disc. —*Scott Yanow*

Red Garland Trio / Nov. 21, 1958 / Original Jazz Classics ✦✦

This session from pianist Red Garland, reissued on LP in Fantasy's *Original Jazz Classics* series but not yet on CD, originally appeared on the Moodsville label. Its slow tempos (only "And the Angels Sing" moves a little) fit well into the theme of that subsidiary's releases but it resulted in the set being a bit sleepy. Bassist Paul Chambers and drummer Art Taylor help out and Garland plays these two blues and four standards well but the lack of variety makes this reissue one of Red Garland's lesser efforts. —*Scott Yanow*

All Kinds of Weather / Nov. 27, 1958 / Original Jazz Classics ✦✦✦

Red Garland was always a consistent pianist and all of his mid- to late '50s Prestige dates are worth acquiring. This CD reissue has six titles having to do with seasons and the weather (such as "Rain," "Summertime" and "Winter Wonderland"). The gimmick served as a good excuse for Garland, bassist Paul Chambers and drummer Art Taylor to explore six superior songs, and their interpretations always swing and uplift the melodies. —*Scott Yanow*

Red in Bluesville / Apr. 17, 1959 / Original Jazz Classics ✦✦✦✦

Pianist Red Garland and his trio (with bassist Sam Jones and drummer Art Taylor) explore six veteran blues-based compositions ranging from Nellie Lutcher's "He's a Real Gone Guy" and "St. Louis Blues" to "Your Red Wagon" and Count Basie's "M Squad Theme." Throughout, Garland modernizes each of the selections with his distinctive chord voicings and he makes the songs sound fresh and new. A solid effort from this very consistent pianist who will always be best remembered for his playing with the classic Miles Davis Quintet. —*Scott Yanow*

Rediscovered Masters, Vol. 2 / Aug. 12, 1959+Mar. 16, 1961 / Original Jazz Classics ✦✦✦✦

The second of two CDs of material released for the first time on a 1977 double LP has music from two separate sessions. Pianist Red Garland, whose distinctive chord voicings are immediately recognizable, is heard on four numbers (including a bonus version of "Satin Doll") from a trio date with bassist Doug Watkins and drummer Specs Wright, as well as on three jams ("Skinny's Blues," "Soft Winds" and "Avalon") with a 1961 quintet also co-starring trumpeter Richard Williams and Oliver Nelson on alto and tenor. Along with virtually all of Red Garland's records, easily recommended for straightahead jazz collectors. —*Scott Yanow*

★ **Red Garland at the Prelude, Vol. 1** / Oct. 1959 / Prestige ✦✦✦✦✦

Originally released as two LPs (*Red Garland at the Prelude* and *Red Garland/ Live!*), this single CD (which has around 77 minutes of music) features a particularly strong trio set by the pianist, bassist Jimmy Rowser and drummer Specs Wright. Garland mostly sticks to standards and the highlights include "Perdido," "Bye Bye Blackbird" (which is reminiscent of the famous Miles Davis version) and two versions of "One O'Clock Jump." Straightahead jazz fans should get this one. —*Scott Yanow*

The Red Garland Trio with Eddie Lockjaw Davis, Vol. 1 / Dec. 11, 1959 / Original Jazz Classics ✦✦✦

In the late 1950s, Prestige started a new subsidiary (Moodsville) that was designed to provide mood music for courting couples. The emphasis on this CD reissue, the very first Moodsville release, is on ballads, matching pianist Red Garland, bassist Sam Jones and drummer Art Taylor with guest tenor Eddie "Lockjaw" Davis on three of the eight tunes. Due to the overly relaxed nature of much of this music and the lack of variety, this is not one of the more essential Red Garland sets, but it is still generally enjoyable. Highlights include "We'll Be Together Again," "When Your Lover Has Gone" and "Blue Room." —*Scott Yanow*

Soul Burnin' / Jul. 15, 1960-Mar. 16, 1961 / Original Jazz Classics ✦✦✦

The music on this CD reissue is drawn from three separate Red Garland sessions but had not been previously put out on CD. Best are two selections ("On Green Dolphin Street" and "If You Could See Me Now") that find the pianist, bassist Peck Morrison and drummer Charlie Persip being joined by Oliver Nelson (on alto and tenor) and trumpeter Richard Williams; the horns in particular are quite inventive during their solos. Three numbers (two standards plus "Soul Burnin'") have Garland, bassist Sam Jones and drummer Arthur Taylor in more conventional but pleasing form, while the spirited closer ("A Little Bit of Basie") matches the pianist with bassist Doug Watkins and drummer Specs Wright. Fine music that will be enjoyed by straightahead jazz fans, although (due to the availability of so many Red Garland sessions) this CD is not essential. —*Scott Yanow*

Bright and Breezy / Jul. 19, 1961 / Original Jazz Classics ✦✦✦

During 1961-62, following a long series of recording for Prestige, pianist Red Garland recorded four LPs for the Jazzland label. His style was unchanged from a few years earlier, and this trio set with bassist Sam Jones and drummer Charlie Persip (reissued on CD in the OJC series) is very much up to par. Highlights include Garland's interpretations of "I Ain't Got Nobody," "Blues in the Closet" and "Lil' Darlin." An enjoyable straightahead session. —*Scott Yanow*

Solar / Jan. 30, 1962 / Original Jazz Classics ✦✦✦

Pianist Red Garland recorded many sessions during 1955-63 and his distinctive chord voicings and relaxed style were always worth hearing. The wild card on this quartet is Les Spann who had the unusual double of guitar and flute; his flute is a major asset on "Where Are You?" and "The Very Thought of You." Garland (along with bassist Sam Jones and drummer Frank Gant) is in fine form throughout these underplayed standards; highlights include "Sophisticated Swing," "Solar" and "This Can't Be Love." —*Scott Yanow*

Red's Good Groove / Mar. 22, 1962 / Jazzland ✦✦✦

Large doses of funk & soul-jazz, plus fine baritone from Pepper Adams and Blue Mitchell on trumpet. —*Ron Wynn*

When There Are Grey Skies / Oct. 9, 1962 / Original Jazz Classics ✦✦✦✦

This set was pianist Red Garland's 25th session as a leader since 1956 but it would be eight years before his next record. Garland's influential style had been fully formed since the mid-'50s and his chord voicings were immediately recognizable. With the assistance of bassist Wendell Marshall and drummer Charlie Persip, Garland explores and updates seven veteran songs (including a previously unreleased "My Blue Heaven") dating from the '20s era. This fine CD is highlighted by such unlikely material as "Sonny Boy," "St. James Infirmary," "Baby Won't You Please Come Home" and a 12-minute "Nobody Knows the Trouble I've Seen." —*Scott Yanow*

The Quota / May 3, 1971 / MPS ✦✦✦

After being very active on records and in clubs from 1955-62, pianist Red Garland went back to his native Texas. He did not return to records until 1971, when he cut "Auf Wiedersehen" and this particular LP, which has not yet been reissued on CD; except for a couple of Japanese dates in 1974, it would be another six years before Garland began making a real comeback. Teamed up with Jimmy Heath (who doubles on tenor and soprano), bassist Peck Morrison and drummer Lenny McBrowne, Garland plays in the same distinctive style he had in the 1950s, not showing any decline or loss of chops. The quartet performs four jazz standards, the title cut (a Heath original), and Leroy Vinnegar's "For Carl." —*Scott Yanow*

Red Alert / Dec. 2, 1977 / Original Jazz Classics ✦✦✦✦

This is an interesting set, featuring pianist Red Garland with a sextet also including cornetist Nat Adderley, both Harold Land and Ira Sullivan on tenor, bassist Ron Carter and drummer Frank Butler. With one of the largest recording groups he ever led, Garland sounds fine, but the material (which includes "The Whiffenpoof Song," "Sweet Georgia Brown," "Stella by Starlight" and "It's Impossible") could certainly have been more inspired. —*Scott Yanow*

Crossings / Dec. 1977 / Original Jazz Classics ✦✦✦

Amazingly enough, this set (reissued on CD) was the first time that pianist Red Garland and drummer Philly Joe Jones recorded together in a trio setting, even though they had both been a part of Miles Davis' first classic quintet. With bassist Ron Carter completing the group, they perform five standards and the bassist's "Railroad Crossing." This is one of Garland's best later dates (Philly Joe often pushes him), and the highlights include "Solar," "Oleo" and "Love for Sale." —*Scott Yanow*

Feelin' Red / May 15, 1978 / Muse ✦✦✦

I Left My Heart . . . / May 15, 1978 / Muse ✦✦✦

Equinox / Aug. 4, 1978-Aug. 5, 1978 / Galaxy ✦✦✦

Stepping Out / Jul. 9, 1979-Jul. 10, 1979 / Galaxy ✦✦✦✦

During three dates in July 1979, pianist Red Garland recorded enough material to fill up three sets; unfortunately, none of the music has yet been reissued on CD. This particular album has some good playing by Garland in a trio with bassist Ron Carter and drummer Ben Riley; guitarist Kenny Burrell helps out on three of the six numbers. The group performs six superior standards, including "Yours Is My Heart Alone," "Have You Met Miss Jones" and Clifford Brown's "Daahoud," and Garland shows that even this late in his career, he was still a fine player with a musical conception of his own. —*Scott Yanow*

So Long Blues / Jul. 9, 1979-Jul. 12, 1979 / Galaxy ✦✦✦✦

Not released until 1984, this LP has "new" material from two Red Garland Galaxy sessions. While "So Long Blues" is from a quintet with pianist Garland, trombonist Julian Priester, tenorman George Coleman, bassist Ron Carter and drummer Ben Riley, the other five selections showcase Garland with Carter, Riley, and (on two occasions) guitarist Kenny Burrell. The biggest surprise is the pianist's vocal on "The Best Man." Otherwise, no real surprises occur, but everyone plays well within the hard bop mainstream. —*Scott Yanow*

Strike Up the Band / Jul. 11, 1979-Jul. 12, 1979 / Galaxy ✦✦✦✦

Pianist Red Garland's final Galaxy set (he only recorded two other records before his death in 1984) is an outing with an all-star quintet: tenor saxophonist George Coleman (in excellent form), trombonist Julian Priester, bassist Ron Carter and

drummer Ben Riley. They stretch out on four jazz standards (including "Straight, No Chaser," "Everything Happens to Me" and "Strike Up the Band") and Carter's "Receipt, Please." The pianist, who had spent much of the past 16 years living in his native Texas, shows that he could still swing with the best. —*Scott Yanow*

Erroll Garner

b. Jun. 15, 1921, Pittsburgh, PA, **d.** Jan. 2, 1977, Los Angeles, CA

Piano / Swing, Bop

One of the most distinctive of all pianists, Erroll Garner proved that it was possible to be a sophisticated player without knowing how to read music, that a creative jazz musician can be very popular without watering down his music, and that it is possible to remain an enthusiastic player without changing one's style once it is formed. A brilliant virtuoso who sounded unlike anyone else, Erroll Garner on medium-tempo pieces often stated the beat with his left hand like a rhythm guitar while his right played chords slightly behind the beat, creating a memorable effect. His playful free-form introductions (which forced his sidemen to really listen), his ability to play stunning runs without once glancing at the keyboard, his grunting and the pure joy that he displayed while performing were also part of the Erroll Garner magic.

Garner, whose older brother Linton is also a fine pianist, appeared on the radio with the Kan-D-Kids at the age of ten. After working locally in Pittsburgh, he moved to New York in 1944 and worked with Slam Stewart's trio during 1944-45 before going out on his own. By 1946 Garner had his sound together and when he backed Charlie Parker on his famous "Cool Blues" session of 1947, the pianist was already an obvious giant. His unclassifiable style had an orchestral approach straight from the swing era but was open to the innovations of bop. From the early '50s Garner's accessible style became very popular and he never seemed to have an off day up until his forced retirement (due to illness) in early 1975. His composition "Misty" became a standard. Erroll Garner, who had the ability to sit at the piano without prior planning and record three albums in one day (all colorful first takes), made many records throughout his career for such companies as Savoy, Mercury, RCA, Dial, Columbia, EmArcy, ABC-Paramount, MGM, Reprise and his own Octave label. —*Scott Yanow*

1944, Vol. 3 / Nov. 3, 1944-Dec. 25, 1944 / Classics ✦✦✦

On this CD, the third Classics set featuring Erroll Garner at the beginning of his career, the pianist is mostly heard during Dec. 22-25, 1944, when he was caught on disc practicing at Baron Timme Rosenkrantz's home. Because there were no time restrictions, Garner really stretches out on a few of the numbers, including the ten-and-a-half-minute "Duke for Dinner" (which has abstract references to many of Duke Ellington's songs) and nine-minute versions of "Variations on a Nursery Rhyme," "I Got Rhythm" and his own "In the Beginning." In addition, there is an eight-minute medley of Christmas songs. In general, Erroll Garner is surprisingly unrecognizable in spots, playing quite impressionistically with only his sly wit being identifiable. The set is rounded off by a previously unreleased version of "Somebody Loves Me" (with a vocal by Inez Cavanaugh) from Nov. 3, 1944 that is actually the earliest documentation of Garner discovered yet. The music is historic, but not as significant as what was to come from the pianist very shortly. —*Scott Yanow*

1944 / Nov. 16, 1944-Dec. 14, 1944 / Classics ✦✦✦

Pianist Erroll Garner's earliest recordings were taped privately at Baron Timme Rosenkrantz's apartment in New York. While Garner practiced, stretched out and tried out new ideas, Rosenkrantz kept a recorder running. The resulting discs were originally not planned for release, but in the early 1950s (with Garner's great popularity), some did come out. This Classics CD, one of four that contain all of the performances, finds Garner performing for as long as ten minutes ("Floating On a Cloud") on one piece. His style was not quite fully formed (it would solidify in 1945) and Garner sounds surprisingly impressionistic on such numbers as "The Clock Stood Still," "Autumn Mood" and "Overture to Dawn." Only on the faster pieces is he fairly distinctive, making this CD (and its follow-up) a true historical curiosity. —*Scott Yanow*

1944, Vol. 2 / Dec. 14, 1944-Dec. 20, 1944 / Classics ✦✦✦

The second in the Classics label's Erroll Garner series has nine unusual piano solos recorded privately at Baron Timme Rosenkrantz's apartment (ranging from the two-and-a-half-minute novelty "Twisting the Cat's Tail" to an extensive eight-minute exploration of "I Hear a Rhapsody"), along with the ten songs that comprised Garner's first officially recorded session. The latter were originally cut as piano solos for the Rex label (later put out by Atlantic), but had bass (John Simmons) and drums (Doc West) overdubbed, which explains why they are better recorded than the piano. Overall, this is an interesting but not overly essential release. —*Scott Yanow*

1944-1945 / Dec. 22, 1944-Mar. 9, 1945 / Classics ✦✦✦✦✦

The fourth in Classics' reissuance of all of the early recordings by the great pianist Erroll Garner has some unusual performances. The first eight numbers were private recordings cut during a jam session at Timme Rosenkrantz's apartment. Garner (who at that point in time only hinted at his emerging distinctive style and showed the influence of Fats Waller) and trumpeter Charlie Shavers constantly inspire each other and are assisted by trombonist Vic Dickenson, altoist Lem Davis, bassist Slam Stewart (in top form), drummer Cliff Leeman and, on one song, clarinetist Hank D'Amico. Those selections are quite extended (two songs exceed ten minutes) and sometimes a little loose but filled with excitement; the ad-lib ending of "Red Cross" is fairly humorous. Wrapping up this CD are Garner's first studio recordings: four selections cut with a trio for the Black & White label and four piano solos made for Signature. Although performed only a short time after the earlier jam session, Garner was already starting to play in his own familiar style. Recommended. —*Scott Yanow*

1945-1946 / Sep. 25, 1945-Feb. 1946 / Classics ✦✦✦✦

The fifth CD in the European Classics label's Erroll Garner reissue series showcases the great pianist on the 21 recordings that he cut in a five-month period during 1945-46. Garner's four trio numbers for Savoy (particularly his hit version of "Laura") helped make him famous. Those are included on this set along with four obscure piano solos for the Disc and Arco labels, 11 numbers for Mercury, and a couple of V-Disc performances. Despite the success of "Laura," Garner at that early point in time was better at medium-tempo numbers. He romps on such tunes as "Indiana," "Lady Be Good," "Bouncin' with Me" and "High Octane." This outing is not quite essential, but it does contain plenty of enjoyable numbers. —*Scott Yanow*

The Elf / Sep. 25, 1945-Mar. 29, 1949 / Savoy ✦✦✦

This set allows one to hear the very distinctive pianist Erroll Garner in his early days. Four tracks are with bassist John Levy and drummer George de Hart in 1945, but the lion's share is with bassist John Simmons and drummer Alvin Stoller from 1949. The medium-tempo pieces are the most enjoyable with Garner's slightly behind-the-beat right hand echoing his on-the-beat left hand. The ballads can sometimes get a bit overly rhapsodic but are still enjoyable. It is no wonder that Garner remained popular for decades without needing to adjust or water down his style. —*Scott Yanow*

Long Ago and Far Away / Jun. 28, 1950-Jan. 11, 1951 / Columbia ✦✦✦

1950-1951. This is great Garner. Unfortunately, the remastering is not as great. —*Michael Erlewine*

Body and Soul / Jan. 11, 1951-Jan. 3, 1952 / Columbia ✦✦✦✦

Too Marvelous for Words, Vol. 3 / May 26, 1954 / EmArcy ✦✦✦✦✦

The third in the Polygram series of overviews. Plenty of majestic performances. —*Ron Wynn*

Erroll Garner Collection, Vols. 4 & 5: Solo Time! / Jul. 7, 1954 / EmArcy ✦✦✦✦

Mambo Moves Garner / Jul. 27, 1954 / Mercury ✦✦✦✦✦

For this lengthy session, pianist Erroll Garner added a conga player (Candido) to his trio (which includes bassist Wyatt Ruther and drummer Eugene Heard) for the first time. Throughout the remainder of his career he would occasionally play in the Latin idiom. This CD reissue (which adds two songs from the same session to the original LP program) finds the pianist in typically enthusiastic form and the highlights include "Mambo Garner," "Night and Day," "Cherokee" and "Sweet Sue." —*Scott Yanow*

The Original Misty / Jul. 27, 1954-Mar. 14, 1955 / Mercury ✦✦✦✦✦

This is a reissue of the first Garner version of Misty made in the early '50s. —*Ron Wynn*

Afternoon of an Elf / Mar. 14, 1955 / Mercury ✦✦✦

This out-of-print LP features a typically exuberant solo set by pianist Erroll Garner. Garner actually recorded 20 selections during the one session, seven of which are on the album. The distinctive pianist introduces three of his originals (including the title cut) and comes up with clever reworkings of four standards, highlighted by a well-disguised "St. James Infirmary" and a witty rendition of "A Smooth One." Few pianists showed as much consistent enthusiasm and inventiveness within a set style as Erroll Garner, and this fine LP is quite enjoyable. —*Scott Yanow*

Solitaire / Mar. 14, 1955 / Mercury ✦✦✦

On March 14, 1955, Erroll Garner sat down at the piano and played one interesting solo after another, resulting in two albums of music. Seven pieces (all but "That Old Feeling" are taken as ballads) were originally released as *Solitaire*; this CD reissue adds four additional selections that are taken at faster paces. Although not essential, the rhapsodic and occasionally wandering but always intriguing set should greatly interest fans. —*Scott Yanow*

★ **Concert by the Sea** / Sep. 19, 1955 / Columbia ✦✦✦✦✦

Concert by the Sea was arguably the finest record pianist Erroll Garner ever made, and he made many—a few outstanding—good recordings. But this live recording (9/19/55) with his trio (Eddie Calhoun, bass; Denzil Best, drums) presented a typical Garner program; it was a mixture of originals, show biz and pop standards delivered with his unique delivery and enthusiasm. The rhythms and brilliant use of tension and release were perfectly captured. And while for many jazz listeners, Garner's deliberate structures were too orchestrated, there was an equal spontaneity in the propulsion of these orchestrations that swung as well as anything. —*Bob Rusch, Cadence*

Other Voices / Sept. 2, 1956-May 31, 1957 / Columbia ✦✦

Among his more pop (and popular) releases when it was issued in 1956. This reissue isn't of the highest caliber; it's merely a decent one. Find the original if possible. —*Ron Wynn*

Dreamstreet & One World Concert / Dec. 18, 1959-Aug. 25, 1962 / Telarc ✦✦✦✦

Two of pianist Erroll Garner's albums for his Octave label have been reissued on full on this single CD from Telarc. Backed by bassist Eddie Calhoun and drummer Kelly Martin, Garner is heard stretching out in the studios and playing in concert at the 1963 Seattle World's Fair. Among the most consistent of jazzmen, Garner typically romps through a variety of standards plus his own "Misty," "Dreamstreet," "Mambo Gotham" and a medley of songs from the play *Oklahoma*. Other highlights of the spirited set include "Just One of Those Things," "Blue Lou," "The Lady Is a Tramp," "The Way You Look Tonight" and "Mack the Knife." —*Scott Yanow*

Dancing on the Ceiling / Jun. 1, 1961-Aug. 19, 1965 / EmArcy ✦✦✦✦✦

The great pianist Erroll Garner is heard on these 11 selections, jamming on standards with bassist Eddie Calhoun and drummer Kelly Martin. One number is from 1964 and another from a year later, but the remainder was performed in 1961; all of the selections were previously unreleased. The music is marvelous and sometimes miraculous, with Garner's distinctive style heard at its best throughout. —*Scott Yanow*

Close-Up in Swing/A New Kind of Love / Jul. 1961-Feb. 1963 / Telarc ✦✦✦✦

Two former LPs were reissued in full on this single CD. The earlier date features pianist Erroll Garner in typically brilliant and witty form with his 1961 trio, which also included bassist Eddie Calhoun and drummer Kelly Martin. Whether it be a sly "My Silent Love," "All of Me," or a joyful "Back in Your Own Backyard," Garner is heard throughout in his prime. The later date is a bit more unusual, for the pianist improvises on ten themes that would be used in the Paul Newman film "A New Kind of Love." Joined by a big band and string orchestra conducted by Leith Stevens, Garner, who never learned to read or write music, contributed several original themes to the score (a few of which are quite catchy) in addition to jamming on such tunes as "You Brought a New Kind of Love to Me," "Louise" and "Mimi." On both former albums, the overall results are quite memorable, which is not a surprise, for Erroll Garner always seemed incapable of playing an uninspired or indifferent solo. —*Scott Yanow*

Easy to Love / July 14, 1961-Aug. 19, 1965 / EmArcy ✦✦✦

1961-1965. This is feathery at times, tenacious at others. —*Ron Wynn*

You Brought a New Kind of Love / Jul. 1963 / Mercury ✦✦✦

Pianist Erroll Garner was at the height of his popularity when he recorded this now-out-of-print LP. Backed by a small string section, brass and woodwinds arranged by Leith Stevens, Garner performs ten songs that were used in the film *A New Kind of Love*, including five of his own compositions and the standards "You Brought a New Kind of Love to Me" and "Louise." Garner plays as well as usual, but these concise performances sound very much like safe film music, making the set recommended primarily to the pianist's most devoted fans. —*Scott Yanow*

Now Playing: A Night at the Movies/Up in Erroll's Room / Jul. 25, 1964+Mar. 19, 1968 / Telarc ✦✦✦✦

Many of Erroll Garner's sessions from the 1960s have been reissued by Telarc. This single CD brings back all of the music from two former LPs. Garner and his quartet (bassist Ike Isaacs, drummer Jimmie Smith and percussionist Jose Mangual) romp through 13 songs taken from movies (including "You Made Me Love You," "I Found a Million Dollar Baby," "It's Only a Paper Moon" and even "Sonny Boy") during the first half of the set while the later session finds the group backed by seven horns arranged by Don Sebesky on nine diverse tunes ranging from swing standards to "The Girl from Ipanema," "Groovin' High" and Garner's lone original "Up in Erroll's Room." All of the Telarc Erroll Garner CDs are easily recommended (the pianist never seems to have made an uninspired record) and this one is no exception. —*Scott Yanow*

A Night at the Movies / Aug. 5, 1964 / MGM ✦✦✦

Takes you into, through, and around the cinema via Garner's adept, crackling riffs and rhythms. —*Ron Wynn*

That's My Kick & Gemini / Apr. 1966-Dec. 21, 1971 / Telarchive ✦✦✦✦

This CD from Telarchive (a subsidiary of Telarc) reissues the complete content of two later Erroll Garner LPs: *That's My Kick* and *Gemini*. The great pianist was still in prime form and, although his sidemen are fine in support (Wally Richardson is on guitar on the first date and the congas of Jose Mangual add a Latin flavor to the music to both sessions), Garner totally dominates the music as usual. He contributed eight of the 19 compositions and his wit is only exceeded by his creativity. —*Scott Yanow*

Magician & Gershwin and Kern / Aug. 5, 1964-Oct. 30, 1973 / Telarchive ✦✦✦

Two of Errol Garner's last albums, *Magician* and *Gershwin and Kern*, are reissued on this single CD. The pianist, heading trios or quartets, is in typically whimsical and hard-swinging form; he never did decline on record. The former session includes several of his originals plus versions of "Close to You" and "Watch What Happens" that manage to uplift those pop tunes; the latter date has consistently superior material. Garner's very spontaneous playing is as usual both unpredictable and quite accessible and these unedited performances were all first takes. No one ever really sounded like Erroll Garner and this highly enjoyable set of formerly rare material gives one a good example of his magical music. —*Scott Yanow*

Carlos Garnett

b. Dec. 1, 1938, Red Tank, Panama Canal Zone

Tenor Saxophone / Avant-Garde, Post-Bop, Hard Bop

An intense tenor soloist, Carlos Garnett seemed to largely disappear from jazz after the late '70s, but re-emerged 20 years later playing better than ever. He grew up in Panama, started playing tenor in 1957 and early on performed calypso and Latin music. In 1962, Garnett moved to New York, working with rock groups and struggling a bit but listening closely to the free jazz saxophonists. He gained some recognition for his work with Freddie Hubbard (1968-69), Art Blakey's Jazz Messengers (1969-70) and Charles Mingus, and had an important stint with Miles Davis in 1972. Garnett also worked with Jack McDuff, Andrew Hill, Gary Bartz and Norman Connors during the era and recorded five albums of his own for Muse during 1974-77 that ranged from exploratory music to attempts at commercialism. Carlos Garnett was musically inactive during much of the 1980s, but started a comeback in 1991, and in 1996 made one of his finest albums (*Fuego en Mi Alma*, for the HighNote label) in a style little changed since the '70s. —*Scott Yanow*

Black Love / Jan. 18, 1974+Jan. 21, 1974 / Muse ✦✦✦

This CD reissues an interesting if not essential set by the passionate saxophonist Carlos Garnett. The five selections (which are augmented by two previously unissued alternate takes) combine together advanced jazz, electronics (particularly from guitarist Reggie Lucas who was with Miles Davis at the time), the voices of Dee Dee Bridgewater (on one of her first dates) and Ayodele Jenkins which are often heard in the ensembles, and funky pop elements. In addition to Garnett (mostly heard on tenor and soprano), trumpeter Charles Sullivan, pianist Allan Gumbs and guitarist Lucas are the main soloists while Bridgewater is well featured on the two versions of "Banks of the Nile." The unpredictable music overall is eccentric, sometimes overcrowded, and very much of the period but it holds one's interest. —*Scott Yanow*

Fire / Jan. 18, 1974-May 1977 / 32 Jazz ✦✦✦

● **Journey to Enlightenment** / Sep. 20, 1974 / Muse ✦✦✦✦✦

Let This Melody Ring on / Jun. 16, 1975+Jun. 18, 1975 / Muse ✦✦✦

Fuego En Mi Alma / 1996 / High Note ✦✦✦✦

Carlos Garnett made his biggest impact in the late '60s and 1970s, when his intense tenor playing was heard on recordings by Art Blakey, Miles Davis and Norman Connors. Garnett spent a lot of time off the scene in the 1980s but emerged in the '90s in fine form, if a bit more conservative. For this 1996 CD, Garnett is joined by pianist Carlton Holmes, bassist Brad Jones and drummer Shingo Okudaira, playing mostly originals (plus Freddie Hubbard's "Little Sunflower") that are spiritually linked to the music of the John Coltrane Quartet. Fortunately, the musicians do not attempt to sound like their predecessors; Garnett has an original tone of his own, and the improvising has its subtle surprises. Worth checking out. —*Scott Yanow*

Kenny Garrett

b. Oct. 9, 1960, Detroit, MI

Alto Saxophone / Post-Bop

Kenny Garrett was one of the last significant graduates of Miles Davis' groups and is one of the potential greats in jazz. He started early on playing in Detroit with Marcus Belgrave and toured with the Mercer Ellington Orchestra before moving to New York in 1980. He made his debut recording for Criss Cross (1984) and was part of the group Out of the Blue before joining Davis for the trumpeter's last few years. Garrett recorded an obscure session for Paddlewheel (1988) and the weak *Prisoner of Love* (1989) and the recommended *African Exchange Student* (1990) as a leader for Atlantic. Since Miles Davis' death, Garrett has led his own groups and recorded for Warner Brothers, justifying Davis' faith in him. —*Scott Yanow*

Introducing Kenny Garrett / Dec. 28, 1984 / Criss Cross ✦✦✦

At the time he recorded this set, altoist Kenny Garrett was 24, had played with Mercer Ellington's big band, and was freelancing in New York. (His association with Miles Davis would not begin for a few more years.) A measure of the strong reputation Garrett already had is that his sidemen include trumpeter Woody Shaw and pianist Mulgrew Miller; bassist Nat Reeves and drummer Tony Reedus complete the quintet. The group performs five of the altoist's hard bop originals, Miller's "Blues in the Afternoon," and a couple of standards. A strong start to what would be a significant career. —*Scott Yanow*

Prisoner of Love / 1989 / Atlantic ✦

Altoist Kenny Garrett's second recording as a leader (following an earlier effort for Criss Cross) is a surprising dud, especially compared to his later (and near-classic) recordings. The first three selections find Garrett sticking to the melody over automatic pilot rhythms in an unsuccessful attempt to obtain a cross between Grover Washington, Jr. and Stanley Turrentine. "Blue Moon" in particular is a turkey with the embarrassing arrangement altering the chord structure for the worse, and the remainder of this album is not much better. The most notable aspect to *Prisoner of Love* is that Miles Davis (who was Garrett's employer at the time) makes two rare appearances as a sideman, but his muted ensemble work on the nursery rhyme melody of "Big Ol' Head" and "Free Mandela" is as forgettable as virtually this entire misfire. —*Scott Yanow*

African Exchange Student / 1990 / Atlantic ✦✦✦✦

Altoist Kenny Garrett, who was then a key member of Miles Davis' group, had one of his strongest early sets as a leader on this Atlantic disc. "Ja-Hed" features his post-bop improvising over the chord changes of "Impressions," is both lighthearted and adventurous on "Mack the Knife" and the title cut has Garrett expertly building up an emotional solo from intense long tones to sound explorations and late-period 'Trane screams. Throughout the CD, Kenny Garrett's alto is the main attraction but the strong rhythm section (comprising pianist Mulgrew Miller, either Charnett Moffett or Ron Carter on bass, Tony Reedus or Elvin Jones on drums and occasional percussionists) should not be overlooked. Whether it be the modal tribute piece "Shaw," the rarely played Coltrane song "Straight Street" or the minor blues "Nostradamus," Kenny Garrett justifies the praise that he received from Miles Davis. —*Scott Yanow*

Black Hope / 1992 / Warner Brothers ✦✦✦✦

Alto saxophonist Kenny Garrett hasn't been as heavily publicized as his fellow Young Lions, but he can play with as much authority, conviction, and sheer energy as anyone. Only some uneven material keeps his 1992 album from being exceptional, and even on the weak songs, Garrett's playing forces you to pay attention. —*Ron Wynn*

Threshold / 1994 / Warner Brothers ✦✦✦

● **Triology** / 1995 / Warner Brothers ✦✦✦✦✦

Pursuance: The Music of John Coltrane / 1996 / Warner Brothers ✦✦✦✦✦

Pursuance: Music of John Coltrane is Kenny Garrett's tribute to John Coltrane. Working with musicians like Pat Metheny, Brian Blade, and Rodney Whitaker, Garrett creates a loving tribute, one that is respectful to Coltrane's legacy but one that doesn't mimick his sound. It's a moving record that reveals more layers every time you listen to it. —*Thom Owens*

Songbook / May 20, 1997 / Warner Brothers ✦✦✦✦

Altoist Kenny Garrett followed up his highly rated *Triology* and *Pursuance* CDs with this quartet workout on eight of his own compositions. With the assistance of pianist Kenny Kirkland, bassist Nat Reeves and drummer Jeff "Tain" Watts, Garrett alternates torrid blowouts with more thoughtful improvisations, playing with consistent passion. As it turns out, the altoist's solos are more memorable than his compositions, so the set is not quite on the level of his previous two, but Garrett's fiery and inventive solos certainly make it worth picking up. —*Scott Yanow*

Jimmy Garrison

b. Mar. 3, 1934, Miami, FL, **d.** Apr. 7, 1976, New York, NY
Bass / Avant-Garde, Post-Bop, Free Jazz

Jimmy Garrison was one of the most advanced bassists of the 1960s, a perfect candidate to play with John Coltrane and Ornette Coleman. He grew up in Philadelphia and came to New York with Philly Joe Jones in 1958. He freelanced for a couple of years with the likes of Bill Evans, Benny Golson, Kenny Dorham and Lennie Tristano and then succeeded Charlie Haden in Ornette Coleman's Quartet (1961). However Garrison will always be associated with John Coltrane (1961-67), not only playing with the classic quartet (which included McCoy Tyner and Elvin Jones) but surviving the tumultuous changes and staying with 'Trane until the end. Garrison's solos (which were thoughtful and slow to build) were not to everyone's taste but his ability to play coherent and inspiring lines in the raging ensembles behind Coltrane and Pharoah Sanders was quite impressive. After Coltrane's death, Garrison played in groups led by Alice Coltrane, Archie Shepp and Elvin Jones before lung cancer cut short his life. —*Scott Yanow*

Mike Garson

b. Jul. 1945, New York, NY
Piano, Keyboards / Post-Bop, Crossover Jazz

Mike Garson, a true virtuoso, has had a very diverse career. Heard at his best with his own groups or with Free Flight, Garson has also toured with David Bowie and for a television movie on Liberace, he performed the music and had his hands used for the playing sequences of the film! He started playing piano when he was seven, studied classical music for ten years, graduated from Brooklyn College, served in the military and then joined a rock group called Brethren that recorded. Garson soon gained experience freelancing with a wide variety of performers including Mel Tormé, Thad Jones and Annette Peacock; he also studied with Lennie Tristano and had an important six-hour lesson with Bill Evans. Garson toured with Bowie during 1972-74, moved to Los Angeles and worked with Freddie Hubbard and Stanley Clarke (1978). He became a busy studio musician (both composing and performing prolifically) and in 1982 joined Free Flight, a group that switches back and forth between classical, straightahead jazz and funkier rhythms. Garson has recorded jazz as a leader for Contemporary (1979), Jazzhounds, Chase and Reference. —*Scott Yanow*

Avant Garson / Nov. 20, 1979-Nov. 21, 1979 / Contemporary ✦✦✦✦

Pianist Mike Garson's debut as a leader shows off his virtuosity and versatility on a set of unaccompanied solos. The music is consistently colorful and full of surprises, ranging from the melodic to bordering on the avant-garde. Highlights include a tribute to Chick Corea, "Over the Rainbow, " "Chopin Visits Brooklyn" and "Avant Gershwin." The Fantasy label is long overdue to release this underrated gem on CD. —*Scott Yanow*

● **Serendipity** / Apr. 9, 1986+Apr. 27, 1986 / Reference ✦✦✦✦

This is a mostly straightahead set featuring Mike Garson's piano in a variety of settings. He takes "I Should Care" and "My Romance" unaccompanied, duets with the brilliant flutist Jim Walker (his musical partner in Free Flight) on "My One and Only Love," plays three songs in a trio with bassist Stanley Clarke and drummer Billy Mintz, and leads a quintet comprising guitarist Peter Sprague, bassist Jim Lacefield, drummer Mintz and either altoist Gary Herbig or flutist Walker through three of his tricky but likable originals. An excellent all-around set, one of Mike Garson's best. —*Scott Yanow*

The Mystery Man / 1990 / Chase Music ✦✦

Keyboardist Mike Garson has proven through the years (on his own projects and in his work with Free Flight) that he is a masterful and highly versatile jazz musician. However this CD has only a few months of interest to jazz listeners, chiefly a loose and lighthearted "Brooklyn Blues" (which features an unusual trio consisting of Garson, altoist Eric Marienthal and cellist Greg Gottlieb) and a relatively straightahead duet with bassist Brian Bromberg on "Without a Song." Otherwise the release comprises mainly new agey ballads (tunes that set a mood but contain little development or depth) and a few upbeat pop originals. Garson is capable of much better. —*Scott Yanow*

The Oxnard Sessions, Vol. 1 / Aug. 1, 1990-Aug. 2, 1990 / Reference ✦✦✦✦

This is a strictly acoustic set by pianist Mike Garson who has had a diverse and productive career. Most of the tracks (which include four alternate takes) feature Garson in a trio with the underrated bassist Brian Bromberg and drummer Billy Mintz. Bob Shepherd (on tenor and alto) and trumpeter Bob Summers help out in a mostly supportive role on two numbers. Garson is the dominant player throughout, sounding a bit like McCoy Tyner on "Without Self," showing sly humor on "Nothin' to Do Blues," giving "Tenderly" (particularly the second version) an investigation worthy of Lennie Tristano, adding some unexpected twists and turns to

"Lady Be Good" and jamming over his own intense bassline in a duet with guitarist Rick Zunigar on "Solar." Recommended. —*Scott Yanow*

The Oxnard Sessions, Vol. 2 / Aug. 18, 1992-Aug. 19, 1992 / Reference ✦✦✦

Mike Garson has invested in star power to punch up *The Oxnard Sessions, Vol. 2.* The disc features a smaller group (piano/bass/drums/sax) and gives Garson a lot more solo room this time out. Drummer Ralph Humphrey shows more facility with a backbeat than Billy Mintz, who does appear on one alternate take. Saxophonist Eric Marienthal, a powerhouse type whose spurts and squeals add some excitement to even his most shrill and pop-oriented solos, also gets room to show his talents. The selections are more jazz and standard-oriented than before, and Garson and his mates demonstrate much more integrity than at any time on the previous release. —*Ron Wynn*

A Gershwin Fantasia / Aug. 23, 1992 / Reference ✦✦✦

Screen Themes '93 / 1993 / Discovery ✦✦

Screenthemes '94 / 1994 / Discovery ✦✦

George Garzone

b. Boston, MA
Tenor Saxophone, Soprano Saxophone/ Post-Bop

A powerful tenor saxophonist whose adventurous flights with his longtime band the Fringe have made him a legend in the Boston area, George Garzone has spent most of his life as a jazz educator. He began on the tenor when he was six, played in a family band and attended music school in Boston. Garzone first formed his trio the Fringe (a group that in the mid-'90s also included founding member Bob Gullotti on drums and bassist John Lockwood) back in 1972. In addition Garzone has guested in many situations, touring Europe with Jamaaladeen Tacuma and gigging with Danilo Perez, Joe Lovano, Jack DeJohnette, Rachel Z and John Patitucci among others. In 1995 he recorded a fine tribute to Stan Getz on NYC called *Alone.* —*Scott Yanow*

Alone / Aug. 22, 1995 / NYC ✦✦✦

● **Four's and Two's** / Apr. 8, 1996-Apr. 9, 1996 / NYC ✦✦✦✦

On all but two numbers—the somber "In Memory of Deanne Nichols" and "To My Papa," which are ballad features for the leader—George Garzone generously uses fellow tenor Joe Lovano as a co-leader throughout his CD. The two talented players blend together quite well (having carved out their own voices from Sonny Rollins, Joe Henderson and other modern stylists), shooting out some fireworks on the title cut, which is based on "Airegin." Of the other more memorable selections, "Have You Met Miss Jones" is given a countermelody worthy of Lennie Tristano; Garzone and Lovano both switch to soprano on the humorously titled "Snow Place Like Home"; and they take "In a Sentimental Mood" as a showcase for their two tenors sans rhythm. Although not particularly innovative, this sax summit is easily enjoyable and finds both George Garzone and Joe Lovano in top form. —*Scott Yanow*

Charles Gayle

b. Feb. 28, 1939, Buffalo, NY
Tenor Saxophone / Free Jazz, Avant-Garde

The logical successor to Albert Ayler (circa 1965), Charles Gayle is a high energy player whose improvisations are filled with extreme emotions and speechlike screams. He did not emerge in the avant-garde scene until the mid-'80s, making his recording debut with three albums cut for Silkheart in 1988 that were cut within a five-day period (April 10-14). Gayle, who recorded frequently for the Knitting Factory label starting in 1992 (he has also made CDs for Black Saint and Victor), is a ferocious tenor player who in recent times has also been playing bass clarinet and fairly basic piano in addition to taking some eccentric vocals full of strange right-wing preaching. Charles Gayle is certainly a talent not to be taken lightly. —*Scott Yanow*

Always Born / Apr. 10, 1988-Apr. 11, 1988 / Silkheart ✦✦✦

Homeless / Apr. 13, 1988-Apr. 14, 1988 / Silkheart ✦✦✦✦

Spirits Before / Apr. 13, 1988-Apr. 14, 1988 / Silkheart ✦✦✦

● **Repent** / 1992 / Knitting Factory ✦✦✦✦✦

There is absolutely no one currently playing tenor (or any other saxophone) coming close to making the kind of music created by Charles Gayle. While it's reminiscent of Albert Ayler's energetic, twisting 1960s free dates, Gayle's saxophone acrobatics and stamina are astonishing. This two-song CD was recorded live and features one number that runs 23 minutes; it's the short tune. "Jesus Christ and Scripture," the second piece, proceeds for over 50 minutes, much of that featuring Gayle's honks, bleats, turnarounds, moans and anguished cries on tenor. After listening closely to this disc, its lack of repetition and gimmickry is commendable.

It's certainly not for all (or even most tastes), but those who listen fairly and intently to Charles Gayle will be rewarded. —*Ron Wynn*

More Live / Jan. 1, 1993-Feb. 22, 1993 / Knitting Factory ✦✦✦✦✦

Tenor saxophonist Charles Gayle plays with such fury and intensity that it seems he won't make it through the performances featured on these two discs. They spotlight his quartet during concerts. Hearing Gayle's overtones, screams, and blistering solos, backed by equally spirited playing from bassists Vattel Cherry and William Parker, and either Michael Wimberly or Marc Edwards on drums, it's easy to forget you're hearing it as they played it, with little pacing or variance in volume. It's impossible not to remember the 1960s and '70s free and loft jazz schools, but it's also appropriate to emphasize that Gayle doesn't sound like anyone else currently active and deserves significant attention beyond tiny jazz publications and sympathetic, but small, audiences. —*Ron Wynn*

Raining Fire / Jan. 21, 1993-Jan. 22, 1993 / Silkheart ✦✦✦✦

Translation / Jan. 21, 1993-Jan. 22, 1993 / Silkheart ✦✦✦✦

Consecration / Apr. 17, 1993-Apr. 18, 1993 / Black Saint ✦✦✦

Kingdom Come / 1994 / Knitting Factory ✦✦✦

Testaments / Jun. 22, 1995-Jul. 11, 1995 / Knitting Factory ✦✦✦

Gayle's fourth release for the Knitting Factory label finds him backed by longtime drummer Michael Wimberley and bassist Wilber Morris. —*Jason Ankeny*

Unto I Am / Nov. 1, 1995 / Victo ✦✦✦

Herb Geller

b. Nov. 2, 1928, Los Angeles, CA

Alto Saxophone, Soprano Saxophone / Bop, Hard Bop

Herb Geller is a survivor of the Los Angeles jazz scene of the 1950s who is playing better than ever in the mid-'90s. Geller played in 1946 with Joe Venuti's Orchestra and in 1949 he traveled to New York to play with Claude Thornhill. In 1951 he moved back to L.A. and married the excellent bop pianist Lorraine Walsh. Geller was a fixture in L.A., playing with Billy May (1952), Maynard Ferguson, Shorty Rogers, Bill Holman and Chet Baker among others, jamming with Clifford Brown and Max Roach and leading a quartet that included his wife (1954-55). Lorraine Geller's sudden death in 1958 eventually resulted in the altoist deciding to leave the country to escape his grief. He played with Benny Goodman off and on between 1958-61, spent time in Brazil and in 1962 moved to Berlin. Geller worked in German radio orchestras for 30 years, played in European big bands and continued to grow as a musician although he was pretty much forgotten in the US. From the early '90s on, Herb Geller has begun returning to the States on a more regular basis and he recently recorded a tribute to Al Cohn for Hep. Geller also recorded as a leader in the 1950s for EmArcy, Jubilee and Atco and in the 1980s and '90s for Enja, Fresh Sound and V.S.O.P. —*Scott Yanow*

Herb Geller Plays / Aug. 6, 1954 + Aug. 9, 1954 / EmArcy ✦✦✦

Other than four titles from a year before, this LP contains altoist Herb Geller's first recordings as a leader. Cut during a period when Herb was based in Los Angeles and regularly working with his wife, the talented but short-lived pianist Lorraine Geller, the music also has either Curtis Counce or Leroy Vinnegar on bass and Lawrence Marable or Eldridge Freeman on drums. Herb Geller was already in his early prime and contributed six originals. The band also performs one of Lorraine's tunes, plus five standards, all in swinging and boppish style. This LP (which has not been reissued lately) is well worth searching for. —*Scott Yanow*

Outpost Incident / Aug. 19, 1955+Aug. 22, 1955 / EmArcy ✦✦✦✦

Last available as a Trip LP in the 1980s, this is an excellent bop set with heated playing from altoist Herb Geller and trumpeter Conte Candoli. The Zoot Sims-inspired tenorman Ziggy Vines (whose only other recording was during Clifford Brown's final gig) holds his own, and the rhythm section (pianist Lorraine Geller, either Red Mitchell or Leroy Vinnegar on bass and drummer Lawrence Marable) is perfect for the time period. The music, a mixture of standards (including "Crazy He Calls Me" and "You'd Be So Nice to Come Home To") and Geller originals, swings hard and contains plenty of exciting solos. Hopefully, Polygram will eventually get around to reissuing their three valuable Herb Geller sets. —*Scott Yanow*

That Geller Feller / Mar. 14, 1957 / Fresh Sound ✦✦✦✦

Stax of Sax / 1958 / Fresh Sound ✦✦✦✦

This somewhat obscure recording by the bop-oriented altoist Herb Geller features him in a 1958 quintet with vibraphonist Victor Feldman, pianist Walter Norris, bassist Leroy Vinnegar and drummer Anthony Vazley. Other than a session for Atco, this was Herb Geller's last American album until 1993; it would be 1975 before he recorded as a leader again. Geller is in fine form on three of his originals and two standards ("Change Partners" and "It Might as Well Be Spring"). Originally cut for Jubilee, this Fresh Sound CD is part of an extensive series that has brought back

many forgotten dates from the 1950s. Bop collectors will enjoy this one. —*Scott Yanow*

Rhythm and Reason / Jan. 13, 1975 / Discovery ✦

Hot House / Nov. 24, 1984 / Circle ✦✦✦✦

Other than one unfortunate set in 1975 (which was both quite commercial and rather confused), altoist Herb Geller did not record as a leader during 1960-83. However, he worked steadily in Germany for decades and continued to improve as a player (even though the jazz world temporarily forgot about him). For his first set after all of that time, Geller is heard live with a German rhythm section (pianist Hartmut Sperl, bassist Bernd Wolf and drummer Achim Brauer) performing five bebop standards, plus Antonio Carlos Jobim's "Triste." The altoist sounds enthusiastic and consistently creative during this somewhat rare but recommended European album. —*Scott Yanow*

Birdland Stomp / Jan. 24-25, 1986 / Fresh Sound ✦✦✦

Jazz Song Book / Dec. 1988 / Enja ✦✦✦

Altoist Herb Geller worked on putting his life story into a musical play for many years. This early attempt finds him performing nine original songs that he had planned at the time to use in the as yet unproduced show. With the assistance of pianist Walter Norris, guitarist John Schroder, bassist Mike Richmond and drummer Adam Nussbaum, Geller (on alto and soprano) sounds fine, but his solos are actually on a higher level than the generally forgettable instrumentals. This CD is not without interest, but has been overshadowed by Herb Geller's superior later recordings. —*Scott Yanow*

● **Herb Geller Quartet** / Aug. 5, 1993-Aug. 6, 1993 / V.S.O.P. ✦✦✦✦✦

This quartet outing with pianist Tom Ranier, bassist John Leitham and drummer Louis Bellson is one of altoist Herb Geller's finest recordings. Geller, whose long period in Europe has resulted in him being somewhat forgotten in the US, has actually improved through the years and was even stronger in the mid-'90s than he had been in the mid-'50s. For this date he contributes five originals (including a tribute to Lenny Bruce "Stand-Up Comic" during which Geller sings) and performs six mostly lesser-known standards, highlighted by "The Peacocks" which has its composer Jimmy Rowles sitting in on piano. This CD is easily recommended to bop collectors for it finds Herb Geller at the peak of his powers. —*Scott Yanow*

Playing Jazz / Jan. 16, 1995-Jan. 20, 1995 / Fresh Sound ✦✦✦✦

Plays Al Cohn Songbook / May 7, 1996 / Hep ✦✦✦✦

The Georgians

f. 1922, **db.** 1929

Group / Classic Jazz, Big Band, Swing

The first small group to be drawn out of a big band and exist interdependently was the Virginians, which included members of the Paul Whiteman Orchestra in the early '20s. The second one was the Georgians, musicians who were part of Paul Specht's commercial big band. Based at the Hotel Alamac, each night when the main ballroom closed and the regular job was over, the Georgians performed for dancers at the Alamac's nightclub, the Congo Room. The septet had a talented and versatile trumpet soloist in Frank Guarente, advanced and surprisingly swinging arrangements by pianist Arthur Schutt, two fine reed players among the four horns (which at one point included trombonist Russ Morgan) and a top drummer in Chauncey Morehouse. Starting in December 1922, the Georgians recorded an excellent series of sides (the first 24 of which have been reissued on a Retrieval CD) that lasted into 1924. The Georgians were a hit when they visited England with Specht in 1923. The group broke up in 1924, but Guarente organized a New Georgians band and toured Europe from 1924-27, recording six titles (under the trumpeter's name) in 1926. Back in the US, the name of the Georgians was used for a few unrelated studio recording groups from 1924-29, including two titles that featured Red Nichols in 1925. British trumpeter Nat Gonella used the Georgians name in the 1930s because of the popularity of his version of "Georgia On My Mind." —*Scott Yanow*

The Georgians / Nov. 29, 1922-Nov. 17, 1923 / Retrieval ✦✦✦✦✦

After the Virginians (a group whose members were drawn from the early Paul Whiteman Orchestra), the Georgians were the first band-within-a-band in jazz. The sextet/septet was taken out of the more commercial Paul Specht Orchestra. This 1997 reissue CD has the first 24 recordings of this underrated group, and it is notable in several ways. Pianist Arthur Schutt's arrangements are fairly inventive for the period, the rhythm section (which also includes drummer Chauncey Morehouse) is subtle, and trumpeter Frank Guarente (the band's musical director) is quite effective both as the lead in the ensembles and in his short solos. Although not as significant as the New Orleans Rhythm Kings or King Oliver's Creole Jazz Band, the Georgians were one of the finest hot dance/jazz bands of the era. Jazz historians and collectors of early 1920s music are well advised to pick up this highly enjoyable set. —*Scott Yanow*

Jane Getz

b. 1948
Piano / Hard Bop, Post-Bop

Jane Getz made a strong but brief impression while playing in New York in the mid- to late '60s and then seemed to disappear until she emerged in Los Angeles in the mid-'90s. The truth is that she never left music, but took a long hiatus from jazz. Considered a prodigy as a child, Jane switched from classical music to jazz when she was nine. She lived in Los Angeles and San Francisco and then at the age of 15 dropped out of high school and traveled to New York City, where within hours she was playing with Pony Poindexter. Getz worked with the who's-who of jazz during her eight years in New York, most notably with Charles Mingus, Stan Getz (unrelated), Rahsaan Roland Kirk, Charles Lloyd and Pharoah Sanders (with whom she recorded for ESP). In the early '70s, Getz moved back to L.A. and became a studio musician. She was signed to RCA under the name Mother Hen and played country music, in addition to appearing on many rock and pop albums (including with Ringo Starr, Harry Nilsson and John Lennon). After 20 years outside of jazz, Getz started playing jazz gigs in Los Angeles, often teaming up with Dale Fielder, where it was obvious that her improvising skills were still very much intact. In 1996, she finally recorded her first jazz album as a leader, *No Relation* (Clarion Jazz). —*Scott Yanow*

● **No Relation** / Jun. 26, 1996-Jun. 27, 1996 / Clarion Jazz ◆◆◆◆◆
Pianist Jane Getz (yes, she is not related to Stan Getz) caused a stir in the mid-'60s when she performed and recorded with Charles Mingus and Pharoah Sanders, even gigging with the other Getz. Unfortunately a few years later she dropped out of jazz altogether and became an obscure legend. However unknown to much of the jazz world, Getz spent the next two decades living in Los Angeles, playing country music and rock quite successfully, recording under the name of Mother Hen and performing behind a variety of pop stars. In the 1990s, she finally returned to jazz. On *No Relation*, the pianist's long overdue recording debut in jazz as a leader, Jane Getz shows that her improvising talents had grown through the years. Seven of the ten songs are her originals (all but "You Don't Know What Love Is," a swinging trio workout on "Come Sunday" and Dale Fielder's "J. Reese Waltz") and the music falls into the area of advanced hard bop. Joined on the majority of the selections by trumpeter Brian Swartz and either Dale Fielder (who plays the uncredited soprano on "Cowboy Music"), Doug Webb or Phil Vieux on tenor, bassist Darek Oleszkiewicz and either Fritz Wise or Russell Bizzett on drums, Getz has an opportunity to accompany the younger horn players before constantly stealing solo honors. Mixing together elements of Bud Powell and McCoy Tyner, Jane Getz proves to be a real powerhouse with consistently inventive ideas. Her release is highly recommended. —*Scott Yanow*

Stan Getz

b. Feb. 2, 1927, Philadelphia, PA, d. Jun. 6, 1991, Malibu, CA
Tenor Saxophone / Cool, Bossa Nova, Post-Bop

One of the all-time great tenor saxophonists, Stan Getz was known as "The Sound" because he had one of the most beautiful tones ever heard. Getz, whose main early influence was Lester Young, grew to be a major influence himself and to his credit he never stopped evolving.

Stan Getz had the opportunity to play in a variety of major swing big bands while a teenager due to the World War II draft. He was with Jack Teagarden (1943) when he was just 16 and this was followed by stints with Stan Kenton (1944-45), Jimmy Dorsey (1945) and Benny Goodman (1945-46); he soloed on a few records with BG. Getz, who had his recording debut as a leader in July 1946 with four titles, became famous during his period with Woody Herman's Second Herd (1947-49), soloing (along with Zoot Sims, Herbie Steward and Serge Chaloff) on the original version of "Four Brothers" and having his sound well-featured on the ballad "Early Autumn." After leaving Herman, Getz was (with the exception of some tours with Jazz at the Philharmonic) a leader for the rest of his life.

During the early '50s Getz broke away from the Lester Young style to form his own musical identity and he was soon among the most popular of all jazzmen. He discovered Horace Silver in 1950 and used him in his quartet for several months. After touring Sweden in 1951 he formed an exciting quintet that co-featured guitarist Jimmy Raney; their interplay on uptempo tunes and tonal blend on ballads was quite memorable. Getz's playing helped Johnny Smith have a hit in "Moonlight in Vermont," during 1953-54 Bob Brookmeyer made his group a quintet and, despite some drug problems during the decade, Getz was a constant pollwinner. After spending 1958-60 in Europe, the tenorman returned to the US and recorded his personal favorite album, *Focus*, with arranger Eddie Sauter's Orchestra. Then

in Feb. 1962 Getz helped usher in the bossa nova era by recording *Jazz Samba* with Charlie Byrd; their rendition of "Desafinado" was a big hit. During the next year Getz made bossa nova flavored albums with Gary McFarland's big band, Luiz Bonfa and Laurindo Almeida, but it was *Getz/Gilberto* (a collaboration with Antonio Carlos Jobim and Joao Gilberto) that was his biggest seller, thanks in large part to "The Girl from Ipanema" (featuring the vocals of Astrud and Joao Gilberto).

Stan Getz could have spent the next decade sticking to bossa nova but instead he de-emphasized the music and chose to play more challenging jazz. His regular group during this era was a pianoless quartet with vibraphonist Gary Burton, he recorded with Bill Evans (1964), played throughout the 1965 Eddie Sauter soundtrack for *Mickey One* and made the classic album *Sweet Rain* (1967) with Chick Corea. Although not all of Getz's recordings from the 1966-80 period are essential, he proved that he was not shy to take chances. *Dynasty* with organist Eddie Louiss (1971), *Captain Marvel* with Chick Corea (1972) and *The Peacocks* with Jimmy Rowles (1975) are high points. After utilizing pianist Joanne Brackeen in his 1977 quartet, Getz explored some aspects of fusion with his next unit which featured keyboardist Andy La Verne. Getz even used an echoplex on a couple of songs but, despite some misfires, most of his dates with this unit are worthwhile. However purists were relieved when he signed with Concord in 1981 and started using a purely acoustic backup trio on most dates. Getz's sidemen in later years included pianists Lou Levy, Mitchell Forman, Jim McNeely and Kenny Barron. His final recording, 1991's *People Time*, (despite some shortness in the tenor's breath) is a brilliant duet set with Barron.

Throughout his career Stan Getz recorded as a leader for Savoy, Spotlite, Prestige, Roost, Verve, MGM, Victor, Columbia, Steeple Chase, Concord, Sonet, Black Hawk, A&M and EmArcy among other labels (not to mention sessions with Lionel Hampton, Dizzy Gillespie and Gerry Mulligan) and there are dozens of worthy records by the tenor currently available on CD. —*Scott Yanow*

Opus de Bop / Dec. 12, 1945-May 5, 1949/ Savoy ◆◆◆
Some of tenor saxophonist Stan Getz's earliest recordings are included on this well-conceived LP. Getz displays a harder sound than one might expect on sextet sides with trombonist Kai Winding and trumpeter Shorty Rogers from late 1945 and on four selections with a quartet from mid-1946. The final four selections (from May 1949) are more typical as Getz (along with fellow tenors Al Cohn and Zoot Sims) plays hard-swinging cool bop; the three tenors can barely be told apart. Bop collectors will want this interesting music. —*Scott Yanow*

Early Stan / Mar. 14, 1949-Apr. 23, 1953 / Prestige ◆◆◆◆◆
This two-LP set includes seven sessions from 1949-50 and one from 1953 that feature the great tenor saxophonist Stan Getz. Getz is heard with a Terry Gibbs septet, in quartets with either pianist Al Haig or Tony Aless, with Haig in a sextet that features vocals from Blossom Dearie, on a couple of collaborations with guitarist Jimmy Raney and in a classic if odd date with four other tenors (Al Cohn, Allen Eager, Brew Moore and Zoot Sims), all of whom sounded identical at the time. This two-fer (which contains several alternate takes) gives one a fine overview into the early days of Stan Getz. —*Scott Yanow*

Stan Getz / Apr. 8, 1949-Feb. 8, 1958 / Prestige ◆◆◆◆◆
A complement to its fellow two-fer *Early Stan*, this two-LP set finds Getz heading quartets from 1949-50 that co-star either pianist Al Haig or Tony Aless, and performing two titles from 1949 with four other tenors (Zoot Sims, Al Cohn, Brew Moore and Allen Eager), all of whom were so influenced by Lester Young at the time that they sound identical. The second half of this set is a reissue of *Stan Getz with Cal Tjader*, a sextet set from 1956 with vibraphonist Tjader, pianist Vince Guaraldi, guitarist Eddie Duran, bassist Scott La Faro and drummer Billy Higgins. Throughout, Getz is in excellent form, making this a recommended set. —*Scott Yanow*

The Brothers / Apr. 8, 1949 / Original Jazz Classics ◆◆◆

Prezervation / Jun. 21, 1949-Jul. 28, 1949 / Original Jazz Classics ◆◆◆

Quartets / Jun. 21, 1949-Apr. 14, 1950 / Original Jazz Classics ◆◆◆◆

The Complete Roost Recordings / May 12, 1950-Dec. 16, 1954 / Blue Note ◆◆◆◆
The Complete Roost Recordings is a three-disc, 59-track box set that contains all of the recordings Stan Getz made for the Roost Record label in the '50s. The set includes all of his officially released sessions—including the date led by guitarist Johnny Smith, the live performances with Count Basie, and a full disc of live performances with his quintet—as well as many unreleased and alternate takes. Roost was the first label Getz recorded for as a leader, and what's surprising about these sessions is how mature he sounds here. He had already arrived at his full, rich tone and was able to improvise with skill and grace. That's what makes this box set so rewarding—it's not only historically important, but it offers a wealth of excellent music. —*Leo Stanley*

Roost Quartets / May 17, 1950-Mar. 1, 1951 / Roulette ✦✦✦✦✦
After leaving Woody Herman's Orchestra, tenor saxophonist Stan Getz became one of the leaders of the "cool school" due to his attractive light tone and his strong jazz abilities. This CD features his 1950-51 quartets. On the first seven selections, Getz is accompanied by pianist Al Haig, bassist Tommy Potter and drummer Roy Haynes; they play such numbers as "On the Alamo," "Yesterdays" and the appealing "Hershey Bar." By late 1950 Getz had a new band, a rhythm section that he had discovered and immediately hired in Connecticut. Although bassist Joe Calloway and drummer Walt Bolden are obscure, pianist Horace Silver later became a major star. On his recording debut (15 performances including three alternate takes), Silver displays a style that was already recognizable and fit in perfectly with Getz. —*Scott Yanow*

☆ **The Complete Recordings of the Stan Getz Quintet with Jimmy Raney** / Aug. 15, 1951-Apr. 23, 1953 / Mosaic ✦✦✦✦✦
This limited-edition three-CD set will be hard to acquire but it is a gem. Tenor saxophonist Stan Getz and guitarist Jimmy Raney had very complementary cool-toned but hard-swinging styles. Their gig at Storyville in Boston resulted in some classic music that, along with five studio sessions, is included in this box. The supporting cast includes pianists Al Haig, Horace Silver, Duke Jordan and Hall Overton; the music was originally recorded for Roost, Clef, Norgran and Prestige. This essential set is filled with exciting performances from Stan Getz when he was first becoming a highly influential force in jazz. —*Scott Yanow*

Live 1952, Vol. 1 / Apr. 15, 1952-Aug. 9, 1952 / Jazz & Jazz ✦✦✦
This Italian import features tenor saxophonist Stan Getz in rare Birdland appearances from April 15, 1952 (with a quintet including pianist Horace Silver, guitarist Jimmy Raney, bassist Charles Mingus and drummer Connie Kay) and Aug. 9, 1952 (with Raney, pianist Duke Jordan, Mingus and drummer Phil Brown). Getz is in excellent form on these eight selections which are highlighted by "Potter's Luck," "Parker 51" (which is really "Cherokee") and "Move." Getz and Raney had a special chemistry and all of their recordings are excellent but this LP will be difficult to locate. —*Scott Yanow*

Move! Live 1952-1953 / Aug. 7, 1952-Jan. 15, 1953 / Natasha ✦✦✦✦
This CD is highly recommended not so much for its historic value (guitarist Jimmy Raney, Stan Getz's most stimulating partner during this period, is absent) but for the consistently stimulating playing of tenor saxophonist Getz. These radio broadcasts from Birdland are well-recorded, Getz is in top form and his supporting cast (pianist Duke Jordan, bassist Bill Crow, drummer Kenny Clarke and on three songs trumpeter Dick Sherman) is excellent. Stan Getz, whether coming up with surprising variations on "Moonlight in Vermont" or romping during the title cut, comes up with many colorful solos. —*Scott Yanow*

The Best of the Verve Years, Vol. 1 / Dec. 12, 1952-Mar. 21, 1967 / Verve ✦✦✦✦
This two-CD sampler is most highly recommended for listeners not familiar with Stan Getz's recordings of the 1950s and '60s. Starting with a version of "Stella by Starlight" that co-stars guitarist Jimmy Raney, this set matches Getz's cool tenor with such artists as trumpeters Dizzy Gillespie and Conte Candoli, trombonist J.J. Johnson, baritonist Gerry Mulligan, pianists Oscar Peterson, Bill Evans and Chick Corea, valve trombonist Bob Brookmeyer and vibraphonist Gary Burton. Also included are his two main bossa nova hits "Desafinado" and "The Girl from Ipanema" along with a couple of tracks from Getz's highly-rated *Focus* album. It's a fine overview of the great tenor's middle years. —*Scott Yanow*

Plays / Dec. 12, 1952-Jan. 14, 1954 / Verve ✦✦✦✦
Tenor saxophonist Stan Getz is in excellent form playing with one of his finest groups, a quintet with guitarist Jimmy Raney and pianist Duke Jordan. Although the music does not quite reach the excitement level of the Getz-Raney Storyville session, this music (particularly the ballads) really shows off the tenor's appealing tone. This CD is rounded out by four titles that Getz cut with a quartet in 1954 that co-starred pianist Jimmy Rowles. —*Scott Yanow*

Life in Jazz: A Musical Biography / Dec. 29, 1952-Mar. 6, 1991 / Verve ✦✦✦
This sampler of Stan Getz's Verve recordings was released at the same time (in 1996) as a definitive biography also titled *A Life in Jazz*. The 11 selections are all excellent but would have been more effective if released in chronological order. There are three numbers from the 1950s, five from the '60s, one from 1987 and two from 1991 including a version of "Night and Day" that is taken from the tenor's final recording session. Highlights include "Billie's Bounce" (a 1957 collaboration with trombonist J.J. Johnson), "Corcovado" from the *Getz/Gilberto* album and "Summertime" with Gary Burton; there is also a guest shot with Abbey Lincoln. All of the selections are available elsewhere but this CD serves as a good introduction to Stan Getz's musical magic. —*Scott Yanow*

Stan Getz at the Shrine / Nov. 8, 1954 / Norgran ✦✦✦✦
Tenor Stan Getz and valve-trombonist Bob Brookmeyer made a mutually beneficial team. Although they had not played together all that much in 1954 (Brookm-

eyer had left Getz's band earlier in the year to join the Gerry Mulligan Quartet), the strong musical communication between the two horns during this CD reissue is obvious. Eight of the ten selections are from a live concert (with pianist John Williams, bassist Bill Anthony and drummer Art Mardigan) while the final two numbers (on what was originally a pair of LPs) were cut in the studio the following day with the same personnel except that Frank Isola was on drums. Highlights of this cool-toned bop music (which, in addition to the solos, has many exciting ensembles) include "Lover Man," "Pernod," "Tasty Pudding" and "It Don't Mean a Thing." —*Scott Yanow*

Hamp and Getz / Aug. 1, 1955 / Verve ✦✦✦✦✦
The cool tenor of Stan Getz and the extroverted vibraphonist Lionel Hampton might have seemed like an unlikely matchup but once again producer Norman Granz showed his talents at combining complementary talents. Hampton and Getz really battle hard on "Cherokee" and "Jumpin' at the Woodside" and, other than a ballad medley, the other selections on this CD (which include two previously unreleased performances) are also heated. Classic music from two of the best. —*Scott Yanow*

East of the Sun: The West Coast Sessions / Aug. 9, 1955-Aug. 2, 1957 / Verve ✦✦✦✦
Four long-out-of-print Stan Getz albums (*West Coast Jazz, Stan Getz and the Cool Sounds, The Steamer* and *Award Winner*) plus two selections originally on samplers and 13 previously unissued performances (mostly alternate takes) are reissued on this three-CD set (the packaging is so ingenious that the three-fer takes up as little space as a single CD). Some songs are preceded by a bit of studio chatter and false starts, an unnecessary frivolity, although the alternates are very good to have. In all cases, the great tenor is joined by pianist Lou Levy and bassist Leroy Vinnegar; trumpeter Conte Candoli is on the first seven selections, while the drum chair is shared by Shelly Manne (in 1955) and Stan Levey (during 1956-57). While Lou Levy is excellent both as a quiet bop soloist and as a sympathetic accompanist on the frequently cooking music, it is for Stan Getz's glorious sound and consistently creative (yet melodic) ideas that this reissue is recommended. —*Scott Yanow*

The Best of the West Coast Sessions / Aug. 10, 1955-Aug. 2, 1957 / Verve ✦✦✦
In 1996 when Verve released a three-CD set that fully documented six sessions from the 1955-57 period by tenor saxophonist Stan Getz, they also came out with this one-CD sampler. Most Getz fans will prefer the former, which has 37 performances (as opposed to the latter's ten), but many of the main highlights are on this disc, including a heated rendition of "Shine," "Four," "A Handful of Stars" and "East of the Sun." The Lou Levy Trio and (on a few numbers) trumpeter Conte Candoli work quite well with the cool-toned tenor. —*Scott Yanow*

In Stockholm / Dec. 1955 / Verve ✦✦✦
This excellent LP finds Stan Getz, who had just recovered from a serious illness, in fine form playing standards with a Swedish rhythm section that includes the talented pianist Bengt Hallberg. One of the lesser-known Getz dates, the great tenor (who was 30 at the time) clearly inspired the quietly swinging rhythm section. —*Scott Yanow*

☆ **Stan Getz and J.J. Johnson at the Opera House** / Sep. 29, 1957-Oct. 7, 1957 / Verve ✦✦✦✦✦
On two Jazz at the Philharmonic concerts, tenor saxophonist Stan Getz and trombonist J.J. Johnson (backed by the Oscar Peterson Trio plus drummer Connie Kay) performed an identical repertoire during the two sets of music, one recorded in mono and the other in stereo. All of the music from those dates (with the exception of one number left out due to lack of space) is included on this very exciting release: two versions apiece of "Billie's Bounce," "My Funny Valentine," "Crazy Rhythm" and "Blues in the Closet" plus one try at "Yesterdays" and "It Never Entered My Mind." Surprisingly Oscar Peterson and guitarist Herb Ellis do not solo at all but Getz and Johnson make a perfect combination and are in peak form. Bebop at its best, it has plenty of uptempo jamming and no shortage of ideas. —*Scott Yanow*

Stan Getz and the Oscar Peterson Trio / Oct. 10, 1957 / Verve ✦✦✦✦
This very enjoyable CD for the first time gathers together all of the music recorded at this timeless session. Tenor saxophonist Stan Getz is joined by pianist Oscar Peterson, guitarist Herb Ellis and bassist Ray Brown for a well-rounded set filled with appealing standards, three Getz originals (two of which are blues) and a fine ballad medley. Everyone is in top form and Getz clearly enjoyed playing with Peterson. —*Scott Yanow*

Live in Europe / 1958 / Jazz Anthology ✦✦✦
Tenor-great Stan Getz spent several years in Europe in the late '50s. This difficult-to-find French import features Getz in a quartet/quintet with pianist Martial Solal, bassist Pierre Michelot, drummer Kenny Clarke and, on two numbers, guitarist Jimmy Gourley. The results are predictably excellent with such songs as "All God's

Children Got Rhythm," "Broadway" and "East of the Sun" among the high points. —*Scott Yanow*

Stan Getz with Cal Tjader / Feb. 8, 1958 / Original Jazz Classics ✦✦✦
W/ Cal Tjader. 1987 reissue, super Latin-jazz summit. Billy Higgins fits in nicely on drums. —*Ron Wynn*

Stan Meets Chet / Feb. 16, 1958 / Verve ✦✦✦
Tenor saxophonist Stan Getz and trumpeter Chet Baker never particularly liked each other and, even though they had musically compatible styles, they only worked together briefly in three periods. Their mutual hostility can be felt in subtle ways on this session which has been reissued on CD. Getz ignores Baker's attempt to state the melody of "I'll Remember April" and he plays it himself several bars after. The two horns do not meet at all on the ballad medley and, since Baker sits out on "Jordu," they only play together on two of the four performances. Getz battles a squeaky reed on "I'll Remember April" and Baker seems a bit subpar in general although he really digs in on "Half-Breed Apache" (a very fast "Cherokee"). So overall this CD (which also includes pianist Jodie Christian, bassist Victor Sproles and drummer Marshall Thompson), even with some good moments, does not live up to its potential. —*Scott Yanow*

Jazz Giants '58 / Aug. 1, 1958 / Verve ✦✦✦✦
This LP contains more than its share of brilliant music. Tenorman Stan Getz meets up with baritonist Gerry Mulligan, trumpeter Harry "Sweets" Edison, the Oscar Peterson Trio and drummer Louie Bellson for three standards and a lyrical ballad medley but it is the well-constructed solos on the blues "Chocolate Sundae" (during which every note seems to fit perfectly) that are most memorable. —*Scott Yanow*

Stockholm Sessions '58 / Aug. 26, 1958-Sep. 16, 1958 / Dragon ✦✦✦✦
This double LP from the Swedish label Dragon is not only very attractive but the music is both rare and quite rewarding. Taken from Stan Getz's stay in Europe, the great tenor is heard with some of Sweden's top jazz musicians of the era including trombonist Ake Persson, expatriate trumpeter Benny Bailey, baritonist Lars Gullin and either Bengt Hallberg or Jan Johansson. The 18 octet/nonet performances include eight alternate takes and find Getz's cool tenor sound fitting in perfectly with the Swedes. —*Scott Yanow*

In Denmark 1958-59 / Dec. 7, 1958-Oct. 25, 1959 / Olufsen ✦✦✦
In late 1958 Stan Getz lived in Denmark and these recordings, cut at live concerts, are the result. The great tenor is heard with three different quartets (three songs feature expatriate Oscar Pettiford on bass) and featured with Ib Glindemann's Orchestra. The music (all jazz standards) is consistently excellent with the cool tenor clearly rejuvenated by his years in Europe. —*Scott Yanow*

Jazz Collector Edition / Dec. 7, 1958-Jan. 29, 1977 / LaserLight ✦✦✦
The packaging faults to this CD (which is part of an extensive reissue series) are rather unfortunate. There is no personnel listing, the recording dates are not given, the breezy liner notes are largely irrelevant and inaccurate (Stan Getz did not spend "two important years with Stan Kenton" nor form his own group directly after leaving Kenton, two songs are mislabelled ("Stan's Tune" is actually "Con Alma" and "Blues in Suburbia" should be called "Meadows") and the program at 44 minutes is the length of an LP. Despite those problems, this CD is generally worthwhile. Tenor saxophonist Stan Getz is heard accompanied on three separate occasions by large European ensembles (the Danish Radio Big Band and the orchestras of Ib Glindemann and Kurt Edelhagen) and he sounds consistently inspired. The first four numbers (highlighted by "Yesterdays" and "Old Folks") are from January 29, 1977, the versions of "Don't Get Around Much Anymore," "Cherokee" and "My Funny Valentine" are from December 7, 1958 (performed during the tenor's long period overseas) and the two mistitled songs date from October 23, 1971. Getz's beautiful tone, lyrical style and ability to swing at any tempo (along with the rarity of the performances) should make this CD of strong interest (despite the packaging) to his many fans. —*Scott Yanow*

Cool Velvet & Voices / Mar. 1960-Dec. 2, 1966 / Verve ✦✦
Two of tenor saxophonist Stan Getz's lesser-known (and least significant) albums are combined on this single Verve CD. Just prior to recording his bossa nova hits, Getz is backed by a string section arranged by Russ Garcia in 1960 on a variety of melodic standards (the *Cool Velvet* portion of this disc) while in 1966 he is joined by both a string section and a vocal choir arranged by Claus Ogerman. Some of the latter performances border on muzak. Although Getz's tone sounds as beautiful as ever, no fire is lit under his playing and his accompaniment is difficult to sit through. —*Scott Yanow*

Stan Getz at Large, Vol. 1 / Jan. 14, 1960-Jan. 15, 1960 / Jazz Unlimited ✦✦✦✦
This music on this CD and the second volume was originally only available as a pair of limited-edition LPs overseas. What makes the first volume of these quartet sessions (with pianist Jan Johansson) special is that much of the material (including "Pammie's Tune," "I Like to Recognize the Tune" and the previously unissued "A New Town Is a Blue Town") is fresh and some of it is quite obscure. Even on "Night and Day" and Dave Brubeck's "In Your Own Sweet Way," Getz's playing is enthusiastic and full of surprising twists. —*Scott Yanow*

Stan Getz at Large, Vol. 2 / Jan. 14, 1960-Jan. 15, 1960 / Jazz Unlimited ✦✦✦✦
The second of two CDs recorded by Stan Getz while in Copenhagen finds the great tenor performing such fresh material as Johnny Mandel's "Just a Child," Harold Land's "Land's End" and "He Was Good to Me" in addition to two previously unreleased selections with a fine quartet featuring pianist Jan Johansson. These very obscure performances are well-recorded and should delight all Stan Getz fans. —*Scott Yanow*

☆ **Focus** / Jul. 1961-Oct. 1961 / Verve ✦✦✦✦✦
Stan Getz's personal favorite recording, this challenging session found the great tenor improvising over a big band performing seven songs composed and arranged by Eddie Sauter. Nothing was written out for Getz but he was up to the challenge, creating beautiful and logical statements, and interacting closely with the orchestra. Music worth hearing several times. —*Scott Yanow*

Stan Getz and Bob Brookmeyer / Sep. 12, 1961-Sep. 13, 1961 / Verve ✦✦✦✦
Shortly after returning to the US (following three years in Copenhagen) Stan Getz had a musical reunion with Bob Brookmeyer. As usual the cool-toned tenor blends in very well with the valve trombonist and, backed by a fine rhythm section (pianist Steve Kuhn, bassist John Neves and drummer Roy Haynes), they perform three Brookmeyer pieces (including one titled "Minuet Circa '61"), two standards and Buck Clayton's "Love Jumped Out." This little-known session is often quite memorable. —*Scott Yanow*

Jazz Samba / Feb. 13, 1962 / Verve ✦✦✦✦✦
This classic session which launched the bossa nova craze in the early '60s was originally recorded for Verve. The reissue from DCC Compact Classics improves the sound a bit and adds the shortened 45 version of "Desafinado" to the original program. The music, which matches Stan Getz's cool tenor with guitarist Charlie Byrd and his lightly swinging group, helped introduce Antonio Carlos Jobim's music to the US through the hit recordings of "Desafinado" and "One Note Samba." It's essential music, no matter in what format one acquires it. —*Scott Yanow*

☆ **The Bossa Nova Years (Girl from Ipanema)** / Feb. 13, 1962-Oct. 9, 1964 / Verve ✦✦✦✦✦
This five-LP box set (which has been reissued on CD) contains nearly all of Stan Getz's classic bossa nova sessions, five wonderful yet diverse LPs (*Jazz Samba, Big Band Bossa Nova, Jazz Samba Encore, Stan Getz/Laurindo Almedia* and *Getz/Gilberto*). The cool-toned tenor is heard on his groundbreaking collaboration with guitarist Charlie Byrd (which resulted in the best-selling "Desafinado"), is showcased with a big band arranged by Gary McFarland (introducing "No More Blues" and "One Note Samba"), stars in recordings with guitarists Laurindo Almeida and Luiz Bonfa and is heard at the famous meeting with composer/pianist Antonio Carlos Jobim, guitarist Joao Gilberto and singer Astrud Gilberto which resulted in the major hit "The Girl from Ipanema." This essential set finishes off with three previously unissued performances from a 1964 Carnegie Hall Concert, concluding with a remake of "The Girl from Ipanema." These recordings stand as proof that it is possible for good music to sell. —*Scott Yanow*

Big Band Bossa Nova / Aug. 27, 1962-Aug. 28, 1962 / Verve ✦✦✦
This is an essential part of his bossa nova period. W/ Gary McFarland. —*Ron Wynn*

Jazz Samba Encore / Feb. 8, 1963-Feb. 27, 1963 / Verve ✦✦✦
Wonderful pairing of Stan Getz and Luiz Bonfa (g). —*Ron Wynn*

★ **Getz/Gilberto** / Mar. 18, 1963-Mar. 19, 1963 / Verve ✦✦✦✦✦
When bossa nova seemed in danger of being written off as a fad, this classic album came out and made bossa nova a permanent part of music. The combination of tenor saxophonist Stan Getz, pianist/composer Antonio Carlos Jobim and guitarist/singer Joao Gilberto had universal appeal (they all worked so beautifully together), and the last-minute addition of Astrud Gilberto, who had never sung professionally before, to "The Girl from Ipanema" made the record a huge hit. The 1997 CD reissue, which also includes such memorable numbers and future standards as "Desafinado," "Corcovado (Quiet Nights of Quiet Stars)" and "So Danco Samba," adds the shortened 45 versions of "Ipanema" and "Corcovado" to the original program. This music has been reissued many times and belongs in everyone's collection. —*Scott Yanow*

Stan Getz with Guest Artist Laurindo Almeida / Mar. 21, 1963 / Verve ✦✦✦
Music that is lush, beautiful, and substantial. —*Ron Wynn*

Stan Getz and Bill Evans / May 5, 1964-May 6, 1964 / Verve ✦✦✦✦

As musically serene and amazing as you'd expect. Getz and Evans are incredible, while Ron Carter (b), Richard Davis (b), and Elvin Jones (d) aren't too bad either. —*Ron Wynn*

Getz Au Go Go Featuring Astrud Gilberto / Aug. 19, 1964 / Verve ✦✦✦

This enjoyable LP, the last album recorded by Stan Getz in his bossa nova period, is not included in the Verve box sets documenting the era. Half of the music features Astrud Gilberto's soft vocals (including versions of "Corcovado" and "One Note Samba") while the remainder of the set is more straightahead, featuring Getz with his quartet which at the time co-starred the young vibraphonist Gary Burton. —*Scott Yanow*

The Canadian Concert of Stan Getz / Mar. 1965 / Can-Am ✦✦✦

This LP is a bit valuable because it documents a group that recorded relatively little, Stan Getz's 1965 quartet with vibraphonist Gary Burton, bassist Gene Cherico and drummer Joe Hunt. Although "Morning of the Carnival" looks back a little at his bossa nova recordings, the remainder of this fine set (taken from a radio broadcast of a Vancouver concert) is straightahead and features fairly advanced improvising. —*Scott Yanow*

A Song After Sundown / Aug. 2, 1966-Aug. 3, 1966 / Bluebird ✦✦

For this unusual CD, Stan Getz and his all-star 1966 quintet (which comprised guitarist Jim Hall, vibraphonist Gary Burton, bassist Steve Swallow and drummer Roy Haynes) are teamed up with The Boston Pops Orchestra under the direction of Arthur Fielder. Getz plays well enough but the arrangements are predictably lightweight with the emphasis on ballads; few surprises occur during this slight disappointment. —*Scott Yanow*

Sweet Rain / Mar. 21, 1967-Mar. 30, 1967 / Verve ✦✦✦✦✦

From someone who made so many classics, this might be his best romantic work overall. —*Ron Wynn*

Dynasty / Jan. 11, 1971-Mar. 17, 1971 / Polydor ✦✦✦✦

This double CD finds tenor saxophonist Stan Getz in an unusual setting, playing in a quartet with organist Eddy Louise, guitarist Rene Thomas and drummer Bernard Lubat. Together they perform advanced improvisations on five Louise songs, two by Thomas, Albert Mangelsdorff's "Mona" and just one standard, "Invitation." The music is often fascinating and really challenges Getz. —*Scott Yanow*

Captain Marvel / Mar. 3, 1972 / Columbia ✦✦✦✦✦

This LP (which should be reissued on CD as soon as possible) was one of Stan Getz's most successful recordings of the 1970s. Teamed up with a younger rhythm section (keyboardist Chick Corea, bassist Stanley Clarke, drummer Tony Williams and percussionist Airto), Getz is in consistently brilliant form on "Lush Life" and five Corea compositions. "Times Lie" and "Five-Hundred Miles High" are memorable but it is this version of "La Fiesta" (a song that perfectly fit Stan Getz's tone) that is truly classic. Highly recommended. —*Scott Yanow*

The Best of Two Worlds / May 21, 1975 / Columbia ✦✦

Stan Getz's reunion with guitarist/vocalist Joao Gilberto does not live up to expectations. Although the veteran tenor saxophonist sounds fine, the material on this LP (generally more modern Brazilian songs than he had recorded previously) is erratic and surprisingly forgettable. Gilberto has plenty of vocals and the large percussion section and guitarist Oscar Castro Neves help out, but this is definitely a lesser effort. —*Scott Yanow*

The Peacocks / Jul. 1975 / Columbia ✦✦✦✦

Although listed under Stan Getz's name, this CD is really a showcase for pianist Jimmie Rowles, an underrated stylist loved by singers and musicians alike. Rowles is heard in exquisite duets with Getz, solo, in a quartet with Getz, bassist Buster Williams and drummer Elvin Jones, and on "The Chess Players" during which the quartet is joined by four vocalists including three from Jon Hendricks' family. Most memorable are the haunting title cut, "Lester Left Town" and several of Rowles' touching vocals. —*Scott Yanow*

The Master / Oct. 1, 1975 / Columbia ✦✦✦

On this LP the great tenor Stan Getz is heard with a quartet comprising pianist Albert Dailey, bassist Clint Houston and drummer Billy Hart. Together they stretch out on four extended performances (all between nine and 11 minutes long) that are highlighted by "Lover Man" and "Invitation." More straightahead than Getz's other Columbia albums of the period, this set finds him really pushing himself. —*Scott Yanow*

☆ **Gold** / Jan. 1977-Feb. 1977 / Inner City ✦✦✦✦✦

This double CD has been reissued on two CDs by Steeple Chase for it finds tenor saxophonist Stan Getz in superb form. His modern quartet (featuring pianist Joanne Brackeen, bassist Niels Pedersen and drummer Billy Hart) is heard live at Copenhagen's Montmartre, celebrating Getz's 50th birthday with some brilliant

playing. The emphasis is mostly on standards but there have been few versions of such songs as "Lady Sings the Blues," "Lush Life," "Lester Left Town" and "Eiderdown" that could compare with the lyricism and creativity of these renditions. This is essential music featuring a master at his best. —*Scott Yanow*

Another World / Sep. 13, 1977 / Columbia ✦✦✦

Stan Getz's recordings with his late-'70s group have often been criticized because Andy La Verne backed the veteran tenor with electric keyboards and the originals by La Verne and bassist Mike Richmond were open to the influence of fusion. On one selection on this out-of-print double LP Getz uses a digital delay to create an echo effort that must have distressed some of his longtime fans, but actually the music heard throughout this set is generally quite rewarding. The musicianship is high and Stan Getz was open to new challenges. And for closeminded beboppers, there are versions included of "Willow Weep for Me" and "Blue Serge" along with the newer material. —*Scott Yanow*

Children of the World / Dec. 20, 1978-Dec. 21, 1978 / Columbia ✦✦

It is not the electronics of Andy La Verne that is bothersome on this LP but the poppish material (which includes the theme from *Evita*) and the excessive amount of keyboardists and guitarists. Stan Getz cannot be blamed for trying something new (he even uses an Echoplex sparingly) and his cool-toned tenor is in fine form but the overall results are rather forgettable. —*Scott Yanow*

Forest Eyes / Nov. 1979 / Jazz Man ✦✦

Stan Getz performs nine songs from the soundtrack of the film *Forest Eyes* with a Dutch orchestra for this fairly obscure LP. The great tenor is in his usual professional form but none of the themes are all that memorable and his backing is fairly anonymous. It's not one of the essential Stan Getz albums. —*Scott Yanow*

The Dolphin / May 1981 / Concord Jazz ✦✦✦✦

Stan Getz's first recording for Concord finds him returning to the strictly acoustic straightahead format, performing six standards with a quartet comprising pianist Lou Levy, bassist Monty Budwig and drummer Victor Lewis. Getz is in particularly fine form on the title cut, "Joy Spring" and "The Night Has a Thousand Eyes." —*Scott Yanow*

Spring Is Here / May 1981 / Concord Jazz ✦✦✦

This CD was recorded at the same sessions that resulted in *The Dolphin* but were not released until after Stan Getz's death. Actually the music (which features pianist Lou Levy, bassist Monty Budwig and drummer Victor Lewis in addition to the leader's tenor) is the equal of the original set, with "How About You," "Easy Living," and "Old Devil Moon" showing off Getz's tone and strong improvising skills at its best. —*Scott Yanow*

Billy Highstreet Samba / Nov. 4, 1981 / EmArcy ✦✦✦

During a period when Stan Getz was recording purely straightahead jazz for Concord, he joined up with keyboardist Mitchel Forman, guitarist Chuck Loeb, bassist Mark Egan, drummer Victor Lewis and percussionist Bobby Thomas, Jr., for this obscure session in France. First released in the US in 1990, this finds the veteran tenor playing "contemporary" jazz, doing a good job of fitting into five Loeb and two Forman originals plus "Body and Soul." Not essential music but a fine example of Getz's flexibility and creative instincts. —*Scott Yanow*

Pure Getz / Jan. 1982 / Concord Jazz ✦✦✦✦

Stan Getz's 1982 band featured the harmonically advanced pianist Jim McNeely, bassist Marc Johnson and drummer Victor Lewis; Billy Hart fills in for Lewis on three numbers. This date sticks (with one exception) to high-quality jazz standards, some of which ("Sippin' at Bell's") are not performed all that often. Getz is particularly swinging on "Tempus Fugit" and quite lyrical on Billy Strayhorn's "Blood Count." —*Scott Yanow*

Poetry / Jan. 12, 1983 / Elektra ✦✦✦

This out-of-print duet LP is as much pianist Albert Dailey's date as Stan Getz's. Getz lets Dailey, who passed away a little over a year later, dominate the music and the lyrical pianist comes up with some fresh ideas during the standards set. "Confirmation," "A Child Is Born" and "Spring Can Really Hang You Up the Most" are high points as are Dailey's unaccompanied solo performances of "'Round Midnight" and "Lover Man." Pity that this album is so difficult to find. —*Scott Yanow*

Line for Lyons / Feb. 18, 1983 / Gazell ✦✦✦✦

This LP (whose contents have since been reissued by Storyville on CD) found trumpeter Chet Baker guesting with Stan Getz's 1983 quartet (which also included pianist Jim McNeely, bassist George Mraz and drummer Victor Lewis). Although Getz and Baker ended up not getting along very well personally, their cool-toned musical personalities fit together perfectly as can be heard on a brief duet version of "Line for Lyons." The remainder of the set finds them successfully revisiting six standards from the 1950s, making one wish it had not been 25 years since their last collaboration. —*Scott Yanow*

The Stockholm Concert / Feb. 18, 1983 / Gazell ✦✦✦✦
Stan Getz and his 1983 quartet (which included pianist Jim McNeely, bassist George Mraz and drummer Victor Lewis) are in good form during this performance in Stockholm. With the exception of Alec Wilder's "The Baggage Room Blues" and Jobim's "O Grande Amor," the repertoire is typical for this period in Getz's career but the veteran tenor was able to come up with fresh statements for such standards as "How Long Has This Been Going On" "We'll Be Together Again," "I'll Remember April" and Billy Strayhorn's heartbreaking "Blood Count." If anything, Getz's tone became even more luscious through the years yet he never seemed to lose his fire. —*Scott Yanow*

Voyage / Mar. 9, 1986 / Black Hawk ✦✦✦
Tenor saxophonist Stan Getz found a perfect accompanist in pianist Kenny Barron, who would regularly play in his group for his last five years. This out-of-print Black Hawk LP finds the pair, along with bassist George Mraz and drummer Victor Lewis, performing two standards and four more recent pieces, including two ("Dreams" and "Voyage") by Barron. The music is difficult to classify (modern bop?) but relatively easy to understand; Getz never coasts. —*Scott Yanow*

Anniversary! / Jul. 6, 1987 / EmArcy ✦✦✦✦
As he did to celebrate his 50th birthday, Stan Getz performed at the Montmartre Club in Copenhagen at the time of his 60th birthday. This enjoyable set (mostly lengthy versions of standards) finds the veteran tenor still very much in his prime and greatly assisted by pianist Kenny Barron, bassist Rufus Reid and drummer Victor Lewis. Worth picking up. —*Scott Yanow*

Serenity / Jul. 6, 1987 / EmArcy ✦✦✦✦
From the same sessions that resulted in *Anniversary,* Stan Getz celebrated his 60th birthday as he had his 50th, with a gig at the Cafe Montmartre in Copenhagen. Joined by pianist Kenny Barron, bassist Rufus Reid and drummer Victor Lewis, Getz (who only had four years left) plays in peak form, really stretching out on lengthy versions of three standards, Victor Feldman's "Falling in Love" and Kenny Barron's "Voyage." His solo on "I Remember You" is particularly strong. —*Scott Yanow*

Yours and Mine: Live at the Glasgow International Jazz Festival / Jun. 29, 1989 / Concord ✦✦✦✦

Soul Eyes / Jun. 29, 1989-Jul. 27, 1989 / Concord Jazz ✦✦✦

Apasionado / 1989-Mar. 2, 1992 / A&M ✦✦
This rather commercial album (the next to last of Stan Getz's long career) is saved only by the great tenor's tone and creativity. The originals by Eddie del Barrio and Herb Albert are quite forgettable and the backup by a variety of studio musicians is anonymous. But somehow the wonderful playing of Stan Getz makes this a worthwhile session despite it all. —*Scott Yanow*

People Time / Mar. 3, 1991-Mar. 6, 1991 / Verve ✦✦✦✦✦
Stan Getz's final recording, a two-CD live set of duets with pianist Kenny Barron that was cut just three months before his death, finds the great tenor in surprisingly creative form despite an occasional shortness of breath. Getz's tone is as beautiful as ever and he does not spare himself on this often exquisite set. His version of Charlie Haden's "First Song" is a highlight but none of the 14 performances are less than great. A brilliant farewell recording by a masterful jazzman. —*Scott Yanow*

Terry Gibbs (Julius Gubenko)

b. Oct. 13, 1924, New York, NY
Vibes / Bop, Latin Jazz
One of the most hyper of all jazzmen (even his ballads are taken mostly double-time), Terry Gibbs is a consistently exciting and competitive vibraphonist. As a xylophonist he won an amateur contest when he was 12. After spending three years in the military during World War II, Gibbs played on 52nd Street, gigged with Tommy Dorsey (1946 and 1948), Chubby Jackson (touring Scandinavia during 1947-48), Buddy Rich (1948), Woody Herman's Second Herd (1948-49) and Benny Goodman (1950-52). Gibbs settled in Los Angeles in 1957, worked in the studios, led jazz orchestras (his late-'50s version was callled the Terry Gibbs Dream Band), was the musical director of *The Steve Allen Show* during the 1960s and in the 1980s and '90s has often teamed up in a quintet with Buddy DeFranco. Terry Gibbs, who recorded as a leader for Prestige, Savoy, Brunswick, EmArcy, Mercury, Verve, Time, Impulse, Dot, Xanadu, Jazz a La Carte and Contemporary (among others), had such fine pianists as his sidemen through the years as Terry Pollard, Pete Jolly (on accordion in 1957), Alice McLeod (in 1963 before she became Alice Coltrane) and John Campbell. —*Scott Yanow*

Jazz Band Ball / Sep. 1957 / V.S.O.P. ✦✦✦
This reissue is unrelated to another V.S.O.P. set simply titled *A Jazz Band Ball.* Terry Gibbs on vibes and marimba matches wits and creativity with Victor Feldman and Larry Bunker, both of whom double on vibes and xylophone. Assisted by

pianist Lou Levy, bassist Max Bennett and drummer Mel Lewis, the intriguing front line essentially plays bop, but with a great deal of color. The interaction between the vibraphonists, who are all featured and occasionally trade off, is the main reason to acquire this very interesting set. —*Scott Yanow*

Launching a New Sound in Music / Feb. 17, 1959 / Mercury ✦✦✦
It is ironic that the Contemporary label came out with five CDs worth of unknown material by the Terry Gibbs Big Band while Polygram has completely neglected its studio sides by the same group. The music on this set, last available as a Trip LP, was the first by Gibbs' "Dream Band," a swinging outfit of top studio musicians who were based in L.A. at the time. This album comprises two arrangements apiece by Bill Holman, Bob Brookmeyer, Manny Albam, Al Cohn, Med Flory and Marty Paich, which pay tribute to Benny Goodman, Artie Shaw, Count Basie, Duke Ellington, Lionel Hampton and Tommy Dorsey. The tunes are mostly overly familiar (including "Stardust," "Cotton Tail," "Begin the Beguine" and "Flying Home") and clock in around three minutes, meaning that the solos are quite concise, but there are some good individual moments from the vibraphonist/leader, trumpeter Conte Candoli, and trombonist Frank Rosolino. —*Scott Yanow*

● **Dream Band, Vol. 1** / Mar. 17, 1959-Mar. 19, 1959 / Contemporary ✦✦✦✦✦
The music on this CD, not released for the first time until 1986, features the formerly little-known Terry Gibbs Big Band, an orchestra that worked fairly regularly in Los Angeles from 1959-62. The repertoire is primarily swing-era standards, but the arrangements (by Bill Holman, Bob Brookmeyer, Al Cohn, Marty Paich and Manny Albam) are fairly modern for the time; the all-star group's ensembles are tight, and such colorful soloists as vibraphonist Gibbs, valve trombonist Bob Enevoldsen, trumpeters Stu Williamson and Conte Candoli, tenorman Bill Holman, pianist Pete Jolly and altoist Joe Maini are heard from. There would be five CDs released by this band; this is an excellent set to start with. —*Scott Yanow*

Dream Band, Vol. 3: Flying Home / Mar. 17, 1959-Mar. 19, 1959 / Contemporary ✦✦✦✦
The third CD in this five-volume series draws its material from the same live sessions that resulted in the first two Terry Gibbs Dream Band releases, but contains all previously unheard performances. Ranging from well-known standards ("Avalon," "I'm Getting Sentimental over You" and "Flying Home") to more recent tunes ("Airegin" and Gibbs' "It Might as Well Be Swing") and originals by arrangers Bill Holman, Bob Brookmeyer and Al Cohn, the music stays consistently colorful and swinging. Gibbs had some of the top L.A.-based players in his big band, which lasted from 1959-62, and among the key soloists on this set are trumpeter Conte Candoli, Bill Holman, Bill Perkins and Med Flory on tenor, and altoists Joe Maini and Charles Kennedy. —*Scott Yanow*

Dream Band, Vol. 2: The Sundown Sessions / Nov. 1959 / Contemporary ✦✦✦✦
The legendary Terry Gibbs Dream Band, a notable unit that from 1959-62 made a few long-out-of-print albums for Mercury and Verve, was well served by the five CDs of previously unreleased material released by Contemporary in the late 1980s. Vol. 2 has charts by Bill Holman, Al Cohn, Manny Albam, Lennie Niehaus and Med Flory on six swing-era songs and four later tunes, including Gibbs' "The Fat Man." Of the soloists featured during this live set, which also resulted in part of Vol. 3, vibraphonist Gibbs, trumpeter Conte Candoli, altoists Joe Maini and Charlie Kennedy, Bill Perkins on tenor and pianist Lou Levy are most notable. Recommended for fans of swinging big bands. —*Scott Yanow*

Dream Band, Vol. 4: Main Stem / Jan. 20, 1961-Jan. 22, 1961 / Contemporary ✦✦✦✦
Unlike the first three CDs released by Contemporary of Terry Gibbs' early-'60s "Dream Band," the music on the fourth and fifth volumes was out previously on Mercury (although it has been out of print for many years). And while the earlier sets focused on swing-era standards, the fourth volume mostly has less common material. Gibbs' all-star orchestra (which includes trumpeter Conte Candoli, high-note trumpeter Al Porcino, trombonist Frank Rosolino, Richie Kamuca and Bill Perkins on tenors, altoists Joe Maini and Charlie Kennedy and drummer Mel Lewis among others) swings hard on such tunes as "Day In, Day Out," "Sweet Georgia Brown," "Too Close for Comfort" and "Ja-Da." It is not at all surprising that the vibraphonist-leader sounds so happy leading his short-lived band. —*Scott Yanow*

The Dream Band, Vol. 5: Big Cat / Jan. 20, 1961-Jan. 22, 1961 / Contemporary ✦✦✦✦✦
Taken from the same live sessions as *Vol. 4* (and last out several decades ago on Mercury) this fifth release by vibraphonist Terry Gibbs' "Dream Band" has plenty of swinging numbers from the 17-piece big band. Mostly comprising West Coast jazz all-stars (including Richie Kamuca and Bill Perkins on tenors, trumpeter Conte Candoli, trombonist Frank Rosolino and drummer Mel Lewis), the orchestra is in top form on such numbers as "Tico Tico," "Billie's Bounce," "Jump the Blues Away" and a few obscure oriignals. The inventive arrangements by Bill Holman,

Manny Albam and Al Cohn insured that Terry Gibbs' Dream Band would have its own sound and the fifth volume may very well be its finest. —*Scott Yanow*

That Swing Thing / Apr. 5, 1961-Apr. 8, 1961 / Verve ✦✦✦
Vibraphonist Terry Gibbs has so much energy that even the ballads on this obscure Verve LP seem hyper. Recorded live at Shelly's Manne Hole, Gibbs, pianist Pat Moran, bassist Jimmy Bond and drummer Gary Frommer romp through such tunes as "Let My People Blow" "Moanin'," "Mannehole March" and even "Three Blind Mice." Fun music, but this will be a difficult album to find. —*Scott Yanow*

Gibbs/Nistico / 1963 / Time ✦✦✦
As one would expect from looking at the lineup (vibraphonist Terry Gibbs, tenor saxophonist Sal Nistico, guitarist Turk Lake, bassist Charlie Andrus, drummer Jake Hanna and pianist Nat Pierce), swing is the thing on this Time release. The odd part is that Pierce mostly plays organ (whose idea was that?), which weighs down the group a bit since his is very much a pianistic style. The nine tunes are all Terry Gibbs originals, and Gibbs, although a masterful vibraphonist, has never been a major composer. However, the enthusiastic solos of the co-leaders keep the music colorful and swinging. —*Scott Yanow*

El Nutto / Apr. 15, 1963 / Limelight ✦✦
This would be a routine Terry Gibbs quartet set except for one fact: the pianist is Alice McLeod, who after getting married would change her name to Alice Coltrane. The third of three albums she recorded with Gibbs (decades later, her son Ravi Coltrane would work for the vibraphonist's son, drummer Gerry Gibbs), McLeod sounds fine on ten obscure tunes, all Gibbs originals. Certainly, none of the songs (which include "El Nutto," "The Nightie Night Waltz," "Hey Pretty" and "Just for Laughs") caught on, and their melodies are not particularly memorable, but the solos of Gibbs and the appearance of the pianist make this album of historic interest. —*Scott Yanow*

Take It from Me / Jan. 16, 1964 / Impulse! ✦✦✦
This is a likable small-group date from vibraphonist Terry Gibbs, who welcomes guitarist Kenny Burrell, bassist Sam Jones and drummer Louis Hayes to his quartet. Gibbs contributed six originals, none of which are that catchy, but he also stretches out on "All the Things You Are" and "Honeysuckle Rose." Gibbs and Burrell work together quite well, and their improvisations and the upbeat mood of the set are superior to the newer melodies. —*Scott Yanow*

Bopstacle Course / Jul. 1974 / Xanadu ✦✦✦✦
Vibraphonist Terry Gibbs' first recording as a leader in eight years is quite exciting. Gibbs, Barry Harris (the foremost exponent in the 1970s and '80s of bebop piano), bassist Sam Jones and drummer Alan Dawson romp through four Gibbs originals, "Body and Soul," "Softly As in a Morning Sunrise," "Manha de Carnaval" and "I'm Getting Sentimental over You." As is usually true of most Terry Gibbs dates, even the ballads are full of plenty of energy. Gibbs and Harris should have a rematch. —*Scott Yanow*

Jazz Party: First Time Together / 1981 / Palo Alto ✦✦✦
Vibraphonist Terry Gibbs and clarinetist Buddy DeFranco teamed up for the first time for this live album, and the matchup was so successful that they have worked together on and off ever since, recording quite a few other sets. Gibbs' hyperactive bebop style clearly inspired DeFranco, who can play a lot of notes himself. With swinging support from pianist Frank Collett, bassist Andy Simpkins and drummer Jimmie Smith, the Gibbs-DeFranco quintet roars through such songs as "Air Mail Special," "Love for Sale" and "Samba Wazoo." This is the most difficult to find of the Gibbs-DeFranco collaborations, since Palo Alto soon went out of business, but it is up to the level of their dates for Contemporary. —*Scott Yanow*

Air Mail Special / Oct. 4, 1981-Oct. 5, 1981 / Contemporary ✦✦✦✦
Air Mail Special, a reissue CD put out in 1990, has seven of the eight songs originally on Palo Alto's *Jazz Party/First Time Together* and three numbers from the Tall Trees release *Now's The Time*. Since both of those labels are extinct, this was a welcome reissue although it would have been preferable to have the two original sets intact. Vibraphonist Terry Gibbs and clarinetist Buddy DeFranco always made for a compatible and mutually inspiring team. Every tune of theirs seems to end up being uptempo or at least doubletime with the vibraphonist constantly pushing the clarinetist. They blend together quite well and their tradeoffs are generally outstanding; on "Blues For Brady" they race through all 12 keys. The rhythm section (pianist Frank Collett, bassist Andy Simpkins and drummer Jimmie Smith) is a bit overshadowed but keeps up with the lead voices on this consistently exciting set. —*Scott Yanow*

The Latin Connection / May 9, 1986+May 10, 1986 / Contemporary ✦✦✦✦
Vibraphonist Terry Gibbs sounds fine on this Latin-jazz date, which also includes altoist Frank Morgan, pianist Sonny Bravo, bassist Bobby Rodriguez and three percussionists, including Tito Puente playing timbales on three of the nine numbers. Most of the tunes are bop and swing standards (such as "Scrapple from the Apple," "Groovin' High," "Good Bait" and "Sing, Sing, Sing") and have excellent

spots for Gibbs, Morgan and the percussion section. A fine date that surprisingly (particularly for Fantasy) was allowed to go out of print. —*Scott Yanow*

Chicago Fire / Jul. 24, 1987-Jul. 26, 1987 / Contemporary ✦✦✦✦✦
This was the second meeting on record by vibraphonist Terry Gibbs and clarinetist Buddy DeFranco (an obscure set for Palo Alto from 1981 was the first), and it officially launched the quintet which would record several additional sets. With the powerful pianist John Campbell, bassist Todd Coolman and Terry's son Gerry Gibbs on drums, the two veterans play heated versions of such tunes as "Rockin' in Rhythm," "Cherokee," "Giant Steps" and "52nd Street Theme." Gibbs and DeFranco always inspire each other, making all of their recordings of strong interest to bop fans. —*Scott Yanow*

Holiday for Swing / Jul. 1987-Aug. 1988 / Contemporary ✦✦✦✦

Kings of Swing / Apr. 13, 1991-Apr. 15, 1991 / Contemporary ✦✦✦✦✦
Recorded at Kimball's East, Emeryville, CA, with the Terry Gibbs, Buddy DeFranco, Herb Ellis Sextet. A late and very nice album of cuts like "Body and Soul" and "Stompin' at the Savoy" that features these kings of swing as fresh today as ever. The CD is 68 minutes. —*Michael Erlewine*

Memories of You / Apr. 13, 1991-Apr. 15, 1991 / Contemporary ✦✦✦✦

Play That Song: Live at the 1994 Floating Festival / Oct. 23, 1994-Oct. 27, 1994 / Chiaroscuro ✦✦✦✦
The most unusual aspect to this Terry Gibbs quartet date (which was recorded live at the 1994 Floating Jazz Festival on board the *S.S. Norway*) is that seven of the nine selections are originals by the vibraphonist-leader. Of these, the most memorable are "Play That Song" (which has a catchy rhythm enthusiastically played by Terry's son Gerry on drums), "Penthouse Groove" (a hard-swinger that lets pianist Uri Caine show off his Oscar Peterson influence), the strong melody of "Sweet Young Song of Love" and the medium-tempo blues "The Fat Man" which inspires Terry Gibbs' most exciting playing. Also in the "cooking" category are the quartet's renditions of Artie Shaw's "Moon Ray" (the clarinetist's most famous original) and "Limehouse Blues." It does seem a bit odd how the theme of "The Beautiful People" is very similar to "What's New" but that is the only real fault to this swinging set. Gibbs and Caine blend together well while never getting in each other's way while bassist Boris Koslo and drummer Gerry Gibbs are excellent in support. Recommended. —*Scott Yanow*

Banu Gibson

b. Oct. 24, 1947, Dayton, OH
Vocals / Classic Jazz
During an era when most female singers who interpret music from the 1920s come across as dated "red hot mamas," camp or satirical, Banu Gibson practically stands alone. She performs music from the 1920s and '30s creatively but within the boundaries of the idiom, giving fresh life and excitement to forgotten tunes and swinging hard with her New Orleans Hot Jazz Orchestra. Growing up in Hollywood, FL, Gibson was trained as a dancer although she studied voice as a child with an opera singer. She gained early experience playing in a Miami club opposite Phil Napoleon (1967-68), touring with Your Father's Mustache (1969-72) and appearing at Disneyland in the *Class of '27* (1972-78). She moved to New Orleans in 1973, commuting to Los Angeles and working in N.O. doing choreography and directing. Gibson learned how to play rhythm banjo and on April 1, 1981, put together her six-piece band which improved steadily throughout the 1980s and became a popular attraction at traditional jazz festivals. Although Banu Gibson has recorded for World, Jazzology and Stomp Off, her most rewarding recordings are for her own Swing Out label and those rank with the top classic jazz of the era. —*Scott Yanow*

Jazz Me Blues / 1974+1980 / World Jazz ✦✦✦
On this out-of-print LP, there are seven selections by the excellent classic jazz singer Banu Gibson from 1980, early in her career, and six by the 1974 version of the World's Greatest Jazz Band. Banu is joined by a pickup group of Los Angeles-based Dixieland musicians, including trumpeter Bill Vogel, the great swing pianist Johnny Varro and drummer Gene Estes; the best are Gibson's spirited versions of "Jazz Me Blues," "Happy Days and Lonely Nights" and "Radio." The WGJB at the time comprised quite an all-star lineup (trumpeter Yank Lawson, Bob Wilber on clarinet and soprano, Vic Dickenson and Benny Morton on trombones, Bud Freeman on tenor, pianist Ralph Sutton, bassist Bob Haggart and drummer Gus Johnson) and mostly sticks to warhorses, but Freeman's workout on "Crazy Rhythm," Sutton's feature on "The Sheik of Araby" and a pair of Dickenson vocals are somewhat memorable. Dixieland fans will enjoy this album. —*Scott Yanow*

On Tour / Nov. 28, 1982 / Jazzology ✦✦
Singer Banu Gibson does her best during this loose concert appearance (from the 1982 Manassas Jazz Festival) and there a few good moments but the poorly organized jam session has plenty of car wrecks as various horn players (including nine

horns on "Swing That Music") consistently crash into each other. Trumpeter Billy Butterfield and clarinetist Johnny Mince are the most notable players in the supporting cast but frankly many of the performances on this LP should not have been released. For much better examples of Banu Gibson's singing, get her Swing Out CDs instead. —*Scott Yanow*

Jazz Baby / Sep. 1, 1983-Dec. 16, 1983 / Stomp Off ✦✦✦
The great classic jazz singer Banu Gibson is heard for the first time with her regular group (the New Orleans Hot Jazz Orchestra) on this Stomp Off LP. Although the group would improve (and swing a lot harder) when eventually the tuba player was replaced by a string bassist, this is an excellent outing. Gibson brings a real understanding of the veteran standards and sounds quite spirited and creative within the idiom on such songs as "Down in Honky Tonk Town," "Changes," "Sweet Man" and "Rose of Washington Square." With fine solos contributed by cornetist Charles Fardella, trombonist Steve Yocum and pianist David Boeddinghaus (the group did not have a clarinetist yet), this was a major first step for Banu Gibson, who would soon be at the top of her field. —*Scott Yanow*

Let Yourself Go / Jan. 1988 / Swing Out ✦✦✦✦✦
Most singers who attempt to interpret tunes from the 1920s come across as either nostalgia acts, campy or corny. Banu Gibson is a major exception for she sings creatively within the idiom, her voice is both powerful and versatile and she swings without "modernizing" or simplifying the style. This CD from her Swing Out label (along with Swing Out 104) is quite definitive for the material is superior (with "Let Yourself Go," "Love Me or Leave Me," an inventive version of "I Got Rhythm" and "Put That Sun Back in the Sky" being among the highlights), there is lots of room for solos from her New Orleans Hot Jazz Orchestra (cornetist Charles Fardella, trombonist David Sager, pianist David Boeddinghaus, bassist James Singleton and drummer Hal Smith) and there are plenty of heated and exciting ensembles. This release is highly recommended to fans of classic jazz. —*Scott Yanow*

● **You Don't Know My Mind** / Jun. 26, 1989-May 2, 1990 / Swing Out ✦✦✦✦✦
Banu Gibson ranks at the top of her field, one of the very few creative singers in the 1990s interpreting music from the 1920s in the older style without directly copying any of the past greats. There are plenty of exciting solos on this CD from cornetist Charles Fardella, trombonist David Sager, the reeds (clarinet, tenor and alto) of Tom Fischer and pianist David Boeddinghaus while the hot rhythm section often sounds like Fats Waller's group. Gibson always swings hard and she has a particularly strong (yet appealing) voice that is quite versatile. The material is highlighted by "I've Got My Fingers Crossed," "I Cover the Waterfront," "Ol' Pappy" and "Truckin' " but each of the 16 selections are quite rewarding. All classic jazz collectors should be aware of Banu Gibson, and this CD (along with Swing Out 103) features her in prime form. —*Scott Yanow*

Livin' in a Great Big Way / May 22, 1990-Jul. 16, 1990 / Swing Out ✦✦✦✦✦
This is an unusual Banu Gibson CD in that, instead of using her regular New Orleans Hot Jazz Orchestra, the talented singer is accompanied by just one of two pianists, John Sheridan or David Boeddinghaus. Gibson's repertoire on this set includes both classics from the pre-bop era and obscurities, and the highlights (among many) are "They All Laughed," "It's Been So Long," "About a Quarter to Nine," "I've Got a Feelin' You're Foolin' " and "I'll See You in My Dreams." Arguably the top classic jazz singer to be active in the 1990s, Banu Gibson's attractive voice and versatile swinging style are very much in evidence throughout this excellent outing. —*Scott Yanow*

Zat You, Santa Claus? / Jan. 12, 1995-Jan. 15, 1995 / Swing Out ✦✦✦✦
The talented classic jazz singer Banu Gibson and her New Orleans Hot Jazz band are in fine form on a set of Christmas songs. Most of the material is swinging (including "Santa Claus Blues," the touching "I'll Be Home for Christmas," "At the Christmas Ball," "Christmas Night in Harlem" and three originals by Gibson and/or John Sheridan), and there is space for concise solos by trumpeter Duke Heitger, trombonist David Sager, pianist David Boeddinghaus and the reeds of Tom Fischer. This is a cheerful set that even sounds good in July. —*Scott Yanow*

Harry "The Hipster" Gibson

b. 1914, New York, NY, d. May 9, 1991, California
Piano, Vocals / Swing, Jive

Harry "The Hipster" Gibson, a talented if eccentric pianist-vocalist, had his brief moment of fame before fading into obscurity. He started out playing on 52nd Street as a stride pianist and in 1944 even performed "In a Mist" at an Eddie Condon Town Hall concert. But it was his crazy compositions (including "Who Put the Benzedrine in Mrs. Murphy's Ovaltine," "Handsome Harry the Hipster" and "Stop That Dancin' Up There") and frantic singing style (predating rock 'n' roll by a decade) that gave him an underground reputation. Gibson's definitive recordings were made for Musicraft in 1944 and 1947 and his unusual showmanship was

captured on a few Soundies during the period. However Gibson's excessive drug use resulted in his quick decline after 1947. He did record a somewhat demented Christmas album in 1974 and some new songs for Progressive in 1986 but largely wasted his great potential. —*Scott Yanow*

● **Boogie Woogie in Blue** / Apr. 21, 1944+Feb. 8, 1946 / Musicraft ✦✦✦✦✦
Harry "The Hipster" Gibson, a talented boogie-woogie and stride pianist, had by 1944 become an infamous personality whose crazy jive talk and humorous vocals often championed a decadent lifestyle. For a few years, he had a strong cult following before fading out in the late '40s. Gibson's best recordings were the dozen sides he cut for Musicraft during 1944 and 1947, and all are included on this definitive release. Among his greatest "hits" were "Handsome Harry the Hipster," "Get Your Juices at the Deuces," "4F Ferdinand, The Frantic Freak," "Who Put the Benzedrine in Mrs. Murphy's Ovaltine," "I Stay Brown All Year Round" and the classic "Stop That Dancin' Up There." Highly recommended. —*Scott Yanow*

Digs Christmas / 1974 / Viper's Nest ✦✦
The potential behind this record (reissued on CD in 1994) was quite promising. The often hilarious vocalist/pianist Harry "The Hipster" Gibson performs 13 Christmas-related songs, but unfortunately, his humor mostly misses the mark and comes across as weak. Gibson plays well enough, with lots of boogie-woogie lines, but such numbers as "I Don't Want a Lot for Christmas," "I Wish My Mother-In-Law Don't Visit Us This Christmas," and "I Saw Mommy Kissing Santa Claus" do not live up to their potential. A couple of songs recorded for the Bicentennial in 1976 (including "That's the Spirit") round out this often tedious and disappointing set. —*Scott Yanow*

Who Put the Benzedrine in Mrs. Murphy's Ovaltine? / 1976+1989 / Delmark ✦✦✦
After his heyday in the mid-'40s, pianist-singer Harry "The Hipster" Gibson faded away from the limelight. He continued playing on a part-time basis and this Delmark CD released for the first time a live performance from 1976 and some studio tracks from 1989. Although the backup bands are not overly impressive (the 1976 group is an amateurish blues-rock band), Gibson proves to still be in his musical prime, taking several fine piano solos. However it is the Hipster's frequently hilarious storytelling (which deals with tales of the drug life) that are most memorable, particularly "Me & Max," "I Got Framed" and "I Flipped My Wig in San Francisco." It makes one regret that Gibson did not do more with his career. —*Scott Yanow*

Everybody's Crazy But Me / 1986 / Progressive ✦✦✦
Harry "The Hipster" Gibson was past his prime when he made this solo set for Progressive in 1986; in fact, his peak years were largely finished by 1948. However, Gibson does take a few worthwhile piano solos, in addition to offering some spaced-out social commentary and remaking "Stop That Dancing Up There." Those listeners who appreciate a wacky sense of humor will probably enjoy such tunes as "Solution for Pollution," "Homegrown," "Keep Venice Nude" and "Male Chauvinistic Pig." But there were so many lost years from this colorful personality, who should have become a household name in the 1950s. —*Scott Yanow*

Astrud Gilberto

b. 1940, Bahia, Brazil
Vocals / Bossa Nova, Brazilian Jazz

Astrud Gilberto is a limited but strangely memorable singer known mostly for her very first recording. At the famous 1963 collaboration between Stan Getz, Antonio Carlos Jobim and her then-husband Joao Gilberto, Astrud was spontaneously asked to sing the English lyrics to "The Girl from Ipanema" even though she was a housewife and not a professional singer. Her cool-toned voice fit the song perfectly and, after it became a giant hit, she unwittingly became a celebrity. Gilberto recorded with Stan Getz again in 1964 and made a series of albums for Verve during 1965-69. Although lightning did not strike again, the easy-listening encounters with string orchestras sold well. Astrud Gilberto has continued singing on a part-time basis, and it is doubtful if she has performed anywhere in the past 33 years without having to sing "The Girl from Ipanema." —*Scott Yanow*

The Essential Astrud Gilberto / Mar. 18, 1963-May 27, 1967 / Verve ✦✦✦✦
This British LP has some of Astrud Gilberto's finest early recordings. The cool-toned bossa nova singer is heard at her best on "The Girl from Ipanema," "Meditation," "Corcovado," "Bim-Bom," "One Note Samba" and "It Might As Well Be Spring." Unfortunately, the liner notes, which do sum up her importance well, say nothing about the exact recording dates or personnel. However, listeners running across this appealing album are advised to pick it up anyway, for it is an excellent sampler. —*Scott Yanow*

The Shadow of Your Smile / Oct. 21, 1964-June 3, 1965 / Verve ✦✦✦

The Silver Collection: The Astrud Gilberto Album / 1965 / Verve ✦✦✦✦✦
Harder to find than *Compact Jazz*, this also repeats about half of the tracks from that collection and makes the major boo-boo of not including "The Girl From

Ipanema." But if you want more Gilberto, this is recommended. It has 25 songs, most of which do not duplicate *Compact Jazz*, all but three dating from 1965, and leans heavily on material by Antonio Carlos Jobim and Luiz Bonfa. —*Richie Unterberger*

The Astrud Gilberto Album / Jan. 27, 1965+Jan. 28, 1965 / Polygram Brazil ✦✦✦
Demure Brazilian vocalist Astrud Gilberto became a hit artist in 1963 with the song "The Girl from Ipanema." She recorded it with her husband Joao Gilberto, plus tenor saxophonist Stan Getz and Antonio Carlos Jobim. The resulting furor eventually got her a solo album, this 1965 work. It's got some charming moments, and she was ideal for the light bossa nova sound. But the jazz content was and still is minimal. —*Ron Wynn*

● **Look to the Rainbow** / Nov. 22, 1965-Feb. 4, 1966 / Verve ✦✦✦✦✦
For this CD reissue the music on singer Astrud Gilberto's LP *Look to the Rainbow* is combined with half of the songs from her following album *A Certain Smile*. The former session was one of the bossa nova singer's best (11 perfectly suitable songs on which her soft voice is accompanied by an orchestra arranged by Gil Evans and Al Cohn) while on the latter she interacts successfully with a trio led by organist Walter Wanderley. —*Scott Yanow*

A Certain Smile, A Certain Sadness / Sep. 20, 1966-Sep. 23, 1966 / Verve ✦✦✦

Beach Samba / May 27, 1967-Jun. 30, 1967 / Verve ✦✦✦
One of Gilberto's less-impressive '60s Verve outings, primarily due to the more pop-oriented song selection. Much of this is just standard pleasant Gilberto: off-hand vocals and a sumptuous Brazil pop-cum-US orchestration feel (Ron Carter and Toots Thielemans are among the sidemen). And some of the pop choices work well, particularly Tim Hardin's gorgeous "Misty Roses." No vocals or arrangements, however, could save the criminally wrong-headed military march of "A Banda (Parade)," or the exasperatingly coochie-coochie duet between Gilberto and her six-year-old son on the Lovin' Spoonful's "You Didn't Have to Be So Nice." Which makes it all the more surprising when the next and concluding track, "Nao Bate O Corocao," has Gilberto cutting loose with confident, sassy scats, as she rarely did before or since. The CD reissue improves matters by adding five bonus cuts from *A Certain Smile, A Certain Sadness*, recorded in 1966 in more authentically bossa nova-style arrangements, anchored by organist Walter Wanderley. —*Richie Unterberger*

Astrud Gilberto with Stanley Turrentine / 1971 / Columbia ✦✦
W/ Stanley Turrentine. 1988 reissue of 1971 set that had some mildly entertaining moments. —*Ron Wynn*

Astrud Gilberto Plus James Last Orchestra / 1986 / Verve ✦✦✦
1987 release. Gilberto still has alluring sound. —*Ron Wynn*

Girl from Ipanema / Jun. 3, 1997 / Prime Cuts ✦✦

The Silver Collection: The Astrud Gilberto Album / Verve ✦✦✦✦
Harder to find than *Compact Jazz*, this also repeats about half of the tracks from that collection and makes the major boo-boo of not including "The Girl from Ipanema". But if you want more Gilberto, this is recommended. It has 25 songs, most of which do not duplicate *Compact Jazz*, all but three dating from 1995, and leans heavily on material by Antonio Carlos Jobim and Luiz Bonfa. —*Richie Unterberger*

Compact Jazz: Astrud Gilberto / Verve ✦✦✦✦
The best compilation of her peak years. Gilberto's brand of breathy boss nova-jazz has a romantic (if slightly cheesy) charm of its own, and these 16 tracks, including "Girl from Ipanema", show her to her best advantage, with support from Stan Getz, Antonio Carlos Jobim, Joao Gilberto, and Gil Evans, among others. —*Richie Unterberger*

Talkin' Verve / Polygram ✦✦✦
Although it's not a definitive overview of Astrud Gilberto's Verve recordings, *Talkin' Verve* is a solid sampler of her years with the label, boasting 16 songs including "Beginnings", "Bim Bom", "Wailing of teh Willow", "Don't Leave Me, Baby", "Stay", "She's a Carioca" and "Windy". In order to be definitive, her recordings with Stan Getz would have to have been included, but as it stands, this isn't a bad introduction to her solo recordings. —*Stephen Thomas Erlewine*

João Gilberto

b. Jun. 1931, Bahia, Brazil
Guitar, Vocals / Bossa Nova, Brazilian Jazz
Joao Gilberto's esteemed colleague Antonio Carlos Jobim always gave Gilberto the credit for starting the bossa nova, which developed from his quiet, syncopated guitar laced with the rhythms of the samba and harmonic sophistication of American cool jazz. Add to that Gilberto's hushed voice and delicate pinpoint enunciation of the Portuguese words and you get an irresistibly seductive combination. Having grown up with both the samba and modern jazz (particularly Gerry Mulligan and

Bud Shank) in his ears, Gilberto moved to Rio de Janeiro in the early 1950s, where he met Jobim and began recording his songs. In 1958, Gilberto's record of his own "Bim Bom" and Jobim's "Chega de Saudade" became a huge hit in Brazil and had the effect of unofficially launching the bossa nova movement. Gilberto was one of the Brazilian artists who performed at Carnegie Hall in the first North American bossa nova concert in 1962. In 1963, Gilberto collaborated with his then-wife Astrud, Jobim, and Stan Getz on the *Getz/Gilberto* album, which thanks to "The Girl from Ipanema" became a major hit (No. 2 on the pop album charts). Since then, the reclusive Gilberto's records have appeared sporadically on Elektra-Musician, Warner Bros., Verve, Tropical—and his rare live appearances are always eagerly awaited by Brazilian music fans. —*Richard S. Ginell*

The Boss of the Bossa Nova / Oct. 19, 1962 / Atlantic ✦✦✦

Gilberto and Jobim / 1960 / Capitol ✦✦✦✦✦
The back cover of this Capitol LP claims "Here's the album that started it all," and to an extent that is true. A year before Stan Getz first met up with Charlie Byrd to launch bossa nova in the US, Joao Gilberto (with backing by an orchestra led by Antonio Carlos Jobim) recorded a dozen bossa nova performances, including "One Note Samba," "Meditation," "Corcovado" and even "I'm Looking over a Four Leaf Clover." But since this record was not heard domestically until after bossa nova caught on, it had less of an impact than one would expect. The emphasis is on Gilberto's voice (and his guitar during the instrumental "Um Abraco No Bonfa") during the very brief renditions, all of which are under two minutes. Since there is less than 21 minutes of music on the LP, the historic set is only recommended when found at a budget price. —*Scott Yanow*

★ **Amoroso/Brasil** / Nov. 17, 1976-1980 / Warner Brothers ✦✦✦✦✦
Two of the influential Joao Gilberto's LPs (*Amoroso* and *Brasil*) are combined on this single CD. The former session is fairly distinctive with Gilberto interpreting four of Antonio Carlos Jobim's compositions (including "Wave" and "Triste") and four other songs (highlighted by "Besame Mucho," "Estate" and an odd 31-bar rendition of "'S Wonderful"). The strings (arranged by Claus Ogerman) are unnecessary but Gilberto proves to be in prime form. The later album also has its moments of interest (including a Brazilian version of "All of Me") and finds Gilberto backed by Johnny Mandel arrangements and assisted by singers Caetano Veloso, Gilberto Gil and Maria Bethania. Overall there is not much variety throughout this gently swinging program but these are a pair of Gilberto's better post-1970 recordings. —*Scott Yanow*

The Brazilliance Music of Rhythm / Nov. 1990 / Rykodisc ✦✦✦
Recent Afro-Latin, bossa nova release by Joao Gilberto, the husband of Astrud Gilberto and a pioneer in jazz/Afro-Latin fusion in the '60s. While his heart's still in the right place, the sound seems a bit limp three decades later, although it's also retained some charm and romantic, sentimental quality. —*Ron Wynn*

The Legendary Joao Gilberto / 1958-1961 / World Pacific ✦✦✦✦✦
It is difficult to overstate or overhype the importance of this CD, for it exhaustively documents the starting point of bossa nova in Brazil prior to the global craze. The building blocks are solidly in place—Joao Gilberto's highly distinctive, pioneering acoustic guitar rhythms, his precisely enunciated vocals (recorded not too closely for a change!), the stripped-down samba-based percussion, Antonio Carlos Jobim's extraordinary songs, and most tellingly on many tracks, Jobim's spare, often-copied backdrops and countermelodies for strings, winds and horns that are so much a part of his compositions. We can eavesdrop on the exact beginning of the bossa nova movement with the 1958 single containing Jobim's "Chega de Saudade" and Gilberto's "Bim Bom"; one can easily see why this quietly revolutionary record hit the Brazilian music scene like a silent cruise missile. Moreover, the second single was "Desafinado," a fully formed masterpiece long before it became an international hit, with Gilberto producing a precision-cut gem of vocal pinpointing. Along with the singles, there are three albums of material squeezed onto one CD, 38 tracks in all, of which only a dozen surfaced in the US on LP at the time. In addition to Jobim's songs, there are plenty of first-rate contributions by Gilberto, Dorival Caymmi, Ary Barroso, Carlos Lyra, and other writers. And perhaps most importantly, besides being historically indispensible and an extraordinary deal for the consumer, this music is an absolute pleasure to hear. —*Richard S. Ginell*

Live In: Montreux / 1991 / Elektra ✦✦✦
The eminence grise of bossa nova steps halfway out of the shadows in a performance that, as always, adds new depth to the word reflective. Guitar of perfect simplicity backs vocals at once provisional-seeming and definitive. The songs themselves mix standards like "Aquarela do Brasil" and "Garota de Ipanema" with less familiar songs. —*John Storm Roberts, Original Music*

Joao / Dec. 22, 1992 / Verve ✦✦✦✦
Recent but classic jazz-bossa is played by one of its defining spirits. Vocally, Gilberto is in fine muttering form, communicating intensely with somebody in his breast pocket, and his guitar is as delicate as ever. This recording expresses the

close links of bossa nova and jazz. *Joao* has Clare Fisher arranging and on some cuts playing keyboards, along with one of those saccharin string sections even the most avant-garde Brazilians love. —*John Storm Roberts*

Dizzy Gillespie (John Birks Gillespie)

b. Oct. 21, 1917, Cheraw, SC, **d.** Jan. 6, 1993, Englewood, NJ
Trumpet Leader, Composer / Bop, Afro-Cuban Jazz, Jump Blues

Dizzy Gillespie's contributions to jazz were huge. One of the greatest jazz trumpeters of all time (some would say the best), Gillespie was such a complex player that his contemporaries ended up copying Miles Davis and Fats Navarro instead, and it was not until Jon Faddis' emergence in the 1970s that Dizzy's style was successfully recreated. Somehow Gillespie could make any "wrong" note fit and harmonically he was ahead of everyone in the 1940s, including Charlie Parker. Unlike Bird, Dizzy was an enthusiastic teacher who wrote down his musical innovations and was eager to explain them to the next generation, thereby insuring that bebop would eventually become the foundation of jazz.

Dizzy Gillespie was also one of the key founders of Afro-Cuban (or Latin) jazz, adding Chano Pozo's conga to his orchestra in 1947 and utilizing complex polyrhythms early on. The leader of two of the finest big bands in jazz history, Gillespie differed from many in the bop generation by being a masterful showman who could make his music seem both accessible and fun to the audience. With his puffed-out cheeks, bent trumpet (which occurred by accident in the early '50s when a dancer tripped over his horn) and quick wit, Dizzy was a colorful figure to watch. A natural comedian, Gillespie was also a superb scat singer and occasionally played Latin percussion for the fun of it, but it was his trumpet playing and leadership abilities that made him into a jazz giant.

The youngest of nine children, John Birks Gillespie taught himself trombone and then switched to trumpet when he was 12. He grew up in poverty, won a scholarship to an agricultural school (Laurinburg Institute in North Carolina) and then in 1935 dropped out of school to look for work as a musician. Inspired and initially greatly influenced by Roy Eldridge, Gillespie (who soon gained the nickname of Dizzy) joined Frankie Fairfax's band in Philadelphia. In 1937 he became a member of Teddy Hill's Orchestra in a spot formerly filled by Eldridge. Dizzy made his recording debut on Hill's rendition of "King Porter Stomp" and during his short period with the band toured Europe. After freelancing for a year, Gillespie joined Cab Calloway's Orchestra (1939-41), recording frequently with the popular bandleader and taking many short solos that trace his development; "Pickin' the Cabbage" finds Dizzy starting to emerge from Eldridge's shadow. However Calloway did not care for Gillespie's constant chance-taking, calling his solos "Chinese music." After an incident in 1941 when a spitball was mischievously thrown at Calloway (he accused Gillespie but the culprit was actually Jonah Jones), Dizzy was fired.

By then Gillespie had already met Charlie Parker who confirmed the validity of his musical search. During 1941-43 Dizzy passed through many bands including those led by Ella Fitzgerald, Coleman Hawkins, Benny Carter, Charlie Barnet, Fess Williams, Les Hite, Claude Hopkins, Lucky Millinder (with whom he recorded in 1942) and even Duke Ellington (for four weeks). Gillespie also contributed several advanced arrangements to such bands as Benny Carter, Jimmy Dorsey and Woody Herman; the latter advised him to give up his trumpet playing and stick to full-time arranging!

Dizzy ignored the advice, jammed at Minton's Playhouse and Monroe's Uptown House where he tried out his new ideas, and in late 1942 joined Earl Hines' big band. Charlie Parker was hired on tenor and the sadly unrecorded orchestra was the first orchestra to explore early bebop. By then Gillespie had his style together and he wrote his most famous composition "A Night in Tunisia." When Hines' singer Billy Eckstine went on his own and formed a new bop big band, Diz and Bird (along with Sarah Vaughan) were among the members. Gillespie stayed long enough to record a few numbers with Eckstine in 1944 (most noticeably "Opus X" and "Blowing the Blues Away"). That year he also participated in a pair of Coleman Hawkins-led sessions that are often thought of as the first full-fledged bebop dates, highlighted by Dizzy's composition "Woody 'n You."

1945 was the breakthrough year. Dizzy Gillespie, who had led earlier bands on 52nd Street, finally teamed up with Charlie Parker on records. Their recordings of such numbers as "Salt Peanuts," "'Shaw Nuff," "Groovin' High" and "Hot House" confused swing fans who had never heard the advanced music as it was evolving and Dizzy's rendition of "I Can't Get Started" completely reworked the former Bunny Berigan hit. It would take two years for the often-frantic but ultimately logical new style to start catching on as the mainstream of jazz. Gillespie led an unsuccessful big band in 1945 (a Southern tour finished it) and late in the year he travelled with Parker to the West Coast to play a lengthy gig at Billy Berg's club in L.A. Unfortunately the audiences were not enthusiastic (other than local musicians) and Dizzy (without Parker) soon returned to New York.

The following year Dizzy Gillespie put together a successful and influential orchestra which survived for nearly four memorable years. "Manteca" became a standard, the exciting "Things to Come" was futuristic and "Cubana Be/Cubana Bop" featured Chano Pozo. With such sidemen as the future original members of the Modern Jazz Quartet (Milt Jackson, John Lewis, Ray Brown and Kenny Clarke), James Moody, J.J. Johnson, Yusef Lateef and even a young John Coltrane, Gillespie's big band was a breeding ground for the new music. Dizzy's beret, goatee and "bop glasses" helped make him a symbol of the music and its most popular figure. During 1948-49 nearly every former swing band was trying to play bop and for a brief period the major record companies tried very hard to turn the music into a fad.

By 1950 the fad had ended and Gillespie was forced due to economic pressures to break up his groundbreaking orchestra. He had occasional (and always exciting) reunions with Charlie Parker (including a fabled Massey Hall concert in 1953) up until Bird's death in 1955, toured with Jazz at the Philharmonic (where he had opportunities to "battle" the combative Roy Eldridge), headed all-star recording sessions (using Stan Getz, Sonny Rollins and Sonny Stitt on some dates) and led combos that for a time in 1951 also featured Coltrane and Milt Jackson. In 1956 Gillespie was authorized to form a big band and play a tour overseas sponsored by the State Department. It was so successful that more traveling followed including extensive tours to the Near East, Europe and South America, and the band survived up to 1958. Among the young sidemen were Lee Morgan, Joe Gordon, Melba Liston, Al Grey, Billy Mitchell, Benny Golson, Ernie Henry and Wynton Kelly; Quincy Jones (along with Golson and Liston) contributed some of the arrangements. After the orchestra broke up, Gillespie went back to leading small groups, featuring such sidemen in the 1960s as Junior Mance, Leo Wright, Lalo Schifrin, James Moody and Kenny Barron. He retained his popularity, occasionally headed specially assembled big bands and was a fixture at jazz festivals. In the early '70s, Gillespie toured with the Giants of Jazz and around that time his trumpet playing began to fade, a gradual decline that would make most of his 1980s work quite erratic. However Dizzy remained a world traveler, an inspiration and teacher to younger players, and during his last couple of years he was the leader of the United Nation Orchestra (featuring Paquito D'Rivera and Arturo Sandoval). He was active up until early 1992.

Dizzy Gillespie's career was very well documented from 1945 on, particularly on Musicraft, Dial and RCA in the 1940s, Verve in the 1950s, Philips and Limelight in the 1960s and Pablo in later years. —*Scott Yanow*

★ **The Complete RCA Victor Recordings 1937-1949** / May 17, 1937-Jul. 6, 1949 / Bluebird ✦✦✦✦✦

This two-CD set dwarfs all previous reissues of the trumpeter's Victor output. Gillespie's pioneering bebop big band made many of their greatest recordings for that label and they are all here including the original version of "Manteca", "Two Bass Hit", "Cubana Be/Cubana Bop", "Good Bait", "Hey Pete! Le's Eat Mo' Meat" and "Jumpin' With Symphony Sid"; among the soloists are tenors James Moody and Yusef Lateef, trombonist J.J. Johnson and the innovative Chano Pozo on congas. In addition, this essential release has Gillespie's three earliest recorded solos (with Teddy Hill's Orchestra in 1937), "Hot Mallets" with Lionel Hampton's all-star group in 1939, a combo session (four songs and three alternate takes) with Don Byas and Milt Jackson in 1946 and the two versions of "Overtime" and "Victory Ball" that Dizzy made with the 1949 Metronome All-Stars. "Overtime" has a tradeoff between trumpeters Gillespie, Fats Navarro and Miles Davis! No jazz collection is complete without this innovative and exciting music. —*Scott Yanow*

Groovin' High [Drive Archive] / Feb. 29, 1945-Feb. 22, 1953 / Drive Archive ✦✦✦

This budget-price Drive Archive CD features trumpeter Dizzy Gillespie during two different periods. He is heard along with Charlie Parker on classic versions of "Groovin' High," "Dizzy Atmosphere" and "All the Things You Are" from 1945. Much rarer are his 1952 Paris recordings with tenor saxophonist Don Byas and pianist Arnold Ross and his 1953 session with strings; during the latter Gillespie virtually ignores the unswinging string arrangements and comes up with melodic variations for the standard melodies. Although not essential, there are some very interesting performances on this boppish CD. —*Scott Yanow*

Oo Bop / Feb. 1945-Feb. 22, 1953 / Tradition ✦✦✦

A ragtag of sessions from 1945, 1946, 1952, and 1953. The 1945 cuts (including "Salt Peanuts") also have Charlie Parker aboard; the ones from 1946 are less innovative and far more commercial-minded, with Alice Roberts on vocals. There's also a number with strings from 1953, and a selection ("Perdido") from the famous 1953 Massey Hall concert with Gillespie, Parker, Bud Powell, Charles Mingus, and Max Roach. There's good stuff here, no doubt, but it's too thematically scattered; it makes more sense to get the material on more focused compilations. —*Richie Unterberger*

Shaw Nuff / Feb. 9, 1945-Nov. 12, 1946 / Musicraft ✦✦✦✦✦
This CD has Dizzy Gillespie's classic Musicraft sides (all except "A Handfulla Gimme"), some of the most famous recordings of his long career. These influential performances (which set the standard for bebop) include "Blue 'n' Boogie" (with tenor saxophonist Dexter Gordon), seven gems with Charlie Parker (highlighted by "Groovin' High," "Hot House" and "Salt Peanuts"), a few numbers with Sonny Stitt and nine big-band recordings including "Our Delight," "Ray's Idea" and the futuristic "Things to Come." If Dizzy Gillespie's career had ended after these recordings, he would still be famous in the jazz world. —*Scott Yanow*

One Bass Hit / May 15, 1946-Nov. 12, 1946 / Musicraft ✦✦✦✦✦
A good reissue spotlighting Gillespie's prime orchestra in the mid '40s. —*Ron Wynn*

Dizzier and Dizzier / Aug. 22, 1947-Jul. 6, 1949 / RCA ✦✦✦
Because all of Dizzy Gillespie's recordings from the 1946-49 period for Victor are already available on a definitive two-CD set, this single disc sampler is rather pointless except possibly for beginners. There are 17 selections taken from this period and some of the classics (such as "Manteca") are actually missing from this reissue. There are some great moments including three of the four numbers from a notable small-group date in 1946 and such tunes as "Two Bass Hit," "Good Bait" and "Hey Pete! Le's Eat More Meat" but this CD can be safely passed by in favor of the earlier release. —*Scott Yanow*

It Happened One Night / Sep. 29, 1947 / Natural Organic ✦✦✦✦
On the night of Sept. 29, 1947, there were three sets of music at Carnegie Hall: the Dizzy Gillespie Big Band, Ella Fitzgerald backed by the orchestra and the Dizzy Gillespie-Charlie Parker Quintet. The second and third parts of the show are included on this very interesting LP. Fitzgerald sounds fine on tunes such as "Lady Be Good" and "How High the Moon," scatting while being backed by the big band. However the reason to search for this set is to get the five titles from Diz and Bird. This version of "Confirmation" has some miraculous Parker. —*Scott Yanow*

Live at Carnegie Hall / Sep. 29, 1947 / Artistry ✦✦✦✦
This LP documents the same concert (but a different set) as *It Happened One Night*. The Dizzy Gillespie Orchestra performs ten selections including several that they never recorded commercially (such as "Relaxin' at Camarillo," "Salt Peanuts," "Hot House" and "Toccata for Trumpet") plus "new" versions of "Cubana Be/ Cubana Bop" and "Things to Come." The leader/trumpeter, who is the main soloist throughout, is in particularly fiery form on this very enjoyable (and somewhat historical) set. —*Scott Yanow*

Bebop Enters Sweden 1947-1949 / Dec. 20, 1947-1949 / Dragon ✦✦✦✦
A rather fascinating LP, *Bebop Enters Sweden* features radio broadcasts from Sweden by three American bop groups. Chubby Jackson & His Fifth Dimensional Jazz Group, an all-star sextet of Woody Herman alumni, performs three numbers and tenor saxophonist James Moody is heard sitting in with trumpeter Gosta Torner's Jam Session Band for three other songs, but the bulk of this set is taken up by Dizzy Gillespie's orchestra. From early 1948, that classic band provides fresh variations on such songs as "Our Delight," "Manteca" and "Ray's Idea." —*Scott Yanow*

Dizzy Gillespie and Max Roach in Paris / Feb. 28, 1948+May 15, 1949 / Vogue ✦✦✦✦
The bulk of this CD from the French Vogue label features the Dizzy Gillespie Orchestra in particularly strong form at a Paris concert. In addition to the leader/ trumpeter, the main soloists are altoist Howard Johnson, Big Nick Nicholas on tenor, pianist John Lewis and Chano Pozo on congas. The highlights of this date (which was formerly made available domestically on LP by Prestige) include "Woody'n' You," "I Can't Get Started," "Good Bait," "Afro-Cuban Drum Suite" (which is really "Cubana Be") and "Things to Come." In addition there are four selections from a 1949 quintet led by drummer Max Roach that stars trumpeter Kenny Dorham, James Moody on tenor and pianist Al Haig. —*Scott Yanow*

Dizzy Gillespie and His Big Band / Jul. 26, 1948 / GNP ✦✦✦✦✦
The Dizzy Gillespie Big Band was the most innovative jazz orchestra of 1946-49, proof that bebop was not exclusively a small-group music. All of its recordings are well worth acquiring and this particular CD gives one a well-rounded picture of the orchestra at a concert before an enthusiastic crowd. With prominence given James Moody's tenor, Cecil Payne on baritone and Chano Pozo on congas (he was killed a short time after this performance) in addition to the remarkable leader/ trumpeter, the Dizzy Gillespie Orchestra is heard at its absolute prime. Versions of "Good Bait," "One Bass Hit" and "Manteca" are among the highlights of this recommended CD. —*Scott Yanow*

Good Bait / Dec. 1948-Jul. 1949 / Spotlite ✦✦✦✦
This LP features the Dizzy Gillespie Orchestra on a pair of extensive radio broadcasts from late 1948 and mid-1949. Considering that its studio recordings were declining during this period (as Capitol records tried to cash in on the "bebop fad") and that the big band would break up altogether in early 1950, these perfor-

mances are quite valuable. But more importantly, with such soloists as altoist Ernie Henry, tenor saxophonist Yusef Lateef and trombonist J.J. Johnson in addition to Dizzy himself, the music is consistently exciting. It's available from the English Spotlite label. —*Scott Yanow*

The Dizzy's Diamonds: The Best of Verve Years / Jun. 6, 1950-Nov. 6, 1964 / Verve ✦✦✦
Many of trumpeter Dizzy Gillespie's recordings for the Verve label in the '50s and early '60s (when he was at the peak of his powers) have inexcusably been out of print for decades. This three-CD set is a sampler of his legacy, with the discs subtitled "Big Band," "Small Groups & Guests" and "In an Afro Cuban, Bossa Nova, Calypso Groove." The programming jumps all over the place and makes little sense but this set serves as a good excuse to acquire 40 performances by the great Gillespie and the many all-stars who recorded with him. Few but the most fanatical veteran Gillespie fans will have had all of these selections in their collection. This will fill a void until Verve gets around to doing a much more comprehensive Dizzy Gillespie reissue program. —*Scott Yanow*

Dee Gee Days: Savoy Sessions / Mar. 1, 1951-Jul. 18, 1952 / Savoy ✦✦✦
During 1951-52, Dizzy Gillespie had his own record label, Dee Gee. Having been forced to break up his big band in 1950 due to the impossible financial situation, he was working regularly with a small group which for a short while included a young tenor named John Coltrane; the future giant's first recorded solo ("We Love to Boogie") is one of the highlights of this CD. Gillespie is heard in a wide variety of novelties, bop romps and ballads on this diverse program. There are many vocals from him and Joe Carroll, a funny parody of Louis Armstrong on "Umbrella Man," and one extended performance on the fiery "The Champ"; all of the other cuts are in the three-minute range. Enjoyable but not essential music. —*Scott Yanow*

Dizzy Gillespie / Mar. 25, 1952-Feb. 22, 1953 / Everest ✦✦✦
This budget LP gives no personnel or date information so one gets what they pay for. Actually the half-hour of music is generally quite rewarding. Dizzy Gillespie is teamed with expatriate tenor Don Byas on "Blue and Sentimental" and fronts a rhythm section for strong versions of "Sleepy Time Down South" and "Blue Moon." The other seven tracks find Gillespie performing with "his Operatic Strings" but the results are much more exhilarating than one might fear. He does not let the arrangements inhibit him and he plays brilliantly throughout. This music deserves better treatment than was given it by Everest (it should be reissued complete and in chronological order with all of the discographical data) but, if found at a cheap price, get this. —*Scott Yanow*

Dizzy Gillespie in Paris, Vol. 2 / Mar. 27, 1952-Feb. 22, 1953 / Vogue ✦✦✦✦✦
The second of two CD volumes of Dizzy Gillespie performances put out by Vogue has the full contents from three of his Paris studio sessions. The great trumpeter heads a quintet that includes tenor saxophonist Don Byas and pianist Arnold Ross on four songs (plus three alternate takes); highlights include Gillespie's playing on "I Cover the Waterfront" and his vocal on the two versions of "Say Eh." The most rewarding of the sets finds him leading a septet on such numbers as "Cripple Crapple Crutch" (which has his classic blues vocal), "Somebody Loves Me" and two versions of "Wrap Your Troubles in Dreams." The final eight selections feature Dizzy Gillespie's regular band of 1953 (with trombonist Nat Peck in baritonist Bill Graham's place). Vocalist Joe Carroll helps out on a couple of the numbers and Gillespie is in particularly memorable form on "My Man" and "'S'Wonderful." This highly enjoyable music is easily recommended. —*Scott Yanow*

On the Sunny Side of the Street / 1952-Feb. 1953 / Moon ✦✦✦✦
On this Moon CD, trumpet great Dizzy Gillespie is heard in three different settings. Four songs (including a 13-minute version of "Perdido") are from his 1952 visit to Paris and have Gillespie's regular group augmented by tenor saxophonist Don Byas, a combination that works quite well. In addition Gillespie and his band play "On the Sunny Side of the Street" later in the year (a version mostly featuring Joe Carroll's vocal) and the trumpeter's quintet performs five numbers during a German concert in 1953. These renditions make for interesting comparisons to Gillespie's more familiar versions of his repertoire made for larger companies during the era. Highlights include "The Champ," "Good Bait," "Perdido," "They Can't Take That Away from Me" and "Manteca." —*Scott Yanow*

Dizzy Gillespie/Gerry Mulligan / 1952-1961 / Europa ✦✦✦✦
The previously unissued performances included on this Italian LP were mostly recorded in Europe and add to the legacy of several of their participants. Trumpet-great Dizzy Gillespie jams five tunes with a group of Europeans plus expatriate tenor Don Byas. Altoist Hubert Fol and the rhythm section from the same date perform a fine version of "Everything Happens to Me" and this LP concludes with a Gerry Mulligan-led jam session that teams the baritonist with trumpeter Ruby Braff and tenor saxophonist Bud Freeman for a fine version of "Rose Room." Nice music, nothing too essential. —*Scott Yanow*

Dizzy Gillespie in Paris, Vol. 1 / Feb. 9, 1953 / Vogue ✦✦✦✦
This CD fully (except for a saxophone feature) documents a Paris concert by Dizzy Gillespie and his quintet with baritonist Bill Graham (the liners mistakenly list him as playing alto and tenor), pianist Wade Legge, bassist Lou Hackney and drummer Al Jones. Actually, singer Joe Carroll (whose overly enthusiastic vocals are an acquired taste) co-stars with Gillespie on many of the selections. There is plenty of joking around but the trumpeter is in consistently inventive form before a very appreciative crowd during a well-rounded show. Highlights include "The Champ," "Good Bait," Sarah Vaughan's guest vocal on "Embraceable You," and "Ooh-Shoo-Bee-Doo-Be." —*Scott Yanow*

Diz and Getz / Dec. 9, 1953+Oct. 16, 1956 / Verve ✦✦✦✦✦
Dizzy Gillespie was at the peak of his powers throughout the 1950s, still the pace-setter among trumpeters. This double CD matches Dizzy with Stan Getz, the Oscar Peterson Trio and drummer Max Roach. Getz, although identified with the "cool" school, thrived on competition and is both relaxed and combative on the uptempo explorations of "It Don't Mean a Thing" and "Impromptu." —*Scott Yanow*

★ **Dizzy Gillespie with Roy Eldridge** / Oct. 29, 1954 / Verve ✦✦✦✦✦
To call this music "classic" would be a great understatement. Producer Norman Granz loved to team together combative musicians in jam sessions, both live and in the studios. Since Roy Eldridge was one of the most competitive of trumpeters and Dizzy Gillespie considered him his original idol, they made a perfect matchup. This two-CD set includes a ballad medley and a few slower pieces, but to hear Gillespie and Eldridge battling on "I've Found a New Baby" and "Limehouse Blues" is to hear two of the very best trying to cut each other. Highly recommended for all jazz collections. —*Scott Yanow*

One Night in Washington / Mar. 13, 1955 / Elektra ✦✦✦
This excellent LP documents a meeting between trumpeter Dizzy Gillespie and a Washington, D.C.-based orchestra in 1955. Gillespie is the only significant soloist on the four-part "Afro Suite" (which includes "Manteca"), a couple of Buster Harding pieces, "Tin Tin Deo," "Caravan" and a group original. The big band is fine (if not distinctive) in support of the great trumpeter. —*Scott Yanow*

Dizzy Gillespie and His Big Band at Birdland / 1956 / Sandy Hook ✦✦✦
This LP (put out by a collector's label) contains a couple of radio broadcasts featuring Dizzy Gillespie's acclaimed big band of 1956, the one that toured the world. With altoist Phil Woods, tenor Billy Mitchell and pianist Walter Davis among the supporting cast, trumpeter Gillespie felt that a big band such as this one was a perfect setting for his music. Among the better selections on this set are "Night in Tunisia," the always humorous "Doodlin'" and "Dizzy's Business." —*Scott Yanow*

The Modern Jazz Sextet / Jan. 12, 1956 / Verve ✦✦✦✦
Producer Norman Granz was a near-genius at matching together jazz musicians in such a way that they would stimulate each other to play above their heads. He always loved jam sessions, but it did not take too much insight to realize that putting trumpeter Dizzy Gillespie and altoist Sonny Stitt together with a strong rhythm section would result in some explosive music. The fireworks really fly on this LP during versions of "Tour de Force," "Dizzy Meets Sonny," "Mean to Me" and "Blues for Bird," with time out taken for a ballad medley. Bebop at its best. —*Scott Yanow*

On Tour with Dizzy Gillespie and His Big Band / Aug. 1956 / Artistry ✦✦✦
The Dizzy Gillespie Big Band of 1956 was caught in concert for this excellent LP. The spirited young orchestra plays such standbys as "The Champ," the humorous "Doodlin'" and "Groovin' High" (featuring altoist Phil Woods) along with Gillespie's showcases "Begin the Beguine" and "Stella by Starlight." This classic ensemble was unfortunately disbanded in early 1958. —*Scott Yanow*

☆ **Birk's Works: Verve Big Band Sessions** / May 25, 1956-Apr. 8, 1957/ Verve ✦✦✦✦✦
Dizzy Gillespie's globetrotting big band of 1956-57 was one of his finest groups, a very exciting orchestra that at various times had such players as trumpeters Gillespie, Joe Gordon and Lee Morgan, trombonists Melba Liston and Al Grey, altoists Phil Woods and Ernie Henry, the tenors of Billy Mitchell, Ernie Wilkins and Benny Golson, and pianists Walter Davis, Jr. and Wynton Kelly. With arrangements contributed by Quincy Jones (who was in the trumpet section), Wilkins, Liston and Golson, this was a classic orchestra. Its three studio albums plus a few numbers only previously out on samplers and nine previously unreleased performances (mostly alternate takes) are on this wonderful two-CD set. The high points are many including "Dizzy's Business," "Jessica's Day," "The Champ," "Cool Breeze," "Birks Works," "Whisper Not," "Stablemates" and "I Remember Clifford." Essential music. —*Scott Yanow*

"Live" 1957 / Jun. 14, 1957 / Jazz Unlimited ✦✦✦
Although not quite up to the exciting level of their Newport Jazz Festival appearance of a month later, this live CD of the Dizzy Gillespie big band gives one a

strong set from the legendary orchestra. In addition to the leader/trumpeter, such soloists as Lee Morgan (who takes the opening trumpet solo on "Night in Tunisia"), altoist Ernie Henry, trombonist Al Grey and Benny Golson on tenor make strong impressions. "Jordu," "I Remember Clifford," a blazing "Cool Breeze" and a humorous "Doodlin'" are among the highlights. —*Scott Yanow*

The Dizzy Gillespie Big Band / Jun. 14, 1957 / Jazz Hour ✦✦✦✦
Recorded less than a month before their exciting appearance at the 1957 Newport Jazz Festival, the Dizzy Gillespie Orchestra is in excellent form on this date from a concert in Chester, PA. Despite there being liner notes, nowhere on this CD is the personnel of the orchestra listed. In addition to the trumpeter/leader, the key soloists are trombonist Al Grey, tenor saxophonist Billy Mitchell and during the first part of "A Night in Tunisia," a young Lee Morgan. Other than an Austin Kromer vocal on "Wonder Why," the performances are generally quite rewarding with this version of the torrid "Cool Breeze" making for an intriguing comparison with the classic rendition from Newport. —*Scott Yanow*

★ **At Newport** / Jul. 6, 1957 / Verve ✦✦✦✦✦
This CD features Dizzy Gillespie's second great big band at the peak of its powers. On the rapid "Dizzy's Blues" and a truly blazing "Cool Breeze," the orchestra really roars; the latter performance features extraordinary solos by Gillespie, trombonist Al Grey and tenor saxophonist Billy Mitchell. In addition to fine renditions of "Manteca" and Benny Golson's then-recent composition "I Remember Clifford," the humorous "Doodlin'" is given a definitive treatment, there is a fresh version of "A Night in Tunisia" and pianist Mary Lou Williams sits in for a lengthy medley of selections from her "Zodiac Suite." This brilliant CD captures one of the high points of Dizzy Gillespie's remarkable career and is highly recommended. —*Scott Yanow*

Talkin' Verve / Jul. 6, 1957-Oct. 26, 1966 / Verve ✦✦
In the 1990s, Verve had several CD reissue programs going on simultaneously. "Talkin' Verve" was one of their more eccentric series, and some of those releases did not have much of a plot or purpose. This particular set draws its material from a wide variety of Dizzy Gillespie recordings (most readily available in more coherent fashion elsewhere), focusing on some of his more danceable performances (sort of). Certainly the lightweight renditions of "Theme from the Cool World," "Walk on the Wild Side," "Kush," "Bang, Bang" and "Swing Low, Sweet Cadillac" are far from classics, either as bebop or Afro-Cuban jazz. So overall, this is a rather frivolous and forgettable reissue. —*Scott Yanow*

Dizzy Gillespie Duets / Dec. 11, 1957 / Verve ✦✦✦✦✦

The Greatest Trumpet of Them All / Dec. 17, 1957 / Verve ✦✦
The title given this LP may very well be true, but this particular session is surprisingly restrained. Dizzy Gillespie is heard in an octet with tenor saxophonist Benny Golson, altoist Gigi Gryce, trombonist Henry Coker and baritonist Pee Wee Moore, but the Golson arrangements seem to inhibit the trumpeter and the repertoire (mostly by Golson and Gryce) fails to inspire Gillespie. For many other jazz musicians this would be a "good" or even "fine" effort, but Dizzy Gillespie has recorded too much classic music for this disappointment to rate very high. —*Scott Yanow*

Sonny Side Up / Dec. 19, 1957 / Verve ✦✦✦✦✦
W/ Sonny Rollins and Sonny Stitt (sax). The dynamic threesome hit some impressive heights, with Stitt at his peak. —*Ron Wynn*

The Ebullient Mr. Gillespie / Feb. 17, 1959-Feb. 20, 1959 / Verve ✦✦✦
Dizzy Gillespie was certainly in good spirits for this long out-of-print session with his sextet, an ensemble also featuring pianist Junior Mance, Les Spann on flute and guitar and the congas of Chino Pozo (a cousin of the late Chano). Gillespie jokes around on "Swing Low, Sweet Cadillac," sings "Umbrella Man" and otherwise emphasizes more mellow material. A pleasing—if not all that essential—date of melodic music from the masterful trumpeter. —*Scott Yanow*

Have Trumpet, Will Excite! / Feb. 17, 1959-Feb. 20, 1959 / Verve ✦✦✦
With his globetrotting big band now in the past, Dizzy Gillespie headed a quintet featuring pianist Junior Mance and Les Spann on flute and guitar for this excellent effort. Gillespie is at his best on such unlikely material as "My Heart Belongs to Daddy," "My Man" and "I Found a Million Dollar Baby." Pity that Verve has allowed so many of its great Dizzy Gillespie recordings (including this one) to be out of print literally for decades. —*Scott Yanow*

Copenhagen Concert / Sep. 17, 1959 / Steeple Chase ✦✦✦
This Steeple Chase CD for the first time releases music from a Sept. 17, 1959, Copenhagen concert featuring trumpeter Dizzy Gillespie and his Quintet of the period (which includes altoist Leo Wright, pianist Junior Mance, bassist Art Davis and drummer Teddy Stewart). Wright (who doubled on flute) was a perfectly suitable musical partner for Gillespie (staying with the group until 1962) and was always able to take assertive solos without trying to steal the spotlight from the trumpeter. Diz is in good spirits throughout these two sets, singing a good-humored "Ooh-Shoo-Bee-Doo-Be" and scatting furiously on "Lady Be Good." His

trumpet chops are in excellent form and his solos are as complex as ever. Highlights include "My Man," "Wheatleigh Hall," "Night in Tunisia" and "Woody 'n You." —*Scott Yanow*

Gillespiana / Carnegie Hall Concert / Nov. 14, 1960-Mar. 4, 1961 / Verve ✦✦✦✦✦
This CD combines two complete and related LPs. When Lalo Schifrin joined Dizzy Gillespie's Quintet in 1960, he was encouraged by Gillespie to write an extended work for him. "Gillespiana" was the result, an impressive five-movement suite that showcased the trumpeter's talents with a large orchestra. The latter half of this CD was recorded at Carnegie Hall the same day that "Gillespiana" was debuted live, but those five pieces are more conventional, highlighted by remakes of "Manteca" and "Night in Tunisia" (the latter as the more involved "Tunisian Fantasy"). Only an overly silly version of "Ool Ya Koo" with Joe Carroll detracts from this otherwise superb release. —*Scott Yanow*

Dizzy Gillespie Quintet in Europe / 1961 / Unique ✦✦
The 1961 Dizzy Gillespie Quintet (with Mel Lewis subbing on drums) is heard at a European concert playing their standard repertoire. This budget LP from Italy (which lacks any liner notes and the exact recording date) has decent versions of "Lady Be Good," "There Is No Greater Love," "The Mooche," "Night in Tunisia" and "Long Long Summer" but there are better examples of this particular group elsewhere. —*Scott Yanow*

☆ **An Electrifying Evening with the Dizzy Gillespie Quintet** / Feb. 9, 1961 / Verve ✦✦✦✦✦
Why isn't the exciting music on this LP available on CD? Dizzy Gillespie (along with altoist Leo Wright, pianist Lalo Schifrin, bassist Bob Cunningham and drummer Chuck Lampkin) were in peak form for this live performance. Their versions of "Kush," "Salt Peanuts" and "The Mooche" are all excellent, but it is "A Night in Tunisia," with its absolutely stunning trumpet break (which lasts half a chorus), that is most memorable. —*Scott Yanow*

Perceptions / May 22, 1961 / Verve ✦✦✦
This unusual session consists of a complex six-movement suite by J.J. Johnson featuring Dizzy Gillespie's trumpet over a brass choir (six trumpets, two trombones, two bass trombones, four French horns and two tubas), bass, drums, percussion and two harps. Often reminiscent of classical music, Johnson's writing allows plenty of room for Gillespie to improvise. The result is a rather unique set of music that is well worth searching for. —*Scott Yanow*

Dizzy on the French Riviera / May 1962-Jul. 1962 / Philips ✦✦✦✦✦
Long out of print, this highly enjoyable LP finds trumpeter Dizzy Gillespie and his quintet joined by guitarist Elek Bacsik and percussionist Pepito Riestria for some joyous explorations of bossa nova rhythms and related material. This extended version of Antonio Carlos Jobim's "No More Blues" is classic and the quintet's renditions of "Long Long Summer," "Desafinado" and "Here It Is" are also memorable. In addition to the trumpeter, altoist Leo Wright and pianist Lalo Schifrin have plenty of solo space. All of Gillespie's Philips recordings should be reissued on CD. —*Scott Yanow*

New Wave / May 1962-Jul. 1962 / Philips ✦✦✦✦✦
It is such a pity that Dizzy Gillespie Philips' LPs have yet to be reissued on CD, for the trumpeter (45 at the time of this recording) was at the peak of his powers in the early '60s. On such songs as "In a Shanty in Old Shanty Town," "Careless Love," "One Note Samba" and the "Theme from *Black Orpheus*," Gillespie and his expanded quintet (with guests Bola Sete or Elec Bacsik on guitar and Charlie Ventura taking a memorable bass sax solo on "No More Blues-Part II") show a great deal of spirit and creativity. Leo Wright (on alto and flute) and pianist Lalo Schifrin are also in fine form throughout this gem. —*Scott Yanow*

Composer's Concepts / Sep. 1962-Apr. 23, 1964 / EmArcy ✦✦✦
This interesting double LP contains Lalo Schifrin's six-movement work for Dizzy Gillespie and a large orchestra titled "The New Continent," three compositions by Tom McIntosh for Gillespie's 1963 quintet and 11 themes from Mal Waldron that were played by Gillespie's group for the soundtrack of *The Cool World*. Little all that memorable occurs but Diz has plenty of fine trumpet solos. —*Scott Yanow*

Something Old, Something New / Apr. 23, 1963 / Philips ✦✦✦✦✦
This out-of-print LP features the 1963 Dizzy Gillespie Quintet at its best. With strong soloing by tenor saxophonist James Moody and pianist Kenny Barron, trumpeter Gillespie was inspired to play at his best. These rapid versions of "Be-Bop" and "Dizzy Atmosphere" are classic, "Good Bait" receives definitive treatment and the logical medley of "I Can't Get Started" and "'Round Midnight" is also quite memorable. The remainder of this essential (but sadly unavailable) set includes three Tom McIntosh compositions and "This Lovely Feeling." —*Scott Yanow*

Dizzy Gillespie and the Double Six of Paris / Jul. 8, 1963 / Verve ✦✦✦
This odd (but successful) matchup finds the Double Six of Paris singing vocalese in French to a dozen bebop classics associated with Dizzy Gillespie. Gillespie with

pianist Bud Powell and a rhythm section take solos that uplift this date; two songs feature his quintet (with James Moody on alto). Not for all tastes, this is a unique addition to Dizzy Gillespie's discography. —*Scott Yanow*

The Cool World/Dizzy Goes Hollywood / Sep. 11, 1963-Apr. 23, 1964 / Verve ✦✦✦✦
This single CD reissues all of the music from two rare Dizzy Gillespie LPs. Dating from 1963-64, the set features the trumpeter's interpretation of the score of the obscure film *The Cool World* (although these are not the actual performances heard in the movie) plus 11 themes from other films. Gillespie, who is joined by James Moody (on tenor, alto and flute), pianist Kenny Barron, bassist Chris White and drummer Rudy Collins, was in peak form during that era and hopefully all of his other Philips recordings will also be reissued by Verve in the future. Although the liner notes deal only with *The Cool World*, the other set is actually of greater interest. Gillespie uplifts such tunes as the "Theme from Exodus," "Moon River," "Days of Wine and Roses," "Never on Sunday" and "Walk on the Wild Side," turning them into swinging jazz. *The Cool World* pieces (all composed by Mal Waldron) are also worth hearing although they are not as memorable overall. This set is a real historical curiosity and, although not essential, it is a release that should please Dizzy Gillespie fans while reminding others of how great a trumpeter he was before his long decline. —*Scott Yanow*

Jambo Caribe / Nov. 4, 1964-Nov. 6, 1964 / Limelight ✦✦✦
This fun LP features Dizzy Gillespie and his quintet plus the percussion of Kansas Fields playing eight rhythmic pieces influenced by melodies from South America. Such tunes as "Fiesta Mo-jo," "Jambo" and "Trinidad, Goodbye" never became standards but "And Then She Stopped" was played by Gillespie in future years. Good music if not one of his classics. —*Scott Yanow*

With Gil Fuller and the Monterey Jazz Festival Orchestra / Oct. 1965 / Blue Note ✦✦✦
For this studio session, Dizzy Gillespie was reunited with arranger Gil Fuller who that year led a specially assembled big band for the Monterey Jazz Festival. A bit of a disappointment, this CD failed to generate the fireworks one might expect. There are some good moments, most notably on "The Shadow of Your Smile," "Groovin' High" and "Things Are Here" (the answer to "Things to Come") but the big band is mostly heard from in a purely accompanying role behind the great trumpeter and little interplay occurs. —*Scott Yanow*

And His Quintet / Nov. 24, 1965 / RTE ✦✦
During this Paris concert (released for the first time on a 1994 CD) the Dizzy Gillespie Quintet of 1965 (with James Moody on tenor and flute, pianist Kenny Barron, bassist Christopher White and drummer Rudy Collins) emphasizes Latin rhythms over straightahead swinging. The great trumpeter never really cuts loose and is often outshone by Moody who has "Umh, Umh" as a flute feature. "Chega de Saudade" is the best performance, "One Note Samba" is listenable but not memorable, "Con Alma" and "Tin Tin Deo" are typical and Gillespie has a moderately humorous vocal on the calypso "Oh Joe." Overall the set is a disappointment. —*Scott Yanow*

Swing Low, Sweet Cadillac / May 25, 1967-May 26, 1967 / GRP/Impulse! ✦✦
Although trumpeter Dizzy Gillespie was in his prime in the mid-1960s, this CD (which is a straight reissue of an Impulse LP) is a disappointment. Gillespie mostly jokes around on "Swing Low, Sweet Cadillac" (a routine he did better in the early 1950s), the brief "Bye" is a waste and Dizzy makes the mistake of singing the forgettable "Something in Your Smile" (from *Dr. Doolittle*). Although the trumpeter has decent solos on the Brazilian "Mas Que Nada" and his lengthy "Kush" and Dizzy's interplay with the audience is sometimes humorous, this effort with his quintet (which includes James Moody on tenor, alto and flute and pianist Mike Longo) is definitely a lesser effort that does not deserve to be continually reissued. —*Scott Yanow*

Live at the Village Vanguard / Oct. 1, 1967 / Blue Note ✦✦✦✦
This double CD reissues material formerly on LPs restoring several of the selections that were originally issued in edited form. A pair of unusual jam sessions, on the first (and more eccentric of the two) trumpeter Dizzy Gillespie is paired with baritonist Pepper Adams, pianist Chick Corea, bassist Richard Davis, either Mel Lewis or Elvin Jones on drums and violinist Ray Nance (who is in particularly adventurous form). The second date substitutes Garnett Brown for Nance and is a bit more conventional. These lengthy performances (all but one of the seven songs are over 11 minutes) contain some loose and rambling moments but also plenty of creative playing by this unusual group of all-stars. —*Scott Yanow*

Reunion Big Band / Nov. 7, 1968 / MPS ✦✦✦✦✦
This little-known LP actually contains one of Dizzy Gillespie's greatest performances of the 1960s. Joined by a particularly strong big band (which includes trombonist Curtis Fuller, altoist Chris Woods, James Moody on tenor, both Sahib Shihab and Cecil Payne on baritones and a screaming trumpet section), Dizzy

Gillespie performs the most exciting version of "Things to Come" ever recorded plus "One Bass Hit" and the more recent "Con Alma," "Frisco" and "The Things Are Here." Although already 51, the trumpeter is heard at his best on this hard-to-find but essential LP. —*Scott Yanow*

Enduring Magic / 1970-1985 / Black Hawk ✦✦✦
This LP contains performances by trumpeter Dizzy Gillespie with the Dwike Mitchell-Willie Ruff duo taken from five separate concerts spanning the years 1970-85. Gillespie always sounded comfortable with this group which featured Mitchell on piano and Ruff playing bass and occasional French horn. The music (which includes "Blue & Boogie," "Take the 'A' Train" and "Love for Sale") is enjoyable, intimate and swinging. —*Scott Yanow*

Dizzy Gillespie and the Dwike Mitchell-Willie Ruff Duo / 1971 / Mainstream ✦✦✦✦
Trumpeter Dizzy Gillespie sounds quite comfortable playing in an intimate setting with pianist Dwike Mitchell and Willie Ruff (who plays bass and occasional French horn). Gillespie explores a couple of recent collaborations with his sidemen plus "ConAlma," "Woody'n You" and Ruff's "Bella Bella." This is one of Gillespie's stronger sets of the '70s; he was 54 years old at the time. —*Scott Yanow*

The Giants of Jazz and Dizzy Gillespie Live / Nov. 2, 1971+Nov. 15, 1974 / Jazz Door ✦✦✦✦
This is an interesting collector's CD that bebop followers will want. The Giants of Jazz was the name for an all-star group that toured during 1971-72 and consisted of trumpeter Dizzy Gillespie, trombonist Kai Winding, altoist Sonny Stitt, pianist Thelonious Monk, bassist Al McKibbon and drummer Art Blakey. The obvious high point of their four selections on this CD (which includes a Winding feature on "Lover Man") is an exciting version of "Blue 'n' Boogie." The second half of the disc features Gillespie in 1974, playing three songs with his pianoless quartet of the period (which co-starred guitarist Al Gafa) and three with guest Sonny Stitt; the latter has fiery solos during the jams on "Groovin' High," "All the Things You Are" and "Wee." —*Scott Yanow*

Giants of Jazz / Nov. 12, 1972 / Atlantic ✦✦✦✦✦
This two-LP set (which should be reissued on CD) features a dream band comprising trumpeter Dizzy Gillespie, Sonny Stitt on alto and tenor, trombonist Kai Winding, pianist Thelonious Monk (in a very rare stint as a sideman), bassist Al McKibbon and drummer Art Blakey. In general, the all-stars perform up to their usual standards on such standards as "Night in Tunisia," "Woody 'n You ," "Tour de Force," "Allen's Alley" and "Blue 'n' Boogie." Monk is well featured on "Blue Monk" and "'Round Midnight" but Stitt steals honors on "Everything Happens to Me." A historic and superlative set. —*Scott Yanow*

The Giant / Apr. 1973 / Accord ✦✦✦
This CD finds trumpeter Dizzy Gillespie at age 55, just beginning to slip. Gillespie plays well enough on these nine selections with a fine rhythm section comprising pianist Kenny Drew, bassist Niels Pedersen, drummer Kenny Clarke and the congas of Humberto Canto; Johnny Griffin's tenor is a major asset on four numbers. Still, the edge is missing on these explorations of standards and recent originals although he is in particularly fine form on the ballads such as "I Waited for You" and "The Girl of My Dreams." —*Scott Yanow*

Dizzy Gillespie's Big Four / Sep. 19, 1974 / Pablo ✦✦✦✦✦
Arguably Dizzy Gillespie's most rewarding recording of the 1970s, this quartet date (with guitarist Joe Pass, bassist Ray Brown and drummer Mickey Roker) finds the 57-year-old trumpeter near peak form on three of his compositions and four standards. These versions of "Tanga" and "Be Bop" are brilliant. —*Scott Yanow*

Afro-Cuban Jazz Moods / Jun. 4, 1975+Jun. 5, 1975 / Original Jazz Classics ✦✦✦
Here we have a summit meeting late in the careers of the pioneering titans of Afro-Cuban jazz—Dizzy Gillespie fronting the Machito orchestra on trumpet, with Mario Bauza as music director, alto saxophonist/clarinetist, and organizing force, and Chico O'Farrill contributing the compositions and arrangements. This could have been just a nostalgic retro gathering 25 years after the fact, but instead, these guys put forth an ambitious effort to push the boundaries of the idiom. The centerpiece is a 15-minute trumpet concerto for Dizzy called "Oro, Incienso y Mirra," where O'Farrill melts dissonant clusters, electric piano comping, and synthesizer decorations together with hot Afro-Cuban rhythms into a coherent, multi-sectioned tour de force. Dizzy, who apparently had never been in the same room with synthesizers before, is magnificent as he peels off one patented bebop run after another over Machito's band and in the gaps between. There is also an equally sophisticated suite of O'Farrill pieces grouped under the title "Three Afro-Cuban Jazz Moods," which mixes rock elements into the rhythms. Parts of "Pensativo" sound as if O'Farrill had been carefully listening to Santana, the teacher learning from the student, as it were. It adds up to a paltry 32 minutes of music, yet one can forgive the short weight, this being all there is of a historic recording session. —*Richard S. Ginell*

The Dizzy Gillespie Big Seven / Jul. 16, 1975 / Pablo ✦✦✦
Recorded at the 1975 Montreux Jazz Festival, this set features trumpeter Dizzy Gillespie (then 58 years old and slightly past his prime) heading an all-star outfit (that also includes vibraphonist Milt Jackson, the tenors of Eddie "Lockjaw" Davis and Johnny Griffin, pianist Tommy Flanagan, bassist Niels Pedersen and drummer Mickey Roker) jamming three standards including a 16-minute version of "Lover, Come Back to Me." There are some fine moments (and some rambling ones) on this generally enjoyable jam session. —*Scott Yanow*

The Trumpet Kings at Montreux '75 / Jul. 16, 1975 / Pablo ✦✦✦✦
Putting competitive trumpeters Dizzy Gillespie, Roy Eldridge, and Clark Terry and an Oscar Peterson Trio with bassist Niels Pedersen and drummer Louis Bellson together before a live crowd at the Montreux Jazz Festival was a typically inspired idea by producer Norman Granz. The trumpeters bring out the best in each other on "There Is No Greater Love," "On the Alamo" and "Indiana," although Peterson does not let himself get upstaged during this exuberant jam session. —*Scott Yanow*

Dizzy's Party / Sep. 15, 1976+Sep. 16, 1976 / Original Jazz Classics ✦✦

Free Ride / Feb. 1, 1977+Feb. 2, 1977 / Original Jazz Classics ✦✦
Recent reissue of a late '70s Pablo session, with Gillespie playing some entertaining originals, backed by the Lalo Schifrin orchestra. The compositions and performances are good, but not great. —*Ron Wynn*

Gifted Ones / Feb. 3, 1977 / Pablo ✦✦
This Norman Granz session got it backwards. Instead of featuring Dizzy Gillespie with the Count Basie Orchestra, Basie is heard with a Gillespie-led quartet. The emphasis is on blues and fairly standard chord changes and, even with bassist Ray Brown and drummer Mickey Roker completing the group, there are no surprises. What should have been a classic encounter is instead fairly routine. —*Scott Yanow*

Montreux '77 / Jul. 14, 1977 / Original Jazz Classics ✦✦✦
It wasn't until the mid-'70s that a trumpeter emerged who could not only emulate Dizzy Gillespie, but display a larger range: Jon Faddis. Unfortunately, Gillespie and his protégé barely recorded together, and this 1977 encounter at the Montreux Jazz Festival is quite disappointing. The trumpeters (plus vibraphonist Milt Jackson, pianist Monty Alexander, bassist Ray Brown and drummer Jimmie Smith) play well enough on "Girl of My Dreams," "Get Happy," "The Champ," and a ballad medley, but amazingly enough, there are no trade-offs between Faddis and Gillespie (the younger trumpeter is much too respectful throughout this session), and few fireworks occur in what should have been an explosive encounter. —*Scott Yanow*

Trumpet Summit Meets Oscar Peterson Big Four / Mar. 1980 / Original Jazz Classics ✦✦✦
W/ Freddie Hubbard, Clark Terry, Joe Pass. Not spectacular, but a satisfying and enjoyable romp by these veterans. —*Ron Wynn*

Digital at Montreux, 1980 / Jul. 19, 1980 / Original Jazz Classics ✦✦
A 1980 date with trumpeter Dizzy Gillespie playing in an unusual trio setting with guitarist Toots Thielemans and drummer Bernard Purdie. Purdie, a consummate funk and R&B percussionist, makes the switch to mainstream material adequately, while Gillespie and Thielemans establish a quick, consistent rapport. —*Ron Wynn*

Musician-Composer-Raconteur / Jul. 17, 1981 / Pablo ✦✦
This double LP is subtitled "Dizzy Gillespie Plays and Raps in His Greatest Concert," an exaggeration to say the least. In reality, this set (which contains some of his humorous joking with the audience) is a fine all-around example of Gillespie at a typical concert in 1981. At the age of 63, he was no longer the powerful trumpeter he once was, but he still had something to contribute. His sextet (with vibraphonist Milt Jackson, James Moody on tenor and alto and the fine guitarist Ed Cherry) stretches out on long versions of "A Night in Tunisia," "Con Alma" and "Olinga" along with four other pieces. —*Scott Yanow*

To a Finland Station / Sep. 9, 1982 / Original Jazz Classics ✦✦✦✦
This unique set finds Dizzy Gillespie (who was nearly age 65) sharing the front line with the great Cuban trumpeter Arturo Sandoval. Backed by a fine Finnish rhythm section, Sandoval and the great trumpeter are both in good spirits playing five of Gillespie's originals including "Wheatleigh Hall" and "And Then She Stopped." Considering that it would be another decade before Sandoval was able to defect from Cuba (and finally play the music he wanted), this recording is of great historic value. —*Scott Yanow*

Closer to the Source / Aug. 24, 1984-Sep. 30, 1984 / Atlantic ✦
It was an open secret that by the 1980s, Dizzy Gillespie was well past his playing prime. A very likable and humorous entertainer and still an expert scat singer, his trumpet playing had unfortunately greatly declined, and in 1984, at the time of this misfire, he was soon to turn age 67. This set of commercial material (with

guest spots by Stevie Wonder, tenor saxophonist Branford Marsalis and bassist Marcus Miller) is quite forgettable—throwaway funk tunes with the parts of the sidemen sounding as if they were phoned in. This LP fortunately went quickly out of print. —*Scott Yanow*

New Faces / 1984 / GRP ✦✦✦
Gillespie was teamed up with Branford Marsalis for this decent effort. His own trumpet playing had faded quite a bit by this time (he was already age 67), but he sounds enthusiastic on five of his compositions (including "Birk's Works"), "Tin Tin Deo," and Mike Longo's "Every Mornin'," trading ideas with such young turks as Marsalis, pianist Kenny Kirkland and bassist Lonnie Plaxico. —*Scott Yanow*

Live at Royal Festival Hall / Jun. 10, 1989 / Enja ✦✦✦✦
Dizzy Gillespie, who was nearing 72 years old at the time of this concert, headed one of his finest big bands during his later years, the United Nation Orchestra. With such stellar sidemen as trumpeters Arturo Sandoval and Claudio Roditi, trombonists Slide Hampton and Steve Turre, altoist Paquito D'Rivera, James Moody on tenor and alto, pianist Danilo Perez and singer Flora Purim, Gillespie was relieved from having to carry this concert by himself and could concentrate on taking short solos and enjoying listening to the band play. Whether it is "Tanga," "And Then She Stopped" or an 18-minute version of "A Night in Tunisia," every selection on this excellent CD works. —*Scott Yanow*

Symphony Sessions / Aug. 26, 1989-Aug. 27, 1989 / Pro Arte ✦✦
Teaming Dizzy Gillespie with a symphony orchestra may have been a good idea in theory but, by the time of the recordings that comprise this CD, he was already nearing the age of 72, and his trumpet playing had declined quite a bit. Since Gillespie is the main soloist throughout this set (in which his quintet with tenor saxophonist Ron Holloway is accompanied by the Rochester Philharmonic Orchestra conducted by John Dankworth), there are many weak moments. Certainly these versions of "Manteca" and "A Night in Tunisia" pale in comparison to the earlier classic recordings, leading one to the conclusion that this matchup should have occurred 20 years earlier. —*Scott Yanow*

Winter in Lisbon / Aug. 1990 / Milan ✦✦
This CD, featuring Dizzy Gillespie playing on the soundtrack of *The Winter in Lisbon* (a film never properly distributed), is only of minor interest. He wrote the nine themes and Slide Hampton put together the arrangements, but, as with most soundtracks, the music sounds incomplete without the picture. Also, Gillespie's playing at this late date in his life was quite erratic. —*Scott Yanow*

Rhythmstick / Mar. 1991 / CTI ✦✦✦

To Diz with Love: Diamond Jubilee Recordings / Jan. 29, 1992-Feb. 1, 1992 / Telarc ✦✦✦
Dizzy Gillespie's final recording, taken from a month he spent featured at the Blue Note in New York, matches the aging giant with such fellow trumpeters as Jon Faddis, Wynton Marsalis, Claudio Roditi, Wallace Roney, Red Rodney, Charlie Sepulveda and the ancient—but still brilliant—Doc Cheatham (who cuts both Diz and Faddis on "Mood Indigo"). Although Gillespie was no longer up to the competition, the love that these fellow trumpeters had for him (and some fine solos) makes this historic CD worth getting. —*Scott Yanow*

To Bird with Love: Live at the Blue Note / Jan. 23, 1992-Jan. 25, 1992 / Telarc ✦✦✦
Taken from a month that Dizzy Gillespie was featured at the Blue Note in New York, virtually at the end of his playing career, the 74-year-old trumpeter is quite erratic on this set of bop standards. However, his supporting cast (heard from in different combinations) includes such major players as altoists Jackie McLean, Antonio Hart and Paquito D'Rivera and tenors Benny Golson, Clifford Jordan and David Sanchez, in addition to a strong trio led by pianist Danilo Perez. The sidemen are in generally fine form and Bobby McFerrin literally came out of the audience to scat on "Oo Pa Pa Da." The good spirits and obvious love that these musicians had for Gillespie make up for his technical lapses. —*Scott Yanow*

Bird Songs: Final Recordings / Jan. 23, 1992-Jan. 25, 1995 / Telarc ✦✦
With this CD, Telarc squeezes another package out of a month-long salute to the jazz master's 75th birthday at New York's Blue Note jazz club, advertising them as Dizzy Gillespie's last recordings (they're not). What it is, is a mixed blessing, an obviously heartfelt tribute to an aging legend by several of his disciples, conservative to a fault in its adherence to the basic bop language that Dizzy and the album's co-honoree Charlie Parker helped invent. Dizzy's solos are like fallen swans; the chops simply weren't there anymore to execute his still-potent ideas, and reviewers in Dizzy's final years found his decline painful to report (many pretended not to notice). Otherwise, the excerpts here present a holiday for saxophones, with Benny Golson, David Sanchez, Clifford Jordan, Antonio Hart, Paquito D'Rivera and Jackie McLean taking turns on the front line, backed by the workmanlike trio of Danilo Perez on piano, George Mraz on bass and Lewis Nash or Kenny Washington on drums. Easily the best of the sax encounters is "Ornithol-

ogy," where a speeding McLean and relatively relaxed D'Rivera engage in a high-flying dialogue, and the first part of Bobby McFerrin's vocal solo is so uncannily like late-period Dizzy that one is fooled. This album and its companions might have worked better as videos, where one could still bask in Dizzy's live presence and thus experience the atmosphere of this celebration more fully. —*Richard S. Ginell*

John Gilmore
b. Sep. 28, 1931, Summit, MS, **d.** Aug. 20, 1995, Philadelphia, PA
Tenor Saxophone / Avant-Garde, Free Jazz
John Gilmore's decision to play almost exclusively within the realm of Sun Ra's Arkestra long frustrated jazz observers who felt that he would have made a bigger impact if he had had a solo career. Gilmore grew up in Chicago and after a stint in the Army (1948-52), he worked with Earl Hines (1952). In 1953 he joined Ra and 40 years later when the bandleader died, Gilmore was still there. His playing in the 1950s was an influence on the developing John Coltrane and Gilmore, who teamed up with Clifford Jordan for a 1957 Blue Note session, did spend 1964-65 with Art Blakey's Jazz Messengers. However other than a few sideman recordings in the 1960s (including with Freddie Hubbard, McCoy Tyner, Andrew Hill and Pete La Roca), Gilmore stuck with Ra, being well featured both on hard bop and free-form material. He briefly headed the Arkestra after Ra's death. —*Scott Yanow*

★ **Blowing In from Chicago** / Mar. 3, 1957 / Blue Note ✦✦✦✦✦
Clifford Jordan's first date as a leader actually found him sharing a heated jam session with fellow tenor John Gilmore. Backed by pianist Horace Silver, bassist Curly Russell and drummer Art Blakey, the two saxophonists square off mostly on obscurities (other than Gigi Gryce's "Blue Lights" and "Billie's Bounce"); the original six selections are joined by the previously unreleased "Let It Stand" on the CD reissue. This was one of Gilmore's few sessions outside of Sun Ra's orbit, and if anything, he slightly overshadows the cooler-toned Jordan. Recommended. —*Scott Yanow*

Adele Girard
b. 1913, **d.** Sep. 7, 1993, Denver, CO
Harp / Swing, Dixieland
Possibly the greatest jazz harpist of all time, Adele Girard showed that it was possible to swing hard on that angelic instrument; only the little-known Casper Reardon had preceded her. Girard played with Harry Sosnick's band and then in 1937 she joined clarinetist Joe Marsala's combo, marrying him the same year. Her swing and Dixieland recordings with Marsala in the 1930s and '40s (although somewhat obscure) are remarkable to hear today. Little was heard of Girard after the mid-'50s but she emerged in 1992 to record a fine album with Bobby Gordon for Arbors. —*Scott Yanow*

George Girard
b. Oct. 7, 1930, New Orleans, LA, **d.** Jan. 18, 1957, New Orleans, LA
Trumpet, Vocals / Dixieland
One of the finest New Orleans jazz players to emerge in the 1950s, George Girard's premature death from cancer cut short a very promising career. He became a professional in 1946 after graduating from high school, played with Phil Zito and then became a key member (along with Pete Fountain) of the Basin Street Six (1950-54). After the breakup of that group, Girard led his own bands and freelanced until bad health forced him to retire in 1956. Girard had an exciting trumpet style and was a rhythmic vocalist whose potential was sadly not realized. In addition to his recordings with the Basin Street Six, Girard led sessions that were later issued by Storyville, GHB and Good Time Jazz in addition to cutting two full albums for Vik. —*Scott Yanow*

● **George Girard** / Sep. 19, 1954-July 1, 1956 / Storyville

Egberto Gismonti
b. Dec. 5, 1947, Carmo, Brazil
Guitar, Piano / World Fusion, Latin Jazz
A versatile and talented musician equally skilled on guitar and piano, Egberto Gismonti has recorded an impressive string of sets for ECM. He started piano lessons when he was six, going on to receive extended classical training and to study in Paris with Nadia Boulanger. Gismonti became interested in "choro" (Brazilian funk music) and had switched his musical course by the late 1960s. He started playing the six-stringed classical guitar in 1967 and in 1973 added an eight-string guitar. Since then, Gismonti has made many recordings and worked with such artists as Airto Moreira and Flora Purim, Nana Vasconcelos, Paul Horn, Jan Garbarek, Charlie Haden, and his own groups. In his native country, Gismonti has been involved in a lot of studio work, including work on over 11 films. Throughout his

career, the multi-instrumentalist has mixed his Brazilian heritage and classical training with jazz, light funk, folk music and ECM-type introspection. —*Scott Yanow*

Danca Das Cabecas / Nov. 1976 / ECM ✦✦✦✦

The initial American release features extended pieces for guitarist and percussionist Nana Vasconcelos. A tour de force, with the pieces segueing together beautifully. —*Michael G. Nastos*

Sol Do Meio Dia / Nov. 1977 / ECM ✦✦✦✦

This is also an excellent record. Gismonti plays an eight-string guitar. —*Michael G. Nastos*

Solo / Nov. 1978 / ECM ✦✦✦✦✦

Sanfona / Nov. 1980+Apr. 1981 / ECM ✦✦✦

These are virtuoso solo performances and group sessions including a suite and Gismonti's famous "Frevo." This is a double-record set full of prominent Brazilian jazz. —*Michael G. Nastos*

Duas Vozes / Jun. 1984 / ECM ✦✦✦

● Danca Dos Escravos / 1989 / ECM ✦✦✦✦✦

Infancia / Nov. 1990 / ECM ✦✦✦✦

Much of this CD is at a quiet volume, but the music is full of tension and inner excitement, with repetition used very effectively. Filled with memorable folk melodies that flow logically (the jubilant main theme of "Infancia" is a high point), the music is quite stimulating, often shifting moods gradually and coming up with unexpected twists. Gismonti (mostly on piano but making two appearances on guitar) is the lead voice in his quintet, and he contributed all of the compositions, so he deserves the main credit for the recording's success; well worth searching for. —*Scott Yanow*

Musica De Sobrevivencia / Apr. 1993 / ECM ✦✦✦

Zig Zag / Apr. 1995 / ECM ✦✦✦

Jimmy Giuffre

b. Apr. 26, 1921, Dallas, TX

Tenor Saxophone, Clarinet / Baritone Saxophone, Soprano Saxophone, Flute, Cool, Avant-Garde

Jimmy Giuffre has had many accomplishments in a long career that has never been predictable. Giuffre graduated from North Texas State Teachers College (1942), played in an Army band during his period in the service and then had stints with the orchestras of Boyd Raeburn, Jimmy Dorsey and Buddy Rich. His composition "Four Brothers" became a hit for Woody Herman, an orchestra that Giuffre eventually joined in 1949.

Settling on the West Coast, the cool-toned tenor started also playing clarinet and occasional baritone. He was with Howard Rumsey's Lighthouse All-Stars (1951-52) and Shorty Rogers' Giants (1952-56), recording with many top West Coast jazz players. In 1956 he went out on his own, forming the Jimmy Giuffre 3 with guitarist Jim Hall and bassist Ralph Pena (later Jim Atlas). Giuffre had a minor hit with his recording of "The Train and the River," a song that he played during his notable appearance on the 1957 television special *The Sound of Jazz*. In 1958 Giuffre had a most unusual trio with valve trombonist Bob Brookmeyer and guitarist Hall (no piano, bass or drums!), appearing in the movie *Jazz on a Summer's Day*. After a couple years of reverting back to the reeds-guitar-bass format, in 1961 the new Jimmy Giuffre 3 featured pianist Paul Bley and bassist Steve Swallow and was involved in exploring the more introspective side of free jazz. From 1963 on Giuffre maintained a lower profile, working as an educator although Don Friedman and Barre Phillips were in his unrecorded 1964-65 group. He popped up on records now and then in the 1970s with diverse trios (including a session with Bley and Bill Connors) and his 1980s unit often utilized the synthesizer of Pete Levin. Giuffre, who started late in life playing flute and soprano and seems to have made a career out of playing surprising music, reunited with Bley and Swallow in 1992. He has recorded as a leader through the years for Capitol, Atlantic, Columbia, Verve, Hat Art, Choice, Improvising Artists, Soul Note and Owl. —*Scott Yanow*

Four Brothers / Feb. 19, 1954-Jan. 31, 1955 / Capitol ✦✦✦

This album has Giuffre's first recordings as a leader, three sessions that resulted in ten selections. Switching between tenor, clarinet and baritone, Giuffre is heard in a quartet and quintet with trumpeter Jack Sheldon and with Sheldon in a pianoless septet also including Shorty Rogers on fluegelhorn, altoist Bud Shank and valve trombonist Bob Enevoldsen. The leader wrote eight of the ten songs (including a remake of his biggest hit "Four Brothers"), several of which show off his growing interest in both folk and classical musics. Fine performances. —*Scott Yanow*

☆ **The Complete Capitol & Atlantic Recordings of Jimmy Giuffre** / Feb. 19, 1954-Dec. 3, 1958 / Mosaic ✦✦✦✦✦

Jimmy Giuffre has always followed his own singular musical path. In the mid- to late '50s, he was increasingly interested in folky melodies, quiet playing and lyrical freedom. This limited-edition 1997 six-CD set has a great deal of formerly rare material (including six previously unreleased performances) that traces his career during a nearly five-year period. The cool-toned Giuffre (switching between clarinet, tenor and baritone) is heard with a few medium-size groups of West Coast all-stars, heading a pianoless quartet that includes trumpeter Jack Sheldon, matching wits with clarinetist Pee Wee Russell ("Blues in E Flat") and cornetist Rex Stewart ("In a Mellotone"), collaborating with the Modern Jazz Quartet, playing songs from *The Music Man,* and leading the Jimmy Giuffre 3. The latter group started out also including guitarist Jim Hall and bassist Jim Atlas, but it is the two projects that match Giuffre with Hall and valve trombonist Bob Brookmeyer (no piano, bass or drums) that are most intriguing. In addition, on one odd date, Giuffre overdubbed four tenors while joined by Hall and Brookmeyer (this time on piano). Although Jimmy Giuffre's influence was quite slight—his quiet experiments were soon overshadowed by the more fiery avant-garde—this music has dated fairly well and rewards repeated listenings. —*Scott Yanow*

Tangents in Jazz / May 1955 / Capitol ✦✦✦

This unusual set has Jimmy Giuffre (on clarinet, tenor and baritone) in a pianoless quartet with trumpeter Jack Sheldon, bassist Ralph Pena and drummer Artie Anton. The music (all but one of the ten numbers are by Giuffre) puts an emphasis on cool tones and relaxed improvising, hinting at folk themes but sounding quite modern for the time. —*Scott Yanow*

Tenors West / Nov. 9, 1955-Nov. 10, 1955 / GNP ✦✦✦

Although this set is often issued under Jimmy Giuffre's name, the tenor saxophonist only actually appears on five of the 11 selections. The first date of what is actually a Marty Paich album features fellow tenor Bob Cooper in an octet with Paich's piano, trumpeter Conte Candoli, baritonist Jack Dulong, valve trombonist Bob Enevoldsen and flutist Harry Klee; both Enevoldsen and Klee play some of the sections on tenor, giving the ensemble a Four Brothers sound. Giuffre replaces Cooper on the later session and does emerge as the most consistently interesting soloist. The real stars are Paich's inventive arrangements. —*Scott Yanow*

The Jimmy Giuffre Clarinet / Mar. 21, 1956-Mar. 22, 1956 / Atlantic ✦✦✦

This continually interesting set finds Jimmy Giuffre sticking exclusively to his cool-toned clarinet, mostly playing in the lower register, in several settings. The thought-provoking and generally relaxed works feature a wide variety of instrumentation. Giuffre takes "So Low" as an unaccompanied solo, duets with Jimmy Rowles' celeste on "Deep Purple," plays a fairly free "Fascinatin' Rhythm" in a Benny Goodman-type trio with pianist Rowles and drummer Shelly Manne, performs with a couple of other trios (including a group consisting of his clarinet, an alto clarinetist and a bass clarinetist), uses three flutes and drums on the atonal "The Side Pipers" and three woodwinds plus bassist Ralph Pena on an atmospheric "My Funny Valentine," concluding with a nonet blues. A very interesting album. —*Scott Yanow*

The Jimmy Giuffre Three, Vol. 46 / Dec. 3, 1956-Dec. 24, 1956 / Atlantic ✦✦✦✦

This disc features the first version of Giuffre's *3*. With guitarist Jim Hall and either Ralph Pena or Jim Atlas on bass, Giuffre is heard on clarinet, tenor and baritone. The generally introverted music is wistful, has a fair amount of variety, and is melodic while still sounding advanced. In addition to the nine original songs (including the earliest recording of Giuffre's classic folk song "The Train and the River"), two previously unreleased tunes (including "Forty-Second Street") were added to the CD reissue. An excellent introduction to Jimmy Giuffre's unique (if not particularly influential) music. —*Scott Yanow*

The Music Man / Jan. 2, 1958-Jan. 6, 1958 / Atlantic ✦✦✦✦

Jimmy Giuffre's four Atlantic albums of 1958 are among his rarest and most satisfying releases. Unlike the other three, this particular set finds Giuffre (tripling as usual on clarinet, tenor and baritone) leading a somewhat conventional band, a seven-horn pianoless nonet. They perform 11 songs from the musical *The Music Man,* best known of which are "76 Trombones," "Gary, Indiana" and "Till There Was You." The arrangements (all by Giuffre) swing, the beauty and joy of the melodies are brought out, and the leader (who takes all of the solos except on "The Wells Fargo Wagon") is in top form. A true rarity. —*Scott Yanow*

Trav'lin' Light / Jan. 20, 1958-Jan. 21, 1958 / Atlantic ✦✦✦✦

In 1958, Jimmy Giuffre led one of the most unusual groups ever, a trio comprising his reeds (clarinet, tenor and baritone), valve trombonist Bob Brookmeyer and guitarist Jim Hall; no piano, bass or drums. —*Scott Yanow*

Four Brothers Sound / Jun. 23, 1958-Sep. 1, 1958 / Atlantic ✦✦✦✦

Western Suite / Dec. 3, 1958 / Atlantic ✦✦✦✦

Ad Lib / Jan. 1959 / Verve ✦✦✦

Seven Pieces / Feb. 25, 1959-Mar. 21, 1959 / Verve ✦✦✦

The Easy Way / Aug. 6, 1959-Aug. 7, 1959 / Verve ✦✦✦✦
A compelling trio date with Jim Hall (g). —*Ron Wynn*

In Person / Aug. 1960 / Verve ✦✦✦

● **1961** / Mar. 3, 1961+Aug. 4, 1961 / ECM ✦✦✦✦✦
One of the most intriguing groups that Jimmy Giuffre led was the trio that he had during 1961-62 with pianist Paul Bley and bassist Steve Swallow. As opposed to the free jazz and high-energy avant-garde players that were beginning to emerge, Giuffre (who stuck exclusively to clarinet) sought to free up his music but with subtlety, a use of space and at a quiet volume. This ECM double CD not only reissues two of the trio's three out-of-print LPs (*Fusion* and *Thesis*) but adds some previously unreleased selections too. The music was still tied (although sometimes loosely) to chordal improvisation but there are spots on these originals by Giuffre, Paul Bley and Carla Bley (plus a dramatic version of the standard "Goodbye") where the performances are nearly as advanced as Ornette Coleman's. The three musicians often act as equals and bassist Steve Swallow (years before he switched permanently to electric bass) is particularly advanced. Thought-provoking music. —*Scott Yanow*

Emphasis, Stuttgart 1961 / Nov. 7, 1961 / Hat Art ✦✦✦✦✦
The 1961 version of the Jimmy Giuffre 3 featured the leader sticking to clarinet and interacting with pianist Paul Bley and bassist Steve Swallow in music that was fairly free but also soft and quiet. While their three studio albums contain plenty of strong moments, this live date (first released by Hat Art on a 1993 CD) really finds the musicians stretching themselves and challenging each other. Although some of the structures are conventional (Paul Bley's "Carla" is a blues) and the players avoid sound explorations, much of their mutual communication borders on the telepathic and plenty of chances are taken. The results are subtle and well worth a close listen. —*Scott Yanow*

Flight, Bremen 1961 / Nov. 23, 1961 / Hat Art ✦✦✦✦

Free Fall / Jul. 10, 1962-Nov. 1, 1962 / Columbia ✦✦✦✦
Fine trio pieces with Paul Bley (p) and Steve Swallow (b). —*Ron Wynn*

Music for People, Birds, Butterflies and Mosquitos / Dec. 1972 / Choice ✦✦
After a decade off from recording, Jimmy Giuffre returned for this little-known set. The music is moody, fairly spontaneous, and melodic, but often wandering and rather insubstantial. Giuffre triples on clarinet, tenor and flute and is joined by bassist Kiyoshi Tokunaga and drummer Randy Kaye for a dozen of his concise originals. None of the songs clock in over 5:37, and although they form a sort of suite, the overall results are not too memorable. —*Scott Yanow*

River Chant / Apr. 1975 / Choice ✦✦

IAI Festival / May 19, 1978 / Improvising Artists ✦✦✦✦
Although four musicians are listed for this date (Jimmy Giuffre, altoist Lee Konitz, guitarist Bill Connors and pianist Paul Bley), these five performances are actually a set of duets featuring Giuffre on tenor, clarinet, bass flute and soprano interacting with the other players. Three songs are duets with Konitz (there is also one apiece with Bley and Connors), including "Blues in the Closet," and these are the main reasons to acquire this disc. The CD reissue is an exact duplicate of the original LP, with just 37 minutes of music, but it is definitely worth hearing. This was the final release by Bley's Improvising Artists label. —*Scott Yanow*

Dragonfly / Jan. 14, 1983-Jan. 15, 1983 / Soul Note ✦✦✦

Quasar / May 3, 1985-May 5, 1985 / Soul Note ✦✦✦
After returning to more active playing in the mid-'70s, Jimmy Giuffre recorded on an occasional basis, generally once every two years. On several of his albums, he featured the keyboards and synthesizers of Pete Levin. With bassist Bob Nieske and drummer Randy Kaye completing the quartet (which was together several years), Giuffre is heard on clarinet, tenor, soprano, flute and bass flute on eight obscure pieces, including four of his originals. Although often electronic, the music has the typical thoughtfulness of Giuffre's relaxed approach and some picturesque moments. —*Scott Yanow*

Momentum, Willisau 1988 / Sep. 3, 1988 / Hatology ✦✦✦✦
A set of live duets and solos by two reed players would not seem to have much potential except maybe in avant-garde jazz, but this recital is actually quite melodic, makes use of space and holds one's interest throughout. Veteran Jimmy Giuffre (heard here on clarinet and soprano) and Andre Jaume (doubling on tenor and bass clarinet) perform obscure and mostly spontaneous originals. The fairly basic themes contrast sound and silence, and the thoughtful renditions contain subtle surprises and fine interplay. A sleeper that is well worth picking up. —*Scott Yanow*

Liquid Dancers / Apr. 24, 1989 / Soul Note ✦✦✦

Diary of a Trio: Saturday / Dec. 1989 / Owl ✦✦✦

Diary of a Trio: Sunday / Dec. 1989 / Owl ✦✦✦

Tyree Glenn
b. Nov. 23, 1912, Corsicana, TX, **d.** May 18, 1974, Englewood, NJ
Trombone, Vibes / Swing
Tyree Glenn, who had the unusual double of trombone and vibes, was an important asset at various times to both Duke Ellington and Louis Armstrong. Glenn started out working in territory bands in Virginia, then moved to the West Coast, playing with groups headed by Charlie Echols (1936) and Eddie Barefield. After playing with Ethel Waters and Benny Carter, he became a longtime member of the Cab Calloway Orchestra (1939-46). Glenn visited Europe with Don Redman's big band (1946). During his association with Duke Ellington (1947-51), he was an effective wa-wa trombonist in the Tricky Sam Nanton tradition and Ellington's only vibraphonist, being well featured on the "Liberian Suite." During the 1950s Glenn worked in the studios, led his quartet at the Embers and freelanced in swing and Dixieland settings. Other than some European dates in 1947, Glenn's only extensive opportunity to record was for Roulette (1957-58 and 1961-62). During 1965-68 he toured with the world with Louis Armstrong's All-Stars. After leaving Armstrong, Tyree Glenn led his own group during his last few years. —*Scott Yanow*

At the Embers / Mar. 28, 1957-Mar. 29, 1957 / Roulette ✦✦✦✦

● **Tyree Glenn at the Roundtable** / 1958 / Roulette ✦✦✦✦
Trombonist Tyree Glenn, who played with both Duke Ellington and Louis Armstrong, was not that well-known as a bandleader, but he did head six now-obscure albums for Roulette from 1957-62, none of which have been reissued on CD yet. For this fairly freewheeling live set, the distinctive trombonist is joined by guitarist Mary Osborne, pianist Hank Jones, bassist Tommy Potter and drummer Jo Jones for likable versions of a dozen standards. A few ("Just a Wearyin' for You," "Wonder Why" and "Marcheta") are lesser known. Glenn sounds in particularly fine form on "Teach Me Tonight," "There Will Never Be Another You" (which finds him switching to vibes), "Royal Garden Blues," and "Limehouse Blues." Fun music, but this will be difficult to find. —*Scott Yanow*

The Trombone Artistry / 1962 / Roulette ✦✦✦

Globe Unity Orchestra
f. 1966 **db.** 1986
Group /Big Band, Free Jazz
Formed in 1966 by pianist Alexander von Schlippenbach to perform his composition "Globe Unity" at the Berlin Jazztage, Globe Unity has been a forum for some of the top free jazz players to get together and engage in collective improvisation. They mostly performed in Germany up until 1974 but have since toured Europe, India, the Far East and Canada. Among its members through the years have been Albert Mangelsdorff, Kenny Wheeler, Evan Parker, Manfred Schoof, Paul Rutherford, Steve Lacy, Peter Brotzmann, George Lewis and Han Bennink. The group (which has recorded for FMP and Japo) has been only occasionally active since celebrating its 20th anniversary in 1986. —*Scott Yanow*

● **Live in Wuppertal 73** / Mar. 25, 1973 / FMP ✦✦✦✦✦

Hamburg '74 / Nov. 19, 1974 / FMP ✦✦✦✦

Evidence / Mar. 31, 1975 / FMP ✦✦✦✦

Pearls / Nov. 25, 1977+Nov. 27, 1977 / FMP ✦✦✦✦✦
The free-jazz big band had a cast of stars: Enrico Rava, Albert Mangelsdorff, Anthony Braxton, and many others. —*AMG*

Jahrmarket / 1977 / Potorch ✦✦✦

Improvisations / Sep. 5, 1977+Sep. 9, 1977 / Japo ✦✦✦

Compositions / Jan. 1979 / Japo ✦✦✦

Intergalactic Blow / June 4, 1982 / Japo ✦✦✦

Don Goldie
b. Feb. 5, 1930, Newark, NJ, **d.** Nov. 25, 1995, Florida
Trumpet / Dixieland
A talented soloist with a wide range, Don Goldie was the son of longtime Paul Whiteman trumpeter Harry Goldfield. Goldie performed with many types of groups including with Buddy Rich and the society band of Lester Lanin before gaining prominence for his playing with Jack Teagarden's Dixieland sextet (1959 until the trombonist's death in 1964). Goldie eventually settled in Miami where in the early '70s he recorded 11 albums for Jazz Forum, many of which were dedicated to the work of one composer. A fixture in Miami clubs and hotels, Don Goldie committed suicide in 1995. —*Scott Yanow*

● **Brilliant** / Jan. 1961 / Argo ✦✦✦✦✦

Trumpet Caliente / Oct. 3, 1962 / Argo ✦✦✦

The Best of Jimmy McHugh / 1977 / Jazz Forum ✦✦✦✦

Don Goldie's obscurity was always a bit puzzling. A brilliant trumpeter with a wide range, an appealing tone and the ability to play Dixieland and swing with drive and creativity, Goldie recorded for Argo and Verve from 1961-62 and then was largely off records until the 1970s. By then, he had settled in Miami, and his return to disc only occurred when he started his own Jazz Forum label. Eight of his records featured jazz interpretations of one composer's work. This particular LP finds Goldie playing seven standards written by Jimmy McHugh, including "When My Sugar Walks Down the Street," "I Can't Give You Anything But Love," and "On the Sunny Side of the Street." With a fine rhythm section (pianist Jack Keller, bassist Mark Trail and drummer Red Hawley), plus the obscure but talented violinist Dick Shepp, Goldie is heard throughout in prime form. A good buy for mainstream fans, but none of the Jazz Forum sets have yet appeared on CD. —*Scott Yanow*

Don Goldie's Dangerous Jazz Band / 1982-Sep. 19, 1988 / Jazzology ✦✦✦✦

Trumpeter Don Goldie and his longtime Florida-based band perform ten hot jazz standards on his Jazzology debut. The other musicians (trombonist Hank Bredenberg, clarinetist Ernie Goodson, pianist Jack Keller, bassist Mark Trail and drummer Red Hawley) are obscure but quite effective in this Dixieland-oriented setting, and Goldie was an underrated great. Highlights include "Hindustan," "Riverboat Shuffle," "Put on Your Old Grey Bonnet" and "I'm Coming Virginia." —*Scott Yanow*

Larry Goldings

b. 1968, Boston
Organ, Piano / Post-Bop

One of the top organists to emerge since Joey De Francesco, Larry Goldings began piano lessons when he was nine. Goldings, who graduated from the New School for Social Research in the late '80s, was Jon Hendricks' accompanist during 1987-89, worked with Jim Hall for three years and (inspired by Jimmy Smith) he led a trio that gave him an opportunity to play organ. He worked on the Hammond B-3 with Maceo Parker and in 1990 recorded his first set for Minor Music. Since then Goldings has toured and recorded with John Scofield and signed with Warner Bros. —*Scott Yanow*

The Intimacy of the Blues / 1991 / Verve ✦✦✦✦

W/ Fathead Newman (sax) and Bill Stewart (b). —*Ron Wynn*

Light Blue / Sep. 1992 / Minor Music ✦✦✦✦

Caminhos Cruzados / Dec. 19, 1993-Dec. 20, 1993 / Novus ✦✦✦✦✦

Listening to this CD, it is surprising to note that few bossa nova records up to now have featured organs. Larry Goldings' subtle style (a laidback Jimmy Smith) perfectly fits the idiom and some of the selections performed on his set are given straightahead sections for variety. The music is mostly easy-listening with an appealing ensemble sound, consistently excellent concise solos from Goldings and guitarist Peter Bernstein, and tasteful backup from drummer Bill Stewart and percussionist Guilherme Franco. The three guest appearances by Joshua Redman make one wish that he were on more tracks for his tenor fits very comfortably into this setting. —*Scott Yanow*

● **Whatever It Takes** / Oct. 1995 / Warner Brothers ✦✦✦✦✦

Larry Goldings is one of the most promising of the younger organists. Although he was originally known as a pianist, Goldings has been mostly concentrating on organ in recent times, including a high-profile stint as a member of John Scofield's quartet. For his Warner Brothers debut, *Whatever It Takes*, Goldings is teamed with guitarist Peter Bernstein and drummer Bill Stewart for ten numbers, five of which include some notable guests. Two songs match together the soulful altos of Maceo Parker and David Sanborn, young tenor giant Joshua Redman is on three other numbers (including "Yipes" which also includes Parker) and there are two appearances by trombonist Fred Wesley. The music features a lot of appealing grooves that look back to the classic Hammond organ era of the 1960s while remaining contemporary. —*Scott Yanow*

Big Stuff / Aug. 20, 1996 / Warner Brothers ✦✦✦

Awareness / Oct. 18, 1996-Dec. 19, 1996 / Warner Brothers ✦✦✦

Larry Goldings has proven to be equally adept on piano and organ. He sticks to the former exclusively on this trio set with bassist Larry Grenadier and veteran drummer Paul Motian. The music mostly emphasizes originals and contains plenty of diversity, with Goldings ranging in style from mid-1970s Keith Jarrett and some abstract post-bop to impressionistic and introspective ballads. Few sparks fly, but the set does hold one's interest and finds the pianist stretching himself. —*Scott Yanow*

Jean Goldkette

b. Mar. 18, 1899, Valenciennes, France, **d.** Mar. 24, 1962, Santa Barbara, CA
Leader / Classic Jazz

Although he was a fine classically trained pianist who emigrated to the US in 1911, Jean Goldkette's importance to jazz is a bandleader in the 1920s. Goldkette actually had over 20 bands under his name by the mid-'20s but it was his main unit (which recorded for Victor during 1924-29) that is the only one remembered today. In 1924 the band included Tommy and Jimmy Dorsey and Joe Venuti, with the legendary cornetist Bix Beiderbecke heard on just one selection ("I Didn't Know"); his inability to sightread at the time kept his first stint with Goldkette quite short. However in 1926 Bix became the orchestra's top soloist and the jazz lineup was fairly impressive with such musicians as Spiegle Willcox, Bill Rank, Don Murray, Frankie Trumbauer, Joe Venuti, Eddie Lang, Steve Brown and Chauncey Morehouse being among the personnel. With Bill Challis working as chief arranger, the orchestra was among the best of the period, even defeating Fletcher Henderson at a Battle of the Bands contest in New York. Unfortunately Goldkette's Orchestra was not allowed to cut loose much in the studios and were saddled with indifferent vocalists who were not part of the band. Best among their recordings are ""My Pretty Girl" and "Clementine"; Steve Brown's swinging bass is a major asset on many of the other numbers, particularly during the final choruses. In 1927 Paul Whiteman hired away most of Goldkette's top jazz players (including Bix and Tram) and the band's later recordings are of lesser interest although Hoagy Carmichael is heard on two vocals. Goldkette, who also helped organize McKinney's Cotton Pickers and the Orange Blossoms (the latter became the Casa Loma Orchestra), dropped out of the jazz business by the early '30s, working as a booking agent and a classical piano soloist. In 1959 Jean Goldkette revived some of the old arrangements (adding some new ones by Sy Oliver) for a Camden "reunion" LP, but few of the sidemen (other than Chauncey Morehouse) were present. —*Scott Yanow*

● **1924-1929** / Mar. 17, 1924-Jan. 14, 1929 / TOM ✦✦✦✦✦

Jean Goldkette's best-known big band was the 1926-27 unit that featured cornetist Bix Beiderbecke and C-melody saxophonist Frankie Trumbauer. However, this very interesting collector's LP (which will hopefully be reissued on CD by the reactivated TOM label) features some of Goldkette's best recordings prior to and right after the Bix era. Unfortunately, no personnel listing or recording dates are given, but the valuable set does span practically Goldkette's entire (if brief) bandleading career. Among the key sidemen on these hot dance band sides are trombonist Tommy Dorsey, Jimmy Dorsey on clarinet and alto, violinist Joe Venuti and trumpeters Sterling Bose and Andy Secrest; the versions of "My Blackbirds Are Bluebirds Now" and "Don't Be Like That" utilize the nucleus of McKinney's Cotton Pickers. —*Scott Yanow*

Dance Hits of the '20s in Stereo / Jul. 13, 1959 / RCA Camden ✦✦✦

Jean Goldkette, whose recording career as a bandleader came to an end in 1929 when he was only 30, was still just 60 when he led his only LP. For this "reunion" date, the only former sideman in the big band is drummer Chauncey Morehouse, but many of the songs (arranged by Sy Oliver) recapture the sound of the legendary orchestra. Best are "Dinah" and "My Pretty Girl," which were transcribed off of the original records. Some of the other tunes (a few of which feature singer Lou Hurst with Debbie and the Diplomats) are a bit too modern in spots, but generally avoid camp or parody in favor of solid swing. An interesting LP which is now a collectors' item. —*Scott Yanow*

Gil Goldstein

b. 1950
Keyboards, Piano, Accordion / Post-Bop

Gil Goldstein, an excellent pianist and synthesizer player, actually started on the accordion. In the late '80s he resumed doubling on it for special occasions such as a recording project for Michel Petrucciani and for his own sessions. Earlier Goldstein had picked up important experience playing with Pat Martino, Jim Hall, Billy Cobham, the Gil Evans Orchestra (starting in 1983) and Wayne Shorter. In 1991 he helped in reconstructing Gil Evans' arrangements for Miles Davis' Montreux Jazz Festival concert and he has recorded as a leader for Chiaroscuro (1977), Muse, Blue Note, World Pacific and Big World. Generally Gil Goldstein's music grooves while utilizing the influences of other cultures (particularly Latin America). —*Scott Yanow*

Pure As Rain / Nov. 14, 1977+Nov. 16, 1977 / Chiaroscuro ✦✦✦

Pianist Gil Goldstein's debut as a leader is mostly an introspective affair emphasizing wistful moods. Goldstein plays quite well and is heard in separate duets with bassist Jeff Berlin and Fred Miller's English horn, in a trio with Berlin and drummer Bob Moses, playing "Without an Anchor" with harmonica great Toots Thielemans, adding the Latin percussion of Ray Barretto to two numbers, and backing a vocal by Mary Eiland. Interesting music that rewards repeated listenings, but this LP has been out of print for quite awhile. —*Scott Yanow*

Sands of Time / May 14, 1980-May 15, 1980 / Muse ✦✦✦

City of Dreams / Mar. 1989-Jul. 1989 / Blue Note ✦✦
This CD suffers from a lack of individuality and an overly relaxed mood. The fine acoustic pianist Gil Goldstein (who adds synthesizer strings and doubles on accordion and plays on "Loro") often sounds as if he is performing impressions of Chick Corea with some nods in the direction of Ramsey Lewis. The new material rarely rises above the level of easy-listening jazz; Bill Evans on a sleepy day. Gil Goldstein is certainly capable of better. —*Scott Yanow*

● **Zebra Coast** / Jun. 6, 1991-Jun. 9, 1991 / World Pacific ✦✦✦

Vinny Golia

b. 1956, New York, NY
Reeds / Avant-Garde
One of the unsung heroes of avant-garde jazz, Vinny Golia has been recording prolifically in Los Angeles (on his Nine Winds label) and staging concerts (ranging from solo improvisations and trios to his Large Ensemble) since 1977. He started out as a visual artist and even designed a Chick Corea album cover (*The Song of Singing*), not taking up the saxophone until he was already 21. Within a short time Golia was playing gigs in settings ranging from blues bands to a folk-rock group and Indian music. He started on the soprano and soon added flute, tenor, piccolo, clarinet, bass clarinet, baritone, bass sax and more, currently playing 19 reeds! In 1973 he moved to Los Angeles, played regularly with John Carter and Bobby Bradford and becoming a force in the underground new music scene. In 1977 Golia founded New Winds and, although the first few records were of his music, the label has since broadened its scope and put out over 70 releases to date that document the L.A. avant-garde jazz scene. Vinny Golia has played in recent times with the saxophone octet Figure 8 (recording for Black Saint), William Parker's big band in New York, Bradford's quartet and his own many diverse groups. —*Scott Yanow*

Spirits in Fellowship / Oct. 1977 / Nine Winds ✦✦✦✦✦
Vinny Golia's debut recording was also the first LP released by his Nine Winds label. Although not as strong a player as he would soon be, Golia already had a very inquisitive musical spirit. With clarinetist John Carter, bassist Roberto Miranda and drummer Alex Cline, Golia (who is heard on tenor, baritone, piccolo, two flutes, two recorders, percussion and the exotic sho) adds a lot of color to the adventurous set. The five originals each have "plots" (such as "the transmutation of negative energy to positive," "the battle of nature vs. machine" and "to say more with less") which are portrayed in very abstract fashion. An interesting release. —*Scott Yanow*

Openhearted / Feb. 7, 1979 / Nine Winds ✦✦✦✦
The second LP from Nine Winds features the versatile avant-gardist Vinny Golia playing six originals that feature him on alto flute, soprano, clarinet, bass clarinet, tenor and baritone. Golia is joined by trumpeter Baikida Carroll, bassist Roberto Miranda, drummer Alex Cline and (on three of the six numbers) guitarist Nels Cline. From sound explorations to free bop, the advanced music always holds one's interest and has plenty of unexpected tone colors. —*Scott Yanow*

In the Right Order / Aug. 25, 1979 / Nine Winds ✦✦✦✦✦
On this fine all-around showcase, a two-LP set from his Nine Winds label, Vinny Golia gets a chance to really stretch out in a trio with bassist Roberto Miranda and drummer Alex Cline. Golia, heard on soprano, alto clarinet, B-flat and E-flat clarinets, bass clarinet, tenor, shakuhachi, sho, baritone sax and bass sax (ten winds in all), performs nine of his complex and fairly open-ended originals. This exploratory music is definitely for open-eared listeners. —*Scott Yanow*

Solo / Jul. 16, 1980 / Nine Winds ✦✦✦
This early effort from Vinny Golia has seven unaccompanied solos, with Golia switching between soprano (which he plays on three of the pieces), bamboo bass flute, bamboo twig flute, bass sax, clarinet, baritone and tenor; seven of the "Nine Winds" he was playing at the time. Golia is careful to vary moods, and his improvisations are generally quite thoughtful, making logical use of space, and are open to a variety of emotions. —*Scott Yanow*

The Gift of Fury / Jun. 6, 1981 / Nine Winds ✦✦✦✦
For this colorful and explorative set, multireedist Vinny Golia performs in a quintet with all of the members of his two trios of the period: trombonist John Rapson, pianist Wayne Peet, bassist Roberto Miranda and drummer Alex Cline. The musicians were among L.A.'s best (Miranda has long been an underrated great), and Golia keeps the proceedings (comprising six of his originals) continually interesting by switching between clarinet, bass clarinet, soprano, tenor, baritone, bass flute and alto flute. Stimulating and unpredictable music. —*Scott Yanow*

Slice of Life / Jun. 6, 1981 / Nine Winds ✦✦✦✦✦
This LP is one of multi-instrumentalist Vinny Golia's strongest early albums. Showcased in a trio with bassist Roberto Miranda and drummer Alex Cline, Golia shows off his individuality and chance-taking playing on tenor, soprano, baritone, various flutes and the hotchiku during four lengthy originals. There is plenty of variety in tonal colors and moods, with Golia displaying consistently inventive ideas and quite a bit of fire. Hopefully this date will be reissued someday on CD. —*Scott Yanow*

Compositions for Large Ensemble / Mar. 14, 1982 / Nine Winds ✦✦✦✦

Facts of Their Own Lives / Jul. 14, 1984 / Nine Winds ✦✦✦✦✦
On an irregular basis, Vinny Golia has led his "Large Ensemble" on and off during the past 15 years. The 1984 concert heard on this live two-LP set has solo space for virtually all of the 15 musicians, including such colorful sidemen as altoist Tim Berne, trombonists John Rapson and Michael Vlatkovitch, pianist Wayne Peet, trumpeter John Fumo and Golia himself (on soprano, baritone and contrabass clarinet). The music is consistently exciting, often dense, and utterly impossible to predict, much different than one normally expects from a big band. —*Scott Yanow*

Goin' Ahead / Mar. 23, 1985-Mar. 24, 1985 / Nine Winds ✦✦✦✦✦
Vinny Golia has recorded in many types of settings on his Nine Winds label, from unaccompanied solos to big-band recordings. Possibly the best setting for the multi-instrumentalist is in a two-horn quintet, where he has another lead voice to play off of, yet gets plenty of solo space for his many horns. On this fine album (consisting of six originals, including pieces dedicated to Bill Evans and Robert Mitchum), Golia mostly sticks to soprano and baritone in musical encounters with such familiar faces as trumpeter John Fumo, pianist Wayne Peet, bassist Ken Filiano and drummer Alex Cline; the band could almost be called the Nine Winds All-Stars. Many moods are explored, and Golia shows how much he had grown as a player during the eight years since he started the label. —*Scott Yanow*

● **Out for Blood** / Sep. 19, 1988 / Nine Winds ✦✦✦✦✦
This is an exciting free-bop album. Vinny Golia (who switches between tenor, baritone, soprano and sopranino) teams up with the witty and extroverted trombonist Mike Vlatkovich, pianist Wayne Peet, bassist Ken Filiano and drummer Alex Cline for frequently explosive interplay on six of his more colorful originals. Although it would have been nice to have liner notes that told the stories behind the unusual song titles (which include "Joey Evans Spies the Mouse," "The Great Adams City Caper" and "I Never Want to Miss Last Fall"), the music itself needs no explanation. Highly recommended to the more open-eared listener, this is one of Vinny Golia's finest recordings to date. —*Scott Yanow*

Pilgrimage to Obscurity / Jul. 1991 / Nine Winds ✦✦✦

Commemoration / Oct. 11, 1991+Apr. 11, 1992 / Nine Winds ✦✦✦✦

On Worldwide & Portable / Dec. 1991 / Nine Winds ✦✦✦

Decennium Dans Axlan / Apr. 11, 1992 / Nine Winds ✦✦✦✦

Haunting the Spirits Inside Them . . . / Apr. 27, 1992 / Music & Arts ✦✦✦

Against the Grain / 1993 / Nine Winds ✦✦✦✦

Tutto Contare / Nov. 20, 1995 / Nine Winds ✦✦✦✦
The Vinny Golia Large Ensemble comprises on this live recording three trumpets, four trombones, tuba, seven reeds, keyboards, three strings, two basses, drums and two percussionists. The huge band performs six of Golia's complex originals. Among the many soloists on the set are the leader on two types of clarinets, trumpeters John Fumo, Rob Blakeslee and Mark Underwood, trombonists Mike Vlatkovich and Eric Jorgensen, David Ocker on clarinet, pianist Wayne Peet, altoist Steve Flower, the tenors of Steve Marsh and Bill Plake and violinist Harry Scoro. However it is the dense ensembles that are most remarkable. The music is consistently atonal yet leaves room for space and develops logically (if not predictably). The sounds are sometimes otherworldly (making it difficult to know who is playing what) and the performances do not swing conventionally but they definitely fit into the area of jazz due to the high level of improvisation. This stimulating set is recommended most to listeners with very open ears. —*Scott Yanow*

11 Reasons to Begin / Mar. 6, 1996 / Music & Arts ✦✦✦

The Art of Negotiation / Mar. 8, 1996-Mar. 9, 1996 / CIMP ✦✦✦

Dante No Longer Repents / Apr. 27, 1996 / Music & Arts ✦✦✦✦

Triangulation / May 22, 1996+Sep. 17, 1996 / Nine Winds ✦✦✦

Benny Golson

b. Jan. 25, 1929, Philadelphia, PA
Tenor Saxophone, Composer, Arranger / Hard Bop
Benny Golson is a talented composer/arranger whose tenor playing has continued to evolve with time. After attending Howard University (1947-50) he worked in Philadelphia with Bull Moose Jackson's R&B band (1951) at a time when it

included one of his writing influences, Tadd Dameron on piano. Golson played with Dameron for a period in 1953 and this was followed by stints with Lionel Hampton (1953-54), Johnny Hodges and Earl Bostic (1954-56). He came to prominence while with Dizzy Gillespie's globetrotting big band (1956-58), as much for his writing as for his tenor playing (the latter was most influenced by Don Byas and Lucky Thompson). Golson wrote such standards as "I Remember Clifford" (for the late Clifford Brown), "Killer Joe," "Stablemates," "Whisper Not," "Along Came Betty" and "Blues March" during 1956-60. His stay with Art Blakey's Jazz Messengers (1958-59) was significant and during 1959-62 he co-led the Jazztet with Art Farmer. From that point on Golson gradually drifted away from jazz and concentrated more on working in the studios and with orchestras including a couple years (1964-66) in Europe. When Benny Golson returned to active playing in 1977, his tone had hardened and sounded much closer to Archie Shepp than to Don Byas. Other than an unfortunate commercial effort for Columbia (1977), Golson has recorded consistently rewarding albums (many for Japanese labels) since that time including a reunion with Art Farmer and Curtis Fuller in a new Jazztet. Through the years he has recorded as a leader for Contemporary, Riverside, United Artists, New Jazz, Argo, Mercury and Dreyfus among others. —*Scott Yanow*

● **New York Scene** / Oct. 14, 1957+Oct. 17, 1957/ Original Jazz Classics ✦✦✦✦✦
Benny Golson's debut as a leader was recorded at a time when he was better known as a composer than a tenor saxophonist. This CD reissue, which adds "B.G.'s Holiday" to the original LP program, features Golson in a quintet with fellow future Jazztet co-leader Art Farmer on trumpet, pianist Wynton Kelly, bassist Paul Chambers and drummer Charlie Persip on five selections, and with the same group plus four horns on three other songs. The set is most significant for including an early version of Golson's "Whisper Not" (which soon became a jazz standard) along with "Step Lightly," as well as for the leader's inventive and swinging arrangements; plus, there are some excellent solos from Golson and Farmer. Overall, this underrated gem served as a strong start to Benny Golson's influential solo career. —*Scott Yanow*

The Modern Touch / Dec. 19, 1957+Dec. 23, 1957 / Original Jazz Classics ✦✦✦✦
Benny Golson's second album as a leader (reissued on CD in the OJC series) is a solid hard-bop date featuring the tenorman in a quintet with trumpeter Kenny Dorham, pianist Wynton Kelly, bassist Paul Chambers and drummer Max Roach. The all-star group performs three Golson originals (none of which really caught on), a pair of Gigi Gryce tunes (best known is "Hymn to the Orient") and the standard "Namely You." Excellent playing on an above-average set that defines the modern mainstream of 1957 jazz. —*Scott Yanow*

The Other Side of Benny Golson / Nov. 12, 1958 / Original Jazz Classics ✦✦✦✦
Tenor saxophonist Benny Golson's third recording as a leader was significant in two ways. It was his first opportunity to work with trombonist Curtis Fuller (the two would be members of the Jazztet by 1960) and it was one of his first chances to really stretch out on record as a soloist; up to this point Golson was possibly better known as a composer. Three of the six originals on this CD reissue of a Riverside date are Golson's ("Are You Real" was the closest one to catching on) but the emphasis is on the solos of the leader, Fuller and pianist Barry Harris; bassist Jymie Merritt and drummer Philly Joe Jones are excellent in support. —*Scott Yanow*

Benny Golson and the Philadelphians / Nov. 17, 1958 / United Artists ✦✦✦

Gone with Golson / Jun. 20, 1959 / Original Jazz Classics ✦✦✦✦
Shortly before the formation of the Jazztet, tenor saxophonist Benny Golson and trombonist Curtis Fuller teamed up for this quintet set with pianist Ray Bryant, bassist Tommy Bryant and drummer Al Harewood. Although Golson contributed three of the six songs ("Blues After Dark" is the best-known one), the emphasis is on his playing; the tenor is quite heated on the uptempo blues "Jam for Bobbie." The CD reissue adds "A Bit of Heaven" (originally on a sampler but part of the same session) to the original program, a fine example of hard bop of the late '50s. —*Scott Yanow*

Groovin' with Golson / Aug. 28, 1959 / Original Jazz Classics ✦✦✦
This is one of at least four recordings that matched up tenor saxophonist Benny Golson and trombonist Curtis Fuller prior to the formation of the Jazztet; ironically, Fuller only stuck around for one Jazztet record before departing. Reissued on CD, the LP-length program has two lesser-known Golson compositions, "Drum Boogie," "I Didn't Know What Time It Was" and "Yesterdays." Three of the tunes are blues, and the two ballads are taken at a medium-tempo pace. With pianist Ray Bryant, bassist Paul Chambers and drummer Art Blakey forming a solid rhythm section, the hard bop music does indeed groove in its own fashion. —*Scott Yanow*

Gettin' with It / Dec. 23, 1959 / Original Jazz Classics ✦✦✦

Turning Point / Oct. 30, 1962-Nov. 1, 1962 / Mercury ✦✦✦
Renamed *Turning Point* upon one of its reissues, this quartet set for tenor saxophonist Benny Golson was the beginning of the close of an era. Within a year, Golson would be working full-time as a writer in the studios, and he de-emphasized his playing until making a comeback in the late 1970s. Golson is heard on this LP for one of the last times playing in his original Don Byas/Lucky Thompson-influenced style. Joined by pianist Wynton Kelly, bassist Paul Chambers and drummer Jimmy Cobb, Golson performs two originals, plus five superior standards, including "How Am I to Know," "Three Little Words" and "Alone Together." A rewarding but sadly out-of-print set. —*Scott Yanow*

Stockholm Sojourn / Jul. 14, 1964 / Original Jazz Classics ✦✦✦
Although the International Jazz Orchestra (which was arranged and conducted by Benny Golson) recorded their parts for this LP on July 14, 1964, some of the soloists were dubbed in later that year. Golson, who does not play at all on this set, seemed inspired by the large instrumentation—a full orchestra with trumpets, trombones, French horns, several English horns doubling on oboes, five reeds, up to six additional flutes and a pianoless rhythm section—and his charts (six of his originals and three standards) are both inventive and full of subtle surprises. Among the many highlights are Golson's reworkings of "Are You Real," "Waltz for Debby" and "I Remember Clifford." This underrated set is recommended. —*Scott Yanow*

Killer Joe / 1977 / Columbia ✦✦
This album broke Golson's long hiatus in America and reintroduced him to the domestic jazz audience, but it wasn't quite the hit for him as for Quincy Jones. —*Ron Wynn*

California Message / Oct. 20, 1980-Oct. 22, 1980 / Baystate ✦✦✦
This set, also available on the Timeless label, was Benny Golson's first album (other than a dismal commercial affair for Columbia) since 1964; he had spent the interim writing full-time for the studios. For this celebratory occasion, Golson reunites with trombonist Curtis Fuller in a septet also including trumpeter Oscar Brashear, trombonist Thurman Green and pianist Bill Mays. The music (seven Golson compositions, including his older "hits" "Blues March," "Whisper Not" and "I Remember Clifford") are not as surprising as his new sound, which had discarded his former roots in Don Byas and Lucky Thompson for a gruffness closer to Archie Shepp. —*Scott Yanow*

One More Mem'ry / Aug. 19, 1981-Aug. 20, 1981 / Timeless ✦✦✦

Time Speaks / Dec. 8, 1982-Dec. 9, 1982 / Timeless ✦✦✦✦
This set is chiefly notable for teaming together for the first time trumpeters Freddie Hubbard and Woody Shaw. Ostensibly a tribute to Clifford Brown, the sextet date (which also features Benny Golson on tenor, pianist Kenny Barron, bassist Cecil McBee and drummer Ben Riley) only has two songs actually played by Brown ("I'll Remember April" and "Jordu"), along with originals by Golson, Shaw and Hubbard ("Blues for Duane"). No matter; it is for the Hubbard-Shaw matchup that this straightahead outing is mostly recommended, as the two trumpeters provide most of the fireworks. —*Scott Yanow*

This Is for You, John / Dec. 1983 / Timeless ✦✦
Tenors Benny Golson (a childhood friend of John Coltrane) and Pharoah Sanders (who played with Coltrane's group during his last two years) team up with pianist Cedar Walton, bassist Ron Carter and drummer Jack DeJohnette for a sincere tribute to the late saxophonist. The material is different than one might expect, with four recent Golson originals, one by Sanders and only two songs ("Greensleeves" and "Vilia") that were actually recorded by Coltrane. Unfortunately, the two tenors do not blend together very well, and Golson's pitch comes across as unreliable; Sanders usually takes solo honors. Overall, this album does not live up to its potential. —*Scott Yanow*

Stardust / Jun. 22, 1987-Jun. 23, 1987 / Denon ✦✦✦✦
This obscure CD, released by Japanese Denon but for a time made available in the US, has tenor saxophonist Benny Golson welcoming trumpeter Freddie Hubbard, pianist Mulgrew Miller, bassist Ron Carter and drummer Marvin "Smitty" Smith to his quintet set. Hubbard was in prime form during this period, and the repertoire (three Golson tunes, an original apiece by Carter and the trumpeter, "Love Is a Many Splendored Thing" and "Stardust") provides inspiration for some excellent hard bop-oriented solos. Worth searching for. —*Scott Yanow*

Live / 1989 / Dreyfus ✦✦✦✦

Domingo / Nov. 11, 1991-Nov. 13, 1991 / Dreyfus ✦✦✦✦✦
Tenor saxophonist Benny Golson reunites with his longtime associate Curtis Fuller for this enjoyable set of hard bop. With assistance from pianist Kevin Hays, bassist James Genus, drummer Tony Reedus and (on "Blues March") trumpeter Jean-Loup Longnon, Golson and Fuller both sound very much in their musical prime. The tenor's sound at this point had become quite a bit harder than previously, at times fairly close to Archie Shepp's, but he swung as hard as ever. Fuller

in contrast is unchanged from his earlier days. Together they play in top form on six of Golson's compositions plus Fuller's "A La Mode" and Dave Brubeck's "In Your Own Sweet Way." —*Scott Yanow*

I Remember Miles / Oct. 5, 1992-Oct. 6, 1992 / Evidence ♦♦♦♦♦
There are a few remarkable recreations on tenor saxophonist Benny Golson's tribute to Miles Davis, particularly "'Round Midnight" and parts of "So What" and "Bye Bye Blackbird." Trumpeter Eddie Henderson (especially when muted) comes very close to duplicating not only the sound but the spirit of Davis while Golson sometimes discards his own strong musical personality to do close impressions of John Coltrane. Trombonist Curtis Fuller, pianist Mulgrew Miller, bassist Ray Drummond and drummer Tony Reedus are also in fine form on a program that not only has five songs associated with 1950s Miles Davis but three Golson originals including "One Day, Forever (I Remember Miles)" which (although worthy) is not in the same league as his earlier classic "I Remember Clifford." This heartfelt tribute album has enough unique moments to make it easily recommended. —*Scott Yanow*

Up Jumped Benny / May 23, 1996 / Arkadia ♦♦♦♦
Benny Golson had not appeared on an American jazz label in a long time, so Bob Karcy of Arkadia Jazz stepped in where others feared to tread, issuing this live gig from a jazz club somewhere in Switzerland on the last day of a tour. Armed with a rhythm section of competent young players (Kevin Hays, piano; Dwayne Burno, bass; Carl Allen, drums), Golson takes his dusky tenor sax tone frequently into Coltrane extended harmonic country when the tempos are up, his head figuratively in the clouds above the occasionally combustible trio. Yet he also ruminates in an almost withdrawn manner at ballad tempo on a lengthy treatment of his jazz standard "I Remember Clifford," concluding with a quiet solo elegy for Brownie based on a tenor (the vocal species) aria from Puccini's *Tosca*. Stanley Crouch's liner notes are full of his usual respect-your-elders blather and the sound quality is boxy, but Golson's fans will feel fortunate to have this. —*Richard S. Ginell*

Benny Golson in Paris / Nov. 17, 1958-Dec. 12, 1958 / Disques Swing ♦♦♦♦
Two sessions were combined and reissued on this 1987 DRG/Swing LP: a United Artists album led by tenor saxophonist Benny Golson and three titles from a date featuring Golson but actually headed by trumpeter Roger Guerin. The former set has Golson teaming up with trumpeter Lee Morgan, pianist Ray Bryant, bassist Percy Heath and drummer Philly Joe Jones on six then-recent jazz tunes, including three songs by Golson (highlighted by "Stablemates") and John Lewis' "Afternoon in Paris." The other date has Golson and Timmons joining Guerin, bassist Pierre Michelot and drummer Christian Garros for "Blues March," "I Remember Clifford" and Timmons' "Moanin'." Although both sessions are rather obscure, the music is excellent hard bop for the period, and the songs are some of the best from the era. —*Scott Yanow*

Eddie Gomez

b. Oct. 4, 1944, San Juan, Puerto Rico
Bass / Post-Bop
Eddie Gomez is a brilliant bassist whose flexibility and quick reflexes make him an ideal accompanist (although his own albums tend to be a bit erratic jazzwise). He grew up in New York and was with the Newport Festival Youth Band during 1959-61. After studying at Juilliard, Gomez played with Rufus Jones' sextet, Marian McPartland (1964), Paul Bley (1964-65), Giuseppe Logan, Gerry Mulligan and Gary McFarland among others. Gomez came to fame during his long period with the Bill Evans Trio (1966-77). He has since worked in a countless number of settings including filling in for Charles Mingus (1978) and with Steps Ahead (1979-84), Benny Wallace, Joanne Brackeen, Jack DeJohnette, Chick Corea and in commercial settings as a studio musician. Eddie Gomez has recorded as a leader for Columbia, ProJazz and Stretch. —*Scott Yanow*

Down Stretch / Jan. 22, 1976-Jan. 23, 1976 / Black Hawk ♦♦♦

Gomez / Jan. 1984-Feb. 1984 / Denon ♦♦♦
Nice, mainstream fare. —*Ron Wynn*

Discovery / Nov. 1985 / Columbia ♦♦♦♦
A powerful recording, it features Michael Brecker on sax and E.W.I., an electronic wind instrument. Musically this album covers jazz and classical and a little avant-garde. —*Paul Kohler*

Trio / Mar. 4, 1986 / Pro Arte ♦♦♦

Power Play / Nov. 1987 / Columbia ♦♦♦

Street Smart / May 1989 / Columbia ♦♦
This outing by bassist Eddie Gomez does not come close to living up to its potential. The strong cast does include several top-notch improvisers (including the

reeds of Dick Oatts, trumpeter Randy Brecker, pianist Kenny Werner and organist Jack McDuff) and the music is often jazzy but there are absolutely no chances taken. The album sounds preplanned, second-by-second. A "contemporary" jazz item with Oatts playing the part of a low budget Michael Brecker is followed by an easy listening original, a salsa performance, a heartfelt ballad and a straight-ahead but uneventful blues. A couple of meaningless funk numbers alternate with a pair of forgettable ballads; all of the music clocks in between 3:52 and 5:38. The lack of spontaneity and excitement makes this a disappointing and passable item. —*Scott Yanow*

● **Next Future** / 1992 / Stretch ♦♦♦♦
Bassist Eddie Gomez is better as a sideman than as a leader on recording dates, but this is one of his stronger efforts in the latter category (even if one has to get used to him taking or sharing virtually all of the melodies). Chick Corea sticks exclusively to an atmospheric synthesizer but otherwise this is a fairly straightahead quintet session featuring Gomez with the Coltranish tenor of Rick Margitza, pianist James Williams, drummer Lenny White and a guest appearance from flutist Jeremy Steig. —*Scott Yanow*

Nat Gonella (Nathaniel Charles Gonella)

b. Mar. 7, 1908, London, England
Trumpet, Vocals / Dixieland
Inspired by Louis Armstrong, Nat Gonella in the 1930s could be considered the Wingy Manone or Louis Prima of England. He started off playing in the jazz-oriented dance bands of Billy Cotton, Roy Fox, Ray Noble and Lew Stone during 1929-34 before leading his own band the Georgians, named thus because his version of "Georgia on My Mind" was popular. Although he visited and played in the US in 1939, Gonella chose to stay in England where he made many records during 1932-42, a few in the mid-'40s and then became less prominent. In 1958 he formed the New Georgia Jazz Band (which recorded frequently during the next three years) and he remained an active and popular figure into the late '70s. Nat Gonella's recordings are worth investigating by swing and Dixieland fans. —*Scott Yanow*

● **Mister Rhythm Man** / Jan. 1934-Mar. 1935 / EMI ♦♦♦♦♦
Swing trumpeter/vocalist Nat Gonella was a popular attraction in England during the 1930s, recording many numbers reminiscent of Wingy Manone and Louis Prima. This imported LP features Gonella with his Georgians, a group ranging in size from eight to eleven pieces. The repertoire includes such numbers as "Don't Let Your Love Go Wrong," "E-Flat Blues," "Basin Street Blues," "Stardust," and four three-song medleys. Fun music that deserves to be reissued in full on CD someday. —*Scott Yanow*

Crazy Valves / Jul. 4, 1934-Sep. 24, 1937 / ASV ♦♦♦♦♦
Nat Gonella was in ways the Wingy Manone of Great Britain. An excellent trumpeter and a spirited singer, Gonella was (like Manone) inspired by Louis Armstrong and played in a similar style, between Dixieland and swing. Unfortunately, not much of his output (which includes hundreds of numbers cut during the 1932-42 period) has been reissued on CD, so one needs to rely on English LPs. This particular album is quite definitive, containing 18 of Gonella's best records from when he was 26-29 years old. Gonella's theme song, "Georgia on My Mind," is here, as are memorable versions of "How'm I Doin'," "Crazy Valves," "Nagasaki," "The Sheik of Araby" and "Trumpetuous." Worth searching for by pre-bop collectors. —*Scott Yanow*

Yeah Man / Jul. 24, 1935-Dec. 1, 1937 / Harlequin ♦♦♦♦
Nat Gonella records have always been a bit difficult to acquire in the US. The British trumpeter/vocalist had plenty of competition during the 1930s and '40s, and even in more recent years, his reissues have mostly been on English LPs such as this one. A fine sampling of numbers from 1935 and 1937, these 16 titles feature Gonella as the lead voice with his swinging 11-piece Georgians. Highlights include "Georgia Rockin' Chair," "St. Louis Blues," "Yeah Man," "Farewell Blues" and "Whatcha Gonna Do When There Ain't No Swing," but each selection has its enjoyable moments. —*Scott Yanow*

How'm I Doin'? / Jan. 10, 1936-Dec. 10, 1936 / Old Bean ♦♦♦♦♦
Englishman Nat Gonella has always been somewhat overlooked in the US since his records have long been rare, but he was one of the best trumpeters of the 1930s, and an enjoyable singer too. He recorded extensively with his Georgians during the swing era, including the 20 titles included on this superior (and generous) British LP. Performing hot standards along with a couple of originals, Gonella is heard in peak form on such tunes as "How'm I Doin'," "Fan It," "The Music Goes Round and Round," "Someone Stole Gabriel's Horn" and "Lady Be Good." No pre-bop collection is complete without at least a couple of Nat Gonella sets; he is well worth discovering. —*Scott Yanow*

Paul Gonsalves

b. Jul. 12, 1920, Boston, MA, **d.** May 14, 1974, London, England
Tenor Saxophone / Bop, Swing
The greatest moment of Paul Gonsalves' musical career occurred at the 1956 Newport Jazz Festival when, to bridge the gap between "Diminuendo in Blue" and "Crescendo in Blue," Duke Ellington urged him to take a long solo, egging him on through 27 exciting choruses that almost caused a riot. That well-publicized episode resulted in Ellington having a major "comeback," and Gonsalves forever earning Duke's graditude.

Gonsalves had already earned a strong reputation during his stints with Count Basie (1946-49) and the Dizzy Gillespie Orchestra (1949-50). Joining Ellington in 1950, Gonsalves' warm breathy tone and harmonically advanced solos were a constant fixture for 24 years (except for a brief time in 1953 when he was with Tommy Dorsey) and he was well featured up until his death, just ten days before Ellington passed on. In addition to his countless number of recorded performances with Ellington, Gonsalves led dates of his own on an occasional basis including for Argo, Jazzland, Impulse (highlighted by a combative meeting with Sonny Stitt), Storyville, Black Lion and Fantasy. —*Scott Yanow*

Cookin' / Aug. 6, 1957 / Argo ✦✦✦✦
With Clark Terry on trumpet. —*Michael G. Nastos*

● **Gettin' Together!** / Dec. 20, 1960 / Original Jazz Classics ✦✦✦✦
The most easily available of tenor saxophonist Paul Gonsalves' infrequent sessions as a leader, this CD is a straight reissue of his original Jazzland LP. Three songs (including two ballads) showcase Gonsalves in a quartet with pianist Wynton Kelly, bassist Sam Jones and drummer Jimmy Cobb, while five other pieces add cornetist Nat Adderley (in his prime during the era) to the band. The music is straightahead and shows that Gonsalves was quite capable of playing with younger "modernists." —*Scott Yanow*

Tell It the Way It Is / Sep. 4, 1963 / Impulse! ✦✦✦✦✦
Tenor saxophonist Paul Gonsalves is heard in peak form throughout this excellent (but thus far out-of-print) Impulse LP. "Body and Soul" features Gonsalves with a quartet which also includes pianist Walter Bishop, bassist Ernie Shephard and drummer Osie Johnson; trumpeter Rolf Ericson and Ray Nance (on violin and trumpet) help out on a lengthy version of Bishop's soulful "Tell It the Way It Is," and four other pieces have altoist Johnny Hodges making the band a septet. A particularly strong outing by all of the musicians. —*Scott Yanow*

Encuentro / Sep. 15, 1968 / Fresh Sound ✦✦✦✦
This little-known CD from the Spanish Fresh Sound label is a reissue of an LP from the defunct Catalyst company. The music consists of one of tenorman Paul Gonsalves' best sets as a leader. Gonsalves and trumpeter Willie Cook are heard featured in Argentina (during a tour by Duke Ellington's Orchestra) with a local rhythm section led by the fine pianist Enrique Villegas. Highlights of this fine mainstream swing set include a nearly ten-minute version of "Perdido," "St. Louis Blues" and "Just Friends." —*Scott Yanow*

Just A-Sittin' and A-Rockin' / Aug. 28, 1970+Sep. 3, 1970 / Black Lion ✦✦✦
This relaxed session gave three of Duke Ellington's finest sidemen rare opportunities to record outside of Ellington's Orchestra: tenor saxophonist Paul Gonsalves, Ray Nance (who had left Ellington a few years earlier) on trumpet, violin and vocal and (for half of this CD) altoist Norris Turney. The emphasis is on slower material but there are a few romps (such as "Stompy Jones") to give the session a bit of variety. Good swinging performances on mostly familiar tunes. —*Scott Yanow*

Paul Gonsalves Meets Earl Hines / Dec. 15, 1970+Nov. 29, 1972 / Black Lion ✦✦✦✦
Most of this CD was recorded at the earlier date. Duke Ellington's longtime tenor, Paul Gonsalves, was a perfect match for the inventive pianist, Earl Hines, who (along with bassist Al Hall and drummer Jo Jones) is in top form on five standards, three by Ellington. The music swings hard and has its surprising moments. The one track from 1972 is a solo version of "Blue Sands" played by its composer Earl Hines. Although not essential, this CD should please the fans of Hines and Gonsalves, two masterful players who had only previously recorded together once, on a date shared by the pianist and Johnny Hodges. —*Scott Yanow*

Babs Gonzales

b. Oct. 27, 1919, Newark, NJ, **d.** Jan. 23, 1980, Newark, NJ
Vocals / Bop
A limited but enthusiastic singer, Babs Gonzales did what he could to popularize bop. He had brief stints with Charlie Barnet and Lionel Hampton and then led his own group (Three Bips and a Bop) during 1946-49, recording 24 numbers during 1947-49 including the earliest version of "Oop-Pop-A-Da" and such songs as

"Weird Lullaby," "A Lesson in Bopology," "Professor Bop" and "Prelude to a Nightmare"; among his sidemen on these dates were Tadd Dameron, Tony Scott, Roy Haynes, James Moody, J.J. Johnson, Julius Watkins, Sonny Rollins (making his recording debut), Art Pepper, Wynton Kelly and even Don Redman. However once the bop "fad" ended, Gonzales became more of a cult figure. He worked with James Moody (1951-53), recorded with Jimmy Smith and Johnny Griffin, ran his own label (Expubidence) and wrote two autobiographies that were more colorful than accurate. —*Scott Yanow*

● **Weird Lullaby** / Feb. 24, 1947-Nov. 23, 1958 / Blue Note ✦✦✦✦✦
Virtually all of singer Babs Gonzales' most important recordings are on this colorful CD. A pioneering bop-oriented scat singer who predated the vocalese masters Eddie Jefferson, King Pleasure and Jon Hendricks, Gonzales sang with enthusiasm and an emphasis on vowels. Babs is featured on eight numbers with his Three Bips and a Bop (pianist-composer Tadd Dameron is in the supporting cast) including the original version of Gonzales' "greatest hit" "Oop-Pop-A-Da." Other sessions are as noteworthy for their unique personnel as for Babs' singing which include tenor saxophonist Sonny Rollins (in his recording debut), trombonists Bennie Green and J.J. Johnson, the French horn master Julius Watkins, altoist Art Pepper, pianist Wynton Kelly, drummer Roy Haynes, Don Redman (on soprano), flutist Albert Soccaras and violinist Ray Nance. The final four numbers (from 1956 and 1958) find Gonzales backed on two songs apiece by the Jimmy Smith Trio and the Bennie Green Quintet (with pianist Sonny Clark). Highlights overall include "Weird Lullaby," "Babs' Dream," "Professor Bop," "Prelude to a Nightmare," "The Continental," "St. Louis Blues" and "'Round Midnight." Essential for bop collectors. —*Scott Yanow*

Jerry Gonzalez

b. Jun. 5, 1949, New York, NY
Trumpet, Percussion / Afro-Cuban Jazz, Post-Bop, Latin Jazz
A multitalented musician, Jerry Gonzalez plays trumpet in the tradition of Miles Davis and Dizzy Gillespie while also being one of the top Latin percussionists. He played in salsa bands as a teenager and freelanced in the 1970s and '80s with (among others) Dizzy Gillespie, Tony Williams, Eddie Palmieri, Tito Puente and McCoy Tyner. In 1980 Gonzales formed the Fort Apache Band, a group that has creatively Latinized all types of challenging jazz compositions including a full set of Thelonious Monk tunes. Gonzales and his important group have recorded for Enja and Sunnyside. —*Scott Yanow*

Ya Yo Me Cure / Jul. 1979-Aug. 1979 / American Clave/Pangaea ✦✦✦
The debut recording as a leader by Jerry Gonzalez features an early version of the trumpeter/Latin percussionist's Fort Apache Band (although it had not been named at this point). The advanced Latin jazz set (which has been reissued on CD) features such notable sidemen as trombonist Steve Turre, Mario Rivera on tenor, pianist Hilton Ruiz, singer Frankie Rodriguez and several percussionists. In addition to three originals by Rodriguez, the hot ensemble Latinizes such unlikely tunes as "Caravan," Wayne Shorter's "Nefertiti," Thelonious Monk's "Evidence" and "The Lucy Theme." Frequently exciting music. —*Scott Yanow*

The River Is Deep / Nov. 5, 1982 / Enja ✦✦✦✦
And the Fort Apache Band. Powerhouse group; strong material. A sparkling session that helped cement Gonzalez's status among the new crop of Latin-jazz stars. —*Ron Wynn*

● **Rumba Para Monk** / Oct. 27, 1988-Oct. 28, 1988 / Sunnyside ✦✦✦✦✦
Jerry Gonzalez has referred to himself as being "bilingual" in that he is equally skilled on trumpet and congas, in bebop and in Latin music. Gonzalez succeeds in his goal of combining the two idioms without watering down either style on this essential Sunnyside CD. The first Afro-Cuban Thelonious Monk tribute has plenty of spots for the percussion of Steve Berrios and Gonzalez, but also contains many strong solos from the leader's often-muted Miles-influenced trumpet, Carter Jefferson's tenor and Larry Willis' very un-Monklike piano. With the exception of "Ugly Beauty," the Latin percussion is an integral part of each performance, giving this set of Monk tunes a very different perspective that is also quite flexible. A highly enjoyable set with the highlights including "Bye-Ya," "Nutty," "Little Rootie Tootie," and "Jackie-ing." —*Scott Yanow*

Obatala / Nov. 6, 1988 / Enja ✦✦✦✦✦
Recorded live in Zurich, this is one of the finest recordings by Jerry Gonzalez's Fort Apache Band. Mixing together bop and post-bop with Latin jazz, Gonzalez's ten-piece group consists of his trumpet and congas, tenor saxophonist John Stubblefield, trombonist Papo Vasquez, pianist Larry Willis and a six-piece rhythm section including four percussionists. Gonzalez and his band show that it is possible to turn even such numbers as "Nefertiti," Miles Davis' "Eighty-One" and Thelonious Monk's "Jackie-ing" into heated Afro-Cuban jazz. Highly recommended. —*Scott Yanow*

Earthdance / Oct. 2, 1990-Oct. 3, 1990 / Sunnyside ✦✦✦✦✦

Red-hot modern Afro-Latin and Latin-jazz, with driving grooves, great playing, and up-to-the-minute rhythms. —*Ron Wynn*

Crossroads / 1994 / Milestone ✦✦✦✦

Pensativo / Apr. 1995-Aug. 1995 / Milestone ✦✦✦✦

The brothers Gonzales, trumpeter/conguero Jerry and bassist Andy, and their dauntless sextet, the Fort Apache Band, serve up an enigmatic collection of pensive Latin jazz that, for all of its intelligence and musicality, just misses ignition. Perhaps one reason for this is Gonzales' often subdued trumpet and fluegelhorn; another is the extensive overdubbing of the percussion instruments at the cost of the spontaneity and fire of Latin rhythms interlocking on the spot. Things come almost to a dead halt with the drifting, eight-minute "A Flower Is a Lovesome Thing"—just ethereal solo horns over Larry Willis' piano—and on the final duet track, "Ruby, My Dear." Nevertheless, one can savor the intriguing triple horn voicings on "Midnight Train" and "Heidi Ho," and "Gonzilla" is a studio tour de force of multiple trumpets, all played by Jerry, with a muted one above wild African drumming. —*Richard S. Ginell*

Fire Dance / Feb. 2, 1996-Feb. 4, 1996 / Milestone ✦✦✦✦

Jerry Gonzales and the Fort Apache Band have an invigorating idea going, fusing the front line of bebop to the unstoppable groove of a Latin rhythm section. Trouble is, whenever they remove the Latin rhythms—which happens most of the time on this compilation from a live gig at Blues Alley in Washington, D.C.—we are left with a standard-issue hard-bop band of the most conventional sort. Gonzales often ruminates thoughtfully in a muted Miles manner circa the 1950s, while John Stubblefield's earthy bebop tenor adds some soul to the mix, and Joe Ford contributes alto and soprano sax. When Gonzales moves over from the trumpet to the congas, some electric moments begin to emerge as he interacts with Steve Berrios on drums or timbales. Ultimately, though, this live CD does not ignite; perhaps this group could have used a seventh man, a regular Latin percussionist, to mix things up all the time. —*Richard S. Ginell*

Jerry Gonzalez & The Fort Apache Band / Feb. 2, 1996-Feb. 4, 1996 / Milestone ✦✦✦

Dennis Gonzalez

b. 1954, Abilene, TX
Trumpet / Avant-Garde, Post-Bop

A talented trumpeter who has recorded a consistently rewarding string of lesser-known dates, Dennis Gonzalez's playing falls between advanced hard bop and free jazz. He moved to Dallas in 1977 and started the Daagnim label for which he recorded frequently with top local players. Starting in 1986 Gonzalez also made several dates for the Silkheart label (utilizing Charles Brackeen on one session) and Konnex. —*Scott Yanow*

Little Toot / Apr. 8, 1985 / Daagnim ✦✦✦

Octet recording with an emphasis on horns and improvisation. Gonzalez has many other fine recordings. If you like creative music, seek them out. —*Michael G. Nastos*

Stefan / Apr. 6, 1986 / Silkheart ✦✦✦

Creative trumpeter and percussionist leads ensemble. All originals and a fresh unconventional sound. —*Michael G. Nastos*

● **Namesake** / Feb. 14, 1987 / Silkheart ✦✦✦✦

Debenge, Debenge / Feb. 11, 1988-Feb. 12, 1988 / Silkheart ✦✦✦

The Earth and the Heart / Jul. 2, 1989-Dec. 30, 1989 / Music & Arts ✦✦✦✦

Catechism / July 14, 1987 / Daagnim ✦✦✦✦

Benny Goodman

b. May 30, 1909, Chicago, IL, **d.** Jun. 13, 1986, New York, NY
Clarinet, Bandleader / Swing, Big Band, Traditional Jazz

The greatest jazz clarinetist of all time, Benny Goodman deserved his title as "The King of Swing." Although not the actual founder of swing, BG's phenomenal success in 1935 launched the swing era and, without watering down his music or displaying an extroverted show-biz personality, he became a major pop star. His eccentricities (being very self-possessed) resulted in some odd incidents and a great deal of misunderstanding through the years, but they were consistent with the fact that Goodman's main interest in life was playing clarinet and that everything else was secondary.

Benny Goodman began on clarinet when he was 11 and he had two years of study with the classically trained Franz Schoepp (whose other students included Jimmy Noone and Buster Bailey). Goodman, who first played in public doing an imitation of Ted Lewis when he was 12, developed fast. By 1923 he was a member of the Musicians Union and playing regularly in Chicago. In August 1925 when he

was 16, Goodman joined Ben Pollack's Orchestra and in December 1926 he made his recording debut with Pollack. Technically gifted from the start, Goodman was a major soloist with Pollack (along with Jimmy McPartland, Glenn Miller and later Jack Teagarden) and had his first opportunities to lead his own recording sessions in 1928 including two songs with a trio. After leaving Pollack in 1929, Goodman worked with Red Nichols' Five Pennies and then became a very busy studio musician, recording a countless number of performances (often in anonymous settings) during 1929-33. He even doubled during this era on alto, baritone and (on one session) trumpet. His own dates in 1933-4 featured Teagarden, Billie Holiday (in her recording debut), Mildred Bailey, Coleman Hawkins and the up-and-coming Gene Krupa. In 1934 Goodman put together his first orchestra, started recording for Columbia and appeared as one of three big bands on the *Lets' Dance* radio series; the show's trademark melody would permanently become his own opening theme. Using Fletcher Henderson arrangements, Goodman's well-rehearsed ensemble showed that it was possible to play both jazz and dance music simultaneously.

But when the radio show ended in May 1935, Benny Goodman's future as a bandleader was far from secure. With Bunny Berigan on trumpet, the band made popular records for Victor of "King Porter Stomp" and "Sometimes I'm Happy." The clarinetist also teamed up with Teddy Wilson and Gene Krupa for the first recordings of the Benny Goodman Trio and then agreed to go on a cross-country tour with the orchestra. After some minor successes and major disasters, the group was well-received in Oakland and then on August 21, 1935, they nearly caused a riot at the Palomar Ballroom in Los Angeles as teenagers went crazy over the band; unknown to BG, his national broadcasts on the *Let's Dance* series had been very popular in California. From that point on, he went from success to success, causing sensations in Chicago and New York. Although Berigan did not stay long with the band, his successors (Ziggy Elman, Harry James and Chris Griffin) formed one of the great trumpet sections, Gene Krupa became the pacesetter among drummers, and pianist Jess Stacy and singer Helen Ward (later Martha Tilton) were major assets. Goodman, by using Teddy Wilson and Lionel Hampton regularly in his quartet, broke boundaries in race relations. He had the most popular band in the world during 1935-38.

The high point to Benny Goodman's success was his historic January 16, 1938, Carnegie Hall concert which was miraculously recorded and released for the first time in the early '50s. "Sing, Sing, Sing" made Krupa such a star that the fact (plus a personality conflict with Goodman) resulted in him being the first of BG's stars to depart. Although BG's popularity was soon matched and then exceeded during the swing era by Artie Shaw and Glenn Miller, his orchestra (even with its turnover) remained a major force. By 1940 James, Wilson and Stacy were gone but Goodman had the pioneering electric guitarist Charlie Christian playing in his new sextet, he had signed with Columbia, the clarinetist was starting to record challenging arrangements by Eddie Sauter and he was using such fine sidemen as Cootie Williams, Georgie Auld and Johnny Guarnieri. As the 1940s advanced, other top players (such as Mel Powell, Lou McGarity, Red Norvo and even a young Stan Getz) and singers (Helen Forrest and Peggy Lee) made contributions and Goodman remained "King of Swing." He even took some time to show the classical music world that he could play their music too.

By 1945 and the rise of bebop, Benny Goodman's music started to be thought of as old-fashioned. BG's own playing rarely changed from that point forward but he remained enthusiastic about performing the old repertoire, and no one played it better. He broke up his band in 1946 and then opened his music temporarily to bebop. Goodman had a 1948 septet with fellow clarinetist Stan Hasselgård and Wardell Gray, used Fats Navarro on one recording and his 1949 orchestra had some very advanced arrangements by Chico O'Farrill in its book. But by the following year, Goodman returned permanently to swing. He led small groups and occasional big bands throughout the remainder of his career. While the orchestras tended to be nostalgic affairs (revisiting the Henderson charts), the combos allowed Goodman to stretch out and display his brilliant style. He had some reunions with his Trio and Quartet, participated in the rather fictional 1956 movie *The Benny Goodman Story* (playing the clarinet solos) and toured the USSR in 1962. Among Goodman's sidemen in the 1950s were Terry Gibbs, Buck Clayton, Ruby Braff, Paul Quinichette, Roland Hanna, Jack Sheldon, Bill Harris, Flip Phillips and Andre Previn. During his last three decades BG often used alumni and even such youngsters as Herbie Hancock and George Benson. Goodman was less active in the 1960s and made no records during 1973-77. He came back in 1978 to play at his 40th-anniversary Carnegie Hall concert before drifting back into retirement again. However in the early '80s Goodman began to show a strong interest in performing and he put together his final big band (which was really founded by Loren Schoenberg), playing on a public television show just a short time before his death.

Due to his continuing popularity, Benny Goodman (still a household name) is represented on more records than any jazz leader other than Duke Ellington. Most of his radio broadcasts and lesser-known recordings from the 1930s and '40s were released on Sunbeam LPs, his output for Victor during the swing era has been fully reissued, his Columbia performances have come out in more piecemeal fashion and there are a countless number of later combo sessions that are available; Music Masters, possessor of BG's private tapes, has thus far come out with ten CDs of previously unreleased material. —*Scott Yanow*

Rare B.G. / Mar. 21, 1928-Dec. 26, 1928 / Sunbeam ♦♦♦♦♦
The collectors' label Sunbeam has dedicated half of its releases to documenting Benny Goodman recordings, often rare ones. This LP includes Goodman's first two trio sides (which are from June 13, 1928, not February 1927, as listed); alternate takes of "Jungle Blues" (which has Goodman's only recorded trumpet solo) and "Room 1411"; vocal-dominated performances by Johnny Marvin, Irene Beasley and the great Annette Hanshaw; and sideman appearances by BG with many overlapping groups, including those called the All-Star Orchestra, the Ipana Troubadours, Mills Musical Clowns, the Lumberjacks and the Dixie Daisies. Throughout, there are many fine examples of jazz and hot dance music from the late '20s. —*Scott Yanow*

A Jazz Holiday / Jan. 23, 1928-Oct. 23, 1934 / Decca ♦♦♦♦
This two-LP set contains some of Benny Goodman's most interesting pre-swing recordings. The many highlights include two sides by his very first trio (from 1928), the satirical "Shirt Tale Stomp," Goodman's only recorded trumpet solo (on "Jungle Blues") and some rare spots on alto and baritone, four classic sides by the Joe Venuti-Eddie Lang All-Star Orchestra (including definitive versions of "Beale Street Blues" and "Farewell Blues" with trombonist/singer Jack Teagarden) and sessions led by Adrian Rollini and Red Nichols (the latter has memorable renditions of "Dinah" and "Indiana" along with a famous version of "The Sheik of Araby"). These many all-star New York bands are full of young and energetic players with BG only 19 on the earliest of these hot sides. Highly recommended in one form or another; some of the material has since been reissued on CD. —*Scott Yanow*

Great Soloists: Featuring Benny Goodman / Mar. 1929-Nov. 22, 1933 / Biograph ♦♦♦
This LP has a grab bag of somewhat rare items, featuring clarinetist Benny Goodman as a sideman during the 1929-33 period. Included are dance sides with Ben Selvin's orchestra, a hot version of "Roll on Mississippi" and strong appearances with Mills Musical Clowns (a pickup group put together by Irving Mills) and Steve Washington's orchestra. Interesting pre-swing sides by the future King. —*Scott Yanow*

Benny Goodman and the Giants of Swing / Apr. 18, 1929-Oct. 23, 1934 / Prestige ♦♦♦♦
This excellent LP collects together some of Benny Goodman's best early recordings, all cut at least a few years before he became known as the King of Swing and also co-starring the great trombonist/singer Jack Teagarden. BG is heard during 1929-31 with Red Nichols' Five Pennies (whose eight selections include "Indiana," "Dinah" and Teagarden's famous vocal on "The Sheik of Araby"), the 1930 session by Irving Mills' Hotsy Totsy Gang that included an ailing Bix Beiderbecke, an Adrian Rollini date from 1934 and four gems by the Joe Venuti-Eddie Lang All-Star Orchestra in 1931. Throughout, Goodman (just barely out of his teens) and Teagarden, along with other talented jazzmen then earning a living as studio musicians, seem overjoyed to be able to play jazz. This is highly enjoyable music that serves as a fine introduction to early pre-swing jazz. —*Scott Yanow*

B.G. & Big Tea in NYC / Apr. 1929-Oct. 1934 / GRP ♦♦♦♦♦
CD reissue of some early '30s material that doesn't feature clarinetist Benny Goodman in a leadership role. Instead, he's in bands under the direction of Red Nichols, Arthur Rollini, and Irving Mills. Yet, he's the star soloist, along with trombonist Jack Teagarden. —*Ron Wynn*

Swinging '34, Vol. 1 / 1934 / Melodean ♦♦♦♦
These two volumes find Benny Goodman and an impressive nine-piece unit (which includes trumpeter Bunny Berigan, trombonist Jack Jenney and drummer Gene Krupa) jamming anonymously under the bandname of "Bill Dodge and His All-Star Orchestra" (even though there was no Bill Dodge). The music, recorded for radio airplay for use between shows, features excellent examples of early swing with plenty of then-recent compositions and, on the first volume, four vocals by Red McKenzie. Collectors will enjoy comparing these performances to the regular studio versions; both are generally enjoyable. —*Scott Yanow*

Swinging '34, Vol. 2 / 1934 / Melodean ♦♦♦♦
This is the second of two LPs documenting music recorded for anonymous radio airplay in early 1934 by Benny Goodman and a particularly strong nonet (including trumpeter Bunny Berigan and trombonist Jack Jenney). The results are swing performed a year before it became wildly popular; these performances hold their own against their more familiar studio versions. —*Scott Yanow*

The Complete Benny Goodman, Vol. 1 (1935) / Apr. 4, 1935-Nov. 22, 1935 / RCA ♦♦♦♦♦
This is the first of eight double LPs that contain all of Benny Goodman's output for Victor during the remarkable 1935-39 period. After recording "King Porter Stomp" and "Sometimes I'm Happy" on July 1, 1935, and then thrilling the crowd at the Palomar Ballroom in Los Angeles on August 21, the Goodman Orchestra became the most popular in the world, not losing its dominance until the rise of Glenn Miller in 1939. This two-fer not only includes the two hits but all of trumpeter Bunny Berigan's solos with Goodman, the debut of the BG Trio (with pianist Teddy Wilson and drummer Gene Krupa), and many other swinging sides, even a hot version of "Jingle Bells." —*Scott Yanow*

☆ **The Birth of Swing** / Apr. 4, 1935-Nov. 5, 1936 / Bluebird ♦♦♦♦♦
This three-CD set includes all of the Benny Goodman big band's recordings from April 1935 through November 1936, a period when the orchestra became the most popular and influential in the world, making both swing and Benny Goodman into household words. Augmented by some alternate takes, this set shows just how solid and musical a unit Goodman had from the start. Key soloists include trumpeters Bunny Berigan and Ziggy Elman, pianist Jess Stacy and the band's excellent singer Helen Ward, but BG usually emerges as the main star, with the tight, swinging ensembles being a close second. In addition to the hits ("King Porter Stomp," "Sometimes I'm Happy," "When Buddha Smiles," "Stompin' at the Savoy," and "Goody-Goody"), even the lesser-known numbers and pop tunes have their strong moments. This music is essential to any serious jazz collection. —*Scott Yanow*

Greatest Hits [RCA] / Apr. 4, 1935-Jul. 6, 1937 / RCA Victor ♦♦♦
This CD was released in 1996 as part of RCA's *Greatest Hits* jazz series, an "introduction to jazz" reissue program. Clarinetist Benny Goodman cut the majority of his most famous recordings for Victor during the period covered by this CD which has 15 mostly famous swing selections including four from his Trio and Quartet. The music is not programmed in chronological order and amazingly enough for a program of this sort, there is no personnel listing for the orchestra! The vocalists (including Helen Ward and Ella Fitzgerald) and trumpeters Bunny Berigan and Harry James are not even identified! The music is quite good (with such highlights as "Stompin' at the Savoy," "King Porter Stomp," "After You've Gone" and "Sing, Sing, Sing") but all of the recordings are easily available on other Bluebird CDs. —*Scott Yanow*

Sing, Sing, Sing / Apr. 4, 1935-Apr. 11, 1939 / Bluebird ♦♦♦
A fine all-around single CD, it sums up Benny Goodman's 1935-39 period on Victor. During this time BG became jazz's and popular music's number one attraction, achieving this impressive feat without watering down his music or emphasizing novelties. All Goodman did was play the music he loved and the audience magically responded and started dancing. This set has most of BG's better-known recordings from the era including "King Porter Stomp," "Goody Goody," "Roll 'Em," "Don't Be That Way," "One O'Clock Jump" and of course the memorable "Sing, Sing, Sing"; it serves as a good beginning for those listeners just beginning to explore Benny Goodman's music. —*Scott Yanow*

Thesaurus, Vol. 1 / Jun. 6, 1935 / Sunbeam ♦♦♦
June 6, 1935, was a very busy day for Benny Goodman and his big band. The group recorded no less than 51 tunes for transcriptions that were leased to NBC radio stations under the pseudonym of the Rhythm Makers Orchestra. Recorded shortly before BG made it big (otherwise they could not have been disguised as a fictional band), these excellent sides are a fine showcase for Goodman and his sidemen which at the time included trumpeter Pee Wee Erwin, pianist Frank Froeba and drummer Gene Krupa among others. This first of three LP volumes is highlighted by a surprisingly effective swing version of "Yes, We Have No Bananas." —*Scott Yanow*

Thesaurus, Vol. 2 / Jun. 6, 1935 / Sunbeam ♦♦♦
The second of three LPs documenting one very busy day in the life of Benny Goodman's orchestra, these transcriptions cut for radio are well recorded and consistently swinging even with the presence of a few fluffs (each performance only received one runthrough). The musicians received just $1 apiece per tune (51 songs were cut that day) so listeners definitely receive their money's worth. A fascinating look at the Benny Goodman Orchestra just before it became wildly successful. —*Scott Yanow*

Thesaurus, Vol. 3 / Jun. 6, 1935 / Sunbeam ♦♦♦
This is the third and final volume of LPs chronicling the 51 songs recorded by the Benny Goodman orchestra for radio transcriptions in one day. This set includes interesting versions of "King Porter Stomp" and "Sometimes I'm Happy" performed less than a month before the hit studio renditions, and captures the King of Swing only a short time before he unexpectedly became a household name. —*Scott Yanow*

Original Benny Goodman Trio and Quartet Sessions, Vol. 1: After You've Gone / Jul. 11, 1935-Feb. 3, 1937 / Bluebird ✦✦✦✦

Although Benny Goodman came to fame as leader of a big swinging orchestra, from nearly the beginning he always allocated some time to playing with smaller groups. On July 13, 1935, the Benny Goodman Trio debuted (featuring drummer Gene Krupa and pianist Teddy Wilson) and 13 months later vibraphonist Lionel Hampton made the unit a quartet. The first interracial group to appear regularly in public, this outlet gave BG an opportunity to stretch out and interact with his peers. The CD *After You've Gone* contains the first ten Trio recordings and the initial 12 studio performances by the Quartet. Helen Ward contributes two fine vocals but the emphasis is on the close interplay between these brilliant players. —*Scott Yanow*

The Complete Small Group Recordings / Jul. 13, 1935-Apr. 6, 1939 / RCA ✦✦✦✦✦

The music of the Benny Goodman Trio and Quartets (with the clarinetist, pianist Teddy Wilson, drummer Gene Krupa and sometimes vibraphonist Lionel Hampton) has been put out many times through the years, including in other, earlier "complete" sets. This 1997 three-CD reissue not only has all of the regular recordings, but 20 alternate takes, two of which were previously unissued. Many of the performances (such as "After You've Gone," "Moonglow," "Dinah" and "Avalon") are quite famous, considered perfect examples of "chamber jazz," and collectors will certainly enjoy hearing many of the alternates. Singers Helen Ward and Martha Tilton, trumpeter Ziggy Elman (on "Bei Mist Bist Du Schoen") and (after Krupa's departure) drummers Dave Tough and Buddy Schutz, bassist John Kirby and pianist Jess Stacy also make appearances. Classic music with many exciting moments from the King of Swing and his famous sidemen. —*Scott Yanow*

The Complete Benny Goodman, Vol. 2 (1935-1936) / Nov. 22, 1935-Jun. 16, 1936 / RCA ✦✦✦✦✦

The second two-LP set in this eight-volume series has all of Benny Goodman's Victor studio sides that were recorded during a seven-month period when the orchestra consolidated and built on its unexpected success. In addition to such popular recordings as "When Buddha Smiles," "Stompin' at the Savoy," and "Goody Goody," there are six selections by the Benny Goodman Trio, many enjoyable vocals from Helen Ward (the best of BG's many singers), and four hot numbers by a combo under Gene Krupa's leadership that match the clarinetist with trumpeter Roy Eldridge and tenor great Chu Berry. Essential music in one form or another. —*Scott Yanow*

Benny Goodman from the Congress Hotel / Dec. 27, 1935-Feb. 10, 1936 / Sunbeam ✦✦✦✦

This five-LP box set houses the same music as the five individual volumes, even including all of the same liner notes, and is overall a gem. Benny Goodman was booked into the Congress Hotel in December 1935 for a one-month stint; the engagement was eventually extended to six months. These well-recorded aircheck are seven separate but continuous broadcasts that contain plenty of strong examples of BG's early band. Unlike his 1937 version, this orchestra only had its leader and pianist Jess Stacy as memorable soloists (although trombonist Joe Harris did a good job in a Jack Teagarden vein), but the ensembles are remarkably tight, Helen Ward's vocals are enjoyable, the band always swung (even on the pop tunes), and the recording quality is quite good. Highly recommended to those who can find this rare box. —*Scott Yanow*

The Complete Benny Goodman, Vol. 3 (1936) / Aug. 13, 1936-Dec. 9, 1936 / Bluebird ✦✦✦✦

The third of eight two-LP sets reissuing all of Benny Goodman's Victor recordings from the swing era, this two-fer has such "killer dillers" as "Down South Camp Meeting," "St. Louis Blues" and two versions of "Bugle Call Rag," in addition to performances by the Benny Goodman Trio and his new Quartet (with vibraphonist Lionel Hampton), Ella Fitzgerald as a guest vocalist and trumpeter Ziggy Elman's first recordings with the band. In all there are 32 performances on this set that prove that Benny Goodman really did deserve the title "The King of Swing." —*Scott Yanow*

The Complete Benny Goodman, Vol. 8 (1936-1939) / Dec. 2, 1936-May 4, 1939 / Bluebird ✦✦✦✦✦

The final volume of this definitive series of Benny Goodman's Victor studio recordings not only contains his recordings from April and May 1939 but digs up a variety of alternate takes (most of them previously unissued) from the 1936-39 period. It is fascinating to hear "new" versions of such songs as "Stompin' at the Savoy," "Sing, Sing Sing," "Avalon" and "Sugarfoot Stomp," especially when one is familiar with the original released renditions. In addition, this two-fer has the two recordings (and one alternate) cut by the Metronome All-Star Band which in 1939 (with such musicians as Bunny Berigan, Jack Teagarden and Tommy Dorsey)

allowed Goodman to reunite with some of his associates from the earlier days. A fitting ending to an essential series. —*Scott Yanow*

Airplay / Dec. 15, 1936-Oct. 11, 1938 / Doctor Jazz ✦✦✦

There are so many CDs and LPs in existence of Benny Goodman radio broadcasts that it seems silly or repetitive to release more but as long as the musical quality stays as high as on this two-LP set, there is no reason to complain. Most unusual is a broadcast in 1937 that took place when Gene Krupa was ill. Benny Goodman and Teddy Wilson perform a duo version of "Body and Soul" and, with the addition of Lionel Hampton, form an unusual clarinet-vibes-piano trio on "Dinah." An excellent set. —*Scott Yanow*

The Complete Benny Goodman, Vol. 4 (1936-1937) / Dec. 30, 1936-Oct. 22, 1937 / Bluebird ✦✦✦✦

The fourth of eight volumes (all are two-LP sets) documenting Benny Goodman's highly influential Victor studio sides, the 1936-37 period covered by this set found BG's amazing popularity still on the rise (he was now a household name), Harry James joining the orchestra and Martha Tilton settling in as the band's regular vocalist. Among the many memorable recordings are "Sing, Sing, Sing," the BG Quartet's "Avalon" and "Sugarfoot Stomp." —*Scott Yanow*

★ **On the Air 1937-1938** / Mar. 3, 1937-Sep. 20, 1938 / Columbia/Legacy ✦✦✦✦✦

In the early '50s, after the unexpectedly large sales of Benny Goodman's 1938 Carnegie Hall concert, Columbia came out with a two-LP set of broadcasts from 1937-39 that also sold well. This recent double-CD set not only includes the music on the original LPs but adds 14 additional tracks only previously put out on collector's labels. *On the Air* really captures the Benny Goodman big band (along with some examples of the Trio and Quartet) at its peak and shows why the original swing orchestras (as opposed to the weak nostalgia bands that are currently around) were so popular with younger people in the 1930s and '40s. These performances are still exciting. —*Scott Yanow*

Roll 'Em, Vol. 1 / Mar. 25, 1937-Nov. 22, 1939 / Columbia ✦✦✦

Columbia has never coherently reissued their valuable 1939-46 Benny Goodman recordings. This LP is a bit confusing for it includes six aircheck performances from 1937-38 that are available elsewhere, along with ten studio recordings from 1939. The liner notes mistakenly say that the guitar solo on "Honeysuckle Rose" is by Arnold Covey; it is actually Charlie Christian. There is some excellent music on this LP but as a sampler it misses the mark. —*Scott Yanow*

Avalon: The Small Bands, Vol. 2 (1937-1939) / Jul. 30, 1937-Apr. 6, 1939 / Bluebird ✦✦✦✦

This second of two CDs reissuing all of Benny Goodman's Trio and Quartet recordings for Victor starts out with eight performances co-starring the magical team of vibraphonist Lionel Hampton, pianist Teddy Wilson and drummer Gene Krupa (including their famous version of "Avalon"), and then finishes off with 14 recordings from the post-Krupa era. The latter have either Dave Tough or Buddy Schutz in the drummer's spot and three cuts (including a classic version of "I Cried for You") add bassist John Kirby. No matter what the personnel, Benny Goodman is in top form on these highly enjoyable classics from his early prime. —*Scott Yanow*

Benny Goodman at the Madhattan Room / Oct. 13, 1937-Jan. 16, 1938 / Sunbeam ✦✦✦✦

Available originally as a dozen individual sets, these late-1937 broadcasts of Benny Goodman's Orchestra, Trio and Quartet from the Madhattan Room of the Pennsylvania Hotel in New York were also put out as this 12-LP box, containing exactly the same program and liner notes as the original sets. There are many highlights with strong solos from Goodman and trumpeter Harry James, exuberant backup by Gene Krupa, features for the Trio and Quartet and plenty of vocals by Martha Tilton. Since this set gives one a valuable look at the Benny Goodman Orchestra as they seem to be counting down to their famous January 1938 Carnegie Hall concert, it sems fitting that the series concludes with two numbers actually from that historic performance that were left out of the Columbia set due to their rough quality. Few bands could withstand the enormous amount of recordings, broadcasts and performances that Benny Goodman's orchestra underwent at the peak of its popularity without losing some of its quality, but the taskmaster clarinetist kept his troops nearly flawless in their ensemble work and they never failed to swing. This is a great set well worth searching for. —*Scott Yanow*

The Complete Benny Goodman, Vol. 5 (1937-1938) / Oct. 29, 1937-Apr. 8, 1938 / Bluebird ✦✦✦✦✦

It was during the period covered by this two-fer that Benny Goodman played his famous Carnegie Hall concert and his orchestra reached its peak. This fifth of eight two-LP sets documenting Benny Goodman's Victor recordings of the '30s has more than its share of memorable performances including "Don't Be That way," "One O'Clock Jump" and two versions of "Life Goes to a Party" plus the last recordings of the Benny Goodman Quartet before Gene Krupa (after a dispute with BG) left the band to form his own orchestra. Other sessions include an unusual one that found some of Count Basie's sidemen (including tenor-great Lester Young) sitting in, and there is also a quartet date with Dave Tough sitting and performing ably in the departed Krupa's place. As with all of the two-fers in this series, this one is highly recommended and deserves to be reissued in full on CD. —*Scott Yanow*

☆ **The Complete 1937-38 Jazz Concert No. 2** / 1937-1938 / Columbia ◆◆◆◆◆
This two-LP series was quickly released after the big success of Benny Goodman's best-selling 1938 Carnegie Hall Concert set. Labelled "No. 2," these excellent aircheck performances have no relation to the Carnegie Hall concert except for the time period. The Benny Goodman Orchestra and small groups often sounded much more exciting live in concert than on their studio recordings and one can really tell from these performances why drummer Gene Krupa was so popular, and a thorn in BG's side. With Harry James, Ziggy Elman and Chris Griffin forming a classic trumpet section, the Benny Goodman Orchestra (with its clean ensembles and hard-swinging sound) had its own distinctive and well-loved style. This double LP (since reissued with additional tracks on CD) contains essential music; listen to Harry James on "St. Louis Blues" for proof of the band's excitement. —*Scott Yanow*

Treasure Chest Series, Vol. 1 / 1937-1938 / MGM ◆◆◆◆
This three-LP series features radio airchecks by the Benny Goodman big band and small groups during 1937-38. Since the producers were quite choosy in designing these programs, there are virtually no weak selections with the big band numbers emphasizing middle and uptempo swing and the Trio and Quartet selections up to the level one would expect of Benny Goodman, Lionel Hampton, Teddy Wilson and Gene Krupa. The first volume contains "When Buddha Smiles," "Dear Old Southland," "Madhouse" and a few quartet performances. The biggest surprise is Lionel Hampton's ad-lib appearance on vibes during the big band's "I Know That You Know." —*Scott Yanow*

Treasure Chest Series, Vol. 2 / 1937-1938 / MGM ◆◆◆◆
The second of three LPs in this superior series continues the issuance of rare (and well-chosen) live performances by Benny Goodman's big band and small groups. Virtually every selection is a gem and there are a few surprises. The big band joins the quartet at the end of a rousing "Avalon" while "Space, Man" finds Lionel Hampton and Jess Stacy sharing the same piano. Overall, this series finds BG and his sidemen at their best —*Scott Yanow*

Treasure Chest Series, Vol. 3 / 1937-1939 / MGM ◆◆◆◆
The third and final LP in this wonderful series of radio airchecks once again features Benny Goodman, his big band and small groups at their best; the producers really cherry-picked the large amount of live documentation to come up with some of the most rewarding performances by BG during one of his prime periods. The biggest surprise of *Volume 3* is the addition of Harry James' trumpet to the quartet on "Twilight in Turkey" but even the selections that should be predictable tend to swing hotter than expected. As a bonus, a 1939 live version of "AC-DC Current" adds a rare performance by guitarist Charlie Christian to his slim discography. Overall this is a great series that deserves to be reissued on CD. —*Scott Yanow*

★ **Benny Goodman Carnegie Hall Jazz Concert** / Jan. 16, 1938 / Columbia ◆◆◆◆◆
One of the great concerts ever captured on record is in itself a turning point in the way jazz is judged by outsiders. Never before had a full jazz concert been held at Carnegie Hall; it is hard to believe that tapes of this momentous event were kept in a closet, forgotten until rediscovered by accident in 1950. There are many, many high points, including exciting versions of "Don't Be That Way" and "One O'Clock Jump," a tribute to the 20 years of jazz that were then on record, a jam-session version of "Honeysuckle Rose" which found sidemen of the orchestras of Duke Ellington and Count Basie interacting with Goodman's stars, exciting performances by the Trio and Quartet and of course "Sing, Sing, Sing" with Gene Krupa's creative (if not too subtle) drumming and Jess Stacy's remarkable ad-lib piano solo. Fortunately this program has been reissued in full on CD and it belongs in every serious music library, capturing Benny Goodman and the swing era in general at its height. —*Scott Yanow*

Wrappin' It Up: The Harry James Years, Part II / Mar. 9, 1938-May 4, 1939 / Bluebird ◆◆◆◆
A "best-of" CD, this Bluebird release is somewhat unnecessary since all of Benny Goodman's recordings for the label have already been reissued in more complete form. However this set, which is sure to frustrate completists, includes rare takes of "The Blue Room," "I'll Always Be in Love with You" and "Louise" along with a previously unissued version of "Undecided." The Benny Goodman Orchestra is featured on 22 selections from the period right after drummer Gene Krupa left the band. Trumpeter Harry James is the main star but there are also good solos from tenors Bud Freeman and Jerry Jerome, pianist Jess Stacy and (on "Ti-Pi-Tin") guest

Lester Young. Benny Goodman (still just 29 at the time) is in prime form and, since the emphasis is on instrumentals, there are plenty of killer dillers included. Highlights include "Ti-Pi-Tin," "Big John Special," "Wrappin' It Up," "Bumble Bee Stomp," "Smoke House" and "Estrellita" but all of the music is rewarding. However more serious collectors will want to get these swing recordings as part of a more complete series. —*Scott Yanow*

The Complete Benny Goodman, Vol. 6 (1938) / Apr. 8, 1938-Oct. 13, 1938 / Bluebird ◆◆◆◆◆
This sixth of eight two-LP sets documenting Benny Goodman's Victor studio recordings finds BG in his post-Gene Krupa era. The classic trumpet section of Harry James, Ziggy Elman and Chris Griffin was still intact but after the Carnegie Hall concert there must have been a feeling of these performances being anticlimatic. Still, there are lots of memorable moments on these big-band and quartet tracks with a liberal amount of Martha Tilton vocals, pop tunes (although superior ones) and jazz standards. The rhythm was now much more subtle (with Dave Tough on drums) but the BG sound in 1938 was not that much different than in 1937 and the music is well worth acquiring. —*Scott Yanow*

The Best of Newhouse / May 10, 1938-Apr. 18, 1939 / Phontastic ◆◆◆◆
This two-LP set owes its existence to Jerry Newhouse who in 1938 was a young swing fan who had just bought a professional record-cutting machine so as to record his favorite musicians off radio broadcasts. The Swedish Phontastic label wisely went through Newhouse's acetates in 1981 and were able to put together this generous package of timeless swing. Mostly dating from 1938, these well-recorded performances do not necessarily shed new light on Benny Goodman's legacy but they offer "new" versions of BG's standards, including a version of "Sing, Sing, Sing" that lets Lionel Hampton stretch out on drums. —*Scott Yanow*

The Complete Benny Goodman, Vol. 7 (1938-1939) / Oct. 13, 1938-Apr. 7, 1939 / Bluebird ◆◆◆◆◆
The seventh two-LP set in this eight-volume series continues the documentation of Benny Goodman's influential studio recordings for Victor in the '30s. High points of this fine two-fer include a version of "Ciribiribin" that predates Harry James' famous recording, the unusual "Bach Goes to Town," a memorable "I Cried for You" by Goodman's quintet (with John Kirby on bass), "Sent for You Yesterday" (featuring a Johnny Mercer vocal) and the big Ziggy Elman hit "And the Angels Sing." Recommended. —*Scott Yanow*

Jumpin' at the Woodside / May 2, 1939-May 9, 1939 / Giants of Jazz ◆◆◆
This well-recorded Giants of Jazz LP finds the Benny Goodman Orchestra in transition. Lionel Hampton had temporarily taken over on drums (giving the band a rhythmic drive more enthusiastic than had been heard since Gene Krupa's departure a year earlier) and, while Krupa himself guests on a hot version of "Chicago" by the Quartet, a small-group performance from the later of these two broadcasts finds BG trying out guitarist George Rose. Although Rose did not catch on, the stage was being unwittingly set for Charlie Christian's arrival later that year. Since these two radio airchecks are complete, some time is wasted with dated talk and novelties but there are enough strong musical moments to make this set worth acquiring. —*Scott Yanow*

Alternate Goodman, Vol. 1 / Aug. 10, 1939-Sep. 13, 1939 / Phontastic ◆◆◆
Although Columbia has never fully reissued Benny Goodman's valuable work for the label during 1939-46, the Swedish Phontastic label did release no less than 12 LPs full of alternate takes and unissued performances from the era, issued chronologically. So, thanks to Phontastic, it is possible to acquire alternate versions of songs while the original takes remains completely unavailable. *Vol. 1* contains "new" versions of such classics as "Jumpin' at the Woodside," "Stealin' Apples," "Bolero," and "Boy Meets Horn." With trumpeters Ziggy Elman and Jimmy Maxwell, trombonist Vernon Brown and tenorman Jerry Jerome among the soloists, it quickly becomes obvious that Benny Goodman (even though his popularity was gradually being exceeded by Glenn Miller) had a great band in 1939. —*Scott Yanow*

Legendary Benny Goodman / Aug. 10, 1939-Sep. 26, 1951 / Columbia ◆◆◆◆
Released by Columbia Special Products back in 1981, this five-LP box set contains an excellent cross-section of Benny Goodman's recordings for Columbia, dating from 1939-42, 1945-46 and a few tracks from 1950-51. Since CBS has never reissued BG's recordings in full, this sampler (which has become hard to find) is the best set from this era put out to date, tracing the evolution of Benny Goodman through his second great band (including a few tracks by the Sextet with guitarist Charlie Christian) to some of the clarinetist's first post-war recordings and a few performances where, instead of being the pacesetter, he was looked upon as a nostalgia act. Throughout BG plays quite well and, even with only five selections to a side (for a total of around 150 minutes on the five LPs) this box is worth bidding for. —*Scott Yanow*

Benny Goodman on V-Disc / Aug. 11, 1939-Oct. 1948 / Sunbeam ✦✦✦✦

Originally released as three separate LPs, this three-LP set is a straight reissue with the same liner notes as the individual Sunbeam records. A wonderful acquisition for the true collector, *Benny Goodman on V-Disc* contains a wide variety of performances that were issued on V-Discs (limited-edition records specially available for servicemen during World War II), and many of the selections were formerly quite rare. Although a few tracks are from 1939-41 and some others date as late as 1948, the bulk of the music is from 1944-46, not one of the King of Swing's better-known periods. Such star soloists as trumpeter Cootie Williams, guitarist Charlie Christian, Gene Krupa, trumpeter Roy Eldridge, vibraphonist Red Norvo and pianist Mel Powell have their spots but the clarinetist consistently gets solo honors. Historical and quite enjoyable performances. —*Scott Yanow*

Fletcher Henderson Arrangements / Aug. 11, 1939-Feb. 23, 1953 / Columbia ✦✦✦

Fletcher Henderson was always Benny Goodman's favorite arranger and the clarinetist constantly went out of his way to give Henderson's danceable and swinging charts a great deal of credit for his own success. This particular LP does not include Henderson's earlier "hits" for Goodman (which were recorded for Victor) but does contain highlights from BG's Columbia years, starting with "Stealin' Apples" (Fletcher's old theme song), "Honeysuckle Rose" (which includes a fine Charlie Christian guitar solo) and "Henderson Stomp," continuing through 1945's "Just You, Just Me" and three performances with vocalist Helen Ward that were recorded in 1953 specifically for this LP (including "I'll Never Say 'Never Again' Again"). Since Henderson had died in late 1952, this fine LP served as a tribute to his writing skills and is a good excuse to hear a variety of classic Benny Goodman big-band recordings. —*Scott Yanow*

The Best of Big Bands / Aug. 16, 1939-Sep. 12, 1945 / Columbia ✦✦✦

This CD, a sampler from Benny Goodman's 1939-45 period with Columbia, unfortunately does not list any recording dates or personnel (inexcusable omissions) but contains worthwhile music from the King of Swing. The 16 performances (not released in chronological order) have arrangements by both Fletcher Henderson and Eddie Sauter, three vocals apiece by Helen Forrest and Peggy Lee and plenty of fine solos from Goodman. Most of the tracks (other than Peggy Lee's hit "Why Don't You Do Right?") are lesser known, making this somewhat ill-conceived set worth acquiring if found at a budget price. —*Scott Yanow*

Alternate Goodman, Vol. 2 / Sep. 13, 1939-Nov. 29, 1940 / Phontastic ✦✦✦

The second of 12 LPs that chronologically release alternate and rare versions of Benny Goodman's Columbia recordings, this one has quite a bit of variety, including Sextet versions of "Flying Home," "Soft Winds" and "I'm Confessin'," the 1940 Metronome All-Star Band (which is dominated by BG alumni) romping through "King Porter Stomp" and a dozen Goodman orchestra performances. Goodman fanatics will want to acquire this entire series. —*Scott Yanow*

★ **Featuring Charlie Christian** / Oct. 2, 1939-Mar. 13, 1941 / Columbia ✦✦✦✦✦

Charlie Christian was not the first electric guitarist but he was its first giant. He elevated the guitar from a member of the rhythm section (where it was often inaudible) to the front line, taking solos that could challenge any saxophonist. His playing was so appealing to his contemporaries that it was not until the emergence of rock in the mid- to late '60s that more advanced guitarists emerged. By then it was over a quarter-century since Christian's premature death from tuberculosis. He spent his only two high-profile years as a member of the Benny Goodman Sextet and 18 of their best recordings are on this CD. Christian and Goodman are joined by Lionel Hampton on the first dozen performances while the final six boast the explosive combination of trumpeter Cootie Williams and Georgie Auld's tenor. The riffing inspires heated yet melodic solos, resulting in classic music that is impossible to dislike. —*Scott Yanow*

Clarinet á la King, Vol. 2 / Dec. 27, 1939-Oct. 2, 1941 / Columbia ✦✦✦

Much more coherent than the first LP in this series (R 139615), *Vol. 2* consists of 16 of Benny Goodman's studio recordings for Columbia that date from late 1939 through 1941. A fine "best-of" (rather than "complete") set, this LP has among its many highlights "Zaggin' with Zig," "Henderson Stomp," the Cootie Williams trumpet feature "Superman," "Solo Flight" (which showcases guitarist Charlie Christian), "The Earl" and the title cut. A fine introduction to Goodman's underrated early-'40s orchestra. —*Scott Yanow*

Greatest Hits / 1939 / Columbia/Legacy ✦✦✦

Columbia's *Greatest Hits* is a solid collection boasting the most familiar versions of such Benny Goodman hits as "Let's Dance," "Clarinet a La King," "Jersey Bounce," "Flying Home," "Slipped Disc," "Air Mail Special," "Benny Rides Again" and "Sing, Sing, Sing (With a Swing)." It's not a perfect collection, but it does offer a good introduction for the curious. —*Stephen Thomas Erlewine*

Featuring Helen Forrest / Mar. 1, 1940-Jun. 4, 1941 / Columbia ✦✦✦

Helen Forrest was considered one of the top band singers of the swing era, earning prestigious stints with the orchestras of Artie Shaw, Benny Goodman and Harry James. Not a jazz singer, her appealing voice and attractive phrasing were considered major assets to any band. This particular CD has 16 of her many recordings with BG during 1939-41; Goodman and his star sidemen (including trumpeter Cootie Williams) provide most of the jazz interest. —*Scott Yanow*

Alternate Goodman, Vol. 3 / Nov. 29, 1940-Jan. 21, 1941 / Phontastic ✦✦✦

The third of 12 LPs put out by the Swedish label Phontastic (like the others) comprises alternate takes and rare studio recordings by the Benny Goodman Orchestra. There are two sextet tracks with trumpeter Cootie Williams, Count Basie and guitarist Charlie Christian, a few Helen Forrest vocals and some advanced instrumentals. Most collectors will take an all-or-nothing approach to this important series. —*Scott Yanow*

Eddie Sauter Arrangements / Dec. 18, 1940-Mar. 17, 1945 / Columbia ✦✦✦✦✦

Here is an LP crying to be reissued on CD. Eddie Sauter was Benny Goodman's most advanced arranger. His writing for BG in the early '40s was much more unpredictable than Fletcher Henderson's and often full of surprises and unusual colors. A dozen of Sauter's greatest arrangements (including "Moonlight on the Ganges," "La Rosita," "Superman" and a remarkable reworking of "Love Walked In") are heard on this set and they really challenge Benny Goodman to come up with fresh ideas. A classic album. —*Scott Yanow*

Solid Gold Instrumental Hits / Dec. 18, 1940-Mar. 17, 1945 / Columbia ✦✦✦

Despite its dumb title (none of these 20 performances were million sellers), this double LP contains many of the high points of what was Benny Goodman's most interesting orchestra. The arrangements of Eddie Sauter and Mel Powell in particular challenged BG (while giving him an entire new book of material) and led to many classic moments. High points include "Air Mail Special," "Clarinet á la King," "Clarinade," "Love Walked In" "String of Pearls" and "Jersey Bounce." —*Scott Yanow*

Alternate Goodman, Vol. 4 / Jan. 28, 1941-Mar. 27, 1941 / Phontastic ✦✦✦

On the fourth of 12 LPs released by the Swedish Phontastic label that issue in chronological order alternate takes and rarities from Benny Goodman's period with Columbia in the '40s, high points include "Perfidia," "Scarecrow," "Solo Flight" (starring guitarist Charlie Christian), Cootie Williams' feature "Fiesta in Blue" and a sextet version of "Airmail Special." —*Scott Yanow*

Alternate Goodman, Vol. 5 / Mar. 27, 1941-Sep. 25, 1941 / Phontastic ✦✦✦

On the fifth volume of a 12-LP series of Benny Goodman alternate takes and rarities, the 1941 Orchestra is heard playing "new" versions of such songs as "Don't Be That Way," "Smoke Gets in Your Eyes," "Clarinet á la King" and "The Earl." Also quite interesting (to hear once) is Peggy Lee's debut on the alternate of "Elmer's Tune"; she sounds scared to death. —*Scott Yanow*

Roll 'Em Live: 1941 / Jul. ??, 1941-Oct. ??, 1941 / Vintage Jazz ✦✦✦✦

Good collaboration with Big Sid Catlett (d). Not-so-good sound quality. —*Ron Wynn*

Featuring Peggy Lee / Aug. 15, 1941-Dec. 10, 1941 / Columbia ✦✦✦✦

When Peggy Lee made her first recording with Benny Goodman's orchestra, she was 19 and scared to death. The result, "Elmer's Tune," is one she probably wished were lost, but the other 15 recordings on this CD (all from 1941) find her improving month by month, struggling gamely through the difficult Eddie Sauter and Mel Powell arrangements. Many of these titles were formerly rare and offer an interesting look at the early Peggy Lee. —*Scott Yanow*

Alternate Goodman, Vol. 6 / Sep. 25, 1941-Nov. 27, 1941 / Phontastic ✦✦✦

The sixth of 12 LPs that contain alternate versions of Benny Goodman's recordings from his period on Columbia in the '40s has several highlights: two versions of "Clarinet á la King," several Peggy Lee vocals (including "Let's Do It") and two titles ("If I Had You" and "Limehouse Blues") by Goodman's new sextet with trombonist Lou McGarity and pianist Mel Powell. True Benny Goodman collectors are advised to pick up these worthy 12 LPs in a hurry. —*Scott Yanow*

Small Groups: 1941-1945 / Oct. 28, 1941-Feb. 4, 1945 / Columbia ✦✦✦✦

When one thinks of Benny Goodman's small groups, it is generally his original Trio and Quartet (with Lionel Hampton, Teddy Wilson and Gene Krupa) or his sextet with Charlie Christian that comes immediately to mind. This superior set dates from a slightly later period and features a sextet with trombonist Lou McGarity and pianist Mel Powell (the clarinet-trombone blend works very well) and his 1944-45 quintet/sextet with vibraphonist Red Norvo. Vocalists Peggy Lee, Jane Harvey and Peggy Mann give this set some variety. The music (and the clarinet playing) is consistently brilliant. —*Scott Yanow*

Alternate Goodman, Vol. 7 / Nov. 27, 1941-Feb. 5, 1942 / Phontastic ✦✦✦

Part of a 12-LP series put out by the Swedish label Phontastic, this set (as with the others) comprises alternate takes and rarities from the Benny Goodman Orchestra during his period with Columbia. As interesting as the big-band alternates are (particularly "A String of Pearls"), it is the two-numbers from the Benny Goodman Sextet (which features trombonist Lou McGarity and pianist Mel Powell) and three performances from the 1941 Metronome All-Star Band that are of greatest interest. —*Scott Yanow*

Alternate Goodman, Vol. 8 / Mar. 10, 1942-Jun. 17, 1942 / Phontastic ✦✦✦

The eighth of 12 LPs of Benny Goodman alternate takes and rarities from the '40s has a hilarious breakdown on "Before" by the big band and four titles from his 1942 sextet (which co-stars trombonist Lou McGarity) and quartet including two contrasting versions of "The World Is Waiting for the Sunrise." As with all of the records in this series, collectors should love comparing these versions to the ones originally approved by Goodman. —*Scott Yanow*

Way Down Yonder (1943-1944) / Dec. 9, 1943-Jan. 1946 / Vintage Jazz ✦✦✦✦

This valuable CD contains performances from 1943-46 originally recorded for World War II servicemen. VJC has fleshed out the original recordings with alternate takes and breakdowns which, due to the high quality of the music, makes this CD even more interesting. Gene Krupa is heard with Goodman's 1943 big band and in a trio with pianist Jess Stacy while the bulk of this set features the BG Quintet with vibraphonist Red Norvo during 1944 including an early version of the classic "Slipped Disc." —*Scott Yanow*

The Complete Capitol Small Group Recordings / Jun. 12, 1944-Dec. 14, 1955 / Mosaic ✦✦✦✦✦

This limited-edition four-CD set fills some gaps in the huge discography of Benny Goodman. The great clarinetist is primarily featured during the 1947-49 period, heading a diverse assortment of small bands. After performing with a quartet on "After You've Gone" in 1944, BG in 1947 utilizes such sidemen as pianists Jess Stacy, Tommy Todd, Jimmy Rowles, Mel Powell and Teddy Wilson (the latter is featured on ten trio performances), Ernie Felice (on accordion), vibraphonist Red Norvo and Goodman's former singer, Peggy Lee, who drops by for previously unissued versions of "Eight, Nine and Ten" and "Keep Me in Mind." Also quite notable are three titles with the "Hollywood Hucksters" that are highlighted by "Happy Blues," which has humorous vocals by Goodman and Stan Kenton. While all of this music falls in the area of swing (with a touch of bop), Goodman's five recordings from 1948-49 are very boppish, featuring tenorman Wardell Gray and either Fats Navarro (on "Stealin' Apples") or Doug Mettome on trumpet. The remainder of this box dates from 1954-55 with Goodman performing trios with Mel Powell, jamming in a sextet with trumpeter Charlie Shavers and having a reunion with vibraphonist Lionel Hampton. All in all, this attractive box has more than its share of highly enjoyable music. —*Scott Yanow*

King of Swing / Jul. 21, 1944-Jan. 14, 1946 / Giants of Jazz ✦✦✦

The Giants of Jazz label consistently released well-recorded LPs of Benny Goodman radio appearances. This one is no exception, giving one a rare (if brief) glance at BG's unrecorded big band of 1944 with trumpeter Roy Eldridge, along with more extended performances by Goodman's orchestra (which featured trombonist Lou McGarity and a young Stan Getz on tenor) and quintet in January 1946. The vocals of Art Lund and Liz Morrow do not hurt either. Fine swing from the tail end of the swing era by its King. —*Scott Yanow*

The Best of Benny Goodman: Capitol Years / 1944-1955 / Capitol ✦✦✦

The Best of Benny Goodman: The Capitol Years is an excellent 18-track overview of the clarinetist's stint at Capitol. He recorded for the label between 1944 and 1955, during which time he played in a wide variety of combinations, from his traditional big band to small trios. This disc captures the variety and vitality of this era, featuring both re-recordings of '30s hits like "Sing, Sing, Sing" and relatively new songs, as well as solo spots from Harry James, Lionel Hampton, Mel Powell and Ruby Braff. It's a good sampler of an underrated time in Goodman's career. —*Leo Stanley*

Slipped Disc (1945-46) / Feb. 4, 1945-Jan. 2, 1946 / Columbia ✦✦✦✦

One of Benny Goodman's greatest combos was the sextet that he led in 1945. With Red Norvo on vibes, either Teddy Wilson or Mel Powell on piano and the humming bass solos of Slam Stewart, this unit had a lot of personality and yet allowed Goodman to operate throughout as the lead voice. This set has 14 performances by this highly enjoyable band, including their hit "Slipped Disc," "Tiger Rag," "Shine," "China Boy" and two versions of "I Got Rhythm." In addition, there are three selections from two of Goodman's sextets in the following year with vibraphonist Johnny White. Great swing music from Benny Goodman who is heard throughout at his best. —*Scott Yanow*

Alternate Goodman, Vol. 10 / Feb. 25, 1945-Jun. 18, 1945 / Phontastic ✦✦✦

The tenth of 12 LPs of Benny Goodman alternate takes and rarities from his period with Columbia contains a variety of odds and ends including three "new" versions of "Gotta Be This or That," two of "Love Walked In" and one apiece of "Clarinade," "Ain't Misbehavin'" and the sextet's "Rachel's Dream." Little did Benny Goodman know that his work in 1945, although hardswinging, was already in danger of slipping behind the times. Despite that, this music is quite enjoyable and timeless. —*Scott Yanow*

Goodman on the Air / May 1945-Dec. 23, 1945 / Phontastic ✦✦✦

Benny Goodman had one of his great years in 1945 when he was still only 36. Although history looks at him as being a bit old-fashioned musically by this time, especially when compared to Charlie Parker and Dizzy Gillespie, in reality BG was still the world's top clarinetist, leader of an exciting (if underrated) big band and at the peak of his commercial fame. The LP *Goodman on the Air*, released by the Swedish Phontastic label, comprises radio airchecks from 1945 featuring both the Goodman Sextet (on five numbers) and big band on selections that might be familiar to the clarinetist's fans (such as "Slipped Disc," "Clarinet á la King" and "King Porter Stomp") but actually differ greatly from their studio versions. Worth searching for. —*Scott Yanow*

Alternate Goodman, Vol. 11 / Aug. 29, 1945-Jan. 30, 1946 / Phontastic ✦✦✦

The next-to-last of 12 LPs released by the Swedish label Phontastic continues the documentation of alternate takes and rarities recorded by Benny Goodman during the 1939-46 period. Goodman had an excellent big band in 1945 as one can hear on such selections as "Just You, Just Me," "Give Me the Simple Life" and "Fascinating Rhythm," but it is his sextet (heard here on five performances) that really stars. Vibraphonist Red Norvo, pianist Mel Powell and bassist Slam Stewart star on such numbers as "Tiger Rag," "Shine," and "China Boy" and really push the clarinetist to some of his best playing. —*Scott Yanow*

Swing Sessions / Oct. 17, 1945-Jan. 11, 1946 / Hindsight ✦✦✦

This CD contains previously unreleased performances by Benny Goodman that were originally recorded for the Armed Forces Radio Service during 1945-46. Four selections feature his short-lived big band of the era and these sport arrangements by Eddie Sauter, Mel Powell and Fletcher Henderson (a reworking of "Somebody Stole My Gal"). In addition to a vocal apiece from Liza Morrow and Art Lund on the orchestra performances, there are solos from trumpeter Bernie Privin and (on two numbers) the young tenor Stan Getz. However, the bulk of this set features Goodman's small group of the era with the clarinetist/leader, vibraphonist Red Norvo and pianist Teddy Wilson getting plenty of solo space. The enjoyable release is not essential but collectors will want to pick it up. —*Scott Yanow*

Alternate Goodman, Vol. 12 / Jan. 23, 1946-Aug. 7, 1946 / Phontastic ✦✦✦

The twelfth and final of the dozen LPs released by the Swedish label Phontastic completes the issuance of Benny Goodman alternate takes and rarities from his valuable period (1939-46) with Columbia. Although there are some fine big-band performances on this set (particularly a two-part version of "Oh, Baby!") it is the small-group performances (which co-star pianist Mel Powell) that are most exciting and foretell BG's future. Collectors are well advised to pick up all 12 of these LPs while they can still be found. —*Scott Yanow*

Undercurrent Blues / Jan. 28, 1947-Oct. 15, 1949 / Capitol ✦✦✦✦✦

During 1947-49 on an irregular basis, clarinetist Benny Goodman's band recorded bebop for Capitol before he permanently switched back to swing in 1950. All of BG's small group recordings from this period have been reissued on a Mosaic set and five are duplicated on this single CD but there are also four previously unissued big-band performances along with six others on this recommended reissue. Goodman and his band interpret a pair of Mary Lou Williams originals and other highlights include "Stealin' Apples" (a septet track with trumpeter Fats Navarro), "Bop-Hop," "Dreazag," "Bedlam" and "Blue Lou." Key soloists include trumpeter Doug Mettome, Wardell Gray on tenor and pianist Buddy Greco while Chico O'Farrill provided most of the big-band charts. It is very interesting to hear the great swing clarinetist adapting to the new music. —*Scott Yanow*

Swedish Pastry / May 24, 1948-Jun. 5, 1948 / Dragon ✦✦✦✦

In 1948 the young Swedish clarinetist Stan Hasselgård so impressed Benny Goodman that BG invited him to join his new septet, a unit that also included tenor saxophonist Wardell Gray and pianist Teddy Wilson. Because of the recording strike and Hasselgård's death before year's end in a car accident, no commercial recordings were made of the two-clarinet combo, but luckily the short-lived septet was captured live at the Cique in Philadelphia during a two-week period. Although Goodman is the dominant soloist, Hasselgård has some solo space and even gets to interact with BG. This was one of Goodman's few bop-oriented bands and so this LP fills a major gap in jazz history. —*Scott Yanow*

Alternate Goodman, Vol. 9 / 194 / Phontastic ◆◆◆
The ninth of 12 LPs of alternate takes and rare items from Benny Goodman's '40s orchestra and small groups has more than its share of strong items. Highlights include an alternate to "Mission to Moscow" and ten performances from BG's combos, including a "new" version of "Slipped Disc." —*Scott Yanow*

Sextet / Nov. 24, 1950-Oct. 22, 1952 / Columbia ◆◆◆◆
In 1950, Benny Goodman formed a new sextet, and although he used a big band for some recordings, the small group was his main outlet for the next couple of years. This CD features this somewhat forgotten unit, a hot swing combo featuring vibraphonist Terry Gibbs and usually pianist Teddy Wilson. Rather than repeat his older hits, the clarinetist clearly enoyed playing other standards not generally associated with him. Excellent and enjoyable music. —*Scott Yanow*

B.G. in Hi-Fi / Nov. 8, 1954-Nov. 16, 1954 / Capitol ◆◆◆◆◆
On this all-around excellent CD, Benny Goodman performs a dozen selections (mostly Fletcher Henderson arrangements) with a big band filled with sympathetic players in 1954 and eight other numbers with a pair of smaller units that also feature pianist Mel Powell and either Charlie Shavers or Ruby Braff on trumpets. Although the big-band era had been gone for almost a decade, Benny Goodman (then 46) plays these swing classics with enthusiasm and creativity and shows that there was never any reason for anyone to write him off as "behind the times." —*Scott Yanow*

An Album of Swing Classics / Mar. 25, 1955-Mar. 26, 1955 / Classic ◆◆◆
In 1955 Benny Goodman led one of his finest groups of the decade, a septet with trumpeter Ruby Braff, Paul Quinichette's tenor, trombonist Urbie Green and pianist Teddy Wilson. This three-LP box set from the Book of the Month Club includes a beautiful booklet and much swinging music. Although most of the 19 songs that Goodman performs are identified with him, these small-group renditions are fresh and lively with BG drawing inspiration from his talented sidemen. Recommended. —*Scott Yanow*

Yale Recordings, Vols. 1-5 / Mar. 26, 1955-Jun. 28, 1967 / Music Masters ◆◆◆◆◆
In his will, Benny Goodman gave to Yale not only all of his band arrangements (over 1,500) but 400 ten-inch master tapes of unreleased studio and concert recordings. Some of the more rewarding sessions have now been issued by Music Masters and this particular box set includes the first five volumes (and a 40-page booklet), six CDs in all (since *Vol. 5* had two CDs by itself) which are also available separately. The music dates from 1955-84 (the second half of Benny Goodman's career) and is taken from quite a few sessions, including a full CD of material by his excellent septet of 1955 (featuring trumpeter Ruby Braff and Paul Quinichette on tenor), big-band performances from 1958 with several vocals by Jimmy Rushing and many selections from a 1959 engagement with a nonet featuring trumpeter Jack Sheldon, trombonist Bill Harris and tenorman Flip Phillips. Although no longer a pacesetter, Benny Goodman remained one of the jazz world's most brilliant performers, making this set well worth acquiring. —*Scott Yanow*

Yale Recordings, Vol. 2: Live at Basin Street / Mar. 26, 1955 / Music Masters ◆◆◆◆◆
The second CD to be compiled from the valuable tapes that Benny Goodman willed to Yale features one of his strongest groups from the '50s, a septet with trumpeter Ruby Braff, tenorman Paul Quinichette and pianist Teddy Wilson. Recorded at the same period as a Book-of-the-Month collection but not duplicating any of the performances, Benny Goodman is heard in top form, clearly inspired by his younger colleagues. Many of the songs are fairly typical of his veteran repertoire but they sound fresh and different in this setting, making this one of the stronger entries in this valuable series. —*Scott Yanow*

Yale Archives, Vol. 1 / Sep. 8, 1955-Jan. 17, 1986 / Music Masters ◆◆◆
Shortly after Benny Goodman's death in 1986, trustees at Yale University's Music Library were surprised to find out that, in addition to memorabilia and over 1,500 arrangements, Benny Goodman had left them around 400 ten-inch master tapes of concert and studio performances that had never been heard before, along with the right to lease these recordings for commercial release. *Vol. 1* of what is now known as BG's Yale Archives is a hodgepodge collection of performances that skip around between 1955 and 1986. Among the dozen selections on this CD are a couple of tunes by BG's 1955 combo with trumpeter Ruby Braff, an example of the group he led briefly in 1959 with trombonist Bill Harris and Flip Phillips' tenor, some okay big-band performances, Goodman's forgotten 1967 septet with trumpeter Joe Newman and tenor saxophonist Zoot Sims, and a version of "Blue Room" played by his last band, Goodman's 1986 orchestra. —*Scott Yanow*

The Benny Goodman Story / Aug. 1955 / Decca ◆◆◆
One of the most successful of the music biography movies of the '50s was *The Benny Goodman Story*. The plot was pure fiction but the music was often quite exciting, helped out by the fact that Goodman himself did all of the clarinet play-

ing. This two-LP set contains the movie's soundtrack with strong "roles" played by pianist Teddy Wilson, vibraphonist Lionel Hampton, drummer Gene Krupa, trumpeters Harry James and Buck Clayton, Stan Getz on tenor, and of course the mighty clarinetist. —*Scott Yanow*

The Benny Goodman Story / Dec. 7, 1955-Dec. 14, 1955 / Capitol◆◆◆
Consumer advisory: In 1955, Universal Pictures released *The Benny Goodman Story*, starring Steve Allen. Goodman himself played the music in the film (which consisted of re-recordings of his old hits), rounding up such former band members as Harry James, Martha Tilton, and Lionel Hampton, and a successful soundtrack LP was issued by Decca. But Goodman wasn't under contract to Decca; he was on Capitol, which rushed him into the studio in December to recut his hits again. Capitol then released this album early in 1956, with the same title as the film and the Decca soundtrack, its cover deceptively declaring that it contained "brilliant new high-fidelity recordings made especially for this album of the selections featured in the motion picture of his life." Pretty sneaky. Forty years later, Capitol reissued the album on CD with the same cover, which indicates that ethics in the record business have not improved (in case you were wondering). That said, the reissue adds five bonus tracks, pushing the album to an hour's length. And though the album is not what it claims to be, it is nevertheless a hot session on which Goodman plays with his usual assurance, and the big band, which features Dick Hyman and Milt Hinton along with guest appearances by James, Tilton, and Ruby Braff, and a version of the quintet featuring Hampton, Mel Powell, George Duvivier, and Bobby Donaldson, are effective. —*William Ruhlmann*

B.G. World Wide / Dec. 14, 1956-Nov. 8, 1980 / TCB ◆◆◆◆◆
This four-CD box set from the European TCB label releases for the first time the music from four Benny Goodman concerts. The great clarinetist is heard at two nostalgic big-band appearances, heading a 13-piece unit in Bangkok, Thailand, in 1956 (with fine solos heard from trumpeter Mel Davis and Budd Johnson on tenor) and a 15-piece orchestra in Santiago, Chile in 1961, a band that also features trumpeter Buck Clayton. However it is the other two performances that are of greatest interest. Goodman plays at his most advanced with an all-star group (which includes trumpeter Jack Sheldon, trombonist Bill Harris, the tenor of Flip Phillips and vibraphonist Red Norvo) during a particularly exciting set from Basel, Switzerland, in 1959 and his solos from Berlin in 1980 in a quintet with four supportive but obscure musicians are surprisingly inspired. In fact the German concert is arguably Goodman's finest recording of his last decade. This well-conceived set (which has a different small booklet for each of the CDs) is highly recommended to Benny Goodman's many fans. —*Scott Yanow*

Yale Recordings, Vol. 4: Big Band Recordings / May 16, 1957-Jun. 17, 1964 / Music Masters ◆◆◆
This fourth volume of material culled from the tapes willed by Benny Goodman to the Yale University Music Library contains a variety of big-band performances taken from no less than five different sessions held over an eight-year period. Such musicians as baritonist Pepper Adams, Bob Wilber (on tenor), Zoot Sims and BG's former vocalist Martha Tilton get their spots. While several Eddie Sauter arrangements are performed, one has to also sit through a weak 1964 session that includes a forgettable version of "People." An interesting if somewhat erratic set. —*Scott Yanow*

Yale Recordings, Vol. 8: / May 16, 1957-Jan. 24, 1961 / Music Masters ◆◆◆◆
The eighth volume of previously unreleased material willed by Benny Goodman to Yale continues the series with some very interesting selections. Martha Tilton gets to redo her hit "Bei Mir Bist Du Schon" in 1958 with a big band, Goodman's clarinet is well featured with a quintet that includes pianist Andre Previn on three tracks, and BG has his last musical encounter with pianist Mel Powell on a pair of medleys. But most unusual are eight selections cut with a nine-piece unit in 1961 that are dominated by songs associated with Hawaii including "On the Beach at Waikiki," "Blue Hawaii," "Sweet Leilani" and "My Little Grass Shack." Bill Stegmeyer's creative arrangements and an all-star lineup actually make this into a highly enjoyable and very surprising session. —*Scott Yanow*

Benny in Brussels, Vol. 1 / May 1958 / Columbia ◆◆◆◆◆
Benny Goodman's successful stint at the 1958 Brussels World Fair served as an excuse for him to record some albums of his new big band. With tenor saxophonist Zoot Sims, trumpeter Taft Jordan and Goodman's new discovery, pianist Roland Hanna (who was then 26), getting some fine solos and Jimmy Rushing taking a personable vocal on "Brussels Blues," BG's backup crew was strong. As for the King himself, although no longer thought of as an innovator, at the age of 49 he was still very much in his prime and he is in fine form throughout these two volumes. —*Scott Yanow*

Benny in Brussels, Vol. 2 / May 1958 / Columbia ◆◆◆◆◆
The second of two LPs recorded by the 1958 Benny Goodman Orchestra, live from the Brussels World Fair, is highlighted by "Stealin' Apples," a Gershwin medley,

Jimmy Rushing's vocal on "Mr. Five by Five" and a rousing rendition of "One O'Clock Jump." Pianist Roland Hanna is strongest among the supporting cast and Goodman clearly enjoyed having a big band again, even if only for a short time. —*Scott Yanow*

Yale Recordings, Vol. 3: Big Band in Europe / May 1958 / Music Masters ✦✦✦✦
The third volume in this important series taken from tapes willed by Benny Goodman to the Yale Music Library focuses on the big band he took to Europe in 1958, a tour that culminated in a week at the Brussels World Fair in Belgium. The orchestra was filled with both young names like Zoot Sims and pianist Roland Hanna and veterans such as trombonist Vernon Brown and trumpeter Taft Jordan. With the great Jimmy Rushing and Ethel Ennis contributing vocals and the ensemble playing a variety of mostly new charts, Benny Goodman had the right to feel inspired. His playing of this "modern swing" is typically brilliant; collectors will want this entire series. —*Scott Yanow*

Benny Rides Again / Sep. 1958-Nov. 1958 / Chess ✦✦✦
Goodman leads a big band again for the majority of this LP with few surprises. The instrumentals (all standards except for the recent "Stereo Stomp") are fine but the unidentified personnel (which has such players as Bob Wilbur, Pepper Adams and Russ Freeman) mostly functions as an anonymous ensemble. Better are the four selections by Goodman and a rhythm section that include pianist Andre Previn. Nice music overall but there are many more essential Benny Goodman sets available elsewhere. —*Scott Yanow*

Happy Session / Nov. 1958 / Columbia ✦✦✦
Recorded after Benny Goodman returned with his 1958 big band from a European tour that included an exuberant stint at the Brussels World Fair, this LP alternates between orchestra performances (the mostly newer compositions include four by a Yugoslavian composer, Bobby Gutesha) and Goodman features with his rhythm section, which co-stars Andre Previn's piano. BG dominates this album and is in excellent form. —*Scott Yanow*

Yale Recordings, Vol. 7: Florida Sessions / Aug. 15, 1959-Aug. 17, 1959 / Music Masters ✦✦✦✦
One of the most interesting bands led by Benny Goodman after the end of the swing era was the forgotten septet featured on this CD. It was essentially a sextet co-led by tenor saxophonist Flip Phillips and trombonist Bill Harris that they willingly let BG take over. Phillips and Harris were alumni of Woody Herman's First Herd and their constant riffing and well-constructed solos really push the competitive clarinetist to play at his best and most fiery. Rather than revisit past glories, during this live gig Benny Goodman and his all-stars play infectious arrangements that perfectly set up the solos, creating exciting new music in the swing tradition. Recommended. —*Scott Yanow*

Legendary Concert / Oct. 28, 1959 / Artistry ✦✦✦✦
In 1959 Goodman (then 50) took over a sextet co-led by two alumni of Woody Herman's First Herd (tenor saxophonist Flip Phillips and trombonist Bill Harris) and eventually expanded it into a short-lived ten-piece group. This LP documents a concert from his European tour and finds the King of Swing successfully exploring both new material and old favorites. The vibes of Red Norvo and trumpeter Jack Sheldon are also strong assets; pity that this group did not stay together longer. —*Scott Yanow*

Yale Recordings, Vol. 5 / Nov. 13, 1959-Jun. 14, 1963 / Music Masters ✦✦✦
The fifth volume of material taken from the tapes that Benny Goodman willed to Yale's Music Library is, for no particular reason, a double-CD set. Two separate and somewhat forgotten Goodman combos are featured: a fine ten-piece unit from 1959-60 that includes trumpeter Jack Sheldon, trombonist Bill Harris and Flip Phillips on tenor, and an otherwise totally unrecorded sextet from 1963. The latter not only features cornetist Bobby Hackett and the young bassist Steve Swallow but the forgotten Modesto Bresano, who contributes some fine tenor and flute. Benny Goodman is in fine form with both of these unjustly obscure combos. —*Scott Yanow*

Together Again! / Feb. 13, 1963-Aug. 27, 1963 / Bluebird ✦✦✦✦
The music on this CD has been reissued several times, including once previously on a Bluebird CD. This was the first full reunion in the studios of the Benny Goodman Quartet (featuring the clarinetist, vibraphonist Lionel Hampton, pianist Teddy Wilson and drummer Gene Krupa) and, although they would get together on an infrequent basis over the next decade, this was their last studio recording. In general, the classic swing stars avoided recreating their past triumphs and instead recorded veteran standards that they had missed the first time around. Krupa's bass drum work (which is meant to fill in for a bassist) gets a bit heavy-handed at times, but the good spirits of the reunion uplift the music. Highlights include "Seven Come Eleven," "I've Found a New Baby," "Runnin' Wild" and the blues "Four Once More." —*Scott Yanow*

Yale Recordings, Vol. 10: / Feb. 13, 1963-Aug. 27, 1963 / Music Masters ✦✦✦✦
One of the most famous jazz groups of all time was the original Benny Goodman Quartet which featured Lionel Hampton, Teddy Wilson and Gene Krupa. Despite its fame, the unit was only actually together for 16 months during 1936-38 and (even with infrequent reunions through the decades) the Quartet only recorded one studio record in later years. This particular CD comprises unreleased material from the three sessions that resulted in a 1963 RCA album. There are second versions of "Who Cares" and "Dearest" and a rehearsal excerpt of the blues "Four Once More" but otherwise the songs are completely different from what was originally released. And with the exception of "Liza," none of the tunes had been previously recorded by the classic quartet. It is quite unusual to hear Goodman, Hampton, Wilson and Krupa interpreting such numbers as "Love Sends a Little Gift of Roses," "Bernie's Tune," "East of the Sun" and "It's All Right with Me." Although there are times when one wishes that there were a bassist added and that Krupa would lay a bit easier on his bass drum, the relaxed music does swing and adds to the very rich legacy of Benny Goodman. This is the tenth release thus far of "new" material that is drawn from the scores of private tapes that the King of Swing willed to the Yale University Music Library. Recommended to BG's many fans. —*Scott Yanow*

Made in Japan / Feb. 25, 1964 / Capitol ✦✦
One could not blame Benny Goodman for getting a bit bored by the mid-'60s. He had achieved astonishing success by 1935 when he just 26 and with the passing of the big-band era a decade later, he was no longer a pacesetter in jazz. Despite possessing a fully formed style, BG led many high-quality groups through the years and continued playing creatively within the swing tradition, but the LP *Made in Japan* is merely a lukewarm affair. Backed by a supportive but faceless rhythm section and limiting the length of the performances (only two exceed four minutes, and three are less than half as long), Goodman plays passable but unmemorable versions of swing standards like "Stompin' at the Savoy" and "Dinah." It's worth acquiring at a budget price but otherwise there are many far superior Benny Goodman CDs currently available. —*Scott Yanow*

Yale Recordings, Vol. 7: Live at the Rainbow Grill / Jun. 3, 1966-Jun. 29, 1967 / Music Masters ✦✦✦
The seventh volume of music taken from the hundreds of tapes that Benny Goodman willed to Yale University covers a period of time when the King of Swing used pickup (although still all-star) groups, combining veterans with younger talents. This CD has nine selections from a septet with trumpeter Joe Newman, Zoot Sims' tenor and guitarist Attila Zoller. There is nothing surprising about the repertoire (BG generally ignored the novelty pop tunes of the '60s) and this particular unit works well. The remaining six numbers find Goodman sharing the front line with trumpeter Doc Cheatham (whose solo style was not as well developed as it would become after he passed his 70th birthday), allocating two vocals to the forgotten Annette Saunders and trying out a new pianist who was subbing for Hank Jones, Herbie Hancock. Even with this unusual personnel, the result is a strong set of solid swing. —*Scott Yanow*

Let's Dance Again / Oct. 28, 1969-Nov. 28, 1969 / Mega ✦✦
What to do with the King of Swing by the late '60s? Benny Goodman had already recorded nearly every worthwhile song from the golden age of popular music (1920-50) and his unchanging (although never stale) swing style was too familiar for most jazz listeners of later eras to fully appreciate. So, for this LP, recorded in London with a big band and an octet filled with English musicians, Goodman was persuaded to emphasize more recent items. BG performs such songs as "Yesterday," "This Guy's in Love with You," "On a Clear Day" and "I Talk to the Trees," in addition to a few remakes of swing standards. Since he primarily sticks to the melody in these short renditions and sounds predictably silly and out-of-place in spots, this album is not one of the high points of Benny Goodman's career. —*Scott Yanow*

Benny Goodman Today / Feb. 20, 1970 / London ✦✦
By 1970 there seemed little new for Benny Goodman to say musically. A major success 35 years earlier and the possessor of a brilliant but unchanging clarinet style, BG was performing less during this period and his big-band projects generally emphasized re-creations of the past. This attractive but routine double LP (which does not list the personnel) features Goodman in a big band mostly comprising Europeans (other than guitarist Bucky Pizzarelli) running through a program not all that different than what he might have presented in 1940; only four of the 20 songs are of newer vintage. A pleasing but not very stimulating set of music. —*Scott Yanow*

On Stage / Mar. 13, 1972 / London ✦✦✦
While Benny Goodman's big-band projects of his later years overly relied on re-creations and revisits to earlier successes, his small-group work gave the clarinetist a much better opportunity to stretch out. This double LP matches the 63-year-

old King of Swing with tenor-great Zoot Sims, vibraphonist Peter Appleyard and a strong rhythm section for an enjoyable set of standards. —*Scott Yanow*

The King Swings / Dec. 8, 1973 / Star Line ✦✦✦

For this fairly rare live session (reissued on CD with one extra selection), Benny Goodman heads a nonet that includes some all-stars (trombonist George Masso, Al Klink on tenor, vibraphonist Peter Appleyard, pianist John Bunch, guitarist Bucky Pizzarelli and bassist Slam Stewart) plus the relatively unknown drummer Joe Corsello and English trumpeter John McLevy. Most of the repertoire is somewhat typical (and greeted enthusiastically by the German audience during the Hamburg concert) but contains a few surprises: Slam Stewart's feature on "Lady Be Good," a rendition of Stephen Sondheim's "Night Waltz," a hot Dixielandish "That's a Plenty," and a rare version of "Bed Mir Bist Du Schon" which finds BG playing the famous Ziggy Elman fralich interlude on clarinet. —*Scott Yanow*

Fortieth Anniversary Concert / Jan. 17, 1978 / London ✦✦✦✦

In 1978 Benny Goodman celebrated the 40th anniversary of his original pioneering Carnegie Hall concert with a new concert at the palace of classical music. From reviews of the actual event, the music and presentation were quite erratic, but this double LP, which only includes the best moments, is on a higher level. In addition to a strong big band, Goodman was joined by vibraphonist Lionel Hampton, pianist Mary Lou Williams, his late-'30s vocalist Martha Tilton, and a newer singer, Debi Craig. With trumpeters Warren Vache and Jack Sheldon (why did he sing "Rocky Raccoon"?) and tenor saxophonist Buddy Tate also getting solo space, Benny Goodman was fairly inspired; he even sings "I Love a Piano." With the exception of a medley, "Loch Lomond" and of course "Sing, Sing, Sing" (which has drummer Connie Kay playing Gene Krupa's famous solo), none of the songs from the 1938 concert were reprised. This set has both historical and musical value and no Benny Goodman collection is quite complete without it. —*Scott Yanow*

Live! Benny: Let's Dance / Oct. 7, 1985 / LaserLight ✦✦✦

This soundtrack from a PBS special is Benny Goodman's last recording. After a period of semi-retirement, Goodman had recently taken over the big band put together by Loren Schoenberg and he had regained his enthusiasm for touring. The big band almost exclusively played early Fletcher Henderson arrangements and boasted such soloists as trumpeters John Eckert and Randy Sandke, trombonist Eddie Bert and Ken Peplowski on tenor. In addition, for the PBS special, such veterans as pianist Dick Hyman and drummer Louis Bellson helped out. Benny Goodman at the age of 76 still swung with the best and his death less than a year after this recording meant that he went out on top. —*Scott Yanow*

Mick Goodrick

b. Jun. 9, 1945, Sharon, PA
Guitar / Post-Bop

One of many significant guitarists to be featured at one time or another with vibraphonist Gary Burton's groups (including Larry Coryell, John Scofield and Pat Metheny), Mick Goodrick has not achieved the fame of the others due to his focusing on a career as a jazz educator. However, Goodrick has long had his own distinctive sound. He started on guitar when he was 12, was inspired to play jazz during Stan Kenton's summer camps, and in 1967 graduated from Berklee College. He was soon teaching at Berklee before spending a period with Burton (1973-76) recording extensively with the vibist. Since then, Goodrick has mostly been a teacher in the Boston area, most notably at the New England Conservatory, although he did tour with Charlie Haden's Liberation Orchestra in 1985 and worked for a period with Jack DeJohnette's Special Edition in the late 1980s. Mick Goodrick has recorded as a leader much too infrequently: an ECM date in 1978 and sessions in the 1990s for CMP, Novus and Ram. —*Scott Yanow*

● In Passing / Nov. 1978 / ECM ✦✦✦✦✦

Guitarist Mick Goodrick once worked alongside Pat Metheny in Gary Burton's band, and they have a similar sound, voicings, and eclectic approach. Goodrick's 1978 debut as a leader was a strong set that had fusion, straightahead, and even almost free pieces. He also headed a strong band, with English saxophonist John Surman at his terse, animated best, plus bassist Eddie Gomez and drummer Jack DeJohnette in fine form. —*Ron Wynn*

Biorhythms / Oct. 1990 / CMP ✦✦

This is a difficult CD to get a handle on. The music ranges from loose funk and nearly free-form interplay to selections that emphasize space and silence as much as music. The sparse sound of the trio does not mask Mick Goodrick's mastery of the guitar, but excitement and fire are kept to a bare minimum on many of the tracks. Bassist Harvie Swartz and drummer Gary Chaffee give Goodrick fine support, and "Groove Test" is a nice cooker, but the 10-minute "Something like That Kind of Thing" wanders aimlessly. A so-so effort. —*Scott Yanow*

Rare Birds / Apr. 12, 1993-Apr. 13, 1993 / RAM ✦✦✦✦

Sunscreams / Jun. 17, 1993 / RAM ✦✦✦

Guitarist Mick Goodrick fits in terms of sound, influences, versatility and tuning into a loose corps that also includes John Abercrombie, John Scofield and Pat Metheny (possibly Bill Frisell). These musicians are comfortable with jazz, fusion, pop or rock, and can even move into international styles of classical. Goodrick's sometimes light, sometimes terse, angular lines, finely constructed solos and voicings are the main attributes on this session. Original material rather than standards dominate the session. —*Ron Wynn*

Jim Goodwin

b. 1943
Cornet / Classic Jazz, Dixieland

An excellent classic jazz cornetist based in Portland, OR, Jim Goodwin deserves much more recognition. Raised in Seattle, he learned jazz on piano and cornet, assisted by his father, drummer Bob Goodwin. He moved to San Francisco in 1969 and often worked with pianist Ray Skjelbred. The cornetist then spent a period in Europe before settling in Portland. Jim Goodwin has recorded an album apiece as a leader for Berkeley Rhythm (1971-77) and Rhythm Masters (1987-88), along with a very enjoyable 1993 Arbors duet CD with pianist Dave Frishberg. —*Scott Yanow*

● Jim Goodwin & Friends / Aug. 1971-Jan. 23, 1978 / Berkeley Rhythm ✦✦✦✦

An excellent trad jazz cornetist who has recorded far too little through the years, Jim Goodwin is heard in a variety of settings on this LP, all but one selection being from 1977-78. Goodwin duets with pianist Burt Bales on "Melancholy Baby," takes a rare piano solo on "You're a Lucky Guy," and jams with such top musicians as pianist Ray Skjelbred, guitarist Marty Grosz, bassist Mike Duffy, and soprano saxophonist Dick Hadlock, among others. Fun music, with the highlights including "I've Got My Fingers Crossed," "A Sailboat in the Moonlight" and "The Love Nest," but this locally released album will be difficult to acquire. —*Scott Yanow*

Taking a Chance / Jun. 15, 1987+Apr. 8, 1988 / Rhythm Masters ✦✦✦✦

Cornetist Jim Goodwin and pianist Ray Skjelbred, who are featured on this set of duets, have teamed up together off and on since they first met in 1967. Skjelbred's style is based in Earl Hines, Joe Sullivan and Art Hodes (as Richard Hadlock accurately states in his perceptive liner notes) while Goodwin, who has a little of Wild Bill Davison's tone (but without the sarcasm and screams) is a solid Chicago player a bit reminiscent of Max Kaminsky. The two make a near-perfect match on their relaxed set of superior standards and they get fairly heated on "Rosetta." Clarinetist Hamilton Carson sits in successfully on four tracks, adding a little bit of Pee Wee Russell's phrasing to the proceedings. The music overall may not startlingly innovative but the improvisations are certainly creative within the boundaries of traditional jazz. This small label release is one to search for by pre-swing jazz fans. —*Scott Yanow*

Bob Gordon

b. Jun. 11, 1928, St. Louis, MO, **d.** Aug. 28, 1955, California
Baritone Saxophone / Cool

Bob Gordon was a fine West Coast bop-oriented baritonist. He played with Shorty Sherock (1946), Alvino Rey's Orchestra (1948-51) and Billy May (1952) before becoming an in-demand session player for jazz dates with the likes of Shelly Manne, Maynard Ferguson, Chet Baker, Clifford Brown (1954), Shorty Rogers, Tal Farlow and Stan Kenton. While on his way to playing at a Pete Rugolo concert in San Diego, Bob Gordon was killed in a car accident. His lone album as a leader has been reissued by V.S.O.P. —*Scott Yanow*

Bob Gordon Memorial / Dec. 1953-May 1954 / Fresh Sound ✦✦✦✦✦

Moods in Jazz / Dec. 1953 / V.S.O.P. ✦✦✦✦

On one of two albums led by baritonist Bob Gordon before his tragic death in a 1955 car crash, the cool-toned baritonist blends in well with trombonist Herbie Harper in a quintet that also includes a no-name rhythm section (pianist Maury Dell, bassist Don Prell and drummer George Redman). The emphasis is on slower tempos, in fact, two of the songs are titled "Slow Mood" (the Eddie Miller composition) and "Slow." This CD reissue of a Tampa set is worth picking up by fans of relaxed straightahead jazz. —*Scott Yanow*

● Meet Mr. Gordon / May 6, 1954+May 27, 1954 / Pacific Jazz ✦✦✦✦✦

A brilliant testimony to the baritone sax player who helped define the cool and bouncy West Coast sound, it was recorded with Jack Montrose (ts). —*David Szatmary*

Bobby Gordon

Clarinet / Swing, Dixieland

Bobby Gordon is best known for his recent Arbors recordings and for his association with Marty Grosz in the Orphan Newsboys. He recorded three early albums for Dot (1962-63) that sought to capitalize on the popularity of folk music and Acker Bilk's string hits. Gordon, who sometimes hints at Pee Wee Russell (although his tone is a lot smoother), has recorded more worthy sets in recent times for Jump and Arbors and currently lives in the San Diego area although he is sometimes coaxed away to play at jazz parties and festivals. —*Scott Yanow*

Plays Bing / May 27, 1997 / Arbors ✦✦✦✦

Clarinetist Bobby Gordon, his cohorts in the Orphan Newsboys (Marty Grosz, Peter Ecklund and Greg Cohen) and other top pre-bop players are heard on this CD performing a variety of songs made famous by Bing Crosby, most of which date from the 1930s. Although Gordon gets top billing, he does not take much more solo space than the other horn players (Peter Ecklund or Randy Reinhart on trumpet, trombonist Dan Barrett and Scott Robinson on tenor, baritone and bass saxes), and the most important participant is actually pianist Keith Ingham, who provided the arrangements. Since Bing Crosby made literally hundreds of songs famous, Ingham had plenty to choose from, and to his credit, he does not stick exclusively to standards; "The Waiter and the Porter and the Upstairs Maid" from the underrated 1940 movie *Birth of the Blues* gets a welcome revival. The charts are often a bit tame, and nothing all that unique occurs, but the music (which includes "Where the Blue of the Night," "I'm an Old Cow Hand," "From Monday On" and "Just One More Chance" among others) is melodic and quite pleasing. —*Scott Yanow*

Dexter Gordon

b. Feb. 27, 1923, Los Angeles, CA, **d.** Apr. 25, 1990, Philadelphia, PA
Tenor Saxophone / Bop, Hard Bop

Dexter Gordon had such a colorful and eventful life (with three separate comebacks) that his story would make a great Hollywood movie. The top tenor saxophonist to emerge during the bop era and possessor of his own distinctive sound, Gordon sometimes was long-winded and quoted excessively from other songs, but he created a large body of superior work and could battle nearly anyone successfully at a jam session. His first important gig was with Lionel Hampton (1940-43) although, due to Illinois Jacquet also being in the sax section, Gordon did not get any solos. In 1943 he did get to stretch out on a recording session with Nat King Cole. Short stints with Lee Young, the Fletcher Henderson Orchestra and Louis Armstrong's big band preceded his move to New York in December 1944 and becoming part of Billy Eckstine's Orchestra, trading off with Gene Ammons on Eckstine's recording of "Blowin' the Blues Away." Dexter recorded with Dizzy Gillespie ("Blue 'n' Boogie") and as a leader for Savoy before returning to Los Angeles in the summer of 1946. He was a major part of the Central Avenue scene, trading off with Wardell Gray and Teddy Edwards in many legendary tenor battles; studio recordings of "The Chase" and "The Duel" helped to document the atmosphere of the period.

After 1952 drug problems resulted in some jail time and periods of inactivity during the 1950s (although Gordon did record two albums in 1955). By 1960 he was recovered and soon he was recording a consistently rewarding series of dates for Blue Note. Just when he was regaining his former popularity, in 1962 Gordon moved to Europe where he would stay until 1976. While on the continent, he was in peak form and Dexter's many Steeple Chase recordings rank with the finest work of his career. Gordon did return to the US on an occasional basis, recording in 1965, 1969-70 and 1972, but he was to an extent forgotten in his native land. It was therefore a major surprise that his return in 1976 was treated as a major media event. A great deal of interest was suddenly shown in the living legend with long lines of people waiting at clubs in order to see him. Gordon was signed to Columbia and remained a popular figure until his gradually worsening health made him semiactive by the early '80s. His third comeback occurred when he was picked to star in the motion picture *'Round Midnight* and, even if his playing by then was past its prime, Gordon's acting was quite realistic and touching. He was nominated for an Academy Award, four years before his death after a very full life. Most of Dexter Gordon's recordings for Savoy, Dial, Bethlehem, Dootone, Jazzland, Blue Note, Steeple Chase, Black Lion, Prestige, Columbia, Who's Who, Chiaroscuro and Elektra Musician are currently available. —*Scott Yanow*

Move / Sep. 4, 1945-Nov. 29, 1948 / Spotlite ✦✦✦✦✦

This very interesting LP is full of historically significant performances from the bebop era. A complement to Spotlite's *The Chase*, the set has alternate takes from three of tenor saxophonist Dexter Gordon's 1947 sessions (which feature trombonist Melba Liston and pianists Jimmy Bunn and Jimmy Rowles), "Blues in Teddy's Flat" from tenor Teddy Edwards, four vocal sides by Earl Coleman (with such sidemen as trumpeter Fats Navarro, Don Lanphere's tenor and pianist Linton Garner), two versions of "Move" by the latter group without Coleman and four obscure numbers from trumpeter Howard McGhee's first date as a leader. This timeless music has plenty of exciting moments. —*Scott Yanow*

● **Long Tall Dexter** / Oct. 30, 1945-Dec. 22, 1946 / Savoy ✦✦✦✦

In the mid- to late '40s, there were three great young tenor saxophonists: Dexter Gordon, Wardell Gray and Teddy Edwards. Of the trio, Dexter Gordon had the greatest influence on upcoming players and was the most bop-oriented. This superb two-LP set contains all 17 selections Gordon cut for Savoy during 1945-47 plus eight alternate takes and a jam session performance (with trumpeter Howard McGhee and altoist Sonny Criss) titled "After Hours Bop." Gordon is heard in a quartet, with several quintets (featuring such major players as pianist Bud Powell, drummers Max Roach and Art Blakey, baritonist Leo Parker and trumpeter Fats Navarro) and in a septet with trumpeter Joe Newman and trombonist J.J. Johnson. Throughout, Gordon holds his own with the slightly older players and gets his career off to a brilliant start. —*Scott Yanow*

Master Takes: The Savoy Recordings / Oct. 30, 1945-Dec. 22, 1947 / Savoy ✦✦✦✦

This single album contains 15 of Dexter Gordon's significant Savoy sides from the prime years of the bop era. Gordon was (along with Wardell Gray and Teddy Edwards) the top young tenor of the period and his fame and influence would soon dwarf his two competitors. These quartet and quintet performances (featuring such top players as pianist Bud Powell, baritonist Leo Parker and trumpeter Fats Navarro) are concise, swinging and advanced for the time. This set is really more for general collectors since all of this music (plus the alternate takes, an additional session and one jam-session number) were included on the two-fer *Long Tall Dexter.* —*Scott Yanow*

★ **The Chase!** / Jun. 5, 1947-Dec. 4, 1947 / Stash ✦✦✦✦✦

During the mid-to-late '40s, Dexter Gordon, one of the top young tenors to emerge during the bop era, had nightly tenor "battles" in Los Angeles clubs with his two bop competitors, Wardell Gray and Teddy Edwards. Fortunately, Gordon also had opportunities to meet up with his fellow tenors on record: "The Chase" (featuring Gray and Gordon) is a classic and "The Duel" (which was recorded twice with Edwards) is close behind. Although issued as part of Stash's budget series, the vintage music on this CD (which has all of Dexter Gordon's recordings for Dial in 1947) is often quite memorable. In addition to battles, Gordon teams up with trombonist Melba Liston in a quintet, leads a couple of his own quartets and "Blues In Teddy's Flat" features Edwards. Since all of the alternate takes are also included, this highly recommended release is quite definitive and recaptures some of the excitement of the period. —*Scott Yanow*

The Hunt / Jul. 6, 1947 / Savoy ✦✦✦

This two-LP set could be called "A Day in the Life of Central Avenue." These four side-long performances are jams featuring a nonet comprising tenors Dexter Gordon and Wardell Gray, trumpeter Howard McGhee, altoist Sonny Criss, trombonist Trummy Young, pianist Hampton Hawes (making his recording debut), guitarist Barney Kessel, either Harry Babasin or Red Callender on bass and Connie Kay or Ken Kennedy on drums. The recording quality is only so-so, but the solos and the many tenor trade-offs are generally quite heated and often exciting. The two-fer preserves the legacy of a brief but colorful era. —*Scott Yanow*

Daddy Plays the Horn / Sep. 1955 / Bethlehem ✦✦✦

One of only two Dexter Gordon recordings from the 1953-59 period, this Bethlehem set (reissued on CD through Evidence) is a fine jam session-flavored date featuring the tenor with pianist Kenny Drew, bassist Leroy Vinnegar and drummer Lawrence Marable. The programming differs from the listing on the liners; the fourth, fifth and sixth songs are actually first, second and third! Gordon is in particularly good form on these four standards and two fairly basic originals and his style was little different than the way he would sound in the 1960s. Recommended to straightahead jazz fans. —*Scott Yanow*

Dexter Blows Hot and Cool / Nov. 11, 1955-Nov. 12, 1955 / Authentic/Dootone ✦✦✦

Little was heard of tenor saxophonist Dexter Gordon on record during the 1950s; in fact this somewhat obscure LP (Savoy in one of their reissue programs also released these performances) was one of Gordon's only three appearances on record (two as a leader) during 1953-59. He fronts a quintet with pianist Carl Perkins, bassist Leroy Vinnegar, drummer Chuck Thompson and the forgotten trumpeter Jimmy Robinson and sounds fairly strong on the straightahead material. Few surprises occur but this collector's item from a dark period in Dexter Gordon's life has its share of fine music. —*Scott Yanow*

The Resurgence of Dexter Gordon / Oct. 13, 1960 / Original Jazz Classics ✦✦✦

Originally put out on Jazzland, this important set was a comeback album by the great tenor Dexter Gordon who had (with the exception of a couple of occasions in 1955) been largely off record since 1952. Teamed up with trombonist Richard Boone), trumpeter Martin Banks and pianist Dolo Coker, Gordon is in excellent form on the six selections, all originals by either the leader or Coker. Because of the large amount of Dexter Gordon recordings from his later years, this CD is not essential but fans should enjoy it. —*Scott Yanow*

Doin' Alright / May 6, 1961 / Blue Note ✦✦✦✦
The title of this Blue Note set perfectly fit at the time, for tenor saxophonist Dexter Gordon was making the first of three successful comebacks. Largely neglected during the 1950s, Gordon's Blue Note recordings (of which this was the first) led to his rediscovery. The tenor is teamed with the young trumpeter Freddie Hubbard, pianist Horace Parlan, bassist George Tucker and drummer Al Harewood for a strong set of music that is highlighted by "You've Changed" (which would become a permanent part of Dexter's repertoire), "Society Red" (a blues later used in the film *Round Midnight*) and "It's You or No One." —*Scott Yanow*

The Complete Blue Note Sixties Sessions / May 6, 1961-May 29, 1965 / Blue Note ✦✦✦✦✦
The Complete Blue Note Sixties Sessions is an attractive six-disc box set featuring all of Dexter Gordon's '60s recordings for the label in chronological order. Such classic albums as *Dexter Calling* and *Go!* were recorded during these years, and they are presented in their entirety, as are two complete sessions that have been previously unavailable on CD and several unreleased alternate takes. For serious Gordon fans and musicologists, it's an essential collection, but its very thoroughness makes it less appealing to casual fans, who would be better off acquiring the individual albums. —*Stephen Thomas Erlewine*

Dexter Calling . . . . / May 9, 1961 / Blue Note ✦✦✦✦
Tenor saxophonist Dexter Gordon recorded seven Blue Note albums during 1960-64 and all are easily recommended. The power and creativity he showed during those performances led to his first successful comeback and display him in prime form. This particular CD (the reissue adds a version of "Landslide" not released at the time) showcases the distinctive tenor with a quartet that also includes pianist Kenny Drew, bassist Paul Chambers and drummer Philly Joe Jones. Gordon and Drew contributed six originals to the date but it is the leader's interpretations of the two standards ("End of a Love Affair" and particularly "Smile") that are most memorable. —*Scott Yanow*

Landslide / May 9, 1961-Jun. 25, 1962 / Blue Note ✦✦✦
Landslide comprises previously unreleased material from three separate Dexter Gordon-led sessions between May 1961 and June 1962. The title track is a *Dexter Calling...* outtake featuring pianist Kenny Drew, bassist Paul Chambers and drummer Philly Joe Jones; it was later added to the CD version of *Dexter Calling...* as a bonus track. Three songs—"Love Locked Out," "You Said It," "Serenade in Blue"—are from May of 1962 and feature trumpeter Tommy Turrentine, pianist Sir Charles Thompson, bassist Al Lucas and drummer Willie Bobo. The remaining three songs—"Blue Gardenia," "Six Bits Jones," "Second Balcony Jump"—were recorded in June of 1962 and feature trumpeter Dave Burns, pianist Sonny Clark, bassist Ron Carter and drummer Philly Joe Jones. All three sessions hold together fairly well, and although nothing on the record qualifies as a masterpiece, nothing is bad, either. In comparison to the released sessions, this material may pale somewhat, but it remains first-rate hard bop and is recommended to Gordon collectors. —*Stephen Thomas Erlewine*

Go! / Aug. 27, 1962 / Blue Note ✦✦✦✦
Dexter Gordon is in hard-swinging yet lyrical form throughout this particularly strong release. Accompanied by pianist Sonny Clark, bassist Butch Warren and drummer Billy Higgins, Gordon is heard at his best on "I Guess I'll Hang My Tears Out to Dry," "Where Are You" and "Three O'Clock in the Morning": three rarely performed standards. All of Dexter Gordon's Blue Note recordings (and in reality 90% of his releases) are recommended to lovers of bop and straightahead jazz. —*Scott Yanow*

A Swingin' Affair / Aug. 29, 1962 / Blue Note ✦✦✦✦
Recorded just two days after his popular album *Go* and using the same personnel (pianist Sonny Clark, bassist Butch Warren and drummer Billy Higgins), tenor-great Dexter Gordon stretches out on two of his originals, Warren's "The Backbone" and (best of all) three standards: "You Stepped Out of a Dream," "Until the Real Thing Comes Along" and the high point "Don't Explain." This CD is well worth getting. —*Scott Yanow*

Cry Me a River / Nov. 28, 1962 / Steeple Chase ✦✦✦
This CD contains two separate European sessions taken from radio broadcasts. Tenor saxophonist Dexter Gordon, who had just moved to Europe, is heard on lengthy versions of "I'll Remember April" and "Cry Me a River" from 1962 with a Danish trio comprising pianist Atli Bjorn, bassist Marcel Rigot and drummer Williams Schioppfe. The two 1964 numbers ("The Thrill Is Gone" and "Suite") are by Bjorn's 1964 trio with bassist Benny Nielsen and drummer Finn Frederiksen; the talented pianist is well showcased. —*Scott Yanow* .

Our Man in Paris / May 23, 1963 / Blue Note ✦✦✦✦
Tenor saxophonist Dexter Gordon, who had recently moved to Europe, is featured on this set with the all-star rhythm section sometimes called "The Three Bosses": pianist Bud Powell, bassist Pierre Michelot and drummer Kenny Clarke. The repertoire is strictly bop standards and Powell in particular is in excellent form. Gordon sounds fine too on such songs as "Scrapple from the Apple," "Stairway to the Stars" and "A Night in Tunisia." —*Scott Yanow*

One Flight Up / Jun. 2, 1964 / Blue Note ✦✦✦
Tenor-great Dexter Gordon and trumpeter Donald Byrd make for an excellent team on this 1964 hard-bop quintet date with pianist Kenny Drew, bassist Niels Pedersen (then only 18) and drummer Art Taylor. The Blue Note LP only contains three selections: an 18-minute rendition of Byrd's "Tanya," Drew's minor-toned "Coppin' the Haven" and a quartet version of "Darn That Dream" that finds Gordon in lyrical form. —*Scott Yanow*

Cheesecake / Jun. 11, 1964 / Steeple Chase ✦✦✦✦
Dexter Gordon's long stint at the Club Montmartre in Copenhagen during the summer of 1964 included weekly radio broadcasts. These live performances have been preserved and released by Steeple Chase on a series of albums. This particular LP features the great tenor with a rhythm section comprising Europe's best (pianist Tete Montoliu, bassist Niels Pedersen and drummer Alex Riel) performing Dexter's "Cheese Cake," "Manha de Carnival" and "Second Balcony Jump." Gordon takes long solos that never seem to run out of ideas, making this set a valuable addition to his lengthy discography. —*Scott Yanow*

King Neptune / Jun. 24, 1964 / Steeple Chase ✦✦✦✦
Dexter Gordon and his European quartet (pianist Tete Montoliu, bassist Niels-Henning Orsted Pedersen and drummer Alex Riel) played a three-month engagement at Copenhagen's Montmartre Club during the summer of 1964. The group had an hour-long radio broadcast every other Thursday night, and the results have been released by Steeple Chase on six CDs. *Cheesecake* was the first, and its follow-up, *King Neptune*, features the quartet and the great tenor stretching out on "Satin Doll," "Body and Soul," "I Want to Blow Now" (which Gordon briefly sings), and the otherwise unknown title cut, a Gordon original that was never recorded elsewhere. All of the releases in this valuable *Dexter in Radioland* series are recommended. —*Scott Yanow*

I Want More / Jul. 9, 1964 / Steeple Chase ✦✦✦✦
Steeple Chase has released on six CDs the radio broadcasts of Dexter Gordon and his 1964 Quartet (with pianist Tete Montoliu, bassist Niels-Henning Orsted Pedersen and on this volume drummer Rune Carlsson) from Copenhagen's Montmartre Club. In addition to the title cut, Dexter and Co. perform "Come Rain or Come Shine," "Where Are You," the fun "I Want to Blow Now" (which Gordon sings) and "Second Balcony Jump." Fans will want all of the releases in this enjoyable and well-recorded series. —*Scott Yanow*

Love for Sale / Jul. 23, 1964 / Steeple Chase ✦✦✦✦
Dexter Gordon and his Quartet of 1964 (pianist Tete Montoliu, bassist Niels-Henning Orsted Pedersen and drummer Alex Riel) had a three-month engagement at the Montmartre Club in Copenhagen, broadcasting on the radio every other Thursday. Steeple Chase has released these consistently exciting (and well-recorded) performances on six CDs. *Love for Sale* features the impressive group jamming on the title cut, "Cherokee," two Gordon originals (including "Big Fat Butterfly" which has the tenor taking a brief vocal) and an emotional rendition of "I Guess I'll Hang My Tears Out to Dry." It's recommended, as are all of the releases in this valuable *Dexter in Radioland* series. —*Scott Yanow*

It's You or No One / Aug. 6, 1964 / Steeple Chase ✦✦✦✦
The fifth of six Steeple Chase CDs taken from the 1964 broadcasts of tenor great Dexter Gordon and his quartet (pianist Tete Montoliu, bassist Niels-Henning Orsted Pedersen and drummer Alex Riel) from Copenhagen's Montmartre Club once again finds Gordon in top form. He performs extended versions of four standards ("Just Friends," "Three O'Clock in the Morning," "Where Are You?" and "It's You or No One") with creativity and the music is quite enjoyable, recommended to bop fans. —*Scott Yanow*

Billie's Bounce / Aug. 20, 1964 / Steeple Chase ✦✦✦✦
Dexter Gordon and his 1964 Quartet (with pianist Tete Montoliu, bassist Niels-Henning Orsted Pedersen and drummer Alex Riel) broadcast from the Montmartre Club in Copenhagen on six occasions and all of the music has been issued on Steeple Chase CDs. This particular set finds the group playing a fairly brief "Night in Tunisia" and long versions of "Billie's Bounce" (over 17 minutes), "Satin Doll" and Gordon's "Soul Sister." The well-recorded performances feature the great bop tenor in peak form and are easily recommended as is this entire *Dexter in Radioland* series. —*Scott Yanow*

After Hours / 1964-1965 / Steeple Chase ✦✦
Tenor saxophonist Dexter Gordon, the fine trumpeter Rolf Ericson and a Danish rhythm section (pianist Lars Sjosten, bassist Sture Norin and drummer Per Hulten) are heard on four rather lengthy performances: "All the Things You Are," "Darn That Dream," an 18-minute "Straight, No Chaser" and a previously unissued nearly 17-minute rendition of "I Remember You." Originating from a club

appearance in Stockholm probably from 1964-65 (this CD lacks liner notes), the music is well played if sometimes a bit long-winded. —*Scott Yanow*

After Midnight / 1964-1965 / Steeple Chase ♦♦
This CD has two rather long performances by a quintet led by Dexter Gordon that also features trumpeter Rolf Ericson, pianist Lars Sjosten, bassist Sture Norin and drummer Per Hulten: a 20-minute version of "Three O'Clock in the Morning" and a 26-minute rendition of Miles Davis' "No Blues." Although not essential, these live radio broadcasts (from an often-overlooked period in the great tenor's career) are enjoyable and worth hearing by straightahead jazz fans. —*Scott Yanow*

Clubhouse / May 27, 1965 / Blue Note ♦♦♦
Although tenor saxophonist Dexter Gordon had moved to Europe in 1962, he made a return visit to the US in 1965 that resulted in both this album and *Gettin' Around*. Gordon teams up with trumpeter Freddie Hubbard, pianist Barry Harris, bassist Bob Cranshaw and drummer Billy Higgins for three of his originals, two obscurities and a standard that ended up being the date's most memorable performance: "I'm a Fool to Want You." The CD reissue is a reproduction of the original LP which was not issued until the mid-'70s. It is excellent music if not quite essential. —*Scott Yanow*

Gettin' Around / May 28, 1965 / Blue Note ♦♦♦♦
Dexter Gordon meets up with vibraphonist Bobby Hutcherson, pianist Barry Harris, bassist Bob Cranshaw and drummer Billy Higgins on this excellent hard-bop date. Recorded during one of the great tenor's infrequent US visits (he had moved to Europe in 1962), Gordon is in excellent form on six diverse selections that range from "Manha de Carnaval" and "Shiny Stockings" to "Heartaches" and Gordon's original "Le Coiffeur." Although underrated during this era due to his residence in Europe, Dexter Gordon was at the peak of his powers throughout this period; all of his Blue Note releases are easily recommended. —*Scott Yanow*

Squirrel: Live at Montmartre / Jun. 29, 1967 / Blue Note ♦♦♦♦

Body and Soul / Jul. 20, 1967 / Black Lion ♦♦♦♦♦
Tenor saxophonist Dexter Gordon recorded three CDs' worth of material during a two-day period at Copenhagen's legendary Montmartre Club; *Take the 'A' Train* and *Both Sides of Midnight* have also been released by Black Lion on CD. Gordon and his impressive quartet (pianist Kenny Drew, bassist Neils-Henning Orsted Pederson and drummer Albert "Tootie" Heath) play versions of "Like Someone in Love," "Come Rain or Come Shine," "There Will Never Be Another You," "Body and Soul" and "Blues Walk" that clock in between nine and 14 minutes. Ironically, Dexter, who was in peak form during his years in Europe, was somewhat forgotten in the US at the time. This set is recommended along with the two other CDs from this well-documented engagement. —*Scott Yanow*

Both Sides of Midnight / Jul. 20, 1967 / Black Lion ♦♦♦♦♦
Tenor saxophonist Dexter Gordon is accompanied by an all-star rhythm section (pianist Kenny Drew, bassist Niels Pederson and drummer Albert "Tootie" Heath) on this enjoyable club recording from Copenhagen's Montmartre. In addition to Ben Tucker's modal "Devilette," Gordon explores four jazz standards, really digging into the material. Bop fans are advised to pick up this excellent CD. —*Scott Yanow*

Live at the Montmartre Jazzhus / Jul. 20, 1967-Jul. 21, 1967 / Black Lion ♦♦♦♦
Three Dexter Gordon CDs (which are also available separately) are housed in this particular Black Lion box. The music included on *Both Sides of Midnight, Body and Soul* and *Take the 'A' Train* were performed live during a two-day period at the legendary Copenhagen club Montmartre by the veteran tenor with pianist Kenny Drew, bassist Niels Pederson and drummer Albert "Tootie" Heath. The 15 standards (including two versions of "Blues Walk") find Dexter in typically exuberant form, stretching out (only two numbers are under eight-and-a-half minutes) and sounding quite relaxed even at the more rapid tempos. Gordon's many fans will want this music in one form or another. —*Scott Yanow*

Take the "A" Train / Jul. 21, 1967 / Black Lion ♦♦♦♦♦
During a two-day period (July 20-21, 1967) tenor saxophonist Dexter Gordon and his quartet (pianist Kenny Drew, bassist Niels Pederson and drummer Albert "Tootie" Heath) recorded enough music to fill up three CDs, all of which have been released by the English Black Lion label. Four of the six standards on this hard-swinging set ("But Not for Me," "Take the 'A' Train," "Blues Walk" and "Love for Sale") are over ten minutes long while the other two ("For All We Know" and "I Guess I'll Have to Hang My Tears Out to Dry") are a little more concise. Throughout, Dexter Gordon is in consistently creative form, making this CD well worth getting by his fans. —*Scott Yanow*

Live at the Amsterdam Paradiso / Feb. 5, 1969 / Affinity ♦♦♦♦
The great tenor Dexter Gordon made so many consistently enjoyable straightahead recordings during 1960-78 that it is difficult to come up with any sets that are not recommended to fans of bebop. This double LP finds Gordon in excellent form, performing four jazz standards along with two of his originals ("Fried

Bananas" and "Junior") with a Dutch trio (pianist Cees Slinger, bassist Jacques Schois and the future avant-garde innovator Han Bennink on drums). Virtually all of Gordon's records from his productive European period find him at his peak and this two-fer is no exception. —*Scott Yanow*

Day in Copenhagen / Mar. 10, 1969 / Polydor ♦♦♦
Unlike many other American expatriates living in Europe, tenor saxophonist Dexter Gordon always managed to play and record with the top musicians while overseas. This excellent sextet session (with trombonist Slide Hampton, trumpeter Dizzy Reece, pianist Kenny Drew, bassist Niels Pedersen and drummer Art Taylor) finds him exploring three Slide Hampton compositions and a trio of standard ballads. The other soloists are fine but Gordon easily dominates the set, playing his brand of hard-driving bop. —*Scott Yanow*

More Power / Apr. 2, 1969+Apr. 4, 1969 / Original Jazz Classics ♦♦♦
Recorded at the same two sessions that also resulted in *The Tower of Power* (a title that predated the R&B group), this set features tenor-great Dexter Gordon in the middle of one of his infrequent visits to the US, during a long period when he lived in Europe. Gordon, joined by James Moody's tenor on two cuts (Moody only solos on Tadd Dameron's "Lady Bird"), is accompanied throughout by pianist Barry Harris, bassist Buster Williams and drummer Albert "Tootie" Heath. The music (three Gordon originals, including the original version of "Fried Bananas," Jobim's "Meditation" and a Tadd Dameron tune) finds Gordon at the peak of his powers, a place he stayed for 15 years even though he tended to be overshadowed by many younger players during this era. —*Scott Yanow*

Power / Apr. 2, 1969+Apr. 4, 1969 / Prestige ♦♦♦
This two-LP set is most notable for helping to introduce (at least in a studio setting) tenor saxophonist Dexter Gordon's catchy original "Fried Bananas" and for his notable rendition of "Those Were the Days" (a song that Gordon successfully uplifted). The two-fer, which combines together music originally released as *The Tower of Power* and *More Power,* is otherwise enjoyable but not overly memorable. James Moody guests on tenor during three of the eight selections but few sparks fly although the rhythm section (pianist Barry Harris, bassist Buster Williams and drummer Albert "Tootie" Heath) is typically excellent. All of this music has been reissued on CD. —*Scott Yanow*

The Tower of Power / Apr. 2, 1969+Apr. 4, 1969 / Original Jazz Classics ♦♦♦
The high point of this boppish CD is a bit of a surprise, tenor Dexter Gordon's emotional rendition of "Those Were the Days." Otherwise fellow-tenor James Moody's guest appearance on "Montmartre" is less exciting than one would hope although the other two quartet performances (with pianist Barry Harris, bassist Buster Williams and drummer Albert "Tootie" Heath) are good. Recorded during an infrequent visit to the US, this recording (along with its companion *More Power)* failed to create much of a stir. —*Scott Yanow*

The Panther! / Jul. 7, 1970 / Original Jazz Classics ♦♦♦♦
Although Dexter Gordon contributed three originals to this American session, it is his rendition of the three standards that are most memorable. The great tenor romps on the familiar line "The Blues Walk," digs into "Body and Soul" (giving this warhorse a fresh new interpretation) and makes a classic statement on "The Christmas Song." With the assistance of pianist Tommy Flanagan, bassist Larry Ridley and drummer Alan Dawson, Gordon is in typically spirited form for this upbeat set. —*Scott Yanow*

Dexter Gordon at Montreux (With Junior Mance) / June 18, 1970 / Original Jazz Classics ♦♦♦♦
Dexter Gordon's set at the 1970 Montreux Jazz Festival is typically exciting with long tenor solos, fine backup (from pianist Junior Mance, bassist Martin Rivera and drummer Oliver Jackson) and a well-rounded repertoire: Gordon's "Fried Bananas," "Sophisticated Lady," Thelonious Monk's "Rhythm-A-Ning," an explorative "Body and Soul," "Blue Monk" and "The Panther." This excellent CD serves as a fine all-around introduction to the music of the great tenor saxophonist. —*Scott Yanow*

Jumpin' Blues / Aug. 27, 1970 / Original Jazz Classics ♦♦♦
Although tenor saxophonist Dexter Gordon seemed to have been largely forgotten in the US during his long residence in Europe, he was playing in prime form during the period and made occasional trips back to America. On this CD reissue, Gordon teams up with pianist Wynton Kelly (one of his last recordings), bassist Sam Jones and drummer Roy Brooks for an obscure original ("Evergreenish"), "The Jumpin' Blues," the veteran ballad "For Sentimental Reasons" and three songs that were long a part of Gordon's repertoire: "Star Eyes," "Rhythm-A-Ning" and "If You Could See Me Now." Dexter Gordon is in fine form on the excellent straightahead bop set. —*Scott Yanow*

The Shadow of Your Smile / Apr. 21, 1971 / Steeple Chase ♦♦♦
Tenor saxophonist Dexter Gordon uplifts four warhorses (a cooking "Secret Love," "Polkadots and Moonbeams," "The Shadow of Your Smile" and "Summertime") in

lengthy and creative renditions. This live set from Stockholm, Sweden, finds Gordon joined by an excellent Swedish rhythm section (pianist Lars Sjosten, bassist Sture Nordin and drummer Fredrik Noren) on an excellent LP of fairly explorative bop. —*Scott Yanow*

Ca' Purange / June 28, 1972 / Prestige ◆◆◆

The harmonically advanced trumpeter Thad Jones is a perfect contrast to the tenor of Dexter Gordon on this enjoyable Prestige LP. Gordon was somewhat forgotten in the US at the time (his "comeback" was still four years away) but is in excellent form on the four numbers, particularly during a passionate version of "The First Time Ever I Saw Your Face." —*Scott Yanow*

Generation / Jul. 22, 1972 / Original Jazz Classics ◆◆◆◆

Veteran tenor saxophonist Dexter Gordon welcomed trumpeter Freddie Hubbard to his recording group several times during his career and each collaboration was quite rewarding. For this Prestige studio set the two horns (who are joined by pianist Cedar Walton, bassist Buster Williams and drummer Billy Higgins) work together quite well on "Milestones" (a second version is included as a bonus track), "Scared to Be Alone," Thelonious Monk's "We See" and Gordon's "The Group." This CD should please collectors. —*Scott Yanow*

Dexter Gordon-Sonny Grey with the Georges Arvanitas Trio / Feb. 16, 1973 / Spotlite ◆◆◆◆

Recorded in Paris during a prime period, tenor saxophonist Dexter Gordon jams on four basic group originals, including his own "Fried Bananas" and "Dexter Leaps Out." The medium to uptempo numbers clock in between 9 and 12 minutes apiece, giving Dexter, trumpeter Sonny Grey and the French rhythm section (pianist Georges Arvanitas, bassist Jacki Samson and drummer Charles Saudrais) plenty of opportunities to stretch out. A fine jam session that was decently recorded. —*Scott Yanow*

Blues á la Suisse / Jul. 7, 1973 / Prestige ◆◆

Tenor-great Dexter Gordon sounds fine on these four extended performances ("Gingerbread Boy," "Blues á la Suisse," "Some Other Spring" and "Secret Love") which (with the exception of the six-minute "Some Other Spring") clock in between ten and 15 minutes apiece. The rhythm section (Hampton Hawes on electric piano, electric bassist Bob Cranshaw and drummer Kenny Clarke) is not as attuned to Gordon's music as one would hope (the electronics do not really blend in well), making this a somewhat average (but still fairly enjoyable) bop session. —*Scott Yanow*

Revelation / 1974 / Steeple Chase ◆◆◆◆

Virtually all of tenor saxophonist Dexter Gordon's Steeple Chase recordings find him in prime form. This music, released for the first time in 1995, is a bit unusual in that Gordon (who usually played in a quartet) is joined by the fiery trumpeter Benny Bailey who has a particularly exciting solo on "At Ronnie 's." The obscure European rhythm section is fine in support of the two lead voices who, in addition to "At Ronnie's," perform Bill Barron's "Revelation," a couple of standards and a two-song ballad medley. Worth picking up. —*Scott Yanow*

The Apartment / May 24, 1974-Sep. 8, 1974 / Steeple Chase ◆◆◆◆◆

While in Europe, tenor sax great Dexter Gordon recorded many sessions with pianist Kenny Drew, bassist Niels Pedersen and drummer Albert "Tootie" Heath. All are worth acquiring and this one is no exception. In addition to three of his originals (including the title tune), the quartet performs the old bop line "Wee-Dot" and Horace Silver's "Strollin" while the ballad "Old Folks" is taken as an emotional Gordon-Pedersen duet. —*Scott Yanow*

More than You Know / Feb. 21, 1975-Mar. 27, 1975 / Steeple Chase ◆◆◆◆

Dexter Gordon's Steeple Chase recordings of the early to mid-'70s are among the most rewarding of his career. This particular session (which finds Gordon backed by a string orchestra arranged by Palle Mikkelborg) is one of the lesser items from this fertile period. Dexter is in memorable form on "Naima" and "More Than You Know" but the backup orchestra has little interplay with Gordon and the lush charts offer few surprises. This set does not quite live up to its potential although Dexter Gordon fans will still find moments to enjoy. —*Scott Yanow*

Strings and Things / May 17, 1976-May 19, 1976 / Steeple Chase ◆◆◆

Veteran tenor saxophonist Dexter Gordon's Steeple Chase recordings of the early to mid-1970s are among the finest of his career, with the exception of this CD. Joined by a large (and mostly unidentified) orchestra arranged by either Esko Linnavalli or Palle Mikkelborg, Gordon is often surrounded by intrusive ensembles filled with dated effects and some electronics. The first three selections are rather unfortunate, particularly Dexter's poor vocal on Antonio Carlos Jobim's "This Happy Madness." Much better is an inventive reworking of "More Than You Know" and a spirited rendition of Thad Jones' "A Good Time Was Had By All," which lets some of the Scandinavian sidemen (including trumpeter Allan Botschinsky and bassist Niels Pedersen) have some solo space before Dexter takes

over with some effective soprano. However, this project overall is surprisingly erratic and weak, done in by the forgettable arrangements. —*Scott Yanow*

☆ Stable Mable / Mar. 10, 1975 / Steeple Chase ◆◆◆◆◆

Dexter Gordon is in frequently exuberant form on this quartet session with pianist Horace Parlan, bassist Niels Pedersen and drummer Tony Inzalaco. The material, which includes "Just Friends," "Misty," "Stablemates" and "Red Cross," is familiar, but the veteran tenor sounds quite inspired throughout the joyous outing. —*Scott Yanow*

Swiss Nights, Vol. 1 / Aug. 23, 1975 / Steeple Chase ◆◆◆◆

The first of three volumes taken from the 1975 Zurich Jazz Festival features tenor saxophonist Dexter Gordon (with his reliable sidemen pianist Kenny Drew, bassist Niels Pedersen and drummer Alex Riel) stretching out on "Tenor Madness," "Wave," "You've Changed" and "Days of Wine and Roses." All of the performances are at least ten minutes long and there are some rambling moments, but in general, the music is quite rewarding. This was one of Dexter Gordon's prime periods. —*Scott Yanow*

Swiss Nights, Vol. 2 / Aug. 23, 1975-Aug. 24, 1975 / Steeple Chase ◆◆◆◆

The second of three CDs taken from Gordon's appearances at the 1975 Montreux Jazz Festival showcases the veteran tenor in peak form. With strong support from the talented rhythm section (pianist Kenny Drew, bassist Niels-Henning Orsted Pedersen and drummer Alex Riel), Dexter is particularly exciting on a nearly 15-minute version of "There Is No Greater Love," "Wave" and Thelonious Monk's "Rhythm-A-Ning"; the latter two songs were issued for the initial time on this six-song CD reissue. Dexter Gordon is heard throughout at his best. —*Scott Yanow*

Swiss Nights, Vol. 3 / Aug. 23, 1975-Aug. 24, 1975 / Steeple Chase ◆◆◆◆

The third of three CDs taken from tenor saxophonist Dexter Gordon's appearances at the 1975 Zurich Jazz Festival has more variety than the other two. There are previously unissued versions of "Tenor Madness" and "Days of Wine and Roses" (the latter has a guest appearance by trumpeter Joe Newman), tender ballad renditions of "Didn't We" and "Sophisticated Lady," an effective vocal by Gordon on "Jelly Jelly," and a rollicking rendition of "Rhythm-A-Ning." With pianist Kenny Drew, bassist Niels Pedersen and drummer Alex Riel offering strong support, Dexter Gordon is heard in enthusiastic, hard-swinging form. —*Scott Yanow*

Something Different / Sep. 13, 1975 / Steeple Chase ◆◆◆◆◆

What is different about this set (recorded in a particularly busy year for Dexter Gordon) is that the veteran tenor is joined by a trio (guitarist Philip Catherine, bassist Niels Pedersen and drummer Billy Higgins) that does not include a pianist. Otherwise, the music is at the same high quality level and in the same modern bop genre as one would expect. In addition to one of his originals and Slide Hampton's "Yesterday's Mood," Gordon stretches out on some standards, making a classic statement on the ballad "When Sunny Gets Blue." All of his Steeple Chase albums (particularly those from the 1975-76 period) are well worth acquiring. —*Scott Yanow*

★ Bouncin' with Dex / Sep. 14, 1975 / Steeple Chase ◆◆◆◆◆

Dexter Gordon recorded nine albums for Steeple Chase during 1975-76 (seven in 1975 alone) and was at the peak of his powers. This particular release finds Gordon joined by pianist Tete Montoliu, bassist Niels Pedersen and drummer Billy Higgins for two of his originals and three jazz standards. Gordon is in superlative form, jamming with enthusiasm and melodic creativity on these familiar chord changes. —*Scott Yanow*

Lullaby for a Monster / Jun. 15, 1976 / Steeple Chase ◆◆◆◆

Recorded shortly before his triumphant return to the US after a dozen years overseas, this Dexter Gordon album features him in a surprisingly sparse setting, accompanied only by bassist Niels Pedersen and drummer Alex Riel. Whether it be the humorous melody "Nursery Blues," Pedersen's title cut or the four jazz standards (of which "Good Bait" was first released on this CD reissue), he is up to the challenge and his lengthy solos never lose one's interest. —*Scott Yanow*

Biting the Apple / Nov. 9, 1976 / Steeple Chase ◆◆◆◆◆

Many of Dexter Gordon's finest recordings were cut in Europe just prior to his triumphant return to the US. This album was recorded just weeks before and it is one of the veteran tenor's best. With strong assistance from pianist Barry Harris, bassist Sam Jones and drummer Al Foster, Dexter plays exciting solos on "I'll Remember April," a warm version of "Skylark" and his two originals, "Apple Jump" and "á la Modal." It is highly recommended, as are all of Dexter Gordon's Steeple Chase recordings from this period. —*Scott Yanow*

Featuring Joe Newman / Nov. 1976 / Monad ◆◆◆

This live set is better than it appears at first glance. The recording quality is excellent and Dexter Gordon (who had recently returned to the US after quite a few years in Europe) is in inspired form, really tearing into his solos with intensity. Trumpeter Joe Newman, who obviously had not played much with Gordon, has to fight to find a place for himself in the ensembles and is sometimes overextended in his solos but his colorful tone is immediately recognizable. The rhythm section is fine in support with drummer Wilbur Campbell really pushing the group and pianist Jodie Christian contributing some excellent solos. Not every number is a classic. Newman's feature on "Ode to Billy Joe" is a bit dull and there are some unfortunate fadeouts with the two parts of "Body and Soul" being lengthy fragments from Dexter Gordon solos, "The Shadow of Your Smile" only comprising Gordon's statement and "Softly" ending during Newman's spot. However Dexter Gordon's heated improvisations on "Tangerine" and "Walkin'" are both quite memorable. So, although not essential, this CD is easily recommended to fans. —*Scott Yanow*

Homecoming: Live at the Village Vanguard / Dec. 11, 1976-Dec. 12, 1976 / Columbia ✦✦✦✦✦
The acclaim that met Dexter Gordon when he returned to the US after 14 years in Europe was completely unexpected. Not only did the jazz critics praise the great tenor but there were literally lines of young fans waiting to see his performances. This double CD, recorded during his historic first American tour, improved on the original double LP with the inclusion of previously unreleased versions of "Fried Bananas" and "Body and Soul." Gordon in a quintet with trumpeter Woody Shaw, pianist Ronnie Mathews, bassist Stafford James and drummer Louis Hayes frequently sounds exuberant on these lengthy performances; all ten songs are at least 11 minutes long. The excitement of the period can definitely be felt in this excellent music. —*Scott Yanow*

Sophisticated Giant / Jun. 21, 1977-Jan. 26, 1979 / Columbia ✦✦✦✦
This excellent Columbia album was recorded less than a year after Dexter Gordon's well-publicized tour of the US following a dozen years spent living in Europe. With assistance from such other major players as trumpeters Woody Shaw and Benny Bailey, vibraphonist Bobby Gordon sounds in superlative form on Woody Shaw's "The Moontrame," four standards and his own "Fried Bananas." In addition to the original program (which features Dexter with an all-star tentet), the 1997 CD reissue adds two 1979 features for vocalese singer Eddie Jefferson ("Diggin' It" and "It's Only a Paper Moon") which were originally released on Gordon's *Great Encounters;* trumpeter Shaw and trombonist Curtis Fuller co-star with Gordon. An excellent acquisition. —*Scott Yanow*

Who's Who in Jazz / Nov. 11, 1977 / Who's Who in Jazz ✦✦
This LP is an unusual one for tenor saxophonist Dexter Gordon. Instead of his usual bop-based group, the backing is more swing-oriented (with vibraphonist Lionel Hampton, pianist Hank Jones, guitarist Bucky Pizzarelli, bassist George Duvivier, drummer Oliver Jackson and Candido on congas) as is the repertoire. Gordon plays a few songs on his less-distinctive soprano sax and the music, although reasonably pleasing, is not up to Gordon's earlier recordings. This odd set is a historical curiosity. —*Scott Yanow*

Manhattan Symphonie / 1978 / Columbia ✦✦✦✦
This LP is one of Dexter Gordon's last great albums. The veteran tenor (assisted by pianist George Cables, bassist Rufus Reid and drummer Eddie Gladden) is in superior form on such classic numbers as "As Time Goes By," "Moment's Notice" and most memorably "Body and Soul"; during the latter he shows what he learned from John Coltrane (who was originally most influenced by Gordon). Until Columbia gets around to reissuing it on CD, this superior LP is well worth searching for. —*Scott Yanow*

Nights at the Keystone, Vols. 1-3 / May 13, 1978-Mar. 24, 1979 / Blue Note ✦✦✦✦
Nights at the Keystone dates from a couple of years after Dexter Gordon had returned triumphantly to America (1978-79). He took strong solos on several lengthy performances. One can fault the occasional excess of song quotes (especially "Laura," which seemed to pop up in every solo) but Gordon's authoritative sound, freshness of ideas and confident explorations easily compensated. Pianist George Cables was often in dazzling form (check out "Tangerine") and was continually inventive. Bassist Rufus Reid and drummer Eddie Gladden were perfect in support. In addition, the ambience of the late, lamented Keystone Korner, San Francisco's top jazz club and possessor of one of the most knowledgeable jazz audiences anywhere, can be felt. —*Scott Yanow*

Great Encounters / Sep. 23, 1978 / Columbia ✦✦✦✦
The two great tenors, Dexter Gordon and Johnny Griffin, battle it out on in exciting fashion on live versions of "Blues up and Down" and "Cake," bop singer Eddie Jefferson and trumpeter Woody Shaw join Gordon and his quartet (pianist George Cables, bassist Rufus Reid and drummer Eddie Gladden) on "Diggin' In" and "It's Only a Paper Moon" and Dexter takes Thelonious Monk's ballad "Ruby My Dear" as his feature. Everything works quite well on this diverse but consistent LP, one of Dexter Gordon's later efforts. —*Scott Yanow*

Gotham City / August 11, 1980-Aug. 12, 1980 / Columbia ✦✦✦
Tenor saxophonist Dexter Gordon was still in fairly good form at the time of this later recording. The veteran great is joined by an all-star rhythm section (pianist

Cedar Walton, bassist Percy Heath and drummer Art Blakey) along with guest appearances from trumpeter Woody Shaw and guitarist George Benson. Although this boppish set is rather brief (just four songs totalling around 37 minutes), the quality of the solos is quite high. —*Scott Yanow*

Jive Fernando / 1981 / Chiaroscuro ✦✦
The recording quality on this LP is not flawless, the liner notes (which do not list the recording date) are somewhat irrelevant and Dexter Gordon's rhythm section (keyboardist George Duke, bassist Ralph Garrett and drummer Oliver Johnson) is not perfectly suited to his music but the great tenor plays fairly well on the four extended performances. This obscure session (not essential but worthwhile) is highlighted by "Blue Monk" and "The Shadow of Your Smile." —*Scott Yanow*

American Classic / Mar. 8, 1982 / Elektra ✦✦
Tenor saxophonist Dexter Gordon's final album (not counting his work on the film *Round Midnight*) is a decent effort if not all that notable. Gordon is assisted by Grover Washington, Jr. (who makes some guest appearances on soprano), pianist Kirk Lightsey, organist Shirley Scott, bassist David Eubanks and drummer Eddie Gladden, sounding best on "Besame Mucho" and "Skylark." Worth picking up but not that essential. —*Scott Yanow*

The Other Side of Round Midnight / July 1, 1985-July 12, 1985 / Blue Note ✦✦✦
Outtakes and alternate cuts from the soundtrack of the film that got Dexter Gordon an Oscar nomination. —*Ron Wynn*

Round Midnight / July 1, 1985-July 12, 1985 / Columbia ✦✦✦

Joe Gordon (Joseph Henry Gordon)

b. May 15, 1928, Boston, MA, **d.** Nov. 4, 1963, Santa Monica, CA
Trumpet / Hard Bop
A fine bop-oriented trumpeter, Joe Gordon's tragic death in a fire cut short any chance he had at fame in the jazz world. He became a professional in 1947 and had stints with Georgie Auld, Lionel Hampton, Charlie Parker (on an occasional basis during 1953-55), Art Blakey (1954) and Don Redman. Gordon was with Dizzy Gillespie's 1956 big band, touring the Mideast and getting a solo on "Night in Tunisia." He was in the Horace Silver quintet, moved back to Boston for a period and then relocated to Los Angeles where he worked and recorded with Barney Kessel, Benny Carter, Harold Land, Shelly Manne, Dexter Gordon and Shelly Manne (1958-60). Joe Gordon, who led dates for EmArcy (1955) and Contemporary (1961), was on one Thelonious Monk recording and spent his last few years as a freelance musician. —*Scott Yanow*

Introducing Joe Gordon / Sep. 3, 1955+Sep. 8, 1955 / EmArcy ✦✦✦✦
Trumpeter Joe Gordon only led two sessions during his short life (he died at age 35). For his debut set, the fine hard-bop trumpeter was matched with tenor saxophonist Charlie Rouse, pianist Junior Mance, bassist Jimmy Schenck and drummer Art Blakey. Most of the tunes are originals based on the chord changes of standards, and Gordon sounds in fine form in this swinging setting. Pity that this EmArcy date (expanded from six songs to eight on the Trip LP reissue) is currently difficult to find. —*Scott Yanow*

● **Lookin' Good!** / Jul. 11, 1961-Dec. 18, 1961 / Contemporary ✦✦✦✦✦
Joe Gordon did not live long, only making it to 35. His second of two recordings as a leader (originally released by Contemporary) finds him on the verge of leading his own group. Gordon wrote all eight of the selections and is joined by the adventurous but obscure altoist Jimmy Woods, pianist Dick Whittington, bassist Jimmy Bond and drummer Milt Turner. Although the solos are generally more memorable than the tunes, this is an excellent effort that hints at what might have been had Joe Gordon lived. —*Scott Yanow*

Danny Gottlieb (Daniel Richard Gottlieb)

b. Apr. 18, 1953, New York, NY
Drums / Post-Bop, Crossover Jazz
A flexible and talented drummer, Danny Gottlieb studied with Mel Lewis and Joe Morello. After graduating from the University of Miami (1975), he did session work in the Miami Beach area. Gottlieb joined Gary Burton's Quartet (1976) at a period when Pat Metheny was the guitarist. When Metheny soon formed his Group, Gottlieb became a charter member (1977-83). In 1981 he teamed up with Metheny's bassist Mark Egan in a band that by 1983 was called Elements. He has worked in many other settings since then including with John McLaughlin in the short-lived later version of the Mahavishnu Orchestra (1984) and Al DiMeola (1985). Gottlieb continues to play on a part-time basis with Elements. —*Scott Yanow*

Aquamarine / 1987 / Atlantic ✦✦✦✦
The debut album from this former Pat Metheny Group drummer features guitarist John Abercrombie. —*Paul Kohler*

Whirlwind / 1989 / Atlantic ✦✦✦

This great follow-up album has an incredible list of sidemen, featuring John Abercrombie (g). —*Paul Kohler*

● **Brooklyn Blues** / Dec. 1990 / Big World ✦✦✦✦

Drummer Danny Gottlieb's third CD as a leader is his most straightahead and rewarding with the trio. Joined by keyboardist Gil Goldstein, flutist Jeremy Steig, guitarist John Abercrombie and bassist Chip Jackson, Gottlieb (who takes a supporting role) plays four group originals and an obscurity, plus Lee Morgan's "Melancholee," Wayne Shorter's "Diana," Scott LaFaro's "Gloria's Step" and Ray Charles' spirited "I Believe to My Soul." It is particularly nice to hear Steig in this type of setting again. —*Scott Yanow*

Dusko Goykovich (Dusan Goykovich)

b. Oct. 14, 1931, Jajce, Yugoslavia
Trumpet, Fluegelhorn / Hard Bop

An excellent bop-based soloist who in recent times has been recording rewarding sets for Enja, Dusko Goykovich played in Yugoslavia and Germany before visiting the US for the first time with Marshall Brown's International Youth Band (playing at the 1958 Newport Jazz Festival). Goykovich attended Berklee (1961-63) and played with the orchestras of Maynard Ferguson (1963-64) and Woody Herman (1964-66) before deciding to return to Germany, leading a group with Sal Nistico (1966). He was with the Kenny Clarke-Francy Boland Big Band (1968-73) and had a 12-piece band with Slide Hampton (1974-75). Miles Davis is his main influence but Dusko Goykovich (who has been quite active during the past two decades in Europe) has his own extroverted style. —*Scott Yanow*

After Hours / Nov. 1971 / Enja ✦✦✦✦

Yugoslavian trumpeter Dusko Goykovich is in excellent form on this hard bop-oriented quartet set. With pianist Tete Montoliu playing up to his usual level and fine support contributed by bassist Rob Langereis and drummer Joe Nay, Goykovich takes stimulating solos on two standards ("A Child Is Born" and "I Love You"), Slide Hampton's "Last Minute Blues," and three basic originals. Easily recommended to straightahead jazz fans. —*Scott Yanow*

● **Soul Connection** / Feb. 1994 / Enja ✦✦✦✦✦

Trumpeter Dusko Goykovich, a fixture in Germany for decades, has had few of his recordings available in the US. This Enja CD is an exception, an excellent quartet/quintet date with pianist Tommy Flanagan, bassist Eddie Gomez and drummer Mickey Roker; tenor saxophonist Jimmy Heath is on five of the nine selections. Goykovich, whose hero was Miles Davis (one of his eight originals on this session is called "Ballad for Miles"), has a mellow tone and a likable swinging style. This relaxed CD is an excellent example of his talents. —*Scott Yanow*

Bebop City / 1995 / Enja ✦✦✦✦

Balkan Blue / 1996 / Enja ✦✦✦

John Graas (John J. Graas)

b. Oct. 14, 1924, Dubuque, IA, d. Apr. 13, 1962, Van Nuys, CA
French Horn / Cool, Third Stream

Along with Julius Watkins, John Graas was one of the first jazz French horn soloists. After playing some classical music, in 1942 he became a member of the Claude Thornhill Orchestra. A period in the Army (1942-45) and stints with the Cleveland Orchestra and Tex Beneke's big band preceded Graas' first high-profile gig, playing with Stan Kenton's Innovations Orchestra (1950-51). After leaving Kenton, he settled in Los Angeles and worked as a studio musician in addition to being used on West Coast jazz dates by Shorty Rogers and others. Graas, an excellent composer who sought to combine together jazz and classical music (predating the Third Stream movement), recorded fairly regularly as a leader during 1953-58, sessions that (with the exception of one V.S.O.P. release) have not been reissued. He died of a heart attack at the age of 37. —*Scott Yanow*

● **International Premiere in Jazz** / Oct. 1956+Mar. 18, 1958 / V.S.O.P. ✦✦✦✦✦

John Graas was a multitalented French horn player not shy to take chances in both his solos and his writing. On this V.S.O.P. CD reissue of two sessions for Andex, Graas performs his 17-minute three-part "Jazz Chaconne No. 1" and four alternate takes with a nonet including altoist Art Pepper, trumpeter Jack Sheldon and flutist Buddy Collette. In addition, Graas' four-movement "Jazz Symphony No. 1" is played by the Rundfunk-Symphony Orchestra with guest soloists taken from the Erwin Lehn band (German musicians who have remained quite obscure). The lack of liner notes is unfortunate for it would have been interesting to hear what John Graas' goals were in writing this music. Overall the performances hold one's attention, particularly the "Jazz Chaconne," and this CD is recommended to adventurous listeners. —*Scott Yanow*

Teddy Grace

b. Jun. 26, 1905, Arcadia, LA, d. Jan. 4, 1992, La Mirada, CA
Vocals / Swing, Blues Jazz

A superior singer whose career was tragically cut short, most of Teddy Grace's recordings have been reissued on a Timeless CD. She became a professional singer in 1931, sang on the radio in the South, worked for Al Katz (1933), Tommy Christian (1934) and Mal Hallett (on and off during 1934-37) and recorded for Decca during 1937-40, using such sidemen as Bobby Hackett, Jack Teagarden, Charlie Shavers, Buster Bailey, Pee Wee Russell and Bud Freeman. Grace became disenchanted with the music business and quit in 1940. She joined the WACs during World War II and after straining herself singing during a busy schedule of bond rallies and shows, she lost her voice. Although Teddy Grace's speaking voice eventually came back in a weakened form, she was unable to sing again and spent the rest of her life outside of music. —*Scott Yanow*

Turn On That Red Hot Heat / Feb. 26, 1937-Sep. 9, 1940 / Hep ✦✦✦✦

Most of singer Teddy Grace's finest recordings are on her Timeless CD. Her Hep disc, which only duplicates one selection ("I'll Never Let You Cry"), primarily focuses on Grace's recordings with the Mal Hallett and Bob Crosby Orchestras. In fact, all except one of her performances from those two associations are included on this release. Although Hallett's band was minor league, he had a strong trumpet section, along with future star pianist Frankie Carle. The Crosby numbers are less interesting than the Bobcats' usual instrumentals, and, truth be told, some of the lesser selections on this set are only of interest for Grace's sincere delivery and sense of swing. However, completists will want this CD, which also includes her one number ("Red Wagon") with Lou Holden's band and the four songs that resulted from the singer's first session as a leader. —*Scott Yanow*

● **Teddy Grace** / Oct. 25, 1937-Sep. 26, 1940 / Timeless ✦✦✦✦✦

Even veteran swing collectors might be unaware of the enjoyable recordings that the unfortunately obscure but very talented Teddy Grace made during her relatively brief career. This valuable CD has 22 of the 30 selections that she made as a leader (leaving off two sessions) and finds Grace very much at ease, whether interpreting swinging lesser-known material, a series of high-quality blues or period pieces. The supporting cast, which includes such notables as cornetist Bobby Hackett, trumpeters Charlie Shavers and Max Kaminsky, trombonist Jack Teagarden, clarinetist Pee Wee Russell, tenor saxophonist Bud Freeman and pianist Billy Kyle among others, speaks for the high esteem in which she was held during the era. —*Scott Yanow*

Stephane Grappelli (Stephane Grappelly)

b. Jan. 26, 1908, Paris, France, d. Dec. 1, 1997, Paris, France
Violin / Swing

One of the all-time great jazz violinists (ranking with Joe Venuti and Stuff Smith as one of the big three of pre-bop), Stephane Grappelli's longevity and consistently enthusiastic playing did a great deal to establish the violin as a jazz instrument. He was originally self-taught as both a violinist and a pianist, although during 1924-28 he studied at the Paris Conservatoire. Grappelli played in movie theaters and dance bands before meeting guitarist Django Reinhardt in 1933. They hit it off musically from the start even though their lifestyles (Grappelli was sophisticated while Django was a gypsy) were very different. Together as the Quintet of the Hot Club of France (comprising violin, three acoustic guitars and bass) during 1933-39 they produced a sensational series of recordings and performances. During a London engagement in 1939, World War II broke out. Reinhardt rashly decided to return to France but Grappelli stayed in England, effectively ending the group. The violinist soon teamed up with the young pianist George Shearing in a new band that worked steadily through the war. In 1946 Grappelli and Reinhardt had the first of several reunions although they never worked together again on a regular basis (despite many new recordings). Grappelli performed throughout the 1950s and '60s in clubs throughout Europe and, other than recordings with Duke Ellington (*Violin Summit*) and Joe Venuti, he remained somewhat obscure in the US until he began regularly touring the world in the early '70s. Since then Grappelli was a constant traveller and a consistent pollwinner, remaining very open-minded without altering his swing style; he recorded with David Grisman, Earl Hines, Bill Coleman, Larry Coryell, Oscar Peterson, Jean Luc Ponty and McCoy Tyner among many others. Active up until near the end, the increasingly frail Grappelli remained at the top of his field even when he was 89. His early recordings are all available on Classics CDs and he recorded quite extensively during his final three decades. —*Scott Yanow*

★ **1935-1940** / Sep. 30, 1935-Jul. 30, 1940 / Classics ✦✦✦✦✦

This Classics CD has all of the recordings made under violinist Stephane Grappelli's name during the 1935-40 period. The earlier selections (with his Hot Four) match his violin with Django Reinhardt's guitar in what was essentially the Quintet of the Hot Club of France. There are also nine duets with Reinhardt; a couple find Grappelli switching to piano. The set concludes in 1940 with Grappelli (in London) leading an octet on two numbers that also feature the young pianist George Shearing. —*Scott Yanow*

1941-1943 / Feb. 28, 1941-Dec. 8, 1943 / Classics ♦♦♦♦♦

This Classics CD reissues some very rare recordings made by violinist Stephane Grappelli: all of his performances as a leader during a difficult three-year period. The violinist had decided to stay in England during World War II (when Django Reinhardt returned to France) and soon had a new group featuring the young pianist George Shearing. This CD has seven sessions with quartets and quintets along with one featuring a larger group that includes other strings and a harp. Although there are vocals on eight of the numbers (by Beryl Davis and Dave Fullerton), the swinging performances and the rarity of the recordings easily compensate. —*Scott Yanow*

Unique Piano Session / 1955 / Jazz Anthology ♦♦♦

Piano was Stephane Grappelli's first instrument and, although he has recorded occasionally on it through the years, this was the first of only two albums to feature Grappelli exclusively on piano. A relaxed stride player, Grappelli mostly performs originals and obscure material with a trio on this interesting but hard-to-find LP. —*Scott Yanow*

Violins No End / May 4, 1957 / Original Jazz Classics ♦♦♦♦

Since Joe Venuti was in the middle of a long off-period, this CD reissue features arguably the two top jazz violinists of the 1950s: Stephane Grappelli and Stuff Smith. Joined by pianist Oscar Peterson, guitarist Herb Ellis, bassist Ray Brown and drummer Jo Jones, the two masterful violinists share four songs ("Don't Get Around Much Anymore," "Chapeau Blues," "No Points Today" and "The Lady Is a Tramp") in a fine studio session that contrasts the styles of the fairly complementary fiddlers. In addition, although this set has been reissued under Grappelli's name, there are three songs from a Paris concert that took place the same day without Stephane. Stuff sounds in peak form on his "Desert Sands," "How High the Moon" and "Moonlight in Vermont." This fun set is easily recommended. —*Scott Yanow*

Feeling + Finesse = Jazz / Mar. 7, 1962-Mar. 9, 1962 / Atlantic ♦♦♦

Although he was very active in France during the 1950s and '60s, violinist Stephane Grappelli recorded relatively little until 1969. This Atlantic LP from 1962 finds Grappelli in good form in a quintet with guitarist Pierre Cavalli, performing a Django-dominated repertoire that is not all that different from what he would be playing 30 years later. —*Scott Yanow*

Two of a Kind / Jan. 23, 1965-Jan. 24, 1965 / Storyville ♦♦♦

Although it is hard to believe, discographies list this session (co-led with fellow violinist Svend Asmussen) as Stephane Grappelli's only recording as a leader during 1963-68. Accompanied by two guitarists, bassist Niels Henning Orsted Pedersen and a drummer, the two violinists (contemporaries whose similar styles matured in the 1930s) sound excellent on the LP, playing four standards, Toots Thielemans' "Blue Lady" and three of their originals. —*Scott Yanow*

Limehouse Blues / Jun. 23, 1969-Jun. 24, 1969 / Black Lion ♦♦♦♦

In 1969 violinist Stephane Grappelli and guitarist Barney Kessel teamed up for a few albums. This CD, in addition to five hot performances that originally came out on LP, has five previously unreleased performances from the same sessions. Throughout, the two principals (backed by rhythm guitarist Nini Rosso, bassist Michel Gaudry and drummer Jean-Louis Viale) are in top form, consistently inspiring each other. —*Scott Yanow*

Meets Barney Kessel / Jun. 23, 1969-Jun. 24, 1969 / Black Lion ♦♦♦♦♦

This excellent set features a logical combination. Violinist Stephane Grappelli originally came to fame through his recordings with guitarist Django Reinhardt. Barney Kessel, although more influenced by Charlie Christian than by Django, was one of the top jazz guitarists of the 1950s and '60s and his style was quite complementary to Grappelli's. The two teamed up for several albums' worth of material in 1969. This CD reissues the former LP *I Remember Django*, adding four additional selections and serving as a perfect introduction to the brilliant playing of Stephane Grappelli. —*Scott Yanow*

Venupelli Blues / Oct. 22, 1969 / Charly ♦♦♦♦♦

Stephane Grappelli and Joe Venuti, arguably the two top violinists in jazz history, only made one recording together, this heated 1969 studio session. With pianist George Wein and guitarist Barney Kessel helping out as part of the supporting four-piece rhythm section, Grappelli and Venuti often romp during the title cut and the six standards that comprise this memorable session. This violin "battle" ends up as a dead heat, a joyous and historic occasion for all concerned. —*Scott Yanow*

Afternoon in Paris / Mar. 1971 / Verve ♦♦♦

This is a typically flawless swing set by violinist Stephane Grappelli. Joined by pianist Marc Hemmeler, bassist Eberhard Weber and drummer Kenny Clare for a session originally cut for MPS, Grappelli mixes together sophisticated ballads with hotter stomps and uplifts the somewhat modern rhythm section. —*Scott Yanow*

Recorded Live at the Queen Elizabeth Hall London / Nov. 8, 1971 / PYE ♦♦♦

The early '70s found veteran violinist Stephane Grappelli recording regularly for a wide variety of labels. One of the most consistent of all jazz performers, Grappelli never made an indifferent record and virtually all of his sets are worth acquiring. On this LP, the violinist is joined by the Alan Clare Trio for a set of familiar but still exciting standards including "How About You," "This Can't Be Love," "Lady Be Good" and "Sweet Georgia Brown." —*Scott Yanow*

Jalousie: Music of the 30s / Jun. 14, 1972-Mar. 7, 1973 / Angel ♦♦

This was the first of three albums that matched together the two great violinists Stephane Grappelli and Yehudi Menuhin. They performed a set of superior standards (mostly from the 1920s and '30s) but unfortunately Menuhin was unable to improvise. The classical violinist does his best but his written parts weigh down the jazz content of this merely pleasant session. —*Scott Yanow*

Homage to Django / Jun. 19, 1972-Jun. 22, 1972 / Classic Jazz ♦♦♦♦

Violinist Stephane Grappelli has recorded many Django Reinhardt tributes during the past few decades. This double LP, which includes many originals co-written by Reinhardt and Grappelli in addition to a few 1930s standards, is one of his best. With the assistance of either Alan Clare or Marc Hemmeler on keyboards, guitarist Ernie Cranenburgh, bassist Lennie Bush and drummer Chris Karan, Grappelli is in top form on such rarely played numbers as "Tears," "Clopin-Clopant," "Are You in the Mood," "Sweet Chorus" and "Fantaisie." This classic music deserves to be reissued on CD. —*Scott Yanow*

Satin Doll / Nov. 12, 1972-Nov. 13, 1972 / Vanguard ♦♦♦

On this double LP, violinist Stephane Grapelli gets away from his usual tribute to the late Django Reinhardt and plays 15 standards including "Mack the Knife," "The Girl from Ipanema," "You Took Advantage of Me" and two versions of "Body and Soul." Accompanied by organist Eddy Louiss, pianist Marc Hemmeler, guitarist Jimmy Gourley, bassist Guy Pedersen and drummer Kenny Clarke, Grappelli is in typically flawless form for these enjoyable swing sessions. —*Scott Yanow*

Stephane Grappelli / Feb. 1973 / PYE ♦♦♦

One of many recordings made by violinist Stephane Grappelli in 1973 (at least eight albums), this budget release does not list personnel (pianist Alan Clare, bassist Lennie Bush and drummer Tony Crombie) or the recording date but it has some excellent music nevertheless. Highlights include "It Don't Mean a Thing," "Crazy Rhythm" and "Avalon." It's not essential but enjoyable. —*Scott Yanow*

Talk of the Town / Mar. 19, 1973 / Black Lion ♦♦

Violinist Stephane Grappelli plays a set of ballads in duet with pianist Alan Clare on this set. Although one wishes there were more variety in tempos and moods (and perhaps a little less taste), the results are pleasant enough and worth picking up for those who love Grappelli's timeless sound. —*Scott Yanow*

Just One of Those Things / Jul. 4, 1973 / Angel ♦♦♦♦♦

This is a typically swinging live set by the great violinist Stephane Grappelli, who is featured in a quartet with pianist Marc Hemmeler, bassist Jack Sewing and drummer Daniel Humair at the 1973 Montreux Jazz Festival. Grappelli, who was experiencing a bit of a renaissance at the time, sounds quite exuberant on many of the tunes, particularly "Just One of Those Things," "All God's Chillun Got Rhythm" and "Them There Eyes." This CD reissue gives listeners a fine example of Grappelli's joyous playing. —*Scott Yanow*

Parisian Thoroughfare / Sep. 5, 1973-Sep. 7, 1973 / Delta ♦♦♦

This collector's CD features violinist Stephane Grappelli in several settings. Grappelli takes a number apiece from 1960 and 1961 (both of which are erratically recorded) with European rhythm sections; performs three selections in a swinging quintet with guitarist Barney Kessel; and plays a heated "After You've Gone" in 1973 with the Diz Disley Trio. But the majority of this CD is from a 1975 set that matches the violinist with pianist Johnny Guarnieri, guitarist Jimmy Shirley (who recorded very infrequently this late in his career), bassist Slam Stewart and drummer Jackie Williams. The all-star encounter, which is full of delightful moments, is the main reason to acquire the set. *Parisian Thoroughfare* also has a unaccompanied Grappelli piano solo on "Sysmo," and during "Flonville," the leader is heard overdubbed on both violin and piano. An interesting package of formerly rare material. —*Scott Yanow*

I Got Rhythm / Nov. 5, 1973 / Black Lion ♦♦♦♦♦

This attractive two-LP set features violinist Stephane Grappelli playing a concert with one of his finest backup groups, The Hot Club of London (comprising guitarists Diz Disley and Denny Wright along with bassist Len Skeat). Together they perform nine standards, three Django Reinhardt tunes and a Gershwin medley with enthusiasm and mostly hard-driving swing. All of this music has since been reissued on a CD (*Live in London*) with one additional track added. —*Scott Yanow*

★ **Live in London** / Nov. 5, 1973 / Black Lion ✦✦✦✦✦
One of the best groups that violinist Stephane Grappelli collaborated with during the second half of his long career has been the Hot Club of London, a unit led by guitarist Diz Disley and usually including a second rhythm guitarist and a bassist. This Black Lion CD reissues the entire contents of a former two-LP set (*I Got Rhythm*) and even has room for a previously unreleased version of "Them There Eyes." Grappelli sounds particularly inspired playing with this group, very comfortable with the drumless setting and free to dominate the proceedings. —*Scott Yanow*

Stephane Grappelli / Bill Coleman / Dec. 1973 / Classic Jazz ✦✦✦✦
Bill Coleman, a fine swing trumpeter, settled in France in the 1930s and, other than during World War II, remained overseas for the remainder of his life. Somewhat underrated in jazz history books, he had a distinctive sound of his own. Coleman's musical reunion with violinist Stephane Grappelli (they had recorded together 35 years earlier) is a celebratory occasion, with spirited versions of nine standards resulting from their long-overdue joint recording. Not yet out on CD, this LP is well worth searching for. —*Scott Yanow*

Stephane Grappelli Meets Earl Hines / Jul. 4, 1974 / Black Lion ✦✦
This unusual duet session by violinist Stephane Grappelli and pianist Earl Hines had the potential for a lot of fireworks but is disappointingly relaxed. The emphasis is on ballads and, although Hines typically takes some chances with time during his solos, the music on the CD is on a whole overly tasteful and safe, well-played but not as memorable as it could have been. —*Scott Yanow*

The Reunion, With George Shearing / Apr. 11, 1976 / Verve ✦✦✦✦✦
Back in 1940 pianist George Shearing made his debut as a sideman with violinist Stephane Grappelli's new band. In 1976, over 30 years since they last played with each other, the two masters had a recorded reunion and they sounded as if they had been performing together for decades. With the assistance of bassist Andy Simpkins and drummer Rusty Jones, Grappelli and Shearing create some musical magic on nine standards and Grappelli's "La Chanson de Rue." —*Scott Yanow*

Tea for Two / Oct. 28, 1977-Oct. 30, 1977 / Angel ✦✦
For the third recorded meeting between violinists Stephane Grappelli and Yehudi Menuhin, the rhythm section is joined by some woodwinds on a few of the selections. Grappelli sounds fine but Menuhin's classical technique did not prepare him to improvise and he weighs down the proceedings a bit, making some of the ballads sound too sweet. This LP is therefore a historical curiosity rather than an essential acquisition. —*Scott Yanow*

Live at Carnegie Hall / Apr. 5, 1978 / Doctor Jazz ✦✦✦
Stephane Grappelli teams up once again with the Diz Disley Trio (which in 1978 comprised Disley and John Ethridge on guitars, along with bassist Brian Torff), and the results are often quite exciting. Grappelli is heard at his best on such songs as "I Can't Give You Anything But Love," "Crazy Rhythm" and even "Chattanooga Choo Choo." Few surprises occur, but this swinging music is enjoyable anyway. —*Scott Yanow*

Uptown Dance / Apr. 1978 / Columbia ✦✦✦✦
On this LP violinist Stephane Grappelli is heard in a different setting than usual, accompanied by a large orchestra arranged by Claus Ogerman. "Uptown Dance" is particularly catchy and most of the other songs, come across quite well. The supporting cast (which has pianist Jimmy Rowles and keyboardist Richard Tee alternating) is a major asset to this enjoyable set. —*Scott Yanow*

Young Django / Jan. 19, 1979-Jan. 21, 1979 / Verve ✦✦✦✦✦
This CD finds veteran violinist Stephane Grappelli joined by bassist Niels Pedersen and guitarists Philip Catherine and Larry Coryell for a memorable tribute to Django Reinhardt. Grappelli has recorded many Reinhardt memorial albums through the years but this one is particularly special for both Coryell and Catherine go out of their way to display the unexpected influence that Reinhardt has had on their styles. The guitarists contribute a song apiece and also enjoy playing seven compositions co-written by Django and Grappelli. —*Scott Yanow*

Live at Tivoli Gardens, Copenhagen, Denmark / Jul. 6, 1979 / Original Jazz Classics ✦✦✦✦
Stephane Grappelli's lone Pablo album matches his violin in trios with guitarist Joe Pass and bassist Niels Pedersen, two masters who could not only keep up with him but often inspired his solos. The repertoire is unsurprising as is the musical excellence but those are not good reasons to pass this set by. Recorded live in Copenhagen, Denmark, the trio brings fresh life to such old standards as "It's Only a Paper Moon," "Let's Fall in Love" and "I Get a Kick Out of You." —*Scott Yanow*

Stephane Grappelli and Hank Jones: A Two-Fer! / Jul. 20, 1979 / Muse ✦✦✦
The title of this Muse release is a bit inaccurate for this is but a single LP (not a two-fer). Actually its name was meant to signify that two giants were teamed up: violinist Stephane Grappelli and pianist Hank Jones. Assisted by bassist Jimmy Woode and drummer Alan Dawson, the duo are in fine form on seven familiar standards and the violinist's "Mellow Grapes." Few surprises occur but this swinging date finds everyone displaying spirit and creativity. —*Scott Yanow*

☆ **Stephane Grappelli and David Grisman Live** / Sep. 7, 1979-Sep. 20, 1979 / Warner Brothers ✦✦✦✦✦
One of the most exciting of the many Stephane Grappelli recordings, this live session (a straight CD reissue of the original LP) teams the veteran violinist with mandolist David Grisman's band, an ensemble that (in addition to its leader) boasts hot solos from Mike Marshall on violin, guitarist Mark O'Connor (who switches to violin to battle Grappelli on a memorable "Tiger Rag") and bassist Rob Wasserman. The first two songs ("Shine" and "Pent-Up House") are taken at breakneck tempos and then, after the group tries to cool off on "Misty," they really burn on "Sweet Georgia Brown" and "Tiger Rag." Essential music with more than its share of great solos. —*Scott Yanow*

Happy Reunion / Feb. 17, 1980-Feb. 18, 1980 / Owl ✦✦✦
This CD's title is a bit ironic, for violinist Stephane Grappelli and pianist Martial Solal (who are heard on a set of duets), although two of France's finest jazzmen, had only recorded together once before, and that was for a single selection in which they overdubbed their parts. This 1980 studio recording finds Solal reining in his adventurous style a bit so as to offer solid support for Grappelli. They perform six standards, two of Solal's pieces and a free improvisation. —*Scott Yanow*

At the Winery / Sep. 1980 / Concord Jazz ✦✦✦
Violinist Stephane Grappelli plays his usual repertoire (standards ranging from Stevie Wonder's "You Are the Sunshine of My Life" to "Chicago" and the Reinhardt-associated piece "Minor Swing") in a quartet with the guitars of John Etheridge and Martin Taylor and bassist Jack Sewing. The music, although a bit predictable, is enjoyable, for Grappelli has never lost his enthusiasm for playing swinging jazz. He performs "Let's Fall in Love" and "Love for Sale" as if he had just discovered those songs. —*Scott Yanow*

Vintage 1981 / Jul. 1981 / Concord Jazz ✦✦✦
For this outing, veteran violinist Stephane Grappelli (then 73) jams a variety of standards (several of which he had not recorded previously) with guitarists Martin Taylor and Mike Gari (in addition to bassist Jack Sewing). Grappelli, who switches to electric piano for Taylor's "Jamie" and adds Stevie Wonder's "Isn't She Lovely" to his repertoire, displays an open mind towards new music while retaining his classic swing style. —*Scott Yanow*

Live in San Francisco / Jul. 7, 1982 / Black Hawk ✦✦✦
This out-of-print LP features violinist Stephane Grappelli in a very comfortable setting with guitarists Diz Disley and Martin Taylor and bassist Jack Sewing; three players who he had recorded with many times in the 1970s and '80s. Performing live at San Francisco's Great American Music Hall, the quartet interprets veteran jazz standards plus the Beatles' "Here, There and Everywhere" and Stevie Wonder's "You Are the Sunshine of My Life." Few surprises occur but the music consistently swings and Grappelli is in excellent form. —*Scott Yanow*

Stephanova / Jun. 1983 / Concord Jazz ✦✦✦✦
For this Concord LP, violinist Stephane Grappelli is joined by guitarist Marc Fosset for a set of sparse but swinging duets. The repertoire, which includes "Tune Up," Grieg's "Norwegian Dance," Grappelli's "Waltz for Queenie" and two Fosset originals, is fresher than usual and Grappelli is up to the challenge. —*Scott Yanow*

Grappelli Plays Jerome Kern / 1987 / GRP ✦✦✦✦
This CD is much more unusual for the GRP label than it is for violinist Stephane Grappelli. Joined by two guitars (Marc Fossett and Martin Taylor), bass, drums and a subtle string orchestra, Grappelli comes up with fresh statements on 11 Jerome Kern songs including such classics as "The Way You Look Tonight," "All the Things You Are," "Pick Yourself Up" and "I Won't Dance." —*Scott Yanow*

Olympia 1988 / Jan. 24, 1988 / Atlantic ✦✦✦
Violinist Stephane Grappelli has recorded so many fine sets during the past two decades that, although virtually all of them are enjoyable, most are not essential. This fine concert performance with a quartet (which also includes the guitars of Marc Fosset and Martin Taylor) is typical of Grappelli's ability to infuse familiar melodies that he has performed a countless number of times with enthusiasm, energy and wit. Pianist Martial Solal and violinist Svend Asmussen make guest appearances but most of the focus is on the great Grappelli, who never seems to have an off day. —*Scott Yanow*

My Other Love / 1990 / Columbia ✦✦✦
This is one of only two full sets from his entire career that features violinist Stephane Grappelli exclusively on his first instrument, the piano. On this solo CD,

Grappelli mostly plays slower and romantic renditions of standards (along with three originals) and shows that he could have made a living for himself through the years on his "Other Love." Tasty music that largely succeeds. —*Scott Yanow*

One on One, With McCoy Tyner / Apr. 18, 1990 / Milestone ✦✦✦✦
Violinist Stephane Grappelli, although a veteran of the swing era, has always kept an open mind towards newer styles even while he has retained his own sound and veteran repertoire. This duet set with pianist McCoy Tyner might seem unlikely at first glance but it works quite well. The duo sticks to standards (including two that are associated with John Coltrane) and find plenty of common ground. The mutual respect they have for each other is obvious and they both sound a bit inspired. —*Scott Yanow*

In Tokyo / Oct. 4, 1990 / Denon ✦✦✦✦
Although 82 at the time of this concert, violinist Stephane Grappelli plays with the fire and enthusiasm of a musician half his age. The repertoire is generally fairly familiar but the music (performed in trios with guitarist Marc Fosset and bassist Jean-Philippe Viret) consistently swings and there is nothing predictable or tired about Grappelli's solos. With Marcel Azzola making a few guest spots on accordion, this fine straightahead set is easily recommended as an example of the youthful Stephane Grappelli. —*Scott Yanow*

So Easy to Remember / 1993 / Omega ✦✦✦
Violinist Stephane Grappelli celebrated his 85th birthday in style, playing the same rollicking, joyful "hot" jazz licks he's made with numerous jazz men throughout his estimable career. Working with a talented veteran crew that includes bassist Ron Carter, guitarists Bucky Pizzarelli and Kenny Burrell and drummer Grady Tate, the group easily but impeccably negotiates a program blending standards, ballads and flagwaving stompers, offering both crisp, superb solos and flawless ensemble performances. It's the kind of date that's so relaxed and professional that it's often unjustly overlooked. —*Ron Wynn*

Live 1992 / Mar. 27, 1992-Mar. 28, 1992 / Verve ✦✦✦✦
Fifty-eight years after the first recordings of The Quintet of the Hot Club of France, its violinist Stephane Grappelli still sounds young on this date. Much of the repertoire on this CD stems from the 1930s (including such pieces as "Minor Swing," "Tears" and "Sweet Chorus," all three of which were co-composed by Grappelli and guitarist Django Reinhardt) but Grappelli has retained his enthusiasm and creativity. Performing in a top-notch quartet with two guitars (Philip Catherine and Marc Fosset) and bassist Niels Pedersen, Grappelli is in excellent form and performs a joyous set of melodic swing. —*Scott Yanow*

Flamingo / Jun. 15, 1995-Jun. 17, 1995 / Dreyfus ✦✦✦✦
This CD features a logical combination of two talented Frenchmen, violinist Stephane Grappelli and pianist Michel Petrucciani, who had never recorded together before. With the assistance of bassist George Mraz and drummer Roy Haynes, the co-leaders romp on a variety of standards. Petrucciani was 32 at the time of this June 1995 set, a mere child compared to the 87-year old Grappelli. Despite his age, Grappelli's violin playing sounds as youthful and enthusiastic as it had been in the 1930s; the 60 years of practice had not hurt. While Petrucciani's music is usually in the Bill Evans post-bop vein, he was happy to visit Grappelli's turf on this occasion, mostly playing veteran standards. On such songs as "Sweet Georgia Brown," "How About You" (here mistitled "I Love New York in June"), "I Remember April" and "There Will Never Be Another You," Stephane Grappelli is both joyful and masterful. Highly recommended. —*Scott Yanow*

Celebrating Grappelli / 1997 / Honest ✦✦✦✦

Milford Graves

b. Aug. 20, 1941, New York, NY
Drums / Free Jazz
Milford Graves has been among the flashiest drummers in the free mode, known for skillful inclusion of Asian and African rhythmic ingredients into his solos. He studied Indian music extensively, including learning the tabla from Wasantha Singh. He has unfortunately not recorded much in recent years, especially on American labels. Graves played congas as a child, then switched to trap drums at 17, before his tabla studies with Singh. During the '60s Graves worked with Giuseppi Logan and the New York Art Quartet. He recorded on ESP in the mid-'60s with Logan, and was an original member of the Jazz Composers' Orchestra Association. Graves also played with Hugh Masekela and Miriam Makeba in the early '60s. His appearance in the Bill Dixon-sponsored concert series "The October Revolution in Jazz" helped introduce Graves to a wider audience. He did two albums of duets with pianist Don Pullen at Yale in 1966. Graves worked regularly with Albert Ayler in 1967 and 1968, performing at the 1967 Newport Festival. He also played with Hugh Glover, and worked in a duo with Andrew Cyrille. During the '70s Graves participated in a series of mid-'70s concerts called "Dialogue of the

Drums" with Cyrille and Rashied Ali, including several shows in Black neighborhoods. Graves taught at Bennington College alongside Bill Dixon in the '70s, and toured Europe and Japan. During the '80s, he played in percussion ensembles with Cyrille, Kenny Clarke and Don Moye. Philly Joe Jones later replaced Clarke. —*Ron Wynn*

● **Milford Graves Percussion Ensemble** / Jul. 1965 / ESP ✦✦✦✦
This CD reissue (rather brief at thirty-four-and-a-half minutes) is of limited interest, for it consists of five pieces featuring Milford Graves and the obscure Sunny Morgan as a drum duo. The songs ("Nothing 5-7," "Nothing 11-10," "Nothing 19," "Nothing 13" and "Nothing") largely live up to their titles. Although one can appreciate the audacity of this music, there is nothing memorable about these spontaneous but directionless performances. Mostly just of historic interest. —*Scott Yanow*

The Graves Pullen Duo / Apr. 30, 1966 / Pullen Graves Music ✦✦✦

Anita Gravine

b. Carbondale, PA
Vocals / Bop, Standards
Considering how exciting an album Anita Gravine's *I Always Knew* was in 1985, it is surprising that she has not caught on yet as one of the top jazz singers. In the mid-'60s she sang with the bands of Larry Elgart, Buddy Morrow and Urbie Green. Gravine made her solo debut with *Dream Dancing* on Progressive in the early '80s; *I Always Knew* really displayed her appealing voice, solid sense of swing and versatility. But since then her only jazz recording, *Welcome to My Dream* (recorded in 1986 but not released on Jazz Alliance until 1993), was a disappointment due to weak material (songs from the Bob Hope/Bing Crosby *Road* pictures) and uninspired arrangements that take the songs much too seriously. Hopefully much more will be heard from Anita Gravine in the future. —*Scott Yanow*

Dream Dancing / Sep. 12, 1983-Sep. 13, 1983 / Progressive ✦✦✦✦

★ **I Always Knew** / Oct. 1984 / Stash ✦✦✦✦✦
One of the top vocal albums of the mid-1980s, everything works on this set. Anita Gravine, who had only recorded once previously as a leader (and would have to wait until 1993 until her third release was put out), takes lots of chances on ten selections and is consistently successful. With such fine musicians as pianist Mike Abene (responsible for the inventive arrangements), bassist George Mraz, drummer Billy Hart and guests like trumpeter Tom Harrell and a string section, Gravine really digs into such songs as "Thanks a Million," "I'm Confessin'" (taken as a duet with Mraz), "Not For All the Rice In China," "Look for the Silver Lining," and a delightful version of "The Coffee Song." This is a gem. —*Scott Yanow*

Welcome to My Dream / Nov. 1986 / Jazz Alliance ✦✦
Anita Gravine is a particularly talented jazz singer but this set (which was released for the first time in 1994) is a surprising dud. Gravine interprets ten songs from the Bing Crosby/Bob Hope road movies but Michael Abene's arrangements for the small big band rob the mostly lightweight ditties of their good-natured humor and they cannot stand the glaring light given them as "contemporary art." Only "Moonlight Becomes You" became a standard and to hear songs such as "Road to Morocco" and "Good-Time Charley" given such serious treatment is unintentionally laughable. Anita Gravine deserves to be recorded under much more logical circumstances. —*Scott Yanow*

Wardell Gray

b. Feb. 13, 1921, Oklahoma City, OK, d. May 25, 1955, Las Vegas, NV
Tenor Saxophone / Bop, Swing
Wardell Gray was one of the top tenors to emerge during the bop era (along with Dexter Gordon and Teddy Edwards). His Lester Young-influenced tone made his playing attractive to swing musicians as well as younger modernists. He grew up in Detroit, playing in local bands as a teenager. Gray was with Earl Hines during 1943-45, recording with him (1945). That same year he moved to Los Angeles and he became a major part of the Central Avenue scene, having nightly tenor battles with Dexter Gordon; their recording of "The Chase" was popular. Gray recorded with Charlie Parker in 1947 and yet his style appealed to Benny Goodman with whom he played the following year. Among his own sessions, his solos on "Twisted" (1949) and "Farmer's Market" (1952) were turned into memorable vocalese by Annie Ross a few years later. Back in New York, Gray played and recorded with Tadd Dameron and the Count Basie septet and big band (1950-51); "Little Pony," his showcase with the Basie orchestra, is a classic. Gray was featured on some Norman Granz jam sessions ("Apple Jam" has a particularly heated solo) and recorded with Louie Bellson (1952-53). Ironically Wardell Gray, who in the late '40s was an inspiration to some younger musicians due to his opposition to drug use, himself became involved in drugs and died mysteriously in Las Vegas on May 25, 1955, when he was just 34. —*Scott Yanow*

Wardell Gray and the Big Bands / Sep. 1945-Sep. 1953 / Official ◆◆◆◆
This very interesting LP features tenor saxophonist Wardell Gray as a sideman with the big bands of Earl Hines, Benny Goodman, Count Basie, and Louie Bellson, plus small groups led by Billy Eckstine and Bellson. Covering virtually his entire short career, the album is full of rarities (particularly the Hines numbers) and has among its highlights "The Hucklebuck," "Little Pony" (a classic with Basie) and "The Jeep Is Jumping." —*Scott Yanow*

One for Prez / Nov. 23, 1946 / Black Lion ◆◆◆◆
On November 23, 1946, tenor saxophonist Wardell Gray recorded five numbers with pianist Dodo Marmarosa, bassist Red Callender and drummer Chuck Thompson. This CD has 16 performances in all, the original five tunes plus 11 alternate takes (including five versions of "How High the Moon," which was retitled at the time as "One for Prez"). The playing is excellent, but the repetition of titles makes the set of primary interest to completists rather than casual listeners. —*Scott Yanow*

Wardell Gray / Stan Hasselgård / Apr. 29, 1947-Sep. 1948 / Spotlite ◆◆◆◆
This historic Spotlite LP has live performances from 1947-48, important years in the history of bop. Wardell Cray is featured in a Los Angeles-based sextet with trumpeter Howard McGhee, altoist Sonny Criss and pianist Dodo Marmarosa for three lengthy versions of bop anthems; the tenor is showcased with the Count Basie Orchestra on six forward-looking selections and he teams up with the doomed clarinetist Stan Hasselgård in a sextet for two jams. The music is reasonably well recorded considering its date and source, and the solos are frequently quite exciting. Jazz historians in particular are advised to search for this one. —*Scott Yanow*

★ **Wardell Gray Memorial, Vol. 1** / Nov. 11, 1949-1953 / Original Jazz Classics ◆◆◆◆◆
Originally released as two LPs and then a two-LP set, tenorman Wardell Gray's Prestige recordings are now available as two CDs that have been expanded by the inclusion of alternate takes only previously available on the collector's Misterioso label. The music on this particular CD is taken from two sessions: a quartet outing with pianist Al Haig, bassist Tommy Potter and drummer Roy Haynes, and a sextet session with pianist Sonny Clark, vibraphonist Teddy Charles and the young altoist Frank Morgan. The former date is highlighted by the famous "Twisted," which Annie Ross would soon record in a vocalese version. This CD actually has four versions of "Twisted" (along with seven of "Southside"), so there is a bit of repetition, but the great tenor Wardell Gray is heard throughout in prime form. —*Scott Yanow*

Wardell Gray Memorial, Vol. 2 / Aug. 27, 1950+Jan. 21, 1952 / Original Jazz Classics ◆◆◆◆◆
The second of two CDs reissuing tenor saxophonist Wardell Gray's Prestige recordings features Gray in three different settings. Nine-minute versions of "Scrapple From the Apple" and "Move" were recorded live in L.A. with trumpeter Clark Terry, altoist Sonny Criss, a boppish rhythm section and (on "Move") the competitive tenor of Dexter Gordon. Otherwise, Gray is heard in the studios with a quartet and a sextet that includes trumpeter Art Farmer and pianist Hampton Hawes. The latter date resulted in "Jackie," which (like "Twisted") would soon become a vocalese hit for Annie Ross. Six alternate takes round out this strong reissue. —*Scott Yanow*

Live at the Haig / Sep. 9, 1952 / Fresh Sound ◆◆◆◆
This decently recorded live session features tenor saxophonist Wardell Gray, trumpeter Art Farmer, pianist Hampton Hawes, bassist Joe Mondragon and drummer Shelly Manne stretching out on eight numbers (most of which clock in at 7-10 minutes). Originally a Xanadu LP, the CD reissue adds "Lady Bird" to the original set, which is highlighted by "The Squirrel," "Jackie," "Donna Lee" and "Get Happy." Because of his consistency and truncated life, every Wardell Gray recording is well worth picking up. —*Scott Yanow*

Great Guitars

Group f. 1973/ Bop
A sporadically recurring supergroup featuring Charlie Byrd, Herb Ellis and Barney Kessel, Great Guitars' portentous name carries enormous expectations. But with world-class talent like these three operating in comfortable mainstream country, the music is usually worthy of the billing, genially swinging and harmonically erudite, with Byrd's classical and Latin influences playing against Ellis' and Kessel's Charlie Christian-grounded solo bop. Founded in 1973, Great Guitars recorded its first live album in July of 1974—it was the fledgling Concord Jazz label's fourth release—and the three would reunite now and then to tour and record four more albums. Though a crippling stroke in 1992 ended Barney Kessel's career, Byrd and Ellis carried on with Great Guitars, adding Ron Escheté to the lineup at the Carl Jefferson tribute concert at the Concord Pavilion in July 1995

and recording a fine reunion album in 1996 with Mundell Lowe and, on five tracks, Larry Coryell. —*Richard S. Ginell*

● **Great Guitars** / Apr. 1976 / Concord Jazz ◆◆◆◆◆
The second Great Guitars album features guitarists Charlie Byrd, Barney Kessel and Herb Ellis matching wits and generally inspiring each other throughout this studio set. The trio, along with bassist Joe Byrd and drummer Wayne Philips, are heard together on four numbers (best are "Lover" and Ellis' "Outer Drive"); Ellis and Kessel duet on "Makin' Whoopee," Byrd has two features to himself, and a medley combines together short versions of "Nuages" and "Goin' Out of My Head" with the typically exuberant "Flying Home." A fine all-around effort. —*Scott Yanow*

Great Guitars at Charlie's Georgetown / Aug. 1982 / Concord Jazz ◆◆◆◆
The Great Guitars' fifth and final recording with their original three guitarists (Charlie Byrd, Herb Ellis and Barney Kessel) is another excellent effort, although a bit lazier than their previous records. Bassist Joe Byrd and drummer Chuck Redd contribute tasteful support. Other than "Get Happy," most of the selections (which include "Where or When," "Opus One," "Old Folks" and even a soulful "When the Saints Go Marching In") are taken at slow to medium tempos, but the interplay between the guitarists is always impressive and swinging. —*Scott Yanow*

Great Guitars at the Winery / July 1980 / Concord Jazz ◆◆◆◆
This exciting live session is fairly definitive of the Great Guitars. With fine support offered by bassist Joe Byrd and drummer Jimmie Smith, guitarists Charlie Byrd, Barney Kessel and Herb Ellis romp on such swinging numbers as "Broadway," "Air Mail Special" and "Straighten Up and Fly Right." As usual, Byrd, with his grounding in classical guitar, is the most distinctive, while Kessel and Ellis constantly pay tribute to Charlie Christian. This combination worked quite well, and each of the Great Guitars' five recordings are easily recommended to fans of bop guitar. —*Scott Yanow*

Straight Tracks / Mar. 13, 1978 / Concord Jazz ◆◆◆◆

The Return of the Great Guitars / Feb. 14, 1996-Feb. 15, 1996 / Concord Jazz ◆◆◆◆
The first recording by the Great Guitars in over a decade has a change in personnel. A serious stroke had ended Barney Kessel's career but Herb Ellis and Charlie Byrd were still very much active. Fellow veteran guitarist Mundell Lowe took Kessel's place, and as a wildcard, on eight of the 13 selections the versatile Larry Coryell is heard on fourth guitar. With fine backup by bassist John Goldsby and drummer Tim Horner, the guitarists swing hard on a variety of bop and swing-oriented tunes including "Things Ain't What They Used to Be," "A Smooth One," "The Lady in Red" and "Seven Come Eleven" in addition to some more recent originals. —*Scott Yanow*

Bennie Green

b. Apr. 16, 1923, Chicago, IL, **d.** Mar. 23, 1977, San Diego, CA
Trombone / Bop, Swing
Bennie Green was one of the few trombonists of the 1950s who played in a style not influenced by J.J. Johnson (Bill Harris was another). His witty sound and full tone looked backwards to the swing era yet was open to the influence of R&B. After playing locally in Chicago, he was with the Earl Hines Orchestra during 1942-48 (except for two years in the military). Green gained some fame for his work with Charlie Ventura (1948-50) before joining Earl Hines' small group (1951-53). He then led his own group throughout the 1950s and '60s, using such sidemen as Cliff Smalls, Charlie Rouse, Eric Dixon, Paul Chambers, Louis Hayes, Sonny Clark, Gildo Mahones and Jimmy Forrest. Green recorded regularly as a leader for Prestige, Decca, Blue Note, Vee-Jay, Time, Bethlehem and Jazzland during 1951-61 although only one further session (a matchup with Sonny Stitt on Cadet in 1964) took place. Bennie Green was with Duke Ellington for a few months in 1968-69 and then moved to Las Vegas where he spent his last years working in hotel bands although he did emerge to play quite well at the 1972 Newport Jazz Festival in New York jam sessions. —*Scott Yanow*

● **Bennie Green Blows His Horn** / Jun. 10, 1955+Sep. 22, 1955 / Original Jazz Classics ◆◆◆◆◆
This is fun music. Bennie Green, one of the few trombonists of the 1950s not to sound somewhat like a J.J. Johnson clone, always had a likable and humorous style. He blends in well with tenor saxophonist Charlie Rouse on these standards, blues and jump tunes, two of which have group vocals. With a fine rhythm section (pianist Cliff Smalls, bassist Paul Chambers, drummer Osie Johnson and Candido on congas), Green and his band show that there is no reason that swinging jazz has to be viewed as overly intellectual and esoteric. This CD (a reissue of the original LP) is a fine example of Bennie Green's talents and winning musical personality. —*Scott Yanow*

With Art Farmer / Apr. 13, 1956 / Original Jazz Classics ✦✦✦

Trombonist Bennie Green and trumpeter Art Farmer (with the assistance of pianist Cliff Smalls, bassist Addison Farmer and drummer Philly Joe Jones) challenge each other on these five selections which include an original apiece by the two horns and Smalls in addition to cheerful renditions of "My Blue Heaven" and "Gone with the Wind." The playing is not flawless on this CD reissue of a rather brief (under 34 minutes) LP but the soloists take chances and the music is often exciting. It's recommended to straightahead jazz fans. — *Scott Yanow*

Walking Down / Jun. 29, 1956 / Original Jazz Classics ✦✦✦✦

The third of Bennie Green's three Prestige albums from 1955-56 features the personable trombonist in a quintet with the young tenor saxophonist Eric Dixon (here showing a strong Paul Gonsalves influence) and an obscure but swinging rhythm section (pianist Lloyd Mayers, bassist Sonny Wellesley and drummer Bill English). The solos are colorful if occasionally stumbling and the arrangements of the four standards and Green's "East of the Little Big Horn" have their share of surprises; "Walkin'" and "The Things We Did Last Summer" are taken at two different tempos while "It's You or No One," normally a ballad, really cooks. This straight CD reissue of the original LP is worth picking up. — *Scott Yanow*

Back on the Scene / Mar. 23, 1958 / Blue Note ✦✦✦

It's evident from the opening pair of Latin-flavored performances that *Back on the Scene* is one of Bennie Green's most diverse efforts. Green's warm, supple tone and fondness for swinging, bop-influenced mainstream jazz and jump blues hasn't disappeared; he's just found new facets in his style. The infectious Latin rhythms on Cole Porter's "I Love You" and "Melba's Mood" are welcome, as is "You're Mine You," which showcases Green's sensitive ballad style. Reviving the standard "Just Friends" emphasizes the trombonist's ties to big band and bop, particularly through tenor saxophonist Charlie Rouse's strong solos. The jumping "Bennie Plays the Blues" and "Green Street" are also terrific, finding Green, Rouse and pianist Joe Knight trading full-bodied solos. Even with this vast array of styles, *Back on the Scene* retains all the good-natured spirit and humor of his earlier Prestige albums. — *Stephen Thomas Erlewine*

Soul Stirrin' / Apr. 28, 1958 / Blue Note ✦✦✦✦

Soul Stirrin' is an invigorating, exciting date from trombonist Bennie Green, showcasing his wide range of skills. His tone is alternately boisterous and reflective—the juxtaposition of the wildly swinging "We Wanna Cook" (complete with shouted vocals) and the gentle "That's All" is startling, demonstrating that Green can vary his robust sound according to the occasion. Green's fluid trombone is at the center stage throughout most of *Soul Stirrin'*, but he also steps aside to shine some light on his extraordinary support group—saxophonists Gene Ammons and Billy Root, pianist Sonny Clark, bassist Ike Isaacs and drummer Elvin Jones. Each musician plays with soul and passion, both on the laidback blues and mambos and the rollicking swing numbers. It's a thoroughly enjoyable record and one that is a good introduction to Green's wonderful, friendly style. — *Stephen Thomas Erlewine*

The Swingin'est / Nov. 12, 1958 / Vee-Jay ✦✦

The emphasis is on the blues and very basic chord changes on this relaxed jam session. With trombonist Bennie Green leading an octet that also includes the tenors of Gene Ammons and Frank Foster, trumpeter Nat Adderley, Frank Wess on tenor and flute and a rhythm section led by pianist Tommy Flanagan, everyone has plenty of opportunities to solo. Due to the similarity of the material plus three alternate takes that have been added to augment the original program, it is advisable to listen to this CD in small doses. — *Scott Yanow*

The 45 Session / Nov. 23, 1958 / Blue Note ✦✦✦✦

Trombonist Bennie Green cut four sessions for Blue Note Records, three of which were released as full-length LPs. At the remaining session, the group cut a series of eight songs that were intended for release as singles—as reissue producer Michael Cuscuna points out, several songs fade out at the end on the master tapes, cutting off solos just as they're beginning to take off. The Japanese issue *The 45 Session* collects all nine masters, including one alternate take of Babs Gonzales' vocal tribute to Bennie, "Encore." Considering the strength of Green's combo—it boasted pianist Sonny Clark, bassist Paul Chambers, tenor saxophonist Eddy Williams and drummer Jerry Segal—it's a bit frustrating to hear the songs in truncated form, but since that's the only way they exist, fans should cherish what we do have. And this is music to cherish. Green's Blue Note recordings are consistently fun, and this is no exception. Each song swings with energy, offering each instrumentalist a chance to shine—the piano-handclap breakdown on "Minor Revelation" is as infectious as the blowing "It's Groovy" or the swinging interpretation of "Why Do I Love You." This is cheery, bluesy, good-natured music, and even if Gonzales' hipster salute to Green has dated a bit, the rest of the music is as appealing today as when it was recorded. — *Stephen Thomas Erlewine*

Walkin' and Talkin' / Jan. 25, 1959 / Blue Note ✦✦✦✦

All of Bennie Green's Blue Note records were rich with joyously swinging blues and bop, highlighted by his warm, friendly tone and good humor. *Walkin' & Talkin'*, his third record for the label, was no exception to the rule. Leading a quintet that features tenor saxophonist Eddy Williams, pianist Gildo Mahones, bassist George Tucker and drummer Al Dreares, Green keeps things light, swinging and immensely entertaining. Mahones wrote three of the six songs, including the swinging opener "The Shouter" and the Latin-tinged "Green Leaves"; Green contributed the bluesy title track, and the group offers two standards—engaging, lightly swinging readings of "This Love of Mine" and "All I Do Is Dream of You." The result is no different than Green's two previous Blue Note records, but it's no less satisfying, and fans of swinging bop should be contented with *Walkin' & Talkin'*. — *Stephen Thomas Erlewine*

Bennie Green / Sep. 27, 1960 / Bainbridge ✦✦✦

Trombonist Bennie Green and tenor saxophonist Jimmy Forrest make a potent team on this fine middle-of-the-road 1960 set. Performing three selections by their pianist Sonny Clark, an obscurity, "Solitude," and "Sometimes I'm Happy," Green and Forrest both display extroverted emotions and plenty of swinging ideas. Also heard from are bassist George Tucker, drummer Al Dreares and Joseph Gorgas on bongos. This Time set was last reissued by Bainbridge, although it was put out on CD in Japan. — *Scott Yanow*

Catwalk / Dec. 1960 / Bethlehem ✦✦✦✦

Trombonist Bennie Green's music was always fun—mostly basic blues, ballads and standards played in a naturally accessible fashion. This obscure Bethlehem LP (not yet reissued on CD) features the distinctive trombonist in two settings. Three songs have a sextet with tenor saxophonist Jimmy Forrest (who sits out on Green's feature on "My Foolish Heart"), organist Skip Hall (a routine player), bassist Bull Ruther, drummer Art Taylor, and Tommy Lopez on conga. The other five numbers feature the same group with altoist Lem Davis added and pianist Mal Waldron taking Hall's place. Fine music that has long been overlooked. — *Scott Yanow*

Benny Green

b. Apr. 4, 1963, New York, NY
Piano / Hard Bop

Although not yet an innovator himself, Benny Green has managed to combine the styles of Bobby Timmons, Wynton Kelly, Gene Harris and especially Oscar Peterson in his playing; his fast octave runs are often wondrous. He grew up in Berkeley and played as a teenager with Joe Henderson and Woody Shaw. After moving to New York he spent important periods with Betty Carter (1983-87) and Art Blakey's Jazz Messengers (1987-89), becoming quite well-known during the latter association. In addition to working with Freddie Hubbard, Green popped up in many bop-oriented settings for a few years before joining Ray Brown's Trio in 1992. At the same time he has worked with his own trio which originally included Christian McBride and Carl Allen. When Oscar Peterson in 1992 was asked to name his protegé for a concert, Green was his choice. Benny Green has recorded for Criss Cross and Blue Note in addition to his work with Ray Brown on Telarc and his earlier Blakey dates. — *Scott Yanow*

Prelude / Feb. 1988 / Criss Cross ✦✦✦

Pianist Benny Green's debut as a leader (the first of two Criss Cross releases) was indeed a prelude to his long string of Blue Note recordings. Already a brilliant player who had been in Betty Carter's group and with Art Blakey's Jazz Messengers for a year, Green was at 24 on the brink of jazz stardom. He holds his own with some notable sidemen (trumpeter Terence Blanchard, tenor saxophonist Javon Jackson, bassist Peter Washington and drummer Tony Reedus), performing Duke Ellington's "Take the Coltrane," a pair of obscurities and two of his originals. The music is advanced hard bop and easily recommended to straightahead jazz fans. — *Scott Yanow*

Lineage / Jan. 30, 1990-Feb. 1, 1990 / Blue Note ✦✦✦✦

Benny Green, 27 at the time of this CD, is a modern jazz classicist who has absorbed the music of many bop-oriented pianists into his own style. Hearing him play Bobby Timmons' "Dat Dere" makes it easy to believe that Green is a graduate of Art Blakey's Jazz Messengers. Whether it be a rendition of "See See Rider" (very much in Red Garland's chordal style), the classic bop of Elmo Hope's "Crazy," a tender "I'll Wait and Pray" (one of three unaccompanied solos) or a lazy "Lil' Darlin'," Green plays quite creatively while remaining within the hard-bop tradition. With the assistance of bassist Ray Drummond and drummer Victor Lewis, Green's octave runs and general good taste are impressive if not innovative. This CD is a good example of his talents. — *Scott Yanow*

In This Direction / Dec. 29, 1988-Jan. 2, 1989 / Criss Cross ✦✦✦✦

For his second album as a leader, pianist Benny Green is showcased in a trio with bassist Buster Wiliams and drummer Lewis Nash. Nearing the end of his two-year stint with Art Blakey's Jazz Messengers, Green had mixed together elements of Bobby Timmons and Oscar Peterson in his own impressive style. He performs two numbers apiece by Buster Williams and Bud Powell (including "I'll Keep Lovin' You"), the standard "What Is There to Say," Thelonious Monk's complex "Trinkle Tinkle," and his own "Dealin' with a Feelin'" on a well-rounded and consistently swinging outing. —*Scott Yanow*

Greens / Mar. 4, 1991-Mar. 5, 1991 / Blue Note ✦✦✦✦
One can judge this CD on two different levels. As far as originality goes, pianist Benny Green at age 27 seemed content on his trio date with bassist Christian McBride and drummer Carl Allen to sound like a close relative of Bobby Timmons, Oscar Peterson, and Gene Harris, with touches of Bud Powell; his style at this point in time was quite derivative. But for upbeat, swinging, soulful music, the set fits the bill. Such songs as "Battle Hymn of the Republic," "Soon," "Cute" and "Shiny Stockings" certainly were not in need of being recorded again, and even Green's originals sound strangely familiar. But the trio's enthusiasm, virtuosity and tightness give the music more life than it probably deserves. —*Scott Yanow*

● **Testifyin'!: Live at the Village Vanguard** / Nov. 1991 / Blue Note ✦✦✦✦✦
A former member of Betty Carter's band, Green shows on this set that the word on him was correct; he's both an aggressive and sensitive stylist, able to rip through songs and make quick, yet correct chord changes. Yet he can also play a passionate ballad and not rush through it, instead developing and then completing his solos impressively. —*Ron Wynn*

That's Right! / Dec. 21, 1992-Dec. 23, 1992 / Blue Note ✦✦✦✦✦
At the time of this 1992 recording, Benny Green had developed into a masterful pianist who thought fast, swung hard and played with soul, mixing together Oscar Peterson, Gene Harris and Bobby Timmons. The only problem was that his music had become somewhat predictable, sticking closely to the boundaries of hard bop circa 1962. In his trio with bassist Christian McBride and drummer Carl Allen, Green is heard in top form for the period (his version of Bud Powell's "Celia" is particularly memorable) and performs a program that is easily recommended to lovers of bop. Benny Green plays with such enthusiasm and joy that it almost sounds as if he had invented the style. —*Scott Yanow*

Place to Be / Mar. 1994-May 1994 / Blue Note ✦✦✦✦
Benny Green continued to show gradual growth throughout the 1990s. For this outing with his 1994 trio (which also includes bassist Christian McBride and drummer Kenny Washington), Green shows off the influence of Oscar Peterson and other predecessors, but also displays his own musical voice during a mixture of originals, jazz standards (including "I Want to Talk About You," "Pensativa" and "The Folks Who Live on the Hill") and lesser-known tunes. Three songs add six horns orchestrated by Green and Bob Belden, and a special highlight is Green's solo rendition of Oscar Peterson's "Noreen's Nocturne." Overall, this CD is an excellent example of Benny Green's playing and writing talents. —*Scott Yanow*

Kaleidoscope / Jan. 28, 1997 / Blue Note ✦✦✦
Pianist Benny Green proves himself to be a seasoned composer on this collection of originals. "The Sexy Mexy" nods to Horace Silver with some crisp unison guitar from Russell Malone. The upbeat "Central Park South" features Stanley Turrentine, while the pianist's hypnotic "Thursday Lullaby" shows off his considerable chops. Ron Carter and Lewis Nash round out the capable rhythm section. —*Ken Dryden*

Bunky Green

b. Apr. 23, 1935, Milwaukee, WI
Alto Saxophone / Hard Bop, Post-Bop
Bunky Green has long had his own sound but unfortunately most of his recordings have gone long out of print as he has conducted a career as an educator (including a term as the president of the International Association of Jazz Educators). After playing locally, in 1960 he had a stint with Charles Mingus. That year Green moved to Chicago where he played with Ira Sullivan, Andrew Hill, Louie Bellson, Yusef Lateef and Sonny Stitt among others. Originally strongly influenced by Charlie Parker, Green spent a period reassessing his style and studying, emerging with a much more distinctive sound. He recorded for Exodus (1960) and Argo (1964-66) but his best work was his mid- to late '70s recordings for Vanguard and a 1989 session for Delos. A self-described "inside/outside" player, Bunky Green has had an influence on the styles of Steve Coleman and Greg Osby. —*Scott Yanow*

Transformations / Nov. 1976 / Vanguard ✦✦✦✦
The first of three recordings that altoist Bunky Green made for Vanguard in the mid- to late 1970s (unfortunately, none have yet been reissued on CD) is a fine all-around effort with Green performing three originals and uplifting three pop songs. Assisted by a rhythm section including pianist Al Dailey and guitarist Billy

Butler, Green sounds fine on this set, displaying a distinctive tone and an inquisitive musical spirit. —*Scott Yanow*

Visions / 1978 / Vanguard ✦✦✦✦
Although much of the material on altoist Bunky Green's Vanguard album is rather unlikely (including "Alone Again Naturally," "The Greatest Love of All," "Never Can Say Goodbye," "I Write the Songs" and even "The Entertainer"), Green's solos uplift and give a new slant to the pop tunes. Green is assisted by an oversized rhythm section that includes guitarist Hiram Bullock. —*Scott Yanow*

Places We've Never Been / Feb. 21, 1979+Feb. 22, 1979 / Vanguard ✦✦✦✦✦
The strongest of Bunky Green's three Vanguard LPs of the mid- to late 1970s, this set finds him exploring six of his challenging yet fairly accessible originals. Green's appealing tone and adventurous style work well with the impressive all-star group (which includes trumpeter Randy Brecker, pianist Albert Dailey, bassist Eddie Gomez and drummer Freddie Waits), and he is in heard in prime form throughout the post-bop release. —*Scott Yanow*

In Love Again / June 27, 1987-June 28, 1987 / Mark ✦✦✦✦
Quintet with trumpeter Willie Thomas. Three by saxophonist Green, one by Thomas, one co-written by the pair, one standard ("You Stepped out of a Dream"). —*Michael G. Nastos*

● **Healing the Pain** / Dec. 13, 1989-Dec. 14, 1989 / Delos ✦✦✦✦✦
In listening to Bunky Green, one can hear where Greg Osby, Steve Coleman and Gary Thomas came from. Green sails in and out of the chord changes and makes most of his solos into a do-or-die situation full of emotional intensity, especially when he plays alto. On this diverse CD (which finds him also performing a bit on soprano), Green shows that he is not afraid to occasionally caress a melody (as on a slow "Everything I Have Is Yours") and frequently emphasizes unexpected notes, particularly during a fascinating verison of "I Concentrate on You." Joined by a fine rhythm section consisting of pianist Billy Childs, bassist Art Davis and drummer Ralph Penland, Green is in top form on what may very well be his definitive recording. Highly recommended. —*Scott Yanow*

Charlie Green

b. 1900, Omaha, NE, **d.** 1936, New York, NY
Trombone / Classic Jazz, Blues Jazz
One of the finest early trombonists and the first strong jazz soloist in the Fletcher Henderson Orchestra (joining slightly before Louis Armstrong), Charlie Green played locally in Omaha (1920-23) before his two stints with Henderson (July 1924-April 1926 and late 1928-spring 1929). A superior blues player who could also swing fairly early, Green starred on several classic Bessie Smith recordings (including one called "Trombone Cholly"), recorded in the 1920s with several other blues singers and also worked with the bands of Benny Carter (1929-31 and 1933), Chick Webb (several times during 1930-34), Don Redman (1932) and at the end with Kaiser Marshall. His premature death was from passing out on his doorstep on a winter night and freezing to death. —*Scott Yanow*

Freddie Green

b. Mar. 31, 1911, Charleston, SC, **d.** Mar. 1, 1987, Las Vegas, NV
Guitar / Swing
Freddie Green was known throughout his long career as the definitive rhythm guitarist. He rarely soloed (briefly on a few records early on), he stuck to acoustic guitar and was often more felt than heard. Although he had originally played banjo, Green was playing guitar in New York in early 1937 when producer John Hammond heard him and immediately recommended him to Count Basie. A quick audition and Green had the job, forming a classic rhythm section with Basie, Walter Page and Jo Jones. After 13 years with the orchestra, Green was not originally included in Basie's small group in 1950 but one night sat down uninvited on the bandstand and never left! He stayed with the band even after its leader's death, making a recording with Dianne Schuur and the Frank Foster-led orchestra in 1987 shortly before he passed on after nearly 50 years of service. Freddie Green also composed "Corner Pocket" (later renamed "Until I Met You" for the vocal version) and "Down for Double." —*Scott Yanow*

● **Natural Rhythm** / Feb. 3, 1955+Dec. 18, 1955 / Bluebird ✦✦✦✦
Since he was not a soloist and spent nearly all of his career as the rhythm guitarist for Count Basie's Orchestra, it is not surprising that Freddie Green led relatively few recording sessions of his own. In fact, other than a Concord album co-led with Herb Ellis and four titles from 1945, Green's only date as a leader was a 12-song RCA set from 1955 with a septet including trumpeter Joe Newman, trombonist Henry Coker, Al Cohn on tenor, pianist Nat Pierce, bassist Milt Hinton and either Jo Jones or Osie Johnson on drums. This single CD has that blues-oriented and lightly swinging set, plus a similar set led by Cohn titled *The Natural Seven*. The latter date has a nearly identical group with Cohn, Green, Newman, trombonist

Music Map

Guitar

The Early Giants
Eddie Lang • Lonnie Johnson

Rhythm Guitarists
Johnny St. Cyr • Eddie Condon
Freddie Green (with Count Basie 1937-87)
Allan Reuss

Chordal Acoustic Guitar Soloists
Carl Kress • Dick McDonough • George Van Eps

The First Great Virtuoso
Django Reinhardt

Other Swing Guitarists
Oscar Aleman • Bernard Addison • Teddy Bunn

Innovative Electric Guitarist
Charlie Christian

Early Electric Guitarists
Eddie Durham (1937 with Kansas City Six)
Floyd Smith (with Andy Kirk)
George Barnes • Oscar Moore • Tiny Grimes
Al Casey • Les Paul

Bop Soloists

Barney Kessel	Tal Farlow
Herb Ellis	Kenny Burrell
Emily Remler	Bruce Forman
Russell Malone	Mark Whitfield

Cool-Toned Soloists

Billy Bauer	Jimmy Raney
Johnny Smith	Jim Hall
Ed Bickert	Joshua Breakstone
Doug Raney	Peter Leitch

Brazilian Acoustic Jazz

Laurindo Almeida	Charlie Byrd
Bola Sete	Egberto Gismonti

1960s Greats

Wes Montgomery	Grant Green
George Benson	Pat Martino
Gabor Szabo	Attila Zoller

Fusion

Larry Coryell	John McLaughlin
Al DiMeola	Steve Khan
Terje Rypdal	Hiram Bullock
Allan Holdsworth	Kazumi Watanabe
Frank Gambale	Scott Henderson

Avant-Garde

Sonny Sharrock	Eugene Chadbourne
Derek Bailey	James "Blood" Ulmer

Two Very Different Masters of Solo Guitar
Joe Pass • Stanley Jordan

Modern Swing

Bucky Pizzarelli	Marty Grosz	Cal Collins
Chris Flory	Frank Vignola	Howard Alden

Other Modern Guitarists

John Abercrombie	Philip Catherine
Cornell Dupree	Eric Gale
Ted Dunbar	Lenny Breau
Joe Diorio	Ralph Towner
Mike Stern	Kevin Eubanks

Crossover
Earl Klugh • Lee Ritenour • Larry Carlton

Three Guitar Innovators of the 1990s
Pat Metheny • John Scofield • Bill Frisell

Frank Rehak, Pierce, Hinton and Johnson. With arrangements provided by Al Cohn, Ernie Wilkins and Manny Albam, the music swings and falls between swing and cool jazz. True to form, there are no solos from Freddie Green. —*Scott Yanow*

Grant Green

b. Jun. 6, 1931, St. Louis, MO, **d.** Jan. 31, 1979, New York, NY
Guitar / Hard Bop, Soul Jazz, Groove

Grant Green was born in St. Louis on June 6, 1931, learned his instrument in grade school from his guitar-playing father and was playing professionally by the age of 13 with a gospel group. He worked gigs in his home town and in East St. Louis, IL until he moved to New York in 1960 at the suggestion of Lou Donaldson. Green told Dan Morgenstern in a *Down Beat* interview "The first thing I learned to play was boogie woogie. Then I had to do a lot of rock and roll. It's all blues, anyhow."

His extensive foundation in R&B combined with a mastery of bebop and simplicity that put expressiveness ahead of technical expertise. Green was a superb blues interpreter, and his later material was predominantly blues and R&B, though he was also a wondrous ballad and standards soloist. He was a particular admirer of Charlie Parker, and his phrasing often reflected it. Green played in the '50s with Jimmy Forrest, Harry Edison and Lou Donaldson.

He also collaborated with many organists, among them Brother Jack McDuff, Sam Lazar, Baby Face Willette, Gloria Coleman, Big John Patton and Larry Young. During the early '60s, both his fluid, tasteful playing in organ/guitar/drum combos and his other dates for Blue Note established Green as a star, though he seldom got the critical respect given other players. He was off the scene for a bit in the mid-'60s, but came back strong in the late '60s and '70s. Green played with Stanley Turrentine, Dave Bailey, Yusef Lateef, Joe Henderson, Hank Mobley, Herbie Hancock, McCoy Tyner and Elvin Jones.

Sadly, drug problems interrupted his career in the '60s, and undoubtedly contributed to the illness he suffered in the late '70s. Green was hospitalized in 1978 and died a year later. Despite some rather uneven LPs near the end of his career, the great body of his work represents marvelous soul jazz, bebop and blues.

A severely underrated player during his lifetime, Grant Green is one of the great unsung heroes of jazz guitar. Like Stanley Turrentine, he tends to be left out of the books. Although he mentions Charlie Christian and Jimmy Raney as influences, Green always claimed he listened to horn players (Charlie Parker and Miles Davis) and not other guitar players, and it shows. No other player has this kind of single-note linearity (he avoids chordal playing). There is very little of the intellectual element in Green's playing, and his technique is always at the service of his music. And it is music, plain and simple, that makes Green unique.

Green's playing is immediately recognizable—perhaps more than any other guitarist. Green has been almost systematically ignored by jazz buffs with a bent to the cool side, and he has only recently begun to be appreciated for his incredible musicality. Perhaps no guitarist has ever handled standards and ballads with the brilliance of Grant Green. Mosaic, the nation's premier jazz reissue label, issued a wonderful collection, *The Complete Blue Note Recordings with Sonny Clark*, featuring prime early-'60s Green albums plus unissued tracks. Some of the finest examples of Green's work can be found there. —*Michael Erlewine and Ron Wynn*

Grant's First Stand / Jan. 28, 1961 / Blue Note ◆◆◆
His first album, with Baby Face Willette on Hammond organ and Ben Dixon on drums. Hard to find. Some of this material was released in Japan. —*Michael Erlewine*

Jazz Profile / Jan. 28, 1961-May 20, 1965 / Blue Note ◆◆◆◆
Jazz Profile compiles highlights from Grant Green's recordings for Blue Note, drawing a rough portrait of his career. The compilation features both soul-jazz and hard-bop cuts, giving a good sense of Green's depth and range. While there isn't anything here that will appeal to collectors, *Jazz Profile* does offer a nice introduction for curious listeners. —*Leo Stanley*

Green Blues / Mar. 15, 1961 / Muse ◆◆◆
With [Frank Haynes on tenor sax, Billy Gardner on piano, Ben Tucker on bass, and Dave Bailer on drums. Originally issued on Jazztime under Dave Bailey's name, and now reissued in this format. This is early Green, his second session, and the music is straightahead mainstream jazz with a bluesy flavor. This material is available on *Reaching Out*, a release on the Black Lion label. —*Michael Erlewine*

Reaching Out / Mar. 15, 1961 / Black Lion ◆◆◆
Green is in fine form as is pianist Gardner (better known as an organist), but the album is perhaps most valuable for the contributions of the obscure tenorman Frank Haynes who died in 1965; his sound will remind some a little of Stanley Turrentine. —*Scott Yanow*

Green Street / Apr. 1, 1961 / Blue Note ◆◆◆◆
Most of guitarist Grant Green's recordings of the 1960s feature him in larger groups, making this trio outing with bassist Ben Tucker and drummer Dave Bailey (a CD reissue of the original LP plus two added alternate takes) a strong showcase for his playing. Green, whose main competitor on guitar at the time was Wes Montgomery, already had his own singing sound and a highly individual hornlike approach. He stretches out on a full set of attractive originals plus "'Round Midnight" and "Alone Together," so this reissue is an excellent introduction to his appealing and hard-swinging style. —*Scott Yanow*

Sunday Mornin' / Jun. 4, 1961 / Blue Note ◆◆◆
Sunday Mornin' is Green's fourth album with Blue Note and his first quartet with a piano rather than a Hammond organ. Sidemen include Kenny Drew (piano), Ben Dixon (drums), and Ben Tucker (bass). The result is a sound that is spacious and crisp—a solid setting for Green's single-note leads. This early Grant Green is straightahead jazz with a bluesy tone, similar to what you will find on his album *Matador*. Tunes include the blues "Freedom March," the gospel-influenced "Sunday Mornin'," the lovely theme from "Exodus," a delicate rendition of Billie Holiday's "God Bless the Child," and a great version of the Miles Davis classic "So What." —*Michael Erlewine*

Grantstand / Aug. 1, 1961 / Blue Note ◆◆◆◆
A quartet session with Yusef Lateef (ts, fl) and vintage Jack McDuff on the Hammond organ. Al Harewood is on drums, with the organ taking up the bass chores.

The 15-minute "Blues in Maude's Flat" is very nice indeed, and "My Funny Valentine" (with Lateef on flute) is just plain lovely. No one does standards like Green. —*Michael Erlewine*

Remembering / Aug. 29, 1961 / Blue Note ◆◆◆◆
Available perhaps in Japan, this early Green date includes Horace Parlan on piano, Wilber Ware on bass, and Al Harewood on drums. Mostly standards. —*Michael Erlewine*

Standards / Aug. 29, 1961 / Blue Note ◆◆◆◆
Standards contains the bulk of a trio session Grant Green recorded with bassist Wilbur Ware and drummer Al Harewood on August 29, 1961 (part of this material had been previously issued on the *Remembering* album). The trio ran through seven standards, including "You Stepped Out of a Dream," "Love Walked In," "I'll Remember April," "All the Things You Are" and "If I Had You," which is also present in an alternate take. All three musicians give remarkably sensitive performances—this context brings out the best in Green, who plays with grace, style and passion, breathing life into these familiar songs. —*Stephen Thomas Erlewine*

Born to Be Blue / Dec. 11, 1961+Mar. 1, 1962 / Blue Note ◆◆◆◆◆
This is the one to get, a taste of what is in the (now out-of-print) Mosaic box set *The Complete Blue Note Recordings of Grant Green with Sonny Clark*. This is vintage Green with Sonny Clark on piano and Ike Quebeck on tenor sax. The combination is mesmerizing. This is the stuff groove addicts dream of—a desert island classic pick. Green is the master of standards and the set includes "Someday My Prince Will Come," "Count Every Star," and "Back in Your Own Back Yard." Aside from being just the best jazz, it makes for great easy-listening music. Grandma will love it too. —*Michael Erlewine*

Gooden's Corner / Dec. 23, 1961 / Blue Note ◆◆◆◆◆
This is an album of real beauty and synergy between Green and pianist Sonny Clark, who along with Sam Jones on bass and Louis Hayes on drums rounds out the quartet. Green, an expert with standards, offers "Moon River," "On Green Dolphin Street," and "Count Every Star." This album was also released on *The Complete Blue Note Recordings of Grant Green and Sonny Clark*. —*Michael Erlewine*

★ **The Complete Blue Note with Sonny Clark** / Dec. 23, 1961-Sep. 7, 1962 / Mosaic ◆◆◆◆◆
Guitarist Grant Green and pianist Sonny Clark recorded together on five separate occasions during the 1961-62 period, but virtually none of the music was released domestically until decades later. These performances were clearly lost in the shuffle, for the solos are of a consistently high quality, and the programs were well paced and swinging. Now, the long-lost music (much of which had been previously available only in Japan) is saved for posterity on this Mosaic limited-edition four-CD box set. Green and Clark blend together well; tenor saxophonist Ike Quebec joins their quartet for one session; and the final two numbers add Latin percussion. All of this music should be enjoyed by hard-bop fans. Includes the Blue Note albums *Gooden's Corner, Nigeria, Oleo, Born to Be Blue* (w/ Ike Quebec), and unissued tracks. —*Scott Yanow*

★ **The Complete Quartets with Sonny Clark** / Dec. 23, 1961-Sep. 7, 1962 / Blue Note ◆◆◆◆◆
Mosaic released a four-disc box set titled *The Complete Blue Note with Sonny Clark* in 1991, rounding up everything that the guitarist and pianist recorded together between 1961 and 1962. Blue Note's 1997 version of the set, *The Complete Quartets with Sonny Clark*, trims Mosaic's collection by two discs, offering only the quartet sessions (the Ike Quebec sessions, *Born to Be Blue* and *Blue and Sentimental*, are available on individual discs). In some ways, this actually results in a more unified set, since it puts Green and Clark directly in the spotlight, with no saxophone to complete for solos, but it doesn't really matter if the music is presented as this double-disc set, the four-disc box or the individual albums—this is superb music, showcasing the gutiarist and pianist at their very best. All of the sessions are straightahead bop but the music has a gentle, relaxed vibe that makes it warm, intimate and accessible. Grant and Clark's mastery is subtle—the music is so enjoyable, you may not notice the deftness of their improvisation and technique—but that invests the music with the grace, style and emotion that distinguishes *The Complete Quartets*. Small-group hard bop rarely comes any better than this. —*Stephen Thomas Erlewine*

The Best of Grant Green, Vol. 1 / 1961-1965 / Blue Note ◆◆◆
While the "best-of" format often leaves quite a bit to be desired in a jazz setting, this set contains good Green material from his most productive period, the early and mid-'60s. There's a nice mix between uptempo and slower numbers, standards and his own compositions, as well as soul jazz and straight mainstream and bop material. Although this isn't as far-reaching or comprehensive as Green's Mosaic set, this set will satisfy the needs of those unfamiliar with his work or listeners who just want a good cross-section of his cuts. —*Ron Wynn*

Nigeria / Jan. 13, 1962 / Blue Note ✦✦✦✦✦

This is a great album with the classic synergy of Green and pianist Sonny Clark, who along with Sam Jones on bass and Art Blakey complete the quartet. This album was also released on *The Complete Blue Note Recordings of Grant Green and Sonny Clark*. Just classic Green. —*Michael Erlewine*

Oleo / Jan. 31, 1962 / Blue Note ✦✦✦✦✦

This is an another excellent album with Green and pianist Sonny Clark, who along with Sam Jones on bass and Louis Hayes on drums make the foursome. The entire album is fine with "My Favorite Things," an old favorite of Green. This album was also released on *The Complete Blue Note Recordings of Grant Green and Sonny Clark*. If you can find this album, or the Mosaic set anywhere, you will be very satisfied. The best. —*Michael Erlewine*

The Latin Bit / Apr. 26, 1962 / Blue Note ✦✦✦✦✦

A good title, these are Latin standards with Grant Green in Latin mode and performing standards like "Tico Tico," "Brazil," "Grenada," "Besame Much," and "Hey There." The group includes Johnny Acea (p), Wendell Marshall (b), Willie Bobo (d), and added percussion from Carlos "Potato" Valdez on conga and Garvin Masseaux on chekere. As an added bonus, Ike Quebec plays on two of the standards. One wonders whether these standards were often played by Green. The brightness of the Latin tunes replaces the more substantial soul-jazz feel Grant fans expect. Still, Green in his prime. —*Michael Erlewine*

Goin' West / Nov. 30, 1962 / Blue Note ✦✦✦

Another Blue Note album yet to be reissued, this one (like *Feelin' the Spirit*) includes Herbie Hancock on piano, Reggie Workman on bass, and Billy Higgins on drums. Includes tunes like (can you believe?) "On Top of Old Smokey" and "Tumbling Tumbleweeds." Only Green could carry this off, but he is "the man" when it comes to standards. —*Michael Erlewine*

Feelin' the Spirit / Dec. 21, 1962 / Blue Note ✦✦✦✦

An entire album of spirituals—all jazz instrumentals. Green, already a bluesy guitarist, lets himself out in the gospel format. The result is an album that remains true to both the soul-jazz and gospel genres. Accompanying Green on this date is Herbie Hancock on piano. Every Grant Green fan loves this unique gospel-toned album. It includes standards like "Just a Closer Walk with Thee,""Nobody Knows the Trouble I've Seen," and "Sometimes I Feel like a Motherless Child." A Grant Green classic.—*Michael Erlewine*

Am I Blue? / May 16, 1963 / Blue Note ✦✦✦✦

A date for Blue Note with Joe Henderson (tenor sax), John Patton (Hammond organ), Johnny Coles (tpt), and Ben Dixon (d). —*Michael Erlewine*

★ **Idle Moments** / Nov. 4, 1963 / Blue Note ✦✦✦✦✦

Excellent mid-sized group album, with Green in good form. Bobby Hutcherson (vibes) in the group produces a somewhat different sound than the usual Green album, so make a note of that. Duke Pearson is there on piano along with Joe Henderson (ts), who is hot. All things considered, the groove is there and this is worth having. —*Michael Erlewine*

Solid / Jun. 12, 1964 / Blue Note ✦✦✦✦✦

Not released until 1979, this set contains more challenging material than many of guitarist Grant Green's other Blue Note sessions. In a state-of-the-art sextet with tenor saxophonist Joe Henderson, altoist James Spaulding, pianist McCoy Tyner, bassist Bob Cranshaw and drummer Elvin Jones, Green performs tunes by Duke Pearson, George Russell ("Ezz-thetic"), Sonny Rollins, Henderson ("The Kicker") and his own "Grant's Tune." Perhaps this music was considered too uncommercial initially or maybe it was simply lost in the shuffle. In any case, this is one of Grant Green's finer recordings. —*Scott Yanow*

Talkin' About! / Sep. 11, 1964 / Blue Note ✦✦✦

A rare trio date for Grant Green with Larry Young (organ) and Elvin Jones (d). Although Green was the leader for this date, it is now available on the Mosaic label as part of *The Complete Blue Note Recordings of Larry Young*. One of the first albums by Larry Young. This is classic Green. —*Michael Erlewine*

His Majesty King Funk / Up with Donald Byrd / Nov. 2, 1964-May 26, 1965 / Verve ✦✦✦

This single Verve CD reissues the complete contents of two unrelated LPs: Grant Green's *His Majesty King Funk* (great title) and *Up with Donald Byrd*. Unfortunately the music overall is not as rewarding as Green and Byrd's work of the period for Blue Note. Green is okay with a quintet that includes tenor saxophonist Harold Vick and organist Larry Young but the material (mainly fairly simple funk riffs) is disappointing. Trumpeter Donald Byrd has a potentially strong group with both Jimmy Heath and Stanley Turrentine on tenors along with pianist Herbie Hancock and guitarist Kenny Burrell. However the three- or four-voice "Donald Byrd Singers" and the arrangements by Claus Ogerman weigh down the date. Each album watered down its music to an extent in hopes of gaining commercial

success but neither really caught on. The results are interesting but somewhat forgettable. —*Scott Yanow*

Street of Dreams / Nov. 16, 1964 / Blue Note ✦✦✦

Vibist Bobby Hutcherson joins Green, Larry Young (organ), and Elvin Jones (d) for this fine release, which is now available on the Mosaic label as part of *The Complete Blue Note Recordings of Larry Young*. This is great soul-jazz Larry Young, and Green is, as usual, just excellent. Contains "Somewhere in the Night" and "Street of Dreams." —*Michael Erlewine*

I Want to Hold Your Hand / Mar. 31, 1965 / Blue Note ✦✦✦✦✦

Tenor saxophonist Hank Mobley joins Green, Larry Young (organ), and Elvin Jones (drums) for this very excellent album, which is now available on the Mosaic label as part of *The Complete Blue Note Recordings of Larry Young* (worth getting while it is still available!). Unlike some of Young's later work, this music is in the soul-jazz vein and under Green's lead. It has groove and great playing from Green and Young. —*Michael Erlewine*

☆ **Matador** / May 20, 1964 / Blue Note ✦✦✦✦✦

This is an exceptional Grant Green album for several reasons. For one, it (along with *Solid*) is one of very few Green outings that are straightahead jazz, rather than out-and-out soul jazz. Second, this is one of John Coltrane's finest bands with Green as the featured soloist rather than Coltrane—McCoy Tyner (p), Bob Cranshaw (b) and Elvin Jones (d). Coltrane had just finished recording his classic album *Crescent* and the band is hot. Green shows a lot of guts to lead this band, not to mention to tackle the Coltrane hit "My Favorite Things," and he pulls it off. Green's soul-jazz fans need not fear that this is too dry. It is a great album and classic Grant Green. —*Michael Erlewine*

Iron City / 1967 / Muse ✦✦✦

Recorded for Muse Records in 1967, as Grant Green was on an extended recording hiatus—it was his only record between 1965's *His Majesty, King Funk*, his only album for Verve, and 1969's *Carryin' On*, his return to Blue Note—*Iron City* actually captures the guitarist in fine form, jamming on six blues and R&B numbers with his longtime cohorts, organist Big John Patton and drummer Ben Dixon. The trio had long ago perfected their interplay, and they just cook on *Iron City*, working a hot groove on each song. Even the slow blues "Motherless Child" has a distinct swing in its backbeat, but most of the album finds the trio tearing through uptempo grooves with a vengeance. Green's playing is a bit busier than normal and he solos far more often than Patton, who lays back through most of the album, providing infectious vamps and lead lines. The two styles intermesh perfectly with Dixon's deft drumming, resulting in a fine, overlooked date that showcases some of Green's hottest, bluesiest playing. —*Stephen Thomas Erlewine*

Carryin' On / Oct. 3, 1969 / Blue Note ✦✦

Grant Green's recording career was just starting to slip at the time of this release although the talented guitarist always played as well as he could under the circumstances. He manages to uplift the dated R&Bish and pop material a bit but his backup band (which includes tenor saxophonist Claude Bartee and either Clarence Palmer or Earl Neal Creque on electric piano) seems content to repeat the same grooves endlessly and play it safe, making this CD reissue of rather limited interest. —*Scott Yanow*

Green Is Beautiful / Jan. 30, 1970 / Blue Note ✦✦✦

Of the five songs included on this CD reissue, the first three are one-chord vamps; none of these renditions were destined to be remembered as classics. "Ain't It Funky Now" makes the set worthwhile for it has tenor saxophonist Claude Bartee doing a close imitation of Eddie Harris and trumpeter Blue Mitchell taking an exciting solo. But the unimaginative material in general does not really inspire guitarist Grant Green and keeps this CD from being too essential. —*Scott Yanow*

Alive! / Aug. 15, 1970 / Blue Note ✦✦

Grant Green was one of the most consistent and versatile guitarists of the 1960s but once 1970 came around his recording career became quite erratic. This CD reissue brings back a rather weak effort with Green's sextet (which at the time included Claude Bartee on tenor, vibraphonist William Bivens and either Ronnie Foster or Earl Neal Creque on organ) playing R&B cliches while laying forever on one chord. There are many more rewarding Grant Green sets than this one. —*Scott Yanow*

The Best of Grant Green, Vol. 2 / May, 21 1971-Apr. 23, 1972 / Blue Note ✦✦✦✦

Grant Green signed to Blue Note for a second time in 1969. Where his first stint with the label was nearly all hard bop, the recordings from his second stay were almost all funky soul-jazz. Predictably, these are sessions that jazz purists have dismissed throughout the years, even though—when judged strictly on the level of funky, groove-oriented dance music—the music is quite strong. During the '80s and '90s, dance and hip-hop fans rediscovered Green's records from the late '70s and sampled his playing and grooves on their own records. Blue Note assembled *The Best of Grant Green, Vol. 2* to capitalize on the popularity of this acid-jazz movement. All of the material on this disc is drawn from albums—*The Final Countdown, Live at the Lighthouse, Visions*—that never received much attention in jazz circles. Nevertheless, fans of this sound will find *The Best of Grant Green, Vol. 2* to be a delight—there's a lot of wonderfully funky, dense grooves on here, and many of the songs have been out of print since their original issue. Hard-bop fans will not be reconsider their negative opinion of this music based on this compilation, but acid-jazz, groove and hip-hop fans will find this disc to be an excellent addition to their Grant Green collection. —*Stephen Thomas Erlewine*

Visions / May 21, 1971 / Blue Note ◆◆◆
Grant Green's early-'70s recordings for Blue Note are continually attacked by jazz critics for being slick, overly commercial sessions that leaned closer to contemporary pop and R&B than hard bop or soul jazz. There's no denying that Green, like many of his Blue Note contemporaries, did choose a commercial path in the early '70s, but there were some virtues to these records, and *Visions* in particular. Often, these albums were distinguished by hot, funky workouts in the vein of Sly Stone or James Brown, but that's not the case here. On *Visions,* the guitarist crafted a set of appealingly melodic, lightly funky pop-jazz, concentrating on pop hits like "Does Anybody Really Know What Time It Is," "Love on a Two Way Street," "We've Only Just Begun" and "Never Can Say Goodbye." Supported by minor-league players, Green nevertheless turns in an elegant and dignified performance—after stating the melody on each song, he contributes typically graceful, memorable solos. Simply put, he sounds fresh, and his playing here is the best it has been since 1965's *His Majesty, King Funk*. Ultimately, *Visions* is a bit laidback, and the electric piano-heavy arrangements are a little dated, but Grant Green never made a commercial pop-jazz album as appealing and satisfying as *Visions*. —*Stephen Thomas Erlewine*

Shades of Green / Nov. 23, 1971-Dec. 17, 1971 / Blue Note ◆◆
A Blue Note date with a large group including horns, reeds, woodwinds, vibes, et al. Consists of standards and even a medley. This is not the old Grant Green. —*Michael Erlewine*

The Final Come Down / Dec. 13, 1971 / Blue Note ◆◆◆
A soundtrack for Blue Note with a very large group, including Harold Vick (sax), Cornell Dupree (g), and Grady Tate (d). —*Michael Erlewine*

Live at the Lighthouse / Apr. 21, 1972 / Blue Note ◆◆◆
There is lot of fat to the live jams heard on this out-of-print Blue Note double LP. With the many dated verbal introductions and overly lengthy one-chord funk vamps, this session should have been edited down to one album. Guitarist Grant Green's group (which includes Claude Bartee on tenor and soprano, vibraphonist Gary Coleman, organist Shelton Lester, electric bassist Wilton Felder, drummer Greg Williams and percussionist Bobbye Hall) is actually quite good and Bartee was an underrated saxophonist. But none of the six selections (which include "Betcha by Golly Wow" and Donald Byrd's "Fancy Free") are all that memorable even if there are lots of good feelings. The overall results in this stretched-out format are far from essential. —*Scott Yanow*

The Main Attraction / Mar. 1976 / Kudu ◆◆◆
Guitarist Grant Green's first album in four years and next-to-last recording as a leader looks attractive from the LP jacket but is actually a distinct disappointment. Joined by studio musicians (including flutist Hubert Laws and tenor saxophonist Michael Brecker), Green plays three rather forgettable and lengthy pieces. Arranger David Matthews tries his best but the material is too weak to be made interesting and the musicians sound as if they were counting off the minutes to lunch. This LP does give one a chance to hear Grant Green near the end of his career (his attractive tone and swinging style were still intact) but the out-of-print album is hardly worth looking for. —*Scott Yanow*

Urbie Green (Urbam Clifford Green)

b. Aug. 8, 1926, Mobile, AL
Trombone / Swing, Bop
A fine jazz player with a beautiful tone who has spent most of his career in the studios, Urbie Green is highly respected by his fellow trombonists. He started playing when he was 12, was with the big bands of Tommy Reynolds, Bob Strong and Frankie Carle as a teenager and worked with Gene Krupa during 1947-50. Green had a stint with Woody Herman's Third Herd, appeared on some of the famous Buck Clayton Jam Sessions (1953-54) and was with Benny Goodman off and on during 1955-57. He played with Count Basie in 1963 and spent a period in the 1960s fronting the Tommy Dorsey ghost band (1966-67) but has mostly stuck to studio work. Urbie Green recorded frequently as a leader in the 1950s up to 1963 (for Blue Note, Vanguard, Bethlehem, ABC-Paramount and Command) and dance-band-oriented records for RCA and Command). He has appeared much less often in jazz settings since then but did make two albums for CTI in 1976-77. —*Scott Yanow*

The Fox /Jun. 1976-Nov. 1976 / CTI ◆◆

Lyrical Language of Urbie Green / Jan. 12, 1955-Jan. 19, 1955 / Bethlehem ◆◆◆◆
If one eliminates trombonist Urbie Green's dance-band records of the '50s and his moody and sometimes gimmicky sessions of the 1960s, he has recorded surprisingly few albums through the years as a leader in a jazz context. This excellent effort was one of his best, a septet session in which Marion Evans provided the arrangements and four of the ten selections. Green is in top form (he has always been quite consistent) and shows off his beautiful tone in a septet with the underrated trumpeter Doug Mettome, Ike Horowitz and Danny Bank on reeds, pianist Jimmy Lyon, bassist Oscar Pettiford and either Osie Johnson or Jimmy Campbell on drums. The intriguing set has been reissued on CD. —*Scott Yanow*

● **Senor Blues** / Jun. 1977 / CTI ◆◆◆◆
Overlooking his commercial efforts for Command and Project 3, Urbie Green did not record as a leader during 1960-75. His first CTI set, *The Fox,* was quite dull, but this encore is on a much higher level. The trombonist displays his beautiful tone and impressive technique while joined by several horns and an expanded rhythm section arranged by David Matthews. Grover Washington, Jr., takes three tenor solos and one on soprano, guitarist John Scofield helps out on two songs, and the material is generally fairly strong. Highlights include "Captain Marvel," Charles Mingus' "Ysabel's Table Dance," and "Senor Blues." —*Scott Yanow*

Sea Jam Blues / May 29, 1995-Jun. 2, 1995 / Chiaroscuro ◆◆◆◆

Dodo Greene

Vocals / Standards
b. Buffalo, NY
Dodo Greene was a R&B-inflected jazz vocalist who only recorded a handful of dates during the early '60s. Her one major record was *My Hour of Need*, a session she cut in 1962 with an impressive stable of Blue Note artists including Ike Quebec, Grant Green, Herbie Lewis, Milt Hinton, Billy Higgins and Al Harewood. Greene was the first vocalist Blue Note signed to an exclusive contract, and she was also the only vocalist the label signed during the '60s, which suggests the lack of success the record achieved.

A native of Buffalo, NY, Dodo began singing as a child. She continued to sing throughout her teens, although she was planning a career in medicine. Her first big break arrived when she filled in for a sick vocalist in Cozy Cole's band. He asked her to join his group, but she refused. Eventually, she decided to pursue a career in music and began singing regularly at venues along the East Coast, as well as Chicago. Slowly, she built up a following among audiences and fellow vocalists like Ella Fitzgerald, Sarah Vaughan and Dinah Washington, and was able to play venues in London and Germany.

Greene recorded her first album for Time Records shortly before she signed to Blue Note in 1962. In April, she recorded the material that comprised *My Hour of Need*. Five months later she returned to the studios to cut a follow-up session. Evidently, *My Hour of Need* was not a success, since those recordings, along with a session she recorded in November, remained unreleased until the 1996 CD reissue of *My Hour of Need*. Greene faded away from the spotlight in the years following the release of her lone Blue Note album. There is no apparent record of her recording again, and she presumably stopped performing live by the early '70s. —*Stephen Thomas Erlewine*

My Hour of Need / Apr. 2, 1962-Nov. 2, 1962 / Blue Note ◆◆◆
This set (reissued on CD) was a very unusual release for Blue Note. Dodo Greene was only the second singer to lead a session for Alfred Lion's label (Sheila Jordan had preceded her) and Greene's mixture of R&B and soulful blues in a voice very reminiscent of late-period Dinah Washington is much more pop- and blues-oriented than the music on any other Blue Note release from the period. What other Blue Note album has a full program of soul ballads clocking in between three to five minutes apiece? Although Dodo Greene (who had recorded one slightly earlier record for Time) was apparently signed to an exclusive contract, her only other Blue Note session (six of its nine numbers conclude this CD) had never been previously released. In reality, the main reason to acquire the relaxed set is for the warm tenor of Ike Quebec (who is perfect in this setting) and the occasional guitar of Grant Green. A true obscurity. —*Scott Yanow*

Sonny Greenwich (Herbert Lawrence Greennidge)

b. Jan. 1, 1936, Hamilton, Canada
Guitar / Avant-Garde
One of Canada's top guitarists, the eccentric playing of Sonny Greenwich is always stimulating and usually surprising. He played locally in Toronto, appeared with Charles Lloyd in New York (1965), toured with John Handy (1966-67) and recorded with Hank Mobley (1967). Greenwich came close to joining Miles Davis in 1969, settled in Quebec (he moved to Montreal in 1974) and has since led sessions for Sackville, PM, Justin Time, and his own Kleo label. —*Scott Yanow*

Bird of Paradise / Nov. 1986 / Justin Time ✦✦✦
Studio date for the eclectic electric guitarist and hermit from Canada. Four originals, two standards. A unique voice on his instrument. —*Michael G. Nastos*

● **Live at Sweet Basil** / 1987 / Justin Time ✦✦✦✦✦
Live club date in New York City. Three originals and one standard with quartet. This man is an unsung hero, revered by guitarists. —*Michael G. Nastos*

Standard Idioms / Nov. 21, 1991+Sep. 15, 1992 / Kleo ✦✦✦✦

Hymn to the Earth / Oct. 1994 / Kleo ✦✦✦
Sonny Greenwich, long considered one of Canada's most consistently creative guitarists, is very relaxed on this recording for his label Kleo. Simple rhythms and vamps are the basis for most of the originals and Greenwich plays quite slow and melodically, letting his notes really ring while constructing improvisations that develop gradually. Backed by a fine rhythm section, Greenwich's melancholy flights are given such titles as "Hymn to the Earth," "Nature Prays" and "Invocation," but the music is not of the one-mood new age variety. Some of the performances could have been briefer and the development a bit quicker but, excepting a throwaway vocal by Ernie Nelson on "Serengeti," Greenwich's latest project (which sometimes crosses over into folk and world music) is rewarding. —*Scott Yanow*

Spirit in the Air / Nov. 1995 / Kleo ✦✦✦
This is one of guitarist Sonny Greenwich's friendlier recordings. Greenwich performs six originals that are mostly melodic ballads with "Far Country" being quite peaceful while "Raga" (which uses the tablas of Guy Thouin) pays tribute to Indian music in relaxed fashion. The fourteen-and-a-half-minute "Black Beauty" (which early on has some background yodelling by Ernie Nelson that is reminiscent of Leon Thomas) is the most eccentric piece but will not disturb conservative listeners and even "Free Form" (a freely improvised piece) is lyrical. In addition to Greenwich's distinctive guitar, the main soloist is James Gelfand on piano and an electric piano that is a throwback to the 1970s. Although certainly not Sonny Greenwich's most innovative set (some of his longtime fans may be disappointed at the mellow nature of the program), this CD is reasonably enjoyable in its own right. —*Scott Yanow*

Sonny Greer

b. Dec. 13, 1895, Long Beach, NJ, **d.** Mar. 23, 1982, New York, NY
Drums / Swing
He was never the greatest timekeeper but Sonny Greer was perfect for Duke Ellington's Orchestra during 1924-51, adding color and class to the rhythm section. He met Ellington in 1919 when he was a member of the Howard Theatre's orchestra in Washington, D.C. Greer visited New York for the first time with Elmer Snowden and was an original member of Duke's Washingtonians which was a five-piece group at its start. Greer's playing grew with the band and his large array of sounds (using a drum set that included a gong, chimes, timpani and vibes) added to the Ellington band's "jungle sound." He was with the orchestra until 1951 when, after a few arguments with Duke over his drinking and increasing unreliability, Greer left to join Johnny Hodges' new group. He later worked with Red Allen, Tyree Glenn and J.C. Higginbotham, in 1967 led his own band and played with Brooks Kerr's trio in the 1970s. —*Scott Yanow*

Al Grey

b. Jun. 6, 1925, Aldie, VA
Trombone / Bop, Swing
Al Grey's trademark phrases and often-humorous use of the plunger mute have long made him quite distinctive. After getting out of the service, he was with the orchestras of Benny Carter (1945-46), Jimmie Lunceford (1946-47), Lucky Millinder and Lionel Hampton (off and on during 1948-53). Grey was a well-featured soloist with the classic Dizzy Gillespie globetrotting orchestra during 1956-57 (taking an exciting solo at the 1957 Newport Jazz Festival on a blazing version of "Cool Breeze"). He was with Count Basie's Orchestra on three separate occasions (1957-61, 1964-66 and 1971-77), led a band with Billy Mitchell in the early '60s and had a group with Jimmy Forrest after leaving Count in 1977. In recent years Grey has performed and recorded often with Clark Terry, made a CD with the Statesmen of Jazz and for a time led a quintet that featured his son Mike Grey on second trombone. Al Grey recorded as a leader for Argo (1959-64), Tangerine, Black & Blue, Stash, Chiaroscuro and Capri and co-led an excellent Pablo date in 1983 with J.J. Johnson. —*Scott Yanow*

Key Bone / Jul. 27, 1972-Jul. 28, 1972 / Black & Blue ✦✦✦✦
Trombonist Al Grey's first session as a leader in seven years, this European date was last available domestically as a Classic Jazz LP. Grey matches wits and swing with altoist/singer Eddie "Cleanhead" Vinson, organist Wild Bill Davis, Floyd Smith (a pioneering electric guitarist who worked with Andy Kirk), and drummer

Chris Columbus. The repertoire comprises basic originals by Grey, Davis and Vinson, including "Person to Person," and finds the trombonist in prime form. —*Scott Yanow*

Grey's Mood / Apr. 3, 1973+Oct. 7, 1975 / Classic Jazz ✦✦✦✦
This excellent set (last available as a Classic Jazz LP) features Al Grey on two sessions in peak form. The trombonist is the lead voice in an octet for four numbers that also feature tenorman Hal Singer, and he joins forces with tenor saxophonist Jimmy Forrest (they were both in Count Basie's band at the time) in a quintet also including pianist Tommy Flanagan for three other tunes. Grey wrote six of the seven numbers, all but one of which are blues. Grey and Forrest would soon leave Basie and team up on a regular basis until the tenor's death. Accessible and swinging music. —*Scott Yanow*

Struttin' and Shoutin' / Aug. 30, 1976 / Columbia ✦✦✦✦
Trombonist Al Grey, a master of the wah-wah mute, had a rare opportunity to record with a major label in 1976. But Columbia almost lost the master, and when it was finally released in 1983, one of the principals (tenor saxophonist Jimmy Forrest) had already passed away. Despite its delayed arrival, this upbeat set (dominated by soulful blues but also including two standards) was worth the wait. Grey and Forrest, the principal soloists, are heard as part of a nonet, although there are brief spots for trumpeter Waymond Reed and pianist Ray Bryant. This out-of-print LP will be hard to find, but it is worth picking up. —*Scott Yanow*

● **Truly Wonderful** / Jul. 19, 1978-Jul. 21, 1978 / Vintage Jazz ✦✦✦✦✦
The short-lived Al Grey-Jimmy Forrest Quintet was formed when the pair left Count Basie's Orchestra in 1977 and it ended upon Forrest's death in 1980. This hard-swinging CD features trombonist Grey (an expert with the plunger mute), the tough-toned tenor Forrest, Shirley Scott (playing piano rather than organ), bassist John Duke and drummer Bobby Durham in live performances from Rick's in Chicago. The straightahead music is quite enjoyable with the highlights including Jay McShann's "Jumpin' Blues," Scott's "Blues Everywhere" and "Take the 'A' Train"; even "You Are the Sunshine of My Life" works. Recommended. —*Scott Yanow*

Live at Rick's / July 19, 1978-July 21, 1978 / Aviva ✦✦✦✦
Starting in 1977 and continuing until Jimmy Forrest's death in 1980, trombonist Al Grey and the thick-toned tenor would co-lead a popular quintet. Only three recordings resulted, of which this set (four of the seven selections would be reissued on a Stash CD along with additional material) is the best known. Although the Stash CD is the better buy, this collector's LP (which also features organist Shirley Scott exclusively on piano, bassist John Duke and drummer Bobby Durham) has versions of "In a Mellotone," "C.B. and Me" and "Salty Papa" that have not yet reappeared and are generally as good as the other selections (two standards, an original and Charlie Parker's "The Jumpin' Blues"). Fine, basic straightahead jazz. —*Scott Yanow*

Out 'Dere / Jul. 2, 1980-Jul. 3, 1980 / Grey-Forrest ✦✦✦✦
Recorded just two months before tenor saxophonist Jimmy Forrest's death, this LP was meant to launch his co-op label with trombonist Al Grey, but instead would be the company's only release. Teamed up with organist Don Patterson, young guitarist Peter Leitch and drummer Charlie Rice, Forrest and Grey make for a mutually compatible team on romps, ballad features (Grey takes "Solitude," while Forrest shows plenty of feeling on "Willow Weep for Me"), and group originals, including a song apiece from Patterson and Leitch. Surprisingly, Jimmy Forrest still seemed in prime form this late in his life. —*Scott Yanow*

Al Grey and Jesper Thilo Quintet / Aug. 1986 / Storyville ✦✦✦✦
Swing is the thing on this excellent effort from trombonist Al Grey, who teams up with a Scandinavian rhythm section and the Zoot Sims-inspired tenor of Jesper Thilo. Grey brought in three basic originals, including one titled "I'm Hungry, Sabrina!"; Thilo shows off his warm tone on "On the Sunny Side of the Street," and the quintet plays three other standards, including "A Night in Tunisia." This CD gives listeners a worthy example of Al Grey's talents in a sympathetic setting. —*Scott Yanow*

The New Al Grey Quintet / May 16, 1988-May 17, 1988 / Chiaroscuro ✦✦✦✦

Al Meets Bjarne / Aug. 5, 1988 / Gemini ✦✦✦✦✦
Veteran trombonist Al Grey teams up with the talented, if obscure, Norwegian tenor player Bjarne Nerem and the Norman Simmons Trio (with pianist Simmons, bassist Paul West and drummer Gerryck King) on this informal session for the Norwegian Gemini label. Nerem's playing is a bit reminiscent of Coleman Hawkins, and he works well with Grey, who is clearly the leader. In addition to two Simmons originals and Grey's blues "Al Meets Bjarne," the quintet performs six swing standards, including "Lester Leaps In," "Tangerine" and "Stompin' at the Savoy", and the results are enjoyable and typically swinging. —*Scott Yanow*

Fab / Feb. 4, 1990+Feb. 7, 1990 / Capri ✦✦✦✦

Christmas Stockin' Stuffer / Aug. 1990-Sep. 1990 / Capri ✦✦✦

Live at the Floating Jazz Festival / Oct. 22, 1990-Oct. 25, 1990 / Chiaroscuro ✦✦✦

Me n' Jack / 1995 / Pullen Music ✦✦✦✦✦

This release from Pullen Music has a very logical matchup between trombonist Al Grey and organist Jack McDuff. The music is blues-oriented, with occasional departures such as "God Bless the Child," and features several excellent soloists on a set of mostly basic originals. Grey's mastery of the plunger mute has long given his swing-to-bop trombone its own distinctive sound. Organist Jack McDuff is quite subtle, yet always swings hard, and his regular tenor saxophonist, Jerry Weldon, is a strong asset. Guitarist Joe Cohn continues to grow as an improviser; bassist Jerome Hunter is fine in support, and drummer Bobby Durham drives the ensembles and has a few drum breaks, most notably on "Deli's Blues," which is dedicated to Art Blakey and purposely reminiscent of "Blues March." The music is accessible, full of high spirits and quite joyful. Highly recommended to straightahead jazz fans. —*Scott Yanow*

Center Piece, Live at the Blue Note / Mar. 23, 1995-Mar. 26, 1995 / Telarc ✦✦✦

Matzoh and Grits / Apr. 22, 1996-Apr. 23, 1996 / Arbors ✦✦✦

Johnny Griffin

b. Apr. 24, 1928, Chicago, IL

Tenor Saxophone / Bop, Hard Bop, Groove

Once accurately billed as "the world's fastest saxophonist," Johnny Griffin (an influence tonewise on Rahsaan Roland Kirk) has been one of the top bop-oriented tenors since the mid-'50s. He gained early experience playing with the bands of Lionel Hampton (1945-47) and Joe Morris (1947-50) and also jammed regularly with Thelonious Monk and Bud Powell. After serving in the Army (1951-53), Griffin spent a few years in Chicago (recording his first full album for Argo) and then moved to New York in 1956. He held his own against fellow tenors John Coltrane and Hank Mobley in a classic Blue Note album, was with Art Blakey's Jazz Messengers in 1957 and proved to be perfect with the Thelonious Monk Quartet in 1958 where he really ripped through the complex chord changes with ease. During 1960-62 Griffin co-led a "tough tenor" group with Eddie "Lockjaw" Davis. He emigrated to Europe in 1963 and became a fixture on the Paris jazz scene both as a bandleader and a major soloist with the Kenny Clarke-Francy Boland Big Band. In 1973 Johnny Griffin moved to the Netherlands but has remained a constant world traveller, visiting the US often and recording for many labels including Blue Note, Riverside, Atlantic, Steeple Chase, Black Lion, Antilles, Verve and some European companies. —*Scott Yanow*

Fly, Mister, Fly / 1947-Nov. 18, 1949 / Saxophonograph ✦✦✦

Nineteen at the time of the earliest recordings on this collector's LP, the great tenor Johnny Griffin is heard as the star soloist with Joe Morris' Orchestra. The band, which started out as a hot jump unit, was by 1949 more in the early R&B vein. Griffin's playing includes some honking choruses and plenty of heat during performances that both swing hard and are quite accessible. Morris was a fair trumpeter himself, and among the more notable sidemen are such then-unknowns as guitarist George Freeman, pianist Elmo Hope (who plays some hot boogie-woogie), drummer Philly Joe Jones and bassist Percy Heath. Music made by early R&B groups such as this one has long been forgotten, but is worthy of a re-evaluation, for there are many fine jazz solos on these rare sides. —*Scott Yanow*

Introducing Johnny Griffin / Apr. 17, 1956 / Blue Note ✦✦✦✦

This CD reissue does not have tenor saxophonist Johnny Griffin's first recording as a leader (he made a few sides for OKeh in 1953 and a full album for Argo a few months earlier in 1956), but it gained Griffin a great deal of attention. Soon billed as "the world's fastest saxophonist," Griffin was also a superior ballad interpreter with a fairly distinctive tone of his own. With strong support given by pianist Wynton Kelly, bassist Curly Russell and drummer Max Roach, Griffin romps on three of his originals, barn-busting versions of "The Way You Look Tonight" and "Cherokee" (the latter two were released for the first time domestically on this CD), and a couple of ballads. Superior music. —*Scott Yanow*

☆ **A Blowing Session** / Apr. 6, 1957 / Blue Note ✦✦✦✦✦

More than just a mere "blowing session," these four jams (on a pair of standards and two Johnny Griffin compositions) match together three very different tenor stylists: Griffin, Hank Mobley and John Coltrane. Although the solos and trade-offs are often quite combative, the result is a three-way dead heat, for each of these tenor greats has a different approach and a distinctive sound. Of all of the 1950s jam sessions, this is one of the most successful and exciting. —*Scott Yanow*

★ **The Congregation** / Oct. 13, 1957 / Blue Note ✦✦✦✦✦

The great tenor saxophonist Johnny Griffin is heard in top form on this near-classic quartet set. Assisted by pianist Sonny Clark, bassist Paul Chambers and drummer Kenny Dennis, Griffin is exuberant on "The Congregation" (which is reminis-

cent of Horace Silver's "The Preacher"), thoughtful on the ballads and swinging throughout. It's recommended for bop collectors. —*Scott Yanow*

Johnny Griffin Sextet / Feb. 25, 1958 / Original Jazz Classics ✦✦✦✦

The great tenor Johnny Griffin made his debut on Riverside with this sextet set which has been reissued on CD in the OJC series. Griffin is teamed with trumpeter Donald Byrd, baritonist Pepper Adams, pianist Kenny Drew, bassist Wilbur Ware and drummer Philly Joe Jones for three obscure tunes, the ballad "What's New" and a cooking version of "Woody'n You." High-quality hard bop from some of the best. —*Scott Yanow*

Way Out! / Feb. 26, 1958-Feb. 27, 1958 / Original Jazz Classics ✦✦✦✦

This formerly obscure quartet set by tenor saxophonist Johnny Griffin (reissued on CD in the OJC series) features the fiery soloist on five little-known originals written by Chicagoans plus a burning version of "Cherokee." Virtually all of Griffin's recordings are worth getting and, with the assistance of pianist Kenny Drew, bassist Wilbur Ware and drummer Philly Joe Jones, the tenor is in superior form for this spirited date. —*Scott Yanow*

The Little Giant / Aug. 4, 1959-Aug. 5, 1959 / Original Jazz Classics ✦✦✦✦

This CD reissue is a bit offbeat, for the set by tenor saxophonist Johnny Griffin features three originals by then-obscure pianist Norman Simmons, a reworking of the pop tune "Playmates," Babs Gonzalez's "Lonely One" and the tenor's "63rd Street Theme." Simmons' arrangements for the three horns (which include trumpeter Blue Mitchell and trombonist Julian Priester) are colorful; the rhythm section (pianist Wynton Kelly, bassist Sam Jones and drummer Albert "Tootie" Heath) is state of the art for the period, and Griffin (who is featured in a trio with Jones and Heath on "The Lonely One") is in fine form. An interesting set of obscure straightahead jazz. —*Scott Yanow*

The Big Soul Band / May 24, 1960-Jun. 3, 1960 / Original Jazz Classics ✦✦✦

Tenor saxophonist Johnny Griffin is showcased with a ten-piece group on this CD reissue of a Riverside LP which is augmented by a previously unreleased version of "Wade in the Water." The repertoire is a bit unusual with some spirituals (including "Nobody Knows the Trouble I've Seen" and "Deep River"), a tune apiece by Bobby Timmons ("So Tired") and Junior Mance, and three originals from Norman Simmons who arranged all of the selections. Trumpeter Clark Terry and trombonists Matthew Gee and Julian Priester have some short solos but the emphasis is on the leader who is in typically spirited and passionate form. —*Scott Yanow*

Studio Jazz Party / Sep. 7, 1960 / Original Jazz Classics ✦✦✦

Joined by trumpeter Dave Burns, pianist Norman Simmons, bassist Vic Sproles and drummer Ben Riley, Griffin blazes through performances of "Good Bait," "Low Gravy" and "Toe-Tappin' " on the fine *Studio Jazz Party*. —*Jason Ankeny*

Griff and Lock / Nov. 4, 1960-Nov. 10, 1960 / Original Jazz Classics ✦✦✦✦

Eddie "Lockjaw" Davis and Johnny Griffin co-led a combo during 1960-62, a perfect outlet for the two very competitive and distinctive tenors. This reissue set (which also features pianist Junior Mance, bassist Larry Gales and drummer Ben Riley) is highlighted by heated versions of James Moody's "The Last Train from Overbrook," "Second Balcony Jump," "I'll Remember April" and "Good Bait." Easily recommended to straightahead jazz fans. —*Scott Yanow*

The First Set / Jan. 6, 1961 / Prestige ✦✦✦✦

Live at Minton's / Jul. 6, 1961 / Prestige ✦✦✦✦

During the night of July 6, 1961, the two-tenor quintet co-led by Johnny Griffin and Eddie "Lockjaw" Davis recorded enough material to fill up four LPs; surprisingly, Fantasy has not yet reissued any of the sets in their Original Jazz Classics series. Two of the albums (*The Tenor Scene* and *The Midnight Show*) were last available as this two-LP set. Griffin and Davis, competitive tenors with different sounds, battle each other on ten selections with the assistance of pianist Junior Mance, bassist Larry Gales and drummer Ben Riley. Highlights of the frequently hard-charging date include "Straight, No Chaser," "Woody'n You," "I'll Remember April," "In Walked Bud" and "Our Delight." Exciting music that deserves to be made more widely available. —*Scott Yanow*

White Gardenia / Jul. 13, 1961-Jul. 17, 1961 / Original Jazz Classics ✦✦✦

Tenor saxophonist Johnny Griffin pays tribute to Billie Holiday, who had died exactly two years earlier, on this ballad-oriented set, which has been reissued on CD. Griffin is joined by a brass section (either five or seven pieces), plus a rhythm section and strings (the latter dominated by cellos), for his warm interpretations of nine songs associated with Billie Holiday, plus his original "White Gardenia." The arrangements, provided by Melba Liston and Norman Simmons, are tasteful, and the lyrical music is well performed, if not overly memorable. Worth checking out. —*Scott Yanow*

Tough Tenor Favorites / Feb. 5, 1962 / Original Jazz Classics ✦✦✦✦

Johnny Griffin and Eddie "Lockjaw" Davis, the two "tough tenors" in question, always made for an exciting team. With pianist Horace Parlan, bassist Buddy

Catlett and drummer Ben Riley completing the quintet for this CD reissue of a Jazzland date from 1962, Griff and Lockjaw are in top form and quite competitive on a variety of standards. Highlights include "Blue Lou," "Ow," "I Wished on the Moon" and "From This Moment On." The main winner in these fiery tenor "battles" is the listener. —*Scott Yanow*

Soul Groove / May 14, 1963+May 16, 1963 / Atlantic ✦✦✦
A soul session with John Patton (or Hank Jones) on the Hammond organ and Matthew Gee on trombone. —*Michael Erlewine*

The Man I Love / Mar. 30, 1967 / Black Lion ✦✦✦✦
Teamed up with pianist Kenny Drew, bassist Niels Pedersen and drummer Albert "Tootie" Heath for a club date at Copenhagen's Montmartre in 1967 (reissued on CD by Black Lion), the great tenor saxophonist Johnny Griffin really stretches out on four numbers: "The Man I Love," "Hush-A-Bye," "Blues for Harvey" and a memorable version of "The Masquerade Is Over." Griffin shows why he was early on billed as "the world's fastest tenor" although he also displays warmth on "Sophisticated Lady." A fine example of Griffin's underrated talents. —*Scott Yanow*

You Leave Me Breathless / Mar. 30, 1967-Mar. 31, 1967 / Black Lion ✦✦✦✦

Blues for Harvey / Jul. 4, 1973-Jul. 5, 1973 / Inner City ✦✦✦✦✦

The Jams Are Coming / Dec. 1975-Oct. 1977 / Timeless ✦✦✦
A nice straightahead date. —*Ron Wynn*

Live in Tokyo / Apr. 23, 1976 / Inner City ✦✦✦✦
The great tenor Johnny Griffin really gets a chance to stretch out on this two-LP set. Joined by pianist Horace Parland, bassist Mads Vinding and drummer Art Taylor for this Tokyo concert, Griffin digs into three standards and a pair of his originals; all except for a rapid "Wee" are at least 16 minutes long. Griffin's long cadenza on "The Man I Love" is a highlight. —*Scott Yanow*

Return of the Griffin / Oct. 17, 1978 / Original Jazz Classics ✦✦✦✦
Johnny Griffin recorded this studio album during his first visit to the US in 15 years. Accompanied by a very supportive trio (pianist Ronnie Mathews, bassist Ray Drummond and drummer Keith Copeland), the great tenor is in frequently exuberant form on such tunes as "Autumn Leaves," his own "A Monk's Dream" and the funky "The Way It Is." Long one of the underrated masters, Johnny Griffin is heard at the peak of his powers on this modern bop session. —*Scott Yanow*

Bush Dance / Oct. 18, 1978-Oct. 19, 1978 / Galaxy ✦✦✦✦✦
Johnny Griffin has (at least since the mid-'50s) been one of the masters of the tenor sax although consistently underrated. This studio session is one of his great achievements, particularly a fascinating (and cleverly constructed) 17-minute version of "A Night in Tunisia." Whether it be his own "The Jams Are Coming" or a lyrical version of the veteran ballad "Since I Fell for You," Griffin (joined here by guitarist George Freeman, bassist Sam Jones, drummer Albert Heath and percussionist Kenneth Nash) is inspired and quite creative throughout this highly recommended gem. —*Scott Yanow*

NYC Underground / Jul. 6, 1979-Jul. 7, 1979 / Galaxy ✦✦✦
This Johnny Griffin quartet session, recorded live at the Village Vanguard, finds the distinctive tenor in generally exciting form. With fine support offered by pianist Ron Mathews, bassist Ray Drummond and drummer Idris Muhammad, Griffin is heard in top form on "Yours Is My Heart Alone," "Sophisticated Lady" (a ballad statement that displays his maturity), Thelonious Monk's "Rhythm-a-ning," and two of his originals. —*Scott Yanow*

To the Ladies / Nov. 27, 1979-Nov. 28, 1979 / Galaxy ✦✦✦
Using the same trio that had joined him on *NYC Underground* (pianist Ron Mathews, bassist Ray Drummond and drummer Idris Muhammad), tenor saxophonist Johnny Griffin sticks exclusively to group originals on this interesting but not essential (and unfortunately out-of-print) LP. Griffin is in excellent form, as usual, but none of the tunes (by the leader, Drummond, and Mathews) caught on; the best is "Soft and Furry," which is taken in three parts. —*Scott Yanow*

Call It Whachawana / Jul. 25, 1983-Jul. 26, 1983 / Galaxy ✦✦✦✦
The emphasis is on ballads and slower tempos on this often-exquisite outing by tenor saxophonist Johnny Griffin. With strong support from the young rhythm section (pianist Mulgrew Miller, bassist Curtis Lundy and drummer Kenny Washington), Griffin is heard at his best on a definitive version of "Lover Man," recalls his days (25 years earlier) with Thelonious Monk on "I Mean You" and introduces two recent originals. Superlative music by a masterful player. —*Scott Yanow*

The Cat / Oct. 26, 1990-Oct. 29, 1990 / Antilles ✦✦✦✦
His latest—a tasty, often impressive, outing. —*Ron Wynn*

3 Dances of Passion / Apr. 29, 1992-Apr. 30, 1992 / Antilles ✦✦✦

Chicago, New York, Paris / Dec. 4, 1994-Dec. 5, 1994 / Verve ✦✦✦✦

Mario Grigorov

b. 1963, Sofia, Bulgaria
Piano / Post-Bop
Three days after arriving in the US in 1992, Mario Grigorov was trying out some instruments in a piano store when Bob James walked in, was very impressed and soon signed him to Reprise! Before that remarkable event took place, Grigorov had had extensive classical training in Bulgaria, Iran, East Germany and Austria. By the time his family relocated to Australia, Grigorov was becoming much more interested in jazz and rock. He had a successful composing and recording company, doing a great deal of scoring for films and television, but felt dissatisfied from an artistic level. Grigorov moved to the US, met James, recorded *Rhymes with Orange* for Reprise and went out on tour. A virtuoso player, Mario Grigorov infuses his complex but generally melodic improvisations with strong indications of both his classical background and his Bulgarian heritage. —*Scott Yanow*

● **Rhymes with Orange** / 1994 / Reprise ✦✦✦✦✦
The classically trained pianist Mario Grigorov (who is joined on some tracks by bassist Brian Bromberg and percussionist Glen Velez) makes his American debut on this impressive effort. A virtuoso with a very strong classical influence but the ability to improvise masterfully, Grigorov reworks "Body and Soul" and performs 11 of his originals. If he sticks to jazz, he has a great future. —*Scott Yanow*

Henry Grimes

b. Nov. 3, 1935, Philadelphia, PA
Bass / Free Jazz, Hard Bop
In 1967 at the height of the free-jazz movement, one of its finest bassists Henry Grimes disappeared, dropping out of music permanently. After attending Juilliard in the 1950s, Grimes toured with Arnett Cobb and Willis Jackson and played with the many talented young players in the Philadelphia scene of the mid-'50s. He was with Anita O'Day and Sonny Rollins in 1957 and a member of Gerry Mulligan's Quartet during 1957-58. A measure of his versatility is that at the 1958 Newport Jazz Festival Grimes played with Benny Goodman's Orchestra, Lee Konitz, Sonny Rollins and Thelonious Monk. After stints with Lennie Tristano and Rollins, Grimes became part of the free-jazz movement, playing with Cecil Taylor (off and on during 1961-66), Perry Robinson, Rollins again, Albert Ayler (1964-66) and Don Cherry, leading one session of his own for ESP (1965). And then in 1967 (for reasons that are still unclear) Henry Grimes, who was still only 31, left jazz. —*Scott Yanow*

Henry Grimes Trio / Dec. 28, 1965 / ESP ✦✦✦✦
The mysterious bassist Henry Grimes, who disappeared altogether in 1967, only led this one recording session; it has been reissued on CD. Although Grimes played in a wide variety of settings in the late 1950s, he was working exclusively in the avant-garde by 1965. Teamed with clarinetist Perry Robinson in one of his earliest recordings and the obscure drummer Tom Price, Grimes gets a fair amount of solo space on these six group originals. However, it is for Robinson's playing that the adventurous but not overly memorable disc is chiefly recommended. —*Scott Yanow*

Tiny Grimes (Lloyd Grimes)

b. Jul. 7, 1916, Newport News, VA, **d.** Mar. 4, 1989, New York, NY
Guitar / Bop, Early R&B Jazz, Jump Blues
Tiny Grimes was one of the earliest jazz electric guitarists to be influenced by Charlie Christian and he developed his own bluish swinging style. Early on he was a drummer and worked as a pianist in Washington. In 1938 he started playing electric guitar and two years later he was playing in a popular jive group, the Cats and a Fiddle. During 1943-44 Grimes was part of a classic Art Tatum Trio which also included Slam Stewart. In September 1944 he led his first record date, using Charlie Parker; highlights include the instrumental "Red Cross" and Grimes' vocal on "Romance Without Finance (Is a Nuisance)." He also recorded for Blue Note in 1946 and then put together an R&B-oriented group, "the Rockin' Highlanders," that featured the tenor of Red Prysock during 1948-52. Although maintaining a fairly low profile, Tiny Grimes was active up until his death, playing in an unchanged swing/bop transitional style and recording as a leader for such labels as Prestige/Swingville, Black & Blue, Muse and Sonet. —*Scott Yanow*

And His Rockin' Highlanders / Dec. 30, 1947-Jan. 12, 1953 / Swingtime ✦✦✦✦
During the period covered by this excellent collector's LP, Tiny Grimes (one of the first guitarists to be influenced by Charlie Christian) led an R&B group featuring the honking tenor of either John Hardee (in 1947) or, later on, Red Prysock. The music is fairly basic, especially compared to the bebop of the period, but also of interest to jazz listeners due to the strong musicianship, spirited performances, and pure fun in these renditions. This LP has 16 of Grimes' best recordings of this era, including "Hot in Harlem," "Annie Laurie," "Flying High," "Rock the House,"

"Loch Lomond" and "Sanctifying the Blues." Well worth picking up by those lucky enough to find this imported record. —*Scott Yanow*

Callin' the Blues / Jul. 18, 1958 / Original Jazz Classics ✦✦✦✦

This CD is a straight reissue of the original LP. Guitarist Tiny Grimes, who led three albums for Prestige and Swingville from 1958-59, welcomed two extroverted horn players (tenor saxophonist Eddie "Lockjaw" Davis and veteran trombonist J.C. Higginbotham), plus pianist Ray Bryant, bassist Wendell Marshall and drummer Osie Johnson, to his heated session. The group plays three original blues and "Airmail Special." Although J.C., who had a long decline, sounds a bit past his prime, plenty of sparks fly throughout the date, particularly from Grimes and Lockjaw. —*Scott Yanow*

● **Tiny in Swingsville** / Aug. 13, 1959 / Original Jazz Classics ✦✦✦✦✦

Guitarist Tiny Grimes was in a bit of obscurity when he had the opportunity to first record for Prestige in 1958. This particular CD (a reissue of the original LP) was the final of his three Prestige albums and it really puts the focus on Grimes' bluish but swinging guitar playing. With the strong assistance of Jerome Richardson (who is in top form on flute, tenor and baritone), pianist Ray Bryant, bassist Wendell Marshall and drummer Art Taylor, Grimes is heard in excellent form on "Annie Laurie," his "Durn Tootin'," "Ain't Misbehavin'," "Frankie and Johnnie" and a couple of original blues. —*Scott Yanow*

Profoundly Blue / Mar. 6, 1973 / Muse ✦✦✦

The veteran swing guitarist Tiny Grimes had relatively few chances to record during the '60s and '70s, particularly for American labels. This enjoyable outing for Muse features Grimes in a sextet with tenor saxophonist Houston Person and pianist Harold Mabern; these versions of "Profoundly Blue" and "Tiny's Exercise" are among the high points. Grimes also takes an effective vocal on the blues "Backslider" although the use of electric bass and congas makes the music seem a bit dated in spots. —*Scott Yanow*

Some Groovy Fours / May 13, 1974 / Classic Jazz ✦✦✦✦

With the exception of a Sonet album from 1977, this was guitarist Tiny Grimes' last recording as a leader. Grimes is surprisingly still in peak form and is well showcased in a quartet with pianist Lloyd Glenn, bassist Roland Lobligeois and drummer Panama Francis. Although there are some blues, as usual, Grimes also gets to stretch out "Lester Leaps In" and "I Found a New Baby," which show how strong a swing-based improviser he could be. This music was last available in the US on a Classic Jazz LP, although it has been reissued on CD in France. —*Scott Yanow*

David Grisman

b. 1945, Hackensack, NJ

Mandolin / Swing, Progressive Bluegrass

David Grisman is normally associated with the bluegrass wing of country music, but his music owes almost as much to jazz as it does to traditional American folk influences. Because he couldn't think of what to call his unique, highly intricate, harmonically advanced hybrid of acoustic bluegrass, folk and jazz without leaning toward one idiom or another, he offhandedly decided to call it "dawg music"—a name which, curiously enough, has stuck. A brilliant mandolinist, with roots deep in the Hot Club Quintette of France, Grisman's jazz sensibilities were strong enough to attract the admiration of the HCQ's Stephane Grappelli, who has toured and recorded with Grisman on occasion.

Grisman was already playing the piano, saxophone and mandolin by the time he was a teenager, taking up the latter at age 16. While attending New York University, he began playing with the Even Dozen Jug Band, which at one time included Maria Muldaur and John Sebastian. He formed the Great American String Band with violinist Richard Greene in 1974 and founded the Quintet in 1976 that became known for the "dawg" hybrid. Grisman's breakthrough album was 1979's *Hot Dawg* for A&M's jazz line, Horizon, featuring Grappelli, whom Grisman had met while scoring the film *King of the Gypsies*. By 1980, the Grisman Quintet included such like-minded virtuoso eclectics as fiddler/guitarist Mark O'Connor, violinist Darol Anger (later of the Turtle Island String Quartet) and bassist Rob Wasserman. In 1987, Grisman recorded with jazz violinist Svend Asmussen, and he has also done lots of session work with artists like Béla Fleck (for whom Grisman's example has paved the way), Judy Collins, John Sebastian, Dolly Parton and James Taylor. —*Richard S. Ginell*

Early Dawg / Mar. 1966-Jun. 1973 / Sugar Hill ✦✦✦

Bluegrass meets jazz. —*Hank Davis*

★ **The David Grisman Quintet** / Nov. 1976-Dec. 1976 / Rhino ✦✦✦✦✦

The David Grisman Quintet's eponymous debut was a stunning achievement, capturing a pivotal point in newgrass history. It was a record that opened up new rhythmic textures and instrumental textures—specifically new, jazzier ways to solo. Grisman—who wrote the majority of the compositions—arranged each num-

ber as a way for his quintet to shine instrumentally, as a way for each musician to demonstrate their innovative skills. It's not traditional bluegrass—these instrumental recordings draw equally from folk, rock and country as they do from bluegrass—but was a thrilling new variation on the form that broke down countless doors for the genre. —*Thom Owens*

Hot Dawg / July 1978- Oct. 1978 / A&M ✦✦✦✦✦

With Stephane Grappelli and a Django-esque sound. —*Hank Davis*

Quintet '80 / 1980 / Warner Brothers ✦✦✦

Throughout his career, mandolinist David Grisman has performed music that crosses between many boundaries, from "new acoustic" folk to bluegrass and swing-oriented jazz. This set features Grisman's string group (which also includes violinist Darol Anger, Mike Marshall on mandolin, guitar and violin, Mark O'Connor on violin and guitar, and bassist Rob Wasserman) playing six of Grisman's diverse originals, an obscure tune, and a brief rendition of John Coltrane's "Naima." The music is excellent, but Grisman's more jazz-oriented projects would be in the future. —*Scott Yanow*

Mondo Mando / Jul. 7, 1981-Jul. 16, 1981 / Zebra ✦✦✦✦

David Grisman's desire to break or extend the boundaries of string music, folk, and bluegrass resulted in recordings that are also of interest to jazz listeners. The mandolinist performs seven colorful originals (including "Dawg Funk"), plus Django Reinhardt's lesser-known "Anouman" with various string players, including Mike Marshall on mandolin, violinists Darol Anger and Mark O'Connor, guitarist Tony Rice, and bassist Rob Wasserman; the Kronos String Quartet helps out on "Mando Mando." Unpredictable and fairly unique music. —*Scott Yanow*

Dawg Grass / Dawg Jazz / 1982 / Warner Brothers ✦✦✦✦✦

After several projects that hinted at his interest in jazz, David Grisman split this album between swing and bluegrass. The four jazz numbers include a big-band outing on "Dawg Jazz," a guest appearance by violinist Stephane Grappelli on "Steppin' with Stephane," an appearance by violinist Darol Anger on "Fumblebee," and a version of "In a Sentimental Mood" with both Grappelli and Anger. The flip side of the LP (not yet issued on CD) finds Grisman's string group, plus guest banjoist Earl Scruggs, stretching the boundaries of the bluegrass idiom on tunes such as "Swamp Dawg," "Dawggy Mountain Breakdown," and "Happy Birthday, Bill Monroe." A diverse and continually interesting set. —*Scott Yanow*

David Grisman's Acoustic Christmas / 1983 / Rounder ✦✦✦✦

Sticking to traditional Christmas songs, mandolinist David Grisman and his impressive string group, plus a few guests (including recorder players on two brief songs and banjoist Béla Fleck), alternate swinging renditions of familiar melodies with ballads. Highlights include "Santa Claus Is Coming to Town," "God Rest Ye Merry Christmas," and "Winter Wonderland." —*Scott Yanow*

Mandolin Abstractions / 1983 / Rounder ✦✦✦

Despite the musicianship and some colorful moments, this duo set by mandolinists David Grisman and Andy Statman (essentially melodic free improvisations) misses a rhythm section. The song titles (which include "Two White Boys Watching James Brown at the Apollo," "Journey to the Center of Twang" and the two-part "March of the Mandolas") are more colorful than the music, and although not without interest, this is one of David Grisman's least memorable recordings. —*Scott Yanow*

Acousticity / June 5, 1984-June 7, 1984 / Zebra ✦✦✦✦

By 1984, David Grisman's "Dawg Jazz" concept was at its prime. Grisman's string group (comprising the leader's mandolin, violinist Jim Buchanan, guitarist Jon Sholle and bassist Rob Wasserman, plus guest drummer Hal Blaine) was flexible enough to play anything from bluegrass and folk music to swing; the latter is emphasized on this spirited set during such numbers as "Acousticity," "Blue Sky Bop," "Dawgalypso," and "Tango for Django." Recommended. —*Scott Yanow*

Home Is Where the Heart Is / 1988 / Rounder ✦✦✦

A more traditional country and bluegrass album than his "dawg" sessions, Rounder issued this Grisman session in 1988. He's playing with J.D. Crowe, Ricky Skaggs, and Doc Watson, among others. There's little jazz here, but there are some superb bluegrass, country, and folk selections, plus marvelous playing. —*Ron Wynn*

Svingin' with Svend / Nov. 5, 1986-May 21, 1987 / Zebra ✦✦✦✦

Despite his popularity, mandolinist David Grisman has made relatively few recordings since this CD. Matched with the great veteran swing violinist Svend Asmussen, Grisman holds his own on one of his most jazz-oriented dates. With guitarist Dimitri Vandellos, bassist James Kerwin and drummer George Marsh completing the quintet, Grisman and Asmussen jam on the title cut, two of the violinist's originals, "It Don't Mean a Thing," "Jitterbug Waltz," Milt Jackson's "The Spirit Feel," and a pair of Django Reinhardt-Stephane Grappelli tunes. Highly recommended. —*Scott Yanow*

Don Grolnick

b. Sep. 23, 1947, New York, NY, d. Jun. 1, 1996, New York, NY
Piano, Keyboards / Post-Bop
Don Grolnick was a subtle and rather underrated pianist throughout his career, but his flexibility and talents were well-known to his fellow musicians. Grolnick played in rock bands while a teenager but was always interested in jazz. He worked in the early fusion group Dreams (1969-71), the Brecker Brothers (starting in 1975) and in the early '80s with Steps Ahead. He has long been a busy session musician often utilized by pop singers. In the 1980s Grolnick appeared in many settings including with Joe Farrell, George Benson, Peter Erskine, David Sanborn, John Scofield, Mike Stern and the Bob Mintzer big band. Don Grolnick is heard at his best on his Hip Pocket debut *Hearts and Numbers* (1986) and on his two Blue Note albums, which have been reissued as a double CD. —*Scott Yanow*

Hearts and Numbers / 1985 / Hip Pocket ✦✦✦✦
A very attractive contemporary project. "Pointing at the Moon" and "More Pointing" make for sprightly music. —*Michael G. Nastos*

● The Complete Blue Note Recordings / Feb. 14, 1989-Dec. 1991 / Blue Note ✦✦✦✦✦
Don Grolnick had such a successful career as a commercial keyboardist, playing with the likes of James Taylor, Linda Ronstadt, Steely Dan and James Brown among others, that it was often forgotten that his roots were in jazz. In 1989, he recorded the album *Weaver of Dreams* and nearly three years later led Nighttown. All of the music from the two dates are reissued on this two-CD set without any additional material. In both cases, Grolnick utilizes an unusual four-horn front line featuring trumpeter Randy Brecker, either Barry Rogers or Steve Turre on trombone and Michael Brecker or Joe Lovano on tenor, and has a prominent bass clarinet (either Bob Mintzer or Marty Ehrlich). The unpredictable arrangements, which cover a wide range of styles, are quite colorful, sometimes hinting at Dixieland and swing, and are open to the influence of Charles Mingus. Grolnick himself (heard throughout on acoustic piano) is well showcased on "A Weaver of Dreams," and his eccentric and joyful reworking of "I Want to Be Happy" is a classic. Well worth exploring. —*Scott Yanow*

Medianoche / 1995 / Warner Brothers ✦✦✦✦

Steve Grossman

b. Jan. 18, 1951, New York, NY
Tenor Saxophone, Soprano Saxophone / Hard Bop, Post Bop
Although he started out playing in fusion-oriented settings, Steve Grossman has developed into an excellent hard bop tenor in the tradition of Sonny Rollins (although he has developed his own sound). Grossman originally started on alto when he was eight, added soprano at 15 and tenor at 16. He started at the top as Wayne Shorter's replacement with Miles Davis, playing in his fusion group from late 1969 up to September 1970. Grossman was with Lonnie Liston Smith in 1971, spent a valuable period (1971-73) as part of Elvin Jones' group and in the mid-'70s was with Gene Perla's Stone Alliance. Steve Grossman has mostly led his own bands ever since, recording as a leader for P.M., Owl, Red and Dreyfus. —*Scott Yanow*

Some Shapes to Come / Sep. 4, 1973-Sep. 6, 1973 / PM ✦✦✦

Perspective / 1979 / Atlantic ✦✦✦

Way Out East, Vol. 1 / Jul. 23, 1984-Jul. 24, 1984 / Red ✦✦✦✦

Way Out East, Vol. 2 / Jul. 23, 1984-Jul. 25, 1984 / Red ✦✦✦✦
Tenor saxophonist Steve Grossman, who played with Miles Davis' electric group in the early 1970s, is very much in a Sonny Rollins vein throughout this excellent trio outing with bassist Juni Booth and drummer Joe Chambers. The title is a play on Rollins' classic *Way Out West* album, although most of the material (which includes 'Trane's Slow Blues," "Soul Trane" and "Like Someone in Love") actually belongs more to the John Coltrane songbook. Grossman's tone echoes Rollins while also hinting at his own developing personality, and his improvisations are consistently impressive. —*Scott Yanow*

Love Is the Thing / May 1985 / Red ✦✦✦✦
Although tenor saxophonist Steve Grossman's main influence by the 1980s was Sonny Rollins, this quartet set could be considered a tribute to John Coltrane. With inspiring support from pianist Cedar Walton, bassist David Williams and drummer Billy Higgins, Grossman interprets such ballads as "Naima," "Easy to Love," "Easy Living" and "I Didn't Know What Time It Was," but is careful to vary the tempos and moods; he also contributes an original, "415 Central Park West." Excellent modern mainstream music from a fine tenorman. —*Scott Yanow*

Steve Grossman Quartet, Vol. 1 / Nov. 1985 / DIW ✦✦✦

Steve Grossman Quartet, Vol. 2 / Nov. 1985 / DIW ✦✦✦

Katonah / Feb. 4, 1986 / DIW ✦✦✦

My Second Prime / Dec. 17, 1990 / Red ✦✦✦✦

Do It / Apr. 29, 1991-Apr. 30, 1991 / Dreyfus ✦✦✦✦✦

● In New York / Sep. 13, 1991-Sep. 14, 1991 / Dreyfus ✦✦✦✦✦

Small Hotel / 1993 / Dreyfus ✦✦✦

Time to Smile / Feb. 12, 1993 / Dreyfus ✦✦✦✦✦
This outing is one of tenor saxophonist Steve Grossman's finest recordings to date. He has mixed together the almost equal influences of John Coltrane and Sonny Rollins to achieve his own style and sound. The program is quite strong with its superior yet generally underplayed standards joined by two of the leader's originals, Elvin Jones' "E.J.'s Blues" and Freddie Redd's "Time to Smile"; also the lineup of musicians would be difficult to top. Pianist Willie Pickens shows a lot of versatility on the hard-bop-oriented music, trumpeter Tom Harrell (who is on around half of the tracks) is as fiery and alert as usual, bassist Cecil McBee has a strong musical personality that comes across even when restricted to accompanying the soloists, and drummer Elvin Jones remains in prime form. The main focus however is mostly on Grossman and he continues to grow as an improviser year-by-year. Highly recommended. —*Scott Yanow*

Marty Grosz (Martin Oliver Grosz)

b. Feb. 28, 1930, Berlin, Germany
Guitar, Vocals / Classic Jazz
One of jazz music's great comedians (his spontaneous monologues are often hilarious), Marty Grosz is a brilliant acoustic guitarist whose chordal solos bring back the sound of Carl Kress and Dick McDonough of the 1930s while his vocals are very much in the Fats Waller tradition. It took Grosz a long time to get some visibility. He grew up in New York, attended Columbia University and in 1951 led a Dixieland band with Dick Wellstood that recorded. Based in Chicago, Grosz did record with Dave Remington, Art Hodes and Albert Nicholas in the 1950s, led sessions of his own in 1957 and 1959 for Riverside and Audio Fidelity and tried his best to coax Jabbo Smith out of retirement (some of their rehearsals were later released on LP) but was fairly obscure until he joined Soprano Summit (1975-79). After that association ended, Grosz became a busy freelancer on the classic jazz scene, playing with Dick Sudhalter, Joe Muryani and Dick Wellstood in the Classic Jazz Quartet and in more recent times heading the Orphan Newsboys, a superb quartet that also includes Peter Ecklund, Bobby Gordon and bassist Greg Cohen. Marty Grosz, a unique personality, has recorded several delightful sets for Jazzology and Stomp Off. —*Scott Yanow*

I Hope Gabriel Likes My Music / Jun. 25, 1981-Jun. 26, 1981 / Aviva ✦✦✦✦
This little-known but very enjoyable LP was one of the first times that the mature Marty Grosz emerged on records outside of his work with Soprano Summit. A good-humored vocalist who sings "Junk Man," "Lonesome Me" and the title cut on this set, Grosz is heard in a quartet with trumpeter Jimmy Maxwell, clarinetist Sam Parkins, and either Jack Six or Pete Campo, and with an octet using the same players plus trombonist Bobby Pring, Dick Meldonian on soprano and tenor, pianist Dick Wellstood, and drummer Freddie Stoll. The music is essentially classic jazz with concise solos and colorful ensembles uplifting such songs as "Serenade to a Wealthy Widow," "When Day Is Done" and "California Here I Come." Easily recommended to Marty Grosz fans. —*Scott Yanow*

Sings of Love & Other Matters / May 20, 1986-May 22, 1986 / Statiras ✦✦✦✦
Marty Grosz, a Fats Waller-inspired vocalist, a masterful chordal acoustic guitarist and a frequently hilarious comedian, is well showcased on this Jazzology CD reissue of a set originally cut for the Statiras label. Featured with his Destiny's Tots (a group not dissimilar to his Orphan Newsboys), Grosz sings such bright numbers as "With Plenty of Money and You," "I'm in the Market for You," "I Wish I Were Twins," "My Very Good Friend the Milkman," "I'm Building Up to an Awful Let-down," and "You've Been Taking Lessons in Love." Hot solos are provided by Dick Meldonian (on tenor, alto and baritone), Dan Barrett (doubling on trombone and cornet), pianist Keith Ingham and bassist Phil Flanigan. Highly recommended to classic jazz fans. —*Scott Yanow*

Marty Grosz and the Keepers of the Flame (And the Imps) / Jan. 29, 1987-Mar. 12, 1987 / Stomp Off ✦✦✦✦✦
For this highly enjoyable effort, guitarist/singer Marty Grosz named his band "The Keepers of the Flames"; he also performs three numbers with his "Imps," a trio also including clarinetist Joe Muranyi and Paul Bacon on comb. The Keepers consist of a quintet/sextet drawn from Grosz, cornetist Peter Ecklund, violinist Andy Stein (who comes close to sounding like Joe Venuti), Bacon, Muranyi, guitarist Frank Vignola, pianist Dick Wellstood and Vince Giordano doubling on bass sax and string bass. The colorful and infectious ensembles, along with the many distinctive soloists, make these mostly ancient standards come alive, and Grosz's vocals are often quite humorous. Among the many highlights are "Miss Annabelle

Lee," "Oh Miss Hannah," "He's the Last Word," "Bessie Couldn't Help It" and "Mandy." —*Scott Yanow*

Swing It! / Jun. 1988-Jul. 1988 / Jazzology ✦✦✦✦✦

On this highly enjoyable CD, guitarist-vocalist Marty Grosz leads an all-star swing group called Destiny's Tots and comprising trumpeter Peter Ecklund, trombonist Dan Barrett, clarinetist Bob Gordon, Loren Schoenberg on tenor, pianist Keith Ingham, bassist Murray Wall and drummer Hal Smith. The majority of the selections (which include "The Skeleton in the Closet," Hoagy Carmichael's "Old Man Harlem," "Little Girl" and "Eye Opener") are obscurities and even the better-known songs (such as "Sunrise Serenade" and "Sonny Boy") are rarely heard in this type of freewheeling but controlled small-group setting. A gem of its kind. —*Scott Yanow*

Extra! / Aug. 1989-Sep. 1989 / Jazzology ✦✦✦✦✦

The Orphan Newsboys (comprising guitarist/vocalist Marty Grosz, cornetist Peter Ecklund, clarinetist Bobby Gordon and bassist Greg Cohen) are a very popular attraction on the classic jazz festival and party circuit. Their ensembles are both cool and exciting, Grosz is a masterful rhythm guitarist and a humorous Fats Waller-influenced singer, and the band is one of the very best in performing small-group swing. This CD was their recording debut as a group; clarinetist/altoist Ken Peplowski and bassist Murray Wall sub on five of the 16 selections. Highlights of the delightful set include "One in a Million," "Milenberg Joys," "Blue Room," "Pardon Me, Pretty Baby" and "My Melancholy Baby." Highly recommended. —*Scott Yanow*

Unsaturated Fats / Jan. 30, 1990-Feb. 22, 1990 / Stomp Off ✦✦✦✦✦

This is a rather unusual CD, for few listeners (including early jazz fanatics) would be able to identify the 18 selections as Fats Waller compositions. Only "Lookin' Good But Feelin' Bad" was actually recorded by Waller and, while "St. Louis Shuffle," "That Rhythm Man" and "If It Ain't Love" were slightly known at one time, it had been quite awhile since anyone recorded "Dixie Cinderella," "Asbestos," "Say Yes" and "Charleston Hound." Grosz (who takes some vocals) doubles on guitar and banjo and is joined by pianist Keith Ingham, cornetist Peter Ecklund, clarinetist Joe Muranyi, trombonist Dan Barrett, bassist Greg Cohen and drummer Arnie Kinsella for the spirited and often-surprising program. —*Scott Yanow*

And Destiny's Tots / Mar. 23, 1992-Jun. 11, 1992 / Jazzology ✦✦✦✦✦

The Orphan Newsboys: Rhythm for Sale / May 20, 1993-Jan. 16, 1996 / Jazzology ✦✦✦✦

Songs I Learned At My Mother's Knee & Other Low Joints / Aug. 10, 1994 / Jazzology ✦✦✦✦

Destiny's Tots is the name that guitarist/singer Marty Grosz gave to some of the freewheeling ensembles he put together during the 1980s and '90s (as opposed to the Orphan Newsboys, which is a set group). On this delightful set, Grosz is heard in three different settings: a trio with clarinetist Dick Meldonian and bassist Greg Cohen and two septets that feature either Peter Ecklund or Randy Sandke on trumpet, Meldonian or clarinetist/altoist Ken Peplowski and Bob Pring or Joel Helleny on trombone. Grosz always puts on a good show, making the music of the 1920s and '30s sound both relevant and good-humored. Among the highlights of this 17-song program (13 of which the leader sings) are "Stompy Jones," "Truckin'," "Dinner for One, Please, James," "The Curse of an Achin' Heart" and "When I Take My Sugar to Tea." —*Scott Yanow*

● **Keep a Song in Your Soul** / Oct. 18, 1994-Oct. 19, 1994 / Jazzology ✦✦✦✦✦

Marty Grosz is quite notable in at least three ways. He is one of the top (and one of the few) rhythm acoustic guitarists, and his chordal solos are always delightful. He sings in a Fats Waller-inspired style. And Grosz is one of jazz's top comedians, able to spin out hilarious, sometimes nonsensical monologues. Two of his three talents are heard on this CD, although he should record a comedy album someday. Grosz leads two different groups during the 1994 sessions. One band has the members of his Orphan Newsboys (trumpeter Peter Ecklund, clarinetist Bobby Gordon and bassist Greg Cohen) along with the reeds of Dan Levinson, pianist Chris Dawson and drummer Hal Smith. The other half of this set features Ecklund, Cohen, trombonist Joel Helleny (whose plunger work is outstanding), Dan Block on clarinet and alto, Scott Robinson on tenor and baritone, pianist Keith Ingham and drummer Artie Kinsella. The repertoire is dominated by obscurities from the 1920s and '30s, with a couple of standards tossed in. Grosz sings on half of the songs. Highlights include "Sentimental Gentleman from Georgia," a cooking version of "Hot Lips," "From Monday On" and "Love Will Find a Way." This is a spirited and enjoyable outing, well worth picking up by hot jazz fans. —*Scott Yanow*

Ring Dem Bells / Feb. 25, 1995 / Nagel-Heyer ✦✦✦✦

For this live concert from Hamburg, Germany, guitarist/vocalist Marty Grosz called his pickup sextet "the Swinging Fools." With trumpeter Jon-Erik Kellso and

Scott Robinson on clarinet, soprano and baritone (who are assisted by pianist Martin Litton, bassist Greg Cohen and drummer Chuck Riggs), Grosz had two contrasting soloists who blended together well and took chances within the Dixieland/swing genre. The leader contributes some excellent chordal acoustic guitar solos and a few humorous vocals. The high points of the date include "Rose of the Rio Grande," "Nobody's Sweetheart," "Old Man Blues," "Swing That Music" and "Ring Dem Bells." An excellent outing. —*Scott Yanow*

On Revival Day / Apr. 21, 1995-Apr. 23, 1995 / Jazzology ✦✦✦✦✦

Guitarist/vocalist/ad-libber Marty Grosz's best-known group is the Orphan Newsboys, a quartet with trumpeter Peter Ecklund, clarinetist Bobby Gordon and bassist Greg Cohen. On this particular CD, recorded at the 1995 Atlanta Jazz Party, Grosz heads his "Sugar Daddies," a septet with Ecklund, Gordon, trombonist Bob Havens, pianist Keith Ingham, bassist Frank Tate and drummer Wayne Jones. Thirteen classic tunes from the 1920s and '30s are swung, with the occasional standard (such as "Bugle Call Rag" and "I Wish I Could Shimmy Like My Sister Kate") joined by such rarely performed songs as "Strut Miss Lizzie," "Sobbin' Blues" (which has some fine whistling from Ecklund), "Little Girl" and a hot version of "Let Me Call You Sweetheart." The ensembles are heated but uncrowded, the solos are concise and meaningful, and Grosz's occasional vocals are always fun. This very likable set is highly recommended to fans of pre-bop jazz. —*Scott Yanow*

GRP All-Star Big Band

f. 1992 db. 1994

Group / Hard Bop

GRP is best known as a label specializing in slick and accessible jazz but in 1992 label heads Dave Grusin and Larry Rosen decided to put together a conventional but star-studded big band comprising their company's top players. Three recordings over a four-year period (and one full-length video) have resulted thus far, featuring such musicians as Arturo Sandoval, Randy Brecker, Chuck Findley, Dave Grusin, Ernie Watts, Bob Mintzer, Dave Valentin, John Patitucci and even Tom Scott, Eric Marienthal, Nelson Rangell and Lee Ritenour playing straightahead charts of jazz standards from the 1950s and '60s. The recordings actually offer few surprises (other than the fact that Scott and company still remember how to play bop) but are enjoyable outings. —*Scott Yanow*

● **GRP All-Star Big Band** / Jan. 12, 1992 / GRP ✦✦✦✦✦

When this CD was released, it was a major surprise. GRP is a label whose initial reputation was made on poppish jazz. However, co-founders Dave Grusin and Larry Rosen always had a love for the sound of big bands and for hard bop. For this set, they gathered together some of the most notable players on their label to play 12 jazz standards dating from the mid-1940s ("Donna Lee") up to the early '70s ("Spain"). The lineup of musicians is quite impressive, comprising trumpeters Arturo Sandoval, Randy Brecker and Sal Marquez, trombonist George Bohanon (who had to be imported since GRP did not have any trombonists), a reed section of Eric Marienthal, Nelson Rangell, Bob Mintzer, Ernie Watts and Tom Scott, bassist John Patitucci, drummer Dave Weckl, and several alternating pianists (Grusin, Russell Ferrante, Kenny Kirkland and David Benoit), plus such guests as guitarist Lee Ritenour, flutist Dave Valentine, vibraphonist Gary Burton, clarinetist Eddie Daniels and percussionist Alex Acuna. On the strictly straightahead set, which has such tunes as "Blue Train," "Sister Sadie," "The Sidewinder" and "Manteca," all of the musicians are featured adequately. It is a particular revelation hearing Marienthal and Rangell sound passable in this setting. Easily recommended to hard-bop and big-band collectors. —*Scott Yanow*

GRP All-Star Big Band: Live! / Jan. 31, 1993 / GRP ✦✦✦

All Blues / Jan. 8, 1994-Jan. 9, 1994 / GRP ✦✦

When one considers the large number of great players that participated in this project (including trumpeters Arturo Sandoval, Randy Brecker and Chuck Findley, trombonist George Bohanon, the reeds of Eric Marienthal, Nelson Rangell, Tom Scott, Ernie Watts and Bob Mintzer, such keyboardists as Dave Grusin, Chick Corea, Ramsey Lewis and Russell Ferrante, bassist John Patitucci, drummer Dave Weckl and guests B.B. King and tenor-great Michael Brecker), the rather predictable results are a disappointment. With the exception of Chick Corea's recent "Blue Miles," this album could have been titled "Warhorses" due to the very familiar material. The arrangements by Michael Abene, Scott, Grusin, Mintzer and Ferrante contain no real surprises (other than some unexpected moments on "Misterioso") and none of the solos are long enough to really build. There is a certain novelty in hearing some of the crossover players like Rangell, Scott and Lewis playing hard-bop tunes such as "Birks Works," "Senor Blues" and "Cookin' at the Continental" but why waste B.B. King on yet another version of "Stormy Monday Blues?" —*Scott Yanow*

George Gruntz

b. Jun. 24, 1932, Basel, Switzerland
Piano, Arranger, Composer, Leader / Post-Bop

George Gruntz's Concert Jazz Band, an orchestra that sticks to originals by band members (both past and present) and the leader's arrangements, has long been one of the most stimulating of all jazz big bands. Gruntz, a fine pianist, played locally in Switzerland and then debuted in the US when he appeared with Marshall Brown's International Youth Band at the 1958 Newport Jazz Festival. His trio in Europe accompanied touring American musicians in the 1960s including Dexter Gordon and Rahsaan Roland Kirk and formed three-quarters of Phil Woods' adventurous European Rhythm Machine (1968-69). Gruntz recorded in many different settings including with the Swiss All-Stars, a four-flute septet, and with Mideast musicians and Jean-Luc Ponty on 1967's *Noon in Tunisia*. In 1972 he formed the Concert Jazz Band which through the years has featured a who's who of top musicians including Benny Bailey, Woody Shaw, Franco Ambrosetti, Dexter Gordon, Herb Geller, Phil Woods, Eddie Daniels, Ray Anderson, Lew Soloff, Chris Hunter, Bob Mintzer and many other Americans and Europeans; they typically have two tours a year and have even performed in China. Gruntz has also recorded with smaller groups and his more recent records have been released by Enja and TCB. —*Scott Yanow*

The Band / May 14, 1976 / MPS ◆◆◆
Live at Schauspielhaus. This 21-piece co-led by The Ambrosettis, drummer Daniel Humair, and Gruntz. "Epitaph" for Ake Persson. No holds barred. —*Michael G. Nastos*

CG-CJB (George Gruntz Concert Jazz Band) / Sep. 22, 1978 / MPS ◆◆◆◆◆
It's a 21-piece band. Stunning music by ensemble. Soloists include Elvin Jones (d), John Scofield (g), Lew Tabackin (sax). Other players, like Woody Shaw (tpt), Jimmy Knepper (tb), and Bennie Wallace (ts), make this band special. —*Michael G. Nastos*

● **25 Years** / Mar. 22, 1981-Apr. 28, 1995 / TCB ◆◆◆◆◆
To celebrate their 25th anniversary, the George Gruntz Concert Jazz Band is featured throughout this CD on what is called "The World's Greatest Unknown Hits." The ten previously unreleased selections are each taken from different concerts, and there are plenty of colorful and rambunctious solos, along with a strong dose of humor. There are spots for the electrified trumpet of Palle Mikkelborg, altoist Chris Hunter, trumpeter Arturo Sandoval, pianist/leader George Gruntz (showcased on a medley of "Kinda Gruntzy" and "Rockin' in Rhythm"), trombonists Jimmy Knepper and Dave Taylor, Joe Daley on euphonium, singer Sheila Jordan (on two odd numbers), French horn player John Clark (who romps on Horace Silver's "Room 608"), altoist Tim Berne, and trombonist Ray Anderson among others. Gruntz has long focused on originals by band members, doing all of the arranging himself, so other than the encores, this colorful set is a bit unusual, since it has renditions of "Rockin' in Rhythm," "The Preacher," and even "The Yellow Rose of Texas." These performances, far from mere leftovers, are quite enjoyable and add new light to the Concert Jazz Band's growing legacy. —*Scott Yanow*

Theatre / Jul. 1983 / ECM ◆◆◆
George Gruntz Concert Jazz Band. This is a 1983 studio date with 18-piece group. Sheila Jordan singing "No One Can Explain It" is a waterfall of emotion. Lots of Dino Saluzzi on bandoneon, brass heavy. Operatic and soaring. —*Michael G. Nastos*

Happening Now! / Oct. 16, 1987-Oct. 17, 1987 / Hat Art ◆◆◆◆
George Gruntz's Concert Jazz Band always has such remarkable personnel in its tours, mixing together some of the top adventurous American and European musicians. For this CD, the soloists include the leader/pianist, trumpeters Kenny Wheeler, Manfred Schoof and Enrico Rava, tenors Joe Henderson and Larry Schneider, Ernst Petrowsky on soprano, Howard Johnson on tuba, trombonists Art Baron and Ray Anderson, and singer Sheila Jordan (who is heard on the title cut); heard in the ensembles but unfortunately not featured are altoist Lee Konitz and trumpeters Marvin Stamm and Franco Ambrosetti. Despite the all-star personnel, the ensembles are quite tight, the material (four originals by Gruntz, plus Henderson's "Inner Urge") is generally complex, and the band lives up to its very high potential. —*Scott Yanow*

● **First Prize** / May 7, 1989-May 8, 1989 / Enja ◆◆◆◆◆
This is a particularly fine outing by George Gruntz's Concert Jazz Band. Trombonist Ray Anderson's "Fishin' with Gramps" is a crackup, and the other material is both complex and full of wit and color. With such soloists as trumpeters Mike Mossman, Franco Ambrosetti, Stanton Davis and Manfred Schoof, Larry Schneider (on tenor and soprano), Howard Johnson on bass clarinet and tuba, altoist Chris Hunter (who sometimes sounds quite close to David Sanborn), Vinny Golia on baritone, and others, there is plenty of variety and many brilliant moments. George Gruntz's 18-piece group was one of the finest of the period, and this sometimes eccentric CD is a perfect introduction to his music. —*Scott Yanow*

Serious Fun / Sep. 21, 1989-Sep. 23, 1989 / Enja ◆◆◆◆
George Gruntz is best known as the leader and arranger of his Concert Jazz Band so this trio date is a real rarity. Gruntz's piano playing, although very much in the tradition, features his own individual voice. Joined by bassist Mike Richmond and drummer Adam Nussbaum (fluegelhornist Franco Ambrosetti makes the group a quartet on "Autumn Again"), Gruntz is in excellent form throughout this enjoyable live set. —*Scott Yanow*

Blues 'n Dues Et Cetera / Jan. 4, 1991-Jan. 29, 1991 / Enja ◆◆◆◆◆
Pianist/composer George Gruntz had led his Concert Jazz Band for nearly 20 years at the time of this Enja CD. Although the personnel changes to a large extent every year, Gruntz's principles for his music (all of which he arranges) have remained the same: utilize flexible virtuosi on a repertoire of originals drawn entirely from the band. This particular release combines such major players as altoist Chris Hunter, guitarist John Scofield, trombonist Ray Anderson, trumpeters Wallace Roney, Jon Faddis, Randy Brecker, Michael Mossman, Marvin Stamm, John D'Earth and Franco Ambrosetti and tenors Bob Mintzer, Bob Malach and Jerry Bergonzi on a diverse and well-rounded set of unpredictable music. Anderson's "Rap for Nap" is particularly odd. It's well worth investigating. —*Scott Yanow*

Live in China / Nov. 11, 1992-Nov. 18, 1992 / TCB ◆◆◆◆
In Nov. 1992 the George Gruntz Concert Jazz Band became one of the very first jazz groups to ever tour China. Gruntz's 16-piece orchestra at the time featured such colorful soloists as trumpeters Lew Soloff, Jack Walrath, Tim Hagans and John D'Earth, trombonist Ray Anderson, altoist Chris Hunter and the tenors of Larry Schneider and Bob Malach. For the tour Gruntz brought along bluesmen Billy Branch (on harmonica) and guitarist Carl Weathersby and they are heard singing and playing on three of the six full-length selections, making this set a little more accessible than usual. Ray Anderson's riotous "Literary Lizard" (during which he challenges Lew Soloff in the upper register), Weatherby's emotional guitar solo on "Carl" and the general spirit of this flexible orchestra makes one wonder what the Chinese thought of this extroverted and often eccentric music. —*Scott Yanow*

Dave Grusin

b. Jun. 26, 1934, Denver, CO
Piano, Composer / Crossover Jazz, Bop, Film Scores

Dave Grusin has been a highly successful performer, producer, composer, record label executive, arranger and bandleader. His piano playing ranges from mildly challenging to competent to routine, but he's an accomplished film and television soundtrack composer. Grusin played with Terry Gibbs and Johnny Smith while studying at the University of Colorado. He was assistant music director and pianist with Andy Williams from 1959 to 1966, and started his television composing career. Grusin recorded with Benny Goodman in 1960, and recorded with a hardbop trio that included Milt Hinton and Don Lamond in the early '60s. He also played and did a session with a quintet including Thad Jones and Frank Foster. Grusin did arrangements and recorded with Sarah Vaughan, Quincy Jones and Carmen McRae in the early '70s. He played electric keyboards with Gerry Mulligan and Lee Ritenour in the mid-'70s, then helped establish GRP Records out of a production company. GRP developed into one of the top contemporary jazz and fusion companies; they were later taken over by MCA. Grusin continued recording through the '80s and '90s, doing numerous projects from fusion and pop to working with symphony orchestras. He's also conducted the GRP big band, continued scoring such films as *The Fabulous Baker Boys*, and doing duet sessions with his brother Don, and with Lee Ritenour. Besides his numerous GRP releases, Grusin's also recorded for Columbia, Sheffield Lab and Polygram. —*Ron Wynn*

One of a Kind / 1977 / GRP ◆◆◆
A fairly typical Dave Grusin date from the early days of GRP, this set features five of the keyboardist/producer's originals. The music is often atmospheric and a bit cinematic, with Grusin assisted by the soprano of Grover Washington and flutist Dave Valentin (along with top rhythm section players) on two songs apiece; "The Heart Is a Lonely Hunter" has Grusin's keyboards joined just by Ron Carter's bass. The music is pleasing, but not too substantial. —*Scott Yanow*

Mountain Dance / Dec. 10, 1979-Dec. 17, 1979 / GRP ◆◆◆

Out of the Shadows / Jan. 1982-Feb. 1982 / GRP ◆◆◆
Lee Ritenour makes an occasional interesting statement. Otherwise, this is routine filler. —*Ron Wynn*

Night-Lines / 1983 / GRP ◆◆◆

Harlequin / 1985 / GRP ◆◆◆◆

Sticks and Stones / 1988 / GRP ◆◆◆◆◆
This set works very well. Dave Grusin and his younger brother Don Grusin use a variety of keyboards to create a series of colorful duets. Other than Dori Caymmi's "Southern Wind," all of the fairly spontaneous yet well-planned performances are

originals by one or both of the brothers. Even listeners who are not that much into electronics will find much of interest on this melodic and funky, yet often unpredictable set. —*Scott Yanow*

The Fabulous Baker Boys / 1989 / GRP ✦✦✦

For one of Dave Grusin's most jazz-oriented film scores, the music used in *The Fabulous Baker Boys* (and included on this CD) has fairly straightahead originals played by a sextet (plus strings) that includes Grusin's keyboards, tenor saxophonist Ernie Watts and guitarist Lee Ritenour. In addition, Mercer Ellington put together a big band to perform "Do Nothin' Till You Hear from Me," the Earl Palmer Trio plays "Lullaby of Birdland," and a 1936 recording of the Benny Goodman Quartet performing "Moonglow" is utilized. But the real surprise of the movie (and the CD) is that actress Michelle Pfeiffer does a credible job singing "Makin' Whoopee" and "My Funny Valentine." —*Scott Yanow*

Migration / 1989 / GRP ✦✦✦

On this diverse and generally interesting (if not essential) CD, keyboardist/composer Dave Grusin performs a five-song suite from his soundtrack of *The Milagro Beanfield War* along with selections by Harvey Mason, his brother Don Grusin, Hugh Masekela, Marcus Miller and himself. Other than the suite (which has a string section), the music is mostly played by smaller groups, with Branford Marsalis on tenor and soprano a major asset on three songs and fluegelhornist Hugh Masekela taking a solo on his own "Polina." —*Scott Yanow*

Bonfire of the Vanities / 1990 / Atlantic ✦✦✦✦

This Dave Grusin-penned soundtrack album (which features Grusin amidst an orchestra) is one of those charming delights that make a fascination with soundtrack albums a worthwhile pursuit. Grusin here takes a straight-faced approach to the satire of the movie, providing a charming score infused with a traditional New York feel. He spends a lot of time defining themes with strings and woodwinds, eschewing brass and percussion most of the time—giving the brief "Master of the Universe" and "Concorde" cues (building out from a fanfare theme) an additional punch. In other places, the cues match their visual basis—"Bronx Exit" mines a bass-propelled funk groove, for example. There's a certain amount of repetitiveness involved in the music, of course, but it's really not a problem with this particular album because of the shifting styles and directions. It's almost unfailing in its charm and quality, and there isn't a song anywhere in sight. The music has a crafty wit that's endearing, and that's much of the result of the quality and craftsmanship involved. Grusin takes his underscoring very seriously indeed, and his attention to detail and desire for good music works very much to the benefit of *Bonfire of the Vanities*. Besides, the "Master of the Universe" theme is one of those great big brassy fanfares that represent what's great about classic movie music. —*Steven McDonald*

The Gershwin Connection / 1991 / GRP ✦✦✦✦

Because many of Dave Grusin's albums have been rather commercial and overproduced, it is often forgotten how excellent a pianist he could be. This CD, which includes a 40-page booklet, features an enjoyable program of George and Ira Gershwin tunes played by a continually changing all-star lineup that includes the leader's piano, clarinetist Eddie Daniels, vibraphonist Gary Burton, altoist Eric Marienthal, trumpeter Sal Marquez, guitarist Lee Ritenour, bassist John Patitucci, drummer Dave Weckl and guest spots for pianist Chick Corea (who duets with Grusin on "'S Wonderful") and Don Grusin. A few of the numbers are given light funk rhythms and made to sound slightly "contemporary" (particularly "I've Got Plenty o' Nuthin'," which has an electric Ramsey Lewis-type groove), but overall, this is a very tasteful and respectful set—a classy package. —*Scott Yanow*

● **Homage to Duke** / 1993 / GRP ✦✦✦✦✦

Although Dave Grusin is best known as a soundtrack composer and for his jazz-pop recordings, he has always had a great admiration for jazz. This CD (released in a fairly deluxe package) gave Grusin an opportunity to pay tribute to Duke Ellington. He performs ten mostly familiar songs associated with Ellington and wisely features fluegelhornist Clark Terry on five of the selections. Other prominent soloists include tenor saxophonist Pete Christlieb, trombonist George Bohanon, tenor saxophonist Tom Scott (returning to his roots), clarinetist Eddie Daniels (on an orchestrated version of "Mood Indigo") and pianist Grusin himself. This is a respectful and well-conceived tribute. —*Scott Yanow*

The Orchestral Album / 1994 / GRP ✦✦

Two for the Road: The Music of Henry Mancini / 1996 / GRP ✦✦✦

Dave Grusin's tribute to Henry Mancini starts out quite strong, with a few fine examples of Grusin's piano playing (particularly "Peter Gunn" and "Mr. Lucky"). Unfortunately, as the set progresses, the music gets more and more routine and closer to easy listening. Grusin is joined by bassist John Patitucci and drummer Harvey Mason, singer Diana Krall does fine on two lazy ballads, a horn section (including trombonist Andy Martin) is heard on two songs, and the obscure harmonica player Tollak Ollestad (sounding like Toots Thielemans) has a pair of

appearances. The use of overdubbed strings on some numbers weighs down the set, and what could have been something special ends up being pleasing but predictable. —*Scott Yanow*

Presents: West Side Story / 1997 / N2K ✦✦✦✦✦

To celebrate the 40th anniversary of the opening of *West Side Story* on Broadway, Dave Grusin revived the score, giving its ten themes fresh arrangements that keep the original melodies in mind but add a stronger dose of jazz and Afro-Cuban rhythms to the music. For the most rewarding recording of this music since Stan Kenton's powerful renditions of the early 1960s, Grusin utilized an all-star big band with strings. Among the key soloists are trumpeter Arturo Sandoval, Bill Evans (who takes several superlative soprano solos), Michael Brecker on tenor, baritonist Ronnie Cuber and flutist Dave Valentin (who is featured on a purposely cute rendition of "I Feel Pretty") plus the pianist/leader, who clearly loves the music. In addition, one song apiece features vocalists Jonathan Butler ("Maria"), Gloria Estefan and Jon Secada. Although one wishes that the singers were more jazz-oriented (or that the entire date were instrumental), the overall result is a very respectful yet creative reworking of the famous score. Highly recommended. —*Scott Yanow*

Don Grusin

b. Apr. 22, 1941, Denver, CO
Keyboards / Crossover Jazz

The younger brother of producer/composer Dave Grusin, Don Grusin is an excellent keyboardist who has had his own solo career. He originally avoided music (not wanting to be in his brother's shadow), becoming an economics professor and not becoming a full-time musician until 1975. At that time he put together a band to tour Japan with Quincy Jones, freelanced in Los Angeles and headed the group Friendship which recorded for Elektra in 1978. Grusin recorded a few albums for JVC in the early '80s, and in 1988 with Sticks and Stones (a collaboration with brother Dave), Don Grusin began recording regularly for GRP, playing music that (although influenced by pop) is also somewhat adventurous within the crossover genre. —*Scott Yanow*

10k-La / Nov. 1980-Dec. 1980 / JVC ✦✦✦

Don Grusin / 1983 / JVC ✦✦✦

Raven / 1990 / GRP ✦✦✦

Zephyr / 1991 / GRP ✦✦✦

No Borders / 1992 / GRP ✦✦

Despite playing many songs with geographic titles and including a map of the world in the liners, keyboardist Don Grusin's release is not about world music. The performances are actually overly safe and uniformly easy-listening with upbeat melodies, highly competent but anonymous players and gentle background vocalists; only "Rai Baby" generates a little heat. There is little excuse for such bland music from such talented musicians as Grusin, altoist Eric Marienthal, guitarist Ricard Silveira and violinist Jerry Goodman, making this date a distinct disappointment. —*Scott Yanow*

● **Native Land** / 1993 / GRP ✦✦✦✦

Don Grusin has truly immersed his musical skills in the growing popularity of "world music," music indigenous to people of different cultures throughout the world. On *Native Land,* Don has crafted a sound of music that drifts from one corner of the world to the other. He is supported by such outstanding instrumentalists as Alex Acuna, drums and percussion, Abraham Laboriel, bass, Ricardo Silveira, guitar, and Judd Miller, with a variety of exotic instruments such as the pennywhistle, fletchorn, oboe, Astorian, tuben and taegum. Always performed with passion and sensitivity, this recording is fresh and daring to be different. —*MusD*

Banana Fish / 1994 / GRP ✦✦✦

Gigi Gryce (Basheer Quism)

b. Nov. 28, 1927, Pensacola, FL, **d.** Mar. 17, 1983, Pensacola, FL
Alto Saxophone / Hard Bop

Gigi Gryce was a fine altoist in the 1950s but it was his writing skills (including composing the standard "Minority") that were considered most notable. After growing up in Hartford, CT, and studying at the Boston Conservatory and in Paris, Gryce worked in New York with Max Roach, Tadd Dameron and Clifford Brown. He toured Europe in 1953 with Lionel Hampton and led several sessions in France. After freelancing in 1954 (including recording with Thelonious Monk), Gryce worked with Oscar Pettiford's groups (1955-57) and led the Jazz Lab Quintet (1955-58), a band featuring Donald Byrd. He had a quintet with Richard Williams during 1959-61 but then stopped playing altogether to become a teacher. During his short career Gigi Gryce recorded as a leader for Vogue (many of the releases have been issued domestically on Prestige), Savoy, Metrojazz, New Jazz and Mercury. —*Scott Yanow*

Nica's Tempo / Oct. 15, 1955-Oct. 22, 1955 / Savoy ✦✦✦✦

Altoist Gigi Gryce is heard in two different settings on this LP-length CD reissue (which should have also contained his four slightly earlier quartet cuts for Savoy). Gryce heads a nonet using the same instrumentation as Miles Davis' "Birth of the Cool" group. Four of the songs are instrumentals ("Kerry Dance" and three of the leader's originals) while "Social Call" and "You'll Always Be the One I Love" feature early vocals by Ernestine Anderson. In addition, Gryce is showcased in a 1955 quartet with pianist Thelonious Monk, bassist Percy Heath and drummer Art Blakey. Although Monk contributed three originals (with the colorful names of "Shuffle Boil," "Brake's Sake" and Gallop's Gallop"), ironically it is the one Gryce contribution ("Nice's Tempo") that became a standard. A fine reissue, one of Denon's better Savoy sets. —*Scott Yanow*

● Gigi Gryce & The Jazz Lab Quintet / Feb. 27, 1957+Mar. 7, 1957 / Original Jazz Classics ✦✦✦✦✦

During 1957 altoist Gigi Gryce and trumpeter Donald Byrd co-led a quintet that sought to extend and come up with new variations to bebop. Unfortunately the group did not survive the year but Gryce and Byrd did combine for several memorable recordings, including an excellent Prestige LP reissued on this CD. Their quintet (with pianist Wade Legge, bassist Wendell Marshall and drummer Art Taylor) turn "Love for Sale" into a jazz waltz (an innovation for 1957), introduce Gryce's best-known composition "Minority," swing "Zing Went the Strings of My Heart" and perform a tricky but memorable blues line "Straight Ahead." This is exciting and still fresh-sounding bebop. —*Scott Yanow*

New Formulas from the Jazz Lab / Jul. 30, 1957-Aug. 1, 1957 / RCA ✦✦✦

Altoist Gigi Gryce and trumpeter Donald Byrd were not able to keep their colorful hard-bop quintet together for long, but in 1957, they did record several worthy albums. With pianist Hank Jones, bassist Paul Chambers and drummer Art Taylor forming a solid rhythm section on this LP, the group plays mostly obscure songs by Lee Sears, Ray Bryant, Jones and Byrd, along with surprisingly just one by Gryce ("Capri"). The overall results give fresh life to 1950s straightahead jazz, although the short life of this group kept it from ever being influential. —*Scott Yanow*

Jazz Lab / Oct. 3, 1957 / Columbia ✦✦✦✦

The Jazz Lab was a quintet co-led by altoist Gigi Gryce and trumpeter Donald Byrd that lasted for much of 1957 but broke up after cutting several recordings. The band, which also included pianist Hank Jones, bassist Wendell Marshall (Paul Chambers subs for him on this LP) and drummer Art Taylor, tried (and partly succeeded) in bringing new life to hard bop through fresh originals and inventive arrangements. This set, which will hopefully be reissued on CD, is highlighted by Gryce's "Blue Lights," "Batland," and Byrd's "Xtacy." Worth searching for. —*Scott Yanow*

Gigi Gryce Quartet / 1958 / Metrojazz ✦✦✦

A fine mainstream date, but probably long gone. —*Ron Wynn*

Sayin' Somethin'! / Mar. 11, 1960 / Original Jazz Classics ✦✦✦✦

Altoist Gigi Gryce's last regular group before moving to Africa and largely retiring from music was the quintet featured on this CD, two other Prestige/New Jazz sessions and an album for Trip. Gryce's alto matched well with Richard Williams' impressive trumpet and, with fine support from pianist Richard Wyands, bassist Reggie Workman and drummer Mickey Roker, the two horns explore mostly blues-based originals by Gryce, Curtis Fuller and Hank Jones. There is more variety than expected and the contrast between Gryce's lyricism and the extroverted nature of Williams' solos make this set fairly memorable. —*Scott Yanow*

The Hap'nin's / May 3, 1960 / Original Jazz Classics ✦✦✦✦

Altoist Gigi Gryce, who would retire from playing altogether within a couple of years, leads his promising 1960 quintet on this CD reissue. Trumpeter Richard Williams and pianist Richard Wyands take fine solos on the six jazz standards (two of which, "Minority" and "Nice's Tempo," were Gryce's best-known tunes) while bassist Julian Euell and drummer Mickey Roker are fine in support. The hard-bop set has its strong moments even though this group was largely forgotten after Gryce's retirement. Worth investigating. —*Scott Yanow*

The Rat Race Blues / Jun. 7, 1960 / Original Jazz Classics ✦✦✦✦

Altoist Gigi Gryce's next-to-last album before permanently dropping out of jazz has been reissued on this CD. With trumpeter Richard Williams, pianist Richard Wyands, bassist Julian Euell and drummer Mickey Roker also part of what was a working quintet, Gryce (underrated as a soloist and a particularly strong composer) had one of his finest bands. The group swings its way through two of Gryce's lesser-known originals and three then-recent obscurities. Interesting and generally fresh straightahead jazz. —*Scott Yanow*

Reminiscin' Gigi Gryce Orch-Tette / Jan. 1961 / Mercury ✦✦✦

This is alternately reflective, dashing, and sentimental. —*Ron Wynn*

Vince Guaraldi (Vincánt Anthony Guaraldi)

b. Jul. 17, 1928, San Francisco, CA, d. Feb. 6, 1976, Menlo Park, CA
Piano, Composer / Cool, Latin Jazz

Vince Guaraldi occupies an unusual place in jazz history. Although not a major pianist, his playing in the late '50s on ballads influenced the new age pacesetter George Winston two decades later, he was an Italian whose work in Latin-jazz impressed many and he became best known for writing the scores for the *Peanuts* television cartoons. Guaraldi was with Cal Tjader's first trio in 1951, gigged with the Bill Harris/Chubby Jackson band (1953), Georgie Auld (1953) and Sonny Criss (1955), toured with Woody Herman's Orchestra (1956-57), gained fame playing with Tjader again (1957-59) and returned to Herman for part of 1959. Guaraldi, who recorded two albums for Fantasy during 1956-57, led his own groups from 1960 on and made seven further records for Fantasy during 1962-66 including a recording of his hit original "Cast Your Fate to the Wind" and his 1965 jazz mass. —*Scott Yanow*

Vince Guaraldi Trio / Apr. 1956 / Original Jazz Classics ✦✦✦

This CD reissue in the OJC series brings back the first full session led by pianist Vince Guaraldi. Teamed with the fine guitarist Eddie Duran and bassist Dean Reilly, Guaraldi swings lightly and with subtle creativity on two group originals and eight standards including "Django," "Chelsea Bridge," "Fascinatin' Rhythm" and "The Lady's in Love with You." Tasteful music. —*Scott Yanow*

A Flower Is a Lovesome Thing / Apr. 16, 1957 / Original Jazz Classics ✦✦✦✦

This is one of pianist Vince Guaraldi's better sets. Showcased in a San Francisco-based trio with guitarist Eddie Duran and bassist Dean Reilly, Guaraldi plays seven standards plus his own "Like a Mighty Rose" tastefully and with light swing, making this a program that is equally successful as both cool jazz and background music. —*Scott Yanow*

Jazz Impressions of Black Orpheus / Apr. 18, 1962 / Original Jazz Classics ✦✦✦✦✦

Here we have Vince Guaraldi's breakthrough album—musically, commercially, in every which way. After numerous records as a leader and sideman, for the first time a recognizable Guaraldi piano style emerges, with whimsical phrasing all his own, a madly swinging right hand and occasional boogie-influenced left hand, and a distinctive, throat-catching, melodic improvisational gift. The first half of the CD is taken up by cover versions of tunes from the Antonio Carlos Jobim/Luiz Bonfa score for the film *Black Orpheus*, recorded just as bossa nova was taking hold in America. These are genuinely jazz-oriented impressions in a mainstream boppish manner, with only a breath of samba from Monty Budwig (bass) and Colin Bailey (drums) in the opening minute of "Samba de Orpheus"; an edited version of this haunting song was issued as a 45 RPM single. But DJs soon began flipping the single over to play the B-side, a wistful, unforgettably catchy Guaraldi tune called "Cast Your Fate to the Wind" that opens the North American half of the album. The tune became a surprise hit; Fantasy redesigned the cover to call attention to it, and Vince was on his way to fame as one of Latin and mainstream jazz's most irresistible composers. The whole album evokes the ambience of San Francisco's jazz life in the 1960s as few others do—and such is this record's appeal that even non-jazz and non-Latin music people have been grooving to this music ever since it came out. —*Richard S. Ginell*

Greatest Hits / 1962-1966 / Fantasy ✦✦✦✦

First released on LP in 1980, this compilation concentrates upon bite-sized samples from Guaraldi's Fantasy catalogue. Naturally, Fantasy includes famous tunes like "Cast Your Fate to the Wind" and "Linus and Lucy" but there are also some superb sleepers ("Star Song," Jobim's "Outra Vez") that display Guaraldi's wonderful melodic gift and the sessions with Bola Sete are touched upon. As a chronicle of Guaraldi's Fantasy days, the set is somewhat incomplete, for it leaves out all material recorded prior to "Cast Your Fate" and Guaraldi isn't given much of a chance to stretch out. But this is definitely the place to start for someone who has not heard this whimsically inventive pianist. —*Richard S. Ginell*

Vince Guaraldi in Person / May 1963 / Fantasy ✦✦✦✦✦

A follow-up to his surprise hit album *Jazz Impressions of Black Orpheus*, this is Guaraldi at his most winning, alternating between a straight jazz trio and the fast bossa nova groove of a Latin-ized quintet. Nothing fancy, just irresistible melodic swinging in either format, although it is the bossa treatments that particularly grab the listener's heart and feet. Best in the set are "Outra Vez," where Vince calmly savors Jobim's beguiling harmonies on top of a frantic bossa beat, and Guaraldi's own quirky tune "Freeway." Mostly recorded in a club setting, this is a defining album for Guaraldi as caught in his natural habitat. —*Richard S. Ginell*

Vince Guaraldi, Bola Sete and Friends / 1963 / Fantasy ✦✦✦

With the first bossa nova wave still raging in North America, Guaraldi returned to the Brazilian groove full-time, this time in tandem with the gentle, classical-influenced yet subtly swinging acoustic guitar of Bola Sete. Reportedly Guaraldi and the Rio-born Sete had played together only once before—the day before the session at Vince's house—but you would never know it the way these guys weld themselves together with the irresistibly ticking beat. Composer Guaraldi serves up the album's brightest gems—the winsome "Star Song" and the slightly sardonic, blues-based groovathon "Casaba"—and there is also a lovely bossa nova treatment of Horace Silver's "Moon Rays." *—Richard S. Ginell*

● **A Boy Named Charlie Brown** / 1964 / Fantasy ✦✦✦✦✦

Originally entitled *Jazz Impressions of aBoy Named Charlie Brown*, this is an important album not only because it is Guaraldi's first *Peanuts* soundtrack, but also because the music heard here probably introduced millions of kids (and their parents) to jazz from the mid-1960s onward. Actually, this music is the score for a documentary on the *Peanuts* phenomenon called *A Boy Named Charlie Brown*, which ran before the first *Peanuts* specials per se appeared on the CBS network. The most remarkable thing, besides the high quality of Guaraldi's whimsically swinging tunes, is that he did not compromise his art one iota for the cartoon world; indeed, he sounds even more engaged, inventive and light-hearted in his piano work here than ever. It must have been quite a delightful shock back then to hear a straightahead jazz trio (Guaraldi, Monty Budwig, bass; Colin Bailey, drums) backing all those cartoon figures and genuine children's voices, a mordant running musical commentary that made its own philosophical points. The music on this album laid the groundwork for much that was to come; here is the first appearance of the well-known bossa nova-influenced "Linus and Lucy," and fans of the series will recognize such themes from future episodes as "Baseball Theme" and "Oh, Good Grief" (which is a rewrite of the Dixiebelles' hit "Down at Papa Joe's"). The original LP came with 12 bonus lithographs of Charles Schulz's celebrated *Peanuts* drawings; the only extra thing the CD issue offers is a gratuitous outtake of "Fly Me to the Moon." *—Richard S. Ginell*

The Latin Side of Vince Guaraldi / 1964 / Fantasy ✦✦✦✦

The Latin side for Vince Guaraldi means a brush with both the Brazilian and Caribbean strains of Latin jazz, garnished now and then by an outboard string quartet and graced by four of his own delightful tunes. On Brazilian numbers like "Corcovado" and Brazilian-treated tunes like "Mr. Lucky" and Guaraldi's lovely "Star Song," Vince has drummer Jerry Granelli deploy his distinctive brushes-and-rimshots bossa nova beat. Jack Weeks supplies bittersweet string arrangements as he tries to grant Guaraldi's wish for a "Villa-Lobos sound," which he does, more or less. Other tunes, like Guaraldi's own happy-go-lucky "Treat Street," "Whirlpool" and Nat Adderley's "Work Song," are treated to gentle cha-cha rhythms. Guaraldi's piano is hauntingly melodic, impulsively swinging and unmistakable for anyone else's, and the sound is much improved over the LP issue—especially in the case of the strings, which sound less seedy on the CD. *—Richard S. Ginell*

A Charlie Brown Christmas / 1965 / Fantasy ✦✦✦✦✦

Though not nearly as essential as *A Boy Named Charlie Brown, A Charlie Brown Christmas* does give you the flavor of the mordant jazz touch that Guaraldi made an indispensable part of the *Peanuts* TV specials (since his death, no one has been able to capture that feeling in subsequent episodes). Sometimes a plaintive children's chorus gets in the way, but the Guaraldi trio still gets in some bright, lively work in "Skating," a wonderfully detached treatment of "O Tannenbaum" and a reprise of "Linus and Lucy." As jazz Christmas albums go, this is one of the more endearing ones, and CD buyers get another out-of-place bonus track, "Greensleeves." *—Richard S. Ginell*

Vince Guaraldi and Bola Sete: From All Sides / May 1965 / Fantasy ✦✦✦

Guaraldi and Sete team up again for another attractive, mostly bossa nova session, this time with a softer-focused rhythm section, shorter tracks, and more Guaraldi tunes (four) on the menu than before. Guaraldi's quasi-Oriental "Ginza" is resurrected and retooled, "The Girl from Ipanema" and "A Taste of Honey" are dutifully covered, and the most amusing track is Vince's tongue-in-cheek, slightly rock-ish cha-cha "The Ballad of Pancho Villa." Although Guaraldi was in somewhat fresher form in his other albums with Sete, this one won't disappoint his fans. *—Richard S. Ginell*

Vince Guaraldi at Grace Cathedral / May 21, 1965 / Fantasy ✦✦✦✦✦

In a year that also saw Duke Ellington, Dave Brubeck and Lalo Schifrin write jazz-based pieces for the church, Vince Guaraldi may have come up with the most effective sacred work of the four. Written for the completion of San Francisco's Grace Cathedral, Guaraldi's Mass fuses his mainstream and Latin idioms comfortably and movingly underneath the plain vanilla Gregorian lines and Anglican plainchant of a 68-voice chorus. Sometimes all Guaraldi does to create a beguiling effect is improvise arpeggios or have his trio engage in a hot bossa nova workout

as the chorus chants on one note. Despite the immense size of the cathedral, this music produces an intimate, unpretentious and undeniably emotional response—and there is plenty of jazz content, particularly when Guaraldi's trio goes it alone for nearly a third of the work in the ruminative "Holy Communion Blues." By all means, check this beautiful, unusual album out. *—Richard S. Ginell*

Vince Guaraldi and Bola Sete: Live at El Matador / 1966 / Fantasy ✦✦✦✦

Despite the co-billing, Sete only appears on the second half of the album, leaving the Guaraldi trio to knock out a crisp series of standard pops of the time ("I'm a Loser," "People," "More") and two memorable Guaraldi originals ("Nobody Else," "El Matador") in its patented mainstream and Latin modes in the first half. When Sete turns up, the set goes all-Brazilian as the two display their blended, intertwined teamwork for the third and last time on records in "Favela" and a brace of tunes from *Black Orpheus*. Though it is only a partial collaboration, this album has a bit more fire than their previous ones, possibly due to the live factor. *—Richard S. Ginell*

Oh, Good Grief! / 1968 / Warner Brothers ✦✦✦

In his first album for Warner Bros., Guaraldi serves up another delightful, though pitifully short (27 minutes) helping of his themes for the *Peanuts* TV specials. By this time, like several other pianists, Guaraldi was actively exploring the new sonic horizons offered by electronic keyboards—and so, he superimposes layers of electric harpsichord on most of these tracks. Some of the old sardonic spontaneity goes over the side, replaced by an overloaded gee-whiz atmosphere that sometimes gets in the way of the quartet's willingness to swing. But the tunes are marvelous, and since so little of Guaraldi's vast *Peanuts* output was ever made available, every millisecond of these jazz waltzes, bossa novas and soulful ruminations on Charlie Brown's world becomes cherishable. *—Richard S. Ginell*

Alma-Ville / 1969 / Warner Brothers ✦✦✦✦

Though Guaraldi had a little over six more years to live, this was his last commercial release; thus we have to rely upon memories of the *Peanuts* specials for his considerable musical growth during the '70s (particularly in his airborne use of electronic keyboards). This time, producer Shorty Rogers imposed some discipline upon Guaraldi's increasingly eclectic pursuits and pulled an engaging straight jazz album from him, where the focus is primarily on his melodic swinging piano work in his usual mainstream and Latin grooves. The sidemen include many of Vince's colleagues from the Fantasy days and top-flight guests, with the pungent guitar of Herb Ellis featured most prominently, and Vince even takes a rudimentary electric guitar solo himself on "Uno Y Uno." Curiously, not a word about Guaraldi's *Peanuts* scores—his primary activity at the time—is mentioned in the liner notes (deliberately, no doubt), and the only hint of a connection is the leadoff tune, "The Masked Marvel." *—Richard S. Ginell*

The Eclectic / 1969 / Warner Brothers ✦✦✦

Here, Guaraldi roams further afield than ever—playing piano and electric harpsichord, experimenting with sleek string backdrops, dabbling with the guitar and yes, he sings, too. Vince's amateur Bohemian vocal charm won't come as any surprise to those who remember "Joe Cool" and "Little Birdie" from his later *Peanuts* scores; here, he sounds rather endearing in a pair of songs by pop/folk singer Tim Hardin ("Black Sheep Boy," "Reason to Believe"). Elsewhere there is enough of the old Guaraldi mainstream and Latin jazz piano here to attract the faithful, particularly the lingering rendition of Jobim's "Once I Loved," and another sardonic original, "Lucifer's Lady." Throughout, Guaraldi generally keeps things at a low-key level, which gives this scattershot album at least a veneer of unity. *—Richard S. Ginell*

Johnny Guarnieri (John Albert Guarnieri)

b. Mar. 23, 1917, New York, NY, d. Jan. 7, 1985, Livingston, NJ
Piano / Swing, Stride

One of the most talented pianists of the 1940s, Johnny Guarnieri had the ability to closely imitate Fats Waller, Count Basie and even Art Tatum. Not too surprisingly he was in great demand during his prime years. Guarnieri started classical piano lessons when he was ten and soon switched to jazz. In 1939 he joined Benny Goodman's orchestra, recording frequently with both the big band and BG's sextet. In 1940 Guarnieri became a member of Artie Shaw's orchestra and gained fame playing harpsichord on Shaw's popular Gramercy Five recordings. After further associations with Goodman (1941) and Shaw (1941-42), he was with Tommy Dorsey (1942-43) and then freelanced. Among Guarnieri's many recordings during this era were important dates with Lester Young ("Sometimes I'm Happy"), Roy Eldridge, Ben Webster, Coleman Hawkins, Rex Stewart, Don Byas and Louis Armstrong ("Jack-Armstrong Blues"). He also recorded frequently as a leader during 1944-47, including one date on which Lester Young was his sideman. Guarnieri joined the staff of NBC in the late '40s, appeared in the Coleman Hawkins/Roy Eldridge television pilot *After Hours* (1961), moved to California in the '60s where he often played solo piano and a few times in the 1970s toured Europe. Guarnieri's later records often found him playfully performing stride in 5/4 time. He recorded as a leader through the years for such labels as Savoy, Majestic, Coral (1956), Golden Crest, Camden, Dot, Black & Blue, Dobre and Taz-Jazz (1976 and 1978). —*Scott Yanow*

Johnny Guarnieri Remembered / Dec. 26, 1939-Sep. 1978 / IAJRC ✦✦✦✦
This LP gives listeners an excellent sampling from the many recordings made over a four-decade period featuring the versatile swing pianist Johnny Guarnieri. Most of the selections are taken from his most prolific period, the 1940s. Guarnieri is heard as a sideman with groups led by Ziggy Elman, Benny Goodman (his sextet's rendition of "I'm Confessin' "), Artie Shaw, Jerry Jerome, Will Bradley, Ben Webster, Benny Morton, Coleman Hawkins, Barney Bigard, Don Byas, and J.C. Heard, and in a variety of jam sessions (including a hot V-Disc version of "Rosetta"), as well as with his own small groups. The latest selection is one on which he backs singer Elma Santa on "Alabamy Bound" in 1978. Excellent small-group swing music with enough rarities for this to be worth picking up by collectors. —*Scott Yanow*

● **1944-1946** / 1944 / Classics ✦✦✦✦✦
In addition to recording prolifically in the 1940s, pianist Johnny Guarnieri led a few record dates. This Classics CD has four septet numbers from 1944 that feature tenor saxophonist Lester Young and trumpeter Billy Butterfield as sidemen, four songs with tenorman Don Byas in superb form, and three trio sessions including two that co-star bassist Slam Stewart. Guarnieri, who was versatile enough to be able to closely emulate Count Basie, Teddy Wilson, Fats Waller and Art Tatum, also had his own swing-based style and is consistently creative throughout the performances. Highlights include "Salute to Fats," "Bowin' Singin' Slam," "Gliss Me Again," "I'd Do Anything for You" and "Make Believe"; all 22 selections are enjoyable. —*Scott Yanow*

Plays Harry Warren / May 7, 1973 / Jim Taylor ✦✦✦
Late in his career, after a long period away from recording (only one album since 1958), pianist Johnny Guarnieri made a series of recordings for small labels during 1973-79. This LP features him interpreting a dozen classic songs by one of the most underrated of all songwriters, Harry Warren. Highlights of the solo set include "Nagasaki," "Lulu's Back in Town," "With Plenty of Money and You" and "Lullaby of Broadway," but all dozen tunes (which clock in between two-and-a-half to five-and-a-half minutes) are given favorable treatment by the brilliant, underrated swing pianist. —*Scott Yanow*

Superstride / Jul. 19, 1976+Jul. 26, 1976 / Taz-Jaz ✦✦✦

Plays the Music of Walter Donaldson / 1978 / Dobre ✦✦✦✦
Although he was recording for small labels late in his career, pianist Johnny Guarnieri was still very much in his prime. An underrated swing stylist whose playing was similar to the way he sounded in the mid-'40s, Guarnieri enjoyed giving attention to talented composers of the early days who were also underrated and overlooked. Walter Donaldson, although hardly a household name, had written dozens of standards, some of which are on this trio LP (on which Guarnieri is given fine support by bassist Ray Leatherwood and drummer Danny Pucillo), including "Makin' Whoopee," "My Blue Heaven," "Little White Lies" and "At Sundown." Worth searching for. —*Scott Yanow*

Gliss Me Again / Mar. 10, 1975 / Classic Jazz ✦✦✦
This delightful session, which was recorded under strenuous circumstances, reunited pianist Johnny Guarnieri with the distinctive bassist Slam Stewart. Guitarist Jimmy Shirley and drummer Jackie Williams complete the quartet, which performs 11 well-known standards (including a medley of "I Left My Heart in San Francisco" and "San Francisco"), plus a pair of Guarnieri's swinging originals. Four selections are taken as unaccompanied solos, but it is the full-group numbers that are most colorful. —*Scott Yanow*

Stealin' Apples / Feb. 26, 1978 / Taz-Jaz ✦✦✦✦
Johnny Guarnieri, who was often overlooked in later years, was one of the great jazz pianists of the 1940s, and fortunately, he was still in top form in the '70s. Guarnieri, who could do close impressions of several pianists, loved to imitate Fats Waller both as a pianist and as a singer. On this well-rounded set, he sings a couple of songs, debuts two never-recorded Waller compositions ("I'm Not Worrying" and "I Found You Out"), takes "I've Got a Feeling I'm Falling" and "Black and Blue" in 5/4 time, and revives a variety of Fats' better-known tunes. Excellent music way overdue to be reissued on CD. —*Scott Yanow*

● **Echoes of Ellington** / 1984 / Star Line ✦✦✦✦✦
Johnny Guarnieri's final recording, cut a year before his death, is the one he considered his finest. This solo date finds the classic swing pianist performing Billy Strayhorn's "Take the 'A' Train" and a dozen Ellington compositions, ranging from warhorses which he casts in a fresh light to the relative obscurities "Birmingham Breakdown" and "Mississippi Moan." A passionate rendition of "Caravan" is a

highlight, helping to make this readily available CD a perfect introduction for listeners wishing to explore the playing of Johnny Guarnieri. —*Scott Yanow*

Lars Gullin (Gunnar Victor Gullin)

b. May 4, 1928, Visby, Sweden, d. May 17, 1976, Vissefjarda, Sweden
Baritone Saxophone / Cool, Bop
One of the top baritone saxophonists of all time and a giant of European jazz, Lars Gullin would be better known today if he had visited the US often and if excessive drug use had not cut short his career. Early on he learned to play bugle, clarinet and piano and was actually a professional altoist until switching to baritone when he was 21. Sounding somewhere between Gerry Mulligan and Serge Chaloff, Gullin played in local big bands in the late '40s and was in Arne Domnerus' sextet (1951-53) but is best known for his own small-group recordings. He played with such touring Americans as Lee Konitz (a major influence), James Moody, Clifford Brown, Zoot Sims and Chet Baker and recorded frequently during 1951-60, with "Danny's Dream" being his most famous composition. Gullin also recorded a bit during 1964-65 but made only one later session (1973). Despite a lot of accomplishments in the 1950s, he did not live up to his enormous potential. Gullin can be heard at his best on five Dragon CDs released as *The Great Lars Gullin, Vols. 1-5*. —*Scott Yanow*

Danny's Dream / Feb. 21, 1951-May 25, 1954 / Metronome ✦✦✦✦✦
Lars Gullin was not only one of the top European jazzmen of all time, but one of the best baritone saxophonists ever. This double LP has eight complete sessions and three out of four songs from a ninth date, which were among the first sets led by Gullin. With such notable sidemen as pianist Bengt Hallberg, trombonist Ake Persson, altoist Arne Domnerus, and lesser-known but talented Swedish players, Gullin (who was 22-26 during the era) is heard throughout in prime form. Many of the songs are his originals, including his best-known melody, "Danny's Dream," and there are a few standards. All bop and cool jazz collectors should be aware of Lars Gullin and own several of his sets. —*Scott Yanow*

The Great Lars Gullin, Vol. 2 / Mar. 11, 1953-Dec. 1, 1953 / Dragon ✦✦✦✦✦
In the mid-1980s, the Swedish Dragon label came out with five LPs of music featuring the great Swedish baritonist Lars Gullin. Only *Vol. 1* has thus far been reissued on CD. The second volume, which has the earliest recordings in the batch, consists of performances that were either previously unreleased or quite obscure at the time. Gullin is heard in quartets and quintets, sometimes as a sideman, including a few very rare appearances on alto which, although worthy, show why he mostly stuck to baritone. The cool-toned bop, reminiscent but not derivative of Gerry Mulligan, should be of great interest to 1950s jazz collectors. —*Scott Yanow*

The Great Lars Gullin, Vol. 5 / May 25, 1954-Jan. 26, 1955 / Dragon ✦✦✦✦
Baritonist Lars Gullin had some of his greatest sessions reissued by Dragon in the mid-1980s on five LPs; only *Vol. 1* has been reissued on CD so far. The fifth set is actually the second chronologically, featuring Gullin on two sets with a pianoless quartet comprising the cool-toned guitarist Rolf Berg, bassist Georg Riedel and either Robert Edman or Bo Stoor on drums. Actually, the group is not entirely pianoless, for when Gullin does not solo, he comps on piano behind the other players. All but one of the compositions are Gullin originals, including his famous "Danny's Dream" (this is its original version). Superior cool jazz from Sweden. —*Scott Yanow*

The Great Lars Gullin, Vol. 3 / Sep. 11, 1954-Jun. 13, 1955 / Dragon ✦✦✦✦
For the third of five Lars Gullin LPs compiled and released by Dragon in the mid-1980s, the classic baritonist is heard in an unusual setting on five numbers (plus an alternate take), being joined by a 16-voice choir group. The music, meant to be an extension on Charlie Parker's "Bird with Strings," has its interesting moments, but is not too essential. Otherwise, Gullin is heard on baritone and piano with a 1956 sextet and on two previously unreleased alternate takes from other sessions. All of the entries in this series are recommended to 1950s jazz collectors. —*Scott Yanow*

★ **Great Lars Gullin, Vol. 1** / Apr. 25, 1955-May 31, 1956 / Dragon ✦✦✦✦✦
Improving upon the original LP in Dragon's Lars Gullin series by adding an additional four-song session, this CD features the legendary Swedish baritonist with four different groups from the 1955-56 period, ranging from a quartet to an octet and featuring trumpeter Chet Baker on four numbers. Throughout, Gullin is heard in prime form, stretching out on his most famous original ("Danny's Dream"), featuring the cool-toned clarinet of Arne Domnerus on "Ma" and holding his own with Baker's quartet. Highly recommended. —*Scott Yanow*

The Great Lars Gullin, Vol. 4 / Jan. 28, 1959-Sep. 2, 1960 / Dragon ✦✦✦✦
All of the great Swedish baritonist Lars Gullin's 1959-60 recordings as a leader (except for two titles cut in Italy) are on this excellent LP. Gullin is the main star in settings ranging from an octet to a quartet, although the fine clarinetist Putte Wickman is present on two numbers. All but three of the 14 selections (plus one

alternate) are Gullin's, and he also wrote the arrangements. The music is very much in the modern mainstream, but does not sound overly derivative of American jazz. Unfortunately, Gullin would not be on records again as a leader until 1964, but he still seems in his prime on these frequently exciting and always swinging performances. —*Scott Yanow*

Lars Gullin Quintet Featuring Bernt Rosengren / May 26, 1975 / Storyville ✦✦✦✦

Baritonist Lars Gullin's next-to-last recording (cut a little less than a year before his early death) features lengthy versions of four songs (two originals plus "I Love You" and "Just Friends") played by Gullin's 1975 quintet, a unit also including Bernt Rosengren on tenor and flute, pianist Lars Sjosten, bassist Bjorn Alke and drummer Fredrik Noren. Although his health was a bit shaky, Gullin still seems in good form, playing in a style not much different from the way he sounded during his prime 20 years earlier. In addition, Rosengren, who is a good foil for the baritonist, has "'Round Midnight" as his ballad feature. —*Scott Yanow*

Trilok Gurtu

b. Oct. 30, 1951, Bombay, India
Percussion / World Fusion
Trilok Gurtu gained some recognition when he became the late Collin Walcott's replacement with Oregon in 1985. He studied classical tabla in India but early on mixed his music with jazz. Gurtu worked in Europe (1973-75), moved to New York (1976) and during the next few years played with Charlie Mariano, Don Cherry, Barre Phillips, Karl Berger and Lee Konitz. He had a duo with Nana Vasconcelos, worked with Jan Garbarek, recorded frequently for ECM, toured with John McLaughlin (late '80s-early '90s) and led his own groups in addition to playing with Oregon. Trilok Gurtu's most recent dates as a leader are for CMP. —*Scott Yanow*

Usfret / 1987-1988 / CMP ✦✦✦
Includes Mother Shobha Gurtu (v), Don Cherry (tpt), Ralph Towner (g, k), L. Shankar (violin), Jonas Helborg (b). —*Michael G. Nastos*

● **Living Magic** / Aug. 1990+Mar. 1991 / CMP ✦✦✦✦✦
With Jan Garbarek (saxes), Nana (per), Daniel Goyone (k). Septet. Indian, Turkish, Scandinavian, and Brazilian world fusion, very well conceived. One of Garbarek's better recent efforts, as collaborator or leader. —*Michael G. Nastos*

Crazy Saints / May 1993-Jun. 1993 / CMP ✦✦✦✦

Bad Habits Die Hard / 1995 / CMP ✦✦✦

Barry Guy

b. Apr. 22, 1947, London, England
Bass, Leader / Avant-Garde, Free Jazz
The leader of an exciting avant-garde big band called the London Jazz Composers Orchestra since 1970, Barry Guy is one of the top free-form string bassists, able to get a wide variety of unusual sounds out of his instrument. Classically trained, Guy has had simultaneous careers in advanced jazz and contemporary classical music. He was in the Spontaneous Music Ensemble with Trevor Watts and John Stevens (1967-70), has played in a variety of adventurous small groups (including Amalgam and Iskra 1903) and has recorded often with Evan Parker, Derek Bailey, and the London Jazz Composers Orchestra, most recently for his Maya label. —*Scott Yanow*

Ode / Apr. 22, 1972 / Incus ✦✦✦✦
The debut recording by bassist Barry Guy's London Jazz Composers Orchestra has been reissued (along with the previously unreleased seventh part) on this double CD. In his seven-part "Ode," Guy attempts the near-impossible by having his 21-piece orchestra, which is filled with very advanced improvisers, perform a largely

atonal work that mixes free improvising with some tightly organized ensembles. With such top British players as trumpeter Harry Beckett, trombonist Paul Rutherford, pianist Howard Riley, guitarist Derek Bailey, altoist Trevor Watts, and Evan Parker on tenor and soprano among the personnel, the music is quite dense, emotional, and exciting, if sometimes confusing. Open-eared listeners wanting to hear an important work by the European avant-garde will find this music very stimulating and well worth several listens. —*Scott Yanow*

Zurich Concerts / Nov. 11, 1987+Mar. 27, 1988 / Intakt ✦✦✦✦
This double LP from the European Intakt label has two very different performances. Bassist Barry Guy's London Jazz Composers' Orchestra, a remarkable 17-piece big band, performs Guy's "Polyhymnia" in 1987 and, with the addition of Tony Oxley on second drums, several Anthony Braxton pieces (in a 57-minute "medley") in 1988. The ensembles are often quite dense and emotional, the line between composition and improvisation is difficult to find, and there are short solos from virtually all of the players, including trombonist Paul Rutherford, altoist Trevor Watts and Evan Parker on tenor. Lovers of avant-garde and free-form jazz will want to be aware of this important orchestra and all of its exciting Intakt recordings. —*Scott Yanow*

Harmos / Apr. 4, 1989-Apr. 5, 1989 / Intakt ✦✦✦✦✦
Although little known except to a select few in the US, the London Jazz Composers' Orchestra (even though it operates on a part-time basis) has been one of the top jazz big bands of the 1980s and '90s. Under bassist Barry Guy's leadership, the very avant-garde ensemble performs his forty-three-and-a-half-minute "Harmos," a work that blends together melody and complete freedom, composed sections with intense improvisations. Among the many soloists heard from are trombonist Paul Rutherford, pianist Howard Riley, Evan Parker on soprano and alto, altoist Trevor Watts, and bassists Guy and Barre Phillips, but it is the spirited and overcrowded ensembles that steal the show. A gem, although certainly not for everyone. —*Scott Yanow*

Double Trouble / Apr. 5, 1989-Apr. 6, 1989 / Intakt ✦✦✦✦✦

Arcus / 1990 / Maya ✦✦✦✦

Theoria / Feb. 1991 / Intakt ✦✦✦✦
Pianist Irene Schweizer guested with Barry Guy's London Jazz Composers' Orchestra for this very complex but exciting recording, a nearly 58-minute rendition of "Theoria." Although Schweizer is the main soloist, nearly everyone else in the 17-piece orchestra has their solo spots, including trumpeter Henry Lowther, trombonist Conrad Bauer, Trevor Watts and Evan Parker on reeds, and bassists Guy and Barre Phillips among the bigger "names." The intense yet somehow logical music should delight fans of freer sounds and could open up some new ears to the real potential of the big band. —*Scott Yanow*

Fizzles / Sep. 1991 / Maya ✦✦✦

● **Study—Witch Gong Game II/10** / Feb. 26, 1994-Feb. 27, 1994 / Maya ✦✦✦✦✦
Bassist Barry Guy teamed up with the 13-piece New Orchestra Workshop (NOW) for this difficult but sometimes wondrous set of avant-garde music. The 16-minute "Study" makes excellent use of an ensemble drone and space in building up and releasing tension while the 52-minute "Witch Gong Game II/10" is quite menacing and sometimes even scary. The wide range of tone colors during some of the denser moments make it difficult to know what notes one is hearing and sometimes even what instruments are being played. Among the individual players are the brilliant pianist Paul Plimley, the very flexible vocalist Kate Hammett-Vaughan, six horns, guitar, cello, three bassists (counting Guy) and drums but it is the intense and sometimes ferocious ensembles that are most memorable. This import from the English label Maya will take several listens to digest. —*Scott Yanow*

Bobby Hackett

b. Jan. 31, 1915, Providence, RI, **d.** Jun. 7, 1976, Chatham, MA
Cornet / Dixieland, Swing, Traditional Pop
Bobby Hackett's mellow tone and melodic style offered a contrast to the brasher Dixieland-oriented trumpeters. Emphasizing his middle-register and lyricism, Hackett was a flexible soloist who actually sounded little like his main inspiration, Louis Armstrong.

When Hackett first came up he was briefly known as "the new Bix" because of the similarity in his approach to that of Bix Beiderbecke, but very soon he developed his own distinctive sound. Originally a guitarist (which he doubled on until the mid-'40s), Hackett performed in local bands and by 1936 was leading his own group. He moved to New York in 1937, played with Joe Marsala, appeared at Benny Goodman's 1938 Carnegie Hall concert (recreating Beiderbecke's solo on "I'm Coming Virginia"), recorded with Eddie Condon and by 1939 had a short-lived big band. Hackett played briefly with Horace Heidt and during 1941-42 was with Glenn Miller's Orchestra, taking a famous solo on "String of Pearls." Next up was a stint with the Casa Loma Orchestra and then he became a studio musician while still appearing with jazz groups. Hackett was a major asset at Louis Armstrong's 1947 Town Hall Concert, in the 1950s he was a star on Jackie Gleason's commercial but jazz-flavored mood music albums and he recorded several times with Eddie Condon and Jack Teagarden. During 1956-57 Hackett led an unusual group that sought to modernize Dixieland (using Dick Cary's arrangements and an unusual instrumentation) but that band did not catch on. Hackett recorded some commercial dates during 1959-60 (including one set of Hawaiian songs and another in which he was backed by pipe organ), he worked with Benny Goodman (1962-63), backed Tony Bennett in the mid-'60s, co-led a well-recorded quintet with Vic Dickenson (1968-70) and made sessions with Jim Cullum, the World's Greatest Jazz Band and even Dizzy Gillespie and Mary Lou Williams, remaining active up until his death. Among the many labels Bobby Hackett recorded for as a leader were OKeh (reissued by Epic), Commodore, Columbia, Epic, Capitol, Sesac, Verve, Project 3, Chiaroscuro, Flying Dutchman and Honey Dew. *—Scott Yanow*

The Hackett Horn / Feb. 16, 1938-Jan. 25, 1940 / Epic ♦♦♦♦♦
This set of 16 songs has been reissued intact several times. It includes 12 of the first 16 songs cut at dates led by cornetist Bobby Hackett, featuring a pair of hot combos and a larger big band (why are the other four rewarding sides always left out?) along with two Bix-associated songs recorded under the sponsorship of bandleader Horace Heidt and a pair of jams from a set led by critic Leonard Feather. Throughout, Hackett (then barely in his mid-20s) shows why his original reputation as "the new Bix" never quite fit. Even this early in his career his pretty tone was distinctive. Among the other stars of these swing/trad performances are trombonists George Brunis and Brad Gowans, and clarinetists Pee Wee Russell and Joe Marsala. *—Scott Yanow*

1943 World Jam Session / Dec. 23, 1943 / Jazzology ♦♦♦
This CD has all of the performances recorded by cornetist Bobby Hackett and his octet for the World Transcription Series including false starts and alternate takes. The programming by Jazzology is a bit screwy but that can be adjusted with one's CD player. Hackett is in good form; his group includes trombonist Ray Conniff, clarinetist John Pepper, Nick Caizza on tenor, pianist Frank Signorelli, guitarist Eddie Condon, bassist Bob Casey and drummer Maurice Purtill. Together they perform nine superior standards including "But Not for Me," "When a Woman Loves a Man," "Embraceable You" and "Sweet Georgia Brown." The fact that the issued versions only take up around 25 minutes means that this CD is mostly recommended to Bobby Hackett completists and to historians rather than more general listeners. *—Scott Yanow*

Jazz in New York / Apr. 15, 1944-Sep. 23, 1944 / Commodore ♦♦♦♦
This CD has plenty of hot traditional jazz as played by a variety of top Condonites who were in their prime in the mid-'40s. The three seperate bands feature overlapping personnel with cornetist Bobby Hackett's octet including trombonist Lou

McGarity and the great baritonist Ernie Caceres, trombonist Miff Mole's Nicksielanders also showcasing Hackett and Caceres, and cornetist Muggsy Spanier's Ragtimers featuring Mole; clarinetist Pee Wee Russell is also heard with all three groups. But even if the individual bands are pickup affairs, a few classic performances resulted, most notably Mole's version of "Peg of My Heart," Spanier's "Angry" and "Alice Blue Gown," and Bobby Hackett's "At Sundown" and "Soon." Fun Dixieland from some of the best. *—Scott Yanow*

Live at the Rustic Lodge / 1949 / Jass ♦♦♦
These radio airchecks feature cornetist Bobby Hackett and clarinetist Tony Parenti sitting in with a fine pickup group in New Jersey for two standards and a lengthy blues medley, the local musicians getting three tunes to themselves, Parenti rejoining them for "That's a Plenty" and the great trumpeter Red Allen dominating "Squeeze Me" and "I Wish I Could Shimmy like My Sister Kate." Nothing unique occurs, but the good feelings generated at the sessions can still be savored (along with the frequently hot music) four decades later. *—Scott Yanow*

Dr. Jazz Series, Vol. 10 / Feb. 7, 1952-Apr. 10, 1952 / Storyville ♦♦♦
Cornetist Bobby Hackett and trombonist Vic Dickenson would team up on a regular basis in the late 1960s, so this set of radio broadcasts is valuable in documenting their musical partnership 15 years earlier. With Gene Sedric (a Fats Waller alumnus) on clarinet, pianist Teddy Roy, and several bassists and drummers, the sextet is heard during radio appearances on the *Dr. Jazz* show in 1952. The repertoire is typical Dixieland (only "There's Danger in Your Eyes, Cherie" and Dickenson's "Solitaire" are departures), and nothing too unpredictable occurs. However, the lyrical Hackett cornet and the sly wit of trombonist Dickenson are two reasons why mainstream fans with an open mind to Dixieland may want to acquire this 1996 disc of previously unreleased performances. *—Scott Yanow*

Dr. Jazz Series, Vol. 2 / Feb. 11, 1952-Apr. 17, 1952 / Storyville ♦♦♦

Coast Concert / Oct. 18, 1955+Oct. 19, 1955 / Capitol ♦♦♦♦♦
In the 1950s, Hackett's pretty tone was often utilized on mood music albums, most notably by Jackie Gleason, but he never lost his ability to play hot jazz. *Coast Concert* finds him leading a particularly strong octet that also featured clarinetist Matty Matlock and both Jack Teagarden and Abe Lincoln on trombones. On nine familiar standards (including tunes such as "I Want a Big Butter and Egg Man," "Basin Street Blues" and "Struttin' with Some Barbecue"), the top-notch players really inspire each other with some heated ensembles and creative solo work. This is one of Hackett's best sessions of the decade. *—Scott Yanow*

Live from the Voyager Room / 1956-1957 / Shoestring ♦♦♦
Cornetist Bobby Hackett is best known for his association with traditional jazz bands but during 1956-57 he led a surprisingly modern outfit that played everything from Dixie standards to Benny Golson arrangements and Bob Wilber originals. The personnel at various times included Wilber (on clarinet and soprano), baritonist Ernie Caceres doubling on clarinet, Tom Gwaltney on clarinet and vibes and Dick Cary on piano and alto horn. Although the group did not catch on commercially, its music still sounds quite fresh and unusual today. This LP from the collector's label Shoestring, the first of two, is well worth acquiring. *—Scott Yanow*

Bobby Hackett's Jazz Band: 1957 / Mar. 30, 1957 / Alamac ♦♦♦
The budget-LP label Alamac dug up a fine aircheck from Bobby Hackett's unusual sextet of 1957. With Hackett's cornet, Johnny Gwaltney on clarinet and vibes, Ernie Caceres doubling on baritone and clarinet, Dick Cary playing piano and E♭ horn and fine backing from John Dengler's tuba and Nat Ray's drums, the band plays fresh versions of swing standards and a couple of originals from Cary. *—Scott Yanow*

Off Minor / Jul. 5, 1957+Jul. 5, 1958 / Vipers' Nest ♦♦♦♦ ·
Although cornetist Bobby Hackett gets top billing, this budget CD is actually split between live sessions headed by Hackett in 1957 and trombonist Jack Teagarden in 1958. The six Hackett selections feature a very interesting group consisting of the leader, Dick Cary (the main arranger) on piano and alto horn, Ernie Caceres doubling on baritone and clarinet, Tom Gwaltney on clarinet and vibes, the tuba of

John Dengler and drummer Buzzy Drootin. Although their versions of "Fidgety Feet" and "Royal Garden Blues" are typical Dixieland rousers, "Caravan" (which features Cary's peck horn in the lead), Duke Ellington's "Lady of the Lavender Mist" and the pianist's original "Handle with Cary" are much more modern than one would expect. In addition the vibes-piano-tuba-drums rhythm section does a fine job with Thelonious Monk's "Off Minor"; it is a pity that Hackett sat out on that song. The latter half of the CD features Jack Teagarden's regular group of the period (with the exciting trumpeter Dick Oakley, clarinetist Jerry Fuller, pianist Don Ewell, bassist Stan Puls and drummer Ronnie Gelb) running through four Dixieland warhorses with spirit and drive. The trumpeter who trades off with Oakley on "Royal Garden Blues" is probably Bobby Hackett. This is a recommended acquisition for trad jazz fans. —*Scott Yanow*

Bobby Hackett at the Embers / Nov. 1957 / Capitol ✦✦✦
Supper-club jazz from the Bobby Hackett Quartet, the music borders between solid swing and easy listening with the accent on ballads (other than a couple of exceptions) and mellow sounds from the pretty cornet of Hackett. Nice music but not all that stimulating. —*Scott Yanow*

Live from the Voyager Room, Vol. 2 / 1957-1958 / Shoestring ✦✦✦✦✦
This second of two Shoestring LPs featuring the cornetist's unusual group in the mid-'50s has a lot of doubling of instruments from the sextet, with the earlier edition finding Bob Wilber playing clarinet, alto, soprano, tenor and vibes, Dick Hafer switching between tenor and baritone, and Dick Cary heard on piano, alto horn and trumpet; the later version has Tom Gwaltney on clarinet and vibes and Ernie Caceres switching between baritone and clarinet. But even more impressive than the number of instruments utilized is the range of music performed during these radio airchecks, spanning from Dixieland and some obscure swing tunes to such songs as "Whisper Not," "Willie The Lion" Smith's "Morning Aire" and Duke Ellington's "The Lady with the Lavender Hair." This group never made it commercially, but its music is well worth checking out, if you can find this LP. —*Scott Yanow*

Hawaii Swings / 1959-1960 / Capitol ✦✦
Because he had a very accessible tone on cornet, Hackett was in demand during the 1950s and '60s for mood music albums in addition to jazz dates. This LP was one of his oddest, for he is heard playing a dozen Hawaiian melodies in a band that includes steel guitar, ukulele, guitar and bongos in addition to a standard rhythm section. Fortunately the majority of the selections are taken uptempo and Hackett has plenty of solo space to romp over the unusual backing, making this a novelty date well worth picking up. It is doubtful that it will be reissued on CD anytime in the next decade. —*Scott Yanow*

Bobby Hackett's Sextet / 1962+Feb. 19, 1970 / Storyville ✦✦✦
This Storyville LP combines two very different sessions led by Hackett. The first side has the soundtrack from a film made for the Goodyear Tire Company in 1962 featuring Hackett, trombonist Urbie Green, clarinetist Bob Wilber and pianist Dave McKenna playing typical Dixieland tunes in spirited if overly concise fashion. The flip side features Hackett with trombonist Vic Dickenson in a quintet in 1970 really pushing themselves on five superior standards, including a version of "String of Pearls" on which Hackett reprises his famous solo of three decades earlier with Glenn Miller. —*Scott Yanow*

Hello Louis / Apr. 28, 1964-May 1, 1964 / Epic ✦✦✦✦
This Hackett album, made in tribute to his idol Louis Armstrong (and obviously recorded after "Hello Dolly" became a huge hit), is somewhat unusual. Marshall Brown's arrangements are a bit modernistic for the concept, soprano saxophonist Steve Lacy (who would soon move permanently to Europe and become a key member of the avant-garde) gets one of his few opportunities to play in a Dixielandish session and this set of Armstrong compositions contains many obscurities. Not all of the music is successful (and none eclipse Satch's original versions) but, due to the many surprises, this is worth searching for. —*Scott Yanow*

Plays Tony Bennett's Greatest Hits / Jun. 22, 1966-Sep. 8, 1966 / Epic ✦✦✦
Throughout his career, Hackett was in demand for a wide variety of studio dates due to his highly appealing tone on cornet. He was utilized by Jackie Gleason for a series of commercially successful mood music albums and spent a period touring with Tony Bennett. In tribute to Bennett, Hackett recorded ten songs associated with the singer. Unfortunately, all of these renditions clock in at three minutes or less, making for a 28-minute LP, and none of the performances wander far from the melodies, which include such dubious material as "Put On a Happy Face," "Stranger in Paradise" and of course "I Left My Heart In San Francisco." Pass this one by. —*Scott Yanow*

Creole Cookin' / Jan. 30, 1967 / Verve ✦✦✦✦✦
This long-out-of-print LP contains one of his finest all-around recordings. The cornetist is featured on 11 Dixieland standards and joined by a 15-piece all-star band arranged by Bob Wilber; Wilber and tenor great Zoot Sims also receive some solo

space on this essential release which is well deserving of reissue on CD. —*Scott Yanow*

Melody Is a Must: Live at the Roosevelt Grill / Mar. 1969-Apr. 1969 / Phontastic ✦✦✦
One of Bobby Hackett's favorite groups was the quintet he co-led with trombonist Vic Dickenson during 1969-71. Fortunately this relatively short-lived unit made more than its share of recordings (all of them live). Hackett and Dickenson both had soft tones and fluent styles that were flexible enough to bring new life and their own brand of sly wit to these veteran songs. This set does not duplicate any of the Chiaroscuro releases. —*Scott Yanow*

Live from Mannasas / Dec. 7, 1969 / Jazzology ✦✦✦
This LP captures a very spirited set starring cornetist Hackett, trombonist Vic Dickenson, clarinetist Tommy Gwaltney and singer Maxine Sullivan cut live at a jazz festival. Cornetist Wild Bill Davison and trombonist George Brunis really make the ensembles overcrowded by sitting in unexpectedly during the final two numbers. The good spirits make up for some loose moments. —*Scott Yanow*

Live at the Roosevelt Grill, Vol. 2 / Mar. 26, 1970-Apr. 10, 1970 / Chiaroscuro ✦✦✦✦✦
For a few months in 1970, cornetist Bobby Hackett led one of the finest working groups of his career, a quintet with co-leader Vic Dickenson on trombone, pianist Dave McKenna, bassist Jack Lesberg and drummer Cliff Leeman. Fortunately, the band's long stint at the Roosevelt Grill Hotel was extensively recorded by producer Hank O'Neal; some of it was issued on LP and much more will probably come out on CD. Hackett and Dickenson made an ideal team, both having mellow tones, fluent styles and sly wits. This CD has the dozen songs on the original LP and five selections never issued before, and is easily recommended to fans of mainstream jazz; highlights include "Thou Swell," "It's Wonderful," "A String of Pearls," "Just You Just Me" and "Easter Parade." —*Scott Yanow*

● **Featuring Vic Dickenson at the Roosevelt Grill** / Apr. 19, 1970-May 1970 / Chiaroscuro ✦✦✦✦✦
The Bobby Hackett/Vic Dickenson Quintet of 1969-71 was one of Hackett's favorite bands of his career. The cornet/trombone front line worked together very well, as did a rhythm section led by pianist Dave McKenna. This particular LP, released long after the group had become history, differs from the previous releases in that all of the songs are Dixieland (rather than swing) favorites but, no matter, the band's sly wit and subtle creativity remained at a high level. —*Scott Yanow*

What a Wonderful World / 1973 / Columbia ✦✦✦
One of Hackett's last studio albums, the cornetist is heard in fine form with three different units ranging from seven to 15 pieces. Teresa Brewer's three vocals are typically unfortunate but Hackett, trombonist Vic Dickenson and clarinetist Johnny Mince keep the music (dominated by Dixieland standards) swinging. —*Scott Yanow*

Strike Up the Band / Aug. 3, 1974 / Flying Dutchman ✦✦✦✦✦
Hackett recorded many excellent performances throughout his life; this LP is one of the more rewarding of his later years. He is teamed successfully with tenor saxophonist Zoot Sims and guitarist Bucky Pizzarelli in a frequently exciting sextet. High points include the uptempo "Strike Up the Band," a revisit to "Embraceable You" (Hackett had cut a famous solo on that standard 34 years earlier) and a variety of standards and basic originals. A consistently stimulating and enjoyable set, it is well deserving of being reissued on CD. —*Scott Yanow*

Charlie Haden

b. Aug. 6, 1937, Shenandoah, IL
Bass, Leader / Free Jazz, Hard Bop, Avant-Garde
What would Ornette Coleman have done in 1959 if Charlie Haden were not around? There was probably not another jazz bassist who fully understood Coleman's radical music that early. Haden's large and distinctive tone, his unhurried approach and his ability to state a pulse without handcuffing the lead voices to a repeated chord structure was unprecedented at the time. He played country music on a regular radio show with his family as a child, arrived in Los Angeles in the mid-'50s and gigged with Art Pepper, Hampton Hawes and Paul Bley during 1957-59. It was with Bley at the Hillcrest Club that Haden first performed with Ornette Coleman and Don Cherry and he soon became an important member of their quartet. Haden traveled with Coleman to New York in 1959 and was with him through 1961 including making some innovative records for Atlantic. He worked with Denny Zeitlin during 1964-66, had several reunions with Ornette through the years (including some later recordings), was part of the Jazz Composers' Orchestra Association in the late '60s and in 1969 formed the Liberation Music Orchestra. Always outspoken against injustice and political repression, Haden's avant-garde orchestra was quite political. He also played often with Keith Jarrett (1967-75) including his excellent quintet that featured Dewey Redman,

recorded with Alice Coltrane (1968-72), led a pair of diverse duet albums (1975-76) and was with Old and New Dreams in the mid- to late '70s. A perennial pollwinner, Haden (who teaches at Cal Arts) had a trio during 1982-83 with Jan Garbarek and Egberto Gismonti and since 1986 has led the comparatively conservative Quartet West (which also includes Ernie Watts, Alan Broadbent and Larance Marable) in addition to occasionally putting together a new version of the Liberation Music Orchestra. Charlie Haden, composer of the standard "First Song," has recorded as a leader for Impulse, Artists House, Horizon, ECM, Verve, Blue Note, Soul Note and Antilles. —*Scott Yanow*

Liberation Music Orchestra / Apr. 27, 1970-Apr. 29, 1970 / MCA ✦✦✦✦✦
For the debut recording of his *Liberation Music Orchestra* (reissued on CD), bassist Charlie Haden blended together his passionate anti-fascist politics with his interests in the Spanish Civil War and avant-garde jazz. The all-star ensemble (cornetist Don Cherry, trumpeter Mike Mantler, tenors Gato Barbieri and Dewey Redman, clarinetist Perry Robinson, trombonist Roswell Rudd, Bob Northern on French horn, Howard Johnson on tuba, guitarist Sam Brown, pianist Carla Bley, drummer Paul Motian and percussionist Andrew Cyrille) is a predecessor of Carla Bley's orchestra and her arrangements are not dissimilar to the path she would follow in the next decade. The repertoire on the memorable set includes four songs from the Spanish Civil War, three Bley originals, two from Haden (including "Song for Che"), a solemn "We Shall Overcome" and Ornette Coleman's "War Orphans." Soundtrack recordings from the 1930s Spanish film *Mouris a Madrid* pop up briefly on a few selections, adding to the political nature of the music. Cherry, Rudd, Barbieri and Haden have short solos but it is the colorful folk melodies and spirited ensembles that make this a memorable recording. —*Scott Yanow*

As Long As There's Music / Jan. 25, 1976 / Artists House ✦✦✦✦
Although one would not immediately associate bassist Charlie Haden with pianist Hampton Hawes, they had performed together on an occasional basis since first meeting in 1957. This Artists House LP, a set of five duets, was their last opportunity to play together because Hawes would pass away the following year. The music includes a fairly free improvisation on "Hello/Goodbye," the duo's interpretation of the title cut, a collaboration on "This Is Called Love" and two originals from the pianist. This quiet and often lyrical set contains a great deal of thoughtful and subtle music by two masters. —*Scott Yanow*

● **Closeness** / Jan. 26, 1976-Mar. 21, 1976 / A&M ✦✦✦✦✦
This one is absolutely essential. One duet apiece with Ornette Coleman (sax), Alice Coltrane (p), Keith Jarrett (p), Paul Motian (d). —*Michael G. Nastos*

Golden Number / Jun. 7, 1976-Dec. 20, 1976 / A&M ✦✦✦✦
The second of two duet sets by bassist Charlie Haden (both have been reissued on A&M CDs) is the equal of the first. Haden teams up with Don Cherry (on trumpet and flutes), tenor saxophonist Archie Shepp (for the excellent "Shepp's Way"), pianist Hampton Hawes (jamming Ornette Coleman's blues "Turnaround"), and Ornette himself, who unfortunately plays trumpet this time around. In general, the music is quite intriguing and has its share of variety. —*Scott Yanow*

Gitane / Sep. 22, 1978 / Verve ✦✦✦
The American bassist meets Gypsy guitarist Christian Escoude. —*Michael G. Nastos*

Magico / Jun. 1979 / ECM ✦✦✦✦
Perhaps it was the presence of bassist Charlie Haden, but this trio set has more energy than one normally associates with the other members of the group (Jan Garbarek on tenor and soprano and Egberto Gismonti doubling on guitar and piano). The trio performs group originals and an obscurity during the picturesque and continually interesting release; this combination works well. —*Scott Yanow*

Folk Songs / Nov. 1979 / ECM ✦✦✦✦
One of the better ECM recordings, this collaboration by bassist Charlie Haden, Jan Garbarek on tenor and soprano, and Egberto Gismonti (switching between guitar and piano) is filled with moody originals, improvisations that blend together jazz and world music, and atmospheric ensembles. This date works well both as superior background music and for close listening. —*Scott Yanow*

The Ballad of the Fallen / Nov. 1982 / ECM ✦✦✦
The second recording by Charlie Haden's Liberation Music Orchestra utilizes a few alumni (the bassist/leader, trumpeters Don Cherry and Mike Mantler, tenor saxophonist Dewey Redman, drummer Paul Motian and pianist Carla Bley), along with other musicians who rose to prominence since the 1969 debut album (Jim Pepper and Steve Slagle on reeds, trombonist Gary Valante, guitarist Mick Goodrick, Sharon Freeman on French horn, and Jack Jeffers on tuba). As with the first set, the music mixes together some melodic but avant-garde explorations with revolutionary themes including songs from the Spanish Civil War, El Salvador, Portugal and Chile. "Too Late," a duet by Bley and Haden, serves as a change of pace. The music is quite credible and emotional, and has dated well. —*Scott Yanow*

☆ **Quartet West** / Dec. 22, 1986-Dec. 23, 1986 / Verve ✦✦✦✦✦
The debut recording by Charlie Haden's Quartet West (comprising the bassist/leader, tenor saxophonist Ernie Watts, pianist Alan Broadbent and, at the time, drummer Billy Higgins) launched the popular acoustic group. Haden now had an opportunity to display his skill in playing bop-based music, along with his strong interest in the mood of film noir. For this CD, the quartet performs three standards plus pieces by Pat Metheny, Ornette Coleman ("The Blessing" and "The Good Life"), Charlie Parker ("Passport") and Haden. The band also gave exposure to the underrated Broadbent and helped push Watts towards his original love of Coltranish jazz. —*Scott Yanow*

Etudes / Sep. 14, 1987-Sep. 15, 1987 / Soul Note ✦✦✦
The very democratic trio of bassist Charlie Haden, drummer Paul Motian and pianist Geri Allen perform sensitive yet often exploratory group improvisations on several originals, Ornette Coleman's "Lonely Woman," and Herbie Nichols' "Shuffle Montgomery." The communication between these three masterful players is quite impressive. —*Scott Yanow*

Silence / Nov. 11, 1987-Nov. 12, 1987 / Soul Note ✦✦✦

In Angel City / May 30, 1988-Jun. 1, 1988 / Verve ✦✦✦✦
The second recording by Charlie Haden's Quartet West is similar to the music that the group (bassist Haden, tenor saxophonist Ernie Watts, pianist Alan Broadbent and drummer Larance Marable) would play for the next decade. Among the highlights of this well-rounded set (one of the band's most definitive releases) is "First Song" (Haden's most memorable composition), Miles Davis' "Blue in Green," and a lengthy exploration of Ornette Coleman's "Lonely Woman." An excellent showcase for Haden in a straightahead setting and for Watts, whose passionate sound perfectly fits the band. Highly recommended. —*Scott Yanow*

Montreal Tapes / Jul. 2, 1989 / Verve ✦✦✦
Performed as one of eight concerts at the 1989 Montreal Jazz Festival that featured bassist Charlie Haden, this trio set teams Haden with pianist Paul Bley and drummer Paul Motian. Playing adventurous but unclassifiable music that falls between bop and the avant-garde, the trio contributes one original apiece and also interprets four Ornette Coleman tunes and Carla Bley's classic "Ida Lupino." The musical communication between the three masterful players is impressive on this generally introspective set. —*Scott Yanow*

Dialogues / Jan. 28, 1990-Jan. 29, 1990 / Antilles ✦✦✦
Jazz bassist Haden meets Portuguese guitarist. Strangely beautiful. —*Michael G. Nastos*

First Song / Apr. 26, 1990 / Soul Note ✦✦✦

★ **Dream Keeper** / Apr. 4, 1990-Apr. 5, 1990 / Blue Note ✦✦✦✦✦
Consensus Album of the Year, with the Liberation Music Orchestra. —*Ron Wynn*

Haunted Heart / Oct. 27, 1991-Oct. 28, 1991 / Verve ✦✦✦✦✦
Charlie Haden loves film as much as music, combining both loves on the critically acclaimed *Haunted Heart*. Haden led his tremendous group Quartet West through 12 numbers, several (like Cole Porter's "Every Time We Say Goodbye," Alan Broadbent's "Lady in the Lake," Arthur Schwartz and Howard Dietz's "Haunted Heart," and even the short introduction) with film ties and/or links. Haden transferred vocals on some numbers from Jeri Southern, Billie Holiday and Jo Stafford into the mix without disrupting or disturbing the group framework. Quartet West has emerged as a premier small combo, and Haden nicely paid tribute to the past without being held hostage to it. —*Ron Wynn*

Always Say Goodbye / Jul. 30, 1993-Aug. 1, 1993 / Verve ✦✦✦✦

Steal Away / Jun. 29, 1994-Jun. 30, 1994 / Verve ✦✦✦
This is an unusual record. Bassist Charlie Haden and pianist Hank Jones perform a variety of spirituals, hymns and folk songs as duets. The traditional music (which includes such tunes as "Nobody Knows the Trouble I've Seen," "Swing Low, Sweet Chariot," "Sometimes I Feel like a Motherless Child" and "We Shall Overcome") are all performed respectfully and with reverence. These melodic yet subtly swinging interpretations hold one's interest throughout and reward repeated listenings. —*Scott Yanow*

Now Is the Hour / Jul. 18, 1995-Jul. 20, 1995 / Verve ✦✦✦✦✦

Night and the City / Sep. 1996 / Verve ✦✦✦
The third in a series of Haden duet projects for Verve in the 1990s finds the increasingly nostalgia-minded bass player working New York City's Iridium jazz club with pianist Kenny Barron. Moreover, it is entirely possible that we are getting a skewed view of the gig; according to Haden, he and his co-producer, wife Ruth, tilted this album heavily in the direction of romantic ballads, eliminating the bebop and avant-garde numbers that the two may have also played at the club. Be that as it may, this is still a thoughtful, intensely musical, sometimes haunting set of performances, with Barron displaying a high level of lyrical sensitivity and Haden applying his massive tone sparingly. Most of the seven tracks are fantasias

on well-known standards, though one of the most eloquent performances on the disc is Barron's playing on his own "Twilight Song." If Haden deliberately set out to create a single reflective mood, he certainly succeeded, although those coming to Haden for the first time through this and most of his other '90s CDs would never suspect that this man once played such a fire-breathing role in the jazz avant-garde. —*Richard S. Ginell*

Beyond the Missouri Sky (Short Stories) / 1996 / Verve ✦✦✦✦
This wistful set of duets features two native Missourians (bassist Charlie Haden and guitarist Pat Metheny) emphasizing their lyrical sides on originals and a wide variety of music that includes folk and country standards, Henry Mancini's "Two for the Road" and the debut of Johnny Mandel's "The Moon Song." Some selections have Metheny adding an extra guitar and orchestral effects with his Synclavier, but the emphasis is on intimate interplay by the two masterful players. Highlights include Haden's "Waltz for Ruth," "First Song" and the standard "He's Gone Away" but every selection fits well into the quiet mood of this worthy project. —*Scott Yanow*

Dick Hafer

b. May 29, 1927, Wyomissing, PA
Tenor Saxophone / Cool

A fine veteran tenor saxophonist who has long been overlooked and underfeatured, Dick Hafer made a strong impression with his 1994 Fresh Sound release *Prez Impressions* (a tribute to Lester Young). He started on clarinet when he was seven, switching to tenor in high school. Hafer's first major job was with Charlie Barnet's bebop orchestra of 1949 (being featured on some recorded solos the same day he joined the band). He next was with Claude Thornhill (1949-50), was briefly back with Barnet and then joined Woody Herman (1951-55), soloing most notably on "Wild Apple Honey." Hafer freelanced in New York, played with Tex Beneke (1955), Bobby Hackett (1957-58), Elliott Lawrence (1958-60) and Benny Goodman (1962) and recorded with Charles Mingus (1963) and Johnny Hartman. He moved to Los Angeles in 1974 and worked steadily but was fairly obscure until the Fresh Sound session. Since then an earlier album (1991) from the cool-toned tenor has been released on Progressive. —*Scott Yanow*

In a Sentimental Mood / Dec. 2, 1991-Dec. 3, 1991 / Progressive ✦✦✦✦
Dick Hafer, a veteran tenor saxophonist best known for his association with Woody Herman's Orchestra in the early 1950s, made a big impression with his 1994 tribute to Lester Young for Fresh Sound (*Prez Impressions*). A fine cool-toned tenor in the Four Brothers tradition, Hafer finally had the opportunity to star in a quartet session. As it turned out, that was Dick Hafer's second opportunity. His Progressive CD, which was released in 1996, was actually recorded back in 1991. For this set, Hafer is joined by Johnny Varro (one of the top swing pianists of the past 30 years), bassist Johnny Leitham and the late drummer Gene Estes for a varied program filled not only with swing and bop standards but Al Cohn's "High on You," Bob Enevoldsen's "Three Bop" and Estes' "Forever After"; the latter is based on "After You've Gone." While Hafer purposely emulated Lester Young on the Fresh Sound date, on his Progressive album he sounds more like himself, playing in the same genre as Zoot Sims and Al Cohn. The mix of swinging pieces and ballads works quite well with the highlights including "The Love Nest," "Lullaby in Rhythm" and "The Man I Love." —*Scott Yanow*

● **Prez Impressions** / Feb. 28, 1994-Mar. 1, 1994 / Fresh Sound ✦✦✦✦✦
Veteran tenor saxophonist Dick Hafer's sudden emergence as a brilliant soloist on his Fresh Sound recording is a very welcome event. A reliable musician for the previous 40 years (mostly as a section player in big bands), Hafer heads a quartet (with pianist Ross Tompkins, bassist Dave Carpenter and drummer Jake Hanna) and displays his own wonderful tenor sound, which not only looks towards Lester Young of the 1930s but Prez of the '50s. Hafer is quite creative within Young's style (not merely copying Prez) and swings hard on ten swing standards and a song apiece by Al Cohn and Zoot Sims. It's a wonderful outing of melodic mainstream music by an often overlooked tenor master. —*Scott Yanow*

Tim Hagans

b. Aug. 19, 1954, Dayton, OH
Trumpet / Hard Bop

Tim Hagans, an excellent hard-bop-oriented trumpeter, was with the orchestras of Stan Kenton (1974-77) and Woody Herman (1977) before moving to Sweden (1977-81) where he played with Sahib Shihab, Ernie Wilkins' Almost Big Band, the Danish Radio Orchestra (which was then directed by Thad Jones) and Dexter Gordon. After returning to the US, he taught at the University of Cincinnati and recorded for the local MoPro label. Hagans taught at Berklee (1984-86) and then in 1986 started working with Joe Lovano and Fred Hersch. Since then he has made records with Bob Belden, Lovano, Rick Margitza, John Hart and the Yellowjackets and has worked with the big bands of Bob Mintzer, Maria Schneider and the Gil Evans

Orchestra. Tim Hagans has recorded two Blue Note albums thus far as a leader. —*Scott Yanow*

From the Neck Down / Apr. 19, 1983-Apr. 20, 1983 / Mo Pro ✦✦✦
Tim Hagans was 28, based in Cincinnati and a member of the Blue Wisp Big Band when he recorded his debut album as a leader. He already had a wide range and a strong hard-bop-based sound. Accompanied by pianist Steve Schmidt, bassist Lynn Seaton and either John Von Ohlen or Marc Wolfley on drums (with altoist Sandy Suskind guesting on "Blues for Scheurer"), Hagans did not yet have an original voice on his horn, but his strong technique and ability to swing make the music (all group originals) well worth hearing. —*Scott Yanow*

No Words / Dec. 3, 1993 / Blue Note ✦✦✦✦
The impressive trumpeter Tim Hagans holds his own with the tenor of Joe Lovano during a sextet session with guitarist John Abercrombie, keyboardist Marc Copland, bassist Scott Lee and drummer Bill Stewart that features nine of his originals. The music is essentially advanced hard bop (Lovano and Abercrombie both sound somewhat inspired) and Hagans displays both an attractive tone and a fertile imagination. It's a strong set of modern mainstream jazz. —*Scott Yanow*

● **Audible Architechture** / Dec. 17, 1994-Dec. 18, 1994 / Blue Note ✦✦✦✦✦
Although Tim Hagans is rightly thought of as a veteran hard-bop player, his adventurous spirit has led to him playing fairly freely on this CD. The programming is quite admirable with three pianoless trios followed by four quartet numbers (that also include tenor saxophonist Bob Belden) alternating with separate trumpet-bass ("You Don't Know What Love Is") and trumpet-drums ("Drum Row") duets before a brief unaccompanied trumpet solo closes the set. At times (particularly on "Jasmine in Three" and "Audible Architecture," a pair of his seven originals) Hagans almost sounds like Don Cherry with technique. Of the highlights, "I Hear a Rhapsody" sets the stage, the loose funk played by bassist Larry Grenadier and drummer Billy Kilson (two underrated talents) on "Garage Bands" accompanies the improvised interplay of the horns, Bob Belden is quite memorable (particularly on "Shorts") and the trumpet-drums duet comes off quite well. Actually there is not a throwaway track among the ten with Tim Hagans in prime physical and creative form. Highly recommended. —*Scott Yanow*

Hubsongs: The Music of Freddie Hubbard / Aug. 1, 1997-Aug. 2, 1997 / Blue Note ✦✦✦
Hub Songs not only functions as a heartfelt, loving tribute to Freddie Hubbard, one of the greatest trumpeters in bop history, but it's a dynamic, engaging session in its own right. Both Tim Hagans and Marcus Printup had established themselves as two of the finest hard-bop trumpeters of the '80s and '90s, and they were well prepared for this session. Working with pianist Benny Green, bassist Peter Washing and drummer Kenny Washing, as well as guest musicians Javon Jackson on tenor sax and Vince Herring on alto sax, the duo manages to recapture the driving spirit of Hubbard's best recordings while stamping each song with individual, adventurous solos. —*Leo Stanley*

Bob Haggart

b. Mar. 13, 1914, New York, NY
Bass, Composer / Dixieland, Swing

One of the last survivors of Bob Crosby's Bobcats, Bob Haggart has been a top bassist for 60 years. Originally a guitarist, Haggart taught himself bass while in high school. He gained fame when he joined Bob Crosby in 1935, not only supplying his supportive and swinging bass but contributing arrangements and writing such songs as "What's New," "South Rampart Street Parade," "My Inspiration" and "Big Noise from Winnetka," the latter a colorful duet with drummer Ray Bauduc. After Crosby broke up his band in 1942, Haggart became a studio musician and was on a countless number of sessions (particularly for Decca). In addition to his studio work, the busy bassist teamed with Yank Lawson for recordings as the Lawson-Haggart Band. Bob Haggart participated in many Bobcat reunions with Bob Crosby, co-led the World's Greatest Jazz Band with Lawson starting in 1968 and has been a steady fixture at many jazz parties and festivals through the years. —*Scott Yanow*

Makes a Sentimental Journey / Nov. 1980 / Jazzology ✦✦✦✦
Other than an obscure set for Command in 1963, this was bassist Bob Haggart's first album as a leader, although he co-led many dates through the years with trumpeter Yank Lawson. Haggart leads an eight-piece group through ten swing and pre-swing standards, including "Mandy Make Up Your Mind," "I Can't Believe That You're in Love with Me," "Someday Sweetheart" and "The Sheik of Araby." In the supporting cast are such notables as the Bix Beiderbecke-inspired cornetist Tom Pletcher, clarinetist Tom Gwaltney, bass saxophonist Spencer Clark, and pianist Dill Jones. Easily recommended to Dixieland and mainstream fans, as are Haggart's two follow-up records for Jazzology. —*Scott Yanow*

Enjoys Carolina in the Morning / Apr. 1981 / Jazzology ✦✦✦✦

On his second of three albums as a leader for Jazzology, bassist Bob Haggart performs ten veteran standards, including six that have cities, states or countries in their titles, plus "Song of the Wanderer." Cornetist Tom Pletcher (best known for his work with the Sons of Bix) is the star soloist, but there are also fine spots for valve trombonist Mike Katz, tenorman Jack Howe, bass saxophonist Spencer Clark, and pianist Dill Jones; in addition, Ron Hockett is joined by fellow clarinetist Bill Rappaport on two numbers. The music has the flavor of a spirited jam session, but is well conceived and logical. —*Scott Yanow*

● **A Portrait of Bix** / Mar. 1986 / Jazzology ✦✦✦✦✦

This is a well-planned set featuring ten songs associated with legendary cornetist Bix Beiderbecke; in addition, a brief rendition of his "In a Mist" is played as both an intro to the date and as a coda. Tom Pletcher was the perfect choice to play cornet, since he has always sounded a lot like Bix. Other musicians on the date include Ron Hockett on clarinet and (in a tribute to Frankie Trumbauer) C-melody sax, Jack Howe on tenor, bass saxophonist Spencer Clark, pianist Mike Katz, drummer Doug James, and Haggart. They mostly avoided the tunes that had Beiderbecke's best-known solos in favor of tunes that he soloed on but are flexible enough to be jammed, including "Dardanella," "Clementine," "There'll Come a Time," and "Somebody Stole My Gal." Highly enjoyable music that is long overdue to be reissued on CD. —*Scott Yanow*

Hag Leaps In / Nov. 6, 1995-Nov. 7, 1995 / Arbors ✦✦✦

Bassist Bob Haggart, 81 at the time of his Arbors trio set, is heard still in prime form, whether accompanying the 74-year-old pianist John Bunch or guitarist Bucky Pizzarelli (a mere 69). The most unusual aspect of Haggart's date is that his group performs "Big Noise from Winnetka" without a drummer, which actually makes the song a bit pointless. Otherwise, the repertoire (swing standards and a few basic originals, including the title cut, which is based on "Lester Leaps In") is conventional and enjoyable. The music consistently swings, the three veterans split the solo space fairly evenly, and everyone plays at their usual high level. —*Scott Yanow*

Jerry Hahn

b. Sep. 21, 1940, Alma, NE
Guitar / Post-Bop

A lesser-known but talented guitarist, Jerry Hahn attended Wichita State University and played in Kansas before moving to San Francisco in 1962. He gained some recognition for his work with John Handy's adventurous band (1964-66) which was the hit of the 1965 Monterey Jazz Festival. Hahn led an album in 1967, toured with the Fifth Dimension the following year and was one of many great guitarists to be part of Gary Burton's group (1968-69). He led the Jerry Hahn Brotherhood in the early '70s and then became a teacher at Wichita State University. Hahn maintained a low profile until 1986 when he moved to Portland and began playing full-time again. In 1993 Jerry Hahn relocated to Colorado, recording his first album in 20 years for Enja. —*Scott Yanow*

Ara-Be-In / Apr. 3, 1967-Apr. 4, 1967 / Arhoolie ✦✦✦

● **Moses** / Sep. 1973 / Fantasy ✦✦✦✦

Jerry Hahn's second album is a fairly definitive effort by the talented but greatly underrated guitarist. Best known as an educator and an alumnus of Gary Burton's group, Hahn shows a lot of potential on this quartet set with organist Merl Saunders, bassist Mel Graves and drummer George Marsh. In addition to his diverse originals, Hahn performs swinging versions of "All Blues" and Clifford Brown's "Joy Spring." It is a double pity that this LP has yet to appear on CD and that Hahn was not more extensively recorded in the 1970s. —*Scott Yanow*

Al Haig

b. Jul. 22, 1924, Newark, NJ, **d.** Nov. 16, 1982, New York, NY
Piano / Bop

One of the finest pianists of the bop era (and one who learned from Bud Powell's innovations quite early), Al Haig was quite busy during two periods of his career but unfortunately was fairly obscure in the years between. After serving in the Coast Guard (playing in bands during 1942-44) and freelancing around Boston, Haig worked steadily with Dizzy Gillespie (1945-46), Charlie Parker (1948-50) and Stan Getz (1949-51) and was on many recordings, mostly as a sideman (including some classic Diz and Bird sessions) but also as a leader for Spotlite, Dawn and Prestige. However (other than little-known dates in 1954 for Esoteric, Swing and Period) Haig did not lead any more albums until 1974. He played fairly often during the 1951-73 period but was generally overlooked. That changed during his last decade when he was finally recognized as a bop giant and recorded for Spotlite, Choice, Sea Breeze, Interplay and several Japanese and European labels. —*Scott Yanow*

Al Haig Meets the Master Saxes, Vol. 1 / 1948 / Spotlite ✦✦✦✦

Al Haig was one of the top bop pianists of the 1945-49 period. This is the first of three albums put out by the British Spotlite label that features Haig (mostly as a sideman) during his prime years. Studio sides and more extended live performances are mixed together throughout the series. For the first LP, Haig is heard in quartets led by tenors John Hardee, Coleman Hawkins (three live numbers, including a nearly seven-minute version of "Stuffy"), and Wardell Gray, plus backing the short-lived bop singer Buddy Stewart on "Shawn" and leading his Five Bops (a sextet with Stewart, trombonist Kai Winding and Al Epstein on tenor) for two songs. The recording quality is reasonable for the period, and Haig keeps up with (and often inspires) the horn players. Bop collectors will want all three sets in this series. —*Scott Yanow*

Al Haig Meets the Master Saxes, Vol. 2 / 1948 / Spotlite ✦✦✦✦

Al Haig Meets the Master Saxes, Vol. 3 / 1948-Sep. 3, 1951 / Spotlite ✦✦✦✦

Live in Hollywood / Aug. 4, 1952 / Xanadu ✦✦✦

Al Haig Quartet / Sep. 1954 / Fresh Sound ✦✦✦

Al Haig Today / July 6, 1965 / Fresh Sound ✦✦✦

Invitation / Jan. 7, 1974 / Spotlite ✦✦✦

Special Brew / Nov. 27, 1974 / Spotlite ✦✦✦✦

Pianist Al Haig and guitarist Jimmy Raney (who are joined on this LP by bassist Wilbur Little and drummer Frank Gant) make for a logical combination, since both had styles that were boppish yet thoughtful. Unfortunately, Haig plays electric piano on four of the eight numbers, which dilutes his individuality a bit. The quartet not only performs three Charlie Parker tunes and a couple of veteran standards, but Eddie Harris's "Freedom Jazz Dance," Herbie Hancock's "Dolphin Dance" and Raney's original "We'll Be Together," showing that they were keeping an open mind beyond bop. Fine music but not essential. —*Scott Yanow*

● **Strings Attached** / Mar. 27, 1975 / Choice ✦✦✦✦✦

A stalwart early bopper, pianist Al Haig returned to the recording spotlight briefly in the mid-'70s with this set, which could just as easily been made in the '40s. Haig's fluidity and ability to navigate blistering passages and make the appropriate chord changes enabled him to survive the turbulent bop era; those skills are now second nature, as he shows with crisp, rippling solos throughout the album. —*Ron Wynn*

Piano Interpretation / Jun. 21, 1976 / Sea Breeze ✦✦✦✦

A fine solo piano set from 1976, with Al Haig displaying the total technical package on standards and bop anthems. He plays some rapid-fire; others, he constructs slowly and carefully, then tears them down and rebuilds the theme with nicely executed, intricate solos. —*Ron Wynn*

Piano Time / Jun. 21, 1976 / Sea Breeze ✦✦✦

The second of two solo piano albums Al Haig made in 1976, both done with exacting precision as well as exuberant force. Haig was disproving the critics who said he was finished, and he showed convincingly that there was still plenty of power in his hands and lots of tricks up his sleeve. —*Ron Wynn*

Interplay / Nov. 16, 1976 / Sea Breeze ✦✦✦

Fine duets featuring pianist Al Haig during a busy period in the mid-'70s. He'd overcome personal problems and was cranking out albums left and right for both domestic and foreign labels. These were cut for Interplay, a small West Coast firm, but then were mostly issued in Japan. They are mostly excellent examples of Haig's surging bop style. —*Ron Wynn*

Manhattan Memories / Feb. 1977-Jul. 1977 / Sea Breeze ✦✦✦

After being largely off records during 1955-73 (just one obscure set in 1965), pianist Al Haig was very active from 1974 up until his death in 1982. This LP has two small group dates showcasing Haig in a trio/quartet setting with bassist Jamil Nasser, either Jimmy Wordsworth or Frank Gant on drums and sometimes guitarist Eddie Diehl. Haig's style was largely unchanged from his earlier prime although he had grown as a player, as he shows on such numbers as Bud Powell's "I'll Keep Loving You," Billy Strayhorn's "My Little Brown Book" and Cedar Walton's "Voices Within Me." —*Scott Yanow*

Expressly Ellington / Oct. 14, 1978 / Spotlite ✦✦✦✦

Pianist Al Haig and his longtime bassist Jamil Nasser are heard co-leading a quartet in London that also includes the fine tenorman Art Themen and drummer Tony Mann. Despite the title, the repertoire is not exclusively by Duke Ellington; of the eight songs, four are by Duke and there is a song apiece from Billy Strayhorn and Juan Tizol, in addition to "Flamingo" and "Body and Soul." Few surprises occur, but the boppish music on this LP is enjoyable and should be of interest to straightahead jazz collectors. —*Scott Yanow*

Plays the Music of Jerome Kern / 1978 / Inner City ✦✦✦

For this tasteful but obscure set (only reissued on CD by the Japanese Trio label), veteran bop survivor Al Haig plays four unaccompanied piano solos, has four duets with bassist Jamil Nasser, and backs singer Helen Merrill on "They Didn't Believe Me." Although Jerome Kern did not care for jazz, his songs have long been viable vehicles for jazz improvisations, and Haig picked out some of the best ones for the date, including "The Way You Look Tonight," "All the Things You Are" and "The Song Is You." —*Scott Yanow*

Bebop Live / May 27, 1982 / Spotlite ✦✦✦✦

Pianist Al Haig's final recording (he died less than six months later) is a live jam session with four fine English jazzmen: altoist Peter King (a superior bop player), Art Themen on tenor and soprano, bassist Kenny Baldock and drummer Allan Ganley. This British LP finds Haig still in fine form, playing in his largely unchanged bop style on six songs from the era, including "Bags Groove," "Night in Tunisia" and "Birks Works"; each of the workouts clocks in between six and ten minutes. A fine ending to a career that lasted longer than it originally looked as if it would. —*Scott Yanow*

Edmond Hall

b. May 15, 1901, New Orleans, LA, **d.** Feb. 11, 1967, Boston, MA
Clarinet / New Orleans Jazz, Swing

It took Edmond Hall a long period to develop his own musical individuality but by the early '40s he had a very distinctive and dirty sound on the clarinet that was immediately recognizable within one note. One of four clarinet playing brothers (including Herbie Hall) that were the sons of an early clarinetist Edward Hall, Edmond worked in many bands in New Orleans (including Buddy Petit during 1921-23) before going to New York in 1928 with Alonzo Ross. He was with Claude Hopkins' Orchestra (1929-35), doubling on baritone and only occasionally sounding like his future self on clarinet. Hall played with Lucky Millinder, Zutty Singleton and Joe Sullivan and had his style together by the time he joined Red Allen in 1940. He was with Teddy Wilson's sextet (1941-44) and turned down an opportunity to be Barney Bigard's successor with Duke Ellington's Orchestra in 1942. In 1944 Hall began working with Eddie Condon (including appearances on his *Town Hall Concert* radio series), he led his own group at Cafe Society, spent a few years based in Boston and then during 1950-55 was in the house band at Condon's club. Edmond Hall toured the world as a member of Louis Armstrong's All-Stars (1955-58), worked in the 1960s now and then with Condon and made his final recording (before his death from a heart attack) at John Hammond's 1967 *Spirituals to Swing* concert. He recorded as a leader for Blue Note (1941-44), Commodore, Savoy, Storyville, United Artists and some smaller labels. —*Scott Yanow*

● **1937-1944** / Jun. 24, 1937-Jan. 25, 1944 / Classics ✦✦✦✦✦

Rompin' in '44 / Dec. 4, 1944 / Circle ✦✦✦

This album has the complete output of clarinetist Edmond Hall's band during a 1944 radio transcription session that resulted in nine song, (the master takes), plus six alternate takes, three incomplete versions and three false starts. The swing-oriented group (which also includes trumpeter Irving Randolph, trombonist Henderson Chambers, pianist Ellis Larkins, bassist Johnny Williams and drummer Art Trappier) only recorded one commercial session, so this set is historically important, but the multiple versions make it difficult to listen to the date straight through. Best are the accepted takes of "Opus 15," "The Sheik of Araby" and the title cut. —*Scott Yanow*

This Is Jazz, Vol. 3 / Sep. 1947-Oct. 1947 / Storyville ✦✦✦

The dozen performances on this Storyville LP are taken from five weekly "This Is Jazz" broadcasts, and although listed under clarinetist Edmond Hall's name, there is plenty of feature space for the other musicians: cornetist Wild Bill Davison, trombonist Jimmy Archey, pianist Ralph Sutton, rhythm guitarist Danny Barker, bassist Pops Foster and drummer Baby Dodds. The Dixieland-oriented music (which has many colorful outbursts from Wild Bill) is currently being reissued completely and in chronological order on CD by Jazzology, so this older album is of only minimal interest, despite the hot music. —*Scott Yanow*

The Edmond Hall All Stars / May 2, 1949-May 15, 1949 / TJ ✦✦✦✦

This obscure LP (the only release by the New Hampshire Library of Traditional Jazz) features clarinetist Edmond Hall's 1949 sextet during radio broadcasts emanating from Boston's Savoy Café. Since this particular outfit did not record, and the recording quality is decent, the music will be enjoyed by Dixieland fans fortunate enough to find it. In addition to the distinctive clarinetist, the band features the promising young cornetist Johnny Windhurst, trombonist Vic Dickenson, pianist Ken Kersey, bassist John Field and drummer Jimmy Crawford playing a diverse and generally fresh set of standards, including "Singin' the Blues," "Robbins Nest," Mary Lou Williams' "Lonely Moments," and "Panama." —*Scott Yanow*

Edmond Hall/Ralph Sutton Quartet, at Club Hangover / Jul. 21, 1954-Jul. 24, 1954 / Storyville ✦✦✦✦

This album (not yet reissued on CD) is a superior showcase for clarinetist Edmond Hall, who is heard in prime form. Joined by the great stride pianist Ralph Sutton, bassist Walter Page and drummer Charlie Lodice, Hall stretches out on such likable Dixieland tunes as "St. Louis Blues," "Oh Baby," "I Found a New Baby" and "Blues My Naughty Sweetie Gave to Me." The music is taken from two well-recorded radio broadcasts originating from San Francisco's Club Hangover. —*Scott Yanow*

Edmond Hall's Last Concert / Apr. 24, 1964+Feb. 3, 1967 / Jazzology ✦✦✦✦

It seems strange to hear clarinetist Edmond Hall sounding so strong and very much in his musical prime during what would be his final performance, but Hall's death just eight days later was due to a sudden heart attack suffered while shoveling snow rather than any long-term illness. This 1996 CD mostly features Hall at a Massachusetts concert in a septet also co-starring cornetist Bobby Hackett. They run through eight Dixieland standards (including "When the Saints Go Marching In") with spirit and swing. The music (which was previously unissued) is joined by three formerly unknown Hall showcases that feature him as the only horn at a 1964 concert. Excellent performances, easily recommended to Dixieland collectors. —*Scott Yanow*

Edmond Hall Quartet in Copenhagen / Dec. 2, 1966-Dec. 7, 1966 / Storyville ✦✦✦✦✦

The great and instantly recognizable clarinetist Edmond Hall is at the peak of his powers on this CD during what would be his final studio dates. Hall, who died just two months later from a heart attack (and whose only later recordings were a few songs at the Spirituals to Swing concert), is heard on three hot numbers with Papa Bue's Viking Jazz Band; "Struttin' with Some Barbecue" is given particularly joyous treatment. Eleven of the other selections really showcase Hall as the only horn with a fine Scandinavian rhythm section; plus, there is an unusual departure in Hall's brief unaccompanied rendition of "It Ain't Necessarily So." Whether it be "Muskrat Ramble," an especially creative "Jazz Me Blues," "Oh Baby" or "The World Is Waiting for the Sunrise," Edmond Hall, who never recorded an uninspired solo, rarely sounded better. He exited on top. —*Scott Yanow*

Jim Hall

b. Dec. 4, 1930, Buffalo, NY
Guitar / Cool, Post-Bop

A harmonically advanced cool-toned and subtle guitarist, Jim Hall has been an inspiration to many current guitarists including some (such as Bill Frisell) who sound nothing like him. Hall attended the Cleveland Institute of Music and studied classical guitar in Los Angeles with Vincente Gomez. He was an original member of the Chico Hamilton Quintet (1955-56) and during 1956-59 was with the Jimmy Giuffre Three. After touring with Ella Fitzgerald (1960-61) and sometimes forming duos with Lee Konitz, Hall was with Sonny Rollins' dynamic quartet in 1961-62, recording *The Bridge*. He co-led a quartet with Art Farmer (1962-64), recorded on an occasional basis with Paul Desmond during 1959-65 (all of their quartet performances are collected on a Mosaic box set) and then became a New York studio musician. He has mostly been a leader ever since and in addition to his own projects for World Pacific/Pacific Jazz, MPS, Milestone, CTI, Horizon, Artists House, Concord, Music Masters and Telarc, Jim Hall recorded two classic duet albums with Bill Evans. —*Scott Yanow*

Jazz Guitar / Jan. 10, 1957+Jan. 24, 1957 / Pacific Jazz ✦✦✦✦

Guitarist Jim Hall's debut as a leader has been reissued in full on this excellent CD. Featured in a drumless trio with pianist Carl Perkins and bassist Red Mitchell, Hall (known for his stint with Chico Hamilton and at the time a member of the Jimmy Giuffre 3) already had a harmonically sophisticated style and a sound of his own. Surprisingly, he sticks mostly to modernized versions of swing standards (including "Stompin' at the Savoy," two versions of "Things Ain't What They Used to Be," and "Seven Come Eleven") rather than playing bop tunes. Excellent music played by the up and coming 26-year-old guitarist. —*Scott Yanow*

Good Friday Blues / Apr. 2, 1960 / Pacific Jazz ✦✦✦

W/ Red Mitchell. Some early, less-restrained Hall material. —*Ron Wynn*

It's Nice to Be with You / June 27, 1969-June 28, 1969 / Verve ✦✦✦

A good late-'60s set reissued under a different title (originally *In a Sentimental Mood*.) —*Ron Wynn*

Where Would I Be? / Jul. 1971 / Original Jazz Classics ✦✦✦✦

Although the rhythm section was more "modern" than he usually used (keyboardist Benny Aranov, bassist Malcolm Cecil and Airto Moreira on drums and percussion), guitarist Jim Hall (who always had a harmonically advanced style anyway) has little difficulty adapting to the fresh setting. Highlights of the well-rounded CD reissue include Hall's "Simple Samba," "Baubles, Bangles and Beads," an unaccompanied "I Should Care" and Milton Nascimento's "Vera Cruz." —*Scott Yanow*

● **Alone Together** / Aug. 4, 1972 / Original Jazz Classics ✦✦✦✦✦

Long considered a classic and a revelation to listeners who had taken guitarist Jim Hall for granted, this set of duets with bassist Ron Carter (reissued on CD) has near-telepathic communication between the two musicians and quiet music full of inner tension and fire. Hall and Carter brought in an original apiece and also collaborated on six standards, including "St. Thomas," "Softly As In a Morning Sunrise," "Autumn Leaves" and "Alone Together." Introspective and thought-provoking music. —*Scott Yanow*

Concierto / Apr. 1975 / Columbia ✦✦✦✦

One of the better late-period CTI records, this CD reissue has an exquisite sextet comprising guitarist Jim Hall, altoist Paul Desmond, trumpeter Chet Baker, pianist Roland Hanna, bassist Ron Carter and drummer Steve Gadd. Their version of "Concierto de Aranjuez" (over 19 minutes long) is a near-classic, and the reissue adds an alternate take of "The Answer Is Yes" and the previously unreleased "Rock Skippin'" to the original program. Hall, Desmond and Baker, in particular, made for a potent and very lyrical team. —*Scott Yanow*

Jim Hall Live! / Sep. 10, 1975+Sep. 11, 1975 / Horizon ✦✦✦✦

This fine club date features guitarist Jim Hall in Toronto with two of the top Canadian jazzmen, bassist Don Thompson and drummer Terry Clarke. The interplay between the three players is sometimes wondrous, and although the five selections are all familiar standards (such as "'Round Midnight," "Scrapple From the Apple" and "The Way You Look Tonight"), Hall makes the music sound fresh and full of subtleties. This enjoyable LP has yet to be reissued on CD. —*Scott Yanow*

Commitment / Jun. 1, 1976-Jul. 1, 1976 / A&M ✦✦✦✦

There is lots of variety on this CD reissue, which features guitarist Jim Hall in several different settings. He has separate duets with pianist Don Thompson (Hoagy Carmichael's delightful "One Morning in May"), his wife Jane Hall (who sings "When I Fall in Love"), pianist Tommy Flanagan, and drummer Terry Clarke. He also overdubs acoustic and electric guitars on his solo "Down the Line," teams up with pianist Flanagan and fluegelhornist Art Farmer on two duets, and uses a slightly larger group on "Lament for a Fallen Matador," a Don Sebesky adaptation of a classical piece that has the haunting voice of Joan LaBarbara. Overall, there is plenty of intriguing music on this recommended set. —*Scott Yanow*

Jim Hall and Red Mitchell / Jan. 20, 1978-Jan. 21, 1978 / Artists House ✦✦✦✦

This lyrical, introverted, and sometimes exquisite set of duets by guitarist Jim Hall and bassist Red Mitchell was originally made for John Snyder's Artist House label and later reissued on CD by MHS. Hall and Mitchell always had big ears, and although the music is at a low volume and the duo stretches out on a bit on their four originals, the Mexican folk song "Blue Dove" and "Fly Me to the Moon," there are no sleepy moments. —*Scott Yanow*

Concerto de Aranjuez / Jan. 18, 1981 / Evidence ✦✦✦

Jim Hall's warm, fluid guitar and full tones are the anchor for this good but often unexciting session pairing him with the David Matthews orchestra. Hall recorded the title track on two other occasions; this third version is nicely orchestrated and produced, and Hall's solo is superbly played but adds little to the interpretation that he had provided before. The orchestra is wisely kept from getting in Hall's way, and his guitar lines are bright, sometimes arresting, and frequently dazzling. What is missing is the inventive spark and extra dimension Hall usually injects into his material. When these tracks were originally cut in 1981, Hall had been away from the studio for three years. —*Ron Wynn*

Circles / Mar. 1981 / Concord Jazz ✦✦✦✦

Most of the music on this date (which emphasizes group originals) features guitarist Jim Hall, bassist Don Thompson and drummer Terry Clarke. The versatile Thompson switches to piano for a duet with Hall on "Circles" and on a quartet version (with Rufus Reid on bass) of "My Heart Sings." Nothing all that exciting or unexpected occurs during the CD reissue (which adds an additional song to the original LP), but virtually all of Hall's recordings (which tend to be harmonically sophisticated and quietly subtle) are worth acquiring. —*Scott Yanow*

Jim Hall's Three / Jan. 1986 / Concord Jazz ✦✦✦

Though Hall dominates, this is a nice trio session. —*Ron Wynn*

These Rooms / Feb. 1988 / Denon ✦✦✦

Jim Hall Trio. W/ a sparkling Tom Harrell (tpt) on three cuts. —*Ron Wynn*

All Across the City / May 1989 / Concord Jazz ✦✦✦✦✦

Jim Hall's successful blend of contemporary and mainstream jazz should appeal to both camps on this well-crafted CD. Hall displays the subtle quiet lyricism that makes his guitar sound instantly identifiable. Gil Goldstein is a perfect choice on keyboards, because he uses synthesizer only to color rather than overpower a song, while avoiding schmaltz. Both "Beja-Flor" and the title track benefit from his contributions. Though his piano is frequently in the background, it matches Hall's hushed, effective guitar lines. Bassist Steve LaSpina and drummer Terry Clarke fre-

quently lay out during the introductions and then enter to add either gentle shadings or full steam, if needed. One of Jim Hall's best CDs. —*Ken Dryden*

Live at Town Hall, Vol. 1 / Jun. 26, 1990 / Music Masters ✦✦✦✦

Live at Town Hall, Vol. 2 / Jun. 26, 1990 / Music Masters ✦✦✦✦

For the second half of a two-part Town Hall concert dubbed "The Jim Hall Invitational," different personnel appears on each selection. Throughout guitarist Jim Hall's adventurous spirit is consistent in its inspiration. The lengthy "Hide and Seek" is a searching group improvisation featuring Hall's quartet (with keyboardist Gil Goldstein, bassist Steve LaSpina and drummer Terry Clarke). The other four performances form a bit of a guitar summit. Hall teams up with guitarists Peter Bernstein and John Scofield on individual tracks (the latter is on Coleman Hawkins' "Sanctity"), a rendition of "My Funny Valentine" without Hall matches together Mick Goodrick and John Abercrombie and all five guitarists jam on the leader's "Careful" which also includes vibraphonist Gary Burton. An interesting and successful outing. —*Scott Yanow*

Subsequently / Jan. 1991 / Music Masters ✦✦✦

Toots Thielemans on guitar and harmonica lends a hand, and things stay loose and breezy, but never detached or predictable. —*Ron Wynn*

Youkali / 1992 / CTI ✦✦

A change of pace album for guitarist Jim Hall. He usually makes relaxed, steady dates, but has turned the heat up for this 1992 date. He's also playing with Grover Washington, Jr., and Donald Harrison, as well as Chet Baker. —*Ron Wynn*

Something Special / Mar. 6, 1993-Jun 8, 1993 / Music Masters ✦✦✦✦✦

Dialogues / Feb. 3, 1995-Feb. 25, 1995 / Telarc ✦✦✦✦✦

Guitarist Jim Hall has long been one of the most open-minded of the important stylists to emerge during the 1950s and his harmonically advanced style remains quite modern while hinting at its foundations in bop. For this Telarc CD, Hall teams up with five major players on two numbers apiece: Guitarists Bill Frisell and Mike Stern, Joe Lovano on tenor, fluegelhornist Tom Harrell and Gil Goldstein on accordion. Bassist Scott Colley and drummer Andy Watson are on the Frisell and Lovano tracks and part of the Harrell and Stern performances. All of the compositions but "Skylark" are Hall's originals and, although they are usually a bit dry, there are some exceptions; "Uncle Ed" and "Frisell Frazzle" are a little nutty. The emphasis throughout is on interplay between the lead voices and advanced improvising. Despite his strong sidemen (Stern and Harrell fare best), Jim Hall ends up as the dominant voice on virtually every selection, making this a set his fans will enjoy. —*Scott Yanow*

Textures / Sep. 17, 1996-Sep. 19, 1996 / Telarc ✦✦✦✦

Now this is really different. Without dropping his electric and acoustic guitars for a minute, Jim Hall reaches back to his early classical studies and joins the Third Stream. The result is an absorbing set of seven Hall compositions that reveal a hitherto unseen, serious, sometimes whimsical side of a musician we all thought we had pegged. A lot of this is rooted in 1950s classical/jazz fusions from Stan Kenton to Gunther Schuller, yet Hall thankfully makes even the most cerebral passages sound attractive, thanks in part to the delicate, still-soft timbres of his electric guitar. Each piece is quite different from that of its neighbor; two ("Fanfare," "Reflections") have surprisingly dense and dissonant writing for a brass septet, another ("Quadrologue") uses pizzicato strings plunking acerbically over a repeated ostinato, still another is an informal "Passacaglia" with isolated interludes for solo classical guitar. The splendidly nostalgic "Sazanami," with steel drum tappings over a Caribbean shaker rhythm, is the closest thing to a strictly jazz-oriented groove on the CD, and a mock "Circus Dance" for oompah-ing brass adds a touch of droll and morose humor at the end of the program. Probably the most original piece is "Ragman," with its contemporary string writing, Middle Eastern flavor, and Joe Lovano rattling around the percussive rhythms on soprano sax. Signing with Telarc—allegedly a safe refuge for aging jazz stars—seems to have brought out the daring explorer in Hall in this and his previous release, *Dialogues*. More power to him. —*Richard S. Ginell*

Panorama: Live at Village Vanguard / 1997 / Telarc ✦✦✦✦

Jim Hall's previous two Telarcs, *Dialogues* and *Textures*, were so adventurous and out-of-perceived-character that this compendium of small-group live dates at the Village Vanguard might seem like a step backwards at a superficial glance. But there is enterprise here too, as the cool, mellow-toned Hall grafts a revolving door full of guest soloists onto his rhythm section (Scott Colley, bass; Terry Clarke, drums), each one of whom offers a different slant on what jazz ought to be. Among the pianists, Kenny Barron's response to the challenge is straightahead bebop on "The Answer Is Yes" and a graceful duet with Hall on "Something to Wish For," while Geoff Keezer takes a more contemporary two-fisted approach. Trombonist Slide Hampton inspires a looser feeling in the rhythm section at a relaxed tempo on "Entre Nous" and some loosey-goosey swing on "No You Don't!," but trumpeter Art Farmer sounds rather limp in "Little Blues." The free-minded alto of Greg Osby is the man most capable of pushing Hall a bit outside of his usual game, as well as provoking the bass and drums, on "Furnished Flats" and "Painted Pig." One can only imagine the fascination of the habitually superattentive patrons of the Vanguard at all of this diversity. —*Richard S. Ginell*

Bengt Hallberg

b. Sep. 13, 1932, Göteborg, Sweden
Piano / Cool, Hard Bop
One of Sweden's top jazz pianists, Bengt Hallberg made his first trio recordings when he was 17. In the 1950s he recorded with Lars Gullin, Arne Domnerus and such traveling Americans as Clifford Brown, Stan Getz and Quincy Jones. He worked as a member of the Swedish Radio Big Band (1956-63) and, although in demand as a writer for films and television, Hallberg has continued playing jazz on a part-time basis (often with Domnerus and Karin Krog) up to the present time, mostly recording for Swedish labels such as Metronome, Sonet and Phontastic. —*Scott Yanow*

Kiddin' on the Keys / Dec. 20, 1959-Dec. 30, 1959 / Dragon ◆◆◆◆
At Gyllene Cirkeln / Dec. 29, 1962-Dec. 30, 1962 / Dragon ◆◆◆◆
Hallberg's Happiness / Mar. 1977 / Phontastic ◆◆◆
The Hallberg Touch / Aug. 1979 / Phontastic ◆◆◆
● **Bengt Hallberg in New York** / Sep. 23, 1982 / Phontastic ◆◆◆◆◆
Hallberg's Yellow Blues / Mar. 25, 1987-Nov. 20, 1987 / Phontastic ◆◆◆
Hallberg's Surprise / Mar. 1987-May 1987 / Phontastic ◆◆◆◆

Lin Halliday

b. 1936, DeQueeney, AR
Tenor Saxophone / Hard Bop
It was fitting that Lin Halliday's first record as a leader was called *Delayed Exposure*, for the talented tenor was already 55. Raised in Little Rock, AR, Halliday has been a professional since graduating high school. He spent time in Los Angeles, playing at sessions under the guidance of altoist Joe Maini. Halliday spent a year in Wisconsin and then in 1958 moved to New York. The following year he was Wayne Shorter's replacement with the Maynard Ferguson Orchestra, and later on he spent time with the groups of Louie Bellson and Philly Joe Jones. After more time in Little Rock, Los Angeles and also Chicago, Halliday settled in Nashville in 1966. The tenor saxophonist worked in the studios and in local clubs until 1978, when an injury put him out of action for two years. After he recovered, he moved permanently to Chicago in 1980, where he became a major fixture in the local jazz scene. A strong hard-bop soloist who can hold his own with anyone in a jam session, Lin Halliday recorded with trumpeter Brad Goode in 1988 and since then has led three CDs of his own for Delmark. —*Scott Yanow*

Delayed Exposure / Jun. 25, 1991-Jun. 26, 1991 / Delmark ◆◆◆◆
Lin Halliday's first album was titled *Delayed Exposure* because the big-toned tenor saxophonist was 55 before given a chance to record as a leader. This fine release showed listeners outside of Chicago what Windy City residents had realized for many years—that he was a passionate, richly expressive hard bopper who never failed to swing. Heartfelt performances of "Woody'n You" and "Serpent's Tooth" leave no doubt that Sonny Rollins is Halliday's primary influence, but also demonstrate that he's very much his own man. Halliday, who tends to be more sentimental than Rollins, shows just how soulful a ballad player he can be on the time-honored standards "The Man I Love" and "Darn That Dream." Halliday enjoys a consistently strong rapport with his Chicago support, which includes multi-hornman Ira Sullivan (who is heard on trumpet, fluegelhorn, flute), pianist Jodie Christian, bassist Dennis Carroll and drummer George Fludas. —*Alex Henderson*

● **East of the Sun** / Nov. 27, 1991 / Delmark ◆◆◆◆◆
On his second album, the muscular tenor saxman Lin Halliday continues to excel by sticking with what he does best: unapologetic hard bop greatly influenced by Sonny Rollins' recordings of the late '50s. The insightful Windy City support he'd enjoyed on *Delayed Exposure* reunites with him on *East of the Sun*—Ira Sullivan (who is heard on trumpet, fluegelhorn, tenor sax and alto flute), pianist Jodie Christian, bassist Dennis Carroll and drummer George Fludas. As intensely as Halliday swings on "I Found a New Baby," his warm and very personal lyricism on "Corcovado," "Indian Summer" and "Will You Still Be Mine" indicate that he's a romantic at heart. Like its predecessor, *East of the Sun* makes us wish a label had offered Halliday a deal 20 or 30 years earlier. —*Alex Henderson*

Where or When / Mar. 23, 1993-Mar. 24, 1993 / Delmark ◆◆◆◆
Delmark Records has done the jazz world an enormous favor by documenting Chicago's rich jazz scene, and in the 1990s the Windy City label has had the excellent taste to record Lin Halliday frequently. The tenor saxman's third album finds him once again joined by muli-hornman Ira Sullivan (who is heard on trumpet, tenor

sax and fluegelhorn) and pianist Jodie Christian—only this time, the bassist is Larry Gray, and the drummer is Robert Barry. As spirited and invigorating as he is on the fast tempos of "My Shining Hour" and Sonny Rollins' optimistic "Pent-Up House," Halliday is wise not to neglect ballads—and his romantic side serves him quite well on "Over the Rainbow" and Duke Ellington's "Sophisticated Lady." Sullivan never fails to swing, and Christian's captivating pianism show us why he's so highly regarded in Chi-Town. —*Alex Henderson*

Chico Hamilton (Forestorn Hamilton)

b. Sep. 21, 1921, Los Angeles, CA
Drums, Leader / Cool, Hard Bop, Post-Bop, Crossover Jazz
Chico Hamilton, a subtle and creative drummer, will probably always be better-known for the series of Quintets that he led during 1955-65 and for his ability as a talent scout than for his fine drumming. Hamilton first played drums while in high school with the many fine young players (including Dexter Gordon, Illinois Jacquet and Charles Mingus) who were in Los Angeles at the time. He made his recording debut with Slim Gaillard, was house drummer at Billy Berg's, toured with Lionel Hampton and served in the military (1942-46). In 1946 Hamilton worked briefly with Jimmy Mundy, Count Basie and Lester Young (recording with Young). He toured as Lena Horne's drummer (on and off during 1948-55) and gained recognition for his work with the original Gerry Mulligan pianoless quartet (1952-53). In 1955 Hamilton put together his first Quintet, a chamber jazz group with the reeds of Buddy Collette, guitarist Jim Hall, bassist Carson Smith and cellist Fred Katz. One of the last important West Coast jazz bands, the Chico Hamilton Quintet was immediately popular and appeared in a memorable sequence in 1958's *Jazz on a Summer's Day* and the Hollywood film *The Sweet Smell of Success*. The personnel changed over the next few years (with Paul Horn and Eric Dolphy heard on reeds, cellist Nate Gersham, guitarists John Pisano and Dennis Budimir and several bassists passing through the group) but it retained its unusual sound. By 1961 Charles Lloyd was on tenor and flute, Gabor Szabo was the new guitarist and soon the cello was dropped in favor of trombone (Garnett Brown and later George Bohanon), giving the group an advanced hard-bop style.

In 1966 Chico Hamilton started composing for commercials and the studios and he broke up his Quintet. However he continued leading various groups, playing music that ranged from the avant-garde to erratic fusion and advanced hard bop. Such up-and-coming musicians as Larry Coryell (1966), Steve Potts (1967), Arthur Blythe, Steve Turre (on bass!) and Eric Person (who played in Hamilton's 1990s group Euphoria) were among the younger players he helped discover. In 1989 Chico Hamilton had a recorded reunion with the original members of his 1955 Quintet (with Pisano in Hall's place) and in recent times he has been making records for Soul Note. —*Scott Yanow*

With Paul Horn / Oct. 2, 1954-Nov. 1956 / Crown ◆◆◆
This budget LP (which does not give personnel listings or recording dates) draws its material from three separate sessions led by drummer Chico Hamilton. Hamilton teams up with guitarist Howard Roberts and bassist George Duvivier for two songs, has two others in a trio with guitarist Jim Hall and bassist George Duvivier, and for the final four numbers is heard in the second version of his famous Quintet (the only selections that actually include Paul Horn). The latter selections feature Horn on various reeds (flute, clarinet, tenor, alto and piccolo), cellist Fred Katz (who wrote the four songs), guitarist John Pisano, bassist Carson Smith and Hamilton. Excellent music that deserves to be fully reissued on CD. —*Scott Yanow*

☆ **The Complete Pacific Jazz Recordings of the Chico Hamilton Quintet** / Nov. 12, 1954-Jan. 12, 1959 / Mosaic ◆◆◆◆◆
The original Chico Hamilton Quintet was one of the last significant West Coast jazz bands of the cool era. Consisting of Buddy Collette on reeds (flute, clarinet, alto and tenor), guitarist Jim Hall, bassist Carson Smith and the drummer/leader, the most distinctive element in the group's identity was cellist Fred Katz. The band could play quite softly, blending together elements of bop and classical music into their popular sound and occupying their own niche. This six-CD limited-edition box set from 1997 starts off with a Hamilton drum solo from a 1954 performance with the Gerry Mulligan Quartet; it contains three full albums and many previously unreleased numbers by the original Chico Hamilton band and also has quite a few titles from the second Hamilton group (which has Paul Horn and John Pisano in the places of Collette and Hall). In addition, there are three titles from the third Hamilton Quintet (with Eric Dolphy on flute and alto) and a 1959 Duke Ellington tribute date that featured both Collette and Horn. Most of these performances were formerly quite rare and never reissued coherently before. Highly recommended to jazz historians and to listeners who enjoy classic cool jazz, but this box is sure to be sold out quickly. —*Scott Yanow*

Spectacular / Aug. 4, 1955-Aug. 5, 1955 / Pacific Jazz ◆◆◆◆
The Chico Hamilton Quintet debuted on this important Pacific Jazz LP. One of the last significant West Coast jazz units, Hamilton's band had Buddy Collette on reeds

(flute, tenor, clarinet and alto), guitarist Jim Hall, bassist Carson Smith, the drummer/leader and, most importantly, cellist Fred Katz. A chamber jazz unit that hinted in spots at classical music, this cool jazz band was quite popular for a few years. Unfortunately, most of Hamilton's early recordings have yet to be reissued on CD, but this LP (which has been repackaged several times) can sometimes be located. Highlights include "A Nice Day," "I Want to Be Happy," "My Funny Valentine" and Chico Hamilton's classic feature on "Blue Sands." —*Scott Yanow*

Zen: The Music of Fred Katz / Nov. 1956 / Pacific Jazz ✦✦✦
The second version of the Chico Hamilton Quintet consisted of three holdovers (drummer Hamilton, cellist Fred Katz and bassist Carson Smith), plus guitarist John Pisano and Paul Horn on alto, flute and clarinet. This obscure LP finds the group performing eight of Katz's originals, including the three-part "Suite for Horn," which adds three trombones and four woodwinds. Some of the music is overly precious and a bit fragile, but there are some swinging moments, making this a worthwhile (if difficult-to-find) Third Stream effort. —*Scott Yanow*

The Chico Hamilton Quintet with Strings Attached / Oct. 26, 1958-Oct. 27, 1958 / Warner Brothers ✦✦✦
Other than two selections put out on a sampler and the soundtrack from the 1958 Newport Jazz Festival, this LP is quite significant for having the first recordings of Eric Dolphy with the Chico Hamilton Quintet. Dolphy's solos (on alto, flute and bass clarinet) are brief, but he already sounded fairly distinctive. The third version of Hamilton's popular Quintet also included the drummer/leader, cellist Nate Gershman, guitarist Dennis Budimir and bassist Wyatt Ruther. On this album, half of the tunes are played by the basic quintet, while the remaining five songs have an added string section. The West Coast jazz chamber music generally holds one's interest, but has been out of print for some time. —*Scott Yanow*

Gongs East / Dec. 29, 1958-Dec. 30, 1958 / Discovery ✦✦✦✦✦
The best known of all the 1950s Chico Hamilton Quintet sets, this is also the only early Hamilton music that has been fully reissued on CD. At the time, the drummer's group also included cellist Nate Gershman, guitarist Dennis Budimir, bassist Wyatt Ruther and the young Eric Dolphy on alto, bass clarinet and flute. Dolphy has quite a few short solos on this rewarding music, and the highlights of the date include "Beyond the Blue Horizon," "Passion Flower," Gerald Wilson's "Tuesday at Two" and the exotic "Gongs East." Recommended. —*Scott Yanow*

Ellington Suite / Jan. 9, 1959+Jan. 12, 1959 / World Pacific ✦✦✦
Drummer Chico Hamilton had a reunion of his original quintet (Buddy Collette on tenor and alto, guitarist Jim Hall, cellist Fred Katz and bassist Carson Smith) plus Paul Horn (on alto and flute) from his second group for a program of Duke Ellington and Billy Strayhorn tunes. A rather obscure set (not yet reissued on CD), this date has fresh versions of a lot of familiar standards including "It Don't Mean a Thing," "In a Mellotone," and a medley of "Take the 'A' Train" and "Perdido." Well worth picking up by listeners fortunate enough to find it, this is one of Hamilton's hardest-swinging sets of the 1950s. —*Scott Yanow*

The Chico Hamilton Special / Nov. 29, 1960-Nov. 30, 1960 / Columbia ✦✦✦✦✦
The fourth version of the Chico Hamilton Quintet only recorded two albums (including one of movie melodies) and was the least known of his early groups. However, this generally excellent album is significant for introducing Charles Lloyd (who here plays flute and alto instead of tenor). The other three musicians (cellist Nate Gershman, pianist Harry Pope and bassist Bobby Haynes) would all remain quite obscure, and this would be the last album in Hamilton's famous string of cello groups before the drummer changed directions. Interesting if not essential music, last available on a mid-1980s Columbia LP. —*Scott Yanow*

Transfusion / 1962 / Studio West ✦✦✦
The first four CDs released by Studio West, a subsidiary of V.S.O.P., are all taken from concise (around three minutes apiece) performances that were made to be used as part of the radio show "The Navy Swings". This particular release features performances by one of drummer Chico Hamilton's most stimulating groups, a quintet comprising Charles Lloyd (on tenor, flute and alto), guitarist Gabor Szabo, trombonist George Bohanon, bassist Albert Stinson and the drummer/leader. Because the individual selections are briefer than usual, in many cases only one soloist is featured on each cut. But overall, there is plenty of solo space for Lloyd (very much playing in a Coltrane vein), Bohanon and Szabo. The mixture of seven standards with nine Lloyd originals works quite well with plenty of variety in moods and tempos. An excellent all-around showcase for this much underrated but very timeless unit. —*Scott Yanow*

Drumfusion / Feb. 19, 1962 / Columbia ✦✦✦

Passin' Thru / Sep. 18, 1962+Sep. 20, 1962 / Impulse! ✦✦✦✦✦
Drummer Chico Hamilton's debut on Impulse featured his fifth Quintet, an advanced hard-bop unit that sometimes hinted a little at the avant-garde. Instead of the trademark cello, the band featured trombonist George Bohanon. With Charles Lloyd (doubling on tenor and flute) and guitarist Gabor Szabo and bassist

Albert Stinson all contributing fresh new voices, this was a major band. Four of the six selections on this appealing LP have since been reissued on the CD *Man from Two Worlds*, the definitive set by the Hamilton-Lloyd band. —*Scott Yanow*

Man from Two Worlds / Sep. 18, 1962+Dec. 11, 1963 / GRP ✦✦✦✦✦
Although it tended to get overlooked at the time, one of drummer Chico Hamilton's finest groups was his 1962-63 quartet/quintet. With Charles Lloyd at his most fiery on tenor and flute and the colorful solos of the up-and-coming Hungarian guitarist Gabor Szabo, this band placed a stronger emphasis on melody and softer sounds than the more avant-garde groups of the time but still pushed away at musical boundaries. Trombonist George Bohanon is also on the final four numbers of this CD reissue which brings back all of the music from Hamilton's *Man from Two Worlds* LP and four of the six numbers originally on *Passin' Thru*. Highlights include the original version of Lloyd's most famous song, "Forest Flower." —*Scott Yanow*

A Different Journey / Jan. 19, 1963-Jan. 31, 1963 / Reprise ✦✦✦
Drummer Chico Hamilton considered this quintet (which also included Charles Lloyd on tenor and flute, trombonist George Bohanon, guitarist Gabor Szabo and bassist Albert Stinson) to be his finest band. This superb LP of material not yet reissued on CD has several memorable melodies (including the closing "Island Blues"), lots of advanced yet logical improvising, and more than its share of variety. The group had its own sound and was quite underrated during its relatively short life. A gem. —*Scott Yanow*

Chic Chic Chico / Jan. 4, 1965 / Impulse! ✦✦✦✦
For this interesting LP, drummer Chico Hamilton is mostly heard with an octet of Los Angeles musicians. The group, comprising trumpet/trombone/tenor man Harold Land, French horn/flute (or piccolo) player and guitarist Gabor Szabo, bassist Albert Stinson, and the drummer/leader, performs originals by Hamilton and Szabo, plus "What's New." The concise performances (which are often tightly arranged) are full of subtleties and fine playing, particularly from the guitarist. The title cut was recorded two months later and is the last recording by Chico Hamilton with his star sideman Charles Lloyd, who is heard on flute. Not essential, but this album has its strong moments. —*Scott Yanow*

El Chico / Aug. 26, 1965-Aug. 27, 1965 / Impulse! ✦✦✦
In 1965, Japanese altoist Sadao Watanabe was Chico Hamilton's regular reed player, and it is for his playing (fairly early in his career) that this LP is most notable. Also heard from is guitarist Gabor Szabo (winding up a long period with Hamilton), bassist Al Stinson, guest trombonist Jimmy Cheatham (on three of the eight songs), and the Latin percussion of Willie Bobo and Victor Pantoja. The band plays a couple of movie themes (including "People"), three Hamilton originals, a group improvisation, and two obscurities. The influences of Latin jazz, bossa nova, and the avant-garde are mixed into the unusual musical blend. —*Scott Yanow*

The Further Adventures of El Chico / May 2, 1966-May 5, 1966 / Impulse! ✦✦✦

The Dealer / Sep. 1966 / Impulse ✦✦✦✦
Drummer Chico Hamilton introduced many top young players during his years as a bandleader, but few probably realize that Larry Coryell made his recording debut with Chico a year before joining Gary Burton's quartet. This CD reissue brings back Coryell's initial appearance on record and at times he sounded oddly like Chuck Berry (especially on "The Dealer"). Also heard on this set are altoist Arnie Lawrence, bassist Richard Davis, organist Ernie Hayes (on two numbers) and, on his spirited boogaloo "For Mods Only," Archie Shepp making a rare appearance on piano. Most of the performances still sound surprisingly fresh, especially the explorative "A Trip," making this an underrated but worthy release. —*Scott Yanow*

The Gamut / 1967 / Solid State ✦✦

The Head Hunters / 1969 / Solid State ✦✦✦

Peregrinations / July 9, 1975-July 10, 1975 / Blue Note ✦✦✦
This unusual LP, the first of three featuring altoist Arthur Blythe with drummer Chico Hamilton's mid-'70s group, has an uncomfortable mixture of advanced jazz and commercial elements. Hamilton is joined by a large rhythm section that includes Steve Turre (on electric bass) and guitarists Barry Finnerty and Joe Beck, along with Blythe, Arnie Lawrence on soprano, the keyboards of Jerry Peters, and several vocalists. The overall effect is a bit weird, dated but with some colorful moments. Definitely a mixed bag. —*Scott Yanow*

Euphoria / Oct. 1988 / Soul Note ✦✦✦✦

Reunion / Jun. 28, 1989+Jun. 29, 1989 / Soul Note ✦✦✦✦✦
In 1989, 34 years after the formation of the somewhat unique Chico Hamilton Quintet, the original members (with one exception) reunited for a tour and this Soul Note recording. In addition to drummer Hamilton, Buddy Collette (heard on flute, clarinet and alto), cellist Fred Katz, bassist Carson Smith, and guitarist John Pisano (Jim Hall's first replacement) complete the group. This studio session only includes one standard remake of "I Want to Be Happy" and comprises then-recent

originals by band members, with two selections ("Brushing with B" and "Conversation") being freely improvised duets by Collette and Hamilton. So, rather than merely being an exercise in nostalgia, this excellent set features the Quintet members as they sounded in the late '80s, creating new music for their classic sound. —*Scott Yanow*

Arroyo / Dec. 11, 1990-Dec. 17, 1990 / Soul Note ✦✦✦✦✦
Throughout his career, drummer Chico Hamilton has had an impressive track record as a talent scout. During 1988-92, he recorded four CDs with the up-and-coming altoist Eric Person, an inventive post-bop player who would have a short stint with the World Saxophone Quartet. Hamilton called this particular group (which also featured guitarist Cary DeNigris and bassist Reggie Washington) Arroyo, and they perform a very well-rounded set on this Soul Note release. The music ranges from Lester Young's "Tickle Toe" and a lengthy reworking of "Alone Together" to six group originals that are sometimes fairly free. A stimulating set that is well worth exploring. —*Scott Yanow*

● **My Panamanian Friend** / Aug. 21, 1992-Aug. 28, 1992 / Soul Note ✦✦✦✦✦
My Panamian Friend is Hamilton's finest outing in several years. Part of the reason may be its purpose, paying tribute to the great Eric Dolphy. Another plus is that eight of the nine songs are Dolphy compositions, among them "Springtime," "South Street Exit," and "Something Sweet, Something Tender." But the prime reason for this disc's success is alto saxophonist/flutist Eric Person. He plays with sensitivity and a tender, yet strong, dynamic approach that proves more intriguing than his performances on his recent session as a leader. Although he's no Dolphy, Eric Person not only pays ample respects, but matures greatly as a player on this session. —*Ron Wynn*

Trio! / May 1, 1992-May 7, 1992 / Soul Note ✦✦✦✦
Dancing to a Different Drummer / Mar. 27, 1993-Apr. 2, 1993 / Soul Note ✦✦✦

Jeff Hamilton

b. Aug. 4, 1953, Richmond, IL
Drums / Bop
A reliable and versatile drummer who sounds equally at home with a big band or combo, Jeff Hamilton has a strong reputation in the jazz world. He attended Indiana University, in 1974 was with the Tommy Dorsey ghost band, played briefly with Lionel Hampton and then spent two years as a member of Monty Alexander's Trio (1975-77). Hamilton was with Woody Herman's Orchestra (1977-78), became a member of the L.A. Four (with whom he made six records) and started recording regularly as a sideman for Concord. During 1983-87 he performed with Ella Fitzgerald, the Count Basie Orchestra, Rosemary Clooney and Monty Alexander. In the 1990s Hamilton toured the world with Oscar Peterson and the Ray Brown trio, gigged with the Clayton Brothers' Quartet and has been a co-leader (with John and Jeff Clayton) of the Clayton-Hamilton Orchestra. Jeff Hamilton has also occasionally led his own trio, recording for Lake Street. —*Scott Yanow*

● **Indiana** / Jan. 1982 / Concord Jazz ✦✦✦✦
A star sideman who has proven to be a supportive and inventive straightahead drummer in both combos and big bands, Jeff Hamilton has had few opportunities to lead his own record dates. His debut, which would not be followed by an encore for a dozen years, is a quintet outing with two great saxophonists (tenorman Bob Cooper and altoist Lanny Morgan), pianist Biff Hannon and bassist John Clayton. Mark Murphy dropped by to sing "Split Season Blues" (dedicated to the odd 1981 baseball season). Hamilton and Clayton took care of most of the writing for a set that has four originals and five fresh versions of standards, including Wayne Shorter's "One by One" and "Girl Talk." Fine and straightforward (but not overly predictable) jazz. —*Scott Yanow*

It's Hamilton Time / 1994 / Lake Street ✦✦✦

Jimmy Hamilton

b. May 25, 1917, Dillon, SC, **d.** Sep. 20, 1994, St. Croix, Virgin Islands
Clarinet, Tenor Saxophone / Bop, Swing
A longtime member of the Duke Ellington Orchestra, Jimmy Hamilton's cool vibratoless tone and advanced style (which was ultimately influenced by bop) initially bothered some listeners more accustomed to Barney Bigard's warmer New Orleans sound but Hamilton eventually won them over with his brilliant playing. As opposed to how he sounded on clarinet, Hamilton's occasional tenor playing was gutsy and emotional. Prior to joining Duke, he had worked with Lucky Millinder, Jimmy Mundy and most noticeably Teddy Wilson's sextet (1940-42) and Eddie Heywood; Hamilton also recorded with Billie Holiday. He was with Ellington for 25 years (1943-68) and was well featured on clarinet on "Air Conditioned Jungle," "Ad Lib on Nippon" and a countless number of other pieces. After leaving Ellington, Hamilton moved to the Virgin Islands where he taught music in public schools. He did return to the US to play with Clarinet Summit in 1981 and 1985

and gigged a bit in New York during 1989-90 but was otherwise little heard from in his later years. Jimmy Hamilton only had a few opportunities to record as a leader, mostly dates for Urania (1954), Everest (1960), Swingville (two in 1961) and a 1985 set for Who's Who. —*Scott Yanow*

Jimmy Hamilton Orchestra / 1954 / Jazz Kings ✦✦✦
Clarinetist Jimmy Hamilton spent most of his prime years as a star soloist with Duke Ellington's Orchestra. He only had infrequent chances to lead his own recording sessions, including two albums in 1954 for Urania. This LP reissue consists of four quintet numbers (during which Hamilton is the only horn), plus four octet numbers with trumpeter Ernie Royal and tenorman Lucky Thompson. Other than "Salute to Charlie Parker" and the clarinetist's "Blues for a Princess," the music comprises melodic standards. The playing time is rather chintzy, but what is here is well played and swinging. —*Scott Yanow*

● **Swing Low Sweet Clarinet** / Jul. 1960 / Everest ✦✦✦✦✦
Rediscovered Live at the Buccaneer / Sep. 24, 1985 / Who's Who in Jazz✦✦✦
After retiring to the Virgin Islands in 1968, not much was heard from Duke Ellington's longtime clarinetist Jimmy Hamilton, other than a couple of brief reappearances to play with Clarinet Summit. He taught locally and worked with a quartet on one of the islands. The release of this LP by Who's Who was therefore a bit of a surprise, for it finds Hamilton playing clarinet and alto in prime form with a quartet also including pianist Gary Mayone, bassist Joe Straws and drummer Delroy Thomas. Hamilton performs five lazy love songs and five tunes associated with Duke Ellington. These would be his last recordings and, although not quite definitive (for that one has to hear Hamilton with Duke's band), this is one of his best solo sets. —*Scott Yanow*

Scott Hamilton

b. Sep. 12, 1954, Providence, RI
Tenor Saxophone / Swing
When Scott Hamilton appeared in the mid-'70s fully formed with an appealing swing style on tenor (mixing together Zoot Sims and Ben Webster), he caused a minor sensation for few other young players during the fusion era were exploring pre-bop jazz at his high level. He began playing when he was 16 and developed quickly, moving to New York in 1976. Hamilton played with Benny Goodman in the late '70s but has mostly performed as a leader, sometimes sharing the spotlight with Warren Vache, Ruby Braff, Rosemary Clooney, the Concord Jazz All-Stars or George Wein's Newport Jazz Festival All-Stars. Scott Hamilton, other than a session apiece for Famous Door and Progressive, has recorded a long string of dates for Concord that are notable for their consistency and solid swing. —*Scott Yanow*

Swinging Young Scott / 1977 / Famous Door ✦✦✦✦
This somewhat obscure effort (not yet out on CD) was probably tenor saxophonist Scott Hamilton's first as a leader, slightly predating his association with Concord. Hamilton was quickly considered a bit of a phenomenon because he was essentially a young swing stylist, a nonexistent species at the time. Already quite recognizable, the 22-year-old heads a quintet that also includes trumpeter Warren Vache, pianist John Bunch, bassist Michael Moore and drummer Butch Miles. They perform a couple of Hamilton's basic originals, a blues, and five standards including Trummy Young's "Thru for the Night" and "Liza." Well worth searching for by mainstream fans. —*Scott Yanow*

● **Scott Hamilton** / Mar. 1, 1977 / Concord Jazz ✦✦✦✦✦
Tenor saxophonist Scott Hamilton's debut for Concord (which has been reissued on CD) alerted the jazz world to the young swing stylist and predated Wynton Marsalis' first record (and the emergence of the Young Lions) by a couple years. Hamilton, who mixed together Zoot Sims and Ben Webster to form his own recognizable tone, already sounded in prime form for this set. Teamed up with trumpeter Bill Berry, pianist Nat Pierce, bassist Monty Budwig and drummer Jake Hanna, Hamilton essentially launched the revival of mainstream jazz with this record. Highlights include "Indiana," "Stuffy," "Broadway" and "Blue Room," but all eight selections are quite enjoyable. —*Scott Yanow*

Scott Hamilton 2 / Jan. 7, 1978 / Concord Jazz ✦✦✦✦
Scott Hamilton's second in a countless string of Concord sets as a leader features the warm tenor performing nine standards (including "Rough Ridin'") and his own "Blues for the Players" with pianist Nat Pierce, guitarist Cal Collins, bassist Monty Budwig and drummer Jake Hanna. Most of the tunes are slow to medium tempo, with "I Want to Be Happy" being the one romp of the date. Superior mainstream jazz played by one of the first Young Lions. —*Scott Yanow*

Grand Appearance / Jan. 23, 1978+Feb. 8, 1978 / Progressive ✦✦✦✦
For this rare outing away from the Concord label, the young tenor saxophonist Scott Hamilton (whose mixture of various swing-based players resulted in his own distinctive sound) is heard on two sets with either Hank Jones or Tommy Flanagan

on piano, bassist George Mraz and drummer Connie Kay. As usual, Hamilton sticks mostly to medium-tempo standards, also playing a few warm ballads, an original blues and a heated rendition of "Crazy Rhythm." The CD reissue of this fine set adds "The Shadow of Your Smile" to the program. —*Scott Yanow*

With Scott's Band in New York / Jun. 26, 1978 / Concord Jazz ✦✦✦

Tenor saxophonist Scott Hamilton is in typically fine form on his third album as a leader for Concord. While Hamilton is equally skillful on ballads and hot stomps, cornetist Warren Vache sometimes takes a few too many chances on the uptempo material although one admires his brave attempts; he fares best on "Darn That Dream." Singer Sue Melikian sounds fine on two short vocals, but it is the instrumentals by the sextet (which includes guitarist Chris Flory and pianist Norman Simmons) that are most memorable. —*Scott Yanow*

Back to Back / Sep. 1978 / Concord Jazz ✦✦✦✦

Veteran tenor saxophonist Buddy Tate and the relative youngster Scott Hamilton make for a potent combination on this spirited set of small-group swing. They contribute an original apiece, perform a ballad medley, and indulge in a lot of interplay and trade-offs on the standards. Backed by pianist Nat Pierce, bassist Monty Budwig and drummer Chuck Riggs, the tenors are in excellent form throughout this upbeat session. —*Scott Yanow*

Skyscrapers / Jul. 1979 / Concord Jazz ✦✦✦✦

Tenor saxophonist Scott Hamilton and cornetist Warren Vache always made for a potent team. They co-lead this nonet set, which also features tenorman Harold Ashby, baritonist Joe Temperley, trombonist George Masso and pianist Norman Simmons. The arrangements by Buck Clayton, Masso and Nat Pierce keep the proceedings swinging, and the musicians all receive a fair amount of solo space, particularly the co-leaders on two originals apiece by Clayton and Pierce, plus four superior standards. An excellent effort. —*Scott Yanow*

Tenorshoes / Dec. 1979 / Concord Jazz ✦✦✦✦✦

Tenor saxophonist Scott Hamilton (who can be overly relaxed and comfortable at times) often sounds at his most heated when playing with pianist Dave McKenna, and all of their collaborations are easily recommended. This Hamilton-McKenna effort with bassist Phil Flanigan and drummer Jeff Hamilton mostly emphasizes ballads (although sometimes at medium tempos), plus a cooking version of "How High the Moon" and Hamilton's original "O.K." A typically swinging and consistent Scott Hamilton record which has been reissued on CD. —*Scott Yanow*

● Scott's Buddy / Aug. 1980 / Concord Jazz ✦✦✦✦

This was the second recorded encounter between tenors Buddy Tate and Scott Hamilton and, despite their vast age difference (41 years), it is difficult to tell from their playing who is the older musician. Hamilton is one of the few hornmen from his generation to make the grade as a major swing stylist and his respect for the elder Tate (who returns the feeling) is obvious. With guitarist Cal Collins, pianist Nat Pierce, bassist Bob Maize and drummer Jake Hanna, the two tenors are in spirited form on these standards and riff-filled originals; this combination works well. —*Scott Yanow*

Apples & Oranges / Jan. 1981+Aug. 1981 / Concord Jazz ✦✦✦

Close Up / Feb. 1982 / Concord Jazz ✦✦✦

Tenorman Scott Hamilton teams up with veteran pianist John Bunch and three top Boston players (guitarist Chris Flory, bassist Phil Flanigan and drummer Chuck Riggs) on this relaxed and well-played, if predictable, set. The high-quality repertoire (which includes two Hamilton originals, "Portrait of Jennie," "Robbins Nest" and Tiny Bradshaw's obscure "Soft") and the tasteful playing should appeal to Hamilton's many fans. —*Scott Yanow*

In Concert / Jun. 1983 / Concord Jazz ✦✦✦

By 1983, Scott Hamilton had evolved from being a novelty (a young swing musician in the 1970s) to a solid part of the mainstream establishment. A certain excitement tended to be lacking from his performances (he never exploded like his idol Illinois Jacquet), and his predictable excellence was starting to be taken a bit for granted. This outing with guitarist Chris Flory, pianist John Bunch, bassist Phil Flanigan and drummer Chuck Riggs (the first of two CDs) has the usual mixture of swinging medium-tempo tunes, warm ballads and a couple of stomps ("I've Found a New Baby" and "One O'Clock Jump"). Well-played and enjoyable music with few surprises. —*Scott Yanow*

Scott Hamilton Quintet in Concert / Jun. 1983 / Concord Jazz ✦✦✦

The Second Set / Jun. 1983 / Concord Jazz ✦✦✦

The second CD taken from the same Tokyo date that resulted in the Concord disc *In Concert* finds tenor saxophonist Scott Hamilton in predictably fine form, swinging on eight standards and playing melodic variations in a swing vein. With pianist John Bunch, guitarist Chris Flory, bassist Phil Flanigan and drummer Chuck Riggs taking concise solos and offering tasteful support, Hamilton is well showcased on

such tunes as "All the Things You Are," "Taps Miller," "All Too Soon" and "Jumpin' the Blues." —*Scott Yanow*

The Right Time / 1986 / Concord Jazz ✦✦✦✦

The choice of some offbeat material uplifts this otherwise fairly typical offering by tenor saxophonist Scott Hamilton's mid-1980s quintet, a group also including pianist John Bunch, guitarist Chris Flory, bassist Phil Flanigan and drummer Chuck Riggs. "Sleep," "If I Love Again," Hoagy Carmichael's "Eventide" and even Cole Porter's "All Through the Night" are not performed all that often, and one does not mind hearing additional versions of "Just in Time" and "Skylark"; the date is rounded out by a pair of Hamilton's originals. Everyone swings as usual, and Hamilton (who has yet to make an inferior recording) is in fine form. —*Scott Yanow*

Major League / May 1986 / Concord Jazz ✦✦✦✦✦

An encore of the swing trio that starred on *No Bass Hit* (a co-op record released under Dave McKenna's name), the matchup of tenor saxophonist Scott Hamilton, pianist McKenna and drummer Jake Hanna is quite exciting. There is no need for a bassist with McKenna's left hand present. Highlights include Buck Clayton's "Swinging at the Copper Rail," "Linger Awhile," "September in the Rain" and "It All Depends on You." Highly recommended. —*Scott Yanow*

Scott Hamilton Plays Ballads / Mar. 1989 / Concord Jazz ✦✦✦

Its title accurately describes the romantic music on this CD. The warm tenor of Scott Hamilton (accompanied by pianist John Bunch, guitarist Chris Flory, bassist Phil Flanigan and drummer Chuck Riggs) brings out a great deal of beauty on 11 ballads, including his own "Two Eighteen" and a variety of veteran melodies. —*Scott Yanow*

Radio City / Feb. 1990 / Concord Jazz ✦✦✦✦✦

Race Point / Sep. 18, 1991 / Concord Jazz ✦✦✦✦

Groovin' High / Sept. 17, 1991 / Concord Jazz ✦✦✦✦✦

Fans of jam sessions and tenor battles will definitely want this CD. Tenors Scott Hamilton, Ken Peplowski and Spike Robinson (constantly pushed by the brilliant rhythm section of pianist Gerry Wiggins, guitarist Howard Alden, bassist Dave Stone and drummer Jake Hanna) take turns raising the temperature on such viable devices as "Blues Up and Down," "Shine," "I'll See You in My Dreams" and "The Jeep Is Jumpin'." Robinson (easily the oldest of the trio of tenors) gets a slight edge and generates the most heat, but the saxophonists actually complement each other quite well. A consistently exciting set. —*Scott Yanow*

East of the Sun / Aug. 1993 / Concord Jazz ✦✦✦

For this Concord CD, tenor saxophonist Scott Hamilton gave the readers of Japan's *Swing Journal* the opportunity to vote on which songs they would like him to record. With the exception of his original "Setagaya Serenade" (a stomping blues that Hamilton took the liberty of performing) and "Autumn Leaves," he had recorded all of these veteran songs previously but Hamilton's melodic improvisations do not copy the earlier versions. With the assistance of an English rhythm section (pianist Brian Lemon, bassist Dave Green and drummer Allan Ganley), Hamilton is in typically swinging form on this fine set of standards and ballads. —*Scott Yanow*

Organic Duke / May 18, 1994-May 19, 1994 / Concord Jazz ✦✦✦

Live at the Brecon Jazz Festival / Aug. 13, 1994 / Concord Jazz ✦✦✦

The 25th Scott Hamilton Concord album does not break any new ground (Hamilton's style was essentially fully formed from the start), but it is up to his usual level. Playing in Wales with a British rhythm section (pianist Brian Lemon, bassist Dave Green and drummer Allan Ganley), Hamilton sounds fine on such tunes as "Way Down Yonder in New Orleans," "I Can't Give You Anything But Love," "Fascinatin' Rhythm" and his own "Blue Wales." Solid mainstream swing. —*Scott Yanow*

My Romance / Feb. 23, 1995 / Concord Jazz ✦✦✦✦✦

Tenor saxophonist Scott Hamilton has recorded so many records as a leader (this CD is his 27th for Concord so far) and been so consistent and unchanging through the years that it is difficult to describe any of his records as definitive. However this particular release is one of his stronger ones of recent times. Hamilton sounds quite inspired jamming on six standards, Blue Mitchell's "Blue Caper," two of Norman Simmons' originals and his own blues "Sugarchile" with a quintet consisting of the talented trombonist Joel Helleny, pianist Simmons, bassist Dennis Irwin and drummer Chuck Riggs. Hamilton takes the title cut as a feature and duets with Simmons on a brief "Just a Gigolo"; otherwise the full group is heard on each song. The biggest surprise of this high-quality mainstream date is an uptempo version of the ballad "Poor Butterfly." The presence of a second horn seems to really push Scott Hamilton to play at his best, making this an easily recommended release. —*Scott Yanow*

Jan Hammer

b. Apr. 17, 1948, Prague, Czechoslovakia

Keyboards, Synthesizer / Fusion

One of the more inventive keyboardists of the early fusion days, Jan Hammer has not played much jazz since the late '70s. He studied at Prague Conservatory and in 1967 played at the Warsaw Jazz Jamboree with Stuff Smith. In 1968 after the Russian invasion of Czechoslovakia, Hammer left for the US. He attended Berklee, worked with Sarah Vaughan (1970-71) and moved to New York where he played with Jeremy Steig and Elvin Jones. Hammer gained fame playing with the Mahavishnu Orchestra during its prime period (1971-73) and with Billy Cobham (1973-75). After leading his own groups (Jeff Beck was a sideman in 1976), he had great success with his score for the television series *Miami Vice* and worked with Al DiMeola in 1982 but has not been heard from much since. —*Scott Yanow*

Make Love / Aug. 30, 1968 / MPS ♦♦♦♦
An excellent example of real jazz-rock. —*Ron Wynn*

● **Like Children** / 1974 / Atlantic ♦♦♦♦♦
The keyboardist and violinist Jerry Goodman away from Mahavishnu. They play all instruments (overdubbed). "Country and Eastern Music" and "Steppings Tones" were high-water marks for this new breed (at the time). —*Michael G. Nastos*

The Early Years / 1974-1979 / Nemperor ♦♦♦
Early Years is a brief but adequate collection that culls eight highlights from Jan Hammer's first handful of records. There are some good moments here, but the collection could have been assembled with a little more care. Nevertheless, fans of Hammer's fusion who aren't very familiar with this music may want to use this as a launching pad to exploring his early years. —*Stephen Thomas Erlewine*

Oh Yeah / 1976 / Nemperor ♦♦♦♦♦
This is an album of fusion at its best. "Magical Dog" and "Red & Orange" are definitive statements. This was the first exposure for violinist Steve Kindler. David Earle Johnson is on congas. —*Michael G. Nastos*

Live / 1977 / Columbia ♦♦♦
A great teamup with Jeff Beck (g). —*Ron Wynn*

Melodies / 1978 / Nemperor ♦♦♦

Here to Stay / 1983 / Columbia ♦♦♦
Fine interaction with Neal Schon (g). —*Ron Wynn*

Escape from Television / 1986 / MCA ♦♦♦♦
When first seen on TV, *Miami Vice* was known as much for the music as the stylish action-packed plots. The man behind the music was Jan Hammer, a well-established rock and jazz-fusion player with experience that includes Jeff Beck, John McLaughlin and Jerry Goodman as bandmates and collaborators. On *Escape* a very strong style of current instrumental music can be found, with the edge of rock music and the smooth, spacey appeal of some of the more progressive new age musicians. —*Backroads Music/Heartbeats*

Beyond the Mind's Eye / 1992 / Miramar ♦♦♦
Beyond the Mind's Eye is Grammy award-winning keyboardist/composer Jan Hammer's first solo album in over five years. The 14 tracks, composed for Miramar's new video album, are different than the Video soundtrack. The audio release is remixed, features extended arrangements, and has a bonus vocal track sung by Chris Thompson of the Manfred Mann Group. Known for his *Miami Vice* music, Hammer provides a potent fusion which is perfect for this arena where modern music meets the visual arts. —*Backroads Music/Heartbeats*

Drive / 1994 / Miramar ♦♦♦
Jan Hammer has once again molded jazz themes into an incredibly approachable work of fusion on *Drive*. After having shown the importance of blending melody with engaging orchestration in such successes as the soundtrack to *Miami Vice*, Hammer has invited Jeff Beck on guitar and Michael Brecker on sax to add another dimension to the meaning of light jazz. Keyboardist Hammer, the radiant star on this album, knows when to step aside to let Beck shine with some tearing and sometimes lilting guitar riffs and Brecker glow in the intimate atmosphere he creates with his saxophone. —*MusD*

Gunter Hampel

b. Aug. 31, 1937, Gottingen, Germany

Vibes, Flute, Piano, Bass Clarinet / Avant-Garde, Free Jazz

Gunter Hampel, a multi-instrumentalist who in addition to vibes, bass clarinet and flute also plays piano and other reeds, has done a fine job of documenting his avant-garde music since 1969 for his own Birth label. He started leading his own band in 1958, has been playing very advanced jazz in Europe since the early '60s and in the early '70s formed his Galaxie Dream Band. Among his sidemen have been his wife, singer Jeanne Lee, Anthony Braxton, Alexander von Schlippenbach,

Willem Breuker, Perry Robinson, Enrico Rava and Mark Whitecage. —*Scott Yanow*

Music from Europe / Dec. 21, 1966 / ESP ♦♦♦♦
Gunter Hampel's second release as a leader and his only one for ESP has been reissued on CD. Hampel (heard on vibes, bass clarinet and flute) teams up with the many reeds of Willem Breuker (soprano, bass clarinet, tenor, alto, baritone and clarinet), plus bassist Piet Veening and drummer Pierre Courbois during three complex and sometimes eccentric originals. The nearly 22-minute "Assemblage" is the main piece, and overall, the music is an interesting combination of composition and very free improvising, giving one an interesting early look at Hampel and Breuker. —*Scott Yanow*

July 8, 1969 / Jul. 8, 1969 / Birth ♦♦♦

All the Things You Could Be If Charles Mingus Was Your Daddy / Jul. 1980 / Birth ♦♦♦♦♦

● **Jubilation** / Nov. 1983 / Birth ♦♦♦♦♦

Fresh Heat: Live at Sweet Basil / Feb. 1985 / Birth ♦♦♦♦♦

Lionel Hampton

b. Apr. 12, 1909, Louisville, KY

Vibes, Leader, Drums, Piano / Swing, Big Band, New York Blues

Lionel Hampton was the first jazz vibraphonist and has been one of the jazz giants since the mid-'30s. He has achieved the difficult feat of being musically open-minded (even recording "Giant Steps") without changing his basic swing style. Hamp started out as a drummer, playing with the Chicago Defender Newsboys' Band as a youth. His original idol was Jimmy Bertrand, a 1920s drummer who occasionally played xylophone. Hampton played on the West Coast with such groups as Curtis Mosby's Blue Blowers, Reb Spikes and Paul Howard's Quality Serenaders (with whom he made his recording debut in 1929) before joining Les Hite's band which for a period accompanied Louis Armstrong. At a recording session in 1930, a vibraphone happened to be in the studio, Armstrong asked Hampton (who had practiced on one previously) if he could play a little bit behind him and on "Memories of You" and "Shine" Hamp became the first jazz improviser to record on vibes.

It would be another six years before he found fame. Lionel Hampton, after leaving Hite, had his own band in Los Angeles' Paradise Cafe until one night in 1936 when Benny Goodman came into the club and discovered him. Soon Hampton recorded with BG, Teddy Wilson and Gene Krupa as the Benny Goodman Quartet and six weeks later he officially joined Goodman. An exciting soloist whose enthusiasm even caused BG to smile, Hampton became one of the stars of his organization, appearing in films with Goodman, at the famous 1938 Carnegie Hall Concert and nightly on the radio. In 1937 he started recording regularly as a leader for Victor with specially assembled all-star groups that formed a who's who of swing; all of these timeless performances (1937-41) were reissued by Bluebird on a six-LP set although thus far in piecemeal fashion on CD.

Hampton stayed with Goodman until 1940, sometimes substituting on drums and taking vocals. In 1940 Lionel Hampton formed his first big band and in 1942 had a huge hit with "Flying Home" featuring a classic Illinois Jacquet tenor spot (one of the first R&B solos). During the remainder of the decade, Hampton's extroverted orchestra was a big favorite, leaning towards R&B, showing the influence of bebop after 1944 and sometimes getting fairly exhibitionistic. Among his sidemen in addition to Jacquet were Arnett Cobb, Dinah Washington (who Hampton helped discover), Cat Anderson, Marshall Royal, Dexter Gordon, Milt Buckner, Earl Bostic, Snooky Young, Johnny Griffin, Joe Wilder, Benny Bailey, Charles Mingus, Fats Navarro, Al Gray and even Wes Montgomery and Betty Carter. Hampton's popularity allowed him to continue leading big bands off and on into the mid-'90s, and the 1953 edition that visited Paris (with Clifford Brown, Art Farmer, Quincy Jones, Jimmy Cleveland, Gigi Gryce, George Wallington and Annie Ross) would be difficult to top although fights over money and the right of the sideman to record led to its breakup. Hampton appeared and recorded with many all-star groups in the 1950s including reunions with Benny Goodman, meetings with the Oscar Peterson Trio, Stan Getz, Buddy DeFranco, and as part of a trio with Art Tatum and Buddy Rich. He also was featured in *The Benny Goodman Story* (1956).

Since the 1950s, Lionel Hampton has mostly repeated past triumphs, always playing "Hamp's Boogie Woogie" (which features his very rapid two-finger piano playing), "Hey Ba-Ba-Re-Bop" and "Flying Home." However his enthusiasm still causes excitement and he remains a household name. Hampton has recorded through the years for nearly every label including two of his own (Glad Hamp and Who's Who) and most recently MoJazz. Despite strokes and the ravages of age, Lionel Hampton as of this writing is still a vital force. —*Scott Yanow*

Lionel Hampton (1929-1940) / Apr. 1929-Dec. 1940 / BBC ♦♦♦

1937-1938 / Feb. 8, 1937-Jan. 18, 1938 / Classics ♦♦♦♦♦

Lionel Hampton's Jumpin' Jive, Vol. 2 / Feb. 8, 1937-Oct. 12, 1939 / Bluebird ✦✦✦

Lionel Hampton's small-group swing sessions of 1937-41 were consistently brilliant but unfortunately the current Bluebird CD reissue program has issued these performances in almost random fashion on three separate CDs, leaving out many strong sides and often dividing up sessions between two overlapping CDs. The second volume has a little of this and a little of that including a hot session featuring altoist Johnny Hodges, a few of tenor saxophonist Chu Berry's best performances (particularly "Sweethearts on Parade") and the alternate take of "When Lights Are Low" but this CD is primarily for beginners; it'll drive Hampton collectors crazy. —*Scott Yanow*

☆ **The Complete Lionel Hampton** / Feb. 8, 1937-Apr. 8, 1941 / Bluebird ✦✦✦✦✦

Although this six-LP box set is now out of print, it is so definitive that it deserves the highest rating. Consisting of all of the sessions led by vibraphonist Lionel Hampton prior to the formation of his popular big band, these hot swing sides feature a who's who of jazz greats from the 1930s including trumpeters Ziggy Elman, Cootie Williams, Jonah Jones, Harry James, Rex Stewart, Red Allen and Dizzy Gillespie, altoists Benny Carter, Johnny Hodges and Earl Bostic, tenors Herschel Evans, Chu Berry, Coleman Hawkins, and Ben Webster, guitarist Charlie Christian and the Nat King Cole Trio among many others. With Hamp on vibes, two-fingered piano and occasional vocals, this set is overflowing with classic performances. It should have been reissued in complete form on CD instead of in the piecemeal fashion that it has thus far partially reappeared. This box has yet to be matched. —*Scott Yanow*

Hot Mallets, Vol. 1 / Apr. 14, 1937-Sep. 11, 1939 / Bluebird ✦✦✦

While the original six-LP box set correctly reissued all of Lionel Hampton's 1937-41 small-group recordings as a leader, the CD reissue program has been rather erratic, dividing up some of these selections in almost random fashion between three CDs, often splitting up sessions between a pair of discs. The first of these three CDs is the strongest, highlighted by "On the Sunny Side of the Street" (featuring altoist Johnny Hodges), "I'm Confessin' " with trumpeter Jonah Jones, and the four master takes from a date with Coleman Hawkins, Chu Berry, Ben Webster, Benny Carter and a young Dizzy Gillespie. Great music but dumb programming. —*Scott Yanow*

1938-1939 / Jan. 18, 1938-Jun. 13, 1939 / Classics ✦✦✦✦✦

1939-1940 / Jun. 13, 1939-May 10, 1940 / Classics ✦✦✦✦✦

Tempo and Swing / Oct. 30, 1939-Aug. 21, 1940 / Bluebird ✦✦✦

The third and final CD in a rather flawed reissue program of Lionel Hampton's early small-group recordings as a leader contains most (but not all) of the recordings from six of Hamp's sessions, featuring such players as trumpeter Ziggy Elman and Benny Carter, tenors Ben Webster and Coleman Hawkins, clarinetist Edmond Hall and the Nat King Cole Trio. Best is the Carter-Hall-Hawkins date which is highlighted by two takes of "Dinah," but this music should have been reissued complete and in chronological order as it had been previously on LP. —*Scott Yanow*

Greatest Hits [RCA] / Oct. 30, 1939-Jun. 30, 1956 / RCA ✦✦

The title of this Lionel Hampton introductory CD is a joke since none of the vibraphonist's hits (such as "Flying Home" and "Hamp's Boogie Woogie") are here, nor is there any personnel listing or reference to these sessions in the vapid liner notes. Such players as trumpeter Ziggy Elman, tenor saxophonist Ben Webster and pianist Nat King Cole are among the sidemen on the nine titles from 1939-40. There are also five unrelated titles from a 1956 session cut in Spain that includes pianist Tete Montoliu on two songs and an 11-piece group on the others; all of these songs are currently available on other Bluebird CDs. Pass this sloppy effort by. —*Scott Yanow*

Steppin' Out (1942-1944) / Mar. 2, 1942-Oct. 16, 1944 / MCA ✦✦✦✦

Released as part of MCA's *Jazz Heritage* series in the early '80s, this LP contains 14 of the 16 selections from Lionel Hampton's 1942-44 sessions including two versions of "Flying Home" (featuring the contrasting tenor sax solos of Illinois Jacquet and Arnett Cobb) and the original recording of "Hamp's Boogie-Woogie." This is classic music played in an exuberant swing style that Hampton has continued to keep alive for the half-century since. —*Scott Yanow*

Hamp / May 26, 1942-Mar. 20, 1963 / GRP/Decca ✦✦✦✦

GRP in 1996 released this attractive two-CD box set which has some (but not all) of the highlights from vibraphonist Lionel Hampton's Decca years. In addition to the original version of "Flying Home" (but surprisingly not "Flying Home No.2") and "Hamp's Boogie Woogie," other high points include four titles from Hampton's 1945 Carnegie Hall concert (including "Red Cross" which features guest trumpeter Dizzy Gillespie), his classic 1947 live rendition of "Stardust," Dinah Washington's "Blowtop Blues," "Hey! Ba-Ba-Re-Bop," "Mingus Fingers" (a futuristic piece featuring bassist Charles Mingus), "Midnight Sun," some riotous big band numbers from 1947 and 1949, "Rag Mop," Little Jimmy Scott's "I Wish I Knew," sextet numbers

with organist Buddy Cole and (skipping ahead 13 years) two cuts from a small group date with trumpeter Charlie Teagarden. After hearing these exciting recordings, it is easy to understand Lionel Hampton's appeal. One really needs about four CD's to get all of Hampton's best recordings from the era but this set is a good start. —*Scott Yanow*

All-American Award Concert at Carnegie Hall / Apr. 15, 1945 / Decca ✦✦✦

Lionel Hampton's 1945 Carnegie Hall concert (available on this LP) is a fine all-round showcase for the band which at the time was evolving rapidly from swing to bop and rhythm & blues. Some of the music on this set is a bit hysterical (including a tenor battle by Arnett Cobb and Herbie Fields) and of course "Flying Home." Dizzy Gillespie makes a memorable guest appearance on "Red Cross" and Dinah Washington sings a fine version of her first hit, "Evil Gal Blues." —*Scott Yanow*

● **1945-1946** / 1945 / Classics ✦✦✦✦✦

The sixth CD in Classics' series of Lionel Hampton records documents his music during a one-year period. Hampton's big band, riding high after "Flying Home," continued to grow in popularity during this era. The vibraphonist's showmanship and his sidemen's extroverted solos generated constant excitement, as can be heard throughout these 20 selections. With the exception of Dinah Washington's lone vocal on "Blow Top Blues" and the original version of "Hey! Ba-Ba-Re-Bop," most of the selections were formerly a bit rare, including a pair of rollicking V-disc performances ("Vibe Boogie" and "Screamin' Boogie"). Hampton is heard on 14 numbers with his big band (which included such key sidemen as trumpeter Joe Morris, tenorman Arnett Cobb, the eccentric Herbie Fields on alto and clarinet, and pianist Milt Buckner), four workouts with a septet, and two tunes (including a pair of vocals) with a rhythm quartet. Bing Crosby guests on so-so versions of "Pinetop's Boogie Woogie" and "On the Sunny Side of the Street" (sounding very much out of place), but otherwise, everything works. Stirring and accessible music. —*Scott Yanow*

● **Midnight Sun** / Jan. 29, 1946-Nov. 10, 1947 / GRP/Decca ✦✦✦✦

Although firmly identified with Benny Goodman and the swing era, vibraphonist Lionel Hampton led one of the most bop-oriented and forward-looking big bands of the mid- to late '40s; for proof of that check out "Mingus Fingers" (by Charles Mingus) on this CD. This set reissues some of Hampton's most boppish sides from 1946-47 along with the original version of "Midnight Sun" and is full of extroverted solos and exciting ensembles. Although tenorman Arnett Cobb (heard in the earlier selections) and pianist Milt Buckner are the best-known sidemen, such musicians as the screaming trumpeters Jimmy Nottingham and Leo "the Whistler" Sheppard and tenors Morris Lane, John Sparrow and the young Johnny Griffin provide their own strong moments. Until Decca gets around to reissuing all of Hamp's big band sides in chronological order, this is one of the sets to get. —*Scott Yanow*

Lionel Hampton with the Just Jazz All Stars / Aug. 4, 1947 / GNP ✦✦✦

Taken from the same concert that produced Lionel Hampton's famous "Stardust" solo, this second LP actually has more Hamp (he dominates all six selections) but never reaches the heights of "Stardust." There are some fine moments from trumpeter Charlie Shavers, altoist Willie Smith and bassist Slam Stewart on such familiar material as "Perdido," "Hamp's Boogie Woogie" and "Flying Home," making it a worthwhile release. —*Scott Yanow*

The Original Stardust / Aug. 4, 1947 / Decca ✦✦✦✦✦

Lionel Hampton's classic live version of "Star Dust" at this "Just Jazz" concert is rightfully acclaimed, and remains one of the high points of his long career. Oddly enough Hampton does not appear on the other three selections included on this LP (which has since been reissued on CD) but these fine renditions of "One 'O'Clock Jump," "The Man I Love" and "Lady Be Good" do benefit from excellent solos by trumpeter Charlie Shavers, altoist Willie Smith, Corky Corcoran on tenor and bassist Slam Stewart. Highly recommended. —*Scott Yanow*

Hot House / 1948 / Alamac ✦✦✦

This budget (and possibly bootleg) LP of Lionel Hampton radio airchecks from 1948 is notable for a few reasons. Charles Mingus is heard throughout on bass, the great bop trumpeter Fats Navarro gets a fine spot on "Hot House" and a young Wes Montgomery takes a rare solo during "Brant Inn Boogie." Other key voices include trumpeters Benny Bailey, Teddy Buckner and the remarkable high-note specialist Leo "the Whistler" Sheppard, altoist Johnny Board and Johnny Sparrow on tenor in addition to the leader/vibraphonist. Since this particular orchestra did not get a chance to record commercially (due to the 1948 recording strike), this set is invaluable to jazz historians. —*Scott Yanow*

The Blues Ain't News to Me / Apr. 17, 1951-Aug. 3, 1955 / Verve ✦✦✦✦

This two-LP reissue contains highlights of two Lionel Hampton big-band Verve recordings in 1951 and a full set from 1955. One of the most popular of all bandleaders, Hampton is in fine form during these selections which are not as hysterical as his live performances of the same era. Mixing rhythm & blues with modern swing and showcasing such soloists as trumpeters Benny Bailey and Wallace Davenport, trombonists Jimmy Cleveland and Al Grey and the tenors of Johnny Board and Eddie Chamblee (along with vocals by Hampton, Sonny Parker, Janet Thurlow and Vicki Lee), this is a fine all-round showcase of Hampton's often-overlooked '50s big band. As an added plus, drummer Buddy Rich drops by for "Air Mail Special" and "Flyin' Home." —*Scott Yanow*

The Complete Quartet / Sep. 10, 1953-Jul. 31, 1955 / Verve ✦✦✦

This out-of-print five-LP box set features the great vibraphonist Lionel Hampton on extensive jams of standards with pianist Oscar Peterson, bassist Ray Brown and drummer Buddy Rich; the final two ballads are from a reunion of Hampton with pianist Teddy Wilson and drummer Gene Krupa (in addition to bassist Red Callender). Few surprises occur and no new ground is broken, but the music is consistently joyful and swinging for all concerned. —*Scott Yanow*

Lionel Hampton in Paris / Sep. 28, 1953 / Vogue ✦✦✦

This CD reissue features a loose jam session dominated by vibraphonist Lionel Hampton. The nine selections (which include such titles as "Real Crazy," "More Crazy" and "More and More Crazy"), in addition to many long solos from Hamp, has some spirited playing by trumpeter Walter Williams (who rarely had an opportunity to stretch out like this on records), trombonists Jimmy Cleveland and Al Hayse, clarinetist Mezz Mezzrow, tenors Alix Combelle and Clifford Scott and guitarist Billy Mackell with suitable backup by pianist Claude Bolling, electric bassist Monk Montgomery and drummer Curley Hamner. The results are not innovative or essential but generally quite fun. —*Scott Yanow*

European Concert, 1953 / Sep. 1953 / IAJRC ✦✦✦

Lionel Hampton led one of his most potentially great big bands during a European tour in 1953 but he managed (for unknown reasons) to sabotage it. When Hamp forbid sidemen to record on a freelance basis overseas and most of the key ones disobeyed his orders, the friction eventually led to the breakup of the band. Considering that the orchestra included trumpeters Clifford Brown and Art Farmer, trombonist Jimmy Cleveland, altoist Gigi Gryce, tenor Clifford Scott, pianist George Wallington and Annie Ross on vocals, the dissolution of the orchestra before it made any commercial recordings is a major tragedy. This IAJRC LP contains part of a concert that the band performed and gives hints as to what might have been. Hampton really hogs the spotlight (he is the only soloist on "How High the Moon") but "Blue Boy" has spots for Farmer, Gryce, Scott and, most importantly, Clifford Brown. —*Scott Yanow*

Wailin' at the Trianon / Jul. 22, 1954 / Columbia ✦✦✦

This LP features the Lionel Hampton big band in 1954 playing some consistently rousing (and occasionally hysterical) music. These live performances include three standards and a trio of fairly basic originals played with plenty of spirit and color if not a great deal of subtlety. It is easy to tell from this LP why Hampton's orchestra continued to be quite popular in an era when big bands were becoming quite rare; his performances mixed together the excitement of R&B and early rock 'n' roll with fine jazz solos. —*Scott Yanow*

★ **Hamp and Getz** / Aug. 1, 1955 / Verve ✦✦✦✦✦

If one were to believe the cliches and stereotypes common in some jazz history books, this matchup should not have worked. By 1955 Lionel Hampton was a veteran swing vibraphonist while Stan Getz was the leader of the "cool school" of young tenors. But what these two masters had in common (in addition to a healthy respect for each other's talents) was the ability to swing as hard as possible. Joined by a fine trio, the duo really rip into "Cherokee" and "Jumpin' at the Woodside" (listen to their blistering trade-offs) and, even with a fine ballad medley, it is these torrid jams that make this a highly recommended disc. —*Scott Yanow*

In Paris 1956 / May 3, 1956 / DRG ✦✦✦

This comparatively relaxed Lionel Hampton session (last available on this '80s LP) finds the great vibraphonist, his longtime guitarist Billy Nackel and drummer Curley Hamner in a sextet also including three fine French jazzmen (pianist Claude Bolling, bassist Paul Rovere and the Coleman Hawkins' inspired tenor of Guy Lafitte). Alternating between ballads, standards and originals, the informal and somewhat loose music swings nicely with strong solos all around. —*Scott Yanow*

Reunion at Newport 1967 / Jun. 30, 1956-Jul. 3, 1967 / RCA/Bluebird ✦✦✦✦

Most of this CD is taken up by a special Newport Jazz Festival concert featuring a big band full of Lionel Hampton's alumni. With trombonist Al Grey, Frank Foster on tenor and a screaming trumpet section that boasted Snooky Young, Jimmy Nottingham, Joe Newman and Wallace Davenport, the explosive nature of the music is not too surprising; the climax is provided by guest Illinois Jacquet on "Flying Home." The remainder of this disc contains half of a very effective 1956 session cut in Spain in which the medium-size group includes a castanet player and two songs match Hampton with the great Spanish pianist Tete Montoliu. —*Scott Yanow*

Lionel / Aug. 13, 1957-Aug. 14, 1957 / Audio Fidelity ✦✦✦

A decent small-group LP from 1957, this set does not list personnel or recording dates and has lengthy but somewhat irrelevant liner notes. However, the music (featuring the great vibraphonist with a sextet including Bobby Plater on reeds, pianist Oscar Dennard and guitarist Billy Mackel) contains swinging renditions of a variety of standards and ballads. Since it is doubtful that this material will be reissued on CD anytime soon, it is worth picking up in its original LP format. —*Scott Yanow*

You Better Know It / Oct. 26, 1964 / Impulse! ✦✦✦✦

Vibist Lionel Hampton's rhythmic abilities haven't been dulled by age, and he displayed his proficiency on this date, which includes the enjoyable bonus track "Moon over My Annie." There was no wasted energy or unnecessary or exaggerated solos; just bluesy, assertive, muscular arrangements, accompaniment, and ensemble segments. Highlights included "Vibraphone Blues," "Trick or Treat" and "Swingle Jingle," in which Hampton shifted from vibes to piano. —*Ron Wynn*

Lionel Hampton & Friends: Rare Recordings, Vol. 1 / Apr. 15, 1965-Nov. 13, 1977 / Telarc ✦✦✦

During the mid- to late '70s, Lionel Hampton sought to recapture the magic of his classic '30s all-star recordings with a series of albums featuring his vibes with musicians whom he normally did not encounter in his travels. This particular CD draws one or two selections apiece from seven of these albums (originally on the Who's Who label), all but one from 1977. The lone exception, a version of "Stardust" from 1965, has quite a lineup (trumpeters Clark Terry and Thad Jones, trombonist J.J. Johnson, Lucky Thompson on soprano and tenor great Coleman Hawkins) and is quite listenable but does not live up to its potential. The same can be said for most of these performances which include meetings with pianists Earl Hines and Teddy Wilson, a workout with baritonist Gerry Mulligan, a version of "Cherokee" featuring Steve Marcus' soprano and drummer Buddy Rich, two selections with Dexter Gordon (who has a rare outing on soprano during "Seven Comes Eleven") and a pair of numbers from what would be bassist Charles Mingus' final recording date. Hopefully, these interesting sessions, even though they do not reach the creative heights of Hampton's earlier recordings, will eventually be reissued on CD complete and in chronological order. —*Scott Yanow*

Lionel Hampton and His Jazz Giants / May 15, 1977 / Black & Blue ✦✦✦

By the time of this 1977 small-group recording, Lionel Hampton had been performing with pickup bands for decades, outfits that usually only lasted as long as particular tours. This studio session found the great vibraphonist reuniting with such alumni as Milt Buckner (sticking here exclusively to organ), the remarkable high-note trumpeter Cat Anderson, guitarist Billy Mackel and the two tenors of Eddie Chamblee and Paul Moen. Performing standards and two basic originals, this is an exuberant and generally extroverted outing that has yet to be reissued on CD. —*Scott Yanow*

Live in Emmen, Holland / May 13, 1978 / Timeless ✦✦✦✦

In addition to new versions of Lionel Hampton's three "greatest hits" ("Flying Home," "Hamp's Boogie-Woogie" and "Airmail Special"), this live nonet session features the veteran swing vibraphonist grappling succesfully with two of John Coltrane's most notable compositions ("Giant Steps" and "Moments Notice") along with songs by Roland Hanna and Joe Henderson. Clearly Hampton, although always closely identified with the swing era, was one of the few members of his musical generation to keep up with later developments in jazz. With strong solos by trumpeter Joe Newman, Paul Moen on tenor, Eddie Chamblee (alternating between alto and tenor) and Wild Bill Davis on organ and piano, this spirited and diverse set is highly recommended. —*Scott Yanow*

Fiftieth Anniversary Concert Live at Carnegie Hall / Jul. 1, 1978 / Sutra ✦✦✦

One has to completely overlook this double LP's inadequate packaging (which makes it appear to be a bootleg or a budget series) in evaluating the music of this loose but rather notable set. The lineup includes such brilliant players as trumpeters Cat Anderson, Doc Cheatham and Joe Newman, tenors Arnett Cobb and Paul Moen, altoist Charles McPherson, clarinetist Bob Wilbur, baritonist Pepper Adams and pianist Ray Bryant. Although little prior preparation seems to have taken place (many of the all-stars had rarely played with Hamp in the past), the results are quite spirited, generally musical and consistently fun. —*Scott Yanow*

Sentimental Journey / Mar. 13, 1985-Mar. 14, 1985 / Atlantic ✦✦

A rather forgettable LP, this set mostly features the okay vocals of Sylvia Bennett on a variety of overplayed swing standards. Lionel Hampton's big band is mostly restricted to background work with occasional short individual spots while Hampton himself is the only soloist on five of the nine selections, including the lone instrumental, "Avalon." The lack of liner notes on this Atlantic LP is surprising since its purpose seemed to be to introduce a new singer. This set can be safely passed by. —*Scott Yanow*

Mostly Blues / Mar. 10, 1988-Apr. 8, 1988 / Music Masters ✦✦✦

Considering that this program features such songs as "Someday My Prince Will Come," "Take the 'A' Train," "Honeysuckle Rose" and "Gone with the Wind," its title is rather inaccurate; in fact only three of the nine songs are actually blues. In any case, vibraphonist Lionel Hampton is in fine form as the dominant soloist in a quintet also including pianist Bobby Scott and guitarist Joe Beck. Even as he entered his 80s, Hampton still displayed youthful vitality and enthusiasm. —*Scott Yanow*

Cookin' in the Kitchen / Jun. 7, 1988-Jun. 15, 1988 / Glad Hamp ✦✦✦

The veteran vibraphonist Lionel Hampton (then 79) leads his young big band through recent originals; only Joe Henderson's "Inner Urge" and the Gene Ammons/Sonny Stitt line "Blues Up & Down" were more than a few years old at the time and, to his credit, Hampton avoids his usual repertoire. The music is often funky and played with spirit although the orchestra occasionally sounds like a somewhat anonymous stage band that had not fully developed its own individual personality yet. Jerry Weldon and Doug Miller have a good tenor battle on "Blues Up & Down," altoist Rob Middleton and his brother Andy (on soprano) are in fine form on "Two Brothers" and Hampton has little difficulty finding fresh statements to make on this modern material. —*Scott Yanow*

Mostly Ballads / Sep. 8, 1989-Nov. 28, 1989 / Music Masters ✦✦

As with the slightly earlier *Mostly Blues* CD, the title of this set is inaccurate. True, Hampton performs such ballads as "I'll Be Seeing You," "Lover Man" and "But Beautiful," but many of these songs are taken at medium tempos and this program also includes three Teo Macero originals that are definitely not ballads. The use of synthesizer on several numbers is not particularly interesting and, although trumpeter Lew Soloff contributes a few fine solos, the most rewarding numbers are the ones that focus on Hampton's highly expressive vibes; he is in fine form throughout. It's an erratic but worthy release from the vital octogenarian. —*Scott Yanow*

Live at the Blue Note / Jun. 11, 1991-Jun. 13, 1991 / Telarc ✦✦✦

For a 1991 gig at the Blue Note in New York, vibraphonist Lionel Hampton headed a nonet full of classic veterans that were termed "the Golden Men of Jazz": trumpeters Clark Terry and Harry "Sweets" Edison, tenors James Moody and Buddy Tate, trombonist Al Grey, pianist Hank Jones, bassist Milt Hinton and drummer Grady Tate. Even with its many loose moments, these great players came up with some notable moments, including James Moody's humorous vocalizing on "Moody's Mood for Love" and particularly fine playing by Terry and Grey; Tate and Edison do show their age a bit, but are welcome participants in what must have been an occasion for celebration. —*Scott Yanow*

Just Jazz: Live at the Blue Note / Jun. 11, 1991-Jun. 13, 1991 / Telarc ✦✦

The second of two volumes by "the Golden Men of Jazz" at the Blue Note in New York, this CD is not at the same level as the first with several almost chaotic spots; listen to how Lionel Hampton tries to hog the spotlight on "Ring Dem Bells." There are some good moments from Clark Terry, James Moody and Al Grey (although Harry Edison and Buddy Tate show their age a bit) but the earlier release, *Live at the Blue Note*, is a much better buy. —*Scott Yanow*

For the Love of Music / 1994-1995 / MoJazz ✦✦

For his debut on the MoJazz label, the ancient vibraphonist Lionel Hampton was featured with several groups, some more suitable than others. Keyboardist Patrice Rushen largely ruins a funky rendition of "Flying Home" and several of the other songs (the insipid "Jazz Me" and Chaka Khan's feature on "Gossamer Wings") are little more than throwaways. Better is Hampton's collaboration with Tito Puente's band on "Don't You Worry 'Bout a Thing" and his original "Mojazz" even if Grover Washington, Jr., sounds as if he is on automatic pilot on "Another Part of Me." Overall this so-so disc can easily be passed by. —*Scott Yanow*

Slide Hampton (Locksley Wellington Hampton)

b. Apr. 21, 1932, Jeannette, PA

Trombone, Arranger / Bop, Hard Bop

Slide Hampton has been a fine trombonist and arranger since the mid-'50s, helping to keep the tradition of bop alive in both his playing and his writing. After working with Buddy Johnson (1955-56) and Lionel Hampton, he became an important force in Maynard Ferguson's excellent big band of 1957-59. He led octets in the 1960s with such sidemen as Freddie Hubbard and George Coleman. After traveling with Woody Herman to Europe in 1968, Hampton settled overseas where he stayed very active. Since returning to the US in 1977, he has led his World of Trombones (which features nine trombonists), played in a co-op quintet called Continuum and been involved in several Dizzy Gillespie tribute projects, recording in the 1990s for Telarc. —*Scott Yanow*

His Horn of Plenty / Oct. 1959 / Strand ✦✦✦✦✦

Mellow-Dy / 1967-1968 / LRC ✦✦✦✦

Trombonist Slide Hampton's writing ability has long overshadowed his skills as a player. This CD reissue sets the record straight by putting the focus on Hampton's boppish and consistently creative trombone. The first three selections (a couple of originals and J.J. Johnson's "Lament") showcase Hampton really stretching out with a quartet also including pianist Martial Solal, bassist Henri Texler and drummer Daniel Humair. The second half of the CD has Hampton joined by tenor saxophonist Nathan Davis, vibraphonist Dave Pike, pianist Hampton Hawes (sounding quite modern), Texler, and Humair for a couple more originals and Hawes' "Us Six." Overall, the advanced straightahead music on this CD comprises one of Hampton's best showcases as a trombonist, and the release is easily recommended. —*Scott Yanow*

World of Trombones / Jan. 8, 1979-Jan. 9, 1979 / Black Lion ✦✦✦✦

Ambitious project with nine trombonists merging their skills under the leadership of Slide Hampton. The list includes both established veterans like Curtis Fuller and Steve Turre and emerging newcomers Janice Robinson and Afro-Latin star Papo Vasquez. Hampton's arrangements are excellent, but there's more emphasis on performance style than real solo development. Pianist Albert Dailey and bassist Ray Drummond were also outstanding. —*Ron Wynn*

● **Roots** / Apr. 1985 / Criss Cross ✦✦✦✦✦

Tremendous 1985 quintet session with trombonist Slide Hampton heading a distinguished group and nicely teaming with tenor saxophonist Clifford Jordan in a first-rate hard-bop front line. The rhythm section's quality isn't far behind, especially pianist Cedar Walton and drummer Billy Higgins. —*Ron Wynn*

Dedicated to Diz / Feb. 6, 1993+Feb. 7, 1993 / Telarc ✦✦✦

Trombonist/arranger Slide Hampton pays tribute to the recently deceased Dizzy Gillespie during a collection mostly consisting of Dizzy's compositions. Hampton utilizes "The Jazz Masters," an all-star medium-size group also including trumpeters Jon Faddis, Roy Hargrove and Claudio Roditi, himself and Steve Turre on trombones, bass trombonist Douglas Purviance, the reeds of David Sanchez, Antonio Hart and Jimmy Heath, pianist Danilo Perez, bassist George Mraz and drummer Lewis Nash. Although there is a certain amount of predictability in their treatments of such tunes as "Bebop," "Tour de Force" and "A Night in Tunisia" (and "Overture" after a few song quotes becomes "Blue & Boogie"), the remarkable lineup of musicians cannot be passed over lightly. —*Scott Yanow*

Herbie Hancock

b. Apr. 12, 1940, Chicago, IL

Piano, Keyboards, Leader, Composer / Post-Bop, Fusion, Pop, Electric Funk, Funk, Hard Bop, R&B

Herbie Hancock will always be one of the most revered and controversial figures in jazz—just as his employer/mentor Miles Davis when he was alive. Unlike Miles, who pressed on relentlessly and never looked back until near the very end, Hancock has cut a zigzagging forward path, shuttling between almost every development in electronic and acoustic jazz and R&B over the last third of the 20th century. Though grounded in Bill Evans and able to absorb blues, funk, gospel, and even modern classical influences, Hancock's piano and keyboard voices are entirely his own, with their own urbane harmonic and complex, earthy rhythmic signatures—and young pianists cop his licks constantly. Having studied engineering and professing to love gadgets and buttons, Hancock was perfectly suited for the electronic age; he was one of the earliest champions of the Rhodes electric piano and Hohner clavinet and would field an ever-growing collection of synthesizers and computers on his electric dates. Yet his love for the grand piano never waned, and despite his peripatetic activities all around the musical map, his piano style continues to evolve into tougher, ever-more-complex forms. He is as much at home trading riffs with a smoking funk band as he is communing with a world-class post-bop rhythm section—and that drives purists on both sides of the fence up the wall.

Having taken up the piano at age seven, Hancock quickly became known as a prodigy, soloing in the first movement of a Mozart piano concerto with the Chicago Symphony at the age of 11. After studies at Grinnell College, Hancock was invited by Donald Byrd in 1961 to join his group in New York City, and before long, Blue Note offered him a solo contract. His debut album *Takin' Off* took off indeed after Mongo Santamaria covered one of the album's songs, "Watermelon Man." In May 1963, Miles Davis asked him to join his band in time for the *Seven Steps to Heaven* sessions, and he remained there for five years, greatly influencing Miles' evolving direction, loosening up his own style, and upon Miles' suggestion, converting to the Rhodes electric piano. In that timespan, Hancock's solo career also blossomed on Blue Note, pouring forth increasingly sophisticated compositions like "Maiden Voyage," "Cantaloupe Island," "Goodbye to Childhood" and the exquisite "Speak like a Child." He also played on many East Coast recording sessions for producer Creed Taylor and provided a groundbreaking score to Michelangelo Antonioni's film *Blow Up,* which gradually led to further movie assignments.

Having left the Davis band in 1968, Hancock recorded an elegant funk album *Fat Albert Rotunda* and in 1969 formed a sextet that evolved into one of the most exciting, forward-looking jazz-rock groups of the era. Now deeply immersed in electronics, Hancock added the synthesizer of Patrick Gleeson to his Echoplexed, fuzz-wah-pedaled electric piano and clavinet, and the recordings became spacier and more complex rhythmically and structurally, creating its own corner of the avant-garde. By 1970, all of the musicians used both English and African names (Herbie's was Mwandishi). Alas, Hancock had to break up the band in 1973 when it ran out of money, and having studied Buddhism, he concluded that his ultimate goal should be to make his audiences happy.

The next step, then, was a terrific funk group whose first album, *Head Hunters,* with its Sly Stone-influenced hit single "Chameleon," became the biggest-selling jazz LP up to that time. Now handling all of the synthesizers himself, Hancock's heavily rhythmic comping often became part of the rhythm section, leavened by interludes of the old urbane harmonies. Hancock recorded several electric albums of mostly superior quality in the '70s, followed by a wrong turn into disco around the decade's end. In the meantime, Hancock refused to abandon acoustic jazz. After a one-shot reunion of the 1965 Miles Davis Quintet (Hancock, Ron Carter, Tony Williams, Wayne Shorter, with Freddie Hubbard sitting in for Miles) at New York's 1976 Newport Jazz Festival, they went on tour the following year as V.S.O.P. The near-universal acclaim of the reunions proved a) that Hancock was still a whale of a pianist, b) that Miles' loose mid-'60s post-bop direction was far from spent, and c) that the time for a neo-traditional revival was near, finally bearing fruit in the '80s with Wynton Marsalis and his ilk. V.S.O.P. continued to hold sporadic reunions through 1992, though the death of the indispensable Williams in 1997 casts much doubt as to whether these gatherings will continue.

Hancock continued his chameleonic ways in the '80s—scoring an MTV hit in 1983 with the scratch-driven, proto-industrial single "Rockit" (accompanied by a striking video); launching an exciting partnership with Gambian kora virtuoso Foday Musa Suso that culminated in the swinging 1986 live album *Jazz Africa;* doing film scores; and playing festivals and tours with the Marsalis brothers, George Benson, Michael Brecker and many others. After his 1988 techno-pop album *Perfect Machine,* Hancock left Columbia (his label since 1973), signed a contract with Qwest that came to virtually nothing (save for *A Tribute to Miles* in 1992), and finally made a deal with PolyGram in 1994 to record jazz for Verve and release pop albums on Mercury. Now well into a youthful middle age, Hancock's curiosity, versatility and capacity for growth have shown no signs of fading. *—Richard S. Ginell*

● **Takin' Off** / May 28, 1962 / Blue Note ✦✦✦✦✦
This CD reissues pianist Herbie Hancock's first album as a leader, a set best known for introducing his catchy song "Watermelon Man." The release not only brings back the original hard-bop-oriented program but adds three previously unissued alternate takes, including one of "Watermelon Man." The all-star quintet (which includes trumpeter Freddie Hubbard, tenor saxophonist Dexter Gordon, bassist Butch Warren and drummer Billy Higgins) sounds consistently inspired with Gordon just starting to be influenced by John Coltrane and Hubbard full of youthful fire. Even at this early stage, Herbie Hancock had his own original voice. *—Scott Yanow*

Jazz Profile / May 28, 1962-Apr. 21, 1969 / Blue Note ✦✦✦
This is a most unusual sampler of Herbie Hancock's Blue Note years, for rather than concentrating on his hits (only "Cantaloupe Island" among the seven numbers qualifies), the CD just gives one an almost random glimpse at Hancock's early work. Each of the selections is from a different album, ranging from the hard bop of "Empty Pockets" (with tenor great Dexter Gordon and trumpeter Freddie Hubbard) to "Eye of the Hurricane," a trio rendition of "The Sorcerer" and the lengthy "I Have a Dream," which is played by an early version of Hancock's late-'60s sextet. *—Scott Yanow*

My Point of View / Mar. 19, 1963 / Blue Note ✦✦✦✦
Takin' Off was an impressive debut effort from Herbie Hancock, and his second record, *My Point of View,* proved that it was no fluke. Hancock took two risks with the album—his five original compositions covered more diverse stylistic ground than his debut, and he assembled a large septet for the sessions; the band features such stellar musicians as trumpeter Donald Byrd, tenor saxophonist Hank Mobley, drummer Tony Williams, guitarist Grant Green, bassist Chuck Israels and trombonist Grachan Moncur III. It's a rare occasion that all seven musicians appear on the same track, which speaks well for the pianist's arranging capabilities. Hancock knows how to get the best out of his songs and musicians, which is one of the reasons why *My Point of View* is a captivating listen. The other is the sheer musicality of the record. Hard bop remains the foundation for Hancock's music, but he explores its limitations, finding its soulful side (the successful "Watermelon Man"

rewrites "Blind Man, Blind Man"), its probing, adventurous leanings (the edgy "King Cobra"), and its ballad side. "The Pleasure Is Mine" is a lovely, simple ballad, while "A Tribute to Someone" takes the form to more challenging territory—it's lyrical, but it takes chances. The closer "And What if I Don't" finds the band working a relaxed, bluesy groove that gives them opportunites to spin out rich, tasteful solos. It's a little more relaxed than *Takin' Off,* but in its own way, *My Point of View* is nearly as stunning. *—Stephen Thomas Erlewine*

Inventions and Dimensions / Aug. 30, 1963 / Blue Note ✦✦✦✦
For his third album, *Inventions and Dimensions,* Herbie Hancock changed course dramatically. Instead of recording another multifaceted album like *My Point of View,* he explored a Latin-inflected variation of post-bop with a small quartet. Hancock is the main harmonic focus of the music—his three collegues are bassist Paul Chambers, drummer Willie Bobo and percussionist Osvaldo "Chihuahua" Martinez, who plays conga and bongo. It is true that the music is rhythm-intensive, but that doesn't mean it's dance music. Hancock has created an improvisatory atmosphere where the rhythms are fluid and the chords, harmonies and melodies are unexpected. On every song but one, the melodies and chords were improvised, with Hancock's harmonic ideas arising from the rhythms during the recording. The result is risky, unpredictable music that is intensely cerebral and quite satisfying. *Inventions and Dimensions* displays his willingness to experiment and illustrates that his playing is reaching new, idiosyncratic heights. Listening to this, the subsequent developments of Miles Davis' invitation to join his quartet and the challenging *Empyrean Isles* come as no surprise. *—Stephen Thomas Erlewine*

Empyrean Isles / Jun. 17, 1964 / Blue Note ✦✦✦✦✦
My Point of View and *Inventions and Dimensions* found Herbie Hancock exploring the fringes of hard bop, working with a big band and a Latin-flavored percussion section, respectively. On *Empyrean Isles,* he returns to hard bop, but the results are anything but conventional. Working with cornetist Freddie Hubbard, bassist Ron Carter and drummer Tony Williams—a trio just as young and adventurous as he was—Hancock pushes at the borders of hard bop, finding a brilliantly evocative balance between traditional bop, soul-injected grooves and experimental, post-modal jazz. Hancock's four original concepts are loosely based on the myths of the Empyrean Isles, and they are designed to push the limits of the band and hard-bop. Even "Cantaloupe Island," well known for its funky piano riff, takes chances and doesn't just ride the groove. "The Egg," with its minimal melody and extended solo improvisations, is the riskiest number on the record, but it works because each musician spins inventive, challenging solos that defy convention. In comparison, "One Finger Snap" and "Oliloqui Valley" (alternate takes of both tracks are included as bonuses on the CD reissue) adhere to hard bop conventions, but each song finds the quartet vigorously searching for new sonic territory with convincing fire. That passion informs all of *Empyrean Isles,* a record that officially established Hancock as a major artist in his own right. *—Stephen Thomas Erlewine*

★ **Maiden Voyage** / Mar. 17, 1965 / Blue Note ✦✦✦✦✦
Less overtly adventurous than its predecessor, *Empyrean Isles, Maiden Voyage* nevertheless finds Herbie Hancock at a creative peak. In fact, it's arguably his finest record of the '60s, reaching a perfect balance between accessible, lyrical jazz and chance-taking hard bop. By this point, the pianist had been with Miles Davis for two years, and it's clear that Miles' subdued yet challenging modal experiments had been fully integrated by Hancock. Not only that, but through Davis, Hancock became part of the exceptional rhythm section of bassist Ron Carter and drummer Tony Williams, who are both featured on *Maiden Voyage,* along with trumpeter Freddie Hubbard and tenor saxophonist George Coleman. The quintet plays a selection of five Hancock originals, many of which are simply superb showcases for the group's provocative, unpredictable solos, tonal textures and harmonies. While the quintet takes risks, the music is lovely and accessible, thanks to Hancock's understated, melodic compositions and the tasteful group interplay. All of the elements blend together to make *Maiden Voyage* a shimmering, beautiful album that captures Hancock at his finest as a leader, soloist and composer. *—Stephen Thomas Erlewine*

Blow Up / Oct. 1966 / Atlantic ✦✦✦

Speak like a Child / Mar. 9, 1968 / Blue Note ✦✦✦✦
Between 1965's *Maiden Voyage* and 1968's *Speak Like a Child,* Herbie Hancock was consumed with his duties as part of the Miles Davis Quintet, who happened to be at their creative and popular peak during those three years. When Hancock did return to a leadership position on *Speak like a Child,* it was clear that he had assmilated not only the group's experiments, but also many ideas Miles initially sketched out with Gil Evans. Like *Maiden Voyage,* the album is laidback, melodic and quite beautiful, but there are noticeable differences between the two records. Hancock's melodies and themes have become simpler and more memorable, particularly on the title track, but that hasn't cut out room for improvisation. Instead,

he has found a balance between accessible themes and searching improvisations that work a middle ground between post-bop and rock. Similarly, the horns and reeds are unconventional. He has selected three parts—Thad Jones' fluegelhorn, Peter Phillips' bass trombone, Jerry Dodgion's alto flute—with unusual voicings, and he uses them for tonal texture and melodic statements, not solos. The rhythm section of bassist Ron Carter and drummer Mickey Roker keeps things light, subtle, and forever shifting, emphasizing the hybrid nature of Hancock's original compositions. But the key to *Speak like a Child* is in Hancock's graceful, lyrical playing and compositions, which are lovely on the surface and provocative and challenging upon closer listening. —*Stephen Thomas Erlewine*

The Prisoner / Apr. 18, 1969-Apr. 23, 1969 / Blue Note ♦♦♦

As one of the first albums Herbie Hancock recorded after departing Miles Davis' quintet in 1968, as well as his final album for Blue Note, *The Prisoner* is one of Hancock's most ambitious efforts. Assembling a nonet that features Joe Henderson (tenor sax, alto flute), Johnny Coles (fluegelhorn), Garnett Brown (trombone), Buster Williams (bass) and Albert "Tootie" Heath (drums), Hancock has created his grandest work since *My Point of View*. Unlike that effort, *The Prisoner* has a specific concept—it's a tribute to Dr. Martin Luther King, evoking his spirit and dreams through spacious, exploratory post-bop. Often, the music doesn't follow conventional patterns, but that doesn't mean that it's alienating or inaccessible. It is certainly challenging, but Hancock's compositions (and his arrangement of Charles Williams' "Firewater") have enough melody and space to allow listeners into the album. Throughout the record, Hancock, Coles and Henderson exchange provocative, unpredictable solos that build upon the stark melodies and sober mood of the music. The tone is not of sorrow or celebration, but of reflection and contemplation, and on that level, *The Prisoner* succeeds handsomely, even if the music meanders a little too often to be judged a complete success. —*Stephen Thomas Erlewine*

Mwandishi: The Complete Warner Bros. Recordings / Oct. 4, 1969-Feb. 17, 1972 / Warner Archives ♦♦♦♦♦

This two-CD set reissues the complete contents of three LPs: *Fat Albert Rotunda*, *Mwandishi* and *Crossings*. The earliest session (extensions of generally memorable funk themes used in a Bill Cosby cartoon) features the keyboardist in a sextet on most selections with tenor saxophonist Joe Henderson, trumpeter Johnny Coles and trombonist Garnett Brown; two songs use a 15-piece group. However the bulk of this set showcases Hancock's regular sextet of the era (which comprised trumpeter Eddie Henderson, Benny Maupin on bass clarinet, alto flute and soprano, trombonist Julian Priester, bassist Buster Williams and drummer Billy Hart); the later session also adds Patrick Gleeson's moog synthesizer. The somewhat unique music is both explorative and loosely funky, avant-garde yet influenced by rock and funk. The results are often quite fascinating but this group (which only recorded one further album for Columbia) was a commercial flop which Hancock would eventually break up in favor of the Headhunters. —*Scott Yanow*

Sextant / 1972 / Columbia ♦♦♦

★ **Headhunters** / 1973 / Columbia ♦♦♦♦♦

Headhunters was a pivotal point in Herbie Hancock's career, bringing him into the vanguard of jazz fusion. Hancock had pushed avant-garde boundaries on his own albums and with Miles Davis, but he had never devoted himself to the groove as he did on *Headhunters*. Drawing heavily from Sly Stone, Curtis Mayfield and James Brown, Hancock devloped deeply funky, even gritty, rhythms over which he soloed on electric synthesizers, bringing the instrument to the forefront in jazz. It had all of the sensibilities of jazz, particularly in the way it wound off into long improvisations, but its rhythms were firmly planted in funk, soul and R&B, giving it a mass appeal that made it the biggest-selling jazz album of all time (a record which was later broken). Jazz purists, of course, decried the experiments at the time, but *Headhunters* still sounds fresh and vital two decades after its initial release, and its genre-bending proved vastly influential on not only jazz, but funk, soul and hip-hop. —*Stephen Thomas Erlewine*

Dedication / Jul. 29, 1974 / CBS/Sony ♦♦♦

This is a unique experiment in the Hancock discography, recorded in Tokyo in just one day during a tour of Japan. Side one contains two introspective, complex solo acoustic piano tracks, "Maiden Voyage" and "Dolphin Dance," which are notable since they date from a period when Hancock was supposedly totally immersed in electronics. Side two has two even more unusual things—"Nobu," a one-man show recorded in real time with the sample-and-hold feature of an ARP 2600 synthesizer providing a rhythm section for Hancock's electric keyboards, followed by "Cantaloupe Island" with a pre-recorded synth bass line. Side two is a fascinating look back at the charms and stringent limitations of mid-'70s analog keyboards, as well as a challenge to Hancock's on-the-wing inventiveness—and despite some inevitable stiffness in the rhythm, he comes through with some colorful work. This would be the first of several Japan-only Hancock albums from the '70s, an indication that

Japanese jazz fans were (and perhaps still are) far more open-minded and free-spending than their American counterparts. —*Richard S. Ginell*

Thrust / Aug. 26, 1974 / Columbia ♦♦♦

This is among Hancock's better R&B/funk/rock works. —*Ron Wynn*

Death Wish / 1974 / One Way ♦♦

Herbie Hancock extends the reach of his *Head Hunters*-vintage electric music into the soundtrack field, with some switchbacks to earlier styles and old-fashioned movie suspense music thrown into the eclectic mix. Jerry Peters provides the requisite orchestral backgrounds, and the wah-wah guitar licks give some indication as to where Herbie's funk music would be going in the future. The main title music is the best track—tense, streaked with Hancock's echo-delayed electric piano and understated orchestrations. A good deal of the record, alas, is filled with listless film cues that are meaningless without the action in front of you. Still, the results are, in general, more intriguing than usual for the film genre. —*Richard S. Ginell*

Flood / Jun. 28, 1975-Jul. 1, 1975 / Sony Japan ♦♦♦♦

Herbie and the Headhunters take to the road in this live double album, recorded and released only in Japan. Contrary to the impression left by his American releases at this time, Hancock was still very much attached to the acoustic piano, as his erudite opening workout on "Maiden Voyage/Actual Proof" with his funk rhythm section makes clear. The electric keyboards, mostly Rhodes piano and clavinet, make their first appearances on Side two, where Hancock now becomes more of a funky adjunct to the rhythm section, bumping along with a superb feeling for the groove while Bennie Maupin takes the high road above on a panoply of winds. Except for "Voyage," the tunes come from the *Head Hunters*, *Thrust* and *Man-Child* albums (another reason why this was not released in the US). "Chameleon" comes with a lengthy outbreak of machine pink noise that attests to Hancock's wide-eyed love of gadgetry. In all, this was a great funk band, not all that danceable because of the rapid complexities of Mike Clark's drumming, and quite often full of harmonic depth and adventure. —*Richard S. Ginell*

Herbie Hancock Trio / Jul. 13, 1977 / Columbia ♦♦♦♦

The first V.S.O.P. tour triggered a flood of recording activity in July 1977, but only a fraction of it was released in the US. This session, recorded in San Francisco just days before the Quintet concerts in Berkeley and San Diego, finds Herbie Hancock, Ron Carter and Tony Williams mixing it up sans the horns—and the results are more reflective and cerebral than the full Quintet concerts. Hancock is thoroughly in control of the agenda while Williams throws in those meter-fracturing flurries that keep everyone on their toes. There is a startling re-interpretation of "Speak like a Child" which is significantly tougher and busier than the wistful Blue Note version, as well as challenging Hancock originals like "Whatcha Waiting For" and "Watch It." This is uncompromising acoustic jazz, commercial anathema in the electronic '70s—and thus, only Japan got to hear it. —*Richard S. Ginell*

V.S.O.P. the Quintet: Tempest in the Colosseum / Jul. 23, 1977 / CBS/Sony ♦♦♦♦♦

Only five days after *The Quintet* concerts in California, V.S.O.P. was caught live again on tape in Tokyo's Den-En Colosseum for another Japanese CBS/Sony release. "Tempest" is a good description, for this CD contains more volatile ensemble playing than its Columbia predecessor; clearly some tighter bonding took place since the trans-Pacific flight. The notion that Freddie Hubbard is filling in for Miles Davis in a reunion of his old quintet does not have much relevance, for Hubbard is always his own man, in command of his reverberant tone quality and idiosyncratic flurries that owe very little to Miles. Only "Lawra" is duplicated from *The Quintet*, and there is the additional treat of hearing Hub-Tones' masterpiece "Red Clay" performed to a turn by this crack quintet. —*Richard S. Ginell*

Sunlight / 1977 / Columbia ♦♦♦

Evening with Chick Corea and Herbie Hancock / 1978 / Columbia ♦♦♦♦♦

In 1978, Chick Corea and Herbie Hancock teamed up for a tour, playing duets exclusively on acoustic pianos. One double LP was issued under each of their names. The *Corea* set has lengthy versions of three of Chick's tunes ("Homecoming," "Bouquet," and "La Fiesta"), Hancock's "Maiden Voyage" and their joint work, "The Hook," in addition to a short piece by Bela Bartok. This collaboration brought out the best in both pianists and restored a bit of credibility to two players who had had great success playing more commercial electronic music. —*Scott Yanow*

Direct Step / Oct. 17, 1978-Oct. 18, 1978 / Columbia ♦♦♦♦

For the rabid audiophiles in Japan, Herbie Hancock went to Tokyo to record a direct-to-disc LP that later became one of the world's earliest CD releases. Due perhaps to the arduous one-take-only nature of the direct-to-disc process, Hancock takes the rare step of using a second keyboardist, Webster Lewis, to handle the multiple electronic textures; the rest of the cast is a quorum of Headhunters (Bennie Maupin, reeds; Paul Jackson, bass; Bill Summers, percussion), plus guitarist Ray Obiedo and drummer Alphonse Mouzon. Understandably, the music sometimes sounds a bit inhibited and structured but there are some refreshingly jarring rhythmic disruptions in "Butterfly," "Shiftless Shuffle" eventually develops a fine road-house groove, and the extended "I Thought It Was You" cuts the original version on *Sunlight*. The excellent LP sound is superior to that of the CD—especially the rock-solid bass and drums. —*Richard S. Ginell*

Feets, Don't Fail Me Now / 1979 / Columbia ✦

Herbie Hancock's electric records up until this point were marked by intelligence and adventure, even at their most earthy. But no, this one doesn't have an ounce of either. Herbie falls hook, line and sinker for the disco fad and submerges his personality underneath the plastic vocals and the idiot four-on-the-floor disco beat. Hancock's own gauzy vocals through a Sennheiser vocoder are embarrassing, and even his synthesizer work sounds coarse and gimmicky. This time, even the purists were right; this is of no interest to jazz listeners and it isn't even good disco. —*Richard S. Ginell*

Live Under the Sky / Jul. 26, 1979 / Columbia ✦✦✦

Herbie Hancock's all-star V.S.O.P. Quintet reunited the Miles Davis group of the mid-'60s (Wayne Shorter on tenor and soprano, pianist Hancock, bassist Ron Carter and Tony Williams), with trumpeter Freddie Hubbard doing his best to fill Davis' shoes. The Japanese outdoors concert (recorded during a rainstorm) heard on this two-LP set finds the talented players in fine form on extended versions of six group originals (only Williams' "Pee Wee" dates from the Miles Davis years); a Hancock-Shorter duet medley on "Stella by Starlight" and "On Green Dolphin Street" is offered as the encore. Few surprises occur, but it is particularly rewarding to hear Wayne Shorter (after years of being in Weather Report) stretching out again. —*Scott Yanow*

Monster / 1980 / Columbia ✦✦

Despite the PR hype about this being Herbie Hancock's first "rock" album, *Monster* is really another disco album, though more varied in texture, somewhat more subtle in execution, and blessedly rid of those vocoder vocals, though not of the real ones. "Saturday Night," despite the distinctive presence of Carlos Santana, sets the album's dancefloor tone. The rock element is supposedly supplied by Hancock on the newly developed Clavitar, where, try as he might to articulate like a guitarist, the sound is still that of a mutated synthesizer. Alphonze Mouzon is wasted on drums, and guitarist Wah Wah Watson has a field day on his eponymous specialty. Most annoying (and defining) track—"Go for It." —*Richard S. Ginell*

Magic Windows / 1981 / Columbia ✦✦✦

This is an improvement over Hancock's disco-era productions since at least it is grounded in Herbie's own '70s funk outings ("Chameleon," etc.) instead of generic dance music. Technically, this is an R&B album—not disco—with funkier, more flexible rhythm sections, more intriguing electronic instrumental decorations by Hancock, and some first-class instrumental contributions by the Brothers Johnson, the Escovedo family and Michael Brecker. Herbie even gives himself solo breaks on "Magic Number" and "Satisfied with Love" that redeem both tracks and there is a spooky foretaste of techno-pop on "The Twilight Clone." True, this album is still dominated by the R&B vocals of Sylvester, Gavin Christopher and Vicki Randle but Hancock's own sonic signatures make this record listenable. —*Richard S. Ginell*

Quartet / Jul. 25, 1981 / Columbia ✦✦✦✦✦

A fine mainstream set that showed detractors Hancock hadn't lost his jazz chops. Wynton Marsalis (tpt) (then reaping a wave of prodigy/discovery headlines) is in the group. —*Ron Wynn*

Lite Me Up / 1982 / Columbia ✦✦

Mr. Hands / 1982 / Columbia ✦✦

Future Shock / 1983 / Columbia ✦✦✦

Herbie Hancock completely overhauled his sound and conquered MTV with his most radical step forward since the Sextet days. He brought in Bill Laswell of Material as producer, along with a fellow named Grand Mixer D.ST playing scratch turntables—and the immediate result was "Rockit," which makes quite a post-industrial metallic racket. Frankly, the whole record is an enigma; for all of its dehumanized, mechanized textures and rigid rhythms, it has a vitality and sense of humor that make it difficult to turn off. Moreover Herbie can't help but inject a subversive funk element when he comps along to the techno-beat—and yes, some real, honest-to-goodness jazz licks on a grand piano show up in the middle of "Auto Drive." —*Richard S. Ginell*

Sound-System / 1984 / Columbia ✦✦✦

In the grand tradition of sequels, *Sound-System* picks up from where *Future Shock* left off—if anything, even louder and more bleakly industrial than before (indeed, "Hardrock" is "Rockit" Mk II with a heavier rock edge). Yet Hancock's experiments with techno-pop were leading him in the general direction of Africa, explicitly so with the addition of the Gambian multi-instrumentalist Foday Musa Suso on half of the tracks. "Junku," written for the 1984 Olympic Games with Suso's electrified kora in the lead, is the transition track that stands halfway between "Rockit" and Hancock's mid-'80s Afro-jazz fusions. Also "Karabali" features an old cohort, the

squealing Wayne Shorter on soprano sax. Despite succumbing a bit to the overwhelming demand for more "Rockits," Hancock's electric music still retained its adventurous edge. —*Richard S. Ginell*

Village Life / 1985 / Columbia ✦✦✦✦✦

This quiet, lovely record, in which the Gambian kora virtuoso Foday Musa Suso is given equal billing, was generally ignored when it came out, probably because it fit no one's preconceived idioms—be this jazz, funk, MTV, or even world music. The only performers are Hancock on a detunable Yamaha DX-1 synthesizer and drum machine and Suso spinning his webs of delicate sound on the zither-like kora, vocalizing a bit and playing a talking drum—all in real time in a Tokyo studio. The results are absolutely mesmerizing, with Herbie aligning himself perfectly within Suso's unusual, complex rhythmic conceptions and folk-like harmonies. On the 20-minute "Kanatente," Hancock does introduce some of his own advanced harmonic ideas, and he contrasts and interweaves them with Suso's deceptively simple lines in a splendid jam session that eventually ends in a dance that can only be described as Gambian funk. This music generates the same feeling of ecstatic well-being as an Indian raga—and even hardcore jazz fans may find themselves seduced against their will. —*Richard S. Ginell*

Perfect Machine / Oct. 1988 / Columbia ✦✦✦

Set upon recapturing the pop ground he had invaded with *Future Shock*, Hancock relies upon many of the former's ingredients for yet another go-round on *Perfect Machine*. High-tech producer Bill Laswell is back, so is scratchmaster D.ST—and armed with a warehouse of mostly digital keyboards, Hancock adds the distinctive bass of Bootsy Collins and the Ohio Players' vocalist Sugarfoot, who always sounds as if he had just swallowed something. The music is mostly thumping, funk-drenched techno-pop which still has some verve, particularly the designated single "Vibe Alive" and the "Maiden Voyage" interlude as heard through an electronic fun-house mirror. But this is not really an advance over Hancock's early-'80s pop projects. This would be Hancock's last album for at least seven years as he concentrated upon film projects and reunions with Miles Davis alumni (there was also an aborted deal with the Qwest label). As such, *Perfect Machine* is an appropriate end to this chapter in his career. —*Richard S. Ginell*

Jazz Africa / Dec. 1986 / Verve ✦✦✦✦✦

Recorded in Los Angeles' Wiltern Theatre one December afternoon as part of the Jazzvisions project, this was released four years later almost as an afterthought to the series—and even many of Hancock's electric music fans weren't aware it was out. A pity, for this is one of the great unheralded Herbie Hancock recordings, a rock-'em, sock-'em, live tour de force that fuses Hancock's electric keyboard work, Foday Musa Suso's kora, incantory vocals, and scraping violin, and a thundering African/Caribbean rhythm section. The CD opens and ends quietly with the delicate, folk-like music introduced on *Village Life* but the record is dominated by two lengthy, madly swinging workouts for Hancock, Suso and the rhythm section, which is anchored by Santana's ageless Cuban-born percussionist Armando Peraza. Though not all of the concert is included here (the laserdisc and VHS versions contain more music), the CD does convey a good deal of the incredible energy level of the live event, where Hancock looked and played like a man possessed. This was a real breakthrough for Hancock, but alas, this perpetual chameleon has yet to pursue this stimulating direction further. —*Richard S. Ginell*

Dis Is Da Drum / 1993-1994 / Mercury ✦✦

New Standard / 1995 / Verve ✦✦✦✦

On first glance this record would not seem to have much promise from a jazz standpoint. Herbie Hancock performs a set of tunes which include numbers from the likes of Peter Gabriel, Stevie Wonder, Sade, Paul Simon, Prince, the Beatles ("Norwegian Wood") and Kurt Cobain. However by adding vamps, reharmonizing the chord structures, sometimes quickly discarding the melodies and utilizing an all-star band, Hancock was able to transform the potentially unrewarding music into creative jazz. Hancock, who sticks to acoustic piano, shows that he is still in prime form, taking quite a few fiery solos. With Michael Brecker on tenor and surprisingly effective soprano, guitarist John Scofield, bassist Dave Holland, drummer Jack DeJohnette and percussionist Don Alias (along with an occasional horn or string section that was dubbed in later), the results are often quite hard-swinging and certainly never predictable. Although it is doubtful that any of these songs will ever become a jazz standard, Herbie Hancock has successfully created a memorable set of "new" music. Well worth investigating. —*Scott Yanow*

Secrets / June 1976 / Columbia ✦✦✦

Having long since established his funk credentials, Hancock continues the direction of *Head Hunters* and its US successors here, welding himself to the groove on electric keyboards while Bennie Maupin again shines sardonic beams of light on a variety of reeds. In "Doin' It," the most successful track, Hancock makes a more overt bid for the dance floor, for the tune is basically one long irresistible groove with a very commercial-sounding bridge. Again Hancock chooses to recompose one of his standards; "Cantelope (sic) Island" is almost unrecognizable, converted into a sauntering, swaggering thing. A streamlining process has set in—the drumming has been simplified, some of the old high-voltage drive has been muted—yet there are still enough enjoyable, intelligently musical things happening here to hold a Hancock admirer's attention. —*Richard S .Ginell*

1+1 / 1997 / Verve ♦♦♦

Beyond category in idiom, audacious in its very idea, Herbie Hancock and Wayne Shorter perform a little over an hour of spontaneous improvised duets for grand piano and soprano sax. That's all—no synthesizers, no rhythm sections, just wistful, introspective, elevated musings between two erudite old friends that must have made the accountants at PolyGram reach for their Mylantas. Hancock's piano is long on complex harmonies of the most cerebral sort, occasionally breaking out into a few agitated passages of dissonance. His technique in great shape, Shorter responds with long-limbed melodies, darting responses to Hancock's lashings, and occasional painful outcries of emotion. The leadoff track, "Meridianne—A Wood Sylph," clearly takes off from a base of Satie to set the reflective mood for nearly the whole CD; only the final, brief "Hale-Bopp, Hip-Hop" offers a hint of comic relief. All of the tunes, save for Michiel Borstlap's "Memory of Enchantment," are Hancock or Shorter originals; some, like Hancock's "Joanna's Theme" (from the film *Death Wish*) and Shorter's "Diana," date back to the '70s. As avidly as this music was awaited and as wildly as it was acclaimed by critics, it doesn't really touch the emotions as deeply as the best of the pair's work together and apart. It stands as a graceful, high-minded anomaly in the output of both, but not something you would expect to pull off the shelf to hear too often. —*Richard S. Ginell*

Captain John Handy

b. Jun. 24, 1900, Pass Christian, MO, **d.** Jan. 12, 1971, New York, NY
Alto Saxophone / New Orleans Jazz

Capt. John Handy (no relation to the modern altoist John Handy) was unusual in the New Orleans revival movement because he played Dixieland alto influenced by R&B. A veteran who had been playing clarinet on and off in New Orleans since the 1920s (often with his group the Louisiana Shakers), Handy (who switched from clarinet to alto in 1928) was virtually unknown to the outside world until he started recording in the 1960s. During that decade he played regularly with Kid Sheik Cola's group and the Preservation Hall Jazz Band, toured Europe and recorded for several labels including GHB, RCA (two interesting records) and the Jazz Crusade label. His enthusiastic and very musical playing made him one of the top New Orleans musicians of the 1960s; "Hindustan" was a favorite feature. —*Scott Yanow*

All Aboard, Vol. 1 / Dec. 6, 1996 / GHB ♦♦♦♦

The first of three LPs featuring altoist Captain John Handy, this heated set also includes some relative youngsters (clarinetist Sammy Rimington, pianist Bill Sinclair, banjoist Dick Griffith and bassist Dick McCarthy), plus three other veterans (trumpeter Kid Thomas Valentine, trombonist Jim Robinson and drummer Sammy Penn). While there are some spirited ensembles, along with solo space for the other horns, Handy quickly emerges as the main star. His heated alto (an unusual ingredient in New Orleans jazz) is heard in top form on his trademark "Hindustan," "Who's Sorry Now," "I Can't Escape from You," "Washington and Lee Swing," and a blues. Fun music. —*Scott Yanow*

    All Aboard, Vol. 2 / Dec. 6, 1996 / GHB ♦♦♦

Capt. John Handy with Geoff Bull and Barry Martyn's Band / Apr. 12, 1966 / Beautiful Dumaine ♦♦♦

● **John Handy's Quintet** / Mar. 21, 1966 / GHB ♦♦♦♦♦

Altoist John Handy was one of the most talented of the veteran New Orleans jazzmen who were active in the 1960s. Always a bit out of place in the New Orleans jazz revival movement due to his instrument and style (which was influenced by R&B and swing), Handy could really stomp up a storm. On this freewheeling date he is well showcased in a quintet with trumpeter Cuff Billett, pianist Pat Hawes, bassist Dave Green and drummer Barry Martyn. The Dixieland and swing standards (including "Rose Room," "Indiana," "Dinah" and "Rosetta") serve as perfect vehicles for Handy's highly expressive solos. This London session is one of Captain John Handy's finest recordings and is highly recommended. —*Scott Yanow*

Introducing Cap'n John Handy / Nov. 15, 1966-Nov. 18, 1966 / RCA ♦♦♦♦♦

This was a slightly unusual but logical recording by New Orleans altoist Captain John Handy. Rather than play in the usual New Orleans jazz setting, Handy was teamed with swing all-stars (including trumpeter Doc Cheatham, trombonist Benny Morton and pianist Claude Hopkins) on slightly more "modern" material than usual (such as "Perdido," "I Would Do Anything For You" and "One O'Clock Jump"). To no one's surprise, the underrated and always heated altoist has little dif-

ficulty swinging up a storm. An LP well worth searching for, which RCA will hopefully rediscover and make available on CD. —*Scott Yanow*

New Orleans and the Blues / Mar. 19, 1968-Mar. 20, 1968 / RCA Victor ♦♦♦

Television Airshots / Mar. 23, 1968+Jun. 4, 1970 / Jazz Crusade ♦♦♦♦♦

Captain John Handy (no relation to the other altoist John Handy) was considered quite controversial in New Orleans jazz settings at one time for he had the audacity to play his R&Bish alto in a style of music where the tenor was still not accepted. This CD from the Jazz Crusade label contains the soundtracks from two television appearances dating from 1968 and 1970 that feature Handy in prime form; the films are presumably (and tragically) lost. A forceful improviser who could usually outswing the competition (his drive in the ensembles is remarkable), Handy's playing is easily the highlight of this disc. The first seven selections showcase him in a very spirited septet that includes trumpeter Punch Miller (a little past his prime) and pianist Dick Wellstood. Although Miller does get a little lost on a blues, his singing (really swinging on "Exactly like You") is a joy and he leads the ensembles well. The band really rocks on "Joe Avery's Piece" (a number that Wynton Marsalis occasionally plays), "Capt's Boogie Woogie" and "Exactly like You." The second group is weakened a bit by trumpeter Kid Sheik Cola (whose sincere but out-of-tune whinnying tone is a liability) but the rhythm section (with drummer Sammy Penn adding colorful sounds) really pushes hard in exciting fashion. This is a very enjoyable CD that is easily recommended to fans of freewheeling classic jazz. —*Scott Yanow*

Craig Handy

b. 1963, Oakland, CA
Tenor Saxophone / Post-Bop

One of the potential greats of the 1990s, Craig Handy's playing ranges from bop to advanced post-bop. Since attending North Texas State University (1981-84) he has worked with Art Blakey's Jazz Messengers, Wynton Marsalis, Roy Haynes and Abdullah Ibrahim and recorded with Elvin Jones and Betty Carter among others. Handy's two Arabesque releases from 1991 and 1993 are quite impressive. —*Scott Yanow*

Split Second Timing / Jun. 18, 1991-Jun. 19, 1991 / Arabesque ♦♦♦♦

Tenor saxophonist Craig Handy's debut as a leader is an impressive effort. The advanced hard-bop music (which also features Handy doubling on alto, pianist Ed Simon, bassist Ray Drummond, drummer Ralph Peterson and three guest appearances by trombonist Robin Eubanks) has fine arrangements by Handy, who also contributed five of the nine pieces. At this point, Craig Handy's sound was almost distinctive (blending together Dexter Gordon, John Coltrane and Sonny Rollins), and he clearly had a great future. Recommended. —*Scott Yanow*

● **Introducing Three for All & One** / Apr. 12, 1993-Apr. 13, 1993 / Arabesque ♦♦♦♦♦

The trio of Craig Handy (on tenor and soprano), bassist Charles Fambrough and drummer Ralph Peterson lives up to its potential during a wide-ranging set. The improvisations are explorative yet melodic and logical while the interplay between these talented players is consistently impressive. Together they explore tributes to Clifford Jordan and George Adams and at times hint at Coltrane, Sonny Rollins and even Grover Washington, Jr. Pianist David Kikoski is heard on four selections but his presence is actually unnecessary. Handy's unaccompanied solo on "West Bank: Beyond the Berlin Wall" is a highlight of this recommended disc. —*Scott Yanow*

John Handy

b. Feb. 3, 1933, Dallas, TX
Alto Saxophone, Tenor Saxophone / Post-Bop, Crossover Jazz

A talented and adventurous altoist whose career has gone through several phases, John Handy started playing alto in 1949. After moving to New York in 1958, he had a fiery period with Charles Mingus (1958-59) that resulted in several passionate recordings that show off his originality; he also recorded several dates as a leader for Roulette. Handy led his own bands during 1959-64 and played with Mingus at the 1964 Monterey Jazz Festival but it was at the following year's festival that he was a major hit, stretching out with his quintet (which included violinist Michael White and guitarist Jerry Hahn) on two long originals. Soon Handy was signed to Columbia where he recorded his finest work (three excellent albums) during 1966-68. Since that time he has performed world music with Ali Akbar Khan, recorded the R&B hit "Hard Work" for Impulse in 1976, gigged and recorded with Mingus Dynasty and in the late '80s led a group (called Class) featuring three female violinists who sing. John Handy (no relation to the Dixieland altoist Capt. John Handy) remains a strong soloist who can hit high notes way above his horn's normal register with ease, but he has mostly maintained a low profile, teaching in the San Francisco Bay Area. —*Scott Yanow*

In the Vernacular / Nov. 1959 / Roulette ✦✦✦✦
Altoist John Handy's debut as a leader (which was last available as part of the two-LP set of the same name) was recorded when he was still a member of Charles Mingus' group. Teamed with trumpeter Richard Williams, pianist Roland Hanna, bassist George Tucker and drummer Roy Haynes, Handy (who doubles on tenor) shows the influence of John Coltrane in spots and also the fury and heat of playing with Mingus. He performs six originals (the best known is "Dance to the Lady"), "I'll Close My Eyes," and a lyrical rendition of "I'll Never Smile Again." Excellent advanced hard-bop music well deserving of being reissued on CD. —*Scott Yanow*

No Coast Jazz / 1960 / Roulette ✦✦✦✦
The second of altoist John Handy's three Roulette albums (none of which are currently available on CD) finds Handy performing six originals with a quartet also including pianist Don Friedman, bassist Bill Lee and drummer Lex Humphries. The altoist already had a fairly original sound (his former employer Charles Mingus would certainly not let him get away with copying Charlie Parker), and although open to the influence of John Coltrane, Handy was getting quite distinctive. The inside/outside music (advanced hard bop that sometimes hints at the avant-garde) still sounds quite fresh. —*Scott Yanow*

Jazz / 1962 / Roulette ✦✦✦
Altoist John Handy's third and final Roulette set (a quartet date with pianist Walter Bishop, Jr., bassist Julian Euell and drummer Edgar Bateman) is highlighted by "From Bird," "East of the Sun" and "Strugglin'." Handy's appealing and already distinctive alto sound, combined with an exploratory style, resulted in this music having plenty of surprising moments. Unfortunately, the session is quite scarce, last available as part of a Roulette double LP that also includes an Art Blakey set. —*Scott Yanow*

★ **Live at Monterey** / Sep. 18, 1965 / Columbia ✦✦✦✦✦
John Handy's performance at the 1965 Monterey Jazz Festival was a sensation and arguably the high point of his career. The altoist, using a quintet that included violinist Michael White, guitarist Jerry Hahn, bassist Don Thompson and drummer Terry Clarke (all of whom were young unknowns at the time) played two lengthy songs: the 27-minute "If Only We Knew" and "Spanish Lady" which lasts a mere 19-minute s. After a brief theme, "If Only We Knew" mostly features unaccompanied solos. Handy's opening statement immediately quieted the crowd which was amazed by the altoist's courage and the logic of the advanced yet tonal music. "Spanish Lady" also has a long Handy statement and builds up to a very exciting conclusion. Even over three decades later, the music sounds fresh, colorful and innovative. The original Columbia LP (which has been long out-of-print) had reversed the order of the songs and even their titles so this Koch CD reissue is very welcome on several levels. Highly recommended. —*Scott Yanow*

The Second John Handy Album / July 7, 1966-Jul. 26, 1966 / Columbia ✦✦✦✦✦
After being the surprise success of the 1965 Monterey Jazz Festival, altoist John Handy recorded three brilliant albums for Columbia before largely adopting a much lower profile. His debut for Columbia is the only one that used the same group that appeared at the festival, a quintet with guitarist Jerry Hahn, violinist Michael White, bassist Don Thompson and drummer Terry Clarke. Handy's five originals use some devices from the avant-garde and also show that he was aware of what was happening in popular music in 1966. Each of the pieces has its share of surprises, and the advanced solos still sound unpredictable today. One of John Handy's most exciting recordings. —*Scott Yanow*

New View / Mar. 19, 1967-Jun. 28, 1967 / Columbia ✦✦✦✦✦
Altoist John Handy's 1967 quintet included vibraphonist Bobby Hutcherson, the up-and-coming guitarist Pat Martino, bassist Albert Stinson and drummer Doug Sides. They really stretch out on three pieces (John Coltrane's "Naima" and a pair of originals), highlighted by Handy's emotional and episodic "Tears of Ole Miss (Anatomy of a Riot)," which clocks in at 23:45. The inside/outside music is quite picturesque, emotional, and ultimately logical. It is a pity that John Handy did not make more of an impact on the mainstream of jazz, but his three Columbia studio albums (which are scarce these days) still sound fresh decades later. —*Scott Yanow*

Projections / Apr. 15, 1968 / Columbia ✦✦✦✦
The third of altoist John Handy's three superb Columbia studio albums finds him fronting a quintet comprising violinist Michael White, pianist Mike Nock, bassist Bruce Cale and drummer Larry Hancock. The talented group plays four originals by Handy, three by Nock and one from White. The music (much more concise in general than on the previous two Columbias) contains plenty of surprises and is difficult to categorize (somewhere between the avant-garde and hard bop), although it does not reach the same heights as *New View*. —*Scott Yanow*

Karuna Supreme / Nov. 1, 1975 / MPS ✦✦

Hard Work / Jan. 1976 / Impulse! ✦✦✦
Other than an MPS set that fused together jazz and Indian music with indifferent results, this album was altoist John Handy's first as a leader since 1968. "Hard

Work" became a surprise hit, and overall, the set is open to the influence of R&B, although there are some strong moments from Handy on both alto and tenor. The backup band includes Hotep Cecil Barnard on keyboards, guitarist Mike Hoffmann, and (on three of the seven numbers) Zakir Hussain on tabla. —*Scott Yanow*

Carnival / 1977 / ABC ✦✦
After the surprise success of *Hard Work*, altoist John Handy was rushed back into the studio with hopes of duplicating that album's sales. As it turned out, this record never did catch on (*Hard Work* was a fluke). Handy is mostly featured here in commercial settings, singing two songs and interacting with an electric rhythm section (which sometimes includes guitarist Lee Ritenour and, in one case, Larry Carlton). Best is a duet version of "All the Things You Are" with pianist Sonny Burke, but that lasts less than three minutes. However, this LP is superior to John Handy's next two strictly-for-the-money projects for Warner Bros. —*Scott Yanow*

Excursion in Blue / Aug. 9, 1988-Aug. 10, 1988 / Quartet ✦✦✦✦
John Handy's first recording as a leader in eight years is one of his very few conventional straightahead sessions. Assisted by either Jim McNeely or Buddy Montgomery on piano, bassist Rufus Reid and either Billy Hart or Eddie Marshall on drums, Handy (doubling on alto and tenor throughout the CD) performs four fairly straightforward originals, plus "My One and Only Love," Sonny Rollins' "Paul's Pal" and "How Deep Is the Ocean." John Handy plays so well throughout this little-known set that one wonders why he has recorded so infrequently throughout his career. Well worth picking up. —*Scott Yanow*

Centerpiece / Apr. 10, 1989-Apr. 13, 1989 / Milestone ✦✦✦
Altoist John Handy had a unique group in the late '80s that he called Class and featured three young female singing violinists. Unfortunately on their one recording, the violin playing is de-emphasized in favor of the vocalizing (making the date much less unusual than it would have been), Handy's solos are fairly brief and the repertoire (four blues and four standards), other than one original blues, have all been recorded too many times in the past. Handy had a good thing going and his Class was one of the hits of the 1989 Monterey Jazz Festival, but this disappointingly routine set does not live up to its potential. —*Scott Yanow*

Jake Hanna

b. Apr. 4, 1931, Boston, MA
Drums / Swing
A superior drummer equally at ease driving a big band or playing in small mainstream combos, Jake Hanna has been a strong asset to a countless number of sessions. He started out playing locally in Boston and worked with Toshiko Akiyoshi (1957), Maynard Ferguson (1958), as the house drummer at Storyville in Boston, with Marian McPartland (1959-61) and most significantly with the Woody Herman Orchestra (1962-64). As a studio musician, he was a regular member of the "Merv Griffin" television program's big band (1964-75), moving with the show to Los Angeles (1970) where he is still based. Hanna co-led a group with Carl Fontana that recorded for Concord in 1975, played with Supersax and has since appeared on many mainstream and swing sessions, becoming a fixture at jazz parties and festivals. He has recorded many dates (mostly as a sideman) for Concord. —*Scott Yanow*

● **Live at Concord** / Jul. 1975 / Concord Jazz ✦✦✦✦✦
The Hanna/Fontana Band was a superior all-star septet that performed at the 1975 Concord Jazz Festival. The lineup of musicians heard here is impressive (drummer Jake Hanna, trombonist Carl Fontana, trumpeter Bill Berry, tenorman Plas Johnson, pianist Dave McKenna, guitarist Herb Ellis and bassist Herb Mickman), and everyone is well featured on the seven swinging and generally swing-era standards. Fontana in particular has been heard in this type of setting too infrequently on record. Highlights include Plas' ballad feature on "Old Folks," "Take the 'A' Train" and Hanna's classic brushwork on "I Found a New Baby." Easily recommended to mainstream jazz collectors. —*Scott Yanow*

Kansas City Express / Apr. 1976 / Concord Jazz ✦✦✦✦
Drummer Jake Hanna has only led a handful of recording sessions through the years, although he has been a sideman on a countless number. This well-played, if conventional, mainstream date with trumpeter Bill Berry, tenor saxophonist Richie Kamuca, pianist Nat Pierce and bassist Monty Budwig is most notable for having four rare late-period vocals by the still viable Mary Ann McCall. Among the high points of the instrumentals are "Robbins' Nest," "It's Sand Man" and "Castle Rock." —*Scott Yanow*

Jake Takes Manhattan / Dec. 14, 1976-Dec. 15, 1976 / Concord Jazz ✦✦✦
Drummer Jake Hanna's third and final set as a leader for Concord is a worthwhile, if not overly memorable, quintet set also featuring trumpeter Danny Stiles, Carmen Leggio on alto and tenor, pianist John Bunch and bassist Michael Moore. The nine swing standards include a typically heated "Northwest Passage," "Lester Leaps

In," "Sultry Serenade" and "Them There Eyes." Overall, the music swings quietly and is relaxed even when played at faster tempos. —*Scott Yanow*

Sir Roland Hanna

b. Feb. 10, 1932, Detroit, MI
Piano / Hard Bop, Swing

A talented pianist with a style diverse enough to fit into swing, bop and more adventurous settings, Roland Hanna was one of the last in an impressive line of great pianists who emerged in Detroit after World War II (including Hank Jones, Barry Harris and Tommy Flanagan). After serving in the Army and studying music at Eastman and Juilliard, Hanna made a strong impression playing with Benny Goodman (1958). He worked with Charles Mingus for a period in 1959 and since then has generally led his own trios. Hanna was an integral part of the Thad Jones/Mel Lewis Orchestra (1967-74) and in 1974 helped found the New York Jazz Quartet (with Frank Wess). He was given knighthood (thus the "Sir") from the President of Liberia in 1970. Sir Roland Hanna has led sessions for many labels including Atco (1959), MPS, Choice, Freedom, Inner City and Music Masters. —*Scott Yanow*

Sir Elf / Apr. 1973-May 1973 / Choice ✦✦✦✦✦
Pianist Roland Hanna's first solo album is one of his finest recordings. Whether it be a tribute to Art Tatum on "You Took Advantage of Me," a nod to Erroll Garner on "There Is No Greater Love," a humorous "Bye Bye Blackbird" or his original "Morning," Hanna is in top form on this well-paced and inventive set. —*Scott Yanow*

● **Perugia** / Jul. 2, 1974 / Freedom ✦✦✦✦✦
Excellent piano solos—some of Hanna's sharpest. —*Ron Wynn*

Sir Elf Plus 1 / Aug. 1974+Jul. 1977 / Choice ✦✦✦✦
While *Sir Elf* from 1973 was a set of unaccompanied piano solos by Roland Hanna, his encore for Choice from four years later sometimes adds bassist George Mraz for a few duets. The solo "Yesterdays" was a leftover (but worthwhile) track from 1974; otherwise, the music is from 1977. Hanna (and occasionally Mraz) is heard on a pair of originals, "Majorca" (based on a Chopin melody), and three standards including "My Shining Hour" and "My Heart Stood Still." Superior modern mainstream music. —*Scott Yanow*

Time for the Dancers / Feb. 17, 1977 / Progressive ✦✦✦
For this trio set with bassist George Mraz and drummer Richard Pratt, the talented pianist Roland Hanna introduces four of his originals, plays Mraz's "Jed," and jams the Charlie Parker blues "Cheryl." The interplay between the players, the wide variety of moods covered, and the general swinging feel of the music makes this a recommended set. —*Scott Yanow*

Glove / Oct. 15, 1977 / Storyville ✦✦✦
Pianist Sir Roland Hanna tears through this live trio studio session, recorded in Japan, without seeming to work up a sweat. He covers six standards on this CD that have "love" in their titles. The opener, "Love for Sale," includes a slow but beautiful, almost Oriental, chimelike introduction that rapidly gives way to an uptempo arrangement. Bassist George Mraz has worked with Hanna regularly and provides solid support and several top-notch solos. The choice of drummer is a mystery, Motohiko Hino, whose enthusiastic but often heavy-handed drumming makes it sound as if he were in competition with the pianist instead of supporting him. —*Ken Dryden*

This Must Be Love / 1978 / Audiophile ✦✦✦
Originally recorded for Progressive and reissued by the Audiophile label, this set matches the talented pianist Sir Roland Hanna with bassist George Mraz and drummer Ben Riley. Together they perform six Rodgers and Hart songs (including "This Can't Be Love," "Thou Swell" and "Dancing on the Ceiling"), along with three of Hanna's originals. The musicians are heard throughout in top form, often speaking in a single voice. Excellent modern mainstream music. —*Scott Yanow*

Bird Tracks / Feb. 22, 1978-Mar. 1, 1978 / Progressive ✦✦✦
Tingling versions of songs by and about Charlie Parker. —*Ron Wynn*

Play for Monk / Apr. 10, 1978+Apr. 12, 1978 / Musical Heritage Society ✦✦✦✦
Roland Hanna, like Thelonious Monk, was influenced by Duke Ellington, although his sound has always been quite a bit different than Monk's. For this CD reissue (recorded four years before Thelonious' death during a period when his music was somewhat neglected), Hanna and bassist George Mraz perform duet versions of ten Monk tunes. Although they interpret some of Thelonious' better-known songs, they thankfully skip over "'Round Midnight" (which would be played to death a decade later) and do credible jobs on "Bye Ya" and "Jackie-ing," in addition to the more familiar "Rhythm-A-Ning," "In Walked Bud" and "Ruby My Dear." This heartfelt CD is well worth picking up. —*Scott Yanow*

Impressions / Jul. 17, 1978-July 19, 1978 / Black & Blue ✦✦✦✦

Swing Me No Waltzes / May 2, 1979 / Storyville ✦✦✦✦
This Storyville set stands a bit apart from most of Sir Roland Hanna's other recordings because it features him on a recital of unaccompanied solos, performing (with the exception of Duke Ellington's "Everything But You") all of his own compositions. An underrated composer whose works deserve to be covered by others (but thus far have not been), Hanna shows off his roots in swing and blues while also stretching himself through some more adventurous moments. Very much a complete pianist, Roland Hanna puts on a particularly strong performance. —*Scott Yanow*

Piano Soliloquy / Jun. 25, 1979-Jun. 26, 1979 / L & R Music ✦✦✦

Roland Hanna Plays the Music of Alec Wilder / 1978 / Inner City ✦✦✦
Alec Wilder wrote many intriguing melodies, of which "It's So Peaceful in the Country" and "I'll Be Around" are easily the best known. Roland Hanna performs 11 of Wilder's songs (including those two) in unaccompanied solos and backs singer/producer Helen Merrill on "Sounds Around the House." Wilder's tunes tended to be a bit quirky (either in the melodies or the chord structures), but Hanna easily brings out the beauty in each piece. This LP has unfortunately been out of print for some time. —*Scott Yanow*

Romanesque / Jan. 13, 1982 / Black Hawk ✦✦✦
Originally made for the Japanese Trio label and released domestically by Black Hawk, this was at least the sixth duet album that pianist Roland Hanna made with bassist George Mraz. Hanna takes seven classical melodies (including "Humoresque," "Reverie," "Swan Lake" and "Yours Is My Heart Alone") and transforms them into swinging and lyrical jazz, respecting the melodies but also coming up with fresh variations. Fine music. —*Scott Yanow*

Gershwin Carmichael Cats / June 19, 1982-July 1982 / CTI ✦✦✦
Pianist Roland Hanna interprets three famous Hoagy Carmichael tunes, two by Gershwin, and (unfortunately) the "Theme from Cats." Each tune on this LP is played with a different instrumentation, ranging from Hanna's duet with bassist Mike Richmond on "Embraceable You" to a trio, quartet, quintet, sextet and (for a poppish rendition of "Cats") ten-piece unit. Best is "Skylark," which has fine spots for trumpeter Chet Baker and guitarist Larry Coryell. —*Scott Yanow*

Round Midnight / Mar. 1987 / Town Crier ✦✦✦✦
Sir Roland Hanna's solo piano CD was recorded in an empty concert hall, which helps to add to the classical ambience of the performance. His quiet, lovely "Prelude," which opens the CD, was originally written for solo cello. "Let Me Try" sounds as if it might have influenced pianist Makoto Ozone. "Blues" gives Hanna an opportunity to let his hair down and display some two-fisted chops. His covers of Sonny Rollins' "Oreo" and the title track are also flawless. —*Ken Dryden*

Duke Ellington Piano Solos / Mar. 22, 1991-Mar. 23, 1991 / Music Masters ✦✦✦✦✦
Includes some exquisite solo work—a moving tribute to Duke Ellington. —*Ron Wynn*

Live at Maybeck Recital Hall, Vol. 32 / Aug. 15, 1993 / Concord Jazz ✦✦✦✦✦
Elegance and artistry are the two qualities that best define both Sir Roland Hanna's piano style and this superb CD, the 32nd in Concord's continuing Maybeck solo series. Hanna devotes half the eight selections to Gershwin compositions, and his interpretations of "Love Walked In," "The Man I Love," "How Long Has This Been Going On" and others are sublime, marvelously crafted and magnificent in their ideas and execution. Seldom will you hear a solo date less self-indulgent and more satisfying. —*Ron Wynn*

Susie Hansen

Violin, Leader / Latin Jazz
One of the few violinists who specialize in playing Latin-jazz, the talented Susie Hansen works frequently with both her jazz and salsa bands in the Los Angeles area. Her father James Hansen was with the Chicago Symphony for 37 years and was her first teacher. Susie studied jazz in Boston with Charlie Banacos, sat in often with Cedar Walton in Chicago and moved to L.A. in 1988. She has led her own bands since 1989, debuting on the Jazz Caliente label in 1993 with *Solo Flight*. —*Scott Yanow*

Annette Hanshaw

b. Oct. 18, 1910, New York, NY, d. Mar. 13, 1985, New York, NY
Vocals / Classic Jazz
One of the first great female jazz singers, in the late '20s Annette Hanshaw ranked near the top with Ethel Waters, the Boswell Sisters and the up-and-coming Mildred Bailey. Unlike her contemporary Ruth Etting, Hanshaw could improvise and swing while also being a strong interpreter of lyrics. She was not quite 16 when she started her recording career and her recordings (1926-34) included such major jazz players as Red Nichols, Miff Mole, Jimmy Lytell, Adrian Rollini, Joe

Venuti, Eddie Lang, Vic Berton, Benny Goodman, Manny Klein, Phil Napoleon, Jimmy Dorsey, Tommy Dorsey and Jack Teagarden. Billed as "The Personality Girl," Annette Hanshaw (whose trademark was saying "That's all" at the end of her record) soon got tired of show business and retired in 1934. She lived outside of music for the rest of her life but fortunately most of her records were reissued on British LPs in the 1970s and '80s. —*Scott Yanow*

The Early Years, Vol. 1 / Sep. 12, 1926-Nov. 1926 / Fountain ◆◆◆◆
Annette Hanshaw was one of the finest singers of the late '20s/early '30s before she retired prematurely. This perfectly put-together LP (the first of three from the British Fountain label) has Hanshaw's first 15 recordings, including four songs cut when she was a month shy of turning 16. Accompanied on various tracks by cornetist Red Nichols, trombonist Miff Mole, clarinetist Jimmy Lytell and pianist Irving Brodsky, Hanshaw also backs herself on two songs on piano. Although quite young, she sounds surprisingly mature on such numbers as "Black Bottom," "My Baby Knows How" and "One Sweet Letter from You," proving to be one of the few singers from this era who could swing. —*Scott Yanow*

The Early Years, Vol. 2 / Sep. 12, 1926-Apr. 1927 / Fountain ◆◆◆◆
On the second of three Annette Hanshaw Fountain LPs (all of which deserve to be fully reissued on CD), the 16-year-old singer (who during this era ended each song with a "That's all!") sounds consistently delightful. On most selections, she is accompanied by pianist Irving Brodsky. Clarinetist Jimmy Lytell helps out on two songs, and three tunes also include the Original Memphis Five. Other than "That's Why I Love You" from September 1926 (a copy of which was not discovered until Vol. 1 had already come out), all of the music is from January-April 1927. Highlights include "He's the Last Word," "I'm Gonna Meet My Sweetie Now," "It All Depends on You" and "Rosy Cheeks." —*Scott Yanow*

★ Lovable & Sweet: 25 Vintage Hits / Sep. 12, 1926-Feb. 3, 1934 / ASV/Living Era ◆◆◆◆◆
Annette Hanshaw was one of the finest jazz singers of the late '20s. All of her recordings deserve to be reissued complete and in chronological order. But in lieu of that, this single CD is an excellent introduction to Hanshaw's talents. Covering virtually her entire career, from when she was still 15 up until just two years before her premature retirement, the disc features Hanshaw in a variety of settings. She accompanies herself on piano on "Falling in Love with You" and is backed by such jazz all-stars as cornetist Red Nichols, trombonist Miff Mole, clarinetist Jimmy Lytell, Tommy Dorsey (on trumpet), clarinetist Benny Goodman, Jimmy Dorsey on clarinet and alto, the orchestras of Will Osborne and Victor Young, and even Frank Ferera's Hawaiian Trio. Highlights of the fine sampler include "Black Bottom," "Big City Blues," "Little White Lies," "Walkin' My Baby Back Home" and "Let's Fall in Love," but these 25 numbers are only the tip of the iceberg. —*Scott Yanow*

The Early Years, Vol. 3 / Jun. 1927-Dec. 1927 / Fountain ◆◆◆◆
The third of three LPs from the British Fountain label continued the documentation of singer Annette Hanshaw's earliest recordings; it is a pity that the series did not continue through the remainder of her career. One of the finest jazz singers of the period (despite only being a teenager), Hanshaw is heard interacting with such sidemen as violinist Joe Venuti, bass saxophonist Adrian Rollini, guitarist Eddie Lang and various studio musicians. Among the more memorable selections are "I'm Somebody's Somebody Now," "Annabelle Lee," and "The Song Is Ended." Highly recommended to 1920s collectors. —*Scott Yanow*

Lovable & Sweet / Sep. 13, 1928-Oct. 31, 1929 / World ◆◆◆◆◆
The first of two generous (20-selection) British LPs that feature singer Annette Hanshaw at the peak of her powers, this release would be essential if it were in print. Hanshaw ranked with Ethel Waters and Connie Boswell as the finest female jazz singers of the time, even though she is continually overlooked today. Backed by a variety of top jazz players (including pianist James P. Johnson, clarinetist Benny Goodman, violinist Joe Venuti, the Dorsey Brothers, and trumpeter Phil Napoleon), the singer performs definitive versions of such songs as "My Blackbirds Are Bluebirds Now," "You're the Cream In My Coffee," "A Precious Little Thing Called Love," "Mean to Me," "I Get the Blues When It Rains" and "Daddy, Won't You Please Come Home." Unlike most other singers of the era, Annette Hanshaw's vocals are as listenable and undated as those of her illustrious sidemen. —*Scott Yanow*

She's Got It / Dec. 13, 1929-Feb. 20, 1931 / World ◆◆◆◆◆
The second of two essential (but difficult-to-find) 20-song, hour-long Annette Hanshaw LPs released by the British World label, this album should excite 1920s collectors. Hanshaw was one of the top jazz singers of the era, as she shows on such numbers as "Cooking Breakfast for the One I Love," "I've Got It," "My Future Just Passed," "Little White Lies," "Body and Soul," and "You're the One I Care For." Among the supporting cast (most of whom get concise solos) are Benny Goodman, Tommy and Jimmy Dorsey, cornetist Muggsy Spanier, and bass saxophonist Adrian Rollini. Highly recommended to fans of the era. —*Scott Yanow*

The Personality Girl 1932-1934 / Aug. 16, 1932-Feb. 3, 1934 / Sunbeam ◆◆◆◆◆
With an exception of an obscure medley from 1936, this LP has Annette Hanshaw's final 16 recordings before she decided to retire; she was only 24 in 1934 when she started to drop out of music. The Sunbeam album lets listeners know how much was lost to jazz when Hanshaw stopped recording, for she ranked with the top female jazz singers of the era, including the Boswell Sisters, Ethel Waters, and Mildred Bailey. Assisted by studio musicians including Jimmy Dorsey, Benny Goodman, Joe Venuti, Eddie Lang and Jack Teagarden, she sings such tunes as "We Just Couldn't Say Goodbye," "Say It Isn't So," "I Cover the Waterfront," "It's the Talk of the Town" and even "This Little Piggy Went to Market" with maturity, wit and swing. —*Scott Yanow*

Fareed Haque

b. 1963, Chicago, IL
Guitar / Post-Bop
Fareed Haque is a flexible guitarist whose own records show off his roots in classical music along with his interest in several styles of jazz. Raised in Chicago, Haque traveled extensively as a youth with his parents who were from Pakistan and Chile; the influence of different countries' folk musics can be heard in his playing. He studied jazz at North Texas State University and classical music at Northwestern University in Chicago. Haque made two records with Paquito D'Rivera and played with Tito Puente, Toots Thielemans and Von Freeman among others. He made his debut as a leader for Sting's short-lived Pangaea label (1988) and has since recorded two sets for Blue Note, toured with Joe Zawinul and performed with Straight Ahead, Joey Calderazzo, Renee Rosnes and Dianne Reeves among others. —*Scott Yanow*

Voices Rising / 1988 / Pangaea ◆◆◆◆
● Manresa / 1989 / IRS ◆◆◆
Guitarist Fareed Haque's second CD as a leader (for the short-lived Pangaea label) puts his classical-sounding acoustic guitar in poppish and funky settings, along with some more lyrical and straightahead sections. Other than "Ain't No Sunshine," all of the music was written by Haque and/or his sidemen, who include electric guitarist John Adair and keyboardist Jim Simon. Well-played but not overly memorable post-bop music that is open to other influences. —*Scott Yanow*

Sacred Addiction / Jun. 21, 1993-Jun. 26, 1993 / Blue Note ◆◆◆
Fareed Haque is a talented classical guitarist heard on this set delving into some poppish numbers, light funk, a little bit of Indian-influenced music and a strong version of Chick Corea's "No Mystery." Not every performance works equally well and there are some premature fadeouts. However Haque's pretty but authoritative sound carries the day and makes this set worthwhile. —*Scott Yanow*

Opaque / Feb. 9, 1995-Feb. 17, 1995 / Blue Note ◆◆◆
Deja Vu / 1997 / Blue Note ◆◆◆◆
Blue Note's 1997 Cover Series had several jazz artists performing "re-creations" (really transformations) of classic pop albums. Acoustic guitarist Fareed Haque tackled the Crosby, Stills, Nash & Young set *Deja Vu*, performing all dozen selections, as well as brief intro and reprise versions of "Teach Your Children," in an instrumental and jazz-oriented setting. Haque, who was greatly assisted by fellow guitarist David Onderdonk (who shared with him the arranging duties) is heard on such numbers as "Teach Your Children," "Woodstock" and "Our House." Some of the renditions sound purposely dated, particularly in their use of sitar and Fender Rhodes, while others are fresher, stretching the pop tunes into funky vamps. This CD is mostly recommended to open-minded listeners who are very familiar with the original versions. —*Scott Yanow*

Paul Hardcastle

b. Dec. 10, 1957, London, England
Keyboards / Dance-Pop, New Wave, Crossover Jazz, Electronic, Contemporary Jazz
Hardcastle is a producer and keyboardist from London. He recorded solo in the mid-'80s, with his "19," a track featuring news reports and other sources on Vietnam, becoming a major hit in Britain. Later, he produced and did remixes for artists such as Ian Dury and Phil Lynott. He sells well in the specialty dance market and occasionally releases records as part of the duo Kiss The Sky (with Jaki Graham), as well as names like the Def Boys, Beeps International, and Jazzmasters. Among his releases: 1985's *Zero One*, 1994's *Jazzmasters II* and 1996's *Hardcastle 2.* —*Steve Huey*

● The Very Best / 1981-1989 / EMI ◆◆◆◆◆
The Very Best is a 14-track collection of Paul Hardcastle's sample-intensive dance music from the '80s. Not only are his two big hits, "19" and "The Wizard," included, but so are 12 other cuts, most of which will be unfamiliar to anyone but dedicated fans; however, this remains the best way for casual fans to get Hardcastle's biggest singles. —*Stephen Thomas Erlewine*

Paul Hardcastle / 1985 / Chrysalis ◆◆◆◆◆

An accomplished songwriter, producer, and keyboard player, Hardcastle enjoyed some mild success on the R&B and dance charts with this self-titled release. He landed two hits on the R&B charts and cut his definitive track, "19," which even got him some pop attention and was his finest track as a performer and composer. —*Ron Wynn*

The Jazzmasters II / 1994 / JVC ◆◆

Essentially background dance music with cooing vocals, quiet and predictable electronic rhythms and some derivative sax solos, the performances on this CD are pleasant but instantly forgettable. Paul Hardcastle plays keyboards, guitar, bass and percussion and is assisted by singer Helen Rogers and the reeds of Phil Todd and Chris Snake Davis. From the jazz standpoint this recording is very weak but it made the so-called "contemporary jazz" charts and has been a big seller. —*Scott Yanow*

● **Hardcastle 2** / 1996 / JVC ◆◆◆

In the early '90s, Paul Hardcastle moved away from the synth-pop and dance material that made him semi-famous during the '80s, choosing to pursue a jazz-fusion direction with his 1994 album, *Hardcastle.* The sequel, *Hardcastle 2,* is very similar in terms of style and content to its predecessor. Keeping vaguely club-oriented dance rhythms as the basis of his music, Hardcastle plays jazzy keyboard and guitar lines that alternate between the jazzy experimentation and jazzy, neo-psychedelic rock fusion (see his cover of Pink Floyd's "Money" for an example). And "jazzy" is the right term—he's approximating the sound of jazz, without delving into the blood and guts that makes the music vital. Consequently, this is music that will please fusion freaks and dance club fanatics, but leave purists feeling cold. At the very least, purists can be (somewhat) heartened by the fact that *Hardcastle 2* boasts the most substantive playing, if not material, that Hardcastle has yet demonstrated on record, and suggests that he could play real jazz if only he chose to. —*Stephen Thomas Erlewine*

John Hardee

b. Dec. 20, 1918, Corsicana, TX, **d.** May 18, 1984, Dallas, TX
Tenor Saxophone / Bop, Swing
John Hardee's time in jazz's major leagues was brief but memorable. The thick-toned tenor (influenced by Coleman Hawkins and Chu Berry) toured with Don Albert (1937-38) and graduated from college in 1941. After a period as a band director at a Texas school and a stint in the Army, Hardee played with Tiny Grimes in 1946 and recorded 18 titles as a leader (1946-48) including eight for Blue Note that were reissued in a Mosaic set; other songs have been released by Savoy and Spotlite. Hardee also had recording dates with Russell Procope, Earl Bostic, Billy Kyle, Helen Humes, Billy Taylor and Lucky Millinder. But in the early '50s he returned to Dallas where he worked in the school system, just playing locally and rarely emerging during his last 30 years. —*Scott Yanow*

Wilbur Harden

b. 1925, Birmingham, AL
Trumpet, Fluegelhorn / Hard Bop
Wilbur Harden is a mystery man in jazz history for he appeared on some important recording sessions (most notably with John Coltrane) and then after 1960 fairly well disappeared. He played R&B with Roy Brown (1950) and Ivory Joe Hunter and then served in the Navy. Harden emerged in 1957 recording with Yusef Lateef and led four record dates for Savoy in 1958; three were with Coltrane (who became the leader on reissues) and one in a quartet with Tommy Flanagan. In 1960 Wilbur Harden (who was one of the first trumpeters to double regularly on fluegelhorn) recorded one title with Curtis Fuller but then ill health forced him to retire at the age of 35. —*Scott Yanow*

Mainstream 1958 / Mar. 13, 1958 / Savoy ◆◆◆◆

● **Tanganyika Suite** / May 13, 1958+Jun. 29, 1958 / Savoy ◆◆◆◆◆

Jazz Way Out / Jun. 24, 1958 / Savoy ◆◆◆◆

The King and I / Sep. 23, 1958-Sep. 30, 1958 / Savoy ◆◆◆◆◆

Bill Hardman

b. Apr. 6, 1933, Cleveland, OH, **d.** Dec. 5, 1990, Paris, France
Trumpet, Fluegelhorn / Hard Bop
A reliable hard bop-oriented trumpeter, Bill Hardman never became famous but he helped out on many sessions. While a teenager Hardman gigged with Tadd Dameron and after graduating high school he was with Tiny Bradshaw (1953-55). He debuted on record with Jackie McLean (1955), played with Charles Mingus (1956) and gained recognition for his work with Art Blakey's Jazz Messengers (1956-58). Hardman worked with Horace Silver (1958), Lou Donaldson (on and off during 1959-66), rejoined Blakey twice (1966-69 and in the late '70s), was with

Mingus again (during parts of 1969-72) and led a group with Junior Cook (1979-81). Bill Hardman had an appealing style in the Clifford Brown tradition and recorded as a leader for Savoy (1961) and Muse. —*Scott Yanow*

What's Up / July 7, 1939 / Steeple Chase ◆◆◆◆

Saying Something / Oct. 18, 1961 / Savoy ◆◆◆

Trumpeter Bill Hardman's debut album as a leader was his only chance to lead a record date until 1978. Teamed up with altoist Sonny Redd, pianist Ronnie Matthews, either Doug Watkins or Bob Cunningham on bass, and drummer Jimmy Cobb, Hardman performs originals and obscurities, with "Angel Eyes" being the only standard. The music overall is solid hard bop, very much of the period but still fairly fresh. This music was last available on a 1986 reissue Savoy LP. —*Scott Yanow*

Home / Jan. 10, 1978 / Muse ◆◆◆◆

Bill Hardman had long been a talented—if not overly original—bop trumpet soloist. Best known for his four stints with Art Blakey's Jazz Messengers, Hardman is in excellent form on a pair of Brazilian pieces, two originals by pianist Mickey Tucker and Tadd Dameron's lesser-known "I Remember Love." There are also fine solos throughout this date by Tucker, tenor saxophonist Junior Cook and trombonist Slide Hampton. —*Scott Yanow*

Focus / Apr. 17, 1980 / Muse ◆◆◆◆

Always a bit underrated and overshadowed, trumpeter Bill Hardman was a solid soloist in the tradition of Clifford Brown. He led three Muse albums during 1978-81, of which this was the second. Matched as usual with his fellow hard-bop stylist, tenor saxophonist Junior Cook, along with trombonist Slide Hampton, pianist Walter Bishop, Jr., bassist Leroy Williams and drummer Stafford James, Hardman is heard in top form on such numbers as Hank Mobley's "Avila & Tequila," Tadd Dameron's "Focus" and "Minority." —*Scott Yanow*

● **Politely** / Jul. 7, 1981 / Muse ◆◆◆◆◆

This quintet date (with trumpeter Bill Hardman, tenor saxophonist Junior Cook, pianist Walter Bishop, Jr., bassist Paul Brown and drummer Leroy Williams) is very much in the bop vein. Despite its title (the name of a Hardman minor blues), much of the session is actually hard-driving. John Coltrane's "Lazy Bird" and Hardman's ballad feature on "Smooch" are highlights of this excellent album. —*Scott Yanow*

Otto Hardwicke

b. May 31, 1904, Washington D.C. **d.** Sep. 5, 1970, Washington D.C.
Alto Saxophone / Swing, Classic Jazz, Big Band
Otto Hardwicke had a sweet tone on alto and a fluid style. Hardwicke grew up with Duke Ellington and was originally a bassist until Duke talked him into switching to C-melody sax in 1920. He was an original member of the Washingtonians and was with Ellington until 1928 when he traveled to Paris, working with Noble Sissle. He had his own band by 1930 but two years later rejoined Ellington. Hardwicke, who took a famous solo on the original version of "Sophisticated Lady" (a standard he co-wrote) was an important player (on alto and occasional baritone and bass saxes) with Ellington prior to 1928 but during 1932-46 he was rarely heard from except in section work; Johnny Hodges got virtually all of the alto solos. Personal differences in 1946 resulted in him leaving the band and, after recording two songs as a leader the following year, Otto Hardwicke retired from music. —*Scott Yanow*

Roy Hargrove

b. Oct. 16, 1969, Waco, TX
Trumpet, Leader / Hard Bop
Roy Hargrove is a hard-bop-oriented young lion who has a great deal of potential. A fine straightahead player who does not sound overly influenced by any of his predecessors, Hargrove's fiery solos resulted in him winning the *Downbeat* Readers' Poll in 1995. He met Wynton Marsalis in 1987 when the trumpeter visited his high school and impressed Marsalis, who let him sit in with his band. With the help of Wynton, Hargrove was soon playing with major players including Bobby Watson, Ricky Ford, Carl Allen and in the group Superblue. Hargrove attended Berklee (1988-89) and in 1990 released his first of four recordings for Novus; he was 20 at the time. He has been touring ever since with his own group which for several years included Antonio Hart. In addition to Novus, Hargrove has recorded for Verve and as a sideman with quite a few notables including Sonny Rollins, James Clay, Frank Morgan and Jackie McLean plus the group Jazz Futures. —*Scott Yanow*

Diamond in the Rough / Dec. 1989 / Novus ◆◆◆◆

Trumpeter Roy Hargrove's debut as a leader found him occasionally recalling Freddie Hubbard but already sounding fairly original in the hard-bop genre. On a quartet version of "Easy to Remember," Hargrove shows restraint and maturity in his lyrical ballad statement while featuring his strong bop chops on most of the other selections. Among the many other up-and-coming voices heard on this 1989 set are pianist Geoffrey Keezer (who contributes three originals and shows what he had picked up from McCoy Tyner), the fluid altoist Antonio Hart and drummer Ralph Peterson, Jr. Tenor saxophonist Ralph Moore, pianist John Hicks and drummer Al Foster are also in the notable supporting cast. The one fault to the CD is that the performances and solos are often a little too brief, with all but "Whisper Not" in the 4-6 minute range. But for a debut, Roy Hargrove can still be proud of *Diamond in the Rough.* —*Scott Yanow*

Public Eye / Oct. 1990 / Novus ✦✦✦

Tokyo Sessions / Dec. 4, 1991-Dec. 5, 1991 / Novus ✦✦✦✦

Trumpeter Roy Hargrove and alto saxophonist Antonio Hart, two of the finest contemporary hard boppers, made a potent team on this CD featuring sessions recorded in Tokyo during 1991. Hargrove's fierce trumpet solos and Hart's bluesy, equally energetic and accomplished answering alto statements fueled nine excellent reworkings of standards and jazz repertory. The quintet performed such established material as Oscar Pettiford's "Bohemia After Dark," Thelonious Monk's "Straight, No Chaser," and Kenny Dorham's "Lotus Blossom," as well as Cole Porter's "Easy to Love," with confidence and in a smooth yet expressive style. It would still be nice to hear Hart and Hargrove doing their own material rather than simply putting their spin on shopworn, though wonderful, anthems. —*Ron Wynn*

The Vibe / 1992 / Novus ✦✦✦✦

The last of trumpeter Roy Hargrove's recordings to feature his longtime altoist Antonio Hart also includes pianist Marc Cary, bassist Rodney Whitaker, drummer Gregory Hutchinson and guest spots for the tenors of Branford Marsalis and David "Fathead" Newman, plus trombonist Frank Lacy and organist Jack McDuff. Hargrove (still just 22) was already on his way to being one of the better hard-bop-based trumpeters in jazz, as he shows on group originals, James Williams' "Alter Ego," Wayne Shorter's "Pinocchio," "Milestones," and "The Things We Did Last Summer." A fine example of Hargrove's rapidly emerging style. —*Scott Yanow*

Beauty & The Beast / Nov. 20, 1992-Nov. 21, 1992 / Novus ✦✦✦✦✦

Trumpeter Roy Hargrove, altoist Antonio Hart and a supportive Japanese rhythm section play Walt Disney on this surprisingly successful set. The ten songs are taken from eight Disney movies, and some are more familiar than others. After a weak start with a rather straight ballad reading of "Beauty and the Beast," "The Bare Necessities" is a delight with its joyful parade rhythms. "Chim Chim Cheree" is given a Coltrane treatment, although it is more straightahead than Trane's 1965 recording, before the appealing chord changes and perky melody of "He's a Tramp," and some heated moments in "The Siamese Cat Song" provide some of the session's high points. Although "When You Wish upon a Star" (a ballad feature for Hargrove) offers no real surprises, "Someday My Prince Will Come" is taken uptempo, while "Kiss the Girl" from *The Little Mermaid* is taken as a medium-tempo blues, "Under the Sea" has a calypso feel, and the closing "Ev'rybody Wants to Be a Cat" could have come from the repertoire of Art Blakey's Jazz Messengers. Throughout this date, Hargrove and Hart are in top form, generally inspired by the fresh material and balancing fire with lyricism. —*Scott Yanow*

Of Kindred Souls / May 1993 / Novus ✦✦✦✦✦

Of all the "Young Lions" to emerge in jazz after the rise of Wynton Marsalis, trumpeter Roy Hargrove is among the most impressive, filling in the major gap left by the early departure of Lee Morgan. On his fifth session as a leader, Hargrove is heard live with his quintet (which also features pianist Marc Cary and Ron Blake on tenor and soprano) with cameo appearances on a selection apiece by altoist Gary Bartz and trombonist Andre Hayward. Hargrove is in excellent form on a set of group originals, a brief ballad medley and the standard "My Shining Hour." All of the trumpeter's releases thus far are worth picking up. —*Scott Yanow*

● **With the Tenors of Our Time** / Dec. 8, 1993-Jan. 17, 1994 / Verve ✦✦✦✦✦

Trumpeter Roy Hargrove has the opportunity of a lifetime on this recording, sharing separate songs with five great tenors: Johnny Griffin, Joe Henderson, Branford Marsalis, Joshua Redman and Stanley Turrentine. Everyone fares well, including Hargrove's group (Ron Blake on tenor and soprano, pianist Cyrus Chestnut, bassist Rodney Whitaker and drummer Gregory Hutchinson). The young trumpeter (who is vying for Lee Morgan's unoccupied chair) keeps up with the saxophonists on this generally relaxed affair; recommended for hard-bop fans. —*Scott Yanow*

Family / Jan. 26, 1995-Jan. 29, 1995 / Verve ✦✦✦✦

Parker's Mood / Apr. 12, 1995-Apr. 14, 1995 / Verve ✦✦✦✦

Sixteen songs associated with (and in 12 cases composed by) Charlie Parker are jammed by a drumless trio consisting of trumpeter Roy Hargrove, pianist Stephen Scott and bassist Christian McBride. To add variety to the set, there are three duets (using all of the possible combinations) and one unaccompanied solo apiece including a Hargrove workout on "Dewey Square." Other highlights include "Klactoveesedstene," "Laura," "Yardbird Suite," McBride's spot on "Red Cross," "Cardboard," and "Star Eyes," but all 16 performances are enjoyable. —*Scott Yanow*

Habana / Jan. 5, 1997+Jan. 6, 1997 / Verve ✦✦✦✦

At last, this highly touted, heretofore conservative young lion makes his move beyond neo-bop toward something new, fresh and potentially important. He had to go to Havana to find it, starting with some jam sessions with Cuba's Los Van Van dance band in February 1996, which led to the formation of an exciting ten-piece US/Cuban band called Crisol. True, this album is a somewhat subdued recorded debut; as heard at the Playboy Jazz Festival in June 1997, Crisol is obviously capable of real thermal combustion. But one can still hear the embryo of its complex fusion of Afro-Cuban rhythm, bop and progressive jazz impulses on this disc. Hargrove himself still seems dazzled by his new discovery, groping a bit for direction in his own solos. But challenged by the asymmetrical rhythms, he takes more chances and jaggedly strikes some fire. Irakere's Chucho Valdes, an awesome pianist and progressive-minded musician, is one of the anchors of the band, and Russell Malone contributes some of his meatiest, most driven guitar work. The tune that remains most indelibly in the memory is trombonist Frank Lacy's "O My Seh Yeh," which opens and closes the CD in neat, bookended fashion. But the most promising track is a smoking arrangement of Kenny Dorham's "Afrodisia," where the heat of this crosscultural exchange rises well above room temperature. One can only hope that US and Cuban politicos will forego their usual roadblocks and allow these meetings to continue. —*Richard S. Ginell*

Rufus Harley

b. May 20, 1936, Raleigh, NC

Bagpipes, Reeds / Soul Jazz, Hard Bop

Jazz's only bagpipe specialist, Rufus Harley proved that jazz can be played on any instrument. He was originally a saxophonist and took up the bagpipes in the early '60s. Harley recorded four albums for Atlantic (*Bagpipe Blues* and *Scotch and Soul*) during 1965-69 and appeared on one selection apiece on albums by Sonny Stitt, Herbie Mann and in 1974 with Sonny Rollins. Otherwise Rufus Harley has not been heard from much during the past 20 years but he certainly made his own place in jazz history. —*Scott Yanow*

● **Scotch and Soul** / Apr. 6, 1966-Apr. 29, 1966 / Atlantic ✦✦✦✦✦

Although Rufus Harley also plays flute, soprano and tenor on this record, it is for his bagpipe playing that the out-of-print album is most notable. The bagpipes tend to be a drone instrument, and Harley cannot surmount the problem of cutting off notes quickly, but he plays his main instrument as well as anyone, and is thus far the only jazz bagpipe player. With the assistance of pianist Oliver Collins, bassist James Glenn, drummer Billy Abner and Robert Gossett on conga, Harley's versions of "Feeling Good" and "Scotch & Soul" are quite unique. —*Scott Yanow*

Bagpipe Blues / 1965 / Atlantic ✦✦✦✦

Tribute to Courage / Apr. 10, 1967-Aug. 10, 1967 / Atlantic ✦✦✦

Everette Harp

b. Aug. 17, 1961, Houston, TX

Alto Saxophone / Crossover Jazz

An emotional R&B-oriented saxophonist, Everette Harp graduated from North Texas State University and played locally in Houston during 1981-88, becoming a studio musician. In 1988 he moved to Los Angeles and was soon playing in major R&B bands (including those of Anita Baker, Sheena Easton and Kenny Loggins). In 1991 Harp toured with George Duke and Marcus Miller and recorded his debut for Manhattan. In 1992 he toured with Rachelle Ferrell and two years later his second album (for Blue Note Contemporary) was released. The popular Everette Harp's background is in gospel and R&B but he sometimes displays the ability to improvise; hopefully a jazz album will be in the future. —*Scott Yanow*

● **Everette Harp** / 1992 / Blue Note ✦✦✦✦

One listen to "Full Circle" from this CD is all one needs to be convinced that David Sanborn is back to his old soulful R&B ways; the only problem is that it's Everette Harp. Harp, who shows virtually no individuality on alto, hints at Kenny G. on soprano and mostly performs derivative instrumentals. A few numbers include routine group soul vocals. The set of R&B is pleasant and well played but is instantly forgettable and strictly-for-the-money dance music. —*Scott Yanow*

Common Ground / 1994 / Blue Note ✦✦

This CD can be dismissed quickly for Everette Harp (principally on alto) seems content to merely ape the sound of David Sanborn but without the sincere emotions or any pretense at creativity or originality. This pop/R&B date is essentially mindless dance music and even Branford Marsalis' one appearance does not help. —*Scott Yanow*

What's Going On / 1997 / Blue Note ✦✦✦

As part of Blue Note's "cover" series, saxophonist Everette Harp and a large group of vocalists (including Kenny Loggins), rhythm section players, and a horn section perform "cover" versions of the nine songs on Marvin Gaye's famous *What's Going*

On record, including the title cut, "Mercy Mercy Me" and "Inner City Blues." Since Harp is an R&B-oriented player, this project makes sense, while containing far fewer revelations than the Charlie Hunter and Fareed Haque entries in the series. Harp rarely wanders much from the melodies, his treatments of the songs are quite optimistic and emotional (if predictable and a bit lightweight), and the saxophonist's fans (and Gaye's too) should enjoy the effort. —*Scott Yanow*

The Harper Brothers

f. 1988, db. 1991
Group / Hard Bop
One of the most hyped jazz groups of the late '80s, the Harper Brothers (co-led by drummer Winard Harper and trumpeter Philip Harper) symbolized what was right and wrong about the Young Lions movement. The musicianship in this hard-bop unit was excellent and the young players respected their elders, but strong originality was lacking (they were largely revisiting the past) and the Harper Brothers received an excess of publicity at the expense of more innovative players. Still, during its five years, the group produced four enjoyable bop albums for Verve and its sidemen (altoist Justin Robinson, tenors Javon Jackson and Walter Blanding, pianists Stephen Scott and Kevin Hays, and bassists Michael Bowie and Nedra Wheeler among them) all had strong starts to their career. Both Winard and Philip Harper have grown musically since the band's breakup. —*Scott Yanow*

● **Harper Brothers** / Jun. 21, 1988 / Verve ✦✦✦✦✦
The debut CD from the Harper Brothers helped give fuel to the "Young Lions" movement and the revival of hard bop. In addition to some straightahead originals, the briefly popular group performs Lee Morgan's "Mogie," a pair of Reuben Brown songs, "Portrait of Jennie" and "Easy to Love." Drummer Winard Harper and trumpeter Phillip Harper (who would improve in later years) are joined in the derivative but swinging group by altoist Justin Robinson, pianist Stephen Scott and bassist Michael Bowie. Recommended for hard bop fans. —*Scott Yanow*

Remembrance / Sep. 8, 1989-Sep. 9, 1989 / Verve ✦✦✦✦
A solid live album from young cats. —*Michael G. Nastos*

Artistry / 1991 / Verve ✦✦✦
1991 session by Winard and Philip Harper, the brothers whose trumpet/sax sound and conception echoed classic late-'50s hard-bop material. This was their next-to-last album as a duo, and it was aided by contributions from Javon Jackson, Kevin Hays, and Nedra Wheeler. —*Ron Wynn*

You Can Hide Inside the Music / Oct. 15, 1991-Oct. 16, 1991 / Verve ✦✦✦
This set by the Harper Brothers is a bit unusual in that the hard-bop unit finds itself often in the position of being a backup group to singer Ernie Andrews, who takes five spirited vocals. Although the Harper Brothers gained quite a bit of publicity during their existence, their lack of originality held them back artistically. Altoist Justin Robinson and Walter Blanding on tenor both display run-of-the-mill tones on this date while trumpeter Phillip Harper often falls into the trap of trying to imitate Lee Morgan's swagger but without his range. Drummer Winard Harper, the strongest member of the group, always did his best to push the band but on the CD the best instrumental is actually a trio rendition of pianist Ray Gallon's "That's the Question." In addition to Ernie Andrews, trumpeter Harry "Sweets" Edison (clearly past his prime) makes two appearances while organist Jimmy McGriff is a strong asset on the vocal piece "She's Got the Blues for Sale." However the star of the date is definitely Ernie Andrews. His name should have received much higher billing with the Harper Brothers properly demoted to supporting cast members. —*Scott Yanow*

Billy Harper

b. Jan. 17, 1943, Houston, TX
Tenor Saxophone / Post-Bop, Hard Bop
An intense tenor saxophonist whose music has stretched the boundaries of hard bop and modal music, Billy Harper graduated from North Texas State College and in 1966 moved to New York. He worked on and off with Gil Evans for the next ten years, was with Art Blakey's Jazz Messengers (1968-70), played with Elvin Jones (1970), Max Roach, the Thad Jones/Mel Lewis Orchestra (recording a notable solo on "Fingers") and Lee Morgan. Harper has recorded as a leader for Strata East, Black Saint, Denon and Soul Note and has maintained a low profile during the past decade but he did record a set for Evidence in 1993. —*Scott Yanow*

Capra Black / Oct. 1973 / Strata East ✦✦✦

● **Black Saint** / Jul. 21, 1975-Jul. 22, 1975 / Black Saint ✦✦✦✦✦
An important document and the first album for the Italian Black Saint label. A potent quartet, with Harper's most familiar themes. This is essential listening in the modal jazz idiom. —*Michael G. Nastos*

Soran-Bushi, Billy Harper / Dec. 15, 1977+Dec. 17, 1977 / Denon ✦✦✦

In Europe / Jan. 24, 1979-Jan. 25, 1979 / Soul Note ✦✦✦

Destiny Is Yours / Dec. 1989 / Steeple Chase ✦✦✦✦

Somalia / Oct. 18, 1993+Oct. 21, 1993 / Evidence ✦✦✦✦✦
The passionate tenor saxophonist Billy Harper had not been heard on record as a leader in quite a few years when this superlative Evidence CD was released in 1995. Harper (who is joined by trumpeter Eddie Henderson, pianist Francesca Tanksley, bassist Louie Spears and both Newman Taylor Baker and Horacee Arnold on drums) brings back the spirit of John Coltrane, performing a very spiritual and generally intense set of music. The five originals are highlighted by the title cut, "Quest" and the nearly 22-minute "Thy Will Be Done." This CD contains some of Billy Harper's finest playing in years. —*Scott Yanow*

Herbie Harper

b. Jul. 2, 1920, Salina, KS
Trombone / Cool
A fine trombonist active in the West Coast jazz scene of the 1950s, Herbie Harper has spent most of his playing time since 1955 as a studio musician although he occasionally re-emerges in the jazz world. After playing with Charlie Spivak's Orchestra (1944-47), Harper settled in Los Angeles where he gigged with Teddy Edwards and had short-time associations with Benny Goodman, Charlie Barnet and Stan Kenton (1950). In addition to recording in the 1950s with June Christy, Kenton, Maynard Ferguson, Benny Carter and Barnet, Herbie Harper led five albums of his own during 1954-57 for Nocturne, Tampa, Bethlehem and Mode. He has mostly worked in the studios since then but has emerged to play with Bob Florence's big band and in the 1980s he recorded for Sea Breeze and with Bill Perkins for V.S.O.P. —*Scott Yanow*

● **Five Brothers** / June 15, 1955 / V.S.O.P. ✦✦✦✦✦
Trombonist Herbie Harper, who has not been heard of much as a leader since the 1950s, has always been a talented bop-based trombonist with an attractive tone. For this quintet set, he is teamed with multi-instrumentalist Bob Enevoldsen (mostly sticking to tenor), guitarist Don Overberg, bassist Red Mitchell and drummer Frankie Capp. The West Coast-styled ensembles still sound appealing. This is one of the obscure Tampa sessions that have been rescued and reissued by V.S.O.P. —*Scott Yanow*

Herbie Harper Quintet / Apr. 21, 1954 / Nocturne ✦✦✦✦
Herbie Harper's debut as a leader features the trombonist in two different quintets with either Jimmy Rowles or Marty Paich on piano, bassist Harry Babasin, drummer Roy Harte and either Bud Shank (on tenor and baritone) or baritonist Bob Gordon. The Harper-Gordon combination in particular works well, and the music bridges the gap between swing and cool jazz. Highlights include "Dinah," "Five Brothers" and "Jeepers Leapers." —*Scott Yanow*

Herbie Harper Sextet / Jun. 1957 / V.S.O.P. ✦✦✦✦
Trombonist Herbie Harper's fifth and final session as a leader in the 1950s is an excellent outing that also features the little-known tenorman Jay Core, guitarist Howard Roberts, pianist Marty Paich, bassist Red Mitchell and either Frank Capp or Mel Lewis on drums. Core and Capp contributed an original apiece and the sextet also plays five superior standards along with a surprising rendition of "Little Orphan Annie." This set for the defunct Mode label (reissued by V.S.O.P.) has plenty of high-quality West Coast jazz. —*Scott Yanow*

Revisited / May 6, 1981-May 7, 1981 / Sea Breeze ✦✦✦
Trombonist Herbie Harper, who led some fine sessions during 1954-57, mostly worked in the studios through the following decades. This 1981 LP was his first as a leader in 24 years. Harper's cool-toned style was unchanged from the 1950s, and his playing on the seven standards was fluent and creative within the genre as ever. Harper is joined by guitarist Jim Nichols, bassist Bob Badgley, and drummer Chuck Piscitello for such songs as "Shadow Waltz," "Keepin' Out of Mischief Now," "All the Things You Are" and a jazz waltz version of "Summertime." —*Scott Yanow*

Herbie Harper/Bill Perkins Quintet / Sep. 14, 1989+Sep. 15, 1989 / V.S.O.P. ✦✦✦✦✦
Trombonist Herbie Harper is best-known for his recordings in the 1950s but this 1989 set shows that decades of studio work had not dulled his style. Teamed in a quintet with Bill Perkins (who switches between tenor, baritone and flute), guitarist Larry Koonse, bassist John Leitham and drummer Larance Marable, Harper mixes together standards and lesser-known tunes including Russ Freeman's "The Wind," Jobim's "Zingaro," "Remember" and Bob Brookmeyer's "Dirty Man." This is a modern cool jazz set that swings at a quiet volume; straightahead jazz fans will enjoy the results. —*Scott Yanow*

Philip Harper

b. May 10, 1965, Baltimore, MD
Trumpet / Hard Bop

A good hard-bop trumpeter who in recent years has become a more adventurous improviser, Philip Harper became well-known during 1988-93 as co-leader (with older brother Winard) of the Harper Brothers. He had previously toured with Art Blakey's Jazz Messengers (where his Lee Morgan-influenced style fit in perfectly) and recorded with Cecil Brooks III, Joe Chambers and Errol Parker. Since the Harper Brothers band broke up (having produced four albums for Verve), the trumpeter has recorded as a leader for Muse and played with the Mingus Big Band. —*Scott Yanow*

Soulful Sin / Feb. 22, 1993 ✦✦✦
● **The Thirteenth Moon** / Jan. 21, 1994 / Muse ✦✦✦✦

Winard Harper

b. Jun. 4, 1962, Baltimore, MD
Drums / Hard Bop

An excellent drummer whose creativity stretches beyond the hard-bop settings in which he is often featured, Winard Harper (along with younger brother Philip) gained a great deal of publicity during 1988-93 as co-leader of the Harper Brothers. Before that band he had gained important experience working with Betty Carter and since then Winard Harper has freelanced and continued to grow as a player. —*Scott Yanow*

● **Be Yourself** / 1994 / Epicure ✦✦✦✦✦

The music on Winard Harper's Epicure release (Art Blakeyish romps, boogaloos, ballads and bop) is straight from vintage Blue Note stylewise although the majority of the songs are actually group originals. But, as with the best revival Dixieland of the 1950s, the musicianship, enthusiasm and creativity of the musicians (within the genre's boundaries) uplift the music beyond the limits of nostalgia. Trumpeter Eddie Henderson is in top form, altoist Antonio Hart is fine in a Cannonball Adderley bag during his three appearances and tenor saxophonist Don Braden takes a major step forward with these performances. In addition, David "Fathead" Newman has two features on tenor, the rhythm section is excellent and the drummer/leader is content to push the other musicians rather than engaging in lengthy solos himself. It's recommended for hard-bop fans. —*Scott Yanow*

Tom Harrell

b. Jun. 16, 1946, Urbana, IL
Trumpet, Fluegelhorn / Hard Bop

Tom Harrell has managed to fight courageously (and thus far successfully) against schizophrenia to become one of jazz's top trumpeters of the 1980s and '90s. On stage he is totally focused on his playing and seems to only come alive when he is improvising. Harrell grew up in Northern California and toured with Stan Kenton (1969), Woody Herman (1970-71) and Horace Silver (1973-77). He moved to New York in the mid-'70s and played during this period with Cecil Payne, Bill Evans (1979), Lee Konitz's Nonet (1979-81) and George Russell (1982). Harrell traveled the world with the Phil Woods Quintet (1983-89) and has since then generally led his own bands, recording for Contemporary and Chesky. His style mixes together the power of Clifford Brown with the lyricism of Chet Baker. —*Scott Yanow*

Aurora/Total / Jun. 24, 1976 / Pinnacle ✦✦✦

Harrell's first album features choice material and Bob Berg (ts). —*Michael G. Nastos*

Play of Light / Feb. 11, 1982 / Black Hawk ✦✦✦✦

Trumpeter Tom Harrell's second set as a leader (his first was an obscure date from 1976 on the Pinnacle label) was recorded shortly before he joined Phil Woods' quintet. Harrell, an underrated composer who writes complex yet logical songs, performs four originals plus Andy La Verne's "Where You Were" and "Everything Happens to Me" on this sadly out-of-print LP. Harrell holds his own with the all-star group (which includes tenor saxophonist Ricky Ford, guitarist Bruce Forman, pianist Albert Dailey, bassist Eddie Gomez and drummer Billy Hart) and performs advanced hard bop. Worth searching for. —*Scott Yanow*

Moon Alley / Dec. 22, 1985 / Criss Cross ✦✦✦✦✦
Open Air / May 26, 1986 / Steeple Chase ✦✦✦✦
Visions / Apr. 18, 1987-Apr. 9, 1990 / Contemporary ✦✦✦✦
Stories / Jan. 26, 1988-Jan. 27, 1988 / Contemporary ✦✦✦✦

One of the joys of hearing Tom Harrell (who sticks here to fluegelhorn) on his own sessions is that his writing tends to be showcased. All seven of the diverse and advanced originals on this release are Harrell's, and he enlisted other top-notch players to interpret them. Tenor saxophonist Bob Berg and pianist Niels Lan Doky have many fine solos, bassist Ray Drummond and drummer Billy Hart are stimu-

lating in support, and guitarist John Scofield helps out on three numbers. This CD (which has one additional selection than the original LP) is an excellent example of Harrell's talents. —*Scott Yanow*

● **Sail Away** / Mar. 22, 1989-Mar. 23, 1989 / Contemporary ✦✦✦✦✦

Tom Harrell emerged in the mid- to-late 1980s as one of the most consistently creative trumpeters in jazz. He wrote all eight compositions for this set (Harrell is a talented and very underrated writer), music that challenges his particularly strong sidemen: pianist James Williams, guitarist John Abercrombie, bassist Ray Drummond, drummer Adam Nussbaum, and sometimes tenorman Joe Lovano and Dave Liebman on soprano. Recorded shortly after Harrell left the Phil Woods Quintet after a long stint, this highly recommended CD finds him on the brink of greater success as a leader. —*Scott Yanow*

Form / Apr. 8, 1990-Apr. 9, 1990 / Contemporary ✦✦✦✦

This was trumpeter Tom Harrell's first recording since ending his long period with Phil Woods' quintet. He performs five originals plus the standard "For Heaven's Sake." Most intriguing are "January Spring" (a lengthy workout just for the theme) which is freely improvised except for the theme) and the cooking "Rhythm Form" which, although loosely based on "I Got Rhythm," sounds as if it could have been written by Ornette Coleman. Throughout the date the contributions of Joe Lovano (on tenor and soprano), pianist Danilo Perez, the fine flutist Cheryl Pyle (on "January Spring") and the mighty Charlie Haden-Paul Motian rhythm team keep the trumpeter quite inspired. —*Scott Yanow*

Passages / Oct. 10, 1991-Oct. 11, 1991 / Chesky ✦✦✦✦

This CD is most notable for featuring ten of trumpeter Tom Harrell's compositions. Few of the melodies from the harmonically advanced originals will stick in one's mind after one or two listens, but the solos are excellent (and in Harrell's case, often exquisite) and the generally melancholy moods of the advanced hard-bop pieces are memorable in their own way. In addition to Harrell, Joe Lovano is in fine form on tenor, soprano and alto, Cheryl Pyle's two guest appearances on flute are a bonus and the rhythm section is supportive and alert with pianist Danilo Perez emerging as a major soloist, taking the title cut as a lyrical free improvisation duet with Harrell. An intriguing and thought-provoking session. —*Scott Yanow*

Upswing / Jun. 11, 1993-Jun. 12, 1993 / Chesky ✦✦✦✦✦
Bottom Line / Nov. 7, 1995 / Mons ✦✦✦
Labyrinth / Jan. 1996 / RCA ✦✦✦✦

Tom Harrell has been gradually gaining recognition as one of the most consistently creative brassmen in jazz. Although his soft tone can sometimes be a little reminiscent of Chet Baker, Harrell's technique is on a higher level and he is a more advanced player. Harrell is heard in fine form throughout this CD which is split between appearances with his impressive quintet and with a nonet/tentet. The trumpeter, who contributed nine of the ten selections, is quite generous in allocating solo space and in keeping his improvisations relatively brief and to the point. The selections display variety within the hard-bop/post-bop idiom, ranging from rhythmic pieces such as "Marimba Song" and "Samba Mate" to the tongue twister "Cheetah" and several numbers which make the augmented group sound like a big band. Of the sidemen, tenor saxophonist Don Braden and pianist Kenny Werner have several good spots, Gary Smulyan's deep-toned baritone (the personnel listing mistakenly has him down as playing bass clarinet) is a highlight of "Blue in One" and Rob Botti's oboe is an important voice on "Majesty." Harrell, who plays both piano and overdubbed fluegelhorn on a solo interpretation of "Darn That Dream," continues to grow as an original improviser. —*Scott Yanow*

Look to the Sky / Jun. 18, 1996 / Steeple Chase ✦✦✦✦
Art of Rhythm / 1997 / RCA ✦✦✦✦✦

Tom Harrell's second album for RCA, *The Art of Rhythm*, continues his streak of adventurous, satisfying records. Enlisting a large cast of guest musicians—including violinist Regina Carter, bassist Andy Gonzalez, tenor saxophonist Dewey Redman, guitarist Mike Stern and drummer Leon Parker—Harrell has concentrated on Latin jazz on *The Art of Rhythm*, and the results are anything but conventional. It's unpredictable, yet enjoyable, music that rewards repeated listens. —*Leo Stanley*

Joe Harriott

b. Jul. 15, 1928, Kingston, Jamaica, **d.** Jan. 2, 1973, London, England
Alto Saxophone / Post-Bop, Avant-Garde

Joe Harriott's music goes virtually unheard today, yet the alto saxophonist exerted a powerful influence on early free jazz in England. The Jamaican-born and raised Harriott played with his countrymen, trumpeter Dizzy Reece and tenor saxophonist Wilton "Bogey" Gaynair, before emigrating to England in 1951. In London, Harriott worked freelance and in the band of trumpeter Pete Pitterson. In 1954, he landed an important gig with drummer Tony Kinsey; the next year he played in saxophonist Ronnie Scott's big band. His first album as a leader was 1959's *Southern Horizon*. Originally a bop-oriented player, Harriott gradually grew away from the conventions of that style. During a 1960 hospital stay, Harriott envisaged a new method of improvisation that, to an extent, paralleled the innovations of Ornette Coleman. Harriott was initially branded a mere imitator of Coleman, but close listening to both men reveals distinct differences in their respective styles. Harriott manifested a more explicit philosophical connection with bebop, for one thing, and his music was more concerned with ensemble interaction than was Coleman's early work. The 1960 album *Free Form*, which included trumpeter Shake Keane, pianist Pat Smythe, bassist Coleridge Goode, and drummer Phil Seaman, illustrated Harriott's new techniques. Beginning in 1965, he began fusing jazz with various types of world folk musics. He collaborated with Indian musician John Mayer on a record—1967's *Indo-Jazz Suite*—that utilized modal and free jazz procedures. The album's traditional jazz quintet instrumentation was augmented by a violin, sitar, tambura, and tabla. Harriott's recorded output was scarce, and virtually none of it remains in print. —*Chris Kelsey*

● **Southern Horizons** / May 5, 1959-Apr. 21, 1960 / Jazzland ✦✦✦✦

Free Forms / Nov. 1960 / Jazzland ✦✦✦✦

Abstract / Nov. 22, 1961-May 5, 1962 / Columbia ✦✦✦
Altoist Joe Harriott, whose fairly free jazz in the early 1960s was sometimes a little reminiscent of both Ornette Coleman and Charles Mingus, was one of the most advanced jazz musicians then working in England. This out-of-print LP (none of Harriott's recordings are easily available in the 1990s) features Harriott and his quintet (which consists of trumpeter Shake Keane, pianist Pat Smythe, bassist Coleridge Goode, either Bobby Orr or Phil Seamen on drums and, on a couple tunes, Frank Holder on bongos). They perform seven of the leader's originals and "Oleo," and the music is consistently unpredictable, although not afraid to swing hard in spots. A reappraisal and rediscovery of Joe Harriott is long overdue. —*Scott Yanow*

Indo-Jazz Suite / Oct. 10, 1965 / Atlantic ✦✦✦✦

Indo Jazz Fusions: The Joe Harriott-John Mayer Do / Sep. 3, 1966-Sep. 4, 1966 / Atlantic ✦✦✦

Allan Harris

b. 1958
Vocals / Standards, Traditional Pop
One of the top male jazz singers to emerge in the 1990s, Allan Harris sometimes sounds a bit like Nat King Cole but also puts his own personality into his spirited rendition of standards. He first recorded for his own Love Productions label and has more recently recorded two sets for Mons: *It's a Wonderful World* (a sextet date with Benny Green, Mark Whitfield and Claudio Roditi) and an ambitious effort on which he is backed by Germany's 54-piece Metropole Orchestra. —*Scott Yanow*

Setting the Standard / 1994 / Love Productions ✦✦✦✦
The debut of singer Allan Harris finds the Nat King Cole-inspired vocalist in a variety of settings that sometimes include three horns and a string section. Not really an improviser, Harris uplifts 11 standards by embracing the strong melodies and giving fresh meaning to their lyrics. Highlights include a swinging "On the Street Where You Live," "You Go to My Head" and a surprisingly jubilant "I Know What I Got." —*Scott Yanow*

● **Here Comes Allan Harris and the Metropole Orchestra** / Oct. 18, 1994-Dec. 20, 1995 / Mons ✦✦✦✦
Allan Harris' third recording and second for Mons features the singer in a memorable meeting with the 54-piece Metropole Orchestra, which is conducted and arranged by Rob Pronk. Harris interprets 15 superior standards with great sensitivity and attention paid to the lyrics, although he always swings. Surprisingly, the strings do not weigh down the melodic music. Highlights include "Mean to Me," Charlie Parker's "Yardbird Suite," "The Folks Who Live on the Hill," "Don't Blame Me" and a cooking "Lookin' at the World Through Rose-Colored Glasses." —*Scott Yanow*

It's a Wonderful World / Oct. 1995 / Mons ✦✦✦✦

Barry Harris

b. Dec. 15, 1929, Detroit, MI
Piano / Bop
One of the major bop pianists of the past 40 years, Barry Harris has long had the ability to sound very close to Bud Powell yet he can also do convincing impressions of Thelonious Monk and has his own style within the bop idiom. He was an important part of the Detroit jazz scene of the 1950s and has been a jazz educator since that era. Harris recorded his first set as a leader while in 1958 and moved to New York in 1960 where he spent a short period with Cannonball Adderley's Quintet. He also recorded with Dexter Gordon, Illinois Jacquet, Yusef Lateef and Hank Mobley and was with Coleman Hawkins off and on throughout the decade

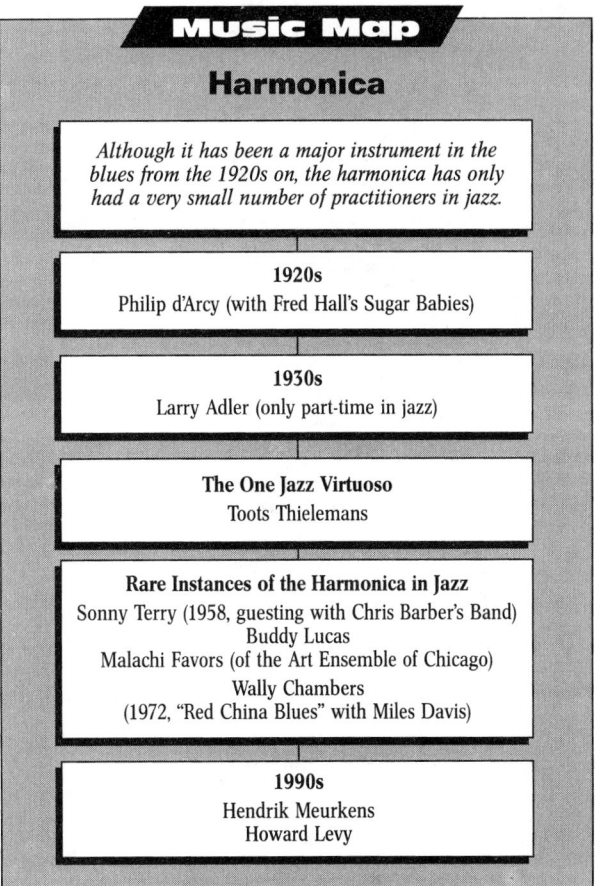

Music Map

Harmonica

Although it has been a major instrument in the blues from the 1920s on, the harmonica has only had a very small number of practitioners in jazz.

1920s
Philip d'Arcy (with Fred Hall's Sugar Babies)

1930s
Larry Adler (only part-time in jazz)

The One Jazz Virtuoso
Toots Thielemans

Rare Instances of the Harmonica in Jazz
Sonny Terry (1958, guesting with Chris Barber's Band)
Buddy Lucas
Malachi Favors (of the Art Ensemble of Chicago)
Wally Chambers
(1972, "Red China Blues" with Miles Davis)

1990s
Hendrik Meurkens
Howard Levy

(including Hawk's declining years). In the 1970s Harris was on two of Sonny Stitt's finest records (*Tune Up* and *Constellation*) and made many recordings in a variety of settings for Xanadu. Barry Harris has mostly been working with his trio during the past 20 years and he has recorded as a leader for Argo (1958), Riverside, Prestige, MPS, Xanadu and Red. —*Scott Yanow*

Barry Harris at the Jazz Workshop / May 15, 1960-May 16, 1960 / Original Jazz Classics ✦✦✦✦
Pianist Barry Harris' second recording as a leader (he led a set for Argo in 1958) finds him at the age of 30 playing in the same boppish style he would have throughout his career. Teamed up with bassist Sam Jones and drummer Louis Hayes, this live CD reissue (which adds three alternate takes to the original LP program) is an excellent example of Harris' playing. Highlights of the enthusiastic straightahead set (which includes three obscure but worthy originals by the pianist) include "Is You Is or Is You Ain't My Baby," "Moose the Mooche" and "Woody 'n You." —*Scott Yanow*

Preminado / Dec. 21, 1960+Jan. 19, 1961 / Original Jazz Classics ✦✦✦✦
This CD reissue (a straight reissue of the original Riverside LP) features the great bop pianist Barry Harris in a trio with bassist Joe Benjamin and drummer Elvin Jones. Jones in particular pushes the pianist, and this fine set has many strong moments, including strong versions of "My Heart Stood Still," Harris' original title cut and "What Is This Thing Called Love"; in addition, Barry Harris takes "I Should Care" as an unaccompanied solo. —*Scott Yanow*

Listen to Barry Harris / Jul. 4, 1961 / Riverside ✦✦✦
Striking solo piano. —*Ron Wynn*

Chasin' the Bird / May 31, 1962+Aug. 23, 1962 / Original Jazz Classics ✦✦✦✦
Barry Harris has long been one of the top interpreters of the piano styles of Bud Powell and Thelonious Monk. This CD reissue of a trio session with bassist Bob Cranshaw and drummer Clifford Jarvis finds him performing near the top of his form. Highlights include "Chasin' the Bird" (during the theme, Harris plays both

countermelodies simultaneously), "'Round Midnight," "The Way You Look Tonight" and three fine originals. This is excellent music that should please bop collectors. —*Scott Yanow*

Luminescence / Apr. 20, 1967 / Original Jazz Classics ✦✦✦
Bebop sessions were comparatively rare in 1967, but pianist Barry Harris and his sextet on this CD reissue perform with the sincerity and enthusiasm that was more closely associated with this music in 1957. The trumpetless group (which also consists of baritonist Pepper Adams, tenor saxophonist Junior Cook, trombonist Slide Hampton, bassist Bob Cranshaw and drummer Lenny McBrowne) performs four of Harris' joyful originals (most of which are based on common chord changes), the ballad "My Ideal" and two Bud Powell tunes, "Dance of the Infidels" and "Webb City." Everyone is in fine form, particularly Harris and Adams, and the pianist's arrangements perfectly fit (and uplift) the music. Highly recommended to bebop collectors. —*Scott Yanow*

Magnificent / Nov. 25, 1969 / Prestige ✦✦✦

Barry Harris Plays Tadd Dameron / Jun. 4, 1975 / Xanadu ✦✦✦✦✦
Barry Harris, arguably the top bebop pianist of the 1970s, '80s and '90s, was particularly in prime form throughout his Xanadu recordings. The perfect player to interpret Tadd Dameron's music (of which he had full understanding), Harris performs eight of the influential composer's songs on this 1975 LP with bassist Gene Taylor and drummer Leroy Williams. Highlights of the highly recommended (but probably difficult-to-find) set include "Hot House," "The Chase," "Casbah" and "Our Delight." —*Scott Yanow*

● **Live in Tokyo** / Apr. 12, 1976+Apr. 14, 1976 / Xanadu ✦✦✦✦
All of pianist Barry Harris' Xanadu records of the 1970s are gems, featuring the bop master in particularly inspired form. Many of the Xanadu artists toured Japan in 1976, resulting in several records including Harris' *Live in Tokyo* and this LP. This album of "leftovers" not released on the other sets sticks to bebop standards. Harris performs four numbers (lengthy explorations of "Like Someone in Love" and "Night in Tunisia," plus two versions of "Ornithology") in a trio with bassist Sam Jones and drummer Leroy Williams. Two other songs ("Groovin' High" and "Blue 'n' Boogie") find the trio joined by altoist Charles McPherson and guitarist Jimmy Raney. Although not containing any real surprises, this swinging straightahead music is quite enjoyable. —*Scott Yanow*

Barry Harris Plays Barry Harris / Jan. 17, 1978 / Xanadu ✦✦✦✦
For this excellent Xanadu set (an LP that was reissued briefly on CD), pianist Barry Harris (not particularly famous as a composer) performs seven of his catchy originals, most of which are based on the chord changes of bop standards. With fine assistance from bassist George Duvivier and drummer Leroy Williams, Harris shows that if he had pursued this path, he might have come up with a few standards of his own creation. "Father Flanagan" (dedicated to pianist Tommy Flanagan) is most memorable. —*Scott Yanow*

The Bird of Red and Gold / Sep. 18, 1979 / Xanadu ✦✦✦✦✦
Although this LP claims to have the recording date of Sep. 18, 1989, and is listed so in some discographies, the album itself came out in 1982, making one assume that it is really from 1979. Unlike most of his other Xanadu LPs (which were generally dedicated to the work of one composer), this solo recital by pianist Barry Harris is a more diverse set. Harris contributed five originals (including his haunting "Nascimento" and the title cut, which he also sings) and also plays some standards and Thelonious Monk's "Pannonica." Superior bop-based music. —*Scott Yanow*

For the Moment / Mar. 2, 1984 / Uptown ✦✦✦✦
Throughout his career, pianist Barry Harris has kept the spirit of bebop and the music of Bud Powell and Thelonious Monk alive in his joyous and creative playing. For this live concert, Harris is heard in a trio with bassist Rufus Reid and drummer Leroy Williams. There is a four-song Thelonious Monk medley, five originals (including "To Monk with Love" and "For the Moment," which Harris played at Thelonious' funeral), "My Heart Stood Still," and a boppish version of the "I Love Lucy Theme." A delightful and enthusiastic set. —*Scott Yanow*

Live at Maybeck Recital Hall, Vol. 12 / Mar. 1990 / Concord Jazz ✦✦✦✦
Barry Harris has long been the perfect bebop pianist. This solo recital finds Harris paying tribute to Bud Powell and Thelonious Monk as well as Art Tatum, not so much in their compositions (although he does perform Bud's "I'll Keep Loving You") but in aspects of their styles that he has enveloped into his own musical personality. Harris is even able to make bebop sense out of a medley consisting of "It Never Entered My Mind" and the themes from *The Flintstones* and *I Love Lucy*. —*Scott Yanow*

Confirmation / Sep. 1, 1991 / Candid ✦✦✦

First Time Ever / Oct. 1, 1996-Oct. 2, 1996 / Evidence ✦✦✦✦

Beaver Harris (William Godvin Harris)

b. Apr. 20, 1936, Pittsburgh, PA, **d.** Dec. 22, 1991, New York, NY
Drums / Avant-Garde, Post-Bop
A greatly undervalued drummer easily on a level with many of his more famous contemporaries, Beaver Harris was one of the avant-garde's most well-rounded musicians. He was accomplished in any and all jazz styles, yet as a bandleader favored the more progressive facets of the music. Harris began playing drums at the age of 20. After his discharge from the army in 1957, he returned to Pittsburgh, where he jammed with famous musicians like Horace Silver and Benny Golson as they passed through town. Harris moved to New York in 1962 and fell in with many of the major figures in the nascent free-jazz movement. From 1966 on, Harris recorded with Marion Brown, Albert Ayler, Gato Barbieri, Roswell Rudd, and Archie Shepp. In 1968, Harris, trombonist Grachan Moncur III, and pianist Dave Burrell formed 360 Degree Music Experience, a cooperative group that served in various guises as Harris' primary creative vehicle for the rest of his life. Harris eventually assumed the group's leadership; members in the '70s and '80s included saxophonists Ken McIntyre, Hamiet Bluiett, and Ricky Ford, steel drummer Francis Brown, bassist Cameron Brown, and pianists Rahn Burton and Don Pullen. Harris worked with Cecil Taylor in the '70s. During his career, Harris also played with a good many straightahead jazzers, including Sonny Rollins, Chet Baker, Thelonious Monk, Charlie Rouse, and Al Cohn. As can be inferred from his group's name, Harris made a conscious attempt to transcend stylistic limitations. Though he was best known as an avant-gardist, Harris' multifaceted style was rooted in jazz's core values, as was evidenced by his work with so many top-rank mainstream players. —*Chris Kelsey*

From Ragtime to No Time / Dec. 11, 1974-Feb. 11, 1975 / 360 ✦✦✦✦
This is a most unusual album. Drummer Beaver Harris was generally most associated with the avant-garde, but on the first side of this LP, he utilizes such trad jazz players as trumpeter Doc Cheatham, clarinetist Herb Hall and valve trombonist Marshall Brown; plus, Maxine Sullivan has two vocals. The four songs are originals by Harris, Roy Burrows and Dave Burrell, and they allow the veteran mainstream musicians to improvise in a more modern setting (with pianist Burrell, Harris and either Ron Carter or Jimmy Garrison on bass). The flip side has a more modern group playing the two-part "Round Trip"; among the musicians are Howard Johnson on baritone and bass clarinet, flutist Keith Marks, a variety of percussionists, and singer Bill Willingham. The idea behind Harris' original version of the 360 Degree Music Experience was to improve communication between several generations of jazz musicians, and this project works quite well. —*Scott Yanow*

● **In: Sanity** / Mar. 8, 1976-Mar. 9, 1976 / Black Saint ✦✦✦✦✦
Recording with 360 Degree Music Experience. Improvisational music with world music touches from percussionist Harris and pianist Dave Burrell. An essential purchase for the adventurous listener. —*Michael G. Nastos*

Live at Nyon / Jun. 14, 1979 / Cadence ✦✦✦✦✦
An ambitious, swinging quintet date, with a welcome appearance from Grachan Moncur III (tb). —*Ron Wynn*

Beautiful Africa / Jun. 23, 1979+Jun. 25, 1979 / Soul Note ✦✦✦✦
A continually intriguing record, this outing by drummer Beaver Harris is most notable for featuring two underrated and often overlooked but talented advanced improvisers: trombonist Grachan Moncur III and Ken McIntyre (heard on alto, bassoon and flute). With pianist Rahn Burton and bassist Cameron Brown completing the quintet, the group plays five complex group originals that clearly inspire the talented players. Recommended to followers of post-bop jazz. —*Scott Yanow*

Negcaumongus / Dec. 7, 1979 / Cadence ✦✦✦✦
Brilliant septet cuts. Ricky Ford (ts) and Don Pullen (p) are magnificent. —*Ron Wynn*

Beaver Is My Name / Nov. 1983 / Timeless ✦✦✦

Well Kept Secret with Don Pullen / 1984 / Hannibal ✦✦✦✦

Benny Harris

b. Apr. 23, 1919, New York, NY **d.** May 11, 1975, San Francisco, CA
Trumpet, Composer, Bop
A minor figure in the bop era who had potential but unfortunately retired from music in 1952, Benny Harris played with Tiny Bradshaw (1939) and twice with Earl Hines' Orchestra (1941 and 1943). He was a fixture on 52nd Street in the early '40s, taking part in many early bop sessions and playing with Benny Carter, John Kirby, Coleman Hawkins, Don Byas and Thelonious Monk. Harris also was part of Boyd Raeburn's band for a period during 1944-45 and recorded with Clyde Hart in December 1944 and with Byas in 1945. The composer of "Ornithology," "Crazeology," "Reets and I" (often performed by Bud Powell) and "Wahoo" (based on "Perdido"), Benny Harris did not play all that much in the mid- to late '40s. He was

with Dizzy Gillespie's big band briefly in 1949 and recorded with Charlie Parker in 1952 but then permanently dropped out of music. —*Scott Yanow*

Bill Harris (William Palmer Harris)

b. Oct. 28, 1916, Philadelphia, PA, **d.** Aug. 21, 1973, Hallandale, FL
Trombone / Bop, Swing

Bill Harris was one of the few modern trombonists of the 1945-60 era who was not influenced by J.J. Johnson. A very distinctive player almost from the start with a strong and highly original wit, Harris became a professional musician in 1938 and toured with the big bands of Gene Krupa, Ray McKinley and Bob Chester. After playing with Benny Goodman (1943-44) and Charlie Barnet and guesting on a couple of Eddie Condon's Town Hall concerts, Harris became famous for his work with Woody Herman's First Herd (1944-46); "Bijou" was a showcase and the trombonist is heard at his best on Herman's many uptempo (and often riotous) performances. One of the few First Herd members to also be in the Four Brothers Second Herd (1948-50), Harris also rejoined Herman a few times during 1956-59. He co-led a band with Charlie Ventura (1947), teamed up with Chubby Jackson (1953) and was a star with Jazz at the Philharmonic during 1950-54. During the second half of the 1950s Harris often collaborated with Flip Phillips and their band formed the nucleus of Benny Goodman's group in 1959. He mostly retired to Florida in the 1960s after a spell in Las Vegas, occasionally leading his own groups and playing with Red Norvo. Bill Harris led dates during 1945-57 for Mercury, EmArcy, Dial, Capitol, Verve, Fantasy and Mode, usually featuring alumni from the Woody Herman Orchestra. —*Scott Yanow*

The Bill Harris Memorial Album / Sep. 30, 1957 / Xanadu ◆◆◆◆
Originally recorded for the Mode label and last reissued by Xanadu in 1983, this was trombonist Bill Harris' last record as a leader (although he lived until 1973). A unique stylist with a wit and sound of his own, Harris is heard in top form with a quintet also including vibraphonist Terry Gibbs, pianist Lou Levy, bassist Red Mitchell and drummer Stan Levey. Bob Dorough dropped by to help Gibbs and Harris on the scat vocal of "Lemon Drop." All eight of the selections are remakes of songs recorded by Harris with Woody Herman's First and Second Herds, but obviously these quintet versions sound a bit different than the original big-band jams. Among the highlights of the sadly out-of-print LP are "Your Father's Moustache," "Apple Honey" and "Early Autumn," in addition to the jubilant "Lemon Drop." —*Scott Yanow*

● **Bill Harris and Friends** / Sep. 1957 / Original Jazz Classics ◆◆◆◆◆
Trombonist Bill Harris led relatively few recording sessions throughout his career, and this is the definitive one. On the quintet set with the great tenor Ben Webster, pianist Jimmy Rowles, bassist Red Mitchell and drummer Stan Levey, Harris' unique tone is showcased throughout "It Might as Well Be Spring"; he jams enthusiastically with Webster on a variety of standards, and verbally jokes around with Ben on a unique version of "Just One More Chance." —*Scott Yanow*

Craig Harris

b. Sep. 10, 1954, Hempstead, NY
Trombone / Avant-Garde

One of the more esoteric trombonists of the avant-garde, Craig Harris has been an original stylist throughout his career. He played in R&B bands early on, graduated from college in 1976 and had stints with Sun Ra (1976-78) and Abdullah Ibrahim (1979-81). During the 1980s and '90s he has worked with the who's who of the avant-garde including David Murray's octet and big band, Henry Threadgill, Lester Bowie's Brass Fantasy, Olu Dara, Cecil Taylor, Sam Rivers, Muhal Richard Abrams and Charlie Haden's Liberation Orchestra. Craig Harris has also led a few of his own groups (best known are Tailgater's Tales and the R&Bish Cold Sweat) and has recorded as a leader for several labels including India Navigation, Soul Note and JMT. —*Scott Yanow*

Aboriginal Affairs / 1983 / India Navigation ◆◆◆◆
Craig Harris, who had spent two years playing with Sun Ra's Arkestra, is a very advanced and generally original trombonist. On his debut as a leader, Harris doubles on the Australian didjeridoo. His septet on this set is filled with like-minded players including avant-garde veteran Ken McIntyre (switching between alto, flute and bass clarinet) and pianist/vocalist Donald Smith. Harris' six originals feature all the members of the group on a program of challenging material that rewards repeated listenings. —*Scott Yanow*

Black Bone / Jan. 4, 1983-Jan. 13, 1983 / Soul Note ◆◆◆◆
Outstanding session led by trombonist Craig Harris from 1983. His robust, vocalized solos were well supported by an all-star quartet including George Adams on tenor sax, Donald Smith on piano, bassist Fred Hopkins, and drummer Charlie Persip. The pieces ranged from respectful covers of standards to rousing, spirited originals. —*Ron Wynn*

Shelter / Nov. 19, 1986-Dec. 1986 / JMT ◆◆◆◆
W/ Tailgaters Tales. This is an aggressive, never-dull session that operates in the stylistic middle ground between jazz, R&B, blues, and rock. —*Ron Wynn*

Tributes / 1985 / OTC ◆◆◆

● **Blackout in the Square Root of Soul** / Nov. 1987 / JMT ◆◆◆◆◆
A first-rate example of a fresh direction in jazz that blends improvisatory zeal, funk, and R&B references. —*Ron Wynn*

Cold Sweat Plays J.B. / Nov. 1988 / JMT ◆◆
Great gutbucket R&B and populist jazz played with fire, zeal and grit. The Godfather would be proud. — *Ron Wynn*

Four Play / Aug. 1990 / JMT ◆◆◆

F Stops / Jun. 24, 1993-Jun. 25, 1993 / Soul Note ◆◆◆

Eddie Harris

b. Oct. 20, 1934, Chicago, IL, **d.** Nov. 5, 1996, Los Angeles, CA
Tenor Saxophone / Soul Jazz, Hard Bop, Groove

Eddie Harris had a diverse and erratic recording career, leading to many observers greatly underrating his jazz talents. Harris has had his own sound on tenor since at least 1960, his improvisations range from bop to free, he was a pioneer with utilizing the electric sax (and was much more creative on it than most who followed), he introduced the reed trumpet, is a fine pianist (one of his first professional jobs was playing piano with Gene Ammons), composed the standard "Freedom Jazz Dance" and, although his vocals are definitely an acquired taste, he is a skilled comedian.

After getting out of the military, Eddie Harris' very first recording resulted in a hit version of "Exodus." His high-note tenor playing (which managed to sound comfortable in the range of an alto or even soprano) was well featured on a series of strong-selling Vee-Jay releases (1961-63). After two outings for Columbia (1964), he switched to Atlantic for a decade. In 1966 Harris started utilizing an electric sax and he debuted the popular "Listen Here" (although the 1967 recording is better known). At the 1969 Montreux Jazz Festival Harris and Les McCann made for a very appealing combination, recording such songs as "Compared to What" and "Cold Duck Time." Harris' later output for Atlantic was streaky, sometimes rock-oriented and occasionally pure comedy. Later in life he recorded generally strong jazz sets for such labels as Impulse, Enja and Steeple Chase while remaining a unique musical personality. —*Scott Yanow*

Jazz for "Breakfast at Tiffany's" / July 1961 / Vee-Jay ◆◆◆◆
Tenor saxophonist Eddie Harris' third album features him exploring 11 themes from Henry Mancini's score for *Breakfast at Tiffany's*. Harris stretches out the most on "Moon River" and the title cut but he does justice to the nine lesser-known themes. This long-out-of-print LP holds one's interest throughout and, although Harris comes up with plenty of fresh ideas, he also never leaves the melody far behind. His unlisted backup group is a septet that includes trombonist Joe Avant, vibraphonist Charles Stepney, pianist Willie Pickens and guitarist Joe Diorio. A fine (if obscure) outing. —*Scott Yanow*

★ **Exodus to Jazz** / Jan. 17, 1961 / Vee-Jay ◆◆◆◆◆
This reissue of tenor saxophonist Eddie Harris' debut as a leader brings back his hit recording of "Exodus" (here heard in both the single and the full-length versions) and a variety of appealing originals. Harris, whose impressive range often puts him in the alto (and even soprano) register, was distinctive from the start. Joined by a fine Chicago-based quintet that also features pianist Willie Pickens and guitarist Joe Diorio, Harris is in top form on this classic session. —*Scott Yanow*

The Artist's Choice: The Eddie Harris Anthology / Jan. 1961-Feb. 20, 1977 / Rhino ◆◆◆
This two-CD sampler from Rhino Records jumps all over the place. Most of tenor saxophonist Eddie Harris' classics are here (including "Exodus," "Listen Here" and "Freedom Jazz Dance") but it is strange that the music was not programmed in strict chronological order since Harris (the master of the electronic sax) did evolve and go through different periods. Actually the recordings from the 1960s tend to be far superior to Harris' later output and it is odd that none of his more successful comedy numbers from later years (or anything after 1977) were included. Although reasonable as an introduction to Eddie Harris' career, many aspects of this wide-ranging artist are missing and nearly all of this music is currently available on other CDs, making this two-fer more of a frivolity than a necessity. —*Scott Yanow*

Mighty like a Rose / Apr. 14, 1961 / Vee-Jay ◆◆◆◆
Tenor saxophonist Eddie Harris' second album, following on the heels of his surprise hit "Exodus," did not have any big sellers but the eight performances are rewarding. This long-out-of-print LP features the same quintet as the earlier date (with guitarist Joe Diorio and pianist Willie Pickens also getting solo space). The highlights include "My Buddy," the theme from *Spartacus*, a couple of originals

and a brief version of the title cut. Harris' distinctive sound has always been well worth hearing; hopefully the revitalized Vee-Jay label will get around to bringing this date back one day. —*Scott Yanow*

Eddie Harris Goes to the Movies / 1962-1963 / Vee-Jay ✦✦✦

With the wine-and-candlelight string backdrops of Dick Marx throwing velvet drapery in back of a lush tenor sax, this LP oozes the mood-music formula so favored by pop record producers in mid-century America. Eddie Harris, to be sure, also follows some sturdy antecedents in this bag—Charlie Parker, for one—and he does well, coming up with some intricately curled bop runs within the limited time frames of each track and imprinting his own distinctive tone and phrasing on each well-worn tune. You can probably guess some of the tried-and-true choices—"Laura," "Moonglow," "Tonight," "On Green Dolphin Street" et al.—most of them slow ballads, or for a change of pace, a mild, perhaps Latin-accented bounce. A period piece, but seductive if you're in the mood. —*Richard S. Ginell*

The Lost Album Plus the Better Half / 1962-1963 / Vee-Jay ✦✦✦✦

This CD contains an LP's worth of unissued material plus half of an album that was released. With a supporting cast that on different tracks includes Ira Sullivan on trumpet, altoist Bunky Green, organist Mel Rhyne and guitarist Joe Diorio among others, the underrated but very distinctive tenor is in consistently spirited form. Eddie Harris stretches out on the rhythm changes of "Cuttin' Out" and the blues "Shakey Jake," (both of which are over 15 minutes long) and is heard on a variety of much shorter performances. A few of the briefer pieces are throwaways but all of Eddie Harris' Vee-Jay recordings are enjoyable and this one is no exception. —*Scott Yanow*

Bossa Nova / 1963 / Vee-Jay ✦✦✦✦✦

When the bossa nova wave came crashing through America, naturally the folks at Vee-Jay thought that their star saxophonist should give it a shot—and this LP came and went with the tide. But far from being a casual response to a fad, this is a great record, one where Harris came to his own comfortable accommodation with the Brazilian idiom without the aid of a single Luiz Bonfa or A.C. Jobim standard. Harris not only retains his own sound, he leans pleasingly into the bossa groove with a lightness of tone and swing that rivals pack leader Stan Getz, and he even stretches out into feverish Coltrane territory in his solo on the ten-minute "Cev y Mar." Credit a young neighborly Argentinian, the endlessly versatile Lalo Schifrin, for the solid piano work, half of the tunes, and the gritty group arrangements, but it is Eddie who comes up with the most beguiling composition, "Lolita Marie." Also guitarist Jimmy Raney checks in on a few tracks with some relaxed bop licks. —*Richard S. Ginell*

Cool Sax, Warm Heart / Jan. 15, 1964-Jan. 16, 1964 / Columbia ✦✦✦

Cool Sax from Hollywood to Broadway / Sep. 22, 1964-Sep. 24, 1964 / Columbia ✦✦✦

Because Eddie Harris had a major hit on his first record with his interpretation of the theme from *Exodus*, for a few years he often included movie themes in his recordings. This date took the concept to the extreme and some of the songs (such as "People," "From Russia with Love," the theme from *Malamondo* and "Who Can I Turn To") are not really worth hearing twice. The better tracks on this quintet outing (which also includes pianist Cedar Walton, guitarist Kenny Burrell, bassist Bob Cranshaw and drummer Billy Brooks) are "Days of Wine and Roses," "On Green Dolphin Street" and four Harris originals. This hard-to-find LP has some good music but is not essential. —*Scott Yanow*

For Bird to Bags / 1965 / Exodus ✦✦✦✦

It is only right that at least on this one occasion tenor saxophonist Eddie Harris recorded for the Exodus label since that was the name of his first hit. Most unusual among the selections is "Salute to Bird" (on which Harris quotes many Charlie Parker tunes) and "Salute to Bags" (during which the leader switches to piano). Harris plays with a Chicago-based quintet featuring Charles Stephney on vibes and piano and guitarist Roland Faulkner; pianist Willie Pickens and guitarist Joe Diorio (who were on Harris' earlier records) make guest appearances. Throughout, Harris (whose mastery of the extreme upper register and immediately recognizable sound are both quite impressive) is in excellent form; pity that this music was last available on a long-out-of-print LP. —*Scott Yanow*

The In Sound/Mean Greens / Aug. 9, 1965-Jun. 7, 1966 / Rhino ✦✦✦✦✦

This CD from Rhino's valuable Atlantic reissue program combines two former LPs from the 1965-67 period. *The In Sound* is among tenor saxophonist Eddie Harris' most significant recordings, highlighted by the original version of his "Freedom Jazz Dance," and including a memorable rendition of "The Shadow of Your Smile," three standards and a blues. Harris is assisted by an all-star rhythm section (pianist Cedar Walton, bassist Ron Carter and drummer Billy Higgins) and, on three selections, trumpeter Roy Codrington. The lesser-known *Mean Greens* set (comprising mostly originals except for Harris' high-note treatment of "It Was a Very Good Year") utilizes the same personnel on the first four numbers and is just as exciting,

with the calypso "Yeah Yeah Yeah" being a high point. The final three performances are more unusual, for Harris switches to electric piano and jams with a Latin rhythm section; included is the original (and somewaht obscure) recording of "Listen Here" which predates his hit version by over a year. Overall this CD is a well-rounded and highly recommended set. —*Scott Yanow*

The Best of Eddie Harris / Aug. 9, 1965-Apr. 19, 1969 / Atlantic ✦✦✦

Part of a massive Atlantic *Jazz Anthology* series in 1970, this LP-turned-CD was skimpy in its day, and now serves as the sketchiest of introductions to this bewilderingly eclectic saxophonist/inventor/pianist/bopper/balladeer/funkmeister—. Even assuming the limited time frame, why were three of Harris' seven Atlantic albums up to that point (*Mean Greens*, *The Tender Storm*, *Silver Cycles*) not even represented, and where is that galvanic swinger "Sham Time"? That said, there is still an awful lot of great '60s jazz on this record anyway: the funky-funky hit version of "Listen Here," two of its soulful successors, "Live Right Now" and "Movin' on Out"; the enduring pretzel-like "Freedom Jazz Dance"; a nice cover of "The Shadow of Your Smile"; and the lush, perhaps even tongue-in-cheek "Theme in Search of a Movie." Buy this only if you cannot afford the far-more-comprehensive two-CD box, *Artist's Choice*. —*Richard S. Ginell*

The Tender Storm / Sep. 19, 1966 / Atlantic ✦✦✦

In a sense, this LP was really the calm before the storm, the album on which Eddie Harris unveiled some new ideas in his act—that would explode on the very next album *Electrifying*—while hewing tightly to a standard acoustic quartet format. Here he starts to use the Varitone amplified saxophone, albeit very discreetly, as he sticks mostly to the doubled octave effects for a suave tone that allows for some slippery swinging. While Harris' soon-to-be-distinctive funk mode is in full bloom on the opening track, "When a Man Loves a Woman," his lovely ballad form from the Vee-Jay days remains intact on "Berkeley Square." The support couldn't be more professional—Cedar Walton (piano), Ron Carter (bass), Billy Higgins or Bobby Thomas (drums)—nor the selections more conventional (contemporary and past standards, plus Harris' title track), which in our conservative jazz climate ought to make this a candidate for reissue. —*Richard S. Ginell*

Excursions / 1966-1973 / Atlantic ✦✦✦✦✦

This double LP has three selections apiece from 1966 and 1968 and six from 1973, all of which were previously unreleased at the time. Eddie Harris is heard in top form on the diverse program, some of which is funky and some of which is purely straightahead. Highlights include "Listen Here Goes Funky," the 16-minute "Turbulence," "Fragmentary Apparitions," "Hey Wado" and "Oleo." Harris switches among tenor, his electrified sax and (on "Turbulence") reed trumpet; his sidemen include guitarist Ronald Muldrow, keyboardists Larry Nash and Richard Abrams, and pianists Jodie Christian and Cedar Walton. This out-of-print set is well worth searching for. —*Scott Yanow*

☆ Electrifying Eddie Harris / Apr. 20, 1967 / Atlantic ✦✦✦✦✦

This is one of tenor saxophonist Eddie Harris' most famous and significant LPs. He displays his mastery of the electronic Varitone saxophone (virtually the only player before John Klemmer to get his own sound on the electric sax) during the memorable "Theme in Search of a Movie" and particularly on his hit version of "Listen Here." A couple of tunes add a pair of percussionists, and "Sham Time" features a horn section in back of Harris; the basic quartet composes the leader, pianist Jodie Christian, bassist Melvin Jackson and drummer Richard Smith. A classic date. —*Scott Yanow*

Plug Me In / 1968 / Atlantic ✦✦✦

One of Eddie Harris' more underrated sessions, this out-of-print Atlantic album finds Harris creatively playing his electrified tenor on a wide variety of tunes, some of which utilize rock-funk rhythms of the period. Although his supporting cast includes such fine players as baritonist Haywood Henry, trumpeter Jimmy Owens and pianist Jodie Christian, the focus throughout is on Harris' distinctive playing. Highlights include "Live Right Now," "It's Crazy" and "Theme in Search of a T.V. Commercial." The only real fault to this enjoyable set is that the playing time is under 27 minutes. —*Scott Yanow*

High Voltage / Oct. 28, 1968-Apr. 19, 1969 / Atlantic ✦✦✦✦

Recorded live at Shelly's Manne Hole in Hollywood and the Village Gate in New York City, Eddie Harris is caught on LP near the peak of his popularity, peddling his electric funk thing with his regular quartet—Jodie Christian (piano), Melvin Jackson (bass) and Billy Hart (drums). His flair for drama shows in the pounding opening cut "Movin' on Out," in which he builds the tension with an escalating series of murky cascades on his Echoplexed electric sax. He can also be playful with the electronics on the repetitively lovely "Children's Song" (which, though credited to Harris, is actually a South African tune called "Mangwene Mpulele," previously covered by Harry Belafonte). And then, when you least expect it, Eddie turns around and adopts a husky Coleman Hawkins-like tenor stance on the retro ballad "Is There a Place for Us?" Fascinating music, and a jazz radio staple in its time. —*Richard S. Ginell*

Silver Cycles / Sep. 4, 1968 / Atlantic ✦✦✦✦✦

Still riding high from "Listen Here," Harris really started experimenting here with a dazzlingly eclectic LP that must have left his new fans wondering just who the real Eddie Harris was. There is good old Latinized funk in the opening cuts, "Free at Last" and "1974 Blues," but what was one to make of the next one, "Smoke Signals," with its interplanetary Echoplexed electric sax and ethereal wordless female voices? Then it's on to a long-limbed Coltrane tribute on pianist Jodie Christian's "Naima"-like "Coltrane's View," a wailing cry of raw pain with a huge band of horns, strings and voices ('I'm Gonna Leave You by Yourself'), another avant-garde electronic extravaganza ("Silver Cycles") and . . . well, you get the point; there's a surprise around every bend. The music is by turns swinging, touching, feverish, detached, nightmarish, and peaceful, bursting with new ideas generated from Harris' plunge into electronics. This album has been unjustly overlooked, probably because Harris was selling a lot of records and getting airplay at the time (a cardinal sin for purists), or perhaps for its free, anything-goes '60s spirit. The sound was always curiously distant on LP and on individual tracks reissued on CD; one wonders if this was due to a damaged or third-hand master tape. —*Richard S. Ginell*

Free Speech / Dec. 15, 1969/ Atlantic ✦✦✦

Eddie Harris, who doubles on electric tenor sax and reed trumpet, is joined by keyboardist Jodie Christian, bassist Louie Spears, drummer Billy Hart and percussionist Felix Henry on this okay session of funky jazz. Harris plays quite well as usual (he can be easily identified within a note or two) but none of his six originals on this out-of-print LP are very substantial. —*Scott Yanow*

Come on Down! / Mar. 3, 1970 / Atlantic ✦✦✦✦

The album title and the weird cover portrait of Eddie with an orange substituting for his head refer to the recording locale—Miami. The rationale might have been to give Miami the same down-home soul appeal that Muscle Shoals and Memphis were enjoying at the time. Certainly Harris got a romping soul-jazz-rock session out of the trip, a bit overloaded on the electric guitar side, but invigorating. Ira Sullivan joins the fracas now and then with some uninhibited trumpet, Donald "Duck" Dunn (from Booker T. & the MGs) is the anchor on bass and supersessionman Cornell Dupree dominates the guitars. The centerpiece is a long, frantic, rowdy R&B remake of "Live Right Now" in which Harris seems to be jooglin' around on electric sax as part of the rhythm section, and "Fooltish" has a loose swaggering appeal. "Really" finds him soulfully crooning through his electric horn for the first time, and "Why Don't You Quit?" builds inexorably to a majestic Echoplex extravaganza. Worth hunting for in the LP bins. —*Richard S. Ginell*

Live at Newport / 1970 / Atlantic ✦✦✦

Eddie Harris hit the 1970 Newport Jazz Festival head on with his satchel of electronic sax gear, funky soul-jazz track record, and a quartet with Jodie Christian now anchored on electric piano. Naturally there would be some funk on display ("Carry on Brother") and guest vocalist Eugene McDaniels, composer of "Compared to What," comes up with a lame, hectoring sequel, "Silent Majority." Yet a good deal of this truncated edition of Harris' Newport set is pitched at a more abstract level. "Don't You Know the Future's in Space" with its tumbling drums and outbreaks of near freeform reed trumpet (a Harris invention), is already in progress when we fade into the track, and "South Side" is a rough-and-tumble jazz sprint, with Harris delivering a complex cerebral solo. These advanced tracks didn't win him any points with the critics of the time, but hindsight reveals that harmonically as well as electronically, Harris was ahead of most of the pack. As a bonus, the LP includes a short post-set speech in which Harris prophesizes that his reed trumpet will be a godsend for brass players (who, alas, completely ignored it). —*Richard S. Ginell*

Second Movement / 1971 / Atlantic ✦✦✦

In 1968 tenor saxophonist Eddie Harris and pianist/vocalist Les McCann recorded the classic *Swiss Movement*. In contrast, their reunion three years later is surprisingly forgettable. Trumpeter Benny Bailey was replaced by strings and woodwinds, McCann takes an excess of vocals and, although Harris has a few fine solos, none of the five selections are at all memorable; when was the last time anyone played "Shorty Rides Again" or "Carry on Brother"? This out-of-print LP is a major disappointment. —*Scott Yanow*

Instant Death / Dec. 7, 1971 / Atlantic ✦✦✦✦✦

This is one of Eddie Harris' stronger Atlantic albums of the 1970s. Harris jamming on "Instant Death" is one of his most satisfying statements on the reed trumpet, guitarist Ronald Muldrow's "A Little Wes" is memorable and even the briefer pieces are worthwhile. In addition to Harris (who mostly plays his electrified tenor) and Muldrow, the group consists of keyboardist Muhal Richard Abrams, bassist Rufus Reid, drummer Billy James and percussionist Henry Gibson. This long-out-of-print LP is long overdue to be reissued on CD. —*Scott Yanow*

Eddie Harris Sings the Blues / Jul. 25, 1972 / Atlantic ✦✦✦

Eddie Harris had sung through his horn prior to this release, but not to such a great extent as on this wide-ranging LP. Here he tries to shape words through the filters of a reed mouthpiece, a slightly noisy wah-wah pedal and electronic amplification, and the results are genuinely expressive despite the aura of gimmickry. Indeed, "Please Let Me Go," thanks to Harris' pleading sax vocal and Richard Evans' string drapery, deliberately and hauntingly evokes Billie Holiday's orchestral sessions from the 1950s. In the category of funk, "Ten Minutes to Four" is almost a reworking of "1974 Blues" in the exotic 10/4 meter and, "Walk with Me" could have been a minor hit single with its catchy tune, wah-wah sax vocals and stentorian brass riffs. Finally, if for no other reason than ego (Harris admitted so himself), he tackles "Giant Steps" at a galloping Latin beat, the scattershot solo with the freak high notes all in his own style. Another fascinating installment in Harris' long Atlantic period. —*Richard S. Ginell*

Eddie Harris in the UK / 1973 / Atlantic ✦✦✦

Following the hip strategy of the time, Eddie Harris flew to London to mix it up with some of Britain's most in-demand rockers—including guitarists Jeff Beck and Albert Lee, pianist Stevie Winwood and drummer Alan White—on this LP. Truthfully, though, most of the results aren't too different from what Harris had been recording at home at the time, with only a hint of a rock edge. If anything, the workmanlike Brits are too much on their best behavior—Beck plays with restraint and taste while Lee is jazzier and a bit flashier—making Harris seem like a wild man by comparison. The most entertaining tune is an EH-patented funkster "Wait a Little Longer," which develops a head of steam and escalates into a freeform brawl, but the designated free workout "Conversations of Everything and Nothing," give or take a few stimulating passages, wanders uncontrollably. —*Richard S. Ginell*

Is It In? / Dec. 16, 1973-Dec. 17, 1973 / Atlantic ✦✦✦✦

Eddie Harris makes a radical turn toward electronic R&B on this popping, enterprising LP of grooves, humorous one-off vignettes, and other eclectic pursuits. Driven by a standard drum kit and tacky-sounding electric bongos, some of Harris' most irresistible grooves ("Funkaroma," "Look Ahere") can be found here. The title track, a Ronald Muldrow/Harris collaboration, is an ingenious self-contained little piece, with a chugging machine-driven rhythm, a catchy guitar riff, and a great brief repeated chorus. Harris resurfaces as a competent piano player (with overdubbed electric sax) on the down-home "House Party Blues" and as usual, he plugs another electronic innovation into his sax on "Space Commercial," an eerie pitch-tracking device designed by Robert Moog, inventor of the Moog synthesizer. —*Richard S. Ginell*

I Need Some Money / Jul. 15, 1974-Dec. 2, 1974 / Atlantic ✦✦✦

No longer content to hide his voice behind a horn and an amp, Eddie Harris finally steps out as a singer in the first of a series of humorous hard-luck songs that would be the flagships of his next few LPs (one reason for this move, perhaps, was the title of this album, but his vocals didn't produce any hits). Harris also fools with an electronic rhythm machine and electronic horn attachments that practically turn his sax into a synthesizer. In any case, the thing he still does best here is ride a groove, the best of which is the extremely danceable "Get on Down," complete with Leon Thomas-like yodeling and a percussive vocal from the erstwhile sax master. "Carnival" also develops a head of steam when it starts to evoke a street celebration. There are indications, though, that Harris' repertoire of funk sax licks is beginning to run a bit thin. —*Richard S. Ginell*

Bad Luck Is All I Have / 1975 / Atlantic ✦✦

Eddie Harris had nearly as many voices as sax timbres—ranging from nasal, sly asides to electronically strangled yowls and even falsetto. But none of these Eddie Harrises, nor the spirited percussive help of Willie Bobo, could save the humdrum, mostly R&B-based material that he created for this album. Even the long list of woes on the title track gets a bit tedious (besides, Loudon Wainwright III did the same thing with a more wry twist). His acoustic piano skills seems to have slipped, too, on the haphazard "Obnoxious," and the lengthy experimental piece at the LP's close, "Abstractions," is hopelessly diffuse. Pass this one right by. —*Richard S. Ginell*

That Is Why You're Overweight / 1975 / Atlantic ✦✦✦

This LP gets off to a terrific start with "It's All Right Now," a fascinating funk loop with a repeated chorus and a solid groove. Then the restless Harris goes all over the place, with soul vocals, comedy vocals (the gluttonous title track would be an enduring part of his act), straight jazz on acoustic piano, a single extravagant production ("Tryin' Ain't Dyin' "), with tenor sax, orchestra and chorus that sounds like his large-scale '60s outings, a bold Coltrane-ish modal piece for big band ("Exempt"), and ultimately just himself on rapid bebop tenor. Some of this stuff hits, some of it misses—in the case of bassist Bradley Bobo's embarrassing lead vocal on "Live Again," badly—and all of it suggests that Harris' curiosity and impatience had him flailing around in search of a direction. —*Richard S. Ginell*

The Reason Why I'm Talking Shit / 1978 / Atlantic ♦♦
One wonders who talked Atlantic Records into issuing this offbeat LP, the jazz world's equivalent of the Elvis talking album. It's a compilation of Eddie Harris comedy monologues before sets at nightclubs in Minneapolis, Evanston, Milwaukee and Redondo Beach, with plenty of sex to go around. Actually, Eddie is fairly droll in his X-rated way, telling the audience what is really on their minds at nightclubs. Still, you get the feeling that all of Side One is frustrating foreplay before the music that never comes. Side Two offers a few snippets of churchy and funky music in between the ha-haahs, and Harris gives his record company a nice little stab-in-the-back at the close. Hard to find—which is just as well. —*Richard S. Ginell*

How Can You Live Like That / Nov. 20, 1976 / Atlantic ♦♦♦
Still mixing up his pitches with erratic success, Eddie Harris comes up with another LP full of abrupt changes of gear. There is electric funk, some sumptuous big-band charts (courtesy of Richard Evans), new electronic attachments for his sax, some sorties into Jamaican reggae on "Love Is Too Much to Touch" and Brazilian samba on "Come Dance with Me," and the reliably funky guitarist Ronald Muldrow is always at hand. The title track is another series of urban complaints, though without humor this time. Side Two is mostly a reunion of the rhythm section that made Eddie's mid-'60s acoustic albums—an inspired Cedar Walton, Ron Carter and Billy Higgins—and they get a chance to stretch out at length like old times on "Nothing Else to Do." Some of this music sounds a bit routine for Harris but the range of idioms is extraordinary and it was apparently recorded in just one day. —*Richard S. Ginell*

The Versatile Eddie Harris / Feb. 8, 1977-Aug. 7, 1981 / Atlantic ♦♦♦♦
This LP has quite a bit of variety from tenor saxophonist Eddie Harris. Most of the selections are from February 20, 1977, although there are also two slightly earlier cuts that feature a rare sideman outing for trumpeter Don Ellis, and a humorous version of "That Is Why You're Overweight" from 1981. Otherwise Harris is showcased with a quartet that includes guitarist Ronald Muldrow. In addition Harris has duets with Muldrow ("No One Would Believe") and drummer Paul Humphrey ("One Man Section") and takes a vocal on "Drams Are for Real." No matter what the setting, the highly original and always funky Eddie Harris is heard in prime form. —*Scott Yanow*

Tale of Two Cities / 1978+May 1983 / Night ♦♦♦♦
This CD from the short-lived Night label features the talented tenor Eddie Harris on two different occasions. From 1978 Harris is caught live at Keystone Korner in San Francisco, playing four superior standards plus his famous hit "Listen Here" while joined by pianist Jack Wilson, bassist Herbie Lewis and drummer Eddie Marshall. The three Chicago cuts from 1983 ("Chicago Serenade," "Sonnymoon for Two" and "Illusionary Dreams") showcase him not only on tenor but electric sax, some reed trumpet, piano and vocals, along with pianist Rob Schneiderman, bassist Louis Spears and drummer Albert "Tootie" Heath. The recording quality is good and Harris sounds somewhat inspired on both occasions, emphasizing his roots in bebop while still sounding contemporary and original. —*Scott Yanow*

I'm Tired of Driving / Apr. 1979 / RCA ♦♦
Eddie Harris' next record company, strangely enough, was RCA, which had little interest in jazz at the time and didn't know what to do with this protean talent. The first try was this somewhat tepid brew of mostly R&B/slanted pop-jazz music with a whiff of disco now and then, utilizing Harris' array of straight and electronically-altered vocals, lots of acoustic tenor sax, and some piano. There is another querulously complaining vocal title track, and a large enough budget for the full Richard Evans strings/big band/voices treatment. Although EH's personal sax sound is always recognizable, and he is more crisply recorded than on any of his Atlantic records, the LP's anonymous, pre-packaged '70s feeling drains much of Harris' personality right out of the studio. —*Richard S. Ginell*

Playing with Myself / 1979 / RCA ♦♦♦
On his second and last RCA LP, Harris strips everything down to just tenor sax and acoustic grand piano—with himself overdubbing on both—in an austere, uncompromising series of sessions in several studios. A bold move, particularly for RCA (which probably didn't give a damn anymore), one that few players would dare attempt and fewer could pull off. For Harris, this is only a partial success; some tracks are wandering and anarchic, others are quite musical and one in particular, the title track, actually swings quite well without a rhythm section. The most consistent problem is that Harris' piano work is unvaried in touch and rather toneless regardless of which piano he is playing, certainly not in the same class as his instantly identifiable tenor sax, which is often magnificent. Some of his more interesting compositions include "Vextious Progressions," which is virtually as convoluted as "Giant Steps," a remake of "Freedom Jazz Dance," a careening marathon

called "What," and a wee burst of muted reed trumpet as a short encore ("I Heard That"). —*Richard S. Ginell*

Sounds Incredible / Mar. 1980 / Angelaco ♦♦♦♦
Starting with this LP, Eddie Harris ended his flirtations with the mass market, choosing to record mostly in a straightahead, bop-rooted manner for a variety of small American and European labels for the rest of his life. His electronic experimentations did not end, though, and he puts them to marvelously musical use here, armed with a good trio—Smith Dobson (piano), James Leary (bass), Eddie Marshall (drums)—and some of his best original material in many years. The two Harris originals that light up the grooves most are the jubilant "Singing My Cares Away," with a great Harris tenor solo combining elements of bop and his patented funk manner, and "You Know It's Wrong," with its wondrous big band-like chorus for massed electric saxes. There is also a really stimulating take on *Fiddler on the Roof's* "Matchmaker" in 6/8 time, and the LP concludes with Eddie playing by himself again, on toneless piano and warm tenor. Worth seeking out. —*Richard S. Ginell*

Steps Up / Feb. 20, 1981 / Steeple Chase ♦♦♦
Some torrid interchanges and dialogs with pianist Tete Montoliu. —*Ron Wynn*

The Electrifying Eddie Harris / Aug. 1982 / Mutt & Jeff ♦♦♦♦
This little-known Eddie Harris LP finds the veteran tenor saxophonist in excellent form, revisiting two of his earlier hits ("Listen Here" and "Theme in Search of a Movie") and introducing four newer pieces. Harris, who is joined by a Los Angeles-based rhythm section (pianist Bill Henderson, bassist Larry Gales and drummer Carl Burnette), was drifting into relative obscurity around this period but he is heard throughout this fine date near his peak. —*Scott Yanow*

Homecoming / 1985 / Spindletop ♦♦♦♦
This is an unusual LP in several ways. The Spindletop label was mostly known for releasing commercial jazz sets, not a challenging outing such as this one. Tenor saxophonist Eddie Harris and pianist Ellis Marsalis participate in seven mostly-adventurous duets, and their unlikely collaboration brought out the best in both players. They contributed two originals apiece in addition to creating interesting versions of "Out of This World," "Darn That Dream" and "Have You Met Miss Jones?" This set is well worth searching for but will probably be hard to find. —*Scott Yanow*

Eddie Who? / Feb. 27, 1986 / Timeless ♦♦♦♦♦
Eddie Harris plays tenor, reed trumpet, piano and takes a few vocals on this well-rounded CD. The trio outing with bassist Ralphe Armstrong and drummer Sherman Ferguson starts out with the humorous "Eddie Who?" and has among its highlights "Daahoud," "Softly as in a Morning Sunrise" and "There Was a Time." In general this is a straightahead outing that shows off Eddie Harris' mastery of the bebop vocabulary. Well worth picking up. —*Scott Yanow*

Live in Berlin / Mar. 24, 1988 / Timeless ♦♦♦
Recent, exemplary Harris material. —*Ron Wynn*

There Was a Time (Echo of Harlem) / May 9, 1990 / Enja ♦♦♦♦♦
Eddie Harris, famous as the master of the electrified sax and for his brand of funky jazz, sticks exclusively to acoustic straightahead music on this rewarding Enja CD. With assistance from pianist Kenny Barron, bassist Cecil McBee and drummer Ben Riley, Harris is heard in peak form on such songs as "Love Letters," "Autumn in New York," "The Song Is You" and a lengthy "Harlem Nocturne." Although Harris has maintained a fairly low profile during the past decade, he is still playing in his prime as this highly recommended CD demonstrates. —*Scott Yanow*

For You, for Me, For Everyone / Oct. 1992 / Steeple Chase ♦♦♦♦
Tenor saxophonist Eddie Harris was scheduled to record a duet set with pianist Jodie Christian but for unknown reasons Christian never showed up. Harris made it a solo showcase by first recording on piano and then overdubbing his tenor. The spontaneous experiment worked quite well as Harris performed four originals, lesser-known songs by Gershwin and Donald Byrd and four standards. The music is thoughtful and melodic but has its fiery moments, serving as a reminder (to those who may have forgotten) that Eddie Harris can really play. —*Scott Yanow*

Funk Project: Listen Here! / Nov. 7, 1992-Nov. 9, 1992 / Enja ♦♦♦

Dancing by a Rainbow / Apr. 3, 1995+Apr. 4, 1995 / Enja ♦♦♦
This 1996 effort features a 12-minute take on one of Harris' more famous compositions, "Mean Greens." —*Jason Ankeny*

Last Concert / Mar. 14, 1996-Mar. 15, 1996 / Act ♦♦♦♦

Freedom Jazz Dance / Mar. 11, 1997 / Music Masters ♦♦♦♦
Eddie Harris' final "authorized" studio date, like most in the last decade and a half of his life, is a conservative acoustic blowing session, trying one last time to capture the minds and hearts of bop-minded purists. Frankly, he never sounded better on tenor than he does here, his tone luminous, the freak high notes perfectly integrated into his uniquely swinging style, his ballad phrasing infused with an even

more poignant singing quality. He had a crack backup piano trio in tow, anchored by his old cohort Billy Hart on drums (who sounds freer than ever), with the emerging Jacky Terrasson on piano and George Mraz on bass. Yet the CD's mainstream idiom is cautious in the extreme—"Joshua Fit the Battle of Jericho" à la 'Trane is about as adventurous as this quartet gets (and EH was into that style when it was current)—and the only Harris original is the title tune, albeit superbly done. As a document of Eddie Harris in full bloom as a hard bopper, this is marvelous, but that was only one side of this bewilderingly multi-faceted, innovative musician—and as such, it is an incomplete memorial. —*Richard S. Ginell*

Gene Harris

b. Sep. 1, 1933, Benton Harbor, MI
Piano / Soul Jazz, Hard Bop, Groove

One of the most accessible of all jazz pianists, Gene Harris' soulful style (influenced by Oscar Peterson and containing the bluesiness of a Junior Mance) is immediately likable and predictably excellent. After playing in an Army band (1951-54) he formed a trio with bassist Andy Simpkins and drummer Bill Dowdy which was by 1956 known as the Three Sounds. The group was quite popular and recorded regularly during 1956-70 for Blue Note and Verve. Although the personnel changed and the music became more R&B-oriented in the early '70s, Harris retained the Three Sounds name for his later Blue Note sets. He retired to Boise, ID, in 1977 and was largely forgotten when Ray Brown persuaded him to return to the spotlight in the early-'80s. Harris worked for a time with the Ray Brown Trio and has led his own quartets ever since, recording regularly for Concord and heading the Phillip Morris Superband on a few tours. —*Scott Yanow*

And the Three Sounds / Jul. 26, 1971 / Blue Note ✦✦✦

Of the Three Sounds / Jun. 29, 1972 / Blue Note ✦✦✦

Yesterday, Today, Tomorrow / Jun. 14, 1973 / Blue Note ✦✦✦

Astral Signal / 1974 / Blue Note ✦✦✦

In a Special Way / Mar. 1976-May 1976 / Blue Note ✦✦

Gene Harris was always funky, right from the start of the Three Sounds until he began a belated solo career in the early '70s, but he never tried to come to terms with contemporary funk quite as explicitly as he did with *In a Special Way*. Teaming with a number of funk and fusion stars, including Earth, Wind & Fire's Philip Bailey and guitarist Lee Ritenour, Harris crafted a record that revels in contemporary soul trends from the mid-'70s—lite funk in the vein of EWF, disco, Philly soul, and vapid fusion. The production is heavy-handed and glossy, filled with drippy strings, thumping bass, wordless backing vocals and silly synthesized effects. Through it all, Harris plays *exactly like he always does*, as if he were oblivious to his surroundings. It makes for some truly bizarre moments: the disco interpretation of Cole Porter's "Love for Sale," the farting synth-bass meshing with disembodied vocals on "Five/Four," the completely botched fuzak and fuzz guitar take on Coltrane's "Naima." Occasionally, Harris plays quite nicely, as on "Rebop" or "Theme for Relana," but his solos just sink into the overproduced murk. There's really no explanation for the heavy-handed gloss of *In a Special Way*—with Harris' piano mixed to the back, it sounds like the work of studio hacks, but there are enough glimpses of his unique musical personality to make it a wasted opportunity. And there's really no explanation for the bevy of children on the cover, either. —*Stephen Thomas Erlewine*

Tone Tantrums / May 1977 / Blue Note ✦✦

Live at Otter Crest / Apr. 24, 1981 / Bosco ✦✦✦

Underrated latter-period Harris on piano with trio. Great extended "Battle Hymn," Basie's repertoire represented in "Shiny Stockings" and "Cute," and reliable Harris' "A Little Blues There." —*Michael G. Nastos*

Hot Lips / May 11, 1982 / JAM ✦✦✦

Pianist Gene Harris was in the early stages of a "comeback" (actually, he never really stopped playing) when he made this now-obscure LP for the obsolete JAM label. The funky and R&B-ish "Hot Lips" had a bit of radio airplay at the time, while most of the other music is both soulful and fairly straightahead. Harris is joined by guitarist Ron Eschete, bassist John Heard, drummer Jimmy Smith and percussionist Ephrain Toro for a worthwhile set whose other highlights include "Everything Must Change," "Meditation" and "Blue Monk." —*Scott Yanow*

The Gene Harris Trio Plus One / Nov. 19, 1985-Dec. 1985 / Concord Jazz ✦✦✦✦✦

This superb album (reissued on CD) solidified pianist Gene Harris' return to the jazz major leagues. Teamed up with bassist Ray Brown, drummer Mickey Roker and tenor saxophonist Stanley Turrentine, Harris stretches out on such songs as Ray Brown's blues "Gene's Lament," "Things Ain't What They Used to Be," "Yours Is My Heart Alone" and "Battle Hymn of the Republic." Harris and Turrentine work together so well on this soulful blues/bop date that one wishes they teamed up much more often. —*Scott Yanow*

Tribute to Count Basie / Mar. 1987-Jun. 1987 / Concord Jazz ✦✦✦

A big-band date that slightly predated pianist Gene Harris' association with the Philip Morris Superband, this CD is ostensibly a tribute to the recently deceased Count Basie, but surprisingly, only two of the eight songs ("Swingin' the Blues" and "Blue and Sentimental") were played by Basie, although one original ("Captain Bill") was written in homage of the bandleader. Harris' 16-piece orchestra does bring back the spirit of Basie's band in spots, with a lightly but steadily swinging rhythm section and such soloists as trumpeters Conte Candoli and Jon Faddis and tenors Plas Johnson and Bob Cooper. But in reality, Harris dominates the solo spotlight, and the music (which includes a memorable version of "When Did You Leave Heaven?") is a bit predictable. —*Scott Yanow*

● **Listen Here!** / Mar. 1989 / Concord Jazz ✦✦✦✦✦

Although often associated with the blues, only one of the ten selections on this quartet set by pianist Gene Harris (who is joined by guitarist Ron Eschete, bassist Ray Brown and drummer Jeff Hamilton) is technically a blues. An excellent all-around showcase for the soulful pianist, Harris sounds in prime form exploring such tunes as "This Masquerade," "Don't Be That Way," Eddie Harris' "Listen Here" and "The Song Is Ended." This CD gives listeners a fairly definitive look at Gene Harris' accessible and swinging style. —*Scott Yanow*

Live at Town Hall / Sep. 23, 1989 / Concord Jazz ✦✦✦✦

This CD documents one of the first concerts by Gene Harris' star-studded big band, an orchestra heard at the beginning of an 80-day world tour. Unlike his earlier big band Basie tribute album, Harris is not the only musician to get significant solo space on this set, although, due to the overflowing lineup, not enough is heard from everyone. The straightforward arrangements (by John Clayton, Frank Wess, Torrie Zito, Bob Pronk and Lex Jasper) balance swingers with ballads. Among the more memorable tracks are Harry "Sweets" Edison's feature (both muted and open) on "Sleepy Time Down South," a pair of fine vocals apiece by Ernie Andrews and Ernestine Anderson, the roaring "Old Man River" and Harris' interpretation of Erroll Garner's ballad "Creme De Menthe." Toss in short solos from the likes of Ralph Moore, James Morrison (on trombone), Frank Wess, Michael Mossman and baritonist Gary Smulyan and the result is a satisfying, swinging and fairly fresh big band date. —*Scott Yanow*

At Last / May 1990 / Concord Jazz ✦✦✦✦✦

A wonderful teamup of Gene Harris with Scott Hamilton. —*Ron Wynn*

Gene Harris and the Philip Morris Superband / Oct. 18, 1990 / Concord Jazz ✦✦✦

When listening to this CD (recorded in Sydney, Australia), it is best to forget about the all-star personnel in Gene Harris' big band since, except for guitarist Kenny Burrell (who has three short solos), none of the sidemen are heard from individually more than twice. There are no torrid tenor battles or trumpet tradeoffs and "Battle Royal" gives six soloists only two choruses apiece, missing the opportunity to generate some fireworks. What this CD does contain is a variety of swinging charts, blues-based material and ballads in the Count Basie style that mostly showcase the soulful and distinctive piano of Gene Harris. There is a strong uniformity to the set, despite using contributions from seven different arrangers, all of whom have a rather conservative approach. In addition to Harris, trumpeter James Morrison has a nice spot on "A Child Is Born," baritonist Gary Smulyan roars a bit on "Lover," altoist Jerry Dodgion imitates Johnny Hodges during "Warm Valley" and trumpeter Harry "Sweets" Edison is fine on his "Centerpiece." But in general this orchestra does not live up to the "Superband" title or the great potential of the personnel. —*Scott Yanow*

Black and Blue / Jun. 29, 1991 / Concord Jazz ✦✦✦✦

Although there are few actual blues on this CD, pianist Gene Harris gives all of the songs (whether complex standards, ballads or near-blues) a bluesy feel, adding soul and a church feeling to each of the melodies. With the assistance of guitarist Ron Eschete, bassist Luther Hughes and drummer Harold Jones, Harris is in typically fine form. —*Scott Yanow*

Like a Lover / Jan. 17, 1992 / Concord Jazz ✦✦✦✦

Live at Maybeck Recital Hall, Vol. 23 / Aug. 3, 1992 / Concord Jazz ✦✦✦✦

The blues piano artistry of Gene Harris is well known to jazz fans, and this rare solo concert CD is worth acquiring. The leisurely "Lu's Blues" is beautifully understated, while "Elephant Blossom Blues" is an uptempo romp in the mold of Oscar Peterson, and "Blues for Rhonda" emphasizes a percussive, boogie woogie-like approach. His approach to standards is also fresh. "Angel Eyes" brings to mind a closing set in an after-hours club, while his jubilant rendition of "Erroll's Theme" shows he has energy to spare. Don't miss this excellent date. —*Ken Dryden*

Brotherhood / Aug. 4, 1992-Aug. 5, 1992 / Concord Jazz ✦✦✦✦✦

A Little Piece of Heaven / Jul. 30, 1993-Jul. 31, 1993 / Concord Jazz ✦✦✦✦

Funky Gene's / May, 25, 1994-May 27, 1994 / Concord Jazz ✦✦✦

It's the Real Soul / Mar. 10, 1995-Mar. 11, 1995 / Concord Jazz ✦✦✦✦

In His Hands / Dec. 9, 1996+Dec. 10, 1996 / Concord Jazz ✦✦✦
Not only is this gospel album a huge change of pace for Gene Harris, it is also a major departure for Concord Jazz, whose mainstream rep is so ingrained that one would have expected Harris to jump labels in order to do this. For Harris, this is not totally unexpected—a lot of his work with the Three Sounds had a strong gospel feeling—but here he goes all the way over and leans into the call-and-response rhetoric with an expansive fervor, while also getting in some blues-drenched licks with the right hand. To drive home the rootsy point, Harris provides backing for the gospel vocals of his daughter Niki and various friends from his Boise, Idaho residence—all of whom do perfectly all right—and Brother Jack McDuff joins in on soulful organ now and then. While many traditional gospel flagwavers are included here, so are some pop songs ("Lean On Me," "Everything Must Change") that obviously have some of that old-time religious flavor. Some of the slower numbers drag on for a while, but the best tracks have a genuine vitality that ought to conquer any jazz-minded listener. —*Richard S. Ginell*

Down Home Blues / Dec. 11, 1996-Dec. 12, 1996 / Concord Jazz ✦✦✦
Having shared some gospel space on parts of Gene Harris' *In His Hands*, Harris and Brother Jack McDuff take the next step and move heavily into the blues on this one, assisted by Ron Eschete on guitar, Luther Hughes on bass and savvy veteran Paul Humphrey on drums. Clearly Harris has the edge on vitality as of these sessions; while Harris can still build up the blues rhetoric to a convincingly shouting climax, McDuff frankly sounds tired and out of gas on "J&G Blues" and several other numbers. Quite often, though, it is Eschete who comes up with the tastiest solos on this disc, and Gene's daughter Niki and Curtis Stigers help out on soul vocals on several tracks. There are also a couple of non-blues standards, "Time After Time" and "You Don't Know What Love Is", McDuff's mellow, Leslie-treated Hammond B-3 lead on the latter tune is his most soulful contribution on the album. —*Richard S. Ginell*

Donald Harrison

b. Jun. 23, 1960, New Orleans, LA
Alto Saxophone, Soprano Saxophone / Post-Bop
A talented post bop altoist with a personal angular style, Donald Harrison came to fame with Art Blakey's Jazz Messengers but has not become a major name in jazz yet despite his talent. He studied at the New Orleans Center for the Creative Arts with Ellis Marsalis, went to Berklee (1979-80), worked with Roy Haynes and Jack McDuff, and was with Blakey during 1982-84, sharing the front line with Terence Blanchard. Harrison and Blanchard co-led a group for a few years, recording frequently before they broke up their band. Donald Harrison returned to the Jazz Messengers for a few brief occasions, led his own groups and recorded as a leader for Candid, making guest appearances on CTI sessions. —*Scott Yanow*

Full Circle / May 14, 1990 / Sweet Basil ✦✦✦

For Art's Sake / Nov. 9, 1990-Nov. 10, 1990 / Candid ✦✦✦
This CD sometimes sounds like a hard bop jam session. Altoist Donald Harrison, who is joined by trumpeter Marlon Jordan (19 at the time), pianist Cyrus Chestnut, bassist Christian McBride and drummer Carl Allen, starts off the live session with "So What" and the "Freddie Freeloader"-like blues "Nut" (which alternates between two different keys). However, the date takes a welcome turn to the left during a 17-minute version of "Softly, as in a Morning Sunrise," which features an explorative Harrison solo, an explosive yet thoughtful improvisation from Jordan, and intense work by the rhythm section. After the leader's showcase on a rather sober interpretation of "In a Sentimental Mood," the quintet does a close impression of the Jazz Messengers on "For Art's Sake" (during which Chestnut imitates Bobby Timmons) before stretching out on "Oleo." This somewhat derivative music may not be essential, but the developing individuality of the young player does pop through here and there, and the solos are well played. —*Scott Yanow*

Indian Blues / May 22-23, 1991 / Candid ✦✦✦
Alto saxophonist Donald Harrison explores another area of his New Orleans heritage, the music of the Mardi Gras "Indians." His solos are more bluesy and R&B-flavored, while the supporting cast includes Dr. John on piano, along with Cyrus Chestnut, drummer Carl Allen, bassist Phil Bowler, percussionists Bruce Cox and Howard Smiley Ricks, and Harrison's father on vocals. —*Ron Wynn*

Power of Cool / 1993 / CTI ✦✦

● **Nouveau Swing** / Apr. 22, 1997 / GRP ✦✦✦✦
On his Impulse! Records debut, Donald Harrison mixes his usual straightahead work with rhythmic elements from tropical climates. Albert Wonsey plays appropriate piano on all tracks, though Harrison employs two different rhythm sections, Christian McBride and Carl Allen for the more conventional tunes and Ruben Rogers and Dion Parson for the others. The others include "Bob Marley," which borrows its rhythmic feel from such later Marley songs as "Exodus"; "Little Flowers,"

which also has a Caribbean lilt; "Septembro," the requisite samba; and "Duck's Groove," the requisite New Orleans second-line number. The concept is slight and inconsistently applied, as if Harrison was looking for something distinctive, but not too challenging. As ever, he is a proficient alto player with a comfortable retro style. —*William Ruhlmann*

Wendell Harrison

b. 1942, Detroit, MI
Clarinet, Tenor Saxophone / Bop
A fine clarinetist and tenor saxophonist, Wendell Harrison has been an important force in Detroit during the past 25 years. He began clarinet when he was seven, started playing tenor in high school and studied with Barry Harris. In 1960 he moved to New York, playing with Jack McDuff, Elvin Jones, Sonny Stitt, Grant Green and Sun Ra in addition to being in Hank Crawford's band for over four years. In 1970 Harrison moved back to Detroit, starting doing session work and became a jazz educator. He has formed several labels (Tribe, Rebirth and WenHa), recording frequently and utilizing such sidemen as Leon Thomas, Marcus Belgrave, Kirk Lightsey, Charles Tolliver and (with his Clarinet Ensemble) James Carter. —*Scott Yanow*

● **Forever Duke** / 1991 / Wen-Ha ✦✦✦✦✦
Clarinetist leads modern ensemble through five Duke tunes and two originals. Guests include Charles Tolliver (tpt) and Harold McKinney (p). There is a brief appearance by a five-piece clarinet ensemble. —*Michael G. Nastos*

Live in Concert / 1992 / Wen-Ha ✦✦✦
This 1992 performance in Detroit's Museum of African-American History includes a big band and the Clarinet Ensemble. Unique music, mostly modern, with three standards. —*Michael G. Nastos*

Rush & Hustle / 1994 / Wen-Ha ✦✦✦✦
This is a fairly unusual record. Wendell Harrison leads his Clarinet Ensemble on six of his colorful originals and the standard "My Shining Hour." The group consists of four clarinets (including Harrison who doubles on tenor), one bass clarinet and two contrabass clarinets; the promising James Carter is among the latter. In addition, a standard rhythm section (with an added percussionist) backs the reeds. Harrison's episodic compositions/arrangements (which range from modern bop, modal and light funk to some free moments) hold one's interest throughout, with the leader and pianists Harold McKinney and Pamela Wise getting their share of solo space. The one disappointment is that the bass clarinet and contrabass clarinets are primarily heard in the ensembles; it would have been nice to hear the two contrabass clarinets trading off. —*Scott Yanow*

Nancy Harrow

b. , New York, NY
Vocals / Standards, Vocal Jazz
Nancy Harrow made a strong impression with her Candid recording *Wild Women Don't Have the Blues* in 1960 but it was a long time before she was a full-time singer. She had studied classical piano extensively from the age of seven before decided to become a dancer and later a jazz singer. After her Candid recording and an album for Atlantic (1962), Harrow raised a family and spent time outside of music. In 1975 Nancy Harrow came back and has recorded frequently since then for Audiophile, Finesse, Inner City, Tono, Gazell and Soul Note. She is a talented and swinging bop-based singer who wrote all of the material for her 1993 *Lost Lady* release. —*Scott Yanow*

● **Wild Women Don't Have the Blues** / Nov. 2, 1960-Nov. 3, 1960 / Candid ✦✦✦✦
Although singer Nancy Harrow made a strong impression with this debut recording (which has been reissued on CD), she did not lead another record date until 1978 other than a lesser-known effort for Atlantic in 1966. Obviously, the years of obscurity were not deserved, for this set is a near-classic. Harrow is heard in her early prime singing such veteran songs as "All Too Soon," "On the Sunny Side of the Street," the seven-minute "Blues for Yesterday," and the title cut (originally done by Ida Cox in the 1920s). A more modern stylist (although influenced by Billie Holiday a little) than the material she performed at the time, Harrow is joined by such top mainstream players as trumpeter Buck Clayton (who provided the arrangements), tenorman Buddy Tate, trombonist Dickie Wells and pianist Dick Wellstood. Highly recommended, Harrow's debut date has plenty of spirit and enthusiasm. —*Scott Yanow*

Anything Goes / Nov. 29, 1978+Dec. 18, 1978 / Audiophile ✦✦✦✦
Nancy Harrow's first record in 16 years features the fine jazz singer accompanied by a sympathetic trio consisting of guitarist Jack Wilkins, bassist Rufus Reid and drummer Billy Hart. For this CD reissue, Harrow recorded four additional songs in 1990 with the same group. The renditions (mostly arranged by Bob Brookmeyer) are generally quite concise—many are under three minutes long—but full of hon-

est emotion and subtle creativity. Highlights include "A Woman's Intuition," "I Wished on the Moon," "Them There Eyes" and "Foolin' Myself." —*Scott Yanow*

Two's Company / May 8, 1984-Jul. 5, 1984 / Inner City ◆◆◆
This set (originally released by Japanese EmArcy but thus far only made available domestically on an Inner City LP) is a set of exquisite duets by singer Nancy Harrow and her longtime guitarist Jack Wilkins. The music should appeal both to jazz vocalist and cabaret collectors, for Harrow's improvisations are quite subtle. She shows great respect for both melody and lyrics and performs mostly older material, such as "Just One of Those Things," "I've Got a Crush on You" and "Easy Living"; the occasional exceptions include Bob Marley's "Is This Love?" Wilkins supports Harrow's voice quite sympathetically and has some short solos on the rather brief (all but one of the dozen songs are under three minutes) but satisfying interpretations. —*Scott Yanow*

Street of Dreams / Apr. 28, 1988-Oct. 17, 1988 / Gazell ◆◆◆

Secrets / Nov. 21, 1990-Jan. 18, 1991 / Soul Note ◆◆◆◆◆

Lost Lady / Jun. 28, 1993-Nov. 29, 1993 / Soul Note ◆◆◆◆

Antonio Hart

b. 1969, Baltimore, MD
Alto Saxophone / Hard Bop, Post-Bop
An excellent altoist who gained recognition for his work with Roy Hargrove, Antonio Hart studied classical saxophone at the Baltimore School for the Arts for four years. He sat in with Art Blakey's Jazz Messengers, toured with Hargrove for a few years and in the mid-'90s formed his own group. Hart, who is most influenced by Cannonball Adderley and Gary Bartz, has recorded for Novus with Hargrove and as a leader on four of his own CDs. —*Scott Yanow*

For the First Time / Feb. 1991-Apr. 1991 / Novus ◆◆◆◆
Based on his debut as a leader, nobody will ever accuse altoist Antonio Hart of suffering from a lack of confidence! The opener, his burning "Majority," starts immediately by featuring Hart trading off with tenor saxophonist Bill Pierce. On the strutting "Big H.M." the 22-year-old altoist welcomes his employer of the time, trumpeter Roy Hargrove, and holds his own. Hart also roars on "Del Sasser" and flourishes on the hard bop material, much of which also features the fine trumpeter Thomas Williams. In addition, Hart's treatments of some standard ballads finds him showing maturity and great restraint, letting the themes tell their story without feeling the need to double-time everything. An impressive debut. —*Scott Yanow*

Don't You Know I Care / 1992 / Novus ◆◆◆◆
It was a measure of Antonio Hart's confidence that he invited fellow alto great Gary Bartz to sit in on "At the Closet Inn" during his second recording date as a leader. It was also a measure of Hart's talents that even at this early stage he was not overshadowed by the intense if underrated Bartz. The nucleus band for this excellent advanced hard bop date consists of pianist Aaron Graves, bassist Rodney Whitaker, drummer Greg Hutchinson, and up-and-coming trumpeter Darren Barrett; trombonist Jamal Haynes and percussionist Kimati Dinizulu are also heard on two songs apiece. Hart performs seven originals, Duke Ellington's "Don't You Know I Care" and Quincy Jones' "Jessica's Day," displaying a fairly original tone and strong creative ideas within the tradition. —*Scott Yanow*

● **For Cannonball & Woody** / 1993 / Novus ◆◆◆◆◆
Altoist Antonio Hart's latest recording starts out with an eerie recreation of the Cannonball Adderley version of "Sticks" from 1968 which, like the original, even has a live audience shouting out encouragement and clapping along more or less in time. After that the music gets more original, featuring trumpeter Darren Barrett (who shows an impressive amount of versatility), either Carlos McKinney or Mulgrew Miller on piano and a guest spot from cornetist Nat Adderley on "Sack O' Woe." In addition to the Adderley tributes, there are several Woody Shaw pieces that generally contain new arrangements for an expanded group, based more on the spirit of the original '70s versions rather than the notes. Antonio Hart is in top form throughout this well-conceived release. —*Scott Yanow*

It's All Good / 1994 / Novus ◆◆◆◆

Here I Stand / Mar. 25, 1997 / GRP ◆◆◆◆◆
One cannot help but be impressed by the versatility that altoist Antonio Hart shows throughout this set. He plays with the intensity of John Coltrane on "The Community," utilizes his soprano on the light reggae groove of "True Friends," jams a boppish rendition of "Flamingo" in a trio with organist Shirley Scott (who plays effective piano on the blues "Like My Own"), sounds like a mixture of Richie Cole and Paquito D'Rivera on the Afro-Cuban "Ven Devorame Otra Vez" (which has a vocal sample of three Latin singers that fits in well), and also plays more advanced music that utilizes three or four other horns (a little reminiscent of Herbie Hancock's "Speak Like a Child"). Overall, Hart's music generally fits into the

modern mainstream, but it avoids being predictable or merely revisiting the past. The only minus to this program is the closing piece, which has an annoying rap by Jessica Care Moore, but that can easily be skipped. Otherwise, this is a well-conceived and highly recommended set, one of Antonio Hart's most rewarding to date. —*Scott Yanow*

Billy Hart

b. Nov. 29, 1940, Washington, DC
Drums / Post-Bop
A flexible drummer who has been a sideman in many different settings, Billy Hart is a creative player most at home playing advanced jazz. He worked early on in Washington D.C. with Buck Hill and Shirley Horn and was with the Montgomery Brothers (1961), Jimmy Smith (1964-66) and Wes Montgomery (1966-68). Hart was a member of Herbie Hancock's challenging sextet (1969-73) and played regularly with McCoy Tyner (1973-74) and Stan Getz (1974-77) in addition to extensive freelancing (including recording with Miles Davis on 1972's *On the Corner*). His own opportunities to lead sessions have been comparatively rare but Billy Hart has led interesting dates for Horizon, Gramavision and Arabesque. —*Scott Yanow*

● **Enchance** / Feb. 24, 1977-Mar. 3, 1977 / A&M ◆◆◆◆◆
A recording just at the edge of all-out. Powerful, pretty, and potent. All originals. An important document. —*Michael G. Nastos*

Oshumare / 1985 / Gramavision ◆◆◆

Rah / Sep. 1987 / Gramavision ◆◆◆
Excellent original compositions. This is very listenable, time after time. Many great soloists and ensemble players. Highly recommended. —*Michael G. Nastos*

Amethyst / May 22, 1993-May 29, 1993 / Arabesque ◆◆◆◆

John Hart

b. Jun. 15, 1961, Fort Belvoir, VA
Guitar / Post-Bop, Hard Bop
A fairly distinctive modern mainstream guitarist, John Hart has impressed many with his fine recordings as a leader for Blue Note and Concord. He began on the guitar when he was 12, graduated from the University of Miami in 1983 and moved to New York City the following year. Among his most significant associations were those with Terumasa Hino, Larry Goldings and particularly Jack McDuff, with whom he toured and recorded. In addition, Hart has been a busy music educator and performed with many top jazz artists, including Jimmy Smith, Lou Donaldson, James Moody, Mike Mainieri, the Maria Schneider Orchestra and Steve Allen, in addition to leading his own groups. —*Scott Yanow*

● **One Down** / Dec. 21, 1988 / Blue Note ◆◆◆◆
John Hart is a talented jazz improviser. Although his sound was not overly distinctive at this early stage, he proves throughout the set (which includes four unaccompanied solos, five trio numbers, one quartet performance and two songs by a quintet) that he is an inventive player. Whether playing the ridiculously complex "Take No Prisoners," a moody ballad (such as his "Deborah"), or the medium-tempo boppish blues "Transcendence," or reinterpreting standards, he never seems to run short of melodic ideas. The musical communication between Hart, bassist Chuck Bergeron and drummer John Riley is quite impressive, and the horns (trumpeter Tim Hagans and tenor saxophonist Rick Margitza) sound heated in their appearances. A strong debut. —*Scott Yanow*

Trust / Apr. 28, 1991 / SomethinElse'◆◆◆
John Hart, a very quiet electric guitarist, is often quite reminiscent of Jim Hall. Working carefully with bassist Michael Formanek and drummer Victor Lewis on this CD, Hart manages to sound thoughtful and introspective not only on the lyrical ballads, but even on the rather fast blues "The Arrival" and a bright version of "Everything I Love." His three unaccompanied features ("Embraceable You," "All the Things You Are" and "Michael's Turn") find the guitarist leaving even more space than on the trio tracks (although "All the Things You Are" really cooks), making an impact with each note. But it is important to listen to these subtle performances at a fairly high volume; otherwise, one might mistake them for background music. —*Scott Yanow*

High Drama / Jun. 12, 1995-Jun. 14, 1995 / Concord Jazz ◆◆◆◆

Bridges / Feb. 5, 1997 / Concord Jazz ◆◆◆
Bridges is John Hart's second release as a leader for Concord, but the young guitarist's first with his true working quartet (saxophonist Chris Potter, bassist Bill Moring and drummer Andy Watson, with whom Hart has been performing for the past five years). Though Hart and Potter are certainly adequate and inventive soloists and the rhythm section proves deftly sympathetic, nothing ever really seems to catch fire in even one of these ten tracks. There's little doubt that new originals such as "Private Eyes" and "Urban Appalachia" are commendable for their taste

and sense of reflective jam. And you really can't argue with the selection of Rodgers & Hammerstein's "It Might as Well Be Spring," Johnny Mandel's standard "Summer Wishes, Winter Dreams" and Antonio Carlos Jobim's "Zingaro" as cover versions. It's not that *Bridges* is bad, because it's not; it's very competently played and full of jazzy, tasteful bop, post-bop and modern chops. It's just that *Bridges* never seems to build any intensity, and that there's so much music that's equally if not more interesting being made out there. —*Chris Slawecki*

Johnny Hartman

b. Jul. 3, 1923, Chicago, IL, d. Sep. 15, 1983, New York, NY
Vocals / Standards, Ballads, Traditional Pop

A superior ballad singer with a warm baritone voice, Johnny Hartman was rediscovered, to an extent, posthumously when some of his recordings were used on the soundtrack of the 1995 Clint Eastwood film *Bridges of Madison County,* but jazz fans had never forgotten him for his classic date with John Coltrane. After military service, Hartman sang with Earl Hines (1947), the Dizzy Gillespie Big Band (1948-49) and Erroll Garner. Although he recorded two Bethlehem albums in 1956, Hartman was generally overlooked during the 1950s. However, his three Impulse albums (1963-64) were well received, particularly the Coltrane collaboration, which was highlighted by the definitive version of "Lush Life" and a memorable "My One and Only Love." But it would be 1977 before he recorded again and, despite some fine later sessions (including for Bee Hive), Johnny Hartman was underrated throughout his lifetime. —*Scott Yanow*

All of Me / Nov. 1956 / Bethlehem ✦✦✦✦

Reissued on CD by Evidence, the original 12-song program has been augmented by four "new" alternate takes but the CD lists the wrong personnel. The warm baritone singer Johnny Hartman is actually accompanied by the Ralph Sharon Trio and trumpeter Howard McGhee on four songs and the Frank Hunter String Orchestra on the remainder of the set. The emphasis is on ballads (always Hartman's strong point) with the highlights including "Blue Skies," "Tenderly," "The Lamp Is Low" and "I Concentrate on You." —*Scott Yanow*

Songs from the Heart / Oct. 1955 / Bethlehem ✦✦✦✦

Johnny Hartman's first full album as a leader (which has been reissued on this CD through the Evidence label) features the singer doing what he does best—interpreting superior ballads. Accompanied by pianist Ralph Sharon, bassist Jay Cave, drummer Christy Febbo and the underrated bop trumpeter Howard McGhee, Hartman sings a dozen top-notch standards, including "What Is There To Say?" "We'll Be Together Again," "They Didn't Believe Me" and "Moonlight in Vermont"; in addition, the CD has six "new" alternate takes. Hartman's deep baritone voice sounds particularly rich throughout the enjoyable set. —*Scott Yanow*

Sittin' in With / 1961 / VGM ✦✦✦

This is a live album that should interest collectors. The warm baritone ballad singer Johnny Hartman is heard on four concise numbers backed by pianist Andrew Hill's trio (with bassist John Mixon and drummer Gene Gamage). In addition there are two lengthy improvisations from Hill that give the innovative pianist an opportunity to stretch out and allows listeners to hear how he sounded prior to his Blue Note recordings. —*Scott Yanow*

Priceless Jazz Collection / Mar. 7, 1963-Sep. 24, 1964 / GRP ✦✦✦

Priceless Jazz Collection is a budget-priced compilation that intends to give neophytes an affordable introduction to Johnny Hartman's Impulse! recordings. Although purists and collectors will find this sampler incomplete and inconsequential, it nevertheless gives new listeners a good idea of Hartman's music during the '60s by featuring such fine cuts as "Lush Life," "These Foolish Things," "They Say It's Wonderful," "I Just Dropped by to Say Hello" and "In the Wee Small Hours of the Morning." —*Leo Stanley*

★ John Coltrane and Johnny Hartman / Mar. 7, 1963 / Impulse! ✦✦✦✦✦

John Coltrane's matchup with singer Johnny Hartman, although quite unexpected, works extremely well. Hartman, who had not recorded since 1956, was in prime form on the six ballads, and his versions of "Lush Life" and "My One and Only Love" have never been topped. Coltrane's playing throughout the session is beautiful, sympathetic and still exploratory; he sticks exclusively to tenor on the date. At only half an hour, one wishes there were twice as much music, but what is here is classic, essential for all jazz collections. —*Scott Yanow*

I Just Dropped by to Say Hello / Oct. 9, 1963+Oct. 17, 1963 / MCA ✦✦✦✦✦

This 1995 GRP CD reissue brings back ballad singer Johnny Hartman's second Impulse session, following his classic collaboration with John Coltrane. Hartman is heard in peak form throughout these 11 pieces, which include "In the Wee Small Hours of the Morning," "Sleepin' Bee," "Stairway to the Stars" and even "Charade." Tenor saxophonist Illinois Jacquet is on five of the songs, guitarists Kenny Burrell and Jim Hall help out on a few tunes, and Hartman is consistently accompanied by

pianist Hank Jones, bassist Milt Hinton and drummer Elvin Jones. This is one of his finest recordings. —*Scott Yanow*

The Voice That Is / Sep. 22, 1964-Sep. 24, 1964 / Impulse! ✦✦✦

Ballad singer Johnny Hartman's third and final Impulse session is not quite on the same level as the first two. Although the earlier of the two sessions has several near-classic performances (including "My Ship," "Waltz for Debby" and "It Never Entered My Mind"), the second date has weaker material, primarily several songs from movies or shows including "Sunrise, Sunset." Hartman is in fine form, whether backed by the Hank Jones quartet or accompanied by an octet arranged by pianist Bob Hammer, but this set is not as essential as his earlier meetings with John Coltrane and Illinois Jacquet. —*Scott Yanow*

The Unforgettable Johnny Hartman / Sep. 1966 / ABC/Paramount ✦✦✦

For Trane / Nov. 29, 1972+Dec. 1, 1972 / Blue Note ✦✦✦

This CD combines parts of two sessions recorded in Tokyo by the warm ballad singer Johnny Hartman. Although titled *For Trane,* the vocal recital only has three songs associated with John Coltrane ("My Favorite Things," "Violets for Your Furs" and "Nature Boy") and the majority of the selections are actually taken from an unrelated session in which Hartman was matched with trumpeter Terumasa Hino. The music alternates between ballads ("Violets for Your Furs" and "The Nearness of You" are high points) and swingers and, although Hartman does not really improvise, his voice (still in its prime at the time) is appealing. Considering his slim discography, Johnny Hartman's fans will definitely want this one. —*Scott Yanow*

Today / 1972 / Perception ✦✦

Today, Johnny Hartman's first record for Perception, was a new beginning of sorts. It just wasn't a very good beginning. Hartman decided to ease his way into the popular mainstream with *Today,* recording such recent pop hits "By the Time I Get to Phoenix," "Games People Play," "Betcha by Golly Wow," "Help Me Make It Through the Night" and "We've Only Just Begun." All of these songs are terrific pop singles, but with the exceptions of "By the Time I Get to Phoenix" and "Help Me Make It Through the Night," they're identified by their performers as much as the songs themselves, and none of them lend themselves to the kind of hushed, sympathetic treatment Hartman has been known to give. Furthermore, the sound of the record is too slick for Hartman, which gives the record an uneasy 'easy-listening' sound. There are moments on *Today* that work, such as the lovely "Summer Wind," but by and large this is a missed opportunity. —*Stephen Thomas Erlewine*

I've Been There / 1975 / Perception ✦✦

Like its predecessor *Today, I've Been There* is a polished collection of contemporary pop and soul hits as sung by the gifted jazz vocalist, Johnny Hartman. "Raindrops Keep Falling on My Head," "If," "Rainy Days and Mondays," "The First Time Ever I Saw Your Face" and "For the Good Times" are all great pop songs, but Hartman is simply not suited for this straightahead style—he is too idiosyncratic to put himself into this straitjacket. As a result, *I've Been There* sounds awkward, with only a few moments rising to the merely pleasurable status. A rare case of a complete dud from Johnny Hartman. —*Stephen Thomas Erlewine*

Live at Sometime / Oct. 13, 1977 / Trio ✦✦✦

Once in Every Life / Aug. 11, 1980 / Bee Hive ✦✦✦✦✦

Johnny Hartman's next-to-last album (he made a record for Audiophile 12 days later) finds the 57-year-old singer still in prime form. His rich baritone voice is joined by a sextet including Frank Wess (on tenor and flute), trumpeter Joe Wilder and pianist Billy Taylor. The ballads range from slow to a brighter medium-tempo pace, and Hartman (particularly on such tunes as "Easy Living," "Wave" and "I Could Write a Book") shows that he still had it this late in his career. Unfortunately, this Bee Hive album has yet to be reissued domestically on CD. —*Scott Yanow*

This One's for Tedi / Aug. 23, 1980 / Audiophile ✦✦✦

And I Thought About You / 1998 / Blue Note ✦✦✦✦

Johnny Hartman has gained posthumous fame as one of the warmest ballad singers of this century. His deep baritone voice is well showcased on this 1997 CD, which emphasizes slower tempos with a couple of exceptions ("Sunday" and "After You've Gone"). Accompanied by a subtle orchestra arranged by Rudy Traylor (the personnel is unknown), Hartman is in such fine form that it seems sad that this obscure effort was his only studio date of the 1957-62 period. Highlights of the brief (33-minute) set include "To Each His Own," "Little Girl Blue" and "There's a Lull In My Life." —*Scott Yanow*

Stan Hasselgård

b. Oct. 4, 1922, Sundsvall, Sweden, d. Nov. 23, 1948, Decatur, IL
Clarinet / Bop, Swing

Stan Hasselgård was (along with Buddy DeFranco and Tony Scott) the first clarinetist to fully explore bebop, and the only one to share the bandstand with Benny Goodman. He played swing in Sweden and recorded with local groups before moving to New York in 1947. Hasselgård sat in with both Dixieland and bop players and recorded in December for Capitol, using Red Norvo and Barney Kessel. For part of 1948 he was in the Benny Goodman Septet along with Wardell Gray and Teddy Wilson and, although a recording strike kept the group off records, broadcasts have been released by Dragon that contrast the two clarinetists' styles. Hasselgård had a quintet with Max Roach later in the year and was planning a new band when he died in a car crash at the age of 26. — *Scott Yanow*

Young Clarinet / Dec. 1940-Nov. 18, 1948 / Dragon ✦✦✦✦
This single album spans clarinetist Stan Hasselgård's entire recording career, starting with what was probably his first session in 1940 (when he was 18) up until a V-disc date in 1948 (with pianist Barbara Carroll and guitarist Chuck Wayne) that was made just five days before his tragic death in a car accident. But, other than two numbers from the November 1948 set, the music on this LP focuses on Hasselgård's beginning years, when he was a swing-oriented clarinetist most influenced by Benny Goodman. He is heard in a variety of obscure studio performances with fellow Swedes, none of whom became famous outside of Europe. Whether it be in a duet or a septet, Hasselgård comes across (in hindsight) as the most sophisticated soloist. A historically important and enjoyable swing set. — *Scott Yanow*

Jazz Clarinet of Ake "Stan" Hasselgård (1945-1948) / Oct. 11, 1945-Nov. 18, 1948 / Dragon ✦✦✦✦✦
One of several Dragon LPs featuring the recordings of the talented but ill-fated clarinetist Stan Hasselgård, this set mostly consists of previously unreleased performances. Hasselgård plays "Blue Skies" and "I Couldn't Sleep a Wink" in 1945 with a Swedish trio, plus two other numbers with a sextet including trumpeter Rolf Ericson; he also performs ten songs with a sextet on a 1947 radio broadcast and is heard just five days before his death at a V-disc session. The latter resulted in an unissued version of "Patty's Idea" (which starts off with Hasselgård doing a verbal imitation of Benny Goodman) and "Cotton Top"; one can hear Hasselgård's immersion in bop. Highly recommended, as are Stan Hasselgård's other Dragon sets. — *Scott Yanow*

The Permanent Hasselgård / Oct. 1945-Nov. 1948 / Phontastic ✦✦✦✦✦
This excellent sampler CD (which does not duplicate the other Stan Hasselgård sets on Dragon) features the brilliant but ill-fated bop clarinetist in a variety of rare performances. The first dozen numbers were recorded in Sweden during 1945-47 (all but three are from 1947) and they trace Hasselgård's development from a Benny Goodman-influenced swing player to one open to the innovations of bop; trombonist Tyree Glenn is a guest on "Sweet Lorraine." The final ten selections are from Hasselgård's year in the US, including some songs from his own combos, a meeting with vibraphonist Red Norvo on "Who Sleeps," four live selections taken from Hasselgård's brief period with Benny Goodman's Septet (a two-clarinet group that also included tenor saxophonist Wardell Gray) and a V-disc recording of "Cotton Top." This enjoyable release is highly recommended to bop collectors who may not be aware of Stan Hasselgård's talents. — *Scott Yanow*

Jammin' at Jubilee / Jan. 5, 1948-Jul. 3, 1948 / Dragon ✦✦✦✦✦
In August 1947, clarinetist Stan Hasselgård left his native Sweden for the US, where he would spend his final year before his premature death in a car accident. This very interesting Dragon LP takes its material from 1948, when a recording strike kept the clarinetist (and virtually all other union musicians) off of records. The mostly live performances feature Hasselgård with a quintet headed by drummer Jackie Mills, jamming with tenorman Wardell Gray and pianist Dodo Marmarosa and as part of the Arnold Ross Quartet (with guest Billy Eckstine on vocals and valve trombone), plus three selections made with Benny Goodman's shortlived 1948 septet. It was during his final year that Hasselgård evolved quickly from a swing clarinetist to a more boppish player (one of the few on his instrument) and began to really sound quite individual. This LP shows the great promise he had. — *Scott Yanow*

● **At Click (1948)** / May 24, 1948-Jun. 5, 1948 / Dragon ✦✦✦✦✦
Were it not for his tragic death in a car accident late in 1948, Stan Hasselgård might be remembered as one of jazz's top clarinetists. He had impressed Benny Goodman to the point that BG used him as part of his septet for a few weeks in 1948. Although no commercial recordings resulted due to a recording strike, the group (which also featured tenor saxophonist Wardell Gray and pianist Teddy Wilson) broadcast regularly from the Click in Philadelphia. Virtually all of the existing joint Goodman-Hasselgård airchecks are included on this Dragon CD, which adds a few more performances to the original program of the LP of the same name. The boppish music is often fascinating and Benny Goodman ("The King of Swing") fits quite well into the advanced arrangements. The recording quality is generally decent and, due to the historic nature of these timeless (and rather unique) performances, very acceptable. — *Scott Yanow*

Greg Hatza

Organ / Soul Jazz, Hard Bop
In the mid-'70s, organist Greg Hatza recorded two albums for Coral and then was virtually forgotten for 20 years before recording *The Greg Hatza ORGANization* in the mid-'90s for Palmetto, showing that he had not lost anything despite the years of obscurity. At the age of five, Hatza had his first piano lessons, but it was a decade later that he discovered the organ and permanently switched instruments, teaching himself. He began working at age 16, played at football player Lenny Moore's club for four years, and recorded his two early records. But after the organ dropped in popularity in the 1970s, Hatza switched for a long period to electric keyboards. However, after hearing Joey De Francesco play in 1993, Hatza was persuaded by the young organist (who was familiar with his records) to return to the organ, and he soon signed with Palmetto. — *Scott Yanow*

The Greg Hatza Organization / Mar. 1993-Apr. 1993 / Palmetto ✦✦✦
Greg Hatza is a Jimmy Smith-influenced organist who had not been on records for over 20 years before the release of this CD. He plays in a timeless style that very much harks back to the 1960s, particularly on the blues and standards. Two of the selections, a slower than usual version of "Moment's Notice" (made a bit funky) and an advanced original ("The Wizard"), find him breaking away from the Jimmy Smith style and displaying his own interesting musical personality. Hatza's backup group features a pair of strong voices in the Jackie McLean-inspired altoist Jim Snidero and versatile guitarist Paul Bollenback, who switches from rock to Wes Montgomery with little difficulty; drummer Gary Jenkins is fine in support, and guest Major Boyd adds his soulful soprano to "From Me to You." All in all, this is enjoyable, swinging music. — *Scott Yanow*

● **In My Pocket** / Mar. 5, 1996 / Palmetto ✦✦✦✦
The return of the organ to prominence in the 1990s has allowed Greg Hatza, who recorded two albums for Coral in the late '60s, to make a full-fledged comeback. For his second Palmetto date, Hatza generally avoids blues (other than "Move Over" and the heated "Jump Street") in favor of more challenging chord changes but fits very securely into the organ tradition. Tenor saxophonist Ralph Lalama and guitarist Paul Bollenback have plenty of concise solos, drummer Gary Jenkins is excellent in support and the selections (nine Hatza originals plus Sam Cooke's "A Change Is Gonna Come") swing quite nicely. The catchy "Rio Nights," a funky "Mr. Nasty" and the soulful jazz waltz "Sister Jason" are among the high points of this recommended disc. — *Scott Yanow*

Hampton Hawes

b. Nov. 13, 1928, Los Angeles, CA, **d.** May 22, 1977, Los Angeles, CA
Piano, Keyboards / Bop, Hard Bop, Crossover Jazz
Hampton Hawes was one of the finest jazz pianists of the 1950s, a fixture on the Los Angeles scene who brought his own interpretations to the dominant Bud Powell style. In the mid- to late '40s he played with Sonny Criss, Dexter Gordon and Wardell Gray, among others on Central Avenue. He was with Howard McGhee's band (1950-51), played with Shorty Rogers and the Lighthouse All-Stars, served in the army (1952-54) and then led trios in the L.A. area, recording many albums for Contemporary. Arrested for heroin possession in 1958, Hawes spent five years in prison until he was pardoned by President Kennedy. He led trios for the remainder of his life, using electric piano (which disturbed his longtime fans) for a period in the early to mid-'70s but returning to acoustic piano before dying from a stroke in 1977. Hampton Hawes' memoirs *Raise Up Off Me* (1974) are both frank and memorable, and most of his records (for Xanadu, Prestige, Savoy, Contemporary, Black Lion and Freedom) are currently available. — *Scott Yanow*

Memorial Album / Feb. 12, 1952 / Xanadu ✦✦✦✦
Other than six songs from a September 1951 session that were released on a Xanadu sampler, this particular Xanadu LP has pianist Hampton Hawes' earliest recording as a leader. Twenty-three at the time of the first dates, Hawes already had his boppish style largely together, showing off the influence of Bud Powell. The recording quality of these live performances is decent and certainly listenable. Hawes is heard on three occasions in 1952 with a trio that includes bassist Joe Mondragon and either Shelly Manne or Larry Bunker on drums. In addition, there are three particularly satisfying numbers from a 1956 engagement with bassist Red Mitchell and drummer Chuck Thompson that displays Hawes' growth through the period. All of the material was initially released on this 1982 LP. — *Scott Yanow*

Piano: East/West / Dec. 1952 / Original Jazz Classics ✦✦✦
This CD reissue has two unrelated early sessions from pianists Hampton Hawes and Freddie Redd. Hawes, heard in a quartet with vibraphonist Larry Bunker, bassist Clarence Jones and drummer Larence Marable, already ranked as one of the top bop-based pianists in 1952. He performs eight straightahead numbers (five bop standards and three originals like "Hamp's Paws"), including a two-minute version of "Move" that lives up to its name. Redd, who recorded much less during his

longer career, stretches out a bit more on four numbers (including three originals) in a trio with bassist John Ore and drummer Ron Jefferson. Excellent music, easily recommended to bop collectors. —*Scott Yanow*

● **This Is Hampton Hawes, Vol. 1** / Jun. 28, 1955 / Original Jazz Classics ✦✦✦✦✦
The first of pianist Hampton Hawes' long string of Contemporary recordings (which, as with most of his output for that label, has been reissued on CD in the Original Jazz Classics series) features him in his early prime in a trio with bassist Red Mitchell and drummer Chuck Thompson. In addition to three of his basic originals, Hawes performs fresh and swinging versions of seven standards, making such overplayed tunes as "I Got Rhythm," "What Is This Thing Called Love?" and "All the Things You Are" really come alive. A gem, the first of many classic Hawes Contemporary dates. —*Scott Yanow*

★ **Four! Hampton Hawes!!!!** / Jan. 27, 1958 / Original Jazz Classics ✦✦✦✦✦
Pianist Hampton Hawes' 1950s recordings for the Contemporary label are at such a high level that they could all be given five stars. This outing with bassist Red Mitchell, drummer Shelly Manne and guitarist Barney Kessel (who is a slight wild card) is also quite successful. Two previously unreleased numbers ("Thou Swell" and "The Awful Truth") have been added to the CD reissue. Highlights of the exciting bop date include "Yardbird Suite," "There Will Never Be Another You" and "Love Is Just Around the Corner." —*Scott Yanow*

For Real! / Mar. 17, 1958 / Original Jazz Classics ✦✦✦✦
Although this was at least Hampton Hawes' 11th record as a leader, it was his first (and one of his relatively few) that included a horn player. The pianist matches quite well with the hard bop tenor of Harold Land (heard in his early prime), and the quartet outing, which also includes drummer Frank Butler, has an extra bonus in the playing of the brilliant bassist Scott LaFaro. Performing three bop standards (including "Crazeology") and three originals (two of which were co-written by Land), pianist Hawes sounds inspired by the other players and is in top form throughout the generally memorable outing. —*Scott Yanow*

The Sermon / Nov. 24, 1958-Nov. 25, 1958 / Contemporary ✦✦✦✦
This set, not yet reissued on CD, was pianist Hampton Hawes' last before he started what would be five years in prison on drug charges. He had been arrested 11 days before and ironically chose to record a set of spirituals (plus a blues) as he awaited trial. Not released until this 1987 LP, the music (played with bassist Leroy Vinnegar and drummer Stan Levey) is full of intense emotion, strong melodies and a little more variety than one might expect. Hawes' treatments of such tunes as "Down by the Riverside," "Nobody Knows the Trouble I've Seen," "When the Roll Is Called up Yonder" and "Joshua Fit de Battle of Jericho" are quite haunting. —*Scott Yanow*

This Is Hampton Hawes, Vol. 2: Trio / Dec. 3, 1955-Jan. 26, 1956 / Original Jazz Classics ✦✦✦✦
Hampton Hawes recorded many superb trio sets in the 1950s, including three with bassist Red Mitchell and drummer Chuck Thompson. This straightahead set (reissued on CD) finds the group exploring seven standards often played by bop musicians (including "You and the Night and the Music," "'Round Midnight" and "Autumn in New York") plus a couple of original blues. Although originally strongly influenced by Bud Powell, Hawes' own personality comes through in this very likable music. —*Scott Yanow*

The Green Leaves of Summer / Feb. 17, 1964 / Original Jazz Classics ✦✦✦✦✦
Pianist Hampton Hawes' first recording after serving five years in prison finds Hawes evolving a bit from a Bud Powell-influenced bop pianist to one familiar with more modern trends in jazz. Reissued on CD, this trio date finds Hawes interacting closely with bassist Monk Montgomery and drummer Steve Ellington (making his recording debut). Hawes had lost nothing of his swinging style while in prison, as can be heard on such numbers as "Vierd Blues," "St. Thomas" and "Secret Love," and he was just starting to hint at moving beyond bop. Recommended. —*Scott Yanow*

Here and Now / May 12, 1965 / Original Jazz Classics ✦✦✦
For this interesting but not essential CD reissue, pianist Hampton Hawes, along with bassist Chuck Israels and drummer Donald Bailey, tries his best to uplift then-current songs (plus his original "Rhonda") including "Fly Me to the Moon," "What Kind of Fool Am I?," "Chim Chim Cheree," and even "People." In general, the treatments are somewhat straightahead ("The Girl from Ipanema" is taken as swing rather than bossa nova), and Hawes' solos transform some of the tunes a bit. —*Scott Yanow*

I'm All Smiles / Apr. 30, 1966-May 1, 1966 / Original Jazz Classics ✦✦✦
The second of two CD reissues taken from a Hampton Hawes engagement at Mitchell's Studio Club in Los Angeles has the pianist interacting closely with bassist Red Mitchell and drummer Donald Bailey. Hawes stretches out on five challenging pieces including "Spring Is Here," "The Shadow of Your Smile" and his own "Searchin." The material was not originally released until 1972, but it is the equal

of Hawes' other album from the dates, *The Séance*. Well worth picking up. —*Scott Yanow*

The Séance / Apr. 30, 1966-May 1, 1966 / Original Jazz Classics ✦✦✦✦✦
Hampton Hawes made many of his finest records for Lester Koenig's Contemporary label. His final sessions before choosing to freelance (he would rejoin Koenig during his last year) resulted in two live albums, both reissued on CD. Teamed up with bassist Red Mitchell and drummer Donald Bailey, Hawes displays the influence of the avant-garde in places, stretching out his improvisations a bit while still showing off his roots in bop. Both CDs are equal in value, and this particular set includes such highlights as "Oleo," "Easy Street" and "My Romance." —*Scott Yanow*

Hamp's Piano / Nov. 1967 / Saba ✦✦✦

Blues for Bud / Mar. 10, 1968 / Black Lion ✦✦✦✦
One of pianist Hampton Hawes' better sets, this CD reissue features Hawes during a European tour in a trio with bassist Jimmy Woode and drummer Art Taylor. Hawes both explores his bebop roots and contributes new material that shows that he was aware of McCoy Tyner and the more advanced players of the era. Among the highlights are "Blues Enough," "Sonora," "Blues for Bud" (which is one of five previously unreleased performances included in the 11 tracks) and "Spanish Steps." Recommended. —*Scott Yanow*

The Challenge / May 7, 1968-May 12, 1968 / Storyville ✦✦✦✦
Although it does not say it anywhere on this LP (originally recorded in Japan for RCA), the "challenge" was that this was Hampton Hawes' first set of unaccompanied piano solos. Although based in bop, Hawes was always much more than a one-handed pianist, and he proves up to the challenge. The repertoire includes jazz standards, three originals, and the current pop tune "Who Can I Turn To?" Throughout the date, the pianist shows that he could create stirring music without the assistance of a rhythm section. Unfortunately, this music (last put out on a Storyville LP) has yet to be reissued on CD. —*Scott Yanow*

Key for Two / Jan. 1968 / Affinity ✦✦✦
A stomping workout with fellow pianist Martial Solal. —*Ron Wynn*

Plays Movie Musicals / Aug. 1969 / Fresh Sound ✦✦
This CD reissues one of pianist Hampton Hawes' more obscure sessions. Trying during the era to widen his repertoire beyond the usual bop standards, Hawes performs eight songs originally written for movies. Some of the tunes, such as "My Man" and "Old Devil Moon," are of a higher quality than others ("People" and "As Long as She Needs Me"). For the set, Hawes was joined by not only bassist Bob West and drummer Larry Bunker, but also a string section arranged by Billy Byers. Formerly available as half of the LP *The Two Sides of Hampton Hawes*, this interesting but very brief (under 29 minutes) and far from essential outing has been reissued on CD by Fresh Sound. —*Scott Yanow*

High in the Sky / 1970 / Fresh Sound ✦✦✦
Originally put out on a Vault LP, then reissued as half of Jaz's two-fer *The Two Sides of Hampton Hawes* and finally reissued on CD by Fresh Sound, this little-known trio set matches pianist Hawes with two of his old friends, bassist Leroy Vinnegar and drummer Donald Bailey. Hawes, whose style had evolved from the 1950s, plays five of his originals (including the nearly 11-minute title cut) and "The Look of Love." He was at the time a post-bop pianist with an open mind toward pop music and the more adventurous side of jazz. Unfortunately, this CD is a bit brief at a little over 36 minutes, but it does give listeners a good example of Hampton Hawes' playing during the important transitional period. —*Scott Yanow*

Trio at Montreux / Jun. 1971 / Fresh Sound ✦✦✦✦
This CD consists of a continuous 57-minute set performed by pianist Hampton Hawes' Trio with bassist Henry Franklin and drummer Mike Carvin. Two songs (Bert Bacharach's "This Guy's in Love with You" and Hawes' "High in the Sky") are fully explored and, despite the extreme length and some wandering sections, the performance holds one's interest throughout. —*Scott Yanow*

A Little Copenhagen Night Music / Sep. 2, 1971 / Freedom ✦✦✦✦
Pianist Hampton Hawes (who is joined by bassist Henry Franklin and drummer Michael Carvin) plays a more boppish repertoire on this live set from Copenhagen's legendary Montmartre than he usually did during the era. Hawes swings his way through spirited versions of "Now's the Time," "'Round Midnight" and "Cheryl," performs his "Spanish Way," and welcomes tenor great Dexter Gordon to a rousing version of "Long Tall Dexter" (which is mistitled on the LP as "Dexter's Deck"). Hopefully, this date (along with *Live at the Montmartre* from the same night) will eventually be combined on a CD set. —*Scott Yanow*

Live at the Montmartre / Sep. 2, 1971 / Freedom ✦✦✦✦✦
Hampton Hawes, a bop-oriented pianist in the '50s, continued to develop and evolve throughout his career without losing his musical identity. For this trio set with bassist Henry Franklin and drummer Michael Carvin, Hawes shows the influ-

ence of McCoy Tyner a bit and, by performing Burt Bacharach's "This Guy's in Love with You" (along with four other group originals), he shows his openness to including some pop material in his repertoire (although his explorative version owes little to the original hit tune). This excellent live session has plenty of close interplay by the tight trio. —*Scott Yanow*

Universe / May 1972-June 1972 / Prestige ◆◆◆

In 1972, Hampton Hawes began to fully explore electric keyboards. Although his longtime fans were not happy with the temporary move, Hawes' music at the time was actually more creative than it was often rated. There are dated and poppish elements to this out-of-print Prestige LP, but also some fine solos from tenor saxophonist Harold Land, trumpeter Oscar Brashear, guitarist Arthur Adams, and the leader. Hawes deserves credit for his willingness to take chances, and even if this album (consisting of seven moody originals) is not as significant as most of his boppish trio dates from the 1950s, it deserves to be re-evaluated, for it is better than often thought. —*Scott Yanow*

Blues for Walls / Jan. 16, 1973-Jan. 18, 1973 / Prestige ◆◆

For a few years (mostly 1972-74), pianist Hampton Hawes spent time exploring electric keyboards. His music became funkier and less distinctive, but his recordings from the era (which are mostly out of print) are certainly quite listenable, if a bit dated in places. This Prestige LP, which has not yet been reissued on CD, finds Hawes teamed with trumpeter Oscar Brashear and reeds of Hadley Caliman, guitarist George Walker, bassist Henry Franklin and drummer Ndugu Chancler for performances of seven of the keyboardist's interesting (if not overly memorable) originals. —*Scott Yanow*

Live at the Jazz Showcase in Chicago / Jun. 10, 1973 / Enja ◆◆◆◆

Although some of Hampton Hawes' early-'70s recordings found him using electric piano (and sounding less distinctive than usual), this live set is purely acoustic. Hawes teams up with bassist Cecil McBee and drummer Roy Haynes for lengthy renditions of "Stella by Starlight," Charlie Parker's "Bluebird," the pianist's "Spanish Moods" and "St. Thomas." Although Hawes resisted any avant-garde influences, his playing on this date often finds him stretching himself past bebop and he is heard throughout in prime form. —*Scott Yanow*

Playin' in the Yard / Jul. 7, 1973 / Prestige ◆◆◆

This live LP (which has not yet been reissued on CD) mostly features Hampton Hawes on electric piano, performing at the 1973 Montreux Jazz Festival in a trio with electric bassist Bob Cranshaw and drummer Kenny Clarke. Hawes interprets three of his originals, Sonny Rollins' catchy "Playin' In the Yard," and "Stella by Starlight." Although well-played, little memorable occurs, and Hawes never did sound as distinctive on keyboards as he did on acoustic piano. —*Scott Yanow*

Northern Windows / Jul. 17, 1974-Jul. 18, 1974 / Prestige ◆◆◆

Recorded Live at the Great American Music Hall / Jun. 10, 1975 / Concord Jazz ◆◆◆◆◆

This album, one of pianist Hampton Hawes' last recordings, is a surprise success. First Hawes, in duets with bassist Mario Suraci, really digs into two rather unpromising pop tunes ("Fly Me to the Moon" and "Sunny") in extended versions ("Sunny" is given over 14 minutes) and brings out surprising beauty in those overdone songs. For the second side of this LP, Hawes performs his own suite for solo piano, an impressive three-movement work that he titled "The Status of Maceo" that has enough variety in its 20-plus minutes to keep one's interest throughout. —*Scott Yanow*

Something Special / Jun. 10, 1976 / Contemporary ◆◆◆◆

This 1994 CD released for the first time a live set (recorded at Half Moon Bay, California) performed less than a year before pianist Hampton Hawes' death. Hawes, in a quartet with guitarist Denny Diaz, bassist Leroy Vinnegar and drummer Al Williams, dominates the music and displays his ability to uplift a couple of pop tunes ("Sunny" and "Fly Me to the Moon"). He also swings creatively through a blues, "St. Thomas" and a pair of his originals. This excellent music gives no hints of Hawes' upcoming demise. —*Scott Yanow*

At the Piano / Aug. 14, 1976 / Original Jazz Classics ◆◆◆◆

Hampton Hawes' final recording found him returning not only to the acoustic piano after having dabbled in electric keyboards from 1972-74, but to producer Lester Koenig and his Contemporary label, where Hawes recorded most of his classic gems of the 1950s. Teamed up with bassist Ray Brown and drummer Shelly Manne, Hawes shows that he was still in prime form. The trio plays two of Hawes' originals, some current and worthwhile pop tunes ("Killing Me Softly With His Song" and "Sunny"), and "Blue in Green" and "When I Grow Too Old to Dream." The excellent LP, which has not yet been reissued on CD, also has in its liner notes a very interesting conversation between Hawes and Koenig from January 20, 1977; both would pass away before the year ended. —*Scott Yanow*

Coleman Hawkins

b. Nov. 21, 1904, St. Joseph, MO, d. May 19, 1969, New York, NY
Tenor Saxophone / Classic Jazz, Swing, Bop

Coleman Hawkins was the first important tenor saxophonist and he remains one of the greatest of all time. A consistently modern improviser whose knowledge of chords and harmonies was encyclopedic, Hawkins had a 40-year prime (1925-65) during which he could hold his own with any competitor.

Coleman Hawkins started piano lessons when he was five, switched to cello at age seven and two years later began on tenor. At a time when the saxophone was considered a novelty instrument, used in vaudeville and as a poor substitute for the trombone in marching bands, Hawkins sought to develop his own sound. A professional when he was 12, Hawkins was playing in a Kansas City theater pit band in 1921 when Mamie Smith hired him to play with her Jazz Hounds. Hawkins was with the blues singer until June 1923, making many records in a background role, and he was occasionally heard on instrumentals. After leaving Smith he freelanced around New York, played briefly with Wilbur Sweatman and in August 1923 made his first recordings with Fletcher Henderson. When Henderson formed a permanent orchestra in January 1924, Hawkins was his star tenor.

Although (due largely to lack of competition) Coleman Hawkins was the top tenor in jazz in 1924, his staccato runs and use of slap-tonguing sound quite dated today. However, after Louis Armstrong joined Henderson later in the year, Hawkins learned from the cornetist's relaxed legato style and advanced quickly. By 1925 Hawkins was truly a major soloist and the following year his solo on "Stampede" became influential. Hawk (who doubled in early years on clarinet and bass sax) would be with Fletcher Henderson's Orchestra up to 1934 and during this time he was the obvious pacesetter among tenors; Bud Freeman was about the only tenor who did not sound like a close relative of the hard-toned Hawkins! In addition to his solos with Henderson, Hawkins backed some blues singers, recorded with McKinney's Cotton Pickers, and with Red McKenzie in 1929 he cut his first classic ballad statement on "One Hour."

By 1934 Coleman Hawkins had tired of the struggling Fletcher Henderson Orchestra and he moved to Europe, spending five years (1934-39) overseas. He played at first with Jack Hylton's Orchestra in England and then freelanced throughout the continent. His most famous recording from this period was a 1937 date with Benny Carter, Alix Combille, Andre Ekyan, Django Reinhardt and Stephane Grappelli that resulted in classic renditions of "Crazy Rhythm" and "Honeysuckle Rose." With World War II coming close, Hawkins returned to the US in 1939. Although Lester Young had emerged with a totally new style on tenor, Hawkins showed that he was still a dominant force by winning a few heated jam sessions. His recording of "Body and Soul" that year became his most famous record. In 1940 he led a big band that failed to catch on, so Hawkins broke it up and became a fixture on 52nd Street. Some of his finest recordings were cut during the first half of the 1940s including a stunning quartet version of "The Man I Love." Although he was already a 20-year veteran, Hawkins encouraged the younger bop-oriented musicians and did not need to adjust his harmonically-advanced style in order to play with them. He used Thelonious Monk in his 1944 quartet, led the first official bop record session (which included Dizzy Gillespie and Don Byas), had Oscar Pettiford, Miles Davis and Max Roach as sidemen early in their careers, toured California with a sextet featuring Howard McGhee and in 1946 utilized J.J. Johnson and Fats Navarro on record dates. Hawkins toured with Jazz at the Philharmonic several times during 1946-50, visited Europe on a few occasions and in 1948 recorded the first unaccompanied saxophone solo, "Picasso."

By the early '50s the Lester Young-influenced Four Brothers sound had become a much greater influence on young tenors than Hawkins' style and he was considered by some to be out of fashion. However, Hawkins kept on working and occasionally recording and by the mid-'50s was experiencing a renaissance. The up-and-coming Sonny Rollins considered Hawkins his main influence, Hawk started teaming up regularly with Roy Eldridge in an exciting quintet (their appearance at the 1957 Newport Jazz Festival was notable) and he proved to still be in his prime. Coleman Hawkins appeared in a wide variety of settings, from Red Allen's heated Dixieland band at the Metropole and leading a bop date featuring Idrees Sulieman and J.J. Johnson to guest appearances on records that included Thelonious Monk, John Coltrane and (in the early '60s) Max Roach and Eric Dolphy. During the first half of the 1960s Coleman Hawkins had an opportunity to record with Duke Ellington, collaborated on one somewhat eccentric session with Sonny Rollins and even did a bossa nova album. By 1965 Hawkins was even showing the influence of John Coltrane in his explorative flights and seemed ageless.

Unfortunately 1965 was Coleman Hawkins' last good year. Whether it was senility or frustration, Hawkins began to lose interest in life. He practically quit eating, increased his drinking, and quickly wasted away. Other than a surprisingly effective appearance with Jazz at the Philharmonic in early 1969, very little of

Hawkins' work during his final three-and-a-half years (a period during which he largely stopped recording) is up to the level one would expect from the great master. However, there are dozens of superb Coleman Hawkins recordings currently available and, as Eddie Jefferson said in his vocalese version of "Body and Soul," "He was the king of the saxophone." —*Scott Yanow*

● **Body & Soul** / Apr. 27, 1927-Jul. 18, 1963 / RCA ✦✦✦✦✦
This single LP is a perfect sampler of the career and talents of Coleman Hawkins. The 16 selections find the great tenor saxophonist in many different settings, ranging from the Fletcher Henderson big band and other groups from the '20s, through the swing and bop years, and concluding with a musical encounter with Sonny Rollins in 1963. Long out of print, this well-conceived LP is still quite valuable. —*Scott Yanow*

The Complete Coleman Hawkins, Vol. 1 / Nov. 14, 1929-Aug. 1940 / RCA ✦✦✦✦✦
This French LP features two of Coleman Hawkins' most important solos from the '20s ("Hello Lola" and "One Hour" with The Mound City Blue Blowers), the complete session from 1939 that resulted in his famous version of "Body and Soul," a hot combo with Benny Carter (on trumpet), a roughly recorded radio aircheck with some all-stars and three songs from his short-lived big band from a pair of broadcasts. Although most of this material has since been reissued, this set does give a well-rounded portrait of the early Coleman Hawkins. —*Scott Yanow*

Three Great Swing Saxophones / Nov. 14, 1929-Aug. 23, 1946 / Bluebird ✦✦✦
This CD is a best-of collection that includes performances showcasing the tenors of Coleman Hawkins and Ben Webster and altoist Benny Carter, mostly from the swing era. Hawk is heard with Fletcher Henderson's Orchestra, playing "One Hour" and "Hello Lola" with the Mound City Blue Blowers, on two versions of "Dinah" with Lionel Hampton, soloing a song with McKinney's Cotton Pickers and performing his famous version of "Body and Soul." Webster is featured with Bennie Moten, Willie Bryant, Lionel Hampton, Duke Ellington (including "Cotton Tail") and Rex Stewart while Carter is heard with McKinney's Cotton Pickers, Mezz Mezzrow, Hampton and with his own bands in 1940-41. Very much a sampler (virtually all of the music is available elsewhere), this set serves as a fine introduction to the early work of these classic players. —*Scott Yanow*

☆ **In Europe 1934-39** / Nov. 18, 1934-May 26, 1939 / Jazz Up ✦✦✦✦✦
In 1934 Hawkins, after 11 years as the star soloist with Fletcher Henderson's pioneering jazz big band, was looking for other worlds to conquer. To satisfy his curiosity he travelled to Europe and for the next five years was a major celebrity overseas, only returning to the US when World War II was about to start. This magnificent three-CD set contains every recording that the great tenor saxophonist made in Europe, 71 in all (including alternate takes). Whether featured in London, Switzerland, Paris or Holland, Hawkins dominates these recordings, which find him in a variety of settings, from duets with pianist Freddie Johnson to medium-sized bands. Benny Carter and Django Reinhardt also make a few notable appearances. This perfectly done set is highly recommended. —*Scott Yanow*

Hawk in Holland / Feb. 4, 1935-Apr. 26, 1937 / GNP ✦✦✦
This enjoyable LP finds Hawkins guesting with the Ramblers, a fine Dutch swing group, in 1935 and 1937. While pianist Freddie Johnson is the only other distinctive soloist (although Annie de Reuver contributes two haunting vocals), the Ramblers do an excellent job of accompanying their American guest on a variety of standards and a couple of Hawk's originals. The closer, "Something Is Gonna Give Me Away," finds the tenorman romping with just the rhythm section and is quite memorable. This material has since been reissued on CD. —*Scott Yanow*

Coleman Hawkins and Benny Carter / Mar. 2, 1935-Aug. 23, 1946 / Disques Swing ✦✦✦
This attractive LP (which contains quite a few photos in its gateway liners) is drawn from four separate recording sessions. Hawkins is heard as the main soloist with Michel Warlop's orchestra in 1935, and he teams up with Benny Carter, two of Europe's best saxophonists (Alix Combelle on tenor and altoist Andre Ekyan), and Django Reinhardt for the famous "Crazy Rhythm" all-star session of 1937. In addition, Benny Carter is heard in Europe in 1938 and with his Chocolate Dandies (featuring trumpeter Buck Clayton and Ben Webster on tenor) in 1946. Superb music, all of which has since been reissued. —*Scott Yanow*

Dutch Treat / Apr. 1936-Jun. 14, 1938 / Xanadu ✦✦✦
It was during his period in Europe (1934-39) that Hawkins smoothed out some rough edges in his tenor playing and really matured as an improviser. This Xanadu LP features some of his European sessions, including a meeting with the Swiss group the Berries and a series of duets and trios with pianist Freddy Johnson. Hawkins is the dominant soloist throughout and in fine form. —*Scott Yanow*

● **Body and Soul** / Oct. 11, 1939-Jul. 9, 1956 / RCA ✦✦✦✦✦
Ignoring past reissues (including a definitive two-CD set from 1995 that had 40 recordings), RCA came out with this 19-selection single CD in 1996; all of the per-

formances were in the previous reissue. If found at a budget price, this CD can act as a fine introduction to the great tenor Coleman Hawkins. Among its high points are two very different versions of "Body and Soul," classic renditions of "When Day Is Done," "The Sheik of Araby," and the modernistic "Half Step Down, Please," an appealing "I Love Paris" and a few numbers with strings and woodwinds. The music dates from 1939-40, 1946-47 and 1956 and is generally beyond criticism. —*Scott Yanow*

1940 / Aug. 4, 1940-Aug. 23, 1940 / Alamac ✦✦✦
The Coleman Hawkins big band only lasted around a year, recording but four songs in the studio. Although Hawkins was a major name in jazz, his orchestra never did catch on, partly because it did not have a strong personality of its own. This Alamac LP is valuable, for it contains performances by the big band from the Savoy Ballroom aired over the radio, including fine versions of "The Sheik of Araby" and "I Can't Believe That You're in Love with Me." Hawkins sounds typically hard-swinging but, other than trumpeter Joe Guy, the rest of the anonymous-sounding band is mostly just used in support of the leader. —*Scott Yanow*

☆ **Classic Tenors: Lester Young & Coleman Hawkins** / Dec. 8, 1943-Dec. 23, 1943 / Flying Dutchman ✦✦✦✦✦
Although this LP is long out of print, its brilliant contents have since been reissued by Bob Thiele on a couple of his labels. Hawkins is featured on eight of the 12 selections. Half come from a fine session with trumpeter Bill Coleman, but it is the other four that are of greatest interest, for they find the tenor saxophonist in a quartet with pianist Eddie Heywood, bassist Oscar Pettiford and drummer Shelly Manne. Their rendition of "The Man I Love" has what is arguably Heywood's finest solo, preceding a lengthy roaring statement by Hawkins. The other tracks ("Sweet Lorraine," "Get Happy" and "Crazy Rhythm") are almost as special. In addition, this LP finishes off with an excellent session from tenor saxophonist Lester Young, trombonist Dickie Wells and trumpeter Bill Coleman. Wells' high-note trombone solo on "I'm Fer It Too" is a crackup. —*Scott Yanow*

Complete Coleman Hawkins on Keynote / Jan. 1944-Dec. 1944 / Verve ✦✦✦✦✦
The 61 songs on these four CDs represent Hawkins' complete output for Keynote Records recorded between January and December of 1944 with Teddy Wilson and Earl Hines as part of the Coleman Hawkins Quintet, the Cozy Cole All-Stars, Coleman Hawkins and His Sax Ensemble and the All-American Four, Charlie Shavers' All American Five, and George Wettling's New Yorkers—Hawkins' and Wettling's first contact went back close to 20 years, to the Roseland Ballroom. At the time, Hawkins had given up trying to make it as the leader of a big band, and had returned to playing with small groups in the clubs along New York's 52nd Street. A joint project of PolyGram and Nippon Phonogram of Japan, this set is loaded with previously unissued takes and tracks from Hawkins' Keynote library, which also features Roy "Little Jazz" Eldridge and Billy Taylor. From the opening bars of two different previously unissued takes of "I Only Have Eyes for You," the set shows its worth, presenting outtakes that are equal in value to any of their released counterparts—Wilson and Hawkins perform superbly on all three versions, with markedly different performances on each, pretty much representing the way all of the outtakes here are fully justified. Each disc has more than its share of worthwhile rarities and previously unreleased cuts, and one leads into the next so well that it is difficult to take in just one of the these four discs at a time. From Disc Two onward, there is also more improvisation than one is accustomed to in jazz recordings if this era, owing to the fact that many of the sessions used the 12-inch master disc format, which allowed for just over five minutes' playing time, nearly 60% more than the usual three minutes-and-change, giving all of the players a chance to stretch out in ways closer to their usual stage and radio performances (though I wouldn't change the various three-minute versions of "Bean at the Met" on Disc One for any amount of money). The sound is generally superb, with an intimate, live-in-the-studio ambience and very little in the way of noise, considering the age of the recordings (no enhanced noise reduction of any kind has been used on this set). —*Bruce Eder*

☆ **Rainbow Mist** / Feb. 16, 1944-May 22, 1944 / Delmark ✦✦✦✦✦
Hawkins was always an open-minded musician. A very advanced player even when he first emerged with Fletcher Henderson's orchestra in the '20s, by the '40s he may have been technically middle-aged but remained a young thinker. For his recording session of February 16, 1944, the great tenor invited some of the most promising younger players (including trumpeter Dizzy Gillespie, bassist Oscar Pettiford and drummer Max Roach) and the result was the very first bebop on records. During their two sessions, the large ensemble recorded six selections including Gillespie's "Woody 'n You ," Hawk's "Disorder at the Border" and a new treatment of "Body and Soul" by the tenorman, which he retitled "Rainbow Mist." Also on this highly recommended CD are four titles matching the tenors of Hawkins, Ben Webster and Georgie Auld (with trumpeter Charlie Shavers added as a bonus) and a session from Auld's big band, highlighted by Sonny Berman's trumpet solo on "Taps Miller." —*Scott Yanow*

Thanks for the Memory / May 17, 1944-Dec. 1, 1944 / Xanadu ◆◆◆◆◆
On this fine LP Hawkins is heard on four separate sessions from 1944, only one of which has since been reissued on CD. The latter is his encounter with fellow tenors Georgie Auld and Ben Webster; that date led to the little-known original recording of "Salt Peanuts." In addition he is heard with the Esquire All-Stars of 1944, on a date actually led by saxophonist Walter "Foots" Thomas and in a matchup with trumpeter Charlie Shavers and Hawk's greatest disciple, Don Byas. Hot swing that looks forward toward the rapidly emerging bebop. —*Scott Yanow*

Hollywood Stampede / Feb. 23, 1945-Jun. 1944 / Capitol ◆◆◆◆◆
Hawkins led one of his finest bands in 1945, a sextet with the fiery trumpeter Howard McGhee that fell somewhere between small-group swing and bebop. This CD contains all of that group's 12 recordings, including memorable versions of "Rifftide" and "Stuffy"; trombonist Vic Dickenson guests on four tracks. This CD concludes with one of Hawkins' rarest sessions, an Aladdin date from 1947 that finds the veteran tenor leading a septet that includes 20-year-old trumpeter Miles Davis. —*Scott Yanow*

Coleman Hawkins/Lester Young / Feb. 1945-Apr. 1946 / Spotlite ◆◆◆◆
Hawkins and Lester Young crossed paths constantly throughout their careers but only recorded together on an infrequent basis. This LP from the English Spotlite label features the two great tenors teaming up with trumpeter Buck Clayton for three songs at a jam session; everyone is in fine form. The other side of this set finds Young and Hawkins individually showcased on three numbers apiece. Lester has the benefit of the Nat King Cole Trio plus Buddy Rich on two of his songs, while part of Hawkins' miniset is with the great quintet that he led with trumpeter Howard McGhee. Rare broadcasts containing classic music that was fortunately well-recorded. —*Scott Yanow*

Hawk Variation / 1945-1957 / Contact ◆◆◆◆
This is an utterly fascinating LP of rare Coleman Hawkins. First the veteran tenor saxophonist is heard on the two-part "Hawk Variation," his initial unaccompanied tenor solo (recorded a couple years before his more famous "Picasso"). Hawkins is also featured backing singer Delores Martin, on two alternate takes from a 1949 Paris session, guest-starring with a Danish band, uplifting four so-so songs recorded with a quartet in 1950, on a radio transcription made with Elliot Lawrence's All-Stars and soloing on two versions of "Walking My Baby Back Home" that were cut with a pickup band that also included cornetist Rex Stewart, trumpeter Cootie Williams and fellow tenor Bud Freeman. Hawkins collectors will have to own this set. —*Scott Yanow*

The Coleman Hawkins Set / Sep. 18, 1949-Oct. 19, 1957 / Verve ◆◆◆
Coleman Hawkins was frequently featured with Norman Granz's *Jazz at the Philharmonic* during 1946-59 and Granz usually made sure that Hawk had a special spot in addition to participating in the jam sessions. This LP finds Hawkins showcased with two different quartets from 1949 and 1950 (both recorded live at Carnegie Hall); three of the six selections were not released until the '80s. The repertoire is familiar ("Rifftide," "Stuffy" and ballads including "Body and Soul") but Hawkins' solos are fresh and creative. The second side of this record features the tenor giant matched with trumpeter Roy Eldridge on two jams and a brief ballad medley. The combative Eldridge always brought out the best in Hawkins and this music is quite exciting. —*Scott Yanow*

Coleman Hawkins and Johnny Hodges in Paris / Dec. 21, 1949-Jun. 20, 1950 / Vogue ◆◆◆◆◆
This CD from the French Vogue label features two unrelated groups, six titles from tenor saxophonist Coleman Hawkins that were formerly on a Prestige LP and a lengthy pair of sessions by altoist Johnny Hodges that were last available in the US on Inner City in the 1970s. Hawkins dominates his sextet date (altoist Hubert Fol and drummer Kenny Clarke are most prominent among the sidemen) and is in superior form on two blues, two ballads and two romps. Hodges allocates much more solo space to his fellow players during his 16 numbers, a wise decision considering that the musicians include Don Byas on tenor, trumpeter Harold Baker, trombonist Quentin Jackson and clarinetist Jimmy Hamilton; all four soloists had their own individual voices. The mixture of bop-tinged jump tunes, blues and ballads is a predecessor to the type of music featured by Hodges' own group a few years later when he temporarily left Duke Ellington's Orchestra to go out on his own. There are lots of highlights to be heard on this highly recommended CD. —*Scott Yanow*

Body and Soul Revisited / Oct. 19, 1951-Oct. 13, 1958 / Decca ◆◆◆
Hawkins had been the dominant tenor saxophonist from the mid-'20s up until 1940, but even though he remained a major force, his influence was waning, due to the emergence of Lester Young and then Charlie Parker. By the early '50s he only recorded on an infrequent basis. Fortunately, a few years later (partly due to the rise of Sonny Rollins whose original hero was Hawk) his fortunes were on the rise again. This Decca CD contains quite a variety of music. There are ten selections of

melodic "mood" music from 1951-53 in which Hawkins mostly sticks to the melody (an exception is an excellent version of "If I Could Be with You"). Then the great tenor is heard in an occasionally exciting session with Cozy Cole's All-Stars; cornetist Rex Stewart steals the show with a couple of colorful solos. The best music on this CD is taken from a 1955 radio broadcast in which Hawkins plays "Foolin' Around" (based on the chords of "Body and Soul") totally unaccompanied and roars on "The Man I Love." This set concludes with three selections (one previously unissued) from a fine session led by clarinetist Tony Scott. —*Scott Yanow*

Disorder at the Border / Sep. 6, 1952-Sep. 13, 1952 / Spotlite ◆◆◆
Although Hawkins' studio recordings from this era were few and generally found him restricted to playing commercial mood music, his concert and club appearances showed him to still be in prime form. This enjoyable LP has the great tenor leading two different quintets at Birdland on broadcasts that were aired just a week apart. The rhythm section features the then-unknown pianist Horace Silver, bassist Curly Russell and either Art Blakey or Connie Kay on drums. More importantly, trumpeters Roy Eldridge and Howard McGhee (heard separately) inspire the competitive Hawkins to play at his best. A short but very thorough interview wraps up this erratically recorded but very interesting release. —*Scott Yanow*

The Hawk Returns / May 27, 1954 / Savoy ◆◆
This CD features Hawkins on a dozen selections (all around three minutes long) performing with an odd group (organ, piano, bass, drums and sometimes a vocal group). Despite the potentially commercial backing, he really digs into the tunes and creates some magic. Pity that this CD only lasts around 36 minutes. —*Scott Yanow*

1954 / Nov. 8, 1954 / Jazz Anthology ◆◆◆
This relaxed session matches the great tenor with a fine sextet that also includes trumpeter Emmett Berry and trombonist Eddie Bert. Hawk and company sound fine on the nine standards, swinging in a mainstream style that might have been out of fashion at the time but still remains timeless and highly enjoyable. —*Scott Yanow*

Masters of Jazz, Vol. 12 / Nov. 8, 1954-Feb. 13, 1968 / Storyville ◆◆◆
A very interesting release, this set has a version of "Honeysuckle Rose" from a Hawkins session in 1954 that usually gets left out of reissues (it was originally released in a sampler), four numbers from a live date in Europe that matches his tenor with a superb rhythm section (pianist Bud Powell, bassist Oscar Pettiford and drummer Kenny Clarke) and two songs from what probably was Hawkins' final studio session. Despite being very ill, he is in surprisingly strong form on the latter (from February 1968), easily playing with more fire and strength than he had in 1966 on *Sirius*, his last complete album. —*Scott Yanow*

Cool Groove / May 10, 1955 / Drive Archive ◆◆◆
One of the rarer Coleman Hawkins sessions has been reissued on this Drive Archive CD. The veteran tenor was somewhat overlooked during the era (prior to a major "comeback" in 1957) but he always played at a consistently high level. On four of the eight selections, Hawk is showcased in a quintet with Joe "Earl" Knight (mostly on piano but also playing some early organ), rhythm guitarist Sidney Gross, bassist Wendell Marshall and drummer Osie Johnson. The remaining four numbers add trumpeter Ernie Royal and trombonist Eddie Bert. Hawkins is in prime form, particularly on "Blue Room," "Running Wild," "The Breeze and I" and "My Own Blues." Although the songs are actually programmed in a slightly different order than is listed, this reissue is worth picking up. —*Scott Yanow*

Hawk in Paris / Jul. 9, 1956-Jul. 13, 1956 / VIK ◆◆◆◆
This CD is a major surprise. Hawkins had always wanted to record with a large string section and he received his wish on the majority of these 12 romantic melodies, all of which have some association with Paris. The surprise is that he plays with a great deal of fire (his doubletiming on "My Man" is wondrous), and that Manny Albam's arrangements mostly avoid being muzaky and quite often are creative and witty. What could have been a novelty or an insipid affair is actually one of Coleman Hawkins' more memorable albums. —*Scott Yanow*

The Gilded Hawk / Oct. 17, 1956-Feb. 8, 1957 / Capitol ◆◆
Jazz musicians often have as one of their cherished goals the desire to record with a full string section. Hawkins, who recorded an excellent string album (*The Hawk in Paris*) earlier in 1956, received his wish a few times. *The Gilded Hawk*, last available as this LP, finds the great tenor being weighed down by Glenn Osser's muzaky arrangements for the strings. Since Hawkins does little other than caress the melodies, nothing significant happens, making this one of the more dispensable Coleman Hawkins. —*Scott Yanow*

The Hawk Flies High / Mar. 12, 1957-Mar. 15, 1957 / Original Jazz Classics ◆◆◆◆◆
The year 1957 was one of the great ones for the veteran tenor saxophonist (who was then 51); he suddenly became rediscovered, even though he had never suffered a period of decline. *The Hawk Flies High* found him playing mostly with bop-

oriented musicians a couple decades his junior (including trombonist J.J. Johnson and trumpeter Idrees Sulieman) and more than holding his own. The memorable "Sanctity" has a particularly classic Hawkins solo, is but each of the six tracks are quite enjoyable. —*Scott Yanow*

Blues Wail: Coleman Hawkins Plays the Blues / Mar. 12, 1957-Dec. 30, 1960 / Prestige ◆◆◆

Tenor great Coleman Hawkins was usually bored with the blues, at least until the period covered by this CD sampler. A master at deciphering complex chord changes, Hawkins found the blues to be overly simple but around 1957 (after 35 years of major league activity) he began to explore the blues more seriously, at least on an occasional basis. This CD has nine performances from as many sessions. The music is consistently excellent (particularly "Juicy Fruit," the lengthy "Blues for Tomorrow," which also features John Coltrane, "Stealin' the Bean" with trumpeter Charlie Shavers and a pair of collaborations with fellow tenor Eddie "Lockjaw" Davis), but it is recommended that listeners (beginners and experts alike) instead acquire the complete sessions, since the blues were only a small aspect of the Coleman Hawkins story. —*Scott Yanow*

Coleman Hawkins, Roy Eldridge, Pete Brown, Jo Jones All-Star / Jul. 5, 1957 / Verve ◆◆◆◆

In 1957 Hawkins underwent a critical renaissance. Fellow musicians and writers alike finally realized that his style (whether currently in fashion or not) was timeless and that the veteran tenor could still blow most of his competitors away. He teamed up with trumpeter Roy Eldridge and altoist Pete Brown for what would be a highly successful set at the Newport Jazz Festival. Their first number ("I Can't Believe That You're in Love with Me") was so explosive it made the rest of the performance (a ballad medley and "Sweet Georgia Brown") anticlimactic. Actually, Brown is just okay on "I Can't Believe" but the long solos of Eldridge and Hawkins are among the most exciting of their career, making this LP well worth searching for. —*Scott Yanow*

Coleman Hawkins Encounters Ben Webster / Oct. 16, 1957 / Verve ◆◆◆◆

W/ Ben Webster. These aren't encounters in the confrontational sense, but a merger of great musical minds. —*Ron Wynn*

The Genius of Coleman Hawkins / Oct. 16, 1957 / Verve ◆◆◆◆

Genius may not be the right word, but "brilliance" certainly fits. At the age of 51 in 1957, Hawkins had already been on records for 35 years and had been one of the leading tenors for nearly that long. This CD matches him with the Oscar Peterson Trio (plus drummer Alvin Stoller) for a fine runthrough on standards. Hawk plays quite well, although the excitement level does not reach the heights of his sessions with trumpeter Roy Eldridge. —*Scott Yanow*

Volume One: Warhorses / Dec. 16, 1957 / Jass ◆◆

Considering the outstanding lineup of players (tenor-great Coleman Hawkins, trumpeter Red Allen and trombonist J.C. Higginbotham among them), this should have been a great session. As it turned out (and is accurately stated in the LP's title), the seven tunes are all overdone standards, most of them from the repertoire of Dixieland bands, like "Bill Bailey," "Battle Hymn of the Republic" and "The Saints." In addition to that liability, there is less than 30 minutes of music on this LP. What is here is fine but not really worth searching for. This music has since been combined with the equally brief LP *High Standards* (Jass 11) on one single CD. —*Scott Yanow*

High and Mighty Hawk / Feb. 18, 1958-Feb. 19, 1958 / Affinity ◆◆◆◆

Although Hawkins had been a major tenor stylist for over 35 years by the time of this recording, he had never felt all that comfortable playing blues, preferring to dig his harmonic talents into more complicated material. For one of the first times, on the lengthy "Bird of Prey Blues" that opens this LP, Hawkins showed that at last he had mastered the blues. His honking and roaring improvisation, although more sophisticated than the usual solos by R&B tenors, captured their spirit and extroverted emotions perfectly. It is the highlight of this otherwise excellent (if more conventional) quintet session with trumpeter Buck Clayton and pianist Hank Jones. —*Scott Yanow*

Blues Groove / Feb. 28, 1958 / Swingville ◆◆◆

Strange as it seems, after over 35 years on the scene, Hawkins seemed to discover the blues in 1958. A harmonic wizard who enjoyed improvising over the most complex chord changes, he finally dug into the blues around this period and learned to emphasize extroverted emotions. This LP finds him jamming joyously on two standards and four blues (including "Marchin' Along") with a sextet that also prominently features guitarist Tiny Grimes. —*Scott Yanow*

Rare Live Performance / Mar. 18, 1958-Oct. 27, 1959 / Jazz Anthology ◆◆◆

This imported LP features Hawkins playing with two different pickup groups during 1958-59. On side one he jams on three familiar but appealing numbers with a sextet that includes trombonist Jimmy Cleveland and tenorman Benny Golson (although the latter is left out of the personnel listing), while the second side finds

Hawk interacting with guitarist Tiny Grimes and a quintet. The music, which might have been taken from television appearances, is predictable but swinging. —*Scott Yanow*

Meets the Sax Section / Apr. 24, 1958 / Savoy ◆◆◆

This studio session for Savoy finds the great Hawkins playing as part of a five-piece sax section. Actually, the other saxophonists and part of the rhythm section were taken from the Count Basie Orchestra and outfitted with arrangements by Billy Ver Planck. They play a variety of little-known but swinging material; the logical charts and high-quality solos make this LP well worth acquiring. —*Scott Yanow*

High Standards / Aug. 7, 1958 / Jass ◆◆

This impressive lineup (tenor great Coleman Hawkins, trumpeter Red Allen and altoist Earl Warren, who for some reasons sticks here to clarinet) should have guaranteed a highly recommended LP, but the very brief playing time (around 27 minutes) and the predictable music make this set a bit of a disappointment. This has since been reissued on a CD along with the equally scanty *Warhorses*. —*Scott Yanow*

Coleman Hawkins and His Friends at a Famous Jazz Party / Oct. 16, 1958-Nov. 6, 1958 / Enigma ◆◆◆

True, this LP looks like a bootleg and it is probably semi-legitimate at best, but the music is quite exciting. Possibly taken from television shows, such musicians as tenor-great Coleman Hawkins, trumpeters Red Allen, Charlie Shavers and Rex Stewart, trombonists J.C. Higginbotham and Dickie Wells, and clarinetist Buster Bailey, among others, star, and for some reason they seem quite inspired, possibly by each other's presence. "Love Is Just Around the Corner" and a "Bugle Call Rag" that teams Shavers and Stewart are among the high points. Probably difficult to find and not too pretty to look at (with a dumb sketch of Hawkins on the front and a totally blank back cover), pick this one up if you see it. —*Scott Yanow*

Soul / Nov. 7, 1958 / Original Jazz Classics ◆◆

This is a decent but not very exciting outing. Then 52, Hawkins uses a typically young rhythm section (including guitarist Kenny Burrell and pianist Ray Bryant) and plays melodically on a variety of originals and standards. This insipid version of "Greensleeves" is difficult to sit through but the rest of this CD is enjoyable if not overly inspiring. —*Scott Yanow*

Hawk Eyes / Apr. 3, 1959 / Original Jazz Classics ◆◆◆◆

Tenor-great Coleman Hawkins tended to be at his best when challenged by another horn player. On this highly enjoyable CD, Hawkins is joined by the superb trumpeter Charlie Shavers and a strong rhythm section that includes guitarist Tiny Grimes and pianist Ray Bryant. With such superior songs as "Through for the Night," "I Never Knew" and "La Rosita," in addition to long jams, plenty of fireworks occur during this frequently exciting session. —*Scott Yanow*

The Immortal Coleman Hawkins / Jul. 3, 1959-Feb. 1, 1963 / Pumpkin ◆◆◆

There are quite a few recordings (mostly, like this one, on LP) of Coleman Hawkins concert appearances during 1957-65, his final prime period. This Pumpkin set finds Hawk matched with his best partner, trumpeter Roy Eldridge, for fiery versions of "Soft Winds" and "Sweet Sue" in 1959. The second half features the veteran tenor saxophonist with a Swedish rhythm section performing two ballads and the jumping "Rifftide." This is a good example of strong late-period Coleman Hawkins. —*Scott Yanow*

Blowin' up a Breeze / Aug. 9, 1959-Jun. 12, 1963 / Spotlite ◆◆◆

This LP has two excellent concert performances by Hawkins. First he is heard at the 1959 Playboy Jazz Festival with a Chicago-based rhythm section performing four standards, including a remake of his old standby "Body and Soul" and a strong version of "Centerpiece." The flip side moves up to 1963 as Hawkins and the Tommy Flanagan trio explore "The Way You Look Tonight" and two ballads. A nice all-around set of strong mainstream jazz comes from one of its pioneers. —*Scott Yanow*

With Red Garland Trio / Aug. 12, 1959 / Original Jazz Classics ◆◆◆

One of Hawkins' better Prestige sessions (originally on its Swingville subsidiary) finds him fronting a then-modern rhythm section for a variety of basic originals, the ballad "I Want to Be Loved" and "It's a Blues World." The lengthy "Bean's Blues" is the high point of this generally relaxed session. —*Scott Yanow*

Dali / 1959-May 1962 / Stash ◆◆◆◆

This Stash CD, despite some silly graphics on the liners, has quite a bit of rewarding music. There are three examples of the fireworks that generally occurred when tenor saxophonist Coleman Hawkins and trumpeter Roy Eldridge met up (taken from a live session in 1959), while the remainder of this disc finds Hawk playing in Brussels in 1962. The veteran tenor is particularly strong on "Disorder at the Border" and "Rifftide," but the high point is a rare unaccompanied solo on "Dali," the fourth and final time that Hawkins recorded an improvisation by himself. It is a pity he never recorded an entire album like that. —*Scott Yanow*

Centerpiece / 1959-Sep. 1, 1962 / Phoenix ✦✦✦

Coleman Hawkins All Stars / Jan. 8, 1960 / Prestige ✦✦✦

"Some Stretching" sums up this set for the Coleman Hawkins Sextet (a pickup group), for it does indeed stretch out on five songs. Hawkins, then 54, was still very much in his prime and he formed an interesting front line with the fine swing trumpeter Joe Thomas and the distinctive trombonist Vic Dickenson. Joined by the Tommy Flanagan Trio, the three horns all take consistently excellent solos on this fine mainstream session. —*Scott Yanow*

In Concert with Roy Eldridge / 1959+1962 / Bandstand ✦✦✦✦✦

The material here dates from the 1959 Newport Jazz Festival and an English show some three years later. The opening Newport track, Benny Goodman's "Soft Winds," is kicked off by Ray Bryant's piano, with Eldridge coming in and then Hawkins, each showing off his differing but ultimately compatible approach to the material, which simmers and boils for 11 minutes. The fidelity is excellent on this and its neighboring track, a hot version of Hawkins' arrangement of "Sweet Sue," despite their live origins. Hawkins' arrangement of "Joshua Fit the Battle of Jericho" is a long, sweet, mellow jam in which the Hawk spreads his wings gradually over the last six minutes, joined by Eldridge in a soaring finale. There's more noise on the British tracks—which include "Autumn Leaves," "If I Had You" and a killer extended jam to Hawkins' "Disorder at the Border"—although the sound is fairly close and intimate. The band on the Newport tracks includes Ray Bryant at the piano, Tommy Bryant on bass, and Oliver Jackson on drums, while the group on the British sides is Tommy Flanagan at the piano, Major Holley on bass, and Eddie Locke on drums. —*Bruce Eder*

At Ease with Coleman Hawkins / Jan. 29, 1960 / Original Jazz Classics ✦✦

Recorded originally for the Prestige subsidiary Moodsville, Hawkins (along with the Tommy Flanagan Trio) sticks exclusively to ballads and slower pieces, all played at a low flame. Although it is nice to hear the veteran tenor interpreting "Poor Butterfly" and "I'll Get By," this CD is more successful as pleasant background music than as creative jazz. —*Scott Yanow*

Bean Stalkin' / Oct. 1960-Nov. 1960 / Pablo ✦✦✦✦

In contrast to Hawkins' sometimes sleepy studio albums from this era, his live performances were generally quite exciting. This set features the great tenor at two European concerts in 1960, performing three fairly heated numbers with a four-piece rhythm section, matching wits with trumpeter Roy Eldridge on "Crazy Rhythm" and leading two all-star jams with Eldridge, fellow tenor Don Byas and altoist Benny Carter. Some of the music is quite fiery, making this a recommended disc. —*Scott Yanow*

In a Mellow Tone / Dec. 30, 1960 / Original Jazz Classics ✦✦✦✦

A superior session with Hawkins, Eddie "Lockjaw" Davis (ts), and others. —*Ron Wynn*

Night Hawk / Dec. 30, 1960 / Original Jazz Classics ✦✦✦✦

Hawkins was one of the main inspirations of his fellow tenor Eddie "Lockjaw" Davis, so it was logical that they would one day meet up in the recording studio. This CD has many fine moments from these two highly competitive jazzmen, particularly the lengthy title cut and a heated tradeoff on "In a Mellow Tone," on which Davis goes higher but Hawkins wins on ideas. —*Scott Yanow*

Jazz Reunion / 1961 / Jazz Man ✦✦✦

The reunion referred to in the title was between tenor saxophonist Coleman Hawkins and clarinetist Pee Wee Russell, two legendary players who had recorded a couple of classic sides back in 1929. Still in their musical primes, both Hawkins and Russell were looking much more toward modern material to explore during this era and, although they revisit "If I Could Be with You," they also perform some Duke Ellington tunes, two of Russell's recent originals and the bop standard "Tin Tin Deo." The septet (which also includes trombonist Bob Brookmeyer, trumpeter Emmett Berry and pianist Nat Pierce) is in excellent form, with Russell consistently taking solo honors. —*Scott Yanow*

The Hawk Relaxes / Feb. 28, 1961 / Original Jazz Classics ✦✦

While Hawkins' recordings in the early '60s for Swingville tended to swing (not too suprisingly), his Moodsville dates were dominated by overly relaxed treatments of ballads. That is the case with this CD, which finds the great tenor saxophonist sounding alright on melody statements of such tunes as "When Day Is Done," "More than You Know" and "Moonglow" but failing to develop his solos very much beyond the opening themes. The sameness of tempos makes this affair chiefly viable as background music, although of a high quality within that genre. —*Scott Yanow*

On Broadway / Jan. 2, 1962-Aug. 16, 1962 / Prestige ✦✦✦

This single CD has all of the music from tenor saxophonist Coleman Hawkins' two LPs *Good Old Broadway* and *Make Someone Happy*, plus two numbers from a third album, *The Jazz Version of No Strings*. In general, Hawkins' output for Prestige tended to be a bit disappointing and lackluster, not due to weak playing on his part (Hawk was still very much in his musical prime) but because of indifferent material and unimaginative frameworks. Joined by pianist Tommy Flanagan, bassist Major Holley and drummer Eddie Locke, Hawkins primarily plays show tunes, with some (such as "Smoke Gets in Your Eyes," "The Man That Got Away" and "Get out of Town") being much more durable than others (such as "Talk to the Trees," "Cry Like the Wind" and "Have I Told You Lately?"). Most of the performances clock in around four minutes, and despite some decent playing, the overall effect lacks much excitement and is a bit forgettable. —*Scott Yanow*

Alive! / Aug. 13, 1962+Aug. 15, 1962 / Verve ✦✦✦✦✦

From the mid-'50s until Coleman Hawkins' death in 1969, the tenor saxophonist frequently teamed up with trumpeter Roy Eldridge to form a potent team. However, Hawkins rarely met altoist Johnny Hodges on the bandstand, making this encounter a special event. Long versions of "Satin Doll," "Perdido" and "The Rabbit in Jazz" give these three classic jazzmen (who are ably assisted by the Tommy Flanagan Trio) chances to stretch out and inspire each other. The remainder of this CD has Eldridge and Hodges absent while Coleman Hawkins (on "new" versions of "Mack the Knife," "It's the Talk of the Town," "Bean and the Boys" and "Caravan") heads the quartet for some excellent playing. Timeless music played by some of the top veteran stylists of the swing era. —*Scott Yanow*

Hawkins! Alive! at the Village Gate / Aug. 13, 1962-Aug. 15, 1962 / Verve ✦✦✦✦

The great Hawkins (who debuted on records 40 years earlier) gets to stretch out on this live outing by his 1962 quartet (which also features pianist Tommy Flanagan). This CD, which as a former LP had lengthy versions of "All the Things You Are," "Joshua Fit the Battle of Jericho" "Mack the Knife" and "Talk of the Town," is augmented by previously unreleased versions of "Bean and the Boys" and "If I Had You," all of which show that Coleman Hawkins in his late 50s was still a powerful force. —*Scott Yanow*

Duke Ellington Meets Coleman Hawkins / Aug. 18, 1962 / Impulse! ✦✦✦✦✦

This CD documents a historic occasion. Although Coleman Hawkins had been an admirer of Duke Ellington's music for at least 35 years at this point and Ellington had suggested they record together at least 20 years prior to their actual meeting in 1962, this was their first (and only) meeting on record. Although it would have been preferable to hear the great tenor performing with the full orchestra, his meeting with Ellington and an all-star group taken out of the big band does feature such greats as Ray Nance (on cornet and violin), trombonist Lawrence Brown, altoist Johnny Hodges and baritonist Harry Carney. High points include an exuberant "The Jeep Is Jumpin'," an interesting remake of "Mood Indigo" and a few new Ellington pieces. This delightful music is recommended in one form or another. —*Scott Yanow*

Desafinado: Bossa Nova and Jazz Samba / Sep. 12, 1962+Sep. 17, 1962 / GRP/Impulse! ✦✦✦✦✦

This set seems to have the word "fad" written all over it, but surprisingly it is a major success. During the era when everyone was trying to cash in on the popularity of bossa nova, tenor-great Coleman Hawkins recorded eight selections with a group consisting of two guitars, bass and three percussionists. In addition to a classic version of "O Pato" and such typical songs as "Desafinado" and "One Note Samba," Hawkins and company even turn "I'm Looking over a Four-Leaf Clover" into a strong bossa. Although this straight CD reissue of a former LP (which was most recently put out with improved sound in 1997) is a bit brief, the music is highly enjoyable. —*Scott Yanow*

Back in Bean's Bag / Dec. 10, 1962 / Columbia ✦✦✦

Hawkins teamed up with the personable trumpeter Clark Terry for this upbeat set of of solid swing. Terry in particular is in exuberant form on "Feedin' the Bean" and a delightful version of "Don't Worry About Me," but Hawkins' playing (particularly on the trumpeter's ballad "Michelle") is also in fine form. The Tommy Flanagan Trio assists the two classic hornmen on this superior LP. —*Scott Yanow*

Today and Now / Sep. 9, 1963+Sep. 11, 1963 / Impulse! ✦✦✦

Of Hawkins' three sessions for Impulse in the early to mid-'60s, this is the most intriguing due to the unusual repertoire. Included are such songs as "Go Lil' Liza," Quincy Jones' recent ballad "Quintessence," "Put on Your Old Grey Bonnet," "Swingin' Scotch" and "Don't Sit Under the Apple Tree." Despite (or perhaps due to) the strange choice of tunes, Hawkins is in inspired form, taking consistently creative solos on the fresh material. —*Scott Yanow*

Wrapped Tight / Feb. 22, 1965-Mar. 1, 1965 / Impulse! ✦✦✦✦

Hawkins' last strong recording finds the veteran, 43 years after his recording debut with Mamie Smith's Jazz Hounds, improvising creatively on a wide variety of material on this CD, ranging from "Intermezzo" and "Here's That Rainy Day" to "Red Roses for a Blue Lady" and "Indian Summer." Best is an adventurous version of "Out of Nowhere" that shows that the tenor saxophonist was still coming up with new ideas in 1965. —*Scott Yanow*

Rifftide / Mar. 1965 / Pumpkin ✦✦✦

Hawkins is heard during this concert performance near the end of his career and shortly before the steep decline that resulted in his death. Joined by the Earl Hines Trio on this LP from the collector's label Pumpkin, Hawkins is in surprisingly good form on five standards, displaying the tone that had made him his main influence on all saxophonists 40 years earlier. —*Scott Yanow*

Supreme / Sep. 26, 1966 / Enja ✦✦

The great tenor Coleman Hawkins started to go downhill in late 1965 (eating too little, drinking too much) and his career became progressively sadder until his death on May 19, 1969. This Enja CD (which composes brand new material taken from a Baltimore club date) has five lengthy performances and strong work from the rhythm section (pianist Barry Harris, bassist Gene Taylor and drummer Roy Brooks) but Hawkins' solos are consistently aimless and occasionally lost. His lines are shorter than in previous years and he seems to be gasping for air to an extent. The ironic part is that the audience is overly enthusiastic, loving every note no matter how desperate Hawkins sounds. Only on the brief closing "Ow" (where the tenor trades off very advanced phrases with Harris) does Coleman Hawkins sound up to par. Skip this set and acquire some of his many valuable earlier recordings instead. —*Scott Yanow*

Sirius / Dec. 20, 1966 / Original Jazz Classics ✦

Hawkins' final studio session is rather sad. Due to an excess of drink and his unwillingness to eat, the great tenor saxophonist went steadily downhill between 1965 and his death four years later. Recorded in late 1966, this quartet set finds Hawk constantly short of breath and unable to play long phrases. He is able to get away with this deficiency on the faster pieces but the ballads are rather painful to hear. Even at this late stage Hawkins still had his majestic tone but this recording is only of historical interest. —*Scott Yanow*

Erskine Hawkins

b. Jul. 26, 1914, Birmingham, AL, d. Nov. 11, 1993, Willingboro, NJ
Trumpet / Swing, Early R&B Jazz, New York Blues

A talented high-note trumpeter and a popular bandleader, Erskine Hawkins was nicknamed "the 20th Century Gabriel." He learned drums and trombone before switching to trumpet when he was 13. While attending the Alabama State Teachers College, he became the leader of the college band, the 'Bama State Collegians. They went to New York in 1934, became the Erskine Hawkins Orchestra, started making records in 1936 and by 1938 were quite successful. With Hawkins and Dud Bascomb sharing the trumpet solos, Paul Bascomb or Julian Dash heard on tenors, Haywood Henry on baritone, and pianist Avery Parrish, this was a solidly swinging band that delighted dancers and jazz fans alike. Hawkins had three major hits ("Tuxedo Junction," "After Hours" and "Tippin' In") and was able to keep the big band together all the way until 1953; some of their later sessions were more R&B-oriented yet never without jazz interest. Hawkins led a smaller unit during his last few decades (the survivors of the big band had a recorded reunion in 1971) and the trumpeter kept on working into the 1980s. —*Scott Yanow*

1936-1938 / Jul. 20, 1936-Sep. 12, 1938 / Classics ✦✦✦✦✦

This excellent CD has the first 24 recordings by trumpeter Erskine Hawkins' Orchestra, which was originally known as the 'Bama State Collegians. From the start, Hawkins had his sound together, with such top soloists as Dud Bascomb and the leader on trumpets, either Paul Bascomb or Julian Dash on tenor, baritonist Haywood Henry, and pianist Avery Parrish. Although there are some vocals from James Morrison, Billie Daniels and Merle Turner, it is the many spirited instrumentals that made Hawkins' big band one of the most popular of the next decade. Among the highlights of this superior set are "Swinging In Harlem," "Uproar Shout," "I Found a New Baby" and "Rockin' Rollers' Jubilee." —*Scott Yanow*

1938-1939 / Sep. 12, 1938-Oct. 2, 1939 / Classics ✦✦✦✦✦

The second in the Classics label's reissuance of all of trumpeter-bandleader Erskine Hawkins' early recordings features the orchestra in its early prime. Although underrated in the history books, Hawkins led one of the finest big bands of the era. Among the more memorable selections in this consistently exciting set are "Weary Blues," "King Porter Stomp," "Swing Out," "Swingin' on Lenox Avenue," "Gin Mill Special," and the original version of "Tuxedo Junction." All of the CDs in the valuable series are highly recommended to swing collectors. —*Scott Yanow*

The Complete Erskine Hawkins, Vol. 1-2 / Sep. 12, 1938-Dec. 20, 1939 / RCA ✦✦✦✦

Before CDs took over, this was one of the finest of all Erskine Hawkins' LP sets, a two-fer with the trumpeter's first 34 Bluebird recordings (although in three cases, the alternate take was substituted for the original). Erskine Hawkins' Orchestra was consistently exciting, overflowing with top jazz soloists, and both danceable and blues-oriented enough to please a wide audience. "Tuxedo Junction" (recorded

a few months before Glenn Miller's version) was the big hit of the period, but nearly all of the instrumentals are equally rewarding. Wonderful music that is also available on Classics CDs. —*Scott Yanow*

★ **The Original Tuxedo Junction** / Sep. 12, 1938-Jan. 10, 1945 / Bluebird ✦✦✦✦✦

This is an excellent one-CD sampler of the music of Erskine Hawkins' Orchestra. Although serious collectors will want to get the comprehensive Classics releases, this is a perfect place for more general listeners to begin. Hawkins' three biggest hits ("Tuxedo Junction," "After Hours" and "Tippin' In") lead off the set which otherwise has highlights from 1938-42. With the exception of 1945's "Tippin' In" (which features some memorable lead alto by Bobby Smith), all of Hawkins' key soloists are here, including the leader and Dud Bascomb on trumpets, either Paul Bascomb or Julian Dash on tenor, baritonist Haywood Henry and pianist Avery Parrish (who made "After Hours" famous). Timeless swing. —*Scott Yanow*

After Hours / Sep. 12, 1938-May 9, 1946 / RCA ✦✦✦

This 1960 LP, which can still be found in collectors' shops, has a dozen of the Erskine Hawkins big band's finest and most popular recordings, including "Tippin' In," "After Hours," "Bear Mash Blues," "Tuxedo Junction" and "Song of the Wanderer." Since then, this music has been reissued many times, including more recently on CD, and, since the personnel listing is not even given here, this generally worthwhile sampler's value has dropped quite a bit through the years. —*Scott Yanow*

1939-1940 / Oct. 2, 1939-Nov. 6, 1940 / Classics ✦✦✦✦✦

The Erskine Hawkins Orchestra was riding high during the era covered by this Classics CD, and their recording of "After Hours" (included among this reissue's highlights), which features pianist Avery Parrish, would keep the momentum going. Such numbers as "Satan Does the Rhumba," "Uptown Shuffle," "Gabriel Meets the Duke" and "Junction Blues" show why the Hawkins band was one of the most popular in Harlem during the 1930s and '40s. —*Scott Yanow*

1940-1941 / Nov. 6, 1940-Dec. 22, 1941 / Classics ✦✦✦✦✦

Although Erskine Hawkins' Orchestra was at its best on instrumentals, it did record a fair amount of vocal numbers during the swing era. The fourth Classics CD to chronologically reissue the trumpeter-bandleader's recordings has 13 vocals among the 22 selections, including six by the indifferent Jimmy Mitchelle, but there are also a bunch of swinging instrumentals (often arranged by Sammy Lowe), including "Soft Winds," "Riff Time," "Blackout" and "Shipyard Ramble," that feature tenors Julian Dash and Paul Bascomb along with trumpeters Dud Bascomb and Hawkins. —*Scott Yanow*

1941-1945 / Dec. 22, 1941-Nov. 21, 1945 / Classics ✦✦✦

All of the recordings cut by the always-underrated Erskine Hawkins Orchestra during a four-year period are reissued on this Classics CD. Actually, there is only one cut from 1941 and seven songs from 1942, so the bulk of the set deals with the 1945 edition of the orchestra. In general the instrumentals are much more rewarding than the vocals, featuring solos by the trumpeter-leader, altoist Bobby Smith (who stars on the hit record of "Tippin' In") and tenor saxophonist Julian Dash. The vocals by James Mitchelle, Ida James, Carol Tucker and Dolores Brown are harmless if forgettable; pianist Ace Harris fares best singing "Caldonia." In addition to "Tippin' In," highlights include "Lucky Seven," "Bear Mash Blues" (a near-classic by Sammy Lowe), "Caldonia," "Good Dip" and "Holiday for Swing." This is the fifth Erskine Hawkins CD from Classics and, due to the consistency of the band, all are recommended. —*Scott Yanow*

Live at Club Soul Sound / May 27, 1971 / Chess ✦✦✦

Trumpeter/bandleader Erskine Hawkins' only recording after 1962 (he lived until 1993) features many of the surviving orchestra alumni—including trumpeter Dud Bascomb, Julian Dash and Paul Bascomb on tenors, and baritonist Haywood Henry—plus a few ringers (such as trumpeter Ernie Royal and altoist Earl Warren), stretching out on surprisingly effective versions of seven swing-era songs. Hawkins' three biggest hits ("Tuxedo Junction," "Tippin' In" and "After Hours") are revisited, and the spirit of the old group is still there despite the passing of a few decades, making this a very successful reunion. Originally cut for the Stang label, this historic and enjoyable swing set was reissued on a 1984 Chess LP. —*Scott Yanow*

Clancy Hayes (Clarence Leonard Hayes)

b. Nov. 14, 1908, Caney, KS, d. Mar. 3, 1972, San Francisco, CA
Banjo, Vocals / Dixieland

Clancy Hayes was one of the finest vocalists of the Dixieland revival movement, much better than the typical musician who feels compelled to sing. He was a steady fixture in San Francisco from 1927 on, appearing regularly on the radio and in clubs. He hooked up with Lu Watters in 1938, performing with Watters' big band for two years and then ten with the Yerba Buena Jazz Band, mostly as a rhythm banjoist and occasionally on drums. He gained his greatest fame while singing with Bob Scobey's group (1950-59). In the 1960s Hayes worked with the Firehouse Five Plus Two, Turk Murphy, in an early version of what would be the

World's Greatest Jazz Band and with his own groups. Clancy Hayes recorded as a leader for Verve (1950), Audio Fidelity (1960), Good Time Jazz (1963), Delmark, ABC-Paramount and Fat Cat Jazz (1969) and helped make songs such as "Oh by Jingo," "Ace in the Hole" and his own "Huggin' and A-Chalkin'" popular in the trad jazz world. —*Scott Yanow*

● **Oh by Jingo** / Aug. 31, 1964 / Delmark ♦♦♦♦♦

Clancy Hayes, a fine banjoist who originally came to fame with Lu Watters' Yerba Buena Jazz Band in the 1940s, was a rarity. Unlike most Dixieland-oriented musicians who choose to sing, Hayes' likable voice was quite strong; he always swung, and his winning personality made his singing a high point whenever he appeared. He recorded frequently with Bob Scobey in the 1950s and led five albums of his own during 1960-66. This CD reissue from 1964 matches Hayes with the Salty Dogs, a hot septet that features cornetist Lew Green, trombonist Jim Snyder, clarinetist Kim Cusack and Jim Dapogny (best known as a pianist) on second cornet and valve trombone. Hayes' nine vocal numbers (which all have heated ensembles and plenty of colorful solos by his sidemen) are joined by three instrumentals plus six new alternate takes. Among the happier performances are "Oh! By Jingo," "Rose of Washington Square," "Beale Street Blues," "Cakewalking Babies" and "My Little Bimbo." The consistently strong musicianship, the enthusiastic playing and singing, the excellent material and Clancy Hayes' memorable voice make this a set that trad jazz collectors will want to go out of their way to pick up. —*Scott Yanow*

Clifford Hayes

Violin / Classic Jazz, Jazz Blues, Prewar Country Blues

A shadowy figure in jazz and blues history, Clifford Hayes was an okay violinist but more significant as a leader of recording sessions. He recorded with Sara Martin (1924) and often teamed up with banjoist Cal Smith in early jug bands including the Old Southern Jug Band, Clifford's Louisville Jug Band, the well-known Dixieland Jug Blowers (1926-7) and Hayes' Louisville Stompers (1927-29). One of the Dixieland Jug Blowers' sessions featured the great clarinetist Johnny Dodds, while pianist Earl Hines was a surprise star with the otherwise primitive Louisville Stompers (a jugless group with a front line of Hayes' violin and Hense Grundy's trombone). Clifford Hayes' last recordings were in 1931 and all of his sessions (plus those of some other jug bands) are available on four RST CDs. —*Scott Yanow*

Clifford Hayes & the Louisville Jug Bands, Vol. 1 / Sep. 16, 1924-Dec. 10, 1926 / RST ♦♦♦♦♦

The first of four volumes from the Austrian RST label that reissue the complete output of several historic jug bands from Louisville features violinist Clifford Hayes in several contexts. In 1924 he led the first jug band on record, backing blues singer Sara Martin on some exuberant performances that overcame the primitive recording quality. In addition, this CD has Hayes leading the Old Southern Jug Band, Clifford's Louisville Jug Band and the Dixieland Jug Blowers; all of the groups greatly benefit from the exciting playing of Earl McDonald on jug. The CD is rounded out by four selections from Whistler's Jug Band. Historic and generally enjoyable music, it's recommended to 1920s collectors. —*Scott Yanow*

● **Clifford Hayes & The Louisville Jug Bands, Vol. 2** / Dec. 10, 1926-Apr. 30, 1927 / RST ♦♦♦♦♦

The second of four CDs in a very valuable series from the Austrian RST label has 12 selections from The Dixieland Jug Blowers (a very spirited sextet with violinist Clifford Hayes, the colorful jug blowing of Earl McDonald and on six numbers, clarinetist Johnny Dodds as a guest), eight from Earl McDonald's Original Louisville Jug Band and four by Whistler's Jug Band (its leader Buford Threlked doubles on guitar and nose whistle). The monologue on the former group's "House Rent Rag" is quite memorable and still humorous. Of the four CDs, this is the most essential one for it finds these historic groups in their prime. —*Scott Yanow*

Clifford Hayes & the Louisville Jug Bands, Vol. 3 / Jun. 6, 1927-Feb. 6, 1929 / RST ♦♦♦♦♦

The third of four CDs from the Austrian RST label has the final ten selections from the Dixieland Jug Blowers along with 14 by Clifford Hayes' Louisville Stompers. Although the former no longer had the powerful jug playing of Earl McDonald, the mysterious H. Clifford was a good substitute and the three-horn septet (which features two guest vocalists) certainly had plenty of spirit. The Louisville Stompers is essentially a stripped-down jugless version of the Jug Blowers, a jazz-oriented quartet comprising violinist Clifford Hayes, trombonist Hense Grundy, pianist Johnny Gatewood and the impressive guitarist Cal Smith, who makes "Blue Guitar Stomp" a classic. The final seven Stompers performances are a bit surprising, for the pianist is the great Earl Hines, who has a few short solos although mostly in a supporting role. All four of the CDs are easily recommended to collectors of the era, for on a whole they contain the complete output of these unusual groups. —*Scott Yanow*

Clifford Hayes & the Louisville Jug Bands, Vol. 4 / Feb. 6, 1929-Jun. 17, 1931 / RST ♦♦♦♦♦

The fourth and final CD in this brief but important series from the Austrian RST label features a number of different jug bands in a variety of roles. There are the three last performances by Clifford Hayes' Lousville Stompers (the two versions of "You're Ticklin' Me" have Earl Hines on piano while "You Gonna Need My Help" features the classic blues singer Sippie Wallace).; the Kentucky Jazz Babies (a quartet with violinist Clifford Hayes and trumpeter Jimmy Strange) do a good job on two numbers, and Phillips' Louisville Jug Band (an odd quartet with Hooks Tifford on C-melody sax and Charles "Cane" Adams playing what is called "walking cane flute") performs eight songs. In addition, Whistler and his Jug Band play two primitive numbers, while violinist Clifford Hayes backs the minstrel singer Kid Coley and reunites with the great jug player Earl McDonald behind the vocals of country pioneer Jimmie Rodgers, Ben Ferguson and John Harris. An interesting set, to say the least; all four CDs in this series are recommended to fans of the era. —*Scott Yanow*

Louis Hayes

b. May 31, 1937, Detroit, MI
Drums / Hard Bop

A superior hard bop drummer best-known for supporting soloists rather than taking the spotlight himself, Louis Hayes led a band in Detroit as a teenager and was with Yusef Lateef during 1955-56. He had three notable associations: Horace Silver's Quintet (1956-59), the Cannonball Adderley Quintet (1959-65) and the Oscar Peterson Trio (1965-67). Hayes often teamed up with Sam Jones, both with Adderley and Peterson and in freelance settings. He led a variety of groups during the 1970s including quintets co-led by Junior Cook and Woody Shaw. Louis Hayes has appeared on many records through the years with everyone from John Coltrane and Cecil Taylor to McCoy Tyner, Freddie Hubbard and Dexter Gordon and has led sessions for Vee-Jay (1960), Timeless (1976), Muse (1977) and Candid (1989). —*Scott Yanow*

Louis Hayes (Feat. Yusef Lateef & Nat Adderley) / Apr. 26, 1960 / Vee-Jay ♦♦♦♦

The 1960 Cannonball Adderley Quintet (with drummer Louis Hayes, cornetist Nat Adderley, pianist Barry Harris and bassist Sam Jones) performs on this Vee-Jay CD reissue with tenor saxophonist Yusef Lateef in Cannonball's place. Although one misses the fiery altoist, the contrast between Nat's exciting (if sometimes erratic) cornet and Yusef's dignified yet soulful tenor make this an above-average session of swinging bop. The high-quality originals are augmented by five "new" alternate takes. —*Scott Yanow*

Breath of Life / Feb. 2, 1974 / Muse ♦♦♦

Ichi-Ban / May 5, 1976 / Timeless ♦♦♦♦

The group that drummer Louis Hayes and tenor saxophonist Junior Cook co-led in early 1976 lasted only a few months, but it was a superior hard bop band. Pianist Ronnie Mathews, bassist Stafford James and percussionist Guilherme Franco were all strong assets, but the real significance of the group was that it starred trumpeter Woody Shaw. This superior set mostly features obscurities (best-known is Thelonious Monk's "Pannonica"), with the highlights being Shaw's "The Moontrane" and bassist Walter Booker's "Book's Bossa." Fortunately, the superior set has been reissued on CD by the Dutch Timeless label. —*Scott Yanow*

● **The Real Thing** / May 20, 1977-May 21, 1977 / Muse ♦♦♦♦♦

For a time in 1977, drummer Louis Hayes co-led a quintet with the great trumpeter Woody Shaw. The band's only studio album (last available as a Muse LP) also features René McLean (tripling on soprano, alto and tenor), pianist Ronnie Mathews, bassist Stafford James, and (on three of the six tunes) guest trombonist Slide Hampton. On three little-known tunes and a trio of group originals, the modern hard bop unit plays concise but meaningful solos; a different combination of musicians gets the solo spotlight on each song. A well-conceived and continually interesting session that deserves to be reissued on CD. —*Scott Yanow*

Variety Is the Spice of Life / 1979 / Gryphon ♦♦♦♦

Although best known for his work as a valuable sideman, drummer Louis Hayes has led some stimulating sessions of his own through the years. This somewhat obscure but valuable LP is most notable for featuring the unique singer Leon Thomas on "Little Sunflower" and "Nisha" and for giving ample solo space to underrated altoist Frank Strozier, who doubles here on flute. With keyboardist Harold Mabern, bassist Cecil McBee and a couple of percussionists rounding out the group, Hayes leads his band through a diverse set that includes "Stardust," "What's Goin' On," "Invitation" and "My Favorite Things." Excellent, advanced straightahead music. —*Scott Yanow*

Light and Lively / Apr. 21, 1989 / Steeple Chase ♦♦♦♦♦

Another good one, with Charles Tolliver (tpt) and Bobby Watson (as). —*Michael G. Nastos*

The Crawl / Oct. 14, 1989 / Candid ♦♦♦♦♦

Veteran modal and post bop stylists from the 1970s are featured on this enjoyable CD. Trumpeter Charles Tolliver, altoist Gary Bartz, tenor saxophonist John Stubblefield, pianist Mickey Tucker and bassist Clint Houston, along with the drummerleader, are all heard in fine form even if Tolliver and to a lesser extent Bartz had not yet lived up to their great early potential. Bartz is brilliant during his feature spot on "Autumn in New York," Tolliver shows that he was still full of strong ideas, Stubblefield sounds quite original on both tenor and soprano, and the rhythm section is superb. In fact, bassist Houston often steals solo honors and his speedy patterns behind the horns are always worth listening to closely. With interesting modal originals to blow on, in addition to a blues and a pair of standards, this live session from 1989 has many memorable moments. — *Scott Yanow*

Una Max / Dec. 19, 1989 / Steeple Chase ♦♦♦♦

Tubby Hayes (Edward Brian Hayes)

b. Jan. 30, 1935, London, England, **d.** Jun. 8, 1973, London, England
Tenor Saxophone, Flute, Vibes / Bop, Hard Bop

One of England's top jazz musicians of the 1950s and '60s, Tubby Hayes was a fine hard bop stylist on tenor and occasionally vibes and flute. A professional at 15, Hayes played with Kenny Baker and in the big bands of Ambrose, Vic Lewis and Jack Parnell during 1951-55. He led his own group after that and started doubling on vibes in 1956. Hayes co-led the Jazz Couriers with Ronnie Scott (1957-59) and appeared in the US a few times during 1961-65. He headed his own big band in London, sat in with Duke Ellington's Orchestra in 1964 and was featured at many European festivals. Heart trouble forced him out of action during 1969-71 and caused his premature death. Tubby Hayes led sessions for Tempo (1955-59), London, Jazzland (1959), Fontana, Epic (a 1961 date with Clark Terry and Horace Parlan), Smash (a 1962 album that matched him with James Moody and Roland Kirk), 77, Spotlite and Mole. — *Scott Yanow*

Tubby Hayes / 1957-Apr. 1972 / IAJRC ♦♦♦♦

One of England's finest jazz musicians, Tubby Hayes was a superior tenor saxophonist who was also quite capable on vibes and flute. This fine LP gives one an overview of Hayes on a variety of mostly previously unissued selections. Hayes plays vibes behind fellow tenor Ronnie Scott on two numbers from the 1957-59 period, is heard with the Harry South Orchestra, heads a quartet that also includes pianist Victor Feldman, leads three versions of his big band, and on his very last recording (Apr. 1972), plays "I Thought About You" with a quartet. This album is an excellent introduction to Tubby Hayes, an excellent musician in danger of being forgotten due to his early death. — *Scott Yanow*

● **New York Sessions** / Oct. 3, 1961-Oct. 4, 1961 / Columbia ♦♦♦♦♦

Tubby Hayes was a superior tenor saxophonist from England who played in the tradition of Zoot Sims and Al Cohn, with just a dash of Johnny Griffin and early John Coltrane. This CD finds Tubby holding his own with a top-notch swinging rhythm section (pianist Horace Parlan, bassist George Duvivier and Dave Bailey) along with guests Clark Terry (on four of the ten selections) and vibraphonist Eddie Costa (on three songs). Whether it be an uptempo rendition of "Airegin" or a tender "You're My Everything," Tubby Hayes shows that he is an underrated legend. The original six selections are joined by four equally rewarding unreleased performances. — *Scott Yanow*

Tubby's Back in Town / Jun. 23, 1962 / Smash ♦♦♦♦

Night and Day / Nov. 7, 1963-Aug. 9, 1966 / Jazz House ♦♦♦♦♦

There are relatively few Tubby Hayes CDs currently available, making this collection of live performances from Ronnie Scott's club in London quite valuable. Hayes was a versatile bop-based performer who during the period covered by the set was showing a bit of the influence of Johnny Griffin and Rahsaan Roland Kirk. Tubby is heard mostly on tenor but doubles on flute during Clark Terry's "The Simple Waltz" and sticks to vibes on "Spring Can Really Hang You Up the Most." The five lengthy performances (all but one are over 13 minutes long) also include some strong playing by Jimmy Deuchar (who is heard on trumpet and mellophonium on one song apiece) and pianists Terry Shannon and Mike Pyne. Reasonably well recorded for club appearances of the mid-1960s, this CD (whose music was initially released in 1996) is easily recommended to straightahead jazz collectors. — *Scott Yanow*

A Tribute: Tubbs / Dec. 1963 / Spotlite ♦♦♦

This highly enjoyable Spotlite LP features tenor saxophonist Tubby Hayes at a concert performing lengthy versions of three boppish originals, plus "All of You." Hayes is teamed with trumpeter Jimmy Deuchar, pianist Terry Shannon, bassist Freddy Logan and drummer Allan Ganley and sounds in prime form, displaying a distinctive tone on the straightahead material. — *Scott Yanow*

Graham Haynes

Cornet / Post-Bop

The son of drummer Roy Haynes, Graham grew up around jazz musicians; his Hollis, Queens, neighborhood was also home to Roy Eldridge, Milt Jackson, and Jaki Byard. The younger Haynes played in the same high school band as bassist Marcus Miller. In 1982, he began an association with saxophonist Steve Coleman; he played on the latter's 1985 debut recording, *Motherland Pulse*, an album which also featured a young Geri Allen. Haynes' work occasionally hints at an experimental nature, but too often he's apt to place his Miles-ian cornet in static, synthesized, funk-oriented contexts that do not enhance or augment the essential lyricism of his work. Haynes is obviously attracted to various world music traditions on records like 1994's *The Griots Footsteps*. — *Chris Kelsey*

● **What Time It Be!** / Mar. 13, 1990-Mar. 14, 1990 / Muse ♦♦♦♦

Nocturne Parisian / Sep. 11, 1991-Apr. 18, 1992 / Muse ♦♦♦♦

Transition / Sep. 1994+Feb. 1995 / Antilles ♦♦♦♦

Where Miles Davis left off in the recording studio just before his death, cornetist Graham Haynes picks up, continuing to explore the controversial marriage between mainstream jazz and hip-hop rhythms. With the swipe of a scratch turntable, John Coltrane's "Transition" is sent reeling into the hip-hop age (who is to say that the ever-curious Coltrane wouldn't be dabbling in hip-hop if he were still alive?), as are a number of Haynes originals. Yet Haynes also has other fusions and revivals on his mind, sometimes reaching back to Miles' nearly forgotten mid-'70s "jungle band" for fuel. "Walidiya" throws Middle Eastern vocals and a sitar into a lengthy, mesmerizing procession, overseen by Haynes' far-off cornet and Steve Williamson's soprano sax. Haynes even successfully revives one of Miles' least-imitated experiments, the wah-wah-pedal trumpet (or in this case, cornet), on "Mars Triangle Jupiter" and "Freestylin.'" — *Richard S. Ginell*

Tones for the 21st Century / 1996 / Verve ♦♦♦

Graham Haynes' view of the future is provocatively put forth on this mostly self-contained CD, where, with the exception of an African harp and a couple of spoken voices, the sounds are made up entirely of his cornet, fluegelhorn, Tibetan trumpet, keyboards and racks of electronics. It is a peaceful vision, bordering on new age at times but also with an element of darkness rarely heard in feel-good electronic mood music. The opening track, "Millennia," is a striking piece for sampled voice, phase-shifted electronic sounds, and fluegelhorn, while "Sadguru" places Haynes' fluegelhorn over Indian tambura-like electronic droning. The lengthiest piece, "Out of Phaze," is exactly what it proclaims, loaded with backwards effects whipping past us, phase shifting, portentous voices, and foggy electronic revolving motifs, ending with a brief, mellow, ghostly visit into the "Spirit World." No doubt to the dismay of some, Haynes' vision apparently excludes any place for jazz, for there is no pulse or jazz feeling in any of these tone poems. But that's beside the point, for these are intelligent, smoothly wrought pieces on their own terms. — *Richard S. Ginell*

Roy Haynes

b. Mar. 13, 1926, Roxbury, MA
Drums / Bop, Hard Bop

A veteran drummer long overshadowed by others but finally, in the 1990s, being recognized for his talents and versatility, Roy Haynes has been a major player for 45 years. He worked early on with the Sabby Lewis big band, Frankie Newton, Luis Russell (1945-47) and Lester Young (1947-49). After some engagements with Kai Winding, Haynes was a member of the Charlie Parker quintet (1949-52); he also recorded during this era with Bud Powell, Wardell Gray and Stan Getz. Haynes toured the world with Sarah Vaughan (1953-58), played with Thelonious Monk in 1958, led his own group and gigged with George Shearing, Lennie Tristano, Eric Dolphy and Getz (1961). He was Elvin Jones' occasional substitute with John Coltrane's classic quartet during 1961-65, toured with Getz (1965-67) and was with Gary Burton (1967-68). In addition to touring with Chick Corea (1981 and 1984) and Pat Metheny (1989-90), Haynes has led his own Hip Ensemble on and off during the past 28 years. When one considers that he has also gigged with Miles Davis, Art Pepper, Horace Tapscott and Dizzy Gillespie, it is fair to say that Roy Haynes has played with about everyone! He led dates for EmArcy and Swing (both in 1954), New Jazz (1958 and 1960), Impulse (a 1962 quartet album with Rahsaan Roland Kirk), New Jazz, Pacific Jazz, Mainstream, Galaxy and more recently Dreyfus, Evidence and Storyville. In 1994 Roy Haynes was awarded the Danish Jazzpar prize. His son Graham Haynes is an excellent cornetist. — *Scott Yanow*

Jazz Abroad / 1956 / EmArcy ♦♦♦

● **We Three** / Nov. 14, 1958 / Original Jazz Classics ✦✦✦✦
Everyone's favorite sideman, drummer Roy Haynes, is heard on this CD leading his first American record date. Since the trio also includes pianist Phineas Newborn and bassist Paul Chambers, and Haynes is modest in taking much solo space himself, the excellent set is most notable for the virtuosic yet reasonably restrained playing of Newborn. Best known among the tunes are "After Hours" and Tadd Dameron's "Our Delight," but all six selections feature strong musical communication by these top-notch players. —*Scott Yanow*

Just Us / Jul. 5, 1960 / Original Jazz Classics ✦✦✦
Considering his stature, drummer Roy Haynes has led relatively few sessions throughout his long career. From 1957-77, he headed just seven albums (none from 1969-77), including this fine trio set. Haynes sounds as if he enjoys accompanying the Red Garland-influenced piano playing of Richard Wyands and the obscure bassist Eddie DeHaas on six of the songs, and has "Well Now" as his feature. Haynes' concise drum solos always hold one's interest, and even though this tasteful date is far from definitive, the music is enjoyable. —*Scott Yanow*

Out of the Afternoon / May 16, 1962+May 23, 1962 / Impulse! ✦✦✦✦✦
For this set, drummer Roy Haynes gathered together a powerful quartet that also featured pianist Tommy Flanagan, bassist Henry Grimes and, most notably, Rahsaan Roland Kirk. Kirk, heard on manzello, tenor, stritch and flute, easily steals the show without trying. He uplifts "Fly Me to the Moon," Artie Shaw's "Moon Ray," "If I Should Lose You" (which would remain in Rahsaan's repertoire for years), and "Some Other Spring"; in addition, the group plays three of Haynes' originals. Fine music made special by Roland Kirk. —*Scott Yanow*

Cracklin' / Apr. 10, 1963 / Original Jazz Classics ✦✦✦✦
Most of drummer Roy Haynes' dates as a leader put the focus on a star soloist. For this CD reissue, Haynes is joined by pianist Ronnie Mathews, bassist Larry Ridley, and the great tenor Booker Ervin. Ervin's unique sound, soulful yet very advanced, is well showcased on "Under Paris Skies" and originals by Mathews, Haynes and Randy Weston ("Sketch of Melba"), along with his own "Scoochie." —*Scott Yanow*

Hip Ensemble / 1971 / Mainstream ✦✦✦✦
This explosive session helped cement the reputations of George Adams (ts) and Hannibal Marvin Peterson (tpt). —*Ron Wynn*

Equipoise / 1972 / Mainstream ✦✦✦

Senyah / 1973 / Mainstream ✦✦✦

Vistalite / Jul. 12, 1977-Jul. 20, 1977 / Galaxy ✦✦✦
The music on this out-of-print LP is an interesting but sometimes uncomfortable mixture of advanced hard bop with electric instruments, aspects of funk, and the influence, in spots, of the avant-garde. Tenor great Joe Henderson is an asset to four of the seven selections (particularly an acoustic quartet rendition of "Invitation"), but most of the other players—including Stanley Cowell, mostly on electric keyboards, Ricardo Strobert on alto and flute, and an oversized rhythm section—sound rather faceless and anonymous. None of the group originals are all that memorable either, making this date a slight disappointment. —*Scott Yanow*

Thank You, Thank You / Jul. 16, 1977-Jul. 20, 1977 / Galaxy ✦✦
Roy Haynes, who came up shortly after Max Roach and Art Blakey, has been a major drummer since the late '40s but has never gotten quite the recognition he deserves. This somewhat obscure outing features Haynes in a variety of settings including a duet with percussionist Kenneth Nash, a pair of quartets with either George Cables or Stanley Cowell on piano, a quintet on the title cut featuring the tenor of John Klemmer and vibraphonist Bobby Hutcherson, and a selection with a two-keyboard septet. The music ranges from poppish to more straightahead with plenty of diverse moods explored. —*Scott Yanow*

True or False / Oct. 30, 1986 / Evidence ✦✦✦✦
After decades of rarely leading any sessions, drummer Roy Haynes in the 1980s and '90s finally received chances to make his own records. This 1986 Paris performance, not released domestically until Evidence put this CD in 1997, finds Haynes inspiring tenorman Ralph Moore (Trane-ish but sounding fairly original), pianist David Kikoski and bassist Ed Howard to some high-quality straightahead playing. The nine selections are consistently rewarding, with highlights including an uptempo "Limehouse Blues," Charlie Parker's "Big Foot," Chick Corea's "Bud Powell," Thelonious Monk's "Played Twice" and Sonny Rollins' exuberant "The Everywhere Calypso." Easily recommended to hard bop collectors. —*Scott Yanow*

Homecoming / Jun. 27, 1992 / Evidence ✦✦✦✦✦

When It's Haynes It Roars / Jul. 25, 1992-Jul. 26, 1992 / Dreyfus ✦✦✦✦✦

Te Vou! / 1994 / Dreyfus ✦✦✦✦✦
Veteran drummer Roy Haynes only has a single short solo on this CD but one suspects that his presence helped solidify and inspire the illustrious sidemen (altoist Donald Harrison, guitarist Pat Metheny, pianist David Kikoski and bassist Christian McBride). Harrison and Metheny are the lead solo voices on a program that

ranges from compositions by Chick Corea, Thelonious Monk (the difficult "Trinkle Twinkle") and Ornette Coleman to three by Metheny. Strong as the other musicians are, Christian McBride often comes close to stealing the show (as can be heard during his solo on Charlie Haden's "Blues M45"). This all-star matchup works quite well. —*Scott Yanow*

My Shining Hour / Mar. 10, 1994-Mar. 13, 1994 / Storyville ✦✦✦✦

Stephanie Haynes

b. California
Vocals / Standards, Traditional Pop, Vocal Jazz
Blessed with a beautiful voice, Stephanie Haynes has appeared regularly in Los Angeles and Orange County clubs during the past 15 years. A classically-trained flutist through college, she sang in jazz clubs in Albuquerque, New Mexico in the late '60s and then performed pop music with a Top 40 group for seven years. However, Haynes rediscovered jazz, moved to Orange County, worked frequently with pianist Kent Glenn (1980-85) and recorded for Ortho, Trend and Holt. In recent years she has often performed adventurous duets with pianist Dave MacKay (including cutting a CD for Why Not) and sung with Bopsicle. —*Scott Yanow*

Here's That Rainy Day / Jul. 27, 1988-Jul. 28, 1988 / Trend ✦✦✦✦

Dawn at Dana Point / Aug. 9, 1992-Aug. 10, 1992 / Holt ✦✦✦
The melodies and lyrics (most of which were composed by Dave Holt) are unfamiliar, but the beautiful voice of Stephanie Haynes (one of the top singers in Los Angeles) makes this CD worth getting. The tasteful backup (from tenor saxophonist Jack Montrose, pianist Pete Jolly, bassist Chuck Berghofer and drummer Nick Martinis) is an added plus on the lightly swinging date of newly composed love songs. —*Scott Yanow*

● **Two on a Swing** / 1993 / Why Not ✦✦✦✦✦
Stephanie Haynes not only possesses a beautiful voice but has the ability to always find the right note, which is fortunate, for pianist Dave MacKay really pushes her on their duet recording, sometimes only barely hinting at the more conventional chords to the standards. The results are full of chance-taking, with the hair-raising accompaniment inspiring Haynes to really stretch herself. The interplay between voice and piano on "Easy to Love" and the witty "Everything but You" are high points on this very satisfying and sometimes unpredictable set. —*Scott Yanow*

Kevin Hays

b. 1968, New York, NY
Piano / Post-Bop
A talented pianist, Kevin Hays grew up in Connecticut and started lessons when he was seven. He made his recording debut with Nick Brignola, toured with the Harper Brothers (1989-90) and worked with Joshua Redman, Benny Golson, Donald Harrison, Roy Haynes and Joe Henderson among others. Kevin Hays recorded three albums with Bob Belden and in 1994 cut his first record as a leader, *Seventh Sense* (Blue Note). —*Scott Yanow*

● **Seventh Sense** / Jan. 12, 1994-Jan. 13, 1994 / Blue Note ✦✦✦✦
Pianist Kevin Hays' style mixes the influences of Bill Evans and McCoy Tyner and he helps define the modern mainstream on this Blue Note disc. The quintet set also features plenty of solo space from vibraphonist Steve Nelson and the excellent tenorman Seamus Blake. Opening with three Hays originals and also including Hindermith's "Interlude" (which finds the group sounding a little like the Modern Jazz Quartet) and such standards as "My Man's Gone Now" and "East of the Sun," the music pays tribute to the past without becoming predictable or overly derivative. It's a fine release. —*Scott Yanow*

Ugly Beauty / May 24, 1994 / Steeple Chase ✦✦✦✦

Sweetear / Aug. 1, 1994 / Steeple Chase ✦✦✦

Go Round / Jan. 21, 1995-Jan. 22, 1995 / Blue Note ✦✦✦✦
Pianist Kevin Hays shows individuality on this CD and he certainly takes chances. The compositions (all but "Invitation" were penned by Hays) must be quite difficult to play because according to the liners, "Daybreak" is 12 bars with a couple of bars in 5/4, "The Run" has sections in 5/4, 4/4 and 3/4 in every chorus, and "Invitation" is completely altered. Both of the tenors (the obscure Steve Hall and Seemus Blake) somehow manage to sound comfortable and creative in this format, which is an extension of the controlled freedom of Wayne Shorter and Andrew Hill. On some tracks Hays plays an electric piano and, with Hall's Shorter-influenced tenor, one thinks of early Weather Report or 1970s Herbie Hancock; Blake adds to the atmosphere by sometimes electrifying his sax. The alert and versatile playing of bassist Doug Weiss and drummer Billy Hart is also quite impressive. This is thought-provoking music that grows in interest over time. —*Scott Yanow*

Crossroad / Dec. 1, 1995 / Steeple Chase ✦✦✦

Andalucia / Dec. 21, 1996+Dec. 22, 1996 / Blue Note ✦✦✦

J.C. Heard (James Charles Heard)

b. Oct. 8, 1917, Dayton, OH, **d.** Sep. 27, 1988, Royal Oak, MI
Drums / Swing, Bop

J.C. Heard was a very supportive drummer versatile enough to fit comfortably into swing, bop and blues settings. He was in vaudeville shows as a dancer in his youth. Heard's first important job playing drums was with Teddy Wilson's big band in 1939. He later worked with Wilson's sextet and with Coleman Hawkins and Benny Carter. Heard was with Cab Calloway's Orchestra (1942-45), recorded with top bop musicians, led his own band at Cafe Society (1946-47), was a member of Erroll Garner's trio (1948) and toured with Jazz at the Philharmonic. During 1953-57 he spent time in Japan and Australia; he freelanced in New York during 1957-66 (including playing with the Coleman Hawkins-Roy Eldridge Quintet and in 1961 with Teddy Wilson's trio) and then in 1966 J.C. Heard moved to Detroit, where he worked as a bandleader and a mentor to younger musicians into the mid-'80s. —*Scott Yanow*

● **The Detroit Jazz Tradition—Alive & Well** / Oct. 6, 1983-Oct. 7, 1983 / Parkwood ◆◆◆◆◆

After moving to Detroit in 1966, not much was heard from drummer J.C. Heard outside of Michigan, although he remained active as a player and an educator. This LP was Heard's first as a leader since 1958 and put the focus on two fine Detroit-area players, pianist Claude Black and a saxophonist named George Benson, and Canadian bassist Dave Young. Together they perform five standards and a couple of Heard's basic originals, plus Black's "Poor People's Bossa Nova." The pianist, making his recording debut, is impressive on his feature "If You Could See Me Now," while Heard does a fine job singing his "J.C.'s Blues." A worthwhile LP showing that Heard, despite his low national profile, had not lost a thing either in his playing talents or his enthusiasm. —*Scott Yanow*

Some of This, Some of That / Dec. 26, 1986 / Hiroko ◆◆◆◆

The only recording of the J.C. Heard Orchestra (a Detroit-based big band that the drummer had founded in 1981) finds the veteran Heard (just two years prior to his death) mostly playing high-quality hard bop with his 13-piece big band. Of the eight songs (best-known are "Nica's Dream" and Woody Shaw's "Sweet Love of Mine"), four are the leader's originals. Among the sidemen, trumpeter Walter Szymanski makes the biggest impression. Pianist Earl Van Riper is the only musician with even a slight "name," but the J.C. Heard Orchestra had a hard-driving and appealing sound. —*Scott Yanow*

Heath Brothers

f. 1975
Group / Hard Bop

Jimmy, Percy and Albert "Tootie" Heath teamed up in 1975 to form the Heath Brothers. Up until then bassist Percy had been busy with the Modern Jazz Quartet, but with the group in "retirement" (temporarily, as it turned out), all three brothers were free to join forces. Originally a quartet with pianist Stanley Cowell but expanding after the addition of guitarist Tony Purrone and Jimmy's son Mtume on percussion, the band recorded for Strata East (1975), four albums for Columbia and two for Island. Tootie Heath left the group early on and was replaced by Akira Tana, although he came back for the final 1983 record. Although the Heath Brothers' music was essentially hard bop, there were occasional departures into jazzy R&B on isolated selections. All of their LPs are worth searching for although none have yet been reissued on CD. —*Scott Yanow*

● **Marchin' On** / Oct. 22, 1975 / Strata East ◆◆◆◆◆

The debut recording by the Heath Brothers—which at the time consisted of Jimmy Heath on tenor, soprano and flute, bassist Percy Heath, drummer Al "Tootie" Heath and pianist Stanley Cowell—was one of their best, but also their most obscure release. Made for the soon-defunct Strata East label, this LP has Jimmy Heath's four-part "Smilin' Billy Suite," an original apiece from Cowell and the two other brothers (including Percy's "Watergate Blues"), and Duke Ellington's "Warm Valley." High-quality hard bop. —*Scott Yanow*

Passing Thru / May 19, 1978 / Columbia ◆◆◆◆

The Heath Brothers' second recording and Columbia debut has an impressive amount of variety. The core group—Jimmy Heath on tenor, soprano and flute, bassist Percy Heath, drummer Albert "Tootie" Heath and keyboardist Stanley Cowell—is joined on some selections by their future guitarist Tony Purrone, percussionist Mtume (Jimmy's son), and a four-piece brass section. With Jimmy's arrangements for the fairly diverse but consistently straightahead set adding color, this LP, which mixes bop standards with more recent originals, is well worth searching for. —*Scott Yanow*

Live at the Public Theater / 1979 / Columbia ◆◆◆◆

The fourth of the Heath Brothers' seven recordings before their breakup in 1983 (they would regroup in 1997) once again puts the focus on Jimmy Heath's writing,

including such originals as "A Sassy Samba" (for Sarah Vaughan), "Cloak and Dagger," and the unusual "For the Public." Along with Jimmy's tenor and soprano, the main soloists are keyboardist Stanley Cowell (who is also a master of the kalimba, the African thumb piano) and guitarist Tony Purrone. Offering tasteful support are bassist Percy Heath, drummer Akira Tana (an unknown at the time) and a couple of percussionists. Unfortunately, none of the Heath Brothers' enjoyable Columbia LPs have yet been reissued on CD. —*Scott Yanow*

In Motion / Jan. 1979-Feb. 1979 / Columbia ◆◆◆

By the time they recorded their second Columbia album (their third overall), the Heath Brothers had changed their personnel a little. Drummer Albert "Tootie" Heath had departed and was replaced by Keith Copeland, while Tony Purrone officially joined as the band's regular guitarist. Holdovers included Jimmy Heath (on tenor, soprano and flute, in addition to providing the arrangements), bassist Percy Heath, and keyboardist Stanley Cowell. In addition, this set often utilizes an eight-piece brass section. The material ranges from "The Voice of the Saxophone" (taken from Jimmy Heath's "Afro American Suite of Evolution") and Percy's "Move to the Groove" to Billy Strayhorn's "Passion Flower." —*Scott Yanow*

Expressions of Life / 1980 / Columbia ◆◆◆

The Heath Brothers' fourth and final Columbia album has a couple of funky tracks ("Dreamin'" and "Use It, Don't Abuse It") with added personnel, but otherwise features the core of Jimmy Heath on tenor and soprano, bassist Percy Heath doubling on cello, keyboardist Stanley Cowell, guitarist Tony Purrone and drummer Akira Tana. Excellent music mostly based in hard bop, with fine versions of Thelonious Monk's "Ruby My Dear," Cowell's "Equipoise" and "Confirmation," but nothing that unusual occurs. —*Scott Yanow*

Brotherly Love / Dec. 29, 1981-Dec. 30, 1981 / Antilles ◆◆◆◆

By their sixth album, the Heath Brothers (consisting of Jimmy on tenor and soprano, Percy Heath on bass, keyboardist Stanley Cowell, guitarist Tony Purrone and drummer Akira Tana) were sticking to their basic hard bop format, with an occasional poppish tune tossed in to give the group variety and possible commercial potential. This excellent set finds the band performing Kenny Dorham's "No End," "Autumn in New York," Percy's "Rejoice," and three originals by Jimmy. With eight years of constant playing, the Heath Brothers had developed into a solid working group with a sound of its own; Jimmy Heath's writing and solos gave the band its own personality. This Antilles set, which has been reissued on CD, is an excellent example of their playing. —*Scott Yanow*

Brothers and Others / May 16, 1983-May 17, 1983 / Antilles ◆◆◆◆◆

The seventh and final Heath Brothers recording before their official breakup, which has been reissued on CD by Antilles, has a different personnel than their previous few. Jimmy Heath (doubling on tenor and soprano), bassist Percy Heath and keyboardist Stanley Cowell are joined by original member and drummer Albert "Tootie" Heath, plus guest trombonist Slide Hampton and violinist Joe Kennedy for two songs apiece. It is Jimmy Heath's distinctive and inventive writing, including four complex originals and all of the arrangements, that gives this enjoyable set its greatest interest, but actually, all of the Heath Brothers recordings (some of which will be difficult to find) are easily recommended to straightahead jazz fans. —*Scott Yanow*

As We Were Saying / Feb. 23, 1997-Feb. 24, 1997 / Concord Jazz ◆◆◆◆◆

During the Modern Jazz Quartet's temporary retirement from 1975-83, bassist Percy Heath teamed up with tenor and soprano great Jimmy Heath and drummer Albert "Tootie" Heath (who left after a few years) to form the Heath Brothers. There had been occasional reunions since then, but this is the first record done under the Heath Brothers name in over a decade, and it finds the musical communication between the three siblings as strong as ever. Joined by either Stanley Cowell or Sir Roland Hanna on piano and such guests as guitarist Mark Elf, trombonist Slide Hampton, trumpeter Jon Faddis (brilliant during his three appearances) and percussionist Mtume (Jimmy's son), the Heaths perform a varied yet continually colorful set. The music is largely bop-oriented and includes six likable originals, "I'm Glad There Is You," "Daydream," and Fats Navarro's "Nostalgia." Although Percy has some solo spots, as do the guests, the main voice throughout is Jimmy Heath, who has long had his own distinctive sounds on tenor and soprano. Without exaggeration, it can be accurately stated that all nine performances on this CD are memorable in their own way. Highly recommended. —*Scott Yanow*

Albert "Tootie" Heath (Albert Heath)

b. May 31, 1935, Philadelphia, PA
Drums / Hard Bop, Post-Bop

The younger brother of Percy and Jimmy Heath, Albert "Tootie" Heath has long been a top hard bop-based drummer with an open mind toward more commercial styles of jazz. After moving to New York (1957) he debuted on record with John Coltrane. Heath was with J.J. Johnson's group (1958-60) and the Jazztet (1960-61), worked with the trios of Cedar Walton and Bobby Timmons in 1961 and recorded many records as a sideman for Riverside during that era. He lived in Europe in 1965-68 (working frequently with Kenny Drew and Dexter Gordon and backing touring Americans) and, after returning to the US, he played regularly with Herbie Hancock's sextet (1968-69) and Yusef Lateef (1970-74). After an additional year in Europe, he joined the Heath Brothers band (1975-78) and then settled in Los Angeles, where Tootie Heath has continued freelancing up to the present time, recently recording with the Riverside Reunion Band. —*Scott Yanow*

Kawaida / Dec. 11, 1969 / Trip ✦✦✦✦
An adventurous octet date with Don Cherry (tpt) and Herbie Hancock (p). —*Ron Wynn*

● **Kwanza (The First)** / Jun. 4, 1973 / Muse ✦✦✦✦
Excellent recording from the Heath Brothers' drummer, with brothers Percy (b) and Jimmy (sax), Curtis Fuller (tb), Ted Dunbar (g), and Kenny Barron (p). —*Michael G. Nastos*

Jimmy Heath

b. Oct. 25, 1926, Philadelphia, PA
Tenor Saxophone, Arranger, Flute, Soprano Saxophone / Hard Bop
The middle of the three Heath Brothers, Jimmy Heath has a distinctive sound on tenor and is a fluid player on soprano and flute and a very talented arranger/composer whose originals include "C.T.A." and "Gingerbread Boy." He was originally an altoist, playing with Howard McGhee during 1947-48 and the Dizzy Gillespie big band (1949-50). Called "Little Bird" because of the similarity in his playing to Charlie Parker, Heath switched to tenor in the early '50s. Although out of action for a few years due to "personal problems," Heath wrote for Chet Baker and Art Blakey during 1956-57. Back in action in 1959, he worked with Miles Davis briefly that year in addition to Kenny Dorham and Gil Evans, and started a string of impressive recordings for Riverside. In the 1960s Heath frequently teamed up with Milt Jackson and Art Farmer and he also worked as an educator and a freelance arranger. During 1975-82 Jimmy Heath teamed up with Percy and Tootie in the Heath Brothers and since then has remained active as a saxophonist and writer. In addition to his earlier Riverside dates, Jimmy Heath has recorded as a leader for Cobblestone, Muse, Xanadu, Landmark and Verve. —*Scott Yanow*

The Thumper / Nov. 27, 1959 / Original Jazz Classics ✦✦✦✦
Jimmy Heath at age 33 made his recording debut as a leader on this Riverside session, which has been reissued on CD in the OJC series. The hard bop tenor saxophonist is in superior form, contributing five originals (of which "For Minors Only" is best known), jamming with an all-star sextet (including cornetist Nat Adderley, trombonist Curtis Fuller, pianist Wynton Kelly, bassist Paul Chambers and drummer Albert "Tootie" Heath) and taking two standards as ballad features. The excellent session of late '50s straightahead jazz is lifted above the normal level by Heath's writing. —*Scott Yanow*

Nice People / Dec. 1959-1964 / Original Jazz Classics ✦✦✦
A compilation of Riverside albums. Well programmed. —*Michael G. Nastos*

Really Big / Jun. 24, 1960-Jun. 28, 1960 / Original Jazz Classics ✦✦✦✦✦
Jimmy Heath's first chance to lead a fairly large group, an all-star ten-piece, found him well featured both on tenor and as an arranger-composer. With such colorful players as cornetist Nat Adderley, fluegelhornist Clark Terry, altoist Cannonball Adderley, and either Cedar Walton or Tommy Flanagan on piano, Heath introduces a few originals (including "Big 'P'" and "A Picture of Heath") and uplifts "Green Dolphin Street," "Dat Dere," and "My Ideal," among others. A well-conceived set that has been reissued on CD. —*Scott Yanow*

The Quota / Apr. 14, 1961+Apr. 20, 1961 / Original Jazz Classics ✦✦✦✦

Triple Threat / Jan. 4, 1962+Jan. 17, 1962 / Riverside ✦✦✦✦

Swamp Seed / Mar. 11, 1963 / Original Jazz Classics ✦✦✦
An early version of the Heath Brothers, with Albert (d) and Percy (b) on board. —*Ron Wynn*

● **On the Trail** / 1964 / Original Jazz Classics ✦✦✦✦✦
Unlike some of his other Riverside recordings, the accent on this Jimmy Heath CD reissue is very much on his tenor playing (rather than his arrangements). Heath is in excellent form with a quintet that also includes pianist Wynton Kelly, guitarist Kenny Burrell, bassist Paul Chambers and drummer Albert "Tootie" Heath. The instantly recognizable hard bop saxophonist performs four standards and three of his own compositions, including the original versions of "Gingerbread Boy" and "Project S." It's a good example of his playing talents. —*Scott Yanow*

The Gap Sealer / Mar. 1, 1972 / Cobblestone ✦✦✦✦
Some of Heath's finest, most aggressive playing. He is a standout on soprano, flute, and tenor. —*Ron Wynn*

Jimmy / Mar. 1, 1972 / Muse ✦✦✦✦
Originally a Cobblestone LP titled *The Gap Sealer*, this was Jimmy Heath's first chance to lead his own record date since the collapse of the Riverside label in 1964. Heath, heard on tenor, soprano and flute, performs four of his originals, a song by percussionist Mtume (his son), and the standard "Invitation." As it turns out, none of the material is all that memorable, and Kenny Barron's use of electric keyboards waters down his distinctive style. Heath, who is also joined by electric bassist Bob Cranshaw, Mtume, and brother Al "Tootie" Heath on drums, stretches himself in places and is in fine form, but this is a fairly forgettable effort overall. —*Scott Yanow*

Love and Understanding / Jun. 11, 1973 / Xanadu ✦✦✦
This is one of Jimmy Heath's more unusual and versatile records, and fortunately it has been reissued on CD. Heath switches between tenor, soprano and flute on a diverse program (five originals plus Duke Ellington's "In a Sentimental Mood") that ranges from hard bop to light funk and R&Bish jazz. Heath's sidemen (trombonist Curtis Fuller, cellist Bernard Fennell, keyboardist Stanley Cowell, electric bassist Bob Cranshaw and drummer Billy Higgins) sound quite inspired by the material and Heath plays at his most inventive throughout the underrated set. —*Scott Yanow*

Time and the Place / Jun. 24, 1974 / Landmark ✦✦✦✦
Although this 1994 CD looks like a reissue, the music was actually released for the first time 20 years after it was recorded. Jimmy Heath, who is heard here on tenor, alto, soprano and flute, played at his prime throughout the 1970s although he tended to be somewhat overlooked in popularity polls. Heath was stretching himself during the era, as can be heard on these obscure pieces; five of his originals plus Kenny Dorham's "No End." Although essentially bop-based, Heath was open to the influences of the avant-garde and fusion and, with a flexible group also including trombonist Curtis Fuller, guitarist Pat Martino, pianist Stanley Cowell, bassist Sam Jones, drummer Billy Higgins and percussionist Mtume, Jimmy Heath consistently takes adventurous yet logical solos. Worth checking out. —*Scott Yanow*

Picture of Heath / Sep. 22, 1975 / Xanadu ✦✦✦✦
As was true of most Xanadu dates, the accent is on bebop during this Jimmy Heath LP. Doubling on tenor and soprano, Heath is heard on five of his better originals, including "For Minors Only," "CTA" and the title cut, plus "Body and Soul." The great tenorman was clearly inspired by the stellar rhythm section (pianist Barry Harris, bassist Sam Jones and drummer Billy Higgins), resulting in one of his best blowing sessions. —*Scott Yanow*

New Picture / Jun. 18, 1985-Jun. 20, 1985 / Landmark ✦✦✦✦
Ten years after his most recent set as a leader, Jimmy Heath (heard here on tenor and soprano) finally had another opportunity to lead an album of his own. This date, reissued on CD, finds Heath playing in a largely unchanged style from his earlier days, although some of his freer flights hint slightly at the avant-garde. With strong support given by pianist Tommy Flanagan, guitarist Tony Purrone (an alumnus of the Heath Brothers), bassist Rufus Reid and drummer Al Foster, Heath performs four originals, "Lush Life," Charlie Parker's "Dewey Square," and "Sophisticated Lady." Three numbers add two French horns, a trombone and a tuba to the ensembles for color; Heath provided the arrangements. A tasteful and swinging effort. —*Scott Yanow*

Peer Pleasure / Feb. 17, 1987-Feb. 18, 1987 / Landmark ✦✦✦✦✦
The most unusual aspect of this CD is that Jimmy Heath, in addition to his usual tenor and soprano, also plays alto (his original instrument) on two of the six numbers. The material pays tribute to John Coltrane, Sonny Rollins, Ben Webster (an Ernie Wilkins original), and Dizzy Gillespie, and "Ellington's Stray Horn" is included along with a Monty Alexander original. Two songs are played by Heath with guitarist Tony Purrone, bassist Stafford James and drummer Akira Tana; pianist Larry Willis makes the group a quintet on one piece, and trumpeter Tom Williams expands the band to a sextet for the three remaining selections. The largely straightahead set benefits from the changing instrumentation and the fresh material, and Jimmy Heath (60 at the time) shows that he was still very much in prime form. —*Scott Yanow*

Little Man, Big Band / Jan. 30, 1992-Mar. 3, 1992 / Verve ✦✦✦✦

You've Changed / Aug. 2, 1994 / Steeple Chase ✦✦✦

You or Me / Dec. 12, 1995 / Steeple Chase ✦✦✦

Percy Heath

b. Apr. 30, 1923, Wilmington, NC
Bass / Bop, Hard Bop, Cool
The oldest of the three Heath Brothers, Percy Heath's association with the Modern Jazz Quartet has been the dominant activity of his career. An excellent soloist and a perfect accompanist with an appealing tone, Percy (who grew up in Philadelphia) was originally a violinist. He switched to bass in 1946, was soon playing

locally and the following year he moved to New York with brother Jimmy to join Howard McGhee's band. Heath played with the who's who of bop (Charlie Parker, Dizzy Gillespie, Thelonious Monk, Fats Navarro, Miles Davis and J.J. Johnson) in various settings and recordings. In 1951 he joined Milt Jackson's Quartet, which in 1952 became the Modern Jazz Quartet. For the next 23 years the MJQ toured and recorded constantly. After its temporary breakup, Percy joined Jimmy and Tootie in the Heath Brothers Band (1975-82), going back to the MJQ (where he is still a key member) when they regrouped in the early '80s. Strangely enough, Percy Heath has never led a record date of his own. —*Scott Yanow*

Chuck Hedges

b. Chicago, IL
Clarinet / Dixieland, Swing
A very talented if often overlooked veteran clarinetist, Chuck Hedges is an exciting player whose music falls between swing and Dixieland. He played in the early '50s with George Brunis, Danny Alvin and Muggsy Spanier in Chicago. Later in the decade he was with Dave Remington, in the 1960s Hedges toured with trumpeter Dick Ruedebusch and in the 1970s and '80s he often played with Wild Bill Davison. Although he has long lived in Milwaukee, Chuck Hedges plays often in Chicago and is a regular at several traditional jazz festivals. He co-led a Jazzology album with Allan Vache (1982) and has recorded as a leader for Arbors and Delmark (1992-93). —*Scott Yanow*

Clarinet Climax / Jun. 1982 / Jazzology ✦✦✦✦
Chuck Hedges' recorded debut as a leader is actually a jam session date that costars fellow clarinetist Allan Vache. Joined by a swinging rhythm section then employed by Jim Cullum's Happy Jazz Band (pianist John Sheridan, Howard Elkins on guitar and banjo, bassist Jack Wyatt and drummer Jim Vaughn), Hedges and Vache battle it out on five extended standards. Considering that they had never played together before this concert, it is remarkable how exciting (and perfectly coherent) the music is, particularly the interplay between the two clarinetists. Such tunes as "Undecided," "China Boy" and "Memories of You" prove to be excellent vehicles for the talented players on this worthy LP. —*Scott Yanow*

The Square Roots of Jazz / Jun. 3, 1983 / Magna Graphic ✦✦✦✦
There is nothing square about the music on this LP, a delight for mainstream jazz collectors. Chuck Hedges, one of the top swing/Dixieland clarinetists of the 1980s and '90s, teams up with trumpeter Johnny Varro (whose style is straight out of Teddy Wilson), bassist Ray Letherwood and drummer Gene Estes for a set of vintage standards. Other than Thelonious Monk's "'Round Midnight," a surprise choice, the music is predictable in its excellence and swing, with highlights including "When You're Smiling," "Have You Met Miss Jones?" and "I Found a New Baby." —*Scott Yanow*

No Greater Love / Dec. 1992 / Arbors ✦✦✦✦
Although he has been a top clarinetist for over 30 years and a popular attraction at classic jazz parties and festivals, clarinetist Chuck Hedges has had relatively few opportunities to lead his own record dates; in fact, this Arbors CD was his first session as a leader in nine years. Pianist Eddie Higgins (showcased on his "Magnolia Rag"), bassist Bob Haggart and drummer Gene Estes are swinging and supportive of Hedges, who is in top form on such numbers as "There Is No Greater Love," "Samba Dese Days," and "Cheek to Cheek." A superior advanced swing date. —*Scott Yanow*

● **Swingtet Live at Andy's** / Mar. 22, 1993-May 3, 1993 / Delmark ✦✦✦✦✦
The talented clarinetist Chuck Hedges is joined by some excellent Chicago-based players (vibraphonist Duane Thamm, guitarist Dave Bany, bassist John Bany and drummer Charles Braugham) for a spirited set of superior swing-based tunes. "Softly as in a Morning Sunrise," "It's Allright with Me," "Breakfast Feud" and "I Don't Wanna Be Kissed" are among the high points of this consistently swinging and very enjoyable music, a bit of a throwback to the 1950s. Hedges has rarely been given the opportunity to lead a record session, so that fact (on top of the high quality of the music) makes this successful effort something special. —*Scott Yanow*

Neal Hefti

b. Oct. 29, 1922, Hastings, NE
Arranger, Composer, Trumpet / Swing
One of the top jazz arranger/composers of the 1950s, Neal Hefti first wrote charts in the late 1930s for Nat Towles. He contributed arrangements to the Earl Hines big band, played trumpet with Charlie Barnet, Horace Heidt and Charlie Spivak (1942-43) and toured with Woody Herman's First Herd (1944-46), marrying Woody's singer Francis Wayne. It was with Herman that Hefti began to get a strong reputation, arranging an updated "Woodchopper's Ball" and "Blowin' up a Storm," and composing "The Good Earth" and "Wild Root." He also took a notable solo during a Lucky Thompson session on "From Dixieland to Bop." However,

Hefti soon relegated his trumpet playing to a secondary status (although he played it on an occasional basis into the 1960s) and concentrated on his writing. He contributed charts to the orchestras of Charlie Ventura (1946), Harry James (1948-49) and most notably Count Basie (1950-62). For Basie he wrote "Little Pony," "Cute," "Li'l Darling," "Whirlybird" and many other swinging songs, often utilizing Frank Wess' flute in inventive fashion. Neal Hefti also led his own bands off and on in the 1950s but in later years concentrated on writing for films, while remaining influenced by his experiences in the jazz world. —*Scott Yanow*

Left and Right / 1956 / Columbia ✦✦✦
Neal Hefti, a fine trumpeter whose swing-based style hinted at bop, became a notable full-time arranger by the late 1940s. However, this obscure LP from the mid-1950s is a real surprise, for Hefti is featured playing trumpet on ten danceable numbers as part of an unidentified sextet. The last (and most extended) example of Neal Hefti's decent abilities on trumpet, this date finds Hefti improvising melodically on such tunes as "That Old Black Magic," "You Do Something to Me," "Mack the Knife," and "I Won't Dance." Not essential music, but certainly a historical curiosity. —*Scott Yanow*

Mark Helias

b. Oct. 1, 1950, Brunswick, NJ
Bass / Avant-Garde
An adventurous and flexible bassist, Mark Helias did not start on his instrument until he was 20. Helias studied at Yale and played locally with such modern players as Leo Smith and Anthony Davis. He recorded with many top avant-garde musicians including Anthony Braxton (1977), Dewey Redman and Muhal Richard Abrams and teamed up with Ray Anderson in the band Bass Drum Bone and the bizarre funk group Slickaphonics (on and off during 1980-83). Helias was also in the band Nu (1985-87) which included Don Cherry, Carlos Ward and Nana Vasconcelos. Starting in 1984 he has led his own series of explorative sessions for Enja. —*Scott Yanow*

Split Image / Aug. 29, 1984 / Enja ✦✦✦✦
With Dewey Redman (ts), Tim Berne (as), Herb Robertson (tpt), and Gerry Hemingway. Six more Helias originals. —*Michael G. Nastos*

● **The Current Set** / Mar. 4, 1987-Mar. 5, 1987 / Enja ✦✦✦✦✦
Septet with Tim Berne (as), Robin Eubanks (tb), Greg Osby (as), Herb Robertson, Victor Lewis, and Nana Vasconcelos (per). Six originals by leader and bassist, all in strong improvisatory flavor, while keeping rhythm intact. "Greetings from L.C." a fave. —*Michael G. Nastos*

Desert Blue / Apr. 1, 1989-Apr. 2, 1989 / Enja ✦✦✦✦

Loopin' the Cool / Dec. 14, 1994-Dec. 15, 1994 / Enja ✦✦✦✦
Although every musician is important on this stimulating session (the tightness of drummer Tom Rainey and percussionist Epizo Bangoura is not to be overlooked), one's attention is generally drawn to the three main voices. Bassist-leader Mark Helias contributed all of the compositions and arrangements and functions both as a member of the rhythm section and as a lead player. Violinist Regina Carter blends in colorfully with Ellery Eskelin's tenor and comes up with many inventive and unpredictable solos. Eskelin, who takes honors throughout the date, at times recalls both Clifford Jordan (in his sound) and prime Archie Shepp (the tonal distortions). The music in general is more conventional than the improvisations but also contains some unexpected moments and hints of both folk and Indian music along with advanced jazz. Easily recommended to adventurous listeners. —*Scott Yanow*

Gerry Hemingway

b. 1955, New Haven, CT
Drums / Avant-Garde
A long-time member of the Anthony Braxton Quartet, Gerry Hemingway has become a leader in his own right during the past decade. A very alert drummer who reacts immediately to the playing of other musicians, Hemingway studied at Wesleyan College and Yale. In the mid-'70s he played often with such advanced musicians as George Lewis, Anthony Davis, Leo Smith and Mark Helias. In 1978 he formed the Auricle label to document his music. Hemingway was a member of BassDrumBone with Ray Anderson and Mark Helias and since the early '80s has been with Braxton's Quartet, Marilyn Crispell's group and (starting in 1985) his own quintet. —*Scott Yanow*

Kwambe / Jan. 10, 1978+Feb. 20, 1978 / Auricle ✦✦✦

Solo Works / Sep. 12, 1978+Jun. 28, 1981 / Auricle ✦✦✦

Tubworks / Dec. 1983-Aug. 1987 / Sound Aspects ✦✦

Outerbridge Crossing / Sep. 1985 / Sound Aspects ✦✦✦✦

● **Special Detail** / Oct. 29, 1990-Oct. 30, 1990 / Hat Art ✦✦✦✦✦
Ambitious, far-reaching mid-'80s session by drummer and percussionist Gerry Hemingway that features Don Byron playing a variety of saxophones in the period before he decided to concentrate on clarinet. He uses an unorthodox trombone/cello pairing instead of a pianist, and buttresses each composition with sympathetic, careful rhythms. —*Ron Wynn*

Down to the Wire / Dec. 8, 1991-Dec. 10, 1991 / Hat Art ✦✦✦✦✦

Demon Chaser / Mar. 2, 1993 / Hat Hut ✦✦✦

Marmalade King / Aug. 1, 1995 / Hat Hut ✦✦✦

Julius Hemphill

b. 1940, Fort Worth, TX, **d.** Apr. 2, 1995
Alto Saxophone, Composer, Soprano Saxophone, Flute / Avant-Garde, Free Jazz
One of the giants of the jazz avant-garde, Julius Hemphill had a distinctive sound and a bluish yet dissonant style and was also a talented arranger/composer. An influence on many forward-thinking young players including Tim Berne and (more indirectly) David Sanborn, Hemphill took lessons on clarinet from John Carter in Ft. Worth, studied music at North Texas State and played locally in Texas in addition to serving in the military. After moving to St. Louis in 1968, Hemphill became a major force in the city, forming the Black Artists Group, founding his own label Mbari and recording two albums later reissued on Freedom. He moved to New York in the mid-'70s, recorded with Anthony Braxton and Lester Bowie in 1974 and was part of the loft jazz scene. Hemphill was a founding member of the World Saxophone Quartet (1976) and became the main writer for the group. He was also closely involved in multimedia events and his own individual projects. After being forced out of the WSQ in 1990 (the group has declined ever since), Hemphill had his own saxophone sextet before his health failed. He recorded as a leader for several labels including Freedom, Sackville, Elektra/Musician and Black Saint. —*Scott Yanow*

★ **Dogon A.D.** / Feb. 1972 / Freedom ✦✦✦✦✦
This historic album features four then-unknowns on three lengthy avant-garde explorations that were quite influential not only in St. Louis (where they were recorded) but eventually on such diverse players as altoists Tim Berne and David Sanborn. Julius Hemphill (on alto and flute), trumpeter Baikida Carroll, cellist Abdul Wadud and drummer Philip Wilson are in superb form, both as soloists and in ensembles where they react to each other instantly. This important music is better to be heard than described. —*Scott Yanow*

Coon Bid'ness / Feb. 19, 1975 / Freedom ✦✦✦✦✦
This historic LP includes a 20-minute performance with altoist Julius Hemphill, trumpeter Baikida Carroll, baritonist Hamiet Bluiett, cellist Abdul Wadud and drummer Philip Wilson ("The Hard Blues") taken from the same session that resulted in *Dogon A.D.* In addition, there are four briefer tracks that feature Hemphill, Bluiett, Wadud, altoist Arthur Blythe, drummer Barry Altschul and the congas of Daniel Zebulon. The music throughout is quite avant-garde but differs from the high-energy jams of the 1960s due to its emphasis on building improvisations as a logical outgrowth from advanced compositions. It's well worth several listens. —*Scott Yanow*

Blue Boye / Jan. 1977 / Mbari ✦✦✦

Roi Boye and the Gotham Minstrels / Mar. 1, 1977 / Sackville ✦✦✦
Psycho-theater drama in the form of the free African-American creative-jazz movement at its height. —*Michael G. Nastos*

Raw Materials and Residuals / Nov. 1977 / Black Saint ✦✦✦✦

Flat out Jump Suite / Jun. 4, 1980-Jun. 5, 1980 / Black Saint ✦✦✦✦
Quartet with Abdul Wadud (cello), Olu Dara on trumpet, and Warren Smith on percussion. Unabashed free music, at times funky. —*Michael G. Nastos*

Georgia Blues / Aug. 1984 / Minor Music ✦✦✦✦

Julius Hemphill Big Band / Feb. 1988 / Elektra ✦✦✦
The only recording by altoist Julius Hemphill at the head of a big band is a mostly very stimulating set of exploratory music. Some of the music wanders a bit, and K. Curtis Lyle's talking on his poem "Drunk on God" is a distraction, but other selections feature colorful solos from many players, including Hemphill (doubling on soprano), guitarist Bill Frisell (well showcased on "Bordertown"), trombonist Frank Lacy, and the tenors of John Stubblefield and John Purcell. This valuable, but increasingly rare CD is particularly notable for giving one a rare chance to hear Hemphill's adventurous big-band arrangements. —*Scott Yanow*

☆ **Fat Man and the Hard Blues** / Jul. 15, 1991-Jul. 16, 1991 / Black Saint ✦✦✦✦✦
After leaving the World Saxophone Quartet, the innovative altoist/composer Julius Hemphill recorded with an unaccompanied sax sextet. This CD features such great players as Marty Ehrlich, Carl Grubbs, the young James Carter, Andrew White and baritonist Sam Furnace along with the leader on 14 of Hemphill's compositions.

These miniatures (all under seven minutes) are most notable for their fresh melodies, logical arrangements and spirited ensembles. —*Scott Yanow*

Live from the New Music Cafe / Sep. 27, 1991 / Music & Arts ✦✦✦✦✦

Oakland Duets / Nov. 13, 1992-Nov. 14, 1992 / Music & Arts ✦✦✦

Five Chord Stud / Nov. 18, 1993-Nov. 19, 1993 / Black Saint ✦✦✦✦✦
Although altoist Julius Hemphill gets top billing on this CD, his heart surgery in 1993 forced him to stop playing. However, this saxophone sextet was his regular group; he contributed six of the eight compositions (the other two are free improvisations) and the chance-taking heard throughout this adventurous music definitely makes most of the performances sound like they came from a Julius Hemphill recording, even if his alto is missed. The sextet has a very strong lineup (altoists Tim Berne, Marty Ehrlich and Sam Furnace, tenors James Carter and Andrew White and baritonist Fred Ho) and the resulting CD contains more than its share of variety. The music ranges from the soulful "Spiritual Chairs" and a boppish "Band Theme" to introspective ballads and wild passionate interplay. Other than Fred Ho (who is not heard from enough), each of the players has his chance to star. The generally fascinating music rewards repeated listenings but one has to have an open mind before putting it on. —*Scott Yanow*

At Dr. King's Table / 1997 / New World ✦✦✦

Bill Henderson

b. Mar. 19, 1930, Chicago, IL
Vocals / Standards
Bill Henderson sings blues, ballads and swing tunes in the tradition of Joe Williams and Ernie Andrews but with his own personality. He started singing professionally in 1952, performed in Chicago with Ramsey Lewis, moved to New York and started recording as a leader in 1958. He had a hit with "Senor Blues" (recorded with Horace Silver); Jimmy Smith's trio backed Henderson on one date; during his period on Vee-Jay (1959-61) his sidemen included Ramsey Lewis, Booker Little, Yusef Lateef and Eddie Harris; and in 1963 Henderson was featured on a full album (for MGM) accompanied by the Oscar Peterson Trio. Although he made one further record in 1965 (for Verve) and was with Count Basie during 1965-66, Bill Henderson never really received the fame that his talents deserved. He settled in Los Angeles, worked as an actor and occasionally led a group containing both pianist Dave MacKay and pianist-vocalist Joyce Collins. Henderson (who recorded a couple of albums for Discovery in the 1970s but very little since) still performs regularly in the Los Angeles area and is in prime form in the mid-'90s. —*Scott Yanow*

★ **Complete Vee-Jay Recordings, Vol. 1** / Oct. 26, 1959-Nov. 21, 1960 / Vee-Jay ✦✦✦✦✦
The first of two CDs that reissue all of singer Bill Henderson's output for Vee-Jay, this set finds Henderson (at the ages of 29-31) virtually at the beginning of his recording career; only a few singles preceded the Vee-Jay sessions. Henderson, a straightforward singer who developed his own sound while being in the tradition of Joe Williams, is heard on this CD in several settings. He is backed by the Ramsey Lewis trio on seven numbers, accompanied by a notable all-star sextet (with trumpeter Booker Little, tenorman Yusef Lateef and arrangements by Benny Golson); joined by a Count Basie-oriented octet arranged by Frank Wess; has the assistance of the MJT + 3 on one number, and is backed by an orchestra on the final two songs. One of the most often overlooked jazz singers of the past 35 years, Bill Henderson is heard throughout the definitive set in top form, particularly on such numbers as "Bye Bye Blackbird," "It Never Entered My Mind," "Moanin'" and "Sleeping Bee." Highly recommended. —*Scott Yanow*

Complete Vee-Jay Recordings, Vol. 2 / Dec. 5, 1960-Apr. 25, 1961 / Vee-Jay ✦✦✦✦✦
It seems odd that Bill Henderson did not make it big, particularly when one considers how few new male jazz singers emerged during the 1960s. This second of two CDs continues the reissuance of all of his 1959-61 recordings for Vee-Jay. Although there are a few lightweight tracks, most of the selections find Henderson swinging lightly or wringing honest emotion out of the ballads. The backup varies greatly, from string orchestras and the Count Basie band to a combo with tenor sophonist Eddie Harris and a quartet headed by pianist Tommy Flanagan. Both volumes are recommended. —*Scott Yanow*

● **Bill Henderson/Oscar Peterson Trio** / Feb. 1963-May 28, 1963 / Verve ✦✦✦✦✦
This CD brings back one of the high points of singer Bill Henderson's career. Because he settled in Los Angeles, Henderson never became a major name, but he was actually one of the top male jazz singers to emerge in the late 1950s. Backed quite sympathetically by the swinging Oscar Peterson Trio (which consisted of pianist Peterson, bassist Ray Brown and drummer Ed Thigpen), Henderson is in prime form on such songs as "All or Nothing at All," "Gravy Waltz," "I've Got a Crush On

You" and "The Folks Who Live on the Hill"; four previously unissued songs round out the fairly definitive collection. —*Scott Yanow*

Live with the Count Basie Band / 1965-1966 / Monad ✦✦✦

Bill Henderson was only with the Count Basie Orchestra for one year and he was barely documented singing with the classic ensemble, so this live CD has its historic value even if, at 26 minutes, it is inexcusably brief. Henderson runs through ten songs from his repertoire of the period, which ranges from the timeless ("If I Could be with You" and "Broadway") to the dated ("You're Nobody 'Til Somebody Loves You" and "Yesterday"). He manages to avoid merely filling in for Joe Williams and, at least during the brief period he was with Basie, Henderson carved out his own niche. The recording quality is decent but it is a pity that there is not twice as much music. —*Scott Yanow*

Live at the Times / Aug. 1975 / Discovery ✦✦✦

Stylized. Some good moments with Joyce Collins (v). —*Ron Wynn*

"Joey" Revisited / 1976 / Monad ✦✦✦

The packaging of this live release is a bit shoddy, with bassist Steve LaSpina's name listed as "Lespina" and keyboardist Dave Mackay's being listed as "Malachai." Singer Bill Henderson is in generally strong voice on 11 songs (including "Tulips or Turnips," which is mistakenly listed as "What Am I to You?"), although his dialogue between tunes should have been cut out. Henderson is accompanied by pianist Joyce Collins (who sings on three songs), Mackay, LaSpina and drummer Jerry Coleman; highlights include "You Better Love Me," "Sweet Georgia Brown," "I Can't Give You Anything but Love" and a surprisingly effective "Royal Garden Blues." The listed date is an estimate, since none is given on the release. This is the band that Henderson used around the period to record similar material for Discovery. Search for those records first. —*Scott Yanow*

Street of Dreams / May 3, 1979 / Discovery ✦✦

Good material, though uneven. —*Ron Wynn*

Tribute to Johnny Mercer / May 5, 1981 / Discovery ✦✦✦✦

Henderson's best among recent Discovery releases. —*Ron Wynn*

Eddie Henderson

b. Oct. 26, 1940, New York, NY
Trumpet / Post-Bop, Fusion

Eddie Henderson was one of the few trumpeters who was strongly influenced by Miles Davis' work of his early fusion period. He grew up in San Francisco, studied trumpet at the San Francisco Conservatory of Music but was trained to be a doctor when he permanently chose music. Henderson worked with John Handy, Tyrone Washington and Joe Henderson in addition to his own group. He gained some recognition for his work with the Herbie Hancock Sextet (1970-73) although his own records (which utilized electronics) tended to be commercial. After Hancock broke up his group, Henderson worked with Art Blakey and Mike Nock, recorded with Charles Earland and later in the 1970s led a rock-oriented group. In recent times he has returned to playing acoustic hard bop (touring with Billy Harper in 1991) while also working as a psychiatrist. —*Scott Yanow*

Realization / Feb. 27, 1973-Feb. 28, 1973 / Capricorn ✦✦

Inside Out / Oct. 1973 / Capricorn ✦✦✦

Few trumpeters in the 1970s sought to emulate the electric innovations of Miles Davis, distorting their tones with electronics. Eddie Henderson was one of the lone exceptions, as he shows on his second recording as a leader, an interesting if somewhat dated effort not yet reissued on CD. Joined by four of the other five members of the Herbie Hancock Sextet of the period (Hancock himself on keyboards, Bennie Maupin on reeds, bassist Buster Williams and drummer Billy Hart in addition to Eric Gravatt on second drums, Bill Summers on congas and the synth of Patrick Gleeson), Henderson performs five of his originals, plus two by Maupin. The rhythmic and spacy music has its strong moments, but is very much of the time period. —*Scott Yanow*

Sunburst / Mar. 1975-Apr. 1975 / Blue Note ✦✦✦

Heritage / 1975 / Blue Note ✦✦✦

Comin' Through / Jan. 1977 / Capitol ✦✦

Mahal / 1978 / Capitol ✦✦

Running to Your Love / 1979 / Capitol ✦✦

● Inspiration / Jul. 8, 1994-Jul. 9, 1994 / Milestone ✦✦✦✦✦

Considering that he has been a potentially great trumpeter for over 25 years, it is surprising that Eddie Henderson has had so few sessions as a leader, and even fewer that are rewarding. This 1994 set may be his very best. Henderson is featured with a quintet that also includes pianist Kevin Hays, vibraphonist Joe Locke, bassist Ed Howard and drummer Lewis Nash; Grover Washington adds his

soprano to two numbers. The emphasis is on straightahead material ranging from bop ("Surrey with the Fringe on Top" and "On Green Dolphin Street") to obscurities by Joe Henderson, Herbie Hancock, Kenny Barron, Billy Harper, Bobby Hutcherson and McCoy Tyner. Throughout, Henderson plays in prime form and he takes the majority of the solo space, making this CD an excellent example of his talents. —*Scott Yanow*

● Dark Shadows / Sep. 1995 / Milestone ✦✦✦✦✦

Although overlooked in jazz polls, trumpeter Eddie Henderson (who made his initial impression during the late 1960s/early '70s) recorded some of his final records as a leader in the mid-1990s. For this set, Henderson works quite well with vibraphonist Joe Locke (who also doubles on his atmospheric marimba) and a fine rhythm section during a variety of challenging pieces, including fairly obscure works by Wayne Shorter, Chick Corea, Joe Henderson, Freddie Hubbard, Locke and Henderson. The closing "The Water Is Wide" has a haunting wordless vocal by Henderson's daughter Lee Menzies; they had not seen each other in 15 years, and it was recorded on the same day that the trumpeter's mother passed away. An intriguing set of post-bop jazz. —*Scott Yanow*

Fletcher Henderson

b. Dec. 18, 1897, Cuthbert, GA, **d.** Dec. 29, 1952, New York, NY
Arranger, Leader, Piano / Classic Jazz, Swing

Fletcher Henderson was very important to early jazz as leader of the first great jazz big band, as an arranger and composer in the 1930s and as a masterful talent scout. Between 1923-39 quite an all-star cast of top young Black jazz musicians passed through his orchestra, including trumpeters Louis Armstrong, Joe Smith, Tommy Ladnier, Rex Stewart, Bobby Stark, Cootie Williams, Red Allen and Roy Eldridge, trombonists Charlie Green, Benny Morton, Jimmy Harrison, Sandy Williams, J.C. Higginbotham and Dickie Wells, clarinetist Buster Bailey, tenors Coleman Hawkins (1924-34), Ben Webster, Lester Young (whose brief stint was not recorded) and Chu Berry, altoists Benny Carter, Russell Procope and Hilton Jefferson, bassists John Kirby and Israel Crosby, drummers Kaiser Marshall, Walter Johnson and Sid Catlett, guest pianist Fats Waller, and such arrangers as Don Redman, Benny Carter, Edgar Sampson and Fletcher's younger brother Horace Henderson. And yet at the height of the swing era, Henderson's band was little-known.

Fletcher Henderson had a degree in chemistry and mathematics, but when he came to New York in 1920 with hopes of becoming a chemist, the only job he could find (due to the racism of the times) was as a song demonstrator with the Pace-Handy music company. Harry Pace soon founded the Black Swan label and Henderson, a versatile but fairly basic pianist, became an important contributor behind the scenes, organizing bands and backing blues vocalists. Although he started recording as a leader in 1921, it was not until January 1924 that he put together his first permanent big band. Using Don Redman's innovative arrangements, he was soon at the top of his field. His early recordings (Henderson made many records during 1923-24) tend to be both futuristic and awkward, with strong musicianship but staccato phrasing. However, after Louis Armstrong joined up in late 1924 and Don Redman started contributing more swinging arrangements, the Fletcher Henderson Orchestra had no close competitors artistically until the rise of Duke Ellington in 1927. By then Henderson's band (after a period at the Club Alabam) was playing regularly at the Roseland Ballroom but, due to the bandleader being a very indifferent businessman, the all-star outfit recorded relatively little during its peak (1927-30).

With the departure of Redman in 1927 and the end of interim periods when Benny Carter and Horace Henderson wrote the bulk of the arrangements, Fletcher himself developed into a top arranger by the early '30s. However, the Depression took its toll on the band and the increased competition from other orchestras (along with some bad business decisions and the loss of Coleman Hawkins) resulted in Henderson breaking up the big band in early 1935. Starting in 1934 he began contributing versions of his better arrangements to Benny Goodman's new orchestra (including "King Porter Stomp," "Sometimes I'm Happy" and "Down South Camp Meeting"), and ironically Goodman's recordings were huge hits at a time when Fletcher Henderson's name was not known to the general public. In 1936 he put together a new orchestra and immediately had a hit in "Christopher Columbus," but after three years he had to disband again in 1939. Henderson worked as a staff arranger for Goodman and even played in BG's Sextet for a few months (although his skills on the piano never did develop much). He struggled through the 1940s, leading occasional bands (including one in the mid-'40s that utilized some arrangements by the young Sun Ra). In 1950 Henderson had a fine sextet with Lucky Thompson but a stroke ended his career and led to his death in 1952. Virtually all of Fletcher Henderson's recordings as a leader (and many are quite exciting) are currently available on the Classics label and in more piecemeal fashion domestically. —*Scott Yanow*

1921-1923 / Jun. 1921-Jun. 11, 1923 / Classics ✦✦✦

This Classics CD reissues the first 23 recordings of Fletcher Henderson and his orchestra. The music is generally fairly primitive but historically it is quite significant since Henderson's group would develop into the first real jazz big band; also, the 1921-22 sides have rarely been reissued. Oddly enough, his only three solo piano recordings date from this period. The earliest orchestra recordings are essentially period dance-band performances but, by the end of this CD, Henderson's big band was already beginning to display a bit of its own musical personality although (needless to say) the best years were still in the future. —*Scott Yanow*

★ **A Study in Frustration/Thesaurus of Classic Jazz** / Aug. 9, 1923-May 28, 1938 / Columbia ✦✦✦✦✦

Formerly a four-LP set, this three-CD box contains some of the finest recordings of the 1920s and '30s. Fletcher Henderson's big band during this period featured many of the top Black jazz soloists including trumpeters Louis Armstrong, Joe Smith, Rex Stewart, Tommy Ladnier, Bobby Stark, Cootie Williams, Red Allen and Roy Eldridge, trombonists Charlie Green, Jimmy Harrison and J.C. Higginbotham, tenors Coleman Hawkins, Ben Webster and Chu Berry, clarinetist Buster Bailey, altoist Benny Carter and guest pianist Fats Waller, among others. With Don Redman and later Benny Carter and Fletcher himself contributing advanced arrangements, Henderson had the leading big band of 1923-27 and one of the best jazz orchestras of the next few years. This is an essential acquisition for all serious jazz collections. —*Scott Yanow*

The Pathe Sessions (1923-1925) / Nov. 26, 1923-Jun. 25, 1925 / Swaggie ✦✦✦✦✦

During the year and a half covered by these 19 selections, Fletcher Henderson's orchestra developed from a fine dance band into the first jazz big band. The quick evolution was caused by the addition of a young cornetist whose legato phrases and sense of swing greatly influenced the other members of Henderson's orchestra and eventually all of jazz: Louis Armstrong. While the first 12 selections on this Australian LP have advanced Don Redman arrangements and some interesting moments from the tenor of Coleman Hawkins, it is the final seven numbers that find the band learning to swing. Armstrong's solos sound several years ahead of everyone else but the band was beginning to catch up. —*Scott Yanow*

Fletcher Henderson (1924-1927) / Jul. 10, 1924-Apr. 24, 1927 / EPM ✦✦✦✦

This French CD contains many of the best recordings from Louis Armstrong's year with Henderson, including such classics as "Copenhagen," "Everybody Loves My Baby," "Mandy Make up Your Mind" and "Sugar Foot Stomp." During this time Henderson added other fine soloists (including trombonist Charlie Green and clarinetist Buster Bailey) and Don Redman's arrangements began to swing. The final six numbers from this 22-selection CD are from the Henderson Orchestra's zenith in 1927, with "Fidgety Feet" and "Variety Stomp" featuring brilliant work from tenor great Coleman Hawkins, trombonist Jimmy Harrison, clarinetist Bailey and trumpeter Tommy Ladnier. A perfect introduction to Fletcher Henderson. —*Scott Yanow*

Fletcher Henderson and Louis Armstrong / Oct. 10, 1924-Oct. 21, 1925 / Timeless ✦✦✦

This rather unusual CD has 24 selections but most of them are shorter excerpts. The focus is on the brilliant solos that Louis Armstrong took while a member of the Fletcher Henderson Orchestra. Since his cornet flights were years ahead of some of the wheezing arrangements and the attempts by the other sidemen, the producers simply cut out the more dated segments and sometimes spliced in several of his solos from different takes of the same song. Where the producers erred was in not including every Armstrong solo with Henderson and, most importantly, not programming the CD in complete chronological order so one could more easily trace the month-by-month growth of this innovative jazzman. Still, this is a historical curiosity and the music is consistently exciting. —*Scott Yanow*

1924-1925 / Oct. 1924-Feb. 1925 / Classics ✦✦✦✦

This excellent European LP contains 14 performances (including three alternate takes) from Armstrong's period with Fletcher Henderson's orchestra. Most of these selections are fairly rare (such as "My Rose Marie," "Twelfth Street Blues" and "Me Neenyah") and only one performance is duplicated from the CD *Fletcher Henderson (1924-1927)*. Almost all of these cuts have memorable Louis Armstrong solos that easily take honors and are state-of-the-art for 1925. —*Scott Yanow*

1925-1926 / Nov. 23, 1925-Apr. 14, 1926 / Classics ✦✦✦✦✦

The Classics series has undergone the admirable task of reissuing on CD in chronological order every selection (although no alternate takes) of Fletcher Henderson's orchestra. This set finds the post-Armstrong edition of this pacesetting big band swinging hard on a variety of standards and obscurities. With cornetist Joe Smith, trombonist Charlie Green, clarinetist Buster Bailey and tenor great Coleman Hawkins contributing many fine solos and Don Redman's often-innovative arrangements inspiring the musicians, at this period Fletcher Henderson's orchestra had no close competitors among jazz-oriented big bands. Even the weaker pop

tunes (like "I Want to See a Little More of What I Saw in Arkansas") have their strong moments. —*Scott Yanow*

☆ **Fletcher Henderson and the Dixie Stompers (1925-1928)** / 1925-1928 / Disques Swing ✦✦✦✦✦

This duplicates the monumental four-LP set *A Study in Frustration* on ten of its 33 songs, but the music is of such high quality that it is worth purchasing for the 23 "new" pieces. The program included all of the titles recorded by Henderson under the band name the Dixie Stompers....The personnel on the inside cover mistakenly listed that of the Chocolate Dandies record. Collectively the Dixie Stompers consisted of cornetists Tommy Ladnier, Rex Stewart, Joe Smith, Russell Smith and Bobby Stark (last three titles), trombonists Charlie Green, Benny Morton and Jimmy Harrison, clarinetist Buster Bailey, Don Redman on clarinet, alto and (on two songs) vocals, Coleman Hawkins on tenor, clarinet and bass sax, altoist Don Pasquale, pianist Fletcher Henderson, Charlie Dixon on banjo, June Cole or Ralph Escudero on tuba and drummer Kaiser Marshall. The music was generally superb and Redman's innovative arrangements made this band often sound futuristic despite the acoustic recordings. The contrast between Ladnier's hot New Orleans cornet and Joe Smith's cool, lyrical style is worth noting, as are the solos by the long-forgotten but very talented Bobby Stark on the final three selections. Buster Bailey played his usual impossible runs on clarinet, the young Hawkins was still learning at this point and Charlie Green was in prime form on the early sides. This was a historically significant set, and is a delight to hear. —*Scott Yanow,*

● **1926-1927** / Apr. 14, 1926-Jan. 22, 1927 / Classics ✦✦✦✦

This CD in Classics' chronological series, which captures the Fletcher Henderson Orchestra at its peak, is overloaded with classics: "Jackass Blues," "The Stampede" (which has a very influential tenor solo by Coleman Hawkins), "Clarinet Marmalade," "Snag It" and "Tozo," among others. In addition to Coleman Hawkins, Tommy Ladnier emerges as a major trumpeter and Fats Waller drops by for his "Henderson Stomp." Eight years before the official beginning of the swing era, Fletcher Henderson's orchestra was outswinging everyone. —*Scott Yanow*

1927 / Mar. 11, 1927-Oct. 24, 1927 / Classics ✦✦✦✦✦

Fletcher Henderson's orchestra was at the peak of its powers during this period, as can be heard on such torrid recordings as "Fidgety Feet," "Sensation," "St. Louis Shuffle," and "Hop Off"; even the overly complex Don Redman arrangement "Whiteman Stomp" (which Paul Whiteman's musicians apparently had trouble learning) is no problem for this brilliant orchestra. Classics' chronological reissue of Henderson's valuable recordings on this CD covers the many high points of the peak year of 1927; only Duke Ellington's orchestra was on the level of this pacesetting big band. —*Scott Yanow*

The Complete Fletcher Henderson (1927-1936) / Mar. 11, 1927-Aug. 4, 1936 / RCA/Bluebird ✦✦✦✦

"Complete" is in this case a relative term, meaning every recording by Fletcher Henderson's orchestra owned by RCA/Bluebird rather than every record he made during this period. A perfectly done two-LP set, these 34 songs include three from 1927 (featuring trumpeters Tommy Ladnier and Joe Smith at their best), 12 varying sides from 1931-32 (during which tenor saxophonist Coleman Hawkins and trumpeters Rex Stewart and Bobby Stark make even the most commercial material into worthwhile music), a session from 1934 with trumpeter Red Allen, and 15 numbers from 1936 that co-star trumpeter Roy Eldridge and Chu Berry on tenor. Throughout, the consistent high quality of the solos and the musicianship (even with some off moments) make one regret that this classic orchestra was not more commercially successful. —*Scott Yanow*

Indispensable / Mar. 1927-Aug. 4, 1936 / RCA ✦✦✦✦✦

This double CD from RCA's *Jazz Tribune* series (a straight reissue of an earlier two-LP set) has highlights from bandleader Fletcher Henderson's Victor recordings. Dating from 1927, 1931-32, 1934 and 1936, several editions of Henderson's orchestra are represented, with such soloists as trumpeters Tommy Ladnier, Bobby Stark, Rex Stewart, Red Allen and Roy Eldridge, trombonists Jimmy Harrison, Benny Morton, Sandy Williams and J.C. Higginbotham, clarinetist Buster Bailey, altoist Edgar Sampson, and tenors Coleman Hawkins, Ben Webster and Chu Berry being among the key soloists; Henderson always used the best. Although not as complete as some series, there are many high points on this two-fer, including two takes apiece of "St. Louis Shuffle" and "Variety Stomp," "Sugar Foot Stomp," "Roll On, Mississippi, Roll On," "Singing the Blues," "Poor Old Joe," "Hocus Pocus," "Jangled Nerves," "Riffin'" and "You Can Depend on Me." An excellent set filled with classics. —*Scott Yanow*

Hocus Pocus / Apr. 27, 1927-Aug. 4, 1936 / Bluebird ✦✦✦✦

This single CD contains 21 of the 34 selections included on *The Complete Fletcher Henderson (1927-1936)*, mostly the hotter numbers, although one regrets the omissions. High points include "St. Louis Shuffle," "Variety Stomp," "Sugar Foot Stomp," the swinging title cut, examples of early Roy Eldridge trumpet and "Strangers," which contrasts a horrendous vocal with some inspired Coleman Hawkins tenor. —*Scott Yanow*

1927-1931 / Nov. 4, 1927-Feb. 5, 1931 / Classics ✦✦✦✦✦
With its high musicianship and many talented soloists (including trumpeters Rex Stewart and Bobby Stark, trombonist Jimmy Harrison, Coleman Hawkins on tenor and altoist Benny Carter), the Fletcher Henderson Orchestra should have prospered during this period, but unaccountably its leader (never a strong businessman) seemed to be losing interest in the band's fortunes and made several bad decisions. The result is that by 1931 Henderson's orchestra was struggling while Duke Ellington's was becoming a household name. This Classics CD, in covering over three years, demonstrates how few recordings this band made (only four songs apiece in both 1929 and 1930), although the quality largely makes up for the quantity. The original band version of "King Porter Stomp" and an explosive "Oh Baby" are the high points of this satisfying collection. —*Scott Yanow*

1931 / Feb. 5, 1931-Jul. 31, 1931 / Classics ✦✦✦✦
Even with such strong players as trumpeters Bobby Stark and Rex Stewart, trombonist Benny Morton and tenor saxophonist Coleman Hawkins, the fortunes of Fletcher Henderson's orchestra were slipping during 1931. With the departure of Don Redman several years earlier, the group's arrangements were less innovative, and the pressure was on to perform commercial songs for the Depression audience. Even the jazz standards (such as "Tiger Rag" and "After You've Gone") are less interesting than those of their competitors, although this new version of "Sugar Foot Stomp" is a classic and the strong solos by the all-star cast make this CD well worth acquiring. —*Scott Yanow*

Tidal Wave / Apr. 10, 1931-Sep. 25, 1934 / GRP/Decca ✦✦✦✦✦
Fletcher Henderson's five Decca sessions are reissued in full on this fine CD. The 1931 and 1934 big bands are showcased. While the former group (heard on eight numbers) features such soloists as trumpeters Bobby Stark and Rex Stewart, trombonist Benny Morton, and Coleman Hawkins on tenor, the later group showcases trumpeter Red Allen, trombonist Claude Jones, clarinetist Buster Bailey and tenor Ben Webster; altoist Benny Carter has a guest appearance on "Liza." Highlights of these early swing performances include "Sugar Foot Stomp," "Singin' the Blues" (which has Rex Stewart paying tribute to Bix Beiderbecke), the atmospheric "Radio Rhythm," "Big John's Special," "Down South Camp Meetin'" and "Rug Cutter's Swing." Excellent music that proves that swing did not begin with Benny Goodman in 1935. —*Scott Yanow*

1931-1932 / Jul. 31, 1931-Mar. 11, 1932 / Classics ✦✦✦
During this period Fletcher Henderson was often stuck recording commercial leftover like "My Sweet Tooth Says I Wanna (but My Wisdom Tooth Says No)", "I Wanna Count Sheep (Till the Cows Come Home)" and "Strangers," but in most cases his all-star orchestra was able to overcome the material. This CD, part of Classics' complete chronological reissue of Henderson's recordings, also finds the orchestra backing Baby Rose Marie on two songs in addition to attempting (with uneven success) to put its stamp on jazz standards made famous by other musicians (such as "12th Street Rag" and "Casa Loma Stomp"). The music is generally quite good if not essential Henderson. —*Scott Yanow*

1932-1934 / Dec. 9, 1932-Sep. 12, 1934 / Classics ✦✦✦✦
Although the Fletcher Henderson Orchestra was struggling and missing opportunities during this era, its recordings greatly improved from the ones in 1931. Henderson had finally developed into a top arranger (as can be heard on "Honeysuckle Rose" and "Wrappin' It Up"), the band was full of top soloists (trumpeter Bobby Stark has his greatest moments on "The New King Porter Stomp") and even if Coleman Hawkins chose to move to Europe (after starring on "It's the Talk of the Town") the band should have been poised to flourish in the swing era. These recordings (from Classics' complete chronological program) prove that swing did not begin with Benny Goodman in 1935. —*Scott Yanow*

1934-1937 / Sep. 25, 1934-Mar. 2, 1937 / Classics ✦✦✦✦✦
In early 1935 Fletcher Henderson broke up his classic orchestra but a year later, with the success of so many other big bands, he formed a new ensemble. This Classics CD includes four songs from 1934, Henderson's entire output from 1936 and his first recording of 1937. The main difference between the two units is that the later one boasted the trumpet of Roy Eldridge and tenor solos from Coleman Hawkins' potential successor, Chu Berry. "Christopher Columbus" became a hit, as did the band's new theme song ("Stealin' Apples"), but the brief bit of glory would not last. However, Henderson's brand of swing music still sounds fresh today and this CD is easily recommended. —*Scott Yanow*

1937-1938 / Mar. 2, 1937-May 28, 1938 / Classics ✦✦✦✦
The Classics chronological reissue of Fletcher Henderson's recordings continues with this disc, which traces the decline of his last "permanent" orchestra. With the departure of Roy Eldridge, Henderson for the first time since the early '20s lacked any major trumpet soloists, although he still featured the fine tenor of Chu Berry

and a variety of up-and-coming players. Unfortunately the band was far overshadowed by other orchestras influenced by Henderson and since the quality of his recordings was declining, the breakup of his group was hardly noticed. The irony is that the founder of the swing era could not survive when his music (as played by Benny Goodman) caught on. —*Scott Yanow*

1938 / Jul. 11, 1938-Jul. 13, 1938 / Jazz Unlimited ✦✦✦
The Fletcher Henderson Orchestra was in decline in 1938 and its breakup would come the following year. However, despite its eventual commercial failure, it was still a first-class swing band at this late point with fine soloists in trumpeter Emmett Berry, trombonist Ed Cuffee, tenor Elmer Williams and clarinetist Eddie Barefield. The two formerly unknown radio broadcasts included on this CD took place a few months after the band's final studio recordings and are generally excellent. Fletcher Henderson was definitely in Benny Goodman's shadow by this time (even if the announcer calls Henderson "the King of Swing") but, as such numbers as "Down South Camp Meeting," "Bugle Blues" and "Panama" show, there was still plenty of life left in this veteran band. —*Scott Yanow*

Fletcher Henderson with Slam Stewart and the Jazz Tones / Oct. 31, 1945-1959 / Sutton ✦✦
This has always been a great mystery LP, not helped by the absence of any liner notes or discographical details. Its title is inaccurate, since it actually consists of separate four-song sessions by Fletcher Henderson and bassist Slam Stewart, plus two tunes from "The Jazz Tones." The Henderson date (from October 31, 1945) was the pianist/arranger's final session with a big band. The music (which has solo spots for trumpeter Emmett Berry, trombonist Vic Dickenson and tenor saxophonist Otis Finch) is worthwhile (particularly a shouting version of "King Porter Stomp"), but the recording quality (which has the orchestra sounding as if it were a half block away from the microphone) is abysmal despite it being a studio recording. Slam Stewart is heard with his 1946 quartet (a group also including pianist Billy Taylor, guitarist John Collins and drummer Harold "Doc" West) in an equally rare session. The "Jazztones" (a phony name) is actually a 1959 septet that includes trumpeter Buck Clayton, clarinetist Pee Wee Russell, trombonist Dickenson and tenor saxophonist Bud Freeman. Its two numbers (which were also put out by Crown) were given incorrect titles ("School's Out" is really "Synthetic Blues," while "Goodbye Big Town" is "Billboard March"). In summary, this long-out-of-print budget LP has good music but horrendous packaging; hopefully it will be reissued properly in the future. —*Scott Yanow*

Fletcher Henderson's Sextet (1950) / Dec. 20, 1950-Dec. 21, 1950 / Alamac ✦✦✦
Recorded only a day or two before a stroke ended his playing career and, soon afterward, his life, this LP contains a broadcast that finds Fletcher Henderson playing mostly standards with a fine sextet. Trumpeter Dick Vance and clarinetist Eddie Barefield were alumni of his orchestra but it is tenor saxophonist Lucky Thompson who takes honors on this spirited session of small-group swing. —*Scott Yanow*

Horace Henderson

b. Nov. 22, 1904, Cuthbert, GA, **d.** Aug. 29, 1988, Denver, CO
Arranger, Piano / Swing
In some ways, it is ironic that Horace Henderson spent his life in his older brother Fletcher's shadow. Horace was a much better pianist and became a skillful arranger early on, but he actually accomplished a lot less during his life than Fletcher and was largely forgotten after the swing era ended. He began studying piano when he was 14 and attended Atlanta University and Wilberforce College, where he had his own student band, the Collegians, which in time became the Horace Henderson Orchestra and, in 1928, the Dixie Stompers. After a period working with Sammy Stewart, Henderson put together a new big band that played regularly in New York in 1929-31 before it was taken over by Don Redman. Henderson worked with Redman until joining his brother's orchestra as a pianist and arranger (1933-34). He briefly led another band, worked with Vernon Andrade, was back with Henderson in 1936, and then had yet another orchestra in 1937-40 that was based in Chicago. Horace Henderson was in the army for parts of 1942-43, rejoined Fletcher for a period, and then worked as accompanist for Lena Horne. He led groups in Los Angeles from 1945-50 and spent later periods playing in Minneapolis, Las Vegas and (from the late '60s on) Denver. However, Horace Henderson, who led recording sessions with his brother's sidemen in 1933 and his own big band in 1940 (plus obscure small-group dates in 1945 and 1951 and a 1954 broadcast with his orchestra released by IAJRC decades later), was more valuable as a contributor of arrangements to other bands. Among those orchestras that benefited from his charts were the Casa Loma Orchestra, and those of Benny Goodman, Charlie Barnet, Tommy Dorsey, Jimmie Lunceford, Earl Hines and, most notably, Fletcher Henderson, who had 30 of his brother's arrangements in the book, including "Hot and Anxious" (which used a riff that later became "In the Mood") and Fletcher's 1936 hit "Christopher Columbus." —*Scott Yanow*

● **Horace Henderson 1940-Fletcher Henderson 1941** / Feb. 27, 1940-Apr. 24, 1941 / Classics ✦✦✦✦

Horace Henderson spent most of his career in the shadow of his brother Fletcher, even though he was actually a superior pianist and a comparable arranger. Other than an all-star session that he headed in 1933, Horace did not make his first recordings as a leader until 1940, when he led a regular (if short-lived) big band. Five sessions resulted in 21 titles, all of which are included on this very enjoyable CD. Most notable among Henderson's sidemen are trumpeter Emmett Berry, tenor-man Elmer Williams, and Ray Nance (shortly before he joined Duke Ellington) on trumpet, violin and the vocal to "They Jittered All the Time." This excellent swing CD, which has plenty of "killer dillers," is rounded off by a four-song session by Fletcher Henderson's 1941 big band, cut shortly before it broke up. Recommended. —*Scott Yanow*

Joe Henderson

b. Apr. 24, 1937, Lima, Ohio

Tenor Saxophone / Hard Bop, Post-Bop

Joe Henderson is proof that jazz can sell without watering down the music; it just takes creative marketing! Although his sound and style are virtually unchanged from the mid-'60s, Joe Henderson's signing with Verve in 1992 was treated as a major news event by the label (even though he had already recorded many memorable sessions for other companies), his Verve recordings had easy-to-market themes (tributes to Billy Strayhorn, Miles Davis and Antonio Carlos Jobim) and as a result he became a national celebrity and a constant pollwinner while still sounding the same as when he was in obscurity in the 1970s!

The general feeling is that it couldn't happen to a more deserving jazz musician. After studying at Kentucky State College and Wayne University, Joe Henderson played locally in Detroit before spending time in the military (1960-62). He played briefly with Jack McDuff and then gained recognition for his work with Kenny Dorham (1962-63), a veteran bop trumpeter who championed him and helped Henderson get signed to Blue Note. Henderson appeared on many Blue Note sessions both as a leader and as a sideman, spent 1964-66 with Horace Silver's Quintet and during 1969-70 was in Herbie Hancock's band. From the start he had a very distinctive sound and style that, although influenced a bit by both Sonny Rollins and John Coltrane, also contained a lot of brand new phrases and ideas. Henderson has long been able to improvise in both inside and outside settings, from hard bop to free form. In the 1970s he recorded frequently for Milestone and lived in San Francisco but was somewhat taken for granted. The second half of the 1980s found him continuing his freelancing and teaching while recording for Blue Note, but it was when he hooked up with Verve that he suddenly became famous. Virtually all of his recordings are currently in print on CD including a massive collection of his neglected (but generally rewarding) Milestone dates. —*Scott Yanow*

Snap Your Fingers / 1962 / Todd ✦✦✦

Early work from the hard bop jazz great, which immediately suggested that Joe Henderson would be around a long time. It took nearly 30 more years before he got his due. The spiraling lines and robust tone have become a staple on the jazz circuit. This set has been reissued on CD. —*Ron Wynn*

The Blue Note Years / Apr. 1, 1963-Feb. 15, 1990 / Blue Note ✦✦✦

Unlike many other box sets currently available, this four-CD package is actually a sampler taken from Joe Henderson's many recordings for Blue Note; all but three selections date from 1963-69. Out of the 36 selections, 26 feature the great tenor as a sideman and some are from sessions not reissued in quite a while. Henderson is instantly recognizable (his distinctive tone has not changed much since 1963) and an asset to each of these performances. Also included in the box is a very attractive 40-page booklet that is highlighted by his complete Blue Note discography. This set is particularly recommended to listeners only vaguely aware of Joe Henderson's powerful music. —*Scott Yanow*

★ **Page One** / Jun. 3, 1963 / Blue Note ✦✦✦✦✦

Tenor saxophonist Joe Henderson's debut as a leader is a particularly strong and historic effort. With major contributions made by trumpeter Kenny Dorham, pianist McCoy Tyner, bassist Butch Warren and drummer Pete La Roca, Henderson (who already had a strikingly original sound and a viable inside/outside style) performs six generally memorable compositions on this CD reissue. Highlights include the original versions of Dorham's "Blue Bossa" and Henderson's "Recorda Me." It's highly recommended. —*Scott Yanow*

Ballads & Blues / Jun. 3, 1963-Nov. 16, 1985 / Blue Note ✦✦✦

This CD is part of a sampler series put out by Blue Note in 1997. Tenor great Joe Henderson is heard playing five ballads and a pair of blues from two different periods of his career. A pair of the selections are taken from his 1963 Page One set with trumpeter Kenny Dorham and pianist McCoy Tyner, "You Know I Care" is a quartet rendition from 1964, and there are three numbers played with a 1985 pianoless trio also including bassist Ron Carter and drummer Al Foster. But best is a classic

(and haunting) rendition of "Lazy Afternoon" taken from a date actually led by drummer Pete La Roca. Although the music is nice, Joe Henderson had too many highlights in his career (even just from his Blue Note dates) for them all to be included on one set. A decent sampler, but more serious collectors will want the readily available complete CDs instead. —*Scott Yanow*

Our Thing / Sep. 9, 1963 / Blue Note ✦✦✦✦

Joe Henderson's second recording as a leader features a very strong supporting cast: trumpeter Kenny Dorham (one of Henderson's earliest supporters), pianist Andrew Hill, bassist Eddie Khan and drummer Pete La Roca. Together they perform three Dorham and two Henderson originals, advanced music that was open to the influence of the avant-garde while remaining in the hard bop idiom. The uptempo blues "Teeter Totter" contrasts with the four minor-toned pieces and, even if none of these songs became a standard, the playing is consistently brilliant and unpredictable. Even at this relatively early stage, Joe Henderson was a potentially great tenorman. —*Scott Yanow*

In 'n Out / Apr. 10, 1964 / Blue Note ✦✦✦✦

Joe Henderson's third Blue Note release (which is here reissued on CD along with the addition of a previously unissued version of the title cut) matches the very distinctive tenor with the veteran trumpeter Kenny Dorham and an unbeatable rhythm section: pianist McCoy Tyner, bassist Richard Davis and drummer Elvin Jones. Henderson—who has always had the ability to make a routine bop piece sound complex and the most complicated free improvisation seem logical—and Dorham provided all of the material and the music still sounds fresh over three decades later. —*Scott Yanow*

Inner Urge / Nov. 30, 1964 / Blue Note ✦✦✦✦✦

The fourth of Joe Henderson's early Blue Note recordings is his first in a quartet setting without trumpeter Kenny Dorham. Henderson (who is accompanied by pianist McCoy Tyner, bassist Bob Cranshaw and drummer Elvin Jones) is in explorative form on three of his originals (including "Inner Urge" and the original version of "Isotope"), Duke Pearson's "You Know I Care" and the standard "Night and Day." The music straddles the boundaries between hard bop and the avant-garde and, while Henderson's improvisations are chordal-based, they are also quite unpredictable and prone to emotional outbursts. This colorful music is highly recommended. —*Scott Yanow*

Mode for Joe / Jan. 27, 1966 / Blue Note ✦✦✦✦✦

Tenor saxophonist Joe Henderson's fifth and final early Blue Note album is his only one with a group larger than a quintet. Henderson welcomes quite an all-star band (trumpeter Lee Morgan, trombonist Curtis Fuller, vibraphonist Bobby Hutcherson, pianist Cedar Walton, bassist Ron Carter and drummer Joe Chambers) and they perform originals by Henderson (including "A Shade of Jade"), Walton and Morgan ("Free Wheelin' "). The advanced music has plenty of exciting moments and the young talents play up to the level one would hope. —*Scott Yanow*

● **The Kicker** / Aug. 10, 1967 / Original Jazz Classics ✦✦✦✦✦

Joe Henderson's first recording for Milestone was very much a continuation of the adventurous acoustic music he had recorded previously for Blue Note. For those listeners who do not wish to invest in the tenor saxophonist's "complete" eight-CD Milestone box set, this single CD is a good place to start in investigating his "middle period" music. Henderson is featured in a sextet with trumpeter Mike Lawrence, trombonist Grachan Moncur III, pianist Kenny Barron, bassist Ron Carter and drummer Louis Hayes on a well-rounded set highlighted by "Mamacita," "Chelsea Bridge," "If," "Without a Song" and "Nardis." —*Scott Yanow*

☆ **The Milestone Years** / Aug. 10, 1967-Sep. 26, 1976 / Milestone ✦✦✦✦✦

Tenor saxophonist Joe Henderson's most famous recordings are his early Blue Notes and his more recent Verves, but in between he recorded exclusively for Milestone and, although he was in consistently fine form in the diverse settings, Henderson was somewhat neglected during his middle years. This massive eight-CD set contains all of the music from Henderson's dozen Milestone LPs plus a duet with altoist Lee Konitz and his guest appearances with singer Flora Purim and cornetist Nat Adderley. The music ranges from Blue Note-style hard bop and modal explorations to fusion and '70s funk, with important contributions made by trumpeters Mike Lawrence, Woody Shaw and Luis Gasca, trombonist Grachan Moncur and keyboardists Kenny Barron, Don Friedman, Joe Zawinul, Herbie Hancock, George Cables, Alice Coltrane, Mark Levine and George Duke among others. Not all of the music is classic (some of the later sets are unabashedly commercial) but none of the 82 selections is dull and the very distinctive Joe Henderson always gives his best. It's highly recommended. —*Scott Yanow*

Tetragon / Sep. 27, 1967-May 16, 1968 / Original Jazz Classics ✦✦✦✦

Joe Henderson's second Milestone recording (which, as with all the others, is currently available on his massive "complete" eight-CD box set) features the great tenor with two separate rhythm sections: Kenny Barron or Don Friedman on piano, bassist Ron Carter and either Louis Hayes or Jack DeJohnette on drums.

Highlights of this LP include the title track, "I've Got You Under My Skin" and "Invitation." —*Scott Yanow*

Four / Apr. 21, 1968 / Verve ✦✦✦✦✦
Released for the first time on this CD in 1994, the previously unknown live session from 1968 features the great tenor Joe Henderson (who was then just a few days short of turning 31) playing for the first and possibly only time with the Wynton Kelly Trio. Henderson, pianist Kelly, bassist Paul Chambers and drummer Jimmy Cobb really stretch out on six standards (including a two-song medley), all of which clock in between 11:47 and 16:05 (except for a three-minute "Theme"). Henderson really pushes the rhythm section (which, although they had not played with the tenor previously, had been together for a decade) and he is certainly inspired by their presence. This is a frequently exciting performance by some of the modern bop greats of the era. —*Scott Yanow*

Straight, No Chaser / Apr. 21, 1968 / Verve ✦✦✦✦
Taken from the same live session that resulted in the Verve CD *Four*, this set (which was released for the first time in 1996) matches the great tenor Joe Henderson with the former Miles Davis rhythm section of pianist Wynton Kelly, bassist Paul Chambers and drummer Jimmy Cobb. Although Henderson had not played with the other musicians before, they blend together quite well and obviously inspired each other. In addition to standards, the quartet also performs a couple of then-recent songs ("Days of Wine and Roses" and "On a Clear Day"), the ancient "Limehouse Blues" and Miles Davis' "Pfrancin'." Recommended. —*Scott Yanow*

Power to the People / May 23, 1969+May 29, 1969 / Milestone ✦✦✦✦✦
This LP (which has been included in Joe Henderson's eight-CD complete Milestone box set) has quite a few classic moments. At that point in time, tenor saxophonist Henderson was a sideman with Herbie Hancock's Sextet, so Hancock was happy to perform as a sideman, doubling on piano and electric piano, with the all-star group, which also includes trumpeter Mike Lawrence, bassist Ron Carter and drummer Jack DeJohnette. Highlights are many, including the original version of "Black Narcissus," "Isotope," a lyrical rendition of "Lazy Afternoon," and the free-form "Foresight and Afterthought." —*Scott Yanow*

If You're Not Part of the Problem . . . . / Sep. 24, 1970-Sep. 26, 1970 / Milestone ✦✦✦✦
This live session from the legendary Lighthouse features a particularly strong version of the Joe Henderson Quintet, which at the time included the leader on tenor, trumpeter Woody Shaw, keyboardist George Cables, bassist Ron McClure and drummer Lenny White. There are excellent remakes of "Mode for Joe" and "Blue Bossa" plus two new originals and a fine rendition of "'Round Midnight." As is typical of Henderson's Milestone recordings, this one did not sell all that well but blame cannot be placed on the musical quality. All of the performances on this LP are included in Joe Henderson's eight-CD Milestone box set. —*Scott Yanow*

In Pursuit of Blackness / Sep. 24, 1970-May 12, 1971 / Milestone ✦✦✦
This Joe Henderson LP features the great tenor with two very different groups. "Invitation" and "Gazelle" are taken from the same live sessions that resulted in his previous album and showcase Henderson's quintet with trumpeter Woody Shaw, keyboardist George Cables, bassist Ron McClure and drummer Lenny White. The remaining three tracks are funkier and freer, adding bassist Stanley Clarke to a rhythm section of Cables and White and featuring the rather ad-lib "Mind over Matter." It's an interesting if slightly erratic set. —*Scott Yanow*

Joe Henderson in Japan / Aug. 4, 1971 / Milestone ✦✦✦✦✦
Tenor saxophonist Joe Henderson toured Japan in the summer of 1971 and performed in Tokyo with an all-Japanese rhythm section (keyboardist Hideo Ichikawa, bassist Kunimitsu Inaba and drummer Notohiko Hino). Henderson really stretches out on two of his compositions ("Out 'n' In" and "Junk Blues"), "'Round Midnight" and Kenny Dorham's "Blue Bossa." The trio gives him strong support and Henderson is heard throughout in top form. The frequently superb performances heard on this LP have been reissued in Joe Henderson's eight-CD "complete" Milestone box set. —*Scott Yanow*

Black Is the Color / Mar. 1972-Apr. 1972 / Milestone ✦✦
For a short period tenor saxophonist Joe Henderson made extensive use of overdubbing. This LP finds him not only playing tenor but adding flute, alto flute, soprano and percussion; he also utilizes extra musicians (most notably David Horowitz on synthesizer and percussionist Airto) to augment his core group of keyboardist George Cables, bassist Dave Holland and drummer Jack DeJohnette. Although the music holds one's interest, it is not up to the same creative level of his earlier Milestone releases; a few of these pieces sound like Henderson was hoping for a hit. —*Scott Yanow*

Multiple / Jan. 30, 1973-Apr. 13, 1973 / Original Jazz Classics ✦✦✦
This CD reissue of the original Joe Henderson LP is one of the few on which the great tenor extensively utilized overdubbing. The main group includes Henderson (who later overdubbed himself on soprano, flute, percussion and even voice), key-

boardist Larry Willis, bassist Dave Holland, drummer Jack DeJohnette and percussionist Arthur Jenkins; later on, guitarists James Blood Ulmer and John Thomas were added to some of the tracks. The music is at times funky, dense and a bit aimless although it is generally quite stimulating. This is not an essential release, but those listeners who stereotype Joe Henderson as a strictly acoustic stylist will find the set particularly interesting. —*Scott Yanow*

The Elements / Oct. 15, 1973-Oct. 17, 1973 / Original Jazz Classics ✦✦
This is one of the odder Joe Henderson recordings. The four lengthy selections not only feature the great tenor saxophonist but the piano and harp of Alice Coltrane (during one of her rare appearances as a sideman), violinist Michael White, bassist Charlie Haden, percussionist Kenneth Nash and Baba Duru Oshun on tablas. The somewhat spiritual nature of the music (Henderson's compositions are titled "Fire," "Air," "Water" and "Earth") and the presence of Alice Coltrane makes these Eastern-flavored performances rather unique if not all that essential: an early example of world music. This LP has been reissued as part of Henderson's eight-CD Milestone box set. —*Scott Yanow*

Canyon Lady / Oct. 1973 / Original Jazz Classics ✦✦✦
This LP has trumpeter Luis Gasca featured as a co-star with tenor saxophonist Joe Henderson. Gasca arranged "Tres Palabras" which is played by a 13-piece group (Oscar Brashear takes the trumpet solo) while the other three originals (two by pianist Mark Levine) use either a sextet or a nonet. Henderson is in fine form on these spirited Latinish performances, which have also been included on his eight-CD Milestone box set. —*Scott Yanow*

Black Narcissus / Oct. 19, 1974-Apr. 1975 / Milestone ✦✦✦
This Milestone LP (which has been included in Joe Henderson's eight-CD Milestone set) is a bit of a mixed bag. The tenor recorded four numbers with pianist Joachim Kuhn's trio in Paris and later had percussion and Patrick Gleeson's synthesizer overdubbed. In addition, there is the odd "Amoeba" (which finds Henderson doubling on synth himself) along with a superior version of "Good Morning Heartache" featuring Henderson, Kuhn, bassist Dave Friesen and drummer Jack DeJohnette. This album has its moments although there are many much more consistent Joe Henderson albums around. —*Scott Yanow*

Black Miracle / Feb. 13, 1975-Sep. 25, 1975 / Milestone ✦✦
Tenor saxophonist Joe Henderson's final Milestone recording has a few attempts at trying to create a hit (including utilizing George Duke's keyboards, overdubbing a horn section and synthesizers and playing Stevie Wonder's "My Cherie Amour") but this LP did not sell any more than Henderson's less commercial efforts. Actually the music is generally fairly good, funky at times but still with searching solos from Henderson. "Soulution" and "Gazelle" are high points. As with his other Milestone recordings, this one has been reissued on CD as part of Joe Henderson's eight-CD box set *The Milestone Years*. —*Scott Yanow*

Barcelona / Jun. 2, 1977-Nov. 15, 1977 / Enja ✦✦✦✦
Tremendous, frenzied trio date by tenor saxophonist Joe Henderson, recently released, with bassist Wayne Darling and drummer Ed Soph. After many years of obscurity, Henderson has become famous in the last few years. But the whirling lines, huge tone, and astonishing solos that he routinely offers on this album have been prized by jazz fans since the early '60s. —*Ron Wynn*

Relaxin' at Camarillo / Aug. 20, 1979+Dec. 29, 1979 / Original Jazz Classics ✦✦✦
Originally on Contemporary, this CD reissue teams the great tenor Joe Henderson with pianist Chick Corea, either Tony Dumas or Richard Davis on bass and Peter Erskine or Tony Williams on drums. The repertoire includes two songs by Corea, Henderson's "Y Todavia La Quiero," the standard ballad "My One and Only Love" and Charlie Parker's "Relaxin' at Camarillo." This informal session has plenty of fine solos from the two principals and is recommended to fans of advanced hard bop. —*Scott Yanow*

Mirror, Mirror / Jan. 1980 / Pausa ✦✦✦✦
Tenor saxophonist Joe Henderson has had a remarkably consistent career. Although he has spent periods (such as the 1970s) in relative obscurity and others as almost a jazz superstar, Henderson's style and sound have been relatively unchanged since the 1960s. This lesser-known LP finds Henderson in typically fine form in an acoustic quartet with pianist Chick Corea, bassist Ron Carter and drummer Billy Higgins. Carter and Corea contribute two songs apiece, Henderson gets to perform his "Joe's Bolero" and the tenor sounds majestic on "What's New?" —*Scott Yanow*

☆ **The State of the Tenor (Live at the Village Vanguard)** / Nov. 4, 1985 / Blue Note ✦✦✦✦✦
The very distinctive tenor saxophonist is heard at his best on this two-CD set recorded live at the Village Vanguard. Accompanied only by bassist Ron Carter and drummer Al Foster, Henderson at times recalls Sonny Rollins, but none of his searching improvisations are predictable. Of the 14 selections, 12 were originally released on two Blue Note LPs, while the renditions of "Stella by Starlight" and "All

the Things You Are" were previously unissued. Highlights of this particularly strong set (recorded over a three-day period) include "Beatrice," several Thelonious Monk tunes (particularly "Friday the Thirteenth" and "Ask Me Now"), "Soulville" and "Isotope." —*Scott Yanow*

Punjab / Nov. 27, 1986 / Arco ◆◆◆

Evening with Joe Henderson / Jul. 9, 1987 / Red ◆◆◆◆
Although Joe Henderson's pianoless trio recordings for Blue Note in 1985 received a fair amount of publicity, this similar date for the Italian Red label has been almost completely overlooked. Joined by bassist Charlie Haden and drummer Al Foster, Henderson is in excellent form, giving "Beatrice," "Invitation," Thelonious Monk's "Ask Me Now" and his own "Serenity" lengthy and rewarding explorations. —*Scott Yanow*

The Standard Joe / Mar. 16, 1991 / Red ◆◆◆◆
For at least his fourth recording in six years heading a pianoless trio, the great tenor Joe Henderson (along with bassist Rufus Reid and drummer Al Foster) is heard on his own "Inner Urge," an original blues, two lengthy versions of "Body and Soul" and three other jazz standards. This Italian import is particularly recommended to listeners not that familiar with Henderson's playing, for he brings new life to these often overplayed compositions. —*Scott Yanow*

★ **Lush Life: The Music of Billy Strayhorn** / Sep. 3, 1991-Sep. 8, 1991 / Verve ◆◆◆◆◆
With the release of this CD, the executives at Verve and their marketing staff proved that, yes indeed, jazz can sell. The veteran tenor Joe Henderson has had a distinctive sound and style of his own ever since he first entered the jazz major leagues, yet he has spent long periods in relative obscurity before reaching his current status as a jazz superstar. As for the music on his "comeback" disc, it does deserve all of the hype. Henderson performs ten of Billy Strayhorn's most enduring compositions in a variety of settings, ranging from a full quintet with trumpeter Wynton Marsalis and duets with pianist Stephen Scott, bassist Christian McBride and drummer Gregory Hutchinson to an unaccompanied solo exploration of "Lush Life." This memorable outing succeeded both artistically and commercially and is highly recommended. —*Scott Yanow*

Big Band / Mar. 16, 1992-Jun. 26, 1996 / Verve ◆◆◆◆
Big Band is a special record in Joe Henderson's catalog. As the first time he has recorded with a big band, it would be noteworthy, but what makes it truly exceptional is how Henderson effortlessly adapts to the setting, not only in the way he plays, but also in the way he can write. Every song on the album has been written and/or arranged by Henderson, and the quality of the music makes one wonder why he didn't venture into the genre earlier. It's a record that proves that big band music can still sound alive and vital, even in the '90s. —*Leo Stanley*

So Near, So Far (Musings for Miles) / Oct. 12, 1992-Oct. 14, 1992 / Verve ◆◆◆◆◆
Joe Henderson's follow-up to his hugely successful *Lush Life* disc is another concept album, this time involving ten songs (including many lesser-known ones) associated with Miles Davis. Henderson only actually played with Davis for a few weekends around 1967 but he shows a great deal of understanding for this potentially difficult music. With particularly strong assistance from guitarist John Scofield, bassist Dave Holland and drummer Al Foster, Henderson revives such forgotten songs as "Teo," "Swing Spring" and "Side Car" in addition to coming up with fresh interpretations of "Miles Ahead," "Milestones" and "No Blues." He is to be congratulated for not taking the easy way out and sticking to the simpler material of Davis' earlier years. —*Scott Yanow*

Double Rainbow: The Music of Antonio Carlos Jobim / Sep. 19, 1994-Nov. 6, 1994 / Verve ◆◆◆◆◆
The third of tenor saxophonist Joe Henderson's tribute CDs on Verve was originally supposed to be a collaboration with the great bossa nova composer Antonio Carlos Jobim, but Jobim's unexpected death turned this project into a memorial. Henderson performs a dozen of the composer's works with one of two separate groups: a Brazilian quartet starring pianist Eliane Elias and a jazz trio with pianist Herbie Hancock, bassist Christian McBride and drummer Jack DeJohnette. In general Henderson avoids Jobim's best-known songs in favor of some of his more obscure (but equally rewarding) melodies and in some cases (such as a very straightahead "No More Blues") the treatments are surprising. Highlights of this very accessible yet unpredictable CD include "Felicidade," "Triste," "Zingaro" and a duet with guitarist Oscar Castro-Neves on "Once I Loved" although all of the performances are quite enjoyable. Highly recommended. —*Scott Yanow*

Porgy and Bess / May 25, 1997-May 28, 1997 / Verve ◆◆◆◆
In general, Joe Henderson's take on *Porgy and Bess* meets the high standards of his latter-day records for Verve. Working with arranger Bob Belden and a wonderful combo—including guitarist John Scofield, pianist Tommy Flanagan, bassist Dave Holland, drummer Jack DeJohnette, trombonist Conrad Herwig and vibraphonist

Stefon Harris—Henderson brings Gershwin's music to life with subtle beauty and grace. Furthermore, he demonstrates his uniqueness—Henderson's *Porgy and Bess* may share the same source as Miles Davis' legendary *Porgy and Bess*, yet it has an original sound, relying less on orchestration than that classic. While this disc is not flawless—instead of enhancing the music, guest spots from vocalists Chaka Khan and Sting actually stop the momentum, calling attention to themselves—it nevertheless is another valuable addition to Henderson's catalog. —*Leo Stanley*

Scott Henderson

b. 1955
Guitar / Fusion

One of the finest fusion (as opposed to crossover) guitarists of the 1980s and '90s, Scott Henderson's explosive playing is often teamed up with electric bassist Gary Willis in their group Tribal Tech. Originally most influenced by rock, Henderson (who grew up in West Palm Beach, FL) played in local funk and rock bands. In 1980 he moved to Los Angeles to attend the Guitar Institute of Technology, studying with Joe Diorio. After graduating he became a teacher himself at GIT. Henderson played with Jeff Berlin and Jean-Luc Ponty and in 1985 toured with the original version of Chick Corea's Elektric Band. During 1987-89 he worked on and off with Joe Zawinul's Syndicate and since then Tribal Tech has been his main band. As a leader Scott Henderson has recorded for Passport, Relativity and Blue Moon. —*Scott Yanow*

Spears / Jun. 1985 / Passport ◆◆◆
Scott Henderson's outlook was perfectly summarized when, in 1991, he told *L.A. Jazz Scene*: "Fusion isn't a dirty word to me. I'm proud to call myself a fusion player." Indeed, real jazz-fusion—spontaneous, risk-taking and improvisatory—is exactly what the electric guitarist passionately and enthusiastically embraces on *Spears*, his debut album. Drawing on such influences as Return to Forever, John McLaughlin and Weather Report, the hard-edged guitarist set the uncompromising tone for his career and that of his band Tribal Tech, which in 1985 included Gary Willis on electric bass, Pat Coil on electric keyboards, Michael Brecker-disciple Bob Sheppard on tenor and soprano sax and flute, Steve Houghton on drums and Brad Dutz on mallets & percussion. Often showing a complex and cerebral sense of melody and harmony, this CD (first released on Passport and reissued by Relativity in 1990) underscores the fact that when fusion is played with integrity, it's very much an extension of the jazz tradition. —*Alex Henderson*

Tribal Tech with Gary Willis / Nov. 19, 1990 / Relativity ◆◆◆◆◆
An interesting, sometimes enchanting, blend of technology, aggressive rhythms, and improvisatory zeal. —*Ron Wynn*

Dr. Hee / Mar. 1987-Apr. 1987 / Relativity ◆◆◆◆
When Scott Henderson recorded his second album with Tribal Tech, *Dr. Hee*, in 1987, commercial "quiet storm" and "smooth jazz" stations had found quite a niche for themselves by spotlighting bland, uninteresting (but commercially successful) fluff. But that type of muzak held no interest whatsoever for Henderson, who stuck to his guns and continued to triumph by offering gutsy, challenging fusion. Henderson isn't one to shy away from abstraction, and some of the songs on *Dr. Hee* (most written by either Henderson himself or his long-time partner, bassist Gary Willis) aren't always terribly easy to absorb. Like so much of the bebop, post-bop and free jazz that came before it, this CD (first released on Passport, then reissued by Relativity in 1990) reveals more and more of its richness with repeated listenings. —*Alex Henderson*

● **Nomad** / Apr. 1988 / Relativity ◆◆◆◆
Like its predecessors, Henderson's third date as a leader is a fine example of how creative and inspired genuine jazz-rock can be. Tough and aggressive yet full of appealing melodic and harmonic nuances, this CD contains not one iota of the type of lightweight smooth jazz or muzak Henderson has often voiced his contempt for. With *Nomad*, Tribal Tech underwent a few personnel changes, and for the first time, recorded an entire album minus a sax. While electric bassist Gary Willis, drummer Steve Houghton and percussionist/mallet player Brad Dutz remained, saxman Bob Sheppard was gone, and keyboardist Pat Coil had been replaced by David Goldblatt. Despite these changes, Tribal Tech's sound (which was essentially guided by Henderson and Willis) remained easily recognizable. The '70s breakthroughs of Weather Report, Return to Forever and John McLaughlin, among others, still had an impact on Tribal Tech, but by 1988, it was even more evident that Henderson was a fine soloist and composer in his own right. —*Alex Henderson*

● **Illicit** / Apr. 1992 / Mesa ◆◆◆◆◆

Face First / Apr. 1993-May 1993 / Mesa ◆◆◆◆

Dog Party / 1994 / Mesa ◆◆◆

Reality Check / Nov. 1994 / Mesa ◆◆◆◆

Tore Down House / 1997 / Mesa ✦✦✦✦✦

Scott Henderson, a ferocious guitarist who is a pacesetter in fusion (the real stuff), has also recorded some intense and adventurous blues-oriented material. On this Mesa release, Henderson's guitar is well-featured on ten of his originals (plus Jaco Pastorius' "Continuum") which range from blues to R&B. With boisterous and sometimes rather humorous vocals contributed by Thelma Houston and Masta Edwards, and fine playing from a group that includes Pat O'Brien on harmonica, saxophonist Albert Wing and the versatile bassist Dave Carpenter, Henderson has constructed an often-riotous set of memorable performances. Some of the titles ("I Hate You," "You Get off on Me" and "Meter Maid") let one know that the guitarist does not take himself too seriously and a few of the vocals have rather funny lyrics that both parody and uplift the music. A typically unpredictable and stimulating set from the masterful guitarist. —*Scott Yanow*

Wayne Henderson

b. Sep. 24, 1939, Houston, TX

Trombone / Soul Jazz, Hard Bop, R&B

Wayne Henderson's trombone teamed up with Wilton Felder's tenor in the Jazz Crusaders to give the group its own trademark sound. A fine hard bop soloist who later in his career chose to become an R&B producer instead, Henderson first played regularly with Felder, Joe Sample and Stix Hooper in Houston in the mid-'50s. By the time they moved to Los Angeles and started recording in 1961 they were known as the Jazz Crusaders. After many records for Pacific Jazz, in 1971 the group changed their name to the Crusaders. With Henderson's decision to quit the band in 1975, the Crusaders lost a great deal of their originality. In the mid-'90s Henderson and Felder had a nostalgic reunion with an enlarged group for a recording on the Par label. —*Scott Yanow*

● **Back to the Groove** / 1992 / Par ✦✦✦✦

Trombonist Wayne Henderson has had a surprisingly sporadic solo career. During his years with the Jazz Crusaders, he only led two record dates of his own, and it was not until a decade after he left the group that he led his third session. Henderson does take some fine solos on this generally rewarding disc, which also features tenor saxophonist Wilton Felder (his old section mate in the Crusaders), keyboardist Rob Mullins and guitarist Dwight Sills. The release, which is subtitled "The Next Crusade," is an extension of Henderson's old band, and the selections range from straightahead (including "Joshua") to soul-jazz and some funkier sounds. Worth picking up, although this CD will probably be difficult to find. —*Scott Yanow*

Jon Hendricks

b. Sep. 16, 1921, Newark, OH

Vocals, Lyricist / Vocalese, Bop

The genius of vocalese, Jon Hendricks' ability to write coherent lyrics to the most complex recorded improvisations is quite notable, as were his contributions to the classic jazz vocal group Lambert, Hendricks and Ross. Hendricks grew up in Toledo, OH, singing on local radio. After a period in the military (1942-46), he studied for the law but eventually switched to jazz. He spent a period of time playing drums before becoming active as a lyricist and vocalist. In 1952 his "I Want You to Be My Baby" was recorded by Louis Jordan. In 1957 Hendricks made his recording debut (cutting "Four Brothers" and "Cloudburst" while backed by the Dave Lambert Singers). Soon he teamed up with fellow singers Dave Lambert and Annie Ross to form their vocal trio, starting off with a recreation (through overdubbing) of some of Count Basie's recordings. Lambert, Hendricks and Ross (after 1962 Yolande Bavan took Ross' place) stayed together up to 1964 and they have yet to be topped as a jazz vocal group, influencing those that would follow (including the Manhattan Transfer). In 1960 Hendricks wrote and directed the show *Evolution of the Blues* for the Monterey Jazz Festival; he would revive it several times during the next 20 years. During 1968-73 he lived and worked in Europe. After returning to San Francisco, Hendricks wrote about jazz for the *San Francisco Chronicle*, taught jazz and formed a group with his wife Judith, children Michelle and Eric and other singers (including for a time Bobby McFerrin) called the Hendricks Family that is active on a part-time basis up to the present. Although he never recorded often enough, Hendricks did cut a classic Denon album featuring McFerrin, George Benson, Al Jarreau and himself recreating all the solos in the original version of "Freddie Freeloader." He also recorded through the years as a leader for World Pacific, Columbia, Smash, Reprise, Arista and most recently Telarc. —*Scott Yanow*

A Good Git-Together / Oct. 1959 / World Pacific ✦✦✦✦

Jon Hendricks' first album as a leader has not been reissued since its 1959 release, but it is a real gem. This rarity features such major sidemen on various tracks as altoist Pony Poindexter, guitarist Wes Montgomery and both Nat and Cannonball Adderley. Hendricks—who, at the time, was riding high in Lambert, Hendricks and

Ross—is in superb form on such numbers as "Everything Started in the House of the Lord," a couple of songs that Hendricks had written for Louis Jordan, Randy Weston's "Pretty Strange," "Social Call" and the jubilant "A Good Git-Together." A near-classic LP long overdue to be reissued on CD. —*Scott Yanow*

Evolution of the Blues / Sep. 21, 1960 / Columbia Special Products ✦✦✦✦

Jazz vocalist and lyricist Jon Hendricks conceived a musical presentation on jazz history for the 1960 Monterey Jazz Festival and called it *Evolution of the Blues*. Columbia subsequently issued this similarly titled album, which features Hendricks' stylized vocals and other presentations linked to the theme. This presentation was revived and presented again in 1975. —*Ron Wynn*

Fast Livin' Blues / Sep. 6, 1961-Sep. 27, 1961 / Columbia ✦✦✦

Jive and blues vocals. Some poignant cuts, some merely enjoyable. —*Ron Wynn*

Salute to Joao Gilberto / 1963 / Reprise ✦✦✦✦

Jon Hendricks idolizes Joao Gilberto—he has spoken fondly of their first meeting, at which they scatted to each other before ever speaking a word—and he wasted little time putting together a tribute album at the height of the first bossa nova wave. It ought to be no surprise that he would display total sympathy with the bossa nova manner here, singing softly and smoothly—and Hendricks' English wordplay is quite faithful to the original tunes and meanings of the Portuguese lyrics, in contrast to his usual whimsical work with jazz improvisations. Hendricks is particularly winning and irresistibly swinging on the rare occasions ("Voce E Eu," "Samba Da Minha Terra") when he scats to the Brazilian rhythm; he should have done more of that here. But then, his versions of Gilberto's repertoire are carefully based on Gilberto's early EMI/Odeon recordings (now available on *The Legendary Joao Gilberto*); even Antonio Carlos Jobim's string and wind charts for the originals are preserved by adapter Johnny Mandel. Alas, the only Hendricks lyric that has become a universal standard is that for Jobim's "Chega De Saudade" ("No More Blues"), and the LP itself is now hard to find. But as Hendricks' only album-length encounter with bossa nova, this is essential. —*Richard S. Ginell*

● **Jon Hendricks Recorded in Person at the Trident** / 1963 / Smash ✦✦✦✦

One of singer Jon Hendricks' better post-Lambert, Hendricks and Ross recordings of the 1960s, this spirited live set has been reissued on CD by Polygram under the Smash subsidiary. Recorded in Sausalito, California with local musicians (the fine but obscure tenor Noel Jewkes, pianist Flip Nunez, bassist Fred Marshall and drummer Jerry Granelli), the CD does an excellent job of summing up Hendricks' music of the era. He performs some hip bop ("Stockholm Sweetnin'"), revisits some L, H and Ross material ("Cloudburst" and "Shiny Stockings"), sings a couple of current tunes ("This Could Be the Start of Something Big" and "Watermelon Man"), performs a touching version of "Old Folks," breaks up the place with his humorous "Gimme That Wine" and revives the ancient ballad "I Wonder What's Become of Sally." Excellent music reissued by Polygram in 1991. —*Scott Yanow*

Cloudburst / Feb. 1972 / Enja ✦✦✦✦

Tell Me the Truth / 1975 / Arista ✦✦✦

Jon Hendricks had not recorded in over a decade when he finally got the chance with Arista. This somewhat obscure effort is quite worthwhile. Hendricks sings eight songs (including "Flat Foot Floogie," "Naima," "On the Trail" and "Blues for Pablo"); all but "Old Folks" have his own lyrics. He is assisted by a fine backup crew and, on "Flat Foot Floogie," the Pointer Sisters. Hendricks is in spirited form throughout this rare LP. —*Scott Yanow*

Love / Aug. 1981-Feb. 1982 / Muse ✦✦✦✦

The first recording to document Hendricks & Company, this underrated album finds vocalese genius Jon Hendricks sharing the vocal duties with Judith Hendricks, Michele Hendricks, Bob Gurland and sometimes Leslie Dorsey while joined by three different rhythm sections, guest trumpeter Harry "Sweets" Edison, and the tenor of Jerome Richardson. The emphasis throughout is on Hendricks' witty and inventive lyrics to such numbers as "Royal Garden Blues," "Lil' Darlin'," "Tell Me the Truth," "The Swinging Groove Merchant" and "In a Harlem Airshaft," among others. Superior bebop singing on a very enjoyable set that has fortunately been reissued on CD. —*Scott Yanow*

Freddie Freeloader / Jun. 7, 1989-Mar. 20, 1990 / Denon ✦✦✦✦✦

This CD would be highly recommended if it were only for Jon Hendricks' brilliant vocalese version of "Freddie the Freeloader," which has Bobby McFerrin singing pianist Wynton Kelly's part, Al Jarreau as Miles Davis, George Benson as Cannonball Adderley, and Hendricks recreating John Coltrane. However, all 13 selections on the very memorable set have their strong moments, and the other guests include the Manhattan Transfer, the Count Basie Orchestra, Wynton Marsalis, Stanley Turrentine, Tommy Flanagan, Al Grey and the Jon Hendricks Vocalstra. "Jumpin' at the Woodside" recalls the Lambert, Hendricks & Ross version, Judith Hendricks sings Louis Armstrong's solos on "Stardust" and "Swing That Music," Turrentine helps to recreate "Sugar," there are a couple of Thelonious Monk tunes, and the exciting proceedings conclude with "Sing, Sing, Sing." Essential music. —*Scott Yanow*

Boppin' at the Blue Note / Dec. 23, 1993-Dec. 26, 1993 / Telarc ✦✦✦✦✦
Jon Hendricks, the genius of vocalese (writing words to fit the recorded solos of jazz greats) has long been one of the top lyricists in music. However, the emphasis during the first seven songs of this live CD is on scatting and heated bop-oriented improvising. Hendricks, assisted by Michelle Hendricks, is joined by quite an all-star horn section: trumpeter Wynton Marsalis, trombonist Al Grey, altoist Red Holloway and tenor Benny Golson, in addition to a supportive four-piece rhythm section. After a warmup on "Get Me to the Church on Time," Jon Hendricks sings some humorous lyrics on "Do You Call That a Buddy?" swings hard on his original boppish "Good Ol' Lady" and gets a bit lowdown on "Contemporary Blues." The biggest surprise of the date is "Everybody's Boppin'" which features scatting by Jon Hendricks, Michele Hendricks and Wynton Marsalis. Wynton is quite effective and typically virtuosic in a manner similar to Dizzy Gillespie. Michele is excellent on an uptempo "Almost Like Being in Love" and "Since I Fell for You," Jon sings the blues on "Roll 'em Pete" and, together with Kevin Burke and Judith, Michele and Aria Hendricks, performs vocalese versions of three Count Basie charts long ago recorded by Lambert, Hendricks And Ross: recreations of recreations. This is Jon Hendricks' best all-round recording in several years and was one of the finest jazz vocal albums to be released in 1995. —*Scott Yanow*

Michele Hendricks

Vocals / Bop
The daughter of Jon Hendricks, Michele has gradually emerged from her father's shadow to carve out a niche of her own. She started singing at the age of eight and often accompanied her dad on road trips, sometimes getting the opportunity to sing with him on stage. After being a dance and drama student in London at Gradison College, Michele joined Jon Hendricks and Family.

She performed with her father's *Evolution of the Blues* show and then from 1981 was part of Hendricks Family, one of the top vocal groups of the 1980s and a logical extension of Lambert, Hendricks & Ross. Michele Hendricks spent a couple years outside of jazz in the mid-1980s trying to decide her eventual musical path, and then in 1987 recorded the first of several excellent bop-oriented dates as a leader for Muse. —*Scott Yanow*

● **Carryin' On** / Apr. 1987 / Muse ✦✦✦✦✦
Michele Hendricks' debut as a leader, which has been reissued on CD, finds Jon Hendricks' daughter carrying on the bebop tradition while infusing the music with her own personality. In addition to a fine rhythm section led by pianist David Leonhardt, Hendricks is joined by tenors Stan Getz ("Old Devil Moon" and "Prelude to a Kiss") and Ralph Moore (for three songs) on separate selections. Michele Hendricks displays a highly appealing and strong ability to swing. Well worth acquiring, as are her two other slightly later Muse releases. —*Scott Yanow*

Keepin' Me Satisfied / May 1988 / Muse ✦✦✦✦
Michele Hendricks' second recording as a leader finds her both reinforcing her roots in bebop and stretching out a bit. With such fine musicians as pianist David Leonhardt, trombonist Slide Hampton, trumpeter Claudio Roditi and tenorman David Newman, Hendricks explores such diverse numbers as "What's Going On?" "Honeysuckle Rose," "Just In Time," "Sassy Strut" and two of her own originals. She also shares the spotlight with her notable father Jon Hendricks on a blazing version of "Everybody's Boppin'." —*Scott Yanow*

Me and My Shadow / Feb. 1990 / Muse ✦✦✦✦✦
On her third and final Muse CD as a leader, Michele Hendricks sounds quite individual performing this well-conceived set. She is accompanied by James Williams or David Leonhardt on piano, bassist Ray Drummond, and drummer Marvin "Smitty" Smith, with three numbers being pianoless. The material ranges from "But Beautiful" and "Misty" to the humorous "Na Na Na," "Me and My Shadow," and Don Pullen's "Spirit Song." Throughout, Michele Hendricks is in consistently creative form, making this a definitive example of her musical talents. —*Scott Yanow*

Ernie Henry

b. Sep. 3, 1926, New York, NY, **d.** Dec. 29, 1957, New York, NY
Alto Saxophone / Hard Bop
Ernie Henry accomplished a lot in a short period of time before passing away prematurely. He had his own sound although his style was clearly heavily influenced by Charlie Parker. He worked during the bop era with Tadd Dameron (1947), Fats Navarro, Charlie Ventura, Max Roach and the Dizzy Gillespie Orchestra (1948-49). He was with Illinois Jacquet's band (1950-52), maintained a low profile for a few years and in 1956 recorded with Thelonious Monk (the *Brilliant Corners* album), worked with Charles Mingus and toured with Dizzy Gillespie's big band (1956-57)

before his death. Ernie Henry led three albums for Riverside during 1956-57. —*Scott Yanow*

Presenting Ernie Henry / Aug. 23, 1956-Aug. 30, 1956 / Original Jazz Classics ✦✦✦✦
Altoist Ernie Henry's first of three sessions as a leader, all of which were made within 16 months of his premature death, served as a strong debut. Joined by trumpeter Kenny Dorham, pianist Kenny Drew, bassist Wilbur Ware and drummer Art Taylor, Henry—who always had a distinctive tone—performs five of his boppish originals, plus "Gone with the Wind" and "I Should Care." Throughout the date, Henry hints strongly at the great potential he had. This set has thus far only been reissued by the OJC series on LP. —*Scott Yanow*

Seven Standards and a Blues / Sep. 30, 1957 / Original Jazz Classics ✦✦✦
Recorded just three months before his unexpected death, this set by altoist Ernie Henry is his definitive album as a leader. Reissued on CD with a second take of "Like Someone in Love" added to the program, Henry, pianist Wynton Kelly, bassist Wilbur Ware and drummer Philly Joe Jones do indeed play seven standards (including "I Get a Kick out of You," "Soon" and "I've Got the World on a String"), plus a Henry blues ("Specific Gravity"). Superior modern mainstream music, but there should have been much more from the potentially significant Ernie Henry. —*Scott Yanow*

● **Last Chorus** / Sep. 23, 1957 / Original Jazz Classics ✦✦✦✦✦
Last Chorus presents Ernie Henry, who died Dec. 29, 1957. Henry's alto playing combined the exigency of the hard alto sound with the big, scooping delivery more associated with the tenor sax and players like Sonny Rollins; a more deliberate sound than fleet register runs. This record found him leading his own groups or in the company of Kenny Dorham or Thelonious Monk. —*Bob Rusch, Cadence*

Deborah Henson-Conant (Deborah Hensen-Conant)

b. , Stockton, CA
Harp / Post-Bop, Crossover Jazz
One of the finest (and one of the very few) jazz harpists in the world, Deborah Henson-Conant combines storytelling and vocals in her entertaining show. She played piano from age ten and started doubling on harp when she was 13. It became her main instrument while she was in college and, although classically trained, she also enjoyed improvising. In 1982 she began seriously playing jazz and the following year started amplifying her harp. In 1989 Henson-Conant was signed to GRP and she recorded three well-received recordings. She has since toured the world and recorded for Laika (a European company) and her own White Cat company. —*Scott Yanow*

● **'Round the Corner** / 1987 / Golden Cage ✦✦✦✦✦
From the jazz standpoint, this is harpist Deborah Henson-Conant's strongest CD to date. Released by her private label, the program features Henson-Conant (who is accompanied by bassist John Lockwood and drummer Bob Gullotti) playing melodic versions of six jazz standards (including "Georgia on My Mind," "Take Five" and "Summertime") plus her own "'Round the Corner." Actually the high point is a delightful "Over the Rainbow" which starts out as an extensive medley of songs from *The Wizard of Oz.* Deborah Henson-Conant is one of the very few harpists who can improvise jazz and this fine set is superior to her better-known (and slightly later) GRP releases. Worth searching for. —*Scott Yanow*

On the Rise / Oct. 1988 / GRP ✦✦✦
The first of Deborah Henson-Conant's three GRP recordings gained her a great deal of attention. One of the very few jazz harpists, Henson-Conant is heard on a diverse program that ranges from funky numbers and a few commercial (but worthy) tracks to quiet ballads. She is joined on various tracks by the members of Elements, performing her originals and Mark Egan's "Eastern Sunlight." Not definitive, but worth picking up. —*Scott Yanow*

Caught in the Act / 1990 / GRP ✦✦✦
One of that rare breed known as jazz harpists, Conat-Henson is an underrated player and gifted composer. She doesn't have her full talents tested here because this set alternates between more expansive, ambitious jazz-based tunes and lighter, Adult Contemporary and pop instrumental fare. But hearing harp in a lead role is interesting, no matter the context. —*Ron Wynn*

Talking Hands / 1991 / GRP ✦✦✦

Budapest / 1992 / Unity ✦✦✦✦
This CD from harpist Deborah Henson-Conant is a mix of funky grooves, folk melodies, world music mood pieces and exuberant jams. Henson-Conant's harp (and occasional voice) shines through the ensembles. The backup crew includes Mark Johnson's tenor and soprano, the co-leaders of Special EFX (guitarist Chieli Minucci and percussionist George Jinda) and bassist Victor Bailey. This atmospheric music, which was actually recorded in Budapest, is one of Henson-Conant's stronger efforts. —*Scott Yanow*

Naked Music / 1994 / Laika ✦✦✦✦

Just for You / Jun. 1, 1994-Jun. 12, 1994 / Laika ✦✦✦✦
Harpist Deborah Henson-Conant teams up with bassist Wolfgang Diekmann and percussionist Davey Tulloch for live versions of ten of her originals. Henson-Conant, who also contributes vocals and humorous introductions, proves to be quite a showperson in addition to being a superior harpist. The music falls somewhere between advanced bop, crossover and even cabaret. No matter what it is called, this release from the German label Laika is colorful and entertaining, not merely a replay of Henson-Conant's GRP recordings. —*Scott Yanow*

Alter Ego / 1996 / Golden Cage Music ✦✦✦✦
Although recorded in the studio, this CD gives listeners a good example of what a live performance by harpist/vocalist Deborah Henson-Conant was like in the mid-1990s. The music ranges from some jazz (particularly "Beck's Blues") to vocal folk ballads and philosophical pieces. Henson-Conant has a pretty voice, and even if her singing is largely outside of jazz, it is full of humor, good cheer and intelligence. Her "Congratulations" (an alternative birthday song) has usually been a crowd pleaser, and her use of overdubbing on a couple tracks to achieve multiple voices is tastefully done. —*Scott Yanow*

Woody Herman (Woodrow Charles Herman)

b. May 16, 1913, Milwaukee, WI, d. Oct. 29, 1987, Los Angeles, CA
Clarinet, Alto Saxophone, Soprano Saxophone , Vocals, Leader / Swing, Bop, Hard Bop, Big Band
A fine swing clarinetist, an altoist whose sound was influenced by Johnny Hodges, a good soprano saxophonist and a spirited blues vocalist, Woody Herman's greatest significance to jazz was as the leader of a long line of big bands. He always encouraged young talent and more than practically any bandleader from the swing era, kept his repertoire quite modern. Although Herman was always stuck performing a few of his older hits (he played "Four Brothers" and "Early Autumn" nightly for nearly 40 years), he much preferred to play and create new music.
Woody Herman began performing as a child, singing in vaudeville. He started playing saxophone when he was 11 and four years later he was a professional musician. He picked up early experience playing with the big bands of Tom Gerun, Harry Sosnik and Gus Arnheim and then in 1934 he joined the Isham Jones orchestra. He recorded often with Jones and when the veteran bandleader decided to break up his orchestra in 1936, Herman formed one of his own out of the remaining nucleus. The great majority of the early Herman recordings feature the bandleader as a ballad vocalist but it was the instrumentals that caught on, leading to his group being known as "the Band That Plays the Blues." Woody Herman's theme "At the Woodchopper's Ball" became his first hit (1939). Herman's early group was actually a minor outfit with a Dixieland feel to many of the looser pieces and fine vocals contributed by Mary Ann McCall in addition to Herman. They recorded very frequently for Decca and for a period the group had the female trumpeter/singer Billie Rogers as one of its main attractions.
By 1943 the Woody Herman Orchestra was beginning to take its first steps into becoming the Herd (later renamed the First Herd). Herman had recorded an advanced Dizzy Gillespie arrangement ("Down Under") the year before, and during 1943 Herman's band became influenced by Duke Ellington; in fact Johnny Hodges and Ben Webster made guest appearances on some recordings. It was a gradual process but by the end of 1944 Woody Herman had what was essentially a brand new orchestra. It was a wild goodtime band with screaming ensembles (propelled by first trumpeter Pete Candoli), major soloists in trombonist Bill Harris and tenorman Flip Phillips, and a rhythm section pushed by bassist/cheerleader Chubby Jackson and drummer Dave Tough. In 1945 (with new trumpeters in Sonny Berman and Conte Candoli), the First Herd was considered the most exciting new big band in jazz. Several of the arrangements of Ralph Burns and Neal Hefti are considered classics, and such Herman favorites as these entered the book: "Apple Honey," "Caldonia," "Northwest Passage," "Bijou" (Harris' memorable if eccentric feature) and the nutty "Your Father's Mustache." Even Igor Stravinsky was impressed and he wrote "Ebony Concerto" for the orchestra to perform in 1946. Unfortunately, family troubles caused Woody Herman to break up the big band at the height of its success in late 1946; it was the only one of his orchestras to really make much money. Herman recorded a bit in the interim and then by mid-1947 had a new orchestra, the Second Herd, which was soon also known as the Four Brothers band. With the three cool-toned tenors of Stan Getz, Zoot Sims and Herbie Steward (who a year later was replaced by Al Cohn) and baritonist Serge Chaloff forming the nucelus, this orchestra had a sound different from that its more extroverted predecessor but it could also generate excitement of its own. Trumpeter/arranger Shorty Rogers and eventually Bill Harris returned from the earlier outfit, and with Mary Ann McCall back as a vocalist, the group had a great deal of potential. But despite such popular numbers as Jimmy Giuffre's "Four Brothers," "The Goof and I" and "Early Autumn" (the latter ballad made Getz into

a star), the band struggled financially. Before its collapse in 1949 such other musicians as Gene Ammons, Lou Levy, Oscar Pettiford, Terry Gibbs and Shelly Manne made important contributions.
Next up for Woody Herman was the Third Herd, which was similar to the Second except that it generally played at danceable tempos and was a bit more conservative. Herman kept that band together during much of 1950-56, even having his own Mars label for a period; Conte Candoli, Al Cohn, Dave McKenna, Phil Urso, Don Fagerquist, Carl Fontana, Dick Hafer, Bill Perkins, Nat Pierce, Dick Collins and Richie Kamuca were among the many sidemen. After some short-lived somall groups (including a sextet with Nat Adderley and Charlie Byrd), Herman's New Thundering Herd was a hit at the 1959 Monterey Jazz Festival. He was able to lead a big band successfully throughout the 1960s, featuring such soloists as high note trumpeter Bill Chase, trombonist Phil Wilson, the reliable Nat Pierce and the exciting tenor of Sal Nistico. Always open to newer styles, Woody Herman's boppish unit gradually became more rock-oriented as he utilized his young sidemen's arrangements, often of current pop tunes (starting in 1968 with an album titled *Light My Fire*). Not all of his albums from this era worked, but one always admired Herman's open-minded attitude. As one of only four surviving jazz-oriented bandleaders from the swing era (along with Duke Ellington, Count Basie and Stan Kenton) who was still touring the world with a big band, in the 1970s Herman welcomed such new talent as Greg Herbert, Andy La Verne, Joe Beck, Alan Broadbent and Frank Tiberi; he also recorded with Chick Corea, had a reunion with Flip Phillips and celebrated his 40th anniversary as a leader with a notable 1976 Carnegie Hall Concert.
Woody Herman returned to emphasizing straightahead jazz by the late '70s. By then he was being hounded by the IRS due to an incompetent manager from the 1960s not paying thousands of dollars of taxes out of the sidemen's salaries. Herman, who might very well have taken it easy, was forced to keep on touring and working constantly into his old age. He managed to put on a cheerful face to the public, celebrating his 50th anniversary as a bandleader in 1986. However, his health was starting to fail and he gradually delegated most of his duties to Frank Tiberi before his death in 1987. Tiberi still leads a Woody Herman Orchestra on a part-time basis but it has never had the opportunity to record. Fortunately Herman was well-documented throughout all phases of his career and his major contributions are still greatly appreciated. —*Scott Yanow*

Blues in the Night / Nov. 8, 1936-Sep. 10, 1941 / Sunbeam ✦✦✦
Woody Herman began his bandleading career on Nov. 8, 1936, making his debut on the radio aircheck heard on the first half of this LP; this broadcast is from the Roseland Ballroom where Herman would play opposite the fairly new Count Basie Orchestra for quite a few months. Isham Jones' fine dance band had broken up shortly before and half of the musicians reorganized (with some newer players) as a co-op orchestra with the likable Herman as the frontman. At 23, Woody Herman was already a fine clarinetist and a good crooner. This very interesting broadcast primarily focuses on standards and Dixieland tunes played in a conventional swing style. The second half of the LP has studio sides mostly dating from 1941, with Bing Crosby heard as a guest singer on "I Ain't Got Nobody" and the Herman band showing that, after five years of existence, they had pretty much developed a style of their own. —*Scott Yanow*

Jukin' with Woody Herman / Apr. 26, 1937-Apr. 2, 1942 / ✦✦✦✦✦
This excellent LP contains 16 studio recordings by Woody Herman's Band That Plays the Blues, dating from 1937-42. Since most of these selections (other than "Get Your Boots Laced Papa!") are rarely issued and the emphasis here is on jazz rather than Herman's ballad and novelty vocals, this LP is well worth searching for. Next to his clarinet, the top soloists are tenorman Saxie Mansfield and trombonist Neal Ried. —*Scott Yanow*

★ **Blues on Parade** / Apr. 26, 1937-Jul. 24, 1942 / GRP ✦✦✦✦✦
This single CD gives a definitive look at Woody Herman's first orchestra, the Decca ensemble he led during 1936-42 billed "the Band That Plays the Blues." Although he also recorded many vocal ballads during this era, the emphasis here is on hot swing with such highlights as the original version of "Woodchopper's Ball," "Blue Prelude," "Blue Flame," the humorous "Fan It" and two takes of "Blues on Parade." Also heard are performances by Herman's early small combos (the Woodchoppers and the Four Chips) along with a Dizzy Gillespie composition/arrangement ("Down Under") that hints at Woody Herman's future. —*Scott Yanow*

First Session / Sep. 23, 1937 / ✦✦✦
This LP features Herman's first orchestra close to its birth, although its title is not really accurate, since the band had already cut some studio recordings. These are radio transcriptions that are superior to his first Decca records. The leader takes four ballad vocals, while the band gets to show off their talents on some of the more jazz-oriented selections. Herman's orchestra had not yet found its own musical personality and would not began to catch on until 1939. This fine LP gives one a look at the Herman legacy near its start. —*Scott Yanow*

The Uncollected Woody Herman and His Orchestra (1937) / Sep. 23, 1937-Nov. 1937 / Hindsight ✦✦✦

These 16 selections are taken from two sessions made for radio transcriptions in 1937; most of the first ten numbers are also included on a Circle LP, although the final six date from two months later. Better than many of Herman's commercial Decca recordings of this period, these 16 jazz-oriented performances are generally quite enjoyable, with tenorman Saxie Mansfield, fluegelhornist Joe Bishop and trombonist Neil Reid being the main soloists next to clarinetist Herman (who also takes two vocals). —*Scott Yanow*

Big Band Bounce & Boogie / Apr. 12, 1939-Nov. 8, 1943 / ✦✦✦✦

Prior to the release of *Blues on Parade*, a CD that duplicates eight of these 16 selections, this LP had been the best all-around set of early Woody Herman available. *The Band That Plays the Blues* did not feature any outstanding virtuosos but was a versatile and enthusiastic outfit that could swing hard when given a chance. On this LP one hears many of the orchestra's best instrumentals, along with a few examples of Herman's crooning style. —*Scott Yanow*

Dance Time: Forty Three / Feb. 1943-Jun. 1943 / First Heard ✦✦✦✦✦

Due to a recording strike by the Musicians Union, very few commercial recordings were made during 1943, including none by Herman's fine orchestra before November. First Heard has filled the gap by releasing this LP, taken from radio broadcasts aired earlier in the year. Of particular interest in this last version of his "Band That Plays the Blues" are the fine trumpet solos of Billie Rogers, the only female trumpeter to hold a regular position in a major American big band. Novelty aside, she does a fine job and also takes two good vocals. In addition to Herman's clarinet and alto spots, other key musicians include Vido Musso on tenor, trombonist Neal Reid and the young pianist Jimmy Rowles. Pity that both Billie Rogers and the big band she formed in 1944 are totally forgotten today. —*Scott Yanow*

Turning Point / Nov. 18, 1943-Dec. 12, 1944 / Decca ✦✦✦✦

This LP has a very accurate title for, during 1943-44, Woody Herman was searching for a new sound. His "Band That Plays the Blues" had been decimated by the draft and Herman was in the mood for a change anyway. These 14 selections from his transition year found him welcoming guests from other bands onto his records (including Ben Webster, Juan Tizol and Johnny Hodges from the Duke Ellington Orchestra, along with tenormen Georgie Auld and Budd Johnson), going through a brief Ellington phase and then encouraging the gradual emergence of the First Herd. Only five members of Herman's November 1943 orchestra were still with him by the time of the last recording on this set (Dec. 12, 1944). The journey between bands and the highly enjoyable music that was created along the way are well worth hearing. —*Scott Yanow*

Woodchopper's Ball, Vol. 1 / Aug. 2, 1944-Aug. 21, 1944 / Jass ✦✦✦✦

1944 was a pivotal year in Herman's career, the year his orchestra gradually evolved into the First Herd, his most exciting band. This CD features music from two radio shows in August (actually rehearsals for the broadcasts) plus performances from two prestigious engagements at the Hotel Pennsylvania in August and the Hollywood Palladium that October. With Flip Phillips' jump tenor and Bill Harris' expressive trombone already emerging as the band's top soloists, and Francis Wayne contributing a few fine vocals, Ralph Burns and Neal Hefti were hurriedly putting together colorful arrangements to challenge the young sidemen. The music on this set, which precedes the Herd's first commercial recordings, could be titled *The Birth of the Herd*. Recommended, particularly to serious Woody Herman fans. —*Scott Yanow*

The Uncollected Woody Herman and His First Herd / 1944 / Hindsight ✦✦✦

Hindsight's second LP of Woody Herman broadcasts (the first volume dated from 1937) is actually taken exclusively from rehearsals for radio shows and finds Herman at an important transition in his career. The old "Band That Plays the Blues" was making way for the First Herd; already tenor saxophonist Flip Phillips and trombonist Bill Harris were in place as the key soloists. Other than "Apple Honey," most of the material heard on this LP was in the earlier band's repertoire, so it makes for very interesting listening for those fans only familiar with the First Herd's studio recordings. —*Scott Yanow*

☆ **Thundering Herds** / Feb. 19, 1945-Dec. 27, 1947 / Columbia ✦✦✦✦✦

This now out-of-print three-LP set is still the best compilation to date of Herman's First and Second Herds. These 48 selections (the cream of his Columbia recordings) include many classics such as "Apple Honey," "Caldonia," "Northwest Passage," "Bijou," "Your Father's Moustache," eight numbers from Woody Herman's Woodchoppers, "Let It Snow," a new rendition of "Woodchopper's Ball," the four-part "Summer Sequence" and the original version of "Four Brothers." Even the lesser items on this set are memorable, making this the number one Herman release to own. Why hasn't it been reissued in total on CD yet? —*Scott Yanow*

★ **Thundering Herds 1945-1947** / Feb. 19, 1945-Dec. 27, 1947 / Columbia ✦✦✦✦

Since the definitive three-LP box set *Thundering Herds* is out of print, this single CD is the best place for listeners to go first when starting to explore the music of Woody Herman. There are 14 selections from what was arguably his best band, his First Herd, and two numbers (including the original version of "Four Brothers") by the Second Herd. A few rarities (such as "A Jug of Wine" and "The Blues Are Brewing") are mixed in with such classics as "Apple Honey," "Northwest Passage," "Bijou," "Your Father's Mustache" and a new version of "Woodchopper's Ball," but there is unavoidably a lot missing from this single disc, a set which will have to suffice until a more complete reissue series comes along. —*Scott Yanow*

The Best of the Big Bands / Feb. 26, 1945-Dec. 22, 1947 / Columbia ✦✦

This CD reissue of classic material from the First and (in two cases) the Second Herd is a bit of a mess. Despite having chatty liner notes, there are no listings of Herman's sidemen or the exact recording dates. Also, some so-so material is mixed in with a few of the First Herd's greatest performances and the whole set is made anonymous by the meaningless title *Best of the Big Bands*. Highlights include "Caldonia," "Laura," "Apple Honey" and "Northwest Passage," so if given a budget price this might serve as a good introduction to Herman, but in general it is advisable to wait until this material comes around again. —*Scott Yanow*

Northwest Passage, Vol. 2 / Feb. 18, 1945-Aug. 22, 1945 / Jass ✦✦✦

Unlike the first volume in this CD series, *Vol. 2* does not find the First Herd in transition but instead in its early prime. Taken from five separate radio broadcasts, these live performances are generally colorful and sometimes quite exciting, although there are more vocals than normal. More for First Herd fanatics and completists than for general collectors. —*Scott Yanow*

The Second Herd—1948 / Mar. 12, 1948-May 12, 1948 / Storyville ✦✦✦✦

Woody Herman's Second Herd came of age during a year (1948) when, due to a recording strike, very few records were made. This CD contains three radio broadcasts and gives listeners a good idea of what it was like to see the big band live. With such major players as trumpeter/arranger Shorty Rogers, trombonist Earl Swope, guitarist Jimmy Raney, baritonist Serge Chaloff and the tenors of Al Cohn, Stan Getz and Zoot Sims, this was a powerhouse unit that was fairly modern for the time. Mary Ann McCall and Woody Herman take occasional vocals, and there are some dance numbers, but it is the jazz tunes (such as "Half Past Jumping Time," "Non Alcoholic," "Tiny's Blues," "The Goof and I" and "Four Brothers") that make this a fairly significant release. —*Scott Yanow*

Roadband (1948) / Mar. 1948-May 12, 1948 / Hep ✦✦✦✦

Woody Herman's Second Herd was one of his finest orchestras but, unlike the First Herd, it was a money loser and the Musicians Union strike of 1948 kept it off commercial recordings for much of that important year. Fortunately, a few LPs of broadcasts (including this one) show just how strong a unit it was. Solos by the likes of tenors Stan Getz, Zoot Sims and Al Cohn and baritonist Serge Chaloff (who together formed the "Four Brothers" that year) plus the vocals of Woody Herman and Mary Ann McCall made this a memorable outfit, which plays at its best on this set imported from Scotland. It is a particular joy to hear the Second Herd performing so much material that they otherwise never recorded. —*Scott Yanow*

★ **Keeper of the Flame: The Complete Capitol Recordings** / Dec. 29, 1948-Jul. 21, 1949 / Capitol ✦✦✦✦

Subtitled *The Complete Capitol Recordings of the Four Brothers Band*, this CD contains 19 selections from Herman's Second Herd, including three songs never before released. Top-heavy with major soloists (including trumpeters Red Rodney and Shorty Rogers, trombonist Bill Harris, tenors Al Cohn, Zoot Sims, Stan Getz and Gene Ammons and vibraphonist Terry Gibbs, not to mention Herman himself) this boppish band may have cost the leader a small fortune but they created timeless music. Highlights include "Early Autumn" (a ballad performance that made Stan Getz a star), the riotous "Lemon Drop" and Gene Ammons' strong solo on "More Moon." —*Scott Yanow*

Third Herd, Vol. 1 / May 30, 1952-Sep. 11, 1953 / Discovery ✦✦✦

During 1952-53, when Herman's Third Herd had trouble landing a recording contract (big bands were out), he formed his own label, Mars Records. This first of two Discovery LPs contains ten of the Herd's records for Mars and the music is spirited, swinging and a bit safer than the sounds created by the first two Herds. Unfortunately, Discovery has thus far not reissued all of his Mars sides and this LP clocks in at under 29 minutes, but the music is excellent and Woody Herman fans will want it anyway. —*Scott Yanow*

Third Herd, Vol. 2 / May 30, 1952-Mar. 30, 1954 / Discovery ✦✦✦

The second of two LP volumes released by Discovery documents some more of the recordings Herman and his Third Herd made for their own label, Mars Records, during 1952-54. This melodic but swinging orchestra had its share of fine soloists (such as trombonist Carl Fontana and the tenors of Arno Marsh and Bill Perkins) along with fine arrangements from Nat Pierce and Ralph Burns. Unfortunately, this

LP only has 31 minutes of music and many of his Mars recordings have been bypassed (they should all be released in chronological order), but more devoted fans will still want it. —*Scott Yanow*

Music for Tired Lovers / Jul. 8, 1954 / Columbia ✦✦✦
In 1954 Woody Herman recorded one of his most unusual sets, a purely vocal album in which he was accompanied by the Erroll Garner Trio. Herman, who originally sang on half of his band's recordings, was always an expressive ballad singer and he does a fine job on such standards as "My Melancholy Baby," "Let's Fall in Love" and "I'm Beginning to See the Light." The humorous photo on this out-of-print LP is an extra bonus. —*Scott Yanow*

The Woody Herman Band / Sep. 1954 / Capitol ✦✦✦✦
When Herman originally formed his Third Herd in 1950 (after the financial collapse of the Second Herd), he put the emphasis on music for the dancing public first and the jazz public second. However, the jazz content was always strong and by 1954 the band was less shy to swing hard. This hard-to-find LP was one of that orchestra's finest recordings, a strong all-around set highlighted by the flag-waver "Wild Apple Honey," several Ralph Burns arrangements and solos by such fine players as tenors Bill Perkins and Dick Hafer, Cy Touff's bass trumpet, Jack Nimitz's baritone (featured on "Sleep") and Herman's alto and clarinet. —*Scott Yanow*

Road Band / Oct. 13, 1954-Jun. 7, 1955 / Capitol ✦✦✦✦
This out-of-print LP finds Herman's Third Herd in its prime. Rather than just revisiting his celebrated past, he and his orchestra primarily perform then-recent material, much of it arranged by Ralph Burns. Highlights include a big-band version of Horace Silver's "Opus De Funk," Burns' "Cool Cat on a Hot Tin Roof," "I Remember Duke" and Bill Holman's reworking of "Where or When." With tenors Richie Kamuca and Dick Hafer, trumpeter Dick Collins and bass trumpeter Cy Touff as the main soloists, the Third Herd had developed into a particularly strong unit by the mid-'50s. —*Scott Yanow*

The Herd Rides Again / Jul. 30, 1958-Aug. 1, 1958 / Evidence ✦✦✦
This CD contains a better-than-expected reunion of Herman's First Herd. Actually, many of the key players from that classic band (such as tenorman Flip Phillips and trombonist Bill Harris) were not on this date, while some of the musicians who did participate were Hermanites from a later era or (in the case of trombonist Bob Brookmeyer and tenor saxophonist Sam Donahue) had never been a part of his bands before. Because the music was generally only a decade old, the results are quite satisfying, with fresh solos and spirited ensembles giving new life to such numbers as "Northwest Passage," "Caldonia" and "Blowin' up a Storm," among others. Certainly Brookmeyer's playing on "Bijou" will not remind anyone of Bill Harris. —*Scott Yanow*

Wildroot / Jul. 30, 1958-Dec. 26, 1958 / Vee-Jay ✦✦✦
Half of these 1958 sessions mix past members of the Herd with new ones, on remakes of old Herman charts. These swing fairly respectably, but more interesting are the four cuts from a December 26, 1958 session with Charlie Byrd as featured guitarist. These have a Latin flavor that pushes the music into more exciting territory; "Bamba Samba" is a particularly lively effort in this direction. —*Richie Unterberger*

Herman's Heat & Puente's Beat / Aug. 1958 / Evidence ✦✦✦✦✦
By 1958, Herman's Third Herd was history and he was back to working with small groups again. For the sessions that this CD comprises, he used two separate studio orchestras filled with musicians (and some alumni) familiar with his music. In addition to the fine straightahead charts (which includes a new version of "Woodchopper's Ball," "Lullaby of Birdland" and "Midnight Sun"), Herman added Tito Puente's five-piece Latin rhythm section to six selections, bringing variety and strong rhythmic excitement to this fine set. —*Scott Yanow*

Woody Herman Sextet at the Round Table / Jan. 26, 1959-Feb. 1, 1959 / Roulette ✦✦✦
By 1959 Herman had broken up his Third Herd and was utilizing a sextet filled with important young players. This live LP from 1959 (the only recording of this group) finds him well featured on both alto and clarinet with a band that also boasts trumpeter Nat Adderley, acoustic guitarist Charlie Byrd and Eddie Costa on piano and vibes. All 12 selections (mixing together standards and forgotten originals) have their enjoyable moments. A rare chance to hear Woody Herman as a key soloist in a small group. —*Scott Yanow*

The Fourth Herd & the New World of Woody Herman / Jul. 31, 1959-Dec. 27, 1962 / Mobile Fidelity ✦✦✦
This CD is quite a bit different from most audiophile releases, for it contains rare rather than famous recordings. 1959's *The Fourth Herd* (which features an all-star group of studio musicians and Woody Herman alumni along with his octet of the time) was only put out briefly by Jazzland, while the music on 1962's *The New World of Woody Herman* was never available commercially before; both were originally cut for the SESAC Transcribed Library and were available only to selected

radio stations on a subscription basis. The earlier session has solo spots for tenors Zoot Sims, Al Cohn and Don Lanphere, trumpeters Nat Adderley and Red Rodney, vibraphonist Eddie Costa, and Herman on clarinet, a bit of alto and two vocals; Cohn and pianist Nat Pierce wrote most of the colorful and diverse arrangements. By the later session (which has charts by Pierce, Gene Roland, Phil Wilson and Bill Chase), Woody Herman once again was leading an exciting big band of his own. Trombonist Phil Wilson, Duke Ellington's tenor Paul Gonsalves (filling in for the temporarily absent Sal Nistico) and Herman are the solo stars and (as with the first date) the music swings hard and contains its share of surprises. —*Scott Yanow*

Live at Monterey / Oct. 3, 1959 / Atlantic ✦✦✦✦
Woody Herman returned to the big band wars in 1959 with these two very successful appearances at the Monterey Jazz Festival. His new band featured such major players as trumpeter Conte Candoli, trombonist Urbie Green, acoustic guitarist Charlie Byrd and a sax section comprising tenors Zoot Sims, Bill Perkins and Richie Kamuca, Don Lanphere on alto and tenor, and baritonist Med Flory, in addition to Herman himself. The all-star orchestra romps through "Four Brothers," "Monterey Apple Tree" and "Skoobeedoobee," and Urbie Green is well featured on the ballad "Skylark" and "The Magpie." Excellent music that signaled a comeback for Woody Herman. —*Scott Yanow*

Woody Herman (1963) / Oct. 15, 1962-Oct. 16, 1962 / Echo Jazz ✦✦✦✦
In 1962 Woody Herman signed a contract with Philips and went on to record some of the finest big-band albums of his long career. Unfortunately, all are currently out of print (none have yet appeared on CD) but most are well worth searching for. This version of Herman's Thundering Herd featured high-note trumpet work by Bill Chase, trombonist Phil Wilson, pianist Nat Pierce and the exciting tenor of Sal Nistico. High points of this fine LP are "Sister Sadie" and "Camel Walk." —*Scott Yanow*

Verve Jazz Masters 54 / Oct. 15, 1962-Sep. 9, 1964 / Verve ✦✦✦✦
Purely by the accidental circumstance of having a relatively small slice of music from which to draw, Verve's Woody Herman *Jazz Masters* volume provides a service by selecting from all five out of print Philips albums that document one of Herman's best bands. This was a zesty, youth-driven outfit, studded with fine musicians like the late trumpeter Bill Chase, tenor player Sal Nistico, pianist-arranger Nat Pierce (who apparently ran the band behind the scenes), trombonist Phil Wilson and drummer Jake Hanna. The repertoire proves that Herman had his ear to the ground by including numbers like a thoroughly energizing, authentic-sounding version of Mingus' "Better Git It in Your Soul." For old time's sake, road father Woody is there with an occasional good-humored vocal like a revivified oldie like "Caldonia." All this unit lacked was the First Herd's extra spark of originality and zeitgeist-inspired exuberance—being exactly in the right place at the right time in history—but it's a close judgment call. In other words, while you wouldn't want this CD as a single-disc introduction to Herman's six-decade career—a First or Second Herd sampler would be a better choice—there's a lot of exciting music to be heard here. —*Richard S. Ginell*

Encore: Woody Herman (1963) / May 19, 1963-May 21, 1963 / Philips ✦✦✦✦
Herman led one of his finest orchestras during 1962-66, a hard-swinging outfit filled with enthusiastic young players such as high-note trumpeter Bill Chase, trombonist Phil Wilson and the exciting tenor saxophonist Sal Nistico. The LP *Encore* has quite a few highlights, including the uptempo blues "That's Where It Is," a Nat Pierce arrangement of Herbie Hancock's "Watermelon Man" and Charles Mingus' "Better Git It in Your Soul" and a remake of "Caldonia." Excellent music that deserves to be reissued on CD. —*Scott Yanow*

Woody's Big Band Goodies / May 21, 1963-Sep. 9, 1964 / Philips ✦✦✦
Herman's Swingin' Herd of the early-to-mid '60s was one of his finest big bands, an ensemble that could compare well with his historic First and Second Herds. Their series of LPs on Philips (all now out of print and well deserving of a complete reissue on CD) are consistently exciting. *Big Band Goodies* consists of some "leftovers" from Encore and three newer selections from 1964. Actually the older tracks are on the same high level as those issued previously. No band with such soloists as trumpeters Bill Chase and Dusko Goykevich, trombonist Phil Wilson and the exciting tenor Sal Nistico—not to mention arrangements by pianist Nat Pierce and a rhythm section propelled by drummer Jake Hanna—should be taken for granted. *Big Band Goodies* finds this orchestra interpreting some older tunes ("Sidewalks of Cuba," "Bijou" and "Apple Honey"), Thelonious Monk's "Blue Monk," and the well-titled "Wailin' in the Woodshed" with equal success. —*Scott Yanow*

Woody Herman (1964) / Nov. 20, 1963-Nov. 23, 1963 / Philips ✦✦✦✦
All of Woody Herman's recordings for Philips (which regrettably remain out of print and unissued on CD) are excellent. He was leading one of the finest orchestras of his long career, playing both current and older tunes with creativity (helped out greatly by Nat Pierce's arrangements) and featuring such talented soloists as trumpeter Bill Chase, trombonist Phil Wilson and tenor great Sal Nistico. The

release ranges from "Deep Purple" and "After You've Gone" to Oscar Peterson's "Hallelujah Time" and even "A Taste of Honey"; everything works. —*Scott Yanow*

Swinging Herman Herd, Recorded Live / Sep. 9, 1964 / Brunswick ♦♦♦
The Swingin' Herd of the early to mid-'60s was one of his great orchestras. This live LP, the final one of Herman's consistently exciting Philips releases, has particularly diverse material, with many pop tunes of the era represented. Although Joe Carroll's two vocals and "Everybody Loves Somebody Sometime" were not the band's most significant moments, there are other performances on this set (particularly "Bedroom Eyes," "Just Squeeze Me" and "Dr. Wong's Blues") that compensate. —*Scott Yanow*

My Kind of Broadway / Nov. 27, 1964-Mar. 13, 1965 / Columbia ♦♦♦
Herman's Swinging Herd of the '60s was so successful they were signed up by their old label, Columbia. Their first CBS release (which, like the others, has yet to be reissued on CD) features jazz interpretations of a dozen songs that debuted in Broadway shows. There are some fine solos and the arrangements try hard but some of the selections (such as "Who Can I Turn To?," "My Favorite Things" and "The Sound of Music") sound out of context in this setting. Nice music but not too essential. —*Scott Yanow*

Woody's Winners / Jun. 28, 1965-Jun. 30, 1965 / Columbia ♦♦♦♦♦
Of the many exciting recordings by the Swinging Herd of the '60s, this is the definitive set. With such soloists as trumpeters Bill Chase, Dusko Goykovich and Don Rader, and tenors Sal Nistico, Andy McGhee and Gary Klein, this orchestra rarely had any difficulty raising the temperature. Recorded live at Basin Street West in late June of 1965, this set finds the enthusiastic band featuring a three-way trumpet battle on "23 Red," reworking "Northwest Passage" (highlighted by Sal Nistico's long tenor solo) and romping on a lengthy version of "Opus de Funk" in addition to interpreting a few ballads and blues. This is a very memorable LP that deserves to be reissued on CD so it can be in every jazz collector's library. —*Scott Yanow*

Jazz Hoot / Jun. 28, 1965-Mar. 23, 1967 / Columbia ♦♦♦
This collector's LP includes unissued and rare items by Herman's Swingin' Herd of the '60s. Several selections (including "Hallelujah Time," "Watermelon Man" and "Greasy Sack Blues") are alternate versions of tunes released on other albums, and a couple others ("The Duck" and "Boopsie") originally came out as singles featuring guitarist Charlie Byrd. All in all a nice set of music that wraps up Herman's '60s recordings for Columbia. —*Scott Yanow*

The Jazz Swinger / Feb. 28, 1966-Jun. 10, 1966 / Columbia ♦
Apparently, the same Columbia executives who tried to get Miles Davis to record an album of forgettable melodies from the film *Dr. Doolittle* and were unsuccessful in persuading Thelonious Monk to record Beatles songs somehow talked Woody Herman into singing songs associated with Al Jolson. Not only did Herman have a singing style much different from Jolson's, but many of the dated lyrics were embarrassing even 30 years ago. As for the arrangements for the orchestra, the more modern they were, the cornier they sounded (particularly Bill Holman's modernization of "Swanee" and "Toot, Toot, Tootsie"). What a mess—the only likable part about this misfire is the album drawing of Herman singing while down on one knee like Jolson; fortunately he was not drawn in blackface. —*Scott Yanow*

Live in Seattle / 1967 / Moon ♦♦♦
The 1967 edition of Woody Herman's Orchestra is captured live in concert on this well-recorded European import. With fine playing from tenor saxophonist Sal Nistico, baritonist Ronnie Cuber, pianist John Hicks and high-note trumpeter Bill Chase, this is an excellent all-around showcase for the band. Some tunes are stronger than others, with "Greasy Sack Blues" and "Jumpin' Blue" being high points, although "Make Someone Happy" and the funky "Hush" are more routine. To Herman's credit, "Four Brothers" is the only one of his older songs to be reprised on this interesting set; the leader sounds good on clarinet, alto and soprano. —*Scott Yanow*

Concerto for Herd / Sep. 1967 / Verve ♦♦♦
1967 found the Woody Herman Orchestra in transition. While tenor saxophonist Sal Nistico and trombonist Carl Fontana were the biggest names, trumpeter Luis Gasca and pianist Albert Daily were up-and-coming players. This LP, recorded live at the tenth annual Monterey Jazz Festival, features the side-long "Concert for Herd," an adventurous work by Bill Holman. In addition, there are three shorter pieces that find Herman and his musicians exploring a variety of music including a boogaloo and a feature for Herman's soprano sax ("The Horn of the Fish"). This fine all-around set has been long out of print. —*Scott Yanow*

Woody / Jul. 29, 1970-Jul. 30, 1970 / Cadet ♦♦
Woody Herman deserved great credit for encouraging his younger musicians to write for his big band and for including new material in his repertoire, but sometimes one was justified in wondering about his judgment. Alan Broadbent's lengthy reworking of "Blues in the Night" is worthwhile and the version of "A Time

for Love" heard on this LP features the brilliant young fluegelhornist Tom Harrell (Herman was always a gifted talent scout). However, the other four poppish songs are rather weak and two have embarrassingly bad lyrics that Herman sings, greatly weakening the album. Not one of the classic Woody Herman records. —*Scott Yanow*

Brand New / Mar. 1971 / Fantasy ♦♦♦
Of all of the big bandleaders who emerged during the swing era, Herman had always been the most receptive to keeping his music modern and attuned to the music younger people were listening to. This unusual LP found him welcoming the great electric blues guitarist Mike Bloomfield to the band for three numbers. The other selections include new originals, Ivory Joe Hunter's "I Almost Lost My Mind" and "After Hours." Keyboardist Alan Broadbent arranged most of the material, although Nat Pierce's chart on "After Hours" was most memorable. With Woody Herman taking a couple of vocals and soloing on clarinet, soprano and alto, this early-'70s release was a surprise success. —*Scott Yanow*

The Raven Speaks / Aug. 28, 1972-Aug. 30, 1972 / Original Jazz Classics ♦♦♦♦♦
The best of his Fantasy releases of the '70s, this well-rounded CD is highlighted by a great jam on "Reunion at Newport" and strong soloing from Herman (on soprano and clarinet), pianist Harold Danko, trumpeter Bill Stapleton and the tenors of Gregory Herbert and Frank Tiberi. The Herman orchestra performs a couple of modern ballads ("Alone Again Naturally" and "Summer of '42"), some blues and a few swinging numbers, showing off their versatility with expertise and spirit. —*Scott Yanow*

Giant Steps / Apr. 9, 1973-Apr. 12, 1973 / Original Jazz Classics ♦♦♦♦
Woody Herman always went out of his way during his long career to encourage younger players, often persuading them to write arrangements of recent tunes for his orchestra. On this LP one gets to hear his band interpret such selections as Chick Corea's "La Fiesta," Leon Russell's "A Song for You," "Freedom Jazz Dance," "A Child Is Born" and "Giant Steps"; what other bandleader from the '30s would have performed such modern material? With strong solo work from tenors Gregory Herbert and Frank Tiberi, trumpeter Bill Stapleton and Herman himself, this is an impressive effort. —*Scott Yanow*

Feelin' So Blue / Apr. 11, 1973-Jan. 7, 1975 / Original Jazz Classics ♦♦♦
This LP has a variety of recordings Herman cut for Fantasy during 1973-75 that had not found a place on his other releases. There are some good moments (notably "Brotherhood of Man") but nothing all that memorable occurs. This is an average release from a jazz institution. —*Scott Yanow*

Thundering Herd / Jan. 2, 1974-Jan. 4, 1974 / Original Jazz Classics ♦♦♦
Of all the big-band leaders of the swing era, Woody Herman went the most out of his way to interpret current material and keep his orchestra young, enthusiastic and modern. For this Fantasy date (reissued on CD in the OJC series), Herman's band not only plays two John Coltrane songs, but material from Frank Zappa ("America Drinks and Goes Home"), Stanley Clarke ("Bass Folk Song") and even Carole King ("Corazon"). This is one of Herman's most successful efforts of the period, for the arrangements (by Alan Broadbent, Bill Stapleton and Tony Klatka) are inventive and generally swinging, with such soloists as Frank Tiberi on tenor, fluegelhornist Klatka and electric keyboardist Andy La Verne keeping the music continually interesting. "Blues for Poland," "Lazy Bird" and the Zappa piece are high points. —*Scott Yanow*

Children of Lima / Oct. 22, 1974-Jan. 7, 1975 / Fantasy ♦♦
This is an unusual album by Woody Herman's Young Thundering Herd. The big band joins with the Houston Symphony Orchestra to perform a pair of Alan Broadbent pieces: the 18-minute "Variations on a Scene" and the five-minute "Children of Lima." In general this "third-stream" effort is not all that interesting and finds the Herman band being weighed down by the strings. The flip side of the LP (not yet reissued on CD) finds the big band two months later playing Broadbent's "Far In" and three pop tunes ("Never Let Me Go," "Where Is the Love?" and Chicago's "25 or 6 to 4"). Despite some good solos by Frank Tiberi on tenor and bassoon and tenorman Gregory Herbert (showcased on "Never Let Me Go") along with a couple of spots for Herman, this is definitely a lesser effort that has not dated well. —*Scott Yanow*

King Cobra / Jan. 7, 1975-Jan. 9, 1975 / Fantasy ♦♦
As the years passed and Woody Herman continued to age, his orchestra's music stayed young and contemporary. Never willing to have a mere nostalgia band, he continued looking ahead for new music without lowering his standards. On this LP from 1975, the big band performs an excellent version of Chick Corea's "Spain," explores material by Tom Scott and Stevie Wonder and sounds fine on "Come Rain or Come Shine." Herman's vocal on "Jazzman" does not come off so well, but occasional misfires are excused when one considers how many chances he took during his productive career. —*Scott Yanow*

40th Anniversary Carnegie Hall Concert / Nov. 20, 1976 / Bluebird ✦✦✦✦
To celebrate his 40th anniversary as a bandleader, Herman had a celebrated concert at Carnegie Hall. For the first half of the program he welcomed back many of his alumni including such veterans as tenors Flip Phillips, Stan Getz, Zoot Sims, Jimmy Giuffre and Al Cohn, the Candoli brothers, trombonist Phil Wilson and singer Mary Ann McCall. Overall, the concert served as a loving tribute to a major jazz figure. The only major flaw was Herman's tendency to call out soloists' names before they finished playing, pretty much ruining this version of "Four Brothers." It was originally available as a two-LP set although the first half has since been reissued on this CD. —*Scott Yanow*

Lionel Hampton Presents Woody Herman / 1977 / Who's Who In Jazz ✦✦✦
This LP contains a rare small-group session from late in his career. Switching among clarinet, soprano and alto, Herman is the lead voice throughout these five extended jams on standards. Joined by a six-piece rhythm section including vibraphonist Lionel Hampton, pianist Roland Hanna and guitarist Al Caiola, he is in fine form on this fun session. —*Scott Yanow*

Road Father / Jan. 3, 1978+Jan. 4, 1978 / Century ✦✦✦✦

Woody Herman and Flip Phillips / Jan. 5, 1978 / Century ✦✦✦
Over 30 years after the First Herd broke up, Flip Phillips had a reunion with Woody Herman for this LP. The emphasis is on ballads and Phillips plays beautifully throughout, but this set lacks variety (only "There Is No Greater Love" is taken at a medium pace). Still, within its limitations and with the orchestra itself mostly playing a supporting role, Phillips and Herman (the latter particularly on alto) blend very well together on this pretty music. —*Scott Yanow*

Plays Chick, Donald, Walter and Woodrow / Jan. 1978 / Century ✦✦✦
In keeping with his policy of featuring his orchestra on modern material, Herman had his band play compositions by Chick Corea (the three movements of "Suite for a Hot Band") and the team of Donald Fagen and Walter Becker (co-leaders of Steely Dan). In reality, the orchestra's solos are more impressive than the compositions, with Tom Scott taking a couple of guest spots and the other strong voices including Joe Lovano and Frank Tiberi on tenors, baritonist Bruce Johnstone and Herman himself on soprano and clarinet. It's a worthy but not particularly memorable effort. —*Scott Yanow*

Woody and Friends at the Monterey Jazz Festival / Sep. 1979 / Concord Jazz ✦✦✦✦
Recorded live at the 1979 Monterey Jazz Festival, Herman and his Young Thundering Herd welcomed trumpeters Woody Shaw and Dizzy Gillespie and trombonist Slide Hampton to the bandstand for "Woody 'n You " and "Manteca," and featured guest Stan Getz on a typically beautiful rendition of "What Are You Doing the Rest of Your Life?" The other side of this LP finds The Herd sounding in spirited form on four standards, with baritonist Gary Smulyan and tenor saxophonist Frank Tiberi (who doubles on bassoon during "Caravan") taking solo honors. —*Scott Yanow*

Presents, Vol. 1: A Concord Jam / Aug. 1980 / Concord Jazz ✦✦✦✦

Live in Chicago / Mar. 1981 / Status ✦✦✦

Woody Herman Presents..., Vol. 2: Four Others / Jul. 1981 / Concord Jazz ✦✦✦✦
The second of three sets that find Herman presenting all-star groups, this one is quite a saxophone summit. The tenors of Al Cohn, Sal Nistico, Bill Perkins and Flip Phillips (referred to as "Four Others") because none of them were on the original recording of "Four Brothers" and each played with a different Herd) and a strong rhythm section form an exciting septet. Al Cohn's arrangements perfectly set up the soloists on these attractive jam tunes. Herman only actually appears on one song, joining the group on alto for "Tenderly," but he must have enjoyed seeing his alumni all still playing at their prime. —*Scott Yanow*

Live at Concord Jazz Festival (1981) / Aug. 15, 1981 / Concord Jazz ✦✦✦
The Woody Herman Orchestra is in fine form during this live performance from the 1981 Concord Jazz Festival. Other than trumpeter Bill Stapleton, none of the sidemen are all that well known over a decade later but they played very well as an ensemble and there are some worthwhile solos on the varied material. Al Cohn guests on "Things Ain't What They Used to Be" and a spirited "Lemon Drop" while the great Stan Getz steals solo honors on "The Dolphin." —*Scott Yanow*

World Class / Sep. 1982 / Concord Jazz ✦✦✦
As with most of the Woody Herman Orchestra's recordings for Concord, this set (taken from concerts in Japan) welcomes guests from Herman's past. In this case tenors Al Cohn, Med Flory, Sal Nistico and Flip Phillips get to star on half of the eight selections, including a remake of "Four Brothers" and Phillips' "The Claw." Phillips has an opportunity to reprise his famous *Jazz at the Philharmonic* solo on "Perdido." The regular Herman sidemen do not sound as distinctive in comparison,

but they play quite well on these attractive arrangements, four of them by pianist John Oddo. —*Scott Yanow*

Presents, Vol. 3: Great American Evening / Apr. 1983 / Concord Jazz ✦✦✦✦
The third and final LP volume in the *Woody Herman Presents* series finds him leading an all-star band, playing clarinet and taking rare late-period vocals on "I've Got the World on a String" and "Caldonia." Actually, there are almost too many talents to hear from during this set, including tenor saxophonist Scott Hamilton, trombonist George Masso, trumpeter/vocalist Jack Sheldon (who does a funny bit on "Leopard-Skin Pill-Box Hat"), Japanese clarinetist Eiji Kitamura, and even whistler Ron McCroby. It all works somehow on this upbeat set of swinging music. —*Scott Yanow*

Fiftieth Anniversary Tour / Mar. 1986 / Concord Jazz ✦✦✦✦✦
This set, which is the best of the Woody Herman Orchestra's Concord recordings, celebrates his 50th year as a bandleader, quite an accomplishment. No guest stars are needed for this set, which shows just how strong a big band he still had. With tenor saxophonist Frank Tiberi gradually taking over leadership duties (today he leads the ghost Woody Herman Orchestra) and trombonist John Fedchock contributing the arrangements, the band was in fine shape even if the leader was aging. Whether it be "It Don't Mean a Thing," John Coltrane's "Central Park West" (a great arrangement) or Don Grolnick's "Pools," every selection is excellent. —*Scott Yanow*

Woody's Gold Star / Mar. 1987 / Concord Jazz ✦✦✦✦
Herman's final recording, made just weeks before his health began to seriously fail, is actually quite good. With future leader Frank Tiberi contributing some strong tenor solos, John Fedchock writing some colorful arrangements for a varied program (ranging from "Rose Room" and "'Round Midnight" to Chick Corea's "Samba Song"), and three guest percussionists on some of the pieces, this is an enjoyable release. Herman takes short solos on three of the pieces, recorded approximately 50 years after he formed his first successful big band. This serves as a fine closer to a significant career. —*Scott Yanow*

Vincent Herring

b. Nov. 19, 1964, Hopkinsville, NY
Alto Saxophone, Soprano Saxophone / Hard Bop
It was only fitting that Vincent Herring gained his first important recognition playing with Nat Adderley, for his sound is strongly influenced by his idol, Cannonball Adderley. Born in Kentucky and raised in California, Herring moved to New York in 1983 and played with a variety of major musicians (including Lionel Hampton, David Murray, Horace Silver and Art Blakey) before joining Adderley (1987-93). Vincent Herring, who has recorded for Landmark and Music Masters, has led his own group since the early '90s. —*Scott Yanow*

American Experience / Apr. 17, 1986-Oct. 1986 / Music Masters ✦✦✦✦
This Music Masters CD, released in 1991, contains altoist Vincent Herring's earliest recordings (some of which predate his association with Nat Adderley). Actually, his Cannonball Adderley-inspired style was already recognizable. Herring is the dominant soloist throughout, with pianists John Hicks and Bruce Barth making significant contributions. The material has a nice balance between fiery pieces and laid-back ballads and most of the solos tend to be concise, melodic and swinging. —*Scott Yanow*

Scene One / Dec. 20, 1988-Dec. 21, 1988 / Evidence ✦✦✦

Evidence / Jun. 29, 1990-Jul. 2, 1990 / Landmark ✦✦✦✦✦
A much sharper, clearer statement than his other release. The compositions are better and the music is more dynamic. —*Ron Wynn*

Dawnbird / Oct. 31, 1991-Feb. 1991 / Landmark ✦✦✦✦✦
Alto saxophonist Vince Herring has steadily developed his own tart, bluesy sound, emerging from the shadow of prime influence Cannonball Adderley. There is more spark, ambition and drive in his playing on this release than on any previous date; he tries new things on each number and isn't afraid to stretch out. He is working with two bands and is consistently excellent with both units, and his sparkling sound overcomes the difference in quality between groups and makes this by far his best release. —*Ron Wynn*

● **Secret Love** / 1993 / Music Masters ✦✦✦✦✦
Altoist Vincent Herring's release is an impressive effort. Although he still sounds fairly close to Cannonball Adderley at times, Herring is continuing to develop as a fine modern bop stylist. Accompanied by a strong rhythm section (pianist Renee Rosnes, bassist Ira Coleman and drummer Billy Drummond), Rosnes explores Kenny Barronis' "And Then Again" and eight standards including Jobim's lesser-known "If You Never," John Lewis' "Skating in Central Park" and Billy Strayhorn's lyrical "Chelsea Bridge." —*Scott Yanow*

Folklore: Live at the Village Vanguard / Nov. 26, 1993-Nov. 28, 1993 / Music Masters ✦✦✦✦

Days of Wine and Roses / Jun. 17, 1994-Jun. 18, 1994 / Music Masters ✦✦✦
Altoist Vincent Herring gained his initial recognition for his ability to emulate Cannonball Adderley while a member of Nat Adderley's quintet. On this CD, a 1994 date made for the Japanese Alfa label and released for the first time in the US in 1997, the emphasis is on slower tempos with just a few moments of heat (particularly Jobim's "Triste"). Pianist Cyrus Chestnut often gains one's attention with both his creative accompaniment and solos; bassist Jesse Murphy and drummer Billy Drummond are fine in support. Herring is in worthwhile form but does not stretch himself much in this setting, playing unadventurous solos on nine very familiar standards, most of which do not need to be revived again (such as "Star Eyes," "Come Rain or Come Shine" and "We'll Be Together Again"). —Scott Yanow

Into the Midnight / 1995 / Music Masters ✦✦✦✦

Change the World / Jan. 13, 1997-Jan. 15, 1997 / Music Masters ✦✦✦
Altoist Vincent Herring teams up with pianist Joey Calderazzo, bassist Richie Goods, drummer Carl Allen and percussionist Daniel Sadownick to perform a rather unusual repertoire for a jazz date. In addition to his original ballad "Timothy" and a couple of obscure pop tunes, Herring interprets a song by Prince and three by Billy Joel. However, by reharmonizing the pieces and opening them up, Herring essentially turns them into jazz. Although nothing here is destined to become a standard in the jazz world, the fresh material does inspire the players a bit, although the results fall short of classic. A change of pace (which seems a bit out of place in this context) is a version of Hank Mobley's "Soft Impressions," which co-stars guest trumpeter Roy Hargrove. —Scott Yanow

Fred Hersch

b. , Cincinnatti, OH
Piano / Post-Bop

A superior soloist, accompanist and interpreter of ballads, Fred Hersch started playing piano when he was four. He moved to New York in 1977 and has worked as a sideman with many players, including Stan Getz, Joe Henderson, Toots Thielemans, Art Farmer, Jane Ira Bloom, Eddie Daniels and Janis Siegel, in addition to leading his own groups. During 1980-86 he taught at the New England Conservatory and has since been on the faculty of the New School. In addition, Hersch has recorded extensively as a leader, including for Sunnyside, Concord, Angel/EMI, Red and Chesky. —Scott Yanow

Thelonious / Feb. 1977 / Nonesuch ✦✦✦✦
Pianist Fred Hersch has a very different style than Thelonious Monk did, and on this solo tribute CD, he does not attempt to closely emulate Monk. Hersch does hint at Thelonious in spots on the 13 Monk compositions, but mostly performs in a sparse, melodic and quietly playful manner. His interpretations of such songs as "In Walked Bud," "Ask Me Now," "Let's Cool One" and "Misterioso" (which he calls "Five Views of Misterioso") are tasteful yet full of subtle invention. A pleasing and respectful effort. —Scott Yanow

Horizons / Oct. 1984 / Concord Jazz ✦✦✦✦
Fred Hersch's debut as a leader was this trio set with bassist Marc Johnson and drummer Joey Baron. Hersch, who mixes together elements of Bill Evans and Tommy Flanagan with his own approach to chordal improvisation, already sounds fairly individual on such numbers as "My Heart Stood Still," Herbie Hancock's "One Finger Snap" and "The Surrey with the Fringe on Top." The superior compositions and Hersch's own logical but fresh style made this an impressive beginning to his productive solo career. —Scott Yanow

Sarabande / Dec. 4, 1986-Dec. 5, 1986 / Sunnyside ✦✦✦✦
Teamed up in a trio with bassist Charlie Haden and drummer Joey Baron, pianist Fred Hersch is heard on this date exploring the modern mainstream of jazz. His thoughtful and exploratory solos on such numbers as Ornette Coleman's "Enfant," Jimmy Rowles' "The Peacocks," "What Is This Thing Called Love?" "Blue In Green" and three of his own originals (including the title cut) are full of subtle and generally swinging surprises. This CD is a fine example of Fred Hersch's playing. —Scott Yanow

E.T.C. / May 19, 1988 / Red ✦✦✦

The French Collection / 1989 / Angel ✦✦✦

Heartsongs / Dec. 4, 1989-Dec. 5, 1989 / Sunnyside ✦✦✦✦✦

Forward Motion / Jul. 22, 1991-Jul. 23, 1991 / Chesky ✦✦✦✦
This subtle set sneaks up on the listener, gradually building in tension and excitement. Pianist Fred Hersch varies the instrumentation on many of the tracks (only six of his originals use the full group) and the CD starts off with several quiet selections. But just as one thinks that they know what to expect on the rest of the session, up pops "Janeology" (a tribute to Jane Ira Bloom that is a rather spaced-out performance based on "Confirmation") and a driving piece dedicated to Joe Henderson, "Phantom of the Bopera" (great title!). Using tenor saxophonist Rich Perry,

cellist Erik Friedlander, bassist Scott Colley and drummer Tom Rainey in different settings (including an unusual cello-piano-percussion trio on "Frevo"), Fred Hersch is heard throughout the continually surprising date playing at the top of his form. —Scott Yanow

Red Square Blue: Jazz Impressions of Russian Composers / Sep. 1, 1992-Oct. 1, 1992 / Angel ✦✦✦
This is an unusual set. Pianist Fred Hersch explores music by Mussorgsky, Gliere, Scriabin, Tchaikovsky, Rimsky-Korsakoff, Liadov and Rachmaninoff, performing jazz improvisations while being respectful to the original themes. With the assistance of bassist Steve La Spina, drummer Jeff Hershfield and (on various tracks) flutist James Newton, Toots Thielemans on harmonica, altoist Phil Woods (also heard on clarinet) and cellist Erik Friedlander, Hersch brings out some unexpected beauty in the melodies. This CD is a follow-up to a 1989 disc (*Jazz Impressions*) on which Hersch and a similar group played their interpretations of themes by French (rather than Russian) classical composers. —Scott Yanow

Dancing in the Dark / Dec. 1992 / Chesky ✦✦✦✦✦

Live at Maybeck Recital Hall, Vol. 31 / Oct. 1993 / Concord Jazz ✦✦✦
Hersch downplays his own compositions, including only two of his pieces among the 11-song program. Hersch sparkles on Thelonious Monk's "In Walked Bud," nicely conveying its unpredictable flavor and quick-shifting harmonic flair. He's equally effective on Ornette Coleman's "Ramblin'," communicating a mood somewhere between frenetic and calculating. He's quite proficient on the shopworn standards "Embraceable You," "Body and Soul," and "You Don't Know What Love Is," but frankly it's more rewarding to hear Fred Hersch tackling his own work or exploring the ambitious fare of Monk or Coleman than putting his stamp on great songs that have been done many times. —Ron Wynn

Fred Hersch Trio Plays . . . / Feb. 16, 1994-Feb. 17, 1994 / Chesky ✦✦✦✦✦
For this enjoyable disc, pianist Fred Hersch (along with bassist Drew Gress and drummer Tom Rainey) creates inventive versions of a dozen songs by 11 jazz composers (including Hersch's tribute to Bill Evans, "Evanessence"). Whether it be "Milestones," "Con Alma," "Moment's Notice," or a pair of Thelonious Monk tunes, Hersch and his trio are heard in top form, and they sound particularly inspired by the superior material. —Scott Yanow

Plays Johnny Mandel: I Never Told You / Sep. 20, 1994-Sep. 21, 1994 / Varese ✦✦✦✦

Point in Time / Mar. 20, 1995-Mar. 24, 1995 / Enja ✦✦✦✦

● **Plays Billy Strayhorn** / Jun. 1995+Aug. 1995 / Nonesuch ✦✦✦✦✦
For this well-rounded tribute to the great Billy Strayhorn (a nearly invisible genius during his lifetime), pianist Fred Hersch performs a dozen of Strayhorn's compositions, mixing together well-known tunes with such obscurities as "Lament for an Orchid," "Ballad for Very Tired and Very Sad Lotus-Eaters" and "Pretty Girl." Hersch takes three numbers as unaccompanied solos (including a beautiful version of "Lotus Blossom"), four trio performances with bassist Drew Gress and drummer Tom Rainey, a duet with singer Andy Bey ("Something to Live For"), three selections in which the trio is joined by a string section, and a piano duet with Nurit Tiles on "Tonk." Although the emphasis is on ballads and great respect is shown for Strayhorn's melodies, Fred Hersch varies the tempos, uses some advanced harmonies, and lets his own musical personality shine through. Highly recommended. —Scott Yanow

Plays Rodgers & Hammerstein / Jan. 1996 / Elektra/Asylum ✦✦✦
Fred Hersch grew up loving the show tunes of Rodgers & Hammerstein, so he took advantage of the opportunity to pay tribute to the songwriters. This solo piano set mixes together some standards (most notably "It Might As Well Be Spring" and "The Surrey with the Fringe on Top") with some lesser-known but worthwhile tunes, including "Loneliness of Evening" and "I Have Dreamed." Hersch's harmonically advanced yet melodic style transforms even the most unlikely tunes into high-quality jazz. —Scott Yanow

Thirteen Ways / 1997 / GM ✦✦✦

Conrad Herwig

b. 1959
Trombone / Post-Bop

Conrad Herwig is one of New York's more prominent young progressive/mainstream trombonists. He has recorded and/or performed with a number of famous leaders, including, but not limited to, Joe Henderson, Jack DeJohnette, and Paquito D'Rivera. Herwig is an alumnus of the famous University of North Texas jazz program, an experience that obviously prepared him well as a big band player. He began his professional career in the early '80s with Clark Terry's big band; stints with Buddy Rich, Toshiko Akiyoshi, Mel Lewis, and others were to follow. Herwig has become an increasingly in-demand sideman in the '90s. He is an accomplished pedagogue, having taught clinics and workshops around the world. Currently, Herwig is on the faculty at William Patterson College in New Jersey. His seventh album as a leader, *The Latin Side of John Coltrane,* emphasizes an affinity for South American idioms. —*Chris Kelsey*

With Every Breath / 1987 / Ken Music ✦✦✦✦

Originally put out as a Sea Breeze LP and then reissued on CD by Ken Music, trombonist Conrad Herwig's debut as a leader finds him matching his wit and creative ability in a quintet with Jim Snidero (who doubles on alto and soprano), pianist Richie Beirach, bassist Ron McClure and drummer Adam Nussbaum. Herwig displays plenty of personality during his solos on five originals and the standard "Alone Together," holding his own with the all-star post-bop group. —*Scott Yanow*

● **New York Hardball** / Jan. 21, 1989-Jan. 22, 1989 / Ken Music ✦✦✦✦✦

Conrad Herwig Quartet. One of the better underpublicized trombonists on the contemporary scene. —*Ron Wynn*

Intimate Conversations / Mar. 11, 1990-Mar. 12, 1990 / Ken Music ✦✦

Throughout this rather dry set of duets (which includes one original and three suites), trombonist Conrad Herwig and pianist Richie Beirach use their knowledge of 20th-century classical music to combine atonal compositions with their improvisational talents. Alhtough one can admire the self-restraint and the musicians' creative use of space, the lack of mood variation results in one's mind wandering. Only a few blasts from Herwig at the beginning of "Opalescent" briefly alter the introspective atmosphere. The net result is a set of advanced background music. —*Scott Yanow*

The Amulet / Apr. 8, 1991-Apr. 9, 1991 / Ken Music ✦✦✦✦

New York Breed / Jan. 4, 1996 / Double-Time ✦✦✦✦

Latin Side of John Coltrane / Mar. 15, 1996-Mar. 16, 1996 / Astor Place ✦✦✦✦

John Coltrane's music has been interpreted many ways since his death in 1967 but rarely in a Latin jazz setting. Trombonist Conrad Herwig, in putting together this project, wisely avoided using any other tenor or soprano saxophonists, instead gathering together several trumpeters, either Ronnie Cuber or Gary Smulyan on baritone, flutist Dave Valentin and a crack Latin rhythm section. By varying the instrumentation and personnel on each selection, Herwig has succeeded in continually casting Coltrane's music in a new light. The opening and closing versions of "Blessing" have Milton Cardona vocalizing a brief prayer. All of the other music (with the exception of Mongo Santamaria's "Afro Blue") consist of 'Trane compositions. Herwig is well showcased, as are trumpeter Brian Lynch and most of the sidemen. The results are quite fresh, often infectious and unpredictable. A fine tribute to the flexibility of John Coltrane's 1960-64 music. —*Scott Yanow*

Eddie Heywood (Edward Heywood, Jr.)

b. Dec. 4, 1915, Atlanta, GA, **d.** Jan. 2, 1989, Miami Beach, FL
Piano / Swing, Pop

The Eddie Heywood Sextet was very popular in the mid-'40s, playing melodic and tightly arranged versions of swing standards. Heywood's father, Eddie Heywood, Sr., was a strong jazz pianist of the 1920s who often accompanied Butterbeans and Susie. He taught piano to his son, who played professionally when he was 14. Heywood, Jr. performed with bands led by Wayman Carver (1932), Clarence Love (1934-37) and, after moving to New York, Benny Carter (1939-40). Heywood led his own group from that period on, backing Billie Holiday on a few occasions starting in 1941. In 1943 Eddie Heywood took several classic solos on a Coleman Hawkins quartet date (most notably "The Man I Love") and put together his first sextet, which also included Doc Cheatham and Vic Dickenson. Their 1944 version of "Begin the Beguine" became a hit and three years of strong success followed. During 1947-50 Heywood was stricken with a partial paralysis of his hands and could not play at all. He made a gradual comeback in the 1950s, mostly performing watered-down commercial music in addition to composing the standard "Canadian Sunset." Despite a second attack of paralysis in the late '60s, Eddie Heywood continued performing into the 1980s. —*Scott Yanow*

Eddie Heywood and His Orchestra / Feb. 19, 1944-Mar. 11, 1944 / Commodore ✦✦✦✦✦

In 1944, pianist Eddie Heywood's sextet, which featured tight arrangements, brief solos and an emphasis on melody, started to catch on big. Their Commodore recordings, particularly a hit version of "Begin the Beguine" (which would later be remade on Decca), made Heywood a household name at the time. All dozen of the group's Commodore performances are on this definitive LP, featuring trumpeter Doc Cheatham, altoist Lem Davis, trombonist Vic Dickenson, bassist Al Lucas and drummer Jack Parker along with the leader. In addition to the catchy rendition of "Beguine," other highlights include "Blue Lou," "I Can't Believe That You're in Love with Me" and "Just You, Just Me." —*Scott Yanow*

John Hicks

b. Dec. 12, 1941, Atlanta, GA
Piano / Post-Bop, Hard Bop

A versatile pianist who is able to retain his own personality whether playing hard bop, free or anything in between, John Hicks has recorded many records throughout his career, both as a leader and as a sideman. After studying music at Lincoln University in Missouri, Hicks attended Berklee and started working as a freelance musician. He moved to New York in 1963 and was a member of Art Blakey's Jazz Messengers (1964-66) and the groups of Betty Carter (1966-68) and Woody Herman (1968-70). He later worked again with Blakey (1973) and Carter (1975-80) in addition to recording with Oliver Lake, Lester Bowie, Charles Tolliver and Chico Freeman (1978-79). From the early '80s on, Hicks has led his own trio and worked regularly with David Murray, Arthur Blythe, Pharoah Sanders and others. As a leader John Hicks has recorded for Strata East, Theresa, Limetree, DIW, Timeless, Red Baron, Concord, Evidence, Novus, Reservoir, Mapleshade and Landmark, among others. —*Scott Yanow*

● **After the Morning** / Jan. 5, 1979-Jan. 6, 1979 / West 54 ✦✦✦✦✦

This first album is a real keeper. Great piano playing throughout. —*Michael G. Nastos*

Some Other Time / Apr. 24, 1981-Aug. 1981 / Evidence ✦✦✦✦

A flexible jazz pianist who can fit in comfortably in settings ranging from bop to fairly free, John Hicks is in excellent form during this straightforward set, which is mostly a trio outing with bassist Walter Booker and drummer Idris Muhammad from 1981. Originally a Theresa LP, the Evidence reissue CD adds "Epistrophy" (which features the same group in 1982), "Night Journey" (the trio in 1984), and "After the Morning," an effective piano duet by John with his wife Olympia Hicks. Two special highlights of the program are John Hicks' solo piano versions of "Ghost of Yesterday" and "Some Other Time." —*Scott Yanow*

In Concert / Aug. 1984 / Evidence ✦✦✦✦

This Evidence CD, which reissues the music on a Theresa LP while adding two "new" selections, has four trio numbers featuring pianist John Hicks with two friends (bassist Walter Booker and drummer Idris Muhammad), an opportunity for vibraphonist Bobby Hutcherson to sit in (on Sonny Rollins' "Paul's Pal"), a Hicks duet with flutist Elise Wood, and a pair of piano solos including a medley of "Some Other Time" and "Some Other Spring." An excellent example of Hicks' playing abilities and an enjoyable set of modern hard bop. —*Scott Yanow*

John Hicks / 1984 / Theresa ✦✦✦

A well-rounded pianist, John Hicks' music on this set ranges from swing (Billy Strayhorn's tender "Star-Crossed Lovers" and "That Ole Devil Called Love") to Walter Davis' hard bop classic "Gypsy Folk Tales" and Hicks' intense "For John Chapman." This LP, which has not yet been reissued on CD, has four trio numbers with vibraphonist Bobby Hutcherson and bassist Walter Booker, a trio of unaccompanied piano solos, and a piano duet version of the leader's "After the Morning" that teams Hicks with his wife Olympia. —*Scott Yanow*

Sketches of Tokyo / Apr. 11, 1985 / DIW ✦✦✦✦

Luminous / Jul. 31, 1985+Sep. 1985 / Evidence ✦✦✦✦

While he is regarded as being among the finest and most intense jazz pianists currently active, John Hicks is also quite versatile. He has a reflective, lyrical bent throughout the 11 songs on this '88 date. Flutist Elise Wood's entrancing, superbly played solos almost demanded that things be less vigorous and more introspective, but the session was not devoid of energy. Hicks offered soothing melodies and warm, lush solos, showing that he could be equally outstanding as a complementary/supporting player. The same held true for bassist Walter Booker, alternating drummers Jimmy Cobb and Alvin Queen, and special guest tenor saxophonist Clifford Jordan. —*Ron Wynn*

Two of a Kind / Jun. 14, 1986-Aug. 4, 1987 / Evidence ✦✦✦

Pianist John Hicks and bassist Ray Drummond had not worked together often when they recorded the 11 tracks on this '80 session. Neither was the consensus star that each is in the '90s, but they were already accomplished soloists. Their union yielded some superb, distinctive playing on this collection of mostly standards. Hicks nicely outlined the basic melodies, then began probing their structure, reworking and restating, finding his own directions and expressing fresh thoughts without distorting the songs. Drummond's heavy yet sometimes barely audible bass lines were both supportive and compelling, at times contrasting Hicks and at other times establishing their own direction. They were a true duo, each player conscious of the other but able to make his own way. —*Ron Wynn*

Eastside Blues / Apr. 8, 1988 / DIW ✦✦✦✦

This album is explosive and substantive, with Curtis Lundy and Victor Lewis. —*Ron Wynn*

Naima's Love Song / Apr. 8, 1988-Apr. 9, 1988 / DIW ✦✦✦✦
Hicks moves into overdrive. Wonderful alto sax from Bobby Watson. —*Ron Wynn*

Power Trio / May 10, 1990 / Novus ✦✦✦✦✦

Is That So? / Jul. 10, 1990 / Timeless ✦✦✦✦✦

Live at Maybeck Recital Hall, Vol. 7 / Aug. 1990 / Concord Jazz ✦✦✦✦✦
Rollicking, thoughtful, unpredictable, and eclectic solo piano. —*Ron Wynn*

Crazy for You / Apr. 3, 1992 / Red Baron ✦✦✦
In the early 1990s, pianist John Hicks participated in many records as a leader for several labels. This trio outing with bassist Wilbert Bascomb, Jr. and drummer Kenny Washington is less substantial than most. Hicks sounds fine on eight Gershwin numbers (including, for no reason at all, two versions apiece of "K-R-A-Z-Y for You" and "I Got Rhythm") that were recorded to tie in with the successful Broadway show *Crazy for You*, but nothing all that surprising or purposeful occurs that justifies yet another recording of these warhorse tunes. —*Scott Yanow*

Friends Old and New / Jan. 14, 1992 / Novus ✦✦✦✦✦
'92 session with pianist John Hicks playing in various combo settings with some excellent musical associates. Bassist Ron Carter, tenor saxophone dynamo Joshua Redman, trumpeter Clark Terry, trombonist Al Grey, and drummer-vocalist Grady Tate are among the friends who join Hicks for some powerhouse numbers. —*Ron Wynn*

Lover Man: Tribute to Billie Holiday / 1993 / Red Baron ✦✦✦
Pianist John Hicks only actually saw Billie Holiday perform once but was enthusiastic about recording this Lady Day tribute. His renditions of ballads and blues (with only "What a Little Moonlight Can Do" being faster than a medium-tempo pace) are tasteful, relaxed, melodic and somewhat predictable. The music (which also features bassist Ray Drummond and drummer Victor Lewis) is consistently excellent but rarely rises above the level of superior background music, lacking the emotional intensity that Holiday could give these songs. The music is solid but not inspired. —*Scott Yanow*

Beyond Expectations / Sep. 1, 1993 / Reservoir ✦✦✦✦

Single Petal of a Rose / 1994 / Mapleshade ✦✦✦✦✦

In the Mix / Nov. 13, 1994 / Landmark ✦✦✦✦

A Piece for My Peace / 1996 / Landmark ✦✦✦✦
Pianist John Hicks has long been a master of the modern mainstream without necessarily blazing any new paths of his own. On this CD he is featured on a pair of solo numbers, a duet with flutist Elise Wood (a sensitive version of Duke Ellington's "Star Crossed Lovers"), a trio rendition (with bassist Curtis Lundy and drummer Cecil Brooks III) of "Mood Swings, a quintet (a blazing version of "My Shining Hour" that has both Bobby Watson and Vincent Herring on altos), and five selections with the full sextet. Four standards follow six obscurities (including Charles Mingus' "Diane"). Hicks, who often shows off the influence of McCoy Tyner's voicings, has never recorded an uninspired record and this one is better than average for him. Due to the variety of moods, instrumental colors and settings, the music is continually interesting and well worth acquiring. —*Scott Yanow*

J.C. Higginbotham (Jay C. Higginbotham)

b. May 11, 1906, Social Circle, GA, d. May 26, 1973, New York, NY
Trombone / New Orleans Jazz, Swing
An extroverted trombonist with a sound of his own, J.C. Higginbotham was heard at his best during the late '20s: early '30s when he was one of the stars with Luis Russell's Orchestra. From that point on he went gradually downhill due to being an alcoholic but he had worthy moments along the way. He started his career playing in territory bands in the Midwest. Higginbotham was with Russell (1928-31) for some classic recordings, including a few sessions backing Louis Armstrong and two songs on which he fronted the orchestra under the title of "J.C. Higginbotham and his Six Hicks." Higginbotham was a featured soloist with the orchestras of Fletcher Henderson, Chick Webb and Benny Carter during the next six years before rejoining Russell's band when it was playing a purely supportive role behind Armstrong (1937-40); he had a few solos on Satch's better records of the period. Having teamed up with Red Allen while with Luis Russell, J.C. happily joined Allen's hot jump band for a long stint (1940-47). Higginbotham spent a few years in obscurity, led his own groups in the mid-'50s and rejoined Allen for a residency at the Metropole that lasted until 1963. He led sessions for Sonet (1962) and Jazzology (1966) but continued to decline until his death. —*Scott Yanow*

Higgy Comes Home / Dec. 1966 / Jazzology ✦✦✦✦
By the time he recorded his only full-length American album as a leader, trombonist J.C. Higginbotham (60 at the time) was a bit past his prime. However, he sounds fairly inspired by the rare opportunity and matches wits with the great tenor Bud Freeman and four lesser-known players (trumpeter Dan Havens, pianist Jimmy Weathers, bassist Bob Rix and drummer Ken Lowenstine). Together they jam ener-

getically on versions of a blues and seven standards, including "Indiana," "Dinah" and "Jingle Bells." This obscure effort is easily recommended to Dixieland and pre-bop collectors. —*Scott Yanow*

Billy Higgins

b. Oct. 11, 1936, Los Angeles, CA
Drums / Hard Bop, Free Jazz
A very adaptable drummer, Billy Higgins came to fame playing with Ornette Coleman's Quartet but proved to be an expert bop player too. He started his career playing R&B and rock in the Los Angeles area, then teamed up with Don Cherry and James Clay in an unrecorded group called the Jazz Messiahs. In the mid-'50s Higgins started rehearsing with Ornette Coleman. He was on Ornette's first records (starting in 1958), came to New York and played with Coleman during 1959-60 before Ed Blackwell (who was actually his predecessor) replaced him. Higgins and Blackwell were both on Coleman's monumental *Free Jazz* album and Higgins would participate in occasional reunions with Ornette through the years. He kept busy during the 1960s, '70s and '80s, freelancing with a countless number of major players, including recordings with Thelonious Monk, Steve Lacy, Sonny Rollins, Lee Morgan, Donald Byrd, Dexter Gordon, Jackie McLean, Hank Mobley, Mal Waldron, Milt Jackson, Art Pepper, Joe Henderson, Pat Metheny and David Murray's big band. From 1966 on Higgins also often played with Cedar Walton's trio and later with the Timeless All-Stars. Based in Los Angeles during most of the 1980s and '90s, Billy Higgins became an inspiration to younger musicians (including the members of the B Sharp Quartet and Black/Note), opening the World Stage as a performance venue and recording label. —*Scott Yanow*

Soweto / Jan. 21, 1979 / Red ✦✦✦✦
Higgins hasn't been a bandleader on many sessions; this date was one of those rare times, as he headed a quartet on this release for the Italian Red label. Higgins played with intelligence, drive and style, keeping things rhythmically tight while principal soloist Bob Berg on tenor saxophone displayed his thick tone and versatility on a program of mainstream and hard bop featuring compositions by Higgins (two of the five), pianist Cedar Walton (two others) and one by Berg himself. This was a welcome entry by a good group that unfortunately didn't work together longer. —*Ron Wynn*

The Soldier / Dec. 3, 1979 / Timeless ✦✦✦
This recording with Cedar Walton (p) presents post-bop standards, well-played. —*Michael G. Nastos*

Bridgework / Jan. 4, 1980-Apr. 23, 1986 / Contemporary ✦✦✦✦
This LP (not yet reissued on CD) features drummer Billy Higgins in a rare leadership role at two unrelated sessions separated by six years. The three titles from 1980 match Higgins with the underrated (and generally underrecorded) but talented tenor James Clay, pianist Cedar Walton and bassist Tony Dumas; they perform Thelonious Monk's "Evidence," a standard, and a Walton tune. The equally rewarding later set (cut in 1986) has Higgins, Walton, tenor saxophonist Harold Land and bassist Buster Williams playing three group originals and a nearly 11-minute rendition of "I Hear a Rhapsody." The music overall is excellent hard bop with some strong moments but no major surprises. —*Scott Yanow*

● **Billy Higgins Quintet** / Apr. 12, 1984-May 29, 1984 / Evidence ✦✦✦✦
Originally released by the tiny Riza label, this CD reissue has one of drummer Billy Higgins' few dates as a leader. Actually, Higgins mostly plays a supportive role as usual, backing saxophonist Gary Bias (heard in top form), pianist William Henderson and bassist Tony Dumas. Bias, Henderson and William James Lee contributed all of the material, which is fresh, generally modal post-bop. Well worth picking up. —*Scott Yanow*

3/4 for Peace / Jan. 27, 1993 / Red ✦✦✦

Once More / May 25, 1980/ Red ✦✦✦

Eddie Higgins

b. Feb. 21, 1932, Cambridge, MA
Piano / Hard Bop, Post-Bop
A solid bop-based pianist, Eddie Higgins has never become a major name but he has been well respected by his fellow musicians for decades. After growing up in New England, he moved to Chicago where he played in all types of situations before settling in to a long stint as the leader of the house trio at the London House (1957-69). Higgins moved back to Massachusetts in 1970 and has freelanced ever since, often accompanying his wife, vocalist Meredith D'Ambrosio, and appearing at jazz parties and festivals. Eddie Higgins has led sessions of his own for Replica (1958), Vee-Jay (1960), Atlantic and more recently Sunnyside; back in 1960 he recorded as a sideman for Vee-Jay with Lee Morgan and Wayne Shorter. —*Scott Yanow*

Eddie Higgins / 1960 / Vee-Jay ✦✦✦✦✦

Soulero / Aug. 25, 1965 / Atlantic ✦✦✦

Pianist Eddie Higgins' third album as a leader (following an obscurity for Replica and a Vee-Jay LP) features his regular Chicago-based trio of the era, a group with bassist Richard Evans and drummer Marshall Thompson. A mainstream pianist with an open ear toward more modern harmonies, Higgins explores such numbers as his "Tango Africaine," "Django," "Beautiful Dreamer" and "Makin' Whoopee" with equal sensitivity and plenty of swing. This worthy LP, unfortunately, will be difficult to find. —*Scott Yanow*

My Time of Day / Oct. 24, 1978-Oct. 25, 1978 / Spinnster ✦✦✦

A relaxed and often thoughtful solo piano date, this LP by Eddie Higgins is high-lighted by a lengthy "West Side Story Medley," three Michel Legrand songs put together in a second medley, and a respectful reworking of Bix Beiderbecke's "In a Mist." Higgins' flexible style has long allowed him to break through many artificial stylistic borders to create accessible music of his own. —*Scott Yanow*

Once in a While / Jun. 6, 1982 / Spinnster ✦✦✦✦

A jam session feel pervades this set. Pianist Eddie Higgins is matched with no fewer than three trumpeters (Pete Minger, who often takes honors, John Swan, and Bill Prince, who doubles on tenor) plus bassist Lew Berryman, drummer Red Hawley and Nancy Weckwerth, who plays French horn on "Stockholm Sweetnin." Minger's work on his ballad feature "Once in a While," which contrasts with the heated "Oleo," is a high point of this long-out-of print, boppish LP. —*Scott Yanow*

By Request / Aug. 5, 1986 / Statiras ✦✦✦✦

Originally a Statiras LP recorded in 1986, when this date was reissued as a CD in 1992, Eddie Higgins went back into the studio and recorded five solos (including his "Magnolia Rag") to increase the release's length. The bulk of the set is the earlier trio date with bassist Milt Hinton and drummer Bobby Rosengarden, which primarily sticks to warhorses that are often requested of Higgins and most other jazz pianists. Highlights include "St. Louis Blues," "A Hundred Years from Today," "Little Rock Getaway," "Indiana" and "Sweet Georgia Brown." A strong all-around set from the underrated mainstream pianist. —*Scott Yanow*

Those Quiet Days / Dec. 21, 1990 / Sunnyside ✦✦✦✦

Nice, sometimes delightful date with pianist Eddie Higgins. Rather than the customary keyboard-bass-drums lineup, he substituted guitarist Kevin Eubanks for a drummer and interacts with bassist Rufus Reid. The results are both satisfactory and revealing; the absence of a percussionist frees everyone to alternate between setting the beat and working off it. —*Ron Wynn*

● **Zoot's Hymns** / Feb. 3, 1994-Feb. 4, 1994 / Sunnyside ✦✦✦✦✦

Pianist Eddie Higgins alternates trio outings (also including bassist Phil Flannigan and drummer Danny Burger) with quartet performances that feature the cool-toned tenor of John Doughten on this consistently swinging set. "Zoot's Hymns" is a Higgins original that sets the tone for the CD (of which many but not all of the songs were formerly performed by Zoot Sims); other highlights include "The Red Door," "In Your Own Sweet Way," "Hi Fly" and "'Tis Autumn." —*Scott Yanow*

In Chicago / Dec. 1, 1995 / Solo Art ✦✦✦

Portrait in Black and White / Mar. 25, 1996-Mar. 26, 1996 / Sunnyside ✦✦✦

Andrew Hill

b. Jun. 30, 1937, Chicago, IL
Piano / Avant-Garde, Post-Bop

Andrew Hill has long been a highly original pianist and composer. Never quite free-form but too advanced to be accepted by bop fans, Hill's complex music has never really caught on, although he is widely respected as an innovative jazz musician. He started on piano when he was 13, studied with the composer Paul Hindemith and throughout the 1950s freelanced in jazz and R&B settings in Chicago. In 1961 Hill moved to New York and became Dinah Washington's accompanist. After a stint with Rahsaan Roland Kirk in 1962, he has mostly worked as a leader. Hill's series of explorative and advanced Blue Note albums (1963-1966) have been reissued in a Mosaic box set; *Point of Departure* (1964) has such sidemen as Kenny Dorham, Eric Dolphy and Joe Henderson and other dates feature John Gilmore, Freddie Hubbard, Sam Rivers and Henderson. Hill also recorded for Blue Note during 1968-70, became an educator and by the mid-'70s was teaching in public schools in California. He has recorded less frequently during the past couple of decades for labels such as Steeple Chase, Freedom, East Wind, Soul Note and Blue Note, but remains a very viable performer who has stuck to his own singular musical vision. —*Scott Yanow*

So in Love / 1955-1956 / Warwick ✦✦✦

★ **Black Fire** / Nov. 8, 1963 / Blue Note ✦✦✦✦✦

Black Fire, Andrew Hill's debut record for Blue Note, was an impressive statement of purpose that retains much of its power decades after its initial release. Hill's music is quite original, building from a hard bop foundation and moving into

uncharted harmonic and rhythmic territory. His compositions and technique take chances; he often sounds restless, searching relentlessly for provocative voicings, rhythms and phrases. *Black Fire* borrows from the avant-garde, but it's not part of it—the structures remain quite similar to bop, and there are distinct melodies. Nevertheless, Hill and his band—comprising tenor saxophonist Joe Henderson, bassist Richard Davis and drummer Roy Haynes—are not content with the limitations of hard bop. Much of the music is informed by implied Afro-Cuban rhythms and modal harmonics, resulting in continually challenging and very rewarding music. Hill's complex chording is thoroughly impressive, and Henderson's bold solos are more adventurous than his previous bop outings would have suggested. Their expertise, along with the nimble, unpredictable rhythm section, help make *Black Fire* a modern jazz classic. —*Stephen Thomas Erlewine*

Smoke Stack / Dec. 13, 1963 / Blue Note ✦✦✦

Trimming away some of the overt Afro-Cuban rhythms that distinguished *Black Fire*, Andrew Hill turned in a dense, cerebral set of adventurous post-bop on his second Blue Note session, *Smoke Stack*. Composed entirely of original Hill compositions, *Smoke Stack* is in the middle ground between hard bop and free jazz—it isn't as loose and dissonant as free, but with its long, winding modal improvisations and hazy song structures, it's a lot less accessible than bop. It also isn't as successful as *Black Fire*, which worked similar territory with edgier results. Part of the problem is that Hill simply meanders throughout most of *Smoke Stack*, wandering off into quietly discordant sections that turn in on themselves. It's subdued music that requires concentration, but doesn't necessarily reward such effort. Even with its faults, *Smoke Stack* is a far from unworthy record—Hill's insular, intellectual style may be occasionally frustrating, but his playing is frequently provocative and challenging, and his backing group of Richard Davis (bass), Eddie Khan (bass) and Roy Haynes (drums) offer sympathetic support. However, it's an album that promises more than it delivers. [Blue Note's CD reissue of *Smoke Stack* included four alternate takes as bonus tracks.] —*Stephen Thomas Erlewine*

☆ **Complete Blue Note Andrew Hill Sessions (1963-66)** / Nov. 8, 1963-Mar. 7, 1966 / Mosaic ✦✦✦✦✦

Andrew Hill was one of the greatest pianists of the '60s, but he never quite received his due. Hill was a skillful, cerebral musician who consciously positioned his music between hard-bop and free. He was at his peak in the mid-'60s, as his playing and composing continued to explore new territory. All of his seminal recordings for Blue Note between 1963 and 1966 are collected on the limited-edition, seven-disc box set *The Complete Blue Note Andrew Hill Sessions (1963-66)*. During those three years, he recorded with an astonishing array of talents, including Eric Dolphy, Freddie Hubbard, Sam Rivers, Joe Henderson, Roy Haynes, Elvin Jones, Tony Williams, Richard Davis, Joe Chambers, John Gilmore and Kenny Dorham. The box features 15 alternate takes, including 10 previously unreleased cuts, and a composition that has never been released. The sheer scope of the set means that it's of interest only to serious jazz collectors, but it proves that Hill was one of the most adventurous and rewarding pianists of the '60s. —*Stephen Thomas Erlewine*

Judgment! / Jan. 8, 1964 / Blue Note ✦✦✦✦✦

Augmenting his rhythm section of bassist Richard Davis and drummer Elvin Jones with vibraphonist Bobby Hutcherson, pianist Andrew Hill records an excellent set of subdued but adventurous post-bop with *Judgment*. Without any horns, the mood of the session is calmer than *Black Fire*, but Hill's compositions take more risks than before. Close listening reveals how he subverts hard bop structure and brings in rhythmic and harmonic elements from modal jazz and the avant-garde. The harmonic structure on each composition is quite complex, fluctuating between dissonant chords and nimble, melodic improvisations. Naturally, Hill's playing shines in this self-created context, but Hutcherson equals the pianist with his complex, provocative solos and unexpected melodic juxtapositions. Jones shifts the rhythms with style and his solos are exceptionally musical, as is Davis' fluid bass. The combination of the band's intricate interplay and the stimulating compositions make *Judgment* another important release from Hill. It may require careful listening, but the results are worth it. —*Stephen Thomas Erlewine*

★ **Point of Departure** / Mar. 31, 1964 / Blue Note ✦✦✦✦✦

The most famous session that pianist Andrew Hill ever led, this avant-garde date matches his distinctive style with quite a cast of players: trumpeter Kenny Dorham, Eric Dolphy (on alto, flute and bass clarinet), tenor saxophonist Joe Henderson, bassist Richard Davis and drummer Tony Williams. The CD reissue adds two "new" alternate takes to the original five-song program, all Hill originals. The complex inside/outside music, which is full of surprising twists, is a classic in its own way and is essential for any representative jazz collection. —*Scott Yanow*

Andrew!!! / Jun. 25, 1964 / Blue Note ✦✦✦✦

Anyone familiar with Andrew Hill's music will find the cover to *Andrew!!!* a little bizarre, to say the least. Hill was one of the most intense and cerebral musicians on Blue Note's roster, incorporating avant-garde and modal techniques into his adventurous post-bop. The cover to *Andrew!!!* apparently is an attempt to humanize Hill—it's a soft-focus close-up of a smiling Andrew Hill, who looks more like a teen idol than a serious jazz musican, and the first-name title is adorned with no less than three exclamation points and a subtitle, "The Music of Andrew Hill," which suggests that it's an album of romantic, easy-listening standards. It's not. *Andrew!!!* is just as adventurous and challenging as any of his other albums, which is to Hill's credit. The pianist leads tenor saxophonist John Gilmore, vibraphonist Bobby Hutcherson, bassist Richard Davis and drummer Joe Chambers through a set of six original songs. Often, the music has a floating, hypnotic quality, which only makes Hill's dissonance, unusual voicings and complex arrangements more compelling than usual. *Andrew!!!*, if anything, is even less accessible than the previous *Point of Departure*, but its restless, searching quality and endlessly provocative music make it just as successful. —*Stephen Thomas Erlewine*

Compulsion / Oct. 8, 1965 / Blue Note ✦✦✦✦
Compulsion continues Andrew Hill's progression, finding the pianist writing more complex compositions and delving even further into the avant garde. Working with a large, percussion-heavy band featuring Freddie Hubbard (trumpet, fluegelhorn), John Gilmore (tenor saxophone, bass clarinet), Cecil McBee (bass), Joe Chambers (drums), Renaud Simmons (conga), Nadi Qamar (percussion) and, for one track, Richard Davis (bass), Hill has created one of his most challenging dates. The extra percussion is largely used for texture, as is the dueling bass on "Premonition," and that's one of the reasons why the record is so interesting—it's a shifting, provocative, occasionally unsettling set of shifting tonal colors. Hill's compositions often seem more like sketches and blueprints instead of full-fledged songs. This, of course, is not a bad thing, since this approach allows the musicians room to improvise and discover evocative new sounds. Overall, *Compulsion* doesn't hold together as well as *Black Fire* or *Point of Departure*, but the session has enough fiery, challenging highlights to make it necessary for Hill fans. —*Stephen Thomas Erlewine*

Grass Roots / Aug. 5, 1968 / Blue Note ✦✦✦✦
Although pianist Andrew Hill's many Blue Note sessions from 1963-66 have been reissued in a limited-edition Mosaic box set, his slightly later projects for the label have not yet come out on CD. One of the best Blue Note albums of 1968 (when the label was starting to seriously decline in quality), this outing matches the unique Hill with tenor saxophonist Booker Ervin, trumpeter Lee Morgan, bassist Ron Carter and drummer Freddie Waits on five of his complex, yet often catchy originals. The themes are sometimes more lyrical and even soulful than one might expect, but the improvisations are as advanced as ever. Well worth searching for. —*Scott Yanow*

Dance with Death / Oct. 11, 1968 / Blue Note ✦✦✦✦
Not released on LP until 1980, this session was probably considered too adventurous for the Blue Note label of 1968, which was far different from the company of a year earlier. The six Hill originals bring out the best in his notable sidemen (trumpeter Charles Tolliver, Joe Farrell doubling on tenor and soprano, bassist Victor Sproles and drummer Billy Higgins), and the music is challenging, falling between advanced hard bop and the avant-garde. Hopefully, the current Blue Note label will eventually release this little-known gem on CD. —*Scott Yanow*

Lift Every Voice / May 16, 1969 / Blue Note ✦✦✦
Andrew Hill incorporates vocals into his concept with ease and skill. —*Ron Wynn*

Invitation / Oct. 17, 1974 / Steeple Chase ✦✦✦
Dashing pieces, first-rate piano. —*Ron Wynn*

Spiral / Dec. 20, 1974+Jan. 20, 1975 / Freedom ✦✦✦✦
After four years mostly off of records, the innovative pianist-composer Andrew Hill re-emerged for this Freedom set, which has since been reissued on CD. The program is split between quintet numbers with altoist Lee Konitz (who doubles on soprano) and trumpeter Ted Curson, and quartet performances that showcase the somewhat forgotten altoist Robin Kenyatta. In addition, "Invitation," the one Hill nonoriginal, is taken as a spontaneous duet with Konitz. Although the music overall does not reach the heights of the pianist's earlier work for Blue Note (or his later sessions), there are enough surprising moments and thought-provoking solos to make this release worth picking up by open-eared listeners. —*Scott Yanow*

Divine Revelation / Jul. 10, 1975 / Steeple Chase ✦✦✦
For this quartet date, the great and innovative pianist/composer Andrew Hill performs "Here's That Rainy Day," his powerful 25-minute opus "Divine Revelation," and three more concise originals with a quartet; an alternate take of "July 10th" was added to the CD reissue. In addition to Hill, bassist Chris White and drummer Leroy Williams, the set features a completely obscure but reasonably talented altoist (Jimmy Vass) who also is heard on soprano and flute and seemed to have really dug into the essence of Andrew Hill's complex but logical music. —*Scott Yanow*

Live at Montreux / Jul. 1975 / Freedom ✦✦✦✦
Beautiful, authoritative solo playing. —*Ron Wynn*

Nefertiti / Jan. 25, 1976 / Inner City ✦✦✦✦
Originally recorded for the Japanese East Wind label and only made available domestically on a 1979 Inner City LP, this trio outing by pianist Andrew Hill also features bassist Richard Davis and drummer Roger Blank. Hill performs six of his unpredictable originals ("Nefertiti" is his tune, not the more famous composition by Wayne Shorter) and, although the music seems slightly more conservative than usual for a Hill set, the music is consistently stimulating; too bad it's so difficult to locate. —*Scott Yanow*

From California with Love / Oct. 12, 1978 / Artists House ✦✦✦✦
One of the major jazz pianists to emerge during the 1960s, Andrew Hill has always performed uncategorizable music that has never been a major commercial success despite (or perhaps because of) its obvious artistic value. The creative pianist is heard on two side-long solo improvisations on this excellent LP, building his solos from fairly simple themes into works of great complexity and individuality. This deluxe LP (which contains an insightful interview and Hill's discography up to that time) is worth the search. —*Scott Yanow*

Faces of Hope / Jun. 13, 1980-Jun. 14, 1980 / Soul Note ✦✦✦✦
Sometimes loping, sometimes soaring solo piano from Andrew Hill, one of several impressive releases he made in the '80s. This time, however, it's neither the arrangements nor the songs that score, but Hill's emphatic execution of them. —*Ron Wynn*

Strange Serenade / Jun. 13, 1980-Jun. 14, 1980 / Soul Note ✦✦✦
Hill enters the '80s on a stirring trio note. —*Ron Wynn*

Shades / Jul. 3, 1986-Jul. 4, 1986 / Soul Note ✦✦✦✦
Pianist Andrew Hill's first recording as a leader in six years was particularly notable for co-starring (and challenging) the underrated tenor Clifford Jordan. The quartet set (with bassist Rufus Reid and drummer Ben Riley) has six of Hill's typically challenging and complex inside/outside originals, a perfect outlet for Jordan and the pianist to interact. Stimulating and unusual music that is difficult to classify as anything but "modern jazz." —*Scott Yanow*

Verona Rag / Jul. 5, 1986 / Soul Note ✦✦✦✦✦
Although Andrew Hill in this solo recital does wonders with the standards "Darn That Dream" and "Afternoon in Paris" and contributes two other superior originals, it is his breakdown of his striding "Verona Rag" that is most fascinating, transforming the piece from a spiritual-type rag into a very advanced improvisation. Hill, a true individualist, embodies the best in creative jazz. —*Scott Yanow*

Eternal Spirit / Jan. 30, 1989-Jan. 31, 1989 / Blue Note ✦✦✦✦✦
Andrew Hill returned to the Blue Note label (where he made many significant releases during 1963-80) for a stimulating quintet date with vibraphonist Bobby Hutcherson, altoist Greg Osby, bassist Rufus Reid and drummer Ben Riley in 1989. The pianist's six originals (which are joined by three alternate takes on the CD), his dense chords behind the other improvisers and his own unpredictable solos are not all overshadowed by his talented sideman, even Osby who is heard in particularly inspired form. There are no weak performances on this superb post-bop effort, Andrew Hill's strongest recording in several years. —*Scott Yanow*

But Not Farewell / Jul. 12, 1990-Sep. 1990 / Blue Note ✦✦✦✦
This is a recommended set of stimulating post-bop jazz. Andrew Hill's highly distinctive piano playing and unusual compositions hint at the past while following their own rules. The feeling of polyrhythms is present in several of Hill's seven compositions on this CD. The tightness of the bass-drum team (Lonnie Plaxico and Cecil Brooks) is quite impressive, as is the blend of Robin Eubanks' warm trombone and Greg Osby's alto. Osby's angular improvisations, which seem out of place in standard bebop, sound perfectly at home in Andrew Hill's music. "Friends" features the altoist's lyricism in a duet with the pianist. Although the final two numbers (including the 13-minute freely improvised "Gone") are solo piano performances, it is the quintet tracks with Osby and Eubanks that are the main reason to acquire this disc. —*Scott Yanow*

Buck Hill (Roger Hill)

b. Feb. 13, 1927, Washington, D.C.
Tenor Saxophone / Hard Bop

Buck Hill received some fame in the 1970s for being a mailman who also plays tenor. He actually began playing professionally in 1943 but always had a day job in Washington, D.C. He recorded with Charlie Byrd (1958-59) but had to wait until the late '70s before getting his own dates. He has since led sessions for Steeple Chase and Muse, displaying a large tone and a swinging style. —*Scott Yanow*

This Is Buck Hill / Mar. 20, 1978 / Steeple Chase ✦✦✦✦
Tenor saxophonist Buck Hill made his debut as a leader with this release, cut when he was already 51. Reissued on CD with an alternate take of "S.M.Y." added, this is a superior quartet set matching Hill with pianist Kenny Barron, bassist Buster Williams and drummer Billy Hart. Hill received some initial publicity because of his

unusual situation, being a mailman during the day and a part-time player at night. However, he certainly sounds like a world-class post-bop player on this date, exploring Williams' blues "Tokudo," two standards ("Yesterdays" and "Oleo"), and three of his own modal yet swinging originals. Recommended. —*Scott Yanow*

● **Scope** / Jul. 8, 1979 / Steeple Chase ✦✦✦✦✦

Buck Hill's second set as a leader, which has been reissued on CD, features the talented tenor (whose longtime day job was being a mailman) on seven of his originals with the same rhythm section that appeared on his debut date: pianist Kenny Barron, bassist Buster Williams and drummer Billy Hart. The tunes are mostly challenging, not being based on bop standards, and clearly inspired the musicians. Hill is heard in top form throughout the underrated but superior session. —*Scott Yanow*

Easy to Love / Jul. 11, 1981–Jul. 12, 1981 / Steeple Chase ✦✦✦✦

Plays Europe / 1982 / Turning Point ✦✦✦✦✦

This live concert in Holland is worth finding. —*Michael G. Nastos*

Capital Hill / Aug. 7, 1989 / Muse ✦✦✦✦

Buck Hill recorded three sets for Steeple Chase during 1978-81, one for a smaller European label and then nothing until 1989. Unlike most of his earlier dates, this Muse CD mostly comprises standards (six out of eight songs) and puts the emphasis on the boppish side of the tenor's style, greatly assisted by pianist Barry Harris, bassist Ray Drummond and drummer Freddie Waits. Hill romps throughout the program, particularly on such numbers as "Tenor Madness," "Stompin' at the Savoy" and "On the Trail." —*Scott Yanow*

The Buck Stops Here / Apr. 13, 1990 / Muse ✦✦✦✦

The Washington D.C. tenor legend with the big buttery sound gives the warhorse "Harlem Nocturne" one of its more inspired readings. Elsewhere on his third Muse outing he shares the solo spotlight with the rarely recorded Johnny Coles, who seldom plays a superfluous note on his warm-voiced fluegelhorn. This is a nicely balanced set of pretty ballads and jaunty originals like Cole's infectious "Wip Wop." —*Les Line*

I'm Beginning to See the Light / Jun. 12, 1991 / Muse ✦✦✦

The latest entry from this mailman turned jazz soloist. Hill's style has soul-jazz seasoning and a bluesy bite. —*Ron Wynn*

Impulse / Jul. 24, 1992 / Muse ✦✦✦✦✦

On Buck Hill's fourth release for Muse, the veteran tenor saxophonist is heard in peak form. This particularly well-rounded set has many high points, including a hard-charging "Blues in the Closet," a couple of rare workouts for Hill's mellow-toned clarinet and a bright rendition of "Sweet Georgia Brown." However, the high point of the quartet date (which also features fine supportive work from pianist Jon Ozmont, bassist Carroll Dashiell and drummer Warren Schadd) is Hill's caressing of the beautiful McCoy Tyner melody "You Taught My Heart to Sing," a song that deserves to become a standard based on this rendition alone. —*Scott Yanow*

Impressions / Mar. 28, 1995 / Steeple Chase ✦✦✦

Teddy Hill

b. Dec. 7, 1909, Birmingham, AL, **d.** May 19, 1978, Cleveland, OH
Leader, Tenor Saxophone / Swing

Though he led a successful big band throughout the 1930s, Teddy Hill is best remembered for managing Minton's Playhouse in Harlem, a nightclub where experimental jam sessions eventually led to the birth of the then-current *lingua franca* of jazz, bebop. Prior to that, his musical career began after moving to New York in 1927, where he joined George Howe's band (which become Luis Russell's within months), staying until 1931. He started his own band in 1934, attracting such sidemen as Roy Eldridge, Chu Berry, Dicky Wells, Bill Coleman and Dizzy Gillespie (who recorded his first solos while with Hill). The band played at the Savoy Ballroom regularly and toured England and France in the summer of 1937, but by 1940, Hill had left the band business in order to manage Minton's. There, such players as Gillespie, Berry, Charlie Christian, Jimmy Blanton, Thelonious Monk and Kenny Clarke jammed after their regular gigs until past the wee hours, working out advanced harmonic innovations. (Indeed, one of the jams recorded by fan Jerry Newman was given the title "Up on Teddy's Hill"). The importance of Minton's waned after World War II, though, and when it discontinued its music policy in 1969, Hill became manager of the Baron Lounge. —*Richard S. Ginell*

● **Dance with His NBC Orchestra** / Feb. 26, 1935-May 1, 1935 / Jazz Archives ✦✦✦✦✦

It would not be an exaggeration to call this French CD "definitive" of Teddy Hill's band, since it includes all 26 of his orchestra's recordings. Hill led an excellent big band during 1935-37 that, although overshadowed by its competitors, featured such major soloists as trumpeters Roy Eldridge, Frankie Newton and Dizzy Gillespie (heard on his very first recording date), trombonist Dicky Wells, and ten-

orman Chu Berry, among others. Although trumpeter Bill Dillard takes nine unfortunate ballad vocals, the other selections are excellent examples of no-nonsense swing. Highlights include "Lookie, Lookie, Lookie, Here Comes Cookie," "Uptown Rhapsody," "At the Rug Cutters' Ball," "China Boy" and "King Porter Stomp." A must for swing collectors. —*Scott Yanow*

Earl Hines

b. Dec. 28, 1903, Dusquesne, PA, **d.** Apr. 22, 1983, Oakland, CA
Piano, Leader, Composer / Classic Jazz, Swing, Big Band

Once called "the first modern jazz pianist," Earl Hines differed from the stride pianists of the 1920s by breaking up the stride rhythms with unusual accents from his left hand. While his right hand often played octaves so as to ring clearly over ensembles, Hines had the trickiest left hand in the business, often suspending time recklessly but without ever losing the beat. One of the all-time great pianists, Hines was a major influence on Teddy Wilson, Jess Stacy, Joe Sullivan, Nat King Cole and even, to an extent, Art Tatum. He was also an underrated composer responsible for "Rosetta," "My Monday Date" and "You Can Depend on Me" among others.

Earl Hines played trumpet briefly as a youth before switching to piano. His first major job was accompanying vocalist Lois Deppe. In 1922, he and his orchestra made their first recordings supporting Deppe. The following year Hines moved to Chicago where he worked with Sammy Stewart and Erskine Tate's Vendome Theatre Orchestra. He started teaming up with Louis Armstrong in 1926 and the two masterful musicians consistently inspired each other. Hines worked briefly in Armstrong's big band (formerly headed by Carroll Dickerson) and they unsuccessfully tried to manage their own club. 1928 was one of Hines' most significant years. He recorded his first ten piano solos including versions of "A Monday Date," "Blues in Thirds" and "57 Varieties." Hines worked much of the year with Jimmy Noone's Apex Club Orchestra and their recordings are also considered classic. Hines cut brilliant (and futuristic) sides with Louis Armstrong's Hot Five, resulting in such timeless gems as "West End Blues," "Fireworks," "Basin Street Blues" and their remarkable trumpet-piano duet "Fireworks." And on his birthday on December 28, Hines debuted with his big band at Chicago's Grand Terrace.

A brilliant ensemble player as well as soloist, Earl Hines would lead big bands for the next 20 years. Among the key players in his band through the 1930s would be trumpeter/vocalist Walter Fuller, Ray Nance on trumpet and violin (prior to joining Duke Ellington), trombonist Trummy Young, tenor saxophonist Budd Johnson, Omer Simeon and Darnell Howard on reeds and arranger Jimmy Mundy. In 1940 Billy Eckstine became the band's popular singer and in 1943 (unfortunately during the musicians' recording strike), Hines welcomed such modernists as Charlie Parker (on tenor), trumpeter Dizzy Gillespie and singer Sarah Vaughan in what was the first bebop orchestra. By the time the strike ended, Eckstine, Parker, Gillespie and Vaughan were gone but tenor Wardell Gray was still around to star with the group during 1945-46.

In 1948 the economic situation forced Hines to break up his orchestra. He joined the Louis Armstrong All-Stars but three years of playing second fiddle to his old friend were difficult to take. After leaving Armstrong in 1951, Hines moved to Los Angeles and later San Francisco, heading a Dixieland band. Although his style was much more modern, Hines kept the group working throughout the 1950s, at times featuring Muggsy Spanier, Jimmy Archey and Darnell Howard. Hines did record on a few occasions but was largely forgotten in the jazz world by the early '60s. Then in 1964 jazz writer Stanley Dance arranged for him to play three concerts at New York's Little Theater, both solo and in a quartet with Budd Johnson. The New York critics were amazed by Hines' continuing creativity and vitality and he had a major comeback that lasted through the rest of his career. Hines travelled the world with his quartet, recorded dozens of albums and remained famous and renowned up until his death at the age of 79. Most of the many recordings from his career are currently available on CD. —*Scott Yanow*

Earl Hines (1928-1932) / Dec. 1928-Jun. 1932 / Classics ✦✦✦✦✦

☆ **Earl Hines** / Feb. 13, 1929-1929 / Raretone ✦✦✦✦✦

Nearly impossible to find now, this LP from the collector's label has all of the music recorded by Earl Hines as a solo pianist (two versions of "Glad Rag Doll") and as a bandleader in 1929. Hines, who would lead orchestras for 20 years, had a particularly strong big band from the start, with George Mitchell and Shirley Clay on trumpets and the reeds of Cecil Irwin. This LP allows one to hear 15 performances of nine songs (there are quite a few very interesting alternate takes) and much of the music is exciting. Pity that the Depression would keep the band out of the studios until 1932, and that this music is not yet available in complete form on CD. —*Scott Yanow*

Swingin' Down / Jul. 1, 1932-Mar. 27, 1933 / Hep ✦✦✦✦

This LP and Hep 1003 contain the entire recorded output of Earl Hines' big band of 1932-33 (including all of the alternate takes), an underrated orchestra. At the time

Hines' featured soloists were trumpeter/singer Walter Fuller, trombonist Trummy Young, and the reeds of Darnell Howard, Omer Simeon and Cecil Irwin, in addition to the brilliant pianist/leader. The fine arrangements (particularly Jimmy Mundy's) show off this band's power. "Blue Drag," "Rosetta," "Cavernism," "Madhouse" and "Swingin' Down" are among the best performances. —*Scott Yanow*

Earl Hines (1932-1934) / Jul. 1932-Mar. 1934 / Classics ✦✦✦✦✦

Deep Forest / Jul. 14, 1932-Oct. 27, 1933 / Hep ✦✦✦✦
This LP and Hep 1018 have all of the recordings of Earl Hines' 1932-33 orchestra (including the many alternate takes). This often overlooked big band featured strong and swinging arrangements (particularly those of Jimmy Mundy) along with fine solos from trumpeter Walter Fuller, trombonist Trummy Young (who joined in mid-1933) and the reeds of Omer Simeon, Cecil Irwin and Darnell Howard. Both of these LPs are well worth searching out, for they offer fine examples of early swing and the sparkling virtuosity of Hines' piano. —*Scott Yanow*

Harlem Lament / Feb. 13, 1933-Mar. 7, 1938 / Portrait ✦✦✦
This excellent LP (which unaccountably leaves out the recording dates of its 16 selections) features the best recordings by Earl Hines' Orchestra during 1932-34 (prior to signing with Decca) and 1937-38. Highlights include the initial version of "Rosetta," such Jimmy Mundy charts as "Cavernism" and "Madhouse," a small-group romp on "Honeysuckle Rose" and early examples of Ray Nance's trumpet on the later tracks. Throughout, the music consistently swings hard and the leader's brilliant piano is a constant joy. —*Scott Yanow*

Earl Hines (1934-1937) / Sep. 1934-Feb. 1937 / Classics ✦✦✦✦

Earl Hines & His Orchestra 1936, 1938 & 1940 / 1936-May 1, 1941 / Alamac ✦✦✦
Sometimes releases from low-budget labels include some very rewarding music. This LP from the 1970s by the long-defunct Alamac label features Earl Hines' only recordings from 1936 (solo piano workouts on "Avalon" and "I Surrender Dear"), two numbers from a radio broadcast from his 1938 big band, guest appearances in 1941 with Henry Levine's Barefoot Dixieland Philharmonic and six numbers that catch his 1940 orchestra live. The recording quality is streaky, but collectors will want this valuable set. —*Scott Yanow*

Earl Hines (1937-1939) / Feb. 10, 1937-Oct. 6, 1939 / Classics ✦✦✦✦✦

Earl Hines (1939-1940) / Oct. 6, 1939-Dec. 2, 1940 / Classics ✦✦✦✦✦

● **Piano Man** / Jul. 12, 1939 Mar. 19, 1942 / Bluebird ✦✦✦✦✦
This sampler of Earl Hines' Bluebird recordings features five brilliant piano solos from the often-breathtaking pianist, "Blues in Thirds" by Sidney Bechet's Trio with Hines and 16 of the better performances from his big band of 1939-42. An excellent purchase for those not familiar with Hines' big-band days, this CD includes such classics as "Piano Man," "Boogie Woogie on St. Louis Blues" and "Jelly Jelly" along with many hot swinging performances from this very underrated orchestra. —*Scott Yanow*

☆ **The Indispensable Earl Hines, Vol. 1 & 2** / Jul. 12, 1939-Dec. 2, 1940 / RCA ✦✦✦✦✦
The best way to acquire the 1939-45 recordings of Earl Hines' exciting big band is to somehow get the two double LPs released by French RCA, for they include all of their performances plus the alternate takes. The first set is highlighted by "Indiana," "Piano Man," "Riff Medley," two takes of "Boogie Woogie on St. Louis Blues," two versions of "Tantalizing a Cuban" and three typically remarkable Hines solo piano performances. Hard-swinging music from one of the swing era's great orchestras. —*Scott Yanow*

☆ **The Indispensable Earl Hines, Vol. 3 & 4** / Oct. 21, 1939-Jan. 12, 1945 / RCA ✦✦✦✦✦
The second of two "complete" two-fers from French RCA in their sadly discontinued *Jazz Tribune* series starts off with two alternate versions of Hines' piano solos and then includes all of his orchestra's recordings from Dec. 1940 through 1942 plus two numbers from 1945 and four more Hines solos. During this period, with Budd Johnson and Franz Jackson starred on tenor and although many of the musicians were lesser-known players (other than the increasingly popular vocalist Billy Eckstine), the orchestra was one of the top swing big bands around. High points include the piano solos, "Jelly Jelly" (Eckstine's first hit), "Windy City Jive," "The Father Jumps" and "Second Balcony Jump." This highly recommended set has unfortunately become difficult to find. —*Scott Yanow*

And the Duke's Men / May 16, 1944-May 14, 1947 / Delmark ✦✦✦
This very interesting Delmark CD has formerly rare selections from three different groups in the mid-'40s. Pianist Earl Hines heads a septet that also features trumpeter Ray Nance, altoist Johnny Hodges, Flip Phillips on tenor and vocalist Betty Roche. Drummer Sonny Greer leads a group of Ellingtonians that includes cornetist Rex Stewart, clarinetist Jimmy Hamilton, trombonist Lawrence Brown and baritonist Harry Carney, and high-note trumpet wiz Cat Anderson is at the helm of a

competent (if somewhat anonymous) big band. All of this music is essentially swing with bop overtones and the 15 performances (originally on the Apollo label) are quite enjoyable. —*Scott Yanow*

Earl Hines / Nov. 4, 1949-Nov. 6, 1949 / GNP ✦✦✦
Pianist Earl Hines visited Paris with the Louis Armstrong Quintet and recorded performances (last available on this LP) with a quintet that included trumpeter Buck Clayton, clarinetist Barney Bigard, bassist Arvell Shaw and drummer Wallace Bishop; in addition, the 14 selections include three piano solos. The music overall is somewhere between Dixieland and swing, mainstream pre-bop jazz that swings easily if in this case a bit predictably. —*Scott Yanow*

Varieties / Dec. 15, 1952-Aug. 21, 1954 / Xanadu ✦✦✦
This Xanadu LP features two very different Earl Hines sessions from the mid-to-early '50s, shortly after leaving the Louis Armstrong All-Stars. Hines is heard on an interesting trio set in which he takes four vocals, switches to celeste on "If I Had You" and romps on "Humoresque." The flip side finds him heading an unusual band with three horns (trumpeter Jonah Jones, trombonist Bennie Green and Aaron Sachs on tenor and clarinet) and three vocalists (the forgotten Lonnie Satin, Helen Merrill on her recorded debut and Etta Jones); Hines himself chips in on "Ella's Fella." It's not essential but a very musical and somewhat unique set. —*Scott Yanow*

Earl Hines at Club Hangover, Vol. 5 / Sep. 10, 1955-Sep. 24, 1955 / Storyville ✦✦
During the mid-'50s the classic jazz pianist Earl Hines, who was considered a very modern player in the '20s and' 30s, was reduced to playing in Dixieland bands in San Francisco so as to earn a living. Fortunately, his groups still featured talented sidemen (on this LP he has trumpeter Marty Marsala, trombonist Jimmy Archey and clarinetist Darnell Howard) and plenty of drive, even if the repertoire (which in this case included "Darktown Strutters Ball," "Ballin' the Jack" and "St. James Infirmary") was uninspired and predictable. Dixieland fans will enjoy this set more than most Hines collectors. —*Scott Yanow*

Another Monday Date / Nov. 1955-Dec. 1956 / Prestige ✦✦✦✦
Two of pianist Earl Hines' finest recordings sessions of the 1950s are included on this CD. One is a tribute to Fats Waller on which Hines (with guitarist Eddie Duran, bassist Dean Reilly and drummer Earl Watkins) explores songs associated with Waller. The other date is Hines' only solo session of the decade and features him playing his own compositions (including "Everything Depends on You," "You Can Depend on Me," "Piano Man" and "My Monday Date") along with "Am I Too Late?" During the 1950s, Hines was somewhat forgotten in jazz, reduced to playing Dixieland dates, so this two-fer is far superior to his other sessions prior to his "comeback" of 1964. —*Scott Yanow*

Earl Fatha Hines and His All Stars, Vol. 2 / 1957-1958 / GNP ✦✦
On the second of two LPs featuring the great pianist Earl Hines with a Dixieland band, it seems strange to hear Hines play such warhorses as "High Society," "That's a Plenty" and "Royal Garden Blues," but the power and enthusiasm of the frequently riotous front line (cornetist Muggsy Spanier, trombonist Jimmy Archey and clarinetist Darnell Howard) causes the music to be quite exciting rather than routine. It's recommended more for Spanier fans than for Hines collectors. —*Scott Yanow*

Earl Fatha Hines and His All-Stars, Vol. 1 / 1957-1958 / GNP ✦✦
Spirited and generally high-powered Dixieland is the order of the day on this first of two LPs. The early modern pianist Earl Hines is a bit out of place in this setting but does his best to fit in with the dominating cornetist Muggsy Spanier, trombonist Jimmy Archey and the hyper clarinet of Darnell Howard. The repertoire is somewhat predictable as are the solos, but the front line's enthusiasm carries the day. —*Scott Yanow*

Earl's Backroom and Cozy's Caravan / Feb. 3, 1958 / Felsted ✦✦✦
This LP of material originally recorded by Stanley Dance in 1958 features quite a few obscure—but talented—players. On half of the program, the Earl Hines Quartet showcases the great pianist (who was in a long period of critical neglect) and the forgotten tenor and baritonist Curtis Lowe. The other session has drummer Cozy Cole leading a group of complete unknowns: trumpeter Lou Jones, Phatz Morris on the unusual double of trombone and harmonica, tenor saxophonist Boe McCain, pianist June Cole, guitarist Dicky Thompson and bassist Pete Compo. They come up with interesting ideas on a blues, "Caravan" and "Margie." —*Scott Yanow*

A Monday Date / Sep. 7, 1961-Sep. 8, 1961 / Original Jazz Classics ✦✦✦
Earl Hines, one of jazz's greatest pianists, was a modern stylist who broke up the usual stride piano pattern of the 1920s with unexpected accents and an uncanny ability to play successfully with time; he had the trickiest left hand in the business. After his orchestra disbanded in 1947 and he spent a few unfulfilling years as a sideman with the Louis Armstrong All-Stars, Hines entered a decade of critical neglect and indifference in which his talents were fairly well forgotten; he found himself playing Dixieland in San Francisco for several years. This particular CD is

a decent Dixieland set with trumpeter Eddie Smith, trombonist Jimmy Archey and clarinetist Darnell Howard. Still, Hines' abilities are somewhat wasted on tunes such as "Bill Bailey," "Yes Sir, That's My Baby" and "Clarinet Marmalade." His renaissance was still three years in the future. —*Scott Yanow*

The Legendary Little Theater Concert / Mar. 7, 1964 / Muse ✦✦✦✦
The great pianist Earl Hines had been fairly well forgotten by the jazz establishment at the time of this concert, relegated to playing Dixieland in San Francisco. However this appearance by his quartet (with bassist Ahmed Abdul-Malik, drummer Oliver Jackson and, on three cuts, tenor saxophonist Budd Johnson) caught the attention of New York critics and suddenly Hines was rediscovered and a hot item again. The momentum would last throughout the remainder of his life and he would never be taken for granted again. Some of the music from his *Little Theater Concert* was issued at the time by Contact, but this two-LP set contains "new" material including five medleys and fresh versions of "Stealin' Apples" and "Rosetta." Hines would record many sets during the next decade that were superior to this one, but this historic gig made them all possible. —*Scott Yanow*

Spontaneous Explorations / Mar. 7, 1964-Jan. 17, 1966 / Contact ✦✦✦✦✦
This two-CD set contains a pair of very exciting sessions by the great pianist Earl Hines. The earlier set, recorded the same day as his historic "comeback" concert at the Little Theater, was Hines' first solo session since 1956 and is full of stunning performances. The later session finds Hines, a veteran of the 1920s, sounding quite comfortable in a trio with two young modernists: bassist Richard Davis and drummer Elvin Jones. The pianist, in fact, sounds quite youthful throughout these classic recordings, taking wild chances and constantly pushing himself. —*Scott Yanow*

Linger Awhile [1964] / Nov. 5, 1964-Nov. 6, 1964 / Bluebird ✦✦✦
After the success of his Little Theater concert earlier in 1964, Earl Hines was suddenly a hot property; he would record frequently during the next decade and practically all of his recordings are worth getting. This CD is a bit unusual, for Hines (usually heard with a trio or solo) leads a quintet also featuring Ray Nance (for four selections) on cornet and violin and Hines' longtime friend Budd Johnson on tenor, soprano and baritone saxophones. The original 12 selections are augmented by six alternate takes and the results are melodic, swinging and quite enjoyable. —*Scott Yanow*

The New Earl Hines Trio / Nov. 9, 1964-Nov. 10, 1964 / Columbia ✦✦
A relaxed and at times lazy set by pianist Earl Hines and his 1964 trio with bassist Ahmed Abdul Malik and drummer Oliver Jackson, the overly concise performances (only one of the dozen songs is over four minutes) contain no real surprises. Hines takes a few pleasing (but forgettable) vocals and since he recorded so frequently during the 1964-77 period, there are many better sets to acquire before this okay LP. —*Scott Yanow*

Earl Hines & Roy Eldridge at the Village Vanguard / Mar. 14, 1965 / Xanadu ✦✦✦
Pianist Earl Hines and trumpeter Roy Eldridge only actually play together on "Blue Moon," but both are in fine form. Hines dominates a couple of lengthy medleys and Eldridge really digs into a nearly 11-minute blues in which he is accompanied by just bass and drums; he is also inspired on a briefer "I Can't Get Started." This LP is worth acquiring, even if Hines and Eldridge barely meet. —*Scott Yanow*

Grand Reunion / Mar. 14, 1965 / Verve ✦✦✦✦
For a session at the Village Vanguard, pianist Earl Hines and his trio were joined part of the time by the great tenor Coleman Hawkins and trumpeter Roy Eldridge. But on this LP, the three giants only actually play together on a fine version of "Take the 'A' Train." Eldridge has "The Man I Love" and "Undecided" as his features (Hines is absent on the latter), Hawkins gets to roar on "Sweet Georgia Brown" and Hines and his trio play a lengthy "Grand Terrace Medley." The music is excellent but not as explosive as one might expect from these competitive players. —*Scott Yanow*

Reunion in Brussels / Mar. 17, 1965 / Red Baron ✦✦✦
The "reunion" on this CD is between pianist Earl Hines and drummer Wallace Bishop who had played with Hines' big band over 20 years earlier. With bassist Rolland Haynes completing the trio, Hines is in good form on a variety of standards (including three medleys), performing a typical mid-'60s set of melodic—but occasionally unpredictable—jazz, one of the many enjoyable examples of his talents currently available. —*Scott Yanow*

Blues in Thirds / Apr. 20, 1965 / Black Lion ✦✦✦✦✦
Earl Hines' solo piano sessions were always a joy. Freed from having to keep a steady rhythm to accommodate a bassist and a drummer, Hines was able to take wild chances with time, with his left hand playing broken patterns rather than sticking to a steady stride. This Black Lion CD augments the eight selections originally released on an LP with two alternate takes and "Black Lion Blues." Hines made many exciting recordings during 1964-77; this set is a good place to start in exploring his frequently dazzling playing. —*Scott Yanow*

Hines (1965) / Apr. 20, 1965 / Master Jazz ✦✦✦✦
Recorded the same day as the CD *Blues in Thirds*, this LP finds Earl Hines in excellent and frequently exciting form playing six standards and two originals as unaccompanied piano solos. Hines was one of the giants and most of his recordings are worth acquiring. —*Scott Yanow*

Live: Aalborg Denmark 1965 / Apr. 22, 1965 / Storyville ✦✦✦
This 1994 CD comprises a previously unreleased trio set by pianist Earl Hines, recorded during a European tour. The music is actually fairly average for Hines at the time, but that means that for most other pianists, it would be considered wondrous. Given steady support by bassist Morten Hansen and drummer Jorgen Kureer, Hines runs through his usual repertoire, including three medleys (one of which comprises Fats Waller-associated songs), "Perdido," "Black Coffee," and Hines' long showcase on "Boogie Woogie on St. Louis Blues." Enjoyable music, if not essential. —*Scott Yanow*

Paris Session / May 27, 1965 / Ducretet Thompson ✦✦✦✦✦
After being somewhat neglected during the 1950s (Hines did not have the opportunity to record any solo piano sets during 1957-63), his rediscovery in 1964 gave the veteran pianist a remarkable renaissance that lasted until his death in 1983. *Paris Session* was his third solo album in less than six weeks but this LP holds its own with his other recordings of the period. Hines sounds quite joyous playing nine standards and his "Sixty Five Foubourg," displaying his distinctive style and chance-taking approach. —*Scott Yanow*

At the Village Vanguard / Jun. 29, 1965-Jun. 30, 1965 / Columbia ✦✦✦
Recorded one year after his "comeback" began, pianist Earl Hines is featured on this live session with his quartet, which at the time featured bassist Gene Ramey, drummer Eddie Locke and on five of the nine selections, the tenor and soprano of Budd Johnson. The tunes are superior and these versions of "Cavernism," "Rosetta" and "Tea for Two" are high points. Most of Hines' post-1964 output is quite enjoyable and this LP is no exception. —*Scott Yanow*

Blues So Low / 1966 / Stash ✦✦
Considering that this is an Earl Hines solo set, it is surprising how routine the music is. Hines performs far too many medleys with unrelated songs and odd song quotes for this to be considered one of his great sessions. A Fats Waller medley is eventful and a collage titled "The Blues and Other Folks," for no particular reason, concludes with a ten-minute version of "Sweet Lorraine." In general, this is a rather trivial performance, with its few inspired moments not occurring often enough to justify its purchase. —*Scott Yanow*

Once Upon a Time / Jan. 10, 1966-Jan. 11, 1966 / Impulse! ✦✦✦
For reasons that are unclear, this LP reissue of an Impulse set drops one of the seven songs ("Black and Tan Fantasy") from the program, reducing the playing time down to a mere 29 minutes. But if one finds this LP at a budget price, it is worth picking up, for the great pianist Earl Hines is featured on three selections with many of the members of the Duke Ellington Orchestra (including on the exciting "Once Upon a Time" and "Cotton Tail"), in a quartet featuring Jimmy Hamilton and with a nonet that also includes clarinetist Pee Wee Russell along with some Ellingtonians. Great music, lousy packaging. —*Scott Yanow*

Dinah / Apr. 29, 1966 / RCA ✦✦✦
This excellent LP finds the great pianist Earl Hines performing solo versions of such superior standards as "Dinah," "Rose Room" (heard in two versions), "Blue Skies" and his own "Blues in Thirds." Hines, who loved to break up the rhythms and take wild chances with time, was generally at his best when performing solo and this set is an example of his pianistic mastery. —*Scott Yanow*

Blues & Things / Jul. 19, 1967 / New World ✦✦✦✦
Originally the initial release from the Master Jazz label, this fine session was reissued on a New World CD in 1997. Pianist Earl Hines and singer Jimmy Rushing had crossed paths many times through the years, but this was their first joint recording; in addition, this was the first official recording by Hines' 1967-69 quartet, a unit also including Budd Johnson on tenor and soprano, bassist Bill Pemberton and drummer Oliver Jackson. Although getting co-billing, Rushing was really a guest on the date, appearing on just four of the nine numbers. Although he sounds a little raspy on "Exactly Like You," Rushing is otherwise in prime form, also singing "Am I Blue," "Save It Pretty Mama" and a rocking "St. Louis Blues." Hines is typically brilliant on his "One Night in Trinidad" and rollicking on the multi-key "Changin' the Blues," while the underrated Johnson shows just how distinctive he was on both of his horns. Recommended. —*Scott Yanow*

Boogie Woogie on St. Louis Blues / 1969 / Prestige ✦✦✦
Pianist Earl Hines loved to play medleys and there are three included on this LP, but they vary in quality. The *Showboat* and *West Side Story* medleys have their moments, even if the fusing together of "Manhattan" and "Slaughter on Tenth Avenue" does not work as well. The program also includes the umpteenth version of Hines' 1939 hit "Boogie Woogie on St. Louis Blues." This material, unreleased until

1982, does not add much to the legacy of Earl Hines but his fans will find enough magic in this music to justify its purchase. —*Scott Yanow*

Earl Hines at Home / 1969 / Delmark ✦✦✦

This interesting solo CD features the great pianist Earl Hines performing four of his lesser-known compositions ("Love at Night Is out of Sight," "Minor Nothing," "Moon Mare" and "The Cannery Walk") in addition to two standards and a vocal version of "It Happens to Be Me." For most pianists, this set would be one of the high points of their career but Hines recorded so many superb albums during the 1964-77 period that this fine date is only average for him. —*Scott Yanow*

☆ **The Quintessential Recording Session** / Mar. 15, 1970 / Halcyon ✦✦✦✦✦

In 1970, Earl Hines was persuaded to do new versions of the eight solo performances that he had recorded at the beginning of his career, 42 years earlier. Some of these songs (most notably "Chimes in Blues," "Chicago High Life" and "Panther Rag") he had rarely played since the 1920s but, after a quick listen to the original recordings, he came up with new and exciting interpretations. This LP contains one of Earl Hines' finest recordings of his comeback years, although unfortunately it is not yet available on CD. —*Scott Yanow*

Earl Hines and Maxine Sullivan / Nov. 1970 / Chiaroscuro ✦✦✦

Fatha and His Flock on Tour / Nov. 1970 / MPS ✦✦✦

This somewhat obscure MPS LP features pianist Earl Hines' working band of 1970. Most notable is singer Marva Josie's effective version of "I Just Wanna Make Love to You" that opens the date (although musically, this Chicago electric blues classic is a bit out of place). Josie also pops up on three other songs (including Hines' "Night in Trinidad"), but makes less of an impact on those numbers. Not enough is heard from Haywood Henry (doubling on baritone and clarinet), and the pianist's solos are not as lengthy or explorative as usual. However, there are some bright moments, most notably "Second Balcony Jump" and three solo Hines features. —*Scott Yanow*

It Don't Mean a Thing If it Ain't Got That Swing! / Dec. 15, 1970-Nov. 29, 1972 / Black Lion ✦✦✦✦

This recommended set teams the great pianist Earl Hines with Duke Ellington's longtime tenor saxophonist, Paul Gonsalves, in a quartet. Since Hines mostly recorded in trios and unaccompanied during his last decade, it is particularly enjoyable to hear him interacting with a horn player. The repertoire includes three Duke Ellington songs, "Over the Rainbow," "Moten Swing" and, from 1972, a piano solo version of "Blue Sands." —*Scott Yanow*

Earl Hines Plays Duke Ellington / Jun. 1, 1971-Dec. 10, 1971 / New World ✦✦✦✦✦

During a four-year period, pianist Earl Hines recorded enough of Duke Ellington's compositions to fill up four LPs. This double CD contains 20 of his better performances including both Ellington's better-known standards and a few obscurities (most notably lengthy versions of "The Shepherd" and "Black Butterfly"). The music is satisfying, although one wishes that New World had reissued all of the music from this extensive project on three CDs. —*Scott Yanow*

Hines Does Hoagy / Jul. 18, 1971 / Audiophile ✦✦✦✦✦

Earl Hines pays tribute to composer Hoagy Carmichael on this inventive set of solo piano. High points of this fine LP include a ten-minute version of "Stardust," "Sky-lark" and "Ole Buttermilk Sky." Pity that Hines did not tackle "Riverboat Shuffle" but chose to mostly stick to Carmichael's classic ballads. One of three albums recorded by the great pianist in a two-day period, this is one of about 50 recommended Hines sets. —*Scott Yanow*

My Tribute to Louis / Jul. 18, 1971 / Audiophile ✦✦✦✦✦

Twelve days after Louis Armstrong died, his old friend Earl Hines recorded a solo tribute to the great trumpeter/vocalist. This Audiophile LP, one of three that Hines recorded in a two-day period, features eight songs associated with Satch including "Struttin' with Some Barbecue," "A Kiss to Build a Dream On," "Someday You'll Be Sorry" and two versions of Armstrong's theme "When It's Sleepy Time Down South." This set should be of particular interest to Earl Hines collectors, for the pianist rarely performed most of these songs, and he gives fresh heartfelt renditions to the standards. —*Scott Yanow*

Comes in Handy / Jul. 19, 1971 / Audiophile ✦✦✦✦✦

Earl Hines' third tribute LP to be recorded in a two-day period, this set features five of W.C. Handy's best-known compositions ("St. Louis Blues," "Ole Miss," "Memphis Blues," "Loveless Love" and "Beale Street Blues") along with three unrelated songs of which "For the Past Masters" is the most touching. So many of Hines' solo sessions are superb that is difficult to call any single one definitive, but this is a highly enjoyable and rather emotional set. —*Scott Yanow*

Plays Duke Ellington, Vol. 2 / Dec. 10, 1971+Nov. 27, 1972 / New World ✦✦✦✦

Partners in Jazz / Feb. 14, 1972 / MPS ✦✦✦✦

With Jaki Byard (p). Piano duets from masters of two styles and generations. Definitive. —*Michael G. Nastos*

Hines Plays Hines / Jul. 29, 1972 / Swaggie ✦✦✦✦✦

During 1971-72, Earl Hines recorded entire sets of the compositions of Louis Armstrong, W.C. Handy, Hoagy Carmichael and Duke Ellington; a George Gershwin program was one year in the future. However, one of the most enjoyable of these tributes is this Swaggie LP featuring Hines' own compositions. The ten songs include a few that became standards (most notably "My Monday Date" and "You Can Depend on Me") and some enjoyable lesser-known tunes (such as "When I Dream of You," "Tosca's Dance" and "I Can't Trust Myself Alone"). Hines (who takes a vocal on "So Can I") is in superior form for this brilliant set. —*Scott Yanow*

★ **Tour de Force** / Nov. 22, 1972-Nov. 29, 1972 / Black Lion ✦✦✦✦✦

Pianist Earl Hines is in top form on this brilliant set of solo piano. This CD (which has three previously unreleased performances along with five of the six numbers from its counterpart LP) and *Tour de Force Encore* greatly expand upon the original set. Whether it be "Mack the Knife," "Indian Summer" or "I Never Knew," Hines is near the peak of his creativity on this CD, taking wild chances with time and coming up with fresh new variations on these veteran standards. —*Scott Yanow*

Tour de Force Encore / Nov. 22, 1972-Nov. 29, 1972 / Black Lion ✦✦✦✦✦

The second of two CDs taken from a pair of solo piano sessions (and greatly expanding upon the original LP that came out), this set features the great pianist Earl Hines near the peak of his powers, stretching out on a variety of stimulating standards including "Who's Sorry Now," "I Never Knew," "Stompin' at the Savoy" and "Mack the Knife." Every jazz collection should have at least a few examples of Hines' stimulating and exciting piano; this CD and *Tour de Force* are perfect examples of his virtuosic powers. —*Scott Yanow*

Earl Hines Quartet / 1973 / Chiaroscuro ✦✦✦

This LP has a fairly loose set by pianist Earl Hines in a quartet with guitarist Tiny Grimes, bassist Hank Young and drummer Bert Dahlander. Their version of "Watermelon Man" is a bit lightweight and some of the ballads have been overdone through the years, but these renditions of "Second Balcony Jump," "Memories of You" and "Showboat Medley" are quite enjoyable. It's not essential but also not a bad acquisition. —*Scott Yanow*

An Evening with Earl Hines / 1973 / Chiaroscuro ✦✦✦

This double LP is valuable as documentation of Earl Hines and his band on a typical gig in 1973. Marva Josie has a few vocals and Tiny Grimes contributes some guitar solos but the leader/pianist is easily the main star, romping on such tunes as "Perdido," "Boogie Woogie on the St. Louis Blues" and "Lester Leaps In." Swinging (if not essential) music. —*Scott Yanow*

☆ **Quintessential Continued** / 1973 / Chiaroscuro ✦✦✦✦✦

In 1970 for the *Quintessential* date, Earl Hines was persuaded to revisit his first eight solo recordings, from 1928. For this sequel (last available on LP), he re-recorded some other selections he had originally cut as solos in 1928 ("73 Varieties" which is a remake of "57 Varieties"), 1929 ("Glad Rag Doll") and 1932 ("Down Among the Sheltering Palms" and "Love Me Tonight"). In addition, Hines performs two pieces his '30s big band used to play ("Deep Forest" and "Cavernism") along with the more recent "Another Child." Perhaps it is the joy of rediscovering the older classics, but Earl Hines was in particularly brilliant form for both of the *Quintessential* sessions; hopefully they will be reissued by Chiaroscuro on CD in the near future. —*Scott Yanow*

★ **Live at the New School** / Mar. 1973 / Chiaroscuro ✦✦✦✦✦

Even though it is not yet available on CD, this LP is a first pick because it features pianist Earl Hines at the absolute peak of his powers. Nine years after his renaissance began, Hines seemed to still be getting more daring in his playing. This version of "I've Got the World on a String" is somewhat miraculous (the chances he takes are breathtaking) and the Fats Waller medley (which features six songs) is definitive. The inclusion of "When the Saints Go Marching In" might not have been necessary and "Boogie Woogie on the St. Louis Blues" is a bit exhibitionistic, but those are minor complaints about a definitive and classic session by a true jazz master. —*Scott Yanow*

Earl Hines Plays George Gershwin / Oct. 16, 1973 / Classic Jazz ✦✦✦✦

This excellent two-LP set features the great pianist Earl Hines interpreting ten of George Gershwin's compositions. Highlights of this solo piano session include extensive explorations of "Embraceable You" and "They Can't Take That Away from Me" (both are over ten minutes) and more concise readings of "They All Laughed" and "Love Walked In." Hines recorded so many rewarding records throughout his career that what would be considered "best" for some is merely "good" for him. This set is worth picking up, if it can still be found. —*Scott Yanow*

Swingin' Away / Dec. 5, 1973+Dec. 7, 1973 / Black Lion ✦✦✦
Pianist Earl Hines recorded dozens of sessions during the 1960s and '70s after his rediscovery. This Black Lion CD differs from most in that he utilizes a sextet. In addition to Hines (who consistently takes solo honors), there are some good spots for trumpeter Doc Cheatham (who was soon to be rediscovered himself), Rudy Rutherford (on clarinet, alto and tenor) and guitarist Jack Wilkins. Buck Clayton contributed three obscure tunes to the date but the band sounds more comfortable on such Hines standbys as "You Can Depend on Me" and "Rosetta." Fine small-group swing from the early '70s. —*Scott Yanow*

Piano Solos / Jan. 29, 1974 / LaserLight ✦✦✦✦
The budget label LaserLight has unearthed an excellent set of Earl Hines piano solos recorded ten years after his rediscovery. Hines was one of the true originals, a chance-taking pianist who loved to play with time and always seemed to make it back safely from his breathtaking flights. He stretches out on six standards (including "Once in Awhile," "Wrap Your Troubles in Dreams" and "Don't Take Your Love from Me") and takes a vocal on his composition "So Can I." This is excellent music that is frequently quite exciting. —*Scott Yanow*

Masters of Jazz, Vol. 2 / Mar. 23, 1974-Mar. 24, 1974 / Storyville ✦✦✦✦
Earl Hines, age 68 at the time of this solo set, is in fine form on these six explorations of standards. He really digs into "Over the Rainbow" and "My Shining Hour" (the latter is nearly 11 minutes long) and is in particularly inventive form on "I've Got the World on a String" and "The Devil and the Deep Blue Sea." One of the giants of jazz piano, Earl Hines was still in his prime for this session which was cut 46 years after his first recording as a leader. —*Scott Yanow*

Live at the New School, Vol. 2 / Apr. 15, 1974 / Chiaroscuro ✦✦✦
Not at the same level as his first Chiaroscuro *Live at the New School* LP (which was titled *I've Got the World on a String*), this Earl Hines solo piano LP has two lengthy medleys (one featuring four of his compositions), a fine version of "Japanese Sandman," "Blue Skies" and "Slaughter on 10th Avenue." The music is excellent enough but just not as classic as some of Hines' other solo sets. —*Scott Yanow*

Earl Hines Plays Cole Porter / Apr. 16, 1974 / New World ✦✦✦✦
This CD reissue of an Earl Hines solo piano session originally made for the Australian Swaggie label is a bit unusual. Hines had apparently not played any of the seven songs (which include such standards as "Night and Day," "What Is This Thing Called Love?" and "I Get a Kick out of You") previously, nor would they enter his repertoire after the session. No matter, Hines interprets the compositions as if he had been familiar with them for decades. His chance-taking improvisations have their hair-raising moments (particularly when he suspends time) and are quite exciting. A superb effort by the immortal pianist who at 71 still seemed to be improving. —*Scott Yanow*

West Side Story / Jul. 2, 1974 / Black Lion ✦✦✦✦
This Black Lion CD reissues a somewhat obscure but highly enjoyable Earl Hines piano solo date from the 1974 Montreux Jazz Festival. Hines proves to be in prime form still, whether digging into a *West Side Story* medley, stretching out on "Don't Get Around Much Anymore" or even playing Burt Bacharach's "Close to You." Even at that late stage of his career, Hines constantly took chances and came up with surprising and consistently fresh ideas. This set is easily recommended, as are virtually all of the pianist's unaccompanied solo albums. —*Scott Yanow*

Earl Hines/Budd Johnson / Jul. 16, 1974 / Classic ✦✦✦
Tenor saxophonist Budd Johnson (who on this LP doubles on soprano) played with the great pianist Earl Hines off and on from the mid-'30s up to the late '70s. This excellent quartet session features the band stretching out on six numbers including three standards, a blues and two Johnson pieces. Solid small-group swing from a pair of classic veterans. —*Scott Yanow*

Live at Buffalo / 1976 / Improv ✦✦✦
During the mid- to late '70s Earl Hines utilized the quartet heard on this LP: Rudy Rutherford on reeds, bassist Harley White, drummer Eddie Graham and the singer Marva Josie. This is a fairly typical set by the unit, with an uptempo opener ("Second Balcony Jump"), some Ellington ("Black and Tan Fantasy"), a Rutherford feature on "The Man I Love," a blues ("Melodica Blues"), a jazz version of the current pop tune "Close to You," Josie's vocal on "A Sunday Kind of Love," the millionth remake of "Boogie Woogie on the St. Louis Blues" and Hines' closing theme "It's a Pity to Say Goodnight." It's not essential but a fine document of Earl Hines' last regular working group. —*Scott Yanow*

The Father of Modern Jazz Piano / Sep. 9, 1977-Dec. 30, 1977 / M.F. Productions ✦✦✦✦
This five-LP box set consists of three albums of piano solos by the great Earl Hines and two LPs on which Hines is joined by tenor saxophonist Budd Johnson, bassist Bill Pemberton and drummer Oliver Jackson. This excellent package is generally available at budget prices, and there are many strong performances. In many ways it is definitive, for Hines is heard performing a wide variety of material, including

solo renditions of "The One I Love," "Can't We Talk It Over?" "The Pearls," "Wolverine Blues," "A Monday Date," a lengthy "Blues in Thirds," "You Can Depend on Me" and of course "Boogie Woogie on the St. Louis Blues." The quartet selections are also consistently excellent. —*Scott Yanow*

Lionel Hampton Presents Earl Fatha Hines / Sep. 26, 1977 / Who's Who ✦✦✦
Although they were both active during the same half-century, pianist Earl Hines and vibraphonist Lionel Hampton rarely had the opportunity to play together. This quintet set from 1977 finds the immortal pair joined by bassist Milt Hinton, drummer Grady Tate and Sam Turner on congas, jamming contentedly on standards like Hampton's "Earl's Pearl" and Hines' "One Night in Trinidad." Few surprises occur, but the music swings hard and is quite enjoyable. —*Scott Yanow*

Earl Hines in New Orleans / Nov. 7, 1977 / Chiaroscuro ✦✦✦
Earl Hines' final solo piano record was reissued on CD in 1996 and its original seven selections have been joined by five equally rewarding (and previously unreleased) numbers. 73 at the time, Hines had lost none of the adventure in his playing, as he shows on such tunes as "I'll See You in My Dreams," "Blue Skies," "Diane," and "Wolverine Blues." A half-century after he started making his original impact, Earl Hines was still one of the most exciting pianists in jazz. —*Scott Yanow*

Honor Thy Fatha / 1978 / Drive Archive ✦✦✦
This CD reissues one of pianist Earl Hines' last recordings, a Direct to Disc album done originally for Real Time and formerly titled *Hits I've Missed*. Hines (with backup from bassist Red Callender and drummer Bill Douglass) performs nine songs, some of which were more familiar than others. Certainly Hines was well acquainted with Fats Waller's "Squeeze Me" and "Ain't Misbehavin,'" Duke Ellington's "Sophisticated Lady" and James P. Johnson's "Old Fashioned Love" but he had never recorded "Misty," Horace Silver's "The Preacher" or "Blue Monk" before. The real wild card track was his rendition of "Birdland," with Red Callender switching to tuba. This interesting CD (well-played but not really essential) adds alternate versions of "Birdland" and "Blue Monk" to the original program. —*Scott Yanow*

Terumasa Hino

b. Oct. 25, 1942, Tokyo, Japan
Trumpet, Fluegelhorn / Hard Bop, Fusion
A fine trumpeter influenced by Freddie Hubbard and Miles Davis, Terumasa Hino has long been one of Japan's best jazz musicians. A professional since 1955, Hino has mostly become known to Americans since the 1970s due to his Enja recordings, although some of his albums were made available domestically by Catalyst, Inner City and Blue Note. He moved to the US in 1975, where he worked with Gil Evans, Jackie McLean, Dave Liebman and Elvin Jones. Hino has spent more time in Japan since the early '80s and has recorded in several different styles ranging from straightahead to fusion. —*Scott Yanow*

Vibrations / Nov. 7, 1971 / Enja ✦✦✦

Taro's Mood / Jun. 29, 1973 / Enja ✦✦✦

Double Rainbow / Feb. 19, 1982 / Columbia ✦✦

Bluestruck / Sep. 19, 1989+Sep. 21, 1989 / Blue Note ✦✦✦✦✦
Terumasa Hino's fiery cornet (which is in the tradition of Freddie Hubbard, Lee Morgan and Woody Shaw) may not be highly individual, but his ideas on this Blue Note CD are creative. Young tenor Rob Scheps is influenced by Joe Henderson although his tone is a bit lighter, and the rhythm section (pianist Onaje Allan Gumbs, either Michel Formanek or Bob Hurst on bass and drummer Victor Lewis) is subtle and tasteful throughout, while altoist Bobby Watson makes a cameo appearance on the final selection. The most distinctive voice is easily guitarist John Scofield, who during this era was quickly emerging as one of the top in his field. All of the tunes on the date are Hino's except Woody Shaw's "Sweet Love of Mine" and "Autumn Leaves." The originals range from the Spanish groove of "Romancero Gitano" to the boppish "Bluestruck" and Terumasa's feature "Alone, Alone and Alone." This may not be an innovative date but neither is it a mere blowing session, for the arrangements of the leader and Don Sickler are very effective in setting off the soloists. Recommended. —*Scott Yanow*

From the Heart / Jan. 17, 1991-Jan. 18, 1991 / Somethin Else'✦✦✦✦
This CD contains the type of music that trumpeter Freddie Hubbard should have been creating during the 1980s and '90s. The originals are both challenging and swinging, Hino utilizes a strong group of individualists and the cornetist's own playing is consistently fiery and explorative, most influenced by Hubbard. Hino uses his regular band of the period (a sextet with tenor saxophonist Roger Byam, guitarist John Hart, pianist Onaje Allan Gumbs, bassist Michael Formanek and drummer Michael Carvin) and their familiarity with each other's playing really shows on the tight but spontaneous session. —*Scott Yanow*

Triple Helix / Apr. 18, 1993 / Enja ✦✦✦

● **Unforgettable** / Apr. 21, 1993-Apr. 22, 1993 / Blue Note ✦✦✦✦✦

Spark / 1994 / Blue Note ✦✦✦✦✦

This is one of trumpeter Terumasa Hino's more interesting releases. Hino often sounds like an exact duplicate of Freddie Hubbard in his prime on the more hard bop-oriented pieces, while mixing in a bit of Miles Davis with Hubbard on the funkier numbers. He is joined by a fine Japanese group (in addition to Jay Hoggard on marimbas and vibes and percussionist Don Alias), which includes two percussionists who keep the rhythms torrid; Hoggard (particularly on marimbas) is a major part of the ensembles. Highlights include memorable versions of Horace Silver's "Song for My Father" (which is given funky Latin rhythms) and Silver's neglected "Calcutta Cutie." Other than the tribute, "Art Blakey," most of the other performances utilize rhythmic vamps while "Suavemente" features the trumpeter's expressive long tones over a synthesizer. Every selection holds one's interest, making this one of Terumasa Hino's most rewarding recordings to date. —*Scott Yanow*

Acoustic Boogie / 1995 / Blue Note ✦✦

One has to wonder what the motivation was behind this record by the Terumasa Hino-Masamui Kikuchi Quintet since there are no liner notes. The rhythm section (which consists of pianist Masamui Kikuchi, bassist James Genus and drummer Billy Kilson) lays down some monotonous and generally quiet grooves on each selection, while occasionally trumpeter Hino, altoist Greg Osby or Kikuchi get around to taking solos. Even for dance music, the results are extremely dull, with no real development or anything approaching excitement occuring. Perhaps this release is meant for the "acid jazz" crowd, but so little happens that one could imagine them falling asleep on the dance floor. —*Scott Yanow*

Milt Hinton

b. Jun. 23, 1910, Vicksburg, MS
Bass / Swing

Bassist Milt Hinton has probably appeared on more records than any other musician in the world and he remains a vital figure in jazz even at the age of 87. He grew up in Chicago and worked with many legendary figures from the late '20s to the mid-'30s, including Freddie Keppard, Jabbo Smith, Tiny Parham (with whom he made his recording debut in 1930), Eddie South, Fate Marable and Zutty Singleton. He was with Cab Calloway's Orchestra and his later small group during 1936-51. Considered the best bassist before the rise of Jimmy Blanton in 1939, Hinton was featured on "Pluckin' the Bass" (1939) and was an ally of Dizzy Gillespie in modernizing Calloway's music.

After leaving Cab, Hinton worked in clubs with Joe Bushkin, had brief stints with Count Basie and Louis Armstrong's All-Stars, and in 1954 became a staff musician at CBS, appearing on a countless number of recordings (jazz and otherwise) during the next 15 years; everything from Jackie Gleason mood music and polka bands to commercials and Buck Clayton jam sessions. By the 1970s Hinton was appearing regularly at jazz parties and festivals and his activities have not slowed down during the past two decades; in 1995 he toured with the Statesmen of Jazz. Although a modern soloist, Hinton has also kept the art of slap bass alive. A very skilled photographer, Hinton has released two books of his candid shots of jazz musicians, including one (*Bass Line*) which has his fascinating memoirs. Milt Hinton has recorded as a leader for Bethlehem, Victor (both in 1955), Famous Door, Black & Blue and Chiaroscuro and as a sideman for virtually every label! —*Scott Yanow*

The Trio / Oct. 17, 1977 / Chiaroscuro ✦✦✦

Although bassist Milt Hinton gets top billing on this album and takes a few solos, pianist Hank Jones is the main soloist and star, with drummer Bobby Rosengarden fine in support. Jones has "Oh What a Beautiful Morning" as a spontaneous solo feature, and other highlights of the good-natured set include "'S'Wonderful," "Mona's Feeling Lonely," "I'll Remember April" and "Hank You, Thank." —*Scott Yanow*

The Judge's Decision / 1984 / Exposure ✦✦✦

For this rather obscure LP, veteran bassist Milt Hinton (74 at the time) teams up with four musicians he considered to be up-and-coming young players: pianist Jay D'Amico, altoist Sam Furnace, tenor saxophonist Mike Walters and drummer Kevin Norton. Although not much has been heard since from Walters and Norton, D'Amico and particularly Furnace have had professional careers. The music ranges from a few originals, including Hinton's "Mona's Feeling Lonely," to four standards, such as "Indiana" and Oscar Pettiford's "Tricotism." Good music with no real surprises. —*Scott Yanow*

Old Man Time / Oct. 3, 1989-Mar. 2, 1989 / Chiaroscuro ✦✦✦✦✦

This double-CD set gave bassist Milt Hinton an opportunity to engage in reunions with many of his old friends from the 1930s. The seven sessions were compiled during a 12-month period and the results are often delightful. The opening "Old Man Time" is sung by Hinton himself, and it is both insightful and humorous. The other highlights include Joe Williams singing "Four or Five Times" (which features some very rare Flip Phillips clarinet), three bass guitar duets with Danny Barker,

appearances by Dizzy Gillespie, Lionel Hampton, Clark Terry, Al Grey, and Ralph Sutton, and the formation of a group called "the Survivors" that has guitarist Al Casey at age 75 being the youngest member; the latter band also includes 85-year-old trumpeter Doc Cheatham, Eddie Barefield, Buddy Tate and even Cab Calloway. A lot of storytelling takes place during the songs and, in addition to the 92 minutes of music, there are two "Jazzspeaks." The 13-minute one features Hinton, Calloway, Cheatham and Barefield reminiscing about their experiences in the early days, while a marvelous 45-minute monologue by the bassist covers most of his long and productive life and is fascinating. Highly recommended. —*Scott Yanow*

Laughing at Life / 1994 / Columbia ✦✦✦✦

Milt Hinton's major label debut as a leader (at age 85), other than a 1955 date for Victor, finds the great bassist utilizing two separate rhythm sections on a variety of standards. In addition to fine solos from pianists Richard Wyands and Derek Smith, there are guest appearances by trumpeter Jon Faddis (who defies his stereotype by sounding closer here to Roy Eldridge than to Dizzy Gillespie) and veteran Harold Ashby, whose warm tenor recalls Ben Webster. Even if Hinton's three vocals are one too many, his singing has its charm. The finale "The Judge and the Jury" adds four other bassists for a very musical tribute to one of the few veterans of the 1920s still to be heard in his prime in the mid-'90s. —*Scott Yanow*

The Trio: 1994 / Jan 14, 1994 / Chiaroscuro ✦✦✦✦

Back to Bass-ics / Sep. 3, 1984 / Progressive ✦✦✦✦

Jutta Hipp

b. Feb. 4, 1925, Leipzig, Germany
Piano / Hard Bop, Cool, Bop

Jutta Hipp had a strangely brief career, dropping out of music altogether shortly after emigrating to the US. She studied painting in Germany and played jazz secretly during World War II. When the Soviets took over East Germany, she fled with her family to Munich. Hipp played locally and in 1952 recorded with Hans Koller. She led her own quintet in Frankfurt in 1953-55 and recorded for several labels, including a session that was later released by Blue Note. Moving to New York in November 1955, Hipp played at the Hickory House for much of the first half of 1956, recording two trio albums for Blue Note. Although originally inspired by Lennie Tristano, she was criticized at the time for being too influenced by Horace Silver; however, a studio album from July 1956 with Zoot Sims finds her showing a fairly original style. Unfortunately, that was her final recording, for Jutta Hipp soon dropped out of music, apparently to return to painting, and little has been heard from her since. —*Scott Yanow*

New Faces—New Sounds from Germany / Apr. 24, 1954 / Blue Note ✦✦✦✦

Jutta Hipp at the Hickory House, Vol. 1 / Apr. 5, 1956 / Blue Note ✦✦✦✦

At the Hickory House is a thoroughly appealing collection of lightly swinging small-combo jazz that draws equally from hard bop and soul-jazz. There's a soulful lilt to Jutta Hipp's playing that keeps it engaging and enjoyable. The rhythm section of Peter Ind (bass) and Ed Thigpen (drums) largely stay out of the way, letting Hipp dictate the tempo and mood of the pieces, and she has a knack for creating infectious, swinging interpretations of jazz and pop standards that are enjoyable and easy to listen to. *Vol. 1* contains such staples as "Dear Old Stockholm," "Billie's Bounce," "Mad About the Boy," "Ain't Misbehavin'" and "These Foolish Things," all of which are performed with verve and style, making the record a wonderful little gem. —*Stephen Thomas Erlewine*

Jutta Hipp at the Hickory House, Vol. 2 / Apr. 5, 1956 / Blue Note ✦✦✦✦

Jutta Hipp at the Hickory House, Vol. 2 has the same infectious spirit and sense of fun as the first volume. Taken from the same date, this ten-track album features such standards as "Moonlight in Vermont," "After Hours," "If I Had You" and "My Heart Stood Still," all of which are given swinging, spirited interpretations by Hipp and her rhythm section of bassist Peter Ind and drummer Ed Thigpen. As with the first volume of *At the Hickory House*, *Vol. 2* is another thoroughly enjoyable set of swinging soul-jazz and should appeal to fans of Horace Silver and the Three Sounds. —*Stephen Thomas Erlewine*

● **Jutta Hipp with Zoot Sims** / Jul. 28, 1956 / Blue Note ✦✦✦✦✦

Jutta Hipp, a talented German pianist, came to the US in the mid-1950s and quickly gained some attention. However, she was soon criticized for sounding too close to Horace Silver and, after recording this final Blue Note album, she gradually dropped out of music. Reissued in 1996 on CD with two extra selections, Hipp's boppish music on the set is very enjoyable and swinging. Oddly enough, she does not sound at all like Silver on the date, making one wonder why she soon left the jazz world. Teamed up with the great tenor Zoot Sims (who dominates the music), the somewhat hesitant trumpeter Jerry Lloyd (who briefly came out of retirement), bassist Ahmed Abdul-Malik and drummer Ed Thigpen, Hipp sounds excellent on a couple of basic originals and such standards as "Violets for Your

Furs," "Almost Like Being in Love" and J.J. Johnson's "Wee Dot." This formerly rare set is well worth picking up by straightahead jazz collectors. —*Scott Yanow*

Hiroshima

f. 1974
Group / World Fusion, Crossover Jazz
Dan Kuramoto (keyboards, sax, flute, shakuhachi), June Okida Kuramoto (koto), and Johnny Mori and Danny Yamamoto (percussion) debuted in 1979 on a self-titled Arista album. After a sophomore work (*Odori*) in 1980, the group signed with Epic and released five albums: *Third Generation* (1983), *Another Place* (1985), *Go* (1987), *East* (1989) and *Providence* (1992). During this period, Hiroshima added bassist Dean Cortez and keyboardist Kimo Cornwell. The band signed with Qwest and released *Hiroshima L.A.* in 1994. —*John Bush*

Hiroshima / 1979 / Arista ✦✦✦

Odori / 1980 / Arista ✦✦

Third Generation / 1983 / Epic ✦✦

Another Place / 1985 / Epic ✦✦
Pseudo-fusion from a sadly popular group. —*Ron Wynn*

Go / 1987 / Epic ✦✦✦
Limited jazz content. —*Ron Wynn*

Ongaku / 1988 / Arista ✦✦
Fusion schlock. —*Ron Wynn*

East / 1989 / Epic ✦✦
At its best, Hiroshima has offered an adventurous and even visionary fusion of jazz, Japanese music, R&B, pop and rock. But sadly, the L.A. band has, since the mid-'80s, failed to live up to its enormous potential and made albums based on commercial considerations more than artistic ones. Focusing on both Asian-influenced pop-jazz and lightweight R&B-pop, Hiroshima generally makes commercial radio airplay its No. 1 goal, takes few risks and delivers one of its weakest, most boring albums ever. While the insistent "Midtown Higashi" packs a bit of a punch and demonstrates the band's strength as composers, most of the other new age-ish instrumentals are nothing more than bloodless, shallow elevator music. And the contrived "urban contemporary" tunes aren't much better. —*Alex Henderson*

Providence / 1992 / Epic ✦✦

L.A. / 1994 / Qwest ✦✦✦
With *L.A.*, Hiroshima once again sells itself short artistically. Except for the riveting "Native Son," Hiroshima plays it safe as usual and avoids anything challenging or adventurous. An excess of production and shortage of improvisation continues to be a definite problem. Nonetheless, *L.A.* isn't a terrible album. In fact, this collection of Asian-flavored pop-jazz instrumentals and relaxed R&B-pop vocals is generally pleasant and likable, and has more heart than the type of drivel dominating 1989's *East*. This CD works well enough as mood music, but the disappointing Hiroshima is capable of more—much more. —*Alex Henderson*

● **The Best of Hiroshima** / 1983-1989 / Epic ✦✦✦✦
The Best of Hiroshima is a ten-track collection that contains a good overview of the fusion group's Epic recordings, including such cuts as "San Say," "One Wish," "Thousand Cranes," "Hawaiian Electric," "Island World," "I Do Remember" and "Time on the Nile." —*Stephen Thomas Erlewine*

Urban World Music / 1996 / Warner Brothers ✦✦✦
Urban World Music captures a revitalized and re-energized Hiroshima, full of new ideas and new ambitions. Although the title suggests that the album is composed of worldbeat explorations, that isn't quite the case. Like any Hiroshima album, *Urban World Music* is filled with fusions, but the music on this particular collection is given a slight, but noticeable, dance-oriented sheen, thanks to producer Robin Millar (who previously worked with Sade and Everything But the Girl). With new lead vocalist Kimaya Sweard in tow, Hiroshima creates a lightly funky sort of jazzy soul numbers, complete with worldbeat flourishes. As always, the gruop has problems writing consistently compelling material, but when they are on, they provide some intriguing sounds and directions. In short, *Urban World Music* suggests more than it delivers, but those suggestions are quite enticing on their own. —*Leo Stanley*

Wishful Thinking / Ampex ✦✦✦

Al Hirt (Alois Maxwell Hirt)

b. Nov. 7, 1922, New Orleans, LA
Trumpet / Dixieland
A virtuoso on the trumpet, Al Hirt is often "overqualified" for the Dixieland and pop music that he performs. He studied classical trumpet at the Cincinnati Conservatory (1940-43) and was influenced by the playing of Harry James. He freelanced

in swing bands (including both Tommy and Jimmy Dorsey and Ray McKinley) before returning to New Orleans in the late '40s and becoming involved in the Dixieland movement. He teamed up with clarinetist Pete Fountain on an occasional basis from 1955 on and became famous by the end of the decade. An outstanding technician with a wide range along with a propensity for playing far too many notes, Hirt had some instrumental pop hits in the 1960s and also recorded swing and country music but mostly stuck to Dixieland in his live performances. He remains a household name although one often feels that he could have done so much more with his talent. Hirt's early Audio Fidelity recordings (1958-60) and collaborations with Fountain are the most rewarding of his career. —*Scott Yanow*

Al Hirt in New Orleans / Dec. 29, 1955 / Coral ✦✦✦✦
Trumpeter Al Hirt's first record as a leader is strictly Dixieland. Hirt was at his best in the mid- to late 1950s before making some very commercial dates. His band of the time (with clarinetist Harry Shields, either Bob Havens or Buddy Castigliola on trombone, pianist Roy Zimmerman, guitarist Joe Capraro, bassist Phil Darois and drummer Paul Edwards) was solid and swinging, while the trumpeter showed off just enough of his technique to make a strong impression. Among the highlights of this excellent LP are "After You've Gone," "Floatin' Down to Cotton Town," "Toot Toot Tootsie Goodbye" and "While We Danced at the Mardi Gras." —*Scott Yanow*

☆ **The Very Best of Al Hirt & Pete Fountain** / 1957 / MGM ✦✦✦✦✦
This is an album that lives up to its name, for both trumpeter Al Hirt and clarinetist Pete Fountain rarely sounded better than they did on this collaboration. With the underrated trombonist Bob Havens, pianist Roy Zimmerman, bassist Bob Coquille and drummer Paul Edwards completing the group, plenty of fireworks are felt. Fountain is very effective switching to tenor on a rollicking "Washington and Lee Swing"; Hirt is exuberant on "South Rampart Street Parade" and "Panama," and each of the dozen selections is full of excitement. The musicians were clearly inspired and rarely sounded more creative. A classic encounter that unfortunately has yet to be reissued on CD. —*Scott Yanow*

Swingin' Dixie, Vol. 3 / 1958 / Audio Fidelity ✦✦✦✦
The third in trumpeter Al Hirt's enjoyable series of Dixieland LPs for Audio Fidelity is the equal of the previous two. Hirt, trombonist Bob Havens, clarinetist Harold Cooper and pianist Ronnie Dupont all take plenty of solo space on the dozen standards. Highlights include "Original Dixieland One Step," "High Society," "Mack the Knife" and "Down by the Riverside," while "Lullaby of Birdland" offers a slight change of pace. Unfortunately, Hirt would soon branch out beyond Dixieland into less interesting (although more lucrative) areas, so his early records (such as this one) are still his best. —*Scott Yanow*

Swingin' Dixie at Dan's Pier 600 in New Orleans, Vol. 1 / 1958 / Audio Fidelity ✦✦✦✦
The first of four Al Hirt Audiophile albums recorded during the same year, this LP finds the trumpeter in prime form before he started making commercial hit records. With trombonist Bob Havens and clarinetist Harold Cooper completing the front line, Hirt runs through an exciting set of Dixieland. This version of "Saints" is quite unusual, for Hirt and his fellow horn players start off trading four-bar phrases and gradually cut it in half again and again until they are trading off every beat. Other highlights include "Tiger Rag," "Fidgety Feet" and "Hindustan." An excellent example of Hirt's Dixieland playing, but, unfortunately, all of his Audio Fidelity releases are long out of print. —*Scott Yanow*

Swingin' Dixie at Dan's Pier 600 in New Orleans, Vol. 2 / 1958 / Audio Fidelity ✦✦✦✦
Trumpeter Al Hirt was heard at his best in the mid- to late 1950s, when his fame was mostly regional. Playing in his native New Orleans, Hirt and his sextet (which includes trombonist Bob Havens and clarinetist Harold Cooper) swing their way through a dozen Dixieland standards on his second of four albums in this series. Hirt's phenomenal technique is clearly in evidence, and he comes up with many exciting ideas on such songs as "Darktown Strutters Ball," "Stumblin'," "Chicago" and "Song of the Wanderer." Worth searching for by Dixieland fans. —*Scott Yanow*

Al (He's the King) Hirt and His Band / Dec. 7, 1960-Dec. 16, 1960 / RCA ✦✦✦
Al Hirt's debut with RCA is generally Dixieland-oriented and much better than what would follow. Hirt is explosive on such numbers as "I Love Paris," "Jazz Me Blues," "Cornet Chop Suey" and "Christopher Columbus," but the renditions are quite brief (all under three minutes) and were clearly recorded with hopes of radio airplay. Trombonist Jack DeLaney and clarinetist Pee Wee Spitelera are fine in a supporting role behind "the King." —*Scott Yanow*

Horn A-Plenty / 1962 / RCA ✦✦✦
Al Hirt sounds fine on this RCA LP, functioning as the dominant soloist while backed by a big band arranged by Billy May. RCA was clearly trying to move Hirt beyond Dixieland, and the virtuoso did his best to respond, although he is (at the most modern) a swing player. The briefness of these performances (only one song barely exceeds three minutes) and the predictability of the charts keep the album

from being too special, although the overall results are pleasing. Among the highlights are "Holiday for Trumpet," "Margie" and "Memories of You." —*Scott Yanow*

Our Man in New Orleans / Sep. 4, 1962-Sep. 5, 1962 / RCA ✦✦✦

Cotton Candy / 1964 / RCA ✦✦✦✦✦

Al Hirt has always seemed a bit overqualified for the music he performs, but his early Dixieland dates have their moments of interest. However, by the early '60s, his career took a much more commercial turn (especially on records), and this LP was one of the low points. Joined by the insipid Anita Kerr Singers and arrangements that would have embarrassed most country-pop singers of the era, Hirt plays consistently corny trumpet on such songs as "Cotton Candy," "Hello Dolly" (a surprisingly weak version), "Walkin' With Mr. Lee" and an unlistenable "12th Street Rag." This album is only worth getting as an example of how bad Al Hirt's taste could be. —*Scott Yanow*

Live at Carnegie Hall / Apr. 22, 1965-Apr. 24, 1965 / RCA ✦✦

By 1965, trumpeter Al Hirt was a commercial success, although from the jazz standpoint most of his output for RCA was becoming increasingly forgettable. Although he was joined by the Gerald Wilson Orchestra for nine of the 13 selections on this live LP, all of the selections (other than a six-minute rendition of "Carnival of Venice") are quite brief, with several under two minutes. Hirt shows off his technique on a variety of showy devices, but every note sounds planned in advance, whether it be "Bye Bye Blues," "Down by the Riverside," or a remake of his hit "Java." —*Scott Yanow*

Super Jazz/Monument / Jan. 12, 1976 / Monument ✦✦✦✦

This double LP features both the Al Hirt and Pete Fountain bands performing live during halftime at the 1976 Super Bowl. Trumpeter Hirt, heard on one of his best recordings in 15 years, leads a sextet featuring longtime clarinetist Pee Wee Spitelera on two lengthy numbers, plus a four-song "Salute to Satchmo." Clarinetist Fountain (at the front of an octet that also stars tenor great Eddie Miller) romps on six swinging numbers, and the two bands jam together on "Perdido," "Basin Street Blues" and "Super Bowl Blues." Dixieland fans will want to pick up this often-overlooked gem. —*Scott Yanow*

● **That's a Plenty** / Mar. 29, 1988-Mar. 31, 1988 / Pro Arte ✦✦✦✦

Trumpeter Al Hirt is represented on relatively few CDs. This particular release finds him heading a septet that also features veteran clarinetist Peanuts Hucko, trombonist James Huggan and keyboardist Dave Zoller. The repertoire is typical Dixieland, along with an occasional swing ballad and a version of Hirt's famous hit "Java." The virtuoso trumpeter, who was 65 at the time, was still in prime form, swinging his way through "That's a Plenty," "Royal Garden Blues," "Bourbon Street Parade" and "The Saints" with flash and excitement. —*Scott Yanow*

Steve Hobbs

b. , Raleigh, NC
Vibes / Hard Bop

One of the more talented vibraphonists to come up in the late '80s, Steve Hobbs' style is bop-based but fairly original. He studied at Berklee, the University of Miami and the University of Northern Colorado in Greeley and freelanced in Denver for six years with such players as Tom Harrell, Joe Bonner, Spike Robinson and Stix Hooper. Hobbs eventually moved back to Raleigh, where he works as an educator but keeps up an active performance schedule. He has thus far recorded as a leader for Cexton, Timeless and Candid. —*Scott Yanow*

Escape / Nov. 11, 1988-Nov. 12, 1988 / Cexton ✦✦✦

Cultural Diversity / Aug. 5, 1991-Aug. 6, 1991 / Timeless ✦✦✦✦

● **Lower East Side** / Jul. 21, 1993-Jul. 22, 1993 / Candid ✦✦✦✦✦

Art Hodes

b. Nov. 14, 1904, Nikoliev, Russia, **d.** Mar. 4, 1993, Harvey, IL
Piano / Dixieland, Blues Jazz

Throughout his long career, Art Hodes was a fighter for traditional jazz, whether through his distinctive piano playing, his writings (which included many articles and liner notes) or his work on radio and educational television. Renowned for the feeling he put into blues, Hodes was particularly effective on uptempo tunes in which his on-the-beat chordings from his left hand could be quite exciting. Born in Russia, he came to America with his family when he was six months old and grew up in Chicago. Hodes had the opportunity to witness Chicago jazz during its prime years in the 1920s and he learned from other pianists. In 1928 he made his recording debut with Wingy Manone but spent most of the 1930s in obscurity in Chicago until he moved to New York in 1938. He played with Joe Marsala and Mezz Mezzrow before forming his own band in 1941. Hodes recorded for Solo Art, his Jazz Record label, Signature, Decca and Black & White during 1939-42, but he made more of an impression with his heated Dixieland recordings for Blue Note

during 1944-45 (all of which have been reissued on a Mosaic box set). During 1943-47 Hodes edited the important magazine *The Jazz Record,* had a radio show and became involved in the moldy fig vs. bebop wars with Leonard Feather and Barry Ulanov; jazz on a whole lost from the latter. In 1950 he returned to Chicago where he remained active locally and made occasional records. Hodes hosted a television series *Jazz Alley* for a time in the 1960s, wrote for *Downbeat* and was a jazz educator. Art Hodes recorded frequently during the 1970s and '80s and was widely recognized as one of the last survivors of Chicago jazz. His later recordings were for such labels as Audiophile, Jazzology, Delmark, Storyville, Euphonic, Muse, Parkwood, Candid and Music & Arts. —*Scott Yanow*

★ **Complete Blue Note Art Hodes Sessions** / Mar. 18, 1944-Dec. 16, 1945 / Mosaic ✦✦✦✦✦

From 1944-45, pianist Art Hodes led nine sessions for Blue Note in addition to being a featured sideman on a quartet date headed by drummer Baby Dodds. This limited edition five-LP box set from Mosaic has all 70 selections, including ten that were previously unissued. Hodes, a veteran of 1920s Chicago who later received recognition for his blues playing, loved playing Dixieland and classic jazz. In settings ranging from a trio to a septet, Hodes inspires and interacts with some of the top trad jazz players of the mid-1940s, including trumpeters Max Kaminsky and (on one session) Wild Bill Davison, trombonists Ray Conniff, Sandy Williams and Vic Dickenson, clarinetists Rod Cless, Edmond Hall, Mezz Mezzrow, Omer Simeon and Albert Nicholas, the great soprano innovator Sidney Bechet, bassists Bob Haggart, Israel Crosby, Pops Foster and Wellman Braud, and drummers Dodds, Danny Alvin and Fred Moore, among others. The music overall is generally straightforward Dixieland with plenty of exciting ensembles and hot solos. A collector's item that (typically for Mosaic) was perfectly conceived. —*Scott Yanow*

The Trios / May 5, 1953-Dec. 10, 1953 / Jazzology ✦✦✦✦

This very enjoyable set features pianist Art Hodes in three different trios with a variety of legendary jazz pioneers. The clarinet spot is filled on four songs apiece by either Darnell Howard, George Lewis, or the forgotten but talented Volly DeFaut. The other position is taken by either drummer Baby Dodds (on one of his very last dates), banjoist Lawrence Marrero, or Jasper Taylor, who may have been the first washboard player back in the early 1920s. The Lewis tracks were privately recorded, while the remaining performances were originally released on a ten-inch Paramount LP. Everyone plays quite well, and the contrasts between the clarinetists' styles make this a particularly special collection. —*Scott Yanow*

Art for Art's Sake / Jun. 12, 1957 / Jazzology ✦✦✦✦

Most of this reissue album (of a set originally released by the tiny Dotted Eight label) features pianist Art Hodes in a trio with bassist Truck Parham and drummer Freddie Moore. While the majority of the numbers are bluesy and thoughtful, a heated "Tiger Rag" with Moore on washboard is a highlight. Three other numbers also include the regular horn section of Chicago's Jazz Ltd. (trumpeter Fred Greenleaf, trombonist Dave Remington and clarinetist Bill Reinhardt), adding contrast and some heat to the fine trad jazz set. —*Scott Yanow*

Plain Old Blues / May 1962 / EmArcy ✦✦✦✦

Friar's Inn Revisited / 1968 / Delmark ✦✦✦✦

The bulk of this excellent album of Dixieland standards features pianist Art Hodes in a sextet with trumpeter Nappy Trottier, trombonist George Brunis (who also sings "Angry") and clarinetist Volly De Faut. Since recording opportunities for these musicians and for traditional jazz in particular were fairly rare in 1968, Delmark documented some very valuable music in this relaxed session. The LP is rounded out by two alternate takes left from a quartet date that Hodes did about the same period of time with the swing veteran clarinetist Barney Bigard. —*Scott Yanow*

Hodes' Art / Oct. 22, 1968-Apr. 23, 1972 / Delmark ✦✦✦

Opportunities for pianist Art Hodes to record in the 1960s were quite rare. In fact, other than a record documenting a concert, Hodes' entire output from 1963-70 was three albums cut for Delmark in 1968; traditional jazz was definitely out of style. This particular Delmark CD has brief moments from a variety of veteran greats. "When My Sugar Walks Down the Street" matches Hodes and his rhythm section with trombonist George Brunis, trumpeter Nappy Trottier and clarinetist Volly De Faut; the clarinetist (a veteran of the early '20s) also plays on "Struttin' with Some Barbecue." In addition to three piano-bass-drums trio numbers, Hodes is heard on six relaxed selections in a trio with clarinetist Raymond Burke (in good form) and veteran bassist Pops Foster. This music is historic and enjoyable. —*Scott Yanow*

Down Home Blues / Jul. 5, 1970 / Jazzology ✦✦✦✦

Although Art Hodes was beginning to record a lot around this period, this LP was his first full-length solo piano date since 1942. The emphasis for the session is on the blues. Hodes does perform a couple of slight departures, too—"Buddy Bolden's Blues" and "Miss Otis Regrets." The pianist's reputation soared during this era for his ability to put lots of feeling into slow, traditional blues; this set is a strong example of his talents in that area. —*Scott Yanow*

Selections from the Gutter / Oct. 5, 1970-Oct. 10, 1970 / Storyville ✦✦✦✦
At the age of 65, pianist Art Hodes was very much in his prime in the early 1970s. This release from Storyville features Hodes on slower blues-oriented material, including a memorable rendition of Hoagy Carmichael's "Washboard Blues," plus a couple of romps (such as "St. Louis Blues") for variety. Five songs add the bass of Jens Solund, but otherwise, this is a solo set with a few particularly haunting moments. —*Scott Yanow*

The Art of Hodes / 1972 / Euphonic ✦✦✦
One of several Art Hodes solo piano albums for Euphonic, this fine LP (none of the Euphonics has yet been reissued on CD) features Hodes alternating slow, bluesy material with hotter tunes like Jelly Roll Morton's "Grandpa's Spells," "Pagin' Mr. Jelly" and even a credible rendition of "The Saints." The biggest departure of the album is "Watermelon Man," a Herbie Hancock song that does have the feeling of vintage jazz. Hodes is in fine form throughout, although technical imperfections with the recording process resulted in a few notes fluttering a bit. —*Scott Yanow*

Up in Volly's Room / Mar. 15, 1972-Apr. 1972 / Delmark ✦✦✦✦
Clarinetist Volly DeFaut made a few notable recordings during the first half of the 1920s, including some with Jelly Roll Morton, and then largely dropped out of music. Fortunately, he never completely gave up playing, and his contributions to these 1972 sessions (reissued on CD) are one of the main reasons to acquire this release. While seven numbers match DeFaut with pianist Art Hodes, bassist Truck Parham and drummer Barrett Deems, there are also four Hodes-Parham duets and versions of "Ja Da" and "Panama Rag" that add trumpeter Nappy Trottier and trombonist George Brunis to the full group. Hodes, who is really rollicking on the more uptempo material, adds a strong blues sensibility to each of the songs. Among the many highlights of the delightful set (mostly comprising Dixieland standards) are "St. Louis Blues," "Struttin' with Some Barbecue," "After You've Gone" and "Volly's Room." —*Scott Yanow*

Home Cookin' / Oct. 31, 1974 / Jazzology ✦✦✦✦
Pianist Art Hodes was well recorded in the 1970s, usually solo or with a rhythm section. This Jazzology release is a change of pace, for it features Hodes leading what was billed as his "Jazz Four . . . Plus Two." Hodes, cornetist Ernie Carson, trombonist Charlie Bornemann and Franz Jackson (on clarinet, tenor and soprano) have plenty of solo space and are well supported by bassist Jimmy Johnson and drummer Hillard Brown. The Dixieland-oriented music is highlighted by "Joshua Fit the Battle of Jericho," "Indiana," "Chicago" and "Washington and Lee Swing," and is easily recommended to fans of the idiom. —*Scott Yanow*

I Remember Bessie / Sep. 19, 1977 / Euphonic ✦✦✦✦
For this solo piano set, the great veteran Art Hodes pays tribute to Bessie Smith and (to a lesser extent) Ma Rainey by performing music that they recorded in the 1920s. Although the emphasis is on slower blues, he also romps on "Alexander's Ragtime Band," "At a Georgia Camp Meeting" and a memorable version of "Cake-walkin' Babies From Home." Virtually every Art Hodes album is well worth picking up by collectors of pre-bop and blues; this increasingly hard-to-find LP is no exception. —*Scott Yanow*

When Music Was Music / 1978 / Euphonic ✦✦✦
On this mellow LP, Art Hodes plays solo piano renditions of ten of his favorite standards. Eight of the songs (including "Cherry," "I'm Comin' Virginia" and "Mood Indigo") are taken at relaxed tempos, while "Truckin'" and "I Know That You Know" are the only stomps. Hodes long had the ability to infuse every song with the blues, and that talent is very much in evidence on this obscure but worthy album. —*Scott Yanow*

Blues Groove / Oct. 1978 / Jazzology ✦✦✦✦
Seventy at the time of this album, pianist Art Hodes is in fine form jamming on standards and a few blues with a fairly obscure supporting cast: cornetist Sammy Duncan, trombonist Charlie Bornemann, clarinetist Herman Foretich, bassist Pepper Himmage and drummer Duncan Souter. Foretich's funny liner notes are almost a good enough reason by themselves to acquire this set, which is highlighted by "Mama's Gone Goodbye," "When My Dreamboat Comes Home" and a heated "Farewell Blues." —*Scott Yanow*

Someone to Watch over Me / Aug. 26, 1981 / Muse ✦✦✦✦✦
After a long period of critical neglect, pianist Art Hodes' career was on the upswing in the early '80s. Rightfully celebrated for his blues solos, Hodes' uptempo romps (check out "Grandpa's Spells" and "Struttin' with Some Barbecue" on this solo set) could be jubilant, with his left hand exuberantly pounding out chords on the beat. This well-rounded set is a fine showcase for his playing talents. —*Scott Yanow*

Apex Blues / Dec. 12, 1944 / Jazzology ✦✦✦
All of the music recorded by pianist Art Hodes for radio transcriptions in a trio with clarinetist Mezz Mezzrow and drummer Danny Alvin on Dec. 12, 1944 was issued on this set. The ten songs (the ten accepted versions plus nine alternate takes, six incomplete attempts, and four false starts) are unfortunately pro-

grammed in a very eccentric fashion, scattered all over the album, so it's difficult to follow the progression of the performances. Also, since Mezzrow's playing is typically erratic, the music is not essential, although it should be of interest to pre-swing collectors. —*Scott Yanow*

South Side Memories / Nov. 29, 1983 / Sackville ✦✦✦
Art Hodes pays tribute to the Chicago of the 1920s on this nostalgic and bluesy set. He performs three fine originals and such vintage standards as "Savoy Blues," "Cake Walkin' Babies From Home" (a real showstopper), "Willie the Weeper" and "The Pearls." One of the most significant survivors of the 1920s still active in the 1980s, Hodes deserved a great deal of credit for helping to keep classic jazz alive and relevant during his last few decades. Recommended. —*Scott Yanow*

The Authentic Art Hodes Rhythm Section / Jun. 7, 1985-Jun. 8, 1985 / Parkwood ✦✦✦✦
The title of this Parkwood set is a bit ironic, since pianist Art Hodes is the entire rhythm section. Hodes performs a pair of duets ("Jelly Roll Blues" and "When It's Sleepy Time Down South") with the great trumpeter Doc Cheatham, and joins Doc in accompanying singer Carrie Smith. The feeling throughout is of 1920s classic blues recordings, helped out by Smith's ability to emulate another Smith, Bessie. Among the more memorable vocal selections are "Big Butter and Egg Man," "There'll Be Some Changes Made" and "Backwater Blues." —*Scott Yanow*

Blues in the Night / Jun. 16, 1985 / Sackville ✦✦✦
Art Hodes recorded so many solo piano albums in the 1970s and '80s that it is difficult to call any particular one definitive, but his Sackville outing is an excellent all-around showcase. The pianist mostly sticks to slower tempos, with "Please Don't Talk About Me When I'm Gone" being an exception, and even if few of the songs on this date are technically blues, Hodes gives each of the tunes a strong blues feeling. A fine effort. —*Scott Yanow*

Solos, Vol. 1 / Apr. 20, 1987-Jul. 10, 1989 / Parkwood ✦✦✦✦
Pianist Art Hodes is heard on two different solo albums on this single CD. First he performs eight Christmas songs, infusing the familiar melodies with a strong dose of blues and rhythm (although the emphasis is on relaxed tempos). The later set has eight of Hodes' blues-oriented originals. Hodes was one of the top pianists in classic jazz with a distinctive voice of his own. This set from his later years is a fine example of his talents. —*Scott Yanow*

Live from Toronto's Cafe Des Copains / 1988 / Music & Arts ✦✦✦✦

Hot 'n' Cool Blues / Feb. 23, 1988+Dec. 11, 1988 / Parkwood ✦✦✦✦

The Music of Lovie Austin / Apr. 17, 1988 / Stomp Off ✦✦✦✦
This is a slightly off-the-wall project that succeeds quite well. In the 1920s, pianist Lovie Austin's Blues Serenaders recorded a series of numbers that usually featured cornetist Tommy Ladnier, clarinetist Jimmy O'Bryant and drummer W.E. Burton. In 1988, veteran pianist Art Hodes (83 at the time) teamed up with three Europeans (cornetist Abbi Hubner, clarinetist Reimer Von Essen and drummer Trevor Richards) to perform new versions of ten of the 16 songs originally recorded by Austin, plus Hodes' "Blues for Lovie Austin." The ensemble-oriented music (mostly blues-oriented obscurities from the mid-'20s) is given very favorable treatment by the four players, all of whom clearly understand the idiom. Classic jazz fans will want this somewhat obscure effort. —*Scott Yanow*

Keepin' out of Mischief Now / Nov. 3, 1988-Nov. 4, 1988 / Candid ✦✦✦✦
For this Candid CD, an 84-year old Art Hodes performs an effective set of solo piano. Renowned for his blues playing, Hodes is actually at his best on more uptempo romps in which his left hand is used to state and push the beat. He plays a wide variety of material during the program, ranging from "See See Rider" and "Struttin' with Some Barbecue" to Duke Ellington's "Saturday Night Function," Horace Silver's "The Preacher" and even "Tennessee Waltz." This is an excellent outing from a veteran great near the end of his career. —*Scott Yanow*

Pagin' Mr. Jelly / Nov. 14, 1988 / Candid ✦✦✦✦✦
Art Hodes was just ten days short of his 84th birthday at the time of this Candid solo piano CD. Hodes had had his own style for quite a few decades by then. A masterful blues player, on the more uptempo tunes, Art's left hand tended to state each beat in doubletime, a very effective device. For this tribute to Jelly Roll Morton, Hodes performs 13 tunes recorded by Morton (eight of which Jelly Roll wrote) along with two of his own originals, a blues and "Pagin' Mr. Jelly," which is partly based on Morton's "King Porter Stomp." The five faster performances really stomp, the three medium-tempo renditions swing and the seven introspective pieces are quite soulful. Recommended. —*Scott Yanow*

Final Sessions / Jul. 30, 1990-Aug. 19, 1990 / Music & Arts ✦✦✦✦
Pianist Art Hodes, one of the leading pianists during the revival years of classic jazz, is surprisingly strong during what would be his final recordings. Already in his mid-'80s, Hodes (three years before his death) explores 13 familiar themes ranging from "Alexander's Ragtime Band" and "Royal Garden Blues" to "America

the Beautiful." Six songs are duets with Jim Galloway on soprano, Hodes teams up with clarinetist Kenny Davern for "Summertime," there are four trios with both horns and also two unaccompanied piano solos. Hodes was a very consistent performer throughout his lengthy career and his last album (available as a 71-minute CD) is well worth hearing. —*Scott Yanow*

Johnny Hodges

b. Jul. 25, 1907, Cambridge, MA, d. May 11, 1970, New York, NY
Alto Saxophone, Soprano Saxophone / Swing, Ballads, New York Blues
Possessor of the most beautiful tone ever heard in jazz, altoist Johnny Hodges formed his style early on and had little reason to change it through the decades. Although he could stomp with the best swing players and was masterful on the blues, Hodges' luscious playing on ballads has never been topped. He played drums and piano early on before switching to soprano sax when he was 14. Hodges was taught and inspired by Sidney Bechet, although he soon used alto as his main ax; he would regretfully drop soprano altogether after 1940. His early experiences included playing with Lloyd Scott, Chick Webb, Luckey Roberts and Willie "The Lion" Smith (1924) and he also had the opportunity to work with Bechet. However, Johnny Hodges' real career began in 1928 when he joined Duke Ellington's Orchestra. He quickly became one of the most important solo stars in the band and a real pacesetter on alto; Benny Carter was his only close competition in the 1930s. Hodges was featured on a countless number of performances with Ellington and also had many chances to lead recording dates with Duke's sidemen. Whether it was "Things Ain't What They Used to Be," "Come Sunday" or "Passion Flower," Hodges was an indispensable member of Ellington's Orchestra in the 1930s and '40s. It was therefore a shock in 1951 when he decided to leave Duke and lead a band of his own. Hodges had a quick hit in "Castle Rock" (which ironically showcased Al Sears' tenor and had no real contribution by the altoist) but his combo ended up struggling and breaking up in 1955. Hodges' return to Duke Ellington was a joyous occasion and he never really left again. In the 1960s Hodges teamed up with organist Wild Bill Davis on some sessions, leading to Davis joining Ellington for a time in 1969. Johnny Hodges, whose unchanging style always managed to sound fresh, was still with Duke Ellington when he suddenly died in 1970. —*Scott Yanow*

Hodge Podge / Mar. 28, 1938-Oct. 14, 1939 / Legacy/Epic ✦✦✦
This is a good set that should have been a great one. Rather than reissue all 43 of altoist Johnny Hodges' small-group dates for Vocalion and OKeh, this CD (which should have been two) only contains 16. The music is often classic small-group swing ("Jeep's Blues," "Hodge Podge" and "Rent Party Blues" are among the high points) and there are several superb examples of Hodges playing soprano (showing off the influence of Sidney Bechet), but many valuable performances are missing. The problem is that the set is a straight reissue (although with some new liner notes) of an Epic LP rather than being an improvement. This important material deserves to be repackaged in a more complete fashion. —*Scott Yanow*

Passion Flower / Nov. 2, 1940-Jul. 9, 1946 / Bluebird ✦✦✦✦✦
For 42 years (with a four-year interruption), altoist Johnny Hodges was the top soloist in Duke Ellington's all-star Orchestra. This excellent CD reissue has the eight selections (plus an alternate take) from Hodges' two Bluebird sessions of 1940-41; among the sidemen on such classics as "Day Dream," "Good Queen Bess," "Passion Flower" and "Things Ain't What They Used to Be" are either Cootie Williams or Ray Nance on trumpet, trombonist Lawrence Brown and Ellington himself. In addition, there are 13 selections by the Duke Ellington Orchestra of 1940-46 that feature Hodges, including "Don't Get Around Anymore," "In a Mellotone," "Warm Valley," "I Got It Bad" and "Come Sunday." This is classic music that has been intelligently repackaged. —*Scott Yanow*

Ellingtonia! / Sep. 3, 1946-Aug. 27, 1964 / Onyx ✦✦✦
This long-out-of-print 1974 Onyx LP has a variety of fine performances featuring altoist Johnny Hodges. The first two titles ("Esquire Swank" and "Midriff") also have the full Duke Ellington Orchestra and spots for high note trumpeter Cat Anderson and trombonist Lawrence Brown. In addition, there are four songs apiece from a 1950 Paris session (featuring trumpeter Harold "Shorty" Baker, trombonist Quentin Jackson and Don Byas on tenor) and a previously unissued four-tune date from 1964 with Anderson, Brown and tenor saxophonist Paul Gonsalves. Johnny Hodges' beautiful alto sound and mastery of blues and ballads is much in evidence on these fine swing sessions. Well worth a search. —*Scott Yanow*

Caravan / Jun. 1947-Jun. 19, 1951 / Prestige ✦✦✦✦
This single CD, which reissues all of the music from a double LP, has a variety of formerly rare sessions from 1947-51. Although the great altoist Johnny Hodges gets top billing, and he leads three sessions from 1947 (featuring such top Ellington stars as trombonist Lawrence Brown, tenorman Al Sears, baritonist Harry Carney and either Taft Jordan or Harold Baker on trumpet), he is actually absent on the second half of the release. With Billy Strayhorn and/or Duke Ellington as leader

and Willie Smith on alto, these enthusiastic swing performances range in personnel from a three-trombone septet to a version of "Caravan" with Ellington on piano and Strayhorn making a rare appearance on organ. Although the music falls just short of classic, Ellington collectors will love these rarities. —*Scott Yanow*

The Rabbit in Paris / Apr. 15, 1950-Jun. 20, 1950 / Inner City ✦✦✦✦
During a European tour by the Duke Ellington Orchestra, alto star Johnny Hodges had an opportunity to lead an octet (mostly comprising Ellington's sidemen) at a few recording sessions. He enjoyed the experience so much that by the following year Hodges left Ellington and for four years was a bandleader himself. The results of the 1950 sessions (which also feature trumpeter Harold Baker, trombonist Quentin Jackson, clarinetist Jimmy Hamilton and guest tenorman Don Byas) are concise (all of the songs clock in around the three-minute mark) but make very good use of each second. The riff-filled originals, standards and Ellington-associated tunes receive swinging treatment by these classic all-stars, making this an LP whose contents deserve to be reissued on CD. —*Scott Yanow*

☆ **The Complete Johnny Hodges Sessions (1951-1955)** / Jan. 15, 1951-Sep. 8, 1955 / Mosaic ✦✦✦✦
As is true of most Mosaic box sets, it would be very difficult to improve upon this reissue. After 22 years, altoist Johnny Hodges left Duke Ellington's Orchestra in 1950 to try to make it on his own as a bandleader. Five years later, he returned to Ellington for the final 15 years of his life after having recorded the music heard on this six-LP set. Hodges' small group, a unit that emphasized blues, ballads and riff-filled romps, was an extension of the Ellington band. Hodges had a big hit with "Castle Rock" (ironically a feature for tenor saxophonist Al Sears), but otherwise had trouble at the end making ends meet. Other notable sidemen on these enjoyable performances include trumpeters Emmett Berry and Harold "Shorty" Baker, trombonist Lawrence Brown and tenors Flip Phillips, Ben Webster, and John Coltrane on one session (during which he unfortunately does not solo); the final session, from Sept. 8, 1955 (after Hodges had already returned to Ellington), also has trumpeter Clark Terry and pianist Billy Strayhorn. Most of this music had been long out of print at the time this 1989 box was released. A highly recommended gem of swinging jazz. —*Scott Yanow*

Used to Be Duke / Jul. 2, 1954+Aug. 5, 1954 / Verve ✦✦✦
Recorded during his five-year "vacation" from Duke Ellington's orchestra, this Johnny Hodges set (reissued on CD) features his band sticking mostly to standards. With trumpeter Harold "Shorty" Baker, trombonist Lawrence Brown, baritonist Harry Carney, pianist Call Cobbs or Richie Powell, bassist John Williams, drummer Louis Bellson and either Jimmy Hamilton or John Coltrane (who unfortunately does not solo) on tenor, Hodges had a particularly strong group. High points include "On the Sunny Side of the Street," the title track and a seven-song ballad medley. This session was also included in Mosaic's six-LP Johnny Hodges set. —*Scott Yanow*

A Man and His Music / 1954-1962 / Storyville ✦✦✦
This Storyville LP features music from four different settings, but unfortunately does not list the recording dates. The bulk of the set has either altoist Johnny Hodges or trumpeter Charlie Shavers backed by the obscure Al Waslon trio on radio broadcasts. Hodges plays his usual repertoire, such as "All of Me," "I Got It Bad" and "Jeep's Blues," in concise (under three minutes apiece) but enjoyable versions. Shavers is flashy during his mini-set, making one wonder why he was so underrated during his career. This worthwhile LP is rounded off by a 1954 concert version of "In a Mellow Tone" from Hodges' band, which includes a rare early solo from John Coltrane, and a version of "I'll Make Fun for You" from the early-'40s John Kirby Sextet. —*Scott Yanow*

At a Dance, in a Studio, on Radio / 1954-1957 / Enigma ✦✦✦✦
Although this is a bootleg album, the music on this LP is historically significant, particularly a couple of titles from 1954 on which tenor saxophonist John Coltrane (the year before he joined Miles Davis) gets to solo; trumpeter Harold "Shorty" Baker and trombonist Lawrence Brown are also in the supporting cast. Although the bulk of the album is a 1954 dance date (probably taken from a radio broadcast) there are also a few titles from March 1957 by the full Ellington band. This is worth picking up, particularly for the early Coltrane solos. —*Scott Yanow*

The Big Sound / Jun. 26, 1957+Sep. 3, 1957 / Verve ✦✦✦✦
No surprises, but the session was as good as one might hope. Gathered here was the Ellington band with Billy Strayhorn at the piano. While it was not an Ellington record, the band brought its solid qualities in backing and the occasional solo to all the fine Hodges features. This was an integrated unit, not some detached studio band for Hodges to blow over, under, around, and through. It was wonderful Hodges and fine Ellington. —*Bob Rusch, Cadence*

A Smooth One / Apr. 7, 1959+Sep. 8, 1960 / Verve ✦✦✦
This attractive double LP from 1979 includes two complete sessions by altoist Johnny Hodges that were previously unissued at the time. Most unusual is that

Hodges contributed 15 of the 19 compositions; the others are "Melancholy Baby," "Lotus Blossom" and two by clarinetist Jimmy Hamilton. Despite the unfamiliar material, the music is very much in the Duke Ellington style, with an emphasis on blues, ballads and riff tunes. In addition to Hodges, the other main soloists are trumpeter Harold "Shorty" Baker, tenor Ben Webster (on the first date) and trumpeter/violinist Ray Nance (on the second). None of this enjoyable music has yet been reissued on CD. —*Scott Yanow*

Masters of Jazz, Vol. 9 / Nov. 22, 1960-Mar. 14, 1961 / Storyville ✦✦✦✦✦
Here is a CD that is highly recommended for swing collectors. Altoist Johnny Hodges and tenor saxophonist Ben Webster team up for a sextet set from 1960, a club appearance that was released for the first time on this set. Their six performances (all are basic Hodges originals) find the pair of veteran swing stylists in prime form. The remainder of the program (three standards plus Hodges' "Good Queen Bess") is played by a septet dominated by Ellington musicians including the leader/altoist, baritonist Harry Carney, trumpeter Ray Nance and trombonist Lawrence Brown. Excellent music that still has not dated. —*Scott Yanow*

At the Berlin Sportpalast / Mar. 1961 / Pablo ✦✦✦✦
This double CD, a straight reissue of a Pablo double LP, documents a fun set. Altoist Johnny Hodges and some fellow members of Duke Ellington's Orchestra (Ray Nance on cornet, violin and vocals, trombonist Lawrence Brown, baritonist Harry Carney, bassist Aaron Bell, drummer Sam Woodyard and guest pianist Al Williams) jam through a typical set of standards and Ellington tunes. Everyone gets featured and, even if there are no real surprises, the musicians are consistently heard in top form. Superior small-group swing by some of the best. —*Scott Yanow*

Blue Hodges / Aug. 23, 1961-Aug. 24, 1961 / Verve ✦✦✦
This out-of-print LP (which has not yet been reissued on CD) is the earliest of several matchups between altoist Johnny Hodges and organist Wild Bill Davis. With the assistance of Les Spann on guitar and flute, bassist Sam Jones and drummer Louis Hayes, Hodges and Davis mostly stick to fresh material, including three then-recent originals by Gary McFarland. Highlights include "Azure Te," "It Shouldn't Happen to a Dream" and "There Is No Greater Love," in addition to some swinging blues. —*Scott Yanow*

Mess of Blues / Sep. 3, 1963-Sep. 4, 1963 / Verve ✦✦✦
In the 1960s altoist Johnny Hodges took a brief time off from Duke Ellington's orchestra to record eight albums with organist Wild Bill Davis. For this, their third collaboration, the duo welcomes guitarist Kenny Burrell, trumpeter Joe Wilder and either Osie Johnson or Ed Shaughnessy on drums. Hodges plays typically beautifully on such numbers as "I Cried for You," "Lost in Meditation" and "Stolen Sweets" and, although no real surprises occur (and the playing time at around a half-hour is quite brief), the performances are up to par. However, the music on this long-out-of-print LP has yet to appear on CD. —*Scott Yanow*

● **Everybody Knows** / Feb. 6, 1964+Mar. 8, 1965 / GRP/Impulse! ✦✦✦✦✦
This excellent single CD has the complete contents of two Impulse LPs: *Everybody Knows Johnny Hodges* and *Inspired Abandon*, which was actually a Lawrence Brown album featuring Hodges. The two similar and equally rewarding swing-oriented albums find Hodges joined by a variety of top Ellington stars, including trumpeters Cat Anderson and Ray Nance, either Harold Ashby or Paul Gonsalves on tenors and trombonist Brown, among others. The renditions of "310 Blues," "The Jeep Is Jumpin'," "Stompy Jones" and "Mood Indigo," in particular, sound quite fresh and inventive. Recommended. —*Scott Yanow*

Johnny Hodges/Wild Bill Davis, Vols. 1 & 2 / Jan. 7, 1965-Sep. 11, 1966 / RCA Jazz Tribune ✦✦✦✦
This enjoyable double-CD from RCA's Jazz Tribune series combines a pair of sessions from altoist Johnny Hodges and organist Wild Bill Davis. The earlier set has the pair joined by two guitarists (Mundell Lowe and Dickie Thompson,) bassist Milt Hinton and drummer Osie Johnson, while the second session has trombonist Lawrence Brown, Bob Brown on tenor and flute, Thompson returning on guitar and drummer Bobby Durham. Another difference between the two dates is that the later album (which has been reissued on CD in the Bluebird series) was recorded in concert. The music generally sticks to standards (many written by Duke Ellington), ballads and an occasional blues. Hodges and Davis were a surprisingly complementary team (their collaborations were a brief vacation from their usual settings) and they seem to inspire each other. Fine swing-based music. —*Scott Yanow*

Wings and Things / Jul. 27, 1965 / Verve ✦✦✦
Altoist Johnny Hodges and organist Wild Bill Davis made quite a few records together during the 1960s, although each of their efforts had slightly different personnel. In the case of this long-out-of-print Verve LP, they are assisted by trombonist Lawrence Brown, guitarist Grant Green, bassist Richard Davis, drummer Ben Dixon and, on three numbers, pianist Hank Jones. With the exception of "Take the 'A' Train" and the two ballads "The Nearness of You" and "Peg o' My Heart," the

material (including three Hodges originals and Duke Ellington's "Imbo") is quite obscure. The group always swings, and it is interesting to hear Hodges in this setting; pity that this LP's music has not yet been reissued on CD. —*Scott Yanow*

Johnny Hodges with Lawrence Welk's Orchestra / Dec. 20, 1965-Dec. 21, 1965 / Dot ✦✦✦
This was one of the oddest matchups and yet ended up being fairly logical. Altoist Johnny Hodges had one of the most beautiful tones ever heard and Lawrence Welk always loved beautiful music. This Dot LP features Hodges on a dozen standards while accompanied by a string section, brass and a rhythm section. The concise and melodic interpretations are indeed pretty and the arrangements (by a dozen different writers) are generally fine. Plus, the album cover (which has a picture of the unlikely duo) is classic. Recommended for the novelty value although this LP may be hard to find. —*Scott Yanow*

Blue Pyramid / Dec. 27, 1965+Jan. 17, 1966 / Verve ✦✦✦
On this collaboration between altoist Johnny Hodges and organist Wild Bill Davis, they are joined by trombonist Lawrence Brown, clarinetist Jimmy Hamilton, guitarist Billy Butler, electric bassist Bob Bushnell, either Herbie Lovelle, Joe Marshall or Johnny Hodges, Jr. on drums and, on the organless "At Dawn," pianist Jimmy Jones. Although the blues feeling (as pointed out in the liner notes) is emphasized throughout the date, many of the songs, including "The Brown Skin Gal in the Calico Gown" and "Stormy Weather," are not blues, but only bluesy. Overall a fine outing, but this LP has been out of print for a couple of decades. —*Scott Yanow*

In a Mellow Tone / Sep. 10, 1966-Sep. 11, 1966 / Bluebird ✦✦✦✦✦
Altoist Johnny Hodges and organist Wild Bill Davis teamed up successfully on quite a few albums in the 1960s. This set, reissued on CD, was their final one and quite possibly their most rewarding. With solo work provided by not only the co-leaders but trombonist Lawrence Brown, obscure tenor Bob Brown, and guitarist Dickie Thompson (drummer Bobby Durham helps out in support), this is a particularly interesting unit. Unlike most of their other collaborations, this outing by Hodges and Davis sticks mostly to better-known material, including a previously unissued version of Duke Ellington's "Squeeze Me But Please Don't Tease Me" and four Hodges originals. Highlights include "It's Only a Paper Moon," "Taffy," "Good Queen Bess" and "In a Mellotone." This release is recommended as a strong (and swinging) example of Johnny Hodges outside of the Duke Ellington Orchestra. —*Scott Yanow*

Triple Play / Jan. 9, 1967-Jan. 10, 1967 / Bluebird ✦✦✦✦
Altoist Johnny Hodges is heard in three different settings on this reissue CD. Such top swing stars as trumpeters Ray Nance, Cat Anderson and Roy Eldridge, trombonists Buster Cooper, Lawrence Brown and Benny Powell, tenors Paul Gonsalves and Jimmy Hamilton, baritonist Harry Carney, pianists Hank Jones and Jimmy Jones (the latter two sometimes together), guitarists Tiny Grimes, Les Spann and Billy Butler, bassists Milt Hinton, Aaron Bell and Joe Benjamin and drummers Gus Johnson, Rufus Jones and Oliver Jackson are heard in nonets with the great altoist. Despite the many changes in personnel, the music is fairly consistent, with basic swinging originals, blues and ballads all heard in equal proportion. As usual, Johnny Hodges ends up as the main star. —*Scott Yanow*

Holly Hofmann

b. Painesville, OH
Flute / Bop
n excellent bop-oriented flutist, Holly Hofmann began on the flute when she was five. She had extensive classical training and in 1984, when she moved to San Diego, Hofmann began playing jazz fulltime. She worked with James Moody, Slide Hampton and Mundell Lowe, among others, before making her recording debut on Capri (1989). Hofmann has since recorded fine straightahead dates for Jazz Alliance (1992) and Azica (1995), led her own groups and played regularly in the San Diego area. —*Scott Yanow*

Further Adventures / Jun. 28, 1989-Jun. 29, 1989 / Capri ✦✦✦✦
Flutist Holly Hofmann's second Capri recording uses the same musicians as her debut: pianist Mike Wofford, bassist Bob Magnusson and drummer Sherman Ferguson. Hofmann, a superior bop-based improviser, performs a wide range of jazz standards and obscurities, including pieces by Ellington and Strayhorn ("Mount Harissa"), Art Pepper ("True Blues"), Djavan, Neal Hefti, Bud Powell, and Thelonious Monk ("Green Chimneys") plus an original apiece by Wofford (the title cut) and Magnusson. The inventive arrangements and high-quality solos make this an excellent CD worth searching for. —*Scott Yanow*

Take Note / Dec. 10, 1990 / Capri ✦✦✦✦✦

Duo Personality / Apr. 1992 / Jazz Alliance ✦✦✦✦
On this intimate record of "jazz chamber music," talented flutist Holly Hofmann performs duets with pianist Mike Wofford, guitarist Mundell Lowe, bassist Bob Magnusson and guitarist/vocalist Ron Satterfield. In addition, she plays on a pair of

trios with these musicians. The well-rounded set, which includes four group origi- nals and six standards, including Lee Morgan's "Speedball," features Hofmann in top form no matter who she is collaborating with. —*Scott Yanow*

● **Tales of Hofmann** / Jul. 19, 1995-Jul. 20, 1995 / Azica ◆◆◆◆◆
Holly Hofmann is such a talented flutist that it is remarkable that she is still not all that well known; certainly she ranks up there with Frank Wess and Lew Tabackin among the bop-oriented players. On her set for Azica, she enlisted a particularly strong supporting cast (trumpeter Bobby Shew, pianist Bill Cunliffe, bassist Bob Magnusson and drummer Victor Lewis) for a set dominated by obscure but supe- rior material. Hofmann's opening cadenza to one of the date's two standards ("Softly, as in a Morning Sunrise") gets the set off to a particularly strong start and virtually all of the tracks that follow are rewarding in one way or another. Among the highlights are Bobby Shew's "Red Snapper" (which deserves to be a standard), Mike Wofford's "Afterthoughts" (a strong modal piece in tribute to John Coltrane), Hoffman's thoughtful "And Now You" and the cooking blues "Bone-Crusher." Throughout, both Shew and Cunliffe (the latter a sympathetic accompanist whose improvisations are consistently strong) get their share of solos, while Magnusson and Lewis are excellent in support. A fine straightahead date. —*Scott Yanow*

Just Duet / Jun. 21, 1996-Feb. 18, 1997 / Azica ◆◆◆◆◆
In 1996-97, flutist Holly Hofmann and pianist Bill Cunliffe often toured as a duet, so it was logical that they would document their musical partnership on a CD. The versatile musicians blend together quite well throughout this set, which ranges musically from some bossa nova ("Conto de Ossanha") and bop ("Powell's Prances") to adaptations of classical themes (Schumann's "Three Romances"), the emotional ballad "Old Folks" and their "High Flutin' Blues." Other than a touch of synthesizer and percussion on the wistful closer ("Home"), the music does not have any overdubs or sweetening; none is needed. Hofmann consolidates her position as one of the top bop-oriented flutists of the 1990s, while Cunliffe (with his occasional striding) continues to surprise. Highly recommended. —*Scott Yanow*

Jay Hoggard

b. Sep. 24, 1954, Washington, DC
Vibes / Avant-Garde, Post-Bop
AJay Hoggard has had a wide-ranging career. One of the top vibraphonists to emerge during the 1970s, Hoggard originally started on piano and saxophone before switching to vibes. By the early '70s he was working in New England with such top avant-garde players as Anthony Davis and Leo Smith. Hoggard moved to New York in 1977 where he played with Chico Freeman and Anthony Davis. In 1978 he recorded a solo avant-garde vibes performance but he followed it up with a more commercial date. Hoggard has worked with such greats as Sam Rivers, Cecil Taylor, James Newton and Kenny Burrell in addition to leading his own group; he has recorded hard bop-oriented dates as a leader for Contemporary, India Navigation and several for Muse. —*Scott Yanow*

Solo Vibraphone / Nov. 18, 1978 / India Navigation ◆◆◆◆◆
The release of this live concert (which has been reissued on CD) helped to intro- duce vibraphonist Jay Hoggard to the jazz world. A more avant-garde oriented player at the time than he would become, Hoggard holds one's interest throughout the six unaccompanied vibe solos, including a previously unissued rendition of "Air Mail Special" played in tribute to Lionel Hampton. Thought-provoking music. —*Scott Yanow*

Days Like These / 1979 / GRP ◆◆
Vibes playing is fine, but it's otherwise forgettable. —*Ron Wynn*

Rain Forest / Nov. 1980 / Original Jazz Classics ◆◆◆
Jay Hoggard's lone date for Contemporary (reissued as an OJC CD) was one of the vibraphonist's finest early sets. The music (all six songs are Hoggard originals) falls into the area of advanced hard bop. Chief among the sidemen are Chico Freeman (heard on tenor, soprano and bass clarinet), keyboardist Kenny Kirkland, and color- ful percussionist Paulinho Da Costa; two songs utilize three vocalists, and there is a strong African feel to some of the ensembles. —*Scott Yanow*

Mystic Winds, Tropical Breezes / 1982 / India Navigation ◆◆◆◆◆
Pianist Anthony Davis (who contributed one of the four originals), co-stars with inventive vibraphonist Jay Hoggard on this adventurous set. Dwight Andrews is heard from on bass clarinet, the great Cecil McBee is on bass, and the remainder of the group includes drummer Billy Hart, percussionist Don Moye and Wilson Moor- man III on tympani. The lengthy interpretations (ranging from 8 to 13 minutes) are episodic and contain more than their share of surprises and atmospheric moments. —*Scott Yanow*

Love Survives / 1983 / Gramavision ◆◆◆◆

Riverside Dance / 1985 / India Navigation ◆◆◆◆
This 1985 LP is an excellent showcase for vibraphonist Jay Hoggard. He performs Thelonious Monk's "Brilliant Corners," Billy Strayhorn's "Lush Life," and five of his

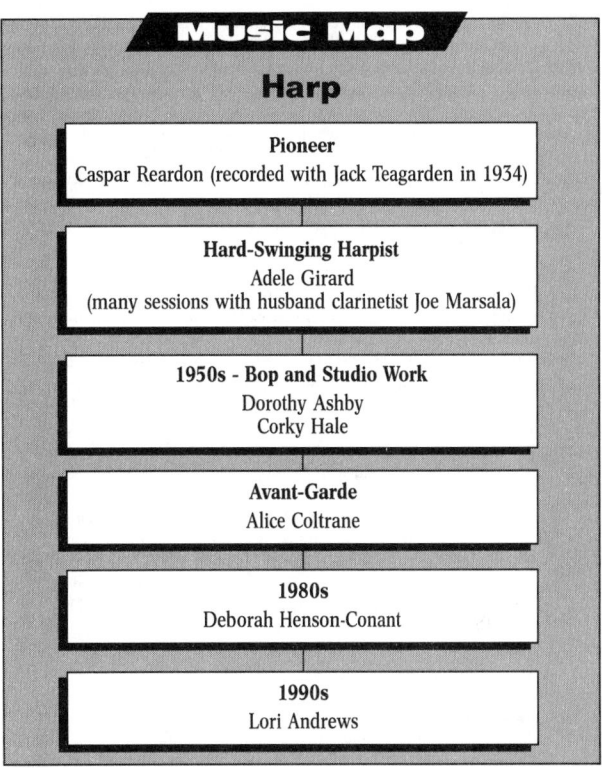

Music Map

Harp

Pioneer
Caspar Reardon (recorded with Jack Teagarden in 1934)

Hard-Swinging Harpist
Adele Girard
(many sessions with husband clarinetist Joe Marsala)

1950s - Bop and Studio Work
Dorothy Ashby
Corky Hale

Avant-Garde
Alice Coltrane

1980s
Deborah Henson-Conant

1990s
Lori Andrews

diverse originals with a quintet also including keyboardist Onaje Allan Gumbs, guitarist Vernon Reid, bassist Jerome Harris and drummer Pheeroan AkLaff. The inside/outside music is never predictable and inspires Hoggard to some of his best playing of the period. —*Scott Yanow*

Overview / Jun. 22, 1989 / Muse ◆◆◆◆
Very good, with Geri Allen (p). —*Michael G. Nastos*

The Little Tiger / Jun. 10, 1990 / Muse ◆◆◆◆◆
An album with the vibraphonist at his best. The title track alone is worth the price. With Benny Green. —*Michael G. Nastos*

● **The Fountain** / Jul. 10, 1991 / Muse ◆◆◆◆◆
Vibraphonist Jay Hoggard has had a diverse recording career, playing everything from very free jazz to a couple of commercial efforts. In the 1990s he seemed to discover straightahead jazz and this quintet session (with guitarist Kenny Burrell and pianist James Weidman) is mostly very much in that idiom. Hoggard is fine on standards such as "Stompin' at the Savoy" (a tribute to Lionel Hampton) and Monk's "Epistrophy" but it is on his originals (the soulful "Sweet Potato" and a fairly free "The Fountain") that Hoggard sounds most individual. —*Scott Yanow*

In the Spirit / May 4, 1992 / Muse ◆◆◆◆

Love is the Answer / Jan. 9, 1994-Feb. 27, 1994 / Muse ◆◆◆◆

Billie Holiday (Eleanora Harris)

b. Apr. 7, 1915, Baltimore, MD, **d.** Jul. 17, 1959, New York, NY
Vocals / Swing, Classic Female Blues, Ballads
Billie Holiday remains (four decades after her death) the most famous of all jazz singers. "Lady Day" (as she was named by Lester Young) had a small voice and did not scat but her innovative behind-the-beat phrasing made her quite influential. The emotional intensity that she put into the words she sang (particularly in later years) was very memorable and sometimes almost scary; she often really did live the words she sang.

Her original name and birthplace have been wrong for years but are listed cor- rectly above thanks to Donald Clarke's definitive Billie Holiday biography *Wish- ing on the Moon*. Holiday's early years are shrouded in legend and rumors, due to her fanciful ghostwritten autobiography *Lady Sings the Blues*, but it is fair to say that she did not have a stable life. Her father Clarence Holiday (who never did marry her mother) played guitar with Fletcher Henderson and abandoned his family early on, while her mother was not a very good role model. Billie essentially grew up alone, feeling unloved and gaining a lifelong inferiority complex that led to her taking great risks with her personal life and becoming self-destructive. Holiday's life becomes clearer after she was discovered by John Hammond singing in Harlem clubs. He arranged for her to record a couple of titles with Benny Goodman in 1933 and although those were not all that successful, it was the start of her career. Two years later she was teamed with a pickup band led by Teddy Wilson and the combination clicked. During 1935-42 she would make some of the finest recordings of her career, jazz-oriented performances in which she was joined by the who's who of swing. Holiday sought to combine together Louis Armstrong's swing and Bessie Smith's sound; the result was her own fresh approach. In 1937 Lester Young and Buck Clayton began recording with Holiday and the interplay between the three of them was timeless.

Lady Day was with Count Basie's Orchestra during much of 1937 but, because they were signed to different labels, all that exists of the collaboration are three songs from a radio broadcast. She worked with Artie Shaw's Orchestra for a time in 1938 but the same problem existed (only one song was recorded) and she had to deal with racism, not only during a Southern tour but in New York too. She had better luck as a star attraction at Cafe Society in 1939. Holiday made history that year by recording the horribly picturesque "Strange Fruit," a strong anti-racism statement that became a permanent part of her repertoire. Her records of 1940-42 found her sidemen playing a much more supportive role than in the past, rarely sharing solo space with her. Although the settings were less jazz-oriented than before (with occasional strings and even a background vocal group on a few numbers) Billie Holiday's voice was actually at its strongest during her period with Decca (1944-49). She had already introduced "Fine and Mellow" (1939) and "God Bless the Child" (1941) but it was while with Decca that she first recorded "Lover Man" (her biggest hit), "Don't Explain," "Good Morning Heartache" and her renditions of "Ain't Nobody's Bizness if I Do," "Them There Eyes" and "Crazy He Calls Me." Unfortunately, it was just before this period that she became a heroin addict and she spent much of 1947 in jail. Due to the publicity she became a notorious celebrity and her audience greatly increased. Lady Day did get a chance to make one Hollywood movie (*New Orleans*) in 1946 and, although she was disgusted at the fact that she was stuck playing a maid, she did get to perform with her early idol Louis Armstrong.

Billie Holiday's story from 1950 on is a gradual downhill slide. Although her recordings for Norman Granz (which started in 1952) placed her once again with all-star jazz veterans (including Charlie Shavers, Buddy DeFranco, Harry "Sweets" Edison and Ben Webster), her voice was slipping fast. Her unhappy relationships distracted her, the heroin use and excessive drinking continued and by 1956 was way past her prime. Holiday had one final burst of glory in late 1957 when she sang "Fine and Mellow" on *The Sound of Jazz* telecast while joined by Lester Young (who stole the show with an emotional chorus), Ben Webster, Coleman Hawkins, Gerry Mulligan and Roy Eldridge, but the end was near. Holiday's 1958 album *Lady in Satin* found the 43-year-old singer sounding 73 (barely croaking out the words) and the following year she collapsed; in the sad final chapter of her life she was placed under arrest for heroin possession while on her deathbed!

Fortunately, Billie Holiday's recordings have been better treated than she was during her life and virtually all of her studio sides are currently available on CD. —*Scott Yanow*

☆ **The Quintessential Billie Holiday, Vol. 1 (1933-1935)** / Nov. 27, 1933-Dec. 3, 1935 / Columbia ◆◆◆◆◆

After years of reissuing her recordings in piecemeal fashion, Columbia finally got it right with this nine-CD *Quintessential* series. All of Lady Day's 1933-42 studio recordings (although without the alternate takes) receive the treatment they deserve in this program. *Vol. 1* has Holiday's first two tentative performances from 1933 along with her initial recordings with Teddy Wilson's all-star bands. High points include "I Wished on the Moon," "What a Little Moonlight Can Do," "Miss Brown to You," and "Twenty-Four Hours a Day." —*Scott Yanow*

Billie Holiday: The Legacy Box 1933-1958 / Nov. 27, 1933-Feb. 19, 1958 / Columbia ◆◆◆

The logic behind this sampler is puzzling. Rather than reissue the very best of Billie Holiday's Columbia recordings on a three-CD box set or a package of her rare alternate takes, CBS tries it both ways by including 60 common selections already available in the *Quintessential* series along with ten rarities that were either unissued or alternates. This otherwise attractive box (which includes a colorful booklet) will drive completists and veteran collectors crazy. The music (mostly from 1933-42 with three weaker performances from 1957-58) is often classic but duplicates more coherent reissues. —*Scott Yanow*

☆ **Billie Holiday: The Voice of Jazz: The Complete Recordings 1933-1940** / Nov. 1933-Oct. 1940 / Affinity ◆◆◆◆◆

Lady Day / Jul. 2, 1935-Jun. 15, 1937 / Columbia ◆◆◆◆

This LP, whose contents have since been reissued on CD, used to be the one definitive set to acquire of early Billie Holiday. The 12 selections are all classics (particularly "What a Little Moonlight Can Do," "If You Were Mine," "Billie's Blues," "I Must Have That Man," "Easy Living," "Me, Myself and I" and "I Cried for You") and find Lady Day joined by such all-stars as pianist Teddy Wilson, trumpeters Roy Eldridge, Bunny Berigan and Buck Clayton, clarinetist Benny Goodman, the tenors of Lester Young and Ben Webster and altoist Johnny Hodges, among others. Wonderful music that is essential to acquire in one form or another. —*Scott Yanow*

If You Were Mine / Jul. 2, 1935-Nov. 28, 1938 / Drive Archive ◆◆

Fourteen of Billie Holiday's studio sides from 1935-38 (most of which were originally under the leadership of pianist Teddy Wilson) are reissued on this Drive Archive CD. Some of the titles are classics (particularly "What a Little Moonlight Can Do" and "Miss Brown to You") while a few are quite obscure. The music is fine but the sound quality is not as good as one would hope, plus these important performances have already been reissued in more definitive fashion on CD by Columbia. This CD does serve as a budget sampler for listeners not yet familiar with Billie Holiday. —*Scott Yanow*

★ **The Quintessential Billie Holiday, Vol. 2 (1936)** / Jan. 30, 1936-Oct. 21, 1936 / Columbia ◆◆◆◆◆

The second of nine volumes in this essential series (all are highly recommended) continues the complete reissue of Billie Holiday's early recordings (although the alternate takes are bypassed). This set is highlighted by "I Cried for You" (which has a classic alto solo from Johnny Hodges), "Billie's Blues" (from Holiday's first session as a leader), "A Fine Romance" and "Easy to Love." Holiday's backup crew includes such greats as pianist Teddy Wilson, baritonist Harry Carney, trumpeters Jonah Jones and Bunny Berigan and clarinetist Artie Shaw. There's lots of great small-group swing. —*Scott Yanow*

Don't Explain / Sep. 29, 1936-Jul. 25, 1958 / Audio Fidelity ◆◆

This three-LP box set is one of the more bizarre Billie Holiday reissues, with virtually all of the discographical information given on its back cover being completely inaccurate. A hodgepodge collection of live performances along with a few (presumably illegal) studio cuts, the recordings jump all over the place, from broadcasts with Count Basie in 1937 to TV appearances, concert performances in the 1950s and the 1936 studio version of "I Can't Pretend"; the latter has dubbed-in phony applause. The recording quality varies from decent to barely listenable. —*Scott Yanow*

★ **The Quintessential Billie Holiday, Vol. 3 (1936-1937)** / Oct. 28, 1936-Feb. 18, 1937 / Columbia ◆◆◆◆◆

The third of nine CDs that document all of Billie Holiday's studio recordings of 1933-42 for Columbia has classic versions of "Pennies from Heaven," "I Can't Give You Anything but Love" (on which she shows the influence of Louis Armstrong) and "My Last Affair," along with Lady Day's first meeting on record with tenor saxophonist Lester Young. Their initial encounter resulted in four songs including "This Year's Kisses" and "I Must Have That Man." All nine volumes in this admirable series (if only the alternate takes had been included!) are highly recommended. —*Scott Yanow*

☆ **The Quintessential Billie Holiday, Vol. 4 (1937)** / Mar. 31, 1937-Jun. 15, 1937 / Columbia ◆◆◆◆◆

The fourth of nine CDs in this essential series of Billie Holiday's studio recordings of 1933-42 features the great tenor Lester Young on eight of the 16 performances. Prez and Lady Day make a perfect match on "I'll Get By" (although altoist Johnny Hodges steals the honors on that song), "Mean to Me," "Easy Living," "Me Myself and I" and "A Sailboat in the Moonlight." Other strong selections without Young include "Moanin' Low," "Let's Call the Whole Thing Off" and "Where Is the Sun?" It's highly recommended along with all of the other CDs in this perfectly done Billie Holiday reissue program. —*Scott Yanow*

★ **The Quintessential Billie Holiday, Vol. 5 (1937-1938)** / Jun. 15, 1937-Jan. 27, 1938 / Columbia ◆◆◆◆

The fifth of nine CDs in the complete reissue of Billie Holiday's early recordings (sans alternate takes), this great set has 18 selections, all but four featuring tenor saxophonist Lester Young and trumpeter Buck Clayton. Among the classics are "Getting Some Fun out of Life," "Trav'lin' All Alone," "He's Funny That Way," "My Man," "When You're Smiling" (on which Prez takes a perfect solo), "If Dreams Come True" and "Now They Call It Swing." All nine volumes in this series are highly recommended, but if one can only acquire a single entry, this is the one. —*Scott Yanow*

☆ **The Quintessential Billie Holiday, Vol. 6 (1938)** / May 11, 1938-Nov. 9, 1938 / Columbia ◆◆◆◆◆

The sixth of nine CDs in this very worthy series traces Billie Holiday's recording career throughout most of 1938. Although not containing as many true classics as

Vol. 5, most of these 18 selections are quite enjoyable, particularly "You Go to My Head," "Having Myself a Time," "The Very Thought of You" and "They Say." All of the sets in this reissue program are recommended, featuring Lady Day when she was youthful and still optimistic about life. —*Scott Yanow*

The Quintessential Billie Holiday, Vol. 7 (1938-1939) / Nov. 28, 1938-Jul. 5, 1939 / Columbia ✦✦✦✦✦

By 1939, when the bulk of these 17 selections were recorded, Billie Holiday was dominating her own recordings, allocating less space for her sidemen to solo. This was not really a bad thing since Lady Day's voice was getting stronger each year. On the seventh of nine CD volumes that reissue all of Holiday's 1933-42 Columbia recordings (other than the alternate takes, which have been bypassed), Holiday sounds at her best on "More than You Know, Sugar" (featuring a superb Benny Carter alto solo), "Long Gone Blues" and "Some Other Spring." It's recommended along with all of the other entries in the *Quintessential* series. —*Scott Yanow*

Billie Holiday / Apr. 20, 1939-Apr. 8, 1944 / Commodore ✦✦✦✦✦

This CD includes all of Billie Holiday's Commodore recordings (the master takes but no alternates): four titles from 1939 (including the still haunting "Strange Fruit" and "Fine and Mellow") and the remainder dating from 1944 when Holiday's voice was at its peak. The latter sessions are highlighted by "I'll Get By," "Billie's Blues," "He's Funny That Way" and "I'm Yours." Pianist Eddie Heywood has many sparkling solos on the 1944 selections. This definitive single CD contains music essential for every jazz collection. —*Scott Yanow*

The Complete Commodore Recordings / Apr. 20, 1939-Apr. 8, 1944 / GRP ✦✦✦

Billie Holiday recorded on four occasions for the Commodore label: once in 1939 (a date that resulted in "Fine and Mellow" and "Strange Fruit") and three sessions in 1944 (dates highlighted by "I Cover the Waterfront," "I'm Yours," "He's Funny That Way," "Billie's Blues," and "On the Sunny Side of the Street"). While the former session has Lady Day joined by a background octet that includes trumpeter Frankie Newton, the Eddie Heywood Sextet forms the nucleus of the later dates. This two-CD set has all 18 selections and no less than 27 alternate takes. Since the great majority of the performances are ballads, and with the exception of pianist Heywood, there are very few instrumental solos, there are no significant differences between the versions. Therefore, this set (as opposed to a single CD of the master takes), even though it is well-conceived, is strictly for completists. —*Scott Yanow*

☆ The Quintessential Billie Holiday, Vol. 8 (1939-1940) / Jul. 5, 1939-Sep. 12, 1940 / Columbia ✦✦✦✦✦

The eighth of nine volumes that feature all of the master takes from Billie Holiday's Columbia recordings of 1933-42 is one of the better sets, although all nine CDs are recommended. High points include "Them There Eyes," "Swing, Brother, Swing," "The Man I Love," "Ghost of Yesterday," "Body And Soul," "Falling in Love Again," and "I Hear Music." Among the variety of all-stars backing her, tenor saxophonist Lester Young makes his presence known on eight of the 18 numbers. —*Scott Yanow*

Control Booth Series, Vol. 1 / Sep. 12, 1940-Mar. 21, 1941 / Jazz Unlimited ✦✦✦

Strictly for completists, this Storyville CD has 25 performances but just ten separate songs; 15 are alternate takes. Slightly more complete than an Affinity box set that covered the 1940 selections, this release surprisingly leaves out one version of "Loveless Love." The music, particularly the originally released versions, is excellent; Lady Day is in fine form, and there are some solos from trumpeter Roy Eldridge, Benny Carter (on clarinet), tenorman Georgie Auld, pianist Teddy Wilson and (on the final session) tenor saxophonist Lester Young. Among the tunes are "I Hear Music," "St. Louis Blues," "Let's Do It" and "Romance in the Dark." Most collectors would be satisfied with just the regular versions, but one can appreciate slight differences in each rendition, particularly from the soloists. —*Scott Yanow*

The Quintessential Billie Holiday, Vol. 9 (1940-1942) / Oct. 15, 1940-Feb. 10, 1942 / Columbia ✦✦✦✦✦

The final volume in this nine-CD series contains all of Billie Holiday's recordings from her final 16 months with the label. Highlights include "St. Louis Blues," "Loveless Love," "Let's Do It," "All of Me" (arguably the greatest version ever of this veteran standard), "Am I Blue," "Gloomy Sunday" and "God Bless the Child." All 153 of Lady Day's Columbia recordings (even the occasional weak item) are well worth hearing and savoring. —*Scott Yanow*

Billie's Blues / Jun. 12, 1942-Jan. 5, 1954 / Blue Note ✦✦✦✦✦

Most of this excellent CD features one of Billie Holiday's finest concert recordings of the 1950s. Recorded in Europe before an admiring audience, this enjoyable set finds Lady Day performing seven of her standards with her trio and joining in for jam session versions of "Billie's Blues" and "Lover Come Back to Me" with an all-star group starring clarinetist Buddy DeFranco, vibraphonist Red Norvo and guitarist Jimmy Raney. These performances (which find Holiday in stronger voice than on her studio recordings of the period) have also been included in Verve's

massive CD box set. This program concludes with Holiday's four rare sides for Aladdin in 1951 (between her Decca and Verve periods), which are highlighted by two blues and "Detour Ahead," and her 1942 studio recording of "Trav'lin' Light" with Paul Whiteman's Orchestra. —*Scott Yanow*

Masters of Jazz, Vol. 3 / Jan. 18, 1944-1949 / Storyville ✦✦✦

This very interesting CD has a variety of mostly rare Billie Holiday live performances from 1944-49. In addition to two selections with the 1944 Esquire All-Stars, Lady Day is heard with Hot Lips Page, accompanied by pianist Teddy Wilson on a 1947 version of "The Man I Love," backed by Percy Faith's string orchestra on "You Better Go Now" and joined by a Red Norvo-led band in 1949 that also includes trumpeter Neal Hefti and the reeds of Herbie Steward. Collectors are advised to search for this set. —*Scott Yanow*

Fine and Mellow / Jan. 18, 1944-Apr. 15, 1959 / Collectables ✦✦✦

This CD contains 20 selections featuring Billie Holiday in a variety of live performances covering a 15-year period. Starting with two songs in 1944, in which she was backed by the Esquire All-Stars, and continuing through TV appearances and club dates, one can hear the gradual aging and decline of Lady Day's voice, which definitely took a turn for the worse between 1955-56. And yet oddly enough the last five numbers, which were performed April 15, 1959 (making them Holiday's final recordings), actually find her sounding stronger than she had in a few years, perhaps in a final gasp of energy. Of great historical value, this set has plenty of strong moments to justify its acquisition. —*Scott Yanow*

★ The Complete Decca Recordings / Oct. 4, 1944-Mar. 8, 1950 / Decca ✦✦✦✦✦

Billie Holiday is heard at her absolute best on this attractive two-CD set. During her period on Decca, Lady Day was accompanied by strings (for the first time), large studio orchestras and even background vocalists, so jazz solos from her sidemen are few. But her voice was at its strongest during the 1940s (even with her personal problems) and to hear all 50 of her Decca performances (including alternate takes and even some studio chatter) is a real joy. Among the high points of this essential set are her original versions of "Lover Man" (Holiday's biggest selling record), "Don't Explain," "Good Morning Heartache," "'Tain't Nobody's Business if I Do," "Now or Never," "Crazy He Calls Me" and remakes of "Them There Eyes" and "God Bless the Child." —*Scott Yanow*

☆ The Complete Billie Holiday on Verve 1945-1959 / Feb. 12, 1945-Mar. 1, 1959 / Verve ✦✦✦✦✦

This is a rather incredible collection, ten CDs enclosed in a tight black box that includes every one of the recordings that Verve owns of Billie Holiday, not only the many studio recordings of 1952-57 (which feature Lady Day joined by such jazz all-stars as trumpeters Charlie Shavers and Harry "Sweets" Edison, altoist Benny Carter and the tenors of Flip Phillips, Paul Quinichette and Ben Webster) but prime performances at Jazz at the Philharmonic concerts in 1945-7, an enjoyable European gig from 1954, her "comeback" Carnegie Hall concert of 1956, Holiday's rather sad final studio album from 1959 and even lengthy tapes from two informal rehearsals. It's a perfect purchase for the true Billie Holiday fanatic. —*Scott Yanow*

Verve Jazz Masters 47: Sings Standards / Feb. 12, 1945-Mar. 1059 / Verve ✦✦✦

Of Verve's countless number of Billie Holiday samplers, this one—which is actually a second helping from the *Jazz Masters* series—is as good as any of them artistically. Like many of its cousins on the shelves, this one takes in the whole cross-section of Holiday's recordings for Norman Granz, from an exuberant 1945 JATP concert all the way to her last poignant sessions with the Ray Ellis string orchestra in 1959. Unlike them, this one does not contain songs with which Billie is inextricably tied, but all of the well-known standards are given the inimitable Holiday stamp, often in league with many of Granz's legendary soloists. Of course, this is the most troubling period for Holiday scholars, for her voice was going downhill fast in the 1950s, yet one has to admit that her Verve recordings often pack an emotional wallop that eclipse most of the earlier ones. A few random highlights: the JATP "All of Me" and "Body and Soul" from the mid-'40s, with Holiday in fresh voice and a whole bunch of star horns wailing in tangled contrapuntal splendor underneath; and a "When It's Sleepy Time Down South" from the Ray Ellis sessions where the combination of Holiday's broken-down voice and exquisite phrasing will break your heart. Verve's thorough discographical entries, here and in the entire Jazz Masters series, are exemplary for what is, after all, an inexpensive sampler for newcomers to jazz. —*Richard S. Ginell*

Billie Holiday at Storyville / Oct. 29, 1951-1953 / Black Lion ✦✦✦

Billie Holiday is in generally good form for this club appearance. On most of the selections she is accompanied by the Carl Drinkard Trio, but six others find her joined by Buster Harding's Trio; the great tenor Stan Getz sits in on three of these numbers, making one wish that he and Lady Day had collaborated more extensively. This set of standards (most of which had been recorded previously by Holiday) are not up to the quality of her Decca output but are enjoyable nevertheless. —*Scott Yanow*

Songs for Distingue Lovers / Jun. 6, 1956–Jun. 7, 1956 / Verve ✦✦✦
A wonderful date. Holiday is nearing the end, but summons her resources and does a highly creditable job. —*Ron Wynn*

Lady in Satin / Feb. 19, 1958–Feb. 21, 1958 / Columbia ✦✦✦✦✦
This is the most controversial of all Billie Holiday records. Lady Day herself said that this session (which finds her accompanied by Ray Ellis' string orchestra) was her personal favorite, and many listeners have found her emotional versions of such songs as "I'm a Fool to Want You," "You Don't Know What Love Is," "Glad to Be Unhappy" and particularly "You've Changed" to be quite touching. But Holiday's voice was essentially gone by 1958, and although not yet 43, she could have passed for 73. Ellis' arrangements do not help, veering close to Muzak; most of this record is very difficult to listen to. Late in life, Billie Holiday expressed the pain of life so effectively that her croaking voice had become almost unbearable to hear. The 1997 CD reissue adds two alternate takes of "I'm a Fool to Want You," part of which were used for the original released rendition, plus the stereo version of "The End of a Love Affair" (only previously released in mono) and examples of Lady Day rehearsing the latter song, including a long unaccompanied stretch. There is certainly a wide range of opinion as to the value of this set. —*Scott Yanow*

The Monterey Jazz Festival with Buddy DeFranco / Oct. 5, 1958 / Black Hawk ✦
Appearing at the first Monterey Jazz Festival, Billie Holiday tried gamely to succeed, but during this live set she often sounds a bit out of it. Accompanied by the Mal Waldron Trio (and on the final few numbers baritonist Gerry Mulligan, altoist Benny Carter and clarinetist Buddy DeFranco), Lady Day struggles through the half-hour set, performing old favorites but often sounding quite weak. The results, as heard on this LP (recorded nine months before her death), are historic but often rather sad. —*Scott Yanow*

Last Recordings / Mar. 3, 1959–Mar. 11, 1959 / Verve ✦✦
In many ways, a sad event. 1988 reissue of an album with Ray Ellis and his orchestra. It's poignant in a tragic way. —*Ron Wynn*

Control Booth Series, Vol. 2 / Mar. 21, 1941–Feb. 10, 1942 / Jazz Unlimited ✦✦✦
This Jazz Unlimited CD (available through Storyville) features multiple takes of Billie Holiday during the last four sessions from her early prime years. Strangely enough, three of the takes, including two masters, are not included on this otherwise complete set. Holiday is heard on such numbers as "All of Me," "God Bless the Child," "Am I Blue," "Gloomy Sunday" and a swinging arrangement of "It's a Sin to Tell a Lie"; other than short spots for trumpeter Emmett Berry and pianist Teddy Wilson (in addition to tenorman Lester Young on "All of Me"), the focus is entirely on Lady Day's voice. The many versions (which include eight that were previously unissued) should greatly interest collectors, but the missing renditions are quite unfortunate. —*Scott Yanow*

Dave Holland

b. Oct. 1, 1946, Wolverhampton, England
Bass / Post-Bop, Avant-Garde
One of the top bassists of free bop and the avant-garde, Dave Holland has long been quite flexible. He started on bass in 1963 and studied extensively in England, playing with many of the top British players including Humphrey Lyttelton, John Surman, Evan Parker, Tubby Hayes, Ronnie Scott and Kenny Wheeler (which is quite a variety!). After playing with the Spontaneous Music Ensemble, he worked with Miles Davis during 1968-70 as Ron Carter's replacement, recording several albums including most notably *Bitches Brew*. He next teamed up with Chick Corea, Anthony Braxton and Barry Altschul in Circle (1970-71) and after Corea's decision to play more accessible music, Holland became a member of Braxton's quartet up until 1976. He also played with Paul Bley (1972-73) and Stan Getz during the period 1973-75. Holland was in Gateway with John Abercrombie and Jack DeJohnette (1975-77), a group that in the mid-'90s had a reunion. The bassist played regularly with Sam Rivers during 1976-80 and in 1982 formed his own group, which through the years has included Kenny Wheeler, Steve Coleman and Robin Eubanks among others. He has been active as an educator, worked with the M-Base players, and toured with Pat Metheny, Herbie Hancock and DeJohnette in a quartet, and has recorded as a leader since 1971 for ECM. —*Scott Yanow*

Music for Two Basses / Feb. 15, 1971 / ECM ✦✦✦

Conference of the Birds / Nov. 30, 1972 / ECM ✦✦✦✦
This was one of bassist Dave Holland's most adventurous sets, an avant-garde outing with both Sam Rivers and Anthony Braxton on reeds, along with percussionist Barry Altschul (Braxton, Altschul and Holland had been members of Circle (with Chick Corea) and were soon to form a quartet that included trumpeter Kenny Wheeler. The contrast between the two masterful reed players on the six Holland originals is the main reason to acquire this minor classic. —*Scott Yanow*

Holland/Rivers / Feb. 18, 1976 / IAI ✦✦✦

Emerald Tears / Aug. 1977 / ECM ✦✦✦✦
As strong and inventive a player as Dave Holland is, he was unable to make this set of unaccompanied bass solos (which have been reissued on CD) of more than minor interest. Performing six of his originals, one by Anthony Braxton and Miles Davis' "Solar," Holland unfortunately avoids infusing the music with any humor or much variety, making this a sleepy session for most listeners. —*Scott Yanow*

Life Cycle / Nov. 1982 / ECM ✦✦✦
Wholly original cello solos in jazz and folk flavors. —*Myles Boisen*

● **Jumpin' In** / Oct. 1983 / ECM ✦✦✦✦✦
Bassist Dave Holland leads one of his most stimulating groups on this superlative quintet date. With the young Steve Coleman on alto and flute, trumpet great Kenny Wheeler, trombonist Julian Priester and drummer Steve Ellington in the band, Holland had a particularly creative group of musicians in which to interpret and stretch out his six originals; Coleman also contributed one composition. This set, which has plenty of variety in moods, tone, colors and styles, is one of Holland's better recordings. —*Scott Yanow*

Seeds of Time / Nov. 1984 / ECM ✦✦✦✦
In the mid-1980s, bassist Dave Holland led his finest group, a quintet with up-and-coming altoist Steve Coleman, trombonist Julian Priester, trumpeter Kenny Wheeler and (on this date) drummer Marvin "Smitty" Smith. The all-star musicians pack plenty of music and concise solos into each performance (nine originals), and the unique group carved out its own niche, not quite free but certainly unpredictable. —*Scott Yanow*

The Razor's Edge / Feb. 1987 / ECM ✦✦✦✦✦
Dave Holland's mid-1980s band played inventive music that was between post-bop and the avant-garde. The group acted as a launching pad for altoist Steve Coleman, gave publicity to the always-underrated trumpeter Kenny Wheeler, and in 1987 also featured trombonist Robin Eubanks and drummer Marvin "Smitty" Smith. The group's three ECM releases are well worth exploring, and this set gives listeners a strong example of their work. —*Scott Yanow*

Triplicate / Mar. 1988 / ECM ✦✦✦✦
Very much a co-op trio, this ECM date matches together bassist Dave Holland, his old associate Jack DeJohnette and altoist Steve Coleman, who spent time in both of their bands. For the well-rounded date, the band performs one song apiece by Coleman and DeJohnette, four by Holland, a traditional "African Lullaby," Charlie Parker's "Segment" and Duke Ellington's "Take the Coltrane." Steve Coleman, who always had an original sound, really excels in this sparse setting. —*Scott Yanow*

Extensions / Sep. 1989 / ECM ✦✦✦✦✦
Dave Holland Quartet. With Kevin Eubanks (g). This was the 1990 *Down Beat* Critic's Album of the Year. Very good band/album music. Percussionist Smitty Smith is unreal. Recommended. —*Michael G. Nastos*

Ones All / May 1993 / Intuition ✦✦✦

Dream of the Elders / Mar. 1995 / ECM ✦✦✦✦
Stylewise, the music on this CD sounds much closer to a mid-'60s Blue Note release than what one might expect from ECM. Although the general sound of the ensembles is light, the music is often filled with inner heat, a little reminiscent of a Wayne Shorter record. Altoist Eric Person and vibraphonist Steve Nelson work well together, bassist Dave Holland takes plenty of solo space, drummer Gene Jackson keeps the momentum flowing and guest vocalist Cassandra Wilson does a fine job on Maya Angelou's poem "Equality." Holland's originals have plenty of variety in moods, while close attention is paid to dynamics. A satisfying and thought-provoking session. —*Scott Yanow*

Major Holley

b. Jul. 10, 1924, Detroit, MI, d. Oct. 25, 1990, Maplewood, NJ
Bass / Swing, Bop
Major Holley was best known for using the Slam Stewart trademark of singing along with his bowed bass solos, although he sang in unison while Stewart vocalized an octave above his bass. Otherwise, Major Holley (known as "Mule") was a fine supportive bassist. He originally played violin and tuba but switched to bass while playing in navy bands. He played with Dexter Gordon, Charlie Parker and Ella Fitzgerald in the mid- to late '40s and in 1950 did a series of duet recordings (never reissued) with Oscar Peterson. After a period working for the BBC in England, he toured with Woody Herman (1958), played with the Al Cohn-Zoot Sims quintet (1959-60) and worked in the studios, in addition to appearing on some jazz recordings and having a stint with Duke Ellington (1964). Major Holley taught at Berklee (1967-70), freelanced in New York, and recorded with everyone from Roy Eldridge and the Lee Konitz Nonet to Quincy Jones; he even met up on two records with Slam Stewart. —*Scott Yanow*

● **Featuring Gerry Wiggins** / Mar. 21, 1974 / Black & Blue ✦✦✦✦

Red Holloway

b. May 31, 1927, Helena, AR

Tenor Saxophone, Alto Saxophone / Bop, Swing, Soul Jazz, Groove

An exuberant player with attractive tones on both tenor and alto, Red Holloway is also a humorous blues singer. Whether it be bop, blues or R&B, Holloway can hold his own with anyone. Holloway played in Chicago with Gene Wright's big band (1943-46), served in the army and then played with Roosevelt Sykes (1948) and Nat Towles (1949-50) before leading his own quartet (1952-61) during an era when he also recorded with many blues and R&B acts. Holloway came to fame in 1963 while touring with Jack McDuff, making his first dates as a leader for Prestige (1963-65). Although he has cut many records in R&B settings, Red Holloway is a strong bop soloist at heart, as he proved in the 1970s when he battled Sonny Stitt to a tie on their recorded collaboration. He has mostly worked as a leader since then but has also guested with Juggernaut and the Cheathams and played with Clark Terry on an occasional basis. —*Scott Yanow*

Cookin' Together / Feb. 2, 1964 / Original Jazz Classics ✦✦✦✦✦

For this set, tenor saxophonist Red Holloway, who was a regular member of organist Jack McDuff's group, used McDuff's sidemen (which included guitarist George Benson) and the organist himself. This Prestige date has thus far only been reissued by the OJC series on LP. The material comprises Burt Bacharach's "Wives and Lovers," "This Can't Be Love," and five Holloway originals, which have more diversity than one might expect. An interesting aspect to the soulful and swinging set is that McDuff made his debut on piano for two songs. —*Scott Yanow*

Brother Red / Feb. 6, 1964-Feb. 7, 1964 / Prestige ✦✦✦✦✦

The 11 selections included on this CD reissue include seven songs from a session headed by tenor saxophonist Red Holloway that used the members of the Jack McDuff Quintet (with the organist, guitarist George Benson, bassist Wilfred Middlebrooks and drummer Joe Dukes), three pieces from a McDuff date in which the lead voices are backed by an orchestra arranged by Benny Golson, and a selection from a sampler. The material varies a bit ("Wives and Lovers" and Holloway's soul ballad "No Tears" are forgettable) but the blues and the uptempo pieces (highlighted by "This Can't Be Love") are quite enjoyable and the underrated saxophonist is in excellent form. —*Scott Yanow*

Red Soul / Dec. 1965 / Prestige ✦✦✦

Good to get, if you can find it. Holloway with Lonnie Smith on organ and George Benson on guitar. Tunes like "Big Fat Lady" and "Good and Groovy." —*Michael Erlewine*

Hittin' the Road Again / 1982 / JAM ✦✦✦

On his first set as a leader since the 1960s, Red Holloway is heard on tenor, alto and baritone, in addition to taking a good-natured blues vocal on "Sylvia Is Her Name." Holloway wrote five of the six songs, none of which caught on, and used L.A.-based musicians (keyboardist Dwight Dickerson, guitarist Shuggie Otis, bassist Richard Reid and either Gerryck King or Jimmy Smith on drums) for this likable but obscure straightahead outing, which has not yet been reissued on CD. —*Scott Yanow*

Nica's Dream / Jul. 7, 1984 / Steeple Chase ✦✦✦✦

Doubling on tenor and alto, Red Holloway shows on this no-nonsense quartet set how strong an improviser he is within the world of bebop. Joined by pianist Horace Parlan, bassist Jesper Lundgaard and drummer Aage Tanggaard, Holloway plays two basic originals and five jazz standards, highlighted by a lengthy "Lover Man," "Love for Sale" and a speedy "Wee." —*Scott Yanow*

Red Holloway and Company / Jan. 1987 / Concord Jazz ✦✦✦✦✦

Saxophonist Red Holloway (equally distinctive on tenor and alto) performs a more diverse program than usual on this Concord CD, infusing such songs as "But Not for Me," "Passion Flower," Thelonious Monk's "Well You Needn't," "Summertime" and two of his originals with plenty of soul and solid swing. Holloway, a masterful interpreter rather than an innovator, is in top form throughout the recommended set, which also features pianist Cedar Walton, bassist Richard Reid and drummer Jimmie Smith. —*Scott Yanow*

● **Locksmith Blues** / Jun. 1989 / Concord Jazz ✦✦✦✦✦

This is a fun set, which is not surprising when one considers that two of jazz's most good-humored players (saxophonist Red Holloway and fluegelhornist Clark Terry) are the co-leaders. The sextet (which also includes pianist Gerald Wiggins, guitarist Phil Upchurch, bassist Richard Reid and drummer Paul Humphrey) plays a colorful set of jazz standards, including "Red Top," "Come Sunday" and "Cotton Tail," and three basic Holloway originals, one of which ("Locksmith Blues") finds Holloway and C.T. clearly enjoying themselves while sharing the vocals. Everyone is heard in top form, making this straightahead CD an excellent example of the co-leaders' talents. —*Scott Yanow*

Live at the Floating Jazz Festival 95 / Nov. 5, 1995-Nov. 9, 1995 / Chiaroscuro ✦✦✦✦

The great Harry "Sweets" Edison joins Holloway and his backing unit—pianist Dwight Dickerson, bassist Richard Reid and drummer Paul Humphrey—on this lively outing recorded at the 1995 Floating Jazz Festival. Featured tracks include "River's Invitation," "Wave," "Well You Needn't" and "Nica's Dream." —*Jason Ankeny*

Ron Holloway

b. 1953, Washington D.C.

Tenor Saxophone / Hard Bop

An excellent tenor saxophonist with an open mind who is best known for his hard bop-oriented performances and recordings, Ron Holloway started playing music in the seventh grade. He worked in R&B and funk bands early on and sat in with such players as Sonny Rollins, Freddie Hubbard and Dizzy Gillespie. After playing with Gil Scott-Heron during 1981-88, Holloway (sounding a bit like Stanley Turrentine) was in Dizzy Gillespie's last band (1989-92). He has recorded several albums as a leader for Milestone. —*Scott Yanow*

Slanted / Aug. 1993-Sep. 1993 / Milestone ✦✦✦✦

● **Struttin'** / Feb. 1995-Apr. 1995 / Milestone ✦✦✦✦✦

Scorcher / Feb. 1996-Mar. 1996 / Milestone ✦✦✦✦

Christopher Hollyday

b. Jan. 3, 1970, New Haven, CT

Alto Saxophone / Hard Bop

One of the "Young Lions" of the late '80s, altoist Christopher Hollyday created a big stir when he appeared on the scene but has maintained a surprisingly low profile during the past couple of years. He started playing alto when he was nine, developed quickly and was playing in clubs when he was 14, the year when he recorded his first album on his own Jazzbeat label. Back then he was heavily influenced by Charlie Parker but a few years later Hollyday sounded almost like a clone of Jackie McLean. In 1988 he took a group into the Village Vanguard and the following year he toured with Maynard Ferguson's big band. During 1989-92, Hollyday recorded four CDs for Novus and was starting to develop his own voice when he was dropped from the label. —*Scott Yanow*

Treaty / Jan. 27, 1985 / Jazzbeat ✦✦✦

Christopher Hollyday's first recording, cut when he was just 14, was issued on his family's private Jazzbeat label. The LP features Hollyday during a period when his biggest influence was Charlie Parker. Hollyday, pianist John Medeski (who would a decade later gain fame with Medeski, Martin & Wood), bassist Nat Reeves and drummer Ron Savage perform some jazz standards, a tune apiece by James Williams and Russ Freeman, and the teenage altoist's "Bop Bop" and "Treaty of Jazz." —*Scott Yanow*

● **Christopher Hollyday** / Jan. 25, 1989-Jan. 26, 1989 / Novus ✦✦✦✦✦

Altoist Christopher Hollyday's first release for Novus (following a few small label sets) immediately made him one of the top Young Lions of the era. 19 at the time, Hollyday was clearly strongly influenced by Jackie McLean (one of his main teachers), but holds his own with an all-star group comprising trumpeter Wallace Roney, pianist Cedar Walton, bassist David Williams and drummer Billy Higgins. Performing two of McLean's originals ("Appointment In Ghana" and "Omega") and five bop standards, the young saxophonist shows plenty of potential and fares quite well. —*Scott Yanow*

On Course / Jan. 16, 1990-Jan. 17, 1990 / Novus ✦✦✦

This 1990 session sounds like a Blue Note date circa 1966 featuring Jackie McLean. At the age of 20, altoist Christopher Hollyday deserved credit for picking a different role model than anyone else in his generation but his advanced originals, creative choice of notes and high energy are consistently overshadowed by his derivative sound. Hollyday does experiment a bit wth the instrumentation, taking "Impromptu," "In a Love Affair" and "Spontaneous" as duets with, respectively, bassist John Lockwood, pianist Larry Goldings and drummer Ron Savage. The young rhythm section is excellent and the compositions (all but a melodic one-chorus version of "Memories of You" and Goldings' blues-with-a-bridge "Hit and Run" are the altoist's) are strong, but Christopher Hollyday at this point did not have an original voice or message of his own. —*Scott Yanow*

The Natural Moment / Jan. 21, 1991-Jan. 22, 1991 / Novus ✦✦✦✦

The progress on this album is evident. —*Michael G. Nastos*

And I'll Sing Once More / Jan. 14, 1992-Jan. 16, 1992 / Novus ✦✦✦✦

By the time he recorded his fourth Novus release, alto saxophonist Christopher Hollyday, who often sounded like a particularly abrasive version of his teacher Jackie McLean, was starting to show some individuality. Then 22, Hollyday is heard on this set with a 14-piece group that includes six brass, Scott Robinson on reeds, violinist Mark Feldman and two Indian percussionists. He performs four originals, two by pianist Kenny Werner and three standards, exploring the area between hard bop and post-bop. Shortly after this set, Hollyday was dropped by Novus and began a long hiatus from recording. —*Scott Yanow*

Bill Holman (Willis Leonard Holman)

b. May 21, 1927, Olive, CA
Arranger, Leader, Tenor Saxophone / Hard Bop, Post-Bop
One of the great arrangers, Bill Holman's dense but hard-swinging charts often have so much of value going on that they reward repeated listenings. After a stint with Charlie Barnet (1950-51), Holman became well-known for his arrangements for Stan Kenton (1952-56) which helped advance the Kenton sound. Although a fine tenor saxophonist, Holman's writing has always overshadowed his playing. He concentrated on studio work by the 1960s but also wrote through the years for Woody Herman, Maynard Ferguson, Gerry Mulligan, Count Basie and Buddy Rich among others. Holman wrote the charts for Natalie Cole's best-selling *Unforgettable* album (1991) and has led his own part-time big band in the Los Angeles area since 1975. Bill Holman recorded as a leader for Capitol, Coral (reissued on Sackville), Andex and Hi Fi during 1954-60 and more recently his Los Angeles band has been documented by JVC. —*Scott Yanow*

The Fabulous Bill Holman / Apr. 25, 1957+Apr. 29, 1957 / Sackville ✦✦✦✦
Bill Holman's second album as a leader was originally released on Coral before being reissued on Sackville in 1979. The masterful arranger is heard taking some rare solos on tenor with a 16-piece group of top West Coast jazz players from the era. For the set, Holman rewrote two standards ("Airegin" and "You and I") and contributed a pair of concise originals, plus the nearly 17-minute "The Big Street." Among the other soloists are trumpeter Conte Candoli, pianist Lou Levy, valve trombonist Stu Williamson, altoists Charlie Mariano and Herb Geller and tenorman Richie Kamuca (who at one point trades off with Holman). The music is fairly advanced for the time period and still sounds fresh decades later. —*Scott Yanow*

In a Jazz Orbit / Feb. 11, 1958-Feb. 13, 1958 / V.S.O.P. ✦✦✦✦
Considering his talents, arranger Bill Holman has led relatively few recording sessions through the years. This formerly rare big-band set from 1958 (originally on the Andex label and reissued on CD by V.S.O.P.) features a 15-piece band filled with West Coast all-stars. Among the soloists on these five standards and four originals are trombonists Frank Rosolino, Carl Fontana and Ray Sims, altoists Charles Mariano and Herb Geller, trumpeter Jack Sheldon, Richie Kamuca on tenor, pianist Victor Feldman and Holman himself on tenor. The leader's arrangements were quite distinctive (although not as complex as they would become) at this fairly early stage and the results are a big band album that still sounds fresh nearly four decades later. —*Scott Yanow*

Jive for Five / May 29, 1958-Jun. 6, 1958 / V.S.O.P. ✦✦✦✦
For a brief time, tenor saxophonist Bill Holman and drummer Mel Lewis led a hard-swinging quintet based in Los Angeles. Trumpeter Lee Katzman, pianist Jimmy Rowles and bassist Wilford Middlebrook complete the group, a band that benefits greatly from the arrangements of Holman. Rowles contributed "502 Blues Theme," Holman brought in two songs, and the unit also performs the obscure "Mah Lindy Lou" and two originals. This LP (originally on the Andex label) serves as proof that not all jazz recordings from Los Angeles in the 1950s are quiet and cool. —*Scott Yanow*

Bill Holman's Great Big Band / Jun. 29, 1960-Jul. 1, 1960 / Capitol ✦✦✦✦
This lesser-known effort from arranger Bill Holman, who is also heard on tenor, was his last recording as a big-band leader for some time. The brevity of the performances (none of the 11 songs are over four minutes long, and several are under three minutes) is disappointing, cutting down on the solo space, but the versions of such unusual material as "Shadrack," "The Moon Is Blue," "June Is Busting out All Over" and "Old Man River" are full of surprises. Among the key soloists are tenorman Bill Perkins, trumpeter Conte Candoli (showcased on "Lush Life"), and trombonist Frank Rosolino. This out-of-print LP is worth searching for. —*Scott Yanow*

The Bill Holman Band / Nov. 30, 1987-Dec. 1987 / JVC ✦✦✦✦
This JVC CD is a reissue of a late-'80s CD. Bill Holman has long been one of the top arrangers in jazz but, because he has not recorded all that many albums and because he is based in L.A., he tends to get overlooked in popularity polls. An innovative writer who features crowded yet swinging ensembles and charts that are both complex and colorful, Holman generally emphasizes originals these days. However, on this record, which was his first full set on record as a leader since 1960, six of the nine selections are standards (including "Just Friends," which was composed by John Klenner, not John Klemmer as listed) and it is interesting to hear what Holman does to such songs as Stevie Wonder's "Isn't She Lovely?" Monk's "I Mean You" (which at one point has four soprano saxophonists trading

off) and the theme from the 1930s movie *Hurricane*, "The Moon of Manakoora." With such soloists as altoist Lanny Morgan, the late great tenor Bob Cooper, trumpeters Bob Summers and Don Rader, and trombonists Rick Culver and Bob Enevoldsen, along with the high note trumpet of Frank Szabo, it is not surprising that the enjoyable disc has plenty of highlights, but actually it is the ensembles that are most notable. The many arranged choruses on "Just Friends" are particularly memorable. —*Scott Yanow*

● **A View from the Side** / Apr. 24, 1995+Apr. 25, 1995 / JVC ✦✦✦✦✦
Although he never seems to win any popularity polls, Bill Holman is among the most respected and unique arrangers of the past 40 years. This CD features his band of the mid-'90s, an outfit that includes many of the top Los Angeles-based musicians. Holman's writing is often colorfully overcrowded (rewarding repeated listenings) yet logical, with the charts progressing and developing from beginning to end rather than repeating the same basic ideas continuously. Whether it be the many complex themes of "No Joy in Mudville," the showcases for tenor saxophonist Pete Christlieb ("But Beautiful") and Bob Efford's bass clarinet ("The Peacocks"), the very advanced "Make My Day" or the rebuilding of "Tennessee Waltz," this JVC release is a consistently memorable set from a masterful arranger who deserves much greater recognition in the jazz world. —*Scott Yanow*

● **Brilliant Corners: The Music of Thelonious Monk** / Feb. 11, 1997+Feb. 12, 1997 / JVC ✦✦✦✦✦

Richard "Groove" Holmes (Richard Arnold Holmes)

b. May 2, 1931, Camden, NJ, **d.** Jun. 29, 1991, St. Louis, MO
Organ / Hard Bop, Soul Jazz, Groove
Revered in soul-jazz circles, Richard "Groove" Holmes was an unapologetically swinging Jimmy Smith admirer who could effortlessly move from the grittiest of blues to the most sentimental of ballads. Holmes, a very accessible, straightforward and warm player who was especially popular in the Black community, had been well respected on the Philadelphia-Southern New Jersey circuit by the time he signed with Pacific Jazz in the early 1960s, and started receiving national attention by recording with such greats as Ben Webster and Gene Ammons. Holmes, best known for his hit 1965 version of "Misty," engaged in some inspired organ battles with Jimmy McGriff in the early 70s before turning to electric keyboards and fusion-ish material a few years later. The organ was Holmes' priority in the mid- to late 80s, when he recorded for Muse. Holmes was still delivering high-quality soul-jazz for that label (often featuring tenor titan Houston Person) when a heart attack claimed his life at the age of 60 in 1991. —*Alex Henderson*

Groove / Mar. 1961 / Pacific Jazz ✦✦✦✦
When the participants on this CD reissue gathered together in March 1961, it was with the objective of recording a Les McCann vocal album. However, the band had such a good time during their warmup that McCann and the others agreed that it would be a crime to waste the opportunity. Organist Richard "Groove" Holmes, whom McCann had recently discovered, was made the leader; a few jump tunes and originals were agreed upon, and the result is a loose, enjoyable jam session. In addition to Holmes' appealing organ and McCann's typically funky piano, a major bonus is the brilliant playing of tenor saxophonist Ben Webster, whose tone was at its most gorgeous during this period. The five songs on the original LP are joined by a number that was last on a sampler, a McCann vocal track ("Next Spring"), and a previously unreleased version of "Just Friends." The spontaneous and soulfully swinging music, which also features trombonist Tricky Lofton, guitarist George Freeman and drummer Ron Jefferson, is easily recommended. —*Scott Yanow*

Groovin' with Jug / Aug. 15, 1961 / Pacific Jazz ✦✦✦✦✦
This CD reissues a logical combination: organist Richard "Groove" Holmes and the soulful, boppish tenor of Gene Ammons. With fine support given by guitarist Gene Edwards and drummer Leroy Henderson, Groove and Jug play soulful versions of standards, blues and ballads, with the highlights including Art Farmer's "Happy Blues," "Hittin' the Jug" and "Exactly Like You." High-quality soul-jazz. —*Scott Yanow*

After Hours / 1962 / Pacific Jazz ✦✦✦✦✦
The original *After Hours* album had Joe Pass on guitar, and Lawrence Marable on drums. This combines most of another album (*Tell It Like It Is*) with Gene Edwards on guitar. This is early Groove Holmes, 13 tracks in all. This is fine soul-jazz and it is clear why many feel that Holmes is the man of the groove, when it comes to the Hammond B-3. —*Michael Erlewine*

Tell It Like It Is / 1961 / Pacific Jazz ✦✦✦
Very fine Hammond B-3 with Holmes, Gene Edwards on guitar, and Holmes' Leroy Henderson on drums. Near the start of his career, this is classy soul jazz. —*Michael Erlewine*

Somethin' Special / Apr. 1962 / Pacific Jazz ✦✦✦

Somethin' Special is a laidback, funky classic which features Richard "Groove" Holmes trading licks with pianist Les McCann, saxophonist Clifford Scott and guitarist Joe Pass, who makes one of his first recorded appearances on this album. It's a fine, infectious album, highlighted by Holmes and McCann's stylish solo. Blue Note's 1997 CD reissue features two bonus cuts, including one that features saxophonist Ben Webster. —*Leo Stanley*

Soul Message / Aug. 3, 1965 / Original Jazz Classics ✦✦✦✦✦

Organist Richard "Groove" Holmes hit upon a successful formula on this Prestige session (reissued on CD in the OJC series), mixing together boogaloo rhythms with emotional solos. His doubletime version of "Misty" became a big hit, and the other selections, including Horace Silver's "Song for My Father" and a pair of soulful originals, are in a similar vein. The lone ballad of the set ("The Things We Did Last Summer") is a fine change of pace. With the assistance of guitarist Gene Edwards and drummer Jimmie Smith, Groove Holmes shows that it is possible to create music that is both worthwhile and commercially successful. —*Scott Yanow*

Misty / Aug. 3, 1965-Aug. 12, 1966 / Original Jazz Classics ✦✦✦✦

Organist Richard "Groove" Holmes in the mid-'60s had a hit with his medium-tempo rendition of "Misty." This CD reissue has the original short version (which was cut as a 45) plus other medium-tempo ballads performed in similar fashion. Holmes and his trio (featuring guitarist Gene Edwards and drummer George Randall) play enjoyable if not overly substantial versions of such songs as "The More I See You," "The Shadow of Your Smile," "What Now My Love?" and "Strangers in the Night," trying unsuccessfully for another pop hit; the organist's sound is more appealing than some of the tunes. —*Scott Yanow*

★ **Blue Groove** / Mar. 15, 1966-May 29, 1967 / Prestige ✦✦✦✦✦

This CD, which reissues two former LPs by Richard "Groove" Holmes (*Get Up & Get It* and *Soul Mist*), showcases the organist in a quintet featuring the tenor of Teddy Edwards and guitarist Pat Martino, with his trio, and (on two standards) with trumpeter Blue Mitchell and tenor saxophonist Harold Vick. Overall, this 73-minute set has many fine solos, spirited ensembles and two well-rounded programs. —*Scott Yanow*

Living Soul / Apr. 22, 1966 / Prestige ✦✦✦

The Groover! / Feb. 14, 1968 / Prestige ✦✦✦

Holmes acquits himself well, if with few surprises, on this trio session with Billy Jackson on drums and either George Freeman or Earl Maddox on guitar. The organist shows his hundred-miles-per-hour capabilities on the frantic opener "Speak Low," but hits a more sensitive groove for "Blue Moon," and gets close to an R&B mood on the longest cut, the eight-minute "The Walrus." This has been reissued with another 1968 session, *That Healin' Feelin',* on the single-disc Prestige CD *Legends of Acid Jazz.* —*Richie Unterberger*

Legends of Acid Jazz / Feb. 14, 1968-Aug. 26, 1968 / Prestige ✦✦✦✦✦

Combines two 1968 albums, *The Groover!* and *That Healin' Feelin',* on one 78-minute disc. Both are solid Holmes sessions, the earlier *Groover* putting Holmes into an organ-guitar-drums trio. *That Healin' Feelin',* a quartet date recorded six months later, retains R&B elements but gets closer to solid straightahead jazz, especially with the sterling contributions of saxophonist Rusty Bryant. —*Richie Unterberger*

☆ **That Healin' Feelin'** / Aug. 26, 1968 / Prestige ✦✦✦✦

Holmes at the helm of a strong quartet, with especially notable contributions from Rusty Bryant (himself a soul-jazz artist of note) on sax and Billy Butler on guitar. The title track and "Irene Court" have especially nimble touches, and "Laura" slows the tempo down for some sensuous soloing by Bryant; the honky-tonk treatment of "See See Rider" gets closest to straight R&B territory. This has been reissued with another 1968 session, *The Groover!,* on the single-disc Prestige CD *Legends of Acid Jazz.* —*Richie Unterberger*

Double Exposure / 1973 / LRC ✦✦

This album contains two albums, one by Groove Holmes and the other by Jimmy McGriff. They do not play together here. Holmes is with Kwasi Jay Ourba on bongo/congas, Garald Hubbard on guitar, Jerry Jemmott on bass, Larry Willis on piano, and drums. Six cuts by McGriff and five by Groove Holmes. The tunes "Catherine" and "Rainy Day" are very nice. —*Michael Erlewine*

Night Glider / 1973 / Groove Merchant ✦✦✦

Groove's Groove / 1977-1988 / 32 Jazz ✦✦✦

There's no rhyme or reason to *Groove's Groove.* The ten songs on the album were recorded at various dates during 1977, 1980 and 1988, all with different lineups. There is one thing holding them together—it's all hot soul-jazz, with exceptionally funky playing from Groove Holmes. Spinning out busy, overloaded lines and chords from his organ, Holmes gets deep into the groove, turning everything into a speedy, bluesy soul-jazz workout—even the standard "Stella By Starlight" is taken

at a breakneck pace. His bandmates, for the most part, follow his lead, turning in funky performances that keep the music in the groove. The playing may be a little too busy for some tastes—Holmes and guitarist Gerald Smith trading skittering, frenzied solos on "Broadway" could make heads spin—but the resulting record burns with energy, and that alone is enough to recommend it. —*Stephen Thomas Erlewine*

Shippin' Out / Jun. 1977 / Muse ✦✦✦✦

After cutting a few albums for Groove Merchant in 1972-73, organist Groove Holmes was largely away from records (other than an odd date for Flying Dutchman) until this set, his Muse debut. Back in a comfortable setting, heading a soul-jazz quintet that also includes tenor saxophonist Dave Schnitter (best known for his association with Art Blakey's Jazz Messengers), guitarist Steve Giordano, drummer Idris Muhammad and Buddy Caldwell on conga, Holmes explores a wider range of songs than usual. In addition to his basic blues "Shippin' Out," the organist swings "Where or When," a faster-than-usual version of "Stella By Starlight," Chick Corea's "Windows" and even a credible interpretation of "Feelings." This fine Muse LP, which would be followed by several other rewarding efforts, has yet to be reissued on CD. —*Scott Yanow*

Good Vibrations / Dec. 19, 1977 / Muse ✦✦✦✦✦

An album of uptempo cookers from his middle period. W/ Houston Person (ts). —*Michael Erlewine*

Broadway / Dec. 2, 1980 / Muse ✦✦✦

W/ Houston Person (ts). Tight band. Later, uptempo but slick. It lacks the space that his early small-combo funk albums have. —*Michael Erlewine*

Blues All Day Long / Feb. 24, 1988 / Muse ✦✦✦✦✦

Blues All Day Long is an example of an artist excelling by sticking with what he does best. Richard "Groove" Holmes was a master of the grittiest of blues and the most romantic of ballads—two of the things that make the album the soul-jazz triumph it is. Whether savoring the richness of the blues on "Groove's Groove" (not to be confused with the gem he recorded on 1965's Soul Message) and "Slo Blooze," displaying his mastery of ballads on "These Foolish Things" or getting unapologetically funky on Benny Golson's "Killer Joe," the spirited Jimmy Smith disciple makes Blues a most welcome addition to his catalogue. Holmes has highly enthusiastic support in big-toned tenor titan Houston Person, trumpeter Cecil Bridgewater, guitarist Jimmy Ponder, drummer Cecil Brooks III and percussionist Ralph Dorsey, all of whom seem quite inspired by the South Jersey native's down-home soulfulness. —*Alex Henderson*

Hot Tat / Sep. 5, 1989 / Muse ✦✦✦✦

Richard "Groove" Holmes had less than two years to live when he recorded *Hot Tat,* but the Hammond B-3 great gives little or no indication that his health was in decline on this enjoyable, though not essential, soul-jazz date. Much of the time, Holmes is in a relaxed mood and generally favors what is essentially mood music—but mood music with integrity. Most of the players heard on 1988's *Blues All Day Long* are employed on this album, including tenor saxophonist Houston Person, trumpeter Cecil Bridgewater, guitarist Jimmy Ponder and percussionist Ralph Dorsey. But this time, Holmes works with bassist Wilbur Bascomb instead of handling all of the bass work himself, and employs Greg Bandy in place of Cecil Brooks III. *Hot Tat* will be of interest primarily to "Groove" Holmes' diehard fans; for more casual listeners, *Blues All Day Long* would be a better introduction to his Muse output. —*Alex Henderson*

Bertha Hope

b. Nov. 8, 1936, Vicksburg, MS

Piano / Hard Bop

Although she recorded three piano duets with her husband Elmo Hope in 1961, few knew that Bertha Hope was a talented pianist until her 1992 Minor Music release *Between Two Kings.* She grew up in California, started studying classical piano when she was three, became interested in jazz through the playing of Bud Powell and in the late '50s worked in Los Angeles clubs with a trio. Bertha was married to Elmo Hope from 1960 up until his death in 1967 but put her own career on hold until emerging in the early '90s. —*Scott Yanow*

In Search Of / Oct. 1990 / Steeple Chase ✦✦✦✦

● **Between Two Kings** / 1992 / Minor Music ✦✦✦✦✦

Elmo's Fire / Jan. 1991 / Steeple Chase ✦✦✦✦

Elmo Hope ((St.) Elmo Sylvester Hope)

b. Jun. 27, 1923, New York, NY, d. May 19, 1967, New York, NY

Piano / Bop, Hard Bop

Overshadowed throughout his life by his friends Bud Powell and Thelonious Monk, Elmo Hope was a talented pianist and composer whose life was cut short by drugs. His first important gig was with Joe Morris' R&B band (1948-51). He recorded in New York as a leader (starting in 1953) and with Sonny Rollins, Lou Donaldson, Clifford Brown and Jackie McLean, but the loss of his cabaret card (due to his drug use) made it very difficult for him to make a living in New York. After touring with Chet Baker in 1957, Hope relocated to Los Angeles. He performed with Lionel Hampton in 1959, recorded with Harold Land and Curtis Counce, and returned to New York in 1961. A short prison sentence did little to help his drug problem and, although he sounds fine on his trio performances of 1966, he died a little over a year later. Elmo Hope's sessions as a leader were cut for Blue Note, Prestige, Pacific Jazz, Hi Fi Jazz, Riverside, Celebrity, Beacon and Audio Fidelity; his last albums were initially released on Inner City. Hope was also a fine composer although none of his songs became standards. *—Scott Yanow*

Elmo Hope Trio / Feb. 8, 1959 / Original Jazz Classics ✦✦✦✦
This CD reissue brings back the music from a Contemporary LP that originally came out on the Hi Fi label. The boppish and fairly original Elmo Hope performs seven of his obscure originals, many of which are well worth reviving, plus "Like Someone in Love" in a trio with bassist Jimmy Bond and drummer Frank Butler. Bop and straightahead jazz fans wanting to hear a talented pianist play fresh tunes should explore Elmo Hope's valuable music. *—Scott Yanow*

★ **Trio and Quintet** / Jun. 18, 1953-Oct. 31, 1957 / Blue Note ✦✦✦✦✦

Hope Meets Foster / Oct. 4, 1955 / Original Jazz Classics ✦✦✦
This decent bop session features tenor saxophonist Frank Foster and pianist Elmo Hope in a quintet with the forgotten trumpeter Freeman Lee (who is on three of the six songs), bassist John Ore and drummer Art Taylor. They perform three of Hope's originals, two by Foster and an uptempo version of "Georgia on My Mind." None of the originals caught on (when was the last time anyone played "Fosterity"?) and nothing that innovative occurs but the music should please bop fans. *—Scott Yanow*

Meditations / July 28, 1955 / Original Jazz Classics ✦✦✦✦
Although Elmo Hope was one of the more interesting jazz composers of the 1950s, the emphasis in his trio set with bassist John Ore and drummer Willie Jones is on Hope's piano playing. Influenced greatly by Bud Powell (his contemporary), Hope performs standards (such as "All the Things You Are" and "Falling in Love with Love") along with some originals, most of which are based on the chord changes of earlier songs. Fans of bop piano and Bud Powell will want this enjoyable CD reissue. *—Scott Yanow*

The All Star Sessions / May 7, 1956-Nov. 14, 1961 / Milestone ✦✦✦✦✦
This single CD reissues all of the music (except for a second take of "Moe, Jr.") formerly on a two-LP set having the same name and catalog number. Before that, the music originally came out on the Prestige album *Informal Jazz* and the Riverside release *Homecoming*. The often-overlooked pianist-composer Elmo Hope is heard in three different settings. He first heads a four-song jam session (two swinging originals and a couple of standards) that has lengthy solos from trumpeter Donald Byrd and the contrasting tenors John Coltrane and Hank Mobley, along with fine support from bassist Paul Chambers and drummer Philly Jones. The 1961 dates consist of a sextet outing with trumpeter Blue Mitchell and the tenors of Jimmy Heath and Frank Foster, plus four numbers played with the trio (which has bassist Percy Heath and drummer Philly Joe Jones). Other than a version of "Imagination," all of the selections from 1961 are Hope's intriguing and ultimately logical originals. Excellent music from an underrated great. *—Scott Yanow*

Homecoming / Jun. 22, 1961+Jun. 29, 1961 / Original Jazz Classics ✦✦✦✦
Probing, introspective piano solos from Elmo Hope on this '61 date issued by Riverside. *—Ron Wynn*

Hope Full / Nov. 9, 1961+Nov. 14, 1961 / Original Jazz Classics ✦✦✦✦
During the early years of the bop revolution, few of its younger pianists recorded unaccompanied solos. Even by 1961, solo albums by the bop musicians were considered a bit unusual, but Elmo Hope (an underrated composer and pianist) fares quite well during this Riverside set, which has been reissued on CD. Hope is joined by his wife Bertha on second piano during three of the eight numbers, most notably on a swinging "Blues Left and Right." Of the solo pieces, Elmo Hope is at his best on "When Johnny Comes Marching Home" and a cocktailish, but appealing, version of "Liza." *—Scott Yanow*

Here's Hope / 1961 / V.S.O.P. ✦✦✦
In 1961, underrated bop pianist Elmo Hope recorded a pair of really obscure albums for the soon-defunct Celebrity and Beacon labels. Both were fortunately reissued by V.S.O.P. in the 1980s on two of their first LPs; hopefully, they will eventually come out on CD. This date, which matches Hope with bassist Paul Chambers and drummer Philly Joe Jones, features the pianist playing six of his compositions, including the catchy "De-Dah," which Clifford Brown had played eight years earlier. The one flaw of the album is that there are only 27 minutes of music, although the quality is quite high. *—Scott Yanow*

High Hope / 1961 / V.S.O.P. ✦✦✦✦
This excellent but little-known effort was originally put out by the quickly obsolete Beacon label. The talented pianist Elmo Hope performs six of his originals, including "Mo's Bluff" and "Crazy," in trios with either Paul Chambers or Butch Warren on bass and Philly Joe Jones or Granville Hogan on drums. Since there are just barely 26 minutes of music and this V.S.O.P. reissue has not yet resurfaced on CD, it is not an essential release, but the music is quite worthwhile and enjoyable. In fact, Elmo Hope's relatively slim discography makes all of his recordings quite valuable due to his talent. *—Scott Yanow*

The Final Sessions / Mar. 8, 1966+May 9, 1966 / Evidence ✦✦✦✦✦
Originally released posthumously on two Inner City LPs and later reissued by Fantasy on a pair of CDs, pianist Elmo Hope's last sessions are best acquired on this double CD, for it includes three alternate takes plus five selections that have been released for the first time unedited (making them slightly longer than previous versions). Hope, who is joined by bassist John Ore and either Clifford Jarvis or Philly Joe Jones on drums, was still in top playing form in 1966, although he would pass away the following year before he turned 44. Somewhat neglected, Hope was a contemporary and friend of Bud Powell and Thelonious Monk and, in addition to his playing, was a talented composer. In fact, out of the 14 selections that he performs, all but three were his originals and several are well worth reviving. Elmo Hope is in surprisingly joyous form throughout the set, sounding both original and accessible to bebop fans. Highly recommended. *—Scott Yanow*

Claude Hopkins

b. Aug. 24, 1903, Alexandria, VA, **d.** Feb. 19, 1984, New York, NY
Piano / Swing, Stride
A talented stride pianist, Claude Hopkins never became as famous as he deserved. He was a bandleader early on and toured Europe in the mid-'20s as the musical director for Josephine Baker. Hopkins returned to the US in 1926, led his own groups and in 1930 took over Charlie Skeete's band. Between 1932-35 he recorded steadily with his big band (all of the music has been reissued on three Classics CDs), which featured Jimmy Mundy arrangements and such fine soloists as trumpeter/vocalist Ovie Alston, trombonist Fernando Arbello, a young Edmond Hall on clarinet and baritone, and tenorman Bobby Sands, along with the popular high-note vocals of Orlando Roberson. The orchestra's recordings are a bit erratic, with more than their share of mistakes from the ensembles and a difficulty in integrating Hopkins' powerhouse piano with the full group, but they are generally quite enjoyable. Mundy's eccentric "Mush Mouth" is a classic and Hopkins introduced his best-known original "I Would Do Anything for You." Although they played regularly at Roseland (1931-35) and the Cotton Club (1935-36) and there were further sessions in 1937 and 1940, the Claude Hopkins Big Band never really caught on and ended up breaking up at the height of the swing era. Hopkins did lead a later unrecorded big band (1944-47) but mostly worked with small groups for the remainder of his career. He played with Red Allen's group during the second half of the 1950s, led his own band during 1960-66 and in 1968 was in the Jazz Giants with Wild Bill Davison. Claude Hopkins led an obscure record for 20th Century Fox (1958) and three Swingville albums (1960-63) but his best later work were solo stride dates for Chiaroscuro and Sackville (both in 1972) and a trio session for Black and Blue in 1974; it is surprising that his piano skills were not more extensively documented. *—Scott Yanow*

● **1932-1934** / May 24, 1932-Jan. 1, 1932 / Classics ✦✦✦✦✦
The first of three Classics CDs that contain all of pianist Claude Hopkins' big-band recordings is the most essential of the trio. Although Hopkins was a masterful stride player, his orchestra never really had its own individual sound, and therefore did not catch on. However, many of the selections on this set (particularly the Jimmy Mundy-arranged instrumentals) are quite memorable, with the eccentric "Mush Mouth" being a classic. Other highlights include Hopkins' theme "I Would Do Most Anything for You," "Three Little Words," "California Here I Come" and "Honeysuckle Rose." In addition to the leader, the main soloists in the band during the era were trumpeter/vocalist Ovie Alston, trombonist Fernando Arbello, up-and-coming clarinetist Edmond Hall, and underrated tenor Bobby Sands, but the most popular member of the orchestra was high-voiced singer Orlando Roberson. Highly recommended to swing and big-band fans, this set of studio recordings also includes 11 numbers not previously out on a collectors' LP. *—Scott Yanow*

1934-1935 / Jan. 11, 1934-Feb. 1934 / Classics ✦✦✦✦✦
The second of three CDs documenting the history of the Claude Hopkins Orchestra does not quite reach the heights of the first set (too many Orlando Roberson high-note vocals and some erratic moments by the musicians) but still has many moments of interest. With trumpeter Ovie Alston (who takes four vocals), trombonist Fernando Arbello, clarinetist Edmond Hall (also heard on baritone), and tenorman Bobby Sands sharing the solo space with pianist Hopkins, some of the selections swing quite hard. Best are "Harlem Rhythm Dance," "Everybody Shuffle,"

"King Porter Stomp," "In the Shade of the Old Apple Tree" and "Zozoi." All of the numbers except for the last three are from 1934. —*Scott Yanow*

Singin' in the Rain / Oct. 18, 1935 / Jazz Archives ✦✦✦✦✦

1935 / Nov. 1935 / Alamac ✦✦✦
The Claude Hopkins big band did not cut any records from March 1935 to January 1937, a period when swing really caught on. All that exists of the orchestra during this period, when it was greatly overshadowed by its competition, are some radio broadcasts that were released on obscure LPs. This budget album emphasizes the group's jazz side, with seven instrumentals and three that have rhythm vocals by Ovie Alston; the band's main soloists during this time were Alston on trumpet, clarinetist Edmond Hall, altoist Hilton Jefferson and Bobby Sands on tenor. Since the recording quality is not always the greatest and this album was cheaply put together, it is not essential, but serious swing collectors may want to search for it. —*Scott Yanow*

1937-1940 / Feb. 2, 1937-Mar. 4, 1940 / Classics ✦✦✦
The third and final Claude Hopkins Classics CD has some really obscure and diverse music. The 1937 Hopkins big band included trumpeter Jabbo Smith and trombonist Vic Dickenson in its lineup, but of the six titles it cut, five are showcases for singer Beverly White; in all, the legendary Smith gets a single chorus. Better are eight titles by trumpeter Ovie Alston's orchestra, which includes Hopkins on piano in 1938 along with some of his sidemen. This CD concludes with six numbers by the pianist's struggling 1940 big band, decent swing performances that preceded the orchestra's complete breakup. A bit of a collector's item. —*Scott Yanow*

Yes Indeed / Mar. 25, 1960 / Swingville ✦✦✦

Let's Jam / Feb. 21, 1961 / Swingville ✦✦✦

Swing Time / May 22, 1963 / Swingville ✦✦✦

Crazy Fingers / 1972 / Chiaroscuro ✦✦✦✦

Soliloquy / May 13, 1972 / Sackville ✦✦✦✦✦
A brilliant stride pianist, Claude Hopkins was captured on record relatively few times after 1940 and rarely on unaccompanied solos, which seemed to be his natural setting. This solo set really allows Hopkins an opportunity to stretch out, and he excels on eight standards and three originals. The frequently exciting yet sometimes thoughtful music is highlighted by "Indiana," "Sugar," "Crazy Fingers" and "Who's Sorry Now?" Recommended. —*Scott Yano*

Fred Hopkins

b. Oct. 11, 1947, Chicago, IL
Bass / Avant-Garde
Fred Hopkins has gained his greatest recognition as bassist with the co-op trio Air, but he has played through the years with most of the top avant-garde musicians and his abilities are well known to his fellow players. He recorded with Kalaparusha Maurice McIntyre in 1970, worked with Henry Threadgill and Steve McCall in the trio Reflection (1971-72), freelanced in Chicago, moved to New York in 1975 and reunited with Threadgill and McCall as Air (1975-mid-'80s); after McCall's departure in 1982 the group (with Pheeroan AkLaff on drums) became known as New Air. Hopkins has also worked and recorded with Anthony Braxton, Marion Brown, Oliver Lake, David Murray, Hamiet Bluiett, Craig Harris, Don Pullen and many others but, strangely enough, he has never led a record session of his own. —*Scott Yanow*

Glenn Horiuchi

b. Feb. 27, 1955
Piano, Keyboards / Avant-Garde, World Fusion
One of the key figures in the mixture of adventurous jazz with Asian melodies and instruments, Glenn Horiuchi has emphasized original compositions that look both backwards and ahead to the future throughout his productive career. After getting a master's in mathematics from UC San Diego, Horiuchi became a major activist in the National Coalition for Redress/Reparations, documenting stories about the internment of Japanese-Americans during World War II and helping to win reparations for the victims. A highly original pianist and composer, the Los Angeles-based Horiuchi (who has written extensively for the theatre) has recorded as a leader for the Soul Note and AsianImprov labels. —*Scott Yanow*

Issei Spirit / Jul. 1988 / Asian Improv ✦✦✦✦
Pianist Glenn Horiuchi's second album as a leader (following his debut *Next Step*) is a strong effort. Horiuchi mixes together his Japanese heritage with inside/outside jazz, creating explorative and unpredictable yet often melodic music. His six originals on this album vary the personnel and range from his unaccompanied solo on "Saburo" and a trio to a two-bass quartet; Rosey Ruey has a brief vocal on "Tear Dem Walls." —*Scott Yanow*

Manzanar Voices / Jun. 1989 / Asian Improv ✦✦✦✦
Glenn Horiuchi's music is generally political (he was heavily involved in the reparations movement for the Japanese-Americans forced to live in prison camps during World War II) and hints strongly at the traditional Japanese taiko rhythm yet also has the improvising and excitement of jazz. On this LP, Horiuchi interacts closely with drummer Leon Alexander and either M'Chaka Uba or Taiji Miyagawa on bass for six of his diverse originals. —*Scott Yanow*

Oxnard Beat / Oct. 1989 / Soul Note ✦✦✦✦✦
Throughout his career, pianist-composer Glenn Horiuchi has consistently (and successfully) combined together Asian music (especially from Japan) with advanced jazz. This widely available set (most of Horiuchi's other recordings have been done for the tiny AsianImprov label) features the pianist, tenor saxophonist Francis Wong (who doubles on flute), bassist Taiji Miyagawa and Leon Alexander (on drums and vibes) stretching on seven of Horiuchi's continually intriguing originals. The taiko rhythm (prevalent in Japanese music) plus some of the advanced harmonies give Horiuchi's recordings their own unique flavor. —*Scott Yanow*

Poston Sonata / Dec. 1991 / Asian Improv ✦✦✦
Glenn Horiuchi, who was heavily involved in the reparations movement for Japanese-American survivors of the ten prison camps in the US, pays tribute to the internees of the camp at Poston, Arizona on this CD. Performing five solos and three duets with Lillian Nakano (who performs on the shamisen, a traditional Japanese instrument), Horiuchi includes remakes of some of his earlier pieces plus the four-part "Poston Sonata." Adventurous music that blends together jazz with Japanese music. —*Scott Yanow*

● **Calling is It and Now** / Sep. 15, 1993 / Soul Note ✦✦✦✦✦

Hilltop View / Aug. 27, 1995+Sep. 2, 1995 / Music & Arts ✦✦✦

Mercy / Sep. 2, 1995+May 26, 1996 / Music & Arts ✦✦✦✦

Paul Horn

b. Mar. 17, 1930, New York, NY
Flute, Alto Saxophone, Clarinet / Hard Bop, Folk-Jazz, World Fusion
When one evaluates Paul Horn's career, it is as if he were two people, pre- and post-1967. In his early days, Horn was an excellent cool-toned altoist and flutist, while in more recent times he has been a new age flutist whose mood music is often best used as background music for meditation. Horn started on piano when he was four and switched to alto at the age of 12. After a stint with the Sauter-Finegan Orchestra on tenor, Horn was Buddy Collette's replacement with the popular Chico Hamilton Quintet (1956-58), playing alto, flute and clarinet. He became a studio musician in Los Angeles but also found time during 1957-66 to record cool jazz albums for Dot (later reissued on Impulse), World Pacific, Hi Fi Jazz, Columbia and RCA, and he participated in a memorable live session with Cal Tjader in 1959. In addition, in 1964 Horn recorded one of the first *Jazz Masses*, utilizing an orchestra arranged by Lalo Schifrin. In 1967 Paul Horn studied transcendental meditation in India and became a teacher. The following year he recorded unaccompanied flute solos at the Taj Mahal (where he enjoyed interacting with the echoes) and in the future would record in the Great Pyramid, tour China (1979) and the Soviet Union, record using the sounds of killer whales as "accompaniment" and found his own label, Golden Flute. Most of Paul Horn's work of the past 20 years is of little interest from the jazz standpoint. —*Scott Yanow*

Plenty of Horn / Oct. 1958 / Dot ✦✦✦
While still a member of the Chico Hamilton Quintet, Paul Horn recorded two albums for the Dot label that were later reissued on Impulse and most recently came out in the late 1970s on this two-LP set. Switching among flute, clarinet and his cool-toned alto, Horn is in excellent form on the wide-ranging material, which reflects the influence of Hamilton's chamber jazz approach but also contains some hard swinging. The settings range from a quartet to a ten-piece group that utilizes a string quartet and a 12-piece mini big band. Among the sidemen are drummer Hamilton, cellist Fred Katz, vibraphonist Larry Bunker and pianist Gerry Wiggins, but most of the emphasis is on Horn's playing (particularly on flute); he also contributed five originals. Worth searching for, this music has not yet been reissued on CD. —*Scott Yanow*

Something Blue / Mar. 1960 / Original Jazz Classics ✦✦✦✦
Years before Paul Horn became famous for his pioneering new age and mood music albums, he was an adventurous bop-based improviser trying to create an alternative to the hard bop music of the era. On this CD reissue of a set cut for Hi Fi, Horn plays alto, flute and clarinet on six complex originals (four are by the leader) in a quintet with vibraphonist Emil Richards, pianist Paul Moer, bassist Jimmy Bond and drummer Billy Higgins. All of the music is fairly episodic, with tricky frameworks and some unusual time signatures being utilized. The results are generally stimulating; Richards is actually the most impressive soloist on the interesting if often dry release. —*Scott Yanow*

The Sound of Paul Horn / Mar. 30, 1961 / Columbia ✦✦✦✦
This sadly out-of-print Columbia LP features Paul Horn at the peak of his jazz powers. Horn, who after 1967 would stick mostly to mood music, was a fine jazz improviser who fell between cool jazz and hard bop. He doubles on alto and flute on six originals (including the lengthy "Mirage for Miles") plus "Without a Song" and "My Funny Valentine." Also in fine form are vibraphonist Emil Richards, pianist Paul Moer, bassist Jimmy Bond and drummer Milt Turner. —*Scott Yanow*

Profile of a Jazz Musician / Aug. 16, 1962-Aug. 17, 1962 / Columbia ✦✦✦✦
In the early 1960s, Paul Horn was a swinging and advanced improviser whose music reflected an interest in third-stream music while remaining tied to the bop/cool tradition. With his regular quintet of the era (which also includes vibraphonist Emil Richards, pianist Paul Moer, bassist Victor Gaskin and drummer Milt Turner), Horn (on alto, flute and bass flute) performs five of his originals, a song by Moer, Dr. Seuss' "Just Because We're Kids" and "Lazy Afternoon." This out-of-print LP was one of Horn's finer jazz dates. —*Scott Yanow*

Cycle / Mar. 17, 1965-Mar. 18, 1965 / RCA ✦✦
One can hear hints of Paul Horn's future directions on this obscure LP. Horn (doubling on alto and flute) shows his interest in Indian music on "Shadows No. 1" and "Shadows No. 2" (which are dedicated to Ravi Shankar) and in the drone feeling that he gives "Chim Chim Cheree." "In the Bag" and "Greensleeves" add a pair of Scottish bagpipes (!) to the quintet (which also includes vibraphonist Lynn Blessing, pianist Mike Lang, bassist Bill Plummer and drummer Bill Goodwin) so this is not an album for everyone. Within three years, Horn would abandon jazz altogether to work on atmospheric mood music. —*Scott Yanow*

Inside the Taj Mahal / Apr. 25, 1968 / Rykodisc ✦✦✦

Inside the Taj Mahal, Vol. 2 / Apr. 25, 1968 / Kuckuck ✦✦✦
Horn's most influential album was captured when Horn slipped into the Taj Mahal one night with his flute and a tape recorder. The resulting set of spontaneous solo flute improvisations took full advantage of the magical resonances of India's famous monument. Each tone Horn plays hangs suspended in space for 28 seconds, and the acoustics are so perfect you can't tell when the original sound stops and the echo takes over. —*Linda Kohanov*

Inside the Great Pyramid / May 1977 / Kuckuck ✦✦✦
The flutist continues his travels, arriving in Egypt to record in the Great Pyramid of Giza. The double-CD set features a powerful introspective suite of 40 spontaneously composed "psalms" created by Horn on piccolo, alto, and C flutes. —*Linda Kohanov*

China / 1978-1986 / Kuckuck ✦✦✦
This exquisite collaboration between Horn and Chinese multi-instrumentalist David Mingyue Liang captures the timeless elegance of oriental music. —*Linda Kohanov*

Inside the Cathedral / Aug. 21, 1983 / Kuckuck ✦✦✦

Traveler / 1985 / Kuckuck ✦✦✦
Originally released in 1987, this album is a striking summation of Horn's many talents. Reverberant solo instrumental episodes are complemented by evocative original compositions involving synthesizers, string quartet, even a boys' choir. —*Linda Kohanov*

The Peace Album / 1988 / Kuckuck ✦✦✦✦✦
This holiday release from 1988 is by one of the greatest flutists of our time. The exquisite elegance of the music comes partly from the uniquely conceived "multi-flute orchestra," in which Horn is the only musician, adding unusual depth and dimension to the performances of these pieces, ranging from "Silent Night" to "We Three Kings" to "Ave Maria." This Celestial Harmonies release is dedicated to the peace inside each one of us and offers sterling performances throughout. —*Backroads Music/Heartbeats*

Brazilian Images / Oct. 1989 / Black Sun ✦✦
Listeners will hear the sounds of flute, saxophone, Chinese bamboo flute, guitar and percussion on this release dedicated to the beautiful spirit of the Brazilian people . . . —*MusD*

Africa / 1994 / Gema ✦✦✦✦✦
West African tradition is upheld in Paul Horn's *Africa*. Horn delicately adds color to the texture of the original compositions by Guinean musician Sekou Camara Cobra. The music falls squarely within the realm of griots—hereditary West African storytellers and minstrels. The jazzy overtones of Horn's flute and saxophone blend well with the syncopated rhythms of Sekou's percussion and guitar work. The songs are sung in the traditional languages of Malinke and Susa. —*MusD*

☆ **Inside Canyon de Chelly** / 1997 / Canyon ✦✦✦✦
Paul Horn, one of the leading proponents of solo improvisational flute, collaborates here with Native American flute player R. Carlos Nakai in a genuinely equal pairing. As with some of Paul Horn's earlier *Inside* albums, this is a field recording,

done in two weeks inside of Canyon De Chelly and capitalizing on its natural acoustics. Listen to "Raven Rendezvous," in which Horn uses his soprano saxophone to "speak" to a raven that happened into the area. The sound of Nakai's Native American flute, echoing the natural sounds of the canyon and its water, is breathtaking on "Within the Rocks." The two of them toss ideas back and forth at times, trying out different tonalities or embellishing what the other has put forth. —*Bob Gottlieb*

Shirley Horn

b. May 1, 1934, Washington, DC
Piano, Vocals / Ballads
A superior ballad singer and a talented pianist, Shirley Horn put off potential success until finally becoming a major attraction while in her 50s. She studied piano from the age of four. After attending Howard University, Horn put together her first trio in 1954 and was encouraged in the early '60s by Miles Davis and Quincy Jones. She recorded three albums during 1963-65 for Mercury and ABC-Paramount but chose to stick around Washington D.C. and raise a family instead of pursuing her career. In the early '80s she began recording for Steeple Chase but Shirley Horn really had her breakthrough in 1987 when she started making records for Verve, an association that continues to the present day. —*Scott Yanow*

Live at the Village Vanguard / Aug. 1961 / Can-Am ✦✦✦
Vocalist-pianist Shirley Horn's earliest recording, this live performance (during a time when Miles Davis was championing her) predates Horn's first studio date by two years. The playing time is a bit brief (33 minutes) and the recording quality is just decent but is Shirley Horn already playing and singing in a recognizable style. Although there are a couple of medium-tempo numbers, the emphasis as usual is on ballads; an instrumental version of "'Round Midnight" gives the historic set (a trio outing with bassist John Mixon and drummer Gene Gammage) some variety. —*Scott Yanow*

Loads of Love / 1963 / Mercury ✦✦✦
Two of pianist-vocalist Shirley Horn's rarest (and earliest) recordings are reissued in full on this single CD. Actually, Horn does not play piano at all, sticking exclusively to vocals, and she had less control over the interpretations (being persuaded to sing some songs at faster-than-usual tempos) than she would later on. The arrangements for the big bands that back Horn were written by Jimmy Jones and Quincy Jones and, although the overall music is enjoyable, Horn would have much preferred to be the pianist behind her own vocals. Since she would only record two other albums during the next 15 years (sticking to playing locally in the Washington D.C. area while raising her daughter), this CD gives one a valuable look at the early Shirley Horn; her distinctive vocal style was already nearly fully formed. —*Scott Yanow*

Travelin' Light / 1965 / ABC/Paramount ✦✦✦
This CD reissue brings back a historic session, vocalist-pianist Shirley Horn's last before she drifted into semi-retirement so she could raise her daughter. Among her sidemen on this date include trumpeter Joe Newman, the flutes of Frank Wess and Jerome Richardson and guitarist Kenny Burrell, but the main star throughout is Horn. Not all of the material is equally strong and none of the very concise dozen performances clock in at even three minutes, so this is not an essential session. But Shirley Horn fans and completists will want the generally enjoyable vocal date. —*Scott Yanow*

A Lazy Afternoon / Jul. 9, 1978 / Steeple Chase ✦✦✦
Brisk, inviting, and well played. —*Ron Wynn*

Violets for Your Furs / Jul. 10, 1981-Jul. 12, 1981 / Steeple Chase ✦✦✦✦

All Night Long / Jul. 1981 / Steeple Chase ✦✦✦
The word about Horn's talents begins to spread in the jazz world. —*Ron Wynn*

Garden of the Blues / Nov. 16, 1984 / Steeple Chase ✦✦✦✦
Tremendous piano, fine compositions. —*Ron Wynn*

I Thought About You / May 12, 1987+May 13, 1987 / Verve ✦✦✦✦✦
This live set (recorded at Hollywood's Vine St. Bar and Grill) was Shirley Horn's "comeback" album after many years in which she purposely maintained a low profile as she raised her daughter. Typical of Horn's music ever since, she sings intimate ballads with her trio (which includes bassist Charles Ables and drummer Steve Williams) and plays very effective piano behind her vocals, taking "Isn't It Romantic" as an instrumental. —*Scott Yanow*

Softly / Oct. 1987 / Audiophile ✦✦✦✦

● **Close Enough for Love** / Nov. 1988 / Verve ✦✦✦✦✦
Shirley Horn's second Verve recording consolidated the success that she had had with her previous release, *I Thought About You*, and resulted in her gaining a large audience for her ballad vocals and solid jazz piano playing. Performing with her usual trio (which includes bassist Charles Ables and drummer Steve Williams) and

guest tenor Buck Hill on five of the 13 tracks, Horn is heard in definitive form throughout these studio sessions. Highlights include "Beautiful Friendship," "Baby, Baby All the Time," "This Can't Be Love," "I Wanna Be Loved," "But Beautiful," "Get out of Town" and "It Could Happen to You." —*Scott Yanow*

You Won't Forget Me / Jun. 12, 1990-Aug. 1990 / Verve ♦♦♦♦
Miles Davis (tpt) and Wynton (tpt) and Branford Marsalis (ts) are part of the guest cast. Great piano and delightful vocals. —*Ron Wynn*

Here's to Life / 1991 / Verve ♦♦♦
Shirley Horn's meeting with a string section and an orchestra arranged by Johnny Mandel has some exquisite moments, although sometimes it is just overly sweet. Horn recorded with her trio (which includes bassist Charles Ables and drummer Steve Williams) first, emphasizing slow ballads. Mandel used the pianist-vocalist's improvisations and chord voicings as the basis for his charts, and trumpeter Wynton Marsalis took guest solos on "A Time for Love" and "Quietly There." Shirley Horn fans will love this CD (which includes such numbers as "Here's to Life," "How Am I to Know?" and "If You Love Me") but no real surprises or contrast occur. —*Scott Yanow*

I Love You Paris / Mar. 7, 1992 / Verve ♦♦♦

Light out of Darkness (A Tribute to Ray Charles) / Apr. 30, 1993-May 3, 1993 / Verve ♦♦♦♦

The Main Ingredient / May 15, 1995-May 18, 1995 / Verve ♦♦♦♦♦

Loving You / Feb. 11, 1997 / Verve ♦♦♦
Shirley Horn continues in a formula that has become very popular for her. De-emphasizing her piano, Horn sings one very slow ballad after another. The intimate music, which features her trio members, percussionist Alex Acuna and most prominently the keyboards and orchestrations of George Mesterhazy, has very little variety and should be listened to in small doses. Horn's singing is full of subtle emotion and sensuality, particularly on such numbers as Jobim's "Someone To Light Up My Life," Lil Green's "In the Dark," "Kiss and Run" and "The Island," but no real surprises occur and the consistently dreamy mood has the potential to become quite sleepy. —*Scott Yanow*

Lena Horne

b. Jun. 30, 1917, New York, NY
Vocals / Swing, Middle-Of-The-Road Pop, Show Tunes, Traditional Pop
An ageless beauty and a very appealing personality, Lena Horne was never really a jazz singer as much as a superior pop vocalist, since she does not improvise. Horne started performing when she was six, sang and danced at the Cotton Club as early as 1934, was with Noble Sissle's Orchestra (1935-36), recorded with Teddy Wilson in the late '30s and sang with Charlie Barnet's big band during 1940-41. She also recorded with Artie Shaw (1941) and made major impressions in the films *Boogie Woogie Dream* (actually a jazz short), *Cabin in the Sky* and especially *Stormy Weather*. Married to arranger-pianist Lennie Hayton, Horne has been a popular attraction since the 1940s but her connection with jazz (even when she sings veteran swing standards) is peripheral. A Bluebird compilation of some of her best early recordings is recommended. —*Scott Yanow*

● **Stormy Weather: The Legendary Lena (1941-1958)** / Jan. 7, 1941-Jun. 9, 1958 / Bluebird ♦♦♦♦♦
Although the very attractive Lena Horne has never really been a jazz singer, her vocals are generally of interest to jazz listeners and she has occasionally recorded in jazz settings. This Bluebird CD is fairly definitive of the first half of her career. Horne sings a pair of ballads with Charlie Barnet's 1941 Orchestra and two songs (including "Don't Take Your Love from Me") with a unique Artie Shaw-led all-star band that includes Benny Carter, Red Allen and a string section. The remainder of the disc features Lena backed by studio orchestras and the results are superior (if sometimes overly dramatic) renditions of standards as rendered by a topnotch cabaret singer. Highlights include "Stormy Weather," "Ill Wind," "Moanin' Low," "As Long as I Live" and "It's All Right with Me." —*Scott Yanow*

Lena Horne at MGM / 1942-1956 / Rhino ♦♦♦♦
Lena Horne appeared in many MGM musicals during the 1940s but almost always in cameos, singing one or two songs and then disappearing. This Rhino CD collects together 23 songs (six of which were actually outtakes) from Horne's films. Although generally not jazz, these swinging middle-of-the-road pop performances are quite enjoyable and give one a well-rounded musical portrait of Lena Horne. Highlights include "Honeysuckle Rose," "Somebody Loves Me," a medley from *Showboat* and "The Lady Is a Tramp." —*Scott Yanow*

More Than You Know / 1946 / Simitar ♦♦♦
Musically, the contents on this CD are excellent. The packaging, however, is quite faulty. There are less than 28 minutes of music (nine selections from 1946 that generally clock in at the most at three minutes apiece), and nowhere are the dates or

personnel given. One of the more jazz-oriented Lena Horne collections, it finds the singer often joined by bands (ranging from a combo to an orchestra) arranged by pianist Phil Moore, with occasional solos from either Karl George or Gerald Wilson on trumpet, Tyree Glenn or Murray McEachern on trombone, tenorman Lucky Thompson and altoist Willie Smith. Horne sounds wonderful on such songs as "More Than You Know," "Old Fashioned Love" and "Glad to Be Unhappy," but the results only add up to about 40% of a CD. —*Scott Yanow*

Lena & Gabor / Oct. 11, 1969 / Gryphon ♦♦♦
Collaboration between Horne and guitarist Gabor Szabo, who proved to be one of her most sympathetic accompanists. They made expert duo recordings, with Szabo's delicate, sometimes emphatic playing smoothly accompanying Horne's distinctive vocals. The '69 session has been reissued on CD. —*Ron Wynn*

The Lady & Her Music [Original Master Recording] / 1981 / Mobile Fidelity ♦♦♦
A two-disc reissue of the album of the Broadway show—which was basically a retrospective of Lena Horne's life and career. The 1981 album was produced by Quincy Jones, who did a masterful job of delivering the show to recorded form. Horne was in fine voice for this, and there isn't a disappointing moment, though some will want to go back to the original versions of much of the material—they should check out *Lena Horne at MGM*, a Rhino release. —*Steven McDonald*

An Evening with Lena Horne / Sep. 19, 1994 / Blue Note ♦♦♦♦♦
It is difficult not to love Lena Horne. Recorded when she was 77, this live CD finds the ageless singer sounding as if she were 57 at the most (and the photo of her on the cover makes her look 47). Horne talks the lyrics a little more than in the past but she cuts loose in spots with power, performs superior standards, takes part of a Duke Ellington-Billy Strayhorn medley as a duet with bassist Ben Brown and is not shy to hold long notes. On six of the songs, 11 horns from the Count Basie Orchestra riff and play harmonies behind her; otherwise Horne is joined by her usual quartet with pianist Mike Renzi and guitarist Rodney Jones. The well-rounded set is Lena Horne's most rewarding recording in years. —*Scott Yanow*

Wayne Horvitz

b. 1955, New York, NY
Keyboards / Avant-Garde
Active as a performer since 1976, Wayne Horvitz has long been a key part of New York's downtown new music scene. In addition to leading his own band, the President, he has worked with John Zorn (on both *Naked City* and a tribute to Sonny Clark), Butch Morris, Billy Bang, Fred Frith, Robert Previte and others, recording his unpredictable music for Elektra/Nonesuch, Black Saint and Sound Aspects. —*Scott Yanow*

Some Order, Long Understood / Feb. 1982 / Black Saint ♦♦♦

This New Generation / 1985 / Elektra ♦♦♦♦
Mid-'80s release that established Horovitz among the prime composers and players on the contemporary improvising scene. He's not among either the traditionalists or the fusion/light jazz crowd, but is part of the New York "downtown" school that utilizes everything from hard bop to rock to contemporary classical. Guitarist Bill Frisell was also an important contributor to the date. —*Ron Wynn*

Nine Below Zero / 1986 / Sound Aspects ♦♦♦

Todos Santos / May 1989 / Sound Aspects ♦♦♦
Explosive, animated session from the late '80s with Horvitz, Butch Morris, and Robert Previte engaging in spirited dialogues that were sometimes nearly chaotic, but always impressive. Horovitz shared space with the duo of Bill Frisell and Doug Wieselman and played compositions done by his wife Robin Holcomb. —*Ron Wynn*

● **Bring Your Camera** / Dec. 11, 1991 / Elektra ♦♦♦♦
A downtown NYC supergroup led by keyboardist Wayne Horvitz hybridizes jazz, rock, improv, and dashes of blues guitar from Elliot Sharp. —*Myles Boisen*

Live in Poland / Feb. 3, 1994 / Cavity Search ♦♦♦♦

Cold Spell / Feb. 18, 1997 / Knitting Factory ♦♦♦

Monologue: Twenty Compositions for Dance / May 5, 1997 / Cavity Search ♦♦♦

George Howard

b. , Philadelphia, PA d. Mar. 20, 1998
Soprano Saxophone / Instrumental Pop, R&B, Crossover Jazz
George Howard's polished fusion of funk, jazz and urban soul helped the soprano saxophonist become one of the most popular contemporary jazz performers of the '80s and '90s. Since he concentrated on groove and overall sound instead of improvisation, Howard never received much attention from jazz critics, but he retained a large audience well into his second decade of performing.

Howard began his musical career in the late '70s. He received his first break when Grover Washington Jr., one of his musical idols, invited him on a tour in 1979. The tour helped establish Howard's name, and in 1982 he released his debut album, *Asphalt Garden*, on Palo Alto. The record was a moderate hit, as was its follow-up, 1984's *Steppin' Out*. It wasn't until the 1985 release of *Dancing in the Sun* that Howard earned a large audience. The album reached No. 1 on the contemporary jazz charts. Following the release of *Dancing In the Sun*, he moved to MCA, where he issued *A Nice Place to Be*, *Reflections*, *Personal* and *Love Will Follow*. All four records were considerable successes on the charts. In 1991, Howard signed to GRP, releasing his debut *Love and Understanding* that year. It was followed by *Do I Ever Cross Your Mind?* in 1992 and *When Summer Comes* in 1993. *A Home Far Away* was released in 1994, and *Attitude Adjustment* was issued in 1996. All of his GRP recordings were quite successful, confirming his place among the most popular contemporary jazz performers of the '90s. His first five years with GRP, plus a selection of his MCA recordings, were summarized on 1997's *The Very Best of George Howard*. Howard returned to recording with *Midnight Mood*, which was released in January 1998 shortly before his premature death from cancer. —*Stephen Thomas Erlewine*

Asphalt Gardens / Jun. 21, 1982+Aug. 31, 1982 / Palo Alto ✦✦✦

Steppin' Out / 1984 / GRP ✦✦

Dancing in the Sun / 1985 / GRP ✦✦

● **The Very Best of George Howard (and Then Some)** / 1985-1997 / GRP ✦✦✦✦✦
Spanning 1985-97, this compilation focuses on George Howard's work for MCA and later, GRP, and shows how little progress the soprano saxman made artistically in the course of 12 years. There are a few worthwhile tracks on this CD, including the haunting "A Home Far Away" and the sensuous R&B-pop number "Find Your Way" (one of two new offerings). But regrettably, the disc underscores the fact that more often than not, Howard chose to resort to formula instead of gambling with inspiration. From 1985's "Love Will Find a Way" (a pointless cover of the Lionel Richie hit) to 1996's "Diane's Blues," the Philly native's blend of pop, R&B and jazz has a homogenized, assembly-line quality and sounds like the work of a poor man's Grover Washington, Jr. It's sad that Howard usually insists on the automatic-pilot approach because—as he demonstrates on "A Home Far Away"—he's capable of much more. —*Alex Henderson*

A Nice Place to Be / 1986 / MCA ✦✦✦

Personal / 1989 / MCA ✦✦
This outing by George Howard contains soul vocals, R&B grooves and the leader's noodling soprano, played without the fire, creativity or originality of his major influence, Grover Washington, Jr. Nothing unexpected occurs and the derivative dance music (the main purpose of which was getting radio airplay) was instantly dated. Very forgettable. —*Scott Yanow*

Love Will Follow / Dec. 30, 1991 / GRP ✦✦✦✦

● **Do I Ever Cross Your Mind?** / 1992 / GRP ✦✦✦✦
Unlike most of the soprano blowers out there in the pop-jazz market, Howard avoids the "Fuzak" plague, and keeps a strong hold on his R&B roots. At the same, time, Howard's 1992 CD stays away from the vocal-dominated tracks, which pop up all the more frequently in this genre. A solid, masterful set of funk/fusion. —*Steve Aldrich*

Love and Understanding / Jan. 13, 1992 / GRP ✦✦✦
George Howard was never a bad musician. In fact, the Philadelphian's live performances often underscore the fact that while he's hardly in a class with Grover Washington, Jr. (his main influence), he can be rather likeable when given the chance to let loose and stretch. But sadly, Howard seldom allows himself to do that in the studio. *Love & Understanding* is typical of so much of his work—overproduced, formulaic and devoid of improvisation. His by-the-book R&B-pop approach is designed to ensure commercial radio airplay, and he's careful to avoid making any type of personal or honest statement. Quite clearly, the album shamelessly wastes the talents of a decent musician. —*Alex Henderson*

When Summer Comes / 1993 / GRP ✦✦

Home Far Away / 1994 / GRP ✦✦✦
George Howard has never claimed to be a jazz artist and his recordings are of minor interest to followers of improvised music. There are a few times on this recording when the soprano saxophonist (who has made a career out of copying Grover Washington, Jr.) sounds like a solo might cut loose, but the electronic rhythms keep that impulse in check. This set is only passable as background music and will immediately disappoint anyone who gives it a close listen. —*Scott Yanow*

Attitude Adjustment / 1995 / GRP ✦✦✦
1995 was a bad year for George Howard. He got a divorce, somebody messed with his car, and there were other unpleasant experiences he doesn't care to specify. Of course, as a popular artist, Howard felt compelled to convey his experience to his

listeners. How to do so in an essentially instrumental medium like jazz? Talk! In "Best Friend," Howard takes his saxophone out of his mouth long enough to mutter about his disintegrating relationship, even quoting Chris Darden: "...but uh...I'm not bitter." In the title track, the "Adjustment Crew" addresses the problem of automotive vandalism, and on the album-closing "Adjusted Attitude," the crew takes on Rush Limbaugh. You say you would rather hear Howard play than listen to his problems? Well, there's some of that on this record, too, in the usual mixture of busy drum tracks and background vocals. Still, you hope next year will be better for him, both personally and musically. —*William Ruhlmann*

Freddie Hubbard (Frederick Dewayne Hubbard)

b. Apr. 7, 1938, Indianapolis, IN
Trumpet, Fluegelhorn / Hard Bop, Post-Bop
One of the great jazz trumpeters of all time, Freddie Hubbard formed his sound out of the Clifford Brown/Lee Morgan tradition and by the early '70s was immediately distinctive and the pacesetter in jazz. However a string of blatantly commercial albums later in the decade damaged his reputation and, in the early '90s (with the deaths of Dizzy Gillespie and Miles Davis), just when Hubbard seemed perfectly suited for the role of veteran master, his chops started causing him serious troubles. Born and raised in Indianapolis, Hubbard played early on with Wes and Monk Montgomery. He moved to New York in 1958, roomed with Eric Dolphy (with whom he recorded in 1960) and was in the groups of Philly Joe Jones (1958-59), Sonny Rollins, Slide Hampton and J.J. Johnson before touring Europe with Quincy Jones (1960-61). He recorded with John Coltrane, participated in Ornette Coleman's *Free Jazz* (1960), was on Oliver Nelson's classic *Blues and the Abstract Truth* album (highlighted by "Stolen Moments") and started recording as a leader for Blue Note that same year. Hubbard gained fame playing with Art Blakey's Jazz Messengers (1961-64) next to Wayne Shorter and Curtis Fuller. He recorded *Ascension* with Coltrane (1965), *Out to Lunch* (1964) with Eric Dolphy and *Maiden Voyage* with Herbie Hancock and, after a period with Max Roach (1965-66), he led his own quintet which at the time usually featured altoist James Spaulding. A blazing trumpeter with a beautiful tone on fluegelhorn, Hubbard fared well in freer settings but was always essentially a hard bop stylist.

In 1970 Freddie Hubbard recorded two of his finest albums (*Red Clay* and *Straight Life*) for CTI. The follow-up, *First Light* (1971), was actually his most popular date, featuring Don Sebesky arrangements. But after the glory of the CTI years (during which producer Creed Taylor did an expert job of balancing the artistic with the accessible), Hubbard made the mistake of signing with Columbia and recording one dud after another; *Windjammer* (1976) and *Splash* (a slightly later effort for Fantasy) are low points. However, in 1977 he toured with Herbie Hancock's acoustic V.S.O.P. Quintet and in the 1980s, on recordings for Pablo, Blue Note and Atlantic, he showed that he could reach his former heights (even if much of the jazz world had given up on him). But by the late '80s Hubbard's "personal problems" and increasing unreliability (not showing up for gigs) started to really hurt him and a few years later his once-mighty technique started to seriously falter. Whether Freddie Hubbard will ever make a serious comeback is open to question, but his fans can certainly enjoy his many recordings for Blue Note, Impulse, Atlantic, CTI, Pablo and his first Music Masters sets. —*Scott Yanow*

Open Sesame / Jun. 19, 1960 / Blue Note ✦✦✦✦✦
Freddie Hubbard's first recording as a leader, *Open Sesame* features the 22-year old trumpeter in a quintet with tenor saxophonist Tina Brooks, the up-and-coming pianist McCoy Tyner, bassist Sam Jones and drummer Clifford Jarvis. The CD reissue adds two alternate takes to the original six-song program and shows that even at this early stage Hubbard had the potential to be one of the greats. On the ballad "But Beautiful" he shows maturity, and other highlights include "Open Sesame," a driving "All or Nothing at All" and "One Mint Julep." It's an impressive start to what would be a very interesting career. —*Scott Yanow*

Ballads / Jun. 19, 1960-May 7, 1964 / Blue Note ✦✦✦
Freddie Hubbard's early years on Blue Note found him quickly developing from a Clifford Brown hard bopper to a more original stylist. This sampler (released as a 1997 CD) finds Hubbard emphasizing his warm sound on seven ballads including "Body and Soul," "But Beautiful" and his own "Lament for Booker." The material is drawn from seven of his excellent Blue Note sessions, all of which are individually available in full. Nice music played with such sidemen as tenors Wayne Shorter, Tina Brooks, Hank Mobley and Jimmy Heath, altoist James Spaulding and pianists Cedar Walton, McCoy Tyner and Herbie Hancock, among others. —*Scott Yanow*

Goin' Up / Nov. 6, 1960 / Blue Note ✦✦✦✦
For his second recording as a leader, trumpeter Freddie Hubbard (22 at the time) performs two compositions apiece by Kenny Dorham and Hank Mobley, the obscure "I Wished I Knew" and his own "Blues for Brenda." Hubbard (featured in a quintet with tenor saxophonist Mobley, pianist McCoy Tyner, bassist Paul Chambers and drummer Philly Joe Jones) takes quite a few outstanding solos, playing

lyrically on the ballads and building his own sound out of the Clifford Brown/Lee Morgan tradition. It's an excellent set of advanced hard bop. —*Scott Yanow*

Hub Cap / Apr. 9, 1961 / Blue Note ✦✦✦
On *Hub Cap,* his third effort as a leader, Freddie Hubbard sticks to the tried-and-true hard bop formula, which is something of a mixed blessing. There's no question that much of this music is enjoyable, but it's not quite up to the standards of its two predecessors. Part of the problem is Hubbard's sextet, which features tenor saxophonist Jimmy Heath, trombonist Julian Priester, pianist Cedar Walton, bassist Larry Ridley and drummer "Philly" Joe Jones. All of the musicians are talented, but only a few are inventive, and that becomes a problem, since it becomes clear that Hubbard is beginning to break free from his influences and develop his own style. In other words, he's capable of more adventurous music than this straightahead hard bop. That said, *Hard Bop* is a very good hard bop date. There is energy to the performances, and Hubbard's vigorous, inspired playing continues to impress, as do some of his original compositions. Only when compared to Hubbard's first two records, or what would come later, does *Hub Cap* seem like a lesser effort. —*Stephen Thomas Erlewine*

Here to Stay / Apr. 9, 1961-Dec. 27, 1962 / Blue Note ✦✦✦✦
This two-LP set, which was released in 1979 as part of United Artists' Blue Note reissue series, brought back trumpeter Freddie Hubbard's early album *Hub Cap,* a sextet session with tenor saxophonist Jimmy Heath, trombonist Julian Priester and pianist Cedar Walton. Although that session (comprising four Hubbard compositions, one of Walton's songs and Randy Weston's "Cry Me Not") is excellent, it is the full album of previously unreleased material from an all-star quintet that is of greatest interest. Hubbard teams up with fellow Jazz Messengers Wayne Shorter (on tenor), Walton, bassist Reggie Workman and (in Blakey's spot) drummer Philly Joe Jones for some advanced hard bop. High points include the fiery "Philly Mignon" and a strong version of "Body and Soul." —*Scott Yanow*

Minor Mishap / Aug. 2, 1961 / Black Lion ✦✦✦✦
This is one of Freddie Hubbard's more obscure sessions of the 1960s. Actually, it was originally led by the forgotten trombonist Willie Wilson (who died in 1963) but has been reissued by Black Lion on CD under Hubbard's name. The 23-year-old trumpeter is teamed with Wilson, baritonist Pepper Adams and the Duke Pearson Trio (with bassist Thomas Howard and drummer Lex Humphries) for originals by Wilson, Pearson, Adams, Donald Byrd and Tommy Flanagan in addition to two standards that feature the trombonist; the reissue adds five alternate takes to the original seven-song program. Hubbard and Adams both have plenty of solos on this excellent hard bop date, one that is worth picking up by straightahead jazz fans. —*Scott Yanow*

★ **Ready for Freddie** / Aug. 21, 1961 / Blue Note ✦✦✦✦✦
Trumpeter Freddie Hubbard really came into his own during this Blue Note session. He is matched with quite an all-star group (tenor saxophonist Wayne Shorter, pianist McCoy Tyner, bassist Art Davis and drummer Elvin Jones in addition to Bernard McKinney on euphonium), introduces two of his finest compositions ("Birdlike" and "Crisis") and is quite lyrical on his ballad feature "Weaver of Dreams." Hubbard's sidemen all play up to par and this memorable session is highly recommended; it's one of the trumpeter's most rewarding Blue Note albums. —*Scott Yanow*

The Artistry of Freddie Hubbard / Jul. 2, 1962 / Impulse! ✦✦✦✦
Trumpeter Freddie Hubbard leads a particularly talented sextet (with trombonist Curtis Fuller, a rare outing away from Sun Ra for tenor saxophonist John Gilmore, pianist Tommy Flanagan, bassist Art Davis and drummer Louis Hayes) on three of his originals and strong versions of "Summertime" and "Caravan." This advanced hard bop music deserves to be reissued on CD. —*Scott Yanow*

Hub-Tones / Oct. 10, 1962 / Blue Note ✦✦✦✦✦
Trumpeter Freddie Hubbard teams up on record with James Spaulding (who doubles on alto and flute) for the first time on this excellent set. With the assistance of pianist Herbie Hancock, bassist Reggie Workman and drummer Clifford Jarvis, the quintet performs four of the trumpeter's originals (including "Lament for Booker" and the title cut) plus an advanced version of the standard "You're My Everything." John Coltrane's modal music was starting to influence Hubbard's conception and his own playing was pushing ahead the modern mainstream without really entering the avant-garde. —*Scott Yanow*

Body and Soul / Mar. 8, 1963-May 2, 1963 / Impulse! ✦✦✦✦
The second of trumpeter Freddie Hubbard's two Impulse albums features the 25-year-old in three separate settings. He is heard along with tenor saxophonist backed with strings ("Skylark," "I Got It Bad" and "Chocolate Shake" are all given beautiful treatments), with a 16-piece band and in a septet with Eric Dolphy and Wayne Shorter. This well-rounded and highly recommended showcase shows why Freddie Hubbard was considered the top trumpeter to emerge during the early '60s. —*Scott Yanow*

Breaking Point / May 7, 1964 / Blue Note ✦✦✦✦✦
This CD reissue (which augments the original five-song program with alternate takes, originally issued on 45s, of "Blue Frenzy" and "Mirrors") brings back the first recording Hubbard cut with his own working band (as opposed to an all-star studio group). On these selections (particularly the memorable "Breaking Point"), Hubbard and his quintet (James Spaulding on alto and flute, pianist Ronnie Matthews, bassist Eddie Khan and drummer Joe Chambers) play music that falls in between hard bop and the avant-garde, stretching the boundaries of the jazz modern mainstream. Their explorative flights are still quite interesting more than three decades later and Hubbard, having broken away from his earlier Clifford Brown and Lee Morgan influences, really sounds very much like himself. —*Scott Yanow*

Blue Spirits / Feb. 19, 1965-Mar. 5, 1966 / Blue Note ✦✦✦✦
This CD, Freddie Hubbard's last Blue Note release of the 1960s (with the exception of the blowing session *The Night of the Cookers*), adds two numbers to the original LP program and features the great trumpeter in three challenging settings ranging from a sextet to an octet. Hubbard uses such sidemen as altoist James Spaulding, tenors Joe Henderson and Hank Mobley, the euphonium of Kiane Zawadi, pianists Harold Mabern, McCoy Tyner and Herbie Hancock, bassists Larry Ridley, Bob Cranshaw and Reggie Workman, drummers Clifford Jarvis, Pete La Roca and Elvin Jones, the congas of Big Black and on one song bassoonist Hosea Taylor. The set comprises seven diverse Hubbard originals and, even though none of the songs caught on to become standards, the music is quite challenging and fairly memorable. —*Scott Yanow*

The Night of the Cookers: Vols. 1 & 2 / Apr. 9, 1965-Apr. 10, 1965 / Blue Note ✦✦
This double CD reissues the two LP volumes titled *The Night of the Cookers.* Since these performances (four lengthy workouts ranging from 19-24 minutes apiece) were taken from a club date that matched together the trumpets of Freddie Hubbard and Lee Morgan (along with James Spaulding on alto and flute, pianist Harold Mabern, bassist Larry Ridley, drummer Pete La Roca and the congas of Big Black), this should have been a classic. However, Morgan sounds quite subpar, the recording quality is just passable, the individual solos are stretched out far too long and the overall results are a major disappointment. —*Scott Yanow*

Backlash / Oct. 19, 1966+Oct. 24, 1966 / Atlantic ✦✦✦✦
Trumpeter Freddie Hubbard led a particularly fine quintet in the mid-'60s that has long been underrated. The edition heard on this Atlantic LP features James Spaulding on alto and flute, pianist Albert Dailey, bassist Bob Cunningham and drummer Otis Ray Appleton. This studio recording is most notable for debuting Hubbard's "Little Sunflower" and also has a good remake of "Up Jumped Spring" along with four other obscure pieces. The music straddles the boundaries between hard bop, soul and the avant-garde and has plenty of unpredictable moments. This is the strongest of Freddie Hubbard's three Atlantic records of the period. —*Scott Yanow*

High Blues Pressure / Nov. 1967 / Atlantic ✦✦✦
For this studio album, Freddie Hubbard expanded his quintet by adding tenor saxophonist Bennie Maupin, Kiane Zawadi on euphonium and the tuba of Howard Johnson. The music is complex but swinging, with fine solos from the trumpeter-leader, altoist James Spaulding, Maupin and pianist Kenny Barron. This LP (which has not yet been reissued on CD) will be hard to find. —*Scott Yanow*

The Black Angel / 1969 / Atlantic ✦✦✦
The most obscure and the last of Freddie Hubbard's three Atlantic LPs of the 1960s (none of which have reappeared yet on CD) features the trumpeter right before he found some commercial success on CTI. He performs three of his originals, Walter Bishop, Jr.'s "Coral Keys" and Kenny Barron's "The Black Angel" with an excellent sextet that includes James Spaulding on alto and flute, Kenny Barron on keyboards, bassist Reggie Workman, drummer Louis Hayes and percussionist Patato Valdes. Although not essential, the music is quite advanced, hard-swinging and explorative. —*Scott Yanow*

The Hub of Hubbard / Dec. 9, 1969 / MPS ✦✦✦✦✦
Trumpeter Freddie Hubbard, whose Atlantic recordings had straddled the boundary between hard bop and the avant-garde, sticks to bebop on this excellent recording. Performing in a quintet with tenor saxophonist Eddie Daniels (no clarinet this time), pianist Roland Hanna, bassist Richard Davis and drummer Louis Hayes, Hubbard is in top form on four selections: "Without a Song," a ridiculously uptempo "Just One of Those Things," "Blues for Duane" and a ballad rendition of "The Things We Did Last Summer." —*Scott Yanow*

A Soul Experiment / 1969 / Atlantic ✦✦

☆ **Red Clay** / Jan. 27, 1970-Jan. 29, 1970 / CTI ✦✦✦✦✦
Freddie Hubbard has long considered this recording to be his best, and with good reason. The trumpeter is heard at the peak of his powers performing five originals (one, "Cold Turkey," was released for the first time on this CD reissue) in a quintet with tenor saxophonist Joe Henderson, keyboardist Herbie Hancock, bassist Ron Carter and drummer Lenny White. "Red Clay" is a classic and the other selections

("The Intreprid Fox," "Suite Sioux" and "Delphia") all feature Hubbard taking colorful solos in a style that blends hard bop with subtle funky rhythms. Classic music of the early 1970s. —*Scott Yanow*

★ **Straight Life** / Nov. 16, 1970 / CTI ♦♦♦♦♦
Recorded between trumpeter Freddie Hubbard's better-known classics *Red Clay* and *First Light*, *Straight Life* is actually arguably Hubbard's greatest recording. Hubbard, joined by an all-star group that includes tenor saxophonist Joe Henderson, keyboardist Herbie Hancock, guitarist George Benson, bassist Ron Carter and drummer Jack DeJohnette, is frequently astounding on "Straight Life" (check out that introduction) and "Mr. Clean," constructing classic solos. The very memorable set is rounded off by the trumpeter's duet with Benson on a lyrical version of the ballad "Here's That Rainy Day." This exciting CD is essential for all serious jazz collections. —*Scott Yanow*

The Best of Freddie Hubbard [Columbia] / 1970-1973 / Columbia ♦♦
Columbia's *Best of Freddie Hubbard* contains eight highlights from his soul-jazz, fusion and funk-jazz recordings for CTI records, including "Lonely Town," "Betcha By Golly, Wow," "The Godfather," "Red Clay" and "Free as a Bird." It's not one of the best periods of Hubbard's career, but this gives a represenative portrait of his time at CTI. —*Stephen Thomas Erlewine*

Sing Me a Song of Songmy / Jan. 21, 1971 / Atlantic ♦♦
This is a strange LP. Trumpeter Freddie Hubbard and his quintet (which consisted of tenor saxophonist Junior Cook, pianist Kenny Barron, bassist Art Booth and drummer Louis Hayes) is joined by a chorus, a string orchestra, several reciters, an organist and a variety of processed sounds emanating from tapes. The thoughts expressed in the music (topical and anti-war messages) are quite sincere but the abstract sounds will be enjoyed by only a limited audience; jazz fans should look elsewhere. —*Scott Yanow*

First Light / Sep. 1971 / CTI ♦♦♦♦♦
The third of Freddie Hubbard's "big three" recordings for CTI (it was preceded by *Red Clay* and *Straight Life*), *First Light* was probably the trumpeter's most popular album. The first of his recordings to utilize the string and woodwind arrangements of Don Sebesky, Hubbard sounds quite inspired by his accompaniment and plays at his best throughout, particularly on "First Light" and "Uncle Albert/Admiral Halsey." The CD reissue by Columbia adds one previously unissued selection ("Fantasy in D") to the original program. —*Scott Yanow*

Sky Dive / Oct. 1972 / Columbia ♦♦♦♦
Freddie Hubbard's fourth CTI recording (and the second one with Don Sebesky arrangements) certainly has a diverse repertoire. In addition to his originals "Povo" and "Sky Dive" (both of which are superior jam tunes), the trumpeter stretches out on the theme from *The Godfather* and Bix Beiderbecke's "In a Mist." The charts for the brass and woodwinds are colorful, there is a fine supporting cast that includes guitarist George Benson, Keith Jarrett on keyboards and flutist Hubert Laws, and Hubbard takes several outstanding trumpet solos. This LP (not yet reissued on CD) is worth searching for. —*Scott Yanow*

In Concert, Vols. 1 & 2 / Mar. 3, 1973 / Columbia ♦♦♦♦
The CTI All-Stars are featured on this enjoyable CD, which presents highlights originally released on two LPs. Trumpeter Freddie Hubbard and tenor saxophonist Stanley Turrentine always made for a potent team and, with the assistance of an all-star rhythm section (guitarist Eric Gale, keyboardist Herbie Hancock, bassist Ron Carter and drummer Jack DeJohnette), the very individual stylists sound in fine form, particularly on "Povo" and "Gibraltar." —*Scott Yanow*

Keep Your Soul Together / Oct. 1973 / Columbia ♦♦♦♦
Trumpeter Freddie Hubbard's CTI recordings have long been underrated and a bit downgraded by writers who get them confused with his much commercial output for Columbia. For this LP (not yet reissued on CD) Hubbard is heard in fine form on four of his originals (highlighted by "Spirits of Trane") with a septet that includes tenor saxophonist Junior Cook, keyboardist George Cables, guitarist Aurell Ray, either Kent Brinkley or Ron Carter on bass, drummer Ralph Penland and Juno Lewis on percussion. The music is sometimes funky but definitely creative jazz with Hubbard heard during his prime period. —*Scott Yanow*

Polar AC / 1974 / CTI ♦♦♦
Trumpeter Freddie Hubbard's sixth and final CTI studio recording has its moments although it is not on the same level as his first three. Hubbard, backed on four of the five songs by a string section arranged by either Don Sebesky or Bob James, is assisted on songs such as "People Make the World Go Round" and "Betcha By Golly, Wow" by flutist Hubert Laws and guitarist George Benson. "Son of Sky Dive" showcases his trumpet with a sextet including Laws and tenor saxophonist Junior Cook. The music is enjoyable but not essential and this LP has yet to appear on CD. —*Scott Yanow*

High Energy / Apr. 29, 1974-May 2, 1974 / Columbia ♦♦♦
One of Freddie Hubbard's few decent efforts during his very commercial period with Columbia, this LP found his quintet (with tenor saxophonist Junior Cook and keyboardist George Cables) joined by a small orchestra and a string section on a set of potentially dismal material. Fortunately, these six performances (particularly "Crisis," "Ebony Moonbeams" and Stevie Wonder's "Too High") are given fairly creative treatment. The leader-trumpeter is in good form and there is solo space given to Ernie Watts (on bass flute, soprano and flute) and tenorman Pete Christlieb in addition to the quintet members. —*Scott Yanow*

Liquid Love / 1975 / Columbia ♦♦
Imagine hearing trumpeter Freddie Hubbard sing! Truth be told, he only joins in on the group vocal of "Put It in the Pocket" but that is about the only historic aspect to this wasteful release. While Hubbard's CTI recordings had perfectly balanced both the artistic and the commercial, much of his Columbia output sounds as if it was recorded strictly for the money. None of the six selections heard on this LP stayed in Hubbard's repertoire long (when was the last time that he performed "Midnight at the Oasis" and "Liquid Love"?) and the funky rhythms do little to uplift the music. George Cables, who plays keyboards on this album and was responsible for some of the arrangements, has his name misspelled "Gables" on the album jacket; was he trying to hide his identity? —*Scott Yanow*

Gleam / Mar. 17, 1975 / Sony ♦♦♦♦
In contrast to his rather commercial Columbia albums of the period, this live double LP from Japanese Sony finds trumpeter Freddie Hubbard really digging into the material, even on such songs as "Put It in the Pocket," "Midnight at the Oasis" and a memorable version of the Stevie Wonder-associated "Too High." Hubbard and his working group of the time (which consisted of tenor saxophonist Carl Randall, keyboardist George Cables, bassist Henry Franklin, drummer Carl Burnett and Buck Clark on congas) are in particularly creative form, especially on "Kuntu" and "Spirits of Trane." —*Scott Yanow*

Windjammer / 1976 / Columbia ♦
This LP is (along with his *Splash* album on Fantasy) probably trumpeter Freddie Hubbard's worst recording. Hubbard, who is joined by a string section, five vocalists and an oversized orchestra, sounds like a parody of himself on these meaningless funk tracks. Why jazz's top trumpeter of the 1970s would allow himself to get sucked into this trashy Bob James production is debatable but there is no debate as to the merit of this fortunately out-of-print LP. This is insincere music that was dated before it was even released. —*Scott Yanow*

Bundle of Joy / 1977 / Columbia ♦♦
Freddie Hubbard's string of commercial albums for Columbia in the mid- to late '70s ruined the trumpeter's reputation. This particular LP is not as bad as some (at least his duet with harpist Dorothy Ashby on "Portrait of Jenny" is pretty and Ernie Watts gets a good tenor solo on "Rahsaan") but it is not one of his finer moments either. With an oversized funky rhythm section, a string section and five "background" vocalists, Hubbard had little to do. Skip this and get his CTI and Blue Note albums instead. —*Scott Yanow*

Super Blue / 1978 / Columbia ♦♦♦
After several terrible sellout albums for Columbia, Freddie Hubbard attempted to rekindle some of the magic from his CTI years on this small group date. With such CTI alumni as flutist Hubert Laws, tenorman Joe Henderson, and even guitarist George Benson (on one selection) helping out, Hubbard shows that he still had the chops (if not necessarily the creativity) to continue being a major jazz trumpeter. Unfortunately, his career has been fairly aimless ever since. —*Scott Yanow*

The Love Connection / Feb. 1979-Mar. 1979 / Columbia ♦♦

Skagly / Dec. 1979 / Columbia ♦♦♦
In general, Freddie Hubbard's Columbia recordings (none of which have been reissued on CD) can be skipped by serious jazz fans because, with the exception of *Super Blue* and to a lesser extent this album, they are overtly commercial and rather insincere efforts. This particular record at least uses the trumpeter's regular quintet of the period (with Hadley Caliman on tenor and flute, the up-and-coming keyboardist Billy Childs, bassist Larry Klein and drummer Carl Burnett), although the title cut has three guests (including keyboardist George Duke) whose role seemed to be to make the music more funky. With the exception of the standard "Theme from *Summer of '42*," none of the other songs (all group originals) caught on but Hubbard takes some good solos during these modern mainstream performances. —*Scott Yanow*

Live at the North Sea Jazz Festival / Jul. 12, 1980 / Pablo ♦♦♦♦
Trumpeter Freddie Hubbard's recording career was rather aimless by 1980 but, as shown by his playing on this live double LP, he was still in prime form. Hubbard and his quintet (which consisted of tenor saxophonist David Schnitter, keyboardist Billy Childs, bassist Larry Klein and drummer Sinclair Lott) play extended versions of five of his compositions plus "The Summer Knows" and "Impressions."

Although these renditions of "First Light" and "Red Clay" will not make listeners forget the original versions, it is gratifying to hear the trumpeter really pushing himself. His reputation had been soiled by his Columbia funk albums but this two-fer shows that in 1980 Hubbard had few competitors among trumpeters. It's well worth searching for. —*Scott Yanow*

Mistral / Sep. 15, 1980-Sep. 19, 1980 / Liberty ✦✦
Compared to his live performances, this studio recording is a disappointment. Altoist Art Pepper and keyboardist George Cables have a few spots but the arrangements are a bit commercial, the originals (three by trumpeter Freddie Hubbard and one apiece from Cables and bassist Stanley Clarke) are forgettable and no one sounds like they are sweating. This LP is one of Hubbard's lesser efforts. —*Scott Yanow*

Splash / 1981 / Fantasy ✦
Outpost / Mar. 16, 1981-Mar. 17, 1981 / Enja ✦✦✦✦
This little-known CD is actually a special outing for Freddie Hubbard. Pianist Kenny Barron, bassist Buster Williams and drummer Al Foster are quite comple-mentary on the diverse material, which includes "You Don't Know What Love Is," two Hubbard originals, Williams' "Dual Force" and Eric Dolphy's "Loss." Through-out, Hubbard is heard in prime form. —*Scott Yanow*

Rollin' / May 2, 1981 / MPS ✦✦✦
Trumpeter Freddie Hubbard and his 1981 quintet (which included Dave Schnitter on tenor and soprano, keyboardist Billy Childs, bassist Larry Klein and drummer Carl Burnett) are in fine form on this live set originally recorded for MPS. The LP consists of seven songs Hubbard often performed during that period, including "One of Another Kind," "Here's That Rainy Day" "Up Jumped Spring" and his heated blues "Byrdlike." Although few surprises occur, the largely straightahead music is quite enjoyable and Hubbard's fans may want to search for this fairly rare item. —*Scott Yanow*

Keystone Bop / Nov. 27, 1981+Nov. 29, 1981 / Prestige ✦✦✦
Trumpeter Freddie Hubbard's Nov. 1981 engagement at San Francisco's legendary Keystone Korner was extensively recorded and the highlights were released on three LPs; the Nov. 29 material has since been reissued on a single CD. Hubbard was matched with tenor saxophonist Joe Henderson, vibraphonist Bobby Hutcher-son, pianist Billy Childs, bassist Larry Klein and drummer Steve Houghton for per-formances that were often fairly lengthy. *Keystone Bop* consists of a 17-minute ver-sion of "One of Another Kind" and nine-minute renditions of Hutcherson's "The Littlest One of All" and the standard "Body and Soul"; both of the latter are on the CD. The results are predictably excellent. The other LPs in this series are *Classics* and *A Little Night Music*. —*Scott Yanow*

Keystone Bop: Sunday Night / Nov. 29, 1981 / Prestige ✦✦✦
This CD reissues an LP and a half's worth of material recorded by Freddie Hub-bard and his sextet (with tenor saxophonist Joe Henderson, pianist Billy Childs, vibraphonist Bobby Hutcherson, bassist Larry Klein and drummer Steve Hough-ton) at the legendary San Francisco club Keystone Korner one night in 1981. The great trumpeter is in excellent form on remakes of three of his compositions ("Birdlike," "Sky Dive" and "The Intrepid Fox"), Hutcherson's "The Littlest One of All" and "Body and Soul." Although few surprises occur, Hubbard fans can be assured that this set finds him in excellent form on a good night. —*Scott Yanow*

Born to Be Blue / Dec. 14, 1981 / Original Jazz Classics ✦✦✦✦
Trumpeter Freddie Hubbard teams up with veteran tenor saxophonist Harold Land and Hubbard's regular rhythm section of the period (keyboardist Billy Childs, bass-ist Larry Klein, drummer Steve Houghton and percussionist Buck Clark) on this fine modern hard bop CD, a straight reissue of the original Pablo LP. Hubbard had hurt his reputation with his very commercial Columbia recordings of the mid- to late '70s so in 1981 he was doing his best to return to his brand of straightahead jazz. This date is highlighted by "Gibraltar," Clifford Brown's "Joy Spring" and a revisit to Hubbard's "Up Jumped Spring." —*Scott Yanow*

Face to Face / May 24, 1982 / Pablo ✦✦✦✦✦
Trumpeter Freddie Hubbard met the Pablo All-Stars for this unique and frequently exciting set. Inspired by the presence of pianist Oscar Peterson, guitarist Joe Pass, bassist Niels-Henning Orsted Pedersen and drummer Martin Drew, Hubbard stretches out on five numbers which include "All Blues," his own "Thermo" and "Portrait of Jenny." A combative player, Hubbard both challenges and is challenged by the remarkable pianist; pity they did not record together more often. This stim-ulating CD is a reissue of the original LP. —*Scott Yanow*

Back to Birdland / Aug. 1982 / Real Time ✦✦✦✦
This well-recorded outing (which has been reissued on CD by Drive Archive) was trumpeter Freddie Hubbard's first worthwhile studio recording (with the exception of *Super Blue*) since the mid-'70s. Essentially a bebop date, Hubbard is teamed with a sextet comprising altoist Richie Cole, trombonist Ashley Alexander, pianist George Cables, bassist Andy Simpkins and drummer John Dentz; altoist Med Flory

sits in on "Byrdlike." Hubbard shows, on such standards as "Shaw Nuff," "Star Eyes" and "Lover Man," that he could still play straightahead jazz with the best of them. Alexander is featured on "Stella by Starlight" and Cole is also in excellent form. —*Scott Yanow*

Sweet Return / Jun. 13, 1983-Jun. 14, 1983 / Atlantic ✦✦✦✦
One of Freddie Hubbard's best albums since the early '70s, this quintet date finds him joined by quite an all-star lineup: Lew Tabackin on tenor and flute, pianist Joanne Brackeen (who has many fine solos throughout the album), bassist Eddie Gomez and drummer Roy Haynes. High points include Hubbard's tender version of "Misty" (at the time he had a particularly lovely tone on fluegelhorn), Brackeen's "Heidi-B" and the quintet's rendition of the standard "The Night Has a Thousand Eyes." —*Scott Yanow*

Life Flight / Jan. 23, 1987-Jan. 24, 1987 / Blue Note ✦✦✦✦
This CD captures the great trumpeter Freddie Hubbard at the age of 48 just before he began to decline. Hubbard is heard in excellent shape on two selections apiece with two separate bands. One group, a sextet with tenor saxophonist Stanley Tur-rentine and guitarist George Benson, recalls the trumpeter's glory days on CTI, although the material ("Battlestar Galactica" and "A Saint's Homecoming Song") was of recent vintage. The other band, a quintet with tenor saxophonist Ralph Moore, looks back towards his earlier Blue Note and Atlantic days; they perform two Hubbard originals ("The Melting Pot" and "Life Flight"). Overall this set (from an era when the veteran trumpeter was being overshadowed by Wynton Marsalis) gives listeners one of the last opportunities to hear Freddie Hubbard in peak form. —*Scott Yanow*

Topsy: Standard Book / Oct. 10, 1989-Oct. 11, 1989 / Triloka ✦✦✦
It was the producer's idea that Freddie Hubbard play all of the nine standards on this CD with a mute in his trumpet. Hubbard was not happy with the restriction, but does his best on the quartet/quintet session with pianist Benny Green, bassist Rufus Reid, drummer Carl Allen and, on three numbers, altoist Kenny Garrett. While it is interesting to hear Freddie Hubbard tackle such material as "Topsy," "As Time Goes By," "Cherokee" and "Love Me or Leave Me," the music is often more mellow than one might hope, even when uptempo. It's a pleasing but not essential release from the Japanese label Alfa/Compose. —*Scott Yanow*

Bolivia / Dec. 13, 1990-Jan. 14, 1991 / Music Masters ✦✦✦
Freddie Hubbard is in decent but not quite prime form on this CD; his tone was starting to decline ever so gradually. His sidemen were quite strong (Ralph Moore on tenor, altoist Vincent Herring, pianist Cedar Walton, bassist David Williams and drummer Billy Higgins), the material is superior (highlighted by "Bolivia," Hub-bard's "Dear John" and a few of his recent Latin-flavored originals) and overall the music is satisfying enough to make this a recommended disc to fans of the modern mainstream. —*Scott Yanow*

Live at Fat Tuesday / Dec. 6, 1991-Dec. 7, 1991 / Music Masters ✦✦
This live double CD is a bit odd. Trumpeter Freddie Hubbard's once beautiful tone was definitely on the decline by this point, which is particularly noticeable on high notes (which often sound painful) and the lone ballad "But Beautiful." Tenor saxo-phonist Javon Jackson seems content to imitate Joe Henderson, while pianist Benny Green, who normally sounds like a mixture of Bobby Timmons, Gene Har-ris and Oscar Peterson, here adopts the heavy tone and chord voicings of McCoy Tyner. Bassist Christian McBride and drummer Tony Reedus play fine in support but these often-lengthy performances are not at all memorable. Better to pick up Freddie Hubbard's earlier sessions instead. —*Scott Yanow*

Blues for Miles / Apr. 3, 1992-Apr. 4, 1992 / Evidence ✦✦✦

Monk, Miles, Trane & Cannon / Aug. 19, 1994-Aug. 20, 1994 / Music Masters ✦✦

Freddie Hubbard & Woody Shaw Sessions / Nov. 21, 1985-Jun. 12, 1987 / Blue Note ✦✦✦

Peanuts Hucko (Michael Andrew Hucko)

b. Apr. 7, 1918, Syracuse, NY
Clarinet, Tenor Saxophone / Swing, Dixieland
Peanuts Hucko has long had a sound on clarinet that is nearly identical to that of Benny Goodman. A fine tenor player in his early days (although he largely gave up the instrument after the 1940s), Hucko's clarinet is an attractive addition to any Dixieland or swing combo. He started out as a tenor saxophonist playing in the big bands of Will Bradley (1939-41), Charlie Spivak (1941-42) and Bob Chester. Hucko was a member of Glenn Miller's Army Air Force Band where he was a star clarinet soloist. After being discharged from the military and playing with Benny Goodman (1945-46) and Ray McKinley (1946-47), Hucko started an on-and-off association with Eddie Condon. He worked in the studios in the 1950s, visited Europe with Jack Teagarden and Earl Hines in 1957, toured the world with Louis Armstrong's All-Stars (1958-60) and in the 1960s often led his own Dixie/swing band. In the 1970s for a period he was the leader of the Glenn Miller ghost orches-

tra and in recent times Hucko has often headed groups featuring his wife, vocalist Louise Tobin. —*Scott Yanow*

Live at Eddie Condon's / 1960 / Chiaroscuro ✦✦✦
Released on a 1977 LP and not yet reissued on CD, this live set features the superior swing clarinetist Peanuts Hucko (who has the ability to sound just like Benny Goodman) in a quartet with pianist Ralph Sutton, the obscure bassist Dante Montucci and drummer George Wettling. The recording quality is decent and certainly listenable, and the music itself is often quite heated. Considering his talents, Hucko has had relatively few chances to lead his own albums—it would be nearly 20 years before his next recording as a leader. This enjoyable mainstream set has among its highlights spirited and hard-swinging versions of "I Found a New Baby," "Stealing Apples" and "Running Wild." —*Scott Yanow*

Peanuts Hucko with His Pied Piper Quintet / 1979 / World Jazz ✦✦✦
When one considers that this album teams together Peanuts Hucko (who often sounds like Benny Goodman) and vibraphonist Peter Appleyard (who when he wants to can sound like a close relative of Lionel Hampton) in a quintet, it is not surprising that much of the music is in the vein of Benny Goodman's small groups. With pianist Ross Tompkins, bassist Arnold Fishkind and drummer Jack Sperling also in the band, this is an infectious set of swing-oriented music. In addition to the Dixieland standard "Riverboat Shuffle" and various swing tunes, included on the album are four little-known but enjoyable Hucko originals. This out-of-print LP is worth searching for. —*Scott Yanow*

Tribute to Louis Armstrong and Benny Goodman / Oct. 24, 1983+Jul. 6, 1986 / Timeless ✦✦✦✦

● **Swing That Music** / 1992 / Star Line ✦✦✦✦
Peanuts Hucko, one of the few swing clarinetists still active in the 1990s, heads a fine octet for this spirited set of standards. With solo contributions made from trumpeter Randy Sandke, Danny Moss on tenor, trombonist Roy Williams, pianist Johnny Varro and vibraphonist Lars Erstrand (not to mention singer Louise Tobin), this set should easily satisfy Benny Goodman fans. Highlights include "Swing That Music," an exciting "Stealin' Apples" and "One O'Clock Jump"; Hucko has a rare vocal on "When You're Smiling." —*Scott Yanow*

Armand Hug

b. Dec. 6, 1910, New Orleans, LA, **d.** Mar. 19, 1977, New Orleans, LA
Piano / Dixieland, New Orleans Jazz, Stride
A superior New Orleans-style pianist, Armand Hug tended to be underrated throughout his life, but his many recordings are still quite enjoyable. Hug spent much of his life in his native New Orleans, where he began playing in public in 1923. He joined Harry Shields' band in 1926, worked a bit with the New Orleans Owls in 1928, and made his recording debut with Sharkey Bonano in 1936. Hug primarily performed as a solo pianist, having long residencies at various clubs and also hosting his own series on local television. Armand Hug recorded as a leader for New Orleans Bandwagon, Capitol, Good Time Jazz, Circle, Paramount, Southland and Golden Crest, along with three fine albums in the 1970s for Swaggie. —*Scott Yanow*

● **Armand Hug & New Orleans Dixielanders/Eddie Miller & The New Orleans Rhythm Pals** / Dec. 11, 1958 / Southland ✦✦✦✦✦
This album has two sessions recorded on the same day. Pianist Armand Hug is heard leading a septet on a four-song session that features trumpeter Mike Lala, trombonist Bob Havens, bass trombonist Emile Christian and clarinetist Harry Shields; Raymond Burke has a guest appearance on "Easy Goin' Blues," playing harmonica! Good as those performances are, it is the four numbers from a quintet outing that are most memorable, for tenor great Eddie Miller and a four-piece rhythm section romp through a mostly-heated miniset highlighted by "Buzzard's Parade." Highly recommended to New Orleans jazz fans. —*Scott Yanow*

Dixieland from New Orleans / Aug. 9, 1959 / GHB ✦✦✦✦
Although the New Orleans revival received strong momentum in the early 1960s when Preservation Hall was opened, there were many fine recordings made in N.O. during the 1950s. On this superior GHB LP, pianist Armand Hug (one of the Crescent City's top keyboardists of the era) jams through eight mostly rarely played tunes including "I Never Knew What a Gal Could Do," "Missouri Two Beat," "All Dressed Up With a Broken Heart" and "Peace in the Valley" (which features gospel singer Sister Elizabeth Eustis). Among the key sidemen are trumpeter Mike Lala (now forgotten but quite underrated), either Sam Head or Bob Havens on trombone and clarinetist Harry Shields. —*Scott Yanow*

Armand Hug of New Orleans / Jun. 6, 1971+Jul. 11, 1971 / Swaggie ✦✦✦✦
This superior LP from the Australian Swaggie label features pianist Armand Hug on a set of unaccompanied solos. Mixed together are three originals (including one called "Four Minute Slow Drag at the Fern"), New Orleans-based obscurities and a few standards (such as "Baby Won't You Please Come Home" and "Someday You'll

Be Sorry"). Hug had a distinctive and swinging style of his own that was influenced by Jelly Roll Morton. He is in top form during the highly enjoyable album. —*Scott Yanow*

Volume Two / May 26, 1974 / Swaggie ✦✦✦✦
Despite its title, this was actually New Orleans pianist Armand Hug's third solo piano LP for the Australian Swaggie label. Hug, one of the finest trad pianists to emerge from N.O. during the 1950s and '60s, performs a few standards but mostly emphasizes obscurities (including the debut of a Nick LaRocca song "Sugar Baby, Be My Love") and among the highlights are his own "Creole Baby Doll," Sidney Bechet's "I Keep Calling Your Name," Paul Mares' "I'm Going Home" and "I Never Knew What a Gal Could Do." This little-known session rewards close investigation, for Hug was quite talented. —*Scott Yanow*

Bix Hug / 1976 / Jazzology ✦✦✦
This record is rather unusual, for it features pianist Armand Hug paying tribute to cornetist Bix Beiderbecke. Hug recreates 17 of Bix's cornet solos, revives Beiderbecke's four impressionistic piano pieces and also plays "Adirondack Sketches, Eastwood Lane." Although laid out like a double LP, all of the music is actually included on a single record and most of the interpretations are quite brief. An interesting if not essential set from the fine New Orleans pianist. —*Scott Yanow*

Spike Hughes (Patrick Cairns Hughes)

b. Oct. 19, 1908, London, England, **d.** Feb. 2, 1987, London, England
Bass / Classic Jazz
Spike Hughes, as a bassist (one of the best in the early '30s), and as an arranger and bandleader, made an important (if little-known) contribution to jazz. He arranged for British dance bands of the late '20s before beginning an excellent series of jazz records in 1930 with his Decca-Dents and Three Blind Mice. Among his sidemen were some of England's top jazz musicians, many of whom rarely had such a good opportunity to get away from playing commercial music; one session found Hughes and his rhythm section backing Jimmy Dorsey. In 1933 Hughes came to New York and recorded with an all-star group whose nucleus was the Benny Carter Orchestra. These recordings featured such greats as Carter, Coleman Hawkins, Chu Berry, Red Allen, Dickie Wells, flutist Wayman Carver and Sid Catlett playing Hughes' colorful arrangements. A multi-talented individual, Spike Hughes unfortunately chose to leave jazz altogether in 1934 to concentrate on classical music and being a journalist. —*Scott Yanow*

● **Volumes 1 & 2** / Mar. 12, 1930-Nov. 5, 1930 / Kings Cross ✦✦✦✦✦
Spike Hughes, a fine bassist and an advanced composer, led a series of enjoyable jazz-oriented performances in his native England during 1930-32. All of the selections have been reissued on a pair of double-CD sets from the British Kings Cross label. The first volume has some of the strongest performances with such soloists as trumpeters Sylvester Ahola, Max Goldberg and Norman Payne, altoist Philip Buchel, clarinetist Danny Polo and Buddy Featherstonhaugh on tenor being heard from. In addition, cornetist Muggsy Spanier guests on one cut and Jimmy Dorsey (doubling on alto and clarinet) is backed by Hughes' "Three Blind Mice" on one full session, really showing off his virtuosity on "I'm Just Wild About Harry." Even if a few of the vocals are quite dated, the often-hot playing throughout this double disc should greatly interest classic jazz collectors. —*Scott Yanow*

● **Volumes 3 & 4** / Nov. 19, 1930-Nov. 20, 1932 / Kings Cross ✦✦✦✦✦
All of bassist/composer Spike Hughes' British recordings of 1930-32 have been reissued on two double CDs by the English Kings Cross label. Although the first set gets a slight edge, both volumes should greatly interest early jazz collectors, for they show that there was quite a bit of jazz talent in England during the early years of the Depression. The 41 numbers on *Vols. 3 & 4* are essentially jazz-influenced dance music, but there are plenty of hot solos along with some indifferent vocals. Well worth searching for. —*Scott Yanow*

★ **1933** / Apr. 18, 1933-Oct. 16, 1933 / Challenge ✦✦✦✦✦
In 1933, British composer/bassist Spike Hughes visited the US and organized three recording sessions that resulted in 14 titles. Hughes used some of the top jazz all-stars of the era (including trumpeter Red Allen, trombonist Dicky Wells, altoist Benny Carter, flutist Wayman Carver and both Coleman Hawkins and Chu Berry on tenors) on selections that he arranged and, on ten occasions, also composed. The music is advanced, picturesque, often moody and generally swinging. A change-of-pace bonus are jammed versions of "Sweet Sue" and "How Come You Do Me Like You Do?" In addition to giving listeners the opportunity to hear both Hawkins and Berry soloing on some of the same songs, these selections find Carver taking a few of his earliest recorded flute solos. The imported CD also includes the eight titles (plus a previously unissued alternate take of "Devil's Holiday") from Benny Carter's big band dates of the year, which seems a logical matchup, since the first four titles use a band similar to Hughes'. Among the highlights overall are "Bugle Call Rag," "Nocturne," "Arabesque," "Donegal Cradle Song," "Swing It" and "Symphony in

Riffs." Highly recommended to vintage jazz collectors. In fact, so pleased was Hughes with the results of his sessions that he immediately retired from jazz to become a full-time critic, feeling that he could not top the heights of these performances. —*Scott Yanow*

Helen Humes

b. Jun. 23, 1913, Louisville, KY, d. Sep. 9, 1981, Santa Monica, CA
Vocals / Swing, Classical Female Blues, Piedmont Blues, Jump Blues, Prewar Country Blues

Helen Humes was a versatile singer equally skilled on blues, swing standards and ballads. Her cheerful style was always a joy to hear. As a child she played piano and organ in church and made her first recordings (ten blues in 1927) when she was only 13 and 14. In the 1930s she worked with Stuff Smith and Al Sears, recording with Harry James in 1937-38. In 1938 Humes joined Count Basie's Orchestra for three years. Since Jimmy Rushing specialized in blues, Helen Humes mostly got stuck singing pop ballads but she did a fine job. After freelancing in New York (1941-43) and touring with Clarence Love (1943-44), Humes moved to Los Angeles. She began to record as a leader and had a hit in "Be-Baba-Leba"; her 1950 original "Million Dollar Secret" is a classic. Humes sometimes performed with Jazz at the Philharmonic but was mostly a single in the 1950s. She recorded three superb albums for Contemporary during 1959-61 and had tours with Red Norvo. She moved to Australia in 1964, returning to the US in 1967 to take care of her ailing mother. Humes was out of the music business for several years but made a full comeback in 1973 and stayed busy up until her death. Throughout her career Helen Humes recorded for such labels as Savoy, Aladdin, Mercury, Decca, Dootone, Contemporary, Classic Jazz, Black & Blue, Black Lion, Jazzology, Columbia and Muse. —*Scott Yanow*

1927-1945 / Apr. 30, 1927-1945 / Classics ♦♦♦♦♦
When she was just 13 and 14 years old, Helen Humes made her recording debut, cutting ten risqué, double-entendre-filled blues, naughty tunes that she later claimed to understand at the time. Until the release of this Classics CD in 1996, those numbers (which have backup in various settings by either De Loise Searcy or J.C. Johnson on piano and juitarist Lonnie Johnson or the guitar duo team of Sylvester Weaver and Walter Beasley) had never been reissued on the same set before. Humes sounds fairly mature on the enjoyable blues sides. Her next session as a leader would not take place until 15 years later, when she was 28 and a veteran of Count Basie's Orchestra. The singer is heard here with groups in 1942 and 1944-45, performing three numbers with altoist Pete Brown's sextet (a band including trumpeter Dizzy Gillespie, who unfortunately does not solo), Leonard Feather's Hiptet (which has some rare solos from trumpeter Bobby Stark) and Bill Doggett's spirited octet. The latter date is highlighted by classic renditions of "He May Be Your Man" and "Be-Baba-Leba." Highly recommended. —*Scott Yanow*

Be-Baba-Leba / Nov. 20, 1944-Nov. 20, 1950 / Savoy ♦♦♦♦
Subtitled "The Rhythm and Blues Years," this highly enjoyable LP features the underrated and always cheerful singer Helen Humes in 1944 for four songs with Leonard Feather's Hiptet (swing-oriented tunes that have been reissued on a Classics CD) and in 1950 with bands led by altoist Marshall Royal, drummer Roy Milton (a late date) and tenor great Dexter Gordon. Humes had a flexible style that could sound quite credible on blues, ballads, swing and early R&B. Among the many superior numbers heard from the 1950 dates are "This Love of Mine," "He May Be Yours," "Be-Baba-Leba" and "Helen's Advice." Hopefully, all of this music will be reissued on CD. —*Scott Yanow*

1947 / Aug. 1947-1948 / Trip ♦♦♦♦
The three sessions on this 1970s Trip LP were originally cut for Mercury but have not yet been reissued on CD by Polygram. That is a pity, for the dozen selections feature Helen Humes in prime form, backed by the type of groups that accompanied Billie Holiday a decade earlier. Trumpeter Buck Clayton, tenor saxophonist John Hardee and (on one session) pianist Teddy Wilson all make their presence known, but Humes is the main star. Able to sing anything from lowdown blues to ballads and swinging stomps with equal skill, Humes is particularly memorable on "Jet Propelled Papa," "They Raided the Joint," "Flippity Flop Flop" and "Married Man Blues." Although it will be difficult to find, this album is worth tracking down. —*Scott Yanow*

Tain't Nobody's Biz-Ness If I Do / Jan. 5, 1959-Feb. 10, 1959 / Original Jazz Classics ♦♦♦♦♦
Helen Humes had not recorded as a leader in seven years when she made the first of three albums for Contemporary, all of which have been reissued on CD in the OJC series. Humes, 45 at the time, was at the peak of her powers, although she never really made a bad record. Accompanied by Benny Carter (on trumpet), trombonist Frank Rosolino, tenor saxophonist Teddy Edwards, pianist Andrew Previn, bassist Leroy Vinnegar and either Shelly Manne or Mel Lewis on drums, the singer is typically enthusiastic, exuberant and highly appealing on such numbers as "You

Can Depend on Me," "When I Grow Too Old to Dream" and "'Tain't Nobody's Biz-ness if I Do." She even sings credible versions of "Bill Bailey" and "When the Saints Go Marching In" on this easily recommended CD. —*Scott Yanow*

★ **Songs I Like to Sing** / Sep. 6, 1960-Sep. 8, 1960 / Original Jazz Classics ♦♦♦♦♦
One of the high points of Helen Humes' career, this Contemporary set (reissued on CD) features superior songs, superb backup and very suitable and swinging arrangements by Marty Paich. Humes' versions of "If I Could Be with You," "You're Driving Me Crazy" and "Million Dollar Secret," in particular, are definitive. On four songs, she is backed by tenor great Ben Webster, a rhythm section and a string quartet; the other numbers find her joined by a 14-piece band that includes Webster and Teddy Edwards on tenors, along with altoist Art Pepper. This classic release is essential and shows just how appealing a singer Helen Humes could be. —*Scott Yanow*

Swingin' with Humes / Jul. 27, 1961-Jul. 29, 1961 / Original Jazz Classics ♦♦♦♦
The third of Helen Humes' three memorable Contemporary releases, all of which are out on CD, features the distinctive singer on a dozen standards that she had missed documenting thus far. With fine backup work by trumpeter Joe Gordon, tenor saxophonist Teddy Edwards, pianist Wynton Kelly, guitarist Al Viola, bassist Leroy Vinnegar and drummer Frank Butler, Humes is in top form on such tunes as "When Day Is Done," "There'll Be Some Changes Made," "Pennies From Heaven" and "The Very Thought of You." One of her better albums. —*Scott Yanow*

Sneakin' Around / Mar. 16, 1974 / Classic Jazz ♦♦♦♦
Helen Humes did both bawdy, double-entendre-laden blues and R&B, and more sophisticated, jazz-tinged numbers during her career. This set, done with Gerald Badini, Gerry Wiggins, Major Holley, and Ed Thigpen, had a little of both, and was spiced up by Humes, singing with equal parts sass and grace. It was originally done for the Black and Blue label and was recently on CD. —*Ron Wynn*

On the Sunny Side of the Street / Jul. 2, 1974 / Black Lion ♦♦♦♦
Several major jazz personalities are heard on this Black Lion reissue CD, recorded live at the 1974 Montreux Jazz Festival. The fine singer Helen Humes sticks to standards and blues while accompanied by either Earl Hines or Jay McShann on piano, tenor saxophonist Buddy Tate, bassist Jimmy Woode and drummer Ed Thigpen. Although Hines and McShann are not the ideal accompanists, Humes fares quite well, winning the audience over with her enthusiasm and sincerity. —*Scott Yanow*

Helen Humes / Sep. 1974 / Audiophile ♦♦♦♦
This lesser-known Helen Humes album features the veteran singer in an intimate setting with pianist Connie Berry, guitarist Charlie Howard and bassist Al Autry. Because she primarily sticks to ballads on the set (including "Wrap Your Troubles in Dreams," "Embraceable You," "A Hundred Years from Today" and a wonderful version of "More Than You Know"), this date lacks the excitement of her best albums. However, Helen Humes fans are well aware that she never made an indifferent or uninteresting record and will want this obscure effort too. —*Scott Yanow*

Talk of the Town / Feb. 18, 1975 / Columbia ♦♦♦♦
Two years into her return from a six-year retirement, Helen Humes was at the height of her fame when she reunited with producer John Hammond to make her lone Columbia album. Joined by Buddy Tate (doubling on tenor and clarinet), guitarist George Benson (a Hammond discovery a decade earlier), pianist Ellis Larkins, bassist Major Holley and drummer Oliver Jackson, Humes is in fine form for a fairly typical mixture of blues, standards and ballads. She sounds particularly inspired during "He May Be Your Man," "Every Now and Then," "If I Could Be With You" and "Deed I Do." —*Scott Yanow*

● **Helen Humes and the Muse All Stars** / Oct. 5, 1979+Oct. 8, 1978 / Muse ♦♦♦♦♦
Helen Humes' return to an active singing career was one of the happier events in jazz of the late '70s. Able to give great feeling and sensitivity to ballads but also a superb lowdown blues singer, Humes flourished musically during her last years. On this excellent release (the CD reissue adds two alternate takes to the original program), Humes matches wits with altoist/singer Eddie "Cleanhead" Vinson on "I'm Gonna Move to the Outskirts of Town" and is in top form throughout. Tenors Arnett Cobb and Buddy Tate (along with a fine rhythm section led by pianist Gerald Wiggins) don't hurt either. An enthusiastic "Loud Talking Woman" and "My Old Flame" are high points. —*Scott Yanow*

Helen / Jun. 17, 1980+Jun. 19, 1980 / Muse ♦♦♦♦♦
Helen Humes was one of the most appealing jazz singers of the late '30s, and of the late '70s. Her comeback in her last few years was a welcome event, and all of her recordings for Muse are recommended. This one finds her backed by a veteran sextet including tenorman Buddy Tate, trumpeter Joe Wilder and pianist Norman Simmons. Her versions of "There'll Be Some Changes Made," "Easy Living" and "Draggin' My Heart Around" are particularly memorable. —*Scott Yanow*

Let the Good Times Roll / Aug. 1, 1973 / Classic Jazz ♦♦♦♦♦
Helen Humes had been retired for several years (and off record since 1961) when she began her comeback with this set. Recorded for the French Black & Blue label

and made available domestically on a Classic Jazz LP, the album mostly features the veteran swing singer doing remakes, some of which top her earlier versions. Louis Jordan's "They Raided the Joint" is an exciting opener and is matched by "That Old Feeling," "Be-Baba-Leba," "He May Be Your Man" and Humes' classic "A Million Dollar Secret." Particularly strong assets in her notable backup group are tenorman Arnett Cobb, guitarists Al Casey and Clarence "Gatemouth" Brown, pianist Jay McShann and organist Milt Buckner. Wonderful music that deserves to be made widely available. —*Scott Yanow*

Bobbi Humphrey

b. Apr. 25, 1950, Marlin, TX
Flute / Crossover Jazz, Instrumental Pop, Jazz Funk, Soul Jazz, Fusion, Mainstream Jazz
Bobbi Humphrey was a jazz flutist whose musical tastes leaned toward fusion and smooth jazz-pop. From the outset of her career, Humphrey was quite popular, winning a large crossover audience with her pop-oriented jazz-fusion. Throughout her career, her popularity exceeded her critical acclaim, although several critics did praise her technique and showmanship. Despite the lack of critical praise, audiences stayed with Humphrey for decades, buying her records and attending her concerts from the Montreux Festival to Carnegie Hall.

Although Bobbi Humphrey was born in Marlin, Texas, she was raised in Dallas. She began playing flute in high school and continued her studies at Texas Southern University and Southern Methodist University. Dizzy Gillespie saw Humphrey play at a talent contest at Southern Methodist and, impressed with what he had heard, he urged her to pursue a musical career in New York City. She followed through on his advice, getting her first big break performing at the Apollo Theatre on Amateur Night. Shortly afterward, she began playing regularly throughout the city, including a gig with Duke Ellington.

Humphrey signed with Blue Note in 1971. Her smooth blend of jazz, funk, pop and R&B fit in well with the new sound of Blue Note, and her six albums for the label—*Flute In, Dig This, Blacks and Blues, Satin Doll, Live at Montreux,* and *Fancy Dancer*—were all successes. In particular, 1973's *Blacks and Blues* was a rousing success, earning her a crossover pop and R&B audience. That same year, she played the Montreux Festival in Switzerland. In 1976, she was named Best Female Instrumentalist by *Billboard.* The following year, she switched record labels, signing with Epic and releasing *Tailor Made* that same year. She also played on Stevie Wonder's platinum album *Songs in the Key of Life* in 1977.

Tailor Made was the first of three albums on Epic Records—*Freestyle* followed in 1978, and *The Good Life* appeared about a year afterward. During the '80s, Humphrey continued to perform regularly, even if she didn't record often. She returned to recording in 1989, releasing *City Beat* on Malaco Records. Five years later, *Passion Flute* appeared on the Paradise Sounds label. —*Stephen Thomas Erlewine*

Flute In / Sep. 30, 1971-Oct. 1, 1971 / Blue Note ✦✦✦✦
Bobbi Humphrey's Best / 1971-1975 / Blue Note ✦✦
Dig This / Jul. 20, 1972+Jul. 21, 1972 / Blue Note ✦✦✦
Blacks and Blues / Jun. 7, 1973+Jun. 8, 1973 / Blue Note ✦✦✦
Satin Doll / Jun. 20, 1974-Aug. 5, 1974 / Blue Note ✦✦✦
Fancy Dancer / Aug. 5, 1975 / Blue Note ✦✦
Tailor Made / 1977 / Epic ✦✦✦
The Best of Bobbi Humphrey [Epic] / 1977-1979 / Epic ✦✦✦
Freestyle / 1978 / Epic ✦✦
Good Life / 1979 / Epic ✦✦✦
● **City Beat** / Jul. 1989 / Malaco ✦✦✦✦✦
A representative effort by flutist Humphrey, who delivers a jazz-pop sound. —*David Szatmary*
Passion Flute / 1994 / Paradise Sounds ✦✦✦

Percy Humphrey

b. Jan. 13, 1905, New Orleans, LA, **d.** Jul. 22, 1995, New Orleans, LA
Trumpet / New Orleans Jazz, Dixieland
Percy and his brother, clarinetist Willie Humphrey, became well known from the 1960s on for their playing in the erratic but enjoyable Preservation Hall Jazz Band. Percy, whose other brother was trombonist Earl Humphrey (1902-1971), was never a major musician, but he played his simple melodic leads with sincerity. He gained his initial recognition working with New Orleans brass bands, including the Eureka Brass Band. Humphrey was with George Lewis during 1951-53 and mostly played locally, became a fixture at Preservation Hall after it opened in 1961, and toured the world with the Preservation Hall Jazz Band, performing until

shortly before his death at the age of 90. Percy Humphrey, who sounded at his best on a Sweet Emma Barrett date in 1961, recorded as a leader for Riverside, Pearl, GHB, Storyville and Smoky Mary, among other labels. —*Scott Yanow*

Percy Humphrey & His Sympathy Five / Jan. 1, 1951-May 11, 1954 / American Music ✦✦✦
Percy Humphrey, the main trumpeter with the Preservation Hall Jazz Band during the 1960s, '70s and '80s, was never that strong a player. This CD starts off with Humphrey as the weak link in his own quintet on six previously unreleased numbers with clarinetist Raymond Burke, trombonist Jack Delaney, pianist Stanley Mendelson and drummer Paul Barbarin in 1954; Delaney often takes solo honors while Humphrey constantly falters. There are also four songs from a Barbarin date in which the drummer heads a septet including Humphrey, clarinetist Willie Humphrey, trombonist Waldron Joseph and guitarist Johnny St. Cyr in 1951, plus three delightful (and previously unknown) tunes from the obscure guitarist-vocalist Blind Gilbert in a trio that includes clarinetist Burke in 1953; "Let Me Call You Sweetheart" is a highlight. Overall this is an interesting historical set that is most highly recommended to New Orleans jazz collectors. —*Scott Yanow*

Sounds of New Orleans, Vol. 1: Paul Barbarin & His Band/Percy Humphrey's Jam Session / 1951-May 16, 1954 / Storyville ✦✦✦✦
Drummer Paul Barbarin always led first-class New Orleans jazz bands. This CD features his 1951 septet (a group that included trumpeter Enrie Cagnolatti, clarinetist Albert Burbank and trombonist Eddie Pierson) on seven hot standards. The second half of this set moves up to 1954 and showcases a pickup group led by trumpeter Percy Humphrey that also features clarinetist Ray Burke, trombonist Joe Avery and pianist Sweet Emma Barrett. Although the latter group is a bit more erratic, their session is historic since several members of the band would later be with the Preservation Hall Jazz Band. —*Scott Yanow*

Percy Humphrey at Manny's Tavern / 1953 / Biograph ✦✦✦
New Orleans: The Living Legends / Jan. 24, 1961 / Original Jazz Classics ✦✦✦
Trumpeter Percy Humphrey's debut as a leader (he was already 56) finds the sincere if limited trumpeter jamming on a variety of traditional New Orleans themes with a group of complementary musicians: trombonist Louis Nelson, clarinetist Albert Burbank, banjoist Emanuel Sayles, bassist Louis James and drummer Cie Frazier. The lack of a piano and a rather predictable rhythm section leave an overly sparse empty feeling in some of the ensembles, although the music (which includes "Milenberg Joys," "We Shall Walk Through the Streets of the City" and "Rip 'Em Up Joe") is spirited and generally enjoyable. "Climax Rag" has been added to the original LP program for the CD reissue. —*Scott Yanow*

● **Climax Rag** / Feb. 24, 1965 / Pearl ✦✦✦✦✦
Percy Humphrey, whose later recordings with the Preservation Hall Jazz Band tended to be quite erratic, is in generally good form on this LP made available through Delmark. Humphrey sounds inspired by the strong New Orleans jazz group (trombonist Jim Robinson, clarinetist Albert Burbank, banjoist George Guesnon, bassist Alcide Pavageau and drummer Cie Frazier) and his renditions of "Climax Rag," "When I Grow Too Old to Dream," "Fidgety Feet" and even "Swanee River" and "Yes Sir, That's My Baby" are quite fun. —*Scott Yanow*

New Orleans to Scandinavia / Sep. 29, 1972 / Storyville ✦✦✦
A Portrait of Percy Humphrey / Sep. 28, 1972-Sep. 29, 1972 / Storyville ✦✦✦
Living New Orleans Jazz / May 26, 1974-May 27, 1974 / Smokey Mary ✦✦✦

Willie Humphrey

b. Dec. 29, 1900, New Orleans, LA, **d.** Jun. 7, 1994, New Orleans, LA
Clarinet / New Orleans Jazz, Dixieland
Since he was the grandson of trumpeter and music teacher Jim Humphrey, the son of clarinetist Willie Humphrey, Sr., and the brother of both trumpeter Percy and trombonist Earl Humphrey, it is not surprising that Willie Humphrey, Jr. became a musician. After some violin lessons, he switched to clarinet when he was 14 and started working locally. Humphrey spent part of 1919-20 in Chicago, where he played with King Oliver and Freddie Keppard, but then returned home, missing his chance to be recorded early in his career. Humphrey spent 1925-32 in St. Louis, playing with Fate Marable and Dewey Jackson, and toured with Lucky Millinder (1935-36), but otherwise lived in New Orleans the remainder of his life. He worked as a music teacher and in a navy band during World War II, and in the 1950s he spent a period working with Paul Barbarin. Willie Humphrey and his brother Percy came to fame performing with the Preservation Hall Jazz Band starting in the 1960s, touring and spreading the joy of New Orleans jazz around the world. Although far from a virtuoso, Willie Humphrey played his simple ensemble-oriented style with spirit; he recorded as a leader for Smoky Mary and late in his career for GHB. —*Scott Yanow*

● **New Orleans Traditional Jazz Legends, Vol. 2** / Sep. 15, 1983-Sep. 16, 1983 / Mardi Gras ◆◆◆◆

Two Clarinets on the Porch / Aug. 21, 1991-Aug. 28, 1991/ GHB ◆◆◆

Alberta Hunter

b. Apr. 1, 1895, Memphis, TN, d. Oct. 17, 1984, Roosevelt, NY
Vocals / Standards, Classic Female Blues

An early blues vocalist in the 1920s, a sophisticated supper club singer in the 1930s and a survivor in the '80s, Alberta Hunter had quite a career. Hunter actually debuted in clubs as a singer as early as 1912, starting out in Chicago. She made her first recording in 1921, wrote "Down Hearted Blues" (which became Bessie Smith's first hit) and used such sidemen on her recordings in the 1920s as Fletcher Henderson, Eubie Blake, Fats Waller, Louis Armstrong and Sidney Bechet. She starred in *Showboat* with Paul Robeson at the London Palladium (1928-29), worked in Paris and recorded straight ballads with John Jackson's Orchestra. After returning to the US, Hunter worked for the USO during World War II and Korea, singing overseas. She retired in 1956 to become a nurse (she was 61 at the time) and continued in that field (other than a 1961 recording) until she was forced to retire in 1977 when it was believed she was 65; actually Hunter was 82! She then made a startling comeback in jazz, singing regularly at the Cookery in New York until she was 89, writing the music for the 1978 film *Remember My Name* and recording for Columbia. After the 1920s, Alberta Hunter recorded on an infrequent basis but her dates from 1935, 1939, 1940 and 1950 have been mostly reissued by Stash, her Bluesville album (1961) is out in the OJC series and her Columbia sets are still available. —*Scott Yanow*

Complete Recorded Works, Vol. 1 (1921-1923) / May 1921-Feb. 1923 / Document ◆◆◆

For completists, specialists and academics, Document's *Complete Recorded Works, Vol. 1 (1921-1923)* is invaluable, offering an exhaustive overview of Alberta Hunter's early recordings. For less dedicated listeners, the disc is a mixed blessing. There are some absolutely wonderful, classic performances on the collection, but the long running time, exacting chronological sequencing, poor fidelity (all cuts are transferred from original acetates and 78s), and number of performances are hard to digest. The serious blues listener will find all these factors to be positive, but enthusiasts and casual listeners will find that the collection is of marginal interest for those very reasons. —*Thom Owens*

● **Young Alberta Hunter: The Twenties** / 1921-1929 / Vintage Jazz Classics ◆◆◆◆◆

This LP gives listeners a strong sampling of singer Alberta Hunter's work in the 1920s. The 14 selections find her joined by such major jazz names as pianists Fletcher Henderson and Eubie Blake, cornetist Louis Armstrong, soprano saxophonist Sidney Bechet and Fats Waller (on organ). Although best known during the era as a classic blues singer, Hunter was always flexible and able to sing a wide variety of material. The best way to acquire all of her 1920s recordings are through her Document CDs but this LP sampler is excellent, with the highlights including "Down Hearted Blues" (her composition which Bessie Smith would make into a big hit in 1923), "Nobody Knows The Way I Feel Dis Morning," "If You Can't Hold the Man You Love" and "I'm Going to See My Ma." —*Scott Yanow*

Complete Recorded Works, Vol. 2 (1923-24) / Feb. 1 1923-Nov. 6, 1924 / Document ◆◆◆

Complete Recorded Works, Vol. 3 (1924-27) / Nov. 1924-Feb. 26, 1927 / Document ◆◆◆

Complete Recorded Works, Vol. 4 (1927-46) / May 20, 1927-1946 / Document ◆◆◆

Classic Alberta Hunter: The Thirties / Mar. 20, 1935-Jan. 1950 / Stash ◆◆◆◆

After returning to the US from England in 1935, Alberta Hunter continued working as a jazz-oriented singer in the US although she maintained a lower profile than in the 1920s. She had just three recording sessions during 1935-40 (all of the music is included on this valuable LP) and eight numbers in 1950 (two of which are here) prior to retiring from music in the mid-1950s to become a nurse. Among the highlights of these 15 selections by the timeless singer are "You Can't Tell the Difference After Dark," a remake of "Downhearted Blues," "Someday, Sweetheart" and "The Castle's Rockin'." In the backup groups on some numbers are trumpeter Charlie Shavers, clarinetist Buster Bailey and either Lil Armstrong or Eddie Heywood on piano, among others. Recommended. —*Scott Yanow*

The Legendary Alberta Hunter: '34 London Sessions / Sep. 24, 1934-Nov. 2, 1934 / DRG ◆◆

This handsome LP is a bit of an oddity. Alberta Hunter, famous as a jazz-oriented blues singer in the 1920s, reinvented herself as a sophisticated stage singer in London. Her 11 recordings with Jack Jackson's society dance orchestra in 1934 are very straight, outside of jazz and somewhat dated today. Whether it be "Two Cigarettes

in the Dark," "Miss Otis Regrets" or "Two Little Flies on a Lump of Sugar," Hunter interprets the romantic ballads like a cabaret singer. So, although this reissue was perfectly done (with extensive liner notes), there is little here to interest jazz listeners. —*Scott Yanow*

Songs We Taught Your Mother / Aug. 16, 1961 / Original Blues Classics ◆◆◆◆

Although Alberta Hunter, who had briefly come out of retirement, gets first billing on this CD reissue, in reality she shares the spotlight with two other veterans of the 1920s: Lucille Hegamin and Victoria Spivey. Each of the singers is featured on four songs apiece while backed by such top players as clarinetist Buster Bailey, trombonist J.C. Higginbotham, and Cliff Jackson or Willie "The Lion" Smith on piano. Hunter is in superior form on such numbers as "You Gotta Reap Just What You Sow" and "I Got a Mind to Ramble," although she would soon be out of music for another 15 years, continuing her work as a nurse. Hegamin (who had not recorded since 1932) was having a brief last hurrah, despite sounding good, and Spivey, reviving her "Black Snake Blues," would soon be launching her own Spivey label. This is a historic and enjoyable set recommended to both classic jazz and blues collectors. —*Scott Yanow*

Chicago: The Living Legends / Aug. 16, 1961 / Original Blues Classics ◆◆◆◆

This CD reissue is notable for two main reasons. It finds Alberta Hunter (who had retired from music in 1956 to become a nurse and who in the interim had only recorded once, two weeks earlier) in peak form on such numbers as "St. Louis Blues," "Downhearted Blues" and "You Better Change." In addition, it was pianist Lovie Austin's first recording in a couple decades; she was nearly 74 at the time and working as pianist at a Chicago dancing school. Austin's "Blues Serenaders" (a quintet also including trombonist Jimmy Archey, clarinetist Darnell Howard, bassist Pops Foster and drummer Jasper Taylor) has some concise solo space on the vocal pieces and takes three numbers (including Austin's "Gallion Stomp") as instrumentals. A well-conceived and historic set. —*Scott Yanow*

Remember My Name / 1977 / Columbia ◆◆◆◆

Although the cover on this album makes it look as if this is a soundtrack album (the singer had written several songs for the film "Remember My Name"), this is actually an important studio album. Alberta Hunter, a veteran of the 1920s who was 82 at the time, was at the beginning of a remarkable comeback after having been out of music for 20 years (working as a nurse). The singer is absolutely delightful and often saucy on such numbers as "You Reap Just What You Sow," "I've Got A Mind To Ramble," "My Castle's Rockin'" and "Downhearted Blues," making this her definitive late-period album. In addition to Hunter and a fine rhythm section (pianist Gerald Cook, guitarist Wally Richardson, bassist Al Hall and either Connie Kay or Jackie Williams on drums), three veteran horn players (trumpeter Doc Cheatham, trombonist Vic Dickenson and tenorman Budd Johnson) help out with short solos. Highly recommended. —*Scott Yanow*

Amtrack Blues / 1978 / Columbia ◆◆◆◆

Alberta Hunter's second recording since launching her remarkable comeback (she was 83 when this album was cut) finds the veteran blues singer (a survivor of the 1920s) still in strong form and full of spirit. Such songs as "Darktown Strutters Ball," "My Handy Man," "Old Fashioned Love" and "I've Got a Mind to Ramble" are given fine treatment by Hunter, who is joined by the Gerald Cook quartet, trombonist Vic Dickenson, trumpeter Doc Cheatham and tenorman Frank Wess on various tracks. Unfortunately none of Alberta Hunter's four Columbia albums have yet been reissued on CD but all are worth searching for. —*Scott Yanow*

Glory of Alberta Hunter / 1981 / Columbia ◆◆◆◆◆

Alberta Hunter's comeback after 20 years off the music scene was quite inspiring. She was (along with Sippie Wallace) virtually the only classic blues singer of the 1920s still active during part of the 1980s, and her four Columbia albums (of which this was the third) are surprisingly strong. With able backing by the Gerald Cook quartet, trumpeter Doc Cheatham, trombonist Vic Dickenson and tenor saxophonist Budd Johnson, Alberta Hunter sings some standards (including "Some of These Days," "The Glory of Love" and "I Cried for You"), a few religious hymns ("Ezekiel Saw the Wheel" and "Give Me That Old Time Religion"), the Yiddish tune "Ich Hob Dich Tzufil Lieba" and her own "Alberta's Blues" and "The Love I Have for You." —*Scott Yanow*

Look for the Silver Lining / 1982 / Columbia ◆◆◆◆

Classic blues singer Alberta Hunter's final recording (made when she was 87, two years before her death) is as powerful as her previous three Columbia albums. The legendary, delightful singer puts plenty of feeling into "Look for the Silver Lining," "He's Funny That Way," "Somebody Loves Me" and four of her originals. As was true of each of her final sets, Hunter is joined by the Gerald Cook quartet and several veteran horn players (trumpeters Doc Cheatham and Jonah Jones, trombonist Vic Dickenson and tenorman Budd Johnson), all of whom sound quite happy to be supporting the ancient yet ageless singer. —*Scott Yanow*

Charlie Hunter

b. 1968, Rhode Island

Guitar / Post-Bop, Acid Jazz, Fusion, Experimental, Jazz Rock

Charlie Hunter, who plays an eight-string guitar, provides his own basslines and leads an otherwise bassless guitar-sax-drums trio. He grew up in Berkeley, CA, and began playing guitar when he was 12. Hunter played in rock bands until forming his trio with tenor saxophonist Dave Ellis and drummer Jay Lane. Although very much a jazz group, the group also displays their interests in funk and rock. In addition to recording for Blue Note with his trio, Hunter works with T.J. Kirk, a band playing the music of Thelonious Monk, James Brown and Rahsaan Roland Kirk that has recorded for Warner Bros. In 1997 Charlie Hunter toured with a two-horn quartet (his guitar not only filled in for a bass but sometimes sounded eerily like an organ) and recorded a suprisingly successful jazz transformation of Bob Marley's reggae classic *Natty Dread. —Scott Yanow*

Charlie Hunter Trio / 1993 / Mammoth ✦✦✦✦

● **Bing, Bing, Bing!** / 1995 / Blue Note ✦✦✦✦✦

It is difficult not to be impressed with the playing of guitarist Charlie Hunter. By using two extra strings, Hunter is able to create his own basslines and have a very self-sufficient bassless (and keyboardless) trio with tenor saxophonist Dave Ellis and drummer Jay Lane that has all of the parts covered. The music on this CD (all originals) crosses over between straightahead jamming to '70s retro funk (à la Eddie Harris) that is infectious enough to fit into an acid jazz setting. However, even at its funkiest, the rhythms are subtle and the improvising reasonably creative, making this a potentially popular group that should still interest jazz listeners. —*Scott Yanow*

Ready . . . Set . . . Shango! / 1996 / Blue Note ✦✦✦✦

Although it is never clear what "shango" is, this set by guitarist Charlie Hunter's quartet is quite accessible and enjoyable. Marketed as some type of new alternative jazz, the music in reality is bop-based and not that far from soul-jazz. The most unusual aspectis that Hunter plays an eight-string guitar, which allows him not only to play bass lines (there is no bassist on the CD) but at times to emulate an organ. Both tenorman Dave Ellis, who would soon start his own solo career, and altoist Calder Spanier have plenty of solo space, while drummer Scott Amendola keeps the music grooving and moving. The nine selections may all be originals, but the music is also tied to the swinging tradition. Recommended. — *Scott Yanow*

Natty Dread / 1997 / Blue Note ✦✦✦✦

As one of the first releases in Blue Note's Cover Series, this CD is quite unusual. Guitarist Charlie Hunter, who on his instrument plays both lead and basslines simultaneously, decided to perform the nine songs from reggae master Bob Marley's 1974 album *Natty Dread.* Hunter and his band members (altoist Calder Spanier, Kenny Brooks on tenor and drummer Scott Amendola) turn the Marley-associated songs into creative jazz and certainly give these themes a fresh slant. On "No Woman, No Cry," Hunter's eight-string guitar hints at Bill Frisell, "Lively Up Yourself" is turned into a shuffle and other songs have the flavor of salsa, gospel, groove music and even hard bop. Although the themes are recognizable, Charlie Hunter has succeeded on this set in coming up with fresh new jazz interpretations of music not played in this context before. Well worth checking out. —*Scott Yanow*

Chris Hunter

b. Feb. 21, 1957, London, England

Alto Saxophone, Flute / Crossover Jazz, Post-Bop

Closely inspired by David Sanborn (who he often sounds like on alto), Chris Hunter is best known in the US for his work with Gil Evans. He started playing music when he was 12 and toured with the National Youth Jazz Orchestra at 19. After playing with Mike Westbrook (1978-79), Hunter became a studio musician in Europe. He first played with Evans in 1983, which led to his moving to New York. In 1984 he toured with Evans, played with the Michel Camilo sextet and began working with Mike Gibbs. He has since recorded as a leader for Atlantic and the Japanese Paddle Wheel label. —*Scott Yanow*

Chris Hunter / May 1986-Jun. 1986 / Atlantic ✦✦✦✦

Robert Hurst III

b. Oct. 4, 1964, Detroit, MI

Bass / Hard Bop

Robert Hurst came to fame for his work with Wynton and Branford Marsalis. He was originally a guitarist but instead later an important bassist in the Detroit jazz scene of the late '70s. He recorded with *Out of the Blue* (1985) and has since recorded with Tony Williams, Mulgrew Miller, Harry Connick, Jr., Geri Allen, Russell Malone and Steve Coleman, among others. Hurst was with Wynton Marsalis' group during 1986-91, switched over to Branford's band and became a member of

the Tonight Show Orchestra. Robert Hurst, a very supportive bassist, debuted as a leader in 1993 with a release on DIW/Columbia. —*Scott Yanow*

● **Robert Hurst Presents: Robert Hurst** / Aug. 20, 1992-Aug. 23, 1992 / DIW/ Columbia ✦✦✦✦

This set finds bassist Robert Hurst leading the Tonight Show All-Stars (with Branford Marsalis on various reeds and pianist Kenny Kirkland) plus trumpeter Marcus Belgrave and guest Ralph Miles Jones III (on bass clarinet and bassoon) through 11 of his originals and a solo bass version of Thelonious Monk's "Evidence." The music is complex and hard-driving but the improvisations are rather cold and sometimes boring. Hurst, a superior bassist, is not a superior composer and his compositions at best set moods. Of the supporting cast, the most distinctive voices are Belgrave and Jones; the latter has a colorful bass clarinet solo on "The Snake Charmer." This is a decent effort but not all that essential. —*Scott Yanow*

One for Namesake / Nov. 18, 1993-Nov. 19, 1993 / Columbia ✦✦✦

Bobby Hutcherson

b. Jan. 27, 1941, Los Angeles, CA

Vibes / Hard Bop, Post-Bop

Although when he first came up vibraphonist Bobby Hutcherson was associated with the avant-garde, he has since settled down into being "merely" a brilliant stylist whose playing falls between hard bop and post bop, rather than becoming an innovator. Hutcherson originally studied piano and then started concentrating on vibes as a teenager. He worked in the L.A. area with Curtis Amy and Charles Lloyd before joining the Al Grey-Billy Mitchell Quintet. Hutcherson moved to New York in 1961, made a big impression with his playing on Eric Dolphy's *Out to Lunch* (1964) and worked with everyone from Jackie McLean, Hank Mobley and Grachan Moncur III to Hank Mobley, Herbie Hancock, Andrew Hill, McCoy Tyner and Grant Green. Whenever an advanced vibraphonist was needed for a recording, Hutcherson got the call. He recorded a series of albums as a leader for Blue Note (1965-77), co-led a quintet with Harold Land (1967-71) and has headed his own groups since, other than his dates with the Timeless All Stars in the 1980s. In addition to Blue Note, Bobby Hutcherson has recorded as a leader for Cadet, Columbia, Timeless, Evidence, Contemporary and Landmark. —*Scott Yanow*

☆ **Dialogue** / Apr. 3, 1965 / Blue Note ✦✦✦✦✦

Vibraphonist Bobby Hutcherson's debut as a leader is still one of his most advanced recordings. Reissued on CD, the six-song program (including an Andrew Hill composition "Jasper" that was only previously out on an obscure 1979 LP) has an all-star group of young greats (trumpeter Freddie Hubbard, Sam Rivers on tenor, soprano, bass clarinet and flute, pianist Andrew Hill, bassist Richard Davis and drummer Joe Chambers in addition to Hutcherson), complex originals by Hill and Chambers and plenty of dynamic solos. The adventurous music falls between post bop and the avant-garde and finds the musicians all sounding quite inspired and challenged. An underrated Blue Note classic. —*Scott Yanow*

Spiral / Apr. 3, 1965+Nov. 25, 1968 / Blue Note ✦✦✦

Not released initially until this 1979 LP, these fine advanced performances deserved a better fate. One song, "Jasper," features an all-star sextet (comprising vibraphonist Bobby Hutcherson, Sam Rivers on tenor and bass clarinet, trumpeter Freddie Hubbard, pianist Andrew Hill, bassist Richard Davis and drummer Joe Chambers) and has been reissued on CD. The other five selections (which have not yet returned) are more in the modal/hard bop vein, matching Hutcherson with his future co-leader tenor saxophonist Harold Land, pianist Stanley Cowell, bassist Reggie Johnson and drummer Chambers. All of the songs are originals by band members and have their unpredictable moments while not forgetting to swing. Intriguing music that hopefully will resurface someday. —*Scott Yanow*

● **Components** / Jun. 14, 1965 / Blue Note ✦✦✦✦✦

This CD reissue spans a wide variety of styles, from hard bop (Bobby Hutcherson's attractive "Little B's Poem") to mostly atonal sound explorations ("Air"). There are four compositions apiece by the vibraphonist/leader and drummer Joe Chambers, with Chambers tending to be freer and more avant-garde. The talented young musicians (trumpeter Freddie Hubbard, James Spaulding on alto and flute, pianist Herbie Hancock, bassist Ron Carter, Chambers and Hutcherson) are up to the challenge and the results are always stimulating. Open-eared listeners are advised to pick up this CD, taken from a period when the versatile Bobby Hutcherson was considered one of the brightest new voices of what was called "the New Thing." —*Scott Yanow*

Happenings / Feb. 8, 1966 / Blue Note ✦✦✦✦

This is an excellent showcase for Bobby Hutcherson, who plays vibes and marimba in a quartet with pianist Herbie Hancock, bassist Bob Cranshaw and drummer Joe Chambers. On the straight CD reissue of the original LP, Hutcherson performs six of his diverse originals (which range from advanced hard bop to the nearly free-form "The Omen") plus Hancock's "Maiden Voyage." Hutcherson's outings on marimba are particularly interesting since they show the influence of modern classical music. His own style would become more conservative and predictable through the years, making Bobby Hutcherson's earlier records the ones to get for adventurous listeners. —*Scott Yanow*

Stick Up! / Jul. 14, 1966 / Blue Note ✦✦✦✦✦

Just being notified as to this set's all-star lineup (vibraphonist Bobby Hutcherson, tenor saxophonist Joe Henderson, pianist McCoy Tyner, bassist Herbie Lewis and drummer Billy Higgins) should cause most veteran jazz collectors to go out of their way to acquire the release. The quintet performs five of Hutcherson's little-known (but worthwhile) compositions plus Ornette Coleman's catchy "Una Muy Bonita." The advanced modal music (which sometimes hints at the avant-garde while holding onto its roots in hard bop) continually keeps one's interest. —*Scott Yanow*

Total Eclipse / Jul. 12, 1967 / Blue Note ✦✦✦✦✦

Although thought of as an avant-garde vibraphonist when he first emerged, Bobby Hutcherson eventually became an important part of the modern mainstream. This set, with its modal originals, is somewhere in between where Hutcherson had been and where he was going. Joined by tenor saxophonist Harold Land (with whom he had just started co-leading a quintet) and the up-and-coming pianist Chick Corea, Hutcherson is in excellent form on four of his originals and Corea's "Matrix." —*Scott Yanow*

Oblique / Jul. 21, 1967 / Blue Note ✦✦✦✦

There is a tension in this modern mainstream performance from 1967 that is often absent from today's music. While still playing music based on hard bop, vibraphonist Bobby Hutcherson and his quartet (which includes pianist Herbie Hancock, bassist Albert Stinson and drummer Joe Chambers) pulled at the chord structures and stretched the boundaries of the music during their improvisations. The two Chambers pieces ("Oblique" and "Bi-Sectional") are the freest and most fascinating recordings but even Hancock's repetitive vamp ("Theme from *Blowup*") is of interest. The four young masters on the CD reissue were quite capable of playing a variety of styles and their versatility, creativity and fire make this CD a standout. —*Scott Yanow*

Patterns / Mar. 14, 1968 / Blue Note ✦✦✦✦

This lesser-known Bobby Hutcherson CD (reissued in 1995) has concise but searching solos from the vibraphonist, James Spaldling (doubling on alto and flute), pianist Stanley Cowell, bassist Reggie Workman and drummer Joe Chambers on originals by Chambers (four), Cowell and Spaulding. All of the musicians worked together often during this period (Chambers is on nine of Hutcherson's ten Blue Note albums) and they make the complex music sound simpler (and perhaps more logical) than it really is. None of the songs caught on although some (particularly Cowell's "Effi" and the drummer's "Patterns," which is heard in two versions) seem eerily familiar. A good example of advanced hard bop. —*Scott Yanow*

Medina / Aug. 11, 1969 / Blue Note ✦✦✦✦

The Bobby Hutcherson-Harold Land Quintet was one of the main unsung groups of this era. Not avant-garde enough to be grouped with the free jazz innovators and owing nothing to fusion, vibraphonist Hutcherson and tenor saxophonist Land seemed to fall between the cracks, as bandleaders if not as solo musicians. This 1969 recording, not released until 1980, teams the co-leaders with pianist Stanley Cowell, bassist Reggie Johnson and drummer Joe Chambers for a variety of complex originals; two apiece by Hutcherson, Cowell and Chambers. The modal music is between hard bop and the avant-garde but can simply be called explorative and unpredictable. —*Scott Yanow*

Now / 1969 / Blue Note ✦✦✦

Now is another exceptional record Bobby Hutcherson cut with the Harold Land quintet. Like their other collaborations, the music falls between the borders of the avant-garde and post-bop, but *Now* is distinguished by the presence of vocalist Gene McDaniels and a vocal chorus, as well as conga player Candido. The chorus doesn't always mesh well with Hutcherson and Land, but the album offers plenty of provocative, challenging moments that make it an essential listen for dedicated fans of the vibraphonist and tenor saxophonist. —*Stephen Thomas Erlewine*

San Francisco / Jul. 15, 1970 / Blue Note ✦✦✦✦✦

This CD reissue is an exact duplicate of the original LP. Vibraphonist Bobby Hutcherson and tenor saxophonist Harold Land co-led a quintet on the West Coast for quite a few years. The remainder of the personnel was often open to change and on this particular release the duo is augmented by keyboardist Joe Sample (normally with the Jazz Crusaders at the time), bassist John Williams and drummer Mickey Roker. The music is often quite advanced yet more accessible than one would expect. There are hints of rock rhythms on a few tracks along with modal melodies influenced by John Coltrane and plenty of rewarding solos from the co-leaders. —*Scott Yanow*

Natural Illusions / Mar. 2, 1972+Mar. 3, 1972 / Blue Note ✦✦

Natural Illusions is one of the rare Bobby Hutcherson dates that finds the vibraphonist flirting with the mainstream and fusion. Hutcherson leads a band that features Ron Carter and George Duvivier alternating on bass, guitarist Gene Bertoncini, pianist Hank Jones, drummer Jack DeJohnette and harpist Gene Bianco. The group plays a selection of standards ("The Folks Who Live on the Hill," "Sophisticated Lady," "Lush Life"), contemporary hits ("The Thrill Is Gone"), and new jazz songs, giving them all a smooth, lush treatment. There's little of the unpredictable phrasing and modal harmonies that distinguished Hutcherson's albums, and the music often sounds conventional, making it one of the lesser efforts in his catalog. —*Stephen Thomas Erlewine*

Live at Montreux / Jul. 5, 1973 / Blue Note ✦✦✦✦✦

By 1973 Blue Note was fairly well a dead label and this often-brilliant advanced hard bop set was only released at the time in Europe and Japan. Now with the CD reissue, Americans can finally hear the mutually inspiring performance of vibraphonist Bobby Hutcherson and trumpeter Woody Shaw. Joined by a fine rhythm section, they create fiery solos on modal originals, with Shaw in particular in prime form. Highly recommended. —*Scott Yanow*

Cirrus / Apr. 17, 1974+Apr. 18, 1974 / Blue Note ✦✦✦

While it doesn't quite match the heights of their early collaborations, *Cirrus* finds Bobby Hutcherson resuming his partnership with tenor saxophonist Harold Land, and the results are quite good. The pair work with pianist Bill Henderson, trumpeter Woody Shaw, bassist Ray Drummond, drummer Larry Hancock, saxophonist/flutist Emmanuel Boyd and percussionist Kenneth Nash on this set of originals. The music is a little smoother than their earlier collaborations, but there are enough captivating, provocative moments to make the reunion a success. —*Stephen Thomas Erlewine*

Linger Lane / 1974 / Blue Note ✦✦

The View from the Inside / Aug. 4, 1976-Aug. 6, 1976 / Blue Note ✦✦✦

Vibraphonist Bobby Hutcherson was one of the last jazz artists to be recording for the Blue Note label (along with Horace Silver) before it finally collapsed. Some of the vibist's later Blue Note albums are forgettable but this LP with Manny Boyd (doubling on tenor and soprano), keyboardist Larry Nash, bassist James Leary and drummer Eddie Marshall has some excellent hard bop music. The material (all by band members except "For Heaven's Sake") is generally melodic but has some fine solos; pity that Blue Note has not yet reissued this LP on CD. —*Scott Yanow*

Knucklebean / 1977 / Blue Note ✦✦✦✦

This little-known gem is from the declining days of Blue Note. Vibraphonist Bobby Hutcherson welcomed his friend trumpeter Freddie Hubbard to his date and Hubbard (who is heard on four of the six selections) almost stole the show. It is particularly nice to hear Hubbard (whose recordings from this era are horrible) playing jazz again. In addition to the leader (who also doubles on marimbas), solo space is given to keyboardist George Cables and the reed players Manny Boyd and Hadley Caliman. This LP is worth searching for since it may be awhile before it returns on CD. —*Scott Yanow*

Highway One / May 1978-Jun. 23, 1978 / Columbia ✦✦✦

With keyboardist George Cables and Bobby Hutcherson contributing all of the compositions, it is not too surprising that this LP has plenty of strong melodies. Hutcherson is heard backed by string and horn sections on one selection apiece but they add to rather than detract from the melodic but not simplistic music. Freddie Hubbard drops by for a cameo on one ballad and flutist Hubert Laws is heard from in spots. A fine (if not overly adventurous) outing. —*Scott Yanow*

Conception: The Gift of Love / Mar. 15, 1979+Mar. 16, 1979 / Columbia ✦✦✦

Vibraphonist Bobby Hutcherson's Columbia releases, although well distributed at the time, are now difficult to find and have not been reissued on CD. This is one of his lesser efforts, a set that matches Hutcherson's quintet (which also includes pianist George Cables, bassist James Leary, drummer Eddie Marshall and percussionist Kenneth Nash) with 13 horns (including flutist Hubert Laws). The seven originals are by band members and pianist Cedar Walton (who produced and arranged the set). Although well played and reasonably challenging, nothing all that memorable occurs. —*Scott Yanow*

Un Poco Loco / 1979 / Columbia ✦✦✦✦

By 1980, vibraphonist Bobby Hutcherson had evolved from a member of the avant-garde into a top exponent of the modern mainstream. This excellent LP (mostly originals and obscurities but highlighted by an inventive version of Bud Powell's classic title cut) features Hutcherson with a top-notch all-star group also including guitarist John Abercrombie, keyboardist George Cables, electric bassist Chuck Domanico and drummer Peter Erskine. Pity that this fine set has been long out-of-print. —*Scott Yanow*

Solo / Quartet / Sep. 28, 1981-Mar. 1, 1982 / Original Jazz Classics ✦✦✦✦✦

This is one of vibraphonist Bobby Hutcherson's most unusual and interesting releases. The first half of the set features Hutcherson all by himself although, by utilizing overdubbing, he almost sounds like Max Roach's M'Boom ensemble. Hutcherson is heard on vibes, marimbas, bass marimba, chimes, xylophone and bells and these three selections are quite fun and energetic. The second half is more conventional, with Hutcherson welcoming pianist McCoy Tyner (in his first sideman appearance in a decade), bassist Herbie Lewis and drummer Billy Higgins for two standards and a pair of the vibraphonist's originals. The quartet set is excellent but it is Bobby Hutcherson's solo performances that are most memorable and unique. —*Scott Yanow*

Farewell Keystone / Jul. 10, 1982-Jul. 11, 1982 / Evidence ✦✦✦✦

Recorded a year before San Francisco's legendary club Keystone Korner (which was open for 11 years) closed, this live set features tenor saxophonist Harold Land with Bobby Hutcherson (who co-led a group with him in the 1970s) and trumpeter Oscar Brashear (who has often teamed up with Land during the past 15 years). With pianist Cedar Walton, bassist Buster Williams and drummer Billy Higgins completing the sextet, it is not surprising that the music is hard bop-oriented and of consistent high quality. Originally out on Theresa, the Evidence CD reissue adds a lengthy version of Harold Land's "Mapenzi" to the original five-song program, all of which are originals by the musicians. Recommended. —*Scott Yanow*

Four Seasons / Dec. 11, 1983 / Timeless ✦✦✦

This set by vibraphonist Bobby Hutcherson is a bit unusual in that, rather than playing complex originals, he interprets seven jazz standards. With the assistance of pianist George Cables, bassist Herbie Lewis and drummer Philly Joe Jones, Hutcherson sounds in top form on such numbers as Thelonious Monk's "I Mean You," "Star Eyes" and "If I Were a Bell." —*Scott Yanow*

Good Bait / Aug. 9, 1984-Aug. 10, 1984 / Landmark ✦✦✦✦

For the debut of Orrin Keepnews' Landmark label, the producer teamed vibraphonist Bobby Hutcherson with pianist George Cables, bassist Ray Drummond, drummer Philly Joe Jones and (as a wild card) Branford Marsalis (who doubles on tenor and soprano). Interpreting tunes by McCoy Tyner ("Love Samba"), Tadd Dameron, Thelonious Monk ("In Walked Bud"), Rodgers & Hart and John Carisi plus two of his better originals ("Highway One" and "Montgomery"), Hutcherson performs a strong set of solid advanced hard bop. —*Scott Yanow*

Vibe Wise / Aug. 9, 1984-Oct. 10, 1985 / 32 Jazz ✦✦✦

Color Schemes / Oct. 1985 / Landmark ✦✦✦✦

On *Color Schemes*, Bobby Hutcherson (vibes) is backed by a top-notch rhythm section for a set of jazz standards and originals. Every selection has its worthwhile points, with the standouts being a bossa nova-flavored version of Joe Henderson's "Recorda-Me." The leader dueted with pianist Mulgrew Miller (who continued to move forward as an impressive soloist, gradually discarding the McCoy Tyner influence) on his ballad "Rosemary, Rosemary," an uptempo rendition of "Remember" and a colorful overdubbed duet with percussionist Airto Moreira ("Color Scheme") that found Hutcherson blending together vibes, marimba and orchestra bells. This is an easily recommended album of high-quality, if conservative, music. —*Scott Yanow, Cadence*

In the Vanguard / Dec. 5, 1986+Dec. 6, 1986 / Landmark ✦✦✦✦✦

Vibraphonist Bobby Hutcherson was once associated with the avant-garde to a certain extent but by the 1970s it was clear he had found his voice in the modern mainstream of jazz. This live set from the Village Vanguard features him on both vibes and marimbas with stellar sidemen: pianist Kenny Barron, bassist Buster Williams and drummer Al Foster. Their repertoire (in addition to Hutcherson's "I Wanna Stand over There") comprises five standards and the results are high-quality modern bebop. The communication between the players is quite impressive. —*Scott Yanow*

Cruisin' the Bird / Apr. 15, 1988+Apr. 16, 1988 / Landmark ✦✦✦✦

Throughout his career, vibraphonist Bobby Hutcherson has recorded one rewarding set after another, always being quite consistent. This date (which as usual can be considered advanced hard bop) finds Hutcherson (who doubles on marimba) interacting with saxophonist Ralph Moore (heard on tenor and soprano), pianist Buddy Montgomery, bassist Rufus Reid and drummer Victor Lewis. Together they perform four of Hutcherson's unpredictable originals plus a trio of standards (including "Come Rain or Come Shine"). Fine music. —*Scott Yanow*

Ambos Mundos / Aug. 1989-Sep. 1989 / Landmark ✦✦✦✦

This Landmark session was a change of pace for vibraphonist Bobby Hutcherson, an Afro-Cuban set in which he uses an expanded group. Five selections (four of his originals plus a song by drummer Eddie Marshall) feature the leader with flutist James Spaulding, guitarist Randy Vincent and a six-piece rhythm section, while "Tin Tin Deo" and "Besame Mucho" are jammed with guitarist Bruce Forman,

bass, drums and two percussionists. Intriguing and consistently exciting music. —*Scott Yanow*

Mirage / Feb. 15, 1991+Feb. 18, 1991 / Landmark ✦✦✦

This quartet date by Bobby Hutcherson works quite well due to the chemistry between the vibraphonist and pianist Tommy Flanagan. They take Thelonious Monk's "Pannonica" and "Love Letters" as exquisite duets and perform eight high-quality selections as a quartet with bassist Peter Washington and drummer Billy Drummond. Among the other highlights are Barry Harris' "Nascimento," Flanagan's "Beyond the Bluebird" and Antonio Carlos Jobim's "Zingaro." Everything clicks on this inspired outing. —*Scott Yanow*

Landmarks / Feb. 12, 1992 / Landmark ✦✦✦

Acoustic Masters II / Mar. 1993 / Atlantic ✦✦✦✦

Dick Hyman

b. Mar. 8, 1927, New York, NY
Piano / Swing, Stride, Classic Jazz

A very versatile virtuoso, Dick Hyman once recorded an album on which he played "A Child Is Born" in the styles of 11 different pianists from Scott Joplin to Cecil Taylor. Hyman can clearly play anything he wants to and during the past two decades he has mostly concentrated on pre-bop swing and stride styles. Hyman worked with Red Norvo (1949-50) and Benny Goodman (1950) and then spent much of the 1950s and '60s as a studio musician. He appears on the one known sound film of Charlie Parker (*Hot House* from 1952), recorded honky tonk under pseudonyms, played organ and early synthesizers in addition to piano, was Arthur Godfrey's music director (1959-62), collaborated with Leonard Feather on some History of Jazz concerts (doubling on clarinet) and even performed rock and free jazz, but all of this was a prelude to his present-day work. In the 1970s Hyman played with the New York Jazz Repertory Company, formed the Perfect Jazz Repertory Quintet (1976) and started writing soundtracks for Woody Allen films. He has recorded frequently during the past 25 years (sometimes in duets with Ruby Braff) for Concord, Music Masters and Reference and ranks at the top of the classic jazz field. —*Scott Yanow*

★ **Jelly and James: Music of "Jelly Roll" Morton and James P. Johnson** / 1973 / Sony ✦✦✦✦✦

With the exception of a version of "Fickle Fay Creep," this single CD has all of the music recorded by Dick Hyman for tribute LPs to Jelly Roll Morton and James P. Johnson. By varying the instrumentation (which ranges from a piano solo and duets to a big band) and by picking musicians who really understand vintage jazz, Hyman put together two classic sets. The Morton date features such musicians as clarinetist Kenny Davern (doubling on soprano), violinist Joe Venuti, trumpeter Pee Wee Erwin and trombonist Vic Dickenson (among others) and the highlights include Hyman's showcase on "Fingerbuster," "King Porter Stomp," "The Crave" and an exuberant "Black Bottom Stomp." The James P. Johnson project is most notable for three duets by Hyman (one on pipe organ) with cornetist Ruby Braff and for excellent orchestrations for both a theatre orchestra and a jazz band. Essential music for any serious prebop collection. —*Scott Yanow*

Charleston / Apr. 29, 1975-May 29, 1975 / Columbia ✦✦✦✦✦

Dick Hyman is a modern day wonder, a pianist who can seemingly recreate the style of practically any jazz keyboardist. Since his favorite era is pre-swing, he has in recent years mostly concentrated on the jazz pioneers. This well-rounded set looks into the music of James P. Johnson, the king of stride pianists and an eminent composer of the 1920s. Hyman casts Johnson's music in several different settings. He takes "Caprice Rag" as a piano solo, joins in three duets with cornetist Ruby Braff (including one outing on organ), uses a fairly straight dance band and an even less adventurous theater orchestra on some tracks, and for three selections features a jazz band that includes Braff, Bob Wilber on soprano and trombonist Vic Dickenson. Although there is not a great deal of improvisation on this program, the expert transcriptions and colorful arrangements pay a glorious tribute to the great James P. Johnson. —*Scott Yanow*

Manhattan Jazz / 1987 / Music Masters ✦✦✦✦✦

Every duet album by pianist Dick Hyman and cornetist Ruby Braff is magical. The two distinctive musicians always seem to react immediately to each other and they consistently play highly expressive versions of prebop standards. This outing has its memorable moments and is highlighted by "Jubilee," "You're Lucky to Me," "I'm Crazy 'Bout My Baby" and "Jeepers Creepers"; Hyman takes "I'm Just Wild About Harry" as an unaccompanied solo. The CD is easily recommended to mainstream collectors. —*Scott Yanow*

Themes and Variations on "A Child Is Born" / Oct. 11, 1977-Oct. 12, 1977 / Chiaroscuro ✦✦✦✦✦

This is a unique and rather successful project. Pianist Dick Hyman, who has long had the ability to play credibly in any jazz style (although he tends to stick to pre-bop), performs Thad Jones' classic ballad "A Child Is Born" in the style of a dozen different pianists, including himself. Hyman infuses his interpretations with occasional humorous song quotes and does a superb job of emulating Scott Joplin, Jelly Roll Morton, James P. Johnson, Earl Hines, Fats Waller, Teddy Wilson, Erroll Garner, George Shearing, Cecil Taylor, Art Tatum and Bill Evans before launching into a 17-minute version in his own style. The results are utterly fascinating, making one wish that the pianist had also chosen Albert Ammons, Bud Powell and McCoy Tyner. Unfortunately this LP has yet to be reissued but it is certainly a unique gem. —*Scott Yanow*

☆ **The Music of Jelly Roll Morton** / Feb. 26, 1978 / Smithsonian ✦✦✦✦✦
Of all the Jelly Roll Morton tribute albums that have been recorded through the years, Dick Hyman's is one of the most rewarding. He utilizes a very suitable septet (with clarinetist Bob Wilber, trumpeter Warren Vache, trombonist Jack Gale, Marty Grosz on guitar and banjo, Major Holley doubling on bass and tuba, and Morton alumnus Tommy Benford on drums) on nine of Morton's best tunes, including two ("King Porter Stomp" and "Wolverine Blues") not recorded by Morton in this format. In addition, there is a close recreation of the quartet piece "Mournful Serenade," a couple of trios with Wilber and Benford, and two piano solos ("Fingerbreaker" and "The Pearls") that give Hyman an opportunity to do his Jelly Roll Mortons impressions. This LP should satisfy all traditional jazz fans. —*Scott Yanow*

Say It with Music / Jan. 1979 / World Jazz ✦✦✦
Although this group's title is silly (The Perfect Jazz [Repertory] Quintet), pianist Dick Hyman did gather together a fine all-star mainstream group comprising trumpeter Pee Wee Erwin, Bob Wilber on various reeds, bassist Milt Hinton and drummer Bobby Rosengarden. On their out-of-print LP they perform concise versions ("How Deep Is the Ocean?" at 4:15 is the longest tune) of ten Irving Berlin compositions. The emphasis is on the melody and the solos are short (Berlin would have enjoyed the set), making the out-of-print LP both pleasing and somewhat predictable. —*Scott Yanow*

Live at Michael's Pub / Jul. 24, 1981-Jul. 25, 1981 / JazzMania ✦✦✦✦
In addition to being piano virtuosos with a mastery of a wide variety of styles ranging from bop and stride to classical music, Dick Hyman and Roger Kellaway share an outrageous sense of humor. During the two live concerts heard on this CD, Hyman and Kellaway play piano duet versions of four jazz standards plus Kellaway's theme from *All in the Family* ("Remembering You"), the "Woody Woodpecker Song" and "Chopsticks." Their treatments of these songs are quite adventurous, with plenty of emotional and atonal outbursts while always keeping the melody in clear sight. The ensembles are often dense but the two pianists listen very closely to each other. In fact, when one changes keys, the other one goes right along and extends the idea. The episodic "Chopsticks" (which is really torn apart) is worth the price of this recording by itself. —*Scott Yanow*

Eubie! / 1983 / Seven Star ✦✦✦✦
Shortly after Eubie Blake's death at age 100, Dick Hyman recorded 11 of Blake's compositions on this set of piano solos. The music ranges from the 1899 "Charleston Rag," hits such as "Memories of You," "I'm Just Wild About Harry" and the touching "I'd Give a Dollar for a Dime" to Blake's final composition, "It Was Well Worth the While." Hyman captures Blake's sound perfectly while also stretching out in his own more virtuosic style. ild Dog," "Black and Blue Bottom," "Wild Cat," Pretty Trix" and "Cheese and Crackers" Are included in this very enjoyable set. —*Scott Yanow*

Kitten on the Keys / 1983 / RCA ✦✦✦✦

Runnin' Ragged / Sep. 1985 / Pro Arte ✦✦✦

At Chung's Chinese Restaurant / Sep. 26, 1985 / Musical Heritage Society ✦✦✦✦

Gulf Coast Blues / Jun. 25, 1986 / Omega ✦✦✦
Considering that Clarence Williams was a fairly basic pianist and that Dick Hyman can play anything on the keyboard, it is a bit surprising that his solo interpretions of a dozen Williams tunes are so successful. Hyman generally does not try to play exactly like the composer-pianist but he sometimes emulates Williams' various groups of the 1920s and '30s (most of these songs were originally recorded by combos) and comes up with fresh variations within the vintage style. Among the highlights are "Organ Grinder Blues," "I'm Goin' Back to Bottomland," "What's the Matter Now?" "Papa De-Da-Da" and "Cushion Foot Stomp." —*Scott Yanow*

Stridemonster! / Jul. 19, 1986 / Unisson ✦✦✦✦✦
This is a particularly exciting set. Dick Hyman and Dick Wellstood meet up on a variety of heated selections and try to outstride each other. Wellstood (just a year before his death) takes "Caravan" as his feature, while Hyman takes "I've Got a Crush on You" solo, but it is the eight collaborations (particularly "Keep off the Grass," "Birmingham Breakdown" and "What's the Use of Being Alone?") that are most memorable. This album was put out by the Canadian Unisson label and is quite exciting. —*Scott Yanow*

The Kingdom of Swing & the Republic of Oop Bop Sh'bam / Jul. 30, 1987 / Music Masters ✦✦✦
This CD, which documents a live concert, has a silly title form. Actually, out of the eight selections, only two ("On Green Dolphin Street" and "Night in Tunisia") have anything to do with bop. In reality this is a mainstream date featuring pianist Dick Hyman with some of his favorite players, including fellow pianist Derek Smith, cornetist Warren Vache, trumpeter Joe Wilder, trombonist Urbie Green, Buddy Tate on tenor and clarinet, bassist Milt Hinton (featured on "Joshua Fit the Battle of Jericho") and drummer Butch Miles. Tate's clarinet outing on "Blue Creek" and Wilder's lyrical solo on "When Your Lover Has Gone" are excellent, but in general (considering the players involved) the results are average and fairly predictable. —*Scott Yanow*

Face the Music: A Century of Irving Berlin / Dec. 8, 1987-Dec. 9, 1987 / Music Masters ✦✦✦✦
Dick Hyman certainly had a lot of songs to choose from for this solo piano CD tribute to Irving Berlin (who made it past 100). Hyman is heard expertly mixing together some of Berlin's better-known tunes (such as "Let's Face the Music," "Easter Parade," "Remember" and "Always") with such notable obscurities as "Lady of the Evening," "How About Me?" and "I'll See You In C.U.B.A." Hyman's total control of the piano and his versatile style (which on this date ranges from stride to swing to Art Tatum) makes the set an obvious success. —*Scott Yanow*

Live from Toronto's Cafe des Copains / 1988 / Music & Arts ✦✦✦✦✦
Most of Dick Hyman's recordings of the 1980s and '90s have been based around specific topics but this is a freewheeling solo club set. The pianist is heard on a wide-ranging repertoire that includes such numbers as "What Is This Thing Called Love," "Lush Life," James P. Johnson's "Snowy Morning Blues," an original theme that he wrote for "The Purple Rose of Cairo," Jelly Roll Morton's "Froggie Moore Rag," "At the Jazz Band Ball" and "I'm Just Wild About Harry." A typically superb outing that (due to its variety) serves as a perfect introduction to Dick Hyman's exciting playing. —*Scott Yanow*

Dick Hyman Plays Fats Waller / Dec. 1988 / Reference ✦✦✦✦
Strange as it seems, pianist Dick Hyman was not present at the recording session that resulted in this CD. Months earlier, Hyman performed 15 Fats Waller songs on the Bosendorfer 2905E Reproducing Piano in New York. A computer floppy disc of the date was sent to California, where it was recorded direct to CD. But more important than the technology involved is the music itself. Sometimes Hyman seems to take these pieces a little too seriously, treating "African Ripples" and "Viper's Drag" as if they were classical music but, to his credit, his treatment of the Waller compositions (mixing in the familiar with obscurities such as an enthusiastic "I'm Goin' to See My Ma" and a very complex version of "Bach up to Me") does not attempt to copy Fats' style. A surprisingly uptempo version of "Stealin' Apples" and a thoughtful rendition of "Ain't Misbehavin'" are among the high points. Recommended. —*Scott Yanow*

Live at Maybeck Recital Hall, Vol. 3: Music of 1937 / Feb. 14, 1989 / Concord Jazz ✦✦✦✦
Dick Hyman is such a versatile pianist that his own style has often been overshadowed by his interpretations of other pianists' work. *Music of 1937*, which features 11 diverse songs premiered in that year, finds Hyman at times hinting at Oscar Peterson (especially on "Where or When"), the stride piano masters, classical music and even the basslines of Dave McKenna, but mostly he plays in his own virtuosic yet very melodic and accessible style. "Loch Lomond" pays tribute to Benny Goodman's rendition, "Thanks for the Memories" is based a bit on Bob Hope's original recording and Art Tatum would have been proud to have cut this version of "In the Still of the Night." The wide range of emotions (from an exuberant "Bob White" to a somber "The Folks Who Live on the Hill") and Hyman's typically brilliant playing on the solo recital make this CD a particular standout. —*Scott Yanow*

Dick Hyman Plays Harold Arlen / Apr. 13, 1989-Apr. 14, 1989 / Music Masters ✦✦✦✦
This CD is very much a piano recital, as Dick Hyman (on a set of unaccompanied solos) demonstrates his love for Harold Arlen's music. Nine of the fourteen selections that Hyman chose to record are very well known, three are somewhat obscure and two are somewhere in between. The accent is on Art Tatum's style during some of the songs, along with a few snatches of Teddy Wilson's relaxed stride. Hyman reproduces the ease with which Tatum threw out impossible-to-play virtuosic runs, and (even more impressive) he hints constantly at Art's advanced harmonies without doing strict imitations. He gives a few of the songs unusual twists ("Stormy Weather" becomes a waltz, "Over the Rainbow" has a bossa nova rhythm, the last part of "A Woman's Prerogative" is played in two keys at once, etc.) but the melodies are never far away. Hyman also takes his first real vocal on record, doing a nice job on the lyrics of "In Your Own Quiet Way" with his obviously untrained voice. A fine outing. —*Scott Yanow*

All Through the Night / 1991 / Music Masters ✦✦✦✦

This Dick Hyman solo set features the brilliant pianist interpreting 11 songs written by Cole Porter. In addition to such famous tunes as "Easy to Love" (which is really explored during a 10-minute version), "Begin the Beguine" and "Night and Day," Hyman revives three fairly unknown numbers from "Kiss Me Kate": "Were Thine That Special Face," "Brush up Your Shakespeare" and "Wunderbar." All of Dick Hyman's solo recitals are well worth acquiring. — *Scott Yanow*

Dick Hyman Plays Duke Ellington / Aug. 23, 1992 / Reference ✦✦✦✦

Performed (as was Dick Hyman's previous Fats Waller project) on a Bosendorfer Reproducing Piano and actually recorded from the piano at a later date (one really cannot tell the difference), this outing finds the great Hyman interpreting 14 of Duke Ellington's compositions. Most intriguing are Ellington's nearly atonal "The Clothed Woman" and "Tonk" in which Hyman somehow duplicates an Ellington-Billy Strayhorn piano duet! Other highlights include the joyous "Drop Me off in Harlem," "Doin' the Voom Voom," "Echoes of Harlem" and "The Gal from Joe's." The recording is as rewarding as one would expect. — *Scott Yanow*

The Gershwin Songbook: Jazz Variations / Sep. 15, 1992-Sep. 16, 1992 / Music Masters ✦✦✦

In 1932 George Gershwin published variations of 18 of his songs, turning some of his classics into more challenging workouts. Sixty years later Dick Hyman recorded the 18 pieces in two versions apiece: first a brief and straight rendition of the original sheet music and then his own versions based partly on Gershwin's 1932 songbook. It would have been interesting to hear Hyman actually perform Gershwin's varitions, for one can only guess how much of his own improvisations are taken from the composer's embellishments. In general the flavor of Gershwin is quite strong throughout this date but Hyman does feel free to insert some obvious departures, such as his hot stride on "Fascinating Rhythm," a bit of Tatum and Tristano on "Strike up the Band," hints of Bix on "Do, Do, Do" and some Errol Garnerisms on "Clap Yo' Hands." Although a tad gimmicky, this CD does have its fascinating moments and plenty of brilliant playing from Dick Hyman. — *Scott Yanow*

● Dick Hyman/Ralph Sutton / 1993 / Concord Jazz ✦✦✦✦✦

The two top living stride pianists, Dick Hyman and Ralph Sutton, are teamed up for an exciting live duo session recorded at Maybeck Recital Hall. Hearing the two masters explore jazz standards (mostly from the pre-1940 era) is analogous to seeing Fats Waller and James P. Johnson sharing the same stage in the 1930s. Somehow Hyman and Sutton leave just enough room for the other one to slip in and the ensembles, although bursting at the seams, are never overcrowded. Sutton has "Everything Happens to Me" as his ballad feature, while Hyman tears into "Old Man River" by himself, but it is the stomps by the duo (such as "Sunday," "Dinah," "The World Is Waiting for the Sunrise" and "I'm Sorry I Made You Cry") that make the session so memorable. This historic encounter is a gem. — *Scott Yanow*

From the Age of Swing / 1994 / Reference ✦✦✦

As the title implies, this is very much a swing set. Pianist Dick Hyman (a master of all prebop styles) has little difficulty emulating Teddy Wilson, Art Tatum and Count Basie (among others) plus his own style, in an octet also featuring trumpeter Joe Wilder, trombonist Urbie Green, altoist-clarinetist Phil Bodner, baritonist Joe Temperley, rhythm guitarist Bucky Pizzarelli, bassist Milt Hinton, drummer Butch Miles and (on three tunes) altoist Frank Wess. The opening and closing numbers are ad-lib blues both titled "From the Age of Swing" while sandwiched in are ten swing-era standards plus a couple of obscure Duke Ellington items. Among highlights are "Topsy," "Them There Eyes," "Rose Room" and "Mean to Me." No real surprises occur but mainstream fans should like this swinging set. — *Scott Yanow*

Swing Is Here / Feb. 28, 1996-Feb. 29, 1996 / Reference ✦✦✦

Pianist Dick Hyman pays tribute to small-group swing with a collection of 15 swing-era tunes. Hyman is joined by vibraphonist Peter Appleyard—who sometimes purposely emulates Lionel Hampton—as well as clarinetist Ken Peplowski (nodding toward Benny Goodman), trumpeter Randy Sandke, veteran tenor man

Frank Wess (whose solos are actually the most modern of the date), guitarist Bucky Pizzarelli, bassist Jay Leonhart and drummer Butch Miles. Nancy Marano contributes a few pleasing vocals. Nothing all that unexpected occurs, and the performances of such numbers as "I Hope Gabriel Likes My Music," "Dickie's Dream" and "Jive at Five" do not dwarf the original recordings. But mainstream fans should enjoy the well-played and often spirited outing. — *Scott Yanow*

Cheek to Cheek / Dec. 17, 1996 / Arbors ✦✦✦

Although Dick Hyman has the ability to play credibly in most jazz styles, he has spent much of the 1980s and '90s performing stride and swing. This release, a trio date with guitarist Howard Alden and bassist Bob Haggart, was a change of pace, for Hyman plays mostly in a more boppish and modern mainstream vein. In the wide repertoire, the pianist ranges from "Django" and a pair of Thelonious Monk tunes to Flip Phillips' "The Claw," Billy Strayhorn's "Lotus Blossom," and two of his originals. The music is excellent, if not overly memorable. — *Scott Yanow*

Phyllis Hyman

b. Jul. 6, 1941, Philadelphia, PA, **d.** Jun. 30, 1995, New York, NY
Vocals / Soul, R&B

Phyllis Hyman began her career as a silky-voiced, jazz-influenced singer, and gradually moved into slick, heavily produced Urban Contemporary ballads and light dance numbers. Hyman won a scholarship to music school and then began her professional career with the group New Direction in 1971. When they disbanded after a national tour, Hyman joined the Miami ensemble All The People. She also worked there with another local group, The Hondo Beat, and appeared in the film "Lenny." That was followed by a two-year stint heading Phyllis Hyman & the P/H Factor, before relocating to New York. Hyman did background vocals on Jon Lucien's *Premonition* LP and built her reputation performing in New York clubs. Norman Connors made her his featured vocalist in the mid-'70s, and she was highlighted on a cover of the Stylistics' "Betcha By Golly Wow," which appeared on Connors' *You Are My Starship* LP. Hyman also sang with Pharoah Sanders and the Fatback Band while cutting two singles as a lead artist. Buddah released *Phyllis Hyman* in 1977, but she really began making an impression when she was signed by Arista the next year. The songs "Somewhere in My Lifetime" and "You Know How to Love Me" both made the R&B Top 20. Hyman got her lone Top 10 hit in 1981 with "Can't We Fall in Love Again?" but her albums did consistently well through the '80s. The production teams of Mtume/Reggie Lucas and Narada Michael Walden/Thom Bell gave her material that showcased her skill with sophisticated ballads. Hyman had more success when she left Arista for Philadelphia International in 1986, with the single "Living All Alone" putting her back in the R&B Top 20. She also sang on fusion and light jazz dates by Joe Sample, Ronnie Foster, and Grover Washington, Jr., a more conventional jazz session for McCoy Tyner, and a pop date with the Four Tops. *Prime of My Life* was her most recent release in 1991. — *Ron Wynn*

The Best of Phyllis Hyman / 1979-1986 / Arista ✦✦✦

Hyman's greatest hits and tracks from a period when she was doing some jazz-influenced songs, as well as the perfunctory Urban Contemporary cuts and Adult Contemporary ballads. — *Ron Wynn*

Under Her Spell: Phyllis Hyman's Greatest Hits / 1986-1989 / Arista ✦✦✦✦✦

Phyllis Hyman's soft, sultry, suggestive voice was featured on several pop-jazz and fusion hits during the 1970s and '80s. Hyman had the mellow, relaxed tone that struck a chord with the emerging urban contemporary and fusion audience. The 10 tracks on this collection include the big hits "You Know How to Love Me," "Somewhere in My Lifetime," her cover of the Stylistics' "Betcha By Golly Wow" and the title track, plus others that weren't commercially prominent, but were equally indicative of her direction during that period. These include "Can't We Fall In Love Again?" with Michael Henderson and "Gonna Make Changes." These songs remain her most successful and most memorable as a solo artist. — *Ron Wynn*

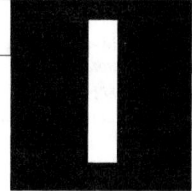

Abdullah Ibrahim (Dollar Brand) (Adolph Johannes Brand)

b. Oct. 9, 1934, Cape Town, South Africa
Piano, Leader / Post-Bop, African Folk Music

A highly individual pianist/composer whose music is influenced by Duke Elling-ton, Thelonious Monk and especially his own South African heritage, Abdullah Ibrahim (who until the 1970s was known as Dollar Brand) performs explorative originals that are full of strong melodies and spirituality. He started on piano when he was seven and was a member of the Jazz Epistles, recording South Africa's first jazz album in 1960. Ibrahim and his future wife, singer Sathima Bea Benjamin, went into self-imposed exile from the apartheid system in 1962, going to Zurich. Duke Ellington heard them perform and arranged for recording ses-sions. Ibrahim was also sponsored by Ellington at the 1965 Newport Jazz Festival and even got to sub for him with his orchestra during a tour. In 1966 Ibrahim worked with Elvin Jones but otherwise he has generally been a bandleader. He has recorded for many labels in settings ranging from being a piano soloist and head of a large band to his septet Ekaya including numerous sessions for Enja. Ibrahim, who visited South Africa in 1976, has returned home several times since its liberation from apartheid. — *Scott Yanow*

Duke Ellington Presents the Dollar Brand Trio / Feb. 1963 / Warner Brothers ◆◆◆◆

Pianist Abdullah Ibrahim (then known as Dollar Brand) was a newcomer to Europe in 1963, having recently left his homeland South Africa. His wife Bea Ben-jamin had persuaded Duke Ellington to see Brand perform, and he was so impressed that he produced Brand on a record date for Reprise with Dollar's trio (which included bassist Johnny Gertze and drummer Makaya Ntshoko), reissued on CD in 1997. Brand, who at the time was very influenced by Thelonious Monk and (to a lesser extent) Ellington, performs five originals plus Monk's "Brilliant Corners." Although his style was not as distinctive as it would become (there is lit-tle heard of his country's folk music), this is a consistently stimulating, exploratory and recommended, if (at 33 minutes) brief set. — *Scott Yanow*

Cape Town Fringe / 1965 / Chiaroscuro ◆◆◆

This little-known quintet set matches the young pianist Abdullah Ibrahim (then known as Dollar Brand) with the tenor of Basil Coetzee, altoist Robbie Jansen, bassist Paul Michaels and drummer Monty Weber on two of his melodic and somewhat spiritual originals ("Cape Town Fringe" and "The Pilgrim"). The Chiar-oscuro LP is brief (just twenty-six-and-a-half minutes) and will be difficult to find, but the themes are well-played and a bit haunting. — *Scott Yanow*

Soweto / 1965 / Chiaroscuro ◆◆◆

This obscure and long-out-of-print Chiaroscuro LP does not have any recording date listed, but it was recorded in Europe in 1965. Pianist Dollar Brand (aka Abdullah Ibrahim) is heard leading two groups comprising mostly fellow expatri-ate South Africans—a quartet with tenor saxophonist Basil Mannenberg and a septet. The three originals ("Soweto," "African Herbs" and "Sathima") are very much in Ibrahim's mature style, full of rich melodies, expert use of repetition and percussive piano. On "African Herbs," he doubles effectively on soprano and elec-tric piano. — *Scott Yanow*

● **Anatomy of a South African Village** / Jan. 30, 1965 / Black Lion ◆◆◆◆

In the mid-1960s, Abdullah Ibrahim (then known as Dollar Brand) was an avant-garde pianist influenced by Thelonious Monk who was not yet displaying much of his South African heritage in his music. This CD reissue is quite valuable for Ibra-him (in a trio with bassist Johnny Gertze and drummer Makaya Ntshoko) per-forms the intriguing title cut, brief versions of "Smoke Gets in Your Eyes" and "Mamma" and a rather hypnotic suite. All of the selections but "Anatomy of a South African Village" were released for the first time on this 1992 CD, one of the better recordings of the early Abdullah Ibrahim. — *Scott Yanow*

The Dream / Jan. 30, 1965 / Freedom ◆◆◆◆

Reflections / Mar. 16, 1965 / Black Lion ◆◆◆

The more familiar one is with the later work of pianist/composer Abdullah Ibra-him, the more interesting they will find this CD reissue. A solo piano set from 1965 (except for a 1968 version of "Honeysuckle Rose"), Ibrahim's roots in Duke Ellington and Thelonious Monk are more apparent in this music than it would be. Still known as Dollar Brand at the time, the pianist's interpretations are often stark (with much use of space), dramatic, dissonant and occasionally out-of-tempo and bitonal. These largely introspective performances do not contain the joyful folk melodies of Ibrahim's later work but they offer a fascinating early look into the music of the important stylist. — *Scott Yanow*

Round Midnight at the Montmartre / Jun. 30, 1965 / Black Lion ◆◆◆

This is an interesting early Abdullah Ibrahim CD, recorded when the pianist-com-poser was still known as Dollar Brand. Teamed with bassist Johnny Gertze and drummer Makaya Ntshoko on six of the eight numbers (two are piano solos), Ibra-him sounds quite advanced, showing off the influence of Thelonious Monk and perhaps Herbie Nichols but not much of his own South African heritage; that would come later. Ibrahim performs six of his originals plus two Monk tunes ("'Round Midnight" and "Light Blue") with originality and a certain amount of unpredictability. — *Scott Yanow*

African Piano / Oct. 22, 1969 / ECM ◆◆◆◆

Pianist Abdullah Ibrahim was still known as "Dollar Brand" when he recorded this solo piano set for ECM and it has been reissued on CD under his original name. The continuous live performance (which is under 39 minutes) explores eight of Ibrahim's originals, none of which are all that memorable. Ibrahim was still in the process of finding his own sound at the time although his improvisa-tions (which use repetition and vamps effectively) have their interesting moments. Still, Ibrahim's later work is more significant. — *Scott Yanow*

Fats Duke and the Monk / Feb. 18, 1973 / Sackville ◆◆◆◆

After a decade of generally intriguing recordings, pianist Abdullah Ibrahim really found his own voice by the early '70s. His lengthy solo set from February 18, 1973, originally released as a pair of Sackville LPs (*Sangoma* and *African Portraits*) has been reshuffled and expanded a bit upon the release of this CD and its companion *Ancient Africa*. One selection apiece from the two albums have been grouped with the previously unreleased "Salaam Peace" to form this disc. Ibrahim is heard on three lengthy medleys; best are "African Portraits" and "Fats, Duke & the Monk" although Fats Waller (who is only represented by a brief "Honeysuckle Rose") gets short shrift on the latter. Ibrahim's passionate solos (which are sometimes joined by his verbal cries) are picturesque, episodic and utterly fascinating on this set even if *Ancient Africa* actually gets the edge. — *Scott Yanow*

Ancient Africa / Feb. 18, 1973 / Sackville ◆◆◆

On Feb. 18, 1973, Abdullah Ibrahim had a busy day, recording two brilliant albums of solo piano. A pair of CD reissues (*Ancient Africa* and *Fats Duke & the Monk*) include all of the material from the LPs *Sangoma* and *African Portraits* although they change the order of the songs around quite a bit; *Ancient Africa* has two pieces from the former album and one from the latter. The superior of the two CDs, *Ancient Africa*, features Ibrahim playing some remarkable music that is rem-iniscent of (but actually historically precedes) Keith Jarrett's famous solo concerts. There are many exciting moments during these picturesque and lengthy improvi-sations, which range from 13 to 21 minutes apiece. Ibrahim combines the sophisti-cation of advanced jazz with the beautiful and often-spiritual melodies of African folk music. Highly recommended. — *Scott Yanow*

African Space Program / Nov. 7, 1973 / Enja ◆◆◆

Poorly recorded, but a great 12-piece group date. — *Ron Wynn*

Ode to Duke Ellington / Dec. 12, 1973 / Inner City ◆◆◆◆

Duke Ellington has long been a major inspiration for Abdullah Ibrahim. This CD, which was formerly available domestically as an Inner City LP, finds Ibrahim dur-ing a solo recital mixing his themes with those of Duke. The net result is that the pianist comes across as a South African Duke Ellington. The music (which includes three medleys and "Impressions on a Caravan") is continually intriguing, with Ibrahim also adding his voice and some tympani to his own "Ode to Duke." —*Scott Yanow*

Good News from Africa / Dec. 10, 1973 / Enja ✦✦✦✦✦

Those not familiar with the probing and soul cleansing sound of pianist Abdullah Ibrahim would do well to check out any of his solo albums or this fine 1973 effort featuring bassist Johnny Dyani. The fully orchestrated and eloquent style of Ibrahim improvising from folk melodies, sometimes dipping into overt jazz colorings, supported by the sympathetic movements of Dyani, speaks much more fully. There was also a lot of coloration with percussion that only occasionally seemed to intrude into the mood of the music, and was quite effective on its own. —*Milo Fine, Cadence*

The Banyana: Children of Africa / Jan. 27, 1976 / Enja ✦✦✦✦

Abdullah Ibrahim sings and plays soprano on "Ishmael" but otherwise sticks to piano on this trio set with bassist Cecil McBee and drummer Roy Brooks. As usual, Ibrahim's folkish melodies (this CD has six of his originals plus a previously alternate take of "Ishmael") pay tribute to his South African heritage and Islam religion without becoming esoteric or inaccessible. Some of the unpredictable music gets a bit intense (Ibrahim is in consistently adventurous form) but his flights always return back to earth and have an air of optimism. An above-average effort from a true individualist. —*Scott Yanow*

Journey / Sep. 1977 / Chiaroscuro ✦✦✦

An excellent nonette with Hamiet Bluiett (baritone sax) and Don Cherry (tpt). —*Ron Wynn*

Autobiography / Jun. 18, 1978 / Planisphere ✦✦✦✦

Recorded live, this two-LP solo set features pianist Abdullah Ibrahim performing songs from his youth, a Duke Ellington medley, "Take the 'A' Train," "I Surrender Dear," Thelonious Monk's "Coming on the Hudson" and some newer pieces, including one ("Khoisan") that he takes as a flute solo. The music is often taken as spontaneous medleys and, although the song titles are often incorrect, this two-fer really does a fine job of summing up Ibrahim's powerful and spiritual music up to 1978. Hopefully, it will be reissued on CD. —*Scott Yanow*

Africa: Tears and Laughter / Mar. 11, 1979-Mar. 12, 1979 / Enja ✦✦✦

This unusual set is powerful but clearly for selected tastes. Pianist Abdullah Ibrahim and saxophonist Talib Qadr, who doubles on soprano and alto, are mostly heard singing and chanting during Ibrahim's religious piece "Ishmael," a heartfelt but difficult-to-listen-to tribute to the pianist's Islamic faith. His other originals, which sometimes find Ibrahim playing soprano, are also quite spiritual, featuring a lot of emphasis on the melody statements and pure religious passion from the quartet, which also includes bassist Greg Brown and drummer John Betsch. A sincere but not essential release. —*Scott Yanow*

Echoes from Africa / Sep. 7, 1979 / Enja ✦✦✦

This is a rather emotional duet set by pianist Abdullah Ibrahim and bassist Johnny Dyani, two masterful musicians from South Africa. Their often introspective music includes three originals (with one piece dedicated to McCoy Tyner) plus a nearly 17-minute improvisation based on a folk melody that also allows one to hear the voices of the two musicians. This moody music has an almost sacred credibility and is quite personal. —*Scott Yanow*

● African Marketplace / Dec. 1979 / Elektra ✦✦✦✦✦

This is one of Abdullah Ibrahim's most colorful band recordings. With a 12-piece group that includes altoist Carlos Ward, trombonist Craig Harris and bassist Cecil McBee along with some lesser-known names, Ibrahim performs eight folklike originals that pay tribute to his life growing up in South Africa. "The Homecoming Song," "Anthem for the New Nation" and especially "The Wedding" (a beautiful hymn) are particularly memorable. —*Scott Yanow*

☆ Live at Montreux / Jul. 18, 1980 / Enja ✦✦✦✦✦

A 1990 reissue of a tremendous concert done in 1980. Carlos Ward and Craig Harris star alongside Ibrahim. —*Ron Wynn*

African Dawn / Jun. 7, 1982 / Enja ✦✦✦✦✦

These are solo versions of his greatest originals, plus Monk tributes. —*Myles Boisen*

Zimbabwe / May 29, 1983 / Enja ✦✦✦✦

This was a nicely blended, somewhat mellow and seemingly quite finished recording by Abdullah Ibrahim with Carlos Ward (alto sax, flute), Essiet Okun Essiet (bass), and Don Mumford (drums) called *Zimbabwe*. Interspaced with non-originals were four Ibrahim compositions, most of which were inspired by the imagery from Ibrahim's South African roots. —*Bob Rusch, Cadence*

Live at Sweet Basil, Vol. 1 / Oct. 1983 / Ekapa ✦✦✦✦

It is a real pity that pianist/bandleader Abdullah Ibrahim's recordings for Black Hawk have been out of print since the collapse of that label. This live LP (which also was originally released on Ibrahim's Ekapa label) has a set of duets by the

pianist and altoist Carlos Ward (who doubles on flute), one of Abdullah's long-term members. The music is episodic, occasionally dramatic and sometimes reverent. Highlights include "The Dream," "For Coltrane" and "Soweto." Incidentally, there was never any Vol. 2. —*Scott Yanow*

☆ Ekaya / Nov. 17, 1983 / Ekapa ✦✦✦✦✦

Pianist/composer Abdullah Ibrahim had one of his strongest groups for this studio date, a septet LP with altoist Carlos Ward, tenor saxophonist Ricky Ford, baritonist Charles Davis, trombonist Dick Griffin, bassist Cecil McBee and drummer Ben Riley. It is always enlightening to hear Ibrahim's originals, of which there are six on this out-of-print LP, being performed by a medium-sized band. There is a great deal of beauty to be heard in these rich melodies; if only this highly enjoyable and spiritual set would be reissued on CD. —*Scott Yanow*

★ Water from an Ancient Well / Oct. 1985 / Tiptoe ✦✦✦✦✦

Also made available domestically at one time by the defunct Black Hawk label, this superior Abdullah Ibrahim recording features the pianist/composer with a very strong septet. Such superior musicians as tenor saxophonist Ricky Ford, altoist Carlos Ward, baritonist Charles Davis and trombonist Dick Griffin are heard at their most creative and emotional on these eight Ibrahim originals. Many of the melodies (particularly "Mandela," "Song for Sathima," "Water from an Ancient Well" and the beautiful "The Wedding" are among Ibrahim's finest compositions. —*Scott Yanow*

South Africa / Jul. 1986 / Enja ✦✦✦✦

Abdullah Ibrahim's spiritual and very melodic South African folk music is always worth hearing and his individuality remains quite impressive. This set, recorded live at the Montreux Jazz Festival, features the pianist (who also plays a bit of soprano and adds his emotional voice to the proceedings) with his longtime altoist Carlos Ward, bassist Essiet Okun Essiet, drummer Don Mumford and vocalist Johnny Classens. The music, dealing with themes related to South African life, is quite personal, unique and surprisingly accessible. —*Scott Yanow*

Mindif / Mar. 7, 1988-Mar. 8, 1988 / Enja ✦✦✦

The music on this CD (all Abdullah Ibrahim originals) was performed and recorded for the soundtrack of a French film, *Chocolat*. The selections are generally fairly brief, and the LP-length set (39 minutes of music) is episodic and a bit incomplete due to the lack of a photo. Ibrahim (heard on piano, flute and voice) is joined by a notable group of players (the tenors of Ricky Ford and Craig Handy, trombonist Benny Powell, bassist David Williams and drummer Billy Higgins), but the overall results, while pleasant, are not as essential as Ibrahim's best work. —*Scott Yanow*

African River / Jun. 1, 1989 / Enja ✦✦✦✦

For this excellent date, pianist Abdullah Ibrahim performs eight of his compositions with a particularly strong group of players: trombonist Robin Eubanks, John Stubblefield on tenor and flute, Horace Alexander Young switching between soprano, alto and piccolo, Howard Johnson on tuba, baritone and trumpet, bassist Buster Williams and drummer Brian Abrahams. But more important than the individual players are the colorful ensembles and the frequently memorable compositions. Highlights include "African River," "Sweet Samba," "Duke 88" and a beautiful version of "The Wedding." —*Scott Yanow*

Mantra Mode / Jan. 1991 / Enja ✦✦✦✦

This was a very special recording for pianist/composer Abdullah Ibrahim because, after nearly 30 years of exile, he was back in Cape Town, South Africa, performing with local musicians. The musicianship is surprisingly high and the African septet does a fine job of interpreting eight of Ibrahim's newer folk melodies. —*Scott Yanow*

Desert Flowers / Dec. 18, 1991 / Enja ✦✦✦

Recent release by pianist and bandleader Abdullah Ibrahim, combining the sweeping township jive rhythms of his native South Africa, swing and gospel piano riffs, and hard-hitting bop solos and progressions. —*Ron Wynn*

Knysna Blue / Sep. 1993-Oct. 1993 / Enja ✦✦✦✦

After decades of self-exile, pianist/composer/bandleader Abdullah Ibrahim finally had an opportunity to return to his native South Africa in the early 1990s. This solo CD was recorded at Cape Town and has seven of his themes, all of which reflect his heritage; in addition, Ibrahim performs Thelonious Monk's "Ask Me Now." An excellent effort that must have been an emotional experience for the unique and masterful Abdullah Ibrahim. —*Scott Yanow*

Incognito

f. 1979, London, England
Group / Acid Jazz, Funk, House

Incognito was formed by Jean Paul Maunick (aka Bluey). Born in Mauritius but raised in London, Bluey caught the crest of the British jazz-funk movement in the mid-'70s and pioneered acid jazz in the '80s. The band's debut album, *Jazz Funk*

(1980), charted in the British Top 30 (and was re-released in the US 15 years later). Among others, Bluey has worked with Jimmy Jam & Terry Lewis, George Duke, Sister Sledge, Stevie Wonder and James Brown. —*John Bush*

Jazz Funk / 1991 / Ensign ✦✦✦

● **Inside Life** / 1992 / Verve/Forecast ✦✦✦✦

Tribes, Vibes and Scribes / 1993 / Verve ✦✦✦

Positivity / 1994 / Talkin Loud ✦✦✦

100 Degrees and Rising / Jun. 6, 1995 / Talkin Loud ✦✦✦
On *100 Degrees and Rising,* the pioneering acid house outfit Incognito turn in another first-rate record, featuring their trademark mixture of jazz, soul, and funk. There's not much to distinguish *100 Degrees* from their previous handful of records, but the band is smooth, accomplished and deep, finding new variations on their trademark sound. —*Stephen Thomas Erlewine*

Remixed / Verve /Forcast ✦✦✦
Incognito Remixed features a number of the group's tracks for Talkin' Loud/Verve remixed by stars like Pete Rock and Roger Sanchez. Some of these 12 songs have previously been released, but the bulk of the disc have never been easily available—most are promotional-only remixes. Frequently these versions, including a steaming "Always Thrree," actually improve on the original take, offering deeper, more textured grooves. In fact, it is arguably the finest, most consistent Incognito album available. —*Leo Stanley*

Beneath the Surface / 1996 / Verve, Forcast ✦✦✦✦
Beneath the Surface finds original lead singer Maysa Leak returning to the Incognito fold. Coincidentally or not, the record finds the group moving deeply into smooth, laidback, jazzy soul. It's a seductive sound and the group executes it well, even though there ironically isn't that much substance beneath the surface. —*Leo Stanley*

Keith Ingham

b. Feb. 5, 1942, London, England
Piano / Swing, Dixieland
A fine swing pianist, Keith Ingham's recent recordings of 1930s vintage songs for the Jump label are quite enjoyable. He started playing professionally in 1964 and worked with Sandy Brown, Bruce Turner and Wally Fawkes (among others) in England during the next decade. In 1974 Ingham recorded with Bob Wilber and Bud Freeman and in 1978 he settled in New York. He had the opportunity to play with Benny Goodman and the World's Greatest Jazz Band and became the musical director and pianist for Susannah McCorkle. Keith Ingham also recorded three albums with Maxine Sullivan, worked with Marty Grosz and Harry Allen, toured with the Eddie Condon Memorial Band and has led sessions for Sackville and Progressive in addition to Jump. —*Scott Yanow*

Fred Astaire Collection / May 21, 1989-May 23, 1989 / Jump ✦✦✦✦

Music of Victor Young / May 21, 1989-May 23, 1989 / Jump ✦✦✦✦

Out of the Past / Dec. 1990 / Sackville ✦✦✦

Donaldson Redux / Jun. 20, 1991-Nov. 25, 1991 / Stomp Off ✦✦✦✦
The tunes of Walter Donaldson (mostly dating from the 1920s) are explored and lovingly investigated on this CD by a group of prebop all-stars headed by pianist Keith Ingham and guitarist/vocalist Marty Grosz. Donaldson, although largely overlooked when lists are made of the great composers, was responsible for such tunes as "My Blue Heaven," "At Sundown," "How 'Ya Gonna Keep 'Em Down on the Farm," "My Baby Just Cares for Me," and "Love Me or Leave Me" (all of which are included in this program along with some lesser-known ditties; he also wrote "Yes Sir, That's My Baby," "Little White Lies," "Makin' Whoopee" and "You're Driving Me Crazy" (which are not performed by this group). Among the talented musicians who are heard on at least a few of the songs (the personnel changes constantly) are cornetist Peter Ecklund, clarinetists Bobby Gordon and Billy Novick, tenor saxophonist Loren Schoenberg, trombonist Dan Barrett, Vince Giordano on bass sax, tuba and bass, violinist Andy Stein, guitarist Frank Vignola, bassist Greg Cohen, Paul Bacon (on comb) and drummers Hal Smith and Arnie Kinsella. This is fun music that is played with spirit. —*Scott Yanow*

Music from the Mauve Decades / Apr. 20, 1993-Apr. 21, 1993 / Sackville ✦✦✦✦✦
1900-1920 was considered "the Mauve Decades," so on this Sackville CD, pianist Keith Ingham (in a trio with clarinetist Bobby Gordon and clarinetist Bobby Gordon) performs 17 songs written during that period. Although one might think that the music would be ragtime-oriented, in reality many of the songs retained their popularity into the 1920s and beyond, including "Glow Worm," "Ida," "My Gal Sal," "Some of These Days" and "Love Nest." The interpretations, which are a little reminiscent of the Benny Goodman Trio, fall into mainstream jazz, between swing and Dixieland. Everyone plays up to par, making this a good acquisition for prebop collectors. —*Scott Yanow*

● **The Keith Ingham New York 9, Vol. 1** / May 9, 1994-May 17, 1994 / Jump ✦✦✦✦✦
This, the first of two CDs, features pianist Keith Ingham and a variety of top mainstream players, heard in different combinations, exploring mostly obscurities from the 1920s and '30s. Such tunes as Alex Hill's "Madame Dynamite," "I'm Gonna Stomp Mr. Henry Lee," "Too Busy," "Learn to Croon" and "Mood Hollywood" are not exactly recorded on a weekly basis in the 1990s. Ingham is joined by such fine players as cornetist Randy Reinhardt, trombonist Dan Barrett (who also plays some effective trumpet), clarinetist Phil Bodner, Scott Robinson on various reeds, guitarist James Chirillo, bassist Murray Wall, Vince Giordano on bass sax and bass, and drummer Arnie Kinsella. The bands range from an octet to several different trios. Highly recommended to fans of the idiom, along with Vol. 2. —*Scott Yanow*

The Keith Ingham New York 9, Vol. 2 / May 9, 1994-May 17, 1994 / Jump ✦✦✦✦✦
The second of two CDs equals the quality of the first volume. Pianist Keith Ingham and a variety of mainstream all-stars (including cornetist Randy Reinhart, Dan Barrett on trombone and trumpet and Phil Bodner and Scott Robinson on reeds), mostly plays obscure gems from the 1920s and '30s. The music falls between swing and Dixieland; among the highlights are "What-Cha-Call-'Em Blues," "Mandy, Make Up Your Mind," "I Never Knew Just What a Girl Could Do" and "That Old Gang of Mine." The settings range from James Chirillo's unaccompanied guitar on "Too Late Now" to an octet. Recommended. —*Scott Yanow*

Back Room Stomp / Jan. 2, 1995-Jan. 3, 1995 / Sackville ✦✦✦✦
Although pianist Keith Ingham and tenor saxophonist Harry Allen are billed as coleaders, the main star of these 14 swing-based tunes is Scott Robinson who is well showcased on clarinet, soprano and baritone. Trumpeter Peter Ecklund also gets some good spots, and the rhythm section (guitarist James Chirillo, bassist Murray Wall and drummer Jackie Williams) is perfect for this style of music. The emphasis is on obscure songs played in the vein of Duke Ellington's small groups of the 1930s and there are plenty of heated moments along with arranged ensembles. Well worth investigating. —*Scott Yanow*

International Sweethearts of Rhythm

f. 1939, **db.** 1949
Group / Big Band, Swing
Probably the finest all-female jazz group, the International Sweethearts of Rhythm was formed in 1939 at the Piney Woods Country Life School in Mississippi. The 17-piece swing group, which was led by singer Anna Mae Winburn, included such fine soloists as tenor saxophonist Viola Burnside and trumpeter Tiny Davis. Eddie Durham and Jesse Stone were among the arrangers. The Sweethearts gradually became popular in the 1940s, appearing on radio broadcasts, touring the US and visiting Europe (1945). The orchestra only made a few records before its breakup in 1949 but a couple of its broadcasts from 1945-46 were released on a Rosetta LP. —*Scott Yanow*

★ **International Sweethearts of Rhythm** / 1945-1946 / Rosetta ✦✦✦✦✦
They were easily the top all-female jazz group before the 1980s, yet the International Sweethearts of Rhythm were barely documented. In the 1940s, they cut a few very obscure 78s that have rarely been reissued. Fortunately, this 1984 LP has 16 selections by the big band taken from a couple of Jubilee radio programs. Although one has to sit through some dated jive chatter from MC Ernie "Bubbles" Whitman, it is worth it to hear the Sweethearts stretching out. Among the key players in this excellent band are leader/vocalist/saxophonist Anna Mae Winburn, trumpeters Tiny Davis (who also sings) and Jean Starr, and the great tenor Vi Burnside. Despite the time period, the orchestra does not show the influence of bop at all and is very solidly in the swing camp. Given extensive liner notes by producer Rosetta Reitz, this album (which will hopefully reappear on CD someday) is well worth searching for and casts light on an important, if often overlooked, big band. —*Scott Yanow*

Irakere

f. 1973
Group / Afro-Cuban Jazz, Latin Jazz
Many of the top Cuban jazz musicians have played in Irakere during the past 30 years including altoist Paquito D'Rivera and trumpeter Arturo Sandoval (before both individually defected). Pianist Chucho Valdes has been the orchestra's longtime leader and its music ranges from Latin-jazz and bop to Cuban folk melodies with an emphasis on infectious rhythms and advanced improvisations. Several of Irakere's records have been made available domestically (including sets for Columbia and more recently Jazz House) but the exciting band was not able to visit the US until 1996. —*Scott Yanow*

● **The Best of Irakere** / June 28, 1978-Apr. 1979 / Columbia/Legacy ◆◆◆◆◆

For today's Latin jazz fans, this is a succinct and nearly complete roundup of Irakere's two North American albums, a brief peek through Cuba's door before politics slammed it shut again for another generation. *Irakere* is represented by four tracks, including the lengthy, uncut "Black Mass" and *Irakere II* by six tracks. The live *Irakere* was an exciting breakthrough, a real advance in the alliance between Afro-Cuban and American jazz that took into account the electronic developments in music since politics isolated Cuba from the US. *Irakere II,* a studio product, is not nearly as startling; the sound and arrangements are slicker, there are strings and voices on some cuts, supertrumpeter Arturo Sandoval was encouraged to show off his pretty tone as well as his fire, and the Cubans even tried to churn out a disco beat on some tracks, negating all of those wild, wonderful Afro-Cuban cross-rhythms. Still, there are passages where the more commercially motivated grooves take off, as in the central section of "Ciento Anos De Juventud," and "Xiomara" is a killer in the old Cuban tradition. Interestingly, when Irakere made their belated American comeback at the Playboy Jazz Festival at Hollywood Bowl in 1996, some of their innovative edge was gone, replaced by overt attempts to get the crowd up on its collective feet. All the more reason to cherish this CD—which has become the only option one has to sample this Cuban band at, and nearly at, its peak. —*Richard S. Ginell*

Chekere Son / May 25, 1979+Jun. 1, 1979 / Milestone ◆◆◆

El Coco / Aug. 3+Aug. 5, 1980 / Milestone ◆◆◆◆

This out-of-print album features the 1980 version of Chucho Valdes' Irakere, a remarkable Cuban band comprising four horns and a six-piece rhythm section. Paquito D'Rivera had defected, but trumpeter Arturo Sandoval was still a key part of the music, along with trumpeter Jorge Varona, tenorman Carlos Averhoff, altoist German Urdeliz and the stirring percussionists. The heated band performs four obscurities (including two by Valdes) and an adaptation of a Beethoven melody. —*Scott Yanow*

Legendary Irakere in London / Oct. 1, 1987 / Jazz House ◆◆◆◆

Homenaje a Beny More / 1989 / Messidor ◆◆◆◆

This record shows off their pop-dance side. It's worth having for the incendiary "Bacalao con Pan" alone. —*Ned Sublette*

● **Live at Ronnie Scott's** / Sep. 1991 / World Pacific ◆◆◆◆

In Irakere's earlier days, this premiere Cuban group often had to disguise the fact that they were playing imperialistic music from the West (i.e. jazz). Maybe now the masquerade is no longer necessary for the music on this definitive CD would

never be mistaken for anything else. Heavily influenced both by Dizzy Gillespie and the rhythms of Cuba and South America, the 11-piece group is in top form interpreting the compositions of its pianist/leader Chuco Valdes (who has a memorable workout on "Mr. Bruce"). Five of the six selections are primaily features for individual players. Throughout this memorable set, the ensemble work is clean and loose, the percussionists keep the proceedings fiery and the soloists are excellent. —*Scott Yanow*

Chuck Israels

b. Aug. 10, 1936, New York, NY
Bass / Cool, Post-Bop

Chuck Israels is still best-known for his work with the Bill Evans Trio (1961-66) but he has been an important educator since the 1970s. A tasteful and supportive bassist, Israels' first recording was the 1958 meeting between John Coltrane and Cecil Taylor. He played with George Russell's sextet (1959-61), was briefly with Eric Dolphy's band and then joined Bill Evans. During the Evans years, Israels also appeared on records led by J.J. Johnson, Herbie Hancock, Gary Burton and Stan Getz. He founded and headed the National Jazz Ensemble (1973-78), a top repertory band that recorded two albums for Chiaroscuro. Since then, Israels has been less active as a player but he did record with the Kronos String Quartet (1984) and Rosemary Clooney (1985) in addition to heading an obscure session for Anima (1991). —*Scott Yanow*

● **National Jazz Ensemble** / 1976 / Chiaroscuro ◆◆◆◆

David Izenon

b. May 17, 1932, Pittsburgh, PA, **d.** Oct. 8, 1979, New York, NY
Bass / Free Jazz, Avant-Garde

A brilliant bassist who was an expert with the bow, David Izenzon's playing with the mid-'60s Ornette Coleman Trio was outstanding. He did not start playing bass until he was already 24. Izenzon worked locally in Pittsburgh until moving to New York in 1961. He played with Paul Bley, Archie Shepp, Sonny Rollins and Bill Dixon, and first joined Ornette's group in October 1961. Izenzon freelanced after Coleman's 1962 Town Hall concert and then played regularly with the innovative altoist during 1965-68. He taught at Bronx Community College (1968-71), played with Perry Robinson and Paul Motian, gained a Ph.D. in psychotherapy (1973) and worked again with Coleman and Motian in 1977 before his early death. —*Scott Yanow*

Jackie & Roy

f. 1946
Vocal Group / Standards, Bop
Singer Jackie Cain (b. May 22, 1928, Milwaukee, WI) and singer/pianist Roy Kral (b. Oct. 10, 1921, Chicago, IL) first joined forces in 1946 and in 1996 they celebrated their 50th anniversary as a vocal duo. Jackie and Roy were with Charlie Ventura's band during 1948-49 (which gave them a great deal of recognition); Lou Stein's "East of Suez" was an unusual feature for their voices. Shortly after leaving Ventura in June 1949, they were married and have worked together on a regular basis ever since. Jackie and Roy had their own television show in Chicago in the early '50s, worked in Las Vegas during 1957-60, settled in New York in 1963 and appeared on some television commercials. They have recorded many spirited jazz performances for a variety of labels through the decades and still perform in the mid-'90s. Roy is the brother of the late singer Irene Kral. *—Scott Yanow*

Star Sounds / Oct. 1979 / Concord Jazz ✦✦✦

High Standards / Feb. 1982 / Concord Jazz ✦✦✦

A Stephen Sondheim Collection / Jul. 24, 1982 / DRG ✦✦✦✦
Jackie Cain & Roy Kral. An excellent live date with solid vocals throughout. Excellent interpretations of Sondheim's stage music by Jackie And Roy. *—Ron Wynn*

● **We've Got It** / 1984 / Discovery ✦✦✦✦✦
The Music of Cy Coleman. Expertly done tributes to Cy Coleman. *—Ron Wynn*

Full Circle / Jan. 14, 1992 / Contemporary ✦✦✦✦✦

Chubby Jackson (Greig Stewart Jackson)

b. Oct. 25, 1918, New York, NY
Bass / Bop, Swing
A fine bassist, Chubby Jackson is best-known for his association with Woody Herman's first two Herds of the mid- to late 1940s where he functioned not only in the rhythm section but as a sort-of cheerleader whose vocal interjections really pushed the band. Although he started on the clarinet when he was 16, Jackson soon switched to bass and was a professional by the time he was 19, playing with many big bands including those led by Raymond Scott, Jan Savitt and Henry Busse. After touring with Charlie Barnet during 1941-43 (sometimes with Oscar Pettiford as the second bassist), Jackson joined Woody Herman's transitional orchestra and was partly responsible for the group, adding many young modernists to the personnel, resulting in the First Herd. Jackson was with Herman during 1943-46 (appearing on many recordings). After Herman broke up the band, Jackson played with Charlie Ventura's septet (1947) and had his own small group that toured Scandinavia. A second tour with Woody (1948) was followed by a period leading his own big band (1948-49), more work with Ventura (1951) and a period co-leading a combo with Bill Harris. Chubby Jackson spent the 1950s as a studio musician, freelancer and a host of his own children's television show. After periods living in Chicago, Las Vegas and Los Angeles, he eventually settled in Florida and has been in semi-retirement although Jackson has occasionally emerged including a stint with Lionel Hampton (1978-79) and with Herman reunion groups. Chubby's son Duffy Jackson (b. Jul. 3, 1953) is a fine drummer who played with Count Basie in the 1970s and has led his own sessions. In addition to his work as a sideman, Chubby Jackson recorded as a leader for Keynote, Prestige, Columbia (1949), Argo, Everest and Crown in addition to some smaller labels. *—Scott Yanow*

Chubby Jackson Sextet and Big Band / Mar. 15, 1950+May 22, 1947 / Prestige ✦✦✦✦✦
Bassist Chubby Jackson has only led record dates on an irregular basis throughout his long career. This LP has two of Jackson's finest studio sessions, a sextet set from 1947 that features trumpeter Conte Candoli and the obscure but fine tenor Emmett Carls, and an all-star 12-piece big band date. The latter set really has an impressive personnel listing, including trumpeter Howard McGhee, trombonists J.J. Johnson and Kai Winding, both Zoot Sims and Georgie Auld on tenors and baritonist Gerry Mulligan in an early outing. On both sessions, the music is extro-

verted bop with plenty of exciting solos by the key players, who are pushed by Jackson's verbal encouragement. *—Scott Yanow*

Cliff Jackson

b. Jul. 19, 1902, Culpepper, WI, **d.** May 24, 1970, New York, NY
Piano / Stride
One of the most powerful stride pianists, Cliff Jackson never became all that famous in the jazz world despite his talent. In 1923 he moved to New York where he played with Lionel Howard's Musical Aces in 1924 and freelanced. Jackson recorded in 1927 with Bob Fuller and Elmer Snowden and then formed a big band (the Krazy Kats) that made some exuberant recordings in 1930 including "Horse Feathers," and "The Terror." After that band broke up, Jackson mostly worked as a soloist in New York clubs. He recorded with Sidney Bechet during 1940-41, cut some solos and Dixieland sides for Black & White (1944-45), made three solos for Disc (1945), led a band for a Swingville session (1961) and recorded solo for Black Lion, Ri-Disc, Jazzology and Master Jazz (1969). Cliff Jackson is also documented in 1966 playing at a festival (on Jazzology) with his wife, Maxine Sullivan. *—Scott Yanow*

● **Cliff Jackson & His Crazy Kats** / Jan. 30, 1930+Feb. 27, 1930 / Retrieval ✦✦✦✦
Pianist Cliff Jackson's Krazy Cats (called "Crazy Cats" on this LP) were a particularly heated Harlem jazz band. They recorded two explosive titles ("Horse Feathers" and "Torrid Rhythm") on Jan. 30, 1930, and returned to the studios a month later to perform ten other numbers, including "The Terror" (heard here in two versions). The ten-piece group featured trumpeter Henry Goodwin, Rudy Powell on clarinet and alto, the leader/pianist, and the forceful tenor of Horace Langhorn, and is well worth discovering by vintage jazz fans. *—Scott Yanow*

Carolina Shout / Dec. 30, 1961+Jan. 16, 1962 / Black Lion ✦✦✦
Cliff Jackson was one of the top stride pianists to emerge in the 1920s so this solo piano disc promises a great deal. But, although Jackson plays these standards and stride classics well enough, his metronomic left hand gets a bit tiring after awhile. He keeps time so perfectly that Jackson often fails to let much life and feeling into his improvisations. However, taken in small doses, these 15 performances (which include an unreleased version of "Squeeze Me" and three "new" alternate takes) do showcase his impressive talents during a period when he did not record very often. *—Scott Yanow*

Parlor Social Piano / Nov. 12, 1968 / Fat Cat Jazz ✦✦✦✦
Pianist Cliff Jackson recorded relatively little during his career—not at all as a leader in the 1950s and just seven dates in the 1960s before his death in 1970. His last full-length LP, this solo set, which has two spirited vocals by producer Johnson "Fat Cat" McRee, features the superior stride pianist still in prime form. The highlights of the obscure album include "Old Fashioned Love," "After You've Gone," "Keep Off the Grass," "Everybody Loves My Baby" and "Carolina Shout." *—Scott Yanow*

D.D. Jackson

b. Jan. 25, 1967, Ottawa, Canada
Piano / Post-Bop
Influenced by his mentor Don Pullen, D.D. Jackson helped the ailing Pullen complete his final work, "Earth Eagle First Circle," in 1995. Jackson started on the piano when he was six and, after growing up in Canada, he earned degrees from the Manhattan School of Music (in jazz) and Indiana University (in classical music); he also had valuable lessons with Pullen and Jaki Byard. D.D. Jackson has played with David Murray, Billy Bang, Nat Adderley, Jane Bunnett, Dewey Redman, and led his own trio, recording for Justin Time. *—Scott Yanow*

● **Peace-Song** / Nov. 25, 1994-Nov. 26, 1994 / Justin Time ✦✦✦✦✦
On his debut as a leader, the 27-year-old pianist D.D. Jackson often plays overcrowded chords in catchy rhythmic phrases that are very reminiscent of the late great pianist Don Pullen, although on some of the slower pieces he shows more originality. Jackson's compositions are sometimes soulful but his inside/outside

playing (on quartets, trios and a solo "Funerale") is quite unpredictable. Tenor saxophonist David Murray throws everything he can into his solo on the opener "Waltz for a New Life," evolving from screams and honks to upper-register screeches; all of his other improvisations seem anticlimatic and almost mellow in comparison. Bassist John Geggie and drummer Jean Martin (who as with the pianist are from Ottawa, Canada) are fine in support but one's attention is constantly drawn to the often-outlandish solos of Murray and Jackson. —*Scott Yanow*

Rhythm Dance / Jan. 15, 1996-Jan. 16, 1996 / Justin Time ✦✦✦✦✦
The intriguing pianist D.D. Jackson teams up with bassist John Geggie (who has an otherworldly bowed bass feature on "Ayse") and drummer Jean Martin for a continually interesting trio set. Jackson's style closely emulates that of his mentor, the late Don Pullen, sometimes featuring clusters of dissonant notes played in rhythmic fashion, which makes his music seem fairly accessible despite its unpredictable nature. Some of Jackson's own musical personality sneaks through at times (particularly on the ballads) and he tends to be more melodic than Pullen. D.D. Jackson will surely become a more individual player as time passes and this excellent outing (which features 11 of his diverse originals interpreted in a wide range of moods) is well worth exploring. —*Scott Yanow*

● **Paired Down, Vol. 1** / Nov. 30, 1996-Dec. 2, 1996 / Justin Time ✦✦✦✦✦

Paired Down, Vol. 2 / Nov. 30, 1996-Dec. 2, 1996 / Justin Time ✦✦✦✦✦

Franz Jackson

b. Nov. 1, 1912, Rock Island, IL
Tenor Saxophone, Clarinet / Dixieland, Swing
One of the last survivors of the pre-swing era, Franz Jackson (a fine tenorman and clarinetist) is still active as of this writing in 1996, having recorded recently for Parkwood with Marcus Belgrave. He worked in the Chicago area starting in 1926 including with Albert Ammons, Carroll Dickerson (1932 and 1934-36), Jimmie Noone (1934), Roy Eldridge (1937) and Fletcher Henderson's Orchestra (1937-38). Jackson travelled to New York with Eldridge (1938-39), played in California with Earl Hines' Orchestra (1940-41) and then worked with Fats Waller (1941) and the Cootie Williams big band (1942). Stints with Frankie Newton (1942-43) and Wilbur DeParis (1944-45) followed and he played in the Pacific on several USO tours. In the mid-'50s after returning to Chicago, Franz Jackson formed his Original Jazz All Stars, a group that lasted for around 20 years. He recorded for Riverside in 1961, Delmark and for his own label Pinnacle; Jackson also recorded with Art Hodes in 1974. He has continued playing regularly in the Chicago area up to the present time. —*Scott Yanow*

Chicago: The Living Legends, Featuring Bob Shoffner / Sep. 5, 1961 / Original Jazz Classics ✦✦✦✦✦
In 1961, Chris Albertson did the jazz world a major service by documenting some of the 1920s and '30s veterans who were still active but had not been heard from on a major label in quite some time. Franz Jackson, featured on this CD reissue exclusively on clarinet, was playing regularly in Chicago at the time. Teamed with trumpeter Bob Shoffner (who had played with King Oliver in the mid-1920s), trombonist John Thomas, pianist Rozelle Claxton, banjoist Lawrence Dixon, Bill Oldham on tuba and drummer Bill Curry, Jackson plays mostly Dixieland standards and tunes from the 1920s, with the exception of his "Blue Thursday." Although this set only shows off one side of Franz Jackson, whose main instrument is really the tenor, it is quite enjoyable and gives listeners a rare late-period look at the still-viable Bob Shoffner. —*Scott Yanow*

Snag It / Aug. 1990 / Delmark ✦✦✦✦
Franz Jackson (77 at the time) is well featured with trombonist Jim Beebe's Chicago Jazz Band on this Delmark CD. With trumpeter Bob Neighbor completing the front line and a fine four-piece rhythm section keeping the music swinging, Jackson (who is heard on tenor, clarinet, soprano and a few vocals) proves to still be in prime form. The repertoire is mostly from the 1920s and '30s, ranging from Dixieland and classic jazz to swing. Highlights include "How'm I Doin'," "High Society," "That Da Da Strain" and "Panama." —*Scott Yanow*

● **Live at Windsor Jazz Festival III** / Jul. 9, 1994 / Parkwood ✦✦✦✦✦
Eighty-one at the time of this 1994 concert, Franz Jackson (a gruff-toned tenor influenced by the style of Coleman Hawkins) was still playing in his prime. The octogenarian is matched with trumpeter Marcus Belgrave and a fine Detroit-based rhythm section that includes veteran drummer Frank Isola for nine standards and a closing blues. Belgrave, a very versatile player capable of playing much more advanced styles of jazz, fits in perfectly in the swing-oriented format, trading off with the older tenor and taking spirited solos. The music is highlighted by "Chicago," "Perdido," a double-time version of "Body and Soul" and "After You've Gone," showing that even in the mid-'90s small-group swing lives. —*Scott Yanow*

Fred Jackson

Tenor Saxophone / Soul Jazz, Fusion
Fred Jackson only released one album and played on a handful of sessions for Blue Note before disappearing from the jazz scene in the mid-'60s. He deserved a better fate. Although he wasn't a wildly original tenor saxophonist, he was a solid journeyman who found a successful common ground between hard bop and earthy soul-jazz on his jazz sessions. His R&B-inflected style worked well on uptempo ravers and slow blues alike, and he had a nice, robust tone. Despite his attributes, he quietly faded away from jazz in the mid-'60s, after his lone album *Hootin' 'n' Tootin'* failed to sell. He returned to R&B and soul, which is where his career began.

Jackson received his big break when he played in Little Richard's band between 1951 and 1953. Toward the end of the '50s, he was invited to join the supporting band for R&B vocalist Lloyd Price. He frequently toured with Price, who was at the peak of his popularity in the late '50s and early '60s, as such singles as "Stagger Lee," "Personality" and "I'm Gonna Get Married" topped the charts. Jackson made his recording debut in 1961, playing on a B.B. King session. Shortly afterward, he cut his first jazz record, appearing in organist Baby Face Willette's band on the album *Face to Face*. Impressed by his performance on the record, Blue Note offered the saxophonist a chance to lead his own session and he accepted, bringing his Price bandmates—guitarist Willie Jones, organist Earl Vandyke and drummer Wilbert Hogan—into the studio on February 2, 1965 to record the album that became *Hootin' 'n' Tootin'.* Two months later, he went back to Van Gelder Studios with his supporting trio and bassist Sam Jones to record his second album. That session was never released, either because *Hootin' 'n' Tootin'* sold poorly or because, as Alfred Lion's notes claimed, that the record was too short for release. The sessions finally appeared in 1998, when they were added as bonus tracks to the CD reissue of *Hootin' 'n' Tootin'.*

Although he wasn't offered the chance to lead another session, Jackson didn't immediately disappear from jazz recording. In June of 1962, he cut a single with John Patton on piano that remains unreleased. The following year, he played on Patton's *Along Came John*, which led to his appearance on Patton's 1964 album, *The Way I Feel*. Throughout the late '60s, he was largely inactive in the recording field. He reappeared in 1971, playing on Bobby Hutcherson's *Head On*. Throughout the '70s, he received constant work as a session man, playing on albums by artists as diverse as Hutcherson, Horace Silver, Jimmy Smith, Carole King, Frank Zappa, Maria Muldaur, Billy Cosby, Terry Callier, Joe Sample, the Whispers, Solomon Burke and Earth, Wind & Fire. He was largely inactive in the '80s and '90s, playing only a handful of sessions by musicians like Dianne Schuur. —*Stephen Thomas Erlewine*

Hootin' 'n' Tootin' / Feb. 5, 1962 / Blue Note ✦✦✦✦✦
Unjustly ignored at the time of its release, Fred Jackson's lone album, *Hootin' 'n' Tootin',* is a thoroughly enjoyable set of funky soul-jazz with hard bop overtones. It is true that Jackson doesn't try anything new on the set, but he proves to be a capable leader, coaxing hot, infectious performances out of guitarist Willie Jones, organist Earl Vandyke and drummer Wilbert Hogan, all of whom were collegues of Jackson in the Lloyd Price band. All of the songs on the album are Jackson originals, and while there are no substantial, memorable melodies, they provide an excellent foundation for the group's smoking interplay. Both the uptempo R&B numbers and the slower blues give the musicians plenty of opportunity to flaunt their chops while working the groove, and the result is a modest but highly entertaining set of earthy, bluesy soul-jazz that should have been heard by a wider audience. Blue Note's 1998 CD reissue adds all of the material from the second and final session Jackson led. All seven tracks from that session are in the same soul-jazz vein and feature the same group, augmented by bassist Sam Jones. Their presence on the reissued *Hootin' 'n' Tootin'* makes an already fine album even better. —*Stephen Thomas Erlewine*

Javon Jackson

b. Jun. 16, 1965, Carthage, MI
Tenor Saxophone / Hard Bop
A fine tenor saxophonist influenced by Joe Henderson, Javon Jackson helps to keep the legacy of Art Blakey and hard bop alive. He grew up in Cleveland and Denver and studied at Berklee (1984-86). Jackson was with the last version of the Jazz Messengers (1987-90) and, since Blakey's death, he has worked with the Harper Brothers, Benny Green, Freddie Hubbard and Elvin Jones. Javon Jackson has recorded as a leader for Criss Cross and Blue Note. —*Scott Yanow*

● **Me and Mr. Jones** / Dec. 16, 1991 / Criss Cross ✦✦✦✦✦

Burnin' / Dec. 20, 1991 / Criss Cross ✦✦✦✦

When the Time is Right / Sep. 7, 1993-Oct. 1, 1993 / Blue Note ✦✦✦✦
This early effort by tenor saxophonist Javon Jackson was produced by Betty Carter. On the well-rounded set, Jackson (who shows the influence of Joe Henderson in his tone and style) performs five jazz standards, including "Love Walked In" and "Sweet and Lovely," and three inventive hard bop originals. He holds his own with altoist Kenny Garrett on two selections, welcomes Dianne Reeves to "I Waited for You" (where she takes a warm ballad vocal), and matches well with pianist Jacky Terrasson and two rhythm sections. A fine effort that stands out from the typical Young Lions output of the era. *— Scott Yanow*

For One Who Knows / Jan. 18, 1995-Jan. 19, 1995 / Blue Note ✦✦✦
This CD only has one fault but it is a major one. It seems that no matter what he plays (whether it be obscure songs by Wayne Shorter, Herbie Hancock, Sonny Rollins and Antonio Carlos Jobim or one of his two originals), Javon Jackson sounds too close to comfort to Joe Henderson; in fact, there are times when the tenor saxophonist sounds identical. That is a real pity for Jackson consistently shows the ability to take chances successfully and his supporting cast (particularly pianist Jacky Terrasson and acoustic guitarist Fareed Haque) is quite strong. The music, essentially advanced hard bop with hints of the avant-garde, is stimulating and generally unpredictable. Now if only Javon Jackson would put away his Joe Henderson records for a few years. *— Scott Yanow*

A Look Within / Feb. 3, 1996-Feb. 4, 1996 / Blue Note ✦✦✦✦
Tenor saxophonist Javon Jackson deserves a lot of credit for stretching himself on this release. Although he can sound very close to Joe Henderson at times, on the set he interprets a wide-ranging repertoire that allows him to avoid falling into the revivalist hard bop category. In addition to a pair of originals (the medium-up blues "Hamlet's Favorite Son" and "Assessment," which is dedicated to Elvin Jones), Jackson performs songs by the likes of Egberto Gismonti, Frank Zappa, Muddy Waters ("Country Girl," which has a vocal by Cassandra Wilson), Freddie Hubbard, Charles Mingus and Hank Mobley (a delightful rendition of "Recado Bossa Nova"). Most of the selections (even the two that include organist Lonnie Smith) utilize a sparse background with the versatile guitarist Fareed Haque, bassist Peter Washington and drummer Billy Drummond leaving plenty of space. This surprisingly modern and subtle program is one of Javon Jackson's finest to date. *— Scott Yanow*

Good People / Jun. 2, 1997 / Blue Note ✦✦✦✦

Milt Jackson

b. Jan. 1, 1923, Detroit, MI
Vibes / Bop, Hard Bop

Before Milt Jackson there were only two major vibraphonists: Lionel Hampton and Red Norvo. Jackson soon surpassed both of them in significance and, despite the rise of other players (including Bobby Hutcherson and Gary Burton), still wins the popularity polls. Jackson (or Bags as he has long been called) has been at the top of his field for 50 years, playing bop, blues and ballads with equal skill and sensitivity.

Milt Jackson started on guitar when he was seven and piano at 11; a few years later he switched to vibes. He actually made his professional debut singing in a touring gospel quartet. After Dizzy Gillespie discovered him playing in Detroit, he offered him a job with his sextet and (shortly after) his innovative big band (1946). Jackson recorded with Dizzy and was soon in great demand. During 1948-49, he worked with Charlie Parker, Thelonious Monk, Howard McGhee and the Woody Herman Orchestra. After playing with Gillespie's sextet (1950-52), which at one point included John Coltrane, Jackson recorded with a quartet comprising John Lewis, Percy Heath and Kenny Clarke (1952), which soon became a regular group called the Modern Jazz Quartet. Although he recorded regularly as a leader (including dates in the 1950s with Miles Davis and/or Thelonious Monk, Coleman Hawkins, John Coltrane and Ray Charles), Milt Jackson stayed with the MJQ through 1974, becoming an indispensable part of their sound. By the mid-'50s Lewis became the musical director and some felt that Bags was restricted by the format but it actually served him well, giving him some challenging settings. And he always had an opportunity to jam on some blues including his "Bags' Groove." However in 1974 Jackson felt frustrated by the MJQ (particularly financially) and broke up the group. He recorded frequently for Pablo in many all-star settings in the 1970s, and after a seven-year vacation the MJQ came back in 1981. In addition to the MJQ recordings, Milt Jackson cut records as a leader throughout his career for many labels including Savoy, Blue Note (1952), Prestige, Atlantic, United Artists, Impulse, Riverside, Limelight, Verve, CTI, Pablo, Music Masters and Qwest. *— Scott Yanow*

In the Beginning / Apr. 1948 / Original Jazz Classics ✦✦✦
This is a very interesting CD, particularly for bop collectors, since it contains very rare early performances by altoist Sonny Stitt and vibraphonist Milt Jackson; some of the titles were originally under trumpeter Russell Jacquet's name. There

are eight songs by a quintet with Stitt, Jacquet and pianist Sir Charles Thompson, what could be considered the first Modern Jazz Quartet records (actually a quintet with Milt Jackson, pianist John Lewis, drummer Kenny Clarke, bassist Al Jackson and Chano Pozo on congas) and five songs from a septet with Jacquet, Stitt, trombonist J.J. Johnson and baritonist Leo Parker. Recorded in Detroit for the tiny Galaxy label, these performances are not essential but they do give listeners an early glimpse at the future stars. *— Scott Yanow*

Bluesology / Jan. 25, 1949-Feb. 23, 1949 / Savoy ✦✦✦✦
This valuable LP collects together a session led by vibraphonist Milt Jackson for Savoy in 1949 (featuring a septet that includes the pioneering jazz French horn of Julius Watkins and tenor saxophonist Billy Mitchell), a sextet set led by drummer Kenny Clarke that has similar personnel (including Watkins, Mitchell and the addition of trumpeter Kenny Dorham) and two songs from a date led by singer Wini Brown. Throughout Jackson shows why he was considered the first important vibraphonist to emerge after Lionel Hampton and Red Norvo. This LP from 1980 is much more coherent (consisting of complete sessions and two alternate takes) than the more recent Savoy CD reissues. *— Scott Yanow*

The First Q / Aug. 24, 1951-Apr. 1952 / Savoy ✦✦✦✦
The early evolution of The Modern Jazz Quartet is traced on this perfectly done LP (far superior to the more recent Savoy CD reissue series). Three four-song sessions that were originally released under vibraphonist Milt Jackson's name are included and these only predate the MJQ by less than a year. Pianist John Lewis is on all of the titles, bassist Ray Brown and drummer Al Jones appear on four apiece and original members bassist Percy Heath and drummer Kenny Clarke are on the other eight. Despite the similarity in personnel, these boppish jams are very much Jackson's dates rather than a co-op, although some of the songs (particularly "Bluesology" and "Softly as in a Morning Sunrise") would soon enter The MJQ's repertoire. *— Scott Yanow*

A Date in New York / Mar. 7, 1954 / Inner City ✦✦✦✦
This European bop session was actually led by pianist Henri Renaud. Milt Jackson has a generous amount of vibraphone solos and is also heard playing piano on three selections; he even takes a vocal on "The More I See You." Tenor saxophonist Al Cohn pops up on four of the performances but the most impressive soloist throughout this out-of-print LP is the great trombonist J.J. Johnson who often steals the show. *— Scott Yanow*

Opus De Jazz / Oct. 28, 1955 / Savoy ✦✦✦
This Savoy CD is a duplicate of the original LP although it lacks the fine liner notes included on the Arista/Savoy 1978 LP. The four selections (which unfortunately total under 34 minutes) are excellent, particularly a fun version of Horace Silver's blues "Opus De Funk" in which vibraphonist Milt Jackson, flutist Frank Wess and pianist Hank Jones have a long tradeoff. The quintet (which also includes bassist Eddie Jones and drummer Kenny Clarke) swings nicely throughout the three blues and lone ballad ("You Leave Me Breathless"). This is not essential, but it is enjoyable music. *— Scott Yanow*

Second Nature / Jan. 5, 1956+Jan. 23, 1956 / Savoy ✦✦✦✦✦
This generous two-LP set combines together all of the music originally released by Savoy on four skimpy albums, over 100 minutes of music recorded in two days. More importantly, the performances are quite exciting with vibraphonist Milt Jackson and tenor saxophonist Lucky Thompson (assisted by bassist Wendell Marshall, drummer Kenny Clarke and either Hank Jones or Wade Legge on piano) making for a perfect team. The standards and basic originals are highlighted by a three-song Duke Ellington ballad medley along with "Soul in 3/4," "Can't Help Lovin' That Man" and "The Lady Is a Tramp." This excellent bop-based music deserves to be reissued in full on CD. *— Scott Yanow*

The Jazz Skyline / Jan. 23, 1956 / Savoy ✦✦✦✦
This session has interest as an example of Milt Jackson's mid-'50s work in a non-Modern Jazz Quartet context. And despite the many critical assertions that the vibist was restrained by pianist John Lewis' direction, his playing here revealed no marked changed. The overall feel of the group (Lucky Thompson, tenor sax; Hank Jones, piano; Wendell Marshall; bass, Kenny Clarke, drums; Jackson, vibes), however, was somewhat more dynamic than that of the MJQ, as Clarke and Jones generally achieved a greater sense of forward momentum than Connie Kay or Lewis. *—Bob Rusch, Cadence*

● **Plenty, Plenty Soul** / Jan. 5, 1957 / Atlantic ✦✦✦✦✦
This superior reissue combines together two sessions led by vibraphonist Milt Jackson. Actually, although Bags is in fine form (and contributed four of the seven selections), he is often overshadowed by rather inspired solos from his sidemen. The first side of this LP, which features a nine-piece group, is highlighted by the contributions of the exuberant altoist Cannonball Adderley while the flip side has a sextet that is not hurt by the solos of tenor saxophonist Lucky Thompson. With

pianist Horace Silver helping out on both dates, these all-star dates still sound fresh and enthusiastic decades later. —*Scott Yanow*

Soul Brothers / Sep. 12, 1957 / Atlantic ✦✦✦✦✦
It is surprising that this set has not yet been issued on CD for it is a real historical curiosity. Not only does vibraphonist Milt Jackson double here on piano but he plays guitar (for the only time on record) during "Bags' Guitar Blues." In addition Ray Charles is heard in a purely instrumental role on piano and, during two songs, on alto sax. Charles' fine playing makes one wonder why he so rarely picked up the horn in later years. Billy Mitchell contributes some fine tenor solos on this boppish/blues material and guitarist Skeeter Best, bassist Oscar Pettiford and drummer Connie Kay offer stellar support. —*Scott Yanow*

Bean Bags / Sep. 12, 1958 / Atlantic ✦✦✦✦
Many of vibraphonist Milt Jackson's Atlantic recordings are long overdue to appear on CD, and that certainly includes this album, a meeting with the great tenor Coleman Hawkins. Assisted by a top-notch quartet (pianist Tommy Flanagan, guitarist Kenny Burrell, bassist Eddie Jones and drummer Connie Kay), Bean and Bags romp through "Stuffy," "Get Happy," a pair of Jackson originals and two fine ballads, with "Don't Take Your Love from Me" being particularly memorable. —*Scott Yanow*

Bags' Opus / Dec. 28, 1958-Dec. 29, 1958 / Blue Note ✦✦✦✦✦
Vibraphonist Milt Jackson welcomes the two future co-leaders of The Jazztet (trumpeter Art Farmer and tenor saxophonist Benny Golson) along with a fine rhythm section (pianist Tommy Flanagan, bassist Paul Chambers and drummer Connie Kay) on this CD reissue. The repertoire (which includes early versions of Golson's "Whisper Not" and "I Remember Clifford" in addition to two standards, a Milt Jackson blues and John Lewis' "Afternoon in Paris") is very much in The Jazztet hard bop vein and Jackson fits in very well with the two lyrical horn soloists. A successful outing by some of the greats. —*Scott Yanow*

★ **Bags and Trane** / Jan. 15, 1959 / Atlantic ✦✦✦✦✦
Vibraphonist Milt Jackson and tenor saxophonist John Coltrane make for a surprisingly complementary team on this 1959 studio session, their only joint recording. With fine backup by pianist Hank Jones, bassist Paul Chambers and drummer Connie Kay, Bags and Trane stretch out on two of Jackson's originals (including "The Late Late Blues") and three standards: a romping "Three Little Words," "The Night We Called It a Day" and the rapid "Be-Bop." This enjoyable music has been included as part of Rhino's *Heavyweight Champion: The Complete Atlantic Recordings* box. —*Scott Yanow*

Statements / Dec. 14, 1961-Aug. 6, 1964 / Impulse! ✦✦✦
Vibraphonist Milt Jackson has been so consistent throughout his lengthy career that his excellence can be taken for granted. This CD reissue of an Impulse LP features Bags with a quartet (including pianist Hank Jones) from 1961 and leading a quintet (with tenor saxophonist Jimmy Heath and pianist Tommy Flanagan) in 1964; the latter was originally half of the LP *Jazz 'n' Samba*. In addition there is a feature for Flanagan in a trio without the vibraphonist that was originally on an Impulse sampler. The blues, ballads, standards and originals are typical of Jackson's recordings as is the high-quality of the swinging music. Nothing too unusual occurs but the results are pleasing. —*Scott Yanow*

Bags Meets Wes / Dec. 18, 1961+Dec. 19, 1961 / Original Jazz Classics ✦✦✦✦✦
His Riverside debut album was a stunner. Wonderful Wes Montgomery Guitar. —*Ron Wynn*

Big Bags / Jun. 19, 1962-Jul. 1962 / Original Jazz Classics ✦✦✦✦
Vibraphonist Milt Jackson is backed by a big band for this change-of-pace release, reissued on CD along with two alternate takes. The Ernie Wilkins and Tadd Dameron arrangements fit the high-quality standards well and Jackson (who contributed two originals) is in top form. There are short solos for cornetist Nat Adderley, trombonist Jimmy Cleveland and the tenors of James Moody and Jimmy Heath but Milt Jackson is the main voice throughout this melodic and always-swinging set. —*Scott Yanow*

Invitation / Aug. 30, 1962-Nov. 7, 1962 / Original Jazz Classics ✦✦✦
Six of the eight selections on this CD (plus two previously unreleased alternate takes) showcase vibraphonist Milt Jackson in an all-star sextet with trumpeter Kenny Dorham, tenor saxophonist Jimmy Heath, pianist Tommy Flanagan, bassist Ron Carter and drummer Connie Kay; the two remaining selections substitute Virgil Jones for Heath, giving the band two trumpets. The music swings (as one would expect from a Milt Jackson date) and the repertoire (three standards, Thelonious Monk's classic ballad "Ruby, My Dear," the obscure "Ruby" and three group originals) gives the set enough variety to hold one's interest throughout. It's not essential but Milt Jackson fans will enjoy this music. —*Scott Yanow*

For Someone I Love / Mar. 18, 1963-Aug. 5, 1983 / Original Jazz Classics ✦✦✦✦✦
The main reasons for this CD reissue's success are Melba Liston's inventive and unpredictable arrangements for the brass orchestra. Vibraphonist Milt Jackson has

nearly all the solos (although trumpeter Clark Terry, trombonist Quentin Jackson, Julius Watkins on French horn and Major Holley on tuba do make their presence known) and seems understandably inspired by the backup orchestra, which consists of four or five trumpets, three trombones, three or four French horns, Holley's tuba and a rhythm section. The well-conceived set (which includes such songs as "Days of Wine and Roses," "Save Your Love for Me," some Duke Ellington ballads and "Bossa Bags") is consistently excellent, making this a highly recommended set. —*Scott Yanow*

Live at the Village Gate / Dec. 9, 1963 / Original Jazz Classics ✦✦✦✦
Vibraphonist Milt Jackson's own sessions outside of The Modern Jazz Quartet tend to be hard-swinging jams through attractive chord changes, a mixture of boppish romps and thoughtful ballad statements. Jackson has frequently worked with tenors and Jimmy Heath, who is well-featured throughout this set (a CD reissue that brings back an earlier LP plus two "new" selections) became an occasional associate. With fine work by pianist Hank Jones, bassist Bob Cranshaw and drummer Al "Tootie" Heath, Milt Jackson is in typically swinging form on some blues, standards, ballads and Jimmy Heath's "Gemini." —*Scott Yanow*

Jazz Round Midnight / Jan. 14, 1964-Jun. 17, 1968 / Verve ✦✦✦
Verve's "'Round Midnight" CD reissue series comprises samplers featuring various artists playing ballads at moderate tempos. Vibraphonist Milt Jackson is heard on this 16-song collection in a variety of settings originally put out on five LPs: *Much In Common, Ray Brown-Milt Jackson, and the Hip String Quartet, In a New Setting* and *Born Free.* The former two sets have been reissued on CD, but the latter three have not reappeared yet. Jackson is featured with a big band that he co-led with bassist Ray Brown and in combos that include such fine players as pianists Hank Jones, Cedar Walton and McCoy Tyner, guitarist Kenny Burrell and tenorman Jimmy Heath. The set overall is not as essential as the complete sessions, but gives a nice overview of the vibraphonist's lyrical talents. —*Scott Yanow*

Jazz 'n' Samba / Aug. 6, 1964-Aug. 7, 1964 / Impulse! ✦✦✦
This is an odd LP. The first session is a conventional one with vibraphonist Milt Jackson, tenor saxophonist Jimmy Heath, pianist Tommy Flanagan, bassist Richard Davis and drummer Connie Kay performing Heath's recent "Gingerbread Boy," Duke Ellington's "I Got It Bad" and a pair of Jackson originals. The flip side substitutes two guitars for Flanagan's piano and uses bossa nova rhythms in hopes of getting a hit. Milt does play well on "I Love You" and Lillian Clark's vocal on "Jazz 'n' Samba" is fine but "The Oo-Oo Bossa Noova" is strictly for those listeners who are nostalgic for *Car 54, Where Are You.* —*Scott Yanow*

In a New Setting / Dec. 1964 / Limelight ✦✦✦
There is nothing all that unusual about the setting presented on this LP by vibraphonist Milt Jackson: a quintet with tenor saxophonist Jimmy Heath (although the inclusion of McCoy Tyner on piano is a surprise). What is new is that five of the 11 selections are under three-minutes long and four others are under four. Jackson frankly states in the liner notes that he has hopes of these performances being singles and getting radio airplay. Fortunately (despite the brevity) the music is very much in the vibist's swinging style and his six originals do not bend excessively in the direction of commercial compromise. But then again, none of these recordings became hits. —*Scott Yanow*

Sunflower / Dec. 12, 1972-Dec. 13, 1972 / CTI ✦✦✦✦✦
Vibraphonist Milt Jackson recorded three albums for CTI in the early '70s; this LP is the best of the trio. The Don Sebesky arrangements for the strings showcase Jackson well, trumpeter Freddie Hubbard and pianist Herbie Hancock make impressions, and the four songs (highlighted by Hubbard's "Sunflower") receive fine treatment. —*Scott Yanow*

Goodbye / Dec. 1972-Dec. 1973 / CTI ✦✦✦
Unlike most CTI albums, this is a small-group date without strings or woodwinds. All but one of the five songs on the LP features vibraphonist Milt Jackson playing standards ("Detour Ahead," "Goodbye," "Old Devil Moon" and "Opus De Funk") as part of a quintet consisting of flutist Hubert Laws, pianist Cedar Walton, bassist Ron Carter and drummer Steve Gadd. The other selection, Jackson's "SKJ," adds trumpeter Freddie Hubbard and substitutes Herbie Hancock and Billy Cobham for Walton and Gadd. The music is all very straightahead; hopefully it will be reissued on CD eventually along with the vibist's *Sunflower* and *Olinga* records. —*Scott Yanow*

Olinga / Jan. 1974 / CTI ✦✦✦
Originally out on the CTI label, this set features vibraphonist Milt Jackson with some of his favorite musicians (pianist Cedar Walton, bassist Ron Carter, drumer Mickey Roker and Jimmy Heath on tenor and soprano) along with an occasional string section. The performances are fairly straightahead for CTI with Bags and company performing the ballad "Lost April," Dizzy Gillespie's "Olinga," a Walton original and three recent songs by Jackson. Although Cedar Walton does not

sound as formidable on electric piano as on acoustic and the other solos overall are a bit safe, this is a nice album. —*Scott Yanow*

Montreux '75 / Jul. 17, 1975 / Pablo ✦✦✦✦

Vibraphonist Milt Jackson teams up with pianist Oscar Peterson, bassist Niels Pedersen and drummer Mickey Roker for a particularly appealing set, one of the few Pablo sessions by the vibist which has not yet been reissued on CD. Pity, for there are many exciting performances (particularly Blue Mitchell's "Funji Mama," "Speed Ball" and "Mack the Knife") and some emotional ballad statements ("Everything Must Change" and "Like Someone like Love"). Bags and O.P. always bring out the best in each other and this well-conceived set is no exception. —*Scott Yanow*

☆ The Big 3 / Aug. 25, 1975 / Pablo ✦✦✦✦✦

This CD (a straight reissue of the original LP) features a rather notable pianoless combo: vibraphonist Milt Jackson, guitarist Joe Pass and bassist Ray Brown. During the Pablo years these three masterful players recorded together in many settings but only this once as a trio. The colorful repertoire (which ranges from "The Pink Panther" and "Blue Bossa" to "Nuages" and "Come Sunday") acts as a device for the musicians to construct some brilliant bop-based solos. —*Scott Yanow*

Feelings / Apr. 12, 1976-Apr. 14, 1976 / Pablo ✦✦

Milt & Strings. Hideous title cut, fine playing, but Hubert Laws is an acquired taste. —*Ron Wynn*

Soul Fusion / Jun. 1, 1977-Jun. 2, 1977 / Original Jazz Classics ✦✦✦✦✦

Pianist Monty Alexander had first appeared on a Milt Jackson record in 1969. Eight years later the great vibraphonist used Alexander's trio (which included bassist John Clayton and drummer Jeff Hamilton, future big band co-leaders) for this spirited Pablo session which has been reissued on CD. Much of the material is obscure (including Jackson's three originals) with Stevie Wonder's "Isn't She Lovely" being the only standard. The music, however, is as straightahead as one would expect from these fine musicians and can be easily recommended to their fans. —*Scott Yanow*

Montreux '77 / Jul. 13, 1977 / Original Jazz Classics ✦✦✦✦

This set from the 1977 Montreux Jazz Festival was very much a spontaneous jam session. Fluegelhornist Clark Terry, who happened to be in town early, was added to vibraphonist Milt Jackson's group at the last moment. When players the caliber of Terry, tenor saxophonist Eddie "Lockjaw" Davis, pianist Monty Alexander, bassist Ray Brown, drummer Jimmie Smith and Jackson get together, one does not have to worry about the lack of rehearsal time. The sextet romps happily through Brown's "Slippery," "A Beautiful Friendship," "Mean to Me," "You Are My Sunshine," the CD's bonus cut "That's The Way It Is" and "C.M.J."; both Terry and Jackson have humorous vocals on the latter. —*Scott Yanow*

Bag's Bag / 1979 / Pablo ✦✦✦✦

Vibraphonist Milt Jackson teams up with pianist Cedar Walton, bassist Ray Brown and (on six of the eight songs) either Billy Higgins or Frank Severino on drums. Together they play group originals and (on the two drumless pieces) a pair of standards. Although the material was largely new, the swinging style is timeless and Milt Jackson typically sounds in top form; has he ever made an indifferent recording? —*Scott Yanow*

Milt Jackson, Count Basie & The Big Band, Vol. 1 / Jan. 18, 1978 / Pablo ✦✦

Milt Jackson, Count Basie & The Big Band, Vol. 2 / Jan. 18, 1978 / Pablo ✦✦

Soul Believer / Jan. 20, 1978-Sep. 19, 1978 / Original Jazz Classics ✦✦✦

As vibraphonist Milt Jackson relates in the liner notes of this CD, he was a singer before he ever played vibes. This is one of his very few vocal albums and Jackson (who also takes some solos) is reasonably effective, displaying a personable voice and a gentle swing in his style. The backup utilizes synthesizers on three of the ten selections (a very unusual event at Pablo) but otherwise the lineup for these ballads and jump tunes comprises old musical friends, most notably pianist Cedar Walton. —*Scott Yanow*

All Too Soon: the Duke Ellington Album / Jan. 1980 / Original Jazz Classics ✦✦✦✦✦

Outstanding tribute by classy band of pros. —*Ron Wynn*

Night Mist / Apr. 14, 1980 / Pablo ✦✦✦✦✦

Most of vibraphonist Milt Jackson's recordings as a leader have been at the head of a quartet or quintet. This spirited set has a variety of "near blues" material being interpreted by an all-star septet featuring such unique voices as trumpeter Harry "Sweets" Edison, the tenor of Eddie "Lockjaw" Davis and altoist Eddie "Cleanhead" Vinson in addition to Jackson, pianist Art Hillery, bassist Ray Brown and drummer Larance Marable. There are plenty of magical moments created on this set by these classic jazzmen. —*Scott Yanow*

Big Mouth / Feb. 26, 1981-Feb. 27, 1981 / Original Jazz Classics ✦✦✦

It is to vibraphonist Milt Jackson's credit that he is able to "overcome" his backing on this CD and play some typically swinging music. Jackson is joined by electric keyboards and electric bass on most selections in addition to a couple of Latin percussionists and as many as four singers. Yet even with the many studio musicians, Jackson's basic bebop approach is unchanged and the repertoire includes several standards (such as "Bags' Groove," "The Days of Wine and Roses" and "I'm Getting Sentimental over You") that he has performed a countless number of times. —*Scott Yanow*

Ain't But a Few of Us Left / Nov. 30, 1981 / Original Jazz Classics ✦✦✦✦

Despite the pessimistic title, all of the members of this particular quartet (vibraphonist Milt Jackson, pianist Oscar Peterson, bassist Ray Brown and drummer Grady Tate) were still active into the mid-'90s. The music is unsurprising but still quite enjoyable and virtuosic as Bags and Co. perform blues, standards and ballads with their usual swing and bop-based creativity. Highlights include the title cut, "Stuffy," "What Am I Here For" and a vibes-piano duo version of "A Time for Love." —*Scott Yanow*

A London Bridge / Apr. 23, 1982-Apr. 24, 1982 / Pablo ✦✦✦✦✦

One of three albums of material recorded by the Milt Jackson Quartet (which consisted of pianist Monty Alexander, bassist Ray Brown and drummer Mickey Roker) during a stay at Ronnie Scott's Club in London, this excellent set features the veterans playing in their usual style (bop, blues and ballad) but with a fresher repertoire than usual including "Impressions," "Good Bait" and Alexander's "Reggae/Later." The pianist often steals the show on this fine set; all three records from this gig are easily recommended. —*Scott Yanow*

Mostly Duke / Apr. 23, 1982-Apr. 24, 1982 / Pablo ✦✦✦✦

The third of three sets released by Pablo from Milt Jackson's engagement at Ronnie Scott's Club in London in 1982 (this CD first came out in 1991) lives up to its title. The great vibraphonist, pianist Monty Alexander, bassist Ray Brown and drummer Mickey Roker play two standards, the leader's "Used to Be Jackson" and six songs associated with Duke Ellington. The music swings hard, Alexander competes with Bags for solo honors and the music should please all straightahead jazz fans. —*Scott Yanow*

Memories of Thelonious Sphere Monk / Apr. 28, 1982 / Original Jazz Classics ✦✦✦✦✦

Milt Jackson and his quartet of 1982 (with pianist Monty Alexander, bassist Ray Brown and drummer Mickey Roker) recorded three albums of material during an engagement at Ronnie Scott's Club in London. Pianist/composer Thelonious Monk had passed away two months earlier and Jackson decided to pay tribute to his old associate. The vibraphonist is in excellent form on four of Monk's standards in addition to a lengthy "Django," his own "Think Positive" and Ray Brown's "Blues for Groundhog." —*Scott Yanow*

Jackson, Johnson, Brown & Company / May 25, 1983-May 26, 1983 / Pablo ✦✦✦✦

The interplay between vibraphonist Milt Jackson and trombonist J.J. Johnson is the main reason to acquire this set. With fine backup from pianist Tom Ranier, guitarist John Collins, bassist Ray Brown and drummer Roy McCurdy, Jackson and Johnson are in top form on a variety of bop standards, including Johnson's "Lament," "Our Delight," "Bags Groove" and "My One and Only Love." Enthusiastic, consistently swinging music from some of the best. —*Scott Yanow*

Soul Route / Nov. 30, 1983-Dec. 1, 1983 / Original Jazz Classics ✦✦✦✦

Vibraphonist Milt Jackson recorded quite extensively during his decade with Norman Granz's Pablo label. This particular release (which has been reissued on CD) is most notable for helping launch the comeback of pianist Gene Harris who had been in obscurity ever since he ended his days with The Three Sounds. Harris' soulful style and expertise with blues fit in perfectly with Milt Jackson's approach and (with fine backup from bassist Ray Brown and drummer Mickey Roker) they play some typically joyful music on some blues, standards and ballads. —*Scott Yanow*

Brother Jim / May 17, 1985 / Pablo ✦✦✦✦

Milt Jackson recorded a couple of dozen albums for Pablo from 1975-85; this CD reissue was the final one before the label drastically slowed down. The vibraphonist's quartet of the period (with pianist Cedar Walton, bassist Bob Cranshaw and drummer Mickey Roker) is augmented by Jimmy Heath and Harold Vick (who both double on soprano and tenor) and, on one song, guitarist Joe Pass. The stimulating instrumentation is sometimes a little unusual (the two sopranos even get to trade off), but the high point is actually Jackson's unaccompanied version of "Lullaby of the Leaves." Enjoyable, swinging straightahead jazz. —*Scott Yanow*

Bebop / 1988 / East West ✦✦✦

The music on this East-West CD (made available through Atlantic) certainly lives up to its title. Vibraphonist Milt Jackson welcomes some of his best musical friends including both veterans and a couple of younger greats: trumpeter Jon Faddis, trombonist J.J. Johnson, Jimmy Heath on tenor, pianist Cedar Walton, bassist John Clayton and drummer Mickey Roker. Together they perform nine classic songs from the bop era with the emphasis on medium and uptempo workouts. Few surprises occur but the hard-swinging music largely comes up to one's expectations. —*Scott Yanow*

The Harem / Dec. 10, 1990-Dec. 11, 1990 / Music Masters ♦♦♦♦
The phrase that can be used to describe a typical recording by vibraphonist Milt Jackson is "predictably excellent." There are no unexpected revelations revealed during this sextet set with flutist James Moody, Jimmy Heath (on soprano and tenor), pianist Cedar Walton, bassist Bob Cranshaw and drummer Kenny Washington (although the soprano-flute blend works very well) but there are also no weak moments either. The group performs three standards and two originals apiece by Jackson, Heath and Walton and the music should please fans of those fine veterans. —*Scott Yanow*

Reverence and Compassion / 1993 / Qwest ♦♦♦♦♦
Vibraphonist Milt Jackson is joined by a top-notch rhythm section (pianist Cedar Walton, bassist John Clayton and drummer Billy Higgins), a six-piece horn section and a large string section on various selections but, despite the potential distractions and competition, Bags' vibes are the stars throughout. The music on this CD is mostly standards along with four Jackson bluish originals and a song apiece from Clayton and Walton. Milt Jackson's style has not changed since the 1950s but he has retained his enthusiasm and creativity and remained a potent force in jazz. —*Scott Yanow*

The Prophet Speaks / 1994 / Qwest ♦♦♦♦♦
Forty-eight years after he first made a major impression on a Dizzy Gillespie recording date, vibraphonist Milt Jackson proves that he was still at the top of his form on this CD. The straightahead date finds his quartet (with pianist Cedar Walton, bassist John Clayton and drummer Billy Higgins) welcoming guests Joshua Redman (whose tenor is on six of the dozen selections) and singer Joe Williams, who helps out on three songs. Redman easily fits into the role that other tenors such as Teddy Edwards and Jimmy Heath have had with Jackson, taking concise solos while allowing the great vibist to be the lead in most of the ensembles. Joe Williams is fine during his three spots, but it is the apparently ageless Milt Jackson who is the main star during this enjoyable set. —*Scott Yanow*

Burnin' in the Woodhouse / 1995 / Qwest ♦♦♦♦
Milt Jackson Quartet / May 20, 1995 / Original Jazz Classics ♦♦♦
The music on this quartet date (which features vibraphonist Milt Jackson, pianist Horace Silver, bassist Percy Heath and drummer Connie Kay) is excellent but the playing time (31 minutes) is fairly disgraceful, particularly when one considers that Jackson did a lot of recording for Prestige; certainly more selections could have been added to make this CD have a decent amount of music. Even the old two-LP set *Opus De Funk* added four selections to the album containing this otherwise enjoyable straightahead set. Quantity aside, Bags and Silver make for a good combination on five standards and Jackson's "Stonewall." —*Scott Yanow*

Sa Va Bella (For Lady Legends) / 1997 / Warner Brothers ♦♦♦♦
Gentleman Milt Jackson pays tribute to a cross section of female singers whom he has admired for over a half a century on this unpretentious straightahead CD. Moreover, Milt is enough of a gentleman not to mention any names in the booklet, presumably so as to not leave anyone out. But you can tell by many of the titles just whom he is referring to; needless to say, "A Tisket a Tasket" cannot refer to anyone else but Ella, "What a Difference a Day Made" is Dinah Washington, etc. Pianist Michael LeDonne, bassist Bob Cranshaw and drummer Mickey Roker make up the first-class, lightly swinging rhythm section, and Etta Jones' smoky vocals decorate three of the tunes as ambassador for her gender. Best of all is when the MJQ stalwart loosens his tie and gets to jam a bit on his own funky "Blues for Queen 'D.'" The great vibraphonists of jazz tend to age very well, and at 74, Jackson is very much on his game here. —*Richard S. Ginell*

Quentin Jackson

b. Jan. 13, 1909, Springfield, OH, d. Oct. 2, 1976, New York, NY
Trombone / Swing
A fixture with Duke Ellington's Orchestra in the 1950s, Quentin Jackson was Duke's best "wah-wah" trombonist (an expert with the plunger mute) since Tricky Sam Nanton. His brother-in-law Claude Jones (who played with McKinney's Cotton Pickers) taught him trombone. Jackson played with Zack Whyte (1930), McKinney's Cotton Pickers (1931), Don Redman's Orchestra (1932-40), Cab Calloway (1940-48) and Lucky Millinder. He took occasional solos with those groups and in the early days was a ballad singer. But most important were his contributions to Duke Ellington's music (1949-60), both as a soloist and in the ensembles. After leaving Duke he toured Europe with Quincy Jones (1960), played with Count

Basie (1961-62), recorded with Charles Mingus (1962), returned to Ellington (1963) and worked with the big bands of Louie Bellson and Gerald Wilson. Quentin Jackson was with the Thad Jones/Mel Lewis Orchestra (1971-75) near the end of his life. His only session as a leader resulted in four titles in 1959 that were reissued by Swing. —*Scott Yanow*

Ron Jackson

b. Philippines
Guitar / Bop
A fine bop guitarist, Ron Jackson has thus far recorded two albums as a leader for Muse. Born in the Philippines (his father was in the military), Jackson grew up near Boston. He attended Berklee starting in 1982 and played electric bass in Paris during 1985-87 (including with Bobby Few, Hal Singer and Leo Wright). Jackson returned to both the US and the guitar in 1987, working with James Spaulding, Jimmy McGriff and with his own groups. He has strong potential for the future. —*Scott Yanow*

● **A Guitar Thing** / Jul. 1991 / Muse ♦♦♦♦♦
Guitarist Ron Jackson's debut as a leader is an impressive outing with pianist Benny Green, bassist Lonnie Plaxico and drummer Cecil Brooks III. Very much a straightahead date, Jackson (who describes himself as a "modern traditionalist") performs standards and originals (of which "On the Edge" is most memorable) with a reasonably original voice. His music always swings. —*Scott Yanow*

Ronald Shannon Jackson

b. Jan. 12, 1940, Fort Worth, TX
Drums, Leader / Free Funk, Free Jazz, Hard Bop, Fusion
Drummer Ronald Shannon Jackson and his Decoding Society of the 1980s learned from the example of Ornette Coleman's Prime Time and are a logical extension of the group. They featured colorful and noisy ensembles, were not afraid of the influence of rock and their rhythms were funky, loud and unpredictable. Jackson played professionally in Texas with James Clay when he was 15. He moved to New York in 1966 where he worked with Byard Lancaster, Charles Mingus, Betty Carter, Stanley Turrentine, Jackie McLean, McCoy Tyner, Kenny Dorham and most significantly Albert Ayler (1966-67) among others. He took time off of the scene and then joined Ornette Coleman's Prime Time (1975-79). Jackson also worked with Cecil Taylor (1978-79) and James "Blood" Ulmer (1979-80). The Decoding Society (formed in 1979) through the years featured many talented and advanced improvisers with the best-known ones being Vernon Reid, Zane Massey, Billy Bang and Byard Lancaster. Jackson also played with the explosive group Last Exit (starting in 1986) and in the early '90s with Power Tools. Ronald Shannon Jackson's music is not for easy-to-offend ears! —*Scott Yanow*

★ **Eye on You** / 1980 / About Time ♦♦♦♦♦
Drummer Roland Shannon Jackson's Decoding Society on this About Time LP comprises quite an all-star lineup: violinist Billy Bang, altoist Byard Lancaster, tenor saxophonist Charles Brackeen, Vernon Reid and Bern Nix on guitars, bassist Melvin Gibbs and percussionist Eraso Vasconcelos. The Decoding Society plays what could be called "free funk," a combination of loud funky rhythms with free jazz and the harmolodics pioneered by Ornette Coleman's Prime Time. Everyone solos together constantly, leading to dense and exciting ensembles that are overflowing with passion. Although this style of jazz (a forerunner of Steve Coleman's groups) never really caught on, the music is quite stimulating and a logical extension of '70s fusion. —*Scott Yanow*

Nasty / Mar. 1981 / Moers ♦♦♦♦
Street Priest / Jun. 13, 1981-Jun. 16, 1981 / Moers ♦♦♦♦
Mandance / Jun. 1982 / Antilles ♦♦♦♦♦
The ensemble-oriented "free funk" music of drummer Roland Shannon Jackson's Decoding Society never can be accused of being overly mellow or lacking in excitement. The 1982 version of his band features trumpeter Henry Scott, Zane Massey on reeds, guitarist Vernon Reid, and both Melvin Gibbs and Bruce Johnson on electric basses. The frenetic and intense ensembles (essentially everyone solos at once) would not be classified as relaxing background music. —*Scott Yanow*

Barbeque Dog / Mar. 1983 / Antilles ♦♦♦♦
Erratic, powerful, and explosive. —*Ron Wynn*

Pulse / Jan. 1984 / Celluloid ♦♦♦♦
Furious, classic jazz-rock in the absolute sense of the term, plus some free and R&B influences filtered through the compositions as well. Drummer Ronald Shannon Jackson has played with Ornette Coleman and Cecil Taylor and led his own Decoding Society band. His music rips and roars, while seamlessly moving through multiple idioms, sometimes blurring and combining them as he goes along. —*Ron Wynn*

Decode Yourself / 1984-1985 / Island ◆◆◆

When Colors Play / Sep. 12, 1986-Sep. 13, 1986 / Caravan of Dreams ◆◆◆◆
Ronald Shannon Jackson's free funk group in 1986 featured quite a bit of talent, most notably Eric Person (alto and soprano) and Zane Massey (tenor and soprano) along with two guitarists, bassist John Moody and Jackson's drums. This obscure LP, recorded live at the Caravan of Dreams, has plenty of intense outbursts and fiery solos, showing that it is possible to play creative funk. —*Scott Yanow*

Texas / Apr. 9, 1987-Apr. 11, 1987 / Caravan of Dreams ◆◆◆
For this explosive studio session, Ronald Shannon Jackson's Decoding Society plays mostly concise but rather crowded originals. Altoist Eric Person (also heard on soprano and flute) and guitarist Cary Denigris would later join Chico Hamilton's band. Also in the sextet are Zane Massey on tenor and soprano, guitarist Masujaa, bassist John Moody, and the drummer/leader. The Decoding Society (along with Ornette Coleman's Prime Time and later on Steve Coleman) showed what fusion and funk could have become if they had not become dominated by pop elements. —*Scott Yanow*

Red Warrior / 1990 / Axiom ◆◆◆
Sprawling drums and guitar highlight this recent session. Produced by Bill Laswell. —*Ron Wynn*

Taboo / 1990 / Venture ◆◆◆
Some dynamic adventures with Vernon Reid (g) venturing outside Living Colour arena. —*Ron Wynn*

Shannon's House / Mar. 19, 1996-Mar. 20, 1996 / Koch ◆◆◆

Willis "Gator" Jackson

b. Apr. 25, 1932, Miami, FL, d. Oct. 25, 1987, New York, NY
Tenor Saxophone / Early R&B Jazz, Hard Bop, Soul Jazz, Groove
An exciting tenor saxophonist whose honking and squeals (although influenced by Illinois Jacquet) were quite distinctive, Willis Jackson was also a strong improviser who sounded perfectly at home with organ groups. He played locally in Florida early on until joining Cootie Williams (on and off during 1948-55). His two-sided honking feature "Gator Tail" with "Cootie" (which earned him a lifelong nickname) was a hit in 1948 and he started recording as a leader in 1950. Jackson was married to singer Ruth Brown for eight years and often appeared on her recordings during this era. His extensive series of Prestige recordings (1959-64) made him a big attraction on the organ circuit. Although generally overlooked by critics, Willis Jackson continued working steadily in the 1970s and '80s. In 1977 he recorded one of the finest albums of his career for Muse, *Bar Wars*. —*Scott Yanow*

● **Call of the Gators** / Dec. 21, 1949-May 2, 1949 / Delmark ◆◆◆◆◆

Please Mr. Jackson / May 25, 1959 / Original Jazz Classics ◆◆◆◆
Willis "Gator" Jackson originally made a strong impression as a honking R&B player, first with the Cootie Williams Orchestra, then with his own popular bands. In 1959, starting with this Prestige set (which has been reissued on CD), Jackson made his mark on soul-jazz. Teamed with the up-and-coming organist Jack McDuff, guitarist Bill Jennings, bassist Tommy Potter and drummer Alvin Johnson, Gator is heard modifying his style a little (gone are most of the screams) in favor of swinging. He performs four group originals, "Come Back to Sorrento," and "Memories of You" with soulful feeling. —*Scott Yanow*

Cool Gator / May 25, 1959-Aug. 16, 1960 / Original Jazz Classics ◆◆◆◆◆
This late 1980s reissue (which has not yet come out on CD) features Willis "Gator" Jackson in one of his earlier jazz sets. Having made his initial reputation as a honking and screaming R&B star, Jackson by 1959 had formed a soul-jazz group that included guitarist Bill Jennings and the young organist Jack McDuff. On this program, the tenor plays a typical set from the era: three standards, the jump tune "A Smooth One," and a couple of his basic originals. Enjoyable and accessible music that swings and contains its share of soul. —*Scott Yanow*

★ **Together Again** / May 25, 1959-Aug. 16, 1960 / Prestige ◆◆◆◆◆
Jackson with Jack McDuff on the Hammond B-3 and Bill Jennings on guitar. —*Michael Erlewine*

Together Again, Again / May 25, 1959-Dec. 31, 1961 / Prestige ◆◆◆
Jackson with Jack McDuff on the Hammond B-3 and Bill Jennings on guitar. Tunes like "Snake Crawl" and "Backtrack" should give you a clue as to the music on this album. —*Michael Erlewine*

Gentle Gator / Jan. 10, 1961-Oct. 30, 1962 / Prestige ◆◆
Tenor saxophonist Willis Jackson is best-known as a passionate and screaming tenorman who puts a lot of emotion into his playing. This CD reissue is a change of pace for it consists of ballads taken from four of "Gator's" Prestige and Moodsville albums of 1961-62. Jackson plays tastefully and sticks close to the melodies, sounding in good form on such songs as "Estrellita," "Girl of My Dreams," "Home" and "They Didn't Believe Me." However, due to the sampler nature of the collec-

tion, the sameness of mood and the overly restrained solos, this CD is of lesser interest. —*Scott Yanow*

Thunderbird / Mar. 31, 1962 / Prestige ◆◆◆◆◆
Great Jackson, robust Freddy Roach organ. —*Ron Wynn*

☆ **Shuckin'** / Oct. 30, 1962 / Prestige ◆◆◆◆◆
His second great album that year. All-star lineup included Kenny Burrell (g), Tommy Flanagan (p). —*Ron Wynn*

Loose / Mar. 26, 1963 / Prestige ◆◆◆
Willis with Carl Wilson on Hammond organ. —*Michael Erlewine*

The Good Life / May 23, 1963 / Prestige ◆◆◆
With Carl Wilson on Hammond organ. —*AMG*

Grease 'n Gravy / May 23, 1963 / Prestige ◆◆◆
Willis Jackson with Carl Wilson on organ. —*Michael Erlewine*

More Gravy / Oct. 24, 1963 / Prestige ◆◆◆
Still more. Jackson with Carl Wilson on Hammond organ. —*Michael Erlewine*

Boss Shoutin' / Jan. 9, 1964 / Prestige ◆◆◆
Willis Jackson with Carl Wilson on Hammond organ. —*Michael Erlewine*

Gator Tails / Mar. 18, 1964 / Verve ◆◆◆
Hot soul-jazz tenor with orchestral backing. —*Ron Wynn*

With Pat Martino / Mar. 21, 1964 / Prestige ◆◆◆◆
Although guitarist Pat Martino (19 at the time) gets second billing on this CD reissue, tenor saxophonist Willis Jackson is the main star throughout. Recorded live at the Allegro in New York on March 21, 1964, this CD releases the complete contents of two Jackson LPs (*Action* and *Live Action*). "Gator Tail" puts on his usual exuberant show with screams and honks being a logical part of his colorful style. The music, fairly basic material with a few standards and blues tossed in, gives listeners a good example of Willis Jackson's music of the 1960s; the quintet also includes trumpeter Frank Robinson, organist Carl Wilson and drummer Joe Hadrick. An enjoyable crowd-pleasing set. —*Scott Yanow*

Smokin' with Willis / Nov. 15, 1965 / Cadet ◆◆◆
Scorching sextet session. —*Ron Wynn*

Star Bag / Mar. 22, 1968 / Prestige ◆◆◆
Willis Jackson with Trudy Pitts on the Hammond B-3. —*Michael Erlewine*

Gatorade / Aug. 1971 / Prestige ◆◆◆
The music on this obscure LP was not released until 1982 and quickly disappeared. Tenor saxophonist Willis Jackson plays funky jazz that is very much of the period with organist Carl Wilson, guitarist Boogaloo Joe Jones, drummer Jerry Potter and Buddy Caldwell on conga. Jackson performs the current pop tunes "Hey Jude" and "The Long and Winding Road," plus a pair of blues (including his "Pow") and a couple of originals. Fun but not overly substantial music. —*Scott Yanow*

West Africa / Oct. 22, 1973 / Muse ◆◆◆
Exuberant title cut. —*Ron Wynn*

Headed and Gutted / May 16, 1974 / Muse ◆◆◆◆
Willis "Gator" Jackson's series of albums for Muse during the 1970s helped keep alive the soulful, tough tenor tradition of Illinois Jacquet, Gene Ammons and (later on) Houston Person. For this particular set, the participation of guitarist Pat Martino made the date more notable than it might have been. With Mickey Tucker on keyboards, electric bassist Bob Cranshaw, drummer Freddie Waits, and Richard Landrum and Sonny Morgan on percussion, Jackson still sounds very much in his prime, particularly on the exciting "Gator Whale." The other selections tend to emphasize ballads ("My One and Only Love" is fairly memorable) and funky jazz, although "The Way We Were" did not really need to be recorded again. —*Scott Yanow*

Plays with Feeling / May 1976 / Cotillion ◆◆◆

In the Alley / 1976 / Muse ◆◆◆
"In the Alley" and "Niamani" are the highlights of this typical but often exciting outing by veteran tenor Willis Jackson. The music includes blues, romps, a ballad, and funky vamps. Jackson is assisted by pianist Sonny Phillips, organist Carl Wilson, guitarist Jimmy Ponder, bassist Jimmy Lewis, drummer Yusef Ali and percussionist Buddy Caldwell. This worthy set has not yet been reissued on CD. —*Scott Yanow*

The Gator Horn / Mar. 8, 1977 / Muse ◆◆◆
Virtually all of tenor saxophonist Willis "Gator" Jackson's albums for Muse in the 1970s (and fortunately, there are many of them) are well worth picking up. Jackson's basic tenor always contained plenty of soul, the potential of exploding and an attractive warm sound. For this fine set, Gator alternates between romps (some of which are funky) and ballads ("You've Changed" and "This Is Always"). Excellent support is contributed by organist Carl Wilson, guitarist Boogaloo Joe Jones,

bassist Dud Bascomb, Jr., drummer Yusef Ali, and Buddy Caldwell on conga. —*Scott Yanow*

Bar Wars / Dec. 21, 1977 / Muse ✦✦✦✦✦
Willis Jackson, a veteran of the jazz-oriented R&B music of the late '40s, was a powerful tenor in the tradition of Gene Ammons. This is a particularly exciting release with Charles Earland pumping away at the organ, guitarist Pat Martino offering a contrasting solo voice and Jackson in top form, wailing away on the uptempo pieces. The CD reissue of the original LP adds two alternate takes to the program. The chord changes might be fairly basic but Willis Jackson plays with such enthusiasm and exuberance that it almost sounds as if he had discovered the joy of playing music. —*Scott Yanow*

Single Action / Apr. 26, 1978 / Muse ✦✦✦✦
Willis Jackson was a tough-toned tenor who came to fame as a honker and screamer with Cootie Williams' big band in the late '40s. Although he calmed down his style a bit through the years, he always has a passionate sound and an accessible style best heard on blues, ballads and standards. This is a CD reissue of a 1978 session that features Jackson with guitarist Pat Martino, organist Carl Wilson and a supportive rhythm section. Although the Barbara Streisand-associated "Evergreen" (heard in two versions) and "You Are the Sunshine of My Life" may not seem like the best material for the tenor, he uplifts the songs. But best are a pair of hard-driving blues and a warm rendition of "Makin' Whoopee." Joe Fields accurately states in the liner notes that Willis Jackson's best recording was his prior Muse release *Bar Wars* but *Single Action* does give one a good example of Jackson playing in a tenor style that (other than Houston Person and now Joshua Redman) is quickly disappearing. —*Scott Yanow*

Lockin' Horns: Willis and Von Live at Laren / Aug. 11, 1978 / Muse ✦✦✦✦
This album has a somewhat unlikely matchup. While Willis "Gator" Jackson's roots are in honking and screaming R&B, and he later became a top-notch soul-jazz player, Von Freeman's unusual tone and exploratory style resulted in him being associated with the avant-garde and post-bop. However, this encounter works well. With organist Carl Wilson, guitarist Boogaloo Joe Jones and drummer Yusef Ali giving strong support, the two tenors challenge each other, romp on "Pow!" and "Willis and Von," and show off their highly original sounds on individual features. Hopefully, this unique set will be reissued on CD. —*Scott Yanow*

Ya Understand Me? / Jan. 26, 1980 / Muse ✦✦✦
With "Groove" Holmes on organ duties, and some tart tenor from Jackson. —*Ron Wynn*

Nothing Butt / Jun. 20, 1980 / Muse ✦✦✦
Tenor saxophonist Willis Jackson got into a routine on his Muse albums, but never lost his enthusiasm and creativity within the genre. This album features Jackson on a current hit ("Just the Way You Are"), a couple of ballads, and three romps ("Nothing Butt," "Hittin' and Missin'," and "Move"). Guitarist Pat Martino is heard in excellent form just before a serious illness; organist Charles Earland is up to his usual groovin' form, and drummer Grady Tate and percussionist Buddy Caldwell keep the music moving. An excellent effort full of enjoyable and fairly accessible music. —*Scott Yanow*

Illinois Jacquet (Jean Baptiste Illinois Jacquet)

b. Oct. 31, 1922, Boussard, LA

Tenor Saxophone, Alto Saxophone, Bassoon / Bop, Swing, Early R&B Jazz, Groove
One of the great tenors, Illinois Jacquet's 1942 "Flying Home" solo is considered the first R&B sax solo and spawned a full generation of younger tenors (including Joe Houston and Big Jay McNeely) who built their careers from his style and practically from that one song!

Jacquet, whose older brother Russell (1917-1990) was a trumpeter who sometimes played in his bands, grew up in Houston and his tough tone and emotional sound defined the Texas tenor school. After playing locally, he moved to Los Angeles where in 1941 he played with Floyd Ray. He was the star of Lionel Hampton's 1942 big band ("Flying Home" became a signature song for Jacquet, Hampton and even Illinois' successor Arnett Cobb), and also was with Cab Calloway (1943-44) and well-featured with Count Basie (1945-46). Jacquet's playing at the first Jazz at the Philharmonic concert (1944) included a screaming solo on "Blues" that found him biting on his reed to achieve high register effects; the crowd went wild. He repeated the idea during his appearance in the 1944 film short *Jammin' the Blues*. In 1945 Jacquet put together his own band and both his recordings and live performances were quite exciting. He appeared with JATP on several tours in the 1950s, recorded steadily and never really lost his popularity. In the 1960s he sometimes doubled on bassoon (usually for a slow number such as "'Round Midnight") and it was an effective contrast to his stomping tenor. In the late '80s Jacquet started leading an exciting part-time big band that thus far has only recorded one album, an Atlantic date from 1988. Through the years, Illinois Jacquet (whose

occasional features on alto are quite influenced by Charlie Parker) has recorded as a leader for such labels as Apollo, Savoy, Aladdin, RCA, Verve, Mercury, Roulette, Epic, Argo, Prestige, Black Lion, Black & Blue, JRC and Atlantic. —*Scott Yanow*

☆ **The Complete Illinois Jacquet Sessions 1945-50** / Jul. 1945-May 22, 1950 / Mosaic ✦✦✦✦✦
This four-CD set has all of the recordings made as a leader by tenor saxophonist Illinois Jacquet during a period when he was at the height of his popularity. After his classic solo made "Flying Home" a major hit for Lionel Hampton in 1942, Jacquet spent time with Cab Calloway's band, was a sensation with Jazz at the Philharmonic and was featured as a star soloist with Count Basie. In 1946 Jacquet went out on his own and his combo (ranging from six to eight pieces) was extremely popular, featuring its leader's hard-swinging solos which utilized a liberal amount of honks and screams. The first real R&B tenorman, Illinois Jacquet was always a much more well-rounded soloist than the specialists who followed him. The 17 sessions that are included on this essential box draws its material from the Aladdin, Apollo, ARA, Savoy and Victor catalogs. Some of the music has been readily available in recent years but this is the best way to acquire the swinging performances. Among Jacquet's most notable sidemen are trumpeters Joe Newman, Emmett Berry (who was actually the leader of one of these dates), Russell Jacquet (who also contributes some bluish vocals) and Fats Navarro (who solos on one song), trombonists Henry Coker, Trummy Young and J.J. Johnson, baritonist Leo Parker, pianists Sir Charles Thompson, Bill Doggett and John Lewis, bassist Charles Mingus, drummers Johnny Otis and Shadow Wilson and (on two songs) singer Wynonie Harris. Fun music. —*Scott Yanow*

☆ **The Black Velvet Band** / Dec. 18, 1947-Jul. 1947 / Bluebird ✦✦✦✦✦
This exciting CD reissues all of tenor saxophonist Illinois Jacquet's Victor recordings of 1947-50. Jacquet was riding high during the period and his octet included at times trumpeter Joe Newman, trombonist J.J. Johnson, baritonist Leo Parker and either Sir Charles Thompson or John Lewis on piano. The 18 performances (all of which have also been reissued in a large but limited-edition Mosaic box set) feature plenty of heated solos by Jacquet (such as "Jet Propulsion," "Riffin' at 24th Street," "Mutton Leg" and "Adam's Alley") plus occasional warm ballads. The CD is rounded off by Jacquet playing "Flying Home" in a guest shot with Lionel Hampton at the 1967 Newport Jazz Festival. Highly recommended to listeners not lucky enough to have the Mosaic set. —*Scott Yanow*

Flies Again / Aug. 11, 1959 / Roulette ✦✦
This CD reissue, which has tenor saxophonist Illinois Jacquet's only session as a leader during 1958-61, is a bit of a disappointment. Jacquet plays well enough and his tone is always endearing but the constant criticism by jazz writers of the 1950s about his honks, squeals and screams led to him leaving some of the extremities (and excitement) out of his solos. Although there are some good buildups here and there, none of the performances explode or stand out. Best is the medium-tempo blues "Teddy Bear," which was possibly conceived as a tribute to the recently deceased Lester Young, while "Bottoms Up" is essentially a routine runthrough on "Flying Home" and "The King" uses the framework of "Jumpin' at the Woodside." All of the other selections are taken at ballad or dance tempos and Jacquet's sidemen are limited strictly to background work. A tame and sometimes simply dull set. —*Scott Yanow*

Illinois Jacquet / Feb. 5, 1962-May 21, 1962 / Epic/Legacy ✦✦✦
This CD reissue, which adds five alternate takes to the original LP program, finds tenor great Illinois Jacquet totally dominating the proceedings. Jacquet is heard in prime form on a few heated romps, is warm on the ballads, does a close imitation of Lester Young on "Pucker Up," and is quite effective during his appearances on alto, especially on "Indiana." The rhythm section, led by pianist Sir Charles Thompson, is very much in the Basie tradition, and the other horns, playing Jimmy Mundy's arrangements, get to riff a lot behind the distinctive leader. The brevity of the performances (only one song exceeds four-and-a-half minutes) and the small amount of solo space given combative trumpeter Roy Eldridge, who would have been an ideal partner for Jacquet, are slight disappointments, but this set is worth picking up. —*Scott Yanow*

Go Power / Mar. 15, 1966-Mar. 17, 1966 / Cadet ✦✦✦
Tenor saxophonist Illinois Jacquet teams up with organist Milt Buckner and drummer Alan Dawson for this live LP that has not yet been reissued on CD. The distinctive tenor roars through "Illinois Jacquet Flies Again" and "On a Clear Day," sounds warm on "Robbins Nest" and "I Want a Little Girl" and is heard throughout in prime form. Buckner's heavy organ sound takes a bit of getting used to (this album would have been much better if he had been on piano) but he does push Jacquet to some fiery playing. —*Scott Yanow*

Bottoms Up / Mar. 26, 1968 / Original Jazz Classics ✦✦✦✦✦
Even in 1968 when the jazz avant-garde was becoming quite influential, tenor saxophonist Illinois Jacquet played in his own timeless style, performing in an

idiom little changed during the past 20 years. With the assistance of pianist Barry Harris, bassist Ben Tucker and drummer Alan Dawson, Jacquet is heard throughout this CD reissue (which adds a previously unissued "Don't Blame Me" to the original program) swinging hard and generally expressing himself in a typically extroverted fashion. "Bottoms Up" (a relative of "Flying Home"), "Jivin' with Jack the Bellboy" and Jacquet's excellent original ballad "You Left Me All Alone" are most memorable. —*Scott Yanow*

The King / Aug. 20, 1968 / Original Jazz Classics ✦✦✦
Tenor saxophonist Illinois Jacquet has never made an indifferent record, and this CD reissue of a Prestige date from 1968 has its strong moments. High points include the rousing, if overly brief "The King," a warm "Blue and Sentimental," and an atmospheric feature on "Caravan" for Jacquet's bassoon. On the other hand, this version of "How High the Moon" does not live up to its potential, and the two other songs ("A Haunting Melody" and "I Wish I Knew How It Would Feel to Be Free") are a bit dated. Two previously unissued alternate takes are included on the still rather brief (41 minutes) CD, which also has worthwhile contributions from trumpeter Joe Newman, pianist Milt Buckner and guitarist Billy Butler. Enjoyable music but not all that essential. —*Scott Yanow*

The Soul Explosion / Mar. 25, 1969 / Original Jazz Classics ✦✦✦✦✦
The great tenor Illinois Jacquet is joined by a ten-piece group that includes trumpeter Joe Newman and Milt Buckner on piano and organ for this 1969 Prestige studio session which has been reissued on CD by the OJC series. Jacquet is in prime form, particularly on "The Soul Explosion" (which benefits from a Jimmy Mundy arrangement), a definitive "After Hours" and a previously unissued version of "Still King." This blues-based set is full of soul but often swings quite hard with the focus on Jacquet's exciting tenor throughout. —*Scott Yanow*

★ **The Blues: That's Me!** / Sep. 16, 1969 / Original Jazz Classics ✦✦✦✦
Tenor saxophonist Illinois Jacquet is heard in top form throughout this quintet set with pianist Wynton Kelly, guitarist Tiny Grimes, bassist Buster Williams and drummer Oliver Jackson. The music, which falls between swing, bop and early rhythm & blues, is generally quite exciting, especially "Still King," "Everyday I Have the Blues" and the lengthy title cut. A particular surprise is a moody version of "'Round Midnight" which features some surprisingly effective Illinois Jacquet on bassoon. This CD reissue is highly recommended. —*Scott Yanow*

The Comeback / Apr. 13, 1971-Apr. 14, 1971 / Black Lion ✦✦✦✦
This is a particularly interesting if not essential set by tenor saxophonist Illinois Jacquet. While Jacquet is in superior form (and does a suprisingly effective imitation of Ella Fitzgerald singing on the humorous "I Wanna Blow Now") and drummer Tony Crombie is fine in support, the most dominant member of the trio is organist Milt Buckner. His "accompaniment" of Jacquet is often roaring and thunderous, sounding like two big bands at once. The trio, which also explores "The King" (Jacquet's feature in the 1940s with Count Basie), "Easy Living," "C Jam Blues," Jacquet's "The Comeback" and "Take the 'A' Train," is a bit out-of-balance and it is a pity that Buckner could not have played a bit of piano or at least let up a little. —*Scott Yanow*

Genius at Work / Apr. 13, 1971-Apr. 14, 1971 / Black Lion ✦✦✦
This live set with organist Milt Buckner and drummer Tony Crombie is quite fun. Tenor great Illinois Jacquet roars throughout "The King," "C Jam Blues" and "Take the 'A' Train," makes a warm ballad statement on "Easy Living," and on "I Wanna Blow Now" he takes an enthusiastic vocal that is highlighted by a suprisingly effective imitation of Ella Fitzgerald. The LP has been long out-of-print but it is worth picking up even if Buckner's organ playing lacks much subtlety. —*Scott Yanow*

Jacquet's Street / Jul. 16, 1976 / Black & Blue ✦✦✦
This is a consistently inspired sextet date featuring the great tenor Illinois Jacquet. Released by the French Black & Blue label and made available in the US by the now-defunct Classic Jazz on an LP (but not yet out on CD), the set teams Jacquet with complementary mainstream players: trumpeter Francis Williams, trombonist Al Cobbs, pianist Milt Buckner, bassist George Duvivier and drummer Oliver Jackson. Jacquet and his sidemen put plenty of spirit into basic jam tunes including "Rock a Bye Basie," "Broadway" and "Taps Miller," coming across like a small-group from Count Basie's Orchestra. Fun and swinging music. —*Scott Yanow*

Jacquet's Got It! / 1988 / Atlantic ✦✦✦✦✦
The Illinois Jacquet big band has been together on a part-time basis for over a decade, yet this is still its only recording. Fortunately, it is a very good one, displaying its leader's love for hard-swinging and exciting performances. The featured sidemen include trombonist Frank Lacy, trumpeters Irv Stokes and Jon Faddis, clarinetist Rudy Rutherford and pianist Richard Wyands, but the great tenor's solos and the exuberant sound of the ensembles are most notable. With arrangements by Wild Bill Davis, Eddie Barefield and Phil Wilson, the highlights include

"Tickletoe," "Stompin' at the Savoy" and "Three Buckets of Jive"; in reality, all eight selections are rewarding. Recommended. —*Scott Yanow*

Ahmad Jamal

b. Jul. 2, 1930, Pittsburgh, PA
Piano / Post-Bop, Cool
One of the few pianists in the 1950s who did not sound like a close copy of Bud Powell, Ahmad Jamal's use of space, ability to gradually increase or decrease the volume with his trio and brilliant use of tension and release were quite original. He greatly impressed Miles Davis (who borrowed from his repertoire and insisted that Red Garland try to sound like him) and Jamal also cut some very popular records without altering his style.

Jamal began playing professionally in Pittsburgh when he was 11. In the late '40s he joined George Hudson's Orchestra. In 1951 he formed his first trio, the Three Strings, a group with guitarist Ray Crawford and bassist Eddie Calhoun. Israel Crosby took Calhoun's place in 1955. One of Jamal's recordings from that year was a version of "Pavanne" that at one point states the melody from John Coltrane's "Impressions," five years before 'Trane "wrote" the song! In 1956 Jamal switched to a piano-bass-drums trio with Walter Perkins replacing Crawford. With Vernell Fournier on drums by 1958, Jamal recorded his most popular album, *Ahmad Jamal at the Pershing,* and his version of "Poinciana" is still famous. The trio broke up in 1962 but Jamal continued growing as a pianist (sometimes doubling on electric piano in the 1970s) and he remains one of the most distinctive (and indirectly influential) pianists in jazz. Ahmad Jamal recorded through the years for Epic, Argo/Cadet, Impulse, Catalyst, 20th Century, Atlantic and Telarc. —*Scott Yanow*

Poinciana / Oct. 25, 1951-Oct. 25, 1955 / Portrait ✦✦✦✦✦
This fascinating 1989 reissue features pianist Ahmad Jamal at the beginning of his recording career. With guitarist Ray Crawford and either Eddie Calhoun or Israel Crosby on bass, Jamal showcases a style that would be a major influence on Miles Davis' music. Jamal's use of space and dynamics was very different than the style of any other jazz pianist of the era. His versions of "Old Devil Moon," "Will You Still Be Mine," "The Surrey with the Fringe on Top" and "A Gal in Calico" inspired Miles to record the songs in a similar fashion, and his "Billy Boy" became the basis of a performance by the Red Garland Trio. Most fascinating is Jamal's inventive interpretation of "Pavanne," for it has a section very reminiscent of "So What" (which was not "composed" by Davis until over two years later) and a melody statement that is exactly the same as John Coltrane's "Impressions." —*Scott Yanow*

Chamber Music of New Jazz / May 23, 1955 / Argo ✦✦✦✦✦

Ahmad Jamal Trio / Oct. 25, 1955 / Epic ✦✦✦✦✦
This long-out-of-print LP contains ten titles from a date by the Ahmad Jamal Trio that were not included on the 1989 reissue *Poinciana.* Jamal was creating quite a stir at the time with his fresh chord voicings and use of space and dynamics. On this album, he performs in a unit with guitarist Ray Crawford and bassist Israel Crosby shortly before he decided to switch to a more conventional piano-bass-drums instrumentation. Among the highlights are "Perfidia," "Love for Sale," "Autumn Leaves" and "They Can't Take That Away from Me." Well worth searching for. —*Scott Yanow*

Ahmad Jamal at the Pershing, Vol. 1 / Jan. 16, 1958-Jan. 17, 1958 / Argo ✦✦✦✦✦

☆ **But Not for Me** / Jan. 16, 1958-Jan. 17, 1958 / Argo ✦✦✦✦✦
The first album by the trio of pianist Ahmad Jamal, bassist Israel Crosby and drummer Vernell Fournier was a big seller partly due to the classic rendition of "Poinciana." The live LP (which unfortunately only has 29 minutes of music) features very tight interplay between the musicians and light but passionate versions of such other songs as "But Not for Me," "Surrey with the Fringe On Top" and "Woody 'n You." A classic that really defined Ahmad Jamal's distinctive sound in many people's minds. —*Scott Yanow*

Ahmad's Blues / Sep. 6, 1958 / Jazz Society ✦✦✦✦✦
This CD reissues most of the music recorded on one night by the 1958 Ahmad Jamal Trio (which consisted of the pianist/leader, bassist Israel Crosby and drummer Vernel Fournier) during a live performance in Washington, DC Originally released as the LP *Ahmad Jamal* plus part of *Portfolio of Ahmad Jamal,* these 16 selections display the uniqueness and tightness of this memorable unit. With great attention paid to dynamics and the use of space yet always swinging (at least lightly), the Ahmad Jamal Trio is heard at its best on such numbers as "It Could Happen to You," "Stompin' at the Savoy," "Squatly Roo," "A Gal in Calico" and "Let's Fall in Love." —*Scott Yanow*

Ahmad Jamal at the Penthouse / Feb. 22, 1959-Feb. 28, 1959 / Argo ✦✦✦
This LP was a change of pace for pianist Ahmad Jamal, whose trio (with bassist Israel Crosby and drummer Vernell Fournier) is joined by a 15-piece string section

arranged and conducted by Joe Kennedy. The interpretations are generally pretty, but with enough variety to hold one's interest. Among the nine selections are Hoagy Carmichael's "Ivy," "Tangerine," "Ahmad's Blues" and "I Like to Recognize the Tune." —*Scott Yanow*

Ahmad Jamal's Alhambra / Jun. 1961 / Argo ◆◆◆◆
Taken from what were probably bassist Israel Crosby's final recordings with pianist Ahmad Jamal (14 months before the bassist's unexpected death), this LP features the classic version of Jamal's Trio (with drummer Vernell Fournier) playing live at the leader's short-lived Chicago club. The interplay between the musicians was often magical, as can be heard on such numbers as "We Kiss in a Shadow," "Love for Sale," "Broadway" and "Isn't It Romantic." —*Scott Yanow*

All of You / Jun. 1961 / Argo ◆◆◆◆
The second of two LPs documenting the Ahmad Jamal Trio's recordings at Jamal's Chicago club (the Alhambra), this out-of-print set also has some of bassist Israel Crosby's last recordings with Jamal before his premature death in 1962. With drummer Vernell Fournier completing the group, Jamal's group had a personal sound of its own, often playing quietly and leaving space but never losing the passion. These versions of "Time on My Hands," "Star Eyes" and "All of You" in particular are well worth hearing. —*Scott Yanow*

The Awakening / Feb. 3, 1970 / Impulse ◆◆◆
The music on this CD has been reissued many times, most recently in 1997. By 1970, pianist Ahmad Jamal's style had changed a bit since the 1950s, becoming denser and more adventurous while still retaining his musical identity. With bassist Jamil Nasser (whose doubletiming lines are sometimes furious) and drummer Frank Gant, Jamal performs two originals (playing over a vamp on "Patterns"), the obscure "I Love Music" and four jazz standards. Intriguing performances showing that Ahmad Jamal was continuing to evolve. —*Scott Yanow*

Free Flight / Jun. 17, 1971 / Impulse ◆◆◆◆◆
This CD reissue from the 1971 Montreux Jazz Festival has one of pianist Ahmad Jamal's finest recordings of the early '70s. Performing with bassist Jamil Sulieman Nasser and drummer Frank Gant, Jamal shows that his basic style has evolved since the 1950s but is still quite recognizable. He uses the electric piano as a double for color and stretches out on three numbers (including a remake of his hit "Poinciana") in addition to playing a five-minute version of Herbie Hancock's "Dolphin Dance." An excellent effort. —*Scott Yanow*

Live At Oil Can Harry's / 1976 / Catalyst ◆◆◆◆
It is a pity that this LP is long out of print (and that the Catalyst label went out of business quite awhile ago), for it gives listeners an excellent example of the playing of pianist Ahmad Jamal in the mid-1970s. His group (comprising guitarist Calvin Keys, bassist John Heard, drummer Frank Gant and Seldon Newton on conga) was temporarily larger than usual, and Jamal stretches out on three originals (including "Effendi") and a lengthy remake of his biggest hit, "Poinciana." —*Scott Yanow*

Intervals / 1979 / 20th Century Fox ◆◆
Ahmad Jamal's recording career became temporarily aimless as the 1970s were ending. This very forgettable LP features Jamal on both electric and acoustic piano, saddled by rather commercial arrangements. The tunes are not always bad (five are by the keyboardist), but the dated pop trappings and Jamal's near-anonymity on electric piano make this a set deserving of being quickly passed by. —*Scott Yanow*

Live at Bubba's / Mar. 20, 1980 / Who's Who ◆◆◆
Although Ahmad Jamal's recording career was erratic at this period, his live performances were as good as his earlier work. Teamed up with bassist Sabu Adeyola and drummer Payton Crossley, Jamal interprets a diverse program highlighted by "Waltz for Debbie" and "I've Never Been in Love Before," although recording "People" was probably a mistake. This worthwhile LP will be difficult to find. —*Scott Yanow*

Ahmad Jamal/Gary Burton in Concert / Jan. 26, 1981 / Personal Choice ◆◆◆◆
From the same concert that resulted in the Chiaroscuro LP *Live in Concert*, this worthy performance (still only available as an out-of-print LP) features the 1981 Ahmad Jamal Trio (consisting of the pianist/leader, bassist Sabu Adeyola and drummer Payton Crossley) stretching out on "Morning of the Carnival" and Chick Corea's "Tones for Joan's Bones." The other three numbers ("One," "Bogata" and "Autumn Leaves") add vibraphonist Gary Burton to the group, and the Burton-Jamal combination works quite well on what was a successful but only one-time collaboration. —*Scott Yanow*

Live in Concert Featuring Gary Burton / Jan. 26, 1981 / Chiaroscuro ◆◆◆◆
Many of Chiaroscuro's later (and more modern than usual) releases quickly went out of print when the label folded, and have not yet been reissued on CD. Recorded at the same Cannes concert that resulted in an equally rewarding set released by the tiny Personal Choice label, this outing is most unusual in teaming

pianist Ahmad Jamal's Trio (which also included bassist Sabu Adeyola and drummer Payton Crossley) with the great vibraphonist Gary Burton on two numbers ("The Night Has a Thousand Eyes" and Duke Ellington's "African Flower"). In addition, Jamal's group is heard performing two obscurities and "My Funny Valentine." Actually, the high point of the set is Gary Burton's somewhat amazing unaccompanied rendition of Jobim's "No More Blues." —*Scott Yanow*

Digital Works / 1985 / Atlantic ◆◆◆
Ahmad Jamal was never as distinctive on electric piano as he was on the acoustic counterpart, making this two-LP set (which finds him doubling) a slight disappointment. Jamal does play well throughout, engaging his sidemen (bassist Larry Ball, drummer Herlin Riley and percussionist Iraj Lashkary) in close interplay, but no new revelations occur on such remakes as "But Not for Me," "Wave" and Jamal's greatest hit, "Poinciana." Good music overall, but not essential. —*Scott Yanow*

Live at the Montreux Jazz Festival / 1985 / Atlantic ◆◆◆◆◆
This live concert was released on a 1986 double LP. Pianist Ahmad Jamal and his quartet (which also includes bassist James Cammack, drummer Herlin Riley and percussionist Selden Newton) dig into three originals, an obscurity, Jack DeJohnette's "Ebony," and a trio of jazz standards (including "Footprints"). This particular group is often reminiscent of Jamal's trios of the '50s, although with more modern bass playing and some denser piano than earlier. Worth picking up by listeners lucky enough to run across the out-of-print two-fer. —*Scott Yanow*

Rossiter Road / Feb. 1, 1986-Feb. 2, 1986 / Atlantic ◆◆◆◆
Few of pianist Ahmad Jamal's many recordings are not worth picking up, and this effort for Atlantic boasts some fresh material and fine playing. Jamal (joined by bassist James Cammack, drummer Herlin Riley and percussionist Manola Badrena) performs seven of his little-known originals and the obscurity "Yellow Fellow." The close musical communication by the players is, as always, the main reason to acquire this release. —*Scott Yanow*

Crystal / 1987 / Atlantic ◆◆◆
There are some magical moments on this quartet set featuring pianist Ahmad Jamal, bassist James Cammack, drummer David Bowles and percussionist Willie White. Jamal's control of dynamics and inventive use of space proved to be as effective as it had been when he first made his mark in the 1950s, although his chord voicings and general style had evolved. Jamal and his group perform ten of his originals with taste, swing and subtle surprises. —*Scott Yanow*

Pittsburgh / 1989 / Atlantic ◆◆◆◆
In an ambitious tribute to his late mother and his hometown, Ahmad Jamal enlists the help of Chicago-based arranger Richard Evans—a more familiar presence in soul-jazz's '60s heyday than in 1989, alas—to decorate five of his compositions and Jimmy Heath's "Mellowdrama," while soloing alone on two others. While Jamal can summon forth all of the bravura resources of his piano technique on pieces like "Foolish Ways" and "Divertimento," he often chooses economy instead, relying on the trademark ostinatos of his rhythm section (James Cammack, bass; David Bowler, drums) for momentum. Evans' orchestrations, always elegant and lean, fit like gloves onto Jamal's compositions, enhancing rather than intruding, often following the contours of the melodic lines. This CD has captured both the character and shaping hand of Jamal and the distinct sound of Evans, and they are a perfect match in this at-times-exquisite piece of work. —*Richard S. Ginell*

Live in Paris '92 / Apr. 3, 1992-Apr. 4, 1992 / Verve ◆◆◆

Chicago Revisited: Live at Joe Segal's Jazz Showcase / Nov. 13, 1992-Nov. 14, 1992 / Telarc ◆◆◆◆
Although it had been more than 40 years since his debut recording, pianist Ahmad Jamal's playing was as viable as ever in the 1990s. Teamed up with bassist John Heard and drummer Yoron Israel for this live Telarc CD, Jamal plays a particularly inspired repertoire that includes "All the Things You Are," Clifford Brown's "Daahoud," John Handy's "Dance to the Lady" and "Be My Love" among its nine selections. Jamal's style had developed since his early days, but his basic approach was unchanged while still sounding quite fresh. This date is an excellent example of Ahmad Jamal's unique sound and highly appealing music in the 1990s. —*Scott Yanow*

I Remember Duke, Hoagy & Strayhorn / Jun. 2, 1994-Jun. 3, 1994 / Telarc ◆◆◆◆
Ahmad Jamal, in paying tribute to Duke Ellington, Billy Strayhorn and Hoagy Carmichael, performs nearly every selection on this CD at a very slow tempo. Or at least his sidemen do, since the pianist often plays doubletime lines, witty quotes from other songs and occasional violent outbursts. In general the music is quite thoughtful and subtle with plenty of surprising ideas and unusual turns. Carmichael gets stiffed a bit (just two songs counting the "Stardust"-inspired "I Remember Hoagy") and a couple of numbers are departures from the theme (including "My Flower," "Never Let Me Go" and "Goodbye") but most of the melo-

dies come from the Ellington/Strayhorn songbook. Throughout, Ahmad Jamal (with the assistance of bassist Ephriam Wolfolk and drummer Arti Dixson) shows that he can sound relaxed, alert and swinging at the slowest of paces, making this a set deserving (and perhaps needing) several listens to fully appreciate. —*Scott Yanow*

The Essence of Ahmad Jamal, Pt. 1 / Oct. 30, 1994-Oct. 31, 1994 / Verve ✦✦✦✦✦
Mostly recorded in Paris, with two additional tracks from New York, this absorbing collection is a testament to the continuing ability of Ahmad Jamal to startle and engage jazz listeners who are tired of Tyner/Evans clones and want to hear something different. An equal mixture of standards and Jamal compositions, some of which move through several contrasting sections, this CD reaches its peaks when Jamal and company dive in and work around a single bass ostinato and a propulsive rhythm groove. Bassists James Cammack (Paris) and Jamil Nasser (New York) provide the former, drummer Idris Muhammad and percussionist Manolo Badrena are in charge of the latter, and a tough-sounding George Coleman turns up on tenor on the New York tracks. One fascinating quirk—Jamal seemed fixated upon Oliver Nelson's "Stolen Moments" at these sessions, for he quotes the tune several times on the album. These sessions were so fruitful that Verve was able to serve up a tasty second helping a year later. —*Richard S. Ginell*

Big Byrd: the Essence, Part 2 / May 13, 1997 / Verve ✦✦✦✦✦
The elements that made *The Essence Part One* such a success—bright, crisp, rhythmically alive piano work often revolving around a tense bass ostinato and propulsive percussion—are abundantly present on *Part Two*, which was drawn from the same Paris and New York sessions but released a year after its predecessor. In no way is this a collection of leftovers; the quality level is so high that one can only conclude that marketing considerations alone prevented *The Essence* from being issued as a double album in the first place. Jamal fields two trios, anchored on bass by James Cammack in the Paris sessions and former colleague Jamil Nasser in the New York ones and by drummer Idris Muhammad on both. Everyone gets an extra jolt of momentum whenever the Afro-Latin percussion of Manolo Badrena goes into action, and violinist Joe Kennedy Jr. adds a potent, slightly raw-edged solo voice to "Manhattan Reflections." A muted, skittering Donald Byrd appears only on the title track—hence its name—which winds its way through several tempo changes and dramatically charged sections over a vast 15-minute timespan. Into his mid-60s, Jamal remained as distinctive and inventive a pianist as ever, with delightful surprises lurking around every bend. —*Richard S. Ginell*

Khan Jamal

b. Jul. 23, 1946, Jacksonville, FL
Vibes / Post-Bop, Avant-Garde
A talented if underrated vibraphonist, Khan Jamal took up the vibes in 1964 and worked early on with the Cosmic Forces and with Byard Lancaster. After further study, Jamal played with Sunny Murray in the late '70s and in the 1980s was with Ronald Shannon Jackson's Decoding Society, the bands of Joe Bonner and Billy Bang and his own groups. He has led sessions for Philly Jazz, Stash, Gazell/Storyville and most notably Steeple Chase. —*Scott Yanow*

Infinity / Dec. 7, 1982-Mar. 14, 1984 / Stash ✦✦✦✦
Although Khan Jamal is an advanced improviser, the sound of his vibes always gives his music a somewhat mellow and accessible air, even when he is at his most adventurous. This Stash LP (three of the five selections have been reissued on the CD *Don't Take No*) matches Jamal with altoist Byard Lancaster (doubling on flute), a Philadelphia-based rhythm section and, on "Infinity" (which dates from 1984), a group that includes Clifton Burton on harmonica and the legendary free drummer Sunny Murray. Jamal contributed four of the five songs, while pianist Bernard Sammul brought in a cooking "The Angry Young Man." Excellent and generally overlooked music. —*Scott Yanow*

Dark Warrior / Sep. 30, 1984 / Steeple Chase ✦✦✦✦
One of the best of vibraphonist Khan Jamal's Steeple Chase albums, this set matches Jamal with the great Charles Tyler (doubling on alto and baritone), the always lyrical bassist Johnny Dyani, and drummer Leroy Lowe. Together they interpret six of Jamal's originals (plus Tyler's "Space Traveller," which was dedicated to Sun Ra), performing colorful inside/outside music full of surprises and variety. —*Scott Yanow*

Three / Oct. 1984 / Steeple Chase ✦✦✦✦
As adventurous as this music sometimes is, the strong lyricism and the attractive sound of the trio (consisting of vibraphonist Khan Jamal, guitarist Pierre Dorge and bassist Johnny Dyani) make the performances fairly accessible. Jamal has long had original styles on vibes and marimba, and he is in top form on four of his songs (including one called "Tjader"), three by Dyani, and Dorge's "Lilli Goes to Town." —*Scott Yanow*

The Traveller / Oct. 31, 1985 / Steeple Chase ✦✦✦✦
Although with its sparse instrumentation (vibraphonist Khan Jamal, bassist Johnny Dyani and drummer Leroy Lowe), this 1985 set may not seem to offer listeners much variety, the wide range of compositions (including Jamal's "Thelonious" and inventive versions of "Equinox" and "Body and Soul") results in the music exceeding expectations. The interplay and constant chance-taking of the players are also major pluses. —*Scott Yanow*

Thinking of You / Oct. 1986 / Storyville ✦✦✦
Vibraphonist Khan Jamal, who sometimes also overdubs on marimba, had a reunion with multireedist Byard Lancaster (heard here on alto, flute, clarinet and bass clarinet) on this intriguing Storyville release. Joined by a frequently heated rhythm section (keyboardist Oliver Collins, thunderous electric bassist Jamaaladeen Tacuma, drummer Billy Hart and percussionist Omar Hill), Jamal performs music that ranges from African-oriented folk songs and the gospelish "Sweet Brown Flower" to Duke Ellington's "In a Sentimental Mood." —*Scott Yanow*

Speak Easy / Sep. 2, 1988 / Gazell ✦✦✦

● **Don't Take No** / Dec. 7, 1982-1989 / Vintage Jazz ✦✦✦✦✦

Bob James

b. Dec. 25, 1939, Marshall, MO
Composer, Arranger, Keyboards / Instrumental Pop, Crossover Jazz, Pop Jazz, Electronic, Avant-Garde
Bob James' recordings have practically defined pop jazz and crossover during the past two decades. Very influenced by pop and movie music, James has often featured R&Bish soloists (most notably Grover Washington, Jr.) who add a jazz touch to what is essentially an instrumental pop set. He actually started out music going in a much different direction. In 1962 Bob James recorded a boppish trio set for Mercury and three years later his album for ESP was quite avant-garde, with electronic tapes used for effects. After a period with Sarah Vaughan (1965-68), he became a studio musician and by 1973 was arranging and working as a producer for CTI. In 1974 James recorded his first purely commercial effort as a leader; he later made big-selling albums for his own Tappan Zee label, Columbia and Warner Bros. including collborations with Earl Klugh and David Sanborn. Listeners who prefer challenging jazz to background dance music will be consistently disappointed by Bob James' post-1965 albums. —*Scott Yanow*

Bold Conceptions / Aug. 13, 1962-Aug. 15, 1962 / Mercury ✦✦✦

Explosions / May 10, 1965 / ESP ✦✦✦
This is a particularly strange release (reissued on CD by ESP). Bob James, nine years before he found his commercial formula and three years after he recorded a fairly straightahead trio date, performs five very avant-garde numbers. Joined by bassist Barre Phillips and drummer Robert Pozar, James plays well enough in this setting, but his use of electronics and distorted tapes are quite distracting and make a large part of the performances barely listenable. —*Scott Yanow*

One / Apr. 1974 / Columbia ✦✦✦
Bob James' first recording for his Tappan Zee label, which has been reissued on CD along with virtually James' entire output by Warner Bros., is typically lightweight. Although Grover Washington, Jr., has two spots on soprano and trumpeter Jon Faddis is in the brass section, James' dated Fender Rhodes keyboard is the lead voice throughout the six pieces, which include two adaptations of classical works. Only a lightly funky version of "Feel Like Making Love" rises above the level of pleasant background music. —*Scott Yanow*

Two / 1975 / Columbia ✦✦
Bob James largely defined pop jazz crossover in the 1970s. This CD, reissued by Warner Brothers, is typical of his output. Mixing together aspects of pop, R&B and classical with just a touch of jazz, James (heard throughout on electric keyboards) put the emphasis on catchy melodies and lightly funky rhythms. The results range from insipid to pleasant, with a brass section, a string section and vocalists (including Patti Austin) utilized to create what is essentially background music. —*Scott Yanow*

Three / 1976 / Columbia ✦✦
Virtually all of keyboardist/arranger Bob James' Tappan Zee catalog has been reissued by Warner Bros. on CD. Unfortunately, the lightweight crossover music has not dated well. James' keyboards often sound gimmicky, the arrangements are danceable but mundane, and, despite two spots for Grover Washington, Jr.'s tenor, little of significance occurs. —*Scott Yanow*

Four / 1977 / CTI ✦✦

Ivory Coast / 1977 / Tappan Zee ✦✦
Psuedo-African flavor does little to bolster standard fuzak. —*Ron Wynn*

Heads / 1977 / Warner Brothers/Tappan Zee ✦✦✦
Ironically, the more clichéd and boring Bob James' albums became, the more they sold. Fluff-oriented dates like *BJ4* were major hits in the steadily growing "quiet storm" market, and the keyboardist wasn't about to tamper with the formula he had perfected. With the calculated *Heads*, he once again threw creativity and artistic integrity to the wind and gave his audience exactly what he thought it wanted: lightweight, innocuous pop jazz that functioned primarily as background music. The talents of Grover Washington, Jr. (tenor and soprano sax) and David Sanborn (alto sax) are wasted on the schlocky and the forgettable. —*Alex Henderson*

Lucky Seven / 1979 / Warner Brothers/Tappan Zee ✦✦✦✦
Successful fusion album by a superstar in the genre. James made an art form of short solos, pop-tinged instrumentals, multitracked vocals by guest stars, and unchallenging tracks. This album utilized all those elements. —*Ron Wynn*

Sign of the Times / 1979 / Warner Brothers/Tappan Zee ✦✦✦
With *Sign of the Times*, Bob James, who had done so much to define so-called "smooth jazz," gave his audience yet another dose of the type of pop/R&B/jazz fluff he'd been successful with. Consistently boring and mindless, the album has all of the things one expects from a Bob James LP–dull arrangements, forgettable melodies and robotic background vocals. —*Alex Henderson*

Touchdown / 1979 / Warner Brothers/Tappan Zee ✦✦✦
Playing uninspired background "muzak" had brought Bob James commercial success, and financially, he certainly had no incentive to change. Despite employing such talent as David Sanborn (alto sax), Hubert Laws (flute), Ron Carter (bass) and Idris Muhammad (drums), *Touchdown* is a bland throwaway. Overproduction is the rule here, and their talents are largely smothered by James' excessive production and trite arrangements. This CD does contain James' likeable "Angela (Theme from Taxi')," but most of the songs on *Touchdown* are pure schlock. —*Alex Henderson*

Double Vision / 1986 / Warner Brothers ✦✦✦✦
This combination works quite well. Poppish keyboardist/arranger Bob James joins with electric bassist Marcus Miller, drummer Steve Gadd, guitarist Paul Jackson, percussionist Paulinho Da Costa and (on two songs) guitarist Eric Gale to accompany the distinctive and always soulful altoist David Sanborn. Sanborn caresses the strong melodies, mostly originals by James and Miller, and plays well with guest vocalist Al Jarreau on "Since I Fell for You." One of the best recordings ever released under Bob James' name (Sanborn gets co-billing) and a big seller. —*Scott Yanow*

Obsession / 1987 / Tappan Zee ✦✦
Date that kept James streak of popular, vapid releases going. —*Ron Wynn*

Grand Piano Canyon / 1990 / Warner Brothers ✦✦✦✦
This CD is more jazz-oriented than most of Bob James' recordings and even takes chances in a few spots. The tunes, mostly by James, contain several strong melodies, including a tribute piece for Sarah Vaughan; among the sidemen are guitarist Lee Ritenour, Kirk Whalum on tenor and soprano, and (in a guest spot) tenor great Michael Brecker. The results overall are still poppish in places, but the diverse instrumentation, which changes from song to song, and the wide range of moods covered make this release of some interest. —*Scott Yanow*

● **Straight Up** / Dec. 20, 1995-Dec. 21, 1995 / Warner Brothers ✦✦✦✦✦
This record is an unexpected treat. Bob James has had a lucrative career writing and playing crossover pop jazz. Although he had actually started his career with a straightahead trio date for Mercury in 1962 and also led a bizarre avant-garde session for ESP in 1965, his career since 1974 has offered very little of interest to consumers who prefer to hear inventive jazz as opposed to pleasant background music. But for this session Bob James returned to the roots then knew he had. Playing in an acoustic trio with bassist Christian McBride and drummer Brian Blade, James contributes five straightforward originals in addition to the standard "Lost April" and interprets tunes by Pat Metheny/Lyle Mays, Horace Silver ("The Jody Grind") and Denny Zeitlin. James plays quite well, takes plenty of chances and sounds influenced a bit by Bill Evans while not hinting at all at his usual pop material. With McBride and Blade contributing consistently stimulating interplay, Bob James has recorded what is certainly the finest jazz album of his career. —*Scott Yanow*

Joined at the Hip / 1996 / Warner Brothers ✦✦✦

Playin' Hooky / 1997 / Warner Brothers ✦✦
Through the years, keyboardist/arranger Bob James has come to symbolize lightweight jazz, performing music that mixes safe, funky rhythms with forgettable melodies and fairly basic improvising. The commercial formula has worked quite well sales-wise, although few of the recordings have stood the test of time very well. This set is in a similar vein, often featuring top studio players sounding quite anonymous. Most of the tunes are James' originals, although there is also a timid exploration of a Chopin melody. Rasheeda displays a sweet and sensuous vocal on the

Gershwin's "Do It Again," but it is undercut by some really dumb, monotonous rhythms. Otherwise, although there are guest spots for the tenor of Boney James and vibraphonist Dave Samuels, nothing much happens. Strictly background music devoid of much beyond "hooks." —*Scott Yanow*

Boney James

b. MA
Soprano Saxophone, Tenor Saxophone / Crossover Jazz, Instrumental Pop
Born in Massachusetts but raised in New York and Los Angeles, Boney James studied clarinet and saxophone in school. After graduation, he worked with several bands and contributed sax, clarinet, keyboards and flute on session and live dates for Morris Day, Ray Parker, Jr., and the Isley Brothers. James' first solo album, *Trust*, appeared on Spindletop Records (it was later re-released by Warner). His next, *Backbone*, reached number five on the contemporary jazz charts. *Seduction* appeared in 1995, followed by *Boney's Funky Christmas* in 1996. —*John Bush*

Trust / 1992 / Spindletop ✦✦✦

● **Backbone** / 1993 / Warner Brothers ✦✦✦✦
Saxophonist Boney James has yet to develop his own musical personality. On this set of obvious dance tracks, James does his best to imitate Grover Washington, Jr., both on tenor and soprano. The material is routine, his backing musicians sound faceless and anonymous, and James does little to uplift the music. Even in the pop music world, Boney James' lack of individuality (if it continues) might eventually cause a problem. —*Scott Yanow*

Seduction / 1995 / Warner Brothers ✦✦✦

Boney's Funky Christmas / 1996 / Warner Brothers ✦✦✦
Working with producer Paul Brown, Boney James' *Boney's Funky Christmas* is an entertaining set of loose, funky and bluesy interpretations of both classic Christmas carols ("The Christmas Song") and more obscure contemporary selections like "A Charlie Brown Christmas" and Donny Hathaway's "This Christmas." Two selections, "This Christmas" and "What Are You Doing New Year's Eve?," are sung by Dee Harvey and Boby Caldwell, respectively, but the star of this show remains Brown and his saxophone, who breathe new life into these holiday cuts. —*Thom Owens*

Sweet Thing / 1997 / Warner Brothers ✦✦✦✦
Although influenced by Grover Washington, Jr., Boney James' own musical personality pops through on his reeds (soprano, alto and tenor) during this R&B-ish dance date. The music is frankly commercial but well played, with some catchy tunes and strong musicianship uplifting the set a bit. Boney James is the main soloist throughout, with Al Jarreau dropping by to sing "I Still Dream." —*Scott Yanow*

Harry James

b. Mar. 15, 1916, Albany, GA, **d.** Jul. 5, 1983, Las Vegas, NV
Trumpet, Leader / Swing
Harry James was the most famous trumpeter of the swing era and his big band was the most popular in the world during 1942-46 (after Glenn Miller went in the Army). A household name even today, James was a talented player with a wide range and impressive technique whose heart was always in jazz even when playing schmaltzy versions of pop melodies or flashy versions of classical themes.

James gained early experience working with his father's circus band, building up his endurance and technique. After playing locally, he made his recording debut while with Ben Pollack's big band (1935-36). Harry James was a star from the time he first joined Benny Goodman's Orchestra (1937-39) and he greatly overshadowed the band's former soloist Ziggy Elman. He had a few record sessions of his own while still with BG and when he formed his own big band in 1939 it was with Goodman's blessing.

The Harry James Orchestra struggled for a time but in 1941 they had their first huge hit with an instrumental version of "You Made Me Love You." Other big sellers followed including "Strictly Instrumental," "Sleepy Lagoon," "I'll Get By," "I Had the Craziest Dream" (one of many Helen Forrest vocals) and the classic "It's Been a Long, Long Time"; James' repertoire also always included his theme "Ciribiribin" and "Two O'Clock Jump." A celebrity who had speaking parts in several movies, Harry James married Betty Grable, added a string section to his band for a few years and was flying high. Even with the end of the big-band era, James was able to keep his orchestra together (although he dropped the strings after 1947). With altoist Willie Smith and tenor saxophonist Corky Corcoran as key soloists, James' postwar bands played a large share of jazz and there was even a period in the late '40s when James sounded open to bop; his solo on "Tuxedo Junction" in 1947 shows that he was well aware of Dizzy Gillespie.

Despite such drummers as Louis Bellson and Buddy Rich, by the 1950s Harry James seemed happy to have his band sound like Count Basie's (helped out by

Ernie Wilkins' arrangements) and to often revisit the past. He remained a popular attraction into the early '80s but failed to advance any further. Perhaps he did not really need to, for no one played Harry James' music better than Harry James! Far too few of his prime Columbia recordings (1941-55) have been reissued on CD. —*Scott Yanow*

1937-1939 / Dec. 1, 1937-Mar. 6, 1939 / Classics ✦✦✦✦✦

Trumpeter Harry James was very consistent in his musical tastes throughout his career. This CD, which has the first 22 selections that James recorded as a leader, starts off with eight numbers in which the trumpeter (still a Benny Goodman sideman at the time) uses many of Count Basie's top sidemen (including trombonist-arranger Eddie Durham, tenor saxophonist Herschel Evans and singer Helen Humes) for swinging performances highlighted by "Life Goes to a Party" and "One O'Clock Jump"; James' bands (particularly from the 1950s on) would often sound like a duplicate of Basie's. In addition, this CD has four tunes from 1938 in which James mostly uses Goodman players (plus baritonist Harry Carney), and he is also heard on the first six numbers by his big band (including "Two O'Clock Jump" and his earliest recording of his theme "Ciribiribin"). However, the hottest performances are four numbers in which James is backed by a boogie-woogie trio featuring either Pete Johnson or Albert Ammons on piano. This enjoyable CD is full of many examples of James' hot swing trumpet and is easily recommended to swing fans. —*Scott Yanow*

And His Great Vocalists / Jan. 5, 1938-May 12, 1952 / Columbia/Legacy ✦✦✦✦

This CD puts the emphasis on Harry James' vocal hits. Such fine singers as Dick Haymes, Helen Forrest, Helen Humes, Kitty Kallen, Art Lund, Rosemary Clooney and even Willie Smith and Betty Grable (among others) are heard from. Among the more famous recordings are "I'll Get By," "I Don't Want to Walk Without You," "I Had the Craziest Dream," "I've Heard That Song Before" and "It's Been a Long Long Time." There are some spots for James' trumpet on these popular numbers but the jazz content is not that strong. When is Columbia going to do a much more complete reissue of Harry James valuable recordings? —*Scott Yanow*

Bandstand Memories: 1938 to 1948 / Apr. 2, 1938-Nov. 30, 1948 / Hindsight ✦✦✦✦✦

This very interesting three-CD set features trumpeter Harry James' Orchestra on a variety of previously unreleased radio broadcast performances. While there are many vocals from Frank Sinatra (in his pre-Tommy Dorsey days), Helen Forrest and Kitty Kallen, it is the instrumentals that are of greatest interest, particularly the earliest tracks which date from the period before James really hit it big. Many of these songs were not recorded commercially by the trumpeter and this strong jazz-oriented set is highly recommended to swing fans. —*Scott Yanow*

The Best of the Big Bands / Feb. 20, 1939-Nov. 13, 1946 / Columbia ✦✦✦

This is very much a hodge-podge set that does not live up to its clichéd title. The recording dates and personnel listing are not included in the chatty liner notes and, although there is some excellent music here (including "Strictly Instrumental," "I Had the Craziest Dream," "You Made Me Love You," "It's Been a Long Long Time" and "Ciribiribin") the programming is not in chronological order and almost seems random. Why hasn't Columbia ever released their many enjoyable and valuable Harry James recordings in complete and coherent fashion? —*Scott Yanow*

Harry James' Greatest Hits / Feb. 20, 1939-Nov. 13, 1946 / Columbia ✦✦✦✦

This sampler LP justifies its name, reissuing 11 popular numbers by Harry James. All of the music has since reappeared on CD but, if found at a good price, this is worth picking up. Most of the hits are here including "Ciribiribin," "You Made Me Love You," "Two O'Clock Jump," "Cherry," "I'll Get By" and "It's Been a Long, Long Time." —*Scott Yanow*

All or Nothing at All / Mar. 28, 1939-Nov. 9, 1939 / Hindsight ✦✦✦

This 17-track, 53-and-a-half-minute disc of air checks chronicles the first year of the Harry James band, when a 23-year-old Frank Sinatra was its featured male vocalist. Sinatra is heard on nine tracks, eight of which are also heard in their studio versions on Legacy/Columbia's *The Complete Recordings*, also released on CD in 1995, and thus make an interesting contrast. The title track, which was the biggest song James and Sinatra enjoyed (albeit not until years later), was even recorded on the same day (Aug. 31, 1939) in the studio for Columbia and at the World's Fair in Flushing, NY, for radio. The set includes one song, "Let's Disappear," that James and Sinatra did not cut for Columbia. Sinatra sounds typically assured, and the arrangements lean more to the "hot" side of swing than those of Tommy Dorsey on which Sinatra would be featured from 1940 to 1942. Eight songs are James band instrumentals, including their theme, "Ciribirin," and such standards as "Avalon" and "Sweet Georgia Brown." Led by James' bravura playing, the orchestra is in fine form, belying their relative lack of success during this period. —*William Ruhlmann*

1939 / Apr. 6, 1939-Oct. 13, 1939 / Classics ✦✦✦✦

The second Harry James CD put out by the Classics label, this set traces the trumpeter's recording career during a six-month period when his big band was struggling financially. It is surprising that James did not catch on immediately, considering how popular he had been with Benny Goodman and since his band at the time was fairly good. Other than the leader, there were no major soloists in the orchestra (altoist Dave Matthews was perhaps best-known), but the arrangements for the instrumentals (including "Indiana," "I Found a New Baby," a surprisingly cooking "Willow Weep for Me" and "Feet Draggin' Blues") were excellent. A little over half of the 23 selections on this reissue have vocals (eight are Frank Sinatra's first appearances on record, including the minor hit "All or Nothing at All"), but the high points are an interesting, unreleased version of "Flash" and "Sleepy Time Gal," which showcases James with just the rhythm section. Recommended for swing fans bored with the usual Harry James greatest-hits sets. —*Scott Yanow*

The Unheard Harry James / Jul. 13, 1939-Feb. 24, 1942 / Blu-Disc ✦✦✦✦

This hard-to-find collector's LP has 16 previously unreleased studio recordings by Harry James with his orchestra (mostly "new" alternate takes). Highlights include a stomping version of "Willow Weep for Me," "Jeffrie's Blues," "Sharp as a Tack," two versions of "Record Session," "B-19" and "Crazy Rhythm." The music is from 1939 and 1941-42 and puts the emphasis on swing although there are a few vocals from Frank Sinatra, Jack Palmer and Dick Haymes. This will be a difficult record to locate but Harry James fanatics will certainly enjoy it. —*Scott Yanow*

The Young Harry James / Oct. 27, 1939-Dec. 13, 1941 / Jazz Archives ✦✦✦✦

Harry James is featured in the early days of his bandleading career (1939 and 1941) on this collector's LP of radio broadcasts. There are five titles from 1939 including a pair of Frank Sinatra vocals and versions of "Flash" and "Two O'Clock Jump." James is showcased in 1941 with the "Chamber Music Society of Lower Basin Street" showing off his technique on Chopin's "Waltz in 'C' Sharp Minor" and swinging hard on "Jeffries' Blues." The second half of this album is highlighted by hot versions of "Flying Home," "Honeysuckle Rose" and "Rose Room"; in addition, Helen Forrest has three vocals. The music on this 1976 LP will hopefully show up on CD eventually for it finds the young trumpeter in prime form. —*Scott Yanow*

● **First-Team Player on the Jazz Varsity** / Feb. 12, 1940-Aug. 12, 1940 / Savoy ✦✦✦✦✦

This perfectly done two-LP set (which should be reissued in full on CD) was put out by Muse on their Savoy subsidiary in 1987. Included are all 31 of the recordings that Harry James and his orchestra recorded for the Varsity label during 1940; if only Columbia had treated their recordings by the great swing trumpeter with as much wisdom. Recorded just prior to when James' Orchestra caught on (it would be the most popular in the world during 1942-45), these sessions have short solos from altoist Dave Matthews, Vido Musso on tenor and pianist Jack Gardner along with vocals from Dick Haymes but one's attention is consistently grabbed by the full ensemble and particularly James' colorful trumpet. Highly recommended if it can be found. —*Scott Yanow*

Harry James & His Orchestra / Mar. 19, 1940+May 22, 1941 / Sunbeam ✦✦✦

This LP from the collector's label Sunbeam features the Harry James Orchestra in two separate radio broadcasts. Although there are some straightforward vocals (three from Dick Haymes and one by Jack Palmer), the emphasis is on jazz and Harry James' trumpet; the lack of a personnel listing is rather unfortunate. Highlights include "Tuxedo junction," "Carnival of Venice," "Cherry" and "Jeffries' Blues." —*Scott Yanow*

Sharp as a Tack / Jun. 18, 1940-Dec. 1953 / Swing Era ✦✦✦✦

Since Columbia has never put out a complete chronological study of Harry James, one has to rely on collections such as this LP to at least gain some of the trumpeter's valuable big-band performances. Sixteen of James' records (dating from 1940-53 and not programmed in chronological order) put an emphasis on the trumpeter's jazz output. Only one song has a vocal and four utilize a string section. Such swinging obscurities as "Prince Charming," "Sharp as a Tack," "Ya Better Stop" and "Circus Days" among many others make this an LP well worth picking up, at least until Columbia starts reissuing this underrated music on CD. —*Scott Yanow*

All the Way / May 1941-Dec. 1954 / Big Band Archives ✦✦✦✦

With the exception of 1941's "Jughead," all of the music on this double-LP is from 1945-48 and 1951-54. A few live appearances mix in with studio recordings and all 29 numbers emphasize the jazz side of Harry James' big band performances; there are no vocals. Among the sidemen are tenorman Vido Musso, altoist Willie Smith, Corky Corcoran on tenor, trombonist Ziggy Elmer and pianists Arnold Ross and Bruce McDonald. Few of these recordings have appeared on CD yet and this collectors' two-fer might be available at a budget price; get it. Highlights include "The Great Lie," "East Coast Blues," the two-part "Moten Swing," "In a Mist" and an extended "King Porter Stomp." —*Scott Yanow*

Harry James and Dick Haymes / 1941 / Circle ◆◆◆

The Uncollected Harry James & His Orchestra, Vol. 1 (1943-1946) / 1943-1946 / Hindsight ◆◆◆◆

The first of six LPs released by Hindsight that make available previously unknown performances from Harry James' Orchestra (mostly from radio airchecks), this set (as with the other five) is easily recommended to swing fans. The 16 numbers span a three-year period and, although the exact recording dates are not given (and probably not known) there is an extensive "probable collective personnel" listing. Helen Forrest has four vocals and the obscure "Songmakers" (which includes Forrest) sings "Between the Devil & the Deep Blue Sea" but otherwise the program comprises instrumentals. The fine set has among its highlights "Indiana," "Body and Soul," "All of Me," "Shorty George" and "Girl of My Dreams." —*Scott Yanow*

The Uncollected Harry James & His Orchestra, Vol. 2 (1943-1946) / 1943-1946 / Hindsight ◆◆◆◆

The second of six Hindsight LPs of Harry James radio transcriptions covers the same period as the first. A special treat of the set is that Helen Ward has four vocals. In addition to the leader/trumpeter (who is in excellent form) there are features for clarinetist Eddie Rosa ("Exactly like You") and pianist Arnold Ross ("How High the Moon") and solo space for altoist Willie Smith and tenorman Corky Corcoran. An excellent set with some of the more memorable numbers including "Blue Turning Grey over You," "G-Flat Special," "Blue Lou" and "I've Found a New Baby." —*Scott Yanow*

The Uncollected Harry James & His Orchestra, Vol. 4 (1943-1946) / 1943-1946 / Hindsight ◆◆◆◆

The fourth of six LPs of Harry James radio appearances put out by Hindsight, this set (as with volumes one and two) covers the war years when James' big band was the most popular in the land. The 16 performances show that, although he had hits with many pop and vocal numbers, James was a particularly strong trumpeter who emphasized jazz in his live sets. Buddy Di Vito and Helen Forrest have two vocals apiece, there are individual features and shorter solos for altoist Willie Smith and the tenor of Corky Corcoran, and Allen Reuss has a rare electric guitar solo on "Honeysuckle Rose." James is in typically exciting form and among the more memorable selections on this program are "Easy Street," "It Must Be Jelly," "Peg of My Heart" and "Mr. Coed." All six entries in the series are easily recommended to swing fans. —*Scott Yanow*

The Uncollected Harry James & His Orchestra, Vol. 5 (1943-1953) / 1943-1953 / Hindsight ◆◆◆◆

The fifth of six LPs of radio performances by Harry James' Orchestra features his big band during three different periods. The first eight numbers (including such songs as "If I Had You," "What Is This Thing Called Love" and "Blue Skies") is from the 1943-46 era when James was at the height of his popularity. Helen Forrest and Buddy Di Vito have a vocal apiece and there are individual features for Willie Smith and Corky Corcoran. There are also seven selections from 1948-49 that are sometimes bop-oriented; singers Gilda Macon and guest Johnny Mercer ("Sugar Blues") are heard on one tune apiece. This fine LP wraps up with a 1953 rendition of "Don't Get Around Much Anymore." All six of the albums in the series are easily recommended to swing collectors. —*Scott Yanow*

★ **Snooty Fruity** / Nov. 21, 1944-Feb. 15, 1955 / Columbia ◆◆◆◆◆

Although altoist Willie Smith is strangely enough given top billing, all 18 selections in this CD actually feature the great swing trumpeter Harry James and his popular bands (of which Smith was a key sideman). Many of James' most exciting jazz performances are on this set including the extended "Tuxedo Junction," "Moten Swing," the "New Two O'Clock Jump," "The Great Lie" and "Stompin' at the Savoy." This essential CD is especially recommended to detractors who think that Harry James was overrated. —*Scott Yanow*

The Uncollected Harry James & His Orchestra, Vol. 6 (1947-1949) / 1947-1949 / Hindsight ◆◆◆◆

During the era covered by this LP (along with *Vol. 4* in the valuable Hindsight series), Harry James' Orchestra and the leader himself were open to the influence of bebop. The arrangements by Ray Conniff, Jimmy Mundy, Neal Hefti, Johnny Richards are generally quite modern and there are many strong solos from the likes of the trumpeter/leader, trombonist Ziggy Elmer, altoist Willie Smith, Corky Corcoran on tenor, clarinetist Eddie Rosa and pianist Bruce MacDonald. Recommended. —*Scott Yanow*

1948-1949 / 1948-1949 / Big Band Landmarks ◆◆◆◆

Few would think of 1948-49 as being Harry James' best period, for his popularity had peaked by 1945 and bop had surpassed swing. However, James was surprisingly open to the influence of bop, he had dropped his string section and vocalists and a variety of modern arrangements (by Neal Hefti, Frank Devenport, Johnny Richards and Jimmy Mundy) often inspired his musicians. With trombonist Ziggy Elmer, altoist Willie Smith, Corky Corcoran on tenor, clarinetist Eddie Rosa and pianist James in peak form, this double LP (which contains rarely heard performances) is highly recommended to big band collectors, even with its lack of liner notes. —*Scott Yanow*

The Uncollected Harry James & His Orchestra, Vol. 3 (1948-1949) / 1948-1949 / Hindsight ◆◆◆◆

Of the six Harry James LPs released by Hindsight in their very interesting series of radio performances, this volume is the most unusual. During the 1948-49 era, the trumpeter/leader and his band were somewhat influenced by bebop (even when playing swing standards) and they had their own sound before slipping back into nostalgia in the 1950s. As usual, the main soloists (along with James) are trombonist Ziggy Elmer, altoist Willie Smith and tenor saxophonist Corky Corcoran along with clarinetist Eddie Rosa and pianist Bruce MacDonald. With modern arrangements provided by Neal Hefti, Johnny Richards and Frank Devenport, the Harry James Orchestra sounds in peak form throughout this highly recommended set. —*Scott Yanow*

One Night Stand / Oct. 25, 1952 / Columbia ◆◆◆

This long out-of-print LP (Columbia has yet to reissue more than a small percentage of its many Harry James recordings) is a jazz-oriented date featuring the trumpeter's 1952 big band. Other than tenor saxophonist Herbie Steward (who is well-featured) there are no major names here among James' sidemen (both altoist Willie Smith and tenorman Corky Corcoran are not on the album) but the music is generally quite enjoyable and swinging. James runs through a colorful version of "The Flight of the Bumble Bee" (with guest accordionist Tommy Gumina) and other highlights include "Memphis Blues," "There They Go," "Feet Draggin' Blues" and "Back Beat Boogie." Not every selection is a classic (there are a couple of throwaways) but this is an album worth picking up, if one is fortunate enough to run across it. —*Scott Yanow*

Swingin' 'n Sweet / 1953-1954 / Giants of Jazz ◆◆◆◆

This is the first of two Giants of Jazz LPs that feature trumpeter Harry James heading an octet rather than his customary big band. Among the sidemen are Herbie Steward on tenor, altoist Willie Smith, valve trombonist Juan Tizol and drummer Buddy Rich. The high points of this enjoyable swing set include "Perdido," "Honeysuckle Rose," "Stardust," "Roll 'Em" and "The Great Lie"; in addition, Rich takes two spirited vocals. This album is worth searching for as is its companion *Saturday Night Swing.* —*Scott Yanow*

Saturday Night Swing / Dec. 1953-Jan. 1954 / Giants of Jazz ◆◆◆◆

This is the second of two Giants of Jazz LPs featuring the Harry James Octet (a small group taken out of the trumpeter's big band) during 1953-54. This setting gave James and his all-stars an opportunity to stretch out a bit. Altoist Willie Smith, tenor saxophonist Herbie Steward and valve trombonist Juan Tizol (featured on "Caravan") get to co-star and drummer Buddy Rich sings "Bewitched, Bothered and Bewildered" quite effectively. An excellent small-group swing outing well-deserving of being reissued on CD; Harry James should have done more. —*Scott Yanow*

1954 / Feb. 18, 1954 / Circle ◆◆◆

Quite a few recordings of Harry James from the mid-'50s have been released through the years. This Circle LP alternates heated swing with nostalgia, instrumentals with Paula Gilbert vocals. Certainly nothing much is added by the release of these versions of "Cherry" and "Sleepy Lagoon" but the leader/trumpeter does take some good solos on "Palladium Party" and "Sugar Foot Stomp." Not essential but a worthwhile acquisition for swing fans. —*Scott Yanow*

Trumpet Blues / Mar. 1955-Apr. 1955 / Drive Archive ◆◆◆

This CD contains previously unreleased performances from Harry James' Orchestra caught live (in stereo) at the Hollywood Palladium in 1955. No real surprises occur but the trumpeter/bandleader is in good form on his usual repertoire with highlights including "Roll 'Em," "Don't Be That Way," "Trumpet Blues" and "You Made Me Love You." —*Scott Yanow*

Harry James in Hi-Fi / Jul. 20, 1955-Jul. 25, 1955 / Capitol ◆◆

More Harry James in Hi-Fi / Nov. 1955-Jan. 1956 / Pausa ◆◆

The emphasis is on recreations of Harry James hits of a decade earlier on this Pausa LP (a reissue of a set originally released by Capitol). Although some of the charts were updated and there are some short solos by altoist Willie Smith and Corky Corcoran on tenor, the results are very predictable. The string section weighs down the music a bit and these renditions of "The Mole," "Strictly Instrumental" and "Street Scene" add little to the earlier versions. A lesser effort. —*Scott Yanow*

Wild About Harry / May 1957 / Capitol ✦✦✦

By 1957, Harry James was in an artistic rut. Although he would occasionally try to come up with fresh material, he never did regain the stature he had in the 1940s. This Capitol LP mostly contains material arranged by Ernie Wilkins and the result is that the James band often sounds like Count Basie's. Buddy Rich's drumming helps uplift the band, altoist Willie Smith, tenorman Corky Corcoran and trombonist Herbie Harper have some good spots and James is in good form, but the music is not all that memorable. —*Scott Yanow*

Harry's Choice / Jun. 1958 / Capitol ✦✦✦

By 1958, Harry James was coasting. For this out-of-print Capitol LP, the trumpeter performs six veteran standards and two fairly basic Ernie Wilkins compositions. James is the main soloist, although there are spots for altoist Willie Smith, trombonist Ray Sims and pianist Jack Perciful. Not much surprising happens on tunes such as "Blues for Sale," "Moten Swing" and "The New Two O'Clock Jump" but swing fans may want to pick this one up if they run across it. —*Scott Yanow*

Verve Jazz Masters, Vol. 55 / 1959–Mar. 10, 1964 / Verve ✦✦✦✦

Although he has surprisingly few CDs currently available, Harry James remains one of the world's most famous trumpeters, more than a decade after his death. This Verve CD is a sampler of his MGM recordings of 1959-64 and, although the claim in the liner notes that this was James' most creative period is nonsense, he does sound versatile and in consistently fine form on the wide-ranging set. Whether it be swing standards, challenging charts by Ernie Wilkins and Ralph Burns (including two that were previously unissued) or a tribute to Louis Armstrong on "Cornet Chop Suey," James is in fine form. But why are all of his MGM records otherwise out-of-print? —*Scott Yanow*

The Spectacular Sound of Harry James / Jan. 19, 1961 / MGM ✦✦✦

This is one of trumpeter Harry James' better dates from the 1960s, an indifferent period for his recordings. He performs Charles Albertine's five-part "Blues Ballet" and five numbers arranged (and four composed) by Ernie Wilkins. Although the tenors of Sam Firmature and Modesto Briseno get to solo on "The Jazz Connoisseur," the emphasis is on the leader's trumpet and the full ensemble of the orchestra. The music swings but is not all that memorable despite James' temporary success at avoiding playing nostalgia and recreations. —*Scott Yanow*

Double Dixie / Jul. 20, 1962 / MGM ✦✦✦✦

The Golden Trumpet of Harry James / Apr. 1968 / London ✦✦✦

Some fine cuts from sessions on London. —*Ron Wynn*

Mr. Trumpet / Jan. 6, 1972–Jan. 8, 1972 / Hindsight ✦✦✦

Considering its opening number, a strong Dixielandish version of "The Sheik of Araby," this CD starts out quite promising but its extreme brevity (just 29 minutes) and some sticky muzaky strings on the ballads result in a lower rating. Trumpeter Harry James is in good form, whether it be on a relaxed "Indiana," a recreation of Benny Goodman's version of "Don't Be That Way" or a swinging "Hot Lips," but every song on this set would have benefited from being twice as long. —*Scott Yanow*

Comin' from a Good Place / Jul. 29, 1976–Jul. 30, 1976 / Sheffield Lab ✦✦✦

This CD reissues one of two direct-to-disc albums that Harry James recorded during a two-day period in 1976 including a pair of previously unreleased alternate takes ("More Splutie, Please" and "Sweet Georgia Brown") from the first LP (*The King James Version*). James plays well enough (although the trumpeter was no longer trying to hit high notes) but the charts (by the likes of Ernie Wilkins, Thad Jones and Bob Florence) offer no revelations and the sidemen (other than drummer Les DeMerle) do not stand out. "Watch What Happens" and "Make the World Go Away" are throwaways but "Moten Swing," "Tuxedo Junction" and "Blues for Sale" have their moments of interest. —*Scott Yanow*

The King James Version / Jul. 29, 1976–Jul. 30, 1976 / Sheffield Lab ✦✦✦

In late July 1976, trumpeter Harry James recorded enough music for two LPs. This particular set gives one a good sampling of his 1976 orchestra and finds James happy to emulate the swing sound of Count Basie. The arrangements, by Ernie Wilkins, Thad Jones, Ray Conniff, Dave Matthews, Rob Turk and Jimmy Haskell, lack any real surprises (other than the fact that James decided to record "Lara's Theme" from *Dr. Zhivago*), and the sidemen, other than drummer Les DeMerle, sound fairly anonymous. James was playing well enough this late in his career, but the solos, arrangements and material are quite routine and predictable. —*Scott Yanow*

Still Harry after All These Years / Mar. 26, 1979–Mar. 30, 1979 / Sheffield Lab ✦✦

This direct-to-disc session (reissued on CD) might have been veteran trumpeter Harry James' final recording. On the merely okay outing with his big band, James alternates swing era standards (such as "Caravan," "Roll 'Em" and "Take the 'A' Train") with forgettable attempts at interpreting new material (such as the theme from *Sanford and Son,* a disco tune called "Dance" and "Help Me Make It Through the Night"). This is not one of Harry James' more significant albums but

it is nice to know that 40 years after he started his first big band, he was still playing well. —*Scott Yanow*

Jon Jang

Piano / Avant-Garde

An important force in the San Francisco Bay Area with his Pan Asian Arkestra and small-group concerts, Jon Jang has had David Murray and James Newton among his sidemen. A leader in the Asian Improv movement (playing inside/outside music influenced by both Charles Mingus and his Chinese heritage), Jang has recorded stirring sets for the RPM (1982), AIR and Soul Note labels and composed adventurous and ambitious works. —*Scott Yanow*

Jang / Nov. 1979–1982 / RPM ✦✦✦✦

This early effort by pianist/composer Jon Jang (which unfortunately has not yet been reissued on CD) finds Jang's writing and conception a bit influenced by Charles Mingus, yet also full of references to his Chinese heritage. The main work, "Are You Chinese or Charlie Chan?/East Wind," is quite political and topical, yet timeless and very musical. The personnel differs on each number, with "Are You Chinese" having the largest group and other tunes including two duets and a trio. Among Jang's key sidemen are tenor saxophonist Francis Wong, baritonist Fred Houn, trumpeter George Sams, cellist Cash Killon, and Mark Izu on the sheng. Intriguing and colorful music. —*Scott Yanow*

Never Give Up! / 1989 / Asian Improv ✦✦✦✦✦

Pianist Jon Jang's Pan Asian Arkestra performs a variety of political works on this CD, including the four movements from his "Reparations Now" concerto, "Never Give Up" (dedicated to Jesse Jackson), and "Let Us Not Forget" (inspired by a speech about the concentration camps in the US during World War II.); they also play "A Night in Tunisia" and the "Butterfly Lovers Song." In addition to Jang, the key soloists in this adventurous yet often melodic set include bassist Mark Izu, Susan Hayase on taiko, tenor saxophonist Francis Wong and trumpeter John Worley. —*Scott Yanow*

Self Defense! / Jun. 21, 1991 / Soul Note ✦✦✦✦✦

Most of the selections on this CD (including "A Night in Tunisia," "Never Give Up," "Butterfly Lovers Song" and the four-part "Concerto for Jazz Ensemble and Taiko") had been recorded on pianist Jon Jang's previous *Never Give Up!* on the AsianImprov label. However, these renditions were cut live, and after two more years of familiarizing themselves with the music, Jang's Pan Asian Arkestera was able to perform versions that were generally superior to the earlier effort. Consisting of three reeds, trumpeter John Worley, trombonist Jeff Cressman, bassist Mark Izu, drummer Anthony Brown and Susan Hayase on taiko (a Japanese drum) along with the pianist/leader, the Arkestra displays a highly original sound, blending together advanced jazz with strong hints of traditional Chinese music. —*Scott Yanow*

Tianenmen! / Feb. 1993 / Soul Note ✦✦✦✦✦

After the Tianenmen Square slaughter in China, pianist Jon Jang wrote the five-part "Tianenmen" to depict the hopes and dreams of the demonstrators, along with the sad reality. This CD has the full work, plus "Butterfly Lovers Song." Jang's adventurous music, which looks both back to the ancient past and towards the future, is expertly interpreted by his unusual group, which includes two musicians utilizing traditional Chinese instruments, flutist James Newton, three reeds, a trumpeter, a trombonist, bassist Mark Izu, percussionist Anthony Brown, and Jang's piano. Emotional and haunting music. —*Scott Yanow*

● **Two Flowers on a Stem** / Jun. 8, 1995–Jun. 11, 1995 / Soul Note ✦✦✦✦✦

Pianist-composer Jon Jang has long created music that combines advanced jazz with aspects of his Chinese heritage. For this superb disc of inside/outside music, Jang utilizes a sextet also featuring the remarkable flutist James Newton, David Murray on tenor and bass clarinet, bassist Santi Debriano, drummer Billy Hart and Chen Jiebing on a haunting cello-like instrument called the erhu. Strong passionate melodies give way to straightahead jamming, free sections and other themes. As with Charles Mingus (one of his influences), Jang's pieces are sometimes quite political and his music often unfolds like an episodic suite. Performing Mingus' "Meditations on Integration," four Jang originals and "Butterfly Lovers Song," the sextet's many colorful voices somehow blend together as one in service to the consistently powerful music. This highly recommended set deserves and rewards repeated listenings. —*Scott Yanow*

Immigrant Suite, Number 1 / Oct. 13, 1995 / Soul Note ✦✦✦

Conrad Janis

b. Feb. 11, 1928, New York, NY

Trombone / Dixieland

An actor on television and films, Conrad Janis has always loved playing Dixieland trombone. His mother Harriet Janis worked closely with critic Rudi Blesh on the definitive book *They All Played Ragtime* and for the Circle label. Conrad Janis played guitar early on but was self-taught on trombone, which he did not start playing until he was already nearly 21. He gigged as a freelancer from the 1950s on between acting jobs, recording on an infrequent basis including early sets for Circle, London and Jubilee. Since the 1980s, Janis has been the leader of the popular Beverly Hills Unlimited Jazz Band. —*Scott Yanow*

● **Conrad Janis & His Tailgate Jazz Band** / Nov. 24, 1950 / GHB ✦✦✦✦

Joseph Jarman

b. Sep. 14, 1937, Pine Bluff, AR
Reeds / Avant-Garde, Free Jazz
A longtime member of the Art Ensemble of Chicago, Joseph Jarman's playing has always been adventurous and utterly unpredictable. He grew up in Chicago, played drums in high school and started on saxophones and clarinet while in the Army. He was in Muhal Richard Abrams' Experimental Band and in 1965 he joined the AACM. Jarman's first album as a leader, 1966's *Song For,* was a very radical statement with an unusual utilization of sound and silence. Although he would record occasional records as a leader for Delmark, India Navigation and Black Saint (including *The Magic Triangle* with Don Pullen and Don Moye), Jarman's main vehicle up until the mid-'90s (when he unofficially left the group) was the Art Ensemble of Chicago where his theatrical performances keep the music from ever getting too conservative or comfortable. —*Scott Yanow*

● **Song For** / Oct. 20, 1966-Dec. 16, 1966 / Delmark ✦✦✦✦✦
This was one of the early classics of the AACM. Altoist Joseph Jarman, who would become a permanent member of The Art Ensemble of Chicago shortly after this recording, is heard in a sextet with trumpeter William Brimfield, the legendary tenor Fred Anderson, pianist Christopher Gaddy, bassist Charles Clark and either Steve McCall or Thurman Barker on drums. The four very diverse improvisations include one that showcases a Jarman recitation, a dirge, the intense "Little Fox Run" and the title cut, which contrasts sounds and a creative use of silence. Overall, this music was the next step in jazz after the high-energy passions of the earlier wave of the avant-garde started to run out of fresh ideas. It's recommended for open-eared listeners. The 1996 CD reissue adds an alternate take of "Little Fox Run" to the original program. —*Scott Yanow*

As If It Were the Seasons / Jun. 19, 1968+Jul. 17, 1968 / Delmark ✦✦✦✦
This set is one of the legendary early AACM releases. Joseph Jarman (heard on alto, bassoon and soprano in addition to fife and recorder) is featured shortly before he became a member of the Art Ensemble of Chicago. Some of his sidemen would become well-known (pianist Richard Abrams, tenors Fred Anderson and John Stubblefield), while others remained obscure or short-lived (bassist Charles Clark, drummer Thurman Barker, flutist Joel Brandon, trumpeter John Jackson and trombonist Lester Lashley). The two lengthy group improvisations (Sherri Scott adds her voice to "Song for Christopher") contrast sound and silence, noise with more conventional sounds, "little instruments" with powerful saxophones. Certainly not for everyone's taste, the truly open-eared will find the innovative results quite intriguing. —*Scott Yanow*

Together Alone / Dec. 1971 / Delmark ✦✦✦
Joseph Jarman and Anthony Braxton play a wide variety of reeds on this duet session, really stretching their range of expressive sounds. The originals are split between the two musicians, but not a lot of magic or close communication occurs, and the improvisations tend to ramble. Overall, a slight disappointment considering the talents involved. —*Scott Yanow*

Egwu-Anwu / Jan. 8, 1978 / India Navigation ✦✦✦

Magic Triangle / Jul. 24, 1979-Jul. 26, 1979 / Black Saint ✦✦✦✦✦

Black Paladins / Dec. 1979 / Black Saint ✦✦✦✦✦

Earth Passage/Density / Feb. 16, 1981-Feb. 17, 1981 / Black Saint ✦✦✦✦
Four advanced improvisers team up to play complex and rather open-ended originals during this adventurous set. Joseph Jarman (on tenor, alto, soprano, piccolo, bass clarinet and various flutes), trombonist Craig Harris (also playing some flute and didgeridoo), bassist Rafael Garrett (heard a bit on clarinet, flute and percussion) and drummer/percussionist Don Moye all communicate very well and are flexible and able to make a great deal of music out of very little. The three-part "Zulu Village" is the highlight of the lesser-known release. —*Scott Yanow*

Calypso's Smile / Mar. 22, 1984+Dec. 1984 / AECO ✦✦✦✦

Connecting Spirits / Jan. 12, 1996 / Music & Arts ✦✦✦✦

Al Jarreau

b. Apr. 12, 1940, Milwaukee, WI
Vocals / R&B, Soft Rock
The only vocalist in history to net Grammy awards in three different categories (jazz, pop and R&B, respectively), Al Jarreau was born in Milwaukee, Wisconsin, on April 12, 1940; the son of a vicar, he earned his first performing experience singing in the church choir. After earning his Masters degree in psychology, Jarreau pursued a career as a social worker, but eventually he decided to relocate to Los Angeles and try his hand in show business, playing small clubs throughout the West Coast. In the mid-1960s, he recorded an LP dubbed *1965* but largely remained an unknown, not re-entering the studio for another decade. Upon signing to Reprise, Jarreau resurfaced in 1975 with the LP *We Got By,* earning acclaim for his sophisticated brand of vocalese and winning positive comparison to the likes of Billy Eckstine and Johnny Mathis. After 1976's *Glow,* Jarreau issued the following year's *Look to the Rainbow,* a two-disc live set that reached the Top 50 on the US album charts. With 1981's *Breakin' Away,* he entered the Top Ten, scoring a pair of hits with "We're in This Love Together" and the title track. After recording 1986's *L Is for Lover* with producer Nile Rodgers, Jarreau scored a hit with the theme to the popular television program *Moonlighting,* but his mainstream pop success was on the wane, and subsequent efforts like 1992's *Heaven and Earth* and 1994's *Tenderness* found greater success with adult contemporary audiences. —*Jason Ankeny*

1965 / Jun. 1965 / Bainbridge ✦✦✦✦✦
More than ten years before he began to receive notice, Al Jarreau sat in with some friends in Illinois and recorded this superb album, his only strictly "pure jazz" recording to date. Accompanied by pianist Cal Bezemer, bassist Gary Allen and drummer Joe Abodeely, Jarreau already sounded quite recognizable. He comes across as a superior jazz singer on such numbers as "My Favorite Things," "A Sleeping Bee" and "One Note Samba," making this little-known LP (not yet reissued on CD) the high point of his jazz career, even though he apparently was not happy with its release over 15 years later. The album shows what could have been had Al Jarreau had the desire to be a jazz singer rather than chasing the money. —*Scott Yanow*

We Got By / 1975 / Reprise ✦✦✦✦✦

Glow / 1976 / Reprise ✦✦✦
A good session, though the gimmicks are kicking in. —*Ron Wynn*

Look to the Rainbow / Jan. 1977-Feb. 1977 / Warner Brothers ✦✦✦✦✦
Singer Al Jarreau's double LP is easily the most jazz-oriented of all of his Warner Bros. recordings. Cut shortly before Jarreau permanently switched to a more mundane version of R&B, these performances feature him as a brilliant scat singer (able to emulate practically any instrument) and a superior ballad interpreter. Joined by vibraphonist Lynn Blessing, keyboardist Tom Canning, bassist Abe Laboriel and drummer Joe Correro, Jarreau is in top form on such numbers as "Better Than Anything," "Look to the Rainbow" and "Take Five." Unfortunately, Al Jarreau essentially started on top, artistically speaking, and has since been intent on emphasizing potential commercial appeal over any possible innovations or chance-taking. —*Scott Yanow*

● **The Best of Al Jarreau** / 1977-1996 / Warner Brothers ✦✦✦✦✦
This is one intelligently programmed greatest-hits album, for after leading with two fine, new 1996 tracks, "Compared to What" and "Goodhands Tonight," the CD actually becomes a cogent chronological account of Jarreau's twenty years with the label—and a most revealing one at that. Early Latin-flavored tracks from the mid-'70s like "Agua de Beber," "Take Five" and "Spain" reveal a unique jazz voice, with extraordinary rhythmic flexibility and an angular, scattershot, unpredictable approach to a tune that must have been as startling to audiences as Lambert, Hendricks and Ross were when they broke through. With "Never Givin' Up" and "Roof Garden," the transition away from jazz begins; by the time we reach the feel-good hit "Mornin'," the productions have become more intricate, polished and comfortable, suitable either for dancing or making out, with little room for the old vocal spontaneity. And things go downhill from there. Curiously, one of Jarreau's best crossover albums, *L Is for Lover,* is ignored, but guest appearances on Bob James/David Sanborn's *Double Vision* ("Since I Fell for You") and *Symphonic Bossa* (a surprisingly lethargic "Like a Lover"), plus the saccharine theme from *Moonlighting,* are included. Jazz listeners who feel that Jarreau's talents have been gradually eroded by avarice in the record industry can present this program as Exhibit A, but at the same time, it serves as a good introduction for the newcomer and a fine refresher course for the faithful. —*Richard S. Ginell*

All Fly Home / 1978 / Warner Brothers ✦✦✦

This Time / 1980 / Warner Brothers ✦✦✦✦
A big hit on the urban, R&B, and fusion landscape. Infrequent jazz vocals. —*Ron Wynn*

Breakin' Away / 1981 / Warner Brothers ✦✦✦✦✦
Some nice R&B-pop cuts on this platinum album. —*Ron Wynn*

Jarreau / 1983 / Warner Brothers ✦✦✦
Pretty pop, R&B, and fusion on this gold album. —*Ron Wynn*

Live in London / Nov. 1984 / Warner Brothers ✦✦✦

L Is for Lover / 1986 / Warner Brothers ✦✦
A 1986 set that is virtually all R&B, fusion, and pop. —*Ron Wynn*

Heart's Horizon / 1988 / Reprise ✦✦✦

Keith Jarrett

b. May 8, 1945, Allentown, PA
Piano, Leader / Post-Bop

One of the most significant pianists to emerge since the 1960s, Keith Jarrett's career has gone through several phases. He gained international fame for his solo concerts, which found him spontaneously improvising all of the music without any prior planning, but he has also led a couple of dynamic quartets/quintets, performed classical music and recently been playing explorative versions of standards with his longtime trio. Although his tendency to "sing along" with his piano now and then is distracting, Jarrett continues to grow as a powerful improviser after 30 years of important accomplishments.

Keith Jarrett started on the piano when he was three and by the time he was seven he had already played a recital. A child prodigy, Jarrett was a professional while still in grade school. In 1962 he studied at Berklee and then started working in the Boston area with his trio. He moved to New York in 1965 and spent four months with Art Blakey's Jazz Messengers. As a member of the very popular Charles Lloyd Quartet (1966-69), Jarrett traveled the world and became well-known; he also began doubling occasionally on soprano (which he would utilize through the 1970s). During 1969-71, he was with Miles Davis' fusion group, playing organ and electric keyboards; Chick Corea was also in the band for the first year. Jarrett can be heard "battling" Corea throughout Davis' *Live at the Fillmore* but is in more creative form on *Live/Evil*.

Upon leaving Miles Davis, Keith Jarrett permanently swore off electric keyboards. He had cut sessions as a leader for Vortex (1967-69) and Atlantic (1971) but starting in November 1971 he recorded extensively for ECM (in addition to some sessions in the 1970s for ABC/Impulse), an association that continues to the present day. In the 1970s Jarrett led two groups, an exciting unit with Dewey Redman, Charlie Haden, Paul Motian and occasional percussionists (often Guilherme Franco) and a European band with Jan Garbarek, Palle Danielsson and Jon Christensen that recorded the popular *My Song*. In addition, starting in 1972 Jarrett began his famous series of improvised concerts, which resulted in such popular recordings as *Solo Concerts*, *Köln Concert* and the mammoth *Sun Bear Concerts*. By the 1980s, Jarrett was performing classical music as much as jazz, but in the 1990s he has recorded extensively (including a six-CD live set) with his "standards trio" that includes Gary Peacock and Jack DeJohnette. Although initially influenced by Bill Evans, Keith Jarrett has had an original and influential style of his own since the early '70s and remains a vital force in jazz. —*Scott Yanow*

Somewhere Before / Oct. 30, 1968-Oct. 31, 1968 / Atlantic ✦✦✦✦
While still a member of the Charles Lloyd Quartet, Keith Jarrett did some occasional moonlighting with a trio, anchored by two future members of Jarrett's classic quartet, Charlie Haden (bass) and Paul Motian (drums). On this CD, Jarrett turns in a very eclectic set at Shelly's Manne-Hole in Hollywood, careening through a variety of idioms where his emerging individuality comes through in flashes. He covers Bob Dylan's "My Back Pages"—which actually came out as a single on the Vortex label—in an attractive, semi-funky style reminiscent of Vince Guaraldi. "Pretty Ballad" delivers a strong reflective dose of Bill Evans, while "Moving Soon" is chaotic free jazz. By the time we reach "New Rag," we begin to hear the distinctive Jarrett idiom of the later trios, but then, "Old Rag" is knockabout stride without the stride. As an example of early, unfocused Jarrett, this is fascinating material. —*Richard S. Ginell*

Foundations / 1968-1971 / Rhino/Atlantic ✦✦✦✦
This two-disc anthology presents formative Jarrett material from the late '60s and early '70s; it doesn't have the depth, emotional intensity, imagination or charm of his Impulse or ECM releases, but still contains some fine tracks. These include two superb songs with Gary Burton, plus a cut with Blakey's Messengers and some odds and ends from unrelated dates. The second disc includes three 1971 tunes by The Jarrett Unit with Haden, Motian and Redman. At this time, the foursome wasn't fully comfortable or used to each other, and there are uncertain, tentative stretches balanced by other periods with all four interacting smoothly. Jarrett is regarded now as an enigma by some and a genius by others; these songs are reminders of a less assured, but in some ways less predictable and wary pianist. —*Ron Wynn*

The Mourning of a Star / Jul. 9, 1971 / Atlantic ✦✦✦
This LP gives one an interesting look at the early Keith Jarrett, who was already performing on an album of the Charles Lloyd Quartet and Miles Davis' early fusion band. He had not yet fully developed his style but he was clearly on his way. These trio performances (with bassist Charlie Haden and drummer Paul Motian) are impressive for the period but the best was yet to come. —*Scott Yanow*

Birth / Jul. 15, 1971-Jul. 16, 1971 / Atlantic ✦✦✦
Very early example of his quirky style and technique. Jarrett is an excellent pianist, but a horrible recorder/soprano saxist. W/ first-rate personnel: Charlie Haden (b), Paul Motian (d), and Dewey Redman (ts). —*Ron Wynn*

Expectations / Oct. 1971 / Columbia ✦✦✦✦
This was the first real indication to the world that Keith Jarrett was an ambitious, multitalented threat to be reckoned with, an explosion of polystylistic music that sprawled over two LPs (now squeezed onto a single CD). Using his classic quartet (Dewey Redman, Charlie Haden, Paul Motian) as a base, Jarrett occasionally adds the biting rock-edged electric guitar of Sam Brown and always-intriguing percussionist Airto Moreira, and indulges in some pleasant string and brass arrangements of his own, along with some grinding organ smears and acceptable soprano sax. Jarrett again turns his early rampant eclecticism loose—from earthy gospel-tinged soul-jazz to the freewheeling atonal avant-garde—yet this time he does it with an exuberance and expansiveness that puts his previous solo work in the shade. "Common Mama," a spicy Latin workout with brass punctuations, "Take Me Back," driving soul-jazz with streaks of electric jazz-rock, and the lengthy, nearly free "Nomads" are the most invigorating tracks. —*Richard S. Ginell*

● **Facing You** / Nov. 10, 1971 / ECM ✦✦✦✦✦
Keith Jarrett's first solo acoustic piano recording remains one of his best. At this point in late 1971, Jarrett had just started improvising completely freely. That does not mean that his solos were necessarily atonal but simply that they were not planned in any way in advance. The music on these eight improvisations are often quite melodic, very rhythmic and bluesy. This set makes for a perfect introduction to Jarrett's many solo piano recordings. —*Scott Yanow*

Works / Nov. 1971-Jan. 1980 / ECM ✦✦
How do you sum up a massive catalogue like Keith Jarrett's output for ECM—which, as of the mid-1990s, numbered over 50 individual discs—on one slim little CD? You can't. Even so, this collection of seven so-called "works"—four of which are actually excerpts of "works"—borders on the bizarre. All the browser gets are three solo piano pieces torn from *Facing You, Staircase* and *The Sun Bear Concerts*, two numbers with Jarrett's European quartet from *My Song*, the second movement of his string quartet, and a swatch from the organ/soprano sax work, "Invocations." There is nothing from the volatile American quartet; the best solo piano recordings, the *Köln Concert* and *Solo Concerts: Bremen/Lausanne*, are ignored; and most astonishingly for an CD reissued in 1992, there is nothing after 1980—which means no *Standards* trio, etc. You would think that ECM might at least fill the CD up to near its capacity but no, this one clocks in at a niggardly 43:09. True, at least the programming is unpredictable (one wonders if a mischievous Jarrett personally supervised the selection). But as an introduction to an important jazz artist, this simply will not do. —*Richard S. Ginell*

Rutya and Daitya / Mar. 1972 / ECM ✦✦✦
Splitting his time between the electric and acoustic pianos and a bit of organ, Jarrett teams up with drummer/percussionist Jack DeJohnette in a series of experimental duets, his only electric session for ECM. The all-acoustic title number ranges all over the lot, from tootling on a bamboo (?) flute to the energizing barrelhouse gospel riffs that would bloom in the solo concerts. Tellingly, there is little in this collaboration that predicts what Jarrett and DeJohnette would do in their Standards Trio of the '80s; rather, it anticipates the exotic third world side of Jarrett's American quartet immediately in the future and adds a finishing flourish to his jazz-rock period. Indeed, the most memorably percolating playing by both musicians turns up in the electric numbers, where Jarrett utilizes the distinctively funky, wah-wah, fuzz-tone approach on electric piano that he developed with Miles Davis. As such, this is a valuable, underrated transition album that provides perhaps the last glimpse of the electric Keith Jarrett as he embarked on his notorious (and ultimately triumphant) anti-electric crusade. —*Richard S. Ginell*

Fort Yawuh / Feb. 24, 1973 / MCA ✦✦✦✦
This live set features pianist Keith Jarrett's finest regular band; all of their recordings are heartily recommended. Jarrett, joined by tenor saxophonist Dewey Redman, bassist Charlie Haden, drummer Paul Motian and percussionist Danny Johnson, performs four diverse originals. The two ballads in particular work well (this group from the start had its own sound) although Redman's playing on Chinese musette might take a bit of getting used to. —*Scott Yanow*

In the Light / Feb. 1973 / ECM ✦✦✦

Even before his solo concerts became popular successes, Keith Jarrett was clearly getting a free hand from ECM founder Manfred Eicher, as this ambitious double album of classical compositions proves. In this compendium of eight works for all kinds of ensembles, the then-28-year-old Jarrett adamantly refuses to be classified, flitting back and forth through the centuries from the baroque to contemporary dissonance, from exuberant counterpoint for brass quintet to homophonic writing for a string section. Though the content is uneven in quality, Jarrett is clearly sincere and skilled enough to exploit his European roots with only a handful of syncopated references to his jazz work. The strongest, most moving individual pieces are the strange, gong-haunted "In the Cave, in the Light" (the probable source of the title of Jarrett's publishing company, Cavelight); "Metamorphosis," with its rich, flowing string lines, prominent solo flute, and free journeys in and out of tonality; and the Bartok-streaked String Quartet. Jarrett himself plays formal solo piano in the eclectic "Fughata" and "A Pagan Hymn," and even conducts the Stuttgart Radio Symphony strings. All of it is richly recorded in the ECM way, making four strings sound like twelve. —*Richard S. Ginell*

★ **Solo Concerts: Bremen and Lausanne** / Mar. 20, 1973+Jul. 1, 1973 / ECM ✦✦✦✦✦

These are the recordings that made Keith Jarrett famous. Originally released as a three-LP set, the two solo piano recitals feature Jarrett freely improvising and never seeming to run out of ideas. A simple figure often develops through repetition and subtle variations into a rather complex sequence and eventually evolves into a new figure. One of the improvisations lasts for three LP sides (64 minutes), while the second concert has two long solos for 30 and 35 minutes, respectively. Despite the length, the music never loses one's interest, making this an essential recording for all jazz collections. —*Scott Yanow*

The Impulse Years 1973-1974 / Feb. 24, 1973-Oct. 10, 1974 / Impulse ✦✦✦✦

The Keith Jarrett American Quartet/Quintet of the 1970s was arguably his finest group, a post-bop unit featuring the pianist/leader, tenor saxophonist Dewey Redman, bassist Charlie Haden, drummer Paul Motian and sometimes Guilherme Franco and/or Danny Johnson on percussion. A highly recommended four-CD set traced the group's final Impulse recordings of 1975-1976. This five-CD box from 1997 reissues all of the music from the sessions that resulted in *Fort Yawuh* (which is expanded to two CDs), *Treasure Island, Death and the Flower* and *Backhand.* The 29 selections (some of which also include guitarist Sam Brown) include nine previously unreleased performances and three songs that are heard for the first time in expanded unedited versions. Although not reaching as many heights as the later Impulse box, there are many strong moments. The music performed by this underrated group (which is heard at its best on the 22 -minute "Death and the Flower" and "Inflight") is inside/outside, hinting at the avant-garde while not shy of using melodies and rhythms. Redman in particular was heard at his best with Jarrett's classic unit. —*Scott Yanow*

Treasure Island / Feb. 27, 1974-Feb. 28, 1974 / Impulse ✦✦✦✦✦

Originally an Impulse LP that surfaced on MCA as a straight reissue on CD, this fine recording features pianist Keith Jarrett's best regular group. Dewey Redman is heard from on tenor, bassist Charlie Haden, drummer Paul Motian and percussionists Guilherme Franco and Danny Johnson are superb in ensembles and guitarist Sam Brown guests on two selections. The emphasis is on the band's sound and Jarrett's rich melodies; he contributed eight originals to this enjoyable modern set. —*Scott Yanow*

Belonging / Apr. 24, 1974-Apr. 25, 1974 / ECM ✦✦✦✦✦

On Keith Jarrett's first recording with his "European" quartet—Jan Garbarek (sax), Palle Danielsson (bass), Jon Christiensen (drums)—he stakes out somewhat less abrasive territory than that which his "American" foursome was exploring at this time. Garbarek sports a neutral, vibratoless tone that occasionally reaches an emotional climax; the rhythm section is supportive and just loose enough. The record operates at its strongest level when Jarrett locks the quartet into his winning gospel mode on "'Long as You Know You're Living Yours" and the tense drive of "Spiral Dance"; the reflective numbers are less compelling. Still, this LP-turned-CD successfully bucked the powerful electric trends of its time and holds up well today. —*Richard S. Ginell*

Luminessence / Apr. 1974 / ECM ✦✦✦✦

Keith Jarrett does not actually play on this CD; rather, he composed three angst-ridden pieces of varying lengths for string orchestra, over which Jan Garbarek improvises on tenor and soprano saxes. The concept is not unlike that of Stan Getz's *Focus*, but this music is far more static, downcast, and free of the pulse of jazz. As was characteristic of his writing then, Jarrett's string parts are mostly turgid and thick-set, indulging in weird, sliding microtones on "Windsong," weighted down by some kind of emotional burden. Particularly when delivering piercing sustained notes on soprano, Garbarek often sounds like a native of the Middle East. The strings are from the Stuttgart Radio Symphony, led by Mladen Gutesha, who faithfully executes Jarrett's dolorous wishes. —*Richard S. Ginell*

Backhand / Oct. 9, 1974-Oct. 10, 1974 / Impulse ✦✦✦✦✦

Recorded at the same sessions as *Death and the Flower,* this set features pianist Keith Jarrett's exciting but underrated American group of the 1970s, a quintet with tenor saxophonist Dewey Redman, bassist Charlie Haden, drummer Paul Motian and percussionist Guilherme Franco. The group (with Jarrett occasionally switching to flute and Redman to the bizarre-sounding musette) is in typically exploratory, yet often melodic form on lengthy renditions of four of Jarrett's inside/outside originals. —*Scott Yanow*

Personal Mountains / 1974 / ECM ✦✦✦✦

It is very much out of character for the prolific Keith Jarrett and his producer Manfred Eicher to hold anything back, yet they've done it here, releasing these live tapes of Jarrett's European quartet ten years after they were recorded. Presumably, they did it in order not to distract attention from *Nude Ants,* which was recorded a week after these concerts, but that never stopped them before from just piling on more discs. In any case, these Tokyo recordings were too good to hide; the quartet had reached an interactive creative high around this time, often burning at the rarified level that *Nude Ants* reached. Jarrett is both lyrically effusive and able to ignite his European colleagues into giving him more swinging support than on earlier sessions. In particular, the title track has a lot of the exploratory fervor of "New Dance" from *Nude Ants,* and "Late Night Willie" gets down deep into the Jarrett gospel feeling. Jan Garbarek is especially forthright in Tokyo on tenor, while his soprano pierces like a beam of sunlight, and Palle Danielsson (bass) and Jon Christensen (drums) are loose, relaxed, and impeccably recorded. Clearly this is one of the peaks of the European quartet's discography. —*Richard S. Ginell*

Shades / 1975 / Impulse! ✦✦✦✦✦

Pianist Keith Jarrett's mid-'70s quintet was the strongest regular group that he ever led and all of its recordings (even some that ramble a bit) are worth picking up. Thanks to its strong start, *Shades* is one of this unit's most rewarding recordings. "Shades of Jazz" has a memorable melody and logical (if unpredictable) improvisations by Jarrett and tenor saxophonist Dewey Redman. The momentum slows down a bit with the gospelish "Southern Smiles" and "Rose Petals" but picks up again with the final number, the rather intense "Diatribe," an excellent vehicle for this classic group. Throughout, bassist Charlie Haden, drummer Paul Motian and percussionist Guilherme Franco keep the band's juices flowing. —*Scott Yanow*

★ **The Köln Concert** / Jan. 24, 1975 / ECM ✦✦✦✦✦

Many critics consider this to be Keith Jarrett's most rewarding solo recording although *Solo Concerts* from the previous year is on the same level. Originally released as a two-LP set, this music is best suited for CD because, while the first 26-minute improvisation fits on one LP side, the second of the two solos (which totals 41 minutes) was programmed over the remaining LP, with side four being only seven minutes long. Logistics aside, the music is quite brilliant with Jarrett (who was improvising freely without any prior planning) developing the most interesting and occasionally startling ideas. The strong, fresh melodies and his bluesy feel make this a very enjoyable outing. —*Scott Yanow*

Death & The Flower / May 1975 / Impulse! ✦✦✦

This set by the Keith Jarrett Quintet (with the leader on piano, soprano and flute, tenor saxophonist Dewey Redman, bassist Charlie Haden, drummer Paul Motian and percussionist Guilherme Franco) contains three of Jarrett's originals. The main selection, the 21-minute "Death and the Flower," develops logically from atmospheric sounds to intense group improvising and back again; it is the main reason to acquire this CD. —*Scott Yanow*

Arbour Zena / Oct. 1975 / ECM ✦✦✦

With saxophonist Jan Garbarek and bassist Charlie Haden along for the ride, Keith Jarrett indulges in three slow, rambling, meditative, vaguely neoclassical concertos for piano and string orchestra. While a few of Jarrett's and Garbarek's passages here and there have a syncopated jazz feeling, this is mostly contemporary classical music, perhaps even somewhat ahead of its time (it might fit in with the neo-Romantic and minimalist camps today). However, although this music can be attractive in small doses, the lack of tempo or texture contrasts over long stretches of time—particularly the nearly 28-minute "Mirrors"—can be annoying if you're not in the right blissful mood. Mladen Gutesha and the Stuttgart Radio Symphony Orchestra perform the string parts with what can only be described as commendable patience. —*Richard S. Ginell*

Mysteries / 1975 / ABC/Impulse! ✦✦✦✦

Another in Impulse's extensive series of Keith Jarrett Quintet recordings, this CD isn't one of the more coherent products of the run. It opens on a faltering note with the hopelessly diffuse and rambling "Rotation," and "Everything That Lives Laments" doesn't really get going until a lyrical Vince Guaraldi-like statement from Jarrett sets the track in motion. "Flame" is certainly novel, with Jarrett on Pakistani flute and Dewey Redman on Chinese musette, which combined with the percussion makes for a diverting India/third world jam. The Coltrane-ish 15-minute title track has passages of meditative beauty and others of listless torpor. For completists only. —*Richard S. Ginell*

Mysteries: Impulse Years 1975–Sep. 9, 1977 / 1975 / Impulse! ✦✦✦✦
At two marathon three-day recording sessions in December 1975 and October 1976, the finest group that pianist Keith Jarrett ever led (his quartet/quintet with tenor saxophonist Dewey Redman, bassist Charlie Haden, drummer Paul Motian and, on the first sessions, percussionist Guilherme Franco) recorded enough material for four memorable albums: *Shades, Mysteries, Byablue* and *Bop-Be*. This four-CD 1996 box set has the complete sessions, including 11 previously unreleased alternate takes. Jarrett's inside/outside music (his unisons with Redman had a unique sound) both held onto the tradition of chordal improvisation and were reminiscent of Ornette Coleman's earlier acoustic groups. There are a few brief exotic sound explorations, but most of the music (best shown on the opening "Shades of Jazz") extends the swinging tradition into complex areas that have yet to be fully explored by others. Continually fascinating music. — *Scott Yanow*

☆ **The Survivor's Suite** / Apr. 1976 / ECM ✦✦✦✦✦
This is one of the finest recordings by pianist Keith Jarrett's mid-'70s group. Jarrett (on piano, soprano and bass recorder), tenor saxophonist Dewey Redman, bassist Charlie Haden and drummer Paul Motian (no percussionist this time) by 1976 were thinking alike during the ensemble's improvisations. "The Survivor's Suite," a 49-minute two-part work, finds the group continually building up and then releasing tension together. There are strong individual solos but it is the interplay between the band members that makes this a particularly memorable outing. —*Scott Yanow*

Eyes of the Heart / May 1976 / ECM ✦✦✦
This live recording features pianist Keith Jarrett (also playing a bit of soprano), tenor saxophonist Dewey Redman, bassist Charlie Haden and drummer Paul Motian performing the 33-minute title cut and an 18-minute piece simply called "Encore." Every recording by this particular group (arguably Jarrett's best working ensemble) is well worth hearing, for they had their own sound and the ability to play both "inside" and "outside" simultaneously, and they were continually full of surprises. Originally released as a two-LP set with the fourth side completely blank, the intriguing music has since been reissued as a single CD. —*Scott Yanow*

Staircase / May 1976 / ECM ✦✦✦✦
The fourth of Keith Jarrett's solo piano albums turns inward, away from the funky, pulsating melodic inventions of its predecessors toward a more reflective, scattered, never-despairing romanticism well removed from the pulse of jazz. As such, it is paradoxically his weakest solo piano album of the '70s and also the most influential, for here is the blueprint for sensitive meandering that the new age piano crowd took off upon in the 1980s. A studio session, *Staircase* is actually only one of four separately titled improvisations on this double album (now on one CD)—the others are "Hourglass," "Sundial" and "Sand"—but their overall moods of repose are so similar that it hardly matters what they are called. One can always admire Jarrett's lovely tone and flexible touch, yet when he gets stuck for ideas, the repetitions finally begin to grate. Maybe he really needs the stimulus of a live audience in order to get the creative and rhythmic juices flowing when flying solo. —*Richard S. Ginell*

Hymns / Spheres / Sep. 1976 / ECM ✦✦
Restlessly searching out new territory for improvisations, Keith Jarrett tackles the massive Karl Joseph Riepp "Trinity" Baroque pipe organ at the Benedictine Abbey in Ottobeuren, Germany. He starts out with a pastoral "Hymn of Remembrance," then embarks upon a long nine-movement series of "Spheres" before closing with a grand "Hymn of Release." The devotee of Jarrett's piano will quickly discover that his organ idiom has nothing to do with his piano performances; he likes slow-moving, pulseless, sometimes dissonant, sometimes reverent or ecstatic smears of sound (which makes practical sense in the hugely reverberant churches where pipe organs are found). In the ninth movement, Jarrett can fool you into thinking that he is playing floating electronic space music (on an eighteenth-century organ!). Yet if one must apply a category, despite the improvisatory element, this double-CD is contemporary classical organ music, much closer to that of Olivier Messiaen than anything in the jazz world—and only intermittently as striking. (Note: on the single CD issue, only "Spheres" is listed.) —*Richard S. Ginell*

Sun Bear Concerts / Nov. 5, 1976–Nov. 18, 1976 / ECM ✦✦✦✦
This gargantuan package—a ten-LP set now compressed into a chunky six-CD box—once was derided as the ultimate ego trip, probably by many who didn't (or couldn't) take the time to hear it all. You have to go back to Art Tatum's solo records for Norman Granz in the '50s to find another large single outpouring of solo jazz piano like this, all of it improvised on the wing before five Japanese

audiences in Kyoto, Osaka, Nagoya, Tokyo and Sapporo. Yet the miracle is how consistently good much of this giant box is. Every concert has truly inspired passages, some admittedly more than others. In the opening Kyoto concert, Jarrett's gospel-driven muse is in full play, up to the level of his peak solo performances in Bremen and Köln, and the Osaka and Nagoya concerts have pockets of first-rate, often folk-like, even profound lyrical ideas. The Tokyo concert takes a while to get in gear, but when Jarrett finally locks into one of his grooving vamps, he carries us along, and there is a memorably melodic encore. In Sapporo, Jarrett breaks from a nicely flowing pattern into a jumpy rhythm that reminds one of C&W guitar fingerpicking, and there's some exuberant barrelhouse stuff and outbreaks of dissonance in Part II. Each concert, ranging from 70 to 78 minutes apiece, is placed on a single CD, while the much briefer sixth disc is reserved for the encores from Nagoya, Tokyo and Sapporo. While *Sun Bear* breaks little ground that his earlier solo piano albums had not already covered, it is nevertheless richly inventive within Jarrett's personal parameter of idioms—and there is little of the torporous meandering that mars most of *Staircase* (recorded only six months before). If price is not a barrier, the Jarrett devotee need not hesitate. —*Richard S. Ginell*

Ritual / Jun. 1977 / ECM ✦✦✦
Keith Jarrett does not actually play on this LP; rather, it is Dennis Russell Davies, a classical pianist and conductor with whom Jarrett collaborates frequently, who performs this 32-minute Jarrett composition on a grand piano. *Ritual* has several of the characteristics of Jarrett's solo improvisations—the repetitive vamps and ostinatos, wistful lyricism, ruminative episodes developing organically out of what preceded them—but without the jazzy/bluesy feeling that runs through the solo concerts. Also, the piece begins in a mournful way unusual for the usually optimistic Jarrett. In any case, it is a thoughtful, absorbing composition, thoroughly tonal harmonically, played with assured technique and appropriate use of classical expressive devices by Davies. Classical listeners as well as Jarrett devotees will find much to savor here. —*Richard S. Ginell*

Silence / Sep. 9, 1977 / GRP ✦✦✦✦
The 1992 CD reissue of the Keith Jarrett "American" Quartet's last recording session combines most of the contents of the LPs *Byablue* and *Bop-Be*, omitting "Yahllah" and "Konya" from the former and "Pyramids Moving" from the latter. (Tellingly, in keeping with conservative '90s tastes—never mind the time-limit excuse—the deleted tracks are the ones which had an experimental Middle Eastern flavor.) Still, this partial sampling of the session indicates that the quartet went out on a high note, still exciting and inventive, the old interplay very much in action, unrepentantly acoustic in an electric era. Like the LP of the same name, "Byablue" brackets the CD with a group version at the beginning and a solo piano benediction at the close, which under these conditions becomes an emotional elegy for the soon-to-be defunct quartet by its leader. —*Richard S. Ginell*

Bop-Be / Nov. 1, 1977 / Impulse! ✦✦✦✦
Here is another helping from the Keith Jarrett "American" Quartet's last recording session—one that is almost as consistent in quality as its predecessor. The happy-go-lucky groove of the title track perfectly expresses its name, with Keith blithely singing along; both Dewey Redman and Charlie Haden get plenty of solo space on Redman's "Gotta Get Some Sleep" and Haden's "Pocket Full of Cherry" (a pun referring to Haden cohort Don Cherry); and Paul Motian remains a marvelously flexible drummer. Moreover, there is another fascinating swatch of Middle Eastern experimentation on "Pyramids Moving." —*Richard S. Ginell*

My Song / Nov. 1977 / ECM ✦✦✦✦✦
In addition to his solo piano concerts and the American group he led that featured tenor saxophonist Dewey Redman, Keith Jarrett was also busy in the mid-'70s with his European band, a quartet comprising Jan Garbarek on tenor and soprano, bassist Palle Danielsson and drummer Jon Christensen. Due to the popularity of the haunting "My Song," this album is the best-known of the Jarrett-Garbarek collaborations and it actually is their most rewarding meeting on records. Jarrett contributed all six compositions and the results are relaxed and introspective yet full of inner tension. —*Scott Yanow*

Byablue / Nov. 1, 1977 / ABC/Impulse! ✦✦✦✦
Amidst rumored tension within the band, Keith Jarrett's "American" Quartet met for one last marathon recording date before disbanding, and Impulse made the most of it by spreading the music out over two separate releases. From the evidence of this, the first and slightly superior LP, the band certainly doesn't sound as if it was ready to break up; the interplay has become telepathic, the musical ideas are still fresh and there is a willingness to experiment. "Rainbow," credited to Margot Jarrett, is top-flight lyrical Keith, while "Trieste" evokes the mood and some of the language of spiritual Coltrane. There is adventure, too; with Dewey Redman and Jarrett wailing on tenor and soprano, respectively, "Konya" sounds almost like a muezzin call to prayer, and "Yahllah" is a rare, brave, moving

merger of jazz and the Middle East. Highly recommended on LP, since the Middle Eastern tracks were deleted from the CD reissue. —*Richard S. Ginell*

Nude Ants / May 1979 / ECM ✦✦✦✦✦

There is a lot of music on this set, including the 30-minute "Oasis." This is a *Live at the Village Vanguard* recording by pianist Keith Jarrett and his European quartet (Jan Garbarek on soprano and tenor, bassist Palle Danielsson and drummer Jon Christensen). The pianist very much dominates the music, but Garbarek's unique floating tone on his instruments and the subtle accompaniment by Danielsson and Christensen are also noteworthy. —*Scott Yanow*

Sacred Hymns / Mar. 24, 1980 / ECM ✦✦✦

Here we have simplicity itself: a series of piano transcriptions of some solemn, now-dark, now-affirmative religious hymns by one G.I. Gurdjieff, with none of the usual flourishes and heady flights usually associated with Keith Jarrett's solo records. Jarrett assumes the proper devotional position, playing with a steady tread but always with attention to dynamic extremes, producing a gorgeously rich piano tone with plenty of bass. The whole record has a serene dignity, even at its loudest levels, that gets to you, and that should be enough for the devout Jarrett following. As for others . . . well, it's definitely not a top ten choice for a basic Keith collection. —*Richard S. Ginell*

Invocations / The Moth and the Flame / 1981 / ECM ✦✦✦

If this schizophrenic double-CD set didn't throw Keith Jarrett's most devoted fans for a loop, nothing ever will. Here we have two radically disparate works involving different timbres, attacks and mindsets, both within themselves and with each other. On "Invocations," a seven-movement suite, Jarrett returns to the massive pipe organ in Ottobeuren, Germany, for a series of sometimes wildly contrasting episodes, ranging from peaceful contemplation to a fourth movement (subtitled "Shock, Scatter") that borders on the comical (people tend to forget that for all of his pretensions, Jarrett does have a sense of humor). Entranced by the abbey's long, long decay time, he brackets the organ movements with some solo meditations on the soprano sax which, pardon the witticism, echo those of Paul Horn. "The Moth and the Flame" finds Jarrett back in a studio with a grand piano, improvising musical still-lifes, rambling aimlessly, or doing his rollicking E-flat ostinato thing familiar from the solo concerts. About all that these two pieces share, with the exception of the E-flat movement from "Moth," is an aversion to a jazz pulse, so although there are plenty of rewarding passages here, casual Jarrett browsers are hereby warned. —*Richard S. Ginell*

Concerts / May 28, 1981-Jun. 2, 1981 / ECM ✦✦✦

By the early '80s, Keith Jarrett was definitely under siege, accused of arrogance, singing along too loudly, rambling eclecticism and other heinous crimes. Indeed, around this time, Jarrett would verbally attack music critics at his solo concerts, and the reflected paranoia is obvious in Peter Ruedi's defensive booklet essay for this three-LP set of music recorded in Bregenz, Austria, and Munich, Germany. This set is not to be confused with the earlier, more consistently inspired *Solo Concerts* triple album which made Jarrett a star, yet the pianist was far from tapped out in these performances. Jarrett is often in his best lyrically funky form, where he makes the most out of a single ostinato idea—particularly at the beginning of the Bregenz concert (side one of the LPs) and in the middle of the Munich concert (side five)—and his touch and exploitation of the dynamics and timbres of a grand piano are always a pleasure to hear. Even the passages of stasis or aimless rippling do not cancel out the treasurable moments, although the string plucking in Munich (side six) may be somewhat gratuitous. In any case, this is far more interesting and elevated music-making than that of the new age navel-gazing imitators cropping up in Jarrett's wake in the early '80s. On the single-CD issue, only the Bregenz concert is included. —*Richard S. Ginell*

Changes / Jan. 1983 / ECM ✦✦✦✦

Unlike the other two Keith Jarrett trio recordings from January 1983, this collaboration with bassist Gary Peacock and drummer Jack DeJohnette does not feature standards. The trio performs the 30-minute "Flying" and a 6-minute "Prism," both of them Jarrett originals. "Flying," which has several sections, keeps one's interest throughout while the more concise "Prism" has a beautiful melody. It is a nice change to hear Jarrett (who normally plays unaccompanied) interacting with a trio of superb players. —*Scott Yanow*

Standards, Vol. 1 / Jan. 1983 / ECM ✦✦✦✦

In January of 1983, Keith Jarrett returned to the trio format and his collaboration with bassist Gary Peacock and drummer Jack DeJohnette resulted in three albums. The first release finds the trio digging into five standards with "God Bless the Child" being dragged out (although not unmercifully) for 15 minutes. The performances, which usually do not swing in a conventional sense, do have a momentum of their own. Jarrett is generous in allocating solo space to Peacock and it is obvious that the three musicians were listening very closely to each other. —*Scott Yanow*

Standards, Vol. 2 / Jan. 1983 / ECM ✦✦✦✦

One of three trio albums that pianist Keith Jarrett recorded with bassist Gary Peacock and drummer Jack DeJohnette during the same month, this second volume of *Standards* gets the edge over the first due to its slightly more challenging material. Jarrett, who has often taken himself a bit too seriously, is surprisingly playful at times in this format. In addition to Jarrett's "So Tender," there are such superior songs explored on this date as Alec Wilder's "Moon and Sand," "If I Should Lose You" and "I Fall in Love Too Easily." Bassist Gary Peacock and drummer Jack DeJohnette listen closely to Jarrett and no matter what direction the pianist turns, they are already there waiting for him. —*Scott Yanow*

Spirits 1 & 2 / May 1985-Jul. 1985 / ECM ✦✦✦

More a technical showcase than a musically worthy enterprise. Jarrett plays 18 instruments, using multitracking to strut his stuff. —*Ron Wynn*

Standards Live / Jul. 2, 1985 / ECM ✦✦✦✦

Standards Live, from 1987, continued at the same high level of previous *Standards Vol. 1 & 2* with pianist Keith Jarrett often recalling his early influence, Bill Evans. The well-integrated trio (Gary Peacock, bass; Jack DeJohnette, drums) plays three frequently performed tunes and three obscurities. The interplay between the players was constantly impressive. —*Scott Yanow*

Still Live / Jul. 13, 1986 / ECM ✦✦✦

Once Keith Jarrett gets into a concept, he likes to keep those tapes rolling. This two-disc live outpouring from a Standards Trio gig at Munich's Philharmonic Hall was the biggest offering from this group up to that time (it wouldn't hold that distinction for long)—and once again, Jarrett treats his brace of pop and jazz standards with unpredictable, often eloquently melodic and structural originality. To cite a pair of highlights: "Autumn Leaves" always seems to bring out an endless flow of invention from Jarrett, and "The Song Is You" gets off to a rollicking start and maintains a nearly relentless energy level for 17 minutes, closing with a Spanish vamp. Again, the rapport with his onetime jazz-rock associate, drummer Jack DeJohnette, and bassist Gary Peacock is total; DeJohnette's mastery of shifting cymbal patterns while maintaining the pulse acts on the trio like a loose tether made of carbon steel. There is a considerable amount of Jarrett vocalizing, though; sometimes he sounds like a tortured animal. CD buyers get "Billie's Bounce" as a bonus. —*Richard S. Ginell*

Changeless / Oct. 9, 1987-Oct. 14, 1987 / ECM ✦✦✦✦

One of only a handful of Keith Jarrett "Standards" Trio records without a standard within earshot, this is a triumph, for Jarrett has successfully brought the organically evolving patterns of his solo concerts into the group format. Each of the first three selections is built upon a constant revolving ostinato, and each evolves from one stage to the next like a Jarrett solo piano improvisation. "Dancing" has a swaying Latin beat in the percussion and bass; "Endless" is full of lyrical invention at a slower tempo; "Lifeline" is catchy and hypnotic; and the fourth number, "Ecstasy," grows out of "Lifeline," closing the album perhaps inevitably with a drawn-out, peaceful piano tremolo. Bassist Gary Peacock and drummer Jack DeJohnette are clearly listening hard, going with the flow. The recordings were taken from four separate concerts in Denver, Dallas, Lexington, KY., and Houston. Jarrett may spout off about society's self-centered soullessness in his querulous liner notes, but he and his trio have clearly backed his words by example, pulling off a genuine collective musical experience. —*Richard S. Ginell*

Dark Intervals / Oct. 1988 / ECM ✦✦✦

This live solo piano concert at Tokyo's Suntory Hall is not a solo concert in the usual freewheeling Jarrett sense. Rather, it sounds like a formal recital of individual compositions, each followed by applause (unlike the improvised concerts where applause only comes at the end of a set). Keith is often in an introspective, even dark mood, with deep growling in the lower bass regions in the closing minutes of "Opening." Yet he can also be quietly affirmative and devotional, always the musician/virtuoso who doesn't flash his technique for its own sake. Of the eight tracks, only "Fire Dance" has some of the jazzy verve associated with the solo concerts. The Jarrett devotee will want this; others should use caution. —*Richard S. Ginell*

Tribute / Oct. 15, 1989 / ECM ✦✦✦✦✦

The Keith Jarrett Standards Trio gets back down to business with two CDs' worth of familiar and perhaps not-so-familiar tunes, recorded in one evening in Cologne, Germany. There is a concept this time, for all the standards carry a dedication to some jazz man or woman who performed them—and they are not predictable choices; Lee Konitz for "Lover Man," "It's Easy to Remember" for John Coltrane, "All of You" for Miles Davis, etc. Almost every number has a reflective solo piano introduction, with one of the notable exceptions being Jarrett's rolling, convoluted opening variations on "All the Things You Are" (Sonny Rollins). "Solar" (the Bill Evans tribute) has challenging, fractured interplay between Jarrett, Jack DeJohnette and Gary Peacock, and it directly segues into Jarrett's own obsessive

"Sun Prayer," which seems to lose its way after a fine start. The other Jarrett composition, "U Dance," a carefree folk-like tune with a rhumba rhythm, closes the concert with a tribute to no one in particular. While the Standards Trio rarely takes anything for granted, transforming everything in its path, the results are not quite as inventive here as on other releases, though disc two is clearly more interesting overall than disc one. Warning to the wary: Keith Jarrett, singer, is in rare groaning form on "I Hear a Rhapsody" and "Solar." *—Richard S. Ginell*

The Cure / Apr. 21, 1990 / ECM ◆◆◆◆

Sure, the Keith Jarrett Trio of the '80s and '90s recorded way too much music for the casual fan to absorb. But one's reservations fade when confronted with the sheer creativity and empathy that the trio displayed in this gorgeously recorded live date at New York's Town Hall. As in several albums before, the emphasis for Jarrett, Gary Peacock and Jack DeJohnette is on standards, save for a sole ostinato-based Jarrett original (the title track). "Bemsha Swing" finds Jarrett at very nearly his best, transforming standard material completely in his own funky manner. In addition, there is a really beautiful rendition of Oscar Levant's "Blame It on My Youth," and an eloquently harmonized "Body and Soul" with generous solo space for Peacock. There is some squeaky vocalizing by Jarrett over some of his solos, but not enough to deter anyone from enjoying this 77-minute outpouring of first-class improvisational jazz. *—Richard S. Ginell*

Paris Concert / 1990 / ECM ◆◆◆◆

The self-imposed quarantine on solo concerts over, Keith Jarrett returned to the improvisatory format that he virtually invented, mellower and more devotional than ever. Indeed, within the 38 minutes of solo improvisation captured at Paris' Salle Pleyel, Jarrett pulls further away from the old rousing (and thoroughly American) gospel, blues and folk roots of earlier concerts toward a more abstract concept. Opening with a soaring, lyrical canonic melody, he rambles through his familiar obsessive hammering, grand tremolos, and the like before topping it off with an ethereal tune that turns somber. There are two encores—Russ Freeman's "The Wind," which begins with a brief swatch of Steve Reich-like minimalism but swiftly turns reflective the rest of the way, and "Blues," a welcome if brief return to one of the pianist's root sources. Again, Jarrett's virtuosic abilities are never in doubt, and he rarely flaunts his technique for its own sake, but one senses that the inspiration level is down; one doesn't come out of the CD all charged up as with many earlier solo concerts. *—Richard S. Ginell*

Book of Ways / Mar. 6, 1991 / ECM ◆◆◆◆

Thanks in no small part to ECM founder Manfred Eicher's patience and indulgence, here we have another of Keith Jarrett's myriad of "special projects"—two CDs of music recorded on a clavichord. This carries Jarrett's anti-electric crusade to a real extreme, the clavichord being a keyboard from J.S. Bach's day, obsolete for over 200 years. The instrument produces a gentle pinging sound like a harpsichord crossed with a zither (the amplified Hohner Clavinet is the closest sound in our time), and Jarrett occasionally tries to stretch the instrument's limited possibilities, hammering percussively on the close-miked strings. Yet for the most part, Jarrett reins in his world-class technique in order to make unpretentiously minimal music on this ancient keyboard. Some of it sounds like folk music, some like new age contemplation, there are convincing neo-baroque musings, and a few of these untitled though numbered selections kick into a higher gear. Sometimes this music is charming; a lot of the time, it gets wearisome. But hey, they also laughed when Keith started putting out massive sets of solo piano . . . *—Richard S. Ginell*

Vienna Concert / Jul. 13, 1991 / ECM ◆◆◆◆

Keith Jarrett feels that this is his finest solo concert; having "courted the flame for a very long time," he writes, this music speaks "the language of the flame itself." Perhaps playing in the European-tradition-encrusted Vienna Staatsoper had an overt influence, for never has a recorded Jarrett solo concert fallen into such a logical, even classical overall structure as this one—all on the wing, mind you. Part I develops in a majestic 41-minute arch, opening with a simple chorale, devotional and trenchant, and suddenly kicking into a daring, complex, agitated toccata without a key center, technically dazzling and darting. That coalesces into a grand tonal passage with inferences of the great European piano concertos before subsiding into a quietly affirmative finale. Part II is shorter and less rigorously structured, surging and ebbing around shimmering tremolos and a brief pulsating rhythm, alternately evoking the Middle East and the medieval Dies Irae. Jarrett's exalted judgment is close to the mark; though more Eurocentric than ever, these are his most impressive solo performances since *Sun Bear.* *—Richard S. Ginell*

Bye Bye Blackbird / Oct. 1991 / ECM ◆◆◆◆◆

This is the Keith Jarrett/Gary Peacock/Jack DeJohnette Trio's elegy for their former employer Miles Davis, recorded only 13 days after the maestro's death. The lonely figure in shadow with a horn on the cover contrasts with the joyous spirit of many of the tracks on this CD, yet there is still a ghostly presence to deal

with—and in keeping with Miles' credo, Jarrett's choice of notes is often more purposefully spare than usual. There is symmetry in the organization of the album, with "Bye Bye Blackbird" opening and the Trio's equally jaunty "Blackbird, Bye Bye" closing the album, and the interior tracks immediately following the former and preceding the latter are "You Won't Forget Me" and "I Thought About You." The centerpiece of the CD is an eighteen-and-a-half-minute group improvisation, "For Miles," which after some DeJohnette tumbling around becomes a dirge sometimes reminiscent of Miles' own elegy for Duke Ellington, "He Loved Him Madly." As an immediate response to a traumatic event, Jarrett and his colleagues strike the right emotional balance to create one of their more meaningful albums. *—Richard S. Ginell*

At the Deer Head Inn / Sep. 1992 / ECM ◆◆◆◆

Keith Jarrett returns to his roots, both musically and physically, on this CD. His first significant jazz gig was at the Deer Head Inn in Allentown, PA (his hometown), and 30 years later Jarrett agreed to perform at the venue again. With the assistance of bassist Gary Peacock and drummer Paul Motian, Jarrett plays six jazz standards (several of which were associated with Miles Davis) plus Jaki Byard's medium-tempo blues, "Chandra." The inventive interpretations give listeners plenty of surprises and variety, making this a very enjoyable outing. *—Scott Yanow*

Bridge of Light / Mar. 1993 / ECM ◆◆◆◆

This is Keith Jarrett's most accomplished collection of classical compositions yet, seated squarely in the American East Coast neoclassical tradition of Samuel Barber, David Diamond, Irving Fine, etc. Jarrett's writing for strings is masterful here; the lines move and interweave instead of being shoveled on as in some pieces of the '70s, and the compositions have shape and direction. Most of all, they share a common feeling of reflection and an unabashed willingness to let the instrumental soloists sing. "Elegy for Violin and String Orchestra" is a particularly gorgeous and inspired piece of music, the "Adagio for Oboe and String Orchestra" is not far behind, and "Bridge of Light for Viola and Orchestra" transfers Jarrett's classical idiom to a full chamber orchestra, now with overtones of late-period Vaughan Williams. Jarrett himself plays the piano on his "Sonata for Violin and Piano," whose third movement hearkens back to the repetitive grooves of the solo concerts. Three of the four works date from 1984, while *Bridge of Light* was written in 1990—and in the orchestral pieces, ECM has given conductor Thomas Crawford and the excellent Fairfield Orchestra glowing sound. Though these works have nothing to do with jazz per se, all Jarrett buffs should investigate this music on its own terms. *—Richard S. Ginell*

At the Blue Note: Saturday, June 4th, 1994, 1st Set / Jun. 4, 1994 / ECM ◆◆◆

As a sampler from Keith Jarrett's huge six-disc omnibus documenting a gig at New York City's Blue Note, ECM extracted one of the discs and put it out on its own. Yet it is enough to demonstrate that Jarrett and his "Standards" trio reached new peaks of creativity and internal telepathy in the 1990s. Not only that, this way is preferable to the usual method of taking fragments of every set and patching them together; those who can't afford the box can still hear how a complete set evolves. The first set of June 4, 1994 is dominated by two marathons, a most inventive twenty-six-and-a-half-minute series of meditations and developing grooves on the subject of "Autumn Leaves" and a twenty-and-a-half-minute resumption of Jarrett's Middle East fusions on "You Don't Know What Love Is/ Muezzin." There is also a romp through Jarrett's own "Bop-Be," which holds its own against any of the established standards. A must-buy for the casual or impecunious Jarrett fan. *—Richard S. Ginell*

Standards in Norway / Oct. 7, 1989 / ECM ◆◆◆

Keith Jarrett has recorded quite a few albums with his "Standards Trio," which also features bassist Gary Peacock and drummer Jack DeJohnette, and virtually all of their releases are enjoyable. The music that they create is in some ways an update of the type of interplay that took place between Bill Evans and his sidemen, where all three musicians often act as equals (although Jarrett, like Evans, has most of the solo space). An uptempo "Love Is a Many-Splendored Thing" is a surprising high point of this disc but also quite memorable are "All of You," "Old Folks" and "How About You?"; none of the eight performances from the concert appearance are throwaways. Jarrett's vocal sounds are more restrained than usual while his piano playing is in peak form. *—Scott Yanow*

☆ Keith Jarrett at the Blue Note: The Complete Recordings / Jun. 3, 1994–Jun. 5, 1994 / ECM ◆◆◆◆◆

The six-CD box set *Keith Jarrett at the Blue Note* fully documents three nights (six complete sets from June 3-5, 1994) by his trio with bassist Gary Peacock and drummer Jack DeJohnette. Never mind that this same group has already had ten separate releases since 1983; this box is still well worth getting. The repertoire emphasizes (but is not exclusively) standards with such songs as "In Your Own Sweet Way," "Now's the Time" "Oleo," "Days of Wine and Roses" and "My

Romance" given colorful and at times surprising explorations. Some of the selections are quite lengthy (including a twenty-six-and-a-half-minute version of "Autumn Leaves") and Jarrett's occasional originals are quite welcome; his twenty-eight-and-a-half-minute "Desert Sun" reminds one of the pianist's fully improvised "Solo Concerts" of the 1970s. Throughout the three nights at the Blue Note, the interplay between the musicians is consistently outstanding. Those listeners concerned about Jarrett's tendency to "sing along" with his piano have little to fear for, other than occasional shouts and sighs, he wisely lets his piano do the talking. —*Scott Yanow*

La Scala / Feb. 13, 1995 / ECM ✦✦✦✦

For this live solo concert (recorded at the Teatro alla Scala in Milano, Italy and released in 1997), pianist Keith Jarrett performs two lengthy improvisations simply titled "La Scala, Parts I and II." Most of the music is quite lyrical and romantic. The first part (which lasted nearly 45 minutes) does have a section using a droning rhythm reminiscent of American Indian music before resolving back into a ballad. The second section (a mere 27 minutes) starts out dissonant, gradually evolves into a peaceful section, and then concludes with the original dissonant ideas. As an encore, Jarrett performs a melodic and very beautiful six-minute rendition of "Over the Rainbow," receiving a well-deserved thunderous ovation at its conclusion. The music overall develops slowly but always holds one's interest, reinforcing one's viewpoint of Keith Jarrett as one of the top pianists of the 1980s and '90s. —*Scott Yanow*

Bobby Jaspar

b. Feb. 20, 1926, Liège, Belgium, d. Feb. 28, 1963, New York, NY

Tenor Saxophone, Flute / Hard Bop, Cool

A fine bop-oriented soloist equally skilled on his cool-toned tenor and flute, Bobby Jaspar's early death from a heart ailment was a tragic loss. As a teenager, he played tenor in a Dixieland group with Toots Thielemans in Belgium. He recorded with Henri Renaud (1951 and 1953) and played with touring Americans including Jimmy Raney, Chet Baker (1955) and his future wife Blossom Dearie. In 1956 Jaspar moved to New York where he worked with J.J. Johnson, was briefly with Miles Davis (1957) and Donald Byrd. He mostly freelanced during the remainder of his career. Bobby Jaspar recorded for Swing, Vogue and Barclay while in Paris and led dates for Prestige, and Riverside while in the US during 1957. —*Scott Yanow*

● **Bobby Jaspar in Paris** / Dec. 27, 1955+Dec. 29, 1955 / Disques Swing ✦✦✦✦✦

Despite its title, this 1986 LP actually features Bobby Jaspar in New York making his first American record. Jaspar teams up with two different rhythm sections (either pianist Tommy Flanagan, bassist Nobil Totah and drummer Elvin Jones or pianist Eddie Costa, guitarist Barry Galbraith, bassist Milt Hinton and drummer Osie Johnson) and mostly plays tenor, but switches to his equally effective flute on three songs and makes a rare appearance on clarinet (his first instrument) for "Clarinescapade." Most of the tunes are straightahead swingers or ballads, and this is an excellent outing well worth reissuing on CD. —*Scott Yanow*

Memory of Dick / Dec. 27, 1955+Dec. 29, 1955 / EmArcy ✦✦✦✦

One of two Bobby Jaspar LPs put out on 1988 CDs, this set finds Jaspar playing in France shortly before he moved to the US. Teamed with guitarist Sacha Distel, pianist Rene Urtreger, bassist Benoit Quersin and drummer Jean-Louis Viale, Jaspar (who plays flute on two songs) swings his way through six jazz standards, an obscurity and his own "Memory of Dick" (for the recently deceased pianist Dick Twardzik). The music is essentially straightahead bebop, the modern mainstream of the period. —*Scott Yanow*

Tenor & Flute / May 23, 1957 / Riverside ✦✦✦✦

● **Bobby Jaspar with George Wallington** / May 23, 1957+May 28, 1957 / Original Jazz Classics ✦✦✦✦✦

This CD reissue, which adds "The Fuzz" to the original six-song LP, is a fine showcase for Bobby Jaspar and acts as an excellent introduction to his playing. A mellow-toned tenor and a fluent flutist who was quite bop-oriented, Jaspar is featured with pianist George Wallington, bassist Wilbur Little, drummer Elvin Jones and (on three numbers) trumpeter Idrees Sulieman. The majority of the tunes (other than "My Old Flame" and "All of You") are originals by group members, straighthead tunes with good blowing changes. Recommended. —*Scott Yanow*

Phenil Isopropil Amine / Dec. 19, 1958 / Verve ✦✦✦

This CD reissues Bobby Jaspar's final studio album (although he lived until 1963). Surprisingly, Jaspar, an excellent tenorman, sticks exclusively to flute, performing in a pair of pianoless groups with either Michel Hausser or Sadi Lallemand on vibes, Paul Roverie or Jymie Merritt on bass, drummer Kenny Clarke, and sometimes percussionist Humberto Canto. Comprising six originals (five by Jaspar) and five jazz standards, this light but not lightweight chamber jazz set should have great appeal to fans of 1950s straightahead jazz. —*Scott Yanow*

The Bobby Jaspar Quartet at Ronnie Scott's (1962) / Jan. 1962 / Mole ✦✦✦

Recorded just a year before his death, this English album (releasing previously unknown music for the first time in 1986) is about the only one released from Bobby Jaspar's final four years. Doubling on tenor and flute while joined by guitarist Rene Thomas, bassist Benoit Quersin and drummer Daniel Humair, Jaspar is heard stretching out on his "Be Like Bud" and five boppish jazz standards. The numbers clock in between seven to ten minutes at this live concert, giving Bobby Jaspar an opportunity to take some of his longest solos on record. Highlights of the spirited set include "Pent-Up House," "Our Delight" and "Oleo." —*Scott Yanow*

Jazz at the Philharmonic

All-Star Groups / Bop, Swing

In 1944 producer Norman Granz organized a concert billed as "Jazz at the Philharmonic" (also JATP) as a fundraiser in Los Angeles. The event, which was recorded, featured Illinois Jacquet, Jack McVea, J.J. Johnson, Shorty Sherock and a rhythm section with Nat King Cole and Les Paul; Jacquet's playing in particular caused a bit of a sensation. After a few more similar events, Granz in 1946 began organizing extensive annual tours using classic swing and bop musicians in a jam-session setting. Although some critics often complained that these events encouraged grandstanding (R&B honking was getting popular during the era), a great deal of rewarding and exciting music resulted and Granz recorded (and later released) much of it on his Verve label. He paid his musicians very well and did his best to fight racism every bit of the way. Among JATP's stars through the years were tenors Flip Phillips (whose solo on "Perdido" became famous), Jacquet, Coleman Hawkins, Lester Young, Ben Webster and Stan Getz, trumpeters Roy Eldridge, Charlie Shavers, Dizzy Gillespie and Harry "Sweets" Edison, trombonists Bill Harris and Tommy Turk, altoists Charlie Parker, Willie Smith and Benny Carter, pianists Hank Jones and Oscar Peterson, a variety of bassists (often Ray Brown) and drummers Louie Bellson, Gene Krupa and Buddy Rich. Ella Fitzgerald started touring with JATP early on, usually having her own separate set and joining in on a finale, and later tours often also included performances by regular groups such as the Oscar Peterson Trio, Gene Krupa's combo, Stuff Smith or Lester Young. After 1957 the annual tours stopped, although there was an attempt to revive JATP in 1967 and Granz kept the spirit of Jazz at the Philharmonic alive on his many jam session-type records for Pablo in the 1970s. —*Scott Yanow*

The First Concert / Jul. 2, 1944 / Verve ✦✦✦✦✦

This single CD contains the seven documented selections from the very first performance of Norman Granz's travelling jam session, Jazz at the Philharmonic. A fairly colorful cast of characters is heard from: trumpeter Shorty Sherock (on the last three numbers), trombonist J.J. Johnson (who is on the first four selections), Illinois Jacquet and Jack McVea on tenors and a strong rhythm section that includes pianist Nat King Cole and guitarist Les Paul. Together they perform six standards and a blues with five of the seven numbers over nine-minutes long. Jacquet's screaming solos (he was the first real R&B tenor player) and the humorous and rather remarkable tradeoff between Cole and Paul on the "Blues" are the high points of this historically significant and very enjoyable release, which ranges from touches of Dixieland through swing, bop and early R&B. —*Scott Yanow*

Bird & Pres: The '46 Concerts / Jan. 1946-Apr. 22, 1946 / Verve ✦✦✦✦

This double LP, which was released by Verve in 1977, contains nine lengthy performances, all taken from 1946 Jazz at the Philharmonic concerts. Altoist Charlie Parker is on all but the first two selections and those seven numbers have been reissued on CD. The main problem with these recordings is that the rhythm section (particularly Lee Young's drumming) is over-recorded and very repetitive and sometimes the mixture of bop and swing stylists (especially on the two numbers without Parker) leads to some uncomfortable ensembles. However, this version of "Lady Be Good" is a classic (especially the solos of pianist Arnold Ross and Bird), and there are some good moments on the other selections by the likes of tenors Lester Young, Coleman Hawkins and Charlie Ventura, altoist Willie Smith, trumpeters Dizzy Gillespie, Howard McGhee, Buck Clayton and Al Killian and pianists Mel Powell and Ken Kersey. —*Scott Yanow*

The Rarest Concerts / Apr. 23, 1946-1953 / Verve ✦✦✦✦

In 1983 Polygram came out with ten LPs that document a variety of concerts by Norman Granz's traveling jam session, which he dubbed Jazz at the Philharmonic. This particular album has three rare performances. "I Found a New Baby" and "I Can't Get Started" are taken from the 1946 tour and feature trumpeter Buck Clayton, the tenors of Coleman Hawkins and Lester Young, pianist Ken Kersey and (on the former song) altoist Willie Smith. However, the reason to search for this LP is for the 22-minute "Concert Blues," which has excellent solos from altoists Willie Smith and Benny Carter, the tenors of Flip Phillips and Ben Webster, trombonist Bill Harris and trumpeters Charlie Shavers and Roy Eldridge; the Oscar Peterson trio and drummer Gene Krupa really drive the horns. —*Scott Yanow*

★ **Bird & Pres** / Sep. 18, 1949 / Verve ✦✦✦✦

Of the ten JATP LPs released by Verve in the early '80s, this one has the most essential music, and its contents have since been reissued on CD. For those who do not have the latest reissue and run across this album, don't let it get away. Not only does this set feature altoist Charlie Parker and the tenors of Flip Phillips and Lester Young, but trumpeter Roy Eldridge, the forgotten but brilliant trombonist Tommy Turk, pianist Hank Jones, bassist Ray Brown and drummer Buddy Rich. "The Opener" and "Lester Leaps In" (both over 12 minutes long) are quite exciting, but it is Charlie Parker's remarkable solo on "Embraceable You" that takes honors. The concluding blues (rightfully called "The Closer") is also quite memorable, for after Eldridge and Rich have a tradeoff, the performance ends temporarily until it is remembered that Bird had not had a chance to play yet. His second breath (which has a countless number of perfectly placed notes) cuts everyone. —*Scott Yanow*

Norgran Blues 1950 / Sep. 16, 1950 / Verve ✦✦✦

The 1950 version of Norman Granz's traveling jam session JATP is featured on this LP, one of ten released by Polygram Classics in 1983. Four fairly basic chord changes ("Norgran Blues," "Lady Be Good," "Ghost of a Chance" and "Indiana") are explored by the all-star lineup (trumpeter Harry "Sweets" Edison, trombonist Bill Harris, the tenors of Flip Phillips and Lester Young, pianist Hank Jones, bassist Ray Brown and drummer Buddy Rich). Due to the absence of JATP regular trumpeter Roy Eldridge, there are less fireworks than usual but the music is still quite enjoyable with Young in fine form and Phillips pleasing the enthusiastic audience. —*Scott Yanow*

The Trumpet Battle 1952 / Sep. 13, 1952 / Verve ✦✦✦✦✦

In 1983 Polygram Classics came out with ten LPs featuring various concerts by Jazz at the Philharmonic, producer Norman Granz's all-star groups. This album is one of the more exciting sets since it features trumpeters Roy Eldridge and Charlie Shavers on a "Jam Session Blues," taking their turns on a five-song ballad medley and most notably participating in "The Trumpet Battle." In addition, altoist Benny Carter (who seems inspired by the jam-session setting) and the tenors of Flip Phillips and Lester Young (along with the Oscar Peterson Trio and drummer Buddy Rich) are not to be overlooked. This classic and memorable music has yet to be reissued on CD. —*Scott Yanow*

Gene Krupa & Buddy Rich / Oct. 11, 1952+Sep. 17, 1954 / Verve ✦✦✦

Drum battles are always much better live than on record. For this Jazz at the Philharmonic LP, the emphasis is on the soloing of both Buddy Rich and Gene Krupa. Rich is heard in 1954 driving an all-star group (with clarinetist Buddy DeFranco, vibraphonist Lionel Hampton and the Oscar Peterson Trio) which climaxes with Hampton apparently jumping on his own set of drums. Gene Krupa in 1952 plays "Drum Boogie" in a trio with altoist Willie Smith and pianist Hank Jones, and at the same concert Rich has a solo on "Cottontail" that is preceded by short spots from trumpeters Roy Eldridge and Charlie Shavers, altoist Benny Carter, and the tenors of Lester Young and Flip Phillips. Krupa joins the band on second drums during a brief version of "Perdido" that is a feature for Phillips' honking and the two drummers have the stage to themselves on a mercifully brief piece accurately titled "The Drum Battle." Of the ten JATP releases, this is the least significant but it still has its fun moments. —*Scott Yanow*

Frankfurt 1952 / Nov. 20, 1952 / Pablo ✦✦✦

This is a previously unreleased concert performance catching the JATP troupe (this time featuring Lester Young, Flip Phillips, Roy Eldridge, Hank Jones, Ray Brown, Max Roach and an uncredited Irving Ashby on guitar) on the last night of their European tour of 1952. After Norman Granz' introductions to an enthusiastic Frankfurt audience, the group kicks off with a swinging version of "How High the Moon" that goes on for some 11 minutes. This is followed by "Undecided," taken at an even faster pace but still clocking in at almost 12 minutes and featuring a extraordinary solos by Eldridge and Young. A "Ballad Medley" is next, spotlighting four selections interpreted as solo turns. Flip Phillips starts thing off with a nice reading of "Deep Purple," segueing into Roy Eldridge's take on "Rockin' Chair." Next up is Hank Jones' nice, understated version of "This Is Always," which sets the stage for Lester Young's stunning "I Cover the Waterfront." The concert closes with an uptempo "Dre's Blues," which speeds up to an almost impossible tempo after Max Roach's drum solo. All in all, another classic entry in this long-standing series that languished in the vaults for far too long. —*Cub Koda*

Hartford, 1953 / May 1953 / Pablo ✦✦✦✦

This CD has some typically exciting performances from Norman Granz's traveling jam session Jazz at the Philharmonic. Actually the JATP All-Stars (trumpeters Charlie Shavers and Roy Eldridge, trombonist Bill Harris, Ben Webster and Flip Phillips on tenors, altoists Benny Carter and Willie Smith, the Oscar Peterson Trio and drummer Gene Krupa) only appear on one song, an enjoyable 15-minute version of "Cotton Tail." The Oscar Peterson Quartet (with guitarist Herb Ellis, bassist

Ray Brown and drummer J.C. Heard) are in excellent form on four selections (including a burning "7 Come 11") and tenor-great Lester Young (accompanied by Peterson's group) shows on three numbers that he was still very much in his prime in 1953. Fans of swinging jazz will want this colorful music, which was released for the first time in 1984 on Pablo (and does not duplicate any of the Verve sets). —*Scott Yanow*

One O'Clock Jump 1953 / Sep. 19, 1953 / Verve ✦✦✦✦✦

In 1983 Polygram Classics released ten LPs taken from Jazz at the Philharmonic concerts. This album is particularly explosive due to the remarkable all-star lineup: trumpeters Roy Eldridge and Charlie Shavers, trombonist Bill Harris, altoists Benny Carter and Willie Smith, the tenors of Flip Phillips, Ben Webster and (on "One O'Clock Jump") Lester Young, the Oscar Peterson Trio plus drummer J.C. Heard. Together they play a 25-minute version of "Cool Blues" (the excitable Eldridge as usual climaxes the proceedings), "The Challenges" (which has a fiery trumpet battle) and "One O'Clock Jump"; the latter two performances are over 13 minutes apiece. This is passionate and competitive music that deserves to be reissued on CD. —*Scott Yanow*

☆ **Tokyo: Live at the...** / Nov. 5, 1983-Nov. 8, 1953 / Pablo ✦✦✦✦✦

This two-CD set (originally out as three LPs) features the contents of a single Jazz at the Philharmonic concert held in Tokyo. There are minisets by the Oscar Peterson Trio with guitarist Herb Ellis and bassist Ray Brown (which is highlighted by "Tenderly" and "Swingin' Till the Girls Come Home") and Gene Krupa (in a trio with altoist Benny Carter and Peterson) along with ten numbers that feature Ella Fitgerald (who scats wildly on "Lady Be Good," "How High the Moon" and the closing "Perdido"). But the real reason to get this set is for the Jazz at the Philharmonic All-Stars (trumpeters Roy Eldridge and Charlie Shavers, trombonist Bill Harris, altoists Willie Smith and Benny Carter, tenors Ben Webster and Flip Phillips, the Oscar Peterson Trio and drummer J.C. Heard) who, in addition to a seven-song ballad medley and a drum feature, stretch out on "Tokyo Blues" and "Cotton Tail." The latter has a witty and explosive trumpet battle by Shavers and Eldridge; Shavers comes out on top. This reissue is highly recommened as a fine example of the excitement of JATP in the mid-'50s. —*Scott Yanow*

The Challenges / Sep. 17, 1954 / Verve ✦✦✦✦✦

1954 was Dizzy Gillespie's first year with Jazz at the Philharmonic and Norman Granz's decision to team the trumpeter with the competitive Roy Eldridge (his former idol) was both inspired and logical. On this LP (one of ten released by Polygram Classics in 1983), the sparks really fly as Diz and Eldridge are joined by the tenors of Ben Webster and Flip Phillips, trombonist Bill Harris, the Oscar Peterson Trio and drummer Louie Bellson; no weak spots in that lineup. Their 16-minute "Jazz Concert Blues" is quite exciting and a lengthy five-song ballad medley has its moments (Gillespie's abstract "Stardust" takes honors) but it is the trumpet battle on "The Challenge" that is most memorable. Until the timeless music is reissued on CD, this hard-to-find LP (JATP at its height) is essential. —*Scott Yanow*

The Exciting Battle: Stockholm '55 / Feb. 2, 1955 / Pablo ✦✦✦✦✦

Blues in Chicago 1955 / Oct. 2, 1955 / Verve ✦✦✦✦

This LP, one of ten released by Polygram in 1983 (and whose contents are not yet available on CD) has its moments of interest. The 20-minute "Blues" features enjoyable solos by five classic horn players: Flip Phillips, Lester Young and Illinois Jacquet on tenors and trumpeters Roy Eldridge and Dizzy Gillespie. In addition, Diz and Young are teamed up in "The Modern Set" while "The Swing Set" features Eldridge, Flip and Jacquet and there is a tasteful five-song ballad medley. Fans of these talented players will want to search for this out-of-print album. —*Scott Yanow*

Jazz at the Philharmonic in Europe, Vol. 3 / Nov. 21, 1957 / Verve ✦✦✦✦

By 1957, the once-popular all-star traveling jam session Jazz at the Philharmonic was primarily performing in Europe but fortunately producer Norman Granz documented some of the concerts. This out-of-print LP matches together trumpeter Roy Eldridge, altoist Benny Carter and the complementary but contrasintg tenors of Coleman Hawkins and Don Byas with pianist Lalo Schifrin, bassist Art Davis and drummer Jo Jones. There are some fireworks on lengthy versions of "Take the 'A' Train," "Indiana" and a blues that is wittily titled "A Jazz Portrait of Brigitte Bardot" along with a four-song ballad medley. Everyone plays up to par and, considering the talent involved, that is saying a lot. —*Scott Yanow*

Jazz at the Philharmonic in Europe / 1958 / Verve ✦✦✦✦✦

This double LP draws its music from one of the final tours of Norman Granz's Jazz at the Philharmonic. Three different all-star groups are heard from, including a septet with trumpeter Dizzy Gillespie, trombonist J.J. Johnson and altoists Benny Carter and Cannonball Adderley (in probably the two altos' only joint recording) for spirited versions of "Bernie's Tune" and "Swedish Jam." There is also a collaboration between Gillespie's group of the era (with altoist Leo Wright and pianist Lalo Schifrin), Johnson and Stan Getz. However, the most memorable selection is a rendition of "All the Things You Are" that, in addition to trumpeter Roy Eldridge, matches together the tenors of Getz, Coleman Hawkins and Don Byas. This generally exciting music has not yet been reissued on CD. —*Scott Yanow*

In London 1969 / Mar. 1969 / Pablo ◆◆◆◆◆

By 1969, producer Norman Granz's Jazz at the Philharmonic was largely a thing of the past in the US, but he put together occasional European tours that resulted in the very interesting and consistently enjoyable music heard on this double CD. Trumpeters Dizzy Gillespie and Clark Terry, tenors Zoot Sims and James Moody, pianist Teddy Wilson, bassist Bob Cranshaw and drummer Louis Bellson form the core group and play two jams and a four-song ballad medley in addition to accompanying blues singer/guitarist T-Bone Walker on three numbers. Teddy Wilson's Trio with Cranshaw and Bellson is in typically flawless form on a few songs and then comes the biggest surprise of the two-fer. The great veteran tenor Coleman Hawkins was in sad shape during the last few years of his life (he would pass away two months after this concert) yet he manages to almost sound as if he were still in his prime, far exceeding any of his post-1965 recordings on "Blue Lou" and three ballads including a partly unaccompanied "September Song" and an emotional rendition of "Body and Soul." Altoist Benny Carter is also heard from and all of the horns join in for a finale, "What Is This Thing Called Love?" This is historic and frequently exciting music. —*Scott Yanow*

At the Montreux Festival / Jul. 16, 1975 / Pablo ◆◆◆◆

Norman Granz and Pablo Records took over a large segment of the 1975 Montreux Jazz Festival and many recordings resulted. This particular CD is a colorful reissue featuring trumpeters Roy Eldridge and Clark Terry, Zoot Sims on tenor, altoist Benny Carter, guitarist Joe Pass, pianist Tommy Flanagan, bassist Keter Betts and drummer Bobby Durham performing four fairly lengthy renditions of standards. Everyone is in fine form but it is the joyful playing of the two complementary but contrasting trumpeters (both of whom can be immediately recognized in a note or two) that makes this a recommended set for fans of straightahead jazz. —*Scott Yanow*

Return to Happiness, Tokyo 1983 / 1983 / Pablo ◆◆◆◆

To commemorate the 30th anniversary of JATP's first visit to Japan, producer Norman Granz put together a new Jazz at the Philharmonic show in 1983. Many of the earlier players were either no longer around or unavailable, but Granz was able to gather a fairly strong all-star crew (Harry "Sweets" Edison and Clark Terry on trumpets, Zoot Sims and Eddie "Lockjaw" Davis on tenors, trombonists J.J. Johnson and Al Grey, pianist Oscar Peterson, guitarist Joe Pass, bassist Niels Pedersen and drummer Louie Bellson) for what would be JATP's final tour. This two-CD set starts off with the all-stars jamming on three lengthy tunes. Each of the horns are also showcased on two short ballads apiece (which by itself totals 33 minutes). The Oscar Peterson Quartet and Ella Fitzgerald both have fine minisets and the proceedings conclude with Fitzgerald scatting with the horns on "Flying Home." Although the music does not reach the heights of JATP's '50s performances, this is a well-conceived, enjoyable and now somewhat nostalgic set. —*Scott Yanow*

Jazz Futures

f. 1991, db. 1991
Group / Hard Bop

This short-lived all-star group toured during part of 1991 and showcased in an intelligent and coherent fashion some of the top Young Lions of the era: trumpeters Roy Hargrove and Marlon Jordan, altoist Antonio Hart, Tim Warfield on tenor, guitarist Mark Whitfield, pianist Benny Green, bassist Christian McBride and drummer Carl Allen. They recorded one fine album for Novus before the future bandleaders all went their separate ways. —*Scott Yanow*

Live in Concert / Jul. 18, 1991+Aug. 18, 1991 / Novus ◆◆◆

When one considers the lineup of talented young musicians (trumpeters Roy Hargrove and Marlon Jordan, altoist Antonio Hart, Tim Warfield on tenor, guitarist Mark Whitfield, pianist Benny Green, bassist Christian McBride and drummer Carl Allen), this CD should have been a classic; instead it is merely good. There is a ballad feature apiece for each of the hornmen, spirited showcases for Green and Whitfield and three group jams. Unfortunately, the ballads are disappointing with none of the horns adding anything new to their interprations of standards. Hargroves fares well on "You Don't Know What Love Is" but Jordan falters a bit on "Stardust." The pianist really romps in an Oscar Peterson groove on "Picadilly Square" and Whitfield is memorable on "Medgar Evers Blues" but the tradeoffs on the closing jam, "Public Eye," are self-indulgent and a bit silly. So overall the results are quite mixed. —*Scott Yanow*

Jazz Passengers

f. 1987
Group / Post-Bop

The Jazz Passengers were founded in 1987 by Roy Nathanson and trombonist Curtis Fowlkes in order to bring lively humor and entertainment back into modern jazz; the name, a takeoff on Art Blakey's Jazz Messengers, signifies that the musicians are merely along for a wild ride. The band also includes percussionist E.J. Rodriguez, bassist Brad Jones (a cohort of Elvin Jones and Muhal Richard Abrams), Steely Dan touring vibist Bill Ware, and guitarist Marc Ribot, who has appeared on albums by noted singer-songwriters Elvis Costello and Tom Waits. Nathanson and Fowlkes met while playing in the pit band for the Big Apple Circus, which gave them the opportunity to play the Charles Mingus music they loved and pay the bills as well. The two joined John Lurie's Lounge Lizards and left after a short time to record a duet album together. They added more and more studio musicians until, eventually, the Jazz Passengers were born. The group made a name for itself in the New York City avant-garde scene centering on the Knitting Factory with its hybrid of Mingus-influenced postbop, dance rhythms, and original tunes complete with lyrics and/or entertaining stories. After five albums on small independent labels, the Passengers finally recorded its major-label debut, *Jazz Passengers in Love*. In 1994, rock singer Deborah Harry started touring and recording with the band. —*Steve Huey*

Implement Yourself / 1990 / New World ◆◆◆◆

Arguably the best group to emerge on the new music/avant-garde scene in many years, Roy Nathanson's Jazz Passengers suffer from both audience ignorance about their talents and meager album distribution due to being on a small label. But they make fine, constantly changing music that's reminiscent of The Art Ensemble in its early days. —*Ron Wynn*

● Live at the Knitting Factory / 1991 / Knitting Factory ◆◆◆◆◆

The Jazz Passengers blend collective improvisation, outside arrangements, free playing and cohesive intragroup interplay better than most hard bop and mainstream jazz groups. They also include other nonjazz elements into their music, from funk to rock and blues. This melange of styles and idioms was on display throughout the 1991 concert captured on this CD. Whether it was the African/Arabic flavor of "Jazz Passengers in Egypt Overture" or the offbeat pace of "Prozak" and "Tikkun," The Passengers don't content themselves with merely executing chord changes and ripping out solos. They take their followers on trips that seldom proceed smoothly, but always result in rewarding experiences. —*Ron Wynn*

Plain Old Joe / 1993 / Knitting Factory ◆◆◆

The Jazz Passengers (which comprises Roy Nathanson on alto, tenor and soprano, trombonist Curtis Fowlkes, violinist Jim Nolet who doubles on guitar, vibraphonist Bill Ware, bassist Brad Jones and drummer E.J. Rodriguez) is an eccentric group with a nutty sense of humor. On this somewhat odd CD, the Jazz Passengers use a great deal of bizarre humor along with interesting combinations of instruments, references to earlier eras of jazz, spoken interludes, vocals by would-be crooner Curtis Fowlkes, noisy sound explorations and some swinging solos. Their version of "If I Were a Bell" is quite silly and "Inzane" lives up to its title. Not everything works but *Plain Old Joe* is certainly not run-of-the-mill music or forgettable. —*Scott Yanow*

In Love / 1994 / Windham Hill ◆◆◆

Individually Twisted / 1996 / 32 Jazz ◆◆◆

On *Individually Twisted*, Deborah Harry became the Jazz Passengers' lead vocalist, and she acquits herself well, helping to turn the album into a thoroughly enjoyable, jazzy hipster pastiche. Elvis Costello also appears on two tracks, including a fun duet with Harry on "Doncha Go 'Way Mad." —*Leo Stanley*

Carter Jefferson

b. 1946, d. Dec. 9, 1993, Krackow, Poland
Tenor Saxophone / Hard Bop

A reliable and advanced soloist who spent most of his career as a sideman, Carter Jefferson is best remembered for his association with Woody Shaw during 1977-80. Jefferson started on clarinet and played alto before settling on tenor, going on tour early in the backup bands of the Temptations, the Supremes and Little Richard. In 1971, he moved to New York to attend New York University and soon spent two years with Mongo Santamaria and a period in 1973 as a member of Art Blakey's Jazz Messengers. After his important stint with Woody Shaw (with whom he recorded several times), Jefferson worked with many top players, including Elvin Jones, Roy Haynes, Cedar Walton, Jerry Gonzalez' Fort Apache Band, Malachi Thompson and Jack Walrath's Masters of Suspense. His premature death in Poland after emergency surgery was a major loss. Carter Jefferson only led one record as a leader, *The Rise of Atlantis,* on the Timeless label in 1978. —*Scott Yanow*

Eddie Jefferson (Edgar Jefferson)

b. Aug. 3, 1918, Pittsburgh, PA, **d.** May 9, 1979, Detroit, MI
Vocals, Lyricist / Vocalese, Bop

The founder of vocalese (putting recorded solos to words), Eddie Jefferson did not have a great voice but he was one of the top jazz singers, getting the maximum out of what he had. He started out working as a tapdancer but by the late '40s was singing and writing lyrics. A live session from 1949 (released on Spotlite) finds him pioneering vocalese by singing his lyrics to "Parker's Mood" and Lester Young's solo on "I Cover the Waterfront." However, his classic lyrics to "Moody's Mood for Love" were recorded first by King Pleasure (1952), who also had a big hit with his version of "Parker's Mood." Jefferson had his first studio recording that year (which included Coleman Hawkins' solo on "Body and Soul") before working with James Moody (1953-57). Although he recorded on an occasional basis in the 1950s and '60s, his contributions to the idiom seemed to be mostly overlooked until the 1970s. Jefferson worked with Moody again (1968-73) and during his last few years often performed with Richie Cole. He was shot to death outside of a Detroit club in 1979. Eddie Jefferson, who also wrote memorable lyrics to "Jeannine," "Lady Be Good," "So What," "Freedom Jazz Dance" and even "Bitches' Brew," recorded for Savoy, Prestige, a single for Checker, Inner City and Muse. —*Scott Yanow*

● **The Jazz Singer** / Jan. 19, 1959-Oct. 29, 1965 / Evidence ✦✦✦✦✦

Eddie Jefferson, one of the great jazz singers and an important pioneer of vocalese, is heard in peak form on this Evidence CD, which reissues an Inner City LP and adds six previously unissued selections to the program. The bulk of the music is from 1959-61 with Jefferson backed by several horns (including trumpeter Howard McGhee and tenor saxophonist James Moody and sometimes three other vocalists). There are many highlights including Jefferson's original classic versions of "Body and Soul" (a tribute to Coleman Hawkins, the "king of the saxophone") and "So What" (dedicated to Miles Davis), a remake of "Moody's Mood for Love" and vocalese adaptations of a few Lester Young and Charlie Parker solos. Most of the unissued tracks are from these sessions, but there is also "Silly Little Cynthia" from 1964 (a duet with pianist Tommy Tucker) and a meeting with guitarist Louisiana Red on 1965's "Red's New Dream." When one considers that Jefferson otherwise did not record during 1963-67, it makes those two numbers not only enjoyable but historic. This CD is highly recommended for all jazz collections. —*Scott Yanow*

★ **Letter from Home** / Dec. 18, 1961-Feb. 8, 1962 / Original Jazz Classics ✦✦✦✦✦

This CD (which augments the original LP program with two alternate takes) is a fine showcase for the vocalese master Eddie Jefferson. Backed by either a tentet or a quintet, which gives solo space to altoist James Moody and the tenor of Johnny Griffin, Jefferson sings his lyrics to such numbers as "Take the 'A' Train," "Billie's Bounce," "I Cover the Waterfront," "Parker's Mood" (the latter differs from the famous lines immortalized by King Pleasure), "A Night in Tunisia" and "Body and Soul," among others. Jefferson is in prime form and these boppish renditions as a whole form a near-classic. —*Scott Yanow*

Body and Soul / 1968 / Original Jazz Classics ✦✦✦✦✦

Eddie Jefferson had not been on record in quite a few years when he recorded this excellent set (reissued on CD) for Prestige. A few of the songs ("Mercy, Mercy, Mercy," "Psychedelic Sally" and "See If You Can Git to That") were attempts to update the singer's style in the mod idiom of the late '60s but the most memorable selections are "So What" (on which Jefferson recreates Miles Davis' famous solo), "Body and Soul," "Now's the Time," "Oh Gee" and "Filthy McNasty"; the latter has very effective lyrics by writer Ira Gitler. Tenorman James Moody, trumpeter Dave Burns and pianist Barry Harris are in the supporting cast of this excellent set. —*Scott Yanow*

Come Along with Me / Aug. 12, 1969 / Original Jazz Classics ✦✦✦✦✦

Vocalist Eddie Jefferson (the founder of vocalese) is in top form throughout this outstanding set, a CD reissue of the original LP. There is a liberal amount of solo space for trumpeter Bill Hardman, altoist Charles McPherson and pianist Barry Harris but it is Jefferson's singing and his witty lyrics to such songs as Horace Silver's "The Preacher," "Yardbird Suite," "Dexter Digs In," "Baby Girl" (based on "These Foolish Things") and even "When You're Smiling" that are the main reasons to acquire this very enjoyable disc. —*Scott Yanow*

Things Are Getting Better / Mar. 5, 1974 / Muse ✦✦✦✦

Singer Eddie Jefferson's first album in five years finds him doing his best to keep up with the times. Somehow he manages to sing Miles Davis' "Bitches Brew" (a nearly impossible melody to make much out of) and he also performs "Freedom Jazz Dance" and "Trane's Blues" in addition to more boppish material (including

an exuberant "Things Are Getting Better," "Night in Tunisia" and "Billie's Bounce"). The Sly Stone tune "Thank You" is the only trivial selection among the eight reissued on this CD while "I Just Got Back in Town" is based on James Moody's improvisation to the ballad "I Cover the Waterfront." The master of vocalese (who was at the peak of his powers during this period) is assisted by trumpeter Joe Newman, Billy Mitchell (on tenor, flute and bass clarinet), keyboardist Mickey Tucker, bassist Sam Jones and drummer Eddie Gladden. A worthy effort. —*Scott Yanow*

Godfather of Vocalese / Mar. 17, 1976 / Muse ✦✦✦✦✦

The innovative scat singer and vocalese lyricist was having a comeback during his final years, teaming up with altoist Richie Cole for spirited performances. The set features Cole, trumpeter Wayman Reed and a fine four-piece rhythm section, but the emphasis is naturally on the singer. Jefferson performs such classics as "I Got the Blues" and "Ornithology," teams up with vocalist Betsy Fersmire on "Keep Walkin'" and "Pinetop's Boogie," and even tackles Herbie Hancock's "Chameleon." —*Scott Yanow*

The Live-Liest / Mar. 26, 1976-Mar. 27, 1976 / Muse ✦✦✦✦

Main Man / Oct. 9, 1977 / Inner City ✦✦✦✦✦

Eddie Jefferson's final recording (cut less than two years before his murder) has many high points. This LP includes classic versions of his funny "Benny's from Heaven," "Moody's Mood for Love" (with the talented singer Janet Lawson helping out), "Body and Soul" (which Jefferson turned into a tribute for Coleman Hawkins), "Jeannine" and the complex "Freedom Jazz Dance." Well worth searching for, hopefully this music will eventually be reissued on CD. —*Scott Yanow*

Thomas Jefferson

b. Jun. 20, 1920, Chicago, IL
Trumpet / Dixieland

One of the finest trumpeters in New Orleans during the 1950s and '60s, Thomas Jefferson played drums and French horn briefly before setting on trumpet. He worked with Oscar Celestin's Tuxedo Orchestra in 1936 and then locally in New Orleans with Sidney Desvignes, Jump Jackson and others. He recorded in the 1950s with Johnny St. Cyr, Santo Pecora and George Lewis. Of Jefferson's own infrequent sessions as a leader, a 1960 date for Southland (in which he is just joined by a rhythm section) is definitive and a 1974 session for Storyville is also excellent. Thomas Jefferson's idol has always been Louis Armstrong. —*Scott Yanow*

From New Orleans / Nov. 12, 1953+Oct. 9, 1960 / Storyville ✦✦✦✦✦

This out-of-print LP features one of the finest trumpeters to emerge in the New Orleans jazz scene of the 1950s. Jefferson performs four songs in a 1953 sextet that also includes trombonist Jack Delaney and clarinetist Raymond Burke. However, it is the other eight selections that are most notable for Jefferson's trumpet and vocals are showcased as the only horn in a quintet with pianist Armand Hug and drummer Monk Hazel. Strongly influenced by Louis Armstrong, Jefferson also had an appealing musical personality of his own which is fully displayed on such numbers as "When You're Smiling," "There'll Be Some Changes Made" and "Someday You'll Be Sorry." This set is really Thomas Jefferson's definitive recording, showing him off at his best. —*Scott Yanow*

● **New Orleans to Midnight** / Nov. 14, 1960 / GHB ✦✦✦✦✦

Thomas Jefferson was one of the finest New Orleans jazzmen to emerge during the 1950s. A talented trumpeter and a fine singer, Jefferson is featured in prime form on this date, a quintet outing with pianist Armand Hug, guitarist Joe Capraro, bassist Sherwood Mangiapane and drummer Monk Hazel. Jefferson's solos on such numbers as "Breeze," "Someday You'll Be Sorry," "There'll Be Some Changes Made" and "In the Shade of the Old Apple Tree," as well as his six vocals (including a near-classic version of "When You're Smiling"), are obviously influenced by Louis Armstrong, but not a direct copy. The music on this highly enjoyable LP, also released on a Storyville album with four additional cuts from an earlier session, has not yet been reissued on CD; it is Thomas Jefferson's definitive date. —*Scott Yanow*

Thomas Jefferson's International New Orleans Jazz Band / Jan. 10, 1974 / Storyville ✦✦✦✦

Considering his talents as a trumpeter and vocalist, it is surprising how few sessions Thomas Jefferson led through the years. With the exception of this album and one set made in 1960 for Southland, Jefferson's few dates have all been made for tiny and long-lost labels. Recorded in Copenhagen with clarinetist Sammy Rimington (doubling on alto) and European musicians, Jefferson sounds typically exuberant throughout the octet outing. Jefferson plays and usually sings on eight standards (including the lesser-known "Mardi Gras" and "Into Each Life Some Rain Must Fall"), most of which qualify as Dixieland warhorses, such as "When

You're Smiling" and "St. Louis Blues." This LP is easily recommended to New Orleans jazz fans. —*Scott Yanow*

Herb Jeffries

b. Sep. 24, 1916, Detroit, MI
Vocals / Ballads, Standards
Although not really a jazz singer, Herb Jeffries is the last surviving member of the 1940 Duke Ellington Orchestra and a fine interpreter of swing songs and ballads. He performed with Erskine Tate in the early '30s, Earl Hines (1931-34) and Blanche Calloway before becoming the first Black cowboy actor in a series of 1930s Westerns. He gained his greatest fame while with Ellington (1940-42), having a big hit in "Flamingo." Jeffries, who recorded with Sidney Bechet in 1940, has worked as a single since leaving Duke in 1942, recording on an occasional basis and remaining active into the mid-'90s. —*Scott Yanow*

● **A Brief History of Herb Jeffries (The Bronze Buckaroo)** / 1934-1995 / Warner Western ◆◆◆◆
Herb Jeffries, who in the late 1990s was the only survivor of the 1940 Duke Ellington Orchestra, is heard on 14 selections on this CD, which covers a six-decade period. There are two tracks from the likable singer's cowboy films of 1938, appearances with Earl Hines' Orchestra (1934) and Sidney Bechet, four numbers with Ellington (including the hit "Flamingo" and "Jump for Joy"), guest shots with Joe Liggins' Honeydrippers, one song taken from a live concert at the Apollo in 1954, and two numbers (including "I'm a Happy Cowboy") from a 1995 session. Throughout, Jeffries is in surprisingly consistent form, displaying a warm baritone. Although not a jazz singer himself, Herb Jeffries sounds quite at home in these diverse settings. A recommended set. —*Scott Yanow*

Say It Isn't So / Jan. 1957 / Bethlehem ◆◆◆
The warm baritone of Herb Jeffries is showcased on a dozen ballads on this CD reissue. Russ Garcia's arrangements for a string orchestra match Jeffries' voice well, but there are no real surprises or variety. Jeffries sounds fine on such tunes as "Say It Isn't So," "When Your Lover Has Gone," "Angel Eyes" and "The End of a Love Affair," although the overall results are rather predictable. —*Scott Yanow*

The Bronze Buckaroo (Rides Again) / 1995 / Warner Brothers ◆◆
This record is a winner, among the finest cowboy albums ever recorded, and maybe the most fascinating. Jeffries does these songs with all manner of jazz inflections, in his singing as well as in the back-up arrangements—there's nothing here that couldn't have fit well in any night club during the 1940s in any part of the country; yeah, there are twangy steel guitars and there's some fiddle back-up, but the dominant presence is Jeffries, with more than half a century of jazz and blues singing behind him. His baritone voice makes for a wonderful (and very different "Tumbling Tumbleweeds"). He gets help from singers as diverse as Michael Martin Murphey, the Sons of the San Joachin, and the Mills Brothers, and it all works magnificently. The running time is a little short at 30 minutes, but the songs are all priceless, for fans of old-style '40s pop (the Mills Bros. etc.) and jazz as well as country and cowboy songs. —*Bruce Eder*

John Jenkins

b. Jan. 3, 1931, Chicago, IL
Alto Saxophone / Hard Bop
John Jenkins, who had a similar sound to Jackie McLean, was most active in 1957 but dropped out of music by the mid-'60s. In 1955 he worked with Art Farmer, led his own group and freelanced around Chicago. Jenkins moved to New York in 1957, played with Charles Mingus, led two albums of his own (on New Jazz and Blue Note) and recorded as a sideman with Donald Byrd, Hank Mobley, Paul Quinichette, Clifford Jordan, Sahib Shihab and Wilbur Ware. Not much has been heard from him since. —*Scott Yanow*

● **Jenkins, Jordan and Timmons** / Jul. 26, 1957 / Original Jazz Classics ◆◆◆◆
Four of the five selections on this CD reissue (which also includes "Tenderly") are obscure jazz originals by altoist John Jenkins, tenor saxophonist Clifford Jordan or trombonist Julian Priester. Inspired by both Charlie Parker and Jackie McLean, Jenkins teams up with Jordan, pianist Bobby Timmons, bassist Wilbur Ware and drummer Dannie Richmond for some bop-oriented improvising. Strange that this would be one of only two sets led by Jenkins. Although the Blue Note CD, recorded just 16 days later, gets the edge, this is an excellent effort, too. —*Scott Yanow*

John Jenkins with Kenny Burrell / Aug. 11, 1957 / Blue Note ◆◆◆◆◆
The second (and best) of John Jenkins' two sessions as a leader features the altoist in a quintet with guitarist Kenny Burrell, pianist Sonny Clark, bassist Paul Chambers and drummer Dannie Richmond. Sounding at times like Charlie Parker (with touches of Phil Woods and Jackie McLean), Jenkins easily keeps up with his better-known sidemen and plays the boppish music with plenty of creativity, emo-

tion and excitement. This 1996 CD reissue adds a pair of "new" alternate takes to the original six-song program which includes three Jenkins originals, one by Burrell and two standards. After listening to the high-quality set, one wonders why John Jenkins did not make it. —*Scott Yanow*

Jazz Eyes / Sep. 10, 1957 / Savoy ◆◆◆

Leroy Jenkins

b. Mar. 11, 1932, Chicago, IL
Violin / Avant-Garde, Free Jazz
Free jazz's leading violinist, Leroy Jenkins has greatly expanded the options and range of sounds and possibilities for stringed instruments in free music. His techniques have included sawing, string bending and plucking. Jenkins plays adventurous phrases and distorted solos, while including elements of blues, bebop and classical in his approach. Jenkins' often lists as influences a diverse group of violinists (Eddie South and Jascha Heifetz) and other instrumentalists (Charlie Parker, Ornette Coleman and John Coltrane among others). Jenkins began playing violin at eight, often at church in Chicago. He was another student of Walter Dyett at Du Sable High, where he also played alto sax. Jenkins graduated from Florida A&M, where he dropped alto and concentrated on violin. He spent about four years teaching stringed instruments in Mobile, Alabama. Jenkins returned to Chicago in the mid-'60s, and divided his time from 1965 to 1969 between teaching in the Chicago public school system and working with the Association for the Advancement of Creative Musicians (AACM). Jenkins was among the AACM musicians who left Chicago for Europe in the late '60s. While in Paris, Jenkins, Anthony Braxton, Leo Smith and Steve McCall founded The Creative Construction Company. He also played with Ornette Coleman there. Jenkins returned to Chicago in 1970, and moved to New York with Braxton shortly after, living and studying at Coleman's New York home for three months. After working briefly with Cecil Taylor and Braxton, Jenkins played with Archie Shepp, Alice Coltrane and Rahsaan Roland Kirk. But more importantly, in 1971 Jenkins, Sirone and Jerome Cooper founded The Revolutionary Ensemble, one of the decade's great trios. They were truly a cooperative venture, with each musician contributing compositions, and their performances often resembling works in progress. All three played several instruments during their concerts. The Ensemble maintained its integrity while making albums that were aesthetic triumphs and commercial flops for six years on various labels. After the trio disbanded, Jenkins made several tours of Europe, led a quintet and a trio featuring Anthony Davis and Andrew Cyrille. During the mid-'80s he served on the board of directors of the Composers' Forum, and was a member of Cecil Taylor's quintet in 1987. Jenkins has presented many free music performances and written numerous pieces for soloists, small groups and large ensembles. A few of his Black Saint and India Navigation sessions are available on CD. —*Ron Wynn*

For Players Only / Jan. 30, 1975 / JCOA ◆◆◆◆

● **Solo Concert** / Jan. 11, 1977 / India Navigation ◆◆◆◆◆
About as adventurous and experimental as violin playing gets. Despite far-out tendencies, Jenkins knows when to come back in and how. —*Ron Wynn*

The Legend of Ai Glatson / Jul. 1978 / Black Saint ◆◆◆◆
Excellent session by dynamic violinist Leroy Jenkins, once part of the wonderful avant-garde trio The Revolutionary Ensemble. Jenkins cut this session in 1978, shortly after the trio's demise, and it's loaded with great violin solos, as well as some unusual, intriguing arrangements and compositions. —*Ron Wynn*

Mixed Quintet / Mar. 22, 1979-Mar. 23, 1979 / Black Saint ◆◆◆◆◆

Lifelong Ambitions / Mar. 11, 1977 / Black Saint ◆◆◆◆◆
Leroy Jenkins, free jazz's greatest violinist, has always worked best in intimate situations with equally talented partners. He certainly had the optimum conditions on this duet date pairing him with outstanding pianist, composer, arranger and conductor Muhal Richard Abrams. The duo played six Jenkins compositions for the session, which was recorded live. Abrams and Jenkins frequently alternated roles, letting each other set the pace, never colliding and forging a highly effective musical partnership. Jenkins' whiplash lines, percussive effects and seamless blend of free and blues influences was capably contrasted by Abrams' driving, soulful piano phrases and solos. —*Ron Wynn*

Urban Blues / Jan. 2, 1984 / Black Saint ◆◆◆◆
Violinist Leroy Jenkins was at the helm of Sting, which played funky and free, did originals and vintage spirituals, and would shift from stretches of collective improvisation to challenging solo exchanges. They were a unique, intriguing group, but sadly didn't last. This 1984 album, reissued on CD, presented them at their best, displaying the breadth of influences, genres, sources and styles that converged and resulted in the work of a great band. —*Ron Wynn*

Leroy Jenkins Live! / Mar. 15, 1992 / Black Saint ✦✦✦
Two CDs that give an overview of Jenkins' earlier tune-oriented and later free playing. Muhal Richard Abrams is a composer who has served as an important musical, spiritual and social influence as president of the AACM (Association for the Advancement of Creative Musicians) founded in Chicago in 1965, by members of his earlier group The Experimental Band. His own work may be heard on "Blu Nlu Blu" (Black Saint 1991) and "Family Talk" (Black Saint 1993) in excellent performances that reach out to the listener. Abrams' recent and daring work, the masterpiece "Duet for Pianos No. 1" has yet to be recorded. —*Blue Gene Tyranny*

Themes & Improvisations / Apr. 9, 1992 / CRI ✦✦✦✦

Santa Fe / 1994 / Lovely Music ✦✦✦
A magnificent CD of violin and viola solos showing the dynamic "pure music" side of this great composer/performer who worked with the AACM in Chicago in the '60s, moved to New York City and founded The Revolutionary Ensemble (they recorded five albums). He has composed many large works played by the Brooklyn Philharmonic, the Cleveland Chamber Symphony, the Albany Symphony, Kronos Quartet, and was included in the Kennedy Center's American Composer series; he recently premiered his opera-for-dance "The Mother of Three Sons" commissioned by the Munich Biennale, and his "Off-Duty Dryad" (1990) was played by The Soldier String Quartet with dancers. He is currently at work on a new opera, which includes three rappers as characters, and a work about the recently uncovered Negro Graveyard in Manhattan. He is a totally engaging performer who keeps the listener on the seat's edge waiting for the next surprising variation and invention. —*Blue Gene Tyranny*

Ingrid Jensen

b. 1967, Vancouver, British Columbia
Trumpet / Hard Bop
One of the most gifted hard bop trumpeters of her generation, Ingrid Jensen was born in Vancouver, British Columbia in 1967. After attending the Berklee College of Music in Boston, she toured Europe with the Vienna Art Orchestra's production "Fe and Males"; following the completion of the tour, she remained abroad, teaching jazz trumpet and becoming, at age 25, the youngest professor at Austria's Bruckner Conservatory. Jensen also toured with Lionel Hampton and His Golden Men of Jazz before returning to the US in 1994, joining the big band Diva; that same year she also recorded her debut LP, the Enja label release *Vernal Fields*. An acolyte of Miles Davis, Art Farmer and Woody Shaw, her second album, *Here on Earth*, appeared in 1997. —*Jason Ankeny*

● **Vernal Fields** / Oct. 11, 1994-Oct. 12, 1994 / Enja ✦✦✦✦
Although trumpeter Ingrid Jensen has a wide range and a potentially fiery style, she holds a great deal in reserve on her debut recording, letting one peek at her emotional intensity now and then but mostly making lyrical statements, Her supporting cast (altoist Steve Wilson, George Garzone on tenor, pianist Bruce Barth, bassist Larry Grenadier and drummer Lenny White) is quite impressive and adds a great deal to the CD without taking the spotlight away from the leader. Ingrid Jensen sounds particularly strong on "Marsh Blues" and the standards "Ev'rytime We Say Goodbye," "I Love You" and an ironic "By Myself" but all nine selections have their moments. The music is basically advanced hard bop where (when she is playing open) sounding like a logical successor to Freddie Hubbard and Woody Shaw while resembling her teacher Art Farmer a bit when utilizing a mute. This is an impressive beginning to what should be an important career. —*Scott Yanow*

Here on Earth / Sep. 19, 1996+Sep. 20, 1996 / Enja ✦✦✦

Papa Bue Jensen

Trombone, Leader / Dixieland, New Orleans Jazz
Leader of the Viking Jazz Band since 1956, Papa Bue Jensen is an excellent Dixieland trombonist who has been active for decades in Denmark. He had recorded with Chris Barber before forming his group (which during 1956-58 was known simply as the New Orleans Jazz Band). Through the years the band has recorded (sometimes for Storyville or Timeless) with such American guests as George Lewis, Wingy Manone, Wild Bill Davison, Edmond Hall, Champion Jack Dupree, Albert Nicholas and Art Hodes. —*Scott Yanow*

● **Greatest Hits** / Nov. 12, 1958-Apr. 15, 1970 / Storyville ✦✦✦✦
The dozen selections on this Storyville CD would not qualify as "hits" but they do a fine job of summing up the Dixieland music of trombonist Papa Bue Jensen's Viking Jazz Band. Programmed in chronological order, there is not much change (either in personnel or in style) from 1958's "Praise of Nyboder" to 1970s "Down by the Riverside" but neither has the band (which includes Finn Otto Hansen on trumpet and clarinetist Jorgen Svare) lost any of its enthusiasm. Highlights of this

likable set include "1919 March," "The Saints," "Lil' Liza Jane" and "Everybody Loves Saturday Night." Recommended for Dixieland fans. —*Scott Yanow*

A Tribute to Wingy Manone / Dec. 1967 / Storyville ✦✦✦✦✦

Down by the River / Sep. 1, 1969-Nov. 30, 1971 / Storyville ✦✦✦✦
The second of two Storyville CD documenting Papa Bue Jensen's Viking Jazz Band during an era when Dixieland was far from popular, this set (subtitled "The Complete Original Recordings, Vol. 2") has all of Jensen's recordings from Dec. 1969-Nov. 1971, except for a German concert released elsewhere by Storyville. The excellent New Orleans-style band (which features trumpeter Finn Otto Hansen, singer Bjarne "Liller" Petersen and clarinetist Jorgen Svare) is heard in top form throughout the set. There are also a few guest appearances from veteran clarinetist Albert Nicholas. Well worth picking up by trad jazz fans, along with Vol. 1 (*Everybody Loves Saturday Night*). —*Scott Yanow*

Live in Copenhagen / Oct. 27, 1975+Sep. 15, 1978 / Storyville ✦✦✦✦
Most of the music from two albums by Papa Bue Jensen's Viking Jazz Band are reissued on this single CD. The seven songs from the earlier session are most notable for the trumpet playing and singing of Theis Jensen, who does a close imitation of Louis Armstrong without falling into satire. His vocals on "Solitude" and "Bye and Bye" come mighty close, and with his trumpet in the lead of a front line also including trombonist Papa Bue Jensen and clarinetist Jorgen Svare, the group often sounds like the Louis Armstrong All-Stars. The later set has Ole Stolle on trumpet, but once again a few vocals close to Satch, this time by banjoist Bjarne "Liller" Petersen, who stars on a surprisingly touching version of "What a Wonderful World." Other highlights include "Stevedore Stomp," "Lazy River," "Bourbon Street Parade" and "Mahogany Hall Stomp." Throughout this highly enjoyable disc, the ensembles are melodic and exciting, the solos show personality, and the overall results are high-quality Dixieland. —*Scott Yanow*

On Stage / Apr. 1982+Sep. 1982 / Timeless ✦✦✦

In the Mood / Oct. 13, 1986-Oct. 14, 1986 / Timeless ✦✦✦
Trombonist Papa Bue Jensen has long led one of the top Scandinavian trad jazz bands. This LP is a bit unusual in that some of the tunes the sextet performs are swing standards (such as "In the Mood," "You'll Never Walk Alone" and "Stardust"), and they also jam such unlikely material as Kris Kristofferson's "Help Me Make It Through the Night" and "Brahms' Lullaby." In general, the set (which also has Sidney Bechet's "Coffee Grinder" and a few New Orleans tunes among its highlights) is successful, as Papa Bue and his band (which includes trumpeter Ole Stolle and clarinetist John Defferary) show that they can swing practically anything. —*Scott Yanow*

Everybody Loves Saturday Night, Vol. 1 / Dec. 16, 1996-Dec. 2, 1969 / Storyville ✦✦✦✦✦
Subtitled "The Complete Original Recordings, Vol 1," this CD has all of the music recorded by trombonist Arne "Papa Bue" Jensen's Viking Jazz Band during a three-year period, other than a couple of lengthy 1968 sessions and an album with trumpeter Wingy Manone. The leader, trumpeter Finn Otto Hansen, and clarinetist Jorgen Svare (showcased on "Home") formed a strong front line; Bjarne "Liller" Petersen contributes occasional vocals, and the CD has four previously unreleased selections among its 18 spirited performances. Highlights include "Jungle Jamboree," "Stevedore Stomp," and "You Rascal You." Easily recommended to Dixieland fans, along with its companion CD *Down By the Riverside*. —*Scott Yanow*

Antonio Carlos Jobim

b. Jan. 25, 1927, Rio de Janeiro, Brazil, **d.** Dec. 8, 1994, New York, NY
Composer, Guitar, Piano, Vocals / Bossa Nova, Brazilian Jazz
It has been said that Antonio Carlos Brasileiro de Almeida Jobim was the George Gershwin of Brazil—and there is a solid ring of truth in that, for both contributed large bodies of songs to the jazz repertoire, both expanded their reach into the concert hall, and both tend to symbolize their countries in the eyes of the rest of the world. With their gracefully urbane, sensuously aching melodies and harmonies, Jobim's songs gave jazz musicians in the 1960s a quiet, strikingly original alternative to their traditional Tin Pan Alley source.

Jobim's roots were always planted firmly in jazz; the records of Gerry Mulligan, Chet Baker, Barney Kessel and other West Coast jazz musicians made an enormous impact upon him in the 1950s. But he also claimed that the French impressionist composer Claude Debussy had a decisive influence upon his harmonies, and the Brazilian samba gave his music a uniquely exotic rhythmic underpinning. As a pianist, he usually kept things simple and melodically to the point with a touch that reminds some of Claude Thornhill, but some of his records show that he could also stretch out when given room. His guitar was limited mostly to gentle strumming of the syncopated rhythms, and he sang in a modest, slightly hoarse yet often hauntingly emotional manner.

Born in the Tijuca neighborhood of Rio, Jobim originally was headed for a career as an architect. Yet by the time he turned 20, the lure of music was too powerful, and so he started playing piano in nightclubs and working in recording studios. He made his first record in 1954 backing singer Bill Farr as the leader of "Tom and His Band" (Tom was Jobim's lifelong nickname), and he first found fame in 1956 when he teamed up with poet Vinícius de Moraes to provide part of the score for a play called *Orfeo do Carnaval* (later made into the famous film *Black Orpheus*). In 1958, the then-unknown Brazilian singer Joao Gilberto recorded some of Jobim's songs, which had the effect of launching the phenomenon known as bossa nova. Jobim's breakthrough outside Brazil occurred in 1962 when Stan Getz and Charlie Byrd scored a surprise hit with his tune "Desafinado"—and later that year, he and several other Brazilian musicians were invited to participate in a Carnegie Hall showcase. Fueled by Jobim's songs, the bossa nova became an international fad, and jazz musicians jumped on the bandwagon, recording album after album of bossa novas until the trend ran out of commercial steam in the late '60s.

Jobim himself preferred the recording studios to touring, making several lovely albums of his music as a pianist, guitarist and singer for Verve, Warner Bros., Discovery, A&M, CTI and MCA in the '60s and '70s, and Verve again in the last decade of his life. Early on, he started collaborating with arranger/conductor Claus Ogerman, whose subtle, caressing, occasionally moody charts gave his records a haunting ambience. When Brazilian music was in its American eclipse after the '60s, a victim of overexposure and the burgeoning rock revolution, Jobim retreated more into the background, concentrating much energy upon film and TV scores in Brazil. But by 1985, as the idea of world music and a second Brazilian wave gathered steam, Jobim started touring again with a group containing his second wife Ana Lontra, his son Paulo, daughter Elizabeth and various musician friends. At the time of his final concerts in Brazil in September 1993 and at Carnegie Hall in April 1994 (both available on Verve), Jobim at last was receiving the universal recognition he deserved, and a plethora of tribute albums and concerts followed in the wake of his sudden death in New York City of heart failure. Jobim's reputation as one of the great songwriters of the century is now secure, nowhere more so than on the jazz scene where every other set seems to contain at least one bossa nova. —*Richard S. Ginell*

★ **Girl from Ipanema: The Antonio Carlos Jobim Songbook** / Feb. 13, 1962-Nov. 16, 1988 / Verve ✦✦✦✦✦

The first of several tribute albums issued just after Jobim's death, this one generally sticks to Jobim's most famous songs as interpreted by several Brazilian and American artists from PolyGram's archives. Jobim himself appears on such obvious choices as the best-selling Stan Getz/Joao and Astrud Gilberto hit "The Girl from Ipanema," and with Astrud on "Agua de Beber" and "Dindi," and again with the late Elis Regina on an "Aguas de Marco" that nearly breaks up with laughter. The American contributions are a mixed bag; Sarah Vaughan's "Corcovado," for example, is rather inappropriately overwrought but Wes Montgomery's "How Insensitive" is a beautiful recording, with Jobim's favored arranger Claus Ogerman in top wistful form. The other jazzers on the CD are Billy Eckstine, Ella Fitzgerald, Oscar Peterson, Shirley Horn and Dizzy Gillespie, proving that Jobim's timelessly aching music attracted quite a diverse cross section of admirers. —*Richard S. Ginell*

● **Wave: Antonio Carlos Jobim Songbook** / Feb. 13, 1962-Nov. 6, 1994 / Verve ✦✦✦✦✦

The sequel to the popular *The Girl from Ipanema* anthology basically reshuffles the deck, duplicating nine of the earlier CD's songs and adding six new ones, using mostly the same performers with a few additions. The new wrinkle is that the artists perform different tunes, a game that one imagines could be continued indefinitely on future issues. Among the highlights: Ella Fitzgerald has a marvelous time bouncing to the rhythms of "So Danco Samba," Wes Montgomery, the consummate musician, scores again with a lovely "Amor Em Paz," Oscar Peterson is a surreal speed demon on "Triste." Lowlight: Sarah Vaughan's awkwardly mannered "The Boy for Ipanema." Again, there is plenty of Stan Getz—along with his tenor sax successor in matters Jobim, Joe Henderson—plus Astrud and Joao Gilberto, Dizzy Gillespie, Toots Thielemans, Charlie Byrd, Herbie Hancock, Chick Corea, Pat Metheny, and Jobim himself. As a jazz buff's introduction to Jobim, either Songbook will do, but Verve's *The Man from Ipanema* triple album is the best, most comprehensively idiomatic choice overall. —*Richard S. Ginell*

The Composer of Desafinado Plays / May 9, 1963-May 10, 1963 / Verve ✦✦✦✦✦

In his first American album, Jobim presents a dozen of his songs, each one destined to become a standard—an astounding batting average. Jobim, who claimed to have been out of practice at the time of the session, merely plays single notes on the piano with one hand, punctuated by chords now and then, sticking to his long, undulating melodies with a few occasional passages of jazz improvisation. Yet it is a lovely idea, not a gesture is wasted. Arranger Claus Ogerman unveils

many of the trademarks that would define his Creed Taylor-produced albums with Jobim—the soaring, dying solo flute and spare, brooding unison string lines widening into lush harmony; flutes doubling on top of Jobim's piano chords—again with an exquisitely spare touch. The songs include "Desafinado," "Corcovado," "Chega de Saudade" (No More Blues), "The Girl from Ipanema," "Meditation," "One Note Samba" and half-a-dozen others (every one of which is included on *The Man from Ipanema*. set) —*Richard S. Ginell*

★ **The Man from Ipanema** / 1963-1964 / Verve ✦✦✦✦✦

Issued nearly a year after Jobim's death, this three-CD set is ground zero, the place to start if you don't have any Jobim in your collection or for anyone who wants a single package of his multifaceted art. The set encompasses not only Jobim's own sporadic work for Verve from 1963 until his final 1994 Carnegie Hall concert and the two A&M albums of 1967 and 1970 (which Verve's parent company PolyGram now owns), but also sessions led by Stan Getz, Joao and Astrud Gilberto in which Jobim appeared as a sideman. Guitarist Oscar Castro-Neves, who selected the music for this set, follows a unique game plan, devoting disc 1 to vocal renditions of Jobim's songs, disc 2 to instrumental versions, and disc 3 to multiple comparisons of a few Jobim standards by different performers. The selections are often adventurous; the cry for environmental reason, "Passarim"—a late Jobim song—actually leads off the set, and the programming digs deeply into Jobim's PolyGram catalogue for such overlooked gems as the bossa waltz "Mojave", the sly "Captain Bacardi" and the self-mocking "Chansong." For casual listening, Discs One And Two flow beautifully, and even Disc Three works, for despite the repetition of tunes, the approaches by Jobim, Getz, the Gilbertos, Elis Regina et. al. are varied enough to keep one's attention. Jobim collectors probably have almost everything on the set anyway, as there are no unreleased tracks other than a humorous uncredited rehearsal of "Aguas de Marco" tacked onto the end of "Vivo Sonhando" on disc 3. But they are certain to be attracted by the unique packaging—a double-spiraled fold-out book containing lots of fascinating interviews and essays, and three discs wrapped in paper cutouts environmentally designed to look like fishes, flowers and leaves. The CD era's most imaginative graphics department has done it again. —*Richard S. Ginell*

Composer / Sep. 1965-1968 / Warner Brothers ✦✦✦

This is a very useful anthology for Jobim collectors, who can now acquire on one CD the entire contents of the Warner Bros. albums *The Wonderful World of Antonio Carlos Jobim* and *A Certain Mr. Jobim*, plus four unreleased tracks from the latter session and the two Jobim-penned songs from *Love, Strings and Jobim*. These sessions, however, do not represent the best of '60s Jobim; they sound like attempts to commercialize the great man by presenting him mainly as an English-language vocalist who thus might sell his songs to American easy-listening consumers. In the *Wonderful World* sessions, Nelson Riddle takes the reins of the orchestra, but the man who could brilliantly reveal Frank Sinatra's soul doesn't quite mesh with Jobim's; the backings are too bright for the composer's dark, yearning undercurrents. The two cuts from *Love, Strings and Jobim* are too brash and vulgar for words (could this really be the work of Eumir Deodato?) but with *A Certain Mr. Jobim*, Jobim is back in the more delicate hands of Claus Ogerman, who lays on the elusive *saudade* shadings most effectively in the four lovely Portuguese-language outtakes. There are generous quotas of Jobim classics here, several forgettable songs, too, but also some instrumental sleepers like the tone poem "Surfboard" (heard twice) and the stunningly beautiful "Estrada de Sol." Jobim nuts will want this, of course, but the Creed Taylor-produced albums from this era are far more musically and emotionally right. —*Richard S. Ginell*

☆ **Wave** / May 22, 1967-May 24, 1967 / A&M ✦✦✦✦✦

When Creed Taylor left Verve/MGM for his own label under the auspices of A&M, he quickly signed Jobim and they picked up right where they left off with this stunningly seductive record, possibly Jobim's best. Jobim contributes his sparely rhythmic acoustic guitar, simple melodic piano style, a guest turn at the harpsichord, and even a vocal on "Lamento," while Claus Ogerman is on board lending a romantically brooding hand with the charts. A pair of instant standards are introduced ("Wave," "Triste") but what makes this album so cherishable are the absolutely first-rate tunes—actually miniature tone poems—that escaped overexposure and thus sound fresh today. The most beautiful sleeper is "Batidinha," where the intuitive Jobim/Ogerman collaboration reaches its peak. One only wishes that this album were longer; 31:45 is not enough. —*Richard S. Ginell*

Francis Albert Sinatra / Antonio Carlos Jobim / 1967 / Reprise ✦✦✦✦✦

Few would have guessed it at the time, but Jobim found his ideal American interpreter—and a marvelously simpatico recording partner—in Frank Sinatra. As Sinatra languorously caresses every Jobim tune, breaking new vulnerable emotional ground with every syllable, the composer is always at his side, gently tugging at his sleeve with his rhythm guitar, occasionally adding an obbligato or countervocal in Portuguese or vocalese. Claus Ogerman's arrangements have never been more gorgeous—and in addition to the Jobim tunes, the team completely transforms three North American standards (you would swear that "I Concentrate on You" was written by a Brazilian on the beach at Ipanema). —*Richard S. Ginell*

Sinatra and Company / Feb. 1969 / Reprise ✦✦✦✦✦

A sequel to the first Sinatra/Jobim was recorded and shelved, and only seven of the ten tracks made it onto side 1 of this 1971 hodgepodge release (the remaining three cuts can be found in that humongous Sinatra suitcase, *The Complete Reprise Studio Recordings*). From the ample evidence here, the phantom sequel was probably even better than its predecessor. Eumir Deodato's arrangements are more outgoing, more varied in mood and more evocative of Brazil, Sinatra sounds even more confidently in command of the idiom, and Jobim, as ever, lays down the fundamental rhythms that gently propel these bossa novas. Indeed, the high point of the whole collaboration is here: the spine-chillingly romantic "This Happy Madness." —*Richard S. Ginell*

Stone Flower / Mar. 16, 1970-May 22, 1970 / Epic/CTI ✦✦✦✦✦

Recorded during the same period as *Tide* with the same producer (Creed Taylor), arranger (Eumir Deodato), and musicians, *Stone Flower* is a stronger record, leading one to speculate that *Tide* may have been released to fulfill Taylor's and Jobim's A&M contracts just as Taylor was forming his own CTI label. Jobim is in a more expansive mood, displaying a swinging samba touch at some length on electric piano in the only non-Jobim song, "Brazil," and Deodato's charts are more subtle and atmospheric. Also, Jobim draws from superior material, pulling away from the bossa nova in the direction of the emerging CTI sound, with excursions into darker Brazilian interiors. Most striking are the exotically-shaped title track (soon to be covered by Latin rock group Santana), the haunting "Children's Games" (better known as "Double Rainbow"), and the frightening "God and the Devil in the Land of the Sun." CD buyers get an extra take of "Brazil" as a bonus. —*Richard S. Ginell*

Tide / May 1970 / Polygram Brazil ✦✦✦

On Jobim's second A&M album, Eumir Deodato takes over the chartmaking tasks—and the difference between him and Claus Ogerman is quite apparent in the remake of "The Girl from Ipanema;" the charts are heavier, more dramatic and structured. Sometimes the arrangements roll back so one can hear, say, the dancing multiphonic flute of wildman Hermeto Pascoal on "Tema Jazz," and the rhythms often veer away from the familiar ticking of the bossa nova. Jobim is his usual understated self, adding very subtle electric piano to his arsenal of acoustic piano and guitar, but the material sometimes falls short of Jobim's tip-top level (dead giveaway: "Tide" is a clever rewrite on the chord changes of "Wave"). Still, it's beautifully made and very musical at all times. —*Richard S. Ginell*

Jobim / Dec. 11, 1972-Dec. 13, 1972 / MCA ✦✦✦

Though this is one of the more obscure Jobim albums, it did introduce what some believe is Jobim's masterpiece, the hypnotically revolving song "Aguas de Marco" (heard here in Portuguese and English versions). Mostly, however, the record lets us in on another side of Jobim, the Debussy/Villa-Lobos-inspired creator of moody instrumental tone poems for films and whatnot, with the instrumental colors filled in by Jobim's old cohort Claus Ogerman. This was supposed to be a breakthrough for Jobim, bursting out of the bossa nova idiom into uncharted territory, yet a lot of this often undeniably beautiful music merely treads over ground that Villa-Lobos explored long before ("Train to Cordisburgo" especially). In any case, Jobim would explore his serious muse with greater success later on. —*Richard S. Ginell*

Elis and Tom / 1974 / Polygram ✦✦✦

Elis Regina, a cool, feminine Brazilian singer who died tragically of cocaine/alcohol poisoning at age 36, made this often deeply affecting album with Jobim in Los Angeles for the Brazilian market only; it was not released in the US until 1989. While there is plenty of bossa nova here, the arrangements at times reflect the more cinematic, more inward directions that Jobim's music was taking, and the lyrics often speak even more harrowingly of heartbreak than ever. Yet this pair can also celebrate Jobim's music, as they do in a rendition of "Aguas de Marco" that nearly collapses in unself-conscious laughter. Throughout, Regina is in the spotlight, with Jobim a supporting, sometimes invisible, always pervasive presence. —*Richard S. Ginell*

Urubu / Oct. 16, 1975-Oct. 23, 1975 / Warner Archives ✦✦✦✦✦

Urubu is the album that MCA's *Jobim* probably aspired to be, a total break away from the bossa nova past that is both ambitious and strikingly original. The shock of dissonant strings, percussive and wind sounds from the Brazilian interior greet us on the first track "Bôto," the first of four songs in which a defiant Jobim throws structural complexities at us and sings in Portuguese only. The second four tracks are an even more radical departure; all are classical orchestral pieces, melancholy and even anguished in tone, owing little or nothing to anyone, streaked with imaginative, even avant-garde orchestral touches from Claus Ogerman. Clearly

we are not on the Ipanema beach anymore, and although this may be rough going for jazz-minded Jobim fans, the payoff is a glimpse into the depths of Jobim's soul. —*Richard S. Ginell*

Terra Brasilis / 1980 / Warner Archives ✦✦✦✦

In some ways, this is a strategic retreat for Jobim after the classical departures of the '70s—a retrospective of past triumphs, including some of the most trod-upon standards ("Ipanema," "Desafinado," "One-Note Samba," etc.), with Claus Ogerman again at hand. But these are thoughtful retoolings, some subtle, some radical, ranging in backing from a lonely piano to elaborate yet sensitive Ogerman orchestral flights that cram more complexity than ever into the spaces (listen to his beguilingly involved take on "Double Rainbow") with only a few overbearing *faux pas*. Jobim's own vocals sound increasingly casual in temperament as he serves them up in an unpredictable mixture of Portuguese, English and scat. And there is much unfamiliar material here, often dressed up in a brooding classical manner. Originally a two-LP set and now on one CD, this is a snapshot of Jobim's view of his output as of 1980; as such, it is not as definitive as Verve's posthumous *The Man from Ipanema* set —*Richard S. Ginell*

E. Convidados / 1985 / Verve ✦✦

Passarim / 1987 / Verve ✦✦✦✦✦

Passarim is Jobim's major statement of the '80s, emerging during a time when Jobim's concerns were turning increasingly toward planet earth issues. The title song is one of Jobim's most haunting creations, a cry of pain about the the the destruction of the Brazilian rainforest that resonates in the memory for hours. Also, by this time Jobim had resumed touring with a large group containing friends and family, and they carry a great deal of the load here, with lots of airy female backup vocals, two worthy songs by Jobim's multi-talented son Paulo and another by flutist/singer Danilo Caymmi. Recorded entirely in Rio, the record's overall sound is very different from Jobim's '60s and '70s work—denser, hazier, still grounded in the samba yet rougher in texture (as is Jobim's voice). Though not as immediately winning as the Creed Taylor-produced albums, this music repays repeated listening—particularly the extended suite from Jobim's score for the film *Gabriela*—and there are samples of Jobim's wry humor in "Chansong" and the bossa nova reworking of "Fascinatin' Rhythm." —*Richard S. Ginell*

Antonio Carlos Jobim and Friends / Sep. 27, 1993 / Verve ✦✦✦✦✦

Jobim made his last Brazilian concert appearance—and the penultimate one of his life—at this warm, star-studded affair in which American jazz musicians jetted down to the Free Jazz Festival in Sao Paulo to pay effusive homage. The miracle is how easily the jazzers were able to capture the yearning essence of Jobim's idiom without really compromising their own distinct styles. Thus Joe Henderson welds his trademark unpredictable flurries into the cool tenor sax bossa nova tradition; Shirley Horn does "Once I Loved" in her own inimitable manner, which matches the mood of the song perfectly; Jon Hendricks' scatting fits the samba like a glove. The pianists go somewhat outside the idiom—Herbie Hancock's modern complexity, Gonzalo Rubalcaba's technical fireworks laced with Afro-Cuban salsa—but they stay within their orbits around the Jobim sun. The composer himself only appears on the last four tracks—he sounds weary and ill—yet he radiates his gentle warmth and spirit throughout the evening. —*Richard S. Ginell*

Alphonso Johnson

b. 1951, Philadelphia, PA

Bass / Fusion, Crossover Jazz, Post-Bop, Funk

After a short stint on trombone, Alphonso Johnson took up the electric bass in 1968. His early gigs included time with Horace Silver, Woody Herman (1972), Chuck Mangione (1973) and Chet Baker. Johnson rose to fame while touring and recording three albums with Weather Report (1974-76). This was followed by stints with Billy Cobham (1976-77), Flora Purim and the Crusaders. Johnson's funky lines on electric bass have been quite influential and in great demand ever since, both in the studios and in the fusion/funk world. —*Scott Yanow*

● **Moonshadows** / 1976 / Epic ✦✦✦✦

Yesterday's Dreams / Sep. 1976 / Epic ✦✦✦

The Best of Alphonso Johnson / 1976-1977 / Epic ✦✦

Spellbound / Jul. 1977-Aug. 1977 / Epic ✦✦✦

Budd Johnson (Albert J. Johnson)

b. Dec. 14, 1910, Dallas, TX, **d.** Oct. 20, 1984, Kansas City, MO

Tenor Saxophone, Soprano Saxophone, Arranger / Swing, Bop

Budd Johnson was a talented and valuable jazz musician for many decades, a behind-the-scenes player and writer who uplifted a countless number of sessions from the 1930s into the '80s. Johnson started off playing in Kansas City in the late '20s with the bands of Terrence Holder, Jesse Stone and George E. Lee. He made his recording debut while with Louis Armstrong's big band (1932-33) and gained attention for his work as tenor soloist and arranger during three stints with the Earl Hines Orchestra (1932-42). One of the first tenor saxophonists to be influenced by Lester Young (although by the 1940s he had a distinctive tone of his own), Johnson had brief stints with Gus Arnheim (1937) and the bands of Fletcher and Horace Henderson (1938) between his periods with Hines. He contributed arrangements to several big bands including those of Woody Herman, Buddy Rich, Boyd Raeburn and Billy Eckstine and was partly responsible for Hines hiring young modernists during 1942-43. He recorded with Coleman Hawkins on the first bebop session (1944), worked with Dizzy Gillespie and Sy Oliver (1947) and in the 1950s led his own groups in addition to touring with Snub Mosley (1952) and Benny Goodman (1957). Johnson was with the big bands of Quincy Jones (1960) and Count Basie (1961-62) before renewing ties with Earl Hines, who he played with on and off again starting in 1964. He formed the JPJ Quartet, which worked on an occasional basis during 1969-75, held his own at the 1971 Newport in New York jam sessions, became a jazz educator and recorded an excellent album with Phil Woods eight months before his death. Budd Johnson led some obscure sessions during 1947-56 in addition to notable albums for Felsted (1958), Riverside, Swingville, Argo, Black & Blue, Master Jazz, Dragon and Uptown. —*Scott Yanow*

Blues a La Mode / Feb. 11, 1958-Feb. 14, 1958 / Affinity ✦✦✦✦
Originally released on the Felsted label and reissued by Master Jazz, this LP features underrated tenor and arranger Budd Johnson with two overlapping groups. Three selections feature Budd with the great trumpeter Charlie Shavers, trombonist Vic Dickenson, Al Sears on baritone, Bert Keyes doubling on piano and organ, bassist Joe Benjamin, and drummer Jo Jones, while three other pieces have Johnson, Shavers, Benjamin, Jones and pianist Ray Bryant. The leader contributed all six numbers and stars in prime form throughout; Shavers and Bryant also fare quite well. This album awaits reissue on CD and is an excellent example of 1950s mainstream jazz. —*Scott Yanow*

And the Four Brass Giants / Sep. 22, 1960+Sep. 6, 1960 / Original Jazz Classics ✦✦✦✦✦
This reissue of a Riverside album, which surprisingly has not yet come out on CD, is a classic. The great Budd Johnson, who takes tenor solos throughout the date and also contributes a bit of clarinet in addition to providing the arrangements, is matched with four distinctive and very different trumpeters: Clark Terry, Harry "Sweets" Edison, Nat Adderley and Ray Nance (who doubles on violin). With Tommy Flanagan or Jimmy Jones on piano, bassist Joe Benjamin and drummer Herb Lovelle, the group performs four swing standards and four of Johnson's swinging originals. The colorful brassmen, Budd's versatile solos, and the inventive arrangements make this a particularly memorable set. Highly recommended. —*Scott Yanow*

★ **Let's Swing** / Dec. 2, 1960 / Original Jazz Classics ✦✦✦✦✦
This CD reissue brings back one of tenor saxophonist Budd Johnson's best showcases. Featured in a quintet with his brother Keg Johnson on trombone, pianist Tommy Flanagan, bassist George Duvivier and drummer Charlie Persip, Budd starts off with a ballad feature ("Serenade in Blue") and performs three originals (including "Downtown Manhattan" and "Uptown Manhattan"), in addition to three other veteran standards. Throughout, Budd Johnson sounds both modern, as if he had come of age as one of the "cool school," and timeless, since he was a major player by the mid-1930s. A fine set. —*Scott Yanow*

The JPJ Quartet / 1969-Jun. 20, 1971 / Storyville ✦✦✦✦
The short-lived (1969-75) JPJ Quartet consisted of Budd Johnson on tenor and soprano, pianist Dill Jones, bassist Bill Pemberton and drummer Oliver Jackson. This valuable CD has six previously unreleased studio performances plus the music from a former Master Jazz LP recorded at the 1971 Montreux Jazz Festival. The quartet plays small-group swing (or mainstream) with melodic creativity. Highlights include Johnson's "Tag Along" (one of six originals by group members), Dill Jones' feature on "Honeysuckle Rose," "Lester Leaps In" and a roaring "The Best Things in Life Are Free." —*Scott Yanow*

In Memory of a Very Dear Friend / Mar. 23, 1978 / Dragon ✦✦✦✦
Veteran tenor saxophonist Budd Johnson (who here takes a vocal on his "Ya Ya Blues") fronts a Swedish rhythm section on this live date that consists of pianist Palle Thomsen, bassist Roman Dylag and drummer Rune Carlsson. Sixty-seven at the time, Johnson was still in his musical prime, and the distinctive tenor is the main reason to purchase this excellent straightahead outing. Highlights include "What Is This Thing Called Love," "Lester Leaps In" and "I Want to Be Happy." —*Scott Yanow*

The Ole Dude and the Fundance Kid / Feb. 4, 1984 / Uptown ✦✦✦✦✦
Veteran tenor saxophonist Budd Johnson (who first emerged 50 years before this recording) was still in fine form when he met up with altoist Phil Woods for this

frequently heated quintet session. During what would be his final recording date (he died later in 1984), Johnson is excellent on the ballads but even better on the faster material, where his interplay and tradeoffs with Woods are a constant joy. There is a lot of spirit in this set; the mutual love and respect felt by the saxophonists is obvious. —*Scott Yanow*

Bunk Johnson (William Geary Johnson)

b. Dec. 27, 1889, New Orleans, LA, **d.** Jul. 7, 1949, New Orleans, LA
Trumpet / New Orleans Jazz
Due to the difference of opinion between his followers (who claimed he was a brilliant stylist) and his detractors (who felt than his playing was worthless), Bunk Johnson was a controversial figure in the mid-'40s when he made a most unlikely comeback. The truth is somewhere in between.

Bunk Johnson, who tended to exaggerate, claimed that he was born in 1879 and that he played with Buddy Bolden in New Orleans but it was discovered that he was actually a decade younger. He did have a pretty tone and, although not an influence on Louis Armstrong (as he often stated), he was a major player in New Orleans starting around 1910 when he joined the Eagle Band. Johnson was active in the South until the early '30s but did not record during that era. Discovered in the latter part of the decade by Bill Russell and Fred Ramsey, he was profiled in the 1939 book *Jazzmen*. A collection was taken up to get Bunk new teeth and a horn. In 1942 he privately recorded in New Orleans and the next year he was in San Francisco playing with the wartime edition of the Yerba Buena Jazz Band. An alcoholic, Johnson's playing tended to be erratic and when Sidney Bechet recruited him for a band in 1945, he essentially drank himself out of the group. In 1946 Bunk led a group that included the nucleus of the ensemble George Lewis would make famous a few years later but Johnson disliked the playing of the primitive New Orleans musicians. He was more comfortable the following year heading a unit filled with skilled swing players and his final album (Columbia's *The Last Testament of a Great Jazzman*) was one of his best recordings. In 1948 the trumpeter (who was only 59 but seemed much older) returned to Louisiana and retired. Many of Bunk Johnson's better recordings have been reissued on CD by Good Time Jazz and American Music. —*Scott Yanow*

★ **Bunk and Lu** / Dec. 19, 1941-Feb. 1944 / Good Time Jazz ✦✦✦✦✦
Included on this historic CD are two rather significant sessions. Lu Watters' Yerba Buena Jazz Band was a major force in launching the Dixieland revival, and their first eight recordings, from their initial session, lead off the disc. Featured are trumpeters Lu Watters and Bob Scobey, trombonist Turk Murphy and clarinetist Ellis Horne on such numbers as "Irish Black Bottom," "Maple Leaf Rag" and "Muskrat Ramble"; pianist Wally Rose's feature on "Black & White Rag" helped start a mini ragtime revival. The second half of the CD has one of legendary trumpeter Bunk Johnson's finest recordings. He is heard leading the wartime version of the Yerba Buena band (which still included Murphy and Horne, in addition to pianist Burt Bales), and Bunk rarely sounded stronger; he is also perfectly in tune for a change. Sister Lottie Peavey takes a fair number of gospel-oriented vocals; Clancy Hayes sings definitive versions of "Ace in the Hole" and "219 Blues," and Johnson himself vocalizes on "Down By the Riverside." But it is for Bunk's trumpet that the latter part of the CD is most notable. —*Scott Yanow*

Bunk Johnson and His Superior Jazz Band / Jun. 11, 1942 / Good Time Jazz ✦✦✦
This CD reissues the first recordings by the legendary Bunk Johnson. Cut in New Orleans on primitive acetates, the trumpeter is teamed with trombonist Jim Robinson and clarinetist George Lewis (both of whom would be in his regular band soon), plus a four-piece rhythm section, for nine numbers. Bunk's playing is primitive, as is Lewis', but also listenable despite the erratic recording quality. Closing this set are nine minutes of "talking records" that feature Johnson reminiscing about the past. In reality, this release is more important historically than musically; get Bunk's final recordings (on Delmark) first. —*Scott Yanow*

Bunk Johnson in San Francisco / Sep. 1943-Jan. 1944 / American Music ✦✦✦

1944 [2nd Masters] / Jul. 29, 1944-Aug. 1944 / American Music ✦✦✦✦✦
Taken from the same five sessions that resulted in the earlier CD *The King of the Blues*, these 14 numbers include six never previously released and a variety of mostly alternate renditions. The erratic but significant trumpeter Bunk Johnson leads what would be the future nucleus of the George Lewis band (with Lewis on clarinet, trombonist Jim Robinson, banjoist Lawrence Marrero and bassist Alcide Pavageau), plus drummer Baby Dodds, through a variety of trad favorites. Highlights include "Walking Through the Streets," "Darktown Strutters Ball," "Panama" and "The Saints." —*Scott Yanow*

Spicy Advice / Jul. 1944 / GHB ✦✦✦
The Bunk Johnson band (which in Los Angeles briefly consisted of the leader/trumpeter, trombonist Floyd O'Brien, clarinetist Wade Whaley, pianist Fred Wash-

ington, guitarist Frank Pasley, bassist Red Callendar and drummer Lee Young) made some radio transcriptions for one day in 1944. All of the music was released for the first time on this 1982 LP. However, there is less than half an hour of playing time on this set; the band does not gel together that well, Bunk is erratic, and the performances (eight songs including one alternate take, three incomplete versions, and a false start) are okay but nothing overly special. Purely for the Bunk Johnson completist. —*Scott Yanow*

King of the Blues / Jul. 1944-Aug. 1944 / American Music ✦✦✦✦
Back in New Orleans during part of 1944-45, the legendary trumpeter Bunk Johnson recorded fairly extensively with his regular group of the period: trombonist Jim Robinson, clarinetist George Lewis, banjoist Lawrence Marrero, bassist Alcide "Slow Drag" Pavageau, drummer Baby Dodds and occasionally the tuba of Sidney Brown. This CD, which launched the rebirth of the American Music label, has 13 performances, including two vocals by Myrtle Jones, three songs not previously released in the US, and two numbers ("Weary Blues" and "How Long Blues") being put out for the first time. In general, Bunk plays very well, and the ensemble-oriented music is quite enjoyable. —*Scott Yanow*

Bunk's Brass Band and Dance Band 1945 / May 14, 1945-May 18, 1945 / American Music ✦✦✦
This CD starts off with a potentially very interesting session, the first-ever recording of a New Orleans brass band. Bunk Johnson heads a group consisting of two trumpeters (the other is Kid Shots Madison), trombonist Jim Robinson, George Lewis on the eerie E-flat clarinet, Isidore Barbarin on alto horn, the baritone horn of Adolphe Alexander, Joe Clark on bass horn, Baby Dodds on snare drum and Lawrence Marrero on bass drum. Unfortunately, the band (particularly Lewis) is generally out of tune, which—despite the power and sincerity of the music—reduces the effectiveness of the recording. The second half of the disc has more conventional performances by Bunk, Lewis and Robinson in a spirited New Orleans jazz sextet, playing numbers such as "Runnin' Wild," "Kentucky Home" and "The Sheik of Araby." —*Scott Yanow*

Bunk Johnson & His New Orleans Jazz Band—New York (1945) / Nov. 21, 1945-Jan. 6, 1946 / Folklyric ✦✦✦✦✦
Some of Bunk Johnson's most exciting performances were recorded when he returned to New York in the fall of 1945. Most of the 15 selections on this LP (some of which have since been reissued on CD) were originally cut for Victor. The veteran trumpeter, who had suddenly become a major name, is featured with clarinetist George Lewis, trombonist Jim Robinson, pianist Alton Purnell, banjoist Lawrence Marrero, bassist Alcide Pavageau and drummer Baby Dodds on a variety of Dixieland standards. Highlights of the very enjoyable release, which features Bunk in prime form, include "You Always Hurt the One You Love," "Sister Kate," "Darktown Strutters Ball" and a definitive version of "When the Saints Go Marching In." —*Scott Yanow*

Bunk Johnson & Mutt Carey in New York / Oct. 3, 1947-Oct. 24, 1947 / American Music ✦✦✦
All 11 selections included here were released for the first time on this 1993 CD. The legendary trumpeter Bunk Johnson is heard with three different groups shortly before he returned permanently to New Orleans. Best are four numbers with an all-star sextet including clarinetist Albert Nicholas and pianist James P. Johnson; during the same day, Mutt Carey (who had recently left Kid Ory's group) is featured with the same band, although the two trumpeters do not actually play together. Bunk is also heard with a pair of pickup groups including either James P. or Dick Wellstood on piano and the soundalike cornetist Jerry Blumberg. The recording quality is a bit erratic on the live performances and the playing is not flawless, so the music is really recommended to New Orleans jazz historians rather than more general Dixieland fans. —*Scott Yanow*

Last Testament / Dec. 23, 1947-Dec. 26, 1947 / Delmark ✦✦✦✦
Bunk Johnson had a rather unlikely career. Completely forgotten and out of music by the late 1930s, he was given a new set of teeth and a trumpet and hailed as a legend. Johnson made an impressive comeback, but excessive drinking resulted in an erratic and short-lived career. Both overpraised by some and dismissed by others, Bunk was actually a fine player when he was at his best. His final recording, reissued on this CD along with two alternate takes, was arguably his best. Utilizing more modern players than his usual New Orleans band (trombonist Ed Cuffee, clarinetist Garvin Bushell, pianist Don Kirkpatrick, guitarist Danny Barker, bassist Wellman Braud and drummer Alphonse Steele), Bunk Johnson performed a wide variety of music ranging from folk songs and swing standards (such as "Out of Nowhere" and "You're Driving Me Crazy") to some rags (most notably "The Entertainer"). Throughout, Bunk sounds at the top of his game, making this CD his definitive release. —*Scott Yanow*

Charlie Johnson (Charles Wright Johnson)

b. Nov. 21, 1891, Philadelphia, PA, **d.** Dec. 13, 1959, New York, NY
Leader, Piano / Classic Jazz
A decent pianist who rarely soloed, Charlie Johnson is of greatest significance for leading his Paradise Ten, an orchestra that had five excellent recording sessions during 1925-29 and played at Smalls' Paradise during 1925-35. Among the sidemen who appear on Johnson's records are trumpeters Jabbo Smith, Thomas Morris, Leonard Davis and Sidney DeParis, trombonists Charlie Irvis and Jimmy Harrison, altoists Benny Carter (who made his recording debut with Johnson in 1927) and Edgar Sampson and tenor saxophonist Benny Waters. In general, their recordings live up to the great potential. Charlie Johnson led his band until 1938 and freelanced until ill health forced his retirement in the 1950s. —*Scott Yanow*

● **The Complete Charlie Johnson Sessions** / Oct. 1925-May 8, 1925 / Hot 'n Sweet ✦✦✦✦✦
Charlie Johnson was never a major pianist, but he led one of the top New York–based jazz bands of the 1925-30 period. All of the recordings by his groups, including ten alternate takes, are on this highly recommended CD. Among the more notable sidemen are altoist Benny Carter (making his recording debut in 1928), tenor saxophonist Benny Waters, the fiery and very exciting trumpeter Jabbo Smith, trombonists Charlie Irvis and Jimmy Harrison, trumpeters Thomas Morris and Sidney DeParis, and singer Monette Moore. Such classic performances as "Don't You Leave Me Here," "You Ain't the One," "Charleston Is the Best Dance After All" and "Walk That Thing" still sound exciting today and make this an essential release for 1920s collectors. —*Scott Yanow*

Freddy Johnson

b. Mar. 12, 1904, New York, NY, **d.** Mar. 24, 1961, New York, NY
Piano / Swing,
An excellent swing-based pianist in the 1930s, Freddy Johnson's peak years were spent in Europe. He worked with Elmer Snowden (1925) and Noble Sissle then first visited Europe in 1928 with Sam Wooding. In 1929 he moved to Paris, leading his own band, working with Arthur Briggs and recording during 1933-34. Johnson spent time in Belgium and Amsterdam, performed often with Coleman Hawkins and Willie Lewis and had a final record session in 1939. Unfortunately, he chose to ignore the dominance of the Nazis, was arrested and spent 1941-44 in a prison camp. After being released and returned to the US, Johnson played with Garvin Bushell and mostly worked as a piano teacher in the 1950s. His sessions as a leader are available on a Classics CD. —*Scott Yanow*

● **1933-1939** / Jul. 8, 1933-Jun. 30, 1939 / Classics ✦✦✦✦✦
Freddy Johnson was a talented swing-oriented pianist who spent the 1930s playing in Europe. This Classics CD contains all five of his sessions, a song ("Wo Ist Der Mann?") on which his band accompanies Marlene Dietrich, plus a date with trumpeter Louis Bacon's septet. In addition to Johnson's many piano solos, the top players are trumpeter Arthur Briggs, Big Boy Goudie on tenor, trombonist Herb Flemming, tenorman Alix Combelle and Bacon. Four songs recorded in 1934 with a Dutch band have delightful vocals from the completely obscure Rosie Poindexter. This CD is a must for collectors of small-group swing. —*Scott Yanow*

Henry Johnson

b. Jan. 28, 1954, Chicago, IL
Guitar / Soul Jazz, Piedmont Blues
A guitarist heavily influenced by his idol Wes Montgomery, Henry Johnson is a fine player with an appealing tone. He has played with the groups of Jack McDuff (1976-77), Sonny Stitt, Hank Crawford, Ramsey Lewis (1979-83) and Joe Williams in addition to recording three albums as a leader for MCA/Impulse during 1987-90. —*Scott Yanow*

● **You're the One** / 1986 / MCA ✦✦✦✦
Henry Johnson's debut as a leader features the guitarist/vocalist (inspired most by Wes Montgomery and George Benson) on a wide variety of material ranging from bop to funkier and more soulful sounds. Backed by five different keyboardists (including his employer Ramsey Lewis on two songs), a pair of bassists and drummer Robert Gates, Johnson is in fine form on this early effort. However, he has not yet lived up to his potential or developed his own voice, despite his continuing promise. —*Scott Yanow*

Future Excursions / 1987 / MCA ✦✦✦
Guitarist Henry Johnson has a highly appealing Wes Montgomery-inspired sound and a likable vocal style. In general, the music on his second release (other than "A Child Is Born" and "When Did You Leave Heaven") is not worthy of him, consisting of somewhat lightweight grooves. Backed by an electronic rhythm section and assisted by James Perkins' tenor, Johnson does his best, but he would sound much more rewarding in a more freewheeling setting. —*Scott Yanow*

Never Too Much / 1990 / MCA ✦✦

A guitarist with an appealing sound influenced by Wes Montgomery and George Benson, Henry Johnson has generally failed to live up to his potential and valued commercial considerations more than artistic integrity. *Never Too Much* isn't very memorable; nor is it one of his worse albums. To be sure, this overproduced jazz/R&B-pop date has its share of schlock and outright dreck—the worst offender being "A Love Like That" (an example of elevator muzak). But Johnson puts his imagination to better use on Luther Vandross' "Never Too Much" and James Taylor's "Don't Let Me Be Lonely Tonight." However, despite some strong points here and there, this CD really isn't worth the price of admission. —*Alex Henderson*

Missing You / 1993 / Heads Up ✦✦✦

Guitarist Henry Johnson, a talented Wes Montgomery clone, performs easy-listening pop-jazz on his Heads Up CD. His solos are pleasant but without adventure and each selection fades out as the performance nears five minutes. The melodic music is enjoyable enough but Henry Johnson is capable of producing much more valuable improvisations than is heard during this set of high-quality background music. —*Scott Yanow*

Howard Johnson

b. Aug. 7, 1941, Montgomery, AL
Tuba, Baritone Saxophone / Post-Bop

One of the top tuba soloists of the past 30 years, Howard Johnson is a very versatile player who not only plays tuba and baritone but other reeds and trumpet. He moved to New York in 1963 where he worked with Charles Mingus (1964-66), Hank Crawford and Archie Shepp. In 1966 he started a 20-year off-and-on association with Gil Evans. Johnson's four-tuba group Substructure performed with Taj Mahal, and in the late '70s he formed a different tuba band called Gravity that in 1996 finally had the opportunity to record (plus play at the Monterey Jazz Festival). Howard Johnson has recorded with Crawford (1983-84), Jack DeJohnette's Special Edition, Jimmy Heath, Bob Moses, George Gruntz's Concert Jazz Band and frequently with Evans' Orchestra among others. —*Scott Yanow*

● **Gravity!!!** / 1995 / Verve ✦✦✦✦✦

Imagine a group that consists of piano, bass, drums and five to seven tubas. Howard Johnson, one of the mightiest tuba players of the past 30 years, has been leading Gravity since 1968 but this is their first recording. Despite the instrumentation, the group plays the music (which ranges from Don Pullen's colorful "Big Alice" and two of Johnson's originals to such standards as "Stolen Moments," "Yesterdays" and "'Round Midnight") with swing, creativity and more variety than one might expect. —*Scott Yanow*

Right Now / Dec. 1, 1996-Dec. 10, 1996 / Verve ✦✦✦✦

The idea of a tuba sextet might seem a bit too daffy a defiance of the laws of gravity, but Hojo's ensemble—nicknamed Gravity—comes up with some surprisingly mellifluous textures on their second album to date. Though the playing sounds staggeringly clumsy on the opening title track, things quickly coalesce thereafter. The tuba harmonies oddly often bear a pleasing kinship with those of Steve Turre's massed conch shells, and the shadow of Gil Evans is everywhere. The eclectic sometime bluesician Taj Mahal—who first worked with Johnson's tuba ensemble back in 1971—revives their long-dormant collaboration by appearing on three tracks, including a Ray Charles-ish "Don't Let the Sun Catch You Crying" (catch the echoes of Evans' "Blues for Pablo" in the tubas) as a perhaps deliberately extreme juxtaposition, Johnson also solos attractively on the tiny pennywhistle on Herbie Hancock's "Tell Me a Bedtime Story," beautifully realized by the group, and moves jaggedly out in front of the band on baritone sax as well. Elegant fun. —*Richard S. Ginell*

J.J. Johnson (James Louis Johnson)

b. Jan. 22, 1924, Indianapolis, IN
Trombone, Composer, Arranger / Bop, Hard Bop

Considered by many to be the finest jazz trombonist of all time, J.J. Johnson somehow transferred the innovations of Charlie Parker and Dizzy Gillespie to his more awkward instrument, playing with such speed and deceptive ease that at one time some listeners assumed he was playing valve (rather than slide) trombone! Johnson toured with the territory bands of Clarence Love and Snookum Russell during 1941-42 and then spent 1942-45 with Benny Carter's big band. He made his recording debut with Carter (taking a solo on "Love for Sale" in 1943) and played at the first JATP concert (1944). Johnson also had plenty of solo space during his stay with Count Basie's Orchestra (1945-46). During 1946-50, he played with all of the top bop musicians including Charlie Parker (with whom he recorded in 1947), the Dizzy Gillespie big band, Illinois Jacquet (1947-49) and the Miles Davis Birth of the Cool Nonet. His own recordings from the era included such sidemen as Bud Powell and a young Sonny Rollins. J.J., who also recorded with the Metronome All-Stars, played with Oscar Pettiford (1951) and Miles Davis

(1952) but then was outside of music, working as a blueprint inspector for two years (1952-54). His fortunes changed when in August 1954 he formed a two-trombone quintet with Kai Winding that became known as Jay and Kai and was quite popular during its two years.

After J.J. and Kai went their separate ways (they would later have a few reunions), Johnson led a quintet that often included Bobby Jaspar. He began to compose ambitious works starting with 1956's "Poem for Brass" and including "El Camino Real" and a feature for Dizzy Gillespie, "Perceptions"; his "Lament" became a standard. Johnson worked with Miles Davis during part of 1961-62, led some more small groups of his own, and by the late '60s was kept busy writing television and film scores. J.J. Johnson was so famous in the jazz world that he kept on winning *Down Beat* polls in the 1970s even though he was not playing at all! However, starting with a Japanese tour in 1977, J.J. gradually returned to a busy performance schedule, leading a quintet in the 1980s that often featured Ralph Moore. In the mid-'90s he remains at the top of his field. J.J. Johnson has recorded as a leader for Savoy, Prestige, Blue Note, RCA, Bethlehem, Columbia, Impulse, Verve, A&M, Pablo, Milestone, Concord and Antilles. —*Scott Yanow*

Mad Bebop / Jun. 26, 1946-Aug. 26, 1954 / Savoy ✦✦✦✦✦

The great trombonist J.J. Johnson is heard in several different settings on this out-of-print but valuable two-LP set. Johnson is featured on three dates from 1946-49 that are greatly expanded by the inclusion of alternate takes; among the sidemen are pianists Bud Powell, John Lewis and Hank Jones, altoist Cecil Payne, baritonist Leo Parker, tenorman Sonny Rollins and drummer Max Roach. In contrast to those early bop sides are eight performances co-led by J.J. Johnson and fellow trombonist Kai Winding in 1954 in a pair of quintets, also including either guitarist Billy Bauer or pianist Wally Cirillo, bassist Charles Mingus (whose presence is definitely felt) and drummer Kenny Clarke. Those selections, highlighted by "What Is This Thing Called Love," "Blues for Trombones" and "Lament," would lead to the popular Jay and Kai group. Overall, excellent music that deserves to be reissued in complete fashion on CD. —*Scott Yanow*

Jay and Kai / Dec. 24, 1947-Aug. 26, 1954 / Savoy ✦✦✦

The music on this Savoy CD is excellent but the packaging is rather dumb. Rather than reissue all 12 selections from a pair of 1954 sessions that led to the birth of the J.J. Johnson-Kai Winding two-trombone quintet (renditions that also include either pianist Wally Cirillo or guitarist Billy Bauer along with bassist Charles Mingus and drummer Kenny Clarke), there are just eight on this CD along with a Johnson track from 1947 ("Yesterdays") and three of the four Winding performances (in a quintet with pianist Lou Stein) from 1952. Sure to frustrate completists, this reissue is still worth picking up if found at a budget price for the music contains plenty of worthy trombone solos. —*Scott Yanow*

The Eminent Jay Jay Johnson, Vol. 1 / Jun. 22, 1953 / Blue Note ✦✦✦✦✦

The CD reissue of the two volumes titled *The Eminent Jay Jay Johnson* straighten out his three Blue Note sessions of 1953-55 and add alternate takes. This particular CD concentrates exclusively on the trombonist's 1953 sextet date with the great trumpeter Clifford Brown, Jimmy Heath (who doubles on tenor and baritone), pianist John Lewis, bassist Percy Heath and drummer Kenny Clarke. The six titles (plus three alternates) are highlighted by "It Could Happen to You," "Turnpike" and a classic rendition of "Get Happy." Although Johnson has a couple of features, Clifford Brown largely steals the show. This CD is well worth getting by listeners who do not have the music on Brownie's own *Complete* Blue Note set. —*Scott Yanow*

The Eminent Jay Jay Johnson, Vol. 2 / Sep. 24, 1954+Jun. 6, 1955 / Blue Note ✦✦✦✦✦

The second of two Blue Note CDs (which differ in their content from the similarly titled LPs) contains two complete sessions that showcase trombonist J.J. Johnson. The first six titles (highlighted by "Old Devil Moon" and "Too Marvelous for Words") feature Johnson in a quintet with pianist Wynton Kelly, bassist Charles Mingus, drummer Kenny Clarke and the congas of Sabu. For the later session, there are also six titles (including "Pennies from Heaven" and "Portrait of Jennie") plus three alternate takes; Johnson is joined by Hank Mobley on tenor, pianist Horace Silver, bassist Paul Chambers and drummer Kenny Clarke. Both of these dates offer listeners excellent examples of the talents of the great trombonist who always played his instrument with the fluidity of a trumpet. Recommended. —*Scott Yanow*

The Finest of J.J. Johnson / Jan. 25, 1955-Jan. 27, 1955 / Bethlehem ✦✦✦✦

It may not be the "finest" but this LP does feature one of the most popular jazz groups of the mid-'50s, the two-trombone quintet co-led by J.J. Johnson and Kai Winding. Both of the players (who are joined by pianist Dick Katz, Milt Hinton or Wendell Marshall on bass and drummer Al Harewood) had similar but generally distinctive styles. On tunes ranging from "Out of This World," "Lover" and "It's All Right with Me" to "Mad About the Boy" and even "Yes Sir, That's My Baby," the unusual band's sound consistently uplifts the themes and the co-leaders' improvising talents keep the music from becoming merely easy-listening. —*Scott Yanow*

Trombone for Two / Jun. 23, 1955-Jun. 24, 1955 / Columbia ✦✦✦✦

The J.J. Johnson-Kai Winding quintet became one of the more unlikely successes of the mid-'50s, recording nine albums during their two years of steady collaborations. Their first Columbia LP (there would be five) has such likable songs as "Give Me the Simple Life," "Trombone for Two," "It's Sand Man," "Let's Get Away from It All" and "This Can't Be Love." With pianist Dick Katz, bassist Paul Chambers (who would soon join Miles Davis) and drummer Osie Johnson, the focus is almost entirely on the competitive but complementary trombonists. The results are bop-based but full of surprises, tasteful but not always predictable. All of this group's albums deserve to be reissued in coherent fashion on CD; this one will be hard to find. —*Scott Yanow*

Jay and Kai Octet / Apr. 1956 / Columbia ✦✦✦

This is an unusual date which has yet to be reissued on CD. The popular two-trombone quintet co-led by J.J. Johnson and Kai Winding was expanded on this album by the inclusion of four additional trombonists and two bass trombonists. On a few of the tunes, some of the players switch to slide trombones and tromboniums. One can hear on this LP the beginnings of the group Winding would lead after 1956, a unit with four trombonists. Highlights include "Night in Tunisia," "Piece for Two Tromboniums," "No Moon at All," "The Surrey with the Fringe on Top," "The Peanut Vendor" and "The Continental." —*Scott Yanow*

The Complete J.J. Johnson Columbia Small Group Sessions / Jul. 24, 1956-Jan. 12, 1961 / Mosaic ✦✦✦✦✦

This seven-CD limited-edition box set from Mosaic is another mind-boggling collection. The masterful trombonist J.J. Johnson recorded steadily for Columbia during the 1956-61 period, heading groups that ranged from quartets to sextets that performed solid hard bop. J.J. is joined on various selections by tenors Bobby Jaspar (doubling on flute) and Clifford Jordan, cornetist Nat Adderley, the young trumpeter Freddie Hubbard, pianists Hank Jones, Tommy Flanagan, Cedar Walton and Victor Feldman, bassists Percy Heath, Wilbur Little, Paul Chambers, Spanky DeBrest, Arthur Harper and Sam Jones, and drummers Elvin Jones, Max Roach, Albert "Tootie" Heath and Louis Hayes. The music was originally issued on nine LPs; plus, there are 21 previously unreleased selections. Johnson's high-quality and consistently inventive playing is quite impressive, making this box a true must for his greatest fans. —*Scott Yanow*

Live at the Café Bohemia / Feb. 1957 / Fresh Sound ✦✦✦

Glittering date with Bobby Jaspar (ts). —*Ron Wynn*

The Great Kai and J.J. / Nov. 4, 1960-Nov. 9, 1960 / MCA/Impulse! ✦✦✦✦✦

This Impulse set (which was given the catalog number of A-1 when it first came out) was the first recorded reunion of trombonists J.J. Johnson and Kai Winding. Given a straight reissue on CD (the original liner notes are reproduced so small as to be largely unreadable), the music still sounds fresh and lively. With pianist Bill Evans, either Paul Chambers or Tommy Williams on bass and Roy Haynes or Art Taylor on drums, the two trombonists are in melodic and witty form on such tunes as "This Could Be the Start of Something Big," "Blue Monk," "Side by Side" and the "Theme from Picnic." Recommended. —*Scott Yanow*

J.J. Inc. / Aug. 1, 1960+Aug. 3, 1960 / Columbia ✦✦✦✦

Trombonist J.J. Johnson's 1960 sextet is featured on this Columbia reissue CD. Most notable among the sidemen is a rather young trumpeter named Freddie Hubbard on one of his first sessions; also helping out are tenor saxophonist Clifford Jordan, pianist Cedar Walton, bassist Arthur Harper and drummer Albert "Tootie" Heath. Seven of the compositions (which are joined by Dizzy Gillespie's "Blue 'n' Boogie") are Johnson's and, although none caught on, "Mohawk," "In Walked Horace" and "Fatback" (which is heard in two versions) are all fairly memorable. The six songs on the original LP are joined by three others from the same dates, two of which were released slightly earlier for the first time on a J.J. Mosaic box set that includes all of this music. A fine straightahead set. —*Scott Yanow*

J.J.'s Broadway / Mar. 12, 1963+Apr. 6, 1963 / Verve ✦✦✦

This is one of the more obscure J.J. Johnson LPs. On six of the ten songs, the great trombonist is joined by four others, while the remaining four tracks (the main reasons to search for this album) feature him in a quartet with pianist Hank Jones, bassist Richard Davis and drummer Walter Perkins. Johnson's writing on the larger group pieces lifts the material, which is all taken from Broadway shows, while his playing on the quartet tracks is up to his usual level. Some of the songs are now forgotten, but "My Favorite Things," "Make Someone Happy" and "Put on a Happy Face" are exceptions. This album has some good music, but it will be very difficult to find. —*Scott Yanow*

Proof Positive / May 1, 1964 / GRP/Impulse! ✦✦✦✦✦

This CD reissue finds trombonist J.J. Johnson in prime form. In fact, his melancholy minor-toned explorations often recall Miles Davis, whose group he had

played with the year before. Backed on six of the seven tracks by pianist Harold Mabern, who at the time was heavily influenced by McCoy Tyner, bassist Arthur Harper and drummer Frank Gant, Johnson gets to really stretch out on "Neo," "Minor Blues" and "Blues Waltz"; "Gloria" was previously available only on an Impulse sampler. Manny Albam's "Lullaby of Jazzland," on which Johnson is joined by guitarist Toots Thielemans, pianist McCoy Tyner, bassist Richard Davis and drummer Elvin Jones, rounds out the excellent set. —*Scott Yanow*

Say When / Dec. 7, 1964-Dec. 5, 1966 / Bluebird ✦✦✦✦

Most of two of trombonist J.J. Johnson's Victor big-band dates (seven of nine numbers from a 1964 album and eight of the nine selections on Johnson's *The Total* LP from 1966) are included on this Bluebird single CD from 1987. In addition to his typically brilliant trombone playing, Johnson did virtually all of the arranging, except for Oliver Nelson's work on his own "Stolen Moments," and contributed nine of the compositions. The emphasis is on the writing with J.J. Johnson and pianist Hank Jones generally being the main soloists; Johnson's reworkings of George Russell's challenging "Stratusphunk" and Miles Davis' "Swing Spring" are among the highlights. —*Scott Yanow*

The Total J.J. Johnson / Nov. 30, 1966-Dec. 5, 1966 / RCA ✦✦✦

All but one selection ("Blue") from this 1966 big-band album has been reissued on CD. J.J. Johnson, the main soloist throughout on trombone, also contributed all the compositions and arrangements for the 13—and 14-piece bands heard on the three sessions. There are short spots for some of the other players, particularly pianist Hank Jones, but the emphasis is on the arranged ensembles, making this project an excellent example of Johnson's often-overlooked writing talents. —*Scott Yanow*

Israel / Feb. 19, 1968-Apr. 16, 1968 / A&M ✦✦

Trombonists J.J. Johnson and Kai Winding had two reunions on A&M LPs in 1968; they had led a very popular two-trombone quintet during 1954-56 before going their separate ways. This date is a bit commercial with a small string section and woodwinds utilized on five of the nine numbers. Still, the beautiful tones of the co-leaders make this a worthwhile set with the highlights including "My Funny Valentine," "Israel," "St. James Infirmary" and "Django." —*Scott Yanow*

Betwixt and Between / Nov. 5, 1968-1969 / A&M ✦✦✦

The second of the three K and J.J. (or J & K) collaborations for A&M's CTI series takes an idea from the first—that of Baroque elaborations—and runs with it. Here, the twin trombonists link each track with a brief interlude—some by Bach, one by Prokofiev (uncredited)—for brass quintet and guitar. Indeed, there are experiments all over this quintessentially '60s project—and purists can't blame it on an outside arranger, for Johnson and Winding do all but one of the charts themselves. A lot of this record has a mild period-rock feeling marked by the edgy guitar of Joe Beck and the wonderfully funky clavinet of, yes, Roger Kellaway (who else would contribute a song entitled "Just a Funky Old Vegetable Bin")—and on one track, the trombonists hide behind the dusky sounds of Varitone octave-multiplying amplifiers. All of this is unified not by the rather self-conscious interludes but by Creed Taylor's immaculate pop-flavored production, so much so that the golden-toned trombonists are almost, but not quite, bit players on their own album. A fascinating, no doubt controversial, record. —*Richard S. Ginell*

Stonebone / Sep. 23, 1969-Sep. 25, 1969 / A&M ✦✦✦✦✦

Oddly, the third of the J & K A&M projects was released only in Japan, though it was given a US catalogue number (SP 3027), and one can only speculate as to why—the diminishing American audience for jazz in 1969, producer Creed Taylor's impending move to start his own label. But the fact is that this is the best album of the three—and the one closest in touch with the crucial improvisatory impulse of jazz. It is a prototype of the CTI formula of the '70s, allowing first-class jazz musicians to groove at length with minimal shaping on the production end to give these tracks drama. Johnson especially enjoys his freedom here, with plenty of room to stretch out joyously. We also hear the fluid inventive guitar of George Benson in full youthful bloom, Herbie Hancock is caught near the beginning of his funky experiments with electronic keyboards (augmented by Bob James and Ross Tompkins on "Recollections") and Ron Carter and Grady Tate have never played better on a Creed Taylor production. If you somehow stumble upon this superb import, grab it or hope that A&M comes to its senses and lets you hear it someday. —*Richard S. Ginell*

Yokohama Concert / Apr. 20, 1977 / Pablo ✦✦✦

Trombonist J.J. Johnson's first recording in eight years (he had spent much of the 1965-76 period working nearly full-time as an arranger/composer) is a live double-LP set with a quintet also including cornetist Nat Adderley, keyboardist Billy Childs, bassist Tony Dumas and drummer Kevin Johnson. Of the 11 songs, only four could be considered standards with "Walkin'" being the only piece not written by Johnson, Adderley or Dumas. The music is challenging and well-played if not overly exciting, but it did result in J.J. Johnson returning to a much busier schedule as a trombonist again. —*Scott Yanow*

Pinnacles / Sep. 17, 1979-Sep. 10, 1979 / Milestone ✦✦✦

After seven years off recording (1970-76), during which he worked full-time writing in the studios, trombonist J.J. Johnson began a successful "comeback" showing that he had lost none of his power or creativity through the years. For this LP (not yet reissued on CD), Johnson teams up on some selections with trumpeter Oscar Brashear and tenor saxophonist Joe Henderson, pianist Tommy Flanagan (who surprisingly plays electric keyboards on half of the selections), bassist Ron Carter and drummer Billy Higgins. Although not quite an essential set, J.J. Johnson is in excellent form on this date, and he contributes four originals; ironically "See See Rider" and "Mr. Clean" are actually the most memorable selections. —*Scott Yanow*

Concepts in Blue / Sep. 23, 1980-Sep. 26, 1980 / Original Jazz Classics ✦✦✦✦

This is a fun set of straightahead jazz. The colorful front line (trombonist J.J. Johnson, fluegelhornist Clark Terry, and Ernie Watts on tenor and alto) obviously enjoyed playing the blues-oriented repertoire and the solos are consistently rewarding. Nothing all that innovative occurs but the results are pleasing. —*Scott Yanow*

★ Things Are Getting Better All the Time / Nov. 28, 1983-Nov. 29, 1983 / Original Jazz Classics ✦✦✦✦✦

J.J. Johnson teams up with fellow trombonist Al Grey for a variety of superior standards and obscurities in a quintet with pianist Kenny Barron, bassist Ray Brown and drummer Mickey Roker. Reissued on CD, this session has many joyful moments, and the interaction between the two very different-sounding trombonists (Grey is hot, while Johnson is cool) on such tunes as "Soft Winds," "It's Only a Paper Moon," "Boy Meets Horn" and the title cut is consistently memorable and enjoyable. Recommended. —*Scott Yanow*

Quintergy: Live / Jul. 1988 / Antilles ✦✦✦✦✦

Trombonist J.J. Johnson, 64 at the time, is heard in top form on this "Live at the Village Vanguard" set. His quintet, which includes Ralph Moore on tenor and soprano, pianist Stanley Cowell, bassist Rufus Reid and drummer Victor Lewis, is perfectly suited to interpret the spirited set of advanced bop. Highlights include Johson's feature on "You've Changed," "Coppin' the Bop," "Lament" and his unaccompanied playing on "It's All Right with Me." Excellent music. Another Antilles CD, *Standards,* comes from the same sessions. —*Scott Yanow*

Standards: Live at the Village Vanguard / Jul. 1988 / Antilles ✦✦✦✦✦

The second of two CDs coming from the same engagement at the Village Vanguard (the first was *Quintergy*), this set features trombonist J.J. Johnson's quintet with Ralph Moore on tenor and soprano, pianist Stanley Cowell, bassist Rufus Reid and drummer Victor Lewis jamming on nine standards, plus the leader's "Shortcake." Johnson is in top form, particularly on "My Funny Valentine," "Just Friends," "Misterioso" and "Autumn Leaves." A good example of the ageless trombonist's talents. —*Scott Yanow*

Vivian / Jun. 2, 1992-Jun. 3, 1992 / Concord Jazz ✦✦✦

The great trombonist J.J. Johnson sticks exclusively to ballads on this ten-song set. Accompanied by pianist Rob Schneiderman, guitarist Ted Dunbar, bassist Rufus Reid and drummer Akira Tana, Johnson's tone sounds at its warmest throughout the CD, which is dedicated to his late wife. Highlights include "Alone Together," "I Thought About You," "How Deep Is the Ocean" and "There Will Never Be Another You," but all of the numbers are rewarding. Due to the lack of variety in tempos and moods, this set is not quite definitive, but collectors will find much to enjoy. —*Scott Yanow*

Let's Hang Out / Dec. 7, 1992-Dec. 9, 1992 / Verve ✦✦✦✦

Forty-nine years after his recording debut, trombonist J.J. Johnson still sounds in peak form on this disc. Most of the numbers on his Verve CD find him accompanied by either Stanley Cowell or Renee Roenes on piano, bassist Rufus Reid and Victor Lewis or Lewis Nash on drums with occasional contributions from trumpeter Terence Blanchard (whose chops sound a little off) and Ralph Moore on tenor and soprano. In addition, tenor saxophonist Jimmy Heath makes a couple of guest appearances and "Beautiful Love" is taken by Johnson as an unaccompanied solo. Despite the strong supporting cast, the great trombonist is the star throughout, particularly on "It Never Entered My Mind," his "Kenya," "It's You or No One" and a tasteful quartet rendition of "I Got It Bad." Excellent music. —*Scott Yanow*

Tangence / Jul. 13, 1994-Jul. 15, 1994 / Verve ✦✦✦✦

Trombonist J.J. Johnson is joined by a string orchestra arranged by Robert Farnon for most of the performances on this CD. Farnon's sweeping scores can sometimes come closer to movie music and muzak than jazz but the high quality of the songs and a few surprising departures, make this CD recommended. Wynton

Marsalis has three guest appearances (including a spirited unaccompanied duet with Johnson on the old Jimmy Lunceford hit "For Dancers Only"), Johnson takes his blues "Opus de Focus" as a duet with bassist Chris Laurence and the trombonist is in particularly fine form on such numbers as "The Meaning of the Blues," "Dinner for One, Please, James," "The Very Thought of You" and his own "Lament." —*Scott Yanow*

Brass Orchestra / Sep. 24, 1996-Sep. 27, 1996 / Verve ✦✦✦✦

J.J. Johnson finds himself at the helm of a dream band here—a full brass orchestra with French horns, euphoniums, tubas and a harp—and gets to exploit its possibilities wherever they might lead. The results are beyond category, where the veteran trombonist's writing has a feathery richness, urbanity, and a depth charge in the bass reminiscent of, but not really indebted to, Gil Evans. There is plenty of straightahead jazz grooving but also several episodes of formal, almost classical writing, as in the suitably joyous "If I Hit The Lottery," and rigorous combinations of both, like the angular tribute to Béla Bartók, "Canon for Bela." The generous Johnson doesn't even appear on a piece he commissioned from Robin Eubanks called "Cross Currents"—Eubanks performs the sputtering trombone solo—nor on Slide Hampton's blazing "Comfort Zone." He also revisits some of his early Third Stream experiments from the '50s and '60s; "Ballad for Joe" derives from his *Poem for Brass* and "Horn of Plenty" and "Ballade" from the *Perceptions* album (the latter two sound a bit staid under the current light). Johnson's own trombone solos are always imaginative, authoritative and irresistibly swinging; at 72, he plays as well here as he ever did. This is a must-buy for all J.J. fans and those who thought that the Third Stream could never rise again. —*Richard S. Ginell*

James P. Johnson

b. Feb. 1, 1894, New Brunswick, NJ, **d.** Nov. 17, 1955, New York, NY
Piano, Composer / Stride, Classic Jazz, Ragtime

One of the great jazz pianists of all time, James P. Johnson was the king of stride pianists in the 1920s. He began working in New York clubs as early as 1913 and was quickly recognized as the pacesetter. In 1917 Johnson began making piano rolls. Duke Ellington learned from these (by slowing them down to half-speed) and a few years later Johnson became Fats Waller's teacher and inspiration. During the 1920s (starting in 1921), James P. Johnson began to record, he was the nightly star at Harlem rent parties (accompanied by Waller and Willie "The Lion" Smith) and he wrote some of his most famous compositions. For the 1923 Broadway show *Running Wild* (one of his dozen scores), James P. composed "The Charleston" and "Old Fashioned Love," his earlier piano feature "Carolina Shout" became the test piece for other pianists and some of his other songs included "If I Could Be with You One Hour Tonight" and "A Porter's Love Song to a Chambermaid."

Ironically, James P. Johnson, the most sophisticated pianist of the 1920s, was also an expert accompanist for blues singers and he starred on several memorable Bessie Smith and Ethel Waters recordings. In addition to his solo recordings, Johnson led some hot combos on records and guested with Perry Bradford and Clarence Williams; he also shared the spotlight with Fats Waller on a few occasions. Because he was very interested in writing longer works, Johnson (who had composed "Yamekraw" in 1927) spent much of the 1930s working on such pieces as "Harlem Symphony," "Symphony in Brown" and a blues opera. Unfortunately, much of this music has been lost through the years. Johnson, who was only semi-active as a pianist throughout much of the 1930s, started recording again in 1939, often sat in with Eddie Condon and was active in the 1940s despite some minor strokes. A major stroke in 1951 finished off his career. Most of his recordings have been reissued on CD. —*Scott Yanow*

Carolina Shout / May 1917-Jun. 1925 / Biograph ✦✦✦

This CD contains 14 of James P. Johnson's piano rolls (cut during an eight-year period) mostly for the QRS company. Although piano rolls generally sound somewhat mechanical (particularly rhythmically), this set is not without interest. There is a version of "Carolina Shout" that originally inspired Duke Ellington and a highlight is a song that few remember that Johnson wrote and he never otherwise recorded, "The Charleston." —*Scott Yanow*

Yamekraw and Other Selections / Jan. 1921-1945 / Smithsonian/Folkways ✦✦✦

This is an odd but very interesting LP. The great pianist James P. Johnson is heard performing his lengthy "Yamekraw" in 1945, an orchestral work that he interprets here as an episodic solo piano performance. On the flip side of the album there are four early recordings that singer/hustler Perry Bradford had something to do with. He sings "Sam Jones Done Snagged His Britches" (probably from the mid-'30s) and "Georgia's Always on My Mind" with the Gulf Coast Seven in 1928; in addition, there are two early instrumentals ("That Thing Called Love" and "Shim-Me King's Blues") by Mamie Smith's Jazz Hounds from 1921. This LP is worth getting primarily for the rare James P. Johnson performance. —*Scott Yanow*

☆ **Harlem Stride Piano** / Aug. 1921-Nov. 18, 1929 / Hot N Sweet'♦♦♦♦♦

This European import consists of the first 24 recordings led by the great stride pianist James P. Johnson plus the piano roll version of his hit "The Charleston." Many of these performances have been formerly issued in haphazard or incomplete fashion but this exciting CD has all of Johnson's dates up until his 1930 solos. There are three early band sides from 1921 (including Johnson's "Carolina Shout"), 13 piano solos ("Snowy Morning Blues," "Riffs" and "Feeling Blue" are particularly memorable) and hot combos that feature such sidemen as cornetists/ trumpeters Louis Metcalfe, Cootie Williams and King Oliver and (on two songs) fellow pianist Fats Waller. The somewhat obscure CD is the perfect way to accumulate these historic performances. —*Scott Yanow*

Father of the Stride Piano / Oct. 18, 1921-Jun. 15, 1939 / Columbia ♦♦♦

This LP gives one a good all-around introduction into pianist James P. Johnson's music, although it does not list the recording dates. There are piano solos from 1921, 1923, 1927 and 1939, a humorous vocal/piano duet with Clarence Williams ("How Could I Be Blue") and four selections from a 1939 septet session with trumpeter Red Allen and trombonist J.C. Higginbotham. Most of this music has since been reissued in more complete fashion on CD. —*Scott Yanow*

Giants of Jazz / Oct. 18, 1921-Apr. 1945 / Time-Life ♦♦♦♦♦

This three-LP box set serves as a near-perfect retrospective of the music of the great stride pianist James P. Johnson. There are two piano solos from 1921 (including his famous "Carolina Shout"), numbers on which the pianist accompanied Bessie Smith and Ethel Waters, some heated combo sides, more classic piano solos (including "Riffs," "What Is This Thing Called Love?" and "Jingles"), jams with clarinetist Pee Wee Russell and trumpeter Frankie Newton and a generous amount of Johnson's 1943-45 performances. The accompanying booklet is definitive, making this a highly recommended set even for collectors who already have the majority of these exciting performances. —*Scott Yanow*

Watch Me Go / Nov. 1921-Oct. 22, 1941 / IAJRC ♦♦♦

This is a perfect LP for collectors for it features the great stride pianist James P. Johnson as an accompanist. Virtually all of the 18 recordings are obscure with the pianist heard backing such singers as Lavinia Turner, Sadie Jackson, Rosa Henderson, Clara Smith, Perry Bradford, Roy Evans, Chick Bullock, Clarence Williams (in 1941) and The Great Day New Orleans Singers. The music is not essential (particularly since Johnson is mostly confined to the background) but veteran collectors of '20s music will love this now-rare LP. —*Scott Yanow*

James P. Johnson & Perry Bradford / Dec. 5, 1921-Mar. 5, 1929 / Arcadia ♦♦♦♦♦

This collector's LP contains 16 consistently heated recordings from the 1920s. The masterful stride pianist James P. Johnson leads his "Harmony Eight" on two numbers from 1921 and is heard on all of his band sides from 1927-29; a special high point is his playing (along with fellow pianist Fats Waller) on "What's the Use of Being Alone?" from a session led by cornetist Johnny Dunn. Rounding out the rather exciting album are six selections that feature vocals by Perry Bradford, two of which offer early examples of the great cornetist Jabbo Smith. 1920s collectors should go out of their way to acquire this set. —*Scott Yanow*

Runnin' Wild (1921-1926) / 1921 / Tradition ♦♦♦

It is not mentioned until the final paragraph of the liner notes of this CD that this set of James P. Johnson solo performances are piano rolls rather than recordings; nowhere does it state that important fact on the outside cover. The most interesting aspect of the reissue is that the great pianist did not otherwise record the majority of the numbers, including his famous "Charleston" (although a longer piano roll version has been released elsewhere). As is true of all piano rolls, the rhythms are a bit mechanical, and some of the playing might have been "enhanced" by additional punching of holes. But in general, these performances do indeed sound like the father of stride piano, even if the CD is less essential than James P.'s actual recordings. —*Scott Yanow*

James P. Johnson 1928-1931 / Mar. 27, 1928-Mar. 25, 1931 / Swaggie ♦♦♦♦

This very enjoyable LP from the Australian Swaggie label has more than its share of classic recordings. Pianist James P. Johnson combines with Fats Waller (on organ), cornetist Jabbo Smith and Garvin Bushell (who switches between clarinet, alto and bassoon) for four melodic selections that were released under the name of The Louisiana Sugar Babes. In addition, Johnson has two piano solos, duets with fellow pianist Clarence Williams on "I've Found a New Baby" and leads a variety of bands that feature vocals from Perry Bradford, Andy Razaf and the "Keep Shufflin' Trio"; among the soloists are trumpeters Cootie Williams, Ward Pinkett, Louis Metcalf and King Oliver. This is timeless music that is essential in one form or another; fortunately, much of it has already been reissued on CD. —*Scott Yanow*

★ **Snowy Morning Blues** / Jan. 21, 1930-Sep. 22, 194 / GRP ♦♦♦♦♦

James P. Johnson was one of the greatest jazz pianists of all time and in the 1920s was considered the "king of the stride piano." This Decca reissue CD contains a

great deal of valuable music. Johnson is first heard on four classic piano solos from 1930 ("You've Got to Be Modernistic" and "Jingles" are particularly memorable) and then on eight Fats Waller-associated tunes in duets with drummer Eddie Dougherty from 1944; the latter performances differ from the eight identical Waller songs that Johnson had recorded earlier in the same year as solos. Since Waller (who had passed away in 1943) was his close friend and former student, there is a lot of emotion in the tributes but also much joy. This highly recommended CD concludes with James P. Johnson romping on eight of his own timeless compositions including "Carolina Shout," "Old Fashioned Love" and "If I Could Be with You." —*Scott Yanow*

● **The Original James P. Johnson 1942-1945** / 1942-1945 / Smithsonian/Folkways ♦♦♦♦♦

One of the masters of jazz piano (and the definitive stride pianist), James P. Johnson came out of his musical isolation of the 1930s (when he was writing extensive works that would unfortunately rarely be performed) to become much more active in jazz in the '40s. This set of 20 piano solos originally cut for the Asch label has eight unreleased tracks and alternate takes. James P. is heard romping through standards (including "Liza" and "St. Louis Blues") and some of his classic originals ("The Dream" and "Snowy Morning Blues"). Most interesting are his lengthier explorations of his "serious" work, including a 12-minute "Yamekraw," and the six-and-a-half-minute "Jazzamine Concerto." Timeless music. —*Scott Yanow*

Ain'tcha Got Music / Jun. 17, 1944-Aug. 1949 / Pumpkin ♦♦♦

Previously unreleased until this LP came out in 1986, these performances feature pianist James P. Johnson during his final period. Johnson takes the title cut unaccompanied, is heard as a guest at Eddie Condon concerts from 1944-47 and (best of all) has five lengthy selections as either solos or duets with drummer Danny Alvin in 1949, shortly before a major stroke put him permanently out of action. Historic value aside, Johnson is heard in prime form on such numbers as "If Dreams Come True," "Over the Waves" and the closing "Liza." This increasingly hard-to-find LP should be of great interest to fans of the innovative stride pianist. —*Scott Yanow*

Victory Stride / Feb. 1992+Jan. 1994 / Music Masters ♦♦♦

James P. Johnson passed away in 1955 and, although he gained fame as the top stride pianist of the 1920s, his ambitious major works were rarely ever performed. During the two years covered by this CD, several of Johnson's most extended suites (much of which was feared to have been lost) were recorded for the first time: "Victory Stride," the four-part "Harlem Symphony," "Concerto Jazz a Mine," the "American Symphonic Suite" and "Drums—A Symphonic Poem"; in addition, The Concordia Orchestra and pianist Leslie Stifelman play an extended version of Johnson's "The Charleston." The music, although technically outside of jazz, should greatly interest jazz collectors for these colorful performances cast new light on the talents of James P. Johnson. —*Scott Yanow*

Lonnie Johnson (Alonzo Johnson)

b. Feb. 8, 1899, New Orleans, LA, **d.** Jun. 16, 1970, Toronto, Canada

Guitar, Vocals / Classic Jazz, Jazz Blues, Acoustic Blues, Country Blues, Piedmont Blues, Prewar Country Blues

Blues guitar simply would not have developed in the manner that it did if not for the prolific brilliance of Lonnie Johnson. He was there to help define the instrument's future within the genre and the genre's future itself at the very beginning, his melodic conception so far advanced from most of his pre-war peers as to inhabit a plane all his own. For more than 40 years, Johnson played blues, jazz, and ballads his way; he was a true blues originator whose influence hung heavy on a host of subsequent blues immortals.

Johnson's extreme versatility doubtless stemmed in great part from growing up in the musically diverse Crescent City. Violin caught his ear initially, but he eventually made the guitar his passion, developing a style so fluid and inexorably melodic that instrumental backing seemed superfluous. He signed up with OKeh Records in 1925 and commenced to recording at an astonishing pace—between 1925 and 1932, he cut an estimated 130 waxings. The red-hot duets he recorded with White jazz guitarist Eddie Lang (masquerading as Blind Willie Dunn) in 1928-29 were utterly groundbreaking for their ceaseless invention. Johnson also recorded pioneering jazz efforts in 1927 with no less than Louis Armstrong's Hot Five and Duke Ellington's orchestra.

After enduring the Depression and moving to Chicago, Johnson came back to recording life with Bluebird for a five-year stint beginning in 1939. Under the ubiquitous Lester Melrose's supervision, Johnson picked up right where he left off, selling quite a few copies of "He's a Jelly Roll Baker" for old Nipper. Johnson went with Cincinnati-based King Records in 1947 and promptly enjoyed one of the biggest hits of his uncommonly long career with the mellow ballad "Tomorrow

Night," which topped the R&B charts for seven weeks in 1948. More hits followed posthaste: "Pleasing You (as Long as I Live)," "So Tired," and "Confused."

Time seemed to have passed Johnson by during the late '50s. He was toiling as a hotel janitor in Philadelphia when banjo player Elmer Snowden alerted Chris Albertson to his whereabouts. That rekindled a major comeback, Johnson cutting a series of albums for Prestige's Bluesville subsidary during the early '60s and venturing to Europe under the auspices of Horst Lippmann and Fritz Rau's American Folk Blues Festival banner in 1963. Finally, in 1969, Johnson was hit by a car in Toronto and died a year later from the effects of the accident.

Johnson's influence was massive, touching everyone from Robert Johnson, whose seminal approach bore strong resemblance to that of his older namesake, to Elvis Presley and Jerry Lee Lewis, who each paid heartfelt tribute with versions of "Tomorrow Night" while at Sun. —*Bill Dahl*

★ **Steppin' on the Blues** / Nov. 4, 1925-Aug. 12, 1932 / Columbia/Legacy ✦✦✦✦✦
Groundbreaking guitar work of dazzling complexity that never fails to amaze—and this stuff was cut in the 1920s! Johnson's astonishingly fluid guitar work was massively influential (Robert Johnson, for one, was greatly swayed by his waxings), and his no-nonsense vocals (frequently laced with threats of violence—"Got the Blues for Murder Only" and "She's Making Whoopee in Hell Tonight" are prime examples on this 19-cut collection) are scarcely less impressive. Johnson's torrid guitar duets with jazzman Eddie Lang retain their sense of legend nearly seven decades after they were cut. —*Bill Dahl*

He's a Jelly Roll Baker / Nov. 2, 1939-Dec. 14, 1944 / Bluebird ✦✦✦✦
This 20-song collection covers 1930s and '40s material in which Johnson primarily performs blues tunes, doing salty, sassy, mournful and suggestive numbers in a distinctive, memorable fashion. His vocals on "Rambler's Blues," "In Love Again," the title cut and several others are framed by brilliant, creative playing and excellent support from such pianists as Blind John Davis, Lil Hardin Armstrong and Joshua Altheimer. This is tight, intuitive music in which Johnson set the tone and dominated the songs. If you're unaware of Lonnie Johnson's brilliant blues material, here's an excellent introduction. —*Ron Wynn*

Losing Game / Dec. 28, 1960 / Bluesville ✦✦✦✦
Johnson recorded prolifically for Prestige's Bluesville during his early-'60s comeback; this 1960 set is a typically gorgeous solo outing that ranges from torchy standards of the Tin Pan Alley species ("What a Difference a Day Makes," "Summertime") to bluesier pursuits of his own creation. —*Bill Dahl*

Blues, Ballads & Jumpin' Jazz / Apr. 5, 1960 / Bluesville ✦✦✦✦✦
This is an unusual CD. In 1960 guitarists Lonnie Johnson and Elmer Snowden (along with bassist Wendell Marshall) teamed up for *Blues and Ballads* which was primarily a showcase for Johnson's blues vocals. This previously unreleased set from the same session has six instrumentals and just four vocals with Snowden generally in the lead. The two guitarists are heard good-naturedly suggesting songs before launching into spontaneous improvisations and the results sound like an intimate concert. Highlights of this fun outing include "Lester Leaps In," "C-Jam Blues" and "Careless Love." —*Scott Yanow*

★ **Blues & Ballads** / Apr. 5, 1960 / Bluesville ✦✦✦✦✦
This combination works quite well. Guitarist-singer Lonnie Johnson was just starting a successful comeback, and here he is teamed up with acoustic rhythm guitarist Elmer Snowden (who had not recorded since 1934) and bassist Wendell Marshall. Johnson sings smooth blues and sentimental ballads with equal skill, and both guitarists have opportunities to display their complementary but distinctive styles. This CD reissue is easily recommended, as is its more instrumental counterpart, *Blues, Ballads, and Jumpin' Jazz, Vol. 2.* —*Scott Yanow*

Idle Hours / Jul. 13, 1961 / Bluesville ✦✦✦✦
Johnson and Victoria Spivey had known one another for decades (they duetted on the ribald "Toothache Blues" way back in 1928), so it's no surprise that their musical repartee on 1961's *Idle Hours* seems so natural and playful. Spivey guests on three tracks (including the title number) and plays piano on her one solo entry. Johnson does the majority of the disc without her, benefitting from pianistic accompaniment by Cliff Jackson. —*Bill Dahl*

Another Night to Cry / Apr. 6, 1962 / Bluesville ✦✦✦
Lonnie Johnson, a talented vocalist and guitarist who chose to spend much of his life playing blues (although in the 1920s he recorded with some of the top jazz stars), had his fifth recording for Prestige/Bluesville (a solo set) reissued on this CD. "Blues After Hours" is an instrumental that shows off his jazz roots and many of the 11 songs (all of which are Johnson originals) have spots for his guitar. Since there is only around 34 minutes on this set (which could have been combined on one CD with the music from another LP) and none of the individual songs even reach four minutes, this is not one of the more essential Lonnie Johnson releases but it does have its strong moments. —*Scott Yanow*

The Complete Folkways Recordings / 1967 / Smithsonian/Folkways ✦✦✦✦
An even two dozen solo performances from late in the legendary guitarist's amazing career (1967), but chock full of stellar moments all the same. Artists of Johnson's versatility were rare even then—he brings a multitude of shadings to "My Mother's Eyes" and "How Deep Is The Ocean," then delivers a saucy "Juice Headed Baby" with the same stunning complexity. —*Bill Dahl*

Blues By / Mar. 8, 1960 / Bluesville ✦✦✦✦
After four years off records and in obscurity, Lonnie Johnson launched his final comeback with this release, which has been reissued on CD. Teamed with tenor saxophonist Hal Singer, pianist Claude Hopkins, bassist Wendell Marshall and drummer Bobby Donaldson, Johnson sings and plays guitar on a variety of blues, showing that the layoff (he was working at the time as a janitor) had not hurt his abilities in the slightest. —*Scott Yanow*

Blues Roots, Vol. 8 (Swingin' with Lonnie) / Oct. 16, 1963 / Storyville ✦✦✦
Backed by pianist Otis Spann, singer/guitarist Lonnie Johnson performs blues and ballads on this well-rounded set. Included are such numbers as his old hit "Tomorrow Night," "See See Rider," "Jelly Jelly" and a lone instrumental, "Swingin' with Lonnie." An above-average outing by the veteran bluesman. —*Scott Yanow*

Stompin' at the Penny / Nov. 1995 / Columbia/Legacy ✦✦✦
This set (reissued on CD) is a bit unusual, for it features bluesman Lonnie Johnson with a Canadian Dixieland band, McHarg's Metro Stompers. In addition to including a few Johnson vocals, he takes credible solos on some trad jazz standards, including "China Boy." Six of the 13 numbers do not have the guitarist, putting the focus on the fine Dixieland band, which includes cornetist Charlie Gall and clarinetist Eric Neilson in addition to the leader on bass. The original LP only sold 1,000 copies, so this reissue brings back music heard by very few at the time; this was Lonnie Johnson's last regular recording, although he did cut a series of numbers for Smithsonian in 1967. —*Scott Yanow*

Marc Johnson

b. Oct. 21, 1953, Omaha, NE
Bass / Post-Bop
Marc Johnson gained his initial reputation as a member of Bill Evans' last rhythm section and his work with Bass Desires (a group featuring both Bill Frisell and John Scofield on guitars) showed off his versatility. While at North Texas State University, Johnson played with a group that included Lyle Mays. He was with Woody Herman's Orchestra (1977), Bill Evans (1978-80), Stan Getz (1981-82) and John Abercrombie (1983) before forming Bass Desires (1985). The latter group recorded two intriguing albums for ECM. In 1989 Marc Johnson made a series of duets with various all-stars for EmArcy, and in 1993 he led the group Right Brain Patrol, a trio with guitarist Ben Monder and percussionist Arto Tuncboyaci that recorded for JMT. —*Scott Yanow*

● **Bass Desires** / May 1985 / ECM ✦✦✦✦
Bass Desires was a rather unusual group, for despite its title and the fact that leader Marc Johnson was a bassist (formerly with the Bill Evans Trio), the main voices were the contrasting guitars of Bill Frisell (who doubled on guitar synthesizer) and John Scofield; drummer Peter Erskine completed the group. This wide-ranging set has four diverse originals, Elmer Bernstein's "A Wishing Doll," a lengthy rendition of John Coltrane's "Resolution," and the folk melody "Black Is the Color of My True Love's Hair." The post-bop music is continually colorful, with Frisell taking honors. —*Scott Yanow*

Second Sight / Mar. 1987 / ECM ✦✦✦
The second release by Bass Desires (a quartet consisting of leader/bassist Marc Johnson, drummer Peter Erskine and the guitars of Bill Frisell and John Scofield) is almost the equal of the first. This advanced unit performs eight group originals that cover a wide variety of moods, from introspective, spacey pieces to ones emphasizing fire and passion. —*Scott Yanow*

2 X 4 / Apr. 17, 1989-Apr. 18, 1989 / Verve ✦✦✦✦✦
Better than average tunes, excellent playing from Gary Burton (vib), Toots Thielemans (harmonica). —*Ron Wynn*

Sound of Summer Running / 1997 / Verve ✦✦✦

Osie Johnson (James Johnson)

b. Jan. 11, 1923, Washington, DC, d. Feb. 10, 1966, New York, NY
Drums / Swing, Bop, Swing-Bop
In the 1950s and the first half of the 1960s, Osie Johnson was one of the most in-demand drummers in New York, making a countless number of recordings and working steadily in the studios. He started working professionally in 1941, was with Sabby Lewis' band in Boston (1942-43) and then was in the military where he played in a Navy band (1944-45). After five years freelancing in Chicago,

Johnson was a member of Earl Hines' band during 1951-53. Stints with Dorothy Donegan and Illinois Jacquet followed before he became a busy session musician, playing and recording with the who's who of mainstream (including Coleman Hawkins, Dinah Washington, Wes Montgomery and Sonny Stitt). In addition to contributing tasteful and supportive drums, Osie Johnson was an occasional composer, arranger and singer, leading sessions for Jazztone (1955) and RCA (1956). —*Scott Yanow*

Swingin' Sounds / Feb. 1955 / Jazztone ✦✦✦

A Bit of the Blues / Apr. 7, 1956+Apr. 28, 1956 / Victor ✦✦✦

Pete Johnson

b. Mar. 25, 1904, Kansas City, MO, **d.** Mar. 23, 1967, Buffalo, NY
Piano / Boogie-Woogie, Blues Jazz
Pete Johnson was one of the three great boogie-woogie pianists (along with Albert Ammons and Meade Lux Lewis) whose sudden prominence in the late '30s helped make the style very popular. Originally a drummer, Johnson switched to piano in 1922. He was part of the Kansas City scene in the 1920s and '30s, often accompanying singer Big Joe Turner. Producer John Hammond discovered him in 1936 and got him to play at the Famous Door in New York. After taking part at Hammond's 1938 *Spirituals to Swing* Carnegie Hall concert in 1938, Johnson started recording regularly and appeared on an occasional basis with Ammons and Lewis as the Boogie Woogie Trio. He also backed Turner on some classic records. Johnson recorded often in the 1940s and spent much of 1947-49 based in Los Angeles. He moved to Buffalo in 1950 and, other than an appearance at the 1958 Newport Jazz Festival, he was in obscurity for much of the decade. A stroke later in 1958 left him partly paralyzed. Johnson made one final appearance at John Hammond's January 1967 *Spirituals to Swing* concert, playing the right hand on a version of "Roll 'Em Pete" two months before his death. —*Scott Yanow*

● **1938-1939** / Dec. 30, 1938-Dec. 1938 / Classics ✦✦✦✦✦
This superlative CD reissue features boogie-woogie pianist Pete Johnson on two classic numbers with singer Big Joe Turner (the original versions of "Goin' Away Blues" and "Roll 'Em Pete"), with inspiring trumpeter Harry James ("Boo Woo" and "Home James"), with his Boogie Woogie Boys (a sextet that includes Turner and trumpeter Hot Lips Page), interacting with fellow pianists Albert Ammons and Meade Lux Lewis (joining Big Joe on "Café Society Rag"), and on a pair of trio numbers. However, it is Johnson's ten unaccompanied piano solos (mostly released previously by Solo Art) that are the rarest and most notable. Taken as a whole, this is Pete Johnson's definitive release, showing that he was much more than just a one-dimensional (although powerful) boogie-woogie specialist. —*Scott Yanow*

King of Boogie / Apr. 16, 1939-May 8, 1939 / Milan ✦✦✦
This sampler of pianist Pete Johnson's 1939-41 recordings has somewhat crummy packaging, which claims that the selections were recorded "at various concerts in France"; actually, these are all studio sides cut in the US. The music—trio and solo performances except for a band number, "627 Stomp"—is excellent, but the 17 numbers are all readily available elsewhere. Fine music which, if found at a budget price, could act as an introduction to the boogie-woogie/blues pianist. —*Scott Yanow*

Master of Blues and Boogie Woogie, Vol. 3 / Dec. 19, 1939-Apr. 1949 / Oldie Blues ✦✦✦
This Dutch LP features pianist Pete Johnson in four different settings spanning a decade of time. Six titles are trio and solo numbers taken from his 1939 Blue Note dates (bassist Abe Bolar is mistakenly listed as playing drums). Much rarer are three songs from a 1946 quintet set with organist Bill Gooden and guitarist Jimmy Shirley, and three songs with a rollicking R&B-ish sextet in 1949. But overall, collectors will prefer to get these performances in complete versions with their original sessions. Good music, but this LP is not essential. —*Scott Yanow*

● **1944-1946** / Feb. 17, 1944-Jan. 31, 1946 / Classics ✦✦✦✦✦
The third "complete" Pete Johnson CD put out by the European Classics label features the great boogie-woogie pianist in three different settings. There are eight formerly rare piano solos from 1944 that cover a variety of moods, five selections with a hot Kansas City octet which includes trumpeter Hot Lips Page, tenorman Budd Johnson and two vocals from the young Etta Jones, and eight intriguing numbers in which Johnson is gradually joined by an additional musician on each track. "Page Mr. Trumpet" is an exciting outing for Hot Lips, and the other top players include clarinetist Albert Nicholas, trombonist J.C. Higginbotham and tenorman Ben Webster. A particularly exciting release. —*Scott Yanow*

Central Avenue Boogie / Apr. 18, 1947-Nov. 29, 1947 / Delmark ✦✦✦
Boogie-woogie pianist Pete Johnson is in excellent form on these selections but this complete reissue of his Apollo recordings does not have much meat. Johnson only cut eight sides for the label so three alternate takes are included plus two

titles (and an alternate) from pianist Arnold Wiley's only Apollo session. The results are enjoyable (particularly Johnson's versions of "Margie" and "Swanee River") although few surprises or real high points occur. —*Scott Yanow*

Plas Johnson (John Johnson, Jr.)

b. Jul. 21, 1931, Donaldsonville, LA
Tenor Saxophone / Soul-Jazz, Hard Bop
Plas Johnson's seductive tenor sound has been utilized on many studio sessions including most notably in the *Pink Panther* film (1963). A more versatile player than one might think, Johnson sounds equally at home in blues, R&Bish and hard bop settings. He recorded a single in New Orleans (1950), moved to Los Angeles and was quickly established as a popular studio musician. Johnson worked with Johnny Otis and Charles Brown, recorded dates as a leader for Tampa (1956-57), Score, Capitol (1958-60), Ava (1964) and Concord (1975-76), worked with the Capp-Pierce Juggernaut and toured with the Gene Harris Superband in 1990. —*Scott Yanow*

Bop Me Daddy / 1956-1957 / V.S.O.P. ✦✦✦
This LP (originally on the Tampa label) is subtitled "Rock 'n' Roll Instrumentals," but is actually an R&B-flavored jazz album. Plas Johnson, whose tenor would be featured anonymously on many hit rock 'n' roll and pop records, is joined by pianist Ray Johnson, bassist Duke Harris and drummer Sharky Hall for a variety of fairly basic melodies. Johnson plays quite melodically and with soul on such numbers as "Makin' Whoopee," "Blue Jean Shuffle" and "Last Call." The music on this LP is pleasing, if not all that essential. —*Scott Yanow*

● **The Blues** / Sep. 1975 / Concord Jazz ✦✦✦✦✦
Throughout most of his career, tenor saxophonist Plas Johnson has worked in the R&B and rock 'n' roll field, adding his virile tenor to many sessions and uplifting the music without receiving that much credit. However, in 1975-76, the busy studio musician was recorded on two occasions as a leader in jazz settings by Concord, with the results show that he is also a superior jazz player. Johnson, teamed up with keyboardist Mike Melvoin, guitarist Herb Ellis, bassist Ray Brown, drummer Jake Hanna and Bobbye Hall on congas for this date, puts plenty of soul and swinging ideas into such songs as "George on My Mind," "Please Send Me Someone to Love" and "Parking Lot Blues." The music is accessible, fairly basic and fun. —*Scott Yanow*

Positively / May 7, 1976+May 8, 1976 / Concord Jazz ✦✦✦✦
This CD reissue brings back one of Plas Johnson's few opportunities through the years to lead his own recording session. The appealing tenor jams through a variety of songs that range from straightahead to soulful, with touches of gospel and even country. Assisted by guitarist Herb Ellis, electric keyboardist Mike Melvoin, bassist Ray Brown, either Jake Hanna or Jimmie Smith on drums, and Bobby Hall on conga, Johnson shows that he was an overlooked transition figure between Stanley Turrentine and Joshua Redman. Highlights include "Lover Man," "My Foolish Heart" and "Careless Love." —*Scott Yanow*

L.A. (1955) / 1983 / Carell Music ✦✦✦
The title of this obscure but worthy LP refers to the style of music rather than the actual recording date. Tenor saxophonist Plas Johnson (who has spent much of his career in the studios, anonymously adding soul to countless recordings) teams up with guitarist Billy Rogers, Art Hillery on organ, and drummer Jimmie Smith during six soulful standards, including "Confessin' the Blues" and "Hard Times," plus Plas' two originals "The Grease Patrol" (an official name for the group) and "Monkey Business." The music is bluesy, swinging, accessible and worth searching for. —*Scott Yanow*

Wayne Johnson

b. 1951
Guitar / Post-Bop, Soul-Jazz
A talented guitarist influenced a bit by Pat Metheny, Wayne Johnson has spent much of his career in the background, doing studio work and touring with Manhattan Transfer. He started playing guitar when he was eight and won several contests while still in school. Johnson attended Berklee during 1972-74, joined the Manhattan Transfer's backup group in 1976, and in 1977 put together a popular trio that recorded for Inner City (1980), ITI (1983), Zebra (1988) and MoJazz (1993). In 1990, Johnson worked with Rickie Lee Jones for a year and has since toured Europe with John Scofield and produced records, in addition to working occasionally with his trio. —*Scott Yanow*

Arrowhead / 1980 / Inner City ✦✦✦

Everybody's Painting Pictures / 1984 / Zebra ✦✦✦

Spirit of the Dancer / 1988 / Zebra ✦✦✦✦

● **Keeping the Dream Alive** / 1993 / MoJazz ✦✦✦✦

Philip Johnston

b. Jan. 22, 1955, Chicago, IL

Alto Saxophone, Soprano Saxophone / Avant-Garde

The twisted avant-jazz of Phillip Johnston first reared its head during the early 1980s, when the composer and saxophonist was a staple of the downtown New York City underground music scene; there he performed with a variety of artists both in and out of the jazz community, among them John Zorn, Eugene Chadbourne, Elliott Sharp, Wayne Horvitz, Butch Morris and the dB's. In addition to commissioned works in conjunction with a number of theatrical and dance productions, Johnston also earned notoriety for his eclectic film work, scoring pictures by directors including Doris Dorrie, Philip Haas and Paul Mazursky; following the 1992 breakup of his group the Microscopic Septet, he soon resurfaced fronting the band Big Trouble, debuting with a self-titled LP on the Black Saint label. After scoring the film noir *The Unknown*, Johnston and Big Trouble returned in 1996 with *Flood at the Ant Farm; Normalology* followed a year later. —*Jason Ankeny*

Big Trouble / Jun. 1992-Jul. 1992 / Black Saint ◆◆◆

Unknown / Nov. 11, 1994 / Avant ◆◆◆

● **Flood at the Ant Farm** / Jul. 25, 1995+Jul. 26, 1996 / Black Saint ◆◆◆◆

The third CD by Philip Johnston's Big Trouble is jazz mixing great musicianship with a touch of madness. He treats Steve Lacy's "Hemline" as if it were penned by Raymond Scott (whose music was adapted for classic Looney Tunes cartoons), and "Bone" sounds like a wild improvisation on a childhood chant. Pianist Joe Ruccek's "Heaven or Hell or Hoboken" has a nifty calypso beat with an intense cacophony of reeds and brass. Johnston is also a gifted composer; his "Pontius Pilate Polka" blends folk dances with swinging Dixieland interludes. "Mr. Crocodile" is a light samba with a touch of reggae. Highly recommended for fans of the great melting pot of jazz. —*Ken Dryden*

Pete Jolly (Peter A. Ceragioli)

b. Jun. 5, 1932, New Haven, CT

Piano / Bop, Cool

A powerful pianist who came to fame on the West Coast in the 1950s, Pete Jolly has been a fixture in Los Angeles for over 40 years. He started on accordion when he was three and began piano when he was eight. He played his first jobs when he was 12. In 1946, his family moved to Phoenix and the following year he joined the Musicians Union and started working extensively in clubs. During a visit to Los Angeles in 1954, Jolly sat in at the Lighthouse, which led to him joining Shorty Rogers' Giants (1954-56). He recorded three albums as a leader for Victor in 1956 (taking rare jazz accordion solos on a few tracks), worked with Buddy DeFranco, Terry Gibbs, Richie Kamuca, Chet Baker and Art Pepper, among others, in the late '50s, and had a surprise hit with "Little Bird" in 1963. Jolly became a busy studio musician in the 1960s but has led his trio with bassist Chuck Berghofer and drummer Nick Martinis regularly in local clubs for over 30 years. In addition to RCA, Pete Jolly has recorded for Metrojazz, MGM, Ava, Charlie Parker Records, Columbia, A&M, Atlas, Holt and V.S.O.P. as a leader. —*Scott Yanow*

The Red Chimney and Sherry's Bar Recordings / Oct. 11, 1960-Feb. 27, 1965 / V.S.O.P. ◆◆◆

Released for the first time in 1994, these straightahead performances are the earliest live recordings by the Pete Jolly Trio. With either Ralph Pena or Chuck Berghofer on bass and drummer Nick Martinis playing on most of the selections, Jolly is in typically exuberant form on a variety of jazz standards including "Oleo," a lengthy "Falling in Love with Love," a humorous "Blues in the Closet" and even "Whistle While You Work." The one flaw to this set is that the noise from the crowd is occasionally distracting, making it advisable to acquire some of Pete Jolly's studio recordings first. —*Scott Yanow*

Little Bird / Nov. 1962+Jan. 1963 / V.S.O.P. ◆◆◆◆

This LP reissue of a release from the obsolete Ava label brings back a hit record. Pianist Pete Jolly, his trio (with bassist Chuck Berghofer and drummer Larry Bunker) and guests (guitarist Howard Roberts and percussionist Kenny Hume) play mostly standards, but it is Jolly's version of the catchy "Little Bird" that caught on. This is a fine all-around straightahead session (highlighted by "Never Never Land," "Spring Can Really Hang You Up the Most" and "Falling in Love with Love") that deserves to be reissued on CD eventually. —*Scott Yanow*

Pete Jolly Trio and Friends / Nov. 1962-Aug. 1964 / V.S.O.P. ◆◆◆◆

This CD contains selections taken from pianist Pete Jolly's three mid-'60s LPs for Ava. Although it would have been preferable to have all of the music complete, this is a fine all-around sampler. The talented bop-based pianist is joined by bassist Chuck Berghofer, guitarist Howard Roberts, either Larry Bunker or Nick Martinis on drums and, on seven of the 16 selections, a string orchestra. All but five of the performances are under three-and-a-half minutes and, although those are

enjoyable enough, it is Jolly's longer explorations ("Falling in Love with Love," "Alone Together," "No Other Love," "Can't We Be Friends" and "I'm Beginning to See the Light") that are most memorable. This CD serves as a good introduction to Pete Jolly's fine playing. —*Scott Yanow*

Sweet September / 1964 / Ava ◆◆◆

Originally this Ava set (reissued in 1987 by V.S.O.P.) was pianist Pete Jolly's follow-up album to his surprisingly popular *Little Bird* LP. Assisted by bassist Chuck Berghofer and drummer Larry Bunker (two of the ten numbers have Nick Martinis on drums and the addition of guitarist Howard Roberts), Jolly mostly performs melodic and easy-listening music, stretching out a bit on "Yours Is My Heart Alone," "There Is No Greater Love" and "Can't We Be Friends." Although trying to be commercial, Jolly cannot help swinging and he sounds better in this format than many others trying to look for a repeat hit. —*Scott Yanow*

Herb Alpert Presents Pete Jolly / 1968 / A&M ◆◆◆◆

Herb Alpert, then at the crest of his fabulously successful roll with the Tijuana Brass, tried to give unsung L.A. hero Pete Jolly—then toiling in the studios—some high-profile exposure-by-association on a trio of albums for his own label, A&M. On their first try, Alpert and Jolly serve up an appealing mix of swinging quartet jazz and period instrumental pop tastefully orchestrated by Marty Paich, very much within the parameters of A&M's enlightened middle-of-the-road direction in its early years. Some soft rock-accented tracks are clearly aimed at airplay (Leroy Anderson's "Serenata," Dori Caymmi's "Like a Lover"), while other Paich orchestrations are a bit tougher and more challenging ("For Carl"), and Neal Hefti's "Lonely Girl" gets an especially lively and erudite workout. Yet whether embroidering the melody or taking off with drummer Earl Palmer, bassist Chuck Berghofer and guitarist John Pisano (on loan from the TJB), Jolly is marvelously inventive and a hard-swinging pianist at all times. This LP is a most attractive marriage between art and commerce—something Alpert was, and remains, very good at. —*Richard S. Ginell*

● **Seasons** / 1969 / A&M ◆◆◆◆◆

This LP, hailed at the time of release and promptly forgotten, is Pete Jolly's masterpiece, a wonderfully emotional electronic tour de force. Almost completely improvised in the studio on a variety of electric and acoustic keyboards, backed by a superb, versatile rhythm section (including drummer Paul Humphrey, guitarist John Pisano and ever-present Chuck Berghofer on bass), *Seasons* unleashes Jolly's imagination, and he creates a marvelous tapestry of sound that both moves the listener and swings spontaneously. Beautifully produced by Herb Alpert, the record is structured as a continuous suite—with only a side break on the LP interrupting the flow—and it comes to an exciting, carefully graded climax on "The Indian's Summer," with Jolly pounding the grand piano and a sudden burst of big-band fireworks courtesy of Bill Holman. There is arch humor in tracks like the scurrying "Bees" and the sauntering "Plummer Park," vivid tone painting in "Rainbows" and "Sand Storm," and aching beauty in "Autumn Festival." Roger Nichols' wistful "Seasons" and the sole standard on the album ("Younger Than Springtime") fit seamlessly into the fabric of Jolly's improvisations, and Jolly uses "Springtime" as a recurring motif. Nothing from Jolly's earlier recordings could prepare the listener for this record, and he has done nothing comparable to it since. If you can find this out-of-print LP, grab it and cherish it. —*Richard S. Ginell*

Give a Damn / Mar. 1970 / A&M ◆◆◆

Next, Herb Alpert placed Pete Jolly in his natural habitat, a nightclub—North Hollywood's legendary Donte's—with a piano trio and what sounds like an over-dubbed quartet of trumpets and trombones. The unnecessary window dressing was probably supposed to help the record sell, which it didn't, and most of the tracks are faded out prematurely. Jolly manages to keep the invention flowing consistently on four then-current hits and two standards (the title track was originally a minor protest hit for Spanky and Our Gang), yet he is often defeated by the ghost horns mimicking his lines. But when Jolly is turned loose on "The Trolley Song" at some length, he responds with some madly uninhibited, uniquely styled, two-fisted swinging to the grooves of bassist Chuck Berghofer and another loaner from the TJB, drummer Nick Ceroli. —*Richard S. Ginell*

25th Anniversary Gem / 1990 / Holt ◆◆◆◆◆

● **Yours Truly** / 1993 / Bainbridge ◆◆◆◆◆

Pete Jolly and his longtime sidemen (Chuck Berghofer has been his regular bassist since the late '50s while drummer Nick Martinis joined up in 1964) perform 11 standards plus his old hit "Little Bird" on this fine outing. The virtuosic pianist dominates the ensembles but the contributions of Berghofer and Martinis (who have to think fast to keep up with him) should not be overlooked. Jolly's total command of the piano and infectious enthusiasm, which can result in some explosive outbursts, do not overshadow his good taste and the self-restraint that he shows on the ballads. —*Scott Yanow*

Yeah! / Oct. 10, 1995-Oct. 11, 1995 / V.S.O.P. ◆◆◆◆

Pete Jolly and his sidemen (bassist Chuck Berghofer and drummer Nick Martinis) celebrated their 21st year as a regularly working trio with this fine V.S.O.P. CD. The musicians sound quite enthusiastic and creative within the boundaries of straightahead jazz, showing that they had not run out of ideas yet. Jolly alternates hot pieces with ballads, standards with obscurities. It is a particular pleasure to hear the powerful pianist interpret such rarely performed songs as George Wallington's "Variations," "Crazeology," Al Cohn's brooding ballad "Ah-Moore" and Shorty Rogers' "Diablo's Dance." Other highlights of the enjoyable set include Horace Silver's "Yeah," "Lullaby of the Leaves" and Zoot Sims' "The Red Door." All those years of playing together have definitely paid off. —*Scott Yanow*

Bobby Jones

b. Oct. 30, 1928, Louisville, KY, **d.** Mar. 6, 1980, Munich, Germany
Tenor Saxophone, Flute / Hard Bop

A minor figure best-known for his association with Charles Mingus in the early '70s, Bobby Jones was a talented tenor saxophonist with a versatile style. He struggled in the musical minor leagues for a long time, playing with the Glenn Miller ghost band (1959), a few months with Woody Herman (1963) and, for a short while, as clarinet with Jack Teagarden. Jones played well with Mingus (1970-72) and recorded albums as a leader for Cobblestone (1972) and Enja (1974), doubling on tenor and clarinet for the latter. He settled in Munich but his emphysema forced him to stop playing and concentrate on arranging before cutting short his life. —*Scott Yanow*

● **The Arrival of Bobby Jones** / Jul. 12, 1972 / Cobblestone ◆◆◆◆◆

The first of Bobby Jones' two sets as a leader features Jones on tenor, soprano and a bit of clarinet in a group including a pair of fellow Charles Mingus alumni (altoist Charles McPherson and pianist Jaki Byard), bassist Richard Davis, drummer Mickey Roker, percussionist Sue Evans and (on "'Stone Bossa" and "Keepin' Up With Jones") guest appearances by Bob Dorough on electric piano. All but one of the seven tunes are by Jones, and these include "Thanks to Trane," "Blues for the Brown Buddha" (dedicated to Charlie Parker), and "As the Crow Flies" (which Jones called "a free-form hillbilly tune"). Although Byard is actually the most impressive soloist throughout the wide-ranging set, Bobby Jones sounds fine on the frequently quirky inside/outside music. —*Scott Yanow*

Hill Country Suite / Aug. 30, 1974 / Enja ◆◆◆◆

The focus is on the short-lived tenor saxophonist Bobby Jones (who doubles on clarinet) throughout this interesting if not essential release. Jones is accompanied by bassist George Mraz and drummer Freddie Waits on his three-part "Hill Country Suite" and three of his other numbers. In addition to Charles Mingus, hard bop and touches of the avant-garde, Bobby Jones' originals were influenced by country and folk music, making for some intriguing sounds. —*Scott Yanow*

Boogaloo Joe Jones

Guitar / Soul-Jazz, Hard Bop

Ivan Jones learned the guitar himself on a three-string instrument that he received as a gift from his father in 1956. He was influenced most by Tal Farlow and Billy Butler, but gravitated toward the R&B juke-joint jazz Butler was popularizing with Bill Doggett. Jones lived in South New Jersey most of his life and worked in and around the Atlantic City area with chitlin-circuit heroes like Wild Bill Davis, Willis Jackson and Charlie Ventura. He made his solo debut on Prestige in 1967, but earned the name "Boogaloo Joe" following a 1969 record of that title. Perhaps the demeaning name distinguished him from the other Jo(e) Jones of jazz, but it suited his style well. While jazz went through some drastic changes during his recording career (1967-76), Jones' sound and style stayed remarkably consistent. His distinctive and likable sound coupled catchy chordal vamps with astonishing rapid-fire single-note playing. He could handle familiar pop covers ("Light My Fire," "Have You Never Been Mellow") and ballads. But he really excelled in the jazz-funk groove and proved himself a first-rate blues player. He recorded with Groove Holmes, Houston Person, Rusty Bryant, Harold Mabern and, most notably, Willis Jackson. Jones, whose distinctive and likable sound never got its due over the course of eight solid Prestige records (and one on his own Joka label in 1975), is finding new life on CD thanks to the apt and rapt attention of the acid-jazz crowd. —*Douglas Payne*

● **Legends of Acid Jazz** / Aug. 4, 1969+Feb. 16, 1970 / Prestige ◆◆◆◆◆

Jones isn't at the top of heap as far as late '60s soul-jazz hybrids go; if you want guitar in particular, you're better off starting with Grant Green (to name one). But if guitar-organ-sax groove jazz is one of the bumps on your backbone, you'll be reasonably pleased with the consistent, slightly laidback mood funk of this set, which combines *Right On Brother* (1969) and *Boogaloo Joe* (1970) onto one CD. —*Richie Unterberger*

Black Whip / Jul. 25, 1973 / Prestige ◆◆◆

Carmell Jones (William Carmell Jones)

b. Jul. 19, 1936, Kansas City, KS, **d.** Nov. 7, 1996, Kansas City, KS
Trumpet / Hard Bop

An excellent hard bop trumpeter, Carmell Jones would probably have been much better-known today if he had not moved to Europe in the mid-'60s at the height of his career. After military service and two years at the University of Kansas, Carmell Jones led a band in Kansas City (1959). The next year he moved to Los Angeles where he recorded a couple of albums as a leader for Pacific Jazz and made records with Bud Shank, Harold Land, Curtis Amy and most significantly Gerald Wilson's Orchestra (1961-63). Jones toured with Horace Silver for a year (1964-65), recording the original version of "Song for My Father" with Silver before moving to Berlin. Although quite active in Europe, Carmell Jones was largely forgotten by the time he moved back to Kansas City in 1980, although a 1982 album for Revelation helped remind a few listeners how good he still was. —*Scott Yanow*

● **The Remarkable Carmell Jones** / Jun. 1961 / Pacific Jazz ◆◆◆◆◆

Of the few records that trumpeter Carmell Jones led throughout his career, his first date was by far his best-known and was generally his most satisfying. Teamed in Los Angeles with tenor saxophonist Harold Land, pianist Frank Strazzeri, bassist Gary Peacock and drummer Leon Pettis, Jones is featured on music that is essentially cool-toned hard bop. In addition to a couple of Jones' originals, there is an obscurity by bassist Jimmy Bond and three other tunes including an 11-minute investigation of Duke Ellington's "I'm Gonna Go Fishing." Jones' Clifford Brown-influenced style blends well with Land, and the music swings throughout in fine fashion. This album (not yet reissued on CD) was reissued by the British Charly label on their Affinity subsidiary in the mid-1980s. —*Scott Yanow*

Dill Jones

b. Aug. 19, 1923, Newcastle Emlyn, Wales, **d.** Jan. 22, 1984, New York, NY
Piano / Stride

An excellent if now somewhat forgotten stride pianist, Dill Jones was born in Wales, studied piano in London and played with Humphrey Lyttelton (1947-48). He led his own trio and worked in the studios and on radio in London during the 1950s. In 1961, Jones moved to New York where he played regularly at Condon's, Ryan's and the Metropole with such players as Yank Lawson, Max Kaminsky, Roy Eldridge, Bob Wilber, Jimmy McPartland and Gene Krupa, fitting right in with the Condon gang. Jones teamed up with Budd Johnson in the JPJ Quartet (1969-74), recorded a solo tribute to Bix Beiderbecke for Chiaroscuro (1972) and worked with the Countsmen and the Harlem Blues and Jazz Band. —*Scott Yanow*

Elvin Jones

b. Sep. 9, 1927, Pontiac, MI
Drums, Leader / Avant-Garde, Post-Bop, Hard Bop

Elvin Jones will always be best-known for his association with the classic John Coltrane Quartet (1960-65) but he has also had a notable career as a bandleader and has continued being a major influence during the past 30 years. One of the all-time great drummers (bridging the gap between advanced hard bop and the avant-garde), Elvin is the younger brother of a remarkable musical family that also includes Hank and Thad Jones. After spending time in the Army (1946-49), he was a part of the very fertile Detroit jazz scene of the early '50s. He moved to New York in 1955, worked with Teddy Charles and the Bud Powell Trio and recorded with Miles Davis and Sonny Rollins (the latter at his famous Village Vanguard session). After stints with J.J. Johnson (1956-57), Donald Byrd (1958), Tyree Glenn and Harry "Sweets" Edison, Elvin Jones became an important member of John Coltrane's Quartet, pushing the innovative saxophonist to remarkable heights and appearing on most of his best recordings. When Coltrane added Rashied Ali to his band in late 1965 as second drummer, Jones was not pleased and he soon departed. He went on a European tour with the Duke Ellington Orchestra and then started leading his own groups which in time became known as Elvin Jones' Jazz Machine. Among his sidemen have been saxophonists Frank Foster, Joe Farrell, George Coleman, Pepper Adams, Dave Liebman, Pat La Barbera, Steve Grossman, Andrew White, Ravi Coltrane and Sonny Fortune, trumpeter Nicholas Payton, pianists Dollar Brand and Willie Pickens, keyboardist Jan Hammer and bassists Richard Davis, Jimmy Garrison, Wilbur Little and Gene Perla among others. Elvin Jones has recorded as a leader for many labels including Atlantic, Riverside, Impulse, Blue Note, Enja, PM, Vanguard, Honey Dew, Denon, Storyville, Evidence and Landmark. —*Scott Yanow*

Elvin! / Jul. 11, 1961-Jan. 3, 1962 / Original Jazz Classics ✦✦✦✦
Drummer Elvin Jones' first full-length album as a leader (reissued on CD in the OJC series) is different than one would expect when you take into consideration that he was a member of the fiery John Coltrane Quartet at the time. This sextet session, which also includes his brothers Thad and Hank on cornet and piano in addition to flutist Frank Wess, Frank Foster on tenor and bassist Art Davis, is straightahead with a strong Count Basie feel. Elvin is still recognizable on the fairly obscure material (only "You Are too Beautiful" qualifies as a standard) and shows that he can cook in the fairly conventional setting. All of the musicians are in fine form and two selections feature the rhythm section as a trio. —*Scott Yanow*

Illumination / Aug. 8, 1963 / Impulse! ✦✦✦✦✦
Sextet with Jimmy Garrison (b), Prince Lasha (as), Sonny Simmons (as), Charles Davis (bar sax), and McCoy Tyner (p). All originals in progressive stance. A jewel. —*Michael G. Nastos*

● **Dear John C.** / Feb. 23, 1965+Feb. 25, 1965 / Impulse! ✦✦✦✦
Drummer Elvin Jones may have been breaking down new rhythmic boundaries at the time with John Coltrane's Quartet but his own sessions as a leader were not all that innovative. This quartet set with altoist Charlie Mariano, bassist Richard Davis and either Roland Hanna or Hank Jones on piano is an example of how the avant-garde of the era was starting to influence the more mainstream players. The music is in general safe but enjoyable with the virtuosic bassist Richard Davis often taking solo honors on what was in reality a modern bop date. —*Scott Yanow*

Heavy Sounds / 1968 / Impulse! ✦✦✦
For this CD reissue, an Impulse session co-led by drummer Elvin Jones and bassist Richard Davis was brought back by MCA. Tenor saxophonist Frank Foster and pianist Billy Green complete the quartet, which performs an erratic but generally interesting set of music including "Shiny Stockings," Foster's funky "Raunchy Rita" and "Elvin's Guitar Blues"; the latter briefly features Jones making his first and only appearance on guitar. The music is essentially advanced hard bop but is not all that essential. —*Scott Yanow*

Live at the Village Vanguard / Mar. 20, 1968 / Enja ✦✦✦✦
In what was probably the first recording by drummer Elvin Jones' working group (and one of his first after the death of John Coltrane), the focus is very much on tenor saxophonist George Coleman. The trio (which also includes bassist Wilbur Little) stretches out on Coleman's "By George," "Laura" and "You Don't Know What Love Is" and is joined by trumpeter Marvin "Hannibal" Peterson for a 15-minute version of "Mr. Jones." The music is very much in the late-'50s/early-'60s modal vein of Coltrane, and although only the length of an LP (just a touch over 40 minutes), the playing on this CD reissue is excellent and reasonably exploratory. —*Scott Yanow*

Puttin' It Together / Apr. 8, 1968 / Blue Note ✦✦✦✦
Joe Farrell (heard on this CD reissue on tenor, soprano and flute) did some of his finest playing while with drummer Elvin Jones' trio during 1968-69. Joined by bassist Jimmy Garrison (in one of his first post-Coltrane recordings), Farrell really digs into group originals, obscurities, "For Heaven's Sake," and Jimmy Heath's "Gingerbread Boy." With Jones pushing him and Garrison sounding quite advanced, Farrell was consistently inspired to play at the peak of his creativity. —*Scott Yanow*

The Ultimate Elvin Jones / Sep. 6, 1968 / Blue Note ✦✦✦✦✦
This is one of Joe Farrell's finest recordings. Switching between tenor, soprano and flute, Farrell had to be good because he was joined in the pianoless trio by bassist Jimmy Garrison and drummer Elvin Jones. The group performs two standards, three Garrison originals and one by Farrell; it is a toss-up as to who takes honors. Farrell is in consistently creative form but Garrison's occasional solos and Jones' polyrhythmic accompaniment are also noteworthy. This LP is long overdue to reappear on CD. —*Scott Yanow*

The Prime Element / Mar. 14, 1969-Jul. 26, 1973 / Blue Note ✦✦✦✦
This two-LP set consists of a pair of unrelated Elvin Jones Blue Note sessions that had not been previously released. The earlier date features Jones in a septet with the tenors of George Coleman and Joe Farrell along with trumpeter Lee Morgan, while the 1973 album has an 11-piece group that includes a large rhythm section, baritonist Pepper Adams and the tenors of Steve Grossman and Frank Foster. The challenging modal material (an extension of John Coltrane's music of the early '60s) and diverse soloists make this two-fer into a rather stimulating listen. —*Scott Yanow*

Poly-Currents / Sep. 26, 1969 / Blue Note ✦✦✦✦
Most of this CD reissue features drummer Elvin Jones leading a sextet full of notables, which also includes the underrated tenor great George Coleman, Joe Farrell on tenor, flute and English horn, baritonist Pepper Adams, bassist Wilbur

Little, and Candid on congas. They stretch out on group originals highlighted by "Mr. Jones" and "Whew." In addition, flutist Fred Tompkins teams up with Farrell's flute, Little and Jones on his own "Yes." Advanced modal hard bop with all of the musicians playing in top form. —*Scott Yanow*

Mr. Jones / Sep. 26, 1969-Jul. 13, 1972 / Blue Note ✦✦✦✦✦

Coalition / Jul. 17, 1970 / Blue Note ✦✦✦✦
Drummer Elvin Jones' Blue Note sessions have long been underrated, partly because the label itself was declining during the era and also partly due to the rise of the avant-garde and fusion, which overshadowed Jones' passionate and advanced hard bop. In 1970, Elvin's band consisted of George Coleman and Frank Foster on tenors (Foster also plays bass clarinet on one number), bassist Wilbur Little, Candido on conga, and the drummer/leader. This was a particularly creative and often intense ensemble, attached to the hard bop tradition but always looking forward. On four group originals (including Coleman's "5/4 Thing") and "Yesterdays," the quintet generates a lot of heat, with the contrast between the tones of Coleman and Foster making this album (not yet reissued on CD) of particular interest. —*Scott Yanow*

Merry-Go-Round / Dec. 15, 1971 / Blue Note ✦✦✦
Inexcusably, there are no date or personnel listings on this LP from Blue Note's declining years, but the music is generally quite worthwhile, if a bit eclectic. The personnel changes throughout the session, despite all the performances being apparently recorded on the same day. The great drummer Elvin Jones is joined by the reeds of David Liebman, Steve Grossman and Joe Farrell; baritonist Pepper Adams is also on two numbers, keyboardists Chick Corea and Jan Hammer generally alternate (although they both appear on a few tunes together), guitarist Yoshiaki Masuo has guest appearances on two songs, and most selections include bassist Gene Perla and percussionist Don Alias. The group mostly plays concise versions of band originals, including Corea's classic "La Fiesta." An interesting set, but Elvin Jones has recorded many more rewarding albums. —*Scott Yanow*

Genesis / 1971 / Blue Note ✦✦✦✦
The graphics are kind of dull on this late-period Blue Note LP, but the music is anything but boring. Elvin Jones' band had expanded during 1969-71 from a pianoless trio to a three-horn quintet. With Dave Liebman and the returning Joe Farrell on tenors and sopranos and Frank Foster contributing some tenor, alto flute and bass clarinet (bassist Gene Perla completes the group), it would not be an overstatement to call this a powerful unit. On five originals by band members (best-known is Jones' "Three Card Molly"), the musicians take long, heated solos that straddle the boundary between hard bop and the avant-garde. Their album (not yet out on CD) has plenty of invigorating music. —*Scott Yanow*

Live at the Lighthouse, Vol. 1 / Sep. 9, 1972 / Blue Note ✦✦✦✦✦
Drummer Elvin Jones 45th birthday (September 9, 1972), was a good excuse to record his group of the period. The results were originally released as a double-LP and have been reissued as two CDs with over an hour of new music added. Jones' pianoless quartet features two masterful saxophonists (both doubling on tenor and soprano) who at the time sounded very close to John Coltrane. Dave Liebman and Steve Grossman were among the first young saxophonists not closely associated with Coltrane who used his style as a starting point in their search for their own musical identities. Their high-powered and sometimes rowdy flights are consistently stimulating. With Gene Perla's alert, sensitive and inventive bass holding the unit together, Elvin Jones was able to play as free as he desired. The first volume (taken from three sets at the Lighthouse) has six fiery selections, four of which were previously unreleased. —*Scott Yanow*

Live at the Lighthouse, Vol. 2 / Sep. 9, 1972 / Blue Note ✦✦✦✦✦
The second of two CDs featuring music recorded at the Lighthouse during a marathon session is the equal of the first. Greatly expanded from the original two-LP set, this disc has a pair of selections from the two-fer ("Sweet Mama" and "The Children, Save the Children") and three performances ("I'm a Fool to Want You," "Britt Piece" and the 28-minute "Children's Merry-Go-Round") that were previously unreleased at the time of this 1990 package. Dave Liebman (on tenor and soprano) is heard in one of his finest pre-Miles Davis recordings; the young tenor Steve Grossman keeps up with him, and bassist Gene Perla acts as a bridge between the fiery saxophonists and explosive drummer Elvin Jones. Exciting and adventurous music that stretches the boundaries of modal hard bop jazz. —*Scott Yanow*

Elvin Jones Is on the Mountain / 1975 / PM ✦✦✦

New Agenda / 1975 / Vanguard ✦✦✦

Elvin Jones Live at the Town Hall / May 1976 / PM ✦✦✦✦
Elvin Jones Live was taken from a John Coltrane Memorial Concert performed at New York's Town Hall, Sept. 12, 1971, and featured his group of that time, Frank Foster on soprano and tenor saxes, Chick Corea's piano, Joe Farrell's sax and flute and Gene Perla's bass on two extended compositions.... This was five strong

individual artists giving exceptionally of themselves, bringing forth a record where the dynamics of the whole were equal to the sum of the parts, making for an exceptional and truly beautiful record. —*Bob Rusch, Cadence*

Summit Meeting / Nov. 18, 1976 / Vanguard ✦✦✦✦

These are some top-shelf sessions w/ James Moody (sax), Clark Terry (tpt). —*Ron Wynn*

Time Capsule / 1977 / Vanguard ✦✦✦

Drummer Elvin Jones' Vanguard recordings of 1975-77, of which this was the final one, generally found him playing with all-stars or augmenting his band with guests. The five obscurities on this LP (three by altoist Bunky Green, who emerges as the date's top soloist) matches Jones with Green, tenor saxophonist George Coleman, the electric piano of Kenny Barron, bassist Junie Booth, guitarist Ryo Kawasaki, and percussionist Angel Allende. Two of the songs ("Frost Bite" and "Digital Display") have bassist Milt Hinton and flutist Frank Wess; the latter piece also adds the soprano of Frank Foster. Overall, the music is worthwhile, although not quite adding up to the sum of its many parts; the set has very little unity despite some individual fireworks. —*Scott Yanow*

Live in Japan 1978 / 1978 / Storyville ✦✦✦✦

This CD is a reissue of a generous 52-minute LP originally put out on the Japanese Trio label and, unfortunately, it does not have any liner notes. Solo identification would have been particularly helpful for both Frank Foster and Pat La Barbera play their tenors in similar John Coltrane-influenced styles during three lengthy tracks: "E.J. Blues," "House That Love Built" and the two part "A Love Supreme." The music is a direct outgrowth of drummer Elvin Jones' days with Coltrane. Bassist Andy McCloud is steady and supportive throughout, while guitarist Roland Prince supplies a chordal base for the tenors. The musicians stretch themselves within the boundaries of Coltrane's music. —*Scott Yanow*

Remembrance / Feb. 3, 1978-Feb. 5, 1978 / MPS ✦✦✦✦

The Elvin Jones Jazz Machine has frequently featured hard-toned tenors who improvise in a style influenced by John Coltrane, modal originals and high-powered performances in which the drummer/leader can push his sidemen. This MPS set is no exception. Pat La Barbera and Michael Stuart double on tenors and sopranos, guitarist Roland Prince offers a contrasting solo voice, and all of the material is obscure with four of the seven songs penned by La Barbera. It's an excellent if somewhat lesser-known outing. —*Scott Yanow*

Love & Peace / Apr. 8, 1978+1982 / Storyville ✦✦✦✦

With the exception of one number ("House That Love Built") from 1978 that matches drummer Elvin Jones with the reeds of Frank Foster and Pat La Barbera, guitarist Roland Prince and bassist Andy McCloud, this CD reissue focuses on an unusual and generally successful reunion session. Drummer Jones and pianist McCoy Tyner have not recorded together that often since leaving John Coltrane's Quartet in late 1965. With Pharoah Sanders (who was part of the reason they departed) on tenor, bassist Richard Davis in the late Jimmy Garrison's spot, and guitarist Jean-Paul Bourelly an added wild card, the musicians avoid Coltrane tunes in favor of newer originals and the standard "Sweet and Lovely." Sanders sounds very much like late-1950s Coltrane; Bourelly is a bit out of place, and Tyner easily takes solo honors. An interesting but not overly memorable outing that was originally cut for the Japanese Trio label and made available in the US by the now-defunct Black Hawk company. —*Scott Yanow*

Very R.A.R.E. / Apr. 8, 1978-Jun. 20, 1979 / Evidence ✦✦✦

The performances heard on this Evidence CD were originally put out by Japanese labels. The first six selections feature the potentially explosive quartet of drummer Elvin Jones, altoist Art Pepper (on four of the numbers), pianist Roland Hanna and bassist Richard Davis. Unfortunately, few sparks occur, a bass-drum feature on "Pitter Pat" is a bit dull and Pepper never really cuts loose. However, the two remaining tracks are much more memorable. Jones' regular quintet of 1978 (with Frank Foster on tenor and soprano, Pat La Barbera on tenor, guitarist Roland Prince and bassist Andy McCloud) stretches out in exciting fashion on the 15-minute "E.J. Blues" and a 26-minute exploration of two of the movements from "A Love Supreme." Those performances (which contrast Foster's Coltrane-inspired tenor with La Barbera's Sonny Rollins-influenced playing) make the CD worth getting. —*Scott Yanow*

Heart to Heart / Aug. 1980 / Denon ✦✦✦✦

Exemplary material, superb Tommy Flanagan (p). —*Ron Wynn*

Earth Jones / Feb. 10, 1982 / Palo Alto ✦✦✦

On this interesting but unfortunately out of print LP, the immortal drummer Elvin Jones teams up with four advanced but very different improvisers: Dave Liebman (doubling on soprano and flute), cornetist Terumasa Hino, pianist Kenny Kirkland and bassist George Mraz. Other than a lyrical version of "Never Let Me Go," the songs were contributed by either Jones ("Three Card Molly") or Liebman, whose "Day and Night" is not surprisingly based on the chord changes of "Night and

Day." The solos are unpredictable but logical, and the blend between the lyrical Hino and Liebman is appealing. —*Scott Yanow*

Brother John / Oct. 1982 / Quicksilver ✦✦✦

This out-of-print album is very much a showcase for saxophonist Pat La Barbera, who doubles on tenor and soprano, for he also contributed five of the eight selections. With drummer Elvin Jones, pianist Kenny Kirkland and bassist Reggie Workman forming a formidable rhythm section, La Barbera is heard throughout in fine form, playing in a style strongly influenced by (but not derivative of) John Coltrane. Unfortunately, this high-quality hard bop set will be difficult to find. —*Scott Yanow*

The Elvin Jones Jazz Machine in Europe / Jun. 23, 1991 / Enja ✦✦✦✦✦

Youngblood / Apr. 20, 1992+Apr. 21, 1992 / Enja ✦✦✦✦✦

Although this superior set features three of the top Young Lions (tenors Joshua Redman and Javon Jackson and trumpeter Nicholas Payton), along with the fine bassist George Mraz, drummer Elvin Jones, 64 at the time, sounds like the youngest member of the group. The well-rounded CD has individual features for Redman ("Angel Eyes"), Payton ("Body and Soul") and Mraz ("My Romance"), along with the leader (the unaccompanied drum solo "Ding-a-Ling-a-Ling"), and has consistently inspired playing from all of the musicians. An excellent effort. —*Scott Yanow*

● It Don't Mean a Thing / Oct. 18, 1993-Oct. 19, 1993 / Enja ✦✦✦✦✦

Elvin Jones has participated in many recording sessions through the years but this CD is one of the most well-rounded sets he has ever led. The lineup of musicians is very impressive: trumpeter Nicholas Payton, Sonny Fortune on tenor and flute, trombonist Delfeayo Marsalis, pianist Willie Pickens, bassist Cecil McBee and vocalist Kevin Mahogany. Everyone plays up to their potential and the material has plenty of variety, ranging from Monk, Ellington and Strayhorn to a traditional Japanese folk song arranged by Elvin's wife Keiko ("A Lullaby of Itsugo Village"), two features for Mahogany (a touching version of "Lush Life" and his scat-filled "Bopsy") and some authentic-sounding R&B (Sam Cooke's "A Change Is Gonna Come"). Payton, Marsalis and Fortune are not on every selection, but each have their chance to shine while pianist Willie Pickens is showcased with the trio on a medley of "A Flower Is a Lovesome Thing" and "Ask Me Now." And as for the drummer, there is still no one around who has captured the sound and spirit of Elvin Jones. —*Scott Yanow*

Etta Jones

b. Nov. 25, 1928, Aiken, SC

Vocals / Standards

An excellent singer who is always worth hearing, Etta Jones grew up in New York and at 16 toured with Buddy Johnson. She debuted on record with Barney Bigard's pickup band (1944) for Black & White, singing four Leonard Feather songs, three of which (including "Evil Gal Blues") were hits for Dinah Washington. She recorded other songs during 1946-47 for RCA and worked with Earl Hines (1949-52). Jones' version of "Don't Go to Strangers" (1960) was a hit and she made many albums for Prestige during 1960-65. Jones toured Japan with Art Blakey (1970) but was largely off record during 1966-75. However, starting in 1976 Etta Jones (an appealing interpreter of standards, ballads and blues) began recording regularly for Muse, often with her husband, the fine tenor saxophonist Houston Person. Some of her finest work has been from the last two decades. —*Scott Yanow*

● Don't Go to Strangers / Jun. 21, 1960 / Original Jazz Classics ✦✦✦✦✦

Etta Jones had been on the jazz scene for over a decade when she recorded this Prestige set (which has been reissued on CD in the OJC series) but it was this album that gave her a breakthrough, specifically the memorable song "Don't Go to Strangers." Actually, Jones is in superb form throughout the other nine songs, too, mixing together the dramatic ability of Abbey Lincoln and some of the expressive qualities of Billie Holiday in the 1950s. With perfectly suitable accompaniment from Frank Wess (doubling on flute and tenor), pianist Richard Wyands, guitarist Skeeter Best, bassist George Duvivier and drummer Roy Haynes, Etta Jones is heard at her early peak on "Yes Sir, That's My Baby" (a warhorse that she greatly uplifts), "Fine and Mellow," "If I Had You" and "Bye Bye Blackbird." —*Scott Yanow*

Etta Jones and Strings / Jun. 9, 1961-Jul. 28, 1961 / Original Jazz Classics ✦✦

On this string session, Etta Jones alternates between sounding like late-period Billie Holiday and Dinah Washington. The dozen songs are mostly ballads including such numbers as "Unchained Melody," "You Don't Know What Love Is," "You Better Go Now" and "All My Life." Although the liner notes talk about how interesting Oliver Nelson's writing is for the string section, in reality the violins greatly water down the jazz content and, with Jones sticking to soulful melody statements, this CD reissue would not be considered one of the high points of her career. —*Scott Yanow*

Something Nice / Sep. 16, 1961-Mar. 30, 1961 / Original Jazz Classics ✦✦✦✦

This CD reissue features singer Etta Jones during two recording sessions in 1960-61. Jones is joined by two separate rhythm sections, and there is a guest appearance for tenor saxophonist Oliver Nelson (on "Easy Living"), two by vibraphonist Lem Winchester, and three from guitarist Wally Richardson. Influenced by Billie Holiday during this era, Jones is at her best during straightforward and sincere renditions of such songs as "My Heart Tells Me," "Till There Was You," "Almost Like Being in Love" and "Canadian Sunset." —Scott Yanow

Lonely and Blue / Apr. 6, 1962-May 4, 1962 / Original Jazz Classics ✦✦✦

Singer Etta Jones often recalls late-period Billie Holiday and Dinah Washington on her CD reissue. The first 11 songs find her accompanied by tenor saxophonist Budd Johnson on four of the songs, guitarist Wally Richardson on seven and the Patti Bown Trio throughout; the final three numbers (bonus tracks), are actually from a date led by tenor-great Gene Ammons and are among the highlights of this set. But overall, despite some fine performances (particularly "You Don't Know My Mind" and "Trav'lin Light"), Jones' lack of individuality at that point in time makes this CD of less importance than her later sets for Muse. —Scott Yanow

Love Shout / Feb. 4, 1963+Feb. 12, 1963 / Original Jazz Classics ✦✦✦✦

Singer Etta Jones' final Prestige album (she would record only once more until 1975) has been reissued on CD in the OJC series. Joined by either a quintet including both organist Larry Young and pianist Kenny Cox or a larger group with the reeds of Jerome Richardson and both Kenny Burrell and Bucky Pizzarelli on guitars, Jones is in excellent form on a wide variety of material. Not only does she perform a rare vocal version of Duke Ellington's "The Gal from Joe's," but she turns "Hi-Lili, Hi-Lo" and "Some Enchanted Evening" into jazz. Other highlights include "Love Walked In," "Like Someone in Love" and "Old Folks." Although Etta Jones' finest work was made for Muse in the 1970s and '80s, the appealing singer is in good form on this LP-length program. —Scott Yanow

Ms. Jones to You / Jan. 7, 1976 / Muse ✦✦✦✦

My Mother's Eyes / Jun. 23, 1977 / Muse ✦✦✦✦

Although by the mid-1970s she had already been a professional singer for 30 years, Etta Jones was in reality just entering her musical prime. Having developed her individuality gradually through the years, she was heard at her very best during her long string of Muse recordings. On this fine date, Jones is joined by her husband (tenor saxophonist Houston Person) and an oversized rhythm section that features keyboardist Sonny Phillips and guitarist Jimmy Ponder. Among the highlights are "The Way You Look Tonight," "Don't Misunderstand," "You Do Something to Me" and "This Girl's in Love with Me." —Scott Yanow

Fine and Mellow / 1987 / Muse ✦✦✦✦

With fine sax from Houston Person. —Ron Wynn

I'll Be Seeing You / Sep. 23, 1987 / Muse ✦✦✦✦

A straightforward and jazz-influenced singer, Etta Jones' series of recordings for the Muse label were among the finest of her career. On this date, as usual, she is joined by her husband, the great soul-jazz tenor saxophonist Houston Person, along with a rhythm section including vibraphonist George Devens and pianist Stan Hope. Jones swings her way through such songs as "Laughing at Life," "Crazy He Calls Me" and "Etta's Blues," and puts plenty of feeling into a faster-than-usual "I'll Be Seeing You." —Scott Yanow

Sugar / Oct. 18, 1989+Oct. 30, 1989 / Muse ✦✦✦✦✦

Christmas with Etta Jones / Jun. 14, 1990-Jun. 15, 1990 / Muse ✦✦✦

The fine vocalist Etta Jones sings nine mostly-familiar Christmas-related songs on this 1990 CD. She is accompanied by one of two groups: a sextet with tenor saxophonist Houston Person, guitarist Randy Johnston and pianist Stan Hope, or an octet with tenorman Bill Easley, fluegelhornist Johnny Coles and keyboardist Horace Ott. Nothing all that memorable occurs on tunes such as "Have Yourself a Merry Little Christmas," "The Christmas Song," "Merry Christmas Baby" and "White Christmas" but the overall results are pleasing. —Scott Yanow

Reverse the Charges / Sep. 19, 1991-Jan. 1991 / Muse ✦✦✦✦✦

At Last / Apr. 21, 1993+Feb. 1, 1995 / Muse ✦✦✦✦

My Gentleman Friend / 1994 / Muse ✦✦✦✦

For this slightly unusual set, veteran singer Etta Jones performs a set of duets with the very supportive yet consistently swinging pianist Benny Green. The tempos vary a bit while Jones generally sticks to the lyrics, adding a soulful touch to each of the standards. The singer displays both maturity and restraint on the somewhat predictable but enjoyable outing which has a late-night feel; highlights include "But Beautiful," "Happiness Is a Thing Called Joe," "You Better Go Now" and "When I Grow Too Old to Dream." —Scott Yanow

Hank Jones

b. Jul. 31, 1918, Vicksburg, MS
Piano / Bop, Swing

The oldest of the three illustrious Jones brothers (which include Thad and Elvin), Hank Jones was also the first of the great Detroit pianists (including Tommy Flanagan, Barry Harris and Roland Hanna) to emerge after World War II, although by then he had long since left town. Jones played in territory bands while a teenager, and in 1944 he moved to New York to play with Hot Lips Page. He had stints with John Kirby, Howard McGhee, Coleman Hawkins, Andy Kirk and Billy Eckstine. Influenced by Teddy Wilson and Art Tatum, Jones' style was also open to bebop and his accessible playing was flexible enough to fit into many genres. He was on several Jazz at the Philharmonic tours (starting in 1947), worked as accompanist for Ella Fitzgerald (1948-53) and recorded with Charlie Parker. In the 1950s Jones performed with Artie Shaw, Benny Goodman, Lester Young, Cannonball Adderley and many others. He was on the staff of CBS during 1959-1976 but always remained active in jazz. In the late '70s, Jones was the pianist in the Broadway musical *Ain't Misbehavin'* and he recorded with a pickup unit dubbed the Great Jazz Trio, which at various times includes Ron Carter, Buster Williams or Eddie Gomez on bass and Tony Williams, Al Foster or Jimmy Cobb on drums. Among the many labels that Hank Jones has recorded for as a leader are Verve, Savoy, Epic, Golden Crest, Capitol, Argo, ABC-Paramount, Impulse, Concord, East Wind, Muse, Galaxy, Black & Blue, MPS, Inner City and Chiaroscuro. —Scott Yanow

Urbanity / Sep. 1947+Sep. 4, 1953 / Verve ✦✦✦✦

This reissue CD has pianist Hank Jones' first recordings as a leader. Jones is heard on six piano solos from 1947 (including "Tea for Two," "Blues for Lady Day" and "Yesterdays") and on four trio numbers from 1953 with guitarist Johnny Smith and bassist Ray Brown. Although he shows hints of his roots in swing (Fats Waller, Art Tatum and a little Nat Cole), Jones at this early point already had his own largely distinctive sound. —Scott Yanow

● **Trio** / Aug. 4, 1955 / Savoy ✦✦✦✦✦

Seminal stuff from Hank Jones, with Kenny Clarke (d), Wendell Marshall (b). —Ron Wynn

Bluebird / Nov. 11, 1955-Dec. 20, 1955 / Savoy ✦✦✦✦

These relaxed cool jazz performances feature pianist Hank Jones in a variety of settings. In addition to drummer Kenny Clarke and either Eddie Jones or Wendell Marshall on bass, "Hank's Pranks" has both Donald Byrd and Manny Dice on trumpets, trumpeter Joe Wilder and flutist Herbie Mann are on a song apiece and Jerome Richardson (doubling on flute and tenor) drops by for two. It's a tasteful set of melodic bop. —Scott Yanow

Relaxin' at Camarillo / Aug. 21, 1956 / Savoy ✦✦✦

Pianist Hank Jones recorded fairly extensively for Savoy during 1955-56, and most of the music was reissued on LPs in the late '70s and early '80s, although the performances have only partially appeared thus far on CD. For his final Savoy session, Jones is teamed with Bobby Jaspar (an excellent tenor player who here sticks exclusively to his fluent flute), bassist Paul Chambers and drummer Kenny Clarke. The music is quiet, but often swings hard. Jones is well featured on three underrated standards ("Moonlight Becomes You," Cannonball Adderley's "Spontaneous Combustion" and a 13-minute rendition of "Relaxin' at Camarillo"), the obscure ballad "Sunday in Savannah," and his own "Minor Contention." This combination of musicians works together quite well. —Scott Yanow

I'm All Smiles / 196 / Verve ✦✦✦

Expressive, charming duets with Tommy Flanagan (p). —Ron Wynn

Hanky Panky / Jul. 14, 1975-Jul. 15, 1975 / Inner City ✦✦✦

Mid-'70s session from an extremely busy period in pianist Hank Jones' career. He was juggling recording dates at four studios, working with various bassists and drummers, and making immaculate trio dates like this one. Everything, from the nicely crafted openings and transitions to his skillful solos and pace, is the work of a genuine master. —Ron Wynn

Solo Piano / Jan. 24, 1976 / All Art Jazz ✦✦✦✦

Also issued at one time as *Have You Met Hank Jones*, this 1979 reissue CD features Jones on 14 unaccompanied piano solos. Despite being a strong two-handed pianist falling into the transition between swing and bop, Jones tends to sound more swinging in a trio format, although these melodic and sometimes rhapsodic solos are also reasonably enjoyable. Highlights include "It Had to Be You," "Let's Fall in Love," "How About You" and "Solo Blues." —Scott Yanow

Rockin' in Rhythm / 1977 / Concord ✦✦✦

Pianist Hank Jones teams up with bassist Ray Brown and drummer Jimmie Smith for this trio set, which has been reissued on CD. An unusual aspect to the music is that on half of the eight standards Jones switches to electric piano; although he does not display as strong a musical personality on that instrument, he plays quite well. Highlights of the boppish set include "My Ship," "Rockin' in Rhythm," "Bag's Groove" and an effective instrumental version of "Your Feet's Too Big." —*Scott Yanow*

Bop Redux / Jan. 18, 1977-Jan. 19, 1977 / Muse ◆◆◆◆

Veteran pianist Hank Jones teams up with bassist George Duvivier and drummer Ben Riley for a set of high-quality explorations of eight bop standards; four apiece by Charlie Parker and Thelonious Monk. Jones is sensitive on the ballads and lightly but firmly swinging on the more uptempo material. Typically tasteful performances come from one of the greats. —*Scott Yanow*

Great Jazz Trio at the Village Vanguard / Feb. 19, 1977+Feb. 20, 1977 / Inner City ◆◆◆◆◆

The name "Great Jazz Trio" is not an overstatement when being applied to a group comprising pianist Hank Jones, bassist Ron Carter and drummer Tony Williams. The all-stars really dig into "Moose the Mooche," "Naima," Claus Ogerman's "Favors" and the Ron Carter blues "12+12." It is a pleasure to hear Williams pushing Jones to come up with some of his most fiery recent playing. —*Scott Yanow*

Just for Fun / Jun. 27, 1977-Jun. 28, 1977 / Original Jazz Classics ◆◆◆◆

Pianist Hank Jones recorded many dates as a leader during the latter half of the 1970s. A superior transitional player whose two-handed style looks towards both swing and bop, Jones is mostly featured on this CD reissue of a Galaxy date in a trio with bassist Ray Brown and drummer Shelly Manne, although three numbers also welcome guitarist Howard Roberts. None of the seven compositions (by Jones, Brown, Pepper Adams, Thad Jones and J.J. Johnson, along with Sara Cassey's title cut) became well-known, but the fine interplay between the musicians and the concise and purposeful solos uplift the tunes. —*Scott Yanow*

Tiptoe Tapdance / Jun. 29, 1977-Jan. 21, 1978 / Original Jazz Classics ◆◆◆

Originally on the Galaxy label, this CD reissue is a rare solo outing by pianist Hank Jones. The emphasis is on ballads and his treatments of these songs (which include three religious pieces) are respectful, melodic and lightly swinging. There is not much variety here but the music (within its limitations) is enjoyable. —*Scott Yanow*

I Remember You / Jul. 1977-Jul. 1978 / Black & Blue ◆◆◆◆

Made for the French Black & Blue label and released in the US on a Classic Jazz LP (but not yet on CD), this outing features pianist Hank Jones emphasizing the swing side of his flexible musical personality. Teamed up with bassist George Duvivier and drummer Oliver Jackson, Jones adds beauty and melodic ideas to such veteran numbers as "You Took Advantage of Me," "Love Walked In," "Like Someone in Love" and (easily the most recent tune) Bobby Timmons' "Dat Dere." A fine set that will be difficult to find. —*Scott Yanow*

Groovin' High / Jan. 25, 1978 / Muse ◆◆◆◆◆

This is essentially a bebop jam session, but due to the participation of cornetist/arranger Thad Jones, the music has its surprises. Pianist Hank Jones (Thad's brother), unrelated bassist Sam Jones, drummer Mickey Roker and tenor saxophonist Charlie Rouse team up in different combinations during seven jazz standards that date back to the bebop era. "Algo Bueno" and "Blue Monk" are features for the rhythm section; "Groovin' High" is an unusual cornet-piano-drums trio made possible by the strength of Hank Jones' left hand; four tunes including "Anthropology," which has a very advanced arrangement for the melody, and a samba version of "Sippin' at Bells," showcase the full group. Although currently out of print, hopefully this superior Muse album will reappear on the 32 Jazz label in time. —*Scott Yanow*

Bluesette / Jul. 1978+Jul. 1979 / Black & Blue ◆◆◆

Ain't Misbehavin' / Aug. 5, 1978-Aug. 6, 1978 / Galaxy ◆◆◆

Hank Jones paying his tribute to Waller. —*Ron Wynn*

In Japan / May 2, 1979 / All Art Jazz ◆◆◆◆

The All Art Jazz label initially released music in Japan before hooking up with Jazz Alliance and in the early 1990s making a few sessions available in the US. This is a typically fine CD from veteran pianist Hank Jones who, with the assistance of bassist George Duvivier and drummer Shelly Manne (both of whom have plenty of short solos), is heard throughout in top form. The tasteful and swinging trio session is highlighted by "Blue Lou," "Cotton Tail," "Polka Dots and Moonbeams" and "Yardbird Suite." —*Scott Yanow*

The Oracle / Mar. 1989 / EmArcy ◆◆◆◆◆

One could excuse Hank Jones if, at the time of *The Oracle*, the 70-year-old pianist chose to stick to revivalist bop, but the biggest surprise of this very democratic date is how modern he plays. Jones is Monkish on "Blues for CM" and often sounds more like a contemporary of McCoy Tyner than of Bud Powell, whom Hank was actually born six years before. Bassist Dave Holland has nearly as much solo space as Jones (along with contributing three compositions), and drum-

mer Billy Higgins gets more space than usual. If there is any fault to this otherwise flawless CD (which also has some underplayed standards such as "Beautiful Love" and "Yesterdays"), it is that there are no individual features. But the interplay between the three musicians is quite impressive. —*Scott Yanow*

Lazy Afternoon / Jul. 1989 / Concord Jazz ◆◆◆◆

Hank Jones, the father of Detroit's piano legacy (preceding Tommy Flanagan, Barry Harris and Roland Hanna) is teamed on this Concord CD with the typically superb bass of Dave Holland, the supportive drumming of Keith Copeland and (on half the songs) Ken Peplowski's alto (with just a touch of his clarinet). Jones performs a diverse yet unified set of standards and originals. His use of celeste on a moody "Lazy Afternoon," his Monkish "Intimidation" and a trio romp on "Speak Low" are among the high points of the excellent release by an ageless master. —*Scott Yanow*

Live at Maybeck Recital Hall, Vol. 16 / Nov. 11, 1991 / Concord Jazz ◆◆◆◆◆

A high point in the career of distinguished pianist Hank Jones was being among the artists tabbed for a solo release in the Maybeck series. While he's always been known as a great accompanist and good trio contributor, his solo skills have sometimes been undervalued. But after hearing him work in this unaccompanied setting, there should be no doubt that Hank Jones is a superb soloist, along with all his other talents. —*Ron Wynn*

A Handful of Keys / Apr. 28, 1992-Apr. 29, 1992 / Verve ◆◆◆◆

There are a playfulness and charm underneath Jones' solos that repeatedly surface throughout his excellent renditions on this disc dedicated to Fats Waller's music. While 10 of the 16 songs are Waller compositions, those that aren't, like "How Come You Do Me Like You Do" and "Your Feet's Too Big," are closely identified with him. Jones' flourishes, expert handling of stride rhythms, and delicate but skillful reworkings not only capture the flavor Waller brought to such songs as "Ain't Misbehavin'," "Honeysuckle Rose" and the title track, but add his character to them with tricky phrases, quick melodies and nimble lines. —*Ron Wynn*

Isham Jones

b. Jan. 31, 1894, Coalton, IA, **d.** Oct. 19, 1956, Hollywood, FL
Composer, Leader / Classic Jazz, Standards

Isham Jones led and broke up several bands during the 1920s and '30s but his greatest legacy is as a songwriter, having composed "It Had to Be You," "On the Alamo," "I'll See You in My Dreams," "The One I Love Belongs to Somebody Else" and "There Is No Greater Love" among others. Although he was originally a saxophonist and pianist, Isham Jones did not take any real solos with his bands. In the early '20s his outfit featured trumpeter Louis Panico, a fairly good soloist for 1921. Jones recorded prolifically during 1920-27 with most selections being jazz-oriented dance band performances. While his 1929-32 recordings are more commercial, the musicianship is high and the melodic renditions are not without interest. Jones' 1932-36 big band became the nucleus of the first Woody Herman Orchestra when Isham Jones decided to temporarily retire. He had another band in 1937 and recorded as late as 1947 but it is for his songs that he will always be remembered. —*Scott Yanow*

● The Panico Period / Oct. 1920-Jan. 17, 1924 / Fountain ◆◆◆◆◆

Isham Jones led one of the most underrated jazz-influenced dance bands of the 1920-24 period. Although the music throughout this British LP (17 titles in all) sounds somewhat primitive compared to what Fletcher Henderson would be playing after 1925, one can hear how advanced Jones' ensemble was when the music is placed in its proper historical context. Far from a "complete" set (Isham Jones recorded quite extensively during the era), this sampler does give one a strong introduction to the orchestra. Chief among the soloists was the talented but soon dated cornetist Louis Panico, one of the first brass stars; his laughing and occasionally crying solos were quite popular during the period. Interesting historical music that (if this release can be found) is easily recommended to vintage music collectors. —*Scott Yanow*

Swinging Down the Lane: 1923-1930 / Jan. 1923-Dec. 15, 1930 / Memphis Archives ◆◆◆◆

Isham Jones was a multitalented individual most renowned for his songwriting abilities (including "It Had to Be You," "I'll See You in My Dreams," "The One I Love Belongs to Somebody Else" and "There Is No Greater Love"). Jones also led a series of superior dance bands on-and-off from 1915-1938. This excellent sampler from the Memphis Archives label has two songs by Isham Jones' band of 1923, 13 from 1924-25, one from 1926 and two from 1930. Although Jones' orchestras were not strictly jazz bands, the 18 selections on this CD focus on his more jazz-oriented recordings and are quite enjoyable. The earlier tracks (particularly "Farewell Blues" and "Memphis Blues" from January 1923) feature improvised ensembles that are a bit reminiscent of the New Orleans Rhythm Kings with some fine trumpet from Louis Panico. By the 1925 performances, arrangements take a greater role but there are always spots for solos; none of the sidemen (other than pianist Roy Bargy) became close to famous, but trumpeter Frank Quartell in particular has some good spots. Overall, this set features hot dance music with strong melodies, high musicianship and the feel of swing. Other highlights include "Nobody's Sweetheart," "It Had to Be You," "Why Couldn't It Be Poor Little Me" (one of two numbers on which Jones was actually directing the Ray Miller band), and "Swinging Down the Lane." —*Scott Yanow*

Vol. 1 / Oct. 8, 1929-Mar. 31, 1931 / Parklane ♦♦♦♦
Isham Jones, best-known as an important songwriter, led a series of interesting bands during the 1920s and '30s. His 1929-31 edition essentially played hot dance music. All but three of the 24 selections on this CD (two alternate takes plus "Stardust") have vocals by either Frank Sylvano, Billy Scott or Eddie Stone, and there are some fine solos by trumpeter Whitey Moeller, trombonist Red Ballard and various lesser-known players. Although the performances just border on jazz, they should be of interest to vintage jazz listeners, particularly "Song of the Blues," "Miss Hannah," "My Baby Just Cares for Me," "Swingin' Down the Lane" and the first-ever ballad recording of "Stardust." —*Scott Yanow*

His Famous Orchestra, 1929-1930 / 1929 / Sunbeam ♦♦♦♦
This collector's LP has 16 fine dance band performances from Isham Jones' late-1920s orchestra. The jazz content is slight (usually just a hot half-chorus solo by a horn after a typical period vocal), but the musicianship is impressive; the performances are certainly danceable for those knowing how to fox trot, and the songs (which include "What's the Use," an early version of "Star Dust," "My Baby Just Cares for Me" and "My Ideal") are of consistently high quality. —*Scott Yanow*

The Great Isham Jones and His Orchestra / Aug. 17, 1932-Jul. 16, 1934 / RCA ♦♦♦♦
Isham Jones' Depression-era orchestra is heard on 16 of their better titles from the era on this excellent but long out-of-print LP in RCA's famous Vintage series. The personnel, which includes trombonist Jack Jenney and some musicians who would later be a part of Woody Herman's first orchestra, is mostly fairly anonymous, although the ensembles are tight and the musicianship is excellent. The emphasis is on dance music, with an occasional jazz-oriented tune (such as "Sentimental Gentleman from Georgia," "China Boy" and "The Blue Room") included for variety. —*Scott Yanow*

Centennial Album / 1935-1937 / Viper's Nest ♦♦♦♦
Isham Jones led first-class dance bands during the 1920-40 era that sometimes were jazz-influenced. This 1994 CD has radio transcriptions taken from two occasions in 1935 and 1937 and emphasizes the jazz side of Jones' music. The 1935 band (which is heard on 17 of the 22 selections) is most notable for including Woody Herman (who has several clarinet solos) and for being the nucleus of the first Herman band a year later. Eddie Stone has three vocals, but it is the swinging instrumentals (including "The Blue Room," "Oh Peter," "King Porter Stomp" and "Sugar Foot Stomp") that are most memorable. The 1937 band, despite having almost completely different personnel, plays in a similar Benny Goodman-inspired vein. Easily recommended to swing fans. —*Scott Yanow*

Featuring Woody Herman / Jan. 24, 1936-Mar. 13, 1936 / Sunbeam ♦♦♦
Before 1936 was over, arranger/composer Isham Jones decided to leave the band business, and the nucleus of his orchestra would soon be taken over by the young Woody Herman. On this collector's LP, one has opportunities to hear jazz-oriented radio performances by Jones' big band near its end in the winter of 1936. Among the key players are trumpeter Chelsea Quealey, trombonist Sonny Lee, tenorman Saxie Mansfield, and Herman himself on alto, clarinet and the vocal on "Old Man Mose." Among the other highlights are "Stomping at the Savoy," "You're Driving Me Crazy" and a private record of "Blues" by a small group headed by Herman and taken from Jones' orchestra. Interesting historical music that has its fun moments. —*Scott Yanow*

Jimmy Jones

b. Dec. 30, 1918, Memphis, TN, **d.** Apr. 29, 1982, Burbank, CA
Piano / Swing
An unusual piano stylist (who sometimes played complex block chords) and a masterful accompanist for singers, Jimmy Jones had his first important job playing and recording with Stuff Smith (1943-45). After working with J.C. Heard (1946-47), he was Sarah Vaughan's pianist (1947-52 and 1954-58) with a two-year illness separating his two long stints. Jones recorded often thoughout the 1950s including "How Hi the Fi" (1954) with Buck Clayton. He worked with Duke Ellington on the 1963 show *My People*, accompanied Ella Fitzgerald (1967-68) and wrote for the studios. In addition to obscure dates as a leader for Session, HRS, Wax, Swing and GNP, and sessions with Stuff Smith, J.C. Heard, Sarah Vaughan and Ella, Jimmy Jones appeared as a sideman on recordings led by many swing all-stars including

Don Byas, Coleman Hawkins, Ben Webster, Johnny Hodges, Clark Terry and Paul Gonsalves. —*Scott Yanow*

Jo Jones

b. Oct. 7, 1911, Chicago, IL, **d.** Sep. 3, 1985, New York, NY
Drums / Swing
Jo Jones shifted the timekeeping role of the drums from the bass drum to the hi-hat cymbal, greatly influencing all swing and bop drummers. Buddy Rich and Louie Bellson were just two who learned from his light but forceful playing, as Jones swung the Count Basie Orchestra with just the right accents and sounds. After growing up in Alabama, Jones worked as a drummer and tap dancer plus carnival shows. He joined Walter Page's Blue Devils in Oklahoma City in the late '20s. After a period with Lloyd Hunter's band in Nebraska, Jones moved to Kansas City in 1933, joining Count Basie's band the following year. He went with Basie to New York in 1936 and with Count, Freddie Green and Walter Page he formed one of the great rhythm sections. Jones was with the Basie band (other than 1944-46 when he was in the military) until 1948, and in later years he participated in many reunions with Basie alumni. He was on some Jazz at the Philharmonic tours and recorded in the 1950s with Illinois Jacquet, Billie Holiday, Teddy Wilson, Lester Young, Art Tatum and Duke Ellington among others; Jones appeared at the 1957 Newport Jazz Festival with both Basie and the Coleman Hawkins-Roy Eldridge Sextet. Jo Jones led sessions for Vanguard (1955 and 1959) and Everest (1959-60), a date for Jazz Odyssey on which he reminisced and played drum solos (1970) and mid-'70s sessions for Pablo and Denon. In later years he was known as "Papa" Jo Jones, and thought of as a wise if brutally frank elder statesman. —*Scott Yanow*

★ **The Essential Jo Jones** / Aug. 11, 1955-Apr. 30, 1958 / Vanguard ♦♦♦♦♦
Jo Jones, one of the most influential drummers of the swing era, did not lead that many record sessions of his own during his career. Producer John Hammond gave him his first two dates when he was working for Vanguard and, with the exception of a second take of "Shoe Shine Boy," all of the music from the two LPs is on this single-CD reissue. The first session is very much in the spirit of Count Basie's band; in fact, Basie himself makes a guest appearance on "Shoe Shine Boy." The other swing-oriented players include trumpeter Emmett Berry, trombonist Freddie Green, tenor saxophonist Lucky Thompson and (on one song apiece) trombonist Lawrence Brown and clarinetist Rudy Powell. The later date is quite a bit different, a trio session with pianist Ray Bryant and bassist Tommy Bryant. There are a liberal amount of drum solos but of greatest interest are the early versions of Ray Bryant's "Cubano Chant" and "Little Susie." —*Scott Yanow*

The Main Man / Nov. 29, 1976-Nov. 30, 1976 / Original Jazz Classics ♦♦♦♦
Sixty-five at the time and still in fine form, drummer Jo Jones had a rare opportunity to lead his own album for Pablo in 1976; the music has since been reissued on an OJC CD. Jones jams through four swing standards and a couple of basic originals with an all-star group including both Harry "Sweets" Edison and Roy Eldridge on trumpets, trombonist Vic Dickenson, tenor saxophonist Eddie "Lockjaw" Davis, pianist Tommy Flanagan, rhythm guitarist Freddie Green and bassist Sam Jones. The music is very much in the Count Basie groove, with purposeful and concise solos, along with some good spots for the leader. —*Scott Yanow*

Our Man Papa Jo! / Dec. 12, 1977 / Denon ♦♦♦♦
The final session for a jazz legend. Drummer Jo Jones was nearing the end when he got together with his old friends, pianist Hank Jones and bassist Major Holley, for this 1982 session. He still managed to play with some degree of authority and anchor the rhythm section, while saxophonist Jimmy Oliver and bassist took care of solo responsibilites. This has been reissued on CD. —*Ron Wynn*

Jonah Jones (Robert Elliott Jones)

b. Dec. 31, 1909, Louisville, KY
Trumpet / Swing, Dixieland
A talented and flashy trumpeter, Jonah Jones hit upon a formula in 1955 that made him a major attraction for a decade; playing concise versions of melodic swing standards and show tunes muted with a quartet. But although the nonjazz audience discovered Jones during the late '50s, he had already been a very vital trumpeter for two decades. Jonah Jones started out playing on a Mississippi riverboat in the 1920s. He freelanced in the Midwest (including with Horace Henderson), was briefly with Jimmie Lunceford (1931), had an early stint with Stuff Smith (1932-34) and then spent time with Lil Armstrong's short-lived orchestra and the declining McKinney's Cotton Pickers. Jones became famous for his playing with Stuff Smith's Onyx club band (1936-40), recording many exciting solos. He gigged with Benny Carter and Fletcher Henderson and became a star soloist with Cab Calloway (1941-52), staying with the singer even after his big band became a combo. Jones played Dixieland with Earl Hines (1952-53), toured Europe in 1954 (including a brilliant recording session with Sidney Bechet) and then led his quartet at the Embers (1955), hitting upon his very successful formula. His shuffle ver-

sion of "On the Street Where You Live" was the first of many hits, and he recorded a long series of popular albums for Capitol during 1957-63, switching to Decca for a few more quartet albums in 1965-67. Jonah Jones recorded a fine date with Earl Hines for Chiaroscuro (1972) and still played on an occasional basis in the 1980s and early '90s. —*Scott Yanow*

Butterflies in the Rain / Oct. 3, 1944 / Circle ♦♦♦

The programming of this LP is quite odd. All of the music was recorded by an impressive late-period swing group (trumpeter/vocalist Jonah Jones, trombonist/vibist Tyree Glenn, Al Gibson on clarinet and baritone, altoist Hilton Jefferson, tenor saxophonist Ike Quebec, pianist Buster Harding, guitarist Danny Barker, bassist Milt Hinton and drummer J.C. Heard) drawn from Cab Calloway's Orchestra. Recorded as radio transcriptions, eight selections resulted. Every drop of music from that day is on the LP. With the exception of "12th Street Rag" (which was completed in one take), the same tunes are heard on both sides of the album, with the first two or three attempts on side one and the remainder (including the accepted versions) on side two. If one wants to hear the full evolution of a performance, they will have to skip around, and listeners who only want to listen to the full-length versions will feel frustrated. In addition to the eight accepted takes, there are 12 false starts, four incomplete numbers and eight full-length alternate takes. Fortunately, there are plenty of fine solos but obviously this release is mostly for completists. —*Scott Yanow*

Jonah's Wail / Jun. 3, 1954+Sep. 22, 1954 / Inner City ♦♦♦♦♦

Originally made for the French Vogue label and released in the US on an Inner City LP, these two Paris sets were cut just two years before trumpeter Jonah Jones would hit it big with his "muted jazz." These performances are quite a bit different. Six numbers (including a pair of alternate takes) match Jones with the great soprano saxophonist Sidney Bechet, and they are remarkably exciting, particularly "When You Wore a Tulip" and "Chinatown My Chinatown" (both of which are heard in two versions). Jones proves to be one of Bechet's finest front line partners, and their competitive ensembles are quite memorable. In addition, Jones is heard in excellent form in a sextet headed by the fine Coleman Hawkins-inspired tenor of Alix Combelle. This music, which is essential for trad and mainstream fans, is long overdue to reappear on CD. —*Scott Yanow*

★ With Dave Pochoney and His All Stars / Jul. 1, 1954-Jul. 7, 1954 / Swing ♦♦♦♦♦

Trumpeter Jonah Jones was in prime form in the mid-1950s when he spent a year in Europe. For the frequently exciting pair of sessions that comprise this LP, Jones is well showcased with some complementary French musicians (gathered together by drummer Dave Pochonet) in settings ranging from a sextet to a ten-piece. The exuberant trumpeter is heard in passionate form on such tunes as "Honeysuckle Rose," "Perdido," and the 10-minute "Jonah Plays the Blues." —*Scott Yanow*

After Hour Jazz / Mar. 20, 1955 / Hall of Fame ♦♦♦♦

Although it last appeared on a budget LP and the date was not given, the music on this set is quite enjoyable. Trumpeter Jonah Jones was installed as the leader upon its reissue by Hall of Fame (the Jazztone date was originally headed by pianist Sammy Price), and Jonah is in excellent form, as are trombonist Vic Dickenson, altoist Pete Brown (on one of his rare sessions of the 1950s), Price, bassist Milt Hinton, and drummer Cozy Cole. Price takes a pair of vocals, and the program of standards, blues and basic originals helps to define mainstream jazz of the 1950s. —*Scott Yanow*

Jonah Jones at the Embers / Feb. 14, 1956-Feb. 29, 1956 / Groove ♦♦♦♦♦

In 1956, Jonah Jones started to become an unlikely commercial success. A veteran swing trumpeter not known to the general public despite being an exciting player, Jones caught on playing frequently muted solos with a quartet at the Embers in New York. His music often featured a shuffle rhythm and mixed Dixieland, swing and show tunes. This first recording by the quartet (also including pianist George Rhodes, bassist John Browne and drummer Harold Austin) was popular, although it would soon be dwarfed by Jones' successes for Capitol. Highlights of the date, which was also released by Groove and Victor but has not yet been reissued on CD, include "It's All Right with Me," "All of You," "High Society" and "At Sundown." —*Scott Yanow*

Muted Jazz / Feb. 22, 1957-Feb. 25, 1957 / Capitol ♦♦♦♦♦

In 1957, trumpeter Jonah Jones hit it big with his version of "On the Street Where You Live," which is included on this LP. Jones' "muted jazz" featured melodic but swinging versions of standards played with a shuffle beat by his quartet nightly at the Embers, and he would keep the attractive—if eventually predictable—formula alive into the late 1960s. In addition to "On the Street Where You Live," this best-selling record has such numbers as "Rose Room," "Undecided," "Too Close for Comfort" and "Royal Garden Blues" played in delightful fashion. —*Scott Yanow*

Swingin' on Broadway / Dec. 1957 / Capitol ♦♦♦♦

Trumpeter Jonah Jones was a hot property in late 1957 due to his hit rendition of "On the Street Where You Live." This follow-up LP had an equally big hit in "Baubles, Bangles and Beads," making Jones a household name for a decade. With shuffling support from pianist George Rhodes, bassist John Brown and drummer Harold Austin, Jones was able to make a lucrative living playing and singing music that did not differ much from what he would have been performing anyway. Other highlights of the LP (which consists of 12 songs from plays) include "The Surrey with the Fringe on Top," "Just in Time" and "I Could Have Danced All Night." —*Scott Yanow*

Jumpin' with Jonah / Jan. 26, 1958-Apr. 26, 1958 / Capitol ♦♦♦♦

Trumpeter Jonah Jones' third Capitol album did not yield any additional hits, but it found him repeating his popular formula of playing Dixieland, swing and show tunes with a shuffle beat. Jones, joined by guest pianist Hank Jones, bassist John Brown and drummer Harold Austin, plays and occasionally sings such numbers as "Bill Bailey," "Jumpin' with Jonah," "A Kiss to Build a Dream On" and "That's a Plenty" with spirit and creative melodic ideas. Pretty good for "pop" music! —*Scott Yanow*

Swingin' at the Cinema / Jun. 1958-Jul. 1958 / Capitol ♦♦♦♦

One in a lengthy series of Capitol albums by trumpeter/vocalist Jonah Jones and his quartet (there were five in 1958 alone), this set finds Jones looking for gold by performing a dozen numbers that originally debuted in Hollywood movies. There were no hits this time around, but the LP sold fairly well. Jones, joined by pianist George Rhodes, bassist John Brown and drummer Harold Austin, uplifts such tunes as "True Love," "Colonel Bogey March," "Three Coins in the Fountain" and "Lullaby of Broadway." —*Scott Yanow*

Jonah Jumps Again / Sep. 1958 / Capitol ♦♦♦

I Dig Chicks / Nov. 14, 1958-Nov. 23, 1958 / Capitol ♦♦♦♦

The cover of this LP gives males three good reasons to "dig chicks." Trumpeter/vocalist Jonah Jones continues his "swinging with a shuffle" formula, performing 11 songs named after women, plus the title cut (which has one of his six vocals of the date). Jones, pianist Teddy Brannon, bassist John Brown and drummer George Foster have a good time romping on such numbers as "Mandy, Make Up Your Mind," "Tangerine," "Blue Lou," "Rosetta" and some lesser-known tunes. The overall results may be a bit lightweight and predictable, but the trumpeter gives this album enough exciting moments to make it worth getting. —*Scott Yanow*

Swingin' 'Round the World / 1958 / Capitol ♦♦♦

Due to his two big hits in 1957, 1958 was a busy year for trumpeter/vocalist Jonah Jones, who recorded five albums for Capitol, including this final effort. Most of Jones' dates were based around themes, and in this case he performed 11 songs having something to do with cities, countries or travel, including "Arrivederci Roma," "A Foggy Day," "Brazil," "Chicago," "Manhattan" and "Song of the Islands." Some of the songs are better served by Jones than others, and his formula with his quartet (which also included pianist Teddy Brannon, bassist John Brown and drummer George Foster) was just starting to run a little thin, although it would continue for another decade. —*Scott Yanow*

Jonah Jones/Glenn Gray / 1961 / Capitol ♦♦♦

Since trumpeter Jonah Jones and bandleader Glen Gray were two of Capitol's biggest jazz-oriented attractions of the late '50s/early '60s, a collaboration seemed logical. Gray's Casa Loma Orchestra (which at this point was really a big band filled with top West Coast studio players) performs a dozen Benny Carter arrangements; tenorman Plas Johnson gets in a few licks, and the swing-oriented repertoire suits Jones' playing just fine on this instrumental LP. Highlights include a remake of "Baubles, Bangles and Beads," "Two O'Clock Jump," "After You've Gone" and "West End Blues." —*Scott Yanow*

Jumpin' with a Shuffle / 1961 / Capitol ♦♦♦♦

Trumpeter/vocalist Jonah Jones was at the peak of his popularity when he recorded this album while appearing in Las Vegas. Sticking mostly to standards rather than songs dug up for a particular concept, this is one of Jones' strongest albums from the Capitol years. With suitable if predictable support from pianist Teddy Brannon, bassist John Brown and drummer George Foster, Jones swings his way through such numbers as "Lazy River," "920 Special," "On the Sunny Side of the Street" and "My Monday Date." —*Scott Yanow*

A Touch of Blue / 1962 / Capitol ♦♦

Trumpeter/vocalist Jonah Jones recorded so many albums for Capitol from 1957-63 that it was always a challenge to come up with new themes for dates, particularly since Jones' smooth style was largely unchanged from the 1940s. In this case, he performs a dozen songs with "blue" or "blues" in their title, joined by his quartet (with pianist Teddy Brannon, bassist John Brown and drummer George Foster) plus a large chorale of "background" singers. The vocalists definitely get in the way, weighing down Jones' versions of such songs as "I Get the Blues When It

Rains," "Blue Turning Grey Over You," "Birth of the Blues," "Blue Skies," etc. A somewhat forgettable record, despite some pleasing moments from the trumpeter. —*Scott Yanow*

And Now, in Person: Jonah Jones / 1963 / Capitol ✦✦✦

Trumpeter Jonah Jones became famous during 1956-57 performing nightly before dancing crowds at the Embers. In 1963, after a long string of albums, he finally had the opportunity to record live. Cut in Los Angeles at the Crescendo, Jones, pianist Andre Persiany, bassist John Brown and drummer Danny Farrar swing their way through nine standards, most of which Jones had recorded before. Such tunes as "It's All Right with Me," "From This Moment On," "Undecided" and "Lullaby of Birdland" receive melodic and shuffling treatment from this very popular (and now underrated) group. The results are a bit slick, but still have their spontaneous moments. —*Scott Yanow*

Back on the Street / Mar. 22, 1972 / Chiaroscuro ✦✦✦✦

By the time trumpeter Jonah Jones teamed up with pianist Earl Hines and tenor saxophonist Buddy Tate for this straightforward sextet date, Jones had been a star with his quartet for 15 years. On what would be one of Jones' last recording sessions from his prime, this Chiaroscuro reissue CD has a bit of slickness associated with the trumpeter's more commercial dates but also some very good jazz playing. Three previously unreleased numbers have been added to the original seven-song program and the music falls between Dixieland and swing with an emphasis on familiar standards. A fine effort. —*Scott Yanow*

Confessin' / Jul. 21, 1978 / Jazz Man ✦✦✦

Recorded a decade after his long-running string of popular albums had run out, this LP finds trumpeter/vocalist Jonah Jones still in good form at the age of 68. Joined by pianist Andre Persiany, bassist Major Holley and drummer J.C. Heard, Jones is heard in Paris playing a seven-song Duke Ellington medley, "The Sheik of Araby," "Love Is Just Around the Corner," "St. Louis Blues" and "I'm Confessin.'" The old shuffling beat had been replaced by solid swing, and the trumpeter plays some heated solos that fall between swing and Dixieland. —*Scott Yanow*

Leroy Jones

b. Feb. 20, 1955, New Orleans, LA
Trumpet / New Orleans Jazz
Heavily influenced by the New Orleans jazz tradition, Leroy Jones has honored his rich heritage while seeking to expand his musical repertoire. He took up trumpet when he joined his elementary school's band. At 13 he joined guitarist Danny Barker's Fairview Baptist Brass Band; Barker also taught Jones privately. He spent four years in the city's popular St. Augustine High School Band. After graduating, he formed the Hurricane Brass Band, which along with the Fairview Band, provided talent for the Dirty Dozen Brass Band. He toured Canada with Eddie "Cleanhead" Vinson and joined Della Reese, leading to international concert tours that eventually resulted in Jones performing in Southeast Asia for a three-year stretch. Recruited by Harry Connick, Jr. for his big band, Jones was Connick's opening act during his 1994 tour. He finally debuted to critical acclaim as a leader in 1995 with his CD *Mo' Cream From the Crop*. —*Ken Dryden*

Mo' Cream from the Crop / 1994 / Columbia ✦✦✦

In his brief liner notes to this CD, Harry Connick, Jr. calls trumpeter Leroy Jones a genius. Jones is no genius (certainly there is nothing on his debut disc that would qualify as original) but he is a fine Lee Morgan-influenced trumpeter and a decent singer. The odd part about this set is that Jones, due to his New Orleans background, is misplaced as a Dixieland trumpeter. He certainly does not have much feel for the music, turning "Tin Roof Blues" into burlesque (with some sounds worthy of Clyde McCoy), playing closing ensembles on "Bourbon Street Parade" that practically define corn and switching the music to bop every third song or so. Trombonist Lucien Barbarin sounds like J.J. Johnson when he does not feel compelled to growl, leaving drummer Shannon Powell (who often plays enthusiastic parade rhythms) as the only musician on the date who belongs in a traditional New Orleans jazz band. There are some enjoyable selections on this disc but the baggage of having to emulate what Jones thinks a New Orleans trumpeter should sound like weighs down the performances. —*Scott Yanow*

● Props for Pops / 1997 / Columbia ✦✦✦✦

Leroy Jones is a fine New Orleans trumpeter based in trad jazz but open to the influence of bop. His clipped phrases give him a distinctive sound, and his vocals are spirited. On this CD, he pays homage to Louis Armstrong by playing several songs associated with Satch, along with a few of his own original tributes. Teamed up with trombonist Craig Klein and a couple of rhythm sections (including pianist Harry Connick, Jr. on two tracks), Jones is in fine form on such numbers as "Struttin' with Some Barbecue," "Jeepers Creepers" and "Ain't Misbehavin,'" sometimes recreating Armstrong's solos and vocals note-for-note and at other times putting in some of his own ideas. A good-humored and successful tribute. —*Scott Yanow*

Oliver Jones

b. Sep. 11, 1934, Montreal, Canada
Piano / Bop
Oliver Jones was already in his 50s when he was discovered by the jazz world. He had started playing piano when he was seven, and at nine he studied with Oscar Peterson's sister, Daisy; the Peterson influence is still felt in his style. Jones played with show bands and worked with pop singer Ken Hamilton (1963-80), much of the time in Puerto Rico. It was not until he returned to Montreal in 1980 that he committed himself to playing jazz full time. Since the mid-'80s Oliver Jones has recorded extensively for Justin Time and established himself as a major modern mainstream player with impressive technique and a hard-swinging style. —*Scott Yanow*

The Many Moods of Oliver Jones / Feb. 1984-Mar. 1984 / Justin Time ✦✦✦✦✦

The Lights of Burgundy / Apr. 1985 / Justin Time ✦✦✦✦✦

Pianist Oliver Jones made an initial stir with the release of this early record. Influenced heavily by Oscar Peterson but already showing his own approach, Jones is teamed with four fellow Canadians: bassist Michel Donato, drummer Jim Hillman, guitarist Reg Schwager and the cool-toned tenor saxophonist Fraser MacPherson. Jones performs four of his originals, including the title cut and "Snuggles," plus six jazz standards such as "Oleo," "In a Mellow Tone" and "Broadway." Jones has been quite consistent throughout his jazz career, making this album (which would win the Canadian Juno award as best jazz record of 1986) worth searching for. —*Scott Yanow*

Speak Low Swing Hard / Jul. 1985-Sep. 1985 / Justin Time ✦✦✦✦

By the time pianist Oliver Jones recorded this set, his sixth release for Justin Time, he was finally gaining recognition in the US for his brilliant playing. A virtuosic pianist, Jones is heard in excellent form on a trio date with bassist Skip Beckwith and drummer Jim Hillman, playing modern mainstream jazz interpretations of such standards as "Soft Winds," "Up Jumped Spring" and "Speak Low," along with his own "Hilly" and a pair of Beckwith originals, including "The Reverend Mr. Jones." —*Scott Yanow*

Requestfully Yours / Nov. 1985 / Justin Time ✦✦✦✦

● Cookin' at Sweet Basil / Sep. 3, 1987 / Justin Time ✦✦✦✦✦

Veteran Canadian pianist Oliver Jones, who was finally becoming famous in the US in 1987, is heard on this live set in NYC playing with bassist Dave Young and drummer Terry Clarke. Jones performs five of his diverse but consistently swinging originals, including "Snuggles," plus "If I Were a Bell" and "My Funny Valentine." An excellent example of the impressive pianist's playing talents. —*Scott Yanow*

Just Friends / Jan. 1989 / Justin Time ✦✦✦✦

Pianist Oliver Jones has recorded over a dozen albums (both LPs and CDs) for the Canadian Justin Time label, and virtually all are recommended. This particular outing finds Jones and his trio (with bassist Dave Young and drummer Nasyr Abdul Al-Khabyyr) welcoming guest fluegelhornist Clark Terry to their date. Performing four of Jones' originals and a quartet of standards (including "Just Friends" and "It Could Happen to You"), C.T.'s joyful presence clearly inspires the other musicians and makes this excellent set even more memorable than a typical Oliver Jones date. —*Scott Yanow*

Northern Summit / Jun. 1990-Sep. 1990 / Justin Time ✦✦✦✦✦

A Class Act / Mar. 1991-May 1991 / Justin Time ✦✦✦✦✦

For this CD, pianist Oliver Jones teams up with bassist Steve Wallace and drummer Ed Thigpen for a slightly more modern program than usual. Influenced by Oscar Peterson but having his own sound within O.P.'s style, Jones performs numbers by Kenny Wheeler, Bill Evans ("Very Early"), Nelson Symonds, Peterson ("Hymn to Freedom") and Thigpen, along with four of his own tunes. Recommended. —*Scott Yanow*

Just 88 / Oct. 19, 1992 / Justin Time ✦✦✦✦✦

Yuletide Swing / May 1994 / Justin Time ✦✦✦✦

Pianist Oliver Jones performs ten familiar Christmas songs on this quartet set with guitarist Richard Ring, bassist Dave Young and drummer Walt Muhammad. Jones sounds quite exuberant on some of the tunes, particularly "Santa Claus Is Coming to Town," "Winter Wonderland" and "Sleigh Ride." A fun session recommended to collectors of Christmas jazz. —*Scott Yanow*

From Lush to Lively / May 31, 1995+Jun. 1, 1995 / Justin Time ✦✦✦

Have Fingers, Will Travel / 1997 / Justin Time ✦✦✦✦

Since bassist Ray Brown is aboard for Oliver Jones' trio set, and his presence often results in pianists sounding a bit like Peterson (think of Gene Harris and Benny Green when they were members of Brown's groups), the shadow of Oscar is felt throughout the date. Drummer Jeff Hamilton (who toured with Peterson) also fits very securely into the style. Oliver Jones is heard in superb form, with his versions of "If I Were a Bell," a thoughtful "I'm Thru with Love," "Without a Song" and "My Romance" being among the highlights. In addition to five familiar standards, Jones performs six of his originals (two blues and four melodic pieces), and it is on those numbers that he tends to sound most individual. This strong straightahead session, as with all of Jones' Justin Time recordings, is easily recommended. —*Scott Yanow*

Philly Joe Jones (Joseph Rudolph Jones)

b. Jul. 15, 1923, Philadelphia, PA, **d.** Aug. 30, 1985, Philadelphia, PA
Drums / Hard Bop

A fiery drummer and a masterful accompanist, Philly Joe Jones came to fame as a key member with the first classic Miles Davis Quintet. After serving in the Army, he moved to New York in 1947, became the house drummer at Cafe Society and played with the who's who of bop (including Charlie Parker, Dizzy Gillespie and Fats Navarro). He worked regularly with Ben Webster, Joe Morris, Tiny Grimes, Lionel Hampton and Tadd Dameron (1953). Jones was with Miles Davis during 1955-58 including the quintet years (1955-56) with John Coltrane, Red Garland and Paul Chambers and the beginnings of the super sextet that also included Cannonball Adderley (recording the classic *Milestones* album). In 1958 he started leading his own groups, recording for Riverside (1958-59) and Atlantic (1960). Jones lived in London and Paris during 1967-72 (performing and recording with some avant-garde players including Archie Shepp). He eventually returned to Philadelphia where he had a fusion group Le Grand Prix, toured with Bill Evans during 1976, recorded for Galaxy in 1977 and 1979 and worked with Red Garland. Starting in 1981 he led the group Dameronia, which revived Tadd Dameron's music. But in reality everything that Philly Joe Jones did after Miles Davis was anticlimactic. —*Scott Yanow*

Blues for Dracula / Sep. 17, 1958 / Original Jazz Classics ✦✦✦✦

Drummer Philly Joe Jones' debut recording as a leader, made shortly after he left Miles Davis' Quintet, starts out with his amusing but overly long monologue on "Blues for Dracula," during which he does his best to imitate Bela Lugosi. The remainder of the set (which has been reissued on CD) is more conventional, with fine playing from cornetist Nat Adderley, trombonist Julian Priester, the great tenor Johnny Griffin, pianist Tommy Flanagan, bassist Jimmy Garrison, and the drummer/leader. Dizzy Gillespie's "Ow" and Cal Massey's "Fiesta" are heard in lengthy versions on the worthwhile but not overly essential release. —*Scott Yanow*

Drums Around the World / May 28, 1959-May 29, 1959 / Original Jazz Classics ✦✦✦

Drummer Philly Joe Jones takes a lot of solo space (including an unaccompanied "The Tribal Message") throughout this CD reissue. He utilizes an all-star group with such soloists as trumpeter Lee Morgan and Blue Mitchell, trombonist Curtis Fuller, Herbie Mann on flute and piccolo, altoist Cannonball Adderley, Benny Golson on tenor, baritonist Sahib Shihab, pianist Wynton Kelly and either Sam Jones or Jimmy Garrison on bass. The music is supposed to showcase styles from around the world including Latin America and the Far East but in general those references are somewhat superficial (including "Cherokee") and come out sounding like hard bop. There is some strong playing, but this set is primarily recommended to fans of Philly Joe Jones' drum solos. —*Scott Yanow*

Showcase / Nov. 17, 1959 / Original Jazz Classics ✦✦✦✦

This is a particularly interesting hard bop-oriented set led by drummer Philly Joe Jones. Most unusual is "Gwen," a Jones ballad that has the leader on both piano and (via overdubbing) drums in a trio with bassist Jimmy Garrison. Otherwise, trumpeter Blue Mitchell, trombonist Julian Priester, tenor saxophonist Bill Barron, either Dolo Coker or Sonny Clark on piano, Garrison, and Jones form a sextet that performs modern tunes by Barron, Priester and Jones, in addition to "I'll Never Be the Same" and Philly Joe's feature on "Gone" (based on the Miles Davis/Gil Evans interpretation of "Porgy and Bess"). A well-conceived, diverse and recommended CD reissue. —*Scott Yanow*

● **Mo' Joe** / Oct. 1, 1968+Oct. 31, 1968 / Black Lion ✦✦✦✦

Although one might think—considering the personnel (which includes trumpeter Kenny Wheeler) and the time period—that this CD reissue contains an avant-garde session, the music is generally straightahead hard bop. Drummer Philly Joe Jones, who has short solos on each of the six selections, is a dominant force even when playing brushes in the ensembles. He contributed two of the six selections (including "Trailways Express," which is a revisit to the Miles Davis arrangement of "Two Bass Hit") and clearly inspires the younger musicians, all of whom were from England; altoist Peter King and tenor saxophonist Harold McNair are particularly impressive. Other highlights include George Gershwin's "Gone, Gone, Gone," a surprisingly cooking version of "Here's That Rainy Day" and Tadd Dameron's "Ladybird." —*Scott Yanow*

Round Midnight / Jul. 18, 1969 / Lotus ✦✦✦

Excellent Italian set with sorely neglected Dizzy Reece on trumpet. —*Ron Wynn*

Mean What You Say / Apr. 6, 1977-Apr. 7, 1977 / Sonet ✦✦✦✦✦

Philly Joe Jones led a quartet (pianist Mickey Tucker, Charles Bowen on soprano and tenor saxes, bassist Mickey Bass) and quintet (add trumpeter Tommy Turrentine) on an April 1977 date called *Mean What You Say*. This was a nice blowing date for Bowen, who at the time had an R&B background and had never before recorded a jazz album ... Mickey Tucker was very strong on this set and at times almost seemed to be the leader with Jones seemingly pushing to assert his position. Still, this was an enjoyable recording with just that little extra added personality to give it an extra edge. —*Bob Rusch / Cadence*

Philly Mignon / Nov. 29, 1977-Dec. 1, 1977 / Galaxy ✦✦✦✦

For this Galaxy LP (which unfortunately has not yet come out on CD), drummer Philly Joe Jones leads a variety of all-stars throughout three obscurities, "Polka Dots and Moonbeams" and "Confirmation." Two songs (including "Polka Dots") feature tenor great Dexter Gordon in a quartet with pianist George Cables, bassist Ron Carter and the drummer/leader. The other three songs match Jones with cornetist Nat Adderley, Ira Sullivan (on tenor or soprano), Cables and Carter. Overall, everyone plays well on this modern hard bop set, making one hope that it will be reissued eventually in the OJC series. —*Scott Yanow*

Drum Song / Oct. 10, 1978-Oct. 12, 1978 / Galaxy ✦✦✦✦✦

Hard bop is spoken here on this straightahead set. Drummer Philly Joe Jones is the leader but the main emphasis is on such soloists as trumpeter Blue Mitchell (heard in one of his last recordings), the tenors of Harold Land and Charles Bowen, pianist Cedar Walton and trombonist Slide Hampton who arranged the four full-band numbers. Hampton (who also contributed two originals) gets "I Wait for You" as his feature while Bowen is showcased on "High Fly." In addition, these versions of "Our Delight" and "Two Bass Hit" have their heated moments. —*Scott Yanow*

Advance! / Oct. 10, 1979-Oct. 12, 1979 / Galaxy ✦✦✦✦

Drummer Philly Joe Jones led a few sets for Galaxy during the 1977-78 period that featured veteran hard bop-oriented players. For this LP (not yet reissued on CD), Jones is matched with trumpeter Blue Mitchell, trombonist Slide Hampton, the tenors of Charles Bowen (who plays one song on soprano) and Harold Land, pianist Cedar Walton and bassist Marc Johnson. "Midnite Waltz" is a change of pace, a trio feature for Walton. Otherwise, the full group plays a pair of obscurities (including Jones' "Trailways"), "Invitation" (always an excellent feature for Land), and "Smoke Gets in Your Eyes." Fine music. —*Scott Yanow*

Quincy Jones

b. Mar. 14, 1933, Chicago, IL
Arranger, Composer, Leader / Bop, Swing, Crossover Jazz, Pop, Traditional Pop

Quincy Jones has had several very successful careers, largely leaving jazz altogether by the early '70s to make his money out of producing pop, R&B and even rap records. His earlier years were much more significant to improvised music. He grew up in Seattle and his first important job was playing trumpet and arranging for Lionel Hampton's Orchestra (1951-53), sitting in a trumpet section with Clifford Brown and Art Farmer. During the 1950s he started freelancing as an arranger, writing memorable charts for sessions led by Oscar Pettiford, Brown, Farmer, Gigi Gryce, Count Basie, Tommy Dorsey, Cannonball Adderley and Dinah Washington among others. He toured with Dizzy Gillespie's big band (1956), started recording as a leader for ABC-Paramount in 1956 and worked in Paris (1957-58) for the Barclay label as an arranger and producer. In 1959, Jones toured Europe with his all-star big band, which was originally put together to play for Harold Arlen's show *Free and Easy*. He kept the orchestra together through 1960, recording for Mercury. In 1961, Jones returned to New York and became the head of Mercury's A&R department, becoming a vice president in 1964. Although he kept on recording throughout the 1960s, Jones' focus shifted to writing for films and television. During 1969-81 he worked for A&M, founding Qwest Records in 1980, a label that has become more active in the 1990s. Among his best jazz compositions have been "Stockholm Sweetnin'," "For Lena and Lennie," "Quintessence," "Jessica's Day" and "The Midnight Sun Never Sets." Although he deserves credit for talking Miles Davis into performing Gil Evans arrangements at the 1991 Montreux Jazz Festival and for signing such artists as Milt Jackson and Sonny Simmons to his Qwest label in the 1990s, very little that Quincy Jones has accomplished during the past 25 years is of any real relevance to jazz. —*Scott Yanow*

★ **This Is How I Feel About Jazz** / Sep. 14, 1956-Feb. 1956 / GRP ✦✦✦✦✦

The music on this CD is from a period when arranger Quincy Jones was a major part of the jazz world, rather than being content just to take bows for it. Six high-quality selections from a 1956 album offer logical, swinging and often distinct arrangements with plenty of solos from the all-star cast (which includes Lucky

Thompson on tenor, altoist Phil Woods and trumpeter Art Farmer); highlights include "Stockholm Sweetnin'," "Walkin'" and "Sermonette." The remainder of the CD reissues two-thirds of a slightly odd collection led and produced (but not arranged) by Jones. Originally titled *Go West, Man*, the LP was designed to show off the talents of West Coast arrangers Jimmy Giuffre, Lennie Niehaus and Charlie Mariano. Three selections have an alto summit featuring Benny Carter, Art Pepper, Herb Geller and Charlie Mariano and there are also some numbers with a sax section; three songs with a trumpet section had to be left out due to lack of space. Although these performances are enjoyable, it is the Quincy Jones charts that are most memorable, making one regret his decision, in the early 1970s, to leave jazz altogether. —*Scott Yanow*

Home Again / Apr. 29, 1958 / Metronome ✦✦✦✦
For this unusual (and now obscure) album, Quincy Jones heads Harry Arnold's Swedish Radio Studio Orchestra. The eight Jones arrangements (some of which would soon be played by his own big band) include "The Midnight Sun Never Sets," "Meet Benny Bailey" and "Doodlin'"; in addition, Arnold contributed "Quincy's Home Again." Among the sidemen are trumpeter Bailey himself (who guests on two numbers), trombonist Ake Persson, altoist Arne Domnerus and pianist Bengt Hallberg. An excellent effort featuring a hard-swinging Swedish band that deserved to be better known in the US. —*Scott Yanow*

The Birth of a Band, Vol. 2 / May 27, 1959+Jun. 16, 1959 / Mercury ✦✦✦
This interesting collector's LP (released in Japan and made available domestically for just a short time) has a variety of rare tracks from the legendary Quincy Jones big band's Mercury sessions. With such top players as fluegelhornist Clark Terry (featured on "Moanin'"), tenorman Zoot Sims, altoist Phil Woods and guitarist Kenny Burrell being featured, and Jones' jazz writing in prime form, this is a particularly strong set. Strange that it has not been coherently reissued on CD yet. In addition to "Moanin'," other highlights include "Daylie Double," "Parisian Thoroughfare," "The Midnight Sun Will Never Set" and "The Preacher." —*Scott Yanow*

☆ **The Birth of a Band, Vol. 1** / Jun. 16, 1959 / Mercury ✦✦✦✦✦
Although this particular big band changed its personnel quite a bit before touring Europe, Quincy Jones began 1959 with high hopes. On one of his finest jazz recordings, Jones' arrangements feature such top players as trumpeter Harry "Sweets" Edison, Zoot Sims and Sam "The Man" Taylor on tenors, altoist Phil Woods and fluegelhornist Clark Terry. Highlights include the title cut, "The Midnight Sun Will Never Set," "Moanin'" and three Benny Golson tunes ("I Remember Clifford," "Along Came Betty" and "Whisper Not"). This music has been reissued on CD. —*Scott Yanow*

The Great Wide World of Quincy Jones / Nov. 4, 1959-Nov. 5, 1959 / EmArcy ✦✦✦✦
Quincy Jones has had such strong success in pop music since the mid-1960s that it is easy to forget just how inventive and distinctive a jazz arranger he was during his prime years. This CD reissue features the Quincy Jones Big Band shortly before they sailed to Europe as part of a Harold Arlen show. Surprisingly, none of the selections are Jones originals, and the arrangements were provided by Ernie Wilkins, Bill Potts, Al Cohn and Ralph Burns. Despite Jones' absence musically (he did conduct the group), the music sounds very much like his work. With such fine soloists as altoist Phil Woods, tenorman Budd Johnson, Les Spann on guitar and flute, Julius Watkins on French horn (on "Everybody's Blues"), trumpeter Art Farmer and two guest spots for trumpeter Lee Morgan, the music (highlighted by "Lester Leaps In," "Cherokee" and "Air Mail Special") featured a top-notch bop-oriented big band. —*Scott Yanow*

Q Live in Paris Circa 1960 / 1960 / Warner Brothers ✦✦✦✦
Quincy Jones' big band of 1960 went to Europe as part of Harold Arlen's ill-fated "Free and Easy" show. When that production died, Jones kept his all-star orchestra together for much of the year before being forced economically to give up. This 1996 CD has a previously unreleased concert performance taped illegally by a fan but now put out legitimately. The recording quality is quite good, and the group (which includes trumpeters Clark Terry and Benny Bailey, trombonists Quentin Jackson, Jimmy Cleveland and Melba Liston, the great French horn soloist Julius Watkins, altoist Phil Woods and Budd Johnson and Jerome Richardson on tenors) was in particularly spirited form that night. All of the mentioned musicians have opportunities to solo, including bassist Buddy Catlett, who really stretches out on "Walkin'" (he was apparently surprised when the band refused to come in); other highlights include the Johnson-Richardson tenor tradeoff on "Birth of a Band," Watkins' playing on "Everybody's Blues" and the swinging "Tickle Toe." This was arguably Quincy Jones' finest band ever. —*Scott Yanow*

Swiss Radio Days Jazz Series, Vol. 1 / Jun. 27, 1960 / TCB ✦✦✦✦✦
Quincy Jones led one of his finest orchestras in 1960. This spirited CD is taken from a live concert (and radio broadcast) from Switzerland. With such soloists as trumpeter Benny Bailey, trombonist Jimmy Cleveland, altoist Phil Woods, Jerome

Richardson on tenor and baritonist Sahib Shihab (among others), the repertoire mostly sticks to bebop. Surprisingly enough, not all of the arrangements heard on the CD are Jones'; there are also swinging charts from Ernie Wilkins, Billy Byers, Melba Liston, Phil Woods and Al Cohn. This well-recorded and previously unissued performance (which came out for the first time in 1994) makes one wish that Quincy Jones would return to jazz someday. —*Scott Yanow*

The Great Wide World of Quincy Jones: Live! / Mar. 10, 1961 / Mercury ✦✦✦✦✦
Quincy Jones' original big band toured Europe under stressful conditions in 1960 before returning home. In 1961, they returned for a tour, and although the personnel had changed a bit, it was still a mighty orchestra. This Japanese LP (which contains music from a Zurich, Switzerland, concert not yet reissued on CD) has six selections, including a 13-minute version of "Stolen Moments" and a nearly nine-minute Phil Woods original, "Banjaluka," along with four shorter pieces. Among the key soloists are trumpeter Freddie Hubbard, Eric Dixon and Budd Johnson on tenors, altoist Woods, trumpeter Benny Bailey (featured on "Moanin'") and trombonist Curtis Fuller. Fine straightahead music from a short-lived but significant jazz orchestra. —*Scott Yanow*

Live at Newport / Jul. 3, 1961 / Trip ✦✦✦
The Quincy Jones Big Band's recorded appearance at the 1961 Newport Jazz Festival was the orchestra's last hurrah before its breakup; the leader would soon become much more involved in the studios. With trumpeter Joe Newman, altoist Phil Woods, trombonist Curtis Fuller and tenorman Eric Dixon as key soloists, this ensemble could hold its own with most of its contemporaries. Jones' arrangements were colorful and distinctive, and the musicianship of the orchestra was quite impressive. It is a pity they could not make it financially. Their final LP has yet to be reissued on CD, but is worth searching for; it was reissued by Trip in the late 1970s. —*Scott Yanow*

The Quintessence / Nov. 29, 1961-Dec. 18, 1961 / GRP/Impulse! ✦✦✦
If it were not for this CD reissue's extreme brevity (under 31 minutes), it would receive a much higher rating. One of arranger/composer Quincy Jones' finest recordings, this 1961 set features such top players as trumpeters Clark Terry, Thad Jones and Freddie Hubbard, Julius Watkins on French horn, and most notably altoist Phil Woods in several big-band settings. Jones' three originals include "Quintessence" and "For Lena and Lennie"; plus, there are reworkings of "Invitation" and pieces by Benny Golson and Thelonious Monk, among others. The music swings, and the solos are logical outgrowths of the arrangements; if only more than one piece were over four minutes long. —*Scott Yanow*

Plays Hip Hits / Apr. 9, 1963-Apr. 11, 1963 / Mercury ✦✦✦
By 1963, Quincy Jones' music was at a crossroads. Still jazz-oriented, Jones' work with a studio big band was clearly aimed at trying to sell records rather than play creative jazz. On this LP, Jones leads an orchestra through a dozen then-recent jazz "hits," including "Comin' Home Baby," "Exodus," "Cast Your Fate to the Wind," "Take Five" and "Watermelon Man." There are some fine short solos by the likes of trumpeter Joe Newman, guitarist Jim Hall, Zoot Sims on tenor, altoist Phil Woods and (on "A Taste of Honey") even Rahsaan Roland Kirk. However, the performances all clock in around three minutes, and the jazz players take solos that often only count as cameos. Pleasant but not particularly substantial music. —*Scott Yanow*

Golden Boy / 1964 / Mercury ✦✦
This Quincy Jones big-band LP finds him exploring a wide variety of material in hopes of finding a hit. Among the selections are "Django," the Beatles' "A Hard Day's Night," "The Sidewinder," a remake of "The Midnight Sun Will Never Set" and three versions of the "Theme from Golden Boy." There are some spots for trumpeters Freddie Hubbard and Joe Newman, altoist Phil Woods, guitarist Jim Hall, and the tough tenor of Eddie "Lockjaw" Davis, but the brevity of the selections (all but "Django" are between two and four minutes) and the conservative nature of many of the charts keep the music from taking any real chances. —*Scott Yanow*

Big Band Bossa Nova / 1964 / Mercury ✦✦
A by-product of the bossa nova fad that followed the success of "Desafinado" (and preceded the famous recording *Getz/Gilberto*), this LP finds Quincy Jones utilizing and exploiting bossa nova rhythms in his arrangements for a big band. It is a little odd that the personnel is not given on the LP, for it includes fluegelhornist Clark Terry, altoist Phil Woods, pianist Lalo Schifrin, guitarist Jim Hall and (on "Soul Bossa Nova") the remarkable Rahsaan Roland Kirk. However, since the selections are all quite brief, and some of the charts are a bit cheesy and inappropriate for the gentle rhythms, this out-of-print LP (although pleasant enough) is of lesser interest. —*Scott Yanow*

The Pawnbroker/The Deadly Affair / 1965-1966 / Verve ✦✦
Two of Quincy Jones earliest film scores (originally released as a pair of LPs) are reissued in full on this single CD. Due to the lack of strong melodies and the

"mood music" nature of most of these selections (which work quite well in the two films but rarely stand alone), this set is of limited interest from the jazz standpoint. *The Pawnbroker,* in addition to a stirring monologue by Rod Steiger taken from the film, has some short spots for trumpeter Freddie Hubbard and trombonist J.J. Johnson in addition to a vocal by Marc Allen; Sarah Vaughan's version of the "Theme from the Pawnbroker" is added to the program. *The Deadly Affair,* which has a vocal by Astrud Gilberto, sometimes features an unidentified tenor saxophonist and is generally of lesser interest. This CD is more for film buffs than for jazz collectors. —*Scott Yanow*

☆ **Walking in Space** / Jun. 1969 / A&M ♦♦♦♦♦
The protean Quincy Jones returned to the recording studio as a leader after a long stretch in Hollywood with this triumphantly contemporary big-band album. He re-established himself firmly with his big-band jazz base while casting a keen eye on the pop scene and the world of electric instruments (even Ray Brown is caught playing superb electric bass here). Q the diplomat also unveils his uncanny ability to attract some of the biggest names in jazz (Freddie Hubbard, Roland Kirk, Hubert Laws, J.J. Johnson, Kai Winding, etc.) as sidemen, a quality that will be put to use again and again in the following decades. For jazz buffs, the long, dramatic title track from the then-raging musical *Hair* is the highlight; Hubbard positively sizzles on muted trumpet and the brash Kirk blasts through the grooving rhythm section under heavy reverb. You also get Q's classic, swaggering arrangement of Benny Golson's "Killer Joe"—practically the definitive version—and a rendition of Edwin Hawkins' freak hit "Oh Happy Day" that bursts with wit and sheer joy. This is one of the great peaks of Creed Taylor's A&M period, and it still sounds spectacular today. —*Richard S. Ginell*

I Heard That! / Jun. 1969-1976 / A&M ♦♦
This two-LP set was supposed to contain a monumental suite tracing the evolution of Black music but since Jones needed more time to work on it (it has yet to emerge!), he put out this stopgap set. One LP contains new material, the other is a retrospective of his previous A&M albums. The first LP is dominated by the generic soul vocals of a Quincy Jones-sponsored creation known as the Wattsline, which is largely saddled with routine soul material after a brief, promisingly funky start ("I Heard That!"). Of the instrumentals, "Midnight Soul Patrol" doesn't quite make it despite the presence of heavyweight funksters like George Duke, Stanley Clarke, Billy Cobham and Alphonso Johnson, but "Brown Soft Shoe" again has Toots Thielemans delivering some classy cameo harmonica. The "greatest hits" disc astutely pulls eight key tracks from all six of Q's earlier A&Ms (though "Gula Matari" and "Walking in Space" are heavily edited)—and frankly, they blow his 1976 music away. —*Richard S. Ginell*

The Best / Jun. 1969-1981 / A&M ♦♦♦
Quincy Jones' A&M recordings, which roam gradually from the maestro's old big-band base to smoothly polished assaults on the pop charts, are given a cursory glance here. Special attention is paid to 1974's *Body Heat*—the big initial plunge into mainstream soul—and the later hit albums *Sounds . . . And Stuff like That* and *The Dude,* at the expense of the early Creed Taylor-produced albums ("Killer Joe" is the sole representative) and transition records like *Smackwater Jack* ("What's Going On," with its anemic vocal by Q, is not the best choice). One reason why this best-of collection does not do justice to its subject is that it barely touches upon the fascinating tracks from all of Jones' A&M phases that feature galaxies of jazzmen. It is decent entertainment, though, for casual listening. —*Richard S. Ginell*

Gula Matari / Mar. 25, 1970-May 1, 1970 / A&M ♦♦♦♦♦
With his second and last album under the Creed Taylor aegis, the complexities of Quincy Jones' Catholic, evolving tastes start to reveal themselves. We hear signs of Q's gradual gravitation toward pop right off the bat with the churchy R&B cover of Paul Simon's megahit "Bridge over Troubled Water," dominated by Valerie Simpson's florid soul vocal and a gospel choir. His "roots" fixation surfaces in the spell-like African groove of the title track, a dramatic tone poem that ebbs and flows masterfully over its 13-minute length. From this point on, it's all jazz; the roaring big band comes back with a vengeance in "Walkin'" where Milt Jackson, Herbie Hancock, Hubert Laws and other jazzers take fine solo turns—and things really get rocking on Nat Adderley's "Hummin'"; Major Holley is a riot with his grumble-scat routine on bass. The whole record sounds like they must have had a ball recording it. —*Richard S. Ginell*

The Best of Quincy Jones, Vol. 2 / Mar. 1970-1981 / A&M ♦♦♦
Musically, this is actually a better collection than *Vol. 1,* digging a little deeper into the A&M files and coming up with some more eclectic material. Some of that extra edge comes from TV land via the streetwise themes from *Sanford and Son* and the now-overlooked first *Bill Cosby Show* ("Hikky-Burr"). Other highlights here are a heavily edited version of the incantory "Gula Matari," the catchy Brothers Johnson debut "Is It Love That's We're Missin'" (from *Mellow Madness*), and the

percolating "Boogie Joe, the Grinder." While this collection isn't a comprehensive Quincy Jones primer either (the closest A&M came was the extra "greatest-hits" disc in the two-LP *I Heard That!*), it is a better bet than its predecessor. —*Richard S. Ginell*

Smackwater Jack / 1971 / A&M ♦♦♦♦
This is where a lot of serious jazz purists get off the train but for the rest of us, this is an exciting journey into Quincy Jones territory where labels are meaningless. Though Q takes us deep into Hollywood and TV with his themes to *Ironside, The Anderson Tapes* and the first *Bill Cosby Show* (with humorous vocals from the Cos' himself), his jazz base remains intact in these fascinating charts, and stellar friends like Freddie Hubbard, Milt Jackson, Toots Thielemans, and Jim Hall are left alone to shine. The centerpiece, "Guitar Blues Odyssey: From Roots to Fruits" is the first of many attempts by Q to summarize musical evolution in one fell swoop. Moreover, this ambitious collage actually works—and it's great fun to hear Thielemans, Hall, Eric Gale and Joe Beck try to mimic guitarists from Robert Johnson to Wes Montgomery to Jimi Hendrix. One can't be quite as enthusiastic about Q's rather weak-kneed vocals on two tracks, but that's about the only stumble in this hugely enjoyable project. —*Richard S. Ginell*

You've Got It, Bad Girl / Oct. 1973 / A&M ♦♦♦
With a predictable combination of movie/TV themes, dreary covers of Top 40 ballads, some jazz and a few striking moments, this is a maddeningly uneven follow-up to *Smackwater Jack.* A magically spooky saunter through the Lovin' Spoonful's "Summer in the City" leads it off, but the record becomes bogged down in easy-listening strings and "soulful" vocals, despite the presence of ace soloists like Phil Woods, Hubert Laws and George Duke. Things do become more exuberant as Stevie Wonder punctuates his "Superstition" on harmonica, and a fussed-over big-band rendition of Dizzy's "Manteca" delivers sporadic kicks. But Q mostly marks time before going completely off the reservation on his next outing. —*Richard S. Ginell*

Body Heat / 1974 / A&M ♦♦♦♦
At the time, this was a breathtaking leap for Quincy Jones, right into the very heart of mainstream commercial soul—and it turned out to be very lucrative, rising to No. 6 on the pop LP charts. Jazz per se has been left far behind but the same musical sensibility, the same brilliant production skills, and the same knack for what will appeal to a wider audience are still at work, and the result is a surprisingly pleasing album. Amazingly, Q still draws a constellation of jazz stars into his studio bands (Herbie Hancock, Frank Rosolino, Hubert Laws, Jerome Richardson, Grady Tate, Bob James), plus soul names like Billy Preston, Bernard Purdie and the soon-to-be-ubiquitous guitarist Wah Wah Watson. The emphasis, though, is first on the honeyed soul vocals from a variety of newcomers, and second on the funky grooves laced with the buzz of now-prized analogue synthesizers and wah-wah guitars. There is one reminder of Q's big-band days, a busy electronic retrofitting of his classic chart of Benny Golson's "Along Came Betty," where one can hear Laws blow at some length. Otherwise, to paraphrase Q himself, if you check your jazz boots at the door, you might enjoy this. —*Richard S. Ginell*

Mellow Madness / 1975 / A&M ♦♦
Released not long after Quincy Jones was operated upon for life-threatening brain aneurysms, the music community was glad to have this album around (you can almost sense Q's own relief as he holds his forehead on the cover). Basically, though, it continues the polished, percolating soul direction that Q initiated with *Body Heat,* alienating purists but entertaining R&B audiences that rushed to buy it. The album is given its commercial edge by two new Jones discoveries, George Johnson (guitar, vocals) and Louis Johnson (bass), who would leap to fame the following year on their own as the Brothers Johnson. One attraction for jazz listeners is Toots Thielemans' "Bluesette," in which the Belgian virtuoso does a nice guitar/whistle cameo and Frank Rosolino blows some fine trombone, but the track is not helped by the overdubbed soul voices. —*Richard S. Ginell*

Roots / 1977 / A&M ♦♦♦
Quincy Jones has been threatening to write a long tone poem sketching the history of Black music for decades now, and he has yet to do it. This project, rushed out in the wake of the 1977 TV mini-series *Roots,* is about as close as he has come. A brief (28 minutes), immaculately-produced and segued suite, *Roots* quickly traces a timeline from Africa to the Civil War, incorporating ancient and modern African influences (with Letta Mbulu as the featured vocalist), a sea shanty, field hollers and fiddle tunes, snippets of dialogue from *Roots* actor Lou Gossett, and some Hollywood-style movie cues. Only a fraction of this music was used in the mini-series; oddly, the most plaintive piece of music, the often-repeated "Roots Mural Theme," is not by Q but by film composer Gerald Fried, who wrote most of the TV score. Though some prominent jazzers (Shelly Manne, Victor Feldman, Ernie Watts, Lee Ritenour, Richard Tee, etc.) turn up in the orchestra, there is

not a trace of jazz to be heard. This is a timely souvenir of a cultural phenomenon, but merely a curiosity for jazz fans. —*Richard S. Ginell*

Sounds & Stuff / 1978 / A&M ✦✦✦

With ears dead-set on the trends of the moment but still drawing now and then on his jazz past, Quincy Jones came up with another classy-sounding pop album loaded with his ever-growing circle of musician friends. Disco was king in 1978 and Q bows low with the ebullient dance hit "Stuff Like That"—which is several cuts above the norm for that genre—along with a healthy quota of elegantly produced soul ballads. Yet amidst the pop stuff, Q still manages to do something fresh and memorable within the jazz sphere with a gorgeous chart of Herbie Hancock's "Tell Me a Bedtime Story." Hancock himself sits in impeccably on electric piano and violinist Harry Lookofsky painstakingly overdubs one of Herbie's transcribed solos on 15 violins. Despite the cast of hundreds that is now de rigeur for Q, the record does not sound overproduced due to the silken engineering and careful deployment of forces. —*Richard S. Ginell*

The Dude / 1980-1981 / A&M ✦✦✦

Now running his own Qwest label and a thousand other things, Quincy Jones still owed one more album to A&M—and he gave them a blockbuster, one that reached No. 10, yielded three hot pop singles and made a star out of soul balladeer James Ingram. "Ai No Corrida," the leadoff track, is the Quincy Jones hit method par excellence—great pacing, superb sound, a catchy tune, a hot Ernie Watts tenor sax solo and you can dance to it, too. Stevie Wonder's irresistible synthesizer hooks lift his "Betcha Wouldn't Hurt Me," and Q and omnipresent composer Rod Temperton are far-seeing enough on the title track to anticipate the rise of rap. But where does all of this pop wizardry, soon to assume mythic dimensions on Michael Jackson's *Thriller,* leave the jazz listener? Yes, Quincy has thought of you too, however briefly, on Ivan Lins' wistful "Velas," where perennial house jazzer Toots Thielemans eloquently returns, taping his part in Belgium. Obviously, though, the main purpose here is to make hit pop singles, and *The Dude* does a fairly good job of that. —*Richard S. Ginell*

Back on Block / 1990 / Qwest ✦✦

Big hit urban-pop release, with virtually no jazz content. —*Ron Wynn*

Listen Up: The Lives of Quincy / 1991 / Qwest ✦✦

Soundtrack of a recent biography/testimonial on Quincy. Some interesting anecdotes, but light on musical highlights. —*Ron Wynn*

Q's Jook Joint / Nov. 1994-1995 / Qwest ✦✦

Originally conceived as a modest big-band project, this inevitably turned into another elaborately megalomaniacal Quincy Jones album, a look back at Q's improbable career as well as an attempt to cover as many bases as possible within the context of a mythical jook-joint atmosphere. Some of the original idea remains intact—sort of—with '90s retrofits of "Let the Good Times Roll" and "Killer Joe" featuring a few members of the original casts (Ray Charles, Hubert Laws) in the leads. But then, the set veers off into the glamorous pop/soul never-never land that Q has perfected, again relying mostly upon remakes of his old productions for himself and others, with time out to play starmaker for a seductive new female singer, Tamia, on "You Put a Move on My Heart." The flaw in this project is built-in; most remakes lack the fresh inspiration of the originals, and few of these tracks approach their predecessors, let alone eclipse them. The Brothers Johnson's "Stomp," helped by the can-rattling cast of the show Stomp and some buoyant rapping, is the sole track that outdoes the original. Check out the brief cameos by Joshua Redman and James Moody, as well as the opening sound collage where the voices of Lester Young, Dizzy Gillespie, Miles Davis, Charlie Parker and Sarah Vaughan can be heard amidst the jive chatter. Q in the mid-'90s is entertaining as always, but not as exuberant nor as innovative, and in the long view, this may not be seen as one of his more successful albums. —*Richard S. Ginell*

Richard M. Jones

b. Jun. 13, 1892, Barton, LA, **d.** Dec. 8, 1945, Chicago, IL
Piano, Leader / Classic Jazz, New Orleans Blues, Acoustic Chicago Blues
The composer of "Trouble in Mind," Richard M. Jones' main significance to jazz was as the leader of an interesting series of recording dates. He played alto horn and cornet with the Eureka Brass Band as early as 1902 and worked as a pianist in New Orleans during 1908-17. After playing with Oscar Celestin (1918), Jones moved to Chicago where he worked for Clarence Williams' publishing company. He recorded as a piano soloist in 1923, accompanied Blanche Calloway and Chippie Hill on record dates (1925-26) and led his Jazz Wizards on sessions of his own during 1925-29; Jones' sidemen included Albert Nicholas, Johnny St. Cyr, Ikey Robinson, Roy Palmer, Omer Simeon and some lesser-known musicians. Richard M. Jones stayed in Chicago for the rest of his life, leading further sessions during

1935-36 and 1944 and working as a talent scout for Mercury in the 1940s. All of his records as a leader have been reissued on two Classic CDs. —*Scott Yanow*

● **1923-1927** / Jun. 1, 1923-Jul. 20, 1927 / Classics ✦✦✦✦

Richard M. Jones was more important as a talent scout and an organizer of bands than as a pianist. This Classics CD features Jones as a soloist on two numbers from 1923 ("Jazzin' Babies Blues" and "12th Street Rag"), with the Chicago Hottentots, backing the mediocre singer Lillie Delk Christian, playing with Nelson's Paramount Serenaders and Willie Hightower's Night Hawks and leading his own Jazz Wizards. Among the other players are clarinetist Albert Nicholas, banjoist Johnny St. Cyr, cornetist Shirley Clay and trombonist Preston Jackson. Although the music is generally not all that classic, this formerly rare material has its strong moments and gives one a good example of middle-of-the-road Chicago jazz of the mid-'20s. —*Scott Yanow*

1927-1944 / Nov. 7, 1927-Mar. 23, 1944 / Classics ✦✦✦

The second of two CDs that reissue every recording led by pianist Richard M. Jones is drawn from three periods and has diverse material. The early band sides are often a bit disappointing, particularly the ones from 1927-28 with clarinetist Artie Stalks and a fairly obscure cast. Two numbers with his "Jazz Wizards" in 1929 are better, due to the participation of trombonist Roy Palmer and clarinetist Omer Simeon. Quite rare are six swinging big-band sides from 1935 on which Jones merely directs (although he does sing "Bring It on Home to Grandma"). Also on this CD are a pair of examples of the pianist singing blues in 1936 (assisted by trumpeter Lee Collins on his famous "Trouble in Mind") and four decent blues-oriented Dixieland numbers from 1944 with trumpeter Bob Shoffner and clarinetist Darnell Howard. The music is not essential overall, but since Classics did include everything, one cannot fault the packaging. —*Scott Yanow*

Rodney Jones

b. Aug. 30, 1956, New Haven, CT
Guitar / Post-Bop, Fusion
An underrated cool-toned guitarist who sounds at his best in straightahead settings, Rodney Jones had his highest visibility during his period with Dizzy Gillespie (1976-79), when he was in his early twenties. Jones had previously worked with Jaki Byard and recorded with Chico Hamilton, and he would follow the association with Gillespie by working for a time as Lena Horne's accompanist. As a leader, Jones has recorded for Timeless (in 1978 and 1981), the RR label, and in the late '80s for Minor Music. —*Scott Yanow*

Articulation / Sep. 1978 / Muse ✦✦✦

When You Feel the Love / Oct. 1980 / Impulse! ✦✦✦

Rodney Jones is an excellent guitarist whose style sometimes hints at George Benson, R&B and soul-jazz. On this fairly rare 1988 CD, Jones gets into the groove on eight of his originals with a group also including keyboardist Kenny Kirkland, electric bassist Marcus Miller, drummer Buddy Williams, percussionist Rick Cutler and the woodwinds of Fred Lipsius. The music is reasonably enjoyable and lightly funky, if not too substantial. —*Scott Yanow*

● **X Field** / 1995 / Music Masters ✦✦✦✦

Sam Jones (Samuel Jones)

b. Nov. 12, 1924, Jacksonville, FL, **d.** Dec. 15, 1981, New York, NY
Bass, Cello / Hard Bop
Sam Jones, a greatly in-demand bassist who often teamed up with drummer Louis Hayes, was also a talented jazz cello soloist. He always took advantage of the fairly rare opportunities he had to lead sessions to create memorable music. He played with Tiny Bradshaw (1953-55), moved to New York in 1955 and worked with the groups of Kenny Dorham, Cannonball Adderley (1957), Dizzy Gillespie (1958-59) and Thelonious Monk among others. While a member of Cannonball Adderley's very successful quintet (1959-65), Jones wrote such originals as "Unit 7" and "Del Sasser" and led three highly recommended albums for Riverside during 1960-62 (all have been reissued in the OJC series) that featured some of his finest cello playing. Sam Jones was with the Oscar Peterson Trio (as Ray Brown's first replacement) during 1966-70 and then freelanced for the remainder of his life, making many recordings including albums of his own for East Wind (1974), Xanadu, Muse, Inner City, Steeple Chase, Interplay and Sea Breeze. —*Scott Yanow*

● **The Soul Society** / Mar. 8, 1960+Mar. 10, 1960 / Original Jazz Classics ✦✦✦✦

Bassist Sam Jones' debut as a leader resulted in one of his finest recordings. On four of the eight selections on the CD reissue of his Riverside set, Jones is well-featured on bass while the other four numbers find him playing very effective cello. The uncredited arrangements for the groups are uniformly excellent and there is solo space for cornetist Nat Adderley, trumpeter Blue Mitchell, Jimmy Heath on tenor, baritonist Charles Davis and pianist Bobby Timmons. The repertoire is superior too with highlights including the debut of Adderley's "The Old Country," a fine jam on "Just Friends," Keter Betts' "Some Kinda Mean," Jones' bowing on "Home" and Bobby Timmons' "So Tired." Actually, all eight selections are memorable on this highly recommended disc. —*Scott Yanow*

The Chant / Jan. 13, 1961+Jan. 26, 1961 / Original Jazz Classics ✦✦✦✦✦
Bassist Sam Jones' Riverside recordings have long been underrated. This CD reissue features Jones on bass and cello for four songs apiece with a particularly strong supporting cast including cornetist Nat Adderley, trumpeter Blue Mitchell, trombonist Melba Liston, altoist Cannonball Adderley (who only takes one solo) and Jimmy Heath on tenor; Victor Feldman and Heath provided the colorful arrangements. Highlights include "Four," "Sonny Boy," Jones' "In Walked Ray" and "Over the Rainbow," but all eight selections in this straightahead set are rewarding. —*Scott Yanow*

Down Home / Aug. 15, 1962-Aug. 16, 1962 / Original Jazz Classics ✦✦✦✦
Bassist Sam Jones, always best known for being a sideman (most notably with Cannonball Adderley's Quintet), recorded three superior Riverside albums as a leader during 1960-62 that have all been reissued on CD in the OJC series. This particular one, the third, features Jones on bass and cello in several settings. Four selections (including Horace Silver's "Strollin'" and "Unit Seven") are with an all star nonet/tentet, while four others showcase Jones' cello in quintets with either Les Spann or Frank Strozier on flute and Israel Crosby or Ron Carter on bass. This is excellent hard bop-based music, but it would be another 12 years before Jones had his next opportunity to be a leader. —*Scott Yanow*

Cello Again / Jan. 5, 1976 / Xanadu ✦✦✦✦
Bassist Sam Jones, who had not recorded on cello in 14 years at the time of this session, sticks exclusively to that instrument throughout this enjoyable, boppish set. Altoist Charles McPherson helps out and almost steals the show on three of the seven selections, but the rhythm section (pianist Barry Harris, bassist David Williams and drummer Billy Higgins) is contentedly subservient to Jones, who takes cello solos on each selection. —*Scott Yanow*

Something in Common / Sep. 13, 1977 / Muse ✦✦✦✦
A fine sextet plus Cedar Walton on piano and Billy Higgins on drums. —*Ron Wynn*

Changes & Things / Sep. 14, 1977 / Xanadu ✦✦✦✦
Bassist Sam Jones' recordings as a leader have generally been underrated, but virtually every one is well-planned and recommended. Although the gathering of the impressive sextet on this Xanadu LP (trumpeter Blue Mitchell, trombonist Slide Hampton, tenor saxophonist Bob Berg, pianist Barry Harris, drummer Louis Hayes, and Jones) could have resulted in a jam session, the music ("Stablemates," Oscar Pettiford's "Laverne Walk" and originals by Jones, Hampton and Mitchell) often has tightly arranged sections and avoids the obvious. The solos are colorful and purposeful, the material fairly diverse, and the results consistently swinging yet rarely predictable. Hopefully, Xanadu will reissue the music on CD someday. —*Scott Yanow*

Visitation / Mar. 1978 / Steeple Chase ✦✦✦
Modern hard bop is explored on this continually interesting set by bassist Sam Jones. Teamed with cornetist Terumasa Hino, tenor saxophonist Bob Berg, pianist Ronnie Mathews and drummer Al Foster, Jones plays a supportive but strong role on tunes by trumpeter Tom Harrell, Mathews and Paul Chambers, plus "My Funny Valentine" (a ballad feature for Hino) and the bassist's famous "Del Sasser." Excellent music. —*Scott Yanow*

The Bassist / Jan. 3, 1979 / Interplay ✦✦✦
Virtually all of Sam Jones' occasional dates as a leader featured him in a purely supportive role with a medium-sized all-star group. This set is a bit different, for Jones is often in the forefront, heading a trio also including pianist Kenny Barron (who switches to electric piano on one song) and drummer Keith Copeland. Barron is actually the dominant soloist during a program consisting of three originals by Jones, two by Barron and the opening Thelonious Monk tune "Rhythm-a-Ning," although Jones has his spots. Well-played post-bop music (not yet reissued on CD) that is most significant for the contributions of Barron. —*Scott Yanow*

Something New / Jun. 4, 1979 / Sea Breeze ✦✦✦✦✦
The short-lived Sam Jones big band made its only recording for Interplay, which was reissued in 1980 on a Sea Breeze LP. The hard-swinging group is heard performing Jones' "Unit Seven" (the bassist was always an underrated composer), "Stella By Starlight" and originals by Pete Yellin, Bob Mintzer and Ernie Wilkins. Many all-stars were in the band, and among those featured are up-and-coming pianist Fred Hersch, trumpeters Richard Williams and John Eckert, Mintzer on tenor, altoist Yellin, trombonist Sam Burtis, and the tenor of Harold Vick (who is showcased on Wilkins' "Tender Touch"). An excellent jazz orchestra that has been long forgotten since Sam Jones' death in 1981. —*Scott Yanow*

Thad Jones (Thaddeus Joseph Jones)

b. Mar. 28, 1923, Pontiac, MI, **d.** Aug. 20, 1986, Copenhagen, Denmark
Trumpet, Cornet, Arranger, Leader, Composer, Fluegelhorn / Bop, Hard Bop
A harmonically advanced trumpeter/cornetist with a distinctive sound and a talented arranger/composer, Thad Jones (the younger brother of Hank and older brother of Elvin) had a very productive career. Self-taught on trumpet, he started playing professionally when he was 16 with Hank Jones and Sonny Stitt. After serving in the military (1943-46), Jones worked in territory bands in the Midwest. During 1950-53, he performed regularly with Billy Mitchell's quintet in Detroit and he made a few recordings with Charles Mingus (1954-55). Jones became well-known during his long period (1954-63) with Count Basie's Orchestra, taking a "Pop Goes the Weasel" chorus on "April in Paris" and sharing solo duties with Joe Newman. While with Basie, Jones had the opportunity to write some arrangements and he became a busy freelance writer after 1963. He joined the staff of CBS, co-led a quintet with Pepper Adams and near the end of 1965 organized a big band with drummer Mel Lewis that, from February 1966 on, played Monday nights at the Village Vanguard. During the next decade, the orchestra (although always a part-time affair) became famous and gave Jones an outlet for his writing. He composed one standard ("A Child Is Born") along with many fine pieces including "Fingers," "Little Pixie" and "Tiptoe." Among the sidemen in the Thad Jones/Mel Lewis Orchestra (which started out as an all-star group and later on featured younger players) were trumpeters Bill Berry, Danny Stiles, Richard Williams, Marvin Stamm, Snooky Young, and Jon Faddis; trombonists Bob Brookmeyer, Jimmy Knepper and Quentin Jackson; the reeds of Jerome Richardson, Jerry Dodgion, Eddie Daniels, Joe Farrell, Pepper Adams and Billy Harper; pianists Hank Jones, and Roland Hanna; and bassists Richard Davis and George Mraz. In 1978 Jones surprised Lewis by suddenly leaving the band and moving to Denmark, an action he never explained. He wrote for a radio orchestra and led his own group called Eclipse. In late 1984, Jones took over the leadership of the Count Basie Orchestra but within a year bad health forced him to retire. Thad Jones recorded as a leader for Debut (1954-55), Blue Note, Period, United Artists, Roulette, Milestone, Solid State, Artists House, A&M and Metronome, and many of the Thad Jones/Mel Lewis Orchestra's best recordings have been reissued on a five-CD Mosaic box set. —*Scott Yanow*

Lust for Life / Mar. 7, 1954-Nov. 4, 1957 / Drive Archive ✦✦✦
The material on this CD had frequently appeared on Everest back in the LP era. Best are three selections featuring the great tenor saxophonist Sonny Rollins ("Sonnymoon for Two," Like Someone in Love" and the "Theme from Tchaikovsky's Symphony Pathetique"). Also on this fine budget set are a selection apiece from trombonists J.J. Johnson and Kai Winding, and performances from several mid-'50s sessions by cornetist Thad Jones including two numbers with bassist Charles Mingus, a quintet set with tenor saxophonist Frank Foster and "The Jones Bash," which features six unrelated musicians all of whom have Jones as their last name. This bop sampler has its strong moments. —*Scott Yanow*

The Fabulous Thad Jones / Aug. 11, 1954-Mar. 10, 1955 / Original Jazz Classics ✦✦✦✦✦
Trumpeter Thad Jones made his debut as a leader for Charles Mingus' Debut label during 1954-55, music that has been reissued as a single CD in the OJC series and as part of a huge 12-CD Mingus Debut box set. The 12 performances (which include two alternate takes) really put the focus on Jones' accessible yet unpredictable style. Half of the music showcases Jones in a quartet with pianist John Dennis, bassist Mingus and drummer Max Roach, while the other six numbers are more in a Count Basie groove with Frank Wess on tenor and flute, pianist Hank Jones, Mingus and drummer Kenny Clarke. The originals tend to be tricky, and even such standards as "I'll Remember April," "You Don't Know What Love Is" and "Get Out of Town" have their surprising moments. —*Scott Yanow*

Detroit-New York Junction / Mar. 13, 1956 / Blue Note ✦✦✦✦
For his first session as a leader for Blue Note, trumpeter Thad Jones ran through five songs, including the standard "Little Girl Blue," with a small group. Jones' time with Debut certainly broke him in, and he is thoroughly professional on this record. Compared to its predecessor, *The Fabulous Thad Jones*, and its successor, *The Magnificent Thad Jones*, *Detroit-New York Junction* pales slightly, but it's nevertheless an excellent set of driving hard bop. —*Stephen Thomas Erlewine*

★ **The Magnificent Thad Jones** / Jul. 14, 1956 / Blue Note ✦✦✦✦✦
This CD reissue has one of trumpeter Thad Jones' finest small-group sessions of the 1950s; the music has also been reissued in full as part of a large Mosaic box set. Jones, who is matched with tenor saxophonist Billy Mitchell, pianist Barry Harris, bassist Percy Heath and drummer Max Roach, performs a couple of his lesser-known but superior originals, two obscurities, a duet with guitarist Kenny Burrell on "Something to Remember You By," "I've Got a Crush On You" (which was not on the original LP) and "April in Paris." The latter in spots purposely

recalls the Count Basie hit recording, in which Thad had played a major part. The music throughout is unpredictable and harmonically sophisticated bop. —*Scott Yanow*

Complete Blue Note/UA/Roulette Recordings of Thad Jones / Mar. 13, 1956-Oct. 31, 1959 / Mosaic ◆◆◆◆◆
The Complete Blue Note/UA/Roulette Recordings of Thad Jones is a wonderful limited-edition, three-disc box set, containing everything the trumpeter recorded for the labels in the late '50s. Jones was a fantastic hard-bop trumpeter and the set captures him in all of his glory and is of interest to serious hard-bop connoisseurs. —*Leo Stanley*

After Hours / Jun. 21, 1957 / Original Jazz Classics ◆◆◆◆
Although Thad Jones' name appears first on this CD reissue, pianist Mal Waldron is actually the session's main force. Waldron contributed all four selections (all of which are worthwhile, even if none caught on) and is a key soloist with the sextet, which also includes trumpeter Jones, Frank Wess on tenor and flute, guitarist Kenny Burrell, bassist Paul Chambers and drummer Art Taylor. Fine straightahead music, very much in the modern mainstream of 1957. —*Scott Yanow*

Mean What You Say / Apr. 26, 1966-May 9, 1966 / Original Jazz Classics ◆◆◆◆◆
A classic set recorded for Milestone and reissued in the OJC series, this date is coled by Thad Jones (heard throughout on fluegelhorn) and baritonist Pepper Adams; pianist Duke Pearson, bassist Ron Carter and drummer Mel Lewis complete the band. The high-quality hard bop unit performs four of Jones' originals, a song apiece by Carter and Pearson, and Burt Bacharach's "Wives and Lovers" and "Yes Sir, That's My Baby." Jones and Adams always made for a potent team, but the rise of the Thad Jones/Mel Lewis Orchestra meant that this particular quintet only lasted a short time. —*Scott Yanow*

☆ **The Complete Solid State Recordings of the Thad Jones/Mel Lewis Orchestra** / May 4, 1966-May 25, 1970 / Mosaic ◆◆◆◆◆
The Thad Jones/Mel Lewis big band was one of the finest jazz orchestras of the late '60s but its Solid State LPs had been long out-of-print for decades before Mosaic wisely reissued all of the music (plus seven previously unissued performances) on this deluxe but limited-edition, five-CD set. With Jones' colorful and distinctive arrangements, such soloists as trumpeters Danny Stiles, Marvin Stamm and Richard Williams; trombonists Bob Brookmeyer and Jimmy Knepper; the reeds of Jerome Richardson, Jerry Dodgion, Joe Farrell, Billy Harper, Eddie Daniels and Pepper Adams; and pianists Hank Jones and Roland Hanna; plus a rhythm section driven by bassist Richard Davis and drummer Mel Lewis, this was a classic band. Highlights among the 42 performances include "Mean What You Say," "Don't Git Sassy," "Tiptoe," "Fingers," "Central Park North" and the original version of "A Child Is Born," but nearly every selection is memorable. —*Scott Yanow*

Presenting Thad Jones: Mel Lewis and the Jazz Orchestra / May 11, 1966 / Solid State ◆◆◆◆
The debut recording of the Thad Jones/Mel Lewis Orchestra, which has been reissued on CD as part of Mosaic's large Thad Jones box, launched a mighty (if part-time) all-star big band. With arrangements by Jones, Bob Brookmeyer and Tom McIntosh and such soloists as baritonist Pepper Adams, pianist Hank Jones, valve trombonist Brookmeyer, Jerome Richardson on various reeds, altoist Jerry Dodgion, and Joe Farrell and Eddie Daniels on tenors (in addition to fluegelhornist Jones), it is not surprising that the orchestra was soon rated near the top. Among the seven selections are four Thad Jones originals (including "Mean What You Say"), "Willow Weep for Me," and Brookmeyer's lengthy "ABC Blues." —*Scott Yanow*

Live at the Village Vanguard / Jun. 1, 1967 / Solid State ◆◆◆◆
The second recording by the Thad Jones/Mel Lewis Jazz Orchestra is the equal of the first. Most memorable are "Little Pixie," Fats Waller's "Willow Tree" and particularly the spirited "Don't Git Sassy." With arrangements by Thad Jones, Bob Brookmeyer and Garnett Brown and an all-star cast that includes trumpeters Snooky Young, Marvin Stamm and Richard Williams; valve trombonist Bob Brookmeyer; the reeds of Jerome Richardson, Jerry Dodgion, Joe Farrell, Eddie Daniels and Pepper Adams (all of whom solo); pianist Roland Hanna; and bassist Richard Davis, among others, this was one of the great big bands. Fortunately, the exciting music on this out-of-print LP has been reissued on CD as part of a very complete Mosaic box set. —*Scott Yanow*

Monday Night / Oct. 17, 1968 / Solid State ◆◆◆
The Thad Jones/Mel Lewis Orchestra was one of the most significant big bands of the late '60s, a most unpromising era for larger jazz orchestras. This live session from the band's regular Monday night gig at the Village Vanguard has strong solos from altoist Jerry Dodgion, Eddie Daniels and Seldon Powell on tenors, trombonist Jimmy Knepper, a bit of plunger trumpet from Jimmy Nottingham, pianist Roland Hanna and trumpeter Richard Williams, in addition to Thad Jones

himself. Most impressive is Bob Brookmeyer's adventurous arrangement of "St. Louis Blues." The contents of this out-of-print LP have been included in the Mosaic box set *The Complete Solid State Thad Jones/Mel Lewis*. —*Scott Yanow*

Basle, 1969 / 1969 / TOB ◆◆◆◆
This live concert, broadcast over Swiss radio and released for the first time on this 1995 CD, features the Thad Jones/Mel Lewis Orchestra at its prime. The remarkable all-star group includes two first trumpeters (Snooky Young and Al Porcino) and such soloists as trumpeters Richard Williams, Danny Moore and Thad Jones; trombonist Jimmy Knepper, Jerome Richardson on soprano, Jerry Dodgion on flute and alto; baritonist Pepper Adam; pianist Roland Hanna; bassist Richard Davis; and tenor great Joe Henderson, whose short stint with the band was long enough to include this European tour. Highlights of the superior set include "Second Race," "The Waltz You Swang for Me," "Don't Get Sassy" and "Groove Merchant." Highly recommended to fans of the band, this Swiss CD can be found with a bit of a search. —*Scott Yanow*

Central Park North / Jun. 17, 1969-Jun. 18, 1969 / Solid State ◆◆◆◆◆
This out-of-print LP (whose music has been reissued in a definitive Mosaic box set) has several classic arrangements, particularly Thad Jones' "Central Park North," the swinging "Big Dipper" and the catchy "Groove Merchant." Soloists include Jerome Richardson on soprano, flute and alto; trumpeters Jimmy Nottingham, Richard Williams, Danny Moore and Jones; pianist Roland Hanna; and tenors Joe Farrell and Eddie Daniels. It's a fine example of the exciting music of one of the top big bands of the late '60s. —*Scott Yanow*

Consummation / Jan. 20, 1970-May 25, 1970 / Blue Note ◆◆◆◆◆
Of the many albums recorded by the Thad Jones/Mel Lewis Orchestra, this was the greatest. Reissued on CD as part of a large Mosaic box set, this set introduced Jones' best-known composition, "A Child Is Born," also has a colorful rendition of his sly "Tiptoe," and finds the big band ripping the roof off during the lengthy and very exciting "Fingers." The all-star cast (which includes fluegelhornist Jones, drummer Lewis, trumpeter Marvin Stamm, trombonist Jimmy Knepper, tenor great Billy Harper, the reeds of Jerome Richardson, Jerry Dodgion and Eddie Daniels, keyboardist Roland Hanna, and bassist Richard Davis, among others) is well served by Thad Jones' inventive and swinging arrangements. A classic. —*Scott Yanow*

Suite for Pops / Jan. 25, 1972-Sep. 1, 1972 / Horizon ◆◆
Despite the sincerity involved, this tribute to Louis Armstrong really does not come off. Thad Jones, in his compositions and arrangements, never quotes or borrows (either directly or abstractly) from Louis Armstrong's music, making this homage little more than namedropping. None of the seven originals or performances are by themselves memorable, despite the all-star nature of the band. There are many much more worthy recordings by the Thad Jones/Mel Lewis Orchestra than this later effort. —*Scott Yanow*

Potpourri / Jun. 1974 / Philadelphia International ◆◆◆
One of the weaker Thad Jones/Mel Lewis big-band sets, this LP finds the impressive orchestra stuck performing a couple of inappropriate Stevie Wonder tunes ("Don't You Worry 'Bout a Thing" and "Living for the City") and the pop song "For the Love of Money," in addition to more suitable material by Marian McPartland ("Ambiance") and four worthwhile originals by Jones. With such notable sidemen as trumpeter Cecil Bridgewater, Ron Bridgewater and Billy Harper on tenors; trombonist Quentin Jackson; baritonist Pepper Adams; keyboardist Roland Hanna; bassist George Mraz; and lead trumpeter Jon Faddis, the music certainly has its moments of interest. But there are a quite few more satisfying recordings by the Thad Jones/Mel Lewis Orchestra than this merely decent LP. —*Scott Yanow*

New Life: Dedicated to Max Gordon / Dec. 16, 1975-Dec. 17, 1975 / A&M ◆◆◆
This LP has extensive packaging (thanks to producer John Snyder) and decent but not overly memorable music. The Thad Jones/Mel Lewis Orchestra's best recordings were for Solid State and Blue Note, although they still boasted an impressive all-star personnel during the mid-1970s. The seven selections (five arranged and composed by Jones and one apiece by Jerry Dodgion and Cecil Bridgewater) do not include any future standards. There are fine solos from the likes of fluegelhornist Jones, Greg Herbert and Frank Foster on tenor, Roland Hanna and Walter Norris on piano, trumpeters Cecil Bridgewater and Waymon Reed, baritonist Pepper Adams, and others, so the music is not without its interesting moments. But in general, the solos and arrangements are more memorable than the melodies. This LP has not yet been reissued on CD. —*Scott Yanow*

Live in Munich / Sep. 9, 1976 / A&M/Horizon ◆◆◆
The last major release by the Thad Jones/Mel Lewis Orchestra before Jones moved to Europe was their strongest in several years. The orchestra was in a state of transition, evolving from an all-star band filled with veterans to a group filled with advanced and hungry young improvisers. Most memorable of the five selec-

tions are "Mornin' Reverend," Jones' fluegelhorn showcase on "Come Sunday," and a definitive 16-minute version of his "Central Park North." Heard on this LP (not yet reissued on CD) are such soloists as pianist Harold Danko, Gregory Herbert on tenor, and Jerry Dodgion on soprano, but it is the sound of the ensemble and the colorful Jones arrangements that make this an album well worth searching for. —*Scott Yanow*

Thad Jones with Mel Lewis, Manuel Desica and the Jazz Orchestra / Dec. 1976 / Pausa ✦✦✦

This is an unusual recording, for it features the Thad Jones/Mel Lewis Orchestra performing Manuel De Sica's five-part "First Jazz Suite." The distinctive sound of the ensemble is intact; baritonist Pepper Adams has a notable solo; Dee Dee Bridgewater takes a vocal, and the big band was still an all-star orchestra at the time. But overall, this obscure set (not yet reissued on CD), which is rounded off by a later live-in-Italy version of Thad Jones' "Little Pixie," is a lesser effort, worthwhile but not essential. —*Scott Yanow*

★ Thad Jones and the Mel Lewis Quartet / Sep. 24, 1977 / A&M ✦✦✦✦✦

This is one of the finest small-group sessions of cornetist Thad Jones' career. With strong and very alert assistance from drummer Mel Lewis (his co-leader in their celebrated big band), pianist Harold Danko and bassist Rufus Reid, Jones plays at his peak on six standards, two of which were issued for the initial time on this CD reissue. Four of the songs are at least nine minutes long (two are over 15 minutes) yet Thad never loses his momentum. The musicians constantly surprise each other and there are many spontaneous moments during this often-brilliant outing. —*Scott Yanow*

Live at Montmartre, Copenhagen / Mar. 21, 1978-Mar. 22, 1978 / Storyville ✦✦✦

Cornetist Thad Jones (pictured on the cover playing valve trombone) does not actually perform on this CD, and he is heard leading the Danish Radio Big Band rather than the orchestra he had co-led with Mel Lewis, but this is a highly recommended set. The 20-piece big band is superb, and they do an expert job of playing such Jones charts as his classic "Tip Toe" (which is given an interpretation as strong as the Jones/Lewis earlier version), "Kids Are Pretty People," "Old Folks" and "A Good Time Was Had By All." Not all of the lead voices are identified, unfortunately, but such top players as Jesper Thilo (heard on alto rather than his usual tenor); Bent Jaedig on tenor; trumpeters Idrees Sulieman and Allan Botschinsky; and trombonist Richard Boone (who takes a typically eccentric vocal on "I Got Rhythm") are among the many soloists. Although a little-known set, this CD is highly recommended. —*Scott Yanow*

Eclipse / Sep. 17, 1979-Sep. 18, 1979 / Metronome ✦✦✦

After moving to Europe in the late 1970s, Thad Jones worked with the Danish Radio Orchestra. In 1979, he formed a European big band in Copenhagen that he called Eclipse. Jones, who was having health problems, is only heard on "Everessence" (where he plays valve trombone), but four of the eight compositions on this set are his, and he also arranged "I Can't Give You Anything But Love." Among the key soloists on the album are several Americans—pianist Horace Parlan, baritonist Sahib Shihab, trumpeter Tim Hagans and trombonist/vocalist Richard Boone—along with trombonist Bjarne Thanning, trumpeter Egon Petersen, altoist Ole Nielsen, Bent Jaedig on tenor, and bassist Jesper Lundgaard (featured on "This Bass Was Made for Walking"). A fine if little-known effort from late in Thad Jones' life. —*Scott Yanow*

Three and One / Oct. 4, 1984 / Steeple Chase ✦✦✦

Thad Jones was 61 at the time of this recording and had made a full-fledged recovery after some health problems, although he was only two years away from his death. He is showcased on cornet throughout the quartet date with pianist Ole Hansen, bassist Jesper Lundgaard and drummer Ed Thigpen, and is heard in very good form. Jones plays two of his originals, Ahmad Jamal's "Night Mist Blues," "My Romance," "My One and Only Love" and "But Not for Me." This date is reminiscent in ways of Jones' Debut session from 29 years earlier, which also found him taking harmonically sophisticated solos in a quartet. Recommended. —*Scott Yanow*

Greetings and Salutations / June 27, 1975-Jan. 29, 1977 / Passport ✦✦✦

In 1975 and 1977, cornetist/arranger Thad Jones and drummer Mel Lewis traveled to Sweden and recorded with the Swedish Radio Jazz Group. The first five selections on this eight-tune CD (which are from 1975) also include the Jones/Lewis Orchestra's first trumpeter, Jon Faddis, who takes one solo and helps out the ensembles. Otherwise, the musicians are mostly obscure (although trumpeter Al Porcino is on the second date and guitarist Rune Gustafsson and altoist Arne Domnerus have achieved some fame) and mostly not overly distinctive. The real stars of the CD are Jones' arrangements, his compositions (six of the eight numbers, including "The Waltz You Swang for Me," a 13-minute version of "Greetings and Salutations," and "My Centennial"), and the expertly played ensembles, which

sometimes fool one into thinking that this is the Thad Jones/Mel Lewis Orchestra. —*Scott Yanow*

Scott Joplin

b. Nov. 24, 1868, Bowie City, TX, **d.** Apr. 1, 1917, New York, NY
Composer, Piano / Ragtime

Ragtime was jazz's direct predecessor (differing from jazz in the absence of blues and improvisation) and Scott Joplin was ragtime's greatest composer. Joplin lived in St. Louis during 1885-93, playing in local bars and clubs. In 1894 he led a band at the Chicago World's Fair and formed the Texas Medley Quartet, which played in vaudeville shows. Relocating to Sedalia, MO, Joplin began having pieces published as early as 1895 and in 1899 his "Maple Leaf Rag" (published by his supporter John Stark) became ragtime's most popular number, selling over 75,000 copies of sheet music during its first year. Joplin soon had many other rags published that helped to make ragtime the pop music of its day, but the tragedy of his life was that his goals were beyond ragtime. He staged a ballet (*The Ragtime Dance*) and two ragtime operas (*The Guest of Honor* and *Treemonisha*) but none were successful, a fact that continually frustrated him. By 1910 Joplin was becoming ill with syphilis and at his death in 1917, ragtime was in the process of being replaced by jazz. Ironically, 57 years after his death, Scott Joplin finally became a household name because his music (most notably "The Entertainer") was used by Marvin Hamlisch in his score for the popular film *The Sting*. Although he never recorded, Scott Joplin's music has been fully documented with "Maple Leaf Rag" becoming a Dixieland jazz standard and pianist Richard Zimmerman (on an excellent five-LP set for Murray Hill) recording everything that Joplin ever wrote. —*Scott Yanow*

● Piano Rags by Scott Joplin / 1970 / Nonesuch ✦✦✦✦✦

A few years before the release of the movie "The Sting" launched a major revival of ragtime, Joshua Rifkin caused a stir with what would be the first of three albums of Scott Joplin piano solos. Although later criticized by some for playing the rags quite straight in a classical approach, Rifkin's straightforward renditions of eight Joplin rags (including "Maple Leaf Rag," "The Entertainer," "The Ragtime Dance" and "Euphonic Sounds") helped introduce these important pieces to a new generation of listeners. All three of his Nonesuch albums are worth picking up as perfect introductions to Scott Joplin's music. —*Scott Yanow*

16 Classic Rags / Oct. 17, 1990 / RCA ✦✦✦✦

Dick Hyman explores some of Scott Joplin's finest rags on this solo piano album. By picking some slower tempos and putting lots of emotion into most of the themes, Hyman's interpretations often have a personality of their own. In addition to "Maple Leaf Rag," "The Easy Winners" "Euphonic Sounds" and "The Ragtime Dance," Hyman plays fairly lengthy versions of "Weeping Willow," "Magnetic Rag" (over five minutes long) and "Lily Queen" without changing a note. —*Scott Yanow*

Clifford Jordan

b. Sep. 2, 1931, Chicago, IL, **d.** Mar. 27, 1993, New York, NY
Tenor Saxophone / Post-Bop, Hard Bop

Clifford Jordan was a fine inside/outside player who somehow held his own with Eric Dolphy in the 1964 Charles Mingus Sextet. Jordan had his own sound on tenor almost from the start. He gigged around Chicago with Max Roach, Sonny Stitt and some R&B groups before moving to New York in 1957. Jordan immediately made a strong impression, leading three albums for Blue Note (including a meeting with fellow tenor John Gilmore) and touring with Horace Silver (1957-58), J.J. Johnson (1959-60), Kenny Dorham (1961-62) and Max Roach (1962-64). After performing in Europe with Mingus and Dolphy, Jordan worked mostly as a leader but tended to be overlooked since he was not overly influential or a pacesetter in the avant-garde. A reliable player, Clifford Jordan toured Europe several times, was in a quartet headed by Cedar Walton in 1974-75 and during his last years led a big band. He recorded as a leader for Blue Note, Riverside, Jazzland, Atlantic (a little-known album of Leadbelly tunes), Vortex, Strata East, Muse, Steeple Chase, Criss Cross, Bee Hive, DIW, Milestone and Mapleshade. —*Scott Yanow*

★ Blowing in from Chicago / Mar. 3, 1957 / Blue Note ✦✦✦✦✦

Clifford Jordan's first date as a leader actually found him sharing a heated jam session with fellow tenor John Gilmore. Backed by pianist Horace Silver, bassist Curly Russell and drummer Art Blakey, the two saxophonists square off mostly on obscurities (other than Gigi Gryce's "Blue Lights" and "Billie's Bounce"); the original six selections are joined by the previously unreleased "Let It Stand" on the CD reissue. This was one of Gilmore's few sessions outside of Sun Ra's orbit, and if anything, he slightly overshadows the cooler-toned Jordan. Recommended. —*Scott Yanow*

Cliff Craft / Nov. 10, 1957 / Blue Note ✦✦✦✦

Happily, Blue Note Records and Michael Cuscuna have reissued this wonderfully relaxed recording, which dates from a very fertile period of the renowned jazz label's history. Tenor saxman Jordan was influenced by and shares influences with Sonny Rollins, Dexter Gordon, John Coltrane and Hank Mobley; the early inspiration of Lester Young can also be heard. On this date, the selection of tunes is pleasantly balanced between three originals, two bebop standards, and Ellington's "Sophisticated Lady." Trumpeter Art Farmer's playing is up to his usual high standard—thoughtful, sensitive and technically brilliant. Pianist Sonny Clark is captured during the most prolific phase of his ten-year recording career; together with bassist George Tucker and drummer Louis Hayes, they create a solid, swinging and simpatico rhythm section. —Lee Bloom

Spellbound / Aug. 10, 1960 / Original Jazz Classics ✦✦✦✦

Tenor saxophonist Clifford Jordan was sponsored by Cannonball Adderley on this set for Riverside, which has been reissued on CD in the OJC series. Jordan did not, at this point have quite the distinctive sound that he would develop by his period with Charles Mingus, but he was already a strong hard bop stylist. Assisted by pianist Cedar Walton, bassist Spanky DeBrest and drummer Albert "Tootie" Heath, Jordan performs four originals ("Toy" is best known), an unusual waltz version of "Lush Life," the ballad "Last Night When We Were Young" and the romping Charlie Parker blues "Au Privave." It's an excellent straightahead outing. —Scott Yanow

Starting Time / Jun. 14, 1961 / Original Jazz Classics ✦✦✦

Reissued in the Original Jazz Classics but thus far just as an LP, this fine set matches together the already distinctive tenor of Clifford Jordan with veteran trumpeter Kenny Dorham, pianist Cedar Walton, bassist Wilbur Ware and drummer Albert "Tootie" Heath. Other than Duke Ellington's "Don't You Know I Care," the group sticks to originals by Jordan, Dorham and Walton. The music is straightahead, and although the tunes are fairly obscure, the solos and high musicianship uplift the music. Recommended to straightahead jazz collectors. —Scott Yanow

Bearcat / Oct. 1961-1962 / Original Jazz Classics ✦✦✦✦

This CD is a straight reissue of the original Jazzland LP. Tenor saxophonist Clifford Jordan, who is joined by pianist Cedar Walton, bassist Teddy Smith and drummer J.C. Moses, is heard in his early prime and displays an original tone while playing in the hard bop style. He stretches out on five of his swinging and fairly advanced originals, "How Deep Is the Ocean," and Tom McIntosh's "Malice Towards None." It would be 1973 before Jordan had another opportunity to be showcased in a quartet format, making this formerly rare set one of his best all-around recordings. —Scott Yanow

These Are My Roots / Feb. 1, 1965-Feb. 17, 1965 / Atlantic ✦✦✦✦

An intriguing concept: Jordan arranging and doing Leadbelly songs. —Ron Wynn

Half Note / Apr. 1974 / Steeple Chase ✦✦✦✦

Tenor saxophonist Clifford Jordan was long an underrated player with a sound of his own and a style that hinted at the avant-garde while being well grounded in hard bop. On this live set (recorded at New York's Half Note), Jordan explores high-quality material (including "Holy Land," "St. Thomas," "Rhythm-a-Ning" and his "The Highest Mountain") with pianist Cedar Walton, bassist Sam Jones and drummer Albert "Tootie" Heath. An excellent example of Jordan's music. —Scott Yanow

The Highest Mountain / Apr. 18, 1975 / Muse ✦✦✦✦

Tenor saxophonist Clifford Jordan teams up with pianist Cedar Walton, bassist Sam Jones and drummer Billy Higgins for this excellent modern hard bop set which has been reissued on CD by Muse. Of the five compositions (which include an original apiece by Jordan, Walton, Jones and Bill Lee), only Thelonious Monk's "Blue Monk" and Jordan's title cut had much life beyond this set but the music is consistently memorable, including Walton's "Midnight Waltz." All of the musicians play up-to-par and Clifford Jordan (who was continually underrated throughout his life) is immediately recognizable as usual. —Scott Yanow

On Stage, Vol. 1 / Mar. 1975 / Steeple Chase ✦✦✦

The first of three CDs featuring tenorman Clifford Jordan and his "Magic Triangle" (pianist Cedar Walton, bassist Sam Jones and drummer Billy Higgins) has fairly lengthy versions of "Pinocchio," "That Old Devil Moon," Walton's "The Maestro," and Jordan's "The Highest Mountain." Recorded live in Amsterdam, the musicians sound inspired by each other's presence, and there are many strong solos from Jordan and Walton. Well worth investigating. —Scott Yanow

Firm Roots / Apr. 18, 1975 / Steeple Chase ✦✦✦✦

One of Jordan's best releases with The Magic Triangle ensemble of Cedar Walton (p), Sam Jones (b), and Billy Higgins (d). —Ron Wynn

Inward Fire / Apr. 5, 1977 / Muse ✦✦✦✦

The Adventurer / Feb. 9, 1978 / Muse ✦✦✦✦

Steady, with consistently interesting and gripping solos. —Ron Wynn

Repetition / Feb. 9, 1984 / Soul Note ✦✦✦✦

Strong leads and good compositions. —Ron Wynn

Dr. Chicago / Aug. 3, 1984 / Bee Hive ✦✦✦✦

This excellent Bee Hive LP features tenor saxophonist Clifford Jordan on three quartet numbers with pianist Jaki Byard, bassist Ed Howard and drummer Vernel Fournier, welcoming trumpeter Red Rodney to two other selections and taking "If I Had You" as a duet with the very versatile Byard. The repertoire is colorful and diverse (three jazz standards, an obscurity, Jordan's bluesy title cut and Fournier's intriguing "Zombie"), and the very consistent Jordan is up to his usual high level. —Scott Yanow

Two Tenor Winner! / Oct. 1984 / Criss Cross ✦✦✦✦✦

Royal Ballads / Dec. 23, 1986 / Criss Cross ✦✦✦✦✦

Brilliant interpretations. —Ron Wynn

Live at Ethell's / Oct. 16, 1987-Oct. 18, 1987 / Mapleshade ✦✦✦✦✦

Tenor saxophonist Clifford Jordan never seemed to record an uninspired record. This Mapleshade CD, cut live at a Baltimore club, matches Jordan with pianist Kevin O'Connell, bassist Ed Howard and drummer Vernel Fournier. In addition to four standards (including "Lush Life" and "'Round Midnight"), Jordan performs Stanley Cowell's "Cal Massey" and three of his own straightahead but diverse originals. Excellent advanced straightahead music from an underrated great. —Scott Yanow

Four Play / 1990 / DIW ✦✦✦✦

Although this CD is technically listed under all four musicians' names (tenor saxophonist Clifford Jordan, pianist James Williams, bassist Richard Davis and drummer Ronnie Burrage), Jordan (who contributed two of the four originals) is primarily the lead voice. His sound was always instantly recognizable and he seemed to be in a good mood for the date, judging by the many song quotes he throws into his solos (espacially on "Hi Fly"). Wiliams sounds at his best on his original jazz waltz "For My Nephews," a tune that also features Davis' bowed bass. Overall, this Japanese CD (which was made available for a time domestically through Columbia) is a good example of the hard bop mainstream of the early 1990s as played by some of its best practioners. —Scott Yanow

Play What You Feel / Dec. 1990 / Mapleshade ✦✦✦✦

Live at Condon's, New York/Down Through the Years / Oct. 7, 1991 / Milestone ✦✦✦✦

With an extraordinary big band. —Michael G. Nastos

Duke Jordan (Irving Sidney Jordan)

b. Apr. 1, 1922, New York, NY

Piano / Bop, Hard Bop

Although he has had a long career, Duke Jordan will always be best-known for being pianist with Charlie Parker's classic 1947 quintet. A little earlier he had worked with the Savoy Sultans, Coleman Hawkins and the Roy Eldridge big band (1946). After his year with Parker (his piano introductions to such songs as "Embraceable You" were classic), Jordan worked with the Sonny Stitt-Gene Ammons quintet (1950-51) and Stan Getz (1949 and 1952-53). He started recording as a leader in 1954, debuting his most famous composition "Jor-du" the following year. Although he worked steadily through the next few decades (writing part of the soundtrack for the French film *Les Liaisons Dangereuses*), Jordan was in obscurity until he began recording on a regular basis for Steeple Chase in 1973. Duke Jordan, who was married for a time to the talented jazz singer Sheila Jordan, has lived in Denmark since 1978 and has recorded through the years for Prestige, Savoy, Blue Note, Charlie Parker Records, Muse, Spotlite and Steeple Chase. Still possessing an unchanged bop style, Jordan remains active in the mid-'90s. —Scott Yanow

Jordu / Jul. 2, 1949+Jan. 28, 1954 / Prestige ✦✦✦✦

The music on this LP has not yet been reissued on CD in the US. The first two titles ("Spider's Webb" and "Strike Up the Band") feature bebop pianist Duke Jordan as a sideman in a quartet with bassist Tubby Phillips and drummer Roy Hall, and led by the talented tenor saxophonist Don Lanphere. The remaining eight selections are from Jordan's debut as a leader, originally cut for the French Vogue label, a 1954 trio set with bassist Gene Ramey and drummer Lee Abrams. The pianist's style changed very little through the years, and virtually all of his recordings are worth picking up for bop fans. This album is perhaps most notable for the inclusion of the initial version of Jordan's most famous original, "Jordu." —Scott Yanow

★ **Flight to Jordan** / Aug. 4, 1960 / Blue Note ✦✦✦✦✦

Duke Jordan, who played regularly with the Charlie Parker Quintet in 1947, has long been known as a superior bebop pianist whose style was touched by the genius of Bud Powell's innovations. This quintet album (which also features trumpeter Dizzy Reece and the young tenor Stanley Turrentine) gave Jordan an opportunity to record six of his originals and, although none became as well-known as his "Jordu," the music has plenty of strong melodies and variety. This is one of Duke Jordan's better recordings and is quite enjoyable. —*Scott Yanow*

East and West of Jazz / Feb. 22, 1962 / Charlie Parker ✦✦

This LP from the long-defunct Charlie Parker label features two unrelated sessions cut on the same day. Pianist Duke Jordan teams up in a quintet with trumpeter Johnny Coles, baritonist Cecil Payne, bassist Wendell Marshall and drummer Walter Bolden for Parker's "Dexterity," a couple of real obscurities, and originals by Payne and Jordan; the latter's "Tall Grass" shows the influence of folk music. The other set showcases pianist Sadik Hakim on five of his compositions (two of which were greatly influenced by his interest in the music of the Near East) in a quartet with guitarist Eddie Wright, bassist Lloyd Buchanan and drummer Kalil Madi. An interesting (if not all that significant) release that promises to be difficult to find. —*Scott Yanow*

Brooklyn Brothers / Mar. 16, 1973 / Muse ✦✦✦✦

A nice session with fellow reed player Cecil Payne. —*Ron Wynn*

The Murray Hill Caper / Apr. 7, 1973-Apr. 23, 1973 / Spotlite ✦✦✦

Pianist Duke Jordan is featured in two different settings on this early Spotlite LP. Unfortunately, the recording quality is not quite state-of-the-art for the period, but the results are certainly listenable. Jordan teams up with baritonist Cecil Payne, bassist David Williams and drummer Al Foster for five of his originals ("Flight to Jordan" is easily the best-known), plus "Night and Day." The second half of the album features Jordan with bassist Lloyd Buchanon and drummer Brian Brake on three of his more obscure but enjoyable originals. This set of fresh bop, although not one of Duke Jordan's most significant releases, is worthwhile. —*Scott Yanow*

Flight to Denmark / Nov. 25, 1973+Dec. 2, 1973 / Steeple Chase ✦✦✦✦✦

Pianist Duke Jordan has recorded a long series of sessions for the Danish Steeple Chase label starting with this 1973 set which has been reissued on CD with four additional selections (three of which are alternate takes). Performing in a trio with bassist Mads Vinding and drummer Ed Thigpen, Jordan plays five of his originals (including "No Problem," "Flight to Denmark" and "Jordu") plus four standards. The pianist's style is easily recognizable (it had not changed much nor lost its enthusiasm since 1947 when he achieved fame playing with Charlie Parker) and this CD is a good example of his talents. —*Scott Yanow*

Two Loves / Nov. 25, 1973+Dec. 12, 1973 / Steeple Chase ✦✦✦✦

Lover Man / Aug. 1975 / Steeple Chase ✦✦✦

Jordan shows his blues side. —*Ron Wynn*

Duke's Delight / Nov. 18, 1975 / Steeple Chase ✦✦✦✦✦

Starting in 1973, pianist Duke Jordan recorded a long series of excellent sets for the European Steeple Chase label; all should be of interest to bop collectors. This CD reissue, which adds an alternate take of the title cut to the original LP program, has five quintet numbers—all Jordan originals—with trumpeter Richard Williams (in excellent form), tenor saxophonist Charlie Rouse, bassist Sam Jones and drummer Al Foster, plus a solo piano rendition of "Solitude." The date lives up to its potential. —*Scott Yanow*

Osaka Concert, Vol. 1 / Sep. 20, 1976 / Steeple Chase ✦✦✦✦

Osaka Concert, Vol. 2 / Sep. 20, 1976 / Steeple Chase ✦✦✦✦

Duke's Artistry / Jun. 30, 1978 / Steeple Chase ✦✦✦✦

Masterful solos. —*Ron Wynn*

The Great Session / Jun. 30, 1978 / Steeple Chase ✦✦✦

Thinking of You / Jul. 11, 1978+Oct. 29, 1979 / Steeple Chase ✦✦✦✦✦

The Duke Jordan set (pianist Jordan, bassist Niels-Henning Orstead Pedersen, drummer Billy Hart) swings nicely in an underplayed fashion. "Foxie Cakes" was taken solo and was interesting for its mix of piano techniques like Thelonious Monk; one begun to hear a more pronounced stride element in his playing. —*Bob Rusch, Cadence*

Wait and See / Nov. 16, 1978+Nov. 17, 1978 / Steeple Chase ✦✦✦✦

Recorded at the same Copenhagen session that resulted in "Tivoli One" and "Tivoli Two," this trio set—reissued on CD with two additional selections—features pianist Duke Jordan, bassist Wilbur Little and drummer Dannie Richmond on seven Jordan originals (including his famous "Jordu"), "Misty" and "Out of Nowhere." Another excellent bop-oriented Duke Jordan session, one of many for Steeple Chase. —*Scott Yanow*

Change a Pace / Oct. 29, 1979 / Steeple Chase ✦✦✦

Duke Jordan, famous as Charlie Parker's pianist in 1947 and long a possessor of a classic bop piano style, fully emerged as a talented composer during his long period with Steeple Chase. On this trio set with bassist Niels Pedersen and drummer Billy Hart, he introduces six new compositions, several of which are worth exploring by other musicians looking for fresh material. Although some of the structures are a bit advanced, Jordan's timeless style is heard throughout in recognizable and prime form. —*Scott Yanow*

Midnight Moonlight / 1979 / Steeple Chase ✦✦✦

Duke in the spotlight. —*Ron Wynn*

Blue Duke / Jun. 8, 1983-Jun. 9, 1983 / RCA ✦✦✦✦

Originally cut for the Japanese Baystate label and then later released by French RCA, this trio set by pianist Duke Jordan (with bassist Harry Memmery and drummer James Martin in Holland) differs from his usual recordings in putting an emphasis on blues, although not exclusively. Jordan performs six of his originals (including "No Problem," "Ben Sugar Blues," "Jordu" and "From Duke to Duke") plus "All the Things You Are," "C Jam Blues" and "St. Louis Blues." The classic bebop pianist's consistency holds up on this set (cut when he was 61), making the obscure LP worth searching for. —*Scott Yanow*

Tivoli One / Nov. 16-Nov. 17, 1978 / Steeple Chase ✦✦✦✦✦

This is a fine all-around trio date for veteran pianist Duke Jordan. Possessor of a rather pure bop style, Jordan (accompanied by bassist Wilbur Little and drummer Dannie Richmond) is in fine form on four of his originals (including a brief rendition of his famous "Jordu" which he uses as a closing theme) and three familiar standards. Bop fans should enjoy this one, along with virtually all of Jordan's Steeple Chase recordings. —*Scott Yanow*

Tivoli Two / Nov. 16-Nov. 17, 1978 / Steeple Chase ✦✦✦✦✦

The second of two recordings, this set also finds the classic bop pianist Duke Jordan being joined by bassist Wilbur Little and drummer Dannie Richmond, live from the Tivoli Gardens in Copenhagen. This time around, Jordan interprets three originals (a lengthy "No Problem," a blues and "Jordu," which functions functions as a closing theme) along with three standards. Jordan is heard at the top of his game during these swinging and probing performances. —*Scott Yanow*

As Time Goes By / Jul. 1985 / Steeple Chase ✦✦✦✦

One for the Library / Oct. 9, 1993 / Storyville ✦✦✦

Duke Jordan has long been one of the top bebop pianists, although living in Europe for many years has resulted in his often being overlooked. On this CD, he performs 18 unaccompanied solos, all but one of which are under four minutes long. Jordan plays six originals and a dozen veteran standards (such as "All The Things You Are," "The Way You Look Tonight," "It's Only a Paper Moon" and "Three Little Words") quite well. The pianist strides and lays down basslines in spots; however, his strength has always been his single-note right-hand lines, and he actually sounds at his best in a trio format. —*Scott Yanow*

Kent Jordan

b. Oct. 28, 1958, New Orleans, LA

Flute / Hard Bop, Crossover Jazz

The son of saxophonist Kidd Jordan and the older brother of trumpeter Marlon Jordan, Kent Jordan's early venture into commercialism on his first two Columbia albums almost ruined his reputation in the jazz world before he had a chance to mature. He had studied at the Eastman School of Music and New Orleans' Center for the Creative Arts, being inspired at the latter by Ellis Marsalis (with whom he recorded). Jordan played and recorded with the groups Jasmine and the Improvisational Arts Quartet before cutting his two Columbia albums (1984 and 1986). His third Columbia album (1988's *Essence*) is much stronger from a jazz standpoint and since that time Jordan has toured with Elvin Jones and shown the jazz world that he can indeed play creative music. —*Scott Yanow*

No Question About It / 1984 / Columbia ✦✦

● **Essence** / 1988 / Columbia ✦✦✦✦

Flutist Kent Jordan's third Columbia set is far superior to his first two rather commercial efforts (*No Question About It* and *Night Aire*). Jordan is well featured on four standards (including "Well You Needn't," which finds him switching effectively to piccolo, and "Moment's Notice"), two tunes by bassist Elton Heron, and Wayne Shorter's "Rio" in a variety of instrumental settings. With such sidemen as pianists Kenny Barron and Billy Childs, guitarist Kevin Eubanks, bassists Dave Holland and Ron Carter, drummers Jack DeJohnette and Al Foster and (on the opening "Curtain Call") trumpeter/brother Marlon Jordan and tenor saxophonist Branford Marsalis, among others, Jordan interacts with an all-star cast. Most of the music is fairly straightahead, and throughout the flutist realizes some of the potential that was wasted on his first two recordings. —*Scott Yanow*

Louis Jordan

b. Jul. 8, 1908, Brinkley, AR, **d.** Feb. 4, 1975, Los Angeles, CA

Alto Saxophone , Vocals, Leader / Swing, Early R&B Jazz, Jump Blues, Urban Blues, East Coast Blues

Effervescent saxophonist Louis Jordan was one of the chief architects and prime progenitors of the R&B idiom. His pioneering use of jumping shuffle rhythms in a small combo context was copied far and wide during the 1940s.

Jordan's sensational hit-laden run with Decca Records contained a raft of seminal performances, featuring inevitably infectious backing by his band, the Tympany Five, and Jordan's own searing alto sax and street corner jive-loaded sense of humor. Jordan was one of the first Black entertainers to sell appreciably in the pop sector; his Decca duet mates included Bing Crosby, Louis Armstrong, and Ella Fitzgerald.

The son of a musician, Jordan spent time as a youth with the Rabbit Foot Minstrels and majored in music later on at Arkansas Baptist College. After moving with his family to Philadelphia in 1932, Jordan hooked up with pianist Clarence Williams. He joined the orchestra of drummer Chick Webb in 1936 and remained there until 1938. Having polished up his singing abilities with Webb's outfit, Jordan was ready to strike out on his own.

The saxist's first 78 for Decca in 1938, "Honey in the Bee Ball," billed his combo as the Elks Rendezvous Band (after the Harlem nightspot that he frequently played at). From 1939 on, though, Jordan fronted the Tympany Five, a sturdy little aggregation often expanding over quintet status that featured some well-known musicians over the years: pianists Wild Bill Davis and Bill Doggett, guitarists Carl Hogan and Bill Jennings, bassist Dallas Bartley, and drummer Chris Columbus all passed through the ranks.

From 1942 to 1951, Jordan scored an astonishing 57 R&B chart hits (all on Decca), beginning with the humorous blues "I'm Gonna Leave You on the Outskirts of Town" and finishing with "Weak Minded Blues." In between, he drew up what amounted to an easily followed blueprint for the development of R&B (and for that matter, rock 'n' roll—the accessibly swinging shuffles of Bill Haley & the Comets were directly descended from Jordan; Haley often pointing to his Decca labelmate as profoundly influencing his approach).

"G.I. Jive," "Caldonia," "Buzz Me," "Choo Choo Ch' Boogie," "Ain't That Just like a Woman," "Ain't Nobody Here But Us Chickens," "Boogie Woogie Blue Plate," "Beans and Cornbread," "Saturday Night Fish Fry," and "Blue Light Boogie"—every one of those classics topped the R&B lists, and there were plenty more that did precisely the same thing. Black audiences coast-to-coast were breathlessly jitterbugging to Jordan's jumping jive (and one suspects, more than a few Whites kicked up their heels to those same platters as well).

The saxist was particularly popular during World War II. He recorded prolifically for the Armed Forces Radio Service and the V-Disc program. Jordan's massive popularity also translated onto the silver screen—he filmed a series of wonderful short musicals during the late '40s that were decidedly short on plot but long on visual versions of his hits (*Caldonia, Reet Petite & Gone, Look Out Sister,* and *Beware,* along with countless soundies) that give us an enlightening peek at just what made him such a beloved entertainer. Jordan also cameoed in a big-budget Hollywood wartime musical, *Follow the Boys.*

A brief attempt at fronting a big band in 1951 proved an ill-fated venture, but it didn't dim his ebullience. In 1952, tongue firmly planted in cheek, he offered himself as a candidate for the highest office in the land on the amusing Decca outing "Jordan for President."

Even though his singles were still eminently solid, they weren't selling like they used to by 1954. So after an incredible run of more than a decade-and-a-half, Jordan moved over to the Mesner brothers' Los Angeles-based Aladdin logo at the start of the year. Alas, time had passed the great pioneer by—"Dad Gum Ya Hide Boy," "Messy Bessy," "If I Had Any Sense," and the rest of his Aladdin output sounds great in retrospect, but it wasn't what young R&B fans were searching for at the time. In 1955, he switched to RCA's short-lived "X" imprint, where he tried to remain up-to-date by issuing "Rock 'n' Roll Call."

A blistering Quincy Jones-arranged date for Mercury in 1956 deftly updated Jordan's classics for the rock 'n' roll crowd, with hellfire renditions of "Let the Good Times Roll," "Salt Pork, West Virginia," and "Beware" benefiting from the blasting lead guitar of Mickey Baker and Sam "The Man" Taylor's muscular tenor sax. There was even time to indulge in a little torrid jazz at Mercury; "The JAMF," from a 1957 LP called *Man, We're Wailin',* was a sizzling indication of what a fine saxist Jordan was.

Ray Charles had long cited Jordan as a primary influence (he lovingly covered Jordan's "Don't Let the Sun Catch You Crying" and "Early in the Morning"), and paid him back by signing Jordan to the Genius' Tangerine label. Once again, the fickle public largely ignored his worthwhile 1962-64 offerings.

Lounge gigs still offered the saxman a steady income, though, and he adjusted his onstage playlist accordingly. A 1973 album for the French Black & Blue logo found Jordan covering Mac Davis' "I Believe in Music" (can't get much loungier than that!). A heart attack silenced this visionary in 1975, but not before he acted as the bridge between the big-band era and the rise of R&B.

His profile continues to rise posthumously, in large part due to the recent acclaimed Broadway musical *Five Guys Named Moe,* based on Jordan's bubbly, romping repertoire and charismatic persona. —*Bill Dahl*

At the Swing Cats' Ball / Jan. 15, 1937-Nov. 1937 / JSP ✦✦✦✦
This very interesting collector's CD features altoist/singer Louis Jordan at the beginning of his career, tracing his progress until right before he hit it big. Jordan is heard in 1937 taking three almost unrecognizable ballad vocals with Chick Webb's Orchestra, backing singer Rodney Sturgis on three tunes, performing two selections from late 1938 with his Elks Rendez-Vous Band (including a hot instrumental, "Honey in the Bee Ball") and jamming a dozen numbers from his two sessions in 1939 with his recently formed Tympany Five. Of the latter, highlights include "Flat Face," "At the Swing Cat's Ball" and "Honeysuckle Rose." Louis Jordan fans will really want this British CD if they do not already have the Classics release 1934-1940. —*Scott Yanow*

☆ **Let the Good Times Roll: The Complete Decca Recordings 1938-54** / 1938-1954 / Bear Family ✦✦✦✦✦
The price of this multidisc import boxed set is indeed a hefty one, but it contains every track the pioneering saxman waxed for Decca—the multitude of hits that inexorably influenced the future of R&B and eventually rock 'n' roll. Bear Family's attention to detail in its presentation is always immaculate, and sound quality follows suit. —*Bill Dahl*

1940-1941 / Mar. 13, 1940+Nov. 15, 1941 / Classics ✦✦✦✦
The second in the Classics label's CD series that reissues all of Louis Jordan's early recordings features the masterful entertainer with his Tympany Five in the period that directly preceded his great commercial successes. Although most of these 26 selections (including "Somebody Done Hoodooed the Hoodoo Man," "After School Swing Session," "Saxa-Woogie" and "De Laff's on You") are quite obscure, the playing by the group is quite infectious and enjoyable. Singers Daisy Winchester and Mabel Robinson are heard on the Mar. 13, 1940 session for a song apiece, but otherwise, the focus is on Jordan and his fine band, which features tenor saxophonist Kenneth Hollon and several trumpeters, including (on one date) Freddy Webster. Recommended to listeners who want to hear more Louis Jordan than just his hit records. —*Scott Yanow*

★ **The Best of Louis Jordan [MCA]** / Nov. 15, 1941-Jan. 1941 / MCA ✦✦✦✦✦
This is a best-of CD collection that actually lives up to its name. Virtually all of Louis Jordan's hits, which musically bridged the gap between small-group swing, R&B and rock 'n' roll, are on this single CD, including "Choo Choo Ch'Boogie," "Let the Good Times Roll," "Ain't Nobody Here But Us Chickens," "Saturday Night Fish Fry," "Caldonia," "Five Guys Named Moe" and "Don't Let the Sun Catch You Cryin'." Serious collectors will want to explore a more complete series, particularly the one part out by Classics, but for a single acquisition, this is the Louis Jordan set to get. Jordan's very likable and good-humored vocals, as well as his hot alto, and the playing of the Tympany Five belong in everyone's music collection. —*Scott Yanow*

1941-1943 / Nov. 15, 1941-Nov. 1941 / Classics ✦✦✦✦✦
During the era covered by this Classics CD (the third in their "complete" Louis Jordan series), Jordan and his Tympany Five became major successes. Among the 24 selections are such hits as "Knock Me a Kiss," "I'm Gonna Move to the Outskirts of Town," "Five Guys Named Moe" and "Is You Is or Is You Ain't My Baby." In addition to the regular Decca recordings, the set includes four numbers originally rejected, plus six Jordan V-Disc performances. Louis Jordan's music (featuring his alto and vocals, plus hot backup work from trumpeter Eddie Roane and a swinging rhythm section) acted as a bridge between small-group swing and early R&B. Highly recommended. —*Scott Yanow*

Five Guys Named Moe: Original Decca Recordings, Vol. 2 / Jul. 21, 1942-May 8, 1952 / Decca ✦✦✦✦✦
Another 18 of the saxist's Decca label classics (although "Five Guys Named Moe" turns up again, in deference to the hit Broadway production). "Is You Is or Is You Ain't (My Baby)," "Jack, You're Dead," "Texas and Pacific," "Boogie Woogie Blue Plate," and "G.I. Jive" are high on the list of gems this time, along with his persuasive 1952 campaign "Jordan for President." —*Bill Dahl*

The Just Say Moe!: Mo' of the Best of Louis Jordan / Jul. 21, 1942-Nov. 6, 1973 / Rhino ✦✦✦✦
A nice across-the-board compilation spanning his Decca, Aladdin, RCA, Mercury, and Tangerine label stints. The Decca standouts include "Don't Worry 'Bout That Mule" and the often-covered "Ain't That Just Like a Woman," while his Mercury

output includes "Big Bess" and "Cat Scratchin." Could have done without the live "I Believe in Music" at the end, though—that isn't the way we want to remember this wonderful performer. —*Bill Dahl*

Five Guys Named Moe / Aug. 1943-1946 / Vintage Jazz Classics ✦✦✦✦

Included on this CD are 27 formerly rare performances by altoist/singer Louis Jordan and his famous Tympany Five. Consisting of radio appearances, plus specially recorded V-discs, the release has quite a few songs not otherwise recorded by Jordan, along with different versions of "Five Guys Named Moe," "Outskirts of Town" and "Caldonia." A special bonus is hearing clarinetist Barney Bigard jam "Rose Room" with the band. The front cover of the CD proclaims "The Father of Rock 'n' Roll," and in ways that is true, although ironically the rise of rock in the mid-1950s knocked Louis Jordan permanently off the pop charts. Recommended. —*Scott Yanow*

1943-1945 / Nov. 22, 1943-Jul. 12, 1945 / Classics ✦✦✦✦✦

Although Louis Jordan's greatest hits are continually reissued, this Classics CD (the fourth in the series) gives listeners an opportunity to hear many of his lesser-known recordings, quite a few of which sound as if they could have been hits, too. Jordan, a fine R&Bish altoist who was an underrated singer and a brilliant comedic talent who knew a good line when he heard one (there are many memorable ones throughout this program), is heard in peak form. The 23 performances are Decca sides (including five not originally released), some V-Discs and the privately recorded "Louis' Oldsmbile Song." Bing Crosby sings duets with Jordan on "My Baby Said Yes" and "Your Socks Don't Match," there are two major hits ("G.I. Jive" and "Caldonia") and among the sidemen are the fine trumpeter Eddie Roane, the forgotten but talented pianist Tommy Thomas, trumpeter Idrees Sulieman (on the January 19, 1945 session) and (for the final two songs) pianist Wild Bill Davis. Other highlights include "You Can't Get That No More," "I Like 'Em Fat Like That," "Deacon Jones" and "They Raided the House." Highly recommended. —*Scott Yanow*

1944-1945 / 1944-1945 / Circle ✦✦✦✦✦

This interesting album features altoist/vocalist Louis Jordan and three versions of his Tympany Five during the 1944-45, when he was reaching the peak of his popularity. With such sidemen as either Eddie Roane, Idrees Sulieman or Aaron Izenhall on trumpet and (on a few numbers) pianist Wild Bill Davis, Jordan and his group are heard recording radio transcriptions for World Broadcasting. Other than "G.I. Jive," the music emphasizes lesser-known tunes and contains plenty of fine solos from Jordan, including the surprisingly advanced "Re-Bop." —*Scott Yanow*

1945-1946 / Jul. 16, 1945-Oct. 10, 1946 / Classics ✦✦✦✦✦

Louis Jordan was at the top of his fame when the 23 recordings reissued on this Classics CD were cut. The influential altoist/singer/entertainer during this era led a version of his Tympany Five that also featured trumpeter Aaron Izenhall, Josh Jackson on tenor and pianist Wild Bill Davis (years before he switched to organ). Among the hits included on the set are "Beware," "Don't Let the Sun Catch You Cryin'," "Choo-Choo Ch'Boogie," "Ain't Nobody Here But Us Chickens," "Let the Good Times Roll" and "Jack You're Dead," but even the lesser-known tracks are entertaining. In addition, a couple of unlikely duets with Ella Fitzgerald ("Stone Cold Dead In the Market" and "Petootie Pie") are quite fun. Recommended to listeners not satisfied with owning only Louis Jordan's hits. —*Scott Yanow*

One Guy Named Louis / Jan. 1954-Apr. 1954 / Blue Note ✦✦✦

It is a strange fact that as rock 'n' roll began to catch on, one of the artists who helped influence its birth was dropping rapidly in popularity. Singer/altoist Louis Jordan, who had had dozens of hits with his Tympany Five while on Decca, recorded 21 songs for Aladdin in 1954 (all of which are included on this CD) and none of them sold well. The strange part is that there is nothing wrong with the music. It compares quite well artistically with his earlier performances; it was just out of style. That fact should not trouble latter-day Jordan fans, for the formerly rare music on this set is witty, swinging and eternally hip. —*Scott Yanow*

Rock 'n' Roll Call / 1955-1956 / RCA ✦✦✦✦

Only a dozen numbers on this disc, but that's all the saxist made during his 1955-1956 pause at RCA's VIK and "X" subsidiaries. The saxist tried hard to keep up with the times, waxing a stomping title track written by Jack Hammer and Rudy Toombs and a Winfield Scott-penned "Slow, Smooth and Easy" and "Let's Do It Up Baby," but the teenagers just weren't buying. No reason we shouldn't! —*Bill Dahl*

No Moe!—Greatest Hits / Oct. 22, 1956-Aug. 1957 / Verve ✦✦✦

With the exception of four numbers taken from a 1957 set in which he heads a quintet co-starring organist Jackie Davis, this CD consists of a dozen songs taken from a 1956 date already reissued (with additional material) on the previously issued CD *Rock 'n' Roll*. Louis Jordan, who had not had a new hit since 1951 (and unfortunately none were in the future) is mostly heard remaking his earlier triumphs such as "Saturday Night Fish Fry," "Ain't Nobody Here But Us Chickens"

and "Choo Choo Ch'Boogie." The music is spirited but the earlier CD is the better purchase. —*Scott Yanow*

Rock 'n' Roll / Oct. 22, 1956-Aug. 1956 / Verve ✦✦✦

Twenty-one-track French import that contains the best of Jordan's 1956-1957 stay at Mercury. Here are the rockin' remakes of his timeless hits, cut with a New York mob including Sam "The Man" Taylor on tenor sax and guitarist Mickey Baker, as well as fresh nuggets like "Big Bess," "Cat Scratchin'," and "Rock Doc." "The JAMF" is a scorching jazz showcase for Jordan's alto, and he does a nice easy-swinging job on "Got My Mojo Working." —*Bill Dahl*

Louis Jordan & Chris Barber / 1962 / Black Lion ✦✦✦

It seems strange that by 1962, altoist/singer Louis Jordan was thought of as a has-been, for he was actually still in his prime. However, Jordan had run out of new hits and seemed very much passé to some listeners. Most of this CD reissue features Jordan sounding quite exuberant and creative on a 1962 set with trombonist Chris Barber's flexible Dixieland band. The nine selections include four remakes (including "Choo Choo Ch'Boogie" and "Is You Is or Is You Ain't My Baby"), a few newer songs, and bright renditions of "Sister Kate" and "Indiana"; Jordan, Barber, trumpeter Pat Halcox and clarinetist Ian Wheeler form a potent front line. Also on the CD are five selections taken from unrelated Barber sessions, including three Duke Ellington songs. Recommended to fans of Dixieland, small-group swing and Louis Jordan. —*Scott Yanow*

I Believe in Music / Nov. 6, 1973 / Evidence ✦✦✦✦

Louis Jordan's final recording (he died 15 months later) has been reissued on this CD, along with six previously unreleased selections. Although Jordan had not been a hitmaker in around 20 years and had been somewhat neglected during the decade before the set, he was still in his musical prime both vocally and instrumentally. The altoist is teamed with tenorman Irv Cox and a rhythm section led by pianist Duke Burrell. There are a few remakes of past hits (including "Caldonia," "Is You Is or Is You Ain't My Baby," "Saturday Night Fish Fry" and "I'm Gonna Move to the Outskirts of Town"), along with newer jump material. Jordan is in good form and high spirits throughout this date. Recommended. —*Scott Yanow*

Marlon Jordan

b. Aug. 21, 1970, New Orleans, LA

Trumpet / Hard Bop

The younger brother of flutist Kent Jordan and the son of avant-garde saxophonist Kidd Jordan, Marlon Jordan gained a great deal of attention early in his career, recording as a leader for Columbia when he was 19, before he had an original sound of his own. He started playing trumpet in the fourth grade and knew Wynton Marsalis (a major influence) and Terence Blanchard when he was a child. Jordan was a featured soloist with the New Orleans Symphony when he was 15, studied at the now-legendary New Orleans Center for Creative Arts and recorded as a sideman with his brother Kent (1987) and Dennis Gonzalez (1988). He cut three albums as a leader for Columbia, toured with Jazz Futures (1991) alongside Roy Hargrove and showed potential. Whether he will someday develop into a jazz giant is not known at this time but Marlon Jordan certainly has the technical skills if not yet the musical individuality. —*Scott Yanow*

For You Only / Dec. 1988 / Columbia ✦✦✦

Trumpeter Marlon Jordan was only 18 when he recorded this set, his debut recording as a leader. Branford Marsalis makes four appearances on tenor; Marlon's brother, flutist Ken Jordan, is heard on the opening "Jepetto's Despair," and there are two duets with bassist/pianist Elton Heron. Four standards (including "Cherokee" and "Stardust") are performed, along with originals by Jordan and Heron. At this point in time, Jordan was heavily influenced by Wynton Marsalis and, to a lesser extent, Miles Davis; he did not yet have a voice of his own. However, Marlon Jordan's playing was reasonably inventive, and he definitely was technically skilled, making this set of both musical and historic interest. —*Scott Yanow*

Learson's Return / 1991 / Columbia ✦✦✦

Marlon Jordan, just 19 at the time of this CD, displays a lot of 1965 Miles Davis in his style. His tenor saxophonist Tim Warfield is most influenced by John Coltrane and Wayne Shorter, the original compositions would not be out-of-place on a vintage Blue Note album and the young rhythm section (pianist Peter Martin, bassist Tarus Mateen and drummer Troy Davis) sounds straight out of the mid-1960s, which is around the time period that they were born. As with most jazz musicians fortunate enough to be documented at an early age, the musicians let their influences show. The music is enjoyable enough with pianist Martin (who ranges from McCoy Tyner to Herbie Hancock and Monk) taking solo honors. Marlon Jordan shows obvious talent and potential but at this early point in his career he was emulating Miles Davis ("Inside the Harem" sounds straight from *Sketches of*

Spain) and Wynton Marsalis ("In a Mellotone" could pass as a dead ringer) much too closely. —*Scott Yanow*

The Undaunted / Jan. 11, 1992-Jan. 12, 1992 / Columbia ◆◆◆

For his third and final Columbia CD, young trumpeter Marlon Jordan (21 at the time) still sounded fairly derivative of inspiration Wynton Marsalis and Miles Davis. His hard bop quintet (which also includes tenor saxophonist Tim Warfield, the brilliant pianist Eric Reed, bassist Tarus Mateen and drummer Troy Davis) is heard performing six of the trumpeter's originals, plus John Coltrane's "Village Blues," with spirit and swing, although not many original ideas. Jordan was one of the youngest of the Young Lions but, even in the late 1990s, he has still plenty of unrealized potential. A good but not essential outing. —*Scott Yanow*

● **Marlon's Mode** /1997 / Arabesque ◆◆◆◆

Trumpeter Marlon Jordan's first recording as a leader in four years finds the 26-year-old still a bit derivative of Wynton Marsalis, but a stronger player overall than he was on his earlier Columbia dates. Jordan's range has expanded; he takes chances in his frequently exciting solos, and his tone is appealing. Actually, his sidemen (most notably clarinetist Alvin Batiste, who is in top form, and Victor Goines on tenor and soprano) sometimes take solo honors during the colorful post-bop date. The repertoire consists of three John Coltrane tunes, two by Miles Davis, "Ballad for Trane" from saxophonist Kidd Jordan (Marlon's father), and "Caravan." Fine music, even though Marlon Jordan has yet to develop into an innovative player. —*Scott Yanow*

Sheila Jordan

b. Nov. 18, 1928, Detroit, MI
Vocals / Bop, Post-Bop

One of the most consistently creative of all jazz singers, Sheila Jordan has a relatively small voice but has done the maximum with her instrument. She is one of the few vocalists who can improvise logical lyrics (which often rhyme!), she is a superb scat singer and is also an emotional interpreter of ballads. Yet despite her talents, Jordan spent much of the 1960s and '70s working at a conventional day job! She studied piano when she was 11 and early on sang vocalese in a vocal group. Jordan moved to New York in the 1950s, was married to Duke Jordan (1952-62), studied with Lennie Tristano and worked in New York clubs. George Russell used her on an unusual recording of "You Are My Sunshine" and she became one of the few singers to lead her own Blue Note album (1962). However, it would be a decade before she appeared on records again, working with Carla Bley, Roswell Rudd and co-leading a group with Steve Kuhn in the late '70s. Jordan recorded a memorable duet album with bassist Arild Andersen for Steeple Chase in 1977 and has since teamed up with bassist Harvie Swartz on many occasions. By the 1980s Sheila Jordan was finally performing jazz on a fulltime basis and gaining the recognition she deserved 20 years earlier. She has recorded as a leader (in addition to the Blue Note session) for East Wind, Grapevine, Steeple Chase, Palo Alto, Black Hawk and Muse. —*Scott Yanow*

☆ **Portrait of Sheila Jordan** / Sep. 19, 1962+Oct. 12, 1962 / Blue Note ◆◆◆◆◆

Sheila Jordan's debut recording was one of the very few vocal records made for Blue Note during Alfred Lion's reign. Accompanied by the subtle guitarist Barry Galbraith, bassist Steve Swallow and drummer Denzil Best, Jordan sounds quite distinctive, cool-toned and adventurous during her classic date. Her interpretations of Oscar Brown Jr.'s "Hum Drum Blues" and 11 standards (including "Falling in Love with Love," "Dat Dere," "Baltimore Oriole" and "I'm a Fool to Want You") are both swinging and haunting. Possibly because of her originality, Sheila Jordan would not record again for over a dozen years, making this highly recommended set quite historic. —*Scott Yanow*

Confirmation / Jul. 12, 1975-Jul. 13, 1975 / Eastwind ◆◆◆◆

Sheila / Aug. 27, 1977-Aug. 28, 1977 / Steeple Chase ◆◆◆◆◆

This was a breakthrough recording for Sheila Jordan. She recorded a superb album for Blue Note in 1962 and then was off records (and only working in jazz on a part-time basis) up until the mid-'70s. She cut two albums for tiny labels and then came this, the first of her vocal-bass duet recordings. While in later years bassist Harvie Swartz would be her frequent musical partner, Jordan's Steeple Chase set features the talented Arild Andersen on bass. The communication between the two often borders on the miraculous and it is a pleasure to hear Sheila Jordan's fresh and original interpretations of such songs as "Lush Life," "On Green Dolphin Street," "Don't Explain" and "Better than Anything." —*Scott Yanow*

Old Time Feeling / Oct. 15, 1982 / Muse ◆◆◆◆

In 1977, Sheila Jordan had recorded an album with only the accompaniment of bassist Arild Andersen. In 1982, she began an occasional duet partnership with bassist Harvie Swartz, and this LP (unfortunately out of print) was their first recorded collaboration as a duo. Jordan's solid sense of swing, subtle creativity, wit

and willingness to take chances are very much in evidence as she walks a tightrope on such numbers as "Sleeping Bee," "Tribute (Quasimodo)," "It Don't Mean a Thing," "Lazy Afternoon" and "Some Other Time." This is a classic set that deserves to be reissued on CD. —*Scott Yanow*

The Crossing / Oct. 1, 1984-Oct. 2, 1984 / Black Hawk ◆◆◆◆◆

Sheila Jordan has recorded fairly infrequently throughout her career but each recording has its very special moments. This Black Hawk LP (not yet reissued on CD except in Japan) has four duets with bassist Harvie Swartz and one with pianist Kenny Barron, as well as backing by Swartz, Barron, and drummer Ben Riley on "Sheila's Blues," and three quintet numbers that add fluegelhornist Tom Harrell to the group. All nine performances are somewhat memorable, with the highlights including an eerie "Inchworm," the autobiographical "Sheila's Blues," "Little Willie Leaps," "Suite for Lady and Prez," and the emotional "It Never Entered My Mind." Well worth searching for. —*Scott Yanow*

Songs from Within / Mar. 1989 / M-A ◆◆◆◆

Sheila Jordan is one of the few singers to record duets frequently with just a string bass, usually Harvie Swartz. Jordan and Swartz interpret a wide variety of standards on their CD along with two originals. Although the always-inventive singer is clearly the lead voice, Swartz is not restricted to merely an accompanying role; he often shares center stage in close interplay with Jordan and his lines are almost as unpredictable as Sheila's. Their versions of such veteran songs as "Waltz for Debbie," "St. Thomas," "My Shining Hour" and "In a Sentimental Mood" sound quite original and fresh. As is the custom with M-A, this CD concludes with a selection taken from another release on the label, a melancholy showcase for Marty Krystall's bass clarinet. —*Scott Yanow*

Lost and Found / Sep. 28, 1989-Sep. 29, 1989 / Muse ◆◆◆◆◆

Every Sheila Jordan recording is special, for the singer is quite unique and puts plenty of feeling and creativity into each performance. Joined by pianist Kenny Barron, bassist Harvie Swartz and drummer Ben Riley for this CD, Jordan uplifts and reinvents such standards as "The Very Thought of You," "Anthropology" and "I Concentrate on You," making each rendition seem fresh and new. —*Scott Yanow*

★ **One for Junior** / Sep. 1991 / Muse ◆◆◆◆◆

This CD is a real gem. Singers Sheila Jordan and Mark Murphy both possess unusual and immediately recognizable voices and are among the top jazz improvisers around. On a typically intelligent and chance-taking program there are many highlights including a humorous conversation between hipsters on "Where or When," a couple of ballad medleys and Jordan's witty lyrics on "The Bird." Assisted by pianist Kenny Barron, bassist Harvie Swartz, drummer Ben Riley and Bill Mays on occasional synthesizer, the two vocalists sound mutually inspired. —*Scott Yanow*

Heart Strings / Mar. 5, 1993-Mar. 6, 1993 / Muse ◆◆◆◆◆

Although sparsely recorded during much of her career, Sheila Jordan has been one of the top jazz singers since 1960. In addition to living the words she sings (à la Billie Holiday), Jordan constantly improvises (few can scat with her sensitivity and swing) and also has the remarkable ability of being able to make up lyrics on the spot that are not only logical but rhyme. Jordan realized a lifelong dream on this Muse CD for she had always wanted to record with a string quartet. Fortunately, the group was given colorful arrangements by pianist Alan Broadbent; in addition, there are two songs with a standard trio that includes Jordan's longtime bassist Harvie Swartz and a duet with Broadbent. The emphasis is on ballads but typically Sheila Jordan makes each of the songs sound like they must have been written specifically for her, even "Look for the Silver Lining" and "Inch Worm." This is a highly recommended gem. —*Scott Yanow*

Stanley Jordan

b. Jul. 31, 1959, Chicago, IL
Guitar / Instrumental Pop, Bop

Stanley Jordan's discovery in the early '80s rightfully earned a lot of headlines in the jazz world for he came up with a new way of playing guitar. Although he was not the first to use tapping, Jordan's extensive expertise gave him the ability to play two completely independent lines on the guitar (as if it were a keyboard) or, when he wanted, two guitars at a time. He had originally studied piano although he switched to guitar when he was 11. After graduating from Princeton in 1981, Jordan played for a time on the streets of New York. Soon he was discovered, had the opportunity to play with Benny Carter and Dizzy Gillespie and, after recording a solo album for his own Tangent label, signed with Blue Note. Since then his career has been surprisingly aimless. Stanley Jordan can play amazing jazz but he often wastes his talent on lesser material, so one has to be picky in deciding which of his recordings to acquire. —*Scott Yanow*

Touch Sensitive / 1982 / Tangent ✦✦✦✦
He first featured the two-handed touch style which he has perfected on this rare independent release. —*Paul Kohler*

● **Magic Touch** / Sep. 1984-Oct. 1984 / Blue Note ✦✦✦✦✦
Other than a little-known independent release in 1982, this Blue Note set has guitarist Stanley Jordan's recording debut. Seven selections are unaccompanied solos, with percussionist Sammy Figueroa added on some of the numbers, and there are three cuts with a rhythm section. Jordan's remarkable tapping technique (which has surprisingly not been emulated much by later guitarists and bassists) allows him to play his instrument like a piano, making most other guitarists sound one-handed. Jordan's playing sounds quite miraculous on such numbers as "Eleanor Rigby," "Freddie Freeloader" his own "Fundance" and Jimi Hendrix's "Angel." —*Scott Yanow*

Cornucopia / Aug. 21, 1986-Mar. 21, 1989 / Blue Note ✦✦✦✦✦
The first half of this CD by the remarkable guitarist Stanley Jordan is so strong that it is a pity that things decline during the latter half. Jordan is quite outstanding on "Impressions" and "Autumn Leaves," emulates B.B. King on "Still Got the Blues", interprets a thoughtful "Willow Weep for Me" and performs a dazzling tour-de-force on the uptempo blues "Fundance"; the latter two are unaccompanied solos that sound like duets or trios. However, a couple of funk pieces (including an unimaginative rendition of "What's Going On") and a new age synthesizer selection are on a lower level. The title cut clocks in at 21:45 and, although it finds Jordan creating "impossible" technical feats on solo guitar, it meanders on indefinitely and gets boring very quickly. This is a frustrating release; get it for the good half if you see it at a budget price. —*Scott Yanow*

Standards, Vol. 1 / Oct. 1986 / Blue Note ✦✦✦✦✦
Guitarist Stanley Jordan (the master of tapping, making his instrument sound like two or three at once) has a wide definition of standards, ranging beyond jazz. His second official Blue Note release therefore not only includes "Georgia On My Mind" and "My Favorite Things," but Paul Simon's "The Sounds of Silence," "Moon River," the Beatles' "Because," and "Silent Night." But no matter what the tune, the main reason to acquire this set of unaccompanied guitar solos is to hear how here remarkable and versatile Jordan's technique is. —*Scott Yanow*

Flying Home / 1988 / EMI ✦✦✦
Stanley Jordan switches largely to funk and pop on this disappointing set. The title cut has nothing to do with Lionel Hampton's trademark song, and Jordan, whose phenomenal tapping technique allows him to play his instrument like a piano, waters down the whole effect by using overdubbing, multiple keyboards and a drum machine. Most of the tunes are his originals (other than "Stairway to Heaven") and fall way outside of jazz, being not even good rock. Pass. —*Scott Yanow*

Street Talk / 1990 / EMI ✦✦

Stolen Moments / Nov. 7, 1990-Nov. 9, 1990 / Somethin' Else ✦✦✦✦✦
This trio set with bassist Charnett Moffett and drummer Kenwood Dennard features the tapping guitarist Stanley Jordan during a typical live show from 1990 playing many songs that he had previously recorded. While "Stairway to Heaven" is treated as very credible rock and "Lady in My Life" gets funky, "Autumn Leaves" really cooks and Jordan fares well on "Stolen Moments" (during which he does a strong imitation of a keyboard) and "Impressions." Jordan's lone original, the rockish "Return Expedition" is, at 15 minutes, way too long and serves primarily as an opportunity for his two fine backup players to take lengthy solos. Jordan's unaccompanied display on the concluding "Over the Rainbow" compensates. An interesting program. —*Scott Yanow*

Bolero / Feb. 15, 1994 / Arista ✦✦
Nobody plays the guitar quite like Stanley Jordan. Defying categorization, *Bolero* is another in a line of Jordan hit releases. After perfecting his skill at playing with two hands on the guitar's fretboard and hammering or tapping the strings to produce melody, countermelody, and rhythm all at the same time, Jordan has gone on to break new musical ground with *Bolero* in fusing jazz, pop and classical. Besides his jazzy version of "Bolero," Jordan mixes original pieces with "Drifting" by Jimi Hendrix and the funk-pop tune "Chameleon." —*MusD*

Taft Jordan (James Jordan)

b. Feb. 15, 1915, Florence, SC, **d.** Dec. 1, 1981, New York, NY
Trumpet / Swing
A fine trumpeter, Taft Jordan was known early in his career (when he joined Chick Webb) as a Louis Armstrong soundalike both on trumpet and vocals. In fact, his recording of "On the Sunny Side of the Street" was so close to Armstrong's live show that when Louis got around to documenting it the following year, some listeners thought he was copying Jordan! Taft Jordan had played and recorded with the Washboard Rhythm Kings before starting his long stint with Webb (1933-42) which continued after the drummer's death when the band was fronted by Ella Fitzgerald. Jordan was (along with Bobby Stark) Webb's main trumpet soloist throughout the 1930s and he gradually developed an original sound of his own. He gained a lot of attention during his period with Duke Ellington (1943-47) although Jordan maintained a lower profile during his last 24 years. He worked at the Savannah Club in New York with Lucille Dixon (1949-53), toured with Benny Goodman (1958), played in show bands and the New York Jazz Repertory Company, and had his own group. Taft Jordan recorded four titles as a leader in 1935 and one album apiece for Mercury, Aamco and Moodsville during 1960-61. —*Scott Yanow*

Mood Indigo / Jun. 30, 1961 / Moodsville ✦✦✦

Vic Juris

b. 1953
Guitar / Post-Bop
Guitarist Vic Juris is best-known for his association with Richie Cole. He made his recording debut with Eric Kloss (1975), gigged with Barry Miles' fusion group and started his off-and-on association with Cole in 1976, appearing on some of the altoist's finest recordings. In addition to recording with Don Patterson, Mel Tormé and Bireli Lagrene, Juris (a fine hard bop-oriented improviser) has played duets with Larry Coryell, been a member of groups led by Dave Liebman and Gary Peacock and recorded as a leader for Muse and Steeple Chase. —*Scott Yanow*

Roadsong / Sep. 19, 1977-Sep. 21, 1977 / Muse ✦✦✦✦
Although best known for his longtime association with altoist Richie Cole, guitarist Vic Juris performs fusion-oriented music during this recording, his first as a leader. Six of the eight selections are Juris originals (the other two songs include Wes Montgomery's "Road Song"), and his interplay with keyboardist Barry Miles, bassist Rick Laird (Jon Burr is on one cut) and drummer Terry Silverlight is impressive. Richie Cole himself drops by to lend his support on two songs. However, despite some fiery solos from the leader, the overall results are not particularly memorable and sound very much of the period. —*Scott Yanow*

Horizon Drive / Jun. 19, 1979 / Muse ✦✦✦

Bleecker Street / Jul. 14, 1981-Jul. 15, 1981 / Muse ✦✦✦
Guitarist Vic Juris shows off his versatility throughout this fairly obscure but worthwhile outing. He swings on Cole Porter's "Everything I Love," sounds soulful à la George Benson on "Bonnie's Song," and takes "Subway" and "Soundtracks" as duets with keyboardists Mick Nock and Gil Goldstein, respectively; the other numbers range from hard bop and funky jazz to touches of fusion. An intriguing set that will unfortunately be difficult to find. —*Scott Yanow*

● **Night Tripper** / Apr. 1994 / Steeple Chase ✦✦✦✦✦
During some of the selections on his Steeple Chase CD, guitarist Vic Juris displays an echoey tone reminiscent of John Scofield while on a few other numbers he has a drier and subtle acoustic sound. Juris' improvising is on a high level, performing "Estate," "Falling in Love with Love," two obscurities and six group originals (four of which are his) with creativity. His sidemen (pianist Phil Markowitz, basssist Steve LaSpina and drummer Jeff Hirshfield) are alert and have quick reactions. Two high points are the eccentric "Dekooning" and a tasteful bossa nova rendition of "Estate," numbers that best show off Juris' impressive flexibility. —*Scott Yanow*

Pastels / May 21, 1996 / Steeple Chase ✦✦✦✦

Moonscape / Oct. 1996 / Steeple Chase ✦✦✦

Music of Alec Wilder / Oct. 24, 1996 / Double-Time ✦✦✦

Max Kaminsky

b. Sep. 7, 1908, Brockton, MA, **d.** Sep. 6, 1994
Trumpet / Dixieland

Max Kaminsky was a reliable Dixieland player who was featured on many sessions with Eddie Condon's gang in the 1940s and '50s. He played early on in Boston and was a veteran of 1920s Chicago where he gigged with Bud Freeman, Frank Teschemacher and Condon. Moving to New York in 1929, Kaminsky had a short stint with Red Nichols and then worked in commercial bands, although he did have opportunities to record with Condon, Benny Carter (1933) and Mezz Mezzrow (1933-34). Kaminsky gained some fame for his work with Tommy Dorsey's Orchestra (1936) including broadcasts with an early version of the Clambake Seven. He was with Artie Shaw briefly in 1938, returned to TD and then was perfectly at home in Bud Freeman's freewheeling Summa Cum Laude Orchestra (1939-40). After periods with Tony Pastor (1940-41) and Artie Shaw's 1942 orchestra, Kaminsky went in the military where he played with Shaw's Navy band throughout the Pacific. Maxie was a star at Eddie Condon's legendary Town Hall concerts (1944-45) and began recording as a leader for Commodore (1944). He alternated between Condon's bands and his own groups, wrote one of the great memoirs (*Jazz Band: My Life in Jazz*), kept an open mind towards newer styles (even jamming with Charlie Parker) while not altering his straightforward approach and toured the Far East with Jack Teagarden (1959). He was a fixture at Jimmy Ryan's for decades and at his death (after a decade of semiretirement) one of the last surviving Condonites. Max Kaminsky recorded as a leader for Commodore, MGM, Victor (1954), Jazztone, Winchester, United Artists, Chiaroscuro (1977) and Fat Cat Jazz. —*Scott Yanow*

Copley Terrace 1945 / 1945 / Jazzology ♦♦♦
This previously unreleased Dixieland set (put out by Jazzology on a 1996 CD) teams trumpeter Max Kaminsky with clarinetist Pee Wee Russell, valve trombonist Brad Gowans, pianist Teddy Roy, bassist John Field and drummer Buzzy Drootin. Taken from radio broadcasts emanating from Boston's Copley Terrace, these private acetates (made by a collector and sometimes a bit worn) contain some excellent playing. The 16 selections are primarily Dixieland warhorses (including "Love Is Just Around the Corner," "Dippermouth Blues," "Basin Street Blues," and "Honeysuckle Rose"), and no real surprises occur, but the spirit of the times definitely comes through. —*Scott Yanow*

Meets the Happy Jazz Band / Feb. 4, 1974-Feb. 5, 1974 / Fat Cat Jazz ♦♦♦♦
Trumpeter Max Kaminsky's first recording as a leader in a decade finds the veteran Condonite jamming with cornetist Jim Cullum Junior's Happy Jazz Band. The rather informal session, which includes two cuts without Kaminsky from the following day's concert, matches Max and Cullum with clarinetist Bobby Gordon, trombonist Mark Hess (who takes an unaccompanied piano solo on "Garage Blues"), pianist Cliff Gillette, banjoist Jim Newell, Buddy Apfel on sousaphone, and drummer Harvey Kindervater. Label producer Johnson McRee takes a vocal on "Spain." The music is Dixieland-ish, but includes a few newer originals like "Jim Cullum Sr. Stomp," "Tex-Max" and "Blanquita." Joyful music that finds the principals in excellent form, but this LP from the defunct Fat Cat label will be difficult to find. —*Scott Yanow*

Two for Tea / Dec. 6, 1975-Dec. 5, 1976 / Fat Cat Jazz ♦♦♦♦
This excellent but hard-to-find LP has live performances from the 1975 and 1976 Manassas Jazz Festivals. It is particularly special because seven of the nine selections showcase trumpeter Max Kaminsky as the only horn in a quartet/quintet. 67 at the time, Kaminsky still sounds fairly strong on a variety of swing and Dixieland standards, including "You Turned the Tables on Me," "On the Sunny Side of the Street" and two versions of "Tea for Two." In addition, there are three loose band numbers with either Wally Garner or Tom Gwaltney on clarinet and Bill Allred or Al Winters on trombone. —*Scott Yanow*

● **When Summer Is Gone** / Nov. 2, 1977-Nov. 3, 1977 / Chiaroscuro ♦♦♦♦♦
Cornetist Max Kaminsky's final record as a leader (he was 69 but still in his musical prime) is a gem and long overdue to be reissued by Chiaroscuro on CD. Joined by guitarist Bucky Pizzarelli, pianist John Bunch, bassist George Duvivier and drummer Ronnie Traxler, Kaminsky performs 11 superior songs, many of which have been rarely played by jazz musicians. He plays quite lyrically on such number as "Poor Little Rich Girl," "Come Down to Earth My Angel," "I'll Follow My Secret Heart" and "Sweet As a Song." The little-known but appealing Mary Eiland takes warm vocals on "When Summer Is Gone" and a touching version of "Blame It On My Youth." A classic of its kind. —*Scott Yanow*

Richie Kamuca

b. Jul. 23, 1930, Philadelphia, PA, **d.** Jul. 22, 1977, Los Angeles, CA
Tenor Saxophone / Cool

An excellent cool-toned tenor who found his own voice in the Lester Young-influenced "Four Brothers" sound, Richie Kamuca tended to be overshadowed by those who came first (such as Stan Getz, Zoot Sims and Al Cohn) but musicians knew how good he was. Kamuca was a soloist with the orchestras of Stan Kenton (1952-53) and Woody Herman (1954-56) and then worked steadily on the West Coast with such groups as those led by Chet Baker, Maynard Ferguson, the Lighthouse All-Stars (1957-58), Shorty Rogers and Shelly Manne (1959-61). He recorded one album apiece as a leader for Liberty, Mode and Hi Fi (1956-57); the latter two have been reissued by V.S.O.P. Moving to New York in 1962, Kamuca worked with Gerry Mulligan, Gary McFarland and Roy Eldridge (1966-71) but was fairly obscure. In 1972 he moved back to Los Angeles to work in the studios but he also played jazz locally with small groups and with Bill Berry's L.A. Big Band. In his later years (1977) before his death from cancer (the day before his 47th birthday), Richie Kamuca recorded three wonderful albums for Concord. —*Scott Yanow*

Richie Kamuca Quartet / Jun. 1957 / V.S.O.P. ♦♦♦
Considering his talent, it is very surprising that tenor saxophonist Richie Kamuca led so few record dates throughout his career—just three during 1956-58 and three for Concord in 1977. This quartet set (a MOD LP reissued by V.S.O.P. on CD) features the excellent cool-toned tenor in a quartet with pianist Carl Perkins, bassist Leroy Vinnegar and drummer Stan Levey. Only the brief playing time (just over 30 minutes) keeps this set from getting a higher rating, for Kamuca is in prime form. Highlights include "Just Friends," "What's New" and "Cherokee." —*Scott Yanow*

West Coast Jazz in Hi Fi / 1959 / Original Jazz Classics ♦♦♦♦
Originally recorded for the Hi Fi label, this CD reissue features tenor saxophonist Richie Kamuca as the main soloist on a variety of standards and basic material arranged by Bill Holman, who plays baritone with the octet. Also heard from are trumpeters Conte Candoli and Ed Leddy, trombonist Frank Rosolino, pianist Vince Guaraldi, bassist Monty Budwig and drummer Stan Levey. The music, although based on the West Coast, is not as cool-toned or as laidback as one might expect. High points of the consistently swinging session include "Blue Jazz" (a Kamuca blues), "Star Eyes," "Linger Awhile" and "Indiana." —*Scott Yanow*

Charlie / 1977 / Concord Jazz ♦♦♦♦
Richie Kamuca's death from cancer at age 47 just months after this final session was a major loss to jazz. One of the top proponents of the Four Brothers sound on tenor, Kamuca always swung and his tone was quite attractive. This particular set is a tribute to Charlie Parker featuring Kamuca's quintet (which includes trumpeter Blue Mitchell, pianist Jimmy Rowles, bassist Ray Brown and drummer Donald Bailey). Most unusual is the fact that Kamuca decided to play alto instead of tenor throughout this set and, although this was clearly not his strongest ax, he solos quite well on this date. The music (bop standards and blues) receives favorable and swinging treatment from the talented veterans. —*Scott Yanow*

● **Richie** / 1977 / Concord Jazz ♦♦♦♦♦
Richie Kamuca, a hard-swinging but cool-toned tenorman, did not lead any record sessions after 1958 until he recorded three albums for Concord in early 1977, ironically just months before his death at age 47 from cancer. This particular set may have been Kamuca's most rewarding. Accompanied by guitarist Mundell Lowe, bassist Monty Budwig and drummer Nick Ceroli, Kamuca is lyrical on the eight

superior standards, taking a surprisingly effective vocal on "'Tis Autumn" and coming up with memorable melodic statements on the other songs. —*Scott Yanow*

Drop Me off in Harlem / Feb. 2, 1977 / Concord Jazz ✦✦✦✦✦

Richie Kamuca's three Concord albums, all recorded within a year of his death, are each highly recommended. This set has inspired instrumentation. Three songs feature the cool-toned tenor in a trio with Herb Ellis (playing acoustic guitar) and bassist Ray Brown, while the remaining five are duets with pianist Dave Frishberg. Kamuca takes a surprising and effective vocal on "Dear Bix" and alternates light romps with lyrical ballads. Highlights of the memorable set include "Drop Me off in Harlem," "Three Little Words" and "Harlem Butterfly." —*Scott Yanow*

Dick Katz (Richard Aaron Katz)

b. Mar. 13, 1924, Baltimore, MD

Piano / Bop

A versatile pianist and arranger, Dick Katz has been responsible for many stimulating and memorable recordings through the years, often as an important sideman and/or producer. He studied at the Peabody Institute, the Manhattan School of Music and Juilliard, in addition to taking piano lessons from Teddy Wilson. In the 1950s, he picked up important experience as a member of the house rhythm section of the Café Bohemia, with the groups of Ben Webster and Kenny Dorham, the Oscar Pettiford big band and later with Carmen McRae. Katz was part of the popular J.J. Johnson-Kai Winding Quintet (1954-55) and Orchestra USA and participated on Benny Carter's classic *Further Definitions* album. He has freelanced throughout much of his career and was a guiding force behind some of Helen Merrill's finest recordings. Katz, who played with Roy Eldridge and Lee Konitz starting in the late 1960s, co-founded Milestone Records in 1966 with Orrin Keepnews. In the 1990s, Dick Katz has worked both as a pianist and an arranger with the American Jazz Orchestra and Loren Schoenberg's big band. Unfortunately, he has not recorded all that frequently as a leader, cutting fairly obscure dates for Atlantic (1957 and 1959), BeeHive (1984) and Reservoir (1992), but the jazz world is well aware of his talents. —*Scott Yanow*

Piano & Pen / Dec. 17, 1958-Jan. 23, 1959 / Atlantic ✦✦✦

● **In High Profile** / May 7, 1984-May 8, 1984 / Bee Hive ✦✦✦✦✦

Through the years, pianist Dick Katz through played an important role behind the scenes on many recording dates, including notable sets by Helen Merrill and Lee Konitz. He has led relatively few sessions of his own, making this quintet outing with Frank Wess (mostly on flute but taking "A Few Bars for Basie" on tenor), trombonist Jimmy Knepper, bassist Marc Johnson and drummer Al Harewood a special occasion. Actually, the horns sit out on four of the eight selections, which are more spontaneous trio features, while the full band tracks sport Katz's colorful arrangements. Highlights of the now out-of-print set include Oscar Pettiford's "Laverne Walk," "Crazy She Calls Me," John Coltrane's "Cousin Mary," and Thelonious Monk's "Friday the 13th." —*Scott Yanow*

3 Way Play / Mar. 26, 1992-Aug. 19, 1992 / Reservoir ✦✦✦✦

The Line Forms Here / May 10, 1995+May 11, 1995 / Reservoir ✦✦✦✦

Fred Katz (Frederick Katz)

b. Feb. 25, 1919, New York, NY

Cello / Third Stream, Cool

Fred Katz's cello playing with the Chico Hamilton Quintet during 1955-58 was largely responsible for the popular cool jazz group's unique sound and atmospheric style. Katz was classically trained (he had studied with Pablo Casals) and worked in orchestras, but also played piano. In the early 1950s, he accompanied several singers, including Lena Horne and Tony Bennett. While with Hamilton, Katz also recorded several albums of his own for Pacific Jazz, Decca and Warner Brothers (1956-58). After leaving Chico (with whom he recorded one final set in 1959), Katz mostly worked outside of jazz, both in classical music and as a professor in anthropology. In 1989, he was part of a Chico Hamilton Quintet reunion, recording for Soul Note and showing that he was still a masterful musician. —*Scott Yanow*

Zen / the Music Of / Nov. 1956 / Pacific ✦✦✦✦

● **Soul Cello** / 1957 / Decca ✦✦✦✦

Fred Katz and Jammers / 1958 / Decca ✦✦✦

4-5-6 / 1958/ Decca ✦✦✦

Folk Songs for Far out Folk / July 21, 1958-Sep. 17, 1958 / Warner Brothers ✦✦✦

Connie Kay

b. Apr. 27, 1927, Tuckahoe, NY **d.** Nov. 30, 1994, New York, NY

Drums / Cool

For two months shy of 40 years (including seven years in which it was on "vacation"), Connie Kay was the drummer/percussionist with the Modern Jazz Quartet. His subtle contributions (showing both restraint and swing) were an invaluable asset to the group. Self-taught on the drums, Kay played in the mid-'40s with Sir Charles Thompson, Miles Davis and Cat Anderson. He was in Lester Young's quintet off and on during 1949-55, a period in which Kay also worked with Beryl Booker, Stan Getz, Coleman Hawkins and Charlie Parker among others. In February 1955 he joined the MJQ, traveling the world with the band up until it called it "quits" in 1974. During that era he also appeared as a guest on small-group dates by Chet Baker, Cannonball Adderley, Jimmy Heath and Paul Desmond/Jim Hall. During 1975-81 Kay worked with Tommy Flanagan, Soprano Summit, Benny Goodman (including his 40th-anniversary Carnegie Hall Concert) and was the house drummer at Eddie Condon's club. He spent his last 13 years back with the MJQ; Mickey Roker filled in when he was ill and Albert "Tootie" Heath took over the drum slot after Connie Kay's death. —*Scott Yanow*

Geoff Keezer

b. Nov. 21, 1970, Eau Claire, WI

Piano / Hard Bop

Geoff Keezer was only 17 when he became the last pianist in Art Blakey's Jazz Messengers (1988-90), a perfect gig for the talented hard bop musician who fit right in with the Horace Silver-Bobby Timmons-Cedar Walton-James Williams-Benny Green tradition. Since Blakey's death, Keezer has recorded steadily as a leader for Sunnyside, Blue Note, DIW/Columbia and Sackville, and played on records led by Art Farmer, Roy Hargrove and Antonio Hart among others. Geoff Keezer has also performed and recorded with the Contemporary Piano Ensemble and in 1997 was a member of Ray Brown's Trio. —*Scott Yanow*

Waiting in the Wings / Sep. 16, 1988-Sep. 17, 1988 / Sunnyside ✦✦✦✦

Pianist Geoff Keezer, only 17 at the time of this CD (his recording debut as a leader), was most strongly influenced in the early days by McCoy Tyner (purposely on his "Babes of McCoyland") but at this point he was already a confident and technically brilliant player with strong signs of developing his own style. His seven compositions are excellent vehicles for improvised solos (each song has its own personality) and his often-stormy piano (heard on five sextet feature, a quintet performance, four trio showcases and an unaccompanied "I Didn't Know About You") pays tribute in its own way to Phineas Newborn, Thelonious Monk and Duke Ellington. Although often confined to short concise solos, Keezer's sidemen are not overshadowed. Bill Pierce, the best known of the players, is coolly passionate on his ballad feature "Pierce on Earth" and he makes a good team with the Freddie Hubbard-inspired trumpet of Bill Mobley. Vibraphonist Steve Nelson recalls Bobby Hutcherson in his early days while bassist Rufus Reid and drummer Anthony Reedus are excellent in support. Recommended. —*Scott Yanow*

Curveball / Jun. 22, 1989 / Sunnyside ✦✦✦

● **Here and Now** / Oct. 3, 1990-Oct. 4, 1990 / Blue Note ✦✦✦✦

Pianist Geoff Keezer, two months shy of his 21st birthday at the time of this session, sometimes recalls McCoy Tyner in his playing with touches of Herbie Hancock, although on a romping version of "Just One of Those Things," his interpretation is pure Bud Powell. Steve Nelson's vibes are most heavily influenced by Bobby Hutcherson and Milt Jackson, while the somewhat dry originals take quirky twists in the best tradition of Wayne Shorter. With bassist Peter Washington and drummer Billy Higgins completing the quartet (altoist Donald Harrison guests on three numbers), this is an excellent (if not innovative) modern mainstream set, a strong showcase for both Keezer and Nelson. —*Scott Yanow*

Live at Maybeck Recital Hall, Vol. 11 / Mar. 10, 1991 / Concord Jazz ✦✦✦✦✦

World Music / Jan. 5, 1992 / Columbia ✦✦✦✦

This CD from the Japanese DIW label, which was made available domestically for a time by Columbia, is not really world music, but advanced hard bop. Pianist Geoff Keezer, a member of Art Blakey's Jazz Messengers at the time, teams up with bassist James Genus, drummer Tony Reedus and sometimes percussionist Rudy Bird on a high-quality set of swinging modern mainstream music. The set ranges from "It's Only a Paper Moon" and "Black and Tan Fantasy" to "Black Is the Color of My True Love's Hair" and originals by Keezer, Thad Jones, Mulgrew Miller and James Williams. A fine release worth searching for. —*Scott Yanow*

Other Spheres / Nov. 19, 1992-Nov. 21, 1992 / DIW ✦✦✦✦

Trio / Nov. 17, 1993 / Sackville ✦✦✦✦

Roger Kellaway

b. Nov. 1, 1939, Newton, MA
Piano / Bop, Hard Bop

A virtuosic pianist whose phenomenal technique rivals Dick Hyman's, Roger Kellaway was initially overlooked in the jazz world. He played piano and bass at the New England Conservatory (1957-59) and actually left school to play bass with Jimmy McPartland. Switching permanently to piano, Kellaway picked up experience working with Kai Winding, Al Cohn/Zoot Sims and Clark Terry/Bob Brookmeyer (1963-65). He recorded with many players including Ben Webster, Maynard Ferguson, Wes Montgomery and Sonny Rollins and in 1966 moved to Los Angeles, where he played with Don Ellis' innovative orchestra. Kellaway became Bobby Darin's musical director, worked in the studios (his piano is heard playing the theme of "All in the Family"), wrote film scores, experimented with electric keyboards, played with Tom Scott and recorded with his popular (but mostly nonjazz) Cello Quartet. Although he gigged locally with Zoot Sims and Harry "Sweets" Edison, it was not until the mid-'80s that Kellaway started playing jazz nearly full-time. His many records since then (for Concord, All Art, Stash and Chiaroscuro) attest to his impressive talents. *—Scott Yanow*

Stride! / 1966 / World Pacific ✦✦✦

The gimmick of this fairly obscure LP by pianist Roger Kellaway is that the virtuosic player strides on many of the pieces. But rather than being a high-quality swing date, Kellaway also plays some current pop tunes (including "Sunny", "It's Lovely Up Here" from *On a Clear Day,* and "Cabaret"), plus a few vintage tunes and Dave Brubeck's "In Your Own Sweet Way." The use of strings and a brass section, along with bassist Red Mitchell and drummer John Guerin, weighs down the set, and Kellaway obviously does not take himself very seriously on this so-so effort, which has more than its share of throwaway performances. *—Scott Yanow*

Say That Again / 1970 / Dobre ✦✦✦

This solo piano LP by Roger Kellaway has strong versions of "Am I Blue," "By Myself" and a ten-minute rendition of "Honeysuckle Rose." They are colorful enough to almost compensate for Kellaway's two vocals (on "I Have the Feeling I've Been Here Before" and "Say That Again") and Gene Lees' typically self-congratulatory liner notes. Worth picking up if found at a budget price. *—Scott Yanow*

Cello Quartet / Jul. 1971 / A&M ✦✦✦✦

Roger Kellaway launched his reputation as a consummate iconoclastic musician with this album, which was considered an elegant breakthrough in its time. He assembled a novel quartet featuring his piano, the late Edgar Lustgarten's classical cello (Kellaway's favorite instrument), Chuck Domanico on bass, and Emil Richards on marimba and percussion, writing pieces using chord symbols and notes without stems to allow for improvisation. The resulting album falls ever so neatly in between the cracks of classical music and jazz, sometimes leaning in the latter direction (e.g., the Latinized groove of "Jorjana No. 2"), but mostly occupying a never-never land of Kellaway's own invention. Lustgarten's lush, dark tone establishes a haunting classical ambience, which creates weird stylistic juxtapositions in pieces like the boogie-based "Esque"; on a few tracks, there is some truly quirky writing for a full studio symphony orchestra conducted by Kellaway. The most memorable of the lot is the instantly winning, deceptively simple "Morning Song" (later published in a version for tuba and piano!), where Kellaway throws in more than a hint of barrelhouse piano. This album became a cult favorite, in and out of print on LP and CD, but never too difficult to locate. *—Richard S. Ginell*

Center of the Circle / 1972 / A&M ✦✦✦✦

Out to shock and surprise everyone who loved the *Cello Quartet* album, Roger Kellaway came up with this strange, often raucous, often brilliant, near-rock 'n' roll follow-up to his earlier quiet breakthrough. But then, in the case of someone who was achieving a measure of fame at the time backing hit rock singles by Melanie ("Brand New Key") and playing the end credits music for the hit TV show *All In the Family,* one should have expected anything. For sheer dazzling fun, it's tough to beat "La Cookeria," a great rave-up full of big band riffs, Kellaway's barrelhouse piano, and fuzz-sustained, wah-wah rock guitar, or the hard-shufflin' "Our Gang Blues," or the fascinating, complex arrangement of the title track (a Melanie tune). Then for sheer chutzpah, there is "Lay Karma Lay," an exuberantly tasteless X-rated ode to carnal joys as presumably sung (?) by the pianist himself. As antidotal interludes to all of this flamboyance and foolishness, Kellaway continues his series of solo piano "On Your Mark, Get Set, Blues" set pieces from *Cello Quartet* with four more installments—the first three in different vintage idioms, the fourth bringing things up to date. Perhaps this was a loopy Kellaway parody of how hit albums were made in 1972; in any case, unlike *Cello Quartet,* it has yet to find its cult. *—Richard S. Ginell*

Nostalgia Suite / Sep. 10, 1978 / Voss ✦✦✦

Taking his *Cello Quartet* idea into a different dimension, Roger Kellaway expanded it into a quintet with the addition of drummer Joe Porcaro, wrote a six-part suite of pieces, and converted this group from something between and beyond categories to a more jazz-oriented band. Finally, Kellaway placed an added burden on the group by recording in the direct-to-disc method, meaning that they had to record each side of the original LP in one continuous, uneditable take. Yet for all intents and purposes, you can hardly hear any tension in their rhythmically alert playing, and Kellaway's unpredictably eclectic spirit—ranging from classic jazz styles to classical dissonance—is still given free rein. Although the accent is on bop, Kellaway frequently reverts to his favorite stride retro-manner, sometimes scatting exuberantly along with his ecstatic piano, and you won't believe Emil Richards' fabulous, perhaps unique bebop chimes solo on "Let's Cook It Right." The valiant cellist Edgar Lustgarten somehow fits comfortably into this jazzier context, though he is present less of the time. One can't resist quoting some of Kellaway's zany titles, which vary in length from "Ungh!" to "May I Interest You in a Little Recreation While You Sleep? They Whispered." This disc was originally issued in direct-to-disc LP form on the Discwasher label; while the CD version technically violates the spirit of D to D, at least it makes this music available to collectors who missed out on the original limited pressing. *—Richard S. Ginell*

Ain't Misbehavin' / Feb. 1986 / Choice ✦✦✦✦✦

Roger Kellaway is a brilliant two-handed pianist whose versatile style and strong sense of humor keep him open to idioms ranging from swing to free, pop to classical. On this date, he digs into six standards. "A Time for Love" and "Here's That Rainy Day" drag a bit, but things improve after that, particularly during a medium-tempo "How Deep Is the Ocean" and an adventurous exploration of "Skylark." One of Kellaway's better jazz dates. *—Scott Yanow*

In Japan / Jun. 5, 1986-Jun. 6, 1986 / All Art Jazz ✦✦✦✦

This CD reissue of a Japanese session is a well-rounded set featuring pianist Roger Kellaway with a trio (also including bassist John Goldsby and drummer Terry Clarke) on five selections, solo on five others and with a quartet (the trio plus trumpeter Valery Ponomarev) for the final two songs. Careful attention to mood variation makes the trio performances particularly rewarding. This enjoyable set is well worth acquiring. *—Scott Yanow*

Fifty-Fifty / Feb. 10, 1987 / Nata ✦✦✦

Pianist Roger Kellaway and bassist Red Mitchell make for a perfectly complementary and mutually inspiring duo on this Stash set. They uplift six jazz standards, stretching out on "Gone with the Wind," "Take the 'A' Train," and an impressionistic "I'll Never Be the Same" for over ten minutes apiece, in addition to creating rollicking versions of "St. Thomas" and "Doxy"; Brad Terry takes a guest whistling vocal on the latter. Recommended. *—Scott Yanow*

Alone Together / Jul. 1988 / Dragon ✦✦✦✦

That Was That / Jan. 21, 1991+Jan. 22, 1991 / Dragon ✦✦✦✦

● **Live at Maybeck Recital Hall, Vol. 11** / Mar. 10, 1991 / Concord Jazz ✦✦✦✦✦

Leave it to Roger Kellaway to come up with one of the most strikingly individual editions of the exhaustive *Live at Maybeck* series. Overall, the disc captures a more reflective side of Kellaway in a typical Maybeck program of mostly standards mixed with a pair of originals. Yet Kellaway's stride-grounded manner still veers off unpredictably and delightfully into the ozone, sometimes invoking Debussy-like whole-tone scales and skirting the lower orbits of bitonality and atonality before neatly extricating himself. His own shuffling stride tune "I'm Still in Love with You" is a match for any of the standards, and he's not afraid to take it outside with flashes of bitonal color. He also gives "Creole Love Call" a similar treatment—which fits the rhythm of the tune—with a rumbling, murky intro deep in the bass. Though this is not one of his more endearingly off-the-wall recordings, it is one of the best we have that is still widely available. *—Richard S. Ginell*

Roger Kellaway Meets Gene Bertoncini and Michael Moore / Feb. 27, 1992-Feb. 28, 1992 / Chiaroscuro ✦✦✦✦

Life's a Take / May 31, 1992 / Concord Jazz ✦✦✦✦✦

To inaugurate Concord's duo series at the Maybeck Recital Hall, Carl Jefferson got the idea of pairing Roger Kellaway with Red Mitchell, who had played together now and then since the 1960s. The fascinating thing about the two is that Kellaway started his career as a bassist and Mitchell started his as a pianist, so naturally there is total empathy at work here, with Mitchell intertwining his instrument with Kellaway's piano as an equal melodic partner instead of a mere time keeper. With a bass player, and a rambunctious one at that, feeding him lines, Kellaway is looser and more apt to flash streaks of wit—which "It's a Wonderful World" does in spades—than on his Maybeck solo recital. His technique, as always, is dazzling, erudite, and all over the keyboard. Although of course no one suspected it at the time, this turned out to be Mitchell's last recording—he died of a stroke less than six months later—and his ironic musings about his jaunty self-penned title track, "Life's a take, and you only get one of them," make this session a bittersweet one. *—Richard S. Ginell*

Sue Keller

b. Jul. 7, 1952, Allentown, PA
Piano / Ragtime, Classic Jazz

A talented ragtime pianist and occasional vocalist who has thus far put out four CDs on her HVR label, Sue Keller started playing piano when she was four. She also studied flute and took voice lessons, played guitar and sang in some school operas. After a wide variety of musical jobs (including playing rock), she started concentrating more on vintage jazz and ragtime. In 1992 Sue Keller established Ragtime Press to publish rags by little-known composers and the HVR label to document her music. —*Scott Yanow*

Kellerized / 1992 / Ragtime Press ◆◆◆◆

On her debut recording, pianist Sue Keller mostly performs material written before 1926, including a few pop songs of the era (such as "Alabamy Bound" and "Waitin' for the Robert E. Lee"), some ragtime tunes, and pieces by Luckey Roberts and James P. Johnson. In addition, Keller debuts her "The Blundering Buffalo" and plays a couple of fairly recent rags. Her stride style and melodic yet rhythmic approach to improvising is quite appealing. —*Scott Yanow*

Nola / 1993 / Ragtime Press ◆◆◆◆◆

Although essentially a ragtime pianist, Sue Keller usually alters the classic compositions a bit, infusing her performances with her own appealing musical personality. Keller has emerged in recent years as an important force not only in keeping ragtime alive but in mixing together both early and recent compositions. Her third CD has many rewarding moments as she sticks mostly to lesser-known material including "Agitation Rag," "Crazy Bone Rag," two Zez Confrey numbers plus four newer rags from the 1970s and '80s. Her singing on a few tracks (closer to Broadway cabaret in style than to jazz) is okay but of lesser importance next to her sparkling and frequently superb piano playing. —*Scott Yanow*

● Ol' Muddy / 1993 / Ragtime Press ◆◆◆◆◆

A superior ragtime/stride pianist who is not too shy to improvise a bit even on classic rags, Sue Keller has recorded several excellent CDs for her Ragtime Press label. Due to the particularly strong material on the release, this CD is a good place to begin exploring Keller's music. In addition to vintage tunes from the 1920s and a variety of rags (both famous and obscure), Keller also performs six newer rags, including her "Cranberry Stomp" and two pieces from Tex Wyndham. A well-rounded set highlighted by such numbers as "The Chevy Chase," "Alligator Crawl," "Castle House Rag" and "New Orleans World's Fair Rag." —*Scott Yanow*

Ragtime Sue / 1994 / Ragtime Press ◆◆◆◆

Sue Keller's fourth release for Ragtime Press finds the pianist not only playing classic rags but popular songs of the early days (including "Alexander's Ragtime Band" and "St. Louis Blues") and, most significantly, five rags written since 1975. She also sings a few of the non-ragtime pieces with a decent and spirited voice. However the emphasis is on her piano playing and Keller manages to bring life to the veteran selections by varying the tempos. This CD contains fresh and enthusiastic renditions that keep ragtime from being just a museum piece. —*Scott Yanow*

I Got What It Takes / 1997 / Ragtime Press ◆◆◆◆

Pianist/singer Sue Keller helps keep ragtime alive in her series of recordings for her Ragtime Press label. This particular collection mixes vintage works (including "Carolina Shout," Scott Joplin's "Gladiolus Rag," Irving Berlin's "International Rag" and James Scott's "Honey Moon Rag") with some material from the 1920s and five works from the 1980s. Keller often plays out of tempo in spots, uses pauses effectively, and puts plenty of feeling into her interpretations. Her occasional vocals on tunes such as "I Got What It Takes" and "After You've Gone" are OK, but it is her piano playing that is most notable. —*Scott Yanow*

Peck Kelley

b. Oct. 22, 1898, Houston, TX, d. Dec. 26, 1980, Houston, TX
Piano / Classic Jazz

For a brief while before the end of the LP era, it was possible for there to be a Peck Kelley section in the jazz section of some record stores. Considering that Kelley avoided leaving Houston throughout his life and went out of his way not to be recorded, it is miraculous that any documentation exists. In the 1920s Kelley led Peck's Bad Boys in Texas, which featured a young Jack Teagarden and Pee Wee Russell. A talented pianist considered advanced at the time, Kelley was supposed to join Russell, Bix Beiderbecke and Frankie Trumbauer at a gig in St. Louis, but union problems prevented that and Kelley used the excuse to stay home. He was constantly offered jobs up north by major bandleaders and celebrities (including Bing Crosby) but turned them all down. In 1983 (a couple years after his death) a double-LP was released by Commodore featuring Kelley in 1957 near the end of his career playing with a sextet. Shortly after, the collector's label Arcadia came out with privately recorded solo and duet performances from 1951 and 1953. On a whole these rough but very interesting recordings prove that Kelley was advanc-

ing with the times, holding onto his roots in stride while showing that he was quite familiar with Lennie Tristano. —*Scott Yanow*

Out of Obscurity / July 12, 1951+1953 / Arcadia ◆◆◆◆

Peck Kelley went out of his way throughout his career to avoid recording. It was only after his death in 1980 that private tapes were released, allowing listeners to hear how the legendary pianist sounded. This double LP has a short interview with Kelley in the early 1970s, a series of piano solos from 1951 and 1953 and five solos by his friend, fellow pianist Lynn "Son" Harrell. A fascinating set that has not yet been reissued on CD, the performances (decently if not flawlessly recorded) show that Kelley had evolved through the years from a stride player to one not unaware of the music of Lennie Tristano and Bud Powell; an extra bonus is a fairly definitive biographical booklet. A couple sessions acquired by Commodore and released elsewhere also shed some light on Peck Kelley's barely documented legacy. —*Scott Yanow*

Jam / Jun. 9, 1957+Jun. 16, 1957 / Commodore ◆◆◆◆◆

Other than a set released by the collectors' label Arcadia, this double-LP has all of the recordings of the legendary pianist and bandleader Peck Kelley. Kelley did his best to remain obscure and unrecorded throughout his life, despite being quite active playing in Texas. These private sessions feature him in a sextet with local players including clarinetist Dick Shannon and guitarist Felix Stagno. Kelley stretches out on 13 standards and a blues, hinting at his roots in 1920s jazz but often sounding surprisingly modern on such numbers a "Limehouse Blues," "Riverboat Shuffle," "You Took Advantage of Me" and "Tea for Two." An important historical release that has not yet been reissued on CD. —*Scott Yanow*

Jon-Erik Kellso

b. 1964
Cornet / Dixieland

An excellent hot jazz trumpeter, Jon-Erik Kellso play that on several Arbors recordings in the mid-1990s, put him near the top of his field. After attending Wayne Street University, he played with the New McKinney's Cotton Pickers and J.C. Heard's Orchestra. Kellso moved to New York in 1989 and was soon working with the who's who of mainstream jazz, including Dan Barrett, Dick Hyman, Kenny Davern, Howard Alden and Marty Grosz. A member of James Dapogny's Chicago Jazz band and Vince Giordano's Nighthawks, Kellso has appeared on record dates, including with Rick Fay and the Magnificent Seven; his debut session as a leader was for Arbors in 1993. —*Scott Yanow*

● Chapter 1 / Apr. 26, 1993-Apr. 27, 1993 / Arbors ◆◆◆◆

Jon-Erik Kellso is a fine young trumpeter who made a strong impression with this early effort for Arbors. Joined by Scott Robinson on tenor, C-melody sax and clarinet, pianist Jeremy Kahn, guitarist Frank Vignola, bassist Milt Hinton and drummer Chuck Riggs, Kellso mostly interprets swing-era standards with a couple of originals and a few obscurities (including Duke Ellington's "Pelican Drag") added for variety. Kellso has a warm tone and a swinging style, making this a fine outing and a good introduction to his playing. —*Scott Yanow*

The Plot Thickens / 1997 / Arbors ◆◆◆

Julie Kelly

b. Oct. 28, 1947, Oakland, CA
Vocals / Standards

A fine singer based in Los Angeles, Julie Kelly studied classical guitar and attended Oakland City College. She lived in Brazil during 1970 and then started seriously performing in 1973. She freelanced in San Francisco (including with John Handy's group), moved to Los Angeles in 1980 and has recorded for Pausa and CMG. Julie Kelly teaches and performs regularly in L.A. —*Scott Yanow*

We're on Our Way / 1985 / Pausa ◆◆◆◆◆

Singer Julie Kelly's first recording includes a true classic, "All My Tomorrows," which features a brilliant trumpet solo from Bobby Ojeda. Kelly also shows plenty of potential on some then-recent tunes, including numbers by Lorraine Feather/David Benoit, Betty Carter, B.B. King and Bob Dorough (an excellent rendition of "Better than Anything"). With arrangements and keyboard work by Steve Kaplan and guest appearances by saxophonists Vince Denham and Gordon Goodwin and trumpeters Ojeda and Frank Szabo, this is a particularly memorable set, the best of Julie Kelly's early recordings. This LP from the defunct Pausa label will hopefully reappear on CD someday. —*Scott Yanow*

Never Let Me Go / 1986 / Pausa ◆◆◆

● Some Other Time / Aug. 13, 1988-Aug. 14, 1988 / Chase Music ◆◆◆◆◆

At first Julie Kelly's voice may sound a bit jarring to some but her singing on this CD will win most listeners over. Kelly slides between notes, sometimes speaks part of the lyrics (as on "Some Other Time") and she takes chances, especially harmonically. Her repertoire on this Chase CD is filled with unusual choices such as two obscure Chick Corea tunes ("Highwire" and "Sounds"), Stevie Wonder's "Part Time Lover," Dave Grusin's "Bahia" and Nat Adderley's underrated classic "The Old Country." Assisted by strong support from a rhythm section led by pianist Tom Garvin and occasional solos from trumpeter Chris Botti and the reeds of Bob Franceschini, Julie Kelly has created her most intriguing and consistent recording. —*Scott Yanow*

Stories to Tell / 1993 / Chase Music ✦✦✦
This CD finds singer Julie Kelly in prime form. With the assistance of Bill Cunliffe on piano and synth, either Tom Warrington or John Clayton on bass, drummer Joe La Barbera and several guests (guitarist Larry Koonse, tenorman Bob Sheppard, trumpeter Clay Jenkins and percussionist Brian Kilgore), Kelly creates fresh interpretations of such songs as "The Surrey with the Fringe on Top," "Long Ago and Far Away," "A Sleepin' Bee" and a boppish "Royal Garden Blues." Most unusual is her transformation of "Tomorrow" (from *Annie*) into jazz. An excellent showcase for the talented singer, who both scats well and interprets lyrics with sensitivity. —*Scott Yanow*

Wynton Kelly

b. Dec. 2, 1931, Jamaica, **d.** Apr. 12, 1971, Toronto, Canada
Piano / Hard Bop
A superb accompanist loved by Miles Davis and Cannonball Adderley, Wynton Kelly was also a distinctive soloist whose decades later would be a strong influence on Benny Green. He grew up in Brooklyn and early on played in R&B bands led by Eddie "Cleanhead" Vinson, Hal Singer and Eddie "Lockjaw" Davis. Kelly, who recorded 14 titles for Blue Note in a trio (1951), worked with Dinah Washington, Dizzy Gillespie and Lester Young during 1951-52. After serving in the military he made a strong impression with Washington (1955-57), Charles Mingus (1956-57) and the Dizzy Gillespie big band (1957), but he would be most famous for his stint with Miles Davis (1959-63), recording such albums with Miles as *Kind of Blue, At the Blackhawk* and *Someday My Prince Will Come*. When he left Davis, Kelly took the rest of the rhythm section (bassist Paul Chambers and drummer Jimmy Cobb) with him to form his trio. The group actually sounded at its best backing Wes Montgomery. Before his early death, Kelly recorded as a leader for Blue Note, Riverside, Vee-Jay, Verve and Milestone. —*Scott Yanow*

Piano Interpretations / Jul. 25, 1951-Aug. 1, 1951 / Blue Note ✦✦✦✦
The obscure music on this CD has rarely been reissued. Pianist Wynton Kelly is heard with a trio (Fred Skeete or Oscar Pettiford on bass and drummer Lee Abrams) at the age of 19 when he was working as an accompanist for Dinah Washington. Featured on this recording a year before he joined Dizzy Gillespie and seven years before his next date as a leader, Kelly in 1951 was already long on his way to achieving his own sound. Influenced most by Bud Powell but also displaying some of the joy of Teddy Wilson's style along with his own chord voicings, Wynton Kelly gives listeners no hints on this enjoyable CD (which has two complete sessions plus three alternate takes) that he was still a teenager. —*Scott Yanow*

Piano / Jan. 31, 1958 / Original Jazz Classics ✦✦✦✦✦
With the exception of an album for Blue Note in 1951, this was pianist Wynton Kelly's first opportunity to record as a leader. At the time he was still a relative unknown but would soon get a certain amount of fame as Miles Davis' favorite accompanist. With guitarist Kenny Burrell, bassist Paul Chambers and (on three of the seven selections) drummer Philly Joe Jones, Kelly performs four jazz standards, Oscar Brown, Jr's "Strong Man" and two of his originals. Kelly became a major influence on pianists of the 1960s and '70s, and one can hear the genesis of many other players in these swinging performances. The CD reissue adds an alternate take of "Dark Eyes" to the original program. —*Scott Yanow*

Kelly Blue / Feb. 19, 1959-Mar. 10, 1959 / Original Jazz Classics ✦✦✦✦✦
Originally cut for Riverside, this set mostly features the influential pianist Wynton Kelly in a trio with his fellow rhythm section mates from the Miles Davis bands, bassist Paul Chambers and drummer Jimmy Cobb. "Kelly Blue" and "Keep It Moving" add cornetist Nat Adderley, flutist Bobby Jaspar and the tenor of Benny Golson to the band for some variety. The CD reissue augments the program with a previously unreleased "Do Nothin' till You Hear from Me" and the alternate take of "Keep It Moving." Kelly was renowned as an accompanist, but as he shows on a set including three of his originals and four familiar standards (including "Softly as in a Morning Sunrise" and "Willow Weep for Me"), he was also a strong bop-based soloist too. A fine example of his talents. —*Scott Yanow*

Kelly Great / Aug 12, 1959 / Vee-Jay ✦✦✦
Pianist Wynton Kelly teams up with trumpeter Lee Morgan, tenor saxophonist Wayne Shorter, bassist Paul Chambers and drummer Philly Joe Jones for a fine advanced hard bop date. There are four originals (all virtually forgotten decades later) by Kelly, Shorter and Morgan but it is the lone standard, a playful version of

"June Night" (which has some puckish Morgan trumpet), that is the standout. At 35 minutes, this CD reissue of a former LP is fairly brief, but what is here on the formerly rare session should satisfy collectors of the style. —*Scott Yanow*

Kelly at Midnight / Apr. 27, 1960 / Vee-Jay ✦✦✦
The problem with this CD reissue is simply that at just over 32 minutes there is not enough of it. The influential pianist Wynton Kelly swings hard and creatively within the bebop tradition with the assistance of bassist Paul Chambers and drummer Philly Joe Jones. Although all three musicians were alumni of Miles Davis' Quintet, Jones had departed before Kelly joined up. However their familiarity with each other's playing is obvious on this brief but enjoyable set. —*Scott Yanow*

★ **Someday My Prince Will Come** / Sep. 20, 1961-Sep. 21, 1961 / Vee-Jay ✦✦✦✦✦
Pianist Wynton Kelly is heard on this CD reissue (the ten songs from the original LP plus five "new" alternate takes) with either bassist Sam Jones and drummer Jimmy Cobb or bassist Paul Chambers and drummer Philly Joe Jones. His light touch and perfect taste are very much present along with a steady stream of purposeful single-note lines that are full of surprising twists. Trumpeter Lee Morgan and tenor saxophonist Wayne Shorter drop by for one song (the blues "Wrinkles"), but otherwise this recommended set (a definitive Wynton Kelly release) showcases magical trio performances. —*Scott Yanow*

It's All Right / Mar. 10, 1964-Mar. 19, 1964 / Verve ✦✦✦
The Wynton Kelly Trio (consisting of the pianist, bassist Paul Chambers and drummer Jimmy Cobb) are augmented by guitarist Kenny Burrell and percussionist Candido on this 1997 CD reissue. The music is essentially easy-listening jazz with concise versions of ten numbers, including a rendition of Charles Lloyd's "One for Joan" that was only previously out in Europe. In addition to the one "new" selection, a few unnecessary false starts for "Kelly Roll" have been included. A brief "The Fall of Love" finds the group joined by a steel drum band, although it makes little impression. The best are "Portrait of Jeannie" and "On the Trail," but overall this effort is not too essential. —*Scott Yanow*

Blues on Purpose / Jun. 25, 1965-Aug. 17, 1965 / Xanadu ✦✦✦✦
Pianist Wynton Kelly is heard on these formerly private tapes from the Half Note (where his trio usually accompanied Wes Montgomery) jamming with bassist Paul Chambers and drummer Jimmy Cobb. Released for the initial time as a 1983 Xanadu LP, the recording quality is only so-so, but Kelly's consistently creative ideas on three standards, plus "Blues on Purpose," "Somebody's Blues" and "Another Blues," are enjoyable and swinging. —*Scott Yanow*

Full View / 1967 / Original Jazz Classics ✦✦✦
Pianist Wynton Kelly's next-to-last set as a leader (he would record a slightly later date for Delmark) featured him at a time when his influence was waning and he was overshadowed by more advanced players. However, Kelly's impact would begin to grow again after his death, when the Young Lions movement began in the early 1980s; certainly pianist Benny Green was greatly touched by Kelly's conception. This Milestone trio set, reissued on CD, matches Kelly with bassist Ron McClure and drummer Jimmy Cobb on a fine program mostly filled with standards but also including the recent Burt Bacharach hit "Walk on By" and Kelly's original "Scufflin'." —*Scott Yanow*

Last Trio Session / Aug. 4, 1968 / Delmark ✦✦✦
The trio led by pianist Wynton Kelly, which also included bassist Paul Chambers and drummer Jimmy Cobb, first functioned as the rhythm section of Miles Davis' Quintet in 1958. In 1963, they left Davis' band and spent time as Wes Montgomery's backup group; the unit stayed together until Chambers' death on Jan. 4, 1969, a run of over ten years (Kelly would pass away two years later). Their final studio session, released for the first time domestically by Delmark in 1988, is unfortunately partly hindered by the inclusion of some unsuitable pop songs (including "Say a Little Prayer for Me," "Watch What Happens," "Light My Fire" and "Yesterday"), but typically, the musicians do their best to swing the tunes. Best are "Kelly's Blues" and "Castilian Waltz." However, this historic set is not too essential overall. —*Scott Yanow*

Stan Kenton

b. Dec. 15, 1911, Wichita, KS, **d.** Aug. 25, 1979, Los Angeles, CA
Piano, Leader, Arranger, Composer / Progressive Jazz, Traditional Pop, Big Band
There have been few jazz musicians as consistently controversial as Stan Kenton. Dismissed by purists of various genres while loved by many others, Kenton ranks up there with Chet Baker and Sun Ra as jazz's top cult figure. He led a succession of highly original bands that often emphasized emotion, power and advanced harmonies over swing, and this upset listeners who felt that all big bands should aim to sound like Count Basie. Kenton always had a different vision.

Stan Kenton played in the 1930s in the dance bands of Vido Musso and Gus Arnheim but he was born to be a leader. In 1941 he formed his first orchestra, which later was named after his theme song "Artistry in Rhythm." A decent Earl Hines-influenced pianist, Kenton was much more important in the early days as an arranger and inspiration for his loyal sidemen. Although there were no major names in his first band (bassist Howard Rumsey and trumpeter Chico Alvarez come the closest), Kenton spent the summer of 1941 playing regularly before a very appreciative audience at the Rendezvous Ballroom in Balboa Beach, CA. Influenced by Jimmie Lunceford (who, like Kenton, enjoyed high-note trumpeters and thick-toned tenors), the Stan Kenton Orchestra struggled a bit after its initial success. Its Decca recordings were not big sellers and a stint as Bob Hope's backup radio band was an unhappy experience; Les Brown permanently took Kenton's place.

By late 1943 with a Capitol contract, a popular record in "Eager Beaver" and growing recognition, the Stan Kenton Orchestra was gradually catching on. Its soloists during the war years included Art Pepper, briefly Stan Getz, altoist Boots Mussulli and singer Anita O'Day. By 1945 the band had evolved quite a bit. Pete Rugolo became the chief arranger (extending Kenton's ideas), Bob Cooper and Vido Musso offered very different tenor styles and June Christy was Kenton's new singer; her popular hits (including "Tampico" and "Across the Alley from the Alamo") made it possible for Kenton to finance his more ambitious projects. Calling his music "Progressive Jazz," Kenton sought to lead a concert orchestra as opposed to a dance band at a time when most big bands were starting to break up. By 1947 Kai Winding was greatly influencing the sound of Kenton's trombonists, the trumpet section included such screamers as Buddy Childers, Ray Wetzel and Al Porcino, Jack Costanzo's bongos were bringing Latin rhythms into Kenton's sound and a riotous version of "The Peanut Vendor" contrasted with the somber "Elegy for Alto." Kenton had succeeded in forming a radical and very original band that gained its own audience.

In 1949 Stan Kenton took a year off. In 1950 he put together his most advanced band, the 39-piece Innovations in Modern Music orchestra that included 16 strings, a woodwind section and two French horns. Its music ranged from the unique and very dense modern classical charts of Bob Graettinger to works that somehow swung despite the weight. Such major players as Maynard Ferguson (whose high-note acrobatics set new standards), Shorty Rogers, Milt Bernhart, John Graas, Art Pepper, Bud Shank, Bob Cooper, Laurindo Almeida, Shelly Manne and June Christy were part of this remarkable project but, from a commercial standpoint, it was really impossible. Kenton managed two tours during 1950-51 but soon reverted to his usual 19-piece lineup. Then quite unexpectedly, Stan Kenton went through a swinging period. The charts of such arrangers as Shorty Rogers, Gerry Mulligan, Lennie Niehaus, Marty Paich, Johnny Richards and particularly Bill Holman and Bill Russo began to dominate the repertoire. Such talented players (in addition to the ones already named) as Lee Konitz, Conte Candoli, Sal Salvador, Stan Levey, Frank Rosolino, Richie Kamuca, Zoot Sims, Sam Noto, Bill Perkins, Charlie Mariano, Mel Lewis, Pete Candoli, Lucky Thompson, Carl Fontana, Pepper Adams and Jack Sheldon made strong contributions. The music was never predictable and could get quite bombastic but it managed to swing while still keeping the Kenton sound.

Stan Kenton's last successful experiment was his mellophonium band of 1960-63. Despite the difficulties in keeping the four mellophoniums (which formed their own separate section) in tune, this particular Kenton Orchestra had its exciting moments. However, from 1963 on, the flavor of the Kenton big band began to change. Rather than using talented soloists, Kenton emphasized relatively inexpensive youth at the cost of originality. While the arrangements (including those of Hank Levy) continued to be quite challenging, after Gabe Baltazar's "graduation" in 1965, there were few new important Kenton alumni (other than Peter Erskine and Tim Hagans). For many of the young players, touring with Stan Kenton would be the high point of their careers rather than just an important early step. *Kenton Plays Wagner* (1964) was an important project but by then the bandleader's attention was on jazz education. By conducting a countless number of clinics and making his charts available to college and high-school stage bands, Kenton ensured that there would be many bands that sounded like his, and the inverse result was that his own young orchestra sounded like a professional college band! Kenton continued leading and touring with his big band up until his death in 1979.

Stan Kenton recorded for Capitol for 25 years (1943-68) and in the 1970s formed his Creative World label to reissue most of his Capitol output and record his current band. In recent times Capitol has begun reissuing Kenton's legacy on CD and there have been two impressive Mosaic box sets. —*Scott Yanow*

Kenton Era / Nov. 1, 1940-Sep. 18, 1953 / Creative World ◆◆◆◆◆

This four-LP set contains a great deal of extraordinary music from Stan Kenton, most of it recorded live in concert or taken from radio transcriptions. Kenton is heard reminiscing about his first 15 years in the business; there are some selections taken from his famous 1941 stint at the Rendezvous Ballroom in Balboa, CA, numbers from rehearsals in 1944, radio airchecks dating from 1944-48, some star-

tling performances by Kenton's Innovations orchestra of 1950-51 and a few swinging numbers from his 1952-53 big band. Virtually all of the music is rare, making this an essential acquisition for collectors. —*Scott Yanow*

Balboa/Summer 1941 / 1941 / Mark ◆◆◆

This LP contains some of the radio transcriptions recorded by Stan Kenton and his orchestra during their early days. Although the album makes it appear that the music might have been performed live in Balboa where the orchestra was creating a bit of a sensation, these are actually noncommercial studio recordings. The emphasis is on the reed section (which included Red Dorris on tenor and altoist Jack Ordean) although trumpeter Chico Alvarez is also heard from. The abstract music, although very different from the style that Stan Kenton would soon develop, was already very original and is worth investigating. —*Scott Yanow*

The Uncollected Stan Kenton & His Orchestra, Vol. 1 (1941) / 1941 / Hindsight ◆◆◆

Hindsight has released six Stan Kenton LPs originating from noncommercial sources. The first volume, taken from various radio transcriptions cut during 1941, gives one an interesting look at the early Kenton orchestra including performances of many songs that were not otherwise recorded by the innovative bandleader. Red Norris (who takes the tenor solos and has two vocals) was Kenton's first star and trumpeter Chico Alvarez has a few good spots on trumpet, but it is the unusual arrangements that gave this orchestra its own unique personality. —*Scott Yanow*

The Uncollected Stan Kenton & His Orchestra, Vol. 2 (1941) / 1941 / Hindsight ◆◆◆

The second of the six Hindsight Stan Kenton LPs covers the same early period as the first. Tenor saxophonist Red Dorris and trumpeter Chico Alvarez are the main soloists while Kenton's arrangements (including the four part "Suite for Saxophones") are the main reason that this orchestra gained such a loyal following. No other big band sounded like it and, although its sound would evolve and change (the emphasis in the early days was on the saxophone section led by altoist Jack Ordean), the performances by Stan Kenton's first orchestra can easily be enjoyed by the fans of his later bands. These formerly rare performances are taken from radio transcriptions and contain many songs not otherwise recorded by Kenton. —*Scott Yanow*

Broadcast Transcriptions 1941-1945 / Aug. 1941-Dec. 1944 / Music & Arts ◆◆◆◆

The music on this CD, 13 selections from 1941 and 17 from 1944, was mostly out previously on Hindsight LPs although the Stan Kenton Mosaic box set does not duplicate any of the performances. These radio transcriptions add to what is known about Stan Kenton's music for the 1941 tracks precede his orchestra's first studio recordings while the later selections are from a little-documented period with six vocals by Anita O'Day. The earlier performances feature the leader's ambitious writing (which made his big band from the start sound quite unique) and short solos from trumpeter Chico Alvarez and tenor saxophonist Red Dorris. The 1944 band had almost completely different personnel with most of the solos taken by trumpeter Buddy Childers and Emmett Carls on tenor (although the young Stan Getz has two spots). Highly recommended to Stan Kenton collectors who do not already have the Hindsight sets. —*Scott Yanow*

The Formative Years / Sep. 11, 1941+Feb. 13, 1942 / Creative World ◆◆◆

It is easy to believe that Stan Kenton's first recordings took place when he signed with Capitol in 1943, but this LP contains his nine earlier performances for Decca. None of the songs were hits even though the band had caused a sensation in 1941 with their engagement in Balboa, CA. With tenor saxophonist Red Dorris and trumpeter Chico Alvarez as the main soloists and altoist Jack Ordean leading the saxophone section (which in the early days was more important to Kenton's sound than the trumpets), this orchestra already stood out from its contemporaries. Highlights among the nine performances on this necessarily brief album (only 27 minutes) are "Gambler's Blues," "Reed Rapture" and "Concerto for Doghouse." This set is essential for all true Stan Kenton fans. —*Scott Yanow*

☆ **The Complete Capitol Studio Recordings of Stan Kenton 1943-47** / Nov. 19, 1943-Dec. 22, 1947 / Mosaic ◆◆◆◆◆

Documenting Stan Kenton's always-controversial but never sleepy music, the seven-CD *Complete Capitol Studio Recordings of Stan Kenton 1943-47* features the orchestra at a time when it was reaching its greatest popularity, evolving from using Kenton's charts into the Pete Rugolo era. In addition to some unreleased tracks, there are also several rare sessions included that were recorded at the time strictly for radio airplay. Most of Kenton's biggest hits ("Artistry in Rhythm," "Eager Beaver," "And Her Tears Flowed like Wine," "Tampico," "Southern Scandal," "Artistry Jumps," "Intermission Riff," "Across the Alley from the Alamo" and "The Peanut Vendor" are here as are many concert works. A classic reissue. —*Scott Yanow*

Milestones / Nov. 19, 1943-Dec. 22, 1947 / Creative World ◆◆◆◆
This LP from Creative World has the original version of Stan Kenton's theme song, "Artistry in Rhythm," his first hit "Eager Beaver," "Artistry Jumps" and eight of his most popular recordings from the 1946-47 period including "Intermission Riff," "Concerto to End All Concertos" and "The Peanut Vendor." This music is essential in one form or another and virtually all of it is available in the four-CD Kenton set *Retrospective*. These performances are still exciting a half-century later. —*Scott Yanow*

By Request, Vol. 3 (1943-1951) / Nov. 19, 1943-Mar. 28, 1951 / Creative World ◆◆◆◆
The third volume in Creative World's *By Request* series mostly sticks to the 1946-47 period with three numbers from 1943-45 and three dating from 1950-51. Highlights include "Harlem Folk Dance," "Southern Scandal," "Unison Riff" and "Dynaflow" and among the soloists are altoist Art Pepper (heard from in two different periods), the tenor of Vido Musso, trumpeter Chico Alvarez and trombonist Kai Winding; in addition there are two vocal tracks for the Pastels and Anita O'Day sings "Gotta Be Gettin.'" This diverse LP fills some important gaps since many of the selections are not reissued that often; most importantly the music is consistently enjoyable. —*Scott Yanow*

★ **Retrospective** / Nov. 19, 1943-Jul. 18, 1968 / Capitol ◆◆◆◆◆
This four-CD set has virtually all of Stan Kenton's most significant recordings from his prime years. Although Kenton completists will prefer to pick up dozens of his individual Creative World releases instead, all other jazz collectors are well advised to get this very well-conceived release. Starting with the original version of "Artistry in Rhythm" from 1943 and continuing through all of the different editions of Kenton's orchestras up to 1968's "How Are Things in Glocca Morra," this set includes not only all of the band's most popular recordings but some of its most inventive and esoteric ones too. Whether it be "Tampico," "Concerto to End All Concertos," "Jolly Rogers," "Art Pepper," "Orange Colored Sky" (with guest Nat King Cole), "All About Ronnie," "Peanut Vendor," and "Maria" or a section of "City of Glass" and a number from the Kenton/Wagner album, the remarkable career of Stan Kenton is covered definitively on this package. It's highly recommended for all jazz collections. —*Scott Yanow*

The Uncollected Stan Kenton & His Orchestra, Vol. 3 (1943-1944) / 1943-1944 / Hindsight ◆◆◆
The Stan Kenton Orchestra, after some initial success, was struggling a bit during the period covered by this Hindsight LP, the third of six volumes. The material performed on these radio broadcasts is certainly eclectic, ranging from such current pop hits as "Paper Doll," "Hit that Jive, Jack" and "Begin the Beguine" to "Eager Beaver" and "In a Little Spanish Town." However the Kenton Orchestra (which was then in a transitional stage) was already quite unique and among the many soloists are a young Stan Getz on tenor (taking a spot on "I Got Rhythm"), veteran tenor Red Dorris and trumpeter Karl George (well featured on "Liza"). Anita O'Day (who was only with the band a brief time) has three vocals and Dolly Mitchell is heard on "Shoo Shoo Baby." —*Scott Yanow*

In Hollywood / May 20, 1944-Dec. 6, 1944 / Mr. Music ◆◆◆◆

Lighter Side / May 20, 1944-Jan. 25, 1955 / Creative World ◆◆◆◆
When one thinks of Stan Kenton's music, humor is not the first word that comes to mind. But the innovative bandleader did record some humorous numbers through the years and 11 are included on this memorable LP. "The Hot Canary" (which features some ridiculous high-note trumpet from Maynard Ferguson) and "Blues in Burlesque" (a hilarious satire of rhythm & blues with a remarkable vocal by Shelly Manne) are classics of a sort but all of these performances stick in one's mind. —*Scott Yanow*

By Request, Vol. 1 (1944-1952) / Dec. 15, 1944-Mar. 20, 1952 / Creative World ◆◆◆◆
Other than three early selections ("Balboa Bash," "Machito" and "Harlem Holiday"), this LP concentrates on the more swinging performances from Stan Kenton's orchestras of 1950-52. Highlights include two charts by Shorty Rogers ("Jolly Rogers" and "Round Robin"), "Blues in Riff" and "Love for Sale." Many notable names have solo space including trombonist Kai Winding,, tenor-great Bob Cooper, altoist Art Pepper, Shorty Rogers and Maynard Ferguson on trumpets, and altoist Bud Shank. It's a strong introduction to the music of Stan Kenton. —*Scott Yanow*

The Uncollected Stan Kenton & His Orchestra, Vol. 4 (1944-1945) / 1944-1945 / Hindsight ◆◆◆
This LP is the fourth in Hindsight's series of Stan Kenton material originally recorded for the C.P. MacGregor radio transcription service and leased to radio stations for airplay only. These performances (which were never available commercially before) feature two different editions of the Stan Kenton Orchestra along with vocal features for Anita O'Day and her successor June Christy. The music is

quite distinctive, standing apart from the swing and bop idioms and highlighted by the arrangements of Pete Rugolo and Gene Roland. Stan Kenton fans will want all six LPs in this enjoyable series. —*Scott Yanow*

Some Women I've Known / Jan. 16, 1945-Sep. 11, 1963 / Creative World ◆◆◆
This fine LP contains 12 performances, two apiece from these six singers with Stan Kenton's Orchestra: Anita O'Day, June Christy, Chris Connor, Jerri Winters, Ann Richards and Jean Turner. With the exception of Connor's "All About Ronnie," none of the recordings are all that familiar and five were actually issued for the first time on this album. Fans of swing-oriented singers will enjoy the valuable set. —*Scott Yanow*

Christy Years / May 4, 1945-Dec. 21, 1947 / Creative World ◆◆◆◆◆
Of all the vocalists who worked with Stan Kenton's Orchestra, June Christy was the most popular and fit the group's music the best. In fact her popularity indirectly helped Kenton finance his more adventurous projects. This LP from Creative World has a dozen of Christy's best recordings including such hits as "Tampico," "Across the Alley from the Alamo," "Shoo Fly Pie and Apple Pan Dowdy" and "How High the Moon." Such soloists as Vido Musso on tenor, trombonist Kai Winding and trumpeter Chico Alvarez also have spots, while altoist Art Pepper pops up on "How High the Moon." —*Scott Yanow*

Encores / Oct. 30, 1945-Dec. 22, 1947 / Creative World ◆◆◆
This LP contains 11 fairly rare and diverse performances from the 1945-47 edition of Stan Kenton's Orchestra. June Christy sings "He's Funny That Way" and such soloists as Vido Musso on tenor, trumpeter Chico Alvarez, trombonist Kai Winding, Bob Cooper on tenor and altoist Art Pepper have spots. None of the selections are considered classics but most (particularly "Painted Rhythm," "Capitol Punishment" and "Abstraction") should delight Kenton collectors. —*Scott Yanow*

Artistry in Rhythm / Oct. 30, 1945-Sep. 4, 1950 / Creative ◆◆◆◆
This sampler from the Creative World catalog consists of 12 performances by Stan Kenton's Orchestra, mostly from 1945-46. There are four June Christy vocals (including "Just A-Sittin' and A-Rockin'"), a pair of features for guest tenor Vido Musso ("Come Back o Sorrento" and "Santa Lucia") and six other pieces (all Kenton and Pete Rugolo arrangements) of which the highlights include "Safranski," "Artisrtry in Bolero" and "Opus in Pastels." It's a fine sampling of Stan Kenton's mid-'40s orchestra. —*Scott Yanow*

Uncollected Stan Kenton & His Orchestra, Vol. 5 (1945-1947) / 1945-1947 / Hindsight ◆◆◆
It was during the period covered by this Hindsight LP that Stan Kenton caught on and became a household name. These radio performances mostly feature arrangements by Pete Rugolo and Gene Roland, although Boots Mussulli contributed a memorable rendition of "I Surrender Dear" and Kenton himself wrote the chart for "Begin the Beguine." Singer June Christy, tenor Vido Musso, trombonist Kai Winding, trumpeter Buddy Childers are the main stars but it is the ensembles and the distinctive arrangements that gave this edition of the Stan Kenton Orchestra its own personality. All of the well-recorded sets in this valuable Hindsight series are recommended to Kenton fans. —*Scott Yanow*

A Concert in Progressive Jazz / Sep. 24, 1947-Sep. 20, 1951 / Creative World ◆◆◆◆◆
This is a fascinating collection of very advanced music. All but two numbers from 1951 ("Theme for Alto" and June Christy's vocal feature on "Come Rain or Come Shine") are from 1947 and all of the charts except for Bob Graettinger's somewhat amazing "Thermopolae" are by Pete Rugolo. This LP contains some of Rugolo's most interesting work (highlighted by "Elegy for Alto," "Monotony," "Lonely Woman," "Cuban Carnival" and "Theme for Alto") and finds Stan Kenton realizing his goal of leading a concert orchestra rather than a dance band. The unique performances (many of which helped Stan Kenton become a cult hero) reward repeated listenings. —*Scott Yanow*

City of Glass / Dec. 6, 1947-May 28, 1953 / Capitol ◆◆◆◆◆
Bob Graettinger was arguably the most radical arranger to ever work in jazz. In fact, it is doubtful if any other big-band leader other than Stan Kenton (who always encouraged adventurous writers) would have used his very complex charts during this era. Graettinger's works, which were influenced by aspects of modern classical music (but were not at all derivative) are all included on this fascinating, if difficult, CD reissue. The four-part "City of Glass," the pieces that comprised "This-Modern World" and a variety of shorter works (including the remarkably dense "Thermopylae") make for some very stimulating listening. This is avant-garde music that still sounds futuristic 45 years later. —*Scott Yanow*

The Innovations Orchestra / Feb. 3, 1950-Aug. 24, 1950 / Capitol ◆◆◆◆◆
The Innovations Orchestra is a double-disc set that combines Stan Kenton's two albums with the Innovations Orchestra, *Innovations in Modern Music* and *Kenton Presents*, along with alternate takes. Kenton assembled the Innovations Orchestra in 1950 at his own expense and although the project sent him into debt, the music

he made was among his best. Featuring such soloists as Art Pepper, Maynard Ferguson, Laurindo Almeida and Bob Cooper, as well as arrangers like Neal Hefti, Shorty Rogers and Pete Rugolo, the two albums retain their power decades after their initial release, and this is the best way to hear the records, whether you're a long time fan or a curious neophyte. —*Leo Stanley*

Innovations in Modern Music / Feb. 3, 1950-Feb. 4, 1950 / Creative World ♦♦♦♦♦

In 1950 Stan Kenton led his most radical band, a 37-piece orchestra with 14 strings and such sidemen as altoists Art Pepper and Bud Shank, Bob Cooper on tenor, trumpeters Shorty Rogers, Chico Alvarez and Maynard Ferguson, trombonist Milt Bernhart, two French horns, a tuba, guitarist Laurindo Almeida, drummer Shelly Manne, Carlos Vidal on congas and singer June Christy. This LP contains some very advanced writing by Pete Rugolo ("Conflict" and "Mirage"), Bill Russo ("Solitaire") and particularly Bob Graettinger ("Incident in Jazz") in addition to features for Kenton's piano ("Theme for Sunday"), June Christy ("Lonesome Road") and Carlos Vidal ("Cuban Episode"). The music is often quite fascinating and very advanced; most of it is has not yet been reissued on CD. —*Scott Yanow*

Kenton Presents / Feb. 3, 1950-Aug. 24, 1950 / Creative World ♦♦♦♦♦

Stan Kenton's most ambitious orchestra was his huge 1950 band. This LP, which mostly contains material not yet reissued on CD, has self-titled showcases for "Art Pepper," "Maynard Ferguson," "June Christy" and "Shelly Manne" in addition to such pieces as "Halls of Brass," "House of Strings" and "Soliloquy." The soloists (which also include trombonist Milt Bernhart) are very impressive but it is the writing (by Shorty Rogers, Bill Russo, Frank Marks, Johnny Richards and Kenton himself) that is most startling, combining together aspects of modern classical music with the most advanced forms of jazz. Although Kenton's Innovations orchestra was a short-lived project and did not influence the future of jazz, its recordings still sound very adventurous over four decades later. —*Scott Yanow*

☆ **The Complete Capitol Recordings of Bill Holman** / Feb. 3, 1950-Sep. 11, 1963 / Mosaic ♦♦♦♦♦

This limited-edition box set is a bit unusual. Rather than reissuing the complete output of a particular artist during a certain era as Mosaic usually does, these four CDs contain all of Stan Kenton's recordings of arrangements by either Bill Holman or Bill Russo. There are three selections from the Innovations band of 1950-51, many recordings from the more swinging 1952-55 period (featuring such soloists as trumpeters Maynard Ferguson and Conte Candoli, trombonist Frank Rosolino, altoists Lee Konitz and Charlie Mariano, tenors Zoot Sims and Bill Perkins and singer Chris Connor) and Holman's three charts for Kenton's mellophonium band of 1961 in addition to less significant vocal features for Ann Richards and Jean Turner. Kenton completists will already have much of this material (only an early version of "All About Ronnie" was previously unissued), but this attractive box (which is overflowing with classics) will still be treasured by true Kentonites. —*Scott Yanow*

Artistry in Jazz / Feb. 5, 1950-Sep. 29, 1965 / Capitol ♦♦♦

This late-'70s LP (released as part of Capitol's *Jazz Classics* series) contains ten previously unissued studio performances by Stan Kenton's Orchestra covering a 15-year period. The highlights are many and the writing (by Gene Roland, Pete Rugolo, Shorty Rogers, Bill Holman, Johnny Richards, Clare Fischer and Kenton) is consistently adventurous. Soloists include such major players as altoist Art Pepper, trumpeter Shorty Rogers, tenor saxophonist Bob Cooper (well-featured on Shorty's "Coop's Solo"), altoist Lee Konitz (heard throughout Holman's "Of All Things"), trumpeter Jack Sheldon and altoist Bud Shank. This valuable music has yet to be reissued since its original release. —*Scott Yanow*

By Request, Vol. 4 (1950-1952) / Sep. 12, 1950-Sep. 11, 1952 / Creative World ♦♦♦

Stan Kenton's 1951-52 orchestra is well featured on the dozen somewhat obscure studio recordings included on this LP. With solo space allocated to altoist Art Pepper, trombonists Frank Rosolino and Milt Bernhart, trumpeter Conte Candoli and Maynard Ferguson, guitarist Laurindo Almeida and altoist Lee Konitz (there are also three vocals by the forgotten Jay Johnson and June Christy sings "Daddy"), bop fans should be interested in searching for this now-rare collection. The music is not essential and there are no classics here, but the set has its strong moments and most of it has not been reissued on CD yet. —*Scott Yanow*

Collector's Choice / Sep. 12, 1950-Feb. 11, 1956 / Creative World ♦♦♦

The emphasis is on standards and melodic material on this enjoyable LP from Creative World. Quite a few of the performances by Stan Kenton's Orchestra are features for talented individuals including the dramatic tenor of Vido Musso ("Santa Lucia" and "Pagliacci"), trumpeter Ray Wetzel ("September Song"), trombonist Milt Bernhart ("Artistry in Tango"), trombonist Carl Fontana ("Sunset Tower" and "Southern Scandal"), trumpeter Chico Alvarez ("Laura") and Maynard

Ferguson ("What's New"), although Shorty Rogers' "Viva Prado" is probably the best-known recording. A worthy collection mostly dating from 1950-51. —*Scott Yanow*

Stan Kenton and His Innovations Orchestra / 1950-1951 / LaserLight ♦♦♦♦

The total amount of time (a little over 38 minutes) is quite brief for this CD but the release is selling for a budget price and the previously unreleased performances are quite valuable. Stan Kenton's Innovations Orchestra (39 members strong counting 16 strings) was the bandleader's most ambitious project with the many brilliant soloists (including altoists Bud Shank and Art Pepper, Bob Cooper on tenor, trumpeters Conte Candoli and Maynard Ferguson) being challenged by the very complex arrangements of Bill Russo, Shorty Rogers and Bob Graettinger among others. This recommended set is highlighted by four selections named after their stars ("Shelly Manne," "Conte Candoli," "Art Pepper" and "Bob Cooper"), Bill Russo's "Improvisation" and Bob Graettinger's dense "Reflections." —*Scott Yanow*

Summer of '51 / 1951 / Garland ♦♦♦♦

When one thinks of Stan Kenton's 1951 music, it is of his huge Innovations Orchestra, which sported a full string section and played very advanced works. However, later in the year Kenton cut back to a conventional 19-piece band, a unit that was only together six months and made few studio recordings. This collector's CD features the all-star orchestra broadcasting from the Hollywood Palladium and it is particularly interesting to hear the unit interpreting some of Kenton's earlier hits. With such distinctive soloists as Maynard Ferguson, Shorty Rogers, Milt Bernhart, Art Pepper and Bob Cooper (plus a couple of vocals by Jay Johnson), the highlights include fresh versions of "Machito," "Eager Beaver," "Collaboration," "Painted Rhythm" and "Intermission Riff." —*Scott Yanow*

Live (1951) / Mar. 1951 / Bandstand ♦♦♦♦

This collector's CD is a bit unusual because it features Stan Kenton's Innovations Orchestra without its string section. Actually the big band mostly sticks to its repertoire of the 1940s on these radio broadcasts, playing fairly straightahead charts that give such players as trumpeters Maynard Ferguson and Shorty Rogers, altoists Art Pepper and Bud Shank, tenor saxophonist Bob Cooper and trombonist Milt Bernhart an opportunity to be featured. Fans of Stan Kenton's earlier groups will find these updated and often-rearranged versions of such songs as "Peanut Vendor," "Eager Beaver," "Southern Scandal," "Intermission Riff" and "Round Robin" quite interesting. —*Scott Yanow*

Portraits on Standards / Sep. 20, 1951-May 6, 1954 / Creative World ♦♦♦♦

While most of Stan Kenton's recordings in the 1950s tend to be complex and sometimes bombastic, his versions of standards could often be sentimental and very melodic. This LP from the Creative World catalog (music originally released by Capitol) alternates between ballads and boppish romps, mostly featuring the 1953-54 orchestra, a band that could often swing hard. With such major soloists as altoist Art Pepper (featured on "Street of Dreams"), trumpeter Conte Candoli, Zoot Sims on tenor, altoist Lee Konitz and trombonist Frank Rosolino, Kenton's orchestra could hold its own with any big band of the period. The arrangements (all by either Bill Russo or Kenton) showcase these talents at their best. —*Scott Yanow*

Live at Cornell University, 1951 / Oct. 14, 1951 / Jazz Unlimited ♦♦♦

This 1993 CD of previously unreleased material features the most adventurous and controversial of Stan Kenton's bands, his Innovations orchestra. Heard in the middle of their second (and sadly final) tour, the 40-piece orchestra (which includes 17 strings) plays such material as "Opus in Pastels," "Dance Before the Mirror" (which is taken from Bob Graettinger's "City of Glass Suite"), "Halls of Brass" and the self-titled pieces "Shelly Manne," "John Graas," "Maynard Ferguson," "Art Pepper" and "Bob Cooper." With such soloists as the screaming trumpeter Maynard Ferguson, Bud Shank (mostly on flute), altoist Art Pepper, John Graas on French horn, tenorman Bob Cooper and trumpeter Conte Candoli, the huge aggregation was top-heavy with talent. However it was the very advanced arrangements and the innovative use of strings that made this a unique if short-lived orchestra. This concert recording has decent sound and some inspired playing that ranks at the level of the band's studio sessions. Highly recommended to Stan Kenton fans. —*Scott Yanow*

23 Degrees North, 82 Degrees South / Sep. 2, 1952-Apr. 23, 1953 / Natasha ♦♦♦

This CD features Stan Kenton's Orchestra on five separate radio broadcasts from 1952-53. Unfortunately the first seven songs (all taken from April 2, 1953) have a distracting hum but otherwise the music is consistently enjoyable. Kenton's band of 1953 was one of his most swinging, featuring a strong rhythm section propelled by drummer Stan Levey and such soloists as tenorman Richie Kamuca, trumpeter Conte Candoli, trombonist Frank Rosolino and altoist Lee Konitz in addition to singer Chris Connor. Konitz in particular is well featured on this CD, which puts the emphasis on standards and hard-swinging. —*Scott Yanow*

● **New Concepts of Artistry in Rhythm** / Sep. 8, 1952-Sep. 16, 1952 / Capitol ✦✦✦✦✦

Stan Kenton's 1952 orchestra was a very interesting transitional band, still performing some of the complex works of the prior Innovations orchestra but also starting to emphasize swing. This CD contains the rather pompous "Prologue" and Bill Holman's complex "Invention for Guitar and Trumpet" (starring guitarist Sal Salvador and trumpeter Maynard Ferguson) but also Gerry Mulligan's boppish "Young Blood" and Bill Russo's features for trumpeter Conte Candoli ("Portrait of a Count"), trombonist Frank Rosolino ("Frank Speaking") and altoist Lee Konitz ("My Lady"). —*Scott Yanow*

Spotlight on Lee Konitz / Dec. 11, 1952-Apr. 30, 1953 / Natasha ✦✦✦✦

This CD contains selections taken from radio broadcasts by one of Stan Kenton's finest orchestras. With such soloists as altoist Lee Konitz (who has many features), trombonist Frank Rosolino and trumpeter Conte Candoli, in addition to five warm vocals by Chris Connor, the Kenton Orchestra uplifts the many standards it interprets, making this one of the more accessible Stan Kenton releases. —*Scott Yanow*

Sketches on Standards / Jan. 28, 1953-Jan. 25, 1955 / Creative World ✦✦✦

This LP contains six Bill Russo arrangements, five from Stan Kenton and one by Lennie Niehaus. The repertoire features many songs not associated with Kenton (such as "Sophisticated Lady," "Pennies from Heaven" and "Over the Rainbow") but the inventive yet melodic treatments certainly sound like the Kenton band. The main soloists are altoist Lee Konitz, guitarist Sal Salvador, trumpeter Conte Canoli and trombonist Frank Rosolino and, although these concise interpretations (none of the dozen performances are much over three minutes) are not essential, the music is quite pleasing. This collection is a change of pace for the Stan Kenton Orchestra. —*Scott Yanow*

By Request, Vol. 5 (1953-1960) / Feb. 11, 1953-Sep. 19, 1960 / Creative World ✦✦✦

It is doubtful that anyone would have requested any of the dozen performances heard on this LP because they are among the more obscure recordings by Stan Kenton's Orchestra. There are no classics here but fans of Kenton's music will be interested in this rare material. Highlights include Chris Connor's vocal on "If I Should Lose You," Lennie Niehaus' alto solo on "I'm Glad There Is You" and three features for Kenton's piano. —*Scott Yanow*

The Definitive Kenton / Jun. 9, 1953-Nov. 18, 1955 / Artistry ✦✦✦✦✦

This double LP from the Artistry label is particularly special because it contains three songs apiece on which Charlie Parker and Dizzy Gillespie guest with the Stan Kenton Orchestra. Although those performances took place on the same day (Feb. 28, 1954), unfortunately Diz and Bird appear separately; Gillespie fares best. However this two-fer would be worth acquiring anyway due to the many swinging concert performances and the consistently exciting solos by such Kenton sidemen as altoist Lee Konitz, trombonist Frank Rosolino, trumpeter Conte Candoli and tenor saxophonist Zoot Sims among others. With Bill Holman and Bill Russo contributing most of the arrangements and drummer Stan Levey driving the band, this is one of the better Stan Kenton collections from the 1950s. —*Scott Yanow*

Kenton '53-Concert in Weisbaden / Sep. 9, 1953 / Astral Jazz ✦✦✦✦

The Stan Kenton Orchestra, on a 1953 tour of Europe, arrived in Weisbaden, Germany, exhausted and a bit late. However, the music quickly revived the band members, and the results can be heard on this small-label CD. The recording quality is quite good, allowing listeners to sample a typical Kenton program from the era. No major new works were premiered, but such talented players as altoist Lee Konitz, tenor saxophonist Zoot Sims and trombonist Frank Rosolino are well featured; trumpeter Conte Candoli, altoist Dave Shildkraut and trombonist Bob Burgess are also heard from. June Christy, back with the band after a three-year absence, has five enjoyable vocals. The enthusiastic crowd obviously inspired the musicians, and this set should please all Kenton fans. —*Scott Yanow*

The European Tour: 1953 / Sep. 16, 1953 / Artistry ✦✦✦✦✦

This CD features Stan Kenton's 1953 orchestra live during a concert from Munich, Germany. This was a particularly strong band with such soloists as trumpeter Conte Candoli, tenor saxophonist Zoot Sims, altoist Lee Konitz and trombonist Frank Rosolino; arrangers Bill Russo and Bill Holman also played in the orchestra (on trombone and tenor) and first trumpeter Buddy Childers and drummer Stan Levey were particularly important assets. There are many highlights to this well-recorded and consistently exciting performance, including a six-song mini-set by singer June Christy, who rejoined Kenton for the historic tour. It's highly recommended. —*Scott Yanow*

By Request, Vol. 2 (1953-1960) / Nov. 30, 1953-Sep. 20, 1960 / Creative World ✦✦✦

This enjoyable LP from the Creative World catalog has selections taken from a seven-year period with the emphasis on the 1954-56 bands. Highlights include "Lover Man" (a feature for altoist Lee Konitz), "Opus in Chartreuse," "Opus in Turquoise" and "Lazy Afternoon." Since this program has performances from several Kenton Orchestras, a wide variety of soloists are heard from including guitarist Laurindo Almeida, tenor saxophonist Bill Perkins, trumpeter Sam Noto, altoist Charlie Mariano and veteran tenor Sam Donahue. The arrangements (by Bill Russo, Bill Holman, Gene Roland and Kenton among others) are generally colorful and the rarity of some of this material makes this set of particular interest to Kenton collectors. —*Scott Yanow*

Contemporary Concepts / Jul. 20, 1955 / Creative World ✦✦✦

This is one of the less important Stan Kenton LP reissues on Creative World. Six veteran standards (all arranged by Bill Holman) and Gerry Mulligan's "Limelight" (with a chart from its composer) were adapted for the 1955 Stan Kenton Orchestra; all but "Limelight" are currently available on CD. The music swings well (with drummer Mel Lewis pushing the rhythm section) and such talented soloists as altoists Charlie Mariano and Lennie Niehaus, tenor saxophonist Bill Perkins, trombonist Carl Fontana and trumpeters Sam Noto and Stu Williamson are well featured. Nothing all that innovative occurs but this accessible set should be of interest to fans of bop (in addition to Kenton's loyal audience) who do not already have the music on CD. —*Scott Yanow*

Kenton in Stereo / Feb. 11, 1956-Feb. 12, 1956 / Creative World ✦✦✦

In the mid- to late '50s many of the surviving big bands (some of which were thrown together just for the occasion) were rerecording their hits in stereo or hi-fi. Stan Kenton was no exception. This set comprises remakes of a dozen of his earlier recordings. Veteran tenor Vido Musso returned to Kenton for the album and he is the chief soloist although there are also spots for trombonist Milt Bernhart, trumpeters Sam Noto and Pete Candoli and altoist Lennie Niehaus. Among the selections are "Intermission Riff," "The Peanut Vendor," "Eager Beaver" and "Concerto to End All Concertos." —*Scott Yanow*

In Concert / Mar. 11, 1956 / Vintage Jazz Classics ✦✦✦✦✦

This double LP features one of Stan Kenton's hardest-swinging orchestras live at a concert in England. Since the rhythm section includes drummer Mel Lewis and bassist Curtis Counce, there was little doubt that the emphasis is on swinging jazz. Boasting soloists of the caliber of trumpeter Sam Noto, altoist Lennie Niehaus, tenorman Bill Perkins and trombonist Carl Fontana, the Kenton orchestra could hold its own with all competitors of the time. The ensemble mostly performs arrangements by Bill Holman, Pete Rugolo and Bill Russo plus two charts from Gerry Mulligan ("Swing House" and "Young Blood") and, although the repertoire is dominated by older material, these well-recorded renditions sound quite fresh and exciting. —*Scott Yanow*

Cuban Fire / May 22, 1956-May 24, 1956 / Blue Note ✦✦✦✦✦

This CD contains one of the classic Stan Kenton albums, a six-part suite composed and arranged by Johnny Richards. The Kenton orchestra was expanded to 27 pieces for these dates including six percussionists, two French horns and six trumpets. With such soloists as tenor-great Lucky Thompson (on "Fuego Cubano,") trombonist Carl Fontana, altoist Lennie Niehaus, Bill Perkins on tenor and trumpeters Sam Noto and Vinnie Tanno, and plenty of raging ensembles, this is one of Stan Kenton's more memorable concept albums of the 1950s. —*Scott Yanow*

Kenton '56 / Nov. 5, 1956 / Artistry ✦✦✦✦

The Artistry label has released several live sets by Stan Kenton's Orchestra from the 1950s and all of these well-recorded sets are highly recommended to Stan Kenton fans. This particular LP originates from a club appearance in San Francisco and finds the 20-piece big band performing arrangements by Bill Holman and Gerry Mulligan along with one by Johnny Richards. At the time Kenton had an all-star saxophone section comprising Bill Perkins and Richie Kamuca on tenors, altoist Lennie Niehaus and baritonist Pepper Adams; all have solo space on this set with Adams showcased on "My Funny Valentine." The other horn players are not as well known but also do well in their spots during the swinging bop-oriented material. The rhythm section (driven by drummer Mel Lewis) really pushes the oversized band to play at its best. —*Scott Yanow*

Rendezvous with Kenton / Oct. 8, 1957-Sep. 10, 1957 / Creative World ✦✦

This LP is one of the less essential Stan Kenton recordings. The 18-piece orchestra is featured playing Joe Coccia's dance arrangements of melodic standards. None of the dozen performances are as long as four minutes (two clock in under two minutes) and the solos generally stick close to the themes. There are some brief spots for trumpeter Sam Noto, altoist Lennie Niehaus, trombonist Kent Larson and the tenor of Bill Perkins but no real excitement occurs. The music is pleasant but not up to the fiery level one would expect of the Stan Kenton Orchestra. —*Scott Yanow*

Back to Balboa / 1958 / Capitol ✦✦✦

For this LP, Stan Kenton's Orchestra performs seven Johnny Richards arrangements and two from Marty Paich along with Bill Holman's "Royal Blue." The 1958 Kenton big band had several excellent soloists and there is a generous amount of individual space for tenor saxophonist Bill Perkins, altoist Lennie Niehaus, trumpeter Sam Noto and trombonist Archie LeCoque among others during a set dominated by modern versions of standards. Well played if not quite essential music. —*Scott Yanow*

By Request, Vol. 6 (1958-1962) / May 15, 1958-Sep. 28, 1962 / Creative World ◆◆

With the exception of one earlier track, the 11 performances on this LP feature Stan Kenton's 1961-62 Mellophonium Band. Actually many of these numbers are a bit lightweight with three Jean Turner vocals, a group "sing-along" on "Beside Balboa Bay" and a couple of melodic standards that have Kenton's piano in the lead. There are a few stronger charts (mostly by Gene Roland) and although this is not one of the essential Stan Kenton albums (who "requested" these songs?), any recording by what was Kenton's last great orchestra is worth hearing. —*Scott Yanow*

The Ballad Style of Stan Kenton / Jun. 12, 1958-Jun. 23, 1958 / Capitol ◆◆◆

Stan Kenton's early arrangements set the tone for his orchestra, but through the years he generally farmed out the writing chores to other talented arrangers who could move the big band forward. However, he did arrange occasional ballad charts, and this 1958 album (reissued on CD in 1997) showcases Kenton's writing. This is an unusual set, for other than some muted trumpet, Kenton's melodic piano is the only soloist. The 13 ballads (a dozen standards and a band original) are given restrained treatments that hint at the band's power without overtly expressing it, and the music is both romantic and danceable. An underrated set. —*Scott Yanow*

Lush Interlude / Jul. 14, 1958-July 15, 1958 / Creative World ◆◆

A 1958 selection with the Kenton Orchestra doing mostly soft, sentimental pieces instead of the surging, frenetic brass works that they were making famous during this period. —*Ron Wynn*

The Stage Door Swings / Sep. 22, 1958 / Capitol ◆◆

Several of Stan Kenton's late-'50s studio recordings do not live up to the potential of his talented orchestra. This is a pleasant set that features Lennie Niehaus' concise (mostly under three minutes) arrangements of then-current show tunes such as "The Party's Over," "Whatever Lola Wants," "Younger than Springtime" and "I Love Paris." Soloists include trumpeter Jack Sheldon, trombonist Ken Larson, Bill Perkins on tenor and Niehaus himself on alto but little exciting happens on what was really a dance-oriented set. —*Scott Yanow*

Kenton Touch / Dec. 23, 1958 / Creative World ◆◆

A 1958 Kenton album that's fairly straightforward and less ambitious than many during that period. The arrangements are standard, the brass section plays with more restraint and less volume, and it's among his best conventional jazz releases. Bill Holman's charts are excellent. —*Ron Wynn*

Kenton Live from the Las Vegas Tropicana / Feb. 2, 1959 / Creative World ◆◆◆◆

The 1959 Stan Kenton Orchestra, which boasted such soloists as trumpeter Jack Sheldon, altoist Lennie Niehaus, Richie Kamuca and Bill Trujillo on tenors and trombonist Ken Larsen, is heard in spirited form on this live LP. Performing arrangements mostly by Gene Roland along with one apiece by Johnny Richards, Niehaus and Kenton, the band plays some surprising material (such as "Tuxedo Junction" and "Street Scene") but mostly comes up with creative, fresh and concise statements. This is admittedly not one of the classic Stan Kenton recordings but is generally superior to his studio recordings of the period. —*Scott Yanow*

Standards in Silhouette / Sep. 21, 1959-Sep. 22, 1959 / Capitol ◆◆◆

This LP is a ballad date by Stan Kenton's 1959 orchestra. Although many of Kenton's top sidemen of a few years earlier had departed, a few of the youngsters in their place included future greats such as trumpeters Rolf Ericson and Bill Chase, trombonist Don Sebesky and baritonist Jack Nimitz. Best known among the soloists is altoist Charlie Mariano. The music (all Bill Mathieu arrangements) is not all that innovative, but the treatments given such songs as "The Meaning of the Blues," "Django" and "I Get Along Without You Very Well" are pleasing and reasonably enjoyable on this relaxed session. —*Scott Yanow*

Viva Kenton / Sep. 22, 1959-Sep. 23, 1959 / Creative World ◆◆◆◆

Stan Kenton added three Latin percussionists to his 18-piece orchestra for this upbeat program. Gene Roland wrote all of the arrangements and composed each of the Latin-flavored tunes, except for "Adios" and "Artistry in Rhythm." Altoist Charlie Mariano, trombonist Don Sebesky and trumpeter Rolf Ericson are among the soloists, and the results, as heard on this LP from the Creative World catalog, are potentially gimmicky but surprisingly successful. —*Scott Yanow*

West Side Story / Mar. 15, 1961-Apr. 11, 1961 / Capitol ◆◆◆◆◆

When the producers of the film *West Side Story* heard a sampling of what the Stan Kenton Orchestra had done to their score, they were disappointed that they had not thought to ask the band to play on the soundtrack. Johnny Richards' arrangements of ten of the famous play's melodies are alternately dramatic and tender

with plenty of the passion displayed by the characters in the story. Soloists include altoist Gabe Baltazar, veteran tenor Sam Donahue and trumpeter Conte Candoli, but it is the raging ensembles that are most memorable about the classic recording. This CD reissue is highly recommended. —*Scott Yanow*

Adventures in Blues / Dec. 7, 1961-Dec. 13, 1961 / Creative World ◆◆◆◆

Arranger Gene Roland composed nine blues-based originals for this LP, featuring himself on soprano and mellophonium along with altoist Gabe Baltazar and trumpeter Marvin Stamm. This is one of the finer recordings by the Mellophonium Band, arguably Stan Kenton's last great orchestra. With the use of 20 horns, Roland was able to get a surprising amount of variety out of the material, making this a Kenton recording well worth investigating. —*Scott Yanow*

Adventures in Jazz / Dec. 11, 1961-Dec. 14, 1961 / Creative World ◆◆◆◆◆

This excellent outing by the 1961 edition of Stan Kenton's orchestra has one classic (Bill Holman's arrangement of "Malaguena"), a superior solo by altoist Gabe Baltazar on "Stairway to the Stars," a feature for Ray Starling's mellophonium ("Misty"), a good workout by veteran tenor Sam Donahue on "Body and Soul," Holman's reworking of "Limehouse Blues" and two colorful Dee Barton composition-arrangements. This well-rounded LP (which also has some solos by trumpeter Marvin Stamm) is one of Kenton's best of the era. —*Scott Yanow*

The Uncollected Stan Kenton & His Orchestra, Vol. 6 (1962) / 1962 / Hindsight ◆◆◆◆

The sixth of Hindsight's six Stan Kenton LPs features his Mellophonium Orchestra, a 22-piece ensemble with 19 horns including a four-piece mellophonium section. These noncommercial recordings (cut strictly for radio airplay) include charts by several arrangers (with Gene Roland and Ray Starling represented the most) and excellent solos from trumpeter Marvin Stamm and especially altoist Gabe Baltazar, who was arguably the last major graduate from Stan Kenton's Orchestras. High points include "Four of a Kind," Lennie Niehaus' arrangement of "Between the Devil and the Deep Blue Sea," a remake of "The Peanut Vendor," "Mellophobia" and Bill Holman's fresh version of "Limehouse Blues." —*Scott Yanow*

Adventures in Time: A Concerto For Orchestra / Sep. 1962 / Capitol ◆◆◆

This LP comprises eight compositions by arranger Johnny Richards that feature Stan Kenton's Mellophonium Orchestra in a variety of time signatures, quite often 5/4 and 7/4. The soloists (altoist Gabe Baltazar, trumpeter Marvin Stamm, Don Menza on tenor and Ray Starling on mellophonium) do their best even if none of the songs are all that memorable by themselves. This worthwhile if not particularly essential release is a bit of a historical curiosity. —*Scott Yanow*

Artistry in Bossa Nova / Apr. 17, 1963 / Creative World ◆◆◆

The 1963 album that marked Kenton's entry into the then-booming bossa nova market. It featured the usual bombastic arrangements with Afro-Latin seasoning. The vocals were not as enticing as those on the Getz albums, but the full brass backdrop proved interesting. —*Ron Wynn*

Artistry in Voices and Brass / Apr. 19, 1963-Sep. 10, 1963 / Creative World ◆◆◆

Another in the series of intricate, unorthodox, and controversial Kenton albums issued in the mid-'60s on his Creative World label. This one matched his usual array of horns with multiple voices. The resulting wave was sometimes arresting, sometimes chaotic, and still seems both advanced and bizarre 30 years later. —*Ron Wynn*

Kenton / Wagner / Sep. 1964 / Creative World ◆◆◆◆◆

This unique album is a surprising artistic success. Stan Kenton and a large studio orchestra filled with many of his alumni perform his adaptations of eight themes from the classical works of Richard Wagner. Somehow Kenton turns Wagner's music into jazz, capturing the intense emotion, pomposity and drama with daring ideas. Not for all tastes, this LP was one of Stan Kenton's last innovative recordings. —*Scott Yanow*

Stan Kenton Conducts the Los Angeles Neophonic Orchestra / Jan. 4, 1965 / Capitol ◆◆

For a relatively brief period the Los Angeles Neophonic orchestra was the world's only permanent resident orchestra devoted to contemporary music. This LP, conducted by the orchestra's inspiration, Stan Kenton, contains music by Hugo Montenegro, Johnny Williams, Allyn Ferguson, Jimmy Knight and Russ Garcia that attempts to combine together aspects of classical with jazz. Much of the time the results are somewhat pompous and stiff although there are several features for altoist Bud Shank; other soloists include Bob Cooper on oboe, trumpeter Gary Barone, vibraphonist Emil Richards and the tenor of Bill Perkins. The music, like the project, had good intentions but is uneven. —*Scott Yanow*

The Compositions of Dee Barton / Dec. 19, 1967-Dec. 20, 1967 / Capitol ◆◆◆

Up until the breakup of his Mellophonium Orchestra in 1963, all of Stan Kenton's big bands had major soloists and future stars. But during his final decade, his orchestras would mostly consist of younger (and one would expect inexpensive) players, few of whom went on to greater heights. This LP consists of seven Dee

Barton charts of his originals. Barton was the band's drummer and, along with tenor saxophonist Kim Richmond (who would later develop into a top arranger himself), is about the only graduate of this particular group to have a significant jazz career. The music is well played but not overly memorable, sort of like this edition of the Stan Kenton Orchestra. —*Scott Yanow*

Live at Redlands University / Oct. 1970 / Creative World ♦♦♦

This double LP is definitive of Stan Kenton's later orchestras. Few of the musicians ever became even minor names; not counting veteran saxophonist Willie Maiden, trumpeters Mike Vax and Warren Gale, trombonist Dick Shearer and drummer John Von Ohlen are the only recognizable players. The arrangements are generally workmanlike and sometimes dramatic but rarely memorable (those of Bill Holman and Willie Maiden excepted), and the old favorite "Peanut Vendor" (here renamed "More Peanut Vendor") gets the most spirited performance. By this point Stan Kenton had so influenced the college stage band movement (and was largely forced for economic reasons to use younger musicians) that his orchestra itself sounded like one of the faceless college orchestras. Still, these versions of "Artistry in Rhythm" and "Granada" make up in emotion for the general lack of creative spontaneity and should satisfy fans of those anonymous student big bands. —*Scott Yanow*

Live at Brigham Young University / Aug. 13, 1971 / Creative World ♦♦

Stan Kenton's young "no-name" big band of the 1970s performs ambitious works by Ken Hanna, Hank Levy, Willie Maiden and Bill Holman on this live double LP. The musicianship is impressive and some of the arrangements are quite dramatic but there's not all that much originality. A lot of soloists are heard from but few of them would have significant jazz careers after their period with Kenton ended; the main exceptions are veteran saxophonist Willie Maiden, trumpeter Mike Vax, trombone Dick Shearer and drummer John Von Ohlen. This set is well played but forgettable. —*Scott Yanow*

Stan Kenton Today / 1972 / Phase 4 ♦♦

The long liner notes in this double LP do not give a complete listing of the personnel of Stan Kenton's 1972 orchestra—an unintentional but understandable omission because Kenton's young band had few original personalities at this point. Other than veteran Willie Maiden (heard here on baritone), the soloists are at best semiobscure. However the musicianship is flawless and the repertoire for this "Live in London" set is dominated by old classics including "Malaguena," "Intermission Riff," "Interlude," "Artistry in Percussion" and naturally "The Peanut Vendor." Fans of college stage bands should enjoy this spirited music. —*Scott Yanow*

Birthday in Britain / Feb. 19, 1973+Feb. 23, 1973 / Creative World ♦♦♦

The Stan Kenton Orchestra of the 1970s featured high-level musicianship, dramatic arrangements, forceful ensembles and workmanlike solos. The 19-piece band heard on this LP is mostly filled with forgotten youngsters; the exceptions are veteran saxophonist Willie Maiden, trombonist Dick Shearer and the then-unknown drummer Peter Erskine. The arrangements are by Hank Levy, Bill Holman (one of his two is "Happy Birthday to You") and Maiden. Well played and sometimes exciting, this music is rarely memorable. —*Scott Yanow*

7.5 on the Richter Scale / Aug. 17, 1973-Aug. 18, 1973 / Creative World ♦♦♦

Solo: Stan Kenton Without His Orchestra / Dec. 1973 / Creative World ♦♦

This LP was Stan Kenton's only solo piano record of his career, and it's a disappointment. Kenton was never a virtuoso but he had an Earl Hines-inspired style and was capable of much better than this introspective and wandering outing. There are some moments of interest as Kenton explores songs one is used to hearing played by his orchestra, but the limited amount of emotions expressed (and the lack of any real swinging) makes this set just passable. —*Scott Yanow*

Stan Kenton Plays Chicago / Jun. 4, 1974 / Creative World ♦♦

Fire, Fury and Fun / Sep. 26, 1974-Sep. 27, 1974 / Creative World ♦♦♦

For this late-period Stan Kenton recording, the bandleader decided to present five of his top soloists from the era: baritonist Roy Reynolds, Tony Campise (mainly on flute), trombonist Dick Shearer, drummer Peter Erskine and Ramon Lopez on congas. Kenton himself is featured on piano during two numbers but none of his sidemen make very strong impressions and the orchestra on a whole sounds like an anonymous college stage band. This is a lesser effort although Erskine (and from the trumpet section Tim Hagans) would become notable in future years. —*Scott Yanow*

Kenton '76 / Dec. 3, 1975-Dec. 5, 1975 / Creative World ♦♦♦

This reasonably enjoyable LP features the Stan Kenton Orchestra during its final period. The ensemble sound remained impressive but among the sidemen only trumpeter Tim Hagans (and to a lesser extent bassist Dave Stone) would go on to greater heights although baritonist Greg Smith is impressive on his feature "A Smith Named Greg." Hank Levy contributed three of the charts, "Tiburon" is Bill Holman's and Kenton's piano is featured on the two ballads "Send in the Clowns"

and "My Funny Valentine." This is not one of the major Stan Kenton albums but the set will be enjoyed by fans of college stage bands. —*Scott Yanow*

Journey into Capricorn / Aug. 16, 1976-Aug. 18, 1976 / Creative World ♦♦♦

Stan Kenton's final studio recording features his young no-name crew (only trumpeter Tim Hagans among the soloists is notable today) showing enthusiasm and impressive musicianship on charts by Hank Levy, Mark Taylor and Alan Yankee. Highlights include Yankee's adaptation of Chick Corea's "Celebration Suite," Levy's "Pegasus" and Hagan's solos. The leader's piano is featured on Stevie Wonder's "Too Shy to Say." This decent LP closed Stan Kenton's rather remarkable career. —*Scott Yanow*

☆ 50th Anniversary Celebration: The Best of Back to Balboa / May 30, 1991-Jun. 2, 1991 / MAMA ♦♦♦♦♦

During the 50th anniversary of Stan Kenton's debut at the Rendezvous Ballroom on Balboa Island in California (an engagement that served as a spectacular beginning to his career), a four-day convention was held to celebrate the late bandleader's legacy, filled with music by his alumni and very interesting panel discussions. The MAMA Foundation put out many of the highlights on this very impressive five-CD set. The first two CDs have 29 selections by an all-star orchestra (which includes among others, trumpeters Conte and Pete Candoli and saxophonists Bob Cooper, Gabe Baltazar, Bud Shank, Bill Perkins and Jack Nimitz) and such guests as Anita O'Day, Maynard Ferguson and Chris Connor; the original arrangers conducted their own work. The next two discs have individual selections for Bob Florence's Limited Edition (a particularly touching medley of "Artistry in Rhythm" and "All the Things You Are"), Maynard Ferguson's Big Bop Nouveau Band, the Lighthouse All-Stars, big bands led by Shorty Rogers, Buddy Childers, Bill Holman, Tom Talbert and Mark Masters and combos headed by Lee Konitz, Bob Cooper, Gabe Baltazar, Bill Perkins and Bud Shank along with The CSULB Vocal Jazz Ensemble. The performances are quite satisfying and cover Kenton's entire career. The final disc actually has over two hours taken from the informative, humorous and often-touching panel discussions; one hour is heard in each speaker simultaneously so one side has to be turned off at a time. This valuable set is essential for all listeners having at least a slight interest in Stan Kenton's music. —*Scott Yanow*

Freddie Keppard

b. Feb. 27, 1890, New Orleans, LA, **d.** Jul. 15, 1933, Chicago, IL
Cornet / New Orleans Jazz, Classic Jazz

One of the New Orleans cornet "kings" (succeeding Buddy Bolden and preceding King Oliver), Freddie Keppard was one of the few innovators of the 1910 era who had a chance to record later on, giving listeners a glimpse of his abilities. Keppard was active from around 1906, leading the Olympia Orchestra and freelancing in New Orleans. In 1914 he helped bring jazz to Los Angeles with his Original Creole Band. After settling in Chicago in the early '20s, Keppard worked with Doc Cook's Dreamland Orchestra (with whom he recorded on several occasions), Erskine Tate, Ollie Powers and Charles Elgar. He could have been the first jazz musician to record (back in 1916) but passed on the opportunity because he was afraid that competitors would steal his ideas. Keppard did record between 1923-27 (his best sides were with his own Jazz Cardinals, particularly "Stockyard Strut") and those performances feature him using a staccato phrasing influenced by brass bands and displaying a spirited tone. Unfortunately Keppard was an alcoholic by the mid-'20s and was soon in a decline just when he should have been entering his prime. He died of tuberculosis in 1933 at the age of 43. All of his recordings are currently available on a single CD put out by the European King Jazz label. —*Scott Yanow*

● The Complete Freddie Keppard 1923/27 / Jun. 23, 1923-Jan. 1927 / King Jazz ♦♦♦♦♦

Freddie Keppard was considered the top cornetist in New Orleans during 1910-14 before he moved up north and was succeeded by King Oliver. Keppard, one of the few early jazzmen to make it onto records, appeared on 25 selections from 1923-27, and all are included on this fascinating CD. Some of the titles (particularly those with Doc Cook's Dreamland Orchestra in 1924) are very primitively recorded and do not contain much Keppard, but the cornetist is heard in fine form on such later numbers as "Messin' Around," "Here Comes the Hot Tamale Man," "It Must Be the Blues" and especially "Stockyard Strut." Among the sidemen are clarinetists Johnny Dodds and Jimmie Noone, trombonist Ray Palmer, pianist Jimmy Blythe and (on two versions of "Salty Dog") blues singer Papa Charlie Jackson. Keppard, whose trumpet breaks often recall military music and aspects of ragtime, is always fascinating to hear, even though he was past his prime by the 1920s. As this CD shows, there was just enough of him on record to give listeners an idea of what 1910 New Orleans jazz probably sounded like. This imported Swiss CD is an essential acquisition for all vintage jazz collectors. —*Scott Yanow*

The Legendary Freddie Keppard—New Orleans Cornet / Jan. 21, 1924-Jan. 1927 / Smithsonian ✦✦✦✦

During his career, pioneering New Orleans cornetist Freddie Keppard (who succeeded Buddy Bolden as the top brassman in the city) appeared on 25 recordings; 15 of the best are on this deluxe LP from the Smithsonian Institution, including "Stockyard Strut," "Messin' Around," both versions of "Salty Dog," and "It Must Be the Blues." Since all of Keppard's recordings are currently available on a CD put out by the King Jazz label, the main reason to get this LP is for the extensive liner notes and seven photos of the legendary player. —*Scott Yanow*

Barney Kessel

b. Oct. 17, 1923, Muskogee, OK
Guitar / Bop, Cool

One of the finest guitarists to emerge after the death of Charlie Christian, Barney Kessel was a reliable bop soloist throughout his career. He played with a big band fronted by Chico Marx (1943), was fortunate enough to appear in the classic jazz short *Jammin' the Blues* (1944) and then worked with the big bands of Charlie Barnet (1944-45) and Artie Shaw (1945); he also recorded with Shaw's Gramercy Five. Kessel became a busy studio musician in Los Angeles but was always in demand for jazz records. He toured with the Oscar Peterson Trio for one year (1952-53) and then, starting in 1953, led an impressive series of records for Contemporary that lasted until 1961 (including several with Ray Brown and Shelly Manne in a trio accurately called "The Poll Winners"). After touring Europe with George Wein's Newport All-Stars (1968), Kessel lived in London for a time (1969-70). In 1973 he began touring and recording with the Great Guitars, a group also including Herb Ellis and Charlie Byrd. A serious stroke in 1992 put Barney Kessel permanently out of action, but many of his records (which include dates for Onyx, Black Lion, Sonet and Concord in addition to many of the Contemporaries) are currently available along with several video collections put out by Vestapol. —*Scott Yanow*

Easy Like, Vol. 1 / Nov. 14, 1953-Dec. 19, 1953 / Original Jazz Classics ✦✦✦✦

Other than four songs apiece released by Onyx and Verve, this CD reissue has guitarist Barney Kessel's first sessions as a leader, performances which launched his longtime association with the Contemporary label. Augmented by two "new" alternate takes, the set features Kessel in boppish form with quintets in 1953 and 1956 featuring either Bud Shank or Buddy Collette doubling on flute and alto. Kessel shows off the influence of Charlie Christian throughout the performances, with the highlights including "Easy Like," "Lullaby of Birdland," "North of the Border" and the accurately titled "Salute to Charlie Christian." —*Scott Yanow*

Kessel Plays Standards / Jun. 4, 1954-Sep. 12, 1955 / Original Jazz Classics ✦✦✦✦✦

Guitarist Barney Kessel teams up with Bob Cooper (mostly on oboe but also doubling a bit on tenor), either Claude Williamson or Hampton Hawes on piano, Monty Budwig or Red Mitchell on bass, and Shelly Manne or Chuck Thompson on drums. Other than his own "64 Bars on Wilshire" and "Barney's Blues," the repertoire on this CD reissue comprises jazz standards. Inventive frameworks and the utilization of Cooper's jazz oboe (a real rarity in jazz of the time) give the otherwise boppish reissue its own personality. —*Scott Yanow*

★ **Barney Kessel, Vol. 3: To Swing or Not to Swing** / Mar. 28, 1955 / Original Jazz Classics ✦✦✦✦✦

Guitarist Barney Kessel's string of recordings for Contemporary in the 1950s included some of the finest work of his career. The unusual repertoire on this set—which includes "Louisiana," "Indiana" and "12th Street Rag," along with four Kessel originals and more usual standards—would by itself make this bop/cool set noteworthy. Add to that a very interesting lineup of players (trumpeter Harry "Sweets" Edison, Georgie Auld or Bill Perkins on tenor, pianist Jimmy Rowles, the rhythm guitar of Al Hendrickson, bassist Red Mitchell, and Shelly Manne or Irv Cottler on drums) and some excellent showcases for Kessel, and the overall results are a CD highly recommended to fans of straightahead jazz. —*Scott Yanow*

Music to Listen to Barney Kessel By / Aug. 6, 1956-Dec. 4, 1956 / Original Jazz Classics ✦✦✦✦

Featured is Kessel's guitar with five woodwinds and a rhythm section. Twelve songs were recorded with Buddy Collette (fl), Andre Previn (p), Shelly Manne (d), Jimmy Rowles (p), Red Mitchell (b), Buddy Clark (b), and others. —*AMG*

The Poll Winners with Ray Brown and Shelly Manne / Mar. 18, 1957-Mar. 19, 1957 / Original Jazz Classics ✦✦✦✦

Because guitarist Barney Kessel, bassist Ray Brown and drummer Shelly Manne all won the *Downbeat*, *Metronome* and *Playboy* jazz polls of 1956, it was decided to team the trio together for this and a few other future recordings. Kessel is generally the lead voice of the pianoless group although Brown and Manne also have plenty of solo space. Together they perform swinging yet quiet versions of a vari-

ety of standards (in addition to the guitarist's "Minor Mood") in a relaxed and thoughtful set, reissued on this CD. —*Scott Yanow*

Let's Cook / Aug. 6, 1957+Nov. 11, 1957 / Contemporary ✦✦✦✦

It is a pity that this excellent session from guitarist Barney Kessel has not yet been reissued on CD. Actually, there are two different sets on this LP. Kessel is matched with vibraphonist Victor Feldman, pianist Hampton Hawes, bassist Leroy Vinnegar and drummer Shelly Manne for a blues-with-a-bridge (the 11-minute "Let's Cook"), Vernon Duke's ballad "Time Remembered" and "Just in Time." The second half of the album has modernized versions of "Tiger Rag" and "Jersey Bounce" as played by the guitarist, tenor saxophonist Ben Webster, trombonist Frank Rosolino, pianist Jimmie Rowles, Vinnegar and Manne. Throughout, Kessel keeps with the other all-stars, swinging hard while paying tribute to the legacy of Charlie Christian. —*Scott Yanow*

The Poll Winners Ride Again / Aug. 19, 1958+Aug. 21, 1958 / Original Jazz Classics ✦✦✦✦

Guitarist Barney Kessel, bassist Ray Brown and drummer Shelly Manne were dubbed "the Poll Winners" when they swept the *Downbeat*, *Metronome* and *Playboy* polls during 1956-57. They recorded several albums together and this CD reissue features the pianoless trio playing a variety of material, some of it a little odd (including "Volare," "Custard Puff," "When the Red, Red Robin Comes Bob, Bob Bobbin' Along" and "The Merry Go Round Broke Down"). This is a good outing, particularly for bop guitarist Barney Kessel. —*Scott Yanow*

Barney Kessel Plays "Carmen" / Dec. 19, 1958+Dec. 23, 1958 / Original Jazz Classics ✦✦✦

This is an unusual set that has been reissued on CD. During an era when many Broadway and movie scores were recorded in jazz settings (thanks in part to the success of Shelly Manne's best selling *My Fair Lady* album), guitarist Barney Kessel chose to interpret nine melodies from Bizet's opera *Carmen*. The guitarist is heard in three different settings: joined by five woodwinds and a rhythm section; with five jazz horns (including altoist Herb Geller and trumpeter Ray Linn) and a trio; and with vibraphonist Victor Feldman in a quintet. Kessel also wrote the arrangements, which pay tribute to the melodies while not being shy of swinging the themes. An interesting if not essential project. —*Scott Yanow*

Some Like It Hot / Mar. 30, 1959-Apr. 3, 1959 / Original Jazz Classics ✦✦✦✦✦

This CD reissue brings back the original Barney Kessel LP of the same name and adds two alternate takes. The release of the movie *Some Like It Hot* served as a good excuse for guitarist Kessel to join together with Art Pepper (switching between alto, clarinet and tenor), trumpeter Joe Gordon, pianist Jimmie Rowles, rhythm guitarist Jack Marshall, bassist Monty Budwig and drummer Shelly Manne to interpret a variety of vintage numbers, most of which date from the 1920s. Such tunes as "I Wanna Be Loved by You," "Runnin' Wild," "Down Among the Sheltering Palms" and "By the Beautiful Sea" are given fairly modern arrangements but still retain the flavor of the 1920s, and it is particularly interesting to hear Gordon and Pepper soloing on these ancient tunes. —*Scott Yanow*

Poll Winners Three! / Nov. 1959 / Original Jazz Classics ✦✦✦✦

From 1956-59, it seemed as if guitarist Barney Kessel, bassist Ray Brown and drummer Shelly Manne won just about every jazz poll. For their third joint recording, which has been reissued on CD, the musicians contributed an original apiece and also performed seven standards. Highlights of the fairly typical but swinging straightahead set include "Soft Winds," "It's All Right with Me," "Mack the Knife" and "I'm Afraid the Masquerade Is Over." —*Scott Yanow*

Barney Kessel's Swingin' Party at Contemporary / Jul. 19, 1960 / Contemporary ✦✦✦

The Poll Winners / Exploring the Scene / Aug. 1960-Sep. 1960 / Contemporary ✦✦✦✦

For one of their better outings, the Poll Winners (guitarist Barney Kessel, bassist Ray Brown and drummer Shelly Manne) perform nine fairly recent jazz standards. It is ironic that this is their only release not yet reissued on CD, since it may very well be their strongest program. The trio performs creative versions of such songs as "Little Susie," "So What," "Doodlin'," "This Here" and Ornette Coleman's "The Blessing." Worth searching for. —*Scott Yanow*

Workin' Out / Sep. 9, 1961-Sep. 10, 1961 / Contemporary ✦✦✦

Autumn Leaves / Oct. 29, 1968-Sep. 19, 1969 / Black Lion ✦✦✦

This CD reissue contains a sleepy trio session by guitarist Barney Kessel, who teams up with bassist Kenny Napper and drummer John Marshall for a variety of current pop tunes (including Burt Bacharach's "The Look of Love" and two Michel Legrand songs) plus a few overly relaxed standards and originals. The CD is rounded out by three bouncy numbers from 1969 that feature Kessel with a big band that includes tenor saxophonist Teddy Edwards and pianist Jimmy Rowles. Overall the lethargic performances function best as superior background music. —*Scott Yanow*

Aquarius: The Music from Hair / Nov. 1968 / Black Lion ✦✦✦
On paper, the pairing of bop guitarist Barney Kessel and the hippie musical *Hair* seems a little unusual, but the results are surprisingly enjoyable. Teaming with guitarist Ike Isaacs, organists Kenny Saloman and Steve Gray, bassist Tony Campo and drummer Barry Morgan, Kessel runs through all the familiar pieces—"Aquarius," "Frank Mills," "Easy to Be Hard," "Good Morning Starshine"—injecting them with a spirited sense of swing. Some of the tunes remain slight, and the guitarist doesn't always sound comfortable with the material, but overall it's a fun, albeit minor, entry in Kessel's catalog. —*Stephen Thomas Erlewine*

Feeling Free / Feb. 13, 1969 / Original Jazz Classics ✦✦✦✦✦
From 1953-61, guitarist Barney Kessel recorded some of the finest albums of his career for the Contemporary label. In 1969, he came back to the company for this single effort, and in the mid-1980s he would return to Contemporary for his final sessions. The 1969 project, which has not yet been reissued on CD, lives up to its title, being one of Kessel's most adventurous dates. He utilized vibraphonist Bobby Hutcherson, bassist Chuck Domanico and drummer Elvin Jones for four fairly free originals, Paul Simon's "The Sounds of Silence," and the pop tune "This Guy's in Love with You." Throughout, Kessel shows that he was familiar with aspects of the avant-garde and that he had a willingness to really stretch himself. An intriguing set. —*Scott Yanow*

★ **Limehouse Blues** / Jun. 24, 1969 / Black Lion ✦✦✦✦✦
Guitarist Barney Kessel and violinist Stephane Grappelli always made for a mutually complementary team. Kessel's background was in Charlie Christian rather than Django Reinhardt (although Django can be felt now and then in his style), but there was always a lot of common ground between him and Grappelli. This LP (whose music has been mostly reissued on CD) also has rhythm guitarist Nini Rosso, bassist Michel Gaudry and drummer Jean-Louis Viale in the quintet. Other than the guitarist's bossa nova "Little Star," the group sticks to swing-era standards, with the highlights including "It Don't Mean a Thing," "Tea for Two" and "How High the Moon." Predictably swinging music. —*Scott Yanow*

Yesterday / Jul. 1973 / Black Lion ✦✦✦✦
This CD reissue has guitarist Barney Kessel's performance at the 1973 Montreux Jazz Festival. Kessel is heard unaccompanied on two ballads (the Beatles' "Yesterday" and his own "In the Garden of Love"), he performs "Laura" in a trio with bassist Kenny Baldock and drummer Johnny Richardson, plays three songs with a quartet also featuring pianist Brian Lemon, uses a quintet on "Bridging the Blues" that also co-stars tenor saxophonist Danny Moss and, for an encore, has a duet with violinist Stephane Grappelli on a delightful version of "Tea for Two." This well-rounded set features Barney Kessel in prime form and is easily recommended to his fans. —*Scott Yanow*

Just Friends / Sep. 1973 / Sonet ✦✦✦
This Sonet recording features guitarist Barney Kessel, bassist Sture Nordin and drummer Pelle Hulten at a live club date in Stockholm. The music is essentially bebop plus a few bossas. Fortunately, Kessel (the main voice throughout) varies the moods and the tempos, so the set (which includes "Just Friends," his original "Going Thru Some Changes" and "Days of Wine & Roses," among others) holds on to one's interest. —*Scott Yanow*

Barney Plays Kessel / Apr. 1975 / Concord Jazz ✦✦✦
Two aspects of this obscure Concord set uplift it beyond the usual straightahead session. All nine selections are originals by guitarist Barney Kessel, and although none caught on as standards, the fresh material does result in some fine solos. The other unusual quality is that the legendary but now little-known Herbie Steward (one of Woody Herman's Four Brothers) sounds in fine form, not on the tenor one might expect, but on alto, soprano and flute. With vibraphonist Victor Feldman, Jimmy Rowles on keyboards, bassist Chuck Domanico, drummer Jake Hanna and percussionist Milt Holland completing the group, the results are quite musical, if not particularly memorable; Steward's rare appearances this late in his career are the main reason to get this set. —*Scott Yanow*

The Poll Winners Straight Ahead / Jul. 12, 1975 / Original Jazz Classics ✦✦✦✦✦
Fifteen years after their last joint recordings, the Poll Winners (a trio with guitarist Barney Kessel, bassist Ray Brown and drummer Shelly Manne) had a reunion for this excellent session, which has been reissued on CD. All three players had grown quite a bit musically since the 1950s and Kessel in particular is heard in excellent form on the three standards and three swinging originals. Overall this is the best all-around recording by the Poll Winners and is easily recommended to bop fans. —*Scott Yanow*

Soaring / Aug. 25, 1976 / Concord Jazz ✦✦✦
Although guitarist Barney Kessel interprets seven standard ballads on this CD reissue (a trio set with bassist Monty Budwig and drummer Jake Hanna), this is not a ballad album. Most of the songs are taken at faster than usual tempos with the emphasis on Kessel's chordal (rather than single-note) solos. The guitarist was

in peak form around this era as can be heard on a romping version of "I Love You," "Star Eyes," "Like Someone in Love" and "Get out of Town." In addition he contributes one of his finest originals, "Seagull," a song that deserves to be revived. This underrated set is well worth exploring. —*Scott Yanow*

Poor Butterfly / 1976 / Concord Jazz ✦✦
Herb Ellis had previously recorded with fellow guitarists Charlie Byrd, Joe Pass and Freddie Green, but this early Concord album (reissued on CD) was his first meeting on records with Barney Kessel. It is of little surprise that the two complementary players (who had both been with the Oscar Peterson Trio at different times in the 1950s) work together quite well. With fine support from bassist Monty Budwig and drummer Jake Hanna, Kessel and Ellis (both generally easy to identify) swing their way through some mostly little-played standards, including "Early Autumn" and "Dearly Beloved," plus a few originals by the co-leaders. Fans of the bop guitar will want this sprightly collaboration. —*Scott Yanow*

Live at Sometime / Feb. 23, 1977 / Storyville ✦✦
Originally available on the Japanese Trio label, this Storyville CD reissue unfortunately has no liner notes. Guitarist Barney Kessel performs a set of overly relaxed warhorses with a couple of quietly supportive sidemen (bassist Kunimitsu Inaba and drummer Tetsujirah Obara) at a Tokyo club. Laurindo Almeida's "Barniana" is the only obscure material on a low-key and lightly swinging date that finds Kessel emphasizing his chordal work on such tunes as "Girl from Ipanema," "Bye Bye Blackbird" and "Willow Weep for Me." Sleepy music. —*Scott Yanow*

Jellybeans / Apr. 1981 / Concord Jazz ✦✦✦
On this fairly typical trio set, guitarist Barney Kessel is joined by bassist Bob Maize and drummer Jimmie Smith. "Stella by Starlight," "St. Thomas" and "Shiny Stockings" generate some heat; there are three Kessel originals and also two veteran ballads. The music swings without giving listeners any real surprises, but Kessel's fans can consider this one of his best Concord recordings. —*Scott Yanow*

Solo / Apr. 1981 / Concord Jazz ✦✦✦
This is an unusual set, the only full-length program of unaccompanied guitar solos recorded by Barney Kessel. Although Kessel was not as skilled in solo work as Joe Pass, the music is relaxed, melodic and tasteful. The interpretations are concise and highlighted by "Brazil," "You Are the Sunshine of My Life," and "Alfie," although "People" could have been skipped. —*Scott Yanow*

Two Way Conversation / Jun. 5, 1973-Oct. 2, 1973 / Sonet ✦✦✦
On this relaxed date, guitarist Barney Kessel and bassist Red Mitchell had a musical reunion; they had played together often in the 1950s. The music includes three Kessel originals, a pair of then-current pop songs ("Alone Again Naturally" and "Killing Me Softly with His Song"), "Summertime" and "Wave." The playing is fine, but no real surprises occur, and some of the subtle interpretations are a bit sleepy. —*Scott Yanow*

Spontaneous Combustion / Feb. 20, 1987-Feb. 22, 1987 / Contemporary ✦✦✦✦
This excellent straightahead set (which has been reissued on CD along with a "bonus" cut, "Shaw Nuff") finds pianist Monty Alexander, along with bassist John Clayton and drummer Jeff Hamilton, lighting a fire under guitarist Barney Kessel and pushing him to some of his more heated playing. Kessel performs four of his better originals plus "'Round Midnight," "Ah, Sweet Mystery of Life," "Everything I Have Is Yours" and "Get Me to the Church on Time," sounding inspired by the company he was keeping. Recommended. —*Scott Yanow*

Red Hot and Blues / Mar. 15, 1988-Mar. 17, 1988 / Contemporary ✦✦✦✦✦
One of guitarist Barney Kessel's final recordings before a stroke put him out of action, this is an excellent quintet session with vibraphonist Bobby Hutcherson, pianist Kenny Barron, bassist Rufus Reid and drummer Ben Riley. Three of Kessel's originals (a pair of blues and a bossa nova) alternate with four standards and Laurindo Almeida's dedication to the guitarist ("Barniana") on this well-paced and consistently swinging set; the uptempo version of "By Myself" is a high point. —*Scott Yanow*

Steve Khan

b. Apr. 28, 1947, Los Angeles, CA
Guitar / Fusion, Post-Bop
The son of lyricist Sammy Cahn, Steve Khan is best known for his fusion records but has proven on a few occasions that he can also play more straightahead. He originally played piano and drums, not starting on guitar until he was 20. After graduating from UCLA in 1969, Khan moved to New York and worked steadily in jazz, pop and R&B settings including with Maynard Ferguson, Buddy Rich, the Brecker Brothers, Joe Zawinul's Weather Update and with fellow guitarist Larry Coryell. In 1981 he formed the quartet Eyewitness, which worked on an occasional basis throughout the 1980s. Steve Khan's most intriguing recordings are a 1980 solo exploration of Thelonious Monk tunes for Novus and a trio outing for Blue Moon named *Let's Call This* (1991). —*Scott Yanow*

Tightrope / 1977 / Columbia ✦✦✦

The Blue Man / Feb. 1978 / Columbia ✦✦✦

This LP features Steve Khan in his fusion period during which his guitar tone was usually a bit distorted and he tended to improvise over funky rhythms. This all-star outing features such players as altoist David Sanborn, tenor saxophonist Michael Brecker, trumpeter Randy Breckner and a large rhythm section with the likes of keyboardists Don Grolnick and Bob James and drummer Steve Gadd. The music is not overly memorable but certainly has spirit and power. —*Scott Yanow*

Arrows / 1979 / Columbia ✦✦

● **Evidence** / Jul. 1980 / Novus ✦✦✦✦✦

Steve Khan gained his initial reputation as a fusion guitarist, so this session (which has been reissued on CD) was a revelation to many when it was released. A rather introspective set of melodic music, the program is highlighted by an eighteen-and-a-half-minute nine-song Thelonious Monk medley that is performed solo. Khan is actually the only performer throughout the date although he uses overdubbing on some cuts ("In a Silent Way" has eight guitars). With its strong melodies (including Wayne Shorter's "Infant Eyes") and subtle but creative playing, this is still one of Steve Khan's most rewarding recordings. —*Scott Yanow*

Eyewitness / Nov. 7, 1981-Nov. 8, 1981 / Antilles ✦✦✦✦✦

Unlike his previous all-star sets, guitarist Steve Khan features his regular group on this album and the results are quite superior. Whether one calls this music fusion or modern funk, the interplay between Khan, electric bassist Anthony Jackson, drummer Steve Jordan and percussionist Manolo Badrena is quite impressive; in fact the four of them share composer credits on three of the five originals. It's one of Steve Khan's best fusion-oriented efforts of the 1980s. —*Scott Yanow*

Blades / Aug. 3, 1982-Aug. 4, 1982 / Passport ✦✦✦

Local Colour / Apr. 1983-May 1987 / Denon ✦✦✦

Good 1987 duo session, in which session and studio ace guitarist Steve Khan went against his reputation and did an album of duets with keyboardist and vocalist Rob Mounsey that weren't just funk and fusion, but mostly jazz-tinged instrumentals. —*Ron Wynn*

Casa Loco / May 21, 1983-May 22, 1983 / Antilles ✦✦✦

Mid-'80s session that blends funk, fusion, and occasional mainstream work by guitarist Steve Khan. Nice production, decent arrangements, and generally fine playing by Khan, although he does few solos. —*Ron Wynn*

Public Access / Jan. 1989 / GRP ✦✦✦

Let's Call This / Jan. 19, 1991-Jan. 20, 1991 / Blue Moon ✦✦✦✦✦

Best known for his fusion recordings, Steve Khan (ten years after recording the purely acoustic solo date *Evidence*) stretches out on this pure jazz date. Accompanied by bassist Ron Carter and drummer Al Foster, Khan explores a variety of superior jazz standards (including songs by Thelonious Monk, Wayne Shorter, Larry Young, Freddie Hubbard and Lee Morgan) along with his own "Buddy System." This is one of Steve Khan's finest recordings to date and is highly recommended to those listeners not familiar with this side of his musical personality. —*Scott Yanow*

Headline / Jan. 12, 1992-Jan. 19, 1992 / Blue Moon ✦✦✦✦✦

Guitarist Steve Khan is heard in two different settings on this CD: in an acoustic trio with bassist Ron Carter and drummer Al Foster on six songs, and jamming with electric bassist Anthony Jackson, drummer Dennis Chambers and percussionist Manolo Badrena on three tunes. Actually, there is a definite unity to the program, and Khan is featured on a variety of jazz tunes including numbers by Larry Young, Ornette Coleman ("The Blessing" and "Turnaround"), Clare Fischer, Wayne Shorter, Thelonious Monk and Joe Henderson. He even plays a song ("Autumn in Rome") by his father, Sammy Cahn. The guitarist consistently stretches himself during these performances (which include a 10-minute version of "All or Nothing at All") and is heard throughout at his most creative. —*Scott Yanow*

Crossings / Dec. 28, 1993-Dec. 30, 1993 / Verve/Forecast ✦✦✦✦

Got My Mental / Sep. 5, 1996-Sep. 6, 1996 / Evidence ✦✦✦✦✦

Franklin Kiermyer

b. Jul. 21, 1956, Montreal, Canada

Drums / Avant-Garde, Free Jazz

Franklin Kiermyer, a fairly obscure drummer, burst on the scene in 1994 with his Evidence CD *Solomon's Daughter*, a remarkably intense quartet date that features Pharoah Sanders at his most ferocious. Kiermyer keeps up with the passion, making one wonder why he was not known before that date. —*Scott Yanow*

● **Solomon's Daughter** / 1994 / Evidence ✦✦✦✦✦

Drummer Franklin Kiermyer may not be a well-known name but this Evidence CD is a real gem. Tenor saxophonist Pharoah Sanders, a powerful screamer who added a lot of fire and intensity to John Coltrane's 1966 quintet, had during the 1980s become much mellower and more melodic both in concert and on records, but this extremely powerful set restored one's faith in his uniqueness. Sanders is heard at the peak of his powers, playing miraculous solos full of screams, shrieks, overtone manipulation and pure emotion. Kiermyer (who wrote all six of the compositions) has the power of an Elvin Jones or a Rashied Ali without really copying their styles; his explosive playing fits in very well with Sanders. Pianist John Esposito and bassist Drew Gress cannot help being overshadowed by the dominant duo but they play quite well and make their contributions felt during the quieter pieces such as "Peace on Earth" and "Birds of the Niles" during which Sanders is quite lyrical and tender. But it is the lengthy blowouts on "If I Die Before I Wake" and "Three Jewels" that really make this set very memorable. "Blowing up a Storm" does not even begin to describe the ferocious music. —*Scott Yanow*

Kairos / Feb. 19, 1995-Feb. 22, 1995 / Evidence ✦✦✦✦✦

Drummer Franklin Kiermyer's debut record, *Solomon's Daughter,* featured some of the most ferocious Pharoah Sanders tenor ever captured and was much more intense than the tenor's usual live performances of the 1990s. Sanders is not on Kiermyer's second Evidence date (*Kairos*) but the explorative music is often in the style of the 1965-66 John Coltrane group in which Pharoah first came to fame. The dynamic Michael Stuart on tenor and occasional piano, pianist John Esposito (who recalls McCoy Tyner a bit) and bassist Dom Richards join the leader for often-raging performances that are quite memorable. Eric Person (on alto and soprano) joins the group on three numbers, one of which also has Sam Rivers on soprano. There are five brief, exotic and somewhat irrelevant selections (including a pygmy chant, a Native American medicine chant and two minutes of Greek bagpipes) but those are fortunately just interludes between the main pieces. Fans of late-period Coltrane will definitely want to pick up this exciting set. —*Scott Yanow*

Rebecca Kilgore

b. Sep. 24, 1948, Waltham, MA

Vocals / Standards, Swing

A self-described "closet musician" who got a rather late start as a jazz professional, Rebecca Kilgore gained confidence after hearing and meeting singer Syd Smith of Wholly Cats. Kilgore eventually replaced Smith in the group and made her record debut in 1981 on an LP called *Doggin' Around.* She became a fan favorite in Portland, Oregon, performing regularly with pianist Dave Frishberg in the Heathman Hotel for several years. Kilgore started gaining national attention with her recordings for Arbors Jazz and her appearances at jazz parties around the US. Her style concentrates on classic songs of the '30s and '40s; her friendly stage presence emphasizes the content of a song across in a swinging, clear, showboat-free manner. In addition to her Arbors CDs, she has recorded with Tall Jazz, drummer Hal Smith and a duo CD with Dave Frishberg for the PHD label. Kilgore married bluegrass musician Peter Schwimmer in 1997 and also has an interest in Western swing and country. —*Ken Dryden*

Looking at You / Apr. 1993 / PHD Music ✦✦✦

Although Rebecca Kilgore can clearly sing jazz, she plays it fairly straight on this duet set with pianist Dave Frishberg (who refrains from singing himself). She uplifts a variety of standards including many lesser-known items, everything from "Brazil" and "Martha" to "Lullaby in Rhythm," "Robin Hood," "Detour Ahead" and the 1920s piece "There Ain't No Sweet Man That's Worth the Salt of My Tears." This set is recommended on the basis of Kilgore's attractive voice, but she is obviously capable of stretching out and challenging herself quite a bit, more than she does here. —*Scott Yanow*

I Saw Stars / Apr. 13, 1994-Apr. 14, 1994 / Arbors ✦✦✦✦✦

Becky Kilgore, a singer based in the Pacific Northwest, is a longtime associate of pianist Dave Frishberg. Frishberg is part of the impressive supporting cast (along with trombonist Dan Barrett, altoist Chuck Wilson, Scott Robinson on tenor, bass sax and clarinet, guitarist Bucky Pizzarelli and bassist Michael Moore) for her solo debut. Kilgore has a nice swing to her style and clearly enjoys reviving such songs as "Happy as the Day Is Long," "A Lonely Coed" and "You Can't Lose a Broken Heart." She has a pleasing voice, gives a liberal amount of space to the soloists (the ensembles often sound a bit like the John Kirby Sextet), and constructs a set of enjoyable music that is heartily recommended to fans of small-group swing. —*Scott Yanow*

● **Not a Care in the World** / Apr. 22, 1997 / Arbors ✦✦✦✦✦

It is obvious on this CD that singer Rebecca Kilgore and pianist Dave Frishberg personally like each other and that they perform music together on a regular basis. Based in Portland, the duo match very well musically. Kilgore has an appealing and straightforward style a little reminiscent of Susannah McCorkle, uplifting songs while varying them only in subtle ways. Frishberg, who may be the top living lyricist, is cast here in the role of a swinging accompanist. Surprisingly, he wrote none of the lyrics, and he does not join Kilgore in any vocal duets. With the occasional assistance of swing guitarist Dan Faehnle, Kilgore explores a wide area of songs, alternating the famous with underplayed obscurities, with Mary Lou Williams' novelty "In the Land of Oo-Blah-Dee" and "An Occasional Man" being among the more memorable numbers. Recommended. —*Scott Yanow*

King Curtis (Curtis Ousley)

b. Feb. 7, 1934, Fort Worth, TX, **d.** Aug. 14, 1971, New York, NY
Tenor Saxophone / R&B, Groove, Hard Bop, East Coast Blues, Southern Soul
King Curtis was the last of the great R&B tenor sax giants. He came to prominence in the mid-'50s as a session musician in New York, recording, at one time or another, for most East Coast R&B labels. A long association with Atlantic/Atco began in 1958, especially on recordings by the Coasters. He recorded singles for many small labels in the '50s—his own Atco sessions (1958-1959), then Prestige/New Jazz and Prestige/TruSound for jazz and R&B albums (1960-1961). Curtis also had a No.1 R&B single with "Soul Twist" on Enjoy Records (1962). He was signed by Capitol (1963-1964), where he cut mostly singles, including "Soul Serenade." Returning to Atlantic in 1965, he remained there for the rest of his life. He had solid R&B single success with "Memphis Soul Stew" and "Ode to Billie Joe" (1967). Beginning in 1967, Curtis started to take a more active studio role at Atlantic—leading and contracting sessions for other artists, producing with Jerry Wexler and later on his own. He also became the leader of Aretha Franklin's backing unit, the Kingpins. He compiled several albums of singles during this period. All aspects of his career were in full swing at the time he was murdered in 1971. —*Bob Porter*

The New Scene of King Curtis / Apr. 21, 1960 / Original Jazz Classics ◆◆◆◆
At first glance, this would appear to be a CD reissue well worth picking up. R&B tenor saxophonist King Curtis is heard in a rare jazz outing, holding his own with cornetist Nat Adderley (in prime form), pianist Wynton Kelly, bassist Paul Chambers and drummer Oliver Jackson on four originals and "Willow Weep for Me." But the single-CD *Soul Meeting* not only contains this entire session, but another related six-song set as well. Only get this particular release if it is found at a budget price. —*Scott Yanow*

● **Soul Meeting** / Apr. 21, 1960+Sep. 18, 1960 / Prestige ◆◆◆◆◆
King Curtis, an influential and greatly in-demand R&B tenorman, made relatively few jazz dates in his career. This CD has two of the best, complete albums originally called *The New Scene of King Curtis* and *Soul Meeting;* the former is also available as a separate CD but should be skipped in favor of this one. Curtis teams up with the passionate cornetist Nat Adderley, pianist Wynton Kelly, either Paul Chambers or Sam Jones on bass and Oliver Jackson or Belton Evans on drums. The music is blues-based bop, with seven basic Curtis originals and four standards. Highly recommended, this set serves as proof that King Curtis could have been a viable jazz player. —*Scott Yanow*

The Best of King Curtis / Aug. 23, 1962-Mar. 11, 1965 / Capitol ◆◆◆◆
The Best of King Curtis collects the bulk of King Curtis' singles for Capitol, plus selected album tracks. Although he didn't have many hits while on Capitol—only "Soul Serenade" hit the charts—this collection demonstrates the depths of Curtis' talents, showcasing his stabs at jazz and blues in addition to his trademark R&B. *Instant Soul* remains a stronger introduction, but for fans that want to dig a little deeper, *The Best of King Curtis* is an excellent purchase. —*Stephen Thomas Erlewine*

Blues at Montreux / July 1971 / Atlantic ◆◆◆◆◆
This live set from the 1971 Montreux Jazz Festival was co-led by tenor saxophonist King Curtis (who tragically would be killed three months later) and veteran blues pianist/vocalist Champion Jack Dupree. With guitarist Cornell Dupree (in excellent form), bassist Jerry Jemmott and drummer Oliver Jackson laying down the foundation, Curtis and Dupree find a great deal of common musical ground. Dupree has quite a few witty vocals (particularly the near-classic "Junker's Blues") while taking choruses of irregular length that keep his sidemen continually guessing. Curtis' distinctive tenor is also heard from, making one truly regret both that this was his final recording and that this LP's music has yet to be reissued on CD. —*Scott Yanow*

King Oliver (Joe Oliver)

b. May 11, 1885, New Orleans, LA, **d.** Apr. 8, 1938, Savannah, GA
Cornet / Classic New Orleans Jazz, Traditional Jazz
Joe "King" Oliver was one of the great New Orleans legends, an early giant whose legacy is only partly on records. In 1923 he led one of the classic New Orleans jazz bands, the last significant group to emphasize collective improvisation over solos, but ironically his second cornetist (Louis Armstrong) would soon permanently change jazz. And while Armstrong never tired of praising his idol, he actually

sounded very little like Oliver; the King's influence was more deeply felt by Muggsy Spanier and Tommy Ladnier.

Although originally a trombonist, by 1905 Oliver was playing cornet regularly with various New Orleans bands. Gradually he rose to the top of the crowded local scene and in 1917 he was being billed "King" by bandleader Kid Ory. A master of mutes, Oliver was able to get a wide variety of sounds out of his horn; Bubber Miley would later on be inspired by Oliver's expertise. In 1919 Oliver left New Orleans to join Bill Johnson's band at the Dreamland Ballroom in Chicago. By 1920 he was a leader himself and, after an unsuccessful year in California, King Oliver started playing regularly with his Creole Jazz Band at the Lincoln Gardens in Chicago. He soon sent for his protégé Louis Armstrong and with clarinetist Johnny Dodds, trombonist Honore Dutrey, pianist Lil Harden and drummer Baby Dodds as a core, Oliver had a remarkable band whose brilliance was only hinted at on records. As it is, the group's 1923 sessions far exceeded any jazz previously recorded; Oliver's three chorus solo on "Dippermouth Blues" has since been memorized by virtually every Dixieland trumpeter.

Unfortunately the Creole Jazz Band gradually broke up in 1924. Oliver recorded a pair of duets with pianist Jelly Roll Morton but otherwise was off records that year. He took over Dave Peyton's band in 1925 and renamed it the Dixie Syncopators; Barney Bigard and Albert Nicholas were among the members. New recordings resulted (including "Snag It", which has a famous eight-bar passage by Oliver) but when the cornetist moved to New York in 1927, his music was behind the times and he made some bad business decisions (including turning down a chance to play regularly at the Cotton Club). Worse yet, his dental problems (caused partly by an early liking of sugar sandwiches) made playing cornet increasingly painful and, on many of his later recordings, Oliver is barely present (although he did a heroic job on 1929's "Too Late"). Pianist Luis Russell took over the Dixie Syncopators in 1929 and, although Oliver's last recordings (from 1931) are superior examples of hot dance music, he was quickly becoming a forgotten name. Unsuccessful tours in the South eventually left Oliver stranded there, working as a janitor in a poolroom before his death at age 52. —*Scott Yanow*

★ **King Oliver's Creole Jazzband 1923-1924** / Apr. 5, 1923-Dec. 6, 1924 / Retrieval ◆◆◆◆◆
The music on this 1997 two-CD import set has been reissued many times, but this is the most complete version yet. Cornetist King Oliver's Creole Jazz Band in 1923 was not only the finest jazz group on record, but the most exciting unit up to that point in time. Although it featured some short solos from the octet (particularly Oliver, 22-year-old cornetist Louis Armstrong, trombonist Honore Dutrey and the great clarinetist Johnny Dodds), the emphasis was on the ensembles. All 37 of the band's recordings are on this two-fer (including such classics as the two versions of "Dippermouth Blues," "Froggie Moore," the two renditions of "Snake Rag," "High Society," "Sobbin' Blues," Chattanooga Stomp," "Buddy's Habits" and three versions of "Mabel's Dream"). In addition, Oliver is heard in 1924 backing the vaudeville team of Butterbeans & Susie and taking two duets with Jelly Roll Morton (including "King Porter Stomp"). This classic New Orleans music is essential for any comprehensive jazz collection. —*Scott Yanow*

Vol. 1 / Mar. 11, 1926-Sep. 17, 1926 / Classic Jazz Masters ◆◆◆◆◆
The first of three LPs reissuing all of cornetist Joe "King" Oliver's recordings for Vocalion and Brunswick with his Dixie Syncopators, this album has four very different versions of "Snag It" and two takes of the hot arrangement "Too Bad." Oliver is in generally fine form on such numbers as "Deep Henderson," the classic "Jackass Blues" and his famous "Sugar Foot Stomp." The personnel is quite strong including second trumpeter Bob Shoffner, trombonist Kid Ory, clarinetists Albert Nicholas and Johnny Dodds and Barney Bigard mostly on tenor. Some of the highlights have been reissued on a Decca CD but better to have all of these valuable performances. —*Scott Yanow*

Sugar Foot Stomp / Mar. 11, 1926-Jun. 11, 1928 / GRP ◆◆◆◆◆
This Decca reissue CD put out by GRP is a fine sampler of King Oliver's 1926-28 recordings with his Dixie Syncopators. The hot jazz dance music is highlighted by several classics ("Too Bad," "Snag It," Jackass Blues," "Sobbin' Blues," "Farewell Blues" and two versions of "Snag It"). With such sidemen as trombonist Kid Ory, clarinetists Albert Nicholas and Omer Simeon and Barney Bigard on tenor and clarinet, Oliver's suppporting cast is quite strong. The cornetist was himself starting to fade during this period but does take a few heated solos and his break on "Snag It" remains quite famous. True King Oliver collectors, though, will want to bypass this one and instead acquire the entries in one of the more comprehensive European complete series. —*Scott Yanow*

Vol. 2 / Apr. 22, 1927-Aug. 13, 1928 / Classic Jazz Masters ◆◆◆◆◆
The second of three LPs reissuing all of King Oliver's Vocalion and Brunswick recordings finds the cornetist playing less than before (his teeth were starting to give him serious problems) but contains worthy solos from trombonists Kid Ory and Jimmy Archey, clarinetist Omer Simeon and Barney Bigard on tenor. At its

worst these performances are of first class dance music and at its best ("Farewell Blues" and "Sobbin' Blues"), the music is timeless. —*Scott Yanow*

Vol. 3 / Aug. 13, 1928-Apr. 15, 1931 / Classic Jazz Masters ✦✦✦

The third and final LP reissuing King Oliver's complete Vocalion and Brunswick recordings can easily be divided into two parts. The first six selections date from the second half of 1928 and include many good examples of '20s dance music; no great solos despite the impressive personnel. The final eight numbers jump to 1931 when cornetist Oliver's chops were completely shot due to serious gum problems. Despite Oliver's near-absence on what would be his final recordings, his orchestra is excellent with trumpeters Ward Pinkett and Dave Nelson, trombonist Jimmy Archey and tenor saxophonist Bingie Madison taking fine solos on an attractive program of future standards. —*Scott Yanow*

● **King Oliver and His Orchestra** / Jan. 16, 1929-Sep. 19, 1930 / RCA ✦✦✦✦

Much more complete than any domestic reissue, this double-CD from French RCA in their Jazz Tribune series (a straight duplication of the earlier two-LP set) features the influential cornetist King Oliver in many of his final recordings. Oliver was finding it increasingly painful to play during this era (in fact Louis Metcalf and Punch Miller substitute for him on the first seven selections) but ironically Oliver had one of his finest bands at the time. Oliver does take a particularly heroic solo on "Too Late" (one of the high points of his career) and on a few other tracks, but the main reason for the performances' success is the high-quality musicianship of Oliver's hot dance band. Such soloists as trumpeters Bubber Miley (featured on "St. James Infirmary") and Red Allen, trombonist Jimmy Archey, altoist Hilton Jefferson and a variety of lesser-known but talented players make each of the 32 recordings well worth hearing. Recommended to fans of pre-swing big bands and classic jazz. —*Scott Yanow*

King Pleasure (Clarence Beeks)

b. Mar. 24, 1922, Oakdale, TN, d. Mar. 21, 1981, Los Angeles, CA
Vocals / Vocalese, Bop

Along with Eddie Jefferson, King Pleasure was one of the early masters of vocalese—a style in which lyrics are written and sung to the solos of jazz instrumentalists. Although Pleasure cited Jefferson as his main influence and said that Jefferson was embracing vocalese before him, Pleasure's sax-like phrasing and scat singing proved equally influential. The charismatic improviser (who recorded for Prestige, Aladdin, Jubilee, HiFi Jazz and United Artists) is best known for his 1952 hit "Moody's Mood for Love," for which Jefferson wrote lyrics to tenor saxman James Moody's 1949 improvisation on the standard "I'm in the Mood for Love." Pleasure was also praised for his interpretations of classics like Lester Young's "DB Blues," Charlie Parker's "Parker's Mood" and Gene Ammons' "Red Top" in the 1950s, and he had a direct or indirect influence on Jon Hendricks, Annie Ross, Bob Dorough, Mark Murphy, Al Jarreau, Lou Lanza and even the Manhattan Transfer. But his recording career didn't last very long. Pleasure was still recording in the early 1960s, but after that, he faded into great obscurity—although the impact of his early work would remain long after his death on Mar. 21, 1981 (only three days before what would have been his 59th birthday). In the late 1990s, one could hear Pleasure's influence on such promising vocalists as Ian Shaw and Lou Lanza. —*Alex Henderson*

● **King Pleasure Sings/Annie Ross Sings** / Oct. 9, 1952-Dec. 24, 1953 / Prestige ✦✦✦✦

The first 12 recordings of King Pleasure's career (which used to comprise the Prestige LP *Original Moody's Mood*) and the second and most famous Annie Ross recording session are on this essential CD. Pleasure's famous vocalese renditions of "I'm in the Mood for Love" (best known as "Moody's Mood for Love," since it was based on a James Moody saxophone solo), "Red Top" (with a young Betty Carter) and "Parker's Mood" (which foretold the death of Charlie Parker more than a year in advance) are included among the music from his five sessions. Ross' date resulted in her two greatest hits, "Twisted" and "Farmer's Market." Both of the singers glide through their tricky lyrics with ease. This innovative music (which also finds Jon Hendricks joining Pleasure on "Don't Get Started") is a must for all serious jazz collections. —*Scott Yanow*

Moody's Mood for Love / 1955-Sep. 5, 1962 / Blue Note ✦✦✦✦

The bulk of this CD reissue contains King Pleasure's final recording session, a 1962 set with unidentified personnel (other than tenor saxophonist Seldon Powell). A few remakes ("I'm in the Mood for Love" and "Don't Get Started") are joined by originals, a couple of straightforward tunes, and some newer vocalese arrangements. In addition, this CD has two previously unreleased numbers and six selections from very rare singles put out by Aladdin and Jubilee during 1956. Highlights overall include "Jazz Jump," "Sometimes I'm Happy," "Mean to Me," "D.B. Blues" and "All of Me." It is easy to acquire the complete King Pleasure, since

everything he recorded has now been reissued on three CDs; all are recommended. —*Scott Yanow*

Golden Days / June 14, 1960 / Original Jazz Classics ✦✦✦

This CD reissue (one of three King Pleasure sets that together contain all of his recordings) has an LP-length session from 1960 (originally put out by HiFi Jazz) that is dominated by spirited remakes of past glories. The vocalese singer revisits such songs as "Moody's Mood for Love," "Don't Get Scared" and "Parker's Mood" with the assistance of tenors Teddy Edwards and Harold Land and pianist Gerald Wiggins. Worth picking up, although the other two King Pleasure releases are generally on a higher and more creative level. —*Scott Yanow*

Nancy King

Vocals / Post-Bop

An adventurous singer with an intriguing sense of humor, Nancy King stretches and extends the bebop tradition. After high school, she worked in San Francisco with Pharoah Sanders, Pony Poindexter and a variety of local players. Resettling in the Pacific Northwest, the underrated Nancy King has had an underground reputation among jazz singers. She can be heard at her best on a pair of Justice recordings she co-led with her frequent musical partner, bassist Glen Moore (as "King and Moore"). —*Scott Yanow*

● **Impending Bloom** / 1991 / Justice ✦✦✦✦✦

Despite the album graphics (which depict a woman, a horse and a fish in the late stages of pregnancy) and the title cut (which deals with a horse in labor, I think), the bulk of this set has nothing to do with childbirth. It does contain more than its share of superb jazz singing by Nancy King, strong interplay between King and bassist Glen Moore, and guest appearances by violinist Rob Thomas, guitarist Jerry Hahn and drummer Lawrence Williams. Nancy King is an inventive singer both with and without lyrics, taking wild chances with a voice that is both lovely and flexible. The three contributions by the songwriting team of Samantha and Glen Moore ("Impending Bloom," "White Duck" and "Man in the Oven") have somewhat bizarre lyrics. Better are King and Moore's fresh reappraisal of a variety of standards, including the singer's unaccompanied "By Myself" and what must be the slowest recorded version ever of "Secret Love." A colorful set. —*Scott Yanow*

Straight into Your Heart / Oct. 15, 1996 / Mons ✦✦✦✦

John Kirby

b. Dec. 31, 1908, Baltimore, MD, d. Jun. 14, 1952, Hollywood, CA
Bass, Leader, Tuba / Swing

John Kirby led one of the most unusual groups during the height of the big-band era, a sextet comprising trumpeter Charlie Shavers, clarinetist Buster Bailey, altoist Russell Procope, pianist Billy Kyle, drummer O'Neil Spencer and his own bass. Although Shavers and Bailey could be quite extroverted, the tightly arranged ensembles tended to be very subtoned and introverted yet virtuosic. Kirby, originally a tuba player, switched to bass in 1930 when he joined Fletcher Henderson's Orchestra. He was one of the better bassists of the 1930s, playing with Henderson (1930-33 and 1935-36) and Chick Webb's big band (1933-35). By 1937 Kirby had his own group at the Onyx Club; Frankie Newton and Pete Brown passed through the band before the personnel was set. With Maxine Sullivan (Kirby's wife at the time) offering occasional vocals, the John Kirby Sextet was quite popular during 1938-42. Shavers' "Undecided" became a hit and the band's abilities to "swing the classics" caught on. The sextet gradually declined in the 1940s. Spencer became ill and was replaced by Specs Powell and later Bill Beason, Kyle was drafted and Procope was replaced by George Johnson. By 1945 (with Shavers' departure to join Tommy Dorsey), the only original members still in the group were Bailey and Kirby himself. The following year the band disbanded and despite some attempts by the bassist to form another similar sextet (including a poorly attended Carnegie Hall reunion in 1950), John Kirby was never able to duplicate his earlier successes. Classics has reissued all of Kirby's prime recordings. —*Scott Yanow*

Boss of the Bass / Dec. 3, 1930-Jan. 15, 1941 / Columbia ✦✦✦

John Kirby was never actually the "boss of the bass," even back in the 1930s, but he was an important bandleader. The second half of this admirable two-LP set features his unique group on 14 of their more rewarding recordings from 1939-41. The complex yet tight arrangements and concise solos by the virtuosi (trumpeter Charlie Shavers, bassist Buster Bailey, altoist Russell Procope, pianist Billy Kyle, drummer O'Neil Spencer and Kirby on bass) gave the John Kirby Sextet a unique sound of its own. The first of these two LPs contains 14 selections featuring Kirby as a sideman with such groups as the Chocolate Dandies, Fletcher Henderson, Chick Webb, Putney Dandridge, Teddy Wilson, Charlie Barnet and Lucky Millinder along with backup work with early versions of his sextet behind singers Midge Williams, Maxine Sullivan and Mildred Bailey. A well-conceived reissue, it contains more than its share of exciting swing performances. —*Scott Yanow*

☆ **1938-1939** / Oct. 28, 1938-Oct. 12, 1939 / Classics ✦✦✦✦

The first of three Classics CDs reissuing all of the John Kirby Sextet's recordings during its prime years (1938-43) has the group's earliest 22 recordings. Although the first five numbers were originally issued as "John Kirby and His Onyx Club Boys," the famous personnel were already in place: bassist Kirby, trumpeter Charlie Shavers (then only 21), altoist Russell Procope, clarinetist Buster Bailey, pianist Billy Kyle and drummer O'Neil Spencer (who took an occasional vocal). The group's unique cool-toned sound, tricky ensembles, and often atmospheric music definitely stood out during an era dominated by loud big bands. There are quite a few classics on this CD, including "Rehearsin' for a Nervous Breakdown," the original version of Shavers' "Undecided," "Dawn on the Desert," "Royal Garden Blues" and "Nocturne." Highly recommended, as are the two other Classics Kirby discs. —*Scott Yanow*

The Biggest Little Band / Oct. 28, 1938-Jan. 15, 1941 / Smithsonian ✦✦✦

☆ **1939-1941** / Oct. 12, 1939-Jan. 15, 1941 / Classics ✦✦✦✦

The second of three Classics John Kirby CDs has 23 more titles in the history of Kirby's unique sextet. The band, comprising trumpeter Charlie Shavers, clarinetist Buster Bailey, altoist Russell Procope, pianist Billy Kyle, drummer O'Neil Spencer and the bassist/leader, performed cool-toned chamber jazz more than a decade before it became popular, and carved out its own unusual niche during the big-band era. The tight ensembles and brief solos brought out the best in each of the players. Highlights of this highly recommended disc include "Humoresque," "Jumpin' in the Pump Room," "Chloe," "Sextet from 'Lucia'" and "Zooming at the Zombie." —*Scott Yanow*

1941 / 1941 / Circle ✦✦✦

Recorded in 1941 when the John Kirby Sextet was at the height of its powers and popularity, this album consists of 14 mostly brief performances cut as radio transcriptions. Clocking in between 1:47 and 3:05, the selections feature concise solos from trumpeter Charlie Shavers, clarinetist Buster Bailey, altoist Russell Procope and pianist Billy Kyle, plus the group's trademark cool sound and flawless work on some rather tricky arrangements. Among the more memorable numbers are "Ida," "Coquette," "Front and Center," "Dawn on the Desert" and "Original Dixieland One Step." —*Scott Yanow*

Biggest Little Band in the Land / May 19, 1941-Aug. 18, 1944 / Classic Jazz ✦✦✦✦

Taken from radio airchecks, this difficult-to-find two-LP set added 24 more performances to the legacy of the John Kirby Sextet. Nat Hentoff's rather general liner notes do not mention the fact that the classic personnel of the sextet (trumpeter Charlie Shavers, altoist Russell Procope, clarinetist Buster Bailey, pianist Billy Kyle, drummer O'Neil Spencer and bassist Kirby) changed during the era, with Spencer's death resulting in Bill Beason getting his spot, and Kyle and Procope departing in favor of Clyde Hart and George Johnson. Even with the changes, the famous Kirby sound remained quite intact, and the arrangements were as tricky and catchy as ever. Among the numbers on this valuable two-fer are "Mr. Haydn Gets Hip," "Bugler's Dilemma," "Rehearsin' for a Nervous Breakdown," "The Peanut Vendor" and "Kansas City Caboose." —*Scott Yanow*

★ **1941-1943** / 1941-Dec. 1943 / Classics ✦✦✦✦

The third John Kirby CD from the European Classics label has 21 performances that trace Kirby's unique sextet from the peak of its popularity in 1941 through the war years. In addition to a dozen songs originally released by Victor, this set has nine rarer numbers that appeared on V-Discs. With trumpeter Charlie Shavers, clarinetist Buster Bailey and altoist Russell Procope, (along with pianist Billy Kyle and drummer O'Neil Spencer), Kirby was able to form an unusual and very distinctive group sound that, although comprising swing virtuosos, looked towards cool jazz of the 1950s. By the later tracks of this CD the band was starting to come apart a bit with first Specs Powell and then Bill Beason replacing the late Spencer, George Johnson ably filling in for Procope and Shavers departing before the final number; the group sound however remained intact and among the many highlights of this CD are "Coquette," "Royal Garden Blues," "Night Whispers," "St. Louis Blues" and "9:20 Special." —*Scott Yanow*

John Kirby and His Sextet / 1941-Jul. 1946 / Alamac ✦✦✦

This budget LP, despite its inaccurate personnel and date listings, has some valuable and rare music from bassist John Kirby. Most of the tunes are taken from radio airchecks, with the exception of a four-song studio date from Apr. 26, 1945, that was originally made for the Asch label. There are four songs from the classic Kirby Sextet (with trumpeter Charlie Shavers, clarinetist Buster Bailey and altoist Russell Procope) and titles from 1943-46, when the horn players included the underrated altoist George Johnson, trumpeters Emmett Bailey and Clarence Berenton and the tenor of Budd Johnson. Recommended for swing collectors; hopefully this interesting music will be reissued on CD. —*Scott Yanow*

1945-1946 / 1945 / Classics ✦✦✦

The fourth and final Classics CD to reissue all of the studio recordings of the John Kirby Sextet features the band's very rare 1945-46 performances, originally released by the Asch, Crown, Disc and Apollo labels. The personnel of the classic unit had changed, with only the bassist/leader and clarinetist Buster Bailey still present on all of the numbers (although altoist Russell Procope and pianist Billy Kyle are on half the selections). Trumpeters Emmett Berry, Clarence Berenton and George Taitt do their best to fill in for the departed Charlie Shavers; drummer Bill Beason was the late O'Neil Spencer's permanent replacement; other musicians making appearances include altoists George Johnson and Hilton Jefferson, tenor saxophonist Budd Johnson (who makes the sextet a septet on six songs) and pianists Ram Ramirez and Hank Jones. The young Sarah Vaughan is featured on four selections (including classic renditions of "You Got to My Head" and "It Might as Well Be Spring"), and the forgotten Shirley Moore takes two vocals. Although the group's sound had not changed and there are some colorful arrangements, Shavers' muted yet fiery trumpet was definitely missed. This valuable release is recommended after acquiring Kirby's first three Classics CDs. —*Scott Yanow*

Andy Kirk

b. May 28, 1898, Newport, KY, d. Dec. 11, 1992, New York, NY
Leader, Bass Saxophone, Tuba / Swing, Bing Band

Andy Kirk was never a major musician (in fact he never really soloed), arranger or personality yet he was a successful big bandleader in the 1930s and '40s. He started playing bass sax and tuba in Denver with George Morrison's band in 1918. In 1925 he moved to Dallas where he played with Terrence Holder's Dark Clouds of Joy. In 1929 he took over leadership of the band (which was renamed Andy Kirk's Twelve Clouds of Joy) and moved to Kansas City. During 1929-30 they recorded some excellent hot performances with such players as pianist/arranger Mary Lou Williams, violinist Claude Williams and trumpeter Edgar "Puddinghead" Battle. Surprisingly Kirk's Orchestra was off records entirely during 1931-35 but in 1936 (the year it relocated to New York) it immediately had a pop hit in "Until the Real Thing Comes Along" featuring the high voice of singer Pha Terrell. In future years such fine soloists as tenor saxophonist Dick Wilson, the early electric guitarist Floyd Smith, Don Byas, Harold "Shorty" Baker, Howard McGhee (1942-43), Jimmy Forrest and even Fats Navarro and (briefly) Charlie Parker would be among Kirk's sidemen. However Mary Lou Williams was the most important musician in the band, both as a soloist and as an arranger. In 1948 Andy Kirk broke up the band (which had recorded mostly for Decca) and in later years ran a hotel and served as an official in the Musicians' Union. A lone "reunion" date in 1956 featured the classic charts but almost none of the original sidemen. —*Scott Yanow*

The Territories, Vol. 1 / Jan. 1927-Dec. 15, 1930 / Arcadia ✦✦✦✦

This collector's LP traces the beginnings of Andy Kirk's Twelve Clouds of Joy. In addition to that big band's first recordings from 1929-30, there are also scarce titles from 1927 by Jeanette James' Synco Jazzers and John Williams. Williams, a baritonist and altoist, was the first husband of pianist Mary Lou Williams, who is heard on the early titles making her recording debut. While the James and Williams numbers are historically significant, it is the initial dates by Kirk's band (which have been reissued on CD) that are most enjoyable. Among the musicians featured on this interesting collection of vintage Kansas City jazz are Mary Lou and violinist Claude Williams. —*Scott Yanow*

● **1929-1931** / Nov. 7, 1929-Mar. 2, 1931 / Classics ✦✦✦✦✦

This highly recommended CD from the European Classics label has all of the early recordings of Andy Kirk's Twelve Clouds of Joy, although unfortunately not the alternate takes. The most famous soloists were pianist Mary Lou Williams (who was also responsible for most of the arrangements), violinist Claude Williams (who unfortunately left Kirk before he had his big success in the mid-1930s) and trumpeter Edgar "Puddinghead" Battle, although the lesser-known players mostly fare fairly well too. The selections are primarily hot vintage Kansas City jazz, including such tunes as "Blue Clarinet Stomp," "Cloudy," "Lotta Sax Appeal," "Mary's Idea" and "Once or Twice." This CD concludes with three numbers from 1931 when Kirk's Orchestra was briefly being used to back singer Blanche Calloway (Cab's older sister). Unfortunately, Kirk's ensemble would not record again for another five years, but these early titles—which give listeners clues as to the big band's evolution—stand alone as fine 1920s jazz. —*Scott Yanow*

● **Mary's Idea** / Mar. 2, 1936-Jan. 3, 1941 / GRP ✦✦✦✦✦

This well-conceived CD has 20 of the most rewarding recordings by Andy Kirk's Orchestra. Ending a five-year period when they were off record, the big band (which had recently relocated to New York from Kansas City) showed that it could outswing most of its competitors, due largely to Mary Lou Williams arrangements and piano playing, the underrated tenor Dick Wilson, and a strong group sound. Pha Terrell's high-pitched vocals helped the band to catch on commercially, but fortunately, he is almost absent from this collection (singing only "What's Your Story, Morning Glory"), which, with the exception of seven selections from 1939-41 (including two small-group numbers led by Mary Lou Williams), concentrates on 1936-37. Among the many highlights are "Walkin' and Swingin'," "Froggy Bottom," "The Lady Who Swings the Band," "Mess-A-Stomp," "Mary's Idea" and "Ring Dem Bells." Highly recommended to listeners who, in skipping the Classics series, want a strong sampling of Andy Kirk's music rather than every single title. —*Scott Yanow*

1936-1937 / Mar. 1936-Jan. 1937 / Classics ✦✦✦✦✦
The Andy Kirk Orchestra ended their five-year hiatus from records in March 1936 in a big way, recording ten titles in their first session alone. Mary Lou Williams' arrangements and several strong soloists (including pianist Williams and tenor saxophonist Dick Wilson) gave the band its own musical personality, and their hit recording of "Until the Real Thing Comes Along" (included on this release) made the group a commercial success for a time. Vocalist Pha Terrell's high voice was always an acquired taste, and many of his vocals (other than the hit and "All the Jive Is Gone") are often difficult to sit through. However, most of the songs on this excellent CD are fairly heated, with highlights including "Walkin' and Swingin'," "Lotta Sax Appeal," "Froggy Bottom," "Christopher Columbus" and "The Lady Who Swings the Band." Listeners who are not completists (and the Classics CD series does skip over alternates anyway) may want to acquire GRP/Decca's single CD *Mary's Idea* instead. —*Scott Yanow*

1938 / Feb. 1938-Dec. 1938 / Classics ✦✦✦✦✦
Andy Kirk's Orchestra was at the height of its popularity during the late 1930s, still riding high from their hit "Until the Real Thing Comes Along." The star of that record, singer Pha Terrell, is on the majority of the songs on this CD (the fourth in Classics' complete reissuance of the master takes of all Andy Kirk recordings from the swing era), but there are some hotter tunes too, most notably "Mess-A-Stomp," "Jump Jack Jump," "Dunkin' a Doughnut" and "Mary's Idea." However, Terrell's dominance of many titles may make many swing fans opt for the GRP/Decca single-disc Andy Kirk sampler instead. —*Scott Yanow*

1937-1938 / Jan. 1937-Jan. 1938 / Classics ✦✦✦✦✦
The third Andy Kirk CD put out by the Classics label (reissuing all of Kirk's swing-era recordings) is primarily for completists, for the then-popular but rather dated singer Pha Terrell is on the majority of the songs. There are some good moments from pianist Mary Lou Williams and tenor saxophonist Dick Wilson (particularly on the instrumentals), with the most memorable numbers being "A Mellow Bit of Rhythm," "Twinklin'," and "The Big Dipper," but Terrell is often difficult to sit through. —*Scott Yanow*

1939-1940 / 1939-1940 / Classics ✦✦✦✦
Andy Kirk's Twelve Clouds of Joy was a top-notch Kansas City swing band that, by 1939, featured the pop vocals of Pha Terrell, the more blues-oriented singing of June Richmond, creative arrangements by Mary Lou Williams, and some excellent soloing from pianist Williams and Dick Wilson on tenor. Most memorable in this entry in Classics' "complete" Andy Kirk CD series are "Floyd's Guitar Blues" (an odd but pioneering electric guitar feature for Floyd Smith), "Wham" and "Scratching in the Gravel." —*Scott Yanow*

1940-1942 / 1940-1942 / Classics ✦✦✦✦✦
The Andy Kirk Orchestra was going through some major changes during the period covered by this CD. Tenor star Dick Wilson died prematurely; pop singer Pha Terrell had left; pianist and chief arranger Mary Lou Williams departed in early 1942 (Ken Kersey was her replacement on piano); and such interesting younger players as trumpeters Harold "Shorty" Baker and Howard McGhee and Al Sears on tenor gave the group a slightly different sound. Actually, the music on this CD (late-period swing) is consistently on a higher level than on most of the previous CDs in the Classics series. Highlights include "The Count," "Hey Lawdy Mama," "Boogie Woogie Cocktail" (featuring Kersey) and Howard McGhee's recording debut on the exciting "McGhee Special." —*Scott Yanow*

1944 / 1944 / Hindsight ✦✦✦
This should be a valuable LP, for Andy Kirk's Twelve Clouds of Joy did not make any commercial recordings during 1944 due to the Musician Union's recording strike. However, the radio transcriptions are quite brief, and there is only a total of 27 minutes of music on the LP. In addition, the chatty Dave Dexter liner notes do not bother identifying the soloists (which may include trumpeter Howard McGhee and Jimmy Forrest on tenor). June Richmond takes two vocals, and there is a certain amount of spirit on the nine performances, but nothing all that unusual occurs, and the extremely brief playing time makes this a passable item despite its historic value. —*Scott Yanow*

Clouds from the Southwest / Mar. 4, 1956-Mar. 12, 1956 / RCA ✦✦✦
There were many reunions of swing-era big bands during the 1950s, but this was certainly one of the most unusual ones. Andy Kirk led a popular and swinging

orchestra during 1929-48, but in 1956, his reunion only included one of his alumni (pianist Ken Kersey)—and only on seven of the 12 numbers. Why Mary Lou Williams and the other survivors were not enlisted for this project is unclear. Last available as a French RCA LP, the music is worthwhile, even though Mary Lou Williams' original charts were updated by Manny Albam, Ernie Wilkins and Al Cohn, and a top-notch orchestra of studio players having nothing to do with Kirk was employed. With such major players as trumpeters Conte Candoli and Joe Newman, trombonist Jimmy Cleveland and Al Cohn on tenor being among the soloists, such vintage tunes as "A Mellow Bit of Rhythm," "McGhee Special," "Froggy Bottom" and "Walkin' and Swingin'" are treated well, but this was certainly a mysterious date. —*Scott Yanow*

Rahsaan Roland Kirk (Ronald T. Kirk)

b. Aug. 7, 1936, Columbus, OH, d. Dec. 5, 1977, Bloomington, IN
Tenor Saxophone, Stritch, Manzello, Flute, Clarinet / Bop, Hard Bop, R&B, Swing, Avant-Garde, New Orleans Jazz

Arguably the most exciting saxophone soloist in jazz history, Kirk was a post-modernist before that term even existed. Kirk played the continuum of jazz tradition as an instrument unto itself; he felt little compunction about mixing and matching elements from the music's history, and his concoctions usually seemed natural, if not inevitable. When discussing Kirk, a great deal of attention is always paid to his eccentricities—playing several horns at once, making his own instruments, clowning on stage. However, Kirk was an immensely creative artist; perhaps no improvising saxophonist has ever possessed a more comprehensive technique—one that covered every aspect of jazz, from Dixie to free—and perhaps no other jazz musician has ever been more spontaneously inventive. His skills in constructing a solo are of particular note. Kirk had the ability to pace, shape, and elevate his improvisations to an extraordinary degree. During any given Kirk solo, just at the point in the course of his performance when it appeared he could not raise the intensity level any higher, he always seemed able to turn it up yet another notch.

Kirk was born with sight, but became blind at the age of two. He started playing the bugle and trumpet, then learned the clarinet and C-melody sax. Kirk began playing tenor sax professionally in R&B bands at the age of 15. While a teenager, he discovered the "manzello" and "stritch"—the former, a modified version of the saxello, which was itself a slightly curved variant of the B-flat soprano sax; the latter, a modified straight E-flat alto. To these and other instruments, Kirk began making his own improvements. He reshaped all three of his saxes so that they could be played simultaneously; he'd play tenor with his left hand, finger the manzello with his right, and sound a drone on the stritch, for instance. Kirk's self-invented technique was in evidence from his first recording, a 1956 R&B record called *Triple Threat*. By 1960 he had begun to incorporate a siren whistle into his solos, and by 1963 he had mastered circular breathing, a technique that enabled him to play without pause for breath.

In his early 20s, Kirk worked in Louisville before moving to Chicago in 1960. That year he made his second album, *Introducing Roland Kirk*, which featured saxophonist/trumpeter Ira Sullivan. In 1961, Kirk toured Germany and spent three months with Charles Mingus. From that point onward, Kirk mostly led his own group, the Vibration Society, recording prolifically with a range of sidemen. In the early '70s, Kirk became something of an activist; he led the Jazz and People's Movement, a group devoted to opening up new opportunities for jazz musicians. The group adopted the tactic of interrupting tapings and broadcasts of television and radio programs in protest of the small number of African-American musicians employed by the networks and recording studios. In the course of his career, Kirk brought many hitherto unused instruments to jazz. In addition to the saxes, Kirk played the nose whistle, the piccolo, and the harmonica; instruments of his own design included the "trumpophone" (a trumpet with a soprano sax mouthpiece), and the "slidesophone" (a small trombone or slide trumpet, also with a sax mouthpiece). Kirk suffered a paralyzing stroke in 1975, losing movement on one side of his body, but his homemade saxophone technique allowed him to continue to play; beginning in 1976 and lasting until his death a year later, Kirk played one-handed. —*Chris Kelsey*

Early Roots / Nov. 9, 1956 / Bethlehem ✦✦✦
Rahsaan Roland Kirk's first recording predated his second by four years and would be a real obscurity until its reissue in the mid-'70s. Kirk at 20 already had a recognizable sound on tenor and, although he had not yet mastered the art of playing two or three horns at once, he did overdub his manzello and stritch on three of the selections released on his debut, hinting at the exciting innovations to come. The music is mostly blues and ballads with a touch of R&B thrown in, a good beginning to a unique career. —*Scott Yanow*

Introducing Roland Kirk / Jun. 7, 1960 / Chess ✦✦✦
Roland Kirk's second recording was his first to get noticed. Playing three horns at once got him some attention but those who listened closely realized that Kirk was

a truly masterful player. Teamed with Ira Sullivan (who himself switched between trumpet and tenor) and a Chicago-based rhythm section, Kirk is in good form on these bop-oriented selections although his great sessions were in the near future. This CD is a straight reissue of the original LP outfitted with newer liner notes. —*Scott Yanow*

☆ **Kirk's Work** / Jul. 11, 1961 / Original Jazz Classics ✦✦✦✦✦

Roland Kirk is in excellent form on this CD reissue of a typically varied (and occasionally amazing) set with organist Jack McDuff, bassist Joe Benjamin and drummer Art Taylor. Kirk mostly sticks to playing tenor and manzello (with highlights including "Three for Dizzy" and "Makin' Whoopee") but takes "Funk Underneath" as a flute feature and tears into the ancient "Skater's Waltz" on both stritch and manzello. McDuff plays well but Roland Kirk dominates the set, displaying an encyclopedic knowledge of music and swinging up a storm. —*Scott Yanow*

We Free Kings / Aug. 16, 1961-Aug. 17, 1961 / Mercury ✦✦✦✦✦

This CD is one of Roland Kirk's finer recordings from his Mercury period. Accompanied by a rhythm section led by pianist Richard Wyands, Kirk on tenor, manzello and stritch (sometimes all three at once) and flute plays some typically miraculous music. Highlights include "Three for the Festival," "Moon Song," "Blues for Alice" and "We Free Kings" but all of the selections contain plenty of Kirk's magic. Twenty years after his death there is still no one around to replace Roland Kirk. This release is recommended to those listeners who do not already have his ten-CD complete Mercury set. —*Scott Yanow*

☆ **Complete Recordings of Roland Kirk** / Aug. 16, 1961-Nov. 17, 1965 / Mercury ✦✦✦✦✦

This ten-CD set not only contains all of the music from Roland Kirk's nine albums for Mercury and Limelight and his guest appearances with Quincy Jones, Tubby Hayes and on one song with organist Eddie Baccus, but quite a few previously unreleased selections (especially from the *Kirk in Copehgen* sessions). Roland Kirk was a unique performer, not only able to play a variety of reed instruments at the same time (including the tenor, flute, clarinet, manzello and stritch) and 20-minute one-breath solos (via circular breathing) but a master of virtually every jazz style from bop and New Orleans to free. Some of his greatest recordings are on this remarkable set, including the entire albums originally titled *We Free Kings, Domino, Reeds and Deeds, Gifts and Messages, I Talk to the Spirits* and *Rip, Rig & Panic*. Such pianists as Richard Wyands, Wynton Kelly, Andrew Hill (including a previously unreleased three-song set from the 1962 Newport Jazz Festival), Harold Mabern, Tete Montoliu, Horace Parlan and Jaki Byard are heard from and the Tubby Hayes date matches together the three reeds of Kirk, Hayes and James Moody in memorable fashion. Although more general collectors may want to start off with a smaller Roland Kirk set, those in-the-know will go out of their way to grab this one before it disappears. —*Scott Yanow*

Talkin' Verve: Roots of Acid Jazz / Aug. 16, 1961-May 2, 1967 / Verve ✦✦✦

This hodgepodge collection has 15 selections mostly taken from Rahsaan Roland Kirk's Mercury recordings of the early 1960s (other than one selection apiece that originally appeared on Limelight or Verve). Although certainly not for completists, this sampling does give listeners a good inkling of Kirk's eclectic talents. Whether jamming in a quartet, playing commercial music with Quincy Jones or jiving around in his colorful and insightful way, Roland Kirk was always a vital force. Highlights include "Hip Chops," "You Did It, You Did It," "A Sack Full of Soul," "Jive Elephant," "Blue Rol" and even "Theme from Peter Gunn." —*Scott Yanow*

● **Does Your House Have Lions: The Rahsaan Roland Kirk Anthology** / Nov. 6, 1961-Mar. 1976 / Rhino ✦✦✦✦

Any listener who feels that Rahsaan Roland Kirk's ability to play three horns simultaneously was a gimmick and that he was a primitive improviser should be forced to listen to this two-CD set. A well-conceived sampler that has highlights from Kirk's Atlantic period (dating from 1965-76 plus an earlier selection from his brief period with Charles Mingus), this anthology is most highly recommended to listeners not familiar with Kirk's musical miracles; more serious collectors will want to get the complete sessions (although there is a previously unavailable version of "Three for the Festival" from 1970 included). In addition to tenor, manzello and stritch, he shows mastery of the baritone, bass sax, the flexaphone, clarinet, flute, nose flute, piccolo, trumpet, English horn, the black mystery pipes, harmonica and various percussion instruments. Although the selections are unfortunately not programmed in chronological order, producer Joel Dorn did a fine job of picking out most of the classic cuts including Kirk's close imitation of both Miles Davis and John Coltrane on "Bye Bye Blackbird," his live versions of "If I Loved You," "The Old Rugged Cross" (complete with a monologue), Kirk's remarkable simultaneous playing of the melodies of "Sentimental Journey" and "Going Home." Not a flawless set (a medley of two unrelated excerpts is a frivolity and "Bright Moments" is unaccountably missing), this two-fer is fine for beginners. —*Scott Yanow*

Domino /Apr. 17, 1962-Sep. 6, 1962 / Mercury ✦✦✦✦

Early-'60s Kirk vehicle in which his inspired blend of show business, hard bop and multi-horn/multiphonic solos hadn't yet jelled. It's conventional, straightahead material, well played but not as imaginative nor as transcendent as Kirk's music would become in the '70s. —*Ron Wynn*

Reeds & Deeds / Feb. 25, 1963-Feb. 26, 1963 / Mercury ✦✦✦✦✦

Roland Kirk Meets the Benny Golson Orchestra / Jun. 11, 1963-Jun. 12, 1963 / Mercury ✦✦✦✦

Kirk in Copenhagen / Oct. 1963 / Mercury ✦✦✦✦✦

I Talk to the Spirits / Sep. 16, 1964-Sep. 17, 1964 / Limelight ✦✦✦✦
Entrancing flute solos. —*Ron Wynn*

Gifts and Messages / Oct. 21, 1964+Nov. 3, 1964 / Jazz House ✦✦✦✦✦

This CD has previously unreleased music featuring the remarkable Rahsaan Roland Kirk in 1964 during a London gig at Ronnie Scott's club. Joined by the talented pianist Stan Tracey, bassist Rick Laird and drummer Allan Ganley, Kirk puts on quite a show. He plays conventionally on tenor in spots (particularly during the opening "Bags' Groove") in addition to wailing on three horns at once and showing off his talents on manzello, stritch, flutes and what he called a saxophonium (a saxophone without a mouthpiece). There is a great deal of humor on this set including many song quotes, a wild version of Tadd Dameron's "On a Misty Night" that is worthy of Richie Cole, some wicked laughing and a few short monologues that are both witty and quite insightful. Although Rahsaan Roland Kirk really had to be seen to be fully appreciated (much of what he did was simply impossible), this CD gives one a fine overview of his unique abilities. —*Scott Yanow*

Rip, Rig and Panic / Now Please Don't... / Jan. 13, 1965+Apr. 1, 1967 / EmArcy ✦✦✦✦

Two of Roland Kirk's albums are combined together on this CD. *Rip, Rig & Panic* is one of the remarkable multi-instrumentalist's greatest recordings; it matches him with pianist Jaki Byard (along with bassist Richard Davis and drummer Elvin Jones), who also has the ability to play in virtually every jazz style. With such titles as "No Tonic Pres," "Once in a While," "From Bechet, Byas and Fats" and the electronic "Slippery, Hippery, Flippery," obviously this is an eclectic (and unique) set. While that session has also been included in the ten-CD complete Mercury box, *Now Please Don't You Cry, Beautiful Edith* is a lesser-known recording (originally on Verve) that has Kirk backed up by pianist Lonnie Smith, bassist Ronald Boykins and drummer Grady Tate. Highlights inclue "Stompin' Ground," "It's a Grand Night for Swinging," "Alfie" and the title cut. —*Scott Yanow*

Slightly Latin / Nov. 16, 1965-Nov. 17, 1965 / Limelight ✦✦✦✦

Now Please Don't You Cry, Beautiful Edith / Apr. 1967 / Verve ✦✦✦✦

This April 1967 recording with Lonnie Smith (piano), Ronnie Boykins (bass), and Grady Tate (drums) presented a solid display of Rahsaan Roland Kirk's talents on tenor, manzello, whistle, strich, and flute in what was perhaps typical of the cornucopia of musical roots and messages that became part of his statements from the '60s up until his death. —*Bob Rusch, Cadence*

Here Comes the Whistleman / Mar. 14, 1965 / Atlantic ✦✦✦✦

The Inflated Tear / Nov. 27, 1967+Nov. 30, 1967 / Atlantic ✦✦✦✦✦

This is a fine all-around set by the remarkable Rahsaan Roland Kirk that has yet to be fully reissued on CD. The LP, from the Atlantic *Jazzlore* reissue series of the early '80s, features Kirk on tenor, manzello, stritch, clarinet, flute, English horn, flexafone and whistle performing a wide variety of colorful originals along with Duke Ellington's "Creole Love Call." Highlights include the memorable "The Black and Crazy Blues," "The Inflated Tear" and "A Handful of Fives." It's one of Kirk's better Atlantic sets. —*Scott Yanow*

Left and Right / Jun. 18, 1968 / Atlantic ✦✦✦✦

This LP features two different sides of the unique Rahsaan Roland Kirk. While the first half of the program is dominated by his nine-part suite "Expansions" (a variety of melodies he had written in the 1950s) and features Rahsaan's intense playing with a variety of guest artists (including Alice Coltrane on harp, baritonist Pepper Adams and trumpeter Richard Williams), the second side generally showcases Kirk on one horn at a time performing six ballads while backed by a string section; he plays beautifully and with melodic creativity. —*Scott Yanow*

Volunteered Slavery / Jul. 7, 1969-Jul. 23, 1969 / Rhino ✦✦✦✦

This straight CD reissue of an Atlantic LP has plenty of variety. Rahsaan Kirk (on tenor, flutes, manzello, stritch and even gong) performs three melodic originals (including the title cut) along with two pop tunes during which he is assisted by "the Roland Kirk Spirit Choir" on background vocals. However it is his performance at the 1969 Newport Jazz Festival (near-riotous versions of "One Ton" and "Three for the Festival" plus a remarkable John Coltrane three-song medley) that is most memorable. —*Scott Yanow*

Rahsaan / Rahsaan / May 11, 1970-May 12, 1970 / Atlantic ✦✦✦✦✦
On this very interesting set, the unique Rahsaan Roland Kirk performs a musical miracle or two. A 17-minute "The Seeker" goes through several musical styles including bop and New Orleans jazz. In addition there are several unusual shorter pieces but it is during a medley that Kirk performs some real magic. At one point he plays two completely different melodies ("Going Home" and "Sentimental Journey") on two different horns at the same time, splitting his lobes so to speak. Topping off that medley is Kirk's perfectly harmonized rendition of "Lover" as played spontaneously by Kirk on three horns at once. —*Scott Yanow*

Natural Black Inventions: Root Strata / Jan. 26, 1971-Jan. 28, 1971 / Atlantic ✦✦✦✦
This is a rather unusual solo LP (not yet available on CD). Other than a couple of percussionists (and piano accompaniment on "Day Dream" by Sonelius Smith), all of the music was created by Rahsaan Roland Kirk without overdubs or edits. He plays tenor, stritch, manzello, clarinets, flutes, black mystery pipes, percussion and various sound effects, often two or three instruments simultaneously. The performances are episodic and colorful with plenty of humor and adventurous moments, worthy of repeated listenings and amazement. —*Scott Yanow*

Blacknuss / Aug. 1971-Sep. 1971 / Atlantic ✦✦✦
The list of songs interpreted by Rahsaan Roland Kirk on this CD (which include such pop/R&B hits as "Ain't No Sunshine," "What's Going On," "Mercy Mercy Me" and "Never Can Say Goodbye") may make this reissue look like a commercial effort but in reality Kirk's versions of these songs are often quite hilarious. The many riotous performances and Princess Patience Burton's crazy vocal on "One Nation" are often crackups. Kirk uplifts, alters, distorts, satirizes and sometimes tears apart these familiar melodies. —*Scott Yanow*

A Meeting of the Times / Mar. 30, 1972-Mar. 31, 1972 / Atlantic ✦✦✦
On first glance this LP combines together a pair of unlikely musical partners; the unique multi-instrumentalist Rahsaan Roland Kirk and Duke Ellington's former ballad singer Al Hibbler. However Rahsaan was very well acquainted with Ellington's music and he plays respectfully behind Hibbler on many of the standards, taking the wild "Carney and Bigard Place" as an instrumental. Hibbler (who did not record much this late in his career) is in good voice and phrases as eccentrically as ever on such songs as "Do Nothin' till You Hear from Me," "Don't Get Around Much Anymore" and "I Didn't Know About You." One leftover selection from Rahsaan's session with singer Leon Thomas ("Dream") rounds out this surprising set. —*Scott Yanow*

I, Eye, Aye Live at Montreux 1972 / Jun. 24, 1972 / Rhino ✦✦✦✦
The amazing Rahsaan Roland Kirk was such a visual artist that sometimes his recordings only hinted at the events that were occuring during his performances. Kirk's appearance at the 1972 Montreux Jazz Festival (which is released on this 1996 CD for the first time) gave him the opportunity to show off some (but certainly not all) of his talents. On the opener "Seasons," Rahsaan plays two flutes together, getting a wide variety of highly expressive sounds while swinging. "Balm in Gilead" (a passionate tribute to Paul Robeson) features Kirk's often-overlooked clarinet," "Volunteered Slavery" (with its "Hey Jude" vamp) gets rather carried away and "Blue Rol No. 2" has Kirk making music on a nose flute. After showing off his circular breathing on "Satin Doll" and "Improvisation," Rahsaan's medley of "Serenade to a Cuckoo" and "Pedal Up" finds him coming up with close impressions of John Coltrane on soprano and Pharoah Sanders' screeching. Rahsaan Roland Kirk was both consistently entertaining and innovative while making music that still sounds fresh and unique. This previously unreleased set should delight Kirk's fans. —*Scott Yanow*

★ **Bright Moments** / Jun. 8, 1973-Jun. 9, 1973 / Rhino ✦✦✦✦✦
This Rhino two-CD set (a straight reissue of an Atlantic two-LP release) is the closest one can come nowadays to hearing what it would be like to see Rahsaan Roland Kirk perform in a club. Kirk, who is joined by a fine four-piece rhythm section for this appearance at San Francisco's legendary Keystone Korner, has colorful (and sometimes very humorous) monologues between the songs and shows off his remarkable virtuosity. Whether it be his emotional renditions of "Prelude to a Kiss" and "If I Loved You," his demonstration of nose flutes on "Fly Town Nose Blues," some authentic New Orleans clarinet playing on "Dem Red Beans and Rice" or a memorable version of his theme "Bright Moments," the music is exciting and unpredictable. This is the definitive Rahsaan Roland Kirk recording of the 1970s and is essential for any serious jazz collection. —*Scott Yanow*

Prepare Thyself to Deal with a Miracle / Oct. 1973 / Atlantic ✦✦✦✦
Although the title of this LP (not yet reissued on CD) is a bit immodest, much of the music lives up to its billing. Not all of the material on side one is all that memorable but how could Rahsaan Roland Kirk play both nose flute and a regular flute simultaneously on "Seasons"? The most remarkable selection is the 21-minute "Saxophone Concerto," which mostly consists of a nonstop one-breath

tenor solo overflowing with creative ideas. There is still no one around in Rahsaan's league. —*Scott Yanow*

The Man Who Cried Fire / 1973-1977 / Night ✦✦✦✦
The best of the releases put out on Joel Dorn's Night Records, this CD has previously unreleased live performances by the amazing Rahsaan Roland Kirk. A few of the numbers are unfortunately just excerpts (including a potentially amazing encounter with the Olympia Brass Band) but there are plenty of highlights. Kirk imitates both Miles Davis and John Coltrane effectively on "Bye Bye Blackbird," performs "Multi-Horn Variations" unaccompanied on three horns, yells humorously through his flute on "You Did It, You Did It," jams in an R&B vein on "Night Train," trades off with singer Jon Hendricks on "Mr. P.C." and is heard making humorous yet insightful comments to the audience. The final selection ("A Visit from the Blues") was Kirk's last recording, an outing on flute just two months before his death. Fans are advised to pick up this valuable and consistently enjoyable CD before it disappears altogether. —*Scott Yanow*

The Case of the 3 Sided Dream in Audio Color / Nov. 1975 / Atlantic ✦✦
The music on this two-LP set (the fourth side is blank except for an odd phone conversation placed near its end) is rather self-indulgent and erratic. Rahsaan Roland Kirk, one of the most talented saxophonists in jazz history, constructed an odd sound collage with dream sequences, some straightforward performances and too many throwaway pieces. On "Bye Bye Blackbird" first he does an excellent imitation of Miles Davis on trumpet and then, switching to tenor, he emulates John Coltrane; unfortunately the power of this performance is greatly lessened by having this cut divided into two sections and placed on different sides. Overall this release is a misfire with only a few moments of interest. —*Scott Yanow*

The Return of the 5000 Lb. Man / 1975-1976 / Warner Brothers ✦✦✦
Rahsaan Roland Kirk's first Warner Bros. album was recorded shortly before he had a serious stroke and is one of the final examples of the unique musician being at full strength. The first portion of this LP ("Theme for the Eulipions," a lighthearted "Sweet Georgia Brown" and a passionate "I'll Be Seeing You") has since been reissued on CD but the interesting second half (Minnie Riperton's "Loving You," vocal versions of "Goodbye Pork Pie Hat" and "Giant Steps" and an excellent version of "There Will Never Be Another You") remains out of print. Kirk (mostly heard on tenor but also playing a bit of flute, harmonica and stritch) puts on a typically remarkable show. —*Scott Yanow*

Kirkatron / 1976 / Warner Brothers ✦✦✦
Shortly after Rahsaan Roland Kirk finished his first album for Warner Brothers, he suffered a major stroke that put him out of action and greatly shortened his life. His second LP for the label actually comprised leftovers from the earlier session plus three songs taken from an appearance at the Montreux Jazz Festival; the latter has been reissued on CD in a sampler but the other selections (which include "Serenade to a Cuckoo," his cover of "This Masquerade," "Sugar," "The Christmas Song" and "Bright Moments") remain out of print. This LP (which finds him mostly sticking to tenor), Kirk's next-to-last album, has enough highlights to make it worth searching for. —*Scott Yanow*

Other Folks' Music / Mar. 1976 / Atlantic ✦✦✦
Rahsaan Roland Kirk's recordings tended to become more eccentric in his later years. He could do so much that he often shot out in several directions at once and that is certainly true throughout this entertaining and consistently colorful LP. Whether it be a samba version of "Donna Lee," the ballad "That's All" (which he plays on reed trumpet) or the haunting "Water for Robeson and Williams," Kirk (who is also heard on tenor, flute, manzello, stritch and harmonica) is successful at everything he attempts on the wide-ranging set of music by "other people." —*Scott Yanow*

Simmer, Reduce, Garnish & Serve / 1976-1977 / Warner Archives ✦✦✦✦
This single CD has selections from Rahsaan Roland Kirk's final three albums. His work on his last record, *Boogie-Woogie String Along for Real,* was quite heroic and miraculous because he had suffered a major stroke that greatly limited his abilities; in fact Kirk had the use of only one of his hands so his playing was sadly restricted. There is a remarkable amount of variety plus a liberal dose of Kirk's humor on this retrospective, ranging from a "Bagpipe Medley" and "Sweet Georgia Brown" (complete with a whistler and Freddie Moore's washboard) to a warm "I'll Be Seeing You" and a tribute to Johnny Griffin, the main influence on Rahsaan's tenor sound. For those listeners who do not already have the three LPs, this is a strong best-of sampler of the saxophonist's final period although his earlier recordings are recommended first. This CD concludes with an emotional and rather touching collage that pays tribute to Kirk's genius and mourns his premature death. —*Scott Yanow*

Boogie Woogie String Along for Real / 1977 / Warner Brothers ✦✦
Rahsaan Roland Kirk's final recording is a bit melancholy. Kirk, making a comeback after a serious stroke, only performs on tenor on this date along with a little

clarinet (on "Make Me a Pallet on the Floor") and harmonica; even he could not play more than one horn at a time with just the use of one hand. Four songs are performed with a veteran rhythm section that includes pianist Sammy Price and guitarist Tiny Grimes, the title cut has Kirk backed by strings and the remainder of the album features pianist Hilton Ruiz and trombonist Steve Turre in the backup group. The music is generally joyful although obviously not on the same powerful level as his pre-stroke recordings. But unlike Richard Nixon (who is "saluted" here on "Watergate Blues"), Rahsaan Roland Kirk was never a quitter and he fought gamely until the end. —*Scott Yanow*

Dog Years in the Fourth Ring / 1965-1975 / 32 Jazz ✦✦✦✦✦
Producer Joel Dorn has long championed the memory of the remarkable Rahsaan Roland Kirk. This three-CD set contains the long-out-of-print Atlantic album *Natural Black Inventions: Root Strata* and two CDs of previously unreleased concert performances. The former features Kirk playing unaccompanied solos (with the exception of a couple of guest percussionists on a few tracks) without any overdubbing. To give one an idea as to how remarkable the results are, Rahsaan is heard utilizing tenor, stritch, manzello, several clarinets, flutes, black mystery pipes, harmonium, piccolo, a music box, tympani, gong, bells, bird sounds and percussion. The music ranges from Dixieland to free and hints strongly at his tremendous talents. The "new" material on the other two CDs is taken from private tapes recorded in 1963 (with Tete Montoliu), 1964 (with the George Gruntz Trio), at a 1970 concert, in Paris and Boston in 1972, Berlin in 1973, and on two occasions in 1975. For those foolish enough to think of Rahsaan Roland Kirk as a gimmicky player, they should hear him do a very close impression of Lester Young on "Lester Leaps In," pay tribute to Sidney Bechet on "Petite Fleur," rip into "Giant Steps," and play pure bop on "Blues for Alice." One of the finest jazz releases of 1997. —*Scott Yanow*

Kenny Kirkland

b. Sep. 28, 1955, Newport, NY
Piano, Keyboards / Post-Bop, Latin Jazz
Closely associated at times with Wynton and Branford Marsalis, Kenny Kirkland has surprisingly only led one CD of his own as of this writing. He started playing piano at age six and later studied at the Manhattan School of Music. Among his early jobs were playing with Michal Urbaniak (on electric keyboards) during 1977, Miroslav Vitous (1979), Terumasa Hino and Elvin Jones. Influenced by Herbie Hancock, Kirkland was well featured while with Wynton Marsalis' band (1981-85) but his departure in 1985 to play pop music with Sting (along with Branford Marsalis) greatly upset Wynton. After leaving Sting in 1986, Kirkland became a session musician and in the early '90s he joined the "Tonight Show" band (under the direction of Branford Marsalis); his only album as a leader is for GRP (1991). —*Scott Yanow*

● **Kenny Kirkland** / 1991 / GRP ✦✦✦✦✦
Keyboardist Kenny Kirkland's long overdue debut as a leader really stretches his talents and is occasionally unpredictable. Virtually each of the performances has its own personality and the personnel and instrumentation differ throughout the release. Among the highlights is "Mr. J.C." (which features some stormy Branford Marsalis tenor), an electric Latin but still boppish update of Bud Powell's "Celia" (taken as a duet with percussionist Don Alias), the sruttin' "Steepian Faith," a driving rendition of Ornette Coleman's "When Will the Blues Leave" that has some free bop alto from Roderick Ward, and Latin versions (with percussionist Jerry Gonzalez) of two standards not normally thought of as belonging to that idiom: Wayne Shorter's "Ana Maria" and Thelonious Monk's "Criss Cross." This highly recommended CD has more than its share of brilliant moments. —*Scott Yanow*

Ryan Kisor

b. Apr. 12, 1973, Sioux City, IA
Trumpet / Post-Bop
One of the youngest of the so-called Young Lions, Ryan Kisor first gained attention when he won the Thelonious Monk Institute of Jazz's first trumpet competition in 1990 at age 17. He had earlier studied trumpet with his father, played with a local band when he was ten, and started studying classical music two years later. Kisor discovered jazz at 14 and developed quickly, playing both jazz and classical music locally. In the summer of 1988, he was inspired at a jazz camp by Clark Terry. After winning the Monk contest, he was signed by Columbia, coming out with a couple of interesting if slightly premature CDs as a leader. Since that time, Ryan Kisor (whose originality has developed gradually) has freelanced around New York, most notably with the Mingus Big Band and the Lincoln Center Jazz Orchestra. —*Scott Yanow*

Minor Mutiny / 1992 / Columbia ✦✦
Minor Mutiny is most significant for documenting the recording debut of Ryan Kisor (the winner of the Thelonious Monk Institute's 1990 trumpet contest), tenor

saxophonist Ravi Coltrane (son of John) and drummer Jeff Siegel. Kisor's first date finds the teenager playing moody originals, including six of his originals and two by the date's producer Jack DeJohnette. The compositions are often not all that interesting, giving a certain melancholy sameness to many of the performances. Kisor's lyrical sound and surprising but logical twists in his solos recall Tom Harrell but he was already on his way to developing his own conception. Coltrane at that point seemed to be mainly influenced by Branford Marsalis with a touch of Michael Brecker. Overall the musicians (which also include keyboardist Michael Cain, bassist Lonnie Plaxico and on two songs drummer Jack DeJohnette) prove to be stronger than the material on this decent and somewhat historic effort. —*Scott Yanow*

● **On the One** / Apr. 13, 1993 / Columbia ✦✦✦✦
A big improvement over his first release, *On the One* features the young trumpeter Ryan Kisor blowing high-powered Art Blakey-type hard bop with a group of impressive up-and-coming musicians including Mark Turner and David Sanchez on tenors, altoist Chris Potter, bassist Christian McBride, drummer Lewis Nash and the "old" man of the group, the 38-year-old pianist Mulgrew Miller. Kisor at this point did not yet have a distinctive voice of his own but he shows much potential for the future. —*Scott Yanow*

Oscar Klein

b. Jan. 5, 1930, Graz, Austria
Trumpet, Guitar / Dixieland, New Orleans, Traditional
An excellent Dixieland trumpeter and an occasional swing guitarist, Oscar Klein (although not well-known in the US) has had a long and productive career in Germany. Klein was an important member of Fatty George's band (1952-57), the Tremble Kids (1957-60) and the Dutch Swing College Orchestra (1959-63). Back with the Tremble Kids off and on during 1963-77, Klein also had the opportunity to play with American musicians passing through Europe, including Albert Nicholas and Wild Bill Davison. Virtually all of his recordings have been made for European labels; most are worth searching for. —*Scott Yanow*

● **Big Four/Jazz for Two** / Apr. 16, 1981-Aug. 21, 1983 / Lino Patruno ✦✦✦✦✦
This wonderful Italian CD will be difficult to locate. The first ten selections are from Apr. 16, 1981 and match the excellent mainstream cornetist Oscar Klein and the fine chordal guitarist Lino Patruno with the soprano sax of Carlo Bagnoli and bassist Marco Ratti. Jazz historians will immediately think of the pair of famous 1940 sets that resulted in eight numbers by the quartet of Sidney Bechet, Muggsy Spanier, guitarist Carmen Mastren and bassist Wellman Braud; Klein and Patruno certainly thought of that band when putting together their session. Bangoli's main influence is clearly Bechet (although his vibrato is not as pronounced); five of the ten songs were also played by the earlier group. The main difference is that Klein does not sound like Spanier, although his style is quite complementary to the format, and the musicians are not trying to copy their predecessors. The interplay between the players on such numbers as "That's a Plenty," "China Boy" and "Chicago" is consistently delightful and full of spirit. The second half of the CD is an intriguing set of duets by Klein and Patruno that were recorded June 14 and Aug. 27, 1983. Patruno switches between his acoustic guitar and banjo, but the main reason these collaborations are of great interest is the contributions of Klein. Rather than just sticking to cornet, he also plays some excellent electric guitar in a swing style that sometimes overlaps with Al Casey and Tiny Grimes, and on "Duo Blues," he jams on harmonica like a 1950s Chicago blues musician. The pair perform seven standards and three basic originals with creativity, swing, and enough variety to hold one's interest throughout. Highly recommended. —*Scott Yanow*

Moonglow / Jan. 6, 1995 / Nagel-Heyer ✦✦✦✦
The liner notes might be in German and the musicians are all Europeans, but the music on this CD will easily communicate to American trad jazz fans. Veteran trumpeter Oscar Klein (who also plays a song apiece quite effectively on clarinet and guitar) heads a fine octet for a live set that also includes clarinetist Werner Keller, trombonist Willy Meerwald, the booting tenor of Engelbert Wrobel, pianist Romano Mussolini, guitarist Lino Patruno, bassist Bob Van Oven and drummer Charly Antolini. Other than a pair of blues ("Oscar's Blues" and "Impromptu Ensemble"), the repertoire comprises swing-era standards. Highlights include an exciting rendition of "Lady Be Good," "Honeysuckle Rose," "All of Me" and "Impromptu Ensemble." This German import is easily recommended to mainstream collectors, as are all of the other Nagel-Heyer releases. —*Scott Yanow*

Randy Klein

b. Sep. 9, 1949, Jersey City, NJ
Vocals, Lyricist / Hard Bop
A fine pianist and a talented lyricist, Randy Klein made a strong impression in 1994 for the song lyrics he contributed to his *Jazzheads* CD. In 1995 he recorded a sensitive set of duets that showcased the sound of bassist Harvie Swartz. Other-

wise he has worked extensively as a composer for films, television and theater. —Scott Yanow

Jazzheads / 1993 / Jazzheads ✦✦✦✦
With the release of this CD, pianist/vocalist Randy Klein takes his place as one of the better jazz lyricists. Six of the eight originals feature his singing and scatting and they deal with such subject matters as avoiding negativity, not wanting to get out of bed to go to work, the need to live in the present, being buried by an excess of information and his love for coffee. The two instrumentals are sensitive duets featuring Klein's piano and bassist Harvie Swartz while the other selections utilize a standard quartet with the tenor of Michael Migliore. On the minus side, the music is not as memorable as the lyrics and therefore it is doubtful if any of these songs will be covered by other musicians. Perhaps for next time Randy Klein should get a musical partner to match his witty words to catchier melodies. —Scott Yanow

John Klemmer

b. Jul. 3, 1946, Chicago, IL
Tenor Saxophone / Hard Bop, Post-Bop, Crossover Jazz
An innovator on the electrified saxophone (using echo effects quite effectively), John Klemmer was also a very strong Coltrane-inspired acoustic tenor saxophonist. He started on tenor when he was 11 in Chicago, toured as a teenager with Ted Weems and made his first recording as a leader in 1967. Klemmer was a key soloist with Don Ellis' innovative big band (1968-70), started electrifying his horn (using an echoplex) and worked on the West Coast. His easy-listening recordings for ABC in the mid-'70s were quite popular, particularly 1975's *Touch,* which found him playing melodies fairly simply. Klemmer alternated the more pop-oriented projects with fiery efforts; his finest jazz album was the two-LP set *Nexus* (mostly reissued on CD), a set of duets and trios with drums and occasional bass. He recorded with Roy Haynes in 1977, cut a few impressive unaccompanied solo saxophone records and then in 1981 dropped out of music altogether due to physical and mental problems. Other than an erratic MCA album in 1989, little has been heard from John Klemmer since. His many recordings for Cadet, ABC/Impulse, ABC, MCA and Elektra are mostly out of print. —Scott Yanow

Involvement / Jun. 1968 / Cadet ✦✦✦

Blowin' Gold / Feb. 1969 / Cadet ✦✦✦
Decent late-'60s set by tenor saxophonist John Klemmer, not as focused nor as exciting as his early-'70s sessions. Klemmer at this point was still finding his own sound and searching for comfortable middle ground between rock, pop, and jazz. —Ron Wynn

All the Children Cried / Sep. 26, 1969 / Cadet ✦✦✦

Eruptions / Aug. 25, 1970 / Cadet ✦✦✦✦

Constant Throb / Aug. 12, 1971 / Impulse! ✦✦✦✦✦

Waterfalls / Jun. 17, 1972 / Impluse! ✦✦✦✦✦
John Klemmer was (along with Eddie Harris) a pioneer and an innovator at utilizing electrical devices on his saxophone. For this live set, Klemmer used an Echoplex on his tenor and soprano and was joined by keyboardist Mike Nock, electric bassist Wilton Feldman, drummer Eddie Marshall, Victor Feldman on percussion and (on two of the eight songs) vocalist Diana Lee. Recorded live on June 17, 1972 (with additional recording added five days later), this CD reissue gives one a good example of Klemmer's playing before his mood music records caught on. He certainly achieved some unusual effects at the time although he never became an influential force. Worth investigating by open-eared listeners. —Scott Yanow

Intensity / Feb. 23, 1973 / Impulse! ✦✦✦✦

Magic and Movement / Jul. 6, 1973 / Impulse! ✦✦✦

Mosaic: The Best of John Klemmer / Jul. 1975-Aug. 1978 / GRP ✦✦✦

Barefoot Ballet / Apr. 1976-May 1976 / MCA ✦✦✦✦

Touch / 1975 / MCA ✦✦✦✦

Arabesque / 1977 / MCA ✦✦✦

Lifestyle / 1977 / MCA ✦✦

Solo Saxophone / 1978 / ABC ✦✦✦✦

Hush / 1978 / Elektra ✦✦✦

★ **Nexus One (for Trane)** / 1979 / Bluebird ✦✦✦✦✦
This CD reissues five of the nine selections from what was arguably tenor saxophonist John Klemmer's greatest recording session. In addition to forceful versions of "Mr. P.C." and "My One and Only Love" that feature Klemmer joined by bassist Bob Magnusson and drummer Carl Burnett, there are three lengthy explorations (of "Softly as in a Morning Sunrise," "Impressions" and his original "Nexus") that are taken as tenor-drums duets. The music is so powerful that listeners should

search for the original double LP that includes three additional trios and a duet on "Four." Klemmer, who was becoming very popular as a melodic pop saxophonist, must have surprised many of his fans with this very explorative document. —Scott Yanow

★ **Nexus for Duo and Trio** / 1979 / Novus ✦✦✦✦✦
At a period of time when John Klemmer had a pop hit with "Touch" and was becoming well known for his electrified renditions of simple melodies, this double LP must have shocked some of his unsuspecting fans. The tenor saxophonist is heard on five jazz standards with bassist Bob Magnusson and drummer Carl Burnett, and on four often-stunning tenor-drums duets with Burnett; four of the performances are over ten minutes long. Quite possibly John Klemmer's finest hour (or really two hours) on record, five of the nine performances have been reissued on CD by Bluebird but, if you can, get the double LP (and the entire program) instead. —Scott Yanow

Brazilia / 1979 / MCA ✦✦✦

Finesse / Dec. 10, 1980 / Elektra ✦✦

Solo Saxophone II: Life / 1981 / Elektra ✦✦✦✦

Music / Mar. 1989 / MCA ✦

Simpatico / 1997 / JVC ✦✦✦✦
When the music on this CD was released for the first time in 1997, it had been a long time since anything had been heard from John Klemmer on records. A superior improviser who was one of the few innovators on the electrified sax (along with Eddie Harris), Klemmer had great commercial success in the mid-1970s with some ballad-oriented mood music recordings that were close to pop. However, by the early '80s, personal problems resulted in him dropping out of music, and other than a 1989 misfire, he had been largely silent during the 1980s and 90s. On this very enjoyable session, Klemmer sticks to his acoustic tenor and is heard performing a set of duets with acoustic guitarist Oscar Castro-Neves. Other than the inclusion of some beach and seagull sounds here and there (added because the duo often played in the Malibu area at the time), the music is unedited and quite spontaneous. Klemmer's pretty tone is often reminiscent of Stan Getz, which is obvious even before getting to his versions of "Early Autumn" and "Moonlight in Vermont," yet his style was always a bit more advanced, and he often pushes himself. Castro-Neves is mostly in a supportive role, adding Brazilian rhythms and his own brand of beauty to the lyrical date. Recommended. —Scott Yanow

Eric Kloss

b. Apr. 3, 1949, Greenville, PA
Alto Saxophone / Hard Bop, Post-Bop
Eric Kloss, a talented high-powered altoist with an open mind towards funk and certain aspects of pop music, recorded a long series of fine albums for Prestige and Muse from the mid-'60s into the late '70s. Blind since birth, Kloss began playing professionally in Pittsburgh in the early '60s. He worked with Pat Martino in 1965, the same year he started recording as a 16-year-old for Prestige. Through the years Kloss used such players on his records as Martino, organist Don Patterson, Jaki Byard, Richard Davis, Alan Dawson, Cedar Walton, Jimmy Owens, Kenny Barron, Jack DeJohnette, Booker Ervin, Chick Corea and Barry Miles in addition to collaborations with Richie Cole and duets with Gil Goldstein. But Eric Kloss seemed to disappear after his 1981 Omnisound album and has not been heard from by the jazz world in quite some time. —Scott Yanow

Introducing Eric Kloss / Sep. 1, 1965 / Prestige ✦✦✦

Love and All That Jazz / Mar. 14, 1966-Apr. 17, 1966 / Prestige ✦✦✦

Grits and Gravy / Dec. 21, 1966-Dec. 22, 1966 / Prestige ✦✦✦✦
Eric Kloss' third recording features the soulful yet adventurous altoist in two different settings. Three brief numbers are performed with a four-piece rhythm section, the reeds of Danny Bank, vibraphonist Teddy Charles and a female vocal group. While those tracks are somewhat lightweight, five other songs (including "Softly as in a Morning Sunrise," "You Don't Know What Love Is," and a ten-minute rendition of "Milestones") match Kloss with pianist Jaki Byard, bassist Richard Davis and drummer Alan Dawson, and are the obvious reasons to search for this LP. As with most of Kloss' output, this album will be a bit difficult to find. —Scott Yanow

First Class Kloss / Jul. 14, 1967 / Prestige ✦✦✦✦

Life Force / Sep. 18, 1967 / Prestige ✦✦✦✦

We're Goin' Up / Dec. 22, 1967 / Prestige ✦✦✦

Sky Shadows / Aug. 3, 1968 / Prestige ✦✦✦✦✦

Consciousness! / Jan. 6, 1970 / Prestige ✦✦✦✦✦

In the Land of the Giants / Feb. 2, 1969 / Prestige ✦✦✦✦✦

To Hear Is to See / Jul. 22, 1969 / Prestige ✦✦✦✦✦

● **Eric Kloss & the Rhythm Section** / Jul. 22, 1969+Jan. 6, 1970 / Prestige ✦✦✦✦

Whatever happened to Eric Kloss? A brilliant player by the time he was 20, Kloss has largely disappeared from the jazz scene since his string of excellent recordings (mostly for Prestige and Muse) stopped in 1981. This particular CD reissue has two complete albums (*To Hear Is to See* and *Consciousness*) that feature Kloss with the Miles Davis rhythm section of the period (keyboardist Chick Corea, electric bassist Dave Holland and drummer Jack DeJohnette); the second session also has the innovative guitarist Pat Martino. It is to Eric Kloss' great credit that he keeps up with his more famous sidemen on the adventurous program, which comprises his seven originals and one song apiece by Pat Martino, Joni Mitchell and Donovan ("Sunshine Superman"). The music blends together aspects of the avant-garde and fusion and rewards repeated listenings. —*Scott Yanow*

One, Two, Free / Aug. 28, 1972 / Muse ✦✦✦✦

Although based in the hard bop tradition, altoist Eric Kloss was always open to the influence of the avant-garde. This stimulating LP, which has not yet been reissued on CD, features Kloss, guitarist Pat Martino, keyboardist Ron Thomas, bassist Dave Holland and drummer Ron Krasinski really stretching out on Carole King's "It's Too Late," "Licea" and the three-part "One, Two, Free." Eric Kloss pushes himself and his sidemen throughout the date, and even if the Fender Rhodes sounds a bit dated, the high musicianship and chance-taking are still exciting to hear. —*Scott Yanow*

Essence / Dec. 14, 1973 / Muse ✦✦✦

Switching between tenor and his usual alto, Eric Kloss teams up with trumpeter Marvin "Hannibal" Peterson and a rhythm section (keyboardist Mickey Tucker, bassist Buster Williams, drummer Ron Krasinski and, on one song, percussionist Sonny Morgan) during versions of three of his originals and one by Barry Miles. "Love Will Take You There" and "Essence" are both over 15 minutes long. The music is very much of the period, advanced post-bop playing with the dual influences of free jazz and early Miles Davis fusion. A fine set that, along with most of Kloss' many Muse releases, is long overdue to be reissued on CD. —*Scott Yanow*

Bodies' Warmth / Jun. 24, 1975-Jun. 25, 1975 / Muse ✦✦✦

Together / Jul. 19, 1976-Jul. 20, 1976 / Muse ✦✦✦

Now / Jan. 4, 1978 / Muse ✦✦✦

Tenor/altoist Eric Kloss recorded often from 1965-81 before disappearing from jazz. His sound was fairly original, he was technically skilled, and, even though his impact was fairly minor, he did record many worthwhile sessions, most of which are currently hard to find. On this LP, Kloss (joined by keyboardist Mike Nock, bassist Mike Richmond and drummer Jimmy Madison) performs six of his originals, none of which caught on. The music is generally lyrical and the leader plays well, even if the rhythm section is fairly anonymous, but little all that memorable occurs. —*Scott Yanow*

Celebration / Jan. 6, 1979-Jan. 7, 1979 / Muse ✦✦✦

The music on this obscure LP (the last in a long string of Eric Kloss Muse recordings) is often funky and in the fusion vein. The altoist is joined by keyboardist Barry Miles (who contributed the only one of the six pieces not written by the leader), guitarist Kenny Karsh, bassist Mike Richmond and drummer Terry Silverlight. The playing is on a high level and the compositions are complex, but the overall music (other than the opening "Celebration") tends to be a bit dull. —*Scott Yanow*

Sharing / Jun. 30, 1981 / Omnisound ✦✦✦✦

The final Eric Kloss recording to date matches the altoist on six lyrical ballads with keyboardist Gil Goldstein. Their interpretations of six originals are generally laidback and lyrical, with the emphasis on melodic development and quieter feelings. The mostly relaxed music does have some heated moments, and the tunes are sometimes quite complex, but this is more introspective than most of Eric Kloss' sessions. —*Scott Yanow*

Earl Klugh

b. Sep. 16, 1954, Detroit, MI
Guitar / Instrumental Pop, Crossover Jazz

An acoustic guitarist with a very pretty tone, Earl Klugh does not consider himself a jazz player and thinks of Chet Atkins as being his most important influence. Klugh played on a Yusef Lateef album when he was 15 and gained recognition in 1971 for his contributions to George Benson's *White Rabbit* record. He played regularly with Benson in 1973, was a member of Return to Forever briefly in 1974 and then in the mid-'70s began recording as a leader. Klugh's popular recordings (for Blue Note, Capitol, Manhattan and Warner Bros.) tend to use light funk beats, stick closely to the melody and put the emphasis on his sound; little surprising ever occurs. —*Scott Yanow*

Magic in Your Eyes / 1976 / Liberty ✦✦✦

Even on this fairly early LP, acoustic guitarist Earl Klugh already had his distinctive sound down, along with his familiar approach to playing lightly funky poppish material. Klugh's tone was always very pretty, and he sounds fine on such tunes as "Magic in Your Eyes," "Cast Your Fate to the Wind" and "Good Time Charlie's Got the Blues," which has a guest appearance by one of his main influences, guitarist Chet Atkins. On most selections, keyboardist Gregory Phillinganes is a key force in the backup band. Unfortunately, Earl Klugh has not developed much from this promising start, and the overall music is a bit superficial, although pleasantly melodic. —*Scott Yanow*

Love Songs / Jan. 1976-Jun. 1981 / Blue Note ✦✦

Although this Blue Note CD is officially a sampler from guitarist Earl Klugh's early years, it is not all that different from the guitarist's regular releases. Klugh has always had a pretty acoustic guitar sound and rarely wanders much from the poppish melodies; nearly all of his recordings to date could be classified as "love songs." The lightweight arrangements (some by Dave Grusin) and the concise nature of the renditions (all of which have fadeouts) were geared towards gaining as much radio airplay as possible. Creating innovative music was not a serious option. Since Earl Klugh succeeded in becoming a steady seller, the strategy worked on a commercial basis, but his performances on this pleasant but instantly forgettable set sound quite dated and lightweight. Useful purely as background music. —*Scott Yanow*

Earl Klugh / 1976 / EMI ✦✦✦✦

The session that portended his light-touch, fusion-pop approach. —*Ron Wynn*

Ballads / 1976-1983 / Manhattan ✦✦✦

While this collection of ballads from past Klugh releases has many pleasant moments, it's so pastoral and calming that each song fades into another one without making much impression. As background music, it's effective. Klugh's solos are well constructed, marvelously articulated, and his lines and phrasing sublime. The material covers an impressive range of genres, from jazz to pop, originals and standards. Those who enjoy untaxing material should find this another delightful Klugh collection; others seeking visceral fare should look elsewhere. —*Ron Wynn*

Finger Paintings / Feb. 1977 / Blue Note ✦✦

Acoustic guitarist Earl Klugh has always had an appealing sound but so many of his recordings are sleepy affairs that do not raise themselves above the level of background music. This early session definitely falls into that category and its reissue as a Blue Note CD reminds one of the swift decline of that label in the 1970s. The melodic music that Klugh creates is quite pleasant but little more than that and the accompaniment by fellow guitarist Lee Ritenour, an anonymous-sounding rhythm section and occasional horns and strings gives listeners no real reason to wake up. —*Scott Yanow*

Dream Come True / 1979 / One Way ✦✦✦

Earl Klugh's pretty guitar sound is well featured on eight selections (seven of his originals plus Burt Bacharach's "Message to Michael"), most of which can be considered high-quality background music. The personnel and instrumentation changes from track to track (keyboardists Darryl Dybka and Greg Phillinganes and electric bassist Marcus Miller make appearances), but the lightweight sounds are fairly consistent throughout this quickly forgotten LP. —*Scott Yanow*

Two of a Kind / 1982 / EMI ✦✦✦✦

Keyboardist Bob James and acoustic guitarist Earl Klugh struck gold with this session, recently reissued on CD. The formula hasn't changed much in succeeding years. Both Klugh and James are capable musicians; they demonstrated on this collection of light, innocuous melodies and occasionally interesting backbeats a high degree of professionalism. Klugh is a first-rate guitarist whose solos are concise and nicely delivered, but frequently sound thin. James' piano and electric keyboard playing is a puzzling combination of flawlessness and lifelessness. —*Ron Wynn*

Wishful Thinking / 1983 / EMI ✦✦✦

With some heavyweight sidemen mixed in, the sound is light, relaxing, jazz-space music. Pleasant stuff. —*Michael Erlewine*

Soda Fountain Shuffle / 1984 / Warner Brothers ✦✦✦

Synthesizer, drum machine backgrounds. Easy-listening programmed light jazz with a touch of space music. One of his most popular. —*Michael Erlewine*

Life Stories / 1986 / Warner Brothers ✦✦✦

Journey / 1986-1995 / Warner Brothers ✦✦

Midnight in San Juan / Mar. 1989-Apr. 1990 / Warner Brothers ✦✦✦
Atmospheric, Latin touches. —*Ron Wynn*

● **Solo Guitar** / 1989 / Warner Brothers ✦✦✦✦

Earl Klugh's long-awaited solo album showcased his pretty sound on the acoustic guitar, giving two-to-three minute melodic readings of superior standards. Some of the pieces (notably "I'm Confessin'") found Klugh playing a relaxed "stride" similiar to some of the guitarists of the '30s. —*Scott Yanow*

Whispers and Promises / 1989 / Warner Brothers ♦♦♦
Standard fusion. Pleasant, lightweight material. —*Ron Wynn*

Late Night Guitar / 1993 / One Way♦♦♦
This is the perfect setting for acoustic guitarist Earl Klugh, playing strong melodies (including such standards as "Smoke Gets in Your Eyes," "Laura," "Mona Lisa" and "Two for the Road") while joined by strings and several horns in an orchestra arranged and conducted by Dave Mathews. As usual for a Klugh session (this one unfortunately has not yet been reissued on CD), the guitarist sticks mostly to the themes and does not improvise much, as he never considered himself a jazz player; but the overall effect is quite pleasing. —*Scott Yanow*

Move / 1993 / Warner Brothers ♦♦
This is a typical set of safe background music by acoustic guitarist Earl Klugh. Klugh has always had an attractive sound but he remains content to record lightweight poppish material with bland sidemen. There is nothing memorable or distinctive about these innocuous performances. —*Scott Yanow*

Sudden Burst of Energy / 1995 / Warner Brothers ♦♦♦

Jimmy Knepper

b. Nov. 22, 1927, Los Angeles, CA
Trombone / Hard Bop
A fine soloist with a distinctive sound not overly influenced by J.J. Johnson, Jimmy Knepper's plays improvisations that are full of subtle surprises. He began on trombone when he was nine, started playing professionally when he was 15 and worked in the big bands of Freddie Slack (1947), Roy Porter (1948-49), Charlie Spivak (1950-51), Charlie Barnet (1951), Woody Herman and Claude Thornhill. Knepper gained fame for his versatile and inventive playing with several of Charles Mingus' groups (1957-62). He also worked with Stan Kenton (1959), Herbie Mann (a 1960 tour of Africa), Gil Evans, Benny Goodman (the 1962 tour of the Soviet Union) and the Thad Jones/Mel Lewis Orchestra (1968-74) in addition to playing in the 1970s with the Lee Konitz Nonet and Mingus Dynasty. Knepper's reputation in the jazz world has remained quite strong although he has not recorded very often as a leader, cutting sessions for Debut, Bethlehem (both in 1957), Steeple Chase (1976), Inner City, Black Hawk, Hep, Soul Note and Criss Cross. —*Scott Yanow*

Idol of the Flies / Sep. 1957 / Bethlehem ♦♦♦♦
Other than a few titles for Debut, this was trombonist Jimmy Knepper's only record date as a leader until 1976. The music is essentially cool-toned bop with six standards and three Knepper originals all being given swinging treatment. Six of the songs feature the trombonist in a quintet with altoist Gene Quill and the young pianist Bill Evans while the other three titles also star trumpeter Gene Roland (who takes a rare vocal on "Gee Baby, Ain't I Good to You") and pianist Bob Hammer. —*Scott Yanow*

● **Cunningbird** / Nov. 8, 1976 / Steeple Chase ♦♦♦♦♦
Trombonist Jimmy Knepper, who had not had the opportunity to lead his own record session in 19 years, is in top form during this quintet outing with tenor saxophonist Al Cohn (a compatible front line partner), pianist Roland Hanna, bassist George Mraz and drummer Dannie Richmond. Knepper contributed all six compositions, which include a couple of haunting ballads, a blues, and a few songs based on the chord changes of standards. However, it is for the excellent solo work of Knepper and Cohn that this hard bop release is most highly recommended. —*Scott Yanow*

Jimmy Knepper in L.A. / Sep. 8, 1977-Sep. 9, 1977 / Inner City ♦♦♦♦♦
For this blowing session, trombonist Jimmy Knepper performs with an all-star quintet comprising Lew Tabackin on tenor and a touch of flute, pianist Roger Kellaway, bassist Monty Budwig and drummer Shelly Manne. These veterans have little difficulty coming up with fresh statements on the six familiar chord changes that they interpret. The hard-charging Tabackin matches very well with Knepper's sly trombone; they should have a rematch someday. —*Scott Yanow*

Primrose Path / Nov. 19, 1980 / Hep ♦♦♦♦

First Place / Feb. 1982 / Black Hawk ♦♦♦♦
Trombonist Jimmy Knepper is well featured on this out-of-print LP from the defunct Black Hawk label, both as a highly original trombonist and as a composer. The six originals (all his) range from tunes based on standards to the more memorable "Distress Dismay," "Fallen Crest" (dedicated to the recently deceased Charles Mingus) and "Idol of the Flies." Knepper is greatly assisted by guitarist Bruce Forman, bassist Mike Richmond and drummer Billy Hart throughout the stimulating, if obscure effort. —*Scott Yanow*

I Dream Too Much / Feb. 1984-Mar. 1984 / Soul Note ♦♦♦♦
With John Clark (French horn), John Eckert (tpt). All brass front line. Includes three Knepper compositions, two standards, one by Hanna. —*Michael G. Nastos*

Dream Dancing / Apr. 1986 / Criss Cross ♦♦♦♦♦
Trombonist Jimmy Knepper teams up with a strong supporting cast (tenor saxophonist Ralph Moore, pianist Dick Katz, bassist George Mraz and drummer Mel Lewis) for fresh renditions of four standards (including "All Through the Night" and a swinging "This Time the Dream's on Me"), plus two of the leader's originals on this Criss Cross set. The music is essentially straightahead hard bop, but Knepper's continually surprising solos uplift the music. —*Scott Yanow*

Moe Koffman (Morris Koffman)

b. Dec. 28, 1928, Toronto, Canada
Flute, Alto Saxophone, Soprano Saxophone / Bop, Pop-Jazz
Moe Koffman became famous for his 1957 hit recording of "Swinging Shepherd Blues," a catchy flute feature. Otherwise, throughout his career Koffman has been a popular soloist whose music ranges from cool-toned bop to jazz interpretations of more poppish material; his commercial successes have sometimes overshadowed his fine improvising talents. Although he has spent most of his life in Canada, Koffman did work with the bands of Sonny Dunham, Ralph Flanagan, Charlie Barnet, Tex Beneke and Jimmy Dorsey in the US during the first half of the 1950s. Later on, Koffman played at George's Spaghetti House in Toronto for over three decades (one week every month), worked extensively in the studios, and has been with Rob McConnell's Boss Brass since 1972. Few of Moe Koffman's records (the earlier sessions were cut for Jubilee, and he made a pair for Duke Street in the mid-'80s) are currently available. —*Scott Yanow*

1967 / 1967 / Just A Memory ♦♦♦
There are some good solos by reed player Moe Koffman on this CD but he was clearly trying to be "with it" by chasing trends of the era. The repertoire (which includes "Comin' Home Baby," "Mercy, Mercy, Mercy," "Watermelon Man" and a remake of Koffman's big seller "Swinging Shepherd Blues") is dominated by jazz hits of the era and Koffman, who sometimes plays two tenors at once (sounding like a one-handed Rahsaan Roland Kirk!), also plays an electrified sax but is best on his flute. The Montreal-based organ-bass-drums rhythm section does their job well and there are enough worthwhile Koffman solos (particularly on the medium-up tempo "Spectacular" which is really "There Will Never Be Another You") to make this set worth picking up if not essential. —*Scott Yanow*

One Moe Time / 1986 / Duke ♦♦♦
Moe Koffman's fluke 1950s hit "Swinging Shepherd Blues" has often obscured the fact that he has long been a fine player. This LP from the Canadian Duke label features Koffman on flute, alto and soprano, along with co-star Ed Bickert on guitar, keyboardist Bernie Senensky, bassist Keiran Overs and drummer Terry Clarke. The music alternates between standards ("Caravan," "My Heart Belongs to Daddy") and originals, including "Paquito," which is dedicated to Paquito D'Rivera. Good (if unsurprising) straightahead music. —*Scott Yanow*

Moe-Mentum / 1987 / Duke ♦♦♦
Using the same personnel that appeared on his previous *One Moe Time* (the leader on flute, alto and soprano, guitarist Ed Bickert, keyboardist Bernie Senensky, bassist Kieran Overs and drummer Barry Elmes), Moe Koffman performs both group originals and a couple standards ("Nature Boy" and "Greensleeves"). The primarily straightahead music is pleasing and most notable for the playing of Bickert. —*Scott Yanow*

● **Featuring Dizzy Gillespie** / 1988 / Soundwings ♦♦♦♦
For a time in 1988, Moe Koffman (tripling on flute, alto and soprano) teamed up regularly with trumpeter Dizzy Gillespie. On this CD, Koffman and his regular group (guitarist Ed Bickert, keyboardist Bernie Senensky, bassist Kieran Overs and drummer Barry Elmes) perform three of Dizzy's tunes, originals by Koffman and Senensky, and "Lush Life" with Gillespie. Diz's trumpet playing was clearly past its prime by 1988, but his scat singing on "Oop-Pop-A-Da" is quite virtuosic and outstanding, easily the high point of this little-known set. —*Scott Yanow*

Charlie Kohlhase

Alto Saxophone, Baritone Saxophone / Post-Bop, Avant-Garde
The Boston-based Kohlhase is an intelligent alto and baritone saxophonist, and an inventive composer with a heady, somewhat sardonic sense of humor. Kohlhase maintains a quintet with personnel that has remained fairly stable throughout its existence. Since its inception in 1989, the group has had only a single change, allowing Kohlhase a consistent outlet for compositional growth and experimentation. Kohlhase's hallmark is an active imagination and a scrupulous attention to detail; his tunes are exceedingly well-crafted, and the band brings them to life with fire and conviction.

Kohlhase started playing saxophone at the age of 18. Though he is mostly self-taught, both as a player and composer, Kohlhase studied at various times with Roswell Rudd, Tom Bergeron, and Stan Strickland. He moved to Boston from Portsmouth, New Hampshire in 1980; he has led his own groups in Boston since 1982. In 1987, he formed the Charlie Kohlhase Quintet with Matt Langley on saxes, Curtis Hasselbring on trombone, John Turner on bass, and Matt Wilson on drums; trumpeter John Carlson replaced Hasselbring in 1992. The quintet toured the Midwest several times in the '90s. Kohlhase has also been associated with the Either/Orchestra since 1987, and has recorded as a sideman with the Mandala Octet and guitarist Mitch Seidman. —*Chris Kelsey*

Research and Development / Aug. 1, 1990-Oct. 15, 1990 / Accurate Jazz ✦✦✦✦✦
Doubling on alto and baritone, Charlie Kohlhase is a versatile player able to sound credible during both inside (hard bop) and outside (avant-garde) improvisations. Teamed up with trombonist Curtis Hasselbring, Matt Langley on tenor, bassist John Turner and drummer Matt Wilson, Kohlhase leads his group through seven of his originals (which include a jazz waltz, a tribute to Johnny Dyani and a Blue Note-type piece), along with a song by Hasselbring, Thelonious Monk's "Off Minor," and "You Go to My Head." The unpredictable but consistently inventive music on this CD rewards repeated listenings. —*Scott Yanow*

● **Good Deeds** / Jan. 12, 1992-Jan. 13, 1992 / Accurate Jazz ✦✦✦✦✦
Charlie Kohlhase, a talented altoist who also has a very deep tone on baritone, is heard on his second CD heading a pianoless quintet that also features Matt Langley's tenor and soprano, trombonist Curtis Hasselbring, bassist John Turner, drummer Matt Wilson and, on two songs, trumpeter Waldron Ricks. Their music is full of subtle (and some not-so-subtle) humor, consistently strong and dynamic soloing, variety and plenty of adventure. One can hear the influence of Charles Mingus in spots but in general the playing is quite original and fresh. Highlights include the Art Blakey tribute "Buhaina Checked Out," the somewhat demented "Cryogenisis," a swinging version of "The End of a Love Affair" and "Floating," which features the four horns without any rhythm section. —*Scott Yanow*

Dart Night / Feb. 26, 1995-Aug. 30, 1995 / Accurate Jazz ✦✦✦✦
With three horns and a piano-less rhythm section, the Charlie Kohlhase Quintet comes ready to blow on this, their second album. The material is cherry-picked from tunes long-standing in the band's set list, and Kohlhase's alto and baritone sax work make an excellent foil for Matt Langley on alto and soprano saxophone and John Carlson on trumpet and fluegelhorn. John Turner on bass and Matt Wilson on drums provide ample support, and despite the lack of a chording instrument behind all the soloing, the music stays cohesive throughout. Highlights include "But I Can't," "Bossa Macabre," "If I Could," "Knee Bop," "I Surely Would" and the almost 12-minute-long "Wraiths." —*Cub Koda*

Lee Konitz

b. Oct. 13, 1927, Chicago, IL

Alto Saxophone, Soprano Saxophone / Cool, Post-Bop
One of the most individual of all altoists (and one of the few in the 1950s who did not sound like a cousin of Charlie Parker), the cool-toned Lee Konitz has always had a strong musical curiosity that has led him to consistently take chances and stretch himself, usually quite successfully. Early on he studied clarinet, switched to alto and played with Jerry Wald. Konitz gained some attention for his solos with Claude Thornhill's Orchestra (1947). He began studying with Lennie Tristano, who had a big influence on his conception and approach to improvising. Konitz was with Miles Davis' Birth of the Cool Nonet during their one gig and their Capitol recordings (1948-50) and recorded with Lennie Tristano's innovative sextet (1949) including the first two free improvisations ever documented. Konitz blended very well with Warne Marsh's tenor (their unisons on "Wow" are miraculous) and would have several reunions with both Tristano and Marsh through the years but he was also interested in finding his own way; by the early '50s he started breaking away from the Tristano school. Konitz toured Scandinavia (1951) where his cool sound was influential and he fit in surprisingly well with Stan Kenton's Orchestra (1952-54), being featured on many charts by Bill Holman and Bill Russo. Konitz was primarily a leader from that point on. He almost retired from music in the early '60s but re-emerged a few years later. His recordings have ranged from cool bop to thoughtful free improvisations and his Milestone set of *Duets* (1967) is a classic. In the late '70s Konitz led a notable Nonet and in 1992 he won the prestigious Jazzpar Prize. He has recorded on soprano and tenor but has mostly stuck to his distinctive alto. Lee Konitz has led consistently stimulating sessions for many labels including Prestige, Dragon, Pacific Jazz, Vogue, Storyville, Atlantic, Verve, Wave, Milestone, MPS, Polydor, Bellaphon, Steeple Chase, Sonet, Groove Merchant, Roulette, Progressive, Choice, IAI, Chiaroscuro, Circle, Black Lion, Soul Note, Storyville, Evidence and Philology. —*Scott Yanow*

Subconscious-Lee / Jan. 11, 1949-Apr. 7, 1950 / Original Jazz Classics ✦✦✦✦✦
This very interesting CD has altoist Lee Konitz's first recordings as a leader, taken from a period of time when he was very much under the musical influence of pianist Lennie Tristano. In fact the program starts off with a quintet date from Jan. 1949 that was actually originally headed by Tristano but features the young altoist. The latter two sessions match Konitz with his fellow Tristano students (including tenor saxophonist Warne Marsh, guitarist Billy Bauer and Tristano-soundalike Sal Mosca on piano). The original style developed by Tristano, Konitz and the others (which was different than bop and cool jazz) still sounds fresh today. —*Scott Yanow*

Ezz-Thetic / Mar. 8, 1951+Sep. 18, 1953 / Prestige ✦✦✦✦
This LP contains important early music from altoist Lee Konitz. There are four little-known selections that team Konitz in a sextet with trumpeter Miles Davis in 1951 (along with such Tritanoites as pianist Sal Mosca and guitarist Billy Bauer); most notable is George Russell's "Ezz-thetic" and Konitz's "Hi Beck." The remainder of this album features the altoist with a quintet in France in 1953 performing four standards that are augmented by four alternate takes. Early examples of cool-toned bop. —*Scott Yanow*

Sax of a Kind / Nov. 19, 1951+Aug. 22, 1953 / Dragon ✦✦✦✦
This is a set that Lee Konitz collectors will definitely want. The distinctive cool-toned altoist is heard in Stockholm in 1951 performing with a variety of fine Swedish players; best known is pianist Bengt Hallberg. The set is rounded off by a version of "Lover Man" that showcases the altoist with Stan Kenton's orchestra in 1953. The recording quality of these radio broadcasts are quite good and Konitz is in top form for the period. —*Scott Yanow*

Konitz Meets Mulligan / Jan. 30, 1953 / Blue Note ✦✦✦✦✦
With Gerry Mulligan Quartet. A simply wonderful pairing of idiosyncratic talents. —*Ron Wynn*

Lee Konitz/Bob Brookmeyer in Paris / Sep. 17, 1953+Jun. 5, 1954 / Vogue ✦✦✦
Two unrelated quintet sessions led by altoist Lee Konitz and valve trombonist Bob Brookmeyer are reissued in full on this Vogue CD. The Konitz set (with guitarist Jimmy Gourley, pianist Henri Renaud, bassist Don Bagley and drummer Stan Levey) has 11 performances of four standards including five of "I'll Remember April." The cool-toned altoist is in fine form for his set as is Bob Brookmeyer who plays one version apiece of four songs with Gourley, Renaud, bassist Red Mitchell and drummer Frank Isola. Bop fans will want this fine straightahead set. —*Scott Yanow*

Jazz at Storyville / Jan. 5, 1954 / Black Lion ✦✦✦✦✦
This excellent CD gives one a definitive look at altoist Lee Konitz at a period of time when he was breaking away from being a sideman and a student of Lennie Tristano and asserting himself as a leader. With pianist Ronnie Ball, bassist Percy Heath and drummer Alan Levitt, Konitz explores a variety of his favorite chord changes, some of which are disguised by newer melodies such as "Hi Beck," "Subconscious Lee" and "Sound Lee." Among the other high points of this well-recorded set are "Foolin' Myself" and a lengthy exploration of "If I Had You." —*Scott Yanow*

Konitz / Aug. 6, 1954 / Black Lion ✦✦✦✦✦
The 1954 Lee Konitz Quartet did not last long but they did record some worthwhile performances that still sound fresh over 40 years later. In addition to eight selections (highlighted by "Bop Goes the Leesel," "Mean to Me," "I'll Remember April" and "Limehouse Blues"), there are six previously unissued alternate takes included on this attractive 1989 CD. Altoist Konitz is ably assisted by pianist Ronnie Ball, bassist Peter Ind and drummer Jeff Morton on cool/bop performances that give one a good sampling of how Konitz sounded in his early prime. —*Scott Yanow*

Jazzlore: Lee Konitz / Warne Marsh / Jun. 14, 1955 / Atlantic ✦✦✦✦
Altoist Lee Konitz and tenor saxophonist Warne Marsh always made for a perfect team. Even by the mid-'50s when they were not as influenced by Lennie Tristano as previously (particularly Konitz), their long melodic lines and unusual tones caused them to stand out from the crowd. On this LP reissue Konitz and Marsh co-lead a particularly strong group that also includes pianist Sal Mosca, guitarist Billy Bauer, bassist Oscar Pettiford and drummer Kenny Clarke. Their renditions of "originals" based on common chord changes along with versions of "Topsy," "There Will Never Be Another You" and "Donna Lee" are quite enjoyable and swing hard yet fall into the category of cool jazz. This set is worth searching for, as are all of the Konitz-Marsh collaborations. —*Scott Yanow*

Lee Konitz / Jan. 17, 1956+Jan. 21, 1956 / Swingtime ✦✦✦✦
These somewhat rare recordings were made in 1956 when altoist Lee Konitz went on tour with the great Swedish baritonist Lars Gullin. Konitz, who also plays tenor on one tune and baritone on two others, works well with this complementary group that includes the tenor of Hans Koller, a second baritonist and a German

rhythm section. Pianist Roland Kovac contributed three of the originals, Konitz brought in three others, Gullin contributed "Late Summer" and the group stretches out on the lone standard "I'm Getting Sentimental over You." The fresh material and interesting combination of saxophonists make this European import LP of above average interest to bop and cool jazz fans. —*Scott Yanow*

Inside Hi-Fi / Sep. 26, 1956+Sep. 16, 1956 / Atlantic ✦✦✦✦

This excellent Atlantic reissue LP (part of their 1987 *Jazzlore* series) feature altoist Lee Konitz with two separate quartets during 1956. Either guitarist Billy Bauer or pianist Sal Mosca are the main supporting voices in groups also including either Arnold Fishkind or Peter Ind on bass and Dick Scott on drums. The most unusual aspect to the set is that on the four selections with Mosca, Konitz switches to tenor, playing quite effectively in a recognizable cool style. The overall highlights of this enjoyable LP are "Everything Happens to Me," "All of Me" and "Star Eyes" but all eight performances are well played and swinging. —*Scott Yanow*

The Real Lee Konitz / Feb. 15, 1957 / Atlantic ✦✦✦✦

Tranquility / Oct. 22, 1957 / Verve ✦✦✦✦

An Image: Lee Konitz with Strings / Feb. 6, 1958 / Verve ✦✦✦

☆ **Live at the Half Note** / Feb. 24, 1959+Mar. 3, 1959 / Verve ✦✦✦✦✦

The music on this two-CD set has a strange history. Pianist Lennie Tristano had a rare reunion with altoist Lee Konitz and tenor saxophonist Warne Marsh (his two greatest "students") during an extended stay at the Half Note in 1959. Tristano took Tuesday nights off to teach and Bill Evans was his substitute but the pianist had a couple of those performances recorded for posterity. Years later while listening to his tapes he was so impressed with Marsh's playing that he sent edited versions (comprising entirely the tenor's solos) to Marsh and somehow they ended up being released in that form by the Revelation label. Finally in 1994 the unedited music was issued by Verve; the consistently exciting playing by Konitz, Marsh and Evans (with backup by bassist Jimmy Garrison and drummer Paul Motian) makes one wonder what took so long. They perform a dozen extended standards (or "originals" based on the chord changes of familiar tunes) with creativity and inspiration. In fact, of all the Konitz-Marsh recordings, this set ranks near the top. —*Scott Yanow*

Lee Konitz Meets Jimmy Giuffre / May 12, 1959-May 13, 1959 / Verve ✦✦✦✦✦

This unusual two-CD set not only reissues the original LP of the same name but three other rare Verve LPs from the 1950s. Altoist Lee Konitz (on "An Image") is showcased during a set of adventurous Bill Russo arrangements for an orchestra and strings in 1958, pops up on half of Ralph Burns' underrated 1951 classic *Free Forms* (the most enjoyable of the four sets) and meets up with baritonist Jimmy Giuffre, whose arrangements for five saxes (including the great tenor Warne Marsh) and a trio led by pianist Bill Evans are sometimes equally influenced by classical music and bop. The least interesting date showcases Giuffre's clarinet with a string section on his five-part "Piece for Clarinet and String Orchestra" and the 16 brief movements of "Mobiles." Overall this third-stream two-fer contains music that is easier to respect and admire than to love although Lee Konitz fans will probably want to acquire the obscure performances. —*Scott Yanow*

You and Lee / Oct. 29, 1959-Oct. 30, 1959 / Verve ✦✦✦

One of the lesser-known Lee Konitz albums, this LP (which has not been reissued yet on CD) features the altoist joined by six brass and a rhythm section for eight Jimmy Giuffre arrangements. The shouting brass contrasts well with Konitz's cool-toned solos and together they perform eight underplayed standards. Guitarist Jim Hall and pianist Bill Evans (who are on four songs apiece) are major assets behind Konitz on this pleasing set. —*Scott Yanow*

Motion / Aug. 29, 1961 / Verve ✦✦✦✦✦

This very spontaneous LP (altoist Lee Konitz had never played before in a trio with bassist Sonny Dallas and drummer Elvin Jones) is quite successful and enjoyable. Konitz and his trio perform five familiar standards, stretching out on such tunes as "I Remember You," "All of Me" and "You'd Be So Nice to Come Home To." The music is searching but melodic, exploratory yet accessible. This is one of Konitz's better albums from the era and is long overdue to be reissued on CD. —*Scott Yanow*

★ **The Lee Konitz Duets** / Sep. 25, 1967 / Original Jazz Classics ✦✦✦✦✦

This CD brings back one of altoist Lee Konitz's greatest sessions. In 1967 he recorded a series of very diverse duets, all of which succeed on their own terms. Konitz is matched with valve trombonist Marshall Brown on a delightful version of "Struttin' with Some Barbecue," matches wits with the tenor of Joe Henderson on "You Don't Know What Love Is," plays "Checkerboard" with pianist Dick Katz, "Erb" with guitarist Jim Hall, "Tickle Toe" with the tenor of Richie Kamuca (Konitz switches to tenor on that cut) and an adventurous and fairly free "Duplexity" with violinist Ray Nance, has three different duets on "Alone Together" and, on "Alpha-numeric," welcomes practically everyone back for a final blowout. The music

ranges from Dixieland to bop and free and is consistently fascinating. —*Scott Yanow*

Zo-Ko-Ma / Mar. 13, 1968-Mar. 14, 1968 / MPS ✦✦✦

Alto Summit / Jun. 2, 1968-Jun. 3, 1968 / Verve ✦✦✦

This unusual album teams together the altos of Lee Konitz, Pony Poindexter, Phil Woods and Leo Wright (along with pianist Steve Kuhn, bassist Palle Danielsson and drummer Jon Christensen) on a variety of challenging material. There are four pieces for the full septet (including one that pays tribute to both Bach and Bird), a pair of quintet performances and a ballad medley that ends in a complete fiasco (it has to be heard to be believed). Despite the latter, everyone fares well on this summit meeting. —*Scott Yanow*

Peacemeal / Mar. 20, 1969-Mar. 21, 1969 / Milestone ✦✦✦✦✦

This Lee Konitz recording is of even greater interest than usual. Altoist Konitz, in a quintet with valve trombonist Marshall Brown, pianist Dick Katz, bassist Eddie Gomez and drummer Jack DeJohnette, performs jazz adaptations of three Bela Bartok piano compositions, a trio of Dick Katz originals, two of his own pieces (including "Subconscious-Lee") and versions of "Lester Leaps In" and "Body and Soul" that include transcriptions of recorded solos by, respectively, Lester Young and Roy Eldridge. A thought-provoking and consistently enjoyable set of music. —*Scott Yanow*

Spirits / Feb. 1971 / Milestone ✦✦✦✦

Altoist Lee Konitz revisits his roots in pianist Lennie Tristano's music on this enjoyable LP from 1971. Four of the nine songs are duets with pianist Sal Mosca (who always sounded a lot like Tristano) while the five other pieces add bassist Ron Carter and drummer Mousie Alexander to the group. Konitz performs three of his own compositions, five by Tristano and one from tenor saxophonist Warne Marsh; typically all of these originals are based closely on the chord changes (and sometimes the melodies) of familiar standards. Despite that lack of originality, this is excellent music and finds altoist Lee Konitz in creative form. —*Scott Yanow*

Jazz a Juan / Jul. 26, 1974 / Steeple Chase ✦✦✦

The always open-minded altoist Lee Konitz teams up with the advanced pianist Martial Solal, bassist Niels Pedersen and drummer Daniel Humair for this adventurous set, recorded live at the 1974 Antibes Jazz Festival. The quartet performs unpredictable and sometimes eccentric versions of five standards plus (on this CD reissue) a previously unissued rendition of Konitz's "Antibes." Solal, whose chord voicings and use of space are quite original, acts as an equal partner with Konitz and the music is often magical and never overly safe. Worth investigating. —*Scott Yanow*

I Concentrate on You / Jul. 30, 1974 / Steeple Chase ✦✦✦✦

Altoist Lee Konitz has always had a desire to play in a wide variety of settings; this duet session with bassist Red Mitchell is a good example. Although Konitz is quite exposed on the 11 Cole Porter songs, he plays in his usual thoughtful and unhurried style, coming up with typically adventurous melodic variations. Mitchell (who switches to piano on "Night and Day") is fine in support and the CD reissue adds three very different alternate takes to the original program. Well worth picking up. —*Scott Yanow*

Lone-Lee / Aug. 15, 1974 / Steeple Chase ✦✦✦✦

This is an unusual release, for it features altoist Lee Konitz playing unaccompanied. He performs lengthy versions of "The Song Is You" (over 19 minutes long) and "Cherokee" (nearly 18 minutes) in swinging but relaxed and fairly free fashion. The improvisations are quite thoughtful and logical yet avoid being predictable and hold onto one's interest throughout. —*Scott Yanow*

Satori / Sep. 30, 1974 / Original Jazz Classics ✦✦✦✦

This is an excellent release that is fairly typical of a Lee Konitz program from the 1970s and '80s. There are a few standards (such as "Just Friends," "Green Dolphin Street" and "What's New"), a few fairly advanced pieces ("Satori" and "Free Blues"), thoughtful improvisations and a bit of hard-swinging. Inspired by the presence of pianist Martial Solal, bassist David Holland and drummer Jack DeJohnette, Konitz stretches himself as usual and comes up with consistently fresh statements while generally playing at a low introspective volume. —*Scott Yanow*

Oleo / Jan. 1975 / Sonet ✦✦✦

The strong interplay between Lee Konitz (who doubles here on alto and soprano), pianist Dick Katz and bassist Wilbur Little is the main reason to search for this Sonet LP. Together they perform eight standards including "I Want a Little Girl," "Oleo," "St. Thomas" and "There Is No Greater Love." In general the improvisations are quite relaxed and thoughtful and, although the results are not all that essential (since there are a lot of Lee Konitz recordings currently available), the altoist's fans will find much to enjoy during these fine performances. —*Scott Yanow*

Chicago 'N All That Jazz / May 6, 1975 / Denon ✦✦✦
This CD is better than it initially appears. Altoist Lee Konitz and his augmented nonet perform eight numbers from the musical *Chicago,* all songs that have been long forgotten ever since. However Konitz (switching between alto and soprano) and his sidemen (who include trumpeter Richard Hurwitz, Dick Katz and Michael Longo on keyboards and bassist Major Holley who also takes a couple of vocals) play with enthusiasm and melodic creativity; some of the themes are quite catchy. The playing time (around 36 minutes) is quite brief and the music is far from essential but the performances are surprisingly pleasing, making this a worthy purchase if found at a budget price. —*Scott Yanow*

Windows / Nov. 6, 1975 / Steeple Chase ✦✦✦
Another good duo, this time with Hal Galper (p). —*Ron Wynn*

Lee Konitz Meets Warne Marsh Again / May 24, 1976 / Pausa ✦✦✦✦
Recorded in London, this quartet date with bassist Peter Ind and drummer Al Levitt is a reunion between the very complementary stylists Lee Konitz on alto and tenor saxophonist Warne Marsh. Their repertoire (common chord changes) and cool jazz styles are not that surprising but both of the saxophonists sound quite inspired to be in each other's presence; they always brought out the best in each other. The melodic and boppish improvisations reward repeated listenings. —*Scott Yanow*

☆ **The Lee Konitz Nonet** / Oct. 13, 1976+Oct. 18, 1976 / Roulette ✦✦✦✦✦
This is a group that should have been able to stay together but it was formed a few years too soon, at the height of the fusion era. Altoist Lee Konitz's nonet (featuring trumpeter Burt Collins, trombonist Jimmy Knepper and keyboardist Andy La Verne among others) reflected its leader's interest in a wide variety of jazz. The music on this out-of-print but valuable LP ranges from swing classics ("If Dreams Come True" and "A Pretty Girl Is like a Melody") and bop ("Without a Song") to Wayne Shorter's "Nefertiti" and a pair of Chick Corea tunes ("Matrix" and "Times Lie"). Sy Johnson wrote most of the arrangements (including a full orchestration of six choruses from Chick Corea's piano solo on "Matrix"). This album is well worth a long search since it is one of Lee Konitz's finest recordings of the 1970s. —*Scott Yanow*

Figure and Spirit / Oct. 20, 1976 / Progressive ✦✦✦✦✦
Altoist Lee Konitz (who doubles on this CD on soprano) teams up with tenor saxophonist Ted Brown, pianist Albert Dailey, bassist Rufus Reid and drummer Joe Chambers for this session. The six songs (originals based on standards by Konitz, Brown and Lennie Tristano) were all performed in one take and although there are a few minor mistakes, the music is quite exciting and spontaneous. Brown was the best possible substitute for Wayne Marsh (Konitz's original choice for the record) and sounds in prime form. It's worth acquiring by fans of straightahead jazz, Lennie Tristano and Lee Konitz. —*Scott Yanow*

Tenorlee / Jan. 7, 1977-Mar. 23, 1978 / Candid ✦✦✦✦
This CD reissue (which adds new versions of "The Gypsy" and "'Tis Autumn" to the original nine-song program) is a bit unusual in that altoist Lee Konitz exclusively plays tenor. Featured in an intimate trio with pianist Jimmy Rowles and bassist Michael Moore, Konitz explores ten superior standards from the swing era plus a brief unaccompanied workout on "Tenorlee." On "Lady Be Good" both Konitz and Rowles quote liberally from the famous 1936 recording by Lester Young and Count Basie. The relaxed, often-lyrical and slightly unpredictable interpretations are quite enjoyable. —*Scott Yanow*

Pyramid / Jun. 11, 1977 / Improvising Artists ✦✦
Reissued on CD by the Black Saint/Soul Note labels, this entry from Paul Bley's IAI label features fairly free playing from an unusual trio comprising Lee Konitz (on alto and soprano), keyboardist Bley and Bill Connors on electric and acoustic guitars. Actually, due to the free nature of the pieces, the music is less exciting than one might hope. Everyone takes chances in their solos but several of the pieces wander on much too long. Overall this session does not reach the heights one might expect from these great players. —*Scott Yanow*

The Lee Konitz Nonet / Sep. 20, 1977-Sep. 21, 1977 / Chiaroscuro ✦✦✦✦✦
The Lee Konitz Nonet was never able to prosper, but they recorded several excellent albums. With such top players as fluegelhornist John Eckert, trombonist Jimmy Knepper and baritonist Ronnie Cuber in the group, and colorful arrangements provided by Sy Johnson, this band's repertoire was as wide as one would expect from a Konitz band. Whether it be the Louis Armstrong-associated "Struttin' with Some Barbecue," a Lester Young-inspired "Sometimes I'm Happy," Charlie Parker's "Chi-Chi," "Giant Steps" or some newer originals, the results are frequently superb. —*Scott Yanow*

Lee Konitz Quintet / Sep. 1977 / Chiaroscuro ✦✦✦
This frequently heated session teams together the great veteran altoist Lee Konitz with the much younger alto saxophonist Bob Mover, who at that point in time sounded like Konitz's clone. Accompanied by pianist Ben Aranov, bassist Mike

Moore and drummer Jim Madison, the two very complementary saxophonists take explorative solos on eight appealing chord changes, constantly challenging each other. Bob Mover would become much more individual within a few years but on this album it is very much like listening to a teacher and his prize student. —*Scott Yanow*

Yes, Yes, Nonet / Apr. 17, 1979 / Steeple Chase ✦✦✦✦✦
It was a tragedy that Lee Konitz's versatile nonet was not able to succeed commercially. Just like its leader, the group was able to stretch from swing standards, bop and cool jazz to freer improvisations and challenging originals. This Steeple Chase release (featuring the nonet when it comprised such fine players as trumpeters Tom Harrell and John Eckert, trombonists Jimmy Knepper and Sam Burtis, baritonist Ronnie Cuber, pianist Harold Danko, bassist Buster Williams and drummer Billy Hart in addition to Konitz on alto and soprano) features the group at its best on such pieces as "Footprints," "Stardust," "My Buddy" and four songs by Jimmy Knepper. It is an excellent outing from a somewhat neglected group. —*Scott Yanow*

Live at Laren / Aug. 12, 1979 / Soul Note ✦✦✦
The 1979 version of Konitz's nonet. Extended examples of Corea's "Matrix" and "Times Lie". —*Michael G. Nastos*

Seasons Change / Oct. 29, 1979 / Circle ✦✦✦
Duets with vibist Karl Berger. —*Michael G. Nastos*

Heroes / 1980 / Verve ✦✦
This CD (and its follow-up *Anti-Heroes*) features the rather odd duo of Lee Konitz (on alto and soprano) and pianist Gil Evans. Since Evans was far from a virtuoso and at best played "arranger's piano" (particularly at this late stage in his life), his accompaniment behind Konitz is quite sparse. The repertoire includes standards, Konitz's "Aprilling," an adaptation of some Chopin and a medley of Evans' "Blues Improvisation" and "Zee Zee." But frankly overall this is a rather uneventful and often dull release that can easily be passed by. —*Scott Yanow*

Anti-Heroes / Jan. 11, 1980-Jan. 12, 1980 / Verve ✦✦
This Verve CD (and its predecessor from the same gigs, *Heroes*) contains duos featuring Lee Konitz on alto and soprano and pianist Gil Evans. Actually the music is rather disappointing; although Konitz plays fairly well on the mixture of standards and obscurities, Evans often wanders and his backing of the saxophonist is sparse and erratic. The results are more important historically than musically. —*Scott Yanow*

Live at the Berlin Jazz Days / Oct. 30, 1980 / MPS ✦✦✦
This Pausa LP contains the music performed at a Lennie Tristano memorial, duets by altoist Lee Konitz (Tristano's greatest student) and pianist Martial Solal. Although the repertoire certainly pays tribute to Tristano's legacy (including such songs as "No. 317 East 32nd Street," "Star Eyes" and Konitz's "Subconsciously"), the altoist had grown quite a bit as an improviser during the previous 30 years and Solal is a major stylist in his own right. Their explorative and spontaneous music covers a wide area of styles from swing and cool-toned bop to freer explorations and lives up to one's expectations. —*Scott Yanow*

Dovetail / Feb. 25, 1983+Feb. 27, 1983 / Sunnyside ✦✦✦✦
Billed as the "Lee Konitz Terzet" (without ever defining what "Terzet" is), this fine trio set features Konitz on alto, tenor, soprano and even a vocal, plus pianist Harold Danko and bassist Jay Leonhart. Konitz states in the liner notes that "we played in a club for one week and found a way to create nice instant arrangements on familiar tunes . . ." That pretty well describes this music, for even the so-called originals by the trio have a close relationship to a familiar standard. The repertoire is certainly a bit offbeat for these modernists, particularly such songs as "I Want to Be Happy," "Sweet Georgia Brown" and "Penthouse Serenade," but the musicians come up with fresh statements on all of the tunes. A continually interesting set, like most of Lee Konitz's recordings. —*Scott Yanow*

Glad, Koonix! / Nov. 5, 1983 / Dragon ✦✦✦✦
Since 1951, altoist Lee Konitz has performed and recorded often in Sweden, where his cool-toned sound has long been popular and influential. On this excellent release from the Swedish label Dragon, Konitz is teamed with the fine trumpeter Jan Allan and a good veteran rhythm section from Sweden. There are two originals by pianist Utsava Goran Strandberg and otherwise the tunes are familiar standards including "Lover Man" (taken as a waltz), "A Child Is Born" (a feature for Allan), Konitz's "Hi Beck," "Cherokee" and "Body and Soul." Somehow Lee Konitz never sounds stale and his solos (even on tunes he had been playing for over 30 years) still have a strong amount of curiosity and wonderment in them. His fans will enjoy this fine straightahead session. —*Scott Yanow*

Dedicated to Lee / Nov. 7, 1983-Nov. 8, 1983 / Dragon ✦✦✦✦✦
Despite its title (a name of a song from 1953), this set from the Swedish Dragon label is actually a tribute to the music of the late baritonist Lars Gullin rather than to Lee Konitz. Most of the selections (all Gullin compositions) feature altoist Konitz with an octet comprising talented but fairly obscure Swedish players. Best known

among the sidemen is trumpeter Jan Allan, who is featured on "Peter of April" in a quintet including Konitz; the altoist has "Happy Again" as his feature. Considering that all of the music is obscure outside of Sweden ("Danny's Dream" is the best-known song) and that the quality is quite high, this set is easily recommended to musicians looking for a fresher bop-based repertoire and to listeners who enjoy discovering "new" material. —*Scott Yanow*

Ideal Scene / Jul. 22, 1986-Jul. 23, 1986 / Soul Note ✦✦✦✦
This Soul Note release features Lee Konitz with his 1986 quartet, a unit that also includes pianist Harold Danko, bassist Rufus Reid and drummer Al Harewood. Konitz, listed as playing soprano on the album but actually sticking exclusively to alto, not only interprets three veteran standards ("Ezz-thetic," "If You Could See Me Now" and "Stella by Starlight") but also three of Danko's then-recent originals and his own "Chick Came Around." The subtle but swinging music is harmonically advanced and full of surprising twists; no predictable bebop here. More than most members of his musical generation, Lee Konitz has continued to keep his music and improvising style fresh and enthusiastic while retaining his own original musical personality through the years. —*Scott Yanow*

Round and Round / 1988 / Music Masters ✦✦✦
The most unusual aspect to this outing by altoist Lee Konitz is that all nine selections are performed in 3/4 time. "Someday My Prince Will Come" and Sonny Rollins' "Valse Hot" were originally waltzes but "Lover Man," "Bluesette" and particularly "Giant Steps" were never recorded in that time signature before. With the assistance of pianist Fred Hersch, bassist Mike Richmond and drummer Adam Nussbaum, Konitz manages to uplift this session above the level of a potential gimmick and finds unexpected beauty in these standards and originals. —*Scott Yanow*

Lee Konitz in Rio / 1989 / M-A ✦✦
Lee Konitz (on alto and soprano) plays well enough on this set but the original material (all composed and arranged by Allan Botschinsky) is somewhat forgettable, the accompaniment (by a Brazilian rhythm section and on some songs a full string section) sounds quite anonymous and little happens in the way of development or surprises. In fact the only unusual aspect to this date is that Konitz was unsuccessful at uplifting the lightweight (if reasonably enjoyable) music. Considering how many more viable Lee Konitz recordings are currently available, this is one of the lesser efforts. —*Scott Yanow*

Konitz in Denmark '89 / Jun. 10, 1989-Jun. 11, 1989 / Rightone ✦✦✦✦
Altoist Lee Konitz has recorded quite a few albums throughout his career in Scandinavia. His cool tone has been very influential in that region of the world and there have been many Scandinavian jazzmen whose styles are compatible with his. For this set, Konitz (who doubles on soprano) joins forces with Jens Sondergaard (who plays alto and baritone), guitarist Morten Hojring, bassist Hugo Rasmussen and drummer Bjarne Rostvold for three standards, two of the altoist's songs, a few group originals and some lesser-known material. Konitz and Sondergaard work well together, making this a date easily recommended to cool jazz fans. —*Scott Yanow*

Zounds / May 23, 1990-May 24, 1990 / Soul Note ✦✦✦
This is a very interesting if occasionally unsettling CD. Lee Konitz (doubling on alto and soprano) and his 1990 quartet (which comprises Kenny Werner on piano and occasional synthesizer, bassist Ron McClure and drummer Bill Stewart) emphasize freely improvised performances throughout the date. Two standards ("Prelude to a Kiss" and "Taking a Chance on Love") are interpreted fairly freely while all of the other selections are group originals; Konitz even takes an unplanned "vocal" (more an example of sound explorations then an attempt at conventional singing) on "Synthesthetics." This is a consistently stimulating and rather unpredictable outing by the talented group. —*Scott Yanow*

Lullaby of Birdland / Sep. 6, 1991-Sep. 7, 1991 / Candid ✦✦✦✦✦

Lunasea / 1992 / Soul Note ✦✦✦✦
Altoist Lee Konitz certainly covers a lot of ground on this Soul Note CD. Performing with his recent discovery Peggy Stern on piano, guitarist Vic Juris, bassist Harvie Swartz, drummer Jeff Williams and percussionist Guilherme Franco, Konitz and his players perform everything from jams in the Lennie Tristano tradition and Brazilian pieces that are almost pop-oriented to free improvisations. Stern is quite impressive throughout the date. Classically trained, she proves from the start that she has a real talent at improvisation and is not afraid to take chances. Konitz sounds inspired by her presence and their interplay makes this an easily recommended set for adventurous listeners. —*Scott Yanow*

And the Jazzpar All Star Nonet / Mar. 27, 1992-Mar. 29, 1992 / Storyville ✦✦✦✦✦
On this diverse and highly enjoyable set altoist Lee Konitz is heard in a variety of settings. Five songs (four of them recently composed) feature Konitz interacting with a fine Danish nonet and on "Subconscious Lee" he is showcased in a quintet with fluegelhornist Allan Botschinsky and pianist Peggy Stern. However it is his six

duets (with Stern, Botchinsky, bassist Jesper Lundgaard and fellow altoist Jens Sondergaard) that are most notable. Konitz, who can play as freely as any avant-gardist, somehow always sounds relaxed and thoughtful, turning these duets into comfortable dialogues. —*Scott Yanow*

Jazz Nocturne / Oct. 5, 1992 / Evidence ✦✦✦✦✦
Although never a poll winner, altoist Lee Konitz has had a more productive and consistently stimulating career than most of his contemporaries, never afraid to improvise fairly freely in his relaxed style. For this Evidence CD, Konitz digs into seven standards with an impressive rhythm section (pianist Kenny Barron, bassist James Genus and drummer Kenny Washington) and constantly comes up with interesting ideas and new twists. There are no phony disguises of familiar tunes with new titles on this date; just creative blowing. Konitz uplifts such often-over-played material as "You'd Be So Nice to Come Home To," "Misty," "Alone Together," "Body and Soul" and "My Funny Valentine" without ever becoming predictable; Kenny Barron is in excellent form too. This CD is recommended as a strong example of Lee Konitz's playing in the 1990s. —*Scott Yanow*

The Jobim Collection / Jan. 6, 1993-Jan. 10, 1993 / Philology ✦✦✦✦
Altoist Lee Konitz and pianist Peggy Stern (who also plays synthesizer on a few of the tracks) sound like they really enjoyed themselves during this set of 14 Antonio Carlos Jobim songs. The emphasis is very much on melodic improvising (one can hear Jobim's themes throughout these performances), but Konitz as usual sounds very much like himself and Stern is consistently inventive both in reharmonizing some of the songs and in her subtle solos. The results are quite delightful and this CD is easily recommended to fans of both bossa nova and Lee Konitz. —*Scott Yanow*

Brazilian Rhapsody / Jan. 28, 1993-Jan. 31, 1993 / Music Masters ✦✦✦
This CD focuses primarily on Brazilian standards performed by the Konitz sextet, except for the Brazilian-flavored "Lunasea," written by Peggy Stern, which features her high school choir. "Berimbau" is swinging and percussive, while the well-known "Insensatez" takes many unexpected turns. "Triste" is also a familiar theme played with relish. Vocalist Adela Dalto makes a strong impression with her guest spot on "A Felicidade." Konitz's duet with the phenomenal acoustic guitarist Romero Lubambo on "Manha De Carnaval" is breathtaking. —*Ken Dryden*

Rhapsody / Jun. 20, 1993-Jul. 14, 1993 / Evidence ✦✦
Lee Konitz's Evidence release has seven selections from the veteran altoist that utilize different all-star personnel. The performances all have a similar commitment to relaxed and melodic freedom but some work better than others. "I Hear a Rhapsody" (featuring a haunting vocal by Helen Merrill) precedes a more abstract "Rhapsody" (titled "Lo-Ko-Mo-and Frizz") that has wandering interplay by Konitz (on alto, soprano and tenor Joe Lovano (switching between tenor, alto clarinet and soprano), guitarist Bill Frisell and drummer Paul Motian. Jay Clayton's beautiful voice and adventurous style is well displayed on "The Aerie" and baritone great Gerry Mulligan sounds reasonably comfortable on a free improvisation with Konitz and pianist Peggy Stern, but a fairly straightforward vocal by Judy Niemack on "All the Things You Are" is followed by an overlong (19-minute) exploration of the same chord changes (renamed "Exposition") by the quartet of Konitz, clarinetist Jimmy Giuffre, pianist Paul Bley and bassist Gary Peacock; their different approaches never really mesh together and this selection is a bit of a bore. The final performance, an extroverted duet by Konitz (on soprano) and fluegelhornist Clark Terry (titled "Flyin'—Mumbles and Jumbles"), adds some badly needed humor to the set. While one can admire Lee Konitz for still challenging himself after all this time, some of the dryer material on the CD (especially the two quartet numbers) should have been performed again; maybe the next versions would have been more inspired. —*Scott Yanow*

Rhapsody II / Jun. 1993-Sep. 1993 / Evidence ✦✦✦
This follow-up to *Rhapsody* is another eclectic mix, with 19 tracks featuring the veteran alto saxophonist in various small-group settings. Baritone sax great Gerry Mulligan and the leader flesh out an inspired duet of "Lover Man" and pianist Peggy Stern joins them for the spacy, extemporaneous "Trio No. 2." The brilliant fluegelhornist Clark Terry is only featured on three very brief improvisations based on "Indiana," which is wasting a great talent. Konitz switches to soprano sax for a moody version of "You Don't Know What Love Is" with vocalist Sheila Jordan and bassist Harvie Swartz. This is an interesting but not essential CD that falls short of its namesake predecessor and *The Lee Konitz Duets* (Original Jazz Classics). —*Ken Dryden*

Strings for Holiday / Mar. 18, 1996+Mar. 19, 1996 / Enja ✦✦✦✦
Always eager to record in new situations, Lee Konitz is showcased on this CD with a string sextet (two violins, violas and cellos), bassist Michael Formanek and drummer Matt Wilson. The cool-toned altoist pays tribute during a dozen songs to both Billie Holiday and (in a more subtle fashion) tenor great Lester Young, two of his early idols. Daniel Schnyder contributed all of the arrangements for the set.

Rather than weighing down the proceedings, Schnyder has the strings adding rich harmonies and phrases that seem to anticipate the leader's phrases, and they even swing. Lee Konitz, who added a vibrato to his sound for the project so he could recreate some of Billie Holiday's feeling, handles the ballads and medium-tempo material beautifully. Highlights include "The Man I Love," "I Cried for You," "All of Me" and "Easy Living." A memorable and heartfelt effort by all concerned. —*Scott Yanow*

It's You / Mar. 1996 / Steeple Chase ✦✦✦✦

Alone Together / Nov. 21, 1996+Nov. 22, 1996 / Blue Note ✦✦✦✦✦
Alone Together, Lee Konitz's first recording for Blue Note, is a special event. The saxophonist teamed up with legendary bassist Charlie Haden and young lion pianist Brad Mehldau, and the trio's set of relaxed bop is astonishing. On paper, the music on *Alone Together*—a collection of standards and originals—should just be straightahead cool bop, but all three musicians are restless and inventive, making even the simplest numbers on the disc vibrant, lively and adventurous. It's a wonderful record, one that makes a convincing argument that Konitz remains a vital force even as he reached his seventieth year. —*Stephen Thomas Erlewine*

Irene Kral

b. Jan. 18, 1932, Chicago, IL., **d.** Aug. 15, 1978, Encino, CA
Vocals / Standards, Ballads
A superb ballad singer who always put both plenty of emotion and subtlety into her often haunting interpretations, Irene Kral stood near the top of her field during her shortened life. The younger sister of singer/pianist Roy Kral (of Jackie & Roy), she debuted as a singer with the Jay Burkhardt Big Band. Freelancing in Chicago (including with a vocal group called the Tattle-Tales), Kral spent nine months singing with Maynard Ferguson's big band in 1957. Next up was an association with Herb Pomeroy's Orchestra. After getting married and settling in Los Angeles, Kral did not work for awhile. However, from 1974-77, she recorded three exquisite albums for Choice and Catalyst, including two duet sets with pianist Alan Broadbent (*Where Is Love* and *Gentle Rain*) that are considered classics; her rendition of "Spring Can Really Hang You Up the Most" is definitive. Sadly, Irene Kral was struck down by cancer at the height of her career at age 46. Her recordings (for United Artists in 1959, a 1963 date for Ava, a Mainstream session in 1965 and the Choice and Catalyst albums) are all currently out of print, although a live set from Sep. 1977 put out by Just Jazz in the mid-1990s is available on CD. —*Scott Yanow*

The Band and I / 1958 / United Artists ✦✦✦✦

Steveireneo! / Feb. 1959 / United Artists ✦✦✦

Better than Anything / Jun. 17, 1963-Jun. 18, 1963 / Ava ✦✦✦✦

Wonderful Life / 1965 / Mainstream ✦✦✦

● **Where Is Love?** / Dec. 1974 / Koch Jazz ✦✦✦✦✦

Gentle Rain / Aug. 1977 / Choice ✦✦✦✦✦

Kral Space / Jun. 1977 / Catalyst ✦✦✦✦✦

Live in Tokyo / Jul. 20, 1977+Jul. 22, 1977 / Trio ✦✦✦✦✦
Irene Kral recordings are unfortunately quite scarce in the late 1990s. The sensitive and subtle singer, who has become legendary since her death, is heard on this Japanese LP accompanied by pianist Alan Broadbent, bassist Kunimitsu Inaba, and either Donald Bailey or Hajime Ishimatsu on drums. Even the medium-tempo tunes come across as ballads, for Kral was always expert at giving each word the most logical emotional interpretation. Highlights include "Angel Eyes," "Everytime We Say Goodbye," "Guess I'll Hang My Tears out to Dry" and "Star Eyes." Worth searching for. —*Scott Yanow*

● **Irene Kral Live** / Sep. 11, 1977 / Just Jazz ✦✦✦✦
Recorded just 11 months before her death, this live set (released for the first time on this 1995 CD) is practically the only Irene Kral recording currently available domestically. Recorded at Half Moon Bay, California, the relaxed date finds Kral accompanied by her favorite pianist, Alan Broadbent (featured on an instrumental version of "I Love You"), bassist Frank De La Rosa and drummer Benny Barth. Although not reaching the emotional heights of her classic studio albums for Catalyst and Choice, Kral's performance does have some magic, particularly the versions of Bob Dorough's "Small Day Tomorrow," "Gentle Rain," "You Are There" and especially "Never Let Me Go." —*Scott Yanow*

Diana Krall

b. , Nanaimo, Canada
Piano, Vocals / Bop, Swing
Singer/pianist Diana Krall got her musical education when she was growing up in Nanaimo, British Columbia, from the classical piano lesson she began at age four and in her high-school jazz band, but mostly from her father, a stride piano player

with an extensive record collection. "I think Dad has every recording Fats Waller ever made," she said, "and I tried to learn them all." Krall attended the Berklee College of Music on a music scholarship in the early '80s, then moved to Los Angeles, where she lived for three years before moving to Toronto. By 1990, she was based in New York, performing with a trio, and singing. After releasing her first album on Justin Time Records, Krall was signed to GRP for her second, *Only Trust Your Heart* and transferred to its Impulse! division for her third, a Nat King Cole Trio tribute album called *All for You*. —*William Ruhlmann*

Stepping Out / 1993 / Justin Time ✦✦✦
Diana Krall's debut recording was a good start for the singer/pianist although at that point she did not stand out from the crowd. A pleasing vocalist a bit in the Ernestine Anderson vein who sings with detached coolness, Krall is also a fine modern mainstream pianist. On this session she is joined by bassist John Clayton and drummer Jeff Hamilton so it is not too surprising that the music swings. Krall sticks mostly to standards and ballads (including her original "Jimmie" and a rather downbeat version of "42nd Street") and shows a lot of potential for the future. —*Scott Yanow*

Only Trust Your Heart / Sep. 13, 1994-Sep. 16, 1994 / GRP ✦✦✦✦

● **All for You** / Oct. 3, 1995-Oct. 8, 1995 / Impulse! ✦✦✦✦✦
Pianist/vocalist Diana Krall pays tribute to the Nat King Cole Trio on her Impulse set. In general the medium and uptempo tunes work best, particularly such hot ditties as "I'm an Errand Girl for Rhythm," "Frim Fram Sauce" and "Hit That Jive Jack." Krall does not attempt to directly copy Cole (either pianistically or vocally) although his influence is obviously felt on some of the songs. The slow ballads are actually as reminiscent of Shirley Horn as Cole, particularly the somber "I'm Through with Love" and "If I Had You." Guitarist Russell Malone gets some solo space on many of the songs and joins in on the group vocal of "Hit That Jive Jack" although it is surprising that he had no other opportunities to interact vocally with Krall; a duet could have been delightful. Bassist Paul Keller is fine in support, pianist Benny Green backs Krall's vocal on "If I Had You" and percussionist Steve Kroon is added on one song. Overall this is a tasteful effort that succeeds. —*Scott Yanow*

Love Scenes / 1997 / GRP ✦✦✦✦
Vocalist/pianist Diana Krall was a very hot property by the time this Impulse CD was released. Teamed in a trio with her regular guitarist Russell Malone and bassist Christian McBride, Krall here mostly emphasizes ballads having something to do with love. She is at her best on "I Don't Know Enough About You," "I Don't Stand a Ghost of a Chance with You" and "How Deep Is the Ocean." However, Krall's earlier Nat King Cole tribute had more variety in tempos and moods and is recommended first. A decent but not essential release. —*Scott Yanow*

Carl Kress

b. Oct. 20, 1907, Newark, NJ, **d.** Jun. 10, 1965, Reno, NV
Guitar / Swing
One of the great guitarists of the 1930s, Carl Kress had a very sophisticated chordal style on acoustic guitar. He originally played banjo before gradually shifting to guitar. Kress played with Paul Whiteman in 1926 and then became a very busy studio musician, recording with all of the top White musicians (including Bix Beiderbecke, Red Nichols' Five Pennies and two classic duets with Eddie Lang) in those segregated days. Kress often teamed up with fellow guitarist Dick McDonough in the 1930s, he co-owned the Onyx Club on 52nd Street for a time and continued working in the studios into the 1960s, playing during his last years in a duo with George Barnes. Most of Carl Kress' solo and duet (with McDonough) recordings from the 1930s are long overdue to be reissued. —*Scott Yanow*

● **Two Guitars (And a Horn)** / 1962 / Vintage Jazz ✦✦✦✦
On the follow-up to *Two Guitars*, the great guitarists George Barnes and Carl Kress once again team up on seven more standards to contrast their single-note lines and unique chord voicings, respectively. The second side of this LP has the duo becoming a trio with the addition of tenor saxophonist Bud Freeman, who contributes the colorfully titled originals "The Eel's Nephew" and "Disenchanted Trout." This timeless small-group swing music is well worth acquiring. Both of these sets should be reissued on CD. —*Scott Yanow*

Ernie Krivda

b. Feb. 6, 1945, Cleveland, OH
Tenor Saxophone / Post-Bop
A brilliant tenor saxophonist with a forceful sound and an original attack that sometimes utilizes staccato phrases, Ernie Krivda has recorded stimulating sessions for Inner City, North Coast Jazz, Cadence and Koch without gaining much fame. He originally played clarinet, switching to alto in high school and later tenor. In 1964 he played for a few months with the Jimmy Dorsey ghost band and he

spent the late '60s playing locally in Cleveland, recording with Bill Dobbins for the Advent label (1969); they co-led a quintet for a few years. Krivda played in Los Angeles with Quincy Jones (1973) and then lived in New York for a period (1976-79). But in general Ernie Krivda (who deserves much greater recognition) has spent the bulk of his career as a vital part of Cleveland's jazz scene. —*Scott Yanow*

Satanic / 1977 / Inner City ♦♦♦♦♦

The explosive tenor saxophonist Ernie Krivda made his recording debut with this brilliant, if now difficult-to-find LP. Thirty-two at the time and temporarily in New York, the Cleveland native performs six of his originals with plenty of fire, creativity and originality. Assisting Krivda is keyboardist Gil Goldstein, electric bassist Jeff Berlin, drummer Bob Moses and percussionist Ray Mantilla. In addition to the memorable music, Krivda's extensive and very frank autobiographical liner notes are a major bonus. —*Scott Yanow*

The Alchemist / Jan. 1978 / Inner City ♦♦♦♦♦

Ernie Krivda has long deserved much greater recognition than he has received, for he has a very original sound on tenor and a versatile style that he employs on exploratory music. His second Inner City LP (which, like the first and third, is long out of print) features Krivda (tripling on soprano and flute), keyboardist Gil Goldstein, bassist Eddie Gomez, drummer Bobby Moses and percussionist Ray Mantilla digging into six of his complex yet generally appealing originals. Challenging music that hopefully will be made available on CD someday. —*Scott Yanow*

The Glory Strut / Dec. 1979 / Inner City ♦♦♦♦

Back in his native Cleveland after a period in New York, the great but generally unheralded tenor Ernie Krivda performs five originals (including a piece dedicated to Horace Silver), "Easy to Love," "Be My Love" and "I Remember Clifford" with a local rhythm section (pianist Dan Naier, bassist Mitchell Cutlip, drummer Ron Godale and sometimes percussionist Skip Hadden). The interpretations are fiery, and Krivda, who sometimes plays staccato runs, is as distinctive and high-powered as usual. —*Scott Yanow*

Live at Rusty's / Sep. 1981 / North Coast Jazz ♦♦♦♦

The Cleveland-based North Coast Jazz label, a short-lived but briefly significant record company, captured the underrated but highly original tenor Ernie Krivda during a live quartet gig with pianist Neal Creque, bassist Juny Booth and drummer Paul Samuels in 1981. Krivda really stretches out on two of his originals (the 14-minute "Irv's at Midnight" and the 19-minute "Song of the Moor"), in addition to playing a warm version of "But Beautiful." Krivda's extroverted sound and exploratory style are heard in fine form on this obscure but worthy LP. —*Scott Yanow*

Fireside Sessions / Oct. 1983+Jan. 1984 / North Coast Jazz ♦♦♦♦

The strength of the Cleveland jazz scene in the mid-1980s is displayed on this advanced hard bop LP. The great tenor Ernie Krivda co-leads the set with trumpeter Kenny Davis, although the then-unknown pianist Allan Farnham (who later hooked up with Concord) would eventually achieve the greatest fame; electric bassist Kyp Reed and drummer Val Kent complete the quintet. On six Krivda originals, one by Davis and a brief "Freedom Jazz Dance," the group digs in and comes up with fresh and fiery statements. —*Scott Yanow*

● Tough Tenor, Red Hot / Nov. 24, 1985 / Cadence ♦♦♦♦♦

Tenor saxophonist Ernie Krivda, whose decision to remain home in Cleveland has resulted in gaining much less recognition than he deserves, is a highly original player with an intense and exploratory style who is not shy of playing conventional chord changes. This live set from Cleveland State University matches Krivda with pianist Chip Stephens, bassist Jeff Halsey and drummer Joe Brigandi on four originals (including "Sarah's Theme," which is dedicated to Sarah Vaughan); in addition, he takes "All the Things You Are" as a duet with Halsey. This excellent LP, which is still available, gives listeners some good examples of Krivda's powerful playing and will hopefully resurface on CD someday too. —*Scott Yanow*

Ernie Krivda Jazz / Jan. 1991-Aug. 1991 / Cadence ♦♦♦♦♦

The legendary, if obscure tenor Ernie Krivda is heard here performing six originals (including "The Bozo" and "Blues for Two," the latter a duet with bassist Jeff Halsey) and three familiar standards ("Autumn Leaves," "Over the Rainbow" and "Love for Sale") with four different bassists, two different drummers, sometimes guitarist Bob Fraser and, during one song, pianist Joe Hunter. In addition, Pete Selvaggio plays accordion on two songs, and there are guest appearances for trombonist Pat Hallaran and a pair of trumpeters on one song. Krivda, who seems incapable of playing an uninspired solo, is typically high-powered and extroverted throughout this post-bop outing. —*Scott Yanow*

The Art of the Ballad / Jun. 1993 / Koch ♦♦♦♦

Golden Moments / Jun. 1995-Aug. 1995 / Koch ♦♦♦

Sarah's Theme / Sep. 11, 1995-Sep. 12, 1995 / CIMP ♦♦♦

Ernie Krivda, a thick-toned tenor who sometimes plays solos filled with staccato runs, resides in Cleveland and has long been an underground legend in the jazz

world. He has mostly displayed his extroverted and hard-driving side on records. This recent set is quite a bit different than expected for it emphasizes lyricism. Krivda, who plays here quite melodically and with legato, is joined by the quiet guitarist Bob Fraser and bassist Jeff Halsey. The brilliant interplay between the two sidemen is by itself worth the price of the disc. Krivda and company dig into four lengthy themes (including the "Autumn Leaves"-based "Sarah's Theme," "Stella by Starlight" and "Ernokee," which uses the chord changes of "Cherokee") and three shorter "Interludes," coming up with inventive and subtle variations. "Ernokee" is the only burner (and even that one sounds relaxed), making this among the most accessible (and certainly the most laidback) of all Ernie Krivda recordings. Recommended. —*Scott Yanow*

Karin Krog

b. May 15, 1937, Oslo, Norway
Vocals / Post-Bop, Avant-Garde

An adventurous singer who is versatile, Karin Krog is able to sing anything from standards to fairly free improvisations. She made her recording debut in 1964, appeared at many jazz festivals in Europe in the mid-'60s and in 1967 came to the US, performing and recording with the Don Ellis Orchestra and Clare Fischer's trio. A world traveler based in Europe, Karin Krog has recorded fairly steadily through the years, using such sidemen as Kenny Drew, Niels-Henning Orsted Pedersen, Jan Garbarek, Ted Curson, Dexter Gordon, Palle Mikkelborg, Steve Kuhn, Steve Swallow, Archie Shepp, Bengt Hallberg and John Surman; she has made records for Philips, Sonet, Polydor and other European labels. —*Scott Yanow*

Jazz Moments / Nov. 11, 1966-Nov. 12, 1966 / Sonet ♦♦♦♦

Joy / Jul. 6, 1968-Oct. 2, 1968 / Sonet ♦♦♦♦

● Some Other Spring / May 1970 / Storyville ♦♦♦♦♦

The talented Norwegian singer Karin Krog sings standards and her own "Blue Eyes" on this enjoyable collaboration with tenor saxophonist Dexter Gordon. Krog, a versatile vocalist, sounds perfectly at home on such tunes as "Some Other Spring," "How Insensitive," "Jelly Jelly" and "Shiny Stockings." Dexter is in excellent form (he had lived in Europe at that point for eight years), and the group is completed by pianist Kenny Drew (who switches to organ on "Blue Eyes"), bassist Niels Pedersen and drummer Espen Rud. This is one of the most accessible Karin Krog releases around and is recommended. —*Scott Yanow*

Hi-Fly / 1976 / Compendium ♦♦♦♦♦

A recording of this most unique vocalist with Archie Shepp (sax). All standards interpreted innovatively. —*Michael G. Nastos*

A Song for You / Jul. 18, 1977-Jul. 19, 1977 / Phontastic ♦♦♦♦

Something Borrowed, Something New / Jul. 1990 / Meantime ♦♦♦

This recent release by Norwegian vocalist Karen Krog has its ups and downs; she's best on the more ambitious, experimental material than doing straight ballads and standards, where deficiences in timing and delivery recur. —*Ron Wynn*

The Kronos Quartet

f. 1973
Group / Avant-Garde, Classical

Few groups so successfully bridged the gap between classical and popular music as the Kronos Quartet. Expanding the parameters of their repertoire to include compositions from rock, jazz and world music, the New York-based artists recorded a body of work virtually unparalleled in its dedication to innovation and range of expression. Comprising David Harrington on first violin, John Sherba on second violin, Hank Dutt on viola and Joan Jeanrenaud on cello, the Kronos Quartet was formed in San Francisco in 1973; though all four members were classically trained, they quickly dispensed with the rigid formalities of their craft, performing their chamber music with all of the impassioned energy commonly associated with rock—even their casual dress flew in the face of the classical establishment. Although Kronos began recording during the late 1970s, they began attracting widespread notice during the middle of the following decade as a result of recordings like 1984's *Monk Suite* (a collection of classical performances of compositions by Thelonious Monk and Duke Ellington) and their 1986 eponymous Nonesuch label debut, which raised many eyebrows via its string-quartet cover of Jimi Hendrix's "Purple Haze." In the years to follow the quartet remained uniquely eclectic and unpredictable, commissioning pieces from modern composers like Philip Glass and John Zorn, performing the works of tango innovator Astor Piazzolla and free-jazz visionary Ornette Coleman, and exploring world music (1992's *Pieces of Africa* exclusively featured music native to the African continent), remaining several paces ahead of their contemporaries at all times. —*Jason Ankeny*

Monk Suite / 1984 / Landmark ♦♦♦♦

The Kronos Quartet, a very open-minded classical string quartet, caused a lot of eyebrows to be raised with this unusual set. They perform eight Thelonious Monk compositions and two Duke Ellington pieces that Monk had recorded. All of the notes played by the strings were written out in advance by arranger Tom Darter but the improvising bassist Ron Carter is a major asset on five of the selections that are placed in a "Monk Suite." In addition, the two Ellington numbers have the Kronos Quartet joined by bassist Chuck Israels and drummer Eddie Marshall. Fortunately the string arrangements are very much in Monk's style, with many of the lines taken directly off of the pianist's recordings. This unique set is worth checking out. —*Scott Yanow*

Complete Landmark Sessions / 1984-1985 / 32 Jazz ✦✦✦✦✦
● **Music of Bill Evans** / 1985 / Landmark ✦✦✦✦✦
For their second and thus far final jazz project, the adventurous Kronos Quartet (a top classical string quartet) performed eight Bill Evans compositions, plus "Nardis" (which Evans always claimed Miles Davis stole from him). Three songs apiece add either guitarist Jim Hall or bassist Eddie Gomez. The members of Kronos (David Harrington and John Sherba on violins, Hank Dutt on viola and cellist Joan Jeanrenaud) do not improvise, but they expertly play Tom Darter's arrangements, some of which (particularly "Peace Piece") are transcriptions of pianist Evans' solos. Overall, this was an intriguing project, as was Kronos' slightly earlier interpretations of Thelonious Monk tunes. —*Scott Yanow*

Gene Krupa

b. Jan. 15, 1909, Chicago, IL, d. Oct. 16, 1973, Yonkers, NY
Drums, Leader / Swing, Dixieland
The first drummer to be a superstar, Gene Krupa may not have been the most advanced drummer of the 1930s but he was in some ways the most significant. Prior to Krupa, drum solos were a real rarity and the drums were thought of as a merely supportive instrument. Krupa, who with his good lucks and colorful playing became a matinee idol, changed the image of drummers forever.

Gene Krupa made history with his first record. For a session in 1927 with the McKenzie-Condon Chicagoans, he became the first musician to use a full drum set on records. He was part of the Chicago jazz scene of the 1920s before moving to New York and worked in the studios during the early years of the Depression. In December 1934 he joined Benny Goodman's new orchestra and for the next three years he was an important part of BG's pacesetting big band. Krupa, whose use of the bass drum was never too subtle, starred with Goodman's Trio and Quartet and his lengthy drum feature "Sing, Sing, Sing" in 1937 was historic. After he nearly stole the show at BG's 1938 Carnegie Hall Concert, Krupa and Goodman had a personality conflict and Gene soon departed to form his own orchestra. It took the drummer a while to realize with his band that drum solos were not required on every song! Such fine players as Vido Musso, Milt Raskin, Floyd O'Brien, Sam Donahue, Shorty Sherock and the excellent singer Irene Daye were assets to Krupa's Orchestra and "Drum Boogie" was a popular number, but it was not until 1941 when he had Anita O'Day and Roy Eldridge that Krupa's big band really took off. Among his hits from 1941-42 were "Let Me off Uptown," "After You've Gone," "Rockin' Chair" and "Thanks for the Boogie Ride." Unfortunately Krupa was arrested on a trumped-up drug charge in 1943, resulting in bad publicity, a short jail sentence and the breakup of his orchestra. In September 1943 he had an emotional reunion with Benny Goodman (who happily welcomed him back to the music world). Krupa also worked briefly with Tommy Dorsey before putting together another big band in mid-1944, one that had a string section. The strings only lasted a short time but Krupa was able to keep his band working into 1951. Tenor saxophonist Charlie Ventura and pianist Teddy Napoleon had a trio hit in "Dark Eyes" (1945), Anita O'Day returned for a time in 1945 (scoring with "Opus No. 1") and, although his own style was unchanged (being a Dixieland drummer at heart), Krupa was one of the first swing big bandleaders to welcome the influence of bebop into his group's arrangements, some of which were written by Gerry Mulligan (most notably "Disc Jockey Jump"). Among the soloists in the second Krupa Orchestra were Don Fagerquist, Red Rodney, Ventura, altoist Charlie Kennedy, tenorman Buddy Wise and, in 1949, Roy Eldridge.

After breaking up his band in 1951, Krupa generally worked with trios or quartets (including such sidemen as Ventura, Napoleon, Eddie Shu, Bobby Scott, Dave McKenna, Eddie Wasserman, Ronnie Ball, Dave Frishberg and John Bunch), toured with Jazz at the Philharmonic, ran a drum school with Cozy Cole and had occasional reunions with Benny Goodman. Gradually worsening health in the 1960s resulted in him becoming semi-retired but Krupa remained a major name up until his death. Ironically his final recording was led by the same person who headed his first appearance on records, Eddie Condon. Gene Krupa's pre-war big-band records are gradually being released by the Classics label. —*Scott Yanow*

1935-1938 / Nov. 19, 1935-Jun. 18, 1938 / Classics ✦✦✦✦✦
The first CD in the European Classics label's "complete" Gene Krupa series starts off with two all-star sessions that preceded the drummer's first dates as a big-band leader. Krupa, Benny Goodman, bassist Israel Crosby (featured on "Blues of Israel")

and sideman from Goodman's 1935 band jam four songs, and from the following year, Krupa is joined by trumpeter Roy Eldridge, tenor saxophonist Chu Berry, pianist Jess Stacy, guitarist Allan Reuss, Crosby and (on two of the four songs) singer Helen Ward. The two instrumentals ("I Hope Gabriel Likes My Music" and "Swing Is Here") are near-classics that are quite heated. Otherwise, this CD has Krupa's first 15 numbers with his big band, a promising outfit which during 1938 also featured tenor saxophonist Vido Musso, pianist Milt Raskin and the vocals of Irene Daye and Helen Ward. Highlights include "Feeling High and Happy," "Stomp" and the previously unissued "The Madam Swings It." —*Scott Yanow*

To Be or Not to Bop / Apr. 1938-1949 / Sounds of Swing ✦✦✦
This collector's LP gathers together a variety of studio recordings by several editions of the Gene Krupa Orchestra. The eight selections from 1938-41 (which include "Prelude to a Stomp," "Foo for Two," Tiger Rag" and a number called "Manhattan Transfer") have all since been reissued on CD by the European Classics label so the two selections from 1946 (which feature trumpeter Red Rodney, altoist Charlie Kennedy and the tenor of Charlie Ventura) and the six tunes from 1949 (when trumpeter Roy Eldridge was back with the band) are of the greatest interest. —*Scott Yanow*

Wire Brush Stomp / May 4, 1938-Aug. 20, 1941 / Bandstand ✦✦✦✦
For this LP, 16 of drummer Gene Krupa's big-band recordings have been gathered together with the emphasis on rarities. Irene Daye and Anita O'Day have some vocals and among the soloists are tenor saxophonists Vido Musso and Sam Donahue and trumpeter Roy Eldridge (the latter on "Watch the Birdie"). Most of the music has since been reissued on CD by Classics but, if found, this LP gives one a good overview of Krupa's underrated swing bands of 1938-41. —*Scott Yanow*

1938 / Jul. 19, 1938-Dec. 12, 1938 / Classics ✦✦✦✦
The second Gene Krupa CD in Classics complete reissuance of his swing-era recordings has 22 titles from Krupa's Orchestra during the latter half of 1938. The big band did not yet have its own personality, but Irene Daye was a fine pop/swing vocalist; Leo Watson is in typically eccentric form singing four good-time numbers; the arrangements of Jimmy Mundy and Chappie Willett generally swing hard; Vido Musso and Sam Donahue get off some fine tenor solos; and the leader/drummer really drives the band. Well worth picking up by swing fans. —*Scott Yanow*

Drummin' Man / Dec. 12, 1938-Jan. 26, 1949 / Columbia ✦✦✦✦✦
This two-LP box set, which came out in the 1960s (but can still be found in some collector's shops), has 32 of the best recordings by Gene Krupa's big band. All of the drummer's hits are here including "Drummin' Man," "Drum Boogie," "Bolero at the Savoy," "Let Me off Uptown," "Rockin' Chair," "After You've Gone," "Leave Us Leap," "Body and Soul," "Opus No. 1" and "Disc Jockey Jump." In addition to Krupa, the stars on these often-classic swing sides include trumpeter Roy Eldridge, singer Anita O'Day, altoist Charlie Kennedy and tenorman Charlie Ventura among others. Since this was the definitive Krupa set, it is a pity that Columbia has not reissued all of the music intact on CD yet. —*Scott Yanow*

1939 / Feb. 26, 1939-Jul. 25, 1939 / Classics ✦✦✦✦
The European label's third Gene Krupa set reissues all of the recordings made by the drummer's big band during a five-month period in 1939. Although working steadily, Krupa's Orchestra had not broken through yet (it was still two years away from its prime period). With Irene Daye contributing ten pleasing vocals among the 22 selections and such soloists as trumpeter Nate Kazebier, trombonist Floyd O'Brien, tenor saxophonist Sam Donahue and pianist Milt Raskin (along with the drummer/leader), the group was starting to show some strong potential, particularly on the instrumentals such as "The Madam Swings It" and "Hodge Podge." Well-played if not overly distinctive swing music. —*Scott Yanow*

1939-1940 / Jul. 24, 1939-Feb. 12, 1940 / Classics ✦✦✦
The fourth CD in the Classics label's "complete" Gene Krupa series contains 23 recordings recorded by the drummer with his big band during a seven-month period. Irene Daye does a generally fine job on her 14 vocals and singer Howard Dulany weighs down one ballad, but naturally the instrumentals are of greatest interest. This period in Krupa's career is generally overlooked in favor of his famous performances with Anita O'Day and Roy Eldridge but there are several gems, including a swinging rendition of "My Old Kentucky Home," "On the Beam," "Symphony in Riffs," the hit "Drummin' Man," "Three Little Words," the two part "Blue Rhythm Fantasy," "The Rumba Jumps" and "Boog It" The main soloists include trumpeter Corky Cornelius, the Artie Shaw-inspired clarinetist Sam Musiker and tenorman Sam Donahue in addition to the colorful leader. —*Scott Yanow*

1940, Vol. 2 / Nov. 2, 1939-Sep. 3, 1940 / Classics ✦✦✦✦
The sixth in the Classics label's chronological reissuance of all the early recordings led by Gene Krupa mostly documents his big band sides of June to Sept. 1940. Unfortunately 12 of the 21 numbers have dominant vocals by the rather routine singer Howard Dulany, greatly lowering the value of this CD. The other nine selec-

tions (which also include three Irene Daye vocals) are on a much higher level with the highlights including "The Sergeant Was Shy," "Washington and Lee Swing," "Who," a previously unreleased "St. Louis Blues" and "Rhumboogie." This CD concludes with a pair of fine instrumentals from earlier periods that were not released at the time. Recommended primarily to swing completists rather than to more general collectors. —*Scott Yanow*

● **Radio Years, 1940** / 1940 / Jazz Unlimited ✦✦✦✦✦
This 1995 CD contains two jazz-oriented radio broadcasts by the early Gene Krupa Big Band. Superior in general to their studio recordings of the era, these performances have plenty of fine solo space for trumpeters Shorty Sherock and Corky Cornelius and tenorman Sam Donohue; the drummer/leader is prominent in the ensembles, and Irene Daye takes seven vocals (there are also nine instrumentals). The announcer (who constantly calls Krupa "America's Number One Drummer Boy") is a bit annoying, but the swinging music is consistently excellent, making this CD a definitive example of Gene Krupa's Orchestra before Anita O'Day and Roy Eldridge joined up. —*Scott Yanow*

Drum Boogie / Jan. 2, 1940-May 21, 1941 / Columbia ✦✦✦✦✦
Gene Krupa's best-known band was the one he led during 1941-42 that featured singer Anita O'Day and trumpeter Roy Eldridge. This fine CD has 16 selections from the orchestra that preceded that group, a big band almost on the same level. Although the programming is not in strict chronological order, the swinging music is consistently enjoyable. With Irene Daye taking some vocals, and solo space for tenorman Sam Donahue and trumpeters Corky Cornelius and Shorty Sherock, many of the best recordings by this outfit are featured including the hit "Drum Boogie," "No Name Jive," "Rhumboogie" and "Blue Rhythm Fantasy." Well worth picking up. —*Scott Yanow*

1940 Vol. 1/ Feb. 19, 1940-Jun. 3, 1940 / Classics ✦✦✦✦
The fifth Gene Krupa CD in Classics' series (which reissues all of the drummer's swing-era studio recordings as a leader) documents Krupa's big band during a four-month period. Of the 22 selections (the majority of which have not been reissued elsewhere), seven have commercial ballad vocals by Howard Dulany, and six have reasonably enjoyable singing from Irene Daye. Of greatest interest are the nine instrumentals (including "Say Si Si," "Manhattan Transfer," "Tuxedo Junction," "Tiger Rag," "No Name Jive" and "Blues Krieg"), although during this era Krupa's orchestra had few major soloists. Tenor saxophonist Sam Donahue plays well, as do trumpeters Shorty Sherock (before he departed in May) and Corky Cornelius, but the Krupa big band's great days were still in the future. Still, swing collectors will want this entire series. —*Scott Yanow*

1940 Vol. 3 / Sep. 17, 1940-Nov. 28, 1940/ Classics ✦✦✦
The seven CD in the Classics label's Gene Krupa reissue series is mostly fairly weak. Despite Krupa's presence, his band at the time was average (only trumpeter Shorty Sherock had much of a reputation as a soloist) and, of the 21 selections on this disc, only three are instrumentals. Irene Daye's nine vocals are certainly listenable, although Howard Dulany's seven ballad features are more routine; Daye and Dulany take "You Forgot About Me" as a vocal duet. The instrumentals ("Hamtramck," "Full Dress Hop" and an excellent version of "Sweet Georgia Brown") are fine, but this CD is only recommended to completists. —*Scott Yanow*

★ **Uptown** / May 8, 1941-May 9, 1949 / Columbia ✦✦✦✦✦
Drummer Gene Krupa's most famous band was his 1941-42 orchestra that featured singer Anita O'Day and trumpeter Roy Eldridge. This definitive CD has 20 selections from that particular unit plus four tunes from Krupa in 1949 when Eldridge had briefly rejoined his band. Virtually all of Krupa's biggest hits are here including "Green Eyes," "Let Me off Uptown," "After You've Gone," "Rockin' Chair," "Thanks for the Boogie Ride" and "That Drummer's Band." This was a classic band, so this is a highly recommended disc for all swing collections. —*Scott Yanow*

Ace Drummer Man / Apr. 1943-Aug. 1947 / Giants of Jazz ✦✦✦✦
This collector's LP has some very interesting music from drummer Gene Krupa that had not been available elsewhere. Nine songs are from a broadcast by Krupa's 1947 big band, a unit that made very few recordings. There are vocals by Dolores Hawkins and Buddy Hughes and fine solos by altoist Charlie Kennedy, Buddy Wise on tenor and trumpeter Ray Triscari. Highpoint of the album are two selections ("Liza" and "Hodge Podge") from a 1943 V-Disc featuring the trio of clarinetist Buddy DeFranco, pianist Dodo Marmarosa and drummer Krupa; these are among DeFranco's very first records. Krupa is heard with tenor saxophonist Charlie Ventura on two songs taken from a different V-disc (including a version of their hit "Dark Eyes") plus on two other tunes that feature singer Anita O'Day with his 1945 big band. None of the music has yet been issued on CD so this LP is well worth searching for by Gene Krupa fans. —*Scott Yanow*

Leave Us Leap / May 30, 1945-1948 / Vintage Jazz ✦✦✦
Much of this CD features drummer Gene Krupa's little-known string orchestra of 1945. Ed Finckel's arrangements are a major asset and there are vocals from Lil-

lian Lane and the G-Noters. Although this group did not last long or develop its own personality, it created some fine music during its short existence. Highlights include "Blue Moon," two versions of "Leave Us Leap" and a feature for trombonist Tommy Pederson on "Moon Tide." In addition there are selections from a slightly later broadcast (without strings) by the big band with tenorman Charlie Ventura and a version of "Disc Jockey Jump" from 1948. An interesting CD, easily recommended to collectors who already have the more obvious releases. —*Scott Yanow*

Gene Krupa: Transcribed / Jan. 1946-Sep. 1946 / IAJRC ✦✦✦✦
This excellent LP deserves to be reissued on CD. The IAJRC collectors' label came out with 16 selections by the 1946 Gene Krupa Orchestra that feature the drummer's big band in top form recording for Capitol's radio transcription service. Trumpeter Red Rodney, tenors Charlie Ventura and Buddy Wise, altoist Charlie Kennedy, trombonist Dick Taylor and pianist Teddy Napoleon are the main soloists while the arrangements were provided by Eddie Finckel, Gerry Mulligan and George Williams. Buddy Stewart and Carolyn Grey take a few vocals and the Krupa Trio (with Ventura and Napoleon) is showcased on "10 Ritchie Drive" and "Limehouse Blues." This obscure music, which is a little boppish in spots (including a number titled "Calling Doctor Gillespie"), puts the focus on one of Gene Krupa's finest big bands. —*Scott Yanow*

1946-1947 / Jan. 1946-Mar. 1947 / Jazz Anthology ✦✦✦✦
The live performances on this French LP feature the 1946-47 Gene Krupa Orchestra, an underrated but talented big band heard at the tail-end of the swing era. Among the main soloists are trumpeters Red Rodney, trombonist Dick Taylor, altoist Charlie Kennedy, pianist Teddy Napoleon and the tenors of Charlie Ventura and Buddy Wise. This obscure music (mostly swing standards) finds the big band a bit influenced by bop, even when playing songs such as "Indiana," "King Porter Stomp" and "Bugle Call Rag." It will take a search but since the music on the LP has not been reissued yet on CD, this fine set is worth bidding for. —*Scott Yanow*

Let Me off Uptown / Apr. 5, 1949-Apr. 12, 1949 / Drive Archive ✦✦✦
Although left out of the history books, drummer Gene Krupa's 1949 big band was very bop-oriented. This Drive Archive CD (which reissues the contents of an Alamac LP) features highlights from three live appearances from an engagement in Hollywood. At the time trumpeter Roy Eldridge was back with the drummer/leader and he can be heard reviving his routine on "Let Me off Uptown" with singer Dolores Hawkins and taking a couple of heated solos (including on "After You've Gone"). Also prominent are trumpeter Don Fagerquist (a fine bop soloist), trombonist Frank Rosolino (who sings "Pennies from Heaven" and "Lemon Drop") and tenor saxophonist Buddy Wise. The recording quality is a bit erratic but the music from this forgotten band is often quite exciting. —*Scott Yanow*

The Original Drum Battle / Oct. 11, 1952 / Verve ✦✦✦
Despite its title and the fact that Buddy Rich is billed as co-leader, this LP only features Rich on one song, a drum battle with Gene Krupa that must have been much more exciting in-person than it is on record. Otherwise Krupa teams up with altoist Willie Smith and pianist Hank Jones for four standards (including "Flying Home" and "Drum Boogie"); one really misses the bass and gets a bit tired of Krupa pounding the bass drum. This set (all of which was recorded at a Jazz at the Philharmonic concert) concludes with tenor saxophonist Flip Phillips being featured on "Perdido." —*Scott Yanow*

Krupa & Rich / May 16, 1955-Nov. 1, 1955 / Verve ✦✦✦
On this CD reissue, drummers Gene Krupa and Buddy Rich only actually play together on one of the seven songs, a lengthy rendition of "Bernie's Tune" that has a six-minute "drum battle." Krupa and Rich do perform two songs apiece with a remarkable all-star band consisting of trumpeters Dizzy Gillespie and Roy Eldridge, tenors Illinois Jacquet and Flip Phillips, pianist Oscar Peterson, guitarist Herb Ellis and bassist Ray Brown. Each of the principals get some solo space, giving this release more variety than one might expect. In addition there are two "bonus cuts" from a Buddy Rich date that feature the drummer with trumpeters Thad Jones and Joe Newman, tenors Ben Webster and Frank Wess, Oscar Peterson, Ray Brown and rhythm guitarist Freddie Green. Excellent music overall if not quite essential. —*Scott Yanow*

Drummer Man / Feb. 15, 1956 / Verve ✦✦✦
Roy Eldridge (trumpet) got the featured billing (along with vocalist Anita O'Day) he deserved on *Drummer Man*, a Feb. 12, 1956, date featuring Gene Krupa fronting a big band. This was a reunion of sorts, but one that worked well, better in some cases than the original. The title's a bit misleading, for although Krupa's propulsions were clearly heard, his soloing was limited to a few features. Still, any drummer or fan of drumming will respond to the ambience of this date. —*Bob Rusch, Cadence*

The Great New Gene Krupa Quartet / Jan. 29, 1964+Feb. 5, 1964 / Verve ✦✦✦
Drummer Gene Krupa's final recording as a leader reunited him with the bombastic tenor saxophonist Charlie Ventura in a quartet with pianist John Bunch and

bassist Nabil Totah. The group mostly performs brief versions of standards including "Come Back to Sorrento," "Take the 'A' Train," "Flying Home" and even "Hello Dolly." Ventura's extroverted playing (on tenor, alto and baritone) is not for everyone's taste but he is in generally good form, and even an aging Krupa still retains his youthful excitement and enthusiasm. This LP will be a difficult one to find. *—Scott Yanow*

Marty Krystall

b. Apr. 12, 1951
Tenor Saxophone, Bass Clarinet / Post-Bop
An intense tenor saxophonist influenced a bit by the sound of Ben Webster but open to adventurous improvisations, Marty Krystall has appeared in several of Buell Neidlinger's groups through the years. He has worked as a studio musician in Los Angeles since the late '70s, helped run the K2B2 label and has recorded with Neidlinger in Krystall Klear and the Buells, Buellgrass (later renamed String Jazz), the group Thelonious and a recent tribute to Herbie Nichols. *—Scott Yanow*

● **Seeing Unknown Colors** / May 1990 / M-A ✦✦✦✦

Joachim Kühn (Joachim Kurt Kuhn)

b. Mar. 15, 1944, Leipzig, Germany
Piano, Keyboards / Avant-Garde, Post-Bop
The younger brother of clarinetist Rolf Kühn, Joachim Kühn has mostly worked in Europe but gained a reputation in the US for his adventurous playing. He has led his own trios since 1962, sometimes worked with his brother and had stints with Jean-Luc Ponty (1971-72), Tony Oxley's quintet in the 1980s and Mike Gibbs. Kühn has recorded for several labels (sometimes on electric keyboards) including MPS, Atlantic and CMP. *—Scott Yanow*

Springfever / Apr. 1976 / Atlantic ✦✦✦✦

Sunshower / Feb. 1978-Mar. 1978 / Atlantic ✦✦✦

I'm Not Dreaming / Mar. 1983 / CMP ✦✦✦✦
An early-'80s quintet work that juggles free, contemporary classical, and mainstream jazz elements. Pianist Kühn plays with more rhythmic energy than on his solo works, and is less concerned with texture and mood. The band includes trombonist George Lewis, cellist Ottomar Borwitzky (who adds a distinctly different sound), plus percussionists Herbert Forsch and Mark Nauseef, who doubles on piccolo and tenor sax. *—Ron Wynn*

Distance / May 1984 / CMP ✦✦✦✦✦
Fine, expressive solo piano by Joachim Kühn from '84, with lots of shimmering melodies, sweeping phrases, and strong rhythms. The album is superbly recorded, and gives Kühn's accomplished technique a great aural portrait. *—Ron Wynn*

From Time to Time Free / Apr. 1988 / CMP ✦✦✦✦
Has intense improvisations from the German veteran pianist. Kühn evokes images of Monk, Nichols, Taylor, and Tyner. J.F. Jenny Clarke is on bass, Daniel Humair on drums. This trio knows each other well. Standouts are "Spy vs. Spy" and "Para." Also a nice version of Coltrane's "India." *—Michael G. Nastos*

Live (1989) / Nov. 27, 1989 / CMP ✦✦✦
Recorded live in Paris, this album includes two standards and four Kühn originals. *—Michael G. Nastos*

Let's Be Generous / Aug. 1990 / CMP ✦✦✦

● **Dynamics** / 1992 / CMP ✦✦✦✦✦
Release by fine European pianist Joachim Kühn, with his usual outstanding solos and keyboard explorations. The songs are generally good, and the production and arrangements, as usual, are first-rate. *—Ron Wynn*

Rolf Kühn

b. Sep. 29, 1929, Cologne, Germany
Clarinet / Post-Bop, Swing
Rolf Kühn's style has evolved through the years. The clarinetist started out playing in German dance bands in the late '40s. He worked with radio orchestras starting in 1952 and moved to the US in 1956. Kühn subbed for Benny Goodman on a few occasions during 1957-58, played in the Tommy Dorsey ghost band (1958) and worked in a big band led by Urbie Green (1958-60). In 1962 Kühn returned to Germany where he has explored more adventurous styles of jazz (including dates with his younger brother, keyboardist Joachim Kühn) but still occasionally shows off his ties to swing. Kühn recorded with an all-star group called "Winner's Circle" (1957), Toshiko Akiyoshi (1958) and as a leader starting in 1953 including a 1956 New York quartet date for Vanguard. *—Scott Yanow*

● **Impressions of New York** / 1967 / Impulse! ✦✦✦✦✦
Although throughout much of his career Rolf Kühn has been a swing-based clarinetist, he also has had an open mind towards much more adventurous jazz, possi-

bly inspired a bit by his younger brother, pianist Joachim Kühn. On this out-of-print but very intriguing LP, the two Kühns, bassist Jimmy Garrison and drummer Aldo Romano perform a 33-minute suite titled "Impressions of New York," which is divided into "Arrival," "The Saddest Day," "Reality" and "Predictions." The music flows with a strong momentum, never losing one's interest. Rolf Kühn easily keeps up with his younger sidemen, and the overall results feature strong development and some surprises. Recommended. *—Scott Yanow*

The Day After / 1972 / MPS ✦✦✦
After a somewhat disastrous day of trying to put together a record (which is outlined with frankness on this LP's liner notes), clarinetist Rolf Kühn decided to use a second day to see if he could salvage the project. Fortunately, Kühn and his sidemen—pianist Joachim Kühn, bassist Peter Warren, drummer Oliver Johnson, percussionist Nana Vasconcelos and guest altoist Phil Woods (showcased on his "Everything in the Garden" and popping up on "CA. 1-9-5-2")—were still in good spirits, and the inside/outside music, which looks towards free jazz while still staying melodic in spots, works quite well. The clarinetist is heard in top form on "Turning Out" and the spontaneously improvised "Sonata for Percussion, Piano and Clarinet." *—Scott Yanow*

As Time Goes By / Apr. 1989 / Blue Flame ✦✦✦✦
Although often overlooked, clarinetist Rolf Kühn's clear tone, obvious virtuosity and creative ideas keep his music consistently stimulating. Rolf's brother, pianist Joachim, takes a strong supportive role on this trio date, while bassist Detlev Beier is also excellent. The group utilizes complex originals, fairly free group improvisational sections, and its own individual sense of swing to make the program memorable. The main performance is the nearly 20-minute "Spontaneous Construction," a multi-sectioned work full of surprising mood and tempo changes. The brief but pretty "When I Fall in Love" features the leader's unaccompanied clarinet, while Rolf Kühn's "Well I Didn't" has a much freer approach before resolving into "When I Fall in Love." "Speed of Speech" is notable for the use of some electronic devices that allow Rolf to state chords. Throughout the date (which also includes two other pieces), the interplay between the three musicians on the unpredictable music is quite impressive. *—Scott Yanow*

Big Band Connection / 1993 / Miramar ✦✦
As noted in the brief liner notes, clarinetist Rolf Kühn utilizes the same instrumentation on this CD as the 1938 Benny Goodman big band (except for the lack of a rhythm guitar), but the orchestra (arranged by Rob Pronk and Barry Ross) actually sounds much closer to Count Basie's in the 1960s than to Goodman's. Kühn draws his players from the NDR Big Band. Unfortunately, except for short spots (most notably on "Sister Sadie"), little is heard from his sidemen except in anonymous ensembles; altoist Herb Geller pops up just twice while pianist Fritz Pauer and trombonist Joe Gallardo make stronger impressions. Rolf Kühn is a talented bop-oriented soloist and has several fine solos, but overall these swinging renditions of tunes such as "Sweet Georgia Brown," "Autumn Leaves" and "Satin Doll" are very safe, middle-of-the-road and without any real surprises. *—Scott Yanow*

Brothers / Jun. 18, 1996 / Intuition ✦✦✦

Steve Kuhn

b. Mar. 24, 1938, New York, NY
Piano / Post-Bop
Steve Kuhn has had an interesting career. A talented jazz pianist, he has worked in many types of settings through the years. He began classical piano lessons when he was five, studied with Madame Chaloff and accompanied her son, baritonist Serge Chaloff, on some gigs when the pianist was 14. He freelanced in Boston as a teenager, graduated from Harvard and moved to New York where he worked with Kenny Dorham's group (1959-60). Kuhn was the original pianist in John Coltrane's Quartet, playing for two months before McCoy Tyner succeeded him. He was with the bands of Stan Getz (1961-63) and Art Farmer (1964-66), lived in Europe (1967-70) and then returned to the US in 1971. Kuhn doubled on electric piano in the 1970s, recorded for ECM and co-led a group with Sheila Jordan in the latter part of the decade. After a period playing commercial music, he formed an acoustic trio in the mid-'80s that has been his main vehicle ever since. Steve Kuhn has recorded as a leader for Impulse (1966), Contact, MPS, BYG, Muse, ECM, Black Hawk, New World, Owl, Concord and Postcards. *—Scott Yanow*

Raindrops (Steve Kuhn Live in New York) / Nov. 1972 / Muse ✦✦✦
Pianist Steve Kuhn's greatest attributes are his steady, sometimes impressive phrasing and interpretative ability; his weak links are a less than intense rhythmic capability and a derivative style. That's overcome on this session mainly because he's playing with a sympathetic rhythm section, and bassist George Mraz in particular helps push the music and increase the energy level. *—Ron Wynn*

Trance / Nov. 11, 1974-Nov. 12, 1974 / ECM ✦✦✦✦

Ecstasy / Nov. 1974 / ECM ✦✦✦✦✦

Motility / Jan. 1977 / ECM ✦✦✦✦

Non-Fiction / Apr. 1978 / ECM ✦✦✦✦

An interesting set of inside/outside music with a bit more energy than the more stereotypical ECM set, this set of five originals is performed by pianist Steve Kuhn (who was really developing his own original sound around this time), Steve Slagle (heard on alto, soprano and flute), bassist Harvie Swartz and drummer Bob Moses. This is a fine release that was soon overshadowed by Kuhn's collaborations with singer Sheila Jordan. —*Scott Yanow*

Playground / Jul. 1979 / ECM ✦✦✦✦✦

After many years off records, Sheila Jordan began to become more active in jazz in the mid-1970s. Her two recordings as part of pianist Steve Kuhn's quartet, of which this was the first, gave her a higher profile and a challenging vehicle for her improvised words and adventurous scat singing. With bassist Harvie Swartz and drummer Bob Moses completing the group, Jordan performs six of Kuhn's originals and lyrics (including "The Zoo" and the 10-minute "Deep Tango") as a member of the quartet, rather than as a dominant vocalist. Intriguing music. —*Scott Yanow*

Last Year's Waltz / Apr. 1981 / ECM ✦✦✦

For a time, singer Sheila Jordan was a regular member of pianist Steve Kuhn's quartet, a group also including bassist Harvie Swartz and drummer Bob Moses. This live set finds the band performing five Kuhn originals, one apiece by Swartz and Steve Swallow, plus "I Remember You," "Confirmation" and a brief medley. Although Jordan functions as a member of the band, her appealing singing is the main reason to acquire this memorable and well-rounded disc. —*Scott Yanow*

Mostly Ballads / Jan. 3, 1984 / New World ✦✦✦✦

For a change of pace, adventurous pianist Steve Kuhn performed a dozen standards (mostly at slower tempos) on this New World release. Half of the selections are duets with bassist Harvie Swartz, while the other songs are unaccompanied piano solos. In addition to such notable tunes as "Body and Soul," "Danny Boy," "'Round Midnight" and "Lover Man," Kuhn cooks a bit on Sonny Rollins' "Airegin." An excellent outing. —*Scott Yanow*

Life's Magic / Mar. 28, 1986-Mar. 30, 1986 / Black Hawk ✦✦✦✦✦

Pianist Steve Kuhn interacts with bassist Ron Carter and drummer Al Foster throughout this stimulating trio outing, which was last available as an LP for the now-defunct Black Hawk label. The musicians perform three standards—Hoagy Carmichael's "Little Old Lady," "Jitterbug Waltz" and "Yesterday's Gardenias"—and four of Kuhn's better originals, including a Foster feature on "Mr. Calypso Kuhn." Fine music that deserves to be reissued on CD. —*Scott Yanow*

Oceans in the Sky / Sep. 20, 1989-Sep. 21, 1989 / Owl ✦✦✦✦

This fairly obscure Owl CD matches together pianist Steve Kuhn, bassist Miroslav Vitous and drummer Aldo Romano for post-bop renditions of three group originals and a variety of standards, including "The Island," "In Your Own Sweet Way" and "The Music That Makes Me Dance." The interplay between the three advanced musicians and their ability to play both inside and outside at the same time are the main reasons to acquire this set. —*Scott Yanow*

Looking Back / Oct. 1990 / Concord Jazz ✦✦✦✦

Live at Maybeck Recital Hall, Vol. 13 / Nov. 18, 1990 / Concord Jazz ✦✦✦✦✦

Years Later / Sep. 1992 / Concord Jazz ✦✦✦✦

Remembering Tomorrow / Mar. 1995 / ECM ✦✦

In a blindfold test it would be easy to identify pianist Steve Kuhn's CD as a stereotypical ECM recording. With its emphasis on space, rather slow development and occasional repetition, the performances of Kuhn, bassist David Finck and drummer Joey Baron (all but one of the 11 pieces are Kuhn's originals) only occasionally rise above the level of background music. There are some heated moments on the sixth song ("All the Rest Is the Same") and the tenth ("Bittersweet Passages"), but most of this set is rather sleepy and melancholy, not living up to the potential of these talented musicians. —*Scott Yanow*

● **Seasons of Romance** / Apr. 12, 1995-Apr. 13, 1995 / Postcards ✦✦✦✦✦

Billy Kyle

b. Jul. 14, 1914, Philadelphia, PA, **d.** Feb. 23, 1966, Youngstown, OH
Piano / Swing

A fluent pianist with a light touch, Billy Kyle never achieved much fame but he always worked steadily. A professional from the time he was 18, Kyle played in the big bands of Tiny Bradshaw and Lucky Millinder and then became an important part of the John Kirby Sextet (1938-42), a perfect vehicle for his style. He was forced to leave the band when he was drafted and, after three years in the military (1942-45), Kyle freelanced, working fairly often with Sy Oliver. He joined Louis Armstrong's All-Stars in 1953 and was there for nearly 13 years until his death. His

playing with Armstrong, although appealing, tended to be very predictable. Billy Kyle had very few opportunities to record as a leader and none during his Armstrong years; just some octet and septet sides in 1937, two songs with a quartet in 1939, and outings in 1946 with a trio and an octet, 17 songs in all! —*Scott Yanow*

● **1937-1938** / 1937 / Classics ✦✦✦✦✦

Pianist Billy Kyle spent most of his career as a sideman (most notably with John Kirby's Sextet and the Louis Armstrong All-Stars) and led few sessions, all of which were formerly rare. That fact makes this CD reissue a major event for small-group swing collectors. Kyle's eight selections from 1937 with his "Swing Club Band" (which hints at the Kirby group) include two vocals apiece by the Palmer Brothers and Leon Lafell, but are notable for the playing of trumpeter Charlie Shavers and altoist Tab Smith on the instrumentals. In addition, Kyle is prominent with the Spencer Trio (a group with clarinetist Buster Bailey and drummer O'Neil Spencer), Timme Rosenkrantz's Barrelhouse Barons (which include cornetist Rex Stewart, trombonist Tyree Glenn, tenorman Don Byas and singer Inez Cavanaugh), and with Jack Sneed and his Sneezers. Sneed was a jazz-influenced calypso singer who was wise enough to use a backup quartet (which included Shavers) taken from the Kirby sextet. Overall, an excellent set. —*Scott Yanow*

1939-1946 / 1939 / Classics ✦✦✦✦

The second of two Classics Billy Kyle CDs has all of the remaining titles the superior swing pianist led during his life (although he lived until 1966). Ten of the 23 numbers are lesser performances, with four featuring the dated organist Bob Hamilton and the vocals of O'Neil Spencer; two are jivey numbers by singer Jack Sneed and his Sneezers, and four others also emphasize O'Neil Spencer's singing along with the organ of Milt Herth. However, the other 13 selections are full of classic swing-oriented performances. The talented British trumpeter Nat Gonella is heard fronting a hot septet also including Kyle, clarinetist Buster Bailey and altoist Benny Carter (their version of "You Must Have Been a Beautiful Baby" is a highlight); Kyle leads a couple of high-quality trio sets from 1939 and 1946, and he also heads a 1946 octet also featuring trumpeter Dick Vance, trombonist Trummy Young, clarinetist Bailey and tenor saxophonist John Hardee. The better half of this CD is so strong that it makes the entire set well worth acquiring despite the organists. —*Scott Yanow*

Charles Kynard

b. Feb. 20, 1933, St. Louis, MO, **d.** Jul. 8, 1979, Los Angeles, CA
Organ / Soul Jazz, Groove

Kynard is an organist whose jazz-funk leanings rival his predecessors and peers, though not eclipsing them. He was solid, though never flashy. He also plays electric bass. Kynard's album *Reelin' with the Feelin'* has been sampled and appears on several acid-jazz releases. —*Michael G. Nastos & Michael Erlewine*

Where It's At / 1963 / Pacific Jazz ✦✦✦

Kynard with funky guitarist Howard Roberts, Clifford Scott (sax), and Milt Turner (d). This is Kynard's first album and it has not been reissued. —*Michael Erlewine*

Charles Kynard / 1971 / Mainstream ✦✦✦✦✦

Kynard's best combo effort. Shows him in a more favorable light as a soul-jazz proprietor. —*Michael G. Nastos*

Professor Soul / Aug. 6, 1968 / Prestige ✦✦✦✦✦

Charles Kynard with Cal Green on guitar and Johnny Kirkwood on drums. This 1968 gem, which has not been reissued, has a rendition of "Christo Redentor." —*Michael Erlewine*

The Soul Brotherhood / Mar. 10, 1969 / Prestige ✦✦✦✦✦

They have got to reissue this one! Here is Kynard with Grant Green on guitar, Blue Mitchell on trumpet, and David "Fathead" Newman on sax. —*Michael Erlewine*

● **Reelin' with the Feelin'** / Aug. 11, 1969 / Prestige ✦✦✦✦✦

Kynard with Wilton Felder on sax, Joe Pass on guitar, Carol Kaye on bass, and Paul Humphrey on drums. This soul jazz date has been being sampled and used in recent acid-jazz albums. —*Michael Erlewine*

Afro-Disiac / Apr. 6, 1970 / Prestige ✦✦✦✦✦

Another Kynard gem that we are waiting for a reissue of. This album features Kynard with Grant Green on guitar and Houston Person on sax. I have not been able to find a copy, but those who know it say that this is the one to hear. I can't wait. —*Michael Erlewine*

Wa-Tu-Wa-Zui / Dec. 14, 1970 / Prestige ✦✦✦

Kynard with Rusty Bryant on sax, Virgil Jones on trumpet, and Melvin Sparks on guitar. —*Michael Erlewine*

Woga / 1972 / Mainstream ✦✦✦

L.A. Four

f. 1974 db. 1982

Group / Cool, Brazilian Jazz

Altoist/flutist Bud Shank and Brazilian acoustic guitarist Laurindo Almeida first teamed up in the 1950s, creating music that predated but strongly hinted at bossa nova. In 1974, they reunited to form the L.A. Four with bassist Ray Brown and drummer Chuck Flores. With Shelly Manne and later Jeff Hamilton replacing Flores on drums, the L.A. Four recorded eight albums for Concord through 1982, breaking up shortly afterward. Their mixture of cool-toned bop, Brazilian-oriented music and ballads was quite attractive. *—Scott Yanow*

The L.A. Four Scores! / Jul. 27, 1974 / Concord Jazz ◆◆◆◆

Altoist Bud Shank (who doubles on flute) and acoustic guitarist Laurindo Almeida first teamed up in 1954 to make a couple of albums called *Brazilliance* that hinted at but greatly predated bossa nova. Twenty years later, Shank and Almeida came together to form the L.A. Four, a quartet also including bassist Ray Brown and drummer Shelly Manne. Their debut recording as a unit was made at the 1974 Concord Jazz Festival, and it finds the appealing musicians blending together well on bossa nova tunes (including "Manha de Carnaval"), Almeida's classical-oriented originals, and some swing. This was a particularly inventive chamber jazz band. *—Scott Yanow*

● **L.A. Four** / Dec. 1975 / Concord Jazz ◆◆◆◆

The second recording and first studio set by the L.A. Four matched together Bud Shank on alto and flute, guitarist Laurindo Almeida, bassist Ray Brown and drummer Shelly Manne for a diverse yet consistently enjoyable program. The selections range from "Dindi" and "Manteca" to "St. Thomas" and a 13-minute exploration of "Concierto De Aranjuez." As usual, the band mixes together bossa nova and Brazilian jazz, some touches of classical music, and cool-toned bop. Recommended as a strong example of the group's appealing sound. *—Scott Yanow*

Going Home / Sep. 29, 1977-Sep. 30, 1977 / East Wind ◆◆◆

Watch What Happens / May 5, 1978 / Concord Jazz ◆◆◆◆◆

For their third recording, the L.A. Four had drummer Jeff Hamilton permanently taking Shelly Manne's place but otherwise utilized their original players (altoist-flutist Bud Shank, guitarist Laurindo Almeida and bassist Ray Brown). Most unusual in their repertoire on this set is Chuck Mangione's "Land of Make Believe," which was a current pop hit. Otherwise, the tunes are the usual mixtures of bossas, classical numbers and standards, including "Summertime," "Mona Lisa" and "Nuages." Tasteful and lightly swinging music. *—Scott Yanow*

Just Friends / 1978 / Concord Jazz ◆◆◆◆

On this rewarding set, the L.A. Four (altoist Bud Shank, acoustic guitarist Laurindo Almeida, bassist Ray Brown and drummer Jeff Hamilton) perform a Bach melody, "Carinhoso" (originally recorded by Shank and Almeida back in 1954), "Just Friends," a "Love" medley ("Love for Sale" and "Love Walked In") and Chick Corea's "Spain." Shank sticks exclusively to alto for the date, leaving his flute in its case, and the result is a more high-powered program than usual. Recommended. *—Scott Yanow*

The Live at Montreux / Jul. 14, 1979 / Concord Jazz ◆◆◆◆◆

The L.A. Four (guitarist Laurindo Almeida, Bud Shank on alto and flute, bassist Ray Brown and drummer Jeff Hamilton) were in their fifth year when they were recorded live at the 1979 Montreux Jazz Festival. The program has two group originals, a samba version of "I Love You," "Just in Time," and a four-song, 14-minute Duke Ellington medley. Fine music, although not containing any real surprises. *—Scott Yanow*

Zaca / Jun. 1980 / Concord Jazz ◆◆◆

The L.A. Four was a "fusion" group that worked quite well, mixing together cool jazz, sambas, bossa nova and classical music. A large reason for the band's success was the sound of acoustic guitarist Laurindo Almeida, although co-leader Bud Shank (doubling on alto and flute) was responsible for many of the more heated moments. With bassist Ray Brown and drummer Jeff Hamilton once again aboard,

the band's sixth Concord release has an interesting variety of strong material. Highlights include Shank's title tune, "Little Boat" and "Secret Love." *—Scott Yanow*

Montage / Apr. 1981 / Concord Jazz ◆◆◆

Montage is a good name for an L.A. Four recording, because the group (Bud Shank on flute and alto, guitarist Laurindo Almeida, bassist Ray Brown and drummer Jeff Hamilton) consistently mixed together different elements to gain its own sound. Included on this date are classical themes by Claude Debussy and Heitor Villa-Lobos, three group originals (including Shank's "Madame Butterball"), "Teach Me Tonight" (taken as a samba), and cooking renditions of "My Romance" and "Squatty Roo." A fine example of the L.A. Four's unique yet very accessible music. *—Scott Yanow*

Executive Suite / Jun. 1982 / Concord Jazz ◆◆◆◆

Eight years after their debut recording, the L.A. Four (guitarist Laurindo Almeida, Bud Shank on alto and flute, bassist Ray Brown and drummer Jeff Hamilton) recorded their eighth and final album. The band and its concept had not run out of gas, but Shank was soon to give up the flute altogether and play a more forceful brand of straightahead jazz. On this last effort, the L.A. Four as usual mixes cool-toned jazz, Brazilian music and classical to form an appealing blend. Two group originals, a few classical themes, "My Funny Valentine" and Antonio Carlos Jobim's "Chega De Saudade" comprise the attractive set. Recommended. *—Scott Yanow*

Pat LaBarbera (Pascel LaBarbera)

b. Apr. 7, 1944, Warsaw, NY

Tenor Saxophone, Soprano Saxophone / Hard Bop

The older brother of Joe La Barbera (drummer with Bill Evans during 1978-80) and arranger/trumpeter John La Barbera, Pat has been a fixture in Toronto since moving to Canada in 1974. He played in a family band early on, attended Berklee (1964-67) and gained recognition for his exciting solos with Buddy Rich's big band (1967-73). After settling in Toronto (where he has done quite a bit of studio work), La Barbera toured with Elvin Jones (1975-78). He has recorded as a leader for PM, Sackville and Justin Time. *—Scott Yanow*

Pass It on / Jan. 19, 1976-June 1976 / PM ◆◆

Pat La Barbera (switching between tenor, soprano and flute) teams up with either Richard Beirach or Don Thompson on piano, bassist Gene Perla and drummer Joe La Barbera for six of his originals. Very influenced by John Coltrane throughout the date, La Barbera's intense flights over the modal material get a little tiring after awhile, despite his obvious talent. A bit of variety is offered on "Cellar Muse" (a duet with his brother Joe), but otherwise, little memorable occurs on this Canadian LP. *—Scott Yanow*

● **Virgo Dance** / Apr. 1987 / Justin Time ◆◆◆◆◆

This Justin Time set is one of Pat La Barbera's better showcases. Listed as playing alto and soprano but actually splitting his time between tenor and soprano, La Barbera teams up with three fellow Canadians (pianist George McFetridge, bassist Neil Swainson and drummer Greg Pilo) to perform advanced standards, including "Footprints," "Miles Ahead" and Steve Swallow's "Eiderdown," plus three group originals. The often intense interpretations are modal-oriented, with La Barbera often closely emulating late-'50s/early-'60s John Coltrane, particularly on tenor. *—Scott Yanow*

JMOG (Jazz Men on the Go) / Dec. 28, 1992-Dec. 29, 1992 / Sackville ◆◆◆◆

"JMOG" stands for "Jazz Men on the Go" because each of the musicians on this CD are talented enough to be constantly in great demand. Tenor saxophonist Pat La Barbera, pianist Don Thompson, bassist Neil Swainson and drummer Joe La Barbera team up on their Sackville release for a set of originals (two apiece from the saxophonist and Swainson and three by Thompson). The music is generally modal-based with Pat La Barbera showing the influence of John Coltrane. In fact, were it not for the sophistication of Swainson's bass playing, much of this session could have taken place in the late '60s instead of 1992. Despite their conflicting schedules, the quartet meshes together quite well with the impressive interplay between Thompson and Swainson, the alert support by Joe La Barbera and the passionate playing of his older brother giving the band a strong identity. The compositions of Pat La Barbera and Swainson tend to be quite serious so Thompson's "Elk the Mooche" (an abstract "Moose the Mooche") is a welcome change of pace. —*Scott Yanow*

Steve Lacy

b. Jul. 23, 1934, New York, NY

Soprano Saxophone / Avant-Garde, Post-Bop, Free Jazz

One of the great soprano saxophonists of all time (ranking up there with Sidney Bechet and John Coltrane), Steve Lacy's career was fascinating to watch develop. He originally doubled on clarinet and soprano (dropping the former by the mid-'50s), inspired by Bechet and playing Dixieland in New York with Rex Stewart, Cecil Scott, Red Allen and other older musicians during 1952-55. He debuted on record in a modernized Dixieland format with Dick Sutton in 1954. However Lacy soon jumped over several styles to play free jazz with Cecil Taylor during 1955-57. They recorded together and performed at the 1957 Newport Jazz Festival. Lacy recorded with Gil Evans in 1957 (they would work together on an irregular basis into the 1980s), was with Thelonious Monk's quintet in 1960 for four months and then formed a quartet with Roswell Rudd (1961-64) that exclusively played Monk's music; only one live set (for Emanen in 1963) resulted from that very interesting group.

Steve Lacy, who is considered the first "modern" musician to specialize on soprano (an instrument that was completely neglected during the bop era), began to turn towards avant-garde jazz in 1965. He had a quartet with Enrico Rava that spent eight months in South America. After a year back in New York, he permanently moved to Europe in 1967 with three years in Italy preceding a move to Paris. Lacy's music evolved from free form to improvising off of his scalar originals. By 1977 he had a regular group that is still together in the mid-'90s, featuring Steve Potts on alto and soprano, Lacy's wife, violinist/singer Irene Aebi, bassist Kent Carter (later succeeded by Jean-Jacques Avenel) and drummer Oliver Johnson; pianist Bobby Few joined the group in the 1980s. Lacy, who has also worked on special projects with Gil Evans, Mal Waldron and Misha Mengelberg among others and in situations ranging from solo soprano concerts, many Monk tributes, big bands and setting poetry to music, has recorded a countless number of sessions for almost as many labels. His early dates (1957-61) were for Prestige, New Jazz and Candid and later on he appeared most notably on sessions for Hat Art, Black Saint/Soul Note and Novus. —*Scott Yanow*

The Complete Steve Lacy / Aug. 8, 1954-Nov. 24, 1954 / Fresco ◆◆◆◆

When soprano saxophonist Steve Lacy joined Cecil Taylor's quartet in 1955, he was best known as a Dixieland-oriented reed player who doubled on clarinet. His earliest period was only documented on a couple of rare ten-inch LPs so, when this double-LP was released by the obscure Fresco label in the late '80s, it was quite noteworthy. In addition to the 16 titles that were on the two LPs, there are 16 previously unissued alternate takes. Lacy is heard in a pair of sextets that were actually led by trumpeter Dick Sutton. Although most of the tunes are either swing or Dixieland standards (including "Sunday," "Jazz Me Blues" and "Avalon"), the music is actually as close to Gerry Mulligan as to Louis Armstrong. The harmonies tend to be advanced and boppish but there are also hints of Dixieland in the ensembles and some of the solos. Very interesting from an historical standpoint (since this was Lacy's debut on records), the music also holds one's interest and fits the title "Progressive Dixieland." —*Scott Yanow*

Soprano Saxophone / Nov. 1, 1957 / Original Jazz Classics ◆◆◆◆◆

A brilliant set. Lacy stakes out his claim as king of soprano sax, years before Coltrane popularizes it. —*Ron Wynn*

Reflections: Steve Lacy Plays Thelonious Monk / Oct. 17, 1958 / Original Jazz Classics ◆◆◆◆◆

Steve Lacy's many recordings of Thelonious Monk tunes through the years are never less than intriguing and always quite respectful to Monk's themes. This set, with bassist Jean-Francois Jenny-Clark, drummer Aldo Romano, and (on four of the six numbers) pianist Michel Graillier, was Lacy's first Paris recording; the French city would be his home base for the next few decades. Lacy explores five of Thelonious' complex compositions, including "Light Blue," "Mysterioso" and "Friday the Thirteenth," plus two versions of Monk's theme "Epistrophy." Lacy thoughtfully digs into the tunes and comes up with fresh and fairly free variations. The music on this Affinity LP (an English label) has not yet reappeared on CD. —*Scott Yanow*

★ **The Straight Horn of Steve Lacy** / Sep. 1960 / Candid ◆◆◆◆◆

Some of soprano saxophonist Steve Lacy's most interesting recordings are his earliest ones. After spending periods of time playing with Dixieland groups and then with Cecil Taylor (which was quite a jump), Lacy made several recordings that dis-

played his love of Thelonious Monk's music plus his varied experiences. On this particular set, Lacy's soprano contrasts well with Charles Davis' baritone (they are backed by bassist John Ore and drummer Roy Haynes) on three of the most difficult Monk tunes ("Introspection," "Played Twice" and "Criss Cross") plus two Cecil Taylor compositions and Charlie Parker's (or is it Miles Davis'?) "Donna Lee." —*Scott Yanow*

Evidence / Nov. 14, 1961 / Original Jazz Classics ◆◆◆◆◆

This early Steve Lacy album teams the great soprano saxophonist with trumpeter Don Cherry, bassist Carl Brown and drummer Billy Higgins for four Thelonious Monk songs, an obscurity by Duke Ellington ("The Mystery Song") and Billy Strayhorn's "Something to Live For." It is quite unusual to hear Cherry, during a period when he was regularly performing with Ornette Coleman's Quartet, playing this kind of standard material. Lacy and Cherry approach these standards from a different angle, bringing new life and opening up new possiblities for these songs. Although the playing time of this CD is brief (under 34 minutes), the quality is quite high. —*Scott Yanow*

School Days / Mar. 1963 / Emanem ◆◆◆◆

During 1961-64 soprano saxophonist Steve Lacy and trombonist Roswell Rudd co-led an unusual quartet that exclusively played the music of Thelonious Monk. Amazingly, no record label was interested in recording the band (despite their high profile) and the eventual breakup led to the group being largely forgotten. In 1975 Emanem came out with this LP, which comprises a decently recorded privately taped live performance from March 1963. Lacy and Rudd are joined by drummer Dennis Charles and (on five of the seven numbers) bassist Henry Grimes. Because Grimes showed up late that day, there are versions of "Bye-Ya" and "Pannonica" that were played without a bass but they still hold together. On such songs as "Brilliant Corners," "Monk's Dream" and "Skippy," the legendary group lives up to one's expectations and really digs into Monk's music. —*Scott Yanow*

Disposability / Dec. 21, 1965-Dec. 22, 1965 / RCA ◆◆◆◆

Forest and the Zoo / Oct. 8, 1966 / ESP ◆◆◆

During the mid- to late '60s, soprano saxophonist Steve Lacy began to really free up his music and perform in avant-garde settings. This ESP CD (a straight reissue of the original LP) was recorded when Lacy was "stranded" in Buenos Aires, Argentina, before he settled permanently in Europe. The adventurous quartet (which also includes trumpeter Enrico Rava, bassist Johnny Dyani and drummer Louis Moholo) performs two lengthy free improvisations (titled "Forest" and "Zoo") that contain their colorful moments along with wandering sections that meander a bit. Overall this date is probably more interesting from a historical standpoint than it is musically. —*Scott Yanow*

Moon / Jul. 1969 / Affinity ◆◆◆

Soprano saxophonist Steve Lacy's first recording as a leader since moving to Europe (except for the obscure *Roba* from three months earlier) was originally cut for the Byg label before being reissued on an Affinity LP. Lacy was in Rome after being "stranded" in South America for quite a time. He had embraced many of the aspects of free jazz, and his interplay with the Italian musicians (trombonist Italo Toni, clarinetist Claudio Volonte, bassist Marcello Melie and drummer Jacques Thollot), as well as cellist Irene Aebi (who would soon become a permanent member of his groups), is intriguing, often dense and quite passionate. Lacy had not yet fully developed his more relaxed, scalar approach to improvising, but his playing is certainly quite distinctive and generally fairly lyrical during performances of five Lacy originals. —*Scott Yanow*

Solo / Aug. 7, 1972-Aug. 8, 1972 / Emanem ◆◆◆◆

Scraps / Feb. 18, 1974+Feb. 21, 1974 / Saravah ◆◆◆◆◆

Saxophone Special / Dec. 19, 1974 / Emanem ◆◆◆◆

This is a chaotic meeting. Some of Europe's best avant-gardists. —*Ron Wynn*

Stabs / Apr. 1, 1975 / FMP ◆◆◆

Axieme / Sep. 1975 / Red ◆◆◆

This solo soprano sax recital by Steve Lacy was performed at a concert in Italy and has its moments of interest, particularly in the way that Lacy uses repetition and develops a couple of his themes. However the four-part work, after a strong start, eventually rambles and ends inconclusively (and apparently without much applause). Lacy shows off his technique and scalar approach but the material is not memorable enough to keep one interested throughout the entire performance. —*Scott Yanow*

Trickles / Mar. 11, 1976+Mar. 14, 1976 / Black Saint ◆◆◆◆◆

One of the early Black Saint albums, this set features a reunion between soprano saxophonist Steve Lacy and trombonist Roswell Rudd; bassist Ken Carter and drummer Beaver Harris complete the quartet. Although Lacy and Rudd had had a group 15 years earlier that exclusively played Thelonious Monk tunes, in this case they perform five of Lacy's diverse originals, stretching themselves on such tunes as "Trickles" and "Robes." The music is less melodic than expected but does have its moments of interest. —*Scott Yanow*

Sidelines / Sep. 1, 1976 / Improvising Artists ✦✦
Soprano saxophonist Steve Lacy and the obscure pianist Michael Smith performed seven of their originals (five by Lacy and two from Smith) for this Improvising Artists set, which has recently been reissued on CD. The music is explorative, thoughtful and a bit dry. It may take listeners a few listens to get into these deliberate collaborations. —*Scott Yanow*

Raps / Jan. 29, 1977 / Adelphi ✦✦✦✦✦
This is a quirky, explosive date with co-conspirator Steve Potts (as). —*Ron Wynn*

Follies / Apr. 11, 1977 / FMP ✦✦✦✦✦

Clinkers / Jun. 9, 1977 / Hat Hut ✦✦✦✦

Stamps / Aug. 27, 1977-Feb. 22, 1978 / Hat Hut ✦✦✦✦✦
Steve Lacy and his quintet are well featured on this double LP that documents two appearances at European festivals. In addition to the soprano/leader, altoist Steve Potts has long been a commanding improviser in his own right and offers a contrasting yet complementary solo voice. Bassist Kent Carter and drummer Oliver Johnson are always alert during this complex music (seven Lacy scalar originals) while Irene Aebi (on cello, violin and occasional background vocal) is more of an acquired taste. Overall this set gives one a good example of Steve Lacy's late-'70s group and its distinctive music. —*Scott Yanow*

High, Low and Order / Dec. 1977 / Hat Art ✦✦✦✦

The Way / Jan. 23, 1979 / Hat Hut ✦✦✦✦
This double-CD reissues the nine numbers from a former double LP, adding three previously unreleased tunes from the same Switzerland concert. The Steve Lacy Five (the leader on soprano, Steve Potts on alto and soprano, Irene Aebi on cello, violin and vocals, bassist Kent Carter and drummer Oliver Johnson) is at its best on scalar-based instrumentals such as the near-classic "Blinks." Some tunes utilize the voices of Aebi and Lacy, and these are often quite eccentric and for more selective tastes. But the many strong solos by Lacy and the highly underrated altoist Potts makes this two-fer of interest for followers of advanced jazz. This was always a well-organized and highly original group. —*Scott Yanow*

Troubles / May 24, 1979-May 25, 1979 / Black Saint ✦✦✦✦✦
This fairly obscure effort from the Steve Lacy Quintet of 1979 features the great soprano saxophonist in typically exploratory yet thoughtful form on five originals. His interplay with the underrated altoist Steve Potts (who doubles on soprano) is the main reason to acquire the set, while violinist/vocalist Irene Aebi's contributions are typically eccentric and an acquired taste. Bassist Ken Carter and drummer Oliver Johnson are stimulating in support of the lead voices. —*Scott Yanow*

Capers / Dec. 29, 1979 / Hat Hut ✦✦✦✦

Ballets / Dec. 18, 1980 / Hat Art ✦✦✦✦

Songs / Jan. 28, 1981-Jan. 29, 1981 / Hat Art ✦✦✦

Herbe de L'oubli / Aug. 13, 1981-Aug. 15, 1981 / Hat Art ✦✦✦✦
Soprano saxophonist Steve Lacy and pianist Mal Waldron have recorded together in a variety of settings through the years, including several duet records. For this set of duos, they stretch out on Waldron's "Hooray for Herbie," Lacy's "Herbe De L'Oubli" and Thelonious Monk's "Epistrophy." Lacy's thoughtful improvising fits well with Waldron's brooding chord voicings on the lesser-known Hat Art release. —*Scott Yanow*

Snake Out / Aug. 14, 1981 / Hat Music ✦✦✦✦

The Flame / Jan. 18, 1982-Jan. 19, 1982 / Soul Note ✦✦✦✦✦
The instrumentation on this set comprising soprano saxophonist Steve Lacy, pianist Bobby Few and drummer Dennis Charles, but the adventurous music certainly does not remind one of the Benny Goodman Trio. On four Lacy originals and one by Few, the musicians take wandering group improvisations that are rarely aimless. By having impressive technique and (just as importantly) open ears, the players constantly react to each other and come up with fresh ideas. An intriguing set. —*Scott Yanow*

★ **Regeneration** / Jun. 25, 1982-Jun. 26, 1982 / Soul Note ✦✦✦✦✦
The consensus album of the year in 1983, it includes one side of Monk and the other of Herbie Nichols' music. Includes Roswell Rudd (tb), Misha Mengleberg (p), Kent Carter (b), and Hans Bennik (d). —*Michael G. Nastos*

Prospectus / Nov. 1, 1982-Nov. 2, 1982 / Hat Art ✦✦✦✦
Although the originals on this two-LP set are dedicated respectively to Miles Davis, Bobby Timmons, Fats Navarro and McCoy Tyner, among others, the music does not sound (except in an abstract way) anything like theirs. Soprano saxophonist Steve Lacy's regular sextet of the period (with Steve Potts on alto and soprano, pianist Bobby Few; Irene Aebi on cello, violin and occasional eccentric

vocals; bassist Jean-Jacques Avenel; and drummer Oliver Johnson) is joined by trombonist George Lewis for seven of the leader's stronger originals, including two lengthy versions of "The Dumps" and a 22-minute rendition of "Cliches." Steve Lacy offered an alternative way to play free jazz, contrasting sound and silence and taking thoughtful and often-scalar improvisations not absent of melody and lyricism, but still quite adventurous and unpredictable. This is one of many excellent recordings of Lacy's music. —*Scott Yanow*

Blinks / Feb. 12, 1983 / Hat Art ✦✦✦✦✦

Futurities / Nov. 1984+Jan. 1985 / Hat Art ✦✦✦✦

Deadline / Mar. 1985 / Sound Aspects ✦✦✦✦
For this project, soprano saxophonist Steve Lacy performs four duets with the little-known pianist Ulrich Gumpert. Lacy's four originals are melodic, while the lengthy improvisations (including a 13-minute "Deadline") tend to be only abstractly connected to the themes. Interesting music, but not essential, particularly when so many more exciting Steve Lacy recordings are currently available. —*Scott Yanow*

The Condor / Jun. 20, 1985-Jun. 24, 1985 / Soul Note ✦✦✦✦
A good sextet date. —*Ron Wynn*

Chirps / Jul. 1985 / FMP ✦✦✦✦

Morning Joy: Live at Sunset Paris / Feb. 16, 1986 / Hat Art ✦✦✦✦✦

One Fell Swoop / Jun. 13, 1986-Jun. 15, 1986 / Silkleaf ✦✦✦
For this date, the thoughtful but adventurous soprano saxophonist Steve Lacy meets up with the fiery baritonist Charles Tyler in a quartet also including bassist J.J. Avenel and drummer Oliver Johnson. Together, they perform three of Lacy's tricky but logical scalar originals, Tyler's "The Adventures Of" and Thelonious Monk's "Friday the 13th." In addition, Tyler (switching to alto) has a fine trio feature with Avenel and Johnson on "Ode to Lady Day." The inside/outside music rewards repeated listenings, and the Lacy/Tyler matchup, helped by their contrasting but complementary styles, works quite well. —*Scott Yanow*

Only Monk / Jul. 29, 1986-Jul. 31, 1986 / Soul Note ✦✦✦✦
Steve Lacy has long been one of the foremost interpreters of pianist Thelonious Monk's music. This set is a solo soprano saxophone recital in which Lacy digs into nine of Monk's compositions. Most of the interpretations are quite concise, with all but the seven-minute "Work" clocking in at under six minutes. As usual, Lacy shows great respect for the melodies, and his improvisations are built off of the themes rather than just the chord changes. The sparse setting allows the soprano master to utilize space effectively and to take his time. The overall results, which are certainly for selective tastes, are often fascinating. —*Scott Yanow*

The Gleam / Jul. 1986 / Silkheart ✦✦✦✦✦
This Silkheart release has one of the finest all-around recordings by Steve Lacy's Sextet. The leader, a longtime master of the soprano sax, is joined by the underrated altoist Steve Potts (who doubles on soprano), pianist Bobby Few, bassist Jean-Jacques Avenel, drummer Oliver Johnson and Irene Aebi on vocals and violin. Aebi's singing, which is always an acquired taste, is as accessible as it ever was on the joyful "Gay Paree Bop"; all five compositions are Lacy originals. Overall, this set gives listeners a particularly strong example of the work of the innovative Steve Lacy Sextet. —*Scott Yanow*

Momentum / May 20, 1987-May 22, 1987 / Novus ✦✦✦✦✦
On Steve Lacy's first album for an American label in over a decade, his sextet is heard on four extensive originals by the great soprano saxophonist. The music is complex yet often melodic and, although Irene Aebi takes typically eccentric vocals on two of the songs, the main reasons to acquire this album are for the thoughtful yet unpredictable solos of Lacy and altoist Steve Potts. —*Scott Yanow*

The Window / Jul. 1987 / Soul Note ✦✦✦✦✦

The Super Quartet Live at Sweet Basil / Aug. 28, 1987-Aug. 29, 1987 / Evidence ✦✦✦
Mal Waldron and Steve Lacy reunited on this four-track set recorded live at Sweet Basil's in 1987. The usually undulating, highly unorthodox Lacy sounds at times almost self-effacing, although his playing retains its sharpness and harmonic edge. But he has played looser, more quirky versions of "Evidence" and "Let's Call This." He seems more in a commemorative than free-wheeling mood. Waldron's snaking, ripping chords and angular piano solos are more aggressive, while bassist Reggie Workman and drummer Eddie Moore alternate between providing concise support and taking their own strong solos. It is a fine date, just not as electrifying as some of Lacy's studio and independent sessions. —*Ron Wynn*

The Door / Jul. 4, 1988-Jul. 5, 1988 / Novus ✦✦✦✦
Steve Lacy's second Novus release uses a variety of different instrumental combinations and each of the selections deserves a comment or two. "The Door" (a whimsical piece built off of the knock of a door) and Thelonious Monk's "Ugly Beauty" (played as a waltz) are performed by the soprano saxophonist's quintet

(consisting of altoist Steve Potts, pianist Bobby Few, bassist Jean-Jacques Avinel and drummer Oliver Johnson). Lacy and Potts take searching improvisations over the strong pulse of the rhythm section. "Cliches" is an overlong duet by Lacy and Avinel with the bassist switching to thumb piano. "Forgetful," a forgotten George Handy ballad originally sung by David Allyn with Boyd Raeburn's orchestra, is played very respectfully by the Lacy-Few duo. The quirky "Blinks" is a four-bar phrase (taken from Kid Ory) that is played up and down a standard scale. Finally there is "Virgin Jungle," the biggest curiosity of the date. Sam Woodyard (Duke Ellington's drummer for many years) was living in Paris and sat in as a second drummer with the group just a month before his death. With violinist Irene Aebi fitting into the role of a slightly spaced Ray Nance, "Virgin Jungle" gets into an Ellington/Juan Tizol groove that works very well. Overall this is a well-conceived and highly recommended set for Steve Lacy fans. —*Scott Yanow*

Anthem / 1989 / Novus ✦✦✦✦
Some of Lacy's most recent material. The playing equals his past standards. —*Ron Wynn*

More Monk / Apr. 18, 1989-Apr. 19, 1989 / Soul Note ✦✦✦✦✦

Hot House / Jul. 12, 1990-Jul. 13, 1990 / Novus ✦✦✦
With Mal Waldron. A 1991 reissue of some fine duets. —*Ron Wynn*

Itinerary / Nov. 26, 1990-Nov. 28, 1990 / Hat Art ✦✦✦✦

Remains / Apr. 29, 1991-Apr. 30, 1991 / Hat Art ✦✦✦✦
On this solo soprano saxophone CD, the remarkable Steve Lacy performs his six-song, half-hour "Time of Tao-Cycle," plus three other originals—including the 18-minute title cut and a blues—and Thelonious Monk's "Epistrophy." The improvising is thoughtful, adventurous, and sometimes wandering, but rarely aimless. For specialized tastes. —*Scott Yanow*

Live at Sweet Basil / Jul. 6, 1991+Jul. 7, 1991 / Novus ✦✦✦✦✦
The Steve Lacy Sextet (comprising the leader on soprano, Steve Potts doubling on alto and soprano, Irene Aebi playing violin and singing, pianist Bobby Few, bassist Jean-Jacques Avenel and drummer John Betsch) had a rare opportunity to appear on a major American label in the early 1990s. This live set is an excellent example of the group's unique music performed live. The versions of Lacy's five scalar originals ("Prospectus," "The Bath," "Morning Joy," "The Wane" and "Blinks") are each at least ten minutes long ("Morning Joy" clocks in over 16) and find the musicians playing with enthusiasm and consistent creativity. Their relaxed but adventurous solo and ensemble work make this a set worth several listens. —*Scott Yanow*

We See / Sep. 1, 1992-Sep. 2, 1992 / Hat Art ✦✦✦✦

Vespers / Jul. 1993 / Soul Note ✦✦✦✦
For this unusual set, soprano saxophonist Steve Lacy's sextet (with Steve Potts on alto and soprano, pianist Bobby Few, bassist Jean Jacques Avenel, drummer John Betsch and vocalist Irene Aebi) is joined by the great tenor Ricky Ford (heard throughout in exciting form) and Tom Varner on French horn. The Lacy originals, which often feature Aebi singing poems, include tributes to Miles Davis, John Carter, Charles Mingus and Stan Getz, among others. The music, as usual, sounds like nothing played by those performers, but does feature lots of interesting tone colors and harmonies and consistently stimulating solos, particularly from Ford and Potter. Well worth exploring. —*Scott Yanow*

5 x Monk, 5 x Lacy / Mar. 26, 1994 / Silkheart ✦✦✦✦✦

Bye-Ya / Mar. 28, 1996-Mar. 29, 1996 / Freelance ✦✦✦✦

Tommy Ladnier

b. May 28, 1900, Florence, LA, d. Jun. 4, 1939, Geneva, NY
Trumpet / Classic Jazz
An exciting trumpeter who can be seen as a bridge stylewise between King Oliver and Louis Armstrong, Tommy Ladnier played early in life in New Orleans and in 1917 moved to Chicago. He worked for a period in St. Louis with Charlie Creath and was part of the Chicago scene in the early '20s, playing with Ollie Powers (1923), Fate Marable and King Oliver (1924-25). He also recorded with a variety of blues singers and Lovie Austin's Blues Serenaders. In 1925 Ladnier visited Europe with Sam Wooding and then became a star soloist with Fletcher Henderson's Orchestra (1926-27), making many excellent records. He returned to Europe with Wooding (1928-29) and worked with Benny Peyton and Noble Sissle (1930-31). Ladnier teamed up with Sidney Bechet on a memorable recording session as the New Orleans Feetwarmers (1932) but work was slow and the duo ran a tailor shop (1933-34) that was more notable for its jam sessions than for its alterations! Ladnier largely dropped out of sight for a few years, leading groups in New Jersey and Connecticut, but was rediscovered in 1938. He recorded the "Panassie Sessions" with Bechet and his new friend Mezz Mezzrow but died suddenly in 1939 from a heart attack. —*Scott Yanow*

Scott LaFaro

b. Apr. 3, 1936, Newark, NJ, d. Jul. 6, 1961, Geneva, NY
Bass / Post-Bop
During his tragically short life, Scott LaFaro quickly developed into one of the most advanced bassists around, competing with Charlie Haden and Charles Mingus. He emphasized high notes, could play with great speed and his interplay with Bill Evans in their trio was mutually stimulating and influential. LaFaro originally played clarinet and tenor before settling on bass while in college. He was with Buddy Morrow's band (1955-56), toured with Chet Baker (1956-57) and worked during the next few years with Ira Sullivan, Barney Kessel, Cal Tjader and Benny Goodman among others. LaFaro joined the Bill Evans Trio in 1959 and, although he would record with Ornette Coleman (including *Free Jazz*) and gig with Stan Getz, the bassist is best remembered for his association with Evans, particularly their Village Vanguard recordings of 1961. The 25-year-old Scott LaFaro's death in a car accident shortly after was a major shock to the jazz world. —*Scott Yanow*

Bireli Lagrene

b. Sep. 4, 1966, Saverene, France
Guitar / Swing, Fusion, Post-Bop
When Bireli Lagrene first emerged in 1980 as a 13-year-old who sounded exactly like Django Reinhardt, he was considered a marvel. Born (like Django) to a Gypsy family, he had been playing guitar since he was four. After a few years and several recordings, Lagrene purposely got away from the Reinhardt influence, playing high-powered rock-oriented fusion and recording with Jaco Pastorius in 1986. He sounded more original but much less interesting during this period. The guitarist has since returned to a quieter form of jazz, playing hard bop versions of standards with hints of his earlier interests in Django and fusion. Bireli Lagrene has recorded thus far for Antilles, Jazzpoint, Blue Note and Dreyfus. —*Scott Yanow*

● **Routes to Django: Live** / May 29, 1980-May 30, 1980 / Antilles ✦✦✦✦✦
Bireli Lagrene's debut on records is extraordinary in a couple of ways. He sounds like an exact duplicate of Django Reinhardt (no easy feat), an accomplishment that is more shocking when one realizes that he was 13 at the time. Already a virtuoso with complete control of his guitar, Lagrene (who like Reinhardt came from a Gypsy family) romps through the swing-oriented set with a variety of lesser-known European musicians including two rhythm guitars, bass and occasional piano, vibes, trumpet and violin. Performances of such tunes as "All of Me," "I've Found a New Baby" and "My Melancholy Baby" are guaranteed to fool even experts on blindfold tests. —*Scott Yanow*

Bireli Swing '81 / Apr. 1981 / Jazzpoint ✦✦✦✦✦
Guitarist Bireli Lagrene spent his teenage years sounding very close in style to Django Reinhardt. For this German import, his second recording, the 14-year-old romps in Djangoish fashion on such tunes as "Djangology," "Lady Be Good" and "Nuages" but also was starting to show some individuality on his own originals. Most of the selections are performed with one or two rhythm guitarists and a bassist, all Europeans. Lagrene has since grown as a player; if only he had had the opportunity this early to record with violinist Stephane Grappelli before his own style changed. —*Scott Yanow*

Fifteen / Feb. 1982 / Antilles ✦✦✦✦✦
Recorded shortly before his playing began to change, this Antilles release features guitarist Bireli Lagrene at the age of 15 jamming in the difficult-to-duplicate style of Django Reinhardt. Lagrene, who was one of the best Reinhardt soundalikes ever, is featured in small groups with other Europeans and sounds at his early best on "Sweet Georgia Brown," "Dark Eyes," "Blues for Bireli" and "I Can't Give You Anything but Love." It is a pity that Lagrene (who is so brilliant in this context) does not play this way very often anymore. —*Scott Yanow*

Stuttgart Aria / Mar. 1986 / Jazzpoint ✦✦✦
By 1986, Bireli Lagrene had decided to search for his own sound in fusion after getting his start as a teenager who very effectively emulated Django Reinhardt. Lagrene (on electric guitar) teams up with Vladislaw Sendeciki on keyboards, drummer Peter Lubke, percussionist Serge Bringolf and (most significantly) the innovative electric bassist Jaco Pastorius. The music (group originals plus "The Chicken," "Donna Lee" and "The Days of Wine and Roses") is often intense and fusion-oriented, and has plenty of heated playing by Lagrene and Pastorius. —*Scott Yanow*

Live Featuring Vic Juris / Jun. 1, 1985-Jun. 2, 1985 / Jazzpoint ✦✦✦
Bireli Lagrene made a major stir when he appeared as a young teenager sounding just like Django Reinhardt. On this German release, the 18-year-old Lagrene is heard for the first time breaking away from his dominant Django influence. Joined by the more high-powered Vic Juris on second guitar, the rhythm guitars of Gaiti Lagrene and Diz Disley, and bassist Jan Jankeje, Lagrene not only performs a pair of Reinhardt tunes and the standard "I Can't Give You Anything but Love,"

but Charlie Parker's "Ornithology," Chick Corea's "Spain" and six originals by either himself or Juris. An interesting transitional album, recorded at a European festival, that has some fire. —*Scott Yanow*

Inferno / 1988 / Blue Note ♦♦
Fans of guitarist Bireli Lagrene's early work probably will not care for this often-passionate CD. Lagrene, who had switched from swing to fusion a few years earlier (and from acoustic guitar to electric), mostly roars throughout seven of his originals (plus Django Reinhardt's "Incertitude"), jamming with tenor saxophonist Bill Evans, keyboardist Clifford Carter, electric bassist Victor Bailey, percussionist Café and one of four drummers. The music is well played but not all that memorable; none of the original themes were destined to catch on. —*Scott Yanow*

Foreign Affairs / Aug. 10, 1988-Aug. 12, 1988 / Blue Note ♦♦♦
Guitarist Bireli Lagrene, who started out as a young teenager very influenced by Django Reinhardt, has made a strong attempt to get away from the Reinhardt gypsy image. On this set, his guitar is often very rock-oriented and, although there are some acoustic moments, the emphasis is on fusion originals. The music is spirited and fun but not performed with a great deal of subtlety. Bireli Lagrene's future development (which direction will he head in next?) should be well worth watching. —*Scott Yanow*

Acoustic Moments / Jul. 1990 / Blue Note ♦♦
Bireli Lagrene, a guitarist who first came up as a remarkable Django Reinhardt clone before getting interested in rock, switches back and forth throughout this CD. He plays some songs acoustically in a classical vein, swings a bit on a couple of standards and then finishes the set with a brief blowout on "Metal Earthquake." Most of the so-called acoustic pieces have electric keyboards and/or synthesizers provided by Koono (there is no actual bass on this set) and one gets the impression that at this point in his career Bireli Lagrene was unsure what direction to go in. The results are interesting but sometimes almost incoherent. —*Scott Yanow*

Standards / Jun. 1992 / Blue Note ♦♦♦♦
This is one of guitarist Bireli Lagrene's better jazz albums of the 1990s. By this time he had pretty much discarded his original Django Reinhardt influence (even on "Nuages" he sounds nothing like Reinhardt) and he took time off from playing rock to perform a dozen familiar standards with bassist Niels Pedersen and drummer Andre Ceccarelli. Lagrene's technique had been admirable from the start and on this studio session his own musical personality was allowed to come to the surface. Highlights include "Softly as in a Morning Sunrise," "Autumn Leaves," "Donna Lee" and "Ornithology." —*Scott Yanow*

Live in Marciac / 1994 / Dreyfus ♦♦♦♦

My Favorite Django / Jan. 1995 / Dreyfus ♦♦♦
When guitarist Bireli Lagrene first debuted as a 13-year-old, he sounded like an exact duplicate of Django Reinhardt. Since that time Lagrene has sought to develop his own individuality but most of his fusion and rock-oriented records have been of lesser interest. For this date he returns to the Reinhardt repertoire (all but "Clair De Lune" are Django compositions) but with a difference. Keyboardist Koona reharmonized most of the songs drastically, aiming for an orchestral sound with his synthesizer with several pieces utilizing his charts for woodwind and string sections. However there is a good use of contrast, including a spontaneous guitar/piano duet on a medium-tempo "Blues for Ike." Lagrene sounds more original than in his early days and he has very impressive technique. Unfortunately the rhythms played by electric bassist Anthony Jackson and drummer Dennis Chambers are unremittingly funky and so unimaginative as to sound as if they were recorded on a different day! One assumes that they were following instructions but, whoever's fault it is, that fatal flaw sinks this effort. The complete lack of swing from the rhythm duo (even on the uptempo "I Got Rhythm"-based "Babik") drains most of the joy and purpose from these songs. Simply put, the original versions by Django Reinhardt are much better. —*Scott Yanow*

Oliver Lake

b. Sep. 14, 1942, Marianna, AR
Alto Saxophone, Flute, Soprano Saxophone / Avant-Garde, Reggae
Oliver Lake is an explosively unpredictable soloist, somewhat akin to Eric Dolphy in the ultra-nimble manner in which he traverses the full range of his main horn, the alto. Lake's astringent saxophone sound is his trademark—piercing, bluesy, and biting in the manner of a Maceo Parker; it was a perfect lead voice for the World Saxophone Quartet, the band with which Lake has made his most enduring mark on jazz.

Lake began playing drums as a child in St. Louis. He first picked up the saxophone at the age of 18. Lake received his bachelor's degree in 1968 from Lincoln University. From the late '60s to the early '70s he taught school, played in various contexts around St. Louis, and led—along with Julius Hemphill and Charles "Bobo" Shaw, among others—a musicians' collective, the Black Artist's Group

(BAG). Lake lived in Paris from 1972-74, where he worked in a quintet comprising fellow BAG members. By 1975, he had (along with most of his BAG colleagues) moved to New York, where he became active on what was called by some the "loft jazz" scene. In 1976, with Hemphill, Hamiet Bluiett, and David Murray, he founded the World Saxophone Quartet. Over the next two decades, that band reached a level of popularity perhaps unprecedented by a free jazz ensemble. Its late-'80s albums of Ellington works and R&B tunes attracted an audience that otherwise might never have found its way to such an esoteric style. Lake continued working as a leader apart from the WSQ and he made excellent small-group albums in the '70s and '80s for Arista/Freedom and Black Saint. In the '80s, Lake led a reggae-oriented band, Jump Up, that had a significant degree of pop success, though its artistic appeal fades in comparison with his jazz work. In the '90s, Lake continued to stretch creatively; a duo album with classically trained pianist Donal Fox sets him free to explore the more fanciful side of his musical personality. Late-'90s concerts with WSQ, his own groups, and such duo mates as the hyper dextrous pianist Borah Bergman show that Lake is still on top of his game. —*Chris Kelsey*

Ntu: The Point from Which Freedom Begins / 1971 / Freedom ♦♦♦♦
Altoist Oliver Lake's debut recording features him with a ten-piece unit in St. Louis. The performances are quite avant-garde, often very loose and influenced by the Art Ensemble of Chicago; Don Moye sits in on congas. In addition to Lake, the other notable players include trumpeter Baikida E.J. Carroll, trombonist Joseph Bowie and drummer Bobo Shaw. Much of this music is hit and miss but it has its successful moments. —*Scott Yanow*

Heavy Spirits / Jan. 31, 1975-Feb. 3, 1975 / Freedom ♦♦♦♦♦
This will be one of the least accessible of altoist Oliver Lake's recordings for most people but repeated listenings reveal a great deal of beauty. The avant-garde master is backed by three violinists on a trio of intense pieces, takes "Lonely Blacks" unaccompanied and performs "Rocket" in an unusual trio with trombonist Joseph Bowie and drummer Bobo Shaw. The other three selections have a more conventional instrumentation (a quintet with trumpeter Olu Dara and pianist Donald Smith) but are almost as challenging. It's worth investigating but listeners will have to have patience in order to fully appreciate this music. —*Scott Yanow*

Holding Together / Mar. 1976 / Black Saint ♦♦♦♦
Driving solos, surging pieces. —*Ron Wynn*

Life Dance of Is / Feb. 16, 1978 / Novus ♦♦♦♦
As is true of some of altoist Oliver Lake's recordings, this out-of-print LP has music that is rather exploratory and purposeful, but sometimes uncomfortable and a bit meandering. Also heard on flute, soprano and, during "Of Is," an odd recitation, Lake utilizes Michael Gregory Jackson on guitar, harmonica and synth, pianist Anthony Davis, sometimes Buster Williams or Leonard Jones on bass, and drummer Pheeroan AkLaff. The leader does play some fine solos, but the outside music is for specialized tastes and is less memorable than one would expect. —*Scott Yanow*

Buster Bee / Mar. 1, 1978 / Sackville ♦♦♦

Shine / Oct. 30, 1978-Oct. 31, 1978 / Novus ♦♦♦
One side neoclassical with strings. Hauntingly beautiful. —*Michael G. Nastos*

Zaki / Sep. 1, 1979 / Hat Art ♦♦♦♦

Prophet / Aug. 11, 1980-Aug. 12, 1980 / Black Saint ♦♦♦♦

Clevont Fitzhubert / Apr. 13, 1981-Apr. 14, 1981 / Black Saint ♦♦♦♦
Altoist Oliver Lake (tripling on soprano and flute), trumpeter Baikida Carroll, pianist Donald Smith and drummer Pheeroan AkLaff engage in fairly free group improvisations during this consistently stimulating set. The themes (five by Lake and one by Carroll) set the moods of the pieces, and the group takes it from there, sometimes going in surprising directions. Worth several listens. —*Scott Yanow*

Jump Up / 1981 / Gramavision ♦♦
Lake steps back to dance music with mixed results. —*Ron Wynn*

Plug It / 1982 / Gramavision ♦♦
This is Lake's least ambitious album conceptually, but it has some good blues and honking R&B-type solos. —*Ron Wynn*

● **Expendable Language** / Sep. 17, 1984+Sep. 20, 1984 / Black Saint ♦♦♦♦♦
This freebop session (which is often quite free but often has a strong pulse) is one of altoist Oliver Lake's more rewarding sessions. Guitarist Kevin Eubanks sometimes seems a bit out of place (generally he plays in more conservative settings) but pianist Geri Allen, bassist Fred Hopkins and drummer Pheeroan AkLaff are quite comfortable thinking on their feet during these spirited performances. —*Scott Yanow*

Dancevision / 1986 / Blue Heron ♦♦
He made a daring attempt to link basic R&B, reggae, and jazz into a seamless mix. It works in some places, but fails in others. —*Ron Wynn*

Gallery / Jul. 1986 / Gramavision ◆◆◆◆

Unlike some musicians associated with the avant-garde, altoist Oliver Lake often sounds at his strongest when backed by a piano-bass-drums rhythm section. This excellent set finds Lake switching between alto, tenor, soprano and flute on six of his stronger originals (including "Olla's Blues," "Sad Louis" and "Gallery") while assisted by pianist Geri Allen, bassist Fred Hopkins and drummer Pheeroah AkLaff; trumpeter Rasul Siddik guests on "Le Sport Suite." Lake's playing is abstract yet related to the themes, and he is heard throughout in top form, making this an easily recommended set for open-eared listeners. —*Scott Yanow*

Impala / 1988 / Gramavision ◆◆◆

The follow-up to Oliver Lake's successful *Gallery* is almost up to the same high level. Joined by pianist Geri Allen, bassist Santi Debriano and drummer Pheeroah AkLaff ("Lef' Sided" adds both Gene Lake and Brandon Ross on drums), Lake performs six diverse originals that could be considered to be free bop. One can hear the connection between this music and straightahead jazz, but Lake's free flights are quite unpredictable, if ultimately logical. Stimulating music. —*Scott Yanow*

Otherside / Apr. 17, 1988-Aug. 1988 / Gramavision ◆◆◆◆

Altoist Oliver Lake is heard in two very separate settings during this set. He is featured with pianist Geri Allen, guitarist Anthony Peterson, bassist Fred Hopkins and drummer Andrew Cyrille on four freebop originals, but of greatest interest are two numbers cut with a passionate and star-filled big band, which includes 16 horns and a rhythm section. Among the key soloists are trombonist Frank Lacy, Mathieu Darriau on tenor and trumpeter Stanton Davis. The often ferocious ensembles are memorable, and the rendition of "Dedication to Dolphy" is particularly noteworthy. Fans of advanced jazz will want to get this underrated release. —*Scott Yanow*

Boston Duets / 1989 / Music & Arts ◆◆◆◆◆

The brilliant avant-garde explorer Oliver Lake (here playing alto, soprano and flute) and the classical pianist Donal Leonellis Fox might seem at first glance to be an odd combination, but this set of duets easily exceeds one's expectations. Fox is fortunately a strong improviser and he not only sets a strong foundation for Lake's flights but often challenges and inspires the saxophonist. Together they play a variety of moody originals plus Thelonious Monk's "Rhythm-a-ning." This set is a surprise success. —*Scott Yanow*

Again and Again / Apr. 1991 / Gramavision ◆◆◆◆

Altoist Oliver Lake (who also plays a bit of soprano on this session) performs eight of his complex but generally accessible ballads with pianist John Hicks, bassist Reggie Workman and drummer Pheeroan AkLaff. Although none of these originals are destined to become standards, they inspire Lake to come up with some of his more lyrical solos. —*Scott Yanow*

Virtual Reality: Total Escapism / Oct. 9, 1991 / Gazell ◆◆◆

Edge-Ing / Jun. 28, 1993-Jun. 29, 1993 / Soul Note ◆◆◆◆

Dedicated to Dolphy / 1996 / Black Saint ◆◆◆◆

Alto saxophonist Oliver Lake doesn't have the multi-instrumental versatility or range of expression of the late Eric Dolphy, but he demonstrates the same controlled passion on this satisfying quintet date. His reworking of Dolphy's quirky "Hat and Beard" is actually brighter-sounding as a result of substituting alto sax for bass clarinet. Pianist Charles Eubanks' bluesy chords on "245" provide inspiration for the leader and the fine young trumpeter Russel Gunn. An excellent salute to Dolphy with a couple of strong Lake originals thrown in for good measure. —*Ken Dryden*

Ralph Lalama

b. Jan. 30, 1951, Pittsburgh, PA
Tenor Saxophone, Flute / Hard Bop

An excellent if underrated tenor saxophonist who often sounds straight from the prime years of Blue Note (most influenced by Hank Mobley and Sonny Rollins), Ralph Lalama has been a valuable soloist on many records. Born to a drummer and a singer, Lalama has been a part of the New York jazz scene since the 1970s. He became a permanent member of the Village Vanguard Orchestra in 1983 (when it was still co-led by Thad Jones and Mel Lewis), was a member of the Metropolitan Bopera House (later the Danny D'Imperio Sextet) and has led several excellent sessions for the Criss Cross label. —*Scott Yanow*

Feelin' and Dealin' / Nov. 23, 1990 / Criss Cross ◆◆◆◆

● **Momentum** / Dec. 22, 1991 / Criss Cross ◆◆◆◆◆

You Know What I Mean / Dec. 26, 1993 / Criss Cross ◆◆◆◆

Dave Lambert

b. Jun. 19, 1917, Boston, MA, **d.** Oct. 3, 1966, Westport, CT
Vocals / Bop, Vocalese

Best-known for being the "Lambert" in the premiere jazz vocal group Lambert, Hendricks & Ross, Dave Lambert was already a veteran singer when that ensemble was formed in 1957. Originally a drummer, Lambert sang with Johnny Long's big band for a year. He was with Gene Krupa's Orchestra (1944-45) and when he sang "What's This" with Buddy Stewart, it was considered the first vocal version of a bop line. On an infrequent basis during the late '40s and early '50s, Lambert led a group of singers. He appeared with Charlie Parker on a Royal Roost broadcast (1949) and his singers backed Bird on his 1953 recordings of "Old Folks" and "In the Still of the Night"—renditions that are somewhat bizarre. Lambert recorded a few numbers with his vocal group for Capitol in 1949 and teamed up with Jon Hendricks (along with two other singers) for the first time in 1955 for an obscure version of "Four Brothers." After Lambert, Hendricks & Ross became popular in 1957, that group dominated his activities although he did record a solo album for United Artists in 1959. He stayed with the ensemble after it became Lambert, Hendricks & Bavan in 1962 (when Annie Ross was succeeded by Yolande Bavan) until its breakup in 1964. The warm-voiced singer's last recording was a scat-filled version of "Donna Lee" performed at a 1965 Charlie Parker memorial concert. Dave Lambert died tragically in 1966, hit by a car while changing a tire. —*Scott Yanow*

Dave Lambert Sings and Swings Alone / 1958-1959 / United Artists ◆◆◆◆◆

Donald Lambert

b. 1904, Princeton, NJ, **d.** May 8, 1962, Newark, NJ
Piano / Stride

Donald Lambert ranks in jazz history as one of the great unknown stride pianists. In the late '20s he was a top pianist appearing regularly at rent parties and clubs in Harlem. However, by the 1930s he preferred to stay in New Jersey, playing in out-of-the-way clubs. He recorded four brilliant solos for Bluebird in 1941 in which he strided various classical themes. Other than privately recorded sets from 1960-62 that were released decades later by Solo Art, IAJRC and two on Pumpkin, that is all the documentation that exists of Donald Lambert. But even with the low quantity, his brilliant technique and appealing ideas come through and one can understand why he was held in such high esteem by his contemporaries (if not why he avoided New York). —*Scott Yanow*

Harlem Stride Classics / 1959 / Pumpkin ◆◆◆◆

Donald Lambert was one of the great stride pianists but unfortunately, other than a short period in New York (1932-36), he mostly played in obscure after-hours clubs in New Jersey. Lambert was persuaded to record for Solo Art in 1961 by Rudi Blesh but otherwise stayed out of the recording studios altogether. Fortunately tapes from his last years (he died in 1962) were released on three albums in the late '70s by the Pumpkin and IAJRC labels. For this LP, Lambert turns such songs as "It's All Right with Me," "The Trolley Song" and "Jingle Bells" into stride, and also performs some classics of the idiom, including "Ain't Misbehavin'," "Keep off the Grass," "Carolina Shout" and "If Dreams Come True." Well worth searching for. —*Scott Yanow*

Meet the Lamb / Jan. 28, 1960-Jan. 2, 1962 / IAJRC ◆◆◆◆◆

An elusive genius, Donald Lambert was a stride pianist on the level of James P. Johnson and Fats Waller but he hardly ever recorded. Luckily tapes from his last two years (1960-62) have been released on Pumpkin and IAJRC albums from the late '70s. This 1976 record has excellent liner notes and a well-rounded program. The recording quality is not state-of-the-art but the solo performances (a drummer sits in on "I Love You Madly") are often quite exciting. Highlights include Lucky Roberts' "Pork and Beans," Willie "The Lion" Smith's "Hold Your Temper," "The Lady's in Love with You," Rachmaninoff's "Russian Rag," James P. Johnson's "Harlem Strut" and "Hallelujah." —*Scott Yanow*

Classics in Stride / 1960 / Pumpkin ◆◆◆◆

The second Pumpkin LP to feature tapes of the great stride pianist Donald Lambert playing in his last years at after-hours clubs in New Jersey is quite valuable, for Lambert otherwise barely recorded at all. The recording quality is so-so but the playing is often spectacular. Lambert is in top form on such numbers as "Anitra's Dance," "Liza," "I Know That You Know" and "Hallelujah." His style and power have rarely been duplicated since his death in 1962 and all of Donald Lambert's few recordings are quite valuable. —*Scott Yanow*

● **Giant Stride** / Mar. 1, 1961 / Solo Art ◆◆◆◆◆

Lambert, Hendricks & Ross

f. 1957 **db.** 1964
Group / Bop, Vocalese

Arguably the greatest jazz vocal group of all time, Lambert, Hendricks & Ross comprised three masterful bop singers who specialized in vocalese: Dave Lambert (1917-1966), Jon Hendricks (b. 1921) and Annie Ross (b. 1930). Originally Lambert and Hendricks tried to record recreations of classic Count Basie performances but they had difficulty coming up with enough talented singers to fill in for all of the horns. However once they discovered Ross, it was decided to just use the three of them and overdub the parts; the result was the classic *Sing a Song of Basie.* Lambert, Hendricks & Ross immediately became a very popular group and during the next few years they recorded several notable albums including a real collaboration with Basie and a collection of Duke Ellington songs. Bad health caused Ross to drop out of the group in 1962 and her replacement Yolande Bavan (the group was renamed Lambert, Hendricks & Bavan) was better in ensembles than as a soloist. When Bavan and Lambert both left the band in 1964, the classic group was history. Lambert, Hendricks & Ross recorded for Impulse, World Pacific and Columbia while Lambert, Hendricks & Bavan made a few albums for RCA. Their influence is still felt in the singing of Manhattan Transfer, the work of the Hendricks Family and in nearly every jazz vocal group formed during the past 30 years. —*Scott Yanow*

★ **Sing a Song of Basie** / Aug. 26, 1957-Nov. 26, 1957 / GRP ✦✦✦✦✦

The premiere jazz vocal group Lambert, Hendricks & Ross made their recording debut on this classic album, which has been reissued on CD by GRP. After unsuccessfully searching in 1957 for a dozen singers who could sing vocalese in a recreation of some famous records by the Count Basie Orchestra, Dave Lambert, Jon Hendricks and Annie Ross decided to overdub their voices several times instead. Utilizing just a rhythm section, the vocalists in note-for-note reproductions of ten Basie records sing the witty and inventive lyrics of Hendricks. Highlights include "It's Sand, Man," "One O'Clock Jump," the uptempo "Little Pony" and "Avenue C." This record was a sensation when it was released and it is still quite enjoyable and unique. —*Scott Yanow*

Sing Along with Basie / 1958 / Roulette ✦✦✦✦

Dave Lambert, Jon Hendricks and Annie Ross had combined their voices to recreate the Count Basie Orchestra on their debut release *Sing a Song of Basie.* For this follow-up (which has not yet been reissued on CD), they actually had the services of the Basie big band itself. The vocal trio (who once again overdubbed their voices in spots several times) performs ten Basie classics including an exciting "Jumpin' at the Woodside," "Tickle Toe," "The King," "Swingin' the Blues" and "Li'l Darlin'." Most memorable is "Going to Chicago Blues," which has L, H & Ross recreating the Basie Orchestra while Joe Williams sings the regular vocal; it is quite fascinating to hear. —*Scott Yanow*

The Swingers! / Oct. 1, 1958+Mar. 1959 / EMI ✦✦✦✦✦

One of the lesser-known sets by the classic jazz vocal group Lambert, Hendricks & Ross, this CD reissue holds its own with their more famous recordings. Assisted by tenor saxophonist Zoot Sims, pianist Russ Freeman and guitarist Jim Hall among others, Dave Lambert, Jon Hendricks and Annie Ross sound at their best on such numbers as "Airegin," "Jackie" (a feature for Ross), "Swingin' 'til the Girls Come Home," "Four" and "Now's the Time." An instrumental ("Clap Hands! Here Comes Charley") from the same dates but originally issued under drummer Sonny Payne's name has been added to the program. The CD is recommended to fans of this unique and influential vocal trio. —*Scott Yanow*

Everybody's Boppin' / Aug. 6, 1959-Mar. 14, 1961 / Columbia ✦✦✦✦✦

Lambert, Hendricks & Ross made their debut on Columbia in 1959, and this CD contains not only all of the music from their first CBS album, but five titles from two later records. This set has many memorable classics from the great singers Dave Lambert, Jon Hendricks (the top vocalese lyricist) and Annie Ross. Highlights include the upbeat "Charleston Alley," a remake of Ross' "Twisted," the heated "Cloudburst," Hendricks' humorous "Gimme That Wine," "Summertime" (a recreation of Miles Davis' version with Gil Evans) and "Come on Home." Although Lambert, Hendricks & Ross only lasted a few years, their influence on other vocal groups was enormous. This set is a perfect place for collectors to begin to explore their vocal magic. —*Scott Yanow*

★ **The Hottest New Group in Jazz** / Aug. 6, 1959-Mar. 9, 1962 / Columbia ✦✦✦✦✦

The immortal jazz vocal group Lambert, Hendricks & Ross recorded five albums during its career: one apiece for Impulse and World Pacific, and three for Columbia. This two-CD set has all of the music from LH&R's Columbia dates (*The Hottest New Group in Jazz, Sing Ellington* and *High Flying*), plus four previously unissued and three very obscure selections. Dave Lambert, Jon Hendricks and Annie Ross were all very talented jazz singers as individuals and masters of vocalese. Virtually every performance of theirs together was special and in the long run

influential. With assistance by the Gildo Mahones Trio, trumpeter Harry "Sweets" Edison (on the earlier album) and altoist Pony Poindexter (during the seven "bonus" tracks), the vocal group is heard in memorable form throughout the two-fer. Among the many highlights are "Twisted," "Cloudburst," Hendricks' hilarious "Gimme That Wine," "Everybody's Boppin'," "Cottontail," "All Too Soon," "Main Stem," "Farmer's Market," "Cookin' at the Continental," "Halloween Spooks" and "Popity Pop." Essential music for all serious jazz collections. —*Scott Yanow*

Swingin' til the Girls Come Home / Sep. 6, 1962-Dec. 21, 1963 / Bluebird ✦✦✦

After Yolande Bavan replaced an ill Annie Ross in 1962, the vocal trio of Lambert, Hendricks & Bavan recorded three albums before disbanding in early 1964. This CD has some of the high points from each of the three albums: a trio date with guest Pony Poindexter on soprano from Basin Street East, an appearance at the 1963 Newport Jazz Festival (which has spots for trumpeter Clark Terry and tenor saxophonist Coleman Hawkins) and a performance from the Village Gate with cornetist Thad Jones and tenorman Booker Ervin. All of the guests get some solo space and the vocalists particularly sound strong on "Doodlin'," "Cousin Mary," "Swingin' till the Girls Come Home," Hendricks' "Gimme That Wine," "Watermelon Man" and "Cloudburst." The Ceylonese singer Bavan definitely gave the group a slightly different sound than it had had with Ross, but she was not as strong a soloist although Bavan fared well in the ensembles. This CD gives one a definitive look at the group and is well worth picking up. —*Scott Yanow*

Lambert, Hendricks and Bavan at Newport / July 5, 1963 / RCA ✦✦✦

Dave Lambert, Jon Hendricks and Yolande Bavan (who had replaced Annie Ross in 1962) recorded three albums during their two years together. This LP has the second date, a successful concert at the 1963 Newport Jazz Festival; four of the eight songs have since been reissued on a sampler CD. In addition to the Gildo Mahones Trio, L,H & B are joined on some songs by trumpeter Clark Terry and tenor saxophonist Coleman Hawkins. Highlights include "One O'Clock Jump," "Watermelon Man," "Cloudburst" and a funny rendition of Hendricks' "Gimme That Wine." All of the records by this group (and its predecessor Lambert, Hendricks & Ross) are well worth acquiring even if Yolande Bavan was not a soloist on the level of an Annie Ross. —*Scott Yanow*

Byard Lancaster (William Byard Lancaster)

b. Aug. 6, 1942, Philadelphia, PA
Alto Saxophone , Flute / Avant-Garde, Post-Bop

A lesser-known avant-gardist who has been based much of his career in Philadelphia, Byard Lancaster is an advanced improviser who is not shy to show the influence of blues and soul in his solos. He played with Sunny Murray starting in 1965 and worked with Bill Dixon (1966-67), Sun Ra (off and on between 1968-71) and McCoy Tyner (1971-77). Lancaster played for a bit with Memphis Slim in Paris but has mostly performed jazz locally. All of his own recordings were for obscure labels (including Vortex, Dogtown, Palm, Philly Jazz and Bellows) but his 1966 ESP date with Sunny Murray has been reissued on CD. —*Scott Yanow*

● **It's Not up to Us** / Dec. 19, 1966 / Vortex ✦✦✦✦✦

A rare recording. Two standards, six originals. —*Michael G. Nastos*

Worlds / 1993 / Gazell ✦✦✦✦

Harold Land

b. Dec. 18, 1928, Houston, TX
Tenor Saxophone / Hard Bop

Harold Land is an underrated tenor saxophonist whose tone has hardened with time and whose improvising style after the 1960s became influenced by (but not a copy of) John Coltrane's. He grew up in San Diego and started playing tenor when he was 16. After working locally and making his recording debut for Savoy (1949), Land had his first high-profile gig in 1954 when he joined the Clifford Brown-Max Roach Quintet. Land performed and recorded with the group until late 1955 when due to family problems he had to return home to Los Angeles (where he has been based ever since). He played with Curtis Counce's band (1956-58), recorded a pair of memorable albums for Contemporary (1958-59), led his own groups in the 1960s and co-led groups with Bobby Hutcherson (1967-71) and Blue Mitchell (1975-78). Harold Land has continued freelancing around Los Angeles up to the present time and has recorded as a leader (in addition to Savoy and Contemporary) for such labels as Jazzland, Blue Note, Imperial, Atlantic, Cadet, Mainstream, Concord, Muse and Postcards. His son Harold Land, Jr., has occasionally played piano with his groups. —*Scott Yanow*

● **Harold in the Land of Jazz** / Jan. 13, 1958-Jan. 14, 1958 / Original Jazz Classics ✦✦✦✦✦

Other than four titles from 1949, this CD reissue has tenor saxophonist Harold Land's first sessions as a leader. Teamed up on the West Coast with trumpeter Rolf Ericson, pianist Carl Perkins, bassist Leroy Vinnegar and drummer Frank Butler,

Land shows that hard bop was very much alive in Los Angeles in the late 1950s. His tone is cooler and softer than it would become later on, but it was already fairly distinctive. Land performs three of his swinging originals, the original version of Perkins' "Grooveyard" (which became a minor standard), an obscurity by Elmo Hope, and the standards "Speak Low" and "You Don't Know What Love Is." The reissue also adds "Promised Land" to the original program. Fine straightahead music. —*Scott Yanow*

The Fox / Aug. 1959 / Original Jazz Classics ✦✦✦✦
Due to his decision to settle in Los Angeles, tenor saxophonist Harold Land has long been underrated. A strong bop stylist who later on would be influenced a great deal by John Coltrane, Land in 1959 had a sound closer to Sonny Rollins. For this excellent straightahead quintet set with trumpeter Dupree Bolton and pianist Elmo Hope, Land performs four of Hope's superior but little-known compositions along with two of his own. This is high-quality hard bop, easily recommended to fans of straightahead jazz. —*Scott Yanow*

West Coast Blues! / May 17, 1960-May 18, 1960 / Original Jazz Classics ✦✦✦✦✦
This reissue (which surprisingly has not yet come out in complete fashion on CD) was originally recorded for the Jazzland label. Tenor saxophonist Harold Land leads an all-star sextet that includes guitarist Wes Montgomery, trumpeter Joe Gordon, pianist Barry Harris, bassist Sam Jones and drummer Louis Hayes. Together, they perform three of Land's originals, "Don't Explain," Charlie Parker's "Klactoveedsedstene," and an early version of Montgomery's "West Coast Blues." The music is as well played and swinging as one would expect from this superior bop group. —*Scott Yanow*

Eastward Ho! Harold Land in New York / Jul. 5, 1960-Jul. 8, 1960 / Original Jazz Classics ✦✦✦✦
Tenor saxophonist Harold Land and trumpeter Kenny Dorham make for a potent front line on this CD reissue, a superior hard bop set. With an obscure and quietly boppish rhythm section (pianist Amos Trice, bassist Clarence Jones and drummer Joe Peters) giving suitable backup, Land and Dorham stretch out on five selections, most notably Cole Porter's "So in Love," "On a Little Street in Singapore" and Land's "O.K. Blues," which was dedicated to producer Orrin Keepnews. A fine effort that serves as a strong example of Harold Land's early work. —*Scott Yanow*

Take Aim / Jul. 25, 1969 / Blue Note ✦✦✦
This little-known Blue Note session by tenor saxophonist Harold Land went unreleased until this 1980 LP and has not yet been reissued on CD. Land and an obscure supporting cast (trumpeter Martin Banks, pianist Amos Trice, bassist Clarence Jones and drummer Leon Pettis) perform five hard bop originals and a lyrical "You're My Thrill." The performances, which are now hard to find, should interest Land collectors and fans of the era's modern mainstream jazz, although overall the results are not that memorable. —*Scott Yanow*

Mapenzi / Apr. 14, 1977 / Concord Jazz ✦✦✦✦
This Concord release was tenor saxophonist Harold Land's first as a leader in a decade, although he had co-led many sessions in the interim with vibraphonist Bobby Hutcherson. Starting in 1975, Land and trumpeter Blue Mitchell worked regularly in a quintet up until Mitchell's death in 1979, but this album was just about their only joint recording. With keyboardist Kirk Lightsey, bassist Reggie Johnson, and drummer Al "Tootie" Heath offering solid support, the group performs four originals by Land (including the title cut and "Rapture"), two songs by Lightsey, and Mitchell's "Blue Silver." Fusion may have been the dominant force at the time, but despite Lightsey doubling on electric piano, this is an excellent example of 1977 hard bop. —*Scott Yanow*

Xocia's Dance (Sue-Sha's Dance) / Oct. 22, 1981 / Muse ✦✦✦✦
An early-'80s reunion between tenor saxophonist Harold Land and vibist Bobby Hutcherson, who co-led some vital West Coast combos in the late '60s and early '70s. Their cohesion and interaction remains intact, as does their solo prowess. Pianist George Cables and drummer Billy Higgins are also terrific. —*Ron Wynn*

A Lazy Afternoon / Dec. 28, 1994-Dec. 31, 1994 / Postcards ✦✦✦✦✦
Harold Land, a long underrated tenor giant based in Los Angeles, is quite melodic yet subtly explorative on his surprising disc. Backed by a string orchestra arranged and conducted by Ray Ellis and a rhythm section led by pianist Bill Henderson, Land explores dozen standards that are highlighted by "Nature Boy," "Invitation" and "You've Changed." He treats the melodies with respect and taste yet is not shy to stretch the music when called for. Harold Land plays beautifully throughout this memorable release. —*Scott Yanow*

Eddie Lang (Blind Willie Massaro)

b. Oct. 25, 1902, Philadelphia, PA, d. Mar. 26, 1933, New York, NY
Guitar / Classic Jazz
The first jazz guitar virtuoso, Eddie Lang was everywhere in the late '20s; all of his fellow musicians knew that he was the best. A boyhood friend of Joe Venuti, Lang

took violin lessons for 11 years but switched to guitar before he turned professional. In 1924 he debuted with the Mound City Blue Blowers and was soon in great demand for recording dates, both in the jazz world and in commercial settings. His sophisticated chord patterns made him a superior accompanist who uplifted everyone else's music and Lang was also a fine single-note soloist. He often teamed up with violinist Venuti (including some classic duets) and played with Red Nichols' Five Pennies, Frankie Trumbauer and Bix Beiderbecke (most memorably on "Singing the Blues"), the orchestras of Roger Wolfe Kahn, Jean Goldkette and Paul Whiteman (appearing on one short number with Venuti in Whiteman's 1930 film *The King of Jazz*) and anyone else who could hire him. A measure of Lang's versatility and talents is that he mostly played the chordal parts on a series of duets with Lonnie Johnson (during which he used the pseudonym Blind Willie Dunn) yet on his two duets with Carl Kress (whose chord voicings were an advancement on Lang's), he played the single-note leads. Eddie Lang, who led some dates of his own during 1927-29, worked regularly with Bing Crosby during the early '30s in addition to recording many sessions with Venuti. His tragic premature death was caused by a botched operation on a tonsillectomy. —*Scott Yanow*

★ **Stringin' the Blues** / Nov. 8, 1926-May 8, 1933 / Columbia ✦✦✦✦✦
This two-LP set (which is long overdue to be reissued on CD) contains a definitive cross-section of the recordings of violinist Joe Venuti and guitarist Eddie Lang. The 32 performances include everything from duets and a few of Lang's meetings with fellow guitarist Lonnie Johnson to examples of Venuti's Blue Four and guest appearances with singer Annette Hanshaw, Clarence Williams, Tommy Dorsey (on trumpet!) and Bing Crosby (on a hot "Some of these Days"). Virtually all of these recordings are superb, with solos also heard from bass saxophonist Adrian Rollini, Don Murray (on clarinet and baritone), cornetist King Oliver, the C-melody sax of Frankie Trumbauer and Jimmy Dorsey (switching between clarinet, alto and cornet). Highly recommended for all collections. —*Scott Yanow*

Handful of Riffs / Apr. 1, 1927-Sep. 27, 1928 / ASV/Living Era ✦✦✦✦

★ **Jazz Guitar** / Apr. 1, 1927-Jan. 15, 1932 / Yazoo ✦✦✦✦✦
Eddie Lang did not lead many sessions during his short life and the great majority are on this Yazoo LP. The most in-demand guitarist of 1925-33, Lang's rare opportunities to head his own dates put the focus on his single-note lines and gave him a chance to be in the spotlight rather than making other players sound good. This LP has two unaccompanied solos (including Rachmaninoff's "Prelude"), duets with pianists Frank Signorelli, Arthur Schutt and Rube Bloom and three of his famous collaborations with fellow guitarist Lonnie Johnson. However, the most memorable tracks are Lang's two exciting duets with guitarist Carl Kress: "Pickin' My Way" and an alternate take of "Feeling My Way." This is highly recommended music from the best jazz guitarist prior to the rise of Django Reinhardt. —*Scott Yanow*

Michael Lang

b. Dec. 10, 1941, Los Angeles, CA
Piano / Hard Bop
Due to his busy schedule in the studios, Michael Lang did not record his first solo album until 1994, after more than 30 years as a professional pianist. He graduated from the University of Michigan in 1963, played with Paul Horn (1964-65) and then moved to Los Angeles and started working in the studios. Lang worked with Stan Kenton's Neophonic Orchestra (1966), Don Ellis (1967) and Tom Scott (1968) and recorded with John Klemmer, Milt Jackson, Ella Fitzgerald, Lee Konitz, Art Pepper, Sarah Vaughan and many others, mostly outside of jazz. Mike Lang always played jazz locally on an occasional basis and finally in 1994 came out with his own album, jazz treatments of Henry Mancini songs for Varese Sarabande. —*Scott Yanow*

● **Days of Wine and Roses** / Sep. 3, 1994+Sep. 15, 1994 / Varese ✦✦✦✦
Michael Lang has worked as a studio pianist for over 30 years but, despite his obvious talent, he had never led a jazz record date until the release of this CD. The theme of the album (which is subtitled "The Classic Songs of Henry Mancini") is certainly a challenging one for, other than "Days of Wine and Roses" (which Lang takes as the leadoff tune), none of Mancini's compositions became jazz standards; after all these songs were written specifically for the movies and not for the improvising musician. The repertoire, other than "Charade" and "Moon River," is dominated by obscurities such as "Whistling Away the Dark" (from *Darling Lili*), "Tom's Theme" (used in the *Glass Menagerie*) and "The Sweetheart Tree" (from *The Great Race*). Six of the songs are taken as piano solos while the other pieces have either Chuck Domanico or Dave Carpenter on bass and Harvey Mason or Joel Taylor on drums assisting Lang. Among the better transformations are turning "Dear Heart" into a soulful ballad, making a hard swinger out of "It's Easy to Say" (from *10*), giving "Charade" a Latin feel and creating an introspective treatment to "Moon River." Some of the melodies are less interesting than others and

there are more moody ballads than romps, but in general Michael Lang uplifts the material and turns it successfully into jazz. —*Scott Yanow*

Don Lanphere

b. Jun. 26, 1928, Wenatchee, WA

Tenor Saxophone, Soprano Saxophone / Bop, Post-Bop

Don Lanphere's career can easily be divided into two periods with a long interlude in between. He came to New York when he was 19 and made some impressive recordings with Fats Navarro in 1949, keeping up with the fiery trumpeter. Lanphere played with Woody Herman's Second Herd (1949), Artie Shaw and the big bands of Claude Thornhill, Charlie Barnet and Billy May. Unfortunately drug use resulted in his arrest and much of 1951-81 found Lanphere either running the family music store in Washington or out of music altogether. An exception was his stint with Woody Herman during 1959-61. However Don Lanphere beat the odds, kicked drugs and made a full comeback starting in 1982. He has since recorded regularly for Hep, developed his style (doubling on soprano) and become a major if somewhat underrated improviser. —*Scott Yanow*

From out of Nowhere / Jun. 1982 / Hep ✦✦✦✦

Stop / Aug. 22, 1983-Jan. 4, 1986 / Hep ✦✦✦✦✦

An excellent all-around set by Don Lanphere (who doubles on tenor and soprano), this release from the Scottish Hep label features Lanphere in several settings. He performs four numbers, including "There's No You" and "The Preacher," in a quintet with trumpeter Jon Pugh, pianist Marc Seales, bassist Chuck Deardorf and drummer Dean Hodges; he explores "Body and Soul" with the same group (without Pugh); he takes "Laura" as a spontaneous duet with bassist Deardorf, and teams up with Pugh on two other straightahead originals in a different quintet with pianist Don Friedman. No matter what the setting, the underrated Don Lanphere is heard throughout in top form. —*Scott Yanow*

Into Somewhere / Dec. 1983 / Hep ✦✦✦✦

Don Love Midge / Oct. 21, 1984-Oct. 24, 1984 / Hep ✦✦✦✦

Don Lanphere/Larry Coryell / Apr. 11, 1990-Apr. 12, 1990 / Hep ✦✦✦✦✦

This combination works quite well. Heard here on soprano, tenor and a rare outing on alto, Don Lanphere matches up with the surprisingly flexible guitarist Larry Coryell in groups ranging from quartets to an octet. The two co-leaders and keyboardist Marc Seales contributed originals, and there are also lyrical versions of such tunes as Bill Evans' "Very Early," "Imagination," "Spring Can Really Hang You up the Most" (a Coryell-Seales duet), "My Ideal" and Horace Silver's "Peace," which has Lanphere and Coryell as a duo. This set has quite a few surprising twists and turns, and shows that the veteran saxophonist was still very much in his musical prime as the 1990s began. —*Scott Yanow*

● **Lopin'** / Dec. 1992 / Hep ✦✦✦✦✦

Don Lanphere, a veteran of the late '40s, really came into his own in the 1980s as can be heard on his recordings for the Scottish Hep label. An inquisitive player who has not forgotten (or felt restricted by) his bop roots, Lanphere is matched with baritonist Denney Goodhew and alto-great Bud Shank on this sextet date. They perform an original apiece from Lanphere and Miller, four by pianist Marc Seales (who leads the fine rhythm section) and three standards. Shank is consistently passionate (really showing emotion on "A Time for Love"), Lanphere is featured on an abstract ballad version of "Have You Met Miss Jones" and Goodhew plays strong enough not to be overshadowed by the better-known saxophonists. This superior modern mainstream release has fresh material and several surprising moments. —*Scott Yanow*

Jazz Worship/A Closer Walk / 1993 / DGL ✦✦✦

Don Still Loves Midge / Jun. 10, 1997-Jun. 11, 1997 / Hep ✦✦✦✦

On this collection of standards and originals—all favorites of his wife, Midge—saxophonist Lanphere alternates between alto, soprano and tenor to tackle renditions of "London by Night," "Just the Way You Are," "The Sky Fell Down" and "Prelude to a Kiss." —*Jason Ankeny*

John LaPorta

b. Apr. 1, 1920, Philadelphia, PA

Clarinet, Alto Saxophone, Tenor Saxophone / Cool

At one point in time John LaPorta looked like he was going to be one of the leading clarinetists in modern jazz. His cool tone and very advanced style (influenced by Lennie Tristano) seemed to be making him the Lee Konitz of the clarinet. He had played with the big bands of Bob Chester (1942-44) and Woody Herman (1944-46) but more importantly recorded with Lennie Tristano in 1947. LaPorta studied with Tristano and six years later was part of the Jazz Composers' Workshop with Charles Mingus and Teo Macero, seeking to bring elements of classical music into jazz. The clarinetist recorded with Mingus in 1954 before the bassist

changed directions and LaPorta led sessions for Debut, Fantasy and Everest during 1954-58. However John LaPorta chose to pursue a career as a teacher (at the Manhattan School of Music and Berklee) and has performed very infrequently during the past 40 years although he does appear on a mid-'90s GM CD. —*Scott Yanow*

Ellis Larkins

b. May 15, 1923, Baltimore, MD

Piano / Swing

Famous for his subtle chord voicings and ability to accompany singers, Ellis Larkins has been in great demand throughout his long career. His parents were musicians (his mother played piano while his father was a violinist), and Larkins was hailed as a prodigy early on, appearing with an orchestra when he was 11. After graduating from the Peabody Conservatory and Juilliard, Larkins was part of Edmond Hall's group in the mid-1940s, recorded with Mildred Bailey, Coleman Hawkins and Dicky Wells, and then worked regularly at the Village Vanguard and the Blue Angel in New York over a 20-year period. His duet records with Ella Fitzgerald and Ruby Braff in the 1950s are masterpieces in subtlety, and he was also a busy studio player. During the 1960s, Larkins worked with singers Joe Williams, Jane Harvey, Georgia Gibbs, and even Eartha Kitt and Harry Belafonte; since then, Larkins has continued playing in New York clubs with a wide variety of singers. He recorded as a leader for Storyville and Decca in the 1950s, for Halcyon and Black & Blue in the 1970s, had additional duets with Braff for Chiaroscuro, and was featured on a couple of dates for Concord, including a 1992 recital at Maybeck Recital Hall. —*Scott Yanow*

A Smooth One / Jul. 21, 1977 / Black & Blue ✦✦✦✦✦

Famed as a subtle accompanist who played harmonically complex chords in a lightly swinging style, pianist Ellis Larkins did not have any opportunities to record a full album as a leader after 1959 until this effort for the French Black & Blue label; it was last available domestically as a Classic Jazz LP. With fine support from bassist George Duvivier and drummer J.C. Heard, Larkins performs five swing-era standards, plus his own "C.E.B." The increasingly rare session gives listeners a good example of Ellis Larkins' tasteful playing. —*Scott Yanow*

● **Live at Maybeck Recital Hall, Vol. 22** / Mar. 29, 1992 / Concord Jazz ✦✦✦✦✦

Due to his work behind the scenes as an accompanist and in the studios, veteran pianist Ellis Larkins has tended to be overlooked. A tasteful and subtle player whose chord voicings are unique, Larkins had a rare opportunity to be heard in a set of unaccompanied solos on this CD. Most of the tunes date from the swing era, and although Larkins is quite melodic (and slower tempos are emphasized), there are some surprises along the way. Highlights include "Howdja Like to Love Me," "Lady Be Good," "Blue Skies," and "Things Ain't What They Used to Be." —*Scott Yanow*

Pete La Roca (Peter Sims)

b. Apr. 7, 1938, New York, NY

Drums / Hard Bop, Latin Jazz

Pete La Roca's decision to leave music in 1968 and become an attorney (under his original name of Pete Sims) cut short a productive career. He started his career playing timbales in Latin bands, changing his name to Pete La Roca at the time. He played drums with Sonny Rollins (1957-early 1959) and had associations with Jackie McLean, Slide Hampton, the John Coltrane Quartet (where he was the original drummer in 1960) and Marian McPartland. La Roca led his own group (1961-62), was the house drummer at the Jazz Workshop in Boston (1963-64) and worked with Art Farmer (1964-65), Freddie Hubbard, Mose Allison, Charles Lloyd (1966), Paul Bley and Steve Kuhn among others. He led two impressive albums: the classic Blue Note record *Basra* with Joe Henderson and *Bliss!,* a Douglas session (reissued on Muse) featuring Chick Corea and John Gilmore. La Roca started playing jazz again in 1979 and has performed on an occasional basis up to the present time. —*Scott Yanow*

● **Basra** / May 19, 1965 / Blue Note ✦✦✦✦✦

It is strange to realize that drummer Pete La Roca only led two albums during the prime years of his career, because this CD reissue of his initial date is a classic. La Roca's three originals ("Basra," which holds one's interest despite staying on one chord throughout, the blues "Candu" and the complex "Tears Come from Heaven") are stimulating but it is the other three songs that really bring out the best playing in the quartet (which comprises tenor saxophonist Joe Henderson, pianist Steve Kuhn and bassist Steve Swallow in addition to La Roca). "Malaguena" is given a great deal of passion, Swallow's "Eiderdown" (heard in its initial recording) receives definitive treatment and the ballad "Lazy Afternoon" is both haunting and very memorable; Henderson's tone perfectly fits that piece. —*Scott Yanow*

Bliss! / May 25, 1967 / Muse ✦✦✦✦

This 1967 quartet session is quite notable in several respects. Although the Muse reissue makes Chick Corea the leader (and the then-unknown pianist is in fine form), it was actually drummer Pete La Roca's date, and he contributes seven now-forgotten but quite intriguing originals. But of greatest interest is the playing of tenor saxophonist John Gilmore, heard during one of his few excursions away from Sun Ra. Fine advanced hard bop. —*Scott Yanow*

● **Swingtime** / Feb. 8, 1997-Mar. 1, 1997 / Blue Note ✦✦✦✦✦

Drummer Pete La Roca (who has gone back to his original name of Pete Sims) had an opportunity in 1997 to lead his first record date in 30 years. Sims, who had become active in jazz again after a long period outside of music, put together a particularly strong band for this CD, utilizing both Dave Liebman and Lance Bryant on sopranos, trumpeter Jimmy Owens, tenor saxophonist Ricky Ford, pianist George Cables and bassist Santi Debriano. Owens and Liebman, especially, sound inspired, while Ford displays a more original tone than he had had previously, although Dexter Gordon's influence can still be felt in some of his phrases. The music is essentially advanced hard bop with plenty of variety. Highlights include a version of "Body and Soul" based on the famous John Coltrane recording, "Susan's Waltz," "Nhon Bashi" and Chick Corea's "Amanda's Song." Even a perky, if slightly out-of-place rendition of "The Candyman" works well. Highly recommended. —*Scott Yanow*

Prince Lasha (William B. Lawsha)

b. Sep. 10, 1929, Fort Worth, TX
Flute / Avant-Garde, Free Jazz

A survivor of the 1960s who has not been heard from in some time, Prince Lasha was an inventive avant-garde flutist who occasionally played alto and clarinet. He played in Texas in an early-'50s band that also included Ornette Coleman. In 1954 Lasha moved to California and languished in obscurity until the 1960s. He recorded two Contemporary albums with Sonny Simmons (1962 and 1967), a 1966 session for British Columbia and as a sideman with Eric Dolphy and the Elvin Jones/Jimmy Garrison Sextet (both of the latter in 1963). After a few more records for small labels (the last one around 1983), Lasha disappeared from the jazz scene. Considering the major comeback that Sonny Simmons had in 1994 after a decade of silence, hopefully Prince Lasha's story will have the same happy ending. —*Scott Yanow*

The Cry / Nov. 21, 1962 / Contemporary ✦✦✦✦✦

Inside Story / 1965 / Enja ✦✦✦✦

Recorded in 1965 but not released domestically until this 1981 LP (Enja had previously put it out in Europe), this obscure set features flutist Prince Lasha in prime form. Assisted by pianist Herbie Hancock, bassist Cecil McBee and drummer Jimmy Lovelace, Lasha performs 7-to 9-minute versions of five of his originals. The inside/outside music has its free moments and solidifies the leader's position as one of the best flutists in the avant-garde movement of the period; he also contributes some credible alto. —*Scott Yanow*

★ **Firebirds** / Sep. 28, 1967-Sep. 29, 1967 / Original Jazz Classics ✦✦✦✦✦

The second of two collaborations by Prince Lasha (on flute, alto and alto clarinet) and Sonny Simmons (alto and English horn), this set has been reissued on CD; when will their 1962 Contemporary recording *The Cry* also come back? Vibraphonist Bobby Hutcherson, bassist Buster Williams and drummer Charles Moffett offer stimulating support and close interplay with the two lead voices, who contributed all five selections. The music is influenced by (but not too derivative of) Ornette Coleman's free-jazz style, and the improvisations are fairly advanced and sometimes quite emotional. Lasha and Simmons made for a potent team, making one wish that they would have a reunion someday. An underrated classic of its kind. —*Scott Yanow*

Last Exit

f. 1986 **db.** 1994
Group / Free Jazz, Avant-Garde

When it comes to avant-garde jazz/rock noise, few bands kicked out the jams better than did Last Exit. A who's-who of jazz players with punk attitudes, Last Exit—guitarist Sonny Sharrock, bassist Bill Laswell, drummer Ronald Shannon Jackson, and saxophonist Peter Brotzmann—could swing, rock, and create an all-out free-jazz din all in the blink of an eye. More important, Last Exit was about the thrill and danger of total improvisation; so much did they believe in this concept that their debut performance in Zurich in 1986 was completely improvised and unrehearsed. Granted, one person's free improvisation is another's tuneless chaos, but Last Exit, due primarily to the skill of its individuals, only infrequently fell off the precipice into the netherworld of arty wanking. These were four men that emotionally, intellectually, and musically belonged together: Sharrock had gotten

his start playing blues, but rebelled against structured, proper guitar technique, preferring to play sheets of atonal metallic distortion; Shannon Jackson grew up playing Texas blues but, through working with players such as Blood Ulmer, explored a percussive world that was not regimented by time and meter; Bill Laswell played and produced rock, funk, and "straight" jazz, and in Last Exit he mashed all of these influences into one feral ball of noise and rhythm; and Peter Brotzmann didn't simply blow sax, he blew it to bits as if his life depended on it.

For a group so driven by improvisation, it is not surprising to find out that much of Last Exit's catalog consists of live recordings. What is inescapable is the band's power; not only did they play ferociously, they played at maximum volume, improvised jazz/rock at Motörhead decibel levels. When angry audience members confronted the band during a gig complaining about the volume, Shannon Jackson not so subtly suggested they take their sorry asses home. The playing is intricate, wildly adventurous, frequently funny, and, perhaps most important, a tribute to musical democracy in action. Any one of these players could take over a tune and dominate, but the reality of Last Exit live was that there was a relaxed, almost intuitive give and take to the performance, as if each musician knew when to blow hard and when to quiet down, when to take the space to solo and when to lay back. What was even more amazing was that Last Exit's audience was becoming younger and less identified with traditional jazz audiences. The band's assaultive approach to improvisation was attractive to punk rockers and adventurous speed-metal fans.

Because of the reputations of the individual players (Brotzmann being the least well known of the group in America), as well as Laswell's position as a big-shot producer (Motörhead, Iggy Pop, Herbie Hancock), Last Exit got a major-label shot with Virgin in 1988. They never became huge, but they continued on devoting touring time in between various solo projects until they called it a career after the tragic death of Sonny Sharrock in 1994. Thankfully, there is plenty of Last Exit to be heard, and, as rumor has it, plenty of live recordings yet to be released. —*John Dougan*

Cassette Recordings '87 / 1987 / Celluloid ✦✦✦

Still live, still pumping big-time improvised noise wail. This one features a take of Jimmy Reed's "Big Boss Man" that sounds like no other version you've ever heard. This is mighty powerful stuff, and those a tad squeamish when it comes to full-bore noisemaking and improvised energy should explore this record only with proper supervision. There's no telling what will happen if you're left alone with these guys for any length of time. —*John Dougan*

Koln / Feb. 12, 1986 / ITM ✦✦✦✦✦

Another live set from the 1986 tour, Koln could well be the best of the bunch. There is an actual song here (Shannon Jackson's aptly titled "Brain Damage," and an opening track, the nearly 20-minute rumble called "Hard School," that scorches from top to bottom. This recording was supposed to come after *Cassette Recordings 87* and before *Iron Path*, but Laswell was involved in some rancorous disagreements with Enemy and the record's release was postponed for a couple of years. But man, was it ever worth the wait. Open up and burn. —*John Dougan*

The Noise of Trouble: Live in Tokyo / Oct. 2, 1986-Oct. 5, 1986 / Enemy ✦✦✦

Last Exit was definitely a noisy group. Consisting of the explosive guitarist Sonny Sharrock, the fiery Peter Brotzmann on tenor and baritone, electric bassist Bill Laswell and drummer Ronald Shannon Jackson, the word "intense" is an extreme understatement to describe the music. With guests Akira Sakata (on alto and clarinet) and pianist Herbie Hancock, the dense ensemble performs a variety of group originals, all pretty much freely improvised. Although it sometimes hints at country-blues and earlier forms of jazz, the music (which is beyond free funk) is certainly quite avant-garde and passionate. —*Scott Yanow*

● **Iron Path** / 1988 / Venture ✦✦✦✦

Their sole major label release, their first studio recording, and a record that iconoclastic critic Chuck Eddy considers one of the 500 greatest heavy metal albums in the history of the universe. But that doesn't mean you should invite all your Deep Purple and Iron Maiden loving friends over for a listening party; they won't be amused. Using the studio to their advantage, Last Exit explore sonic texture on "Prayer" and "The Fire Drum," but never lose sight of the power and energy that makes their live recordings so memorable. If you were to have one Last Exit recording, this might well be the one. But I would add that any one of their live records would enhance your appreciation of this great record immeasurably. —*John Dougan*

Headfirst into the Flames: Live in Europe / 1989 / Mu Works ✦✦✦

Never let it be said that Last Exit didn't take advantage of recording their live shows or playing in front of adoring Europeans. With cover art and song titles courtesy of the late avant-garde British poet Kenneth Patchen, *Headfirst* kicks off with the brain fry of "Lizard Eyes" only to launch into a Sharrock improv called "Don't Be a Cry Baby, Whatever You Do." Brotzmann blows wild and free here, and his squeal and blurt provides a great counterpoint to the rumble of the rhythms and the pummeling sonic overload of Sharrock's guitar. Another piece of blurt that will make your head spin. —*John Dougan*

Bill Laswell

b. Feb. 14, 1950
Bass / Avant-Garde
Bassist/producer Bill Laswell has made important contributions as a performer and producer on jazz, jazz-rock and pop sessions. As a bassist, he played with Material, Curlew and Last Exit, where his pounding riffs and accompaniment were a good match for the slashing riffs of Sonny Sharrock, Peter Brotzmann's outside playing and Ronald Jackson's drumming. Laswell also helped establish record labels OAO and Celluloid. He produced sessions for Herbie Hancock, Material, Curlew, James "Blood" Ulmer, Manu Dibango, Fela Kuti and pop-rock performers Iggy Pop, Motörhead, Laurie Anderson, Gil Scott-Heron, Yoko Ono, Public Image Limited, Mick Jagger and Nona Hendryx. Some of his productions have been controversial; Gil Scott-Heron expressed disdain with Laswell's method of stripping away a lot of his vocals, while his decision to eliminate Fela Kuti's sax solos and substitute others triggered negative comments. Laswell's best playing may be on the album *Baselines*, with John Zorn. He has several sessions available on CD both as a performer and producer. —*Ron Wynn*

Baselines / Mar. 1982 / IRS ✦✦✦
● **Hear No Evil** / 1988 / Venture ✦✦✦✦✦
A wonderful producer and bassist whose albums are more rock and instrumental pop than jazz. —*Ron Wynn*

Psychonavigation / 1994 / Subharmonic ✦✦✦
The brainchild of two ambient music deans (one American, one German), *Psychonavigation* is explained most succinctly by its title. Beautiful synth and looped vocal samples are layered over chill-out percussion and ambling rhythms. There is some diversity: The second track deserts the positive vibe and introduces disturbing vocals. —*John Bush*

Silent Recoil / 1995 / Low ✦✦
For the launch of yet another label, Bill Laswell produced an album with only three tracks of ambient-dub. The lilting atmospherics somehow work when attached to an immense bass line. —*John Bush*

Subsonic, Vol. 2: Bass Terror / 1995 / Sub Rosa ✦✦✦
Instead of a collaboration between Laswell and the ex-member of Scorn, *Subsonic 2* includes a lengthy track from each: Laswell's contribution explores dark percussive ambience, while Bullen uses a dub groove to flavor his ambience. —*John Bush*

Web / 1995 / Subharmonic ✦✦✦
Some of the most abrasive, industrial leaning ambient of either of these composers' careers. Chains rattle, voices whisper menacingly, and dark, dissonant textures and deep bass drones collide on a trio of extended tracks united by the questionably thematic topic of digital communications technology. Difficult but rewarding. —*Sean Cooper*

Sacred System, Chapter 2 / 1997 / Roir ✦✦✦
Laswell continues to explore his dub fetish on *Sacred System: Chapter Two*, teaming with guitarist Nicky Skopelitis, cornetist Graham Haynes, percussionist Bill Buchen and drummer Style Scott to forge a sound also harnessing jazz, Arabic and Indian music. —*Jason Ankeny*

Yusef Lateef (William Evans)

b. Oct. 9, 1920, Chatanooga, TN
Tenor Saxophone, Flute, Oboe / Hard Bop, Post-Bop, New Age
Yusef Lateef has long had an inquisitive spirit and he was never just a bop or hard bop soloist. Lateef, who does not care much for the name "jazz," has consistently created music that has stretched (and even broke through) boundaries. A superior tenor saxophonist with a soulful sound and impressive technique, Lateef by the 1950s was one of the top flutists around. He also developed into the best jazz soloist to date on oboe, an occasional bassoonist and introduced such instruments as the argol (a double clarinet that resembles a bassoon), shanai (a type of oboe) and different types of flutes. Lateef played "world music" before it had a name and his output was much more creative than much of the pop and folk music that passes under that label in the 1990s.

Yusef Lateef grew up in Detroit and began on tenor when he was 17. He played with Lucky Millinder (1946), Hot Lips Page, Roy Eldridge and Dizzy Gillespie's big band (1949-50). He was a fixture on the Detroit jazz scene of the 1950s where he studied flute at Wayne State University. Lateef began recording as a leader in 1955 for Savoy (and later Riverside and Prestige) although he did not move to New York until 1959. By then he already had a strong reputation for his versatility and

for his willingness to utilize "miscellaneous instruments." Lateef played with Charles Mingus in 1960, gigged with Donald Byrd and was well featured with the Cannonball Adderley Sextet (1962-64). As a leader his string of Impulse recordings (1963-66) were among the finest of his career although Lateef's varied Atlantic sessions (1967-76) usually also had some strong moments. He spent some time in the 1980s teaching in Nigeria. His Atlantic records of the late '80s were closer to mood music (or new age) than jazz but in the 1990s (for his own YAL label) Yusef Lateef has recorded a wide variety of music (all originals) including some strong improvised music with the likes of Ricky Ford, Archie Shepp and Von Freeman. —*Scott Yanow*

● **Every Village Has a Song** / May 6, 1949-Mar. 1976 / Rhino/Atlantic ✦✦✦✦
This good two-disc set covers Lateef's tenure at Atlantic as well as featuring formative material from early sessions for Transition, Prestige/Moodsville, Riverside, Impulse, Blue Note and Savoy. The discs show Lateef honing a thick, bluesy, expressive tenor tone in the beginning, evolving into a superior straight jazz player, then expanding his repertoire and choice of instruments and contexts. His flute playing became arguably superior to his tenor, while his solos on oboe, shenai and other previously little-known instruments enabled Lateef to create arresting, fresh and ultimately significant music. While the sampler approach can't fully document his contributions, it's a solid introduction for those unfamiliar with his output. —*Ron Wynn*

Morning / Apr. 5, 1957-Apr. 9, 1957 / Savoy ✦✦✦✦✦
Yusef Lateef's first two sessions as a leader (which were originally released on three LPs) are included in full on this two-LP set. Although he had played with Dizzy Gillespie's big band in the late '40s, Lateef spent a long period in the 1950s studying in Detroit. By the time he emerged with these recordings, he had a fully formed sound not only on tenor but on flute where his style was definitely touched by Eastern music. With a group of fellow Detroiters (trombonist Curtis Fuller, pianist Hugh Lawson, bassist Ernie Farrow, drummer Louis Hayes and Doug Watkins, a fine bassist who here plays percussion) Lateef performs 13 of his originals that range from riffing stomps to modal pieces. —*Scott Yanow*

Gong / Oct. 9, 1957 / Savoy ✦✦✦✦
Quintet of Detroiters, with trumpet by Wilbur Harden. —*Michael G. Nastos*

Other Sounds / Oct. 11, 1957 / Original Jazz Classics ✦✦✦✦
These recordings are among his early African/Middle Eastern fusion efforts, with many exotic instruments. —*Myles Boisen*

The Sounds of Yusef Lateef / Oct. 11, 1957 / Original Jazz Classics ✦✦✦

Cry! / Tender / Oct. 11, 1957+Oct. 16, 1959 / Original Jazz Classics ✦✦✦✦
This well-rounded program, reissued on CD in the OJC program, features Yusef Lateef (tripling on tenor, flute and oboe) heading a quintet also including trumpeter Lonnie Hillyer, pianist Hugh Lawson, bassist Herman Wright and drummer Frank Gant. The music alternates between straightahead pieces and more atmospheric and exotic works. An earlier track ("Ecaps") features Lateef with a different quintet that also includes fluegelhornist Wilbur Harden. —*Scott Yanow*

Yusef at Cranbrook / Apr. 8, 1958 / Argo ✦✦✦

Angel Eyes / Jun. 11, 1959 / Savoy ✦✦✦✦
This double-LP is far superior to most of the piecemeal Yusef Lateef Savoy CD reissues for it has all ten songs that he recorded on one day in 1959. Lateef (on tenor, flute and oboe) is teamed up with the euphonium of Bernard McKinney, pianist Terry Pollard, bassist William Austin and drummer Frank Gant for a typically stimulating and diverse set of music that ranges from the title cut, "Stella by Starlight" and "Poor Butterfly" to "Oboe Blues," "Half Breed" and "Valse Bouk." The unusual blend of Lateef's instruments with McKinney's low brass works quite well and this two-fer (which should be reissued in full on CD) holds one's interest throughout. —*Scott Yanow*

The Three Faces of Yusef Lateef / May 9, 1960 / Original Jazz Classics ✦✦✦✦✦
This is one of Yusef Lateef's most accessible sessions with such famous songs as "Goin' Home," "I'm Just a Lucky So and So" and the ancient standard "Ma, He's Makin' Eyes at Me." Lateef (featured on tenor, flute and oboe) is teamed up with pianist Hugh Lawson, cellist Ron Carter, bassist Herman Wright and drummer Lex Humphries for a set of stimulating music that also includes a few of Lateef's thought-provoking originals. This CD reissue is recommended as are all of his recordings from the era. —*Scott Yanow*

The Centaur and the Phoenix / Oct. 4, 1960+Oct. 6, 1960 / Original Jazz Classics ✦✦✦✦
For this CD reissue of a Riverside date, the great multireedist Yusef Lateef (who switches between tenor, flute, oboe and the argol) is joined on most selections by five other horns (including a bassoonist) and a rhythm section headed by pianist Joe Zawinul. The music has a lot of diversity, from stomps and ballads to Eastern-influenced explorations; two "bonus cuts" from the same date match Lateef with a

four-piece rhythm section that includes pianist Barry Harris and two percussionists. Highlights include "Everyday I Fall in Love," "Summer Song," "Jungle Fantasy" and "The Centaur and the Phoenix." Virtually everything that Yusef Lateef recorded during this era is well worth acquiring. —*Scott Yanow*

Archives of Jazz, Vol. 2 / Oct. 22, 1960 / ALA ✦✦✦
Originally recorded for the Charlie Parker label and reissued on a budget LP, this quintet session matches the great Yusef Lateef (doubling on tenor and flute) with some obscure players (trumpeter Vincent Pitts, pianist John Hormon, bassist Ray McKinley and George Scott or Clifford Jarvis on drums). The performances are generally fairly straightahead with six Lateef originals (including "Outside Blues" and "Trudy's Delight") played along with two of Parker's tunes. The overall results are not essential but comprise a fine outing. —*Scott Yanow*

★ Eastern Sounds / Sep. 5, 1961 / Original Jazz Classics ✦✦✦✦
Although originally issued on the Moodsville label (a subsidiary of Prestige), this classic Yusef Lateef date is not all ballads. Accompanied by pianist Barry Harris, bassist Ernie Farrow and drummer Lex Humphries, Lateef (switching between tenor, oboe and flute) is quite memorable on such pieces as the "Love Theme from *Spartacus*," "Blues for the Orient," "Don't Blame Me" and "The Plum Blossom." He has long been a true original with an active musical curiosity and this set gives listeners a strong example of his work. —*Scott Yanow*

● Into Something / Dec. 29, 1961 / Original Jazz Classics ✦✦✦✦✦
This superior set (which has been reissued on CD) features Yusef Lateef on some straightahead tunes including "When You're Smiling," "I'll Remember April" and "You've Changed." In addition there are some more adventurous and exotic works too, making this a well-rounded program. Lateef is joined by pianist Barry Harris, bassist Herman Wright and drummer Elvin Jones for a particularly memorable performance. —*Scott Yanow*

Jazz Around the World / Dec. 19, 1963-Dec. 20, 1963 / Impulse! ✦✦✦
Yusef Lateef's Impulse recordings of 1963-66 were among the finest of his career. This out-of-print LP, his first effort for Impulse, features Lateef not only on tenor, flute and oboe but bassoon and shanas. Performing with a quintet that also includes trumpeter Richard Williams, pianist Hugh Lawson, bassist Ernie Farrow and drummer Lex Humphries, Lateef plays a variety of folk melodies from other countries along with a few originals and a memorable version (on oboe) of "Trouble in Mind." —*Scott Yanow*

Re-Evaluations: The Impulse Years / Dec. 19, 1963-Jun. 16, 1966 / Impulse! ✦✦✦✦
Multi-instrumentalist Yusef Lateef recorded eight albums for the Impulse label during the 1963-66 period. All are worth acquiring, but as a sampler this two-LP set (which draws its 18 selections from six of the albums) gives one a fine all-around picture of Lateef's many talents. He is heard on his highly appealing tenor, playing flute, jamming "Exactly like You" and an emotional "Trouble in Mind" on oboe, utilizing the exotic shannas and theremin (the latter being an early electronic instrument) and even having a few rare outings on alto. The music ranges from bop and ballads to some avant-garde explorations and mood pieces. —*Scott Yanow*

The Live Session / June 29, 1964 / ABC/Impulse! ✦✦✦✦✦
This out-of-print double LP reissues an earlier album and adds six performances that were previously unreleased. Yusef Lateef (on tenor, flute, oboe, shenai and argol) heads a quintet with trumpeter Richard Williams, pianist Mike Nock, bassist Ernie Farrow and drummer James Black on a set of music ranging from the movie theme "Song of Delilah" and "I Remember Clifford" to a diverse range of original compositions. High points include "Yusef's Mood," "Sister Mamie," "Twelve Tone Blues" and "See See Rider." —*Scott Yanow*

★ Live at Pep's / Jun. 29, 1964 / Impulse! ✦✦✦✦✦
This mid-'60s concert was one of Lateef's finest, as it perfectly displayed his multiple influences and interests. There were hard bop originals, covers of jazz classics like Oscar Pettiford's "Oscarlypso" (a CD bonus track) and Leonard Feather's "Twelve Tone Blues," as well as an unorthodox but effective version of Ma Rainey's "See See Rider." On "Sister Mamie," "Number 7" and drummer James Black's "The Magnolia Triangle," Lateef moved away from strict jazz, although he retained his improvisational flair. Lateef played meaty tenor sax solos, entrancing flute and bamboo flute offerings, and also had impressive stints on oboe, shenai and argol. This was a pivotal date in his career, and those unaware of it will get a treat with this disc. —*Ron Wynn*

1984 / Feb. 24, 1965 / Impulse! ✦✦✦✦
For this live session (which like most of his Impulse recordings has not yet been reissued on CD), Yusef Lateef utilizes several types of flutes along with his oboe and tenor to construct a diverse yet consistently satisfying program. Joined by pianist Mike Nock, bassist Reggie Workman and drummer James Black, Lateef mostly performs originals other than Duke Ellington's obscure "Warm Fire" and

the movie theme "The Greatest Story Ever Told." His use of flutes on the complex "1984" is particularly memorable. —*Scott Yanow*

A Flat, G Flat and C / May 8, 1966-May 9, 1966 / Impulse! ✦✦✦✦
Yusef Lateef (heard on tenor, alto, flute, oboe and the mysterious-sounding theremin) is in explorative and consistently colorful form on this out-of-print LP, one of many Impulse sessions that are long overdue to be reissued on CD. With the assistance of pianist Hugh Lawson, bassist Reggie Workman and drummer Roy Brooks, Lateef performs ten songs (eight are his originals) that are all at least in abstract form related to the blues. Well worth several listens. —*Scott Yanow*

The Golden Flute / Jun. 15, 1966-Jun. 16, 1966 / Impulse! ✦✦✦✦✦
The emphasis is on older tunes and styles on this out-of-print Yusef Lateef Impulse LP. Lateef (switching between tenor, flute and oboe) plays such numbers as "Straighten up and Fly Right," "Ghost of a Chance," "Exactly like You" (on oboe) and "Rosetta" along with some group originals. Lateef has long been a true original and he revitalizes the standards while always swinging and being a bit unpredictable. Well worth searching for, this was Lateef's final Impulse album before switching to Atlantic. —*Scott Yanow*

The Complete Yusef Lateef / May 31, 1967 / Atlantic ✦✦✦✦
Yusef Lateef's first Atlantic album was one of his better ones for the label. Performing on flute, tenor, alto and oboe ("In the Evening"), Lateef is assisted by pianist Hugh Lawson, bassist Cecil McBee and drummer Roy Brooks on a wide-ranging program that ranges from the feel of New Orleans and blues to boogaloo rhythms and the soulful spiritual "Rosalie." This LP is long overdue to be reissued on CD. —*Scott Yanow*

The Blue Yusef Lateef / Apr. 23, 1968-Apr. 24, 1968 / Atlantic ✦✦✦
Yusef Lateef has certainly never been reluctant to take chances throughout his career. On one selection on this CD reissue, he sings/chants in Tagalog, a dialect from the Phillipines. Although that number is unlistenable, Lateef does play some fine tenor and flute during some selections on the date and sometimes utilizes the talents of altoist Sonny Red, trumpeter Blue Mitchell, Buddy Lucas on harmonica, guitarist Kenny Burrell and a good rhythm section. The background vocals of the Sweet Inspirations are a frivolity on two cuts as is a string quartet on "Like It Is," making this album a mixed success. —*Scott Yanow*

Yusef Lateef's Detroit / May 19, 1969-May 20, 1969 / Atlantic ✦✦
The Diverse Yusef Lateef/Suite 16 / Jan. 15, 1970-Nov. 2, 1970 / Rhino ✦✦✦✦
For this single CD Rhino combined together two complete LPs from Yusef Lateef's period on Atlantic. Although there are some period trappings and the use of a vocal group on a few selections, the music sounds fairly fresh and its diversity (ranging from exotic vamps to the adventurous seven-movement "Symphonic Blues Suite") is a major strength. Earl Klugh's solo guitar rendition of "Michelle" is pleasant if out of place and there are some forgettable tracks, but Lateef's willingness to take chances, his highly individual sound on his instruments (tenor, flute, oboe and a rare outing on soprano) and the impressive amount of variety make this a recommended set. —*Scott Yanow*

Part of the Search / Sep. 1, 1971-Dec. 26, 1973 / Rhino/Atlantic ✦✦✦✦
Yusef Lateef's Atlantic albums tended to be erratic affairs with plenty of chances taken and the overall results being a mixed success. This set (reissued on CD) is one of his better efforts from the era. Lateef, doubling on tenor and alto this time, is backed not only by his trio but a big band, string quartet, three background vocalists and a variety of electric keyboardists and guitarists. There are enough good tracks (particularly "Lunceford Prance," "Rockhouse" and "I'm Gettin' Sentimental over You") to make this release worth checking out. —*Scott Yanow*

The Gentle Giant / Jul. 5, 1974-Jul. 6, 1974 / Atlantic ✦✦✦
Yusef Lateef's Atlantic recordings on a whole are much more erratic than his earlier Riverside and Impulse dates. This out-of-print LP has its moments of interest. There is less straightahead swinging than had been heard previously and, along with some exotic pieces, much of this music falls into the R&B field. Lateef, heard on flutes, oboe and tenor, contributes some strong solos but was a nine-minute version of "Hey Jude" really necessary? —*Scott Yanow*

Ten Years Hence / 1975 / Atlantic ✦✦✦✦✦
This double LP was one of Yusef Lateef's last significant recordings. Soon he would take a long hiatus, live in Africa and return with some new age-oriented records. But on this date, a quartet outing with pianist Kenny Barron, bassist Bob Cunningham and drummer Albert "Tootie" Heath, Lateef (on tenor, flute, oboe, sealhorns, shanie, African thumb piano and percussion) is heard in prime form. One song has a string section, another adds horns and background vocals but the emphasis is on the leader, who gets to stretch out with three pieces being over 15 minutes; Lateef really digs into the date's lone standard on "But Beautiful." Worth searching for. —*Scott Yanow*

Doctor Is In & Out / Mar. 1, 1976 / Atlantic ✦✦

Autophysiopsychic / 1977 / CTI ✦✦✦

Autophysiopsychic is probably the single album that many Yusef Lateef fans either love or hate the most. Along with guest soloist Art Farmer on fluegelhorn, guitarist Eric Gale, keyboardist Cliff Carter, drummer Jim Madison and bassist Gary King (except for "Sister Mamie," which features mainstream Steve Gadd and Alex Blake respectively), "Teefski" romps through five fat slices of original funk that have far more in common with the sounds of *Chocolate City* than with the bop sounds of 52nd Street. *Autophysiopsychic* is awash in the soft soul-funk-jazz sound typical of Creed Taylor's (CTI) productions in the 1970s. And even though the backing instrumentation and rhythms are not much more than mainstream R&B and funk shot through with a few oddities, Farmer and Lateef (on tenor and soprano saxes, flute and shanai) lay down solos that bite and swing so momentously that they provide musical merit to this entire project. Each seems to continually prod the other—Lateef more robust and biting, Farmer more fluid and soft—up to the next level. Their turns in "Robot Man" and "Look on Your Right Side" are particularly memorable, especially Farmer's closing solo in "Right Side," which seems to blend New Orleans swing with nursery-rhyme sing-song simplicity. Not the most typical album in Lateef's wide-ranging catalog, but certainly the most fun. —*Chris Slawecki*

In Nigeria / Jul. 19, 1983 / Landmark ✦✦✦

Yusef Lateef had been a musical giant for three decades when this album came out, his first recording in several years. Unfortunately the emphasis here is on setting introspective moods and there is little development in the improvisations. Lateef (on tenor, flutes and vocals) is joined by five African percussionists and a variety of vocalists (including himself) and, despite good intentions, this session is quite forgettable. —*Scott Yanow*

Yusef Lateef's Little Symphony / Jun. 1987 / Atlantic ✦✦

Concerto for Yusef Lateef / 1986 / Atlantic ✦✦

Although Yusef Lateef hates musical categorization, this Atlantic set was accurately released as part of Atlantic's *New Age* series. Lateef (on tenor, soprano, flutes, koto and both acoustic and electric percussion) is joined by two bassists, one guitar, a classical clarinetist and two exotic percussionists to create what is essentially mood music. The 11-movement work simply does not go anywhere and fits securely in the one-mood new age genre. —*Scott Yanow*

Nocturnes / Feb. 1989 / Atlantic ✦✦

Meditations / Feb. 1990 / Atlantic ✦✦

Tenors of Yusef Lateef & Von Freeman / Jul. 1992 / YAL ✦✦✦✦

Yusef Lateef Plays Ballads / 1993 / YAL ✦✦✦

Yusef Lateef Tenors Featuring Rene Mclean / May 1993 / YAL ✦✦✦✦

Woodwinds / Jul. 1993 / YAL ✦✦✦

Metamorphosis / Dec. 1993 / YAL ✦✦

Claiming Open Spaces / 1994 / YAL ✦✦

Tenors of Yusef Lateef & Ricky Ford / 1994 / YAL ✦✦✦✦✦

Veteran tenors Yusef Lateef and Ricky Ford team up for this frequently explosive set. Their seven originals all pay tribute to various tenormen (James Moody, Stanley Turrentine, Sonny Rollins, Jimmy Heath, Wayne Shorter, Joe Henderson and Lateef himself) and the two lead voices, while not copying their inspirations, occasionally insert some of their trademark phrases. Electric bassist Avery Sharpe and drummer Kamal Sabir offer fairly accessible and often-funky backings, but one's main focus is on the intense playing of the two great tenors, who battle it out in fiery fashion. —*Scott Yanow*

Cantata / May 1994 / YAL ✦✦

Suite Life / Dec. 1994 / YAL ✦✦

Andy La Verne

b. Dec. 4, 1947, New York, NY
Piano, Keyboards / Post-Bop

A fine keyboardist who has ranged in styles from Bill Evans to Chick Corea and fusion, Andy La Verne has managed to avoid predictability throughout his career. He began studying as a classical piano student at Juilliard when he was eight. After discovering jazz, La Verne had some important lessons from Bill Evans. He toured with Woody Herman's big band (1973-75), played with John Abercrombie and Miroslav Vitous, and was with Stan Getz's group during 1977-80, often playing electric piano. In the 1980s he performed with the Brubeck-La Verne Trio (which also featured Chris and Dan Brubeck), recorded a tribute to Chick Corea for DMP and became a busy jazz educator. In the 1990s La Verne has concentrated on acoustic piano, recording a solo concert at Maybeck Recital Hall. Through the years Andy La Verne has recorded as a leader for Storyville (1977), Jazzline, Steeple Chase, DMP, Triloka, Concord and some smaller labels. —*Scott Yanow*

Plays the Music of Chick Corea / 1981-1986 / Jazzline ✦✦✦✦

Assisted by John Abercrombie (g), Danny Gottlieb (d), Mark Egan (b), and Marc Johnson (b), pianist La Verne pays tribute to keyboardist/composer Chick Corea. A beautifully executed album, one track features La Verne and Corea playing piano together. —*Paul Kohler*

Liquid Silver / Oct. 1984-Nov. 3, 1984 / DMP ✦✦✦✦

Jazz Piano Lineage / 1988 / DMP ✦✦✦✦✦

On this very interesting set, Andy La Verne performs solo versions of tunes by some of his favorite pianists: Thelonious Monk, Dave Brubeck ("In Your Own Sweet Way"), Richie Beirach, Herbie Hancock, McCoy Tyner ("Passion Dance"), Keith Jarrett, and two apiece by Bill Evans and Chick Corea. In addition, La Verne performs an original and an adaptation of a Debussy melody. Although quite respectful of the themes and the other pianists' styles, La Verne's own musical personality comes through, and his interpretations are full of fresh ideas. Recommended. —*Scott Yanow*

Frozen Music / Apr. 1989 / Steeple Chase ✦✦✦✦

This album features Rick Margitza (ts,ss), Marc Johnson (b), Danny Gottlieb(d). With excellent compositions and playing throughout, it's a must! —*Paul Kohler*

Fountainhead / Jun. 1989 / Steeple Chase ✦✦✦✦

Severe Clear / 1990 / Steeple Chase ✦✦✦✦

Augmented by trumpeter Tim Hagans, this recording finds La Verne in top gear playing some of the most incredible chord voicings. Rick Margitza (ts) is also prominently featured. —*Paul Kohler*

Standard Eyes / Oct. 1990 / Steeple Chase ✦✦✦✦

Pleasure Seekers / Jan. 10, 1991-Jan. 12, 1991 / Triloka ✦✦✦✦

On this CD, keyboardist Andy La Verne performs eight of his own compositions, one song co-written with guitarist Chuck Loeb, and Bud Powell's "Parisian Thoroughfare." La Verne's arrangements for the quartet (which also includes Bob Sheppard on tenor and various reeds, bassist John Patitucci and drummer Dave Weckl) use light funky rhythms and put an emphasis on melodic improvising. With the exception of "Chestnuts" (based on "All the Things You Are"), the chord changes are all new. Somehow the quartet (which had only first come together just a few days earlier) sounds like a regularly working band. Overall, this is a pleasing session of accessible yet reasonably explorative jazz. —*Scott Yanow*

Buy One Get One Free / Apr. 1992 / Steeple Chase ✦✦✦

Universal Mind / 1993 / Steeple Chase ✦✦✦✦

Double Standard / Jan. 11, 1993-Jan. 12, 1993 / Triloka ✦✦✦

Pianist Andy La Verne's idea behind this CD was to play six standards and then six "originals" based on the older tunes but reharmonized and given new melodies. Unfortunately the programming makes little sense, with only one of the newer songs actually following its original source and, because La Verne also reharmonizes the standards, there is less of a contrast between the two pairs of songs than one might expect. The music (quartet performances with Billy Drewes on tenor and soprano, bassist Steve LaSpina and drummer Greg Hutchinson) is generally satisfying with the influence of Bill Evans (and to a lesser extent Chick Corea) felt in the piano solos while Drewes comes across as a light-toned Coltranite. This is overall a good recording that falls short of being special. —*Scott Yanow*

In the Mood for a Classic / Feb. 8, 1993 / Steeple Chase ✦✦✦

● **Live at Maybeck Recital Hall, Vol. 28 (Andy La Verne at Maybeck)** / Apr. 1993 / Concord Jazz ✦✦✦✦✦

The Maybeck Recital Hall series has given many post-bop pianists a rare opportunity to record solo. Andy La Verne, who is normally heard with trios, sounds surprisingly comfortable in the solo setting. His performances on this date are rhapsodic and occasionally wandering as he performs nine standards, Chick Corea's "Impressions for Piano" and his own "Stan Getz in Chappaqua." La Verne reharmonizes the better-known songs and, by often adding vamps, he makes some of the music dark and faintly disturbing; even "Melancholy Baby" and "When You Wish Upon a Star." This is an interesting set of creative jazz. —*Scott Yanow*

Glass Ceiling / Oct. 1993 / Steeple Chase ✦✦✦✦

Spirit of '76 / May 20, 1994 / Four Star ✦✦✦

Serenade to Silver / Jun. 18, 1994 / Steeple Chase ✦✦✦

Time Well Spent / Dec. 15, 1994-Dec. 16, 1994 / Concord Jazz ✦✦✦✦✦

● **Tadd's Delight** / May 7, 1995 / Steeple Chase ✦✦✦✦✦

The music of the late Tadd Dameron remains timeless in the hands of a gifted pianist like Andy La Verne. He integrates lush chords with lively runs into "Good Bait." The pianist makes "Hot House" sound slightly haunting with his sinister introduction. The lyrical, spacious interpretation of "On a Misty Night" is another gem. La Verne's tribute to Dameron, "Tadley Ewing," successfully complements rather than copies the composer's style. —*Ken Dryden*

Where We Were / 1996 / Double-Time ◆◆◆◆

Azar Lawrence

b. Nov. 3, 1953, Los Angeles, CA

Tenor Saxophone , Soprano Saxophone / Post-Bop

Azar Lawrence showed a great deal of potential during his period with McCoy Tyner's Quartet (1973-77) but has not made that strong an impression since. A fine tenor and soprano saxophonist (which he took up in 1970 and 1972 after a few years playing alto), Lawrence performed with Horace Tapscott in Los Angeles. He toured Europe with Clark Terry in 1970 and in 1973 joined Elvin Jones' band. After three months Lawrence decided to switch to Tyner's group and he recorded several impressive albums (on Milestone) while a sideman with the great pianist. Azar Lawrence also recorded three albums as a leader for Prestige during 1974-76 (the last one rather commercial) but has not had further opportunities to head sessions and has maintained a low profile ever since. —*Scott Yanow*

● **Bridge into the New Age** / May 1974+Sep. 1974 / Prestige ◆◆◆◆

Summer Solstice / Mar. 29, 1975+May 1, 1975 / Prestige ◆◆◆

People Moving / Mar. 1976 / Prestige ◆◆

Elliot Lawrence (Elliott Lawrence Broza)

b. Feb. 14, 1925, Philadelphia, PA

Piano, Leader / Swing, Cool

If he had been born ten years earlier, Elliot Lawrence might have been one of the more significant bandleaders of the swing era. As it worked out he was a bit of a prodigy, leading a strong dance band when he was only 20, but by then (1945) the swing era was ending. Lawrence did record steadily as a leader during 1946-60 (for Columbia, Decca, King, Fantasy, VIK and Sesac), sometimes using Gerry Mulligan arrangements, but he mostly worked in the studios. After 1960 Lawrence stopped recording jazz altogether to compose, arrange and conduct for television, films and the theatre. Few of his jazz-oriented sessions are currently available but his hard-to-find music is worth exploring. —*Scott Yanow*

The Uncollected Elliot Lawrence & His Orchestra (1946) / 1946 / Hindsight ◆◆◆◆

Quite young at the time (21), pianist Elliot Lawrence had a first-rate big band in 1946. This set of radio transcriptions (released on LP but not yet on CD) finds Lawrence heading a forward-looking late-period swing band that emphasizes danceable versions of standards. Three of the dozen arrangements are by occasional member Gerry Mulligan, there is solo space for trumpeter Alec Fila and tenorman Frank Lewis, Rosalind Patton takes four vocals and the charts sometimes utilize oboe, bassoon and French horn. Nothing all that startling occurs but there is a showcase for the somewhat forgotten orchestra. —*Scott Yanow*

One Night Stand with Elliot Lawrence / Dec. 9, 1947 / Joyce ◆◆◆

The obscure Elliot Lawrence Orchestra is featured on this radio broadcast from the Hollywood Palladium. Although a personnel listing is given (the no-name band used three trumpets, three trombones, five saxes, guitar, bass, drums and the leader's piano plus French horn and oboe), the actual soloists are not listed; Alec Fila is known to have taken the trumpet solos. With Rosalind Patton and/or Jack Hunter having vocals on five of the nine songs (Lawrence also briefly plays his two themes), not all of the music is jazz. "Bop-Pop" (which finds Lawrence's ensemble exploring bebop) is a highlight. This hard-to-find LP should interest swing collectors but it is not essential. —*Scott Yanow*

● **Elliot Lawrence Band Plays Gerry Mulligan Arrangements** / Mar. 4, 1955-Jul. 5, 1955 / Original Jazz Classics ◆◆◆◆

Elliot Lawrence, who led a swing-oriented big band after the swing era had already passed its prime, primarily worked in the studios in the 1950s. This reissue from the Original Jazz Classics series (which has not yet surfaced on CD) was one of Lawrence's few jazz dates of the decade. Utilizing a dozen Gerry Mulligan charts (seven of the songs were also composed by Mulligan) and an all-star crew of young modernists (including trumpeter Nick Travis, trombonist Eddie Bert, altoist Hal McKusick and Al Cohn on tenor), the results are quite pleasing. Although Mulligan himself does not play, his presence is very much felt on songs such as "The Rocker," "Bweebida Bwobbida," "Strike Up the Band" and "Apple Core." Other highlights include tributes to Zoot Sims ("The Swinging Door") and Lester Young ("Mr. President"). —*Scott Yanow*

Music of Elliot Lawrence / 1956-1957 / Mobile Fidelity ◆◆◆

This Audiophile CD release comprises 22 brief performances (generally two to two-and-a-half minutes apiece) that were originally recorded as radio transcriptions (rather than commercial records). Altoist Gene Quill and tenorman Al Cohn (one of the main arrangers) are the main soloists on the big-band selections while Lawrence (on piano) is also featured in a sextet with guitarist Mary Osborne and Tyree Glenn (who doubles on trombone and vibes). The music ranges from mid-

dle-of-the-road instrumental pop and swing to hints of bop and Dixieland. Although not a major release, this CD does have enjoyable performances and is one of the few Elliot Lawrence recordings currently available. —*Scott Yanow*

Hubert Laws

b. Nov. 10, 1939, Houston, TX

Flute, Piccolo / Hard Bop, Crossover Jazz, Classical, Instrumental Pop

A talented flutist whose musical interest was never exclusively straightahead jazz, Hubert Laws exceeded Herbie Mann in popularity in the 1970s when he recorded for CTI. He was a member of the early Jazz Crusaders in Texas (1954-60) and he also played classical music during those years. In the 1960s Laws made his first recordings as a leader (Atlantic dates from 1964-66) and gigged with Mongo Santamaria, Benny Golson, Jim Hall, James Moody and Clark Terry among many others. His CTI recordings from the first half of the 1970s made Laws famous and were a high point, particularly compared to his generally wretched Columbia dates from the late '70s. He was less active in the 1980s but has come back with a pair of fine Music Masters sessions in the 1990s. Hubert Laws has the ability to play anything well but he does not always seem to have the desire to perform creative jazz. —*Scott Yanow*

The Laws of Jazz / Apr. 2, 1964+Apr. 22, 1964 / Atlantic ◆◆◆◆

Flutist Hubert Laws began his solo career with two little-known LPs for Atlantic, of which this was the first. Joined by pianist Armando Corea (before he became known as Chick), bassist Richard Davis and either Jimmy Cobb or Bobby Thomas on drums, Laws is in fine form during what is essentially a straightahead jazz set. Some of the music is a little funky, but throughout, Laws (who plays piccolo on two of the seven numbers) is in excellent form. Highlights include "Miss Thing," "Bessie's Blues" and his own "Bimbe Blue."—*Scott Yanow*

☆ **Afro Classic** / Dec. 1970 / CTI ◆◆◆◆◆

Hubert Laws' second effort for CTI (following the lesser-known *Crying Song*) made him into a major star in the jazz world. Performing two melodies by Bach, one by Mozart, James Taylor's "Fire and Rain," and the theme from *Love Story*, the flutist plays quite beautifully throughout this classic outing. Don Sebesky's arrangements perfectly frame Laws' flute, and the backup group (an enlarged rhythm section plus bassoonist Fred Alston, Jr.) includes guitarist Gene Bertoncini, vibraphonist Dave Friedman and keyboardist Bob James. —*Scott Yanow*

Crying Song / 1970 / CTI ◆◆◆

The Best of Hubert Laws / 1970-1975 / Columbia ◆◆◆

Some of Hubert Laws' more commercial recordings left much to be desired, but at his best, he's been a highly imaginative soloist who can play jazz, classical and R&B equally well. A fine overview of his CTI efforts of the early to mid-'70s, *The Best of Hubert Laws* is an eclectic and unpredictable CD that finds him offering adventurous interpretations of everything from John Coltrane's "Moment's Notice" to classical pieces by Stravinsky ("The Rite of Spring") and Bach ("Allegro from Concerto No. 3 in D"). While an NAC/smooth jazz artist would play a mindless, note-for-note cover of Maria Muldaur's "Midnight at the Oasis," the flutist insightfully transforms the 1974 pop hit into gritty jazz-funk. Electric keyboardist Bob James performs some excellent solos, which expose and underscore the vacuous and shallow nature of his subsequent work. —*Alex Henderson*

The Rite of Spring / Jun. 1971 / CTI ◆◆◆◆◆

This popular record was considered a bit controversial when it was released in 1972. Don Sebesky's adaptations of classical themes by Debussy, Bach, Faure and Stravinsky (particularly the title cut) were thought of as sacrilegious by some, due to their being placed in funky settings, but the recording was a bit of a hit. One cannot fault flutist Hubert Laws' playing (his CTI years were the most significant of his career), and his rendition of "Pavane" in particular is memorable. Laws is joined by guitarist Gene Bertonicini, vibraphonist Dave Friedman, keyboardist Bob James, bassist Ron Carter, drummer Jack DeJohnette, percussionist Airto, and Wally Kane on bassoon. —*Scott Yanow*

Morning Star / Sep. 1972-Oct. 1972 / CTI ◆◆◆◆

Flutist Hubert Laws is joined by a large string orchestra on this set, which was arranged and conducted by Don Sebesky. Keyboardist Bob James is in the supporting cast, and some unnecessary background vocalists (including Debra and Eloise Laws) are employed on some of the numbers, but the focus is mostly on Laws' brilliant and appealing flute. Highlights include "Let Her Go," "Where Is the Love" and, particularly, "Amazing Grace." The results are pleasing, if not quite essential. —*Scott Yanow*

Carnegie Hall / Jan. 12, 1973 / CTI ◆◆◆◆

This interesting live set features flutist Hubert Laws at the height of his powers and fame. Accompanied by keyboardist Bob James, guitarist Gene Bertonicini, vibraphonist Dave Friedman, bassist Ron Carter, either Freddie Waits or Billy Cobham on drums, and bassoonist Dave Miller, Laws performs a medley of Chick

Corea's "Windows" and James Taylor's "Fire and Rain" (a song he virtually owned), plus a 20-minute version of Bach's "Passacaglia in C Minor." Although the latter two pieces had been recorded previously by Laws, these stretched-out versions are also worth acquiring. Unfortunately, most of Hubert Laws' valuable CTI recordings are not yet out on CD. —*Scott Yanow*

★ **In the Beginning** / Feb. 1974 / CTI ✦✦✦✦

This double LP features flutist Hubert Laws at his finest. The music ranges from classical-oriented pieces to straightahead jazz with touches of '70s funk included in the mix. The supporting cast includes keyboardist Bob James on most tracks, guitarist Gene Bertoncini, bassist Ron Carter, drummer Steve Gadd, three strings and Hubert's brother Ronnie on tenor (his solo on John Coltrane's "Moment's Notice" is arguably Ronnie's best ever on record). Whether it be works by Satie or Sonny Rollins, this recording is one of the most rewarding of Hubert Laws' career. —*Scott Yanow*

Chicago Theme / Feb. 1975-Apr. 1975 / CTI ✦✦✦

Hubert Laws made his finest recordings playing arrangements by Don Sebesky. Unfortunately, starting with this project, Bob James began to take over the writing chores, and the flutist's recordings became much more commercial. Rather than performing with a small group, as he did on his best sessions, Laws is joined by strings and funky rhythm sections playing now-dated commercial grooves. The six selections (which include James' forgettable "Chicago Theme," "Midnight at the Oasis" and Dvorak's "Going Home") are listenable, but nothing special. The only reason to acquire this out-of-print LP is for Laws' still-superb flute playing. —*Scott Yanow*

The San Francisco Concert / Oct. 4, 1975 / CTI ✦✦✦

This live set finds flutist Hubert Laws both looking backwards towards his best CTI recordings and ahead to his generally abysmal output for Columbia. With Bob James doing the arrangements, the music is more overtly commercial than Don Sebesky's earlier work. The adaptations of themes by Bizet and Rimsky-Korsakoff are worthwhile, and Laws does a fine job on the catchy "Feel like Making Love"; the other selection is a forgettable tune by Dave Grusin. Backed by a huge string orchestra, Laws plays quite well, uplifting the material and doing what he can with the charts. This was his final CTI release. —*Scott Yanow*

Romeo and Juliet / 1976 / Columbia ✦✦

Light jazz (with strings, keyboards, voices, etc.) and a classical/Eastern flavor. —*Michael Erlewine*

Land of Passion / 1978 / Columbia ✦✦

How to Beat the High Cost of Living / 1980 / Columbia ✦✦✦

After a series of low-quality commercial releases for Columbia, Hubert Laws came up with this surprisingly worthwhile album. Featured along with acoustic guitarist Earl Klugh, the flutist performed Patrick Williams' music for the film *How to Beat the High Cost of Living*, which starred Susan Saint James, Jane Curtin and Jessica Lange. While the light comedy has been long forgotten and none of these ten selections caught on, the music is largely straightahead, with some strong melodies, and finds Laws and Klugh playing very well. They are backed by a six-piece rhythm section including keyboardist Michael Lang and both Tim May and Mitch Holder on guitars. This out-of-print LP (which probably will not get reissued on CD anytime soon) is well worth acquiring. —*Scott Yanow*

Flute By-Laws / Aug. 25, 1965-Feb . 22, 1966 / Atlantic ✦✦✦✦

The second of two early Hubert Laws Atlantic LPs (not yet reissued on CD) features the flutist with a brass section, a rhythm section that includes pianist Chick Corea, and several percussionists. The music crosses the boundaries between Latin jazz, pop and R&B and consists of six Hubert Laws compositions (none of which stayed in his repertoire too long) and an obscurity. Not overly memorable music, but reasonably pleasing. Laws would next emerge as a leader on records on CTI in late 1970. —*Scott Yanow*

My Time Will Come / 1990-1992 / Music Masters ✦✦

This is a streaky affair, Hubert Laws' first recording as a leader in quite a few years. The great flutist has a reunion with Don Sebesky on a version of "Malaguena" that becomes an imitation of Chick Corea's "Spain," a few of the selections are forgettable funk and "Moonlight Sonata" is ruined by an unbearable rhythm. However, there are some fine performances that feature excellent soloing by Laws and pianist John Beasley. Still, only Hubert Laws' most loyal fans will want this release. —*Scott Yanow*

Storm Then the Calm / 1994 / Music Masters ✦✦✦✦

Ronnie Laws (Ronald Laws)

b. Oct. 3, 1950, Houston, TX
Tenor Saxophone, Soprano Saxophone / Instrumental Pop
The younger brother of Hubert Laws, Ronnie Laws has a nice soulful sound on tenor but has never seriously pursued playing jazz. Throughout his career, which includes early-'70s gigs with Quincy Jones, his brother, Ramsey Lewis, & Earth, Wind and Fire, Laws has been essentially an R&B player. He has led his own albums since 1975 but recorded very little of interest to the jazz world although he is often listed on *Billboard*'s nonsensical "contemporary jazz" chart. —*Scott Yanow*

Pressure Sensitive / Mar. 1975-Apr. 1975 / Blue Note ✦✦

Ronnie Laws has always been an R&B-oriented saxophonist miscast in the jazz world, starting with his early association with the rapidly declining Blue Note label. His debut album (reissued on CD) has a couple of decent melodies (the opening "Always There" is the most memorable), some soulful tenor and soprano playing by the leader in a style heavily influenced by Grover Washington, Jr., and vocals on only one of the eight selections; Laws' attempts to make it as a singer were still in the future. However, this obviously commercial effort (every song fades out before it hits the five-minute mark) can only be recommended in comparison to Ronnie Laws' later more inferior recordings. —*Scott Yanow*

Mirror Town / 1986 / Columbia ✦✦

An R&B/funk vehicle. —*Ron Wynn*

All Day Rhythm / 1987 / Columbia ✦✦✦✦

More for the urban contemporary muzak market. —*Ron Wynn*

In the Groove / 1975-1984 / CEMA ✦✦

In the Groove is a solid, budget-priced sampler that contains nine of Ronnie Laws' biggest crossover hits, including "Stay Awake," "City Girl,' "Just Love," "Fever" and "All the Time." It's not a definitive overview, but it's a good collection for casual fans. —*Stephen Thomas Erlewine*

Fever / Jan. 19, 1976-Mar. 1976 / Blue Note ✦✦✦

True Spirit / 1989 / Par ✦✦

Deep Soul / 1992 / Par ✦✦✦✦

Few of saxophonist Ronnie Laws' recordings are of much interest to jazz fans and, as with his previous sessions, this Par CD is essentially R&Bish dance music. However this time around vocalists are only utilized on two tracks, the funky rhythms are generally surprisingly subtle and on a few occasions Laws actually wanders a bit from the melody. The results are still essentially fluff but for Ronnie Laws about as good as it gets. —*Scott Yanow*

Identity / 1991 / Dar ✦✦

Ronnie Laws showed considerable promise on early efforts like *Pressure Sensitive* and *Fever*, but sadly, all of the tenor and soprano saxman's albums have been motivated by commercial considerations rather than artistic ones. An especially glaring example is *Identity*, a contrived, radio-oriented R&B-pop effort that wastes his talents as an improviser. There are a few bright spots, including the hip-hop-ish "Street Knowledge" and the angular, Miles Davis-influenced "Palisades," but most of the CD consists of mindless, overproduced "smooth jazz." Especially disappointing is "If You Don't Know Me by Now"—Laws could have really soared and made a statement on this Harold Melvin & the Blue Notes classic, but instead, offers a dreadfully bland note-for-note cover. —*Alex Henderson*

Tribute to Legendary Eddie Harris / Oct. 28, 1996-Nov. 15, 1996 / Blue Note ✦✦✦✦

Ronnie Laws' first jazz record (what took so long?) features him performing eight songs associated with the late, great saxophonist Eddie Harris. In some spots Laws (whose other recordings are in the worlds of funk and pop) closely copies his early inspiration and predictably comes out in second place, but when he tries to sound like himself, he comes across as a potentially fine improviser. Laws (who doubles on tenor and soprano) is joined by a rhythm section including pianist Vernell Brown, Jr.; trumpeter Oscar Brashear makes two welcome appearances (particularly on "Cold Duck Time"). Although not essential, this CD (which is highlighted by lightly funky versions of "Freedom Jazz Dance," "Hip Hoppin'" and "Compared to What") is the first Ronnie Laws release recommended for jazz listeners. —*Scott Yanow*

Hugh Lawson (Richard Hugh Jerome Lawson)

b. Mar. 12, 1935, Detroit, MI, d. Mar. 17, 1997, New York, NY
Piano / Hard Bop
One of many talented Detroit pianists of the 1950s (although one of the lesser-known players), Hugh Lawson and his Bud Powell-inspired and piano first gained recognition for his work with Yusef Lateef during the late '50s. He recorded with Harry "Sweets" Edison (1962), Roy Brooks and Lateef on several occasions in the 1960s. In 1972 he was with the Piano Choir (a group with seven pianists!). Lawson

went on tours with Charles Mingus in 1975 and 1977 and made recordings with Charlie Rouse (1977), George Adams and as a leader for Storyville and Soul Note. —*Scott Yanow*

Prime Time / Oct. 20, 1977 / Storyville ✦✦✦✦✦
Pianist Hugh Lawson was 42 when he had his first opportunity to record as a leader. One of the many great pianists who emigrated from Detroit, Lawson spent most of his career overshadowed, but he was an excellent hard bop-based player. Teamed with bassist Bob Cranshaw (heard on acoustic for a change) and drummer Ben Riley, Lawson performs two originals, a few obscurities, Clifford Jordan's "The Highest Mountain," Charles Mingus' "Duke Ellington's Sound of Love," "I Fall in Love Too Easily" and a brief rendition of Bud Powell's "I'll Keep Loving You." A fine straightahead effort. —*Scott Yanow*

● **Colour** / Jan. 1983 / Soul Note ✦✦✦✦
This 1997 CD reissue brings back one of pianist Hugh Lawson's rare opportunities to lead a session of his own. With the assistance of bassist Calvin Hill and drummer Louis Hayes, Lawson performs five of his catchy hard bop-oriented originals (including "Creepy Chicken" and "The Beast from BaliBali"), "If," and a jazz version of "Pictures at an Exhibition." The music is straightahead, but not without its subtle surprises. One of Lawson's finest sets as a leader and easily recommended. —*Scott Yanow*

Janet Lawson

b. Nov. 13, 1940, Baltimore, MD
Vocals / Post-Bop
A brilliant singer who spent a long period off the scene, Janet Lawson is long overdue for much greater recognition. She performed on the radio and regional television as a child. In 1960 she moved to New York where she worked with Art Farmer, Ron Carter, Duke Pearson, Chick Corea and others during the decade. Lawson appeared regularly on Steve Allen's television show (1968-69), worked in theater and in 1976 formed a quintet. She recorded two superb albums in 1980 and 1983 for Inner City and Omnisound. Lawson (an inventive and expressive scat singer with a very wide range) also appeared on records by Eddie Jefferson (1977) and David Lahm (1982). Her father's long-term illness resulted in her leaving music for much of the second half of the 1980s, but in recent years Janet Lawson has worked as a jazz educator and been gigging on the East Coast. —*Scott Yanow*

● **The Janet Lawson Quintet** / Mar. 28, 1980 / Inner City ✦✦✦✦✦
One of the finest jazz singers to emerge in the late '70s, Janet Lawson has surprisingly only led two record sessions to date. A brilliant scatter and a consistently strong improviser, Lawson is joined on this 1980 LP by baritonist Roger Rosenberg (who also plays soprano and flute), pianist Bill O'Connell, bassist Ratzo Harris and drummer Jimmy Madison. The highly appealing vocalist really digs into the six tunes, which include "Jitterbug Waltz," Blossom Dearie's "Sunday Afternoon," "'Round Midnight" and "So High." Lawson should be persuaded to record again. —*Scott Yanow*

Dreams Can Be / May 1983 / Omnisound ✦✦✦✦✦
A wonderful singer who is among the most inventive, Janet Lawson is heard in prime form on her second recording. Joined by her regular group of the time (Roger Rosenberg on baritone, soprano and flute, pianist Bill O'Connell, bassist Ratzo Harris and drummer Jimmy Madison), Lawson stretches out on passionate and unpredictable versions of such tunes as her own "Dreams Can Be," "Hot House," Charles Mingus' "Better Get It in Your Soul" and "Out of This World." Over a dozen years later, Janet Lawson's third record is long overdue. —*Scott Yanow*

Yank Lawson (John Rhea Lawson)

b. May 3, 1911, Trenton, MO, **d.** Feb. 18, 1995
Trumpet / Dixieland, Swing
An exciting Dixieland trumpeter with an appealing tone and strong melodic ideas, Yank Lawson was a popular attraction on the Dixieland scene for decades. He was with Ben Pollack's band during 1933-35 and when it broke up he was one of the many sidemen who became founding members of the Bob Crosby Orchestra. Lawson was featured on many records both with the big band and Bob Crosby's Bobcats during 1935-38. He was with Tommy Dorsey during 1938-39 and had plenty of solo space with Dorsey's Clambake Seven. After a period back with Crosby (1941-42) and with Benny Goodman (1942), Lawson became a studio musician and started leading his own Dixieland sessions. He recorded extensively with Bob Haggart in the Lawson-Haggart band during the 1950s, had reunions with Crosby, played the musical part of King Oliver on Louis Armstrong's *A Musical Autobiography* and had sessions with Eddie Condon, playing at Condon's club regularly during 1964-66. In 1968 he and Haggart put together the World's Greatest Jazz Band, an all-star Dixieland group that was together for ten years. He continued playing with Haggart and other top Dixieland players at festivals and jazz

parties up until his death at age 83. Yank Lawson recorded as a leader through the years for Bob Thiele's various labels (including Signature), Decca, Everest, ABC-Paramount, Project 3, Atlantic, World Jazz Records, Audiophile and Jazzology. —*Scott Yanow*

Louis' Hot 5s and 7s / Jun. 27, 1956 / Decca ✦✦✦✦
Fifteen years before they co-led the World's Greatest Jazz Band, trumpeter Yank Lawson and bassist Bob Haggart led the Lawson-Haggart Jazz Band for a series of recordings. This long-out-of-print LP finds the septet (which also includes trombonist Lou McGarity, clarinetist Bill Stegmeyer, pianist Lou Stein, guitarist George Barnes and drummer Cliff Leeman) playing a dozen numbers originally recorded by Louis Armstrong's classic Hot Five and Seven from 1925-27. While their renditions sometimes hint at the earlier records (even if Barnes' guitar is out of place), the solos are quite fresh and different. Lawson in particular does a fine job on such numbers as "Cornet Chop Suey," "Potato Head Blues" and "Weary Blues." Hopefully someday MCA will get around to digging into their vaults and will unearth this enjoyable effort. —*Scott Yanow*

The Best of Broadway Dixieland Style / 1959 / Signature ✦✦✦✦
During an era when there were many "Jazz Plays Broadway" albums, trumpeter Yank Lawson decided to perform a dozen songs from a variety of musicals rather than just sticking to one score. A few of the numbers on this set are from decades before, including "Makin' Whoopee," "Stormy Weather" and "My Man," while others on the LP are taken from such then-recent shows as *Can Can, Gypsy, My Fair Lady* and *The King and I.* Yank always sounds fine, and on this set, he has an excellent supporting cast (clarinetist Bill Stegmeyer, Bud Freeman on tenor, pianist Lou Stein, bassist Jack Lesberg and drummer Cliff Leeman). However, the brevity of the performances (none longer than 3:14) cuts down on the spontaneity, and since the melodies are played with respect, no real surprises occur. A nice effort, but it is doubtful that this album will be reissued anytime soon. —*Scott Yanow*

The World's Greatest Jazz Band / Jan. 6, 1960 / Everest ✦✦✦
The World's Greatest Jazz Band was formed in the late 1960s by two co-leaders, trumpeter Yank Lawson and bassist Bob Haggart. Although Lawson and Haggart are on this budget LP (along with clarinetist Bill Stegmeyer, tenor saxophonist Bud Freeman, pianist Lou Stein and drummer Cliff Leeman), this is not the WGJB, despite the title. For this interesting effort, Lawson and Haggart perform ten songs having something to do with the Old West, including "South of the Border," "Wagon Wheels," "I'm an Old Cowhand" and "The Yellow Rose of Texas." Fortunately, the songs they picked tend to have worthwhile chord changes suitable for Dixieland, and the overall effect is a lighthearted and generally swinging date. —*Scott Yanow*

Big Yank Is Here / Mar. 29, 1965+Mar. 30, 1965 / ABC ✦✦✦✦

Ole Dixie / May 2, 1966-May 19, 1966 / ABC ✦✦✦✦

Plays Mostly Blues / Mar. 16, 1986 / Audiophile ✦✦✦✦
At the age of 74, Yank Lawson is in fine form on this fairly spontaneous, Dixieland-flavored set. He has a reunion with bassist Bob Haggart (featured on "Whistlin' Cow Blues") and jams with clarinetist Johnny Mince, trombonist George Masso, tenor saxophonist Al Klink, pianist Knocky Parker, and drummer Nick Fatool. The veterans (most of whom date from at least the 1930s) may have mostly had white hair, but their playing still sounds enthusiastic and fresh throughout the session. The repertoire consists of four standards, including "What's New," and four lesser-known tunes, including Haggart's "Dogtown Blues." Easily recommended to trad jazz fans. —*Scott Yanow*

● **That's a Plenty** / Nov. 20, 1943-Feb. 12, 1945 / Dr Jazz ✦✦✦✦✦
This excellent LP (which came out in the mid-1970s but was reasonably available until the early 1990s) features no-nonsense Dixieland from trumpeter Yank Lawson, who was 32-33 during this era. Lawson is heard on four complete sessions with such top players as trombonists Brad Gowans, Miff Mole and Lou McGarity, clarinetists Pee Wee Russell, Rod Cless and Bill Stegmeyer, Joe Marsala on tenor, pianist James P. Johnson, and Yank's longtime friend, bassist Bob Haggart. There is nothing complicated about the music, but the high musicianship, exciting ensembles, and colorful, concise solos make it easily recommended to Dixieland fans. —*Scott Yanow*

Barbara Lea

b. , Detroit, MI
Vocals / Swing, Dixieland
An excellent singer who has been associated with swing and Dixieland, Barbara Lea has never broken through with the general public but she has recorded quite a few worthy albums. She sang with Detroit dance orchestras while in school, performed with the college jazz band (the Crimson Stompers) at Harvard and worked on the East Coast in the 1950s. She recorded for Riverside (1955) and Prestige

(1956-57), using such sidemen as trumpeter Johnny Windhurst and pianists Billy Taylor and Dick Hyman. In the 1960s Lea worked as a stage actress and taught. In the 1970s she sang with Dick Sudhalter and Ed Polcer and recorded in the 1980s for Audiophile including a tribute to her idol and influence Lee Wiley. —*Scott Yanow*

● **Barbara Lea** / Oct. 18, 1956-Oct. 19, 1956 / Original Jazz Classics ✦✦✦✦✦
Singer Barbara Lea's second album (the first is an out-of-print Riverside LP) has been reissued on CD, and it's fairly definitive of her early years. Lea is joined by the great (but ill-fated and now largely forgotten) trumpeter Johnny Windhurst, Dick Cary on either piano or alto horn, sometimes pianist Richard Lowman, guitarist Al Casamenti, bassist Al Hall, and drummer Osie Johnson. Originally a dozen selections, the CD reissue adds an alternate take and an additional title. Lea remains true to the lyrics yet uplifts the material, while the rhythm section swings lightly. Among the many highlights are "Nobody Else but You," "I'm Comin' Virginia," "My Honey's Lovin' Arms" and "Baltimore Oriole." Delightful music by a singer who deserves to be celebrated. —*Scott Yanow*

Lea in Love / Apr. 19, 1957-May 1, 1957 / Original Jazz Classics ✦✦✦✦✦
Singer Barbara Lea often recalls her idol and friend Lee Wiley on this set of love songs. The backup is uniformly tasteful but changes from song to song with such impressive stylists as trumpeter Johnny Windhurst, baritonist Ernie Caceres, Garvin Bushell (on oboe and bassoon), Dick Cary (the arranger on piano and alto horn), guitarist Jimmy Raney and (on a beautiful version of "True Love") harpist Adele Girard making memorable appearances. Lea's straightforward and heartfelt delivery is heard at its best on such songs as "You'd Be So Nice to Come Home To," "Mountain Greenery," "More than You Know" and "Autumn Leaves" (which is partly taken in French). These interpretations are often touching. —*Scott Yanow*

Hoagy's Children / Apr. 27, 1981 / Audiophile ✦✦✦✦✦
A classic of its kind, this wonderful set (which has been reissued on CD) features singer Barbara Lea on seven of the 13 Hoagy Carmichael compositions, pianist Bob Dorough (who vocalizes on six songs, including three that he shares with Lea), cornetist Richard Sudlater (who provided the arrangements), the reeds of Art Baker, bassist Jay Leonhart, and drummer Ronnie Bedford. "New Orleans," "Riverboat Shuffle" and "Little Old Lady" are taken as instrumentals. Surprisingly, the versions of "Stardust" and "Skylark" are among the missing Hoagy tunes, but the versions of "Old Man Harlem," "Hong Kong Blues" (a perfect song for Dorough), and "In the Cool, Cool, Cool of the Evening" are memorable. A well-conceived project. —*Scott Yanow*

Do It Again / Jun. 1983-Nov. 28, 1983 / Audiophile ✦✦✦✦✦
Barbara Lea has long been a fine interpreter of American popular songs from the 1930s and '40s. She is teamed up with some notable players for the November 1983 session (including trumpeter Billy Butterfield, trombonist Vic Dickenson, clarinetist Johnny Mince and a rhythm section led by pianist/arranger Larry Eanet). In addition to those ten songs (which include "Make Believe," "Do It Again," "That Certain Feeling" and "Ace in the Hole"), eight numbers recorded by Lea with pianist Eanet and bassist Steve Novosel from the same year but never released commercially before have been added to the CD reissue. Since Barbara Lea has made relatively few recordings throughout her career and this is a well-balanced set, one can consider this CD somewhat definitive. —*Scott Yanow*

Remembering Lee Wiley / 1976-1995 / Audiophile ✦✦✦✦
Lee Wiley has long been one of Barbara Lea's idols, so her tribute to the swing-era singer is heartfelt and full of sympathy. Lea recorded 11 songs in 1976 and three in 1977 using a trio led by pianist Loonis McGlohon, with guest spots for clarinetist Bob Mitchell. When the music was being made ready for its CD reissue in 1995, Lea got together with McGlohon and a different rhythm section (plus Randy Reinhart on trumpet and trombone) to cut eight more songs. Although Lea lacks Wiley's quiet intensity and understated sensuality, she does an excellent job throughout the ballad-oriented set; highlights include "I Left My Sugar Standing in the Rain," "Time on My Hands," "Down to Steamboat Tennessee," "Sugar" and "Wherever There's Love." —*Scott Yanow*

The Leaders

f. 1985
Group / Post-Bop, Avant-Garde
The Leaders was a veritable supergroup of leftward-leaning, mid-'80s jazz stars. Its front line comprising three of the era's important personalities—trumpeter Lester Bowie, from the decade's most critically acclaimed band, the Art Ensemble of Chicago; alto saxophonist Arthur Blythe, whose Columbia albums of the time almost (but not quite) brought free jazz a measure of popular acceptance; and tenor saxophonist Chico Freeman, who made a series of records that melded the best of mainstream jazz with the passion and originality of the avant-garde. The horns combined with pianist Kirk Lightsey, bassist Cecil McBee, and drummer Famou-

dou Don Moye to make a pair of generally fine, if unspectacular records. Like most (if not all) supergroups, the Leaders existed primarily as a novelty. It seems the band was designed more to attract attention than to exist as an evolving creative entity. The rhythm section also recorded independently for Sunnyside as the Leaders Trio. —*Chris Kelsey*

● **Mudfoot** / Jun. 11, 1986-Jun. 12, 1986 / Black Hawk ✦✦✦✦
The Leaders was formed in the mid-1980s as a vehicle for six notable players (trumpeter Lester Bowie, altoist Arthur Blythe, Chico Freeman on tenor and bass clarinet, pianist Kirk Lightsey, bassist Cecil McBee and drummer Don Moye) to play straightahead advanced jazz. Their debut album, cut for the defunct Black Hawk label, is difficult to find—unfortunately so, for it is an excellent effort. Two songs are group compositions (including the ad-lib "Midnite Train"); Freeman provided a tribute to Eric Dolphy ("Freedom Swing Song"), and the other selections include originals by Blythe and McBee, plus Sam Cooke's "Cupid" (which has a Freeman vocal). Worth searching for. —*Scott Yanow*

Out Here Like This / Feb. 18, 1987-Feb. 19, 1987 / Black Saint ✦✦✦✦✦
The all-star band accurately called the Leaders (trumpeter Lester Bowie, altoist Arthur Blythe, Chico Freeman on tenor, soprano and bass clarinet, pianist Kirk Lightsey, bassist Cecil McBee and drummer Don Moye, although he was always a sideman) developed its own group sound. Performing inside/outside music, the band's Black Saint release features originals by Freeman, Lightsey, McBee and Bowie, plus an obscurity. The trumpeter's straightahead "Zero" is a high point, and all of the musicians play up to their potential. It is particularly interesting to hear Bowie and Blythe excel in this fairly conservative (for them) setting. —*Scott Yanow*

● **Heaven Dance** / May 28, 1988-May 29, 1988 / Sunnyside ✦✦✦✦
This CD is almost worth getting for the bizarre liner notes of Richard Santoro. During this era, pianist Kirk Lightsey (who also plays a bit of flute), bassist Cecil McBee and drummer Don Moye formed the rhythm section of the Leaders, so their set is listed as being by "the Leaders Trio." The musicians perform two Lightsey originals, three by McBee, McBee's "Ode to Wilbur Ware," an obscure Gary Bartz tune, and the standard "This Is All I Ask." Although there is close interplay by the musicians, the pianist is the lead voice, so one can look at this set as being a date by the Kirk Lightsey Trio. Excellent modern mainstream music. —*Scott Yanow*

Unforeseen Blessings / Dec. 19, 1988-Dec. 20, 1988 / Black Saint ✦✦
Although the Leaders is a supergroup comprising trumpeter Lester Bowie, altoist Arthur Blythe, tenor saxophonist Chico Freeman, pianist Kirk Lightsey, bassist Cecil McBee and drummer Don Moye, they fall far short of their potential on this Black Saint CD. Trumpeter Lester Bowie only gets to solo on a tongue-in-cheek version of "Blueberry Hill," and both Blythe and Freeman are very underutilized throughout the date. Pianist Lightsey is the dominant player on the 13 sketches, taking "In a Minute," "Now a Minute" and "Lightish" as unaccompanied solos, "Lucia" as a ballad for the trio and soloing throughout much of the nine minutes of "Heaven Dance." Otherwise there is an unfinished quality to many of the selections, eight of which are under three minutes in length. Other than Lightsey's contributions, this effort is surprisingly forgettable. —*Scott Yanow*

Jeanne Lee

b. Jan. 29, 1939, New York, NY
Vocals / Avant-Garde, Free Jazz
Jeanne Lee combines acrobatic vocal maneuvers with a deeply moving sound and quality that allows her to alternate between soaring, upper register flights and piercing, emotive interpretations. She's extremely precise and flexible, and moves from a song or solo's top end to its middle and bottom accompanying an instrument with a stunning ease. Though many critics have cited Lee as creating free jazz's most innovative vocal approach, she's done very little recording, almost none of it as a leader and even less on American labels. She's best known for her many sessions with Gunther Hampel. Lee studied dance rather than music at Bard College, but while a student there she met Ran Blake. They formed a duo, and she did her first recordings with him, which excited many critics. They toured Europe in 1963. Lee moved to California in 1964, and worked with Ian Underwood and sound poet David Hazelton, whom she later married. She and Hampel established their musical relationship while Lee was in Europe in 1967. Lee recorded with Archie Shepp, Sunny Murray and Hampel in the late '60s, and with Marion Brown, Anthony Braxton, Enrico Rava and Andrew Cyrille in the '70s, while also working with Cecil Taylor. She began composing extensively in the '80s, and has concentrated in recent years on performing her original material, which frequently includes poetic and dance components. Most of her recordings have either been done for European labels or small independents. —*Ron Wynn*

★ **Legendary Duets** / Nov. 15, 1961-Dec. 7, 1961 / Bluebird ◆◆◆◆◆

This is a classic. Singer Jeanne Lee and pianist Ran Blake both made their recording debuts on this set of duets (two songs add bassist George Duvivier), and their interplay is quite memorable. Blake's emotional style makes dramatic use of sound and space, while Lee's haunting vocals also make each note count. The CD reissue (which adds four previously unreleased songs to the original ten-tune program) is highlighted by "Laura," "Where Flamingos Fly," "Evil Blues" and "Sometimes I Feel like a Motherless Child"; included are some very slow ballads ("Lover Man") that are full of inner tension. Fascinating music, highly recommended. — *Scott Yanow*

After Hours / May 25, 1994-May 26, 1994 / Owl ◆◆◆◆

This CD is a bit of a surprise, a standards session featuring the usually adventurous singer Jeanne Lee. The set of duets with pianist Mal Waldron are all taken at very relaxed tempos with only "I Let a Song Go out of My Heart" swinging above a slow-medium pace. Lee mostly emphasizes the lyrics, just scatting sparingly on most tunes (although "Fire Waltz" is totally wordless). Waldron's accompaniment is typically rhythmic, creatively repetitive, brooding and personal. However, it is Lee's haunting and highly expressive voice that really sticks in one's memory. — *Scott Yanow*

Julia Lee

b. Oct. 31, 1902, Boonville, MO, d. Dec. 8, 1958, San Diego, CA

Piano, Vocals / Early R&B Jazz, Swing, Jump Blues

A popular entertainer who recorded frequently for Capitol during 1944-50, Julia Lee, known for her double-entendre songs and rocking piano, was a major attraction in Kansas City. She played piano and sang in her brother George E. Lee's Orchestra during 1920-34, recording with him in 1927 and 1929 (including "If I Could Be with You One Hour Tonight") and cutting two titles of her own in 1929 ("He's Tall, He's Dark and He's Handsome" and "Won't You Come over to My House"). Lee worked regularly as a single in Kansas City after her brother's band broke up. In 1944 she started recording for Capitol and among her sidemen on some sessions were Jay McShann, Vic Dickenson, Benny Carter, Red Norvo and Red Nichols along with many local players. After 1952 Julia Lee only recorded four more songs but she was active up until her death. — *Scott Yanow*

● **Julia Lee and Her Boy Friends** / 1946-1952 / Pausa ◆◆◆◆◆

This 1983 LP from the obsolete Pausa label has a dozen of Julia Lee's better Capitol recordings, all but one from 1946-49. Lee, a fine pianist, tended to sing fairly obvious but cute double-entendre lyrics. Falling between swing-oriented jazz, blues and R&B, the recordings on this set feature such interesting players as sidemen as trombonist Vic Dickenson, altoist Benny Carter, Dave Cavanaugh on tenor, and guitarist Jim "Daddy" Walker, among many others. Highlights include "King Size Papa," "Crazy World," "Snatch and Grab It," and "I Was Wrong" (which has a spot for cornetist Red Nichols). Some, but not all, of this music has since been reissued on CD in samplers. — *Scott Yanow*

Of Lions and Lambs / Jun. 11, 1947-Jul. 2, 1952 / Charly ◆◆◆◆

Julia Lee recorded regularly for Capitol during the 1946-52 period. Although she pops up in some sampler sets, her music has yet to be fully reissued domestically in CDs. This LP from the British Charly label has 16 highlights from Lee's career and duplicates only two songs from an earlier Pausa LP. Lee's basic but effective vocals and good piano playing are matched on ten different sessions with a variety of top players, including trumpeters Ernie Royal, Bobby Sherwood, and Red Nichols, trombonist Vic Dickenson, altoist Benny Carter, Dave Cavanaugh on tenor, guitarist Jim "Daddy" Walker, and many others. Among the more memorable selections are Lee's unaccompanied version of "Nobody Knows You When You're Down and Out," "Tell Me Daddy," "Lotus Blossom," "It Comes in like a Lion," "and "You Ain't Got It No More." — *Scott Yanow*

Kansas City Star / Nov. 1, 1944-Jul. 9, 1952 / Bear Family ◆◆◆◆◆

Peggy Lee

b. May 26, 1920, Jamestown, ND

Vocals / Swing, Pop, Show Tunes, Traditional Pop

Peggy Lee only had a small voice and she never improvised much but her singing often crossed over into jazz and she always swung. She came to fame with Benny Goodman (1941-43) although she was so scared at her first recording session ("Elmer's Tune") that John Hammond urged Goodman to fire her. Goodman knew better and she had a big hit within a year with "Why Don't You Do Right." After marrying Dave Barbour in 1943, Lee retired briefly but was soon a major recording artist for Capitol. During the 1940s and '50s she had quite a few popular records including "It's a Good Day," "Black Coffee," "Manana" and "Fever"; she

also proved to be a talented songwriter. Lee appeared in the Dixieland movie *Pete Kelly's Blues* and recorded *Beauty and the Beat* (1959) with the George Shearing Quintet but then moved farther away from jazz in the 1960s. Peggy Lee's often-atmospheric records from her prime years can be easily enjoyed by jazz fans. — *Scott Yanow*

The Uncollected Peggy Lee (1948) / 1948 / Hindsight ◆◆◆

This enjoyable but very skimpy LP (just 25 minutes) consists of radio transcriptions made by singer Peggy Lee in 1948 with studio bands led by either David Barbour or Billy May. The 12 selections are all under three minutes long (five under two minutes), so there is little time for Lee to do anything other than state the themes. Her voice was in prime form and she sounds enthusiastic on such numbers as "Riding High," "It's a Good Day," "Love Is Just Around the Corner" and "Just One of Those Things," but due to its brevity, this album should only be acquired if found at a budget price. — *Scott Yanow*

Black Coffee / Apr. 3, 1952-Jun. 8, 1956 / MCA/Decca ◆◆◆◆

This attractive two-CD set is an anthology of Peggy Lee's 1952-1956 period with Decca. Much of the music is outside of jazz and more in the genre of period pop and novelties, but Lee sounds cheerful about the whole thing and swings lightly throughout. Some of the later material does give her a chance to show off her jazz chops and among the highlights are "Lover," a duet with Bing Crosby ("Watermelon Weather") and the hit title cut, but jazz listeners will want to be selective. — *Scott Yanow*

Songs from "Pete Kelly's Blues" / May 6, 1955+May 10, 1955 / Decca ◆◆◆◆

Things Are Swingin' / 1958-1959 / Capitol ◆◆◆◆

Many of Peggy Lee's records are not all that strong from a jazz standpoint, but this out-of-print LP is a definite exception. Backed by an orchestra arranged and conducted by Jack Marshall, the emphasis is on swinging renditions of standards; Lee's light, soft voice rarely sounded more appealing. Highlights include such sprightly songs as "It's a Wonderful World," "Lullaby in Rhythm," "Ridin' High" and "You're Mine You." — *Scott Yanow*

● **Beauty and the Beat** / Apr. 28, 1959 / Capitol ◆◆◆◆

For this concert (which has been reissued on CD with two additional tracks), singer Peggy Lee teams up with the 1959 George Shearing Quintet, plus their usual special guest Armando Peraza on conga. Lee sounds quite happy to perform with Shearing—her cool tone fits in very well with the Shearing Quintet's distinctive sound—and she is in excellent form on such tunes as "If Dreams Come True," "All Too Soon," "You Came a Long Way from St. Louis" and her own "There'll Be Another Spring"; there are also three instrumentals, including "Isn't It Romantic?" — *Scott Yanow*

Live at Basin Street East / Feb. 9, 1961+Mar. 8, 1961 / Blue Note ◆◆

This is a lesser Peggy Lee release. Originally it was planned that the singer (at the height of her popularity) would record a live set at Basin Street East in New York. Unfortunately, she caught a cold and her voice was a bit hoarse, so some of the numbers were re-recorded in the studio the following month and spliced quite effectively into the set. However, whether in concert or not, the performances on this CD reissue are rather routine with no chances taken (the dozen sidemen do not get a single solo), and everything sounds fairly well planned in advance. Lee, who is best here on the ballads, never wanders at all from the melodies, and these renditions of her usual repertoire have nothing unique or unusual to offer except perhaps an overly rapid version of "Fever." — *Scott Yanow*

Sings the Blues / 1988 / Music Masters ◆◆◆

By 1988, 68-year-old Peggy Lee did not have much of a voice left. Although she was still determined, physical problems had weakened her, and despite Gene Lees' absurd raving in the liner notes ("Her work has never flagged, the quality of it has never faltered"), this set finds her way past her prime. Actually, the material (only half of which are actually blues) is fairly strong—mostly standards from the 1920s and '30s—and the backup group (a quintet with pianist Mike Renzi and guitarist John Chiodini) does a good job of supporting Lee's quiet and often weak voice. This is one of the better releases from Peggy Lee's later years, but it still pales next to her 1950s recordings. — *Scott Yanow*

Love Held Lightly: Rare Songs by Harold Arlen / Aug. 29, 1988-Sep. 2, 1988 / Capitol ◆◆

The main value of this CD is hearing 14 rare Harold Arlen songs (only "My Shining Hour" qualifies as a standard), including eight being given their first-ever recording. Peggy Lee's voice is quite weak, although still filled with sincere feeling, and the backup group (a nonet with pianist Keith Ingham, trumpeter Glenn Zottola and Ken Peplowski on tenor) is quite jazz-oriented. Lee tries her best, but this release is certainly for selective (and tolerant) tastes. — *Scott Yanow*

Ranee Lee

b. Brooklyn, NY
Vocals / Bop
Although born and raised in Brooklyn, Ranee Lee has lived in Montreal for most of her adult life, and she is best known for her fine recordings for the Canadian Justin Time label. Lee performed as a singer while in high school, toured the US with a local group, and, after she moved to Canada, she starred in the play *Lady Day at Emerson's Bar and Grill*. The influences of Billie Holiday and Dinah Washington can be felt at times in her singing, but Ranee Lee also has her own sound. A measure of her talent is that Milt Hinton and Oliver Jones performed on her first recording (*Deep Song*) and Red Mitchell was a major factor on her second (*Jazz On Broadway*). —*Scott Yanow*

Deep Song / Oct. 1989 / Justin Time ✦✦✦✦
On this excellent CD, one of Ranee Lee's earliest recordings, the singer pays tribute to Billie Holiday with renditions of a dozen songs associated with Lady Day. The Canadian release features Lee joined by pianist Oliver Jones, guitarist Richard Ring, Richard Beaudet on reeds, veteran bassist Milt Hinton and drummer Archie Alleyne; the title cut also includes a string section. Lee manages to recapture Holiday's spirit without resorting to mimicry. This tasteful effort has among its highlights "When a Woman Loves a Man," "Crazy He Calls Me," "Easy Living" and "Them There Eyes." Recommended. —*Scott Yanow*

● **The Musicals: Jazz on Broadway** / Jul. 1991-Aug. 1991 / Justin Time ✦✦✦✦
Contemporary jazz singer tries her hand at ballads, show tunes, and standards, and does a respectable job. The arrangements, production, and background playing are steady and don't overwhelm the vocalist. —*Ron Wynn*

You Must Believe in Swing / Mar. 1996 / Justin Time ✦✦✦

Seasons of Love / Mar. 3, 1997-Mar. 4, 1997 / Justin Time ✦✦✦✦

I Thought About You / May 1994-Jun. 1994 / Justin Time ✦✦✦

Legends of Jazz

f. 1971, **db.** 1988
Group / New Orleans Jazz
Formed and led by drummer Barry Martyn, this New Orleans jazz band featured a variety of ancient players on occasional tours and recordings. The title of their 1978 show (*1000 Years of Jazz*) was not much of an exaggeration! With trumpeter Andrew Blakeney, trombonist Louis Nelson, clarinetist Joe Darensbourg, pianist Alton Purnell, bassist Ed Garland and Martyn forming the original sextet, the Legends recorded two albums for the Crescent Jazz label during 1973-74; the relative youngster Barney Bigard was a guest on the second date. The personnel in future years included trombonist Clyde Bernhardt and bassist Chester Zardis along with lesser-known players and the erratic but spirited group had successful tours of South America and Australia before fading out in the late '80s (the 1988 date is approximate). —*Scott Yanow*

● **The Legends of Jazz [Crescent]** / Oct. 1973 / Crescent Jazz ✦✦✦✦✦
In the early '70s, English drummer Barry Martyn (who was then 32) gathered together a sextet comprising New Orleans jazz veterans, billed them as "The Legends of Jazz" and took them on several tours. This LP, the first release by the Crescent Jazz Productions label, contains some good playing from trumpeter Andrew Blakeney, trombonist Louis Nelson and clarinetist Joe Darensbourg; the rhythm section (comprising pianist Alton Purnell, Martyn and the 88-year-old bassist Edward "Montudi" Garland) also works together quite well. Although the band plays a couple of warhorses, there is also some lesser-known material on the set (including Mike Delay's "Conti Street Parade" and A.J. Piron's "Red Man Blues"), and overall, this joyful album is much better than expected. —*Scott Yanow*

Michel Legrand

b. Feb. 24, 1932, Paris, France
Arranger, Composer, Piano / Pop, Hard Bop, Crossover Jazz, Film Music
Michel Legrand has made his fame and fortune from writing for films but he has done significant work in jazz on an occasional basis. In 1957 he arranged a set of Dixieland and swing standards for a French orchestra (recorded on Philips). In 1958 he used three different all-star groups for the classic *Legrand Jazz* (with such sidemen as Miles Davis, John Coltrane, Phil Woods, Herbie Mann, Bill Evans, Ben Webster, Art Farmer and others. In 1968 he recorded a strictly jazz set with a trio. Legrand has written for albums led by Stan Getz (1971), Sarah Vaughan (1972) and on several occasions for Phil Woods. Several of his songs (such as "What Are You Doing the Rest of Your Life," "Watch What Happens" and "The Summer Knows") have been recorded many times by jazz musicians. —*Scott Yanow*

● **Legrand Jazz** / Jun. 25, 1958-Jun. 30, 1958 / Philips ✦✦✦✦✦
Michel Legrand has spent most of his life as a composer in the studios and for films but this release is a jazz classic. Legrand took 11 famous jazz compositions and arranged them for three different groups. Tenor-great Ben Webster, flutist Herbie Mann, four trombonists and a rhythm section perform pieces by Duke Ellington, Earl Hines, Django Reinhardt ("Nuages") and the Count Basie-associated "Blue and Sentimental." A big band with trumpeters Art Farmer and Donald Byrd and altoist Phil Woods plays "Stompin' at the Savoy," "A Night in Tunisia" and Bix Beiderbecke's "In a Mist." The most famous session has Miles Davis, John Coltrane, Phil Woods, Herbie Mann, pianist Bill Evans, harp, vibes, baritone and a rhythm section performing music by Thelonious Monk, John Lewis, Jelly Roll Morton ("Wild Man Blues") and Fats Waller's "Jitterbug Waltz." Throughout this superlative album, the arrangements are colorful and unusual, making one wish that Legrand had recorded more jazz albums through the years. —*Scott Yanow*

At Shelly's Manne-Hole / Jan. 1968 / Verve ✦✦✦✦✦
Michel Legrand, best known as a film composer, has only made occasional jazz records through the years, but most have been quite worthwhile. This reissue CD brings back a real rarity, a trio session with bassist Ray Brown and drummer Shelly Manne that is arguably Legrand's only jazz date from the 1963-77 period. It is a particularly interesting set, for Legrand takes a rare (if odd) vocal on "My Funny Valentine"; "Los Gatos" is a free improvisation (one of four songs spontaneously "composed" by the musicians on stage), and the pianist shows that he can swing on "Ray's Riff" and "Another Blues." This underrated set is worth investigating. —*Scott Yanow*

Jazz Grand / Mar. 1978 / Gryphon ✦✦✦
For this interesting if out-of-print LP, film producer Michel Legrand leads an impressive big band through a 23-minute exploration of his "Southern Routes" (a jazz suite based on the soundtrack of the film *Les Routes de la Sud*) and then plays piano with a septet on four of his briefer compositions. The latter band has solo work from trumpeter Jon Faddis, altoist Phil Woods and baritonist Gerry Mulligan, all of whom are also featured on the longer piece. Although none of the selections caught on, the colorful arrangements and the excellent solos make this a worthwhile (if difficult-to-find) acquisition, Michel Legrand's first jazz recording in a decade. —*Scott Yanow*

After the Rain / May 28, 1982 / Original Jazz Classics ✦✦✦✦
This high-quality outing (reissued on CD) features composer Michel Legrand faring quite well as a jazz pianist. He performs six of his compositions (only "Pieces of Dream" is well known) with a lyrical septet also including altoist Phil Woods (doubling on clarinet), tenor saxophonist Zoot Sims, trumpeter Joe Wilder, guitarist Gene Bertoncini, bassist Ron Carter, and drummer Grady Tate. The music generally swings, has plenty of fine melodic solos, and gives listeners a taste of some fresh Legrand material. —*Scott Yanow*

Legrand/Grappelli / May 25, 1992-May 27, 1992 / Verve ✦✦✦

Michel Plays Legrand / Sep. 27, 1993-Sep. 28, 1993 / LaserLight ✦✦
Michel Legrand's LaserLight CD boasts quite an all-star band (trumpeter Arturo Sandoval, trombonist Bill Watrous, altoist Bud Shank, Buddy Collette and Hubert Laws on flutes, guitarist John Pisano, bassist Brian Bromberg, drummer Peter Erskine and the leader/pianist) but is surprisingly (and disappointingly) relaxed. The emphasis is on ballads, Legrand sings two dramatic pieces that are outside of jazz, and none of the solos are all that memorable. Sandvoal is overly restrained and, even with some strong moments from Watrous and Laws, this session does not reach the heights one would expect from this cast of musical personalities. —*Scott Yanow*

Peter Leitch

b. 1944, Ottawa, Canada
Guitar / Hard Bop
Peter Leitch has long been one of the top straightahead guitarists in jazz, a fine hard bop-based improviser with a swinging style and an appealing quiet tone. He grew up in Montreal, lived in Toronto during 1977-81, recorded with Oscar Peterson, the Al Grey-Jimmy Forrest Quintet and Sadik Hakim, and debuted as a leader in 1981 on the Jazz House label. Since moving to New York in 1983, Leitch has been a busy freelancer and has recorded a leader for Uptown, Criss Cross, Concord and most frequently for Reservoir. In addition, he has been an occasional and insightful jazz journalist. —*Scott Yanow*

Jump Street / Feb. 9, 1981-Feb. 10, 1981 / Pausa ✦✦✦
Peter Leitch's recording debut as a leader finds the cool-toned guitarist showing plenty of potential. He swings through six songs (five group originals and "Prelude to a Kiss") with pianist George McFetridge, either Neil Swainson or Art Davis on bass, and Terry Clarke or Freddie Waits on drums; trombonist Terry Lukiwski sits in for two songs. The modern mainstream music is still fairly undated, although

this LP from the small Canadian label Jazz House will not be easy to locate. —*Scott Yanow*

Sometime in Another Life / Feb. 6, 1982+Feb. 18, 1982 / Jazz House ✦✦✦✦
Guitarist Peter Leitch's second LP as a leader (released by the Canadian label Jazz House) is a set of mostly lyrical duets with pianist George McFetridge. Leitch, influenced by Grant Green and Kenny Burrell, plus other boppish players, already had an appealing sound and a fluid style. This difficult-to-find LP (which has three Leitch originals, two by the tasteful McFetridge, and "Django") is relaxing, but also full of subtle surprises. —*Scott Yanow*

Exhilaration / Nov. 17, 1984-Dec. 6, 1988 / Uptown ✦✦✦✦
This combination works quite well. The mellow-toned but hard-swinging guitarist Peter Leitch teams up with baritonist Pepper Adams, pianist John Hicks, bassist Ray Drummond and drummer Billy Hart for three Thelonious Monk tunes ("'Round Midnight," "Trinkle Tinkle," and "Played Twice"), two of the guitarist's originals, and "How Deep Is the Ocean." Adams' presence inspires and seems to light a fire under Leitch, who is heard throughout in passionate form. Recommended. —*Scott Yanow*

● **Red Zone** / Nov. 17, 1984-Jul. 20, 1988 / Reservoir ✦✦✦✦✦
This CD reissue not only brings back the six songs from the LP of the same name but adds "It Came Upon a Midnight Clear," a previously unreleased alternate take of "'Round Midnight" from the guitarist's earlier session with baritonist Pepper Adams, and three 1988 unaccompanied guitar solos (a medley of "Lush Life" and "Daydream," "I'm Getting Sentimental over You," and Charlie Parker's "Quasimodo"). The bulk of the set matches Leitch in 1985 with pianist Kirk Lightsey, bassist Ray Drummond and drummer Marvin "Smitty" Smith. The CD as a whole finds the guitarist in prime form playing superior tunes—including "My One and Only Love," Wayne Shorter's "Speak No Evil," Thelonious Monk's "Off Minor" and two of Leitch's own straightahead originals—and is his definitive release thus far. —*Scott Yanow*

On a Misty Night / Nov. 2, 1986 / Criss Cross ✦✦✦✦✦
Peter Leitch, who has an appealing, mellow tone and a boppish style influenced by Kenny Burrell, appears on this set in a pianoless trio with bassist Neil Swainson and drummer Mickey Roker, an instrumentation Burrell helped to popularize in the late 1950s. Leitch is fairly exploratory on songs by Tadd Dameron, Tom McIntosh, Wayne Shorter and Thelonious Monk ("Crepescule with Nellie") plus an original, "Serenata," and a ballad medley of "No More" and "Detour Ahead." Easily recommended to fans of the modern mainstream guitar. —*Scott Yanow*

Mean What You Say / Jan. 1990 / Concord Jazz ✦✦✦✦✦
Guitarist Peter Leitch had worked with pianist John Hicks, bassist Ray Drummond and drummer Marvin "Smitty" Smith on several previous occasions, so it is not surprising to find that they only needed a four-hour session to record this entire CD. The musicians clearly sound very comfortable with each other and, even on the more rapid pieces (such as Hicks' "Time" and "This Is New"), everyone seems very relaxed. Leitch's warm mellow sound is a throwback to the Barney Kessel/Herb Ellis tradition although his tone is distinctive and his ideas are fresh; he takes "In a Sentimental Mood" unaccompanied. John Hicks is up to his usual standards both in his solos and tasteful accompaniment and, with Drummond and Smith in support, there is no weak link to the quartet. A fine example of 1990s bebop as played by some of the best. —*Scott Yanow*

Portraits and Dedications / Dec. 30, 1988-Jan. 24, 1989 / Criss Cross ✦✦✦✦
Trio/Quartet '91 / Feb. 23, 1991-Feb. 24, 1991 / Concord Jazz ✦✦✦✦
From Another Perspective / Jun. 10, 1992 / Concord Jazz ✦✦✦✦
A Special Rapport / Jul. 1, 1993 / Reservoir ✦✦✦✦✦
Duality / Jun. 1, 1994-Jun. 2, 1994 / Reservoir ✦✦✦✦

Colours & Dimensions / Jul. 7, 1995-Jul. 8, 1995 / Reservoir ✦✦✦✦
Guitarist Peter Leitch's soft and inviting tone sometimes hides the fact that he is often a hard-swinging and burning soloist. For this Reservoir CD, he holds his own with such top players as trumpeter Claudio Roditi, altoist Gary Bartz, the reeds of Jed Levy, pianist John Hicks, bassist Rufus Reid and drummer Marvin "Smitty" Smith. The impressive septet performs four of Leitch's originals (including "Song for Jobim") and a song apiece by Bartz, Smith, Harold Land, Charles Mingus ("Duke Ellington's Sound of Love") and Cole Porter ("I Concentrate on You"). This is excellent hard bop music that lives up to its potential. —*Scott Yanow*

Up Front / 1997 / Reservoir ✦✦✦

John Leitham

b. , Philadelphia, PA
Bass / Hard Bop

A talented bassist who has been based in the Los Angeles area since 1983, John Leitham has toured with Woody Herman, George Shearing and most notably with

Mel Tormé. His recordings for USA as a leader feature him in small-group settings and are excellent examples of modern straightahead jazz. —*Scott Yanow*

Leitham Up / May 29, 1989-May 31, 1989 / USA ✦✦✦✦
● **The Southpaw** / Sep. 8, 1992-Sep. 10, 1992 / USA ✦✦✦✦✦
Lefty Leaps In / Apr. 16, 1996-May 22, 1996 / USA ✦✦✦✦✦
Bassist John Leitham's third CD for the USA label features several different overlapping groups. Leitham is heard in a trio with guitarist Barry Zweig and trombonist Bill Watrous; with a quintet that adds pianist Tom Ranier and drummer Jeff Hamilton; in a different trio with Ranier and Hamilton; and with a particularly exciting unit that also features Ranier, drummer Roy McCurdy and both Pete Christlieb and Rickey Woodard on tenors. The music is essentially bop to hard bop, with the highlights including "Long Ago and Far Away," "Oleo," Oscar Pettiford's "Laverne Walk" and "Jordu"; all 11 straightahead selections are quite enjoyable and played well by these expert Los Angeles-based jazzmen. —*Scott Yanow*

Stan Levey

b. Apr. 5, 1926, Philadelphia, PA
Drums / Cool, Bop

Stan Levey, one of the early bop drummers, was greatly in demand in the jazz world of the 1950s. He played with Dizzy Gillespie for the first time in Philadelphia in 1942. Two years later he moved to New York and worked with Charlie Parker, Coleman Hawkins (when his group included Thelonious Monk) and Ben Webster. He toured with Woody Herman in 1945 and was in the Gillespie-Parker Quintet (1945-46). Levey proved to be a superior big-band drummer during his stints with Charlie Ventura, Georgie Auld and Freddie Slack, gaining his greatest recognition while with Stan Kenton's Orchestra (1952-54). Settling in Los Angeles, Levey was with the Lighthouse All-Stars (1954-58) and worked for the next decade as a studio musician. In 1973 he permanently retired from music to run a photography business. Stan Levey led three dates for Bethlehem (1954-56) and one apiece for Liberty and Mode in 1957. —*Scott Yanow*

Stanley the Steamer / Dec. 6, 1954-Sep. 28, 1955 / Affinity ✦✦✦✦
Although drummer Stan Levey is the leader, this album is most significant for the playing of tenor saxophonist Dexter Gordon, who made relatively few recording dates in the 1950s due to drug problems. Dexter is immediately recognizable and even contributed "Stanley the Steamer." Also in fine form on the boppish set are trumpeter Conte Candoli, trombonist Frank Rosolino, pianist Lou Levy and bassist Leroy Vinnegar. The repertoire emphasizes jazz tunes from the previous ten years, including "Max Is Makin' Wax," "Diggin' for Diz," and Miles Davis' "Tune Up." —*Scott Yanow*

Grand Stan / Nov. 1956 / Bethlehem ✦✦✦✦
Drummin' the Blues / Mar. 1957 / Liberty ✦✦✦
● **Stan Levey 5** / Jun. 1957 / V.S.O.P. ✦✦✦✦✦
The excellent bop drummer Stan Levey, who retired from playing in the 1960s to become a full-time photographer, led five record dates during 1954-57 of which this set for MOD (which has been reissued on CD by the V.S.O.P. label) was the last one. Levey gathered together quite an impressive lineup (trumpeter Conte Candoli, Richie Kamuca on tenor, pianist Lou Levy and bassist Monty Budwig) to perform two of Kamuca's originals, three standards and the rarely played "Ole Man Rebop." All of the musicians are in prime form, displaying contrasting but complementary styles. This swinging date is easily recommended. —*Scott Yanow*

Milcho Leviev

b. Dec. 19, 1937, Plovdiv, Bulgaria
Keyboards, Piano / Post-Bop

Milcho Leviev is a virtuosic pianist whose ability to play effortlessly in complex time signatures is quite impressive. He worked early on in Bulgaria, directing the national radio and television big band and leading the quartet Jazz Focus (1965-69) before defecting to the West in 1970, working with Albert Mangelsdorff in Germany. Leviev moved to Los Angeles the following year, becoming a key part of the Don Ellis Orchestra (1971-77), where his ability to play in odd meters was a major asset. He worked with Willie Bobo, John Klemmer, Billy Cobham, Airto Moreira, Art Pepper and Manhattan Transfer before helping to found Free Flight (1980-83). Leviev has freelanced in the L.A. area ever since, recording in recent times for the M-A label. —*Scott Yanow*

Music for Big Band and Symphony Orchestra / Aug. 11, 1977 / Trend ✦✦✦
An interesting if out-of-print collection of Milcho Leviev originals are heard on this scarce LP. The three-part title cut is a third-stream work performed by the Bulgarian Radio Big Band and Symphony Orchestra in 1981. Also heard on the album are a trio version of "Waltz for Maurice" with bassist Ray Brown and drummer Peter Erskine, "Isaac's Touchstone" (which features the leader on electric key-

boards), a collaboration with the soprano of Ray Pizzi on "Sad, A Little Bit," and the original lineup of Free Flight (a virtuosic quartet with flutist James Walker) playing Leviev's famous "Bulgarian Boogie." —*Scott Yanow*

Blues for the Fisherman / Jun. 27, 1980-June 29, 1980 / Mole ✦✦✦✦

Plays the Music of Irving Berlin / Sep. 9, 1982 / Discovery ✦✦✦✦✦

For this solo LP, Milcho Leviev utilizes both acoustic and electric pianos in interpreting nine of Irving Berlin's songs. What is unusual is that Leviev reharmonized and altered most of the tunes, so the songs sound quite complex and almost unrecognizable in spots, although the melodies are still present. Certainly these versions of "What'll I Do," "Alexander's Ragtime Band," "Blue Skies" (which is taken in 7/4 time) and "Cheek to Cheek" sound quite unusual. —*Scott Yanow*

★ **Up and Down** / Sep. 15, 1987 / M-A ✦✦✦✦✦

Originating from a Japanese concert, this CD from M-A teams together pianist Milcho Leviev in duets with the superb bassist Dave Holland. The music ranges from variations of standards to more introspective interplay and stimulating originals by the duo. High points include versions of Leviev's "Up and Down" and Holland's challenging and rather exciting "Jumpin' In." Although the bassist has a fair share of solo space, Leviev's command of the keyboard constantly grabs one's attention; he has long been one of Los Angeles's unheralded treasures. This recommended disc concludes (as do all of M-A's discs) with a selection taken from another CD, a fine performance by pianist Todd Garfinkle. —*Scott Yanow*

Bulgarian Piano Blues / Apr. 1989 / M-A ✦✦✦✦✦

Lou Levy

b. Mar. 5, 1928, Chicago, IL
Piano / Bop, Cool

A superior bop-based pianist who has worked with a countless number of top jazz artists, Lou Levy started on piano when he was 12. He played with Georgie Auld (1947), Sarah Vaughan, Chubby Jackson (1947-48), Boyd Raeburn, Woody Herman's Second Herd (1949-50), Tommy Dorsey (1950), Auld again and Flip Phillips. Levy was outside of music for a few years (1952-54) and then gained a strong reputation as a fine accompanist to singers, working with Peggy Lee (on and off during 1955-73), Ella Fitzgerald (1957-62), June Christy, Anita O'Day and more recently Pinky Winters. Levy also played with Shorty Rogers, Stan Getz, Terry Gibbs, Benny Goodman, Supersax and most of the major West Coast players. Lou Levy has recorded as a leader for Nocturne (1954), RCA, Jubilee, Philips, Interplay (1977) and Verve. —*Scott Yanow*

A Most Musical Fella / Nov. 15, 1956-Jan. 26, 1957 / RCA ✦✦✦

This early effort by pianist Lou Levy (28 at the time) finds him playing superior bop interpretations of seven standards and three straightahead originals. Levy is teamed on the Los Angeles dates with bassist Max Bennett and drummer Stan Levey. Last available as a French RCA LP in 1983, the music is an excellent example of the modern mainstream of the period and still sounds quite stimulating and swinging. —*Scott Yanow*

The Kid's Got Ears / Nov. 27, 1982-Nov. 28, 1982 / Jazzizz ✦✦✦✦

The short-lived Jazzizz label (based in Oregon) lasted long enough to come out with a couple of LPs. This set gave the talented veteran Lou Levy (always a superior bop-based pianist) a rare chance to lead his own date. He performs swinging versions of a variety of standards, plus Al Cohn's "High on You" and "Ding Dong the Witch Is Dead." The latter is one of three unaccompanied piano solos, and in addition, there are three piano-bass duets with John Heard and four trio numbers that add drummer Shelly Manne. A fine if rather obscure set. —*Scott Yanow*

● **Lunacy** / Feb. 9, 1992-Feb. 12, 1992 / Verve ✦✦✦✦✦

Ya Know / Mar. 30, 1993-Apr. 1, 1993 / Verve ✦✦✦✦

This is a rather unusual outing for veteran pianist Lou Levy, since eight of the ten selections have both Eric Von Essen, who doubles on cello, and Pierre Michelot on basses, along with drummer Alvin Queen. The large number of bass solos make this set of more limited interest than expected, but Levy's fine bop-based playing and some excellent originals uplift what could have been a lesser effort. Worth investigating. —*Scott Yanow*

Ron Levy

b. May 29, 1951, Cambridge, MA
Piano, Organ / Blues, Groove, Modern Electric

Ron Levy (born Reuvin Zev ben Yehoshua Ha Levi) was born on May 29, 1951, in Cambridge, MA. Although Levy grew up playing clarinet, he switched to piano at age 13 after attending a Ray Charles concert. Then, influenced by Jimmy Smith, Booker T., and Billy Preston, he picked up on the Hammond organ. Within a few years he was working in the Boston area backing up blues acts. Albert King discovered and hired Levy in 1971 while he was still in high school. They worked

together for 18 months. He then went on to B.B. King's band and worked with King for almost seven years. From 1976 until 1980, Levy worked with the Rhythm Rockers and it was here that he met guitarist Ronnie Earl. Levy joined the Roomful of Blues from 1983 to 1987. Levy's own band, Ron Levy's Wild Kingdom, has recorded a number of fine albums for Black Top, Rounder, and Bullseye, among them 1988's *Safari to New Orleans*, 1993's *B-3 Blues and Grooves* and 1996's *Zim Zam Zoom: Acid Blues on B-3*. —*Michael Erlewine*

Ron Levy's Wild Kingdom / Sep. 1985 / Black Top ✦✦✦

Ten tunes with an all-star cast including Ronnie Earl (guitar), Kim Wilson (harmonica), Greg Piccolo (sax), Wayne Bennett (guitar), and other excellent players. Plenty of fine guitar, keyboards, harmonica, and up-tempo blues music. —*Michael Erlewine*

Safari to New Orleans / 1988 / Black Top ✦✦✦

Ron Levy's piano playing shines throughout *Safari to New Orleans*, but he fails to come up with enough strong songs to make the album memorable. —*Thom Owens*

★ **B-3 Blues & Grooves** / 1992 / Bullseye Blues ✦✦✦✦✦

Ron Levy is one of the finest young masters of the Hammond B-3. Here are 11 soul-satisfying cuts that feature Levy's funky keyboard playing—many written by Levy himself. Those who look for B-3 jams in the soul-jazz vein that are as funky as can be will not be disappointed. This is a great CD to own. —*Michael Erlewine*

Zim Zam Zoom: Acid Blues on B-3 / Mar. 19, 1996 / Bullseye Blues ✦✦✦✦

If you like blues and funky soul-jazz (with just a twist of the future), this is an album to enjoy. Hammond B-3 artist Ron Levy gathers some of the greatest groove players of all time for this steam session, including Melvin Sparks on guitar and the great Idris Muhammad on drums. Call it retro or acid-jazz if you want, but groove lover Levy never stops playing that funky soul-jazz long enough to look back. This album carries the groove tradition on, maintaining that integrity. Produced by Bob Porter. —*Michael Erlewine*

George Lewis

b. Jul. 13, 1900, New Orleans, LA, d. Dec. 31, 1968, New Orleans, LA
Clarinet / New Orleans Jazz

George Lewis never tried to be a virtuoso soloist. He loved to play melodic ensembles where his distinctive clarinet was free to improvise as simply as he desired. When Lewis was inspired and in tune, he could hold his own with any of his contemporaries in New Orleans and he always sounded beautiful playing his "Burgundy Street Blues." To everyone's surprise (including himself), he became one of the most popular figures of the New Orleans revival movement of the 1950s.

It took Lewis a long time to achieve fame. He taught himself clarinet when he was 18 and worked in the 1920s with the Black Eagle Band, Buddy Petit, the Eureka Brass Band, Chris Kelly, Kid Rena, the Olympia Orchestra and other New Orleans groups. He played with Bunk Johnson in Evan Thomas' group in the early '30s but had a day job throughout most of the decade. When Bunk was discovered in 1942, Lewis became part of his band, playing with him on and off through 1945 and getting opportunities to lead his own sessions during 1943-45. However, Johnson was difficult to get along with and a homesick Lewis returned to New Orleans by 1946. He played locally with his own group (featuring trombonist Jim Robinson) and in 1950 was portrayed in an article for *Look*. That exposure led to him recording regularly and by 1952 Lewis was in such great demand that he was soon working before crowds in California and touring Europe and Japan. In addition to Robinson, Lewis' band in its prime years often featured trumpeter Kid Howard, pianist Alton Purnell, banjoist Lawrence Marrero, bassist Alcide "Slow Drag" Pavageau and drummer Joe Watkins. George Lewis, who recorded for many labels (a Mosaic box set of his Blue Note sessions is one of the best reissues), became a symbol of what was right and wrong about the New Orleans revival movement, overpraised by his fans and overcritized by his detractors. At his best he was well worth hearing. —*Scott Yanow*

☆ **Complete Blue Note Recordings** / May 15, 1943-Apr. 11, 1955 / Mosaic ✦✦✦✦

A centerpiece for the dedicated New Orleans collector, it begins with Lewis' "Climax" session in 1943 and ranges through a variety of studio and concert performances over a 12-year period—definitely some of the clarinetist's best work (1943-1944, 1954-1955). —*Bruce Raeburn*

George Lewis of New Orleans / Feb. 26, 1946-Feb. 27, 1946 / Original Jazz Classics ✦✦✦✦

Some great New Orleans standards appear from the Original Zenith Brass Band and the Eclipse Alley Five, featuring Lewis in good company—Isidore Barbarin (Paul's father), Peter Bocage, Jim Robinson, Baby Dodds, and others. —*Bruce Raeburn*

☆ **At Herbert Otto's Party (1949)** / Nov. 23, 1949 / Jazzology ✦✦✦✦✦

George Lewis at his peak is captured while performing for a private party in New Orleans. There's an excellent example of "Burgundy Street Blues," his signature piece. —*Bruce Raeburn*

The Beverly Caverns Sessions / May 26, 1953-May 27, 1953 / Good Time Jazz ✦✦✦✦✦

Clarinetist George Lewis and his usual band of this period (which consisted of trumpeter Kid Howard, trombonist Jim Robinson, pianist Alton Purnell, Lawrence Marrero on banjo, bassist Slow Drag Pavageau and drummer Joe Watkins) are in better-than-average form on this well-recorded live set. Lewis and his group emphasize ensembles on the dozen New Orleans standards and the clarinetist/leader is in surprisingly extroverted form, easily the most impressive soloist. Fans of traditional jazz should go out of their way to pick up this CD. These performances were released for the first time in 1994. —*Scott Yanow*

The Beverly Caverns Sessions, Vol. 2 / May 26, 1953-May 27, 1953 / Good Time Jazz ✦✦✦

The second of two previously unreleased CDs of material from performances in Hollywood by clarinetist George Lewis' band in 1953 is not quite on the same level as his first volume. This 1996 CD finds trumpeter Kid Howard a bit erratic and Lewis occasionally out of tune but the music still has its strong moments. Trombonist Jim Robinson is typically reliable, the rhythm section (pianist Alton Purnell, banjoist Lawrence Marrero, bassist Alcide "Slow Drag" Pavageau and drummer Joe Watkins) is quite strong and some of the more rewarding performances include "In Gloryland," "Red Wing," "Panama" and "When the Saints Go Marching In" (a song that the group really "owned"). But *Vol. 1* definitely gets the edge. —*Scott Yanow*

☆ **Jazz Funeral in New Orleans** / Oct. 26, 1953 / DCC ✦✦✦✦✦

This CD brings back a classic, one of the greatest sessions ever by clarinetist George Lewis. The title of the CD is actually quite inaccurate, for "Just a Closer Walk with Thee" is the only funeral song included on the date, and there is nothing somber about any of the joyful music. Trumpeter/vocalist Kid Howard, who was often very erratic during the era (particularly on radio broadcasts), sounds in top form; the consistent trombonist Jim Robinson is an asset in the ensembles as usual, the rhythm section really drives the group, and clarinetist Lewis often seems to be quite exuberant. Their version of "When the Saints Go Marching In" is definitive, and other highlights include "Ice Cream" and "Panama." This set of prime New Orleans jazz music (last available as a DCC audiophile CD) belongs in every serious jazz collection. —*Scott Yanow*

George Lewis at Club Hangover, Vol. 1 / Nov. 7, 1953+Nov. 14, 1953 / Storyville ✦✦✦

The Sounds of New Orleans, Vol. 7 / Dec. 27, 1953+Jan. 2, 1954 / Storyville ✦✦✦

George Lewis' New Orleans Jazz Band is featured on two well-recorded radio broadcasts on this CD. The clarinetist/leader is generally in fine form as is trombonist Jim Robinson while trumpeter Kid Howard is typically erratic; Howard, drummer Joe Watkins and bassist Alcide Pavageau have spirited (if not necessarily musical) vocals and guest Lizzie Miles sings "Bill Bailey" and "Darktown Strutters Ball" in both English and Creole. Fans of George Lewis' band will want this release but more general collectors can find better sets to acquire first. —*Scott Yanow*

George Lewis' Ragtime Band of New Orleans: The Oxford Series, Vol. 1 / Feb. 21, 1954 / American Music ✦✦✦

These concert performances given at Miami University of Oxford, OH, document Lewis in a particularly relaxed and spontaneous mood. —*Bruce Raeburn*

Jazz at Vespers / Feb. 21, 1954 / Original Jazz Classics ✦✦✦✦

Jazz at the Ohio Union / Mar. 3, 1954 / Disc Jockey ✦✦

Recordings by clarinetist George Lewis' band in the 1950s are maddeningly inconsistent. The same band can perform the same songs during the same week and range from inspired to amateurish. This two-CD set, which documents a complete concert (including announcements) at Ohio State University, should have been much better. Unfortunately, trumpeter Kid Howard was having a very off day, and despite the spirit of the group, too many passages are way out of tune for the 1997 release to be recommended. Lewis and trombonist Jim Robinson do their best (as does the rhythm section, which includes pianist Alton Purnell) and the band runs through its usual repertoire of New Orleans favorites, hymns, ragtime and Dixieland standards (plus a brief "Salute to Ohio State" and "Collegiate"), but Howard largely sinks the effort. —*Scott Yanow*

In Stockholm 1959 / Feb. 10, 1959 / Dragon ✦✦✦✦✦

This is one of the best sessions of clarinetist George Lewis' later years. A Stockholm concert, released for the first time on this CD from the Swedish Dragon label, features Lewis' regular group of 1959, which consisted of trumpeter Avery "Kid" Howard, trombonist Jim Robinson, clarinetist George Lewis, pianist Joseph

Robichaux, bassist "Slow Drag" Pavageau and drummer Joe Watkins. The first half of the set in particular finds all of the musicians in top form, although trumpeter Howard's playing starts getting ragged by the halfway point. Lewis is heard near the peak of his powers on such songs as "Should I," "Burgundy Street Blues," an uptempo "Red Wing," "Runnin' Wild" and "Milenburg Joys." The enthusiastic crowd sounds understandably pleased by the results, an easily recommended set of New Orleans jazz. —*Scott Yanow*

With Papa Bue's Viking Jazz Band / Mar. 24, 1959+Mar. 25, 1959 / Storyville ✦✦✦

New Orleans clarinetist George Lewis teamed up with trombonist Papa Bue Jensen's Copenhagen-based Dixieland band for an LP in 1959 that has been reissued on this CD, along with five previously unreleased alternate takes. Lewis sounds a bit erratic in spots, slipping in and out of tune, and Jensen's band (which includes trumpeter Finn Otto Hansen and Jorgen Svare on second clarinet) was not as strong as it would become. The music, which includes "The Old Rugged Cross," "Listen to the Mocking Bird," "Isle of Capri" and "Salutation March," is full of spirit but not essential. —*Scott Yanow*

George Lewis Plays Hymns / Mar. 10, 1964+Nov. 28, 1964 / Milenburg ✦✦✦✦

This CD reissue brings back the music of a rare LP from the tiny Milneburg label. The popular New Orleans clarinetist George Lewis, backed by pianist Joe Robichaux and bassist Placide Adams, plays 15 traditional spirituals melodically and with plenty of reverence. Lewis' beautiful and heartfelt tone (primitive yet quite effective) caresses such hymns as "His Eye Is on the Sparrow," "Nearer My God to Thee," "I Shall Not Be Moved" and "Lily of the Valley." A special bonus of the reissue is a seven-minute interview from January 5, 1962, that was conducted before a college audience. Lewis is charming and sometimes humorous in answering questions about his life and recent activities. —*Scott Yanow*

Reunion / Jun. 5, 1966 / Delmark ✦✦✦✦

A very fine collaboration with Don Ewell. The 1997 CD reissue adds a new version of "Bucket's Got a Hole in It" and four worthy alternate takes from the same session. —*Ron Wynn*

George Lewis

b. Jul. 14, 1952, Chicago, IL

Trombone , Electronics / Avant-Garde

George Lewis has really had two overlapping careers, being both an avant-garde jazz trombonist and an experimenter with electronics whose work in the latter field is closer to modern classical music. He started on trombone when he was nine, attended Yale and played while still in college with Anthony Davis' sextet. He studied at the AACM school in the early '70s and developed quickly as a player. After two months with Count Basie's Orchestra (1976) he joined Anthony Braxton's exciting quartet where his trombone fit in perfectly with Braxton's reeds; their interplay could often be quite witty. Since then Lewis has played with most of the top avant-garde players (including Roscoe Mitchell, Barry Altschul, Derek Bailey, Evan Parker and Lester Bowie) while simultaneously working on advanced music outside of jazz. His collaboration with John Zorn and Bill Frisell on 1987's *News for Lulu* (for Hat Art) gives one a good example of his trombone playing. George Lewis has also led sessions for Sackville and Black Saint. —*Scott Yanow*

Solo Trombone Album / Nov. 21, 1976 / Sackville ✦✦✦✦

Shadowgraph / 1977 / Black Saint ✦✦✦

Trombonist George Lewis ranks among the more inspired artists working in improvisational circles. He doesn't restrict himself to hard bop and jazz standards; he uses both electric and acoustic instruments, and his compositions are often intricate, yet also allow maximum improvisational freedom. This date, reissued on CD, mixes pieces for large and small groups. The combo pieces are more interesting; the larger pieces are tightly structured and expertly presented, but lack color and tension, despite the fine playing. Lewis limits his own solo space, which is a shame, for he's one of the finest trombonists of his generation. *Shadowgraph, 5* has its flaws, but when it works, it's a reminder of George Lewis' special gifts as a composer and improviser. —*Ron Wynn*

George Lewis / Douglas Ewart / 1978 / Black Saint ✦✦✦

★ **Homage to Charles Parker** / 1979 / Black Saint ✦✦✦✦✦

Both of Lewis' compositions on this album are for an ensemble with Anthony Davis, piano; Douglas Ewart, bass clarinet; George Lewis, tenor trombone and electronics; and Richard Teitelbaum, Polymoog, Multimoog and Micromoog synthesizers. "Blues" (1977) is a "collective orchestration" that builds in a fragmentary style of changing timbres and happy to Tibetan-meditation spirit from material arranged in four basically diatonic choruses, using the essential harmonic sequence of the classic blues form as a starting point . . . but don't expect to hear a traditional "blues" because this music goes to the spirit behind the tune, rather than playing the tune; in the "Homage to Charles Parker" (1978) "the iconography (of the first section) . . . represents the life of Charles Parker—what is known, what is thought to be known, what is dreamed, heard and said—and his 'reality', i.e. birth and death" and the second part is based on the traditional solo with chordal accompaniment form that Charles Parker "brought to a rare level of perfection" and "makes loving inferences as to Parker's afterlife, and points to a new appraisal of world music after his life—one in which Afro-American creative music decisively affirms its place as a living, growing, vital part of world culture." —*Blue* Gene Tyranny

Voyager / Feb. 6, 1993 / Avant ✦✦✦
An interactive composition for computer and acoustic soloists "which analyzes aspects of an improvisor's performance in real time, using that analysis to guide an automatic composing program that generates complex responses to the musician's playing" (Lewis). This procedure results in a vast and continually fascinating range of emotional nuance, from the plaintive to the dense and propelled. Brilliant performances by Lewis on trombone and Roscoe Mitchell on alto and soprano saxophones. —*"Blue" Gene Tyranny*

Changing with the Times / Mar. 15, 1993-Mar. 17, 1993 / New World ✦✦✦✦✦
Innovative pieces, each with a speaker, poet, or singer reflecting on modern living. Titles include "Chicago Dadagram," "So You Say," "The View from Skates in Berkeley," "Airplane," "Epilogue." —*Blue* Gene Tyranny

John Lewis

b. May 3, 1920, La Grange, IL
Piano, Leader, Composer / Bop, Cool, Third Stream
The musical director of the Modern Jazz Quartet for its entire history, John Lewis found the perfect outlet for his interest in bop, blues and Bach. Possessor of a "cool" piano style that (like Count Basie's) makes every note count, Lewis with the MJQ has long helpled make jazz look respectable to the classical music community without watering down his performances.

After serving in the military, Lewis was in the Dizzy Gillespie big band (1946-48). He recorded with Charlie Parker during 1947-48 (including "Parker's Mood") and played with Miles Davis' Birth of the Cool Nonet, arranging "Move" and "Rouge." He worked with Illinois Jacquet (1948-49) and Lester Young (1950-51) and appeared on many recordings during the era. In 1951 Lewis recorded with the Milt Jackson Quartet, which by 1952 became the Modern Jazz Quartet. Lewis' musical vision was fulfilled with the MJQ and he composed many pieces, with "Django" being the best known. In addition to constantly touring with the MJQ during 1952-74, Lewis wrote the film scores to *Odds Against Tomorrow, No Sun in Venice* and *A Milanese Story,* recorded as a leader (including the 1956 cool classic "2 Degrees East, 3 Degrees West") collaborations with Gunther Schuller and records with Svend Asmussen and Albert Mangelsdorff) and worked with Orchestra USA in the mid-'60s. When the MJQ broke up in 1974, Lewis worked as an educator and occasionally recorded as a leader. With the MJQ's rebirth in 1981, he has resumed his former role as its guiding spirit. Most of John Lewis' own projects were recorded for Atlantic. —*Scott Yanow*

★ **Grand Encounter** / Feb. 10, 1956 / Pacific Jazz ✦✦✦✦✦
Also reissued as *2 Degrees East, 3 Degrees West* and occasionally listed under tenor saxophonist Bill Perkins' name, this classic session is the ultimate in cool jazz. Perkins' mellow tone matches quite well with the quiet but inwardly passionate playing of pianist John Lewis, guitarist Jim Hall, bassist Percy Heath and drummer Chico Hamilton. Surprisingly this date has been out of print in recent times but it is sure to reappear on Blue Note eventually. Lewis is featured with the rhythm section on "I Can't Get Started, Hall is added for "Skylark" and the full group plays three standards plus Lewis' memorable (and atmospheric) "2 Degrees East, 3 Degrees West." —*Scott Yanow*

The John Lewis Piano / Jul. 30, 1956-Aug. 24, 1957 / Atlantic ✦✦✦✦
Pianist John Lewis, heard on vacation from the Modern Jazz Quartet, mostly plays introverted interpretations on this out-of-print LP. He duets with drummer Connie Kay and guitarists Barry Galbraith and Jim Hall, only using a full rhythm section (bassist Percy Heath and drummer Kay) on two of the seven selections. The thoughtful and introspective selections include four Lewis originals (best known is "D & E") and three standards (including a tender "It Never Entered My Mind"). —*Scott Yanow*

Afternoon in Paris / Dec. 4, 1956-Dec. 7, 1956 / Atlantic ✦✦✦✦

European Windows / Feb. 20, 1958-Feb. 21, 1958 / RCA ✦✦✦
Although John Lewis plays piano throughout this orchestral album, he only solos on one piece ("Two Degrees East-Three Degrees West"). There are spots for baritonist Ronnie Ross and flutist Gerry Weinkopf but this is very much a third-stream effort. The Stuttgart Symphony Orchestra does not attempt to swing and the charts often lean more towards Western classical music (and the type of music one might

expect from a soundtrack) than jazz. This out-of-print LP is of greater interest from a historical standpoint than it is musically. —*Scott Yanow*

Improvised Meditations & Excursions / May 7, 1959-May 8, 1959 / Atlantic ✦✦✦✦
The emphasis on this fine LP is on John Lewis' piano playing. Taking time off from the Modern Jazz Quartet and his orchestral writing, Lewis performs five standards plus two of his originals ("Delaunay's Dilemma" and "Love Me") in a trio with drummer Connie Kay and either George Duvivier or Percy Heath on bass. A master at playing blues, Lewis' versatility and solid sense of swing can be heard on such songs as his two originals, "Now's the Time," "Yesterdays" and "September Song." —*Scott Yanow*

The Golden Striker / Feb. 12, 1960-Feb. 16, 1960 / Atlantic ✦✦
One of the less interesting John Lewis "third-stream" projects, this LP features Lewis' "Music for Brass." Six of his originals (four songs from his ballet "The Comedy," "Odds Against Tomorrow" and "The Golden Striker") plus four brief "Fanfares" are performed by four trumpets, two trombones, four French horns, a tuba and Lewis' trio. Although the pianist takes a few solos, the music is mostly written out and frankly rather dull. This set has been long out of print. —*Scott Yanow*

● **Wonderful World of Jazz** / Jul. 29, 1960-Sep. 9, 1960 / Atlantic ✦✦✦✦✦
This is one of pianist John Lewis' most rewarding albums outside of his work with the Modern Jazz Quartet. Three numbers (including a remake of "Two Degrees East, Three Degrees West") showcase his piano in a quartet with guitarist Jim Hall, bassist Geroge Duvivier and drummer Connie Kay. A 15-minute rendition of "Body and Soul" has one of tenor saxophonist Paul Gonsalves' finest solos, while "Afternoon in Paris" features a diverse cast with trumpeter Herb Pomeroy, Gunther Schuller on French horn, tenorman Benny Golson, baritonist Jimmy Giuffre and guitarist Jim Hall; altoist Eric Dolphy cuts everyone. This set was reissued in 1988 as part of Atlantic's *Jazzlore* series. —*Scott Yanow*

Jazz Abstraction / Dec. 19, 1960-Dec. 20, 1960 / Atlantic ✦✦✦✦✦
Although John Lewis is listed as the leader (this album's alternate title is "John Lewis Presents Contemporary Music"), the pianist does not actually appear on this record and only contributed one piece ("Django"). On what is very much a Gunther Schuller project, Schuller composed "Abstraction" and was responsible for the adventurous three-part "Variants on a Theme of John Lewis (Django)" and the four-part "Variants on a Theme of Thelonious Monk (Criss-Cross)"; Jim Hall contributed "Piece for Guitar & Strings." One of the most successful "third-stream" efforts, this LP combines avant-garde jazz with aspects of classical music. Among the more notable stars, altoist Ornette Coleman is on "Abstraction" and "Criss Cross" (both of which have been reissued in his Rhino CD box) and multi-instrumentalist Eric Dolphy is on both of the "Variants." Other musicians in the eclectic cast include guitarist Hall, bassist Scott LaFaro, pianist Bill Evans and several classical string players. This is very interesting music that deserves to be reissued in full on CD. —*Scott Yanow*

Original Sin / Mar. 28, 1961-Mar. 31, 1961 / Atlantic ✦✦

A Milanese Story / Jan. 17, 1962 / Atlantic ✦✦✦✦

Essence / May 25, 1962 / Atlantic ✦✦✦

European Encounter / Jul. 2, 1962-Jul. 3, 1962 / Atlantic ✦✦✦✦
Violinist Svend Asmussen (who has had too few of his albums through the decades available in the US) teams up with pianist John Lewis, bassist Jimmy Woode and drummer Sture Kalin on this 1962 session from Stockholm, Sweden. Most notable is the repertoire: six Lewis originals (including "Django") and Ornette Coleman's "Lonely Woman." Asmussen fits in well with Lewis and brings a solid sense of swing to the somewhat complex music. This date was reissued in 1986 as part of Atlantic's *Jazzlore* series. —*Scott Yanow*

Animal Dance / Jul. 30, 1962 / Atlantic ✦✦✦✦

P.O.V. / Jan. 13, 1975-Jan. 17, 1975 / Columbia ✦✦✦
This LP is one of pianist John Lewis' most obscure sessions. Recorded shortly after the Modern Jazz Quartet temporarily broke up, Lewis' set utilizes a jazz rhythm section (with bassist Richard Davis and drummer Mel Lewis) and on some of Lewis' six originals three nonimprovising classical musicians (flutist Harold Jones, violinist Gerald Tarack and cellist Fortunato Arico) display Lewis' interests in bop, cool jazz, classical music and the mixture of the idioms known as Third Stream. None of the originals became standards but, listened to as a whole, they form a pleasing set of music. —*Scott Yanow*

Evening with Two Grand Pianos / Jan. 25, 1979-Feb. 9, 1979 / Little David ✦✦✦✦
This album is an unlikely success. On a set of piano duets by Hank Jones and John Lewis, there is plenty of swing, a liberal dose of good humor and surprisingly uncrowded ensembles. High points of the eight spirited performances include "Stompin' at the Savoy," "Confirmation," "Billie's Bounce" and "I'll Remember

April." It is a pity that this out-of-print LP has not been reissued on CD yet. —*Scott Yanow*

Kansas City Breaks / May 25, 1982-May 26, 1982 / Finesse ✦✦✦
The music on this LP has been reissued several times since its initial release. This was the last record by John Lewis' sextet before it broke up; at the time the Modern Jazz Quartet was beginning to appear again on a fulltime basis. Lewis picked an interesting variety of sidemen (flutist Frank Wess, violinist Joe Kennedy, guitarist Howard Collins, bassist Marc Johnson and drummer Shelly Manne) for his group and together they perform a set of his originals that (tonal variations aside) are not all that different from what one might have heard by the MJQ at the time. "Django," the blues "D&E" and the title cut are among the more memorable selections. The interplay and blend between flute and violin are the main reasons to search for this set. —*Scott Yanow*

Delaunay's Delemma / Oct. 2, 1987 / EmArcy ✦✦✦✦
This is a fun set, a trio outing by pianist John Lewis, bassist Marc Johnson and guitarist Howard Collins that consistently swings, covers a variety of moods and has a strong dose of the blues. An excellent showcase for the leader's piano, the tunes are mostly standards (including Lewis' "Django" and "Concorde") and the set begins and ends with different versions of the same original (titled " . . . And in the Beginning" and "There Was the Blues"). One of John Lewis' better solo dates. —*Scott Yanow*

Midnight in Paris / Dec. 5, 1988-Dec. 6, 1988 / EmArcy ✦✦✦✦✦
A marvelous session. —*Ron Wynn*

Private Concert / Sep. 10, 1990-Sep. 12, 1990 / EmArcy ✦✦✦✦

Meade "Lux" Lewis (Meade Anderson Lewis)

b. Sep. 4, 1905, Chicago, IL, d. Jun. 7, 1964, Minneapolis, MN
Piano / Boogie-Woogie, Piano Blues
One of the three great boogie-woogie pianists (along with Albert Ammons and Pete Johnson) whose appearance at John Hammond's 1938 *Spirituals to Swing* concert helped start the boogie-woogie craze, Meade "Lux" Lewis was a powerful if somewhat limited player. He played regularly in Chicago in the late '20s and his one solo record of the time, "Honky Tonk Train Blues" (1927), was considered a classic. However, other than a few sides backing little-known blues singers, Lewis gained little extra work and slipped into obscurity. John Hammond heard Lewis' record in 1935 and after a search found Lewis washing cars for a living in Chicago. Soon Meade Lux Lewis was back on records and after the 1938 concert he was able to work steadily, sometimes in duets or trios with Ammons and Johnson. He became the first jazz pianist to double on celeste (starting in 1936) and was featured on that instrument in a Blue Note quartet date with Edmond Hall and Charlie Christian; he also played harpsichord on a few records in 1941. After the boogie-woogie craze ended, Lewis continued working in Chicago and California, recording as late as 1962 although by then he was pretty much forgotten. Meade Lux Lewis led sessions through the years that have come out on MCA, Victor, Blue Note, Solo Art, Euphonic, Stinson, Atlantic, Storyville, Verve, Tops, ABC-Paramount, Riverside and Philips. —*Scott Yanow*

Meade Lux Lewis (1939-1954) / 1939-1954 / Story of Blues ✦✦✦
This CD reissue collects together solo, duet and trio sides by the great boogie-woogie pianist Meade Lux Lewis, many of which do not duplicate other readily available collections. Most of the first nine selections surprisingly feature Lewis playing blues with a light stride rather than a boogie bassline. Two titles from 1944 are more typical of what the public expected, while the final three numbers (from 1953-54) are a bit subpar, sloppy if spirited honky tonk music played on a poor piano. This CD is a gap filler for completists but otherwise not too essential. —*Scott Yanow*

● **The Blues Piano Artistry of Meade Lux Lewis** / Nov. 1, 1961 / Original Jazz Classics ✦✦✦✦✦
Boogie-woogie pianist Meade Lux Lewis' next-to-last record was his first recording in five years and his final opportunity to stretch out unaccompanied. This solo Riverside set (reissued by OJC on CD) as usual finds Lewis generally sticking to the blues (with "You Were Meant for Me" and "Fate" being exceptions), mostly performing originals. On a few of the songs Lewis switches effectively to celeste. It apparently only took Meade Lux Lewis two hours to record the full set and the results are quite spontaneous yet well organized, a fine all-around portrait of the veteran pianist in his later period. —*Scott Yanow*

Mel Lewis (Melvin Sokoloff)

b. May 10, 1929, Buffalo, NY, d. Feb. 2, 1990, New York, NY
Drums, Leader / Bop, Post-Bop
Although he was generally reluctant to solo, Mel Lewis was considered one of the definitive big-band drummers, a musician who was best at driving an orchestra

but could also play quite well with smaller units. He started playing professionally when he was 15 and worked with the big bands of Boyd Raeburn (1948), Alvino Rey, Ray Anthony and Tex Beneke. Lewis gained a great deal of recognition in the jazz world for his work with Stan Kenton (1954-57), making the large ensemble swing hard. In 1957 he settled in Los Angeles, became a studio drummer and worked with the big bands of Terry Gibbs and Gerald Wilson. Lewis went to New York to play with Gerry Mulligan's Concert Jazz Band in 1960 and he toured Europe with Dizzy Gillespie (1961) and the Soviet Union with Benny Goodman (1962). In 1965 Lewis formed an orchestra in New York with Thad Jones that grew to be one of the top big bands in jazz. When Jones surprised everyone by suddenly fleeing to Europe in 1979, Lewis became the orchestra's sole leader, playing regularly each Monday night at the Village Vanguard with the band up until his death. Mel Lewis recorded as a leader in the 1950s for San Francisco Jazz Records, Mode (reissued on V.S.O.P.) and Andex and, after Thad Jones left their orchestra, Mel Lewis recorded with his big band for Atlantic, Telarc and Music Masters. —*Scott Yanow*

Mel Lewis Sextet / Jun. 1957 / V.S.O.P. ✦✦✦✦
Mel Lewis, formerly with the Stan Kenton Orchestra (and at the time a busy West Coast studio musician), had a rare opportunity to lead a record date in 1957 when he headed this sextet session for the MOD (Music of the Day) label; it has since been reissued on LP by V.S.O.P. With arrangements by Bob Brookmeyer, Marty Paich and Bill Holman, Lewis and his group (which features Charlie Mariano on alto and tenor, Bill Holman doubling on tenor and baritone, trumpeter Jack Sheldon, pianist Marty Paich, bassist Buddy Clark and the leader/drummer) perform originals by the three arrangers and Sheldon, in addition to the standard "You Took Advantage of Me." The enjoyable boppish music is quite colorful. —*Scott Yanow*

Mel Lewis and Friends / Jun. 18, 1976 / A&M ✦✦✦✦
A rare small-group date led by drummer Mel Lewis, this CD reissues some excellent straightahead music originally put out by A&M's Horizon subsidiary, which was run by producer John Snyder. The liner notes (exact duplications of the LP's) are a bit microscopic, but the music still communicates quite well. Trumpeter Freddie Hubbard is in top form during five selections (including "Moose the Mooche" and a quartet feature on "A Child Is Born"); tenor saxophonist Michael Brecker and Gregory Herbert (mostly on alto) get in their licks; pianist Hank Jones and bassist Ron Carter are typically flawless, and trumpeter Cecil Bridgewater makes a guest appearance on "Sho' Nuff Did." Excellent music. —*Scott Yanow*

Naturally / Mar. 20, 1979-Mar. 21, 1979 / Telarc ✦✦✦✦
This was the first recording by the Mel Lewis Jazz Orchestra, made just a short time after co-leader Thad Jones surprised everyone by suddenly quitting and moving to Europe. Although Jones was gone, the band was still performing his arrangements, and all six of the charts on the set were Thad's; plus, he was the composer of five of the tunes. With such soloists as pianist Jim McNeely, altoist Dick Oatts, trumpeter John Marshall and the tenors of Bob Rockwell and Richard Perry (along with plenty of tight ensembles), it was clear that the orchestra would live on. Worth searching for. —*Scott Yanow*

Live at Village Vanguard / Apr. 1980 / Gryphon ✦✦✦✦
A 1991 reissue of prime sessions, with Lewis at the helm of his longtime big band. High-octane solos and energetic compositions. —*Ron Wynn*

Live in Montreux / Jul. 16, 1980 / Pausa ✦✦✦✦
The 1980 version of the Mel Lewis Jazz Orchestra performs five Herbie Hancock tunes arranged by Bob Mintzer, quite an assignment for the young tenor saxophonist, who was not even a member of the big band. Mintzer's reworkings of such tunes as "Dolphin Dance" and "Speak like a Child" are fresh and unpredictable. Such soloists are featured as pianist Jim McNeely, altoist Dick Oatts, future tenor great Joe Lovano (heard on "Eye of the Hurricane"), and trumpeter Earl Gardner; also in the band at the time (but not featured) is altoist Steve Coleman. It is a pity that this music (originally put out on the European MPS label and made available domestically by the now-defunct Pausa label) is difficult to find. —*Scott Yanow*

Mel Lewis Plays Herbie Hancock / Jul. 16, 1980 / Pausa ✦✦✦✦
Live at Montreux. A first-rate big-band date. —*Ron Wynn*

Mellifuous / Mar. 31, 1981 / Landmark ✦✦✦

Mel Lewis & the Jazz Orchestra / Jan. 7, 1982-Jan. 11, 1982 / Finesse ✦✦✦✦
Recorded live at the Village Vanguard, the Mel Lewis big band (which at the time was in the process of finding its own sound) performs arrangements by Bob Brookmeyer. While letting the band swing and leaving space for such soloists as fluegelhornist Tom Harrell, altoist Dick Oatts, Joe Lovano's tenor, pianist Jim McNeely and altoist Kenny Garrett, Brookmeyer (who sits in on valve trombone during "Goodbye World") nevertheless constructs difficult charts that are more than a little inspired by modern classical music; this version of "My Funny Valen-

tine" is quite eerie. Somehow the Mel Lewis Orchestra sounds relaxed on this rather complex music and the overall results are rewarding. —Scott Yanow

20 Years at the Village Vanguard / Mar. 20, 1985-Mar. 22, 1985 / Atlantic ◆◆◆◆
The Mel Lewis Jazz Orchestra (originally co-led by Thad Jones) celebrated its 20th anniversary with this Atlantic album, one of its very few major-label releases. Although two of Jones' arrangements are on this set ("All of Me" and "Interloper"), the big band had changed quite a bit since his defection in 1979, becoming younger (it was originally an all-star group), less dependent on one arranger, and a bit more influenced by classical music while still swinging. The 1985 version of the band included such notable players as pianist Kenny Werner, altoist Dick Oatts and both Joe Lovano and Ralph Lalama on tenors, but it was more of a team effort without any one player dominating. Excellent modern big-band music. —Scott Yanow

● **The Definitive Thad Jones, Vol. 1** / Feb. 11, 1988-Feb. 15, 1988 / Music Masters ◆◆◆◆◆
Although Thad Jones (who passed away in 1986) had left the big band that he co-led with drummer Mel Lewis back in 1979, some of his charts remained in the orchestra's book. On the first of two CDs taken from an engagement at the Village Vanguard (a third CD, *Soft Lights and Hot Music*, is also from these dates), Lewis leads his men through five Jones arrangements, including "Quietude," "Three in One" (which is 13 minutes long) and the 15-minute stomper "Little Pixie." The soloists include baritonist Gary Smulyan, both Joe Lovano and Ralph Lalama on tenors, altoists Ted Nash and Dick Oatts, trumpeter Glenn Drewes and pianist Kenny Werner. Recommended as a particularly strong example of the Mel Lewis Orchestra. —Scott Yanow

The Definitive Thad Jones, Vol. 2 / Feb. 11, 1988-Feb. 15, 1988 / Music Masters ◆◆◆◆

Soft Lights and Hot Music / Feb. 11, 1988-Feb. 15, 1988 / Music Masters ◆◆◆◆
Recorded at the same sessions that resulted in two other CDs (both of which featured Thad Jones arrangements), this CD has charts by five different musicians, yet the sound of Mel Lewis' Jazz Orchestra stayed consistent. Most unusual is that all but two numbers on this release (originals by Kenny Werner and band pianist Jim McNeely) are standards. Altoist Ted Nash ("Our Love Is Here to Stay" and "It Could Happen to You") has two features; pianist Kenny Werner ("The Touch of Your Lips"), trombonist John Mosca ("How Long Has This Been Going On") and altoist Dick Oatts ("Little Man, You've Had a Busy Day") are also showcased; and there are spots for the tenor of Ralph Lalama, trumpeter Glenn Drews and the up-and-coming tenor Joe Lovano. This fine effort is at the usual high level of the inventive orchestra. —Scott Yanow

The Lost Art / Apr. 11, 1989-Apr. 12, 1989 / Music Masters ◆◆◆◆

To You: A Tribute to Mel Lewis / Sep. 10, 1990-Sep. 12, 1990 / Music Masters ◆◆

Ramsey Lewis

b. May 27, 1935, Chicago, IL
Piano, Keyboards / Soul Jazz, Crossover Jazz, Instrumental Pop, Pop-Soul
Ramsey Lewis has long straddled the boundary between bop-oriented jazz and pop music. Most of his recordings (particularly in the mid-'60s) were very accessible and attracted a large nonjazz audience. In 1956 he formed a trio with bassist Eldee Young and drummer Red Holt. From the start (1958) their records for Argo/Cadet were popular although in the early days they had a strong jazz content. In 1958 Lewis also recorded with Max Roach and Lem Winchester. On the 1965 albums *The In Crowd* and *Hang On Ramsey*, Ramsey made the pianist into a major attraction and from that point on his records became much more predictable and pop-oriented. In 1966 his trio's personnel changed with bassist Cleveland Eaton and drummer Maurice White (later the founder of Earth, Wind and Fire) joining Lewis. In the 1970s Lewis often played electric piano although by later in the decade he was sticking to acoustic and hiring an additional keyboardist. He can still play melodic jazz when he wants to but Ramsey Lewis has mostly stuck to easy-listening pop music during the past 30 years. —Scott Yanow

Consider the Source / 1956-Apr. 1959 / Chess ◆◆◆◆
Consider the Source is a 17-track compilation of recordings made by the Ramsey Lewis Trio between 1956 and 1959 and features performance of standards like "I Love Paris" and "My Funny Valentine." —AMG

Gentleman of Swing / 1956 / Argo ◆◆◆◆
This was pianist Ramsey Lewis' first album, a trio set with bassist Eldee Young and drummer Red Holt. Lewis sounds like a cross between John Lewis and Oscar Peterson, playing melodic and lightly boppish versions of such pieces as "Carmen," Russ Freeman's "The Wind," "Bei Mir Bist Du Schoen," Gerry Mulligan's "Limelight" and a few originals. Five of the nine selections have since been reissued on CD but the full LP is worth getting. Chances are that this historic album

can be picked up fairly inexpensively at a used record store; it is worth taking a chance on. —Scott Yanow

Ramsey Lewis and His Gentlemen of Jazz, Vol. 2 / Feb. 9, 1958 / Argo ◆◆◆◆
This out-of-print LP (some of the contents have since come out on CD in the Decca reissue series) was the second one issued under pianist Ramsey Lewis' name and is taken from the same session as his debut. Joined by his longtime sidemen bassist Eldee Young and drummer Red Holt, Lewis plays a melodic brand of swinging bop. This version of "Delilah" (from the film *Samson and Delilah*) was a minor hit and other highlights include "Please Send Me Someone to Love," "Black Is the Color," "It Ain't Necessarily So" and "On the Street Where You Live." Ramsey Lewis' roots in jazz (which in later years would sometimes be hidden) is very much in evidence throughout this enjoyable trio set. —Scott Yanow

Ramsey Lewis Trio in Chicago / Apr. 1960 / Argo ◆◆◆◆
One of pianist Ramsey Lewis' most satisfying jazz albums of his pre-*The In Crowd* days, this LP features the pianist, bassist Eldee Young and drummer Red Holt jamming a variety of standards (including "Old Devil Moon," "I'll Remember April" and "But Not for Me"), plus "Carmen," "Delilah" and "Folk Ballad." The trio stretches out a little more during the live date than they did in the studio, and they seem inspired by the audience. As with most of Lewis' early Argo/Cadet releases, this has not been reissued yet on CD, but the excellent LP can probably be found in budget bins. —Scott Yanow

More Music from the Soil / Feb. 16, 1961-Feb. 17, 1961 / Cadet ◆◆◆
This is a typically enjoyable and accessible early Ramsey Lewis Trio recording. The pianist, bassist Eldee Young and drummer Red Holt swing their way through such songs as "Around the World in 80 Days," "Since I Fell for You," "Blues for the Night Owl" and "Autumn in New York." On "Hello Cello," Young does a fine job switching to cello. As is true of most of Lewis' Argo recordings, this one has not yet reappeared on CD. —Scott Yanow

The Greatest Hits [Chess] / 1961-1966 / Chess ◆◆◆
From a rock or pop listener's perspective, this is inarguably Lewis' most essential material. This 18-song double album has all four of his Top 40 hits from 1965-66 ("The In Crowd," "Hang on Sloopy," "A Hard Day's Night," and "Wade in the Water"), as well as various other cuts from 1961-66 LPs and singles, dominated by covers of popular Motown, R&B, and pop songs. Its unabashed pop-friendly approach isn't going to impress serious jazzbos, but then, Lewis wasn't pretending to make serious art during this period. He aimed to stake out some pleasant jazz-R&B-pop grooves with good hooks, and—with the help of sidemen like drummer Maurice White (later in Earth, Wind & Fire) and the rhythm section of Eldee Young and Red Holt (soon to form the similar Young-Holt Unlimited)—he succeeded. —Richie Unterberger

Never on Sunday / Aug. 10, 1996-Aug. 11, 1996 / Cadet ◆◆◆
The playing time on this LP (under half an hour) means that the ten selections are a bit briefer than usual. Pianist Ramsey Lewis, bassist Eldee Young and drummer Red Holt had one of the most popular groups in jazz of the era, playing soulful and melodic versions of standards that were both swinging and accessible. Highlights of this LP include "I Got Plenty of Nothing," "The Breeze and I" and "Exactly Like You." —Scott Yanow

Stretchin Out / Feb. 23, 1960-Feb. 24, 1960 / Cadet ◆◆◆◆
The Ramsey Lewis Trio, with bassist Eldee Young and drummer Red Holt joining the leader/pianist, was a hot property in 1960, although it was still five years before "The In Crowd." Their swinging string of albums for Argo (most of which unfortunately have relatively brief playing time, like this 31-minute program) are among Lewis' strongest from the jazz standpoint, balancing a commercial emphasis on melody with jazz improvising and swinging. Later on, the balance would shift towards pop, but Ramsey Lewis' late-'50s/early-'60s work resulted in sets of interest to jazz listeners, including this LP. Highlights include "Little Liza Jane," "My Ship" (which at 4:06 is easily the longest performance of the set), "Put Your Little Foot Right Out" and "A Portrait of Jennie." —Scott Yanow

The Ramsey Lewis Trio at the Bohemian Caverns / Jun. 4, 1964-Jun. 6, 1964 / Cadet ◆◆◆◆
This live set by the Ramsey Lewis Trio resulted in the minor hit "Something You Got," an interesting four-song, 12-minute "West Side Story Medley," and five briefer numbers. One of the last Lewis LPs before the major success of "The In Crowd" pushed him in more overtly commercial directions, this enjoyable album finds the group balancing accessible elements with swinging mainstream jazz. Worth searching for. —Scott Yanow

Bach to the Blues / 1964 / Cadet ◆◆◆
For this set by pianist Ramsey Lewis, bassist Eldee Young (Richard Evans plays bass on two songs when Young switches to cello) and drummer Red Holt, the group performs five original themes based on classical music, along with four blues-oriented tunes. Although a touch lightweight, the music is enjoyable enough

and certainly superior to most of Lewis' output in the 1970s and '80s. —*Scott Yanow*

★ **The In Crowd** / May 13, 1965-May 15, 1965 / Chess ✦✦✦✦✦
This fine live record was a big hit due to the surprise popularity of Ramsey Lewis' version of "The In Crowd," which reached No. 5 on the pop charts. The rest of the LP is fairly typical for Lewis, bassist Eldee Young and drummer Red Holt—soulful and grooving versions of a wide variety of tunes, including "Since I Fell for You," "Tennessee Waltz," the love theme from "Spartacus" and "Come Sunday." Recommended. —*Scott Yanow*

Hang On Ramsey / Oct. 14, 1965-Oct. 17, 1965 / Cadet ✦✦✦
Considering that this album was an obvious follow-up to "The In Crowd," it is surprising that the music is not more commercial; that would happen in the near future. As it was, pianist Ramsey Lewis (assisted as usual by bassist Eldee Young and drummer Red Holt) had another big hit in "Hang on Sloopy," and the set (as with the previous one) was recorded at a club before an enthusiastic crowd. The enjoyable LP also includes a couple of Beatles tunes (their version of "A Hard Day's Night" caught on), "He's a Real Gone Guy," "Billy Boy" and "Hi-Heel Sneakers" among the highlights. This was the final full-length recording by the group before Young and Holt left to form their own band. —*Scott Yanow*

Wade in the Water / Mar. 26, 1996-Jun. 19, 1996 / Cadet ✦✦✦
A major hit in its time, but of dubious quality from a remastering standpoint. —*Ron Wynn*

Maiden Voyage / Apr. 6, 1968-Dec. 1968 / Chess ✦✦✦
This pop-oriented CD reissue brings back the highlights from pianist Ramsey Lewis' two Argo records *Maiden Voyage* and *Mother Nature's Son*. Although Lewis' trio of the time (with bassist Cleveland Eaton and drummer Maurice White) is heard prominently, they are accompanied by strings, voices (including Minnie Riperton) and (on the last four numbers) a large orchestra. There are some good piano solos but the Charles Stepney arrangements (which are lavishly praised in the liner notes) are period pieces as is much of the material, which includes selections from Lennon & McCartney, Bob Dylan, Burt Bacharach ("Do You Know the Way to San Jose") and Aretha Franklin. Even Herbie Hancock's "Maiden Voyage" and Mike Gibbs' "Sweet Rain" sound like pop tunes. One can hear the beginnings of the crossover music of the 1980s and '90s in recordings such as this one but the performances have not dated all that well. —*Scott Yanow*

Down to Earth / Nov. 6, 1958-Dec. 4, 1969 / Mercury ✦✦✦✦
The Ramsey Lewis Trio was popular from the start, cutting four albums of material during 1958, only two years after Lewis began teaming up with bassist Eldee Young and drummer Red Holt. This LP (one of very few by the group in its early days that were not made for Argo or Cadet) has the trio emphasizing folk songs and traditional melodies such as "Dark Eyes," "Come Back to Sorrento," "John Henry" and "Billy Boy." Their concise interpretations (only two songs are longer than 3:15) feature swinging solos by Lewis and respect for the melodies. The music (if not essential) is quite accessible while still being jazz-oriented. Worth picking up. —*Scott Yanow*

Sun Goddess / 1974 / Columbia ✦✦✦✦

The Electric Collection / 1975-1977 / Columbia ✦✦✦
Although slick and commercial, most of the 1970s sides gathered on the 1991 CD *Electric Collection* are decent, creative and tasteful. Ramsey Lewis, who's heard on both acoustic piano and electric keyboards, sounds genuinely inspired on meaty yet accessible material ranging from jazz-funk workouts like "Come Back, Jack," and "The Messenger" to the playful "Blues for the Night Owl." If "Tequila Mockingbird" seems greatly influenced by Earth, Wind & Fire, it's because most of his sidemen on that appealing number are members of the soul/funk powerhouse. To be sure, there are a few duds here, including the dreadful, muzak-like "I'll Always Dream About You" and an unimaginative cover of EWF's "That's the Way of the World." But gratefully, throwaways don't dominate this generally enjoyable, though never outstanding, compilation. —*Alex Henderson*

Tequila Mockingbird / 1977 / Columbia ✦✦
Lightweight. —*Ron Wynn*

Routes / 1980 / Columbia ✦✦✦
Standard Ramsey Lewis vehicle; good-to-routine pop-flavored and soulful material with some rousing piano solos and some not so energetic. Lewis was in the middle of another impressive run, making one hit album after another. —*Ron Wynn*

Live at the Savoy / 1981 / Columbia ✦✦✦

The Two of Us / 1984 / Columbia ✦✦✦
This is great supper club/cabaret fare. Not for serious jazz fans or purists. —*Ron Wynn*

Keys to the City / 1987 / Columbia ✦✦✦
A pop date. —*Ron Wynn*

We Meet Again / 1988-1989 / Columbia ✦✦✦✦
Billy Taylor (p) takes the date, but Lewis shows chops he seldom taps these days. —*Ron Wynn*

Ivory Pyramid / 1992 / GRP ✦✦

Sky Islands / 1993 / GRP ✦✦
Ramsey Lewis has long been content to record lightweight pop/R&B grooves. Occasionally on this set the acoustic pianist (whose backup crew includes guitarist Henry Johnson and keyboardist Michael Logan) sounds like he would like to break away a bit from the predictable but he keeps the impulse in check. There is little to distinguish this CD from his previous few. —*Scott Yanow*

Between the Keys / Dec. 1995-Jan. 1996 / GRP ✦✦
Although Ramsey Lewis gained his initial fame as a jazz pianist, many of his records (including this one) are really more in the R&B field. The soul vocals, acid jazz rhythms and tinkling piano result in superior background music and there are some good moments (such as Grover Washington, Jr.'s soprano on "Sun Goddess 2000") but Ramsey Lewis is capable of much better. A strictly commercial effort that succeeds more as dance music than as creative jazz. —*Scott Yanow*

Dave Liebman

b. Sep. 4, 1946, New York, NY
Soprano Saxophone, Tenor Saxophone , Flute / Avant-Garde, Post-Bop
Dave Liebman has developed over time to become one of the top soprano saxophonists in jazz. A highly individual and explorative (yet versatile) improviser who can stretch from bop to free, Liebman studied early on with Lennie Tristano and Charles Lloyd. He gained important experience playing with Ten Wheel Drive (1970), Elvin Jones (1971-73) and Miles Davis' fusion group (1973-74). Liebman formed Lookout Farm in 1974, the first of several groups (including Quest in the 1980s) that teamed his reeds with pianist Richie Beirach. By the late '80s he had largely dropped the tenor to concentrate on soprano and occasionally flute although he made a rare recording on tenor for Double-Time in 1995. Dave Liebman, who is very active in jazz education and has written several books, has recorded for a countless number of labels through the years as a leader including PM, ECM, Horizon, Timeless, Palo Alto, Impulse, Soul Note, Heads Up, Storyville, Owl, CMP, Red and Candid. —*Scott Yanow*

Open Sky / May 1, 1972-Jun. 10, 1972 / PM ✦✦✦✦
Adventurous pieces. A triumphant exhibition of multi-reed versatility. Tremendous work in a small-combo format. —*Ron Wynn*

Lookout Farm / Oct. 10, 1973-Oct. 11, 1973 / ECM ✦✦✦✦✦
Liebman at the top-of-the-heap as an unabashed improviser. A high-water mark for this period. Completely original post-Tristano piano of Richard Beirach. —*Michael G. Nastos*

Drum Ode / Mar. 1974 / ECM ✦✦✦

Sweet Hands / Jul. 25, 1975-Jul. 30, 1975 / Horizon ✦✦✦
The influence of India upon jazz had not been spent entirely when Dave Liebman and Lookout Farm recorded the first of his Horizon albums, which pursues the East-meets-West direction of his former employer Miles Davis, but without the latter's dramatic thrust. The sweet hands refer to those of tabla player Badal Roy (a fellow Miles alumnus), whose precise Indian rhythmic structures underpin and control the bumpy fusion of Indian music and jazz-funk on "Sweet Hand Roy." Elsewhere, Roy's "Ashirbad" merges into George Harrison's "Within You, Without You," a lovely idea until the track begins to drift. Ever the eclectic, though, Liebman does achieve ignition on "Dr. Faustus," which whips up a jazz-rock-funk frenzy with Richie Beirach's propulsive electric piano and kibitzing clavinet, John Abercrombie's rock guitar, and Liebman's masterful, occasionally Echoplexed saxes. There is also some free jazz grooving on "Napanoch." Fascinating music, if not always convincing. —*Richard S. Ginell*

Forgotten Fantasies / Nov. 18, 1975-Nov. 20, 1975 / Horizon ✦✦✦✦
Fine playing. Not quite as accomplished conceptually. —*Ron Wynn*

Light'n up Please! / May 1976-Sep. 1976 / Horizon ✦✦
Allied with Pee Wee King of James Brown fame, Dave Liebman plunges headlong into funk in the wake of Herbie Hancock's *Headhunters*, but his heart doesn't seem to be in it. At times, he sounds bored playing R&B riffs that he seemed to have outgrown at the time, lapsing into free-jazz flurries in an effort to stay interested, and the rhythm section is leaden. The whole thing is recorded with a dry, airless ambience, possibly emulating *Headhunters* and its sought-after riches—but no, it didn't translate into anything close to a gold record. Leon Thomas makes some fairly ridiculous vocal appearances on the energetic but mindless funk of "Children of the Ghetto" and the pale imitation of a JB groove, "Got to Work." Yet there are a few moments, particularly on "Tranquility of the Protective Aura," where Liebman's lovely soprano is permitted to soar unimpeded. The title of the

album refers either to photography or cigarettes, depending upon which side of the cover you're looking at. —*Richard S. Ginell*

Pendulum / Feb. 4, 1978-Feb. 5, 1978 / Artists House ✦✦✦✦✦

Doin' It Again / Aug. 1979 / Timeless ✦✦✦
Hot playing and exuberant solos. —*Ron Wynn*

Dedications / Sep. 1979 / CMP ✦✦✦✦
Septet performances in 1979 led by saxophonist David Liebman. These mix standards, originals, blues, and ballads, with strong, intense solos from Liebman, fine arrangements and ensemble interaction, and standout contributions from pianist Richie Beirach and bassist Eddie Gomez. —*Ron Wynn*

What It Is / 1980 / Columbia ✦✦✦

If Only They Knew / Jul. 14, 1980 / Timeless ✦✦✦

Sweet Fury / Mar. 23, 1984-Mar. 24, 1984 / From Bebop To Now ✦✦✦✦
Mid-'80s blues, funk, and straightahead sessions featuring tenor saxophonist David Liebman. A fine soloist and underrated composer, Liebman can make standard blues seem intense and loosen up rigid funk material, while stretching out on tenor or soprano and adding some punch to routine mainstream numbers. —*Ron Wynn*

The Loneliness of a Long-Distance Runner / Nov. 1985-Dec. 1985 / CMP ✦✦✦✦✦
David Liebman did it alone (solo and ensemble multi-dubbing) on *The Loneliness of a Long-Distance Runner*. The "distance" on this very personal program conception was one of one's life span, with Liebman viewing the importance of the race being not the finality but the process of the experience. Included with this work are notes by the artist, which may or may not help the listener relate to the music by the suggested imagery of the notes or titles. The multiple overdubs were particularly well integrated, giving much of this a WSQ (World Saxophone Quartet)-like texture under Liebman's bluesy Ornette Coleman-like lines (a lonely woman-like phrase recurs throughout)...The overdubbing added a great textural emotion and conveys the involvement and harmony one expects from a group. Over this the soprano saxman involved himself in some outstanding improvisations, maintaining a tension, passion and involvement that was unfaltering. —*Bob Rusch, Cadence*

★ **Homage to John Coltrane** / Jan. 27, 1987-Jan. 28, 1987 / Owl ✦✦✦✦✦
Reissue in 1991. An intense tribute to one of Liebman's prime influences. —*Ron Wynn*

Midpoint /Apr. 21, 1987-Apr. 22, 1987 / Storyville ✦✦✦✦

The Energy of the Chance / 1988 / Heads Up ✦✦✦

Trio + One / May 1, 1988-May 2, 1988 / Owl ✦✦✦✦✦
Soprano master doing variation of familiar themes and out-and-out original material. With Dave Holland (b) and Jack DeJohnette (d). Very worthwhile new music. —*Michael G. Nastos*

Chant / Jul. 1989 / CMP ✦✦✦✦

☆ **The Tree** / Apr. 24, 1990 / Soul Note ✦✦✦✦✦
This rather interesting set of solo soprano saxophone explorations by David Liebman (one of the greats on that instrument) has an odd concept that works. Liebman plays a six-part suite that has titles of "Roots," "Trunk," "Limbs," "Branches," "Twigs" and "Leaves" and then does a second version, playing the sections in the opposite order. The sections farthest from the "Roots" are the most advanced although all of these movements are fairly free. It's well worth several listens. —*Scott Yanow*

West Side Story Today / Oct. 13, 1990-Oct. 17, 1990 / Owl ✦✦✦✦✦

Classic Ballads / Dec. 1990-Jan. 1991 / Candid ✦✦✦✦
Outstanding straightahead and mainstream date by veteran saxophonist Dave Liebman, dedicated to Natalie Visentin. Liebman is great in any style, but this time sounds more convincing and passionate than on any recent traditional set he's done. It's a trio setting, with pianist Vic Juris and drummer Steve Gilmore. —*Ron Wynn*

Joy / Mar. 19, 1992-Mar. 20, 1992 / Candid ✦✦✦✦✦
David Liebman has recorded several tributes to John Coltrane through the years (even though he really doesn't sound like him) and this Candid CD is one of his most rewarding. Utilizing a strong college orchestra, some guests and (on "After the Rain") the 17 flutes and five bass clarinets of the JMU Flute Choir, Liebman performs six of Coltrane's top compositions from the 1961-66 period. He sticks to soprano except for some Indian flute on "India" and pays tribute to Coltrane's creative spirit rather than just imitating his solos. "Alabama" and "Naima" are passionate ballads, "India" sounds exotic, and the medley of "Joy" and "Selflessness" are free and intense. There are strong individual moments from pianist Butch Taylor and trumpeter John D'Earth although Liebman is the main soloist throughout.

He tackles Coltrane's music on its own terms and the results are fresh and often quite exciting. —*Scott Yanow*

Setting the Standard / May 1992 / Red ✦✦✦✦

Seasons / Dec. 27, 1992-Jan. 19, 1993 / Soul Note ✦✦✦✦✦
David Liebman is at his best in pastoral, ethereal situations. This trio session, recorded in 1992 and '93, contains both lengthy tunes and shorter works in which Liebman's intense soprano sax and flute and more robust tenor solos are nicely supported by Billy Hart's sensitive yet assertive drumming and Cecil McBee's bass work, which provides whatever is necessary, from interaction to competition. The three never become detached or predictable and don't allow the music to lose its edge. The songs don't have a propulsive rhythmic quality, but never lack appeal or distinction. —*Ron Wynn*

Besame Mucho / Mar. 6, 1993-Mar. 7, 1993 / Red ✦✦✦

Miles Away / Mar. 12, 1994-Mar. 13, 1994 / Owl ✦✦✦✦✦
Dave Liebman, who played with Miles Davis' group during 1974-75, pays tribute to the innovative trumpeter throughout this excellent Owl CD. To Liebman's credit he does not ignore Davis' fusion period; in fact he starts out with the most recent composition (Robert Irving's "Code M.D." from 1984) and works his way backwards chronologically. Actually, with Vic Juris often playing rockish guitar and the older tunes being reharmonized, there is a definite unity and freshness to the material. Charles Mingus' moody ballad "Smooch" comes across as quite contemporary while "Solar" sounds like it could have written in the 1970s. Liebman's highly expressive soprano, Juris' echoey guitar and pianist Phil Markowitz are the main soloists, but everyone plays quite well; the inclusion of Caris Visentin's English horn on "Pan Piper" (from *Sketches of Spain*) is a nice touch. Because this project does not merely copy the past but brings some fresh insight to the material, one suspects that even Miles Davis would have liked the results. —*Scott Yanow*

Songs for My Daughter / May 1994 / Soul Note ✦✦✦✦

Voyage / May 1995 / Evidence ✦✦✦

New Vista / Jun. 20, 1996-June 23, 1996 / Arkadia ✦✦
This CD is a disappointment, not because of the repertoire (which ranges from the theme of "Beauty and the Beast" to Jobim, other Brazilian tunes and originals (or the electronic setting) often featuring the synth of Phil Markowitz and Vic Juris' guitar) but because of Dave Liebman's tone. Normally a brilliant soprano saxophonist, Liebman sounds distressingly out of tune on most of the selections, a problem that probably could have been fixed quickly. As it is, one can only hear the potential of what this accessible set could have been. —*Scott Yanow*

Lighthouse All-Stars

f. 1949, db. 1962
Group / Bop, Cool, West Coast Jazz
Bassist Howard Rumsey initiated a jazz policy at the Lighthouse Cafe in Hermosa Beach, CA, in 1949. His Lighthouse All-Stars performed on a nightly basis, and on Sundays there was traditionally a 12-hour jam session. The Contemporary label recorded Rumsey's groups on a fairly regular basis during 1952-57 and such major players as Shorty Rogers, Maynard Ferguson, Rolf Ericson, Stu Williamson, Conte Candoli, Milt Bernhart, Bob Enevoldsen, Frank Rosolino, Jimmy Giuffre, Bob Cooper, Bud Shank, Hampton Hawes, Marty Paich, Claude Williamson, Sonny Clark, Shelly Manne, Max Roach, Stan Levey and guests Miles Davis and Chet Baker were among the participants. The music was essentially bebop with some cooler-toned performances, particularly the ones starring Cooper on oboe or English horn and Shank on flute. The Lighthouse All-Stars only made one record after 1957 (an outing for Philips during 1961-62) before passing into history. In the 1980s the group was revived for some appearances and further Contemporary recordings; the last version featured Shorty Rogers, Cooper (after Coop's death Jack Nimitz took his place), Shank, Bill Perkins, Pete Jolly, Monty Budwig and Larance Marable. —*Scott Yanow*

Mexican Passport / Jul. 22, 1952-Oct. 2, 1956 / Contemporary ✦✦✦
This sampler CD has ten performances that cover a few versions of Howard Rumsey's Lighthouse All-Stars. Each of the songs finds the pacesetting cool jazz outfit featuring Latin rhythms, either by an extra percussionist (Carlos Vidal or Jack Costanzo) or band members banging on percussion when not soloing. There are quite a few one-chord sections in these jams and among the ten numbers are two versions of "Viva Zapata" and three versions of "Witch Doctor." The soloists include many of the top members of Rumsey's groups including Shorty Rogers, Chet Baker, Conte Candoli, Milt Bernhart, Frank Rosolino, Bob Cooper, Herb Geller, Jimmy Giuffre, Bud Shank, Sonny Clark, Hampton Hawes, Claude Williamson, Max Roach and others. But completists will prefer to get the full sessions instead. —*Scott Yanow*

Sunday Jazz á la Lighthouse / Feb. 21, 1953 / Original Jazz Classics ✦✦✦✦✦

For quite a few years in the 1950s, it was a tradition at the Lighthouse for music to be presented on Sundays from 2 p.m. until 2 a.m. The Lighthouse All-Stars formed the core of the all-star group, but quite often other notable players would sit in. This CD reissue presents live performances from one such Sunday. In addition to the usual band members of the time (trumpeter Shorty Rogers, trombonist Milt Bernhart, Bob Cooper and Jimmy Giuffre on tenors, pianist Frank Patchen, bassist Howard Rumsey, and drummer Shelly Manne), trumpeter Maynard Ferguson, pianist Hampton Hawes, and Carlos Vidal on conga have opportunities to be heard. The music is straightahead, generally cool-toned, but with plenty of heat; "Viva Zapata" is a Latin romp. Virtually everyone is featured. Highlights include "Four Others," Rogers' playing on "All the Things You Are" and "Bernie's Tune." —*Scott Yanow*

Lighthouse at Laguna / Jun. 20, 1955 / Original Jazz Classics ✦✦✦✦

Lighthouse All-Stars at Laguna / Jun. 20, 1955 / Original Jazz Classics ✦✦✦✦

In 1955, the Lighthouse All-Stars frequently played away from their homebase. On this live set, they are heard appearing two hours away from the Lighthouse, at the Irvine Bowl in Laguna Beach. The All-Stars of the time (altoist Bud Shank, Bob Cooper on tenor, trombonist Frank Rosolino, pianist Claude Williamson, bassist/leader Howard Rumsey and drummer Stan Levey, but surprisingly no trumpet) perform five numbers, including features for Shank on flute and Rosolino, and support guitarist Barney Kessel on "'Round Midnight." In addition, pianist Hampton Hawes' trio (with bassist Red Mitchell and drummer Shelly Manne) romps on "Walkin'" and a heated "The Champ." This fine all-around survey of the modern jazz mainstream of 1955 is currently available as a CD reissue. —*Scott Yanow*

★ **Music for Lighthousekeeping** / Oct. 2, 1956-Oct. 6, 1956 / Original Jazz Classics ✦✦✦✦✦

The final full-length Contemporary album by the original Lighthouse All-Stars is up to the level of their previous recordings. In fact, if anything, this set is more freewheeling than some of the others. Bassist Howard Rumsey's band at the time consisted of trumpeter Conte Candoli, trombonist Frank Rosolino, Bob Cooper on tenor, pianist Sonny Clark and drummer Stan Levey. Bill Holman and Cooper provided most of the arrangements and five of the eight songs, while Clark brought in a blues, "I Deal." Also on the date are two Count Basie-associated tunes, "Taxi War Dance" and "Topsy." This CD reissue mostly features straightahead music that is more hot than cool. —*Scott Yanow*

Double or Nothin' / Feb. 14, 1957-Feb. 27, 1957 / Liberty ✦✦✦✦✦

In the Solo Spotlight / Aug. 17, 1954-Mar. 12, 1957 / Original Jazz Classics ✦✦✦✦✦

The nine selections on this CD reissue (nearly all the Lighthouse All-Stars' Contemporary recordings are now available in the OJC series) each extensively feature one or two top West Coast jazz players. Bassist Howard Rumsey's group was expanded to an octet, and showcased are trombonist Frank Rosolino ("Funny Frank"), tenor saxophonist Richie Kamuca, trumpeter Conte Candoli, drummer Stan Levey, Bob Cooper on tenor, trumpeter Stu Williamson, valve trombonist Bob Enevoldsen, pianist Claude Williamson, bassist Rumsey (on "Concerto for Doghouse") and altoist Bud Shank. With the exception of the Rumsey feature (composed by Stan Kenton), all of the music was new, with the arrangements provided by pianist Dick Shreve, Bill Holman, Cooper and Williamson. An excellent set. —*Scott Yanow*

Jazz Rolls Royce / Oct. 28, 1957 / Liberty ✦✦✦

Other than an obscure effort for Philips in 1961, this was the final recording by Howard Rumsey's Lighthouse All-Stars. Actually, the 1957 edition of the band (with trumpeter Stu Williamson, trombonist Frank Rosolino, Bob Cooper on tenor, pianist Victor Feldman doubling on vibes, bassist Rumsey, and drummer Stan Levey) is augmented on this obscure LP by ten additional horns. Cooper is the most important force on the date, for not only does he take many fine tenor solos, but he composed five of the six numbers (all but the opening "Strike Up the Band") and provided all of the arrangements. The music, although not innovative, is colorful and swings but will be difficult to locate. —*Scott Yanow*

Jazz Structures / 1961-1962 / Philips ✦✦✦

Jazz Invention / Feb. 12, 1989 / Contemporary ✦✦✦✦✦

To celebrate the 40th anniversary of the first music played at the legendary club the Lighthouse, the Lighthouse All-Stars were reunited for a special concert. Some of the personnel was a little different than in the old days. Howard Rumsey no longer played bass and both trombonist Frank Rosolino and drummer Shelly Manne were no longer around but the group was still filled with plenty of great talent: Tenorman Bob Cooper, altoist Bud Shank, trumpeter Conte Candoli, valve trombonist Bob Enevoldsen, pianist Claude Williamson, bassist Monty Budwig and drummer John Guerin. Together they perform eight songs from the period with spirit and creativity within the genre of cool jazz. As a result of this successful

reunion, Shorty Rogers would be heading the group for the next few years. —*Scott Yanow*

Kirk Lightsey

b. Feb. 15, 1937, Detroit, MI
Piano / Hard Bop, Post-Bop

A pianist who is not a trendsetter but is consistently excellent, Kirk Lightsey long ago developed his own sound within the hard bop tradition. He started playing piano when he was five although he also played clarinet while in high school. Lightsey worked in Detroit and California in the early '60s, often accompanying singers. He gained some attention in 1965 when he recorded with Sonny Stitt and was on five Prestige records with Chet Baker. However Lightsey mostly had low-profile gigs until he toured with Dexter Gordon (1979-83) and became part of the Leaders (starting in the late '80s). Kirk Lightsey has recorded with Jimmy Raney, Clifford Jordan, Woody Shaw, David Murray and Harold Land among others and has led his own sessions for Criss Cross and Sunnyside including piano duets with Harold Danko. —*Scott Yanow*

Lightsey 1 / Sep. 22, 1982+Oct. 5, 1982 / Sunnyside ✦✦✦✦

Long a top interpreter of modern mainstream jazz, pianist Kirk Lightsey was well recorded by the new Sunnyside label in the early 1980s. This solo date features Lightsey (who plays a little bit of flute on "Fresh Air") playing two originals, a pair of songs by Wayne Shorter (including "Fee-Fi-Fum"), Thelonious Monk's tricky "Trinkle Tinkle," an obscurity, and "Never Let Me Go." The pianist is in top form throughout the well-paced program. —*Scott Yanow*

Lightsey 2 / Sep. 22, 1982+Aug. 19, 1983 / Sunnyside ✦✦✦✦✦

For his second Sunnyside release (four of the selections are actually from the same date that resulted in the previous *Lightsey 1*), pianist Kirk Lightsey performs eight stimulating piano solos. The emphasis is on modern jazz originals, including tunes by Tony Williams, Wayne Shorter, Sonny Rollins and Phil Woods ("Goodbye Mr. Evans") plus three of Lightsey's own tunes. In addition, singer Roslyn Burrough makes a guest appearance on "You Are So Beautiful." Excellent music. —*Scott Yanow*

Isotope / Feb.14, 1983 / Criss Cross ✦✦✦✦

Kirk Lightsey has long been an underrated modern mainstream pianist. He has a fine workout on this trio set with bassist Jesper Lundgaard and drummer Eddie Gladden from 1983. Of the six selections, Sonny Rollins' "Oleo" and Joe Henderson's "Isotope" are best known, but the other four tunes (by Johnny Griffin, Wayne Shorter, Tony Williams and the obscure Rudolph Johnson) are rarely performed. The strong interplay between the musicians and the interesting material uplift the set above the average trio date. —*Scott Yanow*

● **Shorter by Two** / Jul. 19, 1983+Jul. 21, 1983 / Sunnyside ✦✦✦✦✦

This CD is an off-the-wall project that was a big success. Kirk Lightsey and Harold Danko perform duo piano versions of 11 Wayne Shorter compositions. They dig into such Shorter tunes as "Ana Maria," "Pinocchio," "Lester Left Town," "Nefertiti," and quite a few obscurities, bringing out unexpected beauty during their very different interpretations of the complex and often haunting material. Highly recommended. —*Scott Yanow*

Everything Happens to Me / Mar. 14, 1983 / Timeless ✦✦✦✦

Pianist Kirk Lightsey and his 1983 trio (with bassist David Eubanks and drummer Eddie Gladden) are joined by trumpeter Chet Baker for six numbers—originals by Wayne Shorter, Joe Henderson, Ray Brown and Dexter Gordon, plus "Everything Happens to Me." Baker sings on "Everything" and "Ray's Idea," and while his vocals are nothing outstanding, his trumpet playing sounds fine. It is particularly interesting to hear Lightsey (usually featured as the lead voice on his own dates) accompanying Baker. —*Scott Yanow*

Lightsey Live / Jun. 28, 1985 / Sunnyside ✦✦✦✦

Pianist Kirk Lightsey is captured in a solo concert on this CD. Most of the material (including Tony Williams' "Pee Wee," Thelonious Monk's "Trinkle Tinkle" and Wayne Shorter's "Fee-Fi-Fo-Fum") had been recorded within the previous few years by Lightsey, but these versions are often quite lengthy (7-11 minutes) and obviously a bit different. In addition, he performs an original and two standards, including "Just One of Those Things." This CD acts as a fine introduction to the high-quality modern mainstream piano of Kirk Lightsey. —*Scott Yanow*

Everything Is Changed / Jun. 4, 1986-Jun. 5, 1986 / Sunnyside ✦✦✦✦

This excellent album finds pianist Kirk Lightsey exploring five standards and his bassist Santi Wilson Debriano's "Nandi" with a solid quartet. Drummer Eddie Gladden is an asset but trumpeter Jerry Gonzales (whose muted statements on four of the six selections recall the lyricism of Miles Davis) often comes close to stealing the show. Lightsey, who sounds particularly strong on the ballads, is the obvious leader and his tasteful yet swinging piano is a joy to hear. —*Scott Yanow*

Kirk 'n' Marcus / Dec. 24, 1986+Dec. 26, 1986 / Criss Cross ✦✦✦✦✦

Although he has gained a little more recognition in the mid-1990s, Detroit-based trumpeter Marcus Belgrave remains an often-overlooked great. For pianist Kirk Lightsey's quintet set, Belgrave is teamed with tenor saxophonist Jean Toussaint, bassist Santi DeBriano, drummer Eddie Gladden and the leader on six little-known pieces; including originals by Kenny Dorham ("Windmill"), DeBriano, Toussaint and a pair from Belgrave. The modern hard bop date has plenty of fine solos and is easily recommended to straightahead jazz collectors. —*Scott Yanow*

From Kirk to Nat / Nov. 28, 1990 / Criss Cross ✦✦✦✦✦

One of the main reasons why this tribute to the Nat King Cole Trio by Kirk Lightsey is a success is that Lightsey (who is from a much later bop-influenced generation) sounds nothing like Cole. Featured in a trio with guitarist Kevin Eubanks and bassist Rufus Reid, Lightsey performs a set of music reminiscent of Cole but several of the songs (including his original "Kirk's Blues," "Never Let Me Go" and "Close Enough for Love") were never actually recorded by Cole; Lightsey takes surprisingly effective vocals on the latter two songs. —*Scott Yanow*

Goodbye Mr. Evans / May 12, 1994 / Evidence ✦✦✦✦

Abbey Lincoln (Anna Marie Wooldridge)

b. Aug. 6, 1930, Chicago, IL

Vocals / Post-Bop, Standards, Avant-Garde

As with her hero Billie Holiday, Abbey Lincoln always means the lyrics she sings. A dramatic performer whose interpretations are full of truth and insight, Lincoln actually began her career as a fairly lightweight supper-club singer. She went through several name changes (including Anna Marie, Gaby Lee and Gaby Wooldridge) before settling on Abbey Lincoln. She recorded with Benny Carter in 1956 and performed a number in the 1957 Hollywood film *The Girl Can't Help It*. Lincoln's first of three albums for Riverside (1957-59) had Max Roach on drums and he was a major influence on her; she began to be choosy about the songs she sang and to give words the proper emotional intensity. Lincoln held her own on her early dates with such sidemen as Kenny Dorham, Sonny Rollins, Wynton Kelly, Curtis Fuller and Benny Golson. She was quite memorable on Roach's *Freedom Now Suite*, showing some very uninhibited emotions. Lincoln's Candid date *Straight Ahead* (1961) had among its players Roach, Booker Little, Eric Dolphy and Coleman Hawkins, and she made some important appearances on Roach's Impulse album *Percussion Bitter Suite*.

Abbey Lincoln and Max Roach were married in 1962, an association that lasted until 1970. They worked together for a while but Lincoln (who found it harder to get work in jazz due to the political nature of some of her music) became involved in acting and did not record as a leader during 1962-72. She finally recorded for Inner City in 1973 and gradually became more active in jazz. Her two Billie Holiday tribute albums for Enja (1987) showed listeners that the singer was still in her prime and she has recorded several excellent sets for Verve in the 1990s. Because she puts so much thought into each of her recordings, it is not an understatement to say that every Abbey Lincoln set is well worth owning. —*Scott Yanow*

Affair / Jul. 1956-Nov. 6, 1956 / Liberty ✦✦✦

This CD reissues the music from Abbey Lincoln's first LP along with two slightly earlier numbers originally available as a single. Lincoln was at the time making the transition from a potential sex symbol and lounge singer to becoming a dramatic jazz interpreter. Her voice was recognizable even at this early stage but some of the ballads are more lightweight than the ones she would be performing in the near future. Backed by anonymous orchestras arranged by Benny Carter, Jack Montrose and Marty Paich, Abbey Lincoln's straightforward delivery was already impressive and pleasing. —*Scott Yanow*

That's Him / Oct. 28, 1957 / Original Jazz Classics ✦✦✦✦✦

This CD reissue brings back singer Abbey Lincoln's second recording and first for Riverside, adding alternate takes of "I Must Have That Man" and "Porgy" to the original LP program. Lincoln is accompanied by quite an all-star roster (tenor saxophonist Sonny Rollins, trumpeter Kenny Dorham, pianist Wynton Kelly, bassist Paul Chambers and drummer Max Roach) and, even this early, she was already a major jazz singer with a style of her own. Abbey Lincoln was careful from this point on to only interpret lyrics that she believed in. Her repertoire has a few superior standards (including several songs such as "I Must Have That Man" and "Don't Explain" that are closely associated with Billie Holiday) plus Oscar Brown, Jr.'s "Strong Man" and "Tender as a Rose"; she takes the latter unaccompanied. "Don't Explain" is slightly unusual in that Paul Chambers is absent and Wynton Kelly makes an extremely rare appearance on bass. All three of Abbey Lincoln's Riverside albums (each of which have been reissued in the OJC series) are well worth several listens. —*Scott Yanow*

It's Magic / Aug. 23, 1958 / Original Jazz Classics ✦✦✦✦✦

Because Abbey Lincoln has always been careful to sing songs that have a deep meaning for her, all of her recordings through the years are memorable in their own way; there are no duds in her discography. Her second Riverside session (and her third recording) has been reissued on this CD in the Original Jazz Classics series. The backup musicians are among the best in jazz at the time (Kenny Dorham or Art Farmer on trumpet, trombonist Curtis Fuller, Benny Golson on tenor, Jerome Richardson or Sahib Shihab on reeds, pianist Wynton Kelly, Paul Chambers or Sam Jones on bass and drummer Philly Joe Jones) and they have opportunities to play short solos. Lincoln is heard at her early best on such numbers as "I Am in Love," "An Occasional Man," "Out of the Past" and Randy Weston's "Little Niles." Recommended. —*Scott Yanow*

Abbey Is Blue / Mar. 25, 1959-Mar. 26, 1959 / Original Jazz Classics ✦✦✦✦✦

Abbey Lincoln's third of three Riverside albums (all of these recommended sets have been reissued on CD) directly precedes her more adventurous work with drummer (and then-husband) Max Roach. With fine backup from trumpeter Kenny Dorham, pianist Wynton Kelly, Les Spann (doubling on guitar and flute), bassist Sam Jones and drummer Philly Joe Jones on seven of the ten numbers and by Roach's regular quintet of the time on the other three selections, Abbey Lincoln is quite emotional and distinctive during a particularly strong set. Highlights include the first vocal version ever of "Afro-Blue," "Come Sunday," Oscar Brown, Jr.'s "Brother, Where Are You," "Softly, As in a Morning Sunrise," "Long as You're Living" and Lincoln's own "Let Up." A very memorable set. —*Scott Yanow*

★ **Straight Ahead** / Feb. 22, 1961 / Candid ✦✦✦✦✦

Reissued several times since it originally came out on a Candid LP, this is one of Abbey Lincoln's greatest recordings. It is a testament to the credibility of her very honest music (and her talents) that Abbey's sidemen on this date include the immortal tenor saxophonist Coleman Hawkins (who takes a memorable solo on "Blue Monk"), Eric Dolphy on flute and alto, trumpeter Booker Little (whose melancholy tone is very important in the ensembles), pianist Mal Waldron and drummer Max Roach. High points include "When Malindy Sings," "Blue Monk," Billie Holiday's "Left Alone" and "African Lady." —*Scott Yanow*

People in Me / Jun. 23, 1973-Jun. 27, 1993 / Inner City ✦✦✦✦✦

The music on this out-of-print LP from the defunct Inner City label was recorded in Japan and has been released by several other record companies since. Abbey Lincoln's first record in a decade, the set features the very original singer joined by a couple of Japanese players (pianist Hiromasa Suzuki and bassist Kunimitsu Inaba) plus drummer Al Foster, percussionist Mtume and the horns (soprano, tenor and flute) of Dave Liebman. Abbey Lincoln wrote or co-composed all eight selections, best-known of which is "People in Me." Every Abbey Lincoln recording is well worth picking up because her sincerity, credibility and talent make each of her dates memorable in their own way. —*Scott Yanow*

Golden Lady / Feb. 4, 1980 / Inner City ✦✦✦✦✦

Throughout her impressive career, singer Abbey Lincoln has successfully matched her talents with some of the most powerful jazzmen. On this out-of-print Inner City LP, Lincoln is joined by trumpeter Roy Burroughs, pianist Hilton Ruiz, bassist Jack Gregg, drummer Freddie Waits and (most notably) tenor saxophonist Archie Shepp (one of his better dates of the 1980s). Lincoln interprets three standards (including "Sophisticated Lady") but most impressive are her three originals, particularly "Caged Bird." Her interplay with Shepp gives proof (if it was still needed) that Abbey Lincoln has long been a major jazz singer. —*Scott Yanow*

Talking to the Sun / Nov. 25, 1983-Nov. 26, 1983 / Enja ✦✦✦✦

A 1990 release of a session with Lincoln singing and accompanied by some prime Young Lions. —*Ron Wynn*

Abbey Sings Billie, Vol. 2 / Nov. 6, 1987+Nov. 7, 1987 / Enja ✦✦✦✦✦

Abbey Lincoln is the perfect person to pay tribute to Billie Holiday. She knew Lady Day during her last years and, like Holiday, Lincoln has always lived the words she sings and chosen to only interpret lyrics that have great meaning to her. Her expressive powers have been quite strong throughout her career and there are plenty of dramatic moments on this disc along with its first volume. Tenor saxophonist Harold Vick, who would die suddenly within days of these sessions, is quite effective as is the supportive rhythm section. Abbey Lincoln shows off her versatility on such diverse numbers as "Gimme a Pigfoot," "Don't Explain" and "Please Don't Talk About Me When I'm Gone." —*Scott Yanow*

Abbey Sings Billie, Vol. 1 / Nov. 6, 1987-Nov. 7, 1987 / Enja ✦✦✦✦✦

Abbey Lincoln's idol has always been Billie Holiday. Although she has never really copied Lady Day and she has long had her own style and sound, the feeling and intensity that Lincoln gives the lyrics she interprets is reminiscent of late-period Holiday. A perfect person to pay tribute to Billie Holiday, Lincoln (on the first of two Enja CDs) is joined by the underrated tenor Harold Vick (who would pass away unexpectedly within a short time after this recording), pianist James

Weidman, bassist Tarik Shaha and drummer Mark Johnson for fresh renditions of standards. Mal Waldron's "Soul Eyes" is taken as an instrumental feature for Vick and other highlights include "What a Little Moonlight Can Do," "Strange Fruit," an emotional "I'll Be Seeing You" and a song perfectly suited for Abbey Lincoln's voice: "Crazy He Calls Me." One of the singer's best recordings of the 1980s and a fine complement to the equally rewarding *Vol. 2. —Scott Yanow*

The World Is Falling Down / Feb. 21, 1990-Feb. 27, 1990 / Verve ✦✦✦✦✦
Abbey Lincoln's first in a series of impressive recordings for Verve matches her unique voice and very credible style with fluegelhornist Clark Terry, the altos of Jackie McLean and Jerry Dodgion, bassist Charlie Haden, drummer Billy Higgins and French pianist Alain Jean-Marie. McLean has all of the alto solos and most of the instrumental arrangements were contributed by Ron Carter. Lincoln has always been expert at picking out superior material to record and all eight numbers on this CD are memorable in their own way, particularly Haden's classic "First Song," a French version of "How High the Moon," "Hi Fly," Michel Legrand's "You Must Believe in Spring" and Lincoln's two originals "The World Is Falling Down" and "I Got Thunder." *—Scott Yanow*

You Gotta Pay the Band / Feb. 25, 1991-Feb. 26, 1991 / Verve ✦✦✦✦
Stan Getz is featured on one of his final recordings during this excellent Abbey Lincoln CD; Getz's cool tenor fits in very well with Lincoln's voice, making one wish that they had met up previously. With pianist Hank Jones, bassist Charlie Haden, drummer Mark Johnson and (on two songs) Maxine Roach's viola completing the group, it is not surprising that Lincoln sounds typically inspired. Actually her version of "Brother, Can You Spare a Dime?" is a bit of a misfire with its dated lyrics (which should have been modified and altered to fit a female). However, "Bird Alone," Freddie Hubbard's "Up Jumped Spring" (given lyrics by Lincoln) and five of her originals more than compensate. Recommended. *—Scott Yanow*

Devil's Got Your Tongue / Feb. 24, 1992-Feb. 25, 1992 / Verve ✦✦✦✦

When There is Love / Oct. 4, 1992-Oct. 6, 1992 / Verve ✦✦✦✦
This CD is a change of pace for Abbey Lincoln. She interprets ten standards (plus four of her originals), all love songs performed as duets with pianist Hank Jones. Although there is some social commentary, the emphasis is on male-female relationships and Lincoln sounds more optimistic than usual. Among the more memorable selections are Duke Ellington's "Black Butterfly," "The Nearness of You," "You Came a Long Way from St. Louis," Fats Waller's "Jitterbug Waltz" and "You Won't Forget Me." *—Scott Yanow*

A Turtle's Dream / May 1994-Nov. 1994 / Verve ✦✦✦✦

Who Used to Dance / Apr. 6, 1996-May 19, 1996 / Verve ✦✦✦
Not everything works on this chance-taking ballad-oriented set (the version of "Tambourine Man" is a bit tedious and overly long), but in general Abbey Lincoln's voice is in excellent form for this period. Her interplay with altoists Frank Morgan, Oliver Lake and Steve Coleman (the latter in excellent form on "Street of Dreams") and a variety of young horn players (plus her regular trio) is colorful, unpredictable, emotional and modern. Among the highlights are "Who Used to Dance" (a feature for the tap dancing of Savion Glover), "Love What You Doin'" and an eccentric "The River." Virtually everything that Abbey Lincoln has recorded during her career is well worth hearing and this 1997 release is no exception. *—Scott Yanow*

John Lindberg

b. Mar. 16, 1959, Royal Oak, MI
Bass / Avant-Garde
A steady, sympathetic accompanist and solid soloist, bassist John Lindberg is best known for his work in the String Trio of New York. Lindberg studied music in Ann Arbor, Michigan, before moving to New York in 1977. He played and recorded in the Human Arts Ensemble with Joseph Bowie and Bobo Shaw in the late '70s, and worked with Anthony Braxton from 1978 to 1985. They performed in both Europe and America. Lindberg was a founding member of the String Trio of New York in 1979, and currently remains with the ensemble. He also worked in a trio with Jimmy Lyons and Sunny Murray in 1980. Lindberg lived and worked in Paris from 1980 to 1983, leading small combos, playing solo and working in a group led by Murray that also featured John Tchicai. Lindberg has recorded as a leader for Cecma, Black Saint, West Wind, ITM and Sound Aspects. *—Ron Wynn*

Give and Take / Nov. 13, 1982-Nov. 14, 1982 / Black Saint ✦✦✦✦

The East Side Suite / Jul. 8, 1983 / Sound Aspects ✦✦✦✦

Trilogy of Works for Eleven Instrumentalists / Sep. 8, 1984-Sep. 9, 1984 / Black Saint ✦✦✦✦
Bassist John Lindberg is best known for his associations with the String Trio of New York and for a time with Anthony Braxton, but, as witness this stimulating set, he also has the potential to be a major bandleader and composer. Lindberg

performs three of his originals (including the 20-minute "Dresden Moods") as part of an 11-piece group also including such notables as trumpeters Hugh Ragin and Mike Mossman, trombonist Ray Anderson and the reeds of Marty Ehrlich and J.D. Parran, among others. The music is coherent yet unpredictable, a little reminiscent of Charles Mingus, yet different and never dull. Well worth checking out by open-eared listeners. *—Scott Yanow*

● **Dodging Bullets** / Jun. 8, 1992-Jun. 9, 1992 / Black Saint ✦✦✦✦✦

Luminosity / Feb. 5, 1992-Aug. 23, 1996 / Music & Arts ✦✦✦

Quartet Afterstorm / Mar. 18, 1994-Mar. 20, 1994 / Black Saint ✦✦✦✦✦

Resurrection of a Dormant Soul / Oct. 15, 1996 / Black Saint ✦✦✦

Paul Lingle

b. Dec. 3, 1902, Denver, CO, d. Oct. 30, 1962, Honolulu, HI
Piano / Dixieland, Ragtime
Paul Lingle was a local legend in San Francisco during the 1940s. A talented stride pianist who also played ragtime, Lingle was a fan of Jelly Roll Morton. He started playing piano when he was six and first worked professionally in San Francisco in the 1920s. Lingle was Al Jolson's accompanist in the late '20s, recording the soundtrack of some of his first sound films. He spent the 1930s working in radio and with Al Zohn's jazz band in San Francisco. During the Dixieland revival of the 1940s, Lingle at first was a piano tuner in Santa Cruz but by 1944 was playing in San Francisco clubs, generally solo. When Leadbelly and Bunk Johnson passed through town, they both asked for him. In 1952 Lingle moved to Honolulu where he continued playing up until his death. Unfortunately he was reluctant to record throughout his career and his only studio session resulted in just eight songs cut for Good Time Jazz in 1952. However, three-and-a-half albums of private tapes from 1951-52 were released posthumously on the Euphonic label that allow listeners to get a fuller picture of Paul Lingle's talent. *—Scott Yanow*

Final Curtain / 1947-1951 / Euphonic ✦✦✦
It is fitting that the final release from the Euphonic label (a 1992 LP) unearths more material by pianist Paul Lingle, for the Lingle recordings put out by Euphonic were probably the company's greatest contribution to jazz. The pianist's only official studio recordings were half an album cut for the Good Time Jazz label, although he lived to be 59. Euphonic fortunately came out with three additional records of live performances by the Jelly Roll Morton-inspired traditionalist. Their final Lingle set features piano solos from three different sources (including some recorded by Turk Murphy) during the 1947-51 period. The recording quality is a bit erratic in spots, but there is so little Lingle available (and he was a consistently exciting soloist) that all of the numbers are well worth having. Among the highlights are "A Bag of Rags," "Ostrich Walk," "Pastime Rag No. 3," and "Black Bottom Stomp." *—Scott Yanow*

● **Dance of the Witch Hazels** / 1951 / Euphonic ✦✦✦✦✦
Pianist Paul Lingle recorded very little throughout his career, and nothing at all after leaving San Francisco for Hawaii in 1953. This LP of live performances (which has decent if not state-of-the-art sound quality) features Lingle at his best. The pianist always had a wide repertoire, and on the set, he digs into such tunes as "Good Gravy Rag," "Strut Miss Lizzie," "Ace in the Hole" and "September in the Rain," plus his own title cut. A fine stride pianist whose style included touches of ragtime and Jelly Roll Morton, Paul Lingle was one of the best in his idiom from 1940-53. *—Scott Yanow*

The Legend of Lingle / 1951 / Euphonic ✦✦✦✦
The second LP of live solos performed by Paul Lingle at the Jug Club features the trad jazz pianist in excellent form, playing obscurities from the 1920s along with a few warhorses. The Euphonic label (which did the jazz world a major favor by documenting the rarely recorded Lingle) only put out LPs, which are all difficult to find now, but in general, they are worth searching for (particularly those by the pianist). The sound quality is only okay during these particular performances, but Paul Lingle's spirited style definitely comes through. Highlights include Scott Joplin's "Original Rags," "Muscle Shoals Blues," "Little Rock Getaway," and "That's a Plenty Rag." *—Scott Yanow*

Vintage Piano / 1951- Oct. 1965 / Euphonic ✦✦✦✦
One of the first releases from the Euphonic label, this obscure release has seven piano solos from Paul Lingle and seven duets by pianist Bill Mitchell and bassist Ken Peterson. The Lingle performances, feature the pianist playing his jazzy versions of rags, blues and standards, including "Good Gravy Rag," "Maple Leaf Rag" and "I've Found a New Baby." The 1965 selections showcase Mitchell, a part-time but talented musician. In addition to his own "Blues for Paul Lingle," Mitchell performs rags by Charles Hunter, Joplin and Tom Turpin, plus numbers by W.C. Handy and Jelly Roll Morton ("The Pearls" and "Grandpa's Spells"). Pre-swing piano collectors will want to search for this hard-to-find LP. *—Scott Yanow*

Ray Linn (Raymond Sayre Linn)

b. Oct. 20, 1920, Chicago, IL, **d.** Nov. 1996, Columbus, OH
Trumpet / Bop, Dixieland
A versatile trumpeter, Ray Linn started out as a modernist and ended up as a revivalist. Linn began his professional career playing with the orchestras of Tommy Dorsey (1938-41) and Woody Herman (1941-42); he would rejoin Herman on three occasions (1945, 1947 and 1955-59). Linn also worked on and off with Jimmy Dorsey (1942-45), Benny Goodman (1943 and 1947), Artie Shaw (1944-46) and Boyd Raeburn (1946). While with Raeburn his solos were quite advanced for the period. Linn became a studio musician after moving to Los Angeles in 1945 but had the opportunity to work with Bob Crosby (1950-51) and many of the top West Coast jazz players in the 1950s in addition to Woody Herman. From the 1960s on he mostly worked in television. Although his sessions as a leader in 1946 (which resulted in eight songs) had such titles as "The Mad Monk" and "Blop Blah," Ray Linn's later albums for Trend (1978) and Discovery (1980) were Dixieland-oriented. —*Scott Yanow*

Chicago Jazz / Sep. 28, 1978 / Trend ✦✦✦
Although Ray Linn had had a diverse career with stints with a variety of modern jazz bands (Boyd Raeburn, the Sauter-Finegan Orchestra and Bill Holman), by the 1970s he was mostly playing Dixieland. This spirited direct-to-disc LP matches Linn's trumpet with Henry Cuesta (doubling on clarinet and baritone), tenor great Eddie Miller, trombonist Bob Havens, pianist Dave Frishberg, bassist Richard Maloof and drummer Jack Davenport on six veteran swing and Dixieland standards, a pair of his originals (including "Bix's Bugle") and Frishberg's "North Hollywood Rotary Parade." Although not essential, the music on this tasteful set is quite enjoyable. —*Scott Yanow*

● **Empty Suit Blues** / Sep. 26, 1980 / Discovery ✦✦✦✦
Ray Linn, who spent much of his career as a fairly modern trumpeter, also enjoyed playing Dixieland and swing. This album, his second and final release for Trend, has an intriguing lineup of players: Linn (who also wrote the arrangements), Gary Foster on clarinet, alto, baritone and flute, veteran Eddie Miller on tenor and clarinet, trombonist Bob Havens, pianist Dave Frishberg, bassist Jim Hughart and drummer Dick Berk. Woody Herman's former vocalist, Mary Ann McCall, does a fine job on three ballads, and the instrumental highlights include "Empty Suit Blues," "I'm Sorry I Made You Cry" and "Struttin' with Some Barbecue." An interesting session that has not yet been made available on CD. —*Scott Yanow*

Jeff Linsky

b. 1952, Los Angeles, CA
Guitar / Bop, Brazilian Jazz, Latin Jazz
An appealing guitarist who specializes in Brazilian and Latin jazz, Jeff Linsky was primarily self-taught although he studied briefly with Spanish guitarist Vicente Gomez and Joe Pass. He lived in Hawaii during 1972-88 before moving to the San Francisco Bay area. Linsky has thus far recorded easily enjoyable albums for Kamei (1991-92), GSP, Concord and Concord Vista. —*Scott Yanow*

Up Late / May 1988 / Concord Jazz ✦✦✦✦
Jeff Linsky's debut for the Concord label is a high-quality Brazilian jazz date. His acoustic guitar sounds perfectly at home in a quietly swinging group that also includes flutist Steve Kujala, bassist John Leitham and both Gary Cardile (who is replaced by Chris Trujillo on three songs) and Louis Conte on percussion. Six Linsky originals, Baden Powell's "Berimbau," "Besame Mucho," and "I Didn't Know What Time It Was" comprise the repertoire, and the music is quite enjoyable. —*Scott Yanow*

Simpatico / 1991 / Kamei ✦✦✦✦

Rendezvous / 1992 / Kamei ✦✦✦✦

● **Solo** / 1992 / GSP ✦✦✦✦✦
A delightful set of music, the dozen unaccompanied solos on this CD feature Jeff Linsky playing an Asturias requinto (a æ-size Spanish guitar). A top exponent of Brazilian jazz and bossa novas, Linsky interprets tunes by Jobim, Bonfa and Caymmi, plus two originals and such standards as "Autumn in New York," "Nature Boy" and "God Bless The Child." The melodic music is accessible and soothing, but also contains plenty of subtle surprises and understated invention by the talented guitarist. Recommended. —*Scott Yanow*

Angel's Serenade / Mar. 2, 1994-Mar. 3, 1994 / Concord Picante ✦✦✦✦✦

California / Jan. 8, 1996-Jan. 9, 1996 / Concord Vista ✦✦✦

Passport to the Heart / Mar. 7, 1997-Mar. 9, 1997 / Concord Jazz ✦✦✦
As might be expected of a disc entitled *Passport to the Heart*, much of the music herein is mellow and romantic in nature. But Linsky is gifted and smart enough that it seldom descends into sloppy sentimentality, nor is it sleep-inducing. The covers are interesting, ranging from a swinging version of Al Jarreau's "Mornin'"

to Chaka Khan's "Through the Fire" and Stevie Wonder's "Summer Soft." But it's on his original compositions that Linsky is most expressive. If it doesn't offer some of the highlights of some of his earlier efforts, such as *California*, it is more consistent throughout. —*Ross Boissoneau*

Melba Liston

b. Jan. 13, 1926, Kansas City, MO
Trombone, Arranger / Bop, Hard Bop
A fine section trombonist, Melba Liston achieved her greatest fame as an arranger, particularly for her projects with Randy Weston. She grew up in California and played with Gerald Wilson's Orchestra starting in 1943. Her most notable recording as a soloist was with Dexter Gordon in 1947. Liston worked with Count Basie (1948-49), Dizzy Gillespie's big band (1949-50), and backed Billie Holiday but then spent a few years outside of music. She toured with and wrote for Dizzy Gillespie's orchestra (1956-57) and visited Europe with Quincy Jones' big band (1959), staying with that orchestra into 1961. Liston then became a freelance arranger, working on sessions led by Weston, Johnny Griffin and Milt Jackson, writing for the studios, teaching and occasionally playing. A serious stroke has confined her to a wheelchair since 1985 but Melba Liston has written for several recent Randy Weston projects. —*Scott Yanow*

And Her Bones / Dec. 22, 1958-Dec. 24, 1958 / Metrojazz ✦✦✦✦

Booker Little

b. Apr. 2, 1938, Memphis, TN, **d.** Oct. 5, 1961, New York, NY
Trumpet / Post-Bop, Avant-Garde
The first trumpeter emerging after Clifford Brown's death to gain his own sound, Booker Little had a tremendous amount of potential before his premature death. He began on trumpet when he was 12 and played with Johnny Griffin and the MJT + 3 while attending Chicago Conservatory. Little was with Max Roach (1958-59) and then freelanced in New York. He recorded with Roach and Abbey Lincoln, was on John Coltrane's *Africa/Brass* album and was well documented during a July 1961 gig at the Five Spot with Eric Dolphy. Little had a memorable melancholy sound and his interval jumps looked towards the avant-garde but he also swung like a hard bopper. Booker Little led four sessions (one album apiece for United Artists, Time, Candid and Bethlehem) but died of uremia at the age of 23, a particularly tragic loss. —*Scott Yanow*

Booker Little 4 and Max Roach / Oct. 1958 / Blue Note ✦✦✦✦✦
This CD reissue features trumpeter Booker Little at the beginning of his tragically brief career. The first six selections find the distinctive soloist playing with a quintet also including the young tenor George Coleman, pianist Tommy Flanagan, bassist Art Davis and drummer Max Roach (who was his regular employer at the time). Little contributed three now-obscure originals and also plays two standards and an early version of Miles Davis' "Milestones." The remainder of the CD has lengthy versions of "Things Ain't What They Used to Be" and "Blue 'n' Boogie" from a jam session that matched Little with fellow Memphis-based players including Coleman, altoist Frank Strozier, and the masterful pianist Phineas Newborn. Overall this forward-looking hard bop set is easily recommended. —*Scott Yanow*

Booker Little / Apr. 13, 1960-Apr. 15, 1960 / Bainbridge ✦✦✦✦✦
Trumpeter Booker Little's second session as a leader (there would only be four) is a quartet outing (with either Wynton Kelly or Tommy Flanagan on piano, bassist Scott LaFaro and drummer Roy Haynes) that puts the emphasis on relaxed tempos. Little's immediately recognizable melancholy sound and lyrical style are heard in top form on "Who Can I Turn To" and five of his originals, some of which deserve to be revived. His jazz waltz "The Grand Valse" (inspired by Sonny Rollins' "Valse Hot") is a high point of this set, which has been reissued by Bainbridge/Time on CD. —*Scott Yanow*

☆ **Out Front** / Mar. 17, 1961-Apr. 4, 1961 / Candid ✦✦✦✦✦
Booker Little was the first trumpet soloist to emerge in jazz after the death of Clifford Brown to have his own sound. His tragically brief life (he died at age 23 later in 1961) cut short what would have certainly been a major career. Little, on this sextet date with multireedist Eric Dolphy, trombonist Julian Priester and drummer Max Roach, shows that his playing was really beyond bebop. His seven now-obscure originals (several of which deserve to be revived) are challenging for the soloists and there are many strong moments during these consistently challenging and satisfying performances. —*Scott Yanow*

Booker Little and Friend / Aug. 1961-Sep. 1961 / Bethlehem ✦✦✦✦✦
A CD reissue of trumpeter Booker Little's *Victory and Sorrow* album for Bethlehem, this release adds two previously unheard alternate takes of "Matilde" to the original program. Little's final recording before he died of uremia at the age of 23, the sextet session also features fine playing by trombonist Julian Priester, tenor saxophonist George Coleman, pianist Don Friedman, bassist Reggie Workman and

drummer Pete La Roca. However, Booker Little is generally the top soloist on the harmonically advanced hard bop date and he is in peak form throughout although he would pass away on October 5 of that year. Of his six originals, "Molotone Music" and "Victory and Sorrow" are most memorable, even if Little's beautiful playing on a quartet version of the date's one standard "If I Should Lose You" is actually the high point. One wonders why this essential set was retitled since it is never clear who the "Friend" was. —*Scott Yanow*

Charles Lloyd

b. Mar. 15, 1938, Memphis, TN
Tenor Saxophone, Flute / Hard Bop, Crossover Jazz

During 1966-69 Charles Lloyd led one of the most popular groups in jazz, a unit that played at the rock palace Fillmore West in San Francisco and toured the USSR. Lloyd's music, although generally a bit melodic, was not watered-down and managed to catch on for several years during a time when jazz was at its low point in popularity. Lloyd played locally in Memphis (including with B.B. King and Bobby Blue Bland) and then in the mid-'50s moved to Los Angeles to attend USC. During his six years in L.A., he gigged around town and played alto with Gerald Wilson's Orchestra. In 1961 he joined the Chico Hamilton Quintet on flute and tenor, making his recording debut and gaining a strong reputation. During 1964-65 he was with the Cannonball Adderley Sextet and then in mid-1965 formed his own group. By 1966 the Charles Lloyd Quartet included Keith Jarrett, Cecil McBee (who was later succeeded by Ron McClure) and Jack DeJohnette and the band was the hit of the 1966 Monterey Jazz Festival, recorded steadily, toured Europe six times and was remarkably popular. Lloyd, whose most famous composition is "Forest Flower," played tenor in a soft-toned version of John Coltrane while his lyrical flute playing is more original. After his group changed personnel in 1969, Lloyd gradually faded out of music, becoming a teacher of transcendental meditation. The few records he made in the 1970s were quite spiritual and bordered on new age. However pianist Michel Petrucciani looked Lloyd up in the early '80s and persuaded him to return to active playing. For a period Petrucciani was in his quartet. By the late '80s Lloyd had a new group with pianist Bobo Stenson, bassist Palle Danielsson and drummer Jon Christensen that regularly recorded for ECM. Charles Lloyd, whose style remains virtually unchanged from the 1960s, has recorded as a leader for Columbia, Atlantic, Kapp, A&M, Blue Note and ECM. —*Scott Yanow*

Of Course, Of Course / Mar. 8, 1965+May 1965 / Columbia ✦✦✦✦
Charles Lloyd's second album as a leader (which has not yet been reissued on CD) teams him with guitarist Gabor Szabo (his old friend from the Chico Hamilton group), bassist Ron Carter and drummer Tony Williams. Although Lloyd was still a member of Cannonball Adderley's group, his playing on the set shows that he was clearly ready to become a leader. Seven of the nine diverse compositions are his originals; he takes "The Things We Did Last Summer" as a duet with Szabo and rips through "Apex," a trio number without the guitarist. Other notable selections include "Goin' to Memphis" and "Third Floor Richard." Whether on tenor or flute, Charles Lloyd was coming into his own rather quickly, and this underrated set is a minor classic. —*Scott Yanow*

Discovery! The Charles Lloyd Quartet / May 27, 1964+May 29, 1964 / Columbia ✦✦✦✦
Charles Lloyd's recorded debut as a leader was made while he was a member of the Cannonball Adderley Sextet. Doubling on tenor and flute, Lloyd teamed up with pianist Don Friedman, either Eddie Khan or Richard Davis on bass, and Roy Haynes or J.C. Moses on drums. This out-of-print LP has among its highlights "Little Piece" (dedicated to Booker Little), "Days of Wine and Roses," "Sweet Georgia Bright," and the initial full-length version of "Forest Flower." Lloyd's Coltrane-inspired sound was already in place, and his flute playing was becoming distinctive. The music is essentially melodic but advanced hard bop, a strong start to an important career. —*Scott Yanow*

Dream Weaver / Mar. 20, 1966 / Atlantic ✦✦✦✦✦
The debut recording by the Charles Lloyd Quartet was recorded shortly before their first European tour. Even at this point, it was becoming obvious that the band was catching on. Lloyd (doubling on tenor and flute), the young pianist Keith Jarrett, bassist Cecil McBee and drummer Jack DeJohnette together had the rare ability to create an accessible and appealing sound while stretching themselves into some exploratory music. This LP (few of their recordings have yet been reissued on CD) has "Autumn Sequence" ("Autumn Leaves" surrounded by two brief Lloyd compositions), a medley of the tenor's "Meditation" and "Dervish Dance," and three other originals by the leader, including "Sombrero Sam." Excellent music. —*Scott Yanow*

● **Forest Flower** / Sep. 8, 1966+Sep. 18, 1966 / Atlantic ✦✦✦✦✦
This classic album is dominated by the Charles Lloyd Quartet's historic appearance at the 1966 Monterey Jazz Festival. In addition to "East of the Sun," Lloyd (on tenor and flute), pianist Keith Jarrett, bassist Cecil McBee and drummer Jack

DeJohnette performed the 17-minute, two-part "Forest Flower," which was the hit of the festival and helped make the group a sensation. Also included on this LP (which has not been fully reissued on CD) are renditions of Jarrett's "Sorcery" and McBee's "Song of Her" that were recorded ten days earlier. This record, one of the high points of Charles Lloyd's career, should be much more widely available. —*Scott Yanow*

Charles Lloyd in Europe / Oct. 29, 1966 / Atlantic ✦✦✦✦
This concert from Oslo, Norway, took place a month after the Charles Lloyd's Quartet's famous engagement at the 1966 Monterey Jazz Festival. Lloyd (playing his distinctive flute and John Coltrane-inspired tenor), pianist Keith Jarrett, bassist Cecil McBee and drummer Jack DeJohnette made for a potent team, somehow creating music that was both accessible and exploratory. None of the six Lloyd originals on this LP caught on, but they do effectively feature the group and contain some strong moments. —*Scott Yanow*

The Flowering / Oct. 29, 1966 / Atlantic ✦✦✦✦✦
Released by Atlantic in 1971 when the Charles Lloyd Quartet was already history, these performances (from the same concert that resulted in *Charles Lloyd in Europe*) contain some excellent remakes ("Love-In/Island Blues" and "Goin' to Memphis"), Gabor Szabo's "Gypsy '66," Cecil McBee's "Wilpan's," and a fine rendition of "Speak Low." Lloyd (whether on tenor or flute), the already impressive pianist Keith Jarrett, bassist McBee, and drummer Jack DeJohnette are heard in enthusiastic form. This set is even a bit better than the *In Europe* album due to the stronger (if more familiar) material. —*Scott Yanow*

Love-In / Jan. 27, 1967 / Atlantic ✦✦✦✦
Very few jazz groups had opportunities to play the Fillmore West, but the Charles Lloyd Quartet fit right in at the rock palace. Creating music that was strangely accessible but without changing their exploratory post-bop style, the band (comprising Lloyd on tenor and flute, pianist Keith Jarrett, bassist Ron McClure and drummer Jack DeJohnette) was probably the most popular jazz group of the era. This album (not yet reissued on CD) features the Quartet live at Fillmore West performing four Lloyd tunes (including "Love-In" and "Memphis Dues Again/Island Blues"), two by Jarrett, and the Beatles' "Here, There and Everywhere." An excellent example of the musical magic of the Charles Lloyd Quartet. —*Scott Yanow*

Charles Lloyd in the Soviet Union / May 14, 1967 / Atlantic ✦✦✦✦✦
The Charles Lloyd Quartet was (along with Cannonball Adderley's band) the most popular group in jazz during the latter half of the 1960s. Lloyd somehow managed this feat without watering down his music or adopting a pop repertoire. A measure of the band's popularity is that Lloyd and his sidemen (pianist Keith Jarrett, bassist Ron McClure and drummer Jack DeJohnette) were able to have a very successful tour of the Soviet Union during a period when jazz was still being discouraged by the communists. This well-received festival appearance has four lengthy performances including an 18-minute version of "Sweet Georgia Bright" and Lloyd (who has always had a soft-toned Coltrane influenced tenor style and a more distinctive voice on flute) is in top form. —*Scott Yanow*

Soundtrack / Sep. 1969 / Atlantic ✦✦✦
The final recording by the original Charles Lloyd Quartet was made shortly before pianist Keith Jarrett left to join Miles Davis and Lloyd broke up the band. With Jarrett, bassist Ron McClure and drummer Jack DeJohnette still aboard, Lloyd (doubling as usual on tenor and flute) performs four of his songs, including "Sombrero Sam" and a nearly 17-minute remake of his greatest hit, here retitled "Forest Flower '69." Worth searching for, although this Atlantic LP (as with most of Lloyd's output) has not been reissued yet in full on CD. —*Scott Yanow*

Warm Waters / 1971 / Kapp ✦✦

Waves / 1972 / A&M ✦✦
After breaking up his popular quartet in 1969, Charles Lloyd largely dropped out of sight. He re-emerged once in a while in the 1970s to record a bit, but those sessions tended to be influenced by his interest in transcendental meditation and were often merely mood music. This CD reissue is mostly forgettable, finding Lloyd on tenor and flute mostly playing relaxing and soothing solos. Three of the eight numbers are of slightly greater interest because of the presence of guitarist Gabor Szabo, but the use of background vocalists on "TM" do not help, and most of the music is quite faceless. —*Scott Yanow*

Weavings / 1978 / Pacific Arts ✦✦✦

Big Sur Tapestry / 1979 / Pacific Arts ✦

Autumn in New York / 1979 / Density ✦✦✦
This little-known effort is better than some of Charles Lloyd's infrequent projects of the 1970s, for he sticks to tenor and interprets eight standards melodically and with taste. The rhythm section (which includes pianist Tom Grant) is rather anonymous; Suzanne Wallach's occasional vocals are forgettable; and Clare Fisher's

string arrangements are not too inventive, but Lloyd does play quite well. In any case, good luck finding this obscure LP. —*Scott Yanow*

Montreux (1982) / Jul. 1982 / Elektra ✦✦✦

Charles Lloyd came out of isolation and retirement in 1982 due to the persuasion of the then-unknown pianist Michel Petrucciani. As can be heard on this concert LP from the 1982 Montreux Jazz Festival, Lloyd's styles and sounds on tenor and flute were unchanged from his glory days in the 1960s. Petrucciani (at that point more influenced by Bill Evans than he would be) was already a monster, while bassist Palle Danielsson and drummer Son Ship Theus are stimulating in support. Lloyd performs three of his newer originals, Bill Evans' "Very Early," and a long remake of his famous hit "Forest Flower." Throughout, Charles Lloyd shows that he was still in his prime. This excellent music will hopefully be reissued on CD. —*Scott Yanow*

A Night in Copenhagen / Jul. 11, 1983 / Blue Note ✦✦✦✦

From 1982-83, pianist Michel Petrucciani was a member of the Charles Lloyd Quartet. Lloyd, coaxed out of retirement by Petrucciani, sounded virtually unchanged from his earlier days; the passion and enthusiasm were still there. The leader is heard on tenor, flute and the exotic Chinese oboe on seven of his originals, including two ("Of Course, Of Course" and "Sweet Georgia Bright") that were released for the first time on this CD reissue. Bassist Palle Danielsson and drummer Son Ship Theus are excellent in support, and the remarkable singer Bobby McFerrin scats quite creatively on "Of Course, Of Course" and "Third Floor Richard." Recommended.— Scott Yanow

Fish out of Water / Jul. 1989 / EMC ✦✦✦

This new release offers quasi-mystical themes, shimmering horn riffs and flute melodies, plus fine keyboard contributions from Bob Stenson and decent, though hardly aggressive, rhythm section work by bassist Palle Danielsson and drummer Jon Christensen. —*Ron Wynn*

Notes from Big Sur / Nov. 1991 / ECM ✦✦✦✦

Acoustic Masters I / Jul. 1993 / Atlantic ✦✦✦✦✦

The Call / Jul. 1993 / ECM ✦✦✦✦

All My Relations / Jul. 1994 / ECM ✦✦✦✦✦

This CD by the Charles Lloyd Quartet avoids fitting into any of the stereotypes that one might have about ECM's recordings. Pianist Bobo Stenson has carved his own identity out of the styles of Bill Evans and Keith Jarrett, drummer Billy Hart is stimulating in support and Anders Jormin provides a walking bass on many of the tracks; a rarity for ECM sessions. The main focus is on Charles Lloyd, whose playing during the past decade has been some of the finest of his career. He mostly sticks to tenor (just playing flute on "Little Peace" and Chinese oboe on the very brief "Milarepa") and, although traces of John Coltrane's sound will always be in his tone, Lloyd comes up with quite a few original ideas. He is best on "Thelonious Theonlyus" (which has a slight calypso feel to it), the episodic "Cape to Cairo Suite" (a tribute to Nelson Mandela), a long tenor/drums duet on "All My Relations" (which is a mix between "Chasin' the 'Trane" and "Bessie's Blues") and the brooding spiritual "Hymne to the Mother." A strong effort. —*Scott Yanow*

Canto / Dec. 1996 / ECM ✦✦✦✦

Since his return to full-time playing a decade earlier, Charles Lloyd has recorded many sets, most with pianist Bobo Stenson. Bassist Anders Jormin and drummer Billy Hart complete the quartet. Lloyd (on tenor and Tibetan oboe, but no flute this time) performs seven of his newer compositions, and the music, which ranges from fiery outbursts to more introspective moments, generally displays more extroverted emotion than is heard on most ECM releases. Lloyd entered the late 1990s in prime form. —*Scott Yanow*

Didier Lockwood

b. Feb. 11, 1956, Calais, France
Violin / Post-Bop, Fusion

Didier Lockwood has had a diverse career, ranging from fusion to swing and advanced hard bop. In the 1980s he was considered the next in a line of great French violinists after Stephane Grappelli and Jean-Luc Ponty but he has maintained a fairly low profile in the 1990s. Lockwood began studying violin when he was six. Ten years later he stopped his formal training and joined a rock group. He played in Paris with Aldo Romano and Daniel Humair among others, met Grappelli and toured with him. He had a fusion group called Surya and recorded with Tony Williams around the same period of time (1979). Didier Lockwood played in the US on several occasions in the 1980s and recorded an acoustic album in 1986 with fellow violinists John Blake and Michal Urbaniak. —*Scott Yanow*

New World / Feb. 20, 1979-Feb. 22, 1979 / Pausa ✦✦✦

Touted as the heir to Stephane Grappelli and Jean-Luc Ponty, Didier Lockwood's debut recording as a leader (which was also released in Europe by the MPS label)

features the 23-year-old violinist in a generally straightahead setting. Joined by pianist Gordon Beck, bassist Niels Pedersen drummer Tony Williams, and a few guests, Lockwood primarily plays post-bop originals, plus "Autumn Leaves," "Giant Steps" and "Pent Up House" (a duet with guitarist John Etheridge). Although an early effort, this obscure LP is still one of Lockwood's best all-around sets. —*Scott Yanow*

Live in Montreux / Jul. 28, 1980-Jul. 30, 1980 / JMS ✦✦✦

Released at the time in Europe by MPS and in the US by the now-defunct Pausa label, the music from violinist Didier Lockwood's 1980 Montreux Jazz Festival set is in both cases out of print. Lockwood, who can play like Stephane Grappelli, here opts for fusion in a sextet that also includes tenor saxophonist Bob Malach and keyboardist Jan Hammer. Lockwood's unaccompanied "Four Strings Bitch" is a highlight of this well-played date. —*Scott Yanow*

● ### Surya / 1980 / Inner City ✦✦✦✦✦

The music on this out-of-print LP ranges from post-bop to fusion-oriented. Violinist Didier Lockwood, who has thus far yet to reach his potential, performs with his regular band of 1980, a high-powered quintet also including pianist Francis Lockwood, electric bassist Sylvain Marc, drummer Jean-My Truong and Luc Plouton on synthesizer. Although none of the group originals are particularly memorable, the musicians are creative within the now-dated format. —*Scott Yanow*

Fasten Seat Belts / Sep. 1981 / JMS ✦✦✦

Violinist Didier Lockwood's early MPS recordings were made available in the US by Pausa, but are currently out of print. His 1981 quartet (which also includes keyboardist Francis Lockwood, electric bassist Jean-Michel Kajdan and drummer Kirt Rust) is joined on some cuts by tenorman Bob Malach. Other than Stevie Wonder's "Isn't She Lovely," all of the music is by band members. Despite some power by the ensembles and creative ideas, nothing very memorable occurs. —*Scott Yanow*

Didier Lockwood Group / Dec. 1983+Jan. 1984 / Gramavision ✦✦✦✦

Out of the Blue / Apr. 1985 / Gramavision ✦✦✦✦✦

Violinist Didier Lockwood showed great potential when he first arrived on the scene, but despite some good sessions, he has not yet become the pacesetter one originally expected. This is one of his better recordings, a quartet outing with pianist Gordon Beck, bassist Cecil McBee and drummer Billy Hart. Other than "'Round Midnight" and an obscurity, all of the music is by either Lockwood or Beck, although much of it is fairly straightahead (as opposed to Lockwood's earlier fusion-oriented dates). Worth searching for. —*Scott Yanow*

1 2 3 4 / May 1987-Jul. 1987 / Nova ✦✦

Lockwood, once an interesting violinist, seems to have lost direction. —*Ron Wynn*

Phoenix 90 / Jun. 1990-Jul. 1990 / Gramavision ✦✦

Storyboard / Apr. 21, 1996-Apr. 25, 1996 / Dreyfus ✦✦✦✦✦

This is a diverse CD that rewards repeated listening. Violinist Didier Lockwood's most rewarding recording in several years also features Joey De Francesco on organ and trumpet, bassist James Genus and guest Steve Wilson (doubling on alto and soprano) on the first three numbers. The biggest revelation of the set is that Lockwood takes a credible alto solo on "Serie B." Performing his originals along with a few obscurities, the violinist shows versatility, sometimes distorting his tone to get a rockish sound and other times swinging hard. The music (well worth checking out) is fresh and contains its share of surprises. —*Scott Yanow*

Lorne Lofsky

b. May 10, 1954, Canada
Guitar / Cool

A talented cool-toned guitarist in the tradition of Jimmy Raney and his fellow Canadian Ed Bickert, Lorne Lofsky gained some recognition in the US due to a 1980 Pablo album and a few tours with Oscar Peterson. Lofsky, who has also recorded as a leader for Jazz Inspiration, has been a sideman on recording sessions with Chet Baker, the Brass Connection, Kenny Wheeler and Bickert, among others. —*Scott Yanow*

It Could Happen to You / 1981 / Pablo ✦✦✦

The cool-toned guitarist Lorne Lofsky made an initial stir in the US with this album, which has yet to be reissued on CD by Fantasy. Recommended to Norman Granz for Pablo Records by Oscar Peterson, Lofsky is in top form jamming mostly standards with fellow Canadians Kieran Overs and Joe Bendzsa on bass and drums, respectively. Fans of Jimmy Raney and Ed Bickert will enjoy this quiet but sometimes passionate straightahead jazz. —*Scott Yanow*

The Quartet of Lorne Lofsky & Ed Bickert and Friends / Jan. 27, 1985 / Unisson ✦✦✦✦

This Unisson LP features a logical combination. Canadian guitarists Lorne Lofsky and Ed Bickert both have quiet sounds, subtle bop-oriented styles, and the ability to swing at any tempo. With bassist Neil Swainson and drummer Jerry Fuller completing the quartet, the co-leaders play mostly lesser-known material, including "Morning Star," Swainson's "Morning Star," Sam Jones' "Bittersuite," and Coleman Hawkins' "Bean and the Boys." In addition, the guitarists perform a duet version of "I Remember You" and have individual features (Lofsky on "Falling Grace" and Bickert during "Crazy, She Calls Me"). A tasteful and enjoyable (if difficult-to-locate) album. —*Scott Yanow*

● **Bill, Please** / 1994 / Jazz Inspiration ✦✦✦✦✦

Lorne Lofsky is a cool-toned guitarist in the tradition of Jimmy Raney and fellow Canadian Ed Bickert. Since Lofsky's sound is not all that exciting, it is fortunate that he is not only an expert bop-based improviser but very good at picking out a repertoire that fits his style. For his trio set with bassist Mike Downes and drummer Jerry Fuller, Lofsky performs four songs by Bill Evans plus numbers by Wayne Shorter, John Lewis, Lennie Tristano ("317 East 32nd") and Ravel along with a few standards. To give variety to the date, four pieces are taken totally by Lofsky who overdubs a second (and sometimes third) guitar with taste. "Subtle creativity" is a phrase that sums up this session as a whole for it takes several playings to fully appreciate the tight musical communication between the trio members along with Lofsky's inventive ideas. —*Scott Yanow*

Julie London

b. Sep. 26, 1926, Santa Rosa, CA
Vocals / Cool, Standards, Pop, Show Tunes, Traditional Pop
A sultry, smoky-voiced master of understatement, Julie London enjoyed considerable popularity during the "Cool Era" of the 1950s. London never had the range of Ella Fitzgerald or Sarah Vaughan, but often used restraint, softness and subtlety to maximum advantage. An actress as well as a singer, London played with heavyweights like Gregory Peck and Rock Hudson in various films, and was married to Jack Webb of *Dragnet* fame for seven years before marrying songwriter Bobby Troup (*Route 66*). London performed her biggest hit, "Cry Me a River," in the Jayne Mansfield film *The Girl Can't Help It*. After recording her last album, *Easy Does It*, in 1967, she continued to act—playing a nurse on the NBC medical drama *Emergency* from 1974-78. Despite her "sex symbol" image—London was known for her sexy LP covers, which make them collector's items—she was surprisingly shy, and left show biz altogether in the late '70s. —*Alex Henderson*

Julie Is Her Name / 1995 / Liberty ✦✦✦✦✦

For a time, Julie London was as famous for her sexy album covers as for her singing. Her debut set is her best, a set of fairly basic interpretations of standards in which she is accompanied tastefully by guitarist Barney Kessel and bassist Ray Leatherwood. "Cry Me a River," from this album, was her biggest hit, and her breathy versions of such numbers as "I Should Care," "Say It Isn't So," "Easy Street" and "Gone with the Wind" are quite haunting. London's LP's have yet to be comprehensively reissued on CD, but can sometimes be found in specialty shops; they certainly stick in one's mind. —*Scott Yanow*

● **Time for Love: The Best of Julie London** / 1955-1965 / Rhino ✦✦✦✦✦

A collection of dusky, atmospheric mood music released as a CD in 1990, *Time for Love* serves as a superb overview of the jazz-pop songstress in her prime. Seductive and personal interpretations of "No Moon at All," "You'd Be So Nice to Come Home To," "Cry Me a River" (a major hit for her) and other classics beautifully demonstrate that, like June Christy and Helen Merrill, London realizes just how effective subtlety can be. While the big-band accompaniment on some sides (including a soul-bearing version of Thelonious Monk's "Round Midnight") is nothing to complain about, London is best served by intimate, minimalist small groups—some boasting only Barney Kessel's guitar and Ray Leatherwood's bass. —*Alex Henderson*

Make Love to Me / 1957 / Liberty ✦✦✦✦

Julie London's concise and melodic versions of standards were quite popular during the latter half of the 1950s. Her subtle sensuality and lightly swinging style made for a potent combination. This album (which has not yet reappeared on CD) matches London's voice with an orchestra arranged by Russ Garcia on standards and a couple of newer tunes, including Bobby Troup's "It's Good to Want You Bad." Among the more memorable selections are "If I Could Be with You," "Alone Together," "I Wanna Be Loved" and "You're My Thrill." —*Scott Yanow*

The Best of Julie / 1957-1960 / Liberty ✦✦✦✦✦

This English Liberty LP from the 1980s has one selection apiece from 13 of Julie London's earlier albums. Although she never thought of herself as a singer, London had a sensuous and surprisingly flexible voice that sounded at its best in intimate jazz settings. Highlights of this set (in addition to the miniature reproductions of London's famed album covers) are her hit "Cry Me a River," "They Can't Take That Away from Me," "Mad About the Boy," "Invitation to the Blues," "The Nearness of You" and "Daddy." This hard-to-find LP serves as a perfect introduction to the magic of Julie London's music. —*Scott Yanow*

Mike Longo

b. Mar. 19, 1939, Cincinnati, OH
Piano / Bop
Mike Longo is best known as a reliable and versatile player who was the pianist with Dizzy Gillespie during 1966-73. He started taking piano lessons when he was three, played professionally when he was 15 and while in high school in Ft. Lauderdale he had the opportunity to play with Cannonball Adderley. In 1960 Longo worked at the Metropole in New York with Red Allen and Coleman Hawkins, he spent 1961 living in Toronto (where he studied with Oscar Peterson) and then returned to New York where he accompanied some singers. Mike Longo recorded with Gillespie during his period with the trumpeter and led a few of his own sessions for Mainstream, Pablo (1976) and Consolidated Artists (1981). —*Scott Yanow*

Talk with the Spirits / Jan. 1976 / Pablo ✦✦✦

Pianist Mike Longo, still best known for his longtime membership in Dizzy Gillespie's group (1966-73), had his recorded debut as a leader on this Pablo LP (not yet reissued on CD). Longo gathered together an impressive sextet also including trumpeter Virgil Jones, tenor saxophonist Harold Vick, guitarist George Davis, bassist Bob Cranshaw and drummer Mickey Roker, and also welcomed Dizzy himself, who made cameo appearances on conga and a vocal, but not on trumpet. The music, five of Longo's originals, is less memorable than the solos, although overall this is a pleasing effort that ranges from lightly funky to straight-ahead. —*Scott Yanow*

New York '78 / 1978 / Consolidated Artists ✦✦✦✦

Solo Recital / Jun. 1982 / Consolidated Artists ✦✦✦

El Moodo Grande / Mar. 15, 1994 / LRC ✦✦✦

Like a Thief in the Night / 1997 / Delta ✦✦✦

● **I Miss You John: Tribute to Dizzy Gillespie** / 1997 / Consolidated Artists ✦✦✦✦

Eddy Louiss

b. May 12, 1941, Paris, France
Organ, Piano / Hard Bop
Eddy Louiss has spent most of his career leading his own group in France but twice has made particularly notable recordings, both on organ. He had sung as a member of the Double Six (1961-63), played piano with Johnny Griffin in the mid-'60s and worked at times with Kenny Clarke and Jean-Luc Ponty. But he is best known for recording *Dynasty* with Stan Getz (1971) and for his recent duet set with pianist Michel Petrucciani (1994) on Dreyfus. —*Scott Yanow*

★ **Eddy Louiss/Michel Petrucciani** / Jun. 14, 1994-Jun. 16, 1994 / Dreyfus ✦✦✦✦✦

Organ-piano duet recordings are quite rare in jazz history, making this successful collaboration rather historical in its own way. It is particularly interesting to hear pianist Michel Petrucciani, who usually dominates his own recordings, being matched up with and inspired by an equal. Organist Eddy Louiss proved to be the perfect choice for this date. The duo performs originals that are often quite boppish along with three standards. Louiss' comping and basslines really push the pianist while Petrucciani (who gets to show off his expert skills as an accompanist) constantly sets a fire under Louiss during this live date. The interplay between the pair is quite exciting and they have plenty of torrid tradeoffs. It's a highly recommended disc. —*Scott Yanow*

Joe Lovano

b. Dec. 29, 1952, Cleveland, OH
Tenor Saxophone, Soprano Saxophone / Post-Bop, Hard Bop
One of the top saxophonists of the 1990s, Joe Lovano still seems to be improving! His tenor tone is based in the tradition but is fairly original, and his chance-taking improvisations are both stimulating and refreshing. His father Tony "Big T" Lovano was a fine tenorman who played in Cleveland. Joe originally started on alto when he was six, switching to tenor five years later. He attended Berklee and then worked with Jack McDuff and Lonnie Smith. After three years touring with Woody Herman's Orchestra (1976-79), Lovano moved to New York, playing regularly with Mel Lewis' Big Band, Paul Motian's various groups (since 1981), Charlie Haden's Liberation Music Orchestra and (in the early '90s) John Scofield in addition to touring Europe with Elvin Jones (1987). Joe Lovano has recorded as a leader for Soul Note, Jazz Club, Label Bleu (reissued by Evidence), Enja, JSL (a date with his father) and a long string of very impressive outings for Blue Note. His 1995 Blue Note set *Rush Hour* features Joe Lovano and his wife, singer Judi Silvano, in top form collaborating with Gunther Schuller on a challenging set of music. —*Scott Yanow*

Tones, Shapes and Colors / Nov. 21, 1985 / Soul Note ✦✦✦✦

Joe Lovano's recorded debut as a leader features the tenor in a quartet with pianist Ken Werner, bassist Dennis Irwin and drummer Mel Lewis. Together, they perform three originals apiece by the leader and Werner. None of the tunes are simple or based on the chords of standards, but although they did not catch on, the interplay by the musicians, the excellent pacing of tempos and moods, and the consistently satisfying solos make this a set worth searching for. —Scott Yanow

Village Rhythm / Jun. 7, 1988-Jun. 9, 1988 / Soul Note ✦✦✦✦

By 1988, it was becoming increasingly obvious that tenor saxophonist Joe Lovano was on his way to becoming a major name in the jazz world. For this advanced hard bop set, he contributed all of the selections other than Charles Mingus' "Duke Ellington's Sound of Love," including a tribute to his father, tenorman Tony "Big T" Lovano. Teamed with trumpeter Tom Harrell, pianist Kenny Werner, bassist Marc Johnson and drummer Paul Motian, Lovano is heard throughout in his early prime, playing inventive and generally concise improvisations that were beginning to become distinctive. —Scott Yanow

Worlds / May 5, 1989 / Evidence ✦✦✦✦✦

Landmarks / Aug. 13, 1990-Aug. 14, 1990 / Blue Note ✦✦✦✦✦

Although the title of this CD makes it sound as if tenor saxophonist Joe Lovano was performing veteran jazz classics on this date, all but one of the ten songs played by his quintet are actually Lovano originals. With strong assistance provided by guitarist John Abercrombie, pianist Ken Werner, bassist Marc Johnson and drummer Bill Stewart, Lovano often sounds like a mixture of Dewey Redman and early John Coltrane on his enjoyable set. His music has enough variety to hold one's interest, Abercrombie is in particularly strong form, and Lovano is consistently creative during the modern mainstream music. —Scott Yanow

Sounds of Joy / Jan. 1991 / Enja ✦✦✦✦

From the Soul / Dec. 28, 1991 / Blue Note ✦✦✦✦✦

Joe Lovano heads a lineup with pianist Michel Petrucciani, bassist Dave Holland, and late drummer Ed Blackwell. It's hard-edged, explosive playing all around, with Blackwell laying down his patented bombs while Petrucciani and Holland converge behind Lovano's dynamic solos. —Ron Wynn

Universal Language / Jun. 26, 1992-Jun. 28, 1992 / Blue Note ✦✦✦✦✦

Universal Language is one of Joe Lovano's most ambitious and successsful albums, an attempt to prove the cliché that music is indeed the universal language. He does this by writing a set of ten original compositions that cover a broad spectrum of sounds and styles, from hard bop to worldbeat-influenced postbop. His band—trumpeter Tim Hagans, drummer Jack DeJohnette, pianist Kenny Werner, vocalist Judi Silvano and bassists Charlie Haden, Scott Lee and Steve Swallow—handle the subtleties of the music expertly, bringing the melodic themes into unexpected territory. Silvano's voice is used as texture, not a lead instrument, which helps give the music complexity and an otherworldly depth. It's an unabashedly adventurous and risky project, and it works frighteningly well. —Stephen Thomas Erlewine

Tenor Legacy / Jun. 18, 1993 / Blue Note ✦✦✦✦

Joe Lovano welcomes Joshua Redman to his sextet set (which also features pianist Mulgrew Miller, bassist Christian McBride, bassist Lewis Nash and percussionist Don Alias) and, rather than jam on standards, Joe Lovano composed five new originals, revived three obscurities and only chose to perform two familiar pieces. By varying the styles and instrumentation (for example "Bread and Wine" does not have piano or bass), Lovano has created a set with a great deal of variety and some surprising moments. The two tenors (who have distinctive sounds) work together fine and some chances are taken. This matchup works well. —Scott Yanow

Quartets / Mar. 12, 1994+Jan. 22, 1995 / Blue Note ✦✦✦✦✦

This double-CD features tenor saxophonist Joe Lovano during two appearances at the Village Vanguard recorded ten months apart. Other than the leader, the pair of quartets are completely different and they bring out two sides of Lovano. The earlier session features the leader in a stimulating pianoless quartet, matching wits and creativity with fluegelhornist Tom Harrell. While the music is closer to Ornette Coleman than to Gerry Mulligan (to name two famous pianoless groups), Harrell's tone more closely resembles Chuck Mangione than Don Cherry although fortunately he is much more inventive. The four Lovano originals are adventurous and all of the musicians sound as if they are stretching themselves. The second disc showcases Lovano in a more conventional quartet. The repertoire (just one original this time) covers John Coltrane, Thelonious Monk, Miles Davis, Charles Mingus and Gordon Jenkins and finds the tenorman displaying his roots in Sonny Rollins. The rhythm section on the later date (pianist Mulgrew Miller, bassist Christian McBride and drummer Lewis Nash) is excellent at accompanying (rather than challenging) Lovano. In both cases Joe Lovano is heard in prime form, making this an easily recommended two-fer. —Scott Yanow

☆ **Rush Hour** / Apr. 6, 1994-Jun. 12, 1994 / Blue Note ✦✦✦✦✦

This is one of the most exciting jazz releases of 1995. Joe Lovano is showcased on four songs backed by a string section, is accompanied by a stringless big band filled with woodwinds and brass during four other pieces, performs Ornette Cole-

man's "Kathline Gray" with a chamber group, takes two songs as duets with his wife Judi Silvano (who contributes wordless vocals), plays his own "Wildcat" as an overdubbed feature for his tenor and drums and does a straightforward version of "Chelsea Bridge" unaccompanied. Gunther Schuller's arrangements for the larger pieces (which include three of his own colorful originals: "Rush Hour on 23rd Street," "Lament for M" and "Headin' out, Movin' In") expertly blend together Gil Evans-type orchestrations with aspects of modern classical music and freer forms of jazz while allowing the music to swing. Silvano's voice is also an asset on three of the orchestra performances and trumpeter Jack Walrath briefly makes his presence felt. However this very well-conceived release would not have succeeded were it not for the talent, versatility and risk taking of Joe Lovano. His improvisations (mostly on tenor) push the boundaries of this already adventurous music. Lovano's sound (which occasionally hints a little at Clifford Jordan) is quite original and, on the basis of this date alone, he must rank as one of the top tenors of the 1990s. —Scott Yanow

Celebrating Sinatra / Jun. 2, 1996+Jun. 3, 1996 / Blue Note ✦✦✦✦✦

Although this project may not seem to have much potential at first glance, tenor saxophonist Joe Lovano's tribute to Frank Sinatra is consistently brilliant and inventive. Since Sinatra recorded countless songs, Lovano had plenty to choose from, and he came up with 13 superior standards. Rather than just play the tunes in conventional swing fashion, Lovano is featured in quite a few different settings, caressing and bending the melodies à la Sonny Rollins. "Chicago" is taken as a duet with drummer Al Foster, eight songs have Judi Silvano's haunting voice mostly singing wordlessly as part of the ensemble, Manny Albam orchestrated eight songs (some of which use woodwinds and a few strings), and other key players include pianist Kenny Werner, bassist George Mraz and Billy Drewes on soprano sax and bass clarinet. No matter how familiar the song (including "I'll Never Smile Again," "I've Got the World on a String," a rollicking "South of the Border" and "One for My Baby"), each performance has plenty of surprising moments. A real gem. —Scott Yanow

Flying Colors / 1997 / Blue Note ✦✦✦✦✦

Flying Colors is an excellent duet album between Joe Lovano and Gonzalo Rubalcaba, capturing the saxophonist and pianist running through a set of adventurous hard bop highlighted by their unpredictable solos and empathetic interplay. —Leo Stanley

Frank Lowe

b. Jun. 24, 1943, Memphis, TN

Tenor Saxophone / Avant-Garde, Free Jazz

A powerful tenor saxophonist whose roots in R&B and bop can often be felt even in his freer improvisations, Frank Lowe has stuck to his own singular musical path throughout his low-profile career. He started playing the tenor when he was 12 and spent some time at the University of Kansas and in San Francisco. He gigged regularly with Sun Ra in New York (1966-68) and worked with many of the top avant-garde players of the era, including Alice Coltrane, drummer Rashied Ali (they made a duo set for Survival in 1973), Archie Shepp and Don Cherry. Frank Lowe, who has recorded as a leader for ESP, Freedom, Black Saint, Marge, Palm, Kharma, Cadence and most recently CIMP, has headed his own bands on an irregular basis during the past two decades and remains an underrecognized free jazz master. —Scott Yanow

Black Beings / 1973 / ESP ✦✦✦

One of the later ESP blowouts, this CD reissue features the tenor of Frank Lowe interacting with Joseph Jarman (heard here on alto and soprano), violinist Leroy Jenkins (operating under the pseudonym of "The Wizard" but quite recognizable), bassist William Parker and drummer Rashid Sinan. Two of the three originals (which include the 25-minute "In Trane's Name") are lengthy and wander a bit, but the intense music is well worth hearing by free-jazz collectors. —Scott Yanow

Fresh / Sep. 1974-Mar. 7, 1975 / Freedom ✦✦✦✦✦

The emphasis is on color and sound on this spirited avant-garde album. Four of the five selections feature the adventurous tenor of Frank Lowe with trumpeter Lester Bowie, trombonist Joseph Bowie, cellist Abdul Wadud and either Steve Reid or Bob Shaw on drums. They perform two Lowe originals and two pieces by Thelonious Monk; these renditions are full of surprises and contrasts. In addition, Lowe is heard with an unknown group of local musicians called "the Memphis Four" on "Chu's Blues" in 1974. Open-eared listeners should find this set to be quite stimulating. —Scott Yanow

The Flam / Oct. 1975 / Black Saint ✦✦✦✦✦

On this free jazz date the powerful tenor Frank Lowe teams up with trumpeter Leo Smith, trombonist Joseph Bowie, bassist Alex Blake and drummer Charles Bobo Shaw for five group originals including the collaboration "Third St. Stomp."

The very explorative and rather emotional music holds one's interest throughout. These often heated performances are better heard than described. —*Scott Yanow*

Doctor Too Much / Nov. 1978 / Kharma ✦✦✦

Lowe and Behold / Dec. 1979 / Musicworks ✦✦✦

Exotic Heartbreak / Nov. 1982 / Soul Note ✦✦✦

Decision in Paradise / Sep. 24, 1984+Sep. 28, 1984 / Soul Note ✦✦✦✦
The all-star lineup (tenor saxophonist Frank Lowe, trumpeter Don Cherry, trombonnist Grachan Moncur III, pianist Geri Allen, bassist Charnette Moffett and drummer Charles Moffett) practically guarantees that this music will be worth hearing. Although a touch more conservative than one might expect (more of an open-minded straightahead set than music emphasizing sound explorations), all six group originals are of interest including Lowe's unaccompanied performance on Butch Morris' "I'll Whistle Your Name" and Moncur's whimsical "You Dig." —*Scott Yanow*

★ **Bodies and Soul** / Nov. 18, 1995-Nov. 19, 1995 / CIMP ✦✦✦✦✦
Frank Lowe led his first record date in 1975 but the explorative tenor saxophonist has never gained more than an underground reputation. A masterful improviser who has retained a free spirit through the years, Lowe's music is actually much more accessible than one might expect. On *Bodies and Soul,* Lowe's sound varies from the gruff roars of prime Archie Shepp to Sonny Rollins. Assisted by bassist Tim Flood (making his recording debut) and veteran drummer Charles Moffett, Lowe explores four originals plus music by John Coltrane ("Impressions"), Pharoah Sanders, Ornette Coleman, Phillip Watson, Don Cherry and even a melodic and unaccompanied version of Johnny Green's "Body and Soul." The free bop music is often quite thoughtful but never predictable and is well worth an investigation. —*Scott Yanow*

Vision Blue / Feb. 19, 1997-Feb. 20, 1997 / CIMP ✦✦✦✦

Mundell Lowe (James Mundell Lowe)

b. Apr. 21, 1922, Laurel, MS
Guitar / Cool, Swing

A reliable cool-toned guitarist who was on many sessions through the years despite never becoming a household name, Mundell Lowe picked up early experience during 1936-40 playing Dixieland in New Orleans and country music in Nashville. He toured with Jan Savitt (1942), Ray McKinley (1945-47), Mary Lou Williams (1947-49), Red Norvo and Ellis Larkins. In 1950 he became a staff musician at NBC although he always played jazz on the side. Lowe was with the Sauter-Finegan Orchestra (1952-53), worked with Benny Goodman on an occasional basis, and recorded as a leader for RCA, Riverside, Camden and Charlie Parker Records. In 1965 Lowe moved to California and worked as a composer for films and television, teaching film composition during 1979-85. He played locally in Los Angeles, often with Richie Kamuca and Benny Carter. Mundell Lowe (who is married to singer Betty Bennett) recorded sets for Famous Door (1974), Dobre (1976) and Jazz Alliance (1992). —*Scott Yanow*

Mundell Lowe Quartet / Aug. 27, 1955+Oct. 4, 1955 / Original Jazz Classics ✦✦✦✦
Most of this set is essentially straightahead bebop with guitarist Mundell Lowe heard in top form on such numbers as "Will You Still Be Mine," "I'll Never Be the Same," "All of You" and "Cheek to Cheek." The wild card here is Dick Hyman who, in addition to piano and some celeste on "The Night We Called It a Day," mostly plays organ. His tone is thin and restrained, almost as if he were playing a cheap electric piano; Jimmy Smith would not make his presence known for another year. However, Lowe is the main voice throughout this fairly colorful Riverside quartet date (also including supportive playing by bassist Trigger Alpert and drummer Ed Shaughnessy), which has been reissued on CD in the *OJC* series. —*Scott Yanow*

Satan in High Heels / Nov. 30, 1961-Dec. 22, 1961 / Charlie Parker ✦✦✦
Mundell Lowe's score for the exploitation flick *Satan in High Heels* is an immensely enjoyable collection of exaggeratedly cinematic jazz. Lowe runs through all sorts of styles, from swinging big band to cool jazz, from laid-back hard-bop to driving bop. He pulls it off because his big band comprises musicians as skilled as Oliver Nelson, Al Cohn, Phil Woods, Urbie Green, Joe Newman and Clark Terry. They help give the music the extra kick it needs, and *Satan in High Heels* winds up as a terrific set of humorous and sleazy, but well-played, mainstream jazz. —*Stephen Thomas Erlewine*

California Guitar / 1974 / Famous Door ✦✦✦✦
Guitarist Mundell Lowe, who recorded regularly as a leader during 1954-62, had not had his own record date for over a decade when he cut this now-obscure LP for the Famous Door label. The three selections from 1972 (two standards and "Famous Door Blues") match the swing-oriented Lowe with the rhythm guitar of Irving Ashby, pianist Jimmy Rowles, bassist Monty Budwig and drummer Donald

Bailey; the other four numbers ("Open House at Arleen's" and three veteran songs) feature Lowe in a quartet with pianist Roger Kellaway, Budwig and Bailey. Throughout, the music is melodic, swinging and a touch predictable, but has enough heat to hold one's interest. —*Scott Yanow*

Guitar Player / Oct. 16, 1976-Oct. 17, 1976 / Dobre ✦✦✦✦
Guitarist Mundell Lowe plays quite well in a sparse trio with bassist Monty Budwig and drummer Nick Ceroli on this LP, swinging melodically. Unfortunately, the song selection is not too inspired (with two obscurities joined by such warhorses as "Scrapple from the Apple," "Satin Doll" and "Prelude to a Kiss"), and no real surprises occur, but it does serve as a fine showcase for Lowe's attractive sound and straightahead style. —*Scott Yanow*

● **Souvenirs** / Nov. 10, 1977+Feb. 27, 1992 / Jazz Alliance ✦✦✦✦
This CD features guitarist Mundell Lowe on two separate occasions. Eight selections are from 1977, and other than an unaccompanied version of his "I Think You Always Knew," these find Lowe leading a trio also including bassist Bob Magnusson and drummer Nick Ceroli. Ceroli passed away before the four numbers from 1992 were cut (two Lowe duets apiece with either pianist Mike Wofford or Magnusson), so this set is subtitled "A Tribute to Nick Ceroli." Lowe mostly sticks to standards, although he contributed two tunes and also performs Al Cohn's "P-Town," Benny Carter's "Souvenirs" and Miles Davis' late-period "Star People." Overall, this CD serves as a particularly strong introduction to the music of the underrated Mundell Lowe. —*Scott Yanow*

Transit West / Jul. 28, 1983-Jul. 29, 1983 / Pausa ✦✦✦
Guitarist Mundell Lowe's "TransitWest," a quartet also including Sam Most on flute and tenor, bassist Monty Budwig and drummer Nick Ceroli, did not last very long, and this LP is quite difficult to find, but the group was an excellent outlet for the guitarist's playing during its brief existence. Four straightahead and often lyrical Lowe originals alternate on the set with five veteran standards including "Old Folks," "Nuages" and "Cottontail." Most of the music swings gently, but with inner passion, and the blend between Lowe and Most is quite attractive. —*Scott Yanow*

Jimmie Lunceford

b. Jun. 6, 1902, Fulton, MS, **d.** Jul. 12, 1947, Seaside, OR
Leader/ Swing

The Jimmie Lunceford Orchestra has always been a bit difficult to evaluate. Contemporary observers rated Lunceford's big band at the top with Duke Ellington and Count Basie but, when judging the music solely on their records (and not taking into account their visual show, appearance and showmanship), Lunceford's ensemble has to be placed on the second tier. His orchestra lacked any really classic soloists (altoist Willie Smith and trombonist Trummy Young came the closest) and a large portion of the band's repertoire either featured the dated vocals of Dan Grissom or were pleasant novelties. And yet, the well-rehearsed ensembles were very impressive, some of the arrangements (particularly those of Sy Oliver) were quite original and the use of glee-club vocalists and short concise solos were pleasing and often memorable. Plus Lunceford's was the first orchestra to feature high-note trumpeters (starting with Tommy Stevenson in 1934) and had a strong influence on the early Stan Kenton Orchestra.

Although he was trained on several instruments and was featured on flute on "Liza" in the 1940s, Jimmie Lunceford was much more significant as a bandleader than as a musician. While teaching music at Manassa High School in Memphis in 1927, Lunceford organized a student band called the Chickasaw Syncopators, recording two songs that year and a pair in 1930. After leaving Memphis, the band (known by then as the Jimmie Lunceford Orchestra) played in Cleveland and Buffalo and cut two songs in 1933 that were not issued until decades later. The breakthrough year was 1934. The orchestra made a strong impression playing at New York's Cotton Club, waxed a few notable songs for Victor and then started recording regularly for Decca. Their tight ensembles and colorful shows made them a major attraction throughout the remainder of the swing era. Among their many hits were "Rhythm Is Our Business," "Four or Five Times," "Swanee River," "Charmaine," "My Blue Heaven," "Organ Grinder's Swing," "Ain't She Sweet," "For Dancers Only," "'Tain't What You Do, It's the Way That Cha Do It," "Uptown Blues" and "Lunceford Special." The stars of the band included arranger Sy Oliver (on trumpet and vocals), Willie Smith, Trummy Young (who had a hit with "Margie") and tenor saxophonist Joe Thomas. In 1939 Tommy Dorsey lured Sy Oliver away (although trumpeters Gerald Wilson and Snooky Young were important new additions), which was a major blow. Unfortunately Lunceford underpaid most of his sidemen, not thinking to reward them for their loyalty in the lean years. In 1942 Willie Smith was one of several key players who left for better-paying jobs elsewhere and the orchestra gradually declined. Jimmie Lunceford was still a popular bandleader in 1947 when he suddenly collapsed; rumors have persisted that he was poisoned by a racist restaurant owner who was very reluctant about feeding his band. After

Lunceford's death, pianist/arranger Ed Wilcox and Joe Thomas tried to keep the orchestra together but in 1949 the band permanently broke up. —*Scott Yanow*

● **Volume 1 (1927-1934)** / Dec. 13, 1927-Sep. 4, 1934 / Masters of Jazz ✦✦✦✦
This valuable French CD contains the first 21 selections recorded by the Jimmie Lunceford Orchestra. Usually in reissue programs such as this one, Lunceford's two numbers leading the Chickasaw Syncopators in 1927 are left out, but fortunately those are included for they show his orchestra in its formative period. There are also two titles from 1930 (which as with the 1927 sides were recorded in Memphis, TN), two songs from 1933 and the first nine performances for Decca in 1934. The band's personnel was already set with such top soloists as altoist Willie Smith, tenor saxophonist Joe Thomas and the pioneering high-note trumpeter Tommy Stevenson; trumpeter-arranger Sy Oliver joined up by 1934. Highlights include "Memphis Rag," "White Heat," "Swingin' Uptown" and the wonderfully titled "Flaming Reeds and Screaming Brass." —*Scott Yanow*

Jimmie Lunceford (1930-1934) / Jun. 6, 1930-Nov. 7, 1934 / Classics ✦✦✦✦✦
The first in Classics' "complete" Jimmie Lunceford series has two titles apiece from 1930 (when the band was based in Tennessee) and 1933 along with its first six sessions for Decca in 1934. Lunceford's band had an immediately recognizable sound by 1934 and, despite the presence of such top soloists as altoist Willie Smith, tenor saxophonist Joe Thomas and high-note trumpeter Tommy Stevenson, it was its arranged ensembles (particularly those of Sy Oliver) that gave the orchestra its musical identity. Among the better selections on this CD are "Flaming Reeds and Screaming Brass," "White Heat," "Swinging' Uptown," "Rose Room," "Miss Otis Regrets" and the band's fresh interpretations of Duke Ellington's "Black and Tan Fantasy" and "Mood Indigo." —*Scott Yanow*

☆ **The Complete Jimmie Lunceford** / May 15, 1933-Dec. 23, 1940 / Columbia ✦✦✦✦✦
The one fault to this magnificent four-LP box set is that it is out of print. Put out by French CBS in 1981, the definitive reissue has all of Jimmie Lunceford's recordings for Vocalion and OKeh including two titles from 1933 and all of his 1939-40 performances (which were cut between two long periods with Decca). The only two personnel changes that took place during 1939-40 were important ones as trumpeters Snooky Young and Gerald Wilson joined Lunceford while arranger-trumpeter Sy Oliver (who was largely responsible for the big band's musical identity) left to join Tommy Dorsey. Lunceford's Orchestra was at its peak during this period and high points of its stay with Vocalion include "'Tain't What You Do," "What Is This Thing Called Swing," "Ain't She Sweet," "White Heat," "Well, All Right Then," "Belgium Stomp," "Wham," "Uptown Blues," "Lunceford Special" and "What's Your Story, Morning Glory?" In addition to Snooky Young, the main soloists are trombonist Trummy Young, altoist Willie Smith and tenor saxophonist Joe Thomas, but the Lunceford sound was very much a group effort, dependent on high musicianship, surprising arrangements and tight ensembles. Not every selection in this box is a classic (Dan Grissom's vocals are an acquired taste) but this is a perfectly conceived reissue. All of the music except for the nine alternate takes have been reissued on CD by the Classics label. —*Scott Yanow*

● **Stomp It Off** / Sep. 4, 1934-May 29, 1935 / Decca ✦✦✦✦✦
While European labels (most notably Classics and Masters of Jazz) reissue every Jimmie Lunceford recording, its domestic counterpart as usual only gives consumers best-of collections. This CD is actually quite good, consisting of highlights from Lunceford's first year with Decca and serving as a fine introduction to his orchestra's music. Nearly all of the 21 numbers are excellent, and among the more colorful selections are reworkings of three Duke Ellington tunes, "Miss Otis Regrets," "Dream of You," two versions of the bubbly "Rhythm Is Our Business," and "Sleepy-Time Gal," which has a remarkable sax section chorus. —*Scott Yanow*

☆ **Volume 2 (1934)** / Sep. 5, 1934-Dec. 18, 1934 / Masters of Jazz ✦✦✦✦✦
Five sessions by the Jimmie Lunceford Orchestra are reissued in full on this French CD including three alternate takes. The big band was in its early prime during the period and these 19 selections include many memorable arrangements by Sy Oliver and Ed Wilcox including "Miss Otis Regrets," "Stomp It Off," "Since My Best Gal Turned Me Down" and "Rhythm Is Our Business." The short solos by altoist Willie Smith (who doubled on clarinet), tenor saxophonist Joe Thomas and muted trumpeter Sy Oliver compensate for the occasional indifferent vocals of Henry Wells. —*Scott Yanow*

1934-1935 / Nov. 7, 1934-Sep. 30, 1935 / Classics ✦✦✦✦✦
The second of Classics' reissuance of all the master takes of Jimmie Lunceford's recordings finds the orchestra gaining in popularity and in power. Among the highlights (most of the songs were arranged by Sy Oliver or Ed Wilcox) are "Since My Beat Gal Turned Me Down," "Rhythm Is Our Business," "Shake Your Head," "Sleepy-Time Gal," "Four or Five Times" and "Swanee River." The high musicianship and clean ensembles (along with the showmanship) are most impressive and the concise solos (particularly from altoist Willie Smith and tenor saxophonist Joe Tho-

mas and trumpeter Sy Oliver) are enjoyable and fit in logically as part of the arrangements. —*Scott Yanow*

For Dancers Only / Sep. 23, 1935-Jun. 15, 1937 / Decca ✦✦✦✦
For this CD, 20 selections by Jimmie Lunceford's highly rated orchestra are reissued. Dating from 1935-37 and not as complete as the Classics series, the release does give listeners a good overview of Lunceford's music. The arrangements by Sy Oliver (including "Swanee River," "My Blue Heaven," "Organ Grinder's Swing" and "For Dancers Only") are generally the most memorable tracks; this CD also contains a previously unissued take of "Ragging the Scale." Among the main soloists are altoist Willie Smith, tenor saxophonist Joe Thomas and trumpeter Oliver. —*Scott Yanow*

1935-1937 / Sep. 30, 1935-Jun. 15, 1937 / Classics ✦✦✦✦✦
Although there have been a few GRP/Decca samplers released domestically, the best way for serious collectors to acquire the recordings of Jimmie Lunceford are by getting the reissue CDs put out by the European labels. On Classics' third Lunceford set, the personnel stays the same (except for one minor change) during the 15-month period that is covered. The well-rehearsed unit continued to grow and develop during this time. Among the high points of the CD are "My Blue Heaven," "Organ Grinder's Swing," "Harlem Shout" and "Slumming on Park Avenue." Although one can do without the occasional Dan Grissom vocals, the concise solos, tricky charts and hip singing of Sy Oliver make this music well worth investigating by fans of the swing era. —*Scott Yanow*

Hollywood '36—Culver City '46—New York '48 / 1936-1948 / Jazz Up ✦✦
This CD features the Jimmie Lunceford orchestra on three separate occasions. The band is heard on a soundtrack from a short film in 1936 (including "Rhythm Is Our Business") and on radio broadcasts from Los Angeles in 1946 (during which they revisit some of their earlier hits) and in New York in 1948 a year after its leader's death; the band's style during the latter is unchanged. Frankly nothing that unique occurs on any of these performances and the recording quality is a bit streaky at times, making this CD of greatest interest to Lunceford completists. —*Scott Yanow*

1937-1939 / Jun. 15, 1937-Jan. 3, 1939 / Classics ✦✦✦✦✦
For this entry in Classics' complete reissuance of Jimmie Lunceford's recordings, the biggest news for the band was the addition of trombonist Trummy Young who, in addition to being a major soloist, had vocal hits in "Margie" and "'Tain't What You Do (It's the Way That You Do It)." Other highlights of this well-rounded CD include "Annie Laurie," "Sweet Sue" and "By the River Saint-Marie." —*Scott Yanow*

Jimmie Lunceford (1939) / Jan. 3, 1939-Sep. 14, 1939 / Classics ✦✦✦✦✦
For this Classics CD, most of the Jimmie Lunceford Orchestra's earlier Vocalion recordings (owned by Columbia) are reissued. The loss of Sy Oliver in August 1939 (he was lured away by Tommy Dorsey) would soon hurt the band but they were still using Oliver's arrangemetns in the last session. "Baby, Won't You Please Come Home," "What Is This Thing Called Swing," a classic rendition of "Ain't She Sweet," "Well, All Right Then" and "Belgium Stomp" are among the more memorable selections on this CD that also has a few typically inferior Dan Grissom ballad vocals. Swing fans will want all of these CDs even if they do not include Lunceford's alternate takes. —*Scott Yanow*

Jimmie Lunceford (1939-1940) / Dec. 14, 1939-Jun. 19, 1940 / Classics ✦✦✦✦✦
The Jimmie Lunceford Orchestra was at the height of its power and fame during the period covered by this Classics CD. Arranger-trumpeter Sy Oliver's defection to Tommy Dorsey hurt but his charts were still in the books and his replacement Snooky Young proved to be a superior first trumpeter and soloist. With altoist Willie Smith, Joe Thomas on tenor and trombonist Trummy Young still around as stars, the band was in top form on such numbers as "Uptown Blues," "Lunceford Special," "Bugs Parade," "What's Your Story, Mornin' Glory" and "Swingin' On C." All of the releases in this series are well worth picking up by swing collectors. —*Scott Yanow*

Jimmie Lunceford (1940-1941) / Jul. 9, 1940-Dec. 23, 1941 / Classics ✦✦✦✦✦
With the loss of arranger-trumpet-vocalist Sy Oliver, Lunceford's band was still fairly strong although it was no longer developing as quickly as it had previously. During the year and a half covered by this CD, such numbers as "Whatcha Know, Joe," "Siesta at the Fiesta," "Yard Dog Maazurka" and the two-part "Blues in the Night" were recorded along with lesser material (including some dreary vocal features for Dan Grissom). Although not essential, this CD is recommended to Lunceford completists. —*Scott Yanow*

Instrumentals Never Before on Record / 1941-1943 / First Time ✦✦✦
The exact recording dates (other than ambiguously stating "1941-1943") are not given on this out-of-print LP. "Yesterdays," a rare feature for the ill-fated trumpeter Freddie Webster, seems to be the earliest selection while the other numbers (performed after alto star Willie Smith had left Jimmie Lunceford's Orchestra to join

Charlie Spivak and later Harry James) are probably from 1943. Taken from radio broadcasts, the material on the album is somewhat valuable for many of these songs were not recorded commercially by Lunceford and this version of his band is lesser known. The leader even makes a rare musical appearance on "Holiday for Strings," playing flute. Tenor saxophonist Joe Thomas was still aboard and the other main soloists were trombonist Fernando Arbello, clarinetist Omer Simeon and altoist Kurt Bradford (who is featured on "Alone Together"). —Scott Yanow

1941-1945 / 1941-1945 / Classics ✦✦✦✦
Jimmie Lunceford's Orchestra was starting to decline during the period covered by this 1996 CD from the European Classics label. There are nine numbers (including a two-part "I'm Gonna Move to the Outskirts of Town") that feature the 1941-42 orchestra, which still included trombonist Trummy Young (who has three vocals, including "Easy Street"), altoist Willie Smith, and tenorman Joe Thomas; unfortunately, Dan Grissom takes three dull vocals, and there is only one instrumental, the accurately titled "Strictly Instrumental." The second half of the set is from 1944-45, and although there are a couple worthwhile tracks (most memorably the two-part "Back Door Stuff" and "Jeep Rhythm"), Joe Thomas was the only major soloist remaining. The music overall is historic, but not as essential as Jimmie Lunceford's earlier performances. —Scott Yanow

Jubilee / 1944 / Joyce ✦✦✦
One and a half broadcasts taken from the *Jubilee* radio series are included on this collector's LP. One has to sit through a lot of nonsensical babble from the host Ernie "Bubbles" Whitman and a not-so-funny comedy routine by Jerry Lester but there are a few worthwhile musical moments. Jimmy Lunceford's big band plays four numbers including a version of "Holiday for Strings" that finds the leader making a rare appearance on flute. In addition the Eddie South Trio plays two numbers (including pianist Billy Taylor's advanced "Mad Monk"), Maxine Sullivan takes two vocals, the Golden Gate Quartet performs "Straighten Up and Fly Right" and Art Tatum has a solo piano version of "Smoke Gets in Your Eyes." Quite a grab bag. —Scott Yanow

1944 / Feb. 8, 1944-Feb. 9, 1944 / Circle ✦✦✦
The Jimmie Lunceford Orchestra was in decline at the time of these wartime radio transcriptions although it was still an impressive outfit. Joe Thomas on tenor and occasional vocals remained the band's main star but most of the orchestra's players were more anonymous (with the exception of Omer Simeon on clarinet and alto) and Claude Trenier's vocals were only a slight improvement on Dan Grissom's in the 1930s. At 32 minutes, this LP is a bit brief although there are some good moments on such tunes as the two-part "Back Door Stuff," "Jeep Rhythm" and "For Dancers Only." However it is better to acquire Lunceford's studio sides (most of which are currently available on European CDs) first. —Scott Yanow

Margie / Apr. 25, 1946-May 1947 / Savoy ✦✦✦✦
The final recordings of the Jimmie Lunceford Orchestra (prior to its leader's death) are included on this excellent CD. The 13 selections (three sessions from 1946-47) generally avoid the influence of bebop and stick to Lunceford's sound and swing style. Tenor saxophonist and vocalist Joe Thomas was the only one of the major Lunceford soloists to still be with the big band although trumpeter Bob Mitchell, clarinetist Omer Simeon and altoist Kurt Bradford (featured on "The 'Jimmies'") also have solo space, such up-and-coming players as trumpeter Joe Wilder and trombonist Al Grey make early appearances and former trombone star Trummy Young returns for four numbers, doing a remake of his hit "Margie." This is a historical and easy-to-enjoy CD overall, put out by Savoy in 1989. —Scott Yanow

Jimmie Lunceford in Hi Fi / May 1958 / Capitol ✦✦✦
After bandleader Jimmie Lunceford's death in 1947, tenor saxophonist Joe Thomas and pianist Ed Wilcox led the "ghost orchestra" for two years before giving up. In 1957 there was a one-time reunion for this LP that featured some of the Lunceford stars (including altoist Willie Smith, tenor saxophonist Joe Thomas, trombonist Trummy Young and singer Dan Grissom) being joined by studio players for recreations of their earlier hits, arranged in the Lunceford style by Billy May. It is a pity that trumpeter-vocalist Sy Oliver did not participate but this is a largely successful retrospect of some of the high points of Jimmie Lunceford's career. —Scott Yanow

Jan Lundgren

b. Mar. 22, 1966, Olofstrom, Sweden
Piano / Hard Bop, Bop
A fine bop-based pianist, Jan Lundgren has visited the US several times since the mid-1990s and been gradually gaining a very strong reputation. Even while undergoing extensive classical piano training, Lundgren was playing jazz locally, and by the time he was 20, he had begun working with Arne Domnerus and Putte Wickman. Lundgren has picked up valuable experience accompanying many visiting Americans (including Herb Geller, Johnny Griffin and Mark Murphy). In 1994, he recorded his debut as a leader for the Four Leaf Clover label. Since then,

Lundgren has recorded separate sets with Herb Geller and Bill Perkins for Fresh Sound and led further albums for Alfa and Four Leaf Clover. —Scott Yanow

Conclusion / May 31, 1994-Jun. 1, 1994 / Four Leaf Clover ✦✦✦✦
The young Swedish pianist Jan Lundgren (28 at the time) teams up with two veterans (bassist Jesper Lundgaard and drummer Alex Riel) for some moody originals and hard-swinging standards on his debut CD. Lundgren does not have an identifiable sound of his own but he does have control over the bop vocabulary and is able to interpret music in styles ranging from bop ("Oleo" and "There Is No Greater Love") and Bobby Timmons-flavored hard bop ("Olivia") to a close imitation of McCoy Tyner ("Conclusion"). Lundgren also has an appealing touch, shows maturity on the ballads (his restraint on "I See Your Face Before Me" is impressive) and with his trio the young pianist constructs a well-paced set. —Scott Yanow

Bird of Passage / Nov. 25, 1995-Nov. 26, 1995 / Four Leaf Clover ✦✦✦✦

● **California Connection** / Jan. 30, 1996-Jan. 31, 1996 / Four Leaf Clover ✦✦✦✦✦
Bebop is spoken throughout this excellent set. Two Swedish musicians (pianist Jan Lundgren and trumpeter Peter Asplund) meet up with a couple of Americans (bassist Dave Carpenter and drummer Paul Kreibich) on a variety of superior standards, plus a couple of jazz interpretations of obscure Swedish songs. Asplund has a bright sound in the Clifford Brown tradition; Lundgren looks towards Bud Powell, and the Americans are quite supportive of the lead voices. To break up the quartet format, Barney Kessel's "Swedish Pastry" is taken by the rhythm trio; Lundgren and Asplund play a duet version of "Sodermalm"; Lundgren is absent on "I Hear a Rhapsody," and "How Deep Is the Ocean" is a piano-bass duet. Other highlights include "Au Privave," "What Is This Thing Called Love" and "When It's Sleepy Time Down South." Recommended to bebop collectors. —Scott Yanow

Carmen Lundy

b. Nov. 1, 1954, Miami, FL
Vocals / Bop, Standards, Post-Bop
The sister of bassist Curtis Lundy, Carmen is a talented singer who is also a composer (writing a good portion of her repertoire), actor and painter. After studying at Miami University, she moved to New York in 1978 where she worked with Ray Barretto and formed her own trio in 1980, using such pianists as John Hicks and Onaje Gumbs. Lundy recorded for Black Hawk (1987) and Sony (1988) and appeared in the plays *Sophisticated Ladies* and *They Were All Gardenias*, portraying Billie Holiday in the latter. In 1991 she moved to Los Angeles and has since recorded for Arabesque (1992) and JVC. Although open to the influences of folk, R&B and pop, Carmen Lundy (who seems to be on the brink of much greater recognition in the mid-'90s) is a strong improviser. —Scott Yanow

Good Morning Kiss / Jan. 1985+Aug. 1985 / Black Hawk ✦✦✦✦
Carmen Lundy's debut album was so strong that it's surprising a follow-up was not released domestically for another six years. This excellent effort for the soon-defunct Black Hawk label uses a variety of personnel, including several horn players (trumpeters Jon Faddis, Cecil Bridgewater and/or Earl Gardner, trombonist Steve Turre and altoist Bobby Watson, who provided the arrangements) on four of the eight selections; the other numbers showcase Lundy with a rhythm section including keyboardist Harry Whitaker. Lundy (who puts the right amount of feeling into "Love for Sale") has both a flexible range and the ability to sing beautiful low notes. She is also a talented composer, as she shows by contributing five of the eight songs. Well worth searching for. —Scott Yanow

Moment to Moment / Apr. 10, 1991-Apr. 18, 1991 / Arabesque ✦✦✦✦

● **Self Portait** / Nov. 1994 / JVC ✦✦✦✦✦
Today's jazz singers have a great deal of difficulty in building a fresh repertoire because so many of the current pop songs are not really transferable to creative music. Carmen Lundy solves the problem on this CD by writing six of her own songs, both lyrics and music. Her talents in that area are impressive and it would not be surprising if a few future standards came out of her repertoire. Lundy's memorable deep voice, which has a wide range, can go very low (as heard on Jobim's "Triste") and on "Firefly" she overdubs a second part, making the performance sound like a male-female duet. A tasteful string section is used on some selections but most songs utilize the core of a strong rhythm section (pianist Cedar Walton, John Clayton or Nathan East on bass and drummer Ralph Penland) plus occasional guests Ernie Watts and Gary Herbig on reeds. Whether interpreting ballads, singing more heated pieces or floating over a funky vamp, Carmen Lundy pays close attention to the lyrics and mood of each song but feels free to improvise spontaneously. This is one of her strongest recordings to date with the high points including "Spring Can Really Hang You up the Most," "Firefly," "Forgive Me" and "My Ship." —Scott Yanow

Old Devil Moon / 1997 / JVC ✦✦✦✦
The deep voice of Carmen Lundy is well showcased on this varied set. With assistance from an impressive backup crew (pianist Billy Childs, fluegelhornist Randy

Brecker, Frank Foster or Bob Mintzer on tenor, and a pair of rhythm sections), Lundy performs six standards, four of her stimulating originals, and Donny Hathaway's "Flying Easy." The music ranges from fairly straightahead to more R&B-oriented, with Carmen Lundy's appealing voice being the main star. —*Scott Yanow*

Brian Lynch

b. , Milwaukee, WI
Trumpet / Hard Bop
A fine hard bop trumpeter with a crackling sound, Brian Lynch started out played locally in Milwaukee from age 16. After graduating from the Wisconsin Conservatory, he spent much of 1980 in San Diego where he played with Charles McPherson. Relocating to New York in 1981, Lynch worked with George Russell, Horace Silver (1982-85) and the Toshiko Akiyoshi Jazz Orchestra in addition to freelancing. In 1987 he was with Frank Wess' Quintet and started playing with Eddie Palmieri. Lynch was the last trumpeter to be a member of Art Blakey's Jazz Messengers (Dec. 1988-Oct. 1990) and he has been in the Phil Woods Quintet since 1992. Brian Lynch has thus far recorded as a leader for Ken Music and Criss Cross. —*Scott Yanow*

Peer Pressure / Dec. 1986 / Criss Cross ✦✦✦✦
Lynch wrote three of the six tracks. Horace Silver (p), T. Turrentine wrote the others. A solid date from a promising musician. One to look for. —*Michael G. Nastos*

Back Room Blues / Dec. 30, 1989 / Criss Cross ✦✦✦✦
Brian Lynch's second Criss Cross release features the fiery trumpeter in a hard bop quintet with tenor saxophonist Javon Jackson, pianist David Hazeltine, bassist Peter Washington and drummer Lewis Nash. Although the musical style might be familiar, the repertoire (five Lynch originals and one by Hazeltine plus the Dizzy Gillespie-associated "I Waited for You") is not. Lynch digs quite ably into the largely straightahead material and the results are predictably swinging and creative within the tradition. —*Scott Yanow*

● **In Process** / 1991 / Ken Music ✦✦✦✦✦
Brian Lynch was the trumpeter in the last edition of Art Blakey's Jazz Messengers. This CD, recorded just a few days after Blakey's death, finds Lynch leading a hard bop date in the Messengers tradition with three other alumni (tenor saxophonist Javon Jackson, pianist Benny Green and bassist Dennis Irwin) aboard, along with altoist Jim Snidero and drummer Anthony Reedus. The trumpeter's wide range and powerful style are well featured on the quartet and sextet tracks. Lynch's lyrical outings on "Flamingo" and "I Should Care," the struttin' minor blues "D.T.M.Y.M." and the driving "After Dark" are among the high points of this fine straightahead set. —*Scott Yanow*

Keep Your Circle Small / 1995 / Sharp Nine ✦✦✦✦

Spheres of Influence / 1997 / Sharp Nine ✦✦✦✦

Jimmy Lyons

b. Dec. 1, 1933, Jersey City, NJ, **d.** May 19, 1986, New York, NY
Alto Saxophone / Free Jazz, Avant-Garde
Jimmy Lyons worked with Cecil Taylor from 1960 until his death in 1986. Although initially influenced by Charlie Parker, Lyons found a niche for his alto in Taylor's dense and passionate music, becoming an indispensable part of the Cecil Taylor Unit for 26 years. He grew up in Harlem and started playing alto when he was 15, being largely self-taught. A relative unknown when he joined Taylor, Jimmy Lyons was from then on always associated with the innovative pianist although he did have opportunities to lead sessions for BYG (1969), Hat Art and Black Saint, often utilizing bassoonist Karen Borca. It is not surprising that for his own dates, Lyons never used a pianist! —*Scott Yanow*

Other Afternoons / Aug. 15, 1969 / Affinity ✦✦✦✦✦
Because he spent virtually his entire career as Cecil Taylor's altoist, Jimmy Lyons had relatively few chances to record as a leader. This Affinity LP was his first opportunity to head a session and Lyons picked a particularly superior group of sidemen: trumpeter Lester Bowie, bassist Alan Silva and drummer Andrew Cyrille. Rather than sounding like the Art Ensemble of Chicago (Bowie's group) or Taylor's Unit, the all-star band comes closer at times to seeming like an updated version of Ornette Coleman's Quartet. The renditions of four originals are quite adventurous and passionate yet thoughtful and logical. An excellent outing that has not yet reappeared on CD. —*Scott Yanow*

● **Jump Up / What to Do About** / Aug. 30, 1980 / Hat Hut ✦✦✦✦✦

Riffs / Sep. 13, 1980-Sep. 14, 1980 / Hat Music ✦✦✦✦
For one of his very infrequent recordings outside of the realm of Cecil Taylor, altoist Jimmy Lyons teams up with the talented jazz bassoonist Karen Borca, bassist Jay Oliver and drummer Paul Murphy for lengthy and rather adventurous versions of "Theme" and "Riffs No. 1/II" plus the brief "Riffs No. 1/I," which serves as

a prelude to the longer "Riffs." It is always intriguing to hear Lyons stretching out without a piano and this set helped make listeners aware of Borca's brilliant playing on the rarely utilized bassoon. —*Scott Yanow*

Something in Return / Feb. 13, 1981 / Black Saint ✦✦✦✦

Burnt Offering / May 15, 1982 / Black Saint ✦✦✦✦

Wee Sneezawee / Sep. 26, 1983-Sep. 27, 1983 / Black Saint ✦✦✦✦

Give It Up / Mar. 1985 / Black Saint ✦✦✦✦
Altoist Jimmy Lyons spent most of his career as a member of Cecil Taylor's Units. For his own projects, it is not too surprising that he chose not to utilize a piano; who could fill in for C.T.? On these occasions, Lyons often teamed up with the adventurous bassoonist Karen Borca and for this set their quartet (with bassist Jay Oliver and drummer Paul Murphy) is joined by the lyrical trumpet of Enrico Rava. They stretch out on four of Lyons' emotional originals, the ensemble work is frequently exciting and the front line boasts three distinctive and rather different (but complementary) solo voices. Highly recommended. —*Scott Yanow*

Humphrey Lyttelton

b. May 23, 1921, Eton, England
Clarinet, Trumpet / Dixieland, Mainstream Jazz
One of the leaders of England's revivalist movement of the late '40s, Humphrey Lyttelton's music gradually evolved into small-group swing and he has alternated between the two idioms throughout his productive career. After serving in the military, Lyttelton played with George Webb's Dixielanders in 1947 and formed his own group the following year. His band (which usually featured clarinetist Wally Fawkes) was one of the pacesetters throughout the 1950s, sometimes growing in size to include two or three saxophonists (including Tony Coe and Joe Temperley). Lyttelton recorded with Sidney Bechet in 1949 and on a few occasions in the early '60s he collaborated with Buck Clayton. Of his many recordings, Lyttelton's dates for Black Lion and a set for Sackville are the easiest to find in the US. Humphrey Lyttelton, who doubles quite effectively on clarinet, founded his own label in the 1980s (Calligraph) and has written several very informative books on jazz. —*Scott Yanow*

Delving Back and Forth with Humph / 1948-1986 / Southern Studios ✦✦✦✦✦
The discovery of nine performances by cornetist Humphrey Lyttelton's earliest band in the mid-1980s resulted in this very good LP. The previously unreleased numbers, which are in surprisingly good technical shape, feature Lyttelton with three overlapping bands in 1948, mixing together 1920s standards with Lyttelton's "Victory House Drag," "Salty Dog" and an offbeat showcase for the cornetist on "Miss Otis Regrets." Among the key sidemen are clarinetist Wally Falkes and pianists George Webb and Pat Hawes. Since there was not enough music to constitute a full release, Lyttelton recorded eight additional numbers in 1986 with a septet also including clarinetist Fawkes, trombonist Keith Nichols and pianist Stan Greig; highlights of the later date include "On Treasure Island," "Chattanooga Stomp" and three recent originals. Despite the passage of many years, Humphrey Lyttelton's sound and basic approach had not changed all that much, so the music is equally rewarding from both periods. Recommended. —*Scott Yanow*

Humphrey Lyttelton in Canada / Jul. 26, 1983-Jul. 27, 1983 / Sackville ✦✦✦✦
For this set, trumpeter Humphrey Lyttelton performs eight of his obscure but rewarding originals with Jim Galloway (doubling on soprano and baritone), guitarist Ed Bickert, bassist Neil Swainson and drummer Terry Clarke. The music is mostly influenced by Duke Ellington and is in the mainstream (rather than New Orleans jazz) idiom. The one exception is "Caribana Queen," a West Indian-flavored song that finds Lyttelton switching to his effective clarinet and holding his own with Galloway. A fun outing. —*Scott Yanow*

Scatterbrains / Dec. 2, 1984 / Stomp Off ✦✦✦✦
On this date, trumpeter Humphrey Lyttelton jams on seven Dixieland standards, plus "Scatterbrain." His band includes several British musicians (including pianist Stan Greig), as well as clarinetist Kenny Davern and guitarist Al Casey. An excellent showcase for the trumpeter (who at age 63 was still in prime form), this joyous outing is highlighted by "Bugle Call Rag," "I Would Do Anything for You," "Fidgety Feet" and Davern's feature on "Oh Baby." —*Scott Yanow*

● **Rent Party** / Aug. 10, 1991-Jan. 4, 1992 / Stomp Off ✦✦✦✦✦
Trumpeter Humphrey Lyttelton and clarinetist Wally Fawkes first met up in 1947 as part of George Webb's Dixielanders in Great Britain. Forty-four years later, they had a reunion on this exciting CD, jamming with a septet also including either John Beecham or Keith Nichols on trombone and pianist Stan Greig. In addition to four originals, the group mostly emphasizes such fresh material as "Gate Mouth," Luis Russell's "Doctor Blues," "Breeze" and "Viper Mad." Lyttelton, at age 70, had lost little, and he also plays some excellent clarinet on three tunes, including an exciting version of "Ole Miss." Recommended to trad jazz fans. —*Scott Yanow*

M'Boom

f. 1970
Group / Post-Bop
In 1970 Max Roach first organized M'Boom, a unique unit composed of percussionists. By utilizing such instruments as marimba, xylophone, tympani, vibes, bells, gongs, drum sets and even a musical saw, Roach leads a very colorful and self-sufficient group. Originally a septet comprising Roach, Warren Smith, Freddie Waits, Omar Clay, Joe Chambers, Roy Brooks and Ray Mantilla, the group grew to ten pieces in later years. A part-time project, M'Boom has recorded for Baystate (1973), Columbia (1979), Soul Note (1984) and Blue Moon (1992) and appeared at the 1994 Monterey Jazz Festival. —*Scott Yanow*

Re: Percussion / Aug. 25, 1973 / Baystate ✦✦✦✦
Max Roach's percussion sextet. Two extended compositions by Joe Chambers. Excellent. —*Michael G. Nastos*

M'Boom / Jul. 25, 1979-Jul. 27, 1979 / Columbia ✦✦✦✦✦
Other than a Japanese release for Baystate in 1973, this CD contains the initial recording by Max Roach's all-percussion unit M'Boom. Featured on the nine selections (all group originals, other than Thelonious Monk's "Epistrophy") are up to eight players, including Roach, Roy Brooks, Joe Chambers, Omar Clay, Fred King, Ray Mantilla, Warren Smith and Freddie Waits, utilizing all types of percussion instruments—vibes, tympani, chimes, timbales, marimba, xylophone, and so on. The colorful sounds are full of surprises, and the music is both consistently stimulating and quite accessible. —*Scott Yanow*

Collage / Oct. 16, 1984-Oct. 18, 1984 / Soul Note ✦✦✦✦
Max Roach, Warren Smith, and Freddie Waits appear on this one. —*AMG*

● **Live at S.O.B.'s New York** / 1992 / Blue Moon ✦✦✦✦✦
Exciting percussion duels, multiple rhythms, and teeming arrangements and performances by the conglomeration of drummers known as M'Boom. This recent release included founding member Max Roach, plus Roy Brooks, Joe Chambers, Omar Clay, Fred King, Ray Mantilla, Warren Smith, and Freddy Waits performing live at the celebrated New York club S.O.B.'s. —*Ron Wynn*

Harold Mabern

b. Mar. 20, 1936, Memphis, TN
Piano / Hard Bop, Groove, Soul-Jazz
One of several excellent hard bop pianists from the Memphis area, Harold Mabern has led relatively few dates through the years but he has always been respected by his contemporaries. He played in Chicago with MJT + 3 in the late '50s and then moved to New York in 1959. Mabern worked with Jimmy Forrest, Lionel Hampton, the Jazztet (1961-62), Donald Byrd, Miles Davis (1963), J.J. Johnson (1963-65), Sonny Rollins, Freddie Hubbard, Wes Montgomery, Joe Williams (1966-67) and Sarah Vaughan. During 1968-70 Mabern led four albums for Prestige, he was with Lee Morgan in the early '70s, and in 1972 he recorded with Stanley Cowell's Piano Choir. In more recent times Harold Mabern recorded as a a leader for DIW/ Columbia and Sackville and toured with the Contemporary Piano Ensemble (1993-95). —*Scott Yanow*

Rakin' and Scrapin' / Dec. 23, 1968 / Prestige ✦✦✦✦
Reissued on LP but not yet CD, this Prestige set features the excellent hard bop pianist Harold Mabern heading a quintet also including trumpeter Blue Mitchell, tenor saxophonist George Coleman, bassist Bill Lee and drummer Hugh Walker. Other than a brief throwaway version of "I Heard It Through the Grapevine" (which finds Mabern switching to electric piano), the music is essentially boppish, with some ballads and blues included. Nothing too substantial occurs, but it is a good modern mainstream effort for the era. —*Scott Yanow*

Wailin' / Jun. 30, 1969+Jan. 26, 1970 / Prestige ✦✦✦✦✦
This CD reissue combines together two sessions (*Workin' & Wailin'* and *Greasy Kid Stuff*) led by pianist Harold Mabern during 1969-70. The first date utilizes trumpeter Virgil Jones, tenor saxophonist George Coleman, bassist Buster Williams

and drummer Idris Muhammad on four challenging Mabern originals and Johnny Mandel's "A Time for Love." However it is the second session that is most memorable for, in addition to Mabern, Williams and Muhammad, it features trumpeter Lee Morgan and flutist Hubert Laws; the latter mostly plays some surprisingly passionate tenor that makes one wish he had performed on tenor more through the years. Excellent advanced hard bop music that hints at fusion. —*Scott Yanow*

Joy Spring / Apr. 25, 1984+Jan. 9, 1985 / Sackville ✦✦✦✦
Harold Mabern, a superior hard bop pianist, had a rare opportunity to perform a set of unaccompanied solos for this Sackville release. Recorded live from Toronto's Café des Copains and originally broadcast on the radio, Mabern performs six jazz standards (including "Joy Spring," "Pent Up House" and Wayne Shorter's "House of Jade") and a pair of bluesy originals. Although Mabern sounds most comfortable in a trio, he has always been enough of a two-handed player to play solo; he readily acknowledges the influences of Phineas Newborn and Ahmad Jamal. —*Scott Yanow*

Straight Street / Dec. 11, 1989 / Columbia ✦✦✦
For a time in the early 1990s, some of the CDs from the Japanese DIW label were made available domestically through Columbia. This trio date by pianist Harold Mabern, bassist Ron Carter and drummer Jack DeJohnette has Mabern originals dedicated to Sonny Stitt and Wayne Shorter, plus some offbeat standards and a pair of rarely performed John Coltrane tunes ("Straight Street" and "Crescent"). The interplay between the musicians is impressive and Mabern is heard throughout in excellent form. He closes the set with a piano solo that he titled "Apab and Others," after Art Tatum, Phineas Newborn, Ahmad Jamal and Bud Powell. This will be a difficult CD to find. —*Scott Yanow*

Philadelphia Bound / Apr. 15, 1991+Feb. 29, 1992 / Sackville ✦✦✦✦

★ **The Leading Man** / Nov. 9, 1992-Apr. 12, 1993 / Columbia ✦✦✦✦✦
A brilliant pianist who continues to develop and has found his own voice in the modern mainstream, Harold Mabern chose consistently superior tunes for his Columbia CD, ranging from Wes Montgomery's "Full House" (featuring guitarist Kevin Eubanks in a duet with the leader) and songs by Wayne Shorter, Coltrane and Bird, to his own "B&B" (a ballad dedicated to Clifford Brown and Booker Little) and the pop tune "Save the Best for Last." Although one can hear aspects of McCoy Tyner's chord voicings in some of Mabern's solos, he has plenty of very individual ideas; check out his near-miraculous playing on "Moment's Notice." With strong support from drummer Jack DeJohnette and either Christian McBride or Ron Carter on bass (in addition to two appearances by trumpeter Bill Mobley), this is one of Harold Mabern's most impressive outings to date and it is highly recommended. —*Scott Yanow*

For Phineas / Jan. 25, 1995 / Sackville ✦✦✦✦

Doug MacDonald

b. Sep. 10, 1953, Philadelphia, PA
Guitar / Bop, Hard Bop
Doug MacDonald is a fine bop-based guitarist in the tradition of Herb Ellis, Barney Kessel and Joe Pass. He was raised in Honolulu and started on guitar when he was 13, having played trombone briefly before. MacDonald moved to Los Angeles in 1984 after a year in Las Vegas and made a strong impression as a freelancer. In 1990, he relocated to New York. Doug MacDonald has played with top musicians including Stan Getz, Sarah Vaughan, Buddy Rich, Hank Jones, Bob Cooper, Bill Holman, Jack Sheldon, and many others, recording with Sheldon, the Clayton-Hamilton Orchestra and as a leader for Cexton and Resurgent; one of the latter is a nonet album. —*Scott Yanow*

● **Doug MacDonald Quartet** / 1990 / Cexton ✦✦✦✦
Although guitarist Doug MacDonald had recorded two other albums for the tiny Sharp Eleven label by this time, it was the release of this CD and his rising prominence in Los Angeles that resulted in him getting a bit of recognition. A superior bop-based guitarist in the tradition of Barney Kessel and Herb Ellis, MacDonald swings through a program filled with jazz standards, holding his own with pianist

Ross Tompkins, bassist Ray Brown and drummer Jake Hanna. Easily recommended to fans of the bop guitar. —*Scott Yanow*

The Doug MacDonald Trio / 1992 / Cexton ✦✦✦✦

Warm Valley / Sep. 28, 1995+Aug. 31, 1995 / Resurgent ✦✦✦✦

Guitarist Doug MacDonald debuted his nonet in 1995. Consisting of trumpeters Buddy Childers and Jack Trott, trombonist Ira Nepus, French hornist Stephanie Mijanovich, Les Benedict on tuba, pianist Jimmie Dykes (the chief arranger along with Childers), bassist Christoph Luty and drummer Jack LeCompte, the modern brass band (which has no reeds) is featured in accompaniment to MacDonald's solos, during colorful ensembles and on individual improvisations. Both of the trumpeters and trombonist Nepus get solo space while Mijanovich is in the lead for "Warm Valley" and MacDonald takes a brief medley of "Golden Earrings" and "You're Blase" unaccompanied. The leader, whose boppish guitar is in the tradition of Barney Kessel, Herb Ellis and Kenny Burrell, is heard throughout the standards in top form. The arrangements hold one's interest, although they tend to be a bit safe, and highlights include "D.B. Blues," "Let's Get Lost" and "Straight, No Chaser." Fine music. —*Scott Yanow*

Organ-Izing / Feb. 26, 1997+Mar. 1, 1997 / Resurgent ✦✦✦✦

Teo Macero

b. Oct. 30, 1925, Glens Falls, NY

Tenor Saxophone, Baritone Saxophone / Avant-Garde, Third Stream

Teo Macero is best known for being a busy jazz producer at Columbia from 1957 until the late '80s, most noticeably for producing Miles Davis' records. However, he has also been an occasional tenor saxophonist who has been involved in some adventurous sessions. After serving in the Navy, Macero came to New York in 1948 where he attended Julliard until he graduated in 1953. That year he became a member of Charles Mingus' Jazz Composer's Workshop. He made several records with Mingus during 1953-55, recorded with Teddy Charles (1956) and led three albums of his own for Debut, Columbia and Prestige (1953-57). Macero's dry tones on tenor and baritone and advanced choice of notes sometimes put him closer to modern classical music than to jazz. In the late '50s he wrote some atonal classical works, but by then he was working full time as a producer. Teo Macero played on a very infrequent basis during the 1960s and '70s, but in 1983 returned as a player to record a tribute to Charles Mingus on Palo Alto; in 1985 he played on one number during a Doctor Jazz date that he fronted. Some of Macero's earlier recordings as a saxophonist have been reissued on a Stash collection. —*Scott Yanow*

The Best of Teo Macero / Dec. 5, 1953-1979 / Vintage Jazz ✦✦✦✦

This CD is not so much "The Best of Teo Macero" as it is "The Nearly Complete Teo Macero." With the exception of his conventional quintet date for Prestige in 1957 and one or two isolated tracks, this reissue has all of Macero's pre-1983 recordings as a leader, tenor saxophonist and composer. Much of the music is essentially contemporary classical originals with jazz musicians sometimes playing the parts and usually getting a little space to improvise. Teo's tenor resembles Warne Marsh a bit. Much of the music will strike some as weird, others as an innovative precursor of Third Stream jazz. Although bassist Charles Mingus and altoist Lee Konitz are on a few tracks, some of the arrangements are overly pretentious and a bit dull, and it is an inexcusable omission that the dates are not listed. This rather esoteric CD is strictly for open-eared modern classical listeners. —*Scott Yanow*

● **Teo Macero with the Prestige Jazz Quartet** / Apr. 1957 / Original Jazz Classics ✦✦✦✦✦

This CD reissue features tenor saxophonist Teo Macero (who would later become much better known as a record producer) in as straightahead a setting as he ever appeared. With stimulating support from pianist Mal Waldron, vibraphonist Teddy Charles, bassist Addison Farmer and drummer Jerry Segal, Macero performs a variety of then-recent ballads, of which only "Star Eyes" (arranged by Hall Overton) did not come from Teo or his associates. The music is advanced but from the jazz tradition, and overall, this set is more noteworthy for Macero's interesting playing than for the tunes themselves. —*Scott Yanow*

Swinging Guys and Dolls / Oct. 19, 1959-Nov. 4, 1959 / Musical Heritage Society ✦✦✦✦

Teo Macero, best known as a veteran producer, has also had a part-time career as a tenor saxophonist and a writer. For this set from 1959, Macero arranged 11 selections from the hit Broadway show *Guys and Dolls* and added two originals of his own that fit in well. Macero only plays tenor on three of the songs, but he uses three different all-star groups that include vibraphonist Teddy Charles, guitarist Jimmy Raney, pianist Dave McKenna, altoist Phil Woods, valve trombonist Bob Brookmeyer, pianist Mose Allison, tenorman Zoot Sims and the French horn of Julius Watkins. Although some of the reworkings are a bit abstract, the melodies

from the Frank Loesser score (which include "If I Were a Bell") are wisely kept in the forefront. A fine effort. —*Scott Yanow*

Time + 7 / 1963-1965 / Finnadar ✦✦✦✦

This album was way ahead of its time. A reissue with Art Farmer (tpt), John La Porta (reeds), Ed Shaughnessy (d), and Mal Waldron (p). —*Michael G. Nastos*

Impressions of Charles Mingus / 1983 / Palo Alto ✦✦✦

Teo Macero worked as a saxophonist with Charles Mingus off and on from the late 1940s through the mid-'50s, and also produced some of his later records. This obscure Palo Alto LP, recorded shortly after Mingus' death, was Macero's first recording as a player (tenor, alto and flute) since 1957, although on most of the selections, his role as a musician is small. However, Macero was responsible for the eight selections which include tributes to Mingus, Thelonious Monk ("Monk's Funk") and Duke Ellington. The music is sometimes reminiscent of Mingus, particularly in his early, more classical-oriented days, and the notable personnel includes saxophonists Dave Liebman, Pepper Adams, John Stubblefield, Al Cohn, and Lee Konitz, trumpeters Jon Faddis and Ted Curson, flutist Dave Valentin, guitarist Ryo Kawasaki, and keyboardists Biff Hannon and Mike Nock, among many others. This will be a difficult album to find. —*Scott Yanow*

Acoustical Suspension / 1984 / Doctor Jazz ✦✦✦✦

Teo Macero, best known as a producer, has only recorded as a tenor saxophonist on a very infrequent basis through the decades. This unusual album has four very different groups performing Macero's originals. Vibraphonist Lionel Hampton and tenor saxophonist Gato Barbieri (an odd couple) are heard on five numbers along with a saxophone section, two keyboards, two guitars and a rhythm section. "Summer Rain" matches together flutist Dave Valentin and soprano saxophonist Dave Liebman, while "Silent Summer" is a piano duet for Mike Nock and Mal Waldron. Macero only pops up on one number, teaming up with Liebman, altoist Carlos Ward, bassist Cecil McBee and Orlando Digirolamo on accordion; quite a quintet. In general, the writing is not as strong as the solos, but this somewhat eccentric album certainly stands out in the crowd. —*Scott Yanow*

Machito (Frank Grillo)

b. Feb. 16, 1912, Havana, Cuba, **d.** Apr. 15, 1984, London, England

Vocals, Leader / Afro-Cuban Jazz, Latin Jazz

Machito played a huge role in the history of Latin jazz, for his bands of the 1940s were probably the first to achieve a fusion of powerful Afro-Cuban rhythms and jazz improvisation. At its roaring best, the band had a hard-charging sound, loaded with jostling, hyperactive bongos and congas and razor-edged riffing brass. Machito was the front man, singing, conducting, shaking maracas, while his brother-in-law Mario Bauza was the innovator behind the scenes, getting Machito to hire jazz-oriented arrangers. The son of a cigar manufacturer, Machito became a professional musician in Cuba in his teens before he emigrated to America in 1937 as a vocalist with La Estrella Habanera. He worked with several Latin artists and orchestras in the late-'30s, recording with the then-dominant Latin bandleader Xavier Cugat. After an earlier aborted attempt to launch a band with Bauza, Machito founded the Afro-Cubans in 1940, taking on Bauza the following year as music director, where he remained for 35 years. After making some early 78s for Decca, the Afro-Cubans really began to catch on after the end of World War II, appearing with—and no doubt influencing—Stan Kenton's orchestra (Machito played maracas on Kenton's recordings of "The Peanut Vendor" and "Cuban Carnival") and recording some exciting sides for Mercury and Clef. Upon Bauza's urging, Machito's band featured a galaxy of American jazz soloists on its recordings from 1948 to 1960, including Charlie Parker (heard memorably on "No Noise"), Dizzy Gillespie, Flip Phillips, Howard McGhee, Buddy Rich, Harry "Sweets" Edison, Cannonball Adderley, Herbie Mann, Curtis Fuller and Johnny Griffin. Playing regularly at New York's Palladium, Machito's band reached its peak of popularity during the mambo craze of the 1950s, survived the upheavals of the '60s and despite the loss of Bauza in 1976, continued to work frequently in the '70s and early '80s when the term "salsa" came into use. The band recorded for Pablo (in tandem with Gillespie) and Timeless in its later years, and was playing Ronnie Scott's club in London in 1984 when Machito suffered a fatal stroke. A documentary film by Carlo Ortiz, *Machito: A Latin Jazz Legacy*, was released in 1987. —*Richard S. Ginell*

★ **Mucho Macho Machito & His Afro** / 1948-1949 / Pablo ✦✦✦✦✦

The most famous (and common) Machito performances feature his infectious Cuban band welcoming guests from the bebop world. This CD is different, for it has 24 selections from the 1948-49 period by Machito's Afro-Cuban Salseros without the assistance of famous names. Utilizing three trumpets (including Mario Bauza), four saxophones, piano, bass, four percussionists, and the vocals of the leader and Gracilea, the high-powered and always danceable band is heard throughout the CD in prime form. Whether playing originals, updated folk songs or jazz standards, Machito's mighty crew was the pacesetter in Latin jazz of the era.

This important release gives listeners a strong example of how the Afro-Cuban jazz band probably sounded live in concert. —*Scott Yanow*

Afro-Cubop / Mar. 26, 1949-May 7, 1949 / Spotlite ✦✦✦✦✦
This LP has formerly rare broadcasts featuring Machito's Orchestra at the height of the bop era. Trumpeter Howard McGhee and tenor saxophonist Brew Moore guest with the heated band on many selections, including "Cubop City" and "How High the Moon," and vibraphonist Milt Jackson drops by for the brief "Boppin' the Vibes." In addition, Moore and singer Harry Belafonte join Machito on "Lean on Me," and there are three special tracks from an unknown Cuban band (possibly Machito's), two songs of which feature guest Charlie Parker. Historic music that is reasonably well recorded; bop collectors will want this album. —*Scott Yanow*

Tremendo Cuban (1949-1952) / 1949-1952 / Tumbao ✦✦✦
Fresh reissue of incendiary late '40s, early '50s sessions. —*Ron Wynn*

☆ **Latin Soul Plus Jazz** / Dec. 17, 1957-Dec. 24, 1957 / Roulette ✦✦✦✦✦
This band, under Machito's sizzling baton, blows up a storm that could wipe Cuba right off the map. Sitting in are jazz heavyweights Cannonball Adderley, Curtis Fuller, Joe Newman, Herbie Mann, Johnny Griffin, Candido Camero, and others. —*Myles Boisen, Roots & Rhythm*

Machito at the Crescendo / 1960-1961 / GNP ✦✦✦✦✦
Machito, one of the most revered artists in the history of Afro-Cuban music, lives up to his well-deserved reputation for giving 200 percent in concert on *At the Crescendo*. Captured live at Hollywood, CA's Crescendo (a legendary, long-gone Sunset Strip nightclub owned by record exec/producer/concert promoter Gene Norman), Machito and his orchestra swing hard and passionately on both fiery, rhythmic salsa like "Ven Conmigo Guajira," "No Tiene Telerana" and "El Columpio" and spirited Latin-jazz interpretations of Sonny Rollins' "Pent-Up House" (wrongly credited to Miles Davis in the CD's liner notes) and Ray Bryant's "Cuban Fantasy." No one with even a moderate interest in Afro-Cuban music should pass up this dynamic performance (reissued on CD in 1990). —*Alex Henderson*

The New Sound Of . . . / 1963 / Tico ✦✦✦
This "New Sound" dated from 1963, when the big bands had been elbowed aside by smaller típico groups, and it consisted largely—and effectively—of the old sound with a lead flutist. This was always a working dance band and some fads and fashions of the time show up, including a "pachanga merengue" no less, but Machito could never be anything but Machito, and Machito's what you get. —*John Storm Roberts, Original Music*

Afro-Cuban Jazz Moods / Jun. 4, 1975-Jun. 5, 1975 / Pablo ✦✦✦

1983 Grammy Award Winner / Feb. 6, 1982-Feb. 7, 1982 / Impulse ✦✦✦✦
As late as the 1980s, Machito continued to field a powerhouse Latin big band, winning belated acclaim in Europe for his well-preserved brand of salsa. Recorded in Holland for the Timeless label two years before Machito's death, the ensemble may not be quite as airtight as it was in the mambo era, but the old energy and drive still bursts through the speakers. Though Machito's voice had grown huskier with age, his enthusiasm is as infectious as ever, and his dusky-voiced daughter Paula Grillo contributes harmonies and a solo vocal on "Caso Perdido." Outstanding among the soloists is the blazing trumpeter Alfredo "Chocolate" Armenteros, who sounds particularly larger than life on the old chestnut "Manicero" (a.k.a. "The Peanut Vendor"), and all eight horns get to play some flashy solos on the extended mambo "Sambia." —*Richard S. Ginell*

Live at North Sea / Jul. 18, 1982 / Timeless ✦✦✦✦
Powerful, great live sessions. —*Ron Wynn*

Fraser MacPherson (John Fraser MacPherson)

b. Apr. 10, 1928, Winnipeg, Manitoba, Canada, **d.** Sep. 28, 1993, Vancouver, Canada
Tenor Saxophone / Swing, Cool
Fraser MacPherson, who took an awful long time before he was discovered by Americans, was one of the top cool-toned tenors (in the "Four Brothers" style) still active in the 1980s. A professional since 1951, he spent over 25 years in Canada playing in the studios and local dance bands. Although he recorded for the CBC between 1962-72 on a few occasions, it was not until a 1975 session for the small West End label was picked up by Concord that MacPherson began to be known outside of Vancouver. He made several records for Concord and Sackville, often teaming up with the equally cool-sounding guitarist Oliver Gannon. Fraser MacPherson toured the Soviet Union four times but ironically rarely had the opportunity to perform in the US. —*Scott Yanow*

Live at the Planetarium / Jul. 16, 1975 / Concord Jazz ✦✦✦✦✦
Although Fraser MacPherson had first recorded as a leader in his native Canada as early as 1962, it was not until the release of this Concord set in 1979 that he became known in the US. Recorded in 1975 at a Vancouver concert in a trio with guitarist Oliver Gannon and bassist Wyatt Ruther, MacPherson displays a "Four

Brothers" tenor tone as he alternately romps and caresses seven standards. Highlights include "Tangerine," "I'm Getting' Sentimental Over You" and "Li'l Darlin'." —*Scott Yanow*

I Didn't Know About You / Dec. 9, 1980 / Sackville ✦✦✦✦
Tenor saxophonist Fraser MacPherson frequently teamed up with guitarist Oliver Gannon in a quartet during the last 20 years of his life. This Sackville release is a bit unusual, for it is a set of tenor-guitar duets. MacPherson's melodic style, Zoot Sims-inspired sound, and quiet approach blend well with Gannon's subtle solos and steady rhythm. They perform 11 standards, mostly from the swing era, including "Do Nothing Till You Hear from Me," "The More I See You," "Mean to Me" and "In a Mellotone." The music is tasteful, relaxed, lightly swinging and satisfying. —*Scott Yanow*

Indian Summer / Jun. 1983 / Concord Jazz ✦✦✦✦
The late Fraser MacPherson's four Concord albums are all equally rewarding. His cool tenor tone, swinging solos and subtle creativity were always a joy to hear. On this particular release, he digs into seven standards, the obscure "Just My Luck," and "Recado Bossa Nova" with guitarist Oliver Gannon, bassist Steve Wallace and drummer Jake Hanna, and the results are up to par. Among the better numbers are "As Long as I Live," "Deed I Do," and "Long Ago and Far Away." —*Scott Yanow*

● **Jazz Prose** / Aug. 1984 / Concord Jazz ✦✦✦✦✦
The reason that this recording by cool-toned tenor saxophonist Fraser MacPherson gets a slight edge over his others is that pianist Dave McKenna is on the date, and he really pushes the mellow tenor. "On a Slow Boat to China" is a rare MacPherson cooker, and "It Could Happen to You" and "There Is No Greater Love" move too. Recorded live at the 1984 Concord Jazz Festival, this well-rounded set also has ballad features for MacPherson ("Darn That Dream"), guitarist Ed Bickert (Jimmy Giuffre's obscure "Happy Man") and McKenna ("I'll Never Be the Same"); bassist Steve Wallace and drummer Jake Hanna complete the excellent quintet. Easily recommended to mainstream jazz collectors. —*Scott Yanow*

Honey and Spice / Mar. 1987 / Justin Time ✦✦✦✦
Although recorded in Montreal, Canada, this album features the same quartet (with guitarist Oliver Gannon, bassist Steve Wallace and drummer John Sumner) that tenor saxophonist Fraser MacPherson used during his notable tours of the Soviet Union. All eight of the selections are veteran songs (Cole Porter's mid-'50s "I Love You Samantha" is the most recent), and the emphasis is on relaxed, slow to medium tempos. MacPherson's cool tone sounds as beautiful as ever and works well with Gannon's quiet guitar. —*Scott Yanow*

Ellington '87 / May 16, 1987 / Sackville ✦✦✦

Encore / 1990 / Justin Time ✦✦✦✦

In the Tradition / Nov. 15, 1991-Nov. 16, 1991 / Concord Jazz ✦✦✦✦
Everything that the mellow-toned tenor Fraser MacPherson played was "in the tradition," but some of the music on this CD reaches back even further than usual. Several of the songs (such as "Louisiana," "Struttin' with Some Barbecue" and "You're Lucky to Me") are from the 1920s, and even the three group originals hint at that early style. MacPherson, whose sound often resembles Zoot Sims and Stan Getz, was one of the last of the "Four Brothers" cool tenors. He is assisted by trombonist Ian McDougall, guitarist Oliver Gannon, bassist Steve Wallace, and drummer John Sumner (all fellow Canadians) throughout the delightful set, one of MacPherson's last before his 1993 death. —*Scott Yanow*

The Mahavishnu Orchestra

f. 1971, **db.** 1975
Group / Fusion
One of the premier fusion groups, the Mahavishnu Orchestra was considered by most observers during its prime to be a rock band, but its sophisticated improvisations actually put its high-powered music between rock and jazz. Founder and leader John McLaughlin had recently played with Miles Davis and Tony Williams' Lifetime. The original lineup of the group was McLaughlin on electric guitar, violinist Jerry Goodman, keyboardist Jan Hammer, electric bassist Rick Laird and drummer Billy Cobham. They recorded three intense albums for Columbia during 1971-73 and then the personnel changed completely for the second version of the group. In 1974 the band consisted of violinist Jean-Luc Ponty, Gayle Moran on keyboards and vocals, electric bassist Ralphe Armstrong and drummer Michael Warden; by 1975, Stu Goldberg had replaced Moran and Ponty had left. John McLaughlin's dual interests in Eastern religion and playing acoustic guitar resulted in the band breaking up in 1975. Surprisingly, an attempt to revive the Mahavishnu Orchestra in 1984 (using Cobham, saxophonist Bill Evans, keyboardist Mitchell Forman, electric bassist Jonas Hellborg and percussionist Danny Gottlieb) was unsuccessful; two albums resulted. However, when one thinks of the Mahavishnu Orchestra, it is of the original lineup which was very influential throughout the 1970s. —*Scott Yanow*

★ **The Inner Mounting Flame** / Aug. 14, 1971 / Columbia ✦✦✦✦✦
This is the album that made John McLaughlin a semi-household word, a furious, high-energy, yet rigorously figured-out meeting of virtuosos that, for all intents and purposes, defined the fusion of jazz and rock a year after Miles Davis' *Bitches Brew* breakthrough. It also inadvertently led to the derogatory connotation of the word fusion, for it paved the way for an army of imitators, many of whose excesses and commercial panderings devalued the entire movement. Though much was made of the influence of jazz-influenced improvisation in the Mahavishnu band, it is the rock element that predominates, stemming directly from the electronic innovations of Jimi Hendrix. The improvisations, particularly McLaughlin's post-Hendrix machine-gun assaults on double-necked electric guitar and Jerry Goodman's flights on electric violin, owe more to the freak-outs that had been circulating in progressive rock circles than to jazz, based as they often are on ostinatos on one chord. These still sound genuinely thrilling today on CD, as McLaughlin and Goodman battle Jan Hammer's keyboards, Rick Laird's bass and especially Billy Cobham's hard-charging drums, whose jazz-trained technique pushed the envelope for all rock drummers. What doesn't date so well are the composed medium—and high-velocity unison passages that are played in such tight lockstep that they can't breathe. There is also time out for quieter, reflective numbers that are drenched in studied spirituality ("A Lotus on Irish Streams") or irony ("You Know You Know"); McLaughlin was to do better in that department with less driven colleagues elsewhere in his career. Aimed with absolute precision at young rock fans, this record was wildly popular in its day, and it may have been the cause of more blown-out home amplifiers than any other record this side of *Deep Purple*. —*Richard S. Ginell*

★ **Birds of Fire** / 1972 / Columbia ✦✦✦✦✦
Emboldened by the popularity of *Inner Mounting Flame* among rock audiences, the first Mahavishnu Orchestra set out to further define and refine its blistering jazz-rock direction in its second—and, no thanks to internal feuding, last—studio album. Although it has much of the screaming rock energy and sometimes exaggerated competitive frenzy of its predecessor, *Birds of Fire* is audibly more varied in texture, even more tightly organized, and thankfully more matched in content. A remarkable example of precisely choreographed, high-speed solo trading—with John McLaughlin, Jerry Goodman and Jan Hammer all of one mind, supported by Billy Cobham's machine-gun drumming and Rick Laird's dancing bass—can be heard on the aptly named "One Word," and the title track is a defining moment of the group's nearly atonal fury. The band also takes time out for a brief bit of spaced-out electronic burbling and static called "Sapphire Bullets of Pure Love." Yet the most enticing pieces of music on the record are the gorgeous, almost pastoral opening and closing sections to "Open Country Joy," a relaxed, jocular bit of communal jamming that they ought to have pursued further. This album actually became a major crossover hit, rising to No. 15 on the pop album charts, and it remains the key item in the first Mahavishnu Orchestra's slim discography. —*Richard S. Ginell*

Between Nothingness and Eternity / Aug. 1973 / Columbia ✦✦✦✦✦
The first Mahavishnu Orchestra's slim catalog is padded out somewhat by this live album, on which the five jazz/rock virtuosos can be heard stretching out at greater length than in the studio. There are only three selections on the disc, each developing organically through a number of sections, and there are fewer lockstep unison passages than on the earlier recordings. McLaughlin is as flashy and noisy as ever on double-necked electric guitar, and violinist Jerry Goodman and keyboardist Jan Hammer are a match for him in the speed department. Yet one really doesn't hear much music on this album; electricity and competitive empathy are clearly not enough. Beyond the personality conflicts that broke up the band, they seem to have been approaching, though not quite reaching, a musical dead end as well. —*Richard S. Ginell*

Apocalypse / Mar. 1974 / Columbia ✦✦✦✦✦
The first recording of the second Mahavishnu Orchestra was a real stretch for John McLaughlin, an encounter with Michael Tilson Thomas and the London Symphony Orchestra. The union wasn't taken seriously at the time, and it ended up harming the reputation of Thomas—a remarkably adventurous young conductor who defied the stuffy classical powers-that-be and thus probably delayed his eventual rise to the top—more than McLaughlin. But those with ears, then and now, beheld a remarkable series of pieces that neatly juxtapose and occasionally combine the combustion of McLaughlin's group with rich, tasteful symphonic statements orchestrated for McLaughlin by Michael Gibbs. The new Mahavishnu-ites, electric violinist Jeac-Luc Ponty and keyboardist/vocalist Gayle Moran, have their moments, but the real focus of this disc is the quality of the symphonic conceptions and how well McLaughlin blends his lyrical and fiery guitar into the mixture. The best stretch is the breathtakingly ethereal opening of "Hymn to Him"; the promise of fusing rock, jazz and classical elements had never been executed so alluringly before—and wouldn't you know, an old experienced hand at introducing classical

textures into rock, the Beatles' George Martin, is the producer. Don't let old, outworn preconceptions on either side of the fence prevent you from checking out this beautiful record. —*Richard S. Ginell*

Visions of the Emerald Beyond / Dec. 4, 1974-Dec. 14, 1974 / Columbia ✦✦✦
As the second album to document the second Mahavishnu Orchestra, this one isn't as, well, apocalyptic as its predecessor, yet it does focus more intently on the band itself. Jean-Luc Ponty's curling electric violin lines help give this Mahavishnu band a more European sound than its predecessor, and some of the orchestral concepts of *Apocalypse* work their way into the picture via comments by a string trio and trumpet/sax duo. This band also had some interest in a bombastic funk direction that may have been borrowed from Mr. "Chameleon" Herbie Hancock, and would later be followed by Mahavishnu Two's drummer, Michael Walden. Gayle Moran's ethereal vocals don't date as badly as those on many jazz-rock records; at least she can sing. Overall, this Mahavishnu edition is more refined and not as aggressive as the first—although they could charge ahead fairly hard, as "Be Happy" and "On the Way Home to Earth" demonstrate—yet they were still capable of making memorable electric music. —*Richard S. Ginell*

Inner Worlds / 1975 / Columbia ✦✦✦

Mahavishnu / Apr. 1984-May 1984 / Warner Brothers ✦✦✦
John McLaughlin resurrected the esteemed old Mahavishnu Orchestra label for his mid-'80s quintet, even getting old mate Billy Cobham to fill the drum slot on the band's first album. But this is an entirely different conception than any of the '70s Mahavishnu outfits. The sound is cooler, less strident, more thoroughly dominated by advanced electronic textures—including a sleekly elegant digital guitar played through a Synclavier. Instead of a violin, Bill Evans contributes some swirling and sometimes bop-flavored work on saxes, and McLaughlin gets mobile but not overly combustible support from keyboardist Mitch Forman and bassist Jonas Hellborg. The homages continue; the opening of "Nostalgia" is exactly that, a throwback to "In a Silent Way" as filtered through digital gear. While this is undeniably progressive-minded, beautifully played electric music, it is not terribly absorbing; the quality of the material and the intensity level aren't too high. —*Richard S. Ginell*

Adventures in Radioland / 1987 / Relativity ✦✦✦
Though issued under the name John McLaughlin and Mahavishnu, this is in fact the last Mahavishnu Orchestra album to date—and clearly by 1986, the name's usefulness in the marketplace had come and gone. More distressingly, the musical inspiration had run out; all that's left is extremely virtuosic playing of empty notes and a lot of high-tech electronic flash, a chrome-plated embalming of what once was a fresh, exciting idea. Sure, McLaughlin's Les Paul Gibson has much of its old rock majesty, his acoustic guitar work its flamenco-derived speed, and he gets some sly, even subtle timbres out of his Synclavier digital guitar. But the background textures are often full of ugly sounds that Mitch Forman contrives from his digital synths, and Danny Gottlieb's work on the Simmons electronic drums sounds like he is beating on trash can lids. Give them credit for political prescience, though; one of the numbers, recorded over three-and-a-half years before the Berlin Wall came down, is called "The Wall Will Fall." —*Richard S. Ginell*

Kevin Mahogany

b. Jul. 30, 1958, Kansas City, MO
Vocals / Standards, Bop

Kevin Mahogany's sudden prominence in the mid-'90s was a relief to many who felt that male jazz singers under the age of 60 were non-existent. His swinging style is reminiscent but not derivative of Joe Williams. Mahogany played piano, clarinet and various saxophones while growing up before deciding to specialize in singing. Mahogany attended Baker University in Kansas and sang locally in some R&B groups. In the early '90s, Kevin Mahogany dedicated himself to jazz and, after two fine albums for Enja, he signed with Warner Bros.; in addition, Mahogany has recorded as a guest on dates by Elvin Jones and arranger Frank Mantooth. —*Scott Yanow*

Double Rainbow / Feb. 27, 1993 / Enja ✦✦✦

● **Songs and Moments** / Mar. 29, 1994-Mar. 30, 1994 / Enja ✦✦✦✦✦
In the 1990s there has been a serious shortage of male jazz singers under the age of 60, making Kevin Mahogany's "arrival" in his second Enja release quite noteworthy. A strong improviser who can not only scat creatively but uplift lyrics, Mahogany may very well end up as a future pollwinner. He is joined on this CD by a six-piece horn section and a strong rhythm section (pianist John Hicks, bassist Ray Drummond and drummer Marvin "Smitty" Smith), plus there are guest appearances by altoist Arthur Blythe and guitarist Kevin Eubanks. The material (which includes Cedar Walton's "Night Flight," "Caravan," "When I Fall in Love" and the title cut by Milton Nascimento) is challenging and diverse. —*Scott Yanow*

You Got What It Takes / May 19, 1995 / Enja ✦✦✦✦✦

Kevin Mahogany's third and final Enja recording (before moving on to Warner Bros.) was his finest and a very definitive set. More jazz-oriented than his first Warner Bros. set, this program matches Mahogany's attractive voice with pianist James Williams (who contributed the tune "Old Times Sake"), bassist Micheal Formanek, drummer Victor Lewis and guest tenor Benny Golson. Singer Jeanie Bryson helps out on the opening "Baby You Got What It Takes," making one wish that the two vocalists would team up more often. Other highlights include Quincy Jones' classic "Stockholm Sweetnin'," "Route 66" (which has some creative scatting by Mahogany), the brief "Yardbird Suite" and "BG's Groove." Throughout this date, Kevin Mahogany (formerly a saxophonist who obviously knows music well) shows just how strong a jazz singer he can be. Highly recommended. —*Scott Yanow*

Kevin Mahogany / Jan. 29, 1996-Jan. 30, 1996 / Warner Brothers ✦✦✦

Kevin Mahogany's debut for Warner Bros. was an obvious attempt to increase his audience. Mahogany sings some fine jazz (including "I'm Walkin'," "Oh Gee" and "Still Swingin'") along with some more R&B-oriented and even poppish material. Mahogany's voice is appealing, so the erratic nature of the repertoire (a few of the selections really don't cut it) is disappointing. Joined by a septet that includes Kirk Whalum on reeds and organist Larry Goldings, Mahogany does uplift most of the songs, permitting one to recommend this CD with reservations. —*Scott Yanow*

Another Time, Another Place / Mar. 4, 1997-May 5, 1997 / Warner Brothers ✦✦✦✦✦

Kevin Mahogany has a big, rich, mellow, bear hug of a voice suitably matched to his physique, and he also has a musical brain, no doubt enriched by his experience as a baritone sax player. Yet this big voice is agile enough to tackle the slippery stream of words in "Cloudburst"—and there are other surprises on his second Warner Bros. album that one normally does not expect from today's mostly conservative jazz vocalists. For one thing, he actually opens the record with a scatting extravaganza called "Big Rub," with solos all around for a band that includes smokin' Joe Lovano on tenor and Cyrus Chestnut on piano. Elsewhere, Mahogany tries a somewhat daring experiment, matching his swinging tune "I Believe She Was Talkin' About Me" with country singer Randy Travis in a duet. Next to Mahogany, Travis has a small voice, and he doesn't dare scat with the master, but this unlikely yet friendly cultural exchange actually has a lot of charm. That and Mahogany's self-penned, marvelously wry take on the record business, "Fix It in the Mix," indicates that he has a real future as a composer. And of course, the big man displays his strengths with standard ballads like "Nature Boy" and "In the Wee Small Hours of the Morning," singing with a gentle finesse that recalls Johnny Hartman. Check it out. —*Richard S. Ginell*

Mike Mainieri

b. Jul. 24, 1938, New York, NY
Vibes, Leader / Post-Bop, Fusion, Crossover Jazz

Mike Mainieri, a talented and distinctive vibraphonist, has had a productive and diverse career. He first played vibes professionally when he was 14, touring with Paul Whiteman in a jazz trio called Two Kings and a Queen. He played with Buddy Rich's bands for a long period (1956-63) and then became a busy studio musician, appearing on many pop records. Mainieri had opportunities to work with Benny Goodman, Coleman Hawkins and Wes Montgomery (1967-68) among many others, and played in the early fusion band Jeremy and the Satyrs. During 1969-72 he led a 20-piece rehearsal group called White Elephant that included the Brecker Brothers and other studio players. In 1979 he formed Steps (which later became Steps Ahead), an all-star jazz-oriented R&B/fusion band that included such players as Mike Brecker, Don Grolnick, Eddie Gomez and Steve Gadd in its original lineup. Mainieri has revived the group several times since with such musicians as saxophonist Bendik, Warren Bernhardt, Elaine Elias, Rachel Z, Mike Stern, Tony Levin, Victor Bailey, Peter Erskine and Steve Smith making serious contributions. In 1992 Mainieri founded the NYC label, in recent times recording the adventurous *An American Diary*. Prior to NYC, Mike Mainieri had recorded as a leader for such labels as Argo (1962), Solid State, Arista, Artists House, Warner Bros. and Elektra. —*Scott Yanow*

Insight / 1967 / Solid State ✦✦✦✦

White Elephant / 1969-1972 / NYC ✦✦

Starting in 1965 and especially during 1969-72, many of the top studio musicians in New York got together after work on a nightly basis to jam and try out new tunes. Because the players' backgrounds were as much in R&B as in jazz and they were very open to the influence of pop and rock, the music on this reissue (which is taken from the sessions) is a mixture of idioms. The musicianship of the 20 or so musicians is impeccable and there are some fine solos (particularly by Mike and Randy Brecker on tenor and trumpet) but the vocals and lyrics (which are on all 16 tracks of this double CD), although not always dominant, range from dated to

embarrassing. Mike Mainieri and Nick Holmes are responsible for the largely forgettable material (none of which caught on) which, in addition to the vocals, emphasizes funky vamps, R&B riffing and danceable rhythms. Although there are some interesting early solos by the Brecker Brothers and guitarist Joe Beck, this set falls far short of its potential; strangely enough, the fine vibraphonist Mainieri is not heard from except on vocals. —*Scott Yanow*

Free Smiles / Jul. 22, 1978 / Novus ✦✦✦

Wanderlust / Feb. 25, 1981-Feb. 26, 1981 / NYC ✦✦✦

● **An American Diary** / Oct. 1, 1994-Oct. 2, 1994 / NYC ✦✦✦✦✦

In addition to a few group originals, vibraphonist Mike Mainieri performs some unusual pieces with his quartet (Joe Lovano on tenor, soprano and alto clarinet, bassist Eddie Gomez and drummer Peter Erskine) on this CD including two folk songs and selections by Leonard Bernstein ("Somewhere"), Frank Zappa ("King Kong"), Aaron Copland ("Piano Sonata"), Roger Sessions ("Piano Sonata No. 1") and Samuel Barber ("Overture to the School for Scandal"). The pianoless quartet (which displays a lot of versatility by Joe Lovano) turns all of the music into creative jazz. The most interesting aspect to this thought-provoking disc is how difficult it is to tell which compositions are taken from classical music and which are new. There is a surprising unity to the potentially difficult material; the performances on the rather moody outing reward repeated listenings. —*Scott Yanow*

Live at Seventh Avenue South / 1996 / NYC ✦✦✦

Adam Makowicz (Adam Matyszkowicz)

b. Aug. 18, 1940, Cesky Tesin, Czechoslovakia
Piano / Bop, Swing

Adam Makowicz made a strong impression when he first came to the US and at the time he was often compared to Art Tatum. Although his technique is nearly on Tatum's level, Makowicz has long had his own style, mixing together different aspects of jazz ranging from swing to hard bop. He started playing jazz in the late '50s and with Tomasz Stanko formed one of the first European free jazz groups, the Jazz Darings. He led his own groups in Warsaw from 1965 on and in 1970 played electric piano in Michal Urbaniak's band. Makowicz also worked with Urszula Dudziak and recorded several albums in Poland before coming to the US in 1977. Although the initial publicity (when he was championed by John Hammond) has long since died down, Makowicz has, if anything, continued to improve as a pianist. He has recorded many records as a leader for such labels as Columbia, Stash, Choice, Sheffield Lab, Novus and Concord. —*Scott Yanow*

Adam / 1977 / Columbia ✦✦✦✦✦

Adam Makowicz's first record since defecting from his native Poland found him sponsored by producer John Hammond and poised for stardom. However, in 1977, Hammond did not have the same power he had with Columbia in earlier decades, and this would be the pianist's only recording for the label; unfortunately, it has not yet been reissued on CD. The solo set finds Makowicz displaying impressive technique (influenced by, but not derivative of, Art Tatum) on five standards and six of his originals, including "Tribute to Erroll Garner" and "Chopin's Willows." Of the standards, "Tea for Two" and "Cherokee" are given the most impressive treatment. A strong start to Makowicz's American years. —*Scott Yanow*

Classic Jazz Duets / 1979 / Stash ✦✦✦✦

For his second American recording, pianist Adam Makowicz teams up on a set of duets with virtuoso bassist George Mraz, tearing into such songs as "This Can't Be Love," "Confirmation" and "Cherokee" (taken at a remarkable tempo). Makowicz would grow as a player in future years, but his technique and ability to think very quickly on his feet were already in place. Mraz easily keeps up, and the two make frequently magical music. —*Scott Yanow*

Handful of Stars / Aug. 20, 1981-Aug. 21, 1981 / Chiaroscuro ✦✦✦✦

Makowicz is joined by bassist George Mraz and drummer Jack DeJohnette on this lively set originally dating back to 1981. —*Jason Ankeny*

The Name is Makowicz (Ma-Ko-Vitch) / Apr. 25, 1983-Apr. 29, 1983 / Sheffield Lab ✦✦✦

Shows technical prowess. —*Ron Wynn*

Moonray / 1986 / Novus ✦✦✦✦

The talented pianist Adam Makowicz is joined by bassist Jamil Nasser, drummer Frank Gant and occasionally harpist Deborah Henson-Conant and vibraphonist Ed Saindon for frequently exciting versions of eight standards on this set. Makowicz, whose musical personality had continued to grow gradually since he first came to the US a decade earlier, is in prime form during virtuosic and creative treatments of such songs as "All of Me," "What Is This Thing Called Love" and "Indiana." RCA is long overdue to reissue this fine album, along with its follow-up, *Naughty Baby*. —*Scott Yanow*

Interface / 1987 / Gazell ✦✦✦

This is one of pianist Adam Makowicz's lesser-known dates, an album cut in Stockholm with two musicians associated with Keith Jarrett: bassist Palle Danielsson and drummer Jon Christensen. Unlike his previous standards-dominated sessions, Makowicz plays eight of his complex originals here, including "Interface," "Didibop," "Opalescence" and "Seamless Dream." None of the tunes caught on as standards, but the pianist's playing is, as usual, consistently outstanding throughout the post-bop trio set. —*Scott Yanow*

Naughty Baby / Jul. 25, 1987-Jul. 27, 1987 / Novus ✦✦✦✦

The most unusual aspect of this typically exciting recital by Adam Makowicz is that on six of the 11 songs, the pianist is joined by two bassists, Dave Holland and Charlie Haden. Drummer Al Foster completes the group, and Haden is the only bassist on the remaining songs. Makowicz explores 11 George Gershwin songs, including "They All Laughed," "Prelude No .2," "Fascinating Rhythm" and "Rhapsody in Blue." Although he shows great respect for the melodies, the pianist does come up with some fresh variations, even on the warhorses. —*Scott Yanow*

Plays Irving Berlin / Sep. 22, 1991-Sep. 23, 1991 / VWC Productions ✦✦✦✦✦

The flamboyant, gifted pianist brought plenty of harmonic flair and spirit to these interpretations. There have been numerous Irving Berlin repertory projects, and this one wasn't very different from the standpoints of song selection, respectful attitude, etc. But as a showcase for Makowicz's pianistic brilliance, it was ideal. —*Ron Wynn*

★ **Live at Maybeck Recital Hall, Vol. 24** / Jul. 19, 1992 / Concord Jazz ✦✦✦✦✦

Some jazz pianists sound best in trios, with their shortcomings appearing during solo recitals, like the series recorded at Maybeck Recital Hall. Such was definitely not the case for Adam Makowicz, who has always been very much a two-handed pianist with phenomenal technique. As if to show what he has, he begins this CD with his own complex original "Tatum on My Mind." After that, he digs into ten well-worn Cole Porter songs that Tatum and others had recorded through the years, coming up with interesting reinterpretations of such tunes as "Get Out of Town," "I Get a Kick Out of You," "You Do Something to Me," "Begin the Beguine" and "Just One of Those Things." Although Makowicz has recorded sessions that contained more variety, his total command of the piano is particularly well displayed throughout this memorable set. —*Scott Yanow*

The Music of Jerome Kern / Sep. 1992 / Concord Jazz ✦✦✦✦✦

Adam Makowicz interprets 11 well-known Jerome Kern compositions on his trio date with bassist George Mraz and drummer Alan Dawson. The pianist's arrangements are full of surprising turns and twists and his unpredictable flights result in some of the familiar songs being given unusual treatments. Stimulating and occasionally exciting music. —*Scott Yanow*

Adam Makowicz / George Mraz / May 22, 1993 / Concord Jazz ✦✦✦✦

The fifth volume in the Concord Duo Series matches pianist Adam Makowciz and bassist George Mraz in a concert at the Maybeck Recital Hall; both musicians are virtuosos originally from Eastern Europe who found fame in the US on what is very much a duo set. Mraz gets nearly as much solo space as Makowicz. Their repertoire mixes together six fresh renditions of standards with four of the pianist's complex originals, and the harmonically advanced music (which features plenty of close interplay) has enough variety to continually hold one's interest. —*Scott Yanow*

My Favorite Things: The Music of Richard Rodgers / Sep. 7, 1993-Sep. 8, 1993 / Concord Jazz ✦✦✦✦✦

Tribute to Art Tatum / 1997 / VWC ✦✦✦✦

Adam Makowicz's original inspiration was Art Tatum. In fact, the classically trained pianist discovered jazz by hearing a Tatum record broadcast over the Voice of America in his native Poland. In 1997, he revisited his "roots" for this CD, performing 13 selections and a melody by Chopin in the style of Art Tatum, no easy feat. Makowicz has always had phenomenal technique and is certainly up to the job on this set of unaccompanied solos, as he shows on such numbers as "Humoresque," "I Know That You Know," "Begin the Beguine," "Caravan" and "Just One of Those Things." —*Scott Yanow*

Russell Malone

b. Nov. 8, 1963, Albany, GA

Guitar / Bop, Swing

A fine guitarist who has made a stir with his Columbia records of the early to mid-'90s, Russell Malone started playing music when he was five. He was with Jimmy Smith's band for two years in the late '80s and since 1989 has often toured with Harry Connick, Jr. Malone's influences range from swing to R&B and he has an appealing bop-oriented approach that often pays tribute to earlier styles. —*Scott Yanow*

Russell Malone / Aug. 19, 1991-Mar. 25, 1992 / Columbia ✦✦✦✦

Russell Malone's debut as a leader is a charming effort that ranges from swing to numbers in which Malone shows off his Wes Montgomery influence. Malone is not only heard with a fairly modern quartet comprising pianist Donald Brown, bassist Robert Hurst III and drummer Yoron Israel, but also in a trio with the great veteran bassist Milt Hinton and drummer Shannon Powell (Malone and Hinton take "St. Louis Blues" as a duet). There are also two duets with pianist Harry Connick, Jr., including a surprising (and effective) vocal by Malone on "I Don't Know Enough About You." A very enjoyable effort with several other surprises along the way. —*Scott Yanow*

● **Black Butterfly** / Mar. 18, 1993-Apr. 29, 1993 / Columbia ✦✦✦✦✦

Junior Mance (Julian Clifford Mance, Jr.)

b. Oct. 10, 1928, Chicago, IL

Piano / Bop, Soul-Jazz

Junior Mance is well known for his soulful bluesy style, but he is also expert at playing bop standards. He started playing professionally when he was ten. Mance worked with Gene Ammons in Chicago during 1947-49, played with Lester Young (1950) and was with the Ammons-Sonny Stitt group until he was drafted. He was the house pianist at Chicago's Bee Hive (1953-54), worked as Dinah Washington's accompanist (1954-55), was in the first Cannonball Adderley Quintet (1956-57) and then spent two years touring with Dizzy Gillespie (1958-60). After a few months with the Eddie "Lockjaw" Davis-Johnny Griffin group, Mance formed his own trio and has mostly been a leader ever since. He has led sessions for Verve, Jazzland, Riverside, Capitol, Atlantic, Milestone, Polydor, Inner City, JSP, Nilva, Sackville and Bee Hive, among other labels. —*Scott Yanow*

Junior Mance Trio at the Village Vanguard / Feb. 22, 1961-Feb. 23, 1961 / Original Jazz Classics ✦✦✦✦✦

Pianist Junior Mance has long been typecast as a soulful blues player so, as if to confuse listeners, he starts off this live set with an uptempo "Looptown," on which he displays technique worthy of Oscar Peterson. Mance's many fans have no reason to despair though for, in addition to a boppish rendition of "Girl of My Dreams," the pianist does perform a generous amount of blues and soulful pieces. Bassist Larry Gales and drummer Ben Riley help out on this reissue LP which has yet to come out on CD. It's a strong outing. —*Scott Yanow*

Harlem Lullaby / Sep. 12, 1966-Nov. 1966 / Atlantic ✦✦✦

Most records by pianist Junior Mance are well worth getting, but this obscure Atlantic LP was a bit of a misfire. One of the problems is that on three of the eight songs, Mance switches to harpsichord, which doesn't work too well. Otherwise, the material, which includes five Mance originals, is blues-oriented but fairly routine, and no one sounds all that inspired. Mance is joined by either Gene Taylor or Bob Cunningham on bass, and Ray Lucas, Alan Dawson or Bobby Thompson on drums. Although there are some good moments (including the title cut), it would be very surprising if Atlantic ever decided to reissue this one. —*Scott Yanow*

The Tender Touch of Junior Mance / Apr. 1, 1983 / Nilva ✦✦✦

Produced by Alvin Queen, this album features duets between Mance and bassist Martin Rivera, a reprise of G. Harrison's "Something," and five standards. They create their own subtle rythms nicely. —*Michael G. Nastos*

For Dancers Only / Jul. 3, 1983 / Sackville ✦✦✦✦

Pianist Junior Mance is heard in prime form on this set of duets with bassist Martin Rivera. He performs two originals (including "Harlem Lullaby"), "Come on Home," and several swing-era standards with bluesy feeling, soul, and swing. Accessible yet creative music, recommended to a wide audience. —*Scott Yanow*

Truckin' and Trakin' / Dec. 13, 1983 / Bee Hive ✦✦✦✦

This album was pianist Junior Mance's first as a leader since 1967 to include a horn. Mance and tenor saxophonist David "Fathead" Newman make for a logical combination, since their soulful styles often straddle the boundary between jazz and R&B. This hard-to-find LP also features bassist Martin Rivera and drummer Walt Bolden offering fine support behind the lead voices. The repertoire—three veteran standards plus "Funky Carnival" (which features Newman's flute), Hank Crawford's "Truckin'" and Mance's "Mean Old Amtrak"—is basic and serves as viable vehicles for the solos of Mance and Newman. Worth searching for. —*Scott Yanow*

● **Mance's Special** / Sep. 14, 1986+Nov. 30, 1988 / Sackville ✦✦✦✦✦

Fine '86 set with pianist Junior Mance running through romping blues, intricate originals, and moving standards and ballads in a solo set. While he's best at blues-tinged material, Mance shows the versatility necessary to do other material, and doesn't substitute cliches and gimmicks for ideas and substance. —*Ron Wynn*

Here 'Tis / 1992 / Sackville ✦✦✦✦

Softly as in a Morning Sunrise / Jul. 21, 1994 / Enja ✦✦✦✦
This 1994 CD gives listeners an excellent example of pianist Junior Mance's playing. Featured in a trio with bassist Jimmy Woode and drummer Bobby Durham, Mance performs a wide-ranging set that includes a few originals, blues, and standards (including "Broadway," "Lady Bird" and the title cut) that he practically turns into the blues. Mance's style, which mixes together bop, R&B and soul-jazz, is quite appealing and is heard in its prime throughout this splendid session. —*Scott Yanow*

At Town Hall, Vol. 1 / Mar. 30, 1995 / Enja ✦✦✦✦
The veteran pianist Junior Mance has long been known for his soulful take on bop and hard bop. For his Enja release, a live quartet set with tenor saxophonist Houston Person, Mance is heard in top form on a pair of swing-era standards and three of his originals, all of which are at least 82 minutes long. Most memorable is "Jubilation" (which lives up to its name), "Small Fry" and a 15-minute version of "I Cried for You." Bassist Calvin Hill and drummer Alvin Queen are fine in support of the two lead voices and it is of little surprise that Mance and Person work together quite well for their styles have long been very complementary. This CD is easily recommended to their fans. —*Scott Yanow*

At Town Hall, Vol. 2 / Mar. 30, 1995 / Enja ✦✦✦

Albert Mangelsdorff

b. Sep. 5, 1928, Frankfurt, Germany
Trombone / Avant-Garde, Free Jazz
The master of multiphonics (playing more than one note at a time on a horn), Mangelsdorff has been a giant of the European avant-garde for the past 30 years. He originally studied violin and worked as a jazz guitarist before taking up the trombone in 1948. He played bop in the 1950s with Hans Koller and local orchestras. In 1958 Mangelsdorff visited the US to play with Marshall Brown's International Youth Band at the Newport Jazz Festival, but his stays in America have always been fairly brief. By the time he recorded an album with John Lewis in 1962, Mangelsdorff was starting to lean towards the avant-garde. He has since recorded unaccompanied solo albums, been documented at a concert with Jaco Pastorius, led trios and worked with the Globe Unity Orchestra and the United Jazz & Rock Ensemble. Of his many records, the John Lewis set and his valuable MPS albums will be difficult to find, but Albert Mangelsdorff's work for Enja and Sackville can be acquired. —*Scott Yanow*

Live in Tokyo / Feb. 15, 1971 / Enja ✦✦✦✦

● **Tromboneliness** / Jan. 1976+Mar. 1976 / Sackville ✦✦✦✦✦
A full album of unaccompanied solo trombone might seem a bit tedious, but Albert Mangelsdorff is on a different level than most trombonists. For one thing, he is a master of multiphonics (playing chords on a horn), and his use of a wa-wa mute is also quite expert. Although an avant-garde master, Mangelsdorff's version of "Creole Love Call" on this solo album is brilliant, as are his seven diverse originals. In addition, there is plenty of humor on these rambunctious performances. —*Scott Yanow*

Trilogue Live! / Nov. 6, 1976 / Pausa ✦✦✦✦✦
Live trio recording for virtuoso German trombonist. Startling sounds. With Jaco Pastorius (b). —*Michael G. Nastos*

Chuck Mangione

b. Nov. 29, 1940, Rochester, NY
Trumpet, Fluegelhorn, Electric Piano / Bop, Instrumental Pop, Pop Jazz, Crossover Jazz
Throughout the 1970s, Chuck Mangione was a celebrity. His purposely lightweight music was melodic pop that was upbeat, optimistic and sometimes uplifting. Mangione's records were big sellers, yet few of his fans from the era knew that his original goal was to be a bebopper. His father had often taken Chuck and his older brother Gap (a keyboardist) out to see jazz concerts, and Dizzy Gillespie was a family friend. While Chuck studied at the Eastman School, the two Mangiones led a bop quintet called the Jazz Brothers that recorded several albums for Jazzland, often with Sal Nistico on tenor. Chuck Mangione played with the big bands of Woody Herman and Maynard Ferguson (both in 1965), and Art Blakey's Jazz Messengers (1965-67). In 1968, now sticking mostly to his soft-toned fluegelhorn, Mangione formed a quartet that also featured Gerry Niewood on tenor and soprano. They cut a fine set for Mercury in 1972, but otherwise Mangione's recordings in the 1970s generally used large orchestras and vocalists (including Esther Satterfield), putting the emphasis on lightweight melodies such as "Hill Where the Lord Hides," "Land of Make Believe," "Chase the Clouds Away" and the huge 1977 hit (featuring guitarist Grant Geissman) "Feels So Good." After a recorded 1978 Hollywood Bowl concert that summed up his pop years and a 1980 two-LP set

that alternated pop and bop (with guest Dizzy Gillespie), Mangione gradually faded out of the music scene. In the 1970s Chuck Mangione recorded for Mercury and A&M; in the 1980s he had a couple of very forgettable Columbia albums and had not been heard from in the '90s until a 1997 comeback tour found him in good form, having a reunion with his "Feels So Good" band. —*Scott Yanow*

The Jazz Brothers / Aug. 8, 1960 / Original Jazz Classics ✦✦✦
Early, non-pop-oriented straight jazz from trumpet and fluegelhorn player Chuck Mangione and his brother Gap. This was long before Chuck Mangione became a successful instrumental pop musician; these sessions are in either West Coast cool or Midwest/East Coast hard bop mode. —*Ron Wynn*

Hey Baby! / Mar. 8, 1961 / Original Jazz Classics ✦✦✦
The early '60s group the Jazz Brothers featured trumpeter Chuck Mangione and pianist Gap Mangione in a quintet also including up-and-coming tenor Sal Nistico (shortly before he joined Woody Herman's orchestra), bassist Steve Davis and drummer Roy McCurdy; lots of young talent in that band. Their second of three recordings (the first has yet to be reissued) has reappeared as this CD. Those only familiar with Chuck Mangione's later work will be surprised to hear him playing bop-oriented music and showing the strong influence of Dizzy Gillespie. Four standards (including "The Night Has a Thousand Eyes" and "Just You, Just Me") alternate with an obscurity and three group originals. The music has spirit, even if it is a bit derivative and predictable. —*Scott Yanow*

Spring Fever / Nov. 1961 / Original Jazz Classics ✦✦✦✦
The third and final recording (originally released as "the Jazz Brothers" and now reissued on CD in the OJC series) features trumpeter Chuck Mangione, pianist Gap Mangione and tenor saxophonist Sal Nistico in a 1961 hard bop quintet. The music is strictly straightahead with four group originals and versions of "What's New" and "Softly as in a Morning Sunrise" being given winning treatments. Even if the overall results are not all that memorable (none of the musicians had distinctive voices yet), the music should please fans of 1950s jazz. —*Scott Yanow*

Recuerdo / Jul. 31, 1962 / Original Jazz Classics ✦✦✦✦
After three recordings co-leading the Jazz Brothers with pianist Gap Mangione, trumpeter Chuck Mangione headed his first solo record date. The CD reissue adds alternate takes of "Solar" and "The Little Prince" to the original LP program. Joined by an all-star rhythm section (pianist Wynton Kelly, bassist Sam Jones and drummer Louis Hayes) plus Joe Romano on tenor, flute and alto, Mangione mostly sticks to bebop on four jazz standards (including Charlie Parker's "Big Foot") and three of his originals. Although only 21 at the time, he holds his own with the illustrious rhythm section and was starting to display his own musical personality. His next recording as a leader would not take place until 1970, and by then he was starting to explore the pop-jazz formula that was to gain him great commercial success. —*Scott Yanow*

● **Chuck Mangione Quartet** / Mar. 1972 / Mercury ✦✦✦✦✦
While Chuck Mangione's projects with orchestras in the 1970s tended to be bland (although bestsellers), his best jazz work came when the fluegelhornist jammed with his quartet, which in 1971 also included Gerry Niewood on soprano and flute, bassist Joel DiBartolo and drummer Ron Davis. This out-of-print LP finds Mangione taking melodic and worthwhile solos on such numbers as "Land of Make Believe," Freddie Hubbard's "Little Sunflower" and "Manha De Carnival." —*Scott Yanow*

Alive! / Aug. 1972 / Mercury ✦✦✦✦✦
Fluegelhornist Chuck Mangione became a household name during the 1970s and '80s due to some pop hits, but this LP (now out of print) actually contains his finest playing. Mangione, who also contributes some background electric piano, teams up here with Gerry Niewood (tripling on tenor, soprano and flute), electric bassist Tony Levin and drummer Steve Gadd. Together they stretch out on lengthy versions of "High Heel Sneakers," "Legend of the One-Eyed Sailor," "Sixty-Miles Young" and "St. Thomas." The fire heard during these performances is a sharp contrast to Mangione's more popular recordings. Well worth searching for. —*Scott Yanow*

Land of Make Believe / 1973 / Mercury ✦✦

Bellavia / 1975 / A&M ✦✦✦

Chase the Clouds Away / 1975 / A&M ✦✦✦

Main Squeeze / 1976 / A&M ✦✦

Feels So Good / 1977 / A&M ✦✦✦✦
Due to the title cut, this was a huge seller when it originally came out. Reissued on CD, this set from fluegelhornist Chuck Mangione (which helped give guitarist Grant Geissman some fame) is actually stronger from the jazz standpoint than Mangione's subsequent dates. The leader has some good solos, as does Geissman and saxophonist Chris Vadala, and the quintet's ensembles are generally both

sparse and attractive. Pity that in ways this was Chuck Mangione's last worthwhile release of new music to date; success did stunt his artistic growth. —*Scott Yanow*

An Evening of Magic, Live at the Hollywood Bowl / Jul. 16, 1978 / A&M ✦✦✦

Children of Sanchez / 1978 / A&M ✦✦

Fun and Games / 1979 / A&M ✦✦

● **Tarantella** / Dec. 27, 1980 / A&M ✦✦✦✦
This two-LP set is an unusual Chuck Mangione record. Taken from a marathon live concert, the fluegelhornist is featured with a big band. The first album has fairly typical performances (including versions of "Legend of the One-Eyed Sailor" and "Hill Where the Lord Hides"), but it is the second half that is most notable. Mangione performs such boppish numbers as "Things to Come," "'Round Midnight" and "Manteca" with guest Dizzy Gillespie, duets with Chick Corea on "My One and Only Love," and stretches out on "All Blues." He also welcomes such old associates as his brother, keyboardist Gap Mangione, plus tenorman Sal Nistico and altoist Joe Romano, so this is certainly not a typical Chuck Mangione A&M pop record. Not yet reissued, this surprising set is recommended. —*Scott Yanow*

Love Notes / 1982 / Columbia ✦✦

Disguise / 1984 / Columbia ✦

Live at the Village Gate / 1987 / Feels So Good ✦✦✦

Manhattan Transfer

f. 1972
Vocal Group / Bop, Pop
The Manhattan Transfer has never stuck exclusively to performing jazz (other than their classic 1985 album *Vocalese*), but they rank as the top jazz vocal group since Lambert, Hendricks and Ross. Tim Hauser put together the first version of the band in 1969 and by 1972 he was joined by Alan Paul, Janis Siegel and Laurel Masse; in 1979 Cheryl Bentyne took Masse's place. The four singers are versatile, blend together well and each have their own distinct personalities. Whether it be doo wop, recent pop tunes or swing standards, the Manhattan Transfer has long been at the top of its field. Since 1975 they have recorded for Atlantic. —*Scott Yanow*

Jukin' / Apr. 8 1969-Feb. 1, 1971 / One Way ✦✦✦
This was the Manhattan Transfer before they become The Manhattan Transfer, an altogether different vocal group from which founder Tim Hauser was the sole holdover. Released by Capitol in the 1970s on LP, and now on a related label in its CD version, *Jukin'* is an accumulation of scraps recorded over a period of two years in New York and Nashville. Back in those days, the Transfer seemed to be one of several hippie groups (like Spanky and Our Gang and Dan Hicks and His Hot Licks) that looked at the past ironically with arched eyebrows, not like the later Transfer which affectionately celebrated old music at its face value. Hence the pure country treatment of "Fair and Tender Ladies," in which there is a strong whiff of condescension in the group's nasal accents; even the doo wop tribute "Guided Missiles" reeks of barely concealed contempt. Then as now, the Transfer was unpredictably eclectic in their tastes, while also very much aware of the then-current rock marketplace. Hauser's version of Fats Waller's "You'se a Viper" bears some resemblance to the later Transfer manner, and one number, "Java Jive," appears in the same arrangement as the one the 1975 Transfer used, if rougher in vocal texture. For all of the careful production, there is a casual looseness about these tracks that is typical of its time, the heyday of the hippie—and as such, today's Transfer fans are in for a surprise if they want to check out the group's beginnings. —*Richard S. Ginell*

The Manhattan Transfer / 1975 / Rhino ✦✦✦
The Manhattan Transfer first came to the general public's attention as a retro act, a nostalgic throwback in an era consumed with nostalgia—the early/mid-1970s—and their debut Atlantic album, as well as their 1975 summer replacement TV series, catered unashamedly to that market. As a result, this record seemed old when it came out, and it still sounds more than a little sappy today, especially when one considers the astonishing growth of the Transfer since. True, "You Can Depend Upon Me" is a lively precursor of vocalese triumphs to come, enlivened by a brief solo from Zoot Sims, and there are subdued reminders of their jazz roots on "Tuxedo Junction." But the object of the latter exercise was to bring back sweet memories, specifically of a wartime era evoked more explicitly by the unctious, sugary rendition of "Candy." Nothing if not eclectic even then, the Transfer also evokes the Ink Spots, 1940s jive, 1950s doo wop, New Orleans funk, even 1975 with the proto-disco "Clap Your Hands." Yet the net results usually seem calculated, not fresh and innocent. Best bet: seek out the originals and sample later Transfer projects first. —*Richard S. Ginell*

Coming Out / 1976 / Atlantic ✦✦
This CD reissue brings back Manhattan Transfer's second Atlantic recording, showcasing the talented singers (Tim Hauser, Alan Paul, Janis Siegel and Laurel Masse)

on a strictly pop affair. The only hints of jazz pop up in Siegel's ballad "Scotch and Soda," and a funky version of "Poinciana," on which Michael Brecker has a cameo on soprano. There is a good amount of variety, and the singing is reasonably impressive, but the spontaneity and feel of jazz is largely absent from this CD and the brief (35 minutes) set is one of the Manhattan Transfer's weakest to date. —*Scott Yanow*

Pastiche / Dec. 1976-Sep. 1977 / Atlantic ✦✦✦
The dictionary definition of "pastiche" is an artistic composition imitating or caricaturing previous works, so given the lack of home-grown material here, it is hard to say what the Manhattan Transfer meant by this title. In any case, this assortment of odds and ends from various eras in American music—recorded in New York, Los Angeles, Nashville and Australia—finds the Transfer casting its lines in search of a direction that it had yet to find. But there are signs that they were getting close. The Transfer's stunning rendition of "Four Brothers," with composer Jimmy Giuffre present in the sax section, marks the beginning of their championing of the words of Jon Hendricks and placed the Transfer in position to claim the long-vacant throne of group vocalese. Otherwise, there are curiosities like a quasi-C&W-tinted rendition of "Love for Sale" staffed by some of Nashville's finest, fairly ordinary covers of rock and R&B numbers, and as yet, only a few traces of real distinction. —*Richard S. Ginell*

Extensions / 1979 / Atlantic ✦✦✦✦
This audiophile CD reissue brings back one of the Manhattan Transfer's more popular sets. Their hit version of "Birdland" opens the program and among the other tunes are "Twilight Tone" and "Trickle Trickle." From the jazz standpoint, the most significant numbers are the catchy "Birdland," "Wacky Dust," Spyro Gyra's "Shaker Song" and "Body and Soul." Although not exclusively in the idiom, this release has enough high points so as to be easily recommended to jazz collectors. —*Scott Yanow*

Mecca for Moderns / 1981 / Atlantic ✦✦✦✦✦
After the deserved artistic, critical and popular success of *Extensions*, the Manhattan Transfer went back to ace producer Jay Graydon for this one, which almost matches its predecessor in its contemporary energy while drawing selectively from the past. Outstanding is the handclapping treatment of the 1965 rock tune "The Boy from New York City" (a No. 7 hit single) and the happily swinging vocalese of the Basie band's "Until I Met You (Corner Pocket)," although their version of Charlie Parker's difficult "Confirmation" isn't nearly as assured. There is also an ample dose of the inventive weirdness that invaded *Extensions:* the African/Caribbean "(Wanted) Dead Or Alive," with its checklist of dictators, that segues right into a tongue-in-cheek secret agent spoof, "Spies in the Night"; or the ambitious, wordless composition "Kafka." No longer a mere nostalgia act, the Manhattan Transfer had not only caught up with the times, they were now slightly ahead of them as well. —*Richard S. Ginell*

Bodies and Souls / 1983-1984 / Atlantic ✦✦✦
In *Bodies and Souls*, the Transfer almost completely abandons its roots in favor of a slick, pop/R&B direction on one side of the LP version while trying a few more interesting experiments with textures and styles on the other (the CD, of course, doesn't make such a sharp divide). Side one (entitled "Bodies") is relentless in its search for another Top Ten hit, enlisting the help of Rod Temperton—then riding high on his red-hot association with Michael Jackson and Quincy Jones—on two tracks, and Stevie Wonder's harmonica on Temperton's slick R&B/disco "Spice of Life." Meanwhile, side two (a.k.a. "Souls") pokes around the electronic world before falling back upon another ebullient collaboration with Jon Hendricks on Fletcher Henderson's "Down South Camp Meeting." The Transfer is so good at vocalese that you wonder why they bothered to chase hits in the manufactured, anonymous pop language of 1983. —*Richard S. Ginell*

Mantra: Live in Tokyo / Nov. 1983-Oct. 1984 / Rhino ✦✦✦✦
FM Tokyo recorded these live performances, Westwood One broadcast them in the States, and *Bop-Doo-Wop* included five of the tracks, but the rest weren't made available to the public until 1996. Backed by their touring sextet of the time, this is certainly a more spontaneous Transfer than that of their carefully produced recordings, genuinely overflowing with the joy of singing with each other. Listen to their ebullient interplay on "Jeannine," with Cheryl Bentyne's chirping voice way up top, for a charge that the group only delivers live. The *raison d'etre* of the concert was to promote their then-new *Bodies and Souls* album—not their best—and there are inevitable small defects in the ensemble singing ("Trickle Trickle" being particularly more than a little ragged and off-mike). But there is also an ebullient treatment of "How High the Moon," in which guitarist Wayne Johnson does a fleet-fingered tribute to Les Paul's version, and another great rendition of "Four Brothers." —*Richard S. Ginell*

Bop Doo Wop / 1983-1984 / Atlantic ✦✦✦✦

This album, released as a stopgap between major projects, is really an anthology of various studio scraps and live remote pickups, no doubt carefully curated and selected by that indefatigable collector, Tim Hauser. The rhythm track for "My Cat Fell in the Well" dates back to 1976's *Coming Out* sessions (the vocals are from 1984); everything else comes from the period of 1983-84, including five performances from a live gig in Tokyo that was more comprehensively documented in 1996's *Live in Tokyo*. In the studio tracks—a mostly eccentric lot—the ebullient Transfer doo wop manner is celebrated again in "Baby Come Back to Me" and a nutty, fast "Unchained Melody." Though this is a peculiar, disjointed collection that only a Transfer collector would love—the brief sum being less than the total of its parts—the parts are certainly worth hearing, and they are certainly a departure away from the contemporary pop-minded *Bodies and Souls*. —*Richard S. Ginell*

● **Vocalese** / 1985 / Atlantic ✦✦✦✦✦

Many of the Manhattan Transfer recordings up to this point showed off their diversity and covered a wide variety of music, including jazz. This set was quite a bit different, for it is dedicated to the vocalese of the great Jon Hendricks. The Manhattan Transfer (singers Cheryl Bentyne, Tim Hauser, Alan Paul and Janis Siegel) perform a dozen songs using Hendricks' lyrics, including "That's Killer Joe," "Rambo," "Ray's Rockhouse" and "Sing Joy Spring." Utilizing their regular band of the period (which includes guitarist Wayne Johnson), the Count Basie Orchestra (directed at the time by Thad Jones), the Four Freshmen (on "To You"), tenorman James Moody, Bobby McFerrin (guesting on "Night in Tunisia"), McCoy Tyner, Dizzy Gillespie (on "Sing Joy Spring"), altoist Richie Cole, and Hendricks himself, among many others, the Transfer gives these boppish tunes definitive vocal treatments. This is one of their finest jazz recordings and a classic of its kind. —*Scott Yanow*

Live '86 / Feb. 20, 1986-Feb. 21, 1986 / Atlantic ✦✦✦

Perhaps feeling that they should have a real up-to-date live album in their satchel after the half-cocked *Bop-Doo-Wopp*—and needing some product anyway after the triumphant *Vocalese* project—the Transfer went back to Tokyo's Nakano Sun Plaza Hall and did another live session. But as in *Bop-Doo-Wopp*, though these performances take up a whole CD this time, you're not hearing the entire project; the rest of the tunes, all older material, can be seen on the video. What is left is mostly a live version of *Vocalese*—eight of its 11 tracks are reprised—which is perhaps redundant, but just the act of hearing the foursome perform these often difficult Jon Hendricks-lyricized selections without a net adds to our respect. "Airegin" is particularly challenging—and yes, they pull it off quite deftly, though without Hendricks' bitter final verse—and "That's Killer Joe" and "Move" have all of the electricity of the studio versions. The rest of the tunes date back to earlier incarnations of the Transfer—"Four Brothers" again, a touch of a cappella doo wop in "Gloria," a fine "Shaker Song"—backed by the Transfer's excellent small combo. Casual listeners who already bought *Vocalese* don't need this, and the fanatics will have to have it in any case, yet those who have neither album will get a good idea of the excitement the Transfer could inspire in their hot 1980s creative period. —*Richard S. Ginell*

Brasil / 1987 / Atlantic ✦✦✦✦

Tim Hauser likes to say that the Manhattan Transfer gets bored easily; hence the exploratory bent that has made them the most interesting vocal group in jazz (and maybe pop, too). Taking advantage of the then-cresting second Brazilian wave in North America while still going their own way musically, *Brasil* is the Transfer's most daring and perhaps most emotionally moving album to date, an original fusion of the Transfer's vigorous vocal blend, Brazilian harmonic warmth, and the textures of American synthesized pop-jazz and the rhythms of both nations. They rely mostly upon five songs from one of Brazil's finest post-bossa nova writers, Djavan, with two more from Ivan Lins and one apiece from Gilberto Gil and Milton Nascimento (the Transfer has impeccable taste in Brazilian writers), while going to all kinds of folk for English lyrics. The oddly percolating "Soul Food to Go," with dada lyrics by, of all people, the notorious Doug Fieger of the Knack, makes a fine, energetic prelude to an album that also frets about Big Brother, the suppression of freedom and the destruction of the Amazon rain forest. Clearly the Transfer had been listening hard not only to the sound, but also to the fury of Brazil's composers; their causes become the Transfer's as well. Djavan's lovely "Capim" has the dual advantage of having both the composer on vocals and a distinguished visitor from the first Brazilian wave, Stan Getz, blowing urbane obligatos. The last cut, "Notes from the Underground," an angry cry of solidarity with a haunting Lins tune and bumping instrumental lines from the Brazilian group Uakti, aches in the memory for hours. Alas, the elusive *Brasil* baffled many of the Transfer's fans and started a long commercial slide for the group. Yet it belongs among their greatest achievements, right alongside *Extensions* and *Vocalese*. —*Richard S. Ginell*

The Offbeat of Avenues / 1991 / Columbia ✦✦

Other than a recreation of the Miles Davis/Gil Evans recording of "Blues for Pablo" (with trumpeter Mark Isham filling in for Miles), this program by the Manhattan

Transfer is completely outside of jazz. It is doubtful if Sarah Vaughan would have much enjoyed "Sassy" (due to the reliance on electronic rhythms) or the poppish material heard throughout the date, despite the talents of the singers. Other than "10 Minutes till the Savages Come" and the Dirty Dozen Brass Band's guest appearance on "Blue Serenade," the set is disappointingly forgettable. —*Scott Yanow*

Tonin' / 1995 / Atlantic ✦✦

The idea here was to turn the Manhattan Transfer loose on a baker's dozen of good old 1960s pop and R&B hits in league either with the original artists or prominent guests from that period and beyond. And yes, it's a stellar list, guaranteed to stir warm and fuzzy memories, and the tunes echo the old lament of an earlier age, "they don't write songs like they used to." For almost any other vocal group, this would be an entertaining coup, yet for the hugely gifted, compulsively adventurous Transfer, this is just a detour into the tent of nostalgia that they had long outgrown (though they would do better in the retro arena with 1997's buoyant *Swing*). Moreover, they really have nothing new to bring to these tunes; they serve as background singers to Smokey Robinson on his "I Second that Emotion," to Felix Cavaliere on his "Groovin'" or—good grief—Phil Collins subbing for Marvin Gaye on "Too Busy Thinking About My Baby." Indeed, "The Thrill Is Gone" can serve as its own epitaph; even with B.B. King's authentic guitar obligato and Ruth Brown's rap, the Transfer's smooth vocal harmonies turn this gritty blues into pap. However gutsy Arif Mardin's productions were in Atlantic's '60s heyday, he just goes through the crisp-sounding motions here. —*Richard S. Ginell*

Swing / 1997 / Atlantic ✦✦✦✦✦

On this continually interesting CD, the Manhattan Transfer revisits tunes from the swing era, in some cases recreating (through vocalese) specific recordings. Benny Goodman's 1935 version of "King Porter Stomp," Bennie Moten's 1932 recording of "Moten's Swing," Glenn Miller's "I Know Why," Charlie Barnet's "Skyliner" and Fletcher Henderson's exciting arrangement of "Down South Camp Meetin'" are among the many highlights. The vocals are superb (particularly Janis Siegel and Cheryl Bentyne), although one wishes that the individual members had more of a chance to improvise within the style. The backup groups are different than one would expect, including the Western swing band Asleep at the Wheel, violinist Mark O'Connor (Stephane Grappelli makes a special appearance on "Clouds"), and steel guitarist Buddy Emmons. Recommended. —*Scott Yanow*

Herbie Mann (Herbert Jay Solomon)

b. Apr. 16, 1930, New York, NY

Flute, Leader / Bop, Soul-Jazz, Afro-Cuban Jazz, Instrumental Pop, Crossover Jazz

Herbie Mann has played a wide variety of music throughout his career. He became quite popular in the 1960s but in the '70s became so immersed in pop and various types of world music that he seemed lost to jazz. Fortunately, Mann has never lost his ability to improvise creatively as he has shown in recent years.

Herbie Mann began on clarinet when he was nine but was soon also playing flute and tenor. After serving in the Army, he was with Mat Mathews' Quintet (1953-54), and then started working and recording as a leader. During 1954-58 Mann stuck mostly to playing bop, sometimes collaborating with such players as Phil Woods, Buddy Collette, Sam Most, Bobby Jaspar and Charlie Rouse. He doubled on cool-toned tenor and was one of the few jazz musicians in the 1950s who recorded on bass clarinet; he also recorded in 1957 a full album (for Savoy) of unaccompanied flute.

After spending time playing and writing music for television, in 1959 Mann formed his Afro-Jazz Sextet, a group using several percussionists, vibes (either Johnny Rae, Hagood Hardy or Dave Pike) and the leader's flute. He toured Africa (1960) and Brazil (1961), had a hit with "Comin' Home Baby" and recorded with Bill Evans. The most popular jazz flutist during the era, Mann explored bossa nova (even recording in Brazil in 1962), incorporated music from many cultures (plus current pop tunes) into his repertoire, and had among his sidemen such top young musicians as Willie Bobo, Chick Corea (1965), Attila Zoller and Roy Ayers; at the 1972 Newport Festival his sextet included David Newman and Sonny Sharrock. By then, Mann had been a producer at Embroyo (a subsidiary of Atlantic) for three years and was frequently stretching his music outside of jazz. As the 1970s advanced, Mann became much more involved in rock, pop, reggae and even disco. After leaving Atlantic at the end of the 1970s, Mann had his own label for a while and gradually came back to jazz. He recorded for Chesky, made a record with Dave Valentin, and in the 1990s founded the Kokopelli label on which before breaking away in 1996 he was free to pursue his wide range of musical interests. Through the years, Herbie Mann has recorded as a leader for Bethlehem, Prestige, Epic, Riverside, Savoy, Mode, New Jazz, Chesky, Kokopelli and, most significantly, Atlantic. —*Scott Yanow*

Herbie Mann Plays / Dec. 1954 / Bethlehem ✦✦✦✦
Flutist Herbie Mann's first recording as a leader (seven selections from 1954 originally on a 10-inch LP plus four others cut in 1956) has been reissued on CD with three alternate takes added on. Even back in 1954, Mann (who doubles here on flute and alto flute) had his own sound. The music (featuring either Benny Weeks or Joe Puma on guitar in a pianoless quartet) is essentially straightahead bop and finds Mann playing quite melodically and with swing. This set is a good example of Herbie Mann's early style before he started exploring various types of world musics. —*Scott Yanow*

The Mann with the Most / Oct. 12, 1955+Oct. 17, 1955 / Bethlehem ✦✦✦✦
This out-of-print Bethlehem LP, reissued in 1977, matches together flutists Herbie Mann and Sam Most in a fine bop program with guitarist Joe Puma, bassist Jimmy Gannon and drummer Lee Kleinman. The music consistently swings lightly and, other than an original apiece from Puma and Most, the selections are all standards; highlights include "Fascinating Rhythm," "Let's Get Away from It All" and "Seven Come Eleven." Most often takes honors, but Mann is also in fine form on these Russ Garcia arrangements. Worth searching for. —*Scott Yanow*

Flute Souffle / Mar. 21, 1957-Mar. 27, 1957 / Original Jazz Classics ✦✦✦✦✦
At the time of this Prestige set (reissued on CD), Herbie Mann was a flutist who occasionally played tenor, and Bobby Jaspar a tenor saxophonist who doubled on flute. Two of the four songs find them switching back and forth while the other two are strictly flute features. With pianist Tommy Flanagan, guitarist Joe Puma, bassist Wendell Marshall and drummer Bobby Donaldson contributing quiet support, the two lead voices constantly interact and trade off during this enjoyable performance. High points are the haunting "Tel Aviv" and a delightful version of "Chasing the Bird." —*Scott Yanow*

When Lights Are Low / Apr. 18, 1957+Apr. 29, 1957 / Portrait ✦✦✦✦
This Portrait LP (a 1988 reissue of an Epic album titled *Salute to the Flute*) found flutist Herbie Mann accompanied for the first time by a big band on five of the nine selections. Prior to 1959, virtually all of Mann's recordings were bop-oriented, and this one is no exception. Whether it be "Little Niles," "When Lights Are Low," "Beautiful Love" or even "Old Honky Tonk Piano Roll Blues," Mann proves to be an excellent bop soloist; other important players on this date include trumpeter Joe Wilder, altoist Anthony Ortega, pianist Hank Jones, guitarist Joe Puma and bassist Oscar Pettiford. This LP will be a difficult one to find. —*Scott Yanow*

Yardbird Suite / May 14, 1957 / Savoy ✦✦✦✦
Although flutist Herbie Mann's reputation suffered in the jazz world in later years due to his interest in other styles of music, during the 1954-58 period he stuck mostly to cool bebop and held his own with the best. This Savoy LP finds him matching ideas with the great altoist Phil Woods, along with vibraphonist Eddie Costa, guitarist Joe Puma, bassist Wendell Marshall and drummer Bobby Donaldson, and the results are quite enjoyable. In addition to his flute flights on three group originals and "Yardbird Suite," Mann fares quite well on tenor during the two other pieces. This hard-to-find album, which has not yet been reissued on CD, is easily recommended to bop fans. —*Scott Yanow*

Great Ideas of Western Mann / Jul. 3, 1957 / Riverside ✦✦✦
This LP contains a slightly unusual and somewhat obscure session. Flutist Herbie Mann decided to record a full album (five standards and his own "A Stella Performance") on the rarely utilized bass clarinet; this was two years before Eric Dolphy rose to fame. Mann essentially plays bop on the bass clarinet while assisted by trumpeter Jack Sheldon, pianist Jimmy Rowles, bassist Buddy Clark and drummer Mel Lewis. High points include "The Theme," "Get Out of Town" and "Is It True What They Say About Dixie." This enjoyable set is long overdue to be reissued in the OJC series. —*Scott Yanow*

Flute Fraternity / Jul. 1957 / V.S.O.P. ✦✦✦
In the 1950s, Herbie Mann frequently shared the spotlight on record dates with other flutists. This V.S.O.P. LP, a reissue of a set originally for Mode and also out for a while on Premier, matches Mann (who here also plays piccolo, clarinet and tenor) with Buddy Collette (switching between flute, clarinet, tenor and alto) in a quintet with pianist Jimmy Rowles, bassist Buddy Clark and drummer Mel Lewis. The results are generally pleasing, if somewhat lightweight, with such obscure tunes as "Here's Buddy," Rowles' "Pop Melody," "Here's Pete" and Mann's "Theme from 'Theme From'" alternating with three standards and Chico Hamilton's "Morning After." The most interesting aspect to this lightly swinging music is the constant switching around of the lead voices on their various horns. —*Scott Yanow*

Hi Flutin' / Jul. 1957 / Mode ✦✦✦✦
The music on this LP has been reissued several times (including on Premier and on CD by Drive Archive). Herbie Mann (flute, alto flute, clarinet and tenor) and Buddy Collette (flute, alto flute, clarinet, tenor and alto) constantly switch instruments on the fairly basic material which mixes together recent works with originals and a couple of standards. With the assistance of pianist Jimmy Rowles, bassist

Buddy Clark and drummer Mel Lewis, Mann and Collette "battle" to a tie, creating light but substantial music. —*Scott Yanow*

Jazz Masters 56 / Aug. 9, 1957-Jul. 26, 1960 / Verve ✦✦✦✦
During the three years that he recorded for Verve, flutist Herbie Mann's playing changed from straight bop to incorporating elements of Latin, African and South American music. This CD reissues all of the music from one former LP (*Flutista*) and several of the selections from two others (*The Magic Flute of Herbie Mann* and *Herbie Mann's Cuban Band*). Whether it be with a standard quartet, backed by a string section, jamming with a sextet that includes two percussionists, or interacting with a brass section, the flutist is heard in explorative form, satisfying his fertile musical curiosity; he even plays bass clarinet and piccolo on one song apiece. Highlights of this excellent overview of Mann's Verve period include "Baia," "Oodles of Noodles" (Jimmy Dorsey's theme song "Contrasts"), "The Peanut Vendor," "Cuban Patato Chip" and "Caravan." —*Scott Yanow*

Just Wailin' / Feb. 14, 1958 / Original Jazz Classics ✦✦✦
This CD reissue of an earlier Prestige LP emphasizes (although does not stick exclusively to) the blues. The sextet has impressive players (flutist Herbie Mann, Charlie Rouse on tenor, guitarist Kenny Burrell, pianist Mal Waldron, bassist George Joyner and drummer Art Taylor) and the material (originals by Waldron, Burrell and Calvin Massey in addition to a brief "Jumpin' with Symphony Sid") is reasonably challenging, but the musicians never really come together as a group. The straightahead jam session has its strong moments and, as long as one keeps their expectations low, the music will be enjoyable despite the lack of major sparks. —*Scott Yanow*

Flute, Brass, Vibes and Percussion / 1960 / Verve ✦✦✦✦✦
In 1960, flutist Herbie Mann put together a very interesting band that was in its brief existence (before Mann's interests shifted elsewhere) one of the top in Afro-Cuban jazz. Utilizing four trumpets (including Doc Cheatham), up to three percussionists and a flute-vibes-bass-drums quartet, Mann performs four standards (including "Dearly Beloved," "I'll Remember April" and "Autumn Leaves") and two originals in a style that was beyond bop and much more African—and Cuban-oriented. This LP (long deserving of being reissued on CD) is quite underrated and is one of the finest of Mann's long career. —*Scott Yanow*

The Best of Herbie Mann / 1960-1969 / Atlantic ✦✦✦
It is probably true that no single LP could definitively sum up all of the directions that Mann explored in the swingin' '60s, but this one—part of a sprawling 1970 Atlantic Jazz Anthology series and transferred intact onto CD—could have done a more thorough job. There are only six selections, two of which are "Comin' Home Baby." Three of the tracks deal with various manifestations of R&B, of which "Memphis Underground" is the most obvious and most subtly percolating choice, and the remaining track is a murky cover of a movie tune, "A Man and a Woman" with Tamiko Jones on vocals. The timing—about 33 minutes—was short for an LP and it is downright stingy for a CD, given the volume and variety of Mann's Atlantic sessions. Still . . . the music is fairly good; there just should have been more of it. —*Richard S. Ginell*

Herbie Mann Anthology / Aug. 3, 1960-Apr. 18, 1992 / Rhino ✦✦
Rhino Records' two-CD retrospective of flutist Herbie Mann's career (subtitled "The Evolution of Mann") is put in a typically attractive box and has fine liner notes, but is somewhat flawed. There are no selections included from Mann's bop years (1954-58), and far too many cuts from the 1970s when his output was much less significant; in fact several of the numbers on the second disc are so dated as to be practically unlistenable. This two-fer does have some of the high points of Mann's career (including "Comin' Home Baby," "Memphis Underground" and "Hold on, I'm Comin'"), but it is better to get the original sessions instead. —*Scott Yanow*

Herbie Mann Returns to the Village Gate / Apr. 26, 1961+Nov. 17, 1961 / Atlantic ✦✦✦✦
By 1961, flutist Herbie Mann was really starting to catch on with the general public. This LP, a follow-up to his hit *At the Village Gate* (two songs are from the same gig while three others actually date from seven months earlier), features Mann in an ideal group with either Hagood Hardy or Dave Pike on vibes, Ahmed Abdul-Malik or Nabil Totah on bass, drummer Rudy Collins and two percussionists. Mann really cooks on four of his own originals, plus "Bags' Groove," blending in the influence of African, Afro-Cuban and even Brazilian jazz. Worth searching for. —*Scott Yanow*

● **At the Village Gate** / Nov. 17, 1961 / Atlantic ✦✦✦✦✦
Remarkably few of flutist Herbie Mann's recordings are available on CD, but fortunately, this one did get reissued. Mann's hit version of "Comin' Home Baby" from this live set became his first big hit. The composer Ben Tucker plays second bass on that cut, and Mann's other sidemen include vibraphonist Hagood Hardy, bassist Ahmed Abdul-Malik, drummer Rudy Collins and Chief Bey and Ray Mantilla on percussion. In addition to "Comin' Home Baby," Mann and his men perform mem-

orable versions of "Summertime" and "It Ain't Necessarily So"; the latter is 20 minutes long. Recommended. —*Scott Yanow*

Nirvana / Dec. 8, 1961-May 4, 1962 / Atlantic ✦✦✦✦

Brazil Blues / 1961-1962 / United Artists ✦✦✦✦

A slightly expanded version of flutist Herbie Mann's 1961-62 group performs African-, Cuban-, and Brazilian-influenced jazz on this appealing LP. With guitarist Billy Bean, vibraphonist Hagood Hardy, Dave Pike on marimba and four percussionists in the backup group, Mann's flute is well featured on tunes ranging from his own "B.N. Blues" and the standard "Brazil" to "One Note Samba." This album will be difficult to find but is worth the search. —*Scott Yanow*

Do the Bossa Nova with Herbie Mann / Oct. 16, 1962-Oct. 19, 1962 / Atlantic ✦✦✦✦

Rather than play a watered-down version of bossa nova in New York studios (which was becoming quite common as the bossa nova fad hit its peak in 1962), flutist Herbie Mann went down to Brazil and recorded with some of the top players of the style. Guitarist Baden Powell and the group of then-unknown pianist Sergio Mendes, which included drummer Dom Um Romao, formed the nucleus for this generally delightful album. Antonio Carlos Jobim himself dropped by to sing two of his compositions, including "One Note Samba," and even on the token jazz standard "Blues Walk," the music is as much Brazilian as it is jazz. This "fusion" works quite well; pity that the performances last appeared on this out-of-print LP. —*Scott Yanow*

Herbie Mann Live at Newport / Jul. 7, 1963 / Atlantic ✦✦✦

My Kinda Groove / Apr. 1964-May 1964 / Atlantic ✦✦✦

Flutist Herbie Mann was always interested in a variety of different grooves. On this out-of-print LP, the music ranges from bossa nova to Latin-jazz. Mann is backed either by an orchestra arranged by Rene Hernandez or Oliver Nelson (one song features fluegelhornist Clark Terry) or a septet with vibraphonist Dave Pike and guitarist Attila Zoller arranged by Oliver Nelson. Although the results are not all that essential, the music is pleasing and typically rhythmic; a good groove. —*Scott Yanow*

Standing Ovation at Newport / Jul. 3, 1965 / Atlantic ✦✦✦✦

Herbie Mann Today / Nov. 18, 1965-Nov. 19, 1965 / Atlantic ✦✦✦

Flutist Herbie Mann has always had wide interests in music. For this hard-to-find LP he is joined by three brass, vibraphonist Dave Pike, bassist Earl May, drummer Bruno Carr and percussionist Patato Valdes (with arrangements by Oliver Nelson) for a wide-ranging program that includes two Beatles songs, a selection from Burt Bacharach and two ancient pieces by Duke Ellington ("Creole Love Call" and "The Mooche"). In general Mann plays quite well, but there is little memorable about this generally commercial effort. —*Scott Yanow*

New Mann at Newport / Mar. 10, 1966+Jul. 10, 1966 / Atlantic ✦✦✦✦✦

A follow-up to his well-received *Standing Ovation at Newport* from 1965, this out-of-print LP features the popular flutist at the 1966 Festival (except for "All Blues," which is from four months earlier) jamming some heated grooves with trumpeter Jimmy Owens, trombonists Joe Orange and Jack Hitchcock, bassist Reggie Workman, drummer Bruno Carr and percussionist Patato Valdes. The material is stronger than was often the case on Mann's albums from this period, with Jimmy Heath's "Project S," Wayne Henderson's "Scratch" and "All Blues" being among the high points. Herbie Mann's 1960s recordings, which are generally superior to what he would be playing a decade later, tend to be underrated because he had become quite popular. This fine date is worth searching for. —*Scott Yanow*

Glory of Love / Jul. 26, 1967-Oct. 6, 1967 / A&M ✦✦

Flutist Herbie Mann is backed by a large rhythm section and a small horn section on this Creed Taylor-produced A&M set (which has been reissued on CD). Actually, the most interesting aspect of the R&B-oriented date (which includes such songs as "Hold On, I'm Comin'," "House of the Risin' Sun" and "Unchain My Heart") is that the up-and-coming flutist Hubert Laws is matched with Mann on several tracks. —*Scott Yanow*

The Wailing Dervishes / Sep. 21, 1967 / Atlantic ✦✦✦✦✦

One of Herbie Mann's more esoteric excursions, *The Wailing Dervishes* chases after a fusion that is extremely rare even today—jazz and the Middle East. Believe it or not, it works—and there are no commercial or ethnic compromises. Mann does not alter his familiar flute improvisational manner one whit, and he enlists the help of an Armenian-descended oud virtuoso, Chick Ganimian, whose folk-like solos on his stringed instrument blend in with, but derive hardly anything rhythmic from, jazz. Mann's regular sidekick Roy Ayers sounds comfortable on vibes, and Moulay "Ali" Hafid contributes the ethnic rhythms of his bongo-like dümbek to the percussion section. We also get a ringer in the form of bagpipes player Rufus Harley, whose guest solo on the blues "Flute Bag" is like the old saw of a dog walking on its hind legs; one applauds that it can be done at all. Recorded live, this LP

is definitely worth hunting for if you want to hear something really different. —*Richard S. Ginell*

☆ **Concerto Grosso in D Blues** / Nov. 1968 / Atlantic ✦✦✦✦✦

Not only is this rare LP one of Herbie Mann's own favorites, it is one of the most moving classical/jazz fusions ever recorded. Right after the 1968 Berlin Jazz Days festival, Mann, his quintet, co-composer/conductor William Fischer and a team of 80 Berlin musicians entered Teldec Studios to record the huge, ambitious title piece, a concerto that successfully spans the decades from Tchaikovsky to Stockhausen, and from New Orleans to free jazz. With some stretches of group improvisation, the piece has structure, memorable yet surprisingly simple motifs, and holds together even when stretched to the limits of coherence by general outbreaks of freeform. To fill out the album, Mann and Fischer came up with three "chamber" pieces that if anything, are even more successful than the main course. The best of the lot, the wistful "My Little Ones" (written for Mann's children), contains what is perhaps Mann's most haunting solo on record, at once loving and soaring, backed perfectly by Fischer's economical writing for double string quartet. Holler at Atlantic and/or Rhino to put this one back in the stores where it belongs. —*Richard S. Ginell*

Live at the Whisky / 1968 / Atlantic ✦✦✦✦

Flutist Herbie Mann had a particularly strong group in the late '60s, a sextet also including vibraphonist Roy Ayers, Steve Marcus on tenor, guitarist Sonny Sharrock, bassist Miroslav Vitous and drummer Bruno Carr. Although this LP is long out of print, and its total length is under a half-hour, the group's side-long jams on "Ooh Baby" and "Philly Dog" are danceable, funky and spontaneous, making this one of Herbie Mann's better sets of the era. —*Scott Yanow*

Memphis Underground / 1969 / Atlantic ✦✦✦

Herbie Mann has always been open to new trends in his music. For this 1969 studio session, he and three other top soloists (vibraphonist Roy Ayers and guitarists Larry Coryell and Sonny Sharrock) went down to Memphis and combined their talents with a top-notch local rhythm section. The music effectively mixes R&B and country rhythms with the lead jazz voices, although the material, which includes "Memphis Underground," "Hold On, I'm Comin'" and "Chain of Fools," is rather weak. —*Scott Yanow*

Push Push / Jul. 1, 1971 / Embryo ✦✦✦✦

Flutist Herbie Mann opened up his music on this date (and during the era) towards R&B, rock and funk music. The results were generally appealing, melodic and danceable. On such songs as "What's Going On," "Never Can Say Goodbye," "What'd I Say" and the title cut, Mann utilizes an impressive crew of musicians, which include guitarist Duane Allman and keyboardist Richard Tee. This out-of-print LP is worth picking up. —*Scott Yanow*

Hold On, I'm Comin' / 1972 / Atlantic ✦✦✦✦✦

This is one of the best Herbie Mann recordings and arguably his most rewarding of the 1970s. This long out-of-print LP features the leader/flutist, David Newman (on tenor and flute), the avant-garde guitarist Sonny Sharrock and a fine backup rhythm section (electric pianist Pat Rebillot, bassist Andy Muson and drummer Reggie Ferguson) stretching out on a variety of R&Bish material including "Respect Yourself," "Memphis Underground" and "Hold On, I'm Comin'." The high quality of the solos and the spirited ensembles (which were inspired by the audience at the 1972 New York Jazz Festival) make this a generally memorable session. —*Scott Yanow*

Mississippi Gambler / Nov. 1972 / Atlantic ✦✦✦

Here comes *Memphis Underground* Mk. III (*Memphis Two-Step* was Mk. II), with much the same cast of grits-and-gravy sessionmen from Memphis and David "Fathead" Newman along for the ride on tenor and flute. Yet this is by no means a retread of the best-selling sound, for Mann explores somewhat different grooves in a bouquet of pop hits and a couple of down-home-flavored Mann originals. Carlos "Patato" Valdes' congas add an alternative Latin flavor to the Memphis stew and Mann tootles along in his by-now-comfortable soul mode. Not essential listening, but good '70s soul-jazz nonetheless. —*Richard S. Ginell*

Turtle Bay / Oct. 1973 / Atlantic ✦✦✦

Herbie Mann goes back to the well of soul on this LP and comes up with another tastefully funky selection of rock/R&B hits mixed with a few originals of his own. Judging by the date of the album, he decided to let some of the early '70s hits simmer for a couple of years before deciding to lay them down. Side One (or, as credited on the label, the Up Side) finds him interacting gracefully with a sextet of New York session men, including the soulful guitarist David Spinozza and Latin percussionist Ralph MacDonald; the sound is a bit slicker than the grooves he got in Memphis, yet it percolates nicely. On Side Two (or the Down Side), a delicately applied string quartet adds a moody texture; though Mann's old cohort Bill Fischer is not the arranger (William Eaton, Pat Rebillot, and Mann do the honors), his influence seems clear. Herbie's own flute work is often low-key, maybe even a bit lazy, but he is audibly sympathetic with the material, unlike others who dutifully tried to swim with the pop currents in those days. —*Richard S. Ginell*

Reggae / 1974 / Atlantic ✦✦✦
Despite its title, most of the music on this out-of-print LP is not actually reggae but a mixture of jazz, R&B and pop. Flutist Herbie Mann, guitarists Mick Taylor and Albert Lee and keyboardist Pat Rebillot combine with the eight-piece Tommy McCook band to create some spirited and danceable (if a bit dated) music. Together they jam on the Beatles' "Ob-La-Di, Ob-La-Da," the traditional "Rivers of Babylon," Moe Koffman's old hit "Swingin' Shepherd Blues" and an 18-minute version of "My Girl." The results are fun, if not all that substantial. —*Scott Yanow*

Discotheque / 1974-1975 / Atlantic ✦✦

Water Bed / 1975 / Atlantic ✦✦

Bird in a Silver Cage / 1976 / Atlantic ✦✦

Herbie Mann with Joao Gilberto & Antonio Carlos Jobim / 1977 / Atlantic ✦✦✦
Nice, more light than emphatic Afro-Latin and jazz mixture by flutist Herbie Mann and composer/vocalist Joao Gilberto from 1977. The two make an effective team, with Gilberto's sometimes sentimental, sometimes impressionistic works effectively supported by Mann's lithe flute solos. —*Ron Wynn*

Brazil: Once Again / 1978 / Atlantic ✦✦
More than 15 years earlier, Herbie Mann was among the first Americans to record in Brazil with local musicians and really explore bossa nova at its roots. In 1978 for this LP he performed music of contemporary Brazil with a bigger accent on its pop music than on its jazz. With Pat Rebillot contributing arrangements and his keyboard work, the music is listenable, but somewhat forgettable. —*Scott Yanow*

Astral Island / 1983 / Atlantic ✦✦
Although Herbie Mann's flute is typically melodic and lively, the music on this out-of-print Atlantic album is generally fairly routine. Mann uses a "contemporary" electric rhythm section on a variety of then-recent Brazilian tunes, his own "Gold Rush" and even the "Theme from Tootsie"; the results were dated within a year of this record's release. —*Scott Yanow*

See Through Spirits / 1985 / Atlantic ✦✦✦
Herbie Mann's return to the Atlantic label in 1985 was only a one-shot deal that got some airplay but not enough sales to convince the now-corporate label to retain its onetime jazz cornerstone. Actually, this is one of the better Mann albums aimed at a contemporary market, mostly of a mild funk mindset with a few so-so guest vocals, yet always intelligent and musical, with Mann flying in customarily fluent form. The best track is a marvelously atmospheric, almost lost-sounding treatment of Marvin Gaye's "Inner City Blues," outfitted with an irresistible repeated electronic counter-theme. As a bonus, the Latinish leadoff track features guest appearances from once and future Mann associates David "Fathead" Newman and Dave Valentin. Except for a duo project with Valentin for GRP, this would be Mann's last album for a big label—and it is well worth searching out. —*Richard S. Ginell*

Jasil Brazz / 1987 / RBI ✦✦✦
Herbie Mann makes another of his periodic returns to Brazilian fare on this CD, but the country the ever-restless flutist visits is contemporary Brazil, not echoes of the bossa nova past. A lovely place it is, too, full of melodic, evocative material from the pens of Djavan and Ivan Lins, inspiring Mann to sail lightly and playfully like a kite above the modern samba beat. This was 1987, so the backing textures are mostly digital synthesizers, but Mark Soskin's touch is light, and he doesn't interfere with the grooves. Trumpeter Claudio Roditi makes a single, somewhat lackluster appearance on the otherwise luscious "Sonhos," Romero Lubambo is the facile guitarist, and soloist and band get to stretch out a lot on the multi-sectioned marathon "Little Chick a Dee." Everything goes down easily, and the result is one of Mann's best albums of that decade. —*Richard S. Ginell*

Opalescence / Dec. 1988-Jan. 1989 / Kokopelli ✦✦
This release by flutist Herbie Mann for his Kokopelli label is a disappointment. With a few exceptions (a remake of "Comin' Home Baby" and the bossa nova "Sir Charles Duke"), most of the Brazilian-based originals are rather forgettable, and the interpretations by Mann and his five-piece rhythm section often border on easy-listening music. The musicianship is high but the creative level is only so-so. —*Scott Yanow*

Caminho De Casa / Mar. 14, 1990-Mar. 16, 1990 / Chesky ✦✦✦
Flutist Herbie Mann and his group of the time (Jasil Brazz) perform contemporary Brazilian music on this CD, including three numbers by Ivan Lins. Some of the treatments are strictly easy listening or close to bossa nova, while others would fit into the "contemporary jazz" category. On the whole, this is a pleasing set, both as background music and for close listenings—one of Mann's better ones from the past 20 years. —*Scott Yanow*

Deep Pocket / Apr. 28, 1992-May 26, 1992 / Kokopelli ✦✦✦
This is a decent set that could have been a great one. Flutist Herbie Mann had a reunion in 1992 with many of his former sidemen (tenorman David "Fathead" Newman, guitarist Cornell Dupree and keyboardist Richard Tee) along with his contemporary pianist-vocalist Les McCann, and they play a wide ranging program of music (highlighted by "Moanin'," "Papa Was a Rolling Stone," "Sunny," "Mercy, Mercy, Mercy" and "Amazing Grace"). But somehow, once one gets beyond the nostalgia, the performances seem workmanlike and surprisingly uninspired, unlike Herbie Mann's live concerts with this group during the period. There are a few worthwhile moments, but this set is recommended mostly for Mann's greatest fans; get his earlier Atlantics instead. —*Scott Yanow*

Peace Pieces / Mar. 15, 1995-Apr. 17, 1995 / Kokopelli ✦✦✦✦✦
In 1961 Herbie Mann recorded an album (*Nirvana*) with the Bill Evans Trio and the experience made a major impression on the flutist. In his first purely straightahead jazz date in many years, Mann pays tribute to Evans by performing eight of his compositions plus one song ("Blue in Green") that the pianist long claimed Miles Davis permanently "borrowed" from him. On some selections, Mann overdubbed his flutes to form an orchestral sound behind his solos, and a few numbers have lyrical solos from Randy Brecker on fluegelhorn. Otherwise, this is essentially a pianoless quartet session (with guitarist Bruce Dunlap and occasional percussion) that finds Mann really digging into the often-complex material. The late Bill Evans, whose influence as a pianist (particularly in his chord voicings) continues to grow each year, has never been thought of as a major composer, but perhaps it is time for a reassessment. This is a highly recommended outing with the highlights, including "Funkallero," "Turn Out the Stars," "Waltz for Debbie" and "Peace Piece." —*Scott Yanow*

65th Birthday Celebration: Live at Blue Note NYC / Apr. 25, 1995-Apr. 30, 1995 / Lightyear ✦✦✦✦✦
To celebrate his 65th birthday, the influential flutist Herbie Mann played for a week at the Blue Note in New York, along with some of his favorite musicians. Among the many guests on this CD are such notables as trumpeters Claudio Roditi and Randy Brecker, altoists David Newman, Paquito D'Rivera and Bobby Watson, fellow flutist Dave Valetin, Tito Puente on timbales and several rhythm sections. Alternating between Brazilian music, vintage funk jazz (such as "Memphis Underground"), a catchy boogaloo blues ("Dippermouth") and a few straightahead tracks ("Au Privavem" and "Jeep's Blues"), the flutist sounds as if he had a great time. The diverse music is consistently infectious and joyful, with all eight selections well worth hearing. Highly recommended. —*Scott Yanow*

Shelly Manne

b. Jun. 11, 1920, New York, NY, **d.** Sep. 26, 1984, Los Angeles, CA
Drums, Leader / Bop, Cool
Shelly Manne made a countless number of records from the 1940s into the 1980s, but is best known as a good-humored bandleader who never hogged the spotlight. Originally a saxophonist, Manne switched to drums when he was 18 and started working almost immediately. He was with Joe Marsala's band (making his recording debut in 1941), played briefly in the big bands of Will Bradley, Raymond Scott and Les Brown, and was on drums for Coleman Hawkins' classic "The Man I Love" session of late 1943. Manne worked on and off with Stan Kenton during 1946-52, also touring with Jazz at the Philharmonic (1948-49) and gigging with Woody Herman (1949). After leaving Kenton, Manne moved to Los Angeles where he became the most in-demand of all jazz drummers. He began recording as a leader (his first session was cut in Chicago in 1951) on a regular basis starting in 1953, when he first put together the quintet Shelly Manne and His Men. Among the sidemen who were in his band during their long string of Contemporary recordings (1955-62) were Stu Williamson, Conte Candoli, Joe Gordan, Bob Enevoldsen, Joe Maini, Charlie Mariano, Herb Geller, Bill Holman, Jimmy Giuffre, Richie Kamuca, Victor Feldman, Russ Freeman, Ralph Pena, Leroy Vinnegar and Monty Budwig. Manne, who had the good fortune to be the leader of a date by the Andre Previn Trio that resulted in a major seller (jazz versions of tunes from *My Fair Lady*), always had an open musical mind, and he recorded some fairly free pieces on *The Three and the Two* (trios with Shorty Rogers and Jimmy Giuffre that did not have a piano or bass, along with duets with Russ Freeman) and enjoyed playing on an early session with Ornette Coleman. In addition to his jazz work, Manne appeared on many film soundtracks and even acted in *The Man with the Golden Arm*. He ran the popular club Shelly's Manne-Hole during 1960-74, kept his music open to freer sounds (featuring trumpeter Gary Barone and tenor saxophonist John Gross during 1969-72), played with the L.A. Four in the mid-'70s and was very active up until his death. Throughout his career, Shelly Manne recorded as a leader for Savoy, Interlude, Contemporary, Jazz Groove, Impulse, Verve, Capitol, Atlantic, Concord, Mainstream, Flying Dutchman, Discovery, Galaxy, Pausa, Trend, and Jazziz in addition to a few Japanese labels. —*Scott Yanow*

Shelly Manne & His Friends, Vol. 1 / Jan. 22, 1944-May 26, 1944 / Doctor Jazz
◆◆◆◆

Although this LP has drummer Shelly Manne as the leader, in reality the 23-year-old was just a sideman on these three four-song sessions; one of the main connecting threads. Manne is heard with clarinetist Barney Bigard and pianist Eddie Heywood in a trio (including fine versions of "Tea for Two," and Bigard's originals "Step Steps Up" and "Step Steps Down"), in another trio with the great altoist Johnny Hodges and Heywood (including a memorable version of "On the Sunny Side of the Street"), and on four rare titles with an Eddie Heywood group that includes Ray Nance on trumpet and violin, clarinetist Aaron Sachs, Don Byas on tenor and bassist John Simmons. These small-group swing performances are quite enjoyable, but unfortunately out of print. —*Scott Yanow*

Hot Skins / 1952 / V.S.O.P. ◆◆◆

This reissue LP of a session originally for the long-defunct Interlude label contains one of drummer Shelly Manne's more obscure dates. Manne teams up with the congas of Carlos Vidal and the bongos of Mike Pacheco in an oversized rhythm section of fairly unknown players; guitarist Tony Rizzi comes the closest to being a household name and pianist Robert Gil, who contributed four of the originals, never became famous. The accent is on Latin polyrhythms and the performances are generally quite likable and accessible, if not all that essential. —*Scott Yanow*

★ **Vol. 1: The West Coast Sound** / Apr. 6, 1953-Sep. 13, 1955 / Original Jazz Classics
◆◆◆◆◆

Drummer Shelly Manne's first sessions for Contemporary contain plenty of definitive examples of West Coast jazz. This CD has four titles apiece from a 1953 septet date with altoist Art Pepper, Bob Cooper on tenor, baritonist Jimmy Giuffre and valve trombonist Bob Enevoldsen, four from a few months later with Bud Shank in Pepper's place, and four other songs from 1955 when Manne headed a septet with altoist Joe Maini and Bill Holman on tenor in addition to Giuffre and Enevoldsen. With arrangements by Marty Paich (who plays piano on the first two dates), Giuffre, Shorty Rogers, Bill Russo, Holman and Enevoldsen, the music has plenty of variety, yet defines the era, ranging from Bill Russo's "Sweets" (a tribute to trumpeter Harry "Sweets" Edison), Giuffre's "Fugue," the Latin folk tune "La Mucura" and updated charts on older swing tunes. Highly recommended and proof (if any is really needed) that West Coast jazz was far from bloodless. —*Scott Yanow*

The Three and The Two / Sep. 10, 1954 / Original Jazz Classics ◆◆◆◆◆

These two sets for the Contemporary label (reissued on CD in the OJC label) are two of the more unusual sessions led by drummer Shelly Manne in the 1950s. *The Three* features trumpeter Shorty Rogers, Jimmy Giuffre alternating on clarinet, tenor and baritone, and Manne; no piano or bass. Some of the six performances (particularly the four originals) are quite free, particularly the completely improvised "Abstract No. 1." Although these selections were not influential, they rank second in chronological order (behind Lennie Tristano's performances of 1949) among free jazz records. The remainder of this set (*The Two*) is a duet between pianist Russ Freeman and Manne and is also quite advanced in spots, although in general it is a more swinging session, while still being unpredictable. Overall, a very interesting reissue. —*Scott Yanow*

Swinging Sounds, Vol. 4 / Jan. 19, 1956-Feb. 2, 1956 / Original Jazz Classics
◆◆◆◆

This early edition of "Shelly Manne & His Men" is a well-integrated unit featuring the light-toned trumpet of Stu Williamson, the cool but hard-driving altoist Charlie Mariano, pianist Russ Freeman and bassist Leroy Vinnegar, in addition to the drummer/leader. The excellent quintet plays one original apiece from each musician except Vinnegar, in addition to Bud Powell's "Un Poco Loco," Sonny Rollins' "Doxy," the standard "Bernie's Tune" and their closing theme, Bill Holman's "A Gem from Tiffany." A consistently swinging and well-rounded LP that is overdue to be reissued on CD. —*Scott Yanow*

Shelly Manne & His Friends, Vol. 1 / Feb. 11, 1956 / Original Jazz Classics ◆◆◆◆

In addition to his regular quintet recordings with "His Men," drummer Shelly Manne recorded a series of trio dates with "His Friends," which generally included pianist Andre Previn and bassist Leroy Vinnegar; eventually Red Mitchell would take over the bass spot. This initial release from the group, as with all of the later sets, is really a showcase for the remarkable piano playing of Previn, who was not even 27 yet, but already had a dozen years of major league experience behind him. The trio largely sticks to standards and jazz tunes on this date with "Tangerine," Johnny Hodges' "Squatty Roo" and "Girl Friend" being among the highlights. —*Scott Yanow*

More Swinging Sounds / Jul. 16, 1956-Aug. 16, 1956 / Original Jazz Classics
◆◆◆◆◆

Drummer Shelly Manne and his 1956 quintet (with trumpeter Stu Williamson, altoist Charlie Mariano, pianist Russ Freeman and bassist Leroy Vinnegar) perform

some challenging material on this CD reissue. The longest piece is Bill Holman's fifteen-and-a-half-minute four-part suite "Quartet" which, despite its potential complexity, actually swings fairly well. In addition, Manne & His Men interpret Johnny Mandel's obscure "Tommyhawk," a Mariano blues number, Charlie Parker's "Moose the Mooche" and Russ Freeman's "The Wind." Shelly Manne deserves great credit for being continually open to new directions and fresh material while staying on his own singular path. —*Scott Yanow*

☆ **My Fair Lady** / Aug. 17, 1956 / Original Jazz Classics ◆◆◆◆◆

This trio set by Shelly Manne & His Friends (which consists of the drummer/leader, pianist Andre Previn and bassist Leroy Vinnegar) was a surprise best-seller and is now considered a classic. Previn (who is really the main voice) leads the group through eight themes from the famous play including "Get Me to the Church on Time," "I've Grown Accustomed to Her Face," "I Could Have Danced All Night" and "On the Street Where You Live." A very appealing set that is easily recommended; an audiophile version has also been released on CD by DCC Jazz. —*Scott Yanow*

Lil' Abner / Feb. 6, 1957-Feb. 23, 1957 / Contemporary ◆◆◆

In a follow-up to their hit recording of music from *My Fair Lady,* Shelly Manne and his Friends (a trio with pianist Andre Previn, bassist Leroy Vinnegar and the drummer/leader) recorded nine songs from the play *Li'l Abner.* Although Johnny Mercer and Gene DePaul wrote the score, none of the songs caught on except for the ballad "Namely You" and this LP (whose music has not been reissued yet on CD) was not a bestseller. The musicians are in fine form, but the melodies are not too memorable (when was the last time anyone played "If I Had My Druthers" or "Progress Is the Root of All Evil"?). Actually, the main reason to search for this album is for the hilarious photo on the cover. —*Scott Yanow*

Bells Are Ringing / Apr. 15, 1958-Jul. 22, 1958 / Original Jazz Classics ◆◆◆

When Shelly Manne & His Friends (a trio starring pianist Andre Previn) had a surprise hit with their interpretations of melodies from *My Fair Lady,* it started a trend towards recording jazz versions of scores from plays. For this LP, Manne's trio (with Previn and bassist Red Mitchell) perform nine songs from the play *Bells Are Ringing.* Although seven of the pieces remained obscure, "The Party's Over" (which is heard twice) and particularly "Just in Time" caught on. As is always the case with this group, Previn's piano is the lead voice and his virtuosity, good taste, melodic improvising and solid sense of swing are chiefly responsible for the music's success. —*Scott Yanow*

Shelly Manne Plays Peter Gunn / Jan. 19, 1959+Jan. 20, 1959 / Original Jazz Classics ◆◆◆◆

Henry Mancini's writing for *Peter Gunn* was quite significant, for it was the first regular television series to utilize jazz as an integral part of its score. Half a year after the show debuted, drummer Shelly Manne, the members of his quintet (trumpeter Conte Candoli, altoist Herb Geller, pianist Russ Freeman and bassist Monty Budwig) and guest vibraphonist Victor Feldman (doubling on marimba) interpreted the *Peter Gunn* theme and nine selections from the show, including "Dreamsville." The enjoyable music (originally made for the Contemporary label) has been reissued as a CD in the Original Jazz Classics series. Mancini encouraged Manne to use the songs as vehicles for extended solos, and the results are swinging, standing apart from the show. Candoli and particularly Geller are in top form for this fairly memorable effort. —*Scott Yanow*

Son of Gunn!! / May 21, 1959-May 26, 1959 / Contemporary ◆◆◆

At the Blackhawk, Vol. 1 / Sep. 22, 1959-Sep. 24, 1959 / Original Jazz Classics
◆◆◆◆

Shelly Manne's Quintet was recorded extensively at San Francisco's Black Hawk club for three nights in 1959. Although not the most significant group that the drummer led, this edition (with trumpeter Joe Gordon, tenor saxophonist Richie Kamuca, pianist Victor Feldman and bassist Monty Budwig) was certainly capable of playing high-quality bebop. Originally their output was released on four LPs; the reissue expanded the music to five CDs. The first volume adds an alternate take of Frank Rosolino's "Blue Daniel" to a set that includes swinging versions of "Blue Daniel," "Poinciana," "Our Delight" and "Summertime." The extended performances are easily recommended to straightahead jazz fans. —*Scott Yanow*

At the Blackhawk, Vol. 2 / Sep. 23, 1959+Sep. 24, 1959 / Original Jazz Classics
◆◆◆◆

Vol. 2 of the five CDs that document drummer Shelly Manne's Quintet at the Black Hawk club in San Francisco during a three-day period adds a new alternate take of Charlie Mariano's "Step Lightly" to the original program ("Step Lightly," "What's New," "Vamp's Blues"). These lengthy performances ("Vamp's Blues" is over 19 minutes long) give trumpeter Joe Gordon, the cool-toned tenor saxophonist Richie Kamuca, pianist Victor Feldman, bassist Monty Budwig and the leader/drummer a chance to really stretch out. Fine 1950s bebop. —*Scott Yanow*

At the Blackhawk, Vol. 3 / Sep. 23, 1959-Sep. 24, 1959 / Original Jazz Classics
◆◆◆◆

Originally released as four LPs, the Shelly Manne's Quintet's three days at San Francisco's Black Hawk club is now documented on five CDs. The third volume adds a second (and longer) version of "Whisper Not" to the original rendition, Cole Porter's "I Am in Love" and the spontaneous 18-minute "Black Hawk Blues." Considering how much music was documented, it is fortunate that trumpeter Joe Gordon, tenorman Richie Kamuca, pianist Victor Feldman, bassist Monty Budwig and drummer Shelly Manne were in top form for this enjoyable gig. The music is high-quality straightforward and uncomplicated bebop. —*Scott Yanow*

At the Blackhawk, Vol. 4 / Sep. 23, 1959+Sep. 24, 1959 / Original Jazz Classics
◆◆◆◆

Shelly Manne's 1959 Quintet (with trumpeter Joe Gordon, tenor saxophonist Richie Kamuca, pianist Victor Feldman, bassist Monty Budwig and the drummer/leader) was not his most important, but it was a hard-swinging unit well versed in bebop. Their three days at the Black Hawk (a popular San Francisco jazz club during this era) was almost completely documented, originally on four LPs and now expanded to five CDs. As with the first three sets, the fourth volume adds an alternate take (of "Cabu") to the original program ("Cabu," "Just Squeeze Me," "Nightingale" and a full-length version of their theme "A Gem from Tiffany"). The lengthy solos are consistently excellent, making this entire series recommended to straightahead fans. —*Scott Yanow*

At the Blackhawk, Vol. 5 / Sep. 23, 1959+Sep. 24, 1959 / Original Jazz Classics
◆◆◆◆

Unlike the first four volumes of this series, which included three or four selections previously released plus a "new" alternate take, the final CD of the extensive documentation of the Shelly Manne Quintet's stint at the Black Hawk club consists entirely of previously unreleased material. Fortunately the performances by trumpeter Joe Gordon, tenor saxophonist Richie Kamuca, pianist Russ Freeman, bassist Monty Budwig and the drummer/leader are the same high level as on the more familiar material. They perform obscure songs by Horace Silver (has anyone else ever recorded his "How Deep Are the Roots?") and Victor Feldman in addition to a trio feature on "Wonder Why," the ballad "This Is Always" and a new version of the band's theme song "A Gem from Tiffany." —*Scott Yanow*

At the Manne-Hole, Vol. 1 / Mar. 3, 1961-Mar. 5, 1961 / Original Jazz Classics
◆◆◆◆◆

On the first of two CDs (both of which are straight reissues of the original LPs), Shelly Manne and His Men are heard in prime form performing live at their home base, Shelly's Manne-Hole. Trumpeter Conte Candoli was in particularly strong form throughout the stint, showing self-restraint, yet playing with power. Tenor saxophonist Richie Kamuca made for a complementary partner while pianist Russ Freeman and bassist Monty Budwig formed an excellent rhythm section with the leader/drummer. For *Vol. 1* they play "Love for Sale," Duke Ellington's fairly obscure "How Could It Happen to a Dream," "Softly as in a Morning Sunrise" and Dizzy Gillespie's uptempo blues "The Champ." This classic music falls between cool jazz and hard bop. —*Scott Yanow*

At the Manne-Hole, Vol. 2 / Mar. 3, 1961-Mar. 5, 1961 / Original Jazz Classics
◆◆◆◆◆

The second of two CDs (originally an LP for Contemporary) features Shelly Manne's Quintet in superior form at the legendary Shelly's Manne-Hole club in Hollywood. Trumpeter Conte Candoli (in top form) and the cool-toned tenor Richie Kamuca work together very well while the contributions of the rhythm section (pianist Russ Freeman, bassist Chuck Berghofer and the drummer/leader) should not be overlooked. Together they perform four standards (highlighted by "On Green Dolphin Street" and "If I Were a Bell") plus their closing theme "A Gem from Tiffany." Both of the volumes are easily recommended. —*Scott Yanow*

Checkmate / Oct. 17, 1961-Oct. 24, 1961 / Contemporary ◆◆◆

This LP from Shelly Manne is a bit different than his other recordings of scores. In the past, it was his trio with pianist Andre Previn that performed music from hit plays (most notably *My Fair Lady*). For this date, it is Manne's regular quintet (with trumpeter Conte Candoli, tenor saxophonist Richie Kamuca, pianist Russ Freeman and bassist Chuck Berghofer) that play seven themes from a now-forgotten television series (*Checkmate*) composed by Johnny Williams. None of the melodies caught on, but at least they gave these fine musicians some fresh material to improvise on. However, this album is not essential, despite some strong solos. —*Scott Yanow*

Sounds Unheard Of! / 1962 / Contemporary ◆◆

In the early days of stereo, there were quite a few demonstration and sound effects records released that were designed to show consumers the wide variety of sounds that could be accurately captured on record. Most of those releases are quite dispensable, and that includes this duet set by guitarist Jack Marshall and drummer

Shelly Manne. On a dozen standards, Marshall's playing serves as interludes between the percussion displays of Manne; the liners give a full description of every device he hits. The music is fairly routine, even if the sound is excellent for the period. It is of little surprise that this set has not been reissued yet on CD. —*Scott Yanow*

2-3-4 / Feb. 5, 1962 / Impulse! ◆◆◆◆

This unusual CD reissue has five selections from a date featuring the great tenor Coleman Hawkins, pianist Hank Jones, bassist George Duvivier and drummer Shelly Manne. Both "Take the 'A' Train" and "Cherokee" find the group at times playing two tempos at once (Manne sticks to doubletime throughout "Cherokee") and showing that they had heard some of the avant-garde players. The most swinging piece, "Avalon," was previously available only on a sampler, while "Me and Some Drums" features Hawkins and Manne in a very effective duet with the veteran tenor making his only recorded appearance on piano during the first half. This CD is rounded off by a pair of trio features for Eddie Costa (with Duvivier and Manne); one song apiece on vibes and drums. A very interesting set with more than its share of surprises. —*Scott Yanow*

My Son the Jazz Drummer / Dec. 17, 1962-Dec. 20, 1962 / Contemporary ◆◆◆

This album is a real rarity. For his final Contemprary LP of this era, drummer Shelly Manne and a sextet (with fluegelhornist Shorty Rogers, Teddy Edwards on tenor, Victor Feldman doubling on piano and vibes, guitarist Al Viola and bassist Monty Budwig) perform jazz versions of ten Jewish and Israeli-based melodies. Best known are such tunes as "Hava Nagila," "Bei Mir Bist Du Shein" and "Exodus." The arrangements by Rogers, Feldman, Edwards and Lennie Niehaus turn the music into modern mainstream jazz circa 1962, looking towards hard bop and the funky soul-jazz that was popular during the era. This long out-of-print historical curiosity is more successful than one might expect. —*Scott Yanow*

Manne, That's Gershwin / Feb. 24, 1965-Feb. 26, 1965 / Discovery ◆◆◆

On this Discovery LP (which reissues a set originally on Capitol), drummer Shelly Manne heads a big band (arranged by John Williams) on seven selections and his usual quintet of the era (with trumpeter Conte Candoli, altoist Frank Strozier, pianist Russ Freeman and bassist Monty Budwig) on the three remaining songs. The Gershwin program includes some of the typical familiar standards but also versions of the lesser-known "By Strauss," "The Real American Folk Song," "Prelude No.2" and "Theme from Concert in F." Although not all that memorable, this music generally swings, leaves space for concise solos and is fairly fresh. —*Scott Yanow*

Perk Up / Jun. 19, 1967-Jun. 20, 1967 / Concord Jazz ◆◆◆◆

This CD reissue brings back one of the oldest recordings ever issued by the Concord label, a set that was already nine years old when it debuted. Drummer Shelly Manne heads a strong quintet comprising trumpeter Conte Candoli, altoist Frank Strozier (who doubles on flute), pianist Mike Wofford and bassist Monty Budwig. Although the musicians are all associated with the West Coast hard bop tradition, there are plenty of moments during this stimulating set when they make it obvious that they had been listening with some interest to some of the avant-garde players, allowing the new innovations to open up their styles a bit. The fresh material (two standards and a pair of originals apiece by Strozier, Wofford and pianist Jimmy Rowles) inspire the soloists and the music is not at all predictable. Worth investigating. —*Scott Yanow*

Outside / Dec. 11, 1969-Dec. 12, 1969 / Contemporary ◆◆◆

Alive in London / Jul. 30, 1970-Jul. 31, 1970 / Original Jazz Classics ◆◆◆

This CD reissue is taken from drummer Shelly Manne's brief avant-garde period. Actually, Manne does not play much different than usual, but his sextet (trumpeter Gary Barone, John Gross on tenor, keyboardist Mike Wofford, guitarist John Morell and bassist Roland Haynes) was open to much freer improvising than one would have heard in Manne's more famous groups of the 1950s. John Gross is easily the most impressive soloist but, in general, the well-intentioned music is not all that memorable. —*Scott Yanow*

Mannekind / 1972 / Mainstream ◆◆

One of the least interesting groups that drummer Shelly Manne led can be heard on this long out-of-print Mainstream LP. Manne tried hard to keep his mind open to the avant-garde and free jazz during this era, but his septet (comprising trumpeter Gary Barone, John Gross on tenor, pianist Mike Wofford, guitarist John Morell, bassist Jeffry Castleman and percussionist Brian Moffatt) only had one distinctive soloist (Wofford) and the group originals (by Wofford and Morell) are uncomfortable and immediately forgettable. Despite a few good solos, this is one of the weaker Shelly Manne albums. —*Scott Yanow*

Hot Coles / 1975 / Flying Dutchman ◆◆◆

This is an interesting, if often-eccentric LP. Drummer Shelly Manne and a variety of L.A.-based musicians of the mid-'70s (including pianist Mike Wofford, bassist Chuck Domanico, Tom Scott on flute and soprano, guitarist Tommy Tedesco, trumpeter Oscar Brashear and Victor Feldman on vibes and piano) perform unusual versions of eight veteran Cole Porter standards. The somewhat spontaneous arrangements are full of unpredictable moments and, even if everything does not work, the surprising nature of the performances holds one's interest throughout. —*Scott Yanow*

Plays Richard Rodgers' Musical "Rex" / May 1976 / Discovery ✦✦

Drummer Shelly Manne, who first started the trend of jazz musicians recording scores from plays with *My Fair Lady* in 1956, 20 years later failed to hit pay dirt with his interpretations of eight forgettable songs from Richard Rodgers' Broadway musical *Rex*. There are some good solos from his sidemen (which include Lew Tabackin on tenor and flute, keyboardist Mike Wofford and bassist Chuck Domanico), but in general, this is a so-so effort with the musicians being defeated by the material. —*Scott Yanow*

Essence / Jul. 5, 1977-Jul. 6, 1977 / Galaxy ✦✦✦✦✦

French Concert / 1977 / Galaxy ✦✦✦✦✦

This is an excellent LP long overdue to be reissued on CD. Drummer Shelly Manne features pianist Mike Wofford (and bassist Chuck Domanico) on two standards ("Softly, As in a Morning Sunrise" and "Body and Soul") before welcoming the great altoist Lee Konitz to the group for four others (highlighted by "What Is This Thing Called Love" and "Take the Coltrane"). This combination of jazzmen works quite well, resulting in music that is both swinging and explorative. —*Scott Yanow*

Double Piano Jazz Quartet at Carmelo's, Vol. 1 / Sep. 12, 1980-Sep. 13, 1980 / Trend ✦✦✦

An unusual 1980 session with drummer Shelly Manne heading a group that includes pianists Bill May and Alan Broadbent and bassist Chuck Domanico, but no brass, reeds, or woodwinds. Manne's crisp, steady drumming teams with Domanico's consistent bass to set the rhythmic foundation, while pianists May and Broadbent alternate solos and interact, complement, or contrast with Manne and Domanico. —*Ron Wynn*

Double Piano Jazz Quartet at Carmelo's, Vol. 2 / Sep. 12, 1980-Sep. 13, 1980 / Trend ✦✦✦

In Zurich / Feb. 1984 / Contemporary ✦✦✦✦

Seven months before his death, drummer Shelly Manne was still in apparently good health for this trio outing with pianist Frank Collett and bassist Monty Budwig, Manne's next-to-last record. Collett has long been an underrated pianist and the LP is a fine outing for him. Highlights of the straightahead set include Miles Davis's "Solar," "Good Bait," "All of You" and a "French Medley" comprising "Where Is Your Heart" (from "Moulin Rouge") and "La Vie En Rose." Tasteful and swinging music. —*Scott Yanow*

Remember / May 4, 1984-Jan. 15, 1985 / Jazzizz ✦✦✦✦

When Shelly Manne died of a heart attack on September 26, 1984, at age 64, it was a major surprise, for he had been in apparently good health. This rather obscure LP from the Jazzizz label (no connection to the similarly-titled magazine) is the drummer's final recording, and it features his last working group, an excellent trio with pianist Frank Collett and bassist Monty Budwig. Highlights of the live set (Manne's final recording) include "Speak Low," "My Romance" and "Hi-Fly." In addition, Collett and Budwig on January 15, 1985, performed Collett's original "Remember" in tribute to the late drummer. Worth searching for. —*Scott Yanow*

Wingy Manone (Joseph Matthews Manone)

b. Feb. 13, 1900, New Orleans, LA, d. Jul. 9, 1982, Las Vegas, NV
Trumpet, Vocals / Dixieland

Wingy Manone was an excellent Dixieland trumpeter whose jivey vocals were popular and somewhat reminiscent of his contemporary, Louis Prima. He had lost his right arm in a streetcar accident when he was ten, but Manone (who Joe Venuti once gave one cuff link for a Christmas present!) never appeared to be handicapped in public (effectively using an artificial arm). He played trumpet in riverboats starting when he was 17, was with the Crescent City Jazzers (which later became the Arcadian Serenaders) in Alabama, and made his recording debut with the group in the mid-'20s. He worked in many territory bands throughout the era before recording as a leader in 1927 in New Orleans. By the following year, Manone was in Chicago and soon relocated to New York, touring with theater companies. His "Tar Paper Stomp" in 1930 used a riff that later became the basis for "In the Mood." In 1934, Manone began recording on a regular basis, and after he had a hit with "The Isle of Capri" in 1935, he became a very popular attraction. Among his sidemen on his 1935-41 recordings were Matty Matlock, Eddie Miller, Bud Freeman, Jack Teagarden, Joe Marsala, George Brunis, Brad Gowans and Chu Berry. In 1940, Manone appeared in the Bing Crosby movie *Rhythm on the River*, he soon wrote his humorous memoirs *Trumpet on the Wing* (1948), and he would later appear on many of Crosby's radio shows. Wingy Manone lived in Las Vegas

from 1954 up until his death, and he stayed active until near the end although he only recorded one full album (for Storyville in 1966) after 1960. —*Scott Yanow*

● **The Wingy Manone Collection, Vol. 1 (1927-1930)** / Apr. 11, 1927-Sep. 19, 1930 / Collector's Classics ✦✦✦✦✦

The Danish Collector's Classics label (which is available through Storyville) has been reissuing all of trumpeter Wingy Manone's recordings as a leader during his prime years on this series of CDs. Manone is heard in 1927 with his "Harmony Kings," in 1928 with his "Club Royale Orchestra" (a quintet), as a sideman with Benny Goodman in 1929, with the Cellar Boys the following year, and heading a group in 1930 under the name of "Barbecue Joe and His Hot Dogs." There are 11 good-humored vocals by Manone (and plenty of his trumpet), along with significant appearances by such sidemen as tenor saxophonist Bud Freeman, drummer Gene Krupa, clarinetist Frankie Teschemacher and pianist Art Hodes (the latter making his recording debut). Of particular interest is "Tar Paper Stomp," which in 1930 has the same basic melody as "In the Mood," which Glenn Miller made famous nine years later. This perfectly-done reissue is highly recommended to classic jazz fans. —*Scott Yanow*

Jazz Heritage: Jam and Jive / Aug. 28, 1930-Mar. 1, 1944 / MCA ✦✦✦

This out-of-print 1983 LP from MCA's *Jazz Heritage* series is inexcusably brief (under a half-hour of music), but does contain some fine performances from trumpeter-vocalist Wingy Manone. There are five titles from 1930, including "Big Butter and Egg Man," "Up the Country Blues" and "Tar Paper Stomp"; the latter uses the same melody as "In the Mood," which had not been "written" yet. There are also two of the six sections of the extended "Jam and Jive" from 1941, and three songs (including a remake of his hit "Isle of Capri") from 1944. If found at a budget price, this Dixielandish set might serve as an introduction to Wingy Manone, but serious collectors can avoid it. —*Scott Yanow*

The Wingy Manone Collection, Vol. 2 / May 2, 1934-Sep. 26, 1934 / Collector's Classics ✦✦✦✦✦

The second of Collector's Classics' complete reissuance of trumpeter-vocalist Wingy Manone's early recordings has some particularly interesting recordings. There are four songs on which Manone utilizes some of the sidemen from Ben Pollack's Orchestra (all of whom would soon join Bob Crosby), he leads a quartet called "The Four Bales of Cotton" on a spirited version of "Shine," and for ten songs is featured with the New Orleans Rhythm Kings, a pickup group featuring the NORK's original trombonist George Brunis and clarinetist Sidney Arodin. The most unusual session took place August 15, 1934, for Manone led a date that also included trombonist Dicky Wells, the then-unknown clarinetist Artie Shaw, tenor saxophonist Bud Freeman, a strong rhythm section and either Teddy Wilson or Jelly Roll Morton on piano; this was Morton's only recording session of 1931-37. Highly recommended to swing and Dixieland collectors as are the other CDs in this series. —*Scott Yanow*

The Wingy Manone Collection, Vol. 3 / Oct. 3, 1934-May 3, 1935 / Collector's Classics ✦✦✦✦✦

The third CD in the Collector's Classics Wingy Manone series covers the trumpeter-singer's recordings during a seven-month period. With the success of his novelty version of "The Isle of Capri" (which is included here along with a previously unissued alternate take), Manone began to record steadily in 1935 and was quite popular. His Dixieland-oriented performances usually included his vocals, some heated but melodic trumpet and short statements from his sidemen which on this CD include trombonist Santo Pecora, clarinetists Matty Matlock or Sidney Arodin and tenor saxophonist Eddie Miller. Among the more memorable selections are "Royal Garden Blues," "She's Crying for Me," "Zero," "Nickel in the Slot," "Love Is Just Around the Corner" and a performance ("Sliphorn Sam") with a Russ Morgan group, although this version of "On the Good Ship Lollipop" is not too essential. —*Scott Yanow*

Wingy Manone Collection, Vol. 4 1935-36 / May 27, 1935-Jan. 28, 1936 / Collector's Classics ✦✦✦✦✦

Trumpeter Wingy Manone recorded fairly frequently during the year covered by this CD, and his sextet/septet includes such top soloists (at one time or another) as clarinetists Matty Matlock and Joe Marsala, tenors Eddie Miller and Bud Freeman and trombonist George Brunis; plus trombone great Jack Teagarden is aboard for one session. With Manone taking spirited vocals on every selection, these Dixielandish performances gained an audience of their own during this early year in the swing era. Highlights of the fourth volume in this highly recommended series (which is reissuing all of Manone's recordings in chronological order) include "Lulu's Back in Town," "I'm Shooting High" and "The Music Goes 'Round and 'Round." —*Scott Yanow*

1936 / Mar. 10, 1936-Jul. 1, 1936 / Classics ✦✦✦✦

The Classics series (along with the unrelated Collectors Classics label) has been reissuing all of trumpeter Wingy Manone's recordings of the 1930s, many of which did not even reappear during the LP era. By 1936, Manone's records were getting a bit predictable, but taken in small doses they are still quite fun. Manone sings on all of the 22 selections except "Panama," verbally urges on his sidemen (which at times include clarinetist Joe Marsala and tenor saxophonist Eddie Miller), and takes some Louis Armstrong-inspired solos. This CD is the fourth Manone set put out by Classics, and has four sessions from a four-month period; highlights include "Is It True What They Say About Dixie," "Dallas Blues," "Swingin' at the Hickory House," "Sing Me a Swing Song" and "Panama." —*Scott Yanow*

Wingy Manone, Vol. 1 / Apr. 9, 1936-Aug. 6, 1940 / RCA ✦✦✦✦
Until the CD era began, this LP from the celebrated RCA *Vintage* series was the best Wingy Manone album around. A sampler of the trumpeter-vocalist's Victor recordings, the 16 numbers on the album jump around chronologically but are fairly consistent. The high points include "Limehouse Blues," "My Honey's Lovin' Arms," "Blue Lou," "Swingin' at the Hickory House," "Mama's Gone, Good-bye" and "Dallas Blues"; among the sidemen are clarinetist Buster Bailey, tenor saxophonist Chu Berry and trombonist George Brunis. —*Scott Yanow*

1936-1937 / Aug. 20, 1936-May 1937 / Classics ✦✦✦✦
The fifth in Classics' complete Wingy Manone series of CDs features the good-humored trumpeter/singer on 21 selections from a nine-month period. A fair amount of Wingy's sidemen are obscure, but they do sometimes include clarinetists Joe Marsala and Matty Matlock and trombonist George Brunis. Manone sings on all of the selections, and even if many of the songs are far from classics, the swinging solos and jubilance of these Dixieland-oriented performances make the music worth hearing. Highlights include "A Good Man Is Hard to Find" (which has Manone interacting with singer Sally Sharon), "In the Groove," "Let Me Call You Sweetheart," "Floatin' Down to Cotton Town" and "You Showed Me the Way." —*Scott Yanow*

1937-1938 / May 1937-1938 / Classics ✦✦✦✦

Wingy Monone and Sidney Bechet: Together at Town Hall / 1947 / Jazz Archives ✦✦✦✦

Wingy Manone / Papa Bue's Viking Jazzband / Oct. 11, 1966 / Storyville ✦✦✦✦✦
Wingy Manone's next-to-last recording session finds the 62-year-old trumpeter/vocalist still in prime form. Teamed up with trombonist Papa Bue's Viking Jazzband (an excellent Danish Dixieland group), Manone sounds happy to be in such sympathetic company. He plays three of his blues and a variety of veteran standards, including "When You're Smiling," "How Come You Do Me Like You Do" and "Black & Blue." This is an enjoyable effort from the formerly popular entertainer, and it seems strange that he would not record again for another nine years. —*Scott Yanow*

Michael Mantler

b. Aug. 10, 1943, Vienna, Austria
Trumpet / Avant-Garde
Never a major trumpeter, Michael Mantler was most important as an organizer of projects and for his work behind the scenes, most notably for the WATT label. After studying at the Vienna Academy of Music and University, he emigrated to the US so as to attend Berklee in 1962. Mantler, who moved to New York two years later, played trumpet for a time with Cecil Taylor, and in the mid-1960s helped in the formation of the Jazz Composer's Guild. He co-led a big band with Carla Bley, toured Europe in 1965-66 with the Jazz Realities group (a quintet including Bley and Steve Lacy), and formed the Jazz Composers' Orchestra Association, a nonprofit organization that performed and recorded new music. Mantler, who married Carla Bley (their daughter is keyboardist Karen Mantler), recorded with Gary Burton (*A Genuine Tong Funeral*) and the JCOA (most notably *Communications*). He was also a part of Charlie Haden's Liberation Music Orchestra. Mantler worked with Bley on her large projects, formed the New Music Distribution Service in 1972, and then the following year founded the label Watt Works with Bley. He has since recorded on an irregular basis for Watt (usually ambitious and somewhat dry works), led an occasional orchestra, and continued running the label. —*Scott Yanow*

No Answer / Jul. 1973-Nov. 1973 / Watt ✦✦✦
Music by Mantler, Don Cherry, Carla Bley, and Jack Bruce with words from Samuel Beckett. —*Michael G. Nastos*

Silence / Jan. 11, 1977 / Virgin ✦✦✦

Movies / Aug. 1979+Mar. 1980 / Virgin ✦✦✦✦

More Movies / Aug. 1979-Mar. 1980 / Watt ✦✦✦✦

Something There / Feb. 1982-Jul. 1982 / Watt ✦✦✦

Alien / Mar. 1985-Jul. 7, 1985 / ECM ✦✦
Ambitious four-part composition that works at times and bombs at others. —*Ron Wynn*

● **Live** / Feb. 1987 / ECM ✦✦✦✦✦
Performance art at its height, with Jack Bruce (b), Don Preston (synth), and Pink Floyd drummer Nick Mason. —*Michael G. Nastos*

Many Have No Speech / Apr. 1987-Dec. 1987 / ECM ✦✦
An intriguing concept with 42-piece Danish Radio Concert Orchestra, rockers, and jazz elements. Not for all tastes. —*Ron Wynn*

Cerco Un Paese Innocente / 1996 / ECM ✦✦✦
Michael Mantler's *Cerco Un Paese Innocente* is a tribute to the Italian writer Giuseppe Ungaretti. Mantler sets Ungaretti's poetry to evocative chamber music that brings new textures and emotions to Ungaretti's words. Not all of the compositions work, but those that do are majestic and the entire effort is quite admirable. —*Thom Owens*

Larance Marable

b. May 21, 1929, Los Angeles, CA
Drums / Hard Bop
Larance Marable is one of the stalwart mainstream drummers on the Los Angeles jazz scene, in demand for his driving cymbal work and exquisite little bombs. Largely self-taught, he started playing bop in the 1950s with a stream of stellar visitors to L.A., including Charlie Parker, Dexter Gordon, Stan Getz, Zoot Sims and Wardell Gray. He recorded with the Montgomery Brothers in 1960 and also appears on records by Chet Baker, George Shearing, Sonny Stitt, Milt Jackson, and several other significant musicians. He recorded as a leader with tenorman James Clay in 1956 for the Jazz West label. In the 1970s, he toured with Supersax and Bobby Hutcherson, and has since worked in L.A. jazz clubs and concert locales. In the late 1980s and 1990s, Marable has been a regular member of Charlie Haden's Quartet West, recording frequently with the group for Verve. —*Richard S. Ginell*

● **Tenorman** / Sep. 1956 / Blue Note ✦✦✦✦✦

Steve Marcus

b. Sep. 18, 1939, New York, NY
Tenor Saxophone, Soprano Saxophone / Hard Bop
A fine saxophonist who is often a bit overlooked, Steve Marcus has led relatively few sessions throughout his career. After attending Berklee he played with Stan Kenton in 1963. He recorded with Gary Burton (1966) and the Jazz Composer's Orchestra, and had stints with Herbie Mann (1967-70) and Woody Herman. He led an early fusion group (the Count's Rock Band) and then gained some attention when he played with Larry Coryell's Eleventh House (1971-73). In 1975, Marcus joined Buddy Rich's Orchestra where he was a star soloist and an important lieutenant up until Rich's death in 1987. Steve Marcus has recorded as a leader for Vortex (1967-69), Storyville (1970) and much more recently Red Baron (1992). —*Scott Yanow*

Steve Marcus and 201 / 1992 / Red Baron ✦✦✦✦
Steve Marcus' Red Baron CD crosses the artificial boundary between traditional and contemporary, mixing together swinging jazz with aspects of fusion. Doubling on tenor and soprano, Marcus and his quintet (with guitarist John Cariddi, Rave Tesar on synthesizer, bassist Vince Fay and drummer Jim Young) perform often rock-ish group originals and "Three Day Sucker," Marcus' longtime feature with the Buddy Rich big band. While his sidemen are both competent and somewhat anonymous, the leader's strong saxophone solos make this effort quite worthwhile. —*Scott Yanow*

● **Smile** / Feb. 16, 1993 / Red Baron ✦✦✦✦✦
This is one of Steve Marcus' best all-around recordings to date. Alternating barn-burning versions of "Oleo," "Confirmation" and "Woody 'n You" with ballads, Marcus tends to play the slower pieces on his lyrical soprano, saving the romps for his passionate tenor. Backed by pianist John Hicks, bassist Christian McBride and drummer Marvin "Smitty" Smith, Marcus is consistenly brilliant within the bebop tradition, although McBride's bowed bass solo on "Confirmation" almost steals the show. —*Scott Yanow*

Rick Margitza

b. Oct. 24, 1961, Detroit, MI
Tenor Saxophone / Post-Bop, Hard Bop
One of the "Young Lions," Rick Margitza is an excellent tenor saxophonist most inspired by Wayne Shorter, Michael Brecker and John Coltrane. He started on the violin when he was four (his grandfather was a cellist and his father a violinist with the Detroit Symphony), studied classical piano for a bit, and also played oboe before switching to tenor in high school. He attended Wayne State University,

Berklee, the University of Miami and finally Loyola University in New Orleans, where he lived and played for four years. Margitza toured with Maynard Ferguson and also Flora Purim and Airto before moving to New York in 1988. He spent part of '88 in Miles Davis' group and then cut three sets as a leader for Blue Note during 1989-91. His 1994 outing for Challenge found Margitza showing increasing individuality. —*Scott Yanow*

Color / Apr. 1989-May 1989 / Blue Note ◆◆◆

Rick Margitza's debut features the playing of a young tenor saxophonist who mixes together the usual influences: Michael Brecker, Wayne Shorter and John Coltrane. In his favor is that Margitza's 11 originals (performed with a septet that includes guitarist Steve Masakowski, pianist Joey Calderazzo and Jim Beard on synthesizers) range from a Coltranish blues to the poppish "Color Scheme," from brooding ballads to uptempo straightahead explorations. The main weak point is that some of Margitza's solos sound as if he they were taken straight from exercise books. Less formal studying and more jamming will probably eventually eliminate that problem, for Margitza certainly had the technique and the power at this early point in his career. —*Scott Yanow*

Hope / Jun. 1990 / Blue Note ◆◆◆

Play any three-minute segment from this CD by tenor saxophonist Rick Margitza and one would swear that this was a Wayne Shorter record from the mid-'70s. Only the superior recording quality and technology would betray the fact that these performances are of more recent vintage. Even though the original songs do not sound familiar, there is nothing on this moody date that stamps it as Rick Margitza's. The young saxophonist tries his best, often overdubbing his tenor and soprano, varying moods in his compositions and sometimes utilizing the voices of Phil Perry and Ed Calle as part of the ensemble, but in general the music is overly dry and Margitza's tones are a near duplicate of Shorter's, especially on tenor. Despite some good playing (especially from guitarist Steve Masakowski and pianist Joey Calderazzo), this was a premature effort from the young saxophonist, who was not quite ready to be leading his own record session. —*Scott Yanow*

● **This Is New** / May 27, 1991-May 28, 1991 / Blue Note ◆◆◆◆

The problem with tenor saxophonist Rick Margitza at this early stage in his career was that he sounded almost exactly like Wayne Shorter with a strong streak of John Coltrane on ballads. Margitza partly overcomes his lack of individuality by giving the standards on his CD some fresh interpretations. The melody of "On Green Dolphin Street" sneaks up about halfway through and then is barely hinted at while the theme of "Just in Time" does not pop up until just before the closing vamp. Margitza displays maturity on "Body & Soul" and "Everything Happens to Me," and is quite stormy on the more uptempo material. Trumpeter Tim Hagans' guest appearance on "Beware of the Dogs" really seems to inspire Margitza and the rhythm section (pianist Joey Calderazzo, bassist Robert Hurst and drummer Jeff "Tain" Watts) is excellent. Now if only Margitza could solve his identity problem! —*Scott Yanow*

Hands of Time / Dec. 17, 1994+Dec. 18, 1994 / Challenge ◆◆◆◆

Work It / Nov. 1, 1995 / Steeple Chase ◆◆◆

Game of Chance / Oct. 15, 1996-Oct. 16, 1996 / Challenge ◆◆◆◆

Kitty Margolis

b. Nov. 7, 1955, San Mateo, CA

Vocals / Bop

One of the most talented of the female jazz singers of the 1990s, Kitty Margolis made a strong impression with her appearances at the Monterey Jazz Festival (starting in 1989). A chance-taking scat singer and a constant improviser, Margolis played guitar for ten years starting when she was 12, performing in folk-rock groups in high school. She attended Harvard (during which she sang in a Western swing band) and San Francisco State University. In 1978 she began to perform as a jazz singer and often collaborated in the early '80s with guitarist/singer Joyce Cooling; among her sidemen were Eddie Henderson and Pee Wee Ellis. By 1986 Kitty Margolis was working regularly in the San Francisco Bay area with her trio, and she had visited Europe on a regular basis. The series of recordings for her Madkat label display the depth of her musical interests and the consistency of her strong (and still developing) talent. —*Scott Yanow*

Live at the Jazz Workshop / 1989 / Madkat ◆◆◆◆◆

This CD (which adds "Too Marvelous for Words" to the original seven-song LP program) was the recording debut of Kitty Margolis, a talented bop-based singer who is both an expert scatter and a constant improviser. With fine backup from pianist Al Plank, bassist Scott Steed and drummer Vince Lateano, Margolis is in excellent early form on a set of high-quality standards with the high points including "I Concentrate on You," "All Blues" and "All the Things You Are." —*Scott Yanow*

● **Evolution** / 1993 / Madkat ◆◆◆◆◆

Kitty Margolis is a brilliant scat singer who is also expert at interpreting lyrics and shows a great deal of enthusiasm in her performances. Her second release for her Madkat label is a wide-ranging set encompassing everything from Brazilian music, blues and Margolis' new lyrics to Wayne Shorter's "Footprints" and Cedar Walton's "Firm Roots," to some standards, ballads and hot scatting ("Anthropology"). The backup crew is fairly impressive too, with Joe Henderson's tenor present on half of the selections, guitarist Joe Louis Walker adding fire to the blues numbers, and pianist Dick Hindman offering sympathetic support throughout. This versatile set is a perfect introduction to one of the most exciting jazz singers of the 1990s. —*Scott Yanow*

Straight Up with a Twist / 1997 / Madkat ◆◆◆◆

Kitty Margolis' third recording for her Madkat label is certainly her most varied and eccentric. Each of the 13 selections has its share of surprises, with Kitty's regular sextet joined by several guest players, most notably including trumpeter Roy Hargrove (heard in a supporting role on three numbers) and Charles Brown (featured in vocal duets with Margolis on a playful version of "The 'In' Crowd" and a barely recognizable "Wouldn't It Be Lovely"). The usually childlike "Gettin' to Know You" is given a complex but logical arrangement that utilizes Kitty's overdubbed voices, the sensuous classic "Fever" is taken in 7/4 time, "The Night Has a Thousand Eyes" gives the singer a chance to shine over Brazilian rhythms, and Thelonious Monk's "In Walked Bud" is made funky, given new lyrics and renamed "In Walked Bean." Other interesting moments include Kitty showing off her bop chops on "My Romance," getting lowdown on "Today I Sing the Blues," and concluding "Speak Low" in surprising fashion by showing off her interest in Indian music with some very odd wordless vocalizing over the closing vamp. Kitty Margolis' continually intriguing set (which is much less bop-oriented than her previous efforts) also has a few misses, but overall is a strong step forward. —*Scott Yanow*

Tania Maria (Correa Reis Maria)

b. May 9, 1948, Sao Luis, Brazil

Vocals, Piano / Latin Jazz, Pop-Jazz

An enthusiastic performer who has the occasional tendency to ramble on too long, Tania Maria has been popular in the US ever since she started recording for Concord in 1980. She studied classical music, moved to Paris in 1974 and relocated to New York in 1981. A spirited singer and a rhythmic pianist, Tania Maria has recorded for Barclay (1978), Accord (1978-79), Concord, Manhattan and World Pacific. —*Scott Yanow*

Piquant / Dec. 1980 / Concord Jazz ◆◆◆◆

Tania Maria's debut American release helped introduce her to US audiences. Joined by a quintet that includes guitarist Eddie Duran, the exuberant vocalist and pianist performs four of her colorful originals, a couple of obscurities, and a song apiece by Jobim ("Triste") and Ivan Lins. Maria's mixture of Latin jazz with Brazilian pop is quite appealing and helped make her a popular star; this was one of her better efforts. —*Scott Yanow*

● **Taurus** / Aug. 1981 / Concord Jazz ◆◆◆◆◆

Tania Maria's second Concord release (which, as with her other output, has been reissued on CD) is still one of her best sets. The repertoire—five of her originals, "Imagine" and "Cry Me a River"—is diverse; the band (a sextet with two percussionists and guitarist Eddie Duran) is excellent, and there is plenty of space for Maria's keyboard work in addition to her exuberant vocals. Throughout the set of Brazilian jazz/pop, Tania Maria is heard in prime form, making this an excellent introduction to her enthusiastic music. —*Scott Yanow*

Come with Me / Aug. 1982 / Concord Jazz ◆◆◆◆◆

In the early 1980s, Tania Maria burst upon the US music scene, playing an exuberant blend of Brazilian pop and jazz. Her first few recordings for Concord Picante (of which this is the third) remain her most rewarding sets. Maria's spirited vocals and hyper keyboard work star throughout the date (which finds her interpreting seven of her originals and "Embraceable You"), supported by a sextet including both Eddie Duran and Jose Neto on guitar. Worth checking out. —*Scott Yanow*

Love Explosion / Sep. 1983-Oct. 1983 / Concord Jazz ◆◆◆

The Wild! / Sep. 1984 / Concord Jazz ◆◆◆◆

Live in concert, Tania Maria has the tendency to stretch out simple rhythmic ideas a bit past their optimal length. Recorded at San Francisco's Great American Music Hall, this club date is mostly fairly well controlled, while living up to its title. Teamed up with a hot Latin quintet (including guitarist Dan Carillo and John Purcell on alto and soprano), Tania Maria clearly enjoys going over the top on some of the numbers (six of the seven are her originals), showing plenty of spirit, although one imagines that the set would have been more exciting experienced live than on record. —*Scott Yanow*

Made in New York / 1985 / Manhattan ◆◆◆

Bela Vista / 1990 / World Pacific ✦✦✦
1990 release, Latin-oriented recordings. —*Ron Wynn*

Forbidden Colors / Nov. 8, 1991 / Manhattan ✦✦✦✦

Outrageous / Apr. 1993 / Concord Picante ✦✦
Tania Maria sticks to Brazilian pop music on her concise but unremarkable program. The entire focus is on her vocals and there is little or no improvising over the repetitious vamps. The closer one listens to the admittedly danceable music, the more tedious it sounds. —*Scott Yanow*

Charlie Mariano

b. Nov. 12, 1923, Boston, MA
Alto Saxophone, Soprano Saxophone, Flute / Bop, World Music
Charlie Mariano's career can easily be divided into two. Early on, he was a fixture in Boston, playing with Shorty Sherock (1948), Nat Pierce (1949-50) and his own groups. After gigging with a band co-led by Chubby Jackson and Bill Harris, Mariano toured with Stan Kenton's Orchestra (1953-55), which gave him a strong reputation. He moved to Los Angeles in 1956 (working with Shelly Manne and other West Coast jazz stars), returned to Boston to teach in 1958 at Berklee, and the following year had a return stint with Kenton. After marrying Toshiko Akiyoshi, Mariano co-led a group with the pianist on and off up to 1967, living in Japan during part of the time and also working with Charles Mingus (1962-63).

The second career began with the formation of his early fusion group Osmosis in 1967. Known at the time as a strong bop altoist with a sound of his own developed out of the Charlie Parker style, Mariano began to open his music up to the influences of folk music from other cultures, pop and rock. He taught again at Berklee, traveled to India and the Far East and in the early '70s settled in Europe. Among the groups Mariano has worked with have been Pork Pie (which also featured Philip Catherine), the United Jazz and Rock Ensemble and Eberhard Weber's Colours. Charlie Mariano's airy tones on soprano and the nagaswaram (an Indian instrument a little like an oboe) fit right in on some new agey ECM sessions, and he also recorded as a leader through the years for Imperial, Prestige, Bethlehem, World Pacific, Candid (with Toshiko Akiyoshi in 1960), Regina, Atlantic, Catalyst, MPS, CMP, Leo and Calig among others. —*Scott Yanow*

★ **Boston All Stars** / Dec. 1951-Jan. 27, 1953 / Original Jazz Classics ✦✦✦✦✦
Altoist Charlie Mariano plays very much in a Charlie Parker style on these early recordings from Boston (eight from 1951 and six from 1953), but his arrangements for the octet (six of the pieces from the former session) are quite original and unpredictable; only trumpeter Joe Gordon among the otherwise obscure personnel ever gained much recognition. The later six selections match Mariano with trumpeter Herb Pomeroy and the brilliant pianist Dick Twardzik in a quintet; Twardzik, with his odd mixture of Bud Powell and Lennie Tristano, consistently steals the show. A historical and generally enjoyable set, it's recommended to bop fans. —*Scott Yanow*

Charlie Mariano Plays / Dec. 21, 1953-Jan. 27, 1955 / Fresh Sound ✦✦✦✦✦
Back in the 1950s, Charlie Mariano was one of the most promising of the bop-oriented altoists. This Fresh Sound CD reissues 16 selections from three sessions originally released by Bethlehem. The personnel is consistent with Mariano joined by pianist Claude Williamson, bassist Max Bennett, drummer Stan Levey, trombonist Frank Rosolino (on eight songs) and the cooltoned trumpeter Stu Williamson (on 11). The repertoire mixes together fairly basic group originals and swinging standards with many fine solos by the horns. An excellent example of Charlie Mariano's playing in the 1950s. —*Scott Yanow*

Charlie Mariano Quartet / Jul. 11, 1954 / Fresh Sound ✦✦✦✦
This Fresh Sound CD reissues a Bethlehem album by altoist Charlie Mariano from 1954, the prime of his bebop period. Mariano, whose alto tone mixes together Benny Carter and Charlie Parker, is accompanied by a quiet and supportive rhythm section comprising pianist John Williams, bassist Max Bennett and drummer Mel Lewis. Switching to tenor on four of the dozen selections, Mariano sounds in excellent form on ten standards, a blues and his own "Floormat." A swinging cool-bop date. —*Scott Yanow*

Blue Stone / Jul. 31, 1971 / Black Lion ✦✦✦
Charlie Mariano, who gained his initial fame for playing bop and cool jazz in the 1950s, by the early '70s was exploring a mixture of world music and funk/R&B. This interesting but now somewhat dated CD reissue finds Mariano switching between alto, soprano, flute and the nagasuram in a quintet with flutist Chris Hinze and a European rhythm section that explores three Mariano originals (including the previously unreleased 18-minute "Blue Stone"), a piece by Hinze and a traditional South Indian folk song. The moody music contains plenty of intriguing colors and some surprising moments. —*Scott Yanow*

Reflections / Mar. 14, 1974-Mar. 15, 1974 / Catalyst ✦✦✦
With Finnish musicians, including saxophonist Eero Koivistoinen. —*Michael G. Nastos*

Helen Twelve Trees / May 6, 1976-May 8, 1976 / BASF ✦✦✦✦

October / Oct. 5, 1977-Oct. 7, 1977 / Inner City ✦✦✦
A '77 session with onetime Charlie Parker imitator Charlie Mariano now as immersed in Asian and Indian music as he ever was in bop. He's working with a European rhythm section that includes keyboardist Rainer Bruninghaus and bassist Barre Phillips. There are some compositions that reflect Mariano's jazz background, while others have everything from classical strains to Asian scales and instruments. —*Ron Wynn*

Innuendo / Jul. 1991-Sep. 1991 / Lipstick ✦✦

Eric Marienthal

b. Dec. 19, 1957, Sacramento, CA
Alto Saxophone, Soprano Saxophone / Crossover Jazz
Every once in a while (generally when he appears as a sideman), Eric Marienthal shows listeners that he can break away from playing crossover and is capable of being a creative improviser. He attended Berklee for two years, went on tour for seven months with Al Hirt, worked in the studios (including being on the staff at Disney) and then in 1986 he met Chick Corea. Soon he was in Corea's Elektric Band and started recording his own dates for GRP.

Eric Marienthal has also toured with David Benoit and Lee Ritenour, in addition to recording with the GRP All-Star Big Band. —*Scott Yanow*

Voices of the Heart / Dec. 1987-Jan. 1988 / GRP ✦✦✦✦
Altoist Eric Marienthal's debut as a leader has four notable guest appearances by his employer, keyboardist Chick Corea, and one spot for guitarist Frank Gambale. Otherwise, he is generally joined by a quintet also including keyboardist Jim Cox, the great bassist John Patitucci, drummer Vinnie Colaiuta, and guitarist Pat Kelley. The ten obscure songs (only two by the leader) are worthwhile, if not overly memorable, but Marienthal's soulful solos are always fun to hear. —*Scott Yanow*

Round Trip / 1989 / GRP ✦✦✦
Doubling on alto and soprano, Eric Marienthal sounds fine on this set, but the repertoire (mostly by band members) is generally less interesting. Joined by three of the members of Chick Corea's Elektric Band (pianist Corea, bassist John Patitucci and drummer Dave Weckl) plus keyboardist Mitchel Forman and a variety of other top studio players, Marienthal shows some individuality in his solos (along with the influence of David Sanborn), but the somewhat commercial music (all clocking in between 4:09 and 5:02) was clearly recorded with potential radio airplay as the chief goal. —*Scott Yanow*

Collection / 1989-1994 / GRP ✦✦✦
This budget-line anthology from saxophonist Eric Marienthal features cameo appearances from the likes of Chick Corea, Jeff Lorber, David Benoit, John Patitucci, Vinnie Colaiuta and Russel Ferrante. —*Jason Ankeny*

● **Crossroads** / 1990 / GRP ✦✦✦✦✦

Oasis / 1991 / GRP ✦✦
Eric Marienthal, a key sideman with Chick Corea's Elektric Band, sticks to R&B-oriented jazz on this 1991 release. His alto playing is often a soundalike of David Sanborn's, while his soprano looks towards Kenny G. and George Howard. The electronic rhythms (programmed by Jeff Lorber or Russell Ferrante) are funky and danceable, but rather lifeless, while many of the originals are little more than rhythmic vamps. Although a talented enough player, at this early stage Eric Marienthal needed more seasoning (and a stronger purpose) before he could be taken seriously as a leader. —*Scott Yanow*

One Touch / 1993 / GRP ✦✦✦

Street Dance / 1994 / GRP ✦✦
Altoist Eric Marienthal plays well enough in parts of this CD, but the material is generally poppish, a bit anonymous and forgettable. Since Marienthal co-wrote many of the songs with producer/keyboardist Jeff Lorber, he inadvertently proves that he is a stronger saxophonist than he is a composer. Vibraphonist Gary Burton makes an unimportant cameo on one song. Marienthal has sounded better elsewhere. —*Scott Yanow*

Easy Street / 1997 / I.E. Music ✦✦✦✦
Considering that this is a commercial CD geared towards radio airplay (all 11 selections clock in between 4-6 minutes), it is surprising how well altoist Eric Marienthal plays. The best is "Half & Half," which is partly straightahead and has some fine soloing. Otherwise, Marienthal stays in an R&B vein, but shows that his own sound has become increasingly distinctive (while still bowing a bit towards Grover Washington, Jr.). The backup group (which mostly provides quietly funky electronic dance rhythms) includes guitarist Lee Ritenour, keyboardist John Beasley and (on

"Secret Passion") keyboardist Jeff Lorber. A good example of Eric Marienthal's continual growth as a player. —*Scott Yanow*

Dodo Marmarosa (Michael Marmarosa)

b. Dec. 12, 1925, Pittsburgh, PA
Piano / Bop

One of the finest pianists of the bop era, Dodo Marmarosa's career was cut short by mental illness. He playeed locally at first and then made strong contributions to the orchestras of Gene Krupa (1942-43), Tommy Dorsey (1944), Charlie Barnet (taking the opening piano solo on the hit "Skyliner") and Artie Shaw (playing with the Gramercy Five). Marmarosa was often teamed with Barney Kessel (with whom he had been with Barnet and Shaw) and both settled in Los Angeles by 1946. Marmarosa recorded with Boyd Raeburn and Lester Young, became the house pianist for the Atomic label, made an important session with Charlie Parker in 1947 (which resulted in "Relaxin' in Camarillo") and worked with his trio. But after a Savoy date in 1950, nothing was heard from him for a decade. Marmarosa resurfaced in Chicago during 1961-62 to record two live outings and a session with Gene Ammons (for Argo and Prestige), but then disappeared, permanently retiring in Pittsburgh. Dodo Marmarosa's 1946-47 recordings have been partially reissued by Onyx and Dial, while live dates surfaced on Jazz Showcase, Swing House and Phoenix. —*Scott Yanow*

● **Up in Dodo's Room** / 1946-Dec. 3, 1947 / Jazz Classics ✦✦✦✦

Dodo Marmarosa was one of the most brilliant pianists to emerge during the bebop era. Unfortunately, he had emotional problems in the 1950s that resulted in his career being cut short, but this reissue CD features Dodo at the peak of his powers. Marmarosa is heard on four unaccompanied piano solos, on five numbers in a trio with cellist Harry Babasin (who plays his instrument like a string bass) and drummer Jackie Mills, on two selections with trumpeter Howard McGhee, and on "Bird Lore" with trumpeter Charlie Parker. In addition, this CD has six alternate takes from Marmarosa's trio session. On such numbers as "Tea for Two," "Bopmatism," "Dodo's Dance" and "Dary Departs," Dodo Marmarosa comes up with one inventive chorus after another, making this his definitive release. —*Scott Yanow*

Pittsburgh 1958 / 1958 / Uptown ✦✦✦✦

All of the music on this 1997 CD was previously unissued, and it is a major find. The legendary but troubled bop pianist Dodo Marmarosa recorded very little after the late 1940s (other than a few dates in the early 1960s), and he has a relatively slim discography for a player of his stature. The bulk of the release is taken from a 1958 live trio date in which Marmarosa is joined by a couple of local Pittsburgh musicians, bassist Danny Matri and drummer Henry Sciullo. The pianist shows plenty of brilliance on the boppish standards, including "Moose the Mooche," "Always," "Cherokee" and "Billie's Bounce." Also on this CD are three numbers from a 1962 radio show (probably Dodo's last recordings) in which Marmarosa interacts with a quintet on some fairly modern tunes, along with a trio number from 1956 and two selections with a quintet in 1957. Overall, the recording quality is decent, while the playing is quite special. An extra bonus are the extensive liner notes, which include a 1995 interview with Marmarosa, plus the decision to lead off the CD with a brief excerpt from the talk. Highly recommended to bop collectors. —*Scott Yanow*

Dodo's Back / May 9, 1961-May 10, 1961 / Argo ✦✦✦✦

Joe Marsala (Joseph Francis Marsala)

b. Jan. 4, 1907, Chicago, IL, **d.** Mar. 3, 1978, Santa Barbara, CA
Clarinet / Swing, Dixieland

An excellent swing clarinetist who could fit into Dixieland settings yet welcomed Dizzy Gillespie to a memorable session in 1945, Joe Marsala was the older brother of trumpeter Marty Marsala (1909-75) and the husband of the great jazz harpist Adele Girard (1913-1993). He freelanced around Chicago starting in the late '20s including with Wingy Manone and Ben Pollack. He recorded with Manone in the mid-'30s, playing with Wingy on 52nd Street during 1935-36. Marsala soon became a leader himself and during the next ten years (much of which was spent playing at the Hickory House), he featured such sidemen as Adele Girard (whom he married in 1937), Buddy Rich (his first important job), Red Allen, Eddie Condon, Joe Bushkin, Dave Tough, Shelly Manne, Max Kaminsky and his brother Marty, among others. He retired from full-time playing in 1948, working instead in music publishing. However Joe Marsala continued playing on an occasional basis into the 1960s. His studio recordings from 1936-42 are all collected on a Classics CD. Other sessions have been released on IAJRC, Aircheck, Jazzology, Savoy, Black & White, Musicraft and a 1957 album for Stereo-O-Craft. —*Scott Yanow*

★ **Joe Marsala 1936-1942** / Jan. 17, 1936-Jul. 6, 1942 / Classics ✦✦✦✦✦

All 21 of clarinetist Joe Marsala's early recordings as a leader are on this enjoyable CD. An excellent swing clarinetist who was flexible enough to play hot on Dixieland records, Marsala's six sessions reflect his versatile musical tastes. Among his more celebrated sidemen on these formerly rare selections are trumpeters Marty Marsala (his brother), Pee Wee Erwin, Bill Coleman and Max Kaminsky, trombonist George Brunis, altoist Pete Brown, violinist Ray Biondi, drummers Buddy Rich and Shelly Manne (both making their recording debuts) and several fine rhythm sections. Eleven of the numbers have the notable addition of Marsala's wife, Adele Girard, the first great jazz harpist. Her hot harp playing on "Bull's Eye" and "I Know that You Know" steals the show. Highly recommended. —*Scott Yanow*

Lower Register / Jan. 17, 1936-Oct. 28, 1944 / IAJRC ✦✦✦✦

This very interesting collector's LP contains a variety of rarities featuring clarinetist Joe Marsala. He is heard with the "Six Blue Chips" in 1936 (a sextet with trumpeter Pee Wee Erwin), and on a studio side apiece with trumpeter Wingy Manone and bandleader Vic Lewis (which also features cornetist Bobby Hackett). In addition, Marsala is featured on radio broadcasts with Manone and Hackett and an "Impromptu Ensemble" with Eddie Condon; plus, there are two numbers that have him leading a quartet featuring his wife, harpist Adele Girard. The flip side of the album is a 29-minute "America Dances" broadcast from August 18, 1939 that has seven songs and an all-star cast: Marsala, trumpeter Marty Marsala, valve trombonist Brad Gowans, Bud Freeman on tenor, harpist Girard (the best in her field), rhythm guitarist Eddie Condon, drummer Dave Tough, and an unidentified bassist. Throughout the album, the music is Dixieland-flavored swing. Recommended to fans of the era. —*Scott Yanow*

Featuring Adele Girard / Oct. 23, 1942+Oct. 30, 1942 / Aircheck ✦✦✦✦

Contained on this album are two full-length radio broadcasts featuring the obscure Joe Marsala big band. While Marsala was an excellent swing clarinetist, and there are some trumpet solos by Max Kaminsky and Marty Marsala, plus featured vocals by Don Darcey and Al Jennings, the real reason to acquire this album is for the occasional harp solos of Adele Girard, whose consistently brilliant playing makes one wonder why she did not become famous in her own right. A strong improviser who could swing, Girard deserved much more fame. Worth searching for. —*Scott Yanow*

Branford Marsalis

b. Aug. 26, 1960, Breaux Bridge, LA
Tenor Saxophone, Soprano Saxophone, Alto Saxophone / Post-Bop, Hard Bop

The oldest of the four musical Marsalis brothers, Branford Marsalis has already had an impressive career. After studying at Southern University and Berklee, Branford toured Europe with the Art Blakey big band in the summer of 1980 (playing baritone), played three months with Clark Terry and then spent five months playing alto with Art Blakey's Jazz Messengers (1981). He mostly played tenor and soprano while with Wynton Marsalis' influential group (1982-85), at first sounding most influenced by Wayne Shorter but leaning more towards John Coltrane at the end. The musical telepathy between the two brothers (who helped to revive the sound of the mid-'60s Miles Davis Quintet) was sometimes astounding. Branford toured with Herbie Hancock's V.S.O.P. II. in 1983 and recorded with Miles Davis (1984's *Decoy*). In 1985 when he left Wynton to join Sting's pop-rock group, it caused a major (if temporary) rift with his brother that made headlines. Marsalis enjoyed playing with Sting, but did not let the association cause him to forget his musical priorities. By 1986 he was leading his own group, which eventually consisted of pianist Kenny Kirkland, bassist Bob Hurst and drummer Jeff "Tain" Watts; sometimes the band was a pianoless trio that really allowed Marsalis to stretch out. After a couple of film appearances (in *School Daze* and *Throw Mama from the Train*), Branford Marsalis became even more of a celebrity when he joined Jay Leno's *Tonight Show* as the musical director in 1992. However, being cast in the role of Leno's sidekick rubbed against Marsalis' temperament and after two years he had had enough. Branford Marsalis, who attempted to mix together hip-hop and jazz in his erratic *Buckshot LeFonque* project, has recorded steadily for Columbia ever since 1983 (including a classical set), and still seems to be searching for his niche. —*Scott Yanow*

Scenes in the City / Apr. 18, 1983-Nov. 29, 1983 / Columbia ✦✦✦✦✦

Branford Marsalis' debut as a leader is ambitious yet consistently successful. On "Scenes of the City," his narrative is in the same spirit of some of Charles Mingus' recordings of the 1950s. Otherwise the music is in the modern mainstream vein with Marsalis (on tenor and soprano) hinting strongly at Wayne Shorter and John Coltrane, along with a touch of Sonny Rollins. The backup crew includes such notable Young Lions as pianist Mulgrew Miller and Kenny Kirkland, bassist Charnett Moffett, and drummers Jeff "Tain" Watts and Marvin "Smitty" Smith, in addition to bassist Ron Carter. It's an impressive start to a notable career. —*Scott Yanow*

Royal Garden Blues / Mar. 18, 1986-Jul. 2, 1986 / Columbia ✦✦✦✦

Branford Marsalis' second album as a leader followed his first by three years and he had grown a lot in the interim. He had switched permanently to tenor (doubling on soprano), left his brother Wynton's group, toured with Sting and begun heading his own group. Although using quartets on each of the seven selections, Marsalis varies the personnel quite a bit, utilizing pianists Ellia Marsalis, Kenny Kirkland, Larry Willis and Herbie Hancock, bassists Ron Carter, Charnett Moffett and Ira Coleman and drummers Ralph Peterson, Al Foster, Marvin "Smitty" Smith and Jeff Watts. One of Branford's more playful albums, the repertoire includes a tribute of sorts to his native New Orleans on "Royal Garden Blues" plus "Strike Up the Band" and recent originals. An excellent outing. —*Scott Yanow*

Renaissance / Dec. 31, 1986-Jan. 28, 1987 / Columbia ✦✦✦✦✦

The high point of Branford Marsalis' third Columbia release as a leader is a 15-minute version of Jimmy Rowles' "The Peacocks" played in a trio with pianist Herbie Hancock and bassist Buster Williams. The remainder of the program matches Marsalis with pianist Kenny Kirkland, bassist Bob Hurst and drummer Tony Williams on a pair of standards ("Just One of Those Things" and a live version of "St. Thomas"), J.J. Johnson's "Lament" and originals by Marsalis and Williams. Although he did not have an immediately recognizable sound on tenor and soprano at this point, it was obvious from nearly the start that Branford Marsalis would have a very significant career. This is one of his better early efforts. —*Scott Yanow*

Random Abstract / Aug. 1987 / Columbia ✦✦✦✦✦

Branford Marsalis (on tenor and soprano) and his 1987 quartet (which also includes pianist Kenny Kirkland, bassist Delbert Felix and drummer Lewis Nash) stretch out on a wide repertoire during this generally fascinating set. Very much a chameleon for the date, Marsalis does close impressions of Wayne Shorter on "Yes and No," John Coltrane ("Crescent City"), Ben Webster (a warm version of "I Thought About You"), Ornette Coleman ("Broadway Falls") and even Jan Garbarek (on a long rendition of Coleman's "Lonely Woman"); the release also includes a jam on Kirkland's "LonJellis," a piece without chord changes. This is one of Branford Marsalis most interesting (and somewhat unusual) recordings to date. —*Scott Yanow*

● **Trio Jeepy** / Jan. 3, 1988-Jan. 4, 1988 / Columbia ✦✦✦✦✦

Branford Marsalis clearly had a lot of fun during this set. On seven of the ten numbers included on the double-LP (the CD reissue actually has one less selection), Marsalis romps on tenor and soprano in a trio with veteran bassist Milt Hinton and drummer Jeff "Tain" Watts; the remaining three numbers have Delbert Felix in Hinton's place. The performances are quite spontaneous (the occasional mistakes were purposely left in) and Marsalis really romps on such tunes as "Three Little Words," "Makin' Whoopee" and "Doxy." On the joyful outing that is also one of Branford Marsalis' most accessible recordings, Milt Hinton often steals the show. —*Scott Yanow*

Crazy People Music / Jan. 10, 1990-Mar. 1, 1990 / Columbia ✦✦✦✦

Branford Marsalis (on tenor and soprano) performs four of his originals, Bob Hurst's "The Dark Knight," Keith Jarrett's obscure "Rose Petals" and "The Ballad of Chet Kincaid" (co-written by Bill Cosby and Quincy Jones) on this outing with his 1990 quartet, an impressive group that also includes pianist Kenny Kirkland, bassist Hurst and drummer Jeff "Tain" Watts. None of the songs would catch on, but Marsalis is heard throughout in prime form, sounding more original than usual and really pushing himself. —*Scott Yanow*

The Beautiful Ones Are Not Yet Born / May 16, 1991-May 18, 1991 / Columbia ✦✦✦✦✦

This set is one of Branford Marsalis' strongest of the 1990s. Marsalis really stretches out on eight numbers, including six of his originals (the other two songs are by bassist Bob Hurst). There is one guest appearance apiece from brother-trumpeter Wynton and tenor saxophonist Courtney Pine, but otherwise Branford is accompanied only by Hurst and drummer Jeff "Tain" Watts. His playing is often reminiscent in style (but not really sound) of John Coltrane; he is more concise and disciplined than in some of his early-'90s concert appearances, and Marsalis is at his most explorative on this inventive blowing session. —*Scott Yanow*

Bloomington / Sep. 23, 1991 / Columbia ✦✦

This live set (part of which was included in the performance film *The Music Tells You*) features Branford Marsalis and his longtime trio (bassist Robert Hurst and drummer Jeff "Tain" Watts) really stretching out on six pieces. Most of the playing is unfortunately very long-winded and rather dull. Marsalis seems content to play the part of a chameleon, doing his impressions of late-period Coltrane, Sonny Rollins and (when he switches to soprano) Ornette Coleman. Also, the music lacks variety and Marsalis is off-mike part of the time. Although the final two selections give this set a much needed dose of humor, it is too little too late. —*Scott Yanow*

I Heard You Twice the First Time / 1992 / Columbia ✦✦✦

Branford Marsalis plays the blues on this interesting, if erratic, CD. Among his many guests are B.B. King (although there is surprisingly no interaction between Marsalis and King), John Lee Hooker, Russell Malone, Linda Hopkins (who comes across very well), Joe Louis Walker and brothers Wynton and Delfeayo. Ranging from hints of field hollers and New Orleans to country blues, a vignette ("Brother Trying to Catch a Cab (On the East Side) Blues") and a few more conventional burnouts, this is an intriguing set that is worth picking up. —*Scott Yanow*

Dark Keys / Jul. 31, 1996-Aug. 1996 / Columbia ✦✦✦

Dark Keys is Branford Marsalis' first major solo album since taking a leave from recording to be the musical director of *The Tonight Show* in 1993. Instead of following through with the hip-hop inclinations of Buckshot LeFonque, Marsalis has returned to traditional jazz, yet this is far from standard bop. Marsalis pushes at the borders of post-bop, adding elements of hip-hop and rock 'n' roll, making for an adventurous and exciting listen. Occasionally, his experiments are unsuccessful, yet they are never less than intriguing. —*Leo Stanley*

Delfeayo Marsalis

b. Jul. 28, 1965, New Orleans, LA
Trombone / Bop, Hard Bop

Imagine being the younger brother of Wynton and Branford Marsalis! It is little surprise that Delfeayo Marsalis took a while before making his debut on records. The son of Ellis Marsalis and the older brother of drummer Jason (1976-), Delfeayo was always interested in engineering and he started off as a busy record producer, studying both trombone and studio production at Berklee. In addition to his producing, Delfeayo has written some of the most absurd liner notes ever seen, raving about his brothers while trying to pretend that he is an impartial observer! More importantly, Delfeayo Marsalis is a fine J.J. Johnson-inspired trombonist who toured with Ray Charles, Art Blakey's Jazz Messengers and Abdullah Ibrahim before recording his first album as a leader in 1992. In recent times he has been a member of Elvin Jones' Jazz Machine. —*Scott Yanow*

● **Pontius Pilate's Dec** / 1992 / Novus ✦✦✦✦✦

Delfeayo Marsalis' long-delayed debut as a leader on records features the young trombonist on ten of his originals. One should ignore the religious titles and the drawings in the liner notes and enjoy the music for what it is: advanced hard bop. Marsalis' idol is J.J. Johnson and his trombone playing is similar to Johnson's style. Among the many artists who make appearances on this set are tenor saxophonist Joshua Redman (for the opening title cut), trumpeter Scotty Barnhart, brothers Branford (soprano on five numbers), Jason (who at the time was a brilliant 14-year-old drummer) and Wynton (whose highly expressive trumpet solo on "The Weary Ways of Mary Magdalene" is one of the high points of his career) and various sidemen from the Marsalis bands. —*Scott Yanow*

Musashi / Jul. 29, 1996-Jul. 30, 1996 / Evidence ✦✦✦✦

Delfeayo Marsalis' long-overdue second recording finds the trombonist still heavily influenced by his idol, J.J. Johnson, but also displaying an increasingly original personality. A quintet date with Mark Gross on alto and soprano and a Japanese rhythm section (plus guest spots for Branford and Ellis Marsalis), the date alternates standards such as "Too Marvelous for Words" and "Summertime" with passionate originals including the intense "Miyamoto Musashi" and "Queen Himiko." Throughout the set, Marsalis shows the willingness to take chances and stretch himself, and the result is consistently stirring post-bop music. —*Scott Yanow*

Ellis Marsalis

b. Nov. 14, 1934, Gert Town, LA
Piano / Post-Bop, Hard Bop

It is a bit ironic that Ellis Marsalis had to wait for sons Wynton and Branford to get famous before he was able to record on a regular basis, but Ellis has finally received his long-overdue recognition. The father of six sons (including Wynton, Branford, Delfeayo and Jason), Ellis Marsalis' main importance to jazz may very well be as a jazz educator; his former pupils (in addition to his sons) include Terence Blanchard, Donald Harrison, Harry Connick, Jr., Nicholas Payton and Kent and Marlon Jordan among others. He started out as a tenor saxophonist, switching to piano while in high school. Marsalis was one of the few New Orleans musicians of the era who did not specialize in Dixieland or rhythm & blues. He played with fellow modernists (including Ed Blackwell) in the late '50s with AFO, recorded with Cannonball and Nat Adderley in the 1960s, played with Al Hirt (1967-70) and was busy as a teacher. Marsalis freelanced in New Orleans during the 1970s and taught at the New Orleans Center for Creative Arts. He recorded with Wynton and Branford on *Father and Sons* in 1982, an album that they shared with Chico and Von Freeman. Since then, Marsalis has recorded for ELM, Spindletop (a duet session with Eddie Harris), Rounder, Blue Note and Columbia. —*Scott Yanow*

The Classic Ellis Marsalis / Jan. 1963–Mar. 1963 / AFO ✦✦✦✦
When one thinks of New Orleans jazz, it is of Dixieland, but in the early '60s there were several talented local modern jazzmen (many of whom eventually went into teaching) who were open to the influence of the more advanced New York jazz. Pianist Ellis Marsalis (the future father of the Marsalis clan, but at the time fairly unknown) heads a quartet on this CD that also includes the forgotten but excellent tenor saxophonist Nat Perrilliat (who was most influenced by John Coltrane of a few years earlier), bassist Marshall Smith and drummer James Black. An LP from the AFO (All for One) label (*The Monkey Puzzle*) has been reissued in full on this CD, along with three numbers later released on a sampler and a previously unissued version of "Night in Tunisia." Black and Marsalis contributed seven of the 11 songs; the quartet also performs Perrilliat's "Little Joy" and three jazz standards. The music falls into the advanced hard bop (as opposed to avant-garde) area with plenty of hard-swinging performances. —*Scott Yanow*

Piano in E–Solo Piano / Jul. 24, 1986 / Rounder ✦✦✦✦
Ellis Marsalis got his time in the spotlight with this fine solo piano session. His mix of swing, Afro-Latin, classical and bebop was spotlighted on superbly crafted versions of Horace Silver's "Nica's Dream" and John Lewis' "Django," as well as Bud Powell's "Hallucinations" and Fats Waller's "Jitterbug Waltz." Marsalis' own originals, "Fourth Autumn" and "Zee Blues," were also expertly written, with charming melodies and smooth, relaxed, yet impressive solos. While he'll probably never get as much publicity as sons Wynton and Branford, Ellis Marsalis certainly deserves high praise for his formidable piano skills. —*Ron Wynn*

A Night at Snug Harbor, New Orleans / Apr. 30, 1989 / Evidence ✦✦✦

Ellis Marsalis Trio / Mar. 18, 1990 / Blue Note ✦✦✦✦
Pianist Ellis Marsalis is in excellent form for this trio outing with bassist Bob Hurst and drummer Jeff "Tain" Watts. The performances fall generally into the medium-tempo range, with Ellis scattering some witty song quotes throughout the lightly swinging renditions. The high points include one of the more delightful versions ever of Johnny Mandel's "Emily," some close interplay during "Little Niles" and a tongue-in-cheek version of "Limehouse Blues" that includes slapped bass, parade rhythms and Marsalis trying in vain to sound Dixielandish. One programming error should be noted: there is no such song as "Just Squeeze Me" and, rather than the one performed being Fats Waller's "Squeeze Me," it is actually Duke Ellington's "Squeeze Me, but Please Don't Tease Me." —*Scott Yanow*

Heart of Gold / Feb. 1991–Jun. 1991 / Columbia ✦✦✦✦✦
Pianist Ellis Marsalis, despite his connections to Ornette Coleman in the 1950s and his home base being New Orleans, is actually at his best when playing lightly swinging bop in a standard trio. Although he spent a period of time as Al Hirt's pianist, his renditions on this CD of such traditional numbers as "Dr. Jazz," "Do You Know What It Means to Miss New Orleans," "I Can't Give You Anything but Love" and "Sweet Georgia Brown" contain no stride or trad elements. Instead, the enjoyable set (which also features Ray Brown or Reginald Veal on bass and either Billy Higgins or Herlin Riley on drums) often displays the influence of Wynton Kelly and players of his generation. As a footnote, "This Can't Be Love" has the recording debut of 14-year-old pianist Jason Marsalis. —*Scott Yanow*

● **Whistle Stop** / Mar. 20, 1993–Jun. 6, 1993 / Columbia ✦✦✦✦
For this CD, veteran pianist Ellis Marsalis performs songs composed by some of the top modern New Orleans players of the 1960s, including drummer James Black, tenor saxophonist Nat Perrilliat, clarinetist Alvin Batiste, saxophonist Harold Battiste and himself. With the exception of Alvin Batiste's tunes (based on "Cherokee" and a Dixielandish blues), the originals have strong melodies, slightly tricky chord structures and sound quite fresh today. Marsalis utilizes his son Branford on tenor and soprano, bassist Robert Hurst and drummer Jeff "Tain" Watts; the young Jason Marsalis sits in on drums during two numbers. Ellis Marsalis is in particularly inventive form on this unusually obscure material. —*Scott Yanow*

Loved Ones / Aug. 14, 1995+Sep. 11, 1995 / Columbia ✦✦✦✦

Wynton Marsalis

b. Oct. 18, 1961, New Orleans, LA
Trumpet, Leader, Composer, Arranger / Post-Bop, New Orleans Jazz, Swing, Bop, Classical
The most famous jazz musician since 1980, Wynton Marsalis made a major impact on jazz almost from the start. In the early '80s it was major news that a young and very talented Black musician would choose to make a living playing acoustic jazz rather than fusion, funk or R&B. Marsalis' arrival on the scene started the Young Lions movement and resulted in major labels (most of whom had shown no interest in jazz during the previous decade) suddenly signing and promoting young players. There had been a major shortage of new trumpeters since 1970, but Marsalis' sudden prominence inspired an entire new crop of brass players. The music of the mid-'60s Miles Davis Quintet had been somewhat over-

shadowed when it was new, but Marsalis' Quintet focused on extending the group's legacy and soon other young lion units were using Davis' late acoustic work as their starting point.

During the past 15 years Wynton Marsalis has managed to be a controversial figure despite his obvious abilities. His selective knowledge of jazz history (considering post-1965 avant-garde playing to be outside of jazz and 1970s fusion to be barren) is unfortunately influenced by the somewhat eccentric beliefs of Stanley Crouch, and his hiring policies as musical director of the Lincoln Center Jazz Orchestra led to exaggerated charges of ageism and racism from local writers. However, more than balancing all of this out is Marsalis' inspiring work with youngsters, many of whom he has introduced to jazz; a few young musicians, such as Roy Hargrove, have been directly helped by Marsalis.

Wynton Marsalis' trumpet playing has been both overcriticized and (at least early on) overpraised. When he first arrived on the scene with the Jazz Messengers, his original inspiration was Freddie Hubbard. However, by the time he began leading his own group, Marsalis often sounded very close to Miles Davis (particularly when holding a long tone), although a version of Miles with virtuosic technique. He was so widely praised by the jazz press at the time (due to their relief that the future of jazz finally seemed safe) that there was an inevitable backlash. Marsalis' sometimes inaccurate statements about jazz of the 1970s and the avant-garde in general made some observers angry, and his rather derivative tone at the time made it seem as if there was always going to have to be an asterisk by his name when evaluating his talents. Some listeners formed permanent impressions of Marsalis as a Miles Davis imitator, but they failed to take into account that he was still improving and developing. With the 1990 recording *Tune in Tomorrow*, Marsalis at last sounded like himself. He had found his own voice by exploring earlier styles of jazz (such as Louis Armstrong's playing), mastering the wa-wa mute and studying Duke Ellington. From that point on, even when playing a Miles Davis standard, Marsalis has had his own sound and has finally taken his place as one of jazz's greats.

The son of pianist Ellis Marsalis, the younger brother of Branford and the older brother of Delfeayo and Jason (the Marsalis clan as a whole can be accurately called "The First Family of Jazz"), Wynton (who was named after pianist Wynton Kelly) received his first trumpet at age six from Ellis' employer, Al Hirt. He studied both classical and jazz and played in local marching bands, funk groups and classical orchestras. Marsalis played first trumpet in the New Orleans Civic Orchestra while in high school. He went to Juilliard when he was 18, and in 1980 he made his first recordings with the Art Blakey Big Band and joined the Jazz Messengers.

By 1981 the young trumpeter was the talk of the jazz world. He toured with Herbie Hancock (a double-LP resulted), continued working with Blakey, signed with Columbia and recorded his first album as a leader. In 1982 Marsalis not only formed his own quintet (featuring brother Branford and soon Kenny Kirkland, Charnett Moffett and Jeff "Tain" Watts), but recorded his first classical album; he was immediately ranked as one of the top classical trumpeters of all time. His quintet with Branford lasted until late 1985, although a rift developed between the brothers (fortunately temporary) when Branford finally quit the band to tour with Sting's pop group. By that time, Wynton was a superstar, winning a countless number of awards and polls.

Marsalis' next group featured pianist Marcus Roberts, bassist Robert Hurst and drummer Watts. Over time, the group grew to become a four-horn septet with trombonist Wycliffe Gordon, altoist Wes Anderson, Todd Williams on tenor, bassist Reginald Veal, drummer Herlin Riley and (by the early '90s) pianist Eric Reed. Marsalis has really developed his writing during the past decade (being influenced by Duke Ellington) and the septet proved to be a perfect outlet for his arranging. Although Wynton Marsalis broke up the band by 1995, many of the musicians still appear in his special projects or with the Lincoln Center Jazz Orchestra.

In 1997 Marsalis' marathon *Blood on the Fields* (which was released as a three-CD set) became the first jazz-based work to win a Pulitzer Prize. With the passing of so many jazz giants during the past few years, Wynton Marsalis' importance (as a trumpeter, leader, writer and spokesman for jazz) continues to grow. —*Scott Yanow*

All American Hero / Oct. 11, 1980 / Who's Who in Jazz ✦✦✦✦
Along with the other Who's Who album, which was simply called *Wynton Marsalis*, this LP features some of the trumpeter's earliest recordings, although in reality it is a live performance by Art Blakey's Jazz Messengers. At the time, the drummer/leader had a particularly strong sextet with altoist Bobby Watson, Billy Pierce on tenor, pianist James Williams and bassist Charles Fambrough. Together with the trumpeter (who was then not quite 19), the group performs a particularly strong set highlighted by "One by One," "My Funny Valentine" (Marsalis' feature) and "ETA." It is interesting to note that his main influence at the beginning of his career was Freddie Hubbard, not Miles Davis. Both of the Who's Who albums contain excellent music. —*Scott Yanow*

Wynton / Oct. 11, 1980 / Who's Who in Jazz ✦✦✦✦

Taken from the same session as his other Who's Who LP, *All American Hero*, this album features Wynton Marsalis at the beginning of his career; only a date with Art Blakey's big band predates the recording. Although released under Marsalis' name, this is really a set by Art Blakey's Jazz Messengers. The already-brilliant trumpeter (seven days shy of his 19th birthday) fits in well with the all-star group (which also includes altoist Bobby Watson, Billy Pierce on tenor, pianist James Williams, bassist Charles Fambrough and the drummer-leader); Wynton's father Ellis makes a guest appearance playing piano on "Jody." Although the packaging of the hard bop set by Who's Who has some misspellings and incomplete personnel, the music is quite rewarding. Marsalis in 1980 had not yet been heavily influenced by Miles Davis (he was in his brief Freddie Hubbard phase). This LP gives one a rare early look at the influential trumpeter as a teenager. —*Scott Yanow*

Wynton Marsalis / Aug. 1981 / Columbia ✦✦✦✦✦

Trumpeter Wynton Marsalis' debut on Columbia, recorded when he was only 19, made it clear from the start that he was going to be a major force in jazz. At the time Marsalis (who was originally a bit influenced by Freddie Hubbard) was starting to closely emulate Miles Davis of the mid-'60s and his slightly older brother Branford took Wayne Shorter as his role model. The inclusion of Davis' rhythm section from that era (pianist Herbie Hancock, bassist Ron Carter and drummer Tony Williams) on four of the seven selections reinforced the image. The three other numbers feature such up-and-coming talents as pianist Kenny Kirkland, Charles Fambrough or Clarence Seay on bass and drummer Jeff "Tain" Watts, helping to launch the rise of the Young Lions. But although not overly original, there is a great deal of outstanding playing on this set, including a definitive version of Tony Williams' "Sister Cheryl" and the long tradeoff between Wynton and Branford on "Hesitation." —*Scott Yanow*

Think of One / 1983 / Columbia ✦✦✦✦✦

Wynton Marsalis' second Columbia recording as a leader features his working band of 1983: brother Branford on tenor and soprano, pianist Kenny Kirkland, either Phil Bowler or Ray Drummond on bass and drummer Jeff "Tain" Watts. They perform the ballad "My Ideal," Duke Ellington's "Melancholia" and Thelonious Monk's "Think of One" along with some group originals. Wynton was deep in his Miles Davis period while Branford (who was still most influenced by Wayne Shorter) was just beginning to come into his own. Of course, Wynton was already a remarkable virtuoso a few years earlier. All of his recordings are worth getting, and this early document has more than its share of brilliant playing. —*Scott Yanow*

Hot House Flowers / May 30, 1984-May 31, 1984 / Columbia ✦✦✦✦

Wynton Marsalis, very much in his Miles Davis period, plays quite melodically throughout this ballad-dominated outing with strings. Branford Marsalis (on tenor and soprano), flutist Kent Jordan, pianist Kenny Kirkland and drummer Jeff Watts are strong assets but it is Wynton's subtle creativity on such songs as "Stardust," "When You Wish Upon a Star," Duke Ellington's "Melancholia" and "I'm Confessin'" that makes this recording special. The arrangements by Robert Freedman generally keep the strings from sounding too sticky and Wynton's tone is consistently beautiful. —*Scott Yanow*

★ **Black Codes (From the Underground)** / Jan. 11, 1985+Jan. 14, 1985 / Columbia ✦✦✦✦✦

This is probably the best Wynton Marsalis recording from his Miles Davis period. With his brother Branford (who doubles here on tenor and soprano) often closely emulating Wayne Shorter and the rhythm section (pianist Kenny Kirkland, bassist Charnett Moffett and drummer Jeff Watts) sounding a bit like the famous Herbie Hancock-Ron Carter-Tony Williams trio, Wynton is heard at the head of what was essentially an updated version of the mid- to late '60s Miles Davis Quintet (despite Stanley Crouch's pronouncements in his typically absurd liner notes about Marsalis' individuality). The music is brilliantly played and displays what the Young Lions movement was really about; young musicians choosing to explore acoustic jazz and to extend the innovations of the pre-fusion modern mainstream style. Marsalis would develop his own sound a few years later, but even at age 23 he had few close competitors. —*Scott Yanow*

J Mood / Dec. 17, 1985-Dec. 20, 1985 / Columbia ✦✦✦✦

When Branford Marsalis and Kenny Kirkland chose to leave Wynton Marsalis' group to make money with Sting, Wynton had to regroup fast. For this quartet recording with bassist Robert Hurst, III, and drummer Jeff "Tain" Watts, the trumpeter met up with pianist Marcus Roberts for the first time, performing originals by Wynton, Roberts, Ellis Marsalis and Donald Brown. Marsalis was still very much under Miles Davis' influence at the time, but at age 24 he had rather remarkable technique. He stretches out in explorative and consistently creative fashion on these seven straightahead and generally unpredictable selections. —*Scott Yanow*

Standard Time, Vol. 1 / May 29, 1986-Sep. 25, 1986 / Columbia ✦✦✦✦

On the first of three volumes, Wynton Marsalis explores ten standards plus two of his originals with his quartet of the period (which consists of pianist Marcus Roberts, bassist Robert Hurst, III, and drummer Jeff "Tain" Watts). Marsalis' tone is quite beautiful on the well-balanced set; even the ballads have their unpredictable moments. Among the more memorable performances are his treatments of "Caravan," "April in Paris," "New Orleans," "Memories of You" and two versions of "Cherokee." —*Scott Yanow*

Live at Blues Alley / Dec. 19, 1986-Dec. 20, 1986 / Columbia ✦✦✦✦✦

This double LP features the great trumpeter Wynton Marsalis and his 1986 quartet, a unit featuring pianist Marcus Roberts, bassist Robert Hurst and drummer Jeff "Tain" Watts. Although Marsalis during this period still hinted strongly at Miles Davis, his own musical personality was starting to finally shine through. With the versatile Marcus Roberts (who thus far has been the most significant graduate from Marsalis' groups), Wynton Marsalis was beginning to explore older material, including on this set "Just Friends," and "Do You Know What It Means to Miss New Orleans" other highlights include lengthy workouts on "Au Privave" and Kenny Kirkland's "Chambers of Tain." This two-fer is recommended, as are virtually all of Wynton Marsalis' recordings. —*Scott Yanow*

Carnival / 1987 / Columbia ✦✦✦✦✦

Although this is not a jazz album, it should be of interest to jazz collectors. Wynton Marsalis switches to cornet and performs virtuosic pieces written for marching bands and wind ensembles, mostly from the 1890-1920 period. Marsalis makes the impossible sound somewhat effortless on such workouts as "Carnival of Venice," "Flight of the Bumblebee" and a couple of Herbert L. Clarke pieces. In addition, he brings out the beauty in some traditional folk songs (including "Sometimes I Feel like a Motherless Child") and wrestles successfully with Paganini's "Moto Perpetuo, Op. II." —*Scott Yanow*

Standard Time, Vol. 2: Intimacy Calling / Sep. 1987-Aug. 1990 / Columbia ✦✦✦✦

Wynton Marsalis' second of three standard albums was actually released after the third volume. On most of the selections, the brilliant trumpeter is heard in excellent form with his quartet (comprising pianist Marcus Roberts, bassist Reginald Veal or Robert Hurst and either Herlin Riley or Jeff Watts on drums); tenorman Todd Williams helps out on "I'll Remember April" and altoist Wes Anderson is also added to "Crepuscule with Nellie." Marsalis' tone really makes the ballads worth hearing, and his unusual choice and placement of notes keeps the music stimulating. This mostly bop-oriented set is rounded off by a jaunty version of "Bourbon Street Parade." —*Scott Yanow*

Thick in the South: Soul Gestures in Southern Blue, Vol. 1 / 1988 / Columbia ✦✦✦✦

The three volumes that Wynton Marsalis subtitled "Soul Gestures in Southern Blue" (of which this CD is the first) are overall rather disappointing. This initial CD is the strongest of the three due to the inclusion of tenor saxophonist Joe Henderson and (on two of the five numbers) drummer Elvin Jones, but overall Marsalis (who was in the final section of his Miles Davis period), although playing quite well, seemed to have hit a dead end. His five compositions lack any memorable melodies and his own virtuosic solos do not have any distinctive qualities; pianist Marcus Roberts occasionally emerges as the top soloist. However, once he had gotten his three-part tribute to the blues out of the way, Marsalis would once again make some giant leaps forward. —*Scott Yanow*

Uptown Ruler: Soul Gestures in Southern Blue, Vol. 2 / 1988 / Columbia ✦✦✦

The second of the three-part "Soul Gestures in Southern Blue" finds Wynton Marsalis at a transitional spot in his career. While his pianist Marcus Roberts had largely found his own style, the trumpeter was still searching and had not yet thrown off the dominant Miles Davis influence. This quintet outing (which also features the tenor of Todd Williams, bassist Reginald Veal and drummer Herlin Riley) lacks any memorable melodies, although the playing is fine. But overall, the music is much more forgettable than Stanley Crouch's rather incredible liner notes. This CD can be safely passed by in favor of Marsalis' more recent projects. —*Scott Yanow*

Levee Low Moan: Soul Gestures in Southern Blue, Vol. 3 / 1988 / Columbia ✦✦✦

Wynton Marsalis' three-part "Soul Gestures in Southern Blue" (of which this CD is the final section) is a disappointment. None of the themes are particularly memorable and, although the individual solos are fine, not much really happens; overall it is a rather weird tribute to the blues. Actually, the main significance to this particular set is that the trumpeter had for the first time put together the nucleus to his septet. Although there was no trombonist yet, altoist Wessell Anderson, tenor saxophonist Todd Williams, bassist Reginald Veal and drummer Herlin Riley were already in place while pianist Marcus Roberts was still a part of Marsalis' group.

But musically this trilogy can be bypassed; get his more recent recordings instead. *—Scott Yanow*

The Majesty of the Blues / Oct. 27, 1988-Oct. 28, 1988 / Columbia ✦✦✦

This is a good album that should have been great. Two lengthy originals ("The Majesty of the Blues" and "Hickory Dickory Dock") find Wynton Marsalis displaying his rapidly developing writing skills, which were being prodded at the time by Duke Ellington and Charles Mingus. His sextet with pianist Marcus Roberts, tenorman Todd Williams and altoist Wes Anderson is in outstanding form on these performances. However, the three-part "New Orleans Function" has two fatal flaws. Marsalis returned to his New Orleans heritage by welcoming the erratic clarinetist Dr. Michael White, veteran banjoist Danny Barker, trombonist Freddie Lonzo and trumpeter Teddy Riley as guests. Unfortunately, an endless "Sermon" about jazz, written by Stanley Crouch and narrated by Reverend Jeremiah Wright, Jr., drones on for 16 minutes and is unspeakably pompous, killing the momentum for the record. In addition, the closing Dixieland blues is led by the frequently faltering Teddy Riley (while Marsalis plays second trumpet) and is much too ragged to have been released. The main reason to acquire this album is for the first two pieces. *—Scott Yanow*

Original Soundtrack from "Tune in Tomorrow" / 1989 / Columbia ✦✦✦✦✦

This soundtrack recording is very significant in the career of Wynton Marsalis. For the first time, the trumpeter displayed a sound of his own; the Miles Davis influence was finally gone. In addition, Marsalis not only debuted with his septet (which consisted of trombonist Wycliffe Gordon, altoist Wes Anderson, Todd Williams on tenor, soprano and clarinet, pianist Marcus Roberts, bassist Reginald Veal and drummer Herlin Riley) but, in writing this score, Marsalis showed how talented an arranger he was; very much in the Duke Ellington tradition, but without resorting to copying. The 16 selections are sometimes a bit fragmented (a few use extra personnel including clarinetist Michael White on six tracks and vocals by Shirley Horn and Johnny Adams), but they hold up very well apart from the movie and have plenty of spirit and humor. *—Scott Yanow*

Standard Time, Vol. 3 / 1990 / Columbia ✦✦✦

On the third of his standards albums, trumpeter Wynton Marsalis meets up with his father, pianist Ellis Marsalis (along with bassist Reginald Veal and drummer Herlin Riley), for 17 standards and three of his originals (including "In the Court of King Oliver"). Wynton, perhaps because of his father's presence, is very respectful of the melodies, sometimes overly so. The result is that this set is not as adventurous as one would like, although Marsalis' beautiful tone makes the music worth hearing. *—Scott Yanow*

Blue Interlude / 1991 / Columbia ✦✦✦✦✦

Wynton Marsalis' septet was the perfect outlet both for his playing and his writing. The impressive young personnel (pianist Marcus Roberts, altoist Wessell Anderson, Todd Williams on tenor, soprano and clarinet, trombonist Wycliffe Gordon, bassist Reginald Veal and drummer Herlin Riley) was flexible enough to sound like a New Orleans parade band or the David Murray Octet, and Wynton's writing also made them occasionally appear to be a small group from the Duke Ellington Orchestra. On this CD the music is quite strong, as are the solos, and the colorful group is heard at their best on a wide variety of challenging material. *—Scott Yanow*

☆ In This House, On This Morning / May 28, 1992-Mar. 21, 1993 / Columbia ✦✦✦✦✦

For this double CD (which has typically absurd liner notes from Stanley Crouch), trumpeter Wynton Marsalis musically depicts in three parts a lengthy Sunday church service with program music composed for each of the traditional activities. The set does take quite a while to get going, with much of the first two parts consisting of introductions and transitions to themes that never seem to arrive. There are some exceptions, particularly Marsalis' violent trumpet distortions on "Call to Prayer," a spirited New Orleans blues, and Todd Williams' tenor solo on another blues. However, it is the third section that is most notable. The 28-minute "In the Sweet Embrace of Life" instrumentally portrays a preacher giving a heated sermon, building up to a very feverish level. Marsalis' model in his writing is clearly Duke Ellington. Trombonist Wycliffe Gordon is an expert with mutes and Todd Williams is able to hint at both Paul Gonsalves on tenor and Dixieland clarinetists on soprano while altoist Wes Anderson and pianist Eric Reed are also major assets to the septet. Due to the memorable final section, this lengthy work is one of the high points of his career thus far. *—Scott Yanow*

☆ Citi Movement / Jul. 27, 1992-Jul. 28, 1992 / Columbia ✦✦✦✦✦

This double CD contains Wynton Marsalis' score for the modern ballet *Griot New York*. Even more than his trumpet playing, his writing skills had developed quickly during the five years prior to this set. Marsalis' superb septet (which included trombonist Wycliffe Gordon, altoist Wes Anderson, Todd Williams on tenor and soprano, pianist Eric Reed, bassist Reginald Veal and drummer Herlin Riley) performs the complex and consistently colorful music, which goes through a wide variety of

styles (including New Orleans jazz, swing, bop, modal music and even some sections bordering on the avant-garde). The results are unpredictable, exciting and quite enjoyable. This is one of Wynton Marsalis' finest recordings to date. *—Scott Yanow*

Live in Swing Town / 1994 / Jazz Door ✦✦✦✦

The Wynton Marsalis Septet is featured live in concert on this European import. Although the release might be a bootleg (since Marsalis has long been signed to Columbia), the music is well recorded and frequently exciting, with the only real fault being the extreme brevity; the CD has only 31 minutes of music. Performed after *Citi Movement* was recorded, the great trumpeter performs his spirited "The Legend of Buddy Bolden" (much of which is taken unaccompanied), "Swingdown, Swingtown," "Highrise Riff" (the latter two also have solo space for altoist Wes Anderson, Walter Blanding on tenor and trombonist Wycliffe Gordon), and "Cherokee," which has an outstanding trumpet solo. The quantity of the music is low but the quality is quite high throughout this surprising disc, which is well worth searching for. *—Scott Yanow*

Joe Cool's Blues / Apr. 12, 1994-Aug. 25, 1994 / Columbia ✦✦✦✦

For this CD, Wynton and Ellis Marsalis perform music both old and new that is heard on the *Peanuts* television specials. Wynton's septet (altoist Wessell Anderson, Victor Goines on tenor, trombonist Wycliffe Gordon, pianist Eric Reed, bassist Benjamin Wolfe and drummer Herlin Riley, in addition to the trumpeter-leader) jam on eight of Marsalis' compositions and the perennial "Linus & Lucy," Ellis Marsalis' trio performs four of Vince Guaraldi's themes and, on "Little Birdie," an all-star group (including three of the Marsalises but not Wynton) back Germaine Bazzle's vocal. The music is reasonably enjoyable but not too substantial, worth getting even if it is not one of Wynton's more significant albums. *—Scott Yanow*

Blood on the Fields / Jan. 22, 1995-Jan. 25, 1995 / Columbia ✦✦✦✦

The music on this three-CD set (released in 1997) won a Pulitzer Prize, but is not without its faults. Trumpeter Wynton Marsalis tells the story of two Africans (singers Miles Griffith and Cassandra Wilson) who are captured, brought to the US and sold as slaves. Because the male had formerly been a prince while the female had been a commoner, he considers himself to be her superior. He asks for but then ignores the advice of a wise man (Jon Hendricks), gets caught trying to escape, discovers what "soul" is, finally accepts the female as his equal and eventually escapes with her to freedom. Marsalis wrote a dramatic, episodic and generally thought-provoking three-hour work, utilizing the three singers plus 15 other musicians (all of whom have significant musical parts to play) in a massive 27-part suite. Hendricks is delightful (and the star of the catchiest piece, "Juba and a O'Brown Squaw"), Wilson has rarely sounded better, and Griffith keeps up with the better-known singers, while the musicians (particularly trombonist Wycliffe Gordon, baritonist James Carter, pianist Eric Reed and, near the work's conclusion, violinist Michael Ward in addition to Marsalis) are quite superb. It should, however, be mentioned that the use of group narration to tell parts of the story does not work that well, the music could have used a stronger and more complicated story (the last hour has very little action), and few of the themes are at all memorable; Marsalis in the mid '90s was a more talented arranger than composer (despite Stanley Crouch's absurd raving in the liner notes). But as is true of all of Wynton Marsalis' recordings, this one deserves several close listenings. *—Scott Yanow*

Jump Start and Jazz / 1996 / Sony ✦✦✦

Hot on the heels of *Blood on the Fields* and the Pulitzer Prize, this pairing of Wynton Marsalis jazz ballets was issued in 1997 with the Sony Classical logo, possibly to avoid direct marketing competition. Another reason is that these ballets, each lasting a few minutes over half an hour, are mostly written-out compositions with jazz rhythm sections and jazz inflections from the players. As in much of Marsalis' writing in the '90s, he reaches back to several pre-bop classic jazz styles to form a synthesis of his own, with the wailing mark of Ellington ever-present in the voicings and harmonies. *Jazz: 6 1/2 Syncopated Movements* is a tightly arranged series of episodes that stalk across the jazz landscape from ragtime to dissonance, sometimes so tightly that it begins to resemble cartoon music. One of the more striking sections is "Trail of Tears," which has subtly smeared harmonies and horse-laughing from the muted brasses, and "Express Crossing" is right in the mold of Ellington's "Daybreak Express," with a nice breakneck muted solo for Wynton. Though burdened with a typically pompous title, *Jump Start—The Mastery of Melancholy* is actually the less pretentious ballet of the two, a suite of ten brief, disconnected big-band pieces in different idioms where the jazz elements come through with more freedom for the rhythm section and the soloists. This work hits its stride only toward the close with "Bebop" for small group (where Wynton burns as he did in his extreme youth) and Harry "Sweets" Edison's delicious cameo on "Jump." Heavily staffed by members of Marsalis' late septet, the Lincoln Center Jazz Orchestra plays both works in precise, crisp fashion, with Marsalis conducting *Jump Start* and playing lead and section trumpet in both ballets. A definite bonus is that this is the first Wynton Marsalis jazz album that does not have liner notes by the insufferable Stanley Crouch. Tony Scherman does the honors gracefully, without preachy polemics and hysterical Wynton-worshipping. —*Richard S. Ginell*

Warne Marsh

b. Oct. 26, 1927, Los Angeles, CA, **d.** Dec. 18, 1987, Hollywood, CA
Tenor Saxophone / Cool
Along with Lee Konitz, Warne Marsh was the most successful "pupil" of Lennie Tristano and, unlike Konitz, Marsh spent most of his career exploring chordal improvisation the Tristano way. The cool-toned tenor played with Hoagy Carmichael's Teenagers during 1944-45 and then after the Army he was with Buddy Rich (1948) before working with Lennie Tristano (1949-52). His recordings with Tristano and Konitz still sound remarkable today with unisons that make the two horns sound like one. Marsh had occasional reunions with Konitz and Tristano through the years, spent periods outside of music, and stayed true to his musical goals. He moved to Los Angeles in 1966 and worked with Supersax during 1972-77, also filling in time teaching. Marsh, who collapsed and died on stage at the legendary Donte's club in 1987 while playing "Out of Nowhere," is now considered legendary. He recorded as a leader for Xanadu, Imperial, Kapp, Mode (reissued on V.S.O.P.), Atlantic, Wave, Storyville, Revelation, Interplay, Criss Cross and Hot Club. —*Scott Yanow*

Live in Hollywood / Dec. 23, 1952 / Xanadu ✦✦✦✦
This privately recorded club appearance (from the Haig in Los Angeles) features the vastly underrated tenor saxophonist Warne Marsh in excellent form. His long melodic lines contrast well with the Bud Powell-inspired playing of pianist Hampton Hawes. Bassist Joe Mondragon and drummer Shelly Manne complete the quartet, which performs seven bop standards. Since Warne Marsh was sparsely recorded during this era, this is a valuable document of his playing. —*Scott Yanow*

Music for Prancing / Sep. 1957 / V.S.O.P. ✦✦✦✦
A swinging date by the master of cool. —*David Szatmary*

The Art of Improvising / 1959 / Revelation ✦✦
Ne Plus Ultra / Oct. 25, 1969-Sep. 14, 1969 / Hat Hut ✦✦✦✦
This was tenor saxophonist Warne Marsh's first recording as a leader since 1960. Teamed up with complementary altoist Gary Foster (who was most influenced by Marsh's former musical partner Lee Konitz), bassist Dave Parlato and drummer John Tirabasso, Marsh runs through some of his favorite chord changes, including "Lennie's Pennies," "Subconscious-Lee" and "You Stepped Out of a Dream." In addition, there is a fairly free group improvisation (the 15-minute "Touch and Go") and a brief rendition of Bach's "Two-Part Inventions No.13." A strong all-around CD reissue that was originally released by the Revelation label. —*Scott Yanow*

Report of the 1st Annual Symposium on Relaxed Improvisation / May 9, 1972 / Revelation ✦✦✦
This LP certainly has an odd name. The music is relaxed but not sleepy, featuring tenor saxophonist Warne Marsh, altoist Gary Foster, pianist Clare Fischer, bassist Paul Ruhland and drummer John Tirabasso. They perform "Bluesy Rouge" and three familiar standards in very spontaneous fashion; this was really a recorded jam session in which no one paid much attention to the presence of the microphones. The recording quality is OK, if not state of the art, and the playing is not flawless, but the music overall is creative and well worthy of a listen by Warne Marsh fans. —*Scott Yanow*

Live at the Montmartre Club: Jazz Exchange, Vol. 1 / Dec. 3, 1975-Dec. 27, 1975 / Storyville ✦✦✦✦
The first of three releases that document a European tour undertaken by tenor saxophonist Warne Marsh and altoist Lee Konitz finds the Lennie Tristano alumni in prime form. Marsh and Konitz often thought alike musically, and this set certainly has its exciting moments. Joined by pianist Ole Kock Hansen, bassist Niels-Henning Orsted Pedersen and either Alex Riel or Svend Erik Norregard on drums, the two classic saxophonists explore "originals" based closely on common chord changes (including "April" and "Background Music"), plus "You Stepped Out of a Dream" and Lester Young's "Pound Cake." Highly recommended, as are the two following volumes. —*Scott Yanow*

Live at the Montmartre Club: Jazz Exchange, Vol. 2 / Dec. 3, 1975-Dec. 27, 1975 / Storyville ✦✦✦✦
In December 1975, tenor saxophonist Warne Marsh and altoist Lee Konitz went on a European tour. Their musical reunion showed that the magic that had existed between them a quarter-century before when they teamed up with their teacher Lennie Tristano was still very much present. Both saxophonists had grown through the years, and on this second of three sets, they are in consistently inventive form. Accompanied by a quiet English rhythm section (guitarist Dave Cliff, bassist Peter Ind and drummer Alan Levitt), the interplay between Marsh and Konitz, who had very complementary yet individual styles, is quite impressive, as are their individual solos on four thinly disguised "originals," "Foolin' Myself," "Darn That Dream"

and a couple of brief "Two-Part Inventions" by Bach. Well worth acquiring. —*Scott Yanow*

Live at the Montmartre Club: Jazz Exchange, Vol. 3 / Dec. 3, 1975-Dec. 27, 1975 / Storyville ✦✦✦✦
This is the third of three CDs recorded live at the Montmartre in Copenhagen, Denmark. Whenever tenor saxophonist Warne Marsh and altoist Lee Konitz got together, fireworks resulted as the two complementary saxophonists always seemed to bring out the best in each other. This 1995 CD has six standards from the original LP plus previously unreleased versions of "Chi-Chi" and "Wow." Except for "Chi-Chi" (which finds Marsh and Konitz joined by guitarist Dave Cliff, bassist Peter Ind and drummer Al Levitt), the two horns are accompanied by pianist Ole Kock Hansen, bassist Niels Pedersen and drummer Svend Erik Norregard. Marsh and Konitz, as usual, get rid of the themes quickly and then engage in advanced chordal improvisation, showing what they learned from Lennie Tristano along with their growth since the late '40s. All three CDs in this series are well worth getting. —*Scott Yanow*

Unissued Copenhagen Studio Recordings / Dec. 1975 / Storyville ✦✦✦✦
All Music / Feb. 21, 1976 / Nessa ✦✦✦✦
Tenor Gladness / Oct. 13, 1976-Oct. 14, 1976 / Disco-Mate ✦✦✦✦✦
The two complementary but distinctive tenors Lew Tabackin and Warne Marsh stretch out on four jams in a quartet with bassist John Heard and drummer Larry Bunker. In addition, Tabackin is heard unaccompanied on "New-Ance," while Marsh has a ballad feature on "Easy"; the unidentified pianist on this track is most certainly Toshiko Akiyoshi. It is a pity that the enjoyable music was last out on this out-of-print LP from the defunct Inner City label, for it finds both Marsh and Tabackin in competitive and creative form. —*Scott Yanow*

How Deep, How High / Apr. 25, 1977-Aug. 8, 1979 / Discovery ✦✦✦✦
For this very interesting LP, the legendary but underrated tenor saxophonist Warne Marsh is heard in two different settings. Marsh and pianist Sal Mosca (who was heavily influenced by Marsh's former teacher Lennie Tristano) perform four duets (two originals apiece), and on the flip side of the album, Marsh, Mosca, bassist Sam Jones and drummer Roy Haynes stretch out during a concert for "Background Music" (based on "All of Me") and "She's Funny That Way." The music ranges from introspective to more driving, but it swings throughout, and Marsh's solos are always intriguing. —*Scott Yanow*

Warne Out / May 15, 1977-Jun. 5, 1977 / Interplay ✦✦✦✦
An album where wit and inventiveness are the theme, from the title to the leads. —*Ron Wynn*

● Star Highs / Aug. 14, 1982 / Criss Cross ✦✦✦✦✦
Tenor saxophonist Warne Marsh and pianist Hank Jones had not performed together before they met up in the studio to make what would be the second release for the Criss Cross label. With bassist George Mraz and drummer Mel Lewis completing the quartet, plenty of sparks fly between the two lead soloists. Marsh plays with more fire than one would expect from the cool-toned tenor; the material (four lesser-known tunes by the leader, one by Jones, "Moose the Mooche," and "Victory Ball") is fresher than usual, and the album can be easily recommended to straightahead jazz collectors. —*Scott Yanow*

A Ballad Album / Apr. 7, 1983 / Criss Cross ✦✦✦✦✦
Although there is a certain amount of tempo variation, this is largely a ballad showcase CD for tenor saxophonist Warne Marsh. With fine support from pianist Lou Levy, bassist Jesper Lundgaard and drummer James Martin, Marsh sounds quite lyrical on eight veteran standards including "I Can't Give You Anything but Love, Baby," "The Nearness of You" and "Emily." The CD reissue adds three alternate takes to the original program. Fine music that is both relaxing and (thanks to Marsh) somewhat unsettling under the surface. —*Scott Yanow*

Newly Warne / Mar. 11, 1985 / Storyville ✦✦✦✦
The great tenor stylist Warne Marsh is backed by his star pupil pianist Susan Chen, bassist George Mraz and drummer Akira Tana for this Storyville CD. To Chen's credit, she chose not to closely emulate Lennie Tristano and instead was developing her own bop-based style. Marsh continued the old Tristano practice of disguising standards as renamed originals but there are some surprising moments, such as Chen's thoughtful solo piano interlude on the second half of "At First Blush" and the brief tenor-drums duet on "Beautiful Love Fades Out." Warne Marsh's tone is as distinctive as ever and, although he had grown through the years, his timeless style was virtually unchanged from the 1950s. —*Scott Yanow*

Posthumous / 1985 / Interplay ✦✦✦
Strong mid-'80s material by tenor saxophonist Warne Marsh that for some reason was not issued until he died in 1987. It featured Marsh in a much looser, fiery style than usual, without the exacting, complex lines and lengthy constructions he usu-

ally employed. He was backed by three good but not great musicians in pianist Susan Chen, bassist George Mraz, and drummer Akira Tana. —*Ron Wynn*

Back Home / Mar. 1986 / Criss Cross ✦✦✦

For one of his final recordings, tenor great Warne Marsh performs with pianist Barry Harris, bassist David Williams, drummer Albert "Tootie" Heath, and (on three of the seven selections) complementary tenorman Jimmy Halperin, who also had lessons with Marsh's former teacher Lennie Tristano. Other than Tadd Dameron's "Good Bait," the other seven songs are "originals" by Marsh or Tristano that not only steal various standards' chord changes, but have titles that point towards the original sources, including "Leave Me," "See Me Now, If You Could," and "Rhythmically Speaking." Warne Marsh's playing was always much more original than his "composing," and the many subtle surprises on this fine set make it a recommended acquisition. —*Scott Yanow*

Warne Marsh and Susan Chen / Jun. 1987 / Interplay ✦✦✦

During the last few years of his life, tenor saxophonist Warne Marsh often teamed up with pianist Susan Chen, who was one of his students. This duet album has 13 generally brief sketches (three of which are under two minutes long) that are allegedly "originals," plus "Skylark." Certainly such songs as "This Thing," "Pennies," "Marvelous Words," "Another You" and "Have You Met" are rather thin disguises for their original sources and chord changes. Despite that odd habit (which was initiated by Lennie Tristano), the music is generally quite rewarding. Warne Marsh was in prime form during the last years of his life, and Susan Chen (who had studied with Tristano for four months) was starting to develop her own style; where has she been since Marsh's 1987 death? This somewhat obscure LP is worth searching for. —*Scott Yanow*

Two Days in the Life Of... / Jun. 4, 1987-Jun. 5, 1987 / Interplay ✦✦✦✦

This was one of tenor saxophonist Warne Marsh's last records. Fortunately, his musical talents were unimpaired and he sounds in prime form. A pianoless quartet (consisting of guitarist Jim Eschete, bassist Jim Hughart and drummer Sherman Ferguson) fits in with Marsh's music very well (Eschete has several excellent solos), mostly performing thinly-disguised standards. Other than the brief playing time (under 40 minutes) and the lack of liner notes, there are no viable criticisms of this CD, for Warne Marsh, just six months before his death, was still in top form and quite distinctive. —*Scott Yanow*

Wendell Marshall

b. Oct. 24, 1920, St. Louis, MO
Bass / Swing

Best known for his excellent work as a supportive bassist with Duke Ellington (1948-55), Wendell Marshall was the cousin of Jimmy Blanton. After attending Lincoln University and serving in the Army, he worked for a few months with Stuff Smith. In 1948 he moved to New York and joined Mercer Ellington. Soon he was with Duke, and his seven years touring with Ellington gave him a strong reputation. Marshall freelanced after 1955 (including recordings with Mary Lou Williams, Art Blakey, Donald Byrd, Milt Jackson and Hank Jones among many others) and eventually was working steadily in Broadway pit bands. Wendell Marshall retired from music in 1968. —*Scott Yanow*

Claire Martin

b. 1967, London, England
Vocals / Standards, Cool, Traditional Pop, Vocal Jazz

Had Claire Martin become a trumpeter instead of a singer, she would have been compared to Miles Davis and Chet Baker rather than Fats Navarro, Clifford Brown or Lee Morgan. Or as an alto saxophonist, she would have had more in common with Lee Konitz and Paul Desmond than Jackie McLean, Phil Woods or Gene Quill. Greatly influenced by the cool-school singers of the 1950s, the young British diva clearly owes an artistic debt to such greats as Chris Connor, June Christy and Julie London—all of whom, like Martin, favored subtlety and restraint over aggression. But her inspirations don't stop there—born in London in 1967 and raised in a rock 'n' roll era, the smoky, seductive Martin has also been influenced by more recent singers ranging from Joni Mitchell to Kate Bush.

Martin was only six when she entered theatrical school, and by her early teens, had been named Best Solo Vocalist twice by the British Arts Awards. Before debuting at Ronnie Scott's in London at 21, Martin supported herself as everything from a singing waitress to a secretary. Martin went on to become one of England's top jazz vocalists, and the British Jazz Awards exalted her as Best New Jazz Artist of 1994 and Best Jazz Singer of 1995. However, she was little known in the US as of late 1996. In October 1996, she visited New York and recorded with American jazz players for the first time, including alto saxophonist Antonio Hart. —*Alex Henderson*

Devil May Care / Mar. 1993 / Linn ✦✦✦

Though it falls short of the excellence of *Old Boyfriends* or *The Waiting Game*, *Devil May Care* is a very respectable effort from a young artist who found her voice early on. True to form, Martin doesn't inundate listeners with obvious choices. Buddy Guy's "Save Your Love for Me" is the only song on this British release that really qualifies as a standard. Otherwise, Martin turns her attention to lesser-known classics ranging from Noel Coward's "If Love Were All" to the free-spirited title song—a '50s classic by the undeservedly obscure vocalese master Bob Dorough. Martin does her share of writing or co-writing this time, the most noteworthy examples being the pointed "Devil's Gonna Get You" and the dusky "On Thin Ice." While *Boyfriends* or *Waiting* would be better starting points for novices, *Devil May Care* is well worth hearing. —*Alex Henderson*

● **Old Boyfriends** / May 24, 1994-May 26, 1994 / Linn ✦✦✦✦

Many jazz singers, young and old, make the mistake of arbitrarily avoiding the pop, rock and R&B songs of the 1960s, '70s and '80s, but for Claire Martin, they're fair game. This outstanding CD finds her demonstrating the jazz potential in such unlikely vehicles as Rupert Holmes' incisive "Partners in Crime" and Tom Waits' "Old Boyfriends"—not exactly songs jazz singers are usually quick to embrace. True to form, she unearths her share of wrongly neglected classics, including Artie Shaw's "Moon Ray" (a major hit for him during the Swing Era) and Burt Bacharach's "Out of My Continental Mind" (associated with Lena Horne). As daring as Martin is in her choice of material, her vocal style is actually quite straight-forward and lucid and not overly abstract. Martin consistently uses subtlety and restraint to maximum advantage and—like Chris Connor and Julie London before her—makes it clear that "cool jazz" certainly doesn't have to be cold. —*Alex Henderson*

The Waiting Game / 1995 / Linn/Honest ✦✦✦✦✦

One thing Claire Martin won't be accused of is having a conventional or unadventurous repertoire. On the superb *The Waiting Game*, she delivers an engaging version of Betty Carter's "Tight" and insightfully turns everything from Thomas Dolby's "The Key to Your Ferrari" to Joni Mitchell's "Be Cool" into acoustic jazz. "You Hit the Spot" and "Better than Anything" aren't standards, but the soulfulness Martin brings to these neglected classics indicates that they deserve to be. The unique and distinctive improvisor doesn't avoid standards altogether—her heartfelt interpretation of "Everything Happens to Me" being a fine example—but thankfully, she's not one to overemphasize them. Consistently, Martin's singing is as strikingly personal as it is expressive. —*Alex Henderson*

Offbeat: Live at Ronnie Scott's Club / Aug. 21, 1995-Aug. 26, 1995 / Linn ✦✦✦✦

To British jazz fans, Ronnie Scott's Club is London's equivalent of the Village Vanguard—the venue improvisers headline when they have "arrived." Claire Martin has headlined Scott's more than once, and was well received during the August 1995 engagement documented on *Offbeat* (her only live CD). Joined by an intimate and tasteful British trio comprising pianist Gareth Williams, bassist Arnie Somogyi and drummer Clark Tracey, the cool-toned singer is as expressive as she is adventurous. Never one to be predictable in her choice of material, she demonstrates that everything from Stevie Wonder's "Make Sure You're Sure" and Paul Simon's "I Do It For Your Love" to Laura Nyro's "Buy and Sell" can work quite well as acoustic jazz. Hopefully, Martin will record more live albums in the future. —*Alex Henderson*

Make This City Ours / 1997 / Honest ✦✦✦✦

Mel Martin

b. Jun. 7, 1942, Sacramento, CA
Alto Saxophone, Tenor Saxophone, Soprano Saxophone / Bop, Post-Bop

The leader of Bebop and Beyond and a versatile bop-based reed player with an open-minded style, Mel Martin has been a fixture in San Francisco since the 1970s. He had his first gig when he was 14 and after attending San Francisco State he dropped out to become a professional musician. Among his early associations were such rock groups as Santana, Azteca, Cold Blood, Boz Scaggs and Van Morrison, in addition to working in the studios. During 1977-78 he led an adventurous fusion band, Listen, a group that recorded two albums for Inner City and included among its sidemen steel drum wizard Andy Narell. In 1983, after recording a duet album (for Catero) with guitarist Randy Vincent, Martin formed Bebop and Beyond, a band that has since recorded for Concord and Blue Moon, including tribute albums to Thelonious Monk and Dizzy Gillespie; Dizzy participated on the latter. Among Bebop & Beyond's sidemen have been Vincent, George Cables, Eddie Marshall and Warren Gale with such guests on their albums as John Handy and Howard Johnson. In addition to recently performing music from the Charles Mingus songbook with Bebop and Beyond, Martin has recorded a solo Enja set of Benny Carter tunes. —*Scott Yanow*

Growing / May 3, 1978 / Inner City ✦✦✦
Mel Martin's second and final album with his short-lived Listen group has some swinging music, but also contains dated electronics and overly complex writing. Most of the selections feature Martin on many overdubbed reeds (including soprano, alto, tenor, baritone, flute, piccolo, clarinet and bass clarinet) along with keyboardist Larry Dunlop, electric bassist Dave Dunaway and drummer George Marsh. Bobbe Norris takes the vocal on the haunting "Yesterday's Song" (one of three songs written by Dunlap). It is doubtful that the music on this long-out-of-print LP will eventually be reissued, for despite the good intentions, nothing all that memorable occurs. —*Scott Yanow*

Other Side Up / Jan. 1983-Mar. 1983 / Catero ✦✦✦✦
A year before the first Bebop and Beyond recording, Mel Martin (heard on alto, soprano, tenor, flutes, piccolo, bass clarinet and piano) teamed up with guitarist Randy Vincent on record for the first time. This set of duets is bop-oriented, with the repertoire including Thelonious Monk's "Trinkle Tinkle," "Sly Mongoose," a free improvisation based on "Trinkle," "Wait 'til You See Her," and three originals. Vincent's distinctive and unusual sound, as well as Martin's versatility, make this obscure LP worth a search. —*Scott Yanow*

● **Plays Benny Carter** / Mar. 2, 1994-Apr. 30, 1994 / Enja ✦✦✦✦✦

Pat Martino (Pat Azzara)

b. Aug. 25, 1944, Philadelphia, PA
Guitar / Post-Bop

One of the most original of the jazz-based guitarists to emerge in the 1960s, Pat Martino made a remarkable comeback after brain surgery in 1980 to correct an aneurysm caused him to lose his memory and completely forget how to play. It took years, but he regained his ability, partly by listening to his older records!

Martino began playing professionally when he was 15. He worked early on with groups led by Willis Jackson, Red Holloway and a series of organists including Don Patterson, Jimmy Smith, Jack McDuff, Richard "Groove" Holmes and Jimmy McGriff. After playing with John Handy (1966), he started leading his own bands and heading sessions for Prestige, Muse and Warner Bros. that found him welcoming the influences of avant-garde jazz, rock, pop and world music into his advanced hard bop style. After the operation, Martino did not resume playing until 1984. Although not as active as earlier, Pat Martino has regained his earlier form, recording again for Muse and Evidence. —*Scott Yanow*

El Hombre / May 1, 1967 / Original Jazz Classics ✦✦✦✦✦
Guitarist Pat Martino's debut as a leader finds the 22-year-old showing off his roots in soul-jazz organ groups while looking ahead at the same time. Joined by organist Trudy Pitts, flutist Danny Turner, drummer Mitch Fine, and both Abdu Johnson and Vance Anderson on percussion, Martino primarily plays a straight-ahead set (five of his originals, "Just Friends," and "Once I Loved"), but already displays a fairly distinctive sound. This CD reissue brings back Martino's impressive start to what would be a productive solo career. —*Scott Yanow*

Strings! / Oct. 2, 1967 / Original Jazz Classics ✦✦✦✦
Guitarist Pat Martino's second recording as a leader (which has been reissued on CD) finds him essentially playing advanced bop. His quintet (with Joe Farrell on tenor and flute, pianist Cedar Walton, bassist Ben Tucker and drummer Walter Perkins) really roars on an uptempo version of "Minority" and is diverse enough to come up with meaningful statements on four of Martino's originals. —*Scott Yanow*

● **East!** / Jan. 8, 1968 / Original Jazz Classics ✦✦✦✦✦
Despite the title and the cover of this CD reissue (which makes it appear that the performances are greatly influenced by music of the Far East), the style played by guitarist Pat Martino's quartet is very much in the hard bop tradition. Martino was already developing his own sound and is in excellent form with pianist Eddie Green, drummer Lenny McBrowne and either Ben Tucker or Tyrone Brown on bass during two group originals, Benny Golson's "Park Avenue Petite," John Coltrane's "Lazy Bird" and the standard "Close Your Eyes." It's a good example of Pat Martino's playing in his early period. —*Scott Yanow*

Baiyina (The Clear Evidence) / Jun. 11, 1968 / Original Jazz Classics ✦✦✦✦
Pat Martino's fourth of five Prestige albums (reissued on CD) contains plenty of intriguing music. The innovative guitarist is joined by Bobby Rose on second guitar, Gregory Herbert on alto and flute (making his recording debut), bassist Richard Davis, drummer Charlie Persip and Reggie Ferguson on tabla, and Balakrishna on tamboura. Together they perform Martino's four-part suite, whose sections are named after aspects of the Koran. The use of Indian instruments, drones and unusual time signatures (including 7/4, 9/4 and 10/8) gives the performances the flavor of early fusion, and some of the effects sound a bit dated. However, the results were not overtly commercial, and the leader gets in several noteworthy improvisations. —*Scott Yanow*

Desperado / Mar. 1970 / Original Jazz Classics ✦✦✦✦
Guitarist Pat Martino's first five recordings as a leader were made for the Prestige label, and this one (the fifth) has been reissued on CD in the Original Jazz Classics series. Martino performs Sonny Rollins' "Oleo" and five of his originals, using the 12-string guitar. The rhythm section (keyboardist Eddie Green, electric bassist Tyrone Brown and drummer Sherman Ferguson) is funky in spots, electric, and swinging when called for. Eric Kloss makes a guest appearance on soprano for the opening "Blackjack," but otherwise, most of the focus is on Martino's consistently inventive playing. —*Scott Yanow*

Footprints / Mar. 24, 1972 / 32 Jazz ✦✦✦✦✦
Originally released by Cobblestone and later by Muse, this 1997 CD reissue from 32 Jazz features the distinctive and exploratory guitarist Pat Martino in a tribute to Wes Montgomery. Martino does not attempt to sound like Wes (although he uses octaves here and there), and only one of the six selections ("Road Song") was actually recorded by Montgomery; the tribute is more heartfelt than imitative. With the intuitive assistance of rhythm guitarist Bobby Rose, bassist Richard Davis and drummer Billy Higgins, Martino stretches out on six selections, including a bluesy original ("The Visit"), "Footprints," and "Alone Together," always sounding like himself and pushing the boundaries of straightahead jazz. —*Scott Yanow*

Head & Heart: Consciousness/Live / Sep. 2, 1972+Oct. 7, 1974 / 32 Jazz ✦✦✦

Live! / Sep. 7, 1972 / Muse ✦✦✦✦✦
For this intriguing club date, guitarist Pat Martino (who by the early '70s had his own distinctive sound) really stretches out on two of his originals (including "Special Door," which clocks in at 17:43) and the pop song "Sunny." With keyboardist Ron Thomas, electric bassist Tyrone Brown and drummer Sherman Ferguson offering alert and forceful support, Martino performs music that falls between advanced hard bop, fusion and the avant-garde without really fitting into any of the genres. Well worth several listens, but this LP is long out of print. —*Scott Yanow*

☆ **Consciousness** / Oct. 7, 1974 / Muse ✦✦✦✦✦
Martino on the way up. Mostly quartet recordings for the brilliant guitarist. "Willow," a dark, understated gem. Contains seven tracks, three by Martino, three standards, and Joni Mitchell's "Both Sides Now." Guitar students should study this one. —*Michael G. Nastos*

Exit / Feb. 10, 1976 / Muse ✦✦✦✦✦
This LP gave listeners a good sampling of mid-'70s Pat Martino. The distinctive yet flexible guitarist teams up with Gil Goldstein (who sticks here to acoustic piano), the great bassist Richard Davis, and drummer Billy Hart. Martino plays more standards than usual (four out of six songs, including "Days of Wine and Roses" and "Blue Bossa"), and, of his two originals, "Three Base Hit" has the spirit and fire of bop. An excellent outing. —*Scott Yanow*

We'll Be Together Again / Feb. 13, 1976-Feb. 17, 1976 / Muse ✦✦✦✦
This out-of-print LP features a set of duets by guitarist Pat Martino and the electric piano of Gil Goldstein. They perform Martino's three-part "Open Road" and six familiar standards, including the title cut, "You Don't Know What Love Is" and "Send in the Clowns." In general, the music is introspective, dreamy and thoughtful, with an attractive blend between the guitar and the keyboard. —*Scott Yanow*

Starbright / Jul. 1976 / Warner Bros. ✦✦✦

Joyous Lake / Jun. 1977 / Warner Bros. ✦✦✦

The Return / Feb. 1987 / Muse ✦✦✦
Pat Martino suffered a brain aneurysm in 1980, and after successful surgery, he was left with musical amnesia. He had to completely relearn how to play guitar, and the process of recovery took a long time. Finally, in 1987, he was ready to play in public and record. Showcased in a trio with bassist Steve LaSpina and drummer Joey Baron, Martino performs lengthy versions of four new originals during a live set from Fat Tuesdays, showing no mercy either for his sidemen or towards himself. Eighty percent back at the time (he would continue to get stronger record by record during the next few years), the guitarist's musical courage is admirable, and the music (which can only be classified as modern jazz) is frequently exciting. —*Scott Yanow*

Interchange / 1994 / Muse ✦✦✦✦✦

The Maker / Sep. 14, 1994 / Evidence ✦✦✦✦✦

All Sides Now / Jun. 1, 1996-Jan. 15, 1997 / Blue Note ✦✦✦✦
Veteran Pat Martino is teamed up with a variety of different fellow guitarists on this interesting if not quite essential release. Martino matches wits with guitarist Charlie Hunter (who on Stevie Wonder's "Too High" often sounds like an organist), Tuck Andress, Kevin Eubanks, Les Paul ("I'm Confessin'"), Mike Stern and Michael Hedges. In addition, Cassandra Wilson sings Joni Mitchell's "Both Sides Now" accompanied by Martino, and rock guitarist Joe Satriani tries to sit in on two numbers (with indifferent results). A decent effort, but not up to Pat Martino's most significant releases. —*Scott Yanow*

Steve Masakowski

b. Sep. 2, 1954, New Orleans, LA
Guitar / Post-Bop

A fine New Orleans guitarist whose advanced improvisations display the influence of his native city's early jazz and R&B scenes (at least rhythmically), Steve Masakowski attended Berklee in 1974. He invented the key-tar in 1978, an early guitar synthesizer. In 1982 he recorded for his own private Prescriptions label and he has since made albums as a leader for Blue Note and appeared as a sideman on dates led by Rick Margitza, Mose Allison, Red Tyler, Tony Dagradi and Johnny Adams, among others. In recent times, Steve Masakowski has toured with Dianne Reeves. —*Scott Yanow*

Friends / Jun. 1984 / Nebula ✦✦✦

Probably best known for his guitar work with tenor sax player Rick Margitza, Masakowski is a fine musician in the jazz and fusion idioms. This recording also features Margitza on several tracks. —*Paul Kohler*

What It Was / Apr. 1993 / Blue Note ✦✦✦✦

Guitar Steve Masakowski has a guitar sound that falls somewhere between Jim Hall and John Scofield. His laidback music (ten of the dozen songs on his Blue Note CD are his originals) is generally unpredictable, moody and full of strong solos. Masakowski's guitar largely dominates his CD, but there are a few good spots for Rick Margitza's tenor. Frankly, Masakowski at this point was a stronger player than composer, but several of the selections (particularly the mysterious "Budapest" and a couple of bossa novas) stick in one's mind. —*Scott Yanow*

● **Direct Axeccess** / Sep. 1994 / Blue Note ✦✦✦✦✦

Steve Masakowski dedicates his Blue Note CD to Joe Pass and his unaccompanied renditions of "Monk's Mood" and "Emily" would have pleased the late guitarist. Masakowski, who is influenced by Pat Martino and to a lesser extent Jim Hall, also pays tribute to Wes Montgomery, Emily Remler and (on a melodic if unadventurous duet version of "New Orleans" with Hank Mackie) Danny Barker. The guitarist's playing is in the modern mainstream idiom and, even if Masakowski's basic sound is not at this point instantly recognizable, his solos are inventive, swinging and versatile. Bassist James Singleton, drummer Brian Blade and (on six of the songs) pianist David Torkanowsky are excellent in support. —*Scott Yanow*

Hugh Masekela (Hugh Ramopolo Masekela)

b. Apr. 4, 1939, Wilbank, South Africa
Trumpet, Fluegelhorn, Vocals / World Fusion, Instrumental Pop, Soul-Jazz

Hugh Masekela has an extensive jazz background and credentials, but has enjoyed major success as one of the earliest leaders in the world fusion mode. Masekela's vibrant trumpet and fluegelhorn solos have been featured in pop, R&B, disco, Afropop and jazz contexts. He's had American and international hits, worked with bands around the world, and played with African, African-American, European and various American musicians during a stellar career. His style, especially on fluegelhorn, is a charismatic blend of striking upper register lines, half valve effects, repetitive figures and phrases, with some note bending, slurs and tonal colors. Though he's often simplified his playing to fit into restrictive pop formulas, Masekela's capable of outstanding ballad and bebop work. He began singing and playing piano as a child, influenced by seeing the film "Young Man with a Horn" at 13. Masekela started playing trumpet at 14. He played in the Huddleston Jazz Band, which was led by anti-apartheid crusader and group head Trevor Huddleston. Huddleston was eventually deported, and Masekela cofounded the Merry Makers of Springs along with Jonas Gwangwa. He later joined Alfred Herbert's Jazz Revue, and played in studio bands backing popular singers. Masekela was in the orchestra for the musical "King Kong," whose cast included Miriam Makeba. He was also in the Jazz Epistles with Abdullah Ibrahim, Makaya Ntshoko, Gwanga and Kippie Moeketsi. Masekela and Makeba, his wife at that time, left South Africa one year before Ibrahim and Sathima Bea Benjamin in 1961. Such musicians as Dizzy Gillespie, John Dankworth and Harry Belafonte assisted him. Masekela studied at the Royal Academy of Music, then the Manhattan School of Music. During the early '60s, his career began to explode. He recorded for MGM, Mercury and Verve, developing his hybrid African/pop/jazz style. Masekela moved to California and started his own record label, Chisa. He cut several albums expanding this formula and began to score pop success. The song "Grazing in the Grass" topped the charts in 1968 and eventually sold four million copies worldwide. That year Masekela sold out arenas nationwide during his tour, among them Carnegie Hall. He recorded in the early '70s with Monk Montgomery and the Crusaders. Masekela moved in a more ethnic direction during the '70s. He traveled to London to play with Nigerian Afrobeat great Fela Kuti and his Africa '70; then came a session with Dudu Pukwana, Eddie Gomez and Ntshoko, among others, that resulted in his finest jazz/African album, *Home Is Where the Music Is.* Masekela toured Guinea with the Ghanian Afropop band Hedzollah Zoundz, then

recorded a series of albums with them both in California and Africa, with guest stints from the Crusaders, Patti Austin and others. Masekela alternated between American and Africa, cutting a successful pop/dance album with Herb Alpert in the late '70s. During the '80s, Masekela returned to South Africa. He visited Zimbabawe and Botswana, and recorded two albums with the Kalahari Band that once more merged jazz-rock, funk and pop. Masekela was part of Paul Simon's Graceland tour in the mid-'80s, while he continued recording and produced sessions by Makeba. Though the jazz content of his work has varied over the years, Hugh Masekela has far more material on the plus side than the negative. —*Ron Wynn*

Trumpet African / 1962 / Mercury ✦✦✦

Striking early recordings. —*Ron Wynn*

● **Lasting Impression of Ooga Booga** / 1965 / Polygram ✦✦✦✦✦

Lasting Impression of Ooga Booga combines Hugh Masekela's two 1965 albums *The Lasting Impressions of Hugh Masekela* and *The Americanization of Ooga Booga* onto one disc. The music on these albums was groundbreaking at the time—few jazz musicians had delved quite as deeply into African rhythms, especially in the fashion of Masekela. He combines the rhythms with freeform jazz structures and pop-rock melodies. Certainly, the music sounds a bit dated several decades after its initial release, but some of it still sounds fresh, funky, and inventive. —*Thom Owens*

Home Is Where the Music Is / Jan. 1972 / Blue Thumb ✦✦✦✦✦

An outstanding blend of Afro-pop and jazz with strong work by Dudu Pukwana (as). —*Ron Wynn*

Main Event / 1978 / A&M ✦✦✦

"Let the good times roll," Herb Alpert seemed to say as he quickly rejoined forces with Masekela for a follow-up LP to their first collaboration earlier that year. Recording live at the Roxy Theatre and on A&M's soundstage without duplicating anything on their earlier studio album, the two horn players (Alpert on trumpet, Masekela on fluegelhorn) are, if anything, looser and more freewheeling than before. Though Alpert is not on quite as sure a jazz footing as Masekela, neither musician tries to blow the other out of the room. The band, containing only one holdover (guitarist Arthur Adams) from the first album, is more attuned to Latin funk/jazz with a South African tinge this time. Again, Alpert and Masekela have mostly fine tunes to work with, none better than "Foreign Natives" and "Shame the Devil" by African trombonist Mosa Jonas Gwangwa, plus Henry Sithole's wistfully haunting "Mama Way" (which has chanted vocals and a string quartet). This album and its predecessor had the effect of recharging Alpert's music, though both are almost forgotten today. —*Richard S. Ginell*

Tomorrow / 1986-1987 / Warner Brothers ✦✦✦

A mixture of live tracks and studio cuts from African trumpeter and fluegelhorn player Hugh Masekela done in 1986 and 1987. It includes some songs done in fusion style, others with African drummers, and some in a rock or funk mode. —*Ron Wynn*

George Masso

b. Nov. 17, 1926, Cranston, RI
Trombone / Swing, Dixieland

An excellent trombonist who currently records for Arbors, George Masso has had a long if somewhat underrated career. Other than some early gigs (including a 1948 association with Jimmy Dorsey), Masso made his living from teaching in schools up until 1973. However, he always played trombone on the side and, soon after becoming a full-time musician, he toured with the Benny Goodman Sextet (1973). Masso worked with Bobby Hackett, Bobby Rosengarden and the World's Greatest Jazz Band (the latter starting in 1975) and recorded with Scott Hamilton, Warren Vache and Woody Herman. He led sessions for Famous Door, World Jazz and Dreamstreet during 1978-83, frequently sharing the front line with tenor saxophonist Al Klink and trumpeter Glenn Zottola. Since then, George Masso has recorded for Sackville and Arbors and become a reliable fixture at jazz parties and classic jazz festivals. —*Scott Yanow*

A Swinging Case of Masso-Ism / Feb. 1981 / Famous Door ✦✦✦✦

Trombonist George Masso's third recording as a leader and second for the now-defunct Famous Door label (none of the recordings have yet been reissued on CD) has him playing six swinging standards and his own title cut with what could have been called the Famous Door All-Stars: Glenn Zottola (who alternates between trumpet and alto), veteran tenor Al Klink, pianist John Bunch, bassist Linc Milliman, and drummer Butch Miles. Masso's warm sound is well featured on such numbers as "So Danco Samba," "For You, For Me, Forevermore" and "It All Depends on You." —*Scott Yanow*

Pieces of Eight / Jul. 1982 / Dreamstreet ✦✦✦✦

For this excellent but obscure LP, trombonist George Masso arranged five selections for a seven-piece band that also includes the underrated trumpeter Glenn Zottola, Al Klink on tenor, guitarist Bucky Pizzarelli, pianist Derek Smith, bassist Bob Haggart and drummer Bobby Rosengarden. In addition to three standards (including a hard-swinging "Broadway" and a beautiful rendition of "It's So Peaceful in the Country"), Masso and his group perform Cole Porter's little-known "Down in the Depths of the 90th Floor" and the leader's "That's the Way It Goes." While those mainstream performances are fine, it is the three Masso-Pizzarelli trombone-guitar duets ("Do Nothing till You Hear from Me," "Solitude" and "Nobody Else but Me") that make this album particularly notable. —*Scott Yanow*

No Frills, Just Music / Oct. 1983 / Famous Door ✦✦✦✦

This fine straightahead LP from the obsolete Famous Door label matches the warm trombone of George Masso with a couple of stimulating horn soloists (trumpeter Glenn Zottola and altoist Chris Woods) and a swinging rhythm section (pianist Derek Smith, bassist Linc Milliman and drummer Ronnie Bedford). Together they perform five familiar standards, including "Stairway to the Stars" and "C Jam Blues," plus Masso's "Destination Stamford, USA." Fine swing-oriented mainstream jazz that deserves to someday be reissued on CD. —*Scott Yanow*

Just for a Thrill / Aug. 1990 / Sackville ✦✦✦✦

The Wonderful World of George Gershwin / Sep. 26, 1992 / Nagel-Heyer ✦✦✦✦

For the initial release on the German Nagel-Heyer label, trombonist George Masso heads an all-star mainstream septet that also includes clarinetist Kenny Davern, trumpeter Randy Sandke, the fine English tenor Danny Moss, pianist Eddie Higgins, bassist Len Skeat and drummer Jake Hanna. Together they jam on eight George Gershwin songs plus Higgins plays a "Porgy and Bess Medley." Although the liner notes (unlike later releases) are in German, the music easily comunicates; highlights include a blazing "Strike Up the Band," "Soon," and eleven-and-a-half-minute versions of "Somebody Loves Me" and "'S Wonderful." —*Scott Yanow*

● **Let's Be Buddies** / Jul. 14, 1993-Jul. 15, 1993 / Arbors ✦✦✦✦✦

Trombone Artistry / Aug. 27, 1994 / Nagel-Heyer ✦✦✦✦✦

This German CD teams together trombonist George Masso, clarinetist Ken Peplowski, pianist Brian Dee, bassist Len Skeat and drummer Jake Hanna. The trombone-clarinet front line works together quite well, and overall, this is one of Masso's finest recordings. Mainstream fans should enjoy the live recording, which is highlighted by "You'd Be So Nice to Come Home To," "More Than You Know," "It All Depends on You" and a burning rendition of "Three Little Words." —*Scott Yanow*

That Old Gang of Mine / 1997 / Arbors ✦✦✦✦

Mark Masters

b. 1958

Arranger, Leader / Post-Bop

One of the finer arrangers in the Los Angeles area, Mark Masters worked for Stan Kenton's Creative World in the 1980s and has led his Jazz Composers Orchestra since the early '80s. His big band has recorded for Sea Breeze (1984 and 1986), Capri (1990) and Focus (1993); the latter a set of Jimmy Knepper compositions. —*Scott Yanow*

Early Start / Jan. 17, 1984-Mar. 27, 1984 / Sea Breeze ✦✦✦✦

Although not too well-known away from the West Coast, Mark Masters' Jazz Composers Orchestra has often displayed its ability to interpret complex music. On their album, the 19-piece big band performs arrangements by Bill Holman ("Out of Nowhere" and "Film at Eleven"), Hank Levy, Dee Barton, Ken Hanna and Don Piestrup. Other than, to a small extent, altoist Danny House, the musicians are far from household names, but they all fare quite well both in ensembles and during their individual solos. Easily recommended to fans of modern big bands and Stan Kenton. —*Scott Yanow*

Silver Threads Among the Blues / Apr. 1, 1985-Jan. 28, 1986 / Sea Breeze ✦✦✦✦✦

The second recording by Mark Masters' Jazz Composers Orchestra finds the impressive and flexible 18-piece big band interpreting arrangements by Lennie Niehaus, Don Piestrup and Hank Levy, plus three by Ken Hanna. Most intriguing is "The Blues in Two Parts," which combines Bill Russo's "Blues: Before and After" and Ornette Coleman's "Blues Connotation." None of the musicians in the orchestra (except possibly trombonist Dick Shearer) are that well known, but they form a powerful group sound and take concise solos that are a logical part of the arrangements. —*Scott Yanow*

Priestess / Dec. 1990 / Capri ✦✦✦✦

● **Jimmy Knepper Songbook** / Feb. 22, 1993-Feb. 23, 1993 / Focus ✦✦✦✦✦

This recording is a bit of a surprise, for it features the Mark Masters' Jazz Orchestra performing eight Jimmy Knepper compositions. Knepper is much better-known for his individual bop-based trombone style than for his writing. However, Masters' colorful arrangements for his 14-piece big band show that Knepper is a talented composer. In general, the melodies are fresher than the chord changes (one can often guess the original sources), but the charts have their unpredictable moments on this continually interesting CD. In addition to such fine soloists as trumpeter Johnny Coles, tenor saxophonist Jerry Pinter, pianist Tommy Gill, Jr., altoist Gary Foster and baritonist Danny House (who is powerful on the blues "Who You"), Knepper himself is a major force throughout the program, soloing on all but two numbers and sounding very much in his prime. A highly recommended straightahead set. —*Scott Yanow*

The Mastersounds

Group / Cool

Vibraphonist Buddy Montgomery (1930-) and electric bassist Monk Montgomery (1921-82) came together to form the Mastersounds (a melodic and easy-listening bop group) with pianist Richie Crabtree and drummer Benny Barth in 1957. The band caught on for a few years, cutting ten records in four years for Pacific Jazz, World Pacific and Fantasy. Wes Montgomery appeared on one of their 1958 albums, a set of songs from the play *Kismet*. After the group disbanded in 1961, they had a brief reunion in 1965. The two Montgomery brothers had numerous opportunities to play with their more famous sibling under Wes' leadership throughout the 1960s. —*Scott Yanow*

Jazz Showcase Introducing the Mastersounds / Sept. 12, 1957 / World Pacific ✦✦✦✦

This is the debut of the lightly swinging quartet distinguished by vibist Buddy Montgomery. It appeals to fans of The Modern Jazz Quartet. —*David Szatmary*

The King and I / Sept. 19, 1957 / World Pacific ✦✦✦

The first of many dates (*Kismet, Flower Drum Song*) that use showtunes as points of departure. —*David Szatmary*

● **Kismet** / Apr. 22, 1958 / World Pacific ✦✦✦✦✦

It is surprising that this record has not yet been reissued on CD, for it is the only album by the Mastersounds (a quartet consisting of vibraphonist Buddy Montgomery, pianist Richie Crabtree, electric bassist Monk Montgomery and drummer Benny Barth) that also features guitarist Wes Montgomery, who was then barely known outside of his native Indianapolis. Wes' presence clearly inspired his two brothers, and his guitar added a fuller and more unusual sound to the band, which otherwise often sounded a bit like the Modern Jazz Quartet. Sticking to songs from the musical *Kismet*, the Mastersounds perform the show's two hits ("Baubles, Bangles and Beads" and "Stranger in Paradise"), plus five lesser-known songs and an overture that is a medley of six tunes. The music is enjoyable and not only features the Mastersounds at their best, but also gives one an early look at Wes Montgomery's already distinctive style. —*Scott Yanow*

Flower Drum Song / Dec. 4, 1958 / World Pacific ✦✦✦✦

Ballads and Blues / Jan. 7, 1959 / World Pacific ✦✦✦✦

For a few years in the late 1950s, the Mastersounds were a popular band. Consisting of vibraphonist Buddy Montgomery, electric bassist Monk Montgomery, pianist Richie Crabtree and drummer Benny Barth, the group was essentially an easy-listening and less classical-oriented version of the Modern Jazz Quartet. On this out-of-print LP, the band performs a "Blues Medley" (which includes among its three songs numbers by Milt Jackson and John Lewis), three originals, "Solar," "How Deep is the Ocean," "Mint Julep," and Dizzy Gillespie's "The Champ." The music is quite accessible, if now difficult to find. —*Scott Yanow*

The Mastersounds in Concert / Apr. 11, 1959 / World Pacific ✦✦✦✦

Having recorded several popular albums of show tunes that sold fairly well, the Mastersounds had an opportunity in 1959 to stretch out on a live album, which unfortunately has been long out of print. On four standards, a three-song ballad medley, and "Two Different Worlds," the quartet (consisting of vibraphonist Buddy Montgomery, pianist Richie Crabtree, electric bassist Monk Montgomery and drummer Benny Barth) are heard throughout in prime form, swinging hard on such songs as "Stompin' at the Savoy," "Love for Sale" and "Star Eyes." —*Scott Yanow*

The Mastersounds Play Horace Silver / 1959-1960 / World Pacific ✦✦✦✦✦

The Mastersounds (Buddy Montgomery on vibes, electric bassist Monk Montgomery, pianist Richard Crabtree and drummer Benny Barth) explore six Horace Silver tunes on this obscure but worthy LP. They were at the height of their success at the time (the quartet would break up in 1961) and sound in fine form on "Nica's Dream," "Doodlin'" and four lesser-known Silver songs. Excellent music that was endorsed by Horace Silver himself; he even wrote the liner notes. —*Scott Yanow*

Happy Holidays from Many Lands / 1960 / World Pacific ✦✦✦

Swingin' with the Mastersounds / Feb. 1961 / Original Jazz Classics ✦✦✦✦

Exquisite, precise swinging jazz, it delivers a light, unique sound. —*David Szatmary*

Date with the Mastersounds / 1961 / Fantasy ✦✦✦✦

This is the last studio date of the distinctive quartet. —*David Szatmary*

Ronnie Mathews (Ronald Albert Mathews)

b. Dec. 2, 1935, New York, NY
Piano / Hard Bop
Ronnie Mathews is a high-quality modern mainstream pianist who has been an asset to a countless number of sessions. Mathews played with Kenny Dorham, Roy Haynes and, more importantly, Max Roach (1963-68) and Freddie Hubbard, and Art Blakey's Jazz Messengers (1968-69 and for a period in 1975). Among his many other musical associations have been the groups of Clark Terry, Louis Hayes, Dexter Gordon (1976) and Johnny Griffin. Ronnie Mathews has led recording sessions for Prestige (1963), East Wind, Bee Hive (1978-79), Red, DIW and Sackville. —*Scott Yanow*

● **Doin' the Thang** / Dec. 17, 1963 / Prestige ✦✦✦✦✦

Roots, Branches and Dances / Dec. 7, 1978 / Bee Hive ✦✦✦

A talented hard bop pianist best known as a sideman, the underrated Ronnie Mathews had a couple of opportunities during 1978-79 to lead record sessions for the Chicago-based Bee Hive label; neither of the LPs have yet been reissued on CD. For the earlier set, Mathews utilized tenor saxophonist Frank Foster (who plays soprano on one number), bassist Ray Drummond, drummer Al Foster and (on two of the six numbers) percussionist Azzedin Weston. Together they perform "It Don't Mean a Thing," "Hi-Fly," Thelonious Monk's "Reflections," Drummond's "Susanita" and a pair of Mathews originals. The music is essentially advanced hard bop with a few surprises tossed in. An intriguing set. —*Scott Yanow*

Legacy / Sep. 21, 1979 / Bee Hive ✦✦✦✦

Pianist Ronnie Mathews assembled an all-star group (tenor saxophonist Ricky Ford, trumpeter Bill Hardman, bassist Walter Booker, Jr. and drummer Jimmy Cobb) for this hard bop set. Mathews had long been a distinctive but underrated player and is heard in prime form on a varied program including two of his songs, a pair of Tex Allen originals, "Suicide Is Painless," "A Child Is Born" and "Once I Loved." The musicians all live up to their potential, making one wish that the Bee Hive releases of the late '70s were available on CD. —*Scott Yanow*

Song for Leslie / Mar. 1, 1980 / Red ✦✦✦

So Sorry Please / 1985 / Nilva ✦✦✦

Selena's Dance / Jan. 1988 / Timeless ✦✦

At Cafe Des Copains / 1989 / Sackville ✦✦✦✦✦

Dark Before the Dawn / Oct. 26, 1990 / DIW ✦✦✦✦

Ronnie Mathews, a veteran pianist long a top improviser in the modern mainstream, was most heavily influenced by McCoy Tyner's chord voicings but developed his own voice. Throughout his trio CD, he is heard in particularly inventive form, especially during a swinging "The End of a Love Affair," a driving version of "One for Trane" and a boppish rendition of "You Leave Me Breathless." The support by bassist Ray Drummond and drummer Billy Higgins is conventional but tasteful, with the focus very much on Mathews' appealing style. —*Scott Yanow*

Matty Matlock (Julian Clifton Matlock)

b. Apr. 27, 1907, Paducah, KY, d. Jun. 14, 1978, Los Angeles, CA
Clarinet / Dixieland, Swing
A fine clarinetist, Matty Matlock also gained a lot of work in the 1950s as an arranger for Dixieland-flavored sessions. He started playing clarinet when he was 12 and performed in a variety of little-known bands, including one led by Jimmy Joy. He was with Ben Pollack's group during 1929-34, and when the orchestra became Bob Crosby's, Matlock stayed on. He became busy as an arranger but continued playing with Crosby off and on until 1942. At that point he moved to Los Angeles and worked in the studios. Matlock worked with Red Nichols and Pollack again and participated in the music for the film and the television series *Pete Kelly's Blues*. Matty Matlock led the Rampart Street Paraders in the 1950s, had many reunions with Bob Crosby, and continued playing into the mid-'70s. Unfortunately, his recordings as a leader for the X, Columbia, Tops and Warner Bros. labels 1954-60 are all long out of print. —*Scott Yanow*

Pete Kelly's Blues / Jun. 7, 1955-Jun. 9, 1955 / Columbia ✦✦✦✦

Dixieland / 1957 / Tops ✦✦✦✦

Clarinetist Matty Matlock recorded a fine series of Dixieland records from 1957-60, but all are currently out of print; fortunately, they can sometimes be found fairly cheaply in used record stores. This particular set has some solid Dixieland performed by Matlock, trumpeter Dick Cathcart, trombonist Abe Lincoln, Eddie Miller on tenor, pianist Stan Wrightsman, rhythm guitarist Al Hendrickson, bassist Phil Stephens and drummer Nick Fatool. The music (mostly Dixieland standards) is played solidly in the Bob Crosby tradition, with Matlock providing some basic arrangements. Highlights include "Jazz Me Blues," "Paper Doll," "Sugarfoot Strut" and "There'll Be Some Changes Made." —*Scott Yanow*

Pete Kelly at Home / 1957 / RCA ✦✦✦✦

The Dixieland Story, Vol. 1 / Apr. 14, 1958-May 14, 1958 / Warner Bros. ✦✦✦✦

The first of two LPs (which were also at one time available as a two-fer) by clarinetist Matty Matlock's Paducah Patrol does not really tell the story of Dixieland, but it serves as a good excuse for the playing of some hot music. Matlock and a variety of West Coast-based studio musicians and Bob Crosby alumni (John Best and Shorty Sherock on trumpets, trombonists Moe Schneider and Abe Lincoln, Eddie Miller on tenor and baritone, pianist Stan Wrightsman, guitarist George Van Eps, bassist Morty Corb and drummer Nick Fatool) perform ten well-known Dixieland tunes, plus Matlock's "Paducah Parade." The leader's writing for some of the ensembles gives his band its own personality and keeps the six horns quite coherent. Among the tunes covered are "Wolverine Blues," "Royal Garden Blues," "South Rampart Street Parade" and "The Saints." —*Scott Yanow*

● **And They Called It Dixieland** / Oct. 22, 1958-Nov. 5, 1958 / Warner Bros. ✦✦✦✦✦

Matty Matlock's Dixieland records of the late '50s were consistently excellent, but the chances are good that Warner Bros. will never get around to reissuing the music on CD. Matlock's Paducah Patrol was an expanded Dixieland band featuring six, rather than three, horns (Shorty Sherock and John Best on trumpets, both Moe Schneider and Abe Lincoln on trombones, tenorman Eddie Miller and the leader's clarinet), along with a four-piece rhythm section. Matlock's inventive arrangements alternated with some free blowing ensembles, and with this many strong soloists, the group usually lived up to its potential. Among the songs joyously explored on this excellent album are "I'm Gonna Stomp Mr. Henry Lee," "Runnin' Wild," "That's a Plenty" and "They Made It Twice as Nice as Paradise and They Called It Dixieland." Trad jazz fans will want this one. —*Scott Yanow*

Four-Button Dixie / Nov. 1958 / Warner Brothers ✦✦✦✦

With a six-horn front line and a band full of West Coast studio musicians, some of whom were alumni of Bob Crosby's Bobcats and all of whom were very adept at Dixieland, Matty Matlock's ten-piece Paducah Patrol had its own sound. The leader's arrangements kept the vintage tunes fresh, and some of the songs on this LP (such as "You've Got to See Mama Ev'ry Night," "Mama's Gone, Goodbye" and "When Buddha Smiles") were not often played in this setting. Among the key soloists are Eddie Miller on tenor and baritone, Shorty Sherock and Johnny Best on trumpets, and trombonist Abe Lincoln, in addition to the clarinetist/leader. Dixieland fans should search for all of Matlock's hard-to-find LPs. —*Scott Yanow*

Gold Diggers in Dixieland / 1959-1960 / Warner Brothers ✦✦✦✦

Although clarinetist/arranger Matty Matlock would live until 1978, this out-of-print LP from 1959-60 was his last date as a leader. Matlock's Paducah Patrol (a ten-piece, six-horn, Dixieland-flavored outfit) was a logical extension of Bob Crosby's Bobcats. The "plot" for the album is that ten of the 12 songs came out of the three films *Gold Diggers of 1933, 1935* or *1937*, or the play *Gold Diggers of Broadway*. Among the numbers are "With Plenty of Money and You," "Lullaby of Broadway," "We're in the Money" and "Tip-Toe Thru the Tulips with Me." Matlock also provided two basic originals ("$1,000,000 Rag" and "Sugar Daddy Strut") in the same vein. Spirited music. —*Scott Yanow*

Keiko Matsui

Piano, Keyboards, Vocals / Crossover Jazz, Fusion, Pop Jazz, Contemporary Jazz
Fusion/new age keyboard player Keiko Matsui grew up in Tokyo, and took her first piano lesson at the age of five. Influenced by Stevie Wonder and Rachmaninov as well as early fusion masters Maurice Jarre and Chick Corea, Matsui began composing while in junior high, but studied children's culture at the Japan Woman's University (Nihon Joshidaigaku). She moved to the Yamaha Music Foundation in Tokyo after graduation and formed Cosmos, recording four albums with the new age group. Her first album as a leader, 1987's *A Drop of Water*, was released in the US two years after the fact on Passport. The LP also featured her touring partner and husband, shakuhachi player Kazu Matsui, and was financed with their honeymoon money. A contract with MCA that year resulted in two albums, *No Borders* and *Under Northern Lights*. Matsui moved to the White Cat label in 1992, and began charting in the Contemporary Jazz charts. Her 1995 album *Sapphire* hit No. 1 on the charts, and its follow-up also reached the Top Ten the following year. —*John Bush*

Night Waltz / 1991 / Sindrome ✦✦

When Keiko Matsui gives herself the occasional chance to stretch out, she reveals a likable sound. But unfortunately, she doesn't stretch out nearly enough on *Night Waltz*—a CD that shows occasional traces of creativity, but is dominated by cumbersome arrangements, overproduction and new age-ish inclinations. The album's stronger pieces, including the haunting "The White Gate" and the Latin-influenced title song, actually have somewhat of a bite. But most of the other cuts are essentially examples of bloodless, unsoulful new age muzak—although new age with a beat. The improvisatory skills of such sidemen as Gerald Albright and Eric Marienthal are shamelessly wasted on *Night Waltz*, which isn't Matsui's worst album, but has many more weaknesses than strengths. —*Alex Henderson*

● **Dream Walk** / 1996 / ULG ✦✦✦

Dream Walk is Keiko Matsui's most balanced and impressive effort to date, highlighting her knack for smooth, soul-inflected material, as well as her effortlessly gorgeous and stylish vocals. —*Rodney Batdorf*

Bennie Maupin

b. Aug. 29, 1940, Detroit, MI

Tenor Saxophone, Bass Clarinet, Flute, Soprano Saxophone/ Post-Bop, Hard Bop, Fusion

Bennie Maupin is best known for his association with Herbie Hancock and his atmospheric bass clarinet playing on Miles Davis' classic *Bitches Brew* album. Maupin started playing tenor in high school and attended the Detroit Institute for Musical Arts, playing locally in Detroit. He moved to New York in 1963, freelancing with many groups including ones led by Marion Brown and Pharoah Sanders. Maupin played regularly with Roy Haynes (1966-68) and Horace Silver (1968-69), recording with McCoy Tyner (1968), Lee Morgan (1970) and Woody Shaw. After recording with Miles, he joined the Herbie Hancock Sextet. When Hancock broke up his group to form the more commercial Headhunters in 1973, Maupin was the only holdover. He led dates for ECM (1974) and a commercial one for Mercury (1976-77) but failed to catch on as a bandleader and has maintained a low profile during the past 15 years. —*Scott Yanow*

Almanac / 1967 / Improvising Artists ✦✦✦

Hard-edged swing and improvisations with Mike Nock, Cecil McBee, and Eddie Marshall. —*Michael G. Nastos*

● **The Jewel in the Lotus** / Mar. 1974 / ECM ✦✦✦✦

Detroit multi-instrumentalist with other members of Herbie Hancock's Mwandishi. Early-period progressive fusion. —*Michael G. Nastos*

Slow Traffic to the Right / 1976 1977 / Mercury ✦✦

Billy May

b. Nov. 10, 1916, Pittsburgh, PA

Arranger, Leader, Trumpet / Swing, Big Band, Orchestra, Traditional Pop, Instrumental Pop

The last survivor of the club of great arrangers who wrote regularly for Frank Sinatra, Billy May has had several varied careers in and out of jazz. His first notable gig was as an arranger/trumpeter with Charlie Barnet (1938-40), for whom he wrote the wah-wah-ing hit arrangement of Ray Noble's "Cherokee." Later, he worked in the same capacities for Glenn Miller (1940-42) and Les Brown (1942) before settling into staff jobs, first at the NBC studios, then at Capitol Records where he led his own studio big band from 1951 to 1954. His arrangements for Sinatra, beginning with *Come Fly with Me* (1957) and ending with *Trilogy* (1979), are often in a walloping, brassy, even taunting swing mode, generating some of the singer's most swaggering vocals. May has also done extensive scoring for television, film and commercials. Although May has been reticent in recent years, he unexpectedly surfaced in 1996 with some typically bright big-band charts for comic Stan Freberg's *The United States of America, Vol. 2* (Rhino)—25 years after his contributions to *Vol. 1!* —*Richard S. Ginell*

A Band Is Born / Jul. 25, 1951-Feb. 8, 1952 / Pausa ✦✦✦✦

In the early 1950s, a period when big bands were becoming extinct, one of the very few to catch on was arranger Billy May's. May utilized a trademark sliding saxophone sound and a rhythm section that sounds like it would have fit in well with Jimmy Lunceford's band. This Pausa LP, which reissues an earlier Capitol set, has some famous performances, including Billy May's renditions of "All of Me," "Fat Man Boogie" and "When My Sugar Walks Down the Street." The short solos are less important than the general sound of the ensembles. This is the one Billy May album to have. —*Scott Yanow*

Sorta Dixie / 1955 / Creative World ✦✦✦

This is a rather silly record. Arranger Billy May pays "tribute" to Dixieland by essentially tearing apart eight trad standards, plus "Sorta Blues." He uses a bewildering assortment of instruments (including many woodwinds, calliope, celeste,

orchestra bells, xylophone, tympani, triangle and harp) in addition to an oversized big band, and turns such songs as "Oh By Jingo," "Sugar Foot Strut," "Panama" and "The Sheik of Araby" into novelty tunes. A cute but far from essential LP. —*Scott Yanow*

★ **The Best of Billy May, Vol. 1** / 1951-1961 / Aerospace ✦✦✦✦✦

Pop-oriented and "sweet" band cuts from the Billy May orchestra, who enjoyed their prominence in the early '50s, before he sold the band to Ray Anthony in 1954. This anthology includes songs with Nat "King" Cole, Frank Sinatra and Jeri Southern, plus George Shearing. —*Ron Wynn*

Jon Mayer

b. 1938, New York, NY

Piano / Hard Bop, Post-Bop

Jon Mayer, a talented bop pianist, has had a long and colorful career while remaining greatly underrated. He had classical piano lessons and attended the High School of Music and Art and the Manhattan School of Music. Mayer picked up early experience playing with Pete La Roca and Ray Draper and jamming in New York clubs. He worked with the Kenny Dorham big band and Tony Scott's Quartet (where he replaced Bill Evans), and also recorded with Jackie McLean (1957's *Strange Blues*) and John Coltrane (*I Talk to the Trees*). Mayer worked in Paris with Chet Baker and in the 1960s and '70s gigged with the Thad Jones-Mel Lewis Orchestra, Kai Winding, Sarah Vaughan, and the Manhattan Transfer, while also doing session work in the studios. In addition, he wrote pop songs recorded by Les McCann, Nancy Wilson, Vicki Carr, and Gladys Knight, among others. Settling in the Los Angeles area in the 1980s, Mayer worked with Freddie Hubbard, McCann, and his own groups. Jon Mayer's first opportunity to record as a leader was a date for Pullen in 1995; he has since used Ernie Watts occasionally in his quartet. —*Scott Yanow*

● **Round up the Usual Suspects** / 1994 / Pullen Music ✦✦✦✦✦

It seems strange considering his talent and accomplishments that pianist Jon Mayer is not better known, and that this was his recording debut as a leader. He recorded with Jackie McLean and John Coltrane during 1957-58, played in Paris with Chet Baker, later performed regularly with the Thad Jones-Mel Lewis big band, Sarah Vaughan and the Manhattan Transfer (among others) and in more recent times worked with Les McCann's Magic Band. For the session, the hard loop-based pianist enlisted a pair of notable players to complete his trio: bassist Ron Carter and drummer Billy Higgins. Mayer performs his original title tune (a medium-tempo blues) plus Tom Harrell's "Because I Love You" and eight superior standards. The interplay between the musicians is quite impressive, the music always swings (even on the slower tempos) and Mayer holds his own with his famous sidemen on a program that includes such tunes as "Soul Eyes," "When I Fall in Love" and "Speak Low." Overall this is an impressive effort. —*Scott Yanow*

Virginia Mayhew

b. Redwood City, CA

Alto Saxophone, Tenor Saxophone, Soprano Saxophone / Post-Bop, Hard Bop

On her Chiaroscuro CD of 1996, Virginia Mayhew displays mature sounds on each of her reeds and a strong improvising style that builds from the tradition, but has plenty of spontaneity and chance-taking; she also shows strong talent as a composer. Mayhew started on clarinet when she was ten, and six years later switched to alto to join her high school jazz band. When she was 20, she moved to San Francisco, where she gained experience studying and playing locally (including with Earl Hines and Frank Zappa). In 1987, she won the New School's first annual Zoot Sims Memorial Scholarship and relocated to New York. Since then, Mayhew has worked with trumpeter Rebecca Franks (they co-led a quintet that played at the 1990 Monterey Jazz Festival and recorded a 1988 date for the Italian Philology label), the Toshiko Akiyoshi Orchestra, the Sahib Shihab big band, Al Grey (she appears on his Capri CD *Fab*), Clark Terry, Terry Gibbs, Kenny Barron and DIVA, among others. In addition to being an educator and a skilled arranger, Virginia Mayhew has frequently led her own groups. She has the potential to develop into a major voice in jazz. —*Scott Yanow*

It's Time for Virginia Mayhew / 1988 / Philology ✦✦✦✦

For a time, altoist Virginia Mayhew and trumpeter Rebecca Franks co-led a quintet. This Italian CD features the horns with either Larry Goldings or Kevin Hays on piano, Sean Smith or Andy Eulau on bass, and drummer Leon Parker. With the exception of Franks' blues "Honeydew" and Horace Silver's lesser-known "Grease Piece," the repertoire comprises standards. Mayhew in particular is in excellent form (she is showcased on "Body and Soul"), and among the highlights are ""Now's the Time," "Yesterdays" and "Just Friends." Recommended to straightahead jazz collectors who can find this obscure effort. —*Scott Yanow*

● **Nini Green** / Aug. 28, 1996-Aug. 29, 1996 / Chiaroscuro ✦✦✦✦✦

Virginia Mayhew is a strong hard bop-based saxophonist with a sound of her own. For her debut as a leader, Mayhew is quite effective on tenor, alto and soprano (although I think she is most distinctive on the alto), heading a sextet also including the fiery trumpeter Ingrid Jensen, pianist Kenny Barron, bassist Harvie Swartz, drummer Adam Cruz and percussionist Leon Parker. The solos of the two horns and Barron are consistently excellent, and all eight selections are quite rewarding. Most impressive (and a major factor in this set being on a much higher level than a jam session) is the leader's writing. Her "Nini Green" is melodic and catchy enough to become a standard, and Barron's sensitive playing during the opening of Mayhew's "Maybe Someday" is quite touching. Virginia's lyrical soprano solo on an extended version of "Good Morning Heartache" and the exciting rendition of the pianist's "Voyage" are two additional highlights. The saxophonist (who also performs three other fine originals and "Invitation") wraps up the date with a closing 2-minute "Jazzspeak," dur ing which she discusses how the session came about. This exciting set is highly recommended. —*Scott Yanow*

Bill Mays

b. Feb. 5, 1944, Sacramento, CA

Piano / Post-Bop

A fine pianist, Bill Mays has often worked behind the scenes, leading to him being a somewhat overlooked jazz improviser. Mays worked in Los Angeles as a studio musician from the late '60s on, accompanying Sarah Vaughan (1972-73) and Al Jarreau (1975), but mostly doing session work. In the early '80s he began to record jazz as a sideman with Howard Roberts, Bud Shank, Bobby Shew, Road Work Ahead and Mark Murphy. He recorded a duet date with Red Mitchell for ITI (1982) and led a quintet album for Trend (1983). In 1984 Mays moved to New York, and since then he has worked with Murphy, Gerry Mulligan, Ron Carter, James Moody, Sonny Stitt, Art Pepper and the Mel Lewis Orchestra, among others. Bill Mays has recorded fairly regularly for DMP (duet records with Ray Drummond) and especially Concord. —*Scott Yanow*

Two of a Mind / Oct. 1982 / ITI ✦✦✦✦

Pianist Bill Mays' recorded debut as a leader was long overdue (he was already 38) and unfortunately doomed to obscurity, since the ITI label did not last long. That is a pity, for this exploratory yet often swinging set teams him in a set of inventive duets with bassist Red Mitchell. The duo stretches out on Jim Hall's "Waltz New" and five familiar standards, coming up with all types of subtle surprises and reactions to each other's ideas. This is an album that yields new revelations each time it is played. —*Scott Yanow*

Tha's Delights / Jan. 24, 1983 / Trend ✦✦✦✦

Kaleidoscope / Oct. 1989 / Jazz Alliance ✦✦✦

The talented but underrated pianist Bill Mays is heard with Dick Oatts (on tenor, soprano and flute), guitarist Peter Sprague, bassist Harvie Swartz and drummer Jeff Hirshfield in a variety of settings throughout a consistently stimulating modern mainstream CD. Mays performs five standards (including "When the Sun Comes Out" and a lyrical rendition of "My Man's Gone Now"), along with four of his diverse originals, with creativity on this excellent outing. —*Scott Yanow*

One to One, Vol. 1 / Dec. 4, 1989-Dec. 5, 1989 / DMP ✦✦✦✦

The ghost of Bill Evans was certainly present during this duo recording. The musical interplay between pianist Bill Mays and bassist Ray Drummond is reminiscent of Evans and his various bassists. Mays and Drummond operate as equals (in fact the bassist seems to control the music as least as much as Mays) and their solo space is split fairly evenly. That is not to say that Bill Mays is merely imitating Evans on this CD, just that his highly impressive session is very much in that tradition; an adventurous rendition of "Skylark" is the high point. —*Scott Yanow*

One to One, Vol. 2 / Dec. 19, 1990-Dec. 20, 1990 / DMP ✦✦✦✦

W/ Drummond. A fine followup to an excellent initial outing. —*Ron Wynn*

● **Live at Maybeck Recital Hall, Vol. 26 (Bill Mays at Maybeck)** / Sep. 1992 / Concord Jazz ✦✦✦✦✦

Bill Mays gets a rare opportunity to record a full CD unaccompanied on his entry in the renowned *Maybeck Recital Hall* series. He mixes together swing standards with a few more recent selections. Mays' brilliant rendition of "A Nightingale Sang in Berkeley Square" (which starts and ends with a very impressionistic fantasy, making one wonder if its swinging middle section was indeed a dream) is most memorable. Also fun are his renditions of "Stompin' at the Savoy," "I'm Confessin'" and a boogie-woogie filled "Jitterbug Waltz." —*Scott Yanow*

An Ellington Affair / Jul. 22, 1994 / Concord Jazz ✦✦✦✦

Mays in Manhattan / May 28, 1996-May 29, 1996 / Concord Jazz ✦✦✦✦

Lyle Mays

b. Nov. 27, 1953, Wausaukee, WI

Keyboards, Piano / Post-Bop, Fusion

Lyle Mays' style is difficult to describe, more atmospheric (with plenty of unique colors) than swinging and an invaluable part of the sound of the Pat Metheny Group. Mays played and composed for the North Texas State University Lab Band in the mid-'70s. He met Metheny in 1975, toured with Woody Herman's Orchestra (1975-76) and then joined Metheny's band, continuing to play with the guitarist's group up to the present time. Lyle Mays (who is also an excellent acoustic pianist) has recorded several albums as a leader for Geffen. —*Scott Yanow*

Lyle Mays / 1985 / Geffen ✦✦✦✦

His best as a leader. Contemporary multikeyboardist, with an original concept. —*Michael G. Nastos*

Street Dreams / 1988 / Geffen ✦✦✦

This is more to the fusion side, but has lots of exceptional playing. —*Ron Wynn*

● **Fictionary** / Apr. 23, 1992 / Geffen ✦✦✦✦✦

Lyle Mays, who came to fame for his electric collaborations with Pat Metheny, surprised many with this superior outing in an acoustic trio setting. On the liner jacket Mays thanks Herbie Hancock, Keith Jarrett and Paul Bley for their inspiration. If one adds in Chick Corea and especially Bill Evans, that should give listeners an idea what to expect. However, to his credit (and with the assistance of bassist Marc Johnson and drummer Jack DeJohnette), Mays avoids performing overly played standards and sticks mostly to originals (including two free improvisations). There is no coasting on this excellent set. —*Scott Yanow*

Cecil McBee

b. May 19, 1935, Tulsa, OK

Bass / Post-Bop, Avant-Garde

A masterful bassist with an authoritative sound and a thoughtful but adventurous style, Cecil McBee uplifts every session he is on. After playing clarinet in his early years, he switched to bass when he was 17. After college, McBee played with Dinah Washington in 1959 before going in the military. After his discharge in 1962 he moved to Detroit, where he played with Paul Winter (1963-64). Relocating to New York in 1964, McBee worked and recorded with many top advanced players including Jackie McLean, Wayne Shorter, Charles Tolliver, the Charles Lloyd Quartet (1966), Yusef Lateef, Sam Rivers, Pharoah Sanders, Alice Coltrane, Abdullah Ibrahim, Sonny Rollins and Chico Freeman, among many others. Among his associations in the 1980s were McCoy Tyner, James Newton, Joanne Brackeen and (from 1984) the Leaders. Cecil McBee has led his own sessions for Strata East (1974), Enja, India Navigation and Palmetto. —*Scott Yanow*

Mutima / May 8, 1974 / Strata East ✦✦✦

Music from the Source / Aug. 2, 1977 / Inner City ✦✦✦✦✦

Other than a 1974 set for Strata East, this post-bop effort was bassist Cecil McBee's earliest recording as a leader. With Chico Freeman (heard on tenor and flute) as the most impressive soloist, McBee performs two originals and a piece by Hal Galper in a sextet that also includes trumpeter Joe Gardner, pianist Dennis Moorman, drummer Steve McCall and Don Moye on conga. The music is spiritual in nature, sometimes quite modal and in the adventurous genre of John Coltrane without being derivative. A fine live set, one of two recorded within a two-day period at New York's Sweet Basil. —*Scott Yanow*

Alternate Spaces / 1979 / India Navigation ✦✦✦✦

Bassist Cecil McBee and Chico Freeman (who triples on tenor, soprano and flute) teamed up many times during the late '70s and '80s. Their collaborations found them playing music that was a spiritual extension on hard bop, adventurous while moving forward. On this LP, they perform five of McBee's originals in a sextet that also includes trumpeter Joe Gardner, the percussive pianist Don Pullen (a major asset to the date), drummer Allen Nelson and percussionist Don Moye. The often melodic but unpredictable music definitely holds one's interest. —*Scott Yanow*

● **Flying Out** / 1982 / India Navigation ✦✦✦✦✦

This is a rather unusual chamber jazz album that finds bassist Cecil McBee interacting with violinist John Blake, cellist David Eyges, cornetist Olu Dara and drummer Billy Hart. Variety is gained by McBee switching to piano on "Truth—A Path to Peace," while "Into a Fantasy" is a classical-oriented string trio with violin, cello and bass, and "Blues on the Bottom" is a more conventional blues. The advanced music and the blending of the unusual colors works quite well. —*Scott Yanow*

Compassion / Apr. 1983 / Enja ✦✦✦✦✦

Performed the day after *Music from the Source* (which was also recorded at Sweet Basil's in New York), this excellent post-bop set features the brilliant bassist Cecil McBee, up-and-coming saxophonist Chico Freeman (heard on tenor and soprano), trumpeter Joe Gardner, pianist Dennis Moorman, drummer Steve McCall and Don Moye on conga. They perform long renditions of a pair of McBee originals, along with Freeman's "Pepi's Samba." The excellent solos, particularly those of Freeman, are adventurous, yet still based in the hard bop/modal tradition. —*Scott Yanow*

Unspoken / Mar. 11, 1997 / Palmetto ✦✦✦✦✦
Bassist Cecil McBee had not led a recording date since the mid-'80s before heading this 1996 session for Palmetto. Rather than being a showcase for his distinctive bass solos, the set is most significant for featuring eight of McBee's diverse originals. The quirky pieces include an eccentric "Pantamine," the tongue-in-cheek humor of "Catfish" (which at one point sounds like Dixieland filtered through Charles Mingus), the driving "Sleeping Giant," a jazz waltz ("Lucia") and the wild blues "Slippin' n' Slidin.'" All of the musicians fare quite well, particularly the passionate Eric Dolphy-inspired altoist Randall Connors and the versatile pianist David Berkman (whose playing ranges from McCoy Tyner to being nearly free on "Inside Out"). Trumpeter James Zollar tends to be more hard bop-oriented (showing humor with a plunger mute), while drummer Matt Wilson constantly pushes and inspires the musicians. The high musicianship and consistent inventiveness of Cecil McBee and his sidemen (along with the interesting tunes) make this a CD worth picking up. —*Scott Yanow*

Christian McBride

b. May 21, 1972, Philadelphia, PA
Bass / Hard Bop
Everyone's favorite young acoustic bassist of the 1990s, Christian McBride's large sound and expertise both with plucked and bowed solos recall Ray Brown and particularly Paul Chambers. He actually started on electric bass when he was eight and took R&B gigs in high school, but by then he was getting more interested in jazz and playing the acoustic bass. McBride studied at Juilliard (starting in 1989) and then played briefly in the bands of Bobby Watson, Benny Golson, Roy Hargrove and Freddie Hubbard. He toured with the Benny Green Trio, played duets with Ray Brown at the 1994 Monterey Jazz Festival, and recorded his debut as a leader for Verve before touring with his own group in 1995. —*Scott Yanow*

● **Gettin' to It** / Aug. 30, 1994-Sep. 1, 1994 / Verve ✦✦✦✦✦

Number Two Express / Nov. 12, 1995-Nov. 17, 1995 / Verve ✦✦✦✦✦
Christian McBride's second recording as a leader is an all-star affair, matching the young bassist in various combinations with either Kenny Garrett or Gary Bartz on alto, Chick Corea or Kenny Barron on keyboards, vibraphonist Steve Nelson, drummer Jack DeJohnette and percussionist Mino Cinelu. The music ranges from fairly straightahead to funky. Both Garrett and Bartz have opportunities to blow hard (pity that they were not teamed up); Chick Corea revives his "Tones for Joan's Bones," and McBride (who contributed all but four of the ten songs) overdubs his basses on Freddie Hubbard's "Little Sunflower." Continually interesting music which contains plenty of variety. —*Scott Yanow*

Fingerpainting: The Music of Herbie Hancock / Apr. 6, 1997-Apr. 8, 1997 / Verve ✦✦✦✦

Steve McCall

b. Sep. 20, 1933, Chicago, IL, d. May 24, 1989
Drums / Avant-Garde
One of the finest drummers in free jazz, Steve McCall was a subtle improviser who could keep a pulse going without actually stating the beat. He played early on with Lucky Carmichael, a blues singer. McCall met Muhal Richard Abrams in 1961 and became a founding member of the AACM in 1965. Based in Chicago, McCall played with hard bop groups, but made more of an impact performing with top avant-garde players including Anthony Braxton, Leroy Jenkins, Joseph Jarman, Roscoe Mitchell and Leo Smith. McCall was in Paris during 1967-70, playing and recording with Braxton, Marion Brown and Gunter Hampel. He returned to Chicago in 1970, was on a session with Dexter Gordon and Gene Ammons, and was in the trio Reflection with Henry Threadgill and Fred Hopkins. After another year in Europe, McCall went to New York in 1975 where he reunited with Threadgill and Hopkins, and they formed the successful avant-garde group Air. McCall was with Air until the early '80s, also recording with Chico Freeman, Arthur Blythe and David Murray. McCall played with Cecil Taylor's Unit in 1985 and performed regularly with Roscoe Mitchell's Quartet up until his death from a stroke. Although he was on a lot of important sessions (including dates with Joseph Jarman, Fred Anderson and Murray's octet), Steve McCall never led an album of his own. —*Scott Yanow*

Paul McCandless

b. Mar. 24, 1947, Indiana, PA
Oboe, Soprano Saxophone, English Horn / Folk-Jazz, Post-Bop
A talented multi-instrumentalist, Paul McCandless is best known for his longtime association with Oregon and for the floating and meditative sounds that he achieves out of his unusual combination of instruments. McCandless played in Paul Winter's band the Winter Consort (1968-73) and then (with Ralph Towner, Glen Moore and Collin Walcott) he left the group to form Oregon. McCandless is still primarily associated with Oregon (which is operating on a part-time basis in the 1990s) although he has also played and recorded with Gallery and Eberhard Weber and has led sessions of his own for Elektra, Landslide and Windham Hill. —*Scott Yanow*

All the Mornings Bring / Jan. 1979 / Elektra ✦✦✦✦
With strings and horns. Quite enjoyable. —*Michael G. Nastos*

● **Navigator** / Feb. 1981 / Landslide ✦✦✦✦✦
Group includes McCandless (on his usual soprano sax, English horn, oboe, bass clarinet), vocalist Jay Clayton and vibist David Samuels, plus Traut and Rodby. —*Michael G. Nastos*

Heresay / 1988 / Windham Hill ✦✦✦
This is a studio date with Art Lande (p) and Trilok Gurtu (per). Atmospheric without being dissipated. Very good record. —*Michael G. Nastos*

Premonition / Oct. 1991-Dec. 1991 / Windham Hill ✦✦✦
Reed player Paul McCandless has a lot of good company on his release *Premonition*. Together, the musicians explore a set of McCandless originals that revisit the lush beauty of his earlier work while forging into new jazz and fusion realms. Underscoring the project is a broad cast of musical partners that include Pat Metheny group members pianist Lyle Mays and bassist/album producer Steve Rodby. Yellowjackets drummer Will Kennedy, guitarist Steve Cardenas, and keyboardist Fred Simon round out the cast. —*MusD*

Skylight / 1996 / ECM ✦✦✦

Les McCann

b. Sep. 23, 1935, Lexington, KY
Piano, Vocals, Keyboards / Soul-Jazz, Hard Bop, Groove
Les McCann reached the peak of his career at the 1968 Montreux Jazz Festival, recording "Compared to What" and "Cold Duck Time" for Atlantic (*Swiss Movement*) with Eddie Harris and Benny Bailey. Although he has done some worthwhile work since then, much of it has been anticlimactic.

Les McCann first gained some fame in 1956 when he won a talent contest in the Navy as a singer that resulted in an appearance on television on *The Ed Sullivan Show*. After being discharged, he formed a trio in Los Angeles. McCann turned down an invitation to join the Cannonball Adderley Quintet so he could work on his own music. He signed a contract with Pacific Jazz and in 1960 gained some fame with his albums *Les McCann Plays the Truth* and *The Shout*. His soulful funk style on piano was influential and McCann's singing was largely secondary until the mid-'60s. He recorded many albums for Pacific Jazz during 1960-64, mostly with his trio, but also featuring Ben Webster, Richard "Groove" Holmes, Blue Mitchell, Stanley Turrentine, Joe Pass, the Jazz Crusaders and the Gerald Wilson Orchestra. McCann switched to Limelight during 1965-67, and then signed with Atlantic in 1968. After the success of *Swiss Movement*, McCann emphasized his singing at the expense of his playing and he began to utilize electric keyboards. His recordings became less interesting from that point on and, after his Atlantic contract ran out in 1976, McCann appeared on records much less often. However, he stayed popular, and a 1994 reunion tour with Eddie Harris was quite successful. A mid-'90s stroke put him out of action for a time and weakened his keyboard playing (his band began carrying an additional keyboardist), but Les McCann returned to a more active schedule during 1996 and was still a powerful singer. —*Scott Yanow*

The Best of Les McCann / Feb. 1960-Dec. 28, 1961 / Pacific Jazz ✦✦✦✦
The Best of Les McCann collects many highlights from the pianist's first sessions for Pacific Jazz Records, including popular selections like "The Shout," "The Shampoo" and "The Truth." Although the sampler nature of *The Best of Les McCann* will frustrate purists, the album nevertheless gives a good sense of what McCann accomplished in his early career and how he effortlessly fused jazz, blues and gospel. Nearly all of the material on this single-disc collection makes its compact disc debut on this compilation —*Stephen Thomas Erlewine*

● **Les McCann Anthology: Relationships** / Feb. 1960-Nov. 1972 / Rhino ✦✦✦✦✦
One of the many two-CD samplers of Atlantic jazz artists put together by Rhino Records, this retrospective has some of the high points of pianist-vocalist Les McCann's career, but is far from perfect. The first CD is purely instrumental, show-

casing McCann with several of his trios and in collaborations with organist Richard "Groove" Holmes, the tenors of Ben Webster and Stanley Turrentine, the Jazz Crusaders and Gerald Wilson's Orchestra. The second half of the two-fer has three selections on which McCann backs singer Lou Rawls (why were these included?) and just two vocals from the pianist. "Compared to What" and "Cold Duck Time" (from his famous meeting with Eddie Harris at the 1968 Montreux Jazz Festival) have been reissued several times, there are no selections from the 1973-95 period and the music is not programmed in strictly chronological order. Taken as a whole, there is plenty of rewarding music on the collection (including "The Truth," "The Shampoo," "A Little 3/4 for God & Co." and "With These Hands"), but McCann's vocalizing and his post-1972 music should not have been neglected. —*Scott Yanow*

The Shout / Jun. 1960 / Pacific Jazz ✦✦✦✦

Les McCann Plays the Truth / Jun. 1960 / Pacific Jazz ✦✦✦✦

Les McCann in San Francisco / Dec. 1960 / Pacific Jazz ✦✦✦✦

Les McCann in New York / 1960-Dec. 28, 1961 / Pacific Jazz ✦✦✦✦✦
The original Les McCann LP of the same name featured the soulful pianist heading a group consisting of Stanley Turrentine and Frank Haynes on tenors, trumpeter Blue Mitchell, bassist Herbie Lewis and drummer Ron Jefferson on five of his originals, including "A Little 3/4 for God & Co." The CD reissue adds a previously unissued sixth song from the session ("Someone Stole My Chitlins"), plus two formerly unknown numbers from a truncated 1960 date in which McCann, Lewis and Jefferson are joined by vibraphonist Bobby Hutcherson (at the beginning of his career) and Curtis Amy on tenor. The music overall is fairly definitive soul-jazz and finds McCann in prime form throughout a spirited instrumental program. —*Scott Yanow*

Les McCann Sings / Aug. 1961 / Pacific Jazz ✦✦✦✦
A super set with Ben Webster (ts) and Groove Holmes on organ. Soul-jazz and blues at their best. —*Ron Wynn*

Les McCann Plays the Shampoo at the Village / Dec. 28, 1961 / Pacific Jazz ✦✦✦

Pretty Lady / 1961 / Pacific Jazz ✦✦✦✦

Les McCann on Time / Jul. 1962-Aug. 1962 / Pacific Jazz ✦✦✦✦✦

The Gospel Truth / 1963 / Pacific Jazz ✦✦✦

Jazz Waltz / 1963 / Pacific Jazz ✦✦✦

Soul Hits / 1963 / Pacific Jazz ✦✦✦✦

But Not Really / Dec. 1964 / Limelight ✦✦✦✦

McCann / 1964 / Pacific Jazz ✦✦✦

Spanish Onions / 1964 / Pacific Jazz ✦✦✦✦

Live at Shelly's Manne-Hole / Dec. 31, 1965 / Limelight ✦✦✦✦

Les McCann Plays the Hits / Sep. 9, 1966-Dec. 28, 1966 / Limelight ✦✦✦

Bucket of Grease / Dec. 27, 1966-Dec. 28, 1966 / Limelight ✦✦✦

Les McCann Live at the Bohemian Caverns / 1967 / Limelight ✦✦✦✦

Les is More / 1967 / Night ✦✦
Joel Dorn's short-lived Night Music label featured private tapes of some of his favorite jazz artists. Pianist/vocalist Les McCann had collected 500 mostly undated private tapes through the years (the dates listed above are estimates) and this CD is drawn from that archive. McCann and his 1967 trio perform the groove tune "Maleah" and "With These Hands" (the latter has McCann's vocal), while "Samia" reunites the pianist with Eddie Harris. There are also a few numbers without McCann. One features singer Roberta Flack (a few months before cutting her first record for Atlantic) and there is an odd collage of L.A. appearances by such artists as Cannonball Adderley, Stanley Turrentine and Carmen McRae, but unfortunately those are just excerpts. "Clapformation" features an excellent R&B alto solo by Gerald Albright from very early in his career, and there is also a later version of McCann's hit "Compared to What." Very much a mixed bag, this CD (which is far from essential) is a historical curiosity at best. —*Scott Yanow*

★ **Much Les** / Jul. 22, 1968-Jul. 24, 1968 / Rhino ✦✦✦✦✦
This straight CD reissue of an Atlantic LP offers one a fairly definitive look at Les McCann in his prime. The pianist/singer develops long funky vamps that swing, sings "With These Hands" and, even with a string section added to four of the six numbers and three also having two percussionists, the emphasis is on McCann's trio with bassist Leroy Vinnegar and drummer Donald Dean. This is high-quality and intelligent groove music. —*Scott Yanow*

★ **Swiss Movement: Montreux 30th Anniversary Edition** / Jun. 22, 1969 / Rhino ✦✦✦✦✦
One of the most popular soul-jazz albums of all time, and one of the best, although Harris (and trumpeter Benny Bailey) had never played or rehearsed with the Les McCann Trio before, and indeed weren't even given the music. Perhaps that sparked the spontaneous funk that comes through clearly on the tape of this show,

recorded at the Montreux Festival in 1969. It's actually much more of a showcase for McCann than Harris, although the tenor saxist's contributions are significant. The sole vocal, a version of Gene McDaniels' "Compared to What," remains McCann's signature tune. It's worth picking up Rhino's *Montreux 30th Anniversary Edition*, as it adds a nine-minute bonus track ("Kaftan") and historical liner notes. —*Richie Unterberger*

Comment / Aug. 19, 1969-Oct. 22, 1969 / Atlantic ✦✦✦

Invitation to Openness / 1971 / Atlantic ✦✦✦✦

Talk to the People / May 1972 / Atlantic ✦✦

Live at Montreux / Jun. 24, 1972 / Atlantic ✦✦✦✦✦
A good two-disc date, with two hot stints by Rahsaan Roland Kirk (reeds). —*Ron Wynn*

Layers / Nov. 1972 / Rhino ✦✦
On this studio session, Les McCann augments his piano with various keyboards and synthesizers, showing the influence of Miles Davis' music of the period. McCann sets solid grooves with his trio (plus two percussionists) but dilutes his sound to a large extent. The music is set up as two lengthy suites, but unfortunately lacks any really catchy melodies. McCann does his best to stretch himself, and there are moments of interest, but this Rhino CD reissue of an Atlantic LP is not all that essential. —*Scott Yanow*

Another Beginning / 1974 / Atlantic ✦✦

Hustle to Survive / 1975 / Atlantic ✦✦

River High, River Low / 1976 / Atlantic ✦✦

Les McCann the Mann / 1978 / A&M ✦✦

Music Box / 1984 / JAM ✦✦✦

On the Soul Side / Jan. 1994 / Music Masters ✦✦✦✦

Listen Up / 1995 / Music Masters ✦✦✦
Pianist/vocalist Les McCann's first recording since a major stroke in early 1995 found him a weakened player, utilizing a second keyboardist on most selections, but still a powerful singer. McCann and his Magic Band were augmented by a quite a few notable guests on this set, including pianist George Duke, guitarist Dori Caymmi, organist Billy Preston, guitarist David T. Walker and tenorman Ernie Watts; steel drummer Andy Narell is featured on "Trinidad." Surprisingly, McCann only sings two numbers (a tender "When I Fall in Love" and "Listen Up"), and his role is fairly minor on the instrumentals, but there are some strong moments from each of the guests. Other highlights include "Someday We'll Meet Again," "A Little 3/4 for God & Co." (a McCann song from the early '60s), and "Bumpin'." Overall, this is a good mixture of jazz, a bit of funk, R&B and the blues. —*Scott Yanow*

Rob McConnell

b. Feb. 14, 1935, London, Ontario, Canada
Valve Trombone, Arranger, Leader / Bop, Swing
Although it has always been a part-time venture (working maybe 30 days a year, counting an annual recording), Rob McConnell's Boss Brass has been one of the finest big bands since the mid-'70s. An excellent soloist, McConnell has played valve trombone in Toronto (both in the studios and in jazz settings) for nearly four decades. During 1965-69 he was in Nimmons 'n' Nine Plus Six (led by Phil Nimmons) and in 1968 formed the Boss Brass. Originally the group comprised brass instruments plus a rhythm section and emphasized pop music. Although it added a saxophone section in 1971, the Boss Brass did not record much jazz until 1976. Comprising many of Toronto's top musicians (including Sam Noto, Guido Basso, Ian McDougall, Moe Koffman, Eugene Amaro, Rick Wilkins, Ed Bickert, Don Thompson and Terry Clarke, among others), the orchestra mostly plays McConnell's swinging but surprising charts. For a period in the late '80s McConnell moved to Los Angeles and the group broke up, but by 1991 it was back together again. Rob McConnell, who has also cut a few small-group dates for Concord, has recorded with his Boss Brass for Pausa, MPS, Dark Orchid, Innovation and Concord. —*Scott Yanow*

The Jazz Album / Apr. 1976 / Pausa ✦✦✦✦
Rob McConnell's Boss Brass began as a big band comprising trumpets, trombones, French horns, and an expanded rhythm section that played commercial music for Canadian radio transcriptions. In 1972, arranger/valve trombonist McConnell added a sax section for the first time, and with this 1976 set (originally released by the Canadian Attic label), he finally began to use the orchestra for jazz charts. As with most of the Boss Brass' early jazz dates, this LP is long out of print, but already found the band sounding quite recognizable. McConnell and his 22-piece orchestra perform three of his originals, plus "Portrait of Jenny" (a feature for fluegelhornist Guido Basso) and "Body and Soul," which showcases guitarist Ed Bick-

ert. Among the other key players are trumpeter Sam Noto and tenorman Eugene Amaro. Excellent big band music. —*Scott Yanow*

Big Band Jazz, Vol. 1 / 1977 / Pausa ✦✦✦
The 1977 version of Rob McConnell's Boss Brass is similar to the arranger/valve trombonist's 1997 band. The personnel includes such standbys as trumpeters Guido Basso and Sam Noto, trombonist Ian McDougall, the tenors of Eugene Amaro and Rick Wilkins, guitarist Ed Bickert, bassist Don Thompson and drummer Terry Clarke. McConnell's conservative charts swing and contain subtle surprises, with "Just Friends," "Street of Dreams," and Bob Brookmeyer's "Dirty Man" being among the better selections. Since many of the Boss Brass' earlier recordings were only made available domestically by the now-defunct Pausa label, this worthy music will be difficult to find. —*Scott Yanow*

Again!, Vol. 1 / 1978 / Pausa ✦✦✦
The first of two sets recorded by Rob McConnell's Boss Brass in 1978 was originally put out by the Canadian Umbrella label, and for a time on LP by the now-obsolete Pausa company. The 17-horn, 22-piece orchestra performs five standards (including a samba version of "Take the 'A' Train"). "Pianist Jimmy Dale is featured on "Everytime We Say Goodbye"; fluegelhornist Guido Basso is showcased on "A Time for Love"; the two French horns are prominent on "My Ship," and the two tenors (Eugene Amaro and Rick Wilkins) battle it out on the blues. Fine straightahead big band music. —*Scott Yanow*

Again!, Vol. 2 / 1978 / Pausa ✦✦✦
The second of two now-hard-to-find Rob McConnell Boss Brass LPs put out domestically by Pausa is a bit unusual in that the side-long, 17-minute, four-song "Pellet Suite" was not arranged by McConnell, but by this composer, trombonist Ian McDougall. In addition, the 22-piece big band performs McConnell's reworkings of Lester Young's "Tickletoe" and "I Hear a Rhapsody." The main soloists include guitarist Ed Bickert, Rick Wilkins on tenor, altoist Jerry Toth, trumpeter Sam Noto, Gene Amaro on tenor, altoist Moe Koffman and McConnell himself on valve trombone. —*Scott Yanow*

Present Perfect / Oct. 29, 1979-Oct. 31, 1979 / Pausa ✦✦✦
The Boss Brass has always featured some of the finest jazz-oriented session players from Toronto, Canada. Valve trombonist Rob McConnell's swinging arrangements give the orchestra its own personality, as can be heard on this obscure Pausa LP, which was originally put out by the European MPS label. The band performs fresh versions of three swing-era standards (including "You Took Advantage of Me"), a lesser-known tune, and a couple of McConnell originals, including "The Waltz I Blew for You." The key soloists include trumpeters Guido Basso and Sam Noto, altoists Jerry Toth and Moe Koffman, Rick Wilkins and Eugene Amaro on tenors, guitarist Ed Bickert, and McConnell (who is featured on "Smoke Gets in Your Eyes"). Worth searching for, as are virtually all of the recordings by this very consistent big band. —*Scott Yanow*

Live in Digital / Dec. 1, 1980-Dec. 3, 1980 / Sea Breeze ✦✦✦
This CD reissue has the six selections originally put out by the Canadian Dark Orchid label and adds three additional numbers from the same sessions. One of the few early Boss Brass albums currently available on CD, this set features McConnell's big band in typically swinging form. "T.O." goes through many styles, from hints of Dixieland to free; trombonist Ian McDougall is featured on Jobim's "Ana Luisa"; altoist Moe Koffman and trumpeter Sam Noto are heard from on "Groovin' High," and the band gets surprisingly funky on "Squib Cakes." A fine all-around showcase for the jazz orchestra. —*Scott Yanow*

Tribute / Dec. 1980 / Pausa ✦✦✦✦✦
For this out-of-print Pausa LP, which was put out in Europe by MPS, arranger Rob McConnell pays tribute to six then-recently deceased jazz greats (Cannonball Adderley, Gary McFarland, Frank Rosolino, Blue Mitchell, Bill Evans and Paul Desmond) by playing a song written by each. With such soloists as altoist Moe Koffman (featured on "Things Are Getting Better"), trumpeters Guido Basso and Sam Noto, altoist Jerry Toth (playing Desmond's "Wendy") and pianist James Dale (heard on Evans' "My Bells"), there are plenty of fireworks heard throughout the date. But actually, the main stars are McConnell's inventive and swinging arrangements. —*Scott Yanow*

All in Good Time / May 1982 / Sea Breeze ✦✦✦✦
Originally put out by the Canadian label Innovation and made available in the US by the short-lived Palo Alto label, this outing by Rob McConnell's 22-piece Boss Brass has eight typically swinging and fresh arrangements by the leader. He reinvents "I Got Rhythm," contributes three originals (including "Phil Not Bill" and "Schlep It Up to Joe"), and uplifts three jazz standards and Loonis McGloohan's "Songbird." As usual, the Boss Brass, which has had very little turnover through the years, features many top soloists, including altoist Moe Koffman, fluegelhornist Guido Basso (showcased on "Close Enough for Love"), the tenors of Rick Wilkins

and Eugene Amaro, and guitarist Ed Bickert, in addition to McConnell on valve trombone. A fine, if little-known effort. —*Scott Yanow*

Atras Da Porta / Dec. 19, 1983+Dec. 20, 1983 / Innovation ✦✦✦
Virtually every release by Rob McConnell's Boss Brass is easily recommended to fans of straightahead and swinging big bands. Put out by the Canadian Innovation label, this release is a bit unusual in that five of the songs are by Latin American composers, two of which were arranged by Jorge Calandrelli; in addition, the 22-piece orchestra plays "Easy to Love," "Autumn in New York," and "Bye Bye Blues." Although the material might be a bit different than usual, the band's distinctive sound is unchanged, and there is plenty of solo space for the usual top-notch players—altoist Moe Koffman, guitarist Ed Bickert, fluegelhornist Guido Basso, and Eugene Amaro on tenor. An interesting set that finds the big band showing a lot of flexibility. —*Scott Yanow*

Old Friends, New Music / May 17, 1984+May 25, 1984 / Unisson ✦✦✦✦
Valve trombonist Rob McConnell has mostly recorded with his big band the Boss Brass since the mid-'70s. This Canadian LP was a fine change of pace, because it features the valve trombonist in a sextet with some other top players from his orchestra: trumpeter Guido Basso, Rick Wilkins on tenor, guitarist Ed Bickert, bassist Steve Wallace and drummer Terry Clarke. Quite typically, McConnell also provided the arrangements for the ensembles, but the emphasis is definitely on the fine soloists. The leader and Wilkins provided two originals apiece, and the other tunes ("Ray's Idea," Thelonious Monk's "Pannonica," Lanny Morgan's "Friends Again" and Jim Hall's "Simple Samba") are rarely performed, so this bop-oriented set has plenty of fresh music. Worth searching for. —*Scott Yanow*

Boss Brass & Woods / Mar. 11, 1985-Mar. 12, 1985 / MCA ✦✦✦✦✦
Rob McConnell's 22-piece Boss Brass welcomes alto great Phil Woods to four of the eight selections on this release, including a remake of Woods' famous feature with Quincy Jones, "Quintessence"; the altoist also tears into "Out of Nowhere." McConnell's swinging arrangements are full of subtle creativity, as shown during fresh versions of "If Dreams Come True" and "Jive At Five," and there are some excellent solos by trumpeter Guido Basso, Rick Wilkins on tenor, and guitarist Ed Bickert, providing two additional reasons to search for this memorable set. —*Scott Yanow*

The Jive 5 / Aug. 1990 / Concord Jazz ✦✦✦✦
Although "Them There Eyes" is taken at a cooking tempo, this CD is mostly a relaxed and lightly swinging date featuring some of Canada's top jazzmen. Valve trombonist Rob McConnell has a mellow sound and is a very fluent soloist. Matched with the Zoot Sims-inspired tenor of Rick Wilkins, lyrical guitarist Ed Bickert, tasteful bassist Neil Swainson and the supportive drumming of Jerry Fuller, McConnell and his crew explore mostly obscure but straightahead material. "Change Partners" is turned into a bossa nova (as is Thad Jones' "Bossa Nova Ova"); "Dream" could serve as the background for a slow romantic dance; and "4 B.C." is a McConnell original written in tribute to Benny Carter. This swinging session straddles the boundary between bop and mainstream jazz. —*Scott Yanow*

The Brass Is Back / Jan. 28, 1991-Jan. 29, 1991 / Concord Jazz ✦✦✦✦✦
More emphasis on post-bop from composers Silver and Kai Winding. Tunes from Don Thompson, R. Wilkins, Roger Kellaway, and McConnell. Two standards. —*Michael G. Nastos*

Brassy and Sassy / 1992 / Concord Jazz ✦✦✦✦✦
This CD can serve as a perfect introduction to Rob McConnell's Boss Brass. The leader's arrangements (plus one by Ron Collier) uplift such standards as "Strike Up the Band," "Things Ain't What They Used to Be" and "Scrapple from the Apple"; trombonist Ian McDougall introduces his three-part, 19-minute "Blue Serge Suit(e)," and many veteran soloists are featured, including the tenors of Eugene Amaro and Rick Wilkins, trumpeters John MacLeod and Guido Basso, guitarist Ed Bickert, and McConnell himself on valve trombone. Throughout, the Boss Brass is heard in prime form. —*Scott Yanow*

● **Our 25th Year** / Mar. 1993 / Concord Jazz ✦✦✦✦✦
Rob McConnell's Boss Brass has produced 25 years of solid music making, most of in the swinging bebop tradition. The music on this Concord CD has more than its share of surprises, such as a bar of 3/4 put in one chorus of "4 B.C.," phrases "borrowed" from Bob Florence and inserted in "Riffs I Have Known," and an inventive version of "Flying Home." Among the other high points are trumpeter Guido Basso's feature on "Imagination," Eugene Amaro's tenor on "What Am I Here For" and a driving "Broadway." This solid effort is recommended to big band fans. —*Scott Yanow*

Trio Sketches / May 20, 1993-May 21, 1993 / Concord Jazz ✦✦✦✦
The trio of valve trombonist Rob McConnell, guitarist Ed Bickert and bassist Neil Swainson creates mellow and melodic bop-based music. While Bickert has one of the quietest guitar sounds around and Swainson is often content to play softly in the background, McConnell's cool tone and accessible style are often in the lead. The results are predictably swinging with plenty of subtle interplay. —*Scott Yanow*

Overtime / 1994 / Concord Jazz ✦✦✦✦✦

Even Canadians Get the Blues / Apr. 23, 1996-Apr. 24, 1996 / Concord Jazz ✦✦✦✦

Three for the Road / Oct. 11, 1996-Oct. 12, 1996 / Concord Jazz ✦✦✦✦

● **Play the Jazz Classics** / May 26, 1997-May 27, 1997 / Concord Jazz ✦✦✦✦✦

Susannah McCorkle

b. Jan. 1, 1946, Berkeley, CA
Vocals / Standards, Traditional Pop

One of the finest interpreters of lyrics active in the jazz world during the 1980s and '90s, Susannah McCorkle does not improvise all that much, but she brings the proper emotional intensity to the words she sings; a lyricist's dream! She moved to England in 1971 where she worked with Dick Sudhalter and Keith Ingham, among others, performing at concerts with such visiting Americans as Bobby Hackett, Ben Webster and Dexter Gordon. McCorkle sang at the Riverboat jazz room in Manhattan during 1975 (gaining a lot of attention) and recorded two albums in England (tributes to Harry Warren and Johnny Mercer) that were released domestically by Inner City. By 1980 she was back in the US, recording a Yip Harburg set and a fourth album for Inner City. After that label folded, McCorkle switched over to Pausa, but by the late '80s was recording regularly for Concord. She has expanded her pre-bop repertoire to include Brazilian songs and blues and in the late '90s Susannah McCorkle is at the top of her field. —*Scott Yanow*

The Songs of Johnny Mercer / Sep. 19, 1977-Oct. 3, 1977 / Jazz Alliance ✦✦✦✦✦
For her second recording and first US release, singer Susannah McCorkle performs 14 songs fortunate enough to have the delightful lyrics of Johnny Mercer. Whether it be the Dixielandish "At the Jazz Band Ball," "Blues in the Night," the touching "Skylark," a "Dream" medley, "One for My Baby" or the novelty "Arthur Murray Taught Me Dancing in a Hurry," McCorkle does full justice to the words she sings. Recorded in London in 1977, the date finds McCorkle joined by such fine English musicians as pianist Keith Ingham, bassist Ron Rubin, drummer Derek Hogg, the tenors of Danny Moss and Duncan Lamont, and the excellent trumpeter Digby Fairweather. —*Scott Yanow*

The Music of Harry Warren / Aug. 23, 1976-1981 / Inner City ✦✦✦✦
Susannah McCorkle's first album, which finds her in 1976 sounding quite pleased to be recording, features the talented singer interpreting 17 of Harry Warren's best songs, many sporting lyrics by Al Dubin. McCorkle's voice is instantly recognizable, and her ability to bring out the beauty in lyrics was already quite impressive. This English session was first released domestically by Inner City in 1981; at the time, McCorkle recorded two additional songs ("Forty Second Street" and "Chatanooga Choo Choo"). Providing some jazz flavor are pianist Keith Ingham, Bruce Turner on alto and clarinet, bassist Len Skeat and drummer Johnny Richardson. —*Scott Yanow*

Over the Rainbow: The Songs of E.Y. Yip Harburg / Jan. 11, 1980+Feb. 19, 1980 / Jazz Alliance ✦✦✦✦✦
Susannah McCorkle's first three recordings focused on the "songbooks" of specific composers or lyricists. For her third project, McCorkle (backed by pianist Keith Ingham, bassist Jack Six and drummer Ronnie Bedford) explored the words of Yip Harburg, who was most renowned for his work on *The Wizard of Oz.* McCorkle not only revisits a few of those classic tunes (including the title cut, "If I Only Had a Heart" and "Ding Dong, the Witch Is Dead") but plenty of obscure works such as "The Begat," "Napoleon" and "Moanin' in the Mornin." McCorkle was very much up for this assignment and she did Yip Harburg's work justice. —*Scott Yanow*

The People That You Never Get to Love / Nov. 16, 1981+Nov. 18, 1981 / Inner City ✦✦✦✦
After recording three "songbooks," the superb singer Susannah McCorkle performed 14 songs by as many composers on this Jazz Alliance CD reissue. Although there are a few older tunes (such as "The Lady's in Love with You," "I Won't Dance" and "I've Grown Accustomed to His Face"), McCorkle emphasizes newer material, including songs by Blossom Dearie ("Bye Bye Country Boy"), Oscar Brown, Jr. ("The Call of the City"), Dave Frishberg (the obscure "Foodophobia") and a tune that has stayed in her repertoire: "The People That You Never Get to Love." With fine backup work from pianist Keith Ingham, guitarist Al Gafa, bassist Steve LaSpina and drummer Joe Cucuzzo, Susannah McCorkle (who has never recorded a weak album) shows off her versatility without losing her strong musical personality, purpose and charm. —*Scott Yanow*

Thanks for the Memory: The Songs of Leo Robin / Dec. 1983-Jan. 1984 / Pausa ✦✦✦✦
After the Inner City label died, the talented singer Susannah McCorkle recorded three albums for Pausa before it too became defunct; all of her early records remain out of print and long overdue to be reissued on CD. For her tribute to lyricist Leo Robin (her first Pausa project), McCorkle beautifully interprets his lyrics to

13 songs, most of which were originally written for the movies. Best known are "Diamonds Are a Girl's Best Friend," "My Ideal," "Beyond the Blue Horizon," "Havin' Myself a Time" and "Thanks for the Memory, " but there are also some fine obscurities on this date too; when was the last time anyone recorded "My Cutie's Due at Two to Two" or "A Little Girl from Little Rock"? —*Scott Yanow*

How Do You Keep the Music Playing? / Jun. 1985 / Pausa ✦✦✦✦✦
Susannah McCorkle's second Pausa album is highlighted by a remarkable version of "There's No Business like Show Business." Usually performed in razzle-dazzle style, the song is drastically slowed down and treated as a dramatic ballad by McCorkle, and she shows that the words are actually quite touching! Also on the diverse set are the singer's fresh interpretations of such tunes as "A Fine Romance," "Where or When," "Cheek to Cheek," "Slap That Bass" and even a tolerable rendition of "By the Time I Get to Phoenix." Backed by the Ben Aronov trio and on a few numbers joined by either tenor saxophonist Al Cohn or guitarist Gene Bertoncini, Susannah McCorkle is in fine form. —*Scott Yanow*

Dream / Dec. 9, 1986-Dec. 10, 1986 / Pausa ✦✦✦✦
Susannah McCorkle, one of the finest jazz-influenced vocalists to emerge during the 1970s and '80s, sings a wide variety of music on her out-of-print Pausa LP. In addition to some prebop material (including Cole Porter's "At Long Last Love," a vocalese version of "All of Me," "I Get a Kick out of You" and Johnny Mercer's title cut), she also tackles tunes by Paul Simon, Oscar Brown, Jr., Antonio Carlos Jobim and Leiber & Stoller. No matter what the style (she is essentially a swing singer), Susannah McCorkle uplifts each song. She is assisted by the Ben Aronov trio, and occasionally guitarist Gene Bertoncini and tenor saxophonist Frank Wess. —*Scott Yanow*

● **No More Blues** / Oct. 1988 / Concord Jazz ✦✦✦✦✦
Susannah McCorkle first emerged in 1976 as one of the top interpreters of lyrics to mature since the 1950s. Since then, she has continued to grow as an expressive singer who brings out hidden beauty in the songs she sings. For her Concord debut, McCorkle is joined by Ken Peplowski (on clarinet and tenor), either Emily Remler or Bucky Pizzarelli on guitar, pianist Dave Frishberg (in a purely instrumental role), bassist John Goldsby and drummer Terry Clarke. Although many of her recordings have been songbooks focusing on one composer or lyricist, she chose superior standards by a wide variety of writers for this date. Highlights include "Fascinating Rhythm," a hot version of Louis Armstrong's "Swing that Music," "P.S. I Love You," "Sometimes I'm Happy," Gerry Mulligan's inspiring "The Ballad of Pearly Sue" and "No More Blues," but all ten numbers are quite rewarding. Highly recommended. —*Scott Yanow*

Sabia / Feb. 1990 / Concord Jazz ✦✦✦✦
Susannah McCorkle speaks Italian, Spanish, German and Portuguese in addition to English; she used to work as an interpreter before she devoted herself to singing. On her second Concord CD, McCorkle sings 10 Brazilian songs plus "Estate," switching between English, Portuguese and Italian. There is no communication problem as far as conveying her feelings and the high quality of the melodies, so this is a more accessible release than one might think. The vocalist's backup group includes pianist Lee Musiker, Scott Hamilton on tenor and guitarist Emily Remler. —*Scott Yanow*

I'll Take Romance / Sep. 15, 1991-Sep. 17, 1991 / Concord Jazz ✦✦✦✦✦
The plot behind this project by the wonderful singer Susannah McCorkle is that she performs fresh interpretations of familiar standards that deal with love; all but the recent "Where Do You Start" were at least 35 years old at the time and some were of much earlier vintage. Backed by a quintet including Frank Wess on tenor and flute, pianist Allen Farnham and guitarist Howard Alden, McCorkle's very attractive voice and impressive interpretive skills are heard at their best. Highlights include the title cut, "A Beautiful Friendship," "Get out of Town," "It Never Entered My Mind," "Taking a Chance on Love" and "I Thought About You." —*Scott Yanow*

From Bessie to Brazil / Feb. 1993 / Concord Jazz ✦✦✦✦
For this Concord release, singer Susannah McCorkle alternates vintage standards and obscurities with some more recent songs such as "The Waters of March," Dave Frishberg's "Quality Time," and Paul Simon's "Still Crazy After All These Years." The bread and butter is still the older tunes, and among the highlights are "The Lady Is a Tramp," "My Sweetie Went Away," "Hit the Road to Dreamland" and a remake of "The People that You Never Get to Love." McCorkle is joined by four horns (including trumpeter Randy Sandke and Ken Peplowski on tenor and clarinet) plus a rhythm section led by her pianist Allen Farnham who also serves as her musical director. A fine all-round showcase for the talented singer. —*Scott Yanow*

From Broadway to Bebop / 1994 / Concord Jazz ✦✦✦✦
Susannah McCorkle covers a lot of ground during this 1994 CD on which she is joined by a four-horn octet under the musical direction of pianist Allen Farnham. Whether it be "Guys and Dolls," "My Buddy," "Moody's Mood," Don Sebesky's recent "I Remember Bill" (for Bill Evans) or even "Don't Fence Me In," McCorkle

brings an intelligent joy to the lyrics. "Chica Chica Boom Chic" (a tribute to Carmen Miranda) is a bit silly, but otherwise this is an excellent set featuring one of the top jazz-influenced interpreters of lyrics to be on the scene in the 1990s. —*Scott Yanow*

Easy to Love: The Songs of Cole Porter / Sep. 6, 1995-Sep. 8, 1995 / Concord Jazz ◆◆◆◆

Susannah McCorkle has long been a lyricist's dream. Rather than distort or alter the words she interprets, McCorkle (who has an immediately appealing and likable voice) brings out the hidden beauty in the lyrics. For her latest Concord disc, Susannah McCorkle sings 14 songs written by Cole Porter whose lyrics were among the most sophisticated of the 1930-60 era. The arrangements by her musical director and pianist Allen Farnham are quite inventive, with exuberant octet numbers (featuring concise but generally memorable solos from trumpeter Randy Sandke, altoist Chris Potter, trombonist Robert Trowers and Ken Peplowski on tenor and clarinet) alternating with more intimate performances including voice-guitar duets with Howard Alden on a slow chorus of "Just One of Those Things," "Why Don't We Try Staying Home" and the sad "Goodbye Little Dream, Goodbye." Among the other highlights are lengthy renditions of "Anything Goes" and "Let's Do It" which find McCorkle singing every stanza that could be found (the former has many obscure topical references), a boisterous version of "It's All Right With Me" and an emotional "Weren't We Fools?" —*Scott Yanow*

Let's Face the Music: The Songs of Irving Berlin / Oct. 28, 1996+Oct. 30, 1996 / Concord Jazz ◆◆◆◆

Susannah McCorkle, who consistently brings out new meanings in the lyrics she interprets, performs 16 Irving Berlin songs (complete with verses and sometimes lesser-known stanzas) on this delightful set. There is solo space for trumpeter Gregory Gisbert, trombonist Conrad Herwig, young tenor great Chris Potter and altoist Jerry Dodgion; the arrangements by Rich DeRosa are surprisingly modern, and McCorkle is heard in prime form. Among the many highlights are a wistful rendition of "Let's Face the Music and Dance," a sensuous "Cheek to Cheek," "Let Yourself Go," and a wonderful closer, a version of "Waiting at the End of the Road" on which the singer is accompanied only by the rhythm guitar of Al Gafa. Although this interpretation of "There's No Business Like Show Business" (greatly slowed down and surprisingly touching) is not quite as classic as McCorkle's version of a decade earlier, this is overall a highly recommended set by a superb singer. —*Scott Yanow*

Roy McCurdy

b. Nov. 28, 1936, Rochester, NY
Drums / Hard Bop

Roy McCurdy will probably always be best known for his important contributions to Cannonball Adderley's Quintet (1965-75), but he has been a tasteful and stimulating participant in many other sessions through the years. Early on, he worked with Chuck and Gap Mangione in the Jazz Brothers (1960-61). McCurdy gained recognition for his playing with the Jazztet (1961-62), Bobby Timmons, Betty Carter (who was fairly obscure during his stint with her in 1962-63), and Sonny Rollins (1963-64) before joining Adderley. The supportive drummer was flexible enough to evolve with Cannonball's popular group during the decade of change. After Adderley's death, McCurdy relocated to the Los Angeles area, where he has played and recorded with the top local musicians ever since. Surprisingly, Roy McCurdy has yet to lead a record session of his own. —*Scott Yanow*

Dick McDonough

b. 1904, **d.** May 25, 1938, New York, NY
Guitar / Classic Jazz, Swing

With the premature death of Eddie Lang in 1933, Dick McDonough and Carl Kress were considered his likely successors both on jazz dates and in the studios. McDonough was already a very busy player. He had started out in 1927 as a banjoist with Red Nichols, had switched over to guitar and appeared on hundreds of sessions, including with the Dorsey Brothers, the Boswell Sisters, Joe Venuti and in more commercial music. His work accelerated with Lang's passing, he occasionally teamed up with Kress, and during 1936-37, McDonough led a notable series of medium-size group recordings, few of which have ever been reissued. McDonough also recorded with Glenn Miller's unsuccessful big band of 1937 and made a notable appearance on an all-star date with Fats Waller, Tommy Dorsey, Bunny Berigan and George Wettling that was issued as "A Jam Session at Victor." A strong acoustic guitarist who emphasized chords in his solos (influencing Marty Grosz decades later), Dick McDonough's alcoholism cut short his life much too early. —*Scott Yanow*

Guitar Genius in the 1930s / 1934-1937 / Jazz Archives ◆◆◆◆

This collector's LP contains some very obscure but worthy performances. Dick McDonough has a couple of hot chordal-based guitar solos from 1934 ("Chasing a

Buck" and "Honeysuckle Rose") and duets with bassist Artie Bernstein on "The Ramble." The other dozen selections (not listed in most discographies) feature a 1937 big band that includes Adrian Rollini on bass sax and vibes, two vocals by Barry McKinley, and both McDonough and Carl Kress on guitars. Virtually every selection by the orchestra has short solos from both acoustic guitarists, and since they were the pacesetters of the era (aside from Django Reinhardt), and guitarists rarely had opportunities to solo during the period in this setting, the performances are quite unique. Highly recommended to swing and pre-bop guitar collectors. Hopefully, this rare music will be reissued on CD. —*Scott Yanow*

Jack McDuff (Eugene McDuffy)

b. Sep. 17, 1926, Champaign, IL
Organ / Soul-Jazz, Hard Bop, Groove

A marvelous bandleader and organist as well as capable arranger, "Brother" Jack McDuff has one of the funkiest, most soulful styles of all time on the Hammond B-3. His rock-solid bass lines and blues-drenched solos are balanced by clever, almost pianistic melodies and interesting progressions and phrases. McDuff began as a bassist playing with Denny Zeitlin and Joe Farrell. He studied privately in Cinncinnati and worked with Johnny Griffin in Chicago. He taught himself organ and piano in the mid-'50s, and began gaining attention working with Willis Jackson in the late '50s and early '60s, cutting high caliber soul-jazz dates for Prestige. McDuff made his recording debut as a leader for Prestige in 1960, playing in a studio pickup band with Jimmy Forrest. They made a pair of outstanding albums, *Tough Duff* and *The Honeydripper*. McDuff organized his own band the next year, featuring Harold Vick and drummer Joe Dukes. Things took off when McDuff hired a young guitarist named George Benson. They were among the most popular combos of the mid-'60s, and made several excellent albums. McDuff's later groups at Atlantic and Cadet didn't equal the level of The Benson band, while later dates for Verve and Cadet were uneven, though generally good. McDuff experimented with electronic keyboards and fusion during the '70s, then in the '80s got back in the groove with the Muse session *Cap'n Jack*. Other musicians McDuff played with in the '60s and '70s include Joe Henderson, Pat Martino, Jimmy Witherspoon, David "Fathead" Newman, Rahsaan Roland Kirk, Sonny Stitt and Gene Ammons. There are only a few McDuff sessions available on CD, though they include the fine sessions with Forrest. His work with Benson has also been reissued on CD. —*Ron Wynn and Bob Porter*

Brother Jack / Jan. 25, 1960 / Prestige ◆◆◆

Rock Candy / Jan. 25, 1960-Oct. 3, 1963 / Prestige ◆◆◆

A '90s compilation covering sessions that Jack McDuff recorded for Prestige in the early '60s, many of which included guitarist George Benson. It also includes material from McDuff's 1960 debut session on Prestige. Gene Ammons and Jimmy Forrest are also featured on some tracks. —*Ron Wynn*

Tough 'Duff / Jul. 12, 1960 / Original Jazz Classics ◆◆◆◆◆

Organist Jack McDuff's second set as a leader teams him with tenor saxophonist Jimmy Forrest, vibraphonist Lem Winchester (an unusual addition for this type of soul-jazz set), and drummer Bill Elliott. This CD reissue finds the group playing fairly basic material, including a pair of McDuff originals, "Smooth Sailing" and "Autumn Leaves." McDuff, Forrest and Winchester have no difficulty chewing up the chord changes, and although no real surprises occur, the results are typically swingin' and groovin.' —*Scott Yanow*

The Honeydripper / Feb. 3, 1961 / Original Jazz Classics ◆◆◆◆◆

This CD reissue is possibly most significant for being guitarist Grant Green's recording debut. Organist Jack McDuff, the tough-toned tenor Jimmy Forrest, Green and drummer Ben Dixon make for a potent and swinging combination. The repertoire (which has three standards and three originals, including "Whap") comprises blues, blues-oriented tunes (including "I Want a Little Girl") and Henry Mancini's "Mr. Lucky." Due to the high-quality solos, which are full of personality, this reissue is highly recommended to fans of the genre. —*Scott Yanow*

Goodnight, It's Time to Go / Jul. 14, 1961 / Prestige ◆◆◆

McDuff on the Hammond B-3 along with Grant Green on guitar and Harold Vick on tenor sax. What more could you ask for? —*Michael Erlewine*

On with It / Dec. 1, 1961 / Prestige ◆◆◆

This forgotten session (organist Jack McDuff's fifth for Prestige as a leader) was not released initially until 1971 and has yet to be reissued on CD. With the exception of "Hey Lawdy Mama" and Ray Charles' "Drown in My Own Tears," the six selections are originals by the leader. In general, with the exception of the ballad "Dink's Dream," the music is essentially bluesy funk with fine tenor solos by Harold Vick (who switches to flute for the ballad), and good backup playing by guitarist Eddie Diehl and drummer Joe Dukes. The results are danceable, yet full of honest feeling and some chance-taking within the boundaries of soul-jazz. Pity that the date is so obscure. —*Scott Yanow*

Brother Jack Meets the Boss / Jan. 23, 1962 / Original Jazz Classics ✦✦✦✦✦
It is not too surprising that this is a very successful soul-jazz/hard bop outing, for it teams organist Brother Jack McDuff with the great tenor Gene Ammons. The quintet (which also includes the notable Harold Vick on second tenor, guitarist Eddie Diehl and drummer Joe Dukes) performs three basic McDuff tunes, Eddie "Cleanhead" Vinson's "Mr. Clean," Horace Silver's "Strollin'," and the still-viable swing standard "Christopher Columbus." Ammons, whose every note was always full of passion, fits in perfectly with McDuff's group; this accessible set has been reissued on CD. —*Scott Yanow*

Screamin' / Oct. 23, 1962 / Original Jazz Classics ✦✦✦✦
Organist Jack McDuff teams up with his regular drummer Joe Dukes, altoist Leo Wright and guitarist Kenny Burrell for a spirited blues-oriented set which has been reissued on CD in the OJC series. "Soulful Drums," featuring Dukes' drum breaks, was a minor hit. Other selections on this generally fine organ date include spirited versions of "He's a Real Gone Guy," "After Hours" and "One O'Clock Jump" even if the title cut does not quite live up to its name. —*Scott Yanow*

Crash! / Jan. 8, 1963+Feb. 26, 1963 / Prestige ✦✦✦✦✦
Organist Jack McDuff has long had a powerful style and the two former LPs that are combined on this single CD offer some strong examples of his accessible playing. In both cases McDuff is joined by guitarist Kenny Burrell (in fact one of the two sets was originally under Burrell's name), drummer Joe Dukes and occasionally Ray Barretto on congas. In addition Harold Vick is on tenor for most selections and Eric Dixon guests on tenor and flute during three songs. Highlights include a driving "How High the Moon," "Love Walked In" and a pair of original blues: "Smut" and "Our Miss Brooks." McDuff and Burrell work together quite well. This 76-minute CD is easily recommended to fans of the jazz organ. —*Scott Yanow*

★ **Brother Jack McDuff Live!** / Feb. 26, 1963+Jun. 5, 1963 / Prestige ✦✦✦✦✦
Good as organist Jack McDuff's studio recordings are from the early '60s, it is his live sets that are truly exciting. This single CD combines together two former in-concert LPs and finds McDuff leading a very strong group that features the young guitarist George Benson, tenorman Red Holloway, drummer Joe Dukes and, on a few numbers, the second tenor of Harold Vick. The material (cooking blues, standards, Latin numbers and originals) has plenty of variety and drive; McDuff really pushes Benson and Holloway, and the music is both accessible and creative. —*Scott Yanow*

Brother Jack Live! at the Jazz Workshop / Oct. 3, 1963 / Prestige ✦✦✦
Organist Jack McDuff enjoyed some pop recognition in 1963, when his combo recorded at The Jazz Workshop featured a young, blazing guitarist influenced by Wes Montgomery. George Benson's torrid licks and blues fills make this among his hottest albums, along with McDuff's always-smoking, relentless organ accompaniment, transitional lines, and solos. —*Ron Wynn*

Dynamic! / Feb. 6, 1964-Feb. 7, 1964 / Prestige ✦✦✦
With George Benson on guitar. —*AMG*

Legends of Acid Jazz / Jul. 1964 / Prestige ✦✦✦✦✦
While these 12 selections were originally released on six different albums between 1965 and 1969, all of them were cut during July 1964: nine at a New York studio session, and three (embellished by Benny Golson big-band arrangements) live at Stockholm. Thus it makes for a thematically coherent compilation, every track featuring a young George Benson on guitar and Joe Dukes on drums; Red Holloway plays tenor sax on all but two songs. It's top-drawer soul-jazz, recommended to those who might find some of McDuff's other releases too homogenous, as his B-3 travels through diverse moods here: the uptempo blues of "Scufflin'," the slow-burning funk of "Our Miss Brooks," R&B/soul in the cover of "I Got a Woman." The closing "Lexington Avenue Line" is the oddest track, though quite a good one, sounding like a movie soundtrack theme with its dramatic strings. —*Richie Unterberger*

Hot Barbeque / Oct. 19, 1965 / Prestige ✦✦✦

Do It Now! / Dec. 15, 1966-May 23, 1967 / Atlantic ✦✦✦
After a long string of Prestige recordings, organist Jack McDuff recorded a few LPs for Atlantic (all of which are currently out of print) in a similar soul-jazz style. The only change was that the length of the tunes tended to fall into the potential radio airplay range of four to six minutes. McDuff and his regular group of the period (Leo Johnson and Danny Turner on reeds, underrated guitarist Melvin Sparks, and drummer Ray Appleton) swing their way through five of McDuff's originals and two obscurities with plenty of spirit, if not a great deal of originality. —*Scott Yanow*

Moon Rappin' / Dec. 3, 1969-Dec. 11, 1969 / Blue Note ✦✦✦
Moon Rappin' is one of "Brother" Jack McDuff's most ambitious efforts, a loose concept album that finds the organist exploring funky and spacy soundscapes. Unlike most McDuff records, there isn't a steady groove that flows throughout the record—the album flies into atmospheric territory that isn't strictly soul-jazz, but

it's far from free. In many ways, *Moon Rappin'* is a fairly typical album of its time, boasting wah guitars, flutes, spacious reverb, long bluesy vamps, orchestras and disembodied backing vocals, but it also stands out from the pack in how it offers some excellent improvisation (including a rare piano spotlight on the title track) and unpredictable moments, like the stuttering organ and nearly-free interludes on "Made in Sweden." It's not strictly funky—it doesn't have the grit of early Brother Jack records, nor does it swing hard—but it proves that McDuff was as adept in adventurous territory as he was with the groove. —*Stephen Thomas Erlewine*

Down Home Style / 1969 / Blue Note ✦✦✦✦
A set of gritty electric funk and soulful blues, *Down Home Style* is an excellent showcase for "Brother" Jack McDuff's gripping, funky style. Inspired more by the tight grooves of Stax Records than bebop, *Down Home Style* features McDuff leading a small group through a number of R&B grooves, ranging from the stuttering "The Vibrator" and dirty funk of "Butter (For Yo Popcorn)" to the slow blues of "Memphis in June." Occasionally, the group is augmented by a punchy horn section, but the record is designed as a showcase for McDuff's wild, intoxicating Hammond organ, and he runs with it, demonstrating every one of his tricks. —*Stephen Thomas Erlewine*

The Re-Entry / Mar. 1988 / 32 Jazz ✦✦✦✦
After a busy recording career in the 1960s, organist Jack McDuff was erratically documented in commercial settings in the 1970s and was in danger of being forgotten when he launched his successful comeback with this Muse album in 1988. At the age of 61, McDuff proved to still be in his prime as he jammed on three originals, two obscurities, and "Laura," with both Houston Person and Ron Bridgewater on tenors, trumpeter Cecil Bridgewater, guitarist John Hart and drummer Grady Tate. The music falls between hard bop and soul-jazz and should satisfy fans of those styles. —*Scott Yanow*

Another Real Good'un / Mar. 1, 1989+Jul. 18, 1990 / Muse ✦✦✦✦

Color Me Blue / May 1991+Mar. 1992 / Concord Jazz ✦✦✦✦✦
Recent cuts showing that organist Jack McDuff can still stomp through bluesy wailers, pound the bass pedals, and lead a hot combo through funky, exuberant numbers. He's heading a group with former band members like guitarist George Benson and drummer Joe Dukes, plus saxophonist Red Holloway, guitarist Ron Eschete and Phil Upchurch, among others. —*Ron Wynn*

Write On, Capt'n / 1993 / Concord Jazz ✦✦✦
This date doesn't pack the same punch as McDuff's 1960s classics, but is mostly enjoyable despite some annoying trumpet from Joey De Francesco (a fine organist and McDuff fan) and McDuff's own arrangements for the large band backing him. Sometimes the two-trumpet/two-sax/trombone front line seems more of a burden than a help. They are good players, but they aren't given enough to do to be exciting and sometimes just seem in the way. While it's great to hear McDuff back on the Hammond B-3, this will not make anyone forget his Prestige dates with George Benson. —*Ron Wynn*

That's the Way I Feel About It / Dec. 16, 1996-Jan. 23, 1997 / Concord Jazz ✦✦✦✦
At times, McDuff demonstrates how soul-jazz organ stars used to make albums back in their '60s heyday, playing then-current pop hits like "The Age of Aquarius" and the theme from "Mission: Impossible" (which, thanks to cinema, was a hit all over again in 1996 when this CD was made). We also hear McDuff trying out his vocal cords for the first time on Louis Jordan's "Saturday Night Fish Fry"; actually, he merely talks the lyrics over the rhythm section—and at 70, he's entitled to this charming lark. Otherwise, this is another fine, home-cookin' soul-jazz session, with McDuff's Hammond B-3 burning at its usual low-intensity, high-blues-content level. Chris Potter dances around the organ on flutes, Andrew Beals and Jerry Weldon offer solid solos on alto and tenor respectively, and the rest of the Heatin' System runs the gamut from Latin to soul-deep grooves. Fans of the genre can buy with peace of mind. —*Richard S. Ginell*

Gary McFarland

b. Oct. 23, 1933, Los Angeles, CA, **d.** Nov. 3, 1971, New York, NY
Vibes, Arranger, Composer / Post-Bop, Hard Bop
Largely forgotten now, Gary McFarland was one of the more significant contributors to orchestral jazz during the early '60s. An "adult prodigy," as Gene Lees accurately noted, McFarland was an ingenious composer whose music could reveal shades of complex emotional subtlety and clever childlike simplicity. While in the army, he became interested in jazz and attempted to play trumpet, trombone and piano. In 1955 he took up playing the vibes. Displaying a quick ability for interesting writing, he obtained a scholarship to the Berklee School of Music. He spent one semester there and with the encouragement of pianist John Lewis, concentrated on large-band arrangements of his own compositions. He attained early notoriety and success working with Gerry Mulligan, Johnny Hodges, John Lewis, Stan Getz, Bob Brookmeyer and Anita O'Day. McFarland began devoting more

attention to his own career by 1963 when he released what is often regarded as his most significant recording, *The Gary McFarland Orchestra/Special Guest Soloist: Bill Evans*. He also recorded in small-group settings which featured his clever vibes playing. The success of his instrumental pop collection, *Soft Samba*, allowed McFarland to form his first performing group. But his recordings thereafter more often than not featured an easy-listening instrumental pop bent. McFarland went on to excellent work with Gabor Szabo, Shirley Scott, Zoot Sims and Steve Kuhn, but only rarely featured his outstanding compositional talents (as in 1968's *America the Beautiful*). He formed the short-lived Skye Records label with Szabo and vibist Cal Tjader in the late '60s and continued to record prolifically. By the late '60s, though, he was forgotten by his initial jazz followers and he died in 1971 after being poisoned in a New York City bar. —*Douglas Payne*

Essence / Sep. 9, 1960-Oct. 5, 1962 / Atlantic ✦✦✦✦✦
First issued in 1964, this successful union of pianist John Lewis' third-stream stylings and Gary McFarland's deft compositions works quite well. There's a unity among each of the songs, despite three recording sessions and differing instrumentation. Freddie Hubbard, Benny Golson, Phil Woods and Eric Dolphy appear. But it is Lewis and guitarist Jim Hall who leave the strongest impression. —*Douglas Payne*

How to Succeed in Business Without Really Trying/Gloomy Sunday and Other Bright Moments / Nov. 6, 1961-Nov. 15, 1961 / Verve ✦✦✦✦✦
Two unrelated big-band albums (which have overlapping personnel) from the same time period are combined on this single CD: Gary McFarland's *How to Succeed in Business Without Really Trying* and Bob Brookmeyer's *Gloomy Sunday and Other Bright Moments*. McFarland's eight arrangements of tunes from the show of the same name is better than expected. The only one of the numbers to catch on was "Brotherhood of Man," but McFarland's charts uplift the material and there are fine solos from such all-stars as fluegelhornist Clark Terry, the tenors of Oliver Nelson and Al Cohn, pianist Hank Jones, guitarist Kenny Burrell, valve trombonist Bob Brookmeyer and altoist Phil Woods, in addition to the leader/vibraphonist. Brookmeyer's set is actually the superior of the two due to the better material. Brookmeyer arranged four of the eight numbers, and there are also charts by Eddie Sauter, Al Cohn, Ralph Burns and McFarland. Featured are such soloists as Clark Terry, Phil Woods, Al Cohn, vibraphonist Eddie Costa and Brookmeyer, among others; highlights include "Caravan," "Gloomy Sunday" (a feature for Woods) and "Detour Ahead." Well worth picking up. —*Scott Yanow*

With Special Guest Soloist Bill Evans / Jan. 24, 1963 / Verve ✦✦✦✦✦
A stirring, beautiful score and certainly one of McFarland's very best. His painterly talents at evoking moods succeed most brilliantly here. The album is like a soundtrack celebrating the excitement of a big urban wonderland. The compositions are first rate, McFarland's occasional vibes playing is simple and perfect. Bill Evans buoys the event with his graceful, individual style. The whole record represents a beautiful moment in jazz and richly deserves to be issued on CD. —*Douglas Payne*

Point of Departure / Sep. 5, 1963-Sep. 6, 1963 / Impulse! ✦✦✦✦✦
This Impulse LP (not yet reissued on CD) was one of vibraphonist Gary McFarland's best recordings. McFarland contributed six of the seven selections (all but the "Love Theme from David and Lisa") and utilizes an all-star sextet filled with colorful soloists: trombonist Willie Dennis, Richie Kamuca on tenor and oboe, guitarist Jimmy Raney, bassist Steve Swallow and drummer Mel Lewis. The music is bop-oriented, but also open to occasional innovations taken from the avant-garde. None of the songs caught on as standards, but they tend to stay in one's mind after finishing the album. —*Scott Yanow*

Soft Samba / Jun. 15, 1964-Oct. 7, 1964 / Verve ✦✦
Very popular in its day and still loathed by jazz lovers that remember it today. No jazz here and little of interest to those outside the bachelor-pad scene. —*Douglas Payne*

The In Sound / Aug. 2, 1965-Aug. 3, 1965 / Verve ✦✦✦✦
A more comfortable mix of McFarland's vocalese pop and jazz than the more successful *Soft Samba*. *The In Sound* is chock full of brief, enjoyable tunes that stick with you. Guitarist Gabor Szabo is a perfect partner and makes a memorable combination with McFarland's mellifluous vibraphone. —*Douglas Payne*

Tijuana Jazz / Oct. 1965 / Impulse! ✦✦✦
Considering the strong lineup of musicians on this LP (Gary McFarland on marimba, both Clark Terry and Joe Newman on trumpets, valve trombonist Bob Brookmeyer, and an expanded pianoless rhythm section), it had the potential to be a classic; even the material is generally good. Unfortunately, the dozen selections are overly concise (the longest clocks in at 4:01), with seven of the tunes being under three minutes long. McFarland's arrangements are fine, but the solos are quite short, and the Mexican-flavored music is not particularly memorable. A blown opportunity. —*Scott Yanow*

● **Profiles** / Feb. 6, 1966 / Impulse! ✦✦✦✦✦
An excellent collection of McFarland originals performed at Lincoln Center by a stellar orchestra of jazz luminaries including Clark Terry, Bob Brookmeyer, Zoot Sims, Phil Woods, Richie Kamuca, Richard Davis, Gabor Szabo, Sam Brown and others. The concert showcases some of McFarland's best writing and there is a welcome spontaneity lacking in McFarland's studio recordings (but several awkward moments are present). *Profiles* deserves to be reissued on CD. —*Douglas Payne*

Simpatico / May 18, 1966+May 20, 1966 / Impulse! ✦✦
Pure Beatlesque pop from two notable figures in 1960s jazz, Gary McFarland and Gabor Szabo. *Simpatico* features its principals' lackluster singing and silly lyrics, but there are occasional hints of their abilities. —*Douglas Payne*

The October Suite / Oct. 14, 1966+Nov. 1, 1966 / Impulse! ✦✦✦
Featuring Steve Kuhn in a chamber-jazz setting, *The October Suite* is similar to the earlier Bill Evans suite, where an inimitable soloist performs McFarland's evocative music. While McFarland doesn't perform here, his simple, lyrical compositional style is in the spotlight. Kuhn has rarely been more sensitively featured. —*Douglas Payne*

Soft Samba Strings / Oct. 27, 1966 / Verve ✦✦
A misleading title that has less to do with *Soft Samba* and more to do with McFarland's similar feature for Zoot Sims (*Waiting Game*). Rather dull, perhaps because a strong soloist like Sims is missing. —*Douglas Payne*

America the Beautiful / 1968 / DCC ✦✦✦
One of Gary McFarland's major works, this orchestral jazz suite (originally on Skye and reissued on CD by the Audiophile DCC label) utilizes a big band and some strings along with the influence of rock, classical and jazz. The six-movement piece is ultimately a bit downbeat about the future of the US as seen from 1968. The emphasis is on the ensembles rather than any individual voices, and the overall results are certainly listenable but less memorable than one might hope, considering the potential scope of the work. —*Scott Yanow*

Scorpio and Other Signs / Jan. 9, 1968 / Verve ✦✦
Another pop collection, this time framed by a rather inconsequential astrological concept. All originals by McFarland. So witty and light it sometimes feels like a jazz album made for children. Short solo spots, some featuring Marvin Stamm. McFarland's vibes take several nice turns here and his vocalese has never sounded more natural. Not available on CD. —*Douglas Payne*

Does the Sun Really Shine on the Moon? / Jan. 29, 1968-Jan. 31, 1968 / Skye ✦✦
By the time of McFarland's debut on his own label, his early jazz fans pretty much gave up on him. This long-forgotten instrumental LP features Jerome Richardson, Marvin Stamm, Sam Brown, Richard Davis, Grady Tate and Warren Bernhardt in roles permitting little that's memorable. —*Douglas Payne*

Today / Sep. 1969 / Skye ✦✦
Top-of-the-pops instrumental covers of "My Cherie Amour," "Everybody's Talking," some background bossa nova and a criminally wasted cast of all-stars: Hubert Laws, Curtis Fuller, Sam Brown, Ron Carter, Grady Tate and Airto. McFarland's cover of the Beatles' "Get Back" is excellent, though. —*Douglas Payne*

Butterscotch Rum / 1971 / Buddah ✦✦
Features the goofball lyrics of cartoonist Peter Smith. Mostly dreadful originals with badly sung beatnik lyrics that verge on the embarrassing. A terrible coda for a genuine talent. —*Douglas Payne*

Bobby McFerrin

b. Mar. 11, 1950, New York, NY
Vocals / Bop, Post-Bop, Pop
A truly remarkable singer, Bobby McFerrin's ability to make rhythmic sounds while inhaling makes his vocals into nonstop flights of constant creativity. By alternating falsetto quickly with deep bass notes (and somehow not getting lost!), McFerrin can sound like two or three singers at once. His quick reactions and wide knowledge of musical styles plus a strong wit make his solo performances not only remarkable but hugely entertaining.

Despite all of that, Bobby McFerrin's career has not yet lived up to his enormous potential. The son of opera signers, McFerrin was trained as a pianist, but by 1977 he had shifted to singing. He worked for a time with Jon Hendricks and then recorded his debut for Elektra Musician in 1982. In 1983 he started doing concerts featuring his unaccompanied solos and his 1984 release *The Voice* is still his finest recording. In 1988 McFerrin had a fluke hit with "Don't Worry, Be Happy" (which was actually on one of his weaker albums), and he seemed somewhat embarrassed by his unexpected commercial success. He maintained a much lower profile, conducting classical orchestras (why?), forming a thus far unrecorded "Voicestra" with other singers, and recording on only an infrequent basis for EMI and Blue Note; a joke-filled encounter with Chick Corea was often closer to performance art than to jazz. Bobby McFerrin is still a major name, but not the influential force (and poll-winner) that he should be. —*Scott Yanow*

Bobby McFerrin / 1982 / Elektra ✦✦✦✦

Bobby McFerrin's debut recording hints at his potential, although the album also largely plays it safe compared to what was to come. The remarkable singer is at his best on the unaccompanied "Hallucinations" and in a duet with drummer H.B. Bennett on "All Feets Can Dance"; also quite worthwhile are his versions of "Dance With Me" and "Moondance." Most of the diverse selections find McFerrin joined by a rhythm section led by pianist Victor Feldman. Phoebe Snow shares the vocal mike with McFerrin on "You've Really Got a Hold on Me." An interesting but not essential release. —*Scott Yanow*

★ The Voice / Mar. 17, 1984-Mar. 26, 1984 / Elektra ✦✦✦✦✦

The Voice was a milestone in jazz history; it was the first time a jazz singer had recorded an entire album solo, without accompaniment or overdubbing, for a major label. Bobby McFerrin's amazing ability to switch back and forth between bass notes and falsetto, along with his talent for jumping octaves made this record quite a virtuoso showcase. For those interested in the potential of the human voice and in an important jazz talent, *The Voice* is recommended without reservation. —*Scott Yanow*

Spontaneous Inventions / 1985 / Blue Note ✦✦✦✦✦

Bobby McFerrin is heard in prime form throughout this date, which was the follow-up to his classic *The Voice*. A few of the numbers are taken unaccompanied, and these include memorable renditions of "Thinkin' About Your Body," "I Hear Music" and "Manana Iguana." Pianist Herbie Hancock duets with McFerrin on "Turtle Shoes"; "Another Night in Tunisia" (taken from the Manhattan Transfer's *Vocalese* album) features McFerrin with the vocal quartet and Jon Hendricks; soprano saxophonist Wayne Shorter interacts with the vocalist on "Walkin'," and an eccentric "Beverly Hills Blues" has "assistance" from comedian Robin Williams. A continually intriguing release with plenty of wit from the innovative singer. —*Scott Yanow*

● The Best of Bobby McFerrin / 1985-1990 / Blue Note ✦✦✦

The highlights of vocal acrobat Bobby McFerrin's eclectic career are featured on this collection, which includes samples of his work with the St. Paul Chamber Orchestra, Chick Corea, the Yellowjackets, Manhattan Transfer and Jon Hendricks; among the selections are "Spain," "Blue Bossa" and the cloying hit "Don't Worry, Be Happy." —*Jason Ankeny*

Simple Pleasures / 1988 / EMI ✦✦✦✦

This CD will always be remembered for including Bobby McFerrin's surprise hit "Don't Worry, Be Happy." Actually, overall, this album is not quite up to the level of his previous two, for instead of taking unaccompanied vocals, the remarkable singer overdubbed his voice many times, which reduces the miraculous nature of his talents. However, McFerrin's renditions of "Drive My Car," "Drive," and "Sunshine of Your Love" (the program is quite diverse), plus the catchy "Don't Worry," are generally unique and worth hearing. —*Scott Yanow*

Medicine Music / 1990 / EMI ✦✦

Play / Jun. 23, 1990 / Blue Note ✦✦✦

In 1990, singer Bobby McFerrin and pianist Chick Corea teamed up for six concerts that were as much about performance art and wacky comedy as about music; to many people's surprise, Corea proved to be as humorous as McFerrin. This CD features musical highlights from a pair of the concerts. Unfortunately, without seeing the performers in person, one is not always sure what the audience is laughing at, particularly during the first three selections. Still, there are some remarkable moments, primarily from McFerrin, who shows that he can switch effortlessly from soaring falsetto to intense basslines; his ideas on "Blue Bossa" are quite impressive. Corea is heard more often as an accompanist than as an equal partner, so McFerrin often steals the show on this interesting but not essential release. —*Scott Yanow*

Hush / Aug. 1991 / Columbia ✦✦✦

Collaboration between celebrated classical cellist Yo-Yo Ma and vocal improviser Bobby McFerrin. Although neither a strictly classical nor jazz session, the two make effective partners, and each manages to showcase the skills that earned them notoriety. —*Ron Wynn*

Bang! Zoom / 1995 / Blue Note ✦✦

Bobby McFerrin has made relatively few recordings since his hit "Don't Worry, Be Happy." Potentially one of the truly great creative vocalists, McFerrin has flashes of brilliance on this Blue Note CD, including a haunting rendition of Miles Davis' "Selim" (taken from the trumpeter's underrated *Live/Evil* set), but the singer's original material is generally forgettable. McFerrin overdubbed extra voices on many selections, which is quite unnecessary considering his range and ability to sing non-stop; he emphasizes dance and R&B rhythms, and there is often little to the songs other than the grooves and the sound of his voice. In addition, the members

of the Yellowjackets are underutilized, although Russell Ferrante co-wrote three of McFerrin's eight songs. A disappointment. —*Scott Yanow*

The Mozart Sessions / Feb. 5, 1996-May 21, 1996 / Sony ✦✦✦

The informal title says a great deal about the contents of *The Mozart Sessions*, which could have been called *Concerti for Piano and Orchestra, Nos. 23 and 20*, since that is, for the most part, what it is. But, of course, the conductors, vocalist Bobby McFerrin and jazz keyboard player Chick Corea, are not your average classical musicians. Nor is there any doubt about the non-traditional nature of the recording, when it starts with McFerrin's patented improvisational vocals followed by Corea's piano inventions under the title "Prelude." So, for a start, purists should be warned away. On the other hand, the more adventurous may be slightly disappointed, since after they get the preliminaries out of the way, McFerrin and Corea, aided and abetted by the St. Paul Chamber Orchestra, turn in pleasant but unexceptional readings of the concerti, with Corea especially eschewing any attempt at dazzle in what are usually showcase pieces. The piano work is fluid and the orchestral accompaniment delicate, but the principals seem sufficiently concerned about getting anything wrong not to really take off. At the end, as Corea once again improvises in tandem with McFerrin's voice, one longs for more of their interaction, perhaps in a less restrictive context. —*William Ruhlmann*

Circlesongs / Apr. 1, 1997 / Sony ✦✦✦✦

Back in the late '80s, Bobby McFerrin unveiled his sensational a cappella vocal group Voicestra, but the peripatetic singer/composer (and now conductor) waited nearly a decade before putting anything out in that concept—and on a classical label yet! Taking the lead, the rubber-voiced McFerrin sets up revolving wordless vocal patterns, and he and the group improvise what amount to eight individual mantras. The songs have no titles—only "Circlesong One," "Circlesong Two," et al—yet they use all kinds of African, Middle Eastern and other vocal or vocal percussive techniques, as well as studio production embellishments, to shape them after the fact. The 12 singers in this Voicestra are a freely eclectic mixture of R&B, gospel, pop and jazz vocalists (including the Manhattan Transfer's Janis Siegel), performance artists, opera and classical singers, yet they blend together in an astonishingly homogenous manner when used in this fashion. The first "Circlesong" is the most immediately fetching, built around a single riff as McFerrin hollers and moans over the shifting voices, but all of them contain some amazing ideas—and at a mere 42 minutes, the album does not wear out its welcome as it might have had McFerrin stretched the music out to the usual CD length. It's hard to figure out what category to put this disc in—maybe next to Ladysmith Black Mambazo on the world music shelf—but labels don't matter in a sound world with this much imagination and heart. —*Richard S. Ginell*

Howard McGhee

b. Mar. 6, 1918, Tulsa, OK, d. Jul. 17, 1987, New York, NY
Trumpet / Bop, Hard Bop

During 1945-49, Howard McGhee was one of the finest trumpeters in jazz, an exciting performer with a sound of his own who, among the young bop players, ranked at the top with Dizzy Gillespie and Fats Navarro. The "missing link" between Roy Eldridge and Fats Navarro (Navarro influenced Clifford Brown, who influenced most of the post-1955 trumpeters), McGhee originally played clarinet and tenor, not taking up trumpet until he was 17. He worked in territory bands, was with Lionel Hampton in 1941 and then joined Andy Kirk (1941-42), being featured on "McGhee Special." McGhee participated in the fabled bop sessions at Minton's Playhouse and Monroe's Uptown House, modernizing his style away from Roy Eldridge and towards Dizzy Gillespie. He was with Charlie Barnet (1942-43), returned to Kirk (where he sat next to Fats Navarro in the trumpet section) and had brief stints with Georgie Auld and Count Basie before traveling to California with Coleman Hawkins in 1945; their concise recordings of swing-to-bop transitional music (including "Stuffy," "Rifftide" and "Hollywood Stampede") are classic. McGhee stayed in California into 1947, playing with Jazz at the Philharmonic, recording and gigging with Charlie Parker (including the ill-fated "Lover Man" date) and having an influence on young players out on the Coast. His Dial sessions were among the most exciting recordings of his career, and back in New York he recorded for Savoy and had a historic meeting on record with Navarro (1948 on Blue Note).

However, drugs began to adversely affect Howard McGhee's career. He traveled on a USO tour during the Korean War, recording in Guam. McGhee also had sessions for Bethlehem (1955-56), but was inactive during much of the 1950s. He recorded some strong dates for Felsted, Bethlehem, Contemporary and Black Lion during 1960-61, and a quartet outing for United Artists (1962), but (with the exception of a Hep big band date in 1966) was largely off records again until 1976. He had a final burst of activity during 1976-79 for Sonet, Steeple Chase, Jazzcraft, Zim and Storyville, but by then Howard McGhee was largely forgotten and few knew about his link to Fats Navarro and Clifford Brown. —*Scott Yanow*

☆ **Trumpet at Tempo** / Sep. 4, 1945-Dec. 3, 1947 / Jazz Classics ♦♦♦♦♦

While the critical jury is still out on his overall contribution to the form, the indisputable fact remains that until the arrival of Dizzy Gillespie and Charlie Parker in California, Howard McGhee was the West Coast trail blazing bebopper in residence. These early sides show him in top form, straddling a bridge between Roy Eldridge and the new sound that was in the wind. Kicking off with a four-side 1945 date for Philo/Aladdin, Howard's bravura tone is well represented and his stratospheric runs on "Mop Mop" sit comfortably alongside his more reflective work on "Stardust." McGhee was also the trumpeter on the ill-fated Bird session that produced "Lover Man." After Parker left the studio, McGhee jammed two tunes with the remaining personnel, "Thermodynamics" and the title cut, his inspired improvisation on the chord changes to "Indiana." The first actual Dial label date with Howard as leader featured Dodo Marmarosa on piano, producing four classics of the idiom: "Midnight at Minton's," "High Wind in Hollywood," "Dialated Pupils," and "Up in Dodo's Room," alternates of which can be found on the companion Dodo Marmarosa collection, *Up in Dodo's Room.* But the bop motherlode comes with the inclusion of 11 tracks (two alternates) from McGhee's final date for the label, held in New York and featuring James Moody on tenor sax, Milt Jackson on vibes, Ray Brown on bass, Hank Jones on piano and J.C. Heard on drums, a classic lineup indeed. Although McGhee's later work could vacillate between brilliant and banal, the potency of these recordings in indisputable. *—Cub Koda*

Maggie: The Savoy Sessions / Feb. 1948-1952 / Savoy ♦♦♦♦

This single CD put out by the Japanese Denon label has 23 of the 27 selections put out a decade earlier on a two-LP set. Worse than the omissions was the decision to duplicate the liner notes and reprint them so small as to be microscopic. The first half of this set is actually quite good, featuring trumpeter Howard McGhee jamming with a talented sextet that co-stars altoist Jimmy Heath and vibraphonist Milt Jackson and with another group that has solo space for Billy Eckstine on his surprisingly effective valve trombone. The remainder of the CD is much weaker, music recorded in Guam by McGhee, trombonist J.J. Johnson and tenor saxophonist Rudy Williams with a pianoless rhythm trio. Guitarist Skeeter Best is not strong enough to make up for the lack of a piano and some of the repertoire (including an attempt at a brief history-of-jazz) does not work that well. It is best to hold on to the original two-LP set. Otherwise, this CD is mostly recommended for the two earlier dates. *—Scott Yanow*

South Pacific Jazz / Jan. 17, 1952 / Savoy ♦♦♦

Originally half of a Savoy two-LP set, this single CD features trumpeter Howard McGhee and a potentially interesting sextet (with trombonist J.J. Johnson and Rudy Williams on tenor) at concerts performed in Guam. After a rather slapdash history-of-jazz segment, the band digs into more familiar music with some hard-swinging results. The lack of a piano leaves a large gap in the ensembles (despite the presence of guitarist Clifton Best) and it is strange to hear Rudy Williams (formerly a swing altoist) as an R&Bish tenor. Although not essential, Howard McGhee fans will want to pick this up if they do not already own the LP two-fer. *—Scott Yanow*

That Bop Thing / Oct. 22, 1955 / Bethlehem ♦♦♦♦

Due to drug problems, trumpeter Howard McGhee did not record all that much in the 1950s. This is among his best all-round sessions of the decade, a quintet outing with baritonist Sahib Shihab (who doubles on alto), pianist Duke Jordan, bassist Percy Heath and drummer Philly Joe Jones. McGhee's crisp and immediately distinctive sound and boppish style were still in prime form at the time, despite his lack of consistent activity, and he contributed five of the 11 selections. The main soloist throughout, McGhee makes this an LP worth searching for (and hopefully reissuing on CD). *—Scott Yanow*

● **Maggie's Back in Town** / Jun. 26, 1961 / Original Jazz Classics ♦♦♦♦♦

Trumpeter Howard McGhee, after spending much of the 1950s only partly active in music (due to drug problems), made a full-fledged comeback in the early '60s, only to find his bop-oriented music out of fashion. This Contemporary set (reissued on CD in the OJC series) was McGhee's finest recording of the period, a quartet outing with the brilliant pianist Phineas Newborn, bassist Leroy Vinnegar and drummer Shelly Manne. Although tenor saxophonist Teddy Edwards is not on the date, two of his compositions (his famous "Sunset Eyes" and a tribute to the trumpeter "Maggie's Back in Town") are fully explored by the quartet. Other titles include three standards plus McGhee's original blues "Demon Chase." This CD is a perfect starting point for listeners not familiar with the underrated (and often overlooked) Howard McGhee. *—Scott Yanow*

Sharp Edge / Dec. 8, 1961 / Black Lion ♦♦♦♦

Trumpeter Howard McGhee had a bit of a renaissance in the early '60s before slipping back into obscurity. This formerly rare session (reissued on CD by Black Lion) has eight selections (plus four previously unreleased alternate takes) from a quintet featuring McGhee, tenor saxophonist George Coleman, pianist Junior Mance, bassist George Tucker and drummer Jimmy Cobb. The trumpeter wrote arrangements

for all of the songs (four of which were his originals) and the writing makes the band sound like a regularly working group rather than having the feel of a loose jam session. McGhee's style, although a bit calmer than he often sounded in his heyday in the 1940s, was still quite boppish and his distinctive crisp sound was unchanged. Fine swinging music. *—Scott Yanow*

Cookin' Time / Sep. 22, 1966 / Hep ♦♦♦♦♦

Fine big-band arrangements and playing. *—Ron Wynn*

Just Be There / Dec. 9, 1976 / Steeple Chase ♦♦♦♦

Other than an album in 1966 and a few isolated numbers in 1970, trumpeter Howard McGhee made no recordings as a leader during 1963-75. In 1976 he started his final three years of recording activity with a date for Sonet and then this obscure effort for Steeple Chase. McGhee shows some age in his playing, but his crisp sound was still intact, as was his bop-oriented style. Recorded in Copenhagen with old friend Kenny Clarke on drums, baritonist Per Goldschmidt, pianist Horace Parlan and bassist Mads Vinding, this set features McGhee performing four of his straightahead originals plus J.J. Johnson's "Wee Dot." The spirit of classic bebop is very much alive on this enjoyable set. *—Scott Yanow*

Jazz Brothers / Oct. 19, 1977 / Storyville ♦♦♦♦

Trumpeter Howard McGhee, who had a final burst of recording activity during 1976-79, made several fine albums during that period. His project for Storyville (which has not yet been reissued on CD) matches his horn with the complimentary tenor of Charlie Rouse, the great bop pianist Barry Harris, bassist Lisle Atkinson, drummer Grady Tate and the conga of Jual Curtis. McGhee contributed all seven compositions (his many originals deserve to be rediscovered, revived and explored by today's improvisers) and provide good vehicles for the musician's solo flights. An excellent if obscure set. *—Scott Yanow*

Live at Emerson's / Mar. 10, 1978-Mar. 11, 1978 / Zim ♦♦♦

Trumpeter Howard McGhee is heard late in his career on this collector's LP playing at a New Jersey club called Emerson's. McGhee and his sextet (which includes both Frank Wess and Charlie Rouse on tenors, pianist Jim Roberts, bassist Lisle Atkinson and drummer Jual Curtis) perform a repertoire that ranges from an opening blues and Jimmy Heath's "Big P." to the forgotten standard "Deep Night," Jobim's "Meditation" and a few McGhee originals. This boppish date will be difficult to find, but it does feature the veteran trumpeter in fairly good late-period form. *—Scott Yanow*

Home Run / Oct. 11, 1978 / Storyville ♦♦♦♦

To celebrate the 30th anniversary (to the day) of his recorded trumpet battles with Fats Navarro, Howard McGhee teams up with fellow trumpeter Benny Bailey in a similar-styled sextet also including Sonny Redd (on tenor rather than his customary alto), pianist Barry Harris, bassist Lisle Atkinson and drummer Bobby Durham. Highlights of this set include McGhee's blues "Get It On," Navarro's "Nostalgia," "Brownie Speaks" and Bailey's "Funky Senor" (which is purposely similar to Horace Silver's "Senor Blues"). Highly recommended to bebop fans, this is one of Howard McGhee's final recording sessions. *—Scott Yanow*

Young at Heart / Oct. 4, 1979-Oct. 6, 1979 / Storyville ♦♦♦

Tenor saxophonist Teddy Edwards was in trumpeter Howard McGhee's group during 1945-47. Over 30 years later they reunited for what would be McGhee's final recording sessions (although the trumpeter lived until 1987). With pianist Art Hillery, bassist Leroy Vinnegar and drummer Billy Higgins completing the group, McGhee and Edwards are in excellent form on a set filled with bop standards composed by Charlie Parker, Thelonious Monk, Oscar Pettiford and Tadd Dameron. Highlights include "Relaxin' at Camarillo," "Blues in the Closet" and "In Walked Bud." A second and less interesting set (*Wise in Time*) came from these same dates. *—Scott Yanow*

Wise in Time / Oct. 4, 1979-Oct. 6, 1979 / Storyville ♦♦

Originating from the same recording sessions (trumpeter Howard McGhee's last) that resulted in its superior companion *Young at Heart*, this set is a bit of a disappointment. McGhee, tenor saxophonist Teddy Edwards, pianist Art Hillery, bassist Leroy Vinnegar and drummer Billy Higgins all sounded fine on the other record, but this album sticks exclusively to ballads, and the results are dragging and a bit dreary. The renditions of such songs as "I Want to Talk About You," "I Remember Clifford" and John Coltrane's "Crescent" do not even come close to comparing with more definitive earlier versions and the musicians sound a bit tired. Skip this set and get *Young at Heart* (and some of Howard McGhee's earlier albums) instead. *—Scott Yanow*

Chris McGregor

b. Dec. 24, 1936, Umtata, South Africa, **d.** May 26, 1990, Ager, France
Piano, Leader / Avant-Garde

A revered and respected bandleader and pianist, South African Chris McGregor's life was changed forever hearing the hymns of the Xhosa people in his father's church of Scotland mission. He'd eventually depart his South African homeland in protest against apartheid, and lead several seminal ensembles of expatriate South Africans. McGregor selected several great players at the 1962 Johannesburg Jazz Festival, among them Mongezi Fesa, Dudu Pukwana, and Johnny Dyani to be in a new band. The Blue Notes as an integrated band were anathema in '60s South Africa, which was ruled by strict apartheid. They left the country in the early '60s on a European tour and never returned. They remained in Switzerland for a year, then moved to London. McGregor led at various times the Chris McGregor Group and the Brotherhood of Breath. This was an African version of Sun Ra's Arkestra or Cecil Taylor's large orchestra, mixing free and avant-garde arrangements with township jive and other African styles. They developed out of a series of big band concerts McGregor had been presenting weekly at Ronnie Scott's club. McGregor moved to France in the mid-'70s, and did solo dates, but periodically revived the Brotherhood of Breath. Its ranks at one time included Pukwana, Fezi, Dyani and Louis Moholo. McGregor died in 1990 of lung cancer. —*Ron Wynn*

● **And the Brotherhood of Breath** / Oct. 1970 / Neon ◆◆◆◆◆
Studio release with excellent compositions, particularly "The Bride." —*Michael G. Nastos*

Live at Willisau / Jan. 27, 1973 / Ogun ◆◆◆◆◆
The pianist/leader with an 11-piece band of South African expatriates and English free-jazz men. Explosive. —*Michael G. Nastos*

Blue Notes for Mongezi / 1975 / Ogun ◆◆◆◆

Live at Toulouse / May 10, 1977 / Ogun ◆◆◆

Country Cooking / Jan. 1988 / Venture ◆◆◆◆

Jimmy McGriff

b. Apr. 3, 1936, Philadelphia, PA
Organ / Soul-Jazz, Hard Bop, Groove

Jimmy McGriff calls himself a blues organ player—and that's the feeling he delivers in his best soul-jazz albums, with plenty of deep, in-the-pocket swing punctuated by grunting chords in the bass. Though both his parents were pianists, McGriff started on bass and sax, picking up piano, vibraphone and ultimately piano as a teenager. After studying at Combe College of Music in Philadelphia and Juilliard, McGriff became an MP in Korea and worked on the Philadelphia police force for two years. After deciding upon music as a career, he studied organ with Jimmy Smith, Richard "Groove" Holmes and Milt Buckner, and scored a hit record "I Got a Woman" in 1963 (number 20 on the pop charts). This led to a string of R&B hit singles for Sue Records, followed by a prolific series of organ sessions for Solid State (where another substantial hit, "The Worm," emerged in 1969), Blue Note, Capitol, Groove Merchant and LRC. In the 1970s, following the trends of the time, McGriff began to turn toward pop and fusion, adopting electronic keyboards with mixed results. But when he signed with Milestone in 1983, McGriff returned to the Hammond B-3 organ and soul-jazz, anticipating the organ jazz revival with a series of strong, gritty albums, some of which feature Hank Crawford as co-leader. After bouncing around on a number of labels and idioms in the '90s, McGriff returned to Milestone in late 1996 with the soulfully sophisticated *The Dream Team*. —*Richard S. Ginell*

☆ **I've Got a Woman** / 1963 / Collectables ◆◆◆◆◆
McGriff's first album is great. The title cut was in the top 20 in 1962. Also on the same album is "M.G. Blues" and "All About My Girl." This session feautures McGriff, Richard Easley on drums and Walter Miller on guitar. Hi-impact early McGriff is the still the best, and this is the album that started it all, on the Sue label. Three cuts available on the Collectable CD *A Toast to Jimmy McGriff's Golden Classics.* —*Michael Erlewine*

One of Mine / 1963 / Collectables ◆◆◆
His second album, again on Sue. This has been reissued on Collectables. This session has McGriff with Morris Dow on lead guitar and harmonic, Larry Frazier on rhythm guitar, and Willie "Saint" Jenkins on drums. It features the title cut and "The Last Minute"—ten high-energy cuts. —*Michael Erlewine*

★ **At the Apollo** / 1963 / Collectables ◆◆◆◆◆
The third album from McGriff on the Sue label was recorded live at New York's Apollo Theater in 1963. It features McGriff, with Rudolph Johnson on tenor sax, Larry Frazier on guitar and Willie Jenkins on drums, and contains a great version of "Red Sails in the Sunset" and "A Thing for Jug." —*Michael Erlewine*

Jimmy McGriff at the Organ / 1963 / Sue ◆◆◆
McGriff with Rudolph Johnson on soprano and tenor sax, Larry Frazier on guitar and Jimmie Smith on drums. This album contains the classic McGriff cut "Kiko," "That's All," and "Hello Betty." This is drum/sax driven McGriff at his best. —*Michael Erlewine*

Toast to Golden Classics / Collectables ◆◆◆◆◆
This is a compilation of ten cuts taken from the six early Sue albums, one or two from each. The sound is bad, but it will give you a taste of the Sue material—all the best cuts. These early Sue albums are now all available on collectables and worth hearing, despite the sound. —*Michael Erlewine*

● **Greatest Hits** / 1963-1971 / Blue Note ◆◆◆◆◆
Blue Note's *Greatest Hits* doesn't limit itself to the recordings Jimmy McGriff made for the label during the late '60s and early '70s. Instead, it culls from his Sue, Veep and Solid State recordings as well, making it a definitive overview of his career as a gritty, funky singles artist. And, as *Greatest Hits* demonstrates, McGriff could create a monster groove, making his singles intoxicating slices of funky jazz. All of his R&B hits—"I've Got a Woman," "All About My Girl," "Kiko," "The Worm"—are here, as are lesser-known singles and terrific album tracks, resulting in a compilation that isn't just a terrific introduction for neophytes, but also a useful retrospective for collectors. —*Stephen Thomas Erlewine*

Topkapi / 1964-1965 / Sue ◆◆
This finds McGriff with pre-recorded tracks with a horn section, guitar, bass, drums and a string section. The material was arranged and directed by Fred Norman. The album consists of 12 movie and TV themes with McGriff and "orchestra." The orchestra sounds like Musak, but McGriff sounds like McGriff. How the two got together beats me. —*Michael Erlewine*

Blues for Mister Jimmy / 1965 / Collectables ◆◆◆
His last date for the Sue label is a trio, McGriff with Larry Frazier on guitar and Jimmie Smith on drums. Nine bluesy tunes including "Turn Blue," a classic McGriff instrumental. —*Michael Erlewine*

Tribute to Count Basie / 1966 / LRC ◆◆◆
Recorded in 1966 with the Jimmy McGriff Big Band, and it is a VERY large group. At the center of all these instruments is the one-man band organ sound of McGriff. This is a salute to Count Basie and includes ten songs that he wrote or made a part of his repertoire. Actually, this works quite well. —*Michael Erlewine*

A Bag Full of Soul / 1966 / Solid State ◆◆◆
McGriff with funk guitarist Thornell Schwartz. —*Michael Erlewine*

The Worm / Sep. 1968 / Solid State ◆◆◆
A high point of soul-jazz and funk. Both commercial and substantial. —*Ron Wynn*

The Funkiest Little Band in the Land / 1968-1974 / LRC ◆◆◆
This is a collection of McGriff with small bands during the years from 1968 to 1974, before he went to the large orchestra format. Produced by Sonny Lester, many of these appeared on the Groove Merchant label. Includes a lot of funky stuff with titles like "Super Funk," "Fat Cakes," "Groove Fly," and "Dig on It." There are 13 cuts and plenty of vintage McGriff. —*Michael Erlewine*

Electric Funk / Sep. 1969 / Blue Note ◆◆◆
The title of *Electric Funk* may lead you to believe that it's a set of unrepentant, rampaging hard funk, but that's not quite the case. The record is laid-back, but undeniably funky, with Jimmy McGriff and electric pianist Horace Ott leading an unnamed group through a set of soul workouts. It's not jazz, it's jazzy soul, and it's among the funkiest of any soul-jazz records from the late '60s, filled with stuttering drum breaks, lite fuzz guitars, elastic bass, smoldering organ and punchy, slightly incongruous horn charts. —*Stephen Thomas Erlewine*

Georgia on My Mind / LRC ◆◆◆
This is a compilation of sixteen selections from six sessions in the late 1960s and early 1970s, tunes from McGriff albums like *Let's Stay Together* (1966 and 1972 versions), *Fly Dude* (1972), and *Groove Grease* (1971). All small or smallish combos. Mostly standards; some few kickers. —*Michael Erlewine*

Black and Blues / 1971 / Groove Merchant ◆◆◆
For this set by Jimmy McGriff, the organist utilizes Bill Easley (one of his discoveries, heard here on alto and tenor) and veteran trombonist Al Grey in his front line, along with guitarist Melvin Sparks and drummer Bernard Purdie. They perform three standards, including long versions of "Don't Get Around Much Anymore" and "Secret Love," along with an obscurity and a couple of basic originals. Even when the chord changes are quite a bit different, the music is infused with the blues and consistently swings, which is typical of a Jimmy McGriff session. —*Scott Yanow*

Jazz Collector Edition / 1971 / LaserLight ◆◆◆
This is a reissue of two 1970s McGriff albums, *Groove Grease* (1971) and *Main Squeeze* (1974) originally released on the Groove Merchant label. The first has McGriff with Jimmy Ponder (g) and Eddie Gladden (d). The second album has mixed personnel including Everett Barksdale (g), Cliff Davis (sax), Murray Wilson (tpt), and Johnny Board (Baritone sax). In general, nice, laid-back playing. —*Michael Erlewine*

Let's Stay Together / 1972 / Simitar ◆◆◆
McGriff with funk guitarist Thornell Schwartz. —*Michael Erlewine*

Come Together / 1973 / Groove Merchant ◆◆
McGriff and Richard Groove Holmes on the same ticket. —*Michael Erlewine*

Main Squeeze / 1976 / Groove Merchant ◆◆◆
McGriff with the funky guitar of Jimmy Ponder and Connie Lester on alto sax. —*Michael Erlewine*

City Lights / Dec. 19, 1980+Feb. 4, 1981 / Jazz America ◆◆◆◆
To a large extent, organist Jimmy McGriff made his mark recording with large bands in the mid- to late 1960s, often for the Solid State label. His career became a bit more aimless in the late 1970s, when the organ was out of fashion, but he returned to prime form on this album. In reality, McGriff's playing was always fairly similar to Jimmy Smith's, and although not that distinctive, he found his own sound within the Smith tradition of groovin' organists. This LP for the short-lived JAM label matches McGriff with four horns (including tenor saxophonist Harold Vick and trumpeter Danny Moore) and a four-piece rhythm section which includes guitarist Jimmy Ponder and drummer Idris Muhammad. The repertoire is fairly typical for soul-jazz, including "Teach Me Tonight" and some funky blues, and the music is pleasing. —*Scott Yanow*

Movin' Upside the Blues / Dec. 19, 1980-June 24, 1981 / JAM ◆◆◆◆
For his second JAM LP, organist Jimmy McGriff is heard on one selection (Kenny Burrell's "All Day Long") left over from the first session (which features a septet including Harold Vick on tenor and trumpeter Danny Moore), plus four numbers from 1981 with altoist Arnold Sterling, guitarist Jimmy Ponder, trumpeter Bill Hardman, and Vick. As usual, most of the music is blues-based, although the inclusion of "Moonlight Serenade" in this soul-jazz setting is a pleasant surprise. —*Scott Yanow*

Countdown / Apr. 27, 1983-Apr. 28, 1983 / Milestone ◆◆◆◆
His first for Milestone. Produced by Bob Porter, McGriff with two saxes, trombone, guitar, and drums for what the liner notes call a "big band sound" combo. Plenty of good funky organ. Some of the numbers are a little too smooth (too many horns) for my taste. —*Michael Erlewine*

Skywalk / Mar. 19, 1984-Mar. 20, 1984 / Milestone ◆◆◆
Organist Jimmy McGriff's second Milestone recording is his only one for the label that has not yet been reissued on CD. Heard with a nonet on three numbers, a quintet on two songs, and an 11-piece outfit during his "Skywalk," McGriff is in his usual fine form on such tunes as "Jersey Bounce" and "Let's Stay Together." Outside of altoist Bill Easley and guitarist Jimmy Ponder, the sidemen are fairly obscure, although quite capable in this setting. —*Scott Yanow*

The Starting Five / Oct. 14, 1986-Oct. 15, 1986 / Milestone ◆◆◆◆◆
Here is McGriff with two terrific blues honkin' sax masters—Rusty Bryant and David "Fathead" Newman. Add Mel Brown and Wayne Boyd on guitar, plus Bernard Purdie on drums, and you have a recipe for funk. Produced by Bob Porter, this is perhaps the best of McGriff's Milestone output. —*Michael Erlewine*

You Ought to Think About Me / June 10, 1985-June 11, 1985 / Headfirst ◆◆◆◆
Although Jimmy McGriff temporarily switched labels from Milestone to Headfirst in 1990, his brand of swinging funk and blues-oriented jazz was virtually unchanged. Utilizing a quintet that includes the reeds of Bill Easley, trumpeter Stanton Wilson and guitarist Rodney Jones, McGriff explores a wide-ranging set filled with originals and such tunes as "The Way You Look Tonight," "America the Beautiful," "Ain't No Mountain High Enough" and a medley of "One O'Clock Jump" and "C Jam Blues." The results are predictably excellent. —*Scott Yanow*

Blue to the Bone / Jul. 19, 1988-Jul. 20, 1988 / Milestone ◆◆◆◆
McGriff with Bill Easley on sax, Melvin Sparks on guitar, Bernard Purdie on drums, and Al Grey on trombone. The trombone is not that often found in the small-organ combo format and may not appeal to everyone. Smooth, yet funky. —*Michael Erlewine & Ron Wynn*

On the Blue Side / May 1990 / Milestone ◆◆◆◆
An updated version of the vintage McGriff formula: bluesy, soulful organ fare with a balance struck between jazz sensibility and a funk/R&B groove. —*Ron Wynn*

In a Blue Mood / 1991 / K-Tel ◆◆
One of his albums on Headfirst, after leaving Milestone and the great production work of Bob Porter. McGriff on organ and keyboards plus a group with synthesizers, sax, guitar, drums, vocals, and what-not make this more pop-oriented fare than organ funk. —*Michael Erlewine*

Right Turn on Blues / Jan. 22, 1994-Jan. 23, 1994 / Telarc ◆◆◆◆◆
There was virtually no prior planning for this meeting between organist Jimmy McGriff and altoist Hank Crawford, but none was needed. The veterans had already recorded four prior albums together, so they simply jammed through blues, ballads and a few basic originals without any difficulty; Crawford could play

this material blindfolded. McGriff sets the grooves expertly with his foot-pedal basswork, with assistance from guitarist Rodney Jones and drummer Jesse Hameen. The overall result is an enthusiastic session of foot-tapping music. No real surprises occur, but lovers of hard-swinging organ combos have nothing to complain about. —*Scott Yanow*

Blues Groove / Jul. 21, 1995-Jul. 22, 1995 / Telarc ◆◆◆◆
Organist Jimmy McGriff and altoist Hank Crawford always make for a potent team. With guitarist Wayne Boyd and drummer Vance James completing the quartet, McGriff and Crawford explore an appealing mixture of blues, soulful ballads and riff tunes. Few surprises occur, but many of the songs (particularly "Movin' Upside the Blues," "The Sermon," "When I Fall in Love" and "Mercy, Mercy, Mercy") are fairly memorable. The fans of these fine players will not be disappointed. —*Scott Yanow*

Dream Team / Aug. 19, 1996 / Milestone ◆◆◆◆◆
Jimmy McGriff moves back to the Milestone label in style with a great soul-jazz quintet, with whom he recorded one of his best Milestone albums, *The Starting Five*. This time, with no apologies to the notorious O.J. Simpson legal staff, he calls his quintet the "Dream Team"—and for this kind of music, indeed they are. McGriff strokes his Hammond XB-3 keys and pedals with a relaxed in-the-pocket feeling; with this group, he doesn't have to push, nor should he. David "Fathead" Newman holds down the tenor chair, Red Holloway (replacing the late Rusty Bryant) is on alto and tenor, Mel Brown plays really tasty guitar, and Bernard Purdie powers the drums. Check out the effortlessly sauntering, hip-swinging boogaloo of "Fleetwood Stroll" or the slow, deeply soulful treatment of Willie Nelson's country standard "Funny How Time Slips Away" or the oooh-ain't-that-funky "McGriffin." Everybody swings, everybody listens intuitively to each other and feels the down-home churchy grooves, and they recorded it all in one day at Rudy Van Gelder's studio. This has the ingredients for ranking as an instant classic in this idiom. —*Richard S. Ginell*

Steppin' Up / Milestone ◆◆◆
Jimmy McGriff with Hank Crawford on alto sax, Jimmy Ponder on guitar, Billy Preston on piano and Vance James on drums—an exellent group. Produced by Bob Porter, this has tunes like "Something for Bubba," and Percy Mayfield's "River's Invitation" that are standouts. This combination of player sis all that you need for some funky jazz. —*Michael Erlewine*

Soul Survivors / Milestone ◆◆◆◆
Can't beat this lineup: McGriff with Hank Crawford on alto sax, George Benson (or Jim Pittsburgh) on guitar, and Bernard Purdie (or Mel Lewis) on drums. This is another of the fine Milestone recordings of McGriff produced by Bob Porter. No disappointments here. Includes versions of "One Mint Julep," "Because of You," and the Crawford original "The Peeper." Very nice. —*Michael Erlewine*

Rosy McHargue

b. Apr. 6, 1902, Danville, IL
C-Melody Saxophone, Clarinet / Dixieland

Although he is somewhat obscure, Rosy McHargue (who turned 96 in 1998) is the third oldest active jazz musician in history, behind Eubie Blake (who made it to 100) and Benny Waters (just a month older than McHargue and still active as of this writing). Always associated with Dixieland and 1920s jazz, Rosy McHargue in his later years developed into a singer with an encyclopedic knowledge of lyrics (including verses and alternate choruses) from many forgotten songs from the 1920s and before. At the age of 15 in 1917, he worked at his first professional engagement (with the Novelty Syncopators) and made his recording debut in 1922 playing "Wow Wow Blues" with Roy Schoenbeck's Orchestra. Other early recordings included dates with the Seattle Harmony Kings (1925), Frankie Trumbauer (1931), Ted Weems (1934) and Jimmy McPartland (1936). McHargue worked with the Wolverines in late 1925 after Bix Beiderbecke had departed, spent a year with the Seattle Harmony Kings and played with Ted Weems from 1934-42. After moving to Los Angeles, he worked briefly with Eddie Miller and Benny Goodman before having longer stints with Kay Kyser (1943-46) and Red Nichols (1947-51). McHargue, who took the purposely cornball clarinet solo on Pee Wee Hunt's unlikely hit version of "Twelfth Street Rag," played and recorded with Pete Dailey, and has been active in Los Angeles' Dixieland scene up until the present time, still appearing at jazz festivals in 1997. He recorded as a leader for Jump (1947 and 1952), Fairmont, Audiophile, Protone (1957) and, much more recently, Stomp Off (1992). —*Scott Yanow*

● **McHargue's Memphis Five** / Dec. 7, 1947 / Jump ◆◆◆◆
Rosy McHargue was already 45 when he had his debut record session as a leader in 1947. This LP contains the eight selections played that day plus five alternate takes. McHargue, sticking to clarinet, joins with cornetist Nick Cochrane (a talented but long-forgotten player), valve trombonist Brad Gowans, bass saxophonist Joe

Rushton, pianist Marvin Ash and drummer Graham Stevenson to play a variety of Dixieland standards and a few obscurities (including "They Called It Dixieland" and "I Wonder What's Become of Joe"). McHargue's occasional arrangements give variety to the set, and this album is easily recommended to fans of trad jazz. —*Scott Yanow*

Rosy McHargue's Ragtimers / Apr. 2, 1952 / Jump ◆◆◆◆◆
Doubling on C-melody sax and clarinet, Rosy McHargue is heard on this LP leading his regular band of the period. For what was just his second album as a leader, McHargue plays high-quality 1920s jazz with cornetist Bob Higgins, trombonist Moe Schneider, pianist Earle Sturgis, bassist Ray Leatherwood and drummer George Defebaugh. In addition to a few standards, there are superior versions of such tunes as "Palasteena," "Singin' the Blues," "Jazzin' the Blues Away" and "That Mysterious Rag," plus a couple of McHargue originals (including "Rosy's Hangover Rag") and a charming vocal by the leader on "Don't Bring Me Posies." The music overall is melodic and often surprisingly lyrical Dixieland-oriented jazz. Rosy McHargue, who was 50 at the time, still had more than four decades of music ahead of him, but this LP (which hopefully will be reissued on CD someday) is one of his finest all-around recordings. —*Scott Yanow*

Echoes of Bix / Jun. 10, 1985-Jun. 11, 1985 / Mabel Label ◆◆◆◆◆
The legendary C-melody saxophonist Rosy McHargue, who had turned 83 a few months earlier, teams up with soprano saxophonist Dave Dolson's Jazzin' Babies for this delightful LP. Some of the tunes (such as "Big Boy," "Clementine" and "Tia Juana") had been recorded in the 1920s by cornetist Bix Beiderbecke; a few others were from the era, and the title cut was a then-recent original by McHargue. Rosy's beautiful tone on C-melody sax, his interplay with the rest of the band (which also includes cornetist Dick Miller and trombonist John Innes), and his occasional vocals make this a charming set well worth searching for. —*Scott Yanow*

Oh How He Can Sing! / Jul. 9, 1992-Nov. 19, 1992 / Stomp Off ◆◆
This should have been a better CD. Ninety-year-old C-melody saxophonist Rosy McHargue still had a beautiful tone and a lightly swinging style, and the band (which includes cornetist Dick Miller, clarinetist Bill Wood and pianist Robbie Rhodes) is excellent. Unfortunately, McHargue chose to emphasize his singing, taking as many as three vocals on some of the tunes. His ability to remember lengthy and obscure lyrics is impressive, and there is some charm to his singing, but because only one of the 18 songs is taken as an instrumental and because there is far too little of McHargue's saxophone playing, the results are quite disappointing. Not too surprisingly, Rosy's singing was often closer to talking, and he sounded his age much more verbally than musically. So this CD, although it is interesting to hear the full lyrics to some of these period pieces, does not live up to its potential. —*Scott Yanow*

Kalaparusha Maurice McIntyre (Maurice McIntyre)

b. Mar. 24, 1936
Tenor Saxophone / Free Jazz
An intense tenor saxophonist who often plays quite freely, Kalaparusha Maurice McIntyre is a natural extension of the high-energy tenors of the mid-'60s. He was a founding member of the AACM and recorded on Roscoe Mitchell's groundbreaking *Sound* album. He played with other members of the AACM and moved back and forth between Chicago and New York without gaining much fame. McIntyre worked with Jerome Cooper and Muhal Richard Abrams in addition to some of Chicago's blues musicians. In the 1980s he was a member of Kahil El Zabar's Ethnic Heritage Ensemble. Kalaparusha Maurice McIntyre has recorded as a leader for Delmark (1969-70), Black Saint (1979) and Cadence (1981). —*Scott Yanow*

● **Humility in the Light of the Creator** / Feb. 5, 1969-Feb. 15, 1969 / Delmark ◆◆◆◆◆
Superb album by multi-instrumentalist McIntyre, one of the lesser-known Chicago musicians who helped form the AACM and has participated in the city's avant-garde jazz movement since its inception. This was his finest album, a work with sweeping, complex, yet also invigorating and visceral compositions. It also has dazzling playing from McIntyre and his associates. —*Ron Wynn*

Peace and Blessings / Jun. 18, 1979 / Black Saint ◆◆◆◆
This obscure set features passionate blowing by Kalaparusha Maurice McIntyre (heard on tenor, flute, clarinet, bass clarinet and percussion) along with the little-known Longineu Parson on trumpet, fluegelhorn, flute, sopranino and recorders, bassist Leonard Jones, and drummer King Mock. The quartet performs five McIntyre originals and one by Parsons, and the emphasis is on intense solos and very free improvising. There is plenty of fire displayed on this spirited set. —*Scott Yanow*

Ram's Run / Mar. 6, 1981 / Cadence ◆◆◆
This album (taken from a live concert) has an unusual instrumentation: tenor (Kalaparusha Maurice McIntyre), alto (Julius Hemphill), trumpet (Malachi Thompson)

and drums (J.R. Mitchell). The music, five McIntyre compositions, contains plenty of intense moments but the lack of a bass or a chordal instrument is a difficult handicap to overcome. The complex performances will certainly challenge listeners who expect all jazz to swing conventionally. —*Scott Yanow*

Ken McIntyre

b. Sep. 7, 1931, Boston, MA
Alto Saxophone, Flute, Bass Clarinet, Bassoon, Oboe / Avant-Garde, Post-Bop
A versatile player with a thoughtful style who can play quite freely, Ken McIntyre has never been a major name in jazz despite his talents. After serving in the military and graduating from the Boston Conservatory, he arrived in New York in 1960 and made a strong impression. He recorded two albums for New Jazz that year, including one in which he held his own against Eric Dolphy. McIntyre also led two now-scarce records for United Artists during 1962-63 (including one titled *Way Way Out*), but became involved in education, teaching in the public schools starting in 1961. He continued playing on a part-time basis (recording with Cecil Taylor in 1966). McIntyre led five albums for Steeple Chase during 1974-78 including his definitive set Hindsight (which finds him spotlighting each of his five horns in a quartet). He also recorded with Craig Harris in 1983 and put together an Eric Dolphy tribute set for Serene in 1991, but Ken McIntyre has never achieved the recognition he deserved. —*Scott Yanow*

Stone Blues / May 31, 1960 / Original Jazz Classics ◆◆◆◆◆
This early effort by Ken McIntyre (who doubles here on alto and flute) grows in interest with each listen. On a couple of his six originals (including a song called "Cornballs"), McIntyre slides humorously between notes, but other selections are much more serious. McIntyre's sidemen are now somewhat obscure (trombonist John Mancebo Lewis, pianist Dizzy Sal, bassist Paul Morrison and drummer Bobby Ward), but they fit well into his conception which at this early stage was essentially advanced bop slightly influenced by the "new thing" music of Ornette Coleman. This interesting set has been reissued on CD. —*Scott Yanow*

Looking Ahead / Jun. 28, 1960 / Original Jazz Classics ◆◆◆◆◆
It was quite fitting that Ken McIntyre had an opportunity to record in a quintet with Eric Dolphy, for his multi-instrumental approach was similar to Dolphy's, although he always had a very different sound. On this CD reissue, McIntyre plays alto on four tunes and flute on two others (his work on bassoon, oboe and bass clarinet would come slightly later), while Dolphy mostly plays alto but doubles on flute on one number and switches to bass clarinet for "Dianna." With pianist Walter Bishop, Jr., bassist Sam Jones and drummer Art Taylor offering concise solos and swinging support, McIntyre somehow almost holds his own with Dolphy on a variety of originals and George Gershwin's "They All Laughed." A very interesting date. —*Scott Yanow*

The Complete United Artists Sessions / Jun. 11, 1962-May 27, 1963 / Capitol ◆◆◆◆
Ken McIntyre, a very underrated multi-reedist, developed fairly original styles on alto, flute, bass clarinet, oboe and bassoon. He made two fairly well-known sessions for New Jazz in 1960 and recorded for Steeple Chase from 1974-78. However, McIntyre's pair of United Artists records from 1962-63 (his only dates as a leader during 1961-73) have been long overlooked. This double CD from 1997 has all of the music from the original LPs, plus eight previously unreleased cuts. All of the selections except "Laura" and "Speak Low" are McIntyre compositions. The advanced hard bop originals (which show the influence of the avant-garde) tend to be complex, sometimes using tricky time signatures, and lack memorable melodies, but they swing. The leader mostly plays his dry-toned alto, with a bit of flute and oboe, and with the exception of a few spots by pianist Jaki Byard, the backup musicians are mostly supportive and do not stand out. One set has McIntyre and a pianoless rhythm section joined by a dozen strings. His string writing is inventive and shows some otherwise unrealized potential. The other selections are either with a quartet or a quintet (the latter with trombonist John Mancebo Lewis). This obscure but stimulating set grows in interest with each listen. —*Scott Yanow*

● **Hindsight** / Jan. 13, 1974 / Steeple Chase ◆◆◆◆◆
Ken McIntyre had not recorded as a leader in 11 years when he cut this quartet set for Steeple Chase, but he was more than ready. The well-rounded program (which on the CD reissue includes a second version of "Body and Soul") features McIntyre on separate features for his alto, flute, bassoon, oboe and bass clarinet. Although often compared to Eric Dolphy early in his career, McIntyre actually has a style of his own, open to the innovations of the avant-garde, but not shy to embrace melodies. With the assistance of pianist Kenny Drew, bassist Bo Stief and drummer Alex Riel, McIntyre is in consistently brilliant form with the highlights being "Lush Life" (on bassoon), "Body and Soul" (taken on bass clarinet) and "Naima" (for his oboe) and a heated alto workout on "Sunnymoon for Two." —*Scott Yanow*

Home / Jun. 23, 1975 / Steeple Chase ✦✦✦✦✦

This excellent outing by multi-reedist Ken McIntyre ranges musically in his ten originals from a blues, the ballad "Charlotte," and a tribute to John Coltrane ("Sea Train") to freer pieces. McIntyre is heard on alto, flute, bassoon, oboe and bass clarinet and is joined by a stimulating rhythm section consisting of pianist Jaki Byard (who plays electric piano on the title cut), bassist Reggie Workman and drummer Andrei Strobert. The post-bop music is consistently inventive and easily recommended. —*Scott Yanow*

Open Horizon / Nov. 19, 1975 / Steeple Chase ✦✦✦✦

Introducing the Vibrations / Oct. 30, 1976 / Steeple Chase ✦✦✦

The Vibrations were a short-lived group led by Ken McIntyre that also included pianist Richie Harper, bassist Alonzo Gardner, drummer Andrei Strobert and Andy Vega on percussion. With trumpeter Terumasa Hino as a guest, this LP has the group's only recording, performing six McIntyre compositions. The leader is heard on one song apiece playing flute, bass clarinet, oboe and bassoon, and he uses the alto on two others. Surprisingly enough, all of the songs were written during the 1956-62 period (all but one are from 1956-59), although most sound fairly adventurous on this interesting if not essential outing. —*Scott Yanow*

Chasing the Sun / Jul. 1978 / Steeple Chase ✦✦✦✦

Tribute / 1991 / Serene ✦✦✦

A welcome set from an extremely underrated multi-sax performer. —*Ron Wynn*

Dave McKenna

b. May 30, 1930, Woonsocket, RI

Piano / Swing

One of the top swing-based pianists of the past 25 years, Dave McKenna's hard-driving bass lines give momentum to uptempo pieces, and his vast knowledge of superior songs from the 1930s has resulted in many rewarding albums of traditional but fresh music. Although talented from the start, McKenna did not achieve that much recognition until he was already in his 40s. He joined the Musicians' Union when he was 15 and picked up early experience playing with Boots Mussulli (1947), Charlie Ventura (1949) and Woody Herman's Orchestra (1950-51). After two years in the military, McKenna had a second stint with Ventura (1953-54) and then worked with a variety of top swing and Dixieland players including Gene Krupa, Stan Getz, Zoot Sims, Al Cohn, Eddie Condon, Bobby Hackett and Bob Wilber (in the late '70s) and was a soloist at piano bars in Massachusetts. McKenna had recorded for ABC-Paramount (1956), Epic (1958), Bethlehem (a two-piano date shared with Hall Overton in 1960) and Realm (1963), but in 1973 McKenna's talents finally began to be more fully documented. He led sets for Halcyon, Shiah, Famous Door, Inner City (with vocalist Teddi King) and four for Chiaroscuro. And then in 1979 with *No Bass Hit* (a trio date with Scott Hamilton and Jake Hanna), McKenna debuted with Concord, finding his home. He has made many sessions for Concord ever since, some as a sideman or with small groups, but the best ones being unaccompanied recitals. In the mid-'90s Dave McKenna is at the top of his field. —*Scott Yanow*

Piano Scene of Dave McKenna / Jul. 22, 1958-Jul. 23, 1958 / Koch ✦✦✦

This CD reissues one of pianist Dave McKenna's first recordings (which is from 1958, not 1995 as it mistakenly states on the back cover). On what was originally an Epic album, the young McKenna displays a strong technique but a musical personality that had not yet become distinctive. McKenna was surprisingly bop-oriented in the late '50s, and was not yet utilizing powerful basslines, so this trio date with bassist John Drew and drummer Osie Johnson is not on the level of his Concords of the 1980s and '90s; only "'Way Down Yonder in New Orleans" gives hints of what is to come. This swinging and reasonably enjoyable set (notable for McKenna's originals "Splendid Splinter" and "Lickety Split") has been greatly expanded by the inclusion of eight alternate takes, but is not too essential. —*Scott Yanow*

Solo Piano / Feb. 24, 1973 / Chiaroscuro ✦✦✦

Prior to 1973, pianist Dave McKenna had not recorded as a leader in a decade, and it was this particular album (now available on CD with two additional songs and a few alternate takes) that helped McKenna gain recognition for his brilliant playing; it would be followed by three other Chiaroscuro dates and a countless number of sets for Concord. A couple of attempts at uplifting current material aside ("Norwegian Wood" and "My Cherie Amour" do not fit McKenna's sound), this solo performance finds McKenna displaying his fully formed swing style on a variety of superior tunes, (including a three-part "Have You Met Miss Jones Sequence." —*Scott Yanow*

Cookin' at Michael's Pub / Feb. 28, 1973 / Halcyon ✦✦✦✦

A fine 1973 album that was issued on Marian McPartland's Halcyon label. Pianist Dave McKenna mixes stride, light boogie, and blues, plus his own devices, and has a style that is both unorthodox and compelling. His odd rhythmic lines, phrasing, and swinging approach were well documented on this one. —*Ron Wynn*

Dave McKenna Quartet Featuring Zoot Sims / Oct. 1974 / Chiaroscuro ✦✦✦✦✦

Prior to his longtime association with the Concord label, pianist Dave McKenna's four Chiaroscuro albums (of which this CD brings back the second) did a great deal to make the veteran mainstream pianist known to the general jazz public. This set features McKenna, bassist Major Holley and drummer Ray Mosca joined by the great swing tenor Zoot Sims, who doubles on soprano. The original nine-song program is augmented by four previously unreleased numbers. Highlights of the fine straightahead date include "Limehouse Blues," "Deed I Do," "Linger Awhile" and two versions of "I Cover the Waterfront." —*Scott Yanow*

Dave "Fingers" McKenna / May 1977 / Chiaroscuro ✦✦✦✦

Pianist Dave McKenna has recorded in a variety of settings through the years, but sounds at his best when playing unaccompanied solos. For this currently out-of-print LP, McKenna decided to play a full set of the type of tunes he might play in a local bar, such as "My Melancholy Baby," "Bill Bailey," "Chloe," "As Time Goes By," and "The Curse of an Aching Heart." As one might expect, the pianist uplifts all of the melodies and brings a lot of swing to the vintage material. Worth searching for. —*Scott Yanow*

McKenna / Oct. 23, 1977 / Chiaroscuro ✦✦✦✦✦

Dave McKenna's fourth and final Chiaroscuro LP (and his second set of unaccompanied piano solos for the label) features him in top form less than two years before he began recording for Concord. McKenna digs into ten of his favorite standards, including familiar material such as "Avalon," "How High the Moon," "Blue Skies" and "What Is This Thing Called Love." He comes up with fresh variations on these numbers and swings up a storm. Often using heated bass lines and subtle wit, Dave McKenna puts on a memorable recital. —*Scott Yanow*

Giant Strides / May 1979 / Concord Jazz ✦✦✦✦✦

Left Handed Compliment / Dec. 1979 / Concord Jazz ✦✦✦✦✦

Dave McKenna is one of the great swing pianists of modern times. His exciting left-hand bassline really propels his faster performances while his encyclopedic knowledge of early American popular songs and general good taste make his ballad performances memorable. This solo outing finds McKenna playing superior tunes with swing and subtle creativity, as usual. —*Scott Yanow*

☆ **No Bass Hit** / Mar. 1979 / Concord Jazz ✦✦✦✦✦

Most pianists are dependent on a bassist to keep the rhythm unless they are playing unaccompanied solos, but not Dave McKenna. McKenna, who has the ability to consistently set a fire under tenor saxophonist Scott Hamilton, teams up with Hamilton and drummer Jake Hanna for this superlative trio set. The eight standards (which include "If Dreams Come True," "Drum Boogie," "I Love You, Samantha" and "Get Happy") consistently swing hard, and there is plenty of excitement. Highly recommended, particularly to lovers of mainstream jazz. —*Scott Yanow*

Piano Mover / Apr. 1980 / Concord Jazz ✦✦✦✦✦

Pianist Dave McKenna teams up with bassist Bob Maize, drummer Jake Hanna and what is called "the Dick Johnson reed section" for a set of standards both fresh and obscure. Johnson, switching between clarinet, alto and flute, works well with McKenna on this small-group swing set; highlights include "Cottontail," "Star Eyes" and Clare Fischer's "Morning." —*Scott Yanow*

Dave McKenna Trio Plays Music of Harry Warren / Aug. 1981 / Concord Jazz ✦✦✦✦✦

Harry Warren has long been one of the most underrated of the great songwriters of the 1930s. On this trio set with bassist Bob Maize and drummer Jake Hanna, pianist Dave McKenna comes up with fresh ideas on such classics as "Nagasaki," "42nd Street," "I Only Have Eyes for You" and "Lulu's Back in Town," perfect material for his swinging style. The interpretations are consistently delightful and also include a three-song medley, "Carnival," and "We're in the Money" among the highlights. Recommended. —*Scott Yanow*

Celebration of Hoagy Carmichael / May 1983 / Concord Jazz ✦✦✦✦✦

This is a perfect idea for a recording project. In a sparkling and consistently delightful solo set, Dave McKenna performs 11 of Hoagy Carmichael's finest compositions, including a medley of "Skylark" and "Georgia on My Mind." With the exception of "One Morning in May," "Moon Country" and "Come Easy, Go Easy Love," all of the numbers rank with Hoagy's greatest hits, but McKenna's renditions of such familiar tunes as "Stardust," "The Nearness of You" and "Lazy River" are full of subtle surprises and his special brand of swing. Highly recommended. —*Scott Yanow*

The Keyman / Aug. 1984 / Concord Jazz ✦✦✦✦✦

The best way to hear pianist Dave McKenna is solo. His joyous left-hand basslines are always enjoyable, as his knack for performing rarely heard but superior songs. On this solo set, McKenna not only revives the Bix Beiderbecke-associated "Singing the Blues" but "I'll Be a Friend with Pleasure" and "Louisiana" too, along with some tender ballads and even a Michael Franks song ("Don't Be Blue"). This fine all-around recording offers many fine examples of Dave McKenna's magical swing piano. —*Scott Yanow*

★ **Dancing in the Dark** / Aug. 1985 / Concord Jazz ◆◆◆◆◆
The great swing pianist Dave McKenna performs 11 selections written by Arthur Schwartz, one of the lesser-known (but very talented) songwriters of the golden age of American popular music. Among the pieces that McKenna joyfully revives are "By Myself," "A Shine on Your Shoes," "I Guess I'll Have to Change My Plan" and "Dancing in the Dark." Bright, melodic treatments of classic music. —*Scott Yanow*

My Friend the Piano / Aug. 1986 / Concord Jazz ◆◆◆◆
Pianist Dave McKenna fills *My Friend the Piano* with constant surprises; rhythm, tempo and key changes that somehow seem logical after the fact. There is a slight emphasis on ballads, but one's attention rarely wanders for the music, although tasteful, is never entirely predictable. —*Scott Yanow*

No More Ouzo for Puzo / Jun. 1988 / Concord Jazz ◆◆◆◆◆
Despite the ambiguous meaning of the title cut (Puzo is for a jazz fan, Charlie Puzo, but "ouzo" is never defined), the music on this quartet set is easy to understand. Pianist Dave McKenna teams up with guitarist Gray Sargent (a new discovery at the time), bassist Monty Budwig and drummer Jimmie Smiths for memorable renditions of a few standards (including an uptempo "Look for the Silver Lining," a sensitive "Smile," and "You Brought a New Kind of Love to Me"), a few obscurities ("I Keep Going Back to Joe's" is not performed too often), and the original title cut. The interplay between McKenna and Sargent, along with the individual solos, make this another excellent entry in the pianist's extensive output for Concord. —*Scott Yanow*

Live at Maybeck Recital Hall, Vol. 2 / Nov. 1989 / Concord Jazz ◆◆◆◆◆
Fine technique, wonderful melodies. —*Ron Wynn*

Shadows 'n Dreams / Mar. 1990 / Concord Jazz ◆◆◆
Nine of the selections on this solo piano CD by the great swing pianist Dave McKenna have "dream" in their titles (such as "I Had the Craziest Dream," "You Stepped Out of a Dream," etc.) while the remaining five are built around the word "shadow." All of the thoughtful performances on McKenna's relaxed set are taken slow to medium-tempo, including his two originals, the brooding waltz "Shadowland" and the bluesy "Dreams 'n' Blue." McKenna plays quite well throughout, but a little more mood variation would have uplifted the pleasing solo session into something special. —*Scott Yanow*

A Handful of Stars / Jun. 15, 1992 / Concord Jazz ◆◆◆◆◆

Concord Duo Series, Vol. 2 / Dec. 16, 1992 / Concord Jazz ◆◆◆◆

Easy Street / May 6, 1994+May 18, 1994 / Concord Jazz ◆◆◆◆◆
The perfect way to hear pianist Dave McKenna is on his solo records; fortunately he has recorded quite a few for Concord. McKenna enjoys performing sets of music with thematic titles. The first seven songs on this date all have something to do with a street (from "Broadway" and "Basin Street Blues" to "Street of Dreams" and "On the Street Where You Live"). After playing his original "Cat's Cradle" and "My Honey's Lovin' Arms," McKenna performs four songs with "Gone" in its title before concluding the program with "Theodore the Thumper." McKenna, one of the top swing pianists of the 1980s and '90s, features his driving baselines on some of the faster pieces. This is an enjoyable set that gives listeners a strong example of Dave McKenna's talents. —*Scott Yanow*

Christmas Ivory / Feb. 18+19, 1997 / Concord Jazz ◆◆◆
This solo set by pianist Dave McKenna is predictably infectious and joyful. Most Christmas songs naturally lend themselves to swinging jazz interpretations, and McKenna has yet to record an indifferent album, particularly when playing unaccompanied solos. He romps through such songs as "Santa Claus Is Coming to Town," "Jingle Bells" and "Sleigh Bells," contributes two originals (including the touching ballad "Snowbound"), and comes up with enough variety in tempos and moods to hold on to one's interest throughout this enjoyable effort. —*Scott Yanow*

You Must Believe in Swing / Apr. 15, 1997 / Concord Jazz ◆◆◆◆◆
On this wonderful set, pianist Dave McKenna and clarinetist Buddy DeFranco, mutual admirers who had rarely played together before, perform ten exciting duets. Because McKenna is an expert at keeping bass lines going, takes hot single-note solos with his right hand, and is a very self-sufficient pianist, there was no need for other musicians. DeFranco, a brilliant clarinetist for over half a century at this point, sounds inspired by the setting. Although one might consider the clarinetist to be boppish while McKenna is swing-oriented, the pianist has played bop before, and DeFranco is a veteran of the Tommy Dorsey Orchestra and Count Basie's early-'50s combos, so there was plenty of overlapping between their styles. On tunes such as "The Song Is You," the exquisite "Autumn Nocturne," "Poor Butterfly" and "Anthropology," the McKenna-DeFranco matchup is particularly magical. Recommended to fans of either of the musicians. —*Scott Yanow*

Red McKenzie

b. Oct. 14, 1899, St. Louis, MO, **d.** Feb. 7, 1948, New York, NY
Vocals, Comb / Classic Jazz
Red McKenzie was virtually jazz's only comb player, putting tissue paper on a comb and making sounds on his "instrument" similar to a kazoo. McKenzie was quite effective playing his "ax," often more so than when he sang sentimental ballads. In 1924 he formed the Mound City Blue Blowers, a trio with Jack Bland on banjo or guitar and Dick Slevin on kazoo. The group was quite popular for a few years, recording a dozen titles (two with guest Frankie Trumbauer and the last six with Eddie Lang making the group a quartet) during 1924-25. McKenzie also recorded under his own name (as leader of the Candy Kids, the exact same quartet!) during 1924-25. The Blue Blowers name was used for two classic titles ("Hello Lola" and "One Hour") in 1929 featuring Coleman Hawkins, Pee Wee Russell and Glenn Miller, along with the leader's comb; further Blue Blowers titles were cut during 1931 (featuring Hawkins, Jimmy Dorsey and Muggsy Spanier) and 1935-36 (often with Bunny Berigan). McKenzie, who recorded as a straight singer in 1931 and was with Paul Whiteman the following year, never did become a major name, but he did front the Spirits of Rhythm (1934) and the Farley-Riley group (1935) on record dates. He was retired during 1939-43, but came back for a brief while, appearing on some of Eddie Condon's Town Hall concerts and recording a few titles during 1944-47; by then the comb was sadly just a memory. —*Scott Yanow*

Just Friends / Sep. 16, 1929-Jun. 12, 1936 / Emanon ◆◆◆
Red McKenzie was more important as a talent scout and comb player in the 1920s than he was as a singer. This collector's LP, however, puts the focus on McKenzie's reasonably pleasing singing. He is heard with the Midnight Airedales (a studio group including cornetist Red Nichols and trombonist Glenn Miller) for two numbers from 1929, on eight selections from 1931 and 1932 (including "Just Friends" and "Can't We Talk It Over," plus an alternate take of "Time on My Hands") with an unknown studio group, and a 1936 radio broadcast with the Jerry Sears orchestra. Vintage jazz collectors will be interested in this music, although the results are more pleasant than essential. —*Scott Yanow*

● **Red McKenzie** / Jul. 12, 1935-Nov. 16, 1937 / Timeless ◆◆◆◆◆
During 1935-37, singer Red McKenzie (who at this point only occasionally contributed some comb playing) recorded 24 selections for the Decca and Variety labels. All of the titles (although not the three alternates) are on this CD. McKenzie is backed by various top studio musicians in the septets, most notably trumpeter Eddie Farley, trombonist Mike Riley, rhythm guitarist Eddie Condon, tenorman Babe Russin, trumpeter Jonah Jones, bass saxophonist Adrian Rollini, cornetist Bobby Hackett, and on eight numbers, the great trumpeter Bunny Berigan (including the earliest version of "I Can't Get Started" Bunny was on). McKenzie's vocals are fine—they don't hurt anyone—while the instrumental backup often steals the show. —*Scott Yanow*

Red McKenzie-Eddie Condon Chicagoans / Dec. 8, 1944 / Jazzology ◆◆◆
This LP contains all of the music recorded for radio transcriptions by an all-star Eddie Condon septet plus singer Red McKenzie. Other than appearances on Condon's Town Hall concerts and four songs from 1947, this was essentially the swan song for McKenzie, who was still just 45 at the time. An okay singer who had spirit, although he could be maudlin on ballads, McKenzie is fine on these titles. Side one of the album has the master takes of ten songs, plus a full alternate of "I've Got the World on a String," featuring Red and Condon with trumpeter Max Kaminsky, trombonist Jack Teagarden, clarinetist Pee Wee Russell, pianist Gene Schroeder, bassist Bob Casey and drummer Joe Grauso; "I Would Do Anything for You," "Basin Street Blues," "Dinah" and "After You've Gone" are highlights. The flip side, which has lots of false starts, incomplete versions and unissued takes, is strictly for collectors, although some of the talking between songs is of interest. —*Scott Yanow*

Ray McKinley

b. Jun. 18, 1910, Fort Worth, TX, **d.** May 7, 1995
Drums, Vocals, Leader / Swing
A top drummer during the swing era and a likable and personable singer who always displayed good humor, Ray McKinley was most significant in the 1940s in several settings. He played at the start of his career in territory bands, with Smith Ballew and then the Dorsey Brothers Orchestra, staying with Jimmy after the battling Dorseys went their separate ways. In 1939 McKinley became the co-leader (in reality if not in its name) of the new Will Bradley Orchestra. His vocals and the boogie-woogie piano playing of Freddie Slack made the band a hit with such numbers as "Beat Me Daddy, Eight to the Bar" and "Celery Stalks at Midnight." By 1942 trombonist Bradley had gotten sick of the repertoire (which also included "Rock-a-Bye the Boogie," "Scrub Me Mama with a Boogie Beat," "I Boogied When

I Should Have Woogied," "Boogie Woogie Conga," "Bounce Me Brother with a Solid Four," "Booglie Wooglie Piggy" and "Fry Me Cookie with a Can of Lard") and the group broke up. McKinley led a short-lived big band and then went in the military, playing in Europe with Glenn Miller's Army Air Force Orchestra and a small group also including Peanuts Hucko and Mel Powell. After Miller's death, McKinley was one of the band's co-leaders. In 1946 he put together his own orchestra which used some very modern arrangements by Eddie Sauter, was open to the influence of bop, and yet had a Dixieland flavor at times. Not too surprisingly, it failed to catch on (although a Savoy LP shows how strong the band could be). Ray McKinley led the Glenn Miller ghost band during 1956-66 and freelanced with small groups and headed another Glenn Miller-type orchestra until drifting into semi-retirement. — *Scott Yanow*

★ **The Most Versatile Band in the Land** / May 7, 1946-1947 / Savoy ✦✦✦✦
Ray McKinley was originally best known as the unofficial co-leader of the Will Bradley Orchestra and as the drummer with Glenn Miller's Army Air Force Band. The big band he led from 1946-49 was therefore quite surprising in how modern the arrangements were. McKinley was a great admirer of Eddie Sauter, and he let the arranger write whatever he wanted for the band. With pianist Lou Stein, clarinetist Peanuts Hucko and guitarist Mundell Lowe among the key soloists, the orchestra played very advanced swing with touches of bop, along with more conventional vocal features for McKinley (who always sang good-humored lyrics), Ann Hathaway, Teddy Norman and Chris Adams. This double-LP (which has unfortunately not yet been reissued in full on CD) contains all 28 recordings made by the 1946-47 edition of Ray McKinley's big band, and there are many unknown classics to be heard. McKinley seems to have had one of the finest jazz orchestras that no one has ever heard of. — *Scott Yanow*

Class of '49 / 1949 / Hep ✦✦✦✦

Featuring the Arrangements and Compositions of Eddie Sauter / Jul. 27, 1949+Dec. 23, 1949 / Golden Era ✦✦✦✦
During 1946-49, drummer Ray McKinley led a surprisingly adventurous big band that often featured the arrangements of Eddie Sauter. This collector's LP has broadcast versions of a dozen instrumentals performed by McKinley's 1949 orchestra, a group that included among its personnel trumpeter Nick Travis and pianist Lou Stein. The real stars are the charts (seven of the 12 are by Sauter), which contain plenty of surprising and stimulating moments. Some, but not all, of these performances have also been issued by the Scottish Hep label. Well worth checking out for fans of mid- to late '40s modern orchestras, such as those led by Woody Herman and Boyd Raeburn. — *Scott Yanow*

McKinney's Cotton Pickers

f. 1926, **db.** 1934
Big Band, Classic Jazz, Swing
William McKinney was a drummer who by 1923 had retired from playing in favor of conducting and managing a big band. In 1926 his outfit became known as McKinney's Cotton Pickers, and the following year they scored a major coup by hiring arranger/altoist/vocalist Don Redman away from Fletcher Henderson. As the band's musical director, Redman put together an outfit that competed successfully with Henderson and the up-and-coming Duke Ellington. The lineup of musicians by the time they started recording in 1928 included Langston Curl, Claude Jones, George Thomas and Dave Wilborn, but it was the advanced arrangements, the tight ensembles and the high musicianship of the orchestra on the whole that was most impressive. There were a few special all-star sessions with such players as Joe Smith, Sidney DeParis, Coleman Hawkins, Fats Waller, and Lonnie Johnson making appearances, and James P. Johnson sat in on one date. Among the more rewarding recordings overall were "Four or Five Times," "It's Tight like That," "It's a Precious Little Thing Called Love" and four future standards that Redman introduced: "Gee Baby Ain't I Good to You," "Baby Won't You Please Come Home," "I Want a Little Girl" and "Cherry."

It was a major blow in 1931 when Don Redman departed to form his own band. Benny Carter took over as musical director, but despite the presence of such fine players as Doc Cheatham, Hilton Jefferson and holdovers Quentin Jackson, Rex Stewart and Prince Robinson, there would only be one final recording session. The Depression eventually did the band in and after much turnover in 1934 the classic group broke up. McKinney organized later versions of the Cotton Pickers, but without making an impression. — *Scott Yanow*

● **1928-1929** / Jul. 11, 1928-Nov. 5, 1929 / Classics ✦✦✦✦
This is the first of three Classics CD's featuring all of the master takes by McKinney's Cotton Pickers, one of the finest big bands of the late 1920s. The inventive arrangements of leader Don Redman (who also plays alto and clarinet in addition to taking some vocals) are even better than the individual solos. Highlighted by such numbers as "Four or Five Times," "Milenberg Joys," "Cherry," "Don't Be like That," "There's a Rainbow 'Round My Shoulder" and a surprisingly hard-swinging

version of "It's a Precious Little Thing Called Love," the Cotton Pickers feature tight ensembles, spirited vocals and concise hot solos. All three of their Classics CD's are well worth picking up. — *Scott Yanow*

☆ **The Complete McKinney's Cotton Pickers, Vols. 1 & 2** / Jul. 11, 1928-Nov. 6, 1929 / RCA ✦✦✦✦✦
During 1979-84 on three double-LPs, French RCA (in their *Jazz Tribune* series) reissued the complete output of McKinney's Cotton Pickers (one of the great big bands of the 1928-31 period). All of the master takes have since been reissued on CD by the Classics label but, due to the inclusion of the alternate takes, the LP series has yet to be equalled. For the first two-fer, there are six rare alternates plus 27 regular takes. Covering the Cotton Pickers' first (and best) year, this set has many highlights including "Four or Five Times," "Milenberg Joys," "Cherry," "Nobody's Sweetheart," "Don't Be like That," "There's a Rainbow 'Round My Shoulder," "I Found a New Baby" and the original version of Don Redman's "Gee Baby Ain't I Good to You." In addition to work with the regular band (which featured such fine players as trumpeters Langston Curl and John Nesbitt, tenorman-singer George Thomas and Redman himself on alto, clarinet and vocals), there are a few numbers on which Redman leads an integrated band that includes sidemen from Jean Goldkette's Orchestra along with an all-star date (continued on the second two-fer) that has such guests as altoist Benny Carter, tenor great Coleman Hawkins and pianist Fats Waller. Essential music. — *Scott Yanow*

● **The Band Don Redman Built** / Jul. 11, 1928-Nov. 3, 1930 / Bluebird ✦✦✦✦✦
While the European Classics label has reissued all of the recordings of McKinney's Cotton Pickers, the American Bluebird label has only come out with this "best of" collection. The 22 selections on their lone CD are consistently excellent, and on the whole does a fine job of summing up the legacy of this legendary early big band, but serious collectors will want the other performances too. So this release is for general listeners; among the more memorable numbers (all of which were arranged by leader Don Redman) are "Four or Five Times," "Cherry," "It's Tight Like That," "I've Found a New Baby," "Gee Baby, Ain't I Good to You" and "I Want a Little Girl." — *Scott Yanow*

1929-1930 / Nov. 6, 1929-Nov. 5, 1930 / Classics ✦✦✦✦✦
On the second of three Classics CDs that releases the complete output of McKinney's Cotton Pickers (but without the alternate takes), there are many classic performances including "Wherever There's a Will There's a Way," "If I Could Be with You," "Honeysuckle Rose," "Baby Won't You Please Come Home" and "I Want a Little Girl." In addition to the band's regular soloists (trumpeters John Nesbitt, Joe Smith and Langston Curl, trombonist Ed Cuffee and tenorman George Thomas), some tunes also feature guests Coleman Hawkins on tenor, altoist Benny Carter and pianist Fats Waller. Timeless classic jazz. — *Scott Yanow*

The Complete McKinney's Cotton Pickers, Vols. 3 & 4 / Nov. 7, 1929-Nov. 5, 1930 / RCA ✦✦✦✦✦
The second of three two-LP sets put out in the French RCA *Jazz Tribune* series of the early '80s, this series is superior to all current CD programs, for it has the complete output (including alternate takes) of one of the great late-'20s bands, McKinney's Cotton Pickers. Led by arranger-altoist-clarinetist-vocalist Don Redman, the group's best performances were generally in 1929 (its later output tended to have commercial vocals), but this two-fer also contains many memorable tracks (plus nine alternate takes). Among the solo stars are trumpeters John Nesbitt and Joe Smith, trombonist Ed Cuffee, George Thomas on tenor and (starting in November 1930) altoist Benny Carter and cornetist Rex Stewart. In addition, there are some songs from an earlier session that has Carter, tenorman Coleman Hawkins and pianist Fats Waller as guests. Superb music that should be of great interest to 1920s collectors. — *Scott Yanow*

McKinney's Cotton Pickers/Don Redman / Nov. 5, 1930-Jan. 17, 1940 / Classics ✦✦✦✦✦
For the final of three Classics CDs, the last recordings of McKinney's Cotton Pickers finds the band beset by commercial influences and declining a bit after the departure of Don Redman (although altoist Benny Carter became its temporary leader and it was still an impressive outfit). The latter part of the CD features Don Redman's Orchestra of 1938-40, a group that, despite its leader's arrangements and some impressive musicianship, never really caught on. The best among Redman's enjoyable swing performances are "'Deed I Do," "Down Home Rag," "Milenberg Joys," a remake of his composition "Baby Ain't I Good to You" and his theme (heard in two versions) "Chant of the Weed." — *Scott Yanow*

The Complete McKinney's Cotton Pickers, Vol. 5: Plus Don Redman & His Orchestra / Dec. 17, 1930-Jan. 17, 1940 / RCA ✦✦✦✦✦
The third of three French RCA two-LP sets released in the early '80s finishes up the McKinney's Cotton Pickers story with the classic big band's final seven songs (plus four alternate takes). Although commercial vocals were starting to dominate, the band (even after leader Don Redman's departure) was still impressive, and picking

altoist-arranger Benny Carter as the new musical director would have been a good move if the band had been able to continue recording after 1931. There are also two titles (and an alternate) from the Carolina Dandies, a group utilizing some of the sidemen from the Cotton Pickers. The latter half of this two fer features Don Redman's swing orchestra of 1938-40, an excellent outfit that never really developed a distinctive sound of its own. Its leader's cheerful vocals and advanced arrangements combined with some good soloists to create some fine swing music, but the band was history by early 1940. The three RCA two-LP reissues are the best way to acquire all of this valuable music since, unlike the later CD reissues, it has all of the two orchestra's alternate takes, but they will be difficult to locate. —*Scott Yanow*

Hal McKusick

b. Jun. 1, 1924, Medford, MA
Alto Saxophone, Clarinet / Cool

A fine cool-toned altoist and an occasional clarinetist, Hal McKusick worked with the big bands of Les Brown, Woody Herman (1943), Boyd Raeburn (1944-45), Alvino Rey (1946), Buddy Rich and Claude Thornhill (1948-49). In the 1950s, in addition to his work with Terry Gibbs and Elliot Lawrence, he was a busy and versatile studio musician. During 1955-58 McKusick recorded nine albums of material as a leader for Jubilee, Bethlehem, Victor, Coral, New Jazz, Prestige and Decca. Those small group recordings, although basically cool bop, sometimes used very advanced arrangements, including charts by George Handy, Manny Albam, Gil Evans, Al Cohn, Jimmy Giuffre and particularly George Russell. McKusick recently released an album, and still tours. —*Scott Yanow*

Hal McKusick Quartet / Feb. 17, 1955 / Fresh Sound ✦✦✦✦

Hal McKusick was a fine journeyman cool-toned bop-based altoist and clarinetist on this 1955 Bethlehem studio date (reissued on CD by Fresh Sound). McKusick is accompanied by guitarist Barry Galbraith, bassist Milt Hinton and drummer Osie Johnson on a variety of straightahead tunes including seven originals by arranger Manny Albam. The music is pleasing, light and swinging. —*Scott Yanow*

● Jazz Workshop / Mar. 3, 1956-Apr. 4, 1956 / Victor ✦✦✦✦✦

The cool-toned altoist Hal McKusick was a flexible, if not all that distinctive soloist. He is heard in four settings on this British LP, ranging from a pianoless quartet to a quintet and an octet. Among the supporting cast are trumpeter Art Farmer, guitarist Barry Galbraith and trombonist Jimmy Cleveland. George Russell (who plays drums on one number) contributed three songs, and the other composers are a who's who of the era: Johnny Mandel, Gil Evans (a version of "Blues for Pablo" that predates Miles Davis' from *Miles Ahead*), Jimmy Giuffre, Manny Albam and Al Cohn. Fine modern mainstream music from the mid-'50s, although this album may be difficult to find. —*Scott Yanow*

Now's the Time / Feb. 4, 1957-Apr. 7, 1958 / GRP ✦✦✦✦

The decision to include just seven of the twelve numbers from Hal McKusick's *Isn't It Romantic* LP and eight of the ten from *Cross Section Saxes* on this CD reissue is unfortunate, making this a so-called "best of" set; why not reissue three McKusick dates (including *Jazz & the Academy*) complete on two CDs so valuable music is not lost? McKusick, a fine cool-toned altoist who sometimes recalls Paul Desmond a bit, also plays some floating atmospheric bass clarinet on these performances. Four of the titles feature a four-sax septet on two arrangements apiece by George Handy and Ernie Wilkins; the latter's interpretation of "Now's the Time" harmonizes Charlie Parker's original recorded solo à la Supersax. Otherwise, McKusick is matched with trumpeter Art Farmer in a quintet/sextet with either Eddie Costa or Bill Evans on piano. The arrangements (by Farmer, Al Cohn, Manny Albam, Jimmy Giuffre or George Russell) are sometimes complex but always lightly swinging, leaving plenty of space for the horns to solo. Recommended to those listeners who do not already have the more complete LPs. —*Scott Yanow*

Triple Exposure / Dec. 27, 1957 / Original Jazz Classics ✦✦✦✦

Two talented but forgotten bop-based improvisers are featured on this quintet set: Hal McKusick (who switches between his Paul Desmond-inspired alto, tenor and cool-toned clarinet) and trombonist Billy Byers. Accompanied by pianist Eddie Costa, bassist Paul Chambers and drummer Charlie Persip, the two horns get rare opportunities to stretch out on material ranging from "Saturday Night" and an early version of Dizzy Gillespie's "Con Alma" to "I'm Glad There Is You" and three McKusick originals. This obscure Prestige session (reissued on CD in the *OJC* series) should interest straightahead jazz fans. —*Scott Yanow*

John McLaughlin

b. Jan. 4, 1942, Yorkshire, England
Guitar, Leader / Fusion, World Music, Post-Bop

A household name since the early '70s, John McLaughlin was an innovative fusion guitarist when he led the Mahavishnu Orchestra and has continued living up to

his reputation as a phenomenal and consistently inquisitive player through the years. He started on guitar when he was 11 and was initially inspired by blues and swing players. McLaughlin worked with Alexis Korner, Graham Bond, Ginger Baker and others in the 1960s, and played free jazz with Gunter Hampel for six months. His first album was a classic (1969's *Extrapolation*) and was followed by an obscurity for the Dawns label with John Surman, a quintet set with Larry Young (*Devotion*) and *My Goals Beyond* in 1970 which was half acoustic solos and half jams involving Indian musicians.

In 1969 McLaughlin moved to New York to play with Tony Williams' Lifetime, and he appeared on two classic Miles Davis records: *In a Silent Way* and *Bitches Brew*. In 1971 McLaughlin formed the Mahavishnu Orchestra, a very powerful group often thought of as rock but having the sophisticated improvisations of jazz. After three influential albums (*The Inner Mounting Flame, Birds of Fire* and *Between Nothingness and Eternity*), the group disbanded in 1973. McLaughlin, who recorded a powerful spiritual album with Carlos Santana that was influenced by John Coltrane, put together a new Mahavishnu Orchestra in 1974 that, despite the inclusion of Jean-Luc Ponty, failed to catch on, and broke up by 1975. McLaughlin then surprised the music world by radically shifting directions, switching to acoustic guitar and playing Indian music with his group Shakti. They made a strong impact on the world music scene (which was in its infancy) during their three years. Since then, McLaughlin has gone back and forth between electric and acoustic guitars, leading the One Truth Band, playing in trios with Al DiMeola and Paco DeLucia, popping up on some mid-'80s Miles Davis records, forming a short-lived third version of the Mahavishnu Orchestra (with saxophonist Bill Evans), recording an introspective tribute to pianist Bill Evans and, in 1993, touring with a rollicking jazz trio featuring Joey De Francesco and drummer Dennis Chambers. Throughout his productive career, John McLaughlin has recorded as a leader for Marmalade, Dawns, Douglas International, Columbia, Warner Bros. and Verve. —*Scott Yanow*

Extrapolation / Jan. 18, 1969 / Polydor ✦✦✦

John McLaughlin's first recording as a leader features the future innovator playing guitar in an English quartet. Although McLaughlin contributed all ten pieces, baritonist John Surman actually dominates this music, often swinging quite hard. The historically significant set, although a lesser-known item in McLaughlin's discography, is quite musical and enjoyable in its own right. —*Scott Yanow*

★ My Goals Beyond / 1970 / Rykodisc ✦✦✦✦✦

After bouncing around on a couple of labels, the CD reissue of this album ultimately ended up on Rykodisc, which has also released an audiophile LP version. The startling thing about this record is that it points the way toward two directions McLaughlin would take in the future—exploring Indian music and the acoustic guitar, and this while he was in the thick of the burgeoning electronic jazz-rock movement. Side one is a John McLaughlin acoustic guitar tour de force, where he thwacks away with his energetic, single-minded intensity on three jazz standards and five originals (including one genuine self-penned classic, "Follow Your Heart"), and adds a few percussion effects via overdubbing. Side two is devoted to a pair of marvelously intricate fusions of Indian rhythms and drones called "Peace One" and "Peace Two," with jazz flights from flutist/soprano saxophonist Dave Liebman, a *simpatico* encounter with future Mahavishnu cohorts Billy Cobham on drums and Jerry Goodman on violin, and Airto blending his sounds seamlessly with the Indian tambura and tabla. Throughout, McLaughlin's acoustic lines faultlessly straddle the line between the subcontinent and jazz, and the ethereal results still hold up beautifully today. —*Richard S. Ginell*

Devotion / 1970 / Restless ✦✦✦✦✦

This often-exciting set, John McLaughlin's third as a leader and predating The Mahavishnu Orchestra by just a year, is actually more in the style of Tony Williams' Lifetime than McLaughlin's later groups. That fact is not all that surprising when one considers that Lifetime's organist Larry Young is an integral of this rockish but explorative set. None of the individual songs (which also feature bassist Billy Rich and drummer Buddy Miles) caught on but McLaughlin's guitar style was already becoming distinctive. —*Scott Yanow*

Love, Devotion and Surrender / 1972 / Columbia ✦✦✦✦

Mahavishnu John McLaughlin and Devadip Carlos Santana came together under the influences of John Coltrane and Sri Chinmoy (the latter of whom McLaughlin would eventually renounce), cut their hair, and joined forces in probably the greatest guitar summit meeting of the jazz-rock era. Their rapport is obvious from the first track, Coltrane's "A Love Supreme"; both guitarists are on fire, flashing their stuff with extraordinary energy and remarkable arhythmic placement of each note. From this point, the two fuse the high-octane virtuosity of the Mahavishnu Orchestra and Tony Williams' Lifetime (present are Billy Cobham and Jan Hammer—on drums!—from the former and Larry Young from the latter) with Santana's thundering Latin percussion team of Armando Peraza and James Mingo Lewis, without either element dominating. The music reaches an ecstatic peak on the lengthy jam

"Let Us Go Into the House of the Lord" (based on the chords of Bobby Womack's "Breezin'"), where Santana's trademark ascending chromatic flurries give way to McLaughlin machine-gun volleys that make more coherent musical sense than anything he was recording with the first Mahavishnu group around this time. Whatever you may think of gurus and Indian religions, there must be something to it if the results of spiritual immersion are as spectacular and fulfilling as the music on this CD. —*Richard S. Ginell*

Electric Guitarist / 1979 / Columbia ✦✦✦✦
This is an album of reconciliation and penance, a series of reunions with several former colleagues from the early jazz-rock days, some of whom had parted on bitter terms with McLaughlin. But there are no egos out of control here; everyone has grown up, and partly as a result, there is a high level of musical inspiration devoid of pointless decibel wars. Jerry Goodman and Billy Cobham of the first Mahavishnu Orchestra show up first, then a genial reunion with Carlos Santana has some of the old fire. From this point, the CD undergoes a clever systematic reduction in numbers—first to five players, then four (the great combination of Chick Corea, Stanley Clarke and Jack DeJohnette), then three (a delightfully loose reunion of Lifetimers Tony Williams and Jack Bruce), then two (a fierce duel with Cobham), and finally just McLaughlin himself delivering the benediction on, of all things, "My Foolish Heart." Jazz is the dominant flavor in these fusions, often in a more restrained manner than the early-'70s sessions, and it pointed the way toward a new musical maturity for McLaughlin the electric guitarist. —*Richard S. Ginell*

Electric Dreams / Nov. 1978-Dec. 1978 / Columbia ✦✦✦
At this point, it is easy to see that the John McLaughlin story has become a peripatetic journey of electric-acoustic switchbacks, with the formation of the One Truth Band that plays on this CD being just another short chapter in the saga. And this time, McLaughlin is thoroughly in charge—there is little of the competitive dueling or tightly drilled, high-volume unison lines of the past; it's the guitarist and his sidemen, although sometimes keyboardist Stu Goldberg steps out with some wicked chops. McLaughlin returns Miles Davis' favor of naming a piece on *Bitches Brew* after him by turning the tables—and indeed, "Miles Davis" often has the loose, jamming feeling (and a quote of "It's About That Time") of the maestro's own jazz-rock sessions. There are also some aftershocks from the Shakti experience on "Love and Understanding." For the most part, though, McLaughlin conforms to the controlled funk and electronic sounds of the times, with generally more restraint and a considerable musical payoff. —*Richard S. Ginell*

Friday Night in San Francisco / Dec. 5, 1986 / Columbia ✦✦✦✦✦

Belo Horizonte / 1981 / Warner Brothers ✦✦✦
This is a diverse and somewhat obscure John McLaughlin outing recorded in France, mostly with French musicians. Classical pianist Katia Labeque makes appearances on acoustic piano and synthesizer; there is a thoughtful version of "Very Early" recorded in tribute to Bill Evans, and a collaboration with flamenco guitarist Paco DeLucia, "Manitas d'Oro." In general, McLaughlin is in fine shape on this worthwhile set, both on acoustic and electric guitars, occasionally showing some fire. —*Scott Yanow*

Passion, Grace and Fire / Oct. 1982-Nov. 1982 / Columbia ✦✦✦✦
Two years after they recorded *Friday Night in San Francisco,* John McLaughlin, Al DiMeola and Paco DeLucia reunited for another set of acoustic guitar trios. If this can be considered a guitar "battle" (some of the playing is ferocious and these speed demons do not let up too often), then the result is a three-way tie. This guitar summit lives up to its title. —*Scott Yanow*

Music Spoken Here / May 1983 / Warner Brothers ✦✦✦
Though this fitfully inspired yet always intelligently musical record is an electric album, McLaughlin is more often heard on acoustic guitar in something resembling his electric manner, along with more pronounced classical and flamenco influences. This quintet, along with bass and drums, contained two keyboard players, Francois Couturier and the noted classical pianist Katia Labeque (who was McLaughlin's companion). Labeque, seated at a Synclavier and a grand piano, has acres of technique and almost no feeling for jazz, though she is adept at providing moody backdrops, and her rapid-fire synth runs and Jarrett-like etudes on the Steinway aren't too far away stylistically from McLaughlin's helter-skelter flurries. In a continued homage to McLaughlin's once and future employer Miles Davis, "Blues for L.W." brazenly quotes "Blues for Pablo," and sometimes the music texturally resembles the heavily synthesized things that Miles would soon be putting out. —*Richard S. Ginell*

Live at the Royal Festival Hall / Nov. 27, 1989 / JMT ✦✦✦✦
The Mahavishnu revival misadventure now over and done with, John McLaughlin fields a quieter, stripped-down trio in London's Royal Festival Hall and gets far more pleasingly musical results. Engaging in interplay at all kinds of tempos with bassist Kai Eckhardt and supported by the fleet, subtle drums and percussion of Trilok Gurtu, McLaughlin concentrates his energies on the acoustic guitar. Now

and then, he flips a switch and plays through a guitar synthesizer whose broad attacks and occasional organ-like timbres often compensate nicely for the lack of a keyboardist. This trio encourages McLaughlin to display a funkier touch on his instrument without giving up any blinding speed; "Pasha's Love" contains unison flurries as furious as any from the first Mahavishnu group, only at a lower volume level. The final "Blues for L.W." (Lech Walesa) climaxes with some vocal Indian syllabic jamming that joyously rounds out the concert. —*Richard S. Ginell*

Mediterranean Concerto / 1988 / Columbia ✦✦✦
Back in the classical arena, McLaughlin conceived an ambitious guitar concerto, unveiling it with the Los Angeles Philharmonic in November 1985, but waited until 1988 to record it with his old colleagues Michael Tilson Thomas and the London Symphony Orchestra. The big difference between this and the music on *Apocalypse* is that McLaughlin dispenses with jazz and rock entirely, writing a neo-Romantic classical piece (lushly orchestrated again by Michael Gibbs) quite obviously modeled in style and sentiment after Joaquin Rodrigo's *Concierto de Aranjuez.* As such, it isn't nearly as important a statement as the bold pan-stylistic fusions of *Apocalypse.* But it is a notable personal achievement, for McLaughlin plays beautifully, and aside from a few awkward moments, the music's Spanish-tinged charms, especially in the first movement, grow richer upon further hearings. The rest of the CD is devoted to duos between McLaughlin and classical pianist Katia Labeque that speak volumes about intimacy and also heavy absorption in Keith Jarrett. —*Richard S. Ginell*

Que Alegria / Nov. 29, 1991-Dec. 3, 1991 / Verve ✦✦✦✦
The John McLaughlin Trio goes into the studio and broadens its stylistic range considerably in another musically satisfying, open-minded outing. Again, McLaughlin sounds rejuvenated and refreshed in this format, as he switches between acoustic guitar and a guitar synthesizer attachment that softens and rounds his attacks while creating some luminous timbres and textures. McLaughlin's on-again, off-again Indian kick rises prominently into view here as Trilok Gurtu's role broadens into that of an all-purpose percussionist, producing some amazing sounds as backdrops. Pastorius-influenced bassist Kai Eckhardt gets downright funky on "1 Nite Stand" but gives way to the equally accomplished Dominque Di Piazza on most tracks. Yes, there is even some fantastic straightahead blues grooving on "Hijacked"—if one may be permitted to use the terms guitar synthesizer and straightahead in the same sentence. —*Richard S. Ginell*

Time Remembered: John McLaughlin Plays Bill Evans / Mar. 25, 1993-Mar. 28, 1993 / Verve ✦✦
Pianist Bill Evans was one of guitarist John McLaughlin's early heroes, so this Evans tribute seemed like a logical idea. Sticking to acoustic guitar, McLaughlin is joined by four other guitarists (along with the acoustic bass guitar of Yan Maresz) to create an unusual instrumentation that often sounds as full as a keyboard. The leader arranged ten of Evans's compositions and his own "Homage" for a largely introverted set of music that has a strong classical feel. McLaughlin lets loose a few times, but more mood and tempo variations would have kept this from being such a sleepy and overly respectful session. —*Scott Yanow*

Tokyo Live / Dec. 16, 1993+Dec. 18, 1993 / Verve ✦✦✦✦
Although it is tempting to think that the Free Spirits (the trio featured on this CD), due to the similarity of the instrumentation (guitarist John McLaughlin, organist Joey De Francesco and drummer Dennis Chambers), would be an updating of Tony Williams' groundbreaking fusion group Lifetime, the reality is somewhat different. McLaughlin may get top billing, but this music sounds very much like a Joey De Francesco-led Jimmy Smith revival date with most of the selections being blues-based. There are some introspective moments for the guitarist (who plays strictly electric here), but De Francesco dominates the ensembles and takes the lion's share of the solo space. The music is enjoyable enough, although none of the compositions (all but Miles Davis' "No Blues" are by McLaughlin) are all that memorable. —*Scott Yanow*

After the Rain / Oct. 4, 1994-Oct. 5, 1994 / Verve ✦✦✦✦
In the early '70s, John McLaughlin was one-third of the supergroup Lifetime with drummer Tony Williams and organist Larry Young. This particular CD from 1994 matches him with drummer Elvin Jones and organist Joey De Francesco, but the music has little in common with Lifetime. Instead, many of the tunes can be considered to be tributes to John Coltrane; Jones' participation certainly reinforces that connection. McLaughlin, back on electric guitar after sveral years sticking almost exclusively to acoustic, is in top form on such numbers as "Take the Coltrane," "My Favorite Things," "Crescent" and "Afro Blue." The improvising is advanced and colorful with De Francesco keeping the proceedings swinging and, even if the results are not quite classic, the collaboration is somewhat unique. —*Scott Yanow*

The Promise / 1995 / Verve ✦✦✦✦✦
John McLaughlin shoots out in many different directions during this very diverse release. He trades off with fellow guitarist Jeff Beck on "Django," jams his own

"Thelonius Melodius" in a trio with organist Joey De Francesco and drummer Dennis Chambers, has a duet with De Francesco (who switches to trumpet) on "No Return," stretches out with tenor great Michael Brecker on the fourteen-and-a-half-minute "Jazz Jungle," collaborates on acoustic guitar with Paco DeLucia and Al DiMeola, plays Indian music with Zakir Hussain and Trilok Gurtu, and interacts with altoist David Sanborn, among others. A good introduction to latter-day John McLaughlin, this colorful set has plenty of surprises. —*Scott Yanow*

Paco DeLucia/John McLaughlin/Al DiMeola / May 1996-Jul. 1996 / Verve ◆◆◆◆

The acoustic guitar trio of John McLaughlin, Al DiMeola and Paco DeLucia can always be relied upon to create quiet but fiery music. The three virtuosos always sound restrained and tasteful (yet inwardly explosive) when they play together. This 1996 effort has three originals apiece from McLaughlin and DiMeola, two by DeLucia and a beautiful McLaughlin-DiMeola duet on "Manha de Carnaval" that makes one wish they would more fully explore bossa nova. Most of the selections are thoughtful, but there are also plenty of explosive outbursts for contrast (along with the jubilant closer "Cardeosa") on the highly arranged yet spontaneous-sounding program. —*Scott Yanow*

The Heart of Things / 1997 / Verve ◆◆◆◆

Although not referred to anymore by name, this is a mid-'90s incarnation of the Mahavishnu Orchestra idea—another quintet fronted by John McLaughlin playing electric jazz-rock with virtuosity to burn. As before, when the name was last floated in the 1980s, it is a very different sound, but closer to the original Mahavishnu blend than the '80s version ever got. There are rapid-fire unison statements as in the old days, but now softer and more complex in texture and definitely lower in volume. Dennis Chambers, a leftover from the McLaughlin organ trio of the early '90s, is probably the most incendiary drummer McLaughlin has featured since Billy Cobham, and he really mixes things up throughout the CD, including a sizzling one-on-one duel with the guitarist on the questionably titled "Acid Jazz." McLaughlin brandishes his technique with the old flash, yet as has been the pattern in his middle age, his tone is mellow and rounded, often heard through the transforming gauze of MIDI electronics. The experienced Jim Beard is responsible for the keyboard textures; Gary Thomas offers capable tenor, soprano and flute leads; Matthew Garrison (son of Jimmy) is the excellent electric bass player, and they are often augmented by the Latin percussion of Victor Williams. Again, one can say that McLaughlin's playing is more musical and charged with greater authority now than a quarter of a century ago, though not as hot in temperature. Even so, this is the warmest his music has been since the Mahavishnu days. —*Richard S. Ginell*

Jackie McLean

b. May 17, 1932, New York, NY
Alto Saxophone / Post-Bop, Hard Bop

Jackie McLean has long had his own sound, played slightly sharp and with great intensity; he is recognizable within two notes. McLean was one of the few bop-oriented players of the early '50s who explored free jazz in the 1960s, widening his emotional range and drawing from the new music qualities that fit his musical personality.

The son of guitarist John McLean (who played guitar with Tiny Bradshaw), Jackie started on alto when he was 15. As a teenager he was friends with such neighbors as Bud Powell, Thelonious Monk and Sonny Rollins. He made his recording debut with Miles Davis in 1951, and the rest of the decade could be considered his apprenticeship. McLean worked with George Wallington, Charles Mingus and Art Blakey's Jazz Messengers (1956-58). He also participated on a string of jam session-flavored records for Prestige and New Jazz which, due to the abysmal pay and his developing style, he has since disowned. Actually they are not bad, but pale compared to McLean's classic series of 21 Blue Note albums (1959-67). On sessions such as *One Step Beyond* and *Destination Out*, McLean really stretches and challenges himself; this music is quite original and intense, yet logical. McLean also appeared as a sideman on some sessions for Blue Note, acted in the stage play *The Connection* (1959-61) and led his own groups on a regular basis. By 1968, however, he was moving into the jazz education field and other than some Steeplechase records from 1972-74 (including two meetings with his early idol Dexter Gordon) and an unfortunate commercial outing for RCA (1978-79), McLean was less active as a player during the 1970s. However, in the 1980s Jackie McLean returned to a more active playing schedule (sometimes with his son Rene McLean on tenor), recording for Triloka and, most recently, Antilles with all of the intensity and passion of his earlier days. —*Scott Yanow*

The Jackie McLean Quintet [Ad Lib] / Oct. 21, 1955 / Ad Lib ◆◆◆

Lights Out / Jan. 27, 1956 / Original Jazz Classics ◆◆◆◆

Altoist Jackie McLean's second session as a leader is reissued on this CD. The music that he makes with trumpeter Donald Byrd, pianist Elmo Hope, bassist

Doug Watkins and drummer Art Taylor is essentially hard bop with fairly simple (or in some cases nonexistent) melody statements preceding two romps through the "I Got Rhythm" chord changes, a pair of blues, a thinly disguised "Embraceable You" and a straightforward version of "A Foggy Day." Enjoyable if not really essential music from the up-and-coming altoist. —*Scott Yanow*

4, 5 and 6 / Jul. 1956 / Original Jazz Classics ◆◆◆◆

This is a well-rounded CD reissue that brings back altoist Jackie McLean's third recording as a leader. McLean has several fine ballad features ("Sentimental Journey," "Why Was I Born," "When I Fall in Love" and Mal Waldron's "Abstraction") welcomes trumpeter Donald Byrd to Kenny Drew's "Contour" and jams on a lengthy version of Charlie Parker's "Confirmation" with a sextet that includes Byrd and tenor saxophonist Hank Mobley. With pianist Waldron, bassist Doug Watkins and drummer Art Taylor offering fine support, this is a strong hard bop set that is tied to the tradition of bebop while looking forward. —*Scott Yanow*

Jackie's Pal / Aug. 31, 1956 / Original Jazz Classics ◆◆◆

The "pal" of altoist Jackie McLean is trumpeter Bill Hardman, a fine hard bop soloist who would be best known for his association with Art Blakey's Jazz Messengers. This CD reissue is very much in the style of Blakey, with the two horns joined by pianist Mal Waldron, bassist Paul Chambers and drummer Philly Joe Jones. Four of the six selections are group originals (by McLean, Hardman or Waldron), and the set is rounded off by Charlie Parker's "Steeple Chase" and the standard "It Could Happen to You"; the latter is a showcase for Hardman. Although not overly memorable, this is a good early outing for McLean and Hardman, and will be enjoyed by straightahead jazz fans. —*Scott Yanow*

McLean's Scene / Dec. 4, 1956-Feb. 15, 1957 / Original Jazz Classics ◆◆◆◆

Altoist Jackie McLean tends to downgrade his Prestige recordings due to the low pay, the little prior preparation and the jam session feel of the music. Although all of the above is true, the music (while not on a par with his Blue Notes of the 1960s) is still fairly worthy, particularly when compared to the output of his contemporaries. McLean never really copied Charlie Parker and was one of the first in his generation to develop his own sound. Three of the six selections on this CD reissue (a pair of standards and a blues) feature McLean with trumpeter Bill Hardman, pianist Red Garland, bassist Paul Chambers and drummer Art Taylor. The remainder of the set is from a marathon quartet set with pianist Mal Waldron, bassist Arthur Phipps and drummer Art Taylor that would result in material that was used as part of five separate albums. McLean is in lyrical form on "Our Love Is Here to Stay" and "Old Folks," while playing with great intensity on his accurately-titled original "Outburst." —*Scott Yanow*

Jackie McLean and Co. / Feb. 8, 1957 / Original Jazz Classics ◆◆◆

Although altoist Jackie McLean's Prestige recordings of the 1950s are not as significant as his Blue Notes from the '60s, he did record quite a bit of enjoyable hard bop material during this era. This CD is unusual for, in addition to a conventional quintet (with trumpeter Bill Hardman, pianist Mal Waldron, bassist Doug Watkins and drummer Art Taylor), the young tuba player Ray Draper is heard on three of the five group originals. Draper played his instrument as part of the front line rather than in the rhythm section and, even if he was not on the level of McLean and Hardman, he gives some needed color to this set. Waldron, who contributed two of the five selections (the others are by McLean, Watkins or Draper), really sets the melancholy mood for much of the music and is an important force behind the scenes. An interesting CD. —*Scott Yanow*

Strange Blues / Feb. 15, 1957-Aug. 30, 1957 / Original Jazz Classics ◆◆◆◆

The last of the Jackie McLean Prestige sessions, this CD reissue has material from two different sets, but fortunately, the music is on a higher level than one might expect of "leftovers." "Strange Blues" is from a marathon quartet set that McLean had with pianist Mal Waldron, bassist Arthur Phipps and drummer Art Taylor as is a rendition of "What's New" that is an alternate version to the one included on *Makin' the Changes*. In addition, "Disciples Love Affair" and "Millie's Pad" match McLean with the tuba of Ray Draper (who contributed both songs), trumpeter Webster Young, pianist John Meyers, bassist Bill Salter and drummer Larry Ritchie, while the incomplete "Not So Strange Blues" is all McLean on an explosive blues with the rhythm section. A generally strong set chiefly recommended to Jackie McLean completists. —*Scott Yanow*

Alto Madness / May 3, 1957 / Original Jazz Classics ◆◆◆

Altoists Jackie McLean and John Jenkins pay tribute to Charlie Parker throughout this blowing session, not just on Parker's blues "Bird Feathers," but in practically every phrase they play. McLean became much more individual within a few years while Jenkins would fade from the scene altogether. This likable jam session also features a fine boppish rhythm section (pianist Wade Legge, bassist Doug Watkins and drummer Art Taylor) and plenty of tradeoffs by the two altoists. —*Scott Yanow*

A Long Drink of the Blues / Aug. 30, 1957 / Original Jazz Classics ✦✦✦✦
This CD reissue begins with what is titled "Take 1" of "A Long Drink of the Blues." After a false start, the musicians argue for two minutes about the tempo; why was this ever released? "Take 2" is a much more successful 20-minute jam featuring Jackie McLean (doubling on alto and tenor), trombonist Curtis Fuller, trumpeter Webster Young, pianist Gil Coggins, bassist Paul Chambers and drummer Louis Hayes. The second half of this reissue is from a quartet session that showcases McLean on three standard ballads with pianist Mal Waldron, bassist Arthur Phipps and drummer Art Taylor. Although not quite as intense as McLean's later Blue Note dates, the ballad renditions show just how mature and original a soloist he was even at this early stage. Despite "Take 1," this CD is worth getting. —*Scott Yanow*

Makin' the Changes / Aug. 30, 1957 / Original Jazz Classics ✦✦✦✦
This CD reissue of a Jackie McLean LP features the altoist in two different settings. On three selections—a rollicking "Bean and the Boys," an uptempo "I Never Knew" and "I Hear a Rhapsody"—McLean teams up with pianist Mal Waldron in a quartet with bassist Arthur Phipps and drummer Art Taylor. The other three numbers ("What's New," "Chasin' the Bird" and McLean's original "Jackie's Ghost") have more of a jam session feel and feature McLean in a sextet with trumpeter Webster Young, trombonist Curtis Fuller, pianist Gil Coggins, bassist Paul Chambers and drummer Louis Hayes. In general, the hard bop music is swinging and fairly advanced, a step above the usual jam sessions of the time. —*Scott Yanow*

Jackie McLean Plays Fat Jazz / Dec. 27, 1957 / Jubilee ✦✦✦

Jackie's Bag / Jan. 18, 1959-Sep. 1, 1960 / Blue Note ✦✦✦✦✦
This very interesting LP was a giant step forward for altoist Jackie McLean, although it was originally released after a couple of his other Blue Note albums. For the first time, McLean shows some of the influence of Ornette Coleman—not in his sound, but in his improvising approach—and his freer style bridged the gap between hard bop and the avant-garde. Three of the songs, highlighted by "Quadrangle" and "Fidel," match McLean in 1959 with trumpeter Donald Byrd, pianist Sonny Clark, bassist Paul Chambers and drummer Philly Joe Jones, while the other numbers, which include "Appointment in Ghana," showcase McLean in a sextet with trumpeter Blue Mitchell, Tina Brooks on tenor, pianist Kenny Drew, Chambers and drummer Art Taylor. Jackie McLean's Blue Note albums were the most significant of his career, and this LP is well worth searching for. —*Scott Yanow*

New Soil / May 2, 1959 / Blue Note ✦✦✦✦✦
This CD reissue adds "Formidable," which was first released on the 1980 LP *Vertigo*, to the original program. A quintet date with trumpeter Donald Byrd, pianist Walter Davis, Jr., bassist Paul Chambers and drummer Pete La Roca, this music is far superior to the jam session-oriented sets that altoist Jackie McLean made for Prestige a few years earlier. Rehearsal time gave the musicians an opportunity to learn the two McLean originals and the four songs contributed by Davis; the latter's "Davis Cup" is the best-known of the pieces. The music is funky but adventurous, beyond hard bop but still tied to chordal improvisation. Stimulating listening. —*Scott Yanow*

Vertigo / May 2, 1959-Feb. 11, 1963 / Blue Note ✦✦✦✦
This 1980 LP released for the first time "Formidable" from a 1959 session and five numbers from a 1963 McLean set. While "Formidable" has a strong quintet (with altoist Jackie McLean, trumpeter Donald Byrd, pianist Walter Davis, bassist Paul Chambers and drummer Pete La Roca), the 1963 session has the recording debut of drummer Tony Williams along with strong contributions from Byrd, pianist Herbie Hancock (then also near the beginning of his career) and bassist Butch Warren. The latter unit sticks to group originals by Byrd, Hancock and McLean and the music ranges from catchy funk and hard bop to strong hints of the avant-garde. The later session has yet to appear on CD, making this LP worth searching for by Jackie McLean collectors. —*Scott Yanow*

Swing, Swang, Swingin' / Oct. 2, 1959 / Blue Note ✦✦✦✦
This set (reissued on CD in 1997) is different from most Jackie McLean Blue Note sessions in that the altoist, other than an original blues, sticks to standards. McLean's quartet outing (with pianist Walter Bishop, Jr., bassist Jimmy Garrison and drummer Art Taylor) is actually more notable for the passion and intensity expressed in every note the leader plays than it is for the actual ideas. Even when performing at a relaxed pace, the instantly recognizable McLean turns up the heat on tunes such as "What's New," "I Remember You" and "I Love You," making every note count. Although not as essential as the Blue Note dates in which he explored new material, this formerly rare set is enjoyable and easily recommended to Jackie McLean fans. —*Scott Yanow*

Capuchin Swing / Apr. 17, 1960 / Blue Note ✦✦✦✦

Bluesnik / Jan. 8, 1961 / Blue Note ✦✦✦✦✦
This is one of the most accessible of altoist Jackie McLean's Blue Note sessions, for the six songs, which have been augmented on the CD reissue by "new" alternate

versions of "Goin' Way Blues" and "Torchin'," are all blues. McLean teams up with the fiery young trumpeter Freddie Hubbard, pianist Kenny Drew, bassist Doug Watkins and drummer Pete La Roca for diverse originals by the leader, Drew and Hubbard that all have the feeling (if not always the exact structure) of the blues. The variety of tempos, moods and styles make this a highly recommended set. —*Scott Yanow*

A Fickle Sonance / Oct. 26, 1961 / Blue Note ✦✦✦✦✦
A remarkable merger of new-thing/avant-garde leanings and hard-bop fluidity and feelings. —*Ron Wynn*

☆ **Let Freedom Ring** / Mar. 19, 1962 / Blue Note ✦✦✦✦✦
This is one of altoist Jackie McLean's most significant recordings. A veteran of the hard bop scene of the 1950s, McLean was one of the few musicians from his generation to embrace aspects of the avant-garde without losing his own musical personality. McLean kept his own intense sound, but opened up his playing to the point where he could improvise without using chord structures or even a steady tempo. His emotional style is heard at its prime on the four selections included on this CD reissue, a quartet date with pianist Walter Davis, bassist Herbie Lewis and drummer Billy Higgins. Although the music is not quite as free as Ornette Coleman's, it is nearly as innovative, particularly when one considers the expanded vocabulary that McLean uses (with screams and honks being integrated logically into his solos). Even on Bud Powell's ballad "I'll Keep Loving You," McLean's playing is very advanced and, in its own way, free. This is a gem that still sounds quite modern. —*Scott Yanow*

Hipnosis / Jun. 14, 1962+Feb. 3, 1967 / Blue Note ✦✦✦✦
This valuable and attractive two-LP set from 1978 issued for the first time a couple of sessions by altoist Jackie McLean that had been lost in the vaults. The 1962 date is fairly boppish, with McLean being teamed with trumpeter Kenny Dorham, pianist Sonny Clark, bassist Butch Warren and drummer Billy Higgins. The emphasis is on blues and straightahead swinging, but even here McLean sounds like he is pushing the boundaries a bit. The later session features McLean, trombonist Grachan Moncur, pianist Lamont Johnson, bassist Scotty Holt and Higgins. Despite some soulful moments, the music sounds ten (rather than five) years more advanced, and is strongly influenced (but not derivative) of the avant-garde players. Despite being overlooked, the music on both of these dates is up to the high level of Jackie McLean's better-known Blue Note dates and is easily recommended to fans of the innovative altoist. —*Scott Yanow*

Tippin' the Scales / Sep. 28, 1962 / Blue Note ✦✦✦✦
This fairly straightahead LP by altoist Jackie McLean was released for the first time in 1984. Due to its boppish nature, as opposed to his more adventurous recordings of the period, it languished in the vaults for over 20 years, but the music is actually quite enjoyable. With assistance from pianist Sonny Clark, bassist Butch Warren and drummer Art Taylor, McLean is in excellent form on two of his originals, three by Clark (including "Nursery Blues" and "Nicely") and the standard ballad "Cabin in the Sky." A fine hard-bop session. —*Scott Yanow*

★ **One Step Beyond** / Apr. 30, 1963 / Blue Note ✦✦✦✦✦
One of the great Jackie McLean records, this album features the innovative altoist performing two of his originals plus a pair by trombonist Grachan Moncur, III. With vibraphonist Bobby Hutcherson (one of his earliest recordings), bassist Eddie Khan and drummer Tony Williams (McLean's discovery) completing the quintet, this was a group that could play the most advanced material with creativity and improvise freely when it fit the music. The solos and ensembles on the "difficult" material are quite memorable, and it is to Jackie McLean's credit that he was not satisfied to spend his entire career playing hard bop; his musical curiosity led him to listening closely to the music of Ornette Coleman and to adapting aspects of free jazz that fit his distinctive sound. —*Scott Yanow*

Destination Out / Sep. 20, 1963 / Blue Note ✦✦✦✦✦
Five very talented and versatile jazzmen (altoist Jackie McLean, trombonist Grachan Moncur, III, vibraphonist Bobby Hutcherson, bassist Larry Ridley and drummer Roy Haynes) explore three of Moncur's originals plus McLean's "Kahlil the Prophet" on this CD reissue of their 1963 Blue Note album. McLean was one of the few players of his generation to be influenced by the free jazz movement, yet he never lost his musical personality or his distinctive sound. The improvisations by these musicians are both thoughtful and passionate, making expert use of space, tricky time changes and emotional intensity. —*Scott Yanow*

It's Time / Aug. 5, 1964 / Blue Note ✦✦✦✦
Altoist Jackie McLean and his sidemen on this excellent quintet set (which also features trumpeter Charles Tolliver, pianist Herbie Hancock, bassist Cecil McBee and drummer Roy Haynes) explore aspects of free jazz (particularly on "Cancellation") without letting go completely of the concepts of chordal improvisation. Strange as it seems, McLean's sound and highly expressive vocabulary are more advanced than his actual notes, while Tolliver's notes are more unpredictable than his Clif-

ford Brown-inspired tone. Ranging from "Cancellation" to the funky "Das' Dat," this is a stimulating LP that has been reissued as part of Mosaic's four-CD Jackie McLean box set. —*Scott Yanow*

☆ **The Complete Blue Note 1964-1966** / Aug. 5, 1964-Apr. 18, 1966 / Mosaic ✦✦✦✦✦

Altoist Jackie McLean has recorded so many fine albums throughout his career, particularly in the 1960s for Blue Note, that Mosaic could have reissued his complete output without any loss of quality. This four-CD limited-edition box set contains six complete LPs worth of material plus one "new" alternate take. The music (which also features trumpeters Charles Tolliver and Lee Morgan, pianists Herbie Hancock, Larry Willis and Harold Mabern, vibraphonist Bobby Hutcherson, bassists Cecil McBee, Bob Cranshaw, Larry Ridley, Herbie Lewis and Don Moore and drummers Roy Haynes, Billy Higgins, Clifford Jarvis, Jack DeJohnette and Billy Higgins) is explorative (showing the influence of Ornette Coleman) but without totally discarding McLean's bebop roots. The performances straddle the boundaries between advanced hard bop and free jazz, with Jackie McLean consistently emerging as the main star; his solos are consistently exciting and full of unexpected twists and turns. —*Scott Yanow*

Action / Sep. 16, 1964 / Blue Note ✦✦✦✦✦

This LP, whose music has been reissued as part of a Mosaic Jackie McLean box set, has several selections that are quite fascinating. McLean (along with trumpeter Charles Tolliver, vibraphonist Bobby Hutcherson, bassist Cecil McBee and drummer Billy Higgins) plays quite free on "Action" (which does not have a specific set of chord changes to follow), a pair of Tolliver ballads ("Plight" is best known) and even the standard "I Hear a Rhapsody" (McLean's feature). Only the bluesy "Hootman" is a bit more conventional, although those solos are also far from predictable. This album is full of exciting music that has long been overshadowed. —*Scott Yanow*

Right Now / Jan. 26, 1965 / Blue Note ✦✦✦✦✦

With the exception of a beautiful ballad version of Larry Willis' "Poor Eric," the music on this CD (which is also available in Mosaic's four-CD Jackie McLean box set) is hard-charging, intense and fairly free. Altoist McLean was at the peak of his powers during this period and, inspired by the versatile rhythm section (pianist Larry Willis, bassist Bob Cranshaw and drummer Clifford Jarvis), he plays explorative versions of his own "Eco," Willis' "Christel's Time" and Charles Tolliver's "Right Now"; an alternate version of the latter is added on for the CD reissue. This CD offers listeners a particularly strong example of Jackie McLean's unique inside/outside music of the 1960s. —*Scott Yanow*

Consequences / Dec. 3, 1965 / Blue Note ✦✦✦✦

Unreleased until 1979, but fortunately currently available in a Mosaic Jackie McLean CD box set, this superior outing features altoist McLean and trumpeter Lee Morgan as equals in a quintet that also includes pianist Harold Mabern, bassist Herbie Lewis and drummer Billy Higgins. The music is more straightahead than on the altoist's better-known gems of the period, but is never predictable. Morgan really challenges McLean on "Bluesanova," and other highlights include McLean's "Consequence" and the calypso feel of "Tolypso." —*Scott Yanow*

Jacknife / Apr. 12, 1966 / Blue Note ✦✦✦✦✦

The dynamic music on this two-LP set was released for the first time in 1975, although it has since been reissued as part of Mosaic's four-CD Jackie McLean box set. It is surprising that the music was originally overlooked, for both of these sessions have more than their share of brilliant moments. Altoist McLean teams up with trumpeters Lee Morgan and Charles Tolliver (the brassmen play two songs apiece and are both on "Soft Blue") along with pianist Larry Willis, bassist Larry Ridley and drummer Jack DeJohnette on the earlier date. Most memorable is Tolliver's atmospheric "On the Nile," but all of the selections (essentially modal hard bop with some influences from the avant-garde) are quite notable. However, it is the later session, a quartet outing with Willis, DeJohnette and bassist Don Moore, that really finds McLean playing at the peak of his expressive powers. His open style makes occasional shrieks, screams and honks fit in logically as part of his improvisations and his solos (check out the lengthy "High Frequency") are quite adventurous, yet logical. This important music is essential, in one form or another, for all followers of advanced jazz. —*Scott Yanow*

Dr. Jackle / Dec. 18, 1966 / Steeple Chase ✦✦✦✦

Jackie McLean was one of the few hard bop stars (John Coltrane was another) who was greatly affected by the avant-garde innovations of the 1960s. His sound did not change, but his solos became freer and much more emotional. By the time he played in Baltimore for the 1966 concert released on this CD, he had greatly opened up his style and had reconciled his roots with free jazz. With the strong assistance of pianist Lamont Johnson, bassist Scotty Holt and drummer Billy Higgins, McLean stretches out on five numbers (including a previously unreleased "Jossa Bossa") which clock in between eight and over fourteen-and-a-half minutes.

From the start the music is quite intense and it may take listeners a few moments to get used to the altoist's abrasive and sharp tone. However, his creative ideas and constant originality win one over fast and, by the time he finished the set with a blues ("Closing"), the logic of Jackie McLean's improvisations is more apparent. The recording quality is sometimes a little distorted, but the power, color and pure courage of the music is memorable. —*Scott Yanow*

Tune Up / Dec. 18, 1966 / Steeple Chase ✦✦✦✦

From the same "live in Baltimore" session that resulted in *Dr. Jackle*, altoist Jackie McLean and his regular quartet of the period (comprising pianist Lamont Johnson, bassist Scotty Holt and drummer Billy Higgins) explore lengthy versions of three standards ("Tune Up," "I Remember You" and a passionate "Smile") along with McLean's original "Jack's Tune." As well as the altoist plays, it is the solos of the underrated and underrecorded pianist, LaMont Johnson, that make this explorative hard bop release most notable. —*Scott Yanow*

New and Old Gospel / Mar. 24, 1967 / Blue Note ✦✦✦✦

This set (which has been reissued on CD) should have been a classic, but it has one fatal flaw. The only recorded meeting between Jackie McLean and Ornette Coleman (instead of matching the two altoists together) features Coleman exclusively on trumpet. Ornette, who had been playing trumpet for only three years at the time, is much weaker on that instrument than on alto and is simply no match for McLean. It is a pity that this set is so flawed because the originals are quite advanced, pianist Lamont Johnson (who is joined by bassist Scott Holt and drummer Billy Higgins) has what is probably his finest recorded performance and McLean (one of the few hard bop veterans to embrace Coleman's innovations) was in the middle of a peak period. But Ornette Coleman's colorful and unpredictable ideas are ill-served by his erratic trumpet technique, sinking this disappointing effort. —*Scott Yanow*

Bout Soul / Sep. 8, 1967 / Blue Note ✦✦✦✦

'Bout Soul does not mean the same thing as soul-jazz, as the opening track "Soul" makes abundantly clear. Written by Grachan Moncur, III, and poet Barbara Simmons, "Soul" is a tonally free tone-poem that features Simmons' spoken recital. It's about what the concept of soul is, not what soul music is, and that should not come as a surprise to anyone acquainted with Jackie McLean's work. Even as his Blue Note contemporaries were working commercial soul-jazz grooves, McLean pushed the borders of jazz, embracing the avant-garde and free jazz. *'Bout Soul* is one of his most explicit free albums, finding the alto saxophonist pushing a quintet—trumpeter Woody Shaw (who sits out "Dear Nick, Dear John"), pianist Lamont Johnson, bassist Scotty Holt, drummer Rashied Ali—into uncompromising, tonally free territory. This is intensely cerebral music that is nevertheless played with a fiery passion. Although the music was all composed, it is played as if it was invented on the spot. Fans of McLean's straightahead hard bop, or even of his adventurous mid-'60s sessions, might find this a little off-putting at first, but *'Bout Soul* rewards close listening. It is one of McLean's best avant sessions. —*Stephen Thomas Erlewine*

Demon's Dance / Dec. 22, 1967 / Blue Note ✦✦✦✦✦

Altoist Jackie McLean's final Blue Note album preceded four and a half years of silence as he withdrew from the New York scene and started working as an educator. McLean was still very much in top form at the time of this hard-to-find LP. Teaming up with trumpeter Woody Shaw, pianist LaMont Johnson, bassist Scott Holt and drummer Jack DeJohnette, McLean is quite passionate and typically intense on two of his originals plus a couple songs apiece from Cal Massey (including "Message from Trane") and Shaw. The modal-oriented music fit the styles of these advanced jazzmen, and the results are quite stimulating and adventurous. —*Scott Yanow*

Live at Montmartre / Aug. 5, 1972 / Steeple Chase ✦✦✦✦

Altoist Jackie McLean's first recording in five years found him exploring two Charlie Parker tunes, Charlie Chaplin's "Smile" and his own "Das Dat." All but the nine-minute "Confirmation" are over 15 minutes long, yet McLean's lengthy solos hold one's interest, as does the playing of pianist Kenny Drew, bassist Bo Stief and drummer Alex Riel. Although not as advanced as some of his Blue Note classics of the 1960s, McLean is in top form and quite explorative during these performances; his sound is certainly instantly recognizable. —*Scott Yanow*

A Ghetto Lullaby / Jul. 18, 1973 / Inner City ✦✦✦

Within a five-day period in 1973, altoist Jackie McLean, who had only made one album (a live set) between 1968-72, cut enough material for five records. This worthy set features his intense style in a quartet with pianist Kenny Drew, bassist Niels Pedersen and drummer Alex Riel, recorded live at Montmartre in Copenhagen. Although the material—Drew's "Callin'," the ballad "Where Is Love," a pair of William Gault songs and McLean's "Jack's Tune"—is not all that memorable, the altoist's passionate solos and very distinctive sound uplift the music and make this an advanced hard-bop set worth acquiring. —*Scott Yanow*

The Meeting / Jul. 20, 1973-Jul. 21, 1973 / Steeple Chase ✦✦✦
Altoist Jackie McLean met with up his idol, tenor saxophonist Dexter Gordon for a couple of club dates, and the result is a pair of hard-swinging if somewhat loose albums; the accompanying set is *The Source*. The pair of saxophonists (along with pianist Kenny Drew, bassist Niels Pedersen and drummer Alex Riel) give four pieces ("On the Trail" and three obscure originals) lengthy renditions with Dexter's "All Clean" being over 17 minutes long. The music falls short of being classic, but is quite spirited and recommended to fans of both Dexter Gordon and Jackie McLean. —*Scott Yanow*

Ode to Super / Jul. 17, 1973 / Steeple Chase ✦✦✦
This matchup between altoists Jackie McLean and Gary Bartz has always been a bit of a disappointment with the solos much stronger than the material. The title cut, "Ode to Super," (which has vocals from the two co-leaders) is taken from a play, and the originals by McLean, Bartz and pianist Thomas Clausen are not too memorable. Only a torrid jam on Charlie Parker's "Red Cross" really works. A more suitable encore by the two greats is long overdue. —*Scott Yanow*

The Source / Jul. 20, 1973-Jul. 21, 1973 / Steeple Chase ✦✦✦
Veteran tenor Dexter Gordon and altoist Jackie McLean teamed up for a few club dates in 1973 and the results have been released on two Steeple Chase albums; the other one is *The Meeting*. Unlike the earlier release, which focused on lesser-known material, *The Source* features the saxophonists on three jazz standards (Miles Davis' "Half Nelson," "I Can't Get Started" and Charlie Parker's "Another Hair-Do") in addition to reviving Dexter Gordon's 1947 composition "Dexter Digs In." The music is a bit loose and long-winded ("Half Nelson" is over 18 minutes long) but recommended to straightahead jazz fans. —*Scott Yanow*

Antiquity / Aug. 1974 / Steeple Chase ✦✦✦

New York Calling / Oct. 30, 1974 / Steeple Chase ✦✦✦
A wonderful session that helped introduce McLean's then-26-year-old son Rene to the jazz audience. —*Ron Wynn*

New Wine, Old Bottles / Apr. 6, 1978-Apr. 7, 1978 / Inner City ✦✦✦✦✦
This out-of-print LP (originally put out by the East Wind label in Tokyo) is a bit different than it appears. Although its title makes it seem as if altoist Jackie McLean is bringing back a variety of older standards, only three of the songs ("It Never Entered My Mind," "'Round Midnight" and "Confirmation") fit into that category. In addition, McLean and his all-star quartet (pianist Hank Jones, bassist Ron Carter and drummer Tony Williams) perform "Bein' Green" and two of the altoist's tunes: "Appointment in Ghana" and "Little Melonae." The music is essentially hard bop with McLean's unique tone indeed giving new life to this swinging yet often introspective music. —*Scott Yanow*

Monuments / Jun. 1979 / RCA ✦
It seems as if nearly every major jazz musician has a dud or two in their discography. This out-of-print LP is the only major flaw in altoist Jackie McLean's long career, a set of electronic rhythms, dumb vocals ("Doctor Jackyll and Mister Funk") and unadventurous playing that is instantly forgettable. It would be quite a few years before Jackie McLean reappeared on records again after this artistic (and commercial) fiasco. —*Scott Yanow*

☆ **Dynasty** / Nov. 5, 1988 / Triloka ✦✦✦✦✦
This is one of the great Jackie McLean albums. After nearly a decade off of records, the veteran altoist teamed up with his son Rene (who triples on tenor, soprano and flute), pianist Hotep Idris Galeta, bassist Nat Reeves and drummer Carl Allen for a very passionate and high-powered live set. Whether it be originals by Rene McLean (including "J. Mac's Dynasty") or Galeta, a very intense version of "A House Is Not a Home" or Jackie's "Bird Lives," this is dynamic and consistently exciting music. The go-for-broke solos (which transcend any easy categories) and Jackie's unique sharp tone make this an essential CD, one of the top recordings to be released in 1990. —*Scott Yanow*

Rites of Passage / Jan. 29, 1991-Jan. 30, 1991 / Triloka ✦✦✦✦✦
Recorded over two years after his "comeback" album, *Dynasty*, but using the same personnel, altoist Jackie McLean once again sounds in prime form. His intensity and passion had not declined through the years, and his sometimes-abrasive tone had, if anything, become even more distinctive. With this particularly strong group (which has son Rene on tenor, alto and soprano, pianist Hotep Idris Galeta, bassist Nat Reeves and drummer Carl Allen), McLean pours his heart out on two of his originals, plus pieces by Rene and Galeta. Outstanding no-holds-barred music. —*Scott Yanow*

Rhythm of the Earth / Mar. 12, 1992-Mar. 13, 1992 / Antilles ✦✦✦✦
The music on this CD is dedicated to the Dogon people of Mali in West Africa. The originals (by altoist Jackie McLean, trombonist Steve Davis and pianist Alan Palmer) are challenging, but swinging, and inspire the members of the septet, which also include trumpeter Roy Hargrove, vibraphonist Steve Nelson, bassist Nat Reeves and drummer Eric McPherson. The sound of the group (with trombone and

vibes) is a throwback of sorts to McLean's mid-'60s recordings on Blue Note, although the music is not quite as explorative. Jackie McLean is in fine form, and it is good to hear Hargrove playing in this advanced setting. Worth checking out. —*Scott Yanow*

The Jackie Mac Attack Live / Nov. 2, 1992+Nov. 3, 1992 / Verve ✦✦✦✦✦
Veteran altoist Jackie McLean is in top form on this live quartet session with pianist Hotep Idris Galeta, bassist Nat Reeves and drummer Carl Allen. He performs two originals by Galeta, Rene McLean's "Dance Little Mandissa," "'Round Midnight" and his own "Minor March" and "Five." The amount of passion and intensity that McLean puts into his improvisations is quite impressive, and 40 years after his recording debut, he remains in prime form. This strong, advanced hard-bop date gives listeners a good example of his abilities. —*Scott Yanow*

Hat Trick / Jan. 28, 1996-Jan. 31, 1996 / Blue Note ✦✦✦✦
Veteran altoist Jackie McLean was not familiar with pianist Junko Onishi's playing until shortly before recording this quartet CD (which also includes bassist Nat Reeves and drummer Lewis Nash), but he was apparently pleased with how she sounded. Onishi's bop-oriented style (which sometimes uses more complex chord voicings) fits in well with McLean, and the results are generally memorable. Jackie McLean, one of the few hard-bop stylists to embrace aspects of the avant-garde, sounds quite advanced on the straightahead program. His distinctive tone is unchanged from the 1960s, and he still displays all of the fire and enthusiasm he had in his early days. McLean really digs into his two durable originals ("Little Melonae" and "Bluesnik"), five standards, Mal Waldron's "Left Alone" and Onishi's "Jackie's Hat" (based on "Sweet Georgia Brown"), making this outing into something quite special. Recommended. —*Scott Yanow*

Fire and Love / 1997 / Blue Note ✦✦✦
Recorded with his vigorous, youthful septet, *Fire and Love* proves that Jackie McLean hasn't lost any of his fire. The program of all original material gives McLean and his band—Rene McLean (tenor saxophone, percussion), Raymond Williams (trumpet, fluegelhorn), Steve Davis (trombone), Alan Jay Palmer (piano), Phil Bowler (bass), Eric McPherson (drums)—the room to stretch out and venture into some risky territory. As with any latter-day McLean album, the music is advanced hard bop played with skill and passion, and it is well worth investigating. [The American and European issues of *Fire and Love* contain two songs that were not included on the original Japanese pressing.] —*Stephen Thomas Erlewine*

René McLean

b. Dec. 16, 1946, New York, NY
Tenor Saxophone, Alto Saxophone, Flute / Hard Bop
The son of altoist Jackie McLean, René studied alto with his father and Sonny Rollins from the age of nine. He played baritone and later alto with Tito Puente for three years in the early '70s, and also worked with Sam Rivers, Lionel Hampton and with his father in the Cosmic Brotherhood. McLean played in the mid-'70s in a quintet with Woody Shaw and Louis Hayes, started touring with Hugh Masekela in 1978, settled in South Africa in 1985, led his own group and, in the late '80s, recorded with his father for Triloka. René McLean has also led his own albums for Steeple Chase (1975) and Triloka (1993). —*Scott Yanow*

● **Watch Out** / Jul. 9, 1975 / Steeple Chase ✦✦✦✦
This session was René McLean's debut as a leader and it found the 28-year-old switching between alto, soprano, tenor and flute. The son of Jackie McLean, René did not yet have a distinctive voice, but he showed much potential for the future. His sextet (with trumpeter Danny Coleman, pianist Hubert Eaves and guitarist Nathan Page) hints at the innovations of the avant-garde while remaining closer to the style of Art Blakey's Jazz Messengers. It's a worthwhile if not overly memorable effort. —*Scott Yanow*

In African Eyes / 1993 / Triloka ✦✦✦

Jim McNeely

b. May 18, 1949, Chicago, IL
Piano / Post-Bop
A harmonically advanced pianist and a developing arranger, Jim McNeely has had a few notable musical associations in his career. After graduating from the University of Illinois, McNeely had a stint with Ted Curson (1976-78) and was an important member of the Mel Lewis Orchestra (1978-84), Stan Getz's Quartet (1981-85) and, during much of the 1990s, the Phil Woods Quintet. McNeely, who has also played with Bobby Watson, Art Farmer, Joe Henderson, and his own trios, in addition to writing for the Carnegie Hall Jazz Band, has led recording sessions for Steeple Chase (1976), Gatemouth, Owl and, much more recently, Concord, a solo Maybeck Recital Hall set in 1992. —*Scott Yanow*

Rain's Dance / Oct. 4, 1976-Oct. 6, 1976 / Steeple Chase ✦✦✦

● **The Plot Thickens** / May 4, 1979+Jun. 27, 1979 / Muse ✦✦✦✦

Originally released on the tiny Gatemouth label, this recording features the harmonically advanced pianist Jim McNeely (who at this early stage was influenced most by McCoy Tyner), Jon Burr or Mike Richmond on bass, drummer Billy Hart, and guest guitarist John Scofield performing six of McNeely's originals. The originals tend to be complex and dry, but the sidemen play the difficult music with relative ease. —*Scott Yanow*

From the Heart / Oct. 1984-Feb. 1985 / Owl ✦✦✦✦

The advanced post-bop pianist Jim McNeely performs five originals, including a blues called "Ernie Banks" and a tribute to Bob Brookmeyer, "Brooklyn Bob," plus "End of a Love Affair," in a trio with bassist Marc Johnson and drummer Adam Nussbaum. McNeely utilizes a synthesizer for color, and fortunately, the electric keyboard does not weigh down the music, which generally swings and has plenty of strong interplay by the three masterful players. One of Jim McNeely's best outings as a leader thus far. —*Scott Yanow*

Winds of Change / Jul. 1989 / Steeple Chase ✦✦✦

Good late '80s trio work by pianist Jim McNeely, joined by bassist Mike Richmond and drummer Kenny Washington. McNeely plays with style and conviction on five originals and does a good reworking of Thelonious Monk's "Bye-Ya." —*Ron Wynn*

East Coast Blow Out / Sep. 1989 / Lipstick ✦✦✦

Live at Maybeck Recital Hall, Vol. 20 / Aug. 14, 1992 / Concord Jazz ✦✦✦✦

Sound Bites / 1997 / Dragon ✦✦✦

Music of Jim McNeely / New World ✦✦✦✦

Jimmy McPartland

b. Mar. 15, 1907, Chicago, IL, **d.** Mar. 13, 1991, Port Washington, NY
Cornet / Dixieland

A solid Dixieland cornetist with his own lyrical sound (influenced by Bix Beiderbecke initially), Jimmy McPartland played the music he loved for over 60 years. The younger brother of guitarist Dick McPartland (1905-1957), Jimmy was a member of the legendary Austin High School Gang in the 1920s. He was Bix Beiderbecke's replacement with the Wolverines during 1925, joined Ben Pollack's band in 1927 and recorded with the McKenzie and Condon Chicagoans during their famous session. McPartland was one of the main soloists (along with Benny Goodman) with Pollack, and he stayed with the band into 1929. He then moved to Chicago, working steadily through the 1930s. While stationed overseas during World War II (1942-44) he met his future wife, the English pianist Marian Turner. McPartland freelanced at Dixieland sessions during the next four decades, working with Eddie Condon, Art Hodes and other Chicago jazz veterans and often leading his own band. Although eventually divorced from Marian McPartland, they were still close friends and occasionally played together, remarrying just a few weeks before Jimmy McPartland's death two days short of his 84th birthday. Many of his best early recordings were collected on an MCA two-LP set in the 1970s. In addition, he recorded as a leader for Harmony, Prestige, MGM, Grand Award, Jazztone, Epic, Mercury, RCA, Design, Jazzology, Halcyon (Marian's label) and Riff. —*Scott Yanow*

★ **Shades of Bix** / Apr. 24, 1936-Feb. 2, 1956 / Brunswick ✦✦✦✦✦

This double LP is long overdue to be reissued on CD. Trumpeter Jimmy McPartland originally succeeded the legendary Bix Beiderbecke with the Wolverines back in 1925. Decades later, although still influenced a bit by Beiderbecke's sound, McPartland had long developed his own musical personality. The first twelve selections on this set (eight from 1953 and the other four from 1956) feature McPartland paying tribute to Beiderbecke by performing a variety of songs associated with him. Such players as trombonist Lou McGarity, clarinetist Peanuts Hucko, tenorman Bud Freeman and baritonist Ernie Caceres help out on some of the numbers, and pianist Marian McPartland is aboard for the later sides. High point is an emotional version of "In a Mist" that utilizes oboe and bassoon in the arrangement. In addition, this two-fer includes McPartland's sessions of 1936 and 1939, superior Dixieland performances that, on four selections, are highlighted by rare solos from altoist Boyce Brown. This highly recommended set is rounded out by eight superior ballads from 1943 and 1946 featuring the mellow cornet of Bobby Hackett. —*Scott Yanow*

Goin' Back a Ways / 1948-1949 / Halcyon ✦✦✦✦

The music on this LP is the earliest example of cornetist Jimmy McPartland and his wife pianist Marian McPartland playing together. The most notable among the other names to be found in these three combos are clarinetist Gene Sedric and trombonist Vic Dickenson. The music is essentially Dixieland (with tunes such as "Come Back, Sweet Papa," "Royal Garden Blues" and "I've Found a New Baby"), but there are also versions of Bix Beiderbecke's "In a Mist" and "How High the Moon." Even at this early stage, Marian McPartland's playing is more modern than the rest of the group, but she fits in well. This hard-to-find LP from Marian's Halcyon label is worth searching for by Dixieland collectors. —*Scott Yanow*

Jimmy McPartland's Dixieland / Feb. 2, 1957+Mar. 5, 1957 / Epic ✦✦✦✦

This difficult-to-find LP has some solid, no-nonsense Dixieland from veteran cornetist Jimmy McPartland, who had already been playing some of these songs for 30 years. Actually, his date does feature some obscurities, including "Third Street Blues," "The Albatross," "Lackadaisy Lazy" and the catchy "Basin Street Stomp" next to the standards "Oh Didn't He Ramble," "Ballin' the Jack," "Original Dixieland One-Step" and "There'll Be Some Changes Made." McPartland's sidemen include either Peanuts Hucko or Ernie Caceres on clarinet, trombonist Tyree Glenn, pianist Dick Cary, bassist Bill Crow, rhythm guitarist Al Casamenti and either Cliff Leeman or George Wettling on drums. The music is very much in the freewheeling Eddie Condon Chicago jazz style and has plenty of spirit. —*Scott Yanow*

The Music Man Goes Dixieland / Dec. 20, 1957-Jan. 16, 1958 / Epic ✦✦✦✦✦

This out-of-print LP, a bit of a collector's item, is a surprise success. Cornetist Jimmy McPartland performs 11 songs from the show *The Music Man*, easily turning the music into Dixieland. Such tunes as "Seventy Six Trombones," "Gary, Indiana" and "Till There Was You" have rarely received more creative and spirited treatment. McPartland does a great job with the monologue on "Ya Got Trouble," Dick Cary (who plays "F" trumpet, alto horn, celeste and piano) did a fine job with the arrangements, and the who's who of Chicago jazz and swing get to participate in the festivities. Among the large supporting cast are trumpeters Max Kaminsky and Charlie Shavers, trombonists Tyree Glenn, Cutty Cutshall and Lou McGarity, clarinetists Peanuts Hucko, Pee Wee Russell and Bob Wilbur, the great tenors Bud Freeman and Coleman Hawkins (who get to play together!), pianists Marian McPartland and Gene Schroeder, guitarists Sal Salvador and Eddie Condon, bassist Bob Haggart and drummers George Wettling and Cliff Leeman; that is only a partial list. This underrated gem is long overdue to be reissued on CD but it may be years before Sony/Columbia/Epic notices. —*Scott Yanow*

Meet Me in Chicago / May 7, 1959 / Mercury ✦✦✦✦

This LP features a novel idea that works well. Two different but compatible Dixieland bands play together and separately, each one coming out of a different speaker. Cornetist Jimmy McPartland's group is a septet with Bud Freeman on tenor, trombonist Vic Dickenson and clarinetist Bob Maheu, while pianist Art Hodes' sextet features trumpeter Nappy Trottier, trombonist George Brunis and clarinetist Pee Wee Russell. They perform a variety of Dixieland and 1920s standards and their battles (particularly when the entire groups trade off choruses) are quite fun. Trad jazz collectors who run across this LP are well advised to pick it up quickly, for it may be decades before it is reissued by Polygram/Mercury. —*Scott Yanow*

Swingin' / Jun. 16, 1973 / Halcyon ✦✦✦

This out-of-print LP from Marian McPartland's Halcyon label was much more valuable before a Jazz Alliance CD reissued five of its seven selections (along with numbers from a slightly earlier album). One of cornetist Jimmy McPartland's last records (although he would live until 1991), the Dixieland session—which also includes some swing standards—finds McPartland in jubilant form in a sextet with his wife Marian on piano, trombonist Vic Dickenson, Buddy Tate on reeds (tenor, clarinet and baritone), bassist Rusty Gilder and drummer Gus Johnson. The live date has typically spirited versions of such tunes as "I Can't Give You Anything but Love," "Dinah" and "Perdido," along with a few unexpected numbers ("Polka Dots and Moonbeams" and "When You Wish upon a Star"). —*Scott Yanow*

One Night Stand / Dec. 22, 1974 / Jazzology ✦✦✦

The next-to-last full-length recording of cornetist Jimmy McPartland is a live set that also includes trombonist Bill Allred, clarinetist Herman Foretich, pianist Dick Wellstood, bassist Gene Mayl and drummer Joe "Spider" Ridgeway. McPartland, who was still in good form at this point, sounds fine on the six Dixieland standards, taking personable vocals on "Way Down Yonder in New Orleans," "Basin Street Blues" and "St. James Infirmary." His wife, pianist Marian McPartland, sits in on "St. James Infirmary" and shares the piano bench with Wellstood on a delightful version of "Royal Garden Blues." —*Scott Yanow*

Marian McPartland (Marian Turner)

b. Mar. 20, 1920, Windsor, England
Piano / Bop, Swing, Post-Bop

Marian McPartland has become famous for hosting her *Piano Jazz* radio program since 1978, but she was a well-respected pianist decades before. She played in a four-piano vaudeville act in England and performed on the European continent for the troops during World War II. In Belgium in 1944 she met cornetist Jimmy McPartland and they soon married. Marian moved with her husband to the US in 1946, where she sometimes played with him even though her style was more modern than his Dixieland-oriented groups. McPartland eventually had her own trio at the Embers (1950) and the Hickory House (1952-60) which until 1957 included drummer Joe Morello. She recorded regularly for Savoy and Capitol during the 1950s and also made sessions for Argo (1958), Time (1960 and 1963), Sesac and Dot. Although divorced eventually from Jimmy, they remained close friends, sometimes played together and remarried just weeks before his death. She formed her own Halcyon label and recorded several fine albums between 1969-77. McPartland also made three albums for Tony Bennett's Improv label during 1976-77 before signing with Concord, where she has been since 1978. The Jazz Alliance label has made available over 30 CD's worth of material from Marian McPartland's *Piano Jazz* show, some of which are quite fascinating and significant. —*Scott Yanow*

Jazz at the Hickory House / Apr. 21, 1952-Oct. 1953 / Savoy ✦✦✦✦
Pianist Marian McPartland spent some of her favorite years leading a trio nightly at the Hickory House in New York. This excellent but out-of-print two-LP set has a little more than half of McPartland's Savoy recordings, including a full album of live performances from the Hickory House. The latter set features McPartland with bassist Vinnie Burke and drummer Joe Morello (before he became famous touring with Dave Brubeck) while the studio sides have Max Wayne or Bob Carter on bass and Morello sharing the drum slot with Mousie Alexander and Mel Zelnick. The emphasis is on sophisticated but swinging renditions of standards, and gives one a strong idea of how Marian McPartland sounded in the 1950s. —*Scott Yanow*

Marian McPartland / 1963 / Bainbridge ✦✦✦
Marian McPartland, who is joined by bassist Ben Tucker and drummer Dave Bailey along with Ralph Dorsey and Bob Crowder on percussion, plays an above-average set of sophisticated bop-oriented jazz. She contributed three forgotten originals, jams on a few standards (including Tucker's hit "Comin' Home Baby") and plays an early Wurlitzer electric piano on three numbers. The music is pleasing, if not all that memorable. —*Scott Yanow*

Interplay / 1969 / Halcyon ✦✦✦✦

Ambiance / Jul. 1970 / Jazz Alliance ✦✦✦
Originally recorded for her Halcyon label and reissued as a Jazz Alliance CD in 1995, this unusual set by pianist Marian McPartland finds her playing quite free in spots. Her interplay with bassist Michael Moore and drummer Jimmy Madison (Billy Hart takes Madison's place on two numbers) is very alert, sometimes almost telepathic, and much more adventurous than one might expect. Five of the 11 selections are by McPartland, and four are by Moore, but even the standards ("What Is This Thing Called Love" and "Three Little Words") sound as if they are being performed by lyrical avant-gardeists. Fascinating music worthy of several listens. —*Scott Yanow*

A Delicate Balance / 1971-1972 / Halcyon ✦✦✦
This release from Marian McPartland's private label features McPartland alternating between piano and electric piano in a trio with bassist Jay Leonhart and drummer Jimmy Madison. She performs a program ranging from two of her originals and "Freedom Jazz Dance" to tunes by the Beatles, Simon and Garfunkle and Alec Wilder ("Jazz Waltz for a Friend"). The relaxed results are not that memorable, but are well played and reasonably enjoyable. —*Scott Yanow*

A Sentimental Journey / 1972-1973 / Jazz Alliance ✦✦✦✦
Marian McPartland (famous as a modern pianist and for her *Piano Jazz* radio show) was initially introduced to the jazz major leagues through her husband, the late Jimmy McPartland, who was a talented Dixieland-oriented cornetist. During 1972-73, the McPartlands recorded two of their concerts which were later released on Marian's Halcyon label. This CD reissue contains 12 of the 14 selections, and these are among Jimmy McPartland's best later recordings. With front lines that include either trombononist Vic Dickenson and tenorman Buddy Tate, or trombonist Hank Berger and clarinetist Jack Maheu, the cornetist performs Dixieland and swing standards with enthusiasm and power, taking an occasional vocal and clearly having a good time. It's recommended for trad fans. —*Scott Yanow*

Plays the Music of Alec Wilder / Jul. 20, 1973-Jul. 21, 1973 / Jazz Alliance ✦✦✦✦
Alec Wilder, whose best-known compositions are "I'll Be Around" and "It's So Peaceful in the Country," wrote quite a few obscure but rewarding melodies, many of which were melancholy and full of subtle surprises. During the latter part of his life, Wilder became good friends with pianist Marian McPartland, who became one of his top instrumental interpreters. On this CD reissue (which was originally on the Halcyon label), McPartland performs five of Wilder's works as duets with bassist Michael Moore, and five others with a trio also including bassist Rusty Gilder and drummer Joe Corsello. In addition to his two "hits," McPartland performs such interesting pieces as "While We're Young," "Trouble Is a Man" and "Where Are the Good Companions," among others. She has always had a real affinity and respect for Wilder's music (while not being shy to improvise away from the melodies), making this one of Marian McPartland's better recordings of the 1970s. —*Scott Yanow*

Maestro and Friend / Jul. 1973 / Halcyon ✦✦✦✦
Violinist Joe Venuti teams up with pianist Marian McPartland for a set of duets, mostly on standards. The music is quite melodic, but has some exciting moments; there are not that many violin-piano duet versions of "That's a Plenty." A tasteful outing by two masterful players. —*Scott Yanow*

Solo Concert at Haverford / Apr. 12, 1974 / Halcyon ✦✦✦
The emphasis is on ballads during this solo piano recital by Marian McPartland. She performs swing standards, a couple of medleys (including one of "Yesterdays" and "Yesterday"), a blues, Alec Wilder's "I'll Be Around" and her own "Afterglow." Nothing that memorable occurs, but this subtle, easy-listening set put out on her private label, Halcyon, is enjoyable enough and recommended to McPartland's fans. —*Scott Yanow*

Concert in Argentina / Nov. 1974 / Jazz Alliance ✦✦✦✦
This Buenos Aires concert, originally released as a two-LP set, features four different but complementary pianists in solo performances: Marian McPartland, Teddy Wilson, Ellis Larkins and Earl Hines. The Jazz Alliance CD reissue unfortunately leaves out a selection or two apiece by each of the keyboardists (it should have come out as a double CD), so the LP version is the more highly recommended format. McPartland shows off her versatility on a Duke Ellington medley, Wilson swings impeccably, Larkins is typically subtle on his ballads and Hines is the most reckless (and exciting) improviser. —*Scott Yanow*

Wanted / May 14, 1977 / Improv ✦✦✦
Taken from a live performance, this LP is a somewhat erratic set of music recorded for Tony Bennett's short-lived Improv label. Pianist Marian McPartland plays "All the Things You Are" with a trio (bassist Brian Torff and drummer George Reed), clarinetist Herb Hall is featured on "Just a Closer Walk with Thee," tenorman Buddy Tate has "Lonely Avenue" as his showcase and the full group (which includes veteran cornetist Jimmy McPartland and the forgotten Spider Martin on tenor) jams on "Royal Garden Blues," "Dinah" and "Undecided." This was one of Jimmy McPartland's final recordings. —*Scott Yanow*

Now's the Time / Jun. 30, 1977 / Halcyon ✦✦✦✦
On this release from Marian McPartland's Halcyon label, the veteran pianist heads a straightahead all-female quintet that also features the excellent guitarist Mary Osborne, altoist Vi Redd, bassist Lynn Milano and drummer Dottie Dodgion. For the live performance they play eight familiar standards including "Now's the Time," "In a Mellotone," "I'll Remember April" and "But Beautiful." This hard-to-find LP is most valuable for its solos by Osborne and Redd, who both made too few records through the years. —*Scott Yanow*

Piano Jazz: McPartland/Williams / Oct. 8, 1978 / Jazz Alliance ✦✦
This CD comprises the very first *Piano Jazz* radio show and, although interesting to hear once, it does not invite repeated listenings. Marian McPartland sounds nervous and she constantly interrupts Mary Lou Williams' talking while Williams seems quite uptight in spots. There is some good playing by Williams (mostly duets with bassist Ronnie Boykins with McPartland occasionally joining in), but overall this set is mostly a historical curiosity. Fortunately, Marian McPartland would improve quickly as a host and most of the other CDs in this valuable series are more easily recommended than this debut effort. —*Scott Yanow*

★ **Piano Jazz: McPartland/Evans** / Nov. 6, 1978 / Jazz Alliance ✦✦✦✦✦
This is one of the finest of all the Marian McPartland *Piano Jazz* radio shows. Bill Evans (less than two years before his death) not only plays in prime form and talks a little about his career, but also explains to McPartland in detail his approach to playing piano. One gets to know not only Bill Evans the musician, but the man too. Musically, Evans performs a brief "Waltz for Debbie," "All of You" and "Reflections in D," McPartland plays "While We're Young," and they duet on five numbers including "In Your Own Sweet Way," "Days of Wine and Roses" and "I Love You." This is a special show well worth hearing several times. —*Scott Yanow*

From This Moment on / Dec. 1978 / Concord Jazz ✦✦✦
This is a relaxed and tasteful trio outing by pianist Marian McPartland, bassist Brian Torff and drummer Jake Hanna that has been reissued on CD. No surprises occur on the pianist's "Ambiance" or the eight standards, and the music never really commands one's attention, but the performances are pleasing, harmonically sophisticated and lightly swinging. —*Scott Yanow*

Portrait of Marian McPartland / May 1979 / Concord Jazz ✦✦✦✦✦
Although she was married to Dixieland trumpeter Jimmy McPartland and entered the jazz big leagues in the 1940s, pianist Marian McPartland has long been a harmonically sophisticated improviser, open to the influence of later stylists including Bill Evans. For this Concord release (which has been reissued on CD), McPartland teams up with the underrated Jerry Dodgion (who doubles on alto and flute), bassist Brian Torff and drummer Jake Hanna for a program that balances thoughtful ballads with a few faster pieces. Highlights include touching versions of "It Never

Entered My Mind" and "Spring Can Really Hang You Up the Most" and spirited jams on "I Won't Dance" and Chick Corea's blues "Matrix." —*Scott Yanow*

At the Festival / Aug. 1979 / Concord Jazz ✦✦✦✦✦
One of Marian McPartland's better all-round sets for Concord, this date features the veteran pianist at the 1979 Concord Jazz Festival. Joined by bassist Brian Torff and drummer Jake Hanna, McPartland plays her own "In the Days of Our Love," plus five diverse standards that range from "Cotton Tail" to Chick Corea's "Windows." For the last three numbers ("Here's That Rainy Day," "On Green Dolphin Street" and "Oleo"), McPartland's trio is joined by the excellent but underrated altoist Mary Fettig Park (when is she going to record an album of her own?). Recommended. —*Scott Yanow*

Live at the Carlyle / Sep. 10, 1979 / Halcyon ✦✦✦✦
Excellent, strong uptempo cuts and ballads, done in the club popularized by Bobby Short. —*Ron Wynn*

Piano Jazz: McPartland/Blake / Dec. 15, 1979 / Jazz Alliance ✦✦✦✦✦
Of the many subjects whom Marian McPartland has welcomed to her *Piano Jazz* radio series, Eubie Blake (easily the oldest at 96) was among the most delightful. In addition to performing his standbys "You're Lucky to Me," an excerpt from "Charleston Rag" and part of "Stars and Stripes Forever" (in duet with McPartland), Blake plays a few very obscure pieces ("Betty Washboard Rag," "Valse Marion," "Dream Rag" and "Falling in Love with Someone"). McPartland performs Blake's "greatest hit" "I'm Just Wild About Harry" solo, and together they duet on "Kiss Me Again," "St. Louis Blues" and "Little Gypsy Sweetheart." The conversation between the two contains some fresh stories and Blake, even at his advanced age, was still quite a lovable character. Recommended. —*Scott Yanow*

Piano Jazz: McPartland/Cowell / Jun. 26, 1981 / Jazz Alliance ✦✦✦✦
There is more music on this edition of Marian McPartland's *Piano Jazz* radio show than usual. Although Cowell talks a little about his beginnings and his compositions, the emphasis is on their playing and McPartland seems inspired by the chance to perform with a challenging modernist. Cowell performs "Top of Your Head Blues," a fresh rendition of "'Round Midnight" and his "Equipoise," McPartland explores "God Bless the Child" and together they jam on "Stella by Starlight," Percy Heath's "Watergate Blues," "Cherokee" and "You Took Advantage of Me"; on the latter Cowell shows what he learned from studying Art Tatum. —*Scott Yanow*

Piano Jazz: McPartland/Wellstood / Jun. 27, 1981 / Jazz Alliance ✦✦✦✦✦
Dick Wellstood, one of the great stride pianists, died in 1987 before his 60th birthday, and his loss is a major one for jazz. The release of his appearance on Marian McPartland's *Piano Jazz* radio show on this CD is therefore a welcome event. Although Wellstood has some interesting conversations with McPartland, it is for his playing that this set is most recommended. Wellstood is in top form on "Ain't Misbehavin'" and medleys of James P. Johnson and Duke Ellington tunes; McPartland takes "Detour Ahead" as her feature, and they duet on "Lulu's Back in Town," "'Deed I Do" and a spirited "Fine and Dandy." This set is easily recommended, particularly to fans of Dick Wellstood. —*Scott Yanow*

Piano Jazz: McPartland/Stacy / Dec. 1, 1981 / Jazz Alliance ✦✦✦✦✦
This is one of the most valuable of the *Piano Jazz* episodes for the great swing pianist Jess Stacy, who had been semiretired since the late '50s, made his final commercial recording in 1977. After stumbling a bit on "Dancing Fool," he is quite modest while discussing his own playing, but he gets stronger as the hour progresses. Although Stacy has four unaccompanied solos and Marian McPartland is fine on her feature "Heavy Hearted Blues," it is their three joyous duets ("Keepin' out of Mischief Now," "I Would Do Anything for You" and "St. Louis Blues") along with the priceless reminiscing that makes this CD highly recommended to swing collectors. —*Scott Yanow*

Piano Jazz: McPartland/Coltrane / Dec. 4, 1981 / Jazz Alliance ✦✦✦✦

Personal Choice / Jun. 1982 / Concord Jazz ✦✦✦✦
This is a fine all-around set for pianist Marian McPartland. With the assistance of bassist Steve LaSpina and drummer Jake Hanna, McPartland interprets seven standards (highlighted by "I Hear a Rhapsody," "A Sleepin' Bee" and Oscar Pettiford's "Tricotism") plus her own "Melancholy Mood." All of Marian McPartland's Concord releases find her in excellent form, swinging in a fairly modern style that really cannot be categorized. —*Scott Yanow*

Piano Jazz: McPartland/Wilson / 1983 / Jazz Alliance ✦✦✦✦
The date listed for this addition of Marian McPartland's *Piano Jazz* show is an estimate, since the first few releases put out on the Jazz Alliance series unfortunately left out that detail. Dave Brubeck and Marian McPartland have known each other since the early '50s and their mutual respect and love is felt in their conversation and reminiscences. With the exception of the opening duet on "St. Louis Blues" and the closing "Take Five," all of the selections performed are Brubeck's compositions. He takes "Thank You" and the brief "Polytonal Blues" solo, and McPartland explores "Summer Song." But the most intriguing tracks are the duets, particularly

"The Duke," "In Your Own Sweet Way" and the ad-lib "Free Piece." This was one of Marian McPartland's better shows. —*Scott Yanow*

Piano Jazz: McPartland/Brubeck / Mar. 1984 / Jazz Alliance ✦✦✦

Piano Jazz: McPartland/Gillespie / Jan. 1985 / Jazz Alliance ✦✦
Dizzy Gillespie was way past his prime when he appeared on Marian McPartland's *Piano Jazz* radio show in 1985. He actually only plays trumpet in duet with McPartland on two songs ("In a Mellow tone" and "Lullaby of the Leaves") and instead performs on piano. Since Gillespie was never a pianist (he used it to compose), his playing is fairly basic on his five piano duets with McPartland; she also takes "For Dizzy" and "Portrait of Diz" unaccompanied. Their conversation, although good-humored and at times informative, does not cover new ground, making this promising matchup a distinct disappointment. —*Scott Yanow*

Willow Creek and Other Ballads / Jan. 1985 / Concord Jazz ✦✦✦
Marian McPartland interprets ten diverse ballads on this album including her own "Willow Creek." The tunes are all quite sophisticated and they range from Stevie Wonder ("All in Love Is Fair"), Ahmad Jamal ("Without You") and Billy Strayhorn (the emotional "Blood Count") to Dave Brubeck and Noel Coward (his haunting "Someday I'll Find You" from "Private Lives"). This is nice music even if there is not much mood variation. —*Scott Yanow*

Piano Jazz: McPartland/Mancini / Mar. 14, 1985 / Jazz Alliance ✦✦✦✦
Henry Mancini saw his role in music as a film and television composer rather than as a songwriter. During his interesting hour on Marian McPartland's *Piano Jazz* radio show, Mancini discusses his life with good humor and modesty. He takes two brief melody choruses (on "Two for the Road" and "Meggie's Theme"), duets with McPartland on several songs (including "The Pink Panther" and a touching version of "Days of Wine and Roses" and enjoys hearing McPartland interpret "Mr. Lucky" and "Charade." Although only one of his songs ("Days of Wine and Roses") really became a jazz standard, Mancini enjoyed jazz and loved to hear improvising musicians develop his themes. This is an enjoyable set worth a few listens. —*Scott Yanow*

Piano Jazz: McPartland/Eldridge / Aug. 18, 1986 / Jazz Alliance ✦✦✦✦
This CD, which contains one of Marian McPartland's celebrated *Piano Jazz* radio shows, features Roy Eldridge in what must be his final recording. Unable to play the trumpet after September 1980 due to heart problems, Eldridge occasionally made rare appearances on piano, drums or as a singer during what was a quiet final decade before his death on February 26, 1989. It must have been a very frustrating time for the competitive trumpeter, but he sounds in good humor during his chat with McPartland. The discussion shoots all over the place but does include a funny story about Eldridge recording "Rockin' Chair," touches on racism in hotels of the 1940s and brings back to life a cutting contest with Rex Stewart. Musicwise, Eldridge sounds basic but effective on some piano duets with McPartland, and Marian takes two solos of her own. But best are Roy's feature (on both vocal and solo piano) on "Une Petite Laitue" and a version of "I Want a Little Girl" that has his charming vocal backed by McPartland. It's a pity that Roy did not record a full album in the latter format. —*Scott Yanow*

Piano Jazz: McPartland/Short / Nov. 10, 1986 / Jazz Alliance ✦✦✦
Bobby Short is a cabaret performer who has always had an interest in swing-oriented jazz. During his appearance on Marian McPartland's *Piano Jazz* radio show, the mutual respect felt by the two pianists is obvious in their conversations and storytelling. Musically, Short plays "Mood Indigo," "I Guess I'll Have to Change My Plans" and "My Shining Hour" solo (singing on the latter), McPartland is featured on "Nobody's Heart" and "Reflections in D" and there are a few duets, highlighted by "Just One of Those Things" and "It Don't Mean a Thing." This relaxed CD is more for Bobby Short fans than for jazz collectors, but it has its interesting moments. —*Scott Yanow*

Plays the Music of Billy Strayhorn / Mar. 1987 / Concord Jazz ✦✦✦✦
Pianist Marian McPartland has always had an affinity for the compositions of Billy Strayhorn, giving his songs the right amount of sensitivity and swing. For this quartet session with altoist Jerry Dodgion, bassist Steve LaSpina and drummer Joey Baron, McPartland explores ten of Strayhorn's best-known originals including "Isfahan," "Lotus Blossom," "Lush Life," "Take the 'A' Train" and "Raincheck." No revelations or innovations occur, but Billy Strayhorn's music is well served by McPartland's interpretations. —*Scott Yanow*

Piano Jazz: McPartland/Hampton / Jan. 11, 1989 / Jazz Alliance ✦✦✦✦
Marian McPartland welcomes vibraphonist Lionel Hampton (in his early 80s) to this edition of her radio show *Piano Jazz*. The talking mostly goes over the usual stories of Hampton's beginnings and his meeting Benny Goodman; it offers no new revelations, but the seven duets (with Hampton switching to piano on three of the numbers) are the real reason to acquire this disc. Hampton had never lost his enthusiasm for playing, and only one of the performances is under four minutes (with "Midnight Sun" being nearly nine). Hampton takes vocals on "Sweet Georgia

Brown" and "Mack the Knife" and sounds quite exuberant jamming with pianist McPartland on "How High the Moon" and "Flyin' Home." —*Scott Yanow*

Piano Jazz: McPartland/Carter / Feb. 20, 1989 / Jazz Alliance ✦✦

This particular episode of Marian McPartland's famed radio series *Piano Jazz* features the great altoist Benny Carter as her special guest, and it should have been a classic. The interview and verbal interplay is interesting, but unfortunately Carter chose (for unrevealed reasons) to stick exclusively to playing piano. Since piano is about his fifth best instrument (he sticks mostly to melody statements), the duets between McPartland and Carter are of much less interest than expected. McPartland does take three songs as a solo (the program sticks exclusively to her guest's compositions), but this CD can be easily skipped without much regret. —*Scott Yanow*

Piano Jazz: McPartland/McCann / Sep. 27, 1989 / Jazz Alliance ✦✦✦✦

Pianist-vocalist Les McCann is heard near the peak of his powers on this edition of *Piano Jazz* from the Jazz Alliance series of CDs. McCann and Marian McPartland have such an interesting discussion (covering such topics as the evolution of "Compared to What," McCann's beginnings and how Erroll Garner inspired him) that it is unfortunate that so much talking takes place during the latter half of the program. Musically, the best selections are the three ballads (particularly "With These Hands") in which McCann gives the lyrics a great deal of sincere feeling. In addition there is a spirited remake of McCann's greatest hit "Compared to What," a pair of solo features for McPartland and three piano duets. Easily recommended to Les McCann's many fans. —*Scott Yanow*

Plays the Benny Carter Songbook / Jan. 1990 / Concord Jazz ✦✦✦✦✦

Two aspects uplift this Concord CD above most "songbooks." Benny Carter is much better known as an altoist and an arranger than as a composer, so his compositions tend to be quite fresh since they have been underplayed through the years. Also, the fact that Carter himself performs on the majority of these selections (which also include bassist John Clayton and drummer Harold Jones) makes the set something special. Highlights include "When Lights Are Low," "I'm in the Mood for Swing," "Key Largo," "Doozy," "Lonely Woman" and "Only Trust Your Heart," but all 11 songs are enjoyable and swinging. —*Scott Yanow*

Piano Jazz: McPartland/Carroll / Jan. 30, 1990 / Jazz Alliance ✦✦✦

Marian McPartland and Barbara Carroll are old friends, having crossed paths many times since the late '40s. They chit-chat during half of Carroll's appearance on *Piano Jazz* about the old days, conversations only worth hearing once. Carroll performs her own "Too Soon," "My Man's Gone Now" and "Old Friends" (which she also sings in a cabaret style), McPartland improvises on "Imagination" and there are also three duets; best is the closing "There Will Never Be Another You." This particular edition of *Piano Jazz* is quite relaxed and lacks any surprises, revelations or excitement. It is a good souvenir for fans of Barbara Carroll, but overall is far from essential. —*Scott Yanow*

Piano Jazz: McPartland/Hyman / Dec. 7, 1990 / Jazz Alliance ✦✦✦✦✦

Dick Hyman is such a brilliant pianist that Marian McPartland sounds shy to play with him during this interesting edition of her *Piano Jazz* radio show. Hyman performs his "Carousel Memories," Fats Waller's "Handful of Keys," "Body and Soul" and McPartland's obscure "Delicate Balance" solo while she does her best on "A Flower Is a Lovesome Thing" and "Skylark." The conversation has its interesting moments (Hyman talks a bit about his movie scores and working with Woody Allen) but it is the competitive interplay on their piano duets ("Gone with the Wind," "This Time the Dream's on Me" and "Lover Come Back to Me") that are most fun. —*Scott Yanow*

Piano Jazz: McPartland/J. Williams / 1991 / Jazz Alliance ✦✦✦✦

Joe Williams easily charms Marian McPartland during his appearance on her *Piano Jazz* radio show; at times she gushes a bit too much. But except for near the end of "Who She Do" when his voice gets a bit raspy, Williams is in good form during the ballad-oriented set. McPartland takes her own impressionistic "Twilight World" and "Prelude to a Kiss" as piano solos and she is at his best on a touching "Embraceable You," "Just Friends" and "I'm Confessin'." —*Scott Yanow*

Live at Maybeck Recital Hall, Vol. 9 / Jan. 20, 1991 / Concord Jazz ✦✦✦✦✦

Great solos, with strong rhythmic work and phrasing. —*Ron Wynn*

Piano Jazz: McPartland/Hinton / Aug. 15, 1991 / Jazz Alliance ✦✦✦✦✦

This is one of the stronger entries in the numerous releases taken from Marian McPartland's *Piano Jazz* radio series. The octogenarian bassist Milt Hinton is a talented storyteller, he takes his autobiographical "Milt's Rap" and "Joshua" (the latter demonstrates his timeless slapping technique) unaccompanied and he plays six enjoyable duets with the pianist/host. McPartland also has a feature solo ("Stranger in a Dream") and her love and respect for the veteran bassist is obvious. —*Scott Yanow*

Piano Jazz: McPartland/Myers / Aug. 29, 1991 / Jazz Alliance ✦✦✦✦

For this edition of Marian McPartland's hour-long *Piano Jazz* radio show she welcomes Amina Claudine Myers. McPartland seemingly has the ability to relate to any jazz pianist and their duets on three standards (including "Mood Indigo") along with a free improvisation work quite well. Myers has three songs to herself (two of which also feature her emotional vocals) and McPartland takes "Windows" and her spontaneously composed "Portrait of Amina" as her showcases. The conversation holds one's interest and contains some fresh anecdotes by Myers. —*Scott Yanow*

★ **With Guest Lee Konitz** / Sep. 6, 1991 / Jazz Alliance ✦✦✦✦✦

This CD has one of the most rewarding of Marian McPartland's *Piano Jazz* radio shows. Guest Lee Konitz proves to be a very thoughtful and sometimes witty guest. Konitz talks about what he learned from Tristano and in turn what he tries to get across to students himself. He clearly enjoys discussing the magic of improvisation. In addition, the music on this program is uniformly outstanding. For "All the Things You Are" the altoist coaxes McPartland to play freely without a chord structure. He takes "Stella by Starlight" unaccompanied, creates some unpredictable duets with McPartland on familiar yet still fresh standards, plays some abstract piano with the host on "Tactile Talk" and sounds beautiful on soprano during "Little Girl Blue;" upon the latter song's conclusion, Konitz admits that he had never played the song before. This CD ranks up there with the Bill Evans show as the most significant of the *Piano Jazz* programs thus far released on CD. —*Scott Yanow*

Piano Jazz: McPartland/Clooney / Oct. 1991 / Jazz Alliance ✦✦✦✦

Rosemary Clooney's appearance on Marian McPartland's famous radio show *Piano Jazz* has some good music and plenty of lively conversation. Clooney talks about her beginnings, she and McPartland discuss such people as Mitch Miller, Billy Strayhorn and Cole Porter and there is plenty of mutual good feeling. Musically, there is only around 20 minutes of music (three piano solos by McPartland and four Clooney vocals including "My Shining Hour" and a touching version of "September Song") so, although enjoyable, this CD is not essential. —*Scott Yanow*

Piano Jazz: McPartland/Richards / Oct. 16, 1991 / Jazz Alliance ✦✦✦✦

Red Richards was one of the least-known guests on Marian McPartland's *Piano Jazz* radio show, but he definitely deserved to be there. A veteran of the swing era who was three days short of his 79th birthday at the time of the show, Richards in the mid-'90s is still a strong prebop pianist. The show gave him a rare chance for wider exposure and he sounds in top form on four solos (including Willie "The Lion" Smith's "Echoes of Spring" and "Someday You'll Be Sorry"). McPartland takes two ballads ("A Hundred Years from Today" and "The Talk of the Town") as her features, and best of all are their three piano duets: "Tangerine," "Keepin' Out of Mischief Now" and "Runnin' Wild." Since Red Richards has been underrated through the decades, his conversations with McPartland are full of rarely-heard anecdotes and fresh material. Recommended. —*Scott Yanow*

Piano Jazz: McPartland/DeJohnette / Dec. 11, 1992 / Jazz Alliance ✦✦✦

This entry from Marian McPartland's Piano Jazz radio series is a bit surprising for drummer Jack DeJohnette switches to piano for all but two selections and bassist Christian McBride makes the duos into trios. Also, most of the music consists of jazz standards from the 1950s, so (with the exception of DeJohnette's "Silver Hollow") there are no examples of his own more advanced compositions. However, the mutual respect felt by McPartland and DeJohnette is obvious and some of the verbal conversations are quite interesting; in addition, the two pianos work together quite well. —*Scott Yanow*

In My Life / Jan. 1993 / Concord Jazz ✦✦✦✦✦

Pianist Marian McPartland displays her versatility throughout this reflective and generally thoughtful CD on such selections as the Beatles "In My Life," John Coltrane's "Red Planet," Ivan Lins' "Velas" and Ornette Coleman's "Ramblin'." Despite the diverse repertoire, McPartland's own flexible style shines through and her individual musical personality is felt in each song. Altoist Chris Potter makes the trio a quartet on half of the selections and he uplifts the session a bit. McPartland's closing wistful solo piano version of "Singin' the Blues" (dedicated to her late husband cornetist Jimmy McPartland) should not be missed. —*Scott Yanow*

Piano Jazz: McPartland/Burrell / Apr. 15, 1993 / Jazz Alliance ✦✦✦✦

This is the 21st of Marian McPartland's *Piano Jazz* radio shows to be issued on CD. The pianist welcomes guitarist Kenny Burrell for an hour of talk (covering briefly his early days, the legacy of Duke Ellington and his current activities) and music. With the exception of the closing "Raincheck," all of the typically tasteful playing emphasizes slower tempos with two Burrell solos, one McPartland feature ("All Too Soon") and five duets. The biggest surprises are on "Listen to the Dawn" (during which Burrell plays piano in duet with McPartland) and the guitarist's effective vocal on "I'm Just a Lucky So and So." —*Scott Yanow*

Piano Jazz: McPartland/Terry / Sep. 21, 1993 / Jazz Alliance ◆◆◆◆
Fluegelhornist Clark Terry is such a delightful person that, even though most of the stories he tells during his appearance on Marian McPartland's *Piano Jazz* radio show are not that new, they are fun to hear anyway. Still very much in his musical prime in 1993, C.T. is in typically upbeat form on seven duets with pianist McPartland, singing "Mumbles" and "Wham!" and showing his top form on such numbers as "The Snapper," a tender "Come Sunday" and "Memories of You." —*Scott Yanow*

Piano Jazz: McPartland/Ellington / Jan. 24, 1994 / Jazz Alliance ◆◆
The problem with this encounter between Marian McPartland and Mercer Ellington is that Ellington was not much of a musician. He plays some "arranger's piano" with McPartland on the opening "C Jam Blues," but otherwise all of the music (barely 22 minutes worth) comprises exclusively McPartland's piano solos; all familiar Duke Ellington, Mercer Ellington or Billy Strayhorn tunes except for her own improvised "Portrait of Mercer Ellington." The conversation (which naturally focuses on Duke) does not contain any really fresh or new stories and this rather disappointing edition of *Piano Jazz* is quite forgettable. —*Scott Yanow*

Piano Jazz: McPartland/McKenna / May 19, 1994 / Jazz Alliance ◆◆◆◆
For this edition of Marian McPartland's radio show *Piano Jazz*, she welcomes Dave McKenna. The mutual respect they feel toward each other is obvious. The music is at its best when the two pianists duet on older material ("Let's Get Away from It All" and "Struttin' with Some Barbecue") and a bit trivial when they take turns on a Stevie Wonder medley. The results overall are not essential but worth hearing once or twice. —*Scott Yanow*

Piano Jazz: McPartland/Brown / Mar. 7, 1995 / Jazz Alliance ◆◆◆
Marian McPartland and pianist-vocalist Charles Brown obviously hit it off, as heard during this CD release of Brown's appearance on McPartland's radio show *Piano Jazz*. The high point of their generally interesting discussion features Brown talking about (and demonstrating) the difference between 1940s West Coast blues and the blues played in Mississippi. Musically, there is not much interplay between the pair with the emphasis placed on solo performances. Brown takes "These Blues," "Is You Is or Is You Ain't Ma' Baby," his early hit "Drifting Blues," "'Round Midnight," "Sweet Slumber" and "Joyce's Boogie" (the latter in the style of Albert Ammons) while McPartland is heard on "Willow Weep for Me" and her own version of "'Round Midnight." The duo only come together musically on "All My Life," "There Is No Greater Love" and "Seven Long Days." Still, this is a fun set and it is particularly interesting to hear Charles Brown play without his band. —*Scott Yanow*

Piano Jazz: McPartland/Peterson / Jan. 30, 1996 / Jazz Alliance ◆◆◆◆

Piano Jazz: McPartland/McShann / Apr. 1996 / Jazz Alliance ◆◆◆

Silent Pool / Jun. 11, 1996-Jun. 12, 1996 / Concord Jazz ◆◆◆
Rather than "Silent Pool," the Marian McPartland selection on this rather sleepy CD that best sums up the music is "Melancholy Mood." Long adept at writing harmonically sophisticated originals, pianist McPartland is featured on a dozen of her compositions with the backing of 20 strings, bassist Andy Simpkins and drummer Harold Jones. Alan Broadbent's string arrangements (a throwback in some ways to the mood music records of the 1950s) are lush, dreamy, always middle-of-the-road and sometimes dull. McPartland plays well as usual on the ballad-oriented set that includes at least three of her best-known originals ("A Delicate Balance," "Ambiance" and "Threnody"), but the unadventurous strings clearly weigh down the music. —*Scott Yanow*

Joe McPhee

b. Nov. 3, 1939, Miami, FL
Tenor Saxophone, Trumpet, Soprano Saxophone / Avant-Garde, Free Jazz
A multi-instrumentalist who plays adventurous solos on both tenor and trumpet, Joe McPhee began on trumpet when he was eight. After serving in the military, he made his recording debut with Clifford Thornton (1967). By 1969 he was doubling on reeds and he cut his first date as a leader. In 1975 the Hat Hut label was started largely to document McPhee's passionate music and, with the exception of a fine Sackville date with Bill Smith (1983), Hat Hut and its successors (Hat Art and Hat Musics) have continued exclusively recording Joe McPhee's highly original music. —*Scott Yanow*

Black Magic Man / Dec. 12, 1970 / Hat Hut ◆◆◆

Survival Unit II / Oct. 30, 1971 / Hat Art ◆◆◆◆◆

The Willisau Concert / Oct. 11, 1975 / Hat Hut ◆◆◆◆

Variations on a Blue Line 'Round Midnight / Oct. 11, 1977 / Hat Hut ◆◆◆◆◆

Old Eyes and Mysteries / May 30, 1979 / Hat Art ◆◆◆◆

Oleo & A Future Retrospective / Aug. 2, 1982 / Hat Hut ◆◆◆◆◆

● **Visitation** / Nov. 6, 1983 / Sackville ◆◆◆◆◆
The versatile Joe McPhee (who on this set plays fluegelhorn, pocket trumpet, tenor and soprano) teams up with Bill Smith's Ensemble (Smith on soprano, sopranino and alto, violinist David Prentice and bassist David Lee) plus drummer Richard Bannard for a stimulating set of avant-garde music. The interplay between these masterful improvisers on group originals and Albert Ayler's classic "Ghosts" is consistently impressive and worthy of a close investigation by the more open-eared segment of the jazz audience. —*Scott Yanow*

Po Music: Oleo / Mar. 24, 1984-Mar. 25, 1984 / Hat Music ◆◆◆◆◆

Po Music: A Future Retrospective / May 1987 / Hat Art ◆◆◆

Linear B / Jan. 9, 1990-Jan. 12, 1990 / Hat Art ◆◆◆

Sweet Freedom: Now What? / Aug. 25, 1995 / Hat Hut ◆◆◆

Legend Street One / Jun. 1, 1996-Jun. 2, 1996 / CIMP ◆◆◆◆◆

Legend Street Two / Jun. 1, 1996-Jun. 2, 1996 / CIMP ◆◆◆◆◆

Inside Out / Jun. 2, 1996 / CIMP ◆◆◆◆◆

Charles McPherson

b. Jul. 24, 1939, Joplin, MO
Alto Saxophone / Bop, Hard Bop
A Charlie Parker disciple who brings his own lyricism to the bebop language, Charles McPherson has been a reliable figure in modern mainstream jazz for the past 35 years. He played in the Detroit jazz scene of the mid-'50s, moved to New York in 1959 and within a year was working with Charles Mingus. McPherson and his friend Lonnie Hillyer succeeded Eric Dolphy and Ted Curson as regular members of Mingus's band in 1961 and he worked with the bassist off and on until 1972. Although he and Hillyer had a short-lived quintet in 1966, McPherson was not a fulltime leader until 1972. In 1978 he moved to San Diego which has been his home ever since. Sometimes he uses his son Chuck McPherson on drums. Charles McPherson, who helped out on the film *Bird* by playing some of the parts not taken from Charlie Parker records, has led dates through the years for Prestige (1964-69), Mainstream, Xanadu, Discovery and Arabesque. —*Scott Yanow*

Be-Bop Revisited / Nov. 20, 1964 / Original Jazz Classics ◆◆◆◆◆
Bebop is the thing on this excellent outing as altoist Charles McPherson and pianist Barry Harris do their interpretations of Charlie Parker and Bud Powell. With trumpeter Carmell Jones, bassist Nelson Boyd and drummer Al "Tootie" Heath completing the quintet, the band romps through such bop classics as "Hot House," "Nostalgia," "Wail" and "Si Si" along with an original blues and "Embraceable You." A previously unissued "If I Love You" is added to the CD reissue. McPherson and Jones make for a potent front line on these spirited performances, easily recommended to fans of straightahead jazz. —*Scott Yanow*

Con Alma / Aug. 6, 1965 / Original Jazz Classics ◆◆◆◆
Altoist Charles McPherson teams up with distinctive tenor Clifford Jordan, pianist Barry Harris, bassist George Tucker and drummer Alan Dawson for jazz classics by Thelonious Monk, Duke Ellington, Charlie Parker, Dizzy Gillespie (a mysterious version of "Con Alma") and Dexter Gordon, in addition to an original McPherson blues, "I Don't Know," which closely recalls "Parker's Mood." McPherson and Harris both have their share of fine solos, but Jordan generally takes honors on this set; he is the only musician who was looking beyond bop and playing in a more original style. —*Scott Yanow*

The Charles McPherson Quintet Live! / Oct. 13, 1966 / Original Jazz Classics ◆◆◆◆
Altoist Charles McPherson and pianist Barry Harris are the stars of this live bop-oriented session. Trumpeter Lonnie Hillyer does his best, although he stumbles a bit on the rapid "Shaw 'Nuff," drummer Billy Higgins and the forgotten bassist Ray McKinney are fine in support and the repertoire (ranging from the funky "The Viper" and "I Can't Get Started" to "Here's That Rainy Day" and the recent "Never Let Me Go") is diverse and challenging. It's an excellent CD overall. —*Scott Yanow*

Siku Ya Bibi / 1972 / Mainstream ◆◆◆
A CD reissue of a 1972 tribute album to Billie Holiday suffers a bit from overproduction and glossy orchestrations, but alto saxophonist Charles McPherson's passionate playing, along with that of pianist Barry Harris and trumpeter Lonnie Hillyer, helps overcome the sappiness and at least brings home the point of Holiday's poignancy as a vocalist. —*Ron Wynn*

Beautiful / Aug. 12, 1975 / Xanadu ◆◆◆◆◆
Xanadu was a perfect label for altoist Charles McPherson, since he was always a bop-based improviser who was perfectly at home jamming straightahead standards. This CD reissue features the talented altoist (who is joined by pianist Duke Jordan, bassist Sam Jones and drummer Leroy Williams) infusing beauty and boppish ideas into such songs as "They Say It's Wonderful," "It Could Happen to You" and "This Can't Be Love." A previously unreleased trio rendition of "All God's Chil-

lun Got Rhythm" (recorded while the musicians were waiting for McPherson to show up) has been added to the CD. Recommended. —*Scott Yanow*

★ **Live in Tokyo** / Apr. 14, 1976 / Xanadu ◆◆◆◆◆
Altoist Charles McPherson, who developed his own sound out of the Charlie Parker style, plays a couple of blues and four standards on this frequently exciting session. With the strong assistance of pianist Barry Harris, bassist Sam Jones and drummer Leroy Williams, McPherson is in top form with the highlights being his feature on "East of the Sun" and a heated "Bouncing with Bud." —*Scott Yanow*

New Horizons / Sep. 28, 1977 / Xanadu ◆◆◆◆
One of the top bop-oriented altoists of the 1960s, '70s, '80s and '90s, Charles McPherson recorded some of his finest records during his period with the Xanadu label. For this quartet set with pianist Mickey Tucker, bassist Cecil McBee and drummer Freddie Waits, McPherson performs four excellent originals ("Promise" and "Dee Blues" are well worth reviving), plus "I'll Never Stop Loving You" and "Samba D'Orfeo." The music is typically swinging and has its exciting moments. —*Scott Yanow*

Free Bop! / Oct. 23, 1978 / Xanadu ◆◆◆◆◆
Entertaining hard-bop workout. This is perhaps his fiercest, most exciting playing as a leader. —*Ron Wynn*

The Prophet / May 1984 / Discovery ◆◆◆
Early '80s bop and hard bop session from veteran alto saxophonist Charles McPherson. This has a more relaxed, stately quality, not as animated nor as much in debt to mentor Charlie Parker as some past releases. McPherson has been one of the less frenzied, mellower bop players, and this quality emerges throughout his solos. —*Ron Wynn*

First Flight Out / Jan. 25, 1994-Jan. 26, 1994 / Arabesque ◆◆◆◆
Come Play with Me / Mar. 2, 1995 / Arabesque ◆◆◆◆◆
Charles McPherson, who will always be best known for his roots in Charlie Parker's style and his period with Charles Mingus, proves on this CD to still be in his musical prime decades later. Although he had rarely played with any of the sidemen heard on his Arabesque release before, the quartet presents a unified sound, as if they were a regularly working group. McPherson performs three veteran standards and six originals with most of the latter being closely related to the blues; "Pretty Girl Blues" sounds like a mixture of a couple of Bird lines and "Fun House" is based on "Limehouse Blues" while the best of the new compositions is the hard bop boogaloo "Marionette." But no matter what the vehicle, McPherson is in top form throughout this fine date and he sounds clearly inspired by the presence of pianist Mulgrew Miller, bassist Santi Debriano and drummer Lewis Nash. —*Scott Yanow*

Carmen McRae

b. Apr. 8, 1920, New York, NY, **d.** Nov. 10, 1994, Beverly Hills, CA
Vocals / Bop, Standards, Traditional Pop
Carmen McRae always had a nice voice (if not on the impossible level of an Ella Fitzgerald or Sarah Vaughan), but it was her behind-the-beat phrasing and ironic interpretations of lyrics that made her most memorable. She studied piano early on and had her first important job singing with Benny Carter's big band (1944), but it would be another decade before her career really had much momentum. McRae married and divorced Kenny Clarke in the 1940s, worked with Count Basie (briefly) and Mercer Ellington (1946-47), and became the intermission singer and pianist at several New York clubs. In 1954 she began to record as a leader and by then she had absorbed the influences of Billie Holiday and bebop into her own style. McRae would record fairly steadily up to 1989 and, although her voice was higher in the 1950s and her phrasing would be even more laidback in later years, her general style and approach did not change much through the decades. Championed in the 1950s by Ralph Gleason, Carmen McRae was fairly popular throughout her career. Among her most interesting recording projects were participating in Dave Brubeck's the Real Ambassadors with Louis Armstrong, cutting an album of live duets with Betty Carter, being accompanied by Dave Brubeck and George Shearing, and closing her career with brilliant tributes to Thelonious Monk and Sarah Vaughan. Carmen McRae, who refused to quit smoking, was forced to retire in 1991 due to emphysema. She recorded for many labels including Bethlehem, Decca (1954-58), Kapp, Columbia, Mainstream, Focus, Atlantic (1967-70), Black Lion, Groove Merchant, Catalyst, Blue Note, Buddah, Concord and Novus. —*Scott Yanow*

Carmen McRae / Oct. 6, 1954-Dec. 1954 / Bethlehem ◆◆◆
This CD reissue has Carmen McRae's first recordings as a leader. McRae is heard on four songs apiece with the Mat Mathews quintet (a group including Herbie Mann on flute and tenor and guitarist Mundell Lowe) and clarinetist Tony Scott's quartet. On the emotional "Misery" Tony Scott switches to piano and is the only accompanist to the singer. Five alternate takes augment this set which emphasizes

ballads. Overall, the music is pleasing but not too memorable, and one wishes there were more variety. —*Scott Yanow*

I'll Be Seeing You / Jun. 14, 1955-Mar. 10, 1959 / GRP/Decca ◆◆◆◆
This two-CD set mostly brings back material from singer Carmen McRae's Decca years that had been bypassed by other reissues. The oversized box, after a memorable version of "Something to Live For" (in which McRae is accompanied by the song's composer Billy Strayhorn), has many orchestra tracks that are weighed down by middle-of-the-road arrangements more suitable to Doris Day than to McRae; only "Whatever Lola Wants" is memorable among the routine ballads of 1955-56. However, things start improving with "Skyliner" and a March 1957 set with just a rhythm section is quite enjoyable; McRae herself contributes some effective piano on swinging renditions of "Perdido" and "Exactly like You." The majority of the later selections use orchestras but the charts are more jazz-oriented and McRae (who was in her mid- to late 30s during the period) had clearly grown as a singer; tenor saxophonist Ben Webster helps out on "Bye Bye Blackbird and Flamingo." Overall this set is worth picking up for fans of Carmen McRae's early years, giving one a fine overview of her talents in the 1950s. —*Scott Yanow*

Here to Stay / Jun. 14, 1955-Nov. 12, 1959 / GRP/Decca ◆◆◆◆◆
One of several CDs that reissue singer Carmen McRae's early Decca recordings, this release draws its material from the 1955 small group album *By Special Request* and a 1959 record with the Ernie Wilkins Orchestra (*Something to Swing About*). McRae excels in both settings. While tenor saxophonist Zoot Sims, trumpeter Richard Williams and pianist Dick Katz get some solo space on the latter album, the former one showcases McRae either with Dick Katz's quartet, accordion player Mat Mathews' quintet (with flutist Herbie Mann) or (on "Something to Live For") with its composer Billy Strayhorn on piano. During an emotional rendition of "Supper Time," McRae herself plays piano. Throughout the 20 selections, the singer is heard in her early prime, hitting high notes that she would not even think of attempting in her later years. Recommended. —*Scott Yanow*

The Greatest of Carmen McRae / Jun. 14, 1955-Nov. 1959 / MCA ◆◆◆◆◆
This two-LP set has 32 of singer Carmen McRae's finest performances from her Decca years. An excellent sampler that features McRae in 19 different settings, this was a fairly definitive set before the CD era. Among the highlights are "Good Morning Heartache," "Something to Live For" (which has the vocalist backed by the song's composer, pianist Billy Strayhorn), "Yardbird Suite" (recorded the day that Charlie Parker passed away), "Isn't It Romantic," "I Was Doing All Right," "Perdido" and "Baltimore Oriole." —*Scott Yanow*

Carmen McRae Sings Great American Songwriters / Jun. 16, 1955-Mar. 4, 1959 / GRP/Decca ◆◆◆◆
Instead of reissuing all of singer Carmen McRae's early records for Decca in chronological order, the GRP program has hedged its bets a bit by coming up with highlights from each of her sessions although, with the various CDs on a whole, nearly everything has being reissued anyway. The 20 numbers on this CD are taken from ten different sessions and find McRae joined by the Mat Mathews Quintet (featuring flutist Herbie Mann), the Ray Bryant trio and several large orchestras. The repertoire is taken from the songbooks of some of the classic American composers (including Gershwin, Porter, Kern, Rodgers & Hart and Arlen) and McRae's interpretations are both respectful and swinging. It is particularly interesting to hear how high her voice could be in the early days. This CD is easily recommended to her fans. —*Scott Yanow*

● **Sings Lover Man & Other Billie Holiday Classics** / Jun. 29, 1961+Jul. 26, 1961 / Columbia ◆◆◆◆◆
This CD reissues one of Carmen McRae's best recordings of the 1960s. McRae always considered Billie Holiday to be her primary influence, so a tribute album was a natural project for her. Joined by her regular trio (pianist Norman Simmons, bassist Bob Cranshaw and drummer Walter Perkins) and three guests (cornetist Nat Adderley, tenorman Eddie "Lockjaw" Davis and guitarist Mundell Lowe), the singer interprets a dozen songs associated with Lady Day. Although Holiday's influence can be felt, McRae already had her own distinctive voice and phrasing, resulting in fresh versions of such songs as "Them There Eyes," "Miss Brown to You," "I Cried for You" and even "God Bless the Child." A coolly emotional version of "Strange Fruit" (in which she is accompanied just by Lowe's guitar) is a highlight. In addition, two songs not originally included on the LP ("If the Moon Turns Green" and the slightly out-of-place but still satisfying "The Christmas Song") were added to the reissue. Recommended. —*Scott Yanow*

Song Time / 1963-1969 / Hindsight ◆◆◆
In the 1960s Carmen McRae did several sessions for a public-service radio series called *The Navy Swings*. They were 15-minute shows, with Navy recruiting spiels between songs, so the performances are miniatures two or three minutes long. The repertoire is familiar from her LPs of the time (when her voice was in its prime),

but the intimate setting of the piano trio rather than the orchestral backdrop makes the rediscovery of these tapes especially welcome. —*Les Line*

Woman Talk / 1964-1966 / Mainstream ✦✦

This is a compilation from sessions done for the Mainstream label featuring the rich, striking McRae vocals backed by a large orchestra conducted by either Peter Matz or Don Sebesky. Her interpretations and delivery are masterful, but these albums lack the intimacy of her small combo works and are more pop-centered than the Atlantic dates. It has been reissued on CD. —*Ron Wynn*

Alive / 1965 / Columbia/Legacy ✦✦✦

Originally on Mainstream, this live session (which has been reissued by Columbia on CD) features the talented singer Carmen McRae at New York's Village Gate with pianist Norman Simmons, bassist Paul Breslin, drummer Frank Severino, guitarist Joe Puma, flutist Ray Beckenstein and Jose Mangual on bongos. The flute and bongos make the music seem a bit dated, as does the inclusion of some forgettable show tunes from the era (including three songs from "The Roar of the Greaspaint—The Smell of the Crowd"). McRae is in prime voice and sounds best on some Billie Holiday-associated tunes, but the set is mostly for her fans rather than general collectors. —*Scott Yanow*

Take Five / Aug. 1965 / Columbia ✦✦✦✦

Around the time that she was participating in Dave Brubeck's Real Ambassadors, singer Carmen McRae appeared at Basin Street East with the backing of Brubeck's trio (no Paul Desmond on this set). The resulting live album finds McRae mostly interpreting the lyrics of Iola Brubeck; all dozen songs except Desmond's "Take Five" are Dave Brubeck originals. This interesting set finds McRae's voice in prime form, and her vocal versions of such songs as "In Your Own Sweet Way," "Ode to a Cowboy," "It's a Raggy Waltz" and "Travellin' Blues" are definitive. —*Scott Yanow*

★ **The Great American Songbook** / Oct. 1972 / Atlantic ✦✦✦✦✦

On this popular two-LP set, singer Carmen McRae interprets songs by Duke Ellington, Cole Porter, Michel Legrand, Warren & Dubin, Henry Mancini and Jimmy Van Heusen, among others, but it is her rendition of a humorous Jimmy Rowles novelty ("The Ballad of Thelonious Monk") that is best remembered. Joined by pianist Rowles, guitarist Joe Pass, bassist Chuck Domanico and drummer Chuck Flores, McRae had what was at the time a rare opportunity to record a live, spontaneous, jazz-oriented set. She sounds quite enthusiastic about both her accompaniment and the strong repertoire, which includes "At Long Last Love," "I Only Have Eyes for You," "Sunday," "I Cried for You" and "I Thought About You." —*Scott Yanow*

Velvet Soul / 1972-1973 / LRC ✦✦✦

Recent reissue of early '70s material on the Groove Merchant label. McRae was doing mix of standards, ballads, a little blues, and some originals, and was also experimenting with some soul-jazz. These are not as well done as her material on some other labels, but are interesting for showing the mood of a label in the transitional '70s. —*Ron Wynn*

It Takes a Whole Lot of Human Feelings / Feb. 1973 / Groove ✦✦✦

Carmen McRae's charming version of Blossom Dearie's "Hey John" is enough of a reason to search for this out-of-print LP by itself. Accompanied by pianist Dick Shreve, Larry Bunker on vibes, guitarist Joe Pass, bassist Ray Brown and drummer Frank Severino, along with some unidentified players, McRae is also in excellent form on "I Fall in Love Too Easily," "Nice Work if You Can Get It," "Straighten Up and Fly Right" and "All the Things You Are." Not all of the selections are of that quality, but overall, this is definitely a worthwhile acquisition for fans of the singer. —*Scott Yanow*

I Am Music / Apr. 1975 / Blue Note ✦✦

Can't Hide Love / May 3, 1976-May 12, 1976 / Blue Note ✦

This is the type of session that killed Blue Note the first time around. Carmen McRae gamely tries to interpret unsuitable and inferior pop tunes ("The Man I Love" and "A Child Is Born" are the only exceptions) and is backed by an all-star but faceless orchestra that is given nothing to do. The trumpet section (which includes Buddy Childers, Bobby Shew, Al Aarons, Snooky Young, Oscar Brashear and Blue Mitchell) is not given a single solo. The title cut is quite ludicrous and songs such as "Only Women Bleed" and "I Wish You Well" do not fit McRae's style at all. Pass on this one and get her earlier Deccas or her later Novus releases instead. —*Scott Yanow*

Live at Bubba's / Jan. 17, 1981 / Who's Who in Jazz ✦✦✦

A fine, rather informal set from Lionel Hampton's label. —*Ron Wynn*

You're Lookin' at Me (A Collection of Nat King Cole Songs) / Nov. 1983 / Concord Jazz ✦✦✦✦

Carmen McRae's tribute to Nat King Cole (which predated the late-'80s revival of Cole's music) has its strong and weak points. She wisely adds Cole's former guitarist John Collins to her regular trio and picked some fine material (including "I'm an

Errand Girl for Rhythm," "I Can't See for Lookin'" and "Just You, Just Me"). However, McRae's phrasing is much different than Cole's, and why did she sing "Sweet Lorraine" without changing any of the words? Despite those reservations, this set has enough strong moments to justify its purchase. —*Scott Yanow*

For Lady Day / Dec. 31, 1983 / Novus ✦✦✦✦✦

Carmen McRae always considered Billie Holiday to be the most important influence not only on her singing, but on her life. Six years before she recorded her monumental tributes to Thelonious Monk and Sarah Vaughan, McRae performed a Billie Holiday set at New York's Blue Note Club that was broadcast over the radio, on the first of two volumes McRae, who talks movingly about Lady Day at the beginning of the set and accompanies herself on piano on "I'm Pulling Through," is heard in prime form, combining the power and range of her earlier years with the emotional depth and behind-the-beat phrasing of her last period. Accompanied by her rhythm section of the time (pianist Marshall Otwell, bassist John Leftwich and drummer Donald Bailey) and occasionally the tenor of Zoot Sims, McRae really digs into the material, interpreting the songs in her own style, but with a knowing nod towards Holiday. This wonderful set is far superior to most of the Billie Holiday tribute albums of recent years and reminds us how much Carmen McRae is missed. —*Scott Yanow*

Any Old Time / Jun. 23, 1986 / Denon ✦✦✦✦✦

This little-known date, recorded for the Japanese Denon label, features singer Carmen McRae with her regular quartet of the time (pianist Eric Gunnison, bassist Scott Colley, drummer Mark Pulice and guitarist John Collins) and guest tenor Clifford Jordan. McRae is heard in prime form performing a variety of top standards, including "Tulip or Turnip," "Have You Met Miss Jones," "Body and Soul" and "Mean to Me." Although recorded in the studio, this excellent outing gives listeners a good idea of how Carmen McRae sounded live. Well worth searching for. —*Scott Yanow*

Carmen McRae-Betty Carter Duets / Jan. 30, 1987-Feb. 1, 1987 / Great American Music Hall ✦✦✦✦✦

This project is an unusual matchup between two very individual vocalists that generally works. Both Carmen McRae and Betty Carter show a lot of good humor during their duets, cracking occasional jokes and often jamming quite spontaneously. With suitable support from pianist Eric Gunnison, bassist Jim Hughart and drummer Winard Harper along with a very enthusiastic audience at San Francisco's Great American Music Hall, Carter usually takes vocal honors while McRae comes up with the most humorous lines. Some of the ensembles are ragged, but this encounter is overall quite successful. The CD reissue adds three previously unreleased selections that feature McRae without Carter. Now if only someone had teamed together Ella Fitzgerald and Sarah Vaughan for a full album. —*Scott Yanow*

Fine and Mellow: Live at Birdland West / Dec. 1987 / Concord Jazz ✦✦✦✦

An excellent live set. McRae handles uptempo and ballads with ease. CD has one bonus cut. —*Ron Wynn*

☆ **Carmen Sings Monk** / Jan. 30, 1988-Feb. 1, 1988 / Novus ✦✦✦✦✦

Carmen McRae, a good friend of Thelonious Monk's, sang 13 of his songs (two of which are also heard in different live versions) on this memorable project. Half of the lyrics are by Jon Hendricks, while the remainder were written by Abbey Lincoln ("Blue Monk"), Bernie Hanighen or, more recently, Sally Swisher and Mike Ferro. On all but the two concert performances, Carmen is assisted by tenor saxophonist Clifford Jordan, pianist Eric Gunnison, bassist George Mraz and drummer Al Foster; Mraz's solos are particularly impressive although everyone is in sensitive form. The live recordings give listeners two more chances to acknowledge the uniqueness of tenor saxophonist Charlie Rouse's tone. As for McRae, her phrasing has rarely sounded better than on this classic set, and it is a particular pleasure to hear her interpret the intelligent lyrics and unusual melodies. "Dear Ruby (Ruby, My Dear)" and "Listen to Monk (Rhythm-a-Ning)" are among the high points of the essential and very delightful CD. An inspired idea and one of the best recordings of Carmen McRae's career. —*Scott Yanow*

Sarah: Dedicated to You / Oct. 12, 1990-Oct. 14, 1990 / Novus ✦✦✦✦✦

The follow-up to the essential *Carmen Sings Monk* is a tribute to the recently deceased Sarah Vaughan that ranks at the same very high level. Carmen McRae's final recording finds the singer backed by the Shirley Horn Trio (unfortunately, Horn turned down McRae's request to sing a bit) on 13 numbers associated with Sassy, plus Carroll Coates' original "Sarah." On such songs as "Poor Butterfly," "Misty," "Tenderly," "I'll Be Seeing You" and even "Send in the Clowns," McRae brings back the spirit (and some of the phrasing) of Sarah Vaughan while still sounding very much like herself. This very well-conceived tribute is a classic of its kind and a perfect swan song for Carmen McRae. —*Scott Yanow*

Jay McShann

b. Jan. 12, 1909, Muskogee, OK

Piano, Vocals / Swing, Piano Blues, Big Band, Jump Blues

The great veteran pianist Jay McShann (also known as "Hootie") has had a long career, and it is unfair to primarily think of him as merely the leader of an orchestra that featured a young Charlie Parker. He was mostly self-taught as a pianist, worked with Don Byas as early as 1931 and played throughout the Midwest before settling in Kansas City in 1936. McShann formed his own sextet the following year and by 1939 had his own big band. In 1940 at a radio station in Wichita, KS, McShann and an octet out of his orchestra recorded eight songs that were not released commercially until the 1970s; those rank among the earliest of all Charlie Parker records (he is brilliant on "Honeysuckle Rose" and "Lady Be Good") and also feature the strong rhythm-section team McShann had with bassist Gene Ramey and drummer Gus Johnson. The full orchestra recorded for Decca on two occasions during 1941-42 but they were typecast as a blues band and did not get to record many of their more challenging charts (although very rare broadcasts have since surfaced and been released on CD by Vintage Jazz Classics). In addition to Bird (who had a few short solos), the main stars were trumpeter Bernard Anderson, the rhythm section and singer Walter Brown. McShann and his band arrived in New York in February 1942 and made a strong impression but World War II made it difficult for any new orchestras to catch on. There was a final session in December 1943 without Parker, but McShann was soon drafted and the band broke up. After being discharged later in 1944, McShann briefly reformed his group but soon moved to Los Angeles where he led combos for the next few years; his main attraction was the young singer Jimmy Witherspoon.

McShann was in obscurity for the next two decades, making few records and mostly playing in Kansas City. In 1969 he was rediscovered and McShann (who had first sung on records in 1966) was soon a popular pianist/vocalist. Sometimes featuring violinist Claude Williams, he has toured constantly, recorded frequently and appeared at many jazz festivals since then, being active into the mid-'90s. Jay McShann, who has recorded through the years for Onyx (the 1940 radio transcriptions), Decca, Capitol, Aladdin, Mercury, Black Lion, EmArcy, Vee-Jay, Black & Blue, Master Jazz, Sackville, Sonet, Storyville, Atlantic, Swingtime and Music Masters, among others, is a vital pianist and an effective blues vocalist who keeps a classic style alive. —*Scott Yanow*

★ **Blues from Kansas City** / Apr. 30, 1941-Dec. 1, 1942 / GRP ✦✦✦✦✦

This CD surpasses all former collections of pianist Jay McShann's early recordings, for it comprises of every commercial side made by McShann during 1941-43, including 11 delightful, if rarely heard, trio and quartet numbers (featuring McShann, bassist Gene Ramey and drummer Gus Johnson), along with four lesser-known vocals by the limited but talented Walter Brown that are normally skipped. The result is as complete a musical picture of Jay McShann's early piano style and his orchestra (at least how they sounded in the studios) as is possible. Altoist Charlie Parker has five influential if brief solos (best is "Sepian Bounce") and trumpeters Orville Minor and Buddy Anderson, altoist John Jackson and Paul Quinichette on tenor also have their spots. However, McShann is clearly the main star of this definitive set by the last of the great Kansas City swing big bands. Highly recommended. —*Scott Yanow*

The Band that Jumps the Blues! / Nov. 15, 1947-1949 / Black Lion ✦✦✦✦

This collector's LP from the British Black Lion label features pianist Jay McShann during his post-war period, when he was often based in Los Angeles and recording for Swingtime. McShann backs singer Jimmy Witherspoon on "Skid Row Blues" (the alternate take is the one included), and vocalist Crown Prince Waterford is on one number. Otherwise, McShann heads medium-size bands from 1948-49 that mostly lack any big names, although the young trumpeter Art Farmer and tenor saxophonist Maxwell Davis make appearances. There are a few vocals by Lois Booker and Maxine Reed, but the emphasis is on ensemble work and concise solos that fall between swing and early R&B. Spirited music, much of which has not been fully reissued on CD yet. —*Scott Yanow*

McShann's Piano / Aug. 1966 / Capitol ✦✦✦✦

Jay McShann's first recording in a decade (and first official full-length LP) is a fine showcase for the pianist, who takes vocals on three of the 11 selections. McShann is accompanied by guitarist Chuck Norris, electric bassist Ralph Hamilton and either Paul Gunther or Jesse Price on drums. The material is mostly blues-oriented (including "Vine Street Boogie," "Confessin' the Blues" and "Dexter Blues"), although there are a few departures, including "Yardbird Waltz," "Moten Swing" and "The Man from Muskogee." Throughout, McShann's blend of swing, stride, boogie and blues is quite appealing, making one wish that this worthy LP was reissued on CD. —*Scott Yanow*

Confessin' the Blues / Mar. 28, 1969 / Classic Jazz ✦✦✦

Pianist Jay McShann sticks to the blues on this enjoyable release, not only welcoming bassist Roland Lobligeois and drummer Paul Gunther but, in a rare (and purely instrumental role) as a sideman, guitarist T-Bone Walker. McShann takes vocals on several of the selections and contributes his accessible brand of blues piano. The results are enjoyable if not essential. A bit more imagination could have gone into picking out a more inventive repertoire. —*Scott Yanow*

The Big Apple Bash / Aug. 3, 1971-Aug. 10, 1971 / New World ✦✦✦✦✦

Pianist Jay McShann has spent much of his career being classified as a blues pianist when in fact he is a flexible swing stylist. On this excellent release, McShann appears with two groups of all-stars. His original "Crazy Legs and Friday Strut" and "Georgia on My Mind" find him joined by Herbie Mann (on flute and tenor), baritonist Gerry Mulligan and a rhythm section that includes guitarist John Scofield. The other selections (two standards, Duke Ellington's "Blue Feeling" and McShann's own "Jumpin' the Blues") are performed by an octet also featuring Mann, altoist Earle Warren, trumpeter Doc Cheatham, trombonist Dicky Wells and Scofield. The unusual grouping of swing, bop and modern stylists is successful (the material is fairly basic) and Janis Siegel's guest appearance for a vocal duet with McShann on "Ain't Misbehavin'" works. —*Scott Yanow*

Going to Kansas City / Mar. 6, 1972 / New World ✦✦✦✦

This set, originally put out on Master Jazz and the Australian Swaggie label, features pianist Jay McShann at the peak of his powers. Teamed up with a couple of fine swing tenors (Buddy Tate, who doubles on clarinet, and Julian Dash), bassist Gene Ramey and drummer Gus Johnson, McShann romps through some forgotten numbers from the book of his 1940s big band (including "Say Forward, I'll March" and "Four Day Rider"), a few Count Basie-associated tunes, and a couple of basic originals, taking two bluesy vocals. The set gives listeners a strong sampling of Jay McShann's accessible and swinging music. —*Scott Yanow*

Man from Muskogee / Jun. 4, 1972 / Sackville ✦✦✦✦✦

Pianist-vocalist Jay McShann was in the early part of his comeback when he recorded this superior quartet session with violinist Claude Williams (a veteran who was also on the verge of finally being discovered), bassist Don Thompson and drummer Paul Gunther in 1972. Reissued on CD, the fine swing date is so enjoyable that it makes one wonder how McShann and especially Williams had remained so obscure for the past 20 years. McShann (who takes four spirited vocals) leads the quartet through veteran standards and a few blues with the highlights including "After You've Gone," "Yardbird Suite," "Hootie Blues" and "Jumpin' at the Woodside." Recommended. —*Scott Yanow*

Kansas City Memories / Jul. 18, 1973+Jul. 31, 1973 / Black & Blue ✦✦✦

Vine Street Boogie / Jul. 3, 1974 / Black Lion ✦✦✦✦

Pianist Jay McShann's solo performance at the 1974 Montreux Jazz Festival still sounds fresh and lively over two decades later. He performs six mostly blues-based originals (including "Hootie Blues," "Confessin' the Blues" and "Yardbird Waltz"), adding an occasional vocal. In addition, because this concert took place shortly after the death of Duke Ellington, McShann performs respectful versions of Duke's "Satin Doll" and "I'm Beginning to See the Light." A fine all-round effort by a classic veteran. —*Scott Yanow*

Crazy Legs and Friday Strut / Jul. 1, 1976 / Sackville ✦✦✦✦✦

Pianist Jay McShann and tenor saxophonist Buddy Tate are well showcased on this set of duets. Tate leaves his clarinet in the case, and McShann refrains from vocalizing. The results are melodic but swinging instrumental duets, with the emphasis on veteran standards. Highlights of this surprising and successful encounter include "My Melancholy Baby," a three-song "Ellington Medley" and "Rock a Bye Basie." —*Scott Yanow*

After Hours / Apr. 12, 1977 / Storyville ✦✦✦

Other than the opening "Doo-Wah-Doo" and the closing "Cherry Red," both of which include guitarist Thomas Muller, bassist Ole Skipper Mosgard and drummer Thorkild Moller, this is a set of unaccompanied piano and vocals by the great veteran Jay McShann. The music is typical for McShann, with veteran blues (such as "After Hours" and "How Long Blues"), the standard "Ace in the Hole," and some swinging boogie-based originals, plus "Yardbird Waltz." A fine all-around effort, although this Storyville LP is a bit obscure. —*Scott Yanow*

The Last of the Blue Devils / Jun. 29, 1977-Jul. 1, 1977 / Atlantic ✦✦

Kansas City Hustle / Jun. 20, 1978-Jun. 21, 1978 / Sackville ✦✦✦✦

Recorded during the same two-day period that resulted in a Fats Waller tribute, this solo recital by pianist Jay McShann finds him playing four swing era standards, three basic blues originals, "Since I Lost My Baby I Almost Lost My Mind" and "'Round Midnight." As usual, McShann drenches the songs he interprets with the blues, while always swinging; his bass lines are always a joy. —*Scott Yanow*

Music Map

Miscellaneous Instruments

A few of the more famous examples of "miscellaneous instruments" being utilized in jazz:

Bagpipes
Rufus Harley

Bass Saxophone
Adrian Rollini
Spencer Clark
Joe Rushton (with Red Nichols in the 1950s)
Charlie Ventura

Celeste
Meade Lux Lewis

C-Melody Sax
Frankie Trumbauer

Comb
Red McKenzie

Conch Shells
Steve Turre

Contrabass Clarinet
Anthony Braxton • James Carter

English Horn
Bob Cooper • Paul McCandless

Goofus and Hot Fountain Pen
Adrian Rollini

Harpsichord
Johnny Guarnieri (with Artie Shaw's Gramercy Five)

Mandolin
Dave Grisman • John Abercrombie

Marimba
Dave Samuels

Mellophone
Dudley Fosdick (in 1920s with Red Nichols)
Hot Lips Page
Don Elliot

Mellophonium
Gene Roland
Ray Starling

Nagaswaram
Charlie Mariano

Piccolo
Alphonse Picou (famous "High Society" solo
later transferred to clarinet)

Puccolo (whistling)
Ron McCroby

Reed Trumpet
Eddie Harris

Sarussophone
Sidney Bechet
(1924 recording of "Mandy Make Up Your Mind")

Siren
Firehouse Five Plus Two
Rahsaan Roland Kirk

Sitar
Collin Walcott

Slide Saxophone
Snub Mosley

Steel Drums
Andy Narell

Tympani
Vic Berton • Max Roach

Vocorder
Herbie Hancock

In His Own Category
Rahsaan Roland Kirk (Stritch, Manzello, trumpophone,
slidesophone, black puzzle flute, black mystery pipes,
claviette, flexafone)

A Tribute to Fats Waller / Jun. 20, 1978-Jun. 21, 1978 / Sackville ◆◆◆
Jay McShann does not sound at all like Fats Waller, but he is effective during this set of unaccompanied piano solos (no vocals) in bringing back to life nine of Waller's tunes, in his own way. A more blues-based improviser than Waller, with a sparser left hand (swing rather than stride), McShann is in spirited form on such numbers as "Honeysuckle Rose," "All My Life," "Lulu's Back in Town" and "I'm Gonna Sit Right Down and Write Myself a Letter." —*Scott Yanow*

Tuxedo Junction / Aug. 24, 1980 / Sackville ◆◆◆
Veteran pianist Jay McShann has recorded extensively for the Canadian Sackville label, and all of those LPs (most have not yet been reissued on CD) are easily recommended to fans of swing and blues piano. This date matches McShann in duets with bassist Don Thompson, interpreting a pair of originals and such standards as "Tuxedo Junction," "Robbins Nest" and "Do Nothing till You Hear from Me." McShann stretches out longer than usual on the tunes and comes up with plenty of fresh ideas, even on songs he has played a countless number of times. —*Scott Yanow*

Swingmatism / Oct. 20, 1982-Oct. 21, 1982 / Sackville ◆◆◆◆

At Cafe Des Copains / Aug. 17, 1983-Sep. 27, 1989 / Sackville ◆◆◆

Just a Lucky So and So / Aug. 24, 1983 / Sackville ◆◆◆◆◆
Pianist/vocalist Jay McShann was having a full-fledged comeback at the time of this Sackville date, which has been reissued on CD. Teamed with Jim Galloway (who doubles on soprano and baritone), bassist Don Thompson and drummer Terry Clarke, McShann is in a particularly good mood on such standards as "When I Grow Too Old to Dream," "Red Sails in the Sunset" and even "On a Clear Day You Can See Forever." This set gives one a good sampling of Jay McShann's timeless playing. —*Scott Yanow*

Airmail Special / Aug. 1985 / Sackville ◆◆◆◆
Pianist Jay McShann, bassist Neil Swainson and drummer Terry Clarke swing up a storm throughout this joyful set. They interpret eight standards, mostly from the 1930s, including "Airmail Special," "Drop Me Off in Harlem," "Blue Lou" and McShann's famous "Jumpin' the Blues." Although few real surprises occur, these renditions are enthusiastic and swinging, and thus very enjoyable. —*Scott Yanow*

Paris All-Star Blues: A Tribute / Jun. 13, 1989 / Music Masters ◆◆◆◆◆
The Jay McShann orchestra of the early 1940s, best known for having among its sidemen Charlie Parker, only lasted a few years, but made its impact on jazz history. In 1989, pianist McShann had a rare opportunity to record with a big band, a truly all-star outfit. Included among the illustrious players on this CD are trumpeters Clark Terry, Terence Blanchard and Carmell Jones, trombonist Al Grey, the tenors of Hal Singer, Jimmy Heath and James Moody, altoists Benny Carter and Phil Woods, bassist Jimmy Woode, drummer Mel Lewis, and vocalist Ernie Andrews, among others. With arrangements by Ernie Wilkins and Nat Pierce, virtually all of the players have opportunities to solo, and one comes away particularly impressed by the versatility of Andrews, who fills the roles of a lot of different singers. Highly recommended. —*Scott Yanow*

Hootie & Hicks/Missouri Connection / Aug. 14, 1992+Aug. 15, 1992 / Reservoir ◆◆◆

Medeski, Martin & Wood

f. 1992
Group / Post-Bop, Soul-Jazz
Organist John Medeski, percussionist Billy Martin, and bassist Chris Wood formed the band that bears their names in New York City in 1992. The members had previously played with such avant-garde jazz groups as the Lounge Lizards, the Mandala Octet, John Zorn's Masada, and Marc Ribot's Shrek. The band's funky version of jazz fusion and deep, improvisatory grooves earned them a stellar reputation on the club circuit as a live act, and their shows are frequently taped and traded by their steadily growing fan base, creating an almost Grateful Dead-like atmosphere. Their 1992 debut, *Notes from the Underground*, featured the band's reinvention of classics by jazzmen like Wayne Shorter and Duke Ellington, and 1995's *Friday Afternoon in the Universe* is the closest they have come to fully capturing the improvisational flair that fires their live performances. —*Steve Huey*

Notes from the Underground / Dec. 15, 1991-Jan. 23, 1992 / Accurate Jazz ◆◆◆◆

Friday Afternoon in the Universe / Jul. 24, 1994-Jul. 26, 1994 / Gramavision ◆◆◆◆◆

● **It's a Jungle in Here** / 1995 / Gramavision ◆◆◆◆◆

Shack Man / 1996 / Gramavision ◆◆◆◆
Medeski, Martin & Wood's *Shack Man* is the best example to date of the trio's cerebral fusion of soul-jazz, hip-hop and post-punk worldbeat. Relying on a laidback, nearly formless groove for most the album, the group never really works up a head of steam, nor does it really catch fire—it simply simmers. None of the musicians

have the skills to take solos, so the record just rolls along on a lazy groove, rarely rising above the level of background music. *Shack Man* is the kind of album that will appeal to soul-jazz beginners, or listeners that don't really have a concept of the genre. For aficionados, the lack of grit in the groove or instrumental abilities makes the record rather tedious. —*Leo Stanley*

Brad Mehldau

Piano / Post-Bop
Brad Mehldau is another of the plethora of young jazz pianists in the '90s who have adopted Bill Evans as their role model. Yet while the influence of Evans still thoroughly dominates Mehldau's introspective manner, harmonic constructions, and preferred format (the piano trio), he is one of the more absorbing and thoughtful practitioners within that idiom, and he is receptive to the idea of using material from the rock era (Paul McCartney's "Blackbird," for example). Though Mehldau's training is primarily classical, his interest in jazz began early. He played in the Hall High School jazz band of Hartford, CT, winning Berklee College's Best All Around Musician award while still in his junior year at high school. He studied jazz at New York's New School for Social Research under Fred Hersch, Junior Mance, Kenny Werner and Jimmy Cobb. Cobb soon hired him to play in his band Cobb's Mob, and Mehldau also played and recorded with the Joshua Redman Quartet before forming his own trio in 1994 and recording his first Warner Bros. album *Introducing* in 1995. —*Richard S. Ginell*

● **Introducing Brad Mehldau** / Mar. 13, 1995+Apr. 3, 1995 / Warner Brothers ◆◆◆◆
Pianist Brad Mehldau's debut as a leader features his straightahead style in trios with either Larry Grenadier or Christian McBride on bass and Jorge Rossy or Brian Blade on drums. The well-rounded set is highlighted by tasteful and swinging versions of five standards (including John Coltrane's "Countdown," "It Might as Well Be Spring" and "From This Moment On") and four of the pianist's originals. This CD (which is sometimes available at a budget price) serves as a fine start to what should be a productive career. —*Scott Yanow*

Art of the Trio, Vol. 1 / Jan. 28, 1997 / Warner Brothers ◆◆◆
At this point in time, pianist Brad Mehldau's style falls between Keith Jarrett and Bill Evans, being heavily influenced by the voicings of the latter and the free yet lyrical improvising of the former. With fine backup work by bassist Larry Grenadier and drummer Jorge Rossy, Mehldau explores five standards (including the Beatles' "Blackbird" and "Nobody Else But Me") and four originals, coming up with melodic yet adventurous ideas. Mehldau displays much potential for the future. —*Scott Yanow*

Myra Melford

b. Jan. 5, 1957, Glencoe, IL
Piano / Avant-Garde
A powerful pianist and a very original composer, Myra Melford studied with Art Lande at Evergreen State College in Washington and with Henry Threadgill in New York. She worked with Leroy Jenkins, co-led a group with flutist Marion Brandis (recording some cassettes for the Nisus label) and made a few albums for Enemy and an outstanding quintet set for Hat Art in 1994. —*Scott Yanow*

Eleven Ghosts / Feb. 11, 1994-Feb. 12, 1994 / Hatology ◆◆◆◆

● **Even the Sounds Shine** / May 5, 1994-May 6, 1994 / Hat Art ◆◆◆◆◆
Pianist Myra Melford is one of the leaders of the avant-garde of the 1990s. Her lengthy compositions are episodic yet logical, building up logically to passionate levels yet leaving room for quieter moments; she is a master of dynamics. Her melodies are strong but her sideman also have the option to improvise fairly freely within the context of the music. On this CD Melford is fortunate to have such versatile players as the powerful trumpeter Dave Douglas, the very impressive Marty Ehrlich on alto, clarinet and bass clarinet, bassist Lindsey Horner and drummer Reggie Nicholson. Despite their presence, Myra Melford is consistently the most interesting improviser and her accompaniment behind the horn solos constantly drive and push her musicians to play at their maximum creativity. Overall this is a memorable set of innovative jazz well deserving of several listens. —*Scott Yanow*

Alive in the House / Oct. 19, 1995 / Hat Hut ◆◆◆◆

The Same River, Twice / Jan. 25, 1996-Jan. 26, 1996 / Gramavision ◆◆◆◆◆

Gil Melle

b. Dec. 31, 1931, New York, NY
Baritone Saxophone / Hard Bop, Computer Music
A true renaissance man, Gil Melle began his career as a post-bop baritone saxophonist who also composed and painted, later branching out into a wide variety of artistic and scientific fields. He abandoned jazz fairly early on in his career, choosing to compose a number of film and television scores and experiment with elec-

tronic music, instead. Then again, Melle's music wasn't strictly jazz—it was a hybrid of jazz, drawn from Duke Ellington in particular, and classical music, which he called "primitive modern." That "primitive modern" music was on display on a series of albums for Blue Note and Prestige in the late '50s. Following that series, Melle only released records sporadically, but he kept amazingly busy, composing scores, pioneering electronic music, building specialized computers and synthesizers, painting, piloting, restoring automobiles and planes, as well as keeping an antiquarian microscopical instrumentation collection.

Melle was born in New York City, where he was raised by a family friend after his parents abandoned him at the age of two. As a child, he began painting (he won several national painting competitions as a preteen) and playing saxophone as a teen. Before he was 16 years old, he was playing several jazz clubs in Greenwich Village. At the age of 19, he signed to Blue Note, becoming the first Caucasian on the label's roster. At Blue Note, he released five 10-inch records before recording his first full-length, 12-inch LP, *Patterns in Jazz*, in 1956. In addition to recording and performing jazz, Melle continued with his artwork, and his paintings and sculptures were displayed at several New York galleries; in addition, his art was featured on his own albums, as well as records by Miles Davis, Sonny Rollins and Thelonious Monk. He left Blue Note shortly after the *Patterns in Jazz* sessions, signing with Prestige. Between 1956 and 1957, he recorded three albums for Prestige—*Primitive Modern*, *Gil's Guests*, and *Quadrama*—before deciding to halt his career as a traditional jazz bandleader.

Melle moved to Los Angeles in the '60s, where he began to compose scores for film and television. Over the next 30 years, he wrote scores for over 125 films. He also began working with electronic music, building his own synthesizers, including (arguably) the first drum machine, and performing with the first all-electronic jazz band, the Electronauts, at the 10th Monterey Jazz Festival. In 1967, he returned to recording with *Tome VI*, an all-electronic jazz album released on Verve. He continued to pioneer electronic music, writing scores for *Night Gallery* and *The Andromeda Strain* entirely with synthesizers, which was unheard of at the time. In addition to writing music for films, he composed several symphonies, which he performed with symphony orchestras in Toronto, London and New Zealand.

As of the mid-'90s, Melle decided to concentrate on the visual arts, in particular his computer-based digital painting, which drew great acclaim from art critics across America. —*Stephen Thomas Erlewine*

● **Patterns in Jazz** / Apr. 1, 1956 / Blue Note ✦✦✦✦✦

Like the modern art that stormed the art world in the '50s, *Patterns in Jazz*, Gil Melle's debut album for Blue Note, is filled with bright, bold colors and identifible patterns that camouflage how adventurous the work actually is. On the surface, the music is cool and laidback, but close listening reveals the invention in Melle's compositions and arrangments of the standards "Moonlight in Vermont" and "Long Ago and Far Away." Part of the charm of *Patterns in Jazz* is the unusual instrumental balance of Melle's bari sax, Eddie Bert's trombone, Joe Cinderella's guitar and Oscar Pettiford's bass. These low, throaty instruments sound surprisingly light and swinging. Compared to the two standards, Melle's original compositions are a little short on melody, but they give the musicians room to improvise, resulting in some dynamic music. Ultimately, *Patterns in Jazz* is cerebral music that swings—it's entertaining, but stimulating. —*Stephen Thomas Erlewine*

Primitive Modern/Quadrama / Apr. 1, 1956-Apr. 26, 1957 / Original Jazz Classics ✦✦✦

This two-fer is an odd mix of jazz arrangements and pseudoclassical third-stream compositions, with the presence of musicians like Shadow Wilson, not usually found in such settings. It is ultimately a mixed message, for Melle fans only. —*Ron Wynn*

Gil's Guests / Aug. 10, 1956-Jan. 18, 1957 / Original Jazz Classics ✦✦✦✦

Baritonist Gil Melle's recordings are usually a bit unusual and this CD reissue is no exception. Melle's nine compositions are performed by one of three sextet/septets featuring either Art Farmer, Kenny Dorham or Donald Byrd on trumpets, Hal McKusick or Phil Woods on alto, guitarist Joe Cinderella, bassist Vinnie Burke, drummer Ed Thigpen and sometimes either Julius Watkins on French horn or Don Butterfield on tuba. The charts are unpredictable and often dramatic, looking ahead towards a musical future that never occurred. Watkins takes solo honors during his three appearances. —*Scott Yanow*

Tome VI / 1967 / Verve ✦✦✦

Waterbirds / 1970 / Jazz Chronicles ✦✦✦

It features more recent experimentation in electronics. —*David Szatmary*

Mindscape / 1991 / Blue Note ✦✦✦

Sergio Mendes

b. Feb. 11, 1941, Niteroi, Brazil

Piano / Latin Pop, Soft Rock, Samba, Bossa Nova

A pianist, composer and bandleader inextricably linked to the bossa nova craze of the 1960s, Sergio Mendes was born on February 11, 1941 in Niteroi, Brazil. After rising to prominence as the leader of the Bossa Nova Trio, he settled in the US in 1964 and worked on recordings by Antonio Carlos Jobim and Art Farmer. A year later Mendes formed Brasil '65, the first incarnation of the group rechristened several months later as the more famous Brasil '66.

In addition to Mendes, Brasil '66—once marketed as "a delicately mixed blend of pianistic jazz, subtle Latin nuances, John Lennon/Paul McCartney style, some Henry Mancini, here and there a touch of Burt Bacharach, cool minor chords, danceable upbeat, gentle laughter and a little sex"—comprised vocalist/percussionist Jose Soares, bassist/vocalist Bob Matthews, drummer Jao Palma and singer Janis Hansen. Most importantly, the group also featured vocalist Lani Hall, the wife of musician and A&M Records cofounder Herb Alpert, who released their debut *Sergio Mendes and Brasil '66* and watched it rise into the Top Ten on the strength of the hit "Mas Que Nada."

Equinox followed the next year, spawning the minor hits "Night and Day," "Constant Rain (Chove Chuva)" and "For Me." In 1968, *Look Around* rocketed Brasil '66 to the Top Five, while *Fool on the Hill* reached the Top Three, launching the hit title track (a Beatles cover) as well as a smash rendition of Simon and Garfunkel's "Scarborough Fair." A cover of Otis Redding's "(Sittin' On) The Dock of the Bay" highlighted 1969's *Crystal Illusions*, which also notched the minor hit "Pretty World."

Apart from a rendition of "Wichita Lineman" which garnered some airplay, 1969's *Ye-Me-Le* fared poorly, barely cracking the Top 75; after 1971's *Stillness* met with virtually no commercial response, Mendes changed the group's name to the more forward-thinking Brasil '77, but to little avail—after the chart failure of 1972's *Primal Roots*, the band's long association with A&M ended, and they moved to the Bell label for 1973's *Love Music*. By 1975's *Sergio Mendes*—his first solo effort—he had moved to Elektra; after re-launching the backing unit with 1977's *Sergio Mendes and the New Brasil '77*, Mendes dropped from sight for several years, re-signing to A&M in the early 1980s.

Also titled simply *Sergio Mendes*, his 1983 A&M comeback was his first Top 40 smash in close to 15 years; the single "Never Gonna Let You Go," which featured vocalists Joe Pizzulo and Leza Miller, was his biggest hit to date, reaching the No. 4 position on the US charts, and the track "Rainbow's End" also received considerable airplay. Despite the Top 40 success of the single "Alibis," the 1984 follow-up *Confetti* did not fare as well as its predecessor, and Mendes again disappeared. At the dawn of the 1990s, he formed the new Brasil '99; as the decade progressed, he began exploring Bahian hip-hop. —*Jason Ankeny*

Swinger from Rio / Dec. 7, 1964-Dec. 9, 1964 / Atlantic ✦✦✦

Four Sider / 1966 / A&M ✦✦✦✦✦

Sergio Mendes & Brasil '66 / 1966 / A&M ✦✦✦✦✦

After bouncing around Philips, Atlantic and Capitol playing Brazilian jazz or searching for an ideal blend of Brazilian and American pop, Sergio Mendes struck gold on his first try at A&M—then not much more than the home of Herb Alpert and the Tijuana Brass and the Baja Marimba Band. He came up with a marvelously sleek, sexy formula—dual American female voices singing in English and Portuguese over a nifty three-man bossa nova rhythm/vocal section and Mendes' distinctly jazz-oriented piano, performing tight, infectious arrangements of carefully chosen tunes from Brazil, the US and the UK. The hit was Jorge Ben's "Mais Que Nada," given a catchy, tight bossa nova arrangement with the voice of Lani Hall soaring above the swinging rhythm section. But other tracks leap out at you as well, the obvious rouser in the Brazilian go-go treatment of the Beatles' "Day Tripper," but also the sultry treatment of Henry Mancini's "Slow Hot Wind" and the rapid-fire "Tim Dom Dom." Miraculously, Mendes' original Brasil '66 still sounds fresh today; Mendes' piano especially appears not to have dated at all. —*Richard S. Ginell*

★ **Greatest Hits of Brasil '66** / 1966-1969 / A&M ✦✦✦

A 1970 release, along with a slew of other A&M greatest-hits collections, *Greatest Hits* takes us through a dozen Sergio Mendes and Brasil '66 tunes from the albums *Herb Alpert Presents* through *Crystal Illusions*. Not all of these were hits—indeed, not all of them were singles—and they are not representative of the wide range of Brazilian material that Mendes cut during this period. But you do get a good idea of how Mendes' winningly sexy blend of American female voices, simplified bossa nova rhythms, and lavish Dave Grusin orchestrations captivated mainstream America in the late 1960s. *Look Around* receives by far the most attention, with five tracks—which is only fitting, since in retrospect, that appears to be Mendes' most irresistibly memorable album. For a more comprehensive overview of Sergio Mendes on CD, though, *Classics Volume 18* is a better bet. —*Richard S. Ginell*

Classics / 1966-1986 / A&M ✦✦✦✦

As an overview of Sergio Mendes in both of his A&M periods, this 1987-vintage CD is a far more useful collection than the older *Greatest Hits. Classics* includes ten out of the 12 selections on *Greatest Hits*, replacing "Day Tripper" and "Night and Day" with "One Note Samba/Spanish Flea," "Bim Bom," and "Song of No Regrets" (a more than fair trade), adding two more from the Brasil '77 albums and jumping to the 1980s with two chartmaking hits. Of course, this collection leaves a large gap between 1972 and 1983, during which Mendes recorded for other labels—and frankly the two totally Americanized 1983-84 tracks, "Never Gonna Let You Go" and "Alibis," are so vastly inferior to his earlier stuff that they seem terribly out of place. Nevertheless, as a result, you get a better representation of the great Brasil '66 records and some tastes of things that have happened since. —*Richard S. Ginell*

Equinox / 1967 / A&M ✦✦✦✦✦

Equinox continues the scrumptiously winning sound that Sergio Mendes cooked up in the mid-'60s, this time a bit more fleshed out with John Pisano's guitar, a slightly thicker texture, and even an imitation sitar (this was, after all, 1967). Again, the mix of American pop tunes old and new and Brazilian standards and sleepers is impeccable (although it didn't yield any substantial hits), and the treatments are smooth, swinging, and very much to the point. While Mendes reaps a predictable harvest from Antonio Carlos Jobim—he was one of the first to discover and record "Triste" and "Wave"—he also likes to explore the work of other outstanding Brazilian writers like Jorge Ben, Joao Gilberto and especially Edu Lobo (whose "For Me," with its bright flashes of combo organ, is one of the album's highlights). Lani Hall's star was just rising at this time, and it is her cool, clear voice that haunts the memory most often. Like its predecessor, *Equinox* is exceedingly brief in duration, yet not a motion is wasted. —*Richard S. Ginell*

The Great Arrival / Jan. 1967 / Atlantic ✦✦✦

Fool on the Hill / 1968 / A&M ✦✦✦✦✦

Having hit upon another smash formula—cover versions of pop-rock hits backed by lavish strings, a simplified bossa nova rhythm, and the leader's piano comping—Sergio Mendes and Brasil '66 produced two more chartbusting singles, again turning to the Beatles for sustenance with the title track (No. 6) and Simon and Garfunkel for "Scarborough Fair" (No. 16). But again, the bulk of the album was dominated by Brazilians—and by one in particular, the hugely gifted Edu Lobo, whose dramatic "Casa Forte" and infectious "Upa, Neguinho" were the best of his four songs. The tracks were longer now, the string-laden ballads (arranged by Dave Grusin) more lavish and moody, and Lani Hall emerged as the vocal star of the band, eclipsing her new partner, Karen Philipp, and spelled on "Lapinha" by future Brasil '77 member Gracinha Leporace. Even though he had become thoroughly embedded in the consciousness of mainstream America, Mendes still managed to have it three ways, exposing first-class tunes from little-known Brazilian talent and making commercial hits that also happened to be fine records. Cultural note: the striking fold-out cover art, depicting Brasil '66 at sunset seated on top of a nude woman, somehow made it past the uptight censors of the day and no doubt boosted sales (it was Mendes' highest-charting album at No. 3). —*Richard S. Ginell*

Look Around / 1968 / A&M ✦✦✦✦✦

Sergio Mendes took a deep breath, expanded his sound to include strings lavishly arranged by the young Dave Grusin and Dick Hazard, went further into Brazil, and out came a gorgeous record of Brasil '66 at the peak of its form. Here Mendes released himself from any reliance upon Antonio Carlos Jobim and rounded up a wealth of truly great material from Brazilian fellow travellers—Gilberto Gil's jet-propelled "Roda," Joao Donato's clever "The Frog," Dori Caymmi's stunningly beautiful "Like a Lover," Harold Lobo's Carnaval-esque "Tristeza," and Mendes himself (the haunting "So Many Stars" and the title track). Mendes was also hip enough to include "With a Little Help from My Friends" from the Beatles' *Sgt. Pepper* LP. As things evolved, though, the one track that this album would be remembered for is the only other non-Brazilian tune, Burt Bacharach's "The Look of Love," in an inventive, grandiose arrangement with a simplified bossa beat. The tune just laid there on the LP until Mendes and company performed it on the Academy Awards telecast in 1968. The performance was a sonic disaster, but no matter; the public response was huge, a single was released, and it become a monster, No. 4 on the pop charts. So much for the reported demise of bossa nova; in Sergio Mendes' assimilating, reshaping hands, allied with Herb Alpert's flawless production, it was still a gold mine. —*Richard S. Ginell*

Crystal Illusions / 1969 / A&M ✦✦✦✦✦

The sound and band that served Sergio Mendes well on *Fool on the Hill* remain intact on *Crystal Illusions*, with few modifications. Dave Grusin is right there with a lush, haunting orchestral chart when needed; Lani Hall is thrust further into the

vocal spotlight, as cool and alluring as ever in Portuguese or English. Mendes remained on the lookout for fresh Brazilian tunes, and he comes up with a coup, one of the earliest covers of a Milton Nascimento tune to reach North America, "Vera Cruz" (with Hall's English lyrics, it becomes "Empty Faces"), as well as Dori Caymmi's "Dois Dias." The two singles, the perky "Pretty World" and sax-streaked cover of Otis Redding's "The Dock of the Bay," are nice slices of Mendes pop, though they were not significant hits. And yes, Mendes and Brasil '66 do take a large risk on the title track, a lengthy, kaleidoscopic treatment of an Edu Lobo tune which, inspired perhaps by "MacArthur Park," shattered radio's time barrier at seven minutes and 50 seconds. Yet while Grusin goes into a psychedelic freakout, we get a rare chance to hear Mendes stretch out a bit on electric piano. Weird and overblown, but wonderful. —*Richard S. Ginell*

Ye-Me-Le / 1969 / A&M ✦✦✦

Perhaps the Sergio Mendes/Brasil '66 sound was at last beginning to show signs of wear, for not only didn't *Ye-Me-Le* produce any hits ("Wichita Lineman" reached a lowly No. 95), it is less enterprising and fresh-sounding than its predecessors. There is a surprising shortage of Brazilian material, which was always Mendes' most valuable contribution in the long run, and more reliance upon routine covers of pop-rock standards like "Easy to Be Hard" and "What the World Needs Now." But there are special moments, like the hypnotic "Masquerade" (no relation to the Leon Russell/George Benson hit), Sergio Mihanovich's haunting "Some Time Ago," and another winning treatment of a Beatles tune, "Norwegian Wood," where Mendes cuts loose a killer solo on electric piano (believe it or not, the 45 RPM single version features more of that solo from the LP). —*Richard S. Ginell*

Pais Tropical / 1971 / A&M ✦✦✦

Changing their name and style with the trends of the decade, Sergio Mendes and Brasil '77 assume a brighter, perhaps more garish sound that tries to get closer to what was happening in North America, even when exploring Brazil (other Brazilians were pursuing a similar goal in tropicalismo, with differing results). Gracinha Leporace had replaced Lani Hall completely on lead female vocals by now; like many Brazilian voices, her grittier, Portuguese-accented tone is a bit off-key and it definitely alters the group's sound. Mendes kept on coming up with great Brazilian material like "Asa Branca," and "Tonga," and Sergio gives himself an extended jazz piano showcase on Edu Lobo's wordless tour de force "Zanzibar." On the North American ledger, there is a pop-rock slice of countercultural social protest, "So Many People" (one of three tunes by the gnome-like Paul Williams), and Tom Scott lends a contemporary pop-jazz hand on some tracks with his funky tenor sax. Ultimately, Brasil '77 never came close to becoming the commercial force that Brasil '66 was, but Mendes kept on tweaking the mixture. —*Richard S. Ginell*

Stillness / 1971 / A&M ✦✦

Stillness is a concept album—the title tune opens and closes it in moody stillness—and a transition piece all at once, for Sergio Mendes seemed to be searching for a viable way out of the Brasil '66 formula. Indeed, "Righteous Life," using a different L.A. rhythm section, is really a folk-rock record, a good one, and a far cry from the bossa-propelled '60s. So is the funky voodoo cover of Stephen Stills' "For What It's Worth" in its own way, though the old Brasil '66 sound does come in very handy in a superb treatment of another folk-rock song, Joni Mitchell's "Chelsea Morning." Yet Mendes also experiments with different, more authentically Brazilian rhythm patterns in a brilliantly propulsive rendition of Gilberto Gil's "Viramundo" and a lovely Oscar Castro-Neves/Sebastiao Neto tone poem, "Celebration of the Sunrise." This would also be Lani Hall's farewell to Sergio Mendes, leaving the band in mid-album on the way to becoming Mrs. Herb Alpert and starting a solo career, to be replaced by the Brazilian Gracinha Leporace, who is now Mrs. Sergio Mendes. Overlooked in its day, *Stillness* is the great sleeper album of Sergio Mendes' first A&M period. —*Richard S. Ginell*

In Concert / 1972 / A&M ✦✦✦✦

Recorded outdoors in Los Angeles' Greek Theatre but released only in Japan, this live album features a thoroughly Brazilian-accented incarnation of Brasil '77. It is revealing to find out how explosive this group could be in live performance, unshackled from the tight structures in the studio. Brazil '77 boils at a particularly high flame in the lengthy "Viramundo" and "Carnival Medley" (the latter a preview of *Primal Roots*), where the percussion section stirs up tremendously energetic grooves and Sergio gets lots of room to exercise his bop-tinged jazz piano chops. There are, of course, a sprinkling of hits ("Fool on the Hill," "The Look of Love," "Mais Que Nada") in renditions close to the studio versions, with an orchestra playing Dave Grusin's arrangements when needed, along with "The Girl From Ipanema" with an authentic Portuguese vocal from Mendes. By this time, Geri Stevens replaced Karen Philipp as the second female voice, and the impeccable guitar of Oscar Castro-Neves had become a permanent feature of the landscape. —*Richard S. Ginell*

Primal Roots / 1972 / A&M ✦✦

This time, Sergio Mendes freed himself from any commercial expectations, plunged deep into Brazil, and came up with a boldly experimental yet beautifully impressionistic album of Brazilian folk and popular music. Many of the tracks here are ritualistic in structure, with call-and-response vocals, sprinkled with native Brazilian percussion instruments like the agogo, cuica, atabaques and the weird single-string berimbau, creating mysterious moods and grooves. Oscar Castro-Neves—whose guitar shines throughout the album—and bassist Sebastiao Neto wrote one gorgeous tune, "After Sunrise," and Mendes adapts folk songs as well as Baden Powell's "Iemanja" and Dori Caymmi's now-well-known "Promessa de Pescador" to the blend of Brasil '77 female vocals and Brazilian tropical sounds. The record is dominated by a single, gigantic 19-minute piece, "The Circle Game," a rambling, multi-sectioned tour de force with extended Brazilian grooves, properly exotic jazz flute solos from Tom Scott, and dissonant improvisations touching on the jazz avant-garde. Understandably, *Primal Roots* remained dear to Mendes' heart even though it was not a sales blockbuster, and it gives credence to the not-often-floated idea of Mendes as innovator, whose uncompromising explorations of world music sounds place this record years ahead of its time. *—Richard S. Ginell*

Love Music / 1973 / Bell ✦✦

Vintage 74 / Jul. 1974 / Bell ✦✦

Sergio Mendes [1975] / 1975 / Elektra ✦✦✦

Homecooking / 1976 / Elektra ✦✦✦

Sergio Mendes and the New Brasil '77 / 1977 / Elektra ✦✦

Misha Mengelberg

b. Jun. 5, 1935, Kiev, Ukraine
Piano / Avant-Garde, Post-Bop
One of Europe's top jazz pianists, Misha Mengelberg (although born in the Ukraine) is actually Dutch. He studied in the Netherlands and was on Eric Dolphy's famous *Last Date* album in 1964. In 1967 Mengelberg was a founder of the Instant Composers Pool (which sponsors performances by the Dutch avant-garde) and formed a duo with Han Bennink. He has since worked with the ICP Orchestra, the Berlin Contemporary Jazz Orchestra and his own groups and he has recorded adventurous tributes to Thelonious Monk and Herbie Nichols with Steve Lacy. *—Scott Yanow*

Regeneration / Jun. 25, 1982-Jun. 26, 1982 / Soul Note ✦✦✦✦✦

In 1982, very few people were aware of the late pianist Herbie Nichols' name, much less playing his music. The versatile avant-garde pianist Misha Mengelberg gathered together a noteworthy group (comprising trombonist Roswell Rudd, soprano saxophonist Steve Lacy, bassist Kent Carter and drummer Han Bennink) to play three songs apiece by Nichols and Thelonious Monk. The musicians very much understood the composers' purposes, and on such numbers as "Monk's Mood," "Friday the 13th," "Blue Chopsticks" and "2300 Skiddoo" (the latter two had never been recorded with a group larger than a trio before), they come up with definitive treatments. Highly recommended. *—Scott Yanow*

★ **Change of Season** / Jul. 2, 1984-Jul. 3, 1984 / Soul Note ✦✦✦✦✦

After recording an album (*Regeneration*) split between Herbie Nichols and Thelonious Monk compositions, pianist Misha Mengelberg decided to devote a full project to the unjustly neglected Nichols. As with the earlier set, this date also includes soprano saxophonist Steve Lacy and drummer Han Bennink, but this time with trombonist George Lewis and bassist Arjen Gorter. For the first time, seven of Nichols' songs (including "House Party Starting," "Hangover Triangle" and "Change of Season") were performed by a medium-size group, rather than just Nichols' trio, and one can appreciate the formerly unheard colors in the pianist's nearly lost music. It is also a particular pleasure hearing Lewis and Lacy improvising on these challenging, yet fairly straightahead pieces. A gem. *—Scott Yanow*

Who's Bridge / Nov. 8, 1994 / Avant ✦✦✦✦

The Root of the Problem / May 17, 1996-May 19, 1996 / Hatology ✦✦✦✦

Don Menza

b. Apr. 22, 1936, Buffalo, NY
Tenor Saxophone, Arranger / Hard Bop, Bop
Don Menza is a powerful tenor saxophonist who, although able effectively to imitate most of the top stylists (from Coleman Hawkins to John Coltrane), has a distinctive sound of his own. Menza started playing tenor when he was 13. After getting out of the Army he was with Maynard Ferguson's Orchestra (1960-62) as both a soloist and an arranger. A short stint with Stan Kenton and a year leading a quintet in Buffalo preceded a period living in Germany (1964-68). After returning to the US he was with Buddy Rich's big band in 1968, recording a famous solo on "Channel One Suite" that utilized circular breathing and was quite classic. He set-

tled in California, and has worked with Elvin Jones (1969), Louie Bellson, as an educator and in the studios. Don Menza, who has made far too few records, recorded as a leader for Saba (1965) in Germany, Discwasher (1979), Realtime and Palo Alto (the latter two in 1981). *—Scott Yanow*

First Flight / Nov. 1977 / Catalyst ✦✦✦

Tenor saxophonist Don Menza's second recording as a leader (which was preceded by an obscure effort in 1965 for the European Saba label) matches his hard-driving style with trombonist Frank Rosolino, pianist Alan Broadbent and a rhythm section often including two percussionists. Five of the seven songs are Menza originals, ranging stylistically from ballads and bop to the joyful "Samba De Rollins." Unfortunately, this spirited LP (made for the long-defunct Catalyst label) will be difficult to locate. *—Scott Yanow*

Horn of Plenty / May 1, 1979-May 2, 1979 / Voss ✦✦✦✦✦

Tenorman Don Menza's regular sextet of the late 1970s (which also includes trumpeter Chuck Findley, trombonist Bill Reichenbach, pianist Frank Strazzeri, bassist Frank De La Rosa and drummer John Dentz) is heard in fine form on two Ellington/Strayhorn standards and originals by Menza, pianist Frank Strazzeri and Marc Levin. Menza's ability to write catchy, fresh-sounding boppish lines and his fiery solos are two strong reasons to search for this little-known but superior LP. *—Scott Yanow*

Burnin' / 1981 / Real Time ✦✦✦✦✦

The only recording by Don Menza's big band of the early '80s features many of the top Los Angeles-based, jazz-oriented session players of the era. Menza contributed four of the six selections and all of the swinging arrangements; best are "Burnin' (Blues for Bird)," "Tonawanda Fats" and the memorable "Dizzyland." With such soloists as altoist Joe Romano, baritonist Jack Nimitz, pianist Frank Strazzeri, trombonist Bill Reichenbach, Menza's intense tenor, and trumpeters Chuck Findley, Ron King, Don Rader, Bobby Shew and Frank Szabo (all of the trumpeters are featured on "Dizzyland"), the Don Menza Big Band was a mighty if now forgotten orchestra. This album features Menza at the peak of his powers. *—Scott Yanow*

Hip Pocket / Oct. 2, 1981-Oct. 3, 1981 / Palo Alto ✦✦✦✦✦

Don Menza tried a change of pace on this album, doubling on alto and baritone instead of his usual tenor. He has had the misfortune to record the majority of his dates for now-defunct labels, and this LP will be a bit hard to find. Menza teams up with tenorman Sal Nistico, trumpeter Sam Noto, pianist Frank Strazzeri, bassist Andy Simpkins and drummer Shelly Manne for music that is as swinging as one would expect from these players. They perform three of Strazzeri's originals, Menza's "Steppin'," an Alec Wilder obscurity, and Charlie Parker's "Quasimodo." Fine modern bop music. *—Scott Yanow*

● **Live at Claudios** / Aug. 24, 1991 / Sackville ✦✦✦✦✦

The fiery tenor saxophonist Don Menza has had too few opportunities to record as a leader through the years. This rare quartet date with pianist Wray Downes, bassist Dave Young and drummer Pete Magadini ranks with Menza's best. He takes hard-driving solos on four jazz standards (including "Confirmation" and Thelonious Monk's "I Mean You"), a couple of blues by drummer Magadini and his own "Rose Tattoo." This live session finds Menza in top form, showing both humor and versatility in his swinging solos. Recommended. *—Scott Yanow*

Johnny Mercer

b. Nov. 18, 1909, Savannah, GA, d. Jun. 25, 1976, Los Angeles, CA
Vocals, Lyricist / Standards, Traditional Pop
Johnny Mercer's main claim to immortality is his incredible songwriting output, penning the lyrics or music and lyrics to roughly 1,500 songs. Marked by a sophisticated, occasionally whimsical mastery of language and rhymes, many of Mercer's songs have become standards regularly covered by jazz artists. Yet Mercer was also a successful singer, with a relaxed, Southern-accented, jazzy, rhythmically agile delivery that resulted in several major hits in the 1940s. At first, Mercer was torn between acting and songwriting, but having failed to land a part in *Garrick Gaities* in 1930, he ended up writing his first hit, "Out of Breath, Scared to Death of You," for the show. His first charted songwriting hit was Ted Lewis' 1933 recording of "Lazybones." By 1938 he was recording duets with Bing Crosby for Decca and the following year, he was on Benny Goodman's Camel Cavalcade radio program as a featured singer. In 1942, he, Glenn Wallichs and Buddy DeSylva founded Capitol Records, which would eventually become an industry behemoth, and Mercer reeled off a string of hits for his label, including "Atchison, Topeka and Santa Fe," "Ac-Cent-Tchu-Ate the Positive," "Candy" and "Personality." "Atchison" is an especially good example of Mercer's flip, catchy, vocal style. While running Capitol, Mercer the talent scout attracted the likes of Nat Cole, Stan Kenton, Jo Stafford, Peggy Lee and Margaret Whiting to the label, where they had their greatest successes. Among Mercer's most durable lyrics—a highly abbreviated list—are those for "One for My Baby," "Blues in the Night," "Come Rain or Come Shine,"

"My Shining Hour," and "Early Autumn," and his many collaborators have included Harold Arlen, Hoagy Carmichael, Duke Ellington, Jerome Kern, Gordon Jenkins, and Harry Warren. He also contributed to the scores of seven Broadway musicals and several films. Following an album with Bobby Darin and collaborations with Henry Mancini in the early '60s, Mercer's career slowed down under the onslaught of rock 'n' roll, but time has since reconfirmed his status as an American popular music giant. —*Richard S. Ginell*

● **Capitol Collectors Series** / Apr. 6, 1942-Mar. 18, 1949 / Capitol ✦✦✦✦
Today we know Johnny Mercer mainly as the genius songwriter from Savannah, GA., and perhaps tend to forget that he was also one of the most prolific hitmaking singers of the 1940s. This excellent compendium of Mercer's hit singles, plus a pair of his most famous songs ("Blues in the Night" and "One for My Baby") from 78 RPM albums, will definitely give you the idea. Though not the owner of an overpowering, world-beating voice–to his everlasting and needless regret–Mercer had his own Southern hipster charm, with slippery grace notes and swinging turns of phrase that any jazzer would envy. An irony for today's audience is that many of Mercer's biggest hits here–"Candy," "Personality," "Baby, It's Cold Outside"–were not written by him, for he truly was a recording star in his own right and not merely a songwriter out to plug his own material. Paul Weston dresses up most of the charts in period big-band garb, decorated with tasty streaks of strings; the Pied Pipers chirp away most of the time, and Benny Goodman's Orchestra and the King Cole Trio chip in on a track apiece. These records are completely saturated in World War II, GI jivey, moon-June, sentimental atmosphere that place them precisely in their time–and as such, they generate gobs of nostalgia. Informative liner notes, a thorough discography of these 20 sides, and repros of some of the original 78s and sheet music round out this appealing package. —*Richard S. Ginell*

The Uncollected Johnny Mercer (1944) / 1944 / Hindsight ✦✦✦✦
A collection of radio transcripts, they were recorded in 1944 with the Paul Weston Orchestra. —*Kenneth M. Cassidy*

Helen Merrill (Helen Milcetic)

b. Jul. 21, 1930, New York, NY
Vocals / Bop, Post-Bop, Cool
A fine singer with a warm expressive voice, Helen Merrill's infrequent recordings tend to be quite special with plenty of surprises and chance-taking. She started singing in public in 1944 and was with the Reggie Childs Orchestra during 1946-47. Merrill, who was married for a period to clarinetist Aaron Sachs, had opportunities to sit in with some of the top modernists of the time including Charlie Parker, Miles Davis and Bud Powell. She was with Earl Hines in 1952 and started recording regularly for Emarcy in 1954. Her collaboration with Clifford Brown was her first classic. She made several notable EmArcy albums during 1954-58 (including one in 1956 that helped bring Gil Evans out of retirement); all have been reissued in a large box. After recording for Atco and Metrojazz in 1959, she moved to Italy for the next four years, touring often in Europe and Japan. Back in the US, Merrill teamed with pianist/arranger Dick Katz for a pair of notable and unpredictable Milestone dates (1967-68) and then moved to Japan where she was quite popular. Helen Merrill returned to the US in the mid-'70s and has since recorded for Inner City, Owl, EmArcy (including a reunion date with Gil Evans) and Antilles. —*Scott Yanow*

☆ **Complete Helen Merrill on Mercury (1954-1958)** / Feb. 1954-Feb. 21, 1958 / Mercury ✦✦✦✦✦
This four-LP box set, whose contents have been partly reissued on CD, has all of singer Helen Merrill's output for Mercury; only two selections for the Roost label in 1953 precede these definitive recordings. Merrill, whose warm voice was always both distinctive and flexible, could hold her own with the best jazz musicians of the era. Best known of her recordings are her classic collaborations with Clifford Brown on seven selections arranged by Quincy Jones (including "You'd Be So Nice to Come Home To" and "Falling in Love With Love"), but almost as significant was a notable album on which she employed the little-known Gil Evans as arranger, a year before he teamed up with Miles Davis for *Miles Ahead*. Other Mercury dates include work with the Johnny Richards Orchestra, arranger Hal Mooney, flutist Bobby Jaspar and pianist Bill Evans. Highlights include "Glad to Be Unhappy," "Spring Will Be a Little Late This Year," "Anyplace I Hang My Hat Is Home," "Where Flamingos Fly" and "The Things We Did Last Summer," but all 62 selections are well worth hearing. Highly recommended. —*Scott Yanow*

● **Helen Merrill with Clifford Brown** / Dec. 22, 1954-Dec. 24, 1954 / EmArcy ✦✦✦✦✦
Every recording by the short-lived trumpeter Clifford Brown is worth exploring, including his three dates with singers: Dinah Washington, Sarah Vaughan, and this CD reissue with Helen Merrill. Reissued as part of box sets headed by Brown and Merrill, the highly enjoyable Brown/Merrill sessions are also available as this sin-

gle CD. Trumpeter Brown is joined by Danny Bank on baritone and flute, and a four-piece rhythm section including pianist Jimmy Jones and guitarist Barry Galbraith; Quincy Jones provided the arrangements. The music is essentially straightahead bop, yet the seven standards (which include "Don't Explain," "You'd Be So Nice to Come Home To" and "Falling in Love with Love") are uplifted by the presence of Merrill (in top form) and Brown. —*Scott Yanow*

You've Got a Date with the Blues / 1959 / Verve ✦✦✦✦
Helen Merrill dates are always something special. This set for Metrojazz, which has been reissued as a Verve CD, matches the cool-toned yet inwardly heated singer with an all-star sextet arranged by Quincy Jones and featuring solos by trumpeter Kenny Dorham and either Frank Wess or Jerome Richardson on flute and tenor. The repertoire includes versions of "You Go to My Head" and "Just Squeeze Me" sung in French, a couple of numbers by producer Leonard Feather, Duke Ellington's "The Blues From Black, Brown and Beige," and a haunting rendition of "The Thrill Is Gone." Recommended. —*Scott Yanow*

The Artistry of Helen Merrill / Mar. 1964-Aug. 1964 / Mainstream ✦✦✦

Something Special / 1967 / Inner City ✦✦✦✦✦
Helen Merrill has never been shy of taking chances. The music on this out-of-print LP features the singer not only joined in various combinations by some top-notch jazzmen, but framed by tricky and unpredictable arrangements by pianist Dick Katz. Merrill duets with guitarist Jim Hall on "Deep in a Dream"; she is backed by Katz alone on "Here's That Rainy Day," takes "You're My Thrill" (a song she owns) accompanied by Katz and bassist Ron Carter, and is otherwise joined by cornetist Thad Jones and drummer Pete La Roca, in addition to Katz, Hall and Carter. Among the other songs given surprising treatment are "It Don't Mean a Thing," "Baltimore Oriole" and "What Is This Thing Called Love." One of Helen Merrill's finest recordings. —*Scott Yanow*

The Feeling Is Mutual / Nov. 1967 / Milestone ✦✦✦✦✦

A Shade of Difference / Jul. 1968 / Landmark ✦✦✦✦✦
Originally put out by the Milestone label and later reissued by Landmark, this is a superior and consistently surprising effort by singer Helen Merrill. With arrangements provided by pianist Dick Katz and adventurous yet sympathetic playing by Thad Jones on fluegelhorn and cornet, flutist Hubert Laws, altoist Gary Bartz (who is only on Ornette Coleman's "Lonely Woman"), Katz, guitarist Jim Hall, either Ron Carter or Richard Davis, on bass and drummer Elvin Jones, this is a particularly strong jazz vocal date. Merrill's voice was at its prime during the era, and her ability to tackle a wide repertoire and to bring new life to standards (including taking "My Funny Valentine" as a fairly free duet with Ron Carter) makes this a highly recommended effort. —*Scott Yanow*

Sposin' / Oct. 21, 1971-Oct. 25, 1971 / Storyville ✦✦✦✦

Helen Merill / John Lewis / May 17, 1976+Sep. 8, 1976 / Mercury ✦✦✦
Helen Merrill's first American record since 1968 (she had spent much time in Japan) is mostly a duet set with pianist John Lewis; three songs also have flutist Hubert Laws, bassist Richard Davis and drummer Connie Kay. The emphasis is on ballads, with all of the nine songs (other than the pianist's "The Singer") being quite well known. The obvious empathy between Merrill and Lewis is well displayed on such numbers as "Django" (which has rarely been sung), "Angel Eyes," "Alone Together" and "Mad About the Boy." An introspective set full of subtle creativity. —*Scott Yanow*

Chasin' the Bird / Mar. 6, 1979+Mar. 9, 1979 / Inner City ✦✦✦✦
The third collaboration between singer Helen Merrill and pianist/arranger Dick Katz is almost at the level of their first two. A tribute both to George Gershwin and Charlie Parker, Merrill performs eight of the former's songs, a couple of which became Bird tunes with new melody lines ("Embraceable You" is transformed into "Quasimodo," while "I Got Rhythm" becomes "Chasin' the Bird"). Baritonist Pepper Adams, guitarist Joe Puma, bassist Rufus Reid and drummer Mel Lewis join Katz in the quintet, and throughout, Merrill is heard still in prime form. Pity that this worthwhile LP is long out of print. —*Scott Yanow*

Casa Forte / Apr. 11, 1980-May 27, 1980 / Inner City ✦✦✦✦

No Tears, No Goodbyes / Nov. 1, 1984-Nov. 3, 1984 / Owl ✦✦✦

Music Makers / Mar. 1986 / Owl ✦✦✦✦
This is an unusual album, for it features the always flexible singer Helen Merrill and keyboardist Gordon Beck on six trios apiece with either soprano saxophonist Steve Lacy or violinist Stephane Grappelli. Most of the selections are standards (exceptions being Merrill's "Music Makers" and Beck's "And Still She Is with Me"), but all of the songs sound quite fresh, partly due to the unusual instrumentation and also partly because of the players' inventiveness. Highlights include "'Round Midnight" and "When Lights Are Low" (both of which include Lacy) and "A Girl in Calico" and "Lady Be Good" with Grappelli. —*Scott Yanow*

Collaboration / Aug. 18, 1987-Aug. 26, 1987 / EmArcy ♦♦♦♦♦

In 1956, a year before *Miles Ahead,* singer Helen Merrill hired the nearly forgotten arranger Gil Evans to write charts for a dozen songs on one of her record dates. In 1987, they had a reunion, and 11 of the 12 numbers (with "Summertime" taking the place of "You're Lucky to Me") were recorded again. Rather than just a re-creation album, this project found Evans writing fresh arrangements, utilizing three very different ten-pieces: one with a woodwind quintet, another with six horns, and a third that included five strings. This inspired outing, one of the most rewarding sets of Helen Merrill's later dates, was also one of Evans' last great dates and one of his few post-1972 classics. Merrill, who was 57 at the time, is in superb form on such numbers as "Where Flamingos Fly," "A New Town Is a Blue Town," "By Myself" and "Anyplace I Hang My Hat Is Home." A highly recommended CD. —*Scott Yanow*

Duets / Dec. 8, 1988-Dec. 9, 1988 / EmArcy ♦♦♦♦

Singer Helen Merrill and bassist Ron Carter explore 11 standards and an original apiece on this intimate and generally enjoyable set. There is not a great deal of variety, and Merrill's voice has sounded stronger elsewhere, but their versions of "I Fall in Love Too Easily," "A Child Is Born," "Autumn Leaves" and "There Is No Greater Love" are somewhat memorable. One has to certainly admire Merrill's constant desire to take chances in her recordings. —*Scott Yanow*

Just Friends / Jun. 11, 1989-Jul. 5, 1989 / EmArcy ♦♦♦♦

This Is My Night to Cry / Sep. 1989 / EmArcy ♦♦♦♦

Clear out of This World / Jul. 31, 1991-Sep. 3, 1991 / Antilles ♦♦♦♦

A 1992 session with jazz vocalist Helen Merrill's smoky, sometimes sensual, sometimes piercing singing supported by a group including pianist Roger Kellaway, bassist Red Mitchell, and drummer Terry Clarke. The songs are carefully crafted, finely executed standards and ballads for adult audiences. —*Ron Wynn*

Louis Metcalf

b. Feb. 28, 1905, Webster Groves, MO, **d.** Oct. 27, 1981, New York, NY
Trumpet / Classic Jazz

Louis Metcalf seemed to be everywhere in the 1920s but was largely forgotten once the Depression hit, despite remaining active into the late '60s. He played with Charlie Creath in St. Louis in the early '20s, moved to New York, backed a variety of classic blues singers and worked with Willie "The Lion" Smith, Sidney Bechet, Elmer Snowden, Charlie Johnson and Sam Wooding. His most important association was with Duke Ellington, recording with Duke in 1926 and being a regular member of his orchestra during 1927-28. Metcalf's solo style was a contrast to the wa-wa playing of Bubber Miley. He also played with Jelly Roll Morton, King Oliver and Luis Russell and recorded with Bessie Smith in 1931. But after that he stopped recording, leading a band in Montreal and working in the Midwest. Metcalf was back in New York for a few years in the late '30s and spent 1946-52 leading the International Band in Montreal. He recorded obscure sides as a leader for Franwill (1954-55), Stere-O-Craft (1958) and Pickwick (1963); an excellent album for Spivey (1966) finds the trumpeter to have been influenced by bop and playing in a surprisingly modern style. But Louis Metcalf will always be best remembered for his short stint with Duke Ellington 40 years earlier. —*Scott Yanow*

I've Got the Peace Brother Blues / Apr. 1966 / Spivey ♦♦♦♦

Trumpeter Louis Metcalf, best known for playing with Duke Ellington's Orchestra back in 1927, was active into the 1970s. He recorded some isolated sides for Franwill, Stere-O-Craft and Pickwick in 1954-55, 1958 and 1963, but his only full-length album was also his final recording, this 1966 LP. Joined by pianist Sonny White, guitarist Jerome Patterson, bassist Al Matthews, drummer Nelson Cannon and (on one song) label president/singer Victoria Spivey. Metcalf plays seven originals, one by Spivey, and two standards in a style that is surprisingly boppish. Although long forgotten by the 1960s, Metcalf had continued to advance with time, and it is a pity that he was not more fully documented. This increasingly rare LP is worth exploring. —*Scott Yanow*

Mike Metheny

b. 1949, Lees Summit, MO
Fluegelhorn / Crossover Jazz, Hard Bop

The older brother of Pat Metheny, Mike Metheny started off as a classical trumpeter. After graduating from the University of Missouri and serving in the Army, he was encouraged by his brother to play jazz. Already 25, Metheny attended Berklee and soon became a member of the faculty. He switched to fluegelhorn which he felt best suited his soft tone and mellow style and has recorded five albums as a leader thus far for Headfirst (1982), MCA/Impulse and Altenburgh (1995). Based in Kansas City, Metheny (who sometimes utilizes the EVI) has also recorded with Karrin Allyson and is a freelance music journalist. —*Scott Yanow*

● **Blue Jay Sessions** / Nov. 1982 / Headfirst ♦♦♦♦♦

Mike Metheny began his career as a classical trumpeter, gradually switching to jazz; his debut recording finds him sticking to the mellow-toned fluegelhorn. This LP is an excellent showcase for Metheny, who performs one original, his brother Pat's "Ivy," a couple of obscurities, and tunes by Paul Desmond ("Wendy") and Nat Adderley ("Games"). The latter piece adds altoist Jim Odgren to the band, but otherwise the tunes mostly showcase Metheny, who is accompanied by guitarist Bill Frisell (mostly sounding fairly restrained), keyboardist Dick Odgren, bassist Rufus Reid and drummer John Riley. A fairly lyrical date that features Metheny displaying an attractive tone and some nice melodic ideas. —*Scott Yanow*

Day In-Night Out / 1986 / Impulse! ♦♦♦

On all but the opening cut (which utilizes a different rhythm section), fluegelhornist Mike Metheny's second recording matches him with his younger brother, guitarist Pat Metheny, keyboardist Dick Odgren, bassist Rufus Reid and drummer Tommy Ruskin. The material (three originals, Charlie Parker's "Segment," and a variety of melodic obscurities) suits Metheny's soft-toned horn and thoughtful solos well. Pity that this set has been out of print for a while. —*Scott Yanow*

Kaleidoscope / Feb. 19, 1987 / MCA ♦♦♦

Mike Metheny's second of two Impulse recordings is mostly electronic, with Brad Hatfield utilizing a variety of then-modern keyboards. The fluegelhornist/leader doubles on a Steiner E.V.I. (electronic valve instrument) on some numbers, which waters down his tone a bit. With bassist Marshall Wood and drummer John Riley completing the quartet, Metheny performs several group originals, Duke Ellington's "Star Crossed Lovers," and Freddie Hubbard's "Straight Life." In general, the music is atmospheric and sometimes a bit dreamy, and sets a thoughtful mood. —*Scott Yanow*

From Then 'til Now / Jul. 1989-Aug. 1990 / Altenburgh ♦♦♦

Street of Dreams / Feb. 27, 1995 / Altenburgh ♦♦♦♦

Pat Metheny

b. Aug. 12, 1954, LeesSummit,MO'
Guitar, Leader, Composer / Post-Bop, Crossover, Avant-Garde

One of the most original guitarists of the past 20 years (he is instantly recognizable), Pat Metheny is a chance-taking player who has gained great popularity, but also taken some wild left turns. His records with the Pat Metheny Group are difficult to describe (folk-jazz? mood music?) but managed to be both accessible and original, stretching the boundaries of jazz and making Metheny famous enough so he can perform whatever type of music he wants without losing his audience.

Metheny (whose older brother is the trumpeter Mike Metheny) started on guitar when he was 13. He developed quickly, taught at both the University of Miami and Berklee while he was a teenager and made his recording debut with Paul Bley and Jaco Pastorius in 1974. He spent an important period (1974-77) with Gary Burton's group, met keyboardist Lyle Mays and in 1978 formed his group which originally featured Mays, bassist Mark Egan and drummer Dan Gottlieb. Within a short period he was ECM's top artist and one of the most popular of all jazzmen, selling out stadiums. Metheny mostly avoided playing predictable music and his freelance projects were always quite interesting. His 1980 album *80/81* featured Dewey Redman and Mike Brecker in a post-bop quintet, he teamed up with Charlie Haden and Billy Higgins on a trio date in 1983 and two years later recorded the very outside *Song X* with Ornette Coleman. Among Metheny's other projects away from the group were a sideman recording with Sonny Rollins, a 1990 tour with Herbie Hancock in a quartet, a trio album with Dave Holland and Roy Haynes and a collaboration (and tour) with Joshua Redman. Although his *Zero Tolerance for Silence* in 1994 was largely a waste (40 minutes of feedback), Pat Metheny has retained his popularity and remained a consistently creative performer. He has recorded as a leader for ECM (starting in 1975) and Geffen. —*Scott Yanow*

Bright Size Life / Dec. 1975 / ECM ♦♦♦♦♦

Pat Metheny's debut studio album is a good one, a trio date that finds him already laying down the distinctively cottony, slightly withdrawn tone and asymmetrical phrasing that would serve him well through most of the swerves in direction ahead. His original material, all of it lovely, bears the bracing air of his Midwestern upbringing, with titles like "Missouri Uncompromised," "Midwestern Nights Dream" and "Omaha Celebration." There is also a sole harbinger of radical matters way down the road with the inclusion of a loose-jointed treatment of Ornette Coleman's "Round Trip/Broadway Blues," proving that *Song X* did not come from totally out of the blue. Besides the debut of Metheny, this CD also features one of the earliest recordings of Jaco Pastorius, a fully formed, well-matched contrapuntal force on electric bass, though content to leave the spotlight mostly to Metheny. Bob Moses, who like Metheny played in the Gary Burton quintet at the time, is the drummer, and he can mix it up, too. —*Richard S. Ginell*

Watercolours / Feb. 1977 / ECM ✦✦✦✦

Pat Metheny emerges on his second album as an ECM impressionist, generally conforming to the label's overall sound while still asserting his own personality. As the title suggests, there are several mood pieces here that are suspended in the air without rhythmic underpinning, a harbinger for the new age invasion still in the future. Metheny's softly focused, asymmetrical guitar style, with echoes of apparent influences as disparate as Jim Hall, George Benson, Jerry Garcia, and various country guitarists, is quite distinctive even at this early juncture. Metheny's long-running partnership with keyboardist Lyle Mays also begins here, with Mays mostly on acoustic piano but also providing a few mild synthesizer washes. Danny Gottlieb is on drums and ECM regular Eberhard Weber handles the bass. This is essentially the first album by the Pat Metheny Group per se, although the band had yet to find its direction in this somewhat diffuse showing. —*Richard S. Ginell*

★ **Pat Metheny Group** / Jan. 1978 / ECM ✦✦✦✦✦

The first recording by Pat Metheny's Group features the innovative guitarist along with keyboardist Lyle Mays, bassist Mark Egan and drummer Dan Gottlieb. The music is quite distinctive, floating rather than swinging, electric but not rockish and full of folkish melodies. The best known of these six Metheny-Mays originals are "Phase Dance" and "Jaco." This music grows in interest with each listen. —*Scott Yanow*

New Chautauqua / Apr. 1979 / ECM ✦✦✦

Always exploring side routes even at this early stage, Metheny goes it all alone here, overdubbing himself on electric six—and 12-string guitars, acoustic guitar, electric bass, and 15-string harp guitar. Yet this record is basically an indulgence, one where Metheny spins his wheels within the context of the impressionistic ECM ambience, creating pretty sounds but only fleeting streaks of memorable music. The album gets off to a great start on the title track, where Metheny's folk influences come to the fore with a strummed acoustic guitar base and electric guitar overhead. But the lengthy "Long-Ago Child/Fallen Star" drifts aimlessly in a dreamy fashion that only a new age navelgazer could love, and he doesn't grab the listener by the lapels again until the lovely vamp of "Sueno Con Mexico" way down the line. Chalk it up to growing pains. —*Richard S. Ginell*

American Garage / Jun. 1979 / ECM ✦✦✦✦✦

The back liner photo gives the impression of a grungy Midwestern garage band, but no, that doesn't describe this sophisticated jazz-rock quartet, which was simultaneously breaking into mass-market acceptance and away from the contemplative ECM stereotype. The arrangements are more structured, the playing often more intense and searching, with a more pronounced rock influence. On the title track, Metheny digs in and displays some authoritative rock-oriented licks and intensity, and the rhythms on "The Search" have a slight, at times asymmetrical Latin feeling. The nearly 13-minute "The Epic" finds the Metheny group developing some real combustion in the improvised sections as Metheny, keyboardist Lyle Mays, bassist Mark Egan and drummer Danny Gottlieb grow tighter as a unit. In hindsight, some of the music seems a bit too tightly conceived to allow adequate breathing room, but this is still high-quality jazz-rock for its time. —*Richard S. Ginell*

● **1980-1981** / May 26, 1980-May 29, 1980 / ECM ✦✦✦✦✦

Pat Metheny's credibility with the jazz community went way up with the release of this package, a superb two-CD collaboration with a quartet of outstanding jazz musicians that dared to be uncompromising at a time when most artists would have merely continued pursuing their electric commercial successes. From the disbanded Keith Jarrett American quartet came bassist Charlie Haden and tenor Dewey Redman—who alternates with and occasionally plays alongside tenor Michael Brecker—and Jack DeJohnette provides more combustible drumming than Metheny had ever experienced on record before. Yet Metheny's off-kilter wandering on solo electric guitar is a comfortable fit for the post-bop rhythmic crosscurrents of this music. Indeed, Haden and Metheny are in total sympathy, perhaps celebrating their mutual Missouri roots, and Metheny's difficult "Pretty Scattered"—which he mockingly described as "Guitar Revenge!"—nearly manages to stump even Redman and Brecker. The first of the "Two Folk Songs" is a great example of the Metheny folk-jazz fusion, with furious strummed guitar underpinning Brecker's melodic line and excursions on the outside and DeJohnette's spectacular drums. Another remarkable track is "Open," a group improvisation that finds DeJohnette shaping the track's direction with a pushing solo and Metheny and the saxes emerging at the end. The two original LPs were organized so that the more distinctive Metheny fusions were on sides one and four and the overt jazz tracks occupied sides two and three. —*Richard S. Ginell*

As Wichita Falls, So Falls Wichita Falls / Sep. 1980 / ECM ✦✦✦

Intelligent, thoughtful compositions, with excellent solos and ensemble work. —*Ron Wynn*

Offramp / Oct. 1981 / ECM ✦✦✦✦✦

If 1980s *As Wichita Falls, So Falls Wichita Falls* was defined by Pat Metheny's charisma, its less accessible but certainly rewarding successor, *Offramp*, finds him leaning more toward the abstract. But as cerebral as Metheny gets on such atmospheric pieces as "Are You Going with Me" and "Au Lait," his playing remains decidedly lyrical and melodic. Clearly influenced by Jim Hall, the thoughtful Metheny makes excellent use of space—choosing his notes wisely and reminding us that while he has heavy-duty chops, he's not one to beat us over the head with them. Even when he picks up the tempo for the difficult and angular title song, he shuns empty musical aerobics. Throughout the CD, Metheny enjoys a powerful rapport with keyboardist Lyle Mays, who also avoids exploiting his technique and opts for meaningful storytelling. —*Alex Henderson*

Travels / Jul. 19, 1982-Nov. 1982 / ECM ✦✦✦✦

Now well into its gliding Brazilian-tinged mode, the Pat Metheny Group hits the road, as this two-CD set catches the band live in Dallas, Philadelphia, Hartford, Sacramento, and Nacogdoches, TX. Percussionist Nana Vasconcelos is still listed as a "special guest," but ever since Wichita Falls, he had not only been a part of the group, he was the transforming element in the Metheny "sound," adding his various shakers, effects and ethereal vocals. Sidekick Lyle Mays gets deeper into floating, glistening synthesizer textures, but he is still able to take formidable and touching solos on acoustic grand piano. Still experimenting with new hardware, Metheny's work on a detuned guitar synthesizer give the "As Wichita Falls, So Falls Wichita Falls" an exotic Balinese-like sound. Other highlights are the hard Brazilian grooves on "Straight on Red" and "Song for Bilbao," as well as the trademark Metheny glide of "Are You Going with Me?"—and the brief title track has a winning guileless simplicity much like that of Keith Jarrett in a prayerful mood. If you liked the popular *Offramp*, you'll fall for this one too, but get the former album first. —*Richard S. Ginell*

Rejoicing / Nov. 29, 1983-Nov. 30, 1983 / ECM ✦✦✦✦✦

Pat Metheny takes a vacation from his "Group" and performs advanced material with bassist Charlie Haden and drummer Billy Higgins. In addition to Horace Silver's "Lonely Woman," Haden's "Blues for Pat" and three Ornette Coleman tunes, the guitarist plays three of his originals including "The Calling," a lengthy exploration of sounds with his guitar synthesizer. Throughout this excellent set, Metheny and his sidemen engage in close communication and create memorable and unpredictable music. —*Scott Yanow*

First Circle / Feb. 15, 1984-Feb. 19, 1984 / ECM ✦✦✦✦

In *First Circle*, the Pat Metheny Group settled into a lineup that has lasted to this writing—with Metheny, keyboardist Lyle Mays, bassist Steve Rodby and new drummer Paul Wertico forming the core quartet. The ever-restless Metheny also mixes up the music, not quite leaving the Brazilian glide behind but coming up with some fascinating permutations always affixed with his personal stamp. "Forward March," the album opener, is a bizarre parody full of detuned instruments and half-cocked trumpet from Mays; one wonders if this was directed at a few silly skirmishes of the day (Grenada? The Falklands?). "The First Circle" has Brazilian elements, but now in the service of a grander architectural context, while nothing could be simpler and yet more sophisticated than the delicate ballad "If I Could." "End of the Game" might be the best track on the record, equipped with a beautiful pop-flavored set of tunes and harmonies, with a rock beat fused to the floating ambience of South America as personified by the new Argentine percussionist/vocalist Pedro Aznar. "Praise," the closer, is an out-and-out rock tune, an affirmative flip side of "Forward March" and the last of a series of delightful surprises. —*Richard S. Ginell*

The Falcon and the Snowman / 1984 / EMI ✦✦✦

Song X / Dec. 1985 / Geffen ✦✦✦✦✦

W/ Ornette Coleman. Metheny pays tribute to a surprising influence, teaming with Ornette Coleman in a collaboration that shocked everyone with its musical effectiveness. —*Ron Wynn*

Still Life (Talking) / 1987 / Geffen ✦✦✦✦✦

While Brazilian music had captured Metheny's attention since the '70s, he placed an especially strong emphasis on Brazilian elements in the late '80s. A master of uniting seemingly disparate elements as a cohesive whole, the imaginative guitarist effectively combines Brazilian-influenced harmonies and rhythm with jazz, folk and pop elements on "So May It Secretly Begin," "Third Wind," "Minuano (Six Eight)" and other celebrated gems included on the CD *Still Life (Talking)*. The Brazilian leanings are put aside on one of Metheny's most unique offerings ever, "Last Train Home," which boasts a charming Western theme that brings to mind a peaceful journey across the Arizona Desert. That may not sound like the description of a jazz piece, but then, making the unlikely a reality is among Metheny's many admirable qualities. —*Alex Henderson*

Letter from Home / Mar. 1989 / Geffen ✦✦✦✦

Picking up where *Still Life (Talking)* leaves off instead of throwing us a curve ball like *Song X*, the equally triumphant *Letter from Home* stresses Brazilian elements with superb results. While a number of these treasures—including "Beat 70," "Have You Heard" and "Every Summer Night"—were light and accessible enough to enjoy exposure on some "smooth jazz" stations, *Letter* contains the type of depth and honesty that's sorely lacking in most "smooth jazz." Metheny has always known the difference between light and lightweight, and even at his most delicate, avoids entering "muzak" territory. True to form, the improvisor doesn't shy away from making extensive use of technology, but is insightful enough to do so in a very warm and soulful fashion. Like *Still Life, Letter from Home* is a fine example of a CD that is both a commercial and an artistic success. —*Alex Henderson*

Question and Answer / Dec. 21, 1989 / Geffen ✦✦✦✦✦

After spending most of 1989 on tour with his regular unit, guitarist Pat Metheny had a few days free and decided to jam in a studio with two of his favorite musicians: bassist Dave Holland and drummer Roy Haynes. Eight hours later they emerged with more than enough material for a CD. Although Metheny had not planned on releasing the performances, the music was too good to let waste in the vaults. Metheny really stretches himself on his five originals, Ornette Coleman's "Law Years" and three standards while the interplay between Metheny, Holland and Haynes is very impressive. They all seem to think alike and delight in stretching the structures without breaking them; the Metheny-Haynes tradeoff on "All the Things You Are" is a highlight. —*Scott Yanow*

Secret Story / Jul. 1992 / Geffen ✦✦✦✦

This intriguing set is quite adventurous in its own way, covering different styles of world music. "Above the Treetops" uses the eerie-sounding Pinpeat Orchestra of the Royal Ballet and the Choir of the Cambodian Royal Palace (!), while other selections find Metheny not only playing electric and acoustic guitars but a Synclavier (to simulate an accordion), piano, electric bass and even an electric sitar. Some of the pieces (which feature keyboardist Lyle Mays) are more typical of the output of Metheny's Group, while a few others that use members of the London Orchestra are closer to soundtrack music than to improvised jazz. Even with all of the variety, there is plenty of fine guitar playing and lots of thought-provoking music from the always unpredictable Pat Metheny. —*Scott Yanow*

Zero Tolerance for Silence / Dec. 16, 1992 / Geffen ✦

I Can See Your House from Here / 1993 / Blue Note ✦✦✦✦

Guitar giants John Scofield and Pat Metheny teamed up for the first time on records for this CD. The collaboration does take awhile to get going and it is not until the fourth cut, the bluish "Everybody's Party," that the sparks begin to fly; fortunately, the momentum does not let up much throughout the remainder of the CD. All of the selections (including two blues) are originals by either of the guitarists and, with the accompaniment of bassist Steve Swallow and drummer Bill Stewart, this varied set generally lives up to expectations. —*Scott Yanow*

Road to You-Live in Europe / 1993 / Geffen ✦✦✦✦✦

When Metheny celebrates his cerebral side, he usually follows up with something more accessible. After his difficult yet rewarding collaboration with John Scofield, *I Can See Your House from Here*, Metheny stressed accessibility with this captivating live album. The primary focus is on his Brazilian-influenced material from *Still Life (Talking)* and *Letter from Home*, and the very cohesive Metheny Group offers characteristically expressive versions of such favorites as "Have You Heard," "Beat 70" and "Better Days Ahead." While he could have offered a wider variety of material and perhaps revisited some of his early gems, everything he does include comes across as honest and heartfelt. Thankfully, Metheny's emphasis on accessibility and crowd-pleasing doesn't come at the expense of his artistic integrity. —*Alex Henderson*

We Live Here / 1994 / Geffen ✦✦✦✦✦

The first Pat Metheny Group recording in five years is a bit unusual in two ways. The band uses "contemporary" pop rhythms on many of their selections but in creative ways and without watering down the popular group's musical identity. In addition, Metheny for the first time in his recording career sounds a bit like his early influence Wes Montgomery on a few of the songs. With his longtime sidemen (keyboardist Lyle Mays, bassist Steve Rodby and drummer Paul Wertico) all in top form, Metheny successfully reconciles his quartet's sound with that of the pop music world, using modern technology to expand the possibilities of his own unusual vision of creative improvised music. And as a bonus, some of the melodies are catchy. —*Scott Yanow*

Quartet / 1996 / Geffen ✦✦✦

Pat Metheny has had such an unpredictable and diverse recording career that it is somewhat surprising that he has been able to hold on to his great popularity during the past two decades. This set with his "Group," a quartet also featuring keyboardist Lyle Mays, bassist Steve Rodby and drummer Paul Wertico, is generally

quite introspective and is a bit unusual. After touring with his band for nearly a year, the guitarist decided not to record the group's current repertoire, but to instead have a very spontaneous session. Metheny and Mays quickly wrote a full set of new originals (some of which were so open as to be nearly free improvisations) that emphasized their acoustic instruments and the quieter side of their musical personalities. Although a few of the 15 songs use a light groove, many of the pieces are either slow ballads or fairly peaceful sound explorations. Whether fans of the Pat Metheny Group will enjoy the music is open to question, but jazz listeners who like to hear relaxed playing by masterful musicians (and who are patient enough to let the performances develop) will find this to be an interesting if moody release. —*Scott Yanow*

Sign of Four / Dec. 12, 1996-Dec. 15, 1996 / Knitting Factory ✦

This matchup was certainly an unlikely one. The innovative avant-garde guitarist Derek Bailey and the popular and influential Pat Metheny were probably not automatically destined to collaborate. But at the Knitting Factory for a few nights in December 1996 with both Gregg Bendian and Paul Wertico on drums and percussion, Bailey and Metheny joined as one titanic force. It was not a matter of meeting halfway; instead, Metheny willingly played Bailey's free-form music on its own terms. The problem with the results, which have been released as a low-priced three-CD set, is that the music is unremittingly intense, and even during the rare quiet moments, there is little sign of development. Essentially a series of sound explorations with no real beginning or end, the 3 hours and 13 minutes are dominated by noise, dense ensembles and feedback. In other words, this is a real bore for jazz purists. —*Scott Yanow*

Imaginary Day / 1997 / Warner Brothers ✦✦✦✦

More than ever, the Pat Metheny Group is into creating thick, exotic, electronic sonic landscapes, and *Imaginary Day* goes even further out on the cutting edges of technology and global influences than its predecessors. The floating Metheny group signature is often present, but with radically reworked textures, and Brazil seems to be off his international itinerary, replaced by whiffs of repetitive Iranian folk music, Balinese gamelan music and other global influences. Indeed, Metheny only sounds something like his familiar soft-focused self on "A Story Within the Story," playing what amounts to a fine hard-bop solo, and the song-like "Across the Sky." At all other times, he expands his sonic palette on various guitar synthesizers and newly minted guitar mutations, at one point assigning an entire solo piece, "Into the Dream," to the 42-string "pikasso guitar," which sounds like a glittering African zither. "The Roots of Coincidence" is a total departure for the group, a gleefully hard-edged, out-and-out rock piece with thrash-metal and techno-pop episodes joined by abrupt jump cuts. Along with his core lineup of Lyle Mays, Steve Rodby and Paul Wertico, Metheny also includes the duo of multi-instrumentalists Mark Ledford and David Blamires adding various horns and things, and four topline percussionists—Mino Cinelu, Dave Samuels, Glen Velez and Don Alias—replacing departing member Armando Marcal. Through all the experiments, the Metheny Group's music remains uplifting, intelligent, and always accessible to the casual and attentive ear in the late '90s, even as it becomes more portentous. The "words" on the cover art and booklet are written in some kind of strange Esperanto alphabet, with symbols and objects replacing each letter, but there are enough translations in plain English to get you through. —*Richard S. Ginell*

The Metronome All-Stars

Group / Swing, Bop

Metronome Magazine had an annual poll during 1939-61 that picked who their readers considered the top jazz instrumentalists on each instrument for that year. Unlike with other magazine polls, *Metronome* actually recorded the all-stars (trying for the actual winners, but usually also including a few runner-ups) on a fairly regular basis, with sessions gathering the victors of the 1939-42, 1945-50, 1953 and 1956 contests. In most cases the group recorded two songs, and there were short solos (generally one chorus) from practically all of the participants. The early groups were swing-oriented while the later ones were filled with top bop players, but sometimes the combination of players was unusual. Highlights included Benny Goodman playing with many of his alumni in 1940 (including Harry James, Jess Stacy and Gene Krupa), Nat "King" Cole and June Christy sharing the vocal mike on "Nat Meets June" (1946), Dizzy Gillespie, Fats Navarro and Miles Davis trading off in 1949 and Billy Eckstine scatting quite effectively in 1953. A jam on "Billie's Bounce" in 1956 wrapped up the valuable series, which was recorded for labels now owned by Columbia, RCA and Capitol. —*Scott Yanow*

● **The Metronome All-Stars [Tax]** / Feb. 7, 1940-Jan. 10, 1950 / Tax ✦✦✦✦✦

The Metronome All-Stars recording sessions of 1939-50 teamed a wide variety of pollwinners (and runner-ups, when the winners were not available). Some of the dates were recorded by RCA and Capitol. The Columbia dates are on this Tax LP, five sessions in all (including all of the alternate takes) from 1940, 1941, 1942,

1946 and 1950. The first three sessions are dominated by top swing players including Harry James, Cootie Williams, Roy Eldridge, Jack Teagarden, Benny Goodman, Benny Carter, Charlie Barnet, Jess Stacy, Count Basie, Charlie Christian and Gene Krupa, among many others. While the 1946 set has vocals by Nat "King" Cole, Frank Sinatra and June Christy (along with contributions from Charlie Shavers, Johnny Hodges and Coleman Hawkins), the final two titles are strictly bebop, with Dizzy Gillespie, Buddy DeFranco, Lee Konitz, Stan Getz, Lennie Tristano and Max Roach among the illustrious personnel. The solos are brief but usually quite colorful, giving listeners a taste of the many remarkable players who were in their prime during the period. —*Scott Yanow*

Metronome All-Stars 1956 / Jun. 26, 1956-Jul. 18, 1956 / Verve ✦✦✦✦✦
This LP features a variety of great jazz players (the 1956 Metronome All-Stars) performing together. Count Basie's Orchestra plays their hit "April in Paris" with Ella Fitzgerald in what was the first meeting on records between Basie and Fitzgerald. "Everyday I Have the Blues" not only has the duo but Joe Williams, the orchestra goes solo on "Basie's Back in Town" and on "Party Blues" Basie and the two singers have fun with a small group taken from the big band. In addition, George Wallington performs a piano solo ("Lady Fair") and a 21-minute "Billie's Bounce" has solos by an impressive assortment of individualists: trumpeter Thad Jones, altoist Lee Konitz, Al Cohn and Zoot Sims on tenors, clarinetist Tony Scott, baritonist Serge Chaloff, trombonist Eddie Bert, vibraphonist Teddy Cohen, guitarist Tal Farlow, pianist Billy Taylor, bassist Charles Mingus and drummer Art Blakey. This would be the final recording by The Metronome All-Stars (a series that started in the late '30s) and the music on this LP still sounds exciting and joyful. —*Scott Yanow*

Metronome All-Star Bands / Mar. 31, 1937-Jan. 3, 1949 / Bluebird ✦✦✦✦✦
During most of the period 1939-50, *Metronome Magazine* put together all-star sessions featuring their pollwinners; when the winners were not available, other high vote-getters were substituted in their place. This fascinating CD starts off with two numbers from an unrelated 1937 all-star group that features trumpeter Bunny Berigan, trombonist Tommy Dorsey and pianist Fats Waller playing "Blues" and a very memorable rendition of "Honeysuckle Rose." In addition, bands from 1939, 1941, 1946 and 1949 (the years that RCA recorded the pollwinners) are represented. While the 1939 group is practically a Benny Goodman reunion band (including Berigan, Harry James, Tommy Dorsey and Jack Teagarden, among many others) and the 1941 outfit combines many top swing players (such as Goodman, James, Cootie Williams, Dorsey, Benny Carter, Coleman Hawkins, Count Basie, Charlie Christian and Buddy Rich), the 1946 grouping utilizes Woody Herman's First Herd as a nucleus (along with Harry Edison, Cootie Williams, Dorsey, Buddy DeFranco, Johnny Hodges, Harry Carney and Teddy Wilson). The final selections, dating from 1949, find the lineup dominated by top beboppers, including trumpeters Dizzy Gillespie, Miles Davis and Fats Navarro (who trade off during a remarkable passage on "Victory Ball"), J.J. Johnson, Kai Winding, DeFranco, Charlie Parker and Lennie Tristano. Solos are brief during all of these performances (sometimes only eight or 16 bars), but practically every musician gets a chance to be heard. The other Metronome sessions have been reissued on a Tax LP, which covers the Columbia sessions, and by Capitol. This CD, which has all of the Victor sessions' alternate takes, is highly recommended to all serious jazz fans. —*Scott Yanow*

Hendrik Meurkens

b. 1957, Hamburg, Germany
Harmonica, Vibes / Bop, Afro-Cuban Jazz, Brazilian Jazz
Ever since he started taking harmonica solos in the mid-'50s, Toots Thielemans has been without any close competition on his instrument, at least until Hendrik Meurkens arrived on the scene. Born in Germany to Dutch parents, Meurkens began as a vibraphonist, not playing harmonica until he heard Thielemans when he was 19. He traveled to the US to study at Berklee and spent time in Brazil in the early '80s during which he immersed himself in Brazilian jazz. Back in Berlin, Meurkens worked in the studios but also recorded with the Danish Radio Orchestra and had his own jazz group. He made a record in Brazil for the Bellaphon label (1989) and since 1991 has recorded several sets for Concord and Concord Picante as a leader in addition to appearing on records as a sideman with Charlie Byrd. —*Scott Yanow*

Samba Importado / Oct. 1989 / Optimism ✦✦✦

Sambahia / Oct. 1990-Dec. 1990 / Concord Jazz ✦✦✦✦
A nice Afro-Latin date that includes alto sax solos from Pacquito D'Rivera.—*Ron Wynn*

Clear of Clouds / 1992 / Concord Jazz ✦✦✦✦
Hendrik Meurkens, who has the unusual double of harmonica and vibes, is featured with two different groups on this enjoyable CD. Six of the 11 selections were cut in Rio de Janeiro with the underrated trumpeter Claudio Roditi and a spirited Brazilian rhythm section, while the other five (also Brazilian-oriented) features

Meurkens' regular band (which includes Mack Godsbury on soprano and flute) from a Berlin session. Meurkens, who has an appealing sound on harmonica (his strongest instrument), contributed six of the numbers, which blend well with such bossa standards as "Mambo Inn," "Estate" and "No More Blues." The music is pleasing, swinging, and finds the key soloists in fine form. —*Scott Yanow*

● **A View from Manhattan** / Jul. 26, 1993-Aug. 4, 1993 / Concord Jazz ✦✦✦✦✦
Hendrik Meurkens secures his position as the second-best jazz harmonica player (behind Toots Thielemans) with this fine release. Unlike his two earlier Concord recordings, Meurkens sticks to straightahead jazz (rather than Brazilian music) on this set, tackling a variety of challenging material (four of the 11 pieces are his originals) with apparent ease. He comes up with fresh statements on such veteran songs as "Whisper Not," "Naima," "Body and Soul" and "Moment's Notice" and his supporting cast (which includes saxophonist Dick Oatts, trombonist Jay Ashby and pianist Mark Soskin) is consistently strong. This CD gives one an excellent example of Hendrik Meurkens' talents. —*Scott Yanow*

Slidin' / 1994 / Concord Jazz ✦✦✦✦
Most of Hendrik Meurkens' previous recordings have a strong emphasis on Brazilian rhythms, but this CD is more of a modern bop date. With pianists Dado Moroni and Mark Soskin trading off, David Finck and Harvie Swartz sharing the bass spot and guitarist Peter Bernstein and drummer Tim Horner present on most selections, the impressive harmonica player Meurkens improvises fairly freely on material ranging from standards such as "Have You Met Miss Jones" and "All of You" to four of his own straightahead originals. The music is moody yet swinging, demonstrating Hendrik Meurkens' continued growth from his earlier discs. —*Scott Yanow*

October Colors / Nov. 7, 1994 / Concord Picante ✦✦✦✦

Poema Brasileiro / May 21, 1996-May 27, 1996 / Concord Picante ✦✦✦✦

Mezz Mezzrow (Milton Mesirow)

b. Oct. 9, 1899, Chicago, IL, d. Aug. 5, 1972, Paris, France
Clarinet, Tenor Saxophone / Dixieland
Mezz Mezzrow occupies an odd and unique place in jazz history. Although an enthusiastic clarinetist, he was never much of a player, sounding best on the blues. A passionate propagandist for Chicago and New Orleans jazz and the rights of Blacks (he meant well but tended to overstate his case), Mezzrow was actually most significant for writing his colorful and somewhat fanciful memoirs *Really the Blues* and for being a reliable supplier of marijuana in the 1930s and '40s. In the 1920s he was part of the Chicago jazz scene, at first helping the young White players and then annoying them with his inflexible musical opinions. Mezzrow recorded with the Jungle Kings, the Chicago Rhythm Kings and Eddie Condon during 1927-28, often on tenor. In the 1930s he led a few swing-oriented dates that featured all-star integrated bands in 1933-34 and 1936-37. The French critic Hugues Panassie was always a big supporter of Mezzrow's playing and Mezz was well featured on sessions in 1938 with Tommy Ladnier and Sidney Bechet; "Really the Blues" is a near-classic. Mezzrow had his own King Jazz label during 1945-47, mostly documenting ensemble-oriented blues jams with Bechet and occasionally Hot Lips Page. After appearing at the 1948 Nice Jazz festival, Mezzrow eventually moved to France where he recorded fairly regularly during 1951-55 (including with Lee Collins and Buck Clayton) along with a final album in 1959. —*Scott Yanow*

● **1928-1936** / Apr. 6, 1928-Mar. 12, 1936 / Classics ✦✦✦✦✦
Mezz Mezzrow was never that strong a player. His technique was weak, and although he played with enthusiasm and was decent on the blues, he fumbled a lot. However, Mezz did appear on a lot of significant recordings through the years, and some are on this Classics CD. Playing tenor, Mezzrow is heard in 1928 with the Chicago Rhythm Kings, the Jungle Kings (the same group under a different name), Frank Teschemacher's Chicagoans and the Louisiana Rhythm Kings. Those six titles by overlapping bands feature such major players early in their careers as cornetist Muggsy Spanier, clarinetist Frank Teschemacher, pianist Joe Sullivan, Eddie Condon (on banjo) and drummer Gene Krupa; Red McKenzie takes a vocal on "There'll Be Some Changes Made." Also on this CD are eight swing-oriented numbers from 1933-34 by a big band headed by Mezzrow and including such top musicians as trumpeter Max Kaminsky, trombonist Floyd O'Brien, altoist Benny Carter, Bud Freeman on tenor and either Teddy Wilson or Willie "The Lion" Smith on piano. Despite the inclusion of such titles as "Free Love" and "Dissonance," the music is essentially no-nonsense swing. This CD is rounded off by four selections from Art Karle and His Boys (mainly showcases for the dated vocals of Chick Bullock, although trumpeter Frankie Newton is in the backup band) and two songs from Mezz's first 1936 session as a leader. The excellent and often essential music is obviously of greatest interest for the contributions of the many all-stars. —*Scott Yanow*

King Jazz, Vol. 1 / Mar. 27, 1945-Aug. 30, 1945 / GHB ✦✦✦✦✦

In 1945, clarinetist and New Orleans jazz propagandist Mezz Mezzrow started recording sessions for his King Jazz label. The music tended to emphasize ensembles, fairly basic chord structures (lots of lowdown blues, some with bridges) and was most notable for featuring the remarkable soprano saxophonist Sidney Bechet. The selections (most of which were recorded two or even three or four times) had been released through the years in often random fashion. However, in 1997, GHB reissued the entire catalog on this two-CD set, plus the three-disc *Volume Two*. Heard in chronological order, the music can finally be enjoyed in its entirety in coherent fashion. The first volume has 11 piano solos by Sammy Price (a fine blues and boogie-woogie player), a pair of numbers in which Price accompanies singer Pleasant Joseph, and four lengthy band sessions. The latter finds Mezzrow and Bechet joined on the first two dates by trumpeter Hot Lips Page, Price, rhythm guitarist Danny Barker, bassist Pops Foster, and drummer Sid Catlett; the final 21 cuts (from Aug. 29 and 30, 1945) find Mezz and Sidney accompanied by pianist Fitz Weston, Foster and drummer Kaiser Marshall; Douglas Daniels takes the vocal on three versions of "Baby, I'm Cuttin' Out." Although there is a certain sameness to the music after a while, and Mezzrow's sincere flights often run out of gas, the playing of Page and especially Bechet greatly uplift the performances and make this a recommended acquisition to classic jazz collectors. —*Scott Yanow*

King Jazz Story, Vol. 1: Out of the Gallion / Mar. 27, 1945-Dec. 20, 1947 / Storyville ✦✦✦✦

The entire output of clarinetist Mezz Mezzrow's King Jazz label has been reissued over five CDs (the four volumes in this series and a Sidney Bechet set), although due to the many alternate takes and the similar sessions, the reissue producers decided not to program the material in strict chronological order. The first volume has three piano solos from Sammy Price, four numbers from a heated septet date with the great soprano Sidney Bechet and trumpeter Hot Lips Page, and 15 selections by various quintets featuring Mezzrow and Bechet. On five instances, Mezzrow is heard years later telling the story behind certain performances. There is a certain sameness to much of the material, but some selections stand out, particularly "Evil Gal Blues" (featuring a vocal by Coot Grant), a two-part "The Blues and Freud," "Ole Miss," "Blues of the Roaring Twenties," "The Sheik of Araby" and the romping "Perdido Street Stomp." —*Scott Yanow*

King Jazz Story, Vol. 2: Really the Blues / Mar. 27, 1945-Dec. 20, 1947 / Storyville ✦✦✦✦

On the second of five CDs (the four sets in this series plus a single Sidney Bechet release) all of the recordings made for Mezz Mezzrow's King Jazz label have been reissued although unfortunately not in chronological order. This CD contains three piano solos by Sammy Price, five selections from the Mezzrow-Bechet septet (featuring trumpeter Hot Lips Page) plus 14 blues-oriented performances that feature clarinetist Mezz and the great soprano Sidney Bechet in a quintet; Mezzrow also introduces five of the numbers. A pair of two-part jams ("Really the Blues" and "Revolutionary Blues") stand out from the 74 minutes of fairly similar material; Bechet is in typically explosive form throughout. —*Scott Yanow*

King Jazz Story, Vol. 3: Gone Away the Blues / Mar. 27, 1945-Dec. 20, 1947 / Storyville ✦✦✦✦

The third of four CDs in this series from the European Storyville label (along with a single Sidney Bechet set) continues the complete documentation of Mezz Mezzrow's King Jazz label, a company dedicated to "the real jazz" according to its clarinetist and president; namely ensemble and blues-oriented jams matching the erratic Mezzrow with the great soprano saxophonist Sidney Bechet. Since it is not programmed in strict chronological order, this reissue has selections from each of the King Jazz sessions including piano solos from Sammy Price (in addition to a Price duet with drummer Sid Catlett), a vocal from Pleasant Joe, jams from an all-star septet with trumpeter Hot Lips Page, lots of performances from the Mezzrow-Bechet quintet and an oddity, a feature on "Caravan" for an unidentified harmonica player. Mezzrow (in segments obviously recorded quite a few years later) introduces some of the selections with an anecdote. All in all, this series is quite enjoyable (even if a bit repetitive) and easily recommended to Dixieland and Bechet fans. —*Scott Yanow*

King Jazz Story, Vol. 4: Revolutionary Blues / Mar. 27, 1945-Dec. 20, 1947 / Storyville ✦✦✦✦

For the fourth of four CD volumes that (along with a single Sidney Bechet release) reissues every recording made by Mezz Mezzrow's King Jazz label, the erratic clarinetist is once again matched with the great soprano saxophonist Sidney Bechet. Not programmed in strict chronological order (unfortunately), this enjoyable CD has three piano solos from Sammy Price, a vocal by Pleasant Joe and many jams (mostly blues) by groups featuring Bechet, Mezzrow and (on two numbers) trumpeter Hot Lips Page; Mezz verbally introduces five of the songs. Much of the basic

material (Mezzrow loved ensemble-oriented blues) is rather similar but Bechet generally makes the results quite exciting. —*Scott Yanow*

King Jazz, Vol. 2 / Sep. 18, 1946-Dec. 20, 1947 / GHB ✦✦✦✦✦

Along with the double-disc *Volume One*, this 1997 three-CD set finishes the complete reissuance of Mezz Mezzrow's King Jazz label. The clarinetist loved New Orleans jazz, particularly its ensembles, and championed the style throughout his career, although he was far from a virtuoso himself. The music on his King Jazz label, not previously released in complete chronological order domestically, includes many multiple takes and plenty of similar blues-based material, but is of particular interest due to the consistently brilliant playing of the great soprano Sidney Bechet. The performances on this reissue are, with one exception, taken from the band sessions of Sept. 18, 1946 and Dec. 18-20, 1947. Featured are Mezzrow and Bechet with two different but equally complementary rhythm sections: pianist Wesley "Sox" Wilson, bassist Wellman Braud and drummer Baby Dodds (Coot Grant has vaudeville-type vocals on the majority of those titles) or pianist Sammy Price, bassist Pops Foster and drummer Kaiser Marshall. The one exception is an interesting, if out-of-place version of "Caravan" featuring an unidentified harmonica player in a trio. The two volumes are the perfect way to explore the spirited music of Mezz Mezzrow's King Jazz label and are highly recommended to jazz historians. —*Scott Yanow*

Really the Blues / Jan. 1, 1947 / Jazz Archives ✦✦✦

To celebrate the release of his book *Really the Blues*, clarinetist Mezz Mezzrow gathered many of his favorite players, many of whom were recording for his King Jazz label at the time, to perform a Town Hall concert. As usual, Mezzrow is the weak point of the music, bragging a bit in places and doing his best on five songs (including two versions of "Really the Blues") with an all-star group consisting of cornetist Muggsy Spanier, trombonist Sandy Williams, the great Sidney Bechet on soprano, pianist Sammy Price, bassist Wellman Braud and drummer Baby Dodds. This collector's LP also has the same group without Mezzrow (an improvement) jamming on a blues and two Dixieland standards, along with a feature for Price (heard in duet with Dodds) and the old vaudeville team of Coot Grant and "Kid Sox" Wesley Wilson (who interact on "You Can't Do That to Me"). The music is fun, but not too essential; this album will be difficult to locate. —*Scott Yanow*

Paris 1955, Vol. 1 / May 20, 1955 / Swing ✦✦✦

The erratic but well-intentioned clarinetist Mezz Mezzrow goes to France for this LP and performs the two-part (slow and fast) "Blues with a Bridge" and two sections of "Minor with a Bridge" (same format) in a quintet with both Peanuts Holland and Guy Longnon on trumpets, pianist Milton Sealey and drummer Kansas Fields. The spontaneous music, which emphasizes ensembles but also has some solo work, generally holds together despite the absence of a bass. This was one of Mezz's last recordings, and the LP is worth searching for by trad jazz fans, for there is plenty of spirit in the music. —*Scott Yanow*

Pierre Michelot

b. Mar. 3, 1928, Saint Denis, France
Bass / Bop, Hard Bop

For decades Pierre Michelot has been the bassist of choice for Americans traveling through France. His supportive playing was always up to par with the American bassists of the 1950s and '60s. Michelot started on bass when he was 16 and through the years played with Rex Stewart (1948), Coleman Hawkins, Django Reinhardt, Stephane Grappelli, Don Byas, Thelonious Monk, Lester Young, Dexter Gordon, Stan Getz, Bud Powell (in a trio with Kenny Clarke), Zoot Sims, Dizzy Gillespie, Miles Davis, Chet Baker, etc. He even appeared in the movie *'Round Midnight* about American jazz musicians living in Paris. —*Scott Yanow*

● **Bass and Bosses** / Dec. 10, 1989-Dec. 11, 1989 / EmArcy ✦✦✦✦✦

Veteran French bassist Pierre Michelot has had very few chances throughout his career to lead record sessions, so this CD is a real rarity. Michelot teams up with the great harmonica player Toots Thielemans, violinist Pierre Blanchard, pianist Maurice Vander and drummer Billy Higgins for a well-rounded program highlighted by Jimmy Rowles' "The Peacocks," "Jitterbug Waltz," "A Child Is Born" and the bassist's feature "Blues in the Closet." Everyone plays well and the unusual combination of instruments make these standards sound quite fresh. —*Scott Yanow*

Palle Mikkelborg

b. Mar. 6, 1941, Copenhagen, Denmark
Trumpet, Composer / Post-Bop, Avant-Garde

Palle Mikkelborg is a fine trumpeter who is best known stateside for his *Aura* suite which in 1984 featured Miles Davis. Self-taught on trumpet, Mikkelborg started working professionally in 1960. He joined the Danish Radio Jazz Group in 1963 and led it during 1967-72. Mikkelborg performed at the 1968 Newport Jazz

Festival in a quintet and worked through the years with such players as Thomas Clausen, Niels-Henning Orsted Pedersen, Terje Rypdal, Abdullah Ibrahim, Jan Garbarek, George Russell, Dexter Gordon, Gil Evans, Karin Krog and George Gruntz's Concert Jazz Band. He has recorded as a leader for Debut, Metronome, Sonet, Storyville and ECM. —*Scott Yanow*

Heart to Heart / 1986 / Storyville ✦✦✦✦

Trumpeter Palle Mikkelborg has not led that many sessions as a leader. This trio outing with keyboardist Kenneth Knudsen and bassist Niels-Henning Orsted Pedersen (comprising six group originals and John Lennon's "Imagine") is atmospheric, moody and sometimes intriguing. The electronics (Mikkelborg also doubles on keyboards) are often colorful and, overall, this is one of the leader's best outings on trumpet. —*Scott Yanow*

Butch Miles

b. Jul. 4, 1944, Ironton, OH
Drums / Swing

A colorful soloist and an impressive technician in the tradition of Buddy Rich and Gene Krupa, Butch Miles graduated from West Virginia State College in 1966 and worked locally in West Virginia. He toured with Mel Tormé (1972-74) and made a strong impression propelling Count Basie's Orchestra (1975-79). After a few months with Dave Brubeck (recording *Back Home* for Concord in 1979) and a year with Tony Bennett, Miles became a busy freelance musician. He has played at many jazz parties and festivals with a countless number of musicians including most notably Gerry Mulligan, Zoot Sims, Woody Herman, Wild Bill Davison, Clark Terry, Scott Hamilton, Warren Vache and Bob Wilber's Bechet Legacy. Butch Miles led seven fine albums for Famous Door (1977-82) that feature swing standards and a couple of records for Dreamstreet including a vocal date. In 1997 Butch Miles toured with the Count Basie Orchestra (under the direction of Grover Mitchell) and showed that he was still a fiery drummer quite skilled at showmanship. —*Scott Yanow*

● **Butch Miles Salutes Chick Webb** / 1979 / Famous Door ✦✦✦✦

The third of seven Butch Miles Famous Door LPs is the first of three to "salute" a swing-era bandleader. Miles, whose biggest influence was Buddy Rich, performs eight numbers associated with Chick Webb, including "Stompin' at the Savoy," "If Dreams Come True," "Blue Lou" and "Clap Hands, Here Comes Charlie." Eddie Barefield (the arranger for the date, heard here sticking to tenor) had been in the Webb orchestra 40 years earlier. He and Miles are joined by altoist Norris Turney, trumpeter Glenn Zottola, pianist John Bunch and bassist Milt Hinton for some solid swing that still communicates fairly well. —*Scott Yanow*

Butch Miles Salutes Gene Krupa / Jan. 1982 / Famous Door ✦✦✦✦

Butch Miles pays tribute to the influential swing drummer Gene Krupa by performing five songs associated with his big band, including "After You've Gone" and "Drum Boogie," plus his own "Samba Rioja (From Butch to Gene)." Tenor saxophonist Jorge Anders provided the arrangements and participates in the sextet along with the drummer/leader, trumpeter Glenn Zottola, trombonist George Masso, pianist John Bunch and bassist Phil Flanigan. Miles puts spirit into his vocal on "Boogie Blues"; Zottola recalls Roy Eldridge on "After You've Gone"; and Anders is fine on his ballad feature "More Than You Know." An excellent mainstream set that unfortunately has not yet been reissued on CD. —*Scott Yanow*

Butch Miles Salutes Count Basie / Aug. 1982 / Famous Door ✦✦✦✦

To perform three songs associated with Count Basie, a pair of swinging originals ("Hail to the Chief" and "Afternoon of Some Basie-Ites") and a three-song ballad medley, drummer Butch Miles utilizes an octet and the arrangements of Jorge Anders. Miles, who has served a couple of notable stints with the Basie Orchestra, is joined by a couple of Basie-associated players (Frank Wess on tenor and rhythm guitarist Freddie Green), plus Anders on tenor, trumpeter Glen Zottola (who also contributes some alto and tenor), trumpeter Marky Markowitz, pianist John Bunch and bassist Milt Hinton. The music is predictably swinging and very much in the Basie tradition. Happily, Basie was still alive upon this album's release to appreciate the tribute. —*Scott Yanow*

More Miles ... More Standards / Apr. 17, 1985-Apr. 18, 1985 / Famous Door ✦✦✦✦

Among the seven LPs that drummer Butch Miles led for the Famous Door label, three were tributes to Chick Webb, Gene Krupa and Count Basie, respectively. The music on his final effort for Famous Door is also very much in the mainstream tradition. The seven standards (including "Lulu's Back in Town," "How High the Moon" and "920 Special") and one blues all contain plenty of concise and swinging solos. Miles is joined by tenor saxophonist Jorge Anders (who provided the arrangements), trumpeter Glenn Zottola (doubling on alto), pianist Derek Smith,

bassist Linc Milliman, and a pair of up-and-coming swing players in guitarist Howard Alden and trombonist Dan Barrett. Enjoyable music that deserves to be reissued on CD someday. —*Scott Yanow*

Jazz Express / Apr. 15, 1986+Apr. 22, 1986 / Dreamstreet ✦✦✦✦

Butch Miles has long been one of the most colorful drummers in the swing/mainstream genre. Fortunately, he does not completely dominate the solo space on his own rewarding recordings, although he does get his say in. This out-of-print LP from the defunct Dreamstreet label is notable for Miles' interesting three-part "Ivory Coast Suite." Playing with a generally more modern group than usual, Miles holds his own with trumpeter Spanky Davis, trombonist George Masso, Gerry Niewood (doubling on tenor and flute), pianist Harold Danko and bassist Brian Torff on selections by Horace Silver, Sammy Nestico, Oliver Nelson, Neal Hefti, Niewood and Torff. This modern mainstream album is worth searching for. —*Scott Yanow*

Cookin' / Nov. 26, 1995 / Nagel-Heyer ✦✦✦✦✦

Drummer Butch Miles leads a first-class mainstream jazz group on this live set put out by the German Nagel-Heyer label. With trumpeter Randy Sandke, tenor saxophonist Harry Allen, guitarist Howard Alden and bassist Frank Tate completing the pianoless quartet, the high-quality swing that results is not unexpected. Terrie Richards helps out with a couple of vocals. The highlights include "Lady Be Good," Flip Phillips' "The Claw," "Them There Eyes" and "Tickle Toe." Worth searching for. —*Scott Yanow*

Lizzie Miles (Elizabeth Mary [Née Landreaux] Pajaud)

b. Mar. 31, 1895, New Orleans, LA, **d.** Mar. 17, 1963, New Orleans, LA
Vocals / Blues, Dixieland, Classic Female Blues

Lizzie Miles was a fine classic blues singer from the 1920s who survived to have a full comeback in the 1950s. She started out singing in New Orleans during 1909-11 with such musicians as King Oliver, Kid Ory and Bunk Johnson. Miles spent several years touring the South in minstrel shows and playing in theaters. She was in Chicago during 1918-20 and then moved to New York in 1921, making her recording debut the following year. Her recordings from the 1922-30 period mostly used lesser-known players, but Louis Metcalf and King Oliver were on two songs apiece and she recorded a pair of duets with Jelly Roll Morton in 1929. Miles sang with A.J. Piron and Sam Wooding, toured Europe during 1924-25 and was active in New York during 1926-31. Illness knocked her out of action for a period but by 1935 she was performing with Paul Barbarin, she sang with Fats Waller in 1938 and recorded a session in 1939. Lizzie Miles spent 1943-49 outside of music but in 1950 began a comeback, and she often performed with Bob Scobey or George Lewis during her final decade. —*Scott Yanow*

Complete Recorded Works, Vol. 1 (1922-23) / Feb. 24, 1922-1923 / Document ✦✦✦✦✦

Complete Recorded Works, Vol. 2 (1923-28) / 1923-1928 / Document ✦✦✦✦✦

Complete Recorded Works, Vol. 3 (1928-39) / 1928-Oct. 7, 1939 / Document ✦✦✦✦✦

With Tony Almerico's Dixieland Band / 1954-1956 / Rondo ✦✦✦

After gaining her initial reputation in the 1920s, Lizzie Miles made a comeback in the 1950s, when she often appeared with Bob Scobey's band. This particular LP is one of several she made for the Cook and Rondo labels late in her career, when her voice was fortunately still in good form. Joined by a spirited New Orleans band including trumpeter Tony Almerico, trombonist Jack Delaney and clarinetist Tony Costa, Miles mostly sticks to warhorses including "Some of These Days," "Bill Bailey," "Waitin' for the Robert E. Lee" and "Darktown Strutters Ball." —*Scott Yanow*

Hot Songs My Mother Taught Me / 1955 / Cook ✦✦✦✦

This is one of the best of Lizzie Miles' 1950s recordings (none of her solo dates have yet been reissued on CD). Eight of the 14 songs find her accompanied by pianist Red Camp; three add the banjo of Albert French; and three are with a Dixieland band headed by trumpeter Tony Almerico. The mostly intimate settings allow the still strong-voiced Miles to put lots of feeling not only into some typical standards, but such numbers as "Take Yo' Finger Off It," "A Cottage for Sale" and "Dyin' Rag." —*Scott Yanow*

● **Queen Mother of the Rue Royale** / 1955 / Cook ✦✦✦✦✦

An unjustly forgotten name in classic blues annals. Lizzie Miles was a great entertainer and versatile song stylist who could handle everything from vaudeville to classic blues to traditional New Orleans jazz. She had passed her prime by these recordings, but was still able to retain her grit and intensity while relying on experience rather than power. —*Ron Wynn*

Ron Miles

b. 1963, Indianapolis, IN
Trumpet / Post-Bop, Avant-Garde

An adventurous trumpeter, Ron Miles has made a strong impression with his Gramavision releases. A resident of Denver since he was 11, he began playing the trumpet seriously in junior high school and studied music at the University of Denver (1981-85) and the Manhattan School of Music (1986). In addition to local gigs, Miles visited Italy in the summer of 1992 with the play *Sophisticated Ladies* and was a member of the Mercer Ellington Orchestra for a couple of years. He played frequently with Bill Frisell during 1994-95, also recording with the guitarist, and worked as Assistant Professor of Music at Denver's Metropolitan Stage College. Ron Miles has recorded for Prolific (1986) and Capri (1990), as well as several advanced sets for Gramavision. With a bit more exposure, the highly original trumpeter/composer could become an important force in jazz in the future. —*Scott Yanow*

Witness / Jan. 31, 1989 / Capri ◆◆◆◆
Trumpeter Ron Miles' recorded debut as a leader is more of a blowing date than his later sets. Teamed up with some of Colorado's top players (Fred Hess on tenor and flute, pianist Art Lande, bassist Ken Walker and drummer Bruno Carr), Miles explores two of his originals, one by Hess, Thelonious Monk's "Ugly Beauty," Billy Strayhorn's "A Flower Is a Lovesome Thing," and Charles Mingus' "Pithecanthropus Erectus"; the latter tune is rarely revived. Miles displays an original tone and an active musical imagination during this excellent post-bop CD from the Denver-based Capri label. —*Scott Yanow*

● **My Cruel Heart** / 1996 / Gramavision ◆◆◆◆◆
● **Woman's Day** / 1997 / Gramavision ◆◆◆◆
This is an eccentric and varied date featuring the consistently inventive trumpeter Ron Miles, guitarist Bill Frisell (his regular employer at the time), bassist Artie Moore and drummer Rudy Royston (along with a few guests added for color). The music ranges from freakout rock to introspective ballads, from rhythmic pieces to some spacier sounds. Miles has an interesting sound, and he contributed all 12 originals, while Frisell certainly makes his presence felt. Stimulating music that is not for everyone's taste. —*Scott Yanow*

Bubber Miley

b. Apr. 3, 1903, Aiken, SC, **d.** May 20, 1932, New York, NY
Trumpet / Classic Jazz

One of the great trumpeters of the 1920s, Bubber Miley was a master with the plunger mute, distorting his sound quite colorfully. He was largely responsible for Duke Ellington's early success and was the most prominent voice in Duke's Jungle Band of 1926-28, teaming up with trombonist Tricky Sam Nanton; Cootie Williams and Ray Nance would follow in the tradition of Miley. He grew up in New York and played professionally starting in 1920. Miley was with Elmer Snowden's Washingtonians as early as 1923 and freelanced on recordings during 1924-26. He was influenced a bit by King Oliver and Johnny Dunn but was quite distinctive by 1926 and an innovator in his own way. Miley co-wrote "East St. Louis Toodle-oo" and "Black and Tan Fantasy" and starred on the majority of Ellington's recordings during 1926-28. Unfortunately, he was an alcoholic, and by early 1929 was becoming increasingly unreliable, leading to Duke reluctantly firing him. Miley worked in France with Noble Sissle, played in the US with society bandleader Leo Reisman (taking a memorable solo on "What Is This Thing Called Love") and formed his own band in 1930, recording six titles. Bubber Miley played in a few shows in 1931 but died the following year of tuberculosis at the age of 29. —*Scott Yanow*

Bobby Militello

b. Mar. 25, 1950, Buffalo, NY
Alto Saxophone, Flute, Tenor Saxophone / Hard Bop

An excellent reed player who has thus far been underrated, Bobby Militello brings back the spirit of Paul Desmond when he performs with the Dave Brubeck Quartet. After playing locally in Buffalo, he toured with Maynard Ferguson (1975-79). Militello freelanced in Buffalo (1981-84) and Los Angeles (1984-92), playing with the Bill Holman and Bob Florence Orchestras. Bobby Militello, who has recorded with Holman, Florence, Ferguson and Charlie Shoemake among others, has played on and off with Brubeck since 1983 (usually alternating with Bill Smith) and has led several of his own albums for Positive. —*Scott Yanow*

● **Easy to Love** / Nov. 9, 1993-Nov. 12, 1993 / Positive ◆◆◆◆◆
Bobby Militello, on both alto and flute, has an opportunity to stretch out during this CD, playing bebop, '60s-type funky jazz and R&Bish ballads; he even takes an enthusiastic vocal on "I Thought About You." Organist Bobby Jones actually dominates the ensembles, contributing strong solos, heated accompaniment of Militello

and four of the ten selections. With drummer Bob Leatherbarrow providing driving rhythms and trumpeter Jeff Jarvis helping out on a few numbers, the set has the feel of a classic hard-bop organ combo, inspiring Bobby Militello to play at his best. —*Scott Yanow*

Straight Ahead / Dec. 19, 1994-Dec. 22, 1994 / Positive Music ◆◆◆◆

Eddie Miller

b. Jun. 23, 1911, New Orleans, LA, **d.** Apr. 1, 1991, Van Nuys, CA
Tenor Saxophone, Clarinet / Swing, Dixieland

Eddie Miller had a beautiful tone on his tenor, similar to Bud Freeman, although his style was much less angular. Miller was a solidly swinging player who fit easily into Dixieland and swing settings. He worked professionally in New Orleans at the age of 16 and in 1930 made his recording debut with Julie Wintz. He was well featured with Ben Pollack's Orchestra (1930-34) and when Bob Crosby took over the ensemble, Miller became one of its main stars. In addition to his many solos with Crosby's Orchestra and the Bobcats, Miller was a superior clarinetist who took a famous solo on "South Rampart Street Parade." Of the songs he wrote, the haunting "Slow Mood" caught on and became a standard. When Crosby broke up the band in 1942, Eddie Miller put together a short-lived orchestra of his own before being drafted. He was discharged from the military early due to illness and settled in Los Angeles in 1945, becoming a studio musician and appearing on many soundtracks for 20th Century-Fox. Miller participated in nearly all of the Bob Crosby reunions and was on many jazz dates in the 1950s. During 1967-76 he worked in New Orleans with Pete Fountain and he was active at jazz parties and festivals into the mid-'80s. Eddie Miller recorded as a leader for Capitol, Jump, Decca, Tops, Southland, Coral, Blue Angel Jazz Club, 77, Famous Door and Magna Graphic Jazz. —*Scott Yanow*

The Uncollected Eddie Miller & His Orchestra (1944-1945) / 1943-1945 / Hindsight ◆◆◆◆
The short-lived Eddie Miller big band only had one studio session, resulting in four numbers, before breaking up. Fortunately, this LP adds 14 additional titles (three with period vocals by Kathy Summers) that were made as radio transcriptions by the swinging outfit in 1944. Miller, one of the top pre-bop tenor saxophonists, is the main soloist throughout the album, and although his band did not have many big names (best known are clarinetist/arranger Matty Matlock, pianist Stan Wrightsman, rhythm guitarist Nappy Lamare and drummer Nick Fatool), it was a fine successor to Bob Crosby's Orchestra, with which Miller had gained his initial fame. —*Scott Yanow*

● **Eddie Miller-George Van Eps** / Mar. 21, 1946-Mar. 8, 1949 / Jump ◆◆◆◆◆

With a Little Help from My Friends / 1968 / Coral ◆
Tenor saxophonist Eddie Miller's only recording as a leader during 1959-70 is a complete waste. The masterful swing tenor, who always had a beautiful tone, was playing with Pete Fountain's group in the late '60s, and Fountain is on about half of this LP. Unfortunately, Miller was persuaded to perform horrendous arrangements with a harpsichord and a string quartet. Miller sticks to the melody during such material as "Alfie," "With a Little Help from My Friends" and the "Theme from Mission Impossible," and even the better tunes ("What's New," "Sophisticated Lady" and "Out of Nowhere") are sunk by the Muzak-y charts. This album is even worse than it looks. —*Scott Yanow*

Portrait of Eddie / 1971 / Blue Angel ◆◆◆◆◆
Considering his skill and popularity, it is surprising how few record dates tenor saxophonist Eddie Miller led during his career—not counting a commercial effort for Coral, this was Miller's first date as a leader since 1958. The well-conceived effort acts as an excellent retrospective of the tenor's career, including material from the 1920s, the Bob Crosby years, Miller's short-lived big band, his work on movie soundtracks, and some jam session favorites. Featured with a ten-piece band of old friends (including Peanuts Hucko or Matty Matlock on clarinet, Dick Cary and Jackie Coon on trumpets, guitarist Nappy Lamare and drummer Nick Fatool), Miller is in prime form throughout the set. Highlights of the collector's LP include "I've Got a Crush on You," "I'm Gonna Stomp Mr. Henry Lee," "Riverboat Shuffle" and "Lazy Mood." —*Scott Yanow*

It's Miller Time / 1979 / Famous Door ◆◆◆◆
For this freewheeling session, veteran swing tenor Eddie Miller teams up with trombonist George Masso, pianist John Bunch, bassist Milt Hinton and drummer Duffy Jackson. As usual, Miller (who always had a beautiful tone) is exquisite on the ballads (which include "Dream") and stomping on the hotter material (such as "Them There Eyes" and "Love Is Just Around the Corner"). In addition to the standards, the quintet performs the leader's "I've Gotta Be on My Way" and Masso's "For Eddie by George." This out-of-print LP finds Eddie Miller (then 68) still at the top of his game. —*Scott Yanow*

Street of Dreams / Feb. 10, 1982 / Delmark ◆◆◆◆

One of the great tenors to come out of the 1930s is teamed with the superior (but under-recorded) swing pianist Johnny Varro, bassist Ray Leatherwood and drummer Gene Estes for this excellent date. The CD reissue finds the group romping on such songs as "I Never Knew," "Avalon," "Linger Awhile" and "Sunday"; Miller's tone on "Street of Dreams" and his haunting ballad "Lazy Mood" is as beautiful as ever. —*Scott Yanow*

Glenn Miller (Alton Glenn Miller)

b. Mar. 1, 1904, Clarinda, IA, d. Dec. 15, 1944, English Channel
Leader, Arranger, Trombone / Swing , Big Band

Glenn Miller led the most popular band in the world during 1939-42 and the most beloved of all the swing-era orchestras. His big band played a wide variety of melodic music (including swing, vocal ballads and novelties) and had tremendous success in every area. Jazz was only part of their music and Miller (like Stan Kenton) was just not interested in swinging like Count Basie. He employed some good horn soloists along the way, but was most concerned in displaying strong musicianship, well-rehearsed ensembles, danceable tempos and putting together an enjoyable and well-rounded show.

Miller grew up in Colorado, attended college for a short time, and in 1926 joined Ben Pollack's new band. He was with the group for two years, contributing arrangements and taking some trombone solos but, after Jack Teagarden was discovered and signed up, Miller took the hint and quit. In 1928 he was a freelance arranger in New York, and he would work most prominently during the next few years with Red Nichols in pit orchestras, as Smith Ballew's musical director and with the Dorsey Brothers. In 1935 he helped organize Ray Noble's American Orchestra and led his first session, but even by 1937, Glenn Miller was still obscure. He was inspired by the success of many new big bands and he put together an orchestra of his own. That venture started out promising with some fine recordings, but it soon failed, partly because it did not have a personality of its own. In mid-1938 Miller tried again, and although he had a recording contract with Bluebird, the first year was mostly a struggle. However, this time around, by having a clarinet double the melody of the saxophones an octave higher, he had his own trademark. An engagement at Glen Island Casino in the summer of 1939 earned the orchestra a regular radio broadcast and soon their recordings of "Moonlight Serenade" (Miller's theme), "Sunrise Serenade" and particularly "Little Brown Jug" became hits, and by the end of the year Glenn Miller was a household name and his band was considered a sensation. During 1939-42 there were many additional hits including "In the Mood," "At Last," "Stairway to the Stars," "Tuxedo Junction," "Pennsylvania 6-5000," "Chattanooga Choo Choo," "A String of Pearls," "Elmer's Tune," "Don't Sit Under the Apple Tree," "American Patrol," "I've Got a Gal in Kalamazoo," "Serenade in Blue" and "Jukebox Saturday Night." There was simply no competition!

From the jazz standpoint, Miller's best soloists were trumpeters Clyde Hurley, Johnny Best and (by 1942) Bobby Hackett. Tex Beneke, who was more famous for his good-natured vocals, was a decent tenor saxophonist who had a lot of short solos. Less tolerable to jazz listeners were the many ballad vocals of Ray Eberle (who often sounded as if he were straining) and the lightweight but cheerful contributions of singer Marion Hutton.

Only Glenn Miller's decision to enlist in the army stopped his orchestra's success. He did the near-impossible and organized the finest military jazz band ever heard, his Army Air Force Band. By 1944, when it had relocated to London, it featured clarinetist Peanuts Hucko, pianist Mel Powell, drummer/singer Ray McKinley, trumpeter Bobby Nichols and sometimes a string section and a vocal group. Their version of "St. Louis Blues March" became famous and this group's broadcasts and radio transcriptions are well worth searching for. Glenn Miller flew across the English Channel in December 1944 with plans of setting up engagements on the Continent. His plane was shot down (quite possibly in error by the Allies) and lost.

The Army Air Force Band stayed together through 1945. There have been many Glenn Miller ghost orchestras since, but all have been stuck in the role of recreating the past, including note-for-note duplications of the recorded solos. The oddest case is Tex Beneke who has spent the past 50 years essentially performing over and over again the same routines that he had done with Miller during a three-year period!

All of Glenn Miller's Bluebird recordings (from 1938-42) have been reissued a countless number of times including in "complete" sets. His band appears quite prominently in two Hollywood movies of the 1940s (*Sun Valley Serenade* and *Orchestra Wives*) that are recommended viewing. —*Scott Yanow*

His Complete Recordings on Columbia Records / Nov. 21, 1928-May 23, 1938 / Everest ◆◆◆◆

This five-LP box set is rather unusual in that, although listed under Glenn Miller's name, the first three albums actually feature Miller as a sideman, mostly playing in the ensembles since he was never a major soloist. There are 25 selections from the Dorsey Brothers Orchestra of 1928-31 and 1934, dance-band performances with a variety of vocalists (including Bing Crosby) and some fine solos from trombonist Tommy Dorsey (who is also heard a little on trumpet), Jimmy Dorsey on clarinet and alto and (on one session) the great trumpeter Bunny Berigan. Miller is also heard with Clark Randall's Orchestra in 1935 (the singer's backup group is really the early Bob Crosby band). The final two discs feature Miller leading a studio group in 1935 (Berigan has a memorable solo on "Solo Hop") and heading his own unsuccessful big band of 1937-38. Although not essential, this appealing set has a great deal of valuable and historic music and will fill some gaps for swing collectors who might have wondered what Glenn Miller did before he hit it big in 1939. —*Scott Yanow*

The Best of the Big Bands: Evolution of a Band / Apr. 25, 1935-May 23, 1938 / Columbia ◆◆◆

The majority of Glenn Miller's early recordings as a bandleader are included on this CD, which is subtitled "Evolution of a Band." Miller heads a studio group (which includes trumpeter Bunny Berigan) on two numbers from 1935 (why weren't all four from that date included?) and on three complete sessions from 1937-38; if the liner notes are to be believed, the final four performances are previously unissued alternate takes. All of the selections from 1937-38 are taken from a period when Miller was struggling to find his sound and, even by the time of "Dippermouth Blues" (from May 23, 1938), he had not found it yet. But although these recordings are not that distinctive, there are some good moments; the vocals by Kathleen Lane and Gail Reese are excellent. —*Scott Yanow*

On the Air / Jun. 25, 1938-Nov. 29, 1941 / RCA Victor ◆◆◆◆

Three LPs (which were originally available separately) are combined in this box set. The performances by Glenn Miller's Orchestra (dance music, vocal features and a bit of jazz) are taken from radio broadcasts and over half of the selections were not recorded by the band commercially. Since most of this music (released for the first time in 1963 and kept in print for many years afterward) has not reappeared on CD, this is a set that Glenn Miller collectors will want to go out of their way to acquire, although more general listeners should get the studio recordings first. —*Scott Yanow*

The Complete Glenn Miller, Vol. 1 / Sep. 27, 1938-Jun. 2, 1939 / Bluebird ◆◆◆◆◆

In 1975 the Bluebird reissue series initiated a "complete Glenn Miller" program of double LPs; it would be completed in 1980 with *Vol. IX* and all of the music has since appeared in a comprehensive set on CD. This first two-fer is particularly interesting for it has two sessions (from Sept. 27, 1938 and Feb. 6, 1939) that predate the beginning of Glenn Miller's phenomenal success. "King Porter Stomp" and a two-part version of "By the Waters of Minnetonka" are from the early days, while the later dates on this set are highlighted by the original versions of "Moonlight Serenade" and "Little Brown Jug." —*Scott Yanow*

Greatest Hits [RCA] / Sep. 27, 1938-Jul. 15, 1942 / RCA Victor ◆◆◆

This CD is part of RCA Victor's extensive but erratic introduction to jazz series. Glenn Miller had so many hits that it would be impossible to fit them on just one CD. Strangely enough, three of the 15 numbers included on this release ("When You Wish Upon a Star," "Moon Love" and "King Porter Stomp") were not big sellers, making the title a bit pointless. The famous renditions of such numbers as "In the Mood," "Chattanooga Choo Choo," "A String of Pearls" and "Little Brown Jug" are among this CD's highlights, but there are better organized "greatest hits" Glenn Miller collections than this one readily available. —*Scott Yanow*

☆ **The Complete Glenn Miller, Vols. 1-13** / Sep. 27, 1938-Jul. 16, 1942 / Bluebird ◆◆◆◆◆

This 13-CD set (which is enclosed in an attractive and compact black box) completely reissues the contents of the nine double-LP series of the same name, all 277 studio recordings (including 20 alternate takes which have been placed on the 13th disc) that were made by Glenn Miller's extremely popular orchestra. In addition to all of the hits and the occasional jazz performances, the misses (and the many Ray Eberle vocals) are also on this set, so general collectors just wanting a taste of Glenn Miller's music would be better off getting a less expensive greatest-hits set. However, true Glenn Miller fans should consider this remarkable reissue to be essential; it's all here. —*Scott Yanow*

★ **The Popular Recordings (1938-1942)** / Sep. 27, 1938-Jul. 15, 1942 / Bluebird ◆◆◆◆◆

Of the many compilations of Glenn Miller hits, this three-disc set strikes the best balance between comprehensiveness and economy. More casual listeners might want to try *Pure Gold*, while true scholars will have to have the *Complete Glenn*

Miller, but this 60-track collection contains the best of the most popular bandleader of the last part of the swing era. — *William Ruhlmann*

Spirit is Willing / Sep. 27, 1938-Jul. 16, 1942 / Bluebird ✦✦✦✦✦
This single CD looks at the jazz side of Glenn Miller, reissuing 22 instrumentals from his prime years. Although Miller did not have a great jazz band, his orchestra was capable of swinging, and at one time or another had such fine soloists as trumpeters Clyde Hurley, Billy May and Johnny Best, tenor saxophonist Al Klink and clarinetist Ernie Caceres. This is an interesting set even if it offers nothing that is not available elsewhere. — *Scott Yanow*

Pennsylvania 6-5000, Vol. 1: The Sustaining Remotes / Dec. 30, 1938-Oct. 7, 1940 / Vintage Jazz ✦✦✦
On the first of three Glenn Miller CDs put out by the Vintage Jazz Classics label, there are three previously unreleased (and complete) radio broadcasts featuring Miller's Orchestra. The first aircheck is of greatest interest, for it is from Dec. 30, 1938, when Glenn Miller's band was still quite unknown. With the exception of the opening theme, none of the nine selections were ever recorded commercially by Miller. The other broadcasts (from Aug. 10, 1939 and Oct. 7, 1940) are more conventional but will be enjoyed by Glenn Miller's many fans. — *Scott Yanow*

● **The Essential Glenn Miller** / Apr. 4, 1939-Jul. 15, 1942 / Bluebird ✦✦✦✦✦
Glenn Miller's 1939-42 Victor recordings have been reissued a countless number of times in many different ways through the years. This two-CD set does an excellent job of repackaging all of his hits plus a variety of vocal numbers in chronological order. The 47 selections sum up Miller's legacy quite well, making this a definitive set for listeners who do not desire everything that Glenn Miller recorded. — *Scott Yanow*

Memorial 1944-1969 / Apr. 4, 1939-Jul. 15, 1942 / RCA Victor ✦✦✦✦✦
Before the CD era, this two-LP set was the definitive Glenn Miller greatest-hits package. All 30 selections were big sellers (there are no duds included) and none of Miller's most popular songs are missing. Programmed in chronological order, the music starts with "Moonlight Serenade" and continues up to "St. Louis Blues March" (which was actually from Miller's Army Air Force Band). Highlights include "Little Brown Jug," "In the Mood," "Pennsylvania 6-5000," "Anvil Chorus," "Chattanooga Choo Choo," "A String of Pearls" and "Serenade in Blue"; in fact every song. — *Scott Yanow*

★ **Legendary Performer** / May 17, 1939-Sep. 24, 1942 / Bluebird ✦✦✦✦✦
On first glance, this CD may appear to be a greatest-hits package, since many of the songs were recorded by Glenn Miller's Orchestra in the studios, but actually the set contains (in chronological order) many of Miller's most historic radio performances. Starting with his theme "Moonlight Serenade" from the band's opening appearance at the Glen Island Casino (when they were unknown), one can experience from song to song the quick rush to success, a New Year's Eve version of "In the Mood," and a classic rendition of "Chattanooga Choo Choo" (with Miller being awarded the first gold record in history), all the way up to the announcement of Miller's entry into the army, a surprise guest appearance by Harry James, and Glenn Miller's emotional farewell to the audience. This is an essential release for anyone with an interest in Glenn Miller's music and life. — *Scott Yanow*

Little Brown Jug, Vol. 3 / Jun. 20, 1939-Dec. 7, 1939 / Vintage Jazz ✦✦✦
The third of three Glenn Miller CDs put out by the VJC label has three previously unreleased radio broadcasts from 1939, the period when Miller began to make it big. With Clyde Hurley contributing some trumpet solos and both Tex Beneke and Al Klink heard on tenors, this well-rounded set has a stronger dose of jazz than usual, along with the usual vocals of Ray Eberle and Marion Hutton. It's a nice set of solid swing from a legendary orchestra. — *Scott Yanow*

The Complete Glenn Miller, Vol. 2 (1939) / Jun. 22, 1939-Oct. 3, 1939 / Bluebird ✦✦✦✦✦
The second of nine double LPs put out by Bluebird in the mid-'70s that reissue the complete studio output of the Glenn Miller Orchestra finds the big band enjoying (and probably very surprised about) its big success. The 33 selections were recorded in just over a three-month period and, although few of the songs were hits, the program does include the original version of "In the Mood" and a fair amount of hot Clyde Hurley trumpet solos. — *Scott Yanow*

The Complete Glenn Miller, Vol. 9 (1939-1942) / Jun. 27, 1939-Jul. 16, 1942 / Bluebird ✦✦✦✦✦
The ninth and final Glenn Miller double LP released by Bluebird in the late '70s finishes the complete reissuance of his studio recordings for Victor. The two-fer starts off with 18 alternate takes from the 1939-42 period and then features Miller's civilian band's last 14 recordings (including "That Old Black Magic," "Juke Box Saturday Night" and "Rhapsody in Blue"). Glenn Miller completists are advised to either pick up the 13-CD box set that is currently available or search for these nine attractive LP sets; the music and packaging is exactly the same. — *Scott Yanow*

Tuxedo Junction (1939-1940) / Jul. 20, 1939-Apr. 5, 1940 / Vintage Jazz ✦✦✦
The second of three Glenn Miller CDs put out by the VJC label, like the other two in this series, contains three complete (and previously unreleased) radio broadcasts. The performances from Glen Island Casino and the Hotel Pennsylvania are fairly typical for the Miller band of the period with sweet vocals by Ray Eberle, spirited ones from Marion Hutton, a bit of jazz and a lot of dance music. Glenn Miller fans will want all three of the VJC CDs. — *Scott Yanow*

The Glenn Miller Carnegie Hall Concert / Oct. 6, 1939 / RCA ✦✦✦✦
The Glenn Miller Orchestra's appearance at Carnegie Hall does not contain any unusual material, sticking to the band's regular repertoire. However, this was an auspicious occasion (showing that after years of struggle Miller had finally arrived) and there are plenty of highlights. Excellent versions of such songs as "Running Wild," "Little Brown Jug," "One O'Clock Jump" and "In the Mood" are the highlights, and there are also two vocals by Ray Eberle and three from Marion Hutton. A good all-around showcase for the band, it is surprising that the music on this LP has yet to be reissued on CD. — *Scott Yanow*

The Complete Glenn Miller, Vol. 3 (1939-1940) / Oct. 9, 1939-Jan. 29, 1940 / Bluebird ✦✦✦✦✦
The third of nine double LPs reissuing all of Glenn Miller's studio recordings for Victor has 32 selections from a four-month period. Despite the busy activity, the closest that Miller came to a hit out of these largely forgotten tunes is "Johnson Rag." Fans of Miller's music will want all of the two-fers (or better yet, the 13-CD set that is currently available), but more general collectors should stick to samplers because many of these numbers (particularly those with Ray Eberle vocals) are quite forgettable. — *Scott Yanow*

Glenn Miller Concert / 1939-1942 / RCA Victor ✦✦✦
This fine LP (released in 1956 but made available into the 1980s) puts the emphasis on the jazz side of Glenn Miller's Orchestra. The 12 instrumentals (taken from radio broadcasts) feature such fine soloists as trumpeters Clyde Hurley, Johnny Best and Bobby Hackett, clarinetist Ernie Caceres, Tex Beneke on tenor and even a bit of the leader's trombone. Highlights include "One O'Clock Jump," a racehorse version of "Tiger Rag," Hackett's playing on "April in Paris," "Everybody Loves My Baby" and "Are You Rusty, Gate." — *Scott Yanow*

For the Very First Time / Jan. 16, 1940-Jul. 14, 1942 / RCA Victor ✦✦✦✦✦
This deluxe (and now hard-to-find) three-LP set has 20 selections plus ten medleys (with usually a tune apiece representing something old, something new, something borrowed and something blue) taken from radio broadcasts during the prime period of the Glenn Miller Orchestra. Most of the material has not been reissued since, and the rare performances of jazz-oriented dance music are both nostalgic and generally swinging. It's a must for Glenn Miller fans who have already heard most of his studio recordings. — *Scott Yanow*

The Complete Glenn Miller, Vol. 4 (1940) / Feb. 5, 1940-Jun. 13, 1940 / Bluebird ✦✦✦✦✦
With the exception of two titles, all of the music reissued on this two-LP set (the fourth volume out of nine) was recorded within a three-month period, a measure of the great commercial success that Glenn Miller was experiencing in 1940. The hits of the two-fer are "Tuxedo Junction" (heard in two versions) and "Pennsylvania 6-5000," but generally even the lesser-known titles (at least the ones without Ray Eberle's vocals) are enjoyable. Glenn Miller fanatics in particular will want this set (or the currently available 13-CD box), although those just hoping to acquire his most popular numbers will probably be better off with a sampler instead. — *Scott Yanow*

The Complete Glenn Miller, Vol. 5 (1940) / Jun. 13, 1940-Nov. 22, 1940 / Bluebird ✦✦✦
Although one thinks of the Glenn Miller Orchestra (the most popular big band in the world during 1939-42) as having one hit record after another, this two-LP set (which covers a five-month period in 1940) does not contain a single one of his best sellers; "Blueberry Hill" and "A Nightingale Sang in Berkeley Square" come the closest. As usual the band plays a mixture of dance music, pop vocals and swing-oriented jazz. This two-LP set (the fifth of nine) is definitely for completists who do not have Miller's 13-CD box set. — *Scott Yanow*

On the Alamo / Jun. 13, 1940-Nov. 3, 1941 / Drive Archive ✦✦✦
The songs might be familiar but these renditions are a little different than usual because this Glenn Miller CD comprises of excerpts from radio broadcasts. The music mostly emphasizes the jazz side of Miller; only four of the 14 selections have vocals, and only two are by their ballad singer Ray Eberle. With Johnny Best contributing some fine trumpet solos, Tex Beneke getting a few good spots for his tenor and such songs being performed as "Everybody Loves My Baby," "Down for the Count" and "Limehouse Blues" (along with "new" versions of some of Miller's hits), this is a fine all-around release by the still very popular bandleader. — *Scott Yanow*

The Complete Glenn Miller, Vol. 6 (1940-1941) / Nov. 22, 1940-May 28, 1941 / Bluebird ✦✦✦✦✦

The sixth two-LP set in the admirable complete Glenn Miller series, unlike *Vol. 5* (which had virtually no hits), finds the orchestra introducing several of their best-loved numbers. Highlights include "Anvil Chorus," "Song of the Volga Boatmen," "Sun Valley Jump," "Perfidia" and "Chattanooga Choo Choo." Miller's repertoire included pop vocals, novelties and jazz, all of it quite danceable and melodic, and this two-fer finds his big band in peak form. —*Scott Yanow*

Glenn Miller in Hollywood / Mar. 1941-May 1942 / Mercury ✦✦✦✦

The Glenn Miller Orchestra appeared in two Hollywood movies during 1941-42: *Sun Valley Serenade* and *Orchestra Wives*. Their performances recorded for both films (including songs not used in the pictures) are included on this rather brief (64-minute) two-LP set. In addition to featuring fine versions of "In the Mood" and "Sun Valley Jump," the former movie introduced the two hits "I Know Why" and "Chattanooga Choo Choo." *Orchestra Wives* was most notable for "I've Got a Gal in Kalamazoo" and "American Patrol." The enjoyable music makes for an interesting contrast to Glenn Miller's more familiar studio recordings of these songs. —*Scott Yanow*

The Complete Glenn Miller, Vol. 7 (1941) / May 28, 1941-Nov. 24, 1941 / Bluebird ✦✦✦✦

The seventh of nine Glenn Miller two-LP sets released by Bluebird during the 1975-80 period has all of the music recorded by the popular bandleader during a six-month period in 1941, 32 selections in all. Highlights include "It Happened in Sun Valley," "Elmer's Tune" and "A String of Pearls." Although this series (or its replacement, a 13-CD box set) is not essential for more general swing collectors, Glenn Miller completists will want this perfectly done series. —*Scott Yanow*

The Complete Glenn Miller, Vol. 8 (1941-1942) / Dec. 8, 1941-Jun. 17, 1942 / Bluebird ✦✦✦✦✦

This two-LP set, the eighth of nine Glenn Miller two-fers to be released by Bluebird in the late '70s, continues the complete reissuance of Miller's Victor recordings. Highlights include "Moonlight Cocktail," "Keep 'Em Flying," "Don't Sit Under the Apple Tree," "American Patrol," "I've Got a Gal in Kalamazoo" and "Serenade in Blue." The mixture of dance music, pop vocals, novelties and swing worked very well for Miller, whose orchestra was the most popular in the world during 1939-42. A more recent 13-CD set also has all of the music in this valuable series. —*Scott Yanow*

Glenn Miller Army Air Force Band / Jul. 17, 1943-Jun. 1944 / RCA Victor ✦✦✦✦✦

Glenn Miller's greatest orchestra was the one he led while in the army, a 30-piece outfit (not counting vocalists) with ten strings that was capable of playing everything from hard-swinging jazz to mood music. This excellent five-LP set features some of the band's finest recorded performances with such soloists as trumpeters Bernie Privin and Bobby Nichols, clarinetist Peanuts Hucko, Hank Freeman on tenor, altoist Vince Carbone and pianist Mel Powell; the vocalists include the Crew Chiefs, Johnny Desmond and drummer Ray McKinley. High points of this hard-to-find but well-worth-the-search box include "Tail-End Charlie," "Anvil Chorus," "In the Mood," "Everybody Loves My Baby," "Sun Valley Jump," "St. Louis Blues March," "Flying Home" and a few medleys. —*Scott Yanow*

☆ **Major Glenn Miller & the Army Air Force Band (1943-1944)** / Oct. 29, 1943-Apr. 22, 1944 / Bluebird ✦✦✦✦✦

During the two years of its existence the Glenn Miller Army Air Force Band (the greatest orchestra he ever led) performed and recorded frequently, although most of its sessions have been difficult to find ever since. The group was filled with talented jazz soloists (including trumpeters Bobby Nichols and Bernie Privin, clarinetist Peanuts Hucko and pianist Mel Powell), had fine singers in Ray McKinley, Johnny Desmond and the Crew Chiefs, and even an occasional 21-piece string section. This CD has many of the best performances by the huge band including "St. Louis Blues March," "Tail-End Charlie," "Anvil Chorus," "Everybody Loves My Baby" and "It Must Be Jelly" and it is highly recommended to swing fans and jazz historians. —*Scott Yanow*

The Glenn Miller V-Disc Sessions: Vol. 1 / Oct. 29, 1943-May 13, 1944 / Mr. Music ✦✦✦✦

Glenn Miller's Army Air Force Band was the finest group that he ever led. Although it did not make any commercially available recordings, the huge outfit did perform 43 songs for V-Discs that were sent to servicemen overseas. The earliest 22 are included on this first of two rewarding CDs. Mood pieces and novelty vocals alternate with some fine jazz, showing the wide variety of music that this impressive group (which often had a full string section) could generate. Highlights include "St. Louis Blues March," "Tail End Charlie," "G.I. Jive," "Stealin' Apples" and "Here We Go Again." Although the exact personnel is not given, clarinetist Pea-

nuts Hucko, pianist Mel Powell and trumpeter Bobby Nichols are all heard from. —*Scott Yanow*

Missing Chapters, Vol. 6: Blue Champagne / Nov. 27, 1943-May 20, 1944 / Avid ✦✦✦✦

The sixth in Avid's extensive Glenn Miller Army Air Force Band series has music that generally predates the performances on the other five releases. Most of the selections were played before the Miller Orchestra left the US and are taken from domestic radio shows. The ensemble's personnel is essentially the same as it would be in England, with the big band having a swinging rhythm section that includes pianist Mel Powell and drummer Ray McKinley, a full string section and some fine jazz soloists in addition to singer Johnny Desmond. The nearly complete "I Sustain the Wings" broadcast of February 19, 1944, opens the CD and it is followed by a variety of other selections taken from broadcasts of the period. Highlights include "Sun Valley Jump," Mel Powell's feature on "Pearls on Velvet," a classic arrangement of "Holiday for Strings," "It Must Be Jelly," "In an 18th Century Drawing Room" and "Snafu Jump." Glenn Miller fans will want all of the CDs in this important series. —*Scott Yanow*

Missing Chapters, Vol. 1: American Patrol / Mar. 10, 1944-Apr. 21, 1944 / Avid ✦✦✦✦✦

This is the first of six CD sets (nine CDs in all) put out by the English Avid label that feature the legendary Glenn Miller Army Air Force Band. Of the 45 numbers on this two-fer, 38 are available domestically on the three-CD RCA set *The Secret Broadcasts*, but completists will prefer to get *Vol. 1* and *Vol. 2* of the Avid series instead, since together they have 19 additional performances. The oversized Miller aggregation (which had a full string section, singer Johnny Desmond and the Crew Chiefs, a swinging rhythm section and such top soloists as pianist Mel Powell, clarinetist Peanuts Hucko and trumpeters Bobby Nichols and Bernie Privin) alternates swing, fresh remakes of Miller's earlier hits, mood music, romantic vocal ballads and patriotic numbers quite effectively. This was a classic band and swing collectors will want all six of the Avid releases. —*Scott Yanow*

Missing Chapters, Vol. 2: Keep 'em Flying / Mar. 10, 1944-May 19, 1944 / Avid ✦✦✦✦✦

The second in Avid's six CD sets featuring Glenn Miller's Army Air Force Band has 47 fine performances. If one combines *Vol. 1* and *Vol. 2* from this British label, one gets all of the music included on RCA's three-CD set *The Secret Broadcasts* (except for a minute and a half rendition of "My Blue Heaven") plus 19 additional performances; more general listeners may want the RCA release while completists should opt for the Avids. In any case, this music is state-of-the-art 1944 swing with more than its share of variety. The spirited performances include swing standards, older Glenn Miller hits from his peacetime orchestra, inventive mood music, ballad vocals from Johnny Desmond and some fresh and jumping jazz originals. —*Scott Yanow*

Secret Broadcasts / Mar. 10, 1944-Jun. 2, 1944 / RCA ✦✦✦✦✦

This superb three-CD set has highlights of the many radio broadcasts made by Glenn Miller's Army Air Force Band while in Great Britain. Miller had a dream orchestra that had a hard-swinging rhythm section (which included pianist Mel Powell and drummer Ray McKinley), top soloists in clarinetist Peanuts Hucko, trumpeters Bobby Nichols and Bernie Privin and some lesser-known saxophonists plus singer Johnny Desmond with the Crew Chiefs and a full string section arranged by Jerry Gray. Glenn Miller completists will prefer the first two volumes of the English Avid label's Miller series, for that duplicates these three CDs while adding another full disc of material, but listeners wanting one definitive set are advised to pick up this release. The music ranges from heated swing (including some remakes of Miller's earlier hits) to mood music, ballad vocals and adventurous performances that hint at what Glenn Miller might have performed during the postwar years if he had lived. —*Scott Yanow*

The Glenn Miller V-Disc Sessions: Vol. 2 / May 20, 1944-Nov. 17, 1945 / Mister Music ✦✦✦✦

The second of two Mister Music CDs that reissue all of the Glenn Miller Army Air Force Band's V-Disc recordings gets the edge over the first due to its stronger jazz content. With top soloists in trumpeter Bobby Nichols, clarinetist Peanuts Hucko and pianist Mel Powell along with singer Johnny Desmond and the Crew Chiefs, Miller's huge orchestra performs such numbers as "Everybody Loves My Baby," "Poinciana," "I Hear You Screamin'," "Sun Valley Jump" and "Holiday for Strings" in addition to worthy remakes of "Little Brown Jug" and "Chattanooga Choo Choo." This CD concludes with five numbers from October-November 1945, long after Glenn Miller's plane went down over the English channel. One can hear the influence of bebop on the group during "Passage Interdit" and "7-0-5," making one wonder what direction Glenn Miller's music would have gone in if he had lived. Recommended. —*Scott Yanow*

Missing Chapters, Vol. 3: All's Well Mademoiselle / Sep. 6, 1944-May 24, 1945 / Avid ✦✦✦✦

The third of six CD volumes featuring Glenn Miller's Army Air Force Band has some of the later performances by the ensemble, including some music recorded after Miller's death. Mostly taken from radio broadcasts, a nearly-complete program from November 17, 1944 is followed by large—and small-band performances from the next few weeks, selections with the orchestra (which was then headed by Ray McKinley) in May 1945 and a broadcast featuring the band's string section on a set of ballads. Although not quite essential, this highly enjoyable program is easily recommended to Glenn Miller fans. The string arrangements are often touching and there are some good jazz solos on the program by clarinetist Peanuts Hucko, pianist Mel Powell and various horn players. —*Scott Yanow*

Missing Chapters, Vol. 5: The Complete Abbey Road Recordings / Sep. 16, 1944-Nov. 27, 1944 / Avid ✦✦✦✦✦

With much fanfare, in 1996 RCA put out *The Lost Recordings*, a two-CD set comprising six Glenn Miller propaganda broadcasts that were unwittingly his final recordings. This particular two-CD set from the English label Avid (which is probably not as widely available domestically) is actually superior, for it contains the complete broadcasts (with opening and closing themes), more dialogue in German and English by Miller and announcer Ilse Weinberger plus four additional selections (including two with Dinah Shore vocals) taken from an unrelated performance from the previous September. The Army Air Force Band purposely sounded closer to Glenn Miller's earlier orchestra on these performances than it usually did in 1944. Not all listeners will be enchanted by the German dialogue and vocals, but the liner notes give a complete translation and Miller does crack a couple of good jokes. As for the music, it gave the large orchestra plenty of opportunities to swing on numbers as "Here We Go Again," "Caribbean Clipper," "Tail End Charlie," "Everybody Loves My Baby" and "Jeep Jockey Jump." In addition, there are some smooth Johnny Desmond vocals, fine dance music and spirited remakes of Glenn Miller's earlier hits. And yes, the Abbey Road Studios used for these broadcasts is the same one immortalized later on by the Beatles. —*Scott Yanow*

Lost Recordings / Oct. 30, 1944-Nov. 27, 1944 / RCA Victor ✦✦✦

This two-CD set has Glenn Miller's legendary final recordings, six propaganda broadcasts recorded in England with his Army Air Force Band and aired in Nazi Germany and throughout Europe. A female announcer speaks (mostly in German) while Miller alternates between German and English and Johnny Desmond sings quite effectively in German. The big band (which also included a full string section) is heard in prime form on swing tunes and some mood music. All of the performances plus additional announcements and versions of Miller's theme "Moonlight Serenade" are included on the English Avid label's Glenn Miller double-CD *The Complete Abbey Road Recordings* (in addition to four selections from an earlier session), so that two-fer will be preferred by completists. —*Scott Yanow*

Missing Chapters, Vol. 4: The Red Cavalry March / Jan. 22, 1945-Jun. 4, 1945 / Avid ✦✦✦✦

Of the six Glenn Miller Army Air Force Band CD sets (nine CDs in all) put out by the English Avid label, this is the only release that focuses exclusively on the orchestra's performances after Miller's death. Recorded during January, April and June 1945, the large ensemble (which includes a big-band instrumentation with several top soloists and a swinging rhythm section plus a large contingent of strings) still sounds in fine form although it was now largely a ghost band. Highlights include swinging renditions of "Song of the Volga Boatmen," "Music Makers," "A String of Pearls," "Everybody Loves My Baby" and "Here We Go Again." —*Scott Yanow*

A Tribute to Glenn Miller / Jun. 5, 1945 / Metronome ✦

This two-LP set features a lengthy broadcast that is supposed to be paying tribute to the late Glenn Miller. Unfortunately, many of the guests (which include comedians, show-biz types and musicians) had little or nothing to do with Miller and no one ever bothers to explain (or even seem to know) what was so significant about the bandleader. There are some good moments, particularly from Count Basie, Louis Prima, Cab Calloway and an emotional Tex Beneke, but so many of the appearances are obviously self-serving and the comedy routines (especially from an obnoxious Milton Berle who does not even mention his work with Glenn Miller in the movie *Sun Valley Serenade*) are poorly dated, that this two-fer is only interesting from a historical standpoint. —*Scott Yanow*

Original Reunion / Apr. 17, 1954 / GNP ✦✦✦✦

Most recordings by the Glenn Miller ghost band are rather stale and predictable recreations, but this concert is surprisingly effective. In 1954, after the successful release of *The Glenn Miller Story*, producer Gene Norman gathered together a big band that was mostly filled with alumni from Miller's Orchestra. Although there was already a ghost band, this was apparently the first time that many of the former members had had a reunion. Although sticking mostly to the old Miller

songs and the original arrangements, the players felt free to improvise fresh new solos and the results are better than expected. With strong contributions made by clarinetist Willie Schwartz, tenors Babe Russin and Eddie Miller (both of whom were ringers) and trumpeters Clyde Hurley and Johnny Best, this well-recorded and nostalgic reunion (which also has a medley from a vocal group) was a success; the CD reissue is worth picking up. —*Scott Yanow*

In the Digital Mood: Gold Limited Edition / 1983 / GRP ✦✦

It had been nearly 40 years since Glenn Miller disappeared over the English Channel when this early GRP CD was recorded, but Miller's music had not dropped in popularity; in fact, this release was one of GRP's biggest sellers. Larry O'Brien, the leader of the Glenn Miller ghost orchestra, put together a strong group of swing stylists and studio musicians to recreate ten of the best-known Miller hits, including "In the Mood," "Chattanooga Choo-Choo," "Little Brown Jug" and "Pennsylvania 6-5000." Fortunately, some of the solos are not mere recreations off of the records, and there are some good short spots for trumpeters Markie Markowitz, John Frosk, Marvin Stamm and Jimmy Maxwell and several reed players. Three selections use a vocal group with Julius LaRosa as the soloist and Mel Tormé (who takes the whistle solo on "Chattanooga Choo-Choo") and Marlene Ver Planck in anonymous roles. But despite the good spirits, this nostalgic music is very predictable, adds nothing new to the Glenn Miller legacy and seems rather pointless considering that Miller's original records are all available. —*Scott Yanow*

Marcus Miller

b. Jun. 14, 1959, New York, NY

Bass / Funk, Pop, Crossover Jazz, Post-Bop, Fusion

Marcus Miller has spent much of his career as an R&B producer, but he is also one of the most talented electric bassists around. He played R&B as a youth and had stints with Bobbi Humphrey (1977) and Lenny White before becoming a studio musician. Miller was an important part of Miles Davis' band during 1981-82 and he collaborated with the trumpeter on several later projects including *Tutu* and the *Music from Siesta*. He also worked on some David Sanborn albums and appeared on the McCoy Tyner/Jackie McLean record *It's About Time* (1985). After Miles Davis' death, Marcus Miller put together his own group which performs many songs in the style of Davis' later band; they have recorded for the PRA label. —*Scott Yanow*

The Sun Don't Lie / 1993 / PRA ✦✦✦

● **Tales** / 1994 / PRA ✦✦✦✦

It is obvious from the music of his group that Marcus Miller badly misses Miles Davis. The funky grooves he uses on this CD sound like a continuation of Davis' later band, Michael "Patches" Stewart contributes muted trumpet in Davis' style, altoist Kenny Garrett is among Miller's sidemen and Miles Davis himself (along with the voices of several other notables in very brief moments) pops up twice on Miller's release. Marcus Miller's electric bass is a major force throughout the music. Samples are used intelligently, a tribute is paid to the late guitarist Eric Gale (Hiram Bullock starts off his solo sounding uncannily like Gale), "Strange Fruit" (a feature for Miller's bass clarinet) gets a revamping and all of the music is both danceable and full of development. A few songs (especially later in the program) ramble on a bit and one wishes that Marcus Miller would drop the funk now and then for variety's sake, but in general his set holds one's interest. —*Scott Yanow*

Mulgrew Miller

b. Aug. 13, 1955, Greenwood, MS

Piano / Post-Bop, Hard Bop

An excellent pianist who plays in a style influenced by McCoy Tyner, Mulgrew Miller has been quite consistent throughout his career. He was with Mercer Ellington's big band in the late '70s and had important stints with Betty Carter (1980), Woody Shaw (1981-83) and Art Blakey's Jazz Messengers (1983-86). For a long period he was a member of the Tony Williams Quintet (1986-94). In addition, Mulgrew Miller has led his own sessions for Landmark (starting in 1985) and Novus. —*Scott Yanow*

Keys to the City / Jun. 28, 1985 / Landmark ✦✦✦✦

Pianist Mulgrew Miller's debut as a leader found his McCoy Tyner-inspired modal style already fully formed. At the time, he was a member of Art Blakey's Jazz Messengers and was starting to become well known in the jazz world. Teamed with bassist Ira Coleman and drummer Marvin "Smitty" Smith, Miller performs four originals, Joe Henderson's "Inner Urge," "Ev'ry Time We Say Goodbye," "Milestones" and an unaccompanied rendition of Duke Ellington's "Warm Valley." A very consistent improviser, all of Mulgrew Miller's are well worth acquiring, including this maiden effort. —*Scott Yanow*

Work / Apr. 23, 1986-Apr. 24, 1986 / Landmark ♦♦♦♦♦
Made about the time he left Art Blakey's Jazz Messengers to go out on his own, Mulgrew Miller's second date as a leader matches his modern mainstream modal style with bassist Charnett Moffett and drummer Terri Lyne Carrington. Once again, the repertoire is a mixture of Miller originals, jazz standards ("Without a Song," "Powell's Prances" and Thelonious Monk's "Work") and an unaccompanied piano solo ("My Man's Gone Now"). And once again, the set is recommended to fans of 1980s/'90s jazz piano. —*Scott Yanow*

Wingspan / May 11, 1987 / Landmark ♦♦♦♦♦
The emphasis on this quintet album is on Mulgrew Miller's compositions; five of the seven numbers (all but Kenny Garrett's "Sonhos Do Brasil" and the standard "I Remember You") are by the pianist/leader. Miller is joined by bassist Charnett Moffett, drummer Tony Reedus, vibraphonist Steve Nelson and altoist Garrett (who plays flute on one song); percussionist Rudy Bird guests on three numbers. The inventive solos on the fairly complex material and the attractive sound of the ensembles make this a worthy release. —*Scott Yanow*

The Countdown / Aug. 15, 1988-Aug. 16, 1988 / Landmark ♦♦♦♦
Mulgrew Miller's fourth Landmark release is a particularly strong all-star date, teaming the pianist with tenor saxophonist Joe Henderson (who sits out on two of the seven numbers), bassist Ron Carter and drummer Tony Williams. Other than a surprisingly effective "What the World Needs Now Is Love," the repertoire comprises originals by Miller (four) and one apiece from Williams and Henderson ("Tetragon"). A high-quality advanced hard-bop set. —*Scott Yanow*

From Day to Day / Mar. 14, 1990-Mar. 15, 1990 / Landmark ♦♦♦♦
Miller takes center stage and shows his Memphis roots in blues and gospel throughout, plus a good touch on the occasional standard. —*Ron Wynn*

Time and Again / Aug. 19, 1991+Aug. 21, 1991 / Landmark ♦♦♦♦
Pianist Mulgrew Miller's recordings are all quite consistent, falling into the modern modal mainstream area, and they are quite creative within the genre. Miller's sixth Landmark recording finds him returning to the trio format with bassist Peter Washington and drummer Tony Reedus. Six of the ten selections are his compositions (including "Tongue Twister," "Woeful Blues," "My Minuet" and an unaccompanied solo rendition of "Song of Today"), while the four remaining songs include the spiritual "Lord, in the Morning Thou Shalt Hear" (taken solo) and Bud Powell's "I'll Keep Loving You." The reliable pianist is in typically fine form on this swinging and fairly exploratory set. —*Scott Yanow*

Hand in Hand / Dec. 16, 1992-Dec. 18, 1992 / Novus ♦♦♦♦♦
Mulgrew Miller, a talented McCoy Tyner-influenced pianist, leads an all-star septet on much of this date. The main stars, however, are Miller's nine diverse originals which range from modal to Monkish. With tenor saxophonist Joe Henderson appearing on five selections, trumpeter Eddie Henderson on six and altoist Kenny Garrett heard throughout the full CD, Miller has a perfect front line to interpret his tricky but logical originals. Vibraphonist Steve Nelson, bassist Christian McBride and drummer Lewis Nash not exactly get overshadowed either. —*Scott Yanow*

● **With Our Own Eyes** / Dec. 21, 1993+Jan. 2, 1994 / Novus ♦♦♦♦♦
The consistent pianist Mulgrew Miller leads his trio (which includes bassist Richie Good and drummer Tony Reedus) through a set dominated by his originals but also including "Body and Soul" and Michel Legran's "Summer Me, Winter Me." The McCoy Tyner influence will probably always remain a significant part of Miller's style but he is such a powerful player in his own right that one really does not mind. His originals on this set range from the modal 6/4 piece "Somewhere Else" and the thoughtful "Dreamin'" to the melancholy "Carousel." As with all of Mulgrew Miller's releases thus far, this one is well worth picking up. —*Scott Yanow*

Getting to Know You / Mar. 20, 1995-Mar. 21, 1995 / Novus ♦♦♦♦

Punch Miller (Ernest Miller)

b. Jun. 10, 1894, Raceland, LA, **d.** Dec. 2, 1971, New Orleans, LA
Trumpet / New Orleans Jazz, Dixieland
A solid New Orleans trumpeter who never really made it big, Punch Miller worked in New Orleans until moving to Chicago in 1926. He played with Al Wynn, Tiny Parham, Freddie Keppard and Jelly Roll Morton in the 1920s, and worked with low-profile jazz and blues groups in Chicago until returning to New Orleans in 1956. He recorded a few numbers for Atlantic in 1962 and toured Japan with George Lewis in 1963. Punch Miller's 1920s recordings as a sideman have been gathered together and reissued on a CD by the RST label. —*Scott Yanow*

● **Punch Miller (1925-1930)** / Jan. 22, 1925-Nov. 12, 1930 / RST ♦♦♦♦♦
The New Orleans cornetist Punch Miller did not lead any record sessions of his own in the 1920s, but the great majority of his recordings as a sideman (with the exception of his dates with Tiny Parham) are on this valuable CD put out by the Austrian RST label. Miller is heard with the vaudeville team of Billy and Mary

Mack, Albert Wynn's Gut Bucket Five, Jimmy Wade's Dixielanders, King Mutt's Tennessee Thumpers, Jimmy Bertrand's Washboard Wizards, Frankie "Half-Pint" Jaxon and Frankie Franko's Louisianians. In addition, there are two numbers by Wynn that have Dolly Jones on cornet instead of Miller. Among the more notable sidemen overall are Barney Bigard (on tenor and clarinet), drummer Sid Catlett, pianists Alex Hill and Jimmy Blythe and clarinetist Darnell Howard. There are more than its share of classic jazz performances on this disc including "When," "She's Crying for Me," "Parkway Stomp," "Shake Your Shimmy" and "Somebody Stole My Gal." This is a reissue that 1920s collectors should go out of their way to acquire, since all of the sessions are complete. —*Scott Yanow*

Lucky Millinder (Lucius Venable Millinder)

b. Aug. 8, 1900, Anniston, AL, **d.** Sep. 28, 1966, New York, NY
Leader / Swing, Jump Blues
Lucky Millinder was essentially a frontman, an occasional singer who conducted several impressive big bands. Millinder grew up in Chicago, worked as a dancer, and became a bandleader in 1931 using his original name of Lucius Venable, which he soon changed. He freelanced until 1934, when he took over leadership of the Mills Blue Rhythm Band, staying into 1938. In 1940, he formed his own orchestra, which worked at the Savoy Ballroom. Most notable among his sidemen were his star attraction, singer/guitarist Sister Rosetta Tharpe, pianist Bill Doggett and, for a brief time in 1942, trumpeter Dizzy Gillespie and altoist Tab Smith. Lucky Millinder fronted bands on record from 1940-52 and on a last session in 1955; the later recordings tended to be more R&B-oriented, although still of interest from the jazz standpoint. A Classics CD has all of Millinder's 1940-42 sessions. Lucky Millinder spent his later years as a liquor salesman and a disc jockey. —*Scott Yanow*

● **1941-1942** / Jun. 27, 1941-Jul. 29, 1942 / Classics ♦♦♦♦♦
All 20 of the Lucky Millinder Orchestra's valuable 1941-42 recordings are on this recommended CD. Millinder himself was not a musician, and his only vocal here is mostly shouting on "Ride, Red, Ride," but he was an effective bandleader and frontman. Other than a couple of World War II propaganda songs, the music on these sessions emphasizes swing, and several notable artists are featured. Sister Rosetta Tharpe (who also played excellent guitar) has six rollicking showcases, and among the soloists are clarinetist Buster Bailey, tenorman Stafford Simon, pianist Bill Doggett and (on the final four songs) altoist Tab Smith and the rapidly emerging trumpeter Dizzy Gillespie. On "Little John Special," Dizzy quotes directly from the as-yet unwritten "Salt Peanuts." Other highlights include "Rock Daniel," "Apollo Jump," "Rock Me," "That's All" and "Mason Flyer." —*Scott Yanow*

1941-1943 / 1941-1943 / Alamac ♦♦♦
Two different versions of Lucky Millinder's Orchestra are featured on this budget LP, which comprises radio broadcast performances from 1941 and 1943. Since Millinder's band did not record all that much, the album is worthwhile, especially since during this era it featured such fine players as trumpeters Freddie Webster and Joe Guy, either George James or Tab Smith on alto, and Stafford Simon or Sam Taylor on tenor. However, Millinder's studio recordings (available on a Classics CD) are the place to start. —*Scott Yanow*

The Lucky Millinder & His Orchestra 1942 / 1942 / Hindsight ♦♦♦

1943-1944 / 1943-1944 / Kaydee ♦♦♦♦
Other than seven selections, the edition of Lucky Millinder's Orchestra heard on this collector's LP did not have an opportunity to record. At the time, trumpeter Joe Guy (who was influenced by the early Dizzy Gillespie), altoist Tab Smith, and tenor saxophonist Sam "The Man" Taylor were the key soloists, although the colorful singer/guitarist Sister Rosetta Tharpe (who is featured on "Rock Me," "Down by the Riverside" and "I Want a Tall Skinny Papa") was the band's main attraction. These 13 swinging performances also include enjoyable versions of "Little John Special," "Is You Is or Is You Ain't My Baby," "St. Louis Breakdown" and "Cherokee" (a showcase for Taylor), among its more memorable selections. Recommended, if it can be found. —*Scott Yanow*

Mills Blue Rhythm Band

f. 1930, **db.** 1938
Group / Big Band, Swing
This fine big band was originally formed by drummer Willie Lynch as the Blue Rhythm Band in 1930 and as the Coconut Grove Orchestra it backed Louis Armstrong on some records. In 1931 Irving Mills became its manager and it was renamed the Mills Blue Rhythm Band. Lynch's departure later that year resulted in Baron Lee fronting the band until Lucky Millinder took over in 1934. The big band recorded frequently during 1931-37 (all of its recordings have been reissued on five Classics CDs) and, although the orchestra never really caught on or developed its own personality, its recordings did document many fine performances.

Among the sidemen were pianist Edgar Hayes, altoist Charlie Holmes, Joe Garland on tenor, drummer O'Neil Spencer, and by 1934 trumpeter Red Allen, trombonist J.C. Higginbotham and clarinetist Benny Bailey; later editions included altoist Tab Smith, pianist Billy Kyle and trumpeters Charlie Shavers and Harry "Sweets" Edison. When it broke up in 1938, Lucky Millinder formed his own big band. —*Scott Yanow*

1931 / Jan. 21, 1931-Jul. 30, 1931 / Classics ◆◆◆◆
The first of five CDs that reissue all of the recordings (other than a few alternate takes) by the Mills Blue Rhythm Band features spirited ensembles, some swinging moments, a few dated vocalists (including Chick Bullock, Dick Robertson and Charlie Lawman), and a no-name orchestra. Trombonist Harry White and pianist Edgar Hayes were the co-leaders, although the orchestra was actually organized by impresario Irving Mills. Since the group's best recordings tended to be in its later years, this CD is not essential, but fans of pre-swing big bands will want all five CDs. —*Scott Yanow*

1931-1932 / Jul. 30, 1931- Sep. 23, 1932 / Classics ◆◆◆◆◆
Although somewhat forgotten, the Mills Blue Rhythm Band was one of the better jazz orchestras of the early 1930s. Classics has reissued all of the big band's recordings over five CDs. In its early days, the band did not have an excess of famous soloists (altoist Charlie Holmes, from the Luis Russell Band was the first "name" to join), but the band improved with time and always featured excellent ensembles (with fine arrangements from trombonist Harry White), along with worthwhile solo statements. The second Classics Blue Rhythm CD is highlighted by "The Scat Song," "Doin' the Shake," "The Growl," "Rhythm Spasm" and "White Lightning." —*Scott Yanow*

● **1933-1934** / Mar. 1, 1933-Dec. 11, 1934 / Classics ◆◆◆◆◆
By 1933, the Mills Blue Rhythm Band was entering its prime period. On the third of Classics' five "complete" CDs by the orchestra, the music is excellent, except for four OK vocals by Chuck Richards. Trumpeter Ed Anderson emerged as a strong soloist during the period; trombonist J.C. Higginbotham joined the band for the final 11 of these 23 selections; the great trumpeter Henry "Red" Allen signed up in time for the last nine numbers; tenor saxophonist Joe Garland was featured on some good spots; and the rhythm section proves that it could hold its own with most others of the time. In addition, guest singer Adelaide Hall is heard on two previously unreleased numbers. Such charts as "Ridin' in Rhythm," "Harlem After Midnight" (heard in two versions), "The Stuff Is Here (And It's Mellow)," "The Growl" and "Swingin' in E Flat" are quite enjoyable. Recommended. —*Scott Yanow*

● **1934-1936** / Dec. 19, 1934-May 20, 1936 / Classics ◆◆◆◆◆
The fourth of the European Classics label's five CDs containing the complete output of the Mills Blue Rhythm Band captures the underrated orchestra at the peak of its powers. Formerly a "no-name" outfit, trumpeter Henry "Red" Allen, trombonist J.C. Higginbotham, clarinetist Buster Bailey and tenor saxophonist Joe Garland were the group's star soloists by this time. In addition, by the last eight numbers on this highly recommended program, altoist Tab Smith was also part of the band. The CD starts off with three numbers on which singer Chuck Richards is backed by a sextet including Allen, Bailey and trombonist Benny Morton. Otherwise, the program features the full orchestra (directed by Lucky Millinder by this time). There are many exciting tracks, along with a few ballad vocal features for Richards, with the more memorable performances including "Spitfire," "Ride Red Ride," "Congo Caravan," "There's Rhythm in Harlem" (which hints at the then-unwritten "In the Mood"), "Truckin'," and "E Flat Stride." This is the best of the five Classics Blue Rhythm releases. —*Scott Yanow*

1936-1937 / May 20, 1936-Jul. 1, 1937 / Classics ◆◆◆◆◆
The fifth and final Classics CD by the Mills Blue Rhythm Band starts out at the same high level as the fourth set. With trumpeter Henry "Red" Allen, trombonist J.C. Higginbotham, altoist Tab Smith and tenor saxophonist Joe Garland in the band (pianist Billy Kyle soon joined up as well), along with a solid rhythm section, the orchestra could swing quite hard, as shown on such numbers as "St. Louis Wiggle Rhythm," "Merry-Go-Round," "Big John's Special" and "Algiers Stomp." However, by 1937 (when the second half of this CD was recorded), Allen, Higginbotham and Garland had departed. The music is still worthwhile, with Smith and young trumpeters Harry "Sweets" Edison and Charlie Shavers in the band, but the enthusiasm was starting to drop. Due to the heavy competition from the many better-known orchestras, the Mills Blue Rhythm Band would soon become a forgotten part of history, but as the five Classics CDs show, the orchestra did create quite a bit of worthwhile music in the 1930s. —*Scott Yanow*

The Mills Brothers

f. Piqua, OH
Vocal Group / Classic Jazz, Swing, Pop, Show Tunes, Traditional Pop
The Mills Brothers became so popular as a middle-of-the-road pop vocal group

that one forgets just how innovative they were in the 1930s. Billed as "Four Boys and a Guitar," they were experts at imitating instruments including trumpet, trombone, tuba and string bass. With the backing of just a guitar, they simulated a full band and amazed listeners. The Mills Brothers (Herbert, Harry, Donald and John Jr.) started out singing in vaudeville and tent shows, were featured on a radio show for ten months in Cincinnati, arrived in New York and by the end of 1931 were an instant hit. They recorded frequently throughout the decade, made appearances in many films (including 1932's *Big Broadcast*) and recorded with Bing Crosby, the Boswell Sisters and Duke Ellington. John Jr.'s death in 1935 was a tragic loss, although John Sr. effectively took his place. However, by 1942 with their hit "Paper Doll," the old sound gave way to a more conventional pop setting. Fortunately, the English JSP label has reissued on six CDs all of the Mills Brothers' early recordings (1931-39), and these feature the group at the peak of their creativity. —*Scott Yanow*

● **Chronological, Vol. 1** / Oct. 12, 1931-Apr. 14, 1932 / JSP ◆◆◆◆◆
The English JSP label, on six CDs, has reissued in chronological order all of the Mills Brothers recordings from the 1931-39 period. Although they became a best-selling middle-of-the-road pop vocal group in the 1940s, the Mills Brothers were most notable during their first decade for their uncanny ability to imitate instruments, particularly trumpet, trombone and bass. Using only a rhythm guitar, the Mills Brothers were able to sound like an instrumental quintet. This first volume has plenty of hot numbers (including "Nobody's Sweetheart," three versions of "Tiger Rag," and a remarkable rendition of "Sweet Sue"), a couple of medleys with the Boswell Sisters, Bing Crosby and the not-so-hot singer Frank Munn, an appearance on a radio commercial and versions of "Shine" and "Dinah" with Bing Crosby. All of these CDs are highly recommended, particularly to listeners not familiar with the Mills Brothers' earliest (and best) period. —*Scott Yanow*

Early Transcripts and Rare Recordings / Oct. 25, 1931-1945 / Broadway Intermission ◆◆◆◆
This LP release from the collector's label Broadway Intermission has a variety of rarities featuring the Mills Brothers. The unique group (which sounds like an instrumental combo despite utilizing four voices and just an acoustic guitar) is teamed with Bing Crosby (on three alternate versions of studio recordings and a radio broadcast), Al Jolson (two songs from the mid-'40s), Dick Powell (two songs from movies), Duke Ellington's Orchestra ("Diga Diga Do"), Cab Calloway and Don Redman's Orchestra ("Doin' the New Lowdown"), Louis Armstrong (classic versions of "W.P.A." and "The Song Is Ended") and on a medley with the Boswell Sisters, Bing Crosby and singer Frank Munn (whose racist song is best forgotten). In addition there are a couple of their unaccompanied records. Except for the radio broadcasts, all of the music has since been reissued on CD but this LP (if located) does give collectors a well-rounded look at the Mills Brothers' collaborations during their early years. —*Scott Yanow*

★ **Mills Brothers: The Anthology (1931-1968)** / 1931-1968 / MCA ◆◆◆◆◆
The Mills Brothers: The Anthology is a comprehensive 48-song overview of the vocal group's career, spanning their entire career and featuring 32 of their biggest hits. Most of their most famous songs—including "Paper Doll," "Glow-Worm," "Lazy River," and "Rockin' Chair"—are included on this double disc set and the sound is the best it has ever been. In short, it is the definitive retrospective of this ground-breaking vocal quartet. —*Stephen Thomas Erlewine*

Chronological, Vol. 2 / May 1932-Feb. 24, 1934 / JSP ◆◆◆◆◆
The second of six CDs from the British JSP label to trace all of the Mills Brothers' recordings from their first eight years on record has 23 performances covering a 21 month period. In addition to their solo records in which the four vocalists are accompanied only by an acoustic guitar, there are collaborations with Duke Ellington ("Diga Diga Do"), Cab Calloway and the Don Redman Orchestra ("Doin' the New Lowdown"), Alice Faye ("Dinah") and Bing Crosby (two versions of "My Honey's Lovin' Arms"); the latter also includes short spots for future bandleaders Benny Goodman, Tommy Dorsey and Bunny Berigan. The studio recordings are augmented by two numbers from a soundtrack of a film. Some of the other high points of this quite fascinating release include "The Old Man of the Mountain," "Bugle Call Rag," a haunting version of "Smoke Rings" and "I've Found a New Baby." The Mills Brothers at their best. —*Scott Yanow*

Chronological, Vol. 5 (1937-38) / Feb. 2, 1933-Aug. 23, 1938 / JSP ◆◆◆◆◆
The fifth of six JSP CDs that reissue all of the Mills Brothers' early recordings in chronological order mostly covers the July 1937-Aug. 1938 period. In addition to particularly memorable renditions of "Organ Grinder's Swing" and "Caravan," there are three enjoyable collaborations with Louis Armstrong of which "The Song Is Ended" is a definite highlight. There is also a broadcast version of "Flat Foot Floogie," two odd numbers that team Louis Armstrong with Harry Mills ("Elder Eatmore's Sermon on Throwing Stones" and "On Generosity") that do not really come off and three earlier numbers (including a medley with the Don Redman Orches-

tra) that had been formerly bypassed in this definitive series. Highly recommended as are all six of these volumes. —*Scott Yanow*

Chronological, Vol. 3 / May 29, 1934-Feb. 20, 1935 / JSP ✦✦✦✦
For the third of six JSP CDs, the Mills Brothers' complete recordings from a nine-month period are reissued in chronological order for the first time. Other than a couple of numbers from film soundtracks with singer-actor Dick Powell ("Out for No Good" and a hot version of "Lulu's Back in Town"), all 23 selections on this set find the Mills Brothers unaccompanied except for the use of a rhythm guitar. As usual for the group in this era, the four singers do a remarkable job of imitating instruments (particularly trumpet, trombone and bass) and their hotter numbers dominate. Highlights of Vol. 3 from JSP's essential series include "Put on Your Old Grey Bonnet," "Nagasaki," "Some of These Days," "I've Found a New Baby" and a remake of "Tiger Rag." —*Scott Yanow*

Chronological, Vol. 6 / May 30, 1935-Aug. 23, 1939 / JSP ✦✦✦✦
The sixth and final CD in the JSP label's Mills Brothers series starts off with a pair of alternate takes from 1935 ("What's the Reason" and "Nagasaki") that had been bypassed earlier, plus two Harry Mills solo recordings made with Andy Kirk's Orchestra in 1936. The remainder of the CD dates from January-August 1939 and has some remakes ("Sweet Sue," "Goodbye Blues," "Smoke Rings" and "Shine") plus many newer songs (including "Jeepers Creepers," "F.D.R. Jones" and "And the Angels Sing"). Within a few years the Mills Brothers would drop their imitations of instruments (which gave the group its unique identity) and suddenly become hugely popular (if much more conventional) in the pop music world. This sixth volume features the group still in their creative prime. All six CDs are highly recommended. —*Scott Yanow*

Chronological, Vol. 4 / Oct. 28, 1935-Jun. 29, 1937 / JSP ✦✦✦✦
It is ironic that the Mills Brothers are chiefly remembered for being a middle-of-the-road pop vocal group that sang conservative music in the 1940s and '50s for they started out as an innovative jazz band. Up until the early 1940s the Mills Brothers brilliantly imitated instruments, sounding like a full ensemble, even though the only "real" instrument they used was an acoustic guitar. Vol. 4 out of the six very valuable CDs compiled by the English JSP label finds the Brothers dealing with a very traumatic experience, the death of John Mills, Jr. (in early 1936) who had supplied the bass parts and been the group's guitarist. John Sr. (the father of the four brothers) took his son's place as a singer while a variety of different guitarists (starting with Bernard Addison) were used. On this CD the group is heard on four numbers from 1935 (John Jr.'s last records) and then resuming with John Sr. from June 23, 1936 forward. The Mills Brothers' sound was largely unchanged and they had a successful collaboration with a young Ella Fitzgerald in 1937 along with four delightful numbers (plus two alternate takes) with Louis Armstrong; in addition, Harry Mills took "I Found the Thrill Again" as a solo feature. Highlights of this enjoyable set include "Shoe Shine Boy," "Pennies from Heaven," "Carry Me Back to Old Virginny" and "In the Shade of the Old Apple Tree" (the last two with Armstrong). —*Scott Yanow*

Irving Mills

b. Jan. 16, 1894, New York, NY, d. Apr. 21, 1985, Palm Springs, CA
Vocals / Classic Jazz
Irving Mills did a great deal to help jazz, making himself a great deal of money in the process. He is most famous for his work as manager for Duke Ellington during 1926-39, helping Duke gain his job at the Cotton Club in addition to securing numerous recording sessions and important engagements; he also wrote the lyrics to some of Ellington's songs including "It Don't Mean a Thing if It Ain't Got That Swing," "Mood Indigo" and "Sophisticated Lady." He had earlier worked with his brother Jack in establishing a music publishing business that became Mills Music, Inc. Mills also promoted Cab Calloway, Benny Carter, Fletcher Henderson, Jimmie Lunceford and Don Redman and appeared as a singer on many sessions (including some with Ellington). He put together all-star recording groups under the names of the Whoopee Makers and Irving Mills' Hotsy Totsy Gang (1928-30) and in 1931 became the manager for an orchestra which he renamed the Mills Blue Rhythm Band. After breaking with Ellington in 1939, Irving Mills maintained a lower profile but stayed active in management and music publishing into the 1960s. —*Scott Yanow*

● **Irving Mills and His Hotsy Totsy Gang, Vol. 1** / Jul. 27, 1928-Jul. 31, 1929 / Retrieval ✦✦✦✦✦
Irving Mills had a multifaceted career as a promoter (most notably for Duke Ellington), manager, occasional vocalist and lyricist. From 1928-30, he led and organized a series of recordings under the title of the Hotsy Totsy Gang. The British Retrieval label reissued all of the music on three definitive LPs in the 1980s. The first album features music from five different studio bands with such young sidemen as cornetist Jimmy McPartland, Dudley Fosdick on mellophone, Jack Pettis on C-melody sax, guitarist Eddie Lang, drummer Ben Pollack, trombonist Jack

Teagarden and clarinetists Benny Goodman and Jimmy Dorsey, among others; Mills sings two songs. Among the hotter numbers are "'Doin' the New Lowdown," "Digga Digga Do," "Futuristic Rhythm" and "Out Where the Blues Began." Four alternate takes are included on this excellent set, which is highly recommended (if it can be found) to 1920s collectors. —*Scott Yanow*

Irving Mills and His Hotsy Totsy Gang, Vol. 2 / Jul. 31, 1929-Jan. 6, 1930 / Retrieval ✦✦✦✦✦
The second of three LPs from the British Retrieval label that reissued all of the recordings released under the name of Irving Mills and His Hotsy Totsy Gang has music recorded during six sessions. These include a couple of test pressings and two rare selections from 1929 that were recorded strictly for radio airplay. Mills introduces the music on the latter, but is otherwise absent. Many all-stars from the era make notable appearances, including trumpeters Phil Napoleon and Manny Klein, trombonist Miff Mole, Bill "Bojangles" Robinson (who sings and tap dances on "Ain't Misbehavin'" and "Doin' the New Lowdown"), and clarinetists Pee Wee Russell and Jimmy Dorsey. An extra bonus is the participation of Hoagy Carmichael, who leads the band through seven of his numbers (including an early upt-empo version of "Stardust," playing piano and singing three songs. All three volumes are recommended, particularly since some of the music has not yet been reissued on CD. —*Scott Yanow*

Irving Mills and His Hotsy Totsy Gang, Vol. 3 / Feb. 6, 1930-May 3, 1931 / Retrieval ✦✦✦✦✦
This was the third of three LPs put out by the English Retrieval label in the early '80s, fully documenting the many overlapping groups that recorded under the name of Irving Mills' Hotsy Totsy Gang. An unknown version of "High and Dry" (only previously out in Argentina) leads off the date and is followed by the last two Hotsy Totsy sessions, including three titles and an alternate that feature cornetist Bix Beiderbecke on his last legs. Other sidemen include trumpeter Manny Klein, clarinetist Benny Goodman, trombonist Jack Teagarden, violinist Joe Venuti and singer Dick Robertson. The second side of this album has three titles (including a test pressing) from the Mills Merry Makers (Jack Teagarden sings "When You're Smiling"), and three songs and two alternates by Irving Mills' Orchestra that are more in the dance band vein. Hopefully, all of the titles will someday become available on CD, but the LPs (which have extensive liner notes) are fairly definitive and should delight 1920s collectors. —*Scott Yanow*

Pete Minger

Trumpet, Fluegelhorn / Bop
A talented bop-based trumpeter, Pete Minger has an attractive sound and a strong improvising style. After attending Tennessee State College and Berklee, Minger spent ten years with Count Basie's Orchestra (1970-80) as a featured soloist. Minger settled in Miami in the early '80s and has freelanced in the area ever since. He has led superior quartet sessions for Spinnster (1983, later reissued on Concord) and Concord (1992). —*Scott Yanow*

Straight from the Source / Oct. 31, 1983 / Spinster ✦✦✦✦✦

● **Minger Paintings** / 1991 / Jazz Alliance ✦✦✦✦✦
Probably the most rewarding record produced by the late Carolyn Leslie for her Spinster label was a superb quartet session featuring Pete Minger's fluegelhorn called *Straight from the Source*. This CD reissue brings back the original date, plus two previously unreleased tracks ("Just One of Those Things" and "Alone Together"). Best known for his association with Count Basie, Minger is heard taking full advantage of the rare chance to stretch out with just a rhythm section (pianist Dolph Castellano, bassist Keter Betts and drummer Bobby Durham), and he digs into the standards and really does stretch himself. An underrated gem. —*Scott Yanow*

Look to the Sky / Aug. 1992 / Concord Jazz ✦✦✦✦
Fluegelhornist Pete Minger had one of his rare chances to lead a record date for this Concord session and he used it to play quiet but spirited bebop in a quartet with pianist John Campbell, bassist Kiyoshi Kitagawa and drummer Ben Riley. While Campbell's solos show the influence of Bud Powell and the bass-drums team is quite supportive, Minger's soft-toned but fluid fluegelhorn is well featured. He is not afraid to push himself and to his credit his occasional mistakes are left on the record. Pete Minger proves to be a master of the bop vocabulary and is in generally excellent form on nine melodic standards along with his title cut. Bop lovers will not be disapointed by this fine CD. —*Scott Yanow*

Mingus Big Band

b. 1991
Group / Post-Bop
A major expansion on Mingus Dynasty, the Mingus Big Band (which often uses more than 20 musicians) has since 1991 explored the great bassist's music at least

once a week. They play regularly at the Time Spot Cafe in New York and their series of recordings for Dreyfus are often rather remarkable. The huge group performs some of Mingus' most complex works with spirit, virtuosity and plenty of color. Such musicians as Randy Brecker, Ryan Kisor, Lew Soloff, Jack Walrath, Phillip Harper, Art Baron, Frank Lacy, Ronnie Cuber, Alex Foster, Craig Handy, Chris Potter, Steve Slagle, John Stubblefield, James Carter, Kenny Drew, Jr., Michael Formanek, and Marvin "Smitty" Smith are among the many involved in this worthy and exciting project. —*Scott Yanow*

★ **Mingus Big Band 93: Nostalgia in Times Square** / Mar. 1993 / Dreyfus ✦✦✦✦✦
There have been many attempts to revisit the music of Charles Mingus ever since his death in 1979 (with several of the groups being called Mingus Dynasty), but this is by far the most successful of all the Mingus tribute albums. The 20-piece Mingus Big Band is an all-star unit comprising mostly younger musicians who have spent several years really studying and getting inside the great bassist's music. Their debut CD has such spirited soloists as baritonist Ronnie Cuber (who introduces "Nostalgia in Times Square" with a memorable story of his first encounter with Mingus), trumpeters Randy Brecker, Ryan Kisor and Jack Walrath, trombonists Art Baron, Frank Lacy and Dave Taylor, altoist Steve Slagle, tenors Chris Potter, Craig Handy and John Stubblefield and pianist Kenny Drew, Jr., among others. The ten Mingus compositions are all given memorable treatments, particularly "Moanin'," the witty and somewhat nutty "Don't Be Afraid, the Clown's Afraid Too" and "Weird Nightmare." The new arrangements by Sy Johnson, Jack Walrath and Ronnie Cuber are quite crowded and very much in the spirit of Mingus. This was one of the top recordings to be released in 1994 and is essential for all serious jazz collections. —*Scott Yanow*

Gunslinging Bird / 1995 / Dreyfus ✦✦✦✦✦
The Mingus Big Band had been together four years when they recorded this set while on a European tour. The musicians had mastered the great bassist's music, resulting in versions of a variety of Mingus classics that rank with the originals. The largely all-star 15-piece band includes such names as trumpeters Randy Brecker, Phillip Harper and Ryan Kisor, trombonist Frank Lacy, baritonist Gary Smulyan, tenor saxophonists Craig Handy, John Stubblefield, and Chris Potter, and pianist Kenny Drew, Jr. Each of the nine performances are exciting, both in the overcrowded ensembles and the solo statements, with the highlights including "Reincarnation of a Lovebird," "Fables of Faubus" (featuring Harper and altoist Steve Slagle), an explosive "Hog Callin' Blues" (showcasing John Stubblefield's highly expressive tenor), and "Started Medley" (based on "I Can't Get Started"). One can understand, listening to this single disc, why the Mingus Big Band began winning polls as jazz's top orchestra shortly afterwards. —*Scott Yanow*

Live in Time / 1996 / Dreyfus ✦✦✦✦✦
Having exhausted most of the late bassist's best-known songs, the Mingus Big Band emphasizes obscurities (such as "Sue's Changes," "Children's Hour of Dream" and "Chair in the Sky"), along with later-period work, on their third release, a double CD. The orchestra really digs into the complex material, and they perform Mingus' almost impossible-to-play originals with joy, swing and constant excitement. Among the many all-stars on this fascinating and highly enjoyable set (all of whom are featured) are trumpeters Randy Brecker, Phillip Harper and Ryan Kisor, trombonists Frank Lacy, Robin Eubanks and Britt Woodman, altoists Gary Bartz and Steve Slagle, Seamus Blake, Mark Shim and John Stubblefield on tenors, Ronnie Cuber or Gary Smulyan on baritone and Kenny Drew, Jr., or John Hicks on piano. The gloriously overcrowded ensembles, the explosive solos and the spirit of Mingus are three of the many reasons to acquire this memorable effort. —*Scott Yanow*

Que Viva Mingus! / 1997 / Dreyfus ✦✦✦
Que Viva Mingus! is an album dedicated to Mingus' considerable output of Latin-influenced jazz. The selections here include well-known Mingus compositions like "Los Mariachis," "Dizzy Moods," "Ysabel's Table Dance," and "Cumbia and Jazz Fusion," as well as some more obscure titles like "Slippers" and "Moods in Mambo," the album's oldest number, dating from 1949. Among the standout soloists are Randy Brecker on trumpet, John Stubblefield on tenor sax, Steve Slagle on soprano and alto saxes, Ronnie Cuber on baritone sax, and Dave Kikowski on piano. This is exciting, joyous, raucous, and still modern-sounding music, as fresh and challenging as the day it was written. And you can even dance to some of it. —*Joel Roberts*

Mingus Dynasty

b. 1979, **db.** 1991
Group / Post-Bop
Started shortly after bassist/leader Charles Mingus' death in 1979, Mingus Dynasty has featured many of his top alumni in spirited concerts and recordings. Not all of the records come up to the level of Mingus' best performances (the bassist is clearly missed) but many recapture his spirit. The group expanded for a 1988 concert to temporarily become "Big Band Charlie Mingus." Among the musicians who

have participated in the Mingus Dynasty project (which has resulted in recordings for Elektra, Atlantic, Soul Note and Storyville) were Jimmy Owens, Randy Brecker, Richard Williams, Jon Faddis, Jimmy Knepper, John Handy, Joe Farrell, Ricky Ford, George Adams, David Murray, Clifford Jordan, Nick Brignola, Don Pullen, Sir Roland Hanna, Jaki Byard, Dannie Richmond, Billy Hart, Kenny Washington and bassists Charlie Haden, Aladar Pege, Mike Richmond, Reggie Johnson, Reggie Workman and Richard Davis. Mingus Dynasty has been eclipsed in recent years by the remarkable Mingus Big Band. —*Scott Yanow*

● **Chair in the Sky** / May 1980 / Elektra ✦✦✦✦✦
After bassist/composer Charles Mingus' death on January 5, 1979, a reunion band featuring some of his former sidemen called Mingus Dynasty was formed. Cut just six months after the bassist's demise, this album was the first Mingus Dynasty recording, and it has its moments. Such alumni as altoist John Handy, trombonist Jimmy Knepper, trumpeter Jimmy Owens and tenorman Joe Farrell met up with two members of Mingus' last major band (pianist Don Pullen and drummer Dannie Richmond), plus bassist Charlie Haden, who ably fills in for the late bandleader. In addition to "Goodbye Pork Pie Hat" (which was becoming popular at the time), the septet performs three numbers from Mingus' collaboration with Joni Mitchell, plus "Boogie Stop Shuffle" and "My Jelly Roll Soul." Handy and Pullen, in particular, fare well in this spirited setting, although one does miss the innovative bassist. —*Scott Yanow*

Live at Montreux / Jul. 18, 1980 / Atlantic ✦✦✦✦
The second Mingus Dynasty recording displays plenty of energy as the music of Charles Mingus (who had passed away 18 months earlier) is kept alive. Of the musicians in the septet, only trombonist Jimmy Knepper (who provided most of the arrangements) was a longtime member of Mingus' bands. Most of the other players (tenor saxophonist Joe Farrell, trumpeter Randy Brecker, pianist Sir Roland Hanna and drummer Billy Hart) had only had short-term associations with Mingus, whose bass spot is filled by both Aladar Page and Mike Richmond. For the recorded concert, they perform six of the bassist's compositions, mixing together some famous tunes (including "Haitian Fight Song" and "Better Git Hit in Your Soul") with a couple of obscurities ("Consider Me, Oh Lord" and "Sketch Two," which was composed during his last year). Although having two bassists in his spot made sense, one does generally miss the presence of Mingus, even if some fireworks occur during these spirited interpretations. —*Scott Yanow*

Reincarnation / Apr. 5, 1982-Apr. 7, 1982 / Soul Note ✦✦✦

Live at the Village Vanguard / May 27, 1984 / Storyville ✦✦✦✦
Of the five musicians on this set (which include trumpeter Randy Brecker, pianist Roland Hanna, bassist Richard Davis and drummer Kenny Washington), only tenor saxophonist George Adams was closely associated with bassist Charles Mingus. Although the programming is a bit odd and a band really needs more than two horns to bring back the spirit of Mingus' music, the CD is better than expected. "Peggy's Blue Skylight" is heard in a one-minute excerpt from Hanna's unaccompanied piano solo. "Mr. Jelly Roll Soul" is a big success, for the rhythm section grasps the feel of early jazz. Brecker has the right ideas in his solo approach and Adams' R&Bish honking tenor also fits in with the joyful mood. Two lengthy ballads (Brecker's feature on "The Man Who Never Sleeps" and a strong version of "Duke Ellington's Sound of Love") precede "Better Get Hit in Your Soul." As an anti-climatic encore, the final two minutes of Adams' feature on "Goodbye Pork Pie Hat" concludes the set. Considering that this CD only has 44-minutes of music, it is unfortunate that the entire versions of "Peggy's Blue Skylight" and "Goodbye Pork Pie Hat" could not have been included. But, that quibble aside, this is a fine tribute to the unique and colorful music of Charles Mingus. —*Scott Yanow*

Mingus' Sounds of Love / Sep. 29, 1987-Sep. 30, 1991 / Soul Note ✦✦✦✦
One of the better Mingus Dynasty projects, it's possibly Dannie Richmond's last recording session. Long-time Mingus sideman Knepper has taken a number of tunes that Mingus wrote for the women in his life and fashioned a coherent session. —*Stuart Kremsky*

Next Generation Performs . . . / Jan. 8, 1988 / Columbia ✦✦✦
Passion and total commitment were the hallmarks of a performance by Charles Mingus; the presence or absence of these qualities determines the success of the various recordings made by the ever-changing Mingus Dynasty band. This 1991 release by a saxophone-heavy septet is kind of a hit-or-miss affair. Some of the pieces have an academic feel, like a first or second run-through. The band starts out a bit hesitant and restrained on a "new" tune, "Sketch Four," derived from a tape of Mingus singing the melody over a metronome. This is followed by a careful reading of "Portrait." But then the group wakes up to bowl you over with a power-house rendition of "Opus Four," first recorded in 1973. Trumpeter and musical director Jack Walrath, who was in Mingus' final bands, is sounding better than ever, with a crackling, shiny sound that cuts through the ensemble. One of the problems here might be too strong a reed section (Craig Handy, George Adams and Alex Fos-

ter all featured on tenor). In the rhythm section, stalwart pianist John Hicks, bassist Ray Drummond, and drummer Marvin "Smitty" Smith keep things popping. Smith in particular seems responsible for some of the better moments as he challenges and pushes the soloists with his everything-but-the-kitchen-sink approach to the trap set. It's good to have 72 minutes of "new" Mingus music, but it could have been better with an extra day's rehearsal and a trombone. *—Stuart Kremsky*

Live at the Theatre Boulogne-Billancourt, Vol. 2 / Jun. 8, 1988 / Soul Note ♦♦♦
This edition of Big Band Charlie Mingus, a large scale version of the ongoing Mingus Dynasty project, includes a number of performers (Jimmy Knepper, Jaki Byard, the late Clifford Jordan and John Handy, among others) who had played in different editions of the Charles Mingus Jazz Workshop. The group also boasts a stellar saxophone section in John Handy, alto; David Murray, tenor and bass clarinet; Clifford Jordan, tenor and soprano; and Nick Brignola, baritone and flute. This disc features four lengthy versions of favorite Mingus compositions. The ensembles are occasionally a bit ragged, and there are the inevitable dull moments that occur in most live recordings, but the spirit is there and the solos are mostly fairly strong, particularly from David Murray and Jaki Byard. *—Stuart Kremsky*

Next Generation Performs Charles Mingus Brand New Compositions / Nov. 13, 1991 / Columbia ♦♦♦♦

Charles Mingus

b. Apr. 22, 1922, Nogales, AZ, **d.** Jan. 5, 1979, Cuernavaca, MX
Bass, Leader, Composer, Piano / Bop, Avant-Garde, Post Bop
Irascible, demanding, bullying, and probably a genius, Charles Mingus cut himself a uniquely iconoclastic path through jazz in the middle of the 20th century, creating a legacy that became universally lauded only after he was no longer around to bug people. As a bassist, he knew few peers, blessed with a powerful tone and pulsating sense of rhythm, capable of elevating the instrument into the front line of a band. But had he been just a string player, few would know his name today. Rather, he was the greatest bass-playing leader/composer jazz has ever known, one who always kept his ears and fingers on the pulse, spirit, spontaneity, and ferocious expressive power of jazz.

Intensely ambitious yet often earthy in expression, simultaneously radical and deeply traditional, Mingus' music took elements from everything he had experienced—from gospel and blues through New Orleans jazz, swing, bop, Latin music, modern classical music, even the jazz avant-garde. His touchstone was Duke Ellington, but Mingus took the sonic blend and harmonies of Ellingtonia much further, throwing in abrasive dissonances and abrupt changes in meter and tempo, introducing tremendously exhilarating accelerations that generated a momentum of their own. While his early works were written out in a classical fashion, by the mid-'50s, he had worked out a new way of getting his unconventional visions across, dictating the parts to his musicians while allowing plenty of room for the players' own musical personalities and ideas. He was also a formidable pianist, fully capable of taking that role in a group—which he did in his 1961-62 bands, hiring another bassist to fill in for him.

Along the way, Mingus made a lot of enemies, causing sometimes violent confrontations on and off the bandstand. A big man physically, he used his bulk as a weapon of intimidation, and he was not above halting concerts to chew out inattentive audiences or errant sidemen, even cashiering a musician now and then on the spot. At one of his concerts in Philadelphia—and a memorial to a dead colleague at that—he broke up the show by slamming the piano lid down, nearly smashing his pianist's hands, and then punched trombonist Jimmy Knepper in the mouth. For a savage physical portrait of the emotions that seethed within him, check out the photo on the cover of Duke Ellington's *Money Jungle;* Mingus looks as if he is about to kill someone. But he could also be a gentle giant as his moods permitted, and that quality can be felt in some of his music.

Mingus felt the lash of racial prejudice very intensely—which, combined with the frustrations of making it in the music business on his own terms, found its outlet in music. Indeed, some of his bizarre titles were political in nature, such as "Fables of Faubus" (referring to the Arkansas governor who tried to keep Little Rock schools segregated), "Oh Lord, Don't Let Them Drop That Atomic Bomb on Me" or "Remember Rockefeller at Attica." But he could also be wildly humorous, the most notorious example being "If Charlie Parker Was a Gunslinger, There'd Be a Whole Lot of Dead Copycats" (later shortened to "Gunslinging Bird").

Born in a Nogales army camp, Mingus was shortly thereafter taken to the Watts district of Los Angeles, where he grew up. The first music he heard was that of the church—the only music his stepmother allowed around the house—but one day, despite the threat of punishment, he tuned in Duke Ellington's "East St. Louis Toodle-Oo" on his father's crystal set, his first exposure to jazz. He tried to learn the trombone at six and then the cello, but he became fed up with incompetent teachers and ended up on the double bass by the time he reached high school. His early teachers were Red Callender and an ex-New York Philharmonic bassist named

Herman Rheinschagen, and he also studied composition with Lloyd Reese. A proto-Third Stream composition written by Mingus in 1940-41, "Half-Mast Inhibition" (recorded in 1960), reveals an extraordinary timbral imagination for a teenager.

As a bass prodigy, Mingus performed with Kid Ory in Barney Bigard's group in 1942 and went on the road with Louis Armstrong the following year. He would gravitate toward the R&B side of the road later in the '40s, working with the Lionel Hampton band in 1947-48, backing R&B and jazz performers, and leading ensembles in various idioms under the name Baron Von Mingus. He began to attract real national attention as a bassist for Red Norvo's trio with Tal Farlow in 1950-51, and after leaving that group, he moved to New York and began working with several stellar jazz performers, including Billy Taylor, Stan Getz and Art Tatum. He was the bassist in the famous 1953 Massey Hall concert in Toronto with Charlie Parker, Dizzy Gillespie, Bud Powell and Max Roach, and he briefly joined his idol Ellington, where he had the dubious distinction of being the only man Duke ever personally fired from his band.

Around this time, Mingus tried to make himself into a rallying point for the jazz community. He founded Debut Records in partnership with his then-wife Celia and Roach in 1952, seeing to it that the label recorded a wide variety of jazz from bebop to experimental music until its demise in 1957. Among Debut's most notable releases were the Massey Hall concert, an album by Miles Davis, and several Mingus sessions that traced the development of his ideas. He also contributed composed works to the Jazz Composers' Workshop from 1953 to 1955, and later in 1955, he founded his own Jazz Workshop repertory group that found him moving away from strict notation toward his looser, dictated manner of composing.

By 1956, with the release of *Pithecanthropus Erectus* (Atlantic), Mingus had clearly found himself as a composer and leader, creating pulsating, ever-shifting compendiums of jazz's past and present, feeling his way into the free jazz of the future. For the next decade, he would pour forth an extraordinary body of work for several labels, including key albums like *The Clown, New Tijuana Moods, Mingus Ah Um, Blues and Roots* and *Oh Yeah;* standards like "Goodbye Pork Pie Hat," "Better Git It in Your Soul," "Haitian Fight Song" and "Wednesday Night Prayer Meeting"; and extended works like *Meditations on Integration* and *Epitaph.* Through ensembles ranging in size from a quartet to an 11-piece big band, a procession of noted sidemen like Eric Dolphy, Jackie McLean, J.R. Monterose, Jimmy Knepper, Roland Kirk, Booker Ervin, and John Handy would pass, with Mingus' commanding bass and volatile personality pushing his musicians further than some of them might have liked to go. The groups with the great Dolphy (heard live on *Mingus At Antibes*) in the early '60s might have been his most dynamic, and *The Black Saint and the Sinner Lady* (1963), an extended ballet for big band that captures the anguished/joyful split Mingus personality in full, passionately wild cry—may be his masterpiece.

However, Mingus' obsessive efforts to free himself from the economic hazards and larceny of the music business nearly undermined his sanity in the 1960s (indeed, some of the liner notes for *The Black Saint* album were written by his psychologist, Dr. Edmund Pollock). He tried to compete with the Newport festivals by organizing his own Jazz Artists Guild in 1960 that purported to give musicians more control over their work, but that collapsed with the by-now-routine rancor that accompanied so many Mingus ventures. A calamitous, self-presented New York Town Hall concert in 1962; another, shorter-lived recording venture, Charles Mingus Records, in 1964-65; the failure to find a publisher for his autobiography *Beneath the Underdog,* and other setbacks broke his bank account and ultimately his spirit. He quit music almost entirely from 1966 until 1969, resuming performances in June 1969 only because he desperately needed money.

Financial angels in the forms of a Guggenheim Fellowship in composition, the publication of *Beneath the Underdog* in 1971, and the purchase of his Debut masters by Fantasy boosted Mingus' spirits, and a new stimulating Columbia album *Let My Children Hear Music* thrust him back into public attention. By 1974, he had formed a new young quintet, anchored by his loyal drummer Dannie Richmond and featuring Jack Walrath, Don Pullen and George Adams, and more compositions came forth, including the massive, kaleidoscopic, Colombian-based "Cumbia and Jazz Fusion" that began its life as a film score.

Respect was growing, but time, alas, was running out, for in fall, 1977, Mingus was diagnosed with amyotrophic lateral sclerosis (Lou Gehrig's disease), and by the following year, he was unable to play the bass. Though confined to a wheelchair, he nevertheless carried on, leading recording sessions, and receiving honors at a White House concert on Jun. 18, 1978. His last project was a collaboration, *Mingus,* with folk-rock singer Joni Mitchell, who wrote lyrics to Mingus' music and included samples of Mingus' voice on the record.

Since his death, Mingus' importance and fame increased remarkably, thanks in large part to the determined efforts of Sue Mingus, his widow. A posthumous repertory group, Mingus Dynasty, was formed almost immediately after his death, and that concept was expanded in 1991 into the exciting Mingus Big Band, which has resurrected many of Mingus' most challenging scores. *Epitaph* was finally reconstructed, performed and recorded in 1989 to general acclaim, and several box sets of portions of Mingus' output have been issued by Rhino/Atlantic, Mosaic and Fantasy. Beyond re-creations, the Mingus influence can be heard on Branford Marsalis' early *Scenes in the City* album, and especially in the big band writing of his brother Wynton. The Mingus blend of wildly colorful eclecticism solidly rooted in jazz history should serve his legacy well in a future increasingly populated by young conservatives who want to pay their respects to tradition and try something different. —*Richard S. Ginell*

The Young Rebel / May 6, 1946-Oct. 16, 1952 / Swingtime ✦✦✦✦

This collector's LP features bassist Charles Mingus in his early days on a variety of mostly very rare recordings. Four advanced selections are by "Baron Mingus" in 1946 and 1949, four are with Earl Hines (although three of those have vocals by Wini Brown) in 1947 and the remaining six tracks include two by Mingus with Lee Konitz in 1952 and an interesting quartet date led by bassist Oscar Pettiford who is heard here exclusively on cello. A bit of a hodgepodge set ranging from swing/bop to more adventurous sounds, this valuable LP should fill some gaps in Mingus collections. —*Scott Yanow*

☆ The Complete Debut Recordings / Apr. 1951-1958 / Debut ✦✦✦✦✦

This mammoth 12-CD box set may not contain Charles Mingus' most significant recordings (those would take place shortly after these sessions) but there is a remarkable amount of exciting and somewhat innovative music in this reissue of all of the dates recorded for Mingus' label Debut. There are duets and trios with pianist Spaulding Givens, a variety of odd third-stream originals (some with vocalist Jackie Paris and altoist Lee Konitz), the famous Massey Hall concert with Charlie Parker and Dizzy Gillespie (heard in two versions, one with Mingus' overdubbed bass), a four-trombone date with J.J. Johnson, Kai Winding, Bennie Green and Willie Dennis, trio sets with pianists Paul Bley, Hazel Scott and the obscure John Dennis, a quintet with trumpeter Thad Jones and Frank Wess on tenor and flute, Miles Davis' "Alone Together" session, a date led by trombonist Jimmy Knepper, a completely unissued 1957 sextet session and, most importantly, a greatly expanded live session with trombonist Eddie Bert and tenor saxophonist George Barrow which found Mingus finally finding himself musically. Many of these performances are now also available in smaller sets, but this attractive box (which has 64 previously unissued tracks among the 169 selections) is the best way to acquire this valuable music. —*Scott Yanow*

Thirteen Pictures: The Charles Mingus Anthology / 1952-1977 / Rhino ✦✦

It is a thankless and impossible task to sum up the career of Charles Mingus on only two CDs; everyone knows that. But Rhino does have the advantage of being a licensing company, and they did roam far afield for material from most of the important sources, to Atlantic, Debut, Impulse!, United Artists, EmArcy, Mingus' custom Jazz Workshop label, even into the hard-to-crack vaults of Columbia. The whole thing was then assembled into a lavish slipcase with extensive, play-by-play notes, but instead of a sensible chronological approach, Rhino scrambles the sequencing into something incomprehensible. Nevertheless, the newcomer to Mingus will get a colorful, varied, even powerful portrait of the irascible composer/bandleader/bassist. In addition to famous signature numbers like "Haitian Fight Song," "Better Get it in Your Soul," "Goodbye Pork Pie Hat" and "Pithecanthropus Erectus," there are a pair of extended works, odd sidetrips like a trio date with Duke Ellington and Max Roach, even a potent example of Mingus as a solo pianist ("Myself When I Am Real"). It might have been an indulgence on co-producer Hal Willner's part to devote more than two-fifths of the space in what was supposed to be a Mingus primer to the huge 28-minute "Cumbia and Jazz Fusion" and a 25-minute live rendition of "Meditations on Integration." But it was a courageous indulgence, for the kaleidoscope of Colombian rhythms, big-band flourishes, extended improvisation, and weird vocal humor makes for a bold entryway into Mingus' world, and "Meditations," despite the poor sound, receives a provocative performance. Oddly, for a label that distributes Atlantic's archival material, Rhino only includes four Atlantic cuts, but with the complete Mingus Atlantic sessions from 1956-1961 now available in another Rhino box, perhaps that was the plan all along. As such, this is about as useful a relatively affordable Mingus sampler as there is on CD, which isn't saying much, actually. —*Richard S. Ginell*

Jazz Composers Workshop / Oct. 31, 1954-Jan. 30, 1955 / Savoy ✦✦✦

The complex music on this LP finds bassist Charles Mingus looking towards contemporary classical music in some of the rather cool-toned arrangements. It was not until later in 1955 that he found the right combination of influences in which to express himself best, but these slightly earlier performances have their moments. Four of the selections feature tenor saxophonist Teo Macero, pianist Wally Cirillo, drummer Kenny Clarke and Mingus in a quartet while the other five tracks showcase a sextet with Macero, George Barrow on tenor and baritone, clarinetist/altoist John La Porta. —*Scott Yanow*

Intrusions / Dec. 1954 / Drive Archive ✦✦✦

Bassist Charles Mingus was at a transitional point in his career when he recorded this music (which was formerly out on Everest). He was about ready to chuck his explorations with modern classical music devices and add a strong emotional feel to his music. For these five selections the unique voices of trumpeter Thad Jones, altoist John LaPorta, Teo Macero on tenor and baritone, cellist Jackson Wiley and drummer Clem DeRosa are mixed together with Mingus' bass and occasional piano to create music tied to bop but utilizing some simultaneous soloing and unusual combinations of sound. The results are not quite essential but they are often fascinating. —*Scott Yanow*

Charles Mingus [Everest] / Dec. 1954 / Everest ✦✦✦

Before bassist/bandleader Charles Mingus hit upon infusing bop with the emotionalism of soulful church music along with other elements, he experimented with various combinations of jazz and classical music. This budget LP features a rather eclectic lineup of musicians (cornetist Thad Jones, Teo Macero on tenor, clarinetist John LaPorta, cellist Jackson Wiley and drummer Clem DeRosa) with the ensemble stretching out on four complex originals and an unusual version of "What Is This Thing Called Love." Jones' solos are the most interesting part of this adventurous and often odd music. —*Scott Yanow*

Chazz / Dec. 12, 1955 / Fantasy ✦✦✦

The Jazz Workshop of 1955 is in superb form, caught in performance at the Caf Bohemia in New York. Max Roach only appears for a "Percussion Discussion" with Mingus, but the forgotten Willie Jones is no slouch either. A typically adventurous set of tunes includes two montages. ("Septemberly" combines "September in the Rain" and "Tenderly," while "All the Things You Can C-Sharp" is a blend of "All the Things You Are," Rachmaninoff's "Prelude in C-Sharp" and "Clair de Lune.") It's a very spirited date, ranking with his best work in the period. A further disc, *Charles Mingus Quintet Plus Max Roach* (Fantasy 86009), derives from the same date; these were combined as Prestige P-24010. And the boxed set of the *Complete Debut Recordings* (Debut 12-CDC-4402-2) includes an additional hour of previously unissued material. —*Stuart Kremsky*

Mingus at the Bohemia / Dec. 23, 1955 / Original Jazz Classics ✦✦✦✦

A live performance at the Club Bohemia in New York, this is the first Mingus recording to feature mostly his own compositions. Some are his future standards. Here are his first attempts at future techniques such as combining two songs into one. His bass playing really stands out. —*Michael Katz*

Plus Max Roach / Dec. 23, 1955 / Original Jazz Classics ✦✦✦✦

Charles Mingus [Prestige] / Dec. 23, 1955 / Prestige ✦✦✦✦✦

This Prestige two-fer combines two LPs recorded at New York's Cafe Bohemia in December 1955, originally known as *Mingus at the Bohemia* and *Mingus Quintet Plus Max Roach*. This is some of his most spirited live work, with a number of experiments in combining themes (e.g., "Septemberly" is a montage of "September" and "Tenderly.") It's an almost totally successful date, with Max Roach adding another dimension to the few tracks he's on. Note that Fantasy's exhaustive Complete Debut Recordings adds no less than 11 more tracks to the original 12. —*Stuart Kremsky*

★ Pithecanthropus Erectus / Jan. 30, 1956 / Atlantic ✦✦✦✦✦

This Atlantic set has the first truly classic Charles Mingus performance, the lengthy title cut which attempts to depict musically the rise and fall of man. Altoist Jackie McLean, tenor saxophonist J.R. Monterose, pianist Mal Waldron and drummer Willie Jones join the bassist/leader for some stirring music with the humorous "A Foggy Day," (complete with sirens and horns honking like automobiles), "Profile of Jackie" and "Love Chant" completing the particularly strong program. —*Scott Yanow*

Passions of a Man: The Complete Atlantic Recordings (1956-1961) / 1956-1961 / Rhino ✦✦✦✦✦

Charles Mingus really came into his own when he signed with Atlantic in 1956. He began incorporating his own musical roots (church music, blues, pre-bop, and his wide range of emotions) along with advanced harmonies to form his own brand of jazz. The bassist/composer opened his music up to collective improvising (with several horn players often soloing together), changing tempos during a performance (sometimes purposely slowing down or speeding up), using stop-time, and urging his musicians to fully express themselves. Mingus' best performances, which could range from tender to explosive, looked both backwards and forwards at the same time. This six-CD set has all of Charles Mingus' Atlantic recordings from 1956-61, including the complete contents of *Pithecanthropus Erectus, The Clown, Blues & Roots, Oh Yeah,* the elusive *Tonight at Noon* and *Mingus at Antibes,* plus four "new" alternate takes from the *Blues & Roots* sessions, four conventional numbers from a date led by vibraphonist Teddy Charles, and a 75-minute interview (which takes up all of the final disc) conducted by Nesuhi Ertegun. Although the latter, which covers Mingus' early years, is really only worth hearing once, the music—some of the finest work of his career—is consistently timeless. The bassist pushed his sidemen so hard to be original that some of them (including tenors J.R. Monterose and Shafi Hadi, trombonist Jimmy Knepper and drummer Dannie Richmond) did their most significant work for Mingus; among the other stars heard on this important set are altoist Jackie McLean, tenorman Booker Ervin, baritonist Pepper Adams, the amazing Rahsaan Roland Kirk, Eric Dolphy (on alto and bass clarinet), and, in a guest spot, pianist Bud Powell. The many highlights include "Pithecanthropus Erectus," "Reincarnation of a Lovebird," "Haitian Fight Song," "Moanin'," "Wednesday Night Prayer Meeting," and "Ecclusiastics." —*Scott Yanow*

The Clown / Feb. 13, 1957-Mar. 12, 1957 / Atlantic ✦✦✦✦
All of Charles Mingus' Atlantic sessions are well worth picking up. "Haitian Fight Song" is a classic, "Reincarnation of a Lovebird" is close, "Blue Cee" gives the principals (which include trombonist Jimmy Knepper and Shafi Hadi on alto and tenor) a chance to stretch out and Jean Shepherd verbally improvises a memorable story on "The Clown." —*Scott Yanow*

Tonight at Noon / Mar. 12, 1957+Nov. 6, 1961 / Atlantic ✦✦✦✦

Mingus Three / Jul. 9, 1957 / Blue Note ✦✦✦
A rather conventional Charles Mingus recording, this trio set mostly features pianist Hampton Hawes (along with drummer Danny Richmond) performing jazz standards and blues along with Mingus' "Dizzy Moods." The music is high-quality bop as one would expect from the talented musicians (Mingus has almost as much solo space as Hawes), and this 1997 CD's contents have been reissued several times through the years. —*Scott Yanow*

★ **New Tijuana Moods** / Jul. 18, 1957-Aug. 6, 1957 / Bluebird ✦✦✦✦✦
Inspired by a somewhat riotous trip to Mexico, this set was one of bassist Charles Mingus' early classics. Virtually all of the musicians (trumpeter Clarence Shaw, trombonist Jimmy Knepper, altoist Shafi Hadi, pianist Bill Triglia and drummer Danny Richmond, plus percussionists Frankie Dunlop and Ysabel Morel) were inspired to play way above their heads by the volatile bandleader. This reissue of an earlier CD reissue appeared even earlier as a two-LP set with alternate takes to all five selections ("Dizzy Moods," the passionate "Ysabel's Table Dance, "Tijuana Gift Shop," "Los Mariachis" and "Flamingo"). This particular CD leaves out the lengthy alternate to "Los Mariachis" due to lack of space, but otherwise has the complete sessions. There are plenty of intense moments, some fairly free improvising in spots, and some of the best playing ever by these musicians. Recommended. —*Scott Yanow*

East Coasting / Aug. 16, 1957 / Bethlehem ✦✦✦✦
One of Charles Mingus' lesser-known band sessions, this set of five of his originals (plus the standard "Memories of You") features his usual sidemen of the period (trombonist Jimmy Knepper, trumpeter Clarence Shaw, Shafi Hadi on tenor and alto and drummer Danny Richmond) along with pianist Bill Evans. The music stretches the boundaries of bop, is never predictable and, even if this is not one of Mingus' more acclaimed dates, it is well worth acquiring, for the playing is quite stimulating. —*Scott Yanow*

A Modern Jazz Symposium of Music and Poetry / Oct. 1957 / Bethlehem ✦✦✦
Despite its title, this CD reissue (made available through Evidence) does not have poetry and is not a "symposium." What it does have is a memorable narration by Lonnie Elders on "Scenes in the City" (one of the best collaborations between the spoken word and jazz), four obscure Charles Mingus compositions for his sextet (which consists of the bassist/leader, trombonist Jimmy Knepper, Shafi Hadi on tenor and alto, either Bill Hardman or Clarence Shaw on trumpet, pianist Horace Parlan and drummer Dannie Richmond) and three previously unreleased performances including a runthrough on Dizzy Gillespie's "Woody 'n' You." An excellent set of challenging yet often accessible music. —*Scott Yanow*

Scenes in the City / Oct. 1957 / Affinity ✦✦✦✦
A lesser effort but still with more than its share of memorable moments, this Mingus set (a reissue of a date for Bethlehem) has plenty of fine solos by trombonist Jimmy Knepper and tenor saxophonist Shafi Hadi, appearances by trumpeters Bill Hardman and Clarence Shaw and a narration by Melvin Stewart on the interesting "Scenes in the City"; one of the better "jazz and poetry" efforts. —*Scott Yanow*

Jazz Portraits / Jan. 16, 1959 / United Artists ✦✦✦✦
This CD, a straight reissue of *Wonderland*, finds bassist/leader Charles Mingus really pushing altoist John Handy and tenor saxophonist Booker Ervin on four lengthy selections, highlighted by "Nostalgia in Times Square" and "No Private Income Blues." The music is advanced bop that looks towards the upcoming innovations of the avant-garde and is frequently quite exciting. —*Scott Yanow*

Wonderland / Jan. 16, 1959 / Blue Note ✦✦✦✦✦
The music on this LP has been reissued on CD as *Jazz Portraits*. Bassist Charles Mingus pushes his quintet (featuring altoist John Handy, Booker Ervin on tenor, pianist Richard Wyands and drummer Danny Richmond) to play with intensity and

creativity on four lengthy selections including "Nostalgia in Times square" and "Alice's Wonderland." —*Scott Yanow*

☆ **Blues and Roots** / Feb. 4, 1959 / Atlantic ✦✦✦✦✦
One of Charles Mingus' finest studio albums, this date finds the bassist utilizing a nonet (including altoists Jackie McLean and John Handy, Booker Ervin on tenor, baritonist Pepper Adams and the trombones of Jimmy Knepper and Willie Dennis) on six diverse but consistently stimulating originals. Highlights including "Wednesday Night Prayer Meeting," "Cryin' Blues," "E's Flat Ah's Flat Too" and especially "Moanin'." Although "My Jelly Roll Soul" does not really work, the other numbers find Mingus successfully looking both backwards (with group improvising, stop-time breaks and church-like harmonies) and forward (with advanced improvisations and a wider use of emotions than was being utilized in bop). —*Scott Yanow*

★ **Mingus Ah Um** / May 5, 1959-May 12, 1959 / Columbia ✦✦✦✦✦
This LP from 1959 is one of Charles Mingus' classics, highlighted by the original versions of "Better Git It in Your Soul," "Goodbye Pork Pie Hat," "Boogie Stop Shuffle" and "Fables of Faubus." Such top-notch musicians as altoist John Handy, tenors Booker Ervin and Shafi Hadi, trombonists Jimmy Knepper and Willie Dennis, pianist Roland Hanna and drummer Danny Richmond gave bassist Mingus one of his strongest units. —*Scott Yanow*

The Complete 1959 CBS Charles Mingus Sessions / May 5, 1959-Nov. 13, 1959 / Mosaic ✦✦✦✦
In 1959 Charles Mingus recorded two tightly edited LPs for Columbia titled *Mingus Ah Um* and *Mingus Dynasty*. Both of those albums are recommended in their original form as is this limited edition four-LP set which restores solos originally cut out and adds numerous alternate takes to these fascinating sessions. Such players as altoist John Handy, tenor saxophonists Booker Ervin and Shafi Hadi, trombonists Jimmy Knepper and Willie Dennis and trumpeters Richard Williams and Don Ellis and pianist Roland Hanna and Horace Parlan are heard on this deluxe set which is highlighted by the original versions of "Better Git It in Your Soul," "Fables of Faubus," "Boogie Stop Shuffle," "Goodbye Pork Pie Hat," and "Song with Orange." —*Scott Yanow*

Mingus Dynasty / Nov. 1, 1959-Nov. 13, 1959 / Columbia ✦✦✦✦✦
This CD is a straight reissue of the original LP and finds bassist Charles Mingus leading two overlapping but different nine and ten piece groups. Much of the music was written for soundtracks of the time but they easily stand out on their own with fine solos from trombonist Jimmy Knepper, Booker Ervin on tenor, altoist John Handy and pianist Roland Hanna uplifting such songs as "Slop," "Song with Orange," "Far Wells, Mill Valley" and two Duke Ellington-associated numbers. The music can also be heard in unedited form (with many solos added back in) on a Mosaic box set. —*Scott Yanow*

Mingus Revisited / May 24, 1960 / EmArcy ✦✦✦✦
This is an LP reissue of a set that was originally titled *Pre Bird* because it features some of the advanced originals that Charles Mingus wrote prior to hearing Charlie Parker. The bassist leads an undisciplined but colorful 25-piece orchestra on three titles including an Eric Dolphy feature on "Bemonable Lady" while the other five tracks are by a ten-piece (including two pianos) band; Lorraine Cousins sings "Eclipse" and "Weird Nightmare." It's an interesting set of typically unconventional music by Mingus. —*Scott Yanow*

★ **Mingus at Antibes** / Jul. 13, 1960 / Atlantic ✦✦✦✦✦
During 1960 bassist Charles Mingus led one of his finest bands, a pianoless quartet with Eric Dolphy (on alto, flute and bass clarinet), trumpeter Ted Curson and drummer Dannie Richmond. For this live concert, the band was augmented by the great tenor Booker Ervin for some stirring music. All of the music is memorable: "Wednesday Night Prayer Meeting," "Prayer for Passive Resistance," "What Love," "Folk Forms I," and "Better Git It in Your Soul." The immortal pianist Bud Powell sits in on a fine version of "I'll Remember April" and Dolphy and Ervin in particular generate a great deal of heat during some of their solos. —*Scott Yanow*

Charles Mingus Presents Charles Mingus / Oct. 20, 1960 / Candid ✦✦✦✦✦
This quartet date is probably among the very finest jazz records ever made. Dolphy and Curson make a great front line and Mingus and Richmond seem to share one mind between them. The absence of a piano keeps everyone on their toes. All first takes recorded in one afternoon, the session is presented as if it were a nightclub set of the period, complete with Mingus' spoken introduction. —*Stuart Kremsky*

☆ **The Complete Candid Recordings** / Oct. 20, 1960-Nov. 11, 1960 / Mosaic ✦✦✦✦✦
Bassist/leader Charles Mingus cut some of his most exciting and rewarding recordings for Candid in 1960, and this superb four-LP set (which unfortunately is a limited edition) contains all of the music except for a couple of alternate takes that showed up later on. Five selections feature the brilliant pianoless quartet of Eric Dolphy (on alto, bass clarinet and flute), trumpeter Ted Curson, Mingus and drummer Dannie Richmond, and these are highlighted by the bass clarinet-bass conversation on "What Love" and the interplay between the four musicians on the very

memorable "Folk Forms No. 1." Other musicians are added to six other selections (including the 19-minute jam "MDM") and five other numbers feature trumpeter Roy Eldridge who is teamed with altoist Dolphy on three of the songs; those pieces originally appeared on The Newport Rebels LP. This is a highly recommended set that promises to be hard to find in the future. —*Scott Yanow*

Mysterious Blues / Oct. 20, 1960-Nov. 11, 1960 / Candid ✦✦✦✦

Although a Mosaic box set claims to have all of Charles Mingus' Candid recordings, this CD, in addition to four duplications from the box, contains three alternate takes not included elsewhere: "Body and Soul" (featuring trumpeter Roy Eldridge and altoist Eric Dolphy), the Dannie Richmond drum solo "Melody from the Drums" and a septet runthrough on "Reincarnation of a Love Bird." A fine introduction into the music of Charles Mingus, this set still cannot compare to the Mosaic box which has the Mingus' pianoless quartet with Dolphy, Richmond and trumpeter Ted Curson, but completists will have to acquire both releases. —*Scott Yanow*

☆ Oh Yeah / Nov. 6, 1961 / Atlantic ✦✦✦✦✦

One of the great Charles Mingus CD's, this Atlantic reissue (which finds Mingus sticking exclusively to piano and vocal shouts throughout) not only features tenor saxophonist Booker Ervin, trombonist Jimmy Knepper, bassist Doug Watkins and drummer Dannie Richmond, but the amazing Rahsaan Roland Kirk on tenor, manzello, stritch, flute and siren. The music is quite emotional and passionate with "Hog Callin' Blues," "Wham Bam Thank You Ma'am" and the explosive "Ecclusiastics" being particularly memorable. —*Scott Yanow*

The Complete Town Hall Concert / Oct. 12, 1962 / Blue Note ✦✦✦

Charles Mingus' Town Hall Concert has long been considered a famous fiasco and the original United Artists LP (which contained just 36 minutes of music and did not bother identifying the personnel) made matters worse. But this Blue Note CD (released in 1994) does its best to clean up the mess. It contains over a half-hour of previously unreleased music and programs the selections largely in the same order as the concert. There are still confusing moments, inconclusive performances and songs cut off prematurely; Mingus was not in a good temper that day. A highlight among the "new" material is an Eric Dolphy alto solo on the second version of "Epitaph." Blue Note is to be congratulated for doing what they could with what they had, but there are still at least a couple dozen Mingus recordings that would be recommended before this one. —*Scott Yanow*

Town Hall Concert / Oct. 12, 1962 / Original Jazz Classics ✦

What a mess. Charles Mingus' Town Hall concert in 1962 (which was to utilize a large band) found him totally unprepared, with writers literally copying out parts on tables during the performance itself. Mingus' volatile personality did not help matters at all and, while the band was jamming the final number, stagehands closed the curtain. Just as well. This LP seeks to preserve some of the highlights of this fiasco, but there is not much of value here other than glimpses of Mingus' mammoth work, "Epitaph." —*Scott Yanow*

The Black Saint and the Sinner Lady / Jan. 20, 1963 / Impulse ✦✦✦✦✦

One of Charles Mingus' most successful longer suites, the six-part "Black Saint and the Sinner Lady" is full of surprising moments with the 11-piece band exploring a wide variety of moods and colors. Of particular note are Quentin Jackson's wa-wa trombone (which lets Mingus hint strongly at Duke Ellington) and Charlie Mariano's passionate alto. —*Scott Yanow*

☆ Mingus, Mingus, Mingus, Mingus, Mingus / Jan. 1963-Sep. 20, 1963 / Impulse ✦✦✦✦✦

This CD features two separate recording sessions with such top players as trumpeter Richard Williams, trombonists Quentin Jackson and Britt Woodman, Dick Hafer and Booker Ervin on tenors, the many reeds of Eric Dolphy and Jerome Richardson, altoist Charles Mariano and pianist Jaki Byard. Of the seven selections (all of which are memorable), high points include "Mood Indigo," the fiery "Hora Decubitus" and the definitive version of "Better Get Hit in Yo' Soul." —*Scott Yanow*

Mingus Plays Piano / Jul. 30, 1963 / Impulse! ✦✦✦✦

Bassist Charles Mingus would never qualify as a virtuoso on the piano, but his technique was reasonably impressive and his imagination quite brilliant. This unique solo piano CD (which was reissued in 1997) has a few standards ("Body and Soul," "Memories of You" and "I'm Getting Sentimental over You") along with some freely improvised originals, most of which are quite fascinating to hear, as if one were listening to Mingus think aloud. —*Scott Yanow*

Paris 1964 / 1964 / Le Jazz/Charly ✦✦✦

Bassist Charles Mingus is back in the limelight. Mosaic and Rhino have recently issued new sets, with Mosaic finally putting out his late '50s Columbia material in the fashion in which it was originally recorded. This concert date featured one of Mingus' greatest bands; it had two saxophonists in Eric Dolphy and Clifford Jordan, plus pianist Jaki Byard and drummer Dannie Richmond. Mingus created expansive, works-in-progress compositions, letting his band react, interact, develop,

tear apart and reconstruct his music. Dolphy and Jordan played intense, animated, surging solos, and Dolphy's furious alto sax and bass clarinet are contrasted by an evocative lyricism on flute. The sound quality is great and the performances unforgettable. —*Ron Wynn*

Concertgebouw Amsterdam, Vol. 1 / Apr. 10, 1964 / Ulysse Musique ✦✦✦✦

Charles Mingus' 1964 sextet was one of his most exciting bands, featuring Eric Dolphy (on alto, bass clarinet and flute) at his very best (just months before his premature death) along with tenor saxophonist Clifford Jordan, trumpeter Johnny Coles, the remarkably versatile pianist Jaki Byard, drummer Dannie Richmond and the bassist/leader. This first of two CDs taken from early in the band's European tour features lengthy versions of "Ow" (which was also called "Parkeriana" by Mingus), "So Long Eric" and "Orange Was the Color of Her Dress." Fascinating music; all of this classic group's live recordings are well worth searching for. —*Scott Yanow*

Concertgebouw Amsterdam, Vol. 2 / Apr. 10, 1964 / Ulysse Musique ✦✦✦✦

The second of two CDs taken from an Amsterdam concert features Charles Mingus' remarkable 1964 sextet (which included Eric Dolphy, Clifford Jordan, Jaki Byard and Johnny Coles) on a half-hour version of "Fables of Faubus," a nearly 23-minute rendition of "Meditation on a Pair of Wire Cutters" and a more concise bass feature on "Sophisticated Lady." The music is quite explorative, episodic, unpredictable and exciting. —*Scott Yanow*

Live in Stockholm 1964: The Complete Concert / Apr. 13, 1964 / Royal Jazz ✦✦✦

More material from the heavily documented Spring 1964 tour of Europe includes an interesting look at the band in rehearsal, complete with a short dialogue between Mingus and Dolphy about Dolphy's plans to stay in Europe after the tour. (He stayed and then died suddenly in Berlin on June 29.) Also notable here is the rather wacky rendition of "When Irish Eyes Are Smiling," a piece Mingus never recorded any other time. The sound is so-so. —*Stuart Kremsky*

Live in Oslo / Apr. 12, 1964 / Jazz Up ✦✦✦✦

It is very fortunate that Charles Mingus' 1964 sextet was so extensively recorded during its European tour for the great Eric Dolphy (who would pass away only a few months later) rarely sounded better and this was one of the strongest groups the volatile bassist ever led. This particular CD was taken from a television broadcast that is miraculously now also available on video. The very talented band really digs into "Fables of Faubus" and "Orange Was the Color of Her Dress" and, after Mingus stops "Ow" prematurely, the group swings hard on "Take the 'A' Train." —*Scott Yanow*

Astral Weeks / Apr. 14, 1964 / Moon ✦✦✦✦✦

The Charles Mingus sextet of 1964 was arguably the bassist's finest group, featuring the remarkable Eric Dolphy on alto, bass clarinet and flute, tenor saxophonist Clifford Jordan, trumpeter Johnny Coles, pianist Jaki Byard, drummer Dannie Richmond and the bassist/leader. Their European tour was well documented with many radio broadcasts later released on CD. This particular set has long versions of "Meditations on Integration" and "Fables of Faubus"; although the latter is nearly 34 minutes long, its episodic and unpredictable nature and colorful solos hold one's interest throughout. All of the group's recordings are quite exciting and this Italian import is a good place to start in exploring this important band's innovative music. —*Scott Yanow*

Revenge! / Apr. 17, 1964 / Revenge ✦✦✦✦

Of all of bassist Charles Mingus' bands, one of the most exciting was the sextet that he took to Europe in 1964. Consisting of the unique Eric Dolphy (on alto, bass clarinet and flute), tenor saxophonist Clifford Jordan, pianist Jaki Byard, drummer Dannie Richmond and trumpeter Johnny Coles, this band really stretched the limits of bebop. Mingus (greatly assisted by Richmond) constantly changed rhythms when the music became too comfortable and was always pushing his sidemen to play above their capabilities. *Revenge*, a two-CD set from the tour, was the first release on Sue Mingus' label. She organized her company so as to combat the many bootleggers who illegally put out music by her late husband without paying anyone. The Revenge two-fer has (despite saying that it is from April 18) the complete Paris concert of April 17. Coles, who unfortunately is not listed in the personnel, just appears on "So Long Eric" (the same version previously out on Fantasy's *The Great Concert of Charles Mingus*) before becoming ill; otherwise, this is a brilliant quintet date of previously unavailable music. While the versions of "Peggy's Blue Skylight" and "Orange Was the Color of Her Dress" have their moments, the band really digs in during the lengthy explorations of "Meditations on Integration," "Parkeriana" (a tribute to Charlie Parker that is quite a bit different than the Fantasy version) and a definitive and very exciting "Fables of Faubus." Eric Dolphy (particularly on alto) was at the peak of his powers during the tour (he died just a couple months later), Clifford Jordan (whose tone was quite distinctive) manages to keep up and Jaki Byard's versatility (going from bop and free to Duke Ellington and stride) is a major asset to the colorful music. A highly recommended release. —*Scott Yanow*

☆ **The Great Concert of Charles Mingus** / Apr. 17, 1964-Apr. 19, 1964 / Prestige ◆◆◆◆◆

This three-LP set is the finest recording by one of Charles Mingus' greatest bands, his sextet with Eric Dolphy (on alto, bass clarinet and flute), tenor saxophonist Clifford Jordan, trumpeter Johnny Coles, pianist Jaki Byard and drummer Dannie Richmond. Taken from their somewhat tumultuous but very musical tour of Europe, most of these rather lengthy workouts actually just feature a quintet because Coles took sick (he is only heard on "So Long Eric" which here is mistitled "Goodbye Pork Pie Hat"), but the playing is at such a high level that the trumpeter is not really missed. "Orange Was the Color of Her Dress" is given definitive treatment and the nearly 29-minute "Fables of Faubus" and Mingus' relatively brief feature on "Sophisticated Lady" are impressive, but it is the passionate "Meditations on Integration" (an utterly fascinating performance) and "Parkeriana" (a tribute to Charlie Parker that features some stride piano from Byard and what may very well have been Eric Dolphy's greatest alto solo) that make this gem truly essential in all jazz collections. —*Scott Yanow*

Mingus in Europe / Apr. 26, 1964 / Enja ◆◆◆◆◆

This CD reissues three selections originally on the LP *Mingus in Europe, Vol. 2* ("Orange Was the Color of Her Dress," "Sophisticated Lady" and "AT-FW-YOU") and also includes two performances ("Peggy's Blue Sky Light" and the nearly 23-minute "So Long Eric") that do not seem to have been issued previously. The 1964 Charles Mingus Quintet (trumpeter Johnny Coles had departed a few days earlier due to illness) teamed together the unique multi-instrumentalist Eric Dolphy, tenor saxophonist Clifford Jordan, pianist Jaki Byard, drummer Dannie Richmond and the bassist/leader in one of the great bands of the 1960s. There are many recordings currently available from their European tour and all are worth acquiring, including this excellent Enja set (at least by Mingus fans not already owning *Vol. 2*). —*Scott Yanow*

Mingus in Europe, Vol. 1 / Apr. 26, 1964 / Enja ◆◆◆◆◆

This LP features the Charles Mingus Quintet during their European tour in 1964. Bassist Mingus, Eric Dolphy (on alto, bass clarinet and flute), tenorman Clifford Jordan, pianist Jaki Byard and drummer Dannie Richmond stretch out on a 37-minute version of "Fables of Faubus" while the briefer "Starting" is a rare Mingus-Dolphy duet. Although this music could be called avant-garde, there is nothing random about the notes picked or the many emotions expressed. —*Scott Yanow*

Mingus in Europe, Vol. 2 / Apr. 26, 1964 / Enja ◆◆◆

This LP, like all of the European concerts that have been documented of the 1964 Charles Mingus Quintet/Sextet, contains plenty of dynamic and unpredictable music, but since three of the four selections (all but Clifford Jordan's "Charlemagne") have since been reissued on an Enja CD, this particular set is not as essential as the others. However, Mingus and Eric Dolphy fans who do not have the CD will find much to enjoy in these four selections, highlighted by the 17-minute "Orange Was the Color of Her Dress." —*Scott Yanow*

Right Now: Live at Jazz Workshop / Jun. 2, 1964-Jun. 3, 1964 / Fantasy ◆◆◆◆

Soon after Charles Mingus finished touring Europe with his band (the unit that featured Eric Dolphy), he recorded this CD, performed live at the Jazz Workshop in San Francisco. With tenor saxophonist Clifford Jordan and drummer Danny Richmond still in the group but Jane Getz replacing pianist Jaki Byard and altoist John Handy filling in for Dolphy on one song, the band performs excellent versions of "Meditations on Integration" and "New Fables," both of which are over 23 minutes long. Although not up to the passionate level of the Mingus-Dolphy Quintet, this underrated unit holds its own. —*Scott Yanow*

Mingus at Monterey / Sep. 20, 1964 / VDJ ◆◆◆◆◆

One of the high points of Charles Mingus' career was his appearance at the 1964 Monterey Jazz Festival. This long-out-of-print double LP contains the entire set: a lengthy Duke Ellington medley, "Orange Was the Color of Her Dress" and a stunning version of "Meditations on Integration" as performed by a 12-piece group featuring such players as altoist Charles McPherson, John Handy (on tenor), trumpeter Lonnie Hillyer and pianist Jaki Byard. This music is well deserving of eventual reissue on CD, for it showcases the bassist/composer/bandleader at the peak of his powers. —*Scott Yanow*

Portrait / 1964-1965 / Prestige ◆◆◆◆◆

This double LP reissues two albums titled *Town Hall Concert* and *My Favorite Quintet*. The earlier set features what was arguably Charles Mingus' finest group, his sextet with Eric Dolphy, tenor saxophonist Clifford Jordan, trumpeter Johnny Coles, pianist Jaki Byard and drummer Dannie Richmond. Heard shortly before leaving for their famous European tour (during which they were fortunately extensively recorded), the all-star group plays long involved versions of "So Long Eric" and "Meditations on Integration." The latter half of this set has a more conventional

rendition of "So Long Eric," a ballad medley and an attempt at humor on "Cocktails for Two" as played by Mingus, Byard, Richmond, altoist Chartles McPherson and trumpeter Lonnie Hillyer. Overall this is a worthwhile and quite enjoyable two-fer, although not quite at the level of Mingus' greatest work. —*Scott Yanow*

Music Written for Monterey, 1965 / Sep. 25, 1965 / JWS ◆◆◆

Following his big success at the 1964 Monterey Jazz Festival, Charles Mingus' appearance the following year was a major disappointment; he walked off after a half hour when he sensed that his time slot was anticlimactic and that the audience was not paying attention. A week later he performed the full program he had originally planned for Monterey at UCLA and this two-LP set (released privately by his East Coasting Records) preserves that concert. Most of the originals use a nine-piece group, although Mingus at one point expels many of the musicians because he felt they had not learned his music well enough; that verbal confrontation is included on the record. There are some strong moments on this set (which often features trumpeter Lonnie Hillyer and altoist Charles McPherson), but this is an erratic, if colorful effort. —*Scott Yanow*

Reincarnation of a Lovebird / Nov. 30, 1970-Nov. 31, 1970 / Prestige ◆◆◆◆

This excellent two-LP set features Charles Mingus and his 1970 sextet (with trumpeter Eddie Preston, altoist Charles McPherson, tenor saxophonist Bobby Jones, pianist Jaki Byard and drummer Dannie Richmond) stretching out on three of the bassist/leader's standards along with his more recent "Love Is a Dangerous Necessity," a version of "I Left My Heart in San Francisco" and a 17-minute version of "Blue Bird" (a Charlie Parker blues). Practically Mingus' only studio recordings of 1965-71, these performances find the great bassist in fine form, pushing his sidemen to make original statements on the distinctive originals. —*Scott Yanow*

With Orchestra / Jan. 14, 1971 / Denon ◆◆

This obscure session found bassist Charles Mingus along with two of his sidemen (tenor saxophonist Bobby Jones and trumpeter Eddie Preston) performing three of the bassist's compositions in Japan with Toshiyuki Miyama and his New Herd, a fine big band. Little all that memorable occurs and there is only around 32 minutes of music so this CD is not all that essential, but Mingus completists will want to pick up this rarity. —*Scott Yanow*

Let My Children Hear Music / Sep. 23, 1971-Nov. 18, 1971 / Columbia ◆◆◆

The CD reissue of the original LP adds one selection ("Taurus in the Arena of Life") to the program of original music. Mingus' unique compositions (mostly recent, although one was written back in 1939) receive sympathetic treatment by a partly unidentified large orchestra and are full of interesting textures, sound explorations and surprises. It makes for a stimulating listen. —*Scott Yanow*

Shoes of the Fisherman's Wife .... / Sep. 23, 1971-Nov. 1, 1959 / Columbia ◆◆◆

Most of the *Mingus Dynasty*, which features the same lineup as *Mingus Ah Um* and has a similar feel but is less driving. Inexplicable inclusion of "Shoes of the ...." from *Let My Children Hear Music*, recorded twelve years later. All great music. —*Michael Katz*

Charles Mingus and Friends in Concert / Feb. 4, 1972 / Columbia ◆◆◆

Most of Charles Mingus' larger-group recordings, particularly in the later part of his career, tended to be unruly and somewhat undisciplined. This two-CD reissue set (which adds five selections to the original two-LP program), which celebrated Mingus' return to jazz after six years of little activity. Such great jazzmen as baritonist Gerry Mulligan, tenor saxophonist Gene Ammons, altoist Lee Konitz, pianist Randy Weston, James Moody (heard on flute) and a variety of Mingus regulars had a chance to play with the great bassist; even fellow bassist Milt Hinton and Bill Cosby (taking a humorous scat vocal) join in. Most of the music is overly loose, but the overcrowded "E's Flat, Ah's Flat Too" and particularly the "Little Royal Suite" are memorable. The "Little Royal Suite," in addition to Ammons, Konitz, Mulligan, Charles McPherson and Bobby Jones, features an 18-year old Jon Faddis (who was sitting in for an ailing Roy Eldridge) stealing the show. —*Scott Yanow*

Mingus Moves / 1973 / Atlantic ◆◆◆◆

On this Atlantic LP, Charles Mingus introduced his new group which at the time included trumpeter Ronald Hampton, tenor saxophonist George Adams, pianist Don Pullen and his longtime drummer Dannie Richmond. Together this excellent quintet performed seven recent compositions including one ("Moves") that features the vocals of Honey Gordon and Doug Hammond. Only three of the pieces are by Mingus, but all of the music is greatly influenced by his searching and unpredictable style. This out-of-print LP is worth searching for. —*Scott Yanow*

Mingus at Carnegie Hall / Jan. 19, 1974 / Atlantic ◆◆◆◆◆

Although Charles Mingus is the leader on this date, it is actually a jam session featuring an all-star cast (the amazing Rahsaan Roland Kirk, trumpeter Jon Faddis, John Handy on alto and tenor, altoist Charles McPherson, tenor saxophonist George Adams, baritonist Hamiet Bluiett, pianist Don Pullen, drummer Dannie Richmond and the bassist-leader) playing rather long versions of "C Jam Blues" and "Perdido." Of the many soloists, Handy shows off his high note alto on "Perdido" and Faddis (who was then 20) plays some of his favorite Dizzy Gillespie licks but Rahsaan Roland Kirk (who at one point imitates George Adams) cuts everyone. This CD is a straight reissue of the original LP and is often quite exciting. —*Scott Yanow*

Changes One / Dec. 27, 1974-Dec. 30, 1974 / Atlantic ✦✦✦✦✦
Charles Mingus' finest recordings of his later period are *Changes One* and *Changes Two*, two Atlantic LPs that have been reissued on CD by Rhino. The first volume features four stimulating Mingus originals ("Remember Rockefeller at Attica," "Sue's Changes," "Devil Blues" and "Duke Ellington's Sound of Love") performed by a particularly talented quintet (tenor saxophonist George Adams who also sings "Devil Blues," trumpeter Jack Walrath, pianist Don Pullen, drummer Dannie Richmond and the leader/bassist). The band has the adventurous spirit and chance-taking approach of Charles Mingus' best groups, making this an easily recommended example of the great bandleader's music. —*Scott Yanow*

Changes Two / Dec. 27, 1974-Dec. 30, 1974 / Atlantic ✦✦✦✦✦
Along with *Changes One* (both Atlantic LPs have been reissued on CD by Rhino), this set is one of Charles Mingus' most rewarding of his later period. Mingus' band (trumpeter Jack Walrath, tenor saxophonist George Adams, pianist Don Pullen and drummer Dannie Richmond) was particularly strong. This set is highlighted by a 17-minute version of "Orange Was the Color of Her Dress," Sy Johnson's "For Harry Carney" and Jackie Paris' vocal on "Duke Ellington's Sound of Love." —*Scott Yanow*

Cumbia and Jazz Fusion / Mar. 31, 1976-May 1, 1977 / Atlantic ✦✦✦✦
As Charles Mingus' career (and life) moved into its final phase, his recordings exclusively featured large (and often potentially unruly) ensembles. This CD, which contains two rather long performances originally recorded as soundtracks for films, is better than most of what followed. "Cumbia & Jazz Fusion" has a large percussion section and quite a few woodwinds along with trumpeter Jack Walrath, tenor saxophonist Ricky Ford and trombonist Jimmy Knepper while "Music for 'Todo Modo'" adds five horns to Mingus' Quintet. The music is episodic but generally holds its own away from the film. —*Scott Yanow*

Three or Four Shades of Blues / Mar. 9, 1977 / Atlantic ✦✦✦
During Charles Mingus' last year of recording, it seemed that much of the jazz world wanted to play with the bassist. This particular LP includes such major stylists as tenor saxophonists George Coleman and Ricky Ford, trumpeter Jack Walrath, guitarists Philip Catherine, John Scofield and Larry Coryell, pianist Jimmy Rowles and even bassists George Mraz and Ron Carter. The music, two remakes and three newer pieces, is occasionally exciting but not as coherent and purposeful as Mingus' best work, which is understandable because the guests were not as familiar with the great bassist's unique music as his regular group. It still makes for some interesting listening though. —*Scott Yanow*

His Final Work / Nov. 6, 1977 / Gateway ✦✦✦
This session represents the final studio performances by Charles Mingus, though not really his final work as he later supervised some Atlantic sessions when he has too weak to perform. Lionel Hampton, who employed a young Mingus in his band in 1947, has gathered a sympathetic band and fashioned, along with arranger/saxophonist Paul Jeffrey, a relatively comfortable and sedate session. Hampton, who has always seemed stuck in the 1930s and 1940s, sounds surprisingly at home in this music, which points out the true character of Mingus' music: modern, progressive, and yet always aware of the tradition. This disc was originally issued on Who's Who. The Gateway issue completes the session by adding one track ("So Long Eric") which had previously appeared on the sampler collection titled *Giants of Jazz—Volume 2* (Who's Who WWLP 21014). The whole session is also available on a CD called *The Sound of Jazz* on Cleo Records, Germany (CLCD 65005). —*Stuart Kremsky*

Lionel Hampton Presents Music of Charles Mingus / Nov. 6, 1977 / Who's Who In Jazz ✦✦✦
Charles Mingus' final recording as a player (before serious illness struck) is a fun session in which his last quintet (with trumpeter Jack Walrath, tenor saxophonist Ricky Ford, pianist Bob Nelums and drummer Dannie Richmond) is joined by vibraphonist Lionel Hampton, baritonist Gerry Mulligan, trumpeter Woody Shaw, Paul Jeffrey (who arranged the music) on tenor and the French horn of Peter Matt. A bit of a jam session, this group performs seven of Mingus' compositions including versions of such songs as "Peggy's Blue Skylight," "Fables of Faubus" and "Duke Ellington's Sound of Love." Nothing that unusual occurs, but good spirits dominate this final effort. —*Scott Yanow*

Something Like a Bird / Jan. 18, 1978-Jan. 23, 1978 / Atlantic ✦✦✦
Although confined to a wheelchair and less than a year from his death, Charles Mingus supervised the recording sessions that resulted in this LP and its companion *Me Myself an Eye*. The music on this set utilizes a 27-piece band (including 11 saxophones and four guitars) on the 31-minute "Something like a Bird" and a

smaller 21-piece orchestra (only nine saxes and three guitars) for "Farewell Farewell." It seems that everyone wanted to play with (or at least for) Mingus during his last few years and such musicians as Lee Konitz, Charles McPherson, George Coleman, Mike Brecker, Ricky Ford, Pepper Adams, Randy Brecker, Jack Walrath, Slide Hampton, Jimmy Knepper, Larry Coryell and bassists Eddie Gomez and George Mraz help out on this spirited if overcrowded music. It's not essential, but certainly colorful. —*Scott Yanow*

Me, Myself an Eye / Jan. 19, 1978-Jan. 23, 1978 / Atlantic ✦✦✦
The companion to *Something like a Bird*, this LP also finds Charles Mingus (who was confined to a wheelchair and only a year away from his death) supervising large orchestras (in this case 23 and 25 pieces) on some of his compositions. "Devil Woman," "Wednesday Night Prayer Meeting" and "Carolyn 'Keki' Mingus" are fairly concise, but "Three Worlds of Drums" is over a half-hour long and has its rambling sections. The music is colorful and spirited, but not as memorable as one might hope. Still, these loose sessions have their moments. —*Scott Yanow*

Chair in the Sky / Jul. 9, 1979+Jul. 10, 1979 / Elektra ✦✦✦
Recorded just six months after the death of Charles Mingus in January 1979, this first release by the ever-changing Mingus Dynasty is in many ways the freshest. Everyone here, except of course for bassist Charlie Haden, had played with Mingus, in some cases (Richmond, Pullen, and Knepper) quite extensively. Included are first-rate versions of three older tunes and three from the final Joni Mitchell sessions. —*Stuart Kremsky*

Live at the Theatre Boulogne-Billancourt, Vol. 2 / Jun. 8, 1988 / Soul Note ✦✦✦
This edition of Big Band Charlie Mingus, a large scale version of the ongoing Mingus Dynasty project, includes a number of performers (Jimmy Knepper, Jaki Byard, the late Clifford Jordan and John Handy, among others) who had played in different editions of the Charles Mingus Jazz Workshop. The group also boasts a stellar saxophone section in John Handy, alto; David Murray, tenor and bass clarinet; Clifford Jordan, tenor and soprano; and Nick Brignola, baritone and flute. This disc features four lengthy versions of favorite Mingus compositions. The ensembles are occasionally a bit ragged, and there are the inevitable dull moments that occur in most live recordings, but the spirit is there and the solos are mostly fairly strong, particularly from David Murray and Jaki Byard. —*Stuart Kremsky*

Epitaph / 1990 / Columbia ✦✦✦
This double CD is a posthumous recording of a long multisectioned work by Charles Mingus that was only hinted at during his ill-fated Town Hall Concert of 1962. Gunther Schuller conducted and reconstructed this massive work which utilizes 30 musicians including many all-stars; the trumpet section alone comprises Wynton Marsalis, Jack Walrath, Randy Brecker, Lew Soloff, Joe Wilder and Snooky Young. "Epitaph" has some strong moments (including sections in which the band performs "Better Git It in Your Soul," "Monk, Bunk & Vice Versa," "Peggy's Blue Skylight," "Wolverine Blues" and "Freedom") but on a whole the music is somewhat unsatisfying and inconclusive. Still, there are enough moments of interest to make this set recommended even if the presence of Mingus is missed. —*Scott Yanow*

Next Generation Performs . . . / 1991 / Columbia ✦✦✦
Passion and total commitment were the hallmarks of a performance by Charles Mingus; the presence or absence of these qualities determines the success of the various recordings made by the ever-changing Mingus Dynasty band. This 1991 release by a saxophone-heavy septet is kind of a hit-or-miss affair. Some of the pieces have an academic feel, like a first or second run-through. The band starts out a bit hesitant and restrained on a "new" tune, "Sketch Four," derived from a tape of Mingus singing the melody over a metronome. This is followed by a careful reading of "Portrait." But then the group wakes up to bowl you over with a powerhouse rendition of "Opus Four," first recorded in 1973. Trumpeter and musical director Jack Walrath, who was in Mingus' final bands, is sounding better than ever, with a crackling, shiny sound that cuts through the ensemble. One of the problems here might be too strong a reed section (Craig Handy, George Adams and Alex Foster all featured on tenor). In the rhythm section, stalwart pianist John Hicks, bassist Ray Drummond, and drummer Marvin "Smitty" Smith keep things popping. Smith in particular seems responsible for some of the better moments as he challenges and pushes the soloists with his everything-but-the-kitchen-sink approach to the trap set. It's good to have 72 minutes of "new" Mingus music, but it could have been better with an extra day's rehearsal and a trombone. —*Stuart Kremsky*

Bob Mintzer

b. Jan. 27, 1953, New Rochelle, NY
Tenor Saxophone, Bass Clarinet / Post-Bop
A versatile soloist influenced by Michael Brecker on tenor, Bob Mintzer gained experience playing with Deodato, Tito Puente (1974), Buddy Rich, Hubert Laws and the Thad Jones/Mel Lewis Orchestra (1977). In addition to leading his own

bands starting in 1978, Mintzer worked with Jaco Pastorius, Mike Mainieri, Louie Bellson, Bob Moses and the American Saxophone Quartet. He has guested with several Philharmonic Orchestras and led a fine big band in New York since the mid-'80s. Mintzer, a member of the Yellowjackets since 1991 (where his bass clarinet in particular adds a great deal of color to the group), has recorded regularly for DMP for the past decade. —*Scott Yanow*

Incredible Journey / Feb. 1985-Apr. 1985 / DMP ✦✦✦

● **The First Decade** / 1985-1995 / DMP ✦✦✦✦✦

Camouflage / Jun. 1986 / DMP ✦✦✦✦
Good '86 big band set led by tenor saxophonist and bass clarinetist Bob Mintzer, a fine player and arranger. These recordings are in a conventional format, with polished ensemble sections and good, occasionally great solos. They are well produced and mastered, but the material and style tend to be conservative. —*Ron Wynn*

Spectrum / Jan. 1988 / DMP ✦✦✦✦✦
Included is an all-star lineup of R. Brecker, P. Erstine, D. Grolnick, B. Malach, L. Gaines, and 14 other players. This is big-band jazz at its finest. The recording was made live to two-track digital, and the music, exceptional from start to finish, deserves it. —*Paul Kohler*

Urban Contours / Feb. 24, 1989-Mar. 5, 1989 / DMP ✦✦✦✦
This set mixes small- and big-band sessions. —*Ron Wynn*

The Art of the Big Band / Sep. 22, 1990-Sep. 23, 1990 / DMP ✦✦✦
A great technical recording, with good sidemen but unadventurous music. —*Ron Wynn*

I Remember Jaco / Mar. 6, 1991-Mar. 7, 1991 / Novus ✦✦✦✦
Bob Mintzer, mostly on tenor but also playing a bit of bass clarinet (on "A Method to the Madness") and EWI, pays tribute to the late, great electric bassist Jaco Pastorius on this CD. Mintzer had worked with Pastorius in his "Word of Mouth" Orchestra. Surprisingly, Mintzer only plays one Pastorius tune ("Three Views of a Secret") and instead performs seven originals inspired by feelings he had about his experiences with the bassist. With either Jeff Andrews and/or Michael Formanek on bass, former Pastorius associate Peter Erskine on drums and keyboardist Joey Calderazzo, the music is never less than excellent, and Jaco would have enjoyed it. However, the ties to the bassist's music are not as strong as one would expect, and the overall results are worthwhile, but not overly memorable. —*Scott Yanow*

Departure / Sep. 11, 1991-Sep. 17, 1991 / DMP ✦✦✦✦

One Music / Oct. 2, 1991-Oct. 5, 1991 / DMP ✦✦✦✦
This saxophonist's best small-group work, with fellow Yellowjackets. The best cuts are the title and "Look Around." Ventures funky and creative into neo-bop modes. —*Michael G. Nastos*

Only in New York / Nov. 20, 1993-Nov. 21, 1993 / DPM ✦✦✦

Big Band Trane / Dec. 15, 1995-Dec. 16, 1995 / DMP ✦✦✦✦
When one hears of an album titled *Big Band Trane*, it is assumed that the music will either be of songs by John Coltrane orchestrated for a full big band or pieces performed in his style. As it turns out, the Bob Mintzer Big Band only plays three tunes that have anything to do with the great tenor ("My Favorite Things," "A Love Supreme-Acknowledgment" and "Impressions") along with seven unrelated Mintzer originals. The leader himself does not solo on any of the 'Trane pieces and, despite some fiery soprano by Roger Rosenberg on "My Favorite Things," those three songs are disappointingly routine with the orchestra sounding like a professional college stage band. The originals are much better, particularly "Run for Your Life" (which is a little reminiscent of Thad Jones' "Fingers"), the funky "One People" (a good feature for Mintzer's tenor), "Ancestors," "Softly Spoken" and "Trane's Blues." With such soloists as Mintzer, Bob Malach on tenor, pianist Phil Markowitz, trumpeters Randy Brecker, Marvin Stamm and Michael Mossman and altoist Pete Yellin, there are many moments of interest on this modern straightahead disc, but the title was a definite mistake! —*Scott Yanow*

Billy Mitchell

b. Nov. 3, 1926, Kansas City, MO
Tenor Saxophone / Hard Bop
A hard-swinging tenor saxophonist (who is no relation to the crossover keyboardist of the same name), Billy Mitchell made his mark in several settings. He worked in Detroit with Nat Towles' band and in the late '40s he played with Lucky Millinder's Orchestra in New York. In 1949 Mitchell recorded with Milt Jackson, worked in the big bands of Milt Buckner and Gil Fuller and toured with Woody Herman's Second Herd for two months. He spent the first half of the 1950s playing locally in Detroit and then was with Dizzy Gillespie's big band during 1956-57, taking a memorable solo on "Cool Breeze" at the 1957 Newport Jazz Festival. Mitchell was with Count Basie's Orchestra during 1957-61 and in the early '60s led a sextet with Al Grey that featured a young Bobby Hutcherson. He played again

with Basie during 1966-67, worked as an educator and recorded frequently on Xanadu in the late '70s, but has been less prominent since then. Billy Mitchell cut sessions as a leader for Dee Gee, Jubilee, Smash, Catalyst and Xanadu. —*Scott Yanow*

This Is Billy Mitchell Featuring Bobby Hutcherson / Oct. 29-30, 1962/ Smash ✦✦✦✦
Tenor saxophonist Billy Mitchell's second album as a leader (following a 1960 Jubilee date) was last available as a Trip LP in the early '80s. Although the tenor saxophonist is in typically fine form on six obscurities and two standards ("Sophisticated Lady" and "You Turned the Tables on Me"), this record's main significance is that it features the young vibraphonist Bobby Hutcherson, who was virtually at the beginning of his career. Five of the eight songs also include trumpeter Dave Burns, pianist Billy Wallace, bassist Herman Wright and drummer Otis Finch, while the other numbers have organist Sleepy Anderson in place of Wallace and Burns. Mainstream hard bop of the era. —*Scott Yanow*

Now's the Time / 1976 / Catalyst ✦✦✦✦
Billy Mitchell's first album in 13 years is decent, but not all that special. The live set features Mitchell on tenor, soprano and alto performing a pair of lengthy blues and two fairly basic originals. He is joined by guitarist Roland Prince, pianist Wes Belcamp, bassist Earl May and either Ron Turso or Al Beldini on drums. An unidentified trumpeter (no great thrill) sits in on "Now's the Time." Mitchell sounds fine, but nothing that special occurs on this long-out-of-print LP. —*Scott Yanow*

● **Colossus of Detroit** / Apr. 18, 1978 / Xanadu ✦✦✦✦✦
Veteran tenor saxophonist Billy Mitchell could not ask for a better rhythm section than he has here (pianist Barry Jones, bassist Sam Jones and drummer Walter Bolden). Mitchell was careful to pick out a superior program of songs highlighted by a few classic ballads (including "Unforgettable," which in 1978 had been largely forgotten) and Joe Henderson's "Recordame." The results are quite boppish and one of Mitchell's better recordings of the past 20 years. —*Scott Yanow*

Night Flight to Dakar / Mar. 14, 1980-Mar. 19, 1980 / Xanadu ✦✦✦✦

De Lawd's Blues / Jun. 26, 1980 / Xanadu ✦✦✦✦
For this excellent quintet outing with trumpeter Benny Bailey (making a rare American recording), pianist Tommy Flanagan, bassist Rufus Reid and drummer Jimmy Cobb, tenor saxophonist Billy Mitchell performs two originals and tunes by Reid ("Perpetual Stroll"), Bailey and Dolo Coker. Despite the mostly obscure material, the interpretations are purely straightahead, falling between bop and hard bop in style. The musicians all play up to par on Mitchell's third and final Xanadu album as a leader. —*Scott Yanow*

Blue Mitchell (Richard Allen Mitchell)

b. Mar. 13, 1930, Miami, FL, **d.** May 21, 1979, Los Angeles, CA
Trumpet / Hard Bop
Owner of a direct, lightly swinging, somewhat plain-wrapped tone that fit right in with the Blue Note label's hard bop ethos of the 1960s, Blue Mitchell tends to be overlooked today, perhaps because he never really stood out vividly from the crowd, despite his undeniable talent. After learning the trumpet in high school—where he got his nickname—he started touring in the early '50s with the R&B bands of Paul Williams, Earl Bostic and Chuck Willis before returning to Miami and jazz. There, he attracted the attention of Cannonball Adderley, with whom he recorded for Riverside in 1958. That year, he joined the Horace Silver Quintet, with whom he played and recorded until the band's breakup in March 1964, polishing his hard bop skills. During his Silver days, Mitchell worked with tenor Junior Cook, bassist Gene Taylor, drummer Roy Brooks and various pianists as a separate unit and continued recording as a leader for Riverside. When Silver disbanded, Mitchell's spinoff quintet carried on with Al Foster replacing Brooks and a young future star named Chick Corea in the piano chair. This group, with several personnel changes, continued until 1969, recording a string of albums for Blue Note. Probably aware that opportunities for playing straightahead jazz were dwindling, Mitchell became a prolific pop and soul sessionman in the late '60s, and he toured with Ray Charles from 1969 to 1971 and blues/rock guitarist John Mayall in 1971-73. Having settled in Los Angeles, he also played big-band dates with Louie Bellson, Bill Holman and Bill Berry; made a number of funk and pop-jazz LPs in the late '70s; served as principal soloist for Tony Bennett and Lena Horne; and kept his hand in hard bop by playing with Harold Land in a quintet. He continued to freelance in this multi-faceted fashion until his premature death from cancer at age 49. —*Richard S. Ginell*

☆ **Big Six** / Jul. 2, 1958-Jul. 3, 1958 / Original Jazz Classics ✦✦✦✦✦
Trumpeter Blue Mitchell was a virtual unknown when he recorded this Riverside album, his first as a leader. Now reissued on CD in the Original Jazz Classics series, Mitchell is heard in excellent form in an all-star sextet with trombonist Curtis Fuller, tenor-great Johnny Griffin, pianist Wynton Kelly, bassist Wilbur Ware and

drummer Philly Joe Jones. In addition to some group originals, obscurities and the standard "There Will Never Be Another You," the group also plays the earliest recorded version of Benny Golson's "Blues March," predating Art Blakey's famous recording. —*Scott Yanow*

Out of the Blue / Jan. 1959 / Original Jazz Classics ✦✦✦✦✦

This early recording by Blue Mitchell finds the distinctive trumpeter in excellent form in a quintet also featuring tenor saxophonist Benny Golson (who contributed "Blues on My Mind"), either Wynton Kelly or Cedar Walton on piano, Paul Chambers or Sam Jones on bass and drummer Art Blakey. The consistently swinging repertoire includes a surprisingly effective version of "When the Saints Go Marching In." "Studio B," recorded in the same period but formerly available only in a sampler, has been added to the program. It's an enjoyable date of high-quality hard bop. —*Scott Yanow*

Blue Soul / Sep. 1959 / Original Jazz Classics ✦✦✦✦✦

This CD reissue bring back one of trumpeter Blue Mitchell's better sessions from his early period, his third recording as a leader for Riverside. Six of the selections also feature trombonist Curtis Fuller (in excellent form) and the tenor of Jimmy Heath in a sextet with pianist Wynton Kelly, bassist Sam Jones and drummer Philly Joe Jones; the arrangements were provided by Heath and Benny Golson. The other three numbers are more informal and showcase Mitchell in a quartet with Kelly and the two Joneses. Excellent hard bop with the repertoire consisting of "The Way You Look Tonight," "Polka Dots and Moonbeams," "Nica's Dream" and two originals apiece from Golson, Heath and Mitchell. —*Scott Yanow*

Blue's Moods / Aug. 24, 1960-Aug. 25, 1960 / Original Jazz Classics ✦✦✦✦

Of trumpeter Blue Mitchell's seven Riverside recordings (all of which have been reissued as CDs in the Original Jazz Classics series), only this set (along with three numbers on *Blue Soul*) feature Mitchell as the only horn. Joined by pianist Wynton Kelly, bassist Sam Jones and drummer Roy Brooks, the trumpeter is typically distinctive, swinging and inventive within the hard bop genre. He performs four standards, Ronnell Bright's "Sweet Pumpkin," the obscure "Avars," and a pair of originals in fine fashion. —*Scott Yanow*

Smooth as the Wind / Dec. 27, 1960-Mar. 30, 1961 / Original Jazz Classics ✦✦✦✦

Trumpeter Blue Mitchell is in excellent form on this very interesting session, which has been reissued on CD. Mitchell is accompanied by a brass section, a rhythm section and strings. The arrangements (seven by Tadd Dameron and three from Benny Golson) are generally quite stimulating, inspiring the trumpeter to come up with many fresh melodic solos. The repertoire includes two songs that Mitchell played regularly with Horace Silver's Quintet, a pair of superior Tadd Dameron tunes (including the title cut) and six standards. By varying tempos and moods, Dameron and Golson helped create one of the better soloist-with-strings jazz dates. —*Scott Yanow*

A Sure Thing / Mar. 7, 1962-Mar. 28, 1962 / Original Jazz Classics ✦✦✦✦

Trumpeter Blue Mitchell is well featured on this CD reissue with a nonet arranged by Jimmy Heath. The music is straightahead but, thanks to Heath's arrangements, sometimes unpredictable. Best is Mitchell's solo on "I Can't Get Started," "Hootie's Blues" and a quintet workout (with Heath, pianist Wynton Kelly, bassist Sam Jones and drummer Albert "Tootie" Heath) on "Gone with the Wind." —*Scott Yanow*

Cup Bearers / Aug. 28, 1962+Aug. 30, 1962 / Original Jazz Classics ✦✦✦✦✦

Trumpeter Blue Mitchell and four-fifths of the Horace Silver Quintet (with Cedar Walton in Silver's place) perform a variety of superior songs on this CD reissue including Walton's "Turquoise," Tom McIntosh's "Cup Bearers," Thad Jones' "Tiger Lily" and a couple of standards. The music swings hard, mostly avoids sounding like a Horace Silver group, and has particularly strong solos from Mitchell, tenor saxophonist Junior Cook and Walton; excellent hard bop. —*Scott Yanow*

Step Lightly / Aug. 13, 1963 / Blue Note ✦✦✦✦

Trumpeter Blue Mitchell's Blue Note debut went unissued for 17 years, only coming out on this 1980 LP (not yet reissued on CD). The set must have been lost in the shuffle, for the music is consistently excellent. Mitchell, tenor saxophonist Joe Henderson, altoist Leo Wright, pianist Herbie Hancock, bassist Gene Taylor and drummer Roy Brooks perform four originals and obscurities, plus lyrical versions of "Sweet and Lovely" and "Cry Me a River." Worth searching for. —*Scott Yanow*

★ **The Thing to Do** / Jul. 30, 1964 / Blue Note ✦✦✦✦✦

This Blue Mitchell date is a classic, particularly the opening "Fungii Mama," which is really catchy. The trumpeter's quintet of the period (which includes tenor saxophonist Junior Cook, the young pianist Chick Corea, bassist Gene Taylor and drummer Al Foster) also performs two Jimmy Heath tunes and a song apiece by Joe Henderson ("Step Lightly") and Corea. The record is prime Blue Note hard bop, containing inventive tunes, meaningful solos, and an enthusiastic but tight feel. Highly recommended. —*Scott Yanow*

Down with It / Jul. 14, 1965 / Blue Note ✦✦✦✦

Down With It is a fairly standard bop and soul-jazz session from Blue Mitchell. Leading a quintet that features a young Chick Corea on piano, tenor saxophonist Junior Cook, bassist Gene Taylor and drummer Al Foster, Mitchell creates a laid-back atmosphere which makes R&B covers like "Hi-Heel Sneakers" or the lite bossa nova of "Samba De Stacy" roll along nicely. Just as often, the record is so relaxed that it fails to generate much spark, but each of the soloists have fine moments that make the session worthwhile for jazz purists. —*Stephen Thomas Erlewine*

Bring It on Home to Me / Jan. 6, 1966 / Blue Note ✦✦✦✦

Boss Horn / Nov. 17, 1966 / Blue Note ✦✦✦✦

Heads Up / Nov. 17, 1967 / Blue Note ✦✦✦

Collision in Black / Sep. 11, 1968-Sep. 12, 1968 / Blue Note ✦✦✦

Bantu Village / May 22, 1969-May 23, 1969 / Blue Note ✦✦✦

Soul Village / Mar. 1971 / Mainstream ✦✦✦

In general, Blue Mitchell's five Mainstream albums from 1971-74 are not on the same level as his best Blue Notes, but they tend to be worthwhile. His debut for Mainstream features the trumpeter's regular group of 1971, a quintet with tenor saxophonist Jimmy Forrest (who had just come out of retirement), pianist Walter Bishop, Jr., bassist Larry Gales and drummer Doug Sides. On the LP, they play a pair of originals apiece by Mitchell and Bishop and Benny Golson's "Are You Real" with swing and a bit of soul. —*Scott Yanow*

Blue's Blues / 1972-1974 / Mainstream ✦✦✦

At the time that this Mainstream LP was recorded, Blue Mitchell was the featured trumpeter with John Mayall's blues group. Mayall returned the favor for Blue's set, playing harmonica with an electric octet headed by Mitchell. Among the sidemen are Herman Riley (on tenor and flute), keyboardist Joe Sample and guitarist Freddy Robinson. The material (all obscure originals) is primarily blues-oriented, and the music overall is listenable and funky, but not particularly memorable. Just an average date from these fine musicians. —*Scott Yanow*

Graffiti Blues / 1973-1974 / Mainstream ✦✦

A new reissue of a 1973 mainstream session that was part funk, part pop, and far too tame. —*Ron Wynn*

Many Shades of Blue / 1974 / Mainstream ✦✦

Stratosonic Nuances / 1975 / RCA ✦✦

Considering that this record features trumpeter Blue Mitchell, tenor saxophonist Harold Land and (in guest spots) pianists Cedar Walton and Hampton Hawes, one might have expected great things. Unfortunately, the music is quite commercial (obviously recorded with potential record sales in mind) and is sunk by dull and instantly dated arrangements by Wade Marcus (who uses a five-piece horn section). Other than Thelonious Monk's "Nutty" (the only cut not arranged by Marcus), the music—which includes songs by Barry White and Stevie Wonder in addition to two Mitchell arrangements—is immediately forgettable. —*Scott Yanow*

Live / Feb. 1, 1976 / Just Jazz ✦✦✦✦

This excellent session (recorded at Half Moon Bay in 1976 but not released until this 1995 CD) features trumpeter Blue Mitchell with four Northern California musicians: the obscure Coltrane-influenced tenor saxophonist Mike Morris, pianist Mark Levine, bassist Kenny Jenkins and drummer Smiley Winters. The repertoire is fresh, consisting of a nearly 17-minute "Pleasure Bent," the warm ballad "Portrait of Jenny," a song called "Sweet Smiley Winters" that is really a "Sweet Georgia Brown" line penned decades earlier by Coleman Hawkins, Levine's "Something Old, Something Blue" and a brief "Blues Theme." Mitchell is heard in prime form throughout the enjoyable straightahead set which contains a few subtle surprises. —*Scott Yanow*

Last Dance / Apr. 28, 1977-Apr. 30, 1977 / JAM ✦✦✦

For one of his final recordings, trumpeter Blue Mitchell returned to a small group format and came up with an underrated gem. This out-of-print LP features Mitchell with altoist Dick Spencer, pianist Victor Feldman, bassist John Heard and drummer Dick Berk performing five jazz standards and the basic original "Getting' Sentimental Over Blue." Blue's tone is particularly pretty on "Portrait of Jenny." An excellent set that deserves to be reissued on CD someday. —*Scott Yanow*

Summer Soft / 1977 / Impulse! ✦✦

Although there are some fine players on this LP (including trumpeter Blue Mitchell, pianist Cedar Walton and tenors Harold Land, Herman Riley and Eddie Harris), they are largely wasted on inferior material and commercial arrangements. Mitchell's great recordings were in his early days for Riverside and Blue Note. By 1976, major labels were rarely recording straightahead sets, and Blue Mitchell's talents and distinctive sound were misused on projects such as this one. —*Scott Yanow*

Grover Mitchell

b. Mar. 17, 1930, Whatley, AL

Trombone, Leader / Swing

Grover Mitchell is a soulful and expressive soloist who is best known for his association with swing greats and has an appealing, very likable tone that was influenced by Tommy Dorsey. Born in Whatley, AL. and raised in Pittsburgh, he moved to the West Coast in the early '60s. Mitchell played with Duke Ellington's orchestra in 1961 before working with Lionel Hampton briefly in 1962. That year, he joined Count Basie's orchestra, where he stayed until 1970. Mitchell rejoined Basie in 1980 and remained with him until his death in 1984. It was in the early '70s that Mitchell started writing music for television and films, including the hit 1972 film *Lady Sings the Blues* (which starred Diana Ross as Billie Holiday). He began leading his own bands in the 1970s, which have included a big band that recorded for Jazz Chronicles in the 1970s and a Basie-ish orchestra that recorded for Stash throughout the second half of the 1980s. Mitchell has also recorded for Ken, and since 1995, he has been leading the Basie "ghost orchestra." —*Alex Henderson*

Meet Grover Mitchell / Aug. 27, 1978+Mar. 18, 1979 / Jazz Chronicles ✦✦✦

It is not too surprising that the debut recording by Grover Mitchell's big band sounds a bit like Count Basie's. The trombonist/arranger was a member of Basie's band from 1962-70 and would have two future stints (including one as the orchestra's leader). This particular out-of-print LP from a small Los Angeles label features Mitchell's arrangements for a 16-piece big band; eight of the ten songs are his originals. Among the key sidemen are trumpeters Al Aarons, bass trombonist Jimmy Cheatham, the reeds of Buddy Collette, Jackie Kelso and Charlie Owens and pianist Jeannie Cheatham. Fine, swinging music, but this album will be difficult to find. —*Scott Yanow*

The Devil's Waltz / Jul. 20, 1980+Aug. 3, 1980 / Jazz Chronicles ✦✦✦

Live at the Red Parrot / Apr. 20, 1984-Apr. 21, 1984 / Hemisphere ✦✦✦✦

Trombonist/arranger Grover Mitchell was with Count Basie's big band from 1962-70 and 1980-84. During the second period, when the Basie band was off, he often put together an orchestra of his own using some of Count's sidemen. This somewhat obscure LP, recorded five days before Basie's death, features the 14-piece Grover Mitchell Orchestra swinging in a Basie groove. The charts (by Eric Dixon, Frank Foster and Bobby Plater) all move, with the emphasis on originals and basic originals. Among the key soloists are altoist Danny Turner (showcased on "It's a Wonderful World"), baritonist Joe Temperley (heard from on "Street of Dreams"), and tenors Kenny Hing and Eric Dixon. —*Scott Yanow*

Grover Mitchell & His Orchestra / Sep. 26, 1987 / Stash ✦✦✦✦

● **Truckin'** / Sep. 26, 1987 / Stash ✦✦✦✦✦

In the 1980s, the Grover Mitchell Big Band was one of the more underrated jazz orchestras. Influenced by, but not limited to, the swing of Count Basie, the 12-piece version heard on this Stash release performs arrangements by Eric Dixon, Wild Bill Davis (who plays piano on the record), Ernie Wilkins, Cecil Bridgewater and Frank Foster. Among the main soloists in the band are Davis, trumpeters Bridgewater and John Eckert, altoist Norris Turney (who is showcased on "Azure Te"), Doug Lawrence on tenor and soprano and Mitchell himself on trombone. Easily recommended to fans of swinging big bands. —*Scott Yanow*

Hip Shakin' / Jun. 18, 1990-Jun. 19, 1990 / Ken Music ✦✦✦

Red Mitchell (Keith Moore Mitchell)

b. Sep. 20, 1927, New York, NY, **d.** Nov. 8, 1992, Salem, OR

Bass / Cool, Hard Bop

A talented bassist who was always in great demand, Red Mitchell was originally a pianist and he doubled on piano on an occasional basis throughout his career. He switched to bass when he was a member of an army band in Germany. Mitchell played with Jackie Paris (1947-48), Mundell Lowe, Chubby Jackson's big band and Charlie Ventura (1949), toured with Woody Herman's Orchestra (1949-51) and was a member of the popular Red Norvo Trio (1952-54). He played with the Gerry Mulligan Quartet (1954) and then settled in Los Angeles where, during 1954-68, he played with nearly everyone, from West Coast jazz stars (particularly Hampton Hawes) to recording with Ornette Coleman (1959) and being a member of the studio orchestra of MGM. He also co-led a quintet with Harold Land during 1961-62 that recorded for Atlantic. In 1968 Mitchell moved to Stockholm where he led groups, played with European jazzmen and accompanied visiting Americans including Dizzy Gillespie and Phil Woods. Mitchell made occasional visits to the US, and shortly before he died he moved to Oregon. In addition to the Atlantic date, Red Mitchell led albums for Bethlehem (1955), Contemporary, Pacific Jazz, Mercury, Steeple Chase, Caprice, Gryphon, Phontastic, Enja and Capri, in addition to a few smaller European labels. —*Scott Yanow*

● **Presenting Red Mitchell** / Mar. 26, 1957 / Original Jazz Classics ✦✦✦✦✦

Bassist Red Mitchell, who had led two fairly obscure sessions for Bethlehem in 1955, came up with a gem on his lone Contemporary set as a leader (which has been reissued as this CD). Based in Los Angeles at the time, Mitchell utilized pianist Lorraine Geller and two up-and-coming players: James Clay (who splits his time between tenor and flute) and, in one of his first recording sessions, drummer Billy Higgins. The quartet performs then-recent tunes by Miles Davis, Sonny Rollins and Clifford Brown ("Sandu"), a pair of Mitchell originals, "Scrapple from the Apple" and "Cheek to Cheek." Despite Higgins' and (to a lesser extent) Clay's connections with Ornette Coleman, the music is strictly high-quality modern mainstream bop of the era. Easily recommended to collectors of straightahead jazz. —*Scott Yanow*

● **Hear Ye!** / Oct. 14, 1961 / Atlantic ✦✦✦✦✦

In the early '60s bassist Red Mitchell and tenor saxophonist Harold Land co-led a quintet in Los Angeles. The group did not catch on but they did record one Atlantic set which has been reissued on CD. In addition to the co-leaders, the quintet included trumpeter Carmell Jones, pianist Frank Strazzeri and drummer Leon Pettis and, although their original program of six songs comprised group originals, the music falls easily into the hard-bop area with plenty of fine solos and swinging ensembles. The CD reissue adds two previously unreleased tracks including a lone standard, "I'm Old Fashioned." This is a fine effort from a group that deserved greater recognition at the time. —*Scott Yanow*

Red Mitchell Meets Guido Manusardi / 1971 / Pausa ✦✦✦

Originally recorded for an Italian label (although it was made in Stockholm) and only released domestically as an LP from the now-defunct Pausa record company, this set of duets matches the brilliant bassist Red Mitchell with the relatively obscure Italian pianist Guido Manusardi. They stretch out on "God Bless the Child," "Bye Bye Blackbird," their original "Blue Sleepy People" and one lesser-known piece. The interplay between the two musicians is impressive (they were working together regularly at the time), and this was very much an equal musical partnership, with Manusardi often backing the bassist. Subtle and mostly quiet music. —*Scott Yanow*

Hot House / Apr. 18, 1980-Apr. 19, 1980 / Storyville ✦✦✦✦

Bassist Red Mitchell and tenor saxophonist Warne Marsh teamed up several times in the 1980s, including for this duet album. Rather than disguise the song titles (a practice that Marsh had learned from Lennie Tristano), the duo performs straightforward yet exploratory renditions of eight standards, plus Mitchell's original "Undertow." Marsh in particular was in prime form during the era, and although the session would have been a bit more exciting if a third musician (piano, guitar or drums) had been added, since the sound is fairly constant throughout the date, the results are quite musical and creative. —*Scott Yanow*

Red Mitchell-Warne Marsh Big Two, Vol. 1 / Apr. 18, 1980-Apr. 19, 1980 / Storyville ✦✦✦

Released for the first time on this 1996 CD, this set documents a live duo date by tenor saxophonist Warne Marsh and bassist Red Mitchell. As usual, Marsh stretches out with continually fresh variations over common chord changes, but the lack of a drummer and a pianist is felt in a certain lack of momentum. Mitchell plays as well as usual, taking quite a few short solos, but the absence of tonal variety makes the performance of less interest than one might expect. —*Scott Yanow*

Talking / Jan. 10, 1989-Jan. 11, 1989 / Capri ✦✦✦✦✦

This Capri CD has trio playing of the highest order. Bassist Red Mitchell welcomes pianist Kenny Barron and drummer Ben Riley, and surprisingly only performs three standards along with Thelonious Monk's "Locomotive"; the remainder of the program comprises a Kenny Barron song and five originals from the multitalented Mitchell. The close communication between these three players is quite impressive and the music always swings. —*Scott Yanow*

Roscoe Mitchell

b. Aug. 3, 1940, Chicago, IL

Multiple Reeds, Alto Saxophone, Tenor Saxophone, Flute, Soprano Saxophone / Avant-Garde, Free Jazz

One of the top saxophonists to come out of Chicago's AACM movement of the mid-'60s, Roscoe Mitchell is a particularly strong and consistently adventurous improviser long associated with the Art Ensemble of Chicago. After getting out of the military, Mitchell led a hard-bop sextet in Chicago (1961) which gradually became much freer. He was a member of Muhal Richard Abrams' Experimental Band and a founding member of the AACM in 1965. Mitchell's monumental *Sound* album (1966) introduced a new way of freely improvising, utilizing silence as well as high energy and "little instruments" as well as conventional horns. Lester Bowie and Malachi Favors were on that date and Mitchell's 1967 follow-up *Old/Quartet*. With the addition of Joseph Jarman and Philip Wilson (who was later succeeded by Don Moye), the Art Ensemble of Chicago was born. The colorful unit was one of the most popular groups in the jazz avant-garde, and Mitchell was an integral part of the band. Roscoe Mitchell (who, in addition to his main horns, plays clarinet, flute, piccolo, oboe, baritone and bass saxophones) also was involved in individual projects through the years and has recorded as a leader for Delmark, Nessa, Sackville, Moers Music, 1750 Arch, Black Saint, Cecma and Silkheart in settings ranging from large ensembles to unaccompanied solo concerts. —*Scott Yanow*

☆ **Sound** / Aug. 10, 1966+Aug. 26, 1966 / Delmark ✦✦✦✦✦
This innovative set helped introduce the sound and music of the AACM to record, and it just preceded the formation of the Art Ensemble of Chicago. Altoist Roscoe Mitchell joined with trumpeter Lester Bowie, trombonist Lester Lashley, tenor saxophonist Maurice McIntyre, bassist Malachi Favors and drummer Alvin Fielder to perform five numbers (two released for the first time on this 1996 reissue CD) that were quite a bit different than most of the high energy avant-garde releases of the time. Utilizing silence as part of the music, sometimes playing "little instruments" (which ranged from toys to percussion devices), and sometimes hinting at earlier styles while improvising very freely, Mitchell performed music that was both fascinating and sometimes difficult to listen to. The two versions of "Ornette" on this set are fine examples of freebop, while the two lengthy versions of "Sound" ramble on in intriguing fashion. A classic of its kind. —*Scott Yanow*

Old / Quartet / May 18, 1967-May 25, 1967 / Nessa ✦✦✦✦

Congliptious / Feb. 4, 1968+Mar. 11, 1968 / Nessa ✦✦✦
Simply a standout quartet date. Mitchell honks, bleats, and dashes full steam ahead. Issued as Roscoe Mitchell and Ensemble. —*Ron Wynn*

The Roscoe Mitchell Solo Saxophone Concerts / Oct. 22, 1973-Jul. 12, 1974 / Sackville ✦✦✦✦✦
Roscoe Mitchell is a founding member of the Art Ensemble of Chicago and has only had occasional dates as a leader through the years. This is one of his most rewarding, although listeners accustomed to full rhythm sections and conventional swinging might find this one hard to get into. Mitchell proves to be a brilliant architect of sound, frequently building up a simple idea to unimagined heights of complexity. Performing on soprano, alto, tenor and bass saxophones at the three festivals at which this music is taken from, Roscoe Mitchell demonstrates why he is considered one of the masters of avant-garde jazz. This solo set is only topped by his 1976-77 Nessa recording *Nonaah*. —*Scott Yanow*

Quartet / Oct. 4, 1975-Oct. 5, 1975 / Sackville ✦✦✦
With pianist Muhal Abrahms, trombonist George Lewis, and guitarist A. Spencer Barefield. Very challenging listening. —*Michael G. Nastos*

★ **Nonaah** / Aug. 23, 1976-Feb. 22, 1977 / Nessa ✦✦✦✦✦
This is arguably Mitchell's best solo statement. It includes a full-side treatment of the title cut, solo works, duos, and an incredible alto number with Mitchell, Henry Threadgill (as), Joseph Jarman (reeds), and the undervalued Wallace McMillan (b). —*Ron Wynn*

Duets with Anthony Braxton / Dec. 13, 1977 / Sackville ✦✦✦✦

L-R-G / The Maze / SII Examples / Jul. 27, 1978-Aug. 17, 1978 / Nessa ✦✦✦✦
Free improvisation. Definitive statement from Art Ensemble saxophonist and composer. One piece is all horns, another all percussion, and one is solo. This one is for open ears only. —*Michael G. Nastos*

Snurdy McGurdy and Her Dancin' Shoes / Dec. 11, 1980+Dec. 12, 1980 / Nessa ✦✦✦✦
This album is more upbeat and humorous, less dense and intense than some past Mitchell dates, but the music's just as ferocious. —*Ron Wynn*

3x4 Eye / Feb. 18, 1981-Feb. 19, 1981 / Black Saint ✦✦✦
Roscoe Mitchell has continued to head his Sound Ensemble, and this 1981 session presented them doing two extensive numbers and two shorter pieces. The longer works had fiery solos and intricate unison sections, while "JoJar" featured Mitchell's group in a looser, more relaxed posture, and "Variations on a Folk Song" alternated between jagged, flamboyant solos and simple statements. This wasn't among his most intense or combative dates, but Mitchell and the Sound Ensemble were still well worth hearing. —*Ron Wynn*

And the Sound and Space Ensembles / Jun. 1983 / Black Saint ✦✦✦✦

The Flow of Things / Jun. 29, 1986-Sep. 7, 1986 / Black Saint ✦✦✦✦✦
High-energy, kinetic pieces. Jodie Christian (p) opens the eyes of doubters —*Ron Wynn*

Live at the Knitting Factory / Nov. 1987 / Black Saint ✦✦✦✦

After Fallen Leaves / Oct. 1989 / Silkheart ✦✦✦✦

Duets & Solos / Mar. 15, 1990 / Black Saint ✦✦✦✦

This Dance Is for Steve Mc Call / May 1992 / Black Saint ✦✦✦✦

Sound & Space Ensembles / Jan. 28, 1993 / Black Saint ✦✦✦

Hey Donald / May 23, 1994-May 25, 1994 / Delmark ✦✦✦✦✦
Since Roscoe Mitchell (who on this set made his return to the Delmark label after 28 years) is best known as a free jazz pioneer and a longtime member of The Art Ensemble of Chicago, the straightahead nature of a few of the selections will surprise some of his followers. "Walking in the Moonlight" is a sly and witty strut, "Jeremy" a melodic ballad for the leader's flute and "Hey Donald" could have come from the Sonny Rollins songbook. But Mitchell has not forsaken his innovative style. On "Dragons" his soprano playing (with its circular breathing) sounds very African, there are four free duets with bassist Malachi Favors, and the blowouts on "Song for Rwanda" and "See You at the Fair" are fairly adventurous. In general, Mitchell (who is joined by a versatile rhythm section comprising pianist Jodie Christian, bassist Favors and drummer Tootie Heath) saves the more boppish pieces for his tenor while on soprano his intense sound creates a drone effect reminiscent of a bit of bagpipes. All in all, his release for Delmark should keep listeners guessing. —*Scott Yanow*

Sound Songs / Oct. 9, 1994 / Delmark ✦✦✦✦

Hank Mobley

b. Jul. 7, 1930, Eastman, GA, d. May 30, 1986, Philadelphia, PA
Tenor Saxophone / Hard Bop
Accurately described by critic Leonard Feather as "the middleweight champion of the tenor" due to his sound (not as light as Lester Young's or as heavy as Sonny Rollins'), Hank Mobley tended to be taken for granted during his career but recorded a long string of valuable albums for Blue Note. He first gained attention for his work with Max Roach (on and off during 1951-53) and Dizzy Gillespie (1954). An original member of the Jazz Messengers (1954-56), Mobley joined Horace Silver when the pianist broke away from Art Blakey to form his own group (1956-57). Mobley was back with Blakey for a bit in 1959 and spent an unhappy period with Miles Davis (1961-62), but mostly worked as a leader in the 1960s. He was in Europe during much of 1968-70 and recorded with Cedar Walton in 1972, but by the mid-'70s was largely retired due to bad health. Hank Mobley led isolated dates for Savoy, Prestige and Roulette, but it is for his 25 Blue Note albums (recorded during 1955-70) with the who's who of hard bop (including such sidemen as Horace Silver, Art Blakey, Lee Morgan, Milt Jackson, Art Farmer, Donald Byrd, Bobby Timmons, Sonny Clark, Kenny Dorham, Pepper Adams, Wynton Kelly, Freddie Hubbard, Grant Green, Philly Joe Jones, Herbie Hancock, Andrew Hill, Barry Harris, Curtis Fuller, McCoy Tyner, Billy Higgins, James Spaulding, Jackie McLean, Blue Mitchell, Cedar Walton, Ron Carter and Woody Shaw) that he will be best remembered. —*Scott Yanow*

Hank Mobley Quartet / Mar. 27, 1955 / Blue Note ✦✦✦✦
This debut of Mobley on Blue Note includes Horace Silver on piano and Doug Watkins on bass, plus someone named Art Blakey on drums. —*Ron Wynn*

The Jazz Message of Hank Mobley, Vol. 1 / Jan. 30, 1956 / Savoy ✦✦✦
Other than a Blue Note date from the previous year, this CD contains tenor saxophonist Hank Mobley's first two sessions as a leader. With trumpeter Donald Byrd, either Hank Jones or Ronnie Ball on piano, Wendell Marshall or Doug Watkins on bass, drummer Kenny Clarke and (on three numbers) the unusual altoist John LaPorta, Mobley performs a mixture of originals and standards. The results (highlighted by "There'll Never Be Another You," "When I Fall in Love" and "Budo") are a swinging hard bop date. Nothing all that unusual occurs and the CD clocks in at an average LP's length, but the swinging music is easily recommended to straightahead jazz fans and (unlike many of Denon's Savoy reissues), these two sessions are brough back complete. —*Scott Yanow*

Messages / Jul. 20, 1956+Jul. 27, 1956 / Prestige ✦✦✦✦
With the exception of Hank Mobley's original "Alternating Current," which was left out due to lack of space, this single CD has all of the music from the two Prestige LPs *Mobley's Message* and *Hank Mobley's Second Message;* a two-LP set from 1976 which had the same *Messages* title and catalog number, but also the complete program, is actually the preferred acquisition, but will be difficult to locate. The first session mostly features the fine tenor Hank Mobley jamming on four superior bop standards, including "Bouncing with Bud," "52nd Street Theme" and "Au Privavem," and his own "Minor Disturbance" in a quintet with trumpeter Donald Byrd, pianist Barry Harris, bassist Doug Watkins and drummer Art Taylor; altoist Jackie McLean has a strong cameo on "Au Private." The second set, recorded a week later, is less of a jam session, with Mobley, trumpeter Kenny Dorham, pianist Walter Bishop, bassist Doug Watkins and drummer Art Taylor essaying three of Mobley's now-obscure compositions, Benny Harris' "Crazeology" and the standards "These Are the Things I Love" and "I Should Care." The two dates give one a good example of Hank Mobley's playing prior to becoming a regular Blue Note artist, where he would create his greatest work. —*Scott Yanow*

The Jazz Message of Hank Mobley, Vol. 2 / Jul. 23, 1956+Nov. 7, 1956 / Savoy ♦♦♦♦

Hank Mobley / Nov. 25, 1956 / Blue Note ♦♦♦

Hank Mobley and His All-Stars / Jan. 13, 1957 / Blue Note ♦♦♦♦
This CD is a straight reissue of a Hank Mobley LP that features the "Who's Who" of late-'50s hard bop: the tenor-leader, vibraphonist Milt Jackson, pianist Horace Silver, bassist Doug Watkins and drummer Art Blakey. The quintet performs five Mobley compositions (best is the lyrical "Mobley's Musings"), songs that are generally more interesting for their chord changes than for their melodies, which is probably why none of them became standards. One's attention is constantly drawn to the inventive solos and Art Blakey's roaring "accompaniment." An above-average effort from some of the best. —*Scott Yanow*

Hank Mobley Quintet / Mar. 9, 1957 / Blue Note ♦♦♦♦♦
Tenor saxophonist Hank Mobley teamed up with a couple of his more notable employers (pianist Horace Silver and drummer Art Blakey) plus trumpeter Art Farmer and bassist Doug Watkins for this superior Blue Note album which has been reissued (along with two alternate takes) on CD. Mobley's "Funk in Deep Freeze" is the most memorable selection, but on a whole, the six compositions (all Mobley originals) display his underrated writing talents. It is a particular joy to hear the inspired playing of Silver and Blakey on this lesser-known but consistently stimulating hard bop set. —*Scott Yanow*

Hank / Apr. 21, 1957 / Blue Note ♦♦♦♦

Curtain Call / Aug. 18, 1957 / Blue Note ♦♦♦

Poppin' / Oct. 20, 1957 / Blue Note ♦♦♦♦
Poppin' was one of many sessions tenor saxophonist Hank Mobley recorded in the late '50s and early '60s, but remained unreleased until the late '70s and '80s. It's hard to say why this album sat on the shelves, since it as good as the other records he cut at the time. Leading a sextet featuring trumpeter Art Farmer, baritone saxophonist Pepper Adams, pianist Sonny Clark, bassist Paul Chambers and drummer Philly Joe Jones, Mobley plays a selection of five originals and contemporary jazz songs with passion and vigor. All of the musicians turn in fine performances (Clark in particular stands out with his lithe solos and tasteful accompaniment), and the result is a winning collection of straightahead hard-bop that ranks as another solid addition to Mobley's strong catalog. —*Stephen Thomas Erlewine*

Peckin' Time / Feb. 9, 1958 / Blue Note ♦♦♦♦♦
Tenor saxophonist Hank Mobley, who throughout his career was overshadowed by more influential tenors such as Sonny Rollins and John Coltrane, was himself a talented and fairly original player and a fine composer; many of his originals deserve to be revived. For this Blue Note session, which in its CD reissue includes three alternate takes, Mobley, trumpeter Lee Morgan, pianist Wynton Kelly, bassist Paul Chambers and drummer Charlie Persip interpret four of the tenor's songs, including "High and Flighty" and the 12-minute "Gil-Go Blues," along with the standard "Speak Low." The results are high-quality hard bop, the modern mainstream of the era. —*Scott Yanow*

★ **Soul Station** / Feb. 7, 1960 / Blue Note ♦♦♦♦♦
Other than his 1955 debut for Blue Note, this set (reissued on CD) was tenor saxophonist Hank Mobley's first opportunity to record as leader of a quartet without any other competing horns. With the stimulating support of pianist Wynton Kelly, bassist Paul Chambers and drummer Art Blakey, Mobley is in peak form on four of his originals (of which "This I Dig of You" is best-known), "Remember" and the ballad "If I Should Lose You." Mobley's improvisations are melodic and thoughtful, yet always swinging and full of inner fire. This CD serves as a perfect introduction to the playing and writing abilities of this underrated talent. —*Scott Yanow*

Roll Call / Nov. 13, 1960 / Blue Note ♦♦♦♦♦
This set, reissued on CD, differs from tenor saxophonist Hank Mobley's *Soul Station* release of nine months earlier in that although he uses the same impressive rhythm section (pianist Wynton Kelly, bassist Paul Chambers and drummer Art Blakey), Mobley also welcomes young trumpeter Freddie Hubbard. Hubbard actually steals the show on a few of the numbers, but since five of the pieces are Mobley originals, including such forgotten gems as "Roll Call," "My Groove Your Move" and "A Baptist Beat," the tenorman obviously set up this date partly as a way of featuring the fiery Hubbard. Art Blakey took note of the trumpeter's talents and hired him to replace Lee Morgan with the Jazz Messengers a year later. Overall, this is an excellent hard bop date and, as is true of all of Hank Mobley's Blue Note albums, it is easily recommended to fans of straightahead jazz. —*Scott Yanow*

Workout / Mar. 26, 1961 / Blue Note ♦♦♦♦♦
This is one of the best known Hank Mobley recordings, and for good reason. Although none of his four originals ("Workout," "Uh Huh," "Smokin'," "Greasin' Easy") caught on, the fine saxophonist is in top form. He jams on the four tunes, plus "The Best Things in Life Are Free," with an all-star quintet of young modern-

ists—guitarist Grant Green, pianist Wynton Kelly, bassist Paul Chambers and drummer Philly Joe Jones—and shows that he was a much stronger player than his then-current boss Miles Davis seemed to think. This recommended CD reissue adds a version of "Three Coins in the Fountain" from the same date, originally released on *Another Workout*, to the original LP program. —*Scott Yanow*

Another Workout / Mar. 26, 1961+Dec. 5, 1961 / Blue Note ♦♦♦♦
This LP has material from 1961 that for no real reason went unreleased until 1985. One song, "Three Coins in a Fountain," is from the same session that resulted in tenor saxophonist Hank Mobley's famous *Workout* session with guitarist Grant Green, pianist Wynton Kelly, bassist Paul Chambers and drummer Philly Joe Jones. The other five numbers—three obscure Mobley originals, plus "I Should Care" and "Hello Young Lovers"—are from the previously unheard December 5, 1961 session with the same personnel except for Green. Hank Mobley was in a prime period around this time, and all of his Blue Note recordings are well worth picking up. —*Scott Yanow*

No Room for Squares / Mar. 7, 1963+Oct. 2, 1963 / Blue Note ♦♦♦♦
By 1963, Hank Mobley, whose tenor tone perfectly fit the hard bop modern mainstream music of the late '50s and early '60s, had altered his sound slightly to get a harder tone, influenced to an extent by John Coltrane. This CD reissue differs quite a bit from the original LP program, adding alternate takes of "No Room for Squares" and "Carolyn," along with two previously unissued selections ("Comin' Back" and "Syrup and Biscuits") while dropping two songs from the LP which were cut at a slightly earlier session. Mobley leads a top-notch quintet with trumpeter Lee Morgan, pianist Andrew Hill, bassist John Ore and drummer Philly Joe Jones through a set of high-quality, if obscure, originals written by either the leader or Morgan. The music is as satisfying and adventurous, as one would expect. —*Scott Yanow*

Straight No Filter / Jul. 7, 1963-Feb. 4, 1965 / Blue Note ♦♦♦♦♦
Straight No Filter consists of the last remaining unissued Hank Mobley-led Blue Note recordings. The first half of this disc is often superb with several brilliant solos from Mobley, McCoy Tyner (piano) and the still underrated Lee Morgan (trumpet). —*Scott Yanow*

The Turnaround / Feb. 4, 1965 / Blue Note ♦♦♦♦
The CD reissue of Hank Mobley's *The Turnaround* is different from the original LP in that two songs from a March 7, 1963 date were dropped, while two previously unissued ones from February 4, 1965 were added. Most intriguing about this quintet set with trumpeter Freddie Hubbard, pianist Barry Harris, bassist Paul Chambers and drummer Billy Higgins are the six likable but complex Mobley compositions. A very underrated writer, many of Hank Mobley's originals deserve to be revived, including these six ("Pat 'n' Chat," "Third Time Around," "Hank's Waltz," "The Turnaround," "Straight Ahead" and "My Sin"). Rather than stick to the standard 32-bar format heard on most pre-1970 songs, Mobley's pieces utilize choruses of 44, 20 and 50 bars while still sounding logical. All of the musicians play up to par on these advanced hard bop tunes. —*Scott Yanow*

Dippin' / Jun. 18, 1965 / Blue Note ♦♦♦♦♦
All of tenor saxophonist Hank Mobley's Blue Note recordings are recommended for his harmonically advanced, tricky, yet logical originals, in addition to consistently fine soloing from some of the top modern mainstream players of the era; these albums helped define the Blue Note sound of the 1960s. For this date, a straight CD reissue of the original LP, Mobley, trumpeter Lee Morgan, pianist Harold Mabern, bassist Larry Ridley and drummer Billy Higgins perform four of the tenorman's originals, the highly appealing "Recado Bossa Nova" and the standard ballad "I See Your Face Before Me." An excellent outing, even if no "hits" resulted. —*Scott Yanow*

A Caddy for Daddy / Dec. 18, 1965 / Blue Note ♦♦♦♦
Hank Mobley was a perfect artist for Blue Note in the 1960s. A distinctive but not dominant soloist, Mobley was also a very talented writer whose compositions avoided the predictable, yet could often be quite melodic and soulful; his tricky originals consistently inspired the young all-stars in Blue Note's stable. For this CD, which is a straight reissue of a 1965 session, Mobley is joined by trumpeter Lee Morgan, trombonist Curtis Fuller, pianist McCoy Tyner, bassist Bob Cranshaw and drummer Billy Higgins (a typically remarkable Blue Note lineup) for the infectious title cut, three other lesser-known but superior originals, plus Wayne Shorter's "Venus di Mildew." Recommended. —*Scott Yanow*

A Slice of the Top / Mar. 18, 1966 / Blue Note ♦♦♦♦♦
This is one of tenor saxophonist Hank Mobley's more intriguing sessions, for the talented composer had an opportunity to have four of his originals, plus the standard "There's a Lull in My Life," performed by an octet in the cool-toned style of Miles Davis' "Birth of the Cool" nonet, arranged by Duke Pearson. Although recorded in 1966, this date was not released until 1979 and unfortunately has not yet been reissued on CD. Mobley, who continued to evolve into a more advanced

player throughout the 1960s, fits right in with such adventurous players as altoist James Spaulding, trumpeter Lee Morgan (with whom Mobley recorded frequently), pianist McCoy Tyner, bassist Reggie Workman and drummer Billy Higgins. The inclusion of Kiane Zawadi on euphonium and Howard Johnson on tuba adds a lot of color to this memorable outing. *—Scott Yanow*

Hi Voltage / 1967 / Blue Note ✦✦✦✦

This is a typically enjoyable Hank Mobley date from the last great year of music from Blue Note, 1967. The talented tenor, who contributed all six compositions, is teamed with trumpeter Blue Mitchell, altoist Jackie McLean, pianist John Hicks, bassist Bob Cranshaw and drummer Billy Higgins (all Blue Note veterans except Hicks), and everyone plays up to par. The music sticks to advanced hard bop with hints of funk, bossa nova and modal tunes. Strange that none of these selections, which include the ballad "No More Goodbys," "Bossa De Luxe" and "Flirty Gerty," caught on. *—Scott Yanow*

Third Season / Feb. 24, 1967 / Blue Note ✦✦✦✦

Tenor saxophonist Hank Mobley recorded frequently for Blue Note in the 1960s (six albums from 1967-70) and, although overshadowed by the flashier and more avant-garde players, Mobley's output was consistently rewarding. For this over-looked session, which was not issued until 1980 and has yet to resurface on CD, a regular contingent of top Blue Note artists (Mobley, trumpeter Lee Morgan, altoist James Spaulding, pianist Cedar Walton, bassist Walter Booker and drummer Billy Higgins) are joined by a wild card, guitarist Sonny Greenwich. The music is mostly in the hard bop vein, with hints of modality and the gospellish piece "Give Me That Feelin'," but Greenwich's three solos are a bonus and the performances of five Mobley originals and one by Morgan are up to the usual caliber of Blue Note's releases. Pity that this one has been lost in the shuffle; it is one to search for by Hank Mobley fans. *—Scott Yanow*

Far Away Lands / Mar. 26, 1967 / Blue Note ✦✦✦✦

Of all the Blue Note artists of the 1960s, tenor saxophonist Hank Mobley may very well be the most underrated. A consistent player whose style evolved throughout the decade, Mobley wrote a series of inventive and challenging compositions that inspired the all-stars he used on his recordings while remaining in the genre of hard bop. For this lesser-known outing, Mobley teams up with trumpeter Donald Byrd, pianist Cedar Walton, bassist Ron Carter and drummer Billy Higgins for four of his songs (given such colorful titles as "A Dab of This and That," "No Argument," "The Hippity Hop" and "Bossa for Baby"), along with a song apiece from Byrd and Jimmy Heath. An excellent outing, fairly late in the productive career of Hank Mobley. *—Scott Yanow*

Reach Out / Jan. 19, 1968 / Blue Note ✦✦

Reach Out was one of the few times Hank Mobley left behind driving, aggressive hard bop, choosing to concentrate on lightly grooving bop and soul-jazz instead. Essentially, the session resulted in the most commercially oriented record he made, complete with two pop covers ("Reach Out (I'll Be There)," "Goin' Out of My Head") and a laidback, swinging vibe. That wouldn't necessarily be a bad thing, but the band—an impressive lineup of Woody Shaw (trumpet, fluegelhorn), George Benson (guitar), Lamont Johnson (piano), Bob Cranshaw (bass) and Billy Higgins (drums)—sounds constrained by the material and their desire to make the music appeal to a wide audience. Things rarely are worse than on "Reach Out," where the group not only fails to lay down a groove, but they often sound on the verge of falling apart, especially during Higgins' poorly timed breaks. They recover shortly afterward, but no one sounds particularly enthusiastic, including Mobley. In fact, Mobley's presence on the record feels strangely minimal. Only during "Good Pickin's"—a laidback bop original that's easily the best thing here—does he come alive, weaving a spell with long, liquid lines, but its subtle grace just illustrates the problems with this curiously bland record. *—Stephen Thomas Erlewine*

The Flip / Jul. 12, 1969 / Blue Note ✦✦✦

Hank Mobley recorded his second-to-last session in Paris in 1969 with a combination of European and American musicians. The sextet on *The Flip* featured Mobley, trumpeter Dizzy Reece, trombonist Slide Hampton, pianist Vince Benedetti, bassist Alby Cullaz and drummer Philly Joe Jones. Unlike its predecessor, *Reach Out*, there's little attempt to commercialize Mobley's sound, and he sticks to straightahead hard bop throughout the session. On the whole, the date isn't bad, but it isn't particularly distinguished, boasting adequate, unmemorable original compositions and fine, workmanlike performances. Hardcore fans looking to complete a Mobley collection should seek the record out, but most listeners will be satisfied with the stronger Mobley albums that are more readily available. *—Stephen Thomas Erlewine*

Thinking of Home / Jul. 31, 1970 / Blue Note ✦✦✦✦✦

For what would be his final of over 20 Blue Note albums, tenor saxophonist Hank Mobley uses a sextet that also includes trumpeter Woody Shaw, the obscure guitarist Eddie Diehl, pianist Cedar Walton, bassist Mickey Bass and drummer Leroy Wil-

liams for a typically challenging set of advanced hard bop music. For the first and only time in his career, Mobley recorded a "Suite" (consisting of "Thinking of Home," "The Flight" and "Home at Last"); the remainder of the set has three of his other attractive originals plus Mickey Bass' "Gayle's Groove." This music was not released for the first time until 1980 and has not popped up yet on CD. It is only fitting that Hank Mobley would record one of the last worthwhile Blue Note albums before its artistic collapse (it would not be revived until the 1980s) for his consistent output helped define the label's sound in the 1960s. Mobley's excellent playing and the adventurous solos of Woody Shaw make this hard-to-find LP (his last as a leader) one to hunt for. *—Scott Yanow*

The Modern Jazz Quartet

f. 1952

Group / Cool, Third Stream

Pianist John Lewis, vibraphonist Milt Jackson, bassist Ray Brown and drummer Kenny Clarke first came together as the rhythm section of the 1946 Dizzy Gillespie Orchestra and they had occasional features that gave the overworked brass players a well-deserved rest. They next came together in 1951, recording as the Milt Jackson Quartet. In 1952, with Percy Heath taking Brown's place, the Modern Jazz Quartet (MJQ) became a permanent group. Other than Connie Kay succeeding Clarke in 1955, the band's personnel was set. In the early days, Jackson and Lewis both were equally responsible for the group's musical direction, but the pianist eventually took over as musical director. The MJQ has long displayed John Lewis' musical vision, making jazz seem respectable by occasionally interacting with classical ensembles and playing concerts at prestigious venues, but always leaving plenty of space for bluesy and swinging improvising. Their repertoire, in addition to including veteran bop and swing pieces, introduced such originals as Lewis' "Django" and Jackson's "Bags' Groove." The group recorded for Prestige (1952-55), Atlantic (1956-74), Verve (1957), United Artists (1959) and Apple (1967-69) and, in addition to the many quartet outings, they welcomed such guests as Jimmy Giuffre, Sonny Rollins, the Beaux Arts String Quartet, a symphony orchestra conducted by Gunther Schuller, singer Diahann Carroll (on one piece), Laurindo Almeido, a big band and the Swingle Singers. Although the musicians all had opportunities to pursue individual projects, in 1974 Milt Jackson tired of the constant touring and the limitations set on his improvising and he quit the group, causing the MJQ to have a final tour and break up. In 1981 Jackson relented and the Modern Jazz Quartet (which has recorded further albums for Pablo and Atlantic) became active again although on a more part-time basis. Connie Kay's health began to fade in the early '90s (Mickey Roker often filled in for him) and after his death in 1995, Albert "Tootie" Heath became his replacement. *—Scott Yanow*

MJQ: 40 years / Dec. 22, 1952-Feb. 3, 1988 / Atlantic ✦✦✦✦✦

To celebrate The Modern Jazz Quartet's 40th anniversary as a group, Atlantic came out with an attractive four-CD box set that has selections (programmed in chronological order) that cover the group's long career. Most of the selections come from the Atlantic catalog although they have leased a few numbers owned by other labels and, with the exception of four songs from a Japanese concert and one previously unissued performance, all of the music is readily available elsewhere. But this well-conceived set serves as a perfect introduction for new listeners and as a fine retrospective of this important group's legacy. All of the best-known compositions are included and they find vibraphonist Milt Jackson, pianist John Lewis, bassist Percy Heath and drummer Connie Kay (along with a few notable guests) playing at their peak. *—Scott Yanow*

MJQ / Dec. 22, 1952+Jun. 16, 1954 / Original Jazz Classics ✦✦✦✦

Two different groups are heard from on this CD reissue. The original Modern Jazz Quartet (with vibraphonist Milt Jackson, pianist John Lewis, bassist Percy Heath and drummer Kenny Clarke) performs four numbers at the first recording session of the MJQ. In addition there are four selections from a pickup group led by Jackson that also includes pianist Horace Silver and trumpeter Henry Boozier; the latter date introduced Silver's "Opus de Funk." Overall this somewhat brief CD has swinging music that bop fans will want to get. *—Scott Yanow*

☆ Django / Jun. 25, 1953-Jan. 9, 1955 / Original Jazz Classics ✦✦✦✦

Although it had recorded one prior session, the Modern Jazz Quartet really came into its own during the three dates that comprise this CD reissue. Highlights include the original versions of John Lewis' "Django," "Milano," "Delauney's Dilemma" and the four-part "La Ronde Suite." In addition to vibraphonist Milt Jackson, pianist John Lewis and bassist Percy Heath, these performances have the last studio appearances of drummer Kenny Clarke with the group. *—Scott Yanow*

Concorde / Jul. 2, 1955 / Original Jazz Classics ✦✦✦✦

This CD reissue is most significant for having the first recordings of drummer Connie Kay as a regular member of the Modern Jazz Quartet. His subtle style fit in perfectly with vibraphonist Milt Jackson, bassist Percy Heath and pianist John Lewis. Highlights of this rather brief (around 33 minutes) CD are a four-song "Gershwin

Medley," "Softly as in a Morning Sunrise" and "Ralph's New Blues." Excellent and somewhat historic music, although the brevity of this set makes one wish that it were combined on CD with Prestige's other MJQ sessions. —*Scott Yanow*

Fontessa / Jan. 22, 1956+Feb. 14, 1956 / Atlantic ✦✦✦✦✦
This LP has a particularly strong all-around set by the Modern Jazz Quartet. While John Lewis' "Versailles" and an 11-minute "Fontessa" show the seriousness of the group (and the influence of Western classical music), other pieces (such as "Bluesology," "Woody 'n You" and a pair of ballads) look towards the group's roots in bop and permit the band to swing hard. —*Scott Yanow*

Modern Jazz Quartet at Music Inn / Aug. 28, 1956 / Atlantic ✦✦✦✦
The first of two albums the Modern Jazz Quartet recorded at the Music Inn in Lenox, MS, this LP (reissued as part of Atlantic's *Jazzlore* series in 1982) is highlighted by "Oh Bess, Oh Where's My Bess," "Two Degrees East, Three Degrees West," "A Morning in Paris" and "England's Carol" which is the MJQ's reworking of "God Rest Ye Merry, Gentlemen." Clarinetist Jimmy Giuffre sits in with the group successfully on three numbers; best is "Fun." This is a worthwhile outing that has not yet been reissued on CD. —*Scott Yanow*

No Sun in Venice / Apr. 4, 1957 / Atlantic ✦✦✦
This LP has six John Lewis compositions that were used in the French film *No Sun in Venice*. The music is quite complex and disciplined, making this set of lesser interest to fans who prefer to hear Milt Jackson playing bebop-oriented blues. However, the versatile group was perfect for this type of music and these thought-provoking performances reward repeated listenings.—*Scott Yanow*

The Modern Jazz Quartet / Apr. 5, 1957 / Mobile Fidelity ✦✦✦✦
The audiophile label Mobile Fidelity in 1994 came out with a rare LP, a reissue of a 1957 Modern Jazz Quartet session originally on Atlantic. The emphasis is very much on the MJQ's bebop roots and vibraphonist Milt Jackson stars on a five-song ballad medley and several standards including "Night in Tunisia" and his own "Bags' Groove." Fine straightahead music; this group could always swing. —*Scott Yanow*

Third Stream Music / Aug. 23, 1957-Jan. 15, 1960 / Atlantic ✦✦✦✦✦
This Atlantic LP has some unusual performances by the Modern Jazz Quartet. Two selections ("Da Capo" and "Fine") combine The MJQ (which comprises vibraphonist Milt Jackson, pianist John Lewis, bassist Percy Heath and drummer Connie Kay) with the Jimmy Giuffre Three (Giuffre on clarinet and tenor, guitarist Jim Hall and bassist Ralph Pena), on "Exposure" six chamber classical musicians add color, and a pair of other numbers ("Conversation" and the very successful "Sketch") match the MJQ with the Beaux Arts String Quartet. There is plenty of thought-provoking music on this out-of-print album, even if the idea of creating a "Third Stream" between jazz and classical music never came to pass. —*Scott Yanow*

Modern Jazz Quartet and Oscar Peterson Trio at the Opera / Oct. 19, 1957 / Verve ✦✦✦✦
This frequently exciting LP has three lightly swinging performances by the Modern Jazz Quartet ("Now's the Time," "'Round Midnight" and "D&E Blues") and five from the Oscar Peterson Trio (which at the time consisted of the pianist/leader, guitarist Herb Ellis and bassist Ray Brown). While the Modern Jazz Quartet sounds much more introverted than the more exuberant Oscar Peterson Trio, the two popular groups have more similarities than differences. Polygram has reissued the Peterson material on CD, but not yet the songs from the Modern Jazz Quartet. —*Scott Yanow*

The Historic Donaueschingen Jazz Concert / Oct. 27, 1957 / Pausa ✦✦✦
Although given top billing, the Modern Jazz Quartet is actually only featured on half of this reissue LP of material from the MPS label. The MJQ performs three complex John Lewis originals composed for the French film *No Sun in Venice* along with the more straightforward "J.B. Blues." Arranger Eddie Sauter leads a German orchestra on three pieces that are influenced by contemporary classical music, utilize quite a few percussive devices and feature the tenor of Hans Koller. In addition, writer Andre Hodeir directs a smaller group through his complicated "Paradoxe II" and Duke Jordan's "Jordu." Overall, this set is not all that essential (the move towards a "Third Stream" between jazz and classical music never really caught on) but has its interesting moments. —*Scott Yanow*

At Music Inn, Vol. 2 / Aug. 3, 1958+Sep. 3, 1958 / Atlantic ✦✦✦✦
This Mobile Fidelity CD reissues an Atlantic album by the Modern Jazz Quartet. Vibraphonist Milt Jackson, pianist John Lewis, bassist Percy Heath and drummer Connie Kay perform a pair of Lewis originals (the rather dry "Midsommer" and "Festival Sketch"), Charlie Parker's "Yardbird Suite" and a three-song ballad medley; the latter features Milt Jackson exclusively. The most unusual aspect to this set is that the great tenor Sonny Rollins joins the quartet for "Bags' Groove" (during which he is quite witty) and "Night in Tunisia." Rollins is quite creative and fits in naturally with the group. This very well-recorded reissue from the audiophile Mobile Fidelity label is worth picking up. —*Scott Yanow*

Pyramid / Aug. 22, 1959+Jan. 15, 1960 / Atlantic ✦✦✦✦✦
This is a strong LP from the Modern Jazz Quartet with inventive versions of John Lewis' "Vendome," Ray Brown's "Pyramid," Jim Hall's "Romaine," Lewis' famous "Django," and cooking jams on "How High the Moon" and "It Don't Mean a Thing." The MJQ had become a jazz institution by this time, but they never lost their creative edge, and their performances (even on the remakes) are quite stimulating, enthusiastic and fresh. —*Scott Yanow*

Odds Against Tomorrow / Oct. 9, 1959 / Blue Note ✦✦✦✦
The Modern Jazz Quartet never actually recorded for Blue Note, but their United Artists date was reissued on this Blue Note CD. The MJQ (vibraphonist Milt Jackson, pianist John Lewis, bassist Percy Heath and drummer Connie Kay) perform six of Lewis' compositions which were used in the film *Odds Against Tomorrow*. Best known is "Skating in Central Park," but all of the selections have their memorable moments and it is good to hear this classic unit playing such fresh material. —*Scott Yanow*

European Concert / Apr. 11, 1960-Apr. 13, 1960 / Atlantic ✦✦✦✦✦
This live double LP does an excellent job of summing up the first eight years of the Modern Jazz Quartet. Vibraphonist Milt Jackson, pianist John Lewis, bassist Percy Heath and drummer Connie Kay perform remakes of 15 high-quality songs that were permanent parts of their repertoire, everything from the inevitable hits ("Django," "Bluesology" and "Bags' Groove") to "La Ronde," "Vendome," "Odds Against Tomorrow" and "Skating in Central Park." Needless to say, the solos are not close duplicates of the original versions even if some of the frameworks are similar; the audience is understandably enthusiastic. This is a definitive set that is long overdue to be reissued in full on CD. —*Scott Yanow*

Dedicated to Connie / May 27, 1960 / Atlantic ✦✦✦✦✦
After drummer Connie Kay passed away, this previously unreleased concert, recorded in Slovenia in 1960, was issued on a double CD and dedicated to him. The Modern Jazz Quartet (which also includes pianist John Lewis, vibraphonist Milt Jackson and bassist Percy Heath) is heard in surprisingly inspired form playing their usual repertoire of the time. Highlights include a 23-minute medley of John Lewis compositions, "Bag's Groove," "It Don't Mean a Thing," "Django," "How High the Moon" and "Skating in Central Park." Lewis has stated that the group never played better than during this concert. Although that statement is debatable, the MJQ certainly sounds in prime form throughout the easily recommended release. —*Scott Yanow*

The Modern Jazz Quartet and Orchestra / Jun. 3, 1960+Jun. 4, 1960 / Atlantic ✦✦✦✦

The Comedy / Oct. 20, 1960-Jan. 24, 1962 / Atlantic ✦✦
This is the type of album that led many bop purists to criticize the Modern Jazz Quartet (and John Lewis in particular) for being overly influenced by Western classical music. The LP has seven of Lewis' compositions, episodic works arranged in a suite that portrays characters from a fictional Italian comedy based in the 1500s; singer Diahann Carroll guests fairly effectively on "La Cantatrice." Despite being tied to a story, there are some strong improvisations from pianist Lewis and vibraphonist Milt Jackson on this unusual material. The release is not that essential, but it is quite interesting. —*Scott Yanow*

Lonely Woman / Jan. 24, 1962-Feb. 2, 1962 / Atlantic ✦✦✦
This LP (last put out by Atlantic in 1987 as part of their *Jazzlore* reissue series) is best known for having one of the first "covers" of an Ornette Coleman tune, a fine adaptation of "Lonely Woman." Otherwise the set is less significant with six lesser-known John Lewis originals and Gary McFarland's "Why Are You Blue?" being given uplifting but not overly memorable treatments by The MJQ. —*Scott Yanow*

A Quartet Is a Quartet Is a Quartet / May 17, 1963 / Atlantic ✦✦✦

In a Crowd / Sep. 1963 / Douglas ✦✦✦✦

Collaboration with Almeido / Jul. 21, 1964 / Atlantic ✦✦✦✦✦
When Atlantic gets around to reissuing their many Modern Jazz Quartet records on CD, this should be one of the first to come back. The MJQ (vibraphonist Milt Jackson, pianist John Lewis, bassist Percy Heath and drummer Connie Kay) were joined for this 1964 session by the great acoustic guitarist Laurindo Almeido and the music is very memorable. Their version of "One Note Samba" (which starts out with Almeido playing unaccompanied) is a classic, the guitarist fits into the four John Lewis compositions quite comfortably, and "Concierto De Aranjuez" is given lengthy and inventive treatment. —*Scott Yanow*

Plays George Gershwin's "Porgy and Bess" / Jul. 23, 1964-Jul. 26, 1964 / Atlantic ✦✦✦✦
This is one of the lesser-known Modern Jazz Quartet recordings. The MJQ (pianist John Lewis, vibraphonist Milt Jackson, bassist Percy Heath and drummer Connie Kay) interpret seven themes from Gershwin's *Porgy & Bess* and the results are predictably excellent. The ballads (especially "My Man's Gone Now," "I Loves You

Porgy" and "Oh Bess, Oh Where's My Bess") are the most memorable selections on this pleasing and respectful LP. —*Scott Yanow*

Jazz Dialogue / May 25, 1965 / Atlantic ✦✦✦
This is an unusual record in the Modern Jazz Quartet's discography for it matches the MJQ (vibraphonist Milt Jackson, pianist John Lewis, bassist Percy Heath and drummer Connie Kay) with an all-star big band that comprises a dozen horns and guitarist Howard Collins. Unfortunately, the orchestra (which has a fairly impressive lineup) is used exclusively for backup of the rhythm section and none of the horns have any solos. The music, which is highlighted by new versions of such standbys as "Django," "Ralph's New Blues" and "The Golden Striker," is enjoyable enough, although this LP does not live up to its potential. —*Scott Yanow*

Blues at Carnegie Hall / Apr. 27, 1966 / Mobile Fidelity ✦✦✦✦
On this Mobile Fidelity CD reissue of a live Atlantic set from 1966, The Modern Jazz Quartet performs eight blues-based compositions. In addition to such familiar pieces as the inevitable "Bags' Groove," "Ralph's New Blues" (dedicated to jazz critic Ralph Gleason) and "The Cylinder," there are a few newer pieces (including "Home" which is similar to Lee Morgan's hit "The Sidewinder") included for variety. This predictable but consistently swinging set is particularly recommended to fans of vibraphonist Milt Jackson. —*Scott Yanow*

Place Vendôme / Sep. 27, 1966-Oct. 30, 1966 / Verve ✦✦✦
W/ The Swingle Singers. This is a good departure for MJQ. —*Ron Wynn*

Live at the Lighthouse / Mar. 1967 / Atlantic ✦✦✦✦
This fairly obscure LP by the Modern Jazz Quartet features fresh material and improvisations that are both swinging and creative. Pianist John Lewis' "The Spiritual" and "Baseball" along with vibraphonist Milt Jackson's "Novamo" and "For Someone I Love" comprise half the program; there are also excellent ballad renditions of "The Shadow of Your Smile" and "What's New." The MJQ plays up to its usual level, and really none of the classic group's recordings should be passed by. It is a pity that few of the MJQ's Atlantic LPs have been reissued on CD yet. —*Scott Yanow*

Under the Jasmin Tree / Dec. 12, 1967 / Apple ✦✦✦
A more unlikely match of artists and label you will rarely find—the dignified, classically influenced, indelibly Afro-American Modern Jazz Quartet and the Beatles' Apple Corps, Ltd. But Apple in its Rocking Sixties heyday was one of the most daringly eclectic labels on the scene—and as the sole jazz act on the roster, the MJQ was given complete artistic freedom, with no electric guitars or period psychedelia apart from the misleading cover art. The program is more or less standard, poised, painstakingly structured, gently swinging MJQ fare, the group's contrapuntal interplay as telepathic as ever. The most distinctive of John Lewis' compositions are the revolving minor-key theme of "Three Little Feelings, Part One" (part of a three-movement suite), while "The Blue Necklace" has a bell going off like that of a cash register, and Milt Jackson is clearly in his element on the gospel-ish "The Jasmin Tree." An extremely rare LP even when it was in print—the Beatles' rock audience ignored it, the MJQ's fans couldn't find it—the album is now available on CD as part of EMI's extensive Apple reissue series. —*Richard S. Ginell*

Space / 1969 / Apple ✦✦✦
The Modern Jazz Quartet took a hiatus from Atlantic Records to record two LPs for the Beatles' Apple label. Despite the switch, the MJQ's music remained unchanged; it was too classic to alter. This out-of-print album has among its selections a pair of obscure John Lewis originals ("Visitor from Venus" and "Visitor from Mars"), vibraphonist Milt Jackson's ballad feature on "Here's That Rainy Day" and the lengthy "Adagio from Concierto de Aranjuez." Overall, this is an average but worthy outing from a group whose excellence could always be taken for granted. —*Scott Yanow*

Plastic Dreams / May 1971 / Atlantic ✦✦✦
This is a streaky LP. The low points are the rather repetitious "Variations on a Christmas Theme" and "England's Carol" (the latter is based on "God Rest Ye Merry, Gentlemen"). However, "Walkin' Stomp" is quite memorable as is the tango "Plastic Dreams" and "Trav'lin." Two selections add a five-piece brass section to the classic group (John Lewis on piano and harpsichord, vibraphonist Milt Jackson, bassist Percy Heath and drummer Connie Kay). Despite its faults, this generally enjoyable album deserves to be reissued on CD. —*Scott Yanow*

Legendary Profile / 1972 / Atlantic ✦✦✦
The Modern Jazz Quartet had been together 20 years at the time of this lesser-known Atlantic LP. Vibraphonist Milt Jackson and pianist John Lewis introduced two new songs apiece for this date and the quartet (with bassist Percy Heath and drummer Connie Kay) also performs Tim Hardin's "Misty Roses" and the pop song "What Now My Love." Nothing all that unusual happens except that Lewis for the first time with the MJQ doubles on two songs on electric piano. Despite that, the classic sound was still intact and the style remained unchanged. —*Scott Yanow*

In Memoriam / Nov. 5, 1973-Nov. 6, 1973 / Little David ✦✦
The Modern Jazz Quartet's last studio album before their breakup (which fortunately ended up just being a hiatus) in some ways shows why the group fell apart. All of the music on this LP (two works by John Lewis and a remake of "Adagio from the Guitar Concerto: Concierto de Aranjuez") is classically oriented. One can imagine that vibraphonist Milt Jackson (who usually preferred playing bebop) was getting a bit bored. The MJQ is accompanied by an orchestra conducted by Maurice Peress and, despite some stimulating moments, the music is often quite dry. It's one of the classic group's lesser releases. —*Scott Yanow*

Blues on Bach / Nov. 26, 1973+Nov. 27, 1973 / Atlantic ✦✦✦✦
This LP has an interesting concept, alternating four original blues with five adaptations of melodies from classical works by Bach. The Modern Jazz Quartet had long been quite adept in both areas and, despite a certain lack of variety on this set (alternating back and forth between the two styles somewhat predictably), the music is largely enjoyable. Vibraphonist Milt Jackson, pianist John Lewis (doubling here on harpsichord), bassist Percy Heath and drummer Connie Kay were still all very much in their musical prime during the 21st year of the MJQ's existence. —*Scott Yanow*

★ **The Last Concert** / Nov. 25, 1974 / Atlantic ✦✦✦✦✦
The Modern Jazz Quartet broke up after the concert documented on this double CD. It would be nearly seven years before the group got back together again but it certainly went out on top. Mostly revisiting their greatest hits, the MJQ is heard on this two-fer playing inspired versions of such songs as "Softly as in a Morning Sunrise," "Bags' Groove," "Skating in Central Park," "Confirmation," "The Golden Striker," and of course, "Django." This set is a real gem (the music is essential for all serious jazz collections), featuring vibraphonist Milt Jackson, pianist John Lewis, bassist Percy Heath and drummer Connie Kay at their very best. —*Scott Yanow*

Reunion at Budokan / Oct. 19, 1981-Oct. 20, 1981 / Pablo ✦✦✦✦
After a seven-year "vacation," the Modern Jazz Quartet came back together in 1981 for a special reunion that ended up beginning another 14 plus years of playing together on at least a part-time basis. It is somehow fitting that on this Pablo LP (which has music taken from a Japanese concert) seven of the eight selections (all but John Lewis' "Odds Against Tomorrow") were remakes of songs that the MJQ had played in 1974 at their *Last Concert*. The revivals of "Softly as in a Morning Sunrise" and the group's two biggest "hits," "Bags' Groove" and "Django," are among the highlights of this excellent release. —*Scott Yanow*

The Best of the Modern Jazz Quartet [Pablo] / 1981-1985 / Pablo ✦✦✦
Decent overview of late-period Modern Jazz Quartet sessions that were recorded for Pablo in the early '80s, after pianist John Lewis, vibist Milt Jackson, bassist Percy Heath, and drummer Connie Kay renewed their musical association in 1982 following a lengthy absence. They only made a few albums for Pablo in the mid-'80s before returning to Atlantic, but both were excellent. —*Ron Wynn*

Together Again at Montreux Jazz / Jul. 25, 1982 / Pablo ✦✦✦✦
This CD reissue features the revived Modern Jazz Quartet during their 30th year (counting a seven-year "vacation"), playing some of their usual repertoire—such as "Django," "The Cylinder," and "Bags' Groove," which for some reason was renamed "Bags' New Groove"—before an appreciative audience at the 1982 Montreux Jazz Festival. In reality, this release adds little to the MJQ's legacy, since all of the songs but vibraphonist Milt Jackson's "Monterey Mist" had been recorded before (some of them many times), but it does show that the band still had its enthusiasm and the ability to make the veteran material sound fresh and swinging. —*Scott Yanow*

Echoes / Mar. 6, 1984 / Pablo ✦✦✦✦✦
If proof were needed that the Modern Jazz Quartet was back together permanently after a seven-year hiatus (1974-81), it is this CD for the six selections were all fairly new (as opposed to more runthroughs of their earlier hits). Pianist John Lewis contributed three compositions (including the appealing "That Slavic Smile" and "Sacha's March"), vibraphonist Milt Jackson wrote two and bassist Percy Heath brought in his lighthearted "Watergate Blues." With drummer Connie Kay as usual rounding out the group, the MJQ's return was one of the happiest events in jazz of the 1980s. —*Scott Yanow*

Topsy: This One's for Basie / Jun. 3, 1985-Jun. 4, 1985 / Pablo ✦✦✦✦
Despite the title of this CD, the music on this 1985 studio set from the Modern Jazz Quartet is not a program of Count Basie tunes (with the exception of "Topsy") although Basie apparently liked the John Lewis composition "D and E." The other unrelated music is highlighted by an unaccompanied feature for vibraphonist Milt Jackson ("Nature Boy"), "Reunion Blues" and three more complex pieces from pianist John Lewis. Overall this CD gives listeners a fine example of the music of the MJQ during the 1980s. —*Scott Yanow*

Three Windows / Mar. 16, 1987-Mar. 20, 1987 / Atlantic ✦✦✦
The New York Chamber Symphony accompanies the Modern Jazz Quartet on this fine orchestral set. As usual, the writing of John Lewis (who contributed all five compositions) dominates in this type of setting. The material includes three fairly recent originals plus "Three Windows" (which blends together three themes from Lewis's score for the French film *No Sun in Venice*) and the perennial "Django." Nice music overall, although this is not one of the most essential MJQ releases. —*Scott Yanow*

For Ellington / Feb. 1, 1988-Feb. 3, 1988 / East West ✦✦✦✦
This is a tribute album that works quite well. The Modern Jazz Quartet is heard at their best on such Duke Ellington tunes as "Rockin' in Rhythm," "Jack the Bear" and "Ko-Ko." Also quite noteworthy are their two newer pieces, John Lewis' "For Ellington" and Milt Jackson's "Maestro E.K.E." which perfectly capture the spirit of Ellington's music. The ballads sometimes get a little sleepy, but on a whole this is a very enjoyable release. —*Scott Yanow*

Celebration / Jun. 17, 1992-Jul. 16, 1993 / Atlantic ✦✦✦✦✦
As part of their 40th anniversary, the Modern Jazz Quartet welcomed ten guest artists to their CD: Bobby McFerrin (brilliant on "Billie's Bounce"), Take Six, Phil Woods, Wynton Marsalis (who gets to show off his technique on "Cherokee"), Illinois Jacquet, Harry "Sweets" Edison, Branford Marsalis, Jimmy Heath, Freddie Hubbard and Nina Tempo. As usual vibraphonist Milt Jackson and pianist John Lewis also have plenty of solo space and bassist Percy Heath is perfect in support. Since drummer Connie Kay was ailing in 1992 (but back in action the following year), Mickey Roker fills in on seven of the 13 selections. With the exception of "Django" (which features Phil Woods), and "Bags' Groove," the music sticks to bop standards rather than MJQ standbys. It's an enjoyable and varied set. —*Scott Yanow*

Charles Moffett

b. Sep. 6, 1929, Fort Worth, TX, d. Feb. 14, 1997
Drums / Avant-Garde, Free Jazz
Charles Moffett is most significant for being the drummer with Ornette Coleman's 1965-67 trio and for being the father of a remarkable musical family that includes bassist Charnett, drummer Codaryl, vocalist Charisse, trumpeter Mondre and tenor saxophonist Charles, Jr.!

    Charles Moffett, Sr. actually started out as a trumpeter, playing with Jimmy Witherspoon and other groups as a teenager. He switched to drums while in college. Moffett worked as a high school teacher in Texas (1953-61) but also played with jazz and R&B bands on the side. He first joined Ornette Coleman in 1961 but the altoist soon went into retirement for three years. Moffett worked with Sonny Rollins in 1963, recorded with Archie Shepp (*Four for Trane*) and led his own group which included Pharoah Sanders and Carla Bley. When Coleman began playing again, Moffett was a part of his classic trio which also included bassist David Izenzon; a couple of Blue Note records resulted. In 1970 he moved to Oakland where he directed a music school and played locally with Steve Turre and Prince Lasha. He later played with Frank Lowe in New York and continued teaching. Charles Moffett recorded two albums as a leader: a Savoy set in 1969 that featured him also playing trumpet and vibes and a 1974 outing for LRS with his children. —*Scott Yanow*

The Gift / 1969 / Savoy ✦✦✦✦
This largely successful reissue CD brings back an obscure session led by Charles Moffett who here mostly plays vibes and a bit of trumpet in addition to drums. He is teamed up with the underrated (and largely forgotten) tenor saxophonist Paul Jeffrey, bassist Wilbur Ware and drummers Dennis O'Toole and seven-year old Codaryl Moffett. On some selections both O'Toole and Codaryl play drums and the latter proves to be able to hold his own even at such a young age; in fact Codaryl contributed two of the five originals. The songtitle "Avant Garde Got Soul Too" fairly well sums up this adventurous but often surprisingly melodic set. —*Scott Yanow*

Charnett Moffett (Charnet Moffett)

b. Jun. 10, 1967, New York, NY
Bass / Post-Bop, R&B
A virtuosic bassist who is equally skilled on acoustic and electric, Charnett Moffett has thus far been a better sideman than leader. His own recordings (for Manhattan, Blue Note and Evidence) to this point have had an excess of bass features while failing to develop a group sound. The son of drummer Charles Moffett, Sr., and the younger brother of drummer Codaryl, singer Charisse, trumpeter Mondre and tenor saxophonist Charles, Jr., (all of whom have guested on his records), Charnett started on bass early and appeared at age eight on a family record in 1974 for LRS. He later studied at Julliard and was in Wynton Marsalis' quintet when he was 16, playing with the trumpeter regularly during 1983-85. Moffett,

who appeared on 17 records before he turned 20, has worked with Tony Williams, Slide Hampton, Mulgrew Miller, Monty Alexander, Sonny Sharrock, Stanley Jordan, David Sanborn, Arturo Sandoval, Diane Reeves among many others and played regularly with Ornette Coleman during 1993-95. —*Scott Yanow*

Net Man / 1976 / Blue Note ✦✦✦
A brilliant bassist, Charnett Moffett shares a fault with Ron Carter: their own records have a great excess of bass solos. Moffett's debut as a leader features him with diverse groups ranging from duets to quartets and including such fine players as tenor saxophonist Michael Brecker, keyboardist Kenny Drew, Jr., guitarist Stanley Jordan, drummer Al Foster, Kenny Kirkland on keyboards and several of his relatives (including his father, drummer Charles Moffett). Unfortunately, Charnett (who wrote all eight songs except "Mona Lisa" and "Softly as in a Morning Sunrise") dominates the solo space, and most of his improvisations, although technically impressive, are just not all that interesting. —*Scott Yanow*

Beauty Within / 1987 / Blue Note ✦✦
Charnett Moffett is a virtuosic bassist with very impressive chops but this Blue Note release is largely a waste. The dense electronic ensembles never seem to develop beyond the melody statements and the sidemen (most of them being Moffett's siblings) fail to display any originality. Since Charnett wrote all six of the compositions and produced the date himself, the blame for the disappointing fluff rests with the leader. —*Scott Yanow*

Nettwork / 1991 / Manhattan ✦✦
Charnett Moffett features his overdubbed piccolo bass guitar throughout this disc (doing his best imitation of a guitar) as virtually the only lead and solo voice over an electronic background that also includes his funky electric bass and Kenny Kirkland's synthesizer. The music is danceable and reasonably creative within its limits (the grooves are certainly likable), but this set will be of much more interest to funk fans than to jazz collectors. —*Scott Yanow*

● **Planet Home** / Nov. 26, 1994-Nov. 27, 1994 / Evidence ✦✦✦✦✦
Still Life / 1997 / Evidence ✦✦✦

Miff Mole (Irving Milfred Mole)

b. Mar. 11, 1898, Roosevelt, NY, d. Apr. 29, 1961, New York, NY
Trombone / Classic Jazz, Dixieland
For a period in the 1920s, Miff Mole was (prior to the emergence of Jack Teagarden) the most advanced trombonist in jazz. He had gained a strong reputation playing with the Original Memphis Five (starting in 1922) and his many recordings with Red Nichols during 1926-27 found him taking unusual interval jumps with staccato phrasing that perfectly fit Nichols' style. However, in 1927 he started working as a studio musician and Mole concentrated less on jazz during the next couple of decades. He played with Paul Whiteman during 1938-40 and was with Benny Goodman in 1943. By the time he returned to small-group jazz in the mid-'40s (working with Eddie Condon and leading a band at Nick's), Mole sounded like a disciple of Teagarden and his style was no longer unique, although his record of "Peg of My Heart" was popular. Miff Mole's health was erratic by the 1950s and he was largely forgotten by the greater jazz world by the time he died in 1961. His best recordings as a leader were when he led his Molers during 1927-30 although there was a four-song session in 1937 and later albums released by Jazzology, Commodore, Storyville and Argo. —*Scott Yanow*

Miff Mole's Molers—1927 / Jan. 26, 1927-Sep. 1, 1927 / EMI ✦✦✦✦✦
Trombonist Miff Mole gained some fame in the 1920s for his many recordings with cornetist Red Nichols. At a time when many other trombonists had a much more percussive approach, Mole had an unusual style full of staccato runs, unpredictable interval jumps and impressive technique. Mole led a series of sessions during the 1927-30 period with his Molers, which overlapped personnel with Nichols' bands, utilizing some of the top white studio players of the era. This superior British LP contains all 12 numbers cut at the trombonist's sessions of 1927, plus four tunes on which the band backs the popular singer Sophie Tucker. With Nichols, either Jimmy Dorsey or Pee Wee Russell on clarinet, usually pianist Arthur Schutt, guitarist Dick McDonough and drummer Vic Berton being among the key sidemen (bass saxophonist Adrian Rollini is an asset on the final six numbers), the music is quite advanced for the time, particularly in its arrangements. Highlights include "Alexander's Ragtime Band," "Hurricane," "Davenport Blues," Tucker's "After You've Gone," "Imagination" and "Original Dixieland One-Step." —*Scott Yanow*

● **Miff Mole's Molers 1928/30** / Jul. 27, 1928-Feb. 6, 1930 / Swaggie ✦✦✦✦✦
Other than two titles from July 6, 1928, this LP from the Australian Swaggie label has all of the selections led by top studio trombonist Miff Mole during 1928-30. One of the first trombonists to liberate his instrument from a background percussive role, Mole was a virtuoso with a colorful, if odd style that was soon overshadowed by Jack Teagarden. The 17 selections on this album (which includes five

alternate takes) feature such top players as trumpeter Phil Napoleon (cornetist Red Nichols is on the first two numbers), Jimmy Dorsey or Fud Livingston on reeds, pianist Arthur Schutt and sometimes bass saxophonist Adrian Rollini, among others. The arrangements are tricky and unpredictable, adding to the excitement of the intriguing music. Among the better tracks are "Crazy Rhythm," two versions of "That's a Plenty," "After You've Gone" and three renditions of "Navy Blues." —*Scott Yanow*

And His "World Jam Session" Band—1944 / Feb. 9, 1944 / Jazzology ✦✦✦

All of the music that trombonist Miff Mole recorded for the World Broadcasting System on Feb. 9, 1944 is on this album. The performances were made for use as radio transcriptions (since a Musicians Union recording strike was in force). Mole, the rarely heard trumpeter Sterling Bose, clarinetist Pee Wee Russell, rhythm guitarist Eddie Condon, pianist Gene Schroeder, bassist Bob Casey and drummer Joe Grauso perform ten Dixieland-oriented songs in all. In addition to the master takes, one hears eight false starts, three incomplete takes and two alternate versions—obviously, not all of the extracts are essential (the false starts should not have been issued). Best are Mole's classic version of "Peg o' My Heart" (which only took one version to perfect), "At the Jazz Band Ball," and "I Would Do Anything for You." Mole sounds fine although his original style of the 1920s had been replaced by a more derivative Jack Teagarden-influenced approach. —*Scott Yanow*

The Immortal Miff Mole / Nov. 14, 1958-Nov. 15, 1958 / Jazzology ✦✦✦✦

Although one of the top trombonists of the 1920s and a busy studio musician during the next decade, Miff Mole was largely forgotten by the time he recorded this final effort. Despite being in declining health (he died two years later), Mole sounds fine on the Dixieland set, which includes such tunes as "Fidgety Feet," "For Me and My Gal," "Wolverine Blues" and "Who's Sorry Now." Featured are pianist Frank Signorelli, bassist Jack Lesberg, drummer Chauncey Morehouse, either Jack Palmer or Lee Castle on trumpet and Joe Dixon or Jimmy Lytell on clarinet. A special highlight of the LP (not yet reissued on CD) is "Miffology," a very spontaneous six-minute blues in which the musicians did not realize they were being recorded; they were delighted when the truth became known. Worth searching for by Dixieland fans. —*Scott Yanow*

Grachan Moncur III

b. Jun. 3, 1937, Miami, FL

Trombone / Avant-Garde, Free Jazz

One of the first trombonists to explore free jazz, Grachan Moncur, III, is still best known for his pair of innovative Blue Note albums (1963-64) which also featured Lee Morgan and Jackie McLean on the first session and Wayne Shorter and Herbie Hancock on the later date. The son of bassist Grachan Moncur, II, who played with the Savoy Sultans during 1937-45, Grachan, III, started on trombone when he was 11. He toured with Ray Charles (1959-62) was with the Jazztet (1962) and in 1963 played advanced jazz with Jackie McLean. Moncur toured with Sonny Rollins (1964) and played and recorded with Marion Brown, Joe Henderson and Archie Shepp, matching up with fellow trombonist Roswell Rudd in the latter group. He also was part of the cooperative band 360 Degree Music Experience with Beaver Harris. Grachan Moncur, who has also recorded as a leader for BYG (1969) and JCOA (1974), has continued playing challenging music up to the present day and has been an educator. Some of his more recent associations have been with Frank Lowe (1984-85), Cassandra Wilson (1985) and the Paris Reunion Band. —*Scott Yanow*

Evolution / Nov. 21, 1963 / Blue Note ✦✦✦✦✦

Trombonist Grachan Moncur, III's debut as a leader is a little ironic now, since he is no longer as well known as his sidemen: trumpeter Lee Morgan, altoist Jackie McLean, vibraphonist Bobby Hutcherson, bassist Bob Cranshaw and drummer Tony Williams. However, Moncur contributed five originals (including one called "Monk in Wonderland"), plays brilliantly, and sets the tone and moods for this often swinging but exploratory avant-garde set. Well worth several listens. —*Scott Yanow*

● Some Other Stuff / Jul. 6, 1964 / Blue Note ✦✦✦✦✦

Grachan Moncur, III, was one of the top trombonists of the jazz avant-garde in the 1960s although he had only a few chances to lead his own record sessions. This 1964 set (which has been reissued on CD) was one of his finest, a quintet outing with bassist Cecil McBee, two of the members of the Miles Davis Quintet (pianist Herbie Hancock and drummer Tony Williams) and tenor saxophonist Wayne Shorter a just brief time before he joined Miles. The group performs four of Moncur's challenging originals including "Nomadic" (which is largely a drum solo) and "The Twins" which is built off of one chord. None of the compositions caught on, but the strong and very individual improvising of the young musicians is enough of a reason to acquire the advanced music. —*Scott Yanow*

New Africa / Aug. 11, 1969 / Actuel ✦✦✦✦

Also put out in Europe by the BYG and Actuel labels, this British LP is fairly adventurous, featuring the originals and trombone of Grachan Moncur, III. He matches ideas with altoist Roscoe Mitchell, pianist Dave Burrell, bassist Alan Silva, drummer Andrew Cyrille and (on one of the four pieces) his former boss, tenor saxophonist Archie Shepp. Three of the selections are a bit reminiscent of the John Coltrane Quartet in their modality, but it is during the four movements of the continuous "New Africa" that Moncur can be heard at his dynamic best. —*Scott Yanow*

Echoes of Prayer / Apr. 11, 1974 / JCOA ✦✦✦✦

Trombonist Grachan Moncur, one of the unsung heroes of the avant-garde, has recorded far too infrequently as a leader through the years. This obscure LP, his fourth major project, preceded a long period in obscurity. The Jazz Composers Orchestra commissioned the lengthy four-movement piece "Echoes of Prayer" from Moncur, and the all-star orchestra performs the work with its composer. Among the soloists during the many sections are Moncur, altoist Carlos Ward, both Cecil McBee and Charlie Haden on basses, Pat Patrick on flute, trumpeter Marvin Hannibal Peterson, violinist Leroy Jenkins and clarinetist Perry Robinson. Also on the album are a dance ensemble (who play percussion) and the voices of Jeanne Lee and Mervine Grady. The music is quite advanced, sometimes fairly dense, and will take a few listens to fully digest. —*Scott Yanow*

T.S. Monk (Thelonious Monk, Jr.)

b. Dec. 27, 1949, New York, NY

Drums, Leader / Hard Bop, Post-Bop

Although it took him a while before he decided to dedicate himself to playing jazz, T.S. Monk (Thelonious Monk, Jr.) has already accomplished a lot. He started out playing trumpet, and piano before switching to drums when he was 13, taking some lessons from Max Roach. His first public performance was with his father Thelonious Monk on a television show in 1970. He toured with his father's quartet during 1970-71 and then played with the fusion band Natural Essence, the Paul Jeffrey Big Band and had an R&B group called T.S. Monk that had a few hits. In 1986 he established the Thelonious Monk Institute of Jazz, an organization that not only celebrates Monk, Sr.'s music but has an annual competition that has resulted in fame for some of its winners. His work with the Institute inspired the drummer to return to jazz. He played in Clifford Jordan's big band and with Walter Davis before putting together his own sextet which has had stable personnel since the late '80s. Monk's group often performs obscure jazz originals from the 1960s hard bop era with accurate transcriptions contributed by its trumpeter/arranger Don Sickler. Monk himself is an excellent drummer who sounds a little reminiscent of Tony Williams. —*Scott Yanow*

Take One / Oct. 16, 1991 / Blue Note ✦✦✦✦

Drummer T.S. Monk's debut as a leader in jazz found him discarding his earlier R&B-ish music in favor of heading an impressive hard bop revival group. With trumpeter Don Sickler transcribing obscure songs from 1960s-era records, Monk and his band were able to perform little-played numbers by Kenny Dorham, Hank Mobley, Idrees Sulieman, Elmo Hope, Walter Davis, Jr., Clifford Jordan, Donald Brown and Tommy Turrentine in addition to three by Monk's father Thelonious. Sickler and Monk are joined in the consistently exciting group by altoist Bobby Porcelli, Willie Williams on tenor, pianist Ronnie Mathews and bassist James Genus. The T.S. Monk Sextet was just beginning its long life with this recording; all of its CDs are highly recommended to hard bop fans. —*Scott Yanow*

Changing of the Guard / 1993 / Blue Note ✦✦✦✦✦

Drummer T.S. Monk's sextet has quickly become one of the top repertory bands of hard bop. They revive quite a few obscurities on their Blue Note CD, including such forgotten compositions as J.J. Johnson's "Kelo," Clifford Jordan's "Middle of the Block," and Idrees Sulieman's "Doublemint," songs that are not exactly performed every day. They also perform more recent compositions by the likes of James Williams, Bobby Watson, Donald Brown and some of the band members. Trumpeter Don Sickler's arrangements and transcriptions insure that the band plays the songs properly. With consistently inventive solos from Sickler, altoist Bobby Porcelli (who often takes honors), Willie Williams on tenor and soprano, pianist Ronnie Mathews and bassist Scott Colley, there is no weak link to this excellent sextet. The band adds to rather than merely copies the tradition. —*Scott Yanow*

● The Charm / 1995 / Blue Note ✦✦✦✦✦

T.S. Monk, by successfully keeping his sextet together as a regularly working outfit for several years, has been able to form a recognizable group sound in the hard bop tradition. Trumpeter Don Sickler's skills at transcribing charts from records has been a major asset and the band's emphasis on obscurities has resulted in a very fresh repertoire; certainly Buddy Montgomery's "Budini," Melba Liston's "Just Waiting" and even Walter Davis, Jr.'s "Gypsy Folk Tales" would never qualify as standards. In addition to the older material (which includes an offbeat version of

Thelonious Monk's "Bolivar Blues"), pianist Ronnie Mathews and altoist Bobby Porcelli have contributed newer pieces that fit the group's style. Although sometimes overlooked, T.S. Monk's sextet (which also includes Willie Williams on tenor and soprano and bassist Scott Colley) has no weak links and is one of the most consistently satisfying jazz groups around in the mid-'90s. Their fine disc is easily recommended. — *Scott Yanow*

Monk on Monk / Feb. 6, 1997-Feb. 27, 1997 / N2K ♦♦♦♦♦

To celebrate what would have been his father Thelonious Monk's 80th birthday, drummer T.S. Monk put together an all-star group (an expanded version of his sextet) and toured, performing an all-Thelonious program. Just prior to the beginning of the live performances, T.S. and his band recorded this CD. The music is excellent, but there are so many guest artists making cameo appearances (including trumpeters Roy Hargrove, Clark Terry, Arturo Sandoval and Wallace Roney, Wayne Shorter on soprano, tenors Grover Washington Jr. and Jimmy Heath, pianists Herbie Hancock and Geri Allen, bassists Ron Carter, Christian McBride and Dave Holland and singers Dianne Reeves and Kevin Mahogany) that one never really gets to hear Monk's band very much. Considering that T.S.'s unit includes altoist Bobby Watson and singer Nnenna Freelon (both of whom are only heard from briefly), it is a pity that he opted for so many unnecessary guests. There are good versions of such tunes as "Little Rootie Tootie" (which has a very effective Grover Washington Jr. tenor solo), "Crepuscule With Nellie" (one of the few renditions of a band actually stretching out on this theme), and "Bright Mississippi," plus the debut of a recently discovered Monk composition ("Two Timer"), so this set is recommended. But one is left looking forward to hearing the actual T.S. Monk ensemble interpret the songs. — *Scott Yanow*

Thelonious Monk

b. Oct. 10, 1917, Rocky Mount, NC, **d.** Feb. 17, 1982, Weehawken, NJ
Piano, Composer, Leader / Bop, Post-Bop

The most important jazz musicians are the ones who are successful in creating their own original world of music with its own rules, logic and surprises. Thelonious Monk, who was criticized by observers who failed to listen to his music on its own terms, suffered through a decade of neglect before he was suddenly acclaimed as a genius; his music had not changed one bit in the interim. In fact, one of the more remarkable aspects of Monk's music was that it was fully formed by 1947 and he saw no need to alter his playing or compositional style in the slightest during the next 25 years.

Thelonious Monk grew up in New York, started playing piano when he was around five and had his first job touring as an accompanist to an evangelist. He was inspired by the Harlem stride pianists (James P. Johnson was a neighbor) and vestiges of that idiom can be heard in his later unaccompanied solos. However, when he was playing in the house band of Minton's Playhouse during 1940-43, Monk was searching for his own individual style. Private recordings from the period find him sometimes resembling Teddy Wilson but starting to use more advanced rhythms and harmonies. He worked with Lucky Millinder a bit in 1942 and was with the Cootie Williams Orchestra briefly in 1944 (Williams recorded Monk's "Epistrophy" in 1942 and in 1944 was the first to record "'Round Midnight"), but it was when he became Coleman Hawkins' regular pianist that Monk was initially noticed. He cut a few titles with Hawkins (his recording debut) and, although some of Hawkins' fans complained about the eccentric pianist, the veteran tenor could sense the pianist's greatness.

The 1945-54 period was very difficult for Thelonious Monk. Because he left a lot of space in his rhythmic solos and had an unusual technique, many people thought that he was an inferior pianist. His compositions were so advanced that the lazier bebop players (although not Dizzy Gillespie and Charlie Parker) assumed that he was crazy. And Thelonious Monk's name, appearance (he liked funny hats) and personality (an occasionally uncommunicative introvert) helped to brand him as some kind of nut. Fortunately, Alfred Lion of Blue Note believed in him and recorded Monk extensively during 1947-48 and 1951-52. He also recorded for Prestige during 1952-54, had a solo set for Vogue in 1954 during a visit to Paris and appeared on a Verve date with Bird and Diz. But work was very sporadic during this era and Monk had to struggle to make ends meet.

His fortunes slowly began to improve. In 1955 he signed with Riverside and producer Orrin Keepnews persuaded him to record an album of Duke Ellington tunes and one of standards so his music would appear to be more accessible to the average jazz fan. In 1956 came the classic *Brilliant Corners* album, but it was the following year when the situation permanently changed. Monk was booked into the Five Spot for a long engagement and he used a quartet that featured tenor saxophonist John Coltrane. Finally the critics and then the jazz public recognized Thelonious Monk's greatness during this important gig. The fact that he was unique was a disadvantage a few years earlier when all modern jazz pianists were expected to sound like Bud Powell (who was ironically a close friend), but by 1957

the jazz public was looking for a new approach. Suddenly Monk was a celebrity and his status would not change for the remainder of his career. In 1958 his quartet featured the tenor of Johnny Griffin (who was even more compatible than Coltrane), in 1959 he appeared with an orchestra at Town Hall (with arrangements by Hall Overton), in 1962 he signed with Columbia and two years later was on the cover of *Time*. A second orchestra concert in 1963 was even better than the first, and Monk toured constantly throughout the 1960s with his quartet which featured the reliable tenor of Charlie Rouse. He played with the Giants of Jazz during 1971-72 but then in 1973 suddenly retired. Monk was suffering from mental illness and, other than a few special appearances during the mid-'70s, he lived the rest of his life in seclusion. After his death it seemed as if everyone was doing Thelonious Monk tributes. There were so many versions of "'Round Midnight" that it was practically a pop hit! But despite the posthumous acclaim and attempts by pianists ranging from Marcus Roberts to Tommy Flanagan to recreate his style, there was no replacement for the original.

Some of Thelonious Monk's songs became standards early on, most notably "'Round Midnight," "Straight, No Chaser," "52nd Street Theme" and "Blue Monk," Many of his other compositions have by now been figured out by other jazz musicians and are occasionally performed including "Ruby My Dear," "Well You Needn't," "Off Minor," "In Walked Bud," "Misterioso," "Epistrophy," "I Mean You," "Four in One," "Criss Cross," "Ask Me Now," "Little Rootie Tootie," "Monk's Dream," "Bemsha Swing," "Think of One," "Friday the 13th," "Hackensack," "Nutty," "Brilliant Corners," "Crepuscule with Nellie," "Evidence" and "Rhythm-a-Ning," Virtually all of Monk's recordings (for Blue Note, Prestige, Vogue, Riverside, Columbia and Black Lion) have been reissued and among his sidemen through the years were Idrees Sulieman, Art Blakey, Milt Jackson, Lou Donaldson, Lucky Thompson, Max Roach, Julius Watkins, Sonny Rollins, Clark Terry, Gerry Mulligan, John Coltrane, Wilbur Ware, Shadow Wilson, Johnny Griffin, Donald Byrd, Phil Woods, Thad Jones and Charlie Rouse. His son Thelonious Monk, Jr. (T.S. Monk) has helped keep the hard bop tradition alive with his quintet and has headed the Thelonious Monk Institute, whose yearly competitions succeed in publicizing talented young players. — *Scott Yanow*

☆ **The Complete Blue Note Recordings** / Oct. 15, 1947-Apr. 14, 1957 / Mosaic ♦♦♦♦♦

Shortly after Mosaic's limited-edition four-LP box set of pianist/composer Thelonious Monk's Blue Note recordings ran out of stock, Blue Note reissued Monk's entire output plus his recently discovered 1958 live performance with John Coltrane on this four-CD package. The music is unique, highly influential and timeless. Monk did not record all that often for Blue Note during 1947-52 (six sessions) but the number of classics is quite impressive: "Ruby My Dear," "Well You Needn't," "Off Minor," "In Walked Bud," "'Round Midnight," "Evidence," "Misterioso," "Epistrophy," "I Mean You," "Four in One," "Criss Cross," "Straight, No Chaser," and "Ask Me Now." Add to that his two appearances on a 1957 Sonny Rollins date along with the remarkable Coltrane session and the result is a set that should be in every jazz collection. — *Scott Yanow*

The Vibes Are On / Feb. 16, 1948-Nov. 15, 1952 / Chazzer ♦♦♦

Although Thelonious Monk is now considered one of the giants of jazz, up until his breakthrough in 1957 Monk's music was considered far too advanced and eccentric even for followers of bop. Therefore, there are relatively few recordings of the pianist/composer during his early years outside of his Blue Note studio sides. This bootleg LP contains a rare broadcast from 1948 that finds him in a quartet with trumpeter Idrees Sulieman, bassist Curly Russell and drummer Art Blakey performing three songs in his unique style. In addition, this set has ten fine solos from pianist Art Tatum during the 1950-51 period and a rare version of "Blue 'n' Boogie" performed on Nov. 15, 1952 by an octet starring altoist Charlie Parker and trumpeter Dizzy Gillespie. This obscure release is well worth going out of one's way to acquire. — *Scott Yanow*

Thelonious Monk/Herbie Nichols / Mar. 6, 1952-Oct. 15, 1955 / Savoy ♦♦♦

This was a gap-filler when it first came out. Thelonious Monk is heard on four selections from a 1955 quartet date with altoist Gigi Gryce, bassist Percy Heath and drummer Art Blakey. Check out Monk's songtitles: "Brake's Sake," "Shuffle Boil" and "Gallop's Gallop." Herbie Nichols, who only recorded three other albums of material as a leader, is heard on a comparatively light session with guitarist Danny Barker, bassist Chocolate Williams and drummer Shadow Wilson in 1952; Williams sings two of the blues. Although these dates are not essential, Monk and Nichols collectors will find this LP quite valuable. — *Scott Yanow*

Thelonious Monk and Joe Turner in Paris / Mar. 1952+Jun. 7, 1954 / Vogue ♦♦♦♦

This French Vogue reissue CD combines together two unrelated solo piano sets. The nine performances by Thelonious Monk are a bit familiar since these renditions (which are highlighted by "'Round Midnight," "Well You Needn't," "We See" and "Hackensack") had been previously reissued by GNP/Crescendo and Mosaic.

However, the 13 selections (including three alternate takes) by Joe Turner (no relation to singer Big Joe Turner) are much rarer. Turner, a talented American stride pianist who spent most of his life living in France, had only recorded ten songs as a leader prior to this 1952 session and is in top form for such numbers as "Hallelujah," "Between the Devil and the Deep Blue Sea," "Wedding Boogie" and three versions of "Tea for Two." This CD is easily recommended to jazz piano collectors who do not already have the Monk selections. —*Scott Yanow*

Thelonious Monk Trio / Oct. 15, 1952-Sep. 22, 1954 / Original Jazz Classics ◆◆◆◆◆

Half of Thelonious Monk's Prestige recordings are reissued on this CD in the Original Jazz Classics series. With either Percy Heath or Gary Mapp on bass and Art Blakey or Max Roach on drums, Monk introduces such compositions as "Little Rootie Tootie," "Bye-Ya," "Monk's Dream," "Twinkle Tinkle," "Bemsha Swing" and "Reflections." Although Monk was suffering from lack of work and a complete lack of recognition from the public, his music was virtually the same as it would be five years later, when he was suddenly "discovered." Brilliant performances. —*Scott Yanow*

Monk / Nov. 13, 1953-May 11, 1954 / Original Jazz Classics ◆◆◆◆

Thelonious Monk's Prestige recordings (reissued on three LP-length CDs) have been somewhat neglected through the years but, with the exception of a date for Vogue, they are the only documentation that exists of the unique pianist-composer's work as a leader during the latter half of 1952 through 1954. This set has four numbers (including Monk's originals "We See," "Locomotive" and the catchy "Hackensack") featuring Monk with trumpeter Ray Copeland (an underrated player), tenor saxophonist Frank Foster, bassist Curly Russell and drummer Art Blakey. However, it is "Let's Call This" and the two versions of "Think of One" that are best known, for Monk teams up with the French horn wizard Julius Watkins, bassist Percy Heath, drummer Willie Jones and the great tenor Sonny Rollins. Every Thelonious Monk recording is well worth getting, although this one is not quite essential. —*Scott Yanow*

Thelonious Monk and Sonny Rollins / Nov. 13, 1953-Oct. 25, 1954 / Original Jazz Classics ◆◆◆◆

This CD wraps up Thelonious Monk's recordings for Prestige and makes a fine complement to the OJC CDs *Monk* and *Thelonious Monk Trio*. Tenor saxophonist Sonny Rollins (in exuberant form) gets co-billing, and two of the songs ("The Way You Look Tonight" and "I Want to Be Happy") are actually from his own Prestige date; Monk was not a sideman for just anyone. The original version of "Friday the 13th" (which features Rollins and the French horn of Julius Watkins) and trio renditions (with bassist Percy Heath and drummer Art Blakey) of Monk's compositions "Work" and "Nutty" are also included on this excellent release. —*Scott Yanow*

☆ Complete Black Lion and Vogue / Jun. 7, 1954-Nov. 15, 1971 / Mosaic ◆◆◆◆◆

This four-LP limited-edition box set from Mosaic contains the nine piano solos recorded by Thelonious Monk while in Paris on June 7, 1954 (most of which have also been issued by GNP Crescendo) and, more importantly, his complete marathon London session of Nov. 15, 1971. The latter, split between solo and trio performances (with bassist Al McKibbon and drummer Art Blakey) was (other than a record with the Giants of Jazz) Monk's final recording and found the unique pianist in brilliant form, really romping on some of his solos. Although the majority of the songs are his originals, the emphasis on this essential music is on the piano playing. Those critics and listeners who feel that Monk was a limited musician should give these final performances a very close listen. —*Scott Yanow*

Plays Duke Ellington / Jul. 21, 1955+Jul. 27, 1955 / Original Jazz Classics ◆◆◆◆◆

For Thelonious Monk's Riverside debut, producer Orrin Keepnews decided that it would be best to make the somewhat forbidding pianist-composer seem a bit more accessible to the jazz world. Rather than have Monk play his own complex originals, this time around the pianist (in a trio with bassist Oscar Pettiford and drummer Kenny Clarke) interpreted eight Duke Ellington compositions. The results are very interesting with Monk bringing out new angles and ideas to such songs as "Mood Indigo," "Caravan," "It Don't Mean a Thing" and "Sophisticated Lady." A special highlight is an eerie investigation of "Black and Tan Fantasy." This CD reissue (whose music is also on Thelonious Monk's huge Riverside box) is recommended. —*Scott Yanow*

☆ The Complete Riverside Recordings / Jul. 21, 1955-Apr. 21, 1961 / Riverside ◆◆◆◆◆

Although this 15-CD box set is not inexpensive, this is the most essential of all of Thelonious Monk's releases. It was during his years with Riverside that Monk achieved the fame he had long deserved. Producer Orrin Keepnews was wise enough to feature the unique pianist/composer in a wide variety of settings and they are all here: separate trio sessions comprising Duke Ellington songs and standards, meetings on record with Sonny Rollins (including "Brilliant Corners"), John Coltrane, Coleman Hawkins, Gerry Mulligan and Johnny Griffin, the beginnings of

Monk's Quartet with Charlie Rouse, a truncated (and previously unissued) session with Shelly Manne, Monk's famous Town Hall concert of 1959 and a full date of unaccompanied piano solos. Most of this music has also been made available on Milestone two-LP sets and single CDs, but this is the best (and most complete) way to acquire these classics. —*Scott Yanow*

The Unique Thelonious Monk / Mar. 17, 1956+Apr. 3, 1956 / Original Jazz Classics ◆◆◆◆

The second recording that pianist-composer Thelonious Monk made for Riverside (reissued on CD in the Original Jazz Classics series) was a standards session. With the assistance of bassist Oscar Pettiford and drummer Art Blakey (and at the assistance of producer Orrin Keepnews), Monk explores seven veteran standards, some of which (such as "Liza," "Honeysuckle Rose" and "Just You, Just Me") would occasionally pop up in his repertoire in the future. Monk makes these tunes (which also include "Memories of You," "Darn That Dream," "Tea for Two" and "You Are Too Beautiful") sound fresh and unusual. —*Scott Yanow*

Straight, No Chaser: Thelonious Monk / Sep. 1956-1968 / Columbia ◆◆◆◆

This CD, taken from the soundtrack of the fascinating film *Straight, No Chaser*, contains a great deal of previously unissued material by Thelonious Monk. Three songs were released before but the other eight numbers (two solos from 1956 and the remainder from 1967-68) are "new," including rehearsal and club performances and two numbers from Monk's otherwise forgotten octet of 1967. It's a real bonus for collectors and a fine complement to the highly recommended film. —*Scott Yanow*

● Brilliant Corners / Dec. 17, 1956-Dec. 23, 1956 / Original Jazz Classics ◆◆◆◆◆

Thelonious Monk's classic third recording for Riverside (which has been reissued on CD in the OJC series) features five of his originals. The impossible-to-play "Brilliant Corners" finds the pianist in an all-star quintet with tenor saxophonist Sonny Rollins (who co-stars), altoist Ernie Henry, bassist Oscar Pettiford and drummer Max Roach. They also investigate Monk's "Pannonica" (which has the pianist doubling on celeste) and the eccentric "Ba-lu Bolivar Ba-Lues-Are." In addition, Monk plays "I Surrender Dear" unaccompanied, and there is a swinging version of "Bemsha Swing" from the earlier session with Rollins, Roach, bassist Paul Chambers and the pleasant trumpet of Clark Terry. All of the music on this LP-length CD is also available as part of Thelonious Monk's huge *Complete on Riverside* box set. —*Scott Yanow*

Thelonious Himself / Apr. 5, 1957-Apr. 16, 1957 / Original Jazz Classics ◆◆◆◆

This OJC CD reissues a mostly-solo set by pianist Thelonious Monk. Monk's hesitant stride and thoughtful yet very unpredictable flights are always a joy to hear. He performs a variety of swing standards (including "April in Paris" and "I'm Getting Sentimental over You"), his blues "Functional" and as a "bonus" track there is an alternate take of "'Round Midnight" from the earlier date. The one non-solo track is "Monk's Mood," a ballad that finds Monk joined by tenor saxophonist John Coltrane and bassist Wilbur Ware. The overall results are not quite essential but they should greatly interest Thelonious Monk fans who do not have his huge Riverside box set. —*Scott Yanow*

★ Monk's Music / Jun. 25, 1957-Jun. 26, 1957 / Original Jazz Classics ◆◆◆◆◆

This CD reissue has a unique session in which pianist Thelonious Monk heads quite an all-star group: tenors John Coltrane and Coleman Hawkins, altoist Gigi Gryce, trumpeter Ray Copeland, bassist Wilbur Ware and drummer Art Blakey. The only time that Coltrane and Hawkins recorded together, the date is highlighted by a lengthy version of "Well You Needn't" that finds both tenors in top form (even if Monk has to shout out Coltrane's name at one point to get his attention). Hawkins is showcased on a tender rendition of "Ruby, My Dear" and three alternate takes help extend the time of the CD. —*Scott Yanow*

★ Thelonious with John Coltrane / Jun. 25, 1957-Jul. 1957 / Original Jazz Classics ◆◆◆◆◆

Thelonious Monk finally came to fame in the summer of 1957 when he performed regularly with his quartet (featuring the tenor of John Coltrane) at the Five Spot. Unfortunately the Monk-Coltrane musical partnership was not extensively documented, but this CD reissue includes three brilliant recordings with a quartet also including bassist Wilbur Ware and drummer Shadow Wilson: "Ruby My Dear," "Trinkle Tinkle" and "Nutty." 'Trane perfectly fit into Monk's music and it was a mutually beneficial relationship. Also on the CD is Monk piano solo on "Functional" and alternate takes of "Off Minor" and "Epistrophy" that match together Monk, Coltrane, the veteran tenor Coleman Hawkins, altoist Gigi Gryce and trumpeter Ray Copeland. Highly recommended, particularly for the quartet tracks, although true Monk collectors should acquire his huge *Riverside* box set instead. —*Scott Yanow*

☆ Discovery! At the Five Spot / 1958 / Blue Note ◆◆◆◆◆

The collaboration between pianist Thelonious Monk and tenor saxophonist John Coltrane was considered (along with the 1943 Earl Hines big band with Charlie

Parker and Dizzy Gillespie and the music of the pioneering jazz cornetist Buddy Bolden) to be one of the three lost wonders of jazz history. Although they recorded a trio of quartet numbers in the studios (which are included in various Milestone and Riverside reissues), there was apparently no documentation of their lengthy gig at the Five Spot in 1957, until a tape that Coltrane's wife had recorded was recently discovered. This CD has the results, five songs performed by Monk, Coltrane, bassist Ahmed Abdul-Malik and drummer Roy Haynes at the Five Spot. High points of this somewhat miraculous find include "Trinkle Tinkle," "In Walked Bud" and "I Mean You"; there are also shorter versions of "Epistrophy" and "Crepuscule With Nellie." —*Scott Yanow*

Misterioso / Aug. 7, 1958 / Original Jazz Classics ✦✦✦✦✦
Tenor saxophonist Johnny Griffin's hard-driving style perfectly fit pianist-composer Thelonious Monk's music and his 1958 quartet (with bassist Ahmed Abdul-Malik and drummer Roy Haynes) was well documented during one night at the Five Spot Cafe; a second CD (*Thelonious in Action*) is taken from the same evening. Of the two releases, this one gets the edge due to Griffin's memorable improvising on a heated version of "In Walked Bud." Other high points include "Nutty," "Let's Cool One" and "Evidence." —*Scott Yanow*

Thelonious in Action: Recorded at the Five Spot Cafe / Aug. 7, 1958 / Original Jazz Classics ✦✦✦✦✦
One of the most exciting groups that pianist-composer Thelonious Monk ever led was his 1958 quartet with tenor saxophonist Johnny Griffin, bassist Ahmed Abdul-Malik and drummer Roy Haynes. During one night at the Five Spot Cafe they recorded enough music to fill up two CDs; all of the performances are also on Monk's large Riverside box set. *In Action*, a companion to *Misterioso*, shows that Griffin was possibly even a more perfect sideman for Monk than John Coltrane had been the year before. Highlights include "Rhythm-a-Ning," "Blue Monk," "Evidence" and "Blues Five Spot." —*Scott Yanow*

☆ **The Thelonious Monk Orchestra at Town Hall** / Feb. 28, 1959 / Original Jazz Classics ✦✦✦✦✦
Pianist Thelonious Monk's appearance with a tentet at a 1959 Town Hall concert was a major success. With Hal Overton contributing arrangements of Monk's tunes (including a remarkable transcription of Monk's original piano solo on "Little Rootie Tootie") and solos provided by trumpeter Donald Byrd, trombonist Eddie Bert, altoist Phil Woods, Charlie Rouse on tenor and baritonist Pepper Adams, this date was a real standout. The program (plus three additional numbers) has also been included in Monk's huge Riverside box set but, for more budget-minded consumers, this CD is a must. There would only be one other recorded occasion (Thelonious Monk's 1963 Philharmonic Hall concert) when the unique pianist was as successfully featured with a larger ensemble. —*Scott Yanow*

Five by Monk by Five / Jun. 1, 1959-Jun. 2, 1959 / Original Jazz Classics ✦✦✦✦
The title on this CD reissue refers to the fact that five musicians perform five Thelonious Monk compositions. In addition to the five titles ("Straight, No Chaser," "Jackie-ing," "Played Twice," "I Mean You" and "Ask Me Now") there are two "bonus cuts" (alternate versions of "Played Twice." This was one of tenor saxophonist Charlie Rouse's first sessions with Monk (he would be his regular tenor soloists for the next decade) and gave cornetist Thad Jones a rare chance to play with the unique pianist-composer; his style fit right in. —*Scott Yanow*

Alone in San Francisco / Oct. 21, 1959-Oct. 22, 1959 / Original Jazz Classics ✦✦✦✦✦
This CD reissue brings back one of Thelonious Monk's best solo piano sessions. Monk's sparse style and hesitating stride were quite distinctive and his chord voicings (even when playing a conventional triad) always sounded quite unique. In addition to such originals as "Pannonica," "Ruby, My Dear" and "Blue Monk," Monk has off-the-wall interpretations of "You Took the Words Right Out of My Heart" and two versions of the obscure "There's Danger in Your Eyes, Cherie." Recommended. —*Scott Yanow*

At the Blackhawk / Apr. 29, 1960 / Original Jazz Classics ✦✦✦✦
Thelonious Monk's 1960 quartet (which also includes tenor saxophonist Charlie Rouse, bassist John Ore and (for a brief period) drummer Billy Higgins is augmented on this live session by two guests: trumpeter Joe Gordon and the tenor of Harold Land. The extra horns uplift the date and add some surprising moments to what otherwise might have been a conventional but still spirited live session. Highlights include "Let's Call This," "Four in One" and a swinging version of "I'm Getting Sentimental over You." —*Scott Yanow*

April in Paris / Apr. 18, 1961 / Milestone ✦✦✦
The pianist/leader and tenor saxophonist Charlie Rouse are in fine form even if the solos by bassist John Ore and drummer Frankie Dunlop are somewhat pedestrian. This is good but not essential music with lengthy runthroughs on seven Monk originals (plus three standards). —*Scott Yanow*

Two Hours with Thelonious / Apr. 18, 1961-Apr. 21, 1961 / Riverside ✦✦✦
Thelonious Monk's final recordings for Riverside before signing with Columbia resulted in this two-LP set, which contains lengthy runthroughs of Monk's standard repertoire by his quartet at concerts in Milan and Paris. While the leader/pianist's solos are excellent and tenor saxophonist Charlie Rouse is in fine form, the spots for bassist John Ore and drummer Frankie Dunlop sound quite routine (Ore simply walks during his solos) and unnecessary. All of the material has been previously recorded in more definitive versions but this long out-of-print two-fer is still quite enjoyable if not overly memorable. —*Scott Yanow*

Thelonious Monk in Italy / Apr. 21, 1961 / Original Jazz Classics ✦✦✦
Pianist-composer Thelonious Monk's final Riverside recording before signing with Columbia (reissued on CD in the OJC series) was cut during a concert in Italy, part of an extensive European tour that also resulted in recordings from Paris three days earlier. All eight of the songs (which include "Straight, No Chaser," "Bemsha Swing" and "Rhythm-a-Ning") had been recorded in more definitive fashion earlier and, although Monk and his tenor Charlie Rouse sound fine, the bass and drum solos of bassist John Ore and drummer Frankie Dunlop on practically every song are consistently dull and unimaginative. This is not one of Thelonious Monk's more significant dates, but his fans will still find moments to enjoy. —*Scott Yanow*

Thelonious Monk Quartet in Copenhagen / May 15, 1961 / Storyville ✦✦✦✦
Although pianist/composer Thelonious Monk and his quartet (which also includes tenor saxophonist Charlie Rouse, bassist John Ore and drummer Frankie Dunlop) were well recorded during their European tour of 1961 (including the day after in Stockholm), their Copenhagen concert was released for the first time on this 1996 CD. The group performs eight typical Monk standards, including "Jackie-ing," "Well You Needn't" and a lengthy "Blue Monk," and Thelonious takes "Body and Soul" as a piano solo. The music does not contain any major surprises, but both the playing and the recording quality are at high levels (this was originally a radio broadcast), and these variations on Monk tunes should interest the pianist's many collectors. —*Scott Yanow*

Live in Stockholm (1961) / May 16, 1961 / Dragon ✦✦✦
This two-LP set from the Swedish label Dragon features the Thelonious Monk Quartet just prior to the pianist signing with Columbia. Taken from a radio broadcast, these performances feature ten Monk compositions plus "I'm Getting Sentimental over You" and brief piano solos on "Just a Gigolo" and "Body and Soul." As with the other Monk European recordings from this tour, the solos of bassist John Ore and drummer Frankie Dunlop are run of the mill, but Monk and tenor saxophonist Charlie Rouse are in excellent form. —*Scott Yanow*

Monk's Dream / Oct. 31, 1962-Nov. 6, 1962 / Columbia ✦✦✦✦
Most of Thelonious Monk's recordings for Columbia featured his regular working quartet which at the time of his debut consisted of tenor saxophonist Charlie Rouse, bassist John Ore and drummer Frankie Dunlop. The music on this LP is fairly typical of his repertoire of the period, five originals (only "Bright Mississippi" had not been recorded before) and three standards, two of which are taken as brief piano solos. However, despite a certain amount of predictability, the playing is consistently excellent and enthusiastic; even if the jazz world was starting to catch up to Monk, his highly original music stood on its own merits. —*Scott Yanow*

Always Know / Nov. 2, 1962-Feb. 14, 1968 / Columbia ✦✦✦✦
Thelonious Monk fans in particular are advised to search for this valuable two-LP set, for it contains a variety of unissued material from the pianist/composer's six-year period with Columbia. Monk is heard on three piano solos, with his regular working quartet, heading a trio on "Easy Street" and at his renowned Lincoln Center concert with a nonet on "Light Blue" and "Bye Ya." The music on this two-fer is at the same consistent high level as his Columbia recordings of the 1960s and contains some surprising moments. —*Scott Yanow*

Criss-Cross / Nov. 6, 1962-Mar. 29, 1963 / Columbia/Legacy ✦✦✦✦✦
This CD reissue of the Columbia LP adds a previously unissued version of "Pannonica" to the original program along with updated liner notes. The high-quality repertoire (which includes "Hackensack," "Tea for Two," "Criss-Cross" and "Rhythm-a-Ning") and some consistent solos from the leader/pianist and tenor saxophonist Charlie Rouse make this a CD worth picking up. —*Scott Yanow*

The Composer / Nov. 6, 1962-Nov. 20, 1968 / Columbia ✦✦✦
This CD contains a fine cross-section of Thelonious Monk's performances of his own originals during the 1960s, drawing its material from five separate sessions. All of the music (even a then-previously unreleased version of "Blue Monk") is currently available elsewhere but, for listeners just beginning to explore Monk's music, this set (which contains 11 of his compositions performed solo, by his quartet that included tenor saxophonist Charlie Rouse or with Oliver Nelson's orchestra) can serve as a fine introduction to the unique innovator. —*Scott Yanow*

Greatest Hits / Mar. 29, 1963-Nov. 19, 1968 / Columbia/Legacy ✦✦✦
Although *Greatest Hits* samplers of jazz artists, particularly hard bop musicians, usually don't work particularly well, Columbia's attempt at compiling a Thelonious Monk *Greatest Hits* album actually suceeds in offering a good sampling of his some of his most familiar material. The collection contains many of his best-known songs, including "Well You Needn't," "Misterioso," "'Round Midnight," "Ruby, My Dear," "Blue Monk" and "Straight, No Chaser." While this doesn't find Monk at his most adventurous, it does include some of his most accessible performances, and that makes it a good entry point for the curious. —*Stephen Thomas Erlewine*

Tokyo Concerts / May 21, 1963 / Columbia ✦✦✦✦
This two-LP set of material (all but "Evidence" was only previously out in Japan) features the Thelonious Monk Quartet (with tenor saxophonist Charlie Rouse, bassist Butch Warren and drummer Frankie Dunlop) romping through Monk's usual repertoire (eight familiar originals, a brief piano solo on "Just a Gigolo" and the standard "I'm Gettin' Sentimental over You"). The solos are fresh and, even if no real surprises occur, the enthusiasm and joy of this music makes it recommended even to Monk collectors who already have most of his recordings. —*Scott Yanow*

Monterey Jazz Festival '63 / Sep. 21, 1963-Sep. 22, 1963 / Storyville ✦✦✦✦
This double CD contains pianist/composer Thelonious Monk's two sets at the 1963 Monterey Jazz Festival, music that was unreleased until 1994. Monk, tenor saxophonist Charlie Rouse, bassist John Ore and drummer Frank Dunlop perform lengthy versions of two standards ("I'm Getting Sentimental over You" and a nearly 19-minute "Sweet and Lovely") and seven of Thelonious' originals. Nothing all that unusual occurs (outside of the two-beat feel that Ore gives "I Mean You") but Monk and Rouse have plenty of fine solos. An above-average effort. —*Scott Yanow*

Live at the Village Gate / Nov. 12, 1963 / Xanadu ✦✦✦✦
This LP released for the first time an above-average date by pianist Thelonious Monk and his 1963 quartet (tenor saxophonist Charlie Rouse, bassist John Ore and drummer Frankie Dunlop). The recording quality is decent and, although the repertoire is conventional for Monk's groups (four originals and two brief solo versions of "Body and Soul"), both Monk and tenor saxophonist Charlie Rouse take consistently inventive solos while Ore and Dunlop are fine in support. A lengthy version of "I'm Getting Sentimental over You" is most memorable. —*Scott Yanow*

☆ **Big Band and Quartet in Concert** / Dec. 30, 1963 / Columbia ✦✦✦✦✦
This is one of pianist-composer Thelonious Monk's greatest recordings and represents a high point in his career. Performing at Philharmonic Hall in New York, Monk is heard taking an unaccompanied solo on "Darkness on the Delta" and jamming with his quartet (which had Charlie Rouse on tenor, bassist Butch Warren and drummer Frank Dunlop) on fine versions of "Played Twice" and a previously unreleased rendition of "Misterioso." However, this two-CD set has its most memorable moments during the six full-length performances by a ten-piece group. Monk's quartet was joined by cornetist Thad Jones, trumpeter Nick Travis, Steve Lacy on soprano, altoist Phil Woods, baritonist Gene Allen and trombonist Eddie Bert. Jones and Woods have plenty of solos and, although Lacy surprisingly does not have any individual spots, his soprano is a major part of some of the ensembles. Most remarkable is "Four in One" which, after one of Monk's happiest (and very rhythmic) solos, features the orchestra playing a Hal Overton transcription of a complex and rather exuberant Monk solo taken from his original record. This two-CD set is a gem and can be considered essential for all jazz collections. —*Scott Yanow*

It's Monk's Time / Jan. 29, 1964-Mar. 9, 1964 / Columbia ✦✦✦✦
For this Thelonious Monk LP, the unique pianist-composer and his quartet (which at the time had tenor saxophonist Charlie Rouse, bassist Butch Warren and drummer Ben Riley) play some fresher material than normal including "Stuffy Turkey," "Shuffle Boil" and "Brake's Sake" in addition to a few old standbys. Monk takes "Nice Work if You Can Get It" and "Memories of You" as eccentric piano solos. The album gives one a good example of Monk's group of the 1960s. —*Scott Yanow*

Solo Monk / Oct. 31, 1964 / Columbia ✦✦✦✦✦
One of Thelonious Monk's more delightful solo piano sets, this CD reissue (which adds a previously unreleased version of "Introspection" to the original twelve-song program) has many memorable moments. "Dinah" is given a heated yet sparse stride, "I'm Confessin'" is heard in a charming version and Monk originals "Ruby, My Dear" and the beautiful "Ask Me Now" hold their own with such veteran tunes as "I Surrender Dear" and "I Hadn't Anyone till I Love." A highly enjoyable yet thought-provoking set of music that was performed with a liberal dose of humor. —*Scott Yanow*

Straight, No Chaser / Nov. 14, 1966-Jan. 10, 1967 / Columbia/Legacy ✦✦✦✦
For this CD reissue of one of Thelonious Monk's Columbia LPs, two previously unissued performances ("Green Chimneys" and the alternate take of "I Didn't Know About You") were added to the original set, and three edited selections were restored to their original length (including the addition of over five minutes to

"Japanese Folk Song"). Because there was a sameness to most of Monk's Columbia albums of the 1960s (as opposed to his Riversides of the 1950s, which used different personnel on each record), they have tended to be underrated and overlooked through the years. Thelonious' quartet of 1966-67 (which also included tenor saxophonist Charlie Rouse, bassist Larry Gales and drummer Ben Riley) was very familiar with his music and, by being knowledgeable supporting players (particularly Gales and Riley), they made the unique pianist/composer quite comfortable. As for Monk, he is in top form on this lengthy (over 75 minutes) program, often taking long solos and stretching himself. Recommended. —*Scott Yanow*

Nonet: Live! / Nov. 3, 1967 / Le Jazz ✦✦✦✦
Pianist/composer Thelonious Monk led a quartet throughout the 1960s, but on a European tour in 1967 his group was expanded with the addition of several top horn players. This CD, which contains all of the music from a Paris concert, features Monk with his regular tenor Charlie Rouse, bassist Larry Gales and drummer Ben Riley on a couple of songs, adds trumpeter Ray Copeland to make the band a quintet and for a few numbers they are joined by trombonist Jimmy Cleveland, altoist Phil Woods and tenor saxophonist Johnny Griffin; in addition fluegelhornist Clark Terry sits in and stars on "Blue Monk." Monk had only recorded with this large a group on two prior occasions, making this rare recording a historical curiosity; more importantly the music (six of his originals) is excellent. —*Scott Yanow*

Underground / Dec. 14, 1967-Feb. 14, 1968 / Columbia ✦✦✦✦✦
This LP has a remarkable photo of Thelonious Monk on its cover in which the eccentric pianist-composer is depicted in a colorful setting as a revolutionary; it has to be seen to be fully appreciated. On his next-to-last Columbia album (and final quartet album with his longtime tenor Charlie Rouse) Monk plays some very interesting material including such originals as "Ugly Beauty," "Green Chimneys," "Raised Fourth" and "Boo Boo's Birthday." A special treat is vocalist Jon Hendricks' guest spot singing his own words to "In Walked Bud." —*Scott Yanow*

Monk's Blues / Nov. 19, 1968+Nov. 20, 1968 / Columbia ✦✦
One of the most unusual sessions of Thelonious Monk's career found the pianist-composer and his quartet (with old standby Charlie Rouse on tenor) being joined by 11 additional horns, guitar and percussion on a set arranged by Oliver Nelson. Nelson's charts do not really fit Monk's style that closely but they do challenge the composer now and then. In addition to remakes of a variety of Monk's originals (including "Let's Cool One," "Little Rootie Tootie," "Brilliant Corners" and "Trinkle Tinkle"), the band plays a pair of forgotten Teo Macero compositions. This CD reissue adds "new" versions of "Blue Monk" and a Monk piano solo version of "'Round Midnight." This would be Thelonious Monk's swan song for Columbia and, although a bit of an oddity, Monk fans will probably want to pick this one up too. —*Scott Yanow*

The Complete London Collection / Nov. 15, 1971 / Black Lion ✦✦✦✦✦
This attractive box houses three previously released Black Lion CDs recorded at pianist/composer Thelonious Monk's final sessions as a leader; only a few dates with the Giants of Jazz were left in the future for Monk, who would soon retire altogether. Heard in unaccompanied piano solos and in a trio with bassist Al McKibbon and drummer Art Blakey, Monk is in surprisingly exuberant form, still very much at the peak of his powers. Although most of this music was last available in a "complete" Mosaic LP box set, there are actually three additional alternate takes included in the very enjoyable and somewhat definitive set. Highlights include "Little Rootie Tootie," "Meet Me Tonight in Dreamland," "Blue Sphere," "Criss Cross," "The Man I Love" and "Evidence," but all 29 selections are well worth hearing. This is essential music for all serious Thelonious Monk collections; the solo performances in particular are quite memorable. —*Scott Yanow*

J.R. Monterose (Frank Anthony Monterose, Jr.)

b. Jan. 19, 1927, Detroit, MI, **d.** Sep. 16, 1993, Utica, NY
Tenor Saxophone / Hard Bop

J.R. Monterose (not to be confused with fellow tenor Jack Montrose) is most famous for a gig that he personally did not enjoy, playing with Charles Mingus in 1956 and recording on Mingus' breakthrough album *Pithecanthropus Erectus*. He grew up in Utica, NY, played in territory bands in the Midwest and then moved to New York City in the early '50s. Monterose played with Buddy Rich (1952) and Claude Thornhill and recorded with (among others) Teddy Charles, Jon Eardley and Eddie Bert. After leaving Mingus (whom he did not get along with), Monterose played with Kenny Dorham's Jazz Prophets and recorded a strong set for Blue Note as a leader. Although he performed into the 1980s (doubling on soprano in later years), Monterose never really became famous. In addition to his Blue Note date he led sets for Jaro (a 1959 session later reissued by Xanadu), Studio 4 (which was reissued by V.S.O.P.), a very obscure 1969 outing for the Dutch label Heavy Soul Music (1969) and during 1979-81 albums for Progressive, Cadence and two for Uptown. —*Scott Yanow*

● **J.R. Monterose** / Oct. 21, 1956 / Blue Note ✦✦✦✦
J.R. Monterose's first session as a leader was a thoroughly enjoyable set of swing-ing, straightahead bop that revealed him as a saxophonist with a knack for power-ful, robust leads in the vein of Sonny Rollins and Coleman Hawkins. With a stellar supporting group of pianist Horace Silver, trumpeter Ira Sullivan, bassist Wilbur Ware and drummer "Philly" Joe Jones, Monterose has recorded a set of bop that swings at a measured pace and offers many delightful moments. Throughout the session, Monterose sounds vigorous, whether he's delivering hard-swinging solos or waxing lyrical. With his bluesy vamps and soulful solos, Silver is equally impressive, while Sullivan's spotlights are alternately punchy and skilled; similarly, the rhythm section is tight, letting the music breathe while keeping the groove. In fact, the quality of the music is so strong, *J.R. Monterose* qualifies as one of the underappreciated gems in Blue Note's mid-'50s catalog. —*Stephen Thomas Erlewine*

Straight Ahead / Nov. 24, 1959 / Xanadu ✦✦✦✦✦
Originally released by the very obscure Jaro label, this excellent session was saved and reissued by Xanadu on a 1975 LP. The talented but underrated tenor saxo-phonist J.R. Monterose has a rare opportunity to stretch out in a quartet with pia-nist Tommy Flanagan (who would become a longtime friend), bassist Jimmy Garri-son and drummer Pete La Roca. Monterose, whose recording sessions were few and far between during his career, is in top form on five of his offbeat yet logical originals and two standard ballads, sometimes showing a Sonny Rollins influence, but mostly sounding fairly distinctive. —*Scott Yanow*

In Action with the Joe Abodeely Trio / Nov. 1964 / Bainbridge ✦✦✦✦
The LP that launched the V.S.O.P. label is a reissue of a real rarity by the obscure but talented tenor J.R. Monterose, originally cut for Studio 4. With good backing from pianist Dale Oehler, bassist Gary Allen and drummer Joe Abodeely, Monterose displays a unique tone and the ability to play creatively within the advanced hard bop idiom. Considering how well he plays on this set (which has not yet been reissued on CD), it is surprising to realize that this was one of only two sessions (with the other set being even less known) led by J.R. Monterose dur-ing a 20-year period. Worth a search. —*Scott Yanow*

Live in Albany / May 8, 1979 / Uptown ✦✦✦
Other than two obscure efforts in 1964 and 1969, tenor saxophonist J.R. Monterose had not led an album in nearly 20 years when he made this LP for the Uptown label in 1979. Teamed up with pianist Hod O'Brien, bassist Teddy Kotick and drum-mer Eddie Robinson, Monterose does his best, although he does sound a bit rusty in spots. He stretches out on long versions of three jazz standards ("The Shadow of Your Smile," "Ruby My Dear" and "Just Friends") and his own "Lu-an." Truth be told, this album is probably more valuable for the definitive liner notes on J.R. Monterose's career than for the music, which is well intentioned, but a bit erratic. —*Scott Yanow*

A Little Pleasure / Apr. 6, 1981+Apr. 7, 1981 / Uptown ✦✦✦✦
This was intimate and somewhat stimulating quiet club-like music. Pianist Tommy Flanagan's fluency as he spread improvised melodic lines effortlessly over the bar lines was a wonder to hear as were his lush chordal voicings. Tenor and soprano saxophonist J.R. Monterose was more noteworthy for the sincere feeling inherent in his playing than for technical skills. Together they were an interesting pair, play-ing off one another with sensitivity and grace. —*Milo Fine, Cadence*

Bebop Loose & Live / Dec. 4, 1981 / Cadence ✦✦✦✦
Tenor saxophonist J.R. Monterose's final recording has some strong moments. He performs a very long (over 18-minute) version of "Blue Bossa" with pianist Larry Ham, bassist Pat O'Leary, drummer Tom Melito and high-powered fellow tenor Hugh Brodie. While Brodie has his own "Kiamesha" as a feature, Monterose is the only horn on lengthy renditions of "Green Dolphin Street" and "What's New." In better shape than he had been for his Uptown set of 1979, J.R. sounds fairly distinc-tive and pushes himself. Unfortunately, he never did emerge from obscurity. —*Scott Yanow*

Buddy Montgomery (Charles F. Montgomery)

b. Jan. 30, 1930, Indianapolis, IN
Piano, Vibes / Hard Bop
The youngest of the three Montgomery Brothers, Buddy Montgomery has long been a reliable if underrated vibraphonist and pianist. He became a professional in 1948 and the following year toured with Big Joe Turner. He played piano with Slide Hampton in his native Indianapolis, served in the army and then was a member (on vibes) of the popular Mastersounds with his brother Monk. Buddy had a brief stint with Miles Davis (playing vibes) in 1960 and frequently played with brothers Wes and Monk (under the guitarist's leadership) in the 1960s. He moved to Milwaukee in 1969, becoming a local fixture and an educator. In the early '80s Montgomery moved to Oakland where he has recorded for producer

Orrin Keepnews on Landmark and with the Riverside Reunion Band. Buddy Montgomery's earlier dates as a leader were for World Pacific (1957), Fantasy, Riv-erside, Milestone and Impulse (1969). —*Scott Yanow*

The Two-Sided Album / Feb. 28, 1968 / Milestone ✦✦✦

This Rather than That / Sep. 10, 1969+Jan. 1971 / Impulse! ✦✦✦

Ties / 1977 / Bean ✦✦✦
This LP is a real obscurity. Pianist Buddy Montgomery, who up to this point had only led two record dates of his own, sticks to piano and performs five of his origi-nals and brother Wes' "Road Song." The personnel changes practically from song to song, and Montgomery is heard with three different trios (best known among the sidemen is bassist Rufus Reid), plus a sextet on two numbers including tenor saxo-phonist Harold Land and trumpeter Oscar Brashear. The music is mostly straighta-head hard bop and is decently recorded and well-played, if not essential. Good luck finding it, though. —*Scott Yanow*

Ties of Love / 1986 / Landmark ✦✦✦
By 1986, Buddy Montgomery had not recorded as a leader for many years, and because he is so well respected, his first Landmark outing became quite an all-star affair. Heard mostly on piano but also switching to vibes for two songs, Montgom-ery is joined on various tracks by trumpeter Claudio Roditi, David "Fathead" New-man on tenor and flute, guitarist Ted Dunbar, bassists Ron Carter and John Heard, drummers Marvin "Smitty" Smith and Billy Higgins, and a couple of percussion-ists. In addition, tenor saxophonist Eddie Harris jams on "Stablemates" and "Ties," and Marlena Shaw takes vocals on "Ties" and "All the Things You Are." Despite all of the guests, the leader (who contributed five of the eight songs) does not get bur-ied in the proceedings and holds his own with his friends. —*Scott Yanow*

● **So Why Not?** / 1988 / Landmark ✦✦✦✦✦
There is a lot of variety on this outing by Buddy Montgomery. The first four selec-tions find him playing synthesizer with a fair amount of personality; Montgomery also doubles on vibes during "Waterfall" and acoustic piano on "So Why Not." Those numbers also include tenor saxophonist David "Fathead" Newman, a solid rhythm section, and guest spots for trumpeter Warren Gale and guitarist Jim Nichols. However, Montgomery is best showcased on the final four pieces, mostly acoustic trio selections with bassist Ron Carter and drummer Ralph Penland; per-cussionists are added to "Budini" (one of five of the leader's originals on the date), while "My Funny Valentine" finds Montgomery playing vibes and synth. All in all, this is a well-conceived and consistently intriguing straightahead outing by the underrated Buddy Montgomery. —*Scott Yanow*

Live at Maybeck Recital Hall, Vol. 15 / Jul. 14, 1991 / Concord Jazz ✦✦✦✦

Here Again / 1997 / Sharp Nine ✦✦✦✦✦
Since achieving major success in the 1960s with the Montgomery Brothers band, and (along with brother Monk on bass) backing brother Wes on some of the guitar great's most popular albums, Buddy Montgomery has been heard from only occa-sionally. This trio album on Sharp Nine shows him still in fine form both as a com-poser and gently swinging pianist. If the album has one weakness, it is the relative sameness of the compositions and tempos. Even the usually uptempo chestnut "That Old Black Magic" is transformed here into an almost unrecognizable slow ballad. Still, with solid backing from bassist Jeff Chambers and drummer Ray Appleton, Montgomery has made a fine album of quiet, soulful piano music. —*Joel Roberts*

Monk Montgomery (William Howard Montgomery)

b. Oct. 10, 1921, Indianapolis, IN, **d.** May 20, 1982, Las Vegas, NV
Bass / Hard Bop, Crossover Jazz
The oldest of the three Montgomery brothers, Monk Montgomery has the distinc-tion of being the first significant jazz electric bassist, starting on the instrument in 1953. He actually did not start playing bass until he was already 30, but was soon strong enough to play with Lionel Hampton's Orchestra (1951-53). He played in the Montgomery-Johnson Quintet in Indianapolis with his brothers Wes and Buddy (along with tenor saxophonist Alonzo Johnson and drummer Robert Johnson) during 1955-56. Monk moved to Seattle, was joined by Buddy, and they formed the Mastersounds, a popular quartet (1957-60). He played occasionally with his brothers in the 1960s (including a short-lived group called the Montgom-ery Brothers), freelanced, was with Cal Tjader in 1966 and in 1970 settled in Las Vegas. Montgomery played locally (including with Red Norvo's trio during 1970-72), was a disc jockey and led obscure sessions for the Chiss (1971) and Philadel-phia Int. (1974) labels. During his last years he was active as the founder of the Las Vegas Jazz Society. —*Scott Yanow*

It's Never Too Late / 1969 / MoJazz ✦✦
This was one of electric bassist Monk Montgomery's rare opportunities to lead his own date. Reissued on CD by MoJazz, the problem with this session is that Mont-gomery is virtually the only soloist on all ten songs, and the overall music will bore

even the most ardent fans of the electric bass. The arrangements are commercial and, although Montgomery plays well on such tunes as "Bluesette," "My Cherie Amour" and "How High the Moon," among others, the results are largely forgettable. —*Scott Yanow*

● **Reality** / 1974 / Philadelphia International ✦✦✦

Wes Montgomery (John Leslie Montgomery)

b. Mar. 6, 1925, Indianapolis, IN, **d.** Jun. 15, 1968, Indianapolis, IN
Guitar / Hard Bop, Crossover Jazz

Wes Montgomery was one of the great jazz guitarists, a natural extension of Charlie Christian whose appealing use of octaves became influential and his trademark. He achieved great commercial success during his last few years, only to die prematurely.

It had taken Wes a long time to become an overnight success. He started to teach himself guitar in 1943 (using his thumb rather than a pick) and toured with Lionel Hampton during 1948-50; he can be heard on a few broadcasts from the period. But then Montgomery returned to Indianapolis where he was in obscurity during much of the 1950s, working a day job and playing at clubs most nights. He recorded with his brothers vibraphonist Buddy and electric bassist Monk during 1957-59 and made his first Riverside album (1959) in a trio with organist Mel Rhyne. In 1960 the release of his album *The Incredible Jazz Guitar of Wes Montgomery* made him famous in the jazz world. Other than a brief time playing with the John Coltrane Sextet (which also included Eric Dolphy) later in the year, Wes would be a leader for the rest of his life.

Montgomery's recordings can be easily divided into three periods. His Riverside dates (1959-63) are his most spontaneous jazz outings, small-group sessions with such sidemen as Tommy Flanagan, James Clay, Victor Feldman, Hank Jones, Johnny Griffin and Mel Rhyne. The one exception was the ironically titled *Fusion!*, a ballad date with a string section. All of the Riverside recordings have been reissued in a massive 12-CD box set. With the collapse of Riverside, Montgomery moved over to Verve where during 1964-66 he recorded an interesting series of mostly orchestral dates with arranger Don Sebesky and producer Creed Taylor. These records were generally a good balance between jazz and accessibility, even if the best performances were small-group outings with the Wynton Kelly Trio or Jimmy Smith. In 1967 Wes signed with Creed Taylor at A&M and during 1967-68 he recorded three best-selling albums that found him merely stating simple pop melodies while backed by strings and woodwinds. His jazz fans were upset but Montgomery's albums were played on AM radio during the period, he helped introduce listeners to jazz and his live performances were as freewheeling as his earlier Riverside dates. Unfortunately, at the height of his success, he died of a heart attack. However, Wes Montgomery's influence is still felt on many young guitarists. —*Scott Yanow*

Fingerpickin' / Dec. 30, 1957+Apr. 22, 1958 / Pacific Jazz ✦✦✦✦
Guitarist Wes Montgomery first recorded in the late '40s during his brief period with Lionel Hampton before returning to Indianapolis. He next emerged on record on December 30, 1957, for a Pacific Jazz set with local musicians including his two brothers, vibraphonist Buddy and electric bassist Monk. This CD reissues the complete album (which usually has appeared in piecemeal fashion) and finds Wes already quite recognizable. The fairly standard hard bop music (which usually features Buddy's vibes as the lead voice) is also of interest due to the presence of trumpeter Freddie Hubbard who at age 17 was making his recording debut; he sounds a bit nervous. In addition to this set, the CD has three songs from the one session that Wes made with his brothers' popular group, the Mastersounds. He actually appeared on the full album (a set of music taken from the film *Kismet*) but these are the only titles that include guitar solos. Although this reissue on a whole is not essential, the music is generally enjoyable and the CD will fill some gaps in one's Wes Montgomery collection. —*Scott Yanow*

Far Wes / Apr. 1958-Oct. 1959 / Pacific Jazz ✦✦✦✦✦
This historical CD contains some of guitarist Wes Montgomery's first recordings; in fact only three small-group songs predate these performances. The then-obscure guitarist is heard in two different quintets, both of which include his brothers Buddy (on piano) and Monk (playing electric bass). The earlier set has Harold Land's tenor as a lead voice while altoist Pony Poindexter takes his place on the later date, Wes' sound was already quite recognizable and he contributes six originals which alternate with Harold Land's "Hymn for Carl" and four standards. —*Scott Yanow*

Guitar on the Go / Oct. 5, 1959+Nov. 27, 1963 / Original Jazz Classics ✦✦✦
The final Riverside release of Wes Montgomery material (before the important label went completely bankrupt) was similar to his debut four years earlier; a trio with organist Melvin Rhyne and an obscure drummer (this time George Brown). The CD reissue even includes one leftover track from the earliest session ("Missile Blues") along with newer jams and a pair of "bonus tracks": an alternate take of

"The Way You Look Tonight" and a brief "Unidentified Solo Guitar" piece. In general the music swings hard (particularly the two versions of "The Way You Look Tonight") and is a worthy if not essential addition to Wes Montgomery's discography. He would have a few straightahead dates for Verve, but this release was really the end of an era. —*Scott Yanow*

Wes Montgomery Trio / Oct. 5, 1959-Oct. 6, 1959 / Original Jazz Classics ✦✦✦✦
Wes Montgomery's first of many sessions for Riverside matched his guitar with organist Melvin Rhyne and drummer Paul Parker for some straightahead swinging. Highlights include "Yesterdays," "'Round Midnight" and Montgomery's originals "Missile Blues" and "Jingles." This CD reissue adds two alternate takes to the original program. —*Scott Yanow*

☆ **The Complete Riverside Recordings** / Oct. 5, 1959-Nov. 27, 1963 / Riverside ✦✦✦✦✦
Wes Montgomery recorded exclusively for the Riverside label during the four years covered by this massive 12-CD box set and, although his later albums for Verve and particularly the pop-jazz A&M dates sold many more copies, it is for his Riverside dates that his legacy was primarily formed. Virtually unknown at the time of his debut on Riverside, Montgomery soon became a major influence whose style is still copied in the 1990s. The guitarist is heard in quite a few different settings on this box including in trios with organist Melvin Rhynbe, a quartet with pianist Tommy Flanagan, as a sideman on different sessions with Nat Adderley, Harold Land and Cannonball Adderley, performing with his brothers Buddy and Monk, holding his own with pianist George Shearing, vibraphonist Milt Jackson and tenor great Johnny Griffin and (for an album ironically titled *Fusion*) playing with strings for the first time. All in all there are a tremendous amount of rewarding performances included in this essential set, most of which show why Wes Montgomery is still considered one of the all-time great jazz guitarists. —*Scott Yanow*

★ **The Incredible Jazz Guitar of Wes Montgomery** / Jan. 26, 1960+Jan. 28, 1960 / Original Jazz Classics ✦✦✦✦✦
This is one of Wes Montgomery's greatest recordings, a classic that really alerted the world about the talents of the guitarist. In a quartet with pianist Tommy Flanagan, bassist Percy Heath and drummer Albert Heath, Wes introduced his originals "West Coast Blues," "Four on Six," and "D-Natural Blues," performed his "Mister Walker" and stretched out on "Airegin," the ballad "Polka Dots and Moonbeams," "In Your Own Sweet Way" and "Gone with the Wind." All of the unique qualities of Wes Montgomery's style are on display on this essential CD reissue which is also available as part of his 12-CD Riverside boxed set. —*Scott Yanow*

Groove Brothers / Jul. 1960-Dec. 1961 / Milestone ✦✦✦✦
It always seemed strange (considering their popularity) that guitarist Wes Montgomery and the group the Mastersounds (which featured his brothers Buddy and Monk) were never able to successfully (on a commercial basis) combine forces. This two-LP set consists of Wes' recordings with his brothers' group: the full album titled *Groove Yard* and half of two other Fantasy records. With Buddy on piano and vibes, Monk on bass and alternating drummers, the music is consistently excellent with the emphasis on attractive chord changes (including two originals apiece by Buddy and Wes) and solid swinging. Most of this rewarding music has since been reissued on CD. —*Scott Yanow*

Movin' Along / Oct. 11, 1960 / Original Jazz Classics ✦✦✦✦
Because it was recorded between two of Wes Montgomery's best-known albums (*Incredible Jazz Guitar* and *So Much Guitar*), this particular CD is a bit underrated. The great guitarist is teamed with flutist James Clay (who switches to tenor on Wes' "So Do It"), pianist Victor Feldman, bassist Sam Jones and drummer Louis Hayes for four standards (highlighted by Clifford Brown's "Sandu" and "Body and Soul"), Sam Jones' "Says You" and two Montgomery originals. The reissue also adds a pair of alternate takes to the fine program. Wes Montgomery made many of his finest jazz recordings originally for Riverside and this is an often-overlooked gem. —*Scott Yanow*

Encores, Vol. 1: Body and Soul / Oct. 12, 1960-Dec. 19, 1961 / Milestone ✦✦✦✦
In the wake of its massive *The Complete Riverside Recordings* box, Fantasy rounded up 13 of the 16 newly released Wes Montgomery outtakes from that set, added a few stray alternates from earlier LP issues, and produced a pair of intelligently programmed CDs that prove just how staggeringly gifted an improviser Montgomery was. Arranged in chronological order, *Volume One* opens with three alternate takes from the somewhat overlooked *Movin' Along* album, continues with two versions of "Doujie"—one with Buddy Montgomery on vibes instead of piano—from *Groove Yard*, and concludes with four from *Bags Meets Wes*. Everything is worth hearing, for Wes hardly ever misses, and the few times where he does—as in the second chorus of "Blue Roz"—are cancelled out by marvelous newly revealed passages. Indeed, the solo on "Movin' Along" is more beautiful than that on the take Wes approved, and the different, extended, octave-rich tag on "So Do It" is wonderful (too bad producer Orrin Keepnews audibly cuts in and stops

the music). The *Bags Meets Wes* outtakes have the advantage of the crack Philly Joe Jones/Sam Jones/Wynton Kelly rhythm section, as well as an inspired Milt Jackson on vibes. —*Richard S. Ginell*

The Alternative Wes Montgomery / Oct. 12, 1960-Nov. 27, 1963 / Milestone ◆◆◆◆

This CD has 12 "alternate" versions of songs recorded in a variety of settings by guitarist Wes Montgomery during his period with Riverside. Montgomery's sidemen include tenor saxophonist Johnny Griffin, organist Mel Rhyne, vibraphonist Milt Jackson, the flute of James Clay, pianists Wynton Kelly, Buddy Montgomery and Victor Feldman and (on "Tune Up") a string section. The two-LP set that this succeeded actually had two additional selections; all of the material is also available in more definitive form on Wes Montgomery's 12-CD boxed set. In any case, the mistakes and flaws (such as they are) are minor on these performances and this CD gives one a good introduction into Montgomery's early recordings. —*Scott Yanow*

So Much Guitar / Aug. 4, 1961 / Original Jazz Classics ◆◆◆◆◆

This CD contains one of Wes Montgomery's finest recordings, a Riverside date that showcases the influential guitarist in a quintet with pianist Hank Jones, bassist Ron Carter, drummer Lex Humphries and the congas of Ray Barretto. All eight performances are memorable in their own way with "Cottontail," "I'm Just a Lucky So and So" and a brief unaccompanied "While We're Young" being high points. —*Scott Yanow*

Recorded Live at Jorgies Jazz Club / Aug. 19, 1961 / VGM ◆◆◆◆

The tiny VGM label came out with two valuable Wes Montgomery LPs back in the 1980s. This first volume features the influential guitarist stretching out on four pieces in a quartet with brothers Buddy (on piano and vibes) and Monk (bass) along with drummer Billy Hart. These versions of "All of You," Milt Jackson's "Heartstrings," "Summertime" and Wes' "Bock to Bock" range from six to 14 minutes, are reasonably well-recorded and contain stirring improvisations that have not yet surfaced on CD. Fans of the guitarist should go out of their way to find this one. —*Scott Yanow*

Live at Jorgies and More / Aug. 19, 1961-1968 / VGM ◆◆◆

The second of the tiny VGM label's two Wes Montgomery LPs picks up where the first one left off, with a pair of performances (an unknown original "Starlight" and an incomplete version of "'Round Midnight") from a live date in 1961. In addition, this LP is filled out by two numbers from a 1968 TV appearance and a pair of lengthy interviews that actually take up more than half of the record. This interesting but not really essential set is strictly for Wes Montgomery's greatest fans. —*Scott Yanow*

● Full House / Jun. 25, 1962 / Original Jazz Classics ◆◆◆◆◆

This live set is notable for teaming guitarist Wes Montgomery and the Wynton Kelly Trio (comprising pianist Kelly, bassist Paul Chambers and drummer Jimmy Cobb) with the fiery tenor Johnny Griffin. As with the OJC release, six selections (highlighted by "Blue 'n' Boogie" and Wes' "S.O.S.") are augmented by "Born to Be Blue" and a pair of alternate takes. —*Scott Yanow*

Encores, Vol. 2: Blues'n'boogie / Jun. 25, 1962-Nov. 27, 1963 / Milestone ◆◆◆◆

Encores, Volume Two continues the roundup of Wes Montgomery's cherishable alternate takes, eight of the ten of which were previously available only on the 12-CD box. The album picks up the three additional tracks from the live *Full House* sessions not included on the CD version, moves on to an extensive five-tune sampling of Wes' sole Riverside album with strings, *Fusion!*, and concludes with a pair of organ-trio outtakes from 1963. The *Full House* section reaches a peak with a burning rendition of "Blue 'n' Boogie," while "Cariba" is audibly less well organized than the approved take. The alternate versions of the *Fusion!* tracks are as lovely as the approved ones (the string fluff at the close of "Prelude to a Kiss" notwithstanding), and it is a pleasure to have another, brisker take of the best chart on the session, "Tune-Up." Of the final two tracks, the most valuable is the remake of "Movin' Along" in the organ-trio format, which sounds better without the dry, toneless flute of James Clay. For collectors who have hunted down all of the original LPs or CDs and find the 12-CD box a bit expensively redundant, or for newcomers who want an introduction to the Riverside recordings, this and *Encores, Volume 1* are highly recommendable. —*Richard S. Ginell*

Fusion! Wes Montgomery with Strings / Apr. 18, 1963-Apr. 19, 1963 / Original Jazz Classics ◆◆◆◆

Although most Wes Montgomery fans associate his playing with strings with his later A&M and Verve recordings, the influential guitarist actually fronted a string section for the first time on this Riverside date from 1963 which had the ironic name of *Fusion!*. As with his later albums, Montgomery's guitar solos here are brief and melodic, but the jazz content is fairly high even if the emphasis is (with the exception of "Tune-Up") on ballads. This CD has three additional performances

than the original LP and is worth picking up; the music is quite pretty and pleasing. —*Scott Yanow*

Boss Guitar / Apr. 22, 1963 / Original Jazz Classics ◆◆◆

Guitarist Wes Montgomery's string of brilliant straightahead jazz recordings for the Riverside label was near its end when he recorded this trio outing with organist Mel Rhyne and drummer Jimmy Cobb. The music swings hard and is highlighted by "Besame Mucho," "Days of Wine and Roses," "Canadian Sunset" and "The Breeze and I." This CD from the *Original Jazz Classics* series adds two alternate takes to the eight LP performances. Enjoyable if not essential. —*Scott Yanow*

Portrait of Wes / Oct. 10, 1963 / Original Jazz Classics ◆◆◆◆

Wes Montgomery's first recordings for Riverside were in a trio with organist Mel Rhyne and ironically his final albums for the struggling (and soon to be bankrupt) label were with Rhyne again. The brilliant guitarist is in fine form on these appealing tunes with the highlights including "Freddie the Freeloader," "Blues Riff" and "Moanin.'" As is true with most of Montgomery's CD reissues, there are a couple of "bonus" cuts (alternates of "Blues Riff" and "Moanin'") added to bring the playing time up a bit. All of this music is also available as part of Wes Montgomery's 12-CD Riverside box set. —*Scott Yanow*

Movin' Wes / Nov. 11, 1964+Nov. 16, 1964 / Verve ◆◆◆

Wes Montgomery's debut for Verve, although better from a jazz standpoint than his later A&M releases, is certainly in the same vein. The emphasis is on his tone, his distinctive octaves and melody statements. Some of the material (such as "People" and "Matchmaker") are pop tunes of the era and the brass orchestra (arranged by Johnny Pate) is purely in the background but there are some worthy performances; chiefly the two-part "Movin' Wes," "Born to Be Blue" and "West Coast Blues." —*Scott Yanow*

Talkin' Verve: Roots of Acid Jazz / Nov. 18, 1964-Sep. 23, 1966 / Verve ◆◆

The title of this compilation tries to make Montgomery viable for a younger generation, but it's not exactly "acid jazz." Rather, it's an anthology of some of Montgomery's better pop- and soul-oriented material from the mid-'60s. The 16 tracks show Montgomery in both orchestral and small combo settings, a few cuts taken from his collaborations with Jimmy Smith. Purists have long disdained this phase of Montgomery's career. But those who don't measure work by how straightahead it is will find much to enjoy here, in either the cuts with Oliver Nelson's orchestra, or the less elaborate sessions with the likes of Smith, Grady Tate, Ron Carter, and Ray Barretto. —*Richie Unterberger*

Verve Jazz Masters 14 / Nov. 1964-Sep. 16, 1966 / Verve ◆◆◆◆◆

Shedding the temptation of bop purist revisionism that creeps into most assessments of Wes Montgomery, this *Jazz Masters* volume gives newcomers a good cross-section of his Verve recordings, the orchestral Wes along with the small-group Wes. The sequencing, though out of chronological order, is quite clever and musical. Someone who has never heard Montgomery before will be drawn in most enticingly with Wes' brief yet unforgettably catchy hit with Oliver Nelson, "Goin' Out of My Head." That is followed by the burnin' "Impressions" with the Wynton Kelly Trio live at the Half Note, which in turn gives way to a luscious *Bumpin'* outtake with strings, "My One and Only Love," the Latin-grooving "Tequila" . . . and the sequence rolls on smoothly and with considerable diversity from there. There are omissions—nothing from the two albums with Jimmy Smith, nothing from the A&M catalog (which Verve's parent corporation PolyGram owns and could have easily drawn from). But one can still get an idea of how Wes' awesome technical facilities and magical melodic touch dazzled the musicians and wooed the general public of his time. If you don't watch yourself, buying this CD might lead to a full-blown Wes addiction. —*Richard S. Ginell*

The Silver Collection / Mar. 16, 1965-Sep. 28, 1966 / Verve ◆◆◆

One of the earliest Wes Montgomery collections to appear on CD (1984), this minimally (and at one point, misleadingly) annotated item concentrates mostly upon the guitarist's Verve small-group performances. Verve relies heavily upon the two albums Wes made with Wynton Kelly (*Smokin' at the Half Note* and *Willow Weep for Me*), adding a few tracks from the two he made with Jimmy Smith (*Dynamic Duo* and *Further Adventures*) and closing with a sole reminder of Wes' orchestral-backed work, *Bumpin's* glorious "Here's That Rainy Day." As such, we hear Montgomery stretching out with an eloquence and depth of tone that had actually deepened since his more critically celebrated Riverside period. Be warned: though the jewel box and disc claim that "Portrait of Jennie" is Track 9, the selection is actually "13 (Death March)" from the *Dynamic Duo* album—a superior choice that gives you a nice Oliver Nelson big-band chart and more playing time as a bonus. Also, on "Misty," the Claus Ogerman arrangement for winds and brass that was over-dubbed after Wes' death and stripped from the track later has been restored here. —*Richard S. Ginell*

Impressions / Mar. 27, 1965 / Affinity ✦✦✦✦

Right in the middle of his Verve period, Wes Montgomery took off on his only European tour, stopping at Paris' Theatre des Champs Elysees for a concert that yielded several imported LPs from 1978 onward. Armed only with the serviceable piano trio of Harold Mabern (piano), Arthur Harper (bass) and Jimmy Lovelace (drums), Montgomery demonstrates to all doubters that commercial success had not affected his ability to play straightahead, swinging, small-group jazz one iota. The tune mislabeled "Wes' Rhythm" (actually "Twisted Blues") is an extraordinary example of Montgomery stretching out—starting with just Wes, bass and drums and developing into full, shouting call-and-response chords and octaves. "Four on Six" is another driving example of the Montgomery improvisational formula while "Impressions" is looser and more wayward than the famous live version with the Wynton Kelly Trio. Mabern's post-bop and modal ideas sometimes run somewhat ahead of his technique, but he does contribute a challenging uptempo piece, "To When." The live remote recording quality, though mono, is excellent on this LP; you'll hear every detail clearly. —*Richard S. Ginell*

Solitude / Mar. 27, 1965 / Affinity ✦✦✦✦

Here's more from the memorable 1965 Paris concert where Montgomery allowed himself the freedom to stretch out and re-explore the hard bop idiom that wowed the connoisseurs in the beginning. There is some mislabeling to watch out for; the track entitled "Mister Walker" is actually "Jingles" taken at a furiously burning speed and "To Django" is really a mellow treatment of "The Girl Next Door." The high point of the LP is the extended small-group treatment of Wes' bossa nova version of "Here's That Rainy Day," in which he comes up with some lovely ideas that he would use two months later when he recorded it with strings. Finally on "'Round Midnight," Johnny Griffin sits in with an intimate ballad tone and a few of his lightning runs, though Wes is still the center of attention. If anything, the sound here is even better than that on *Impressions*. —*Richard S. Ginell*

Live in Paris / Mar. 27, 1965 / France Concert ✦✦✦✦

A third album of music from Wes Montgomery's Paris concert emerged from France a decade after the Affinity LPs. This sampling from the concert adds two more numbers in which Johnny Griffin sits in with the band while "Twisted Blues" and "Jingles" are duplicated from the Affinity LPs. Again, one is captivated and drawn in by Wes' extraordinary combination of bop dexterity, unorthodox guitar technique and intuitive musicality when turned loose in a concert situation. Griffin explodes midway through his solo on "Full House" (you can hear Wes say "Wow!" after the wild ovation), Dizzy Gillespie's "Blue 'n' Boogie" is loaded with inventive octave work from the guitarist and everyone goes out with a brief encore of "West Coast Blues." The album notes are paltry and badly translated from the French, but the sound again is superb. Since this collection was made available on CD and LP, this is probably the easiest way for Wes fans to acquire a piece of this invaluable music until someone gathers together the entire concert on two CDs. —*Richard S. Ginell*

Bumpin' / May 1965 / Verve ✦✦✦✦✦

Wes Montgomery's second Verve album was the best of his orchestral performances. With arrangements by Don Sebesky, Montgomery had opportunities to stretch out on a couple of the selections (most notably on the title cut and "Here's That Rainy Day") and, even though the jazz is not up to the level of his freewheeling Riverside performances, this set is a good compromise between the demands of the jazz and pop worlds. Plus some of the melodies are quite memorable. —*Scott Yanow*

Smokin' at the Half Note / May 1965-Sep. 22, 1966 / Verve ✦✦✦✦✦

This set contains the very best recordings that guitarist Wes Montgomery recorded for Verve. Actually, most of these performances originally came out with woodwinds and brass arranged by Claus Ogerman added so as to make the music more commercial, but fortunately the overdubs were tossed out for this reissue. For nearly the last time in his career, Montgomery got a chance to stretch out with a very complementary trio (pianist Wynton Kelly, bassist Paul Chambers and drummer Jimmy Cobb) and he really digs into the nine standards (which include his "Four on Six"). This record stands as proof that Wes Montgomery never did decline as a jazz improviser even while his recordings became much more pop-oriented. This music is highly recommended. —*Scott Yanow*

● **Impressions: the Verve Jazz Sessions** / May 1965-Sep. 16, 1966 / Verve Jazz Masters ✦✦✦✦

The two-CD set *Impressions: The Verve Jazz Sessions* salvages Wes Montgomery's straight jazz sessions for Verve, leaving the pop-oriented covers and orchestral sessions to the original albums. There are selected numbers from albums like *Movin' Wes, Goin' Out of My Head* and *California Dreaming*, illustrating that those albums were hardly worthless—each track proves that Montgomery's touch remained elegant and supremely tasteful. The second disc is devoted to the complete sessions for *Smokin' at the Half Note*, the legendary recording Montgomery

made at Van Gelder Studios in 1965 with bassist Paul Chambers, pianist Wynton Kelly and drummer Jimmy Cobb. The music on the record is easily among Montgomery's finest, and this is the first time that all the music from the sessions has been collected in one place. That alone makes it worthwhile for hardcore collectors, but the set also makes an excellent summation of his Verve years for less dedicated fans, since it rounds up his very best work on one attractive set. —*Stephen Thomas Erlewine*

Just Walkin' / May 1965-Sep. 1966 / Verve ✦✦✦✦

Now hard to find, this posthumous 1971 LP gave Wes Montgomery fanatics eight previously unreleased selections from the guitarist's Verve period, all worth cherishing. Though the discographical annotations are very sketchy, it isn't hard to deduce where these tracks came from. Four of the eight are from the *Tequila* sessions, including an entirely new song "Wives and Lovers" and outtakes of "Tequila," "Bumpin' on Sunset," and "The Big Hurt," (the latter two are small-group performances minus the orchestrations of the official takes). A gorgeous rendering of "My One and Only Love" and gently swinging "Just Walkin'," both with superb Don Sebesky charts, are from *Bumpin'* and "Sunny" is a wonderfully relaxed variation on the one from the *California Dreaming* album, entirely different in concept and groove. The closer is a long, thoughtful "'Round Midnight" from the Jimmy Smith sessions, equipped with an often jarringly dissonant Oliver Nelson chart. While a few of Montgomery's solos are marginally inferior to those actually issued, his overall levels of taste and musicality are still tremendously high. —*Richard S. Ginell*

Willow Weep for Me / Aug. 1965 / Verve ✦✦✦

Recorded at the Half Note Club in NYC in the Summer and Autumn of 1965. W/ Wynton Kelly (p), Paul Chambers (b), and Jimmy Cobb (d). Includes brass and woodwinds arrangements by Claus Ogerman on three cuts. —*Michael Erlewine*

Goin' out of My Head / Dec. 7, 1965-Dec. 22, 1965 / Verve ✦✦

Guitarist Wes Montgomery had a hit with this version of "Goin' out of My Head," but musically it is little more than a pleasant melody statement. Accompanied by a wasted all-star big band given dull arrangements by Oliver Nelson, Montgomery mostly sticks to playing themes, even those as dull as "Chim Chim Cheree" and "It Was a Very Good Year." Recordings like this one disheartened the jazz world but made him a household name and a staple on AM radio. Heard three decades later, the recording is at its best when serving as innocuous background music. —*Scott Yanow*

Ultimate Wes Montgomery / 1965-1966 / Verve ✦✦✦

Although serious fans and collectors will have little use for the disc, *Ultimate Wes Montgomery* is a solid collection of 12 highlights from the guitarist's Verve recordings as selected by George Benson. For the curious neophyte, the disc offers a good overview of Montgomery's time at the label, featuring the guitarist in a variety of different settings, including combos with Wynton Kelly, Oliver Nelson and Jimmy Smith. Certainly, the disc should be thought of as an introduction, not the final word, but on that level it works very well. Among the featured numbers are "Baby, It's Cold Outside," "Caravan," "West Coast Blues," "'Round Midnight," "Mi Cosa" and "Four on Six." —*Stephen Thomas Erlewine*

Tequila / Mar. 17, 1966-May 18, 1966 / Verve ✦✦✦

Wes Montgomery on two of the songs included on this LP ("Tequila" and "The Thumb") had an opportunity to jam a bit while backed by just bassist Ron Carter, drummer Grady Tate and the congas of Ray Barretto. The other six selections utilize a string section arranged by Claus Ogerman but, even with a throwaway version of "What the World Needs Now Is Love," there are memorable renditions of "Bumpin' on Sunset" and "How Insensitive" that uplift this album quite a bit beyond the guitarist's later A&M recordings. —*Scott Yanow*

California Dreaming / Sep. 14, 1966-Sep. 16, 1966 / Verve ✦✦

Wes Montgomery's last album for Verve (other than an exciting collaboration with Jimmy Smith) is a so-so orchestral album featuring arrangements by Don Sebesky. The material (which includes "Sunny" and "California Dreaming") is strictly pop fluff of the era and the great guitarist has little opportunity to do much other than state the melody in his trademark octaves. This record was perfect for AM radio of the period. —*Scott Yanow*

Further Adventure of J. Smith and W. Montgomery / Sep. 21, 1966 / Verve ✦✦✦

A Day in the Life / Jun. 6, 1967-Jun. 26, 1967 / A&M ✦✦✦

By the time Wes Montgomery recorded this album (his debut for A&M), he was a major name in the pop world. Montgomery's melodic renditions of current pop hits caught on and were played regularly on Top 40 radio. In most cases the guitarist did little more than play the melody, using his distinctive octaves, and it was enough to make him saleable. Of his three A&M recordings, *A Day in the Life* (the first one) was by far the best and, although the jazz content is almost nil, the results are pleasing as background music. "Windy" was a bit of a hit; the other selections (which find Montgomery backed by muzaky strings arranged by Don

Sebesky) include "Watch What Happens," "California Nights," "Eleanor Rigby" and the title cut. —*Scott Yanow*

Classics, Vol. 22–Wes Montgomery / Jun. 1967-May 1968 / A&M ◆◆◆◆
Unlike other greatest-hits collections of Wes Montgomery's A&M material, this one actually burrows into the vaults and comes up with five unreleased tracks—all with small combos—from the great guitarist's tragically brief final period. Aside from the unreleased goodies, this release is a fine single-CD survey that reveals for all with open ears just how good the music in Montgomery's much-maligned A&M/CTI period really was. Almost all of the great jazzmen were superb melodists and Wes was one of the best; he could charm stones with the way he caresses and swings the pop hits of his day. But more than that, his improvised solos in octaves are concise, beautifully formed mature statements, each note perfectly placed and set in Don Sebesky's and Eumir Deodato's lovely orchestrations. Of the five new cuts, the Miriam Makeba hit "Pata Pata" strikes the most fire as Montgomery propulsively stretches out in octaves at some length and "Hello Young Lovers" offers a brilliantly fleet solo in 3/4 time. "My Favorite Things," which Wes referred to in his last interview just before his death, sounds unfinished; you can sense the spaces where the orchestra was probably supposed to come in. Still, any additional Montgomery music that we can get is worth hearing, especially in the final days when every note counted. —*Richard S. Ginell*

Down Here on the Ground / Dec. 20, 1967-Jan. 26, 1968 / A&M ◆◆
Guitarist Wes Montgomery's three A&M records (of which this was the second) are strictly dated pop music. He sticks to melody statements (with a liberal use of his trademark octaves) on such songs as ""I Say a Little Prayer for You," "Georgia on My Mind," a couple of Lalo Schifrin movie themes and the Tijuana Brass' "Wind Song." At least Montgomery was able to make a good living during his last few years, but jazz fans are advised to avoid this one altogether. —*Scott Yanow*

Road Song / May 7, 1968-May 9, 1968 / A&M ◆
Wes Montgomery's final record (before his death from a heart attack at age 45) is, as with his two previous A&M releases, pure pop. The great guitarist sticks to simple melody statements (with a lot of octaves thrown in) while backed by Don Sebesky's unimaginative arrangements for an orchestra; commercially the combination was a big success. Unless one really has the desire to hear such songs as "Greensleeves," "Fly Me to the Moon," "Yesterday" and "Scarborough Fair" played perfectly straight, this strictly for-the-money effort can be safely passed by. —*Scott Yanow*

Tete Montoliu (Vincente Montoliu)

b. Mar. 28, 1933, Barcelona, Spain, d. Aug. 24, 1997, Barcelona, Spain
Piano / Hard Bop
An outstanding pianist from Spain, Tete Montoliu was born blind. He learned to read music in Braille when he was seven and developed impressive technique on piano. He recorded with Lionel Hampton in 1956, had his first session as a leader in 1958 and played with the touring Roland Kirk in 1963. Through the years he also worked with such visiting Americans as Kenny Dorham, Dexter Gordon, Ben Webster, Lucky Thompson and even Anthony Braxton. Tete Montoliu's visits to the US were very infrequent, but his Steeple Chase albums (starting in 1971) are generally available; he also cut one date for Contemporary (1979) and recorded for Enja and Soul Note. —*Scott Yanow*

Lush Life / Sep. 25, 1971 / Steeple Chase ◆◆◆◆
Recorded at the same solo session that resulted in *That's All*, this set finds the great pianist Tete Montoliu performing his fresh and virtuosic intepretations of six standards, plus two versions of Perry Robinson's "Margareta" and his own original "Dia Inolvidabli." A typically excellent and swinging set. —*Scott Yanow*

That's All / Sep. 25, 1971 / Steeple Chase ◆◆◆◆◆
The virtuosic Spanish pianist Tete Montoliu is usually heard from in trio settings, making this rare solo outing particularly special. Montoliu digs into eight familiar standards (including "You Go to My Head," "'Round Midnight," "A Child Is Born" and "Giant Steps") and to his credit comes up with fresh new variations. Montoliu's style has Bud Powell's bop approach as its foundation but also incorporates the more modern chord voicings of McCoy Tyner and Bill Evans. This album is a fine example of his talents. —*Scott Yanow*

Body and Soul / 1971 / Enja ◆◆◆◆

Music for Perla / May 26, 1974 / Steeple Chase ◆◆◆

● **Tete!** / May 28, 1974 / Steeple Chase ◆◆◆◆◆
The great Spanish pianist Tete Montoliu has recorded many rewarding sessions for Steeple Chase. This trio outing (with bassist Niels Pedersen and drummer Albert "Tootie" Heath) is a typically excellent date. In addition to the lesser-known "Theme for Ernie," Montoliu performs five well-known jazz standards in his own modern jazz style, combining together aspects of Bud Powell, McCoy Tyner and Bill Evans. —*Scott Yanow*

Catalonian Fire / May 1974 / Steeple Chase ◆◆◆◆

Tete a Tete / Feb. 15, 1976-Feb. 16, 1976 / Steeple Chase ◆◆◆◆

Tootie's Tempo / Feb. 1976 / Steeple Chase ◆◆◆◆

Catalonian Folksongs / Dec. 9, 1977 / Timeless ◆◆◆
For this set of piano solos, Tete Montoliu (a native of Spain who, if he had played regularly in the US, would have been much more famous in the jazz world) plays lyrical versions of ten obscure songs, most of which were composed by the Spanish singer-guitarist Juan Manuel Serrat. The melodies are sometimes haunting, sometimes just sentimental, but Montoliu consistently brings out their beauty during his concise interpretations. This import from the Dutch Timeless label was made available by Muse for a time in a 1979 LP. —*Scott Yanow*

Lunch in L.A. / Oct. 2, 1979 / Contemporary ◆◆◆◆◆
For what was probably his only session for an American label, the great pianist Tete Montoliu is heard in top form on a couple of basic originals ("Blues Before Lunch" and "Blues After Lunch"), "Airegin," "Sophisticated Lady" and a lengthy "I Want to Talk About You." On "Put Your Little Foot Right Out," he matches wits quite effectively with Chick Corea for a piano duet. Excellent playing, but the music on this LP has not yet been reissued on CD by Fantasy. —*Scott Yanow*

Catalonian Nights, Vol. 1 / May 30, 1980 / Steeple Chase ◆◆◆◆
In 1980, bassist John Heard and drummer Albert "Tootie" Heath traveled to Barcelona, Spain, to perform and record with the masterful Spanish jazz pianist Tete Montoliu. This live set has fairly long versions of Milt Jackson's basic "D&E," "Ladybird," "Autumn in New York" and "Blue Bossa." Although not an innovator, Montoliu (like Oscar Peterson, whose phenomenal technique he approached) was a master of the modern mainstream and of chordal improvisation. He digs into these songs and comes up with consistently fresh and swinging ideas. —*Scott Yanow*

The Music I Like to Play, Vol. 1 / Dec. 1, 1986 / Soul Note ◆◆◆◆
Pianist Tete Montoliu performs six familiar standards, vibraphonist Bobby Hutcherson's "Little B's Poem" and his own "Don't Smoke Any More" as virtuosic yet thoughtful and relaxed solo interpretations. One of the underrated greats (due to his residing in his native Spain throughout his career), Montoliu recorded fairly frequently throughout his career in Europe and was quite consistent. This album gives one a fine example of his talented playing. —*Scott Yanow*

The Music I Like to Play, Vol. 2 / Dec. 1, 1986 / Soul Note ◆◆◆◆

The Music I Like to Play, Vol. 3 / Jan. 28, 1990 / Soul Note ◆◆◆◆

The Music I Like to Play, Vol. 4 / Jan. 28, 1990 / Soul Note ◆◆◆◆

A Spanish Treasure / Jun. 27, 1991 / Concord Jazz ◆◆◆◆◆
Tete Montoliu has long been one of the most talented pianists in jazz but, because he lives in Spain, he tends to be overlooked. A fine bop-based stylist, Montoliu generally offers few surprises to listeners but always swings. This CD is a typical outing for the pianist, featuring ten jazz standards, fine backup work by bassist Rufus Reid and drummer Akira Tana, and enjoyable improvisations from the virtuosic leader. Most of the performances are fairly concise, falling into the three- to seven-minute range except for a lengthy exploration of "What's New." Highlights include creative versions of the rarely played "Israel" and "Tricotism," "Like Someone in Love" (which is taken as a jazz waltz) and a treatment of "All of You" that finds the 58-year old Montoliu sounding a bit like Chick Corea. —*Scott Yanow*

Jack Montrose

b. Dec. 30, 1928, Detroit, MI
Tenor Saxophone / Cool
Jack Montrose has long been a fine tenor saxophonist and in the 1950s he was an important arranger in West Coast jazz. After graduating from Los Angeles State College (1953) he worked with Jerry Gray, Art Pepper (whom he collaborated with on some memorable sessions), Red Norvo, Shorty Rogers, Mel Tormé and others in L.A. Montrose recorded with Clifford Brown in 1954 (providing the arrangements) and led some excellent albums for Atlantic, World Pacific and RCA during 1955-57. However, the 1960s found him out of fashion. Montrose played at strip joints in Los Angeles, did studio work and then moved to Nevada in 1966, working with show bands. In 1986 he made a recording for Slingshot with Pete Jolly, and Jack Montrose has resurfaced on an occasional basis since, playing in a similar cool-toned style to how he sounded in the 1950s. —*Scott Yanow*

With Bob Gordon / Mar. 11, 1955+Mar. 12, 1955 / Atlantic ◆◆◆◆

● **Jack Montrose Sextet** / Jun. 24, 1955 / Pacific Jazz ◆◆◆◆◆
The second of five albums led by tenor saxophonist Jack Montrose during 1955-57 has long been out of print, which is unfortunate, because this is probably his most rewarding. A talented arranger, Montrose had a sextet (rather than his usual quartet/quintet) to write for on this project. With trumpeter Conte Candoli, baritonist Bob Gordon (on one of his last dates before his death in a car accident), pianist Paul Moer, bassist Ralph Pena and drummer Shelly Manne aboard, the level of

musicianship was high. Montrose's colorful arrangements for five of his originals and three standards (which fit very much in the West Coast jazz genre) swing and are quite effective in setting off the solos. Well worth searching for. —*Scott Yanow*

The Horn's Full / Sep. 10, 1956-Sep. 11, 1956 / RCA ♦♦♦♦♦

Although a somewhat obscure set which has not yet been reissued on CD, this outing by tenor saxophonist Jack Montrose was put out by Fresh Sound in the 1980s. Montrose, an excellent improviser who was also a talented arranger, teams up with vibraphonist Red Norvo, either Barney Kessel or Jim Hall on guitar, Lawrence Wooten or Max Bennett on bass and Mel Lewis or Bill Dolney on drums to perform six of his originals and five swing-era standards. The music is greatly uplifted by Montrose's inventive arrangements and has many concise solos. Despite the quality, Montrose would not have his next opportunity to lead a record date for 28 years. —*Scott Yanow*

Better Late than Never / 1986 / Slingshot ♦♦♦

Tenor saxophonist Jack Montrose had been off records a long time (and had not led his own record date since 1957) when he had the opportunity to record for the short-lived label Slingshot. Joined by the Pete Jolly Trio (which consists of the pianist, bassist Chuck Berghofer and drummer Nick Martinis), Montrose plays ten worthy if obscure songs by producer/composer David Holt. The music on this hard-to-find LP is moody, sometimes picturesque and generally swinging. —*Scott Yanow*

Let's Do It / Sep. 10, 1990-Sep. 11, 1990 / Holt ♦♦♦♦

A fine tenor saxophonist and arranger, Jack Montrose has long deserved to be known much better. The 1960s and '70s were lean years for him, and he had long since settled in Las Vegas when he recorded this quintet CD with trombonist Bill Watrous and the Pete Jolly Trio. As is usual with the selections cut for the Holt label, all of the songs are David Holt compositions. Some are more memorable than others, but the consistently fine solos, the leader's arrangements, and the rare chance to hear Montrose stretch out make this a recommended CD. —*Scott Yanow*

James Moody

b. Mar. 26, 1925, Savannah, GA

Tenor Saxophone, Flute, Alto Saxophone / Bop, Hard Bop

James Moody has been an institution in jazz since the late '40s, whether on tenor, flute, occasional alto or yodelling his way through his "Moody's Mood for Love."

After serving in the air force (1943-46), he joined Dizzy Gillespie's bebop orchestra and began a lifelong friendship with the trumpeter. Moody toured Europe with Gillespie and then stayed overseas for several years, working with Miles Davis, Max Roach and top European players. His 1949 recording of "I'm in the Mood for Love" in 1952 became a hit under the title of "Moody's Mood for Love" with classic vocalese lyrics written by Eddie Jefferson and a best-selling recording by King Pleasure. After returning to the US, Moody formed a septet that lasted for five years, recorded extensively for Prestige and Argo, took up the flute and then from 1963-68 was a member of Dizzy Gillespie's quintet. He worked in Las Vegas show bands during much of the 1970s before returning to jazz, playing occasionally with Dizzy, mostly working as a leader and recording with Lionel Hampton's Golden Men of Jazz. Moody, who has alternated between tenor (which he prefers) and alto throughout his career, has an original sound on both horns. He is also one of the best flutists in jazz. James Moody has recorded as a leader for Blue Note, Xanadu, Vogue, Prestige, EmArcy, Mercury, Argo, DJM, Milestone, Perception, MPS, Muse, Vanguard and Novus. —*Scott Yanow*

The Beginning and End of Bop / Oct. 19, 1948 / Blue Note ♦♦♦♦♦

The idea of the music on this LP signifying the beginning and end of bebop is inaccurate and a bit silly. What is actually here are two unrelated but enjoyable enough straightahead dates. Side one has six titles from tenor saxophonist James Moody with an octet drawn from the Dizzy Gillespie orchestra and featuring the compositions and arrangements of Gil Fuller. Of those numbers, "Cu-Ba" and "The Fuller Bop Man" are best known; there are plenty of short spots throughout for altoist Ernie Henry, baritonist Cecil Payne and trumpeter Dave Burns. The flip side has four selections from a sextet headed by pianist George Wallington who also contributes two of the originals. With trumpeter Dave Burns, trombonist Jimmy Cleveland and tenor saxophonist Frank Foster taking solos, Wallington's session also has more than its share of interesting moments. The Moody material has since been reissued on CD but the Wallington date remains out of print. —*Scott Yanow*

In the Beginning / Apr. 30, 1949-May 15, 1949 / Inner City ♦♦♦♦

This out-of-print Inner City LP contains material from the Vogue label, some of which has since been reissued on CD. Tenor saxophonist James Moody is heard in Europe on three songs with the Max Roach Quintet (which includes the drummer/leader, trumpeter Kenny Dorham, pianist Al Haig and bassist Tommy Potter). There are also two numbers from this unit as a quartet without Moody. The second side finds the tenor in Zurich heading an octet. Most unusual about those relatively

boppish performances is that the sidemen include trumpeter Trummie Young (no relation to trombonist Trummy Young) and altoist Red Allen (no relation to the New Orleans trumpeter of the same name). James Moody sounds distinctive and creative within the bop idiom throughout the enjoyable sessions. —*Scott Yanow*

James Moody & His Swedish Crowns / Oct. 6, 1949-Oct. 18, 1949 / Dragon ♦♦♦♦♦

This Dragon LP features James Moody's Swedish sessions of 1949, highlighted by his famous "Moody's Mood for Love" (which was turned into a vocalese classic by Eddie Jefferson and King Pleasure a few years later). Moody's cool-toned tenor and alto were influential in Sweden and he was really developing his own sound and style during this period. Among his sidemen on the 15 selections are altoist Arne Domnerus, pianist Gosta Theselius and many obscure but talented musicians. The music is quite boppish as can be ascertained by the titles of three of Moody's originals: "Three Bop Mice," "I'm in the Mood for Bop" and "The Flight of the Bopple Bee." Highly recommended and due to be reissued on CD. —*Scott Yanow*

James Moody and Frank Foster in Paris / Jul. 13, 1951-Jul. 13, 1954 / RCA ♦♦♦♦

James Moody, alternating between alto and tenor, is well featured on two of the three sessions (20 selections in all) included on this reissue CD. Moody joins trumpeter Roger Guerin, pianist Raymond Fol, bassist Pierre Michelot and drummer Pierre Lemarchand for a ballad-oriented session that includes "I Cover the Waterfront," "More than You Know" and "This Is Always." Moody is also showcased fronting the same rhythm section plus strings and woodwinds on six French ballads and his melodic improvisations are quite lyrical and subtle. This CD is rounded out by a quartet set led by tenor saxophonist Frank Foster who utilizes a fine French rhythm section in 1954 for three mostly hard-swinging standards and three originals. Since most of these performances were formerly quite rare, this CD should delight both veteran collectors and straightahead jazz fans. —*Scott Yanow*

The Moody Story [Trip] / Sep. 1951-Jun. 15, 1952 / Trip ♦♦♦♦

The music on this out-of-print Trip LP has yet to be reissued on CD. The ten selections are taken from four different sessions from 1951-52 and feature James Moody (who doubles on tenor and alto) mostly with a sextet/septet; the sidemen generally include trumpeter Dave Burns, pianists Sadik Hakim or John Acea and baritonist Cecil Payne. A highlight is "The James Moody Story," which has an interesting vocal by Babs Gonzales with the assistance of Moody himself. This excellent bop-oriented music deserves to be rediscovered. —*Scott Yanow*

Moody's Mood for Blues / Jan. 8, 1955-Jan. 28, 1955 / Original Jazz Classics ♦♦♦♦

In the mid-'50s James Moody led a four-horn septet that played music falling somewhere between bop and R&B. The danceable rhythms and riffing made its recordings somewhat accessible, but the solos of Moody (on tenor and alto) and trumpeter Dave Burns also held listeners' interests. Vocalese master Eddie Jefferson has two guest appearances (on "Workshop" and "I Got the Blue,") and Iona Wade sings "That Man o' Mine" in a Dinah Washington-influenced style but the emphasis is on Moody's solos and the ensembles; the leader's two versions of "It Might as Well as Be Spring" (one on tenor, the other on alto) are highlights of this enjoyable CD reissue. —*Scott Yanow*

Hi-Fi Party / Aug. 23, 1955-Aug. 24, 1955 / Original Jazz Classics ♦♦♦♦♦

For a period in the mid-'50s, tenor saxophonist James Moody (who doubled on alto) was able to keep together a swinging septet that played bop in a fairly accessible way. On this CD reissue of two 1955 sessions, Moody and his group (which includes the fine trumpeter Dave Burns, trombonist William Shepherd, baritonist Pee Wee Moore, pianist Jimmy Boyd, bassist John Lathan and drummer Clarence Johnson) perform swinging versions of fairly obscure originals including the lengthy "Jammin' with James" (which has a long tradeoff between Moody and Burns, Benny Golson's "Big Ben" and "There Will Never Be Another You." The high point is Eddie Jefferson's one appearance, singing his alternate lyrics to Charlie Parker's famous solo on "Lady Be Good" which he renamed "Disappointed." —*Scott Yanow*

Wail, Moody, Wail / Dec. 12, 1955 / Original Jazz Classics ♦♦♦♦

James Moody's mid-'50s band was a septet featuring four horns including the leader's tenor and alto. The bop-based group had plenty of spirit (as best shown here on the 14-minute title cut) if not necessarily a strong personality of its own. This CD (a straight reissue of the original LP plus two additional titles from the same session) is accessible, melodic and swinging; trumpeter Dave Burns is the best soloist among the sidemen. —*Scott Yanow*

★ Everything You've Always Wanted to Know About Sax / Feb. 1956+1961 / Cadet ♦♦♦♦♦

Two-fer date with Eddie Jefferson (v) on some tracks. Also with Tom McIntosh (tb), Howard McGhee (tpt), Hank Jones (p), and Kiane Zawadi (euphonium/tb). —*Michael G. Nastos*

Moody's Mood for Love / Dec. 14, 1956+Jan. 13, 1957 / Argo ◆◆◆◆
A strong version of the "Moody's Mood for Love", with a vocal by the late Eddie Jefferson (v). —*Ron Wynn*

Return from Overbrook / 1956-Sep. 1958 / GRP/Chess ◆◆◆◆◆
Two of James Moody's better albums from the 1950s are reissued in full on this single Chess CD: *Last Train from Overbrook* and *Flute 'n' the Blues*. The former session features Moody (on tenor, alto and flute) backed by ten horns and a four-piece rhythm section on a variety of strong straightahead material (including the title cut, "What's New," "Tico-Tico" and "The Moody One") while the latter is a septet outing that also has solos by trumpeter Johnny Coles, trombonist William Shepherd and baritonist Pee Wee Moore, along with three memorable vocals from Eddie Jefferson. Recommended. —*Scott Yanow*

James Moody [Argo] / Aug. 1959 / Argo ◆◆◆

Hey! It's James Moody / Dec. 29, 1959 / Argo ◆◆◆

Great Day / Jun. 17, 1963-Jun. 18, 1963 / Chess ◆◆◆◆◆
Some good, sometimes excellent sax and flute work from the always reliable James Moody. This was a period in which he was dabbling sometimes in soul-jazz and other times in hard bop, but mostly played mainstream, straightahead originals, standards, and ballads. —*Ron Wynn*

Moody and the Brass Figures / 1967 / Milestone ◆◆◆◆

Don't Look Away Now / Feb. 14, 1969 / Original Jazz Classics ◆◆◆◆◆

The Blues and Other Colors / 1969 / Original Jazz Classics ◆◆◆◆

Never Again / Jun. 8, 1972 / Muse ◆◆◆◆◆
The "Never Again" title refers to James Moody's pledge to stick to tenor and not play alto anymore. He did not reach that goal 100% in the future but did successfully shift his emphasis to tenor which he plays exclusively on this superior Muse LP. Joined by organist Mickey Tucker, electric bassist Roland Wilson and drummer Eddie Gladden, Moody is heard in top form, swinging quite hard. Highlights include "Secret Love," "St. Thomas" and an adventurous version of "Freedom Jazz Dance." Highly recommended. —*Scott Yanow*

Feelin' it Together / Jan. 15, 1973 / Muse ◆◆◆◆
James Moody has an opportunity to show off his versatility on this CD reissue. He switches between tenor, alto and flute (excelling on all three instruments) with a quartet comprising pianist Kenny Barron (who also plays some surprisingly distinctive electric piano and a bit of electric harpsichord), bassist Larry Ridley and drummer Freddie Waits. The music ranges from modern bebop ("Anthropology" and "Autumn Leaves") to spacey ballads and the eccentric "Kriss Kross." Stimulating music. —*Scott Yanow*

Something Special / Jul. 1, 1986-Jul. 2, 1986 / Novus ◆◆◆◆
For his debut on Novus, James Moody (switching between tenor, alto and flute) performs four of Tom McIntosh's moody originals, the standard "More Than You Know" and an updated version of "I'm in the Mood For Love." With strong assistance from pianist Kirk Lightsey, bassist Todd Coolman and drummer Idris Muhammad, Moody takes some chances during this date and stretches himself, showing that he was not content to rely on bebop cliches. All of James Moody's recordings are worthwhile and this one is certainly above-average. —*Scott Yanow*

Moving Forward / Sep. 10, 1987-Nov. 18, 1987 / Novus ◆◆◆◆◆
For this strong blowing date (which has arranged passages by Tom McIntosh), James Moody and his group (pianist Kenny Barron, whose name is misspelled twice in the liners as "Darron," bassist Todd Coolman, drummer Akira Tana and Onaje Allan Gumbs who plays synthesizer on three of the six numbers) perform four strong standards, Jimmy Heath's "A Summer Afternoon" and Moody's "What Do You Do." The leader, who takes a good-humored vocal on the latter, is in consistently fine form on tenor, alto and flute, really stretching out on "The Night Has a Thousand Eyes" and "Giant Steps." Moody was always immediately identifiable and is heard throughout in prime form. —*Scott Yanow*

Sweet and Lovely / Mar. 11, 1989-Mar. 13, 1989 / Novus ◆◆◆◆
James Moody sticks to standards on his third Novus release, including "My Melancholy Baby," "Sweet and Lovely," "Confirmation" and "My Ideal." He uses his rhythm section of the period (pianist Marc Cohen, bassist Todd Coolman and drummer Akira Tana) and welcomes guest Dizzy Gillespie on "Con Alma" and the exuberant "Get the Booty." Moody (tripling as usual on tenor, alto and flute) is the solo star throughout and sounds very much in prime form, whether swinging hard or playing lyrically on ballads. —*Scott Yanow*

Honey / Oct. 1, 1990-Oct. 3, 1990 / Novus ◆◆◆◆
The most unusual aspect to this Novus CD is that James Moody, in addition to his usual tenor and alto, also plays a bit of soprano. Joined by pianist Kenny Barron, bassist Todd Coolman and drummer Akira Tana, Moody alternates between interpreting standards and group originals, sounding quite beautiful on "When You

Wish Upon a Star." Even at age 65, he was still very much in his musical prime. —*Scott Yanow*

Moody's Party / Mar. 23, 1995-Mar. 26, 1995 / Telarc ◆◆◆◆

Young at Heart / 1996 / Warner Brothers ◆◆◆◆
With *Young at Heart*, James Moody interprets the core songs of Frank Sinatra's repertoire as if it were a songbook itself. The results are surprisingly effective, demonstrating the wonderful, lucid tones of Moody's saxophone, as well as the flexibility and depth of the songs themselves. On the album, Moody is supported by a small band, which is occasionally augmented by a full orchestra. —*Thom Owens*

Moody Plays Mancini / Feb. 4, 1997-Feb. 5, 1997 / Warner Brothers ◆◆◆◆
As popular and well known as Henry Mancini was when he was alive, only after his death in 1994 have the substantial musical tributes been coming—and the tunes included on this graceful disc were suggested by the composer himself. Mancini was, of course, a product of the big band era—and thus, steeped in jazz—and his movie themes often make gratifying basic material for ballad improvisations. With only Gil Goldstein's electronic keyboards (used sparingly and strictly in a jazz context), Todd Coolman's bass, and Terri Lyne Carrington's drums to back him up, Moody's tenor, alto and soprano solos are consistently warm, melodic, and easy to assimilate, with a few nudges outside the changes on "Charade." Appropriately, he also chooses to use the flute on the sly, sauntering *Pink Panther* theme and "Soldier in the Rain." The sentimental "Moon River" was the only tune Mancini did not recommend, but it was from Moody's wife's favorite film, and it gives Moody a chance to exercise his deep, endearingly rusty bass voice. —*Richard S. Ginell*

Brew Moore (Milton Aubrey Moore, Jr.)

b. Mar. 26, 1924, Indianola, MS, **d.** Aug. 19, 1973, Copenhagen, Denmark
Tenor Saxophone / Cool
Brew Moore once said that "Anyone who doesn't play like Lester Young is wrong," a philosophy he followed throughout his career. In the early '50s he recorded on a session with fellow tenors Stan Getz, Al Cohn, Zoot Sims and Allan Eager; at the time they all sounded identical. Moore was the only one of the five who did not change his sound through the years. During 1942-48 he worked with local bands in New Orleans and Memphis, moving to New York in 1948 and playing with Claude Thornhill's Orchestra (1948-49). During the next few years he freelanced, working with Machito, Kai Winding and Gerry Mulligan among others. In 1954 he moved to San Francisco where he led his own groups and played with Cal Tjader. Moore, whose cool sound became out of fashion, moved to Copenhagen in 1961 and, other than three years in New York (1967-70), stayed overseas until his death. He recorded as a leader for Savoy (1948-49), Fantasy (1955-57), Jazz Mark, Debut, Steeple Chase, Sonet and Storyville. —*Scott Yanow*

Brew Moore Quintet / Aug. 1955-Feb. 22, 1956 / Original Jazz Classics ◆◆◆◆◆
An excellent cool-toned tenor saxophonist proud of the influence of Lester Young, Brew Moore only recorded on an infrequent basis during his career. He did make two albums for Fantasy that were reissued on LPs in the Original Jazz Classics series (although not yet on CD). The three dates included on this set were all cut in San Francisco with local (and now obscure) musicians: trumpeter Dick Mills, pianist John Marabuto, bassist Max Hartstein, drummer Gus Gustofson and an unidentified guitarist. Marabuto contributed three originals; Mills wrote "Rotation," and the other four songs are familiar standards. Moore plays well (despite a hectic lifestyle, he was fairly consistent on records) and the music is relaxed and swinging. —*Scott Yanow*

Brew Moore / Nov. 5, 1957-1958 / Original Jazz Classics ◆◆◆◆
Brew Moore lived in San Francisco during the latter half of the 1950s, playing mostly with local musicians. On five of the six selections included on this LP (reissued in the 1980s, but not yet on CD) Moore is matched with his fellow tenor Harold Wylie, pianist John Marabuto, bassist John Mosher and drummer John Markam. The music is pleasing and fairly typical of the era's cool jazz, but not overly memorable, just another night's work. "Dues Blues" is taken from a slightly later concert matching Moore with vibraphonist Cal Tjader, pianist Vince Guaraldi, bassist Dean Reilly and drummer Bobby White. A decent but not essential release. —*Scott Yanow*

Svinget 14 / Sep. 26, 1962 / Black Lion ◆◆◆◆◆
For this Black Lion reissue CD, the cool-toned tenor Brew Moore is accompanied by a strong European rhythm section (pianist Bent Axen, the teenaged bassist Niels Henning Orsted Pedersen and drummer William Schiopffe) plus (on two songs apiece) altoist Sahib Shihab, the great baritonist Lars Gullin or vibraphonist Louis Hjulmand; the opening two songs showcase Moore without the guests. Although the music is essentially straightahead cool bop, there are only two jazz standards ("You Stepped Out of a Dream" and Oscar Pettiford's "Laverne Walk") among the eight numbers with the majority being originals by group members. A highlight is "The Monster" which matches Moore with the passionate alto of Shihab and shows

the influence that the avant-garde was starting to have on the mainstream players. Overall this is a particularly strong outing for the underrated (and somewhat forgotten) Brew Moore, who easily holds his own with his sidemen (including Gullin). —*Scott Yanow*

If I Had You / Apr. 15, 1965 / Steeple Chase ✦✦✦✦
In the context of 1965 jazz, Brew Moore was very much out of place. A cool-toned tenor whose hero was Lester Young, Moore was able to carve out his own sound, but he seemed a decade behind many of the pacesetters of the mid-'60s. He spent his last years in Europe and after 1962 was only captured on record on three occasions, all live dates: a pair of radio broadcasts cut two weeks apart in 1965 (and both reissued on CD by Steeple Chase) and a marathon 1971 date that resulted in releases for Storyville and Sonet. Brew Moore's neglect is quite unfortunate for, on evidence of this particular outing in Copenhagen with pianist Atli Bjorn, bassist Benny Nielsen and drummer William Schiopffe, Moore still had a lot to offer. He stretches out quite successfully on four swing-oriented tunes (including the blues "Svinget 14" and Fats Waller's "Zonky") along with a shorter rendition of "Blue Monk." —*Scott Yanow*

● **I Should Care** / Apr. 29, 1965 / Steeple Chase ✦✦✦✦✦
Recorded two weeks after his other Steeple Chase set *If I Had You*, the legendary but always somewhat overlooked tenor saxophonist Brew Moore (a disciple of Lester Young) is heard taking extended solos on four numbers during this radio broadcast from Copenhagen's Montmartre Jazzhus. The Steeple Chase CD features Moore along with pianist Atli Bjorn, bassist Benny Nielsen and drummer William Schiopffe sounding in top form on his "Brew's Blues," the standard "I Should Care," "Manny's Tune" (based on "Indiana") and particularly "In a Mellotone." This set (which gets the edge over *If I Had You*) serves as a strong introduction to the talented but generally forgotten Brew Moore. —*Scott Yanow*

Brew's Stockholm Dew / Feb. 25, 1971 / Sonet ✦✦✦✦
Veteran tenor saxophonist Brew Moore, who died in 1973, spent most of his last dozen years living in Scandinavia. His last recordings resulted in two LPs (the other was released by Storyville) made during the same night. Teamed with pianist Lars Sjosten, bassist Sture Nordin and drummer Fredrik Noren, Moore is in fine form on "Old Folks," Tony Fruscella's "Baite," a pair of Sjosten's originals and his own "Brew's Stockholm Dew." Moore stayed true to his roots in Lester Young-style swing up until the end. —*Scott Yanow*

No More Brew / Feb. 25, 1971 / Storyville ✦✦✦✦
Recorded the same night as music that was released by Sonet, this final recording by the cool-toned tenor Brew Moore (who always wanted to play as much like his idol Lester Young as possible) features seven- to nine-minute versions of "It Could Happen to You," "Manny's Tune" (by Moore's pianist of the late '50s, John Marabuto), his own "No More Brew" and "Blue Monk." The tenorman was in his musical prime right up to his accidental death (falling down a flight of stairs) two years later, playing relaxed, swinging solos. —*Scott Yanow*

Glen Moore

b. Oct. 28, 1941, Portland, OR
Bass, Piano / Post-Bop, Folk-Jazz
One of the longtime members of Oregon, Glen Moore's playing tends to be on the introspective side, thoughtful and melodic improvisations that are open to the influence of folk, classical and ethnic music. He started on bass when he was 13 and freelanced in New York in the mid-'60s. Moore recorded with Nick Brignola in 1967, played part-time with the Paul Bley Synthesizer Show during 1969-71, was with Paul Winter's Consort in 1970 and then left to help form Oregon. In addition to his work with the eclectic group, Glen Moore recorded with Annette Peacock, Larry Coryell, Ralph Towner and Zbigniew Seifert plus some nonjazz dates. He has also led dates for Enja, Elektra and Audioquest and performed duets with singer Nancy King (as King and Moore); the duo has recorded for Justice. —*Scott Yanow*

Introducing Glen Moore / Feb. 1, 1979 / Elektra ✦✦✦
● **Forces of Flight** / Aug. 1, 1995 / ITM ✦✦✦✦

Oscar Moore

b. Dec. 25, 1912, Austin, TX, d. Oct. 8, 1981, Las Vegas, NV
Guitar / Swing
An excellent guitarist influenced after 1939 by Charlie Christian, Oscar Moore was an invaluable part of the Nat "King" Cole Trio during 1937-47, appearing on virtually all of Cole's records during the period. He also recorded with Lionel Hampton, Art Tatum (1941), the Capitol Jazzmen and Lester Young. Unfortunately, Moore's post-Cole career was not that successful. He played with his brother Johnny Moore in the Three Blazers from 1947 to the mid-'50s (the group declined in popularity

after pianist/singer Charles Brown left) and he recorded three records for Verve and Tampa during 1953-54, but then was largely outside of music with the exception of a 1965 Nat Cole tribute album. —*Scott Yanow*

● **Oscar Moore Quartet** / 1954 / V.S.O.P. ✦✦✦✦
Although he was a pioneering electric guitarist and gained a certain amount of fame playing with the original Nat "King" Cole Trio, Oscar Moore had relatively few opportunities to record in the 1950s. This CD reissue of a set originally cut for Tampa features Moore in a quartet with pianist Carl Perkins, bassist Joe Comfort and Mike Pacheco on bongos. Sticking mostly to standards (including the "Samson and Delilah Theme," Moore is in fine form for this set of melodic and easy-listening music that always swings. —*Scott Yanow*

Oscar Moore Quartet with Carl Perkins / 1954 / V.S.O.P. ✦✦✦
Guitarist Oscar Moore, who will always be best known for his years with the Nat "King" Cole Trio, had a couple of opportunities to record as a leader in the mid-'50s, but despite the worthy music, his solo career never caught on. This CD reissue of a Tampa LP matches the swing guitarist with pianist Carl Perkins, bassist Joe Comfort and drummer Lee Young for a brief easy-listening set of standards and basic originals. Nice music. —*Scott Yanow*

We'll Remember You, Nat / Mar. 1966 / Surrey ✦✦✦✦

Ralph Moore

b. Dec. 24, 1956, London, England
Tenor Saxophone / Hard Bop
Ralph Moore, who has lived in the US since 1970, is a fine tenor saxophonist influenced by John Coltrane but possessing a slightly softer tone. He attended Berklee (during that period he had opportunities to play with James Williams and Kevin Eubanks), moved to New York in 1981 and worked with many veteran players including Horace Silver (1981-85), Roy Haynes, Dizzy Gillespie, Freddie Hubbard, Jimmy Knepper, Bobby Hutcherson and Kenny Barron. Ralph Moore debuted on record as a leader in 1985 for Reservoir, recorded several fine albums for Landmark, Criss Cross, Savoy and Mons (with the L.A. Jazz Summit), toured extensively with J.J. Johnson and since 1995 has been a member of the Tonight Show Orchestra in Los Angeles. —*Scott Yanow*

Round Trip / Dec. 21, 1985 / Reservoir ✦✦✦✦
The feel of this set (the debut as a leader by tenor saxophonist Ralph Moore) is very much in the style of Art Blakey's Jazz Messengers. That should not be a surprise, for even though Moore did not play with Blakey (the closest he came was with Horace Silver), trumpeter Brian Lynch and pianist Benny Green certainly did. With guitarist Kevin Eubanks, bassist Rufus Reid and drummer Kenny Washington completing the sextet, Moore leads the band through two originals, Eubanks' "Round Trip," Lynch's "Back Room Blues," and a pair of jazz standards. A fine hard bop date and an excellent start to Ralph Moore's solo career. —*Scott Yanow*

623 C Street / Feb. 27, 1987+Dec. 31, 1987 / Criss Cross ✦✦✦✦
For his second set as a leader, the focus is almost entirely on tenor saxophonist Ralph Moor, who switches to soprano on two of the six numbers. Accompanied by pianist David Kikoski, bassist Buster Williams and drummer Billy Hart, Moore performs group originals, Wayne Shorter's "Black Diamond" and Bud Powell's "Un Poco Loco." Displaying a tone on tenor similar to John Coltrane's, Moore's note choices are more original than his sound. A solid modern mainstream set. —*Scott Yanow*

Rejuvenate / Feb. 19, 1988 / Criss Cross ✦✦✦✦✦
The group assembled for tenor saxophonist Ralph Moor's quintet date is perfect for his John Coltrane-inspired sound: trombonist Steve Turre (who also plays conch shells), pianist Mulgrew Miller, bassist Peter Washington and drummer Marvin "Smitty" Smith. The all-star lineup performs originals by Moore, Turre and Miller in addition to the title cut and "It Might as Well Be Spring" (a ballad feature for the tenor). The two horns blend together very well and consistently inspire each other; the rhythm section is state-of-the-art for this type of modern hard bop music, and the overall results are swinging and at times a bit adventurous. Recommended. —*Scott Yanow*

● **Images** / Dec. 15, 1988+Dec. 17, 1988 / Landmark ✦✦✦✦
The particularly strong material and the all-star lineup (tenor saxophonist Ralph Moore, trumpeter Terence Blanchard, pianist Benny Green, bassist Peter Washington and drummer Kenny Washington) make this a particularly enjoyable set from the tenorman. Although still displaying the inspiration (soundwise) of early-'60s John Coltrane, Moore had developed an increasingly original style within the modern mainstream throughout the 1980s. Highlights of this excellent set include J.J. Johnson's "Enigma" (a ballad feature for Moore), Hank Mobley's "This I Dig of You," and Moore's "Blues for John" (written in tribute to Coltrane). One of Ralph Moore's more significant recordings to date. —*Scott Yanow*

● **Furthermore** / Mar. 3, 1990+Mar. 5, 1990 / Landmark ✦✦✦✦✦

One of the best among the Young Lion tenor saxophonists makes an aggressive, explosive statement. —*Ron Wynn*

Who It Is You Are / Apr. 5, 1993-Apr. 6, 1993 / Savoy ✦✦✦✦

For this fairly relaxed modern mainstream session, Ralph Moore sheds some of the John Coltrane influence he displayed on earlier dates. He features his attractive tone and melodic ideas on a set of superior material, mostly underplayed standards. The rhythm section (pianist Benny Green, bassist Peter Washington and drummer Billy Higgins) is as supportive and tasteful as one would expect, with Green occasionally taking solo honors. Whether it be classic ballads such as "Skylark" and "Some Other Time," the pianist's memorable gospel/jazz number "Testifyin'" or the danceable Latin stomp "Esmeralda," this is an enjoyable set of middle-of-the-road modern jazz. —*Scott Yanow*

Airto Moreira

b. Aug. 5, 1941, Itaiopolis, Brazil

Percussion / Crossover Jazz, Fusion, Brazilian Jazz, Worldbeat, Latin Jazz

The most high-profile percussionist of the 1970s and still among the most famous, Airto Moreira (often simply known by his first name) helped make percussion an essential part of many modern jazz groups; his tambourine solos can border on the amazing! Airto originally studied guitar and piano before becoming a percussionist. He played locally in Brazil, collected and studied over 120 different percussion instruments and in 1968 moved to the US with his wife, singer Flora Purim. Airto played with Miles Davis during part of 1969-70, appearing on several records (most notably *Live Evil*). He worked with Lee Morgan for a bit in 1971, was an original member of Weather Report and in 1972 was part of Chick Corea's initial version of Return to Forever with Flora Purim; he and Corea also recorded the classic *Captain Marvel* with Stan Getz. By 1973 Airto was famous enough to have his own group, signed to CTI and appearing on Purim's sessions. Since then he has stayed busy, mostly co-leading bands with his wife and recording as a leader for many labels including Buddah, CTI, Arista, Warner Bros, Caroline, Rykodisc, In & Out and B&W. Not all of his music as a leader would be called jazz, but Airto remains a very impressive player. —*Scott Yanow*

● **Free** / Apr. 1972-May 1972 / CTI ✦✦✦✦✦

Other than a couple of obscure efforts for Buddah in 1970, this was percussionist Airto's debut as a leader, and this is still his most famous record. A brass section arranged by Don Sebesky is heard on two tracks, and such all-stars as keyboardist Chick Corea, flutist Hubert Laws, the reeds of Joe Farrell and even pianist Keith Jarrett and guitarist George Benson make worthwhile appearances. Flora Purim joins Airto in the one vocal piece ("Free"), and "Return to Forever" receives an early recording. The music combines together jazz, Brazilian music and aspects of fusion and funk quite successfully. —*Scott Yanow*

The Best of Airto / April 1972-1974 / Columbia ✦✦✦✦✦

Without a doubt, Airto put a new face on Brazilian music in the wake of the bossa nova movement, bringing back the frantic complexity of the samba translated into his own frenzied yet controlled electronic/multi-percussion idiom. Here we truly have some of the best of his early work in the US as a leader for the CTI label, where Airto proves that he couldn't be suppressed even by the guiding hand of Creed Taylor. The set kicks off with a pair of great, sizzling tracks from the *Free* album, with Airto feverishly driving bands manned by Chick Corea on electric piano, Keith Jarrett on acoustic piano, and other American all-stars. From there, we move to the *Fingers* album, which features Airto's own band, yet maintains virtually the same level of excitement with a deeper Brazilian streak. The rare *Virgin Land*, released on the CTI subsidiary Salvation, sports a different cast of characters (notably Stanley Clarke and George Duke), but again is dominated by the ebullient percussionist's propulsive drumming and scatting. Finally, we hear the two Airto tracks from the old jerry-built *Deodato/Airto in Concert* LP in vastly superior sound, with Airto and Flora Purim whipping up the crowd at New York's Felt Forum with a primal display of wild native vocals and pushing rhythm. Of this music, only the two tracks from *Free* are otherwise available on CD, so Brazilian jazz addicts ought to be running to the stores for this one. —*Richard S. Ginell*

Fingers / Apr. 1973 / CTI ✦✦✦✦

Vocals by Flora Purim. Potent, uplifting music. Many familiar themes. —*Michael G. Nastos*

Virgin Land / 1974 / CTI ✦✦✦

Identity / 1975 / Arista ✦✦✦

Promises of the Sun / 1976 / Arista ✦✦

I'm Fine / 1977 / Warner Brothers ✦✦

Three-Way Mirror / 1985 / Reference ✦✦✦✦

Percussionist Airto Moreira, his wife, vocalist Flora Purim, and Joe Farrell (heard on flute, soprano and tenor) had teamed up several times through the years, most notably in the original version of "Return to Forever." Farrell would pass away just eight months after this album, but is still heard in fine form on the interesting set. Purim has vocals on three of the seven numbers (only "The Return" actually features Flora, Airto and Farrell playing together); Airto plays as much drums as percussion, and the music ranges from Brazilian jazz and slightly poppish to unclassifiable post-bop playing. Among the others musicians in the quartet/quintet settings are guitarist Jose Neto, pianist Kei Akagi and bassist Mark Egan. An atmospheric and at times haunting effort. —*Scott Yanow*

The Other Side of This / 1988 / Rykodisc ✦✦✦✦✦

Using voice, drum, whistle, chime, shakers, rattle, tambourine, and digeridoo, Airto and company make music that comes from all regions and belongs to none. These are songs for ritual and healing, based on many cultures. The mood is ethereal, yet because of the predominance of percussion, also powerful. New age music with punch. —*Steven McDonald*

Joe Morello

b. Jul. 17, 1928, Springfield, MA

Drums / Hard Bop, Cool

A brilliant drummer, Joe Morello played early on with Phil Woods and Sal Salvador. He had short stints during 1952-53 with Johnny Smith, Stan Kenton's Orchestra and Gil Melle, but really gained a strong reputation for his work with the Marian McPartland trio (1953-56); he also played during the period with Tal Farlow and Jimmy Raney. Morello gained fame as a member of the Dave Brubeck Quartet during 1956-67, making it possible for Brubeck to experiment with unusual time signatures. Due to his failing eyesight (he went blind in 1976) Morello has mostly worked as a drum instructor since (Danny Gottlieb was a student) but still plays and participates in reunions with Brubeck and McPartland. He has led sessions for Score (1956), RCA (1961-62), Ovation (1969) and DMP (1993-94). —*Scott Yanow*

Joe Morello Sextet / Jan. 3, 1956 / Intro ✦✦✦✦✦

● **Joe Morello** / Jun. 6, 1961+Nov. 13, 1962 / Bluebird ✦✦✦✦✦

It's About Time features ten songs with the word "time" in their title. Of these, five of the six quintet selections (starring Phil Woods and a young Gary Burton) and two of the four other songs (which have the quintet augmented by a brass section) are here, along with a totally unreleased big-band session from the following year. With Manny Albam contributing the arrangements, *It's About Time* is a pleasant surprise, a hard-driving set of swinging music. —*Scott Yanow*

Going Places / Apr. 1, 1993+Apr. 2, 1993 / DMP ✦✦✦✦

Drummer Joe Morello is in prime form for this rare opportunity to record as a leader. Morello takes a drum solo on the "*Mission: Impossible* Theme" and shares a duet with bassist Gary Mazzaroppi on "Autumn Leaves"; he also propels the solid rhythm section, which includes pianist Greg Kogan, while Ralph Lalama contributes tenor solos very much in the vein of 1950s Sonny Rollins. The strong repertoire and a certain amount of variety make this CD into an enjoyable bop date. —*Scott Yanow*

Morello Standard Time / 1994 / DMP ✦✦✦✦

Drummer Joe Morello's second date as a leader for DMP (and only third since 1962) uses the same lineup of musicians as the previous one: tenor saxophonist Ralph Lalama, pianist Greg Kogan and bassist Gary Mazzaroppi. Although a powerful drummer, Morello is mostly content to feature his sidemen, particularly the up-and-coming Lalama, whose style fits perfectly into late '50s hard bop. Highlights of the often delightful bop set include "Paper Moon," "Bye Bye Blackbird," "Doxy" and "Take Five." —*Scott Yanow*

Frank Morgan

b. Dec. 23, 1933, Minneapolis, MN

Alto Saxophone / Bop, Hard Bop

It is a real rarity for a jazz musician to have his career interrupted for a 30-year period and then be able to make a complete comeback. Frank Morgan showed a great deal of promise in his early days, but it was a long time before he could fulfill his potential. The son of guitarist Stanley Morgan (who played with the Ink Spots), he took up clarinet and alto early on. Morgan moved with his family to Los Angeles in 1947 and won a talent contest, leading to him recording a solo with Freddie Martin. Morgan worked on the bop scene of early-'50s Los Angeles, recording with Teddy Charles (1953) and Kenny Clarke (1954) and leading his own album for GNP in 1955. But then 30 years of darkness intruded. A heroin addict (following in the footsteps of his idol Charlie Parker), Morgan was arrested for possession of drugs and was in and out of jails for decades. He performed locally on an occasional basis, but it was not until 1985 when he had an opportunity to lead his second date. Morgan managed to permanently kick drugs and after an initial period during which he sounded very close to Charlie Parker, he developed his own bop-based style. Frank Morgan has recorded a string of excellent sets for Contemporary, Antilles and Telarc and has become an inspiring figure in the jazz world. —*Scott Yanow*

★ **Frank Morgan** / 1955 / GNP ✦✦✦✦✦
In 1955, when altoist Frank Morgan recorded his debut as a leader, he was being hyped as "the new bird." Unfortunately, he followed in Charlie Parker's footsteps mostly by becoming an irresponsible drug addict. Thirty years passed before he cut his second album and seriously began his successful comeback. The GNP album features Morgan back at the beginning, performing four numbers with Machito's rhythm section and six other songs with a septet that also includes tenor saxophonist Wardell Gray (heard on his final recordings). Trumpeter Conte Candoli is a major asset on both of these boppish dates, while Frank Morgan shows why he was rated so high at this point in his career. —*Scott Yanow*

● **Easy Living** / Jun. 1985 / Original Jazz Classics ✦✦✦✦✦
After nearly 30 years off the scene, altoist Frank Morgan made a remarkable comeback. Despite his years in prison and obscurity, he had not lost anything in his playing; in fact, he had grown as an individual. Teamed with pianist Cedar Walton, bassist Tony Dumas and drummer Billy Higgins, Morgan (still just 51) digs into songs by Walton, McCoy Tyner, Wayne Shorter and Antonio Carlos Jobim that had not been written when he had last recorded; in addition, he plays versions of three standards that recall his main inspiration, Charlie Parker. Morgan's improbable comeback after such a long period was fortunately permanent. This set (originally released by Contemporary) has been reissued on CD in the Original Jazz Classics series, and in addition to being a historic date, the music is excellent. —*Scott Yanow*

Lament / Apr. 1986 / Contemporary ✦✦✦✦
Frank Morgan's comeback (he had gone 30 years between recordings) was a major story in the mid-'80s. For his third record as a leader (which only followed his second by less than a year), the altoist is once again matched up with pianist Cedar Walton and drummer Billy Higgins, although this time Buster Williams is on bass. Morgan mixes together a few older tunes ("Perdido," Miles Davis' "Half Nelson" and J.J. Johnson's "Lament") with Lee Morgan's "Ceora," Wayne Shorter's "Black Diamond," an obscurity, and his "Thank You Blues." The music is high-quality bop, with Morgan shedding much of his Charlie Parker influence to display his own distinctive sound. —*Scott Yanow*

Double Image / May 21, 1986-May 22, 1986 / Contemporary ✦✦✦✦
This set of duets features altoist Frank Morgan (making such a successful comeback that he led three albums during 1986 alone) and pianist George Cables (who would also record notable duets with Art Pepper). Most of the material is of fairly recent vintage, but even the two potential warhorses ("All the Things You Are" and "After You've Gone") sound fresh and new in this sparse yet very complete setting. —*Scott Yanow*

Bebop Lives! / Dec. 14, 1986+Dec. 15, 1986 / Contemporary ✦✦✦✦✦
Altoist Frank Morgan pays tribute to his bebop beginnings on this live set from the Village Vanguard. He matches wits with fluegelhornist Johnny Coles, pianist Cedar Walton, bassist Buster Williams and drummer Billy Higgins. Morgan takes "Come Sunday" as his ballad feature, really putting a lot of emotion into the piece, and performs five bop standards (including a version of "A Night in Tunisia" that was added to the CD version of this release) and Jackie McLean's "Little Melonae" with the full group. The music often swings hard, and Morgan, although initially influenced strongly by Charlie Parker, sounds quite original, pushing at the tradition. —*Scott Yanow*

Quiet Fire / Mar. 26, 1987-Mar. 28, 1987 / Contemporary ✦✦✦✦

Major Changes / Apr. 1987 / Contemporary ✦✦✦✦
Although associated with bebop, altoist Frank Morgan emerged on records in 1985 as a forward-thinking soloist with a gradually evolving sound of his own (despite being in his early 50s). On this worthy set, he is joined by the McCoy Tyner Trio (which consists of the masterful pianist, bassist Avery Sharpe and drummer Louis Hayes) for mostly modern material. Tyner contributed three originals, including "Frank's Back," and the quartet also digs into "How Deep Is the Ocean," "Emily," "All the Things You Are," "So What" and even "Theme from *Love Story*." Morgan's lyricism works quite well with Tyner's powerful chords, and the results are consistently memorable. —*Scott Yanow*

☆ **Yardbird Suite** / Jan. 10, 1988+Jan. 11, 1988 / Contemporary ✦✦✦✦✦
Altoist Frank Morgan explores the bebop roots on this infectious set, playing six bop-era standards (four by his idol Charlie Parker) and "Skylark." With stimulating support from pianist Mulgrew Miller, bassist Ron Carter and drummer Al Foster, Morgan pays tribute to Bird, yet does not copy him (although he has the ability to

sometimes sound very similar to Parker). This spontaneous session (which includes such songs as "Yardbird Suite," "Scrapple from the Apple" and "Star Eyes") has its subtle surprises and is often hard-swinging. Recommended. —*Scott Yanow*

Reflections / Jan. 11, 1988+Jan. 12, 1988 / Contemporary ✦✦✦✦
Altoist Frank Morgan leads an all-star group on this excellent hard bop set. With tenor saxophonist Joe Henderson, vibraphonist Bobby Hutcherson, pianist Mulgrew Miller, bassist Ron Carter and drummer Al Foster also in the sextet, it is not surprising that Morgan sounds a bit inspired. The musicians all play up to their usual level, performing "Caravan" (which was added to the CD version) and Sonny Rollins' "Sonnymoon for Two," plus a song apiece by Thelonious Monk ("Reflections"), Miller, Hutcherson, Henderson and Carter. Recommended. —*Scott Yanow*

Mood Indigo / Jun. 26, 1989-Jun. 27, 1989 / Antilles ✦✦✦✦✦
This ballad-oriented set features veteran altoist Frank Morgan on four duets with pianist George Cables, interacting with either Cables or Ronnie Mathews on piano, bassist Buster Williams and drummer Al Foster on the other selections, and welcoming trumpeter Wynton Marsalis to "Bessie's Blues" and "Up Jumped Spring." Every Morgan recording is well worth picking up (the altoist has been very consistent in the studio), but this one purposely has less mood variation than most and is often a bit melancholy. —*Scott Yanow*

Jazz 'Round Midnight / Jun. 26, 1989-Nov. 27, 1993 / Verve ✦✦✦
This sampler CD from Verve has ten ballad-oriented performances featuring altoist Frank Morgan that are taken from four Antilles albums (*A Lovesome Thing, Listen to the Dawn, You Must Believe in Spring* and *Mood Indigo*). Serious collectors will want to pick up his complete sets, but those listeners who enjoy hearing Morgan's Charlie Parker-influenced alto at slower tempos may enjoy this overview. There are duets with guitarist Kenny Burrell and pianists Kenny Barron and Barry Harris, a vocal by Abbey Lincoln (on the passionate but somewhat unsuitable "Ten Cents a Dance") and cameos by trumpeter Roy Hargrove and Wynton Marsalis. —*Scott Yanow*

A Lonesome Thing / Sep. 5, 1990-Sep. 6, 1990 / Antilles ✦✦✦
Altoist Frank Morgan's unlikely comeback after 30 years off the scene was a successful fact by 1990. For this Antilles CD he is heard with a fine rhythm section (pianist George Cables, bassist David Williams and drummer Lewis Nash) and welcomes trumpeter Roy Hargrove to three songs. Guest singer Abbey Lincoln takes vocals on "Ten Cents a Dance" (lacking Ruth Etting's desperate hopelessness) and "Wholey Earth." Morgan plays a brief sweet version of "When You Wish Upon a Star" and performs several introspective ballads. There are no barnburners on the date, but overall the music is rewarding. —*Scott Yanow*

You Must Believe in Spring / Mar. 10, 1992-Mar. 11, 1992 / Antilles ✦✦✦✦
A '92 release by marvelous alto saxophonist Frank Morgan, whose life story and triumph over heroin addiction and imprisonment was one of the '80s' great success tales. Morgan's biting, yet sensitive and rich alto has rightly been traced to Charlie Parker, but Morgan long ago rid his style of any imitative excesses. He was excellently supported on this program of duets by an amazing lineup of rotating pianists: Kenny Barron, Tommy Flanagan, Barry Harris, Roland Hanna, and Hank Jones. —*Ron Wynn*

Listen to the Dawn / Apr. 19, 1993-Nov. 27, 1993 / Antilles ✦✦✦✦

Love, Lost & Found / Mar. 7, 1995-Mar. 9, 1995 / Telarc Jazz ✦✦✦✦

Bop / Aug. 19, 1996-Aug. 21, 1996 / Telarc ✦✦✦✦
Although all eight selections on this CD have been played many times before (the only song not a boppish warhorse is John Lewis' "Milano"), altoist Frank Morgan makes each of the pieces sound fresh. As producer John Snyder is quoted in the liner notes, this is bop without cliches. Morgan, who is assisted by pianist Rodney Kendrick, drummer Leroy Williams and either Curtis McLaurin or Ray Drummond on bass, digs into such songs as "Well You Needn't," "A Night in Tunisia" and an 11-minute version of "Half Nelson," coming up with some surprising twists and plenty of viable ideas. A fine effort. —*Scott Yanow*

Lanny Morgan (Harold Lansford Morgan)

b. Mar. 30, 1934, Des Moines, IA
Alto Saxophone / Bop

A superb altoist who is a bit underrated due to living in Los Angeles and not leading that many sessions of his own, Lanny Morgan grew up in L.A. He worked (starting in 1954) in the big bands of Charlie Barnet, Si Zenter, Terry Gibbs and Bob Florence, served in the military (which prevented him from joining Stan Kenton) and then spent the 1960-65 period playing with Maynard Ferguson's Orchestra. After freelancing in New York, he returned to Los Angeles in 1969. Morgan became a busy studio musician, a permanent member of Supersax and a reliable soloist in big bands led by Bill Berry, Bob Florence and Bill Holman. Lanny Morgan has led fine albums for Palo Alto (1981), V.S.O.P. (1993) and Contemporary (1996) and he still has few peers on "Cherokee." —*Scott Yanow*

It's About Time / Sep. 1982 / Palo Alto ◆◆◆◆

Having already been a highly skilled player for over 20 years, altoist Lanny Morgan's recorded debut as a leader was long overdue. The seven selections—four boppish originals, including the "Just Friends"-based "Friends Again," and three standards—match Morgan (who also plays a bit of soprano) with guitarist Bruce Forman, pianist Lou Levy, bassist Monty Budwig and drummer Nick Ceroli; Don Rader's fluegelhorn is added to the title cut. The music is heated bebop, with Morgan's runthrough of "Ko Ko" being a highlight. Such a pity that this Palo Alto LP (which has extensive liner notes by Herb Wong) has not yet been reissued on CD. —*Scott Yanow*

★ **The Lanny Morgan Quartet** / Jun. 11, 1993+Jun. 13, 1993 / V.S.O.P. ◆◆◆◆◆

Altoist Lanny Morgan, despite being a very talented bop-based improviser and a greatly in-demand sideman, has had relatively few opportunities to record as a leader through the years—only two. This quartet set with pianist Tom Ranier, bassist Bob Maize and drummer Frankie Capp is his definitive recording. Morgan is in particularly creative and fiery form on such songs as "Subconscious Lee," "Bloomdido," "After You've Gone" and a song he practically owns, "Cherokee." None of the nine tunes (eight jazz standards plus Tom Garvin's "Flash") are throwaways and this is a CD highly recommended to bop fans. —*Scott Yanow*

Pacific Standard Time / Sept. 1996-Oct. 1996 / Contemporary ◆◆◆◆◆

One of the great bebop altoists, Lanny Morgan can always be relied upon to enthusiastically dig into standards, preserving the melodies and chord changes but coming up with consistently fresh variations. On this Contemporary set, Morgan is joined by three of L.A.'s finest (pianist Tom Ranier, bassist Dave Carpenter and drummer Joe La Barbera), who give him stimulating and swinging support. Lanny mostly sticks to well-known standards, but somehow they sound new. "Stella by Starlight" is taken much faster than normal, "In the Still of the Night" cooks, "Body and Soul" is his ballad feature, "Spring Can Really Hang You Up the Most" is turned into a fast samba, and a blazing "It's You or No One" wraps up the ten-song session. There is not a throwaway track or routine moment in the 67 minutes of music, which is easily recommended to straightahead jazz fans. —*Scott Yanow*

Lee Morgan

b. Jul. 10, 1938, Philadelphia, PA, d. Feb. 19, 1972, New York, NY
Trumpet / Hard Bop

One of the great jazz trumpeters of the 1960s, Lee Morgan was the natural successor to Clifford Brown, making an impact on the scene shortly after Brownie's death and at first playing in a very similar style. He was a bit of a prodigy, working professionally in Philadelphia when he was 15 and joining Dizzy Gillespie's orchestra when he was barely 18. Morgan led his first Blue Note session later that year and he would record his first two classic albums for the label during 1957-58: *The Cooker* and *Candy*. Morgan was with Gillespie's band into 1958 when he became a member of Art Blakey's Jazz Messengers (1958-61), touring and recording extensively with the group and sharing the front line with Benny Golson, Hank Mobley and finally Wayne Shorter. Drug problems resulted in him quitting the band in 1961 and maintaining a low profile in Philadelphia until 1963. When Morgan came back, his first recording was his biggest hit, "The Sidewinder." He entered his greatest period, recording one memorable album after another, writing "Ceora" and "Speedball" and spending a second period with Blakey (1964-65). Morgan's playing became more adventurous and by the end of the decade he was exploring modal music, using some avant-garde elements and opening his playing to the influence of funk. On February 19, 1972 he was fatally shot by a girlfriend, ending his life at the age of 33. Lee Morgan recorded many records throughout his career as a sideman and he led 25 albums for Blue Note (coincidentally the same number as Hank Mobley) plus sessions for Vee-Jay, Roulette, Jazzland and Trip. —*Scott Yanow*

Presenting Lee Morgan / Nov. 4, 1956 / Blue Note ◆◆◆

Trumpeter Lee Morgan's debut as a leader finds him sounding surprisingly mature at the age of 18. On this LP, Morgan welcomes his fellow Philadelphian altoist Clarence Sharpe and an all-star rhythm section (pianist Horace Silver, bassist Wilbur Ware and drummer Philly Joe Jones) for six hard bop selections; best known among the compositions are Benny Golson's "Reggie of Chester" and Donald Byrd's "Little T." Although at this point Morgan was heavily influenced by Clifford Brown (who had died only a few months earlier), his playing was already quite impressive. —*Scott Yanow*

Complete Blue Note Lee Morgan Fifties Sessions / Nov. 4, 1956-Feb. 2, 1958 / Mosaic ◆◆◆◆◆

This four-CD limited-edition box set from Mosaic reissues trumpeter Lee Morgan's first six albums as a leader: *Indeed, Volume Two, Volume Three, City Lights, The Cooker* and *Candy*. There are also four additional selections from the sessions. Just 18 and 19 during this period, Lee Morgan was already far along towards developing a sound of his own that was originally influenced by Clifford Brown, and playing regularly with Dizzy Gillespie's big band. Morgan was joined by the obscure altoists Clarence Sharpe and Kenny Rodgers on his first two albums (along with tenor saxophonist Hank Mobley, pianist Horace Silver, Wilbur Ware or Paul Chambers on bass and either Philly Joe Jones or Charlie Persip on drums), but it was on his third record (a sextet set featuring Benny Golson's writing) that he began to sound mature, particularly on the early version of "I Remember Clifford." Although joined by trombonist Curtis Fuller and tenorman George Coleman on *City Lights*, Morgan was heard at his best on the final two dates: a quintet outing with baritonist Pepper Adams and pianist Bobby Timmons (highlighted by "A Night in Tunisia") and a quartet showcase with pianist Sonny Clark. Overall, the performances are not quite as essential as Lee Morgan's upcoming Blue Note albums and sessions with Art Blakey, but there is a great deal of rewarding hard bop music to be heard on these dates. —*Scott Yanow*

A-1—The Savoy Sessions / Nov. 5, 1956-Nov. 7, 1956 / Savoy ◆◆◆

Trumpeter Lee Morgan, then 18 and at the beginning of his career (his recording debut as a leader resulted in a Blue Note album the day before his brief stint with Savoy began), co-led this session with tenor saxophonist Hank Mobley. Pianist Hank Jones, bassist Doug Watkins and drummer Art Taylor form a tasteful rhythm section behind the lead voices who are in fine form on Fats Navarro's "Nostalgia," originals by Mobley and Watkins, and a four-song ballad medley. Although not essential, this hard bop-oriented LP gives one a good early look at Lee Morgan when he was just 18. —*Scott Yanow*

Lee Morgan, Vol. 2 / Dec. 2, 1956 / Blue Note ◆◆◆◆

Trumpeter Lee Morgan's second recording as a leader (which has been reissued in his four-CD "complete on Blue Note" Mosaic box set) is as notable for the writing of Benny Golson (who composed and arranged four of the six selections) as for the solos of the leader. The set is highlighted by the debut version of "Whisper Not." Actually, Morgan, tenor saxophonist Hank Mobley, pianist Horace Silver, bassist Paul Chambers, drummer Charlie Persip and the obscure altoist Kenny Rodgers all play quite well. Morgan was just 18 and starting to come out of the shadow of his early influence Clifford Brown. An above-average hard bop set. —*Scott Yanow*

Dizzy Atmosphere / Feb. 1957 / Original Jazz Classics ◆◆◆◆

This somewhat obscure Lee Morgan set (originally cut for Specialty and made available on CD in the OJC series) features the trumpeter with other then-current members of the Dizzy Gillespie big band: trombonist Al Grey, tenor saxophonist Billy Mitchell, baritonist Billy Root, pianist Wynton Kelly, bassist Paul West and drummer Charlie Persip. With arrangements provided by Benny Golson and Roger Spotts, the music is modern bop for the period. Highlights include the ten-and-a-half-minute "Dishwater," "Over the Rainbow" and what was probably the first-ever version of Golson's "Whisper Not." Morgan plays extremely well throughout the spirited set, and he was just 18 at the time. —*Scott Yanow*

Lee Morgan, Vol. 3 / Mar. 24, 1957 / Blue Note ◆◆◆◆

Although trumpeter Lee Morgan (then only 18) was the nominal leader of this set, tenor saxophonist Benny Golson contributed all five of the compositions and did the arrangements for the sextet (which also includes altoist Gigi Gryce, pianist Wynton Kelly, bassist Paul Chambers and drummer Charlie Persip). Most notable among the songs is the original version of "I Remember Clifford"; Morgan was the perfect trumpeter to play the tribute to Clifford Brown, who had died in a car crash a year earlier. This CD reissue (a fine hard bop date) adds an alternate take of "Tip-Toeing" to the original program. —*Scott Yanow*

City Lights / Aug. 25, 1957 / Blue Note ◆◆◆◆

Benny Golson's writing for this date uplifts it beyond most of the jam session sets of the period. Trumpeter Lee Morgan (then 19) is in excellent form, holding his own with his impressive sidemen (trombonist Curtis Fuller, George Coleman on tenor and alto, pianist Ray Bryant, bassist Paul Chambers and drummer Art Taylor). Highlights include "City Lights," "You're Mine You" and "Just By Myself." This fine session has been reissued as part of Lee Morgan's four-CD Mosaic box set. —*Scott Yanow*

The Cooker / Sep. 29, 1957 / Blue Note ◆◆◆◆◆

The trumpeter, then just 19, teams up with baritonist Pepper Adams, pianist Bobby Timmons, bassist Paul Chambers and drummer Philly Joe Jones for a particularly strong set that is highlighted by a lengthy and fiery "Night in Tunisia," "Lover Man" and a rapid rendition of "Just One of Those Things." Morgan plays remarkably well for his age (already ranking just below Dizzy Gillespie and Miles Davis), making this an essential acquisition. —*Scott Yanow*

★ **Candy** / Nov. 18, 1957 / Blue Note ◆◆◆◆◆

Lee Morgan's only quartet album is one of his best. Although only 19 at the time, Morgan already had a mature style, a sound influenced by Clifford Brown and a near-complete mastery of the bop vocabulary. With the strong assistance of pianist Sonny Clark, bassist Doug Watkins and drummer Art Taylor, Morgan is very expressive and creative on this CD reissue, particularly on such songs as "Candy," "Since I Fell for You," "All the Way" and even "Personality." —*Scott Yanow*

Here's Lee Morgan / Feb. 2, 1960-Feb. 8, 1960 / Vee-Jay ♦♦♦♦

This CD reissue has its original six songs expanded to 11 with the inclusion of five alternate takes. The music is good solid hard bop that finds Lee Morgan (already a veteran at age 21) coming out of the Clifford Brown tradition to display his own rapidly developing style. Matched with Clifford Jordan on tenor, pianist Wynton Kelly, bassist Paul Chambers and drummer Art Blakey, Morgan's album could pass for a Jazz Messengers set. —*Scott Yanow*

Leeway / Apr. 28, 1960 / Blue Note ♦♦♦♦

This date was one of trumpeter Lee Morgan's more obscure Blue Note sessions, but fortunately, it has been reissued on CD. Matched with altoist Jackie McLean, pianist Bobby Timmons, bassist Paul Chambers and drummer Art Blakey, Morgan interprets two of Calvin Massey's compositions, McLean's "Midtown Blues" and his own blues "The Lion and the Wolff." The music is essentially hard bop with a strong dose of soul; the very distinctive styles of the principals are the main reasons to acquire this enjoyable music. —*Scott Yanow*

Minor Strain / May 12, 1960+Jul. 1960 / Roulette ♦♦♦

Lee Morgan shares this CD reissue with fellow trumpeter Thad Jones. Morgan's three selections feature a quintet with tenor saxophonist Wayne Shorter, pianist Bobby Timmons, bassist Jimmy Roser and drummer Art Taylor. While that hard bop group democratically performs one original apiece from Morgan, Timmons and Shorter, Thad Jones' date has four of his songs plus a previously unissued alternate take of "Subtle Rebuttal"; best known is "Tip Toe" which was later recorded by the Thad Jones/Mel Lewis Orchestra. Jones' septet is filled with Count Basie sidemen (trombonist Al Grey and tenors Billy Mitchell and Frank Wess) along with a fine rhythm section (pianist Hank Jones, bassist Richard Davis and drummer Osie Johnson) and is more swing-oriented than the Morgan group, but the two sets are equally rewarding. —*Scott Yanow*

Expoobident / Oct. 14, 1960 / Vee-Jay ♦♦♦

Trumpeter Lee Morgan is heard on this CD reissue (which augments the original LP with four additional alternate takes) when he was 22 and near the end of his first stint with Art Blakey's Jazz Messengers. Morgan heads a first-class hard bop quintet that also includes tenor saxophonist Clifford Jordan, pianist Eddie Higgins, bassist Art Davis and drummer Blakey and together they perform two standards and five originals. The results are not as essential as Morgan's best Blue Note albums but this set swings and should please fans of hard bop. —*Scott Yanow*

Take Twelve / Jan. 24, 1962 / Original Jazz Classics ♦♦♦♦

This CD reissue (which adds an alternate take of "Second's Best" to the original LP program) was trumpeter Lee Morgan's only recording during an off-period that lasted from mid-1961 to late 1963. Morgan (who sounds in fine form) leads a quintet with tenor saxophonist Clifford Jordan, pianist Barry Harris, bassist Bob Cranshaw and drummer Louis Hayes through four of his originals, Jordan's "Little Spain" and the title cut, an Elmo Hope composition. The superior material uplifts the set from being a mere "blowing" date but it generally has the spontaneity of a jam session. It's one of Lee Morgan's lesser-known dates. —*Scott Yanow*

★ The Sidewinder / Dec. 21, 1963 / Blue Note ♦♦♦♦♦

This album is trumpeter Lee Morgan's best-known recording; the catchy title cut became a hit, launched the boogaloo fad and is still performed decades later. The CD reissue (which adds an alternate take of "Totem Pole" to the original set) finds Morgan at the peak of his powers (where he would remain for the next four or five years) as the leading trumpeter in hard bop. The young (and already immediately recognizable) tenor Joe Henderson, pianist Barry Harris, bassist Bob Cranshaw and drummer Billy Higgins also make strong contributions to this well-rounded program which includes four other memorable Morgan originals: "Totem Pole," "Gary's Notebook," "Boy, What a Night" and "Hocus-Pocus." —*Scott Yanow*

Jazz Profile / 1963-1969 / Blue Note ♦♦

Trumpeter Lee Morgan was one of Blue Note's most important artists in the 1960s. This CD sampler has six rewarding numbers that are easily available elsewhere, not representing the "best" of Lee Morgan but just random spots in his busy recording career. His big hit "The Sidewinder" is naturally here, but the other choices ("C.T.A.," "Trapped," "Twilight Mist," "Our Man Higgins" and "The Procrastinator") were not inevitable. Surprisingly, "Candy" and "Ceora" are absent, as are Morgan's later, more modal explorations. This CD works as an introduction, but anyone with a few Lee Morgan sets can feel free to pass it by. —*Scott Yanow*

☆ Search for the New Land / Feb. 15, 1964 / Blue Note ♦♦♦♦♦

This set (the CD reissue is a duplicate of the original LP) is one of the finest Lee Morgan records. The great trumpeter contributes five challenging compositions ("Search for the New Land," "The Joker," "Mr. Kenyatta," "Melanchole" and "Morgan the Pirate"); songs that deserve to be revived. Morgan, tenor saxophonist

Wayne Shorter, guitarist Grant Green, pianist Herbie Hancock, bassist Reggie Workman and drummer Billy Higgins are all in particularly creative form on the fresh material and they stretch the boundaries of hard bop (the modern mainstream jazz of the period). The result is a consistently stimulating set that rewards repeated listenings. —*Scott Yanow*

Tom Cat / Aug. 11, 1964 / Blue Note ♦♦♦♦

It seems strange that the music on this CD was not released initially until 1980. Trumpeter Lee Morgan had had an unexpected hit with "The Sidewinder," so his more challenging recordings were temporarily put aside. As it turns out, this was one of Morgan's better sets from the 1960s and he had gathered together quite an all-star cast: altoist Jackie McLean, trombonist Curtis Fuller, pianist McCoy Tyner, bassist Bob Cranshaw and drummer Art Blakey. They perform "Rigormortis," McCoy Tyner's "Twilight Mist" and three of the trumpeter's originals including the title cut. The advanced hard bop music still sounds fresh decades later, despite its initial neglect. —*Scott Yanow*

Rumproller / Apr. 21, 1965 / Blue Note ♦♦♦

To follow up on his unexpected boogaloo hit "The Sidewinder," Lee Morgan recorded Andrew Hill's somewhat similar "The Rumproller," but this time the commercial magic was not there. However, the trumpeter, tenor saxophonist Joe Henderson, pianist Ronnie Mathews, bassist Victor Sproles and drummer Billy Higgins all play quite well on the title cut, two of Morgan's songs (the bossa nova "Eclipso" is somewhat memorable), a ballad tribute to Billie Holiday and Wayne Shorter's "Edda." This album is worth picking up, but it is not essential. —*Scott Yanow*

The Gigolo / Jun. 25, 1965+Jul. 1, 1965 / Blue Note ♦♦♦♦♦

Lee Morgan was the leading trumpeter in hard bop during the 1960s and he recorded quite a few classic albums for Blue Note. This is one of them. The CD reissue (which adds an alternate take of the title cut to the original five-song program) features Morgan at his best, whether playing his memorable blues "Speed Ball," an explorative ballad version of "You Go to My Head," a lengthy "The Gigolo" or his other two originals ("Yes I Can, No You Can't" and "Trapped"). There are no weak selections on this set and the playing by the leader, Wayne Shorter on tenor, pianist Harold Mabern, bassist Bob Cranshaw and drummer Billy Higgins is beyond any serious criticism. —*Scott Yanow*

☆ Cornbread / Sep. 8, 1965 / Blue Note ♦♦♦♦♦

This session (reissued on CD by Blue Note) is best known for introducing Lee Morgan's beautiful ballad "Ceora," but actually all five selections (which include Morgan's "Cornbread," "Our Man Higgins," "Most like Lee" and the standard "Ill Wind") are quite memorable. The trumpeter/leader performs with a perfectly complementary group of open-minded and talented hard bop stylists (altoist Jackie McLean, Hank Mobley on tenor, pianist Herbie Hancock, bassist Larry Ridley and drummer Billy Higgins) and creates a Blue Note classic that is heartily recommended. —*Scott Yanow*

Infinity / Nov. 16, 1965 / Blue Note ♦♦♦♦

Although recorded in 1965, this excellent Lee Morgan Quintet session (which features the trumpeter with altoist Jackie McLean, pianist Larry Willis, bassist Reggie Workman and drummer Billy Higgins) was not released until 1980 on this LP and then went quickly out of print. It deserved much better fate. The music, although tied to the hard bop tradition, is challenging and (with the exception of the closing uptempo blues "Zip Code") tricky, really challenging the talented players. This is an album worth searching for (and one that Blue Note should reissue). —*Scott Yanow*

Delightfulee / Apr. 8, 1966+May 27, 1966 / Blue Note ♦♦♦♦♦

This classic set by trumpeter Lee Morgan was reissued on LP in 1984 but has not yet appeared on CD. Of the four quintet numbers with tenor saxophonist Joe Henderson, pianist McCoy Tyner, bassist Bob Cranshaw and drummer Billy Higgins, the instantly likable "Ca-Lee-So" is the most memorable, although the other three Morgan originals ("Zambia," "Nite Flite" and "The Delightful Deggie") also find the trumpeter in excellent form. An unusual aspect to this collection is that there are also two ballads ("Yesterday" and "Sunrise Sunset") that have a nonet playing Oliver Nelson arrangements behind Morgan's lyrical horn; Tyner and tenor saxophonist Wayne Shorter have opportunities to take concise solos. —*Scott Yanow*

Charisma / Sep. 29, 1966 / Blue Note ♦♦♦♦

This set (reissued on CD in 1997) was one of trumpeter Lee Morgan's lesser-known Blue Notes, but it is quite rewarding. The notable sextet (which also includes altoist Jackie McLean, Hank Mobley on tenor, pianist Cedar Walton, bassist Paul Chambers and drummer Billy Higgins) performs originals by Morgan, Walton and Duke Pearson, including particularly catchy versions of the funky "Hey Chico" and Pearson's memorable "Sweet Honey Bee" (which should have become a hit). The three horns, all of whom sound quite individual, each have their exciting moments, and the results are quintessential mid-1960s hard bop. —*Scott Yanow*

The Rajah / Nov. 29, 1966 / Blue Note ✦✦✦

This long-lost Lee Morgan session was not released for the first time until it was discovered in the Blue Note vaults by Michael Cuscuna in 1984; it has still not been reissued on CD. Originals by Cal Massey, Duke Pearson ("Is That So") and Walter Davis, in addition to a couple of surprising pop tunes ("What Not My Love" and "Once in My Lifetime") and Morgan's title cut, are well played by the quintet (which includes the trumpeter/leader, Hank Mobley on tenor, pianist Cedar Walton, bassist Paul Chambers and drummer Billy Higgins). Much of the music is reminiscent of the Jazz Messengers and that may have been the reason that it was lost in the shuffle, for Morgan was soon investigating modal-oriented tunes. Despite its neglect, this is a fine session that Lee Morgan and hard bop fans will want. —*Scott Yanow*

Standards / Jan. 13, 1967 / Blue Note ✦✦✦

Standards is a previously unreleased session capturing Lee Morgan leading a septet—featuring Wayne Shorter, Pepper Adams, James Spaulding, Herbie Hancock, Ron Carter and Mickey Roker—through a selection of six standards ("Blue Gardenia" is repeated as an alternate take), as arranged by Duke Pearson. The septet never gets unwieldy, thanks to Pearson's clever arrangements, which give everyone room to move. Even though every musician has their own moment on *Standards*, the session appropriately functions as a showcase for Morgan's exceptional, lyrical ballad style. His playing is beautiful and moving, making *Standards* a minor gem in his catalog. —*Stephen Thomas Erlewine*

Sonic Boom / Apr. 14, 1967 / Blue Note ✦✦✦✦

This well-rounded LP was not released until 1979 and then remained in print only for a brief time. In addition to the great trumpeter Lee Morgan and a fine rhythm section (pianist Cedar Walton, bassist Ron Carter and drummer Billy Higgins), the set is a bit special, for it allows the often R&B-associated tenor David "Fathead" Newman an opportunity to stretch out in a more challenging setting than usual. Highlights include the funky "Fathead," the complex "Sneaky Pete," Morgan's lyricism on "I'll Never Be the Same" and the infectious rhythms on "Mumbo Jumbo." This is an undeservedly obscure session. —*Scott Yanow*

The Procrastinator / Jul. 14, 1967 / Blue Note ✦✦✦✦✦

This out-of-print double LP from 1978 released for the first time a pair of "lost" Lee Morgan albums. The music (from 1967 and 1969) falls into the category of advanced hard bop with the influence of the avant-garde and modal jazz mixing in with the trumpeter's roots in Art Blakey's brand of hard bop. The earlier date has a particularly impressive lineup of talent (tenor saxophonist Wayne Shorter, vibraphonist Bobby Hutcherson, pianist Herbie Hancock, bassist Ron Carter and drummer Billy Higgins) while the later album is not exactly a throwaway since it features trombonist Julian Priester, George Coleman on tenor, pianist Harold Mabern, bassist Walter Booker and drummer Mickey Roker. There are many highlights to this enjoyable (but now difficult-to-locate) two-fer as Morgan and his contemporaries perform 12 group originals plus the lone standard "Stormy Weather." —*Scott Yanow*

The Sixth Sense / Nov. 10, 1967 / Blue Note ✦✦✦

For this lesser-known Lee Morgan LP, the trumpeter was starting to stretch beyond hard bop into more modal areas while retaining his easily recognizable sound. None of Morgan's originals (which are performed along with pianist Cedar Walton's "Afreaka" and Cal Massey's "The Cry of My People") caught on, but the music is creatively performed by the trumpeter, altoist Jackie McLean (who was always a perfect musical partner), the obscure tenor Frank Mitchell, Walton, bassist Victor Sproles and drummer Billy Higgins. —*Scott Yanow*

Taru / Feb. 15, 1968 / Blue Note ✦✦✦✦

Trumpeter Lee Morgan performs two funky boogaloos, a ballad and three complex group originals on this out-of-print LP whose music was first released in 1980. This is a transitional date with the hard bop stylist leaning in the direction of modal music and even anticipating aspects of fusion. His sextet (which includes Bennie Maupin on tenor, guitarist George Benson, pianist John Hicks, bassist Reggie Workman and drummer Billy Higgins) is quite advanced for the period and inspires Morgan to some fiery and explorative playing. —*Scott Yanow*

Caramba / May 3, 1968 / Blue Note ✦✦✦

Until its 1996 reissue, this was one of the most obscure of all Lee Morgan Blue Note albums. A transitional effort that finds the trumpeter gradually moving beyond hard bop into more modal music, the date starts out with the surprisingly derivative title cut which is very similar to Eddie Harris' "Listen Here." Of the other selections, "Soulita" has the catchiest melody while Cal Massey's slow ballad "A Baby's Smile" was previously unreleased. While Morgan and his fine rhythm section (pianist Cedar Walton, bassist Reggie Workman and drummer Billy Higgins) are in typically swinging form, *Caramba* is most notable for featuring the young Bennie Maupin. Sticking exclusively to tenor, Maupin (who would be much more

distinctive within a year) mixes together Joe Henderson and Wayne Shorter in winning fashion. Although not essential, this CD is a welcome reissue. —*Scott Yanow*

Live at the Lighthouse / Jul. 10, 1970-Jul. 12, 1970 / Blue Note ✦✦✦✦✦

Formerly a double-LP with four lengthy explorations, this release came back in 1966 as a three-CD set with 12 performances! Lee Morgan's next-to-last recording, features trumpeter's regular quintet of the period (with Bennie Maupin on tenor, flute and bass clarinet, pianist Harold Mabern, bassist Jymie Merritt and drummer Mickey Roker). The music is very modal-oriented and probably disappointed many of Morgan's longtime fans, but he had gotten tired of playing the same hard bop-styled music that he had excelled at during the past decade and was searching for newer sounds. The influence of the avant-garde and early fusion is also felt in spots, but the trumpeter's sound was still very much intact and he takes some fiery solos that still sound lively decades later. —*Scott Yanow*

Lee Morgan / Sep. 17, 1971-Sep. 18, 1971 / Blue Note ✦✦

The final recording by Lee Morgan, this double LP has its moments but is somewhat erratic with some modal-oriented selections that ramble on too long and a forgettable debut (on "Croquet Ballet") for the trumpeter's discovery, flutist Bobbi Humphrey. Morgan (who was still just 33) is in generally good form and his band (with Billy Harper on tenor, keyboardist Harold Mabern, Jymie Merritt or Reggie Workman on bass and drummer Freddie Waits) is quite stimulating, but the music has an uncomfortable and incomplete feel to it. It does leave one wondering what Lee Morgan would have done next had he lived. —*Scott Yanow*

Butch Morris (Lawrence Morris)

b. Feb. 10, 1947, Long Beach, CA
Cornet, Conductor / Avant-Garde

In recent years, Butch Morris has worked on what he calls "conduction." By utilizing a vast array of hand signals, he is able to push an improvising ensemble in any direction he wants without actually playing an instrument. Morris is actually a fine mellow-toned cornetist although his playing has often taken second place behind his writing. The brother of bassist Wilber Morris, Morris played with Horace Tapscott, Bobby Bradford and Frank Lowe in California in the early '70s, worked in New York in 1975 with Charles Tyler, Hamiet Bluiett and David Murray, lived in Paris during 1976-77 (recording with Steve Lacy) and returned to the US, Morris has been closely associated with David Murray during the past 20 years, playing in his octet and conducting his big band. Butch Morris has led sessions for Kharma, Sound Aspects and New World, including a recent ten-CD set of his "Conductions." —*Scott Yanow*

Current Trends in Racism in Modern America / Feb. 1985 / Sound Aspects ✦✦✦✦✦

● **Dust to Dust** / Nov. 18, 1990-Nov. 20, 1990 / New World ✦✦✦✦✦

A fine large-group recording. The ensemble has several top players, including Wayne Horvitz (k), Marty Ehrlich (reeds), and John Purcell (reeds). Morris conducts and supervises with his usual skill. —*Ron Wynn*

James Morrison

b. Nov. 11, 1962, Australia
Trumpet, Trombone / Bop, Swing

A natural musician able to play many instruments in numerous styles, James Morrison has made a strong impression every time he has played in the US. Born into a musical family, Morrison began on the cornet when he was seven and was soon also playing trombone, tuba and euphonium. Within a few years, he was also playing alto sax and leading a Dixieland band. He worked steadily as a teenager and at the age of 18 joined Don Burrows' quintet, touring Australia and the Far East. In 1987, he visited the US as a member of Red Rodney's group and was soon a popular fixture on the European jazz festival circuit. Two years later, a pair of his albums (*Postcards from Down Under* and *Swiss Encounter*) were released on Atlantic at the same time in the US, and he toured with Gene Harris' Philip Morris Superband as a trombonist. To show off his versatility, on his 1991 album *Snappy Doo* (which also includes a rhythm section), Morrison overdubbed himself on four trumpets, four trombones, five saxophones and piano. In addition to playing music (he has the ability to trade fours with himself on trumpet and trombone), James Morrison does stunt flying, climbs mountains and drives a racing car. —*Scott Yanow*

Swiss Encounter/Live at the Montreux Jazz Festival / Jul. 1988 / East West ✦✦✦✦

On his jazz waltz "My Delight," James Morrison plays trombone with such ease and authority that he could be excused if he chose to stick exclusively to that instrument. Actually, that would be a shame, for Morrison is an equally talented trumpeter (sounding a little like Clifford Brown), altoist and pianist; he also flies planes and climbs mountains. On *Swiss Encounter*, Morrison doubles on trumpet and trombone, demonstrating his wide range and mastery of bop. Pianist Adam Makowicz, whose viruosity is often taken for granted, clearly enjoyed playing with Morrison, creating intense and witty solos that fit in well with his co-leader's powerful flights; bassist Buster Williams and drummer Al Foster complete the quartet. On "Blues for Judy," Morrison uses multiphonics expertly on trombone and at one point trades two-bar phrases between both his trumpet and trombone! This somewhat obscure release (which was originally made available through Atlantic) is well worth searching for. —*Scott Yanow*

Postcards from Down Under / 1989 / Atlantic ◆◆◆
A collaboration between James Morrison and artist Ken Done, this fairly obscure Atlantic set finds Morrison and pianist Garry Dial performing nine originals that were inspired by Done's paintings; in a few cases, Done reversed the process by creating a painting based on his impressions of Morrison's music. The performances (featuring the leader on trumpet, fluegelhorn, trombone, the EVI, baritone horn and organ, Dial, guitarist Steve Brien, electric bassist Victor Rounds and drummer John Morrison) are solid, sometimes impressionistic and generally straightahead, although none of the individual songs would catch on. —*Scott Yanow*

● **Snappy Doo** / 1990 / Atlantic ◆◆◆◆◆
This is an impressive outing. James Morrison, who is equally skilled on trumpet and trombone (exhibiting wide ranges, a skill at improvising in a personal bop style, and a witty sense of humor), creates his own big band on six selections, augmenting his main axes by overdubbing on euphonium, alto, tenor, baritone and piano while joined by guitarist Herb Ellis, bassist Ray Brown and drummer Jeff Hamilton. In addition, Morrison's arrangement of "Le Belleclarie Blues" shows off his writing talents. The wide variety of music (mixing together standards and originals) makes for a very colorful set, and Morrison displays his own personality on each of his many axes. Working within the tradition, James Morrison is heard finding his own unique niche. —*Scott Yanow*

The Pure Genius of James Morrison / May 13, 1991 / Shanachie ◆◆◆

Jelly Roll Morton (Ferdinand Joseph Lemott)

b. Oct. 20, 1890, New Orleans, LA, **d.** Jul. 10, 1941, Los Angeles, CA
Piano, Composer, Leader / Classic New Orleans Jazz, Traditional Jazz
One of the very first giants of jazz, Jelly Roll Morton did himself a lot of harm posthumously by exaggerating his worth, claiming to have invented jazz in 1902. Morton's accomplishments as an early innovator are so vast that he did not really need to stretch the truth.

Morton was jazz's first great composer, writing such songs as "King Porter Stomp," "Grandpa's Spells," "Wolverine Blues," "The Pearls," "Mr. Jelly Roll," "Shreveport Stomp," "Milenburg Joys," "Black Bottom Stomp," "The Chant," "Original Jelly Roll Blues," "Doctor Jazz," "Wild Man Blues," "Winin' Boy Blues," "I Thought I Heard Buddy Bolden Say," "Don't You Leave Me Here," and "Sweet Substitute." He was a talented arranger (1926's "Black Bottom Stomp" is remarkable), getting the most out of the three-minute limitations of the 78 record by emphasizing changing instrumentation, concise solos and dynamics. He was a greatly underrated pianist who had his own individual style. Although he only took one vocal on records in the 1920s ("Doctor Jazz"), Morton in his late-'30s recordings proved to be an effective vocalist. And he was a true character.

Jelly Roll Morton's pre-1923 activities are shrouded in legend. He started playing piano when he was ten, worked in the bordellos of Storyville while a teenager (for which some of his relatives disowned him) and by 1904 was traveling throughout the South. He spent time in other professions (as a gambler, pool player, vaudeville comedian and even a pimp) but always returned to music. The chances are good that in 1915 Morton had few competitors among pianists and he was an important transition figure between ragtime and early jazz. He played in Los Angeles during 1917-22 and then moved to Chicago where for the next six years he was at his peak. Morton's 1923-24 recordings of piano solos introduced his style, repertoire and brilliance. Although his earliest band sides were quite primitve, his 1926-27 recordings for Victor with his Red Hot Peppers are among the most exciting of his career. With such sidemen as cornetist George Mitchell, Kid Ory or Gerald Reeves on trombone, clarinetists Omer Simeon, Barney Bigard, Darnell Howard or Johnny Dodds, occasionally Stomp Evans on C-melody, Johnny St. Cyr or Bud Scott on banjo, bassist John Lindsay and either Andrew Hilaire or Baby Dodds on drums, Morton had the perfect ensembles for his ideas. He also recorded some exciting trios with Johnny and Baby Dodds.

With the center of jazz shifting to New York by 1928, Morton relocated. His bragging ways unfortunately hurt his career and he was not able to always get the sidemen he wanted. His Victor recordings continued through 1930 and, although some of the performances are sloppy or erratic, there were also a few more classics. Among the musicians Morton was able to use on his New York records were

trumpeters Ward Pinkett, Red Allen and Bubber Miley, trombonists Geechie Fields, Charles Irvis and J.C. Higginbotham, clarinetists Omer Simeon, Albert Nicholas and Barney Bigard, banjoist Lee Blair, guitarist Bernard Addison, Bill Benford on tuba, bassist Pops Foster and drummers Tommy Benford, Paul Barbarin and Zutty Singleton.

But with the rise of the Depression, Jelly Roll Morton drifted into obscurity. He had made few friends in New York, his music was considered old-fashioned and he did not have the temperament to work as a sideman. During 1931-37 his only appearance on records was on a little-known Wingy Manone date. He ended up playing in a Washington D.C. dive for patrons who had little idea of his contributions. Ironically, Morton's "King Porter Stomp" became one of the most popular songs of the swing era, but few knew that he wrote it. However, in 1938 Alan Lomax recorded him in an extensive and fascinating series of musical interviews for the Library of Congress. Morton's storytelling was colorful and his piano playing in generally fine form as he reminisced about old New Orleans and demonstrated the other piano styles of the era. A decade later the results would finally be released on albums.

Morton arrived in New York in 1939 determined to make a comeback. He did lead a few band sessions with such sidemen as Sidney Bechet, Red Allen and Albert Nicholas and recorded some wonderful solo sides, but none of those were big sellers. In late 1940 an ailing Morton decided to head out to Los Angeles but, when he died at the age of 50, he seemed like an old man. Ironically, his music soon became popular again as the New Orleans jazz revivalist movement caught fire and, if he had lived just a few more years, the chances are good that he would have been restored to his former prominence (as was Kid Ory).

Jelly Roll Morton's early piano solos and classic Victor recordings (along with nearly every record he made) have been reissued on CD. —*Scott Yanow*

★ **Jelly Roll Morton** / Jun. 9, 1923-Feb. 2, 1926 / Milestone ◆◆◆◆◆
The legendary Jelly Roll Morton recorded many of his finest piano solos for Gennett and Paramount during 1923-24 and all 20 (counting a second version of "New Orleans Joys") are on this essential CD; high points include the original versions of "King Porter Stomp," "Grandpa's Spells," "Wolverine Blues" and "The Pearls." in addition there are four early (and surprisingly primitive) band performances (including a version of "Mr. Jelly Lord" from 1926) and two piano-cornet duets with King Oliver. This single CD differs from the earlier two-LP set in that it leaves out a few of Morton's less significant 1924 band sides but includes the Oliver duets and the second "New Orleans Joys." —*Scott Yanow*

★ **Ferd "Jelly Roll" Morton** / Jul. 17, 1923-Apr. 20, 1926 / Retrieval ◆◆◆◆◆
This CD reissue from the British Retrieval label has Jelly Roll Morton's first 24 piano solos. The earlier 20 have been issued several times by Milestone but it is convenient to have all 24 (dating from 1923-24 and 1926) together. Morton, who had a very distinctive style, was one of the early jazz giants and his piano playing (a major transition between ragtime and New Orleans jazz) tends to be a bit underrated. Highlights of this delightful set include "Grandpa's Spells," "Wolverine Blues," "Froggie Moore," "Shreveport Stomps" and two versions apiece of "King Porter Stomp" and "The Pearls." Classic music. —*Scott Yanow*

Rarities, Vol. 2 / Oct. 19, 1923-Aug. 1934 / Rhapsody ◆◆◆◆◆
This LP gives Jelly Roll Morton collectors some of the odds and ends that they might have missed in only acquiring the Victor and Milestone releases. The legendary pianist/composer is heard in 1923 on two primitive numbers with a quintet, on the obscure "Soap Suds" in 1926, performing four hot numbers with cornetist Johnny Dunn's band in 1928, participating in his only recordings from the 1931-37 period (two songs with Wingy Manone in 1934), playing four superb piano solos in 1926 (including a definitive version of "King Porter Stomp"), and leading groups behind singers Edmonia Henderson in 1926 and Frances Hereford in 1928. This highly enjoyable set has more than its share of gems. —*Scott Yanow*

Piano Rolls / Sep. 1924-Dec. 1924 / Nonesuch ◆◆◆◆◆
Piano rolls generally sound rather wooden, with square rhythms and a honky-tonk feel; the displays of virtuosity are sometimes impossible for one pianist to perform due to excessive hole punching. Jelly Roll Morton's 11 piano rolls of 1924 (which had previously been put out on LP by Biograph and Everest) often had more life than others of the period, but still sounded a bit mechanical. Using modern techniques during 1996-97 (including the Yamaha Disklavier), producer Artis Wodehouse was able to make Morton's piano rolls sound much more alive than they had previously for this CD. The interpretations almost pass for 1920s piano recordings, and Morton's feel comes across better than in previous versions of the rolls. Of the 11 selections, it is possible that "Sweet Man" was not performed by Jelly Roll (although his name was on the original roll), for the style sounds a bit different. But the other numbers (highlighted by "Shreveport Stomps," "Grandpa's Spells," "King Porter Stomp" and "Mr. Jelly Lord") definitely bring back the spirit of Jelly Roll Morton. —*Scott Yanow*

Jelly Roll Morton 1926-1934 / Sep. 15, 1926-Aug. 15, 1934 / ABC ✦✦✦
This CD, using Robert Parker's innovative enginnering, brings 16 of pianist Jelly Roll Morton's better Victor recordings to life. This is a good sampling of Morton's sessions, although it is not recommended to completists. Highlights include "Black Bottom Stomp," "Grandpa's Spells," "Beale Street Blues" and "You Need Some Loving," the latter with cornetist Johnny Dunn's band. —*Scott Yanow*

☆ **Jelly Roll Morton Centennial: His Complete Victor Recording** / Sep. 15, 1926-Sep. 28, 1939 / Bluebird ✦✦✦✦✦
This five-CD set contains the very best band recordings of Jelly Roll Morton's career. There are 111 performances in this reissue including all of the alternate takes. Bypassed are the pianist's recordings with the vaudevillian clarinetist Wilton Crawley, singers Lizzie Miles and Billie Young and two songs he performed on a radio broadcast in 1940; otherwise all of his Victor recordings are here. The classics (most from the 1926-28 period) include the remarkable "Black Bottom Stomp," "Grandpa's Spells," "The Pearls," "Wolverine Blues" (a trio with clarinetist Johnny Dodds and drummer Baby Dodds), "Shreveport Stomp," "Low Gravy," "Strokin' Away" and "I Thought I Heard Buddy Bolden Say," but listeners will have their own favorites. In general, this is New Orleans jazz at its best with Jelly Roll Morton (as with the best jazz composer/bandleaders) creating his own world of music. —*Scott Yanow*

Anamule Dance / May 23, 1938-Jun. 7, 1938 / Rounder ✦✦✦✦✦
The second of four CDs that reissue the music (but not the verbal monologues) that pianist/composer Jelly Roll Morton recorded for the Library of Congress is, like the other volumes, filled with memorable performances that are sometimes (due to time limitations) incomplete or heard in excerpts. The most interesting selections on this disc are the lengthy "Winin' Boy Blues," Morton's playful "The Anamule Dance," "Mr. Jelly Lord" and a lengthy (and somewhat filthy) version of "Make Me a Pallet on the Floor." —*Scott Yanow*

Kansas City Stomp: The Library of Congress Recordings, Vol. 1 / May 23, 1938-Jun. 7, 1938 / Rounder ✦✦✦✦✦
Pianist/composer Jelly Roll Morton, one of the pioneers of New Orleans jazz, was down and out in 1938 when Alan Lomax found him playing in a Washington D.C. dive. Lomax, realizing that Morton had seen and heard many timeless incidents that would otherwise be forgotten, started interviewing him for the Library of Congress on a wire recorder. Released originally on eight LPs, these discussions found Morton talking about the old days and peppering his talk with piano solos. Rounder has reissued all of the music (and done a fine job of correcting the speed) on four CDs but unfortunately decided to leave out Morton's often-fascinating monologues. This first CD has many strong moments including Morton's demonstration of the piano styles of many forgotten players, his depiction of a New Orleans funeral, his famous demonstration of how "Tiger Rag" evolved from being a quadrille into becoming jazz and comparisons of "Maple Leaf Rag" as played as ragtime and the way Morton preferred it. —*Scott Yanow*

The Pearls / May 23, 1938-Jun. 7, 1938 / Rounder ✦✦✦✦✦
The third of four CDs taken from pianist Jelly Roll Morton's *Library of Congress* recordings is highlighted by the nearly half-hour "Murder Ballad" (a sexual fantasy by Morton about women's prisons), "King Porter Stomp," a two-part "Wolverine Blues" and a seven-minute version of "The Pearls." All four of these releases are recommended to collectors of early jazz, although the LP equivalent (which runs to eight volumes) also includes all of his storytelling. —*Scott Yanow*

Winin' Boy Blues / Jun. 7, 1938-Dec. 14, 1938 / Rounder ✦✦✦✦✦
The fourth and final CD in Rounder's *Library of Congress* series has the later recordings from this extensive program, including two numbers from six months after the original discussions had concluded. Morton, who is heard very briefly on guitar on "L'il Liza Jane," takes fine piano solos on such numbers as "Freakish," "Pep," "Ain't Misbehavin'" and a medley of "Spanish tinge" songs including "The Crave." This fascinating series (which Rounder pitch corrected) is recommended to collectors of early jazz. —*Scott Yanow*

Last Sessions—Complete General Recordings / Dec. 14, 1939-Jan. 30, 1940 / GRP ✦✦✦
This CD contains Jelly Roll Morton's final studio recordings (the only existing later performances by Morton are a couple of tunes from a radio broadcast) and supercedes an earlier two-LP Atlantic set. The main reason to acquire this 1997 CD is Morton's 13 classic piano solos, which include five vocals, his first on record other than the much earlier "Dr. Jazz" and the *Library of Congress* sides. Only ten of the solos were originally released, so this is a very complete reissue. Morton, despite ailing health, was in very good form for the sessions, and his versions of "The Crave," "King Porter Stomp," "Winin' Boy Blues," "Buddy Bolden Blues" and "Don't You Leave Me Here" are quite memorable. In addition, he is heard heading three band dates that, despite the presence of trumpeter Henry "Red" Allen and clarinetist Albert Nicholas, do not quite live up to their potential. They did introduce Jelly

Roll's "Sweet Substitute" (a future standard) and include a hot rendition of "Panama," but such songs as "Get the Bucket" and "Mama's Got a Baby" have not been revived since. Still, this set is highly recommended for the solo performances, Jelly Roll Morton's final contribution to the music he claimed to have founded. —*Scott Yanow*

Bob Moses

b. Jan. 28, 1948, New York, NY
Drums, Composer / Avant-Garde, Post-Bop

A fine drummer, Bob Moses has received his strongest recognition as a colorful and adventurous arranger/composer for large ensembles. He played as a teenager with Rahsaan Roland Kirk (1964-65), formed the early fusion group Free Spirits with Larry Coryell (1966) and toured with Gary Burton's quartet (1967-69). Moses collaborated with Dave Liebman in the trio Open Sky, recorded with Gary Burton in the mid-'70s and worked with Jack DeJohnette's Compost, Pat Metheny (recording *Bright Size Life*), Mike Gibbs, Hal Galper, Gil Goldstein, Steve Swallow, the Steve Kuhn-Sheila Jordan group (1979-82), George Gruntz's Concert Jazz Band and Emily Remler (1983-84). He recorded as a composer for his own Mozown label in 1975 but Moses' reputation as a writer rests primarily with his Gramavision releases, especially *When Elephants Dream of Music* (1982), *Visit with the Great Spirit* (1983) and 1994's *Time Stood Still*. —*Scott Yanow*

★ **When Elephants Dream of Music** / Apr. 11, 1982-Apr. 12, 1982 / Gramavision ✦✦✦✦✦
Although best known as a flexible and tasteful drummer, Bob Moses displayed a great deal of talent on this exciting project as a composer and arranger. He utilized a particularly colorful cast of characters, including altoist David Gross, Jim Pepper on tenor, cornetist Terumasa Hino, trombonist Barry Rogers, flutist Jeremy Steig, vibraphonist David Friedman, guitarist Bill Frisell, keyboardist Lyle Mays, electric bassist Steve Swallow, Howard Johnson on electric contrabass clarinet and tuba, and the voices of Sheila Jordan and Jeanne Lee, among many others. Some of the music is quite lyrical and laidback, and there are tributes to Miles Davis and Billy Strayhorn, but it is the rambunctious and hilarious "Everybody Knows You When You're Up and In" (his answer to "Nobody Knows You When You're Down and Out") that is most memorable. Highly recommended. —*Scott Yanow*

Visit with the Great Spirit / 1983 / Gramavision ✦✦✦✦
Bob Moses, formerly known as a tasteful and flexible drummer, really came into his own as a composer/arranger during his period with Gramavision. This ambitious effort has seven of his diverse and colorful originals. Such distinctive voices as trumpeter Tiger Okoshi, soprano saxophonist David Liebman, tenorman Bob Mintzer, altoist David Sanborn, guitarists Bill Frisell and John Scofield and tuba player Howard Johnson (not to mention various percussionists and background singers) are utilized by Moses in imaginative ways. *When Elephants Dream of Music*, Moses' previous release, is still his definitive recording, but this album comes close, making one wish that Bob Moses could record in this type of setting on at least an annual basis. —*Scott Yanow*

The Story of Moses / 1987 / Gramavision ✦✦✦✦

Danny Moss

b. Aug. 16, 1927, Redhill, England
Tenor Saxophone

A talented veteran swing-oriented tenor, Danny Moss has been an important part of the British jazz scene since the early 1950s. He started playing professionally when he was 16 and through the years has worked with the who's-who of England's jazz community, including Vic Lewis, Ted Heath (1953-55), Johnny Dankworth (1957-61), Alex Welsh and Humphrey Lyttelton (1962-64). A fine thick-toned tenor stylist in the tradition of Coleman Hawkins, Moss has often been called upon to perform with traveling American jazzmen, most notably Buck Clayton in the mid-'60s. He has led his own groups on and off since the 1960s, in addition to extensive freelancing (including working with the Pizza Express All-Stars in the 1980s and with his wife, singer Jeannie Lamb). Danny Moss, who moved to Australia in 1989 but still plays often in Europe, has recorded as a leader for Columbia (1966), 77, Flyright and, more recently, the Nagel-Heyer label. —*Scott Yanow*

● **Weaver of Dreams** / Nov. 17, 1994 / Nagel-Heyer ✦✦✦✦✦
An excellent English tenor saxophonist, Danny Moss had a rare opportunity to record as a leader for the Nagel-Heyer during late 1994 in what was his 50th year as a professional musician. Accompanied by pianist Brian Lemon, bassist Len Skeat and drummer Butch Miles, Moss digs into 14 standards, alternating stomps with ballads. He is a fine player who, due to being based in Europe, tends to get overlooked in the US when one discusses top swing stylists of the 1990s. Moss'

quartet outing is easily recommended to fans of straightahead mainstream jazz. —*Scott Yanow*

Michael Mossman

b. Oct. 12, 1959, Philadelphia, PA

Trumpet / Hard Bop

A fine hard bop trumpeter with a wide range, Michael Mossman has proven to be an asset to many swinging sessions. A flexible player, he toured Europe in 1978 with an orchestra led by Anthony Braxton and played on two tours with Roscoe Mitchell. But Mossman was in more logical surroundings when he was with Lionel Hampton (1984) and during the one month he played with Art Blakey's Jazz Messengers. He played with Machito and Gerry Mulligan in 1985 and then toured and recorded with Out of the Blue (OTB). Mossman played lead trumpet with Toshiko Akiyoshi's Jazz Orchestra, was in Horace Silver's group (1989-91) and was a member of Gerry Mulligan's Rebirth of the Cool Band (1992). In addition he toured with Dizzy Gillespie's United Nation Orchestra, the Philip Morris Superband and Slide Hampton's Jazz Masters Orchestra. He has also played with the Latin jazz bands of Michel Camilo, Mario Bauza and Eddie Palmieri. Michael Mossman co-led sessions for EGT and Red and had a 1995 release on Claves. —*Scott Yanow*

● **Granulate** / Apr. 1990 / Red ✦✦✦✦

Spring Dance / Jul. 26, 1995 / Claves Jazz ✦✦✦

Abe Most

b. Feb. 27, 1920, New York, NY

Clarinet / Swing

A superior swing clarinetist who has spent much of his career either in the studios or recreating the work of Artie Shaw and Benny Goodman, Abe Most is the older brother of flutist Sam Most. He joined Les Brown in 1939, spent 1942-45 in the military and was briefly with Tommy Dorsey in 1946. He moved to Los Angeles in the late '40s where he has worked steadily as a studio musician. Abe Most frequently plays in local clubs (sometimes with his brother) and classic jazz festivals but despite his talent has recorded as a leader much too infrequently. He led obscure sessions for Superior (1946), Trend (1954), Annunciata (1978) and Camard (1984). —*Scott Yanow*

The Most (Abe, That Is) / 1978 / Camard ✦✦✦✦

● **Swing Low Sweet Clarinet** / Sep. 21, 1984 / Camard ✦✦✦✦✦

Other than six numbers in 1946, four in 1954, and a very obscure 1978 LP, this set was clarinetist Abe Most's first real opportunity to stretch out on records as a leader. Most, who is joined by pianist Hank Jones, bassist Monty Budwig and drummer Jake Hanna, performs a few standards, his "Babenu" (dedicated to tenorman Babe Russin and based on the chords of "I've Found a New Baby") and his original title cut. In addition, on a medley of "Manha de Carnaval" and "Samba de Orpheus," Most switches to flute and interacts with his brother, flutist Sam Most. An excellent swing set that has not yet been reissued on CD. —*Scott Yanow*

Live! / Sep. 3, 1994+Jun. 23, 1995 / Camard ✦✦✦✦✦

Abe Most has long been one of the top swing clarinetists around, but he has made relatively few recordings as a leader through the years. Fortunately, the Camard label captured Most during two concerts for this CD. Joined by pianist Ray Sherman, bassist Eugene Wright, drummer Jack Sperling and (on one of the two dates) vibraphonist Peter Appleyard, Abe Most plays five songs associated with Benny Goodman including heated renditions of "Undecided" and "Air Mail Special." Since Appleyard has long had the ability to sound just like Lionel Hampton whenever he wants, this is very much a BG Quartet tribute. The other outing allows Most a chance to show off his roots in Artie Shaw although his own individuality peeks through. With Ray Sherman (an underrated great) also contributing some strong solos, this small-label release is well worth picking up. These veterans should not be taken for granted. —*Scott Yanow*

Sam Most

b. Dec. 16, 1930, Atlantic City, NJ

Flute, Tenor Saxophone / Bop, Cool

One of the first great jazz flutists, a cool-toned tenor and a fine (if infrequent) clarinetist, Sam Most is the younger brother of clarinetist Abe Most. He picked up early experience playing with the orchestras of Tommy Dorsey (1948), Boyd Raeburn and Don Redman. By the time he led his first session (1953), Most was a brilliant flutist (among the first to sing through his flute) and he briefly had the jazz field to himself. Most recorded fine sessions for Prestige, Debut (reissued on Xanadu), Vanguard and Bethlehem during 1953-58, doubling on clarinet. He also worked in different settings with Chris Connor, Paul Quinichette and Teddy Wilson. After playing with Buddy Rich's Orchestra (1959-61), he moved to Los Ange-

les and became a studio musician. Sam Most worked with Red Norvo and Louie Bellson, gained some new prominence with his Xanadu recordings of 1976-79 and became a local fixture in Los Angeles, sometimes playing in clubs with his brother. —*Scott Yanow*

Bebop Revisited, Vol. 3 / Apr. 27, 1951-Dec. 29, 1953 / Xanadu ✦✦✦✦✦

Xanadu's *Bebop Revisited* series reissued many valuable recordings that were not originally on LPs. The third volume has four titles from a quintet (arranged by Tom Talbert) featuring trombonist Kai Winding, tenor saxophonist Warne Marsh and two vocals from Melvin Moore, another four songs from a septet headed by trumpeter Tony Fruscella and also starring altoist Herb Geller and Phil Urso on tenor, and seven performances from an all-star unit led by flutist Sam Most, who also plays plenty of clarinet on this date; trumpeter Doug Mettome, trombonist Urbie Green and pianist Bob Dorough (in his pre-singing days) are major assets on the latter session. Most takes solo honors with his Benny Goodman tribute "Notes to You" but there are many highlights to these formerly obscure sessions. —*Scott Yanow*

But Beautiful / 1976 / Catalyst ✦✦✦✦

Although he was one of the pioneers of the jazz flute and remained one of its finest exponents, Sam Most did not have an opportunity to record as a leader after 1958 until this Catalyst session. The enjoyable LP also includes fine work from pianist George Muribus, bassist Putter Smith and drummer Will Bradley, Jr., although Most is easily the main star. He plays his cool-toned tenor on two tracks, but it is his flute that is most individual; check out his interpretation of "I've Grown Accustomed to Your Face" on this LP, if you can find it. —*Scott Yanow*

★ **Mostly Flute** / May 27, 1976 / Xanadu ✦✦✦✦✦

Sam Most, who had only led one record date since 1958, headed four albums for Xanadu from 1976-79, of which this was the first. A brilliant flutist who was one of the pioneers of the instrument in jazz, Most switches to clarinet (where he is an equally talented bop player) on two of the seven selections during this high-quality set. Teamed up with guitarist Tal Farlow, pianist Duke Jordan, bassist Sam Jones and drummer Billy Higgins, Most makes the most difficult ideas sound effortless. Highlights are two numbers ("Street of Dreams" and "Body and Soul") that are flute/guitar duets. —*Scott Yanow*

Flute Flight / Dec. 28, 1976 / Xanadu ✦✦✦✦✦

Sam Most, one of a handful of truly great flute players, is in fine form on this quartet session with pianist Lou Levy, bassist Monty Budwig and drummer Donald Bailey. He has a classic duet with Levy on "It Might as Well be Spring," plays beautifully on "Last Night When We Were Young," switches to clarinet for "Am I Blue," demonstrates his ability to sing along with his flute on "The Humming Blues" and really cooks during "Flying Down to Rio." A fine all-round showcase for Sam Most's underrated talents. —*Scott Yanow*

From the Attic of My Mind / Apr. 25, 1978 / Xanadu ✦✦✦✦

Flutist Sam Most contributed eight of the compositions to this enjoyable quintet date. With tasteful support from pianist Kenny Barron, bassist George Mraz, drummer Walter Bolden and percussionist Warren Smith, Most could have easily taken the laidback approach often favored by flutists, but instead he digs in and comes up with some fiery statements. None of the originals (which includes blues, ballads and blowing devices) caught on elsewhere, but they work well on this set. —*Scott Yanow*

Flute Talk / Jan. 23, 1979-Jan. 24, 1979 / Xanadu ✦✦✦✦

Essentially a blowing session, the flutes of Sam Most and Joe Farrell are in the forefront of this enjoyable straightahead date. Pianist Mike Wofford, bassist Bob Magnusson, drummer Roy McCurdy and percussionist Jerry Steinholtz are quite supportive of the flutes. Most and Farrell play a few standards (including a creative version of "When You Wish upon a Star"), some straightforward originals and on "Leaves" they freely improvise around each other in an interesting (if overly brief) duet. —*Scott Yanow*

Bennie Moten

b. Nov. 13, 1894, Kansas City, MO, **d.** Apr. 2, 1935, Kansas City, MO

Piano, Leader / Classic Jazz, Big Band

Bennie Moten is today best remembered as the leader of a band that partly became the nucleus of the original Count Basie Orchestra, but Moten deserves better. He was a fine ragtime-oriented pianist who led the top territory band of the 1920s, an orchestra that really set the standard for Kansas City jazz. In fact it was so dominant that Moten was able to swallow up some of his competitors' groups, including Walter Page's Blue Devils, most of whom eventually became members of Moten's big band. Moten formed his group (originally a sextet) in 1922 and the following year they made their first recordings. Among Moten's 1923-25 sides for OKeh was the original version of his greatest hit "South." During 1926-32 Moten's Orchestra recorded for Victor and, although none of his original musicians became famous, the later additions included his brother Buster on occasional jazz accordion, Harlan Leonard, Jack Washington, Eddie Durham, Jimmy Rushing, Hot Lips Page (starting in 1929) Count Basie. So impressed was Moten by Basie's playing that Count assumed the piano chair for recordings from that point on (although in clubs Moten would generally play a feature or two). The most famous Bennie Moten recording session was also his last, ten songs cut on December 13, 1932 that find the ensemble strongly resembling Basie's five years later. In addition to Hot Lips Page, Durham, Washington and Basie, the band at that point also starred Ben Webster, Eddie Barefield and Walter Page, and one of the high points was the debut of "Moten Swing."

Tragically, Bennie Moten died in 1935 from a botched tonsillectomy operation. Buster Moten briefly took over the band, but many of its top members (along with some important additions like Lester Young) eventually gravitated towards Count Basie. —*Scott Yanow*

Bennie Moten (1923-1926) / Sep. 1923-Dec. 13, 1926 / Classics ✦✦✦✦

1923-1927 / Sep. 1923-Jun. 1927 / Classics ✦✦✦✦

Pianist Bennie Moten led one of the finest jazz bands on record in the 1920s, a group that included many of the top musicians of the Midwest. On the first of four Classics CDs—all of which are recommended to vintage jazz collectors—that reissue the master takes of all of Moten's recordings, the band quickly evolves from a sextet in 1923 to a solid 11-piece orchestra. Despite a few novelty effects (including clarinetist Woody Walder occasionally getting weird sounds by playing only the mouthpiece of his horn), even the most primitive numbers on this set are quite enjoyable. Highlights include the original version of "South" (Moten's big hit), "Goofy Dust," "Thick Lip Blues" and "Sugar." —*Scott Yanow*

South (1926-1929) / Dec. 13, 1926-Jul. 17, 1929 / Bluebird ✦✦✦✦✦

Bennie Moten led one of the finest of the territory bands of the 1920s. Trumpeter Ed Lewis, trombonist Thurmon Hayes, the young baritonist Jack Washington and pianist Moten himself were excellent soloists (even if Woody Walder's spots on clarinet and tenor were erratic), the head arrangements were generally quite colorful, and the band had a spirit of its own. This CD from the early '90s reissues 22 of the 39 master takes recorded by Moten's orchestra prior to the arrival of Count Basie, managing to include all of the essential sides such as "Sugar," an inventive version of "Twelfth Street Rag," the delightful "Get Low-Down Blues" and the orchestra's big hit, "South." A solid introduction to the music of Bennie Moten. —*Scott Yanow*

1927-1929 / Jun. 11, 1927-Jun. 17, 1929 / Classics ✦✦✦✦✦

During the period covered by this second of four Classics CDs, Bennie Moten's Kansas City Orchestra was at the peak of its powers, dominating the jazz scene of the Midwest. There were not a lot of famous names in the group yet, but the soloists were colorful, and the band's ensembles could really rock in a pre-swing manner. The main players at the time included cornetist Ed Lewis, Harlan Leonard on various reeds, baritonist Jack Washington and Moten himself on piano. Highlights include "Moten Stomp," "Kansas City Breakdown," "Get Low-Down Blues," "Terrific Blues" and the remake of the band's hit "South." —*Scott Yanow*

1929-1930 / Jul. 18, 1929-Oct. 29, 1930 / Classics ✦✦✦✦✦

From 1929-30, the Bennie Moten Orchestra could hold its own with fellow big bands like Fletcher Henderson, Paul Whiteman and McKinney's Cotton Pickers, although it was the least known nationally of the four. The third of four Classics CDs completely reissuing Moten's recordings finds the young Count Basie taking over the piano slot and such stars joining the band as singer Jimmy Rushing and (by 1930) trumpeter Hot Lips Page. With cornetist Ed Lewis, Eddie Durham on trombone and guitar, clarinetist Harlan Leonard and Buster Moten (on accordion) also heard from, this was a mighty orchestra, as displayed on such numbers as "New Goofy Dust Rag," "The Jones Law Blues" and "New Vine Street Blues." The four imported Classics sets are certainly more complete than the two CDs put out domestically by Bluebird. —*Scott Yanow*

★ Basie Beginnings (1929-1932) / Oct. 23, 1929-Dec. 13, 1932 / Bluebird ✦✦✦✦✦

Bennie Moten's orchestra, arguably the top territory band at the time Count Basie joined as second pianist in 1929, had been reasonably well represented on records since 1923. This does have the cream of Moten's 1929 and 1930 sessions, plus seven of the ten songs cut at their superb Dec. 13, 1932 date. Moten himself never again appeared on records after Basie joined. —*Scott Yanow*

1930-1932 / Oct. 29, 1930-Dec. 13, 1932 / Classics ✦✦✦✦✦

The final of the four "complete" Bennie Moten Classics CDs, which contain all of the orchestra's recordings except for a dozen alternate takes, has the band's final selections from 1930 (including some vocals by Jimmy Rushing) and then all of the music from Moten's classic final session of Dec. 13, 1932. With trumpeter Hot Lips Page, trombonist Dan Minor, Eddie Durham (the main arranger) on trombone and guitar, baritonist Jack Washington, Ben Webster on tenor, bassist Walter Page and pianist Count Basie, the orchestra at times almost sounds like the Count Basie big

band of 1937. "Toby," the original version of "Moten Swing," "The Blue Room," "Milenberg Joys," "Lafayette" and "Prince of Wails" are among the many memorable selections. Highly recommended. —*Scott Yanow*

Paul Motian (Stephen Paul Motian)

b. Mar. 25, 1931, Philadelphia, PA
Leader, Drums / Post-Bop, Avant-Garde

Paul Motian is a subtle drummer who is equally important as the leader of several rather stimulating bands and quite a few colorful recording sessions. Born in Philadelphia, Motian grew up in Providence, RI. After moving to New York in 1955 he played with many top jazz musicians from a wide variety of styles including Tony Scott, Gil Evans, Art Farmer, Lee Konitz, George Russell, Stan Getz, Lennie Tristano, Thelonious Monk, Coleman Hawkins and Roy Eldridge. As a member of Bill Evans' most famous trio (the one with Scott LaFaro), Motian helped define the role of the modern drummer in that type of intimate setting. He remained with Evans after LaFaro's death (Chuck Israels took over as bassist) until 1963. Motian then played with Paul Bley's Trio (1963-64) and he later had a long-term musical relationship with Keith Jarrett, starting in 1966 and including work with Jarrett's quintet in the 1970s. Motian also freelanced and among the many musicians that he worked with were Mose Allison, Charles Lloyd, Charlie Haden's Liberation Music Ensemble and Carla Bley. Motian began leading his own groups in 1977 and these included a trio with Joe Lovano and Bill Frisell and the Electric Bebop Band in the 1990s with Joshua Redman and two guitarists. He has recorded many albums as a leader (starting in 1972) for ECM, GM, Soul Note and JMT, including collaborations with Lee Konitz. —*Scott Yanow*

Conception Vessel / Nov. 25, 1972-Nov. 26, 1972 / ECM ✦✦✦✦

This is Motian's debut as a leader. It includes ambitious cuts with guitarist Sam Brown and also features pianist Keith Jarrett. —*Ron Wynn*

Tribute / May 1974 / ECM ✦✦✦✦

This effort by drummer Paul Motian does not say who the "tribute" is for. Two numbers (the leader's "Victoria" and "Song for Che") feature the trio of guitarist Sam Brown (an underrated player), bassist Charlie Haden and Motian; the remaining three songs (a pair of Motian originals and Ornette Coleman's "War Orphans") add the second guitar of Paul Metzke and the fiery alto of Carlos Ward. Fine post-bop music that contains more energy than many ECM recordings. —*Scott Yanow*

Dance / Sep. 1977 / ECM ✦✦✦✦✦

Although drummer Paul Motian is the leader of this trio set with the brilliant bassist David Izenzon, it is Charles Brackeen, heard on tenor and soprano, who is generally the solo star. Motian's six originals (which include "Waltz Song," "Kalypso," "Asia" and "Lullaby") contain plenty of variety and generally live up to their titles. —*Scott Yanow*

Le Voyage / Mar. 1979 / ECM ✦✦✦✦

● Psalm / Dec. 1981 / ECM ✦✦✦✦✦

The eight compositions by drummer Paul Motian on this ECM release (which is available on CD) are rather dry and none caught on as future standards. But the playing by Motian's sidemen (tenors Joe Lovano and Billy Drewes, bassist Ed Schuller and especially the remarkable guitarist Bill Frisell) uplifted the music and gave this group a strong personality of its own. Although the results are not all that memorable, the music should please adventurous listeners. —*Scott Yanow*

The Story of Maryam / Jul. 27, 1983-Jul. 28, 1983 / Soul Note ✦✦✦✦

Misterioso / 1983-Jul. 1986 / Soul Note ✦✦✦✦✦

Although often overlooked, drummer Paul Motian led one of the most inventive jazz bands of the mid-'80s. His quintet, which featured the tenors of Joe Lovano and Jim Pepper, guitarist Bill Frisell and bassist Ed Schuller, could play anything from swinging advanced hard bop and Ornette Coleman-type free bop to spacier improvising. An underrated composer, Motian contributed seven of the nine numbers for this date; the quintet also performs Thelonious Monk's "Misterioso" and "Pannonica." Frisell is featured on "Byablue" (which had earlier been recorded by Keith Jarrett); the two tenors (Pepper doubled on soprano) work together quite well, and the band definitely had its own sound. Of its three recordings, this is a strong one to start with. —*Scott Yanow*

Jack of Clubs / Mar. 26, 1984-Mar. 28, 1984 / Soul Note ✦✦✦✦

Starting in the early '80s, drummer Paul Motian led a series of fascinating bands, usually pianoless and featuring the highly original guitarist Bill Frisell. For this outing, Motian and Frisell are teamed with the tenors of Jim Pepper and Joe Lovano plus bassist Ed Schuller. The drummer's seven originals feature lots of variety in moods, ranging from witty to introspective and showcasing the colorful players at their best. Frisell (who is featured on "Lament") in particular sounds perfectly at home with Motian's group. —*Scott Yanow*

It Should Have Happened a Long Time Ago / Jul. 1984 / ECM ◆◆◆◆

Tenor/guitar/drums trios are not too common since there are few guitarists around (other than Bill Frisell) who can make up for the absence of both a keyboard and a bass. With Joe Lovano providing some fine tenor solos, Frisell adding fire along with a wide variety of unique sounds and Paul Motian playing some stimulating drums, this is a surprisingly self-sufficient trio. Motian provided all seven originals on the worthy set which has been reissued on CD by ECM. —*Scott Yanow*

Circle the Line / Jun. 1986 / GM ◆◆◆◆

One Time Out / Sep. 21, 1987-Sep. 22, 1987 / Soul Note ◆◆◆◆◆

The key to this unusual trio is not the muscular tenor of Joe Lovano or the propulsive timekeeping of the drummer/leader but the remarkable guitarist Bill Frisell. Able to somehow produce sounds from this guitar that could be mistaken for a keyboard or a steel guitar, in styles ranging from heavy metal and avant-garde jazz to country music, Frisell is the reason that the trio can sound like a full band despite not having a keyboardist or a bassist. The music, which includes seven Motian originals along with "Monk's Mood" and "If You Could See Me Now," features both intense three-way free improvisations and introspective spacey ballads. Few of the tunes themselves will stick in one's mind (although "Morpion" could be an imaginary meeting between 1966 John Coltrane and Jimi Hendrix), but it is the basic sound of the unique group that makes the CD of great interest. —*Scott Yanow*

Monk in Motian / Mar. 1988 / JMT ◆◆◆◆◆

This is an utterly fascinating tribute to the music of Thelonious Monk. Most of the selections feature the unusual trio of tenor saxophonist Joe Lovano, guitarist Bill Frisell (who with his wide range of original sounds is really a one-band band) and drummer Paul Motian. Tenor saxophonist Dewey Redman and pianist Geri Allen are guests on two songs apiece and fit in quite well with the sparse but very complete trio. Among the ten Monk songs explored, taken apart and given surprising treatment are "Evidence," "Bye-Ya," "Ugly Beauty" and "Trinkle Tinkle." Recommended to open-eared listeners. —*Scott Yanow*

Paul Motian on Broadway, Vol. 1 / Nov. 1988 / JMT ◆◆◆◆◆

The quartet of tenorman Joe Lovano, guitarist Bill Frisell, bassist Charlie Haden and drummer Paul Motian digs into nine show tunes from the 1930s and 40s, reinventing them in colorful fashion. The key to the rewarding project is Frisell, whose versatility and wide range of highly original sounds make the overall results sound quite unique. Among the highlights of the memorable set are unusual versions of "Liza," "They Didn't Believe Me" and "Last Night when We Were Young." —*Scott Yanow*

Paul Motian on Broadway, Vol. 2 / Sep. 1989 / JMT ◆◆◆◆◆

This followup to volume 1 is just as well done. —*Ron Wynn*

Bill Evans: Tribute to the Great Post-Bop Pianist / May 1990 / JMT ◆◆◆◆◆

An excellent quartet date featuring sensational guitar by Bill Frisell and nice tenor sax from Joe Lovano. —*Ron Wynn*

Motian in Tokyo / Mar. 28, 1991-Mar. 29, 1991 / JMT ◆◆◆◆

On Broadway, Vol. 3 / Sep. 1991 / JMT ◆◆◆◆◆

Paul Motian & the Electric Bebop Band / Apr. 1992 / JMT ◆◆◆◆

Trio Ism / Jun. 1993 / JMT ◆◆◆◆

Reincarnation of a Love Bird / 1994 / Verve ◆◆◆

Mound City Blue Blowers

f. 1923, db. 1925

Group / Classic Jazz

The Mound City Blue Blowers were an unlikely success. Originally comprising Red McKenzie on comb and tissue paper (which sounded like a kazoo), Dick Slevin on an actual kazoo, and Jack Bland on banjo, the unique band's initial recording in 1924 ("Arkansas Blues" and "Blue Blues") became a big hit. The group recorded 12 titles in all during 1924-25, including two with guest Frankie Trumbauer on C-melody sax and with guitarist Eddie Lang firming up the rhythm on the final six numbers. McKenzie made additional sessions as a vocalist under his own name, while the Mound City title was retired for a few years. However, in 1929, McKenzie used the name for four selections recorded with all-star groups. While "Tailspin Blues" and "Never Had a Reason to Believe in You" featured trombonist/vocalist Jack Teagarden, "Hello Lola" and "One Hour" are considered classic. Coleman Hawkins took a historic ballad solo on the latter, trombonist Glenn Miller rarely sounded hotter than on "Hello Lola," and both clarinetist Pee Wee Russell and McKenzie on comb were in top form. A 1931 date with cornetist Muggsy Spanier, clarinetist Jimmy Dorsey and Hawkins was mostly a feature for McKenzie's vocals, but Red's contributions to the final Mound City Blue Blowers recordings (25 songs cut during 1935-36) are actually quite minor—a few vocals and not enough comb playing. Nappy Lamare, the Top Hatters, Spooky Dickenson

and Billy Wilson actually do most of the singing, but the reason that these last Mound City performances (all available on a single Classics CD) are of great interest are the trumpet solos of either Bunny Berigan or Yank Lawson and Eddie Miller on tenor and clarinet. —*Scott Yanow*

1935-1936 / May 9, 1935-Feb. 17, 1936 / Classics ◆◆◆◆

The Mound City Blue Blowers originally made history with a dozen high-quality novelty recordings during 1924-25 that featured the trio of Red McKenzie's comb, Dick Slevin's kazoo and banjoist Jack Bland; guitarist Eddie Lang solidified the rhythm on their later six numbers. However, other than McKenzie's participation, those dates had little to do with the 25 recordings on this Classics CD, the last issued under the Mound City Blue Blowers' name. In fact, other than taking four vocals on the first date, McKenzie makes only cameo appearances on kazoo during the remainder of the program, although he had clearly organized the bands. The six sessions feature overlapping personnel with some hot playing from either Bunny Berigan (on four of the dates) or Yank Lawson on trumpet and Eddie Miller or Forrest Crawford on tenor and clarinet. In addition to McKenzie, guitarist Nappy Lamare has eight vocals; there are also five from Billy Wilson, four from Spooky Dickenson and two by a vocal group. Only "High Society" and "Muskrat Ramble" are instrumentals, although there are strong solos on nearly every number. The music falls between Dixieland and small-group swing and is most notable for the playing of Berigan. —*Scott Yanow*

Alphonse Mouzon

b. Nov. 21, 1948, Charleston, SC

Drums / Fusion, Crossover Jazz, Post-Bop

A talented drummer whose music stretches from jazz to fusion, rock, funk and pop, Alphonse Mouzon made his first record date in 1969 with Gil Evans. After freelancing in New York, Mouzon was with Roy Ayers during 1970-71, was the original drummer with Weather Report (1971-72), played with McCoy Tyner and then during 1973-75 was with Larry Coryell's Eleventh House. He has since freelanced, worked with Al DiMeola, George Benson, Herbie Hancock (1979-82) and led his own groups, leading dates for Blue Note, MPS, Optimism and Pausa plus his own Tenacious label. —*Scott Yanow*

The Essence of Mystery / 1972-1973 / Blue Note ◆◆◆

Some frenetic drumming and good jazz/rock arrangments. —*Ron Wynn*

● **Funky Snakefoot** / Dec. 10, 1973-Dec. 12, 1973 / Blue Note ◆◆◆◆

One of the few intelligent uses of funk and soul in a '70s instrumental setting (at least from a fusion standpoint). After this album, he became more pop oriented. —*Ron Wynn*

Mind Transplant / Dec. 4, 1974-Dec. 10, 1974 / Blue Note ◆◆◆

The Man Incognito / Dec. 1975+Jan. 1976 / Blue Note ◆◆

Virtue / Nov. 1976 / Pausa ◆◆◆

Back to Jazz / 1985 / Pausa ◆◆◆◆

Throughout his career, drummer Alphonse Mouzon has been featured in many different settings. Some of his own recordings as a leader have been purposely commercial, but this date (originally released by Pausa and reissued by Mouzon on his Tenacious label) is more jazz-oriented. Most selections feature the fine altoist Doug Norwine (where has he been since?), in a quartet with Mouzon, pianist Jeff Daniels (doubling on synth) and bassist Welton Gite; on many of the numbers, Mouzon and Daniels also utilize synths, and "Peace on Earth" has vocal appearances by the drummer's two children. There is also a brief feature ("Space Commander") for Mouzon's electronic percussion. An interesting set worth picking up. —*Scott Yanow*

Love, Fantasy / 1987 / Optimism ◆◆

With such titles as "Baby Let Me Do It," "Get Down with the Funk" and "Shake It Baby," it is not surprising to find out that much of this date by drummer Alphonse Mouzon is R&B-oriented. Three numbers are dominated by vocals, and Mouzon utilizes electronic percussion in places. However, there are some good alto solos from Brandon Fields, and the band fares well on "Milestones." A mixed bag, originally put out by Optimism and now available as a CD on the drummer's Tenacious label. —*Scott Yanow*

The Survivor / 1992 / Tenacious ◆◆◆

Early Spring / 1993 / Optimism ◆◆◆

Drummer Alphonse Mouzon covers a lot of ground on this set, ranging from poppish R&B to straight jazz. Two selections have soulful vocals; Mouzon takes a pair of occasionally self-indulgent selections as features for his many overdubbed instruments; and the four instrumental quartet numbers feature either Gary Meek or Ronnie Laws on soprano or (in two cases) the heated tenor of Ernie Watts (who is best on "Seven Steps to Heaven"). —*Scott Yanow*

On Top of the World / 1994 / Tenacious ◆◆◆

The Night is Still Young / Apr. 23, 1996 / Tenacious ✦✦✦✦
This CD can easily be divided into two sections. The first five originals are acoustic numbers with trumpeter Sal Marquez, either Ernie Watts or Ralph Moore on tenor, bassist Tony Dumas and Alphonse Mouzon on both drums and overdubbed piano; altoist Eric Marienthal makes a guest appearance on "A Promise Kept." The selections were all recorded in celebration of the drummer's new daughter. The remaining eight performances find Mouzon playing drums, piano, organ, acoustic bass and sometimes trumpet, fluegelhorn and strings (without using computers). Three of these numbers add a guest—either Marienthal or Gerald Albright on alto or tenor. Mouzon proves to be an effective "one-man band" on music ranging from sambas to funk, and the program overall holds one's interest. —*Scott Yanow*

Bob Mover

b. Mar. 22, 1952, Boston, MA
Alto Saxophone, Soprano Saxophone / Hard Bop, Cool
When Bob Mover had his highest visibility in the late '70s, he played in a style very similar to Lee Konitz (with whom he recorded in 1977). Mover worked with Ira Sullivan when he was 1, 6 and after moving to New York in 1969 he freelanced in the local scene. Mover played with Charles Mingus briefly in 1973, was with Chet Baker during 1973-75 and started leading his own group in 1976. He had two recording sessions in 1977 (one apiece for Choice and Vanguard) and two for Xanadu in 1981; the latter dates found him beginning to develop his own individuality. —*Scott Yanow*

On the Move / Feb. 1977 / Choice ✦✦✦
Bob Mover's first session as a leader matches his alto and soprano with trumpeter Tom Harrell, pianist Mike Nock, guitarist Peter Sprague, bassist George Mraz, drummer Jeff Pappez and singer Jay Clayton on four lengthy performances: three Mover originals and "Darn That Dream." The use of Clayton's voice as a part of the ensembles gives the band an unusual sound. Mover sounded fairly strong, if a bit derivative at this point (he was 24), but Harrell generally takes solo honors. This session has not yet been reissued on CD. —*Scott Yanow*

Bob Mover / May 1979 / Vanguard ✦✦✦✦
Bob Mover was very strongly influenced by Lee Konitz at this point in time. Doubling on alto and soprano, he does play quite well on a variety of standards, including "We'll Be Together Again" and "Milestones." The supporting cast is quite strong (trumpeter Claudio Roditi, pianist Kenny Barron, bassist Ron McClure, drummer Ben Riley and percussionist Rafael Cruz), and overall, this is a fine hard-bop set (not yet reissued on CD) that was a solid step forward for the saxophonist. —*Scott Yanow*

● **In the True Tradition** / Jun. 23, 1981 / Xanadu ✦✦✦✦✦
Altoist Bob Mover, who originally sounded quite a bit like Lee Konitz, fully displays his individuality on this passionate trio set. Accompanied by bassist Rufus Reid and drummer Bobby Ward, Mover is free to be as explorative as he likes on the high-quality material which includes two originals, a pair of ballads, "Poinciana" and Thelonious Monk's "Evidence." This is one of Mover's finest recordings to date. —*Scott Yanow*

Things Unseen! / Jun. 23, 1981-Dec. 21, 1982 / Xanadu ✦✦✦✦✦
One selection on this album is a song left over from Mover's Xanadu debut *In the True Tradition;* the altoist is heard jamming with bassist Rufus Reid and drummer Bobby Ward on "Jimmy Garrison's Blues." Otherwise, this album mostly features Mover with pianist Albert Dailey, bassist Ray Drummond and drummer Ward on a variety of standards. Tenor saxophonist Steve Hall sits in on "Twardzik" during which Mover switches to soprano. A high point on the album is the duet between Dailey and Mover on a lengthy rendition of "Yesterdays." Overall this set offers high-quality modern bebop. —*Scott Yanow*

The Night Bathers / Jan. 22, 1986 / Justin Time ✦✦✦
When one considers the instrumentation (alto, piano and guitar) and the personnel (Bob Mover, Paul Bley and John Abercrombie), it is not surprising that this date is full of thoughtful, chance-taking and often lyrical improvisations. Most of the selections are either duets or unaccompanied solos, and although there are some melodies, the music was pretty much all improvised on the spot. An intriguing set. —*Scott Yanow*

Television / 1997 / Unidisc ✦✦✦

Famoudou Don Moye

b. May 23, 1946, Rochester, NY
Percussion, Drums / Avant-Garde, Free Jazz
When Don Moye joined the Art Ensemble of Chicago in 1970, he filled the gap that had been there since Philip Wilson left the group a couple years earlier to tour with the Butterfield Blues Band. Moye fit in perfectly, never just functioning as a timekeeper or an accompanist but becoming an equal partner in the innovative avant-garde quintet. He had studied at Wayne State University, toured Europe with the group Detroit Free Jazz and played with Steve Lacy before joining the Art Ensemble in Paris. In addition to his activities with the band, Moye has recorded with the Black Artists Group, performed with Randy Weston, recorded with Joseph Jarman, Don Pullen, Cecil McBee, Hamiet Bluiett, Julius Hemphill, Chico Freeman and Lester Bowie's Brass Fantasy (among others) and since 1984 has been a member of the Leaders. He also recorded an unaccompanied percussion date for the Art Ensemble label AECO in 1975. —*Scott Yanow*

Sun Percussion / Mar. 27, 1975 / AECO ✦✦✦✦
Quintessential solo recording (all percussion) from an Art Ensemble standout. —*Michael G. Nastos*

Milano Strut / Dec. 1978 / Black Saint ✦✦✦

● **Black Paladins** / 1981 / Black Saint ✦✦✦✦✦
Adventurous concept pieces, excellent percussive foundations, and adept playing. —*Ron Wynn*

Afrikan Song / 1996 / AECO ✦✦✦✦

George Mraz

b. Sep. 9, 1944, Czechoslovakia
Bass / Hard Bop
George Mraz has been a greatly in-demand bassist for straightahead dates ever since he emigrated to the US in 1968. After a brief time playing violin and alto, Mraz studied bass at the Prague Conservatory and gigged at a club in Munich for a year. In 1968 he attended Berklee and he soon toured with Oscar Peterson (1970-72). After moving to New York, Mraz became a member of the Thad Jones/Mel Lewis Orchestra (1973-76), worked with Stan Getz (1974-75) and has since played with most of the top jazz players including Walter Norris, Pepper Adams, Roland Hanna, Zoot Sims, Tommy Flanagan, John Abercrombie, Carmen McRae, Jimmy Rowles, Stephane Grappelli and countless others. Other than an obscure duo date with Roland Hanna for Trio in 1976, George Mraz surprisingly did not have an opportunity to lead his own sessions until the mid-'90s when he signed with Milestone. —*Scott Yanow*

My Foolish Heart / Jun. 11, 1995-Jun. 12, 1995 / Milestone ✦✦✦✦
● **Jazz** / Sep. 1995-Oct. 1995 / Milestone ✦✦✦✦✦
Bottom Lines / 1997 / Milestone ✦✦✦✦

Idris Muhammad (Leo Morris)

b. Nov. 13, 1939, New Orleans, LA
Drums / Post-Bop, Crossover Jazz, Soul-Jazz
An excellent drummer who has appeared in many types of settings, Idris Muhammad became a professional when he was 16. He played primarily soul and R&B during 1962-64 and then spent 1965-67 as a member of Lou Donaldson's band. He was the house drummer at Prestige Records (1970-72), appearing on many albums as a sideman. Of his later jazz associations, Muhammad played with Johnny Griffin (1978-79), Pharoah Sanders in the 1980s, George Coleman and the Paris Reunion Band (1986-88). He has recorded everything from post bop to dance music as a leader for such labels as Prestige, Kudu, Fantasy, Theresa and Lipstick. —*Scott Yanow*

Legends of Acid Jazz / Nov. 2, 1970-Sep. 20, 1971 / Presige ✦✦
Drummer Idris Muhammad's first two albums as a leader (*Black Rhythm Revolution!* and *Peace and Rhythm*) are reissued in full on this single CD. While the former set has a few worthy tracks (including Muhammad's colorful feature "Soulful Dreams"), the latter recording is marred by a pair of soul vocals and inferior R&B material. Trumpeter Virgil Jones and saxophonist Clarence Thomas get in their spots and the music is danceable, but overall this lightweight collection is a lesser effort and the pseudo-psychedelic graphics make the back cover largely unreadable. —*Scott Yanow*

Power of Soul / Nov. 1974 / Kudu ✦✦✦
Drummer Idris Muhammad performs a selection apiece by Joe Beck, Grover Washington, Jr., Bob James and Jimi Hendrix (the title cut) on this R&B-ish jazz date. James plays keyboards and provided the arrangements, but the overall music is not excessively commercial. The septet (which also includes trumpeter Randy Brecker and guitarist Beck) is most notable for featuring Washington (doubling on tenor and soprano) in his early days and in top form. —*Scott Yanow*

● **Kabsha** / 1980 / Theresa ✦✦✦✦✦
Drummer Idris Muhammad's strongest jazz date as a leader, this outing was originally made for Theresa. The CD reissue adds two alternate takes to the original six-song program. Muhammad is joined by bassist Ray Drummond and either Pharoah Sanders or George Coleman on tenors; surprisingly, the two saxophonists only play together on the two takes of Coleman's "GCCG Blues." Muhammad, who

had often been heard in funky or more commercial settings, really excels in this sparse setting, showing off what he learned from hearing bands in his native New Orleans. In addition, both the underrated Coleman and Sanders are heard in top form, stretching out on originals, basic pieces and "I Want to Talk About You" (during which Pharoah Sanders lets out a few trademark screams so everyone knows that he is not John Coltrane). Highly recommended. —*Scott Yanow*

My Turn / 1993 / Lipstick ♦♦♦

Included are strong instrumental tunes with great contributions by well-known guest stars. The vocal tunes, including "Free" with vocals by Hiram Bullock, might not be to everyone's taste. Idris plays with a sideman attitude—he does not dominate the band, but delivers a solid groove which serves the music. Overall, the album is a strange mixture between jazz and pop tunes. —*Alex Merck*

Gerry Mulligan

b. Apr. 6, 1927, New York, NY, d. Jan. 20, 1996, Darien, CT

Baritone Saxophone, Arranger, Composer, Leader, Piano / Cool

The most famous and probably greatest jazz baritonist of all time, Gerry "Jeru" Mulligan was a giant. A flexible soloist who was always ready to jam with anyone from Dixielanders to the most advanced boppers, Mulligan brought a somewhat revolutionary light sound to his potentially awkward and brutal horn and played with the speed and dexterity of an altoist.

Mulligan started on the piano before learning clarinet and the various saxophones. His initial reputation was as an arranger. In 1944 he wrote charts for Johnny Warrington's radio band and soon was making contributions to the books of Tommy Tucker and George Paxton. He moved to New York in 1946 and joined Gene Krupa's Orchestra as a staff arranger; his most notable chart was "Disc Jockey Jump." The rare times he played with Krupa's band was on alto and the same situation existed when he was with Claude Thornhill in 1948.

Gerry Mulligan's first notable recorded work on baritone was with Miles Davis' *Birth of the Cool* nonet (1948-50), but once again his arrangements ("Godchild," "Darn That Dream" and three of his originals "Jeru," "Rocker" and "Venus de Milo") were more significant than his short solos. Mulligan spent much of 1949 writing for Elliot Lawrence's orchestra and playing anonymously in the saxophone section. It was not until 1951 that he began to get a bit of attention for his work on baritone. Mulligan recorded with his own nonet for Prestige, displaying an already recognizable sound. After he traveled to Los Angeles, he wrote some arrangements for Stan Kenton (including "Youngblood," "Swing House" and "Walking Shoes"), worked at the Lighthouse and then gained a regular Monday night engagement at the Haig. Around this time, Mulligan realized that he enjoyed the extra freedom of soloing without a pianist. He jammed with trumpeter Chet Baker and soon their magical rapport was featured in his pianoless quartet. The group caught on quickly in 1952 and made both Mulligan and Baker into stars.

A drug bust put Mulligan out of action and ended that Quartet but, when he was released from jail in 1954, Mulligan began a new musical partnership with valve trombonist Bob Brookmeyer that was just as successful. Trumpeter Jon Eardley and Zoot Sims on tenor occasionally made the group a sextet and in 1958 trumpeter Art Farmer was featured in Mulligan's Quartet. Being a very flexible player with respect for other stylists, Mulligan went out of his way to record with some of the great musicians he admired. At the 1958 Newport Jazz Fetival he traded off with baritonist Harry Carney on "Prima Bara Dubla" while backed by the Duke Ellington Orchestra, and during 1957-60 he recorded separate albums with Thelonious Monk, Paul Desmond, Stan Getz, Ben Webster and Johnny Hodges. Mulligan played on the classic *Sound of Jazz* television special in 1958 and appeared in the movies *I Want to Live* and *The Subterraneans*.

During 1960-64 Mulligan led his Concert Jazz Band which gave him an opportunity to write, play baritone and occasionally double on piano. The orchestra at times included Brookmeyer, Sims, Clark Terry and Mel Lewis. Mulligan was a little less active after the big band broke up but he toured extensively with the Dave Brubeck Quartet (1968-72), had a part-time big band in the 1970s (the Age of Steam), doubled on soprano for a period, led a mid-'70s sextet that included vibraphonist Dave Samuels and in 1986 jammed on a record with Scott Hamilton. In the 1990s he toured the world with his excellent "no-name" quartet and led a rebirth of the Cool Band that performed and recorded remakes of the Miles Davis Nonet clasics. Up until the end, Gerry Mulligan was always eager to play.

Among Mulligan's compositions were "Walkin' Shoes," "Line for Lyons," "Bark for Barksdale," "Nights at the Turntable," "Utter Chaos," "Soft Shoe," "Bernie's Tune," "Blueport," "Song for Strayhorn," "Song for an Unfinished Woman" and "I Never Was a Young Man" (which he often sang). He recorded extensively through the years for such labels as Prestige, Pacific Jazz, Capitol, Vogue, EmArcy, Columbia, Verve, Milestone, United Artists, Philips, Limelight, A&M, CTI, Chiaroscuro, Who's Who, DRG, Concord and GRP. —*Scott Yanow*

The Arranger / May 21, 1946-Apr. 20, 1957 / Columbia ♦♦♦♦

This LP includes some of Gerry Mulligan's charts for the orchestras of Gene Krupa ("How High the Moon" and "Disc Jockey Jump") and Elliot Lawrence ("Between the Devil and the Deep Blue Sea" and "Elevation") in addition to featuring his own 1957 big band ("Thruway," "All the Things You Are," "Mullenium" and "Motel"). The Krupa performances are near-classic, the forgotten Lawrence band is in top form and Jeru's specially assembled orchestra features solos from baritonist Mulligan, trumpeters Jerry Lloyd and Don Joseph, trombonist Bob Brookmeyer, tenor saxophonist Zoot Sims and altoist Lee Konitz. Excellent music, although most of it has since been reissued on CD. —*Scott Yanow*

Legacy / 1949-1996 / N2K ♦♦♦

Mulligan—Baker / Aug. 1951-1965 / Prestige ♦♦♦♦♦

This double LP is full of valuable recordings. The classic Gerry Mulligan pianoless quartet with trumpeter Chet Baker is heard on eight gems including "Line for Lyons," "Lady Is a Tramp" and their hit version of "My Funny Valentine." In addition, Gerry Mulligan performs with his unusual tentette of 1951 (which featured two baritones and maracas) and Jeru and Allen Eager head a sextet on a 17-minute version of his original "Mulligan's Too." This two-fer concludes with four numbers taken from Chet Baker's many quintet sessions of 1965 with tenor saxophonist George Coleman and pianist Kirk Lightsey. Most of this music has since appeared on CD, but this was a well-packaged set and does not duplicate Mulligan's remarkable Mosaic box. —*Scott Yanow*

Mulligan Plays Mulligan / Sep. 27, 1951 / Original Jazz Classics ♦♦♦♦

Gerry Mulligan's first session as a leader and one of the first to showcase his baritone was recorded in New York shortly before he relocated to Los Angeles and formed his famous pianoless quartet with Chet Baker. There is a piano on this set (George Wallington) but Mulligan's writing (all seven selections are his) for a two-baritone nonet that also features trumpeter Nick Travis and tenor saxophonist Allan Eager is already in his influential "cool style"; best known among the originals is "Bweebida Bwobbida." Two numbers on the CD reissue feature a smaller unit out of the group with "Mulligan's Too" being an extended workout for the leader and Eager. —*Scott Yanow*

☆ **Pacific Jazz and Capitol Recordings** / Jun. 10, 1952-Jun. 10, 1953 / Mosaic ♦♦♦♦♦

This five-LP box set, as its title states, contains all of the Gerry Mulligan Quartet's recordings for Pacific Jazz and Capitol, everything that that classic group ever recorded other than the material issued by Prestige and a half-record recorded for GNP/Crescendo. Unfortunately, this is a limited-edition set that is now out of print, but it is well worth bidding on in auctions, for not only does it have all of the Mulligan Quartet's other recordings, but also 15 previously unissued performances, all of the sides on which altoist Lee Konitz sat in with the quartet and the eight recordings by the 1953 Gerry Mulligan Tentette. These highly influential performances set the standard for West Coast cool jazz, made trumpeter Chet Baker a star and remain some of the high points of Gerry Mulligan's very productive career. —*Scott Yanow*

☆ **The Complete Pacific Jazz Recordings of the Gerry Mulligan Quartet with Chet Baker** / Jun. 10, 1952-Dec. 17, 1957 / Pacific Jazz ♦♦♦♦

Baritonist Gerry Mulligan's pianoless quartet of 1952-53 with trumpeter Chet Baker was one of the most popular groups of the period and an influential force on West Coast jazz. Mulligan's interplay with Baker looked back towards the collective improvisation of Dixieland but utilized up-to-date harmonies. This four-CD set overlaps with a previous (and now out-of-print) five-LP Mosaic box. In addition to all of the Pacific Jazz (as opposed to Fantasy and GNP/Crescendo) recordings of the Mulligan Quartet (including the hit version of "My Funny Valentine"), this box has a few slightly earlier titles that find Mulligan gradually forming the group (even utilizing pianist Jimmie Rowles on two songs), tunes from live sessions in which altoist Lee Konitz made the band a quintet, the 1957 Mulligan-Baker set called *Reunion* and an Annie Ross date from the same period (leaving out the numbers that have Art Farmer in Baker's place). Despite both musicians remaining active for over 30 years, Mulligan and Baker only teamed up again on one occasion, for a 1970s Carnegie Hall concert released by CTI. The consistently delightful music on this box (much of which is classic) is highly recommended for all jazz collections. —*Scott Yanow*

Jazz Profile / Jan. 29, 1953-Dec. 5, 1957 / Blue Note ♦♦

Part of Blue Note's 1997 CD reissue series, this set has nine numbers taken from baritonist Gerry Mulligan's Pacific Jazz years. He meets up with trumpeter Chet Baker on two quartet numbers (including "My Funny Valentine") and in a ten-piece, joins valve trombonist Bob Brookmeyer in a quartet and a sextet (with the swinging tenor of Zoot Sims), and plays three originals in an octet arranged by Bill Holman (released originally as *The Mulligan Songbook*). The music is excellent, but the sequencing (which jumps around chronologically) is almost random, hitting some of Jeru's early high points almost by accident. —*Scott Yanow*

Gerry Mulligan Quartet with Chet Baker / May 7, 1953-Jun. 1953 / GNP ◆◆◆
The first side of this LP has the six rarest studio performances by the Gerry Mulligan quartet, excellent music that does not duplicate the Mosaic box or Jeru's Prestige output. The quartet with trumpeter Chet Baker sounds at the top of its form on such songs as "Varsity Drag," "Speak Low," "Half Nelson," "Lady Bird," "Love Me or Leave Me" and "Swing House." The second half of this set is not on the same level, finding the Buddy DeFranco quartet of 1953 hampered by the Herman McCoy Swing Choir on six numbers, all of which have "Star" in its title. This budget set inexcusably leaves off any personnel or date listing but is worth picking up for the Mulligan performances. —*Scott Yanow*

Gerry Mulligan in Paris, Vol. 1 / Jun. 1, 1954+Jun. 3, 1954 / Vogue ◆◆◆◆◆
Formerly available in piecemeal fashion, this CD (and *Vol. 2*) has all of the music recorded at baritonist Gerry Mulligan's Paris concerts of June 1954. This particular unit (with valve trombonist Bob Brookmeyer, bassist Red Mitchell and drummer Frank Isola) was one of Jeru's finest, for his own wit, swing and cool-toned creativity were matched by Brookmeyer. High points include "Walkin' Shoes," "Love Me or Leave Me," "My Funny Valentine" and "Five Brothers," but every selection is quite enjoyable. The audience is rightfully enthusiastic. —*Scott Yanow*

Gerry Mulligan in Paris, Vol. 2 / Jun. 3, 1954-Jun. 7, 1954 / Vogue ◆◆◆◆◆
In June 1954, the Gerry Mulligan Quartet (with the leader/baritonist, valve trombonist Bob Brookmeyer, bassist Red Mitchell and drummer Frank Isola) performed at five all-star concerts, four of which were recorded. Only previously available in fragmented form, the very accessible yet chance-taking music has now been reissued in full on two CDs by the French Vogue label. The second volume is highlighted by "Laura," "Five Brothers," "Love Me or Leave Me," "Line for Lyons" and "Motel," but it is no exaggeration to say that every performance is well worth hearing. Both sets are highly recommended, for this cool-toned but witty and hard-swinging music is very enjoyable. —*Scott Yanow*

California Concerts, Vol. 1 / Nov. 12, 1954 / Pacific Jazz ◆◆◆◆◆
This CD documents a concert by Gerry Mulligan's Quartet when the baritonist's group featured trumpeter Jon Eardley, bassist Red Mitchell and drummer Chico Hamilton. Half of these ten selections were either previously unissued or only available as part of obscure samplers. The music, comprising standards, some blues and a few Mulligan originals, is quite enjoyable, swinging lightly and with plenty of interplay between the horns. —*Scott Yanow*

California Concerts, Vol. 2 / Dec. 14, 1954 / Pacific Jazz ◆◆◆◆◆
The second of two CDs in this series mostly consists of previously unissued material taken from a high school concert featuring the Gerry Mulligan Quartet (which at the time featured trumpeter Jon Eardley) plus two guests (valve trombonist Bob Brookmeyer and tenor saxophonist Zoot Sims). This swinging and often witty cool bop music is quite enjoyable and highly recommended. —*Scott Yanow*

Mainstream, Vol. 2 / Sep. 21, 1955-Sep. 22, 1955 / EmArcy ◆◆◆
The Gerry Mulligan Sextet of 1955-56 only released three LPs at the time, but decades later, the revived EmArcy label came up with two more albums of material, alternate takes that feature completely different solos than the more familiar versions. Mulligan's band at the time of the second volume included trumpeter Jon Eardley, valve trombonist Bob Brookmeyer and Zoot Sims on tenor, in addition to bassist Peck Morrison and drummer Dave Bailey. This infectious set is highlighted by "The Lady Is a Tramp," "Broadway," and "Bernie's Tune," all of the music previously unissued. —*Scott Yanow*

Presenting the Gerry Mulligan Sextet / Sep. 21, 1955-Oct. 31, 1955 / EmArcy ◆◆◆◆
The short-lived Gerry Mulligan sextet of 1955-56 recorded three albums before disbanding. This particular out-of-print LP features baritonist Mulligan, trumpeter Jon Eardley, valve trombonist Bob Brookmeyer and Zoot Sims on tenor performing such songs as "Nights at the Turntable," "Broadway," "The Lady Is a Tramp" and "Bernie's Tune." Fun swinging music that is still quite accessible. —*Scott Yanow*

A Profile of Gerry Mulligan / Sep. 21, 1955-Sep. 26, 1956 / Mercury ◆◆◆◆
The second of three LPs recorded by the 1955-56 Gerry Mulligan sextet before it broke up, this fine out-of-print set features such excellent players as baritonist Mulligan, valve trombonist Bob Brookmeyer, Zoot Sims on tenor and either Jon Eardley or Don Ferrara on trumpet. Highlights include "Makin' Whoopie," a Duke Ellington medley and "Westward Walk." Excellent music from one of the top West Coast jazz groups; this band was actually based in New York. —*Scott Yanow*

Mainstream of Jazz / Sep. 22, 1955-Sep. 26, 1956 / EmArcy ◆◆◆◆
One of three LPs recorded by the Gerry Mulligan Sextet of 1955-56, this set includes plenty of lesser-known songs including "Mainstream," "Igloo" and "Lollypop." With such strong soloists as baritonist Mulligan, the always swinging tenor of

Zoot Sims, valve trombonist Bob Brookmeyer and trumpeter Jon Eardley, this was a classic West Coast style jazz band and each of its recordings are worth acquiring. —*Scott Yanow*

Mainstream, Vol. 3 / Oct. 31, 1955-Jan. 25, 1956 / EmArcy ◆◆◆◆
Gerry Mulligan's 1955-56 Sextet recorded three LPs that were released at the time. Nearly three decades later two additional albums (*Mainstream, Vols. 2 and 3*) were issued that included previously unknown alternate takes. Naturally, the solos by the talented players (which include baritone-saxophonist Mulligan, Zoot Sims on tenor, valve trombonist Bob Brookmeyer and trumpeter Jon Eardley) are different than on the master takes. The music (highlighted by "Broadway," "The Lady Is a Tramp" and "Westwood Walk") is quite enjoyable. All of this band's recordings are recommended; hopefully they will appear on CD eventually. —*Scott Yanow*

At Storyville / Dec. 6, 1956 / Pacific Jazz ◆◆◆◆◆
This live concert from the Storyville Club in Boston features Gerry Mulligan's Quartet in late 1956. Baritonist Mulligan had found a perfect partner in valve trombonist Bob Brookmeyer and (with the sympathetic support of bassist Bill Crow and drummer Dave Bailey) they romp through a variety of standards and group originals including such odd titles as "Bweebida Bwobbida," "Utter Chaos" (their theme song) and "Bike up the Strand." A fine all-round performance from this cool-toned bop unit. —*Scott Yanow*

Blues in Time / Aug. 2, 1957+Aug. 27, 1957 / Mobile Fidelity ◆◆◆
This CD from the audiophile label Mobile Fidelity brings back a classic Verve set that matches together baritonist Gerry Mulligan and altoist Paul Desmond. With bassist Joe Benjamin and drummer Dave Bailey completing the pianoless quartet, Mulligan and Desmond are clearly inspired, battling each other and coming up with consistently witty and inventive solos. Although there are five "originals" on this set (along with "Body and Soul" and Mulligan's "Line for Lyons"), all are based on the chord changes of common songs including "Stand Still" ("My Heart Stood Still") and "Battle Hymn of the Republican" ("Tea for Two"). Mulligan's baritone and Desmond's alto fit together perfectly and they bring out the best in each other, making this a highly recommended set for all jazz collections. —*Scott Yanow*

Mulligan Meets Monk / Aug. 12, 1957-Aug. 13, 1957 / Original Jazz Classics ◆◆◆◆
In the late '50s/early '60s, baritonist Gerry Mulligan participated in several recorded "meetings" with jazz musicians who he admired. For this set (reissued on CD in the OJC series), Mulligan teams up with pianist Thelonious Monk (whom shares co-leadership), bassist Wilbur Ware and drummer Shadow Wilson on a surprisingly successful date. Monk and Mulligan blend together quite well on what was essentially Thelonious' repertoire of the era including "'Round Midnight," "Rhythm-a-Ning," "Sweet and Lovely" and "I Mean You"; the CD reissue also includes three alternate takes and has plenty of joyful spirit. —*Scott Yanow*

Gerry Mulligan Meets Stan Getz / Oct. 22, 1957 / Verve ◆◆◆

Reunion with Chet Baker / Dec. 3, 1957-Dec. 17, 1957 / EMI-Manhattan ◆◆◆◆
The Gerry Mulligan Quartet of 1952-53 was one of the best-loved jazz groups of the decade and it made stars out of both the leader and trumpeter Chet Baker. Mulligan and Baker had very few reunions after 1953, but this particular CD from 1957 is an exception. Although not quite possessing the magic of the earlier group, the music is quite enjoyable and the interplay between the two horns is still special. With expert backup by bassist Henry Grimes and drummer Dave Bailey, these 13 selections (plus two new alternate takes) should please fans of both Mulligan and Baker. —*Scott Yanow*

Songbook / Dec. 4, 1957-Dec. 5, 1957 / Blue Note ◆◆◆◆◆
Until it was reissued on CD, this was one of the rarer Gerry Mulligan albums. The original program consisted of seven Mulligan compositions played by a five-sax octet (including the leader on baritone, altoist Lee Konitz, Allen Eager and Zoot Sims doubling on tenor and alto, Al Cohn on tenor and baritone and a rhythm section consisting of guitarist Freddie Green, bassist Henry Grimes, and drummer Dave Bailey). The session has a few surprise touches, giving listeners the rare opportunity to hear Eager and Sims soloing on alto and Cohn doubling on baritone. This was Allen Eager's first recording in several years and would be the last one of his prime (Eager's next album would be for Uptown in 1982); he had other interests outside of music. Perhaps the biggest surprise of the date is that the clever, witty and swinging arrangements are not by Mulligan but by Bill Holman. The CD reissue is rounded off by four selections from a largely unissued ("The Preacher" came out as an edited sampler) session featuring Mulligan with drummer Dave Bailey and a string quartet led by bassist Vinnie Burke. The performances are not chamber music but fairly conventional if spirited bop. Cellist Calo Scott trades off a bit with Jeru and guitarist Remo Palmieri makes one wonder what ever happened to him. Highly recommended for Gerry Mulligan fans. —*Scott Yanow*

I Want to Live / May 24, 1958 / United Artists ✦✦✦✦

Baritonist Gerry Mulligan and a group of West Coast all-stars were heard throughout the soundtrack of the Susan Hayward movie *I Want to Live*. Although not a soundtrack, this LP features six themes from the movie (all composed by Johnny Mandel) performed by the same musicians, who this time around get an opportunity to really stretch out. Since the band comprises Mulligan, trumpeter Art Farmer, altoist Bud Shank, trombonist Frank Rossolino, pianist Pete Jolly, bassist Red Mitchell and drummer Shelly Manne, virtually all of the music is quite interesting with plenty of fine solos and hard swinging. —*Scott Yanow*

☆ **What Is There to Say?** / Dec. 17, 1958-Jan. 15, 1959 / Columbia ✦✦✦✦✦

The last of the pianoless quartet albums that Gerry Mulligan recorded in the 1950s is one of the best, featuring the complementary trumpet of Art Farmer, bassist Bill Crow and drummer Dave Bailey along with the baritonist/leader. This CD reissue of the LP is a little skimpy on playing time but makes every moment count. Virtually every selection is memorable with "What Is There to Say," "Just in Time," "Festive Minor," "My Funny Valentine" and "Utter Chaos" being the high points. Highly recommended both to Mulligan collectors and to jazz listeners who are just discovering the great baritonist. —*Scott Yanow*

The New Gerry Mulligan Quartet (May 19, 1959) / May 19, 1959 / Tax ✦✦✦✦

Baritonist Gerry Mulligan's 1958-59 pianoless quartet with trumpeter Art Farmer, bassist Bill Crow and drummer Dave Bailey did not last that long and only cut one studio album, making this live CD rather valuable. Six of the numbers from the quartet's studio record are heard in fresh versions; plus, there are two selections ("I Can't Get Started" and "Spring Is Sprung") that find Mulligan switching to piano. However, it is the former performances (particularly "As Catch Can," "Just in Time" and a lengthy "Blueport") that are of greatest interest. The interplay between Mulligan and Farmer in the near-classic group makes this an easily recommended set for straightahead jazz collectors. —*Scott Yanow*

★ **Gerry Mulligan Meets Ben Webster** / Nov. 3, 1959-Dec. 2, 1959 / Mobile Fidelity ✦✦✦✦✦

Baritone-saxophonist Gerry Mulligan, a modern who loved to jam with the older musicians, always had a flexible style. He had the opportunity (due to his popularity) to record with several of the major active saxophonists of the 1950s and '60s. This CD finds him sharing the spotlight with the great veteran tenor Ben Webster. Their original six-song LP program is, on this reissue, augmented by five additional selections that were previously unissued but are played at the same high quality. The nearly 77-minute program (during which Mulligan and Webster are joined by pianist Jimmy Rowles, bassist Leroy Vinnegar and drummer Mel Lewis) is full of solid swing, some witty improvising and a few beautiful ballads. —*Scott Yanow*

A Night in Rome, Vol. 2 / 1959 / Fini Jazz ✦✦✦

The Concert Jazz Band / May 28, 1960-Jul. 27, 1960 / Verve ✦✦✦✦

This out-of-print Verve LP has the first recording by Gerry Mulligan's Concert Jazz Band, his 13-piece unit of the early '60s. In addition to the baritonist-leader (who also provided the arrangements), the other key soloists include tenor saxophonist Zoot Sims and valve trombonist Bob Brookmeyer; drummer Mel Lewis propels the ensembles. Highlights include "Bweebida Bwobbida," a chart on Django Reinhardt's "Manoir Des Mes Reves" that recalls Claude Thornhill, a remake of "My Funny Valentine" and a hard-swinging version of "I'm Gonna Go Fishin'." All of the Concert Jazz Band recordings deserve to be reissued on CD. —*Scott Yanow*

Gerry Mulligan Meets Johnny Hodges / Jul. 1960 / Verve ✦✦✦✦

Another one of Gerry Mulligan's encounters with fellow saxophonists, this LP matches the flexible baritonist with the impeccable alto of Johnny Hodges. They contributed three originals apiece to this relaxed date and their tones proved to be quite complementary. Accompanied by pianist Claude Williamson, bassist Buddy Clark and drummer Mel Lewis, Mulligan and Hodges make for a very potent team. —*Scott Yanow*

And the Concert Jazz Band / Nov. 19, 1960 / RTE ✦✦✦✦✦

At a time when all of the important Verve recordings by Gerry Mulligan's Concert Jazz Band of 1960-63 are long out of print, this previously unissued concert performance (a two-CD set made available by the European RTE label) helped to fill the gap. There are many exciting moments among the 14 selections, including hot versions of "You Took Advantage of Me," "Apple Core," "Moten Swing," and "Bweebida Bwobbida"; the ballads include "Body and Soul" and "My Funny Valentine." With the leader's baritone, trumpeter Conte Candoli, valve trombonist Bob Brookmeyer and tenor saxophonist Zoot Sims all getting plenty of solo space and drummer Mel Lewis driving the ensembles, the 14-piece big band is heard at its best. One of the high points is the 21-minute, medium-tempo blues "Spring Is Sprung," which finds Mulligan soloing and comping on piano. Highly recommended. —*Scott Yanow*

The Gerry Mulligan Concert Jazz Band on Tour / Nov. 1960 / Verve ✦✦✦✦

☆ **Gerry Mulligan and the Concert Jazz Band at the Village Vanguard** / Dec. 1960 / Verve ✦✦✦✦✦

Of all the recordings made by Gerry Mulligan's Concert Jazz Band in the 1960s, this is the definitive one. There are many high points including "Body and Soul" (which has fine solos from the baritonist-leader and valve trombonist Bob Brookmeyer), "Come Rain or Come Shine" and the swinging "Let My People Be," but "Blueport" takes honors. On the latter, after hot solos by Mulligan, trombonist Willie Dennis and Jim Reider on tenor, Mulligan and trumpeter Clark Terry have a lengthy trade-off that is quite hilarious with a countless number of quotes from different songs; at one point they trade off cities. Not yet out on CD, this music is essential. —*Scott Yanow*

Holiday with Mulligan / Apr. 10, 1961-Apr. 17, 1961 / DRG ✦✦

Baritone-saxophonist Gerry Mulligan and actress Judy Holliday were an "item" around the time of this recording. Their one meeting on record features Holliday doing some effective singing on 11 songs, mostly lesser-known standards plus four songs co-written by the two leaders. Unfortunately, Mulligan's Concert Jazz Band is largely wasted, being restricted to anonymous accompaniment of Holliday, making this CD of greater historical value than of interest to jazz listeners. —*Scott Yanow*

Presents a Concert in Jazz / Jul. 10, 1961-Jul. 11, 1961 / Verve ✦✦✦✦

For the third record by his Concert Jazz Band, baritonist Gerry Mulligan recorded concert works by the likes of George Russell ("All About Rosie"), Gary McFarland ("Weep" and "Chuggin'") and Johnny Carisi ("Israel") in addition to two of his own compositions. With strong solos from Mulligan, valve trombonist Bob Brookmeyer, Don Ferrara and Nick Travis on trumpets and altoist Gene Quill, this LP offers a set of excellent music from the legendary big band. —*Scott Yanow*

Jeru / Jun. 30, 1962 / RCA ✦✦✦

While Gerry Mulligan was famous in the 1950s for leading pianoless quartets, he never had anything against pianists; in fact he often played piano himself. This 1962 quintet session finds Jeru utilizing the strong talents of pianist Tommy Flanagan along with bassist Ben Tucker, drummer Dave Bailey and the congas of Alec Dorsey to play seven songs (all but "Get out of Town" are somewhat obscure). Mulligan is in fine form and, even if the music on this LP is not all that essential, it is quite enjoyable. —*Scott Yanow*

And His Quartet / Oct. 6, 1962 / RTE ✦✦✦

Originally broadcast over French radio and released for the first time in 1994, this performance from 1962 finds Gerry Mulligan and his sidemen (valve trombonist Bob Brookmeyer, bassist Bill Crow and drummer Gus Johnson) generally sounding inspired throughout their spirited set. Mulligan is first heard taking a fine blues solo on piano during "Spring Is Sprung" before Brookmeyer enters to make the trio a quartet; Jeru also plays piano on "Darn That Dream" while Brookmeyer accompanies the baritonist on "Subterranean Blues." The one disappointment to the set is that the two horns only interact on "Five Brothers" and "Blueport" (other than the brief closing theme "Utter Chaos"), but even on the piano pieces there is enough creativity, wit and charm to continually hold one's interest and the tradeoff on "Blueport" is a high point. —*Scott Yanow*

Gerry Mulligan (1963) / Dec. 18, 1962-Dec. 21, 1962 / Verve ✦✦✦

The final recording by Gerry Mulligan's Concert Jazz Band before he had to break it up is one of its lesser efforts but still quite worthwhile. With originals by Bob Brookmeyer, Gary McFarland and the baritonist/leader (in addition to the standards "Little Rock Getaway" and "My Kind of Love"), this is a high-quality if rather brief program. Trumpeter Clark Terry and guitarist Jim Hall co-star with Mulligan in the solo department. It is a pity that this orchestra could not prosper; all five of its recordings are worth getting. —*Scott Yanow*

Night Lights / Sep. 12, 1963-Oct. 3, 1963 / Verve ✦✦✦

This is a rather relaxed LP featuring baritonist Gerry Mulligan and some of his top alumni (trumpeter Art Farmer, trombonist Bob Brookmeyer, guitarist Jim Hall, bassist Bill Crow and drummer Dave Bailey) exploring three of his own songs (including "Festive Minor"), Chopin's "Prelude in E Minor," "Wee Small Hours" and "Morning of the Carnival" (from *Black Orpheus*). The emphasis is on ballads and nothing too innovative occurs, but the results are pleasing and laidback. —*Scott Yanow*

If You Can't Beat 'em, Join 'em / Jul. 22, 1965-Jul. 28, 1965 / Limelight ✦✦

Feelin' Good / Oct. 10, 1965-Oct. 22, 1965 / Limelight ✦✦

Something Borrowed, Something Blue / Jul. 19, 1966 / Limelight ✦✦✦

This unusual quintet set finds Gerry Mulligan playing alto rather than baritone on four of the six selections. Tenor saxophonist Zoot Sims co-stars and, with the assistance of a fine rhythm section (pianist Warren Bernhardt, bassist Eddie Gomez and drummer Dave Bailey), the complementary horns explore Bix Beiderbecke's "Davenport Blues," the standard "New Orleans," "Sometime Ago" and three obscure but worthwhile Mulligan originals. This forgotten collector's item (the LP has not been available for decades) features swinging music with plenty of fine moments. —*Scott Yanow*

Jazz Fest Masters / Jun. 1969 / Scotti Bros. ✦✦✦✦

This is an easy CD to miss since it was part of the Scotti Bros. *Jazzfest Masters,* a series probably destined for complete obscurity. Recorded at the 1969 New Orleans Jazz Festival, this set is highlighted by three wonderful chance-taking performances by a quartet comprising baritonist Gerry Mulligan, altoist Paul Desmond, bassist Milt Hinton and drummer Alan Dawson, a brilliant unit that otherwise never recorded. Their version of "Line for Lyons" is classic. Two other songs (including a brief "Take Five") have pianist Jaki Byard making the group a quintet and there are a pair of features for Mulligan with the University of Illinois Orchestra. The final selection showcases altoist Al Belleto with The Loyola University Jazz Band on "What's New." But the reason to acquire this CD is for the unique Mulligan-Desmond quartet. —*Scott Yanow*

Age of Steam / Feb. 1971-Sep. 1971 / A&M ✦✦✦✦

During the 1952-65 period baritonist Gerry Mulligan was one of the most famous musicians in jazz but he spent the following five years at a lower profile, recording relatively little and not leading any significant bands. *Age of Steam* was a comeback record of sorts (although he had never declined), giving Jeru the opportunity to lead a big band again. The ensemble performs eight of his recent originals (the best known is "K4 Pacific"), featuring solos by Mulligan (who was now doubling on soprano), Tom Scott on tenor and soprano, Bud Shank on alto and flute, valve trombonist Bob Brookmeyer and trumpeter Harry "Sweets" Edison. The highly enjoyable music (last available on this A&M CD in 1988) still sounds fresh and spirited. —*Scott Yanow*

Carnegie Hall Concert / Nov. 24, 1974 / CTI ✦✦✦

At this 1974 concert baritonist Gerry Mulligan and trumpeter Chet Baker had one of their very rare reunions; it would be only the second and final time that they recorded together after Mulligan's original quartet broke up in 1953. Oddly enough, a fairly contemporary rhythm section was used (keyboardist Bob James, vibraphonist Dave Samuels, bassist Ron Carter, drummer Harvey Mason and, in one of his first recordings, guitarist John Scofield). However, some of the old magic was still there between the horns; and, in addition to two of Mulligan's newer tunes, this set (the first of two LP volumes) also includes fresh versions of "Line for Lyons" and "My Funny Valentine." —*Scott Yanow*

Carnegie Hall Concert, Vol. 2 / Nov. 24, 1974 / CTI ✦✦✦

On the second of two LP volumes, Gerry Mulligan and Chet Baker renew ties for only the second and final time since Mulligan's classic quartet disbanded in 1953. In addition to "Bernie's Tune" and the standard "There Will Never Be Another You," Baker, Mulligan and a young rhythm section (which includes guitarist John Scofield and keyboardist Bob James) perform two newer songs by Jeru. This is is a historically significant and musical set by a pair of masters who should have had more reunions. —*Scott Yanow*

Gerry Mulligan Meets Enrico Intra / Oct. 16, 1975-Oct. 17, 1975 / Pausa ✦✦✦

An unusual entry in baritonist Gerry Mulligan's discography, this LP (recorded in Italy during a two-year stay) finds Mulligan teaming up with pianist Enrico Intra, the reeds of Giancarlo Barigozzi and an Italian rhythm section to play four new compositions, one of his and the other three by Intra. Jeru (who also plays some soprano in addition to his customary baritone) sounds quite creative stretching out on these obscure but rewarding originals. —*Scott Yanow*

Idol Gossip / Nov. 1976 / Chiaroscuro ✦✦✦

This somewhat forgotten studio session finds Gerry Mulligan, 25 years after he first achieved fame with his quartet, playing six of his fairly recent compositions along with a version of "Waltzing Mathilda." With vibraphonist Dave Samuels and a four-piece rhythm section accompanying him, Mulligan performs such songs as "Walk on the Water," "Idol Gossip" and "Strayhorn 2;" the latter a reworking of his "Song for Strayhorn." Jeru proves to still be in prime form and plays a bit of soprano sax on this date along with his distinctive baritone. —*Scott Yanow*

Lionel Hampton Presents Gerry Mulligan / Oct. 29, 1977 / Who's Who ✦✦✦

Walk on the Water / Sep. 1980 / DRG ✦✦✦

Baritonist Gerry Mulligan has had few opportunities to record with a big band since his Concert Jazz Band broke up in 1963, a real pity considering how talented a composer and arranger he has been. This DRG LP features a strong orchestra (with such soloists as trumpeter Tom Harrell, altoist Gerry Niewood, pianist Mitchel Forman among others) performing several of Jeru's compositions (including "For an Unfinished Woman," "Song for Strayhorn" and "Walk on the Water"), Forman's "Angelica" and Duke Ellington's "Across the Track Blues" along with the standard "I'm Getting Sentimental over You." —*Scott Yanow*

La Menace / 1982 / DRG ✦✦

Little Big Horn / 1983 / GRP ✦✦✦

On one of the first relatively straightahead sessions for GRP, baritonist Gerry Mulligan (accompanied by a rhythm section led by Dave Grusin's keyboards with an occasional horn section) performs six of his then-recent compositions, including the title cut. Strangely enough, the most memorable selection is "I Never Was a Young Man" which has a rare but very effective Mulligan vocal. Otherwise, the music is good but not classic. —*Scott Yanow*

Soft Lights and Sweet Music / Jan. 1986 / Concord Jazz ✦✦✦✦

Starting in the late '50s, Gerry Mulligan recorded a series of encounters with fellow saxophonists that included such immortals as Stan Getz, Paul Desmond, Johnny Hodges and Ben Webster. In 1986 he resumed the practice for this one date on which his baritone is matched with the tenor of the young great Scott Hamilton. The music, which includes warm ballads and fairly hot romps (five of the seven songs are Mulligan originals), consistently swing and are quite enjoyable. —*Scott Yanow*

Symphonic Dreams / Feb. 6, 1987-Feb. 7, 1987 / Intersound ✦✦✦

Gerry Mulligan meets a symphony orchestra on this unusual CD. The Houston Symphony (under the direction of Erich Kunzel) performs the seven sections of "The Sax Chronicles" (compositions of Harry Freedman based on Mulligan themes written in the style of a variety of classical composers), two shorter pieces by the classic jazzman ("Song for Strayhorn" and "K-4 Pacific") and a classical work written by Jeru: "Entente for Baritone Sax and Orchestra." The music fits the category of Third Stream and could be called jazzy classical music. It's worth a close listen. —*Scott Yanow*

Lonesome Boulevard / Mar. 1989-Sep. 1989 / A&M ✦✦✦✦

The 1989 Gerry Mulligan Quartet (with pianist Bill Charlap, bassist Dean Johnson and drummer Richie De Rosa) is well featured on this enjoyable set, performing "Splendor in the Grass" and nine recent Gerry Mulligan compositions including "Lonesome Boulevard," "The Flying Scotsman" and "Good Neighbor Thelonious." Baritonist Mulligan deserves great credit for the consistency of his recordings during the previous 40 years. This CD is easily recommended for the leader remained very much in his prime. —*Scott Yanow*

Re-Birth of the Cool / Jan. 29, 1992-Jan. 31, 1992 / GRP ✦✦✦✦

In the summer of 1991 Gerry Mulligan decided to revisit Miles Davis' *Birth of the Cool* recordings. He discussed it with Miles Davis himself who said he might be interested in participating, but sadly Davis died a few months later. With Wallace Roney (the perfect sound-alike) in the trumpeter's place, baritonist Mulligan got the band's original pianist and tuba player (John Lewis and Bill Barber), used his own bassist (Dean Johnson) and drummer (Ron Vincent), and found able substitutes in altoist Phil Woods (unfortunately Lee Konitz was unavailable to play his old parts), trombonist Dave Bargeron and John Clark on French horn. This GRP CD brings back the dozen *Birth of the Cool* recordings of 1949-50 with Mel Tormé taking Pancho Hagood's vocal on "Darn That Dream." Although the charts are the same (and it is a particular pleasure to listen to them with the improved recording quality), the solos are all different and in many cases have been lengthened; no need to stick to only three minutes apiece. This fascinating disc is most highly recommended to veteran jazz collectors who know the original *Birth of the Cool* records. —*Scott Yanow*

Paraiso-Jazz Brazil / Jul. 5, 1993-Jul. 7, 1993 / Telarc ✦✦✦

Dream a Little Dream / 1994 / Telarc ✦✦✦✦

Baritonist Gerry Mulligan had at the time of this recording been a jazz giant for 45 years. His slightly bubbly baritone sound has always been distinctive and he never had difficulty jamming with anyone. In the 1990s Mulligan's regular trio has included pianist Ted Rosenthal, bassist Dean Johnson and drummer Ron Vincent. The sidemen work together very well on this quartet date (Bill Mays fills in for Rosenthal on two songs) and form a solid foundation for Mulligan to float over. The baritonist performs a variety of superior standards such as "Home," "They Say It's Wonderful" and "My Shining Hour," revives "My Funny Valentine" and revisits a few of his originals (including "Walking Shoes" and "Song for Strayhorn"). This is a fine example of Gerry Mulligan's playing. —*Scott Yanow*

Dragon Fly / Mar. 12, 1995-Jun. 27, 1995 / Telarc ✦✦✦

On what was probably Gerry Mulligan's last studio album (recorded less than a year before his death), the great baritonist is heard still in prime form. He contributed all ten compositions and the emphasis is on lyricism and slower tempos; only three songs are taken above a medium pace. There are fine cameos by Grover Washington, Jr., on tenor and soprano (during the first two numbers), cornetist Warren Vache and trumpeter Ryan Kisor. In addition, guitarist John Scofield and vibraphonist Dave Samuels (who both played with Jeru in the 1970s) are on many of the tracks and pianist Dave Grusin is on some, although there is no identification as to which songs. A five-piece brass section was overdubbed on a later occasion. But even with the guests, the focus is generally on Gerry Mulligan and his longtime quartet. The music is thoughtful and tasteful, although it is doubtful if any of the tunes will ever catch on as standards. This is a tasteful if not quite essential final effort by Mulligan, who seems to have ended his very important career quite peacefully. —*Scott Yanow*

Jimmy Mundy

b. Jun. 28, 1907, Cincinnati, OH, **d.** Apr. 24, 1983, New York, NY
Arranger / Swing

One of the finer arrangers of the swing era, Jimmy Mundy never became a big name to the general public, but musicians of the era certainly knew who he was. He played tenor in various local bands and when he was hired by Earl Hines in 1932, he originally played in the orchestra. However, it was his charts (including his original "Cavernism," "Everything Depends on You" and "Copenhagen") that gave him a strong reputation. In 1936 he became a staff arranger for Benny Goodman, writing arrangements for such pieces as "Bugle Call Rag," "Jumpin' at the Woodside," "Swingtime in the Rockies," "Solo Flight" and "Sing, Sing, Sing." He also wrote charts for Count Basie, Gene Krupa, Paul Whiteman, Dizzy Gillespie (1949) and Harry James, among many others, and remained active into the 1970s. Jimmy Mundy led relatively few sessions: a small-group date in 1937, four songs by his short-lived orchestra in 1939, there are a few existing broadcasts of his 1946 Los Angeles band and he led two obscure Epic albums during 1958-59. —*Scott Yanow*

Mike Murley

b. 1962, Canada
Tenor Saxophone / Post-Bop

An excellent tenor saxophonist with a sound of his own, Mike Murley has been an important force in Canadian jazz since the early 1980s. He has recorded as a sideman with Time Warp, the Shuffle Demons, Brian Dickinson, Barry Elmes and Kevin Dean (among others), and led dates of his own for Unity and Counterpoint. Mike Murley has played and recorded with such name musicians as Kenny Wheeler, Randy Brecker and John Abercrombie. In 1988 (the year he spent in New York), Murley played often with Jack McDuff, but throughout his career, most of his work has taken place in Canada, where he has become an increasingly influential figure. —*Scott Yanow*

The Curse / Nov. 1987 / Unity ◆◆◆◆
In one of the first releases by the Unity label, four excellent Canadian jazzmen (tenor saxophonist Mike Murley, cornetist John MacLeod, bassist Jim Vivian and drummer Barry Elmes) come together to perform five of Murley's originals, plus Mal Waldron's "Soul Eyes." Three of the songs are dedicated to Duke Ellington, Elvin Jones and Ornette Coleman ("Orny"). The music is largely freebop with some complex structures, fairly free improvising, and strong interplay between the horn soloists and the rhythm section. Worth searching for by collectors of advanced hard bop. —*Scott Yanow*

● **Two Sides** / Feb. 1990-Mar. 1990 / Unity ◆◆◆◆◆

Time & Tide / Mar. 1992 / Unity ◆◆◆

Departure / Feb. 15, 1994-Feb. 16, 1994 / Cornerstone ◆◆◆
Mike Murley, one of the top saxophonists in Canada, has been careful to document his music fairly extensively for a variety of local labels. He is well showcased on this quartet outing with pianist Dave Restivo, bassist Jim Vivian and drummer Ted Warren, performing five of his tricky but logical originals (including "Dig Diz" and the four-part "Suite Sixties") and "Someone to Watch Over Me." Murley (who doubles here on tenor and soprano) has a distinctive tone, and his style is between hard bop and fairly free jazz. Excellent music. —*Scott Yanow*

Conversation Piece / Oct. 3, 1995-Oct. 4, 1995 / Cornerstone ◆◆◆◆◆
Mike Murley may not be a household name outside of Canada, but his many recordings are consistently stimulating and fresh. On this CD with pianist Dave Restivo, bassist Jim Vivian, drummer Ted Warren and (on four of the eight selections) the Kenny Wheeler-inspired trumpeter John MacLeod, Murley consistently shows off his versatility. He purposely plays "I've Got You Under My Skin" (the only standard of the date) in the style of Sonny Rollins, performs some hard bop originals (in some cases showing off the influence of Joe Henderson), sounds quite tender on Cedar Walton's waltz "Touch Her Soft Lips and Part" and switches to his playful soprano on Thelonious Monk's "Green Chimneys." The medium-tempo blues "L'Homard Blue" wraps up the advanced, straightahead date in swinging fashion. —*Scott Yanow*

Mark Murphy

b. Mar. 14, 1932, Syracuse, NY
Vocals / Post-Bop

A creative singer who has spent his entire career dedicated to jazz, Mark Murphy's wilder flights may not always succeed (sometimes his scatting in live performances can get a bit out of control) but they are never dull or predictable. Murphy began performing when he was 16, recorded his first album (for Capitol) in the late '50s, appeared on some television shows and then spent 1963-72 overseas, performing on radio and television and recording in Europe. Since returning to the US, Murphy has recorded a steady string of stimulating sets for Muse, even incorporating the stories and beat poetry of Jack Kerouac quite effectively on his *Bop for Kerouac* album. Mark Murphy has recorded throughout his career for Capitol, Riverside, Fontana, Saba, Audiophile and Muse. —*Scott Yanow*

This Could Be the Start of Something / May 28, 1959 / Capitol ◆◆◆
Mark Murphy's first album was originally put out by Capitol and was last available as a 1985 Pausa LP. Backed by various West Coast all-stars (including trumpeters Conte and Pete Candoli, either Bill Holman or Richie Kamuca on tenor, and a rhythm section headed by pianist Jimmy Rowles), Murphy sings well, if conventionally. The 13 standards include six concise songs (such as "The Lady Is a Tramp" and "Falling in Love with Love") while the second part of the album is a lengthy medley. Bill Holman provided the swinging arrangements. A good start to a major career. —*Scott Yanow*

● **The Best of Mark Murphy** / 1959-1960 / Capitol ◆◆◆◆◆
The Best of Mark Murphy is an excellent overview of the three albums Murphy recorded for Capitol in the late '50s that proves he was one of the more underrated singers of his era. Murphy is an inventive vocalist, putting new spins on songs like "Day In-Day Out," "Kansas City," "This Could Be the Start of Something Big," "I Only Have Eyes for You," "Witchcraft," "The Old Black Magic," "Cheek to Cheek" and "Lucky in Love." He may scat, improvise or twist the melody too much for some tastes, but the music is always intriguing, especially for fans of jazz vocalists. The 17-track compilation offers a good taste of his style and a good indication of his talents. [*The Best of Mark Murphy* represents the first time any of his Capitol material has been released on compact disc.] —*Stephen Thomas Erlewine*

Playing the Field / 1960 / Capitol ◆◆◆
The third of Mark Murphy's three Capitol LPs (all of which are long out of print) features the singer performing six songs apiece with an unidentified big band arranged by Bill Holman and an unknown trio (why was the personnel not listed?). Murphy is swinging, already displaying an individual voice, although the renditions are generally brief. Highlights include "Put the Blame on Mame," "Swinging on a Star," "Honeysuckle Rose" and "As Long as I Live." —*Scott Yanow*

Rah / Sep. 1961-Nov. 1961 / Original Jazz Classics ◆◆◆◆◆
Mark Murphy was in his early prime when he recorded this superb Riverside set, which has been reissued on CD. With Ernie Wilkins providing the arrangements for a brass ensemble and a rhythm section, Murphy sings 11 superior songs that fit his increasingly chance-taking style. Among the many highlights are "Angel Eyes," "Spring Can Really Hang You Up the Most," "Milestones" and "Doodlin'." Highly recommended. —*Scott Yanow*

That's How I Love the Blues / Oct. 1, 1962-Dec. 28, 1962 / Original Jazz Classics ◆◆◆◆◆
Despite the high quality of this release (currently available on a reissue CD) and the previous Riverside album, Mark Murphy would soon emigrate to Europe, not recording in the US again until 1972. The word "blues" (or in one case, "blue") is in the title of all 12 songs performed on the set. Not all of the numbers are technically blues (including "Blues in My Heart" and "The Meaning of the Blues"), but the great majority are. However, there is a good amount of variety; Al Cohn's charts for a couple of trumpets and a six-piece rhythm section (which includes both piano and organ) are swinging, and Murphy is in top early form. Highlights include "Going to Chicago Blues," "Senor Blues," "Fiesta in Blue" and "Blues in the Night." —*Scott Yanow*

Stolen & Other Moments / Nov. 20, 1972-Dec. 17, 1991 / 32 Jazz ◆◆◆◆

Bridging a Gap / Oct. 1973 / Muse ◆◆◆◆
The celebrated bop, ballads, standards, and scat vocalist sings with customary verve, clarity, and confidence, backed by a combo featuring Mike and Randy Brecker, Ron Carter, and more. —*Ron Wynn*

Mark 2 / May 1975 / Muse ◆◆◆
Strong, individualistic material featuring Murphy doing scat, interpretations, and reworkings of jazz and pre-rock pop tunes with his vivid delivery and dynamic manner. This was his second album for Muse under a unique arrangement that saw him cut several sessions for straight fee rather than royalties in exchange for complete artistic freedom. —*Ron Wynn*

Mark Murphy Sings / Jun. 17, 1975-Jun. 19, 1975 / Muse ✦✦✦✦✦
This CD reissue brings back one of singer Mark Murphy's best all-round sessions. Most memorable are his renditions of Freddie Hubbard's "Red Clay" (here renamed "On the Red Clay"), "Body and Soul" and "Canteloupe Island." Joined by a fine rhythm section led by keyboardist Don Grolnick along with occasional contributions from altoist David Sanborn, tenor saxophonist Michael Brecker and trumpeter Randy Brecker, Murphy is heard throughout in prime form, constantly stretching himself. —*Scott Yanow*

Stolen Moments / June 1, 1978 / Muse ✦✦✦✦✦
One of singer Mark Murphy's most famous records, this album finds him at the peak of his powers. This version of the title cut is considered a classic, and other high points of this gem include Murphy's interpretations of "Farmer's Market," Jobim's "Waters of March" and "Like a Lover." Joined by three horns (including altoist Richie Cole) and a fine San Francisco-based rhythm section led by pianist Smith Dobson, Mark Murphy consistently comes up with creative ideas. Essential music. —*Scott Yanow*

Satisfaction Guaranteed / Nov. 21, 1979 / Muse ✦✦✦✦✦
Good 1979 session with vocalist Mark Murphy putting his stamp on old standards and new tunes, scatting, vocalizing, and extending them in his fiery, dynamic way. His backing band included veteran trombonist Slide Hampton, plus alto saxophonist Richie Cole and baritone saxophonist Ronnie Cuber. —*Ron Wynn*

Bop for Kerouac / Mar. 12, 1981 / Muse ✦✦✦✦✦
This is an unusual recording. Singer Mark Murphy teams up with a fine sextet (featuring altoist Richie Cole and guitarist Bruce Forman) and alternating bop standards with readings from Jack Kerouac books. Since Kerouac was a big jazz fan in the 1950s and his interest in the music influenced the rhythms of his writing, this "poetry and jazz" set works surprisingly well. It also helps that Mark Murphy is heard at the peak of his powers. —*Scott Yanow*

The Artistry of Mark Murphy / Apr. 2, 1982-Apr. 3, 1982 / Muse ✦✦✦✦✦
Mark Murphy's string of Muse recordings contains most of his greatest work. This excellent album, which finds the jazz singer joined by a septet including trumpeter Tom Harrell, Gerry Niewood on reeds and keyboardist Ben Aranov, has many strong selections. Murphy's "Trilogy for Kids" is an inventive medley of "Babe's Blues," "Little Niles" and "Dat Dere." Other memorable numbers include "The Odd Child" (George Wallington's "Godchild" given Murphy's words), "Moody's Mood" and "Autumn Nocturne." Recommended. —*Scott Yanow*

Brazil Song (Cancoes do Brazil) / Aug. 2, 1983-Mar. 22, 1984 / Muse ✦✦✦
Sings the Nat "King" Cole Songbook / Oct. 8, 1983 / Muse ✦✦✦✦
This album (along with *Vol. 2*) finds Mark Murphy performing a rather unusual tribute to Nat "King" Cole. He utilizes the instrumentation of the King Cole Trio (piano, guitar and bass) but sings duets with each of the musicians individually, rather than using all of the players at once. Guitarist Joe LoDuca, keyboardist Gary Schunk and bassist Bob Magnusson are fine in support of the singer. Murphy explores such Cole-associated tunes as "Nature Boy/Calypso Blues," "'Tis Autumn" and "Lush Life." It would have been nice if all of the musicians could have played together a bit, but the strong material and Murphy's interpretive skills hold one's interest throughout. —*Scott Yanow*

Sings the Nat "King" Cole Songbook, Vol. 2 / Oct. 8, 1983 / Muse ✦✦✦✦
The second of two albums finding Mark Murphy paying tribute to Nat "King" Cole once again features him performing duets with keyboardist Gary Schunk, guitarist Joe LoDuca and bassist Bob Magnusson. Since Cole had recorded such a vast number of songs, Murphy mostly avoided the obvious hits, opting for particularly strong material that fits his chance-taking style. This date includes a medley of "Walkin' My Baby Back Home" and "Breezin' Along with the Breeze," as well as such tunes as "Blue Gardenia" and "More than You Know." —*Scott Yanow*

Living Room / Dec. 20, 1984-Dec. 21, 1984 / Muse ✦✦✦✦
For this date, Mark Murphy mixes together a few standards (including "There'll Be Some Changes Made" and a medley of "Misty" and "Midnight Sun," which features Grady Tate also singing) with some offbeat material (Abbey Lincoln's "Living Room," Dave Frishberg's "Our Love Rolls On" and a three-song L.A. medley). This time around, Murphy is joined by a sextet including trumpeter Ted Curson, tenorman Gerry Niewood and keyboardist David Braham. The rather humorous, Louis Jordan-associated "Ain't Nobody Here But Us Chickens" is a highlight. —*Scott Yanow*

Beauty and the Beast / Sep. 10, 1985-Nov. 23, 1986 / Muse ✦✦✦✦✦
Mark Murphy takes plenty of chances on this date. He recites the words he wrote to Wayne Shorter's "Beauty and the Beast" before singing the song, also finding something new to say on "I Can't Get Started" and interpreting such numbers as McCoy Tyner's "Effendi," "Along Came Betty" and "Vocalise"; the latter is based on a melody by Rachmaninoff. Murphy is assisted by a quintet that includes key-

boardist Bill Mays, trumpeter Brian Lynch and violinist Lou Lausche. A very interesting and colorful set. —*Scott Yanow*

Kerouac Then and Now / Nov. 1986 / Muse ✦✦✦✦✦
On this CD, Mark Murphy sings music that he thinks writer Jack Kerouac would have liked in addition to reading excerpts from two of the novelist's works and recreating a classic comedy routine by Lord Buckley. Among the songs Murphy performs (with the assistance of pianist Bill Mays, Steve LaSpina or John Goldsby on bass and drummer Adam Nussbaum) are a painfully slow and highly expressive version of Billy Strayhorn's "Blood Count," Richie Cole's tribute to Eddie Jefferson, a vocalese rendition of "Take the 'A' Train," the classic Thelonious Monk ballad "Ask Me Now," a descriptive "Lazy Afternoon" and a ballad medley. However, it is Mark Murphy's narratives that make this set most unique and memorable. —*Scott Yanow*

September Ballads / Sep. 15, 1987-Nov. 22, 1987 / Milestone ✦✦✦✦
On this date, Mark Murphy performs recent songs by a wide variety of artists, including the team of Pat Metheny and Lyle Mays, Michael Franks, Chick Corea ("Crystal Silence") and others. Unfortunately, the material overall is proof that at least for singers, they don't write them like they used to. Murphy sounds fine, and there are some notable musicians in the backup band (including fluegelhornist Art Farmer, guitarist Larry Coryell and pianist Larry Dunlap), but the overall results are just not that memorable. —*Scott Yanow*

What a Way to Go / Sep. 1990 / Muse ✦✦✦
I'll Close My Eyes / Dec. 16, 1991-Dec. 17, 1991 / Muse ✦✦✦✦
Night Mood / Dec. 31, 1991 / Milestone ✦✦✦
Mark Murphy made his Milestone debut with a set featuring him singing the music of Ivan Lins. Joined by the members of Azymuth and (on some numbers) altoist Frank Morgan and fluegelhornist Claudio Roditi, Murphy (54 at the time) is heard in fine voice on the mostly unfamiliar material, faring quite well even though the style is different than one would expect from the singer. —*Scott Yanow*

Turk Murphy (Melvin Edward Alton Murphy)

b. Dec. 16, 1915, Palermo, CA, **d.** May 30, 1987, San Francisco, CA
Trombone, Leader / Dixieland
Turk Murphy led one of the most popular bands of the San Francisco Dixieland movement. After playing with various big bands (including Mal Hallett and Will Osborne), Murphy first gained fame for his work with Lu Watters' highly influential Yerba Buena Jazz Band (1940-47). He formed his own group in 1947 and after 13 years they found a permanent home at Earthquake McGoon's; it also toured occasionally. Although not thought of as a virtuoso trombone soloist and his occasional singing was just passable, Murphy's ensemble work was superior. He put together a stimulating repertoire filled with obscurities and favorites from the 1920s (along with some newer originals) and his bands were always very musical; among his sidemen through the years were trumpeters Don Kinch, Bob Short and Leon Oakley, clarinetist Bob Helm, pianists Wally Rose, Pete Clute and Ray Skjelbred and singer Pat Yankee. Turk Murphy and his beloved group made many records for such labels as Good Time Jazz, Fairmont, Columbia (1953-56), Verve, Dawn Club, Roulette, RCA, Motherlode, Atlantic, GHB, MPS, Stomp Off and Merry Makers. —*Scott Yanow*

Turk Murphy's Jazz Band Favorites / May 31, 1949-April 1, 1952 / Good Time Jazz ✦✦✦✦✦
All of trombonist Turk Murphy's Good Time Jazz recordings of 1947-52 (all the studio sides he led prior to 1953) are now available on two CDs. The first volume has material from five different sessions and is filled with likable and swinging performances. In addition to the leader, the bands include either Bob Scobey or Don Kinch on trumpet, Bob Helm or Bill Napier on clarinet, and on piano either the legendary Burt Bales, Skip Anderson or Wally Rose. The music is essentially Dixieland, with some of the highlights being "When My Sugar Walks Down the Street," "Struttin' with Some Barbecue," "Trombone Rag," "Down by the Riverside" and "Cakewalkin' Babies from Home" (the latter has Clare Austin on vocals). —*Scott Yanow*

● **Turk Murphy's Jazz Band Favorites, Vol. 2** / Dec. 31, 1947-Jul. 10, 1951 / Good Time Jazz ✦✦✦✦✦
The second of two CDs reissuing all of trombonist Turk Murphy's performances for Good Time Jazz starts out with the very first session Murphy led: four hot numbers (including "Shake That Thing" and "Kansas City Man Blues") which feature a quintet also including trumpeter Bob Scobey, clarinetist Bob Helm, pianist Burt Bales and banjoist Harry Mordecai. The other selections generally find Murphy heading a septet with either Scobey or Don Kinch on trumpet. The music overall is hard-driving, straightforward Dixieland, played with an eye towards the past but not imitative of past versions. Both CDs are highly recommended to trad jazz collectors. —*Scott Yanow*

San Francisco Jazz, Vol. 2 / May 8, 1950-Jul. 10, 1951 / Good Time Jazz ◆◆◆◆

At the Italian Village / 1952-1953 / Merry Makers ◆◆◆◆
After the breakup of Lu Watters' Yerba Buena Jazz Band in late 1950, San Francisco had a lot more talent in the traditional jazz area than it did actual employment. Fortunately, a Sunday afternoon concert held Jan. 6, 1952, at the Italian Village night club that featured trombonist Turk Murphy was so successful that the venue became a haven for classic jazz for the next two years. The music, never before released, debuted on this very enjoyable CD. Not only was Murphy reunited with such Watters alumni as pianist Wally Rose and clarinetist Bob Helm, but this date was one of the earliest performances of housewife-turned-singer Claire Austin who would have a successful career through the rest of the decade. Murphy's septet (with trumpeter Don Kinch) performs a dozen hot jazz selections (four with powerful vocals by Austin in the Bessie Smith tradition) and the CD is rounded out by nine numbers from 1953 featuring a trumpetless quintet with Murphy, Helm and Rose. This very spirited CD is highly recommended for Dixieland fans. —*Scott Yanow*

Barrelhouse Jazz / Aug. 12, 1953 / Columbia ◆◆◆◆
By 1953, trombonist Turk Murphy's band was hitting its stride. Its first record date after signing with Columbia features the solid sextet (Murphy, trumpeter Don Kinch, clarinetist Bob Helm, pianist Wally Rose, banjoist Dick Lammi and Bob Short on tuba) mostly playing obscure tunes (including "Daddy Doo," "King Chanticleer," "The Torch" and Murphy's "Five Aces") along with fresh renditions of "Creole Belle," "Frankie and Johnny," "The Pearls" (which has Murphy switching to washboard) and the always-rousing "Panama." Unfortunately, Turk Murphy's series of Columbia records (unlike his earlier Good Time Jazz dates) have yet to be reissued on CD, but all are worth searching for. —*Scott Yanow*

When the Saints Go Marching In / Aug. 30, 1953-Dec. 14, 1953 / Columbia ◆◆◆◆
Unlike his previous Jelly Roll Morton project, this LP from Turk Murphy's trad jazz band mostly sticks to standards and warhorses. Murphy, trumpeter Bob Short, clarinetist Bob Helm, pianist Wally Rose, banjoist Dick Lammi and Freddie Crewes on tuba romp through such typical numbers as "St. Louis Blues," "Bill Bailey," and "The Saints," plus a rowdy "I Wished I Was in Peoria." The music overall is quite fun and spirited, if not containing any subtle surprises. Recommended to Dixieland fans, although this LP may be hard to locate. —*Scott Yanow*

Music of Jelly Roll Morton / Aug. 31, 1953-Sep. 14, 1953 / Columbia ◆◆◆◆◆
Turk Murphy's Jazz Band was the perfect group to revive and interpret Jelly Roll Morton's music in 1953. The trombonist really studied the early tunes and came up with enthusiastic, fresh, yet respectful interpretations. The sextet (also including either Don Kinch or Bob Short on trumpet, clarinetist Bob Helm, pianist Wally Rose, banjoist Dick Lammi and Freddie Crewes or Short on tuba) performs 16 Morton tunes highlighted by "Kansas City Stomps," "Mr. Jelly Lord," "Shreveport Stomp," "Milenberg Joys" and "The Pearls." During an era when there were many amateur groups playing Dixieland warhorses for partying audiences, Turk Murphy's band was generally on a much higher level altogether. Unfortunately, this LP (reissued in the 1970s) will probably be difficult to find. —*Scott Yanow*

Live at Easy Street, Vol. 1 / Nov. 7, 1958 / Dawn Club ◆◆◆◆
Trombonist Turk Murphy's band played at Easy Street (a club he owned for a time) in San Francisco regularly during the fall and winter of 1958. Three albums of radio broadcasts were issued, and this is the first LP. Murphy and his septet (which at the time included cornetist Bob Short, Jack Crook on clarinet and bass sax, pianist Pete Clute, banjoist Dick Lammi, Al Conger on bass and tuba, and drummer Thad Vandon) are heard on two of their weekly broadcasts, performing six selections on each show, in addition to their theme, "Bay City." The music mixes King Oliver and Jelly Roll Morton classics with a few standards and gives listeners a good idea of how the band sounded live during this period. Among the selections of this worthwhile release are "Sobbin' Blues," "Canal Street Blues," "Milenburg Joys" and "When You and I Were Young Maggie Blues." —*Scott Yanow*

Turk Murphy at the Round Table / Apr. 5, 1959 / Roulette ◆◆◆
For this spirited live set, Turk Murphy and his band (a sextet featuring the leader/trombonist, trumpeter Bob Short, clarinetist Bob Helm and pianist Pete Clute) perform a couple of originals ("Red Flannel Rag" and "Daybreak Blues"), some 1920s material ("Chicago Breakdown" and "Down Home Rag"), and Dixieland standards. Murphy and Pat Yankee take a couple vocals apiece and share the mike on two others. Nothing that unusual occurs, but the music has plenty of spirit, drive and enthusiasm. —*Scott Yanow*

Let the Good Times Roll / 1962 / RCA ◆◆◆◆
Trombonist Turk Murphy's lone recording for RCA would also be his band's last studio album until 1972. The addition of cornetist Ernie Carson to the sextet (which at the time also included clarinetist Bob Helm, pianist Pete Clute, Bob Short on tuba, and, surprisingly, Frank Capp on drums) gave the group a powerful soloist.

Pat Yankee takes vocals on five of the 11 numbers (including a vocal duet apiece with Turk Murphy and Ernie Carson), and overall, this is a fairly satisfying and well-rounded LP. Highlights include "Struttin' with Some Barbecue," an unusual version of "Bilbao Song" which has Clute switching to calliope, "Tiger Rag," and "Wild Man Blues." Worth a search by Dixieland fans. —*Scott Yanow*

● **The Earthquake McGoon Recordings** / 1972-1973 / Merry Makers ◆◆◆◆◆
This highly enjoyable Dixieland CD reissues all of the music from the earlier Merry Maker LP *Turk Murphy's San Francisco Jazz Band* and seven of the dozen selections (leaving out four vocals plus "Harlem Rag") from *Vol. 2*. Trombonist Murphy's group made very few recordings during the 1960s (their music was considered out of style) but fortunately was better documented during the following decade. His sextet (featuring the powerful cornetist Leon Oakley, clarinetist Phil Howe, pianist Pete Clute, Jim Maihack on tuba and either Dick Speer or Carl Lunsford on banjo) was particularly strong in the early '70s and these live renditions of 1920s material (with many tunes from the repertoire of King Oliver and Jelly Roll Morton) are played with spirit, authenticity and quite a bit of excitement. Recommended. —*Scott Yanow*

Frisco Jazz Band, Live! / June 1973 / MPS ◆◆◆
Trombonist Turk Murphy's Frisco Jazz Band was having an upsurge of popularity in the early '70s. This version of the band (featuring cornetist Leon Oakley, clarinetist Bob Helm and pianist Pete Clute) was well documented and a particularly strong ensemble group. Their album, recorded in Europe at the 1973 Heidelberg Jazz Festival, will be hard to find, but contains some fine performances. The 11 songs range from a few famous tunes (including "Dr. Jazz," "St. James Infirmary" and "Panama") and tunes from the books of King Oliver and Jelly Roll Morton to "Big Bear Stomp" and "Fifty Miles of Elbowroom." —*Scott Yanow*

The Many Faces of Ragtime / Jan. 1973 / Atlantic ◆◆◆◆
For their first major label release since the 1950s, the Turk Murphy Jazz Band performs a dozen rags. Although emphasizing Pete Clute's piano, the ragtime-based works (by Scott Joplin and James Scott, plus four obscurities and Murphy's "Little John's Rag") are turned into melodic trad jazz. Cornetist Leon Oakley (a major asset to the band), the leader/trombonist, and clarinetist Phil Howe all have worthwhile solo spots, and the overall results, although not pure ragtime (since there is improvising), is quite respectful to the composer's themes. Unfortunately, Atlantic has not yet reissued this enjoyable music on CD. —*Scott Yanow*

Southern Stomps / May 30, 1980-1986 / Stomp Off ◆◆◆◆
This Stomp Off release collects previously unreleased selections by Turk Murphy's Jazz Band from five different occasions: a 1980 concert and studio sets from 1984-86. On the former date (which resulted in four numbers including "Maple Leaf Rag" and "Flat Foot"), the band featured the leader/trombonist, cornetist Bob Shulz, veteran clarinetist Bob Helm and pianist Pete Clute. The studio sides also have Shulz in addition to clarinetist Lynn Zimmer and pianist Ray Skjelbred (the band's top soloist) and are highlighted by "New Orleans Stomp," "Some Sweet Day" and "Mandy." An excellent sampling of trad jazz from Turk Murphy's last groups. —*Scott Yanow.*

Turk at Carnegie / Jan. 10, 1987 / Stomp Off ◆◆◆◆◆
Less than five months before he died, veteran trad jazz trombonist Turk Murphy was honored with a night at Carnegie Hall. This album has the highlights. The Jim Cullum Band (featuring the leader on cornet, clarinetist Allan Vache and pianist John Sheridan) is in fine form on Jelly Roll Morton's "Freakish" and "Washboard Blues." The Hot Antic Jazz Band from France, a very talented sextet that features the players doubling and tripling on instruments, performs three obscurities and "Turk's Blues." Turk Murphy's final group, a septet mostly filled with unknowns (including cornetists Bob Schulz and clarinetist Ron Deeter) plus guest cornetist Lew Green performs five spirited numbers. As a climax, all three groups combine to play an eight-minute version of Murphy's theme song, "Bay City." Although Turk Murphy was weakened at the time from cancer (this would be one of his last performances), he plays well throughout the emotional and historic performance. —*Scott Yanow*

David Murray

b. Feb. 19, 1955, Berkeley, CA

Tenor Saxophone, Bass Clarinet / Avant-Garde, Post-Bop, Free Jazz
A giant of the avant-garde, David Murray has long had a distinctive tone on tenor and the willingness to play anything from completely free improvisations to bop. Among the most recorded of all jazzmen, Murray's trademark is his sudden leaps into the upper register of his horn.

He started on alto when he was nine and played tenor in a soul group that he led as a teenager. In Southern California Murray often gigged with Bobby Bradford and Arthur Blythe and then in 1975 he moved to New York. He was an original member of the World Saxophone Quartet in 1976 and worked as a sideman with Sunny Murray, James "Blood" Ulmer, Jack DeJohnette's Special Edition and Clarinet Summit, playing bass clarinet in the latter. However, Murray is best known as a leader whose groups have ranged from freewheeling quartets to a spirited big band and an acclaimed octet. He started recording as a leader in 1976 and has since made sessions for Adelphi, India Navigation, Circle, Marge, Red, Horo, Palm, Cadillac, Black Saint, Hat Hut, Cecma, Enja, Portrait, Red Baron and DIW. In 1991 David Murray was awarded the prestigious Danish Jazzpar prize. —*Scott Yanow*

Low Class Conspiracy / May 14, 1976+Jun. 29, 1976 / Adelphi ✦✦✦
This LP contains tenor saxophonist David Murray's first full-length album as a leader. At 21, Murray already had remarkable technique and these explorations with bassist Fred Hopkins and drumer Phillip Wilson are quite adventurous. The opening "Extremininity" is an intense unaccompanied tenor feature, Hopkins takes "Dedication to Jimmy Garrison" as his showcase and the other three pieces are full of interplay by the full trio. None of the compositions themselves are that memorable and some listeners may find Murray's screams and screeches (which he would modify a bit in later years) to be a bit too emotional, but this was a strong first effort. —*Scott Yanow*

Flowers for Albert / Jun. 16, 1976 / India Navigation ✦✦✦✦✦
David Murray, who was 21 at the time, shows a lot of promise on this early recording. The explorative tenor saxophonist joins with trumpeter Olu Dara, bassist Fred Hopkins and drummer Phillip Wilson for five adventurous pieces (three were released for the first time on this 1997 double-CD). In addition, Murray duets with Hopkins on "Ballad for a Decomposed Beauty" and collaborates with Wilson on their duet "Roscoe." The music is often quite free but it also takes its time, showing high energy in well-chosen spots. Since this period David Murray has lived up to his great potential. —*Scott Yanow*

Solo Live, Vol. 1 / 1977 / Cecma ✦✦✦
Ever since emerging on the scene in 1976, tenor saxophonist David Murray has recorded an enormous number of records. In fact, this LP from the Italian Cecma label was already his fourth set of unaccompanied solos. Murray, who doubles here on bass clarinet, tears into five of his originals (best known are "Sweet Lovely" and "Flowers for Albert"). The improvising is quite free, exploratory, and sometimes violent, although there are a few strong melodies. Along with *Vol. 2*, which is partly from the same Swiss concert, this album is a real rarity. —*Scott Yanow*

Solo Live, Vol. 2 / 1977 / Cecma ✦✦✦
This LP from the small Italian Cecma label has two unaccompanied tenor solos by David Murray that are taken from the same concert as *Vol. 1*. While those flights are quite emotional, the flip side of the LP, taken from Aug. 1980, has Murray, for one of the first times in his extensive recording career, tackling a pair of jazz standards—"Body and Soul" and Thelonious Monk's "We See"—in addition to his own, themeless "Untitled." Murray shows some maturity on those tunes, although he does improvise quite freely once the themes are stated. A collector's item. —*Scott Yanow*

Live at the Lower Manhattan Ocean Club, Vols. 1 & 2 / Dec. 31, 1977 / India Navigation ✦✦✦
This double CD, which packages together the two original LPs, captures David Murray's quartet (trumpeter Lester Bowie, bassist Fred Hopkins and drummer Phillip Wilson) in high spirits. The six selections (four are over ten minutes and "For Walter Norris" exceeds 21) are full of spirit, looseness, humor, screams and screeches. Some of it rambles on too long (and Murray's soprano on "Bechet's Bounce" is quite silly) but it generally holds on to one's attention. —*Scott Yanow*

Interboogieology / Feb. 1978 / Black Saint ✦✦✦
For this fairly early recording, avant-garde tenor saxophonist David Murray teams up with cornetist Butch Morris, bassist Johnny Dyani and drummer Oliver Johnson for some fairly free improvisations, with the originals written by either Murray or Morris. Two of the numbers also utilize the adventurous voice of Marta Contreras. The results are stimulating if not essential; a lesser but still interesting effort. —*Scott Yanow*

Murray's 3D Family / Sep. 3, 1978 / Hat Art ✦✦✦✦✦

Sweet Lovely / Dec. 4, 1979-Dec. 5, 1979 / Black Saint ✦✦✦✦
David Murray's string of recordings for Black Saint were among the most rewarding of his career. This one differs from many in that the adventurous tenorman improvises in a sparse trio with bassist Fred Hopkins and drummer Steve McCall. Murray stretches out on four of his originals (which clock in between eight and twelve-and-a-half minutes) and shows plenty of fire but also a healthy dose of lyricism. This is exciting music very much in the avant-garde. —*Scott Yanow*

☆ **Ming** / Jul. 25, 1980+Jul. 28, 1980 / Black Saint ✦✦✦✦✦
His octet was always the perfect setting for tenor saxophonist David Murray, large enough to generate power but not as out of control as many of his big band performances. Murray contributed all five originals (including "Ming" and "Dewey's Cir-

cle") and arrangements, and is in superior form on both tenor and bass clarinet. The "backup crew" is also quite notable: altoist Henry Threadgill, trumpeter Olu Dara, cornetist Butch Morris, trombonist George Lewis, pianist Anthony Davis, bassist Wilbur Morris and drummer Steve McCall. These avant-garde performances (reissued on CD) are often rhythmic enough to reach a slightly larger audience than usual, and the individuality shown by each of these major players is quite impressive. Recommended. —*Scott Yanow*

Home / Oct. 31, 1981+Nov. 1, 1981 / Black Saint ✦✦✦✦✦
Although David Murray has recorded in many different settings throughout his busy career, his octet has always been perfect for his talents. More disciplined than his big band, yet containing more tone colors than his smaller combos, the octet allowed Murray to be exploratory yet occasionally look backwards. This set, his second with the band, has quite an all-star lineup: Murray on tenor and bass clarinet, altoist Henry Threadgill, trumpeter Olu Dara, cornetist Butch Morris, trombonist George Lewis, pianist Anthony Davis, bassist Wilber Morris and drummer Steve McCall. All of the brilliant players have their opportunities to make strong contributions to Murray's five originals (best known of which is "3-D Family"), and the leader's writing is consistently colorful and unpredictable. Recommended. —*Scott Yanow*

★ **Murray's Steps** / Jul. 14, 1982-Jul. 19, 1982 / Black Saint ✦✦✦✦✦
The octet is the perfect vehicle for David Murray as an outlet for his writing, a showcase for his compositions and as an inspiring vehicle for his tenor and bass clarinet solos. For the third octet album (all are highly recommended) Murray meets up with altoist Henry Threadgill, trumpeter Bobby Bradford, cornetist Butch Morris, trombonist Craig Harris, pianist Curtis Clark, bassist Wilber Morris and drummer Steve McCall; quite a talented group of individuals. Their interpretations of four of Murray's originals ("Murray's Steps," "Sweet Lovely," "Sing Song" and "Flowers for Albert") are emotional, adventurous and exquisite; sometimes all three at the same time. —*Scott Yanow*

Morning Song / Sep. 25, 1983-Sep. 30, 1983 / Black Saint ✦✦✦✦
For David Murray, this is a fairly straightforward quartet date. Joined by pianist John Hicks, bassist Reggie Workman and drummer Ed Blackwell, Murray performs three of his lesser-known originals, Butch Morris' "Light Blue Frolic," "Body and Soul" and "Jitterbug Waltz." Doubling on tenor and bass clarinet, Murray as usual has a tendency to jump into the extreme upper register a bit too much at unexpected times, disrupting a relatively mellow mood on a few occasions. But one cannot deny his musicianship, and there are some exciting moments to be heard during this program. —*Scott Yanow*

Live at Sweet Basil, Vol. 1 / Aug. 24, 1984-Aug. 26, 1984 / Black Saint ✦✦✦
The David Murray Big Band tends to be a bit undisciplined, with plenty of rambunctious and overcrowded ensembles. The high point of this first of two releases is easily the 12-minute "Bechet's Bounce," an often nutty and frequently hilarious "tribute" to Sidney Bechet that improves the longer it is played. The Dixieland-esque structures are better understood by some of the musicians than others, and this performance is quite erratic but certainly memorable. Otherwise, the big band (which includes in its all-star cast cornetist Olu Dara, trombonist Craig Harris, altoist Steve Coleman and drummer Billy Higgins, plus Murray on tenor and bass clarinet) digs into Murray's "Lovers," "Silence" and "Duet for Big Band." —*Scott Yanow*

Live at Sweet Basil, Vol. 2 / Aug. 24, 1984-Aug. 26, 1984 / Black Saint ✦✦✦
The David Murray Big Band tends to be both erratic and colorful. Their second of two sets has the 11-piece all-star crew (conducted by Butch Morris) performing five of the leader's originals, including "Dewey's Circle." There are some strong moments, plenty of dense ensembles, and a strong group spirit that makes one wish that the group had recorded a little more coherently in the studios during this period. —*Scott Yanow*

Children / Oct. 1984-Nov. 1984 / Brass Star ✦✦✦✦
This intriguing set combines several strong personalities (David Murray on tenor and bass clarinet, guitarist James "Blood" Ulmer, pianist Don Pullen, bassist Lonnie Plaxico and drummer Marvin "Smitty" Smith) in performances that are avant-garde, close to free bop and sometimes hinting at Charles Mingus, M-Base and harmolodics. The quintet performs a nearly 15-minute version of "All the Things You Are" and three Murray originals, including "David—Mingus." The somewhat noisy performances are fairly spontaneous and, thanks to Pullen's rhythmic style, a little more accessible than one might expect, despite being quite adventurous. —*Scott Yanow*

I Want to Talk About You / Mar. 1, 1986 / Black Saint ✦✦
Throughout this CD it seems as if tenor saxophonist David Murray and his rhythm section (pianist John Hicks, bassist Ray Drummond and drummer Ralph Peterson) are not communicating at all; at least their musical objectives differ greatly. While Murray uses a ballad ("Heart to Heart"), a mysterious mood piece ("Quad"), an R&B

blues ("Red Car"), the title cut and the funky "Morning Song" as points of departure for his wild upper register flights, the backing trio plays all of the selections quite conventionally. The result is that David Murray often sounds very silly, as if he had decided to play whatever he wanted to no matter what the other musicians did, or was it the other way around? John Hicks consistently acts as if Murray were not even there and there is no reaction or feedback by the sidemen to the tenorman's explorations. —*Scott Yanow*

In Our Style / Sep. 3, 1986-Sep. 4, 1986 / DIW ✦✦✦✦
David Murray, doubling on tenor and bass clarinet, interacts with drummer Jack DeJohnette and (on two of the seven selections) bassist Fred Hopkins for a set of originals by Murray, DeJohnette and Butch Morris. The duo/trio explore a variety of moods with Murray's extroverted and advanced solos generally serving as the lead voice. Although an avant-garde set, this Japanese import has its mellow and melodic moments before the fire takes over again. —*Scott Yanow*

The Hill / Nov. 1986 / Black Saint ✦✦✦✦

Hope Scope / May 12, 1987 / Black Saint ✦✦✦✦✦
The perfect setting for the innovative David Murray is the octet that he leads on an irregular basis. This spirited set has tributes to Ben Webster and Lester Young but is at its best when the full ensemble (trumpeters Hugh Ragin and Rasul Siddik, trombonist Craig Harris, altoist James Spaulding, pianist Dave Burrell, bassist Wilber Morris and drummer Ralph Peterson, Jr., along with the leader on tenor and bass clarinet) get to improvise together. This is one of their strongest all-round recordings with "Hope Scope" being a particular high point. —*Scott Yanow*

The Healers / Sep. 26, 1987 / Black Saint ✦✦✦✦
This set of duets by David Murray (doubling on tenor and bass clarinet) and pianist Randy Weston is a bit of a surprise. Rather than performing standards or some of Weston's "hits," the duo stretches out on three obscurities by the two musicians (only Weston's "Blue Moses" is slightly known) and Butch Morris' "Clever Beggar." Weston provides a solid harmonic and rhythmic foundation for Murray's thick-toned but sometimes screeching flights, and the combination works fairly well. —*Scott Yanow*

Spirituals / Jan. 1988 / DIW ✦✦✦
David Murray mostly sticks to spirituals on this Japanese import, a quartet outing with pianist Dave Burrell, bassist Fred Hopkins and drummer Ralph Peterson, but that does not mean that all of the improvising is mellow and melodic. There are some peaceful moments on tunes such as "Amazing Grace" and a spirited "Down by the Riverside," but Murray's playing is so violent on "Abel's Blissed Out Blues" as to be almost satirical. A mixed success from the masterful tenor. —*Scott Yanow*

Ming's Samba / Jul. 20, 1988 / Portrait ✦✦✦✦
Although David Murray had already recorded a countless number of sessions as a leader by the late '80s, *Ming's Samba* was his first on a large American label. Using an "in the tradition" rhythm section comprising pianist John Hicks, bassist Ray Drummond and drummer Ed Blackwell, Murray tears through the calypso "Ming's Samba," pays tribute to the joy (if not the style) of Fats Waller ("Rememberin' Fats"), plays a warm breathy ballad solo à la John Klemmer ("Nowhere Everafter"), has fun on the humorous tango "Spooning" and shows off the expected Eric Dolphy influence (although Eric never slap-tongued) on bass clarinet during "Walter's Waltz." Hicks has several brilliant solos on the complex material, Drummond is superlative in his backing of Murray (check out "Walter's Waltz") and the colorful Blackwell proves to be a perfect foil for the leader. A recommended release although this set will probably be difficult to find. —*Scott Yanow*

New Life / 1988 / Black Saint ✦✦✦✦
The David Murray Octet (which at the time consisted of the leader on tenor and bass clarinet, trumpeters Baikida Carroll and Hugh Ragin, trombonist Craig Harris, altoist John Purcell, pianist Steve Colson, bassist Wilbur Morris and drummer Ralph Peterson) stretches out on four of its leader's originals. The tunes ("Train Whistle," "Morning Song," "New Life" and "Blues in the Pocket") are each fairly memorable—the themes are stronger than usual—and, as usual, the octet features the right combination of adventurous solos and colorful writing. Recommended. —*Scott Yanow*

☆ **Special Quartet** / Mar. 26, 1990 / Columbia ✦✦✦✦✦
When one reads the personnel on this CD, the potential seems enormous: tenor saxophonist David Murray, pianist McCoy Tyner, bassist Fred Hopkins and drummer Elvin Jones. Murray was a good choice for the tenor slot, because, although influenced by John Coltrane's adventurous spirit, he has never sounded like Coltrane, coming closer to the Ben Webster/Paul Gonsalves tradition but with a style of his own. In addition to Trane's "Cousin Mary" and "In a Sentimental Mood" (which Coltrane had recorded with Duke Ellington, and Murray takes as a duet with Tyner), the music includes three of the tenor's originals, including "3D Family") and a Butch Morris song. The fresh material really pushes Tyner, who mostly

sticks to standards with his own trio, while Jones sounds as passionate as usual. A successful outing full of mutual inspiration; easily recommended. —*Scott Yanow*

Shakill's Warrior / Mar. 1, 1991-Mar. 2, 1991 / Columbia ✦✦✦✦
Tenor saxophonist David Murray has recorded so many CDs during the past 20 years that it is difficult to keep up with them. This one finds him in mostly restrained form, updating the tenor/organ soul-jazz tradition with Don Pullen (who sticks exclusively to organ), guitarist Stanley Franks and drummer Andrew Cyrille. The music, with the exception of some typical Murray outbursts into the extreme upper register, is generally respectful and soulful, one of Murray's mellower efforts. Unfortunately, Columbia has since ended its association with DIW so this release will be a difficult one to find. —*Scott Yanow*

David Murray Big Band, Conducted by Lawrence "Butch" Morris / Mar. 5, 1991-Mar. 6, 1991 / Columbia ✦✦✦✦
The David Murray big band, which can be undisciplined and even a bit out of control, is never dull. This generally brilliant effort has quite a few high points. "Paul Gonsalves" recreates the tenor's famous 1956 Newport Jazz Festival solo and has some heated playing from the ensemble. While "Lester" does not really capture the style of Lester Young, "Ben" does bring back the spirit of Ben Webster. "Calling Steve McCall" is a heartfelt tribute to the late drummer (although the poetry does not need to be heard twice) and trombonist Craig Harris' singing on "Let the Music Take You" is so-so, but the colorful "David's Tune" and the eerie "Instanbul" are more memorable. This disc is easily recommended to listeners with open ears. —*Scott Yanow*

The Jazzpar Prize / Mar. 16, 1991-Mar. 17, 1991 / Enja ✦✦✦✦✦
David Murray was the winner of the second annual Jazzpar award in 1991. While in Copenhagen to pick up his cash prize, Murray recorded this superlative set with Pierre Dorge's New Jungle Orchestra. The ten-piece band (which includes guitarist Dorge, pianist Horace Parlan, trumpeter Harry Beckett and a variety of top European players) serves as an excellent outlet for Murray, who doubles on tenor and bass clarinet. Their joint interpretations of three of his pieces—including a gospel medley with a vocal by Donald Murray), two spirited Dorge originals (one is called "David in Wonderland") and Duke Ellington's "In a Sentimental Mood"—are colorful and often memorable. The performances are avant-garde, but not afraid of using melodies and straightahead rhythms when it best suits the music. —*Scott Yanow*

Black and Black / Oct. 7, 1991 / Red Baron ✦✦✦✦
In general, tenor saxophonist David Murray's Red Baron recordings are not on the same level of his Black Saints albums; the settings tended to be more conservative and the material not as strong. This outing with pianist Kirk Lightsey, bassist Santi Debriano, drummer Roy Haynes and trumpeter Marcus Belgrave is better than most of his Red Baron releases. The material is fairly basic (including "Duke's Place" and the two-note "C Jam Blues" theme, which is listed as being composed by four people), Murray tends to play fairly freely despite the boppish rhythm section, and the closing "Head Out" (the longest of the five lengthy jams) has plenty of fiery intensity. Not essential but worth picking up by David Murray fans. —*Scott Yanow*

Fast Life / Oct. 16, 1991-Oct. 17, 1991 / DIW/Columbia ✦✦
This CD is a bit of a mixed bag. The great tenor David Murray is joined by pianist John Hicks, bassist Ray Drummond and drummer Idris Muhammad and is heard at his best on two relatively straightahead pieces, "Luminous" and "Off Season." But Branford Marsalis guests on two other selections and those are much more erratic, with rambling solos by the two tenors and a lot of aimless high energy. Wrapping up this set are a calypso and the lightweight "Intuitively," making the net results less than one might hope. —*Scott Yanow*

Live '93 / 1993 / Sound Hills ✦✦✦✦
This trio session, cut in Germany, was also produced by Murray, and it's yet another example of his rampaging tenor and almost as impressive bass clarinet technique. On the latter instrument, his skills have evolved rapidly; he demonstrates on the title track a newly developed range, creativity and depth. Meanwhile, his tenor, especially his fluidity in the upper range, vocalisms, tone and ideas are so authoritative that his excellence is now taken for granted. The only negative aspect involves the recording time; according to the information on the jacket, this date is only slightly more than 30 minutes. But it's actually over 72, which makes you wonder whether they put the right concert in the wrong CD cover or the wrong information with the right concert. —*Ron Wynn*

Body and Soul / Feb. 11, 1993-Feb. 12, 1993 / Black Saint ✦✦✦✦✦
No matter how many albums Murray issues, he never coasts or goes through the motions. This is mainly a quartet date, although Murray shows on the title track his ability to back a singer as Taana Running gives a moving vocal, complete with her original lyrics. Otherwise, these are either spirited uptempo numbers or equally energized ballads. Murray's sweeping tenor sound remains a marvel, and few can

match him in controlling drive, pitch and volume. Drummer Rashied Ali has not lost the rippling intensity from his days with John Coltrane; he and Murray conclude things in a dazzling duo performance on "Cuttin' Corners" deliberately intended to evoke memories of the Coltrane/Ali album *Interstellar Space.* —*Ron Wynn*

Jazzosaurus Rex / Aug. 18, 1993 / Red Baron ✦✦✦
Two songtitles on this CD ("Jazzosaurus Rex" and "Dinosaur Park Blues") try to make a connection between David Murray's music and the recent movie *Jurassic Park* but, despite that dubious attempt at commercialism, this is actually a fairly typical Murray modern mainstream outing. Accompanied by pianist John Hicks, bassist Ray Drummond and drummer Andrew Cyrille, Murray's playing is consistently exciting whether tearing into the rhythm changes of "The Eternal Triangle," playing ferocious doubletime lines on his "Mingus in the Poconos" or showing off his huge tone on "Chelsea Bridge." The poet G'ar's narration on a blues "Now He's Miles Away" (a tribute to Miles Davis) is a bit trivial but only a minor flaw for this worthwhile David Murray set. —*Scott Yanow*

Saxmen / Aug. 19, 1993 / Red Baron ✦✦
On this Red Baron CD tenor saxophonist David Murray allegedly pays homage to six saxophonists (Lester Young, Sonny Rollins, Charlie Parker, Charlie Rouse, Sonny Stitt and John Coltrane) but much of the time he does not even seem to realize who he is paying tribute to. Not only does Murray not imitate or emulate his predecessors, he often ignores the outlines of the songs themselves. On "Lester Leaps In" his ferocious solo (with its sudden upper-register outbursts) is unintentionally humorous. He is a bit more involved with Thelonious Monk's "Bright Mississippi" and "Broadway," but on the only ballad of the day "Central Park West," Murray's solo gets downright silly during its second half, ruining the peaceful meditative mood of the song with some self-indulgent upper-register ramblings. The rhythm section (pianist John Hicks, bassist Ray Drummond and drummer Andrew Cyrille) largely ignores the tenor's improvisations, making this one of David Murray's more forgettable recordings. —*Scott Yanow*

Dark Star: The Music of the Grateful Dead / Jan. 17, 1996-Jan. 18, 1996 / Astor Place ✦✦✦
The avant-garde tenor and bass clarinetist David Murray had an opportunity to sit in with the Grateful Dead in 1993 and was quite impressed. With Jerry Garcia's death, Murray was inspired to put together this tribute album but often it sounds as if two bands were playing at once without closely listening to each other. Murray and the horns (which include veteran altoist James Spaulding, the very impressive high-note acrobatics of trumpeter Hugh Ragin, either James Zoller or Omar Kabir on second trumpet and the adventurous trombonist Craig Harris) romp through some rowdy and very emotional ensembles while organist Robert Irving, III, (a Miles Davis alumnus) leads the rhythm section through groovin' R&B riffs that seem to ignore the lead voices. The results are often quite silly as the horns screech and squawk while the rhythm churns on. There are two exceptions. The 16-minute "Dark Star" builds slowly to a ferocious level and finds the group acting as one while the closing "Shoulda Had Been Me" is a tenor-guitar duet between Murray and Bob Weir that works quite well. So overall this is a mixed bag, most highly recommended to listeners who have a high tolerance level and a strong sense of humor. —*Scott Yanow*

Fo Deux Revue / Jun. 3, 1996-Jun. 4, 1996 / Justin Time ✦✦✦

Sunny Murray (James Marcellus Arthur Murray)

b. Sep. 21, 1937, Idabel, OK
Drums / Free Jazz, Avant-Garde
An important early free drummer, Sunny Murray was one of the first to play without keeping a steady rhythm or pulse (interacting directly with the lead voices) although he was always perfectly capable of playing more conventionally. He started on drums when he was nine and in 1956 moved to New York. Murray picked up early experience gigging with Red Allen, Willie "The Lion" Smith, Jackie McLean and Ted Curson. He made a giant stylistic leap when he started playing with Cecil Taylor (1959-64) and was the perfect "accompanist" for Albert Ayler (1964-67). Murray also worked with Don Cherry, Ornette Coleman and John Tchicai during the period. He spent 1968-71 in France, playing and recording with

Archie Shepp and freelancing. In the 1970s Murray moved to Philadelphia and led bands usually called the Untouchable Factor. For a time in the 1980s his quintet included Steve Coleman, Grachan Moncur, III, pianist Curtis Clark and bassist William Parker and he had a recorded reunion with Taylor in 1980. Sunny Murray has led dates for Jihad (a 1965 session with Albert Ayler as a sideman), ESP, Shandar, Pathe, BYG, Kharma, Philly Jazz, Marge, Moers Music and Circle although he has maintained a lower profile during the past decade. —*Scott Yanow*

Sunny's Time Now / Nov. 1965 / Jihad ✦✦✦

● **Sunny Murray** / Jul. 23, 1966 / ESP ✦✦✦✦✦
Drummer Sunny Murray's second date as a leader (following by eight months an almost-unknown set for Jihad that featured Don Cherry and Albert Ayler as sidemen) finds Murray leading a high-powered free-jazz quintet. Best known among the sidemen are altoist Byard Lancaster and bassist Al Silva, although second altoist Jack Graham and trumpeter Jacques Coursil also play important roles in the music. Performing lengthy versions of three Murray originals and one by Graham, the band is fairly coherent but also full of fire and chance-taking solos. In ways, this is a typical ESP free-form blowing session, and certainly will be most enjoyed by open-eared listeners. —*Scott Yanow*

Applecores / 1978-1979 / Philly Jazz ✦✦✦

Live at the Moers Festival / Jun. 3, 1979 / Moers ✦✦✦

13 Steps on Glass / Jan. 23, 1996 / Enja ✦✦✦
Tenor saxophonist Odean Pope and bassist Wayne Dockery join Murray on this 1996 effort. —*Jason Ankeny*

Amina Claudine Myers

b. Mar. 21, 1942, Blackwell, AR
Piano, Organ / Avant-Garde
A very original pianist who displays her gospel roots when she plays organ or sings, Amina Claudine Myers started studying music when she was seven. She sang with gospel groups in school. After moving to Chicago Myers taught in the public schools, played with Gene Ammons and Sonny Stitt and joined the AACM. She moved to New York in 1976 (where she would record with Lester Bowie and Muhal Richard Abrams), formed her own group, spent a few years in the early '80s in Europe and toured with Charlie Haden's Liberation Music Orchestra in 1985. Amina Claudine Myers has recorded a diverse variety of music as a leader for Sweet Earth, Leo, Black Saint, Minor Music and Novus. —*Scott Yanow*

Poems for Piano: The Piano Music of Marion Brown / Jul. 26, 1979 / Sweet Earth ✦✦✦✦

Song for Mother Earth / Oct. 9, 1979 / Leo ✦✦✦✦✦
Duets with percussionist Pheeroan AkLaff. Sounds like a bigger group. Excellent. —*Michael G. Nastos*

★ **Salutes Bessie Smith** / Jun. 19, 1980-Jun. 22, 1980 / Leo ✦✦✦✦✦
Vocal perfection and landmark recording for this keyboardist and singer. Desert-island music. —*Michael G. Nastos*

The Circle of Time / Feb. 3, 1983+Feb. 4, 1983 / Black Saint ✦✦✦✦

Jumping in the Sugar Bowl / Mar. 1984 / Minor Music ✦✦✦✦
Intense, provocative mixture of outside and inside sensibilities. Myers at times ranges and attacks the keyboard, then will change direction and display a soulful, gospel-influenced style. The constantly shifting session keeps things interesting, and there are some fine solos as well. —*Ron Wynn*

Country Girl / Apr. 1986 / Minor Music ✦✦✦

Amina / Nov. 1987 / Novus ✦✦✦

In Touch / 1988 / Novus ✦✦
An album that surprised some fans when it was issued, due to the reputations of everyone involved. Myers has been a fierce soloist and adventurous composer and worked in experimental, on-the-edge contexts for much of her career, but turned to fusion and light pop on this date, playing more synthesizer than anything else. It was well produced and effectively played, but guitarist Jerome Harris had a larger role than Myers. —*Ron Wynn*

Najee

f. , New York, NY

Soprano Saxophone, Tenor Saxophone / Instrumental Pop, Crossover Jazz

One of the best selling instrumentalists of the late 1980s and early to mid-1990s, Najee has been a consistent favorite in the "quiet storm" and so-called "smooth jazz" markets. Often compared to Kenny G., George Howard and Dave Koz, the New Yorker has been greatly influenced by Grover Washington, Jr.—although he hasn't been nearly as adventurous. Heavily produced and quite formulaic, Najee's albums have tended to avoid improvisation and strive for commercial radio airplay above all else. Debuting in 1987 with *Najee's Theme*, Najee was an immediate hit in the new adult contemporary (NAC) market. Similiar pop/urban/jazz dates like 1988's *Day by Day* and 1990s *Tokyo Blue* did nothing to jeopardize his niche on "smooth jazz" radio. On stage, Najee takes some risks and stretches out more—in fact, he has been quoted as saying he'd like to record a straightahead jazz or hard bop album eventually. But financially, Najee has had little incentive to pursue such a project. *—Alex Henderson*

Najee's Theme / 1987 / EMI ♦♦

Day by Day / 1988 / EMI ♦♦

Tokyo Blue / 1990 / EMI ♦♦♦♦

Just an Illusion / 1992 / EMI ♦♦

Share My World / 1994 / EMI ♦♦♦

● **Songs from the Key of Life** / 1995 / EMI ♦♦♦♦♦

Ray Nance

b. Dec. 10, 1913, Chicago, IL, **d.** Jan. 28, 1976, New York, NY

Cornet, Violin, Vocals / Swing

Ray Nance was a multi-talented individual. He was a fine trumpeter who not only replaced Cootie Williams with Duke Ellington's Orchestra but gave the "plunger" position in Duke's band his own personality. In addition Nance was one of the finest jazz violinists of the 1940s, an excellent jazz singer and even a dancer. He studied piano, took lessons on violin and was self-taught on trumpet. After leading a small group in Chicago (1932-37) spending periods with the orchestras of Earl Hines (1937-38) and Horace Henderson (1939-40) and a few months as a solo act, Nance joined Duke Ellington's Orchestra. His very first night on the job was fully documented as the band's legendary Fargo concert. A very valuable sideman, Nance played a famous trumpet solo on the original version of "Take the 'A' Train" and proved to be a fine wah-wah player. His violin added color to the suite "Black, Brown and Beige" (in addition to being showcased on numerous songs) and his singing on numbers such as "A Slip of a Lip Will Sink a Ship" and "Tulip or Turnip" was an added feature. Nance was with Ellington with few interruptions until 1963; by then the returning Cootie Williams had taken some of his glory. The remainder of Nance's career was relatively insignificant with occasional small group dates, gigs with Brooks Kerr and Chris Barber (touring England in 1974) and a few surprisingly advanced sideman recordings with Jaki Byard and Chico Hamilton. *—Scott Yanow*

● **Body and Soul** / May 1969 / Solid State ♦♦♦♦♦

Tricky Sam Nanton

b. Feb. 1, 1904, New York, NY, **d.** Jul. 20, 1946, San Francisco, CA

Trombone / Classic Jazz, Swing

One of the most colorful trombonists of all time, Tricky Sam Nanton's expertise with the plunger mute (emitting a large assortment of growls and colorful tones) was a major part of Duke Ellington's original sound and has rarely been duplicated since (although Quentin Jackson sometimes came close). He gained early experience playing with bands led by Cliff Jackson and Elmer Snowden and recorded with Thomas Morris, but after mid-1926 Nanton was only heard with Duke Ellington's Orchestra and small groups; he never led a record date of his own. Nanton made a perfect team with trumpeter Bubber Miley and, when Miley

was replaced by Cootie Williams in 1929, Nanton helped to inspire the younger trumpeter. Nanton was well-featured on many classic recordings (including "East St. Louis Toodle-oo" and "Black and Tan Fantasy") and was a major attraction with Ellington up until his premature death in 1946. *—Scott Yanow*

Marty Napoleon (Matthew Napoli Napoleon)

b. Jun. 2, 1921, New York, NY

Piano / Swing

The nephew of trumpeter Phil Napoleon and the younger brother of fellow pianist Teddy Napoleon, Marty Napoleon gained his greatest fame for playing with Louis Armstrong's All-Stars during two stints. Napoleon was actually a fairly versatile player whose style generally fell between swing and bop. Originally a trumpeter, heart troubles caused him to switch to piano. Napoleon picked up early experience playing with the big bands of Chico Marx, Joe Venuti, Lee Castle, Charlie Barnet and Gene Krupa (1945). Napoleon worked with his uncle's Memphis Five in the early '50s, was part of Charlie Ventura's Big Four and was with Louis Armstrong from 1952-53. In addition to having a two-piano quartet with brother Teddy in 1955, working with Coleman Hawkins, Charlie Shavers and Red Allen, and freelancing, Napoleon frequently led his own trios. He rejoined Louis Armstrong during the trumpeter's twilight years (1966-68 and on and off in 1968-71) and semi-retired in the 1980s. Other than a four-song 1955 trio date for Bethlehem, Marty Napoleon never led a record session, in spite of his talents. *—Scott Yanow*

Phil Napoleon

b. Sep. 2, 1901, Boston, MA, **d.** Sep. 30, 1990, Miami, FL

Trumpet / Classic Jazz, Dixieland

Although often overlooked, Phil Napoleon was one of the top trumpeters active in New York during 1921-25. At a time when most so-called hot players in the Big Apple were still playing staccato and halting lines (not being up to the level of their Chicago counterparts), Napoleon's warm sound and legato phrasing "swung" (before the word had been coined). Classically trained, Napoleon decided to play popular music. By 1921 he was recording frequently with many overlapping groups (most notably the Original Memphis Five, Ladd's Black Aces, the Carolina Cotton Pickers and later on the Charleston Chasers), appearing on literally hundreds of excellent melodic jazz records where his appealing tone and solid lead were a major asset. Although a slight influence on Red Nichols and Bix Beiderbecke (as much for his professionalism and consistency as for his tone), Napoleon never did become a big name. He worked in the studios during the 1930s and '40s, leading his own big band briefly in 1938 and spending part of 1943 with Jimmy Dorsey. In 1949 he emerged with a new version of the Original Memphis Five, playing Dixieland for seven years at Nick's. Napoleon eventually moved to Miami, opened a club called Napoleon's Retreat and played regularly during his declining years. *—Scott Yanow*

Featuring the Original Memphis Five / Dec. 23, 1926-Apr. 5, 1929/ IAJRC ♦♦♦♦

This collector's LP from the International Association of Jazz Record Collectors contains some fairly rare performances from Phil Napoleon, one of the most underrated trumpeters of the 1920s. There are six titles taken from Napoleon's sessions of 1926-27, in which he led a big band; "Tiger Rag" and "Clarinet Marmalade" are among the highlights of those hot dance band performances. There are also eight selections from the Original Memphis Five's sessions of 1927-29, the last recordings by that very prolific recording group except for a final session in 1931. In addition to Napoleon (who was on hundreds of titles with similar bands in the 1920s), this version of the Memphis Five has either Miff Mole or Tommy Dorsey on trombone, plus Jimmy Dorsey on alto and clarinet; four of the songs feature vocals by either Dick Robertson or Scrappy Lambert. Excellent melodic jazz from the second half of the 1920s. *—Scott Yanow*

1929-1931 / May 14, 1929-Nov. 24, 1931/ Old Masters ♦♦♦♦

Trumpeter Phil Napoleon started recording quite early, and from 1921 on, he was on a countless number of records. He actually did not lead his first dates (under his own name) until 1926. This collector's LP from the TOM label features the fine trumpeter in several settings. Five numbers are with Napoleon's Emperors in 1929; there is one selection with Miff Mole's Molers, six with the Hot Air Men, and the four numbers cut at the final date by the Original Memphis Five (although Napoleon would use that group title in later years). This LP unfortunately does not have any liner notes (the back cover is completely blank), but there are some excellent performances on the album. In addition to Napoleon, such top players as trombonists Tommy Dorsey and Miff Mole, Jimmy Dorsey on alto and clarinet, violinist Joe Venuti and guitarist Eddie Lang are among those making strong contributions. Collectors will want this vintage music, most of which has not yet appeared on CD. — *Scott Yanow*

Live at Nick's NYC / 1949-1950 / Jazzology ✦✦✦

Phil Napoleon is one of the unsung heroes of jazz history. He was arguably the first trumpeter based in New York to swing, recording excellent small-group jazz with an attractive tone and a legato style as early as 1921, a time when most other brassmen in the city were emphasizing staccato phrases. This particular CD (previously unreleased material put out in 1996) features Phil Napoleon and his 1949-50 sextet from a variety of live club performances. With the exception of the fine drummer Tony Spargo (a member 30 years earlier of the Original Dixieland Jazz Band), the sidemen are obscure with clarinetist Phil Olivela a main soloist and trombonist Andy Russo mostly sticking to colorful work behind the other players. Of the eighteen tracks, all but seven are medleys comprising two-four songs and the emphasis throughout is on ensembles. Napoleon, who only takes a few solos, offers a strong and lyrical melodic lead, showing that he knew how to say a lot in a short period of time. The performances are nostalgic (most of the songs date from the 1920s), quite danceable and swinging. The only lowpoint is Spargo's occasional whistling (which is far off mike) although he makes up for it with a hot kazoo solo. — *Scott Yanow*

From 1950s Broadcasts / 1953 / Take Two ✦✦✦

Despite his prominence in the 1920s and his long career, Phil Napoleon recorded much too infrequently after 1929. This album features the early-1950s version of his Memphis Five, a sextet that also included trombonist Harry DiVito, clarinetist Gail Curtis, and the up-and-coming pianist Johnny Varro. The 16 selections are mostly Dixieland warhorses and are concise, clocking in between 1:53 and 3:10. The music was originally made as radio transcriptions and released for the first time on this 1978 LP. Enjoyable renditions with few surprises but infectious spirit. — *Scott Yanow*

● Phil Napoleon and the Memphis Five / Oct. 1959 / Capitol ✦✦✦✦

Although he would continue playing into the 1980s, trumpeter Phil Napoleon's last recordings were his three Capitol LPs of 1959-60 (none of which have been reissued on CD yet). The first studio record is quite strong, matching Napoleon with clarinetist Kenny Davern, pianist Johnny Varro and trombonist Harry DiVito in a sextet. The Dixieland band is heard in fine form on such numbers as "Milenberg Joys," "After You've Gone," "Wolverine Blues" and "St. Louis Blues." — *Scott Yanow*

In the Land of Dixie / 1960 / Capitol ✦✦✦✦

Although he played superior jazz-oriented dance music in the 1920s, Phil Napoleon mostly stuck to Dixieland in his later years. On the second of his three Capitol LPs, Napoleon and his sextet (which includes clarinetist Kenny Davern and pianist Johnny Varro) emphasizes such standards as "Fidgety Feet," "Shim-Me-Sha-Wabble," "Runnin' Wild" and "Ballin' the Jack," although the inclusion of a few obscurities ("Anything," "Just Hot" and "Something Comfort") was a good idea. Worth searching for by Dixieland fans. — *Scott Yanow*

Andy Narell

b. Apr. 18, 1954, New York, NY
Steel Drums / World Fusion, Crossover Jazz, Post-Bop

Andy Narell introduced the steel drums to jazz as a solo instrument, playing not only Caribbean and Latin melodies, but R&B, funk and some straightahead jazz. After graduating from the University of California, Berkeley, in 1973, he founded the Hip Pocket label (which became associated with Windham Hill) and has recorded on a regular basis both as a leader and as a sideman ever since. In 1995 Andy Narell became a co-leader of the Caribbean Jazz Project along with Paquito D'Rivera and Dave Samuals, a perfect outlet for his virtuosic and colorful playing. — *Scott Yanow*

Hidden Treasure / Jan. 1979 / Inner City ✦✦✦

Narell is among the rare steel drummers active in jazz as well as traditional Caribbean music. He manages to find ways to blend the two, and also injects elements of pop, rock, and fusion into his albums. These intriguing compositional touches and different musical elements take some weight off the songs, which are mostly routine. — *Ron Wynn*

Stickman / Jun. 1980-Jul. 1980 / Hip Pocket ✦✦✦✦

Andy Narell's second release as a leader (following a long-out-of-print effort for Inner City) was reissued as a 1989 CD. Narell virtually introduced the steel drums to jazz, and this diverse recording (which ranges from Brazilian jazz to touches of rock, post-bop jazz and even a "Celtic Folk Song") was a strong force in making him a well-known name in the jazz world. Narell also plays some keyboards and drums on the date and is joined on the worthwhile effort by guitarist Steve Erquiaga, electric bassist Rich Girard and drummer/percussionist Kenneth Nash. — *Scott Yanow*

Light in Your Eyes / Jan. 1983-Mar. 1983 / Hip Pocket ✦✦✦✦

One of Andy Narell's most exciting and unpredictable albums, *Light in Your Eyes* ranges from the exuberant to the quietly introspective. Narell, who embraces electric keyboards and acoustic piano in addition to his main instrument the steel pans, is undeniably inspired on everything from the driving post-bop number "A Stitch in Time" to the poetic, South American-influenced "The Strayaway Child" to the somewhat Joe Sample-ish title song. World music has long been one of the charismatic Narell's strong points, and on this fine CD, he looks to locations ranging from Africa to South America to Trinidad (where the steel pans originated) for inspiration. — *Alex Henderson*

● Slow Motion / Jan. 1985-Mar. 1985 / Hip Pocket ✦✦✦✦✦

More often than not, the steel pans are used for playing the traditional sounds of Trinidad; but Andy Narell has successfully utilized them in a variety of non-traditional ways. On the ambitious and highly eclectic fusion release *Slow Motion*, elements of everything from Afro-Cuban salsa to Brazilian samba to African music are fair game for the adventurous, even visionary improviser (who is also heard on electric keyboards). Sometimes cerebral and sometimes romantic—sometimes intense and sometimes reflective—*Slow Motion* is one CD that cannot be accused of predictability. For those exploring Narell's music for the first time, this album would be an excellent starting point. — *Alex Henderson*

The Hammer / 1987 / Windham Hill ✦✦✦✦✦

Steel drummer Andy Narell contributed five of the six originals on this excellent set—all but the title cut, which is sung by its composer David Rudder. Joined by his regular band of the period (guitarist Steve Erquiaga, bassist Keith Jones, drummer William Kennedy and percussionist Kenneth Nash), Narell once again shows how surprisingly flexible steel drums can be in jazz, pop, rock, and of course calypso settings. Any album that includes the title "Brontosaurus Ballet" is certainly worth exploring. — *Scott Yanow*

Little Secrets / 1989 / Windham Hill ✦✦✦

Though not among Andy Narell's best albums, *Little Secrets* is a decent jazz/pop/R&B/world release that has more pluses than minuses. Clearly overproduced and overarranged, the album could have done without Narell's pointless overdubs—nonetheless, he doesn't outright smother the material, and gives himself enough room to blow, stretch and improvise. The CD's most noteworthy offerings include "Don't Look Back" (which begins with an Asian feel before taking on more of an Afro-Cuban flavor), the hauntingly introspective "The Songlines" and the hypnotic "Heads or Tails." — *Alex Henderson*

Down the Road / 1992 / Windham Hill ✦✦✦✦

Andy Narell is the Jimmy Smith of the steel drums, an innovative player who has been responsible for introducing his instrument to jazz. On this CD Narell shows off the surprising versatility of his instrument, not only playing spirited Latin jams and calypsos but also heartfelt ballads and more complex works. The lively yet diverse date is a strong example of Andy Narell's talents. — *Scott Yanow*

Fats Navarro (Theodore Navarro)

b. Sep. 24, 1923, Key West, FL, **d.** Jul. 7, 1950, New York, NY
Trumpet / Bop

One of the greatest jazz trumpeters of all time, Fats Navarro had a tragically brief career yet his influence is still being felt. His fat sound, which combined aspects of Howard McGhee, Roy Eldridge and Dizzy Gillespie, became the main inspiration for Clifford Brown, and through Brownie greatly affected the tones and styles of Lee Morgan, Freddie Hubbard and Woody Shaw.

Navarro originally played piano and tenor before switching to trumpet. He started gigging with dance bands when he was 17, was with Andy Kirk during 1943-44 and replaced Dizzy Gillespie with the Billy Eckstine big band during 1945-46. During the next three years Fats was second to only Dizzy among bop trumpeters. Navarro recorded with Kenny Clarke's Bebop Boys, Coleman Hawkins, Eddie "Lockjaw" Davis, Illinois Jacquet, and most significantly Tadd Dameron during 1946-47. He had short stints with the big bands of Lionel Hampton and Benny Goodman, continued working with Dameron, made classic recordings with Bud Powell (in a quintet with a young Sonny Rollins) and the Metronome All-Stars, and a 1950 Birdland appearance with Charlie Parker was privately recorded.

However, Navarro was a heroin addict and that affliction certainly did not help him in what would be a fatal bout with tuberculosis that ended his life at age 26. He was well-documented during the 1946-49 period and most of his sessions are currently available on CD, but Fats Navarro (who would have turned 72 in 1995) could have done so much more! —*Scott Yanow*

☆ **Fat Girl** / Sep. 6, 1946-Dec. 5, 1947 / Savoy ✦✦✦✦✦
This out-of-print two-LP set features trumpeter Fats Navarro's Savoy recordings which have thus far only been reissued on CD in piecemeal fashion. The ill-fated Navarro is heard at the peak of his powers, whether teamed with trumpeter Kenny Dorham, altoist Sonny Stitt and pianist Bud Powell in an octet, interacting with the equally fiery tenor saxophonist Eddie "Lockjaw" Davis, or jamming with pianist Tadd Dameron in quintets featuring baritonist Leo Parker, altoist Ernie Henry or tenor saxophonist Charlie Rouse. Among the classic bebop recordings included on this hard-to-find but essential two-fer are "Webb City," the well-titled "Hollerin' and Screamin'," "Fat Girl," "E*f* Pob," "A Bebop Carol," "Nostalgia" and "Fats Blows." —*Scott Yanow*

★ **Fats Navarro and Tadd Dameron: The Complete Blue Note and Capitol Recordings** / Sep. 26, 1947-Aug. 8, 1949 / Blue Note ✦✦✦✦✦
Many valuable performances from the height of the bop era are included on this double-CD. Subtitled "The Complete Blue Note and Capitol Recordings" and comprising 23 songs and 13 alternate takes, the reissue features the great trumpeter Fats Navarro in peak form with three groups headed by pianist/arranger Tadd Dameron, in trumpet battles with one of his major influences, Howard McGhee, and on a remarkable all-star quintet with pianist Bud Powell and the young tenor Sonny Rollins; among the other sidemen are altoist Ernie Henry, tenors Charlie Rouse, Allen Eager, Wardell Gray and Dexter Gordon and vibraphonist Milt Jackson. In addition to such gems as "Our Delight," "Lady Bird," "Double Talk," "Bouncing with Bud," "Dance of the Infidels" and "52nd Street Theme," Fats is heard with the 1948 Benny Goodman septet ("Stealin' Apples"), and Dameron leads a group with the 22-year old Miles Davis. On a whole, this double-CD has more than its share of essential music that belongs in all historical jazz collections. —*Scott Yanow*

Prime Source / Sep. 26, 1947-Aug. 8, 1949 / Blue Note ✦✦✦✦✦
The music on this out-of-print two-LP set is classic; fortunately all of the performances have since been reissued on CD. The great bop trumpeter Fats Navarro is featured in a couple of Tadd Dameron groups (which also include altoist Ernie Henry and tenors Charlie Rouse, Wardell Gray and Allen Eager), in a famous set of trumpet battles with his main influence Howard McGhee ("Double Talk" is particularly exciting) and on a remarkable quintet session with pianist Bud Powell and the young tenor Sonny Rollins. Brilliant and historic music. —*Scott Yanow*

Fats Navarro with Tadd Dameron / 1948 / Milestone ✦✦✦✦
On this CD reissue are all of the contents of a former two-LP set. Trumpeter Fats Navarro is featured on ten of the thirteen selections with pianist-arranger Tadd Dameron's Orchestra; the other three songs have trombonist Kai Winding in his place. With tenor saxophonist Allan Eager and (on six of the numbers) altoist Rudy Williams as the other key soloists, the boppish music is quite enjoyable. The recording quality of the live performances is decent for the time and the material (all but five are Dameron originals) is consistently of high quality. This valuable CD is easily recommended for bop collectors as is virtually every record that Fats Navarro made in his brief life. —*Scott Yanow*

Buell Neidlinger

b. Mar. 2, 1936, New York, NY
Bass, Cello / Avant-Garde, Post-Bop, Free Jazz
Throughout his career, bassist Buell Neidlinger has played such a wide variety of styles that one can only conclude he can play anything. He started out studying classical cello and also learned trumpet and piano before settling on bass. After moving to New York in 1955, Neidlinger played with Dixieland and mainstream bands and with such top players as Rex Stewart, Vic Dickenson, Coleman Hawkins and Eddie Condon. That same year he joined Cecil Taylor's Quartet, a unit that only worked sporadically during the next six years. Neidlinger was certainly inspired by the challenging music, making several records with Taylor, including a Candid set (reissued in expanded form by Mosaic) that was originally put out under his leadership. He also worked with the Jimmy Giuffre 3, Steve Lacy, Gil Evans, Freddie Redd, and six months as an accompanist for Tony Bennett. In 1962, Neidlinger started a two-year stint as a member of the Houston Symphony Orchestra; by the mid-'60s he was a busy studio musician in New York, and during the next ten years, he played everything from fusion with Jean-Luc Ponty and Frank Zappa rock dates to classical sessions with Stravinsky. After moving to Los Angeles (where he has worked in the studios up to the present day), Neidlinger formed a musical partnership with tenor saxophonist Marty Krystall. On their K2B2 label, Neidlinger and Krystall have recorded with a jazz-oriented bluegrass

group (Buellgrass), some post-bop, a Thelonious Monk tribute, and remarkable interpretations of Herbie Nichols' music (*Blue Chopsticks*) that features Buell on cello with a string trio and two horns. —*Scott Yanow*

Ready for the 90s / 1960-1989 / K2B2 ✦✦✦✦
Four of the five selections on this LP have some adventurous playing from a quartet consisting of tenor saxophonist Marty Krystall, trumpeter Warren Gale, bassist Buell Neidlinger and drummer Billy Higgins. Krystall, who has mostly worked in the studios of Los Angeles, remains an underrated talent who (like Benny Wallace) has been influenced by both Ben Webster's tone and Eric Dolphy's improvising approach while developing his own style. The music includes an original that uses two Stravinsky themes and one piece based a bit on "Night in Tunisia." Rounding off the album is a 1961 performance of "P.O." by pianist Cecil Taylor, Neidlinger and drummer Dennis Charles that has been reissued on a Mosaic box set. In fact, three of the four 1979 numbers have since come out on the Neidlinger CD *Rear View Mirror*, so this album is only for completists who want to get the additional cut ("Modern Gizz"). —*Scott Yanow*

Marty's Garage / Jan. 9, 1961-1973 / K2B2 ✦✦✦✦
Five of the seven selections on this LP from the small K2B2 label features bassist Buell Neidlinger and tenor saxophonist Marty Krystall (who takes one piece on bass clarinet) playing in quartets with trombonist Glenn Ferris and either Billy Elgart or Deborah Fuss on drums; in one case keyboardist Don Preston is in Ferris' place. The music is post-bop (somewhere between hard bop and the avant-garde) and most notable for the fine playing of Krystall. Two other numbers are historical and were released for the initial time on this album. From 1961, Neidlinger plays a duet with tenorman Archie Shepp, and the duo is joined by pianist Cecil Taylor and drummer Dennis Charles on a version of "Section C." An interesting release that has not yet been reissued on CD, although the two earlier tracks have been repackaged by Mosaic. —*Scott Yanow*

Rear View Mirror / Sep. 6, 1979-Nov. 1986 / K2B2 ✦✦✦✦✦
This CD has selections taken from four prior releases on bassist Buell Neidlinger's K2B2 label: three numbers apiece from *Ready for the '90s, Thelonious, Big Day at Ojai* and four from *Our Night Together*. In each case, the bassist is teamed with the underrated tenor saxophonist Marty Krystall. Most of the tunes features a quartet or trio and such fine players as trumpeter Warren Gale, organist Jerry Peters, pianist John Beasley and drummers Peter Erskine, Billy Higgins and Billy Osborne make strong contributions. The final three numbers are the most unusual, featuring versions of "Stardust," "Jumpin' Punkins" and "Happy Go Lucky Local" played by Buellgrass, a group consisting of mandolin, harmonica, violin, tenor, bass and drums. Other highlights include "Igor's Blues" and a memorable version of Thelonious Monk's "Little Rootie Tootie." Although one regrets the missing selections from the four original LPs, this CD gives one a well-rounded picture of bassist Neidlinger's activities during a seven-year period. —*Scott Yanow*

Big Day at Ojai / Aug. 23, 1981 / K2B2 ✦✦✦✦✦
One of the most unusual groups of the early '80s was a band accurately titled Buellgrass. On this live LP, bassist Buell Neidlinger heads a unique sextet also including the late Peter Ivers on harmonica, Andy Statman on mandolin and clarinet, violinist Richard Greene, Marty Krystall on reeds (tenor, soprano and various clarinets) and drummer Peter Erskine. The group mixes the sounds of jazz, blues and bluegrass, and can be heard on this valuable album playing songs associated with Duke Ellington plus Thelonious Monk's "Epistrophy," "Billie's Bounce," "Stardust" and "Tennessee Waltz." Since only three of the eight numbers have thus far been reissued on CD (as part of *Rear View Mirror*), this LP is well worth acquiring, if only to hear the blend between harmonica, mandolin, violin and tenor. —*Scott Yanow*

Swingrass '83 / Feb. 1984 / Antilles ✦✦✦✦✦
Although here renamed "Swingrass," the band on this LP is the same as the one that was called "Buellgrass" (and heard on a K2B2 LP a year earlier), except that Fred Tackett is added on guitar. The unusual mixture of players (bassist/leader Buell Neidlinger, Peter Ivers on harmonica, mandolinist Andy Statman, violinist Richard Greene, Tackett, Marty Krystall on reeds, and drummer Peter Erskine) performs unique renditions of three songs apiece by Duke Ellington and Thelonious Monk, plus a couple of group originals. Certainly these versions of "Mainstem," "Skippy" and "Little Rootie Tootie" are different than any heard previously. A memorable set that has yet to be reissued on CD. —*Scott Yanow*

★ **Locomotive** / Jun. 24, 1987-Jun. 25, 1987 / Soul Note ✦✦✦✦✦
The 1987 version of String Jazz (whose ancestor was Buellgrass) consisted of bassist Buell Neidlinger, longtime musical friend Marty Krystall on tenor saxophone, violinist Brenton Banks, John Kurnick on mandolin and drummer Billy Osborne. Neidlinger's band performs seven Thelonious Monk songs, three by Duke Ellington plus Mercer Ellington's "Jumpin' Punkins." Although several of the selections had been recorded by Neidlinger during the past decade, these renditions sound

quite a bit different. Krystall is a powerful soloist; the obscure string players fare quite well, and such tunes as "Rockin' "In Rhythm," "Skippy," "I Mean You" and "Boo Boo's Birthday" are all given fresh renditions. Recommended. —*Scott Yanow*

Thelonious / Jun. 1988 / K2B2 ✦✦✦✦

The one album by the short-lived group Thelonious finds bassist Buell Neidlinger, Marty Krystall (doubling on tenor and alto), pianist John Beasley and drummer Billy Osborne performing eight of the lesser-known Thelonious Monk compositions. Beasley mostly avoids sounding like Monk; under Neidlinger's direction, the quartet plays the complex numbers with the correct chords and melody lines, and Krystall shows that he is a particularly skilled soloist. Among the highlights are "Trinkle Tinkle," "Locomotive" and "Ask Me Now." Three of the selections have been reissued as part of the CD *Rear View Mirror*, but otherwise, the music is only available on this somewhat rare LP. —*Scott Yanow*

Big Drum / Jun. 6, 1990 / K2B2 ✦✦✦✦

Blue Chopsticks / Jul. 6, 1994-Jul. 7, 1994 / K2B2 ✦✦✦✦✦

Herbie Nichols, a highly original pianist and composer, had a short life shrouded in obscurity, yet he did make a strong impression on his occasional bassist Buell Neidlinger. While Nichols only had the opportunity to record some of his pieces in piano-bass-drums trios, Neidlinger's memorable tribute does not utilize any of those three instruments. With Marty Krystall on reeds, Hugh Schick on trumpet, violinist Richard Greene, Jimbo Ross on viola and Neidlinger sticking to cello, 11 of Nichols' originals are given colorful, often humorous and spirited interpretations. One of the finest releases of 1995, this CD is full of surprises and unusual tone colors. Highlights include "Blue Chopsticks," "The Gig," "Love, Gloom, Cash, Love" and "The Lady Sings the Blues," but each selection is well worth hearing. A gem that belongs in every jazz recording collection. —*Scott Yanow*

Oliver Nelson

b. Jun. 4, 1932, St. Louis, MO, d. Oct. 27, 1975, Los Angeles, CA

Arrange., Alto Saxophone, Tenor Saxophone, Composer, Leader/ Post-Bop, Hard Bop, Groove

Oliver Nelson was a distinctive soloist on alto, tenor and even soprano, but his writing eventually overshadowed his playing skills. He became a professional early on in 1947, playing with the Jeter-Pillars Orchestra and with St. Louis big bands headed by George Hudson and Nat Towles. In 1951 he arranged and played second alto for Louis Jordan's big band and followed with a period in the Navy and four years at a university. After moving to New York, Nelson worked briefly with Erskine Hawkins, Wild Bill Davis and Louie Bellson (the latter on the West Coast). In addition to playing with the Quincy Jones' Orchestra (1960-61), Nelson recorded six small-group albums and a big-band date between 1959-61 which gave him a lot of recognition and respect in the jazz world. *Blues and the Abstract Truth* (from 1961) is considered a classic and helped to popularize a song that Nelson had included on a slightly earlier Eddie "Lockjaw" Davis session, "Stolen Moments." He also fearlessly matched wits effectively with the explosive Eric Dolphy on a pair of quintet sessions. But good as his playing was, Nelson was in greater demand as an arranger, writing for the big-band dates of Jimmy Smith, Wes Montgomery and Billy Taylor among others. By 1967 when he moved to Los Angeles, Nelson was working hard in the studios, writing for television and movies. He occasionally appeared with a big band, wrote a few ambitious works and recorded jazz on an infrequent basis, but Oliver Nelson was largely lost to jazz a few years before his unexpected death at age 43 from a heart attack. —*Scott Yanow*

Meet Oliver Nelson / Oct. 30, 1959 / Original Jazz Classics ✦✦✦✦

Oliver Nelson's debut as a leader found him at the age of 27 already a distinctive and skilled tenor saxophonist. For this quintet set (reissued on CD in the OJC series), Nelson teams up with the veteran trumpeter Kenny Dorham, pianist Ray Bryant, bassist Wendell Marshall and drummer Art Taylor for four of his originals, plus the ballads "Passion Flower" and "What's New." Although none of these Nelson tunes caught on, this was an impressive beginning to a short but productive career and gives a strong example of the multi-talented Nelson's tenor playing. —*Scott Yanow*

Takin' Care of Business / Mar. 22, 1960 / Original Jazz Classics ✦✦✦✦✦

Oliver Nelson would gain his greatest fame later in his short life as an arranger/composer, but this superior session puts the emphasis on his distinctive tenor and alto playing. In a slightly unusual group (with vibraphonist Lem Winchester, organist Johnny "Hammond" Smith, bassist George Tucker and drummer Roy Haynes), Nelson improvises a variety of well-constructed but spontaneous solos; his unaccompanied spots on "All the Way" and his hard-charging playing on the medium-tempo blues "Groove" are two of the many high points. Nelson remains a vastly underrated saxophonist and all six performances on this recommended CD reissue (four of them his originals) are excellent. —*Scott Yanow*

Screamin' the Blues / May 27, 1960 / Original Jazz Classics ✦✦✦✦✦

Oliver Nelson (on tenor and alto) meets Eric Dolphy (alto, bass clarinet and flute) on this frequently exciting sextet session with trumpeter Richard Williams, pianist Richard Wyands, bassist George Duvivier and drummer Roy Haynes. Although Dolphy is too unique and skilled to be overshadowed in a setting such as this, Nelson holds his own. He contributed five of the six compositions (including "Screamin' the Blues," "The Meetin'" and "Altoitis") and effectively matches wits and creative ideas with Dolphy. This CD reissue (also available as part of a huge Eric Dolphy box set) is recommended, as is the follow-up record *Straight Ahead.* —*Scott Yanow*

Images / May 27, 1960+Mar. 1, 1961 / Prestige ✦✦✦✦

This out-of-print double-LP has the music from two albums that have since been reissued on CD in the OJC series: *Screamin' the Blues* and *Straight Ahead.* In both cases Oliver Nelson (doubling on alto and tenor) meets up with the remarkable Eric Dolphy (who switches between flute, bass clarinet and alto). The rhythm section is the same on both dates (pianist Richard Wyands, bassist George Duvivier and drummer Roy Haynes) while trumpeter Richard Williams also appears on the former session. Any musician would sound like a conservative (or a straight man) next to Dolphy but Nelson fares well and he contributed all but two of the dozen compositions. The music (except for some of Dolphy's flights) is essentially straightahead hard bop. Both of these sessions have since been reissued on CD, separately under Nelson's name and as part of a giant Eric Dolphy box set. —*Scott Yanow*

Nocturne / Aug. 23, 1960 / Original Jazz Classics ✦✦✦

This relaxed set (originally on the Prestige subsidiary Moodsville) puts the emphasis on ballads and slower material. Nelson (switching between alto and tenor) is joined by vibraphonist Lem Winchester, pianist Richard Wyands, bassist George Duvivier and drummer Roy Haynes for four standards and three of his originals (including the swinging "Bob's Blues"). Everyone plays well but the intentional lack of mood variation keeps this release from being all that essential. —*Scott Yanow*

Soul Battle / Sep. 9, 1960 / Original Jazz Classics ✦✦✦✦✦

This intriguing session matches together three powerful tenor players: Oliver Nelson, King Curtis (in a rare jazz outing) and Jimmy Forrest. With fine backup work by pianist Gene Casey, bassist George Duvivier and drummer Roy Haynes, the tenors battle to a draw on a set of blues and basic material (including a fine version of "Perdido"). This CD reissue adds one selection ("Soul Street") from the same date to the original LP program and is easily recommended to fans of big-toned tenors and straightahead swinging. —*Scott Yanow*

★ **Blues and the Abstract Truth** / Feb. 23, 1961 / Impulse! ✦✦✦✦✦

This was Oliver Nelson's finest recording and one of the top jazz albums of 1961, a true classic. The lineup is an inspired one: Nelson on tenor and alto, Eric Dolphy doubling on alto and flute, a young trumpeter named Freddie Hubbard, baritonist George Barrow for section parts, pianist Bill Evans, bassist Paul Chambers and drummer Roy Haynes. The contrasting voices of the soloists really uplift these superior compositions which are highlighted by "Stolen Moments" (a future standard), the fun "Hoe-Down" and "Yearnin'." Dolphy cuts everyone but Nelson and Hubbard are also in top form. —*Scott Yanow*

Straight Ahead / Mar. 1, 1961 / Original Jazz Classics ✦✦✦✦✦

This CD reissue brings back a very interesting quintet set matching Oliver Nelson (on alto and tenor) and Eric Dolphy (tripling on alto, flute and bass clarinet). With the assistance of pianist Richard Wyands, bassist George Duvivier and drummer Roy Haynes, the two reedmen battle it out on six compositions (five of Nelson's originals plus Milt Jackson's "Ralph's New Blues"). Although none of Nelson's tunes caught on, this is a fairly memorable date. It certainly took a lot of courage for Oliver Nelson to share the front line with the colorful Eric Dolphy, but his own strong musical personality holds its own on this straightahead date. —*Scott Yanow*

Main Stem / Aug. 25, 1961 / Original Jazz Classics ✦✦✦✦

Unlike most of Oliver Nelson's recordings, this one has the feel of a jam session. A CD reissue of a Prestige set, Nelson (on tenor and alto) teams up with trumpeter Joe Newman (in exciting form), pianist Hank Jones, bassist George Duvivier, drummer Charlie Persip and Ray Barretto on congas for two superior standards ("Main Stem" and "Tangerine") and four of Nelson's more basic originals. The spirited solos of Nelson and Newman are strong reasons to get this colorful session. —*Scott Yanow*

Afro-American Sketches / Sep. 29, 1961+Oct. 10, 1961 / Original Jazz Classics ✦✦✦✦✦

This CD reissue brings back Oliver Nelson's first big-band date as a leader. Meant as a folk album paying tribute to the history of blacks in America, there are such songs as "Jungleaire," "Emancipation Blues," "Going Up North" and "Freedom

Dance." Among the soloists are flutist Jerry Dodgion, trumpeter Joe Newman and Nelson himself on tenor and alto. Even this early, Nelson's writing had its own sound; his seven-part suite is well worth hearing. —*Scott Yanow*

Fantabulous / Mar. 19, 1964 / Argo ✦✦✦✦✦
This somewhat obscure Oliver Nelson date (which was also released on Chess) features Nelson heading a 12-piece group that includes such fine players as altoist Phil Woods, trumpeters Art Hoyle and Snooky Young and pianist Patti Bown. Nelson (on tenor) is generally the main soloist and two of the eight songs (six of which are his compositions) are somewhat known: "Hobo Flats" and "Teenie's Blues." This LP is long overdue to be reissued. —*Scott Yanow*

More Blues....the Abstract Truth / Nov. 10, 1964-Nov. 11, 1964 / MCA ✦✦✦
Unlike the original classic *Blues and the Abstract Truth* set from three years earlier, Oliver Nelson did not play on this album. He did contribute three of the eight originals and all of the arrangements but his decision not to play is disappointing. However, there are some strong moments from such all-stars as trumpeter Thad Jones, altoist Phil Woods, baritonist Pepper Adams, pianist Roger Kellaway and guest tenor Ben Webster (who is on two songs). The emphasis is on blues-based pieces and there are some strong moments, even if the date falls short of its predecessor. —*Scott Yanow*

Sound Pieces / 1966 / Impulse! ✦✦✦✦
This CD reissue features Oliver Nelson in two very different settings. Although best known as an altoist and a tenor saxophonist, Nelson sticks exclusively to soprano throughout the set. He leads a 20-piece big band on three of his compositions which, although interesting, are not overly memorable. Best are five other numbers (two of which were originally issued on the record *Three Dimensions*) that showcase Nelson's soprano playing with a quartet also includes pianist Steve Kuhn, bassist Ron Carter and drummer Grady Tate. Although one would not think of Nelson as a soprano stylist, his strong playing actually put him near the top of his field on such numbers as "The Shadow of Your Smile," "Straight, No Chaser" and his own "Patterns." —*Scott Yanow*

Musical Tribute to JFK: The Kennedy Dream / Feb. 16, 1967-Feb. 17, 1967 / Impulse! ✦✦✦
Ever passionate about politics, Oliver Nelson launches eight heartfelt orchestral jazz compositions from memorable sections of John Kennedy's speeches about equality and positive change. Nelson is occasionally heard singing on soprano and tenor. But one's attention is inevitably drawn to Nelson's compositional ability, particularly with strings. "The Rights of All," "Let the Word Go Forth" and "The Artists' Rightful Place" are standout pieces that also allow an opportunity to savor some of the fine talent: Phil Woods, Hank Jones, George Duvivier and Grady Tate. Deserves to be issued on CD. —*Douglas Payne*

Black, Brown and Beautiful / Mar. 17, 1970-1974 / Bluebird ✦✦✦✦✦
The bulk of this CD has a 1970 session that teams together arranger Oliver Nelson, altoist Johnny Hodges and (on three of the songs) singer Leon Thomas. The big band also includes pianist Earl Hines and the program is highlighted by "Empty Ballroom Blues," "Welcome to New York" and "Creole Love Call"; all of the songs were composed by either Duke Ellington, Nelson or Thomas. That near-classic session is augmented by three numbers from a couple of later dates that feature Nelson's alto playing. Recommended. —*Scott Yanow*

Berlin Dialogue for Orchestra / Nov. 5, 1970 / Flying Dutchman ✦✦✦✦✦
Oliver Nelson wrote two four-part suites specifically to be played by the Berlin Dream Band in 1970: "Berlin Dialogue for Orchestra" and "Impressions of Berlin." The only "names" among the personnel are trumpeter Carmell Jones, trombonist Slide Hampton and Ake Persson and altoist Leo Wright; Nelson is also featured a bit on alto. None of the individual pieces caught on but taken as a whole, this out-of-print LP should please big-band collectors and serves as a good example of Oliver Nelson's writing style. —*Scott Yanow*

Swiss Suite / Jun. 18, 1971 / Flying Dutchman ✦✦✦✦
Recorded at the 1971 Montreux Jazz Festival, this big-band outing features a mostly all-star band and altoist Oliver Nelson (who wrote all of the arrangements and compositions) and trumpeter Danny Moore on remakes of "Stolen Moments," "Black, Brown and Beautiful" and "Blues and the Abstract Truth." However, it is the nearly 27-minute "Swiss Suite" that dominates this album; and, although tenorman Gato Barbieri has a couple of raging solos, it is a five-minute segment when guest altoist Eddie "Cleanhead" Vinson plays the blues that is most memorable. Vinson's classic spot alone is worth the price of this hard-to-find LP. —*Scott Yanow*

Oily Rags / 1974 / Flying Dutchman ✦✦
This out-of-print LP is one of the lesser Oliver Nelson albums. Mostly playing alto (with one number on soprano), Nelson fronts an English group whose roots are in rock. Nelson plays well and there are some good moments (particularly on Jobim's

"Meditation"), but most of the backup musicians sound quite anonymous and little significant occurs. —*Scott Yanow*

Skull Session / 1975 / Flying Dutchman ✦✦
Hardly up to snuff for the talented and overworked Nelson, who was busy scoring TV shows at the time. "Skull Session" is a fun little dabble in electronic funk. But the rest seems beneath Nelson's abilities, as it takes his signature sounds, adds disco, dumbs down the themes and finishes it off with pedestrian solos from L.A. studio musicians. —*Douglas Payne*

Stolen Moments / Mar. 6, 1975 / Inner City ✦✦✦✦✦
A beautiful swan song from the immensely talented Oliver Nelson featuring his terrific alto. Features an excellent West Coast small group with Bobby Bryant, Jerome Richardson, Buddy Collette, Bobby Bryant Jr., Jack Nimitz, Mike Wofford, Chuck Domanico amd Shelly Manne (d). —*Douglas Payne*

Steve Nelson

b. 1955, Pittsburgh, PA
Vibes / Hard Bop
Steve Nelson developed in the 1990s into one of the most promising vibraphonists around, influenced by Milt Jackson but gradually developing his own sound. After gigging with Grant Green in the early '70s, Nelson picked up important experience playing with Kenny Barron, James Spaulding, Bobby Watson and David "Fathead" Newman and has played in a countless number of settings in recent times. Nelson has recorded as a leader thus far for Criss Cross, Red and Sunnyside. —*Scott Yanow*

Communications / Dec. 30, 1987 / Criss Cross ✦✦✦✦

Live Session, Vol. 1 / Jul. 1989 / Red ✦✦✦

Live Session, Vol. 2 / Jul. 1989 / Red ✦✦✦

● **Full Nelson** / Aug. 8, 1989 / Sunnyside ✦✦✦✦✦

Roger Neumann

b. Minot, ND
Arranger, Leader, Tenor Saxophone / Bop
A colorful arranger, Roger Neumann has released only two albums by his "Rather Large Band" (one in 1983 and the other in 1993, both for Sea Breeze) but they are both memorable. A jazz educator based in Los Angeles with experience playing tenor with Woody Herman (1967), Bob Crosby and Anita O'Day, Neumann has contributed arrangements for his wife-singer Madeline Vergari, Buddy Rich, Count Basie, Ray Brown and even the Beach Boys! —*Scott Yanow*

● **Introducing Rodger Neumann's Rather Large Band** / Apr. 1983-Jun. 1983 / Sea Breeze ✦✦✦✦✦
One of the most underrated arrangers around, Roger Neumann had a rare opportunity to record his big band in 1983; surprisingly, the orchestra's second instrumental date would not take place for another decade. Neumann, who is featured on tenor during "Emily," heads a 19-piece big band on this highly recommended album that includes among its personnel the then-unknown altoist Eric Marienthal, trombonists Herbie Harper and Bob Enevoldsen, pianist Tom Ranier and the tenors of Herman Riley and Bob Hardaway. Neumann's ensemble performs three jazz standards, a romping "Flintstones," and a three-part suite dedicated to Blue Mitchell ("They Called Him 'Blue'") that has solos from each of the five trumpeters. Each of the swinging performances is memorable in its own way, and this album is well worth searching for. —*Scott Yanow*

Instant Heat / Nov. 22, 1993-Nov. 24, 1993 / Sea Breeze ✦✦✦✦✦
It is very surprising that this Sea Breeze CD was Roger Neumann's first release since 1983 for his arrangements are colorful, fairly original and hard-swinging. In addition to all of the charts, he wrote eight of the new set's dozen compositions, plays some fine tenor and is very generous in allocating solo space to his 17 sidemen; in fact every musician (including the six subs) gets at least one chance to be heard. The fresh versions of "Good Bait," "Stompin' at the Savoy," "For Heaven's Sake" and Chick Corea's "Children's Song, No. 2" alternate with Neumann's unpredictable originals and the music is consistently enjoyable. This CD is highly recommended to big-band fans as was the earlier Sea Breeze recording *Introducing Roger Neumann's Rather Large Band*. —*Scott Yanow*

New & Used Consensus

f. 1995
Group / Avant-Garde
A group which attempted to find common ground between the polar opposites of notated and improvised music, the New York-based quintet New & Used Consensus marked a convergence of players from intriguingly diverse backgrounds. Trumpeter Dave Douglas was the leader of the Tiny Bell Trio and a member of

John Zorn's Masada, and played with Mark Dresser, Don Byron and Dr. Nerve; bassist Kermit Driscoll was the longtime bass player in the Bill Frisell Band and performed with Zorn and Wayne Horvitz; violinist Mark Feldman played with the Billy Hart Sextet, the Ray Anderson Sextet and Anthony Davis' Epistime; drummer/percussionist Tom Rainey recorded with Kenny Warner, Mark Helias and the Fred Hersch Group; and saxophonist Andy Laster led his own group, Hydra, and was a member of Lyle Lovett's Large Band. —*Jason Ankeny*

New & Used Consensus / Jan. 23, 1996 / Knitting Factory ♦♦♦
The music of the New & Used Consensus draws on the varied stylistic backgrounds of its players on this 1996 release, which combines mainstream jazz improvisation with the compositional structures of everything from klezmer to avant-noise. —*Jason Ankeny*

New Orleans Owls

f. 1925, db. 1927
Group / Classic Jazz
The New Orleans Owls, an excellent if now obscure band, recorded 18 spirited sides during 1925-27. Although none of its sidemen (other than Nappy Lamare) became famous, the ensemble effectively bridged the gap between the New Orleans Rhythm Kings and late '20s dance bands. All of their enjoyable recordings were made available recently on a Frog CD from England. —*Scott Yanow*

★ The Owls' Hoot / Mar. 26, 1925-Oct. 26, 1927 / Frog ♦♦♦♦♦
The New Orleans Owls were a spirited seven-to-nine piece band whose hot jazz and interesting arrangements made it a legendary group to early jazz collectors. Its entire output, 18 selections from five sessions, is reissued on this highly enjoyable CD from the English label Frog. The Owls did not have any famous musicians (other than guitarist Nappy Lamare on the final date) but its versions of such songs as "Stomp Off, Let's Go," "Tampeekoe," "White Ghost Shivers" and "Brotherly Love," in particular, are memorable. In addition to those classic sides, The New Orleans Rhythm Kings' final recordings (two takes apiece of "She's Cryin' for Me" and "Everybody Loves Somebody Blues") and the recordings of John Hyman's Bayou Stompers (two versions apiece of a pair of songs that, in addition to the standard instrumentation, includes the harmonica of Alvin Gautreaux) wrap up this thoroughly enjoyable disc. —*Scott Yanow*

New Orleans Rhythm Kings

f. 1922, db. 1925
Group / Classic Jazz, Traditional Jazz
The New Orleans Rhythm Kings (NORK) were the finest jazz group to be on record in 1922 and the White band has served as proof that, even that early, Blacks were not the only ones that could play jazz with individuality and integrity. The key members of the group (leader-cornetist Paul Mares, trombonist George Brunis and clarinetist Leon Roppolo) were childhood friends from New Orleans. In 1922 they started a 17-month residency at the Friar's Inn Nightclub in Chicago and in August they made their first recordings. Although Mares (unlike Nick LaRocca of the Original Dixieland Jazz Band) was modest about his own playing, saying that he was very influenced by King Oliver, he actually sounded quite a bit different and had a voice of his own. Roppolo was the first significant soloist on record while Brunis would have a long career playing Dixieland. The changing rhythm sections sometimes included the first great jazz bassist Steve Brown (although largely inaudible on his early session), drummer Ben Pollack (a future bandleader) and, on a pair of memorable sessions in 1923, pianist Jelly Roll Morton. Among the future standards introduced by the NORK were "Farewell Blues," "Panama," "That's a Plenty" and "Tin Roof Blues" (the latter included a famous Brunis trombone solo). The band broke up in 1924 when Mares and Roppolo returned to New Orleans. With Santo Pecora on trombone they regrouped for a fine session in January 1925 but Roppolo was already suffering from mental problems; the group's final date two months later was without Roppolo who would soon be institutionalized for the remainder of his life. Mares came back for one further session in 1935 but seemed happy in retirement, leaving the legacy of the NORK to history. —*Scott Yanow*

● New Orleans Rhythm Kings and Jelly Roll Morton / Aug. 29, 1922-Jul. 18, 1923 / Milestone ♦♦♦♦♦
This single-CD reissues all of the music on the earlier double-LP of the same title (and catalog number) except for some alternate takes although it confuses matters a bit by adding a "new" alternate of "Milenberg Joys." The New Orleans Rhythm Kings were the best group on record during 1922 and all of its earliest recordings are on this essential release. With the solid cornet of Paul Mares, the excellent ensemble playing of trombonist George Brunis and the superb soloing of clarinetist Leon Roppolo, the NORK was the most advanced jazz band of its time. The recordings on the CD include sessions as an octet, a quintet and a tentet; some of the latter performances showcase the innovative pianist-composer Jelly Roll Mor-

ton. Highlights include "Tiger Rag," "Maple Leaf Rag," the original versions of "Farewell Blues," "That's a Plenty," "Bugle Call Rag" and "Tin Roof Blues" (the latter having Brunis' most famous trombone solo) plus the Morton sides (including "Clarinet Marmalade," "Mr. Jelly Lord" and "Milenberg Joys"). Classic and historic music. —*Scott Yanow*

New Orleans Rhythm Kings 1934-1935 / Sep. 12, 1934-Feb. 20, 1935 / Swaggie ♦♦♦♦
The New Orleans Rhythm Kings, a very significant early classic jazz group, broke up permanently in 1925. The name was revived during 1934-35 for three sessions that included the NORK's original trombonist George Brunis. Those 13 titles are joined by four songs from a Wingy Manone session dating from the same period on this LP (plus a previously unreleased version of "Royal Garden Blues") released by the Australian Swaggie label. Although recorded during the formative period of swing, freewheeling Dixieland is emphasized. Such top players as trumpeters Wingy Manone and Muggsy Spanier, trombonists George Brunis and Santa Pecora, clarinetists Sidney Arodin and Eddie Miller and drummer Gene Krupa are heard in spirited form and on the final session singer Red McKenzie has five vocals. This excellent music will hopefully be reissued on CD someday. —*Scott Yanow*

The N.Y. Hardbop Quintet

f. 1990
Group / Hard Bop
This excellent group was formed in 1990 as a quartet comprising trumpeter Joe Magnarelli, pianist Keith Saunders, bassist Bim Strasberg and drummer Eddie Ornowski. In 1991, the band became a quintet with the addition of tenor saxophonist Jerry Weldon; Ornowski departed in 1996 and was replaced by Clifford Barbaro. Its repertoire and style does stick to hard bop (stylewise of the Lee Morgan/Hank Mobley era), but the many originals and the fresh renditions of standards keep the group from sounding derivative. The New York Hardbop Quintet performs regularly in (surprise!) New York, but has also toured the West Coast several times. Ironically, all of their recordings thus far have been made for the Swiss TCB label. —*Scott Yanow*

● The Clincher / Apr. 21, 1994-Apr. 22, 1994 / TCB ♦♦♦♦♦
In some ways the New York Hardbop Quintet is similar to a creative Dixieland group of the 1950s, performing in a style that was at its prime 30 years earlier. But by contributing some new material (six of the nine selections on this CD are group originals), displaying very strong musicianship and coming up with consistently inventive solos, the group has its own purpose for existing rather than just as a vehicle for recreating the past. It is true that none of the musicians have strikingly new sounds (trumpeter Joe Magnarelli is in the Lee Morgan/Freddie Hubbard tradition, Jerry Weldon on tenor mixes together early Coltrane, Hank Mobley and Stanley Turrentine, and the rhythm section could easily pass for one from 1966), but the music is quite enjoyable. There is a lot of power in the various soloists' playing and chances are they will all develop their own distinctive voices in the future. As for now, this is a heated and very likable disc of hard-swinging jazz. —*Scott Yanow*

Rokermotion / Mar. 4, 1996-Mar. 5, 1996 / TCB ♦♦♦♦♦
A casual listen to some of the music on this CD may cause one to believe that it is a previously unissued Blue Note date by Lee Morgan and Hank Mobley, except that much of the material is new and the musicians do not really sound like exact duplicates of the early hard-bop greats. Very much living up to their group name, the fine players (tenorman Jerry Weldon, trumpeter Joe Magnarelli, pianist Keith Saunders, bassist Bim Strasberg and veteran drummer Mickey Roker) are quite creative within the older genre, much of which falls into the 1955-60 period (with occasional nods towards the mid-'60s). Performing six originals plus a lyrical "More than You Know" and a reharmonized "East of the Sun" on their third release, the members of the quintet take consistently swinging solos and the spontaneous-sounding ensembles are quite clean and exciting. Whether it be the boogaloo "Little Jake" (which finds Weldon hinting at Stanley Turrentine), a jazz waltz ("The Hip Naz") or the uptempo "Waat" (based on "The Way You Look Tonight"), this European import has many fine moments and is well worth searching for by straightahead jazz fans. —*Scott Yanow*

New York Jazz Quartet

f. 1972, db. 1982
Group / Post-Bop, Cool
The original New York Jazz Quartet was founded by pianist Roland Hanna in the early 1970s and consisted of flutist Hubert Laws, bassist Ron Carter and drummer Billy Cobham. That particular group went nowhere, but in 1974, Hanna had better luck with a lineup of flutist Frank Wess, bassist Carter (eventually replaced by George Mraz) and drummer Ben Riley; Richard Pratt and Grady Tate sometimes

subbed for Riley. The straightahead band (which lasted into the early 1980s) tended to emphasize originals and recorded for the Japanese Salvation label, Enja, Sonet and Beehive (1981). —*Scott Yanow*

In Concert in Japan, Vol. 1 / Apr. 2, 1975 / Salvation ✦✦✦

● **In Concert in Japan, Vol. 2** / Apr. 2, 1975 / Salvation ✦✦✦✦✦

Surge / Feb. 19, 1977 / Enja ✦✦✦✦✦

Song of the Black Knight / Oct. 29, 1977 / Sonet ✦✦✦✦✦
In 1977, the New York Jazz Quartet, a part-time quartet most active from 1975-81, consisted of Frank Wess on tenor, flute and soprano, pianist Roland Hanna, bassist George Mraz and drummer Richard Pratt. The band essentially performed modern mainstream jazz, with the originals of Hanna and Wess consistently challenging the players to come up with fresh statements. On this set, there are four Hanna tunes (including "Time for the Dancers" and the lengthy title cut), plus a pair of Wess compositions. Excellent music that swings but avoids predictability. —*Scott Yanow*

Blues for Sarka / May 17, 1978 / Enja ✦✦✦✦

Oasis / Feb. 13, 1981 / Enja ✦✦✦

The New York Jazz Quartet in Chicago / Jul. 27, 1981 / Bee Hive ✦✦✦✦
The New York Jazz Quartet gave pianist Roland Hanna, Frank Wess (doubling on tenor and flute), bassist George Mraz and drummer Ben Riley an opportunity to collaborate and, although the group did not develop any innovations, it did record several excellent albums. This Bee Hive album is one of their more extroverted affairs with particularly fine playing on Wess' "Four the Hard Way," Thad Jones' "H and T Blues" and the ballad "You Don't Know What Love Is." —*Scott Yanow*

New York Voices

f. 1987
Group / Bop
One of the best (and only) jazz vocal groups of the 1990s, the New York Voices use a repertoire that includes bop songs from the vocalese tradition, plus adaptations of more recent material from the jazz and pop worlds. Leader Darmon Meader (who also plays reeds and the EWI) had taken a vocal group to Europe in 1986 through Ithaca College, using the name of the New York Voices. The following year the group became official, consisting of a rhythm section and five singers: Meader (who also plays reeds and EWI), Caprice Fox, Kim Nazarian, Sara Krieger (later succeeded by Lauren Kinhan) and Peter Eldridge. They have recorded an enjoyable series of CDs for GRP. —*Scott Yanow*

New York Voices / 1989 / GRP ✦✦✦

● **Collection** / 1989-1993 / GRP ✦✦✦✦

Hearts of Fire / 1991 / GRP ✦✦✦

What's Inside / 1993 / GRP ✦✦✦✦

Sing the Songs of Paul Simon / Jun. 1997 / RCA Victor ✦✦✦✦
As Paul Simon was preparing his first Broadway musical, *The Capeman*, the New York Voices assembled *New York Voices Sing the Songs of Paul Simon*, a song-and-dance production of Simon's biggest hits. As a musical experience, the New York Voices turned out a better, richer album than Simon, whose *Songs from the Capeman* was curiously stillborn. *The Songs of Paul Simon*, however, is full of life, teeming with energy and bursting with melody. Produced by Joel Moss and featuring cameos by Christian McBride, Gil Goldstein and Russell Malone, the project features familiar numbers like "Cecilia," "Loves Me Like a Rock," "Me and Julio Down By the Schoolyard" and "Still Crazy After All These Years," but it also showcases wonderful album tracks like "One Man's Ceiling (Is Another Man's Floor)" and "Baby Driver." The arrangements are brighter and brassier than Simon's originals, but there's a real charm to the performances that makes it a thoroughly entertaining experience, one that's much more fun and engaging than *The Capeman*. —*Stephen Thomas Erlewine*

Phineas Newborn

b. Dec. 14, 1931, Whiteville, TN, d. May 26, 1989, Memphis, TN
Piano / Hard Bop
One of the most technically skilled and brilliant pianists in jazz during his prime, Phineas Newborn remains a bit of a mystery. Plagued by mental and physical problems of unknown origin, Newborn faded from the scene in the mid-1960s, only to re-emerge at irregular intervals throughout his life. Newborn could be compared to Oscar Peterson in that his bop-based style was largely unclassifiable, his technique was phenomenal, and he was very capable of enthralling an audience playing a full song with just his left hand.

He started out working in Memphis R&B bands with his brother, guitarist Calvin Newborn, and recorded with local players including B.B. King in the early

1950s. Brief stints with Lionel Hampton and Willis Jackson preceded a period in the military (1952-54). After moving to New York in 1956, Newborn astounded fans and critics alike. Although he worked briefly with Charles Mingus (1958) and Roy Haynes, Newborn usually performed at the head of a trio or quartet. His early recordings for Atlantic (1956), Victor, Roulette and Contemporary are quite outstanding. Unfortunately, after the mid-'60s, Newborn's profile dropped sharply, and although there were further recordings for Contemporary (1969), Atlantic (1969), Pablo (1976) and the Japanese Philips (1977) label, and although he still sounded strong when appearing in public, the pianist was in danger of being forgotten by most of the jazz world during his last decade. Spending most of his time in Memphis, he was an inspiration to many younger pianists including James Williams, Harold Mabern, Mulgrew Miller, Donald Brown and Geoff Keezer, who after Newborn's death would dedicate their work to the Contemporary Piano Ensemble to Phineas. Fortunately, the episode of Jazz Scene USA that features Phineas Newborn in 1962 has been made available on a video by Shanachie. —*Scott Yanow*

Piano Artistry of Phineas Newborn, Jr. / May 3, 1956-May 4, 1956 / Atlantic ✦✦✦✦✦
Phineas Newborn's first record (other than two slightly earlier songs) introduced to the jazz world a major talent. Blessed with a phenomenal technique and the ability to think very fast, Newborn immediately became one of jazz's top pianists, and would remain at the top until health problems forced him to become much less active. On this CD reissue, he explores seven jazz standards, including tunes by Bud Powell ("Celia"), Charlie Parker, Clifford Brown and John Lewis, plus his own "Newport Blues." Joined by bassist Oscar Pettiford, drummer Kenny Clarke and occasionally his brother Calvin Newborn on guitar, Phineas Newborn is in superb form for his debut. —*Scott Yanow*

Phineas' Rainbow / Oct. 16, 1956-Oct. 22, 1956 / Victor ✦✦✦✦

While My Lady Sleeps / Apr. 23, 1957-Apr. 3, 1958 / Bluebird ✦✦✦✦
This CD reissue mostly comprises a 1957 set featuring the virtuosic pianist Phineas Newborn backed by a string orchestra led by Dennis Farnon. Although not as vital as his usual trio dates and Farnon's string arrangements are not too inspiring, the music is pleasing and finds Newborn in his early prime. Particularly noteworthy are his versions of Eddie Miller's "Lazy Mood," "While My Lady Sleeps" and "Bali Hai." Also on this set are three quartet numbers and an unaccompanied rendition of "What's New" from the RCA album *Fabulous Phineas*. —*Scott Yanow*

Phineas Newborn Plays Jamaica / Sep. 7, 1957-Sep. 9, 1957 / RCA ✦✦✦

Piano Portraits / Jun. 17, 1959 / Roulette ✦✦✦✦

I Love a Piano / Oct. 26, 1959-Oct. 29, 1959 / Roulette ✦✦✦✦✦

☆ **The World of Piano** / Oct. 16, 1961-Nov. 21, 1961 / Original Jazz Classics ✦✦✦✦✦
Phineas Newborn's Contemporary debut (he would record six albums over a 15-year period for that label) was made just before physical problems began to interrupt his career. This CD reissue has two trio sessions and finds Newborn joined by either bassist Paul Chambers and drummer Philly Joe Jones or bassist Sam Jones and drummer Louis Hayes. Actually, the accompaniment is not that significant, for the virtuosic Newborn is essentially the whole show anyway. He performs five jazz standards and three obscurities by jazz composers on this superb recital; highlights include "Cheryl," "Manteca," "Daahoud" and "Oleo." —*Scot Yanow*

★ **The Great Jazz Piano of Phineas Newborn Jr.** / Nov. 21, 1961-Sep. 12, 1962 / Original Jazz Classics ✦✦✦✦✦
This recording lives up to its title. Phineas Newborn at his prime had phenomenal technique (on the level of an Oscar Peterson), a creative imagination and plenty of energy. These trio sessions (with Leroy Vinnegar or Sam Jones on bass and either Milt Turner or Louis Hayes on drums) feature Newborn displaying plenty of heat and fresh ideas on compositions by Bud Powell, Bobby Timmons, Benny Golson, Duke Ellington, Thelonious Monk, Sonny Rollins and Miles Davis and two of his own. This is piano jazz at its highest level. —*Scott Yanow*

Newborn Touch / Apr. 1, 1964 / Original Jazz Classics ✦✦✦✦
This CD reissue adds an alternate take and an unissued selection to the original program. Pianist Phineas Newborn's only recording of the 1963-68 period, the trio outing with bassist Leroy Vinnegar and drummer Frank Butler, finds Newborn's virtuosic style unchanged from the late '50s. As is usual on his Contemporary recordings, the pianist explores superior jazz compositions, in this case interpreting a song apiece by Benny Carter, Russ Freeman, Hampton Hawes, Art Pepper, Ornette Coleman ("The Blessing"), Carl Perkins, Frank Rosolino, Leroy Vinnegar, Jimmy Woods and Barney Kessel. Newborn's remarkable control of the piano was still unimpaired, and he is heard giving Oscar Peterson a run for his money. —*Scott Yanow*

Harlem Blues / Feb. 12, 1969-Feb. 13, 1969 / Original Jazz Classics ✦✦✦✦
The superb trio (pianist Phineas Newborn, bassist Ray Brown and drummer Elvin Jones) had never played together before but it didn't matter. They had little trouble

finding common ground. The virtuosic pianist (still in peak form) leads the way on such pieces as his "Harlem Blues," "Ray's Idea" (composed decades earlier by Brown) and Horace Silver's "Cookin' at the Continental." —*Scott Yanow*

Please Send Me Someone to Love / Feb. 12, 1969-Feb. 13, 1969 / Original Jazz Classics ◆◆◆◆

On two days in 1969, pianist Phineas Newborn recorded enough material for two albums (the other is titled *Harlem Blues*), which is fortunate because these were his only recordings of the 1965-73 period. Unfortunately, neither set has been reissued on CD yet. Newborn, who is joined by bassist Ray Brown and drummer Elvin Jones, performs a blues and bop set which includes such tunes as "Rough Ridin'," "He's a Real Gone Guy," "Little Niles" and his own "Brentwood Blues." The emphasis generally is on vintage tunes, and Newborn shows throughout that he was still very much in his musical prime. —*Scott Yanow*

Solo Piano / 1974 / Atlantic ◆◆◆◆

Back Home / Sep. 17, 1976-Sep. 18, 1976 / Contemporary ◆◆◆◆

On one of Phineas Newborn's final recordings (although he would live until 1989), the brilliant but ill pianist is reunited with the rhythm team that he had recorded with in 1969: bassist Ray Brown and drummer Elvin Jones. Actually, despite his health problems, Newborn was always superlative on records, and his playing on five straightahead standards (including "No Moon at All" and "Love for Sale") and three of his originals is excellent, making one wish that this late effort would be reissued on CD. —*Scott Yanow*

Look Out: Phineas Is Back / Dec. 7, 1976-Dec. 8, 1976 / Original Jazz Classics ◆◆◆◆◆

Phineas Newborn was one of the great jazz pianists, possessing phenomenal technique and mastery of the bebop vocabulary, but various illnesses plagued him throughout the 1960s and '70s. On what would be one of his final sessions, Newborn is in surprisingly strong form playing in a trio with bassist Ray Brown and drummer Jimmie Smith. Highlights include "Abbers Song" (a rapid runthrough on "I've Got Rhythm" chord changes), "A Night in Tunisia," a previously unreleased version of "Just in Time" that appeared for the first time on this CD reissue and a creative version of Stevie Wonder's "You Are the Sunshine of My Life." —*Scott Yanow*

Tivoli Encounter / Jul. 16, 1979 / Storyville ◆◆◆

David "Fathead" Newman

b. Feb. 24, 1933, Dallas, TX

Flute, Tenor Saxophone, Alto Saxophone / Soul-Jazz, Hard Bop, Groove

As a teenager, David Newman played professionally around Dallas and Fort Worth with Charlie Parker's mentor, Buster Smith, and also with Ornette Coleman in a band led by tenor saxophonist Red Connors. In the early '50s, Newman worked locally with such R&B musicians as Lowell Fulson and T-Bone Walker. In 1952, Newman formed his longest-lasting and most important musical association with Ray Charles, who had played piano in Fulson's group. Newman stayed with Charles' band from 1954-64, while concurrently recording as a leader and a sideman with, among others, his hometown associate, tenor saxophonist James Clay. Upon leaving Charles, Newman stayed in Dallas for two years. He then moved to New York, where he recorded under King Curtis and Eddie Harris; he also played many commercial and soul dates. Newman returned to Charles for a brief time in 1970-71; from 1972-74 he played with Red Garland and Herbie Mann. Newman parlayed the renown he gained from his experience with Charles into a fairly successful recording career. In the '60s and '70s, he recorded a series of heavily orchestrated, pop-oriented sides for Atlantic, and in the '80s he led the occasional hard-bop session, but Newman's metier was as an ace accompanist. Throughout his career he recorded with a variety of non-jazz artists; Newman's brawny, arrogant tenor sound graced the albums of Aretha Franklin, Dr. John, and many others. It is, in fact, Newman's terse, earthy improvisations with Ray Charles that remain his most characteristic work. —*Chris Kelsey*

★ **House of David Newman: David "Fathead" Anthology** / 1952-1989 / Rhino ◆◆◆◆◆

There have not been many saxophonists and flutists more naturally soulful than David "Fathead" Newman. This two-disc set captures Newman at his best. He never really was an album artist; each LP has had its nuggets, and that's what this captures. It has Newman wailing the blues, then stretching out in the Ray Charles band. He covers a Beatles tune, then an Aaron Neville number. He backs Aretha Franklin and pays homage to the great Buster Cooper. This is one anthology that can be recommended without hesitation. —*Ron Wynn*

Fathead: Ray Charles Presents David Newman / Nov. 5, 1958 / Atlantic ◆◆◆◆◆

The talented David Newman, who alternates on this album between tenor and alto, made his debut as a leader at this session. Since he was in Ray Charles' band at the time, Newman was able to use Charles on piano along with Hank Crawford

(here called Bennie Crawford) on baritone, trumpeter Marcus Belgrave, bassist Edgar Willis and drummer Milton Turner. The music is essentially soulful bebop with the highlights including "Hard Times," "Fathead," "Mean to Me" and "Tin Tin Deo." Everyone plays well and this was a fine start to David "Fathead" Newman's career. —*Scott Yanow*

It's Mister Fathead / Nov. 5, 1958-Mar. 4, 1964 / 32 Jazz ◆◆◆

Straight Ahead / Dec. 21, 1960 / Atlantic ◆◆◆◆

Bigger & Better (The Many Facets of David Newman) / Mar. 5, 1968-Mar. 7, 1968 / Atlantic ◆◆◆

In the late '60s, Newman's resolutely soulful, bluesy and funky tenor sax was transplanted from swinging, gritty combo dates and relocated on a pair of sessions with crossover (some might say sellout) written all over them. Newman performed many pop, soul, and rock covers, backed by strings or large ensembles and often both. His playing was no less stalwart, gritty, and expressive on either tenor or flute, but his arrangements were usually sedate orchestrations or subdued big band charts. Atlantic never emasculated Newman; they just handicapped him a bit, and his playing makes most of this album acceptable listening. —*Ron Wynn*

Captain Buckles / Nov. 3, 1970-Nov. 5, 1970 / Atlantic ◆◆◆◆

An improvement over David Newman's preceding projects, this soulful but relatively straightahead effort teams him with trumpeter Blue Mitchell, guitarist Eric Gale, bassist Steve Novosel and drummer Bernard Purdie in a pianoless quintet. Switching between tenor, alto and flute, Newman performs four originals, a song by Mitchell, Geroge Harrison's "Something," and the standard "I Didn't Know What Time It Was." However, this LP has become a bit scarce. —*Scott Yanow*

Lonely Avenue / Nov. 2, 1971-Nov. 4, 1971 / Atlantic ◆◆◆

An OK but not too essential LP, this effort by David Newman (heard on tenor and flute) leans more to the R&B side, featuring Newman with an oversized rhythm section that includes vibraphonist Roy Ayers (who also plays keyboards), Bags Costello on organ and piano, and guitarist Cornell Dupree. The tunes, mostly recent originals (also the traditional "Precious Lord") are interpreted soulfully by Newman, but little memorable occurs. —*Scott Yanow*

Back to Basics / May 1977-Nov. 1977 / Milestone ◆◆◆◆

A '91 CD reissue of a late '70s session by tenor saxophonist and flutist David Newman, which emphasized his patented soul-jazz and blues while matching Newman with different players on various tracks, rather than having a fixed rhythm section. The top guest stars included keyboardists Hilton Ruiz and George Cables and guitarist Lee Ritenour. —*Ron Wynn*

Concrete Jungle / Nov. 1977 / Prestige ◆◆

A versatile performer, David "Fathead" Newman has appeared through the years in both straightahead and commercial settings. This LP (whose contents have been partly reissued on Newman's *Back to Basics* CD) is definitely in the latter category. Newman, who splits his time here almost equally between alto, soprano, tenor and flute, is accompanied by an electronic rhythm section including keyboardist Pat Rebillot and guitarist Jay Graydon and a string orchestra arranged by William Fischer. The songs range from tunes written by McCoy Tyner and Buddy Johnson ("Save Your Love for Me") to Stevie Wonder, Bob Marley and Marvin Gaye. The net result unfortunately can be summed up as "a whole lot of nothing." The music was instantly dated, overproduced, and not up to Newman's usual level. —*Scott Yanow*

Resurgence / Sep. 23, 1980 / Muse ◆◆◆◆

David "Fathead" Newman's first freewheeling recording in a number of years showed that he was certainly capable of playing creative soul-jazz and bop when inspired. Newman is joined by the underrated trumpeter Marcus Belgrave, guitarist Ted Dunbar, pianist Cedar Walton, bassist Buster Williams and drummer Louis Hayes. The best are "Everything Must Change," Hank Crawford's "Carnegie Blues" and Walton's "To the Holy Land." An excellent effort. —*Scott Yanow*

Still Hard Times / Apr. 1982 / Muse ◆◆◆◆◆

Saxophonist in his prime. Tuneful and exuberant. —*Michael G. Nastos*

Heads Up / Sep. 16, 1986-Sept. 18, 1986 / Atlantic ◆◆◆

For this superior showcase, tenorman David Newman (who also plays some alto and flute) jams on four jazz standards and his own "Heads Up" and "For Buster" while joined by a top-notch rhythm section consisting of vibraphonist Steve Nelson, pianist Kirk Lightsey, bassist David Williams and drummer Eddie Gladden. Although often placed in more tightly arranged settings throughout his career, Newman really excels in a small-group format, where his soulful tones and expertise at jamming over common chord changes are best displayed. This was one of his better sets, even though the album is not very well known. —*Scott Yanow*

Fire! Live at the Village Vanguard / Dec. 22, 1988-Dec. 23, 1988 / Atlantic ◆◆◆◆

For this excellent all-around date, David Newman and a fine rhythm section (pianist Kirk Lightsey, vibraphonist Steve Nelson, bassist David Williams and drummer Marvin "Smitty" Smith) are joined by tenor saxophonist Stanley Turrentine on "Wide Open Spaces" (a tune that years earlier Newman had recorded with fellow tenor James Clay), altoist Hank Crawford on "Lonely Avenue" and both Mr. T. and Crawford on two other songs. In addition, Newman takes "Filthy McNasty" as a flute feature and is showcased on the opening "Old Devil Moon." An enjoyable set of soulful, straightahead jazz. —*Scott Yanow*

Blue Head / Sep. 3, 1989 / Candid ✦✦✦✦✦
The distinctive tenors David Newman and Clifford Jordan make for a potent team on this live jam session set which finds Jordan sitting in with Newman's quartet (which includes guitarist Ted Dunbar, pianist Buddy Montgomery, bassist Todd Coolman and drummer Marvin "Smitty" Smith). The six performances each clock in between 11 and 15 minutes with plenty of stretching out for the two veteran saxophonists, guitarist Dunbar and pianist Montgomery. "Fathead" mostly alternates between tenor and alto while Jordan switches to his rarely heard soprano on "Blues for David." The good-natured tenor tradeoffs on "Strike Up the Band" are in the tradition of Sonny Stitt and Gene Ammons, Newman's "Blue Head" is strongly reminiscent of "Goodbye Pork Pie Hat" and his alto playing on a medium-tempo "Willow Weep for Me" takes solo honors. Of the other cuts, "What's New" is a tasteful feature for Dunbar's guitar and Jordan's "Eyewitness Blues" wraps up the fine performance with a 32-bar romp. Easily recommended to straightahead jazz fans. —*Scott Yanow*

Return to the Wide Open Spaces / 1990 / Amazing ✦✦✦✦✦
For this live concert recorded at the Caravan of Dreams in Fort Worth, a mostly all-star group of Texas jazzmen (plus pianist Ellis Marsalis from New Orleans) was gathered together. The music, which includes four blues and three standards among its nine selections, lacks any real surprises. Most of the numbers have solos by "Fathead" Newman on alto, James Clay's tenor, veteran baritonist Leroy Cooper, the lesser-known trumpeter Dennis Dotson and guitarist Cornell Dupree or Marsalis. In addition, the pianist gets a pair of solo features, and Newman is also heard on tenor and flute. Strangely enough, "Fathead" never gets around to dueling with Clay. Some better planning and the utilization of a few charts (rather than the funcitonal frameworks) would have elevated the pleasing date to a much higher level. —*Scott Yanow*

Mr. Gentle Mr. Cool / 1994 / Kokopelli ✦✦✦✦✦
David "Fathead" Newman is in excellent form on this tasteful program of 11 Duke Ellington compositions. Performing in a sextet with trombonist Jim Pugh, pianist David Leonhardt, bassist Peter Washington, Ron Carter on piccolo bass and drummer Lewis Nash, Newman splits his time between tenor and alto and takes a flute solo on "Azure." The music contains few real surprises (other than the utilization of both bass and piccolo bass) but swings nicely and has fine melodic solos. —*Scott Yanow*

Under a Woodstock Moon / Jun. 15, 1996-Jun. 17, 1996 / Kokopelli ✦✦✦✦
Veteran David Newman is heard in fine form on his excellent CD, switching between tenor, alto and flute. He is joined by a supportive rhythm section (which includes vibraphonist Brian Carrott and pianist David Leonhardt) and occasionally four strings for a cheerful set of ballads and originals. The project is listed as "a personal tribute to the rhythms of Mother Nature," and all of the song titles (other than the original calypso "Amandla") have something to do with either the seasons or the sky, but fortunately, the date is far from being a reverent set of new age music. In fact, despite the mostly relaxed tempos, it is one of David Newman's stronger straightahead efforts and is easily recommended, particularly for Newman's appealing tenor playing. Highlights include "Up Jumped Spring," "Spring Can Really Hang You up the Most," "A Nightingale Sang in Berkeley Square," and the title cut. —*Scott Yanow*

Joe Newman

b. Sep. 7, 1922, New Orleans, LA, d. Jul. 4, 1992, New York, NY
Trumpet / Swing

Joe Newman, one of the very few musicians (other than Freddie Green) to play for long periods with Count Basie's orchestras of both the 1940s and '50s, had an unclassifiable trumpet style. Influenced early on by Louis Armstrong and more prominently by Harry "Sweets" Edison, Newman was a mainstream player who was versatile enough to hold his own with Count Basie's younger (and generally boppish) sidemen. Born to a musical family in New Orleans, Newman not only played with the college band at Alabama State College, but took over its leadership. He gained important early experience playing with Lionel Hampton's big band (1941-43) before joining Basie (1943-47). He was a featured sideman with Illinois Jacquet's popular group and also worked with J.C. Heard. Newman's second period with Basie (1952-61) gave him his greatest fame, as he shared solo space with Thad Jones. The trumpeter also recorded extensively during this era as a leader for Vanguard, Storyville, Jazztone, Savoy, Coral, Roulette, Swingville and

Mercury; his four near-classic RCA sessions have been reissued as a two-CD set. After leaving Basie, Newman toured the Soviet Union with Benny Goodman (1962), freelanced around New York, and became involved in Jazz Interactions (a nonprofit organization that educated youth about jazz), serving as its president starting in 1967. In later years, Joe Newman fared well at the 1972 Newport in New York jam sessions, guested with the New York Jazz Repertory Company, toured with Benny Carter, and led sessions for Black & Blue and Concord. —*Scott Yanow*

★ **The Complete Joe Newman** / Feb. 8, 1955-1956 / RCA ✦✦✦✦✦
Trumpeter Joe Newman, best-known for his playing with Count Basie's Orchestra, led four albums for RCA during 1955-56. This generous two-CD set reissues all the music from these dates and has plenty of swinging performances. The first disc puts the focus on Newman and tenor saxophonist Al Cohn in a pair of octets with arrangements by Ernie Wilkins, Manny Albam and Cohn. The second disc starts out with a tribute to Louis Armstrong, a dozen of Satch's songs modernized for a big band; Newman takes a few rare vocals. The final session matches Newman with flutist Frank Wess in a two-guitar septet arranged by Wilkins. While most of the other two-fers in this French RCA Jazz Tribune series are reissues of earlier two-LP sets, this one was newly compiled and has 48 splendid examples of Basie-ish swing. Highly recommended. —*Scott Yanow*

I Feel Like a Newman / Apr. 1956 / Black Lion ✦✦✦✦
Trumpeter Joe Newman, some Basie men, and a few other sympathetic sidemen play an enjoyable set of 1950s swing on this CD reissue. Six of the ten numbers team Newman with trombonist Billy Byers, altoist Gene Quill, tenorman Frank Foster, pianist John Lewis (a perfect fill-in for Count Basie), guitarist Freddie Green, bassist Milt Hinton and drummer Osie Johnson, while the other selections have Newman playing in a quintet with Frank Wess (who doubles on tenor and flute) and pianist Sir Charles Thompson. Whether it be a veteran standard or a newer song by Ernie Wilkins or Manny Albam, the music always swings and the talented musicians are in fine form. —*Scott Yanow*

Locking Horns / Apr. 10, 1957 / Roulette ✦✦✦✦

Featuring Shirley Scott / Jan. 13, 1958-Jan. 17, 1958 / MCA ✦✦✦✦
This decent LP reissue from MCA's Jazz Heritage series only includes ten of the 11 selections on the original LP, inexcusably leaving out "There's a Small Hotel." The initial release was called *Soft Swingin' Jazz*, and the description generally fits, since trumpeter Joe Newman uses a mute most of the time. He also sings three numbers and is backed by the easy-listening organ of Shirley Scott, bassist Eddie Jones and drummer Charlie Persip. With the exception of "The Farmer's Daughter" and the organist's "Scotty," most of the material dates from the swing era. The interpretations are melodic and cheerful. —*Scott Yanow*

Jive at Five / May 4, 1960 / Original Jazz Classics ✦✦✦
Originally put out on the Swingville label, this CD reissue is very much in the Count Basie vein. That fact is not too surprising when one considers that the quintet includes three members of Basie's men: trumpeter Joe Newman, tenor saxophonist Frank Wess and bassist Eddie Jones. Joined by the complementary pianist Tommy Flanagan and drummer Oliver Jackson, Newman and his friends swing their way through four vintage standards and a couple of the leader's original blues in typical fashion. —*Scott Yanow*

Good N' Groovy / Mar. 17, 1961 / Original Jazz Classics ✦✦✦✦
This was the second of Joe Newman's three dates he led under the Swingville banner. For this session he was in the very fine company of Frank Foster (tenor sax), Tommy Flanagan (piano), Eddie Jones (bass) and Bill English (drums). —*Bob Rusch, Cadence*

Joe Newman at Count Basie's / 1962 / Mercury ✦✦✦✦
Last available as a Trip LP in the 1970s but well worth reissuing on CD someday, this live session teams trumpeter Joe Newman in a quintet with the underrated tenor Oliver Nelson (who has an immediately recognizable sound), pianist Lloyd Mayers, bassist Art Davis and drummer Ed Shaughnessy. They perform various standards (the one listed as "Someone to Love" is actually "Please Send Me Someone to Love"), Newman's tune from the Count Basie book ("The Midgets"), and "Wednesday Blues." Nothing unexpected occurs, but the combination of Newman's swing-based trumpet and Nelson's forward-looking tenor work quite well. —*Scott Yanow*

In a Mellow Mood / 1962 / Stash ✦✦✦
The performances on this LP (featuring trumpeter Joe Newman, pianist Ross Tompkins, bassist Russell George and drummer Roy Lundberg), although recorded in 1962, were not released initially until 20 years later. As the title suggests, the emphasis is on slower, relaxed tempos. Newman sounds fine, but few sparks occur on tunes such as "The Lady's in Love with You," "You Are My Sunshine" and two Billy Taylor songs. Fine music, but not too essential; get Newman's earlier RCA recordings instead. —*Scott Yanow*

I Love My Baby / Jul. 20, 1978 / Black & Blue ◆◆◆◆

Also made available on the Italian budget label I Ganti Del Jazz, this little-known effort finds veteran trumpeter Joe Newman (55 at the time) stretching out quite effectively on four standards and two originals. In what was his first opportunity to lead a recording session since 1962, Newman and his top-notch rhythm section (pianist Hank Jones, bassist George Duvivier and drummer Alan Dawson) swing their way through such songs as "Softly As in a Morning Sunrise," "Paper Moon" and "Fiddy's Moods." —Scott Yanow

Hangin' Out / May 1984 / Concord Jazz ◆◆◆◆

The paths of trumpeters Joe Newman and Joe Wilder crossed occasionally through the years. They were both born in 1922, both had stints with Count Basie's Orchestra (although Newman was there much longer), and both had a countless number of sideman appearances on records (although neither led an excess of recording dates). They came together to co-lead this set, a quintet outing with pianist Hank Jones, bassist Rufus Reid and drummer Marvin "Smitty" Smith. As expected, the results are swinging, lyrical, melodic and well-balanced. Highlights include Newman's "The Midgets," "Secret Love" and the trumpeters' interpretation of "Battle Hymn of the Republic." —Scott Yanow

Frankie Newton (William Frank Newton)

b. Jan. 4, 1906, Emory, VA, d. Mar. 11, 1954, New York, NY
Trumpet / Swing

Trumpeter Frankie Newton, whose mellow and thoughtful style sometimes seemed somewhat out-of-place in the swing era, had a relatively brief but artistically rewarding career. He had stints with Lloyd Scott (1927-29), Cecil Scott (1929-30), Chick Webb, Elmer Snowden, Charlie Johnson and Sam Wooding and appeared on Bessie Smith's final recording session in 1933. Newton worked with Charlie Barnet's short-lived integrated band in 1936 and Teddy Hill before briefly becoming closely associated with bassist John Kirby and his associates. The eventual John Kirby Sextet would have been the logical place for the trumpeter but a falling out in 1937 ended up with the younger Charlie Shavers getting the spot in the commercially successful group. Newton instead played for Mezz Mezzrow and Lucky Millinder, led a few record dates (including participating in a set for Hugues Panassie) and worked at Cafe Society, accompanying Billie Holiday on several of her records (most notably "Strange Fruit"). As the 1940s progressed, Newton became less interested in music and gradually faded from the scene, painting more than playing, dying a forgotten and underutilized talent. —Scott Yanow

At the Onyx Club / May 5, 1937-Apr. 12, 1939 / Tax ◆◆◆◆

The lyrical trumpeter Frankie Newton offered a contrast to the blazing solos of Roy Eldridge. Newton could play high notes but much of the time he was more interested in expressing himself gently and with intelligent subtlety. This LP contains eight selections from recording sessions led by Newton (these have since been reissued on a Classics CD) and some of his backup work with singers Maxine Sullivan and Midge Williams when he was associated with John Kirby's early group. There are a few inferior vocals on Newton's own recordings but also such fine performances as "Who's Sorry Now," "Frankie's Jump" and "Jam Fever"; altoists Pete Brown and Tab Smith (on different dates) are the most memorable of Newton's sidemen. Other high points of these swing dates include Maxine Sullivan's "Loch Lomond" (a major hit) and Midge Williams' version of "The Lady Is a Tramp." —Scott Yanow

James Newton

b. May 1, 1953, Los Angeles, CA
Flute / Avant-Garde, Third Stream, Post-Bop

Newton is a thoroughly contemporary artist, making elegant, sometimes eccentric, always high-minded albums that reflect a wide variety of jazz and classical influences without giving a fig about what happens to be popular at a given time. Besides producing a lovely tone quality, his flute work is highly resourceful, making use of flutter-tonguing, birdlike effects and simultaneous vocal/flute lines, trying to push the envelope of his instrument. As a composer, Newton finds wellsprings of inspiration in John Coltrane, Charles Mingus and Duke Ellington—the latter whose music he transformed completely on the adventurous *The African Flower* album—and he writes charts for all kinds of combinations of instruments.

Newton's first musical experiences were on the electric bass as part of a Motown cover band in San Pedro, which he quit to form a Jimi Hendrix-style trio. However, he also picked up alto and tenor saxophones while in high school, not discovering the flute until he was 16. Heavily influenced by Eric Dolphy (to whom he has been compared) and Roland Kirk, Newton began to lean toward the avantgarde in jazz while studying classical music at Cal State Los Angeles. Soon after moving to Pomona, he joined a local band, Black Music Infinity, that was led by then-free-jazz drummer Stanley Crouch, with Arthur Blythe and David Murray as co-conspirators. Feeling the competitive heat on saxes, Newton decided to concen-

trate totally on the flute at age 22. A year after graduation (1978), he made a move to New York with Murray, where he hooked up with Anthony Davis on three LPs, played in Cecil Taylor's big band, and started recording as a leader on several small and large labels. He moved back to San Pedro in 1982 and started teaching jazz history, composition and jazz ensemble at the California Institute of the Arts in Valencia. Over the years, Newton has also written several classical commissions for various-sized ensembles, and in 1990, he published a book, *Improvising Flute*. Alas, not enough of his recordings are currently available to give one a decent idea of his wide-ranging tastes. —Richard S. Ginell

Solomon's Sons / Jan. 16, 1977 / Circle ◆◆◆

From Inside / Jul. 27, 1978-Jul. 29, 1978 / BV Haast ◆◆◆◆

Crystal Texts / Nov. 27, 1978 / Moers ◆◆◆

Paseo Del Mar / 1978 / India Navigation ◆◆◆◆

James Newton's first American date as a leader finds him paying some tribute to Eric Dolphy, Thelonious Monk ("Monk's Notice") and Duke Ellington (on the one non-original, Duke's "Heaven") while also stretching jazz forward. Matched up with pianist Anthony Davis, cellist Abdul Wadud (who often functions in the role of a bass) and drummer Phillip Wilson, Newton is at his most adventurous on lengthy renditions of "Lake" and "San Pedro Sketches." It was obvious at the time that James Newton would be an important force in jazz for many years to come. —Scott Yanow

Mystery School / 1979 / India Navigation ◆◆◆◆◆

James Newton explores many moods and tone colors with this unusual album. The instrumentation (flutist Newton, clarinetist John Carter, bassoonist John Nunez, Charles Owens on oboe and English horn and the veteran Red Callender on tuba) by itself would give Newton's originals a sound of its own but the complex arrangements (which give more than adequate space for improvisations) display the influences of both modern classical music and jazz. —Scott Yanow

Axum / Aug. 1981 / ECM ◆◆◆

James Newton's set of unaccompanied flute solos is generally more intriguing and diverse than one might expect. An expert at multiphonics (often humming through his flute in order to get more than one note at a time), Newton is also very strong at constructing logical yet utterly unpredictable improvisations. His playing on nine of his originals covers a fair amount of ground, and he alternates between three different types of flutes (his regular horn, alto flute and bass flute). Still, the results are more for specialized tastes. —Scott Yanow

James Newton / Oct. 1982 / Gramavision ◆◆◆◆◆

Flutist James Newton teams up with six distinctive players on this continually interesting set: violinist John Blake, trombonist Slide Hampton, vibraphonist Jay Hoggard, pianist Anthony Davis, bassist Cecil McBee and drummer Billy Hart. The five selections include Billy Strayhorn's beautiful "Daydream," Davis' "Persephone" (a 17-bar piece), and three of the flutist's originals. The variety in the music ranges from an atonal "The Crips" to "Budapest," which recalls Charles Mingus, and the high quality of the players makes this thoughtful presentation a recommended set. —Scott Yanow

Portraits / 1982 / India Navigation ◆◆◆◆◆

Luella / 1983 / Gramavision ◆◆◆◆◆

Most recordings by flutist James Newton are quite spontaneous in their improvising, but well-planned as a whole. This outing features Newton with three string players (violinists John Blake and Gayle Dixon and cellist Abdul Wadud) and a four-piece rhythm section (vibraphonist Jay Hoggard, pianist Kenny Kirkland, bassist Cecil McBee and drummer Billy Hart). Each of the five numbers has its purpose, including "Mr. Dolphy" (a tribute to Eric Dolphy), Wayne Shorter's moody "Anna Maria," and a three-part suite about South Africa ("Diamonds Are for Freedom"). Well worth several listens. —Scott Yanow

Echo Canyon / Sep. 5, 1984-Sep. 7, 1984 / Celestial Harmonies ◆◆◆

Excellent playing of Newton's compositions for solo flute. —Ron Wynn

Water Mystery / Jan. 1985 / Gramavision ◆◆◆◆◆

The five musicians of James Newton's wind ensemble featured on *The Mystery School* in 1982 (flutist Newton, bassoonist John Nunez, Charles Owens on English horn and soprano, clarinetist John Carter and Red Callender on tuba) are joined by oboist Greg Martin, bassist Roberto Miranda, percussionist Anthony Brown, April Aoki on harp and Allan Iwohara on koto for a rather colorful set. There are two tributes to Billy Strayhorn (including a version of "Star Crossed Lovers"), one for George Russell, a remake of "The Crips" and a pair of features for the koto. A very interesting program of adventurous yet quite logical explorations. —Scott Yanow

★ **The African Flower** / Jun. 24, 1985-Jun. 25, 1985 / Blue Note ◆◆◆◆◆

This wonderful set finds flutist James Newton creating fresh interpretations of seven songs written by Duke Ellington and/or Billy Strayhorn. His ensembles include violinist John Blake, altoist Arthur Blythe, cornetist Olu Dara, vibraphonist

Jay Hoggard, pianist Roland Hanna (who has long had the ability to emulate Ellington's chord voicings and touch), bassist Rick Rozie, percussionist Anthony Brown and either Pheeroan akLaff or Billy Hart on drums. In addition, Milt Grayson (who has sung with Ellington) takes a guest vocal on "Strange Feeling." Whether romping through "Cottontail," reviving "Virgin Jungle" (heard in an 11-minute version) or taking an unaccompanied flute flight on "Sophisticated Lady," James Newton's tribute set is quite memorable and a real gem. —*Scott Yanow*

Romance and Revolution / Aug. 20, 1986-Aug. 21, 1986 / Blue Note ✦✦✦✦✦
The great flutist James Newton pays tribute to Charles Mingus and (more indirectly) Eric Dolphy on his "Forever Charles" and a rare remake of Mingus' "Meditations On Integration." Newton interacts with both Steve Turre and Robin Eubanks on trombones, along with pianist Geri Allen, bassist Rick Rozie and drummer Pheeroan akLaff, bringing back the spirit of Mingus. In addition, there is a rendition of Ornette Coleman's "Peace" played with cellist Abdul Wadud, Rozie and akLaff, and a lengthy original ("The Evening Leans Toward You") that covers a wide range of moods. A stimulating set. —*Scott Yanow*

Albert Nicholas

b. May 27, 1900, New Orleans, LA, d. Sep. 3, 1973, Basle, Switzerland
Clarinet / New Orleans Jazz
A superb clarinetist with an attractive mellow tone, Albert Nicholas had a long and diverse career, and his playing was always consistently rewarding. He studied with Lorenzo Tio, Jr., in New Orleans and played with cornet legends Buddy Petit, King Oliver and Manuel Perez while in his teens. After three years in the Merchant Marine he joined King Oliver in Chicago for much of 1925-27, recording with Oliver's Dixie Syncopators. He spent a year in the Far East and Egypt, arriving in New York in 1928 to join Luis Russell for five years. Nicholas, who had recorded in several settings in the 1920s, sounded perfectly at home with Russell, taking his solos alongside Red Allen, J.C. Higginbotham and Charlie Holmes. He would later rejoin Russell when the pianist had the backup orchestra for Louis Armstrong a few years later and Nicholas also worked with Jelly Roll Morton in 1939 (he had recorded with Morton previously in 1929). Things slowed down for a time in the early '40s but the New Orelans revival got him working again in the mid-'40s with Art Hodes, Bunk Johnson and Kid Ory; by 1948 the clarinetist was playing regularly with Ralph Sutton's trio at Jimmy Ryan's. In 1953 Nicholas followed Sidney Bechet's example and moved to France where, other than returning to the US for recording sessions in 1959 and 1960, he happily remained for his final 20 years. —*Scott Yanow*

With the All Star Stompers, This Is Jazz, Vol. 2 / Mar. 1947-Aug. 1947 / Storyville ✦✦✦
This release features clarinetist Albert Nicholas on performances taken from Rudi Blesh's famed "This Is Jazz" radio series of 1947. Nicholas was not technically the leader on the 13 numbers, although he is the only horn player on "Me Pas Lemme Ca," "Albert's Blues" and "South Side Shake." The other selections also feature cornetist Wild Bill Davison and trombonist George Brunis with the rhythm sections including either Charles Queener, Dan Burley, Joe Sullivan, James P. Johnson or Joe Sullivan on piano, rhythm guitarist Danny Barker, bassist Pops Foster and either Baby Dodds or Freddy Moore on drums. The music essentially comprises Dixieland standards, and the playing is fine (Wild Bill is consistently exciting), but all of the performances will eventually be reissued in more complete form in Jazzology's "This Is Jazz" CD series. —*Scott Yanow*

Albert Nicholas-Mezz Mezzrow / Oct. 30, 1951+Nov. 28, 1953 / Jazztone ✦✦✦✦
This out-of-print LP from the 1950s has separate sessions led in Paris by expatriate clarinetists (both of whom are heard in two-clarinet septets). Albert Nicholas, a superior New Orleans stylist, performs five numbers with Andre Reweliotty's Orchestra, and these are highlighted by a surprisingly exciting version of "Moonglow," "Sensation" and "Confessin." The erratic clarinetist Mezz Mezzrow is heard sitting in with Claude Luter's band, and the results in their ensemble-oriented set include a jubilant rendition of "Jingle Bells," "Blues As We Like 'Em" and "Christopher's Rockin'" (which is really "Christopher Columbus"); trumpeter Guy Longnon and clarinetist Luter are major assets. The song listing in the liner notes is partly incorrect, but the one on the album itself is accurate. Dixieland fans should pick this album up if they are lucky enough to run across it, for the music is quite enjoyable and full of spirit. —*Scott Yanow*

★ **New Orleans-Chicago Connection** / Jul. 19, 1959+Jul. 27, 1959 / Delmark ✦✦✦✦✦
Like Sidney Bechet, clarinetist Albert Nicholas moved permanently to France later in his career. Although he was there 20 years (from 1953 until his death in 1973), Nicholas never received Bechet's fame, but he seemed to prosper overseas, no longer having to be concerned with Americans' lack of interest in traditional jazz. This particular album, one of two cut by Nicholas during a rare 1959 visit to the States, teams the melodic clarinetist with the great pianist Art Hodes, bassist Earl

Murphy and drummer Freddy Kohlman. They jam through a set of standards and blues, and the results are enjoyable. The 1997 CD reissue not only has the original 11 selections, but nine alternate takes and a previously unissued "Careless Love" from the same sessions. Highly recommended. —*Scott Yanow*

All-Star Stompers / Jul. 30, 1959-Jul. 31, 1959 / Delmark ✦✦✦✦
From 1956 on, clarinetist Albert Nicholas made his home in Europe. He only recorded in the US again during a 1959 visit, which resulted in a pair of Delmark releases. This particular set matches Nicholas with pianist Art Hodes' band, which at the time included trumpeter Nappy Trottier, trombonist Floyd O'Brien and the then-unknown guitarist Marty Grosz. The music (seven Dixieland standards, "You Gotta See Your Mama Every Night," and "How Long Blues") is predictable but excellent, with some spirited moments and joyous ensembles. Nicholas is in typically prime form throughout. —*Scott Yanow*

With Alan Elsdon's Band, Vol. 1 / Feb. 1, 1967 / Jazzology ✦✦✦✦
Clarinetist Albert Nicholas (who was 66 at the time) was still in prime form when he performed at a British concert from 1967 that was released for the first time on this 1995 CD. Nicholas is featured with an English Dixieland septet led by trumpeter Alan Elsdon and (best of all) on a few quartet numbers including "Rose Room," an emotional "Black & Blue" and "Lover Come Back to Me." Nicholas (who could sometimes resemble Barney Bigard) had his own sound but he spent most of his last two decades living in Europe, largely forgotten by Americans. Classic jazz collectors will want to pick up this superior set. —*Scott Yanow*

With Alan Elsdon's Band, Vol. 2 / Feb. 1967 / Jazzology ✦✦✦✦
The second of two CDs taken from an English concert featuring clarinetist Albert Nicholas, this set matches him with trumpeter Alan Elsdon's very able septet. The music comprises essentially Dixieland standards (including a heated "Royal Garden Blues," "China Boy," "I Found a New Baby" and "Rosetta") and features Nicholas in superior late-period form. Spirited performances. —*Scott Yanow*

● **Baden 1969** / 1969 / Sackville ✦✦✦✦✦
Recorded just four years before his death, this CD in 1997 released for the first time a Swiss concert putting the focus on the great (if underrated) clarinetist Albert Nicholas, who is heard throughout in top form. Nicholas plays his usual repertoire of the era, standards from the 1920s and '30s, but is well showcased as the only horn in a quartet also including pianist Henry Chaix, bassist Alain Du Bois and drummer Romano Cavicchiolo. Highlights include "Rosetta," "Please Don't Talk About Me When You're Gone," "Rose Room" and "I Found a New Baby." —*Scott Yanow*

A Tribute to Jelly Roll Morton / Aug. 1970 / Storyville ✦✦✦✦✦
Eight of the 11 selections on this fine LP feature clarinetist Albert Nicholas (who had recorded with Jelly Roll Morton on a couple of occasions) heading a quartet including pianist Bobby Greene, bassist Jens Solund and drummer Knud Ryskov Madsen. Sticking mostly to Jelly Roll tunes, plus three that Morton had recorded ("Someday Sweetheart," "Mamie's Blues" and "Tiger Rag") but not actually composed, Nicholas shows that the passing of time (he was 70) and his many years in Europe had not dulled his enthusiasm and abilities. In addition, Greene performs a solo piano version of "King Porter Stomp"; pianist Art Hodes is featured on "Grandpa's Spells" from a couple months later; and Papa Bue's Viking Jazz Band romps through "Doctor Jazz." Recommended to vintage jazz collectors. —*Scott Yanow*

Herbie Nichols

b. Jan. 3, 1919, New York, NY, d. Apr. 12, 1963, New York, NY
Composer, Piano / Post-Bop
Few jazz musicians have had as frustrating a career as Herbie Nichols. A very original composer and pianist, Nichols' music was largely unknown not only during his lifetime but still up to the present day. After serving in the Army during 1941-43, he played with many different groups including those led by Herman Autrey, Hal Singer, Illinois Jacquet and John Kirby (1948-49). Although he recorded his originals in trios for Blue Note and Bethlehem during 1955-57, those records were largely overlooked. Nichols spent most of his career making his living not in bop bands but with Dixieland groups, playing music that was unchallenging but sometimes paid the rent. He was just beginning to gain a following with younger musicians (including Roswell Rudd, Archie Shepp, Steve Swallow and Bill Watrous) when Nichols was fatally stricken with leukemia. Decades later Mosaic released all of his Blue Note recordings (including many previously unissued) in a box set. A chapter in A.B. Spellman's *Four Lives in The Bebop Business* in definitive fashion tells the Herbie Nichols story and there have been recent tribute albums by Misha Mengelberg and Buell Neidlinger (the latter's *Blue Chopsticks* interpreted Nichols' originals with two horns, violin, viola and cello!). But with the exception of "Lady Sings the Blues" (which Billie Holiday had recorded), Herbie Nichols' music is still fairly obscure. —*Scott Yanow*

The Art of Herbie Nichols / May 6, 1955-Apr. 19, 1956 / Blue Note ✦✦✦✦
An anthology collecting some pieces by neglected and overlooked pianist Herbie Nichols. Nichols had one of the truly unique styles in all of jazz piano history and didn't really borrow from or imitate anyone. This single disc doesn't match either an earlier Blue Note two-record set, now deleted, or the outstanding Mosaic set, but it's a fine introduction to Nichols' music. —*Ron Wynn*

☆ **The Complete Blue Note Recordings** / May 6, 1955-Apr. 19, 1956 / Mosaic ✦✦✦✦✦
A reissue of the 48 Herbie Nichols recordings formerly out on the limited edition five-LP Mosaic box set, this three-CD package from 1997 has the pianist/composer's greatest work. Nichols was largely neglected during his lifetime; only in the late '90s did the highly original musician start receiving some of the recognition he deserved. Although his originals were often quite orchestral in nature, Nichols only had the opportunity to record in a trio format; the five sessions on this box (30 songs plus 18 alternate takes) feature either Al McKibbon or Teddy Kotick on bass and Art Blakey or Max Roach on drums. The music (all originals except George Gershwin's "Mine") is virtually unclassifiable, and although largely straightahead, sounds unlike anything produced by Herbie Nichols' contemporaries. Essential music. —*Scott Yanow*

● **The Bethlehem Session** / Nov. 1957 / Affinity ✦✦✦✦✦
Herbie Nichols was one of the tragedies of jazz, a very original pianist and composer who could not find regular employment for his thought-provoking music and ended up playing in anonymous Dixieland bands. He only recorded three complete albums as a leader and his *Bethlehem* date was his last. With perfectly suitable accompaniment from bassist George Duvivier and bassist Danny Richmond, Nichols introduces nine of his originals in addition to performing the standard "Too Close for Comfort." —*Scott Yanow*

Red Nichols (Ernest Loring Nichols)

b. May 8, 1905, Ogden, UT, d. Jun. 28, 1965, Las Vegas, NV
Cornet, Leader / Dixieland, Classic Jazz
Overrated in Europe in the early 1930s when his records (but not those of his black contemporaries) were widely available and then later underrated and often unfairly called a Bix imitator, Red Nichols was actually one of the finest cornetists to emerge from the 1920s. An expert improviser whose emotional depth did not reach as deep as Bix or Louis Armstrong, Nichols was in many ways a hustler, participating in as many recording sessions (often under pseudonyms) as any other horn player of the era, cutting sessions as Red Nichols and his Five Pennies, the Arkansas Travelers, the Red Heads, the Louisiana Rhythm Kings and the Charleston Chasers among others, usually with similar personnel!

Nichols studied cornet with his father, a college music teacher. After moving from Utah to New York in 1923 Nichols, an excellent sightreader who could always be relied upon to add a bit of jazz to a dance band recording, quickly became in great demand. His own sessions at first featured trombonist Miff Mole and Jimmy Dorsey on alto and clarinet, playing advanced music that utilized unusual intervals, whole tone scales and often the tympani of Vic Berton along with hot ensembles. Later in the decade, his sidemen included such young greats as Benny Goodman, Glenn Miller, Jack Teagarden, Pee Wee Russell, Joe Venuti, Eddie Lang, Adrian Rollini, Gene Krupa and the wonderful mellophone specialist Dudley Fosdick among others; their version of "Ida" was a surprise hit. Although still using the main name of the Five Pennies, Nichols' bands were often quite a bit larger and by 1929 he was alternating sessions featuring bigger commercial orchestras with small combos. At first Nichols weathered the depression well with work in shows, but by 1932 his long string of recordings came to an end. He headed a so-so swing band up until 1942, left music for a couple of years and for a few months in 1944 was with Glen Gray's Casa Loma Orchestra. Later that year he reformed the Five Pennies as a Dixieland sextet and, particularly after bass saxophonist Joe Rushton became a permanent member, it was one of the finer traditional jazz bands of the next 20 years. Nichols recorded several memorable hot versions of "Battle Hymn Of the Republic," the best being in 1959. That same year a highly enjoyable if rather fictional Hollywood movie called *The Five Pennies* (and featuring Nichols' cornet solos and Danny Kaye's acting) made Red into a national celebrity at the twilight of his long career. Nichols' earlier sessions are just now being reissued on CD in piecemeal fashion but none of his later albums are in print yet. —*Scott Yanow*

Real Rare Red / Nov. 22, 1922-Oct. 1935 / Broadway Intermission ✦✦✦✦
This collector's LP lives up to its title. The first two numbers, by the Syncopated Five, were cornetist Red Nichols' earliest recordings. Only 25 copies were originally printed and just two were known to exist at the time that this album was released. Nichols is also heard in a variety of other settings including with Freddie Rich, Billy Wynne's Greenwich Village Inn Orchestra, with Jack Albin, backing singer Peggy English (on a memorable version of "High, High, High Up in the

Hills"), with Don Voorhees, the Captivators, the Louisiana Rhythm Kings and in three cases with his own band (including a song from a 1935 movie short). This LP is one for true Red Nichols fans to search for, along with its equally rewarding second volume. —*Scott Yanow*

The Sounds of New York, / Jun. 5, 1924-Nov. 18, 1930 / RCA ✦✦✦✦
Perhaps the most remarkable aspect of this long out-of-print French RCA LP from the *Black and White* series is that it proudly states "Vol. 200!" Cornetist Red Nichols has guest spots with George Olsen's Music, Howard Lanin's Ben Franklin Dance Orchestra and Paul Whiteman ("I'm Coming Virginia"), but is mostly showcased with his own groups including his Big Ten (from 1930) and "Red and Miff's Stompers." With such sidemen as trombonist Miff Mole, Jimmy Dorsey on clarinet and alto, pianist Arthur Schutt, drummer Vic Berton and clarinetists Benny Goodman and Pee Wee Russell, Nichols is not the only strong soloist on these dates but he certainly was the main instigator. Fortunately most of this music has been reissued since this fine 1960s album came out. Highlights include two versions apiece of "Delirium" and "Davenport Blues," the heated "Feeling No Pain" and "Make My Cot Where the Cot-Cot-Cotton Grows." —*Scott Yanow*

Real Rare Red, Vol. 2 / Jul. 21, 1925-Oct. 10, 1927 / Broadway Intermission ✦✦✦✦
With 20 selections on this collector's LP (most quite rare), there is over an hour of music from the 1925-27 period featuring cornetist Red Nichols. Nichols is heard taking solos with the Seven Missing Links, the Cotton Pickers, Sam Lanin, the Hottentots, Arnold Brilhart, Mike Markel, Frank Signorelli, Joe Candullo, Lee Morse's Blue Grass Boys, the Arkansas Travellers and Meyer's Dance Orchestra. The acoustically recorded performances range from hot jazz to dance music and trombonist Miff Mole is often the co-start —*Scott Yanow*

Rhythm of the Day / Oct. 1925-Feb. 1932 / ASV/Living Era ✦✦✦
A '92 reissue of prime mid-'20s and early '30s Red Nichols cuts. Many are among the songs that such players as Benny Goodman, Artie Shaw, and others listened to closely and learned from during their youth. This is among the better Nichols reissues available. —*Ron Wynn*

Red Nichols and Sam Lanin's Orchestra / Jan. 20, 1926-May 4, 1928 / Broadway Intermission ✦✦✦✦
Sam Lanin led literally hundreds of record sessions in the 1920s, playing music that fell between jazz and dance. He utilized cornetist Red Nichols on many of the dates, including the 16 numbers from 1926-28 (all but one from 1926-27) that are on this now-rare LP. The personnel is mostly unidentified, although in some cases it features trombonists Miff Mole, Abe Lincoln or Glenn Miller and altoist Jimmy Dorsey. Under a variety of pseudonyms (including the Melody Sheiks, the Arkansas Travelers, the OKeh Melodians and the New York Syncopators), Lanin is heard leading similarly enjoyable groups. The excellent recording quality (for the period) of these performances is an added plus. —*Scott Yanow*

Red & Miff / Nov. 4, 1926-Jan. 5, 1931 / Saville ✦✦✦✦✦
This English LP, which contains 20 selections and a full hour's worth of music, has eight numbers featuring trombonist Miff Mole with Roger Wolfe Kahn's Orchestra and 12 selections from sessions led by cornetist Red Nichols, four of which also co-star Mole. All but four tunes are from the 1926-28 period. Highlights include "Clap Yo' Hands," "Where the Wild, Wild Flowers Grow," "Delirium," "Feeling No Pain," "Sugar" and "Make My Cot Where the Cot-Cot-Cotton Grows." This somewhat rare album is a delight for 1920s collectors. —*Scott Yanow*

● **Red Nichols and His Five Pennies, Vol. 1** / Dec. 8, 1926-Jun. 20, 1927 / Swaggie ✦✦✦✦✦
The first of five albums from the Australian Swaggie label that reissues all of the performances (including alternate takes) from Red Nichols' Five Pennies of 1926—June 1929 shows just how radical and unusual Nichols' music was during 1926-27. The use of whole tone phrases, unpredictable frameworks and Vic Berton's colorful tympani gave these performances a personality of their own that stood far apart from Dixieland. Trombonist Miff Mole, Jimmy Dorsey (doubling on clarinet and alto), pianist Arthur Schutt, guitarist Eddie Lang and (on two songs apiece) violinist Joe Venuti and bass saxophonist Adrian Rollini form the all-star cast for such classic performances as "Washboard Blues," "Buddy's Habits" and "Boneyard Shuffle." All five albums in this series (which came out in the late '80s) are highly recommended to 1920s collectors. —*Scott Yanow*

Red & Ben / Dec. 9, 1926-Sep. 18, 1928 / Broadway Intermission ✦✦✦✦
This collector's LP is split between the Wabash Dance Orchestra (a ten-piece group led by cornetist Red Nichols) and Ben Pollack's Californians. While the former band (which includes trombonist Miff Mole, pianist Arthur Schutt and drummer Gene Krupa) offers fine examples of hot dance music, Pollack's ensemble (heard in its first five recordings) has the recording debuts of clarinetist Benny Goodman and trombonist Glenn Miller. Most notable are "He's the Last Word" and "Waitin' for Katie." The LP is rounded off by the All-Star Orchestra's rendition of "I'm More

Than Satisfied" (which also includes BG). Worth searching for, since not all of this material has been reissued on CD. —*Scott Yanow*

Red Nichols and His Five Pennies, Vol. 2 / Jun. 20, 1927-Mar. 2, 1928 / Swaggie ✦✦✦✦✦

The second of five LPs from the Australian Swaggie label to reissue all of the early recordings led by cornetist Red Nichols has 12 titles plus four alternate taken from six sessions from 1927-28. With the exception of the last two titles, Nichols utilizes groups ranging from seven to ten musicians. His writing for trumpet trios (that also include Leo McConville and Manny Klein) results in many memorable choruses that really spark the ensembles. With such sidemen as trombonist Miff Mole, Dudley Fosdick on mellophone, Jimmy Dorsey, Pee Wee Russell or Fud Livingston on clarinet and drummer Vic Berton (who doubled on tympani), these greatly underrated performances rank with most of the best jazz of the era. Highlights include "Riverboat Shuffle," "Ida" (which was a million-seller), "Nobody's Sweetheart," "My Gal Sal" and "Avalon." The last two songs are more in the symphonic jazz category, featuring period vocals by Scrappy Lambert and more commercial (but still charming) arrangements for the 13-piece group. All five albums in this definitive series are well worth acquiring by 1920s collectors. —*Scott Yanow*

Red Nichols and His Five Pennies, Vol. 3 / Mar. 2, 1928-Oct. 2, 1928 / Swaggie ✦✦✦✦✦

The music on the third of five LPs in Swaggie's Red Nichols series alternates between "symphonic jazz" (which often has vocals by Scrappy Lambert and huge groups modeled a bit on Paul Whiteman) and more freewheeling performances by Nichols' oversized Five Pennies. No matter what the setting, the music on this album (all but one cut dates from a three-month period) is delightful and swinging in its own way. In addition to the cornetist/leader, other key players include trumpeters Leo McConville and Manny Klein in the colorful brass trios with Nichols, trombonist Miff Mole, Dudley Fosdick on mellophone, Fud Livingston and Jimmy Dorsey on reeds, pianist Arthur Schutt and drummer Vic Berton. "Panama," "There'll Come a Time," "Margie," "Original Dixieland One-Step" and "A Pretty Girl Is like a Melody" are especially memorable. —*Scott Yanow*

Red Nichols and His Five Pennies, Vol. 4 / Oct. 2, 1928-Mar. 20, 1929 / Swaggie ✦✦✦✦✦

This is the fourth of five Swaggie LPs documenting cornetist Red Nichols' sessions as a leader during 1926-29 including all the known alternate takes. Although his band was usually known as the Five Pennies, Nichols' ensemble was generally seven-to-ten pieces except when expanded to become a concert orchestra. With the exception of the alternate take of "A Pretty Girl Is like a Melody," all of the performances on this album are from February and March 1929. Nichols uses such players as trombonist Glenn Miller, Dudley Fosdick on mellophone and the reeds of Benny Goodman, Fud Livinston and Jimmy Dorsey on a variety of heated numbers including "Who's Sorry Now," "Chinatown, My Chinatown" and "Alice Blue Gown." There are also three songs by Nichols with his Louisiana Rhythm Kings (which uses similar personnel) and his ten-piece group "the Captivators" which has fine period vocals from Scrappy Lambert. Collectors of 1920s music will enjoy all five albums in this valuable series. —*Scott Yanow*

Featuring Benny Goodman 1929-31 / Feb. 1, 1929-Feb. 19, 1931 / Sunbeam ✦✦✦✦

This Sunbeam album has 16 of the hotter performances by Red Nichols and his Five Pennies from the 1929-31 period; only the four earliest numbers were on Swaggie's "complete" five-LP series. The young clarinetist Benny Goodman is a major asset during these advanced Dixieland sides, but there are also fine solos by the cornetist/leader, trombonists Miff Mole and Jack Teagarden and Dudley Fosdick on mellophone (he was really in a class by himself in the late '20s), while Gene Krupa's drumming is quite prominent on some tunes. Vocals are taken by Scrappy Lambert, Harold Arlen and Wingy Manone but the emphasis is on the fine instrumentalists. Worth searching for. —*Scott Yanow*

Red Nichols and His Five Pennies, Vol. 5 / Apr. 18, 1929-Jun. 11, 1929 / Swaggie ✦✦✦✦✦

The fifth and probably final album in the Australian Swaggie label's very valuable "complete" Red Nichols series alternates freewheeling jazz performances with longer (42 minute) renditions of symphonic dance music which also has its charm. Of the former, these versions of "Indiana," "Dinah" and "On the Alamo" are famous, and there are also hot numbers ("I'm Walking Through Clover" is a highlight) from Nichols' quintet/sextet called the Louisiana Rhythm Kings. In addition, there are four selections by a 23-piece ensemble that are clearly modeled after Paul Whiteman and shift back and forth between dance music and jazz sections. Collectors of 1920s music will want all five albums in this important series which unfortunately comes to a close in June 1929, several volumes short. —*Scott Yanow*

Radio Transcriptions 1929-30 / Aug. 29, 1929-Aug. 25, 1930 / IAJRC ✦✦✦✦

In 1929 cornetist Red Nichols became one of the first jazz bandleaders to record music strictly for radio airplay. The "Brunswick Brevities" generally consisted of a theme song, announcement and one hot number. Five of these "broadcasts" plus Nichols' ten appearances on the "*Heat*" program are included on this historically valuable CD from the collectors' IAJRC label. In addition to Nichols, such musicians as trombonists Glenn Miller and Jack Teagarden, clarinetists Jimmy Dorsey, Pee Wee Russell and Benny Goodman, bass saxophonist Adrian Rollini, tenors Babe Russin and Bud Freeman, pianist Joe Sullivan and drummer Gene Krupa are among the sidemen. In addition there are some poppish vocals by Scrappy Lambert, Dick Robertson and Roy Evans, although the majority of the cuts are instrumentals, including hot versions of "That's a Plenty," "After You've Gone, "The Sheik of Araby" and "Sweet Georgia Brown." An interesting highlight is a four-song medley (played as a mystery quiz) that is performed by the instrumentation of three trumpets, harp and piano. Recommended to classic jazz and Red Nichols collectors. —*Scott Yanow*

Red Nichols and His Five Pennies, 1929-1932 / Oct. 22, 1929-Feb. 18, 1932 / IAJRC ✦✦✦✦

This enjoyable LP has highlights from cornetist Red Nichols' recordings of 1929-32. Although released under the title of the "Five Pennies," the groups range from six to 12 pieces. Utilizing many of the top young White players of the era, Nichols included among his sidemen trumpeter Charlie Teagarden, trombonists Glenn Miller and Tommy Dorsey, Jimmy Dorsey, Babe Russin and Benny Goodman on reeds, and Gene Krupa or Dave Tough on drums. The emphasis is on hot jazz, and the high points include "Hallelujah," "Fan It," "Honolulu Blues," "Yaaka Hula Hickey Dula" and "Clarinet Marmalade." Until the music is released completely and in chronological order, this album is one of the best sets around documenting this important period in Red Nichols' career. —*Scott Yanow*

The Louisiana Rhythm Kings and Red and His Big Ten / Jan. 20, 1930-Jan. 5, 1931 / TOM ✦✦✦✦

This collector's LP (which looks like a bootleg due to its blank back cover and its incomplete personnel listing) has some hot performances from a pair of groups headed by cornetist Red Nichols. The Louisiana Rhythm Kings' dozen songs alternate obscurities with future standards. There are so-so vocals by Wesley Vaughan and solos from Nichols, trombonist Glenn Miller, Babe Russin on tenor, bass saxophonist Adrian Rollini and Jimmy Dorsey doubling on clarinet and alto. The LP concludes with four selections from "Red and His Big Ten" which has similar personnel along with the addition of clarinetist Benny Goodman. Excellent music, much of which is not readily available elsewhere. —*Scott Yanow*

Rockin' in Rhythm / Jun. 18, 1934-Oct. 2, 1939 / Sounds of Swing ✦✦✦

Cornetist Red Nichols made his biggest impact in the late '20s when he recorded hundreds of colorful jazz numbers, but by the mid-'30s he was becoming largely forgotten. Nichols' big band, which is heard on this LP in 1934 ("Rockin' in Rhythm"), 1937 and 1939, did not have a strong personality or purpose of its own. In fact, other than pianist Billy Maxted and guitarist Mike Bryan (who have minor roles on a few of the songs), none of the sidemen ever became known for much. The music overall is routine swing with some hints of Nichols' Dixieland past but little memorable occurs despite some good playing. It would be a decade before Red Nichols made a full-fledged comeback; he treaded water during the swing era. —*Scott Yanow*

1936 / Nov. 30, 1936 / Circle ✦✦

There is relatively little of Red Nichols' cornet on this set of radio transcriptions. Of the dozen tunes, an average vocal group called the Songcopators dominates seven of the selections. The emphasis throughout is on dance music and even such numbers as "Milenberg Joys," "Bugle Call Rag" and "Organ Grinder's Swing" are uneventful. Frank Driggs deserves great credit for the honesty that he shows in his liner notes. Although the melodic music is certainly not objectionable, nothing occurs that makes this set of any interest to anyone but Red Nichols completists. —*Scott Yanow*

Class of '39 / Mar. 31, 1939-Oct. 30, 1939 / Broadway Intermission ✦✦✦✦

Although he had been an important name in the music world in the late '20s, by 1939 when Red Nichols went on the road with his own big band, the cornetist was largely forgotten. His orchestra did not have a strong personality of its own and none of its sidemen went on to prominence in later years. This LP from the Broadway Intermission label has radio airchecks from Nichols' 1939 Orchestra. Although not at all original (even some of its tunes such as "Sunrise Serenade" and "Moonlight Serenade" were other group's hits), the Nichols outfit was quite musical and the leader sounds in generally fine form. Swing collectors will be interested in this somewhat rare LP by Red Nichols' obscure big band. —*Scott Yanow*

Red Nichols and His Five Pennies / 1944-1946 / Tops ✦✦✦

After the breakup of his big band and a sideman stint with the Casa Loma Orchestra, cornetist Red Nichols put together a new edition of his Five Pennies and returned to Dixieland. This obscure LP finds Nichols during 1944-46 leading a sextet that also includes clarinetist Heinie Beau and tenor saxophonist Herbie Haymer; the personnel and recording dates are inexcusably not given. Although not up to the level of Nichols' band of a few years later (when bass saxophonist Joe Rushton was a key member), this freewheeling unit is enjoyable enough, particularly on such tunes as "Should I," "At Sundown," "Whispering" and "Melancholy Baby." —Scott Yanow

At the Jazz Band Ball / Apr. 18, 1947-Oct. 12, 1960 / Broadway Intermission ✦✦✦✦

This collectors' LP features the underrated cornetist Red Nichols on a variety of previously unissued live performances. Nine of the 15 selections showcase his 1959 sextet which also included bass saxophonist Joe Rushton, trombonist Pete Beilman and clarinetist Bill Wood; highlights include "At the Jazz Band Ball," "American Patrol" and "Panama." There is also a version of "Ostrich Walk" with a larger band from 1956, a medley from 1960, three tunes (including "Jazz Me Blues") by his 1951 group and one song ("Lonesome and Lovesick") dating from 1947. The recording quality on this 1987 LP is excellent and Red Nichols fans will definitely want to search for this fine set. —Scott Yanow

Red Nichols & His Five Pennies / 1948-Mar. 16, 1949 / Jump ✦✦✦✦

This excellent LP features two versions of cornetist Red Nichols' Five Pennies with such sidemen as either Matty Matlock or Rosy McHargue on clarinet, trombonist King Jackson, tenorman Don Lodice and the great bass saxophonist Joe Rushton. Nichols' band had its sound down by this time as can be heard on fresh renditions of "That's a Plenty," "Eccentric," "Carolina in the Morning" and particularly a near-classic version of "Battle Hymn of the Republic." This LP may be a bit hard to find but is worth the search for Dixieland fans. —Scott Yanow

Red Nichols and His Five Pennies / 1949 / Jazzology ✦✦✦✦

Taken from radio transcriptions, this CD has twice as much music as the earlier Jazzology LP of the same name. In 1949, cornetist Red Nichols was making a successful comeback leading a new Five Pennies group, a spirited Dixieland sextet. Nichols' unusual solo style—which tended to be thoughtful, sometimes utilized whole-tone phrases, and often sounded thought out in advance—gave the band its own sound, as did the bass saxophone of the mighty Joe Rushton. With trombonist King Jackson and clarinetist Reuel Lynch taking worthy solos and pianist Bobby Hammack and drummer Rollie Culver contributing colorful support, this was one of the better trad-style bands of the era. These well-recorded transcriptions (19 selections in all) include memorable versions of such tunes as "Battle Hymn of the Republic," "I've Found a New Baby," "Indiana," "Ida" and "Sunday," among others. The only minuses are the breezy and often inaccurate liner notes, but the music is definitely worth getting by pre-swing jazz fans. —Scott Yanow

Red Nichols and That Man from Dixieland / 1950-1951 / Take Two ✦✦✦

The music on this LP is drawn from radio broadcasts dating from 1950-51. Cornetist Red Nichols (who takes a vocal on "Sheik of Araby") had a strong sextet during this period which consisted of clarinetist Rosy McHargue, trombonist King Jackson, bass saxophonist Joe Rushton, pianist Bobby Hammock and drummer Rollie Culver. Guest singer Dottie O'Brien has four decent vocals but the group sounds at its best on such instrumentals as "Bugle Call Rag," "Sunday," "Carolina in the Morning" and "Clarinet Marmalade." However, due to the brevity of many of these performances, this set is not all that essential. —Scott Yanow

Syncopated Chamber Music / Feb. 8, 1953-Feb. 9, 1953 / Audiophile ✦✦✦✦✦

The time is a bit brief on this LP (just a little over 31 minutes) but the quality is quite high. Cornetist Red Nichols (who used two different groups during the two-day period) lives up to the title's name, playing exquisite versions of such songs as "Three Blind Mice," "Candlelights," "I Can't Believe That You're in Love with Me," "Manhattan Rag" and even "Easter Parade." Although the individual solos of Nichols, clarinetist Matty Matlock, bass saxophonist Joe Rushton and either King Jackson or Ted Veseley on trombone are excellent, it is the unpredictable arrangements (which have inventive use of space, dynamics and unusual harmonies) that make this a particularly memorable set. —Scott Yanow

In Love with Red / May 1, 1955-Mar. 6, 1956 / Capitol ✦✦

This LP is an unusual release by cornetist Red Nichols whose Five Pennies were greatly augmented for the occasion by strings, woodwinds and (on three of the dozen selections) a vocal group. Overall Nichols' brand of Dixieland is purposely watered down and the music ranges from schlock to novelties with only a few worthwhile jazz moments (most notably "Manhattan Rag"). Nichols completists will want this set anyway, but this LP is one of his less essential efforts. —Scott Yanow

Hot Pennies / Sep. 7, 1956+Sep. 10, 1956 / Capitol ✦✦✦

For this LP, cornetist Red Nichols expanded his Five Pennies from six pieces to twelve, allowing him to arrange some colorful ensembles while still retaining the flavor of Dixieland. With a backup crew that includes trombonist King Jackson, the great bass saxophonist Joe Rushton and clarinetist Heinie Beau, Nichols revisits such veteran songs as "Louisiana," "Maple Leaf Rag," "Ida" (a big hit for him in the 1920s) and "Farewell Blues." The music is enjoyable but will be difficult to find, since Capitol has yet to reissue any of their many Red Nichols records on CD. —Scott Yanow

All Time Hits! / Sep. 7, 1956-Aug. 29, 1959 / Pausa ✦✦✦✦✦

Throughout the 1950s, cornetist Red Nichols usually utilized a sextet which he called his Five Pennies. On this LP of material taken from sessions for Capitol, Nichols is heard on all but one of the ten numbers with groups having from ten to fourteen pieces. This rendition of "Battle Hymn of the Republic" is a true classic, using a brilliant arrangement that investigates the warhorse at three different tempos; a similar approach given "When the Saints Go Marching In" is much less successful. Other highlights include "Margie," "Ida, Sweet as Apple Cider," "Avalon" and "Indiana." This important music deserves to be reissued on CD. —Scott Yanow

Red Nichols and the Five Pennies at Marineland / Oct. 10, 1958 / Capitol ✦✦✦✦

Reissued by the audiophile label Mobile Fidelity on LP, this Red Nichols set is a bit unusual in that it is a live session. The cornetist and his Five Pennies (which includes the great bass saxophonist Joe Rushton, clarinetist Bill Wood and trombonist Pete Beilman) plays one of their typical sets of the period. Nichols had a wide repertoire which included Dixieland standards (including "St. Louis Blues," "Fidgety Feet" and "Carolina in the Morning") and such unusual numbers as the exciting "Entry of the Gladiators," "Silver Threads Among the Gold" and "Lassus Trombone." This date is a fine outing for all of the players. —Scott Yanow

Parade of the Pennies / Nov. 1958 / Capitol ✦✦✦✦

For part of this LP, cornetist Red Nichols (with the assistance of clarinetist Heinie Beau's arrangements) revisited his earlier "hits" with successful remakes of such songs as "Buddy's Habits," "Japanese Sandman," "Avalon" and "Washboard Blues." In addition there are three newer songs co-written by Nichols and Beau. Red's Five Pennies are augmented by Jackie Coon's mellophone, a couple of reeds and the percussion (including tympani) of Ralph Hansell. This is an excellent album well deserving (along with most of Nichols' hard-to-find Capitol LP's) of being reissued on CD. —Scott Yanow

Dixieland Dinner Dance / Aug. 28, 1959-Aug. 29, 1959 / Capitol ✦✦✦

Because this album was ostensibly recorded as a "Dixieland dinner dance," there are more ballads and dance music than usual on the LP by cornetist Red Nichols and his Five Pennies. With bass saxophonist Joe Rushton most prominent among the supporting cast of the sextet, such tunes as "Johnson Rag," "Satan Takes a Holiday" and "American Patrol" are among the high points along with a couple of tasteful medleys. Nice music but this set will be difficult to find. —Scott Yanow

Blues and Old Time Rags / Oct. 22, 1963+Oct. 28, 1963 / Capitol ✦✦✦

Cornetist Red Nichols' final record was this obscure effort which, as with all of his Capitol LPs, has not been reissued on CD. Nichols and the last version of his Five Pennies perform brief renditions of 11 rags and blues with a couple of Dixieland standards (including "Milenberg Joys") tossed in. None of the music on this final effort is particularly memorable but it is pleasing overall and serves as a good ending to Nichols' 40 years on record. —Scott Yanow

Lennie Niehaus

b. Jun. 11, 1929, St. Louis, MO
Arranger, Alto Saxophone / Cool, Bop, Film Music
An excellent altoist and jazz arranger in the 1950s (most notably for Stan Kenton), Lennie Niehaus in more recent times has won fame for his work scoring the music for Clint Eastwood films. After graduating from college, Niehaus played alto and occasionally wrote for Kenton (1951-52) before being drafted into the Army (1952-54). Upon his discharge Kenton welcomed Niehaus back and he worked for the bandleader on-and-off for the rest of the decade. Niehaus, who led and played alto on six albums between 1954-57 (five for Contemporary) had a cool tone a bit reminiscent of Lee Konitz. By the 1960s his playing had gone by the wayside as Niehaus concentrated on writing for films. Although he largely left jazz at that time, his work on *Play Misty for Me* and particularly *Bird* for Clint Eastwood allowed one to once again admire his jazz writing. —Scott Yanow

☆ **The Lennie Niehaus, Vol. 1: The Quintet** / Jul. 2, 1954-Jul. 9, 1954 / Original Jazz Classics ✦✦✦✦✦

Although best known as an arranger, Lennie Niehaus has also been a talented cool-toned altoist. Three different four-song sessions are combined on this reissue LP (which has not yet been reissued on CD), featuring Niehaus in quintets. Eight songs match him with tenorman Jack Montrose (himself a fine arranger), baritonist Bob Gordon, bassist Monty Budwig and drummer Shelly Manne, while the four numbers from 1956 use Stu Williamson on valve trombone and trumpet, pianist Hampton Hawes, bassist Red Mitchell and Manne. The tight arrangements, concise solos and soft tones practically epitomize West Coast-style cool jazz, and these performances are full of subtle surprises. —*Scott Yanow*

Lennie Niehaus, Vol. 2: The Octet, Pt. 1—Zounds! / Aug. 23, 1954 / Original Jazz Classics ✦✦✦✦✦

The CD reissue of this enjoyable set is simply titled *Zounds!* Arranger/altoist Lennie Niehaus utilizes the instrumentation of alto, tenor, baritone, trumpet or French horn, trombone, piano or tuba, bass and drums on these concise miniatures; only Hampton Hawes' "The Sermon" is over four minutes in length. The performances (eight from 1954 and four from 1956) comprise five swinging Niehaus originals and seven jazz standards with plenty of short solos and inventive writing from the leader, whose alto playing remains underrecognized. Recommended. —*Scott Yanow*

The Lennie Niehaus, Vol. 3: The Octet, Pt. 2 / Jan. 11, 1955-Feb. 15, 1955 / Original Jazz Classics ✦✦✦✦✦

For this CD reissue, Lennie Niehaus contributed five originals (including "Rick's Tricks" and "Circling the Blues") plus creative reworkings of six veteran standards and an obscurity called "Yes, Yes, Honey." The lineup of musicians is virtually a who's who of West Coast jazz (altoist Niehaus, tenor saxophonist Bill Holman, baritonist Jimmy Giuffre, trumpeter Stu Williamson, valve trombonist Bob Enevoldsen, pianist Pete Jolly, bassist Monty Budwig and drummer Shelly Manne), and the charts are both swinging and filled with some subtle surprises and occasional unusual tone colors. Well worth checking out, as are Niehaus' other valuable Contemporary sessions of the 1950s. —*Scott Yanow*

★ **Lennie Niehaus, Vol. 4: The Quintets and Strings** / Mar. 16, 1955-Apr. 25, 1955 / Original Jazz Classics ✦✦✦✦✦

This CD reissue brings back one of Lennie Niehaus' finest recordings of the 1950s. His alto is featured throughout the dozen selections and the varied settings (Niehaus is backed by a string quartet, a standard rhythm section and sometimes two other saxophonists in addition to performing four numbers with a standard quintet) gives him an opportunity to show off his writing abilities. Niehuas varies tempos a lot (the strings are often heard on faster material), there is solo space for the tenor of Bill Perkins, baritonist Bob Gordon and Stu Williamson on trumpet and valve trombone, and the leader's boppish alto is heard at the peak of his playing powers. Bop collectors can consider this disc to be essential. —*Scott Yanow*

Lennie Niehaus, Vol. 5: The Sextet / Jan. 9, 1956-Jan. 12, 1956 / Contemporary ✦✦✦✦

Judy Niemack

b. Mar. 11, 1954, Pasadena, CA
Vocals / Post-Bop, Bop

A talented and adventurous jazz singer, Judy Niemack has long had an underground reputation in jazz, although in recent times she has finally begun to receive recognition for her abilities. She sang regularly in school, starting at age seven in a church choir, and at 17 decided to become a professional singer. After meeting Warne Marsh the following year, Niemack became dedicated to jazz. She attended Pasadena City College, had several years of classical study, and also attended the New England Conservatory in Boston and the Cleveland Institute of Music, in addition to private lessons with Warne Marsh. In 1977, she moved to New York and the following year made her recording debut for Sea Breeze.

Since that time, Niemack has freelanced with many top advanced musicians, including Toots Thielemans, James Moody, Lee Konitz, Clark Terry, Kenny Barron, Fred Hersch, Kenny Werner, Joe Lovano and Eddie Gomez, among others, written lyrics to other musicians' compositions (in addition to writing songs of her own), and has toured Europe regularly. In addition, she has been a top jazz educator, teaching throughout Europe. Judy Niemack, a colorful improviser, has thus far recorded as a leader for Sea Breeze, Stash and Freelance. —*Scott Yanow*

By Heart / Feb. 13, 1978-Feb. 16, 1978 / Sea Breeze ✦✦✦✦

Two of Warne Marsh's top students, singer Judy Niemack and Australian trumpeter Simon Wettenhall, teamed up for this fine quartet set with bassist Eddie Gomez and drummer Skip Scott. Tenor saxophonist Marsh himself guests on Niemack's "Way Low" and "I'll Remember April." The interplay between voice and trumpet makes this a very impressive debut, although Wettenhall soon slipped into obscurity. When performing swing standards (whose interpretations are a bit influenced by Marsh and Lennie Tristano) or one of their five originals (including Wettenhall's "Tune for Bix"), the chance-taking Niemack shows a great deal of potential for the future. —*Scott Yanow*

Blue-Bop / Sep. 1988 / Freelance ✦✦✦✦

One does not usually encounter such songs as Cedar Walton's "Bolivia," "Dizzy Atmosphere" and "Moanin'" on vocal albums, but Judy Niemack has always been a very instrumental-oriented jazz singer. Whether scatting, stretching out words, or singing unexpected notes, Niemack (who should be much better-known) is consistently brilliant on this CD from the French Freelance label. She is assisted by Walton, bassist Ray Drummond, drummer Joey Baron and (on three of the 14 numbers) trombonist Curtis Fuller throughout the consistently swinging and often adventurous set. Recommended. —*Scott Yanow*

Long as You're Living / Aug. 18, 1990-Aug. 20, 1990 / Freelance ✦✦✦✦✦

Heart's Desire / 1992 / Stash ✦✦✦✦✦

Straight Up / Aug. 16, 1992-Aug. 17, 1992 / Freelance ✦✦✦✦

Mingus, Monk & Mal / Mar. 6, 1995 / Freelance ✦✦✦✦

● **Night and the Music** / Aug. 21, 1996-Aug. 23, 1996 / Freelance ✦✦✦✦✦

It is difficult not to be impressed by Judy Niemack, who has a very appealing voice with a wide range, the ability to express a wide range of emotions; plus, she swings, indulges in chance-taking improvisations, and writes her own lyrics to the melodies of jazz classics. On this well-conceived set, Niemack, who is joined by pianist Kenny Werner, bassist Ray Drummond, drummer Billy Hart and sometimes guitarist Jean-Francois Prins (cellist Erik Friedlander sits in on one song), performs a wide range of material. After really stretching out on "You and the Night and the Music," she sings some humorous lyrics ("It's Over Now") to Thelonious Monk's "Well You Needn't" (listing all of the things her former boyfriend shouldn't bother doing because it's over), pays tribute to Monk on "A Crazy Song to Sing" (her words to "Misterioso"), sounds quite emotional on "Turn Out the Stars," revives "My Favorite Things," shows frustration on "You Belong to Her" (based on "Stolen Moments"), and infuses "What Is This Thing Called Love" with Lee Konitz's "Subconcious-Lee." In addition, Niemack performs a couple of her originals, sounds quite sad on "Goodbye" and is romantic on the closing "La Chanson Des Vieux Amants." This unpredictable yet consistently satisfying set is a gem. —*Scott Yanow*

Jack Nimitz

b. Mar. 5, 1928, Chicago, IL
Baritone Saxophone

Although he has had a long and productive career, Jack Nimitz has long been underrated, not getting a chance to lead his own record session until a 1995 set for Fresh Sound, when he was already 65. He started on the clarinet when he was 12, switching to alto two years later and gigging locally at 15. In 1949, Nimitz started specializing on the baritone, and soon was playing with such territory bands as those led by Bob Astor, Johnny Bothwell and Daryl Harpa. From 1952-53, he was back in Washington D.C. before touring with Woody Herman (Oct. 1953-Sept. 1955) and a few months with Stan Kenton (1955-56). He was a regular in the house band at the Savoy and then spent an additional year with Kenton (1958-59). Settling in Los Angeles, Nimitz became a busy studio musician and also played with Bill Berry, Benny Carter, Gerald Wilson, Supersax (since its beginning in 1972), Bill Perkins' Big Band, Bud Shank, Frank Strazzeri's Woodwinds West, the Lighthouse All-Stars, and any other high-quality jazz group that needed a talented baritonist. —*Scott Yanow*

● **Confirmation** / May 18, 1995-May 19, 1995 / Fresh Sound ✦✦✦✦✦

Baritonist Jack Nimitz has been part of a countless number of records through the years including with the orchestras of Woody Herman and Stan Kenton, in the studios since 1959 and with Supersax. But until producer Dick Bank decided to put Nimitz at the head of a quartet session for Fresh Sound (*Confirmation*), he had never had the opportunity to lead his own record date. Teamed up with pianist Lou Levy, bassist Dave Carpenter and drummer Joe La Barbera, Nimitz explores a dozen superior songs, ranging from standards ("I'm Getting Sentimental Over You" and "A Handful of Stars") and bop tunes ("Half Nelson" and "Confirmation") to a lyrical "Lost in the Stars," alternating hard swingers with tender ballad statements. This particularly strong straightahead Fresh Sound date is highly recommended. —*Scott Yanow*

Sal Nistico

b. Apr. 2, 1948, Syracuse, NY, **d.** Mar. 3, 1991, Berne, Switzerland
Tenor Saxophone / Bop, Hard Bop

Sal Nistico's explosive tenor solos with Woody Herman in the mid-'60s helped make that edition of Herman's Herds into a success. Originally an altoist, Nistico switched to tenor in 1956 and played with R&B bands for three years. He gigged with and made his recording debut in 1959-60 with the Jazz Brothers, a band also including Chuck and Gap Mangione. But it was while he was with Herman in 1962-65 that Nistico made history. In 1965 he spent five months with Count Basie.

He returned to Count in 1967 and to Herman on several occasions (1968-70, 1971, 1981-82) although without the impact of the first stint. Otherwise the tenor freelanced throughout his career, playing with Don Ellis and Buddy Rich but mostly working with pickup groups. Nistico recorded for several labels as a leader including Riverside, Red and Beehive. — *Scott Yanow*

Heavyweights / Dec. 20, 1961 / Jazzland ✦✦✦✦✦
Recorded shortly before he made history with his contributions to Woody Herman's Orchestra, the recorded debut of tenor saxophonist Sal Nistico as a leader is quite impressive. It is surprising that this LP has not yet been reissued in the Original Jazz Classics series for Nistico (who is matched with cornetist Nat Adderley, pianist Barry Harris, bassist Sam Jones and drummer Walter Perkins) really romps through most of the seven tunes. Adderley is also heard in prime form on the superior bop date, which has among its highlights Harris' "Mamblue," "Just Friends" and "Au Privave." — *Scott Yanow*

Neo Nistico / Nov. 3, 1978 / Bee Hive ✦✦✦✦
Sal Nistico only led three sessions for American labels during his career (along with five for European companies), which is surprising, considering how exciting a bop-oriented soloist he was. For this Bee Hive LP (which has not yet been reissued on CD), Nistico heads a sextet filled with notables (trumpeter Ted Curson, baritonist Nick Brignola, pianist Ronnie Mathews, bassist Sam Jones and drummer Roy Haynes). They jam through a pair of Nistico's originals, Wayne Shorter's "Fee-Fi-Fo-Fum," and three standards including an oddly voiced but roaring "Anthropology." The soloists are all in fine form during the obscure but worthy session. — *Scott Yanow*

● **Empty Room** / 1988 / Red ✦✦✦✦✦

Jimmie Noone (Jimmy Noone)

b. Apr. 23, 1895, New Orleans, LA, **d.** Apr. 19, 1944, Los Angeles, CA
Clarinet / Classic New Orleans Jazz

Considered one of the three top New Orleans clarinetists of the 1920s (with Johnny Dodds and Sidney Bechet), Jimmie Noone had a smoother tone than his contemporaries that appealed to players of the swing era (including Benny Goodman). He played guitar as a child and at age 15 took clarinet lessons from Lorenzo Tio, Jr., and Sidney Bechet (the latter was only 13!). Noone developed quickly and he played with Freddie Keppard (1913-14), Buddy Petit and the Young Olympia Band (1916) which he led. In 1917 he went to Chicago to join Keppard's Creole Band. After it broke up the following year he became a member of King Oliver's band, staying until he joined Doc Cook's Dreamland Orchestra (1920-26). Although Noone recorded with Cook, it was when he started leading a band at the Apex Club that he hit his stride. By 1928 he had pianist Earl Hines and altoist Joe Poston in the unusual quintet (Poston stuck to playing melodies behind Noone) and was recording for Vocalion, creating classic music including an early version of "Sweet Lorraine" (his theme song) and "Four or Five Times." Noone worked steadily in Chicago throughout the 1930s (although he received less attention from the jazz world), he used Charlie Shavers on some of his late-'30s recordings and welcomed the young singer Joe Williams to the bandstand; unfortunately they never recorded together. In 1944 Noone was in Kid Ory's band on the West Coast and seemed on the brink of greater fame when he unexpectedly died. Thanks to European reissue series, Jimmie Noone's recordings are readily available on CD. His son Jimmie Noone, Jr., suddenly emerged out of obscurity in the 1980s to play clarinet and tenor with the Cheathams. — *Scott Yanow*

The Swing Era / Oct. 15, 1923-Jun. 5, 1940 / Best of Jazz ✦✦✦
The Classics label specializes in reissuing the complete output of various top prebop jazz groups. Their *Best of Jazz* series does the opposite, summing up an artist's career on one CD. This 22-selection set covers the career of clarinetist Jimmie Noone. He is heard in 1923 with King Oliver ("Chattanooga Stomp"), on two songs from 1926 with Doc Cook's Dreamland Orchestra (which also features cornetist Freddie Keppard) and with his own Apex Club Orchestra during 1928-30, 1933-34, 1936-37 and two songs from 1940. Although five experts picked out the numbers, the later pieces are not as worthy as the 1928 sides. This CD does achieve its purpose, including such highlights of Jimmie Noone's career as "A Monday Date," "Sweet Lorraine," "My Daddy Rocks Me" and "Apex Blues," but more serious collectors will want everything else too, making the Classics reissues a wiser buy. — *Scott Yanow*

★ **Apex Blues** / May 16, 1928-Jul. 1, 1930 / Decca ✦✦✦✦
This CD reissues the first dozen selections from clarinetist Jimmie Noone's Apex Club Orchestra (all of the numbers with pianist Earl Hines although not the four alternate takes) plus eight slightly later numbers. Noone had an unusual quintet/sextet in which altoist Joe Poston constantly stated the melody (but never actually had any solos), giving the band an unique sound for the period. Many of Noone's greatest recordings are on this CD (including "I Know That You Know," "Four or

Five Times," "Apex Blues," "My Monday Date," "Sweet Lorraine" and "My Daddy Rocks Me with One Steady Roll") although serious collectors will prefer to get the more complete two CDs from the Classics label instead. — *Scott Yanow*

Jimmie Noone and His Orchestra / May 16, 1928-Dec. 11, 1940 / IAJRC ✦✦✦
This LP from the collectors IAJRC label has 16 selections featuring clarinetist Jimmie Noone. The performances are programmed in chronological order and most of the recordings are lesser known. All but the first two and the last four are from 1929-31 and highlights include the 1929 version of "Apex Blues," "That Rhythm Man," "Three Little Words" and "Shine." All of this music has since been reissued on CD but, taken as a sampler, this is a well-conceived introduction to the work of the fine New Orleans clarinetist. — *Scott Yanow*

Oh! Sister Ain't That Hot! / Jul. 23, 1928-Jul. 29, 1930 / MCA ✦✦
he music may be hot on this LP but the chintzy playing time (around 27 minutes) sinks this effort. A sampling of clarinetist Jimmie Noone's 1929-30 recordings (with "It's Tight like That" and an alternate version of the title cut dating from 1928), the music is fine but there simply is not enough of it to justify this album's acquisition at anything but a cheap price; besides, all of the recordings have been reissued in more complete form on CD. — *Scott Yanow*

Volume Two 1928-1929 / Aug. 25, 1928-Jun. 21, 1929 / Swaggie ✦✦✦✦
The second of six LPs that document all of clarinetist Jimmie Noone's sessions as a leader traces his career from 1928's two versions of his theme song "Sweet Lorraine" (which he helped popularize) through one number ("Anything You Want") dating from June 1929. Due to the four alternate takes, 11 somewhat rare selections and the excellent liner notes, this series is the best Jimmie Noone reissue program to date, but these albums from the Australian Swaggie label are becoming increasingly difficult to locate. Joined by altoist Joe Poston, usually pianist Alex Hill and a fine rhythm section (along with cornetist George Mitchell on five performances), Noone is heard in prime form throughout these tracks. Highlights include "It's Tight like That," "St. Louis Blues" and the aforementioned "Anything You Want." — *Scott Yanow*

Volume Three 1929 / Jul. 11, 1929-Oct. 21, 1929 / Swaggie ✦✦✦✦✦
The best Jimmie Noone reissue series (due to the inclusion of alternate takes and its consistently excellent liner notes) resulted in six hard-to-find LPs put out by the Australian Swaggie label. *Volume Three* covers a six-month period when the clarinetist (an inspiration to Benny Goodman) was at the height of his fame. Most selections have vocals (either by Mae Alix, Helen Savage or an unknown male) but there is also plenty of room for Noone's flights on clarinet which are usually backed by altoist Joe Poston playing the melody. A few tunes find the two-horn sextet augmented by two horns, and pianist Zinky Cohn (a remarkable soundalike of Earl Hines) is on all 16 selections. High points include "Am I Blue," two versions of "Apex Blues," "My Melancholy Baby" and a classic rendition of "My Daddy Rocks Me with One Steady Roll." — *Scott Yanow*

Volume Four 1929-1930 / Nov. 19, 1929-Jul. 1, 1930 / Swaggie ✦✦✦✦
The fourth of six LPs put out by the Australian Swaggie label continues the documentation of clarinetist Jimmie Noone's recordings as a leader, including his rare alternate takes. Because pop singer Elmo Tanner (who is tolerable) is on eight of the 17 numbers, this album is not as valuable as the previous three volumes. However, Georgia White on "When You're Smiling" is better, and there is plenty of solo space for Noone (who is generally backed by either Joe Poston or later on Eddie Pollack playing the melody) and Earl Hines soundalike Zinky Cohn. Best are "El Rado Scuffle," "I Lost My Gal from Memphis" and the two previously unissued versions of "San." — *Scott Yanow*

● **Jimmie Noone 1930-1934** / May 16, 1930-Nov. 23, 1934 / Classics ✦✦✦✦✦
The fourth of five CDs that reissue the complete output of clarinetist Jimmie Noone's recordings as a leader (but not all of his alternate takes) covers a four-year period with 13 numbers from 1930, six from 1931, four from 1933 and the final two dating from 1934. The performances generally find Noone backed by multireedist Eddie Pollack (who stuck mostly to the melody) and challenged by Zinky Cohn whose style sounds remarkably close to Earl Hines. There are a lot of vocals on these sides which are surprisingly rewarding including Georgia White's debut ("When You're Smiling"), Elmo Tanner (best-known for his later work with Ted Weems), Pollack (who is joined by Noone on "You Rascal You"), May Alix, Art Jarrett and two early numbers from Mildred Bailey. Earl Hines makes a surprise guest appearance on one of the 1931 sessions. Recommended to early jazz collectors. — *Scott Yanow*

● **Jimmie Noone 1934-1940** / Nov. 23, 1934-Dec. 11, 1940 / Classics ✦✦✦✦✦
On the fifth of Jimmie Noone's five CDs on the Classics label, the New Orleans clarinetist is heard on his final 24 selections as a leader (with the exception of a slightly later live session). The first six numbers close the book on his Apex Club Orchestra, featuring Eddie Pollack (in Joe Poston's old place) playing the melody on alto and sometimes baritone behind Noone's solos; trumpeter Jimmy Cobb and pianist Zinky Cohn get some solo space. Noone is also heard in 1936 with a free-

wheeling New Orleans group featuring trumpeter Guy Kelly and trombonist Preston Jackson, holding his own the following year with the dynamic young trumpeter Charlie Shavers and altoist Pete Brown, and doing his best in 1940 to overcome the weak cornet playing of Natty Dominique. The final four numbers (also from 1940) are dominated by Ed Thompson's dated vocals. No matter what the setting, Noone (who passed away in 1944) is heard in prime form. —*Scott Yanow*

Caecilie Norby

b. 1965, Denmark

Vocals / Pop, Standards, Cabaret, Traditional Pop

Caecilie Norby is a singer with an unusual repertoire that not only includes some jazz standards, but a few pop tunes of the past 30 years (including "Spinning Wheel" and "The Look of Love"). She has a strong voice and a style that shows potential. Born in Denmark to parents active in the classical music world, Norby's background is actually in rock, recording with Frontline in 1985 and spending 1986-93 as half of the rock group One Two. However, she also sang occasionally with a small jazz group in clubs, and pianist Niels Lan Doky was impressed enough to offer to produce her first jazz record. Caecilie Norby, whose greatest musical influence is early Nancy Wilson, has thus far recorded two sets released domestically by Blue Note. —*Scott Yanow*

Caecilie Norby / Sep. 17, 1994-Oct. 2, 1994 / Blue Note ♦♦

This recording should not be on the Blue Note label. Caecilie Norby has a strong voice and the ability to sing some absurdly complex melodies but her style falls between pop and cabaret. When Norby takes a second chorus, the approach is virtually identical to the previous one. Despite the presence of some top jazz players (trumpeter Randy Brecker, pianist Niels Lan Doky, tenorman Rick Margitza and drummer Billy Hart among them), there are no surprises and Norby's vocals lack any purpose or adventure. Skip. —*Scott Yanow*

● **My Corner of the Sky** / 1997 / Blue Note ♦♦♦

Danish singer Caecilie Norby's first recording to be released in the US is quite a mixed bag. At times, Norby comes across as Nancy Wilson, going over the top in places and not showing much subtlety; on Irving Berlin's classic "Suppertime," she does not seem to know what she is singing about, sounding quite upbeat about a lynching. Some other selections are poppish (including odd revivals of "The Look of Love" and "Spinning Wheel"), but there are places (such as on "Just One of Those Things" and Wayne Shorter's "African Fairytale") where Norby shows potential as a jazz singer. She is assisted by a strong cast of Americans and Scandinavians (including pianists Dave Kikoski and Joey Calderazzo, keyboardist Lars Jansson, drummer Terri Lyne Carrington, trumpeter Randy Brecker and, on "Spinning Wheel," tenor saxophonist Michael Brecker), but Caecilie Norby's more significant work probably lies in the future. —*Scott Yanow*

Walter Norris

b. Dec. 27, 1931, Little Rock, AR

Piano / Post-Bop

Walter Norris is a brilliant pianist, a virtuoso whose improvisations can be both very complex harmonically yet often remain melodic. He would be better-known in the US if he had not spent so much time in Germany. Norris worked with Howard Williams in Arkansas (1944-50) as a teenager, was in Houston with Jimmy Ford (1952-53), led his own trio in Las Vegas (1953-54) and then settled in Los Angeles. He was on quite a few sessions during the latter half of the 1950s, most notably with Jack Sheldon, Frank Rosolino and Herb Geller, in addition to Ornette Coleman's first record (1958); he did his best to fit into the latter setting, but (other than Paul Bley at the Hillcrest Club), it was the last time for decades that Coleman would use a pianist! Norris was the music director of the Playboy Club during 1963-70, and was with the Thad Jones/Mel Lewis Orchestra during 1974-76. After a stay in Scandinavia and a brief stint with Charles Mingus, Norris moved to Berlin in 1977 where he has taught and been performing ever since. In the 1990s Walter Norris visited the US several times, recording dates for Concord and displaying his impressive musical growth of the past 20 years. —*Scott Yanow*

Drifting / Aug. 1974-May 1978 / Enja ♦♦♦♦

A '92 reissue of an excellent mid-'70s session by pianist Walter Norris, whose few records are worth having. He's a slashing, more unorthodox player with both free and hard bop ties. His patterns, solos, and phrases aren't among the easiest to follow, but bassist George Mraz and drummer Aladar Page manage to find a comfort zone after some early problems. —*Ron Wynn*

Synchronicity / May 5, 1978 / Inner City ♦♦♦♦♦

Winter Rose / Jun. 18, 1980-Sep. 1980 / Enja ♦♦♦♦♦

Stepping on Cracks / Jul. 17, 1978 / Progressive ♦♦♦♦

A late '70s date with some energetic, if at times nearly chaotic, piano solos from Walter Norris. Norris blends blues, gospel, free, and hard bop elements in his playing, which is filled with crackling runs and unorthodox lines. He's backed by his favorite bassist, George Mraz, and drummer Ronnie Bedford. —*Ron Wynn*

Lush Life / 1990 / Concord Jazz ♦♦♦♦♦

Pianist Walter Norris has the knack for making the most overplayed standards sound fresh. By reharmonizing the chord structures and altering the melodies a bit, he was able to reinvent most of the repertoire on this CD, including a notable "new" version of the title cut. Parts of "My Foolish Heart" are so free as to be almost unrecognizable, and even "On Green Dolphin Street" sounds unusual while swinging hard. With fine support from bassist Neil Swainson and drummer Harold Jones, Walter Norris revitalizes the jazz mainstream with inventive explorations. —*Scott Yanow*

Live at Maybeck Recital Hall, Vol. 4 / Apr. 1990 / Concord Jazz ♦♦♦♦♦

A harmonically advanced and a consistently explorative player, Walter Norris' rhapsodic improvisations often replace the conventional chords of standards with more complex voicings and sometimes wander unpredictably. His 1990 solo set at Maybeck Recital Hall is a perfect place to begin exploring Walter Norris' music. Highlights include the pianist's "Scrambled" (which is a radical reworking of "I Got Rhythm"), "The Song Is You" and "Body and Soul." —*Scott Yanow*

● **Sunburst** / Aug. 13, 1991-Aug. 14, 1991 / Concord Jazz ♦♦♦♦♦

After struggling for years to get some exposure, when pianist Walter Norris made a critically acclaimed solo release for Concord, he was suddenly in demand. This date has the added bonus of superb tenor solos from the great Joe Henderson. He and Norris threaten but don't totally overwhelm bassist Larry Grenadier and drummer Mike Heyman. —*Ron Wynn*

Love Every Moment / Sep. 30, 1992-Oct. 1, 1992 / Concord Jazz ♦♦♦♦

Red Norvo (Kenneth Norville)

b. Mar. 31, 1908, Beardstown, IL

Vibes, Xylophone, Leader / Cool, Swing

Red Norvo was an unusual star during the swing era, playing jazz xylophone. After he switched to vibes in 1943 Norvo had a quieter yet no less fluent style than Lionel Hampton. Although no match for Hamp popularity-wise, Norvo and his wife, singer Mildred Bailey, did become known as Mr. and Mrs. Swing!

Red Norvo has had a long and interesting career. He started on marimba when he was 14 and soon switched to xylophone. Active in vaudeville in the late '20s as a tap dancer, Norvo joined Paul Whiteman's Orchestra in the early '30s (meeting and marrying Mildred Bailey). He recorded some extraordinary sides in the early to mid '30s that showed off his virtuosity and imagination; two numbers (the atmospheric "Dance of the Octopus" and "In a Mist") had Benny Goodman playing bass clarinet! Norvo led his own bands during 1936-44 which, with its Eddie Sauter arrangements (particularly in the early days), had a unique ensemble sound that made it possible for one to hear the leader's xylophone. In 1944 Norvo (who by then had switched permanently to vibes) broke up his band and joined Benny Goodman's Sextet. Through recordings and appearances, he showed that his style was quite adaptable and open to bop. Norvo welcomed Charlie Parker and Dizzy Gillespie to a 1945 record date, was part of Woody Herman's riotous first Herd in 1946 and recorded with Stan Hasselgård in 1948. At the beginning of the 1950s Norvo put together an unusual trio with guitarist Tal Farlow (later Jimmy Raney) and bassist Charles Mingus (later Red Mitchell). The light yet often speedy unisons and telepathic interplay by the musicians was quite memorable. Norvo led larger groups later in the decade, had reunions with Benny Goodman and made many fine recordings. The 1960s found Red Norvo adopting a lower profile after he had a serious ear operation in 1961. He worked with the Newport All-Stars later in the decade and from the mid-'70s to the mid-'80s was once again quite active, making several excellent recordings. However, his hearing eventually worsened and a serious stroke put Red Norvo out of action altogether after 55 years of music. —*Scott Yanow*

Red Norvo / Apr. 8, 1933-Jan. 18, 1957 / Time-Life ♦♦♦♦

Red Norvo had a lengthy and diverse career which is perfectly summed up in the 40 performances included on this three-LP Time/Life box set. This definitive set certainly covers a lot of ground (although it leaves off the music from Norvo's last 25 years on record), his brilliant xylophone showcase on 1933's "Knockin' on Wood" and his early all-star recordings through the small groups he led at the beginning of the swing era, Norvo's unique big band (which featured the vocals of his wife Mildred Bailey), all of the music from a particularly memorable Teddy Wilson quartet session (with Harry James and bassist John Simmons) through the war years, collaborations with the Benny Goodman Sextet and Woody Herman and his brilliant trios in the 1950s before concluding with 1957's "Just a Mood." Its attractive booklet is another reason to acquire this valuable set, even by listeners who already have the majority of the recordings. —*Scott Yanow*

★ **Dance of the Octopus** / Apr. 18, 1933-Mar. 16, 1936 / Hep ✦✦✦✦✦

The first 26 selections that xylophonist Red Norvo ever led are on this essential (and generous) CD. Among the many illustrious sidemen are future bandleaders Benny Goodman (heard on bass clarinet during memorable versions of "In a Mist" and "Dance of the Octopus"), Jimmy Dorsey, Artie Shaw, Jack Jenney, Charlie Barnet and Bunny Berigan, in addition to Chu Berry, Teddy Wilson and Gene Krupa. While the first half of the program features all-star groups, the later tracks are prime examples of small-group swing with arranger Eddie Sauter's mellophone, trumpeter Stew Pletcher and Herbie Haymer's tenor playing key roles. This readily available CD from the Scottish label Hep contains more than its share of classic performances and is essential. —*Scott Yanow*

Red Norvo and His Big Band Featuring Mildred Bailey / Aug. 1936-Mar. 1942 / Sounds of Swing ✦✦✦✦

This collector's LP contains 16 big-band performances from Red Norvo's impressive band, all but 1942's "Jersey Bounce" are from 1936-39. Mildred Bailey has five vocals and the sidemen include trumpeters Stew Pletcher and Jimmy Blake, clarinetist Hank D'Amico and tenors Herbie Haymer and Jerry Jerome. Since quite a few of these titles have not been reissued much since (a complete Red Norvo big-band series is needed on CD), this sampler is well worth picking up since it does contain some of the highlights of this often-overlooked band. —*Scott Yanow*

Red Norvo, Featuring Mildred Bailey / Mar. 22, 1937-Jul. 28, 1938 / Portrait ✦✦✦✦

This CD reissue by Columbia in their Legacy series is a bit of a hodgepodge, covering a two-and-a-half-year period in the bandleading career of xylophonist Red Norvo. Unfortunately the music is not programmed in chronological order, but since most of these largely enjoyable 18 titles (including two never previously released) have rarely been reissued, this sampler will have to do until a more "complete" session comes along. Norvo's band during this period not only featured the occasional vocals of his wife, Mildred Bailey, but fine solo work from the tenor of Herbie Haymer, clarinetist Hank D'Amico and trumpeter Stew Pletcher in addition to the leader. The biggest key in Norvo's orchestra achieving a sound of its own, however, were the distinctive and inventive arrangements of Eddie Sauter. This CD contains great music that deserves to be reissued more coherently. —*Scott Yanow*

Red Norvo and Mildred Bailey / 1938 / Circle ✦✦✦

This LP of radio transcriptions features Red Norvo's 1938 big band. The Eddie Sauter arrangements are consistently inventive and allow the orchestra to play quite quietly at times so its leader's xylophone could be heard not only as a solo instrument but in the ensembles. Mildred Bailey and Terry Allen contribute occasional vocals while the most impressive soloist next to Norvo is clarinetist Hank D'Amico. The band's distinctive sound and ability to swing hard at a light volume makes its music quite delightful and accessible. —*Scott Yanow*

Red Norvo Orchestra Live from the Blue Gardens / Jan. 4, 1942 / Music Masters ✦✦✦✦

Red Norvo's 1942 big band only recorded two songs and was otherwise completely undocumented. However, a tape of a radio broadcast was saved by trombonist Eddie Bert through the years and released on CD in 1992 by Music Masters. Although, other than Bert and singer Helen Ward, Norvo's sidemen are quite obscure, he had a very interesting band throughout this period; the largest he ever led. Norvo (who plays xylophone here but would switch permanently to vibraphone the next year) leads an orchestra comprising three trumpets, three trombones, five reeds (including Sam Spumberg who tripled on tenor, oboe and English horn), a standard rhythm section and up to four vocalists. With colorful arrangements provided by Johnny Thompson, Norvo and his quietly powerful crew perform a variety of standards from the era plus five originals by the leader. This appealing and rather historical set is easily recommended to swing collectors. —*Scott Yanow*

Red Norvo, Vol. 1: The Legendary V-Disc Masters / Oct. 28, 1943-May 17, 1944 / Vintage Jazz ✦✦✦✦

This CD from the VJC label features vibraphonist Red Norvo's V-disc sessions of 1943-44. Most of the music (which includes some breakdowns and alternate takes) finds Norvo leading an octet that includes trumpeter Dale Pearce, trombonist Dick Taylor, clarinetist Aaron Sachs and the tenor of Flip Phillips. Carol Bruce has three vocals and Helen Ward takes two, but the high points are instrumental versions of "1-2-3-4 Jump," "Seven Come Eleven" and "Flyin' Home." The last three titles (from 1944) feature Norvo leading a quintet with clarinetist Aaron Sachs. Overall, this CD contains plenty of fine examples of late swing, just before the influence of bop began to be felt on the principal's styles. Recommended to fans of the era. —*Scott Yanow*

Legendary Trio, Vol. 2: The Norvo-Mingus-Farlow Trio / Oct. 28, 1943-1950 / Vintage Jazz ✦✦✦✦✦

With the exception of two titles and an alternate take featuring singer Helen Ward that were left over from Red Norvo's five-disc sessions of 1943 (which were otherwise reissued in full on Vol. 1), this CD comprises 30 concise performances by Red Norvo's brilliant 1949-50 trio which, in addition to the vibraphonist/leader, also includes guitarist Tal Farlow and bassist Charles Mingus. These radio transcriptions (which do not duplicate the group's studio recordings) contain melodic but often speedy versions of standards. The near-telepathic communication between the three brilliant players and the very appealing sound of the group make this an easily-recommended disc for lovers of straightahead jazz and vibes. —*Scott Yanow*

Improvisations on Keynote / Jul. 27, 1944-Oct. 10, 1944 / Mercury ✦✦✦

As nice a cross-section of mid '40s Norvo cuts as is available. It was culled from the massive Keynote box. —*Ron Wynn*

Time in His Hands / May 28, 1945-Aug. 22, 1945 / Xanadu ✦✦✦

Three of vibraphonist Red Norvo's more obscure studio sessions are released in full on this excellent Xanadu LP. A dozen of the selections (taken from two dates) feature Norvo with the great singing bassist Slam Stewart, pianist Johnny Guarnieri (who does a funny Fats Waller vocal imitation on "Honeysuckle Rose"), drummer Morey Feld and either Bill DeArango or Chuck Wayne on guitar. The quintet performances show the influence of bop while remaining essentially advanced swing. The remaining four numbers find Norvo with a conventional rhythm section that welcomes baritonist Harry Carney, Charlie Ventura on tenor and both Johnny Bothwell and Otto Hardwick on altos. Very much a spontaneous session, these Duke Ellington-flavored performances are also quite enjoyable. —*Scott Yanow*

Fabulous Jam Session / Jun. 6, 1945 / Stash ✦✦✦✦✦

This is a famous recording session that deserves the very complete treatment it receives on this CD from the Stash label. On June 6, 1945, vibraphonist Red Norvo and an all-star swing rhythm section (comprising pianist Teddy Wilson, bassist Slam Stewart and either Specs Powell or J.C. Heard on drums) joined jump tenor Flip Phillips and the two great bop innovators, altoist Charlie Parker and trumpeter Dizzy Gillespie. This mixture of swing and bop stylists recorded four songs ("Hallelujah," "Get Happy," "Slam Slam Blues" and "Congo Blues"), and those recordings and eight alternate takes are included on this exciting album. The performances point out the evolutionary (as opposed to revolutionary) nature of bop from swing, but also its differences. It is fascinating to hear and rewards repeated listenings. —*Scott Yanow*

Norvo / May 29, 1947-Dec. 18, 1947 / Pausa ✦✦✦✦✦

This Pausa LP, which contains recordings originally issued by Capitol, features Red Norvo in several very interesting settings. The first three selections have the vibraphonist with an all-star group that includes altoist Benny Carter, trumpeter Charlie Shavers and his old boss Benny Goodman. The band was dubbed the Hollywood Hucksters. In addition to two straightforward performances, Benny Goodman and Stan Kenton have hilarious vocals on "Happy Blues." Norvo also performs with a variety of notable players, including tenors Jimmy Giuffre and Dexter Gordon (on a very memorable version of "I'll Follow You" and "Bop") and with Benny Carter and tenor Eddie Miller on two other songs. A special event occurs when Norvo switches back to the xylophone (his original instrument) for six selections that utilize oboe, flute, French horns, bass clarinet and bassoon. Their version of "Twelfth Street Rag" is somewhat unique. Worth searching for. —*Scott Yanow*

☆ **Red Norvo Trio with Tal Farlow and Charles Mingus at the Savoy** / May 3, 1950-Apr. 13, 1951 / Savoy ✦✦✦✦✦

Although vibraphonist Red Norvo had been on records for nearly 20 years and had been a pacesetter in both swing and bop, it was when he formed his trio with guitarist Tal Farlow and bassist Charles Mingus in 1950 that he found the perfect setting for his vibes. The interplay between the three masterful musicians on the 25 performances included on this Savoy double-LP (issued by Arista in 1976) is quite memorable with many classic performances. Highlights include "Little White Lies," "Swedish Pastry," "Godchild," "Move" and "Deed I Do," among many others. This two-fer is highly recommended particularly since Savoy has not yet released all of the music on CD. —*Scott Yanow*

The Red Norvo Trios / Sep. 1953-Oct. 1955 / Prestige ✦✦✦✦✦

Although the most famous of Red Norvo's vibes/guitar/bass trios featured guitarist Tal Farlow and bassist Charles Mingus, he continued the appealing format for a few years after his sidemen departed. This CD features Norvo with guitarist Jimmy Raney and bassist Red Mitchell on 15 enjoyable performances from 1953-54 and is rounded off by four songs from 1955 when Farlow rejoined Norvo and Mitchell. —*Scott Yanow*

With Jimmy Raney and Red Mitchell / Mar. 1954 / Original Jazz Classics ◆◆◆◆
This CD reissues an album by the 1954 version of the Red Norvo Trio which consists of vibraphonist Red Norvo, guitarist Jimmy Raney and bassist Red Mitchell. Although not quite reaching the heights of the earlier version with Tal Farlow and Charles Mingus, the close interplay between the musicians on cool-toned bop versions of such songs as "Just One of Those Things," "Crazy Rhythm" and "Bernie's Tune" is consistently hard-swinging yet light, adventurous yet accessible. An enjoyable set. —*Scott Yanow*

● **Just a Mood** / Sep. 17, 1954-Jan. 18, 1957 / Bluebird ◆◆◆◆◆
Vibraphonist Red Norvo was among the most flexible of improvisers from his generation. On this Bluebird CD, Norvo is heard with three very different groups. He interacts with trumpeter Harry "Sweets" Edison, tenor saxophonist Ben Webster and pianist Jimmy Rowles in a swing-oriented sextet; their performances are highlighted by the memorable "Just a Mood." In addition, Norvo plays four songs that have the word "Blue" in their titles with a quintet that is an outgrowth of his trio of a few years earlier (this group consists of flutist Buddy Collette, guitarist Tal Farlow, Monty Budwig or Red Callender on bass and drummer Chico Hamilton) and four "Rose" songs with the who's who of West Coast Jazz: trumpeter Shorty Rogers, clarinetist Jimmy Giuffre, pianist Pete Jolly, Farlow, Callender and drummer Larry Bunker. No matter what the setting, Norvo fits in quite comfortably and the consistent high quality of the formerly rare music makes this a highly recommended set to bop collectors. —*Scott Yanow*

Music to Listen to Red Norvo By / Jan. 26, 1957-Mar. 2, 1957 / Contemporary ◆◆◆
Although vibraphonist Red Norvo is the leader of this sextet date, clarinetist Bill Smith (who contributed the 20-minute four-movement "Divertimento") often sets the tone for the music. His work has classical elements to it, but the five shorter pieces (by Jack Montrose, Barney Kessel, Lennie Niehaus, Duane Tatro and Norvo) are much more jazz-oriented. Norvo's light-toned sextet (which consists of his vibes, flutist Buddy Collette, clarinetist Bill Smith, guitarist Barney Kessel, bassist Red Mitchell and drummer Shelly Manne) was not a regularly working unit, but it sounds well-integrated and tight during the complex, but generally swinging, music which has not yet been reissued on CD. —*Scott Yanow*

Hi Five / Jan. 29, 1957-Feb. 2, 1957 / RCA ◆◆◆
This is one of the most obscure Red Norvo LPs and this quintet (with the leader's vibes; Bob Drasnin on flute, clarinet and alto, guitarist Jimmy Wyble, bassist Bob Carter and drummer Bill Douglass) has been long-forgotten. However, their version of cool jazz (a little reminiscent of the Chico Hamilton Quintet in atmosphere) always swings and features plenty of subtle creativity and fine solos from the lead voices. Maybe someday RCA will get around to reissuing the music and rescuing it from their vaults. —*Scott Yanow*

Norvo...Naturally / May 2, 1957 / V.S.O.P. ◆◆◆◆
Originally released on the obscure Rave label and later reissued by V.S.O.P. on this LP, this enjoyable set from vibraphonist Red Norvo features his 1957 quintet: Bob Drasnin on flute and alto, guitarist Jimmy Wyble, bassist Buddy Clark and drummer Bill Douglass. The music is essentially cool-toned bop that swings hard but lightly—an excellent setting for Norvo's vibes. In addition to two of Red's originals ("Spiders' Web" and "Scorpion's Nest"), the band performs six superior (if somewhat overplayed) standards. The results make one wonder why Jimmy Wyble and Bob Drasnin never became much better known. —*Scott Yanow*

The Forward Look / Dec. 31, 1957 / Reference ◆◆◆◆
The music on this CD, taken from a New Year's Eve concert, had never been issued prior to the release of this CD by Reference in 1991. With Jerry Dodgion (mostly on alto and flute), guitarist Jimmy Wyble, bassist Red Wooten and drummer John Markham being his sidemen, this was a well-integrated group despite the lack of major names. Norvo's vibe playing was in its prime and he is in excellent form during a wide-ranging set that ranges from "My Funny Valentine" and "When You're Smiling" to Quincy Jones' "For Lena and Lennie" and "How's Your Mother in Law"; the repertoire includes quite a few obscurities. This surprisingly well-recorded CD is well worth picking up as an example of Red Norvo's playing in the latter half of the 1950s. —*Scott Yanow*

Windjammer City Style / 1958 / Dot ◆◆
This is a real historical curiosity. Vibraphonist Red Norvo and his augmented group perform nine songs from what was billed as a "history-making film" but is in reality a long-forgotten movie called *Windjammer*. The ensemble—consisting of Norvo's vibes; Jerry Dodgion on alto and flute; Marvin Koral switching between alto, flute and clarinet; guitarist Jimmy Wyble; pianist Bernie Nierow; bassist Red Wooten and drummer Karl Kiffe—uplifts the folkish melodies as best they can but fail to make any of them memorable. The LP, therefore, is of interest only to Red Norvo completists. —*Scott Yanow*

Red Norvo Quintet / 1962 / Studio West ◆◆◆◆
This CD, taken from radio transcriptions cut for the radio show "The Navy Swings," features vibraphonist Red Norvo's group in 1962, which by itself is rather notable, for Norvo made no other recordings as a leader from 1960-68. Red's quintet (which also includes guitarist Al Viola, pianist Jack Wilson, bassist Jimmy Bond and drummer Bill Goodwin) plays very much in the cool-toned but often heated style of his earlier trios. Mavis Rivers and Ella Mae Morse take a total of three vocals, but it is the 11 instrumentals (counting four alternate takes) that are particularly memorable, most notably "Spider's Web," "Lena and Lenny" and "Rhee, O, Rhee." —*Scott Yanow*

Swing That Music / Oct. 1969 / Affinity ◆◆◆◆

Vibes à la Red / 1974-1975 / Famous Door ◆◆◆

The Second Time Around / 1975 / Famous Door ◆◆◆◆
After making only one recording as a leader between 1960-73, vibraphonist Red Norvo cut three albums for Famous Door during 1975-77, launching a bit of a comeback. This LP, his second Famous Door release, is an excellent effort. The veteran vibraphonist plays seven veteran swing standards plus his own blues "A Long One for Santa Monica" with pianist Dave McKenna, bassist Milt Hinton, drummer Mousey Alexander and (on four of the seven numbers) Kenny Davern on soprano. These small-group swing performances (which some would call "mainstream") are quite enjoyable, but because the Famous Door label is obsolete, this LP will be difficult to find. —*Scott Yanow*

Red in New York / 1977 / Famous Door ◆◆◆◆
Red Norvo's third and final recording as a leader for the short-lived Famous Door label is most notable for being one of the earliest recordings of tenor saxophonist Scott Hamilton. In addition, vibraphonist Norvo was glad to once again have the services of his favorite pianist of the era, Dave McKenna, along with bassist Richard Davis and drummer Connie Kay. Together they perform seven swing standards, ranging from "Hindustan" and "All of Me" to "Undecided." Everyone plays up to par, and Red Norvo, 46 years after his recording debut, is still in his musical prime. This LP will be hard to find, but is worth the search. —*Scott Yanow*

Live at Rick's Cafe Americain / 1978 / Flying Fish ◆◆◆
This jam session was supposed to be led by violinist Joe Venuti, but his unexpected death led to vibraphonist Red Norvo (in view of his seniority) becoming the nominal leader. The all-star group (which also includes guitarist Buddy Tate on tenor, trombonist Urbie Green, pianist Dave McKenna, bassist Steve LaSpina and drummer Barrett Deems) plays loosely but coherently on lengthy versions of "On Green Dolphin Street," "Undecided" and "Just Friends" in addition to a more concise "Here's That Rainy Day" and a two-song ballad medley. Nothing all that historic occurs, but there are many fine solos from the principals during these informal jams. —*Scott Yanow*

Red and Ross / Jan. 1979 / Concord Jazz ◆◆◆◆◆
Vibraphonist Red Norvo, 48 years after his first recording, sounds in fine form on this live set with pianist Ross Tompkins, bassist John Williams and drummer Jake Hanna. Tompkins, who takes the opening "Whisper Not" as his feature, fits in well with the masterful vibist and their two-chorus duets in the middle of "The One I Love" and "All of Me" (during which the bass and drums drop out) are the high points of a spirited and consistently swinging session. —*Scott Yanow*

Just Friends / Aug. 8, 1983-Aug. 9, 1983 / Stash ◆◆◆◆
For what would be one of vibraphonist Red Norvo's final recordings (his recording debut was in 1931, 52 years earlier), Norvo teams up quite effectively with guitarist Buck Pizzarelli (an old friend), pianist Russ Kassoff and bassist Jerry Bruno. The seven standards plus John Pizzarelli's "Blues for Red" make for a well-rounded session, balancing ballads such as "My Old Flame" and "I Thought About You" with stomps including "Just Friends" and "Sweet Georgia Brown." Although serious hearing problems and a major stroke would soon end Red Norvo's career, this fine record serves as proof that the great vibraphonist never did decline before his forced retirement. —*Scott Yanow*

Sam Noto

b. Apr. 17, 1930, Buffalo, NY
Trumpet, Fluegelhorn / Bop

An excellent bop soloist, Sam Noto's late-'70s recordings for Xanadu briefly gave him a high profile in the US. Best-known in his early days as a big-band player, Noto was with Stan Kenton (1955-58), Louie Bellson (1959), back with Kenton (1960) and twice with Count Basie during 1964-67. He spent much of 1969-75 working in Las Vegas where he became acquainted with Red Rodney. Rodney used Noto on a 1974 recording, and although he moved to Toronto in 1975 (where he worked in the studios and regularly with Rob McConnell's Boss Brass into the early '80s), Noto gained some fame for his many recordings with Xanadu.

Although appearing on records less often since then, Sam Noto remains quite active in Toronto. —*Scott Yanow*

● **Entrance!** / Mar. 1975 / Xanadu ✦✦✦✦✦
An excellent trumpeter who had long been overlooked, Sam Noto finally at age 44 had an opportunity to lead his own record date in 1975. In fact, he would head four sessions for Xanadu during a three-year period, all of which are easily recommended, although not yet available on CD. This set is of particular interest, because Noto is the only horn in a quartet also featuring pianist Barry Harris, bassist Leroy Vinnegar and drummer Lenny McBrowne. Mixing a few originals with standards, Noto's performance is pure bebop, with the highlights including "Fats Flats," "Entrance" and "Nostalgia." —*Scott Yanow*

Act One / Dec. 1, 1975 / Xanadu ✦✦✦✦
For his second of four Xanadu dates as a leader, the excellent bop trumpeter Sam Noto meets up with his old friend Joe Romano (who sticks here to tenor), pianist Barry Harris, bassist Sam Jones and drummer Billy Higgins. They perform five of Noto's originals, some of which are based on the chord changes of familiar standards, and a beautiful three-song ballad medley. All of the musicians play up to par, making one wish that Noto's Xanadu sets would be reissued on CDs. —*Scott Yanow*

Notes to You / May 18, 1977 / Xanadu ✦✦✦✦
With such tunes as "Quasinoto" and "Cross Chris," one might think that Sam Noto's third Xanadu date was filled with standards, but actually, "'Round Midnight" is the only one of the six songs not composed by the trumpeter. The boppish music finds Noto, tenor saxophonist Joe Romano, baritonist Ronnie Cuber, pianist Jimmy Rowles, bassist Sam Jones and drummer Freddie Waits in excellent form, jamming effortlessly over the sometimes complex chord changes. A fine outing not yet available on CD. —*Scott Yanow*

Noto-Riety / Oct. 17, 1978 / Xanadu ✦✦✦✦✦
The Canadian trumpeter Sam Noto and flutist Sam Most make for a surprisingly effective blend during this enjoyable straightahead date. Noto contributed all six selections and they cover a variety of tempos and grooves in the bebop tradition. With a rhythm section of pianist Dolo Coker, bassist Monty Budwig and drummer Frank Butler, the music can be guaranteed to always swing. —*Scott Yanow*

2-4-5 / Nov. 2, 1986-Jun. 12, 1987 / Unisson ✦✦✦✦
Sam Noto, who was born in Buffalo, has spent much of the past 20 years based in Toronto, Canada. This was his first date as a leader for a Canadian label, and it has more than its share of variety. The excellent bop trumpeter takes three very effective duets with bassist Neil Swainson ("Beautiful Love," "Easy Living" and Bud Powell's "Dance of the Infidels") and is featured on his "Blue Haze" and "I Remember Clifford" with a fine quartet (pianist Gary Williamson, bassist Steve Wallace and drummer Bob McLaren); he also welcomes tenor saxophonist Pat La Barbera. —*Scott Yanow*

to four quintet numbers (a pair of originals plus a song apiece by Charlie Parker and Sonny Stitt). Noto is heard throughout in superior form, making one wonder why he has not led more record dates through the years. Recommended. —*Scott Yanow*

Adam Nussbaum

b. Nov. 29, 1955, New York, NY
Drums / Post-Bop
A very versatile drummer who generally plays in advanced settings, Adam Nussbaum is considered a major asset no matter where he appears, and, one of the finest jazz drummers of the 1990s. Although he started on piano, bass and alto, he eventually settled on drums. Nussbaum studied at the Davis Center and City College of New York, and by 1978 was making a strong impression in the jazz world, playing regularly with both Dave Liebman and John Scofield (1978-83). Other important associations through the years include Stan Getz (1982-83), Gil Evans, the George Gruntz Concert Jazz Band, Gary Burton, Steve Swallow, Michael Brecker, Don Grolnick, Sonny Rollins, Art Pepper, Joe Henderson, John Abercrombie, Sheila Jordan, Lee Konitz and Eddie Daniels, along with countless others. —*Scott Yanow*

NuYorican Soul

f. 1996
House, Acid Jazz
Better known as the dance production team Masters at Work, Kenny "Dope" Gonzalez and Lil' Louis Vega became NuYorican Soul for an EP in 1996 and an eponymous full-length one year later. Much like Guru's jazz-rap fusion project *Jazzmatazz*, *NuYorican Soul* united jazz legends with newer talents in a celebration of jazz, R&B and dance, with most tracks including Latin styles befitting the heritage of Gonzalez and Vega. —*John Bush*

NuYorican Soul / 1997 / Giant Step/Blue Thumb ✦✦✦✦
All-star albums are usually dodgy affairs, but the combined talents—and more importantly, production experience—of Masters at Work proves to keep *NuYorican Soul* from being overburdened with cooks. Roy Ayers, George Benson and Jazzy Jeff contribute prominently to four tracks, and vocalists Jocelyn Brown and India are heard as well, but over half of the album comprises of instrumental tracks—several which include Tito Puente on vibes and timbales, flutist Dave Valentin, trumpeter Charlie Sepulveda, organist/arranger Hilton Ruiz and trombonist Steve Turre. In keeping with Masters at Work's heritage, most of the album is Latin in feel and jazzy in composition, but with ever-present synths and piano runs that belie their heavy dance heritage. If *NuYorican Soul* is one of the best all-star dance albums to date, it is for lack of competition. —*John Bush*

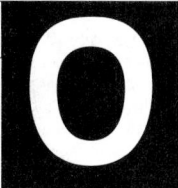

Jimmy O'Bryant

b. 1896, Arkansas, **d.** Jun. 24, 1928, Chicago, IL
Clarinet / Classic Jazz, Blues

Of all the clarinetists in the 1920s, Jimmy O' Bryant probably came closest to duplicating the sound (if not the genius) of Johnny Dodds. O' Bryant worked with the Tennessee Ten (1920-21), in a group co-led by Jelly Roll Morton and W.C. Handy (1923) and briefly with King Oliver (1924), but he is best remembered for his recordings with Lovie Austin's Blues Serenaders and his own Washboard Band; all of the latter have been reissued on two RST CDs. Jimmy O'Bryant's early death robbed him of any chance of gaining lasting fame but his fine (if sometimes primitively recorded) performances as a leader give one a good idea as to his abilities. —*Scott Yanow*

Jimmy O'Bryant (Vol. 2) & Vance Dixon (1923-1931) / Oct. 3, 1923-Jun. 12, 1931 / RST ♦♦♦♦

The second of two Jimmy O'Bryant CDs released by the Austrian RST label features the early and long-obscure clarinetist (who sometimes sounded a bit like Johnny Dodds) on the last nine recordings made by his ironically titled "Famous Original Washboard Band." These trio performances feature O'Bryant, pianist Jimmy Blythe and either Jasper Taylor or W.E. Buddy Burton on washboard; Burton plays effective banjo on "Sugar Babe" and other highlights include "Milenberg Joys," "My Man Rocks Me" and "Shake That Thing." The latter half of this set has recordings by clarinetist and altoist Vance Dixon (who makes O'Bryant seem famous in comparison) with Deppe's Serenaders in 1923 ("Congaine" also features pianist Earl Hines), in duos and trios from 1926-27, backing blues singer Hattie McDaniels (the future actress) on two numbers in 1929 and leading his own group on four novelties from 1931 (including "Laughing Stomp"). Although not as essential as the more significant 1920s recordings, this CD (along with *Jimmy O'Bryant—Vol. 1*) is certainly worth exploring by fans of the era. —*Scott Yanow*

● **Vol. 1 (1924-1925)** / Nov. 1924-Jul. 1925 / RST ♦♦♦♦

On the first of two CDs released by the Austrian RST label, clarinetist Jimmy O'Bryant, a long-forgotten, but talented, player who died in 1928, is featured with his ironically titled "Famous Original Washboard Band" (a trio/quartet with pianist Jimmy Blythe, Jasper Taylor on washboard and guest cornetist Bob Shoffner) on 19 selections. In addition, O'Bryant and Blythe accompany singer Sodarisa Miller during two songs and O'Bryant, cornetist Tommy Ladnier and pianist Lovie Austin assist blues singer Julia Davis on two others. O'Bryant, who in his best moments sounds close to the great Johnny Dodds, was not a major soloist although he might have grown into a stronger talent were it not for his premature death. The primitive recording quality of these early performances may put some off, but O'Bryant plays quite well and many of his originals have not been revived and are worth investigating. 1920s jazz fans will want this CD along with the second volume. —*Scott Yanow*

Anita O'Day (Anita Belle Colton)

b. Oct. 18, 1919, Kansas City, MO
Vocals / Bop, Swing, Traditional Pop

One of the finest singers to emerge from the swing era, Anita O'Day at her prime was a masterful scat singer and a true improviser whose interpretations of standards uplifted and altered even the most familiar songs. After struggling through dance marathons and discovering that she could sing, O'Day picked up valuable experience performing with Max Miller's group in Chicago. Her big break was hooking up with the Gene Krupa Orchestra. During her two years with the drummer's big band (1941-43), O'Day had hits in "Let Me Off Uptown," "Thanks for the Boogie Ride," and "Bolero at the Savoy." She was with Stan Kenton for a year (1944-45), scoring with "And Her Tears Flowed like Wine." When she decided that Kenton's progressive jazz did not suit her, she recommended June Christy as her successor; Christy, Chris Connor and Helen Merrill would all spend the early parts of their careers trying to emulate O'Day.

After a period back with Krupa (during which she recorded popular versions of "Opus No. 1" and "Boogie Blues"), O'Day went out on her own. She recorded for Signature in 1947 and London in 1950 but did not appear on records on a regular basis until she began her association with Verve in 1952. The singer's finest recordings were for Verve during 1952-63, both with big bands and small groups. Very open to the innovations of bebop, O'Day was one of the top singers of the decade, captured at the peak of her powers at the 1958 Newport Jazz Festival in the film *Jazz on a Summer's Day* during which she performed memorable renditions of "Sweet Georgia Brown" and a scat-filled "Tea for Two." She also appeared briefly in *The Gene Krupa Story*. However, heroin addiction (which she fully outlined in her 1981 memoirs *High Times Hard Times*) took its toll and after 1963 O'Day's life was quite erratic. In 1970 she made a strong comeback at the Berlin Jazz Festival and by the mid-'70s was recording regularly for her Emily label. Anita O'Day's voice has gradually deteriorated through the years, particularly after the mid-'80s, but her prime recordings from the 1950s are quite enjoyable and rank with the best of the era. —*Scott Yanow*

Hi Ho Trailus Boot Whip / 1947 / Flying Dutchman ♦♦♦♦

The music on this LP has been circulating on Bob Thiele's various labels for decades. Comprising the first ten selections recorded by Anita O'Day as a leader, these diverse selections find O'Day (when she was 27) singing in several different settings. Two songs (including the atmospheric "Ace in the Hole") are performed with Alvy West's Little Band (a sextet including an accordion player) while the other eight numbers (highlighted by the eccentric title cut, a multi-tempoed "What Is This Thing Called Love" and "How High the Moon") have the singer joined by larger orchestras arranged by either Sy Oliver or Ralph Burns. Highly enjoyable music. —*Scott Yanow*

Anita O'Day 1949-1950 / Sep. 11, 1949-Dec. 27, 1950 / Tono ♦♦♦

This is an interesting LP for it has 15 formerly rare Anita O'Day recordings from 1949-50, material originally cut for the Gem and London labels (prior to her signing with Verve). O'Day, who was 29 and 30 during this period, handles the wide variety of songs (ranging from bop and dated novelties to a calypso and "Tennessee Waltz") with humor and swing, mostly uplifting the occasionally indifferent material. Most of the musicians in the four backup bands are obscure or not featured but there are short spots for guitarist George Barnes and trombonist Will Bradley. Although not essential, this LP is a must for Anita O'Day collectors. —*Scott Yanow*

● **Verve Jazz Masters 49** / 1952-1963 / Polygram ♦♦♦♦♦

This is an excellent one-disc roundup of Anita O'Day's output for Clef, Norgan and Verve—arguably her most important, most experimental period—and it is especially valuable because Anita and her manager Alan Eichler made the selections themselves. It was during this decade of activity that O'Day made the transition from a spent former big-band thrush to an acclaimed jazz diva, despite the turmoil in her personal life and her feeling that she was playing second-fiddle to Ella in Norman Granz' recording stable. The selection is remarkably wide-ranging, sampling from twelve of O'Day's sixteen albums for Granz and his successor at Verve, Creed Taylor, with lots of loosely swinging mid- and uptempo numbers and ballads that can be alternately world-wise and innocent. Among the many highlights that illustrate the diversity of O'Day's Verve period are "No Soap, No Hope Blues," from O'Day's first rare ten-inch album for Granz; her saucy remake of "Boogie Blues" with the innovative Gary McFarland orchestra; and the sexy, swaggering title track of "Waiter, Make Mine Blues." Anyone seeking an entryway into the tough yet vulnerable song world of Anita O'Day will get a lot of helpful direction from this album. —*Richard S. Ginell*

Anita O'Day Swings Cole Porter with Billy May / Jan. 22, 1952-Aug. 17, 1960 / Verve ♦♦♦♦

Most of this CD reissue is taken from sessions in April 1959 on which Anita O'Day interprets Cole Porter songs while accompanied by some rather rambunctious big-band arrangements from Billy May. While her emotional range is wider than Ella Fitzgerald's (who had previously recorded her much better-known *Cole*

Porter Songbook), strangely enough O'Day's voice does not sound as strong on the Billy May set as it does on the six "bonus" cuts which are Cole Porter songs she recorded on other occasions (from 1952-60). Still this CD does have its moments with highlights including "I Get a Kick out of You," "All of You," "It's Delovely," "You're the Top" and two versions of "Love for Sale." — *Scott Yanow*

An Evening with Anita O'Day / Apr. 15, 1954-Aug. 11, 1955 / Verve ✦✦✦✦
A combination of three sessions with three different small backing groups available currently on a Japanese CD—this is an early revealing example of Anita O'Day's growth as a jazz artist since her days as a big band thrush. Her virtuosity at fast tempos is right on the dot, and she is fearlessly willing to take wide-open liberties with the melodies. The tune of "The Man I Love," for instance, is completely taken apart and personalized; you wouldn't even recognize it were it not for the words. O'Day also shows us her vulnerable side in a remarkable on-the-edge performance of "You Don't Know What Love Is," and she gives listeners a rare taste of her songwriting in "Anita's Blues." Barney Kessel and Tal Farlow sit in on guitar on four tracks apiece; the other four are with piano trio. Low-key, modestly produced, this is best heard as directed—in the evening. — *Richard S. Ginell*

Anita / Dec. 6, 1955-Dec. 8, 1955 / Verve ✦✦✦✦✦
This CD is a straight reissue of the original LP with singer Anita O'Day heard in prime form. Accompanied by an orchestra conducted and arranged by Buddy Bregman, O'Day is heard near the peak of her powers on such songs as "You're the Top," "Honeysuckle Rose," an emotional rendition of "A Nightingale Sang in Berkeley Square" and "As Long as I Live." One of her better recordings, this CD is recommended. — *Scott Yanow*

Pick Yourself Up with Anita O'Day / Dec. 15, 1956+Dec. 17, 1956 / Verve ✦✦✦✦✦
For this well-rounded CD reissue that adds nine cuts to the original program, Anita O'Day, in her prime period, is mostly heard accompanied by Buddy Bregman's Orchestra, but there are also a few tracks on which she is joined by a jazz combo featuring trumpeter Harry "Sweets" Edison. Highlights include "Don't Be That Way," "Stompin' at the Savoy," "Pick Yourself Up," "Sweet Georgia Brown" and "I Won't Dance." Virtually all of Anita O'Day's 1950s recordings are recommended—for her drug use had not yet affected her voice and her creativity was generally at its height. — *Scott Yanow*

★ **Anita Sings the Most** / Jan. 31, 1957 / Verve ✦✦✦✦✦
Anita O'Day recorded many rewarding albums in the 1950s when her voice was at its strongest, and this collaboration with the Oscar Peterson Quartet (comprising pianist Peterson, guitarist Herb Ellis, bassist Ray Brown and drummer John Poole) may very well be her best. Not only is the backup swinging, giving a *Jazz at the Philharmonic* feel to some of the songs, but O'Day proves that she could keep up with Peterson. "Them There Eyes" is taken successfully at a ridiculously fast tempo, yet the singer displays a great deal of warmth on such ballads as "We'll Be Together Again" and "Bewitched, Bothered and Bewildered." While Peterson and Ellis have some solos, O'Day is never overshadowed (which is saying a lot) and is clearly inspired by their presence. The very brief playing time (just 33 minutes) is unfortunate on this straight CD reissue of the original LP, but the high quality definitely makes up for the lack of quantity. A gem. — *Scott Yanow*

Anita O'Day Sings the Winners / Apr. 2, 1958-Apr. 3, 1958 / Verve ✦✦✦✦✦
For this CD, which is greatly expanded from the original LP, Anita O'Day sings standards associated with other musicians, including "Four" (Miles Davis), "Early Autumn" (Stan Getz), "Four Brothers" (Woody Herman), "Sing, Sing, Sing" (Benny Goodman and Gene Krupa) and "Peanut Vendor" (Stan Kenton). Some of the material is unusual for a singer to interpret, but O'Day, one of the top jazz vocalists of the decade, improvises when the lyrics are not that strong (or barely exist). The backup by the Russ Garcia Orchestra is not all that memorable, but the focus is entirely on the vocalist, and O'Day really comes through. — *Scott Yanow*

Anita O'Day at Mr. Kelly's / Apr. 27, 1958 / Verve ✦✦✦✦✦
Caught live with just her piano trio at Chicago's famous now-defunct nightclub, Anita O'Day is in an ebullient mood as she tosses off a series of standards and novelties. Whether this is an accurate snapshot of her live act is open to question; the stage business in between numbers seems rather formal and one doesn't really feel the excitement of a live performance. Yet O'Day is clearly in a creative mood, whether allowing her vulnerability to show in the torchy ballads or reveling in the boppish uptempo workouts. Her vocal on "Tea For Two" is a virtuoso deconstruction, full of satiric quotes and rhythmic shifts at a warp-speed tempo. Fleet-fingered Joe Masters decorates the fills with assorted bop runs on the slightly-out-of-tune house piano. — *Richard S. Ginell*

Cool Heat / Jul. 1959 / Verve ✦✦✦✦✦
This LP, which ought to be reissued on CD, finds Anita O'Day's swinging singing backed by cool-toned arrangements from Jimmy Giuffre. Although the orchestra is surprisingly anonymous, the ensembles fit O'Day's voice well on tunes such as

"Mack the Knife," "Gone with the Wind," "Come Rain or Come Shine," "The Way You Look Tonight" and even "Hooray for Hollywood." All of O'Day's recordings for Verve in the 1950s are recommended, and this out-of-print set is no exception. — *Scott Yanow*

Trav'lin' Light / Jan. 18, 1961-Jan. 19, 1961 / Verve ✦✦✦✦✦
A tribute to Anita O'Day's idol Billie Holiday—who had died less than two years before the making of this LP—O'Day's performances here are more notable for what she didn't borrow from her vocal role model. Selections like the title track finds her generating a slightly bitter tone quality and languorous phrasing in the manner of Holiday, but most of this beautiful record finds O'Day going her own way in a more forthright, less vulnerable manner. While O'Day's version of "God Bless the Child" doesn't really make it, just about everything else is marvelous. Half of the tracks feature a small group led by guitarist Barney Kessel while the other half—the more effective tracks, actually—feature now-exuberant, now-exquisite arrangements for big band by Johnny Mandel that make haunting use of muted brass at ballad tempos. This was O'Day's favorite among her Norgran/Verve albums. — *Richard S. Ginell*

All the Sad Young Men / Oct. 16, 1961 / Verve ✦✦✦✦✦
When Creed Taylor took over the production reins from Norman Granz when the latter sold Verve to MGM, he continued to place Anita O'Day in imaginative settings that challenged her creativity. On this LP, she was served with a collection of brilliant, difficult big band charts, courtesy of a 27-year old emerging master named Gary McFarland who mixed instrumental voices and tempo changes in querulous, turbulent combinations. Even a truly odd pick like "You Came a Long Way from St. Louis" is enlivened with sprouting shafts of outlaw muted brass and reeds. Another highlight is the contemporary update of O'Day's old flagwaver with the Krupa band, "Boogie Blues," complete with one of her patented flip upturned glissandos at the end. This album must have been a traumatic experience for O'Day, for as she tells the story, the tapes of McFarland's arrangements arrived by mail from New York and she had to overdub her vocals in an empty studio in Los Angeles. Yet is a tribute to O'Day's abilities that she makes it all sound easy, exhibiting a freedom in phrasing and improvising that is extraordinary even for her. — *Richard S. Ginell*

Time for Two / Feb. 26, 1962-Feb. 28, 1962 / Verve ✦✦✦✦✦
In another experiment, producer Creed Taylor teams O'Day with the alternately Latin and bop-grounded quartet of vibraphonist Cal Tjader—and he gets some amazing performances from this team. O'Day sounds as if she is delighted with Tjader's polished Afro-Cuban grooves, gliding easily over the rhythms, toying with the tunes, transforming even a tune so locked into its trite time as "Mr. Sandman" into a stimulating excursion. Indeed, O'Day's freewheeling phrasing becomes downright sexy on "That's Your Red Wagon" and Dave Frishberg's delicious parody of a spoiled honeybunch, "Peel Me a Grape." Also, thanks to Taylor's obsession with good engineering and tasteful applications of reverb, O'Day's voice sounds much fuller and more attractive in his productions than on her Norman Granz-produced albums. — *Richard S. Ginell*

☆ **Anita O'Day and the Three Sounds** / Oct. 12, 1962-Oct. 15, 1962 / Verve ✦✦✦✦✦
Once Upon a Summertime / Jun. 1963-Mar. 19, 1976 / Glendale ✦✦✦
This LP is definitely a transitional one for Anita O'Day. Four of the dozen performances are taken from June 1963. Her trio joins the singer on four of her "hits" ("Sweet Georgia Brown," "Boogie Blues," "Tea for Two" and "A Nightingale Sang in Berkeley Square"), which were O'Day's final recordings until 1970 due to personal problems. The remainder of this set is from 1975-76, with several trios backing O'Day on a repertoire dominated by swing standards. Although her voice was not as young, O'Day was still in good form at that point, making this album a worthwhile acquisition for her fans. — *Scott Yanow*

Recorded Live at the Berlin Jazz Festival / Nov. 7, 1970 / MPS ✦✦✦
Singer Anita O'Day's first recording in seven years finds her still possessing a decent voice at 50 and the ability to swing and improvise creatively. Backed by pianist George Arvanitas, bassist Jacky Samson and drummer Charles Saudrais, O'Day is at her best on "Honeysuckle Rose," a medley of "Yesterday" and "Yesterdays," and "Street of Dreams," although some of the more recent material (her own "Soon It's Gonna Rain" and "Sunny") is of lesser interest. — *Scott Yanow*

I Get a Kick Out of You / Apr. 25, 1975 / Evidence ✦✦✦✦
At 55 Anita O'Day was having a bit of a renaissance, having kicked drugs and become more active in the 1970s. This live in Japan set (reissued on CD by Evidence) finds the singer stretching out on nine numbers ("Gone with the Wind" is nearly 11 minutes long) and carefully choosing a tune or two from each of six decades (1920s to the '70s). Of the latter "What Are You Doing the Rest of Your Life" and Leon Russell's "A Song for You" (given a definitive treatment) are effective; other highlights include "Undecided," "I Get a Kick out of You" and "Opus One." This is one of O'Day's best recordings of the 1970s. — *Scott Yanow*

My Ship / Jun. 30, 1975 / Emily ♦♦♦

One in a string of six albums that jazz vocalist Anita O'Day made while performing in Japan during the mid-'70s. These were done as she was returning to the stage after a bout with drugs and alcohol. This was also issued on her own label. —*Ron Wynn*

Anita O'Day Live / Sep. 1976 / Star Line ♦♦♦♦♦

Anita O'Day is heard in excellent form on this 1976 concert, released for the first time in 1993. Highlights of this CD include a version of "Tea for Two" that finds O'Day trading one-bar phrases with three of her sidemen, a touching rendition of "A Nightingale Sang in Berkeley Square," a jubilant rendering of "Honeysuckle Rose," and versions of "A Song for You" and "You Are the Sunshine of My Life" that actually top the original recordings. In addition, the late tenor Fraser MacPherson proves to be a perfect foil for O'Day's chance-taking vocal flights. With the exception of pianist Al Wold having trouble with the rapid tempo of "S'Wonderful," the rhythm section also plays quite well. This is one of the best Anita O'Day CDs available. —*Scott Yanow*

Live at Mingo's / Oct. 22, 1976 / Emily ♦♦♦

A solid album by vocalist Anita O'Day that was done in the mid-'70s, but was initially only available in Japan. She subsequently released it on her own label, but it' has still not seen widespread distribution and may be tough to find. Her voice was once again in vivid, expressive form after her successful battle with drug and alcohol problems. —*Ron Wynn*

Mello Day / 1978 / GNP Crescendo ♦♦♦

For this studio set, Anita O'Day performs with the Lou Levy trio and guests Ernie Watts on reeds, percussionist Paulinho Da Costa and either Laurindo Almeido or Joe Diorio on guitar. She mostly sticks to fresher material, some of it of more recent vintage than usual. High points include "Lost in the Stars," "You're My Everything," "Them There Eyes," "Limehouse Blues" and several bossa nova pieces. This LP, although not essential, is worth picking up. —*Scott Yanow*

Angel Eyes / 1978-1979 / Emily ♦♦♦

An outstanding set featuring recordings done by vocalist Anita O'Day in Japan between 1975 and 1978. They're standards and ballads, well-known and obscure, and show that she had come all the way back as a vocalist, overcoming a battle with alcohol and other drugs that sidelined her during the '60s. —*Ron Wynn*

Anita O'Day, Live at the City / Sep. 29, 1979-Sep. 30, 1979 / Emily ♦♦

This LP documents a typical live performance by Anita O'Day, who was 59 at the time. Although there is some good music (her renditions of Johnny Mandel's "Hershey Bar," "Emily" and "Four Brothers"), there is also a lot of loose chit-chat and filler. Although Nat Hentoff raves about O'Day's performance, this hard-to-find LP, which also features pianist Norman Simmons, bassist Rob Fisher, drummer John Poole and Greg Smith on baritone and flute, is a historical curiosity rather than an essential acquisition. —*Scott Yanow*

A Song for You / 1984 / Emily ♦♦♦

Good, but not definitive, mid-'80s Anita O'Day material. The songs are well-chosen, but neither her treatments nor the backing arrangements and production match the classic albums from the '50s or even her comeback work in the '70s. —*Ron Wynn*

In a Mellow Tone / Mar. 13, 1989-Mar. 15, 1989 / DRG ♦♦♦

It is extremely difficult for a vocalist to hide his or her age while singing. Anita O'Day, 69 at the time of this recording, no longer sounded like she had in 1959, but this was actually her best all-around set in several years. O'Day still retained her highly appealing phrasing and most of her range; she still took chances (her version of "I Cried for You" is a good example), and she sounded happy to be alive, having beaten the odds. Gordon Brisker's creative arrangements for the backup group (which consists of his tenor and flute, pianist Pete Jolly, bassist Brian Bromberg, drummer Frank Capp, percussionist Dave Black, and on a few songs the harp of Corky Hale) allow room for plenty of concise solos. On "Anita's Blues," one can almost feel the years dropping away as O'Day hints at her recordings from the 1940s. This fine CD is definitive of Anita O'Day's later years and worth investigating. —*Scott Yanow*

At Vine St.: Live / Aug. 2, 1991-Aug. 3, 1991 / DRG ♦♦

At age 71, Anita O'Day was way past her prime when she performed this live date at the now-defunct Vine St. club. The songs had all been recorded earlier by O'Day in versions more rewarding than these, although she tries her best. Gordon Brisker on tenor and flute leads the backing quintet, which also includes pianist Pete Jolly and does what it can to hold O'Day up. At least she didn't feel compelled to record "Let Me Off Uptown" this late in her career. —*Scott Yanow*

Rules of the Road / 1993 / Pablo ♦

This CD should not have been released. Anita O'Day at age 73 had no voice left. Although the backup group (a big band led by Jack Sheldon) is excellent and the arrangements by Buddy Bregman (with the exception of a corny interpretation of

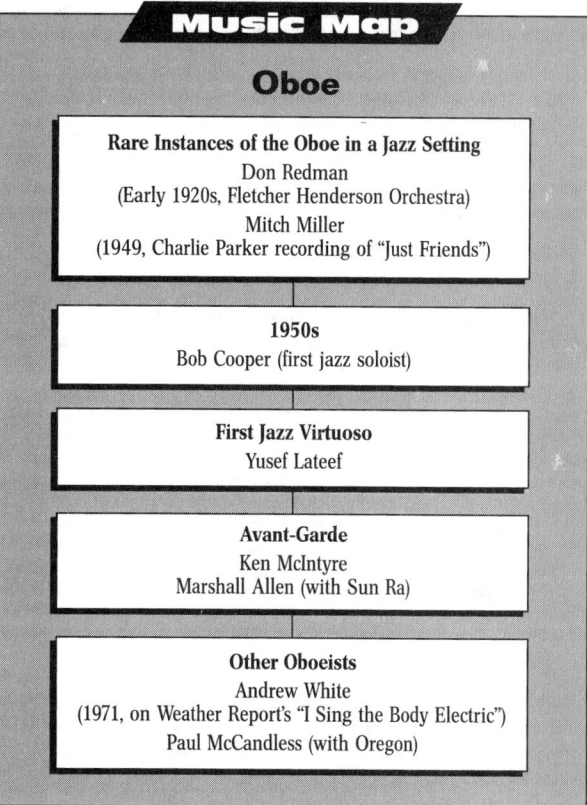

"Shaking the Blues Away") are fine, but the ambitious program is sunk by O'Day's wavering voice which is out of tune more often than not. Jack Sheldon's trumpet solos (and participation in a vocal with O'Day on "I Told Ya I Love Ya, Now Get Out") are the only highlights of this unfortunate effort. —*Scott Yanow*

Chico O'Farrill (Arturo O'Farrill)

b. Oct. 28, 1921, Havana, Cuba
Arranger / Bop, Latin Jazz, Afro-Cuban Jazz

Chico O'Farrill was right in the thick of the Afro-Cuban and Latin waves that hit jazz in the late '40s and '50s. His sophisticated writing for Latin big bands of the early '50s was often bold, brassy and tense, yet he could also achieve a delicate, almost classical ambience in such pieces as "Angels' Flight," and work capably in larger forms (the groundbreaking *Afro-Cuban Jazz Suites*).

O'Farrill took up the trumpet while in military school in Georgia, returning to Cuba as a full-fledged jazz fan after hearing the top American big bands. He studied composition in his native Havana and led his own band there before moving to New York City in 1948, where he soon made a name for himself writing music for Benny Goodman ("Undercurrent Blues"), Stan Kenton ("Cuban Episode") and Machito (*Afro-Cuban Jazz Suite*). From 1951 to 1954, O'Farrill made six fiery 10-inch albums of Latin and American big band jazz for Clef and Norgran, all of which have been reissued on a Verve 2-CD set, *Cuban Blues*. He also appeared with his own band at Birdland and toured the US. Toward the end of the decade, he moved to Mexico City, returning to New York in 1965 to work as arranger and music director of the TV series "Festival of the Lively Arts" and to write arrangements for Count Basie. Though he continued to write pieces for Machito, Kenton, Gato Barbieri and Dizzy Gillespie into the '70s, there were no recording sessions under O'Farrill's name from 1966 until 1995, when he came roaring back on the scene, his imagination and vigor miraculously intact, with the outstanding *Pure Emotion* CD (Milestone). O'Farrill has also put his classical training to use by writing pieces for symphony orchestra like *Three Cuban Dances* and *Symphony No. 1*. —*Richard S. Ginell*

● **Cuban Blues: Chico O'Farrill Sessions** / Dec. 21, 1950-Apr. 16, 1954 / Verve ♦♦♦♦♦

For any and all Latin jazz collectors, casual or serious, this is a fabulous deal, gathering together no less than six exceedingly rare Chico O'Farrill Clef and Norgran

10-inch albums, plus one under Machito's name, on a slimline two-CD set. It will also come as a revelation to anyone who might scoff at anything associated with the 1950s mambo craze, for these discs reveal O'Farrill as a sophisticated, even daring arranger/composer who reached beyond merely providing a beat for dancers. Many of these charts—whether for the brief, dance-oriented Latin numbers, ultra-familiar standards such as "Malaguena" and "The Peanut Vendor," or jazz tunes—are loaded with intricate figures and striking harmonies obviously gleaned from classical study, all crisply executed with a brash, shiny edge by his Afro-Cuban groups and bands staffed by American jazzmen. Occasionally, he even conjures a delicate, classical ambience from a number like "Angels' Flight" (named after Los Angeles' legendary downtown funicular). The apotheosis of O'Farrill's experiments are his two full-blown, groundbreaking *Afro-Cuban Jazz Suites*. The first features Flip Phillips and the redoubtable Charlie Parker as soloists within the Machito band, and the second is even bolder in its zigzag journey through the classical, Latin and jazz camps. Yet for all of his erudition, O'Farrill never forgets to ask for madly percolating Afro-Cuban grooves from his rhythm teams—which clinches the deal for any Latin music fan. —*Richard S. Ginell*

Nine Flags / Nov. 10, 1966-Nov. 14, 1966 / Impulse! ✦✦✦
One of arranger Chico O'Farrill's few jazz recordings of the 1954-94 period, this LP pays tribute to nine different countries, which were represented at the time by Nine Flags fragrances. The ten pieces (which include "The Lady from Nine Flags") have originals influenced by the music of Brazil, England, France, Germany, Hong Kong, Ireland, Italy, Spain and Sweden. The overall music is quite different from O'Farrill's usual Afro-Cuban jazz outings. He features three different groups ranging from a septet to a 15-piece orchestra, assigning solo space to such fine players as trombonist J.J. Johnson, fluegelhornists Art Farmer and Clark Terry and guitarist Larry Coryell (one of his earliest recordings). None of the individual songs caught on, and the interpretations are usually quite concise, but this LP (which has not yet been reissued) is generally quite fun. —*Scott Yanow*

Pure Emotion / Feb. 1995 / Milestone ✦✦✦✦✦
After not having led a recording session under his own name in 29 years, O'Farrill came from seemingly out of nowhere to lead a terrific Afro-Cuban big band date on this CD. O'Farrill claims that he turned down offers to lead standard seven- or eight-piece salsa bands on records over the years, preferring to wait until a big band opportunity came along—and clearly, he was bursting with accumulated charts dating from the 1960s through the 1990s. Not too much has changed since O'Farrill's exciting string of albums for Clef in the 1950s; if anything, his arranging hand has become surer, more sophisticated, thoroughly in touch with a wide variety of influences. Most striking of all is how O'Farrill was able to build a fire underneath the musicians in the band, which includes leaders in their own right like trombonist Robin Eubanks, conguero Jerry Gonzalez and drummer Steve Berrios, as well as Tito Puente's tenor sax/flute player Mario Rivera and O'Farrill's son, Arturo Jr., on piano. The most ambitious track is also the most entertaining one, an extended 1964 O'Farrill composition called "Variations on a Well-Known Theme" ("La Cucaracha"!) that deftly welds together various big band idioms, near-parodies of Muzak and television writing, and Afro-Cuban percussion workouts. Latin jazz fans will be pulverized and delighted by this recording. —*Richard S. Ginell*

Tiger Okoshi (Toru Okoshi)

b. Mar. 21, 1950, Ashita, Japan
Trumpet / Fusion, Hard Bop
Tiger Okoshi is a versatile trumpeter who has played both fusion and fairly straightahead jazz. A resident of the US since 1972, Okoshi first gained attention playing with Gary Burton; he also had a stint with George Russell's Living Time Orchestra in the early '90s and recorded with Bob Moses. Okoshi has recorded regularly as a leader for JVC including an unusual Louis Armstrong tribute album, *Echoes of a Note*, on which he drastically modernized some Dixieland standards. —*Scott Yanow*

Tiger's Baku / Nov. 1980-Apr. 1981 / JVC ✦✦✦✦

Face to Face / 1989 / JVC ✦✦✦

That Was Then, This Is Now / Aug. 1990 / JVC ✦✦✦
Fusion, funk, some mainstream, and light bop are the ingredients for this recent release by Japanese trumpeter Tiger Okoshi. He plays in a high-note, piercing style similar to Terusima Hino, but lacks his harmonic command. The arrangements, production, and mastering are fine, as would be expected. —*Ron Wynn*

Echoes of a Note (A Tribute to Louis "Pops" Armstrong) / Mar. 14, 1993+Mar. 16, 1993 / JVC ✦✦✦

● **Two Sides to Every Story** / Jun. 21, 1994-Jun. 22, 1994 / JVC ✦✦✦✦✦
This set is a rare straightahead outing for trumpeter Tiger Okoshi. Some of the post-bop music is reminiscent of the mid-'60s Miles Davis Quintet although Oko-

shi (who does hint at Davis here and there) is also influenced by Kenny Dorham and Freddie Hubbard. The rhythm section of pianist Gil Goldstein, bassist Dave Holland and drummer Jack DeJohnette is quite strong (swinging but advanced) and guitarist Mike Stern is more restrained than usual. Together the group blends together well and Okoshi (on two standards and a variety of originals) is in excellent form. —*Scott Yanow*

Old and New Dreams

f. 1976, **db.** 1987
Group / Post-Bop, Free Jazz, Avant-Garde
A virtual reincarnation of Ornette Coleman's first ensembles, the cooperative Old and New Dreams brought together trumpeter Don Cherry, tenor saxophonist Dewey Redman, bassist Charlie Haden, and drummer Ed Blackwell to reinterpret the master's early repertoire. By the time of their first album in 1978, ECM's *Old and New Dreams*, all four musicians were leaders with their own projects; this perhaps explains the intermittent nature of their ensuing collaboration (three albums in ten years). The quality of the group's recordings was uniformly high; the two ECM albums benefit from that label's characteristic clarity of sound. With the deaths of Cherry and Blackwell in the '90s, further collaborations of course became impossible. However, the band's limited yet superb output is an important complement to the work they did under Coleman's leadership in the late '50s and early '60s. —*Chris Kelsey*

Old and New Dreams [1] / Oct. 1976 / Black Saint ✦✦✦✦✦
A wonderful album that qualifies as an Ornette Coleman repertory release. Trumpeter Don Cherry, tenor saxophonist Dewey Redman, bassist Charlie Haden, and drummer Ed Blackwell all played with Coleman extensively, and they take his compositions and brilliantly put their own twists on them. —*Ron Wynn*

● **Old and New Dreams [2]** / Aug. 1979 / ECM ✦✦✦✦
The second recording by Old and New Dreams was, like its first from three years earlier, named after the group. Trumpeter Don Cherry, tenor saxophonist Dewey Redman, bassist Charlie Haden and drummer Ed Blackwell made for a mighty team, performing high-quality free bop in the tradition of the Ornette Coleman Quartet (of which they were all alumni). In addition to two of Ornette's tunes (including a lengthy exploration of "Lonely Woman") and an original of their own. Stirring music in a setting that always brought out the best in each of these musicians. —*Scott Yanow*

Playing / Jun. 1980 / ECM ✦✦✦
This Austrian concert CD features the four notable Ornette Coleman alumni (trumpeter Don Cherry, tenor saxophonist Dewey Redman, bassist Charlie Haden and drummer Ed Blackwell) stretching out on three of Ornette's tunes, plus a song apiece from Cherry, Redman and Haden. Although Cherry's chops were not quite in peak form anymore, Redman is consistently stirring. Recommended, as are Old and New Dreams' other three releases. —*Scott Yanow*

One for Blackwell / Nov. 7, 1987 / Black Saint ✦✦✦✦
In Nov. 1987, a three-concert Ed Blackwell Festival was held in Atlanta, Georgia. The festival served as a good excuse to reunite the members of Old and New Dreams (trumpeter Don Cherry, tenor saxophonist Dewey Redman, bassist Charlie Haden and drummer Blackwell), a quartet comprising Ornette Coleman alumni. The unit interprets three rarely-performed Ornette Coleman compositions and a tune apiece by Blackwell and Redman. All of the musicians are in top form on this no-changes music, creating fresh and intuitive melodies with both freedom and hints of the tradition. —*Scott Yanow*

Sy Oliver (Melvin James Oliver)

b. Dec. 17, 1910, Battle Creek, MI, **d.** May 28, 1988, New York, NY
Arranger, Trumpet, Vocals / Swing
Sy Oliver's melodic yet sophisticated arrangements helped define the Jimmy Lunceford sound in the 1930s and modernized Tommy Dorsey's band in the '40s. A fine trumpeter (excellent with a mute) and a likable vocalist, Oliver made his recording debut with Zack Whyte's Chocolate Beau Brummels in the late '20s and also worked with Alphonse Trent. Joining Lunceford in 1933, Oliver was responsible for such memorable charts as "My Blue Heaven," "Ain't She Sweet," "Organ Grinder's Swing," and "'Tain't What You Do" among many. It was a major blow to Lunceford when Oliver jumped at the chance to make a lot more money arranging and occasionally singing for Tommy Dorsey. The hiring of Sy Oliver was a major help for Tommy Dorsey in getting Buddy Rich to join his band. Oliver's arrangement of "On the Sunny Side of the Street" was his biggest hit for Dorsey. After a brief attempt at leading his own orchestra in 1946, Oliver became a freelance arranger and producer for the remainder of his long career. As late as 1975-80 he was regularly leading a band but Sy Oliver will always be best-known for his classic Lunceford charts. —*Scott Yanow*

● **Oliver's Twist & Easy Walker** / Jul. 7, 1960+Oct. 18, 1962 / Mobile Fidelity ◆◆◆◆
During the 1950s and '60s, arranger Sy Oliver's groups reflected its leader's loyalty to the swing era and lack of interest in newer jazz styles. This audiophile CD from Mobile Fidelity reissues two rare Oliver albums that were originally recorded as radio transcriptions. The 24 concise performances range from folk melodies such as "Oh, Them Golden Slippers," "I'm a Little Teapot" and "Arkansas Traveler" to swing compositions. Trumpeter Charlie Shavers is the star of the earlier set while the tenor of Budd Johnson takes honors on the second session. Overall the music is a bit lightweight but enjoyable enough. —*Scott Yanow*

Johnny O'Neal

b. Oct. 10, 1956, Detroit, MI
Piano / Post-Bop, Soul-Jazz
A fine pianist influenced by Oscar Peterson, Johnny O'Neal actually started his career playing gospel piano in church while a teenager. Inspired by Peterson, Art Tatum and Bud Powell, O'Neal started exploring jazz in 1976, impressed Ray Brown, and through Brown's recommendation joined Milt Jackson's group. Other important jobs followed (with Sonny Stitt, Eddie "Lockjaw" Davis and Buddy DeFranco), and in 1982, O'Neal moved to New York and soon recorded his debut with Concord. After playing regularly with Clark Terry, he was a member of Art Blakey's Jazz Messengers (1982-83) and has mostly led his own groups ever since. Johnny O'Neal has recorded as a leader for Concord, Parkwood and Justin Time (1995), taking three effective vocals on the latter set. —*Scott Yanow*

● **Coming Out** / 1983 / Concord Jazz ◆◆◆◆◆
Johnny O'Neal was 26 when he recorded this set, his recording debut as a leader. Since bassist Ray Brown had helped encourage him, it was only right that the pianist asked Brown to join his trio (which also includes drummer Frank Severino) for the album. O'Neal, a member of the Jazz Messengers at the time, often sounds close to Oscar Peterson (his main influence) on a fine program whose highlights include "It Could Happen to You," "Sometimes I'm Happy" and Brown's "Devastation Blues." Even the trio's version of "Just the Way You Are" comes across well on this straightahead set. —*Scott Yanow*

Live at Baker's Keyboard Lounge / Jul. 13, 1985 / Parkwood ◆◆◆◆◆
For the second time in a little over three months, pianist Johnny O'Neal recorded an album for Parkwood with bassist Dave Young and drummer Terry Clarke. The live set has plenty of spirit, with O'Neal exploring standards ranging from Wayne Shorter's "Fe Fi Fo Fum" and Blue Mitchell's catchy "Fuji Momma" to Cedar Walton's "Ugetsu" and "The Battle Hymn of the Republic." A fine outing well deserving of being reissued on CD. —*Scott Yanow*

Soulful Swinging / May 1985 / Parkwood ◆◆◆◆◆
Pianist Johnny O'Neal, a native of Detroit, teams up with Canadian bassist Dave Young and (on four of the seven numbers) drummer Terry Clarke during a well-rounded set. Although largely self-taught, O'Neal often sounds a bit like his idol Oscar Peterson. Highlights of the continually swinging trio set include a nine-minute version of "You're Looking At Me," "Night Mist Blues" and "Ain't Misbehavin'." This small-label release (which has not yet reappeared on CD) is O'Neal's definitive recording to date. —*Scott Yanow*

On the Montreal Scene / Oct. 10, 1995 / Justin Time ◆◆◆◆◆
Pianist Johnny O'Neal displays several sides to his musical personality on this CD. On some tunes, particularly the uptempo romps, he sounds very influenced by Oscar Peterson, yet he also has his own brand of soul, which comes to the forefront on the ballads. During two numbers ("While the Blood Is Running Warm" and, most logically, "Come Sunday"), O'Neal comes across as a top-notch gospel pianist. His forceful and sincere vocalizing on three songs is an acquired taste, but O'Neal is effective on the closing blues. The straightahead music, which sometimes co-stars guitarist Russell Malone, has several surprises, including what may be the only instrumental version ever of the Gene Krupa-Anita O'Day hit "Let Me Off Uptown," a somber "Happy Days Are Here Again," and a colorful interpretation of "Come Sunday." Well worth checking out. —*Scott Yanow*

Junko Onishi

b. Apr. 16, 1967, Kyoto, Japan
Piano / Post-Bop
With the release of her 1993 Blue Note debut *Cruisin'*, pianist Junko Onishi has arrived as one of the most promising of Japan-born jazz musicians. Growing up in Tokyo, Onishi received classical piano lessons but became quite interested in jazz. She studied at Berklee and after three years she moved to New York. Already a well-developed player, Onishi worked with Joe Henderson, Betty Carter, Kenny Garrett and Mingus Dynasty before recording her debut as a leader. She considers her style to be based on Duke Ellington, Thelonious Monk and Ornette Coleman. —*Scott Yanow*

Cruisin' / Apr. 21, 1993-Apr. 22, 1993 / Blue Note ◆◆◆◆◆
On her debut, pianist Junko Onishi (who is accompanied by bassist Rodney Whitaker and drummer Billy Higgins) shows a great deal of creativity. She builds up her "Eulogia" gradually and colorfully with impressive use of the piano's lower register. When she tackles Ornette Coleman's "Congeniality," Onishi manages to be both free and melodic and the pianist also comes up with something fresh to say on "Caravan." In general her tricky frameworks, self-restraint, use of space and careful attention to dynamics and pacing are impressive and show quite a bit of maturity. —*Scott Yanow*

● **Live at the Village Vanguard** / May 6, 1994-May 8, 1994 / Blue Note ◆◆◆◆◆
This is a memorable set. When pianist Junko Onishi performs songs from the likes of Charles Mingus ("So Long Eric"), John Lewis ("Concorde") and Ornette Coleman ("Congeniality"), she interprets each of the tunes as much as possible within the intent and style of its composer. "So Long Eric," although performed by her trio, gives one the impression at times that several horns are soloing together. Polyrhythms are utilized part of the time; Ornette's "Congeniality" has a strong pulse but fairly free improvising, while "Concorde" sounds both distinguished and full of blues feeling, like John Lewis himself. Onishi's exploration of "Blue Skies" uplifts the warhorse through the use of colorful vamps and an altered melody, she takes the slow ballad "Darn That Dream" as a medium-tempo stomp and her original "How Long Has This Been Goin' On" is brooding but not downbeat and swings hard without losing its serious nature. There is not a weak selection in the bunch and the interplay between Onishi, bassist Reginald Veal and drummer Herlin Riley is quite impressive. —*Scott Yanow*

Piano Quintet Suite / Jul. 7, 1995-Jul. 11, 1995 / Blue Note ◆◆◆◆
Pianist Junko Onishi's CD has the feel of a Charles Mingus date, a condition helped out by the inclusion of two Mingus tunes, Billy Strayhorn's "Take the 'A' Train" (here attributed mistakenly to Duke Ellington) and the episodic "Piano Quintet Suite." Onishi is a strong pianist who retains tight control over her colorful sidemen yet gives them freedom within the structures before reining them in. Trumpeter Marcus Belgrave (a Mingus alumnus) excels in this setting and takes a surprise vocal on "Take the 'A' Train" (to an extent imitating Ray Nance imitating Betty Roche) while Japanese altoist Elichi Hayashi hints at but does not directly copy Jackie McLean. Bassist Rodney Whitaker really swings, drummer Tony Rabeson is excellent in support and two of the high points are a fresh new version of "Orange Was the Color of Her Dress" and "Naturally" which is based on "Lullaby of Birdland." This spirited music is easily recommended. —*Scott Yanow*

Oregon

f. 1970
Group / Post-Bop, Folk-Jazz
One of the earliest and finest exponents of world jazz, Oregon began life in 1970 as an offshoot of the Paul Winter Consort, in which the group's original members had played. From the beginning, the band eschewed most jazz conventions. Percussionist Collin Walcott played tabla, sitar, and dulcimer, among other instruments, but did not use a trap set; bassist Glen Moore doubled on clarinet, viola, and piano; and its front line was formed by a double-reedist (Paul McCandless) and an acoustic guitarist (Ralph Towner). The band's music differed from much of what had heretofore been considered jazz. The concept of blues and swing was given a much-reduced prominence in favor of other, less literal forms of tonal and rhythmic organization. For example, Indian ragas would occasionally replace chord changes, and talas would supplant swing time. The group's dynamic approach was quieter than typical by jazz standards, and their overall aesthetic somewhat introspective. Improvisation was central to the band's work, however, and in this sense their music is rooted most firmly in the jazz tradition. Oregon's music is characterized by a heightened method of ensemble interaction, a rapt attention to timbral contrast, and an openness to any and all cultural influences. After Walcott's death in a car accident in 1984, the group disbanded for a time, before eventually replacing him with the percussionist Trilok Gurtu. —*Chris Kelsey*

Our First Record / 1970 / Vanguard ◆◆◆◆◆
The acoustic band Oregon shocked and surprised the jazz world when they debuted in 1970. They blended many influences and styles easily, but also had an ambitious improvisational bent that made them tough to characterize. This in many ways remains their most intriguing release. —*Ron Wynn*

Music of Another Present Era / 1972 / Vanguard ◆◆◆◆◆

Distant Hills / Jul. 2, 1973-Jul. 5, 1973 / Vanguard ◆◆◆◆◆

Crossing / 1973-Oct. 1984 / ECM ◆◆◆

Winter Light / Jul. 16, 1974-Aug. 7, 1974 / Vanguard ◆◆◆◆◆

In Concert / Apr. 8, 1975-Apr. 9, 1975 / Vanguard ◆◆◆◆

Together / Jan. 1976 / Vanguard ✦✦✦✦

Violin / 1977 / Vanguard ✦✦✦✦✦

Out of the Woods / Apr. 1978 / Discovery ✦✦✦✦

● **Roots in the Sky** / April 1979 / Discovery ✦✦✦✦✦
A '92 CD reissue of their '79 album, among their only releases ever issued by a major label. It was characteristically free-wheeling and eclectic, with long stretches of classical, Asian, African, and jazz coming together, and the group mixing structured ensemble work with surging free solos. —*Ron Wynn*

Moon and Mind / 1978 / Vanguard ✦✦✦✦

Oregon in Performance / Nov. 29, 1979-Nov. 30, 1979 / Elektra ✦✦✦✦

Oregon / Feb. 1983 / ECM ✦✦✦✦✦

Ecotopia / Mar. 1987 / ECM ✦✦✦
New percussionist Trilok Gurtu makes an impact within the group. —*Ron Wynn*

45th Parallel / 1988 / Portrait ✦✦✦✦
Oregon bothers jazz people because a) they're difficult to categorize, and b) they radiate endlessly cheerful vibes bordering on vacuous new age while maintaining a sharp improvisational edge. So goes this high-profile appearance on Columbia's spinoff label, which sometimes stays within the bounds of post-bop jazz yet is more likely to go veering off in contemplative folk-like, Asiatic, Spanish, or even neo-classical directions. Ralph Towner handles both the piano and various guitars and synthesizers with equal facility, while Paul McCandless' reed work evokes the pure white light of Paul Winter; Glen Moore continues to man the bass; Trilok Gurtu alternates between tabla and traps; and Nancy King checks in with a bout of eccentric scatting on "Chihuahua Dreams." This is intriguing, free-thinking stuff, always intelligent, evidently durable, yet the music misses the spark of true inspiration that could have made it memorable. —*Richard S. Ginell*

Always, Never and Forever / 1992 / Intuition ✦✦✦✦

Northwest Passage / Sep. 1996-Oct. 1996 / Intuition ✦✦✦✦

Original Dixieland Jazz Band

f. 1917, **db.** 1923
Group / Classic Jazz
The first jazz group to ever record, the Original Dixieland Jazz Band in 1917 made history. They were not the first group to ever play jazz (Buddy Bolden had preceded them by 22 years!), nor was this White quintet necessarily the best band of the time, but during 1917-23 (particularly in their earliest years) they did a great deal to popularize jazz. The musicians learned about jazz from their fellow New Orleans players (including King Oliver), but happened to get their big break first. In 1916 drummer Johnny Stein, cornetist Nick LaRocca, trombonist Eddie Edwards, pianist Henry Ragas and clarinetist Alcide "Yellow" Nunez played together in Chicago. With Tony Sbarbaro replacing Stein and Larry Shields taking over for Nunez, the band was booked at Resenweber's restaurant in New York in early 1917. Their exuberant music (which stuck exclusively to ensembles with the only solos being short breaks) caused a major sensation. Columbia recorded the ODJB playing "Darktown Strutters Ball" and "Indiana" but was afraid to put out the records. Victor stepped in and recorded the group playing the novelty "Livery Stable Blues" (which found the horns imitating barnyard animals) and the "Dixie Jass Band One Step" and quickly released the music; "Livery Stable Blues" was a huge hit that really launched the jazz age. During the next few years the ODJB would introduce such future standards as "Tiger Rag," "At the Jazz Band Ball," "Fidgety Feet," "Sensation," "Clarinet Marmalade," "Margie," "Jazz Me Blues" and "Royal Garden Blues." The group (with J. Russel Robinson taking the place of Ragas who died in the 1919 flu epidemic and trombonist Emile Christian filling in for Edwards) visited London during 1919-20 and they once again caused quite a stir, introducing jazz to Europe. However, upon their return to the US, the ODJB was considered a bit out of fashion after the rise of Paul Whiteman and in 1922 the New Orleans Rhythm Kings (a far superior group). By 1923 when many of the first Black jazz giants finally were recorded, the ODJB was thought of as a historical band and, due to internal dissension, they soon broke up. In 1936 LaRocca, Shields, Edwards, Robinson and Sbarbaro (the latter, the only musician to have a full-time career by then) had a reunion and did a few final recordings together before LaRocca permanently retired. Although the cornetist's arrogant claims that the ODJB had invented jazz are exaggerated and tinged with racism, the Original Dixieland Jazz Band did make a strong contribution to early jazz (most groups that recorded during 1918-21 emulated their style), helped supply the repertoire of many later Dixieland bands and were an influence on Bix Beiderbecke and Red Nichols. —*Scott Yanow*

1917/1923 / Jan. 30, 1917-Apr. 20, 1923 / Jazz Archives ✦✦✦✦
This French import CD has 24 titles by the Original Dixieland Jazz Band, partly duplicating some other sets (including the Bluebird release) but also includes a

few real rarities. Among the latter are versions of "Darktown Strutters Ball" and "Indiana" that rank as the very first jazz records ever made; the liner notes claim that these are from a slightly later remake session (May 31, 1917) but logic and the esteemed discographer Brian Rust place them at January 30. Also quite rare are the four titles ("Some of These Days," "Toddlin' Blues," "Tiger Rag" and "Barnyard Blues") from the ODJB's final recording sessions in 1922-23 before their breakup and the group's 1917 Aeolian recordings which are joined by highlights from their better-known output for Victor. Fascinating early music by easily the best group on records during 1917-21. —*Scott Yanow*

Sensation! / Feb. 26, 1917-Nov. 24, 1920 / ASV/Living Era ✦✦✦✦
This set reissues 18 of The Original Dixieland Jazz Band's recordings. A cross-section of their output (rather than a complete set), the release starts off with their hit version of "Livery Stable Blues," includes such classics as "Tiger Rag" and "Sensation," reissues some of the superior performances that were cut in London during 1919-1920 including "I've Lost My Heart in Dixieland," and concludes with "Margie." It's a fine introduction to this pioneering jazz band. —*Scott Yanow*

★ **75th Anniversary** / Feb. 26, 1917-Jun. 7, 1921 / Bluebird ✦✦✦✦
The Original Dixieland Jazz Band was the first jazz group to record. Although their two earliest titles for Columbia ("Darktown Strutters Ball" and "Indiana") have not been reissued in a long time. All of The ODJB's output for Victor (including "Livery Stable Blues" which was the first jazz recording to ever be released) is on this definitive CD. This colorful group, which stuck exclusively to ensembles with no solos, introduced such standard tunes as "Original Dixieland One Step," "At the Jazz Band," "Fidgety Feet," "Sensation," "Clarinet Marmalade," "Margie," "Jazz Me Blues," "Royal Garden Blues" and "Tiger Rag," all of which are included on this release. It's an essential acquisition for any serious jazz library. —*Scott Yanow*

The Complete Original Dixieland Jazz Band / Feb. 26, 1917-Sep. 25, 1936 / RCA ✦✦✦✦✦
This double-CD has all of the Victor recordings of the first jazz group to record, the Original Dixieland Jazz Band. The five-piece New Orleans band, which essentially stuck exclusively to ensembles, set the standard for 1917-21 jazz. Their "Livery Stable Blues" (which found the horns imitating barnyard animals) was a big hit and the ODJB introduced such future Dixieland standards as "Original Dixieland Onestep," "At the Jazz Band Ball," "Fidgety Feet," "Sensation," "Clarinet Marmalade," "Jazz Me Blues," "Royal Garden Blues" and "Tiger Rag." The 23 numbers from 1917-21, which are rounded out by the humorous "Bow Wow Blues (My Mama Treats Me like a Dog)" were reissued in a single CD by Bluebird. This twofer also has the ODJB's "comeback" recordings of 1936. Six titles are by the original five plus eight very rare titles which find the ODJB forming the nucleus of a musical if not too distinctive big band. Important historical music. —*Scott Yanow*

Original Dixieland Jazz Band / Louisiana Five / Aug. 17, 1917-Mar. 1919 / Retrieval ✦✦✦
This English LP has the seven selections that the Original Dixieland Jazz Band cut for Aeolian in 1917 (which do not duplicate their recordings during the same period for Victor) and the first eight sides by the Louisiana Five from 1918-19. The ODJB titles are excellent, particularly these versions of "Barnyard Blues" (a remake of "Livery Stable Blues"), "Tiger Rag" and "Look at 'Em Doing It Now." However, the Louisiana Five, a trumpetless quintet featuring clarinetist Alcide "Yellow" Nunez and trombonist Charles Panelli, is not at the same level and is quite primitive even for the period. The packaging by Retrieval is flawless but this music is primarily for specialists. —*Scott Yanow*

In England / Sep. 1917-Jan. 21, 1924 / EMI Pathe ✦✦✦✦✦
The original Dixieland Jazz Band's visit to England during 1919-20 caused a sensation and did much to help popularize and even "legitimize" jazz. More importantly for history, the ODJB cut some of their finest recordings while overseas. These very well-recorded documents (some of which are around four rather than three minutes long) feature the ODJB at their best. The performances still do not include any real solos (sticking exclusively to ensembles) but many of the melodies are quite strong. Of their 17 London recordings (all of which are on this CD), high points include "At the Jazz Band Ball," "Tiger Rag," "Tell Me," "I'm Forever Blowing," "Sensation, Bubbles" (one of the first jazz waltzes), "I've Lost My Heart in Dixieland" and "Alice Blue Gown." This CD is rounded out by five real obscurities from English bands cut between 1917-24. Spirited as they are, those groups demonstrate that the ODJB were really the pacesetters for the era. —*Scott Yanow*

1943 / Dec. 3, 1943 / GHB ✦✦✦✦
After a brief comeback the year before, the Original Dixieland Jazz Band was finished by 1937 with cornetist Nick LaRocca's retirement. However, in 1943 multi-instrumentalist Brad Gowans, who had extensively studied their music, gathered together some of the ODJB alumni (trombonist Eddie Daniels, drummer Tony Sbarbaro and one of their later pianists Frank Signorelli) to revisit the old reper-

toire and frameworks. Gowans, who sticks here to clarinet (coming up with a fairly good imitation of Larry Shields' style), enlisted cornetist Wild Bill Davison who, although he does his best to recreate LaRocca's style, sounds rather restrained as he tries to hide his own extroverted musical personality. The quintet is featured on this LP on a set of radio transcriptions and everything is here (including alternate takes and false starts); ten fine performances resulted from this interesting experiment. —*Scott Yanow*

Original Dixieland Jazz in Hi-Fi / Oct. 3, 1957 / Paramount ✦✦✦
Around 1956-57 trumpeter Don Fowler and clarinetist George Phillips, two musicians from the Pacific Northwest, recreated the Original Dixieland Jazz Band on this rather unique LP. Using trombonist George Phillips, pianist George Ruschka and drummer Darrell Renfro, they perform a dozen ODJB selections note-for-note from the original recordings of 40 years earlier. It must have taken a great deal of work and research to get this down correctly, but somehow the bizarre project works. This LP will be very difficult to find and it is doubtful that it will be reissued in the near future. —*Scott Yanow*

The Original Memphis Five

f. 1917, **db.** 1931
Group / Classic Jazz
Founded in 1917 by trumpeter Phil Napoleon and pianist Frank Signorelli, this excellent New Orleans jazz quintet made a ton of records between 1921-31, including many under different names (such as Ladd's Black Aces and the Carolina Cotton Pickers). Napoleon, trombonist Miff Mole (who in 1922 was succeeded by Charles Panelli), clarinetist Jimmy Lytell, Signorelli and drummer Jack Roth were regular fixtures in the early days. Starting in 1926 the personnel changed fairly frequently with cornetist Red Nichols, drummer Ray Bauduc, Mole and (during one session apiece in 1928, 1929 and 1931), Tommy and Jimmy Dorsey making appearances. The original Memphis Five's music was melodic, swinging and very jazz-oriented. Unfortunately most of their hundreds of recordings have not been reissued on CD yet. —*Scott Yanow*

★ **Collection, Vol. 1: 1922-1923** / Apr. 22, 1922-Dec. 10, 1923 / Collector's Classics ✦✦✦✦✦
Phil Napoleon was arguably the best trumpeter on record during 1921-22, and one of the first jazz musicians to swing. Possessor of an attractive and clear tone along with impressive technique, Napoleon's melodic lead was heard on a countless number of sides by the original Memphis Five and other groups with similar personnel. Despite its title, this CD actually starts out with the nine selections recorded by Jazzbo's Carolina Serenaders, a quintet with Napoleon, trombonist Miff Mole, several different clarinetists, pianist Frank Signorelli and drummer Jack Roth. The set also has two numbers from the Southland Six (a similar group with Napoleon, trombonist Charles Panelli and clarinetist Jimmy Lytell) in addition to five sessions from the original Memphis Five. Throughout, Napoleon and his musicians sound as if they have evolved way ahead of the original Dixieland Jazz Band and show the influence of the New Orleans Rhythm Kings, but do not sound like a copy of either. This ensemble-oriented music does not include dated vocals, novelties (other than the weak "barking" on "That Barking Dog—Woof! Woof!"), military staccato phrasing or doo-wacka-doo nonsense, and this CD fills an often overlooked gap in jazz history. —*Scott Yanow*

Kid Ory (Edward Ory)

b. Dec. 25, 1886, La Place, LA, **d.** Jan. 23, 1973, Honolulu, HI
Trombone / Classic New Orleans Jazz, Dixieland
Kid Ory was one of the great New Orleans pioneers, an early trombonist who virtually defined the "tailgate" style (using his horn to play rhythmic bass lines in the front line behind the trumpet and clarinet), and who was fortunate enough to last through the lean years so he could make a major comeback in the mid-'40s. Originally a banjoist, Ory soon switched to trombone and by 1911 was leading a popular band in New Orleans. Among his trumpeters during the next eight years were Mutt Carey, King Oliver and a young Louis Armstrong, and his clarinetists included Johnny Dodds, Sidney Bechet and Jimmie Noone. In 1919 Ory moved to California and in 1922 (possibly 1921) recorded the first two titles by a Black New Orleans jazz band ("Ory's Creole Trombone" and "Society Blues") under the band title of "Spike's Seven Pods of Pepper Orchestra." In 1925 he moved to Chicago, played regularly with King Oliver and recorded many classic sides with Oliver, Louis Armstrong (in his Hot Five and Seven) and Jelly Roll Morton among others.
The definitive New Orleans trombonist of the 1920s, Ory (whose "Muskrat Ramble" became a standard) was mostly out of music after 1930, running a chicken ranch with his brother. However, in 1942 he was persuaded to return, and after a stint with Barney Bigard's group, he formed his own band. Ory's group was featured on Orson Welles' radio show in 1944 and the publicity made it possible for the band to catch on. The New Orleans revival was in full swing and Ory

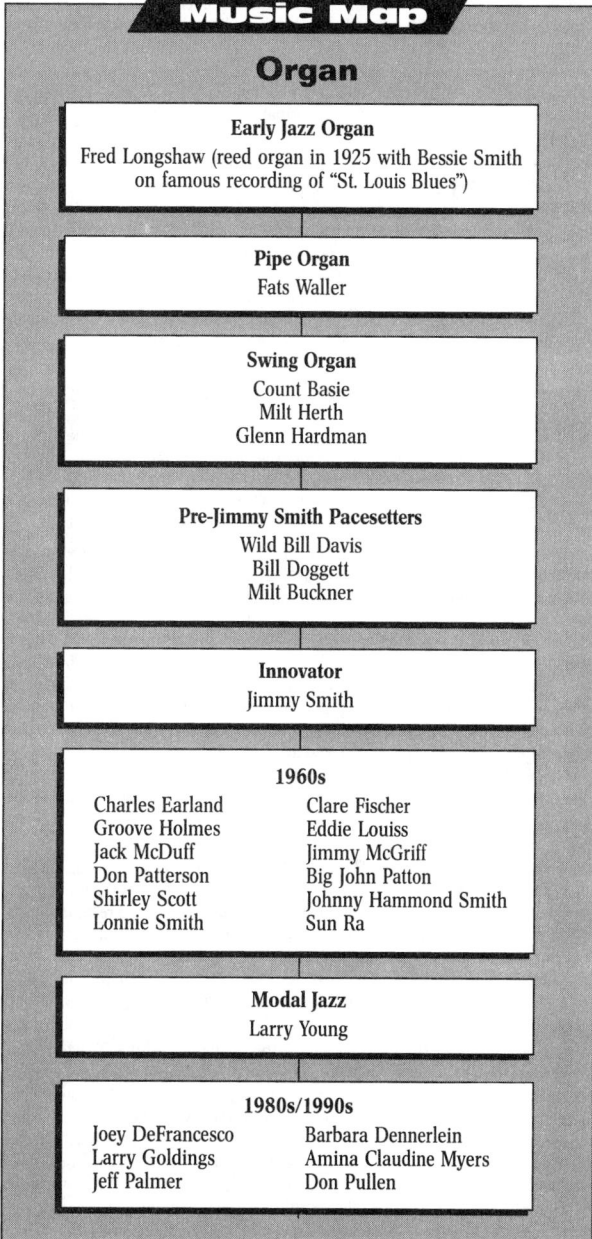

Music Map
Organ

Early Jazz Organ
Fred Longshaw (reed organ in 1925 with Bessie Smith
on famous recording of "St. Louis Blues")

Pipe Organ
Fats Waller

Swing Organ
Count Basie
Milt Herth
Glenn Hardman

Pre-Jimmy Smith Pacesetters
Wild Bill Davis
Bill Doggett
Milt Buckner

Innovator
Jimmy Smith

1960s

Charles Earland	Clare Fischer
Groove Holmes	Eddie Louiss
Jack McDuff	Jimmy McGriff
Don Patterson	Big John Patton
Shirley Scott	Johnny Hammond Smith
Lonnie Smith	Sun Ra

Modal Jazz
Larry Young

1980s/1990s

Joey DeFrancesco	Barbara Dennerlein
Larry Goldings	Amina Claudine Myers
Jeff Palmer	Don Pullen

(whose group included trumpeter Mutt Carey and clarinetists Omer Simeon or Darnell Howard) was still in prime form. He appeared in the 1946 film *New Orleans* (and later on in *The Benny Goodman Story*) and worked steadily in Los Angeles. After Mutt Carey departed in 1948, Ory used Teddy Buckner, Marty Marsala, Alvin Alcorn (the perfect musician for his group) and Red Allen on trumpets. His Dixieland bands always boasted high musicianship (even with the leader's purposely primitive style) and a consistent level of excitement. They recorded regularly (most notably for Good Time Jazz) up to 1960 by which time Ory (already 73) was cutting back on his activities. He retired altogether in 1966, moving to Hawaii. —*Scott Yanow*

Kid Ory's Creole Jazz Band / Mar. 15, 1944-1945 / Folklyric ✦✦✦
This historically significant LP features Kid Ory's New Orleans-styled jazz band on airchecks from the Orson Welles radio show. It was these performances that resulted in a renaissance in Ory's career after more than a decade of obscurity. The tailgate trombonist shares the front line with trumpeter Mutt Carey and clarinetist

Jimmie Noone on the first five selections. Noone's sudden death resulted in him being replaced first by Wade Whaley and Barney Bigard before Joe Darensburg became the band's permanent clarinetist. The final five numbers on this set originate from a different series of broadcasts in early 1945. Overall the music on this LP is better than the recording quality which tends to be a bit shaky and Ory's Good Time Jazz sets from the 1950s are actually his definitive recordings. —*Scott Yanow*

Kid Ory (1944-1945) / Aug. 1944-Nov. 1945 / Good Time Jazz ✦✦✦✦✦
Trombonist Kid Ory led one of the finest and most consistently exciting New Orleans jazz bands of the 1944-60 period. This CD contains 16 selections from 1944-45 when, after a decade out of music, Ory was making what would be a very successful comeback. These studio sides feature veteran trumpeter Mutt Carey and either Omer Simeon or Darnell Howard on clarinet along with a fine rhythm section and Ory's trombone. Highlights include "Blues for Jimmie Noone," "Panama," "Do What Ory Said," "Maryland, My Maryland," "1919 Rag" and "Ory's Creole Trombone." This is fun and often hard-swinging music. —*Scott Yanow*

Kid Ory / Oct. 15, 1946-Jul. 6, 1950 / Columbia ✦✦✦✦
This out-of-print LP features two different versions of trombonist Kid Ory's Creole Jazz Band. The earlier selections (which are highlighted by "Tiger Rag," "Eh, La Bas" and "Bill Bailey") feature trumpeter Mutt Carey and clarinetist Barney Bigard while the sides from 1950 have solos from the strong trumpet of Teddy Buckner and the reliable clarinetist Joe Darensbourg; their eight recordings include "Savoy Blues," "Mahogany Hall Stomp" and "At a Georgia Camp Meeting." Pity that Columbia has kept this enjoyable set unavailable for three decades. —*Scott Yanow*

Kid Ory at the Green Room, Vol. 1 / Feb. 10, 1947 / American Music ✦✦
Recently released for the first time, this is the first of two volumes that document Kid Ory's 1947 band live during a gig. Recorded without the knowledge of the musicians (which include trombonist Ory, trumpeter Mutt Carey and clarinetist Joe Darensbourg), most of the music they played on that particular evening is on these CDs. The first volume is the weaker of the two as the New Orleans jazz band is saddled with requests for swing standards that do not fit their style that well; Ory grudgingly ran through 13 of these tunes as quickly as possible before playing six songs that fit better in his band's repertoire. The music has its moments but the recording quality is just so-so and it takes awhile for Mutt Carey to get warmed up. The second volume is much better. —*Scott Yanow*

Kid Ory at the Green Room, Vol. 2 / Feb. 10, 1947 / American Music ✦✦✦✦
Far superior to the first volume, this CD continues the documentation of a 1947 gig for Kid Ory's Creole Jazz Band. At the time the trombonist's group included trumpeter Mutt Carey (who would leave the band right after this engagement ended) and clarinetist Joe Darensbourg. This group seemed to improve with each song so, by the second half of the night, they were in hot form. The recording quality varies but is listenable (with the crowd becoming more enthusiastic and probably drunker as the night progressed). The band runs through some of their favorite tunes, including "Do What Ory Said," "Eh, La Bas," "1919 March," "High Society" and "Oh! Didn't He Ramble." Ory fans are advised to pick this one up. —*Scott Yanow*

Edward Kid Ory and His Creole Band at the Dixieland Jubilee / 1948 / GNP ✦✦✦
This LP features a typically consistent performance from Kid Ory's popular New Orleans band. Teddy Buckner contributes some impressive trumpet solos, clarinetist Joe Darensbourg is a strong asset and the audience is quite enthusiastic. Nothing unusual occurs but this joyous music (highlighted by "Shine," "Tiger Rag," "Muskrat Ramble" and "Maryland, My Maryland") is enjoyable, if not up to the level of Ory's Good Time Jazz studio recordings. —*Scott Yanow*

King of the Tailgate Trombone / 1948-1949 / American Music ✦✦✦✦
Consisting of previously unissued live performances from two editions of Kid Ory's Creole Jazz Bands, these relatively well-recorded jams should satisfy any lover of New Orleans jazz. Clarinetist Joe Darensbourg (who is on all of the selections) is in good form, trumpeter Andrew Blakeney (heard on 11 of the 15 numbers) has rarely sounded better and trumpeter Teddy Buckner (who stars during the last four songs), although not as expert an ensemble player as some of Ory's sidemen have been, takes some outstanding solos. The Dixieland standards that Ory performs include romping versions of "Panama," "Mahogany Hall Stomp," "Sugar Foot Stomp," "High Society" and "Sweet Georgia Brown." —*Scott Yanow*

At the Beverly Cavern / 1951 / Sounds ✦✦✦
This set consists of broadcast versions of ten songs performed by Kid Ory's New Orleans Jazz band featuring the leader's trombone, cornetist Teddy Buckner and either Joe Darensbourg or Pud Brown on clarinet. Unlike many of the other New Orleans revival groups, this ensemble was very consistent and, although this music is not essential, they are in typically fine form on this fairly obscure LP. —*Scott Yanow*

☆ **Live at Club Hangover, Vol. 1** / May 9, 1953-May 16, 1953 / Dawn Club ✦✦✦✦
This is the first of several Dawn Club LPs documenting the 1953-54 version of Kid Ory's Creole Jazz Band. Consisting of two broadcasts, this set features trombonist Ory, cornetist Teddy Buckner and clarinetist Joe Darensbourg (along with a fine rhythm section) joyfully jamming on a variety of Dixieland standards. One song on each broadcast features the duet of pianist Meade Lux Lewis and drummer Smoky Stover. It's recommended for New Orleans jazz collectors. —*Scott Yanow*

This Kid's the Greatest! / Jul. 17, 1953-Jun. 18, 1956 / Good Time Jazz ✦✦✦✦✦
This CD features selections from some of Kid Ory's finest New Orleans jazz bands, spanning a three-year period; these studio performances never found their way onto the other Good Time Jazz sets. Such excellent players as the colorful cornetist Teddy Buckner (a superior soloist although not as gifted an ensemble player) and his replacement Alvin Alcorn, clarinetists Pud Brown, Bob McCracken, George Probert and Phil Gomez, pianists Lloyd Glenn, Don Ewell and Cedric Haywood, bassists Ed Garland, Morty Corb and Wellman Braud and drummer Minor Hall all make strong contributions on a variety of Dixieland standards including "Milneberg Joys," "Bill Bailey" and "How Come You Do Me like You Do." Quite spirited and very musical New Orleans jazz. —*Scott Yanow*

Kid Ory Plays the Blues / Oct. 3, 1953-Feb. 5, 1955 / Storyville ✦✦✦✦
During the 1950s trombonist Kid Ory, who would turn 70 in 1956, led his finest bands. Among the pacesetters in the New Orleans revival, Ory's groups were always in tune and featured both colorful ensembles and strong soloists. This Storyville LP has strong solos from either Teddy Buckner or Alvin Alcorn on trumpet and Bob McCracken, George Probert or Phil Gomez on clarinet. The rhythm section of pianist Don Ewell, bassist Ed Garland and drummer Minor Hall was one of the best in the idiom. Most of the songs in this series of live broadcasts from the Hangover Club in San Francisco are blues (some just have "blues" in the title) but there is enough variety to make this a recommended set. —*Scott Yanow*

Sounds of New Orleans, Vol. 9 / May 8, 1954-Feb. 26, 1955 / Storyville ✦✦✦✦✦
Although trombonist Kid Ory had formerly used the veteran Mutt Carey and the nearly virtuosic Teddy Buckner as his trumpeters, Alvin Alcorn (who joined the Creole Jazz Band in 1954) proved to be his perfect partner. Alcorn's lyrical but passionate tone was well-featured on solos but it was his ensemble work (building up a song to several climaxes and expertly utilizing dynamics) that made him ideal for this band. This series of broadcasts from Kid Ory's main gig, the Hangover Club in San Francisco, features superior and rather exciting versions of such songs as "Eh, La Bas," "Maryland, My Maryland" "Mahogany Hall Stomp" and "Original Dixieland One Step." Fans of New Orleans jazz will love this CD. —*Scott Yanow*

★ **Kid Ory's Creole Jazz Band (1954)** / Aug. 9, 1954-Aug. 10, 1954 / Good Time Jazz ✦✦✦✦✦
Although some Kid Ory fans might disagree, the veteran trombonist led his finest bands (at least the ones that recorded) in the 1950s. The one heard on this CD is really quite definitive, featuring the brilliant ensemble player (and distinctive soloist) Alvin Alcorn on trumpet, the talented clarinetist George Probert and an excellent rhythm section (pianist Don Ewell, guitarist Bill Newman, bassist Ed Garland and drummer Minor Hall). Their versions on this set of "That's a Plenty," "Gettysburg March," "Clarinet Marmalade" and even "When the Saints Go Marching In" are true classics of New Orleans jazz. This joyous and exciting music is essential for all serious jazz collections. —*Scott Yanow*

Creole Jazz Band / Nov. 30, 1954-Dec. 2, 1954 / Good Time Jazz ✦✦✦✦✦
Trombonist Kid Ory, already 68 at the time of this recording, was at the peak of his powers in the mid-'50s. This particular version of his Creole Jazz Band was one of the finest, featuring trumpeter Alvin Alcorn and clarinetist George Probert, talented soloists who were also superb group players. Alcorn generated a lot of excitement perfectly placing long notes near the end of each ensemble chorus. This Good Time Jazz CD is almost up to the level of its 1954 and 1956 counterparts, highlighted by torrid versions of "Shake That Thing," "Royal Garden Blues" and "Indiana." —*Scott Yanow*

★ **Legendary Kid** / Nov. 22, 1955-Nov. 25, 1955 / Good Time Jazz ✦✦✦✦✦
One of trombonist Kid Ory's greatest recordings, this consistently exciting CD features trumpeter Alvin Alcorn, clarinetist Phil Gomez and a strong rhythm section that includes bassist Wellman Braud and Ory's longtime drummer Minor Hall. These versions of "Mahogany Hall Stomp," "There'll Be Some Changes Made," "At the Jazz Band Ball" and "Shine" are all gems, giving listeners some of the very best in New Orleans jazz, and showing that the music need not be played haltingly by over-the-hill musicians; one can capture its spirit and joy without sacrificing musicianship. Every jazz collection should have this music. —*Scott Yanow*

Favorites! / Jun. 1956-Jul. 1956 / Fantasy ✦✦✦✦✦
This single CD contains 15 of the 17 selections performed by Kid Ory's 1956 Creole Jazz Band that were originally issued on a double LP. Trombonist Ory, trumpeter Alvin Alcorn and clarinetist Phil Gomez make for a very tight but spontane-

ous front line, featuring strong melodic solos and exciting ensembles that paid close attention to dynamics and gradually building up the excitement level. New Orleans jazz at its best. Highlights include "Do What Ory Says," "Jazz Me Blues," "Original Dixieland One-Step," "Panama," "Maryland, My Maryland," "1919 Rag" and "Bugle Call Rag." —*Scott Yanow*

Kid Ory Favorites! / Jun. 1956-Jul. 1956 / Good Time Jazz ✦✦✦✦

Trombonist Kid Ory recorded what were arguably his finest recording sessions for Good Time Jazz. This double LP features Ory, trumpeter Alvin Alcorn and clarinetist Phil Gomez (one of his strongest front lines) on 17 selections that epitomize the best in New Orleans jazz. Highlights include "Do What Ory Says," "Jazz Me Blues," "Original Dixieland One Step," "Panama," "Maryland, My Maryland," "1919 Rag" and "Bugle Call Rag." Two selections ("Mood Indigo" and "Toot, Toot, Tootsie") have been left off the single-CD reissue. —*Scott Yanow*

At the Jazz Band Ball 1959 / Nov. 11, 1959 / Rhapsody ✦✦✦✦

Trombonist Kid Ory (a New Orleans traditionalist) and trumpeter Henry "Red" Allen (New Orleans-born but always looking forward in his playing) make for a frequently explosive combination on this set of Dixieland standards. With clarinetist Bob McCracken and a fine rhythm section helping out, the music on this LP is often quite exciting and heated. —*Scott Yanow*

The Kid Ory Storyville Nights / Dec. 5, 1961 / Verve ✦✦✦

Mary Osborne

b. Jul. 17, 1921, Minot, ND, **d.** Mar. 4, 1992, Bakersfield, CA
Guitar / Bop, Swing

Mary Osborne was a whiz of an electric guitarist—a forthright, madly swinging, inventive player in whom one can hear her original musical inspiration, Charlie Christian, as well as the grace notes and humor of Les Paul. In addition, she was one of only a handful of women in her day who were able to make a dent in jazz's gender barrier, although she did not achieve the recognition that ought to have been her due. Osborne was a versatile musician as a child, playing the violin in a school orchestra and performing on violin, guitar, bass, as well as singing and dancing, in a trio at age 15. Having heard Charlie Christian play with Al Trent's band in Bismarck, North Dakota, she decided to focus upon the electric guitar, on which she became one of jazz's earliest exponents. She toured with a laundry list full of bands—Buddy Rogers, Dick Stabile, Terry Shand, Joe Venuti, and Russ Morgan among them—and with the encouragement of producer/critic Leonard Feather, she recorded with Mary Lou Williams, the Beryl Booker Trio, Coleman Hawkins, Mercer Ellington, Ethel Waters and Wynonie Harris. She was also featured on Jack Sterling's daily CBS radio program from 1952 to 1960. Sometime later, Osborne settled with her husband in Bakersfield, California, where she continued to play gigs now and then. Yet she remained a formidable guitarist late in life; in an appearance with Lionel Hampton at the 1990 Playboy Jazz Festival, she virtually stole the show. She can be heard to good advantage on the Williams and Booker tracks of Bluebird's *The Women: Classic Female Jazz Artists* CD. —*Richard S. Ginell*

● A Memorial / 1959-1981 / Stash ✦✦✦✦✦

Guitarist Mary Osborne led relatively few sessions during her career, just a few titles in the mid to late '40s, a Warwick LP in 1959 and a Stash album that had titles from 1959 and 1981. This Stash CD reissues the full Warwick set plus the Stash songs from 1981 (although not the ones from 1959). The earlier selections feature Osborne's bop-oriented style with a quintet also including rhythm guitarist Danny Barker, pianist Tommy Flanagan, bassist Tommy Potter and drummer Jo Jones. The newer pieces are by a trio with bassist Steve Laspina and drummer Charlie Persip. Despite the 22 years that passed between the sessions, Osborne's appealing and swinging style was completely unchanged and she is in consistently fine form on these mostly-veteran standards. Recommended. —*Scott Yanow*

Now and Then / 1959-1981 / Stash ✦✦✦✦

One of the rare recordings by guitarist Mary Osborne, who was unable to get the exposure she merited due to simple and basic sexism within the industry. Her style was very influenced by Charlie Christian and marked by a nice, swinging feel and full-toned approach. —*Ron Wynn*

Greg Osby

b. Aug. 3, 1960, St. Louis, MO
Alto Saxophone, Soprano Saxophone / Avant-Garde, Free Funk

One of the finest talents to emerge in jazz during the 1980s, Greg Osby's own recordings are often frustrating to listen to. His chance-taking approach is admirable but mixing rap with jazz (as he occasionally does) is analogous to slabbing bacteria on one's bread! Osby studied jazz at Howard University (1978-80) and attended Berklee. He worked in New York with Woody Shaw, Jon Faddis, Ron Carter, Dizzy Gillespie and most notably Jack DeJohnette's Special Edition (1985).

A member of the so-called M-Base scene (essentially an extension of the free funk of Ornette Coleman's Prime Time), Osby has recorded as a leader for JMT and Blue Note but some of his finest playing can be heard on Andrew Hill's records. —*Scott Yanow*

● Greg Osby and Sound Theater / May 1987-Jun. 1987 / JMT ✦✦✦✦✦

This early effort by altoist Greg Osby (who doubles on soprano) matches him with pianist Michele Rosewoman, guitarist Kevin McNeal, bassist Lonnie Plaxico and either Terri Lyne Carrington or Paul Samuels on drums; two songs add Fusako Yoshikda on koto. The performances (mostly Osby originals) are complex, somewhat abrasive, and in the M-Base genre, swinging in their own funky fashion and following a different logic than bebop. Osby plays quite well, and the music grows in interest with each listen. —*Scott Yanow*

Mind Games / May 1988 / JMT ✦✦

Season of Renewal / Jul. 1989 / JMT ✦✦

The free funk altoist Greg Osby's *Season of Renewal* is a strange mixture of avant-garde explorations by the leader (doubling on alto and soprano) and rather inflexible funk rhythms. The mostly wordless vocals by Amina Claudine Myers (who sounds semi-operatic during her two appearances) and Cassandra Wilson add to the odd sounds. The originals, none of which contain much of a melody, never get beyond setting mysterious moods, most of them not assisted by the inappropriate rhythms from the notable supporting cast (which includes guitarist Kevin Eubanks, keyboardist Renee Rosnes and bassist Lonnie Plaxico). If Osby's solos could have been isolated from the "backing," or if the drumming were a lot freer, this music would be quite intriguing. But as it came out, the results are consistently annoying and difficult to sit through. —*Scott Yanow*

Man-Talk for Moderns, Vol. X / Oct. 1990-Nov. 1990 / Blue Note ✦✦

There are several problems with this disappointingly lightweight release. Greg Osby chose to mostly feature his anonymous-sounding soprano instead of his much more distinctive alto. The rhythms on the funky grooves are so predictable and insipid that they could have been played by the sidemen in their sleep and none of the originals are the least bit memorable. Altoist Steve Coleman drops by on "Balaka" to heat things up a little, but, considering how mundane much of this dance music is, Osby sure seems to take it awful seriously. And what's the title of this CD mean, if anything? Better to catch Greg Osby on Andrew Hill's records instead. —*Scott Yanow*

3-D Lifestyles / May 4, 1993 / Blue Note ✦

Greg Osby is a hugely talented altoist but this attempted mixture of rap and jazz is a disaster. Not only does rap that is filled with meaningless name dropping and profanity plague all but one selection, but Osby's alto sounds like an anemic version of Sadao Watanabe. The monotone delivery of the rappers is extremely annoying to hear as is the uninspired playing of Osby. —*Scott Yanow*

Art Forum / 1996 / Blue Note ✦✦✦✦

Greg Osby, who has recorded in a variety of settings (sometimes using hip-hop rhythms and rap), sticks to acoustic jazz on this relaxed, dry and often melancholy set, performing seven originals and two standards. In addition to the basic quartet/quintet (which sometimes utilizes the vibes of Bryant Carrott), five other musicians (most notably the acoustic guitar of Marvin Sewell) add color to some of the ensembles. Osby (who also plays some fine soprano in a sound derived from Wayne Shorter) has long had a very original improvising style, and his subtle solos on the date are continually interesting, although pianist James Williams (in top form) sometimes steals honors. None of the originals have particularly memorable melodies, but this CD acts as a good introduction to Greg Osby's playing. —*Scott Yanow*

Further Ado / 1997 / Blue Note ✦✦✦✦

This jazz (as opposed to funk- and rap-oriented) date from altoist Greg Osby has some fine blowing from the leader, trumpeter Tim Hagans, tenor saxophonist Mark Shim and pianist Jason Moran on ten of Osby's originals and "Tenderly." The solos are actually much more interesting than the moody but generally abrasive (and somewhat dull) melodies. The music falls into the post-bop vein, but it would be preferable to hear Greg Osby uplift some more worthy material than these exploratory, but rather boring, pieces. —*Scott Yanow*

Harold Ousley

b. Jan. 33, 1929, Chicago, IL
Tenor Saxophone, Flute / Groove, Soul-Jazz

A competent funk and soul-jazz saxophonist and flutist, Harold Ousley's bluesy playing on organ combo dates, rock 'n' roll tunes and backing vocalists was stronger than much of what he did when leading groups. His albums were often uneven, both in terms of compositional quality and playing. Ousley began his professional career in the '40s, and at one point backed Billie Holiday. During the '50s, he played with King Kolax and Gene Ammons and worked in circus bands.

Ousley backed Dinah Washington at the 1958 Newport Jazz Festival, an engagement that led to him winning a recording deal. He traveled to Paris the next year with a song revue, then worked with Clark Terry, Howard McGhee, Machito and Joe Newman in the '60s. Ousley began leading his own groups and recording with organ combos, notably Brother Jack McDuff, in the mid-'60s. He worked with Lionel Hampton and Count Basie in the '70s. Ousley currently has no releases available on CD. —*Ron Wynn*

Tenor Sax / 1961 / Bethlehem ✦✦✦✦

Sweet Double Hipness / Mar. 28, 1972 / Muse ✦✦✦

● **The People's Groove** / 1972 / Muse ✦✦✦✦✦

Out of the Blue (OTB)

f. 1984 **db.** 1989
Group / Hard Bop
Founded in 1984, Out of the Blue was devised as a vehicle to feature some of Blue Note's top young jazz talents. Their repertoire emphasized hard bop-oriented originals that extended the Blue Note legacy of the 1960s. The original lineup of OTB consisted of trumpeter Michael Philip Mossman, altoist Kenny Garrett, tenorman Ralph Bowen, pianist Harry Pickens, bassist Robert Hurst and drummer Ralph Peterson, all of whom have gone on to have significant careers. The group recorded four albums from 1985-89 and went on several well-received tours before eventually breaking up when its members developed their own solo careers. Other musicians who were part of OTB were bassist Kenny Davis (who joined in time for their third album), altoist Steve Wilson, pianist Renee Rosnes and drummer Billy Drummond. —*Scott Yanow*

● **Out of the Blue** / Jun. 7, 1985-June 8, 1985 / Blue Note ✦✦✦✦✦
Out of the Blue was formed by Blue Note Records as a way to showcase some of its top young talent. The lineup of players in the original version of the band (trumpeter Michael Mossman, altoist Kenny Garrett, tenor saxophonist Ralph Bowen, pianist Harry Pickens, bassist Robert Hurst and drummer Ralph Peterson) has certainly lived up to its potential. OTB was a strong training ground for the talented musicians. Similar in concept to Art Blakey's Jazz Messengers, the sextet performs seven group originals on their debut recording; everyone but Mossman contributed a song, with Hurst and Garrett represented twice. The music swings hard and, despite being a touch derivative, works quite well. —*Scott Yanow*

Inside Track / Jun. 19, 1986-Jun. 20, 1986 / Blue Note ✦✦✦✦✦
The second of four recordings by Out of the Blue, a band that helped spotlight the talents of its up-and-coming members (trumpeter Michael Mossman, altoist Kenny Garrett, tenorman Ralph Bowen, pianist Harry Pickens, bassist Robert Hurst and drummer Ralph Peterson), features the sextet playing two originals apiece by Mossman, Bowen and Peterson, plus "Hot House." The music is essentially hard bop, and it is particularly interesting to hear Garrett stretching out shortly before he joined Miles Davis' band. Excellent music, although nothing too innovative occurs. —*Scott Yanow*

Live at Mt. Fuji / Aug. 31, 1986 / Blue Note ✦✦✦✦
During its four albums, Out of the Blue was the perfect representative of the Young Lions, featuring Art Blakey-type hard bop by up-and-coming players. Not an innovative group by any means, OTB did give the musicians an opportunity to be showcased in the early stages of their career. For this live concert, two Bud Powell songs ("Parisian Thoroughfare" and "Blue Pearl") are performed by pianist Harry Pickens (in fine form), bassist Kenny Davis (a recent replacement for Bob Hurst) and drummer Ralph Peterson (who would soon be heading his own band). The second half of the program has three group originals, all previously recorded but here stretched out a bit, performed by the same rhythm section plus trumpeter Michael Mossman, altoist Kenny Garrett and Ralph Bowen on tenor. Fine straight-ahead music. —*Scott Yanow*

Spiral Staircase / Jan. 24, 1989-Jan. 25, 1989 / Blue Note ✦✦✦✦
This release from the co-op hard bop group Out of the Blue was most notable for adding pianist Renee Rosnes to the strong lineup (trumpeter Michael Philip Mossman, altoist Steve Wilson, tenor saxophonist Ralph Bowen, bassist Kenny Davis and drummer Billy Drummond). Rosnes wrote the opening selection (the driving "North of the Border") and at this point was not only a strong soloist inspired by

McCoy Tyner but an excellent accompanist behind the horns. Trumpeter Michael Mossman is the most impressive soloist in the group, playing in the Freddie Hubbard/Lee Morgan tradition. Four of Mossman's originals make up the majority of the program; Bowen and Wilson also contributed a song apiece. This OTB release finds the group moving a bit beyond their original role model (Art Blakey's Jazz Messengers) to create a fresh "in the tradition" hard bop-based style of their own. —*Scott Yanow*

Jimmy Owens

b. Dec. 9, 1943, New York, NY
Trumpet / Hard Bop
A fine hard bop soloist, Jimmy Owens has never achieved much fame. He started on trumpet when he was ten and later on studied trumpet with Donald Byrd. Owens has played as a sideman with many major players including Lionel Hampton (1963-64), Hank Crawford (1964-65), Charles Mingus, Herbie Mann, Duke Ellington, Gerry Mulligan, Count Basie, the Thad Jones/Mel Lewis Orchestra and the Dizzy Gillespie reunion band (1968). He played on Billy Cobham's *Spectrum* album in 1973, worked extensively in Europe, was one of the founders of the Collective Black Artists, was closely involved with the Jazzmobile in New York and served on several arts commissions. But playing-wise, Jimmy Owens has not lived up to his potential yet. —*Scott Yanow*

Makoto Ozone

b. Mar. 25, 1961, Kobe, Japan
Piano / Post-Bop
A premier jazz musician in Japan, Ozone has made a successful transition to America, where he became equally prominent in this nation's improvisational community. He began on organ at four, then took up piano as a teenager. He went to Berklee in 1980 and studied composing and arranging. He was noticed by Gary Burton and later recorded with him and was part of his band. Ozone's striking ability (especially on mid-tempo pieces) and impressive technique made him a big hit at the Kool Jazz Festival. His 1984 debut recording featured Burton and bassist Eddie Gomez. It was a stunning example of complete knowledge and mastery of the full jazz piano spectrum. Ozone later worked with European pianist Michel Petrucciani and spent extensive time studying classical music. —*Ron Wynn*

Makoto Ozone / Jun. 23, 1981-Jun. 24, 1981 / CBS ✦✦✦
Pianist Makoto Ozone, who was a member of Gary Burton's group at the time, invited the great vibraphonist to his recording debut as a leader, a trio outing with bassist Eddie Gomez. Twenty-three at the time, Ozone already had impressive technique and a generally introspective style that meshed well with Burton. The group performs five of Ozone's originals (including the two-part "Endless Season"), and even if the results are sometimes a bit sleepy, the pianist does show a lot of potential. —*Scott Yanow*

After / Oct. 1986 / Columbia ✦✦✦✦
An improvement on his debut set as a leader, this Columbia album finds pianist Makoto Ozone playing three quartet numbers with Bill Pierce (who doubles on tenor and soprano), bassist Eddie Gomez and drummer Tommy Campbell, a trio cut without Pierce, a duet with Gomez and two unaccompanied piano solos. Ozone's seven originals feature tight interplay between the musicians, some fire contributed by Pierce, and a display of more diverse moods than his earlier album. —*Scott Yanow*

Now You Know / 1987 / Columbia ✦✦✦
Makoto Ozone is a pianist who often emphasizes introspective moods, yet has an impressive amount of technique. On this effort for Columbia, he is heard in a variety of settings ranging from a duet with flutist Steve Kujala to a quintet with Kujala, guitarist John Abercrombie, bassist Marc Johnson and drummer Peter Erskine. Ozone's seven originals are sometimes a bit dry, but the post-bop improvising by the group (and the close communication between Ozone, Johnson and Erskine) is worth hearing. —*Scott Yanow*

● **Starlight** / Nov. 1989-Dec. 1989 / JVC ✦✦✦✦

Breakout / Dec. 12, 1995 / Verve ✦✦✦✦

Trio / Jan. 7, 1997+Jan. 8, 1997 / Verve ✦✦✦✦

Hot Lips Page (Oran Thaddeus Page)

b. Jan. 27, 1908, Dallas, TX, **d.** Nov. 5, 1954, New York, NY
Trumpet, Vocals / Swing, Dixieland, Blues

One of the great swing trumpeters in addition to being a talented blues vocalist, Hot Lips Page's premature passing left a large hole in the jazz world; virtually all musicians (no matter their style) loved him. Page gained early experience in the 1920s performing in Texas, playing in Ma Rainey's backup band. He was with Walter Page's Blue Devils during 1928-31 and then joined Bennie Moten's band in Kansas City in time to take part in a brilliant 1932 recording session. Page freelanced in Kansas City and in 1936 was one of the stars in Count Basie's orchestra but, shortly before Basie was discovered, Joe Glaser signed Hot Lips as a solo artist. Although Page's big band did alright in the late '30s (recording for Victor), if he had come east with Basie he would have become much more famous. Page was one of the top sidemen with Artie Shaw's Orchestra during 1941-42 and then mainly freelanced throughout the remainder of his career, recording with many all-star groups and always a welcome fixture at jam sessions. —*Scott Yanow*

● **1938-1940** / Mar. 10, 1938-Dec. 3, 1940 / Classics ◆◆◆◆◆

After Hours in Harlem / 1941 / Onyx ◆◆◆◆

Dr. Jazz Series, Vol. 6 / Dec. 21, 1951-Mar. 7, 1952 / Storyville ◆◆◆◆◆
There are not that many recordings from the later part of Page's career, which makes this CD (comprising radio broadcasts) of great interest. Page is heard on a variety of Dixieland and swing standards with quite an assortment of all-stars including cornetist Wild Bill Davison, trombonists Lou McGarity and Sandy Williams, clarinetists Pee Wee Russell, Bob Wilber, Eddie Barefield, Cecil Scott and Peanuts Hucko, pianists Red Richards, Dick Cary, Joe Sullivan and Charlie Queener and drummer George Wettling (who was actually the leader of these groups). Page is in exuberant form whether singing tunes such as "When My Sugar Walks Down the Street" and a riotous "St. Louis Blues" or leading the ensembles. This is one of his best recordings currently available and is often quite exciting. —*Scott Yanow*

Walter Page

b. Feb. 9, 1900, Gallatin, MS, **d.** Dec. 20, 1957, New York, NY
Bass / Swing

One of the finest bassists of the swing era, Walter Page rarely soloed but his four-to-the-bar walking behind soloists set the standard for bassists in the 1930s before the rise of Jimmy Blanton. A longtime resident of Kansas City, Page was with Bennie Moten in the early days (1918-23) and then during 1925-31 led the Blue Devils, Moten's main competition. Unfortunately Page's group only made two recordings and by 1931 Moten had achieved his goal of stealing most of the band's top players, including Page himself. After Moten's death in 1935, Walter Page achieved fame as part of Count Basie's unbeatable rhythm section (along with the pianist/leader, rhythm guitarist Freddie Green and drummer Jo Jones) during 1935-42 and 1946-1949. He spent his remaining years playing with Eddie Condon's Dixieland bands and with his friends from the swing world including Hot Lips Page, Jimmy Rushing and various Basie alumni. Page collapsed on the way to filming *The Sound of Jazz* and died shortly after at the age of 57. —*Scott Yanow*

Marty Paich

b. Jan. 23, 1925, Oakland, CA, **d.** Aug. 12, 1995, Santa Ynez, CA
Piano, Arranger / Bop, Cool

A fine pianist, Marty Paich was much better-known as an arranger, responsible for several famous sessions in the 1950s (most notably Art Pepper's *Modern Jazz Classics*). After serving as arranger for the US Army Air Force Band (1943-46), Paich studied music extensively. Starting in 1952, he became an important fixture in the West Coast jazz scene. Paich worked with Peggy Lee and both the Shelly Manne and Shorty Rogers bands during 1953-54. He led a few dates in the 1950s as a pianist but it was his arrangements for Pepper, Stan Kenton, the Dave Pell Octet and Mel Tormé (the latter utilizing his ten-piece "Dektette") that gave him fame in the

jazz world. After 1960 Marty Paich mostly worked in the studios, but in 1988 he put together a new Dektette to accompany Tormé. —*Scott Yanow*

● **Marty Paich Quartet, Vol. 9** / Aug. 1956 / V.S.O.P. ◆◆◆◆◆
This CD from V.S.O.P. reissues a fairly obscure Tampa LP featuring pianist Marty Paich (better-known as an arranger), altoist Art Pepper, bassist Buddy Clark and drummer Frank Capp; this music has also been issued under Pepper's name. Pepper and Paich would have several notable collaborations during the next few years, but this was their first. Pepper is generally the main star (particularly on such numbers as "You and the Night and the Music," "Over the Rainbow" and "All the Things You Are") while Paich (who has several fine piano solos) contributes three of the eight songs to this cool-toned, but hard-swinging, set. —*Scott Yanow*

Jazz for Relaxation / Aug. 1956-Sep. 1956 / V.S.O.P. ◆◆◆
This V.S.O.P. CD, a straight reissue of a Marty Paich date for Tampa, repeats the packaging faults of the original LP. Although it is a quintet date, the only personnel listed are the pianist/leader, bassist Joe Mondragon and vibraphonist Larry Bunker; guitarist Howard Roberts and drummer Frank Capp go unacknowledged but certainly not unheard. The scanty liner notes claim that this is music to relax by and that all of the tunes are uptempo; actually the first tune ("Dool's Blues") is quite slow! But overlooking those discrepancies, the unfortunately brief program is actually quite enjoyable, showcasing Paich the pianist (rather than the arranger) in prime form. Roberts and Bunker also have plenty of solos and the boppish repertoire (five standards, two originals and Count Basie's obscure "Jump for Me") continually holds one's interest. —*Scott Yanow*

Marty Paich Trio / Jun. 1957 / Mode ◆◆◆
Marty Paich became so well-known as an arranger in the 1950s that his piano playing became secondary. This LP reissue of a session for the Mode label was Paich's only trio set. With the assistance of bassist Red Mitchell and drummer Mel Lewis, Paich plays tasteful versions of three standards, Jack Montrose's "A Dandy Line" and four of his own originals. The music is subtle and quiet but swinging and reasonably enjoyable. —*Scott Yanow*

I Get a Boot Out of You / Jun. 30, 1959-Jul. 12, 1959 / Warner Brothers ◆◆◆◆◆
A good showcase for the orchestrations and arrangements of Marty Paich, one of the top arrangers and conductors during the '50s and '60s. —*Ron Wynn*

New York Scene / Jan. 1959 / Discovery ◆◆◆◆◆

Joanie Pallatto

Vocals / Bop, Post-Bop

An excellent singer, Joanie Pallatto (along with her partner pianist Bradley Parker-Sparrow) has run the Chicago jazz label Southport since 1981. Pallatto has several fine releases of her own with such guests as Bob Dorough, Howard Levy, and Von Freeman. —*Scott Yanow*

● **Passing Tones** / Dec. 1944-May 1995 / Southport ◆◆◆◆◆
Joanie Pallatto, who (with pianist/producer Bradley Parker-Sparrow) founded and runs Southport (one of the top Midwest jazz record labels), has a versatile and very jazz-oriented style. Her scatting sometimes recalls Sheila Jordan; she has a strong voice for ballads and her adventurous spirit allows her to tackle material ranging from "In a Mellow Tone" (during which she interacts quite successfully with tenor saxophonist Von Freeman), "All Blues," "Blue in Green" (for which she wrote the lyrics) and "Save Your Love for Me" to Bob Dorough's "Nothing Like You." Other highlights include Sparrow's "Live" which, in addition to solos from the composer's thunderous piano (a bit reminiscent of Don Pullen) and trumpeter Brad Goode, has some close harmony and hot scatting by Pallatto and April Alosio, a duet with bassist John Whitfield on a pleading "Get out of Town" and an Ellington tribute "Looking for Duke." With the other musicians including pianist Willie Pickens and drummer Robert Shy, this is a particularly memorable effort. —*Scott Yanow*

Who Wrote This Song? / Aug. 1991-1994 / Southport ◆◆◆◆
Joanie Pallatto, a talented Chicago-based singer who with pianist Bradley Parker-Sparrow runs the Southport label, is heard on a wide variety of material and styles

on this CD which has sessions from a three-year period. Ranging from a duet with Sparrow and a vocal collaboration with Bob Dorough on "Along Came Betty" to songs with an electric rhythm section, a string quartet and a vocal quartet, Pallatto certainly takes a lot of chances on this disc. The more successful numbers tend to be the intimate ones; among the other sidemen are guitarist Fareed Haque and pianist Howard Levy. —*Scott Yanow*

Two / Mar. 24, 1997-Jun. 16, 1997 / Southport ✦✦✦✦
Vocalist Joanie Pallatto and pianist Marshall Vente make for a perfect match on this fairly introspective duo set. The pair interpret a wide variety of material (including "Still Crazy After All These Years," "Swinging on a Star," an excellent rendition of "As Time Goes By," "Light My Fire," "Morning of the Carnival" and "My Ship"), and the communication between the two is consistently impressive. One song flows easily to another, and although some more tempo variation might have been beneficial, the beauty of Pallatto's voice and the sensitivity of Vente's piano style shine through. —*Scott Yanow*

Jeff Palmer

b. 1951, Jackson Heights, NY
Organ / Hard Bop
A fine organist who has carved out his own voice from the dominant Jimmy Smith influence, Jeff Palmer started out on accordion. He switched to organ when he was around 15 and was completely self-taught, never having been a pianist. Palmer has played with such guitarists as Grant Green, George Benson, John Scofield and John Abercrombie, and recorded as a leader for Statiras, Soul Note, AudioQuest and Reservoir. —*Scott Yanow*

Laser Wizard / Jul. 16, 1985 / Statiras ✦✦✦✦

Abracadabra / 1987 / Soul Note ✦✦✦✦
Sound explorations are emphasized throughout this release with Jeff Palmer's atmospheric organ, the varied tones of John Abercrombie's guitar synthesizer, David Liebman's very passionate soprano and Adam Nussbaum's drums interacting over a variety of patterns. All of the compositions are group originals with five by Palmer and one apiece from the other three musicians. Whether it be the funky beat of "Hip Slick," the free jamming of "Mr. Adam," the spacey title cut or the almost new age feel of "Mr. John," the themes are less important than the setting of moods and the advanced improvising. —*Scott Yanow*

Ease On / Sep. 1992 / Audioquest ✦✦✦✦

Island Universe / Mar. 8, 1994 / Soul Note ✦✦✦✦✦
Although the instrumentation on this CD might lead one to think that the music on the session is a typical organ date from the 1960s (with alto used instead of tenor), the first moments of the opening "All Cracked Up" immediately changes one's expectations. Organist Jeff Palmer does his best to blow away any thoughts of Jimmy Smith as he plays harmonically advanced and sometimes nearly atonal improvisations. The music is quite adventurous (although often swinging) with plenty of fiery interaction between the musicians. Altoist Arthur Blythe's highly original tone (which sometimes sounds halfway between Cannonball Adderley and Eric Dolphy) fits in perfectly with Palmer and the eccentric soloing of guitarist John Abercrombie. It is a particular joy to hear the legendary drummer Rashied Ali (still best-known for being a member of John Coltrane's Quintet during 1966-67) playing at the peak of his powers after nearly 30 years of general obscurity. But it is Jeff Palmer who deserves the bulk of the credit for this set's success. He contributed all ten pieces and is one of the few organists around today who has managed to escape from the dominant Jimmy Smith influence, developing a style that is even beyond Larry Young. The music on his CD is sometimes quite dark and mildly disturbing but it is also quite often extroverted and full of wild spirits; even "Amerigo" (which is basically a blues) is unpredictable. Jeff Palmer's best recording thus far, *Island Universe* is highly recommended. —*Scott Yanow*

● **Shades of the Pine** / Sep. 14, 1994 / Reservoir ✦✦✦✦✦
Jeff Palmer is a talented organist whose style (as with virtually all organists) is influenced by Jimmy Smith. For this CD he performs nine similar blues, all of which are given strong solos by the leader, tenor saxophonist Billy Pierce and guitarist John Abercrombie; drummer Marvin "Smitty" Smith is consistently swinging in support. Despite the sameness of the repertoire (all but Thelonious Monk's "Ba-lue Bolivar Ba-lues-are" are by Palmer), the cooking music holds one's interest and is quite enjoyable. —*Scott Yanow*

Charlie Palmieri

b. 1927, New York, NY, **d.** 1988, New York, NY
Piano / Latin Jazz, Salsa
The older brother of Eddie Palmieri, Charlie Palmieri was every bit as gifted a pianist as his sibling, very percussive and responsive to rhythm while also flashing florid passages that were clearly the product of a classical education. His piano

studies began at seven, and he attended the Juilliard School of Music, turning pro at 16. He started the group "El Conjunto Pin Pin" in 1948, and then played in a series of ensembles—including those of Tito Puente, Tito Rodriguez and Pupi Campo—before forming his own Charanga Dubonney group in 1958. As music director of the Alegre All Stars while recording for the Alegre label in the 1960s, Palmieri stimulated competition among Latin labels like Tico and Fania, which formed their own all-star bands in response. Like many Latin jazz artists of the time, Palmieri flirted with the popular Latin boogaloo style in the 1960s and made some records for major labels like RCA Victor and Atlantic. He endured a mental near-breakdown in 1969, but rebounded to work again for Puente on his *El Mambo de Tito Puente* television program, and he also found a second career as a historian and teacher of Latin music and history at various New York colleges in the 1970s. Palmieri moved briefly to Puerto Rico from 1980 to 1983, and after suffering a severe heart attack and stroke upon his return to New York, he recovered to lead various Latin combos, including Combo Gigante. One of his last recordings was a galvanizing cameo appearance on Mongo Santamaria's "Mayeya" in 1987 (now on Mongo's *Afro Blue: The Picante Collection* [Concord Picante]), and he appeared in England for the first time in 1988 shortly before his death. Almost all of Palmieri's work is hard to find through domestic channels, but Messidor's *A Giant Step* is available on CD. —*Richard S. Ginell*

Tribute to Noro Morales / 1956 / Alegre ✦✦✦✦✦

Charanga / 1960 / United Artists ✦✦✦

Pachanga at the Caravana Club / 1961 / Alegre ✦✦✦

Latin Bugalu / 1968 / Atlantic ✦✦✦✦

The Giant of the Keyboard / 1972 / Alegre ✦✦✦✦✦

Adelante Gigante / 1975 / Alegre ✦✦✦✦✦
Eddie Palmieri always said his elder brother was the better player, and by the time of his death, Charlie Palmieri was well enough known outside the barrio to get an obituary in the *New York Times*. This classic mid-'70s album has all his usual taste, classic piano (and in a couple of places organ) along with his favorite lead singer, Vitin Aviles, and a tight band. —*John Storm Roberts*

Perdido / 1977 / Alegre ✦✦✦✦

A Giant Step / 1984 / Messidor ✦✦✦✦✦
The late Charlie Palmieri always wanted to do a piano-plus-rhythm album, and in 1984 he got, and royally profited from, the chance. Tracks range from the classic danza "Bajo las Sombras de un Pino" through Puente's "Tito à la King" through Irving Berlin's "Be Careful, It's My Heart." The sidemen are two generations of heavy, and Palmieri's own playing runs from magnificent to superb. —*John Storm Roberts, Original Music*

● **Impulsos** / 1995 / Mpl ✦✦✦✦✦
The late Charlie P. was a greater pianist than his brother, as deeply musical, as universally loved, and with far more sense. He picked musicians by talent not fame, and they blew their hearts out for him. This mid-'70s session has the swing, as hot as EPs but more benign; the jazz solos and tipico ensembles. —*John Storm Roberts*

Eddie Palmieri

b. Dec. 15, 1936, New York, NY
Piano, Leader / Latin Jazz, Afro-Cuban Jazz, Salsa
Eddie Palmieri is one of the foremost Latin jazz pianists of the last half of the century, blessed with a technique that fuses such ubiquitous jazz influences as the styles of Herbie Hancock, Thelonious Monk and McCoy Tyner into a Latin context. No purist, he has also shown a welcome willingness to experiment with fusions of Latin and non-Latin music. However, despite a number of stints with major labels and numerous industry awards and nominations, he has yet to break into the American record scene in a big way.

Like his older brother Charlie, Eddie started playing at an early age (eight) and studied classical piano while also playing drums. He made his professional debut with Johnny Sequi's orchestra in 1955 and eventually joined Tito Rodriguez's popular band in 1958-60. In 1961, Palmieri formed his highly influential band La Perfecta, whose flute and twin- or triple-trombone front line made American jazz musicians like Herbie Mann take notice; he also scored heavily in an excellent 1966 collaboration with Cal Tjader, *El Sonido Nuevo* (Verve). After La Perfecta split up in 1968 due to financial problems, Palmieri played with the Tico and Fania All-Stars, recorded with Alfredo "Chocolate" Armenteros, Cachao, and Justa Betancourt, and, like his brother, cut some Latin boogaloo sessions. Around the mid-1960s, Palmieri began formal studies of arranging, and the Monk influence became more pronounced in his piano work. While recording for the Latin Coco label in the mid-1970s, Palmieri started to mix salsa with R&B, pop, rock, Spanish vocals and jazz improvisation. Brief affiliations with Columbia in the late 1970s and Capitol (in league with David Sanborn) in the late 1980s failed to produce an

American breakthrough hit, though the latter attempt was aimed squarely at the burgeoning "jazz-lite" market. His sole listed CD as a leader in American catalogs (as of this writing) is the jazz-oriented *Palmas* (1993) for the normally classical Nonesuch label. —*Richard S. Ginell*

Mozambique / 1965 / Tico ✦✦✦✦✦

Eddie Palmieri first hit in the '60s with his classic two-trombone sound. This is one of his finest albums; unassuming, joyous, punchy, and sharp, it has the outstanding Ismael Quintana on vocals and Manny Oquendo on timbales. —*John Storm Roberts*

El Sonido Nuevo / Oct. 1966 / Verve ✦✦✦

The meeting of vibist Cal Tjader and pianist Eddie Palmieri yielded a fresh, innovative sound. This date was one of those magical ones in which every cut was masterful, showing how carefully Tjader and Palmieri navigated the line between tasteful pop covers and searing Afro-Latin workouts. The disc has six bonus cuts culled from various Tjader sessions that display his versatility. While they're entertaining, the disc's real meat comes in the nine songs that match Tjader and Palmieri, supported sometimes by a three-trombone/flute front line with bass and percussion and at other times by an orchestra. The CD also has extensive liner notes and excellent remastering. —*Ron Wynn*

Champagne / 1968 / Tico ✦✦✦✦

Champagne was a transitional album from 1968, one that retained tracks with the two-trombone Perfecta but had others that looked forward—an off-center piano solo here, some blazing solo trumpet, a melody that is "Un Dia . . ." in embryo, a touch of proto-Latin-funk. —*John Storm Roberts, Original Music*

★ Sun of Latin Music / 1973 / Coco ✦✦✦✦✦

This album almost perfectly combines Palmieri's experimentalism with the devastating swing that kept him ahead on the street. The "Un Dia Bonito" suite got most attention, but "Una Rosa Española," a one-cut mini-history of salsa, is enchanting. —*John Storm Roberts*

Unfinished Masterpiece / 1979 / Coco ✦✦✦✦✦

The late-'70s *Unfinished Masterpiece* caused a huge quarrel because he couldn't or wouldn't get it done to his own satisfaction (Coco finally put it out anyway, thus the title). Unfinished or no, it's classic Palmieri from his late Golden Age and long unavailable. —*John Storm Roberts*

Sueno / 1982 / Intuition ✦✦✦

The '80s *Sueno*, produced by poly-buff Kip Hanrahan, went nowhere much, perhaps because Capitol didn't know what to do with it. But it's another example of what made Palmieri one of the great salsa bandleaders. —*John Storm Roberts*

Palmas / 1994 / Elektra ✦✦✦

Palmieri's new release featuring his Latin-jazz ensemble lacks the tension between his off-the-wall creativity and the strength of salsa tradition, but is as usual extra. His famous "working-on-it" piano solo now opens more Boulez than Debussy and slouches brilliantly towards salsadom. For the rest, very fine soloing and a tightness rare in contemporary jazz, Latin or otherwise, and a vocal by Eddie Junior. —*John Storm Roberts, Original Music*

Arete / 1995 / RMM ✦✦✦✦✦

Pianist/composer Eddie Palmieri has long been a giant of Afro-Cuban (or Latin) jazz. While some recordings in this idiom lean too far in one direction—not enough jazz improvising or, in other cases, a percussion section that sounds as if it were added on as an afterthought—Palmieri has struck a perfect balance. In trumpeter Brian Lynch, trombonist Conrad Herwig and altoist Donald Harrison, he has three strong soloists who match well with the trio of percussionists. In addition to Palmieri, bassist John Benitez and drummer Adam Cruz (the latter is on just four of the eight Palmieri originals) are flexible enough to play both swing and Latin. A strong plus to this date are the compositions/arrangements of Palmieri, which pay close attention to varying moods, instrumental colors and grooves. Consistently complex and unpredictable, the music is still always quite accessible and enjoyable, thanks to the percussionists. —*Scott Yanow*

Paragon Ragtime Orchestra

f. 1985

Group / Ragtime

In 1985 Rick Benjamin stumbled across priceless arrangements of the Arthur Pryor Orchestra, which had been lost for 65 years. After acquiring the vast amount of music, Benjamin formed the 15-piece Paragon Ragtime Orchestra, an ensemble that, during the past decade, performed works ranging from rags and early popular music to novelties and even satires of classical music. They have thus far recorded three excellent sets for Newport Classic and Dorian Discovery that show that there was always more to ragtime than piano solos! —*Scott Yanow*

★ On the Boardwalk / 1986 / Newport Classics ✦✦✦✦✦

Although ragtime is primarily thought of as music played by solo pianists, during the ragtime era there were many orchestras that performed the lively syncopated style using full orchestrations. Educator Rick Benjamin in 1985 accidentally discovered most of the existing library of The Arthur Pryor Orchestra (which was about to be thrown away) and formed The Paragon Ragtime Orchestra so as to bring the music back to life. In addition to a string quintet, the band uses two cornets, a trombone, two clarinets, a flute, tuba, string bass, drums and percussion on this CD, their recording debut. The colorful charts range from Scott Joplin and W.C. Handy to obscurities, pop tunes of the era, a "George M. Cohan medley" and "An Operatic Nightmare: Desecration Rag No. 2." This is delightful and timeless music that was almost permanently lost. —*Scott Yanow*

The Whistler and His Dog / 1988 / Newport Classics ✦✦✦✦✦

The second CD by Rick Benjamin's Paragon Ragtime Orchestra (which comprises a string quartet, two cornets, one trombone, two clarinets, flute, bass, drums and percussion) is the equal of the first. Using arrangements originally part of the Arthur Pryor Orchestra, this nonimprovising but very syncopated ensemble performs a wide variety of music from the 1905-1920 period, everything from "Dynamite Rag" and "Smiles" to "The Whistler and His Dog" and a waltz medley titled "Old Chestnuts." The little-known music should greatly interest followers of classic jazz since it is its direct predecessor. —*Scott Yanow*

That Demon Rag / Mar. 2, 1992-Mar. 3, 1992 / Dorian ✦✦✦✦

The Paragon Ragtime Orchestra is one of the premiere bands in the esoteric but very accessible idiom of orchestrated ragtime (as opposed to solo pianists). Consisting of a string quartet, two clarinets, two cornets, one trombone, a flutist doubling on piccolo, a bassist and a versatile drummer, this ensemble is directed by its founder Rick Benjamin. Its third recording has quite a variety of mostly obscure music among its 19 pieces including Arthur Pryor's "A Cakewalk Contest," two of Scott Joplin's lesser-known rags, "Ragtime Travesty on 'Il Trovatore'" (which satirizes classical music), Eubie Blake's "Chevy Chase Foxtrot," the "Spirit of Independence" march and a couple of popular numbers. This pre-jazz music (which has no improvisation but plenty of syncopation) is colorfully performed and should greatly interest fans of early American music, jazz and ragtime alike. —*Scott Yanow*

Tiny Parham (Hartzell Strathdene Parham)

b. Feb. 25, 1900, Winnipeg, MB, **d.** Apr. 4, 1943, Milwaukee, WI

Piano / Classic Jazz

Tiny Parham (who was actually rather large) was most significant as an arranger/bandleader in Chicago who recorded many memorable sides from 1927-30. After growing up in Kansas City, Parham toured the Southwest with a territory band and then settled in Chicago in 1926. In addition to accompanying blues singers and cutting sides with Johnny Dodds, Parham recorded extensively with "His Musicians," bands that mostly consisted of now-obscure Chicago players; best known are cornetist Punch Miller and (in 1930) bassist Milt Hinton. Parham's arrangements were often atmospheric, and such numbers as "The Head-Hunter's Dream," "Jogo Rhythm," "Blue Melody Blues," "Blue Island Blues," "Washboard Wiggles" and "Dixieland Doin's" were particularly memorable. After 1930, Parham spent the remainder of his life playing in theatres, often on organ after the mid-'30s, only recording three further titles in 1940 before his premature death. Before the end of the LP era, Swaggie had reissued all of Parham's recordings (including alternate takes); the master versions have since been compiled on two Classics CDs. —*Scott Yanow*

● Complete Recorded Works / 1926-Jul. 2, 1928 / Document ✦✦✦✦✦

Hot Chicago Jazz from the Late 1920s / Jul. 2, 1928-Nov. 11, 1930 / Folklyric ✦✦✦✦✦

There's a late-'20s small-group sound of which many are particularly fond: a small-group sound whose sonorities are bracketed by trumpet and tuba. Pianist Parham's 1928-1930 recordings feature it fairly strongly. Many of them also feature Punch Miller, a fine trumpeter overshadowed—like Jabbo Smith and so many others—by Armstrong. In its mix of solo and head arrangements, as the notes point out, this group uncannily blends the small-group ethos with something of the big bands that were beginning to dominate the scene. —*John Storm Roberts, Original Music*

Barbara Paris

b. Oct. 2, 1954, Denver, CO

Vocals / Standards

Barbara Paris is an excellent jazz vocalist able to make even warhorses sound fresh through her enthusiasm and subtle creativity. She grew up in a musical family and as a child played violin, piano, and then guitar. Barbara gained early experience as a folk singer while a teenager, but soon discovered jazz. However, music was put on the side for a time, as she worked as a hairdresser. The singer dates her first real jazz performance as having taken place on April 3, 1989. Barbara was encouraged by Eddie Shu, a tenor saxophonist formerly with Gene Krupa, and Claude Tissendier, a saxophonist with Claude Bolling's Orchestra. She worked in Europe with Tissendier and for five years off and on with pianist Joe Bonner in Colorado. Barbara Paris has recorded three fine CDs for her Perea label and is a welcome fixture in the Colorado jazz scene, occasionally singing on both the East and West Coasts and in Europe. —*Scott Yanow*

Where Butterflies Play / 1992-1993 / Perea ✦✦✦✦
Barbara Paris, who has a lovely sweet voice and a gentle straightfoward style, is based in Boulder, CO. On this CD her singing is featured in three different settings. Paris performs four ballads (including Harold Vick's "Where Butterflies Play" and "Do You Know What It Means to Miss New Orleans") in duets with pianist Joe Bonner, interprets two Jobim pieces plus "How Deep Is the Ocean" while accompanied by guitarist Mitchell Long and concludes the set with four songs in which she is joined by the talented pianist Ellyn Rucker, the Stan Getz-inspired Richie Chiaraluce on tenor and bassist Dean Ross. The one fault to this program is that the tempos tend to be similar; only the closing pieces with the quartet ("Star Eyes" and "April in Paris") cook a bit. However, the sincerity and appealing simplicity of Barbara Paris' style easily compensate. —*Scott Yanow*

Happy Talk / Apr. 1994 / Perea ✦✦✦✦
Singer Barbara Paris does the near-impossible on this disc, tackling a set of music dominated by veteran standards and making them sound fresh and alive. Certainly "All of Me," "He May Be Your Man" (which uses some phrases identified with Joe Williams) and "But Not for Me" have not exactly been underrecorded through the years, but Paris' subtle creativity and highly appealing phrasing (along with a strong voice), manages to give new life to these warhorses. The supporting cast (pianist Joe Bonner, bassist Kenny Walker, drummer Mike Whitted and Richie Chiaraluce on tenor, alto and flute), although Bonner is the only one with a national reputation, are some of the best musicians based in Colorado. Highlights of the program include "Everything Happens to Me," "April in Paris," "Whisper Not" and "I Fall in Love Too Easily." This CD is easily recommended to listeners who enjoy swinging bop-based vocalists. —*Scott Yanow*

● **Day by Day** / Apr. 24, 1996 / Perea ✦✦✦✦
Singer Barbara Paris' third CD for her Perea label was her best thus far. The appealing vocalist swings her way through some offbeat material ("Accent on Youth," "Copacobano" and "No Voot No Boot"), her own "Paris Blues," and a variety of straightahead standards with the assistance of pianist Llew Matthews, bassist John B. Williams and drummer Roy McCurdy (Nancy Wilson's rhythm section of the time), plus guest Rich Chiaraluce on tenor and flute. A fun set of spirited, straightahead music. —*Scott Yanow*

Charlie Parker

b. Aug. 29, 1920, Kansas City, KS, **d.** Mar. 12, 1955, New York, NY
Alto Saxophone , Composer, Leader / Bop
One of a handful of musicians who can be said to have permanently changed jazz, Charlie Parker was arguably the greatest saxophonist of all time. He could play remarkably fast lines that, if slowed down to half speed, would reveal that every note made sense. Bird, along with his contemporaries Dizzy Gillespie and Bud Powell, is considered a founder of bebop; in reality he was an intuitive player who simply was expressing himself. Rather than basing his improvisations closely on the melody as was done in swing, he was a master of chordal improvising, creating new melodies that were based on the structure of a song. In fact Bird wrote several future standards (such as "Anthropology," "Ornithology," "Scrapple from the Apple," and "Ko Ko" along with such blues as "Now's the Time" and "Parker's Mood") that "borrowed" and modernized the chord structures of older tunes. Parker's remarkable technique, fairly original sound and ability to come up with harmonically advanced phrases that could be both logical and whimsical were highly influential. By 1950 it was impossible to play "modern jazz" with credibility without closely studying Charlie Parker.

Born in Kansas City, KS, Charlie Parker grew up in Kansas City, MO. He first played baritone horn before switching to alto. Parker was so enamored of the rich Kansas City music scene that he dropped out of school when he was 14 even though his musicianship at that point was questionable (with his ideas coming out faster than his fingers could play them). After a few humiliations at jam sessions, Bird worked hard woodshedding over one summer, building up his technique and mastery of the fundamentals. By 1937 when he first joined Jay McShann's Orchestra, he was already a long way towards becoming a major player.

Charlie Parker, who was early on influenced by Lester Young and the sound of Buster Smith, visited New York for the first time in 1939, working as a dishwasher at one point so he could hear Art Tatum play on a nightly basis. He made his recording debut with Jay McShann in 1940, creating remarkable solos with a small

group from McShann's Orchestra on "Lady Be Good" and "Honeysuckle Rose." When the McShann big band arrived in New York in 1941, Parker had short solos on a few of their studio blues records and his broadcasts with the orchestra greatly impressed (and sometimes scared) other musicians who had never heard his ideas before. Parker, who had met and jammed with Dizzy Gillespie for the first time in 1940, had a short stint with Noble Sissle's band in 1942, played tenor with Earl Hines' sadly unrecorded bop band of 1943 and spent a few months in 1944 with Billy Eckstine's orchestra, leaving before that group made their first records. Gillespie was also in the Hines and Eckstine big bands and the duo became a team starting in late 1944.

Although Charlie Parker recorded with Tiny Grimes' combo in 1944, it was his collaborations with Dizzy Gillespie in 1945 that startled the jazz world. To hear the two virtuosos play rapid unisons on such new songs as "Groovin' High," "Dizzy Atmosphere," "Shaw 'Nuff," "Salt Peanuts" and "Hot House" and then launch into fiery and unpredictable solos could be an upsetting experience for listeners much more familiar with Glenn Miller and Benny Goodman. Although the new music was evolutionary rather than revolutionary, the recording strike of 1943-44 resulted in bebop arriving fully formed on records, seemingly out of nowhere.

Unfortunately, Charlie Parker was a heroin addict ever since he was a teenager and some other musicians who idolized Bird foolishly took up drugs in the hope that it would elevate their playing to his level. When Gillespie and Parker (known as "Diz & Bird") traveled to Los Angeles and were met with a mixture of hostility and indifference (except by younger musicians who listened closely), it was decided to return to New York. Impulsively Parker cashed in his ticket, ended up staying in L.A. and, after some recordings and performances (including a classic version of "Lady Be Good" with Jazz at the Philharmonic), the lack of drugs (which he combated by drinking an excess of liquor) resulted in a mental breakdown and six months of confinement at the Camarillo State Hospital. Released in January 1947, Parker soon headed back to New York and engaged in some of the most rewarding playing of his career, leading a quintet that included Miles Davis, Duke Jordan, Tommy Potter and Max Roach. Parker, who recorded simultaneously for the Savoy and Dial labels was in peak form during the 1947-51 period, visiting Europe in 1949 and 1950 and realizing a lifelong dream to record with strings starting in 1949 when he switched to Norman Granz's Verve label.

But Charlie Parker, due to his drug addiction and chance-taking personality, enjoyed playing with fire too much. In 1951 his cabaret license was revoked in New York (making it difficult for him to play in clubs) and he became increasingly unreliable. Although he could still play at his best when he was inspired (such as at the 1953 Massey Hall Concert with Gillespie), Bird was heading downhill. In 1954 he twice attempted suicide before spending time in Bellevue. His health, shaken by a very full if brief life of excesses, gradually declined and when he died in March 1955 at the age of 34, he could have passed for 64!

Charlie Parker, who was a legendary figure during his lifetime, has if anything grown in stature since his death. Virtually all of his studio recordings are available on CD along with a countless number of radio broadcasts and club appearances. Clint Eastwood put together a well-intentioned if simplified movie about aspects of his life (*Bird*). Parker's influence, after the rise of John Coltrane, has become more indirect than direct but jazz would sound a great deal different if Charlie Parker had not existed. The phrase "Bird Lives" (which was scrawled as graffiti after his death) is still very true. —*Scott Yanow*

The Complete "Birth of Bebop" / May 1940-Dec. 29, 1945 / Stash ✦✦✦✦✦
This is the type of Charlie Parker CD that is essential for Bird collectors but less important to more casual jazz fans. The contents of this set should amaze Parker fanatics: Bird's initial private recording of May 1940 (unaccompanied versions of "Honeysuckle Rose" and "Body and Soul" cut in a private recording booth); four remarkable studio-quality selections from 1942 (including "Cherokee") in which the altoist is just backed by rhythm guitar and quiet drums; rehearsal and jam session numbers from 1943 with Bird on tenor (including an amazing seven-minute version of "Sweet Georgia Brown" by the trio of Parker, trumpeter Dizzy Gillespie and bassist Oscar Pettiford); and three lengthy cuts from a late-1945 broadcast by Diz and Bird with a sextet. These important recordings fill a major gap, giving one many clues as to how Charlie Parker sounded before he emerged fully formed on records in 1945. —*Scott Yanow*

Early Bird (1940-1944) / Aug. 1940-1944 / Stash ✦✦✦✦✦
This Stash CD contains some remarkable performances by the young Charlie Parker with pianist Jay McShann's Orchestra. First Bird is heard at the age of 20 with an octet from McShann's big band playing six standards and a blues; his solos on "Lady Be Good" and particularly "Honeysuckle Rose" are classic. Then, after Parker's early version of "Cherokee" from 1942 with the house band at Monroe's Uptown House, one gets to hear what Bird really sounded like on a typical night with Jay McShann's big band. Parker's studio recordings with McShann's Orchestra were three-minute affairs that generally gave him a chorus at the most but, on this

1942 broadcast, Bird really stretches out on a few of the songs, particularly "I'm Forever Blowing Bubbles," and shows just how advanced a player he was at that early stage. This CD concludes with the 1944 McShann big band (after Bird had departed) in fine form on a radio aircheck and, as a bonus strictly for completists, a very scratchy (and almost unlistenable) version of "I Got Rhythm" from August 1940 by McShann with Bird. —*Scott Yanow*

The Charlie Parker Story, Vol. 1 / Nov. 1940-Feb. 26, 1947 / Stash Budget ◆◆◆◆
This budget CD release from Stash has some of the highlights of Charlie Parker's career, tracing in chronological order his evolution during 1940-47. The most interesting of the 13 selections are the first six: "Lady Be Good" from 1940 with a small group from Jay McShann's band; Bird playing "I'm Forever Blowing Bubbles" on the radio with the full McShann orchestra; jam session versions of "Body and Soul," "Cherokee" and "Sweet Georgia Brown" from 1942-43 (the latter song has Parker on tenor with a trio comprising trumpeter Dizzy Gillespie and bassist Oscar Pettiford) and a Bird and Diz broadcast version of "'Shaw Nuff." The remainder of the set is more familiar, drawing from Parker's Dial studio recordings of 1946-47. Overall, this CD (and the second volume) gives listeners an interesting introduction to Charlie Parker's music, although all of these performances are available in more complete form elsewhere. —*Scott Yanow*

☆ **Complete Savoy Studio Sessions** / Sep. 15, 1944-Sep. 24, 1948 / Savoy ◆◆◆◆◆
This three CD box set contains all of the recordings Charlie Parker made for the Savoy label and it is overflowing with gems and an almost countless number of alternate takes. Bird was one of the most important jazzmen of all time and nearly every note he recorded (in the studios if not live) is well worth hearing. This box starts off with his sideman date with Tiny Grimes in 1944, contains Parker's famous "Ko Ko" session of 1945 (with a young Miles Davis on trumpet and highlighted by "Now's the Time" and "Billie's Bounce") and continues through his 1947-48 quintet sessions with a more mature Miles Davis, either Bud Powell, John Lewis or Duke Jordan on piano, bassists Tommy Potter, Curly Russell or Nelson Boyd and drummer Max Roach. Together they recorded such classics as "Donna Lee," "Chasin' the Bird," "Milestones" and "Parker's Mood." Every scrap that the great altoist cut for Savoy is in this box. —*Scott Yanow*

Every Bit of It / Jan. 1945-Dec. 1945 / Spotlite ◆◆◆◆◆
This very interesting double LP from the English Spotlite label contains many of Charlie Parker's lesser-known recordings from 1945. Bird is featured with trumpeter Dizzy Gillespie not only on the five songs recorded by blues singer Rubberlegs Williams but backing trombonist Trummy Young's vocals (real rarities), three numbers featuring Sarah Vaughan and on a session with guitarist/jokester Slim Gaillard; "Slim's Jam" is a classic of its kind. In addition, Parker participates on a half-hour broadcast by Cootie Williams' orchestra (although he only solos on the lone sextet number "Floogie Boo") and on four hot titles with pianist Sir Charles Thompson, trumpeter Buck Clayton and tenor saxophonist Dexter Gordon. —*Scott Yanow*

● **Yardbird Suite: The Ultimate Collection** / Feb. 28, 1945-Sep. 26, 1952 / Rhino ◆◆◆◆◆
Subtitled "The Ultimate Charlie Parker Collection," this two-CD set from 1997 is highly recommended to listeners who wish to become acquainted with the immortal bebop altoist's music, although veteran collectors will find no previously unissued gems among the 38 selections. Bird is featured as a sideman on six classic performances with Dizzy Gillespie in 1945 and on most of his greatest studio sides as a leader; the program draws its music from the Savoy, Dial and Verve catalogs. In addition, Parker is heard on a 1951 radio broadcast with Gillespie and Bud Powell and for a few numbers from his 1952 Rockland Palace concert. Missing are examples of his early work with Jay McShann, broadcasts from the Royal Roost during 1948-49, the original string version of "Just Friends" and an example from his 1953 Massey Hall Concert, but perhaps a third CD would have been needed for all that! Perfect for beginners. —*Scott Yanow*

Yardbird in Lotus Land / Dec. 29, 1945-Apr. 1946 / Spotlite ◆◆◆◆
This LP from the fine English label Spotlite contains several remarkable radio broadcasts featuring the immortal altoist Charlie Parker. First Bird is heard with trumpet great Dizzy Gillespie in a quintet (with one number adding vibraphonist Milt Jackson) from Los Angeles on Dec. 29, 1945 during their famous stint at Billy Berg's. These versions of "Shaw 'Nuff," "Groovin' High" and "Dizzy Atmosphere" are four to six minutes long and really let the soloists stretch out. A briefer "Salt Peanuts" is also heard from the same group. Bird then participates on a ballad medley with fellow altoists Willie Smith and Benny Carter, plays "Ornithology" while joined by the Nat King Cole Trio and Buddy Rich, and finally performs five numbers with trumpeter Miles Davis in a quintet; all of these performances took place in Los Angeles before Parker was hospitalized. —*Scott Yanow*

Bebop's Heartbeat / Dec. 29, 1945-Sep. 29, 1947 / Savoy ◆◆◆◆
Half of this LP consists of the odd but famous Slim Gaillard session in which the guitarist/personality was joined by altoist Charlie Parker and trumpeter Dizzy Gillespie for four songs (highlighted by the humorous "Slim's Jam"). The flip side contains more essential music, the appearance by Diz and Bird at Carnegie Hall on Sept. 29, 1947. These renditions of "A Night in Tunisia," "Dizzy Atmosphere," "Groovin' High" and "Ko Ko" (despite the so-so recording quality) are brilliant, but Parker's solo on "Confirmation" really takes honors. —*Scott Yanow*

☆ **Bird: Complete on Verve** / Jan. 28, 1946-Dec. 10, 1954 / Verve ◆◆◆◆◆
As a leader, Charlie Parker recorded for Savoy and Dial during 1945-48 and then for Verve exclusively (at least in the studios) during 1949-54. This remarkable ten-CD box set, which adds quite a bit of material to an earlier ten-LP set, contains all of these recordings plus Bird's earlier appearances with Jazz at the Philharmonic. The JATP jams are highlighted by Parker's perfect solo on "Lady Be Good," a ferocious improvisation on "The Closer" and a solo on "Embraceable You" that tops his more famous studio recording. In addition, this box has all of the "Bird and Strings" sides; his meetings with Machito's Cuban orchestra; the 1950 session with Dizzy Gillespie and Thelonious Monk, small-group dates (including a 1951 meeting with Miles Davis); odd encounters with voices and studio bands; the famous "Jam Blues" with fellow altoists Johnny Hodges and Benny Carter; and his final recordings, a set of Cole Porter tunes. The fact-filled 34 page booklet is also indispensable. Highly recommended. —*Scott Yanow*

● **Confirmation: The Best of the Verve Years** / Jan. 28, 1946-Dec. 10, 1954 / Verve ◆◆◆◆◆
Anyone daunted by the expense of acquiring the 10-disc *The Complete Charlie Parker on Verve* may well have their prayers answered by this 2-CD distillation of the big box. It covers a wide stretch of material from Parker's career, going back to the first JATP concert in 1946 and stretching almost to the end of his Norman Granz period. One might prefer a chronological approach—which the box takes—to the wild skipping around from session to session and idiom to idiom that occurs here. But the set does touch all of the bases of the Verve catalogue—the JATP concerts, the string sessions, the Afro-Cuban experiments, the big band treatments, the botched Gil Evans session, and of course, the small combo formats that Parker usually worked within. As part of a basic Charlie Parker collection, which would also include samplings from the Dial and Savoy periods, these CDs are essential as an overview of the diverse formats that Parker explored while recording for Granz. —*Richard S. Ginell*

☆ **Complete Dial Sessions** / Feb. 5, 1946-Dec. 17, 1947 / Stash ◆◆◆◆◆
Charlie Parker recorded for Dial during the same period he was cutting his better-known sides for Savoy. This four-CD set contains his 89 Dial recordings including all of the alternate takes. The innovative altoist is heard with Dizzy Gillespie on "Diggin' Diz," playing definitive versions of "Moose the Mooche," "Yardbird Suite" and "Ornithology" in a septet; struggling during his tragic "Lover Man" date; on excerpts from a poorly recorded live session; backing singer Earl Coleman and interacting with the Erroll Garner Trio; playing his classic "Relaxin' at Camarillo" (four versions); and finally leading several sessions with his classic quintet (which included trumpeter Miles Davis, pianist Duke Jordan, bassist Tommy Potter and drummer Max Roach) recording such gems as "Dewey Square," "Embraceable You," and "Scrapple from the Apple." The final session adds the great trombonist J.J. Johnson to the group for more classic music. Essential music, highly recommended for all jazz collections. —*Scott Yanow*

In a Soulful Mood / Mar. 28, 1946-Dec. 17, 1947 / Music Club ◆◆◆◆
In seven recording sessions spaced over a year and a half's time, Charlie Parker changed the face of jazz forever. The sessions he recorded between March of 1946 into December of the following year for the Los Angeles-based Dial Record label set the pace for the new bebop style, with every solo that emerged from Bird's horn taken apart by every horn man like a fine watch. Dipping into the well spring of sides that Bird stockpiled for the label and choosing the takes that find him in a reflective spirit, this compilation goes a long way to be a nice bebop novice primer as well. Parker's work on "Lover Man," "Ornithology," "Yardbird Suite," "Scrapple from the Apple," and "Relaxin' at Camarillo" are the sides that truly set the pace in the evolution of the new style, while his ballad playing on "All the Things You Are," "Out of Nowhere," "My Old Flame," and "Embraceable You" is nothing short of breathtaking. The personnel on any of these tracks is truly a who's who of jazz, with Miles Davis, Dodo Marmarosa, Howard McGhee, Errol Garner, Barney Kessel, Max Roach, Wardell Gray, and J.J. Johnson all contributing mightily on various sides to making these Bird's most fully realized studio recordings. Although these tracks have been reissued exhaustively ad infinitum where every note blown and every take has been put under the jazz microscope, this compilation makes great listening and, with 18 tracks and a 56-minute running time, a budget-priced disc that offers astounding value as well. —*Cub Koda*

The Charlie Parker Story, Vol. 2 / Mar. 28, 1946-1954 / Stash Budget ✦✦✦✦
The second of two CDs in this budget series has a few of the highlights from Charlie Parker's brief but remarkable career. Six of the 13 selections are taken from his Dial recordings, there is a stunning version of "Ko Ko" from a 1949 Carnegie Hall Concert and a variety of live appearances from the 1949-54 period that are mostly drawn from radio and television broadcasts. All of the music is available in more complete form on a variety of Stash releases, but these two volumes can serve as a good introduction to Bird's music for general collectors who just want a taste of the master's magic. —*Scott Yanow*

At the 1946 JATP Concert / May 27, 1946 / Verve ✦✦✦✦✦
An exciting, no-holds-barred jam session with several all-time greats going after each other in an instrumental battle. This 1946 date featured Charlie Parker, Lester Young, Dizzy Gillespie, Coleman Hawkins, Buck Clayton, and Buddy Rich, among others, taking turns showing their mettle. The '92 CD reissue brings things up front with some glorious remastering. —*Ron Wynn*

The Legendary Dial Masters, Vol. 1 / 1946-1947 / Stash ✦✦✦✦
The recordings of alto saxophonist Charlie Parker made for the Dial label in the late '40s are among bop's most storied and vital. He helped establish the genre's vocabulary, playing with the verve, fury, and harmonic excellence that forever altered jazz's course and that of alto saxophonists. Parker worked with Miles Davis, Dizzy Gillespie, Lucky Thompson, and many others while cutting several sessions in California for a label owned by Ross Russell. While they have been reissued on vinyl by England's Spotlite label in nearly complete form, and in a haphazard manner by Warner Bros., this 1989 disc collects 25 seminal master takes from 1946 and 1947. Every solo deserves close scrutiny, as Parker and company turn theory and tradition inside out. —*Ron Wynn*

☆ **The Legendary Dial Masters, Vol. 2** / 1946-1947 / Stash ✦✦✦✦✦

Lullaby in Rhythm / Feb. 1, 1947-Sep. 20, 1947 / Spotlite ✦✦✦
This LP contains music from two radio broadcasts that feature a remarkable all-star band: altoist Charlie Parker, trumpeter Dizzy Gillespie, clarinetist John LaPorta, pianist Lennie Tristano, guitarist Billy Bauer, bassist Ray Brown and drummer Max Roach. In addition to playing bop standards of the period, to answer a request the ensemble performs a rather hilarious version of "Tiger Rag." The matchup of Tristano and his sidemen with Bird and Diz does not always work but it is fascinating to hear. In addition, there are a few excerpts from live sessions featuring poorly recorded but interesting Parker solos. —*Scott Yanow*

The Dean Benedetti Recordings of Charlie Parker / Mar. 1, 1947-Jul. 1, 1948 / Mosaic ✦✦
The packaging is impeccable, this seven-CD box set has a definitive 48-page booklet and the recording quality is as good as possible, so why the "Poor" rating? Dean Benedetti, a fanatical Charlie Parker disciple, recorded Bird extensively during three periods in 1947-48 but did his best to turn off his wire recorder whenever anyone but Parker was soloing. He became legendary, as did his long lost acetates, and Mosaic has done what it could to make the excerpts coherent but the results are still quite unlistenable. None of the performances on this large set are complete; guests such as Thelonious Monk and Carmen McRae are introduced, play or sing two notes and then are cut off. And, although Parker seems to play well, these performances reveal no new secrets and add nothing to his legacy. —*Scott Yanow*

Diz N Bird at Carnegie Hall / Sep. 29, 1947 / Roulette ✦✦✦✦
Nine years after Benny Goodman's groundbreaking concert, bebop finally came to Carnegie Hall. Most notable on this 1997 CD (which contains music that has been reissued many times, often incoherently) is the meeting between altoist Charlie Parker and trumpeter Dizzy Gillespie. Joined by the underrecorded piano of John Lewis, bassist Al McKibbon and the slightly overrecorded drums of Joe Harris, Bird and Diz generate some real fireworks on five songs, and Parker's rendition of "Confirmation," the CD's high point, is definitive and memorable. The remainder of the set (ten selections including "Cool Breeze," "One Bass Hit," "Cubano-Be, Cubano-Bop" and "Things to Come") features the Gillespie big band in typically spirited form. Of particular interest are a few numbers ("Relaxin' at Camarillo," which was arranged by George Russell, "Hot House," and "Toccata for Trumpet") that were never recorded in the studio by the big band. Classic bebop. —*Scott Yanow*

Anthropology / Nov. 8, 1947-Sep. 1948 / Spotlite ✦✦✦
This LP mostly consists of a radio broadcast from Nov. 8, 1947 that features an all-star band dubbed Barry Ulanov and His All-Star Metronome Jazzmen. Altoist Charlie Parker, trumpeter Fats Navarro, clarinetist John LaPorta, Allen Eager on tenor, pianist Lennie Tristano, guitarist Billy Bauer, bassist Tommy Potter, drummer Buddy Rich and Sarah Vaughan who sings "Everything I Have Is Yours." Each of the key musicians has their features including Bird on "Donna Lee" and Navarro throughout "Fats Flats." This set concludes with three numbers taken from a live performance by pianist/composer Tadd Dameron's Orchestra featuring the tenors of Allen Eager and Wardell Gray; the heated solos somehow overcome the poten-

tially distracting surface noise. Bop collectors will want to pick up this LP. —*Scott Yanow*

With Dizzy Gillespie & Miles Davis / 1947-1950 / Stash ✦✦
This CD from Stash's budget series has some "new" Charlie Parker performances but, as veteran collectors well know when confronted with Bird discoveries, the main question must always be "What condition is it in?" Unfortunately, the answer in this case is "Not good." The great altoist is heard playing with the Dizzy Gillespie big band on ten songs in addition to five selections with his own quintet (when Miles Davis was his trumpeter) and one obscurity from 1950. However, the music (recorded by customers in the audience on low budget-tape recorders) is generally incomplete since the tapes were often turned off at the conclusion of Parker's solos. Although Stash's engineers did what they could to correct the pitch and clean up the music, the results are still difficult to listen to, at least until one gets used to them. It is very interesting to hear Bird with Gillespie's orchestra (a collaboration otherwise never recorded) and to listen to Parker playing such unlikely songs as "Things to Come," a fairly lengthy "'Round Midnight," "Good Bait" and "Manteca." But this release is only for true Charlie Parker fanatics. —*Scott Yanow*

☆ **South of the Border: The Verve Latin-Jazz Sides** / Jan. 1948-Jan. 23, 1952 / Verve ✦✦✦✦✦
Verve gathers together all of the master takes of Charlie Parker's recordings with the swinging band of Afro-Cuban jazz pioneer Machito, along with ten other Latinized numbers that he cut in 1951-52. Besides illustrating the willingness of producer Norman Granz to experiment and take Parker out of a small-group bebop straitjacket, this CD shows that Bird's improvisational style changed hardly at all in a Latin setting. He continued to run off his patented lightning bop licks over the congas and bongos and they just happened to interlock with the grooves quite snugly, although he did adapt his phrasing of the tunes themselves to suit their rhythmic lines. Included here is the spectacular "No Noise" that he cut as a guest with Machito and tenorman Flip Phillips in 1948, as well as Chico O'Farrill's epic *Afro-Cuban Jazz Suite* (also with Machito). For those who do not have the 10-CD *The Complete Charlie Parker on Verve*—where all 14 selections can be found—this is an inexpensive way to hear Parker in a refreshingly different context at very nearly the top of his form. —*Richard S. Ginell*

The Band That Never Was / Mar. 1948 / Spotlite ✦✦✦
In 1950 arranger Gene Roland briefly ran a huge 25-piece rehearsal band. The orchestra did not last very long but on April 3 they recorded three numbers plus a lot of excerpts and those are included on this LP. Most notable is the fact that Charlie Parker pops up briefly on these songs, along with trombonist Jimmy Knepper and tenors Al Cohn and Zoot Sims, but the music is mostly of historical interest. Side two of this LP features the Charlie Parker quintet with trumpeter Miles Davis live from the Three Deuces in March 1948, playing quite well. —*Scott Yanow*

Bird on 52nd Street / Jul. 1948 / Original Jazz Classics ✦✦
Altoist Charlie Parker plays quite brilliantly on this live set (reissued on CD in the Original Jazz Classics series) with trumpeter Miles Davis, pianist Duke Jordan, bassist Tommy Potter and drummer Max Roach but the recording quality is consistently crummy and sometimes borders on the unlistenable. In fact, if it featured any other player but Bird, the music would certainly have not been released. For true Charlie Parker completists only. —*Scott Yanow*

☆ **Bird at the Roost: Vol. 1** / Sep. 4, 1948-Jan. 1, 1949 / Savoy ✦✦✦✦✦
Among the most rewarding live recordings of Charlie Parker are his performances on a regular series of broadcasts that emanated from the Royal Roost during 1948-49. Muse, in its Savoy series, released all of this valuable music on two double LPs and a single album; some of it has since appeared on CD. This first volume has six of these radio airchecks (with Symphony Sid Torin announcing) and finds Parker and his quintet (either Miles Davis or Kenny Dorham on trumpets, Tadd Dameron or Al Haig on piano, Curley Russell or Tommy Potter on bass and Max Roach or Joe Harris on drums) getting the opportunity to stretch out on four- to five-minute versions of songs such as "Groovin' High," "Big Foot," "Ornithology," "Slow Boat to China" and "East of the Sun" among others. A special highlight occurs when Bird answers a request on the December 25 broadcast and does a brilliant reworking of "White Christmas." Highly recommended. —*Scott Yanow*

Sessions Live, Vol. 2 / Dec. 12, 1948-Sep. 26, 1952 / Zeta ✦✦
This CD features Charlie Parker during live appearances from two periods. The first eight selections are taken from his Royal Roost broadcasts of 1948-49, music that is available in more coherent fashion elsewhere but is well worth hearing, featuring Miles Davis on one version of "Hot House" and Kenny Dorham elsewhere. The second half of this disc originated from the Rockland Palace Dance Hall in 1952, is poorly recorded (lots of audience noise) and has been reissued by many labels through the years. Bird is heard with a four-piece rhythm section (with strings added on "Laura") and plays reasonably well. —*Scott Yanow*

Sessions Live, Vol. 1 / 1948-1950 / Zeta ✦✦

An '89 CD reissue of late '40s and early '50s tracks with alto sax great Charlie Parker cut live at two seminal locations, Birdland and the Royal Roost. Some have been previously issued on separate live recordings from the same places. Miles Davis, Kenny Dorham, Max Roach, Fats Navarro, Art Blakey, Curley Russell, and Bud Powell are among the participants. —*Ron Wynn*

☆ **Bird at the Roost: Vol. 2** / Jan. 1, 1949-Feb. 19, 1949 / Savoy ✦✦✦✦✦

This double LP, the second of three volumes, continues the documentation of Charlie Parker's Royal Roost broadcasts, performances that allowed his quintet (with trumpeter Kenny Dorham, pianist Al Haig, bassist Tommy Potter and usually drummer Max Roach) to stretch out on such songs as "Scrapple from the Apple," "Hot House," "Barbados," "Groovin' High" and "Oop Bop Sh'Bam." The immortal altoist is heard at his peak throughout and is in consistently brilliant form, giving one a good idea as to what his live performances from the era must have been like. —*Scott Yanow*

Rara Avis / Feb. 21, 1949-1954 / Stash ✦✦✦✦

This CD released for the first time the soundtrack of two of Charlie Parker's appearances on television. Some of the music and talking is trivial and loose but a few of the performances are quite unique and Bird is heard with a variety of intriguing groups. From 1949 Parker plays a fine version of "Lover" and helps trumpeter Shorty Sherrock on "I Can't Get Started" but is drowned out by Sidney Bechet on an uptempo blues. From 1952 Bird gets featured on "Anthropology" and participates in a "Bop vs. Dixieland" blues with trumpeters Max Kaminsky and Miles Davis, trombonists Kai Winding and Will Bradley and clarinetist Joe Marsala; everyone gets to solo. This interesting CD concludes with Bird in fine form in 1954 with a quintet that also includes trumpeter Herb Pomeroy, material not available elsewhere. —*Scott Yanow*

Bird at the Roost: Vol. 3 / Feb. 26, 1949-Mar. 12, 1949 / Savoy ✦✦✦✦✦

Some of Charlie Parker's finest live recordings were performed at the Royal Roost and broadcast on the radio during 1948-49. Savoy, on two double LPs and this single album, released all of the music in chronological order. *Vol. 3* contains the final three broadcasts with Bird's quintet of the period (trumpeter Kenny Dorham, pianist Al Haig, bassist Tommy Potter and drummer Max Roach) being augmented by such special guests as vibraphonist Milt Jackson, tenor saxophonist Lucky Thompson and bop singers Dave Lambert and Buddy Stewart. Highlights include "Half-Nelson," "Cheryl," "Anthropology" and a 6-minute version of "Chasin' the Bird." Highly recommended along with the two earlier volumes. —*Scott Yanow*

Bird in Paris / May 8, 1949-Nov. 1950 / Spotlite ✦✦

During the last five or six years of his life, Charlie Parker's live performances were frequently recorded and later on many of these sessions were released posthumously. This LP documents Charlie Parker's first visit to France and mostly comprises a quintet performance (with trumpeter Kenny Dorham, pianist Al Haig, bassist Tommy Potter and drummer Max Roach) originally recorded on a portable disc machine; the recording quality is quite erratic and there are breaks in a few of the songs where the fan had to turn the disc over. This LP concludes with part of an overcrowded blues (that is chiefly notable as the only example of a song boasting solos from both Bird and soprano great Sidney Bechet) and a broadcast version of "Ladybird" from the following year that features Parker with a French orchestra. It's a very interesting set from a historical standpoint but this LP is not all that essential. —*Scott Yanow*

Charlie Parker with Strings: The Master Takes / Nov. 30, 1949-May 22, 1953 / Verve ✦✦✦✦✦

When producer Norman Granz decided to let Parker record standards with a full string section (featuring Mitch Miller on oboe!), the purists cried sellout, but nothing could be further from the truth. There's a real sense of involvement from Bird on these sides, which collects up all the master takes and also includes some live tracks from Carnegie Hall which—judging from the sometimes uneasy murmurings of the crowd—amply illustrates just how weirdly this mixture of bop lines against "legit" arrangements was perceived. The music on this collection is lush, poetic, romantic as hell and the perfect antidote to a surfeit of jazz records featuring undisciplined blowing. There's lots of jazz, but there's only one Bird. —*Cub Koda*

★ **Charlie Parker & Stars of Modern Jazz at Carnegie Hall (Christmas 1949)** / Dec. 25, 1949 / Jass ✦✦✦✦✦

This Carnegie Hall concert can be considered the height of the bebop era. Among the top young modernists heard near their early peaks are pianist Bud Powell, trumpeter Miles Davis, baritonist Serge Chaloff, altoist Sonny Stitt, trombonist Kai Winding, tenor saxophonists Stan Getz and Warne Marsh, pianist Lennie Tristano, altoist Lee Konitz and Sarah Vaughan. But while their performances are consistently outsanding, Charlie Parker and his quintet (which includes trumpeter Red Rodney, pianist Al Haig, bassist Tommy Potter and drummer Roy Haynes) steals

the show. Bird and Rodney rarely sounded more fiery than on their five songs and Parker's incredible solo on this version of "Ko Ko" might very well be his best. This CD is highly recommended for all collections. —*Scott Yanow*

One Night in Chicago / 1950 / Savoy ✦✦

Another LP primarily for Charlie Parker fanatics, this live performance finds Bird playing with some top Chicago musicians (the obscure Claude McLin on tenor, guitarist George Freeman, pianist Chris Anderson, bassist Leroy Jackson and drummer Bruz Freeman). Most of the selections are not quite complete although they offer a rare chance to hear Bird play songs not in his repertoire (including "There's a Small Hotel," "These Foolish Things" and "Keen and Peachy") but the recording quality is much worse than one would hope. It's interesting music but not really worth hearing more than once or twice. —*Scott Yanow*

Live at Birdland (1950) / Feb. 14, 1950 / EPM ✦

A major disappointment, this CD from its outside looks like a promising sextet session with Charlie Parker, trumpeter Red Rodney and trombonist J.J. Johnson, but whoever recorded these bootlegs shut off their machine whenever Bird was finished soloing, cutting off Rodney and Johnson after a few notes and virtually ruining the performances. In addition, the recording quality is fairly shaky and Bird really does not say anything all that new. This should not have been released. —*Scott Yanow*

Bird at St. Nick's / Feb. 18, 1950 / Original Jazz Classics ✦✦

Veteran Charlie Parker collectors generally know that they should avoid all but his most famous live sessions. It is not that Parker plays bad on this CD reissue (in fact his solo on "Confirmation" is quite miraculous) but, as is often the case with these privately recorded sets, the recording quality is horrible. Bird (with trumpeter Red Rodney, pianist Al Haig, bassist Tommy Potter and drummer Roy Haynes) plays quite well but these versions only hint at what the music must have sounded like. —*Scott Yanow*

Bird & Diz / Jun. 6, 1950 / Verve ✦✦✦✦✦

This session features quite a group: Charlie Parker on alto, trumpeter Dizzy Gillespie, pianist Thelonious Monk, bassist Curly Russell and drummer Buddy Rich. They perform five Bird originals along with "My Melancholy Baby" and there are also seven alternate takes included on this CD. This music is available as part of the Verve ten-CD box but this particular release is quite enjoyable by itself. Bird and Monk never recorded together otherwise. —*Scott Yanow*

One Night at Birdland / Jun. 30, 1950 / Columbia ✦✦✦✦

The recording date may be suspect (trumpeter Fats Navarro died of tuberculosis only a week later) and the recording quality is not state of the art but the music on this two-LP set is often quite brilliant. Charlie Parker is teamed with Navarro, pianist Bud Powell, bassist Curley Russell and drummer Art Blakey for extended (usually six- to ten-minute) versions of 13 songs including "'Round Midnight" (the only time that Bird ever recorded a Thelonious Monk tune), "Move," "Out of Nowhere" and "Ornithology." The all-star lineup clearly inspired each other, making this two-fer well worth searching for. —*Scott Yanow*

Apartment Sessions / Jun. 1950 / Spotlite ✦✦

This LP is strictly for Charlie Parker collectors because the music was privately recorded, the technical quality is streaky and Bird's solos were nearly all that was documented at these two jam sessions from 1950. Parker was in fine form on those days but there are many more essential Bird recordings available. —*Scott Yanow*

Bird with Strings / Aug. 23, 1950-Nov. 14, 1952 / Columbia ✦✦✦

During 1949-54, Charlie Parker often recorded and performed with a string section. This LP contains a cross section of Bird's live performances from 1950-52 and, although the string arrangements are the same as for the studio recordings, Parker's solos are quite a bit different. Pity there's no live version of "Just Friends," his most successful string recording. It's not quite essential music but worth picking up. —*Scott Yanow*

The Bird You Never Heard / Aug. 28, 1950-Jan. 18, 1954 / Stash ✦✦

This CD features Charlie Parker caught live in 1954 with a quintet including Herb Pomeroy, as part of an unknown group in 1950, with pianist Bud Powell, bassist Charles Mingus, drummer Art Taylor and Candido on congas on two songs from 1953 and sitting in with the Chet Baker Quartet in 1953 (although only Bird's solos from the latter were recorded). The recording quality is streaky and these leftover performances from routine gigs are recommended only for Charlie Parker completists. —*Scott Yanow*

In Sweden / Nov. 24, 1950 / Alamac ✦✦

This LP from the budget label Alamac finds Charlie Parker in brilliant form playing with asmall group filled with talented young Swedish players (including trumpeter Rolf Ericson). Unfortunately, the poor recording quality of this live performance lowers the rating quite a bit although listeners who really love Bird will want this one. —*Scott Yanow*

Summit Meeting at Birdland / Mar. 31, 1951-May 9, 1953 / Columbia ✦✦✦✦✦
This LP features the quintet of altoist Charlie Parker, trumpeter Dizzy Gillespie, pianist Bud Powell, bassist Tommy Potter and drummer Roy Haynes performing stirring versions of four bebop standards; "Blue 'n' Boogie" and "Anthropology" receive definitive and very exciting treatment. The flip side features Bird on "Groovin' High" with Milt Buckner's trio (the only time that Parker recorded with an organist) and on a few songs with pianist John Lewis, bassist Curly Russell, drummer Kenny Clarke; percussionist Candido sits in for "Broadway." The recording quality is acceptable and Bird's playing is exceptional. This recommended music should be reissued on CD. —*Scott Yanow*

The Happy Bird / Apr. 12, 1951 / Charlie Parker ✦✦✦
The weak recording quality hurts this LP a bit but it does offer extended performances of "Scrapple from the Apple" (over 15 minutes), "I Remember April" and "Lullaby in Rhythm" (mislabelled "I May Be Wrong") in addition to a short blues. These jam sessions, in addition to altoist Charlie Parker, feature solos from tenor saxophonist Wardell Gray, pianist Dick Twardzik and trumpeter Benny Harris; bassist Charles Mingus and drummer Roy Haynes are fine in support. Not essential music but recommended if seen at a budget price. —*Scott Yanow*

Live: Boston, Brooklyn . . . 1951 / Apr. 1951-Jun. 1951 / EPM ✦✦
Some of Charlie Parker's more fanatical fans followed him around constantly, taping his live performances but usually turning off their recorders whenever Bird's sidemen soloed. The results are poorly recorded excerpts from often-routine gigs. This CD, which features Parker on three separate occasions in 1951, is better than some of the bootleg releases in this idiom but of very limited interest except to Charlie Parker completists who have to have every note of his that has survived. —*Scott Yanow*

Bird with the Herd: 1951 / Aug. 1951 / Alamac ✦✦✦
As is often the case with Charlie Parker's live recordings from the 1950s, this rare performance has erratic sound and bad balance. Still this session, which finds Bird sitting in with Woody Herman's Third Herd, is quite unique. Parker is the main soloist throughout the budget LP, getting a chance to play some fresh material like "The Goof and I," "Four Brothers," and "Lemon Drop," and to interact with a big band. —*Scott Yanow*

Boston (1952) / Dec. 14, 1952-Jan. 18, 1954 / Uptown ✦✦✦✦
Alert Charlie Parker fans were delighted when this 1996 CD came out for it includes two previously unreleased (and well-recorded) radio broadcasts featuring the masterful altoist. Parker is in fine form during his two appearances at Boston's Hi Hat. With Symphony Sid as the disc jockey (he gets Bird to say a few words here and there), Parker romps through his usual repertoire, finding something fresh to say on songs that he had already been playing at least five years. Seven selections feature him in 1952 with trumpeter Joe Gordon, pianist Dick Twardzik, bassist Charles Mingus and drummer Roy Haynes, while four others (three are repeated titles from the earlier date) are from 1954 with trumpeter Herbie Williams, pianist Rollins Griffith, bassist Jimmy Woode and drummer Marquis Foster completing the group. Although both trumpeters (particularly Gordon) sound fine, Charlie Parker easily steals the show. The extensive liner notes, which fully discuss all of the engagements that Bird had in Boston throughout his career, are an added plus. —*Scott Yanow*

Inglewood Jam / Jun. 16, 1952 / Time Is ✦✦
This CD's historic value outweighs the below-par recording quality. Trumpeter Chet Baker is heard shortly before he joined Gerry Mulligan's quartet participating on a jam session with altos Charlie Parker and Sonny Criss. They play lengthy versions of four songs and there are plenty of heated moments on this bop set. It's recommended to listners who do not demand state-of-the-art sound. —*Scott Yanow*

The Complete Legendary Rockland Palace Concert 1952 / Sep. 26, 1952 / Jazz Classics ✦✦✦✦
Charlie Parker's Rockland Palace Concert of 1952 has been released in piecemeal fashion several times through the years, always with terrible sound. This two-CD set is a bit of a revelation for the sound quality, although still far from state-of-the-art, is greatly improved (and pitch-corrected) and the original 19 performances during the busy night for Bird have been expanded to 31. It should be mentioned that the 14 songs on the second disc are in a different order than is listed, although all of the tunes mentioned are included. This particular concert is notable in that the great altoist is heard not only leading a trumpetless quintet (with pianist Walter Bishop, guitarist Mundell Lowe, bassist Teddy Kotick and drummer Max Roach) but is joined on the majority of the numbers by a small string section and an oboeist. Although the strings stick to playing written-out arrangements, Bird's flights are full of surprises. Parker, other than a few unintentional honks and squeals in places, was in typically brilliant form and shows that his repertoire of the era was a lot more diverse than one might expect. Among the songs heard on this two-fer are rare versions of "Stardust," "Sly Mongoose," "This Time the Dream's on Me"

and a pair of Gerry Mulligan originals ("Turnstile" and "Rocker"), in addition to a bunch of standards. And, as one listens to Parker's fiery and explorative solos, it becomes obvious that while many of the players influenced by Bird performed bebop, Charlie Parker simply played himself. —*Scott Yanow*

One Night in Washington / 1953 / Elektra ✦✦✦✦
Charlie Parker had a rare chance to play with a big band during this Washington, DC, concert. Appearing without any rehearsal or even with music in front of him, Bird performed eight numbers with the orchestra, anticipating where the arrangements would go and not missing a cue. His brilliant playing on this out-of-print LP demonstrates to all listeners why he was considered one of the giants of jazz. The recommended set concludes with Red Rodney in the early '80s reminiscing a bit about his time with Charlie Parker. —*Scott Yanow*

Charlie Parker at Storyville / Mar. 10, 1953-Sep. 22, 1953 / Blue Note ✦✦✦
This LP contains two broadcasts featuring Charlie Parker at Boston's Storyville club in 1953. One set finds him accompanied by the Red Garland Trio (two years before Garland became famous playing with Miles Davis) while the other one also features trumpeter Herb Pomeroy and a trio led by pianist Sir Charles Thompson. The recording quality is just so-so but Bird was in fine form for these sessions, playing hot versions of his usual repertoire. —*Scott Yanow*

Yardbird: DC-53 / Mar. 1953-Apr. 1953 / VGM ✦✦✦
This LP contains a couple of live sessions from late in Charlie Parker's career. He is heard on three selections with a fairly large big band that probably includes Zoot Sims on tenor, and guitarist Charlie Byrd, along with four numbers performed with a trio. Bird is in better form than the recording quality, making this set of primary interest to his long-time collectors. —*Scott Yanow*

★ **Jazz at Massey Hall** / May 1953 / Original Jazz Classics ✦✦✦✦✦
The music on this CD features the famous Massey Hall Concert, which teamed together (for the last time on records) the unbeatable team of altoist Charlie Parker and trumpeter Dizzy Gillespie along with pianist Bud Powell, bassist Charles Mingus and drummer Max Roach. The full quintet performs six of their standards; listen to Bird burn on "Salt Peanuts" as a reaction to Gillespie's clowning. This is timeless and highly recommended music. —*Scott Yanow*

Bird at the Hi-Hat / Dec. 18, 1953-Jan. 24, 1954 / Blue Note ✦✦✦✦
One of the better examples of late-period Charlie Parker, this CD contains performances by Bird with a Boston-based quintet (featuring trumpeter Herbie Williams). The repertoire was already largely eight years old but Parker still played such standbys as "Ornithology," "Groovin' High" and "Out of Nowhere" with enthusiasm and creativity. Previously out as a pair of Phoenix LPs, this set should delight Bird's fans. —*Scott Yanow*

Bird / 1988 / Columbia ✦✦✦
This set has the soundtrack of Clint Eastwood's film *Bird*. Arranger Lennie Niehaus managed to isolate Charlie Parker's original alto solos (some from studio sessions and a few from rarer club appearances) and re-recorded them with contemporary bop-based musicians. The effect is rather eerie and generally works, allowing such musicians as pianists Monty Alexander, Barry Harris and Walter Davis, Jr., bassists Ray Brown, Chuck Berghofer and Ron Carter, drummer John Guerin and trumpeters Jon Faddis and Red Rodney to play with Bird. Worth acquiring if only for the novelty value since this setting did not allow Parker the opportunity to react to the other musicians. —*Scott Yanow*

Errol Parker (Raph Schecroun)

b. 1930, Oran, Algeria
Piano, Drums, Leader / Avant-Garde

Errol Parker's music, though largely overlooked by the jazz establishment, is quite fresh and original. Utilizing polytonality (playing in two keys at once), simultaneous soloing and his own drumming (which achieves an African sound by substituting a conga for the snare drum), Parker's tentet sounds unlike any other group. Mostly self-taught on piano, he moved to Paris in 1947 to study sculpture but was soon playing jazz. Parker (under his original name Raph Schecroun) recorded on sessions led by Kenny Clarke, James Moody and Django Reinhardt and played off and on with Don Byas during 1956-58. He recorded some commercial music on organ in 1960 and then, to escape from an exclusive contract so as to record jazz versions of Top 40 material on piano, he used the pseudonym Errol Parker. The latter records sold so well that he permanently changed his name. A car accident in 1963 cut short his commercial success and forced Parker to change his style. After moving to New York in 1968 he formed the Errol Parker Experience which featured two horns. Because he was not satisfied with any other drummers, he began doubling on drums himself and the first few records for his Sahara label find Parker playing (via overdubbing) both piano and drums. In 1982 while teaching at the Williamsburg Music Center, he formed a big band that eventually became his tentet. Due to the eight horns he utilizes, Parker stopped playing piano except for solo engagements and stuck to drums. His recordings (which includes a solo piano tribute to Thelonious Monk) have utilized such sidemen as Robin Eubanks, Wallace Roney, Donald Harrison, Steve Coleman, Graham Haynes, Phillip Harper, Byard Lancaster and Jimmy Owens among others. —*Scott Yanow*

Baobab / Mar. 1978-Apr. 1978 / Sahara ✦✦✦

Doodles / 1979 / Sahara ✦✦✦✦

Tentet / Apr. 26, 1982 / Sahara ✦✦✦✦✦

Algerian-born pianist/percussionist in an original mode. Extraordinary creative music, live in "rehearsal" at the Williamsburg Music Center in Brooklyn. —*Michael G. Nastos*

● **Tribute to Thelonius Monk** / May 4, 1982 / Sahara ✦✦✦✦✦

Solo piano, although no tunes by Monk. —*Michael G. Nastos*

Compelling Forces / 1985 / Cadence ✦✦✦✦

Errol Parker Tentet / Apr. 9, 1991 / Sahara ✦✦✦✦✦

Errol Parker's unusual music (which uses bitonality and simultaneous soloing) has never really caught on due to its complexity, but it is well worth exploring. This fine CD finds Parker sticking to drums and utilizing such top players as trumpeter Phillip Harper, altoist Donald Harrison, and guitarist Cary De Nigris. Together the seven-horn pianoless ten-piece ensemble creates unusual versions of "A Night in Tunisia" and "Ol' Man River" and six originals by the leader. —*Scott Yanow*

Remembering Billy Strayhorn / Sep. 7, 1994+Sep. 28, 1994 / Sahara ✦✦✦✦

Evan Parker

b. Apr. 5, 1944, Bristol, England
Soprano Saxophone, Tenor Saxophone / Avant-Garde, Free Jazz

Among Europe's most innovative and intriguing saxophonists, Evan Parker's solos and playing style are distinguished by his creative use of circular breathing and false fingering. Parker can generate furious bursts, screeches, bleats, honks and spiraling lines and phrases and his solo sax work isn't for the squeamish. He's one of the few players not only willing but anxious to demonstrate his affinity for late-period John Coltrane. Parker worked with a Coltrane-influenced quartet in Birmingham in the early '60s. Upon resettling in London in 1965, Parker began playing with Spontaneous Music Ensemble. He joined them in 1967 and remained until 1969. Parker met guitarist Derek Bailey while in the group, and the duo formed The Music Improvisation Company in 1968. Parker played with them until 1971, and also began working with the Tony Oxley Sextet in the late '60s. Parker started playing extensively with other European free music groups in the '70s, notably The Globe Unity Orchestra as well as its founder Alexander von Schlippenbach's trio and quaret. Parker, Bailey and Oxley co-formed Incus Records in 1970 and continued operating it through the '80s. Parker also played with Chris McGregor's Brotherhood of Breath, other groups with Bailey and did duet sessions with John Stevens and Paul Lytton as well as giving several solo concerts. Parker's albums as a leader and his collaborations are all for various foreign labels; they can be obtained through diligent effort and mail order catalogs. —*Ron Wynn*

Collective Calls / Apr. 15, 1972-Apr. 16, 1972 / Urban ✦✦✦✦

● **Saxophone Solos** / Jun. 17, 1975-Dec. 9, 1975 / Incus ✦✦✦✦✦

Monoceros / Apr. 30, 1978 / Incus ✦✦✦✦✦

Ra 1+2 / Jun. 6, 1978 / Moers ✦✦✦✦

Six of One / Jun. 18, 1980 / Incus ✦✦✦✦✦

Incision / Mar. 1981 / FMP ✦✦✦

Hook, Drift and Shuffle / Feb. 4, 1983 / Incus ✦✦✦

Conic Sections / Jun. 21, 1989 / Ah Um ✦✦✦✦✦

Hall of Mirrors / Feb. 1990 / MM&T ✦✦✦

Process and Reality / 1991 / FMP ✦✦✦✦

The Redwood Session / Jun. 18, 1995 / CIMP ✦✦✦✦✦

This live set was the initial release by the mostly avant-garde CIMP label. Evan Parker (on soprano and tenor) interacts with bassist Barry Guy and drummer Paul Lytton on four lengthy, free sound explorations. Parker generally dominates, achieving a wide variety of sounds out of his horns. The closing "Then Paul Saw the Snake" is the actual high point because trumpeter Joe McPhee sits in, making the trio a dynamic quartet and the music a little more accessible. Those listeners with very open ears should find this set of interest. —*Scott Yanow*

Mars Song / Oct. 24, 1996 / Victo ✦✦✦

Leo Parker

b. Apr. 18, 1925, Washington, DC, d. Feb. 11, 1962, New York, NY
Baritone Saxophone / Bop, Hard Bop

Leo Parker was the proud owner of a big, beefy baritone sax tone and a fluent technique that struck a great match between the gritty, down-home feeling of R&B and the advanced harmonies of bebop. At first, he studied alto in high school, even recording with Coleman Hawkins' early bebop band at age 18 on that instrument in 1944. But upon joining the legendary Billy Eckstine bop band in 1944-45 and '46, Parker switched to baritone and began to garner notice. He worked with Dizzy Gillespie's band on 52nd Street in 1946 and Illinois Jacquet's group in 1947-48, and recorded with Fats Navarro, J.J. Johnson, Dexter Gordon and Sir Charles Thompson—scoring a hit with Thompson, "Mad Lad," on the Apollo label. Parker seemed to be on his way, but drug problems—an epidemic in the bop community—kept interfering with his career, and he recorded only sporadically in the 1950s. In September and October 1961, Parker began a comeback on the Blue Note label with two lively albums that successfully combined his blues, gospel and bop backgrounds. But only a few months later, a heart attack felled him at the age of 36. —*Richard S. Ginell*

The Baritone Great (1951-1953) / Jul. 7, 1951-Aug. 10, 1953 / Chess ✦✦✦✦

Let Me Tell You 'Bout It / Sep. 9, 1961 / Blue Note ✦✦✦✦

This session (reissued on CD) was a comeback record of sorts for Leo Parker. Briefly one of the leading bebop baritone saxophonists (and an alumnus of Billy Eckstine's legendary orchestra), Parker shifted to rhythm and blues in the early 1950s and then mostly dropped out of sight until he recorded this set. After cutting a second album, he died of a heart attack at age 36 on Feb. 11, 1962. A guttural player who emphasized the lower register of the baritone and was influenced by Illinois Jacquet, Parker (who is joined by obscure sidemen) sounds in top form during his varied program which includes several hard swingers, the gospellish funk of the title cut and two selections not on the original LP: "The Lion's Roar" and a second version of "Low Brown." —*Scott Yanow*

● **Rollin' with Leo** / Oct. 12, 1961+Oct. 20, 1961 / Blue Note ✦✦✦✦✦

Baritonist Leo Parker was in the early stages of a comeback when he recorded this, his second Blue Note album of 1961. Tragically, he died just four months later at the age of 36. Performing with a fairly obscure cast (trumpeter Dave Burns is the best known of his sidemen), the full-toned baritonist (who was most influenced by Illinois Jacquet and Charlie Parker) is in excellent form on these basic blues, ballads and jump tunes. —*Scott Yanow*

Leon Parker

Drums / Post-Bop

Leon Parker consistently shows that less is more by making a great deal of music on a greatly reduced drum set sometimes consisting of only a snare drum, bass drum and a cymbal. Parker started playing drums when he was three and became serious when he was around 11. At 15 he playing in a local youth jazz band, and two years later he started studying classical percussion. After graduating from high school, Parker moved to New York City, taking lessons with Barry Harris and freelancing. During a regular gig as a leader at Augie's, he began minimizing his drum set, learning to play entire sets using just a cymbal. He made his recording debut with Harvie Swartz, toured with Sheila Jordan and gigged with Kenny Barron. Parker spent 1989 with his wife Lisa (a flutist), playing throughout Spain and Portugal. Back in New York, he became part of the regular band at the Village Gate. The colorful drummer toured and recorded with Dewey Redman, worked with David Sanchez and was part of the Jacky Terrasson Trio in the mid-1990s. Leon Parker has thus far recorded as a leader for Epicure and Columbia. —*Scott Yanow*

● **Above & Below** / 1994 / Epicure ✦✦✦✦✦

Belief / 1996 / Epicure ✦✦✦

Leon Parker has gained some fame for his ability to create a great deal of sounds out of a very small drum set. This interesting but not essential CD features intimate music ranging from quiet folk songs with influences from several cultures to a bit of straightahead jazz; "Close Your Eyes" has some fine alto work by Steve Wilson in a pianoless trio. Other voices include trumpeter Tom Harrell, trombonist Steve Davis, flutist Lisa Parker and bassist Ugonna Okegwo. Nice music that makes one look forward to Leon Parker's future projects. —*Scott Yanow*

William Parker

Bass / Avant-Garde, Free Jazz

In the early '90s, the direct musical heirs of Taylor, Ayler, and Coleman were mostly ignored by New York jazz critics, who found more to like about the hard bop revivalists who dominated major-label recording. Hence, the public visibility of musicians devoted to an "energy music" aesthetic was minimal. Despite its low profile, however, that strain of free jazz was kept alive by a fairly large group of Lower East Side musicians, many of whom gathered around the music's pre-eminent bassist, William Parker. Parker was the scene's major catalyst for musical activity. With his wife, dancer Patricia Nicholson, and other downtown free players such as drummer Jackson Krall and pianist Mark Hennen, Parker founded the Improvisers Collective, an organization that presented free jazz in combination with other types of spontaneous performance. Beginning in 1994 (and continuing in one form or another as of this writing), the collective produced a well-received series of concerts and festivals that featured some of the city's finest free impro-visers—saxophonists Marco Eneidi, Sabir Mateen, and Daniel Carter, trumpeter Lewis Barnes, and pianist Cooper-Moore, to name a few. Parker was the fulcrum of the collective; he played in nearly all of its various ad hoc groups, and led the Collective's enormous big band, which later recorded under Parker's name as the Little Huey Creative Music Ensemble.

As a bassist, Parker is possessed of a formidable technique, albeit an unconventional one. Unlike a great many jazz bassists, Parker was not formally trained as a classical player, though he did study with three of the finest jazz players of the '60s: Jimmy Garrison, Richard Davis, and Wilbur Ware. Consequently, Parker's style is based on a tradition of self-expression and experimentation. His arco work is possibly the most fascinating aspect of his idiom; Parker excels at the creation of dense, hyperactive streaks of color, gleaned from the inherent harmonic properties of the instrument. At bottom, he is a textural player. Lyricism plays a secondary role in his work, with or without the bow. Parker's pizzicato style is overwhelmingly percussive, in intent and effect. Though he does, to an extent, serve as a harmonic anchor in his groups, his more important role is as a source of energy. Parker drives a band like few other bassists; in combination with a powerful drummer, a Parker-led rhythm section is an inexorable force.

Parker grew up in New York City. Very early in his career he formed an association with Cecil Taylor; Parker played Carnegie Hall with the pianist in the early '70s. Parker released his first album as a leader in 1979. *Through the Acceptance of the Mystery Piece* (on Parker's own Centering Records) featured saxophonists Charles Brackeen and Jemeel Moondoc and violinist Billy Bang. Parker became Taylor's regular bassist in the '80s. He played on several of the pianist's European records, and on Taylor's most recent domestic major-label release, 1989's *In Florescence*, on A&M. Parker left Taylor in the early '90s and began working more often as a leader. He recorded a big-band record for his own label, then began releasing a series of CDs for other companies, significantly Black Saint. Besides his activities as a leader and community organizer, Parker would continue to work as a sideman through the mid-'90s; he remained the bassist of choice for downtown free players like David S. Ware, Matt Shipp, and Rob Brown. —*Chris Kelsey*

Through Acceptance of the Mystery Piece / Feb. 1974-Jan. 21, 1979 / Centering ✦✦✦

● **In Order to Survive** / Apr. 11, 1993+Jun. 28, 1993 / Black Saint ✦✦✦✦

The Listeners / Dec. 1995 / New World ✦✦✦

Testimony / Feb. 13, 1996 / Zeroin ✦✦✦

Compassion Seizes Bed-Stuy / Jul. 9, 1996 / Homestead ✦✦✦✦✦

Sunrise in the Tone World / 1997 / Aum Fidelity ✦✦✦✦

Horace Parlan

b. Jan. 19, 1931, Pittsburgh, PA
Piano / Hard Bop

Horace Parlan has overcome physical disability and thrived as a pianist despite it. His right hand was partially crippled by polio during his childhood, but Parlan's made frenetic, highly rhythmic right-hand phrases part of his characteristic style, contrasting them with striking left hand chords. He's also infused blues and R&B influences into his style, playing in a stark, sometimes somber fashion. Parlan has always cited Ahmad Jamal and Bud Powell as prime influences. He began playing in R&B bands during the '50s, joining Charles Mingus' group from 1957 to 1959 following a move from Pittsburgh to New York. Mingus aided his career enormously, both through his recordings and his influence. Parlan played with Booker Ervin in 1960 and 1961, then in the Eddie "Lockjaw" Davis-Johnny Griffin quintet in 1962. Parlan played with Rahsaan Roland Kirk from 1963 to 1966, and had a strong series of Blue Note recordings in the '60s. He left America for Copenhagen in 1973, and gained international recognition for some stunning albums on Steeple Chase, including a pair of superb duet sessions with Archie Shepp. He also recorded with Dexter Gordon, Red Mitchell, and in the '80s Frank Foster and Michal Urbaniak. He also has recorded extensively for Steeple Chase, Enja and Timeless in the 1980s. —*Ron Wynn*

Movin' and Groovin' / Feb. 29, 1960 / Blue Note ✦✦✦✦
Horace Parlan's debut album for Blue Note, *Movin' and Groovin'*, is a thoroughly impressive affair, establishing Parlan as a distinctive hard bop stylist. Working with

bassist Sam Jones and drummer Al Harewood, Parlan steals the show, playing hard-driving, bluesy bop and lyrical ballads. If it weren't for the inventive chord voicings and percussive right-hand attack, it would be impossible to tell that he was missing two fingers on his right hand, since his playing is remarkably agile and fluid. Parlan sounds vital on swinging blues, slow ballads and straightahead bop, and Jones and Harewood provide appropriately empathetic support on this collection of standards, blues, bop, jazz and originals. Everything swings, no matter the tempo, and the end result is a fine debut from a distinctive pianist. —*Stephen Thomas Erlewine*

Us Three / Apr. 20, 1960 / Blue Note ✦✦✦✦
Despite difficulties left over from polio (the fourth and fifth fingers of his right hand are largely unusable), Horace Parlan has been able to carve out a long-term career as a pianist. His chord voicings, although sometimes a little sparse, are quite effective, and occasionally he uses his left hand to play single-note lines. This 1997 CD reissue is a fairly conventional set featuring Parlan with bassist George Tucker and drummer Al Harewood. The musicians work quite well together, often functioning on an equal basis (particularly on the title cut), and they swing their way through three of Parlan's originals and four standards (including "I Want to Be Loved" and "Walkin'"). Horace Parlan was a popular Blue Note artist during the era, recording seven albums for the label from 1960-63 (all but one from 1960-61), but this is virtually his only set thus far reissued on CD. —*Scott Yanow*

Speakin' My Piece / Jul. 16, 1960 / Blue Note ✦✦✦✦✦
Horace Parlan had a gift for relaxed, swinging hard bop which placed his piano in a central, yet unassuming role. *Speakin' My Piece* is one of the first albums to find Parlan getting all the ingredients right, from his own subtle playing to soliciting fine contributions of his backing band. Stanley Turrentine, in fact, turns out to be an excellent complement to Parlan, playing in a similarly tasteful style. Five of the six numbers are band originals, and each number is quite similar—bluesy, gently swinging hard bop. No one pushes too hard on *Speakin' My Piece*, preferring to create an intimate atmosphere with milder numbers and performances. Such an approach gives each muscian—Parlan, Turrentine, bassist George Tucker, drummer Al Harewood—a chance to shine with lyrical, melodic solos and/or sympathetic support, resulting in a charmingly low-key session. —*Stephen Thomas Erlewine*

Headin' South / Dec. 4, 1960 / Blue Note ✦✦✦✦
On the surface, *Headin' South* is another set of bluesy soul-jazz, but it actually finds the Horace Parlan trio stretching out a little. Adding conga player Ray Barretto to his usual rhythm section of bassist George Tucker and drummer Al Harewood, Parlan decides to take chances with his standard-heavy repertoire. "Summertime" features some evocative bowing from Tucker, and the solo sections on "The Song Is Ended," "Prelude to a Kiss" and "My Mother's Eyes" offer probing, intriguing tonal textures that make the selection of Ahmad Jamal's "Jim Loves Sue" understandable. Barretto's "Congalegre" is a fun, Latin-inflected number, and Parlan's "Headin' South" is a strong, swinging blues, but the slow blues "Low Down" is nearly undone by his incessant circular arpeggio, which lasts for over a minute. Still, that's not nearly enough to sink the record, which is another understated but solid effort from Horace Parlan. —*Stephen Thomas Erlewine*

On the Spur of the Moment / Mar. 18, 1961 / Blue Note ✦✦✦✦
Again working with his longtime rhythm section of George Tucker (bass) and Al Harewood (drums), Horace Parlan manages to make *On the Spur of the Moment* distinctive by emphasizing the rhythmic side of his hard bop. Tenor saxophonist Stanley Turrentine and trumpeter Tommy Turrentine help give the quintet a bluesy edge, which the band exploits to an appealing effect throughout these six, mostly original, compositions. There are a few ballads, and even when things are at their hottest, Parlan's understated playing is a cue for the group to keep it tasteful, but that relaxed atmosphere is part of the reason why *On the Spur of the Moment* is another winning effort from the underrated pianist. —*Stephen Thomas Erlewine*

Up and Down / Jun. 18, 1961 / Blue Note ✦✦✦✦✦
By adding guitarist Grant Green and tenor saxophonist Booker Ervin to his standard rhythm section of bassist George Tucker and drummer Al Harewood, pianist Horace Parlan opens up his sound and brings it closer to soul-jazz on *Up and Down*. Green's clean, graceful style meshes well with Parlan's relaxed technique, while Ervin's robust tone and virile attack provides a good contrast to the laidback groove the rhythm section lays down. Stylistically, the music is balanced between hard bop and soul-jazz, which are tied together by the bluesy tint in the three soloists' playing. All of the six original compositions give the band room to stretch out and to not only show off their chops, but move the music somewhat away from generic conventions and find new territory. In other words, it finds Parlan at a peak, and in many ways, coming into his own as a pianist and a leader. —*Stephen Thomas Erlewine*

● **Happy Frame of Mind** / Feb. 15, 1963 / Blue Note ✦✦✦✦

Happy Frame of Mind finds Horace Parlan breaking away from the soul-inflected hard bop that had become his trademark, moving his music into more adventurous, post-bop territory. Aided by a first-rate quintet—trumpeter Johnny Coles, tenor saxophonist Booker Ervin, guitarist Grant Green, bassist Butch Warren, drummer Billy Higgins—Parlan produces a provocative set that is grounded in soul and blues but stretches out into challenging improvisations. None of the musicians completely embrace the avant-garde, but there are shifting tonal textures and unpredictable turns in the solos which have been previously unheard in Parlan's music. Perhaps that's the reason why *Happy Frame of Mind* sat unissued in Blue Note's vaults until 1976, when it was released as part of a double-record Booker Ervin set, but the fact of the matter is, it's one of Parlan's most successful efforts, finding the perfect middle ground between accessible, entertaining jazz and more adventurous music. —*Stephen Thomas Erlewine*

Arrival / Dec. 21, 1973-Dec. 22, 1973 / Steeple Chase ✦✦✦✦✦

No Blues / Dec. 10, 1975 / Steeple Chase ✦✦✦✦

Frankly Speaking / Feb. 5, 1977 / Steeple Chase ✦✦✦✦

Blue Parlan / Nov. 13, 1978 / Steeple Chase ✦✦✦✦

The Maestro / Nov. 26, 1979 / Steeple Chase ✦✦✦

Musically Yours / Nov. 26, 1979 / Steeple Chase ✦✦✦

Pannonica / Feb. 11, 1981 / Enja ✦✦✦✦✦

Good early -80s trio session with pianist Horace Parlan working alongside bassist Reggie Johnson and drummer Alvin Queen. The material, mostly standards with some originals and ballads, isn't overly ambitious, but Parlan's dense, strong blues-influenced solos and good interaction among the three principals keeps things moving. —*Ron Wynn*

Like Someone in Love / Mar. 1983 / Steeple Chase ✦✦✦✦

Glad I Found You / Jul. 30, 1984 / Steeple Chase ✦✦✦✦✦

Straightahead blowing date. Eddie Harris (ts) almost outdoes Parlan. —*Ron Wynn*

Little Esther / Mar. 1987 / Steeple Chase ✦✦✦

Hi-Fly / Sep. 23, 1997 / Steeple Chase ✦✦✦

Joe Pass (Joseph Anthony Passalaqua)

b. Jan. 13, 1929, New Brunswick, NJ, d. May 23, 1994, Los Angeles, CA
Guitar / Bop

Joe Pass did the near-impossible. He was able to play uptempo versions of bop tunes such as "Cherokee" and "How High the Moon" unaccompanied on the guitar. Unlike Stanley Jordan, Pass used conventional (but superb) technique, and his *Virtuoso* series on Pablo still sounds remarkable two decades later.

Joe Pass had a false start in his career. He played in a few swing bands (including Tony Pastor's) before graduating from high school and was with Charlie Barnet for a time in 1947. But after serving in the military, Pass became a drug addict, serving time in prison and essentially wasting a decade. He emerged in 1962 with a record cut at Synanon, made a bit of a stir with his *For Django* set, recorded several other albums for Pacific Jazz and World Pacific and performed with Gerald Wilson, Les McCann, George Shearing and Benny Goodman (1973).

However, in general Pass maintained a low profile in Los Angeles until he was signed by Norman Granz to his Pablo label. *Virtuoso*, in 1973, made him a star and he recorded very prolifically for Pablo, unaccompanied, with small groups, on duo albums with Ella Fitzgerald and with such masters as Count Basie, Duke Ellington, Oscar Peterson, Milt Jackson and Dizzy Gillespie. Pass remained very active up until his death from cancer. —*Scott Yanow*

The Best of Joe Pass: Pacific Jazz Years / Feb. 1961-Sep. 1964 / Pacific Jazz ✦✦✦

Guitar great Joe Pass' first three years on the Pacific label are the subject of this best-of collection, which offers material cut with his own quartet as well as recordings with Gerald Wilson's Orchestra, Richard "Groove" Holmes, Les McCann and the Sounds of Synanon. —*Jason Ankeny*

The Complete "Catch Me!" Sessions / 1963 / Blue Note ✦✦✦✦✦

Joe Pass' first session as a leader finds the 34-year-old guitarist already playing in a fairly recognizable, boppish style. Pass, who had somehow survived his drug addiction of the 1950s, is well featured in a quartet with pianist Clare Fischer (who doubles on organ), Albert Stinson or Ralph Pena on bass and Colin Bailey or Larry Bunker on drums. This 1980 reissue (unfortunately not yet reissued on CD) is called "complete" because the original eight selections are joined by an alternate take of the original and a version of "Days of Wine and Roses." Excellent bop that largely launched Joe Pass' career, although fame was a decade away. —*Scott Yanow*

Great Movie Themes / 1963 / World Pacific ✦✦

Joy Spring / Feb. 6, 1964 / Blue Note ✦✦✦✦✦

Joe Pass was near the beginning of his career (after a decade of fighting drug addiction) when he recorded the live quartet session included on this CD reissue. The great guitarist was in his early prime, nine years before he started recording for Pablo. Pass is immediately recognizable on the straightahead bebop date and is supported by a fine rhythm section that includes pianist Mike Wofford, bassist Jim Hughart and drummer Colin Bailey. The group stretches out on five standards (the renditions are six-and-a-half to ten-and-a-half minutes apiece) but never runs out of inventive ideas. Easily recommended. —*Scott Yanow*

For Django / Oct. 1964 / Pacific Jazz ✦✦✦✦

Long considered a classic, guitarist Joe Pass' fourth date as a leader (not yet available on CD) finds him performing music that was composed by Django Reinhardt, was part of his repertoire, or is one of two more recent tributes (John Lewis' "Django" and Pass' "For Django"). Pass is joined by the rhythm guitar of John Pisano, bassist Jim Hughart and drummer Colin Bailey; the quartet would reunite in the 1980s. Although Pass was actually more strongly influenced by Charlie Christian than by Reinhardt, and he had already formed his own style, he has no difficulty fitting into the music. Highlights include "Rosetta," "Nuages" and "Limehouse Blues." —*Scott Yanow*

A Sign of the Times / 1965 / World Pacific ✦✦

The Stones Jazz / 1966 / World Pacific ✦✦

Simplicity / 1967 / Pacific Jazz ✦✦✦

An aptly titled release, as guitarist Joe Pass offers smooth, fluent songs, crisp, polished solos, and sentimental material, and does everything with a modicum of effort and intensity. —*Ron Wynn*

Living Legends / Aug. 20, 1969 / Discovery ✦✦✦

Guitar Interludes / Aug. 29, 1969-Apr. 14, 1970 / Discovery ✦✦✦

● **Guitar Virtuoso** / Jan. 30, 1973-Aug. 12, 1992 / Pablo ✦✦✦✦✦

Norman Granz liked to record his artists a lot, and Joe Pass was one of the most prolifically recorded of all of them over the last two decades of his life. As this lavishly boxed, four-CD distillation of his Pablo sessions proves, Pass was probably the guitar-playing equivalent of Art Tatum on the Granz roster—not only for his vast output, but also for the all-encompassing, almost orchestral way in which he got around his instrument. The set is divided equally into four sections—disc one for his astounding solo electric and acoustic guitar sides, disc two for studio recordings with various groups, disc three for various live recordings solo and with groups, disc four the delicate Ella Fitzgerald and other duo partner sessions and quartet pieces backing Sarah Vaughan. Though the box is not in chronological order—which is not necessary here, since Pass was essentially a finished, non evolving artist when he joined Pablo—Jim Ferguson's helpful commentary on the sessions is chronologically organized, balancing out Benny Green's personalized disc-by-disc analysis of the tracks. While the stunning intricacy of the solo tracks form the cornerstone of Pass' reputation, the most immediately winning ones are the informally swinging group sessions that Pass made with the driving supporting guitar of John Pisano at his side. A couple of tracks with a modern Brazilian rhythm section also stand out, as does the supercharged "Sweet Georgia Brown" with Oscar Peterson and Niels-Henning Orsted Pedersen, and the set's lengthiest item, a fond ten-minute take out on "Stompin' at the Savoy" live at Donte's club in North Hollywood, CA. The latter track and a scant two others are the only ones new to CD, and there are no unreleased goods to be heard, but with five hours of Pass taken a little at a time, this box will wear very well over the years. —*Richard S. Ginell*

Virtuoso, Vol. 4 / Nov. 1973 / Pablo ✦✦✦✦✦

The fourth in the series that gave guitarist Joe Pass a forum to show things that weren't always evident on his many studio dates. Everything, from the elaborate and sophisticated solos to his choices of material, reflected his commitment to excellence, and every release he made for the line was superb. —*Ron Wynn*

★ **Virtuoso, Vol. 1** / Dec. 1973 / Pablo ✦✦✦✦✦

This is the album that made Joe Pass famous. On what was actually his second set of unaccompanied guitar solos ("*Virtuoso No.4*" from a month earlier was released years later), Pass shows that it is possible to play unaccompanied versions of such uptempo tunes as "How High the Moon," "Cherokee" and "The Song Is You" on guitar. Pass not only performs the melodies and heated solos, but provides bass lines and harmonies while using a conventional technique (unlike Stanley Jordan's later tapping). Pass would record many unaccompanied recordings and perform at numerous solo concerts during the next 20 years; this is the set that started it all, and it is a certified classic. An essential CD. —*Scott Yanow*

Joe Pass at Akron University / 1974 / Pablo ✦✦✦✦

Most of the material on this concert was familiar, but remained fresh. Of the newer work, "Bridgework" was a blues with a bridge, "Tarde" a Milton Nascimento ballad and "Time In," a key-switching blues. Joe Pass retained his position as one of the masters of the jazz guitar with this album. —*Scott Yanow, Cadence*

Portraits of Duke Ellington / Jun. 21, 1974 / Pablo ✦✦✦✦✦

Recorded just a month after Duke Ellington's death, this tribute album (reissued on CD) features guitarist Joe Pass (just beginning to become famous), bassist Ray Brown and drummer Bobby Durham jamming on eight Ellington tunes and "Caravan" (which was penned by one of Duke's key sidemen, Juan Tizol). The interplay between the three musicians is quite impressive, and Pass' mastery of the guitar is obvious (he didn't really need the other sidemen). Highlights include "In a Mellotone," "Don't Get Around Much Anymore" and "I Got It Bad." Recommended. —*Scott Yanow*

Live at Dante's / Dec. 8, 1974+Dec. 9, 1974 / Pablo ✦✦✦✦

During a period when he was receiving renown as an unaccompanied solo guitarist, the release of this double LP reminded listeners that Joe Pass could also swing hard in a trio setting. Accompanied by the electric bass of Jim Hughart and drummer Frank Severino, Pass mostly explores standards including a few ("What Have They Done to My Song," "A Time for Love" and "You Are the Sunshine of My Life") that were fairly recent at the time. The performances are as excellent as one would expect. In fact, considering how many albums he did for Pablo (a few dozen), it is remarkable to realize that every one of them are quite rewarding. —*Scott Yanow*

Montreux '75 / Jul. 17, 1975+Jul. 18, 1975 / Original Jazz Classics ✦✦✦✦✦

Outstanding solo guitar by Joe Pass, done at the '75 Montreux Festival to an appreciative audience. Pass plays with more energy than on his studio works, doing the usual standards, ballads, and mainstream fare, but also demonstrating an exuberance and joyful flair that's more understated on most occasions. —*Ron Wynn*

Virtuoso, Vol. 2 / Sep. 14, 1976+Oct. 26, 1976 / Pablo ✦✦✦✦✦

The second of Joe Pass' solo guitar albums for Pablo finds the remarkable Pass exploring more recent standards than one might expect. In addition to a few warhorses, there is also "Feelings" (which he somehow manages to make tolerable), "If," two Chick Corea songs ("Five Hundred Miles High" and "Windows") and even "Giant Steps." Pass' mastery of the guitar is obvious throughout this enjoyable set. —*Scott Yanow*

Quadrant Toasts Duke Ellington / Feb. 2, 1977 / Original Jazz Classics ✦✦✦✦

There's a bit more intensity here, thanks to the presence of Milt Jackson (vib), Ray Brown (b), and Mickey Roker (d). —*Ron Wynn*

Virtuoso, Vol. 3 / May 27, 1977+Jun. 1, 1977 / Original Jazz Classics ✦✦✦✦✦

A '92 CD reissue of the third in a series recorded in 1977. Guitarist Joe Pass, whose talent is often taken for granted due to the introspective, relaxed nature of his sessions, displayed his full range and technical skills on a three-volume set designed to highlight those abilities. This third volume was no less a standout than the previous two. —*Ron Wynn*

Montreux '77: Live! / Jul. 15, 1977 / Original Jazz Classics ✦✦✦✦

An '89 CD reissue of a '77 release that was originally included in the Pablo Live series. The digital remastering accents the shadings, voicings, and melodic counterpoint that are Pass' strong points. He's doing familiar material, but adding twists and turns that the receptive, aware audience greatly appreciated. —*Ron Wynn*

Tudo Bem! / May 8, 1978 / Original Jazz Classics ✦✦✦

Afro-Latin and Brazilian material done by guitarist Joe Pass, as he shows his fluency in this idiom. The songs are mostly solid, and even on those that are less than impressive, Pass' steady playing and fluid sound makes them tolerable. —*Ron Wynn*

Chops / Nov. 19, 1978 / Original Jazz Classics ✦✦✦✦✦

I Remember Charlie Parker / Feb. 17, 1979 / Original Jazz Classics ✦✦✦✦

This is a worthy reissue of Pass' late '70s tribute to Charlie Parker. —*Ron Wynn*

Northsea Nights / Jul. 1979 / Pablo ✦✦✦✦

Guitarist Joe Pass and bassist Niels Pedersen, a pair of talented virtuosi, are typically outstanding on this live set of standards. With the exception of their ad-lib "Blues for the Hague," all of the material would qualify as overdone through the years (such as " 'Round Midnight" and "Stella by Starlight") but the duo makes these veteran pieces sound fresh and new again. —*Scott Yanow*

All Too Soon / Feb. 21, 1980 / Original Jazz Classics ✦✦✦✦

Solid, nicely played standards, originals, blues, and ballads by guitarist Joe Pass. He seldom plays in an exuberant fashion, preferring a smooth, relaxed, yet also intricately crafted solo approach. His full notes and elaborate voicings are technically impressive, although sometimes a lack of thematic variety results in his albums all sounding the same. —*Ron Wynn*

Checkmate / Jan. 12, 1981 / Pablo ✦✦✦✦

George, Ira & Joe (Joe Pass Loves Gershwin) / Nov. 23, 1981 / Pablo ✦✦✦✦

There aren't many better matches than the lush, innocent songs of George Gershwin and Joe Pass' equally sentimental, spinning guitar phrases embellishing Gershwin's music. Certainly these songs have been done by countless jazz greats, and Pass doesn't necessarily add anything new. But his takes are wonderfully played, and his choices of material are first-rate. —*Ron Wynn*

Eximious / May 25, 1982-Jul. 8, 1982 / Pablo ✦✦✦✦✦

We'll Be Together Again / Oct. 23, 1983 / Pablo ✦✦✦✦

Live at Long Bay Beach College / Jan. 20, 1984 / Pablo ✦✦✦✦

During the '80s, the Pablo label instituted a series of live albums by their prime stars. This one featured guitarist Joe Pass, and like several Pass dates done in concert, there was more energized playing. Pass' big, sustained tones, carefully constructed solos, and generally impressive technique were demonstrated with a minimum of flair. —*Ron Wynn*

Whitestone / Feb. 28, 1985-Mar. 1, 1985 / Pablo ✦✦✦

Here's nothing new or fresh, but still solid Pass. —*Ron Wynn*

Blues for Fred / Feb. 2, 1988-Feb. 3, 1988 / Pablo ✦✦✦✦

The Pass guitar is impressive as always, though the songs are erratic. —*Ron Wynn*

One for My Baby / Dec. 28, 1988 / Pablo ✦✦✦✦

Virtuoso guitarist Joe Pass didn't need sidemen on any recording, but when he used them, he chose wisely. Tenor saxophonist Plas Johnson, keyboardist Gerald Wiggins and drummer Tootie Heath had not recorded with Pass previously, but along with bassist Andy Simpkins, they achieve a perfect first-take sound on each track. The title cut features Pass with Johnson's bluesy sax and a soft organ and brushed background. Two Pass originals are lengthy blues vehicles with plenty of solo space for all. "I Remember You" is an unlikely choice that developed from Wiggins' jamming in the studio; the ballad is a relaxing detour from the blues that dominate the CD. Joe Pass was without peer on guitar the last 20 years of his life; his playing here won't disappoint. —*Ken Dryden*

Summer Nights / Dec. 1989 / Pablo ✦✦✦✦

This recent Pass boasts impeccable guitar but sometimes undistinguished cuts. —*Ron Wynn*

Joe Pass in Hamburg / Apr. 23, 1990-Feb. 21, 1992 / Blue Jackel ✦✦✦✦

Appassionato / Aug. 9, 1990-Aug. 11, 1990 / Pablo ✦✦✦✦

Guitarist Joe Pass reunited with the same musicians he had used on his classic 1963 album *For Django* for this relaxed exploration of a dozen jazz standards: rhythm guitarist John Pisano, bassist Jim Hughart and drummer Colin Bailey. Alternating romps with ballads, Pass is in typically fine form throughout with "Relaxin' at Camarillo," "Red Door" and "That's Earl, Brother" receiving rare revivals. This CD is one of literally dozens of worthy Joe Pass Pablo recordings. —*Scott Yanow*

Duets / Feb. 16, 1991-Feb. 17, 1991 / Pablo ✦✦✦

A pair of guitarists with a great deal of affection for each other's styles, showcased here in a set of delicate duets that allow both to shine equally. There's never any false flash or glamour, only charm and style. —*Steven McDonald*

Virtuoso: Live! / Sep. 13, 1991-Sep. 15, 1991 / Pablo ✦✦✦✦✦

This continuation of the virtuoso series spotlighting guitarist Joe Pass' skills differed from the others in that this time he was recorded live. The extra ingredient seemed to make Pass play with even more brilliance; he executed difficult runs, octave jumps, and phrases with verve, while his interpretations of standards and harmonic maneuvers were often amazing. —*Ron Wynn*

Live at Yoshi's / Jan. 30, 1992-Feb. 1, 1992 / Pablo ✦✦✦✦✦

An inspired and exciting set by jazz's guitarist nonpareil, it ranges from a blistering race through Sonny Rollins' "Oleo" to the gentle duet with Pass' longtime partner Pisano on "Alone Together." "Swingin' Till the Girls Come Home" is a feature for Budwig, the great West Coast bass player who died shortly after this set. It's one of the best of the many Joe Pass albums. —*Les Line*

Live at Yoshi's, Vol. 2 / Jan. 30, 1992-Feb. 1, 1992 / Pablo ✦✦✦✦✦

Far from being a casual collection of rejects, there is plenty of mellow gold from Joe Pass on this posthumously released second volume from what must have been a memorable gig at this Oakland, California night spot. The two-guitar quartet format was an optimum showcase for Pass' nimble, melodic bop electric guitar, for the greatly unsung fellow guitarist John Pisano offers inspired harmonic, rhythm or obligato support at all times, giving Pass an extra push from underneath. On "I Remember You" and "What Is This Thing Called Love?," Pisano even gives Pass some solo chases which generate a lot of steam, and the gentle semi-bossa nova treatment of Neal Hefti's "Repetition" also bring out the best in both. Bassist Monty Budwig (subbing for Jim Hughart) and drummer Colin Bailey are also in superb form throughout this can't-miss outing. The sound quality is OK, though hum can be heard in some quiet stretches. —*Richard S. Ginell*

Joe Pass & Co. / Jan. 1992 / Pablo ✦✦✦✦

Six Sting Santa / Feb. 4, 1992 / LaserLight ✦✦✦✦

This is one of guitarist Joe Pass' more obscure late-period records. Pass and his regular working quartet of the early '90s (rhythm guitarist John Pisano, bassist Jim Hughart and drummer Colin Bailey) perform a variety of famous Christmas-related songs, plus his own "Happy Holiday Blues." The tasteful renditions swing and include quartet pieces, some two-guitar duets and a few unaccompanied solos from the great Pass, resulting in one of the better Christmas albums around. —*Scott Yanow*

● **Songs for Ellen** / Aug. 7, 1992-Aug. 20, 1992 / Pablo ✦✦✦✦✦

This posthumous CD is novel because it features Joe Pass exclusively on acoustic guitar, and it is obvious that he enjoyed every minute of these sessions. "The Shadow of Your Smile" is no longer easy listening fodder, as Pass turns it into a miniature master class in swing. "Star Eyes" is accented by the soft squeaks of Pass' fingers gently weaving their intricate magic. Most of the works of Joe Pass tended to be improvised blues, so the title track is an exception—a simple yet elegant ballad written for his wife. "Blues for Angel" highlights his matchless mastery of slow blues. The boppish blues "Satellite Village" is a perfect closer. The good news is that there are several more unreleased sessions by Joe Pass that will follow this superb collection. —*Ken Dryden*

My Song / Feb. 2, 1993-Feb. 4, 1993 / Telarc ✦✦✦✦

During his last years, guitarist Joe Pass often used the same unit on a regular basis that he had utilized to record his classic *For Django*, back in 1963. For this pleasing effort John Pisano offers some suitable rhythm guitar while bassist Jim Hughart and drummer Colin Bailey are typically tasteful in support. Tom Ranier is an important addition to the quartet, having one outing apiece on tenor, clarinet and soprano while playing piano on the remaining tracks. Joe Pass naturally emerges as the main star, interpreting the nine standards and two of his originals with taste, hard-driving swing and creativity within the bop tradition. Pass made so many recordings during the 20 years preceding this date that it is difficult to call any one of them "definitive" but this is an excellent group effort. —*Scott Yanow*

Roy Clark & Joe Pass Play Hank Williams / 1994 / Buster Ann Music ✦✦✦✦✦

At first glance, this project, which would be Joe Pass' final recording, might seem a bit unlikely. Pass is teamed up with country guitarist Roy Clark to play a set of Hank Williams tunes, but the date is actually quite successful. Clark has long been a closet jazz player; many of Williams' tunes have attractive chord changes, and Pass had his longtime rhythm section (rhythm guitarist John Pisano, bassist Jim Hughart and drummer Colin Bailey) serving as a solid foundation. Such songs as "Hey, Good Lookin'," "Your Cheatin' Heart," "Long Gone Lonesome Blues" and "There'll Be No Teardrops Tonight" work quite well in this setting. Since Clark (a brilliant guitarist himself) had long been a Joe Pass fan, the results are both competitive and complementary. Recommended. —*Scott Yanow*

Jaco Pastorius (John Francis Pastorius)

b. Dec. 1, 1951, Norristown, PA, d. Sep. 21, 1987, Fort Lauderdale, FL
Bass / Fusion, Post-Bop

Jaco Pastorius was a meteor who blazed onto the scene in the 1970s, only to flame out tragically in the 1980s. With a brilliantly fleet technique and fertile melodic imagination, Pastorius made his fretless electric bass leap out from the depths of the rhythm section into the front line with fluid machine-gun-like passages that demanded attention. He also sported a strutting, dancing, flamboyant performing style and posed a further triple-threat as a talented composer, arranger and producer. He and Stanley Clarke were the towering influences on their instrument in the 1970s.

Though born in Pennsylvania, Pastorius grew up in Fort Lauderdale, where he played with visiting R&B and pop acts while still a teenager, and built a reputation as a local legend. Everything started to come together for him quickly once he started playing with another rookie fusionmeister, Pat Metheny, around 1974. By 1976, he had been invited to join Weather Report, where he remained until 1981, gradually becoming a third lead voice along with Joe Zawinul and Wayne Shorter. Outside Weather Report, he found himself in constant demand as a sessionman and producer, playing on Joni Mitchell, Blood Sweat and Tears, Paul Bley, Bireli Lagrene and Ira Sullivan albums—and his first eponymous solo album for Epic in 1976 was hailed as a tour de force. From 1980 to 1984, he toured and recorded with his own band, the innovative Word of Mouth that fluctuated in size from a large combo to a big band.

Alas, Pastorius became overwhelmed by mental problems, exacerbated by drugs and alcohol, in the mid-'80s, leading to several embarrassing public incidents (one was a violent crackup onstage at Hollywood Bowl in mid-set at the 1984 Playboy Jazz Festival). Such episodes made him a pariah in the music business and toward the end of his life, he had become a street person, reportedly sighted in drug-infested inner-city hangouts. He died in 1987 from a physical beating sustained

while trying to break into the Midnight Club in Fort Lauderdale. Though almost totally forgotten at the time of his death, Pastorius was immediately canonized afterwards (Miles Davis even wrote a tune "Mr. Pastorius" in his honor)—too late for him to have received therapy or help. —*Richard S. Ginell*

Jaco / Jun. 16, 1974 / Improvisng Artists ✦✦✦

This live recording is quite historic for it has the earliest documentation of both electric bassist Jaco Pastorius and guitarist Pat Metheny. Recorded by keyboardist Paul Bley for his Improvising Artists label (without the knowledge of his sidemen which also included drummer Bruce Ditmas), this CD reissues the same relatively brief program as was on the LP. Metheny is actually a minor figure on this date (the recording quality keeps him from sounding distinctive) but Pastorius' raging solos and heated accompaniment inspired Bley to make him the leader of this date. The program consists (with one exception) of songs by either Paul or Carla Bley and generally holds one's interest. —*Scott Yanow*

★ **Jaco Pastorius** / Aug. 1976 / Epic ✦✦✦✦✦

This is one of the most astonishing solo debuts in jazz history, particularly when you realize that this was a 24-year-old barely out of Fort Lauderdale. From the bold opening track "Donna Lee," with only Don Alias' congas as accompaniment, Jaco's electric bass takes command, a rapid, fluid, dancing, rounded-toned force that threads its way obsessively into your brain. The presence of heavywight help like Herbie Hancock, Hubert Laws, Lenny White and Wayne Shorter doesn't faze Jaco a bit; he dominates his musicians at all times. Nor is this strictly a jazz-rock date, for Jaco tries his hand at writing big band brass charts, string arrangements, and Caribbean steel drum music, as well as 1960s post-bop in Hancock's sophisticated idiom—and he scores well everywhere. And there is a flash of startling originality in "Okonkolé Y Trompa," where a French horn intones a pastoral tune over sequencer-like tattoos from Jaco and the congas—a beautiful vision of peace without new age flaccidity. Look no further for the basic source of the Jaco legend. —*Richard S. Ginell*

The Birthday Concert / Dec. 1, 1981 / Warner Brothers ✦✦✦✦

On an irregular basis in the early 1980s, the innovative electric bassist Jaco Pastorius led a big band that he called Word of Mouth. This excellent CD documents Pastorius' 30th birthday party, a concert at which he was joined by the Peter Graves Orchestra (consisting of 14 horns, two steel drums and two percussionists) plus drummer Peter Erskine, Don Alias on conga, and both Michael Brecker and Bob Mintzer on tenors. Brecker co-stars with Pastorius on a strong program that is highlighted by "The Chicken," a burning rendition of "Invitation," and "Liberty City." The music is full of spirit and joy, featuring Pastorius at the peak of his powers just before his tragic decline. —*Scott Yanow*

Word of Mouth / Dec. 1981 / Warner Brothers ✦✦✦✦

Bassist Jaco Pastorius' Word of Mouth orchestra was an unfulfilled dream, a worthy concept that did not last long enough to live up to its potential. Its debut album was released without a listing of the personnel, so here it is: Wayne Shorter, Michael Brecker and Tom Scott on reeds, trumpeter Chuck Findley, the easily recognizable Toots Thielemans on harmonica, Howard Johnson on tuba, drummers Jack DeJohnette and Peter Erskine and percussionist Don Alias. The music ranges from The Beatles' "Blackbird" and some Bach to Jaco originals that cover straightahead jazz, Coltranish vamps and fusion. Next to the bassist/leader, Thielemans emerges as the main voice. It's worth checking out but not essential. —*Scott Yanow*

Invitation / Dec. 1983 / Warner Brothers ✦✦✦✦

More big-band music live in Japan. Look for the CD with more tracks. —*Michael G. Nastos*

Honestly: Solo Live / Mar. 1986 / Big World ✦✦✦✦

Bassist Jaco Pastorius' throbbing, booming electric bass lines made him both a celebrity and a marked man during his lifetime. This Italian date caught Pastorius in peak form; both his speed and facility were unequaled, and he truly approached his instrument like a lead guitar, strumming, zipping through passages, and executing incredible runs. —*Ron Wynn*

Live in Italy / Mar. 1986 / Jazzpoint ✦✦✦

While this bears Pastorius' name as a leader, guitarist Bireli Lagrene comes close to making it his own work. The usually dominating Pastorius takes a more supportive position, while Lagrene ranges, roams, and soars, ripping off swinging solos that reflect his debt to Django Reinhardt. Drummer Thomas Borocz, although playing sensitively and with power, almost gets left behind by the Lagrene/Pastorius team. —*Ron Wynn*

John Patitucci

b. Dec. 22, 1959, New York, NY
Bass / Fusion, Post-Bop

One of the top bassists of the 1990s (on both acoustic and electric), Patitucci's speed, very clear tone and versatility are quite impressive. He started playing bass when he was 11, grew up in Northern California and in 1978 moved south near Los Angeles. He played with Gap Mangione (1979) while going to college and during 1982-85 worked in Los Angeles with Tom Scott, Robben Ford, Stan Getz, Larry Carlton, Dave Grusin, Ernie Watts, Freddie Hubbard and others in addition to becoming a studio musician. In 1985 he gained a high profile when he joined Chick Corea as a regular member of both the Elektric and Akoustic bands. Patitucci toured and recorded extensively with Corea and has made a series of his own diverse sessions for GRP and Stretch (although he is not as strong a composer as he is a bassist). John Patitucci left the Elektric Band in the early '90s but has continued working with Corea on an occasional basis. —*Scott Yanow*

John Patitucci / Dec. 1987 / GRP ✦✦

Stepping out from the shadows of Chick Corea's Elektric and Akoustic bands, Patitucci made a pleasing solo debut here largely on the strength of his brilliant up-front soloing on electric and acoustic basses. Adept at the popular funk slapping manner on electric bass, darting fluidly and jaggedly up high on the Smith/Jackson five-string bass, Patitucci always executes with the moves and body English of a bass player even when his instrument is up in the guitar range. Patitucci's compositions are fairly good, too; thoughtful and not too reliant upon jazz-rock cliches. He gets a lot of expert help from a variety of hot sidemen, including the astonishing Chick himself (who also produced the package), Chick's drummer Dave Weckl, other drummers like Peter Erskine and Vinnie Colaiuta, and the heated tenor sax of Michael Brecker. Without a doubt, this first opus enhanced Patitucci's developing reputation at the time. —*Richard S. Ginell*

On the Corner / 1989 / GRP ✦✦

Sketchbook / 1990 / GRP ✦✦✦

● **Heart of the Bass** / 1991 / Stretch ✦✦✦✦✦

Fusion standout John Patitucci flashes the speed, facility, and flash that's made him the darling of the contemporary jazz set. He's joined by the man whose band has showcased him, pianist Chick Corea, plus percussionist Alex Acuna and other guest stars. The songs are fairly routine, but Patitucci and Corea's performances elevate them. —*Ron Wynn*

Another World / 1993 / GRP ✦✦✦✦

John Patitucci has quickly developed into one of the world's great bassists, both on acoustic and electric. He is not on the same level as a composer but is steadily improving as witness the music on ths fine release. There are many bass solos as one would expect (Patitucci's high-note flights often sound like a guitar) but he does leave space for his sidemen, most notably keyboardist John Beasley (who has two numbers without the bassist), trumpeter Jeff Beal and one selection apiece for the steel drums of Andy Narell and Mike Brecker's tenor. A few tracks are throwaway funk but there are enough surprise twists and unusual improvisations to make this a recommended disc even for adventurous listeners. —*Scott Yanow*

Mistura Fina / Jun. 23, 1994-Aug. 20, 1994 / GRP ✦✦✦

John Patitucci, a brilliant bassist best known for his fusion playing with Chick Corea's Elektric Band, leans strongly in the direction of Brazilian pop music on this CD. Most of the selections have vocals and, although Patitucci takes a lot of excellent acoustic bass solos (and there are occasional solo spots for keyboardist John Beasley and saxophonist Steve Tavaglione), this CD is more in the world music than fusion vein. The vocalists include Joao Bosco, Dori Caymmi, Kleber Jorge, Ivan Lins, Cathy Brandolino and Kevyn Lettau. —*Scott Yanow*

One More Angel / Nov. 19, 1995-Oct. 18, 1996 / Concord Jazz ✦✦✦

Pat Patrick

b. Nov. 1929, d. Dec. 31, 1991, Moline, IL

Baritone Saxophone, Alto Saxophone, Flute / Avant-Garde, Early Free, Progressive Big Band, Modern Creative

Pat Patrick, like John Gilmore, spent virtually his entire career with Sun Ra's Arkestra, leading to him being somewhat underrated. Patrick had a particularly appealing sound on baritone and, although he did not lead any record sessions of his own, he was one of the better baritonists of the 1950s and '60s. As a child he studied piano, drums and trumpet before switching to saxophones. At Du Sable High School in Chicago he first met John Gilmore. Patrick recorded with John Coltrane (*Africa Brass*), played briefly with Duke Ellington, was a member of a little-known version of Thelonious Monk's quartet (1970) and in 1974 he recorded with the Jazz Composer's orchestra. But otherwise, Pat Patrick from 1954 on and off until his death, was closely associated with Sun Ra where he was a reliable sideman. —*Scott Yanow*

Don Patterson

b. Jul. 22, 1936, Columbus, OH, d. Feb. 10, 1988, Philadelphia, PA

Organ / Soul-Jazz, Hard Bop, Groove

Columbus, Ohio-born Don Patterson began his musical career as a pianist, inspired by Erroll Garner. A solid soul-jazz, blues and hard bop organist with a pianistic background, Patterson didn't utilize the pedals or play with as much rhythmic drive as some other stylists, but developed a satisfactory alternative approach. Patterson's organ solos were smartly played, and more melodic than explosive. He switched from piano in 1956 after hearing Jimmy Smith. Patterson made his organ debut in 1959, and worked with Sonny Stitt, Eddie "Lockjaw" Davis, Gene Ammons and Wes Montgomery in the early '60s. He recorded with Ammons, Stitt and Eric Kloss in the early and mid-'60s. Patterson worked often in a duo with Billy James and made several recordings in the '60s and '70s as a leader. He and Al Grey worked together extensively in the '80s. Patterson recorded as a leader for Prestige and Muse. He has one session available on CD. —*Ron Wynn and Michael G. Nastos*

Goin' Down Home / Jan. 22, 1963 / Cadet ✦✦✦✦

Trio with Patterson on the Hammond B-3, Paul Weeden on guitar and Billy James on drums. Includes the Nat Adderley tune "Worksong." —*Michael Erlewine*

Legends of Acid Jazz / May 12, 1964 / Prestige ✦✦✦✦

Among all the practitioners of soul-jazz during the genre heyday of the late 1960s into the 1970s, Hammond B-3 organ groovemeister Don Patterson and modern Texas tenor Booker Ervin (also a veteran of jazz ensembles led by Randy Weston and Charles Mingus) are among those usually overlooked. Yet the pair teamed up to release several albums during that time that were, if not standards of the genre precisely, full of vitality and fever—Ervin's playing, especially, often sounded so emotional and combustible that it seemed like he was suffering a nervous breakdown through his horn, perhaps a residue of his time with Mingus. *Legends of Acid Jazz: Don Patterson / Booker Ervin* surfs the cream of three mid-'60s recording sessions: in a trio setting with drummer Billy James, all five selections from *The Exciting New Organ of Don Patterson*, including one of Miles Davis' early signature tunes, "Oleo" (actually a Sonny Rollins composition); the title track from *Hip Cake Walk*, a 17-minute monument to the soulful power of organ that endured as Patterson's most-beloved hip-swiveler (featuring Leonard Houston on alto sax); and "Love Me with All Your Heart" from *Patterson's People. Legends of Acid Jazz: Don Patterson / Booker Ervin* suffers only slightly from a program that leans heavily toward the mainstream—"Love Me with . . ." goes more than six minutes, and "When Johnny Comes Marching Home" nearly eleven. —*Chris Slawecki*

The Boss Men / Dec. 28, 1965 / Prestige ✦✦✦

Don Patterson with Sonny Stitt on alto sax and Billy James on drums. —*AMG*

Mellow Soul / May 10, 1967 / Prestige ✦✦✦

A trio date with David Fathead Newman on sax and flute plus Billy James on drums. —*AMG*

Four Dimensions / Aug. 25, 1967 / Prestige ✦✦✦

Patterson with Houston Person (sax), Pat Martino (g), and Billy James (d). —*AMG*

● **Dem New York Blues** / Jun. 5, 1968+Jun. 2, 1969 / Prestige ✦✦✦✦✦

Despite claims to the contrary, organist Don Patterson was very much of the Jimmy Smith school, a hard-driving player with fine improvising skills but lacking a distinctive sound of his own. This CD (which reissues two complete LPs) features Patterson in prime form in a quintet with trumpeter Blue Mitchell, Junior Cook on tenor and guitarist Pat Martino, and with a separate group that features trumpeter Virgil Jones and both George Coleman and Houston Person on tenors. Although "Oh Happy Day" is a throwaway, Patterson's spirited renditions of the blues and standards make this a fairly definitive example of his talents. —*Scott Yanow*

Funk You / Sep. 24, 1968 / Prestige ✦✦✦✦

With Charles McPherson on alto sax, Sonny Stitt on alto/tenor, Pat Martino on guitar, and Billy James on drums. —*AMG*

Brothers Four / Sep. 15, 1969 / Prestige ✦✦✦✦

The Genius of the B-3 / Oct. 30, 1972 / Muse ✦✦✦✦✦

A fine album (fast and slow) with Patterson in excellent form. There is some very nice soul-jazz here. CD clocks out at 43 minutes. —*Michael Erlewine*

These Are Soulful Days / Sep. 17, 1973 / Muse ✦✦✦✦✦

Quartet with this great Hammond B-3 organist, Jimmy Heath (sax), Pat Martino (g) and A. Heath (d). —*Michael G. Nastos*

Movin' Up / Jan. 31, 1977 / Muse ✦✦✦✦

Competent, sometimes animated soul-jazz from organist Don Patterson. Although not as blues-oriented as Jimmy McGriff or Jack McDuff, nor as ambitious as Charles Earland, Patterson plays catchy, clever tunes with good solos and interesting rhythm hooks. —*Ron Wynn*

Why Not / Jan. 26, 1978 / Muse ✦✦✦

Big John Patton

b. Jul. 12, 1935, Kansas City, MO

Organ / Hard Bop, Soul-Jazz, Groove

Big John Patton was not nearly as well-known as other warriors in the organ jazz field of the 1960s, yet he could be counted upon for a reliable, even fervent collection of blues and bop-saturated licks and steady bass lines on the Hammond B-3. Mostly self-taught with some rudimentary instruction from his mother, Patton started playing piano in 1948, eventually landing a gig with the Lloyd Price touring band from 1954 to 1959 before moving to New York. Once there, he began to make the transition from piano to organ, learning a lot from two future recording mates, drummer Ben Dixon and guitarist Grant Green. He recorded with Lou Donaldson for Blue Note from 1962 to 1964 and, after impressing Blue Note founder Alfred Lion, made the first of a string of albums as a leader for the label in 1963. Interestingly, many of his albums, though scheduled for release, never saw the light of day until after Blue Note's resurrection in 1985. When the Hammond B-3 and soul-jazz went out of fashion in the 1970s, Patton's career went into eclipse as well, and he settled in East Orange, NJ. But shortly after he started recording again in 1983, Patton was rediscovered by a younger generation, particularly the avant-garde figure John Zorn, who began using his sound out of its usual context on recordings like *The Big Gundown* and *Spillane*'s "Two-Lane Highway." —*Richard S. Ginell*

Along Came John / Apr. 5, 1963 / Blue Note ✦✦✦✦

By the time John Patton recorded *Along Came John*, his debut as a leader, he had already become a familiar name around the Blue Note studios. He, guitarist Grant Green, and drummer Ben Dixon had become the label's regular soul-jazz rhythm section, playing on sessions by Lou Donaldson, Don Wilkerson and Harold Vick, among others. They had developed an intuitive, empathetic interplay that elevated many of their sessions to near-greatness, at least in the realm of soul-jazz. That's one of the reasons why *Along Came John* is so successful—the three know each other so well that their grooves are totally natural, which makes them quite appealing. These original compositions may not all be memorable, but the band's interaction, improvisation and solos are. Tenor saxophonists Fred Jackson and Harold Vick provide good support, as well, but the show belongs to Patton, Green and Dixon, who once again prove they are one of the finest soul-jazz combos of their era. —*Stephen Thomas Erlewine*

Blue John / Jul. 11, 1963-Aug. 2, 1963 / Blue Note ✦✦✦✦✦

This is a fairly bright bit of soul-jazz, not quite as heavy as your normal soul-jazz session. There is nice guitar by Grant Green. The trumpet of Tommy Turrentine and the stritch (two saxophones braced together) of George Braith are not your usual soul-jazz instruments. The dual-horn sound of the stritch ends up sounding too much like honking car horns for my taste. It is hard to stay in the groove in the middle of the freeway. But any John Patton is worth having. —*Michael Erlewine*

The Way I Feel / Jun. 19, 1964 / Blue Note ✦✦✦

For his third album, Big John Patton decided to expand his band to quintet. Retaining the services of his longtime colleagues, guitarist Grant Green and drummer Ben Dixon, he hired tenor saxophonist Fred Jackson (who also played on *Along Came John*) and trumpeter Richard Williams. The combination of two horns can occasionally overshadow the groove Patton, Green and Dixon lay down, but for the most part, the musicians augment the music instead of detracting from it. Nevertheless, the combo never manages to match the peaks of *Along Came John* and *Blue John*. There are several fine moments on the record, and Green and Patton are typically enjoyable, but the record overall is a slight disappointment after its two predecessors. —*Stephen Thomas Erlewine*

Oh Baby / Mar. 8, 1965 / Blue Note ✦✦✦✦

Patton's fourth album for Blue Note. Big John Patton with Grant Green on guitar and Harold Vick on tenor sax. With tunes like "Fat Judy" and "Good Juice," there is no worry about there being a groove. The addition of a trumpet (Blue Mitchell) means you have a horn section, and this tends to be a little much now and again. Although a little on the light side, thanks to Patton and Green, the groove does go down. —*Michael Erlewine*

★ **Let 'em Roll** / Dec. 11, 1965 / Blue Note ✦✦✦✦✦

Patton with Grant Green (guitar), Otis Finch (drums) and Bobby Hutcherson (vibes). Grant Green provides just superb assistance. While vibes is not a usual instrument for soul-jazz sessions, this album works anyway and the groove is established. Grant Green and Patton are just a great combination. —*Michael Erlewine*

Got a Good Thing Goin' / Apr. 29, 1966 / Blue Note ✦✦✦✦✦

Grant Green always brought out the best in Big John Patton. Almost any record that featured the guitarist and organist was dominated by their scintillating inter-

---

Music Map

Percussion

Prior to the bop era, percussionists were not utilized in jazz.

Pioneers

Chano Pozo (with Dizzy Gillespie 1947-48)

Jack Costanzo
(with Stan Kenton and Nat King Cole Trio 1947-50)

Giants of Latin Jazz

Machito

Cal Tjader (bongos early in his career)

Mongo Santamaria

Willie Bobo

Tito Puente

Poncho Sanchez

Brazilian

Airto Moreira   Guilherme Franco

Paulhino Da Casto   Dom Um Romao

Nana Vasconcelos

Other Important Percussionists

Ray Barretto

Carlos Vidal

Babatunde Olatunji

Big Black

Candido

Armando Peraza
(regular guest with George Shearing Quintet)

Sabu Martinez

Potato Valdez

Ralph MacDonald

Mtume

Don Alias

Alex Acuna

Kahil El'Zabar (Ethnic Heritage Ensemble)

Mino Cinelu

Marilyn Mazur

Don Moye

Badal Roy

Tabla and Other Percussion with Oregon

Collin Walcott

Trilok Gurtu

Two Important Percussion-Oriented Groups

Fort Apache Band (Jerry Gonzalez)

Max Roach's M'Boom
(nine percussionists including Roach, Roy Brooks, Joe Chambers, Ray Mantilla and Warren Smith)

---

play, and it always sounded like they were trying to top each other's blistering, funky solos. Patton and Green rarely sounded better than they did on *Got a Good*

Thing Goin', a 1966 session that functioned as a showcase for the pair's dynamic interaction and exciting, invigorating solos. In particular, the duo's mastery is evident because there are no horns to stand in the way—only drummer Hugh Walker and conga player Richard Landrum provide support, leaving plenty of room for Green and Patton to run wild. All five numbers—two originals by Patton and Green, two pop covers ("Ain't That Peculiar," "Shake") and Duke Pearson's "Amanda"—are simple blues and soul-jazz songs that provide ample space for the guitarist and organist to stretch out. And they do stretch out—as a pair, they have never sounded so fiery or intoxicating. Fans of hard bop may find the songs a little too simple, but hot, uptempo soul-jazz rarely comes any better than it does on *Got a Good Thing Goin'. —Stephen Thomas Erlewine*

That Certain Feeling / Mar. 8, 1968 / Blue Note ✦✦✦
It took Big John Patton nearly two years to return to the studio as a leader following the sessions that produced the exceptional *Got a Good Thing Goin'.* When he finally cut its sequel, *That Certain Feeling,* the musical climate had changed just enough to make a difference in his music. Where *Got a Good Thing Goin'* was down and dirty, *That Certain Feeling* was smooth. That's not to say that it didn't groove—it was just cleaner, which means that the groove wasn't as infectious or hot as before. Still, Patton and his band—guitarist Jimmy Ponder, tenor saxophonist Junior Cook and drummer Clifford Jarvis—play very well, and there are moments when everything comes together and it just cooks. And those are the moments that make *That Certain Feeling* worth a search. —*Stephen Thomas Erlewine*

Boogaloo / Aug. 9, 1968 / Blue Note ✦✦✦
Big John Patton with a trumpet and sax, drums, and conga. Harold Alexander (sax) plays a little out for a standard soul-jazz session and the combination of the horns amounts to what it should be—a horn section. For me, this never gets down to the business of being soul music. The groove is weak or not there. —*Michael Erlewine*

Understanding / Oct. 25, 1968 / Blue Note ✦✦
Patton with saxman Harold Alexander and drums. Alexander is playing sax that is just a tad too "out" for an organ combo than is standard for soul-jazz, thus turning the sound toward something other than a real groove. If you like progressive sax, you might be able to stay in the groove. Not me, the sound keeps popping me out. I like to get in the groove and ride. —*Michael Erlewine*

Accent on the Blues / Jun. 9, 1969+Aug. 15, 1969 / Blue Note ✦✦✦
Most John Patton albums are hard-driving, edgy soul-jazz and funk, and the title of *Accent on the Blues* makes the record seem like it would be no different than his other sessions. Of course, that isn't the case. *Accent on the Blues* is among the most atmospheric music Patton has ever made. While it stops short of being free, it's hardly funky soul-jazz, and that may disappoint some fans of his rip-roaring style. Nevertheless, the album is a rewarding listen, primarily because it displays a more reflective side of his talent, demonstrating that he can hold his own among the likes of guitarist James "Blood" Ulmer and saxophonist Marvin Cabell. —*Stephen Thomas Erlewine*

Memphis to New York Spirit / Jun. 9, 1969+Oct. 2, 1970 / Blue Note ✦✦✦
Although it was scheduled for release two times, *Memphis to New York Spirit* didn't appear until 1996, over 25 years after it was recorded. The album comprises the contents of two separate sessions—one recorded in 1970 with guitarist James "Blood" Ulmer, drummer Leroy Williams and saxophonist/flutist Marvin Cabell; the other recorded in 1969 with Cabell, Williams, and saxophonist George Coleman—that were very similiar in concept and execution. Patton leads his combo through a selection of originals and covers that range from Wayne Shorter and McCoy Tyner to the Meters. Though the group is rooted in soul-jazz, they stretch the limits of the genre on these sessions, showing a willingness to experiment, while still dipping into the more traditional blues and funk reserves. Consequently, *Memphis to New York Spirit* doesn't have a consistent groove like some other Patton records, but when it does click, the results are remarkable; it's a nonessential but worthy addition to a funky soul-jazz collection. —*Stephen Thomas Erlewine*

Soul Connection / Jun. 7, 1983 / Nilva ✦✦✦

Blue Planet Man / Apr. 12, 1993-Apr. 13, 1993 / Evidence ✦✦✦

Minor Swing / May 30, 1995 / DIW ✦✦✦

Les Paul (Rhubarb Red)

b. Jun. 9, 1915, Waukesha, WI
Guitar / Swing, Pop, Traditional Pop
Les Paul has had such a staggeringly huge influence over the way American popular music sounds today that many tend to overlook his significant impact upon the jazz world. Before his attention was diverted toward recording multilayered hits for the pop market, he made his name as a brilliant jazz guitarist whose exposure on coast-to-coast radio programs guaranteed a wide audience of susceptible young musicians. Heavily influenced by Django Reinhardt at first, Paul eventually devel-

oped an astonishingly fluid, hard-swinging style of his own, one that featured extremely rapid runs, fluttered and repeated single notes, and chunking rhythm support, mixing in country & western licks and humorous crowd-pleasing effects. No doubt his brassy style gave critics a bad time, but the gregarious, garrulous Paul didn't much care; he was bent on showing his audiences a good time. Though he couldn't read music, Paul had a magnificent ear and innate sense of structure, conceiving complete arrangements entirely in his head before he set them down, track by track, on disc or tape. Even on his many pop hits for Capitol in the late '40s and early '50s, one can always hear a jazz sensibility at work in the rapid lead solo lines and bluesy bent notes—and no one could close a record as suavely as Les. And of course, his early use of the electric guitar and pioneering experiments with multitrack recording, guitar design and electronic effects devices have filtered down to countless jazz musicians. Among the jazzers who acknowledge his influence are George Benson, Al DiMeola, Stanley Jordan (whose neck-tapping sound is very reminiscent of Paul's records), Pat Martino and Bucky Pizzarelli.

Paul's interest in music began when he took up the harmonica at age eight, inspired by a Waukesha ditchdigger. Paul's only formal training consisted of a few unsuccessful piano lessons as a child—and although he later took up the piano again professionally, exposure to a few Art Tatum records put an end to that. After a fling with the banjo, Paul took up the guitar under the influences of Nick Lucas, Eddie Lang and regional players like Pie Plant Pete and Sunny Joe Wolverton, who gave Les the stage name Rhubarb Red. At 17, Les played with Rube Tronson's Cowboys and then dropped out of high school to join Wolverton's radio band in St. Louis on KMOX. By 1934, he was in Chicago, and before long, he took on a dual radio persona, doing a hillbilly act as Rhubarb Red and playing jazz as Les Paul, often with an imitation Django Reinhardt quartet. His first records in 1936 were issued on the Montgomery Ward label as Rhubarb Red and on Decca backing blues shouter Georgia White on acoustic guitar. Dissatisfied with the electric guitars circulating in the mid-'30s, Paul, assisted by tech-minded friends, began experimenting with designs of his own.

By 1937, Paul had formed a trio, and the following year, he moved to New York and landed a featured spot with Fred Waring's Pennsylvanians, which gave Les nationwide exposure through its broadcasts. That job ended in 1941 shortly after he was nearly electrocuted in an accident during a jam session in his Queens basement. After a long recovery period and more radio jobs, Paul moved to Hollywood in 1943, where he formed a new trio that made several V-Discs and transcriptions for MacGregor (some available on LaserLight). As a last-minute substitute for Oscar Moore, Paul played in the inaugural Jazz at the Philharmonic concert in Los Angeles on July 2, 1944; his witty chase sequence with Nat Cole on "Blues" and fleet work elsewhere (now on Verve's *Jazz at the Philharmonic: The First Concert*) are the most indelible reminders of his prowess as a jazzman. Later that year, Paul hooked up with Bing Crosby, who featured the Trio on his radio show, sponsored Les' recording experiments, and recorded six sides with him, including a 1945 No. 1 hit, "It's Been a Long, Long Time." On his own, Paul also made several records with his Trio for Decca from 1944 to 1947, including jazz, country and Hawaiian sides, and backed singers like Dick Haymes, Helen Forrest and the Andrews Sisters. Meanwhile, in 1947, after experimenting in his garage studio and discarding some 500 test discs, Paul came up with a kooky version of "Lover" for eight electric guitars, all played by himself with dizzying multispeed effects. He talked Capitol Records into releasing this futuristic disc, which became a hit the following year. Alas, a bad automobile accident in Oklahoma in January 1948 put Les out of action again for a year and a half; as an alternative to amputation, his right arm had to be set at a permanent right angle suitable for guitar playing. After his recovery, he teamed up with his soon-to-be second wife, a young country singer/guitarist named Colleen Summers whom he renamed Mary Ford, and reeled off a long string of spectacular multilayered pop discs for Capitol, making smash hits out of jazz standards like "How High the Moon" and "Tiger Rag." The hits ran out suddenly in 1955, and not even a Mitch Miller-promoted stint at Columbia from 1958 to 1963 could get the streak going again. After a bitter divorce from Ford in 1964, a gig in Tokyo the following year, and an LP of mostly remakes for London in 1967, Paul went into semiretirement from music.

Aside from a pair of wonderfully relaxed country/jazz albums with Chet Atkins for RCA in 1976 and 1978, and a blazing duet with DiMeola on "Spanish Eyes" from the latter's 1980 *Splendido Hotel* CD, Paul has been long absent from the record scene (some rumored sessions for Epic in the '90s have not materialized). However, a 1991 four-CD retrospective, *The Legend and the Legacy,* contained an entire disc of 34 unreleased tracks, including a breathtaking electrified tribute to the Benny Goodman Sextet, "Cookin'." More significantly, Paul began a regular series of Monday night appearances at New York's Fat Tuesday's club in 1984 (from 1996, Les held court at the Iridium club across from Lincoln Center), attended by visiting celebrities and fans for whom he became an icon in the '80s. Arthritis has slowed Les' playing down in recent years, and his repertoire is largely unchanged from the '30s and '40s. But at any given gig, one can still learn a lot from the Wizard of Waukesha. —*Richard S. Ginell*

The Complete Decca Trios—Plus (1936-1947) / May 11, 1936-Jul. 25, 1947 / MCA ◆◆◆◆◆

The Complete Decca Trios—Plus is a double-disc, 50-track collection containing all of the recordings Les Paul made for Decca between 1936 and 1947, including all of his released and unreleased masters, plus several tracks he cut with fellow Decca recording artists. These are the recordings that earned Paul's reputation as an excellent guitarist and they show his extraordinary range. He could play jazz and Hawaiian music, swing with big bands or subtly support singers like Bing Crosby, Helen Forrest and the Andrews Sisters. All of that is featured here, on a collection that is essential for anyone with an interest in Paul or the history of the electric guitar. —*Stephen Thomas Erlewine*

Les Paul Trio / 1947 / LaserLight ◆◆◆◆

Along with the 1944 JATP concert, this bargain-priced collection of 21 MacGregor radio transcriptions from 1947 is the best example we have of Les Paul's abilities as a jazz guitarist. Though one can still hear the formative Django Reinhardt harmonic influence in the single-string runs, Les' showboating style is fully formed here, marked by humor and mind-boggling speed, but also a lyrical gift in ballads like "Stardust." The songs, mostly standards and uncredited public domain material, are all rather brief, but that imposes a welcome discipline on the solos, although Les did tend to repeat certain ideas from song to song at that time. The CD box fails to name the members of the trio, but one can surmise from the year that Paul Smith is on piano, Cal Gooden is on rhythm guitar and Bob Meyer is on bass; and they make a nifty, tightly-knit foursome. —*Richard S. Ginell*

☆ **The Legend and the Legacy** / Feb. 1948-Dec. 23, 1957 / Capitol ◆◆◆◆◆

If you're going for the big gulp, you could do no better than this excellent four-disc box set, which covers all the highlights of Les and Mary's tenure with the label. Sparkling sound abounds throughout (even on the old acetate masters like "Lover"), with the first three discs covering not only the best issued Capitol masters, but three of Les and Mary's radio shows for NBC and assorted catchy radio commercials for Robert Hall clothiers and Rheingold Beer! The fourth disc in the set features no less than 34 previously unreleased tracks (most worked up for the *Les Paul & Mary Ford at Home* television show) with absolutely no letdown in the quality, musical or otherwise. Combined with all this great music is a booklet that is exemplary in its scope, chock-full of great photos, the best liners you could ask for on Les and Mary by Stephen K. Peeples and, best of all, a track-by-track running commentary from Les himself, right down to what guitar he used. Exhaustive and illuminating, both legend and legacy are served well here. —*Cub Koda*

16 Most Requested Songs / Jul. 13, 1958-Oct. 5, 1961 / Columbia ◆◆◆

Paul and Ford were coming to the end of both their personal and professional partnership when these sides were recorded for Columbia between 1958 and 1961. Their reign on the charts was finishing, too; only a couple of these ("Put a Ring on My Finger" and "Jura") made the lower reaches of the Top 40. Their Columbia output hasn't played too well with critics, and while you should certainly head for the Capitol material first, this disc is hardly disgraceful. Paul's guitar chops and double-tracking wizardry are still much in evidence, all imbued with that hollow reverb that sounds like no one else. Some of this has a pop-rockabilly feel, as if the team was trying to be a bit trendy, out of commercial desperation; nonetheless, those tunes, as well as Les' instrumental showcases, have worn better than the pop ballads that fill out the rest of the compilation. Includes one previously unissued cut, "I Am My Love's." —*Richie Unterberger*

Les Paul Now / 1968 / London ◆◆◆

Les Paul was coaxed briefly out of his musical retirement in 1967 to put together an album for London's audiophile Phase Four label—and who better than this audio pioneer? But rather than use the opportunity to redefine himself as a progressive force in a different decade, Les meekly responded with a series of remakes of his earlier Capitol hits—this time without the help of now-ex-wife Mary Ford. The tracks he originally recorded with Mary are rearranged completely for multiple guitars; only the spectacular "Tennessee Waltz" gains in the translation. The solo tracks for Capitol are remade with all kinds of fascinating stereo effects, but, with the exception of "Caravan," otherwise follow the original blueprints with a few embellishing touches. The only two bits of new material are credited to a writer named Manners: "The System," which went nowhere as a single, is a rare example of Les playing rock 'n' roll, and "Los Angeles" is just a rewrite of Les' hit "Meet Mr. Callaghan." While it was nice to find Les back in action at the time, this record sounds like warmed-over goods. This album was re-released under the title *Multi-Trackin'.* —*Richard S. Ginell*

Chester and Lester / 1977 / RCA ◆◆◆◆◆

After eight years away from the microphones, Les Paul joined forces with country music's Chet Atkins in a marvelously relaxed, tasty session of cross-cultural jam-

ming. The sound of the backup band may be Nashville country, but the tunes, mostly drawn from Paul's repertoire, are jazz and pop standards ("Caravan," "It's Been a Long, Long Time," "Avalon," etc.). Both players improvise, duel and converse with the spontaneity of jazz always in the air—and unlike almost all of Les' recordings since 1947, there is no overdubbing except on "Caravan" and "Lover, Come Back to Me." You won't have any problem telling Chester and Lester apart on these tracks; Les' bright, almost metallic sound and twirling, yet now more economical flurries are a world away from Chet's mellow fingerpicking, lightly tarted with echo. Yet the two styles play brilliantly off each other; one potent example occurs as Chet superimposes the theme from "Picnic" from his repertoire over Les' statement of "Moonglow." A lot of the between-takes session chatter is intentionally left in, with Les' hotfoot voice trading quips with Chet's Tennessee drawl. On "Avalon," heard in two consecutive takes at different speeds, the dialogue is particularly funny, as Atkins mockingly tries to browbeat his old idol. This album (now on CD) had the effect of putting Les Paul well on the road toward canonization by young rock guitarslingers who noticed his name on Gibson instruments. —*Richard S. Ginell*

Guitar Monsters / 1978 / RCA ◆◆◆

Chester and Lester went at it again in Nashville after the success of their first encounter, and the results are just about as marvelous. Reportedly, there was a lot of tension at these sessions, with Les being in a particularly foul mood and suffering from a cold, but it didn't seem to affect the splendid playing on tunes like "Limehouse Blues," the rollicking "It Don't Mean a Thing" and nine others. The tension may have given a bit of a real-life edge to the hilarious mutual joshing of "I'm Your Greatest Fan," but who can say? The choice of tunes again falls mostly in Paul's territory, with old standbys like "Over the Rainbow," "Brazil" and "I Surrender Dear," but Atkins gets in Ralph Flanagan's lovable "Hot Toddy," and there is even a countrified take on Antonio Carlos Jobim's "Meditation." Atkins suavely handles both acoustic and electric guitars on the sessions, while Les' brittle, everywhere-at-once electric guitar is heard for the last time (so far) on a full-length album. Tracks from this album, along with those of *Chester and Lester*, can be heard on the CD *Masters of the Guitar Together* (Pair PDC-2-1230). —*Richard S. Ginell*

Mario Pavone

b. 1939, Connecticut
Bass / Avant-Garde

An adventurous bassist never shy of taking chances, Mario Pavone did not start playing his instrument until he was 24, teaching himself except for a few lessons. Pavone graduated from the University of Connecticut in 1964 as an engineer, but that summer he toured Europe with Paul Bley. He was working as an engineer for a time, but when John Coltrane died in 1967, he attended the funeral and was inspired to switch permanently to music. Pavone had opportunities to jam with Albert Ayler and Archie Shepp and has played with Bill Dixon off and on since the early '70s. One of the co-founders of the Creative Musicians' Improviser's Forum, a Connecticut organization similar in ways to Chicago's AACM, Pavone has worked with many top avant-garde musicians, including Leo Smith, Dewey Redman, Marty Ehrlich and Anthony Braxton. He organized his own label (Alacra), leading three sets between 1979-88. Mario Pavone has also recorded as a leader for New World and with Thomas Chapin and Dixon. —*Scott Yanow*

Shodo / Jun. 1982 / Alacra ◆◆◆

Toulon Days / Nov. 17, 1991-Nov. 18, 1991 / New World ◆◆◆◆

Song For / Feb. 28, 1993-Mar. 1, 1993 / New World ◆◆◆◆

● **Dancer's Tales** / 1997 / Knitting Factory ◆◆◆◆◆

Cecil Payne

b. Dec. 14, 1922, New York, NY
Baritone Saxophone, Flute / Bop, Hard Bop

Although he was one of the finest baritone saxophonists to emerge from the bop era, Cecil Payne has been underrated and frequently overlooked throughout his long career. Payne, who played guitar, alto and clarinet (and spent 1943-46 in the military) first played baritone with Clarence Briggs' band in 1946, giving up alto around the same period (after making his recording debut on the smaller horn with J.J. Johnson). Payne made his reputation as a key member of Dizzy Gillespie's classic bebop big band (1946-49), appearing on virtually all of the orchestra's famous recordings. Payne played with Tadd Dameron, James Moody and with the popular Illinois Jacquet band (1952-54), but then spent a period working at a day job. He returned to music in 1956, starting a long-term association with Randy Weston, and he had periods with Machito (1963-66), Woody Herman (1966-68) and Count Basie (1969-71), but despite appearing on many records over a five-decade period, fame (except among musicians) has always eluded Cecil Payne. He led dates as a leader for Decca (1949), Savoy (1956-57), the Charlie Parker label (1961-62), Spotlite, Strata East (1969-70), Muse and Empathy. —*Scott Yanow*

Patterns / May 19, 1956-May 22, 1956 / Savoy ◆◆◆◆
Fine late-'50s hard bop session featuring baritone saxophonist Cecil Payne. This was one of two strong albums that matched Payne with pianist Duke Jordan, who was then establishing his own reputation as an aggressive soloist and good accompanist. These are mostly short, tartly played, and well-written and arranged pieces. —*Ron Wynn*

Night at the Five Spot / Aug. 12, 1957 / Savoy ◆◆◆◆

Cecil Payne Performing Charlie Parker / Mar. 1961 / Charlie Parker ◆◆◆
Baritonist Cecil Payne is one of the great bebop veterans, but he tends to be overlooked, since he didn't record that much as a leader. This obscure LP finds Payne matched up with trumpeter Clark Terry, pianist Duke Jordan, bassist Ron Carter and drummer Charlie Persip for renditions of six Charlie Parker songs, plus Payne's "Communion." The swinging interpretations (highlighted by "Shaw Nuff," "Relaxin' at Camarillo" and "The Hymn") are strictly straightahead and are most notable for the interplay between Payne and Terry. —*Scott Yanow*

Brookfield Andante / Nov. 5, 1966 / Spotlite ◆◆◆◆◆
This LP is an excellent showcase for the underrated bop baritonist Cecil Payne. Accompanied by a sympathetic British rhythm section (pianist Joe Palin, bassist Alan Cooper and drummer Ron Parry), Payne had a rare opportunity during the live session in 1966 to be the only horn and to stretch out on four of his originals (they clock in between 9:18 and 12:05). The waltz "Brookfield Andante" and "The Opener" are highlights of the easily recommended set. —*Scott Yanow*

● **Zodiac** / 1969-1970 / Strata East ◆◆◆◆◆
Outstanding quintet date featuring Kenny Dorham (tpt), but hard to find. —*Ron Wynn*

Brooklyn Brothers / Mar. 16, 1973 / Muse ◆◆◆◆◆
With Duke Jordan (p) & Trio. Excellent mainstream jazz. —*Michael G. Nastos*

● **Bird Gets the Worm** / Feb. 2, 1976 / Muse ◆◆◆◆◆
Some of Payne's most vibrant, expressive playing. Good ensemble and compositions. —*Ron Wynn*

Bright Moments / Jul. 19, 1979+Jul. 20, 1979 / Spotlite ◆◆◆

Casbah / Dec. 1, 1993 / Stash ◆◆◆◆◆

● **Scotch and Milk** / Sep. 2, 1996-Sep. 3, 1996 / Delmark ◆◆◆◆◆

Nicholas Payton

b. 1973, New Orleans, LA
Trumpet / Hard Bop, New Orleans Jazz
One of the brightest new trumpet stars of the 1990s, Nicholas Payton combines references to his New Orleans heritage with the Young Lions' brand of hard bop and a warm sound. His father Walter Payton, a top bassist, and his mother (a classical pianist) encouraged his interest in music and he received his first trumpet when he was four. Payton developed quickly and at age nine he had opportunities to sit in with the Young Tuxedo Brass Band. One day when Payton was 12, Wynton Marsalis called to speak to his father; Nicholas spontaneously played his trumpet over the phone, impressing Marsalis, who in the future would recommend him to other bandleaders. Payton worked steadily in New Orleans while in high school, he graduated from the New Orleans Center for Creative Arts and studied with Ellis Marsalis. In 1992 he toured with Marcus Roberts, in 1994 he toured Europe with Jazz Futures II, and in addition Payton toured with Elvin Jones and worked with the Jazz at Lincoln Center program. He has recorded with Jones, as a leader on Verve and with the New Orleans Collective on Evidence. —*Scott Yanow*

● **From This Moment** / Sep. 11, 1994-Sep. 12, 1994 / Verve ◆◆◆◆
The young trumpeter Nicholas Payton is featured on this CD as the only horn in a sextet also including guitarist Mark Whitfield, pianist Mulgrew Miller and vibraphonist Monte Croft. Best are Payton's melodic and very mature statements on the veteran standards "You Stepped out of a Dream," "It Could Happen to You," "From This Moment On" and "Taking a Chance on Love." His six originals are less memorable but overall this is a pleasing date that finds the trumpeter showing a great deal of potential. Payton's tone, mixing aspects of Freddie Hubbard, Wynton Marsalis and New Orleans jazz in a postbop setting, is quite appealing. —*Scott Yanow*

Gumbo Nouveau / Nov. 28, 1995-Nov. 30, 1995 / Verve ◆◆◆◆◆
Only 22 at the time of this CD, Nicholas Payton had already quickly developed into a major trumpeter. Possessing a fat tone that is sometimes reminiscent of Freddie Hubbard, by the mid-1990s Payton had become New Orleans' latest significant contribution to jazz. On his second Verve release, Payton interprets and modernizes ten songs associated with his hometown and/or Louis Armstrong. Fortunately, Payton generally retains the flavor and joy of the original versions even while he transforms much of the music into hard bop. To cite a few examples, "Whoopin'

Blues" has parade rhythms, sendoffs worthy of Lionel Hampton and beboppish solos, "Way Down Yonder in New Orleans" is taken as a slow and lightly swinging ballad and "I Gotta Right to Sing the Blues" is turned into a jazz waltz. "Li'l Liza Jane" becomes a largely unrecognizable hard bop romp and this version of the "Saints" is a bit melancholy. But "Wild Man Blues" is a tour-de-force for the trumpeter, and the duet between Payton and pianist Anthony Wonsey on "Weather Bird" has the leader liberally quoting from Louis Armstrong's classic version. Throughout the date Nicholas Payton is the lead voice, pianist Wonsey is the main supporting player, and there are solos from altoist Jesse Davis and tenor saxophonist Tim Warfield. New Orleans jazz purists may not care for all of the updating, but the overall results are fresh and likable. Recommended. —*Scott Yanow*

Gary Peacock

b. May 12, 1935, Burley, ID
Bass / Bop, Swing-Bop, Free Jazz, Avant-Garde
A subtle but adventurous bassist, Gary Peacock's flexibility and consistently creative ideas have been an asset to several important groups. He was originally a pianist, playing in an Army band while stationed in Germany in the late '50s. Peacock switched to bass in 1956, staying on in Germany after his discharge to play with Hans Koller, Attila Zoller, Tony Scott and Bud Shank. In 1958 he moved to Los Angeles where he performed with Barney Kessel, Don Ellis, Terry Gibbs and Shorty Rogers and (most importantly) Paul Bley among others. After moving to New York in 1962, Peacock worked with Bill Evans (1962-63), the Paul Bley trio, Jimmy Giuffre, Roland Kirk and George Russell. In 1964, after a brief stint with Miles Davis, Peacock started an assocation with Albert Ayler, also playing with Roswell Rudd and Steve Lacy. Peacock alternated between Ayler and Paul Bley for a time and returned briefly to Miles Davis in the late '60s. After a period in Japan (1969-72), Peacock studied biology (1972-76), worked with Bley, and off and on from the late '70s has played (and recorded) in a trio with Keith Jarrett and Jack DeJohnette. —*Scott Yanow*

Tales of Another / Feb. 1977 / ECM ◆◆◆◆
Bassist Gary Peacock contributed all six originals to this set, which also features pianist Keith Jarrett and drummer Jack DeJohnette. These musicians (who are equals) have played together many times through the years and their support of each other and close communication during these advanced improvisations is quite impressive. It's a good example of Peacock's music. —*Scott Yanow*

Shift in the Wind / Feb. 1980 / ECM ◆◆◆◆
Bassist Gary Peacock teams up with the underrated pianist Art Lande and drummer Eliot Zigmund for a set of group originals that emphasize close communication between the trio members, really an extension on the innovations of Bill Evans. The interplay between these masterful musicians is more significant than the actual compositions and rewards repeats listenings. —*Scott Yanow*

December Poems / Dec. 1977 / ECM ◆◆◆

Voice from the Past: Paradigm / Aug. 1981 / ECM ◆◆◆

Guamba / Mar. 1987 / ECM ◆◆◆◆
Good late-'80s session with bassist Gary Peacock heading a group that has saxophonist Jan Garbarek and trumpeter Palle Mikkleborg taking the lead, and Peacock working with drummer Peter Erskine in the rhythm section. The only defect comes from ECM's occasional tendency to introduce new age themes and production values into the mix. —*Ron Wynn*

Partners / Dec. 1989 / Owl ◆◆◆◆

Cosi Lontano . . . Quasi Dentro / Jan. 25, 1991 / ECM ◆◆◆

Tethered Moon / Nov. 16, 1991-Nov. 18, 1991 / Evidence ◆◆◆◆◆

● **Oracle** / May 1993 / ECM ◆◆◆◆◆
This set of duets by bassist Gary Peacock and guitarist Ralph Towner, as one might expect from an ECM album, makes expert use of space and has its quiet moments. But there is a surprising amount of ferocious interplay between the two musicians. They may play at a consistently low volume but the set of originals has a few rather passionate grooves and a little more energy than one would have predicted. —*Scott Yanow*

Just So Happens / Oct. 19, 1994 / Postcards ◆◆◆

Curtis Peagler

b. Sep. 17, 1929, Cincinnati, OH, d. Dec. 19, 1992, Beverly Hills, CA
Alto Saxophone, Tenor Saxophone / Bop, Swing
A fine, swinging saxophonist, Curtis Peagler was an asset to many different groups through the years. His alto sound was influenced by Charlie Parker, Eddie "Cleanhead" Vinson and, to a lesser extent, Louis Jordan. At 13 he started on the C-melody sax and soon joined the Sons of Rhythm on alto. Prior to being called up by the Army in 1953, Peagler worked with territory bands and backed singer Big

Maybelle. After being discharged in 1955, he attended Cincinnati Conservatory for two years and played locally; in 1960, with the assistance of Eddie "Lockjaw" Davis, he started recording for Prestige. Peagler then recorded with Lem Winchester and joined his Modern Jazz Disciples, which recorded for Columbia. He moved to Los Angeles in 1962 to freelance, and spent 1966-67 and 1969 with Ray Charles. He did some studio work and toured with Count Basie for seven years (1971-78). Peagler then resettled in Los Angeles, freelanced, founded the Sea Pea Records label, and recorded as a leader for Sea Pea and Pablo, also guesting on dates by Harry "Sweets" Edison and Big Joe Turner. Curtis Peagler spent his last decade as a member of the Cheathams' Sweet Baby Blues Band, recording with the Kansas City swing-oriented group for Concord before heart trouble shortened his life. —*Scott Yanow*

For Basie and Duke / 1982 / Sea Pea ✦✦✦✦

● **I'll Be Around** / 1986 / Pablo ✦✦✦✦✦

Duke Pearson (Columbus Calvin Pearson, Jr.)
....

b. Aug. 17, 1932, Atlanta, GA, d. Aug. 4, 1980, Atlanta, GA
Piano, Arranger / Hard Bop

Duke Pearson was an accomplished, lyrical, and logical, if rather cautious, pianist who played a big part in shaping the Blue Note label's hard bop direction in the 1960s as a producer. He will probably be best remembered for writing several attractive, catchy pieces, the most memorable being the moody "Cristo Redentor" for Donald Byrd, "Sweet Honey Bee" for himself and Lee Morgan, and "Jeannine," which has become a much-covered jazz standard.

Pearson was introduced to brass instruments and the piano as a youth, and his abilities on the latter inspired his uncle, an Ellington admirer, to give him his nickname. Dental problems forced Pearson to abandon the brass family, so from there, he worked as a pianist in Atlanta and elsewhere in Georgia and Florida before moving to New York in 1959. There, he joined Donald Byrd's band, the Art Farmer/Benny Golson Sextet, and served as Nancy Wilson's accompanist. In 1963, he arranged four numbers for jazz septet and eight-voice choir on Byrd's innovative *A New Perspective* album; one of the tunes was "Cristo Redentor," which became a jazz hit. From 1963 to 1970, Pearson was in charge of several recording sessions for Blue Note, while also recording most of his albums as a leader. He also led a big band from 1967 to 1970 and again in 1972, hiring players like Pepper Adams, Chick Corea, Lew Tabackin, Randy Brecker and Garnett Brown. Pearson continued to accompany vocalists in the 1970s, such as Carmen McRae, but he spent a good deal of the latter half of the decade fighting the ravages of multiple sclerosis. —*Richard S. Ginell*

Tender Feelin's / Dec. 6, 1959 / Blue Note ✦✦✦

Tender Feelin's is an appropriate title for Duke Pearson's second album for Blue Note. The record is a lovely, relaxed collection of ballads, standards and jazz staples, with a few originals thrown in for good measure. Since Pearson sticks to the trio format, supported by bassist Gene Taylor and drummer Lex Humphries, the mood of the album remains intimate and low-key. Pearson flourishes in this setting, whether he's playing blues, romantic ballads or surprisingly lyrical improvised solos. Pearson would later explore more adventurous territory, as well as funkier grooves, but *Tender Feelin's* remains a wonderfully understated, romantic mainstream jazz record. —*Stephen Thomas Erlewine*

Bags Groove / Aug. 1961 / Black Lion ✦✦✦✦

Pianist Duke Pearson sounds a lot like Bud Powell in spots during this trio outing with bassist Thomas Howard and drummer Lex Humphries (particularly on "I'm an Old Cowhand") but shows more individuality in his writing. His most famous song "Jeannine" is heard in one of its earliest versions and Pearson's other two originals "Say You're Mine" and "Le Carrousel" are both somewhat memorable. For the CD reissue of Duke Pearson's third trio session in two years, the original six-song program is augmented by three previously unreleased alternate takes. Recomended for straightahead jazz collectors. —*Scott Yanow*

Dedication / Aug. 2, 1961 / Prestige ✦✦✦✦✦

This is among Pearson's finest '60s sessions. Includes sterling solos by Freddie Hubbard (tpt) and Pepper Adams (sax). —*Ron Wynn*

Hush! / Jan. 12, 1962 / Jazztime ✦✦✦✦

● **Wahoo** / Nov. 24, 1964 / Blue Note ✦✦✦✦✦

A truly wonderful advanced hard bop date, *Wahoo* captures pianist Duke Pearson at his most adventurous and creative. With the exception of Donald Byrd's closing "Fly Little Bird Fly," Pearson wrote all of the material on this six-song album, and his compositions are clever, melodic and unpredictable without being cloying or inaccessible. He has assembled a first-rate sextet to perform the material, enlisting trumpeter Byrd, tenor saxophonist Joe Henderson, bassist Bob Cranshaw, alto saxophonist/flutist James Spaulding, and drummer Mickey Roker. Even the subdued "Wahoo" and "ESP" search out new territory with their subtle themes and explor-

atory solo sections. The key to the success of *Wahoo* is that Duke Pearson is a gifted arranger, creating nimble, challenging arrangements that are accessible, but reveal more details upon each listen. As a pianist, he has moved beyond his initial Bud Powell influence and reveals new aspects of his technique. Henderson, Byrd and Spaulding are equally impressive, helping elevate *Wahoo* to one of the finest sophisticated hard bop dates Blue Note released in the mid-'60s. —*Stephen Thomas Erlewine*

Sweet Honey Bee / Dec. 7, 1966 / Blue Note ✦✦✦✦

Pianist/composer Duke Pearson leads an all-star group on this runthrough of seven of his compositions. The musicians (trumpeter Freddie Hubbard, altoist James Spaulding, tenorman Joe Henderson on tenor, bassist Ron Carter, drummer Mickey Roker and the pianist/leader) are actually more impressive than many of the compositions, although the swinging minor-toned "Big Bertha" deserved to become a standard. The frameworks are quite intelligent, with everyone not soloing on each selection and the improvisations are concise and clearly related to each tune's melody and mood. Although not quite essential, this CD reissue has some rewarding music. —*Scott Yanow*

★ **The Right Touch** / Sep. 13, 1967 / Blue Note ✦✦✦✦✦

Duke Pearson rises to the challenge of writing for an all-star octet (with trumpeter Freddie Hubbard, trombonist Garnett Brown, altoist James Spaulding, Jerry Dodgion on alto and flute, Stanley Turrentine heard on tenor, bassist Gene Taylor, drummer Grady Tate and the leader/pianist), contributing colorful frameworks and consistently challenging compositions. The set is full of diverse melodies (the CD reissue has a previously unissued take of "Los Malos Hombres") played by a variety of distinctive soloists; many of these songs deserve to be revived. This is one of the finest recordings of Duke Pearson's career. —*Scott Yanow*

Introducing Duke Pearson's Big Band / Dec. 1967 / Blue Note ✦✦✦✦

Duke Pearson had always displayed a flair for arranging, even on small combo albums, so it shouldn't have come as a surprise that he would attempt his own big band record. What is a surprise is how successful *Introducing Duke Pearson's Big Band* actually is. Pearson leads 13 other musicians through a selection of nine songs, including four originals, two contemporary jazz tunes by Chick Corea and Joe Sample, and three standards. His originals are continually unpredictable and memorable, and his arrangements, especially of the standards, are provocative and intriguing. While it might not appeal to fans of Pearson's wonderful small-group hard bop sessions, it is unquestionably an experiment that works, and one that confirms his remarkable skills and talents. —*Stephen Thomas Erlewine*

The Phantom / Jun. 24, 1968+Sep. 11, 1968 / Blue Note ✦✦✦

After his big band experiment, Duke Pearson returned to a smaller group setting, but he didn't scale back his ambitions. *The Phantom* finds Pearson writing an ambitious set of post-bop that expands the boundaries of the music with Latin percussion and complex harmonies derived from the avant-garde. His supporting band is fairly large, featuring Jerry Dodgion (flute), Bobby Hutcherson (vibes), Sam Brown (guitar), Al Gafu (guitar), Bob Cranshaw (bass), Mickey Roker (drums), Patato Valdez (conga) and Victor Partajo (conga), but they're agile, bringing a spark and energy to the difficult arrangements. The results aren't always successful, but they are intriguing and worth investigating. —*Stephen Thomas Erlewine*

I Don't Care Who Knows It / Jun. 24, 1968-Feb. 13, 1970 / Blue Note ✦✦✦✦

The sessions that comprise *I Don't Care Who Knows It* date from 1969 and 1970 (with one stray track from a 1968 session with Bobby Hutcherson), when Duke Pearson was experimenting with Latin jazz, soul-jazz and funk; they are also the second-to-last dates the pianist ever recorded for Blue Note. Working with a fairly large group that included bassist Ron Carter, drummer Micey Roker, saxophonists Jerry Dodgion, Frank Foster, Lew Tabackin, trumpeter Burt Collins, trombonist Kenny Rupp and occasionally vocalist Andy Bey, Pearson plays the electric piano throughout the majority of the album. As expected, the music swings with an understated funk, with the band alternating between standard hard-bop and mellow, soulful grooves. On the whole, *I Don't Care Who Knows It* is fairly uneven—the sessions don't set well together, but work well as individual sets. Nevertheless, there is enough good material here to make it worthwhile for soul-jazz, Latin-jazz and, especially, Pearson afficianados. —*Stephen Thomas Erlewine*

Now Hear This! / Dec. 2, 1968-Dec. 3, 1968 / Blue Note ✦✦✦✦

Duke Pearson returned to a big band setting for *Now Hear This!*, once again proving his agility and inventiveness as an arranger and leader. Working with a larger band than before—the total number of musicians weighs in at 17—Pearson nevertheless keeps things clean and uncluttered. His compositions, as well as the songs he covers, cover a broad range of emotions, styles and tonal colors, with lush ballads taking the center stage. Even if much of this music is beautiful, Pearson's arrangements take chances and are unconventional, which means it rewards close listening as well. —*Stephen Thomas Erlewine*

Merry Ole Soul / Aug. 20, 1969 / Blue Note ✦✦

How Insensitive / Apr. 11, 1969+Apr. 14, 1969 / Blue Note ✦✦

Like most Blue Note artists, Duke Pearson moved toward commercial-oriented soul-jazz in the late '60s. At least, *How Insensitive* was supposed to be commercial. Pearson simplified his original compositions, chose standards like "Stella By Starlight," and covered contemporary pop songs like Jobim's "Lamento." He also assembled a large band with rock instrumentation like electric guitars, bass, electric pianos, and drum kits. Most importantly, he hired the New York Group Singers' Big Band—a group of singers that are arranged like a horn section (males are the trombones, females are alto saxes, etc.)—to sing on each song. The vocalists may be technically gifted—in particular, Andy Bey has a rich voice—but their presence on these arrangements is quite bizarre, especially since they take center stage. Each song on *How Insensitive* boasts extravagant, layered arrangements that flirt with schmaltz, but the voicings and attack are so unusual, the result is a weird variation on easy listening. There is little opportunity for Pearson to showcase his tasteful playing through improvisation, yet the arrangements are so off-kilter, the music never quite works as background music. In other words, it's a very interesting failure and one of the strangest by-products of Blue Note's late-'60s commercialization. —*Stephen Thomas Erlewine*

It Could Only Happen with You / Mar. 13, 1970 / Blue Note ✦✦✦

On *It Could Only Happen with You,* his final album for Blue Note, Duke Pearson followed the conventions of the time and cut a smooth, commercially oriented jazz album that made allusions to traditional and contemporary pop, hard bop, soul-jazz and bossa nova. The results are a bit muddled, but the album is more coherent than its predecessor, *How Insensitive,* even with its flaws. Pearson's playing remains tasteful, but he tends to get lost among the guitars, flutes, trumpets, trombones, bass, and Flora Purim's vocals. Although the record is a pleasant artifact of its time, it's a rather sad, undistinguished way to close out Pearson's career. —*Stephen Thomas Erlewine*

Niels-Henning Ørsted Pedersen

b. May 27, 1946, Osted, Denmark

Bass / Bop, Hard Bop

A virtuoso who mostly has played in bop-oriented settings, Niels Pedersen has been in great demand since he was a teenager. One of many superb European bassists to emerge during the 1960s, Pedersen originally studied piano before starting to play bass with Danish groups when he was 14. He had to reluctantly turn down Count Basie's offer to join his orchestra when he was just 17 but worked steadily as the house bassist at the Club Montmartre and as a member of the Danish Radio Orchestra. Whenever American jazzmen passed through Scandinavia, they asked for Pederson; during the 1960s he played with Sonny Rollins, Bill Evans, Roland Kirk, Dexter Gordon, Bud Powell and even Albert Ayler (although the latter's session was not too successful). In the 1970s Pedersen was featured in a duo with Kenny Drew. Starting in the mid-'70s he was an occasional member of the Oscar Peterson Trio and he recorded several dates as a leader for Steeple Chase. Pedersen also recorded in many different settings for Pablo Records during the era. He has remained very active up to the current time. —*Scott Yanow*

Jaywalkin' / Sep. 9, 1975+Dec. 10, 1975 / Steeple Chase ✦✦✦✦

Live at Montmartre, Vol. 2 / Oct. 1977 / Steeple Chase ✦✦✦

● **Dancing on the Tables** / Jul. 1979+Aug. 1979 / Steeple Chase ✦✦✦✦✦

The Viking / May 1983 / Pablo ✦✦✦✦

The Art of the Duo / Feb. 10, 1991 / Enja ✦✦✦

Ambiance / Dec. 13, 1993-Dec. 14, 1993 / Dacapo ✦✦✦

Although the Danish Radio Big Band appears on this CD, the main soloist is bassist Niels-Henning Orsted Pedersen. NHOP, who was the regular bassist with the group during 1964-82, appears as the lead soloist on every selection while Thomas Ovesen plays bass with the ensembles. This unusual situation (bass with orchestra) has the potential for boredom but Pedersen's creative and virtuosic playing, a fair amount of variety in the generally straightahead repertoire and the high musicianship of the big band holds one's interest. Tenor saxophonist Bob Rockwell gets featured in a few spots while the traditional folk song "O, Tysta Ensambet" is a duet by NHOP and pianist Ole Koch Hansen, the orchestra's conductor. This CD is worth exploring. —*Scott Yanow*

Those Who Were / 1997 / Polygram ✦✦✦✦✦

Those Who Were is a typically tasteful, swinging album from Niels-Henning Orsted Pedersen, finding the bassist working through a set of standards and recently written bop. Pedersen's supple playing steals the spotlight, but he does lay back on occasion to let saxophonist Johnny Griffin and vocalist Lisa Nilsson shine, lending a warm, friendly air to this charming recording. [Pedersen is supported by guitarist Ulf Wakenius and drummers Alex Riel and Victor Lewis on *Those Who Were.*] —*Stephen Thomas Erlewine*

Dave Pell

b. Feb. 26, 1925, New York, NY

Tenor Saxophone, Leader / Cool, Swing

Dave Pell started out touring with the Tony Pastor, Bob Astor and Bobby Sherwood bands as a teenager before moving to California in the mid-'40s. He found work with Bob Crosby on the latter's Ford radio show in 1946, then played with the Les Brown band from 1947 to 1955. Drawing from the ranks of the Brown band, he began leading his own groups in 1953, usually in an octet format, augmented by guests like Pepper Adams, Benny Carter, Mel Lewis, Red Mitchell, Marty Paich and Art Pepper. He also played as a sideman on records by Shorty Rogers, Pete Rugolo, Benny Goodman and Gene Krupa in the 1950s, while recording under his own name for Atlantic, Kapp, Coral, Capitol and RCA Victor. His primary focus of activity in the 1950s and '60s was in the record business, working as a producer for the budget Tops label in the '50s and Liberty (where he supervised a few hit pop-rock records for Gary Lewis & the Playboys) and briefly Uni in the '60s. He formed a group in the late '70s called Prez Conference, a variation on the theme of Supersax as a tribute to Lester Young, recording two albums for GNP/Crescendo. In the '80s and '90s, Pell revived his octet for recordings on the Fresh Sound (1984) and Headfirst (1988) labels and sporadic live dates in the Los Angeles area, including an appearance at the Jazz West Coast festival in 1994. —*Richard S. Ginell*

Prez and Joe / 1979 / GNP ✦✦✦✦✦

Dave Pell's Prez Conference was to Lester Young what Supersax is to Charlie Parker. Pell's short-lived group featured harmonized Lester Young solos recreated by three tenors and a baritone; their matchup with singer Joe Williams is quite enjoyable. Since Young was in Count Basie's orchestra when Jimmy Rushing was the vocalist, Joe Williams has a rare opportunity to give his own interpretation to Rushing and Billie Holiday classics like "I May Be Wrong," "You Can Depend on Me," "If Dreams Come True" and "Easy Living." A delightful and swinging date. —*Scott Yanow*

● **Live at Alfonse's** / Feb. 25, 1988-Feb. 26, 1988 / Headfirst ✦✦✦✦✦

Ken Peplowski

b. May 23, 1959, Cleveland, OH

Clarinet, Tenor Saxophone / Dixieland, Swing, Traditional Pop

One of the top clarinetists of the 1990s and a very talented tenor player, Ken Peplowski has helped keep the tradition of small-group swing (and occasionally Dixieland) alive. He made his professional debut at ten and played locally in Cleveland. After spending 1978-80 touring with the Tommy Dorsey ghost orchestra (directed by Buddy Morrow), Peplowski settled in New York, freelanced in a variety of settings and played with Benny Goodman. By 1987 he was a Concord artist and has since recorded frequently for that label, backing Mel Tormé and Rosemary Clooney and leading his own sets including brilliant duets with guitarist Howard Alden. —*Scott Yanow*

Double Exposure / Dec. 1987 / Concord Jazz ✦✦✦✦✦

Ken Peplowski's debut as a leader has plenty of brilliant playing. Peplowski, doubling on clarinet and tenor, is joined by guitarist Ed Bickert, pianist John Bunch, bassist John Goldsby and drummer Terry Clarke. Although the repertoire includes Charlie Parker's "Segment" and Hank Mobley's obscure "High and Flighty," Peplowski comes across as a superior swing specialist, particularly on such numbers as "I Would Do Anything for You," "Jubilee" and "Careless Love." A superb start to an important career. —*Scott Yanow*

Sonny Side / 1989 / Concord Jazz ✦✦✦✦✦

Switching between tenor, clarinet and alto, Ken Peplowski is hard-swinging and consistently brilliant throughout this quintet set with guitarist Howard Alden, pianist Dave Frishberg, bassist John Goldsby and drummer Terry Clarke. The music is mostly mainstream swing, with the highlights including "Ring Dem Bells," "When I Take My Sugar to Sea," Sonny Stitt's "Sonny Side" and "Hallelujah." As if to show that he is aware of later styles, Peplowski also does a good job on Rahsaan Roland Kirk's "Bright Moments," Thelonious Monk's "Ugly Beauty" and Miles Davis' "Half Nelson." Recommended. —*Scott Yanow*

Mr. Gentle and Mr. Cool / Feb. 1990 / Concord Jazz ✦✦✦✦✦

In the late '80s, Ken Peplowski (30 at the time of this Concord CD) became one of the brightest stars in mainstream swing. He switches between clarinet, tenor and alto on this set, sounding best on the former, where he is a logical extension of Benny Goodman (utilizing some fluid Buddy DeFranco-like bop ideas). On "Body and Soul," Peplowski and pianist Hank Jones do a close impression of B.G. and Teddy Wilson, and Ken really cooks on an uptempo "You Do Something to Me." In contrast, Peplowski's tone on alto (which he otherwise rarely plays) is a bit dull, particularly on the bossa nova "Follow Your Heart," but he is much stronger on tenor; his encounters with guest Scott Hamilton on two-tenor versions of "Makin' Whoopee" and an uptempo "When Day Is Done" are high points. Joined by a great rhythm section (comprising Hank Jones, guitarist Bucky Pizzarelli, bassist Frank Tate and drummer Alan Dawson), Peplowski is in excellent form throughout the enjoyable set. —*Scott Yanow*

Illuminations / Nov. 20, 1990-Nov. 21, 1990 / Concord Jazz ✦✦✦✦
Ken Peplowski on clarinet and tenor is a superb swing-based soloist who has taken elements from several classic players, fusing them together in his own strangely familiar but fairly original style. Peplowski's clarinet solo on this CD's version of the cooking "June Night" seems to shout out "Benny Goodman Lives!" "If We Never Meet Again," "Alone Together" and a delightful rendition of "Panama" are taken as stirring duets with guitarist Howard Alden. Other selections feature Peplowski in a quintet also including pianist Junior Mance, bassist Dennis Irwin and drummer Alan Dawson. The leader's tenor on "Jim Dawgs" and the romantic "Nancy" are additional highlights of this easily recommended mainstream set. —*Scott Yanow*

The Natural Touch / Jan. 14, 1992-Jan. 15, 1992 / Concord Jazz ✦✦✦✦✦
Ken Peplowski has been one of the most consistent performers in the "new mainstream" movement of the 1990s. Whether playing his fluent clarinet or warm tenor, Peplowski sounds quite comfortable as a creative swing player. As usual, this date with pianist Ben Aronov, guitarist Frank Vignola, bassist Murray Wall and drummer Tom Helito includes a couple more recent tunes (including Thelonious Monk's "Evidence" and originals by Aronov and Vignola), but it is the swing standards (such as "The One I Love Belongs to Somebody Else," "Evenin'," and "I Thought About You") that are most memorable. —*Scott Yanow*

● **Concord Duo Series, Vol. 3** / Dec. 1992 / Concord Jazz ✦✦✦✦✦
Clarinetist Ken Peplowski and guitarist Howard Alden have a rare musical ESP. that enables them to weave intricate lines around each other as they soar through a great mix of overlooked standards and older jazz works on this live date. Peplowski's lyricism is stimulated by Alden's seemingly endless variations on "Blue Room," and the duo transforms "In the Dark" from a piano solo into an impressionist suite for their two instruments. But it is the spirited version of "Chasin' the Bird," complete with Peplowski's whimsical pun-filled introduction, that displays the depth of their playing. There is no loss of momentum when Peplowski switches to tenor sax. His vibrato-filled approach to "Changes" is reminiscent of Coleman Hawkins, while "S'posin'" highlights Alden's imaginative lines. The guitarist winds up the concert with stride-like guitar on "Just One of Those Things," which drives his partner's clarinet to a sizzling climax. —*Ken Dryden*

Steppin' with Peps / Mar. 1993 / Concord Jazz ✦✦✦✦✦
Ken Peplowski is in top form on this consistently exciting swing-based release. Whether playing clarinet (where his Benny Goodman influence is touched by the coolness of Tony Scott) or romping on tenor (mixing together Don Byas with touches of Paul Gonsalves), Peplowski excels throughout this well-planned yet spontaneous session. The dozen performances have many highlights including the interplay of Peplowski and guitarist Howard Alden on "The Courtship," a very beautiful version of "Lotus Blossom" (with Joe Wilder's lyrical trumpet), a hot version of "The Lady's in Love with You" and a reasonably "free" version of Ornette Coleman's "Turn Around." Trumpeters Randy Sandke and Joe Wilder appear on several numbers and the rhythm section (with Alden, pianist Ben Aronov, bassist John Goldsby and drummer Alan Dawson) is excellent but Ken Peplowski emerges as the main star on this memorable set. —*Scott Yanow*

Live / 1994 / Concord Jazz ✦✦✦✦

It's a Lonesome Old Town / Jan. 3, 1995-Jan. 4, 1995 / Concord Jazz ✦✦✦✦

The Other Portrait / Mar. 1996-Apr. 1996 / Concord Jazz ✦✦✦✦
Recorded in Bulgaria with the Bulgarian National Symphony, this is a very different release for clarinetist Ken Peplowski. Although he does play brief unaccompanied versions of "Milestones," "Anthropology," "Single Petal of a Rose" and Jimmy Hamilton's "Duet," Peplowski also performs Witold Lutoslawski's "Dance Preludes," Darius Milhaud's "Concerto for Clarinet & Orchestra" (originally written for Benny Goodman), Plamen Djurov's "Cadenza" (which finds Peplowski switching to tenor), and Ornette Coleman's "Lonely Woman." In general, Peplowski's playing emphasizes his cool tone and strong technique. He pulls off the surprising classical-oriented set fairly well. —*Scott Yanow*

A Good Reed / Jan. 22, 1997+Jan. 23, 1997 / Concord Jazz ✦✦✦✦

Art Pepper

b. Sep. 1, 1925, Gardena, CA, d. Jun. 1, 1982, Panorama City, CA
Alto Saxophone, Clarinet / Cool, Post-Bop, Bop
Despite a remarkably colorful and difficult life, Art Pepper was quite consistent in the recording studios; virtually every recording he made is well worth getting. In the 1950s he was one of the few altoists (along with Lee Konitz and Paul Desmond) that was able to develop his own sound despite the dominant influence of Charlie Parker. During his last years, Pepper seemed to put all of his life's experiences into his music and he played with startling emotional intensity.

After a brief stint with Gus Arnheim, Pepper played with mostly Black groups on Central Avenue in Los Angeles. He spent a little time in the Benny Carter and Stan Kenton orchestras before serving time in the military (1944-46). Some of Pepper's happiest days were during his years with Stan Kenton (1947-52), although he became a heroin addict in that period. The 1950s found the altoist recording frequently both as a leader and a sideman resulting in at least two classics (*Plays Modern Jazz Classics* and *Meets the Rhythm Section*) but he also spent two periods in jail due to drug offenses during 1953-56. Pepper was in top form during his Contemporary recordings of 1957-60 but the first half of his career ended abruptly with long prison sentences that dominated the 1960s. His occasional gigs between jail terms found him adopting a harder tone influenced by John Coltrane that disturbed some of his longtime followers. He recorded with Buddy Rich in 1968 before getting seriously ill and rehabilitating at Synanon (1969-71). Art Pepper began his serious comeback in 1975 and the unthinkable happened. Under the guidance and inspiration of his wife Laurie, Pepper not only recovered his former form but topped himself with intense solos that were quite unique; he also enjoyed occasionally playing clarinet. His recordings for Contemporary and Galaxy rank with the greatest work of his career. Pepper's autobiography *Straight Life* (written with his wife) is a brutally honest book that details his sometimes-horrifying life. When Art Pepper died at the age of 56, he had attained his goal of becoming the world's great altoist. —*Scott Yanow*

Surf Ride / Feb. 7, 1952-Dec. 24, 1953 / Savoy ✦✦✦
The music on this Savoy CD (put out by Nippon Columbia) is quite brilliant, but the packaging leaves a lot to be desired. The recording dates are all incorrect, there are only 12 performances included (around 37 minutes) and none of the sessions are reissued in complete form. Two of the dates, quartet outings with either Russ Freeman or Hampton Hawes on piano, have just three of their four numbers reissued while only six of the eight songs from the altoist's classic session with tenor saxophonist Jack Montrose are here. Even if the four missing selections had been included, the program would have totaled around 49 minutes. The somewhat random nature of this set is unfortunate, for Pepper is in superior form throughout with highlights including "Tickle Toe," "The Way You Look Tonight" and his earliest recordings of such originals as "Susie the Poodle," "Straight Life" and "Surf Ride." Get the more definitive LP sets instead. —*Scott Yanow*

The Early Show: A Night at the Surf Club, Vol. 1 / Feb. 12, 1952 / Xanadu ✦✦✦✦
Altoist Art Pepper was 26 when he led the quartet heard on this Xanadu LP at the Surf Club in Hollywood. The earliest documentation of Pepper as a bandleader is this album and its follow-up, *The Late Show*. Even at this early stage Pepper largely had his own sound (he never chose to copy Charlie Parker) and he was a creative improviser. The sound quality of these tapes is not state-of-the-art, but the performances by Pepper (who also plays some effective clarinet on "Rose Room"), pianist Hampton Hawes, bassist Joe Mondragon and Larry Bunker on drums and vibes are consistently excellent. The repertoire, standards and Pepper "originals" based on fairly common chord changes, is typical of the era but Pepper's often-brilliant solos already put him near the top of his field. —*Scott Yanow*

The Late Show: A Night at the Surf Club, Vol. 2 / Feb. 1952 / Xanadu ✦✦✦✦
The follow-up to *The Early Show*, this Xanadu LP is quite valuable for it continues the documentation of Art Pepper's earliest recording as a bandleader. Saved on an amateur tape recorder from the audience at Los Angeles' Surf Club, these performances have erratic recording quality, but the music is quite exciting. Pepper, joined by pianist Hampton Hawes, bassist Joe Mondragon and Larry Bunker on drums and vibes, performs bop standards and a variety of his originals that were based on the chord changes of familiar tunes. Even at this early stage, Art Pepper's talents and individuality were obvious. —*Scott Yanow*

Discoveries / Oct. 8, 1952-Aug. 25, 1954 / Savoy ✦✦✦✦✦
This double-LP reissues two of altoist Art Pepper's earliest studio dates as a leader. On four songs he is joined by pianist Russ Freeman, bassist Bob Whitlock and drummer Bobby White, a quiet trio that allows Pepper to dominate such songs as "Everything Happens to Me" and "Tickle Toe." In addition, Pepper matches harmonies and wits with tenor saxophonist Jack Montrose (along with pianist Claude Williamson, bassist Monty Budwig and drummer Larry Bunker) on eight exuberant numbers including the earliest recording of Art's famous "Straight Life." But that is not all, for the second of these two LPs contains previously unissued alternate takes of all but one of the 11 pieces. Because Pepper and Montrose were in very good form during the performances, they are well worth hearing twice. In fact, a slightly later LP (titled *Rediscoveries*) would add 14 more versions to the legacy of these two exciting sessions. This highly enjoyable music has unfortunately only been reissued on CD thus far in random fashion. —*Scott Yanow*

Rediscoveries / Oct. 8, 1952-Aug. 25, 1954 / Savoy ✦✦✦✦
This valuable Savoy LP, put out by Muse in 1986, has 14 previously unissued alternate takes taken from two Art Pepper sessions. The great altoist is heard with a

quiet West Coast trio (pianist Russ Freeman, bassist Bob Whitlock and drummer Bobby White) and with a quintet co-starring tenor saxophonist Jack Montrose. The Pepper-Montrose matchup is particularly exciting but Pepper is actually in fine form on all of the performances; it is difficult to believe that these were all rejected takes. The remainder of the two productive sessions were released on a two-LP set around the same period titled *Discoveries*, and most of this music (particularly the alternate takes) has not been reissued on CD yet. —*Scott Yanow*

Art Pepper Quartet, Vol. 1 / Mar. 31, 1953 / Time Is ✦✦✦
This CD contains a live performance from early in altoist Art Pepper's career in which he is joined by pianist Sonny Clark, Harry Babasin on bass and cello, and drummer Bobby White. Recorded at the legendary Lighthouse, the music is better than the recording quality. Pepper and Clark have many fine solos on the six standards and Art's "Brown Gold" (based on "I Got Rhythm") but this CD (there never was a Vol. 2) is strictly for collectors. —*Scott Yanow*

Mucho Calor / 1956 / V.S.O.P. ✦✦✦
This V.S.O.P. LP brings back an obscure session from the long defunct Andex label that was probably recorded around 1956. The emphasis is on Latin jazz with altoist Art Pepper, trumpeter Conte Candoli and tenor saxophonist Bill Perkins, pianist Russ Freeman, bassist Ben Tucker and drummer Chuck Flores interacting with the percussion of Jack Costanza and Mike Pacheko. With arrangements by Bill Holman, Johnny Mandel, Benny Carter and Pepper, the music is quite jazz-oriented if a touch lightweight. Worth investigating by fans of the idiom. —*Scott Yanow*

☆ **The Complete Pacific Jazz Small Group Recordings of Art Pepper** / Jul. 26, 1956-Aug. 12, 1957 / Mosaic ✦✦✦✦
This superior three-LP box set reissues all of altoist Art Pepper's small-group dates for the Pacific Jazz label. Virtually all of the music has since been reissued on CD (part of it as *The Artistry of Pepper* and part of it under trumpeter Chet Baker's name), but the Mosaic box, which has an attractive booklet, is the definitive treatment of this chapter in Pepper's musical story. The great altoist is heard in a sextet with Baker and tenor saxophonist Richie Kamuca, on a version of "Tenderly" with Chet Baker's big band, with Baker and tenor Phil Urso in a different sextet, sharing the spotlight with tenor saxophonist Bill Perkins in a quintet and heading a nonet playing arrangements by Shorty Rogers. The music is very much in the cool/bop tradition, but Art Pepper is instantly recognizable (he never sounded that much like Charlie Parker) and even at this early stage, he was at the top of his form. All 26 performances are quite enjoyable and swinging, making this hard-to-find set worth the search. —*Scott Yanow*

Early Art / Aug. 6, 1956-Jan. 14, 1957 / Blue Note ✦✦✦✦✦
This excellent two-LP set contains some of the lesser-known recordings of altoist Art Pepper in the 1950s, all of his performances for the Intro and Jazz West labels. Pepper is heard on five selections in a quintet that includes vibraphonist Red Norvo and pianist Gerald Wiggins, ten songs with trumpeter Jack Sheldon and eight numbers in a quartet with pianist Russ Freeman. Highlights include "Straight Life," "Tenor Blooz" (on which Pepper switches to tenor), "Broadway," "Patricia" and "When You're Smiling." This high-quality, cool-toned bop music deserves to be better known and eventually reissued in complete form on CD. —*Scott Yanow*

The Return of Art Pepper: The Complete Art Pepper Aladdin Recordings / Aug. 6, 1956-Jan. 1957 / Blue Note ✦✦✦
Blue Note's *The Return of Art Pepper: The Complete Art Pepper Aladdin Recordings* compiles the 13 final masters that the alto saxophonist recorded for Aladdin between August 1956 and January 1957. These are titled *The Return of Art Pepper*, since they were recorded shortly after he completed a jail sentence in 1956. As a result, Pepper's chops are a little rusty, but you can hear that he still has a passion for playing, and he does improve over the course of these tracks. For serious Pepper fans, it's worth a listen, but for less dedicated fans, there are better places to become acquainted with his work. —*Stephen Thomas Erlewine*

The Art Pepper Quartet / Aug. 1956 / Tampa ✦✦✦
Originally released on the defunct Tampa label and then on CD by the small V.S.O.P. label, this straight reissue in the OJC series features the great altoist Art Pepper with pianist Russ Freeman, bassist Ben Tucker and drummer Gary Frommer. Despite the inclusion of five alternate takes, there is still only around 41 minutes of music but the quality is high; even with his erratic lifestyle, Pepper never made a bad record. Highlights include Art's original "Diane," "Besame Mucho" and "Pepper Pot." Fine music, but not essential when one considers how many gems Art Pepper recorded during his rather hectic life. —*Scott Yanow*

Val's Pal / Nov. 23, 1956 / V.S.O.P. ✦✦✦
The music on this V.S.O.P. CD, which originally came out on the Tampa label in the 1950s, has since been reissued by Fantasy in its OJC series. Altoist Art Pepper, who is assisted by pianist Russ Freeman, bassist Ben Tucker and drummer Gary Frommer, is in excellent form during the 41 or so minutes. The seven selections are aug-

mented by five alternate takes. Although not an essential release, these versions of "Diane," "Pepper Pot" and "Besame Mucho" (the latter a song that Art would perform frequently in the late '70s) are somewhat memorable. —*Scott Yanow*

The Way It Was / Nov. 26, 1956-Nov. 23, 1960 / Original Jazz Classics ✦✦✦✦✦
Despite his very erratic lifestyle, altoist Art Pepper never made a bad record. This collection is better than most. The first four titles team together Pepper with tenor saxophonist Warne Marsh, pianist Ronnie Ball, bassist Ben Tucker and drummer Gary Frommer for generally intriguing explorations of four standards. One can feel the influence of Lennie Tristano (with Pepper in Lee Konitz's place) although Pepper had his own sound and a more hard-swinging style. The success of the Pepper-Marsh front line makes one wish that they had recorded together again. The other three selections are leftovers from a trio of classic Pepper albums and all are quite worthwhile. Pepper is heard backed by three separate rhythm sections which include pianists Red Garland, Dolo Coker or Wynton Kelly, either Paul Chambers or Jimmy Bond on bass and Philly Joe Jones, Frank Butler or Jimmy Cobb on drums. Overall this album sticks to bop standards and finds Art Pepper in top form. —*Scott Yanow*

The Artistry of Pepper / Dec. 11, 1956-Aug. 12, 1957 / Pacific Jazz ✦✦✦✦✦
This CD starts off with four selections from a date led by tenor saxophonist Bill Perkins that features altoist Art Pepper; the remainder of the quintet comprises pianist Jimmy Rowles, bassist Ben Tucker and Mel Lewis. While they perform boppish versions of two standards and a pair of Pepper originals, the remainder of the CD has a particularly strong set that showcases Pepper in a nonet arranged by Shorty Rogers. The music in the latter date are all Rogers originals and there are alternate takes of "Diablo's Dance " and "Popo" to round out the program. The other soloists include trumpeter Don Fagerquist, Bill Holman on tenor, baritonist Bud Shank, valve trombonist Stu Williamson and pianist Russ Freeman. Highly recommended to fans of Art Pepper and West Coast jazz. —*Scott Yanow*

★ **Meets the Rhythm Section** / Jan. 19, 1957 / Original Jazz Classics ✦✦✦✦✦
This Contemporary album is one of Art Pepper's greatest recordings. Although he was reportedly nervous to be playing with Miles Davis' rhythm section (pianist Red Garland, bassist Paul Chambers and drummer Philly Joe Jones), the altoist is quite inspired on the nine high-quality tunes. In addition to some bop standards, this album introduced Pepper's "Straight Life," recast the Dixieland tune "Jazz Me Blues" in a modern setting and also includes Pepper's "Waltz Me Blues." The combination of musicians worked very well, making this one of the top jazz albums of a great jazz year, 1957. —*Scott Yanow*

Omega Alpha / Apr. 1, 1957 / Blue Note ✦✦✦✦
The music on this Blue Note LP has always been somewhat obscure. Originally released by Omegatape only on prerecorded tapes, it did not make its debut on an American LP until this 1980 album. It was a strange twist of fate, for the music for altoist Art Pepper (who was in one of his prime periods) was in top form throughout the date, playing "Surf Ride," "Webb City" and five familiar standards with pianist Carl Perkins, bassist Ben Tucker and drummer Chuck Flores. Highlights include "Surf Ride," "Fascinatin' Rhythm" and "Body and Soul." —*Scott Yanow*

★ **Art Pepper + Eleven: Modern Jazz Classics** / Mar. 14, 1959-May 11, 1959 / Original Jazz Classics ✦✦✦✦✦
This is a true classic. Altoist Art Pepper is joined by an 11-piece band playing Marty Paich arrangements of a dozen jazz standards from the bop and cool jazz era. Trumpeter Jack Sheldon has a few solos, but the focus is very much on the altoist who is in peak form for this period. The CD reissue adds two additional versions of "Walkin'" and one of "Donna Lee" to the original program. Throughout, Pepper sounds quite inspired by Paich's charts, which feature the band as an active part of the music rather than just in the background. Highlights of this highly enjoyable set include "Move," "Four Brothers," "Shaw Nuff," "Anthropology" and "Donna Lee," but there is not a single throwaway track to be heard. Essential music for all serious jazz collections. —*Scott Yanow*

Gettin' Together / Feb. 29, 1960 / Original Jazz Classics ✦✦✦✦✦
As a sort of follow-up to Art Pepper's matchup with Miles Davis' trio in the 1957 classic *Art Pepper Meets the Rhythm Section*, Pepper utilizes Davis' sidemen on this 1960 near-classic. In addition to pianist Wynton Kelly, bassist Paul Chambers and drummer Jimmy Cobb, trumpeter Conte Candoli makes the group a quintet on four of the eight numbers. The CD reissue adds "The Way You Look Tonight" (formerly only available on another LP) and an alternate take of the title cut to the original repertoire. This time around, rather than emphasizing standards, Pepper performs just three ("Softly, As in a Morning Sunrise," Thelonious Monk's "Rhythm-A-Ning" and "The Way You Look Tonight") and includes three originals of his own: "Diane," "Bijou the Poodle" and "Gettin' Together." The music is all very straightahead and bop-oriented, but as usual, Pepper brings something very personal and unique to his playing; he sounds like no one else. —*Scott Yanow*

Smack Up / Oct. 24, 1960-Oct. 25, 1960 / Original Jazz Classics ◆◆◆◆◆

The title of this recording (which has been reissued on CD with two takes of the otherwise unknown "Solid Citizens" added) is ironic and inadvertently truthful. Within a short period, Art Pepper would begin spending many years in jail due to his heroin addiction; this was his next-to-last album of this period. Despite the bleak future, the great altoist (who never seemed to make an uninspired record during his unstable life) is in excellent form in a quintet with trumpeter Jack Sheldon, pianist Pete Jolly, bassist Jimmy Bond and drummer Frank Butler. Highlights of this fine album include Harold Land's title cut, the 5/4 blues "Las Cuevas De Mario" and Ornette Coleman's "Tears Inside." —*Scott Yanow*

Intensity / Nov. 23, 1960-Nov. 25, 1960 / Original Jazz Classics ◆◆◆◆◆

This album, reissued on CD with an additional song, "Fine Points," was altoist Art Pepper's final one of his early period and was released when he was already serving a long prison sentence due to his addiction to heroin. Assisted by pianist Dolo Coker, bassist Jimmy Bond and drummer Frank Butler, Pepper was just starting to show the influence of John Coltrane and Ornette Coleman in his style, freeing up his playing and displaying a greater intensity during his improvisations. Ironically, Pepper sticks to swinging standards such as "I Can't Believe That You're in Love with Me," "Gone with the Wind" and "I Wished on the Moon" as points of departure on the interesting and largely enjoyable set. Excluding a 1973 recording with Mike Vax's big band, it would be 15 years before Art Pepper led another record date in the studios. —*Scott Yanow*

Art Pepper Quartet in San Francisco (1964) / May 8, 1964-Jun. 1964 / Fresh Sound ◆◆◆

For altoist Art Pepper, the 1960s were largely a waste with long periods spent in prison due to his narcotics addiction. He spent most of 1964 between prison terms and even tried to make a musical comeback. This CD from the Spanish Fresh Sound label features Pepper with pianist Frank Strazzeri, bassist Hersh Hamel and drummer Bill Goodwin playing a few originals on a television show (Pepper is interviewed briefly by Ralph Gleason) and performing two lengthy numbers at The Jazz Workshop in San Francisco. Many of the altoist's longtime fans were disappointed by his playing during this period, for Pepper had become very influenced by John Coltrane and fearful that, if he did not sound like 'Trane, he would be regarded as old fashioned. Actually, Art Pepper, who plays with more intensity here than he often did in the 1950s, sounds fairly good during these sets, although the recording quality is not always the greatest, and his fans (along with jazz historians) will find these rare performances quite interesting. —*Scott Yanow*

I'll Remember April: Live at Foothill College / Feb. 14, 1975 / Storyville ◆◆◆◆

Altoist Art Pepper was at the beginning of his successful (if relatively brief) seven-year renaissance when he performed at the concert documented on this Storyville CD. Recorded six months before his first official comeback record (*Living Legend*), the great altoist is heard playing with a quartet comp of Tommy Gumina on polychord (an organ-sounding accordion), bassist Fred Atwood and drummer Jimmie Smith. Pepper is in excellent form on lengthy versions of his "Foothill Blues," "I'll Remember April," and "Cherokee," and is quite passionate on a four-and-a-half-minute version of "Here's That Rainy Day." Gumina mostly stays out of the way, and the audience sounds quite happy to get an opportunity to hear the legendary altoist sounding so strong. —*Scott Yanow*

Living Legend / Aug. 9, 1975 / Original Jazz Classics ◆◆◆◆

Art Pepper, one of the major bop altoists to emerge during the 1950s, started his comeback with this excellent set. After 15 years filled with prison time and fighting drug addiction, Pepper was finally ready to return to jazz. Accompanied by three of his old friends (pianist Hampton Hawes, bassist Charlie Haden and drummer Shelly Manne), Pepper displays a more explorative and darker style than he had previously. He also shows a greater emotional depth in his improvisations and was open to some of the innovations of the avant-garde in his search for greater self-expression. Although this recording would be topped by the ones to come, the music (five Pepper originals and an intense version of "Here's That Rainy Day") is quite rewarding. —*Scott Yanow*

The Trip / Sep. 15, 1976+Sep. 16, 1976 / Original Jazz Classics ◆◆◆◆◆

Although some listeners prefer altoist Art Pepper's playing of the 1950s, when he re-emerged in 1975, there was a much greater emotional intensity to his improvisations, and his solos used a wider vocabulary with nonmusical and emotional sounds being added to his ideas as punctuations. This strong quartet date (with pianist George Cables, bassist David Williams and drummer Elvin Jones) finds Pepper performing Michel Legrand's "The Summer Knows," lesser-known tunes by Woody Shaw and Joe Gordon and three originals of his own; the CD reissue also has an alternate take of "The Trip." Powerful music. —*Scott Yanow*

A Night in Tunisia / Jan. 23, 1977 / Storyville ◆◆◆◆

Altoist Art Pepper was nearing the turning point in his career at the time that he performed at the concert at Half Moon Bay, CA, that is included on this Storyville

CD. He had been back on the scene for two years and had not quite broken through to the wider jazz audience yet, but major successes were in the near future. It is obvious from his talking to the audience that Pepper was still unsure about his future, but his playing on this date (with a pickup group comprising pianist Smith Dobson, bassist Jim Nichols and drummer Brad Bilhorn) finds him in top form, creating emotional versions of "A Night in Tunisia" and his three originals "Mr. Yohe," "The Trip" and "Lost Life." Since there are only 40 minutes of music on the CD and this was not one of Pepper's strongest groups, the release is not essential, but fans of the unique altoist will want to pick up these interesting performances. —*Scott Yanow*

No Limit / Mar. 26, 1977 / Original Jazz Classics ◆◆◆◆◆

Art Pepper's third recording in his comeback years was recorded in a studio but has the emotional intensity and chance-taking improvisations of his live concerts of the period. Joined by his regular group (pianist George Cables, bassist Tony Dumas and drummer Carl Burnett), Pepper performs lengthy versions of three of his originals (including the modal "My Laurie") and "Ballad of the Sad Young Men." "Mambo de la Pinta" is a little unusual because Pepper overdubbed himself on tenor to join his alto in the ensembles. Throughout this album (and during his final ten years), Art Pepper played every note as if it might be his last one. The passion displayed on this particular album is enough of a reason by itself to acquire it. —*Scott Yanow*

Tokyo Debut / Apr. 5, 1977 / Galaxy ◆◆◆◆◆

After Art Pepper returned to the scene in 1975, it took him two years to get noticed outside of Los Angeles. His initial visit to Japan was a major turning point, and music from one of the very well-received concerts was released for the first time on this 1995 CD. Pepper performs four numbers—"Cherokee," his original "The Spirit Is Here," a passionate "Here's That Rainy Day" and a speedy workout on "Straight Life"—with a quintet comprising Clare Fischer (who unfortunately sticks exclusively to electric piano), bassist Rob Fisher, drummer Peter Riso and percussionist Poncho Sanchez. For the final three numbers—"Manteca," "Manha De Carnaval" and "Felicidade"—the group is joined by vibraphonist Cal Tjader (this is the only time he ever recorded with Pepper) and guitarist Bob Redfield. The unexpected enthusiasm of the crowd really got to Pepper and his improvisations (even though he is not playing with his regular group) are quite inspired. Memorable music. —*Scott Yanow*

Thursday Night at the Village Vanguard / Jul. 28, 1977 / Original Jazz Classics ◆◆◆◆◆

Art Pepper's appearances at the Village Vanguard in 1977 were a major success, making the brilliance of the West Coast-based altoist obvious to the New York critics. His historical stint at the Vanguard was originally made available on four LPs (all reissued as CDs with one additional selection added on each disc) and more recently in more expanded form as a nine-CD boxed set. The single CD reissue of the Thursday night portion features the great altoist on lengthy versions of "Valse Triste," a particularly passionate version of "Goodbye," "Blues for Les," "My Friend John" and "Blues for Heard." In addition to Pepper, his trio—pianist George Cables, bassist George Mraz and drummer Elvin Jones—is also in top form, and the music is consistently stimulating and emotional. —*Scott Yanow*

Friday Night at the Village Vanguard / Jul. 28, 1977-Jul. 30, 1977 / Original Jazz Classics ◆◆◆◆◆

The second of four releases taken from altoist Art Pepper's very successful stint at the Village Vanguard in July 1977 has been reissued on CD with one extra track, "A Night in Tunisia." Pepper, who is greatly assisted by a highly sympathetic rhythm section (pianist George Cables, bassist George Mraz and drummer Elvin Jones) is at his best on "Caravan," which finds him doubling on tenor, and on an intense rendition of "But Beautiful." All of this music is currently available as part of a massive nine-CD box set that really documents the historic engagement. —*Scott Yanow*

☆ **The Complete Village Vanguard Sessions** / July 28, 1977-July 30, 1977 / Contemporary ◆◆◆◆◆

The Complete Village Vanguard Sessions is an exhaustive box set that contains all 45 takes from Art Pepper's legendary stay at the Village Vanguard. Any serious Pepper fan will find a lot to treasure here, but the sheer size of the set makes it intimidating for less dedicated listeners. —*Leo Stanley*

Saturday Night at the Village Vanguard / Jul. 30, 1977 / Original Jazz Classics ◆◆◆◆◆

The CD reissue of this release, the third of four single sets that document Art Pepper's well-received engagement at the Village Vanguard, adds "For Freddie" to the original three-song program. The other selections, which feature pianist George Cables, bassist George Mraz and drummer Elvin Jones in addition to the altoist/leader, are intense interpretations of "You Go to My Head," Pepper's "The Trip" and a 16-minute version of "Cherokee." The altoist was entering his peak period and the entire gig has also been fully documented on a massive nine-CD box set. —*Scott Yanow*

More for Less / Jul. 28, 1977-Jul. 30, 1977 / Original Jazz Classics ✦✦✦✦✦
The fourth of four CD reissues taken from Art Pepper's three nights at the Village Vanguard in July 1977, as with the other releases, adds one selection ("Scrapple from the Apple") to the music of the original LP; all of the performances on this and the other sets have since been made available as part of a massive nine-CD box set. The great altoist was clearly excited to be playing at the famous New York club, and his rhythm section—pianist George Cables, bassist George Mraz and drummer Elvin Jones—consistently stimulates his imagination. This release has more variety than usual, for in addition to his alto playing (including a memorable unaccompanied solo on "Over the Rainbow"), Pepper switches to clarinet for the lengthy "More for Les" and interprets the ballad "These Foolish Things" on tenor. The nine-CD set is essential for Art Pepper fanatics, but those just wanting a taste of the great altoist's talents will be satisfied with this release. —*Scott Yanow*

San Francisco Samba: Live at Keystone Korner / Aug. 6, 1977+Aug. 8, 1977 / Contemporary ✦✦✦✦
Art Pepper was a tormented genius, and when his demons became too much to bear, he would exorcise them through his horn. By 1977, his playing was becoming more bluesy, punctuated with shouts, wails, squalls, shrieks, whimpers, moans and cries; emotions at his fingertips, art and life fused as one. These are four extended performances (none of them under 11 minutes long) taken from Pepper's stand at San Francisco's Keystone Korner the week after his historic Village Vanguard sessions in New York. Pepper is letting *all* of his emotions out on these numbers, with unabashed, high-energy drumming from Eddie Marshall keeping things moving at a frothy level of excitement on the opener, "Blue Bossa" and the closing "Samba Mom Mom," two of the best examples of Art's impassioned and extended Latin groove playing. Pianist George Cables is saluted on the bluesy "Art Meets Mr. Beautiful," Pepper's pet name for his regular collaborator for the last five years of his life, a swinging romp taken at a fairly brisk pace. A moving rendition of the ballad "Here's That Rainy Day" (which Pepper handles as a request) follows this flag-waver and sports some alternately reflective and wild playing in its extended version. —*Cub Koda*

Live in Japan, Vol. 1 / Mar. 14, 1978 / Storyville ✦✦✦✦
Art Pepper concluded a very successful tour of Japan with a concert in Yamagata that was recorded and released on two Storyville CDs. The first CD has just 38 minutes of music, but the quality is quite high. Pepper (with pianist Milcho Leviev, bassist Bob Magnusson and drummer Carl Burnett) performs lengthy versions of two originals ("Ophelia," "My Laurie") and "Besame Mucho"; the latter was a request from his Japanese friends that was very well received and became a permanent part of his repertoire. The recording quality is excellent and Pepper is in explorative and somewhat inspired form. —*Scott Yanow*

Live in Japan, Vol. 2 / Mar. 14, 1978 / Storyville ✦✦✦
The second of two CDs taken from the final night of Art Pepper's 1978 Japanese tour features the great altoist (along with pianist Milcho Leviev, bassist Bob Magnusson and drummer Carl Burnett) exploring two of his originals ("The Trip," and "Red Car"), a lyrical version of Michel Legrand's "The Summer Knows" and an intense rendition of "Caravan." None of the Storyville sets have been reissued elsewhere, and each adds to the remarkable legacy of Art Pepper whose second career (covering 1975-82) was arguably even greater than his first. —*Scott Yanow*

Among Friends / Sep. 2, 1978 / Discovery ✦✦✦✦
Art Pepper mostly sticks to standards on this Discovery LP, but he brings out new life in the veteran songs, particularly on such ballads as "'Round Midnight," "What's New" and "Besame Mucho." With the assistance of pianist Russ Freeman, bassist Bob Magnusson and drummer Frank Butler, the great altoist (who is heard just prior to signing an exclusive contract with the Galaxy label) is also in top form on such pieces as "What Is This Thing Called Love" and "I'll Remember April." An excellent (if not quite essential) release. —*Scott Yanow*

☆ **Complete Galaxy Recordings** / Dec. 1, 1978-Apr. 14, 1982 / Galaxy ✦✦✦✦✦
Altoist Art Pepper was at the height of his career during his final five years. A brilliant improviser in the 1950s, by the late '70s the many dark experiences he had had in life were reflected in a deep emotional intensity in his playing. He played each solo as if it might be his last and his passion was brutally honest. This giant 16-CD Galaxy set features Pepper at the peak of his powers. Most of the performances are in a quartet setting although there is a session with strings, five unaccompanied alto solos (he also plays clarinet on a few tracks) and a pair of CDs in which Pepper duets with pianist George Cables. Although more general collectors may want to acquire some of the individual sessions first (most of which are available separately on CD), the more dedicated jazz fans are advised to save their money and acquire this essential package. —*Scott Yanow*

Art Pepper Today / Dec. 1, 1978+Dec. 2, 1978 / Original Jazz Classics ✦✦✦✦
Altoist Art Pepper, in the midst of a successful comeback, recorded this excellent set (also included in full in his massive Galaxy box set) for Galaxy. With pianist Stanley Cowell, bassist Cecil McBee and drummer Roy Haynes, Pepper performs a definitive version of his intense ballad "Patricia"; other highlights include "Miss Who," "Lover Come Back to Me" and "Chris' Blues." The CD reissue also has a second alternate version of "These Foolish Things." —*Scott Yanow*

Laurie's Choice / 1978-1981 / LaserLight ✦✦✦✦
Although it has come out on a budget label, these four performances (taken from concert appearances in 1978, 1980 and 1981) had never previously been released before. With support from either George Cables or Milcho Leviev on piano, David Williams or Bob Magnusson on bass and drummer Carl Burnett, the great altoist Art Pepper is in excellent form on an emotional "Kobe Blues," an intense version of "Patricia" and hard-swinging renditions of "Allen's Alley" and his own "Straight Life." —*Scott Yanow*

So in Love / Feb. 23, 1979-May 26, 1979 / Artists House ✦✦✦✦
This deluxe release from the classy (but long defunct) Artists House label, as with all of Art Pepper's recordings of his comeback years, is easily recommended. Actually, all of this music has been reissued in greatly expanded form in Pepper's massive 16-CD Galaxy box set. The original LP has lengthy versions of "So in Love," "Stardust," "Straight, No Chaser" and two Pepper originals ("Diane" and "Blues for Blanche"). Assisted by two equally talented rhythm sections (pianists Hank Jones and George Cables, bassists Ron Carter and Charlie Haden, and drummers Al Foster and Billy Higgins), Pepper is in excellent form throughout the album, giving these songs heartwrenching interpretations. —*Scott Yanow*

Artworks / May 25, 1979-May 26, 1979 / Galaxy ✦✦✦
The performances on this Galaxy LP are essentially outtakes and leftovers from Art Pepper's 1979 sessions for Artists House. However, the quality is quite high, making one wonder why this material was not released until 1984. "Body and Soul" and "You Go to My Head" are particularly special, for they are unaccompanied alto solos, and on "Anthropology," Pepper has a rare outing on clarinet. The remaining numbers—"Desafinado," "Donna Lee" and "Blues for Blanche"—feature the great altoist with pianist George Cables, bassist Charlie Haden and drummer Billy Higgins. All of the highly enjoyable and bop-based but explorative music has since been reissued on CD in Pepper's 16-CD Galaxy box set. —*Scott Yanow*

Tokyo Encore / Jul. 16, 1979-Jul. 23, 1979 / Dreyfus ✦✦✦✦✦
It is not obvious looking at the outside of this CD but the music from this live performance is also included in Art Pepper's 16-CD Galaxy set. However those Pepper fans unable to afford the larger box are advised to acquire this Dreyfus single CD for the altoist is heard in superb form. Accompanied (and inspired) by pianist George Cables, bassist Tony Dumas and drummer Billy Higgins, Pepper stretches out on six superior pieces that are highlighted by "Besame Mucho," "Straight Life" and one of the greatest versions ever recorded of "Over the Rainbow." —*Scott Yanow*

Landscape / Jul. 1979 / Original Jazz Classics ✦✦✦✦✦
Altoist Art Pepper was in inspired form during this Tokyo concert, which has also been reissued as part of a huge "complete" Galaxy box set. This particular single-CD features Pepper (along with pianist George Cables, bassist Tony Dumas and drummer Billy Higgins) on memorable versions of "True Blues," "Sometime" (during which Pepper switches to clarinet), "Landscape," "Avalon," "Over the Rainbow," "Straight Life" and the CD "bonus" cut "Mambo de la Pinta." Throughout, Pepper's intensity and go-for-broke style are exhilarating. —*Scott Yanow*

★ **Straight Life** / Sep. 21, 1979 / Original Jazz Classics ✦✦✦✦✦
Altoist Art Pepper recorded many albums for the Galaxy label during 1979-82, all of which have been reissued in a massive 16-CD "complete" box set. This single CD is fairly definitive and serves as a perfect introduction to Pepper's second (and most rewarding) period. Not only is there a superior version of Pepper's famous title cut but several (emotional and explorative) renditions of "September Song" and "Nature Boy." Filling out this quartet set (which also features pianist Tommy Flanagan, bassist Red Mitchell and drummer Billy Higgins) are "Surf Ride," "Make a List" and "Long Ago and Far Away." Brilliant music. —*Scott Yanow*

Winter Moon / Sep. 3, 1980-Sep. 4, 1980 / Original Jazz Classics ✦✦✦✦✦
Ever since Artie Shaw and Charlie Parker, most jazz musicians have had a desire to record at least once in their lives with strings, often considering it a prestigious honor. Altoist Art Pepper finally had his chance on this album and fortunately the string arrangements (by Bill Holman and Jimmy Bond) do not weigh down the proceedings. Pepper sounds quite inspired performing seven strong compositions highlighted by Hoagy Carmichael's "Winter Moon," "When the Sun Comes Out" and a clarinet feature on "Blues in the Night." This material (plus four alternate takes and two other songs from the same sessions) is included in the massive Art Pepper Galaxy box set. —*Scott Yanow*

One September Afternoon / Sep. 5, 1980 / Original Jazz Classics ✦✦✦
This is one of the lesser-known Art Pepper Galaxy sessions. In addition to pianist Stanley Cowell, bassist Cecil McBee and drummer Carl Burnett, guitarist Howard Roberts helps out on two songs. Three alternate takes are added to the original six-tune program, which is highlighted by "There Will Never Be Another You" and a passionate rendition of "Brazil." —*Scott Yanow*

Arthur's Blues / 1981 / Original Jazz Classics ✦✦✦✦
A '92 CD reissue of another sparkling late-'80s session from alto saxophonist Art Pepper, this one a quartet date with a blues theme. Pepper's jagged, turbulent solos expressed the rage and despair he felt knowing he was nearing the end and still had many things he wanted to say. He's backed by what had become his regular band: pianist George Cables, bassist David Williams, and drummer Carl Burnett. —*Ron Wynn*

● **Art Pepper with Duke Jordan in Copenhagen 1981** / Jul. 3, 1981 / Galaxy ✦✦✦✦
This was the first and last time Pepper worked with Jordan, and came about because Pepper's usual pianist, George Cables, was unable to make the dates at Club Montmartre in Copenhagen. To Pepper's dismay, Danmarks Radio decided to record the first gig of the Montmartre series. Pepper need not have worried—the show was a rousing success, with the band tackling a set of standards (and a couple of Pepper originals) with such verve and determination that relatively simple tunes turned into astounding solo workouts (there are several drum and bass solos to be heard on this record), the amazing highlight of which is a shot at "Besame Mucho" that rounds out 22 minutes. Art Pepper was in the process of dying at the time this recording was made, but there's no lack of energy, no loss of vitality. A two-CD live jazz set that's well worth having and should not be overlooked. —*Steven McDonald*

Art Lives / Aug. 13, 1981-Aug. 15, 1981 / Galaxy ✦✦✦✦
The music on this LP is from altoist Art Pepper's well-documented engagement at the Maiden Voyage club in Los Angeles in 1981. All of the music has since been reissued on CD as part of his giant 16-CD set. Pepper, pianist George Cables, bassist David Williams and drummer Carl Burnett are heard at their best on "Allen's Alley," and "Samba Mom Mom." A special highlight is a passionate duet by Pepper and Cables on "But Beautiful." —*Scott Yanow*

Roadgame / Aug. 15, 1981 / Original Jazz Classics ✦✦✦✦✦
Altoist Art Pepper's 1981 appearances at Los Angeles' now-obsolete Maiden Voyage club were fully documented, resulting in three LPs and a greatly expanded program that is included on Pepper's massive "complete" Galaxy box set. This particular release, the only one thus far to be made available as a single CD, has Pepper and his quartet (with pianist George Cables, bassist David Williams and drummer Carl Burnett) performing "Roadgame" (an alternate take has been added to the CD reissue), "Road Waltz," an intense "Everything Happens to Me" and "When You're Smiling"; on the latter, Pepper switches to clarinet. Although only a year away from his death, the great Art Pepper was still very much in his prime for this memorable outing. —*Scott Yanow*

Art 'n' Zoot / Sep. 27, 1981 / Pablo ✦✦✦✦
This historic music, which was released for the first time on this 1995 CD, features an exuberant session by a notable group of veteran all-stars, recorded live at UCLA in 1981. Altoist Art Pepper is heard on a lyrical and emotional version of "Over the Rainbow" (the only selection that has Charlie Haden on bass). Tenor great Zoot Sims swings on "In the Middle of a Kiss," "Broadway" and "The Girl from Ipanema"; the latter two songs also feature guitarist Barney Kessel. But the main reason to acquire this disc is to hear Sims and Pepper jamming together on "Wee" and "Breakdown Blues." The rhythm section of pianist Victor Feldman, bassist Ray Brown and drummer Billy Higgins is as tight, alert and hard-swinging as one would expect, and it is a joy to hear this rare encounter by the two great saxophonists. It is only a pity that Pepper and Sims did not record together more extensively during their careers. —*Scott Yanow*

Goin' Home / May 11, 1982-May 12, 1982 / Original Jazz Classics ✦✦✦✦✦
Art Pepper's final recording sessions comprised duets with pianist George Cables. Pepper, who splits his time almost evenly here between alto and clarinet, is in surprisingly strong form considering that he only had a month left to live. He is heard at his best on "Goin' Home," "Don't Let the Sun Catch You Cryin'," "Isn't She Lovely" and "Lover Man," really pouring out his emotions into the ballads. Two alternate takes were added to the CD reissue, although for the complete picture, one has to acquire Art Pepper's 16-CD Galaxy box set which contains plenty of otherwise unissued performances. —*Scott Yanow*

Tete-A-Tete / May 11, 1982-May 12, 1982 / Original Jazz Classics ✦✦✦✦✦
Altoist Art Pepper's final recordings resulted in two albums worth of duets with pianist George Cables; the music was reissued in expanded form on Pepper's 16-CD Galaxy box set, but otherwise, this LP is out of print. Highlights of these relaxed but passionate encounters include "Over the Rainbow," "Body and Soul,"

"The Way You Look Tonight" and "You Go to My Head." Pepper never did decline on record, and although he died in June 1982 (just a month after the last of these duets), he is prime form throughout the emotional performances. —*Scott Yanow*

Darn That Dream / May. 23, 1982 / Drive Archives ✦✦✦
Altoist Art Pepper and tenor saxophonist Joe Farrell teamed up for the first and only time on this CD. With pianist George Cables, bassist Tony Dumas and drummer John Dentz also participating, Pepper and Farrell are in good form. They interact on a blues, "Sweet Lorraine," "Mode for Joe" and "Who Can I Turn To," but the high points are their two individual features; Farrell has "Someday My Prince Will Come" and Pepper really tears into "Darn That Dream." —*Scott Yanow*

Jim Pepper

b. 1941, Oregon, d. Feb. 10, 1992, Portland, OR
Tenor Saxophone, Flute / Post-Bop, World Fusion
Jim Pepper will always be best remembered for his popular recording of "Witchi-Tai-To," a peyote chant put to music. Pepper, who is definitively profiled in the hour-long documentary *Pepper's Pow Wow* (available on video), infused advanced jazz with the influence of his Native American heritage. The son of a father who also played saxophone, Pepper early in life loved to tap dance. He largely taught himself both tenor and clarinet, developing a soulful sound and keeping his style open to both free expression and the influence of world music. Pepper grew up in Oklahoma and moved to New York in the mid-1960s. He was a major part of one of the first fusion groups, Free Spirits, which made a record for ABC/Paramount in 1967. Pepper, who played in the "Everything Is Everything" band in the late '60s, was encouraged by Ornette Coleman and Don Cherry to put more of his heritage into his music. Jim Pepper worked with Cherry, Dewey Redman, Charlie Haden's Liberation Music Orchestra and his own bands. He recorded with Paul Motian and Bob Moses and led a session apiece for Europa (1984) and Enja (1987). Pepper passed away at the age of 50 from lymphoma. —*Scott Yanow*

● **Comin' and Goin'** / Jan. 4, 1987 / Antilles ✦✦✦✦✦
Dakota Sound / Jan. 1987 / Enja ✦✦✦✦

Danilo Perez

b. Dec. 29, 1966, Panama
Piano / Post-Bop, Latin Jazz, Afro-Cuban Jazz
A brilliant pianist who has combined the bebop tradition with his Panamanian heritage, African elements and a willingness to take chances, Danilo Perez's improvisations are fascinating to watch develop. In concert he has been known to have his quartet improvising in four different time signatures simultaneously with surprisingly coherent results and his originals tend to develop as they go along with surprising results. Perez started playing piano in Panama at age eight and in 1985 moved to Boston to study at Berklee. He played with Jon Hendricks (1987) and Claudio Roditi (1988) and has had a longtime association with Paquito D'Rivera. Danilo Perez gigged and recorded with Dizzy Gillespie during the trumpeter's last years and has headed several sessions as a leader for Novus and most recently Impulse. —*Scott Yanow*

Danilo Perez / Sep. 1992 / Novus ✦✦✦✦✦
● **The Journey** / Dec. 1993 / Novus ✦✦✦✦✦
Panamonk / Jan. 3, 1996-Jan. 4, 1996 / Impulse! ✦✦✦✦✦
This is one of the more interesting Thelonious Monk tribute albums of the 1990s. Pianist Danilo Perez does not really sound much like Monk except in a couple places on purpose, but he has clearly learned from Monk's music, particularly in his use of space and quirky dissonances. The trio performances range from respectful ballads and Latinized treatments of Thelonious tunes to originals that somehow fit logically into the mood of the set. Perez takes " 'Round Midnight" and the two brief versions of "Monk's Mood" (which open and close the CD) unaccompanied, interacts closely with bassist Aishai Cohen on the other pieces, welcomes the haunting wordless vocal of Olga Roman to "September in Rio" and utilizes either Terri Lyne Carrington or Jeff Watts on the nine trio pieces. The music overall is adventurous, rhythmic and quite joyful. A memorable outing by the talented Danilo Perez. —*Scott Yanow*

Bill Perkins (William Reese Perkins)

b. Jul. 22, 1924, San Francisco, CA
Tenor Saxophone, Baritone Saxophone, Soprano Saxophone, Flute / Cool, Hard Bop, Post-Bop
Among the "coolest" of the West Coast tenor players of the 1950s, Bill Perkins in later years became a bit influenced by John Coltrane and modernized his style in a personal way. A flexible and versatile musician who also plays baritone, alto, soprano and flute, Perkins is best-known for his work on tenor. Born in San Francisco, he grew up in Chile, moved to Santa Barbara and served in the military in

World War II. After studying music and engineering, he played in the big bands of Jerry Wald, Woody Herman (1951-53 and 1954) and Stan Kenton (1953-54 and 1955-58). Perk started recording as a leader in 1956 (most notably *Grand Encounter* with John Lewis) including sets with Art Pepper and Richie Kamuca. During the 1960s, he had a dual career as a studio musician and a recording engineer and during 1970-92 he was a member of the "Tonight Show" band. In recent years, Perkins has played baritone and tenor with the Lighthouse All-Stars and been a member of the Bud Shank Sextet, in addition to heading his own sessions for a variety of labels. —*Scott Yanow*

Tenors Head-On / Jul. 1956-Oct. 29, 1956 / Pacific Jazz ✦✦✦✦

The Lester Young-influenced tenors of Bill Perkins (who has since developed a more Coltrane-oriented style) and Richie Kamuca are matched on this CD reissue. The music is hard-swinging but light-toned runthroughs on standards with the two complementary tenors both in excellent form. The material is taken from two former LPs and feature a pair of all-star rhythm sections (pianist Pete Jolly, bassist Red Mitchell and Stan Levey or pianist Hampton Hawes, Mitchell and drummer Mel Lewis). Lovers of bebop and solidly swinging music will find much to enjoy on the set including some rare (if conventional) bass clarinet and flute from Perkins on a colorful version of "Sweet and Lovely." —*Scott Yanow*

Just Friends / Oct. 29, 1956 / Pacific Jazz ✦✦✦

Quietly There / Nov. 23, 1966-Nov. 30, 1966 / Original Jazz Classics ✦✦✦✦

This set by multi-reedist Bill Perkins (who switches between tenor, baritone, bass clarinet and flute) has been reissued on CD with one extra selection. On what was one of the earliest tributes to film composer Johnny Mandel, Perkins was careful to not only perform ballads such as "Emily," "A Time for Love" and "The Shadow of Your Smile" but to add some variety by also playing a few of Mandel's more obscure medium-tempo numbers. Still, the results are generally fairly relaxed and tasteful on a quintet set with pianist Victor Feldman (who also plays some cheesy-sounding organ and vibes), guitarist John Pisano, bassist Red Mitchell and drummer Larry Bunker. —*Scott Yanow*

Front Line / Nov. 20, 1978 / Storyville ✦✦✦✦

Although Bill Perkins (switching between tenor, flute and baritone) gets top billing, this CD reissue is just as significant for the participation of baritone great Pepper Adams (who contributed three of the six originals) and Gordon Goodwin (playing tenor and soprano) who wrote two of the other songs. The performances are quite melodic with concise solos, tasteful ensembles and close attention paid to color and dynamics. The strong West Coast rhythm section (pianist Lou Levy, bassist Bob Magnusson and drummer Carl Burnette) does an expert job of accompanying the soloists. Several of the originals deserve to become standards, especially Adams' "Dylan's Delight." A fine straightahead set that, due to the fresh material, is a cut above the usual jam session. —*Scott Yanow*

Many Ways to Go / Mar. 1980 / Sea Breeze ✦✦✦

Journey to the East / Nov. 19, 1984-Nov. 22, 1984 / Contemporary ✦✦✦✦

I Wished on the Moon / Nov. 23, 1989+Apr. 25, 1990 / Candid ✦✦✦✦✦

Remembrance of Dino's / May 21, 1990 / Interplay ✦✦✦✦

Our Man Woody / Jan. 8, 1991-Sep. 1991 / Jazz Mark ✦✦✦✦

● Frame of Mind / May 20, 1993-May 21, 1993 / Interplay ✦✦✦✦✦

It is typical of Bill Perkins' adventurous spirit that on his Interplay CD, a session on which he had complete control (including repertoire and sidemen), Perk would perform ten challenging pieces: four Frank Strazzeri originals and compositions by Mike Stern, Duke Pearson, Jimmy Heath, Thelonious Monk, Billy Strayhorn and trumpeter Clay Jenkins. A couple of the pieces are blues but, due to the tricky frameworks, this was far from a routine jam session. Perkins' tenor (he switches to baritone on "You Know I Care") blends in well with Jenkins while the rhythm seciton (pianist Strazzeri, either Tom Warrington or Ken Filiano on bass and drummer Bill Berg) benefits from the inclusion of vibraphonist Bob Leatherbarrow on four of the selections. A wide variety of moods are covered on a rather modern set that serves as an excellent showcase for Bill Perkins. —*Scott Yanow*

Perk Plays Prez / Jun. 26, 1995-Jun. 27, 1995 / Fresh Sound ✦✦✦✦

Back in the 1950s, Bill Perkins had one of the coolest sounds of all tenors, a soft tone greatly influenced by Lester Young. Through the years Perkins continued to evolve, sometimes developing ideas inspired by John Coltrane while never losing his own musical personality. For this 1995 studio set, Perkins returns to his roots. In a quartet with pianist Jan Lundgren, bassist Dave Carpenter and drummer Paul Kreibich, Perkins performs a variety of classic swing standards in the style of Prez (circa 1936-42), recreating note-for-note Lester Young solos and then building up improvisations in his own style while stretching but purposely not breaking through the boundaries of swing. Perkins' ability to emulate Young is quite impressive, and his tightrope act between copying the past and coming up with fresh statements is successful. Jan Lundgren, who normally plays in a boppish style, not

only brings back the spirit of Count Basie but that of Johnny Guarnieri and sometimes Duke Ellington, too. Drummer Kreibich is tasteful in support and bassist Carpenter contributes several speedy solos. Among the many highlights are "Shoe Shine Boy," "Pound Cake," "Taxi War Dance" and "Easy Does It." The brief closer "I Left My Baby" has guest Jack Sheldon taking the vocal while Perkins (without the rhythm section) plays softly behind him. It is a pity that Lester Young's music from the 1950s is ignored and that Doug Ramsey, in his otherwise worthwhile liner notes, repeats the inaccurate notion that Young's post-war recordings paled next to his earlier ones. But, that minor reservation aside, this is a set that should delight both mainstream and Lester Young fans. —*Scott Yanow*

Carl Perkins

b. Aug. 16, 1928, Indianapolis, IN, **d.** Mar. 17, 1958, Los Angeles, CA
Piano / Hard Bop

A fine bop-oriented pianist who overcame a slightly crippled left hand (due to polio), Carl Perkins was a victim of his drug problems, passing away when he was just 29. After stints with Tiny Bradshaw and Big Jay McNeely, he became a fixture on the West Coast. Perkins was with Oscar Moore's trio (1953-54) and briefly played with an early version of the Max Roach-Clifford Brown quintet (1954) but is best-known for his association with Curtis Counce (1956-58). Perkins, who composed one jazz standard ("Grooveyard"), recorded with Counce, Chet Baker, Jim Hall, Art Pepper and as a leader for Savoy (1949), Dootone (1956) and Pacific Jazz (1957), but did not live long enough to realize his potential. —*Scott Yanow*

Ivo Perelman

b. Jan. 12, 1961, Sao Paulo, Brazil
Tenor Saxophone / Avant-Garde

The intense Brazilian tenor player Ivo Perelman combines together the emotional fire of an Albert Ayler with a strong respect for melodies. Originally a classical guitar player, Perleman also played cello, piano, trombone and clarinet before settling on tenor. His passionate style made it difficult for him to catch on at first but Perelman has recorded successful albums for K2B2, Enja, Ibeji, GM, Leo Lab and Cadence with such players as Airto, Flora Purim, Elaine Elias, Buell Neidlinger and Joanne Brackeen in the supporting cast. —*Scott Yanow*

● Ivo / Apr. 4, 1989+May 4, 1989 / ITM ✦✦✦✦✦

For his recording debut, Ivo Perelman performs seven folk melodies, five of which are traditional Brazilian children's songs. A powerful tenor player whose style and sound at times recalls Albert Ayler (without the vibrato), Gato Barbieri and Clifford Jordan, Perelman uses the simple melodies as points of departure and places to land after his intense and fairly free but melodic improvisations. The first three songs co-feature vocalist Flora Purim who is at the top of her game on the haunting "Nesta Rua" and the lighthearted but explorative "O Cravo E A Rose." Two of the other pieces have Perelman dueting with pianist Elaine Elias. The two bassists John Patitucci and Buell Neidlinger work together quite well, Don Preston takes a wild synthesizer solo on "O Cravo E A Rosa" and both drummer Peter Erskine and percussionist Airto are colorful in support. But the main star throughout the CD is Ivo Perelman whose distinctive sound, relative ease in the falsetto register and creative spirit were already impressive at this early point in his career. —*Scott Yanow*

The Children of Ibeji / May 22, 1991-Jul. 10, 1991 / Enja ✦✦✦✦

Soccer Land / 1994 / Ibeji ✦✦✦✦

Man of the Forest / Jan. 3, 1994-Jan. 4, 1994 / GM ✦✦✦✦✦

Ivo Perelman, who has been thought of as a Brazilian Albert Ayler (although that is a simplification and a denial of his originality), fuses together Brazilian music (the playing of his percussionists) with creative jazz in this unusual tribute to the compositions of the Brazilian classical composer Heitor Villa-Lobos. Actually Perelman just uses Villa-Lobos' motifs as a point of departure but one could call the results world fusion since Perelman's mixture creates some startling jazz. Pianist Joanne Brackeen makes her presence felt during her three appearances (including the modal waltz "Veleiro" and the ballad "Rasga O Coracao") while the interaction between the tenor, the accordion of Dom Salvador and the percussionists on "Cantiga Caico" is delightful. Ivo Perelman has an intense sound, complete control of his instrument and an emotional style a little like Archie Shepp in his prime. His passionate music deserves close attention. —*Scott Yanow*

Tapeba Songs / 1996 / Ibeji ✦✦✦

Blue Monk Variations / Feb. 2, 1996 / Cadence ✦✦✦

While waiting at a studio for another musician to show up, tenor saxophonist Ivo Perelman warmed up by playing three versions of "Blue Monk" and three variations based abstractly on the Thelonious Monk tune. Because his spontaneous playing was quite intriguing, it was decided to release the performances on a CD, even though there were only 36 minutes of music. These unaccompanied flights are often quite free and emotional, and although for selected tastes, they generally hold one's interest. —*Scott Yanow*

Revelation / Oct. 10, 1996 / CIMP ◆◆◆◆

En Adir / 1997 / Music & Arts ◆◆◆

Sound Hierarchy / Music & Arts ◆◆◆

Tom Peron

Trumpet / Hard Bop

A fixture in Northern California, trumpeter Tom Peron in 1982 became a member of pianist Jessica Williams' quartet. A bop-oriented player with a wide range, Peron recorded two albums for his own Tomcat label, teamed up with drummer Bud Spangler for a Monarch release and has appeared on records by Joe Gilman and Kitty Margolis. —*Scott Yanow*

● **Interplay** / 1994 / Monarch ◆◆◆◆

Trumpeter Tom Peron, who co-leads this quartet set with drummer Bud Spangler, is a fine bop-based improviser whose first important early musical association was with the great pianist Jessica Williams. Williams is also on this date (along with bassist John Wiitala) and occasionally steals solo honors. However, the main significance to the CD is the excellent playing of Peron, who contributes two originals and really digs into the five standards. Whether taking solo flights open or muted à la Miles Davis, Tom Peron displays a lot of potential for the future. Highlights include the tricky "Trumpeter's Revenge," "Oleo," an uptempo "We See" and a lengthy investigation of "Summertime." —*Scott Yanow*

Dedication / Jun. 24, 1996 / Monarch ◆◆◆◆

P.J. Perry

b. Dec. 2, 1941, Calgary, Alberta, Canada

Alto Saxophone / Bop, Hard Bop

The son of tenor saxophonist Paul Guloien (who used the professional name of Paul Perry), P.J. Perry began his musical career playing alto in his father's band when he was 14. Within a year, P.J. was freelancing in Vancouver. Despite getting several offers to play in the US (including from Terry Gibbs when he was 18), Perry has spent most of his career in Canada (with a few short periods in Europe), performing with all of the top Canadian jazz players and in the studios. Combining together aspects of Art Pepper, Sonny Stitt and Phil Woods in his own passionate style, P.J. Perry has recorded for CBC, Gramaphone, Little Mountain Records and, more recently, Unity (1989) and Jazz Alliance (1990). —*Scott Yanow*

● **My Ideal** / Oct. 1989 / Unity ◆◆◆◆◆

Rich Perry

b. , Cleveland, OH

Tenor Saxophone / Post-Bop

A fine young veteran tenor player, Rich Perry went on the road in 1975 with the Glenn Miller ghost band. In 1976 he moved to New York and joined the Thad Jones/Mel Lewis Orchestra. Since then he has played with a wide variety of top players including Chet Baker, Machito, Bob Moses, Jack McDuff, Billy Hart, Eddie Gomez, Tom Harrell, the Mel Lewis big band and Harold Danko. Rich Perry first recorded as a leader in 1993 for Steeple Chase. —*Scott Yanow*

● **To Start Again** / Apr. 1993 / Steeple Chase ◆◆◆◆◆

On his debut as a leader, Rich Perry (a longtime member of the Mel Lewis Orchestra) often recalls Warne Marsh, playing harmonically advanced lines that are full of unusual twists. Occasionally he also sounds a little like Eddie Harris and Stan Getz but, in general, his dry yet fairly colorful improvisations are quite original. With strong assistance from pianist Harold Danko, bassist Scott Colley and drummer Jeff Hirshfield, Perry is in top form on a set dominated by obscure material including two Thad Jones songs, Antonio Carlos Jobim's attractive "Retrato Em Braco E Preto" and originals by Maria Schneider, Danko and himself. This modern mainstream jazz contains plenty of fire along with a variety of moods. —*Scott Yanow*

Beautiful Love / 1994 / Steeple Chase ◆◆◆◆

Charlie Persip

b. Jul. 26, 1929, Morristown, NJ

Drums / Hard Bop

An excellent drummer both in big bands and combos, Charli Persip changed his name from Charlie in the early '80s. He had early experience playing locally in New Jersey and with Tadd Dameron (1953) but gained his initial recognition for his work with Dizzy Gillespie's big band and quintet (1953-58). In 1959 he formed his own group, the Jazz Statesmen, which featured a young Freddie Hubbard. Persip appeared on many record sessions in the 1950s and '60s with such players as Lee Morgan, Dinah Washington, Red Garland, Gil Evans, Don Ellis, Eric Dolphy,

Roland Kirk, Gene Ammons and Archie Shepp among others. He was with Billy Eckstine during 1966-73, was the main drum instructor for the Jazzmobile in the mid-'70s and has led his Superband (a part-time big band) since the early '80s, recording several dates. —*Scott Yanow*

● **Charles Persip and the Jazz Statesmen** / Apr. 2, 1960 / Bethlehem ◆◆◆◆

Drummer Charlie Persip has not had that many opportunities to lead sessions through the years; in fact, this album was his only one until 1980. His quintet includes up-and-coming players (trumpeter Freddie Hubbard, tenor saxophonist Roland Alexander, pianist Ronnie Matthews and bassist Ron Carter, whom one assumes he could not hold on to for long). The music (even the originals) is essentially mainstream bop with some strong solos from the horns and several spots (most notably on "The Champ") for the leader. Trumpeter Marcus Belgrave subs for Hubbard on one of the five cuts. —*Scott Yanow*

Superband / 1980 / Stash ◆◆◆◆◆

In Case You Missed It / Sep. 12, 1984-Sep. 13, 1984 / Soul Note ◆◆◆

No Dummies Allowed / Nov. 19, 1987+Nov. 25, 1987 / Soul Note ◆◆◆◆

With the exception of the drummer/leader, trumpeter Jack Walrath and the up-and-coming altoist Sue Terry and pianist Darrel Grant, Charlie Persip's Superband was full of obscure names in the late '80s. However, the drummer's sidemen were all quite talented. The arrangements on their CD are quite modern (often emphasizing dense ensembles) yet swing. Walrath's "Revenge of the Fat People" sounds a bit like Charles Mingus (often featuring simultaneous improvisations), Sue Terry does a fine job of weaving together three tunes for an unlikely Billie Holiday medley, and the high-powered "Vital Seconds" is highlighted by a brief spot for Pablo Calajero's passionate baritone. Walrath has solos on several pieces (he is best on the stromy "Thurway Traffic") and other impressive voices include Orpheus Gaitanopoulos' tenor, Sayyd Abdul Al-Khabyyr's alto and pianist Grant. Charlie Persip deserved great credit for keeping this rather uncommercial orchestra together for over ten years. —*Scott Yanow*

Eric Person

Alto Saxophone, Soprano Saxophone / Post-Bop

Eric Person was one of the more well-rounded young players to arrive on the scene in the late-'80s. Early on, the keen-toned saxophonist showed a desire to explore. He possesses an expressive (if somewhat harsh) tone, and seems comfortable with most jazz styles, though his strength is as a modal/free player. Person hails from St. Louis, the son of Thomas Person, a local tenor sax player who naturally exerted a heavy influence on his son. His father started Eric on the saxophone; later, he studied with Lloyd Smith, and at the St. Louis Conservatory of Music. Person moved to New York in 1982 and began to accrue sideman experience with a number of famous leaders, including pianist John Hicks and drummers Ronald Shannon Jackson and Chico Hamilton. Person also has spent time with the small bands of guitarist Kelvin Bell and pianist Michele Rosewoman, and the big band of McCoy Tyner; in 1993, he also became one of the several altoists that have filled Julius Hemphill's vacated chair in the World Saxophone Quartet. —*Chris Kelsey*

● **Prophecy** / Mar. 7, 1992-Feb. 23, 1993 / Soul Note ◆◆◆◆◆

This session featuring both originals and interpretations of compositions by Wayne Shorter and John Coltrane, has many interesting and compelling moments, but also contains long stretches where Person's technical brilliance can't prevent the listener from becoming weary hearing an array of scales, phrases, honks and repeated riffs. The most exciting moments are his elaborations of Coltrane's "Up Against the Wall" and the 13-minute "Interstellar Space Suite," where Person's dynamic, aggressive statements offer an energetic updating and skillful presentation of vintage material. His own tunes are more erratic, but Person is a first-rate player. —*Ron Wynn*

Arrival / Aug. 1992 / Soul Note ◆◆◆◆◆

No More Tales to Tell / Jun. 24, 1996+Jun. 25, 1996 / Soul Note ◆◆◆◆

Houston Person

b. Nov. 10, 1934, Florence, SC

Tenor Saxophone / soul-jazz, Hard Bop, Groove

In the 1990s Houston Person has kept the soulful thick-toned tenor tradition of Gene Ammons alive, particularly in his work with organists. After learning piano as a youth, Person switched to tenor. While stationed in Germany with the army, he played in groups that also included Eddie Harris, Lanny Morgan, Leo Wright and Cedar Walton. Person picked up valuable experience as a member of Johnny Hammond's group (1963-66) and has been a bandleader ever since, often working with his wife, singer Etta Jones. A duo recording with Ran Blake was a nice change of pace but most of Houston Person's playing has been done in blues-oriented organ groups. He has recorded a consistently excellent series of albums for Muse. —*Scott Yanow*

Goodness! / Aug. 25, 1969 / Original Jazz Classics ✦✦✦✦
Tenor saxophonist Houston Person was still a relatively new name at the time he recorded this set, his sixth session for Prestige. The funky music (which includes the hit title song) emphasizes boogaloos, danceable rhythms and repetitious vamps set down by the rhythm section (organist Sonny Phillips, guitarist Billy Butler, electric bassist Bob Bushnell, drummer Frankie Jones and Buddy Caldwell on congas), but it is primarily Person's passionate tenor solos that will come the closest to holding on to the attention of jazz listeners. The music is generally quite commercial and is certainly not recommended to bebop purists, although it has some strong moments. But overall these performances succeed more as background music than as creative jazz. —Scott Yanow

The Truth! / Feb. 23, 1970 / Prestige ✦✦✦

Legends of Acid Jazz / Oct. 12, 1970-Apr. 9, 1971 / Prestige ✦✦✦✦✦
Houston Person was among the guttiest of the gutbucket saxophonists of the soul-jazz golden age—for proof, look no further than *Legends of Acid Jazz: Houston Person*, which compiles two of the saxman's most popular releases, *Person to Person!* and *Houston Express* (both originally released in 1970). *Express* featured the "funk-master general" of the tenor saxophone with a tight, pocket-sized ensemble (including guitarist Grant Green and drummer Idris Muhammad), while, on *Person!*, his supporting ensemble expanded to include trumpet players Cecil Bridgewater and Thad Jones, guitarist Billy Butler and another kindred spirit and prince of funk on his instrument, Motown bassist Gerry Jemmott. *Legends of Acid Jazz: Houston Person* provides a high-voltage cover version extravaganza, including "(For God's Sake) Give More Power to the People" (the Chi-Lites), "Close to You" (the Carpenters), "Yester-Me, Yester-You, Yesterday" (Stevie Wonder), "Young, Gifted and Black" (Aretha Franklin), "Just My Imagination" (the Temptations), and "Lift Every Voice and Sing," which Person describes in his liner notes as the "Black national anthem." Person and friends turn every one of these, and others such as his own "Up at Joe's, Down at Jim's" and his trademark "The Houston Express" into stinging, swinging, original-sounding opuses of funk. —Chris Slawecki

Island Episode / Apr. 9, 1971-Jan. 12, 1973 / Prestige ✦✦✦
All of the music on this 1997 CD was previously unreleased. Eight of the nine selections date from 1973 and match the great soul-jazz tenor Houston Person with a Latin-oriented band that also includes trumpeter Victor Paz, Hank Jones (on electric piano), guitarist Jimmy Ponder, bassist Andy Gonzalez, an unidentified drummer, percussionist Jerry Gonzalez and Nicky Marrero on timbales. Although there are dated aspects to the music, Person fares well. The other selection is from 1971, a funky number with a medium-size group that includes organist Ernie Hayes. Overall, a worthwhile set, if not essential. —Scott Yanow

Stolen Sweets / Apr. 29, 1976 / Muse ✦✦✦✦✦
First-rate soul-jazz, funk, blues, and ballads by tenor saxophonist Houston Person. Vocalist Etta Jones wasn't on this session, so things were mostly uptempo and cooking, with plenty of robust tenor from Person, tasty guitar by Jimmy Ponder, swirling organ riffs and support from Sonny Phillips, and percussion and rhythmic assistance from Frankie Jones and Buddy Caldwell. —Ron Wynn

The Big Horn / May 20, 1976 / Muse ✦✦✦✦
Reliable soul-jazz, nicely played ballads, and good standards are tenor saxophonist Houston Person's forte, and he demonstrates that repeatedly on this '76 quintet set. Pianist Cedar Walton is the type of no-nonsense, consistent player whose skills are often taken for granted, while bassist Buster Williams and drummer Grady Tate are equally unassuming veterans. —Ron Wynn

Wildflower / Sep. 12, 1977 / Muse ✦✦✦✦
Not everything tenor saxophonist Houston Person does depends on funky, raw, upbeat arrangements and grooves. This session from '77 did have some of that, but it also had some straightahead hard bop and mainstream cuts. Trumpeter Bill Hardman, who wasn't making many albums by this point, was a most welcome addition, while Sonny Phillips on organ and guitarist Jimmy Ponder were familiar Person session men at this time. —Ron Wynn

Lost & Found / Sep. 12, 1977-Jun. 15, 1991 / 32 Jazz ✦✦✦✦
This single CD from 1997 has all of the music recorded by tenor saxophonist Houston Person for his 1977 album *Wildflower*, plus a completely unissued session from 1993. The latter teams the soulful Person with the classic pianist/vocalist Charles Brown in a quintet also including guitarist Danny Caron, bassist Red Callender and drummer Gaylord Birch. It is a particular pleasure hearing Brown fare so well in a jazz setting. The earlier date has five fairly long jams, with Person joined by trumpeter Bill Hardman, guitarist Jimmy Ponder, the underrated organist Sonny Phillips, drummer Idris Muhammad and percussionist Larry Killian. In addition to a couple of familiar standards ("Ain't Misbehavin'" and "My Romance"), the title cut, and a Phillips original, the band debuts a previously unknown Tadd Dameron ballad titled "Dameron." All in all, this is a well-rounded CD easily recommended to fans of soul-jazz, hard bop and Charles Brown. —Scott Yanow

The Nearness of Houston Person / Nov. 1977 / Muse ✦✦✦
Intimate, nicely played late '70s session by tenor saxophonist Houston Person that balances robust soul-jazz and blues with stately ballads and standards featuring vocalist Etta Jones. When things heat up, organist Charles Earland helps punctuate Pearson's solos. Then, when Jones steps out front, it's Person who puts the accents behind her singing. —Ron Wynn

Suspicions / Apr. 24, 1980 / Muse ✦✦✦
Some robust funk and fine soul licks, plus solid mainstream fare. —Ron Wynn

Very Personal / Aug. 29, 1980 / Muse ✦✦✦✦✦
A departure for tenor saxophonist Houston Person, normally a soul-jazz, blues, funk, and ballads player. This is more mainstream jazz and hard bop, with Person working alongside pianist Cedar Walton, trombonist Curtis Fuller, bassist Buster Williams, and drummer Vernell Fournier. All those who felt that Person couldn't play bop changes were left looking silly when this came out in 1980. —Ron Wynn

The Talk of the Town / Jan. 23, 1987 / Muse ✦✦✦
Marvelous standards and ballads, with excellent trumpet solos by Cecil Bridgewater. —Ron Wynn

● **Basics** / Oct. 12, 1987 / Muse ✦✦✦✦✦
A good session, with blues and bop leanings. —Ron Wynn

Something in Common / Feb. 23, 1989 / Muse ✦✦✦✦
Houston Person is one of the last in a long line of thick-toned tenors who display soul in every note they play while bassist Ron Carter's versatility is legendary (it seems as if he has spent half of his life in recording studios). Their duet CD, although not inevitable, works out quite well. Carter not only sets the rhythms behind Person but sometimes plays chords (à la Count Basie guitarist Freddie Green) or the melody in unison with the tenor, continually keeping the music flowing in an unhurried and relaxed fashion. None of the selections (seven standards plus "Blues for Two") are taken faster than medium tempo and Person has been chewing up these chord changes for years, so the main attractions of this date are the instrumentation and the strong interplay between Person and Carter. The results are both relaxed and successful. —Scott Yanow

The Party / Nov. 14, 1989 / Muse ✦✦✦✦✦
Good soul-jazz and blues session, with young lion organist Joey De Francesco providing the funky undercurrent to tenor saxophonist Houston Person's thick, authoritative solos, and Randy Johnston and Bertell Knox filling the spaces on bass and drums, plus Sammy Figueroa adding some Afro-Latin fiber for additional support. —Ron Wynn

Why Not! / Oct. 5, 1990 / Muse ✦✦✦✦
Houston Person's warm tenor tone, effortless swing, and skill at playing with organists have been taken for granted through the years, since he breaks no new boundaries and is very consistent. On this CD, he forged a new partnership with the young organist Joey De Francesco, and they work together perfectly on a set of blues, ballads and standards. Randy Johnston adds some nice George Benson-ish guitar solos; Sammy Figueroa's congas are an added plus, and trumpeter Phillip Harper (despite his entrance in the wrong key on "Namely You") tries his best to fill in for Lee Morgan. —Scott Yanow

Marvin "Hannibal" Peterson

b. Nov. 11, 1948, Smithville, TX
Trumpet / Avant-Garde
One of the more intriguing avant-garde trumpeters, Marvin Peterson is also able to play very credible hard bop. After playing trumpet in the North Texas State University band, he moved to New York in 1970. Among his most important associations were with Rahsaan Roland Kirk, Gil Evans (1973-1980), Pharoah Sanders, Elvin Jones and his own bands. Although he has never received the recognition he deserves, the performances of Marvin "Hannibal" Peterson are always stimulating and unpredictable. —Scott Yanow

In Antibes / Jul. 20, 1977 / Inner City ✦✦✦
This live blowout features trumpeter Marvin "Hannibal" Peterson, George Adams on tenor and flute, cellist Diedre Murray, bassist Steve Neil and drummer Makaya Ntshoko stretching out on two 19- to 21-minute jams. "Ro" has some of Adams' intense tenor although he switches to his less impressive flute on "Swing Low Sweet Chariot." There are some strong moments on this set but also lots of rambling. This music was probably better experienced live than on this LP. —Scott Yanow

● **The Angels of Atlanta** / Feb. 15, 1981+Feb. 19, 1981 / Enja ✦✦✦✦✦
Although the Harlem Boys Choir is occasionally utilized and Pat Peterson takes a soulful vocal on "The Inner Voice," this CD is very much trumpeter Marvin "Hannibal" Peterson's date. The explorative trumpeter is heard at his absolute peak, taking lengthy and fiery improvisations that show off not only his virtuosity but his

emotional range. The superlative band (tenor saxophonist George Adams, pianist Kenny Barron, cellist Diedre Murray, bassist Cecil McBee and drummer Dannie Richmond) really inspires Peterson who stretches the boundaries of his music towards gospel and soul without watering down the jazz content. This well-balanced set is one of Hannibal's finest recordings. —*Scott Yanow*

Oscar Peterson

b. Aug. 15, 1925, Montreal, Canada
Piano, Leader / Bop, Swing
Oscar Peterson is one of the greatest piano players of all time. A pianist with phenomenal technique on the level of his idol, Art Tatum, Peterson's speed, dexterity and ability to swing at any tempo have long been amazing. Very effective in small groups, jam sessions and in accompanying singers, O.P. is at his absolute best when performing unaccompanied solos. His original style does not fall into any specific idiom. Like Erroll Garner and George Shearing, Peterson's distinctive playing formed during the mid- to late '40s and fell somewhere between swing and bop. Peterson has been criticized through the years because he uses so many notes, has not evolved much since the 1950s, and has recorded a remarkable number of albums. Perhaps it is because critics ran out of favorable adjectives to use early in his career; certainly it can be said that Peterson plays 100 notes when other pianists might use ten, but all 100 usually fit, and there is nothing wrong with showing off technique when it serves the music. As with Johnny Hodges and Thelonious Monk, to name two, Peterson spent his career growing within his style rather than making any major changes once his approach was set, certainly an acceptable way to handle one's career. Because he was Norman Granz's favorite pianist (along with Tatum) and the producer tended to record some of his artists excessively, Peterson has made an incredible number of albums. Not all are essential, and a few are routine, but the great majority are quite excellent, and there are dozens of classics.

Oscar Peterson started classical piano lessons when he was six and developed quickly. After winning a talent show at 14, he began starring on a weekly radio show in Montreal. Peterson picked up early experience as a teenager playing with Johnny Holmes' Orchestra. From 1945-49, he recorded 32 selections for Victor in Montreal. Those trio performances find Peterson displaying a love for boogie-woogie, which he would soon discard, and the swing style of Teddy Wilson and Nat King Cole. His technique was quite brilliant even at that early stage, and although he had not yet been touched by the influence of bop, he was already a very impressive player. Norman Granz discovered Peterson in 1949 and soon presented him as a surprise guest at a Jazz at the Philharmonic concert. Peterson was recorded in 1950 on a series of duets with either Ray Brown or Major Holley on bass; his version of "Tenderly" became a hit. Peterson's talents were quite obvious, and he became a household name in 1952 when he formed a trio with guitarist Barney Kessel and Brown. Kessel tired of the road and was replaced by Herb Ellis the following year. The Peterson-Ellis-Brown Trio, which often toured with JATP, was one of jazz's great combos from 1953-58. Their complex yet swinging arrangements were competitive—Ellis and Brown were always trying to outwit and push the pianist—and consistently exciting. In 1958, when Ellis left the band, it was decided that no other guitarist could fill in so well, and he was replaced (after a brief stint by Gene Gammage) by drummer Ed Thigpen. In contrast to the earlier group, the Peterson-Brown-Thigpen Trio (which lasted until 1965) found the pianist easily the dominant soloist. Later versions of the group featured drummers Louis Hayes (1965-66), Bobby Durham (1967-70), Ray Price (1970) and bassists Sam Jones (1966-70) and George Mraz (1970).

In 1960, Oscar Peterson established the Advanced School of Contemporary Music in Toronto, which lasted for three years. He made his first recorded set of unaccompanied piano solos in 1968 (strange that Norman Granz had not thought of it) during his highly rated series of MPS recordings. With the formation of the Pablo label by Granz in 1972, Peterson was often teamed with guitarist Joe Pass and bassist Niels Pedersen. He appeared on dozens of all-star records, made five duet albums with top trumpeters (Dizzy Gillespie, Roy Eldridge, Harry "Sweets" Edison, Clark Terry and Jon Faddis) and teamed up with Count Basie on several two-piano dates. An underrated composer, Peterson wrote and recorded the impressive "Canadiana Suite" in 1964 and has occasionally performed originals in the years since. Although always thought of as a masterful acoustic pianist, Peterson has also recorded on electric piano (particularly some of his own works), organ on rare occasions, and even clavichord for an odd duet date with Joe Pass. One of his rare vocal sessions in 1965, *With Respect to Nat,* reveals that Peterson's singing voice was nearly identical to Nat King Cole's.

A two-day reunion with Herb Ellis and Ray Brown in 1990 (which also included Bobby Durham) resulted in four CDs. Peterson was felled by a serious stroke in 1993 that knocked him out of action for two years. Since then, he has gradually returned to the scene, although his left hand has been weakened. But even when he is not 100 percent, Oscar Peterson remains a classic improviser, one of the finest musicians that jazz has ever produced.

The pianist has appeared on an enormous number of records through the years. As a leader, he has recorded for Victor, Granz's Clef and Verve labels (1950-64), MPS, Mercury, Limelight, Pablo and Telarc. —*Scott Yanow*

The Complete Young Oscar Peterson / Apr. 30, 1945-Nov. 14, 1949 / RCA ◆◆◆◆◆
This double CD reissues the complete contents of two valuable LPs, the first 32 studio recordings of the great pianist Oscar Peterson. Recorded in Montreal, Canada, with local musicians during 1945-49 before his fame spread worldwide, these trio performances let one hear how Peterson sounded before he fully discovered bop and formed his own distinctive sound; the pianist already had his remarkable virtuosity, along with a taste for boogie-woogie that he later lost. Sticking mostly to swing standards and rollicking blues, Peterson sounds more touched by the style of Teddy Wilson than he would later on. Fascinating and enjoyable music, highly recommended for all serious jazz collections. —*Scott Yanow*

1951 / Mar. 8, 1951-Jul. 13, 1951 / Just a Memory ◆◆◆◆◆
Recorded for the Canadian Broadcasting Corporation and little heard since then, these radio transcriptions (reissued on CD by Just a Memory) feature the brilliant Oscar Peterson when he was just 25, only two years after being "discovered" by Norman Granz. Peterson performs 20 concise duets with Canadian bassist Austin Roberts; only three songs are over three minutes, and five are under two. Although Peterson's style was fairly bop-oriented during this era, he sticks mostly to swing standards. O.P.'s virtuosity was already quite developed, and he rips into such songs as "Flying Home," "I've Got Rhythm," "Seven Come Eleven," "Air Mail Special" and "Get Happy," making every moment of the brief performances count. This melodic and enjoyable set is recommended even to Oscar Peterson fans who already have over 100 of his records. —*Scott Yanow*

The Trio Set / Sep. 13, 1952+Sep. 19, 1953 / Verve ◆◆◆◆
This LP features two versions of the Oscar Peterson Trio, heard during a pair of Jazz at the Philharmonic Carnegie Hall concerts. The 1952 performance has five jazz standards including a famous version of "Tenderly"; guitarist Barney Kessel and bassist Ray Brown somehow manage to keep up with Peterson on heated renditions of "C Jam Blues" and "Seven Come Eleven." The second trio, with Herb Ellis in Kessel's place, features complex arrangements and spontaneous improvising on such songs as "Swingin' on a Star" and "Swingin' Till the Girls Come Home"; the concert was the latter unit's earliest recording. This LP gives one a definitive look at these two classic groups. —*Scott Yanow*

The Gershwin Songbooks / Nov. 1, 1952-Aug. 1, 1959 / Verve ◆◆◆
In what was a giant undertaking (even for producer Norman Granz), pianist Oscar Peterson recorded ten songbook albums during 1952-54 and when his trio changed, nine more in 1959. Both of his George Gershwin projects (one from 1952 and the other in 1959) have been reissued in full on this single CD. The earlier date matches the brilliant O.P. with guitarist Barney Kessel and bassist Ray Brown, while the 1959 session has Brown and drummer Ed Thigpen. The songbook series found Peterson playing concise (around three-minute) versions of tunes and he always kept the melody in the forefront. The results are not innovative or unique but they are tasteful and reasonably enjoyable. Since five of the songs are played by both groups, a comparison between the two units is interesting. —*Scott Yanow*

The Song Is You: The Best of the Verve Songbooks / Dec. 1952-Aug. 1, 1959 / Verve ◆◆◆
Pianist Oscar Peterson has made a remarkable number of records through the years and his two songbook series for Verve (each recording features the songs of a different composer) were extensive, to say the least. During 1952-54 he cut ten albums (113 songs), and in 1959 he added nine more records (108 songs), in addition to his regular busy activities. Because these were easy-listening sets with concise interpretations that always kept the melodies of the composers close by, they are not considered Peterson's greatest work but they are enjoyable in their own right. This particular two-CD set has some of the highlights from these marathon projects, most of which (the Gershwin songbooks excepted) had never been out on CD before. Peterson teams up with guitarist Barney Kessel and bassist Ray Brown on nine numbers from 1952, features Herb Ellis in Kessel's place on 13 other songs and concludes with ten selections from his 1959 trio with Brown and drummer Ed Thigpen. In all, 32 of the 221 selections are on this two-fer and, although one hopes that these projects will be completely reissued someday (which would be a mammoth undertaking), this melodic set is quite pleasing. —*Scott Yanow*

Compact Jazz: Oscar Peterson and Friends / 1952-1961 / Polygram ◆◆
This bogus anthology skims the surface of Peterson collaborations with giants like Lester Young, Milt Jackson, and Sonny Stilt. Get original sessions if you can find them. —*Ron Wynn*

☆ **At Zardis'** / Nov. 8, 1955 / Pablo ◆◆◆◆◆
The group that Oscar Peterson led between 1953-58 with guitarist Herb Ellis and bassist Ray Brown was one of the great piano trios of all time. It was never so

much a matter of Peterson having two other musicians accompany him as it was that they could meet the pianist as near-equals and consistently inspire him. And unlike most trios, O.P.'s had many arranged sections that constantly needed rehearsals and were often quite dazzling. This live double CD from 1955 has previously unreleased (and unknown) performances of 31 songs (28 standards plus three of Peterson's originals) that were released for the first time in 1994. The pianist is often in typically miraculous form, Ellis (whether playing harmonies, offering short solos or getting his guitar to sound like a conga by tapping it percussively) proves to be a perfect partner, and Brown's subtle but sometimes telepathic contributions should not be overlooked either. —*Scott Yanow*

Oscar Peterson Plays Count Basie / Dec. 27, 1955 / Clef ✦✦✦✦✦
On the face of it, pianist Oscar Peterson (whose virtuosity always allowed him to play an infinite amount of notes) and Count Basie (who made inventive use of silence and space by emphasizing single rhythmic sounds) would seem to have had little in common. However, they both swung and there was a definite overlapping in their repertoire. Peterson's Basie tribute is a near-masterpiece. With guitarist Herb Ellis, bassist Ray Brown and guest drummer Buddy Rich all playing quite sympathetically, O.P.'s arrangements make the nine Basie-associated songs (along with Peterson's original "Blues for Basie") all sound quite fresh and lightly swinging. Quite a few of these renditions (particularly "Easy Does It," "9:20 Special," "Broadway" and "One O'Clock Jump") are instantly memorable. This CD reissue is highly recommended. —*Scott Yanow*

☆ **At the Stratford Shakespearean Festival** / Aug. 8, 1956 / Verve ✦✦✦✦✦
This CD contains what is considered by most listeners to be the finest recording of the Oscar Peterson-Herb Ellis-Ray Brown trio, a group that lasted from 1953-58. Although the soloing was always quite passionate and spontaneous, it was the very complex arrangements that really made this unit sound unique. The live CD adds two selections ("Nuages" and the 13-minute "Daisy's Dream") to the original program, and contains particularly memorable renditions of "Falling in Love with Love," "How About You," "Swinging on a Star," "How High the Moon" and "52nd Street Theme." Essential music from a classic band. —*Scott Yanow*

The Oscar Peterson Trio And . . . / Jul. 7, 1957 / Verve ✦✦✦✦✦
The Oscar Peterson Trio (with guitarist Herb Ellis and bassist Ray Brown) is heard in excellent form on four selections recorded at the 1957 Newport Jazz Festival, which are highlighted by "Will You Still Be Mine" and a dazzling "52nd Street Theme." In addition, the trio (plus drummer Jo Jones) back trumpeter Roy Eldridge on "Willow Weep for Me," altoist Sonny Stitt during "Autumn in New York" and jam with both the hornmen on heated versions of "Monitor Blues" and "Roy's Son." Eldridge and Stitt were always very competitive and their tradeoffs on the latter song is quite exciting. This LP (which can generally be found at a budget price) is well worth picking up. —*Scott Yanow*

☆ **At the Concertgebouw** / Sep. 29, 1957+Oct. 9, 1957 / Verve ✦✦✦✦✦
Although the music on this CD was originally said to be recorded in Europe, it actually comes from a Chicago concert, and the five additional selections (last issued on an LP shared with The Modern Jazz Quartet), supposedly performed in Chicago, are from an appearance in Los Angeles. But, despite the geographical mixups, the music is consistently brilliant and often wondrous. The Oscar Peterson-Herb Ellis-Ray Brown Trio had been together for over four years and these would be among their last (and finest) recordings. The very tricky arrangements sandwiched remarkable solos with pianist Peterson sounding especially inspired. Together with their *Stratford Shakespearean* CD of the previous year, this set features the Trio at the peak of their powers. Highlights include "The Lady Is a Tramp," "Budo," "Daahoud," "Indiana" and "Joy Spring." —*Scott Yanow*

Oscar Peterson Plays 'My Fair Lady' / Nov. 20, 1958-Jan. 1960 / Verve ✦✦✦
This CD combines together the Oscar Peterson's Trio's interpretations of two scores from Broadway shows, one very well-known and the other long forgotten. The performances of seven songs from *My Fair Lady* (at least three of which are now considered standards) is the one recording done by Peterson and bassist Ray Brown with drummer Gene Gammage, a transitional member of the Trio between the long stints of guitarist Herb Ellis and drummer Ed Thigpen. The nine themes from *Fiorello* have remained obscure but the pianist and his sidemen uplift those melodies with their usual swinging treatment. Overall the music on this reissue is consistently enjoyable. —*Scott Yanow*

A Jazz Portrait of Frank Sinatra / May 18, 1959 / Verve ✦✦✦
Pianist Oscar Peterson's Frank Sinatra tribute features his trio (with bassist Ray Brown and drummer Ed Thigpen) playing easy-listening jazz versions of a dozen songs associated with the singer. The renditions are all under four minutes and are highlighted by "Come Dance with Me," "Just in Time," "I Get a Kick out of You" and "How About You." This is not one of Oscar Peterson's most essential dates but it is swinging and enjoyable. —*Scott Yanow*

Oscar Peterson Plays the Irving Berlin Songbook / Jul. 14, 1959-Aug. 9, 1959 / Verve ✦✦✦
Oscar Peterson's *Songbooks* have received mixed reviews through the years. The second time the pianist indulged in this project, he, bassist Ray Brown and drummer Ed Thigpen recorded nine albums in a month. Obviously, not much planning went into the individual songs. Since the emphasis was on easy-listening jazz, the interpretations of the dozen Irving Berlin compositions included on this out-of-print LP are fairly melodic and safe, if swinging. Nothing unexpected occurs, but the music is reasonably pleasing, if lacking in emotional depth; certainly this is one of the happier versions of "Supper Time" (whose lyrics deal with a lynching) yet recorded. —*Scott Yanow*

Oscar Peterson Plays the Jerome Kern Songbook / Jul. 14, 1959-Aug. 9, 1959 / Verve ✦✦✦
Within a one-month period the Oscar Peterson Trio (with bassist Ray Brown and their new drummer Ed Thigpen) recorded nine different *Songbooks,* 108 selections in all. Not too surprisingly this music had a minimum of prior planning and few arranged passages, making it on a lower level than the typical music played by Peterson's prior trio with guitarist Herb Ellis. The 12 numbers performed for the *Jerome Kern* LP (which has not yet been reissued on CD) are given melodic and consistently swinging treatments with such songs as "I Won't Dance," "The Song Is You" and "Pick Yourself Up" among the better selections heard on this pleasing program. —*Scott Yanow*

Jazz Soul of Oscar Peterson/Affinity / Jul. 21, 1959-Sep. 27, 1962 / Verve ✦✦✦✦✦
This 1996 single CD reissues the complete contents of two former LPs by the Oscar Peterson Trio (consisting of pianist Peterson, bassist Ray Brown and drummer Ed Thigpen) in 1959 and 1962. Although the pianist is virtually always the lead voice, Brown and Thigpen both make strong (if subtle) contributions to the music. Highlights include "Liza," "Con Alma," "Waltz for Debby," Brown's "The Gravy Waltz" and "Yours Is My Heart Alone." An above-average release (and rather generous at 74 minutes) from the much-recorded Oscar Peterson. —*Scott Yanow*

Oscar Peterson Plays the Harry Warren Songbook / Jul. 14, 1959-Aug. 9, 1959 / Verve ✦✦✦
This LP is one of nine different *Songbook* LPs recorded by the Oscar Peterson Trio (with bassist Ray Brown and drummer Ed Thigpen) within one month. Peterson performs six songs apiece by Harry Warren (including "Lullaby of Broadway," and "I Only Have Eyes for You") and Vincent Youmans (highlighted by "More than You Know" and "Without a Song") with his usual swinging approach. Very much an ad-lib one-take set, the music is given respectful melodic treatment while being updated to the late '50s. The results are not essential but the pianist's many fans will enjoy his *Songbooks.* —*Scott Yanow*

Oscar Peterson Plays Porgy and Bess / Oct. 12, 1959 / Verve ✦✦✦✦
Oscar Peterson and his trio (with bassist Ray Brown and drummer Ed Thigpen) explore ten of the stronger themes from George Gershwin's *Porgy & Bess* on this CD reissue. It is true that Peterson's version of "Summertime" will not make one forget the classic rendition by Miles Davis with Gil Evans but, as is true with all of these performances, Peterson makes the melodies sound like his own. "It Ain't Necessarily So" and "I Got Plenty o' Nuttin'" are among the more memorable selections. —*Scott Yanow*

Bursting Out with the All-Star Big Band/Swinging Brass / Nov. 5, 1959-Jun. 24, 1962 / Verve ✦✦✦✦
Oscar Peterson's first two full-length big band albums are reissued in full on this single CD. *The Swinging Brass* date has arrangements for 11 horns plus Peterson's Trio (which includes bassist Ray Brown and drummer Ed Thigpen) while *Bursting Out* has the same trio joined by a large orchestra arranged by Ernie Wilkins. There are a couple of short spots for James Moody, Norris Turney and (on "Manteca") Cannonball Adderley but basically the two big bands back the trio. The performances are conservative, tasteful and melodic with Oscar Peterson showing off both his masterful technique and the tightness of his group. —*Scott Yanow*

London House Sessions / Jul. 27, 1961-Aug. 6, 1961 / Verve ✦✦✦✦
Oscar Peterson's week-long engagement at Chicago's London House was initially partially released as four LPs: *The Trio, The Sound of the Trio, Put on a Happy Face* and *Something Warm.* This five-CD set greatly expands upon the program, reissuing the four albums and 30 previously unissued selections. Peterson, bassist Ray Brown and drummer Ed Thigpen worked together quite well, with O.P. easily the dominant force, but this very extensive set is mostly for Peterson completists and his greatest fans, because a certain sameness pervades the music after awhile. —*Scott Yanow*

The Trio [Verve] / Sep. 1961-Oct. 1961 / Verve ✦✦✦✦
Oscar Peterson's Trio with bassist Ray Brown and drummer Ed Thigpen lacked the competitiveness of his earlier group with Brown and guitarist Herb Ellis and the later daring of his solo performances, but the pianist was generally in peak form

during this era. He sticks to standards on this live CD (a good example of the Trio's playing), stretching out "Sometimes I'm Happy" creatively for over 11 minutes and uplifting such songs as "In the Wee Small Hours of the Morning," "Chicago" and "The Night We Called It a Day." Few surprises occur, but Peterson plays at such a consistently high level that one doesn't mind. —Scott Yanow

Very Tall / Dec. 1961 / Verve ♦♦♦♦

Pianist Oscar Peterson and vibraphonist Milt Jackson met up for the first time on record during this studio session,which has been reissued on CD. Peterson here is often content to let Jackson be the main voice during many of the ensembles, although he also works at pushing the vibist to play at his most swinging. With the assistance of bassist Ray Brown and drummer Ed Thigpen, Peterson and Jackson are sensitive on the two ballads and really romp throughout "Green Dolphin Street," "Work Song," "John Brown's Body" and "Reunion Blues." —Scott Yanow

West Side Story / Jan. 24, 1962-Jan. 25, 1962 / Verve ♦♦♦

The Oscar Peterson Trio (comprising pianist Peterson, bassist Ray Brown and drummer Ed Thigpen) do a fine job of interpreting six melodies from West Side Story in addition to a closing reprise of the themes. Originally recorded for Verve, this well-recorded reissue is brief on time (31 minutes) and not all that essential, but it swings nicely and is quite enjoyable. —Scott Yanow

Live at the London House / Sep. 27, 1962 / Verve ♦♦♦

Two former LPs are combined on this CD reissue: Something Warm and Put on a Happy Face. All of the music was recorded at the London House in Chicago in 1962 by the Oscar Peterson Trio (with the pianist/leader, bassist Ray Brown and drummer Ed Thigpen), and the emphasis is on swinging versions of standards, although Oscar also contributes three originals among the 13 selections. Few surprises occur, but no disappointments either. Peterson has long been among the most consistent of pianists, and whether it be "There Is No Greater Love," "Autumn Leaves," "Old Folks" or even "Put on a Happy Face," he usually finds something fresh and swinging to play. —Scott Yanow

Night Train, Vol. 1 / Dec. 15, 1962-Dec. 16, 1962 / Verve ♦♦♦♦♦

Although the repertoire on this CD reissue by the Oscar Peterson Trio (with bassist Ray Brown and drummer Ed Thigpen) is fairly typical (with such veteran standards as "C Jam Blues," "Bags' Groove," "Easy Does It" and "I Got It Bad"), Peterson and his sidemen sound fairly inspired. Actually, the high points are the final two selections: Duke Ellington's "Band Call" and the original version of O.P.'s "Hymn to Freedom." This CD gives one a definitive look at the 1960s Oscar Peterson Trio. —Scott Yanow

☆ **Exclusively for My Friends** / 1963-Apr. 1968 / Verve ♦♦♦♦♦

Oscar Peterson has stated that he feels his MPS recordings are his finest. That is quite a statement considering the huge amount of records that the pianist has produced through the past 50 years. This four-CD set reissues the music from six of his MPS LPs: Action, Girl Talk, The Way I Really Play, My Favorite Instrument, Mellow Mood and Travelin' On. While some of the performances feature the 1963 trio he had with bassist Ray Brown and drummer Ed Thigpen, most of the music dates from 1967-68 and matches O.P. with bassist Sam Jones and either Louis Hayes or Bobby Durham on drums. A special treat is Oscar Peterson's first unaccompanied solo album, which fills up the final CD. Peterson's many fans know what to expect in this set while other listeners need to discover him to realize what all of the fuss was about. Quite simply, Oscar Peterson has long been one of the greatest pianists the world has ever known; this reissue offers plenty of proof. —Scott Yanow

☆ **Oscar Peterson Trio Plus One** / Aug. 17, 1964 / Verve ♦♦♦♦♦

This is a true classic. Fluegelhornist Clark Terry, who long has had the happiest sound in jazz, performs ten enthusiastic and generally hard-swinging songs with the Oscar Peterson Trio (which at the time included bassist Ray Brown and drummer Ed Thigpen). Terry is quite exuberant on such pieces as "Brotherhood of Man" and "Mack the Knife" and even the ballads ("They Didn't Believe Me" and "I Want a Little Girl" among them) are full of excitement. This session, though, is best known for having introduced Clark Terry's humorous "Mumbles" vocals, which can be heard on that piece, and "Incoherent Blues." This delightful and essential release has fortunately been reissued on CD. —Scott Yanow

Canadiana Suite / Sep. 9, 1964 / Limelight ♦♦♦♦

The remarkable pianist Oscar Peterson had never been thought of that much as a composer, making this set of eight of his compositions a bit of a surprise when it was originally released. Now available on CD, Peterson's tribute to his native Canada includes several noteworthy pieces of which "Hogtown Blues" and "Wheatland" are best known. With his 1964 trio (featuring bassist Ray Brown and drummer Ed Thigpen), Peterson swings hard but often with sensitivity throughout the enjoyable set. —Scott Yanow

We Get Requests / Oct. 19, 1964-Oct. 20, 1964 / Verve ♦♦

Pianist Oscar Peterson has long been such a consistent performer that none of his records are throwaways, but this particular CD reissue is weaker than most. Since several of the songs are the type that in the mid-'60s would get requested (such as "People," "The Girl from Ipanema" and "The Days of Wine and Roses"), the program would not seem to have much potential but Peterson mostly uplifts the material (although not much could be done with "People") and adds a few songs (such as his own "Goodbye J.D." and John Lewis' "D. & E.") that probably no one asked for. Overall, this is an average although reasonably enjoyable Oscar Peterson session, featuring bassist Ray Brown and drummer Ed Thigpen. —Scott Yanow

Eloquence / May 29, 1965 / Limelight ♦♦♦

This was the last album that pianist Oscar Peterson and bassist Ray Brown recorded with Ed Thigpen before the drummer departed from O.P.'s trio after six years of steady work. The music heard during this "live from Copenhagen" concert is excellent although, discounting brief selections at the beginning and end of the program, the six songs only total around 37 minutes for the CD reissue. Peterson is in particularly strong form on "Misty," "Django," a cooking "Autumn Leaves" and "Moanin'." —Scott Yanow

Exclusively for My Friends: The Lost Tapes / May 1965-Oct. 30, 1968 / Verve ♦♦♦

In 1995, this CD came out with a dozen previously unheard titles by pianist Oscar Peterson from his famed "Exclusively for My Friends" private party performances made for MPS in the 1960s. Peterson is heard on four songs with bassist Ray Brown and drummer Ed Thigpen, while on the remaining eight, he heads a trio also including bassist Sam Jones and drummer Bob Durham. The emphasis throughout is on O.P.'s virtuosity and melodic improvisations. Although the release does not add anything surprising to Peterson's legacy, his playing is up to the level of his other sets of the period; highlights include "Gravy Waltz," "Three O'Clock in the Morning," an 11-minute exploration of "Tenderly" and even "Put on a Happy Face." —Scott Yanow

The Canadian Concert of Oscar Peterson / Aug. 25, 1965 / Can-Am ♦♦♦♦

Drummer Louis Hayes (who replaced Ed Thigpen) made his recording debut with the Oscar Peterson Trio on the radio broadcast which has been released on this LP. The program (highlighted by "My One and Only Love," "Hallelujah Time," "Corcovado" and "Younger than Springtime") is typical for Peterson during the era and the music is very well-played and consistently swinging. —Scott Yanow

With Respect to Nat / Oct. 28, 1965 / Limelight ♦♦♦♦♦

This LP (which is long overdue to be reissued on CD) is quite unusual. Recorded shortly after Nat "King" Cole's death, pianist Oscar Peterson takes vocals on all but one of the program selections, sounding almost exactly like Cole. Peterson, who rarely ever sang, is very effective on the well-rounded program whether backed by a big band (arranged by Manny Albam) on half of the selections, or recreating both the spirit of the Nat "King" Cole Trio and his own group of the late '50s during a reunion with guitarist Herb Ellis and bassist Ray Brown. —Scott Yanow

Blues Etude / Dec. 3, 1965+May 4, 1966 / Verve ♦♦♦♦

This CD reissue finds pianist Oscar Peterson at a transitional point in his career. Louis Hayes was the new drummer in his trio and, although veteran Ray Brown is on bass during the earlier of the two sessions, by 1966 he would depart after 15 years and be replaced by Sam Jones. However, the basic sound of the Oscar Peterson Trio remained unchanged (O.P. was the dominant voice anyway) and the personality of the group remained intact. Peterson contributed three originals (including the hard-swinging title cut) to this program and also sounds typically fine on "Let's Fall in Love," "The Shadow of Your Smile," "If I Were a Bell" and a definitive version of "Stella By Starlight." —Scott Yanow

☆ **My Favorite Instrument** / Apr. 1968 / Verve ♦♦♦♦♦

Oscar Peterson recorded a remarkable amount of albums during his career but surprisingly this was his first full record of unaccompanied piano solos. Some observers consider his MPS recordings to be his best (quite a few are collected in the four-CD reissue Exclusively for My Friends, including this one). The solo LP features Peterson (freed from the constraints of his trio) stretching out on nine familiar standards, really tearing into a few of them including "Perdido," "Bye Bye Blackbird," "Lulu's Back in Town" while giving "Little Girl Blue" a beautiful lyrical treatment. A prelude to his outstanding Pablo recordings, My Favourite Instrument is one of Peterson's top albums of the 1960s. —Scott Yanow

Hello, Herbie / Nov. 5, 1969-Nov. 6, 1969 / MPS ♦♦♦♦♦

Guitarist Herb Ellis still considers this to be one of his personal favorite recordings. Ellis was reunited with his old boss Oscar Peterson and, with the assistance of O.P.'s trio of the period (with bassist Sam Jones and drummer Bobby Durham), the two lead voices often romp on the jam session-flavored set. Most of the chord changes are fairly basic (including three blues and "Seven Come Eleven") and Peterson was clearly inspired by Ellis' presence (and vice versa). This frequently exciting LP has been reissued several times but not yet on CD. —*Scott Yanow*

Tristeza on Piano / 1970 / Verve ✦✦✦

At the beginning of this set, Oscar Peterson so overwhelms the normally gentle "Tristeza" that it almost becomes a parody. Fortunately, the remainder of the bossa nova-flavored CD reissue is more tasteful and, even if Peterson is overly hyper in spots, he is able to bring out the beauty of such songs as George Gershwin's "Porgy," Antonio Carlos Jobim's "Trieste" and "Watch What Happens" in addition to stomping through the straightahead "You Stepped out of a Dream." —*Scott Yanow*

Oscar's Choice / Nov. 1970 / MPS ✦✦✦✦

Pianist Oscar Peterson is in his usual hard-swinging form on this LP which features one of his more obscure trios (with bassist George Mraz and drummer Ray Price). In addition to such standards as "I'm Old Fashioned," "All the Things You Are" and "Too Close for Comfort," Peterson explores "Greensleeves," Johnny Griffin's "The Jamfs Are Coming" and (the biggest surprise) James P. Johnson's "Carolina Shout" which actually sounds much closer to "Little Rock Getaway." —*Scott Yanow*

☆ Tracks / Nov. 1970 / Verve ✦✦✦✦✦

Pianist Oscar Peterson is frequently astounding on this solo set. After nearly 20 years of mostly performing with trios, O.P. sounds quite liberated in this setting, throwing in some hot stride, unexpected changes in tempos and keys, and surprises whenever he thinks of it. "Give Me the Simple Life," "Honeysuckle Rose" and the ironically titled "A Little Jazz Exercise" are quite remarkable yet Peterson also leaves space for some sensitive ballads. This LP, one of Oscar Peterson's finest recordings, is long overdue to show up on CD. —*Scott Yanow*

Two Originals: Walking the Line & Another Day / Nov. 1970-Dec. 1970 / Verve ✦✦✦✦

This CD features one of the lesser-known versions of the Oscar Peterson Trio, taken from a period when the great pianist was joined by bassist George (then known as Jiri) Mraz and drummer Ray Price. The CD reissues all of the music from their two MPS albums (*Walking the Line* and *Another Day*) except for a version of "Just Friends" left off due to lack of space. Peterson dominates the music more than he had with the Ray Brown-Ed Thigpen (or even the succeeding Sam Jones-Bobby Durham) Trio, sounding in fine form. No real surprises occur other than the inclusion of James P. Johnson's "Carolina Shout," and this particular unit would make no further recordings. Worth picking up, but not essential. —*Scott Yanow*

Reunion Blues / Jul. 1971 / MPS ✦✦✦

Pianist Oscar Peterson joins up with his old friends, vibraphonist Milt Jackson and bassist Ray Brown, in addition to his drummer of the period, Louis Hayes, for a particularly enjoyable outing. After a throwaway version of the Rolling Stones' "I Can't Get No Satisfaction," the all-star quartet performs Jackson's title cut, Benny Carter's ballad "Dream of You" and four standards. Although not up to the excitement of Peterson's best Pablo recordings of the 1970s, this is an enjoyable LP. —*Scott Yanow*

Great Connection / Oct. 1971 / Verve ✦✦✦✦

This matchup between Oscar Peterson, bassist Niels Pedersen and drummer Louis Hayes directly precedes Peterson's recordings for Pablo. The pianist is in typically brilliant form on the LP, performing six standards (including "Soft Winds" and "On the Trail") along with his own "Wheatland." It is not too surprising that Peterson would want to record frequently with Pedersen in future years. —*Scott Yanow*

History of an Artist, Vol. 1 / Dec. 27, 1972 / Pablo ✦✦✦✦✦

It was only fitting that Oscar Peterson's first of his many recordings for Norman Granz's Pablo label would revisit the instrumental combinations he had utilized in the past. This two-CD set has all of the music originally included on three LPs (a two-album set plus a single record) and showcases the great pianist in duets with bassist Ray Brown, in trios that also include guitarists Irving Ashby, Barney Kessel and Herb Ellis, and with other trios that feature such alumni as bassists Sam Jones, George Mraz and Niels-Henning Orsted Pedersen, guitarist Joe Pass and drummers Bobby Durham and Louis Hayes. The only fault with this consistently inventive and hard-swinging program is that the formats (particularly those on the second disc) are not in strictly chronological order. But musically the music (which also features Peterson taking "Lady of the Lavender Mist" as an unaccompanied solo) is superb. —*Scott Yanow*

History of an Artist, Vol. 2 / Dec. 27, 1972 / Pablo ✦✦✦✦

The second of the two volumes during which pianist Oscar Peterson looks back at his earlier associations is a single LP that has since been reissued along with the first album as part of a two-CD set. Unfortunately, the chronology is shuffled a bit on this program but there are some strong performances. Peterson duets with bassist Ray Brown on a remake of their early hit "Tenderly," teams up with guitarists Barney Kessel and Herb Ellis for a pair of trios, interacts with drummer Bobby

Durham and either Sam Jones or George Mraz on bass, and performs "Reunion Blues" with his then-current musical partners: guitarist Joe Pass and bassist Niels Pedersen. —*Scott Yanow*

Oscar Peterson Featuring Stephane Grappelli / Feb. 22, 1973+Feb. 23, 1973 / Prestige ✦✦✦✦✦

This two-LP set, whose music has not yet resurfaced on CD, teams together pianist Oscar Peterson with violinist Stephane Grappelli, bassist Niels Pedersen and drummer Kenny Clarke. It is an understatement to say that there are no weak spots in that quartet. The brilliant musicians perform a dozen swing standards plus their original "Blues for Musidisc" and the music is often quite exciting; Peterson sounds thrilled to be playing with Grappelli, and vice versa. —*Scott Yanow*

The Good Life / May 16, 1973-May 19, 1973 / Original Jazz Classics ✦✦✦✦

Taken from the same live sessions that resulted in *The Trio*, this CD reissue of a Pablo album features three remarkable virtuosos: pianist Oscar Peterson, guitarist Joe Pass and bassist Neils-Henning Orsted Pedersen. Although not quite reaching the heights of the other set, this CD features some typically extraordinary solos and interplay from these musicians. Highlights include Peterson's "Wheatland," the blues "For Count" (which is referred to in the liner notes as "Miles") and "The Good Life." —*Scott Yanow*

★ The Trio / May 16, 1973-May 19, 1973 / Pablo ✦✦✦✦✦

Guitarist Joe Pass and bassist Niels Pedersen both play well on these live performances but the reason to acquire this set is for the remarkable Oscar Peterson. The pianist investigates several jazz styles brilliantly on "Blues Etude" (including stride and boogie-woogie), plays exciting versions of his "Chicago Blues" and "Easy Listening Blues," tears into "Secret Love" and shows honest emotion on "Come Sunday." Peterson really flourished during his years with Norman Granz's Pablo label and this was one of his finest recordings of the period. —*Scott Yanow*

Oscar Peterson & Harry Edison / Dec. 21, 1974 / Original Jazz Classics ✦✦✦✦✦

The third of Oscar Peterson's five duet albums with great trumpeters (the other encounters feature Dizzy Gillespie, Roy Eldridge, Clark Terry and Jon Faddis) teams the masterful pianist with the great swing stylist Harry "Sweets" Edison. The trumpeter, who uses repetition to great degree and had pared his style down to a relatively few notes, matches well with the virtuosic Peterson on these seven standards and their two simple originals "Basie" and "Signify." Together Edison and O.P. give the impression that their chance-taking improvisations are completely logical and a lot easier to play than they really are. —*Scott Yanow*

In Russia / Nov. 17, 1974 / Pablo ✦✦✦✦

Although the music of this two-CD set took place at a concert in the Soviet Union, it is a fairly typical recital by pianist Oscar Peterson with no obvious reference to the exotic location. Peterson takes five selections unaccompanied, performs four others as duets with bassist Niels Pedersen and adds drummer Jake Hanna to the nine remaining numbers. Other than three originals, all of the music comprises veteran standards and, although no real surprises occur, the results are what one would expect from the great Oscar Peterson, who alternates hard swingers with sensitive ballad renditions. —*Scott Yanow*

Oscar Peterson and Dizzy Gillespie / Nov. 28, 1974-Nov. 29, 1974 / Pablo ✦✦✦✦✦

This album was the first of five projects in which pianist Oscar Peterson dueted with a trumpeter. Now reissued on CD, the encounter finds Dizzy Gillespie (then 57) in good form for the period, interacting with Peterson on such pieces as "Caravan," "Autumn Leaves," "Blues for Bird" and two of Gillespie's originals that have become standards: "Dizzy Atmosphere" and "Con Alma." It's a worthy acquisition for fans of Peterson and Gillespie. —*Scott Yanow*

Jousts / Nov. 28, 1974-Jun. 5, 1975 / Pablo ✦✦✦✦

This CD contains nine previously unissued performances from the sessions that resulted in Oscar Peterson's five duet albums with great trumpeters. Clark Terry, Roy Eldridge, Dizzy Gillespie and Harry "Sweets" Edison are heard on two songs apiece, while Jon Faddis pops up on one duet. Eldridge's combative "Crazy Rhythm" and Faddis' "Oakland Blues" are high points, although fans of this interesting series will want all of this often heated music. —*Scott Yanow*

The Giants / Dec. 7, 1974 / Pablo ✦✦✦✦

This is a typically exciting set by a trio comprising three giants whose consistent excellence was always taken for granted: pianist Oscar Peterson, guitarist Joe Pass and bassist Ray Brown. They perform a swinging repertoire of standards and blues, and a special treat is O.P.'s rare outing on organ during "Blues for Dennis" and "Sunny." —*Scott Yanow*

Oscar Peterson & Roy Eldridge / Dec. 8, 1974 / Original Jazz Classics ✦✦✦✦✦

Part of his five sessions that featured duets with different trumpeters, pianist Oscar Peterson's matchup with trumpeter Roy Eldridge (reissued on CD) has its strong moments. Eldridge did not quite have the range of his earlier years but his competitive streak had not mellowed with age. Peterson pushes Eldridge to his limit and the music is generally quite exciting. Highlights include "Little Jazz," "Sunday" and "Between the Devil and the Deep Blue Sea." —*Scott Yanow*

☆ **Oscar Peterson Et Joe Pass a Salle Pleyel** / Mar. 17, 1975 / Pablo ✦✦✦✦✦
This double LP (whose contents have not yet been reissued on CD) has more than its share of remarkable music. Pianist Oscar Peterson takes seven performances (including a five-song Duke Ellington medley and racehorse renditions of "Indiana" and "Sweet Georgia Brown") unaccompanied, and guitarist Joe Pass follows with five solo selections of his own. But it is when Peterson and Pass team together for the final six numbers that the sparks really fly, particularly on "Honeysuckle Rose" and "Blues for Bise"; the results are often quite wondrous. This is essential music from two of the best. —*Scott Yanow*

Oscar Peterson & Clark Terry / May 18, 1975 / Original Jazz Classics ✦✦✦✦
Pianist Oscar Peterson and fluegelhornist Clark Terry always made for a perfect matchup. Their duet set (one of five Peterson made during this period) is quite friendly, witty and hard-swinging. C.T. generally sets the joyous mood and on numbers such as "On a Slow Boat to China," "Shaw 'Nuff," "No Flugel Blues" and "Mack the Knife," the warm-toned fluegelhornist shows that he was one of the few who could truly keep up with the remarkable pianist. —*Scott Yanow*

Oscar Peterson & Jon Faddis / Jun. 5, 1975 / Original Jazz Classics ✦✦✦✦✦
In the mid-'70s, Oscar Peterson recorded duet albums with veteran trumpeters Dizzy Gillespie, Roy Eldridge, Clark Terry and Harry "Sweets" Edison. He paid the young Jon Faddis a huge compliment by also recording a set with him. Faddis, very much under Gillespie's influence but already displaying a wide range, clearly enjoyed the challenge and, on a set of standards and basic material, he often tears into the songs with reckless abandon. The Peterson-Faddis encounter is generally quite exciting and a high point in the early career of Jon Faddis —*Scott Yanow*

Porgy and Bess / Jan. 26, 1976 / Original Jazz Classics ✦✦
This is a strange duet album (a Pablo LP reissued on CD in the OJC series). For a set of ten melodies taken from George Gershwin's famous *Porgy and Bess,* Joe Pass sticks to acoustic guitar while the great pianist Oscar Peterson, for the first and only time in his career, records exclusively on the clavichord, an instrument from the 1600s that preceded the piano. The clavichord comes across as a mix between a harpsichord and a primitive stringed instrument, and apparently, it cannot be played all that fast. The results are novel at first but rather limited on the whole, making one wonder whose bright idea this was. —*Scott Yanow*

Jam Montreux (1977) / Jul. 14, 1977 / Original Jazz Classics ✦✦✦✦
One of many Pablo albums taken from the 1977 Montreux Jazz Festival, this outing teams together pianist Oscar Peterson, bassist Niels Pedersen and drummer Bobby Durham with tenorman Eddie "Lockjaw" Davis and trumpeters Clark Terry and Dizzy Gillespie. The talented (and very competitive) players really dig into the opening uptempo blues ("Ali and Frazier") and they continue cooking on "If I Were a Bell," "Bye Bye Blues" (which has been added to the CD reissue), "Things Ain't What They Used to Be" and "Just in Time." As often happens in this type of situation, the musicians mutually inspire each other; this is one of Dizzy Gillespie's better sessions of the 1970s. There are no losers during these battles. —*Scott Yanow*

Live-Montreux '77 / Jul. 15, 1977 / Original Jazz Classics ✦✦✦✦
This is an interesting CD, one of many taken from the concerts sponsored by Pablo Records at the 1977 Montreux Jazz Festival. Pianist Oscar Peterson is teamed in an unusual trio with both Ray Brown and Niels Pedersen on basses. Sticking to standards and two blues on the boppish set, Peterson allows both of his sidemen plenty of solo space, permitting listeners to compare the large tone of Brown with the speedy fingers of Pedersen. —*Scott Yanow*

Satch & Josh Again / Sep. 20, 1977 / Pablo ✦✦✦✦

Timekeepers / 1978 / Pablo ✦✦✦✦
The pairing of pianists Count Basie and Oscar Peterson might seem unlikely, given their stylistic differences. Basie's notoriety resulted from his ability to say a lot with a little, while Peterson has been celebrated as a modern technical master, whose solos were full of riveting phrases, lines, and statements. Yet the duo made effective partners on this reissued 1978 session and often played against their reputations. Basie has several solos where he demonstrates impressive technique, while Peterson, often accused of overkill, shows he can utilize restraint and delicacy with as much flair as bombast and flash. —*Ron Wynn*

The Paris Concert / Oct. 5, 1978 / Pablo ✦✦✦✦
Pianist Oscar Peterson made so many recordings for Norman Granz's Pablo label (and was so consistent) that while all of his records are recommended, it is difficult to pick out any one as the definitive or essential release. This two-CD set (a straight reissue of the original two-LP release) features Peterson with an all-star trio, a unit comprising guitarist Joe Pass and bassist Niels Pedersen. Just 16 days later Peterson would record *The London Concert* with a different trio. This time around he mostly sticks to standards but includes three songs associated with Benny Goodman (including the riff-filled "Benny's Bugle"), features Pass (who contributed his

original "Gentle Tears") unaccompanied on "Lover Man" and really romps with his fellow virtuosoes on such numbers as "Ornithology," "Donna Lee" and "Sweet Georgia Brown." —*Scott Yanow*

The London Concert / Oct. 21, 1978 / Pablo ✦✦✦✦
This two-CD set, which reissues a Pablo two-LP release, features pianist Oscar Peterson in a strong and supportive trio with bassist John Heard and drummer Louis Bellson. Although his sidemen get some solo space, the focus is primarily on the remarkable pianist on a variety of standards, his own "Hogtown Blues" and a six-song Duke Ellington medley. Whether it be on rapid stomps or sensitive ballads, this trio (which was in reality an all-star pickup group) sounds as if they had worked together regularly for years. —*Scott Yanow*

The Silent Partner / Mar. 14, 1979 / Original Jazz Classics ✦✦✦
This fairly obscure Oscar Peterson LP is unusual for the all-star septet (which includes altoist Benny Carter, fluegelhornist Clark Terry, Zoot Sims on tenor, vibraphonist Milt Jackson, bassist John Heard and drummer Grady Tate) plays pianist Peterson's score from the film *The Silent Partner.* Although none of the eight themes caught on independently, the rather distinctive playing of the great stylists (along with the swinging rhythm section) makes the music stand alone from the movie. —*Scott Yanow*

Night Child / Apr. 11, 1979-Apr. 12, 1979 / Pablo ✦✦✦
This is a most unusual album for Oscar Peterson because the pianist not only performs six of his own compositions but he plays the great majority of time on electric piano. With the assistance of guitarist Joe Pass, bassist Niels Pederson and drummer Louie Bellson, he keeps his own musical personality despite the change in "axes" and, although the results are not essential, this setting does cast a fresh light on Peterson's creativity. —*Scott Yanow*

Skol / Jul. 6, 1979 / Original Jazz Classics ✦✦✦✦
Pianist Oscar Peterson and violinist Stephane Grappelli meet up on this Scandinavian concert. The "backup" crew (guitarist Joe Pass, bassist Niels Pedersen and drummer Mickey Roker) is not too bad either. In addition to a closing blues (which is highlighted by tradeoffs from Peterson and Grappelli), the quintet performs five veteran standards with creativity and swing. This CD, a straight reissue of a Pablo LP, contains plenty of fine music. —*Scott Yanow*

Digital at Montreux / Jul. 16, 1979 / Pablo ✦✦✦
The title is fairly generic but this duet set from pianist Oscar Peterson and bassist Niels Pedersen has plenty of excellent music from two of the best. Peterson and Pedersen perform six standards and a well-conceived five-song Duke Ellington medley. Few real surprises occur but the duo plays up to one's high expectations. —*Scott Yanow*

The Personal Touch / Jan. 28, 1980-Feb. 19, 1980 / Pablo ✦✦✦
This is a somewhat unusual Oscar Peterson record (a CD reissue) in a number of ways. Peterson (along with fluegelhornist Clark Terry, bassist Dave Young, drummer Jerry Fuller and either Peter Leitch or Ed Bickert on guitar) performs 13 songs either written or popularized by Canadians. In addition, he sings the majority of the tunes on his own Nat "King" Cole-influenced voice and contributes two new songs of his own. The repertoire includes some familiar standards ("Some of These Days," "I'll Never Smile Again," "The World Is Waiting for the Sunrise" and "Sweethearts on Parade"), jazz versions of a few pop tunes (including "Spinning Wheel") and a few obscurities. —*Scott Yanow*

Live at the North Sea Jazz Festival / Jul. 13, 1980 / Pablo ✦✦✦✦✦
This double LP matches and mixes together four masterful musicians: pianist Oscar Peterson, guitarist Joe Pass, bassist Niels Pedersen and harmonica great Toots Thielemans. Together they perform O.P.'s "City Lights" and ten veteran standards with creativity, wit and solid swing. There are a few miraculous moments as one would expect from musicians of this caliber and the results are generally quite memorable. Recommended although this music has not yet surfaced on CD. —*Scott Yanow*

A Royal Wedding Suite / Apr. 15, 1981-Apr. 25, 1981 / Pablo ✦✦✦
To celebrate the marriage of Prince Charles and Lady Di of England, Oscar Peterson composed a ten-song suite that he performs on this LP while accompanied by an unidentified string orchestra arranged by Rick Wilkins. Not too surprisingly, Peterson (who doubles here on electric piano) proves to be a talented composer and, even if none of the individual pieces caught on (or was ever apparently recorded again by the pianist), the music is quite satisfying. —*Scott Yanow*

Nigerian Marketplace / Jul. 16, 1981 / Pablo ✦✦✦✦
For this trio set with bassist Niels Pedersen and drummer Terry Clarke, the great pianist Oscar Peterson (appearing at the 1981 Montreux Jazz Festival) performs a medley of "Misty" and "Waltz for Debby," three standards, his own "Cakewalk" and the debut of "Nigerian Marketplace," the first section of an extended suite not yet completed at the time. This is a well-rounded set (reissued on CD) that finds the remarkable Oscar Peterson in typically swinging and prime form. —*Scott Yanow*

The Oscar Peterson Big 4 in Japan '82 / Feb. 20, 1982-Feb. 21, 1982 / Pablo ◆◆◆◆

For this two-LP set, pianist Oscar Peterson teams up with guitarist Joe Pass, bassist Niels Pedersen and drummer Martin Drew for a strong program comprising 11 standards, six Peterson originals and Pedersen's "Future Child." The music is essentially straightahead bop with some impressionistic moments and with the rapid pieces being outnumbered by the sensitive ballads. Highlights include " 'Round Midnight," "Move," "Nigerian Marketplace" and a medley of Peterson's "Hymn to Freedom" and "The Fallen Warrior." —*Scott Yanow*

Two of the Few / Jan. 20, 1983 / Original Jazz Classics ◆◆◆◆◆

This CD reissue brings back a unique duet recording featuring pianist Oscar Peterson and vibraphonist Milt Jackson. One would expect the instrumentation to feature mostly ballads but the opposite is true as O.P. and Bags romp through quite a few uptempo pieces. Highlights include "Lady Be Good," "Limehouse Blues," "Reunion Blues" and "Just You, Just Me." This is a successful and highly enjoyable outing. —*Scott Yanow*

Tribute to My Friends / Nov. 8, 1983 / Pablo ◆◆◆◆

Pianist Oscar Peterson recorded so many albums for Pablo during 1972-83 that it must have been rather difficult for him to come up with fresh material and ideas for records. However, this CD, which features songs associated with nine of his associates (ranging from Louis Armstrong and Billie Holiday to Dizzy Gillespie, Ella Fitzgerald and Lester Young) features a variety of tunes that Peterson had not played that much through the years. With the assistance of guitarist Joe Pass, bassist Niels Pedersen and drummer Martin Drew, Peterson sounds inspired on such themes as "Blueberry Hill," "Stuffy," "Cottontail" and even "A Tisket, a Tasket." —*Scott Yanow*

If You Could See Me Now / Nov. 9, 1983 / Pablo ◆◆◆◆

Oscar Peterson recorded a countless number of albums for Norman Granz's Pablo label during 1972-83 before Granz decided to call a halt (which was temporary) to his company's operations. This set was the pianist's last before a three-year hiatus and it finds his quartet of the period (with guitarist Joe Pass, bassist Niels Pedersen and drummer Martin Drew) in typically swinging form on Miles Davis' "Weird Blues," a pair of Peterson originals, two veteran ballads and a ridiculously rapid "Limehouse Blues," which is taken as a Peterson-Pass duet. —*Scott Yanow*

Oscar Peterson with Harry Edison & Eddie Vinson / Nov. 12, 1986 / Pablo ◆◆◆◆◆

During Nov. 12-14, 1986, pianist Oscar Peterson recorded three albums worth of material for Norman Granz's Pablo label. This particular CD features the great pianist with his quartet (bassist Dave Young, drummer Martin Drew and guest guitarist Joe Pass) along with trumpeter Harry "Sweets" Edison and altoist Eddie "Cleanhead" Vinson. The strictly instrumental set has many fine solos on appealing tunes such as "Stuffy," "Broadway" and the lengthy blues "Slooow Drag." This boppish session gave Vinson a rare chance to really stretch out and he was up for the challenge. —*Scott Yanow*

Live / Nov. 12, 1986+Nov. 14, 1986 / Pablo ◆◆◆◆

Pianist Oscar Peterson's stint at the Westwood Playhouse in Los Angeles in Nov. 1986 resulted in two CDs' worth of material. Peterson's quartet (with guitarist Joe Pass, bassist David Young and drummer Martin Drew) performs an interesting medley of "Perdido" and "Caravan," plays sensitively on "If You Only Knew," explores the pianist's "City Lights" and performs a three-part "The Bach Suite," which is climaxed by "Bach's Blues." Enjoyable music, it's recommended to Peterson's many fans. —*Scott Yanow*

Time After Time / Nov. 12, 1986+Nov. 14, 1986 / Pablo ◆◆◆◆

Pianist Oscar Peterson's final Pablo album (after a countless amount of appearances as both a leader and a sideman) features his quartet (which at the time included guitarist Joe Pass, bassist David Young and drummer Martin Drew) on the second of two CDs (along with *Oscar Peterson Live*) recorded during an engagement at Los Angeles' Westwood Playhouse in Nov. 1986. For the well-rounded set Peterson performs two of his originals, the blues "Soft Winds," a solo ballad medley and, as a climax, a burning version of "On the Trail." —*Scott Yanow*

The Legendary Oscar Peterson Trio Live at the Blue Note / Mar. 16, 1990 / Telarc ◆◆◆◆

Pianist Oscar Peterson had a reunion with guitarist Herb Ellis and bassist Ray Brown at a well-publicized get-together at New York's Blue Note in March 1990. The trio (his regular group of the late '50s) was augmented by Peterson's late-'60s drummer Bobby Durham for spirited performances. Rather than using their complex arrangements of the past, the pianist and his alumni simply jammed through the performances and the results are quite rewarding. On the first of four CDs released by Telarc, the quartet performs "Honeysuckle Rose," a ballad medley, three of the pianist's originals and "Sweet Georgia Brown." As this and the other CDs in the series show, the magic was still there. —*Scott Yanow*

Last Call / Mar. 16, 1990-Mar 17, 1990 / Telarc ◆◆◆◆

The third of four Telarc CDs to be released from an Oscar Peterson reunion engagement at New York's Blue Note Club matches together the great pianist with guitarist Herb Ellis, bassist Ray Brown and drummer Bobby Durham. Although the veterans did not rehearse together beforehand, the repertoire is fresh with five standards being balanced by five Peterson originals including "Bach's Blues," "Wheatland" and "Blues Etude." The performance is as strong as one would expect although the inclusion of Durham's drums makes the music less exciting and risky than the late-'50s trio recordings. It's worth picking up as are the other Oscar Peterson Telarc releases from this now-legendary engagement. —*Scott Yanow*

Encore at the Blue Note / Mar. 16, 1990-Mar. 18, 1993 / Telarc ◆◆◆◆

The fourth CD taken from a reunion engagement at the Blue Note by Oscar Peterson, guitarist Herb Ellis, bassist Ray Brown and drummer Bobby Durham, this set is up to the same level as the other three. The O.P. Trio of the late '50s (along with Peterson's drummer of a decade later) jam through five standards (including a heated "Falling in Love with Love") and four of Peterson's originals, highlighted by a medley of his "Goodbye Old Girl" and "He Has Gone." —*Scott Yanow*

Saturday Night at the Blue Note / Mar. 17, 1990 / Telarc ◆◆◆◆

Oscar Peterson reunited with guitarist Herb Ellis and bassist Ray Brown for this well-recorded engagement, which has resulted in four CDs being released by Telarc. The inclusion of drummer Bobby Durham did make the music a bit safer, and rather than revisit their classic complex arrangements, the ensemble jammed on the songs, so one does not hear the startling octaves that were present in the Trio's work of the late '50s. However, the repertoire on this CD (which includes two standards, Milt Jackson's "Reunion Blues" and five of Peterson's originals) is fresh and fairly challenging. Enjoyable music, it's recommended to the pianist's fans. —*Scott Yanow*

The More I See You / Jan. 15, 1995-Jan. 16, 1995 / Telarc ◆◆◆◆◆

After Oscar Peterson suffered a severe stroke in the spring of 1993, it was feared that he would never again play on a professional level, but two years of intense therapy resulted in the masterful pianist returning to what sounds on this Telarc CD like near-prime form. For the all-star date, Peterson tears into seven standards and two blues and outswings all potential competitors. Altoist Benny Carter at 87 sounds like he is 47 (if Carter had retired back in 1940 he would still be a legend) and fluegelhornist Clark Terry (now 74) proves to be not only (along with the remarkable 90-year-old Doc Cheatham) the finest trumpeter over 70 but one of the top brassmen of any age. The cool-toned guitarist Lorne Lofsky and drummer Lewis Nash are also strong assets while bassist Ray Brown (a year younger than Peterson at a mere 68) displays his typical limitless energy. On appealing tunes such as "In a Mellow Tone," "When My Dream Boat Comes Home" and a medium-up version of "For All We Know," the musicians all play up to their usual high level, making this a joyous comeback album for the great Oscar Peterson. —*Scott Yanow*

An Oscar Peterson Christmas / Jan. 15, 1995-Jul. 30, 1995 / Telarc ◆◆◆

Oscar Peterson takes it easy during his relaxed set. He had not completely recovered from his stroke but he was still an impressive pianist. Peterson, who is assisted by guitarist Lorne Lofsky, bassist David Young, and drummer Jerry Fuller, is joined by a 20-piece string section arranged and conducted by Rick Wilkins. The 14 holiday tunes (which include "God Rest Ye Merry Gentleman," "White Christmas," "Santa Claus Is Coming to Town" and "Have Yourself a Merry Little Christmas") are given tasteful and lightly swinging treatments and there are guest appearances by vibraphonist Dave Samuels and fluegelhornist Jack Schantz. But no real surprises or chance-taking occurs and the music is mostly just pleasant. —*Scott Yanow*

Meets Roy Hargrove & Ralph Moore / Jun. 11, 1996-Jun. 12, 1996 / Telarc ◆◆◆◆

Oscar in Paris / Jun. 25, 1996 / Telarc ◆◆◆

Nonpareil pianist Oscar Peterson may have lost the use of his left hand following his stroke, but he's still got more technique and swing than most of the pianists out there. If you doubt that, check out this recording made in Paris in 1996 with his quartet. Peterson is a treasure, and his takes on these originals and standards offer ample evidence. —*Ross Boissoneau*

Tribute / 1997 / Telarc ◆◆◆

Oscar Peterson, who suffered a stroke in 1993, has since made a partial comeback. Although his left hand is weakened, the pianist's right hand is as powerful as ever, and he is able to mostly cover up his deficiencies. This live tribute CD makes it clear that many jazz fans and musicians are delighted to have Peterson back on the scene again. O.P. performs "Anything Goes" in a quartet with guitarist Herb Ellis, bassist Ray Brown and drummer Lewis Nash, joins with fellow pianist Benny Green on a couple of quintet numbers, and welcomes such top players as vibraphonist Milt Jackson, singer/pianist Shirley Horn, tenor saxophonist Stanley Turrentine (they had never played together before), Roy Hargrove (whose tender fluegelhorn solo on "My Foolish Heart" is a highlight), the Manhattan Transfer and fluegelhornist Clark Terry. Few real surprises occur (Horn's "Here's to Life" is out-of-place and Terry's "Mumbles" routine goes on too long) but overall, the straighta-head music is quite pleasing and heartfelt. —*Scott Yanow*

Ralph Peterson

b. May 20, 1962, Pleasantville, NJ
Drums, Leader / Post-Bop, Hard Bop
During his relatively brief period in the spotlight, Ralph Peterson has already distinguished himself not only as a superior drummer but as an important band-leader, too. It was natural that Peterson would be a drummer, for four of his uncles and a grandfather played drums. He started at age three and, after attending Rutgers and settling in New York, he became a constantly working drummer. In addition to sessions with OTB, David Murray and the Terence Blanchard-Donald Harrison group, Ralph Peterson has led several diverse and adventurous sessions for Blue Note and Evidence, all of which are recommended. —*Scott Yanow*

Triangular / Apr. 20, 1988-Aug. 22, 1988 / Blue Note ✦✦✦✦✦
This is a consistently simulating trio session by the creative drummer Ralph Peterson. On "Bemsha Swing," Peterson's drumming is straight from a New Orleans parade band while "Just You, Just Me" (which features pianist Geri Allen doing her witty impressions of Thelonious Monk) has the trio playing the opening and closing melody choruses in three different tempos simultaneously. "Move" really cooks and each of the five originals (bassist Essiet Essiet's "Splash," three diverse Peterson compositions and the fairly free improvisation "Triangular") have their own personalities. Although Allen is the lead voice, the musical communication between the members of the group results in each musician having an equally important role. Highly recommended. —*Scott Yanow*

V / Apr. 1988 / Blue Note ✦✦✦✦
Some tremendous hard bop and modern jazz material from a session led by drummer Ralph Peterson, featuring trumpeter Terence Blanchard, pianist Geri Allen, and bassist Phil Bowler. —*Ron Wynn*

Volition / Feb. 27, 1989-Feb. 28, 1989 / Blue Note ✦✦✦✦✦
Ralph Peterson's drumming is as consistently explosive as Art Blakey's, making it very difficult for soloists to relax or goof off; otherwise he'll bury them. On this heated CD, he gathered an all-star crew of young greats: trumpeter Terence Blanchard, Steve Wilson on alto and soprano, pianist Geri Allen and bassist Phil Bowler. The solos throughout the high-powered session are concise, telling a quick story, and even the ballads "On My Side" and "The Benevolent One" are stormy. Peterson's sidemen are up to the challenge, making this a superior example of music that is both post-bop and swinging jazz. —*Scott Yanow*

Ralph Peterson Presents the Fo'tet / Dec. 22, 1989-Dec. 23, 1989 / Blue Note ✦✦✦✦✦
An album where this tremendous young drummer unveils a strong lineup of contemporary talent and turns it loose on a hard-bop menu. —*Ron Wynn*

● **Ornettology** / Aug. 7, 1990-Aug. 9, 1990 / Somethin' Else ✦✦✦✦
This CD was a change of pace from drummer Ralph Peterson's Fo'tet dates. Although it looks back at two different styles of the late 1950s (the sparse instrumentation and light feel of the later West Coast jazz groups, particularly Chico Hamilton's sextet, and the chordal freedom of early Ornette Coleman), Peterson's quartet displays a unique sound of its own. Clarinetist Don Byron shows a great deal of versatility in his solos, and his light sound on clarinet contrasts with his Dolphyisms on bass clarinet. Vibraphonist Bryan Carrott and bassist Melissa Slocum are superior ensemble players, although not distinctive solo voices at this point, while Peterson's drumming can serve as a perfect example of subtlety and quiet heat. The performances are exploratory, yet relaxed. Best are the delightful title cut, a somber yet optimistic "Nemesis," the intense "Status Flux," a fast "I Mean You" and a new investigation of Ornette Coleman's "Congeniality," but every selection has its strong moments. This CD concludes with a credible Ralph Peterson cornet solo on "There Is No Greater Love," just one of many surprises included on the highly recommended set. —*Scott Yanow*

Art / Mar. 18, 1992-Mar. 20, 1992 / Blue Note ✦✦✦✦

The Reclamation Project / Nov. 28, 1994-Nov. 29, 1994 / Evidence ✦✦✦✦
All of drummer Ralph Peterson's recordings have an identity of their own. For this album, his first release in three years, the talented young drummer leads an unusual quartet comprising soprano saxophonist Steve Wilson, vibraphonist Bryan Carrott (who doubles on marimba) and bassist Belden Bulloch. Peterson's ten originals explore many moods and grooves but always swing, even when the time signature is complex. The memorable sound of the ensemble and the strong improvising skills of the players are two additional reasons to acquire this explorative but reasonably accessible CD. —*Scott Yanow*

Fo'tet Plays Monk / Nov. 20, 1995+Dec. 18, 1995 / Evidence ✦✦✦✦✦
Drummer Ralph Peterson's recordings are always stimulating and somewhat surprising. For this set, his Fo'tet consists of the leader, soprano saxophonist Steve Wilson, vibraphonist Bryan Carrott and bassist Belden Bullock. Their tribute to Thelonious Monk features the unit (which does not include a pianist) playing nine Monk tunes (including such difficult numbers as "Skippy," "Played Twice," "Criss Cross" and "Four in One"), plus a couple of originals, "Monkin' Around" and "Spherically Speaking." The light sound of the group contrasts with the "heavy" nature of the complex improvisations, and overall, this is a high-quality outing (adding to the jazz tradition rather than just copying the past) that is well worth several listens. —*Scott Yanow*

Michel Petrucciani

b. Dec. 28, 1962, Orange, France
Piano / Post-Bop
Michel Petrucciani has overcome the effects of *osteogenensis imperfecta* (a bone disease that greatly stunted his growth) to become a powerful pianist. Originally greatly influenced by Bill Evans and to a lesser extent Keith Jarrett, Petrucciani has since developed his own individual voice. He started by playing in the family band with his guitarist father and bassist brother. At the age of 15 he had the opportunity to play with Kenny Clarke and Clark Terry, and at 17 he made his first recording. Petrucciani toured France with Lee Konitz in a duo (1980) and moved to the US in 1982. At that time, he coaxed Charles Lloyd out of retirement and toured with his quartet, a mutually beneficial relationship. Petrucciani has since then been a strong attraction in the US, usually playing with a quartet (sometimes featuring Adam Holzman's synthesizer for color) or as a soloist; in 1986 he recorded at Montreux with Jim Hall and Wayne Shorter. Although Petrucciani's ability to overcome his affliction is admirable, his impressive playing stands by itself. —*Scott Yanow*

Michel Petrucciani / Apr. 3, 1981-Apr. 4, 1981 / Owl ✦✦✦

Toot Suite / May 25, 1982 / Owl ✦✦✦

Oracle's Destiny / Oct. 18, 1982 / Owl ✦✦✦✦

● **100 Hearts** / Jun. 1983 / George Wein Collection ✦✦✦✦✦
If it were not for Michel Petrucciani's good taste, it is likely that his impressive technique would dominate his solos. As it is, the pianist has been able to use his technique in surprising ways, avoiding the obvious and showing self-restraint while coming up with ingenious ideas in his improvisations. This solo album, his first for an American label, finds Petrucciani exploring pieces by Ornette Coleman, Charlie Haden and Sonny Rollins in addition to two of his own songs and a lengthy wandering medley that somehow incorporates "Someday My Prince Will Come," "All the Things You Are," "A Child Is Born" and Bill Evans' "Very Early" into a collage. A very impressive outing. —*Scott Yanow*

Live at the Village Vanguard / Mar. 16, 1984 / George Wein Collection ✦✦✦✦
This double LP finds pianist Michel Petrucciani often showing the influence of Bill Evans. His interplay with bassist Palle Danielsson and drummer Eliot Zigmund (an Evans alumnus) is consistently impressive and these eight performances (all but two are between eight and 12 minutes long) never lose their momentum. It's recommended for lovers of piano trios. —*Scott Yanow*

Note 'n Notes / Oct. 5, 1984 / Owl ✦✦✦✦

Cold Blues / Jan. 11, 1985 / Owl ✦✦✦✦✦
A '91 CD reissue featuring outstanding pianist Michel Petrucciani in duets with bassist Ron McClure. While some accuse Petrucciani of too much flash and not enough soul, his expressive phrasing and often dazzling solos reflect a complete knowledge and mastery of the keyboard, while bassist McClure adds enough depth and bottom to keep things from getting too spacy. —*Ron Wynn*

Pianism / Dec. 20, 1985 / Blue Note ✦✦✦✦✦
The virtuosic pianist Michel Petrucciani was at his best throughout this dazzling set. Although frequently recorded in recent years, *Pianism* rankes among Petrucciani's most satisfying releases because he emphasizes emotion over his remarkable technique. —*Scott Yanow*

The Best of the Blue Note Years / 1985-1991 / Blue Note ✦✦✦
The single-disc *Best Of* outing is a mixed blessing. The 12 performances include the wonderful "Bimini" from *Power of Three*, as well as trio and quartet takes from arguably his best release, *Pianism*, and six cuts with him playing acoustic and electric keyboards on the same composition. But the disc gives a grab-bag feel for Petrucciani the composer and improviser; we can't tell how his approach evolved, or chart his growth or stagnation. In addition, the company doesn't even provide complete recording information, omitting the dates for the tracks. A final insult are the ridiculously exaggerated, incomplete liner notes in which Petrucciani is placed in the company of Louis Armstrong, Duke Ellington and Count Basie, an absurd

comparison. This isn't the way to celebrate or document a musician's contributions to a label. —*Ron Wynn*

Power of Three / Jul. 14, 1986 / Blue Note ✦✦✦✦✦
It was logical that Michel Petrucciani (piano) and Jim Hall (guitar) would eventually play together. Both are masters of chordal improvisation and possessors of harmonically rich and introverted styles. At the 1986 Montreux Jazz Festival, the pair, plus soprano saxophonist Wayne Shorter (on three of the five songs), worked together perfectly. Hall and Petrucciani in particular communicated very well on the altered blues "Careful" (where their comping behind each other's solos was exquisite) and on a lengthy and well-constructed version of "In a Sentimental Mood." —*Scott Yanow*

Michel Plays Petrucciani / Sep. 24, 1987-Dec. 10, 1987 / Blue Note ✦✦✦✦
Tackling his own material, with nary a vintage standard within earshot, Petrucciani combines his assertive, driving, mainstream piano with two different trios on two separate occasions. The first half of the program features the hard-swinging combination of bassist Gary Peacock and drummer Roy Haynes, augmented on "One For Us" by the slightly withdrawn guitar of John Abercrombie. The second half finds bassist Eddie Gomez and drummer Al Foster providing somewhat smoother, perhaps more conventional support, occasionally with a Latin twinge, and Abercrombie and percussionist Steve Thornton sit in on one number apiece. Petrucciani's compositions are certainly worthy pieces, but as always, the pianist's direct, intelligently probing solos leave the source material way behind; he's an improviser through and through. —*Richard S. Ginell*

Music / 1989 / Blue Note ✦✦✦✦
Music was a slight departure from pianist Michel Petrucciani's usual Bill Evans-influenced recordings of the period. Petrucciani uses synthesizers (his and Adam Holzman's) on all but two selections, but these are very much in the background, making the ensembles sound a little larger than they actually are. Petrucciani's ten originals range from romantic ("Memories of Paris") and manic ("My Bebop Tune") to charming ("Lullaby") and funky ("Play Me") with a generous supply of Latin-tinged pieces and one rhythmic vocal by Tania Maria; Joe Lovano (on soprano) and the accordion of Gil Goldstein make one appearance apiece. Worth investigating. —*Scott Yanow*

Playground / 1991 / Blue Note ✦✦✦✦
Pianist Michel Petrucciani, who during the early part of his career was heavily influenced by Bill Evans, gradually developed his own sound. By 1991 he was using Adam Holzman on synthesizer with his quintet (which on this date also includes bassist Anthony Jackson, drummer Omar Hakim and percussionist Steve Thornton) to play colors behind his piano. In addition, Petrucciani was backed by funky rhythms and emphasized his own original compositions. Rather than selling out to blatant commercialism, Petrucciani had actually found his own voice within the "contemporary" setting. The music on his CD is of consistently high quality (despite a few too many fadeouts). Highlights include "Miles Davis' Licks" (a blues that utilizes some of Davis' late-period nursery rhyme melodies), the intense "Brazilian Suite No. 3," a playful jam on "Laws of Physics" and the Keith Jarrett-ish "P'tit Louis." Actually, all 11 of Michel Petrucciani's originals are worth hearing and, despite the brief playing time (39 minutes) of this CD, it is recommended. —*Scott Yanow*

Live / Nov. 1991 / Blue Note ✦✦✦

Promenade with Duke / 1993 / Blue Note ✦✦✦

Marvellous / 1994 / Dreyfus ✦✦

Oscar Pettiford

b. Sep. 30, 1922, Okmulgee, OK, d. Sep. 8, 1960, Copenhagen, Denmark
Bass, Cello / Bop
Oscar Pettiford was (along with Charles Mingus) the top bassist of the 1945-60 period and the successor to the late Jimmy Blanton. In addition, he was the first major soloist on the cello. A bop pioneer, it would have been very interesting to hear what Pettiford would have done during the avant-garde '60s if he had not died unexpectedly in 1960. After starting on piano, Pettiford switched to bass when he was 14 and played in a family band. He played with Charlie Barnet's band in 1942 as one of two bassists (the other was Chubby Jackson) and then hit the big time in 1943 participating in Coleman Hawkins' famous "The Man I Love" session; he also recorded with Earl Hines and Ben Webster during this period. Pettiford co-led an early bop group with Dizzy Gillespie in 1944 and in 1945 went with Coleman Hawkins to the West Coast, appearing on one song in the film *The Crimson Canary* with Hawkins and Howard McGhee. Pettiford was part of Duke Ellington's Orchestra during much of 1945-48 (fulfilling his role as the next step beyond Jimmy Blanton) and worked with Woody Herman in 1949. Throughout the 1950s he mostly worked as a leader (on bass and occasional cello), although he appeared on many records both as a sideman and a leader, including with Thelonious Monk

in 1955-56. After going to Europe in 1958, he settled in Copenhagen where he worked with local musicians plus Stan Getz, Bud Powell and Kenny Clarke. Among Pettiford's better-known compositions are "Tricotism," "Laverne Walk," "Bohemia After Dark" and "Swingin' Till the Girls Come Home." —*Scott Yanow*

The Oscar Pettiford Memorial Album / Mar. 10, 1949+Mar. 13, 1954 / Prestige ✦✦✦✦
This out-of-print LP features bassist Oscar Pettiford on two different occasions. He is heard on four songs under the leadership of baritonist Serge Chaloff (these have since been reissued on a Mosaic CD set) and with such fine players as trumpeter Red Rodney, tenor saxophonist Al Cohn and vibraphonist Terry Gibbs; Pettiford was with Woody Herman's Orchestra at the time. While those pieces are quite concise, of greater interest are six performances (including the 9-minute "Burt's Pad") from a 1954 sextet date with trombonist Kai Winding, Cohn and guitarist Tal Farlow. The bassist is well featured on "Stardust," and on "Rhumblues," Pettiford overdubbed himself on cello. Interesting bop-oriented music. —*Scott Yanow*

Discoveries / Feb. 21, 1952-Oct. 1957 / Savoy ✦✦✦✦✦
This 1986 LP is filled with previously unreleased performances including alternate takes from Savoy sessions that featured bassist Oscar Pettiford. Actually, seven of the 14 numbers are from 1952 and find Pettiford playing some very effective cello while accompanied by a rhythm section including Charles Mingus on bass. In addition, Pettiford is heard in a couple of groups with accordionist Mat Mathews, trios with either Eddie Costa or Hank Jones on piano, and a jam session on "No Knox Blues" with tenorman Paul Quinichette. Hopefully, all of this enjoyable music (along with the master takes) will be reissued on CD. —*Scott Yanow*

The New Oscar Pettiford Sextet / Dec. 29, 1953-Aug. 22, 1959 / Original Jazz Classics ✦✦✦✦✦
This LP reissue (not yet out on CD) from the Original Jazz Classics series brings back five selections from a Debut ten-inch LP, plus two later tracks. While the latter matches bassist Oscar Pettiford in a trio with vibraphonist Louis Hjulmand and pianist Jan Johansson (recorded in Europe in 1959), the bulk of the set features a swinging sextet with an unusual instrumentation: Pettiford on cello, tenor saxophonist Phil Urso, Julius Watkins on French horn, pianist Walter Bishop, bassist Charles Mingus and drummer Percy Brice. It is a pity that Pettiford (who composed four of the five pieces) could not have kept this group together, because it had a unique sound and would have been an excellent showcase for Pettiford's skills on cello. Its one existing recording is certainly worth hearing. —*Scott Yanow*

First Bass / Jun. 1953-Jul. 5, 1960 / IAJRC ✦✦✦✦✦
The remarkable Oscar Pettiford, arguably the top bassist in jazz during 1945-60 (Charles Mingus was his closest competitor) and the first great jazz cellist (preceded only by Harry Babasin) is showcased on 14 formerly rare titles on this CD from the collectors' IAJRC label. Pettiford is heard on four fascinating titles with Babasin in which the two cellists are backed by a rhythm section, as part of a small group with vibraphonist Lionel Hampton, in a trio with guitarist Attila Zoller, jamming with pianist Phineas Newborn in 1958 (on "Yardbird Suite" they are joined by altoist Lee Konitz and tenorman Zoot Sims) and with top European players on three numbers from 1960. Whether playing bass or cello, Oscar Pettiford is well-featured on each selection yet his strong soloing and creative ideas keep the music from ever becoming dull or predictable. Highly recommended for bop collectors. —*Scott Yanow*

The Finest of Oscar Pettiford / Aug. 12, 1955 / Bethlehem ✦✦✦✦
This reissue LP does not necessarily have the "best" of bassist Oscar Pettiford; in fact, its original title was *Another One*. But the music performed by Pettiford's octet (a young group including trumpeter Donald Byrd, trombonist Bob Brookmeyer and altoist Gigi Gryce) is excellent and fits securely in the hard bop mainstream of the era. The bassist contributed four of the songs on the date (including "Bohemia After Dark" and "Oscalypso") and is well showcased throughout. Worth searching for. —*Scott Yanow*

★ **Deep Passion** / Jun. 11, 1956-Sep. 6, 1957 / Impulse! ✦✦✦✦✦
Two former LP's by big bands led by bassist Oscar Pettiford (who doubles on cello) are reissued in full on this single CD. The arrangements by Gigi Gryce, Lucky Thompson and Benny Golson feature a lot of concise solos, an inventive use of the harp (either by Janet Putnam or Betty Glamann) and colorful ensembles. Among the many soloists are trumpeter Art Farmer, trombonists Jimmy Cleveland and Al Grey, the French horn of Julius Watkins, the tenors of Thompson or Golson and the bassist-leader. This formerly rare music is highly recommended to straight-ahead jazz fans for it is full of fresh material and subtle surprises. —*Scott Yanow*

Oscar Pettiford and his Birdland Band / May 26, 1957 / Spotlite ✦✦✦✦
Throughout his all-too-short career, bassist Oscar Pettiford had a desire to lead a big band. For 18 months during 1956-57, he kept one going on a part-time basis, resulting in a pair of albums. This LP from the British Spotlite label contains music from a couple of radio broadcasts with Pettiford (who doubles on cello), featuring

such fine players as trumpeter Donald Byrd, trombonist Al Grey, altoist Gene Quill and Jerome Richardson on tenor with a band that included Betty Glamann on harp and two French horns. Mostly group originals arranged by Gryce, the music is excellent and swinging, making one regret that the Pettiford Orchestra could not make it financially. —*Scott Yanow*

Vienna Blues: The Complete Sessions / Jan. 9, 1959+Jan. 12, 1959 / Black Lion ◆◆◆◆◆

After moving to Europe in Sept. 1958, bassist Oscar Pettiford recorded extensively during the last two years of his life. On this CD reissue, Pettiford doubles on cello and is joined by tenor saxophonist Hans Koller, up-and-coming guitarist Attila Zoller and drummer Jimmy Pratt. With the exception of "All the Things You Are," "Stardust" and "There Will Never Be Another You," all of the songs were written either by the leader or Koller. Good mainstream bop with hints (particularly in Zoller's playing) of more advanced styles. —*Scott Yanow*

Montmartre Blues / Aug. 22, 1959-Jul. 6, 1960 / Black Lion ◆◆◆◆

The great bassist Oscar Pettiford spent his last year playing in Europe before his unexpected death on September 8, 1960. Except for four songs cut in August, this CD contains Pettiford's final recordings. Teamed with a young group of Europeans (most impressive is pianist Jan Johansson and trumpeter Allan Botschinsky) who were clearly pleased to be playing with him, Pettiford has a fair amount of solo space on ten numbers with "Willow Weep for Me" being his feature. Five of the tunes are Pettiford originals including the title cut, "Laverne Walk" and his answer to Miles Davis' "So What" which he titled "Why Not? That's What!" This is a fine set of boppish music that makes one wonder what Oscar Pettiford might have accomplished in the 1960s had he lived. —*Scott Yanow*

Flip Phillips (Joseph Edward Filipelli)

b. Feb. 26, 1915, New York, NY

Tenor Saxophone, Bass Clarinet / Bop, Swing, East Coast Blues, Jump Blues

Flip Phillips, who angered some critics early on because he gained riotous applause for his exciting solos during Jazz at the Philharmonic concerts, has been an excellent tenor saxophonist for over 50 years, equally gifted on stomps, ballads and standards. He played clarinet regularly in a Brooklyn restaurant during 1934-39, was in Frankie Newton's group (1940-41) and spent time in the bands of Benny Goodman, Wingy Manone and Red Norvo. However, it was in 1944 that he had his breakthrough. As a well-featured soloist with Woody Herman's Herd (1944-46), Phillips became a big star. His warm tenor was most influenced by Ben Webster but sounded distinctive even at that early stage. He toured regularly with Jazz at the Philharmonic during 1946-57, scoring a bit of a sensation with his honking solo on "Perdido" and holding his own with heavy competition (including Charlie Parker and Lester Young). He occasionally co-led a group with Bill Harris and that band was the nucleus of the ensemble that Benny Goodman used in 1959. Phillips then retired to Florida for 15 years, playing on just an occasional basis, taking up the bass clarinet as a double and making only a sporadic record date. But by 1975 he was back in music full-time making quite a few records and playing at festivals and jazz parties. Even as he passed his 80th birthday, Flip Phillips has lost none of the enthusiasm or ability that he had a half-century earlier. —*Scott Yanow*

★ **A Melody from the Sky** / Sep. 1944-Nov. 1945 / Doctor Jazz ◆◆◆◆◆

This CD is a straight reissue of a Flying Dutchman LP and has all four of tenor saxophonist Flip Phillips' recording sessions as a leader prior to 1949. At the time he was a key member of Woody Herman's First Herd and these performances have short solos from other Herman sidemen (including trombonist Bill Harris and Neal Hefti on trumpet) although Phillips is the main star. His jumping tenor was already quite distinctive whether on romps or ballads. "Sweet and Lovely" and "Stompin' at the Savoy" are high points of this definitive early Flip Phillips set. —*Scott Yanow*

Flip in Florida / May 1963 / Onyx ◆◆◆◆

Tenor saxophonist Flip Phillips' only session as a leader during 1955-74 was this obscurity which was originally released on a tiny label and reissued by Onyx a decade after the fact. Phillips, who enjoyed having a much lower profile than previously, had relocated to Florida by 1954. Fortunately his powers were still in peak form for this quartet set which finds him accompanied by local musicians for a set dominated by standards. Phillips makes his debut playing bass clarinet on "Satin Doll," "The Girl from Ipanema" and "Just Say I Love Her" while featuring his stomping warm tenor to the other pieces. —*Scott Yanow*

Phillips's Head / Aug. 1975 / Choice ◆◆◆

Flipenstein / Jul. 20, 1981 / Progressive ◆◆◆◆◆

A very overlooked hot date on a rather obscure label. —*Ron Wynn*

The Claw: Live at the Floating Jazz Festival / 1986 / Chiaroscuro ◆◆◆◆◆

Veteran tenor Flip Phillips is heard leading a jam session during what was dubbed the 1986 Floating Jazz Festival since the music took place on the S.S. Norway somewhere in the Caribbean Sea. Phillips and his fellow tenors Buddy Tate, Al

Cohn and Scott Hamilton (along with pianist John Bunch, guitarist Chris Flory, bassist Major Holley and drummer Chuck Riggs) clearly had a good time stretching out on the five pieces (which all sport fairly basic chord changes); fluegelhornist Clark Terry dropped by and joins in on three of the pieces. Unfortunately, the liner notes do not tell who solos when but veteran collectors should be able to tell the tenors apart. The only minus to this CD is a surprisingly boring monologue by Phillips (one of Chiaroscuro's few unsuccessful "Jazzspeaks") at the conclusion of this disc. However, his nine minutes of talking is preceded by 64 minutes of hot jamming, making this CD easily recommended to fans of Jazz at the Philharmonic and straightahead jazz. —*Scott Yanow*

A Sound Investment / Mar. 1987 / Concord Jazz ◆◆◆◆◆

W/ Scott Hamilton (ts). An excellent, sympathetic collaboration. A standout pairing of this top swing-era stylist and a modern disciple. —*Ron Wynn*

● **Real Swinger** / May 1988-Jun. 1988 / Concord Jazz ◆◆◆◆◆

Live at the 1993 Floating Jazz Festival / Nov. 1, 1993+Nov. 3, 1993 / Chiaroscuro ◆◆◆◆

Flip Phillips was 79 at the time of this live performance but proves to still be very much in his musical prime. Joined by a rhythm section comprising fellow veterans (pianist Derek Smith, guitarist Bucky Pizzarelli, bassist Milt Hinton and drummer Ray Mosca), Phillips gives standards and riff tunes warm and often hard-swinging treatment. Other than a few tasteless (if humorous) jokes, this is a flawless release that serves as a definitive portrait of Flip Phillips in his later years. —*Scott Yanow*

Pieces of a Dream

f. 1975

Group / Crossover Jazz, R & B

Comprising bassist Cedric Napoleon, drummer Curtis Harmon and keyboardist James Lloyd, Pieces of a Dream was founded in 1975 in Philadelphia when the principal members were all teenagers. Originally somewhat jazz-oriented, Pieces of a Dream has mostly emphasized R&B, although they usually include a few jazz numbers in their performances. Grover Washington, Jr., produced their first three albums (all for Elektra during 1981-83); they have since recorded for Manhattan. Saxophonist Ron Kerber became a member in the 1990s. —*Scott Yanow*

● **The Best of Pieces of a Dream** / 1982-1989 / Blue Note ◆◆◆◆◆

The Best of Pieces of a Dream is an excellent 14-track collection that contains highlights from the fusion group's '80s recordings for Manhattan Records. Among the selections are "Keep It Smooth," "Baby It's Your Turn Now," "Cool Side," "Mt. Airy Groove," "Rising to the Top," "Warm Weather" and "Shadow of Your Smile." It's both a good introduction to the group's sound and an excellent summation of their peak years. —*Stephen Thomas Erlewine*

In Flight / Jun. 1, 1993 / Manhattan ◆◆◆

Pieces of a Dream can always be counted on to offer lightweight jazz-influenced R&B that is pleasing as long as one does not listen too closely or have overly high expectations. This set has several forgettable vocals, some sax solos by Ron Kerber and Marian Meadows that attempt to sound like Grover Washington, Jr., and consistently danceable rhythms. —*Scott Yanow*

Goodbye Manhattan / 1994 / Blue Note ◆◆◆◆◆

This is one of Pieces of a Dream's better efforts. Saxophonist Ron Kerber looks towards Grover Washington, Jr., (on soprano) and David Sanborn (during his alto spots) for inspiration, and the keyboardists recall Ramsey Lewis. But, even with the inclusion of a few throwaway rhythm tracks and some Eva Cassidy pop vocals, some of these selections do contain strong improvising within the R&B genre. Nothing too innovative occurs but the results are mostly quite listenable and always danceable. —*Scott Yanow*

Pieces / Mar. 19, 1997-Jun. 3, 1997 / Blue Note ◆◆◆◆

Despite their long string of R&B-ish recordings, it is difficult to completely write off Pieces of a Dream from a jazz standpoint. The group does lay down some attractive grooves, and every once in a while they sound as if they are interested in playing Ramsey Lewis-type jazz. Keyboardist James Lloyd in particular shows potential throughout this CD, and there are worthwhile contributions from a couple of the guests (Grover Washington Jr. and Hubert Laws who sit in on a song apiece). But in general, this is a set of fairly simplistic R&B dance music and throwaway vocals, at its best when programmed strictly in the background. —*Scott Yanow*

Bill Pierce

b. Sep. 25, 1948, Hampton, VA

Tenor Saxophone, Soprano Saxophone / Hard Bop

Bill Pierce is an excellent saxophonist who also works as an educator. He started off his career in Boston playing R&B with such stars as Stevie Wonder and Marvin Gaye. However, he is essentially a hard bop player as he showed during stints with James Williams (1979-80 and 1984-85) and a high profile association with Art

Blakey's Jazz Messengers (1980-82); with the latter he shared the front line with Wynton Marsalis and Bobby Watson. From 1986-94 Pierce was a regular member of Tony Williams' Quintet, somehow making himself heard over the leader's very loud drumming! He has led several of his own dates for Sunnyside. —*Scott Yanow*

● **William the Conqueror** / May 29, 1985-May 30, 1985 / Sunnyside ✦✦✦✦✦
It is the powerful tenor of Billy Pierce that makes this a highly recommended album. —*Scott Yanow*

Give and Take / Jun. 6, 1987+Oct. 24, 1987 / Sunnyside ✦✦✦✦

Equilateral / Jan. 2, 1988 / Sunnyside ✦✦✦✦

One for Chuck / Apr. 6, 1991-Apr. 7, 1991 / Sunnyside ✦✦✦✦✦

Epistrophy / Dec. 22, 1992 / Evidence ✦✦✦✦✦

Rio / May 25, 1994-May 26, 1994 / Sunnyside ✦✦✦✦

Billie & De De Pierce

Group / New Orleans Jazz, Blues Jazz
Pianist Billie Pierce and cornetist De De Pierce made a charming and musical duo ever since they were married in 1935. Billie was a fine barrelhouse pianist and blues singer, while De De played basic but effective cornet and was also a passionate vocalist. Although Billie (who had worked previously with Buddy Petit and George Lewis) and De De recorded an album for Center in 1953, both of the Pierces were somewhat obscure into the early 1960s. De De went blind in the '50s and retired for a time, but by 1959, he was back in action as the Pierces recorded for Folklyric. Sessions for Jazzology, Riverside and American Music (the latter released posthumously in 1996) featured the Pierces at their best. They were also involved in the early Preservation Hall Jazz Band, recording for Atlantic (a 1962 date with George Lewis), the Preservation Hall label and Rarities. —*Scott Yanow*

Nat Pierce

b. Jul. 16, 1925, Somerville, MA, d. Jun. 10, 1992, Los Angeles, CA
Piano / Swing, Bop, Progressive Big Band, Big Band
Nat Pierce had a long, distinguished, somewhat low-profile career as a champion of latter-day big-band swing, serving as the co-leader of Los Angeles' crack Frank Capp-Nat Pierce Juggernaut and an arranger for several well-known big bands and solo artists. His scores created an irresistible force when allied with a swinging, pushing drummer like Capp, often hewing tightly to the loping drive and tight ensemble of the post-1950s Count Basie orchestra. Likewise, Pierce's spare, tasty piano style not only has been compared to that of Basie, he also subbed very capably—indeed, almost indistinguishably—for the great man off and on from the late 1950s until Basie's death in 1984. Pierce studied music at the New England Conservatory of Music back home in Massachusetts, worked with local Boston bands, and ran his own part-time big band featuring Charlie Mariano from 1949 to 1951. Having already started shopping arrangements to Basie and Woody Herman, he joined Herman's Third Herd in 1951 as pianist/arranger, remaining until 1955. Afterwards, Pierce settled in New York City, where he became a busy freelance arranger, recording pianist, and occasional leader of bands, working with Ruby Braff, Lester Young, Ella Fitzgerald, Quincy Jones, Coleman Hawkins, Pee Wee Russell and Lester Young. Two of his most famous projects took place in 1957—writing the arrangements for *The Sound of Jazz* television show, and playing piano with the Basie rhythm section on the first ear-opening Lambert, Hendricks and Ross album, *Sing a Song of Basie*. In 1961, Pierce rejoined Herman and played a major role in lifting the band into one of its peak periods, serving as chief arranger, road manager and talent scout until 1966. Afterwards, he resumed his freelancing ways, arranging for Anita O'Day, Carmen McRae, Earl Hines and others, working with the bands of Louie Bellson and Bill Berry, reuniting with Herman, and substituting for Basie and Stan Kenton on occasion. In 1975, four years after a move to Los Angeles, Pierce joined forces with Capp to form the Capp-Pierce Juggernaut, which drew its personnel from the best Los Angeles session players out to decompress from their studio gigs. The band recorded a number of swinging albums for the Concord Jazz label, sometimes with guest vocalists like Joe Williams and Ernestine Anderson. Pierce continued to co-lead the Juggernaut off and on until his death, while also making a brief appearance in the 1977 film *New York, New York*, touring Europe in 1980 and 1984 as a member of the Countsmen, and recording frequently for Concord as a sideman for Scott Hamilton, Jake Hanna and others. —*Richard S. Ginell*

The Boston Bust-Out / Dec. 1947-1950 / Hep ✦✦✦✦✦
Boston had a strong but greatly underpublicized bop scene in the late '40s. This Hep CD, which adds a previously unreleased session plus one extra cut to the original LP, features pianist/arranger Nat Pierce, altoist Charlie Mariano and trombonist Sonny Truitt both in big bands and combos. The other personnel is mostly fairly obscure although baritone great Serge Chaloff is showcased on two numbers and there are three fairly straight vocals by Teddi King. The rare studio recordings

range in influences from Dizzy Gillespie to Claude Thornhill and the Miles Davis Nonet; highly recommended for bop collectors. —*Scott Yanow*

★ **The Nat Pierce-Dick Collins Nonet** / Jan. 27, 1954 / Original Jazz Classics ✦✦✦✦✦
One side features the driving West Coast bop of saxist Charlie Mariano, and the other features trumpeter Dick Collins and his more expansive sound. —*David Szatmary*

5400 North / May 21, 1978 / Hep ✦✦✦✦

Dave Pike

b. Mar. 23, 1938, Detroit, MI
Vibes / Hard Bop
Dave Pike has been a consistent vibraphonist through the years without gaining much fame. He originally played drums and is self-taught on vibes. Pike moved with his family to Los Angeles in 1954 and played with Curtis Counce, Harold Land, Elmo Hope, Dexter Gordon, Carl Perkins and Paul Bley among others. After moving to New York in 1960, he put an amplifier on his vibes. Pike toured with Herbie Mann during 1961-64, spent 1968-73 in Germany (recording with the Kenny Clarke-Francy Boland big band) and then resettled in Los Angeles, playing locally and recording for Timeless and Criss Cross. —*Scott Yanow*

Dave Pike / Nov. 1961 / Portrait ✦✦✦✦

Jazz for the Jet Set / Oct. 26, 1965-Nov. 2, 1965 / Atlantic ✦✦✦

Times out of Mind / Oct. 13, 1975-Oct. 14, 1975 / Muse ✦✦✦
Vibraphonist Dave Pike's debut for Muse (which has been reissued on CD) has generally strong individual playing although the material (five group originals plus a brief version of the bop standard "Wee") and use of electronics sound a bit dated. Pike teams up with keyboardist Tom Ranier (who also plays some alto and tenor), guitarist Ron Eschete, either Luther Hughes or Harvey Newmark on bass, drummer Ted Hawke and (on three of the six numbers) guitarist Kenny Burrell. Nothing all that memorable occurs during this lesser effort. —*Scott Yanow*

On a Gentle Note / Nov. 1, 1977 / Muse ✦✦✦✦

Let the Minstrels Play on / Mar. 22, 1978-Mar. 23, 1978 / Muse ✦✦✦
Some Afro-Latin, some fusion and things in between from vibist Dave Pike. Pike is a good player, but sometimes his arrangements bog down between pop and jazz. His style is more reminiscent of Red Norvo, with its lighter, less aggressive and flowing lines. —*Ron Wynn*

Moon Bird / 1981 / Muse ✦✦✦

● **Pike's Groove** / Feb. 5, 1986 / Criss Cross ✦✦✦✦✦

Bluebird / Oct. 1988-Nov. 1988 / Timeless ✦✦✦

Courtney Pine

b. Mar. 18, 1964, London, England
Tenor Saxophone, Soprano Saxophone / Post-Bop
For a while, Courtney Pine appeared as if he were going to be the next Wynton Marsalis. While Marsalis, in the mid-'80s, was doing close impressions of mid-'60s Miles Davis, Pine's impressive playing was nearly identical to John Coltrane's of the same era. Since then, Pine has received less publicity (at least in the US) and his importance has diminished a bit. He played with reggae and funk bands while in school and has always had a strong interest in several forms of music outside of jazz. He played with John Stevens in the early '80s, formed the Jazz Warriors (an open-minded big band) a few years later and started leading his own small groups. In 1986 he toured with George Russell's Orchestra and sat in with Art Blakey's Jazz Messengers but since then, despite some fine records for Antilles, Pine's career has seemed a bit directionless. —*Scott Yanow*

● **Journey to the Urge Within** / Jul. 21, 1986-Jul. 23, 1986 / Antilles ✦✦✦✦✦
This early Courtney Pine recording (the tenor saxophonist was 22 at the time), features some of the most promising Black English jazz musicians of the time including Pine (who also plays some bass clarinet and soprano), singer Cleveland Watkiss (who often is reminiscent of Bobby McFerrin), vibraphonist Orphy Robinson and pianist Julian Joseph. While most of these players have not yet lived up to their potential (Pine remains an expert Coltrane imitator), this disc has its share of strong music. The emphasis is on Courtney Pine's originals, which cover a wide span of emotions and grooves. —*Scott Yanow*

Destiny's Song and the Image of Pursuance / Jul. 29, 1987-Aug. 1, 1987 / Antilles ✦✦✦✦

The Vision's Tale / Jan. 17, 1989-Jan. 19, 1989 / Antilles ✦✦✦
At 26, Courtney Pine in 1989 seemed to be on his way to being one of the top tenors in jazz, although at that point he was still heavily influenced by John Coltrane. This set was a bit of a departure for Pine, who often displays a wild extroverted

Music Map

Piano

Ragtime
Scott Joplin
Tony Jackson
Eubie Blake

New Orleans Jazz Innovator
Jelly Roll Morton

Stride Piano
James P. Johnson	Fats Waller	Luckey Roberts
Donald Lambert	Cliff Jackson	Herman Chittison

Stride Pianists Who Later Became Modern
Duke Ellington   Mary Lou Williams

Boogie-Woogie
Jimmy Yancey	Albert Ammons
Pete Johnson	Meade Lux Lewis

Unclassifiable Innovators
Earl Hines   Art Tatum

Swing
Teddy Wilson	Joe Sullivan	Jess Stacy
Bob Zurke	Count Basie	Billy Kyle
Nat King Cole	Mel Powell	Eddie Heywood
Jay McShann	Johnny Guarnieri	

Founder of Bop Piano
Bud Powell

Bop
George Wallington	Al Haig	Duke Jordan
Dodo Marmarosa	Hampton Hawes	Joe Albany

Very Individual Pianists Beyond Bop
Thelonious Monk	Erroll Garner
Lennie Tristano	Oscar Peterson

1950s
Dave Brubeck	John Lewis
George Shearing	Hank Jones
Barry Harris	Tommy Flanagan
Roland Hanna	Billy Taylor
Lou Levy	Russ Freeman
Claude Williamson	Pete Jolly
Jimmy Rowles	Marian McPartland
Ellis Larkins	Elmo Hope
Walter Bishop, Jr.	Walter Davis
Kenny Drew	Red Garland
Wynton Kelly	Sonny Clark
Phineas Newborn	Gerald Wiggins
Ray Bryant	Mal Waldron
Randy Weston	Martial Solal
Ahmad Jamal	

Funky Hard Bop
Horace Silver	Bobby Timmons
Les McCann	Ramsey Lewis
Junior Mance	Gene Harris
Joe Zawinul	

Revival
Art Hodes	Wally Rose
Ralph Sutton	Dick Wellstood
Dick Hyman	Johnny Varro
Dave McKenna	Dave Frishberg
James Dapogny	Judy Carmichael
Reginald Robinson	Don Ewell
Ray Sherman	

Main Influences on Today's Acoustic Pianists
Bill Evans   McCoy Tyner

Avant-Garde
Cecil Taylor	Herbie Nichols
Paul Bley	Sun Ra
Andrew Hill	Ran Blake
Horace Tapscott	Muhal Richard Abrams
Dave Burrell	Don Pullen
Misha Mengelberg	Anthony Davis
Amina Claudine Myers	Vyacheslav Ganelin Giorgio
Gaslini	Irene Schweizer
Yosuke Yamashita	Marilyn Crispell
Myra Melford	Alexander Von Schlippenbach
Paul Plimley	Matthew Shipp

Post-Bop
Herbie Hancock	Chick Corea
Keith Jarrett	Cedar Walton
Kenny Barron	Jaki Byard
Monty Alexander	Walter Norris
Toshiko Akiyoshi	Steve Kuhn
Roger Kellaway	Horace Parlan
Clare Fischer	Mike Garson
Abdullah Ibrahim	Kirk Lightsey
Tete Montoliu	Alan Broadbent
Joanne Brackeen	Richie Beirach
Adam Makowicz	Hal Galper
George Cables	James Williams
Donald Brown	Larry Willis
Harold Mabern	Stanley Cowell
John Hicks	Michel Petrucciani
Mulgrew Miller	Hilton Ruiz
Danilo Perez	Geri Allen
Michele Rosewoman	Billy Childs
Bill Cunliffe	Fred Hersch
Kenny Kirkland	Benny Green
Geoff Keezer	Marcus Roberts
Jim McNeely	Renee Rosnes
Cyrus Chestnut	Stephen Scott
Jacky Terasson	Kenny Drew, Jr.
Gonzalo Rubalcaba	Chucho Valdes

style, and was (if anything) overly respectful to the standards that he interprets. Perhaps this was due to the presence of pianist Ellis Marsalis who leads a trio consisting of bassist Delbert Felix and drummer Jeff Watts. Pine sounds restricted to the melody with only slight variations on some of the numbers including "In a Mellow Tone," "Skylark" and "God Bless the Child." He does cut loose a bit on a few of the other pieces, but his solos in general are much briefer than usual. The best moments are Pine's outings on both tenor and soprano on "A Raggamuffin's Stance," "I'm an Old Cowhand" and a stormy Coltrane-ish "Giant Steps." It is a pity that the rest of the album is not of that same intensity. In addition, Delfeayo Marsalis' self-righteous and pompous liner notes are a definite minus. — *Scott Yanow*

Within the Realms of Our Dream / Jan. 20, 1990-Jan. 21, 1990 / Antilles ✦✦✦✦✦

Closer to Home / 1992 / Antilles ✦✦✦

A '92 release by British saxophonist Courtney Pine, who with each album moves more towards the musical center. He's working with pop, rock, and reggae compositions and musicians, but at the same time still playing forceful, frequently dynamic tenor and soprano solos. It's not really fusion, nor is it the kind of uncompromising jazz that he once championed. — *Ron Wynn*

Underground / Sep. 16, 1997 / Antilles ✦✦✦✦

John Pisano

b. Feb. 6, 1931, New York, NY
Guitar / Bop

There have been few jazz musicians as modest and self-effacing as John Pisano, an excellent guitarist who has often been quite happy to be in the background. He started playing guitar when he was 14 and, after performing in an Air Force band (1952-55), he gained some recognition as Jim Hall's replacement in the popular Chico Hamilton Quintet (1956-58). Pisano settled in Los Angeles and became a well-respected studio musician who, among other assignments, recorded duets with Billy Bean, played in the Joe Pass Quartet (recording the legendary *For Django* album), worked with Peggy Lee (1960-69) and was a member of Herb Alpert's Tijuana Brass (1965-69). Pisano had a reunion with Joe Pass (touring with him from 1989 until Pass' death in 1994), sticking almost exclusively to rhythm guitar. A collection of collaborations with various associates (*Among Friends*) was released on Pablo in 1995. Recently, he has been performing with singer Jeanne Pisano (his wife) in a group called the Flying Pisanos. — *Scott Yanow*

● **Among Friends** / Feb. 15, 1991-Dec. 9, 1994 / Pablo ✦✦✦✦✦

Though John Pisano made some albums as a co-leader with Billy Bean in the late '50s, Willie Ruff in 1970, and Joe Pass in 1991, until this release, the overly modest guitarist had never appeared as a leader on a record date. One could almost say that he still hasn't, for this album contains a series of duets with six other guitarists. Be that as it may, Pisano at last gets a chance to display his melodically tasty, often hard-swinging post-bop oriented licks on electric and acoustic guitars, easily the equal or better of any of his guests. The 1991 tracks are intricate duets with his late sparring partner Pass; everything else was assembled from sessions held throughout the summer and fall of 1994. There are several fine Pisano originals, "Berry Drive," "D'Joe" (where Pisano's guitar burns especially brightly), "Blue Note Samba" and "Blues for E.S.M.," which remind us of this unsung composer's large contribution to the success of the Tijuana Brass during his tenure there. Pisano's fellow guitarists here are Pass, Dori Caymmi, Lee Ritenour, Ron Affif, Ted Greene and Phil Upchurch—and on "Maos de Afeto," Pisano plays all the guitars himself, with Caymmi on wordless vocals. — *Richard S. Ginell*

Conversation Pieces / 1991-1994 / Pablo ✦✦✦✦

This follow-up album to Pisano's 1995 outing for Pablo, *Among Friends*, finds him once again exploring new terrain on a batch of originals and old standards. His guitar work is joined by guest turns from Lee Ritenour, Phil Upchurch, Dori Caymmi, Joe Diorio, Gene Bertoncini and Ted Greene. With Chuck Domanico, Jim Hughart, Chuck Buerghofer and Jose Marino alternating on bass duties and Colin Bailey, Claudio Slon and Joe La Barbera taking turns manning the drum kit, this is an album that ranges from quiet bebop to moody takes of obscure standards to bits of funk that all find Pisano in rare form. Highlights include the originals "You Were Meant for Me," "Blues for Joe," "Ribbit" and "Jo-Wes," as well as his takes on "Captain Bacardi," "Body and Soul" and Noel Coward's "I'll Follow My Heart." — *Cub Koda*

Bucky Pizzarelli (John Paul Pizzarelli, Sr.)

b. Jan. 9, 1926, Paterson, NJ
Guitar / Swing

A superior guitarist who swing musicians in particular appreciate, Bucky Pizzarelli has been a fixture in jazz and the studios since the early '50s. Self-taught, Pizzarelli has long been a master of the seven-string guitar. He toured with Vaughn Monroe before and after a stint in the military. In 1952 Pizzarelli joined the staff of NBC

and 12 years later he switched to ABC; in addition he worked with the Three Sounds (1956-57) and had several tours with Benny Goodman. In the 1970s he was more active in jazz, co-leading a duo with George Barnes and working with Zoot Sims, Bud Freeman and Stephane Grappelli among many others. Pizzarelli has since kept up a busy recording schedule and plays often at jazz parties. Bucky has also recorded with his son John Pizzarelli on an occasional basis since the early '80s. — *Scott Yanow*

Plays Bix Beiderbecke Arrangements by Bill Challis / May 3, 1972-Jun. 30, 1972 / Monmouth ✦✦✦✦✦

Buck and Bud / Feb. 1977 / Flying Dutchman ✦✦✦✦✦

Cafe Pierre Trio / Aug. 25, 1982-Aug. 26, 1982 / Monmouth ✦✦✦✦

● **Complete Guitar Duos** / Mar. 19, 1984-Apr. 1984 / Stash ✦✦✦✦✦

Fine guitar vehicle for Bucky Pizzarelli and John, Jr. They team on both uptempo and slow tunes, with some originals, but mostly interpretations of both jazz and non-jazz items. This is wonderful for guitar devotees. — *Ron Wynn*

Solo Flight / 1986 / Stash ✦✦✦

John Pizzarelli

b. Apr. 6, 1960, Paterson, NJ
Guitar, Vocals / Swing

The son of the fine guitarist Bucky Pizzarelli, John Pizzarelli has become a popular attraction, singing swing era standards in a charming voice and developing into a fine guitarist himself. Taught guitar by his father, John sat in with Bucky and Zoot Sims at a 1980 concert and has played duets with the older Pizzarelli on an occasional basis ever since. He worked with Tony Monte's trio starting in 1986 and then in 1990 started his own solo career, usually heading drumless trios. John Pizzarelli's voice has developed with time, displaying both charm and self-effacing humor, and his regular group is capable of playing swing tunes at rather rapid tempos. He has recorded as a leader for Chesky, Stash and Novus, and in 1997 appeared in the Broadway production of Johnny Mercer songs called *Dream*. — *Scott Yanow*

I'm Hip / May 1983 / Stash ✦✦✦

One Night with You / Nov. 1988-Feb. 1990 / Chesky ✦✦✦✦

My Blue Heaven / Feb. 6, 1990-Feb. 7, 1990 / Chesky ✦✦✦

All of Me / 1991 / Novus ✦✦✦

This CD is a middle-of-the-road showcase for the pleasant but somewhat limited vocals of John Pizzarelli. Dick Lieb's big band and string arrangements occasionally border on Muzak and are extremely predictable. The tunes (most from the swing era) are superior, but Pizzarelli's treatments pale next to the originals (particularly Nat King Cole), and very little is heard from the leader's guitar. John Pizzarelli would improve as a singer within the next few years so; despite his charm, this project is dispensable. — *Scott Yanow*

Naturally / 1993 / Novus ✦✦✦✦

Dear Mr. Cole / 1994 / Novus ✦✦✦✦

John Pizzarelli's tribute to Nat King Cole features him in a drumless trio with pianist Benny Green and bassist Christian McBride on all but one selection. Pizzarelli is fine as a rhythm guitarist but since he sings on most of the selections and his voice is merely average, this session (which includes 18 selections, most of which were originally associated with Cole) is of less interest than one might hope. At least Pizzarelli has a cheerful style and does not seem to take himself too seriously. Green has many forceful solos but the leader's limited vocal abilities keep this recording from being too essential. — *Scott Yanow*

New Standards / 1994 / Novus ✦✦✦✦

● **After Hours** / Jan. 16, 1996 / Novus ✦✦✦✦✦

Our Love is Here to Stay / 1997 / RCA ✦✦✦✦✦

John Pizzarelli's singing has improved through the years, he has become a particularly strong guitarist (very adept at fast tempos), and his likable personality has remained as constant as his love for swing-era tunes. Joined by a swinging big band arranged by Don Sebesky in the style of Count Basie, Pizzarelli and his trio (with pianist Ray Kennedy and bassist Martin Pizzarelli) play enthusiastically on a set of swingers and ballads. Although the slower material is fine, it is the romps (particularly "Avalon," "Little Girl," "Rhythm Is Our Business" and the instrumental "Say Hey Kid") that are most memorable. An enjoyable outing. — *Scott Yanow*

Lonnie Plaxico

b. Sep. 4, 1960, Chicago, IL
Bass / Post-Bop

Although he became associated for a time with the M-Base musicians, Lonnie Plaxico has been a very flexible bassist throughout his career. Early on he played with Chet Baker, Sonny Stitt and Junior Cook. After spending time in Wynton Marsalis' band (1982), Plaxico worked with Dexter Gordon and Hank Jones before joining Art Blakey's Jazz Messengers in the mid-'80s. He recorded with Dizzy Gillespie and David Murray and led his own sessions for Muse starting in the late '80s. In recent times Lonnie Plaxico has performed with everyone from Steve Coleman and Greg Osby to Bud Shank, Cassandra Wilson and Don Byron. —*Scott Yanow*

● **Plaxico** / Sep. 13, 1989 / Muse ✦✦✦✦✦

Iridescence / Dec. 13, 1990 / Muse ✦✦✦

Short Takes / May 4, 1992-Jun. 6, 1992 / Muse ✦✦✦

With All Your Heart / May 19, 1993 / Muse ✦✦✦✦

Paul Plimley

b. 1953, Vancouver, B.C., Canada
Piano / Avant-Garde
One of Canada's finest musicians, pianist Paul Plimley has built a fresh style that was originally influenced by Cecil Taylor. In 1977 he became a member of the New Orchestra Quintet, he studied with Cecil Taylor in 1979 and was often teamed with bassist Lisle Ellis until Ellis moved in the 1990s to the Bay Area. Plimley has recorded for several labels (including Nine Winds, Music & Arts and Hat Art) and remains a vital force in Canada. —*Scott Yanow*

Both Sides of the Same Mirror / Nov. 1989 / Nine Winds ✦✦✦✦

Paul Plimley/Lisle Ellis/Andrew Cyrille Trio / Nov. 3, 1990 / Music & Arts ✦✦✦✦✦

● **When Silence Pulls** / 1992 / Music & Arts ✦✦✦✦✦

Kaleidoscopes / Apr. 8, 1992-Apr. 9, 1992 / Hat Art ✦✦✦✦
This is a very interesting concept that is partly successful. Pianist Paul Plimley and bassist Lisle Ellis perform ten Ornette Coleman tunes (including two versions of the title cut); never mind that Coleman never used a piano. However, because the duo's interpretations are very free and sometimes only refer to the themes in an abstract way, these performances are not as exciting as they would have been if the melodies had been used as the basis for the improvisations. —*Scott Yanow*

Everything in Stages / Apr. 3, 1995-Apr. 7, 1995 / Songlines ✦✦✦✦

Noir / Nov. 1, 1995 / Victo ✦✦✦

Ed Polcer

b. Feb. 10, 1937, Paterson, NJ
Cornet / Dixieland, Mainstream Jazz
Best known for leading the house band at the third and final version of the Eddie Condon club, Ed Polcer is a solid Dixieland (or Chicago jazz) soloist and a fine ensemble player. He studied at Princeton University and, after graduating in 1958, played at Ryan's and other New York clubs while pursuing a career outside of music. In 1969, Polcer joined Red Balaban's group, becoming co-leader in 1975. The cornetist, who worked with Benny Goodman (1972), Jane Harvey and Cathy Chamberlain, has been a popular figure at jazz parties and classic jazz festivals during the past couple of decades. Polcer can be heard in excellent form on an album he led for Jazzology in 1982 and on *A Salute to Eddie Condon* (a 1993 concert put out by the Nagel-Heyer label). —*Scott Yanow*

Ben Pollack

b. Jun. 22, 1903, Chicago, IL, **d.** Jun. 7, 1971, Palm Springs, CA
Drums, Leader / Classic Jazz, Swing, Dixieland
More important as a talent scout than as a musician, loaded with ambition but cursed with a large capacity for envy, Ben Pollack was one of the forefathers of the big-band era, yet to his everlasting chagrin, he did not profit much from it. His Dixieland-oriented jazz bands of the late 1920s and early 1930s became incubators for an impressive parade of White jazz talent; Glenn Miller, Benny Goodman, Jack Teagarden, Jimmy McPartland, Harry James, Bud Freeman, Charlie Spivak, Yank Lawson and Muggsy Spanier were among the graduates. As a drummer, he was very much respected—Goodman once said that Pollack was one of the first drummers to hit all four beats in a measure—but played less and less as the years wore on. After playing drums in various Chicago school and professional bands in his teens, Pollack joined the New Orleans Rhythm Kings in the early 1920s, making his earliest records for Gennett in 1922-23. He gained early experience in running bands by reorganizing the Bastin band in Los Angeles; he toyed with the idea of returning to his family's fur business in Chicago (but not for long), and formed the first of his own bands in May 1926. Working mostly in Chicago and New York City and recording for Victor, Pollack's bands became moderately successful, but the hot young talent that Pollack rounded up—particularly Goodman—became very impatient with Pollack's old-fashioned singing and commercially oriented shows. Once

the early crew of stars had left, Pollack resurfaced with another hot band of post-Dixielanders like Lawson, Matty Matlock and Eddie Miller. But in Dec. 1934, this band broke up acrimoniously in California, allegedly over Pollack's favored star treatment of his then-girlfriend, singer Doris Robbins. Most of the band's members regrouped under the leadership of Bob Crosby and went on to become a hit act. Pollack's resentment grew as he watched the Crosby band, Goodman, Miller and Harry James achieve fame and fortune—and he even filed a $5 million lawsuit against Goodman, Victor Records, Paramount Pictures and Camel Cigarettes for what he felt were lost earnings (the suit went nowhere). Many years later, he somehow managed to find the inner strength to play himself in the film *The Benny Goodman Story* (1956).

In the meantime, Pollack carried on, leading his own bands until 1942 when he organized an orchestra for comedian/"pianist" Chico Marx to front, recruiting, among others, a 16-year-old singer/drummer/pianist named Mel Tormé. By 1943, he was running his own booking agency and the short-lived Jewel record label in Los Angeles, and through the 1960s, he sporadically organized Dixieland-revival bands such as the Pick-A-Rib Boys. However, Pollack eventually wound down his musical activities to concentrate on running a restaurant in Palm Springs—and the ailing, still-embittered bandleader ended his life by hanging himself in his bathroom. A CD of Pollack's latter-day Pick-A-Rib Boys is available on the Jazzology label. —*Richard S. Ginell*

Benny Goodman with Ben Pollack, 1926-1931 / Dec. 17, 1926-Mar. 2, 1931 / Sunbeam ✦✦✦✦
This is a particularly interesting and unusual Ben Pollack LP, for the 16 selections are all alternate takes. Pollack led important big bands from 1926-34, and among his key sidemen on these 16 selections are clarinetist Benny Goodman (who took his first recorded solos on the Dec. 17, 1926 session), trombonist Glenn Miller, cornetist Jimmy McPartland, trumpeter Charlie Teagarden, tenorman Eddie Miller and trombonist Jack Teagarden. Not all of the selections are classics (since Pollack does take vocals on half of the numbers), but there are memorable versions of "He's the Last Word," "Wang Wang Blues" and "Beale Street Blues" (which features Jack Teagarden's vocal). Worth searching for by 1920s collectors. —*Scott Yanow*

Futuristic Rhythm / Oct. 15, 1928-Nov. 29, 1929 / Saville ✦✦✦✦✦
With the exception of five lesser numbers that were bypassed and a few alternate takes, this generous 20-song British LP has all of the music recorded by Ben Pollack's Orchestra during a 13-month period. The band at the time included such notables as cornetist Jimmy McPartland, trombonist Jack Teagarden and clarinetist Benny Goodman, and alternated between hot jazz choruses and dance band charts. The lineup did include three strings, and vocals were taken by the underrated Belle Mann, Dick Robertson, Gene Austin, the not-so-hot Ben Pollack, Scrappy Lambert and Smith Ballew. However, the jazz content is generally high, and these often overlooked recordings should greatly interest vintage specialists. —*Scott Yanow*

Ben Pollack and His Orchestra 1933-1934 / Dec. 28, 1933-May 29, 1934 / VJM ✦✦✦
Drummer Ben Pollack led a series of very interesting bands from 1926-38, but virtually all got away from him. The group heard on the 16 selections included on this "complete" British LP has the bulk of what would soon be Bob Crosby's Orchestra, including such players as trumpeter Yank Lawson, clarinetist Matty Matlock, Eddie Miller on tenor and clarinet, and guitarist Nappy Lamare. Unfortunately, all but three numbers have vocals (most of them quite indifferent and dated), and the band rarely cuts loose. Pollack excessively featured his girlfriend Doris Robbins at the expense of the jazz content, and eventually the musicians broke away. One can hear plenty of unrealized potential on these interesting, if not exactly essential performances. —*Scott Yanow*

Ben Pollack Big Band / 1938 / Golden Era ✦✦✦✦
This collector's LP features the little-known 1938 Ben Pollack Orchestra, a band most notable for the inclusion of cornetist Andy Secrest who—nine years after he filled in for Bix Beiderbecke with Paul Whiteman's big band—still sounded a bit influenced by Bix. The music is essentially Benny Goodman-style swing with an emphasis on original riff tunes (including "Rug Cutter's Delight" and "Stomping at the Motel"); there are six vocals among the 16 selections. —*Scott Yanow*

● **Ben Pollack and His Pick-A-Rib Boys** / Apr. 25, 1950-May 3, 1950 / Jazzology ✦✦✦✦✦
By 1950, drummer Ben Pollack was regularly playing Dixieland in the Los Angeles area. His "Pick-A-Rib Boys" recorded 20 selections as radio transcriptions (all included on this CD), and these brief performances (none longer than 2:40) pack a lot of music into a short period of time. Trumpeter Dick Cathcart, trombonist Moe Schneider, clarinetist Matty Matlock, pianist Ray Sherman, bassist Walt Yoder and Pollack himself romp through a variety of Dixieland standards, tunes from the 1920s, and a few oddball items including "San Antonio Shout," "The Third Man Theme" and Matlock's "Echo in the Cavern." —*Scott Yanow*

Herb Pomeroy (Irving Herbert Pomeroy III)

b. Apr. 15, 1930, Gloucester, MA
Trumpet / Bop

Herb Pomeroy has spent most of his career as an important and influential educator. The result has been that his own trumpet playing was underrated and not very well documented during his prime years.

Pomeroy studied music at Schillinger House in Boston, which later became the Berklee School of Music. Always based in Massachusetts, the boppish trumpeter gigged with Charlie Parker (a couple of concerts were later released), Lionel Hampton, and Stan Kenton (1954). He recorded with Serge Chaloff and as a leader for the Transition label (1955). Pomeroy began teaching at Berklee in 1955 and was on its faculty for 40 years, touching the careers of scores of young jazz greats. In addition, he taught at the Lenox School of Music for a couple years and usually led a local orchestra filled with his students. Herb Pomeroy, who also recorded as a leader of big band sets for Roulette (1957), United Artists (1958) and Shiah (1980), began to concentrate more on his own playing upon his retirement from teaching. In late '96 he made an Arbors CD with singer Donna Byrne. —*Scott Yanow*

Jazz in a Stable / Mar. 13, 1955 / Transition ✦✦✦

Life is a Many Splendered Gig / Jun. 3, 1957-Jun. 4, 1957 / Fresh Sound ✦✦✦✦

Band in Boston / 1958 / United Artists ✦✦✦✦

Detour Ahead / 1958 / United Artists ✦✦✦✦

● Pramlatta's Hips / 1980 / Shiah ✦✦✦✦

This is Always / Apr. 1996 / Daring ✦✦✦✦

Valery Ponomarev

b. Jan. 20, 1943, Moscow, Russia
Trumpet / Hard Bop

The first major Russian jazz musician to make an impression in the US, Valery Ponomarev has always had an attractive tone, a swinging style and a strong interest in keeping the hard bop legacy of Clifford Brown alive. He played as regularly as possible in the Soviet Union, recording for the Melodiya label and appearing at jazz festivals until defecting in 1973.

Four years later, he joined Art Blakey's Jazz Messengers, a perfect outlet for his style, from 1977-80; he recorded nine albums with Blakey for such labels as Roulette, Timeless and Concord. Ponomarev has since freelanced, usually leading his own quintets and recording extensively for Reservoir. —*Scott Yanow*

Means of Identification / Apr. 14, 1985 / Reservoir ✦✦✦✦✦

● Trip to Moscow / Apr. 11, 1988 / Reservoir ✦✦✦✦✦

Profile / May 2, 1991 / Reservoir ✦✦✦✦✦

Live at Sweet Basil / Jul. 16, 1993 / Reservoir ✦✦✦✦

Live at Vartan Jazz / Feb. 10, 1995-Feb. 11, 1995 / Vartan Jazz ✦✦✦✦

The hard bop trumpeter Valery Ponomarev, who was always most inspired by Clifford Brown and Lee Morgan, is in excellent form on this 1995 outing. However, the recording quality is just OK in spots, leading to a slightly lower rating than the music deserves. Ponomarev is teamed with drummer Ben Riley and three lesser-known players—the fine tenor Francesco Bearsetti, pianist Sid Simmons and bassist Kenny Walker. With the exception of "Autumn in New York" and Kenny Dorham's "N.Y. Theme," all nine selections are the trumpeter's originals. The music swings and is well played, making this small-label release worth acquiring by straightahead jazz fans who have Ponomarev's Reservoir releases. —*Scott Yanow*

A Star for You / Apr. 3, 1997 / Reservoir ✦✦✦✦

Jean-Luc Ponty

b. Sep. 29, 1942, Avranches, France
Violin / Post-Bop, Fusion, Crossover Jazz

It has been a long, fascinating odyssey for Jean-Luc Ponty, who started out as a straight jazz violinist only to become a pioneer of the electric violin in jazz-rock in the '70s and an inspired manipulator of sequencers and synthesizers in the '80s. At first merely amplifying his violin in order to be heard, he switched over to electric violin and augmented it with devices that were associated with electric guitarists and keyboardists, like Echoplex machines, distortion boxes, phase shifters, and wah-wah pedals. Classically trained, with an unquenchable ability to swing when he wants to, and consumed by a passion for tight structures and repeating ostinatos, Ponty has been able to handle styles as diverse as swing, bop, free and modal jazz, jazz-rock, world music and even country, mixing them up at will. Starting in 1977, he also pioneered the use of a five-string electric violin with a low C string. Undoubtedly, he rivals Stephane Grappelli for the title of the most prominent and influential European jazz violinist.

Ponty's father—the director of the school of music in Avranches and a violin teacher as well—got Jean-Luc started on violin at the age of five, and his mother tutored him on piano. He left school at 13 in order to practice six hours a day in the hope of becoming a concert violinist. At 15, he was accepted into the Paris Conservatoire, ultimately winning the *premier prix* at age 17. He played with the Concerts Lamoureux Orchestra for three years, during which time, thanks to the influence of Grappelli and Stuff Smith, he became interested in jazz. Oddly enough, Ponty began playing jazz first on the clarinet and tenor sax, waiting until 1962 to apply it to the violin. After a hitch in the French Army (1962-64), Ponty went completely over to the jazz camp, leading quartets and trios in Europe, recording with Grappelli, Smith and Svrend Asmussen on *Violin Summit*, and visiting the US for the first time in 1967 at a Monterey Jazz Festival workshop. Enriching himself with diverse American experiences in 1969, Ponty recorded with Frank Zappa, joined the George Duke Trio, and upon his return to France, formed the free-jazz Jean-Luc Ponty Experience (1970-72) before settling in the US and rejoining Zappa's Mothers of Invention. He toured and recorded with the Mahavishnu Orchestra in 1974-75 and then set out on his own, compiling a long series of solo albums on Atlantic that pulled away from the more volcanic aspects of fusion toward a more lyrical, European, yet still exciting extension of Mahavishnu's idioms. In 1983, after his records began to sound increasingly formulaic, Ponty switched gears and recharged his creative batteries on the synthesizer. Starting with the *Individual Choice* album, he began constructing attractive revolving patterns of electronic sounds with the help of sequencers, producing backdrops for his violin that were elegantly indebted to Europop influences. He took this direction with him when he signed with Columbia in 1987, but on 1991's *Tchokola* album, Ponty was on the move again, throwing out the sequencers and recording with West African musicians who provided him with new ostinato patterns to play with. —*Richard S. Ginell*

Sunday Walk / Jun. 1967 / BASF ✦✦✦✦

Live at Donte's / Mar. 1969 / Blue Note ✦✦✦✦✦

In October 1969, violinist Jean-Luc Ponty recorded a notable live set with keyboardist George Duke, bassist John Heard and drummer Dick Berk that gained him a lot of exposure in the US. He had actually played at Donte's in Los Angeles with Duke (on acoustic piano), Heard and drummer Al Cecchi the previous March. Four of the songs came out on a 1981 LP. This CD reissues that program and then doubles it with four more songs from the same engagement. This is a release that is recommended to listeners who are not interested in Ponty's many fusion projects for his playing here is relatively straightahead and sounds influenced by the work of the mid-1960s Miles Davis Quintet, and not just because he performs Ron Carter's "Eighty-One." Also of great interest are the solos of Duke, who would eventually become a funk keyboardist and then a pop producer. In this context, he sounds like a mixture of McCoy Tyner and Herbie Hancock. —*Scott Yanow*

Electric Connection / Mar. 3, 1969-Mar. 4, 1969 / Pacific Jazz ✦✦✦

King Kong: Ponty Plays Zappa / Mar. 14, 1969-Mar. 15, 1969 / World Pacific ✦✦✦✦

Cantaloupe Island / Mar. 1969 / Blue Note ✦✦✦✦

Experience / Sep. 1969 / Pausa ✦✦✦✦✦

Open Strings / 1973 / BASF ✦✦✦✦

Upon the Wings of Music / Jan. 1975 / Atlantic ✦✦✦✦✦

Jean-Luc Ponty, who at the time was still with the second version of The Mahavishnu Orchestra, is heard playing his own brand of fusion on this excellent recording, which set the standard for his music of the next decade. With keyboardist Patrice Rushen, Dan Sawyer or Ray Parker on guitars, bassist Ralphe Armstrong and drummer Ndugu, the violinist performs eight of his highly arranged but spirited originals. His early Atlantic recordings (of which this is the first) remain underrated for their important contributions to the history of fusion. —*Scott Yanow*

● Le Voyage: The Jean-Luc Ponty Anthology / May 25, 1975-Mar. 1993 / Rhino ✦✦✦✦✦

One of the leaders of fusion, electric violinist Jean-Luc Ponty's years on Atlantic are well-covered on this two-CD sampler. All but the final two numbers date from the 1975-85 period. Ponty's music can be heard evolving from high-powered fusion to a somewhat mechanical group sound in which his sound is so synthesized as to seem closer to a keyboard than a violin; Ponty's 1993 album *No Absolute Time* returned a bit to his roots. Most of the more memorable selections from the violinist's Atlantic years are on this attractive and well-conceived reissue (including "Bowing-Bowing," "Renaissance," "New Country," "Mirage," "No Strings Attached" and "Stay with Me"). In addition to Ponty, other key soloists include keyboardists Patrice Rushen and Allan Zavod and guitarists Daryl Stuermer and Allan Holdsworth. A fine overview. —*Scott Yanow*

Aurora / Dec. 1975 / Atlantic ◆◆◆◆

This CD reissue has state-of-the-art (for 1975) high-powered fusion that differs surprisingly little from the music that Jean-Luc Ponty has mostly played throughout the 1980s and '90s. The violinist's quintet (which includes guitarist Darryl Stuermer, keyboardist Patrice Rushen, bassist Tom Fowler and drummer Norman Fearrington) displays impeccable musicianship and lots of energy. The group was often so tight that the violin, keyboards, guitar and (to a lesser extent) the electric bass had similar tones, sometimes making it difficult to tell who was soloing at a particular moment. Listeners open to the sound of electronics and funky grooves should be very impressed by the spirited music, which combines the adventure of jazz with the sound of rock. —*Scott Yanow*

Imaginary Voyage / Jul. 1976-Aug. 1976 / Atlantic ◆◆◆

As of 1976, Jean-Luc Ponty's variations on the Mahavishnu Orchestra theme were still fresh and imaginative, cast in a distinctively different, more lyrical, more controlled framework. Ponty's instrumental lineup is identical to that of Mahavishnu—electric violin, guitar, keyboards, bass, drums—but he turns the emphasis on its head, with all commands coming directly from the violin (his) and less competitive crossplay emanating from his colleagues. For starters, "New Country" is a lively jazz-rock hoedown, one of those periodic C&W sidetrips that some fusioneers attempted for a lark, and "The Gardens of Babylon" is a wonderfully memorable tune, the beginnings of which grow out of "New Country." The last half of the CD is taken up by the title composition, a strong four-part suite that hangs together with barely a sag in interest over its 20-minute span. —*Richard S. Ginell*

Enigmatic Ocean / Jun. 1977-Jul. 1977 / Atlantic ◆◆◆◆◆

Consistently imaginative, *Enigmatic Ocean* is one of Jean-Luc Ponty's finest accomplishments. The French violinist recorded his share of fusion gems during the 1970s, and this album is at the top of the list. Often aggressive but sometimes reflective and moody, this CD is as unpredictable as it is adventurous. Ponty has plenty of room to stretch out, let loose and blow, and electric guitarists Allan Holdsworth and Daryl Stuermer contribute some inspired solos as well. Also quite impressive is the insightful and passionate drumming of Steve Smith, who went on to lead the superb fusion band Vital Information. Ponty takes one risk after another, and all of them pay off beautifully. —*Alex Henderson*

Cosmic Messenger / 1978 / Atlantic ◆◆◆◆

Here is more elegant, European-flavored jazz-rock from the French virtuoso, pretty much in the same mold as in previous Atlantic albums but with gradually tightening control over every parameter of performance. Ponty's analog-delay special effects on the title track are spectacular, and the album is loaded more than ever with revolving electronic arpeggios as Ponty's own involvement with the ARP synthesizer grows. But there is still plenty of his fluid, slippery electric violin soloing to be heard within the tight structures of these pieces, and the tunes themselves are often fairly good. In addition, this fusion express finds its way into the funk on "The Art of Happiness," and there are some tricky rhythmic experiments on some tunes. —*Richard S. Ginell*

A Taste for Passion / Jun. 1979-Jul. 1979 / Atlantic ◆◆◆

Despite the title, this release is more subdued than its predecessors on the shelves, more tightly controlled, more conventional in instrumentation. Ponty temporarily pulls back on electronic display for its own sake, even permitting some acoustic instruments to take the fore, and the recorded sound is drier and less lustrous. Nevertheless, Ponty's urbane Euro-sensibility can still be felt strongly in these carefully conceived and "orchestrated" jazz-rock compositions for his six-piece group. "Beach Girl," with its locomotive-driven chorus surrounded by folk-like passages, is the most memorable tune of the lot. If you can overlook the dated timbres of the ARP (a long-defunct company) synthesizers and the flat acoustics that place this music squarely within its decade, this music can still give pleasure to today's CD fans. —*Richard S. Ginell*

Civilized Evil / Jul. 6, 1980 / Atlantic ◆◆◆

All of the titles here make some kind of reference to cosmic issues of good and evil on the planet Earth, but the suggestive wordplay doesn't make this music much different from that on Jean-Luc Ponty's previous Atlantics. Ponty plays with his accustomed fluid virtuosity; the five-piece group ranges from standard Ponty fusion to mild funk; the rhythm section is sometimes more grandly recorded than before; and occasionally, one can hear some embryonic sequenced structures that would be explored further on in the decade. But one still gets the overall impression that Ponty has been around this block a few too many times; what was once fresh and musical has ossified into formula. —*Richard S. Ginell*

Mystical Adventures / Aug. 1981-Sep. 1981 / Atlantic ◆◆◆

Individual Choice / Mar. 1983-May 1983 / Atlantic ◆◆◆

Here is Ponty's radical break with his past, one that further tightened his control over his craft while ironically liberating his muse. In laying out his attractive new music on synthesizers and sequencers, emphasizing revolving ostinato patterns,

Ponty rejuvenated his melodic gift, and as a result, even in this controlled setting, his violin solos take on a new freshness and exuberance. Except for two tracks, Ponty does without a formal rhythm section—and on two other tracks, he goes it completely alone. Indeed, he does best of all when he has no one but himself to play with on "Computer Incantations for World Peace" and the lovely mood piece "Eulogy to Oscar Romero." Guest interloper George Duke (a fellow refugee from Frank Zappa's band) contributes a Minimoog solo to "In Spiritual Love," where Ponty provides his own percussive backing on rhythm computer. Even if one grumbles on principle about the reduction of spontaneity in Ponty's music over the Atlantic years, the musical end here absolutely justifies the means. Don't miss it. —*Richard S. Ginell*

Open Mind / Jul. 5, 1984 / Atlantic ◆◆◆

Ponty embarks on more experiments in the future-is-now world of synthesizers and sequencers, where the painstakingly programmed machines often seem to generate an irresistible momentum of their own. As on *Individual Choice*, Ponty's melodies are immediately appealing in an almost Continental manner, whether spelled out on violin, violectra, or on the sequenced synths that set up the ostinato underpinning. Ponty has even less help than before—no more than one or two supporting players on a few tracks. One of them is George Benson, who does his flavorful jazz/funk thing over Ponty's rhythm computer on "Modern Times Blues"; the other is Chick Corea, who appears on two tracks. This is almost as essential as *Individual Choice*, and in some ways, even more confident and assured. —*Richard S. Ginell*

Fables / Jul. 1985-Aug. 1985 / Atlantic ◆◆◆

Apparently Ponty was lonely for some company in the studio, for he brought in a full rhythm section (Scott Henderson, guitar; Baron Browne, bass; Rayford Griffin, drums) to accompany his impressive battery of electric violins, keyboards, drums and sequencers. The sound has opened up considerably, but again, Ponty continues to explore the high-tech, electronic, sequenced ostinato world that he opened the door to on *Individual Choice*. The music floats, gleams, and rocks along to sometimes rigid grooves in this mostly successful attempt to merge the sequencer-driven Ponty of the '80s with his jazz-rock incarnation of the '70s. It's a very even album, without any extreme peaks or dips, and Ponty dispenses with his sidemen entirely on the final two tracks, the last of which concludes the CD on a gently percolating electronic groove. —*Richard S. Ginell*

The Gift of Time / 1987 / Columbia ◆◆

The act of switching to Columbia did not have a substantial impact upon Jean-Luc Ponty—not yet, at least—for his debut with the label found him mining the repeating, sequencer-driven lode that he was exploring while on Atlantic. But there are two areas where there is a difference: the material is superior to that of *Fables*, more memorable and immediately winning in melodic and arpeggiated content, and the sound quality is considerably improved over that of much of his Atlantic output. The rhythm section of *Fables* returns, with Pat Thomi replacing Scott Henderson on guitar, and as before, they take a definite back seat to their leader's violins, synthesizers and electronic devices. Other points of note: "Between Sea and Sky" has a slightly Jamaican feel, and the lovely "Introspective Perceptions" (another of Ponty's notoriously portentous word pairings) is exactly what the title says it is, appropriately recorded solo. —*Richard S. Ginell*

Storytelling / 1989 / Columbia ◆◆◆◆

When this CD came out, it was violinist Jean-Luc Ponty's strongest in several years. Most of the originals have dense ensembles full of rhythmic patterns set by the keyboards for Ponty to play over. With the exception of "Chopin Prelude No. 20" (a violin improvisation in which the violinist is backed by just Clara Ponty's sober chordal piano), this date falls into the funky fusion area. The enthusiastic high-energy playing, colorful solos (Ponty is in splendid form) and catchy melodies make this a very worthwhile session; Grover Washington (on soprano) and keyboardist Patrice Rushen make guest appearances. —*Scott Yanow*

Tchokola / 1991 / Epic ◆◆◆

Every eight years, it seems, Jean-Luc Ponty picks himself up, gives himself a good shake, and switches direction. In 1967, he made his first life-changing visit to the US; 1975 found him going solo permanently as a jazz/rock icon; 1983 marked a switch to sequencer music; and in 1991, Ponty discovered African music. Taking advantage of the huge interest in African music in France, Ponty recorded his electric violin over the churning, hypnotic grooves of a coterie of visiting West African musicians in Paris, and the results are delicious. In one sense, not that much has changed, for while Ponty has thrown out the sequencers and electronic gizmos, his music remains grounded in repeated ostinato patterns—those provided by the Africans. Ponty dabbles in all kinds of grooves—the Nigerian juju, Cameroon's makossa (there is an especially swinging example of that on "Mouna Bowa"), the Afro-French Caribbean zouk, the sabar from Senegal, West Africa's mandingo, and a few others. On top of these, Ponty imposes his own distinctive melodic ideas on acoustic or electric violin, gingerly negotiating his way over the bumps of the tricky rhythms. At times, one feels that even this endlessly pliable virtuoso is not quite comfortable with these exotic idioms, but the music is so infectious that it usually sweeps him—and us—right along. Now, about 1999 . . . —*Richard S. Ginell*

Live at Chene Park / Jun. 29, 1996 / Atlantic ◆◆◆◆

Odeon Pope

b. Oct. 24, 1938, Ninety Six, South Carolina
Tenor Saxophone / Post-Bop
A fiery and often intense tenor saxophonist, Odeon Pope has been an important member of Max Roach's Quartet since 1969. Pope grew up in Philadelphia, took some important musical lessons from Ray Bryant, and had short associations with organist Jimmy McGriff and Art Blakey's Jazz Messengers. He first began teaming up with Roach in the late 1960s, although it would be another decade before he became a regular part of his group. Pope led Catalyst, a band that made four records in the '70s, and he put together the Saxophone Choir in 1977. Falling into the post-bop genre, the latter band consists of eight saxophones and a rhythm section and has been a part-time unit ever since. But Odeon Pope, who has recorded consistently stimulating dates as a leader for Moers and Soul Note, is best known for his many appearances and recordings with Roach, whom he officially joined in 1979. —*Scott Yanow*

Almost Like Me / Aug. 25, 1982 / Moers ◆◆◆◆

● **The Saxophone Shop** / Sep. 30, 1985-Oct. 1, 1985 / Soul Note ◆◆◆◆◆
Odeon Pope's "Saxophone Choir" is well titled. The tenor saxophonist is joined by three altos and three tenors (along with a standard rhythm section) for six of his originals and two other songs that he arranged. The saxophonists primarily function as "background singers," making their voices heard mostly as accompanists for the leader. It's an interesting concept. —*Scott Yanow*

The Ponderer / Mar. 12, 1990 / Soul Note ◆◆◆◆◆

Out for a Walk / Oct. 1990 / Moers ◆◆◆◆◆

Epitome / Oct. 4, 1993-Oct. 14, 1993 / Soul Note ◆◆◆◆

Art Porter

b. Little Rock, Arkansas **d.** Nov. 23, 1996, Thailand
Alto Saxophone, Soprano Saxophone / Crossover Jazz, Instrumental Pop, Soul
Crossover saxophonist Art Porter doubles on alto and soprano, and got his start playing in the early '90s on albums by Jeff Lorber, Tom Grant and Ramsey Lewis. For his debut as a leader—1992's *Pockey City* on Verve/Forecast—Porter looked to Lorber as well as Paulinho Da Costa, Buzz Feiten and Paul Pesco for support. Much of the same lineup appeared on his subsequent albums for Verve, with programs that maintained contemporary fusion/R&B. —*John Bush*

Pocket City / 1992 / Verve/Forecast ◆◆◆
A '92 session mixing fusion, R&B, and light jazz by Art Porter with a host of guest stars and participants, including Jeff Lorber, Paul Jackson, Jr., Buzz Feiten, Paul Pesco, Paulinho Da Costa, and Valeri Davis. There are also some vocals and elaborate production. —*Ron Wynn*

Straight to the Point / 1993 / Verve/Forecast ◆◆◆

● **Undercover** / 1994 / Verve/Forecast ◆◆◆◆

Lay Your Hands on Me / 1996 / Verve/Forecast ◆◆◆◆
This was Art Porter's final recording before his death in a tragic boating accident. Alternating between alto and soprano, Porter gets off some excellent solos, but this is primarily a crossover date (few of the ten originals are memorable) that is weakened by three throwaway R&B vocals and most successful as background music. However, despite the rather routine electronic backing, Porter shows that he really could play and was a fine R&B-influenced saxophonist who might very well have developed into an important force. —*Scott Yanow*

Chris Potter

b. Jan. 1, 1971, Chicago, IL
Alto Saxophone, Tenor Saxophone / Post-Bop
Although often overlooked in popularity polls, the talented and often adventurous Chris Potter shows a great deal of potential. His first instrument was the piano but when he was ten he began playing tenor and alto. At 18 he moved to New York and spent four years playing with Red Rodney's Quintet, mostly alto but impressing listeners with an occasional piano feature. Since then, he has performed with the Mingus Big Band, Paul Motian, Marian McPartland and John Patitucci among others and led his own dates for Criss Cross and Concord. —*Scott Yanow*

Presenting Chris Potter / Dec. 29, 1992 / Criss Cross ◆◆◆◆

● **Concentric Circles** / Dec. 1993 / Concord Jazz ◆◆◆◆◆
Only 23 at the time of this Concord CD, Chris Potter shows a great deal of originality in his explorative styles on alto and soprano while on tenor he alternates between sounding like John Coltrane (his "Dusk" is not all that different than "Naima") and Dewey Redman. All but two songs on this set are his originals and on some pieces Potter utilizes some overdubbing. Essentially a quintet session, this CD also contains some fine chance-taking solos from pianist Kenny Werner and guitarist John Hart with the music ranging from modal to freebop. —*Scott Yanow*

Pure / Jun. 14, 1994-Jun. 15, 1994 / Concord Jazz ◆◆◆◆

Concord Duo Series, Vol. 10 / Oct. 9, 1994 / Concord Jazz ◆◆◆◆

The Jazz Mentality: Show Business Is My Life / Oct. 17, 1994 / Koch ◆◆◆◆
Although the name of this group might lead one to think that it is a protest against the restrictiveness of "the jazz mentality," the brief liner notes make it clear that these four musicians are proud to be jazz artists. Chris Potter, a young giant, is the best-known player in this group, and he displays fairly original post-bop sounds on tenor, alto and soprano, but the rhythm section (pianist Steve Elmer, bassist Ralph Hamperian and drummer Myles Weinstein) is strong too. The music is advanced and fairly straightahead modern jazz. Among the highlights of the live set are "Show Business Is My Life" (a medium-tempo strut with a solid theme), "Quiet Moments" (one of six Steve Elmer originals), Bobby Timmons' funky jazz waltz "This Here" (listed as "Dis' Here"), which has a swinging Potter alto solo, Elmer's trio feature on "Solar," and numbers on which Potter emulates (at least part of the time) Dexter Gordon and Jackie McLean. Although not essential, this colorful set (which displays the continual growth of Chris Potter) has enough strong moments to make it easily recommended to collectors of the idiom. —*Scott Yanow*

Sundiatta / Dec. 12, 1995 / Criss Cross ◆◆◆◆

Moving In / Feb. 6, 1996-Feb. 7, 1996 / Concord Jazz ◆◆◆◆

● **Unspoken** / May 21, 1997-May 23, 1997 / Concord Jazz ◆◆◆◆
Working with drummer Jack DeJohnette, bassist Dave Holland and guitarist John Scofield, saxophonist Chris Potter recorded his most adventurous record to date with *Unspoken*. Although his powerhouse rhythm section sometimes overwhelms him, Potter flexes more creative muscle throughout *Unspoken*, resulting in an engaging, frequently provocative listen. —*Leo Stanley*

Bud Powell (Earl Powell)

b. Sep. 27, 1924, New York, NY, **d.** Jul. 31, 1966, New York, NY
Piano / Bop
One of the giants of the jazz piano, Bud Powell changed the way that virtually all post-swing pianists play their instruments. He did away with the left hand striding that had been considered essential earlier and used his left hand to state chords on an irregular basis. His right often played speedy single-note lines, essentially transforming Charlie Parker's vocabulary to the piano (although he developed parallel to Bird). Tragically, Bud Powell was a seriously ill genius. After being encouraged and tutored to an extent by his friend Thelonious Monk at jam sessions in the early '40s, Powell was with Cootie Williams' orchestra during 1943-45. In a racial incident, he was beaten on the head by police; Powell never fully recovered and would suffer from bad headaches and mental breakdowns throughout the remainder of his life. Despite this, he recorded some true gems during 1947-51 for Roost, Blue Note and Verve, composing such major works as "Dance of the Infidels, "Hallucinations" (also known as "Budo"), "Un Poco Loco," "Bouncing with Bud," and "Tempus Fugit." Even early on, his erratic behavior resulted in lost opportunities (Charlie Parker supposedly told Miles Davis that he would not hire Powell because "he's even crazier than me!") but Powell's playing during this period was often miraculous. A breakdown in 1951 and hospitalization that resulted in electroshock treatments weakened him but Powell was still capable of playing at his best now and then, most notably at the 1953 Massey Hall Concert. Generally, in the 1950s his Blue Notes find him in excellent form while he is much more erratic on his Verve recordings. His warm welcome and lengthy stay in Paris (1959-64) extended his life a bit but even here Powell spent part of 1962-63 in the hospital. He returned to New York in 1964, disappeared after a few concerts, and did not live through 1966. In later years, Bud Powell's recordings and performances could be so intense as to be scary, but other times he sounded quite sad. However, his influence on jazz (particularly up until the rise of McCoy Tyner and Bill Evans in the 1960s) was very strong and he remains one of the greatest jazz pianists of all time. —*Scott Yanow*

● **Early Years of a Genius (1944-1948)** / Jan. 1944-Dec. 19, 1948 / Mythic Sound ◆◆◆◆◆
This set is the first of ten CDs of privately recorded Bud Powell recordings owned by his friend Francis Paudras. Powell's greatest fans will want all of the releases, but some are better than others. *Vol. 1* is the most historic for ten selections feature the innovative pianist at age 20 in 1944 as a sideman with trumpeter Cootie Williams' Orchestra and there are some unique moments. Powell plays a duet with Wil-

liams on "West End Blues," joins in with Williams' sextet (which also includes altoist Eddie "Cleanhead" Vinson and tenorman Eddie "Lockjaw" Davis) on "Smack Me" and backs guest Ella Fitzgerald on two numbers in addition to playing six songs with the full big band. This valuable set concludes with versions of "Perdido" and "Indiana" that Powell performed at the Royal Roost on Dec. 19, 1948, with an all-star group including trumpeter Benny Harris, trombonist J.J. Johnson, altoist Lee Konitz and clarinetist Buddy DeFranco among others. Bop collectors will have to get this one. —*Scott Yanow*

Bud Powell Trio Plays / Jan. 10, 1947+1953 / Roulette ✦✦✦✦✦
All of the music on this single CD is included in the Blue Note four-CD "complete" set (the best way to acquire these important performances); however, listeners who do not have the larger reissue will not go wrong by getting this CD. The first eight selections (which find the pianist joined by bassist Curley Russell and drummer Max Roach) are from Bud Powell's first trio date, and he is in prime form on such numbers as "I'll Remember April," "Someboy Loves Me" and "Bud's Bubble." The second session (with bassist George Duvivier and drummer Art Taylor in 1953) does not quite reach the same heights, but it does contain some fine playing from the founder of bop piano. —*Scott Yanow*

☆ **Complete Blue Note and Roost Recordings** / Jan. 10, 1947-Dec. 29, 1958 / Blue Note ✦✦✦✦✦
Although pianist Bud Powell recorded some great albums elsewhere (most notably his first couple of sessions for Verve), on a whole his Blue Note records were his most significant and definitive. This four-CD set has all of the music from his five Blue Note albums, his two sessions for the Roost label and all known alternate takes. Powell literally changed the way that the piano is played in jazz and this magnificent set has more than its share of classics. In addition to the many trio performances, trombonist Curtis Fuller sits in on three numbers, there are a few solo cuts and one date features Powell at the head of a quintet with trumpeter Fats Navarro and the young tenor Sonny Rollins. Although there are a few faltering moments in the later dates, this essential release (unlike the similar Verve reissue) is quite consistent. —*Scott Yanow*

Jazz Profile, Vol. 8 / Jan. 10, 1947-Dec. 29, 1958 / Blue Note ✦✦✦
This is an effective single-CD sampling of the innovative pianist Bud Powell, although collectors will want to get the much more valuable four-CD "complete" Blue Note set, which is easily available. Powell is heard in trios dating from 1947 (originally out on Roulette), 1951, 1953 and 1958. In addition, he takes the intriguing "Bud on Bach" solo and jams "Wail" and "Dance of the Infidels" with a 1949 quintet also including trumpeter Fats Navarro and tenor saxophonist Sonny Rollins. Not all of the classics are here (including "Tempus Fugit," "Celia," "Bouncing with Bud" and "Un Poco Loco"), but the release can act as an introduction to beginners not familiar with the founder of bebop piano. —*Scott Yanow*

New York All Star Sessions / Dec. 19, 1948-1957 / Bandstand ✦✦✦✦
This LP contains a variety of live recordings featuring Bud Powell, mostly during his prime years. Three of the selections (from a Christmas 1949 Carnegie Hall Concert) have been reissued on CD by Jass but otherwise the performances are quite rare. Highlights include a version of "Dance of the Infidels" from 1953 with Charlie Parker, "Woody 'n You" from the same year with Dizzy Gillespie and two songs from a Dec. 1948 all-star group that includes trumpeter Benny Harris, trombonist J.J. Johnson, clarinetist Buddy DeFranco and altoist Lee Konitz. Although not essential, this collector's LP should greatly interest bop fans. —*Scott Yanow*

Complete Bud Powell on Verve / Jan. 1949-Sep. 13, 1956 / Verve ✦✦✦✦✦
This five-CD deluxe set contains an impressive 150-page booklet and reissues every scrap of music that the innovative pianist Bud Powell recorded for Verve. The first disc has the best music, four truly outstanding sessions from 1949-51. The other performances (trio sides from 1954-56) are much more erratic, particularly the alternate takes, with gems followed by completely lost solos. Bop fans will want this set but more general collectors are advised to pick up The Blue Notes first. —*Scott Yanow*

★ **The Amazing Bud Powell, Vol. 1** / Aug. 8, 1949-May 1, 1951 / Blue Note ✦✦✦✦✦
The CD reissue of the two LPs titled *The Amazing Bud Powell* puts the important recordings in chronological order (which it wasn't in the LP version) and adds some alternate takes; all of the music has also been included in a definitive four-CD box set. Although the latter is the best way to acquire the important performances, this CD gives one a strong sampling of pianist Bud Powell at his best. Powell is heard on a classic session with trumpeter Fats Navarro and tenor saxophonist Sonny Rollins (which is highlighted by exciting versions of "Dance of the Infidels," "52nd Street Theme" and "Bouncing with Bud") and in a trio for "Over the Rainbow" and three versions of his intense "Un Poco Loco." —*Scott Yanow*

The Complete Bud Powell Blue Note Recordings (1949-1958) / Aug. 8, 1949-Dec. 29, 1958 / Mosaic ✦✦✦✦✦

The Amazing Bud Powell, Vol. 2 / May 1, 1951-Aug. 14, 1953 / Blue Note ✦✦✦✦
These two CD volumes (all of the music has also been reissued on a definitive, "complete" Blue Note Bud Powell four-CD set) differ from the original two LPs in that, in addition to the inclusion of some alternate takes, they are programmed in strict chronological order. The influential bebop pioneer (who not only set the standard for bop pianists but largely invented the style) is heard on fine trio performances from 1951 (with bassist Curly Russell and drummer Max Roach) and 1953 (during which he is matched with bassist George Duvivier and drummer Art Taylor). Highlights include "A Night in Tunisia," "Reets and I," "I Want to Be Happy" and "Glass Enclosure." —*Scott Yanow*

Inner Fires / Apr. 5, 1953 / Elektra ✦✦✦✦
This LP features trio performances by pianist Bud Powell, bassist Charles Mingus and drummer Roy Haynes that were recorded live at a Washington, DC club;hey were released for the first time in 1982. Powell is in consistently exciting form (this was one of his good nights) and the musicians sound inspired and creative during the set of bop-oriented standards. This now out-of-print LP concludes with a couple of excerpts from Bud Powell interviews held in 1963, giving listeners a rare chance to hear his voice. —*Scott Yanow*

Jazz at Massey Hall, Vol. 2 / May 15, 1953 / Original Jazz Classics ✦✦✦✦

Burning in the USA (1953-1955) / 1953-Sep. 1955 / Mythic Sound ✦✦✦
The second of ten CDs of previously unknown and privately recorded Bud Powell performances released by his friend Francis Paudras has a variety of rewarding and fairly exciting renditions. Most of the selections (from 1953 and 1955) are with trios (often matching the pianist with bassist Oscar Pettiford and Art Blakey or Roy Haynes on drums) but there is a rare outing with a big band ("Big Band Blues") and two selections ("Woody 'n You" and "Salt Peanuts") with trumpeter Dizzy Gillespie, bassist Charles Mingus and drummer Max Roach that are listed as being recorded at the famous Massey Hall concert in 1953; the year is right but the location is probably wrong since that concert was fully documented by the Debut label. Bud Powell fanatics are advised to search for all ten of the Mythic Sound releases, although more general listeners should pick and choose; this is not one of the most essential ones. —*Scott Yanow*

Strictly Powell / Oct. 5, 1956 / RCA ✦✦✦✦
Bud Powell's two dates for RCA in 1956-57 are better than expected. Although troubled, Powell actually plays better here than on his Verves of the period. Backed by bassist George Duvivier and drummer Art Taylor, the pianist is heard in fine form during a program of mostly medium-tempo and slower performances, particularly on "There'll Never Be Another You," "Time Was," "They Didn't Believe Me" and five of his originals. There are no extra cuts on the LP-length CD reissue but Bud Powell collectors who own his classic Blue Note dates should give this music a listen. —*Scott Yanow*

Time Was / Oct. 5, 1956+Feb. 11, 1957 / Bluebird ✦✦✦
Pianist Bud Powell's two recording sessions for Victor during 1956-57 resulted in 22 selections; this CD contains 18 of them. Powell was not in the best of shape during this period and he is erratic in these trio outings with bassist George Duvivier and drummer Art Taylor. Quite frequently a brilliant chorus is followed by one in which Powell gets lost, making the performances very interesting, to say the least. —*Scott Yanow*

Swingin' with Bud / Feb. 11, 1957 / RCA ✦✦✦✦
The immortal pianist Bud Powell's two RCA sets from 1956-57 have been unjustly neglected through the years. Superior to his Verve releases from the time (although not on the same level as his Blue Notes), Powell is in generally good form on this trio session with bassist George Duvivier and drummer Art Taylor. Highlights include "Like Someone in Love," "Salt Peanuts," "Shaw 'Nuff" and "Oblivion" (the latter is one of four Powell originals on the program). The set is not essential but is easily recommended to bop collectors. —*Scott Yanow*

The Amazing Bud Powell, Vol. 3 / Aug. 3, 1957 / Blue Note ✦✦✦✦✦
Bud Powell's playing in the late '50s (just prior to his move to Paris) found the troubled pianist in erratic form, often struggling to make it through songs he had written. However, his three Blue Note recordings from the era (which include the slightly later *Time Waits* and *The Scene Changes*) feature Powell in surprisingly inspired form; all of the releases have since been reissued on a comprehensive CD set. *Bud!* (which is subtitled *The Amazing Bud Powell, Vol. 3*) has five trio performances with bassist Paul Chambers and drummer Art Taylor (highlighted by "Bud on Bach" and "Some Soul") and three standards on which the group is joined by trombonist Curtis Fuller. This strong bop set is well worth getting. —*Scott Yanow*

Bud Plays Bird / Oct. 14, 1957-Jan. 30, 1958 / Roulette ✦✦✦✦
Previously unissued until 1996, this trio session by pianist Bud Powell with bassist George Duvivier and drummer Art Taylor is better than his Verve recordings of the period if not quite up to the level of his earlier classic Blue Note dates. Actually, it is a mystery how such excellent music could be unknown and go unreleased for so

long. Powell performs 13 Charlie Parker compositions (including two versions of "Big Foot") and Dizzy Gillespie's "Salt Peanuts." Although there are some minor missteps, the music is quite enjoyable and generally hard-swinging with the more memorable performances including "Straw 'Nuff," "Yardbird Suite," "Confirmation" and "Ko Ko." —*Scott Yanow*

Cookin' at Saint Germain (1957-1959) / 1957-1959 / Mythic Sound ✦✦✦✦
For the third of ten CDs taken from tapes donated by Francis Paudras, pianist Bud Powell is heard in generally excellent form. Most of his performances (all of which were recorded in Paris in 1957 or 1959) feature the bebop innovator in a trio with bassist Pierre Michelot and drummer Kenny Clarke; four of the songs add the always-joyous trumpet of Clark Terry and three of those pieces also feature Barney Wilen on tenor. The sound quality is decent and Bud Powell was definitely "on" for these jams. —*Scott Yanow*

Groovin' at the Blue Note (1959-1961) / 1957-Dec. 17, 1961 / Mythic Sound ✦✦✦✦
The fifth of ten Bud Powell CDs taken from the private tapes of Francis Paudras features the innovative pianist in fine form. Best are three selections (over half of the music) on which Powell, bassist Pierre Michelot and drummer Kenny Clarke are joined by the always-swinging tenor Zoot Sims. All of the music on this release was recorded at the Blue Note club in Paris including a version of "How High the Moon" from 1957 that has trumpeter Dizzy Gillespie and Barney Wilen on tenor making Powell's trio a quintet. This is one of the better releases in the valuable series. —*Scott Yanow*

Time Waits / May 25, 1958 / Blue Note ✦✦✦✦
This set from pianist Bud Powell (which has been reissued on CD in a "complete" four-CD set) is most notable for having the debut versions of seven of Powell's compositions; most memorable are "Time Waits," "Monopoly" and especially "John's Abbey." With bassist Sam Jones and drummer Philly Joe Jones completing the trio, Powell is in surprisingly fine form throughout the enjoyable session, creating music that is far superior to his later Verve recordings. —*Scott Yanow*

The Scene Changes / Dec. 29, 1958 / Blue Note ✦✦✦✦
This CD reissue of pianist Bud Powell's final Blue Note session (the music is also available in a definitive four-CD set) adds an alternate take of "Comin' Up" to the original nine-song program; all are Powell originals. While none of the tunes caught on as standards, most (particularly "Cleopatra's Dream," "Crossin' the Channel" and "The Scene Changes") are memorable. All of Bud Powell's Blue Note records (including this trio outing with bassist Paul Chambers and drummer Art Taylor) feature the innovative pianist in top form. —*Scott Yanow*

Bud in Paris / Dec. 12, 1959-Oct. 14, 1960 / Xanadu ✦✦✦
Pianist Bud Powell's move to France in 1959 helped revive his career, getting him away from the pressures and temptations of New York and probably lengthening his life by a few years. This Xanadu LP features some privately recorded performances with his trio (which includes bassist Pierre Michelot and drummer Kenny Clarke), a pair of heated duets ("Idaho" and "Perdido") with tenor great Johnny Griffin and four quartets with the tenor of Barney Wilen (along with Michelot and Clarke). The recording quality is decent if not of studio quality, but the passion in the playing generally comes through and Powell's fans will want to search for this one. —*Scott Yanow*

The Complete Essen Jazz Festival Concert / Apr. 2, 1960 / Black Lion ✦✦✦✦✦
Pianist Bud Powell is heard in top form throughout this CD, playing six selections with his all-star trio (which also includes bassist Oscar Pettiford and drummer Kenny Clarke) and three songs on which the trio is joined by the great tenor Coleman Hawkins. There is plenty of classic bebop throughout the concert performance with Powell mostly sticking to standards (along with his original "John's Abbey"); Hawkins is best on "Stuffy." This release is recommended as a fine example of the playing of these classic masters. —*Scott Yanow*

A Tribute to Cannonball / Dec. 15, 1961 / Columbia/Legacy ✦✦✦✦
Not released until 1979, and then under tenor saxophonist Don Byas' name, this 1997 CD reissue has pianist Bud Powell listed first as a co-leader with Byas. In any case, the music (produced by Cannonball Adderley, but certainly not a tribute to him) features Byas and Powell in a quintet with trumpeter Idrees Sulieman, bassist Pierre Michelot and drummer Kenny Clarke. Other than two Pierre Michelot songs, including two versions of "Jackie My Little Cat," the repertoire is filled with bebop standards such as "Good Bait," a memorable "Jeannine" and "Just One of Those Things." Both Byas (who had hardly recorded since 1955) and the erratic Powell are heard in superior form. A previously unheard alternate take of "Cherokee" (which is missing its very beginning) has a real surprise in a solo by the producer—apparently, altoist Adderley could not resist the opportunity to jam with Byas and Powell. —*Scott Yanow*

A Portrait of Thelonious / Dec. 17, 1961 / Columbia ✦✦✦✦
This CD reissue is one of the most rewarding Bud Powell recordings to come from his period in France. Powell (along with bassist Pierre Michelot and drummer Kenny Clarke) explores four of Thelonious Monk's tunes, Earl Bostic's "No Name Blues" and the standard "There Will Never Be Another You" but it is the final two numbers ("I Ain't Foolin'" and "Squatty") that really find the bop master at his most spirited and swinging. This very rewarding CD releases for the first time the alternate take (a faster rendition without a clear melody) of "Squatty," a song that (based on its original version) deserves to be revived. One oddity: The applause heard throughout this release was added on later because this was actually a studio album. —*Scott Yanow*

Relaxin' at Home (1961-1964) / 1961-1964 / Mythic Sound ✦✦
The fourth of ten CDs in the Mythic Sound series of privately recorded Bud Powell performances is the least significant. Powell is heard playing solo piano quite loosely at Francis Paudras' home, the recording quality is erratic and (despite some creative outbursts) some of the selections are throwaways. From the historic standpoint there are a few unique renditions including Powell playing (and singing) "The Christmas Song" and a brief version of "La Marseillaise." But overall, this CD is strictly for Bud Powell completists. —*Scott Yanow*

Round Midnight at the Blue Note / 1962 / Dreyfus ✦✦✦
The music on this CD (released for the first time in 1994) features a group accurately dubbed "the Three Bosses." Comprising pianist Bud Powell, bassist Pierre Michelot and drummer Kenny Clarke, this was a tight trio that lived up to its potential. The innovative pianist is in excellent form, performing four Thelonious Monk tunes along with four jazz standards. High points include "Shaw Nuff" and "Night in Tunisia." The only problem is the brevity of this CD, which at 35 minutes should have been twice as long. —*Scott Yanow*

At the Golden Circle, Vol. 1 / Apr. 19, 1962 / Steeple Chase ✦✦✦
Bud Powell sounds as if he enjoyed his engagement at the Golden Circle in Stockholm, Sweden. Five CDs have been released from two of his nights at the club and they find him playing in generally good form. Accompanied by a couple of local musicians (bassist Torbjorn Hultcrantz and drummer Sune Spangberg), Powell on the first volume is at his best on "Move," "Relaxin' at Camarillo" and an emotional "I Remember Clifford"; two of the other three songs are brief sketches that are under two minutes long. None of the sets are essential (the first volume clocks in at just 33 minutes) but they will easily be enjoyed by Bud Powell fans. —*Scott Yanow*

At the Golden Circle, Vol. 2 / Apr. 19, 1962 / Steeple Chase ✦✦✦
The second of five CDs taken from a gig by Bud Powell in Stockholm in which he was joined by a pair of obscure local players (bassist Torbjorn Hultcrantz and drummer Sune Spangberg) has its strong moments. Highlights include Thelonious Monk's "Hackensack," "Moose the Mooche," "Star Eyes" and particularly a 15-minute version of Oscar Pettiford's "Blues in the Closet." The entire series is worth picking up by listeners who enjoy bop-based piano; Powell is generally in fine form. —*Scott Yanow*

At the Golden Circle, Vol. 3 / Apr. 19, 1962 / Steeple Chase ✦✦✦
The third of five CDs that document two nights from pianist Bud Powell's 1962 appearances at the Golden Circle in Stockholm, makes up for its low quantity (just 34 minutes) with some high quality. Powell and the two local musicians (bassist Torbjorn Hultcrantz and drummer Sune Spangberg) stretch out on a version of "Swedish Pastry" that is over 18 minutes, sound quite emotional on "I Remember Clifford" and jam a shorter "I Hear Music." This five-CD series should really have been three sets but it contains some valuable music and enjoyable playing. —*Scott Yanow*

At the Golden Circle, Vol. 4 / Apr. 23, 1962 / Steeple Chase ✦✦✦
The fourth of five CDs taken from two nights that Bud Powell performed at Stockholm's Golden Circle, has repeats of some tunes from the earlier date (April 19) but the playing is completely different. Accompanied by bassist Torbjorn Hultcrantz and drummer Sune Spangberg, Powell generally sounds in fairly good form for the period with the highlights including "Moose the Mooche," "Blues in the Closet" and Powell's own "John's Abbey." —*Scott Yanow*

At the Golden Circle, Vol. 5 / Apr. 23, 1962 / Steeple Chase ✦✦✦
The fifth and final CD from pianist Bud Powell's 1962 stay at the Golden Circle in Stockholm has as its high points versions of "52nd Street Theme" and "Straight, No Chaser" (the latter lasts 20 minutes); on the minus side is a throwaway (and off-mike) Powell vocal on "This Is No Laughin' Matter." On a whole, this series is not as essential as the Blue Notes, but has its strong moments and is worth picking up by lovers of bop piano and the troubled but brilliant Bud Powell. —*Scott Yanow*

Bouncing With Bud / Apr. 26, 1962 / Delmark ✦✦✦✦✦
This Delmark CD is an excellent set by the great pianist Bud Powell in a trio with the teenage bassist Niels Pederson and drummer William Shiopffe. Recorded in Copenhagen, the session features Powell exploring seven bop standards (including

his own "Bouncing with Bud") and "The Best Thing for You." All eight selections (which put the emphasis on faster material other than "I Remember Clifford") showcase Bud Powell during his European renaissance period, giving pianists a definitive lesson in playing bop. —*Scott Yanow*

Bud Powell in Paris / Feb. 1963 / Reprise ✦✦✦✦

Considering how late it was in his career, Bud Powell was in surprisingly good spirits at this live session with bassist Gilbert Rovere and drummer Kansas Fields. The innovative pianist stretches out on nine bop standards including two he had written ("Reets and I" and "Parisian Thoroughfare"); in addition, there are previously unreleased versions of "Indiana" and "B-Flat Blues." Far superior to most of his 1955-58 sessions, this was one of Powell's best late-period recordings; he is in near-prime form throughout. —*Scott Yanow*

Writin' for Duke (1963) / Feb. 1963 / Mythic Sound ✦✦✦

In Feb. 1963, Duke Ellington sponsored a Reprise recording date by Bud Powell (in a trio with bassist Gilbert Rovere and drummer Kansas Fields) that resulted in the album *Bud in Paris*. This set, released as part of Mythic Sound's ten-CD series of privately recorded sessions featuring the innovative bop pianist, comprises outtakes and previously unreleased songs from that studio date. There are many highlights to the excellent session including performances of some of Powell's lesser-known originals ("Bud's Blue Bossa," "Tune for Duke," "For My Friends," "Get It Back," "Trapped," "Free" and "Rue de Clichy"), a few of which deserve to be revived. Also memorable are an emotional "I Got It Bad" and a strong version of "Dear Old Stockholm." —*Scott Yanow*

Strictly Confidential / 1963-1964 / Black Lion ✦✦

These informal performances find the great but ill-fated pianist Bud Powell playing a series of relaxed solos in Francis Paudras' apartment in Paris. The recording quality is just ok and there are some missteps in Powell's solos but there are also moments of interest, particularly his striding on a few of the numbers. This CD is particularly recommended to Bud Powell collectors, although more general listeners should pick up his Blue Notes first. —*Scott Yanow*

The Invisible Cage / Jul. 31, 1964 / Black Lion ✦✦✦

This rather late Bud Powell session is better than expected and probably his last worthwhile recording. Performed shortly before he returned to New York and only two years prior to his death, Powell is at his best on the uptempo material and at his most erratic on the intense ballads. Accompanied ably by bassist Michel Gaudry and drummer Art Taylor, the innovative pianist (even with a few missteps) is mostly in excellent form, particularly on "Like Someone in Love," "Blues for Bouffemont" and his calypso "Una Noche con Francis." —*Scott Yanow*

Blues for Bouffemont / Jul. 1964-Aug. 1964 / Black Lion ✦✦✦

Teeming, sometimes ragged but always blistering piano tracks from Bud Powell, recorded in 1964. These were done in recognition of Powell's stint at Bouffemont following his near breakdown. He and drummer Art Taylor are the dominant musicians, while either Michel Gaudray or Guy Hayat on bass and other drummer Jacques Gervais are competent, but not in Powell or Taylor's class. —*Ron Wynn*

Salt Peanuts / Aug. 1964 / Black Lion ✦✦✦

In Aug. 1964, pianist Bud Powell and his friend/guardian Francis Paudras went on vacation to Edenville on the coast of France. Powell played at a small club each night in a very relaxed atmosphere. This CD contains some of the performances, four songs with a trio (that includes bassist Guy Hayat and drummer Jacques Gervais) and, best of all, three hot numbers that feature tenor great Johnny Griffin who makes the group a quartet. The recording quality is a little erratic on this set but Powell often sounds quite inspired. —*Scott Yanow*

Holidays in Edenville (1964) / Aug. 10, 1964-Aug. 12, 1964 / Mythic Sound ✦✦✦

On the eighth of ten CDs in Mythic Sound's valuable series of privately recorded Bud Powell performances, the masterful pianist is heard playing informally in a small club on the coast of France shortly before he made the fatal decision to return to the US. These previously unreleased selections feature Powell with a young trio (bassist Guy Hayat and drummer Jacques Gervais) and (on two of the ten songs including a 17-minute version of "Hot House") joyfully welcoming the great tenor Johnny Griffin to the bandstand. The recording quality is sometimes a little erratic but Powell is in suprisingly strong form this late in his career; this set should be checked out by bop collectors. —*Scott Yanow*

Award at Birdland (1964) / Oct. 1, 1964 / Mythic Sound ✦✦✦

When pianist Bud Powell returned to the US after five relatively happy years in France, he played a successful engagement at Birdland and then had a quick decline before passing away in 1966. This CD from the Mythic Sound label was Powell's last hurrah—he would only record one more studio album in his career—and it features him playing in a trio with bassist John Ore and drummer J.C. Moses at Birdland. The set begins with Powell receiving an obscure award (and saying a few words) before he performs a dozen numbers; all are standards except for his own "Monopoly." Although not the strongest Bud Powell set available (and

the recording quality is quite erratic), this interesting release hints at what might have been and shows that Powell could still play well this late in his troubled life. —*Scott Yanow*

Ups and Downs / 1964-1965 / Mainstream ✦✦

This CD reissue of the Mainstream LP states in Nat Hentoff's liner notes that the performances are from the mid-'50s and that pianist Bud Powell is heard at the peak of his powers. Wrong on both counts. Actually ,this set comprises Powell's final recordings, dating from late 1964 to early 1965, shortly following his return to New York after several years of relative security in Paris. The great bop innovator had declined greatly since his prime days but actually plays better than one might expect. The bassist and drummer have never been identified. This set is important historically but obviously there are many more rewarding Bud Powell recordings to acquire first. —*Scott Yanow*

Mel Powell (Melvin Epstein)

b. Feb. 12, 1923, New York, NY
Piano, Arranger / Swing

One of the finest swing pianists and a prodigy, Mel Powell was playing piano and writing important arrangements for Benny Goodman by the time he was 18. He had previously played with Bobby Hackett, George Brunis and Zutty Singleton (1939), was the intermission pianist at Nick's and worked in the short-lived Muggsy Spanier big band. During his stay with BG, Powell and the clarinetist struck up a lifelong friendship; among his arrangements for Goodman were "The Earl," "Mission to Moscow," "Clarinade" and "Jersey Bounce." After a period working for the CBS orchestra under Raymond Scott (1942), Powell was one of the stars of the Glenn Miller Army Air Force Band. Powell, whose style was reminiscent of Teddy Wilson's, recorded with Goodman during 1945-47, led a few record dates (his first one was in 1942) and worked in the studios. However, after studying with Paul Hindemith at Yale (1952), he switched his career and became a classical composer. Powell did record some superior jazz dates for Vanguard during 1953-55 and sat in with Bobby Hackett in the mid-'60s but was otherwise occupied completely outside of jazz. After decades of work as a well-respected serial composer, Mel Powell returned to jazz for cruises in 1986 and 1987 that were recorded by Chiaroscuro. However a muscular disease in his legs has since knocked him out of action. —*Scott Yanow*

Unavailable Mel Powell / Dec. 10, 1947-Dec. 31, 1947 / Pausa ✦✦✦✦✦

● Return of Mel Powell / Oct. 21, 1987 / Chiaroscuro ✦✦✦✦

The first jazz recording by pianist Mel Powell since 1955 (in the interim he gained a strong reputation as a modern classical composer), this CD also signalled the rebirth of Hank O'Neal's Chiaroscuro label in 1989. Recorded at the Floating Jazz Festival aboard the S.S. Norway, the set features Powell with altoist Benny Carter, guitarist Howard Alden, bassist Milt Hinton and drummer Louie Bellson performing six standard swing-era songs. Amazingly Powell, who had rarely played jazz or much piano during the previous three decades, sounds in near-prime form and the music is quite delightful. This CD concludes with a 20-minute "Jazzspeak" in which Powell discusses his life and his earlier decision to leave jazz. —*Scott Yanow*

Chano Pozo

b. Jan. 7, 1915, Havana, Cuba, d. Dec. 2, 1948, New York, NY
Percussion / Afro-Cuban Jazz, Latin Jazz, Salsa

Chano Pozo played a major role in the founding of Latin-jazz which was essentially a mixture of bebop and Cuban folk music. He gained his musical background from Cuban religious cults. After moving to New York in 1947, he met Dizzy Gillespie who enthusiastically added him to his bebop big band. Among his features with Dizzy were "Cubana Be/Cubana Bop," "Tin Tin Deo" and "Manteca"; Pozo co-wrote the latter two. Unfortunately Chano Pozo had a hot temper and he was killed in a Harlem bar a month shy of his 34th birthday. —*Scott Yanow*

Preservation Hall Jazz Band

f. 1961
Group / New Orleans Jazz, Dixieland

During the 1950s, although the traditional jazz scene in New Orleans had many top players, there was no one center for the city's veteran greats to play. In 1961, art dealer Larry Borenstein opened a building he called Preservation Hall. The young tuba player Allan Jaffe ran the hall and organized tours for the musicians who often performed there, naming the band after the venue. In the early days, the key musicians included, at various times, trumpeters Kid Thomas Valentine, Punch Miller or De De Pierce, trombonists Louis Nelson or Jim Robinson, clarinetists George Lewis, Albert Burbank or Willie Humphrey, and pianists Joseph Robichaux, Billie Pierce or Sweet Emma Barrett. By the early 1970s, trumpeter Percy Humphrey, his brother Willie on clarinet, and trombonist Jim Robinson (who, after his death in 1976, was succeeded by Frank Demond) usually comprised the front line. The deaths of the Humphreys and Percy's occasional fill-in Kid Sheik Colar in the mid-1990s would seem to signal the end of this group. In general, the group's best recordings were their early ones under the leadership of Barrett and the Pierces; they also cut three hit-and-miss albums for Columbia during 1976-92. The Preservation Hall Jazz Band's worldwide tours resulted in a great deal of goodwill, permitting supporters to somehow ignore the group's very erratic musicianship. —*Scott Yanow*

☆ **New Orleans, Vol. 1** / 1976-1977 / Columbia ✦✦✦✦✦

★ **The Best of Preservation Hall Jazz Band** / 1976-1987 / Columbia ✦✦✦✦✦

New Orleans, Vol. 2 / Dec. 3, 1981-Dec. 4, 1981 / Columbia ✦✦✦✦

New Orleans, Vol. 3 / 1982 / Columbia ✦✦✦

New Orleans, Vol. 4 / 1987 / Columbia ✦✦✦

Andrè Previn (Andreas Ludwig Priwin)

b. Apr. 6, 1929, Berlin, Germany
Piano / Cool, Bop

One of the most versatile musicians on the planet, Andre Previn has amassed considerable credentials as a jazz pianist, despite carving out separate lives first as a Hollywood arranger and composer, and then a world-class classical conductor, pianist and composer. Always fluid, melodic and swinging, with elements of Bud Powell, Oscar Peterson and Horace Silver mixed with a faultless technique, Previn hasn't changed much over the decades but can always be counted upon for polished, reliable performances at the drop of a hat.

He started piano lessons in his native Berlin before the Nazi threat forced his family to move to Paris in 1938 and the US the following year. Settling in Los Angeles, the wunderkind Previn began working as a jazz pianist, an arranger for MGM, and a recording artist for Sunset Records while still in high school—and by his 18th year, his first recordings for RCA Victor had racked up substantial sales. Originally swing-oriented, Previn discovered bop in 1950 just before his induction into the Army. Upon returning to Los Angeles, Previn went into overdrive, gigging as a jazz pianist, scoring films and playing chamber music. Forming a smooth boppish trio with Shelly Manne and Leroy Vinnegar, Previn scored a huge crossover hit with an album of jazz interpretations of *My Fair Lady*, which in turn led to a series of like-minded albums of Broadway scores and kicked off an industry trend. By 1962, Previn started to make the transition away from Hollywood toward becoming a full-time classical conductor, dropping his jazz activities entirely. He stayed away from jazz for 27 years, with the exceptions of a handful of sessions with Ella Fitzgerald and classical violinist/dabbler Itzhak Perlman. Indeed, in 1984, he was quoted as saying that jazz was "an expendable art form" for him. But in March 1989, shortly before resigning from the Los Angeles Philharmonic in a dispute with management, Previn returned to jazz with a trio album for Telarc with Ray Brown and Joe Pass, showing that he had not lost an iota of his abilities. Since then, he has returned frequently to the studio as a jazz pianist for Telarc, Angel, Deutsche Grammophon and DRG when not freelancing as a conductor or composing classical scores. —*Richard S. Ginell*

Previn at Sunset / Oct. 13, 1945-May 31, 1946 / Black Lion ✦✦✦✦✦

The Fats Waller Song Book / June 24, 1953 / Simitar ✦✦✦✦
This LP-length CD reissue from 1997 features pianist Andre Previn and an unidentified rhythm section (probably bassist Buddy Clark and drummer Shelly Manne) performing eight Fats Waller songs and Previn's likable "Fatstuff." The pianist, whose style by the mid-1950s was much closer to Dave Brubeck than to Waller, sounds fairly modern on such tunes as "Ain't Misbehavin'," "Honeysuckle Rose" and "Black and Blue," but shows respect for the melodies. The music swings competently in a West Coast jazz fashion, and Previn's solos are quite spontaneous. —*Scott Yanow*

Li'l Abner / Feb. 6, 1957 / Contemporary ✦✦✦

Double Play! / Apr. 30, 1957+May 11, 1957 / Original Jazz Classics ✦✦✦✦
Pianists Andre Previn and Russ Freeman team up with drummer Shelly Manne in a trio to play eight of their originals (along with the standard "Take Me out to the Ball Game"), all given titles having to do with baseball. This was advertised as the first time that two pianists recorded what was then modern jazz together. Previn and Freeman had very complementary styles, making it difficult to know who was playing what when although a complete play-by-play is included. —*Scott Yanow*

Pal Joey / Oct. 28, 1957-Oct. 29, 1957 / Original Jazz Classics ✦✦✦✦

Gigi / Apr. 7, 1958-Apr. 8, 1958 / Original Jazz Classics ✦✦✦

Andre Previn Plays Vernon Duke / Aug. 12, 1958-Aug. 30, 1958 / Original Jazz Classics ✦✦✦✦

● **Jazz: King Size** / Nov. 26, 1958 / Original Jazz Classics ✦✦✦✦✦
The multitalented Andre Previn is heard on this straight CD reissue of a Contemporary LP as the leader of a trio with bassist Red Mitchell and drummer Frankie Capp. Previn always had his own swing/bop piano style and he is in top form on two of his originals (including the bluish "Much Too Late") and four superior standards. This fine release gives one an excellent example of Previn's skills as a jazz pianist. —*Scott Yanow*

Andre Previn Plays Jerome Kern / Feb. 26, 1959+Mar. 10, 1959 / Original Jazz Classics ✦✦✦✦✦
For this solo piano session (a Contemporary date which has been reissued on CD), the remarkably versatile Andre Previn interprets ten Jerome Kern songs including several ("Sure Thing," "WhipPoor-Will," "Go Little Boat" and "Put Me to the Test") that are quite obscure. Sometimes he treats the melodies with great respect while other performances find him stretching the themes and coming up with fresh variations; "They Didn't Believe Me" is a high point. This is a well-rounded set with plenty of surprises along with consistently tasteful playing, one of Previn's better jazz efforts. —*Scott Yanow*

West Side Story / Aug. 24, 1959-Aug. 25, 1959 / Original Jazz Classics ✦✦✦✦

Like Previn! / Feb. 20, 1960-Mar. 1, 1960 / Original Jazz Classics ✦✦✦✦
This trio set for Contemporary (reissued on CD in the OJC series) differs from other Andre Previn sessions in that all eight of the selections were composed by the pianist. With fine assistance from bassist Red Mitchell and drummer Frankie Capp, Previn is in consistently swinging form on his originals and, even if none of the songs caught on, they make for a solid and varied set of bop-oriented music. —*Scott Yanow*

Andre Previn Plays Harold Arlen / May 4, 1960-May 5, 1960 / Contemporary ✦✦✦
This solo piano set from Andre Previn is a bit unusual for he recasts ten Harold Arlen compositions (all but "For Every Man There's a Woman" and "Coconut Sweet" are quite well-known) by reharmonizing the chords and modernizing the melodies. Most of the songs are taken at slow tempos and the set (which has been reissued on CD) has a consistently melancholy and thoughtful mood throughout. —*Scott Yanow*

A Touch of Elegance / Nov. 9, 1960-Dec. 18, 1962 / Columbia/Legacy ✦✦✦
This CD draws its material from five of pianist Andre Previn's Columbia albums of the 1961-62 period. Three of the five albums (13 of the 18 selections on this sampler) feature Previn's piano backed by string orchestras on well-played but easy-listening music that rarely wanders from the melody. Two other songs are taken from a quartet set with trombonist J.J. Johnson while three pieces feature guitarist Herb Ellis and these are more adventurous. But overall, the music on this CD is overly safe; tasteful but predictable. —*Scott Yanow*

After Hours / Mar. 29, 1989 / Telarc ✦✦✦✦✦
Although Andre Previn had not recorded a regular jazz album in 27 years at this point in time (discounting a pair of Itzhak Perlman sessions featuring Previn's compositions), the great majority of the performances on this trio set with guitarist Joe Pass and bassist Ray Brown are first takes. Previn took time off from his busy schedule in the classical music world to return briefly to jazz, his first love. The results are often magical. Previn, Pass and Brown play together as if they had been touring as a group for years. The pianist is generous with solo space and Pass' solos are sometimes exhilarating. For Previn, it is as if the previous three decades did not occur for he plays in a style little changed from 1960, displaying an Oscar Peterson influence mixed in with Lennie Tristano and Bill Evans' chording, performing ten standards and his own "One For Bunz." Highly recommended. —*Scott Yanow*

Uptown / Mar. 9, 1990-Mar. 10, 1990 / Telarc ✦✦✦✦
This was Andre Previn's second album after his long, symphonically enforced absence from jazz, and it sounds noticeably more fluid and relaxed than his first. No longer apprehensive about dusting off his old skills, Previn is delightfully confident and breezy (dig his sly turns on "Come Rain or Come Shine" and "C Jam Blues"), taking some chances as he rephrases and paraphrases a collection of revivified standards, mostly Arlen and assorted Ellingtonia. Even if Previn, that noted wit, sometimes sounds as if he is kidding the pants off these old tunes, it's great to hear him having such a good time playing jazz again. Mundell Lowe is Previn's new guitar partner, and Ray Brown returns on bass; both are right at home in this refined brand of chamber jazz grooving. Adding to the CD's appeal are some marvelously (and typically) graceful liner notes by Mel Powell, an old pal of Andre's and a lively fellow defector from the jazz piano ranks to the classical world. —*Richard S. Ginell*

Old Friends / Aug. 24, 1991 / Telarc ✦✦✦✦
Andre Previn's "jazz comeback" has been a welcome event even though he clearly regards his jazz playing as an occasional affair. It is to Previn's great credit that when he plays improvised music he sounds like a fulltime jazz pianist. This trio

outing with guitarist Mundell Lowe and bassist Ray Brown was his third jazz date of the period and features the veteran players swinging standards lightly but with passion. A medley has unaccompanied solos by each of the musicians; other highlights include cooking versions of "Stompin' at the Savoy," "One O'Clock Jump," "Topsy" and "Sweet Georgia Brown" in addition to some heartfelt ballad renditions. —*Scott Yanow*

What Headphones? / Oct. 5, 1993 / Angel ✦✦✦✦✦
This is Andre Previn's best album since his return to jazz at the close of the 1980s, and also the most surprising and unpredictable one of his entire jazz life. Rather than play it safe with a conservative trio and a brace of standards, Previn exercises his considerable arranging and compositional skills, lets his curiosity about other idioms roam freely, throws in some Ellington, and does everything with disarming ease and tasty humor. Previn's usual cohorts, Mundell Lowe on guitar and Ray Brown on bass, do form the base of operations, but this time, Previn adds some wonderfully hip little charts for three brass players and teams up with the amateur Antioch Gospel Choir, a local (Bedford Hills, NY) group that Previn took a shine to. Among other treats, the choir inspires Previn to take off on a down-home gospel blues "You Are My All"; it's great to hear Previn unwind and dig in like this. Indeed, Previn's playing shows greater streaks of wit and cannier use of space than ever before, and his self-penned title track has a wild theme, almost avant-garde in its erudite looniness. In addition, Warren Vache (trumpet) and Jim Pugh (trombone) get to contribute several fine solos on their own. *What Headphones?* proves beyond a reasonable doubt that Andre Previn is not only an unbelievably talented musician, but also tremendous fun to spend some time with. —*Richard S. Ginell*

Play Show Boat / 1995 / Deutsche Grammophon ✦✦✦✦
Performing in a style a bit reminiscent of Oscar Peterson, pianist Andre Previn plays eight selections from the play *Show Boat*, six of which are standards plus the obscure "Life on the Wicked Stage" and "I Might Fall Back on You." In addition, Previn contributed three newer pieces with the uptempo blues "Lickety Split" having his most impressive solo. Although the partly bitonal treatment given the usually sweet "Make Believe" takes a bit away from the memorable melody, Previn's interpretations of the other pieces are melodic, respectful and swinging. Guitarist Mundell Lowe has an occasional solo and bassist Ray Brown and drummer Grady Tate are typically excellent in support. This fine bop-oriented date shows that Andre Previn (who has spent most of the past three decades in the classical music world) is still the top part-time jazz pianist around. —*Scott Yanow*

Jazz at the Musikverein / Jun. 24, 1995 / Deutsche Grammophon ✦✦✦✦
Here is an example of crossover marketing '90s style—a classical conductor/jazz pianist signed to the classical Deutsche Grammophon label, whose previous jazz album issued on DG got lost in the shops and whose next disc was prudently shifted over to PolyGram's jazz line, Verve. The occasion was a rare jazz concert in Vienna's legendary, acoustically marvelous symphony hall, the Musikvereinsaal, where Previn—who normally leads the Vienna Philharmonic there—enraptured the Viennese with his piano/guitar/bass trio. According to Previn, one member of the Philharmonic was astonished to learn that the music was made on the wing ("You improvised in public?!", he exclaimed). Well, it wasn't that big a deal for Previn and his usual cohorts Mundell Lowe (guitar) and Ray Brown (bass), who turn in an amiable collection of mostly vintage standards that they probably know in their sleep. Previn is as fluid, witty and melodically inventive as ever in his bop-derived, light-fingered manner, with occasional side trips into stride and Brubeck-like chordal perorations, and there is one flippant, blues-based Previn original entitled "Hi Blondie." The lack of a drummer becomes an asset in this golden mellow hall; a drum kit would have upset the acoustical balance. Andre even gets a chance to make a speech to the audience, but alas, it's in German with no translation (wish we could figure out what he was saying that made the Viennese chuckle). —*Richard S. Ginell*

Bobby Previte

b. Jul. 16, 1957, Niagara Falls, NY
Drums / Avant-Garde
An adventurous drummer and bandleader, Bobby Previte's openminded approach has resulted in some consistently stimulating (if unpredictable) music with some of New York's finest, including John Zorn, Bill Frisell and Wayne Horvitz. His 1990 set of music for the Moscow Circus is particularly memorable. Previte has recorded as a leader for Gramavision, Sound Aspects and Enja, heading such groups as Empty Suits and Weather Clear, Track Fast. —*Scott Yanow*

Bump the Renaissance / Jun. 1985 / Sound Aspects ✦✦✦✦
● **Claude's Late Morning** / 1988 / Gramavision ✦✦✦✦✦
Empty Suits / May 1990 / Gramavision ✦✦✦✦✦
Weather Clear Track Fast / Jan. 7, 1991-Jan. 8, 1991 / Enja ✦✦✦✦✦

Music of the Moscow Circus / Aug. 1991 / Gramavision ✦✦✦✦✦
In 1991 Bobby Previte was given a most unusual assignment: to create a new score of music for the Moscow Circus. Previte, an innovative composer who learned from Gil Evans the joy of combining together acoustic and electronic instruments, was up to the challenging task. The result is a generally fascinating soundtrack, music that stands up by itself but makes one very curious to see how it fits into the circus routines. The music ranges from an electronic opening overture that wittily hints at some past circus themes, several hypnotic new age pieces written to accompany death-defying feats and six brief "clown segments," which are purposely chaotic. Violinist Mark Feldman has some moments in the spotlight and cornetist Herb Robertson gets to lead the riotous clown interludes, but the bulk of the credit for this episodic, colorful and somewhat unique score's success lies with the composer. —*Scott Yanow*

Hue & Cry / Dec. 1993 / Enja ✦✦✦✦✦
Too Close to the Pole / Apr. 27, 1996-Apr. 29, 1996 / Enja ✦✦✦✦
From its opening eccentric fanfare (which pops up briefly in other selections) through the wild group vocal on "Save the Cups" and "3 Minute Heels" (which sounds like Indian music for belly dancers), drummer Bobby Previte's Weather Clear, Track Fast band on this Enja release is continually colorful, cinematic (one can easily imagine crazy adventures occurring) and unpredictable. Although quite advanced, the expert use of repetition, complex but catchy rhythms, and echoey call and response riffing results in a complete lack of forgettable or routine moments. In addition to the six listed selections, there is an odd extra "bonus": an unidentified seventh song that is a five-part, fifteen-minute suite mostly featuring Andrew D'Angelo's bass clarinet. Although there are strong individual heroics from the sextet (such as Janie Saft's organ and retro Fender Rhodes playing, Andy Laster's versatile flights on baritone and Previte's stirring percussive work), it is the chance-taking spirit of the musicians and their performances as a whole that make this a memorable release well worth several listens. —*Scott Yanow*

Ruth Price

b. Apr. 27, 1938, Phoenixville, PA
Vocals / Standards
A talented singer whose wide expressive qualities do justice to any lyrics that she chooses to interpret, Ruth Price has made relatively few recordings throughout her career. Originally a dancer, she attended ballet school in 1952. However by 1954 she was singing with Charlie Ventura and, after freelancing in Philadelphia, she worked as a singer and dancer in New York. Price moved to Hollywood in 1957, recorded a fine album with Shelly Manne (reissued in the Original Jazz Classics series) but didn't cut her second album as a leader until 1983 (for ITI). She toured with Harry James (1964-65) but in recent years has become best-known for running one of Los Angeles' top jazz clubs, the Jazz Bakery. —*Scott Yanow*

● **Ruth Price with Shelly Manne at the Manne-Hole** / Mar. 3, 1961-Mar. 5, 1961 / Original Jazz Classics ✦✦✦✦✦
Singer Ruth Price, on this early set, falls somewhere between swinging jazz, middle-of-the-road pop and cabaret. She does not improvise much but her strong and very appealing voice uplifts the diverse material that she interprets (including "Dearly Beloved," "Shadrack," "Crazy He Calls Me" and "Look for the Silver Lining") and she brings great sincerity to Leonard Bernstein's "Who Am I." Backed by Shelly Manne's Quintet (with plenty heard from pianist Russ Freeman but just guest spots on tenor by Richie Kamuca and one lone appearance by trumpeter Conte Candoli), Price is in fine form for her debut recording as a leader, which has been reissued on CD in the *OJC* series. —*Scott Yanow*

Lucky to Be Me / Jan. 1983 / ITI ✦✦✦✦

Sammy Price

b. Oct. 6, 1908, Honey Grove, TX, d. Apr. 14, 1992, New York, NY
Piano / Boogie-Woogie, Swing, Jump Blues, Early R&B Jazz, Piano Blues
Sammy Price had a long and productive career as a flexible blues and boogie-woogie-based pianist. He studied piano in Dallas and was a singer and dancer with Alphonso Trent's band during 1927-30. In 1929 he recorded one solitary side under the title of "Sammy Price and his Four Quarters." After a few years in Kansas City, he spent time in Chicago and Detroit. In 1938, Price became the house pianist for Decca in New York and appeared on many blues sides with such singers as Trixie Smith and Sister Rosetta Tharpe. He led his own band on records in the early '40s which included (on one memorable session) Lester Young. Price worked steadily on 52nd Street, in 1948 played at the Nice Festival with Mezz Mezzrow, spent time back in Texas and then a decade with Red Allen; he was also heard on many rock 'n' roll-type sessions in the 1950s. In later years, he recorded with Doc Cheatham and Sammy Price and was active until near his death, 63 years after his recording debut. —*Scott Yanow*

1929-1941 / Sep. 29, 1929-Dec. 10, 1941 / Classics ✦✦✦✦✦
This single CD from the European Classics label collects all of pianist Sammy Price's postwar recordings as a leader. Despite its title, only two titles preceded the 1940-41 period: "Blue Rhythm Stomp" by Price's Four Quarters in 1929, and "Nasty But Nice," which finds Price on the same day accompanying trombonist Bert Johnson. Otherwise, the music features Price's Texas Blusicians, New York-based septets and octets put together especially for recordings. The emphasis is on blues, with Price taking several vocals, but such notable guests as altoist Don Stovall, trumpeters Shad Collins and Emmett Berry and (on four songs) tenor great Lester Young uplift the music. Recommended to small-group swing collectors. —Scott Yanow

● **And the Blues Singers** / 1929 / Wolf ✦✦✦✦✦
When the Austrian Wolf logo decided to pay tribute to pianist Sammy Price's prolific legacy as both leader and sideman, they really did it up right. Ninety-four sides on four discs dating from 1929 to 1950 spotlight Price's rippling ivories behind a plethora of vocalists—Peetie Wheatstraw, Harmon Ray, Bea Booze, Johnny Temple, Monette Moore, Scat Man Bailey, and a great many more—as well as some very tasty instrumentals of his own. —Bill Dahl

Rib Joint/Roots of Rock & Roll / Oct. 17, 1956-Mar. 24, 1959 / Savoy ✦✦✦✦✦
Here's a two-LP set that truly deserves immediate CD reissue. Price led a mighty New York R&B combo through three Savoy Records sessions in 1956-57 that elicited some sizzling instrumentals: "Rib Joint" (here in two takes), "Back Room Rock," "Juke Joint," "Chicken Out," "Ain't No Strain" (sidemen included guitarist Mickey Baker and saxman King Curtis). A slightly more restrained 1959 date sans sax that comprises the second LP is no less joyful. —Bill Dahl

Blues and Boogies / Nov. 14, 1969 / Black & Blue ✦✦✦✦✦
Price is heard here on solo piano and vocal, playing eight Price originals and "See See Rider." It is good to hear him alone on this rare solo album, recorded in France. —Michael G. Nastos

★ **Fire** / May 1, 1975 / Black & Blue ✦✦✦✦
The Texas blues and jazz pianist plays in good-time and old-time format with the basic trio of J.C. Heard (d), Carl Pruitt (b), and guests Ted Buckner (tpt), The Mighty Flea (Gene Connors, tb), and Doc Cheatham (tpt). Includes ten Price originals. —Michael G. Nastos

Boogie & Jazz Classics / May 25, 1975 / Black & Blue ✦✦✦✦✦
Price, a delightful, romping pianist in the vintage barrelhouse and boogie-woogie genres, interpreted, reworked, and remade a series of traditional blues and jazz tunes on this fine 1975 release. Everything, from song selection to solos, is wonderful. —Ron Wynn

Just Right / Nov. 2, 1977 / Black & Blue ✦✦✦
A sextet with George Kelly (sax) and Freddie Lonzo (tb) plays two of Price's tunes, five standards (two by W.C. Handy), and one by trumpeter Johnny Lettman. —Michael G. Nastos

Sweet Substitute / Nov. 1, 1979 / Sackville ✦✦✦✦

Paradise Valley Duets / Feb. 26, 1988-Feb. 28, 1988 / Parkwood ✦✦✦✦✦
Recorded live in Windsor, this album features J.C. Heard (d), George Benson (g), and Marcus Belgrave (tpt) playing nine standards and one blues from Price and Belgrave. This is a delight. One whole side features Price and the legendary drummer Heard. Precious Texas piano stomps and jazz. —Michael G. Nastos

King of Boogie-Woogie / Jul. 22, 1995 / Storyville ✦✦✦
On this odd CD reissue, pianist Sammy Price seems intent on becoming the Muhammad Ali of jazz. He brags throughout the liner notes about how he is the king of boogie-woogie and might very well (based on his five vocals on the date) also be the king of the crooners. In reality, Price's piano playing on the basic material (lots of blues and a few standards) is fine, while his vocals are a novelty at best. With backup work from bassist Arvell Shaw and drummer Panama Francis, this is a decent but not particularly riveting set. —Scott Yanow

Julian Priester

b. Jun. 29, 1935, Chicago, IL
Trombone / Avant-Garde, Post-Bop

Julian Priester has long been a flexible and adventurous trombonist who has not yet achieved the fame he deserves. He originally studied piano, baritone horn and finally trombone. Prior to moving to New York in 1958 he worked with Muddy Waters, Bo Diddley, Sun Ra (1954-56), Lionel Hampton and Dinah Washington (1957). Priester gained recognition for his playing with Max Roach (1958-61) during a period when the drummer often used Booker Little and Eric Dolphy. He played in a wide variety of settings throughout the 1960s including six months with Duke Ellington (1969-70). Priester's highest profile gig was with Herbie Hancock's sextet during 1970-73 with whom he toured and recorded. Moving to San

Francisco in the mid-'70s, he experimented with electronic music while still playing trombone, recording with Stanley Cowell and Red Garland. Most of the first half of the 1990s was spent with Dave Holland's quintet and later in the decade he worked with George Gruntz and Sun Ra. —Scott Yanow

● **Keep Swinging** / Jan. 11, 1960 / Original Jazz Classics ✦✦✦✦
Trombonist Julian Priester sounds very much under the influence of J.J. Johnson during his debut as a leader, a Riverside date reissued on CD in the Original Jazz Classic series. The repertoire comprises four Priester originals, one apiece by Jimmy Heath (whose tenor makes the group a quintet on five of the eight songs) and baritonist Charles Davis, and two standards. Priester is heard in his early prime on a warm version of "Once in a While" and plays solid hard bop with pianist Tommy Flanagan, bassist Sam Jones, drummer Elvin Jones and sometimes Heath on this swinging modern mainstream session. —Scott Yanow

Spiritsville / Jul. 12, 1960 / Jazzland ✦✦✦
Love, Love / Jun. 28, 1974-Sep. 12, 1974 / ECM ✦✦✦
Polarization / Jan. 1977 / ECM ✦✦✦
Hints on Light & Shadow / Nov. 14, 1996+Nov. 15, 1996 / Postcards ✦✦✦
This is an unusual set. Trombonist Julian Priester and Sam Rivers (alternating between tenor, soprano, flute and piano) perform a set of duets that also sometimes include the oddball electronics of Tucker Martine. The nine originals are mostly freely improvised; some strong themes do emerge, and there is some excellent interaction between Priester and Rivers (two underrated giants). However, Martine's electronics are occasionally so bizarre as to be distracting. —Scott Yanow

Prima Material

f. 1994
Group / Avant-Garde, Free Jazz

Prima Material is a downtown New York City quintet centered around the free-time, free-jazz brilliance of John Coltrane's last drummer, Rashied Ali. Ali plays with this band as he did with the master—powerfully, with a hyper-rhythmic drive matched by few contemporary percussionists. The band's front line consists of tenor saxophonist Louis Belogenis and altoist Allan Chase, a nicely complementary pair of improvisers. The band's original lineup featured two bassists, William Parker and Joe Gallant. Parker eventually left the group, to be replaced by pianist Greg Murphy, whose percussive agility raised the intensity still another notch. Originally formed to play Coltrane's latest, most expressionistic compositions, the band has also gone on to interpret the works of Albert Ayler. —Chris Kelsey

Peace on Earth / 1994 / Knitting Factory ✦✦✦✦
Most tributes to John Coltrane focus either on his "sheets of sound" work of the late '50s or his early Impulse recordings. For this spirited outing, the emphasis is on Trane circa 1965, the year his music began emphasizing atonality. With Coltrane's last drummer Rashied Ali and the basses of William Parker (best known for his association with Cecil Taylor) and Joe Gallant playing at their most creative, the rhythm section certainly keeps the music stimulating. Louie Belogenis (on tenor) and Allan Chase (doubling on soprano and alto) have plenty of intense but not forbidding solos, showing that they have learned from Coltrane's innovations but avoiding mere imitation and not feeling compelled to blow the roof off the entire time. Actually, the most exciting soloist, altoist John Zorn, is only on two of the five selections, but he makes a strong impression. Other than the eight-minute ballad "Alabama," the other four Coltrane compositions ("Spiritual," "Peace on Earth," "Brazilia" and "India") are each given very lengthy treatment, between 16-19 minutes apiece. The fact that this exciting set continually holds on to one's interest is evidence of how compelling the music is, making this a recommended release for listeners who are open to post-bop sounds. —Scott Yanow

Meditations / Jun. 23, 1995 / Knitting Factory ✦✦✦✦✦
"Meditations" was the most successful recording that John Coltrane made with fellow tenor Pharoah Sanders. For the "remake" 30 years later, drummer Rashied Ali (who was on the original date along with Elvin Jones) meets up with tenor saxophonist Louie Belogenis, altoist Allan Chase, pianist Greg Murphy and bassist Joe Gallant. They revisit the lengthy and intense five-section suite, creating plenty of fireworks. Fortunately, Belogenis and Chase (although inspired by 'Trane's explorative approach) do not sound at all like Coltrane or Sanders, so this powerful version stands on its own. —Scott Yanow

● **Bells** / May 17, 1996 / Knitting Factory ✦✦✦✦✦
On May 1, 1965 at Town Hall, the innovative tenor saxophonist Albert Ayler performed his 21-minute original "Bells" with his quintet (trumpeter Donald Ayler, altoist Charles Tyler, bassist Lewis Worrell and drummer Sonny Murray); the results were released at the time as a one-sided LP on ESP. Thirty-one years later the adventurous quintet Prima Material played a stretched-out rendition of "Bells" that was three times longer than Ayler's original version. The band (heard live at the Knitting Factory) retained all of the themes and, while not copying any of the

original solos, brought back the spirit of the earlier recording. Comprising drummer Rashied Ali (an important survivor from the 1960s who is fortunately still in prime form), a pair of fiery saxophonists (co-leaders Louie Belogenis on tenor and altoist Allan Chase), the percussive pianist Greg Murphy and bassist Joe Gallant, Prima Material both salutes the past and builds on the earlier innovations. An extended Belogenis-Ali duet and the rambunctious interpretations of Ayler's march-like themes are highlights of their spirited performance, which is easily recommended to adventurous listeners. —*Scott Yanow*

Louis Prima

b. Dec. 7, 1911, New Orleans, LA, **d.** Aug. 24, 1978, New Orleans, LA
Trumpet, Vocals / Dixieland, Swing, Early R&B Jazz, Traditional Pop, Jump Blues
Louis Prima became very famous in the 1950s with an infectious Las Vegas act co-starring his wife (singer Keely Smith) that mixed together R&B (particularly the honking tenor of Sam Butera), early rock 'n' roll, comedy and Dixieland. Always a colorful personality, Prima was leading a band in New Orleans when he was just 11. In 1934 he began recording as a leader with a Dixieland-oriented unit and soon he was a major attraction on 52nd Street. His early records often featured George Brunis and Eddie Miller, and Pee Wee Russell was a regular member of his groups during 1935-36. Prima, who composed "Sing, Sing, Sing" (which, for a period, was his theme song), recorded steadily through the swing era, had a big band in the 1940s and achieved hits in "Angelina" and "Robin Hood." In 1954 he began having great success in his latter-day group (their recordings on Capitol were big-sellers and still sound joyous today), emphasizing vocals and Butera's tenor, but he still took spirited trumpet solos. Although he eventually broke up with Keely Smith, Louis Prima (who played a character in Walt Disney's animated film *The Jungle Book* in 1966) remained a popular attraction into the 1970s. —*Scott Yanow*

1934-1935, Vol. 1 / Sep. 27, 1934-Apr. 8, 1935 / TOM ✦✦✦
On the first of four Louis Prima LP's released by the collector's label titled The Old Masters (TOM), the popular musician is heard on his initial recordings. At the time Prima and fellow trumpeter-vocalist Wingy Manone were major entertainers on New York's 52nd Street. Unfortunately, none of the records in this series give exact personnel and dates (discographies have to be consulted) but Prima's sidemen for the freewheeling performances (which are halfway between Dixieland and swing) are quite impressive including trombonist George Brunis, clarinetist Sidney Arodin, tenor saxophonist Eddie Miller and pianist Claude Thornhill. Highlights of the goodtime performances include "Jamaica Shout," "'Long About Midnight," "Breakin' the Ice" and "Let's Have a Jubilee." —*Scott Yanow*

1935-1936, Vol. 2 / Apr. 3, 1935-Nov. 30, 1935 / TOM ✦✦✦✦
The second of four Louis Prima LP's put out by the TOM (The Old Masters) label continues the chronological reissuance of the trumpeter-vocalist's earliest recordings. Personnel and exact dates are not given on the record (which looks like a bootleg) but it is worth noting that on all but the first two songs (which have Eddie Miller), Pee Wee Russell is the clarinetist. Prima, who is the main star, fortunately gave Russell plenty of solo space (the other players are lesser-known). Highlights include "Chinatown, My Chinatown," "Basin St. Blues," "I'm Shooting High" and "I've Got My Fingers Crossed," but in general, all 16 selections are enjoyable and show that Louis Prima was an appealing entertainer from the start. —*Scott Yanow*

1936, Vol. 3 / Feb. 28, 1936-Nov. 16, 1936 / TOM ✦✦✦✦✦
On the third of four Louis Prima albums on this obscure label (which has reissued all of the trumpeter-vocalist's earliest recordings but unfortunately does not provide recording dates or personnel), Louis Prima is heard with a septet on six numbers and with his short-lived big band on ten others. A constant force during the performances (and functioning as a co-star) is the unique clarinetist Pee Wee Russell, the only "name" player among the sidemen. Among the high points are "Dinah," "Alice Blue Gown," "Cross Patch," "Mr. Ghost Goes to Town" and the earliest version of Prima's most famous composition, "Sing, Sing, Sing" (from Feb. 28, 1936). All of these albums are highly recommended to swing collectors but will probably be difficult to find. —*Scott Yanow*

1937-1938, Vol. 4 / May 20, 1937-May 16, 1938 / TOM ✦✦✦✦
The fourth and final LP in the TOM label's Louis Prima series has 16 titles cut during a one-year period. With the departure of clarinetist Pee Wee Russell, Prima's sidemen (which include altoist George Moore, tenor saxophonist Joe Catalyne, clarinetist Meyer Weinberg and pianist Frank Pinero) lack any recognizable names but the swing/Dixieland music is quite consistent. Prima alternated ballads with stomps and his personable vocals and New Orleans-oriented trumpet keep the performances interesting. Best are "Fifty-Second Street," "Tin Roof Blues" (the lone instrumental), "Now They Call It Swing" and "Rosalie." —*Scott Yanow*

Plays Pretty for the People / Feb. 1944-Jan. 1947 / Savoy ✦✦✦✦
This CD contains a cross-section of Louis Prima's big band recordings of the mid-1940s. While Prima had a fine orchestra (which featured some vocals from Lily

Ann Carol), the leader was essentially the whole show. A masterful entertainer who became popular during the swing era, Prima sang well and also played fine New Orleans trumpet. Not all of his humor has dated well, but most of the 20 selections on this fine CD still can communicate to today's listeners. High points include "Robin Hood," "Angelina," "Brooklyn Boogie" and "Chinatown, My Chinatown." This is one of the few Louis Prima swing era CDs available. —*Scott Yanow*

Angelina / Jun. 1950 / Viper's Nest ✦✦✦✦
Swing may have been dead by 1950 but one cannot tell that from this excellent CD, which has three radio broadcasts from the Louis Prima big band. Prima, an exciting performer, shows his versatility on a diverse program and takes quite a few hot trumpet solos while his wife Keely Smith (just 22 at the time) is heard on some ballads. However, it is the sound of Prima's excellent and hard-swinging orchestra that is the biggest revelation; it is a pity that the personnel is unknown. The repertoire ranges from swing (the driving "Boogie in the Bronx" is most notable) and a few Dixieland numbers to versions of Prima's hits (such as "Robin Hood" and "Angelina") and some standards. Taken from Prima's second of three periods (after he broke up his regular Dixieland band of the 1930s and a few years before he hit it big in Las Vegas), this set is quite definitive of his music of the time. —*Scott Yanow*

★ **Capitol Collectors Series** / Apr. 19, 1956-Feb. 23, 1962 / Capitol ✦✦✦✦✦
What Louis Prima accomplished musically in the company of Sam Butera and the Witnesses and vocalist Keely Smith is in hard evidence on this excellent 26-track compilation. All the classics are aboard ("Angelina-Zooma Zooma," "That Old Black Magic," "I've Got You Under My Skin," "Buona Sera"—which includes a great snippet of studio chatter kicking it off—"Oh Marie" and the obligatory "Just a Gigolo/I Ain't Got Nobody") with excellent liner notes from Scott Shea and crisp transfers of the original masters. Although this duplicates several tracks with Rhino's *Zooma! Zooma!* compilation (now long out of print), with the addition of several singles and unissued tracks, this stands as the best single-disc collection available of Prima's tenure with Capitol Records. The perfect place to start your Louis Prima collection. —*Cub Koda*

☆ **The Wildest!** / Jan. 1957 / Capitol ✦✦✦✦✦
Although Louis Prima had been popular for 20 years before recording this LP, this set was his biggest breakthrough to mass appeal. The trumpeter-vocalist, his wife-singer Keely Smith and the group (the Witnesses) headed by the R&Bish tenor Sam Butera made for explosive music that was perfectly captured on this classic disc. The mixture of Prima's humor, Dixieland, early rhythm and blues, Keely Smith's fine voice and the honking tenor made this unit a big hit in Las Vegas. The two medleys ("Just a Gigolo/I Ain't Got Nobody" and "Basin Street Blues/When It's Sleepy Time Down South") are often jubilant and the individual features are at the same level. Memorable music. —*Scott Yanow*

The Call of the Wildest / Jul. 1957 / Capitol ✦✦✦✦✦
Louis Prima's second Capitol LP with Keely Smith, Sam Butera and the Witnesses is just as exciting as his first. The trumpeter-vocalist was a natural entertainer and comedian, and all of his skills are on evidence during this spirited program. The honking tenor of Sam Butera, Keely Smith's appealing voice and the mixture of Dixieland and R&B results in some remarkable and very accessible music. Highlights include the medley of "When You're Smiling" and "The Sheik of Araby," trombonist Red Blount's feature on "Blow, Red, Blow," "Pennies From Heaven," "The Birth of the Blues" and "When the Saints Go Marching In." What a band. —*Scott Yanow*

The Wildest Show Art Tahoe / Jan. 1958 / Capitol ✦✦✦✦✦
This was the third straight classic album by trumpeter-singer Louis Prima with his wife-singer Keely Smith and the spirited R&B tenor saxophonist Sam Butera; it is as exciting as the first two. Recorded live in Lake Tahoe, the band romps through four medleys (including "On the Sunny Side of the Street/Exactly Like You" and "Don't Worry 'Bout Me/I'm in the Mood for Love"), Keely's feature on "A Foggy Day," Butera's showcase on "Come Back to Sorrento" and trombonist Red Blount's extroverted rendition of "How High the Moon." Toss in a few vocal duets and the results are quite memorable. All three of these Capitol records (which have thus far only been reissued on CD in samplers) are highly recommended for they document a unique group at the height of its power. —*Scott Yanow*

Plays Pretty for the People / 1963-1964 / Jazz Band ✦✦✦✦
Although Louis Prima and Keely Smith had split up by the time of the two live performances that comprise this collector's LP, Prima (on vocals and occasional trumpet) was still in fine form. Teamed with a future wife (singer Gia Mione) and still using R&B tenor Sam Butera and the Witnesses (which featured the extroverted trombonist Little Red Blount), Prima mixes together his older hits (including "Buona Sera," "Robin Hood" and "Sing, Sing, Sing") with some Dixieland standards and more recent material. The recording quality is decent and, even with Smith's absence, Prima sounds quite happy to be performing. —*Scott Yanow*

Marcus Printup

b. 1967, Convers, GA
Trumpet / Post-Bop, Hard Bop
A talented trumpeter with a lot of potential, Marcus Printup was discovered by Marcus Roberts at the University of North Florida in 1991. Printup started on trumpet in the fifth grade, played funk as a teenager, and in college was part of a ten-piece band called Soul Reason for the Blues. Since that time he has toured and recorded with Roberts, played with the Lincoln Center Jazz Orchestra, recorded with Carl Allen, performed with Betty Carter, and cut two excellent albums as a leader for Blue Note. —*Scott Yanow*

● **Song for the Beautiful Woman** / Dec. 6, 1994-Dec. 7, 1994 / Blue Note ✦✦✦✦

Unveiled / Feb. 18, 1996-Feb. 19, 1996 / Blue Note ✦✦✦✦
Marcus Printup gained his initial recognition for his playing with pianist Marcus Roberts' group. His second Blue Note recording as a leader features his attractive trumpet in a quintet with Roberts, the Paul Gonsalves-inspired tenor of Stephen Riley, bassist Reuben Rogers and the young drummer Jason Marsalis. Printup, at this point, already had a fairly orignal sound of his own, which was slightly influenced by Wynton Marsalis. His technique is impressive on the date, as is his warmth and consistently creative ideas. Printup contributed seven mostly straight-ahead originals to the well-rounded and continually interesting modern mainstream set (including the brooding ballad "When Forever Is Over," the catchy "Leave Your Name and Number" and the funky title cut). "M & M," a major/minor blues duet with pianist Roberts which looks back to the 1920s, is a definite highlight. Printup also performs jazz standards by Miles Davis (a swinging "Dig"), Benny Golson and Wayne Shorter, along with an emotional version of the traditional "Amazing Grace." This CD gives one an excellent sampling of Marcus Printup's hard bop-oriented playing. —*Scott Yanow*

Russell Procope

b. Aug. 11, 1908, New York, NY, **d.** Jan. 21, 1981, New York, NY
Alto Saxophone, Clarinet / Swing
An excellent altoist, Russell Procope became much better-known as a New Orleans-style clarinetist during his Duke Ellington years. He studied violin for eight years before switching to clarinet and alto. Procope recorded with Jelly Roll Morton in 1928 and had important stints with the big bands of Benny Carter (1929), Chick Webb (1929-31), Fletcher Henderson (1931-34), Tiny Bradshaw (1934-35), Teddy Hill (1935-37) and Willie Bryant. However, it was as a member of the John Kirby Sextet (1938-43) during which he exclusively played alto that Russell Procope did his finest work, playing brilliant solos with a distinctive tone that perfectly fit the music. After a period in the Army and a reunion with Kirby (1945), Procope became a member of the Duke Ellington Orchestra in 1946, staying (except for a short period in 1961 with Wilbur DeParis) until Ellington's death 28 years later in 1974. Because of Johnny Hodges' presence, Procope had very few alto solos, serving instead as a section player and occasional clarinet soloist whose warm tone contrasted with that of the cooler Jimmy Hamilton; Procope was underutilized but secure and happy during his Ellington years. Later in the 1970s he played with Brooks Kerr's group. —*Scott Yanow*

The Persuasive Sax of Russell Procope / 1956 / Dot ✦✦✦✦

Pucho & His Latin Soul Brothers

f. 1959 **db.** 1973
Group / Latin Jazz, Salsa
In the 1960s, no one combined more or less equal elements of jazz, Latin music, soul, and funk as well as Henry "Pucho" Brown (b. Nov. 1, 1938). A somewhat forgotten figure until quite recently, Pucho never achieved the wide recognition of some other Latin-jazz performers exploring similar territory, such as Mongo Santamaria, Willie Bobo, and Cal Tjader. The timbales player and bandleader also may have been too eclectic, or too open to outside influences, to achieve much recognition within the jazz community. What's a weakness in one circle's view, however, is a strength for other listeners. As a result, Pucho has a wider appeal than many straight jazz performers. Fans of R&B, rock, and Latin music can immediately connect with him, especially as he's always made sure to play music that's hot and danceable. His accessibility, however, has by no means compromised the quality of his material or his Latin Soul Brothers bands, which have featured fine and versatile players. Contrary to the assumptions of many listeners, Pucho himself is not Latino, but African-American. As a Harlem teenager, he cultivated loves for jazz, rhythm & blues, and mambo. In the late '50s, he served for several years in the band of pianist Joe Panama. When the group broke up in 1959, Pucho formed a band of his own, recruiting several alumni from Panama's outfit. Even before he'd cemented his reputation on record, Pucho's band attracted notice from top Latin jazzmen. Willie Bobo took several musicians from Pucho's band for his own group,

as did Mongo Santamaria. One of the musicians that Santamaria lured away, in fact, was a young Chick Corea.

Pucho began recording in 1963, and really hit his stride between 1966 and 1970, when he cut over half a dozen albums for Prestige. On these he helped pioneer a style termed Latin boogaloo, which mixed jazz, New York-style Latin music, R&B/soul, and the sort of funk that was just emerging from James Brown and other performers. Pucho wasn't afraid to mix up his material on his LPs, which placed originals by Brown and the Latin Soul Brothers next to covers of tunes by Herbie Hancock, the Temptations, the Beatles, Duke Ellington, and John Barry.

This ensured a certain erratic flavor, but the groove was almost always on the money. The Latin Soul Brothers were at their best when they went for the hottest and funkiest grooves, as on their fine version of "Cantaloupe Island," or eccentrically titled originals like "Soul Yamie" and "Vietnam Mambo." Once in a while, he even used engagingly raw soul vocals, as on the infectiously good-natured "Shuckin' and Jivin'," which could have been an R&B hit. The Latin Soul Brothers certainly couldn't have been accused of predictability, incorporating straight modern jazz chops, psychedelic flourishes, and soul-jazz organ grooves into their repertoire when the mood suited them. The constant factor was the active Latin percussion section, featuring conga, bongos, and Pucho's own timbales.

When his brand of Latin-soul-jazz fusion started to fall from commercial grace in the early '70s, Pucho disbanded the Latin Soul Brothers. For the next 20 years, he made his livelihood by performing conventional Latin music in the Catskill Mountain resorts of New York State. In the early '90s, however, Pucho's back catalog began to generate interest in Britain, where he was a hit with the acid jazz crowd, and where several albums were reissued by the Ace label. Happily, he made a return to Latin-soul-jazz-funk with his 1995 comeback effort, *Rip a Dip*, which found his skills intact. —*Richie Unterberger*

Tough! / Feb. 15, 1966-Nov. 10, 1966 / Prestige ✦✦✦✦✦
A bit more jazz- and pop-oriented than some of his later sessions, with covers of "Yesterday," "The Shadow of Your Smile," "And I Love Her," "Walk on By," and "Goldfinger." However, when Pucho decides to pull out the funky grooves—as he does on "Cantaloupe Island," "Vietnam Mambo," and "Strange Thing Mambo"—he and the Latin Soul Brothers can smoke. Even at its slightest, this is decent mood music. At its best, it's significantly more than that. The CD reissue is a good deal, adding the entirety of the 1966 LP *Saffron and Soul*. —*Richie Unterberger*

★ **The Best of Pucho & the Latin Soul Brothers** / 1966-1970 / Ace ✦✦✦✦✦
Not only the best overview of Pucho's work, but one of the best Latin jazz recordings available, and certainly one of the best in the nowadays-obscure sub-genre of Latin-jazz-soul. Contains 17 tracks from his 1966-70 heyday, intelligently weighted towards his most dance groove-oriented original material and covers, and eliminating the routine pop covers that filled out some of his LPs. "Canteloupe Island," "Soul Yamie," "Shuckin' and Jivin'," "Maiden Voyage," and "Strange Thing Mambo" are all among his very best cuts. With a running time of 76 minutes, it's a good deal even at import prices. —*Richie Unterberger*

Legends of Acid Jazz: The Best of Pucho & His Latin Soul Brothers / Aug. 9, 1967-Jan. 12, 1970 / Prestige ✦✦✦✦✦
This is an entirely different set than the British import compilation on Ace called *The Best of Pucho & the Latin Soul Brothers;* only six tracks are found on both CDs. Which one you prefer totally depends on your individual taste. Soul and rock fans will be far better off with the Ace collection, which concentrates far more heavily on his soul-jazz, R&B, and psychedelic-influenced numbers. The Prestige set focuses on his more sedate, straight jazz side, with tracks taken from his 1967-70 albums (there's nothing from his first two Prestige records, which have been combined onto one CD on the *Tough!* reissue). This is nicely atmospheric stuff with a Latin lilt, but not Pucho at his funkiest and most adventurous. It's also wholly instrumental, with none of the unhoned but energetic vocals that occasionally adorned his material on cuts like "Shuckin' and Jivin.' " —*Richie Unterberger*

Rip a Dip / Jun. 1995 / Milestone ✦✦✦
Pucho's comeback, after more than 20 years of absence from the studio, pretty much picks up without skipping a beat, though it doesn't match the fire of his best '60s work. He leads an 11-member band (augmented by several guest contributions) through an accomplished and typically versatile set, which ranges from James Brown's "Sex Machine" and Ellington's "Caravan" to Afro-Cuban percussion interludes. —*Richie Unterberger*

Tito Puente

b. Apr. 20, 1923, New York, NY
Leader, Percussion, Timbales, Vibraphone / Latin Jazz, Afro-Cuban Jazz, Salsa
By virtue of his warm, flamboyant stage manner, longevity, constant touring, and appearances in the mass media, Tito Puente is probably the most beloved symbol of Latin jazz today. But more than that, Puente has managed to keep his music remarkably fresh over the decades; he can still steal the show at any given jazz fes-

tival. As a timbales virtuoso, he combines mastery over every rhythmic nuance with old-fashioned showmanship—watching his eyes bug out when taking a dynamic solo is one of the great treats for Latin jazz fans. A trained musician, he is also a fine, lyrical vibraphonist, a gifted arranger, and plays piano, congas, bongos and saxophone. His appeal continues to cut across all ages and ethnic groups, helped no doubt by Santana's best-selling cover versions of "Oye Como Va" and "Para Los Rumberos" in 1970-71, and cameo appearances on "The Cosby Show" in the 1980s and the film *The Mambo Kings* in 1992. His brand of classic salsa is generally free of dark undercurrents, radiating a joyous, compulsively danceable party atmosphere. Rooted in Spanish Harlem, of Puerto Rican descent, Puente originally intended to become a dancer but those ambitions were scotched by a torn ankle tendon suffered in an accident. At age 13, he began working in Ramon Olivero's big band as a drummer, and later he studied composing, orchestration and piano at Juilliard and the the New York School of Music. More importantly, he played with and absorbed the influence of Machito, who was successfully fusing Latin rhythms with progressive jazz. Forming the nine-piece Piccadilly Boys in 1947 and then expanding it to a full orchestra two years later, Puente recorded for Secco, Tico and eventually RCA Victor, helping to fuel the mambo craze that gave him the unofficial—and ultimately lifelong—title "King of the Mambo," or just "El Rey." Puente also helped popularize the cha-cha-cha during the 1950s, and he was the only non-Cuban who was invited to a government-sponsored "50 Years of Cuban Music" celebration in Cuba in 1952. Among the major-league congueros who played with the Puente band in the '50s were Mongo Santamaria, Willie Bobo, Johnny Pacheco and Ray Barretto, which resulted in some explosive percussion shootouts. Not one to paint himself into a tight Latin music corner, Puente's range extended to big band jazz (*Puente Goes Jazz*), and in the '60s, bossa nova tunes, Broadway hits, boogaloos, and pop music, although in later years he tended to stick with older Latin jazz styles that became popularly known as salsa. In 1982, he started reeling off a string of several Latin jazz albums with octets or big bands for Concord Picante that gave him greater exposure and respect in the jazz world than he ever had. An indefatigable visitor to the recording studios, Puente recorded his 100th album *The Mambo King* in 1991 amidst much ceremony and affection (an all-star Latin music concert at Los Angeles' Universal Amphitheatre in March 1992 commemorated the milestone), and he kept adding more titles to the tally throughout the '90s. He also appeared as a guest on innumerable albums over the years, and such jazz stars as Phil Woods, George Shearing, James Moody, Dave Valentin and Terry Gibbs have played on Puente's own recent albums. —*Richard S. Ginell*

● **50 Years of Swing: 50 Great Years & Tracks** / 1946-1995 / RMM ✦✦✦✦✦
50 Years of Swing: 50 Great Years & Tracks is a three-disc, 50-song collection chronicling Tito Puente's immensely popular and influential career. Over the course of the collection, Puente's groundbreaking fusions of Latin rhythms and bebop can be heard, as well as his forays into straight jazz and worldbeat, making *50 Years of Swing* a box set of enormous worth. It's one of the raw samplers that educates as it entertains. —*Stephen Thomas Erlewine*

El Timbral / 1949-1951 / Grey Cliff ✦✦✦
Tito Puente's early mambo band is well featured on 25 selections reissued for this CD. In general, the music is not all that jazz-oriented (the horns do not solo), and the emphasis is on danceable rhythms, shouting ensembles and the vocals of Vicentico Valdez and Bobby Escoto. So rather than being Afro-Cuban jazz, Tito Puente's music was leaning much more towards spirited Latin dance music during the era. However, the exciting percussion and catchy melodies make this collection of strong musical interest (in addition to its historic value). —*Scott Yanow*

● **El Rey del Timbal: The Best of Tito Puente** / Nov. 23, 1949-Jan. 28, 1989 / Rhino ✦✦✦✦✦
Summarizing Tito Puente's numerous accomplishments on a single CD would be impossible. *El Rey De Timbal*, a 1997 disc spanning 1949-87, barely scratches the surface—but for Puente, a five-CD box set would also only scratch the surface. But this gem-laden collection does illustrate just how remarkably consistent the salsa legend was during the course of 38 years. *El Rey De Timbal* kicks into high gear with 1949's "Ran-Kan-Kan" before treating us to such essential 1950s recordings as "Cao-Cao Mani Picao," "Cual Es Tu Idea," "Agua Limpia Todo" and "Oye Mi Guaguanco." Live versions of "Separala Tambien" and "A Gozar Timbero" from 1960 are superb, as is 1961's exuberant "T.P. on the Strip." Though salsa dominates the disc, Puente's Latin jazz output for Concord Picante in the 1980s is well represented by "El Rey De Timbal" and "Machito Forever." Diehard Puente fans will notice that "Ban Ban Quiere," "Oye Como Va" and other essential hits are missing, but then, no one said *El Rey De Timbal* was all-inclusive. Again, it barely scratches the surface, but what a marvelous surface it is. —*Alex Henderson*

Cuban Carnival / 1955-1956 / BMG / ✦✦✦✦✦
While the music that came to be termed "salsa" originated in Cuba, Puerto Ricans have been among its strongest supporters. One New York-reared puertoriqueno who soared to the top of the salsa world in the 1950s was timbale player/vibist Tito

Puente. Boasting such early Puente gems as "Cual Es La Idea," "Oye Mi Guanguanco" and "Yambecua," the exuberant, infectious *Cuban Carnival* is essential listening for anyone with even a casual interest in Afro-Cuban music. Many of the players Puente employs in his driving orchestra—including Mongo Santamaria, Willie Bobo and Carlos "Patato" Valdez—would become among the most celebrated percussionists in Latin music. Whether the style is mambo, son, cha-cha or rhumba, *Cuban Carnival* is outstanding from start to finish. —*Alex Henderson*

Puente Goes Jazz / 1956 / RCA ✦✦✦

Top Percussion / 1957 / BMG ✦✦✦✦✦
A stunner from Puente's golden age, this 1957 recording brought together Tito, Mongo, Willie Bobo, Aguabella, and Julito Collazo on percussion with vocalists that included Mercedita Valdez, in seven wonderful cuts of traditional and (then) contemporary Afro-Cuban skin-on-skin. Then as an unexpected gift, there is a seven-minute Latin-jazz suite featuring Puente's considerable jazz-arranger head and a powerful band with Doc Severinson on lead trumpet. —*John Storm Roberts*

★ **Dance Mania** / 1958 / BMG ✦✦✦✦✦
Many have long despaired of finding anything from the days of Puente's young prime, and here's one of his two best albums reissued in CD. This was Puente's big band at the height of its powers, one of the great documents of New York Latin music and the sort of thing that established the man's claim to be one of the creators of big-band mambo. —*John Storm Roberts*

New Cha Cha/Mambo Herd / 1958 / LaserLight ✦✦✦✦
Tito Puente and Woody Herman teamed in the late '50s with spectacular results. Puente's blazing timbales and splendid Afro-Latin rhythms were easily adapted into the Herman swing mode. Puente, Ray Barretto, Gilbert Lopez, Ray Rodriquez and/or Willie Rodriquez simply laid down a barrage of beats, rhythmic patterns and textures, while Herman and his band did their solos and unison arrangements directly over them, easing into the intervals and letting the grooves direct them. Herman himself was still wailing away on clarinet and alto sax, teaming with Puente to ensure that the beat never clashed with the front line. LaserLight's remastering is fine, and they have used the original 1958 liner notes. A pivotal event in jazz and Afro-Latin music. —*Ron Wynn*

On Broadway / Jul. 1982 / Concord Picante ✦✦✦✦✦
The great Latin bandleader Tito Puente has long been one of the pioneers in fusing bebop with very danceable Latin music. On this Concord disc, Puente plays vibes and timbales and utilizes an 11-piece band featuring trumpeter Jimmy Frisaura, Mario Rivera on tenor, soprano and flute, pianist Jorge Dalto and an infectious rhythm section. Jazz standards (including "Sophisticated Lady," "Bluesette" and even Freddie Hubbard's "First Light") alternate with Latin numbers. —*Scott Yanow*

Oye Como Va: The Dance Collection / Jul. 1, 1982-Jun. 13, 1996 / Concord Jazz ✦✦✦✦
Given Tito Puente's staggeringly prolific output on recordings, obviously no single disc can sum it up, so Concord Picante sensibly calls this compendium a "dance" collection. With the aim to keep the mambos, guajiras and cha-chas moving and grooving foremost in mind, there is still a great deal of variety in this CD—powerhouse big-band sounds, classic eight-piece salsa ensembles, lots of burning jazz solos from such firebrands as sax veteran Mario Rivera, and even a touch of the Orient on "Chang." In a bit of a surprise, there are several welcome featured marimba solos for Tito, along with his standard timbales explosions and animated vibraphone spots. Though Puente has a fairly deep backlog of Picante material from which to choose, the live 1984 *El Rey* album receives far more attention than its cousins—four uninterrupted cuts to close the album. But the concentration is worth the space, for we hear one of his hottest versions of "Oye Como Va," as well as other potent examples of how Puente could and still can fire up an audience. The whole package is a testament to Puente's apparently unquenchable vitality in what would be anyone else's dotage—and believe me and Concord Picante, you definitely can dance to this. —*Richard S. Ginell*

☆ **El Rey** / May 1984 / Concord Picante ✦✦✦✦✦
This is a fun set. In the 1980s and '90s, Tito Puente's three-horn, four-percussion nonet perfectly balanced Latin music and boppish jazz. What is most unusual about the CD reissue is that, in addition to his spirited playing on timbales, the emphasis is on Puente's vibes. Inspired by Lionel Hampton but also having his own percussive style, Puente sounds creative on his "second instrument," making one wish that he played it more on other projects. The repertoire is highlighted by the crowd-pleaser "Oye Como Va," an interesting reworking of Eddie Heywood's "Rainfall," "Giant Steps" and "Equinox." —*Scott Yanow*

Mambo Diablo / May 1985 / Concord Picante ✦✦✦✦

Sensacion / 1987 / Concord Picante ✦✦✦✦
It includes "Jordu" and "'Round Midnight" as well as a "Guajira for Cal" (Tjader). Terry Gibbs is a guest artist on two cuts. —*John Storm Roberts, Original Music*

Un Poco Loco / Jan. 1987 / Concord Picante ✦✦✦✦✦
One of his best for the label. Puente's playing in both large and small contexts. —*Ron Wynn*

Salsa Meets Jazz / Jan. 1988 / Concord Picante ✦✦✦✦✦
Excellent, maybe his best on the label. Phil Woods (as) joins the party and soars. —*Ron Wynn*

Goza Me Timbal / Jul. 31, 1989-Aug. 1, 1989 / Concord Picante ✦✦✦✦
This Concord CD was Tito Puente's 99th as a leader and the music is particularly strong. Four jazz standards alternate with a quartet of Puente's originals and Chucho Valdes' "Cha Cha Cha," all of which are potentially good vehicles for jazz improvisations (although "Ode" and "Lambada" are dominated by group vocals). There are plenty of fine solos throughout by the five horn players and the three- or four-piece percussion section keeps the rhythms infectious. In the world of Latin-jazz, Tito Puente has had few peers. —*Scott Yanow*

Out of This World / Dec. 1990 / Concord Picante ✦✦✦

The Mambo King: His 100th Album / 1991 / RMM ✦✦✦✦
Puente's 100th album is a celebration of that fact, with a procession of vocalists, most of whom—like Celia Cruz—were professionally associated with him at one time or another. That doesn't make for a very tight concept, but recordings by musicians of his generation didn't have concepts, they had music. So does this one, including a minor riot with Celia Cruz riding a big, burly mambo arrangement by a band full of just everybody, and a wonderful "El Bribon del Aguacero" with Chocolate Armenteros on trumpet. —*John Storm Roberts*

Mambo of the Times / Dec. 1991 / Concord Jazz ✦✦✦✦
Through his consistently infectious series of recordings for Concord Picante, Tito Puente reinforced his position as one of the most important leaders of Latin jazz. On this CD (which is exciting, danceable and quite surprising within the boundaries of the genre), Puente and his 11-piece unit (which includes trumpeter Charlie Sepulveda and tenorman Mario Rivera) play at their best. "Things to Come" is a strong opener, Fats Waller's "Jitterbug Waltz" gets an off-the-wall but successful transformation and even "Passion Flower" and "If You Could See Me Now" (neither of which would normally be thought of in this context) work well. All five horns have their opportunities to star (the flute tradeoff on "The Best Is Yet to Come" is impressive) and the rhythm section shows that it can compete favorably with that of any other Latin band. Other than the remarkably juvenile liner notes from jazz wannabee Bill Cosby, this is a highly recommended set. —*Scott Yanow*

In Session / 1993 / Bellaphon ✦✦✦✦✦
This outing from Tito Puente is a throwback to Latin-jazz of the 1950s and '60s. Very much a jazz session, most of the selections feature fine solos from trumpeter Charlie Sepulveda and the muscular tenor of Mario Rivera, flutist Dave Valentin and pianist Hilton Ruiz. Drummer Ignacio Berroa and three percussionists really push the ensembles and Puente (on timbales and vibes) has plenty of fine spots. As a bonus, James Moody drops by to do a lively version of his "Moody's Mood for Love" (complete with yodeling). It's an excellent Latin-jazz set. —*Scott Yanow*

Tito Puente & His Latin Jazz All Stars / 1993 / Concord Jazz ✦✦✦✦
This Concord Puente date offers a frenetic mix of furious Latin jazz and danceable cuts, among them "Vaya Puente" and "Master Timbalero," as well as the more ambitious "Nostalgia in Times Square" and "Espresso Por Favor." Puente not only plays vibes, marimba, timbales and percussion, but drives a band that has three sterling rhythmic contributors in Johnny Rodriquez, Jose Madera and Jose Rodriguez, as well as superior saxophonists Mario Rivera and Bobby Porcelli, and capable pianist Sonny Bravo. The band plays straight dance music, intricate bop and big band swing. The ageless Puente continues issuing versatile, first-rate sessions, and this disc adds another chapter to his remarkable legacy. —*Ron Wynn*

Royal 'T' / Jan. 18, 1993+Jan. 19, 1993 / Concord Jazz ✦✦✦✦✦
Tito Puente has long championed Latin-jazz, a combination of Latin percussion and rhythms with bebop-oriented jazz. This release from the Concord Picante label serves as a perfect introduction to his music. For this date, Puente (who performs on timbales and marimba) uses six horns, piano, bass, synthesizer and three other percussionists to play everything from "Donna Lee" and "Stompin' at the Savoy" to his own originals. Soloists include the many reeds (including piccolo) of Mario Rivera, trumpeter Tony Lujan, trombonist Art Velasco and, of course, the percussion section. One of Tito Puente's better recordings of recent times. —*Scott Yanow*

Jazzin' / 1995 / RMM Tropijazz ✦✦✦✦
Although the great Latin bandleader Tito Puente gets first billing and the Count Basie Orchestra "guests" on three of the ten selections, the obvious star of this set is singer India. Her emotional delivery borders sometimes on going over the top but India is quite skilled as an interpreter of lyrics (both in English and in Spanish), as a scatter and as a Latin jazz singer. She alternates standards with newer tunes and is assisted by such soloist as Puente (on vibes, marimbas and timbales), pianist Hil-

ton Ruiz, altoist Bobby Porcelli, Mario Rivera on tenor and flutist Dave Valentin. This CD is a fine effort with plenty of spirit and exciting moments. —*Scott Yanow*

Special Delivery / Jun. 11, 1996-Jul. 13, 1996 / Concord Picante ✦✦✦✦✦
Tito Puente, the godfather of Latin jazz, celebrated 50 years in music with this sizzling CD. "Be-Bop" is launched with a duel between trumpeters Bobby Shew and Maynard Ferguson. Underrated alto saxophonist Bobby Porcelli and tenorman Mario Rivera make this version of "Stablemates" a keeper. The rarely heard "Venus De Milo" is revived with a warm tribute to composer Gerry Mulligan by baritone saxophonist Mitch Forman. *Special Delivery* is big-band Latin jazz at its best. —*Ken Dryden*

Dudu Pukwana

b. Jul. 18, 1938, Port Elizabeth, South Africa, **d.** Jun. 28, 1990, London, England
Piano, Organ, Alto Saxophone / Avant-Garde

A fiery, inspirational alto saxophonist, Dudu Pukwana's wailing leads and indomitable spirit brilliantly fused township jive, free music and honking R&B. Pukwana actually began on piano, taking lessons from his father at age ten. He joined Tete Mbambisa's Four Yanks as a teen in the late '50s after the family moved from Port Elizabeth to Cape Town, South Africa. He also started learning saxophone from Nick Moyake, and listening to imported American jazz and R&B records. Chris McGregor invited Pukwana to join the Blue Notes, an integrated band in the early '60s. He'd eventually depart his homeland with the rest of the band, settling temporarily in Switzerland, then later in London. Pukwana stayed with McGregor's groups until 1969, when he joined Hugh Masekela's Union of South Africa in America. After they disbanded in 1970, Pukwana returned to England and formed his own band. They were initially Spear, and later Assegai. Pukwana also worked with Keith Tippett's Centipede, Jonas Gwangwa, Traffic, the Incredible String Band, Gwigwi Mrwebi, Sebothane Bahula's Jabula, Harry Miller's Isipingo, and the Louis Moholo Unit. Pukwana recorded with Mrwebi in 1970, and made two albums with Assegai before founding a new edition of Spear in 1972. He also played that year on Masekela's *Home Is Where the Music Is* Chisa session. The new Spear, which included Mongezi Feza, Moholo and Miller, plus Bixo Mngqikana, made some excellent albums, among them *In the Townships* and *Flute Music*, before they disbanded in 1978. Pukwana formed the big band Zila, recorded with them, and continued heading the group until his death of liver failure in 1990. Sadly, none of Pukwana's sessions are available in America on CD. —*Ron Wynn*

In the Townships / Aug. 25, 1973-Nov. 10, 1973 / Earthworks ✦✦✦
Exciting Afro-pop, fusion, and jazz set led by the frenetic saxophonist who was a premier soloist among the class of expatriate South African musicians. Pukwana leads a crew of fellow exiles through songs that both celebrate and commemorate their background, with lots of dashing solos and flashy rhythms as well. —*Ron Wynn*

● **Diamond Express** / 1975 / Freedom ✦✦✦✦✦
An early-'70s recording of this saxophonist, with the late trumpeter Mongezi Feza, in their last meeting before Feza died of pneumonia. Squeaky sax and ensemble in an unabashed mood. South African free jazz. —*Michael G. Nastos*

Zila / 1981 / JIKA ✦✦✦✦
A live date at the 100 Club in London, with a larger ensemble and great soloists. —*Michael G. Nastos*

Don Pullen

b. Dec. 25, 1941, Roanoke, VA, **d.** Apr. 22, 1995, East Orange, NJ
Piano, Organ, / Avant-Garde, Post-Bop

Don Pullen developed a surprisingly accessible way of performing avant-garde jazz. Although he could be quite free harmonically, with dense, dissonant chords, Pullen also utilized catchy rhythms, so even his freest flights generally had a handle for listeners to hang on to. The combination of freedom and rhythm gave him his own unique musical personality.

Pullen, who came from a musical family, studied with Muhal Richard Abrams (with whom he played in the Experimental Band) and in 1964 made his recording debut with Giuseppi Logan. In the 1960s, he recorded free duets with Milford Graves, led his own bands, and played organ with R&B groups, backing Big Maybelle and Ruth Brown, among others. Although he worked with Nina Simone (1970-71) and Art Blakey's Jazz Messengers (1974), Pullen became famous as the pianist with Charles Mingus' last great group (1973-75). From 1979-88, he co-led a notable inside/outside quartet with tenor saxophonist George Adams that was in some ways an extension of Mingus' band. In later years, Pullen led his African-Brazilian Connection and recorded with Kip Hanrahan, Roots, John Scofield, David Murray, Mingus Dynasty and Jane Bunnett, among others. His last project found the always-searching pianist seeking to fuse jazz with native American music. Although his life was too short, Don Pullen fortunately did make a fair amount of recordings as a leader including for Sackville (1974), Horo, Black Saint, Atlantic (his funky "Big Alice" became a near-standard) and Blue Note —*Scott Yanow*

Tomorrow's Promises / 1976-1977 / Atlantic ✦✦✦✦✦

Long overdue to be reissued on CD, this early Don Pullen LP helped introduce him to jazz listeners. The pianist is heard in a variety of settings including a duet with multireedist George Adams on "Last Year's Lies and Tomorrow's Promises," and in two groups with Adams and trumpeter Hannibal Marvin Peterson. Actually the most accessible and memorable piece is the rollicking "Big Alice" which also features violinist Michal Urbaniak and trumpeter Randy Brecker. Pullen, a very rhythmic avant-gardist who can play inside or outside, was well-served by this release. —*Scott Yanow*

The Sixth Sense / Jun. 1985 / Black Saint ✦✦✦✦✦

Breakthrough / Apr. 30, 1986 / Blue Note ✦✦✦✦✦

With George Adams Quartet. Pianist Don Pullen and sax/flute/vocalist George Adams (both ex-Mingus players) with drummer Dan Richmond at their creative zenith. —*Michael G. Nastos*

New Beginnings / Dec. 1988 / Blue Note ✦✦✦

Although it may be a bit of a simplification, on *New Beginnings* pianist Don Pullen sets up fairly simple structures (some of which could be grooves for Ramsey Lewis) and then, after stating the theme, tosses in playful runs that are often quite outside, essentially putting his original style from the 1960s in a slightly commercial 1980s setting. Pullen plays quite rhythmically during his more intense phrases and displays a sly sense of humor. Both bassist Gary Peacock and drummer Tony Williams get a generous amount of solo space on the trio date and they are not overshadowed by the leader's often-fanciful flights. However, the set does have one strong fault: at under 28 minutes, it is way too brief. —*Scott Yanow*

Random Thoughts / Mar. 23, 1990 / Blue Note ✦✦✦✦✦

As bent upon pianistic mayhem as Don Pullen often seemed, this was one of his more user-friendly discs, despite having only a bass and drums between himself and tender-eared listeners. Quite often, Pullen starts a piece as if it were a conventional piano trio number, but before long, he's piling up his trademark keyboard-shuffling glissandos, playing the instrument as if it was a big, glittering, percussive crashing board. Yet everything always swings, thanks to Pullen's own early gospel leanings, Lewis Nash's loosey-goosey traps work and James Genus' flexible bass. Among the most ingratiating pieces is "Indio Gitano," a mesmerizing series of Spanish Phrygian couplets that groove irresistibly in 5/4 time, and "626 Fairfax" is notable for the way Pullen's glissandos fit seamlessly into the piece's swinging and harmonic contexts. Don't let Pullen's identification with the avant-garde scare you away from this engaging CD, for he manages to make even fearsome things seem approachable. —*Richard S. Ginell*

● **Kele Mou Bana** / Sep. 25, 1991+Sep. 26, 1991 / Blue Note ✦✦✦✦✦

This CD features pianist Don Pullen's "African-Brazilian Connection." Always a very percussive player, Pullen gets to romp with two percussionists on this date while altoist Carlos Ward flies over the top and bassist Nilson Matta keeps the foundation solid. The repertoire comprises originals and, even in its freer moments, the rhythms keep the music quite accessible. —*Scott Yanow*

Ode to Life / June 29, 1993 / Blue Note ✦✦✦

Pianist Don Pullen's second recording by his African-Brazilian Connection (which includes bassist Nilson Matta, two percussionists and altoist Carlos Ward) is dedicated to the memory of the late tenor saxophonist George Adams. The music is more subdued than is usual on a Pullen disc, with the harmonies being less dissonant and the mood often melancholy and reflective but occasionally joyous. This is one of Pullen's more accessible and introspective sessions. —*Scott Yanow*

Sacred Common Ground / 1994 / Blue Note ✦✦

This was pianist Don Pullen's final recording. A colaboration between the seven-voice Native American Chief Cliff Singers and Pullen's African Brazilian Connection (a sextet with altoist Carlos Ward and trombonist Joseph Bowie), these performances are definitely not for jazz purists. Most of the music features the vocalists singing in their traditional manner. Pullen and his group have a few interludes where they get to stretch out and there are occasional instances where the two groups actually play off of each other. But because the singers really do not improvise, this well-intentioned project is a mixed success. —*Scott Yanow*

Flora Purim

b. Mar. 6, 1942, Rio de Janeiro, Brazil
Vocals / Fusion, Brazilian Jazz, Latin Jazz

Influenced by both traditional Brazilian singers and the improvisations of American jazz divas like Ella Fitzgerald and Sarah Vaughan, Flora Purim was one of the most adventurous singers of the 1970s. After meeting and marrying her husband, percussionist Airto Moreira, in their native Brazil, Purim moved with him to the US in the late 1960s. Though she worked with Stan Getz and pianist Duke Pearson before the decade ended, it wasn't until joining Chick Corea, Joe Farrell, Stanley Clarke and Moreira in the original Return to Forever in 1972 that she became well known in the States. Purim showed considerable promise on Forever classics like "500 Miles High" and "Light as a Feather" and lived up to it when she went solo with 1973's *Butterfly Dreams*. Ranging from superb to passably decent, Purim's Milestone dates of the mid- to late '70s kept her quite visible in the jazz world. Purim's work grew erratic and uneven in the 1980s, and she wasn't recording as often (though she did provide one album for Virgin and three with Moreira for Concord's Crossover label). Purim didn't record very often in the early to mid-'90s either, but she continued to be highly regarded in Brazilian jazz circles. —*Alex Henderson*

★ **Butterfly Dreams** / Dec. 1973 / Original Jazz Classics ✦✦✦✦✦

A wonderful release that she's seldom equalled since. Joe Henderson (sax), George Duke (p), and Airto (per). —*Ron Wynn*

Stories to Tell / May 1974-Jul. 1974 / Original Jazz Classics ✦✦✦✦

500 Miles High / Jul. 6, 1974 / Milestone ✦✦✦✦✦

Fine album by Purim from the period when she was a dominant Afro-Latin vocalist. She cut this with husband Airto; it's a blend of light romantic songs, Afro-Latin tunes, and easy-listening instrumentals. Purim's singing, which grew in range, depth, and impact during this period, keeps things interesting, as does presence of Milton Nascimento. —*Ron Wynn*

Open Your Eyes / 1976 / Milestone ✦✦✦

Purim's finest hour includes the title track that is Flora at her soaring, swooping best. There is great instrumental backing from George Duke (p) and friends. —*Michael G. Nastos*

That's What She Said / 1977 / Milestone ✦✦✦

One of Latin vocalist Flora Purim's final albums for Milestone in an impressive mid- and late '60s release series. She was mixing light pop, fusion, and more conventional Latin and Afro-Latin material into her albums, while working with her husband Airto, bassist Ron Carter, and trumpeter Oscar Brashear. Despite some overproduction, Purim's voice is still strong and impressive on this release. —*Ron Wynn*

Encounter / Apr. 1976 / Milestone ✦✦✦✦

Purim teamed with fellow Afro-Latin vocalist and instrumentalist Hermeto Pascoal, as well as Airto, on this album. It had more interesting rhythmic elements due to Pascoal's presence; the vocal contrast was also intriguing. —*Ron Wynn*

Nothing Will Be as It Was . . . Tomorrow / 1976 / Milestone ✦✦✦

With lots of string, synth, and vocal arrangements, this includes classics such as the title track, "You Love Me Only," and "Bridges" (written by Milton Nascimiento). Support comes from keyboardists Patrice Rushen and George Duke, and Airto (per). —*Michael G. Nastos*

Humble People / 1985 / Concord Jazz ✦✦✦✦

An all-star band supports Flora and Airto Moreira (per) through jazz, funk, and Latin pop. Guests include David Sanborn (as), Joe Farrell (ts), Milton Cardona (per), and Jerry Gonzalez (per). This is one of Purim's better later-period albums. —*Michael G. Nastos*

The Magicians / Mar. 1986-Apr. 1986 / Crossover ✦✦✦

One of mainstream-minded Concord's few so-called crossover projects—hence the separate label—this isn't a very successful venture, a hodgepodge of this and that, recorded with a flat commercial sheen. Misleadingly, the CD opens with Flora singing the blues on the Cheathams' "Sweet Baby Blues," upon which Airto plays straight traps. But while "Garimpo" gets the album back on the Latin track, the energy and quirky inventiveness of the Moreiras is mostly out to lunch, buried under the in-your-face sound and dissipated among a variety of instrumental lineups. "Jump" does get some sharp Brazilian funk going, and the title track has some of the old Airto craziness, but the rest is not going to light too many fires. —*Richard S. Ginell*

Ike Quebec

b. Aug. 17, 1918, Newark, NJ, **d.** Jan. 16, 1963, New York, NY

Tenor Saxophone / Swing, Early R&B Jazz, Groove, Hard Bop, Soul-Jazz

Influenced by Coleman Hawkins and Ben Webster but definitely his own person, Ike Quebec was one of the finest swing-oriented tenor saxman of the 1940s and '50s. Though he was never an innovator, Quebec had a big, breathy sound that was distinctive and easily recognizable, and he was quite consistent when it came to came to down-home blues, sexy ballads and uptempo aggression. Originally a pianist, Quebec switched to tenor in the early 1940s and showed that he had made the right decision on excellent 78s for Blue Note and Savoy (including his hit "Blue Harlem"). As a sideman, he worked with Benny Carter, Kenny Clarke, Roy Eldridge and Cab Calloway. In the late '40s, the saxman did a bit of freelancing behind the scenes as a Blue Note A&R man and brought Thelonious Monk and Bud Powell to the label. Drug problems kept Quebec from recording for most of the 1950s, but he made a triumphant comeback in the early 1960s and was once again recording for Blue Note and doing freelance A&R for the company. Quebec was playing as authoritatively as ever well into 1962, giving no indication that he was suffering from lung cancer, which claimed his life at the age of 44 in 1963. —*Alex Henderson*

☆ **Complete Blue Note Recordings** / Jul. 18, 1944-Sep. 23, 1946 / Mosaic ◆◆◆◆◆
This limited-edition four-LP box set from Mosaic has all of the early Blue Note recordings of tenors John Hardee and Ike Quebec. The little-known Hardee's three sessions are all from 1946 (one is under the leadership of guitarist Tiny Grimes) and find him in top form on a variety of swing-based originals, along with a few standards. In addition to Grimes, the sidemen include trombonist Trummy Young, guitarist Jimmy Shirley and pianists Marlowe Morris and Sammy Benskin. Hardee would eventually settle in Texas as a full-time educator. In contrast, Ike Quebec, who is showcased on five dates (including 11 previously unissued performances), would achieve a bit of fame (his recordings of "Blue Harlem" and "If I Had You" gained some attention) before drugs forced him off the scene in the 1950s; he would make a brief comeback in the early '60s prior to his premature death. Quebec's early Blue Note dates are superior examples of small-group swing and have solo space for some notable stars: guitarist Tiny Grimes, pianist Ram Ramirez, trumpeters Jonah Jones, Buck Clayton and Shad Collins and trombonists Tyree Glenn and Keg Johnson. This 1984 box is certainly definitive but promises to be difficult to find. —*Scott Yanow*

☆ **Complete Blue Note 45 Sessions** / Jul. 1, 1959-Feb. 13, 1962 / Mosaic ◆◆◆◆◆
During his comeback years (1959-62) after a decade mostly off the scene, tenor saxophonist Ike Quebec recorded frequently for Blue Note. He started off with a session aimed at the '45' jukebox market and, although he eventually made a few full-length albums for the label, Quebec cut four '45' dates over a two-year period. This limited-edition (and now out-of-print) three-LP Mosaic box set has all of the jukebox sessions. Most of the 26 selections clock in between four and seven minutes and have long melody statements in addition to concise and soulful solos. Quebec, who was in consistently prime form during his last period, is joined by groups featuring either Skeeter Best or Willie Jones on guitar and Edwin Swanston, Sir Charles Thompson or Earl Van Dyke on organ. Fun and generally danceable music. —*Scott Yanow*

Ballads / Sep. 25, 1960-Mar. 21, 1962 / Blue Note ◆◆◆
Tenor saxophonist Ike Quebec always had a big, warm sound, and he was particularly expert on ballads. This 1997 sampler CD surprisingly does not have any examples of his early work on Blue Note in the mid- to late 1940s, instead concentrating on selections from four of Quebec's seven late-period Blue Note albums, a few songs originally issued as 45s, and "Born to Be Blue," which is taken from an album by guitarist Grant Green. The eight ballads are all standards and put the focus very much on Quebec, making for a fine mood album even if acquiring the full sessions (all but "It Might As Well Be Spring" are currently available on CD) is preferable. —*Scott Yanow*

Heavy Soul / Nov. 26, 1961 / Blue Note ◆◆◆◆
The thick-toned tenor Ike Quebec is in excellent form on this CD reissue of a 1961 Blue Note date. His ballad statements are quite warm and he swings nicely on a variety of medium-tempo material. Unfortunately, organist Freddie Roach has a rather dated sound, which weakens this session a bit; bassist Milt Hinton and drummer Al Harewood are typically fine in support. Originals alternate with standards with "Just One More Chance," "The Man I Love" and "Nature Boy" (the latter an emotional tenor-bass duet) among the highlights. —*Scott Yanow*

The Art of Ike Quebec / Nov. 26, 1961-Oct. 5, 1962 / Blue Note ◆◆◆
Tenor saxophonist Ike Quebec recorded six albums for Blue Note during his last period before passing away in Jan. 1963. This single CD has at least one selection from each of the records (11 in all) that, when taken as a whole, gives one a good idea as to how strong Quebec was still sounding. Although his fans will want to get the individual records (four of the six are currently available on CD's), this is an excellent sampler. Among the other players are organist Freddie Roach, guitarists Grant Green and Kenny Burrell, pianist Sonny Clark, drummer Art Blakey and Billy Higgins, trombonist Bennie Green and tenor great Stanley Turrentine. —*Scott Yanow*

It Might As Well Be Spring / Dec. 9, 1961 / Blue Note ◆◆◆◆
Working with the same quartet that cut *Heavy Soul*—organist Freddie Roach, bassist Milt Hinton and drummer Al Harewood—Ike Quebec recorded another winning hard bop album with *It Might as Well Be Spring*. In many ways, the record is a companion piece to *Heavy Soul*. Since the two albums were recorded so close together, it's not surprising that there a number of stylistic similarities, but there are subtle differences to savor. The main distinction between the two dates is that *It Might as Well Be Spring* is a relaxed, romantic date comprising standards. It provides Quebec with ample opportunity to showcase his rich, lyrical ballad style, and he shines throughout the album. Similarly, Roach has a tasteful, understated technique, whether he's soloing or providing support for Quebec. The pair have a terrific, sympathetic interplay that makes *It Might as Well Be Spring* a joyous listen. —*Stephen Thomas Erlewine*

● **Blue and Sentimental** / Dec. 16, 1961+Dec. 23, 1961 / Blue Note ◆◆◆◆◆
Of tenor saxophonist Ike Quebec's six Blue Note albums from the 1961-62 period, this is the definitive one. The CD reissue (which adds "new" versions of "That Old Black Magic" and "It's All Right with Me" to the original LP program) mostly features Quebec in a quartet with guitarist Grant Green, bassist Paul Chambers and drummer Philly Joe Jones; "Count Every Star" has Quebec joined by Green, pianist Sonny Clark, bassist Sam Jones and drummer Louis Hayes. Although some of the renditions are medium-tempo swingers, it is the soulful ballad versions of "Blue and Sentimental" and "Don't Take Your Love from Me" that are most memorable. Recommended. —*Scott Yanow*

Congo Lament / Jan. 20, 1962 / Blue Note ◆◆◆

Easy Living / Jan. 20, 1962 / Blue Note ◆◆◆◆◆
This CD reissue (which adds three songs to the original LP) is really two sets in one. The first five selections are a blues-oriented jam session that matches together the contrasting tenors of Ike Quebec and Stanley Turrentine with trombonist Bennie Green, pianist Sonny Clark, bassist Milt Hinton and drummer Art Blakey. However it is the last three numbers ("I've Got a Crush on You," "Nancy with the Laughing Face" and "Easy Living") that are most memorable; ballad features for Quebec's warm tenor. All in all this set gives a definitive look at late-period Ike Quebec. —*Scott Yanow*

With a Song in My Heart / Feb. 5, 1962+Feb. 13, 1962 / Blue Note ◆◆◆

Soul Samba / Oct. 5, 1962 / Blue Note ◆◆◆
This CD reissues veteran tenor saxophonist Ike Quebec's final recording as a leader, cut a little more than three months before his death. Recorded during a period when seemingly everyone was making a bossa nova record, Quebec's effort is a bit unusual in that none of the musicians (guitarist Kenny Burrell, bassist Wendell Marshall, drummer Willie Bobo and percussionist Garvin Masseaux) were associated with Brazilian (as opposed to Afro-Cuban) jazz. While Quebec

emphasizes warm long tones (reminiscent of Coleman Hawkins) in a romantic fashion, his sidemen play light and appealing bossa rhythms. The result is high-quality melodic Brazilian dance music (despite the lack of any Jobim songs) with Burrell in particular being quite effective; the pleasing program concludes with three previously unissued alternate takes. —*Scott Yanow*

Alvin Queen

b. Aug. 16, 1950, New York, NY
Drums / Hard Bop
A crisp, powerful and swinging drummer, Alvin Queen hasn't recorded as often as his talents merit, but what he's done is consistently engaging and demanding. Queen worked with George Benson and Stanley Turrentine, then traveled to Europe with Charles Tolliver's quartet. During the '70s he worked with the group Music Inc. co-led by Tolliver and Stanley Cowell. Queen departed America in 1979 for Switzerland, and established Nilva Records. Queen toured France with Plas Johnson and Harry Edison and recorded with John Collins and Junior Mance in the '80s, while working in Zurich with a trio led by Wild Bill Davis and recording with another led by Lonnie Smith. He also did his own dates. Queen has no sessions currently available on CD, but can be heard on reissues by Music Inc. —*Ron Wynn and Michael G. Nastos*

In Europe / Feb. 8, 1980 / Nilva ✦✦✦✦
Quintet with drummer Queen at the helm. Mainstream, bordering on progressive. —*Michael G. Nastos*

Glidin' and Stridin' / 1982 / Nilva ✦✦✦

● **A Day in Holland** / Aug. 1984 / Nilva ✦✦✦✦✦

Uptown / Aug. 24, 1985-Aug. 25, 1985 / Nilva ✦✦✦✦✦
Drummer Alvin Queen's recordings for his European Nilva label have yet to be reissued on CD. This is one of the better releases thanks to strong group originals and the notable sidemen: trumpeter Terence Blanchard, trombonist Robin Eubanks, Manny Boyd on tenor, alto and soprano, pianist John Hicks and bassist Ray Drummond. The music is essentially advanced hard bop; drummer Queen sounds inspired and he pushes the other players to solo at their best. This underrated LP is excellent. —*Scott Yanow*

Quest

f. 1981
Group / Post-Bop
Quest is nominally a cooperative band that includes saxophonist Dave Liebman, pianist Richie Beirach, drummer Billy Hart, and at various times, bassists George Mraz and Ron McClure. As befitting the catholic skills of its straw boss, Liebman, the group's range is exceptionally broad. The individual members are comfortable in all of modern jazz's guises, but the band's collective strength lies in the realm of post-Coltrane modality. The band's eponymously named first album was recorded in 1981 for Palo Alto LP but Liebman's liner notes have been dropped for no real reason. 1986's *Quest II* and 1988's *Natural Selection*, both with McClure. The 1990 CMP album, *Of One Mind*, emphasizes the band's affinity for creative free improvisation. In general, Quest's music reflects a creative empathy shared by its members; the close rapport enjoyed by Liebman and Beirach stems from a musical relationship that goes back more than two decades. The assuredness with which Quest goes about its business results in a music of great depth and intensity. —*Chris Kelsey*

Quest / Dec. 28, 1981-Dec. 29, 1981 / Palo Alto ✦✦✦✦✦
Quest was the name of the quartet that Dave Liebman (who is heard here on soprano and alto flute) had with pianist Richie Beirach, bassist George Mraz and drummer Al Foster. The music on their CD reissue was previously available as a Palo Alto LP but Liebman's liner notes have been dropped for no real reason. "Dr. Jekyll and Mr. Hyde," Foster's tribute to Miles Davis, sounds nothing like the trumpeter's music but builds up expertly in passion and intensity with Liebman's soprano taking honors. Mraz's "Wisteria" is a memorable ballad, Lieb's soprano is explosive on "Softly s in a Morning Sunrise" and Beirach's tender ballad "Elm" (a tribute to the late violinist Zbigniew Seifert) gets fairly adventurous during its latter half. Liebman's hyper "Napanoch" and an atmospheric and floating version of Ornette Coleman's "Lonely Woman" complete this superior postbop release. —*Scott Yanow*

Quest II / Apr. 17, 1986 / Storyville ✦✦✦✦
Quartet set with Liebman, Richie Beirach (p), Ron McClure (b), and Billy Hart (d). —*Ron Wynn*

Natural Selection / Jun. 1988 / Pathfinder ✦✦✦
Quest sometimes played reflective, ethereal pieces that were close to the material done by such bands as Oregon. At other times, they could be funky, loud, free or explosive, particularly Liebman, who played soprano with passion, frequently daz-

zling skill, and verve. Beirach's piano solos avoided the trap of recycling hard bop ideas and ranged from soothing melodies to energetic statements. The lack of predictability and set structure made Quest one of the 1980s more enjoyable bands, and this CD shows why their music defied rigid categorization. —*Ron Wynn*

● **Of One Mind** / Jul. 1990 / CMP ✦✦✦✦
Quest, the quartet co-led by soprano saxophonist David Liebman and pianist Richie Beirach, recorded many sessions during the 1980s. This CD differs from the others in that the music comprises free improvisations with just a little discussion taking place beforehand to plan strategy. Since the group (which also includes bassist Ron McClure and drummer Billy Hart) worked together frequently through the years, the individual members were able to follow each other's thoughts and ideas with only subtle hints. Each song evolves logically if not predictably. The episodic 17-minute "Passages" is the most interesting performance, containing a spacey section, a lyrical Beirach-McClure duet, a spot for Hart's drums and a fiery closing ensemble. Intriguing music. —*Scott Yanow*

Gene Quill (Daniel Eugene Quill)

b. Dec. 15, 1927, Atlantic City, NJ, **d.** Jan. 1989, Atlantic City, NJ
Alto Saxophone / Bop, Cool
In the 1950s, the alto sax didn't get much louder than that played by Gene Quill, a hard-edged soloist who could rival Jackie McLean and frequent partner Phil Woods when it came to intensity, enthusiasm, and hard bop aggression. Like Gene Ammons & Sonny Stitt or Dexter Gordon & Wardell Gray on tenor, Woods and Quill (known as "Phil & Quill") often engaged in celebrated alto battles that exemplified musical sportsmanship at its finest. Because Quill was so tireless and energetic a player in the 1950s (when his battles with Woods were documented by Prestige and RCA), the altoist was a natural sideman for such high-volume jazzmen as Gene Krupa, Quincy Jones and Buddy DeFranco. But Quill, who recorded for Roost and Dawn on his own dates, certainly had no problem playing melodically, and he was in very melodic settings when employed in Claude Thornhill's big band and Gerry Mulligan Concert Jazz Band from 1960-62. Ironically, a man who, to many, epitomized hard bop, became softer and more introspective in the '60s, sometimes bringing to mind the "cool" and lyrical alto playing of Lee Konitz and Art Pepper without sounding like he was consciously imitating either. Quill was in extremely poor health during the last years of his life, when he suffered brain damage and partial paralysis. Regrettably, most of Quill's work as a leader wasn't reissued on CD in the US in the late 1980s or early to mid-1990s. —*Alex Henderson*

Three Bones and a Quill / 1958 / Fresh Sound ✦✦✦✦

Paul Quinichette

b. May 17, 1916, Denver, CO, **d.** May 25, 1983, New York, NY
Tenor Saxophone / Swing
Paul Quinichette was known throughout his career as the "Vice Prez" because he sounded so similar to Lester Young. While most of Young's other followers emulated his 1930s style, Quinichette sounded like Lester Young of the then-present day (the 1950s). After getting experience with Nat Towles, Lloyd Sherock and Ernie Fields, Quinichette was featured with Jay McShann during 1942-44. He played on the West Coast with Johnny Otis (1945-47), traveled to New York with Louis Jordan and performed with Lucky Millinder (1948-49), Red Allen and Hot Lips Page. Quinichette was with Count Basie during 1952-53 (when Basie had reformed his orchestra), worked with Benny Goodman in 1955, recorded with Billie Holiday and held his own on a session with John Coltrane. Otherwise Quinichette mostly led his own group in the 1950s, recording several excellent (if obviously derivative) records. He left music in the late '50s to become an electrical engineer, returning to jazz briefly in the early- to mid-'70s, playing with Sammy Price, Brooks Kerr and Buddy Tate before being forced to retire due to poor health. —*Scott Yanow*

The Vice President / Oct. 5, 1951-Jul. 1952 / Trip ✦✦✦✦
Twelve of the fifteen selections recorded at tenor saxophonist Paul Quinichette's first sessions as a leader were reissued on this late-'70s Trip LP. Quinichette, a near-perfect soundalike of Lester Young in the 1950s, was with Count Basie's new orchestra at the time. Six selections find the tenor joined by Basie himself (on piano and organ) along with such Basie-ites as trumpeter Buck Clayton, trombonist Dickie Wells, guitarist Freddie Green, bassist Walter Page and drummer Gus Johnson. The other selections include two on which Quinichette is joined by trumpeter Joe Newman, trombonist Henry Coker and altoist Marshall Royal and four on which his five-piece rhythm section includes pianist Kenny Drew and organist Bill Doggett. With the exception of "I'll Always Be in Love with You," all of the songs are fairly basic and swinging Quinichette originals; hopefully Polygram will reissue this music on CD eventually. —*Scott Yanow*

● **Cattin' with Coltrane and Quinichette** / Aug. 14, 1952-May 17, 1957 / DCC
✦✦✦✦✦

The often-overlooked Paul Quinichette (who sounded very similar to Lester
Young) is heard at his best on this audiophile CD. Four selections (three Mal Waldron originals plus "Sunday") match Quinichette with fellow tenor John Coltrane
(one should have no difficulty telling them apart!) during a 1957 date that has
been reissued frequently; pianist Waldron, bassist Julian Euell and drummer Ed
Thigpen complete the quintet. Much rarer are two other numbers ("Exactly Like
You" and a previously unreleased "Tea for Two") without Coltrane from the same
session, plus three previously unknown performances ("Green Is Blue," "You
Belong to Me" and "Birdland Jump") from August 14, 1952, that match Quinichette
with pianist Kenny Drew, rhythm guitarist Freddie Green, bassist Gene Ramey
and drummer Gus Johnson. Paul Quinichette is in prime form throughout the
fairly definitive release of swinging mainstream music. —*Scott Yanow*

Moods Featuring Paul Quinichette / Nov. 4, 1954+Nov. 22, 1954 / EmArcy ✦✦✦
This out-of-print album (which was last reissued in the 1970s on a Trip LP) has the
cool-toned tenor Paul Quinichette showcased on two separate four-song sessions
playing six early Quincy Jones compositions, plus a pair of swing standards. The
earlier date matches Quinichette with flutist Sam Most, pianist Sir Charles
Thompson, two guitars, bassist Paul Chambers and drummer Harold Wing. The
November 22 session finds Quinichette joined by flutist Herbie Mann, pianist
Jimmy Jones, bassist Al Hall and three Latin percussionists. The mixture of

straightahead and Afro-Cuban jazz works quite well, but all of Paul Quinichette's
fine EmArcy/Mercury dates remain out of print. —*Scott Yanow*

The Kid from Denver / Jul. 16, 1956-Aug. 1959 / Biograph ✦✦✦
The great Lester Young soundalike Paul Quinichette is well-featured on this reissue CD. He is heard on two numbers with a sextet led by trumpeter Gene Roland,
playing two other songs with Roland's septet and on eight selections with his own
ten-piece group (which is filled with players from the world of Count Basie). Best
are two numbers ("Honeysuckle Rose" and "Pennies from Heaven") that feature
Quinichette backed by Basie's rhythm section plus pianist Nat Pierce. There are
not that many Paul Quinichette albums currently available, making this CD a
rather definitive look at the underrated (if not particularly original) tenor. —*Scott
Yanow*

On the Sunny Side / May 10, 1957 / Original Jazz Classics ✦✦✦✦
This CD reissue adds a previously unreleased version of "My Funny Valentine" to
the original four-song program. The swing-based tenor Paul Quinichette is heard
with a more modern group of players than usual: trombonist Curtis Fuller, both
Sonny Red and John Jenkins on altos, pianist Mal Waldron, bassist Doug Watkins
and drummer Ed Thigpen. Waldron's three originals (highlighted by "Cool-Lypso")
allow plenty of room for swinging, and Quinichette (who also performs "On the
Sunny Side of the Street") sounds comfortable interacting with the younger musicians. An enjoyable and underrated release. —*Scott Yanow*

Sun Ra (Herman "Sonny" Blount)

b. May 22, 1914, Birmingham, AL, **d.** May 30, 1993, Birmingham, AL

Piano, Keyboards, Organ / Avant-Garde, Free Jazz

Of all the jazz musicians, Sun Ra was probably the most controversial. He did not make it easy for people to take him seriously, because he surrounded his adventurous music with costumes and mythology that both looked backwards towards ancient Egypt and forwards into science fiction. In addition Ra documented his music in very erratic fashion on his Saturn label, generally not listing recording dates and giving inaccurate personnel information so one could not really tell how advanced some of his innovations were. It has taken a lot of time to sort it all out (although Robert Campbell's Sun Ra discography has done a miraculous job). While there were times when Sun Ra's aggregation performed brilliantly, on other occasions they were badly out of tune and showcasing absurd vocals. Near the end of his life, Ra was featuring plate twirlers and fire-eaters in his colorful show as a sort of Ed Sullivan for the 1980s!

But despite all of the trappings, Sun Ra was a major innovator. Born Sonny Blount in Birmingham, AL (although he used to claim he was from another planet), Ra led his own band for the first time in 1934. He freelanced at a variety of jobs in the Midwest, working as a pianist/arranger with Fletcher Henderson in 1946-47. He appeared on some obscure records as early as 1948 but really got started around 1953. Leading a big band (which he called the Arkestra) in Chicago, Ra started off playing advanced bop but was early on open to the influences of other cultures and experimenting with primitive electric keyboards and playing free long before the avant-garde got established. After moving to New York in 1961, Ra performed some of his most advanced work. In 1970 he relocated his group to Philadelphia and in later years alternated free improvisations and mystical group chants with eccentric versions of swing tunes, sounding like a spaced out Fletcher Henderson Orchestra. Many of his most important sidemen were with him on and off for decades (most notably John Gilmore on tenor, altoist Marshall Allen and baritonist Pat Patrick). Ra, who recorded a pair of fine solo piano albums for JAI, has been well served by Evidence's extensive repackaging of many of his Saturn dates, which have at last been outfitted with correct dates and personnel details. Sun Ra's vast legacy remains both confusing and vast. *—Scott Yanow*

Sound Sun Pleasure / 1953-1958 / Evidence ♦♦♦♦♦

Sun Ra's kaleidoscope of sounds was just taking shape in the 1950s and early '60s when the 13 tracks comprising this CD were recorded. His Astro-Infinity Arkestra included several emerging musicians who would later become major stars, like baritone saxophonist Charles Davis, Bob Northern on fluegelhorn and James Spaulding, who is featured on various reeds. The great jazz violinist Stuff Smith is even along on "Deep Purple," providing a dazzling, bluesy solo right at home in The Ra mix. *—Ron Wynn*

The Singles / Sep. 1954-1982 / Evidence ♦♦♦♦♦

The eccentric and innovative bandleader/keyboardist Sun Ra recorded and released a series of 45 rpm singles that are unknown to most of his fans on his Saturn label. The very limited-edition records were sold by the band at concerts, never distributed and quickly forgotten until the Evidence label put together this intriguing two-CD set, which contains all of the singles that have been found thus far. Programmed in chronological order, the generally concise pieces usually find Ra with a small group taken from his orchestra, and there are many solos by Ra on such exotic keyboards as the Mini-moog, harmonium, Wurlitzer electric piano (in 1956!), the Gibson Kalamazoo organ, clavinet and the Rocksichord. The biggest surprise is that Ra backed several doo wop groups in the mid-1950s; plus, there are a few numbers without Ra, most notably two excellent blues by guitarist/vocalist Lacy Gibson. Not every selection is classic (some are quite odd), but taken as a whole, the two-fer gives one a valuable alternate look at the unique bandleader. *—Scott Yanow*

Super-Sonic Jazz / 1956 / Evidence ♦♦♦♦

This Evidence CD reissues one of bandleader Sun Ra's first recordings, a legendary album that was only out previously on his small Saturn label. A highly recommended set for listeners who think of Ra as purely an avant-garde player, the music contains several straightahead blues and fine solos from tenor saxophonist John Gilmore, baritonist Charles Davis, trumpeter Art Hoyle and trombonist Julian Priester among others. One can tell by listening to Ra's adventurous piano solos (particularly on "Advice to Medics") and some of the arrangements here that he was not going to stay closely tied to the bobop tradition for long. Fascinating music. *—Scott Yanow*

Sun Song / Jul. 12, 1956 / Delmark ♦♦♦♦

Other than the title cut (a spacey electronic fantasy that concludes this CD reissue), the music on the early effort from Sun Ra and his Arkestra is mostly fairly conventional. Although the leader offers some slightly left-of-center piano, Robert Herndon has a couple of colorful tympani solos, and there are some futuristic song titles (such as "Call for All Demons," "Street Named Hell" and "Brainville"), the music could otherwise pass for a typical "territory band" of the mid-'50s. Most notable among the soloists are tenor saxophonist John Gilmore (an influence on John Coltrane), baritonist Pat Patrick and trombonist Julian Priester. This is a historic set that only hints in spots at Ra's upcoming innovations. *—Scott Yanow*

Angels & Demons at Play/The Nubians of Plutonia / 1956-1960 / Evidence ♦♦♦♦♦

Sun Ra ambles between vigorous hard bop, ambitious, adventurous free jazz, and African and Afro-Latin material on the 15 selections featured on this set of '50s and early-'60s tracks. The first half was recorded in 1956 and 1960 and includes originals from Ronnie Boykins and Julian Priester, plus futuristic organ from Ra on "Music From the World Tomorrow" and hard-blowing solos from John Gilmore and Marshall Allen. The second half consists of rehearsal tapes from 1960 with the Arkestra steadily progressing and moving beyond conventional jazz modes into multiple rhythms, chants, and twisting, roaring arrangements spiced by vividly expressive solos. Plus, like every other disc in the series, it is superbly remastered. *—Ron Wynn*

We Travel the Spaceways / Bad and Beautiful / 1956-1961 / Evidence ♦♦♦♦♦

The opening numbers range from the humorous and futuristic bent of "Interplanetary Music" and "We Travel the Spaceways" to the more musically expansive "New Horizons" and "Space Loneliness." Trumpeter Phil Cochran and the superb horn section of Marshall Allen, John Gilmore and Pat Patrick sometimes remain in the maze and sometimes explode with short but peppery solos. The other songs mix bop and swing tunes with more experimental fare like "Ankh" and "Exotic Two," where Patrick, Gilmore, Ra and Allen soar while bassist Ronnie Boykins and drummer Tommy Hunter maintain the rhythmic center. *—Ron Wynn*

Sound of Joy / Nov. 1957 / Delmark ♦♦♦♦

This reissue, prior to the release of many of Sun Ra's Saturn albums on Evidence CDs, was often thought of as Ra's second recording although now several earlier dates have appeared. The music from Sun Ra's Chicago-based band of the 1950s (some of the performances also appear on Evidence's *Planet Earth/Low Ways*) is quite interesting, because its ties to the bop and swing traditions are much more obvious than they would be in the near future. Ra's eccentric piano and occasional electric keyboard look forward as do some of the harmonies and Jim Herndon's colorful tympani. Two previously unissued cuts (which have also surfaced on an Evidence set) augment the original LP program. *—Scott Yanow*

Jazz in Silhouette / 1958 / Evidence ♦♦♦

This is the CD to put on for bop fans who long ago have written off Sun Ra as a bizarre eccentric. Ra's 1958 tentet was a mighty outfit (with such top players as trumpeter Hobart Dotson, trombonist Julian Priester, altoists James Spaulding and Marshall Allen, tenor great John Gilmore and baritonists Pat Patrick and Charles Davis) and the tunes (all written or co-composed by Ra) are among his strongest; several deserve to be revived. The bop-oriented music only has occasional hints of Ra's upcoming avant-garde explorations (particularly "Ancient Aiethopia"), "Saturn" sounds like a Charles Mingus tune, and "Blues at Midnight" is a rare uptempo straightahead Ra blues. This is the best album from Ra's early Chicago period and is highly recommended. —*Scott Yanow*

Planet Earth / Interstellar Low / 1958-1960 / Evidence ✦✦✦✦✦
This Evidence CD reissues two rare albums originally put out by bandleader Sun Ra on his Saturn label. Taken as a whole it shows Ra's Arkestra evolving from its roots in bop and swing into a unique entity of its own. The first four titles (from 1956), despite Ra doubling on electric keyboards, are fairly conventional. Art Hoyle has a few fine trumpet solos and the twin baritones of Pat Patrick and Charles Davis battle it out on the boppish "Two Tones." The three numbers from 1958 are much more advanced, utilizing some modal vamps, and the final seven selections (from 1960) are generally avant-garde. The group has "vocals" on a couple of pieces, most successfully the memorable "Rocket Number Nine Take Off for the Planet Venus," which also contains an explosive John Gilmore tenor solo. This excellent CD can be used as a way of getting bebop fans interested in Sun Ra's explorative music. —*Scott Yanow*

Holiday for Soul Dance / 1960 / Evidence ✦✦✦✦✦
Sun Ra never concerned himself with the issues of innovation vs. preservation that seem to be the rage in current jazz circles. Instead, his music was both futuristic and classic, embracing the past and anticipating the future. A prime example is this fine eight-track collection of pre-rock standards done in 1968 and 1969. Of course, Ra didn't simply cover these numbers in a reverential manner; instead, he and the Astro-Infinity Arkestra stomp, romp, twist, strut and cut through a collection ranging from "But Not For Me" to "Early Autumn" and "Body and Soul." —*Ron Wynn*

Fate in a Pleasant Mood/When the Sun Comes Out / 1960-1963 / Evidence ✦✦✦✦✦
Sun Ra left Chicago for New York in the early '60s, and half the sessions on this disc were done at the Choreographers' Workshop in New York during 1962 and 1963. The first half were done in Chicago with Marshall Allen and John Gilmore in the solo forefront on alto sax, flute, tenor sax, and clarinet. Ra's teeming piano, Ronnie Boykins' fluid, throbbing bass lines, and Jon Hardy's drums were at the rhythmic core as the orchestra executed both short bursts and extensive dialogues. Ra turned even further outside on the second set; his space/futuristic concept was solidifying musically and his keyboard work growing more piercing and ethereal. —*Ron Wynn*

Cosmic Tones for Mental Therapy/Art Forms of Dimensions Tomorrow / 1961-1963 / Evidence ✦✦✦
Two of Sun Ra's rarer private recordings for his Saturn label are reissued in full on this single CD. *Cosmic Tones for Mental Therapy* is one of his odder dates, with Ra playing the Clavioline (an early synthesizer) and the "astro space organ" in a group sometimes consisting of as many as three bass clarinets (including John Gilmore), altoist Marshall Allen (doubling on oboe), baritonist Pat Patrick, bass, drums, percussion and log drums. The excessive use of echo devices really gives the atmospheric music a strange sound. The other album (*Art Forms of Dimensions Tomorrow*) is a little more conventional (three reeds, two brass, bass, drums and Ra's keyboards) but also fairly free. In general the music on these two sets is unsettling, inconclusive and rambles a bit but also holds one's interest. —*Scott Yanow*

Other Planes of There / 1964 / Evidence ✦✦✦✦✦
Performing five originals with a 13-piece group consisting of one trumpet, three trombones, five reeds, bass, two drums and his own piano, Sun Ra plays some surprisingly well-organized and episodic music on this reissue CD. The improvising is often quite free and the longest performance (the 22-minute "Other Plane of There") is actually the most memorable, because it contains some rather intriguing sections. However, the CD on a whole is not all that essential—some of the pieces ramble on in spots and do little more than set up unusual atmospheres and odd moods. —*Scott Yanow*

The Magic City / 1965 / Evidence ✦✦✦✦
It is safe to say that no city ever got the kind of tribute Sun Ra paid his Birmingham, Alabama, hometown with this 1965 selection. The 27-minute title cut ambles, clashes, and slides toward completion as Ra's movements, segues, and sections alternate between blistering dialogues and emphatic solos, especially Marshall Allen playing piccolo with the same abandon and spiraling intensity as an alto sax, flute, or oboe. But Ra leads them right back through another intense outing, the nearly 11-minute "The Shadow World." After these two pieces, the band sounds more relaxed on the last two cuts. —*Ron Wynn*

The Heliocentric Worlds of Sun Ra, Vols. 1 & 2 / Apr. 20, 1965 / ESP ✦✦✦

Monorails and Satellites / 1966 / Evidence ✦✦✦
Sun Ra's first solo piano session (there would be two later ones for Improvising Artists) finds him exploring seven originals plus the standard "Easy Street" in an eccentric and sometimes rambling fashion. The pieces (none of which stand that

well individually) fit together as a sort of suite, but it is for Ra's playing (which is a different form of avant-garde piano than Cecil Taylor or Paul Bley) rather than any of the originals that this formerly rare set (reissued on CD by Evidence) is most notable. —*Scott Yanow*

★ **Atlantis** / 1967-1969 / Saturn ✦✦✦✦✦
Sun Ra was soaring far and wide on these late-'60s sessions, most notably the 20-minute-plus title cut. This was one of his earliest dates on nothing but electric keyboards, and his manipulation of sounds, noise, whirling phrases, and rhythms was creative and innovative. The other shorter pieces move from somber, almost morose arrangements on *Mu* to the teaming beats of *Bimini* and the otherworldliness of both the Saturn and Impulse versions of *Yucatan*. As usual, Ra's band meshes hard bop, bebop, cool, free, and swing elements, with John Gilmore, Marshall Allen, and company alternately wailing, colliding with, and complementing the master's dashing clavinet, synthesizer, and organ journeys. An essential and excellent set. —*Ron Wynn*

Out There a Minute / 1968-1969 / Blast First ✦✦✦✦
The 13 selections on this CD by a small group taken from Sun Ra's Arkestra are generally both explorative and introspective. The combo includes tenor saxophonist John Gilmore, altoist Marshall Allen, baritonist Pat Patrick, an occasional trumpeter and trombonist (the personnel is not listed), Ra's organ, piano and primitive electric keyboards plus a bassist, drummer and some percussionists. The performances are mostly short sketches that set spacey moods and then fade out; Ra's piano sounds surprisingly like Thelonious Monk in spots. The odd echo devices and spooky keyboards give this eccentric music much atmosphere. The violent ensemble number "Other Worlds" and the lengthy "Next Stop Mars" are changes of pace (sounding like the 1966 John Coltrane Quintet) while many of the other pieces would work well as soundtracks to a science fiction movie. Although not essential, these futuristic sounds from the past hold one's interest. —*Scott Yanow*

My Brother the Wind, Vol. 2 / 1969-1970 / Evidence ✦✦✦
Although considered a classic by some of his fans, this CD release of music originally put out on Sun Ra's Saturn label is actually quite erratic. The band numbers (utilizing a 15-piece group with eight horns, two drums and three percussionists) are generally worthwhile and more melodic than one would expect from Ra during the 1960s; he was just beginning his updated swing period. But several selections feature Ra simply fooling around on his moog synthesizer and "intergalactic" organ, and those rambling performances are often quite tedious. Overall this is very much a mixed bag and falls short of being essential. —*Scott Yanow*

Space Is the Place / 1972 / Evidence ✦✦
Here is a genuine bonus—some previously unissued cuts. *Space is the Place* is the soundtrack to a film that was made but never released, and the tunes are among his most ambitious, unorthodox, compelling compositions. Between June Tyson's declarative vocals, chants and dialogue and Ra's crashing, flailing and emphatic synthesizer and organ fills, and with such songs as "Blackman/Love in Outer Space," "It's After The End of the World" and "I Am the Brother of the Wind," this disc offers aggressive, energized, uncompromising material. —*Ron Wynn*

Cosmos / Aug. 1976 / Inner City ✦✦✦
A hard-to-find, alternately chaotic and tightly organized mid-'70s session that was issued on the Cobra label. Sun Ra provided some stunning organ and synthesizer moments, while leading the Arkestra through stomping full-band cuts, peeling off various saxophonists for skittering, screaming dialogues and mixing in single and group backing vocals. —*Ron Wynn*

A Quiet Place in the Universe / 1976-1977 / Leo ✦✦
This loose concert performance (reissued on CD with two extra selections) is largely a waste. The nearly 19-minute "I Pharoah" is mostly a chant/recitation by Sun Ra that quickly becomes tedious. Pat Patrick's alto feature on a much briefer "I'll Never Be the Same" is okay as is the closing "Space Is the Place," but "Images" is a rather dull duet by French hornist Vincent Chancey and Ra on organ, and "Love in Outer Space" is mostly a drum showcase. There are many better Sun Ra albums currently available so skip this one. —*Scott Yanow*

Voice of the Eternal Tomorrow / The Rose Hue Mansions of the Sun / Sep. 17, 1980 / Saturn ✦✦✦
This unfortunately out-of-print album has all the spectacular excitement of a live Sun Ra event. "Voice of the Eternal Tommorrow" is a sequence of astonishing solos by members of the Arkestra, and the end solo by Sun Ra is so "out there" that the audience sits in stunned silence before applauding respectfully. "The Rose Hue Mansions of the Sun" begins with a high energy loose-chordal hymn by the group and then launches into another incredible 20-minute solo by Sun Ra punctuated by the band...Sun Ra demonstrates a mastery of electronic modulation and the alternation between solo and the various Arkestra entrances leads unceasingly into the most unpredictable zones. —*Blue* Gene Tyranny

Strange Celestial Road / 1980 / Rounder ✦✦✦

Sun Ra's Arkestra romps through three extensive pieces on this session, including the 12-minute-plus "Say" and 16-minute concluding "I'll Wait for You." Ra led the band through swing-based movements, free sections, and segments interspersing funk and pop elements with African-influenced rhythms. The band included two special guests, trombonist Craig Harris and Vincent Chancy on French horn, plus the regulars—saxophonists Marshall Allen and John Gilmore, twin bassists Richard Williams and Steve Clarke, vibists Harry Wilson and Damon Choice and vocalist June Tyson. The array of colors, instrumental contrasts, beats and sounds are vintage Ra, who also adds contributions on various keyboards. Each Sun Ra session had its own unique quality, and that was true on this date as well. —*Ron Wynn*

Blue Delight / Dec. 5, 1988 / A&M ✦✦✦✦

Although Sun Ra's stage shows of the late 1980s often found his music almost buried by the trappings, this CD (which features Ra's band joined by several notable players) has no such problem; the visual aspect is absent and there is no chanting or light show. Four of the eight performances feature Ra and his Arkestra exploring standard material with enthusiasm and hot swing. The title cut is a medium uptempo blues with the pianist-leader doing an excellent job of filling in for Count Basie. The other main soloists on the date are tenor saxophonist John Gilmore (who sounds as if he had listened to several Lee Konitz albums earlier in the day), a rare appearance by trumpeter Tommy Turrentine (who had long been retired), trombonist Julian Priester and guitarist Carl LeBlanc. Ra's newer material allows some freer playing but the structures are also fairly basic, especially the two-chord vamp of "Sunrise" and the repetitive patterns on "They Dwell on Other Places." The drive of bassist John Ore and the two drummers (Billy Higgins and Earl "Buster" Smith) deserves a large amount of credit for this date's success, inspiring the rest of the band to swing in its own eccentric way. —*Scott Yanow*

Somewhere Else / Dec. 1988-Nov. 1989 / Rounder ✦✦✦✦✦

Both small-group and larger Arkestra sessions are included on this recent anthology of late-'80s Sun Ra material. The tune "Priest" includes slashing drum support from Billy Higgins and Buster Smith, twin bass interplay from John Ore and Jerib Shahid, Julian Priester's whiplash trombone and Ra's equally dynamic piano solos. Other numbers include appearances by Don Cherry on pocket trumpet, James Spaulding on alto sax and flute teaming with fellow alto stylist Marshall Allen and tenor saxophonist John Gilmore, plus the vocal cries, swoops and hollers of June Tyson, and Ra's delightful piano and swirling synthesizer. These selections show that Ra hadn't exhausted his creative faculties by the late '80s. —*Ron Wynn*

Salute to Walt Disney / May 29, 1989 / Leo ✦✦

In 1989, avant-garde bandleader Sun Ra frequently played sets of music dominated by songs taken from Walt Disney movies. Since Ra did not believe in having any barriers between musical styles and in his later years often paid tribute in his own way to the past, the unlikely concept somehow seemed logical. The music on this offbeat CD was documented by an audience member with a tape recorder, so the balance is not always state-of-the-art, although the results are quite listenable. Ra's Intergalactic Arkestra had a particularly unusual instrumentation during this European tour, with three altoists (tenor great John Gilmore is absent), James Jackson doubling on bassoon and oboe, just one trumpet (the excellent Michael Ray), two trombones, and a five-piece rhythm section, plus occasional vocals by June Tyson. Actually, there are group vocals on several of the pieces, which include exuberant versions of "Zip a Dee Doo Dah," "High Ho! High Ho!" and "Whistle While You Work." Although Marshall Allen's alto is overly violent on "Someday My Prince Will Come" and there are some rambling moments (some of the vocals were obviously more fun live than on record), this performance generally holds one's interest. Ra has a few piano interludes, and Noel Scott's alto flights are fairly boppish. It helps greatly to have an open mind towards the avant-garde (there are some messy ensembles and out-of-tune passages during the exuberant set), but even if Walt Disney might not have fully approved (he would have preferred a Dixieland treatment), the crazy results are generally quite memorable. —*Scott Yanow*

Purple Night / Nov. 1989 / A&M ✦✦

At its best, Sun Ra's orchestra on this CD uses a simple repetitive riff as a basis for lengthy performances that vary dynamics and build up gradually in intensity. At its worst (the 19-minute "Of Invisible Theme"), the ensemble rambles on aimlessly, almost as if it were creating a sound effects record. unfortunately, their versions of "Love in Outer Space" and "Stars Fellon Alabama" are quite silly with the former featuring a "glee club" vocal while the latter displays Ra's lack of a singing voice. Another minus is the sudden mood change during an otherwise lyrical piano-bass duet on "Journey Towards the Stars" caused by a surprise entrance from Marshall Allen's out-of-tune alto. Cornetist Don Cherry (always muted), James Spaulding on flute and alto, John Gilmore on tenor and trombonist Julian Priester get some solo space but most impressive is John Ore's busy and versatile

bass playing and Ra's frequently Monk-ish piano. However, the minuses easily outweigh the good points on this disc. —*Scott Yanow*

At the Village Vanguard / Nov. 1991 / Rounder ✦✦✦✦

Sun Ra often pulled small units out of the larger Arkestra, and that was the case on this 1991 concert recorded live at the Vanguard. He led a sextet with Chris Anderson on piano, John Gilmore's rugged, soaring tenor sax taking the featured soloist role, and bassist John Ore and Buster Smith completing the rhythm section. Bruce Edwards provided guitar fills and accompaniment, while Ra offered synthesizer coloration, textures and swirling support. Ra's lines seem to flag a bit on the opening cut, "'Round Midnight," but he's worked out the kinks by the second number, "Sun Ra Blues," and for the remainder of the session adds looping countermelodies and phrases to Anderson's themes and statements. —*Ron Wynn*

Tribute to Stuff Smith / Sep. 1992 / Soul Note ✦✦✦✦

Forty years before recording this very interesting CD, keyboardist Sun Ra made his debut on records on a duet with violinist Stuff Smith, playing a haunting version of "Deep Purple." For this CD (one of Ra's final sessions) the quartet workout with violinist Billy Bang finds Ra doing a new version of "Deep Purple" and performing a variety of tunes associated with Smith. Actually Ra was a bit hemmed in by the concept—his conception of time was different than Bang's so there is a certain amount of tension in the music. Also, Billy Bang has a much rougher and a freer style) than Stuff Smith but the end results are well worth hearing. —*Scott Yanow*

Michael Rabinowitz

b. Nov. 27, 1955, Bethany, CO
Bassoon / Post-Bop, Hard Bop

Although the bassoon had been used in jazz on a rare basis since Don Redman and Frankie Trumbauer in the 1920s, Michael Rabinowitz is the first jazz musician ever to specialize on the difficult instrument. He played clarinet in junior high school but switched to bassoon in high school. He played locally in New Haven, studied with Sal Mosca, and after college spent two years in Europe. Upon his return, he recorded on part of an Ira Sullivan Muse record (1981) and with Eddie Buster. Rabinowitz moved to New York in 1986, was part of the avant-garde group Mosaic in 1988, and performed Charles Mingus' "Epitaph" with Gunther Schuller in 1989. Michael Rabinowitz has led his own groups throughout the 1990s, showing on quartet recordings for Cats Paw and Jazz Focus that the bassoon can effectively assume the role of an improvising saxophonist. —*Scott Yanow*

● Gabrielle's Balloon / Nov. 16, 1995 / Jazz Focus ✦✦✦✦✦

There have been very few jazz bassoonists throughout jazz history. Garvin Bushell and Frankie Trumbauer occasionally played it in the 1920s, and in later years Illinois Jacquet, Yusef Lateef and Frank Tiberi all made strong statements on the difficult instrument. But until the rise of Michael Rabinowitz, there were no major full-time jazz bassoonists. On his Jazz Focus set, Rabinowitz is joined by pianist John Hicks, bassist Ira Coleman and drummer Steve Johns. The music (which consists of six standards and four originals) is essentially hard bop, with such songs as "Bernie's Tune," "The Night Has a Thousand Eyes" and "Have You Met Miss Jones" being given swinging and creative interpretations. The bassoon often resembles a baritone sax, although having a slightly different sound, and Michael Rabinowitz is quite fluent in the jazz vocabulary. Due to the scarcity of jazz bassoon records, this disc is not only an enjoyable set but quite historic. —*Scott Yanow*

Boyd Raeburn (Boyde Albert Raeburn)

b. Oct. 27, 1913, Faith, SD, **d.** Aug. 2, 1966, Lafayette, LA
Leader, Bass Saxophone / Bop

Boyd Raeburn was never much of a soloist but his short-lived big bands in the mid-'40s featured some of the most advanced arrangements of the time, particularly those of George Handy. Raeburn actually started out leading commercial orchestras in the 1930s, but it was not until 1944 that his music became relevant to jazz. That year he had a forward-looking swing band that included at various times such players as Benny Harris, the Johnny Hodges-influenced Johnny Bothwell, Serge Chaloff, Roy Eldridge, Trummy Young and Handy on piano playing arrangements from George Williams, Eddie Finckel and Handy. The group overall was influenced by Count Basie but they were also the first to record Dizzy Gillespie's "Night in Tunisia"; Dizzy even guested with the band. By 1945 Raeburn's music became much more radical with George Handy's charts (which were sometimes influenced by modern classical music) dominating the repertoire. Vocalists David Allyn and Ginnie Powell (Raeburn's wife) cheerfully sang while all types of dissonant events occurred behind them! Even though it was a constant struggle to keep the orchestra together, Raeburn's band actually grew in size during 1946 with reed players doubling on woodwinds and the addition of French horns and a harp. Such players as Lucky Thompson, Dodo Marmarosa, Ray Linn and Buddy DeFranco were among the many who passed through the band.

Johnny Richards was the key arranger in 1947, but by the end of the year the band was no longer recording and Raeburn soon went back to performing dance music. His pleasant Columbia records of 1956-57 are of little interest but Boyd Raeburn's earlier bands are represented on sessions for Musicraft and Savoy, radio transcriptions put out by Circle and broadcasts released by IAJRC and Hep. —*Scott Yanow*

One Night Stand with Boyd Raeburn / Jan. 1944+Aug. 7, 1945 / Joyce ✦✦✦
Other than two titles from 1943, this collector's LP from the Joyce label has the earliest documentation of the Boyd Raeburn Orchestra. At the time Raeburn's big band was going in a transition from being a rather commercial outfit to a swing orchestra. Although Ted Travers has two vocals, the band mostly plays in a Count Basie vein on this radio broadcast, performing such tunes as ("920 Special," "Blue Skies" and "It's Sand Man." Unfortunately, the personnel is not given (and was probably not known). This LP ends up with four tunes from the 1945 Raeburn band, a much more radical outfit that played arrangements by George Handy. Although David Allyn and Barbara Jane take a vocal apiece, the accompaniment by the orchestra is rather advanced; best is the instrumental "Hip Boyds." This album will be a difficult record to locate. —*Scott Yanow*

Rare 1944-46 Broadcast Performances / May 27, 1944-Jul. 1946 / IAJRC ✦✦✦✦
Three editions of Boyd Raeburn's short-lived series of orchestras are featured on this IAJRC LP which contains music from several radio broadcasts. The 1944 big band is most notable for guest Roy Eldridge soloing on two songs including an early version of Dizzy Gillespie's "Night in Tunisia" (a real collector's item). The orchestra in 1945 was much more advanced (as one can hear on George Handy's arrangements of "Laura" and "Out of Nowhere") and featured such soloists as tenor saxophonist Frankie Socolow, trumpeter Tommy Allison and altoist Hal McKusick. The group from the following year only appears on three vocal pieces (including two by Ginnie Powell) but there are spots for pianist Dodo Marmarosa and trombonist Ollie Wilson. Boyd Raeburn fans will want to go out of their way to acquire this valuable record. —*Scott Yanow*

Boyd Raeburn and His Orchestra 1944 / Jun. 13, 1944-Aug. 21, 1944 / Circle ✦✦✦
On the first of two Circle CDs taken from Lang-Worth Radio Transcriptions that feature Boyd Raeburn's Orchestra, Raeburn's transitional band is well showcased. Succeeding his undocumented sweet orchestra of the late '30s and preceding his radical 1945 group, this big band essentially played advanced swing with most arrangements contributed by Eddie Finckel or George Williams. There are some dated vocals by Don Darcy and a couple from Marjorie Wood (including "Who Started Love," which has the only George Handy arrangement on the set), and solos from altoist Johnny Bothwell, trumpeter Benny Harris and trombonist Earl Swope. Among the more memorable numbers are "Hep Boyds," "Boyd Meets the Duke" and an early version of "A Night in Tunisia." —*Scott Yanow*

1944-1945 / Jun. 22, 1944-Jan. 17, 1945 / Circle ✦✦✦
The second of two Circle CDs featuring the 1944 Boyd Raeburn Orchestra's transcriptions for Lang-Worth has arrangements by Eddie Finckel, George Williams, Milt Klee, Johnny Mandel and one from George Handy. Raeburn's big band would become much more adventurous later in 1945 but there are some strong moments throughout this set, particularly "Is You Is or Is You Ain't Ma Baby" (which features the vocal of trombonist Trummy Young), "Two Spoos in an Igloo" and two appearances for guest trumpeter Dizzy Gillespie ("Barefoot Boy with Cheek" and a vocal version of "A Night in Tunisia" called "Interlude"). There are also some period vocals by Don Darcy and Marjorie Wood and a few features for the Johnny Hodges-inspired alto of Johnny Bothwell. This is fine late-period swing music although not as unique as Raeburn's recordings of the next two years. —*Scott Yanow*

The Unissued Boyd Raeburn: 1945 / 1945 / Joyce ✦✦✦✦✦
The year 1945 was fascinating for the Boyd Raeburn Orchestra, for it was the period when the big band quickly evolved from a swing-oriented unit into a unique if eccentric and short-lived outfit. This valuable LP from the Joyce label (which will probably be difficult to locate) has some arrangements by Eddie Finckle and Johnny Mandel but it is the many George Handy charts that are most memorable. On tunes such as "Tonsillectomy," "Rip Van Winkle," "Yerxa" and "Dalvatore Sally" (thanks to Handy), the Raeburn Orchestra sounds as advanced as that of Stan Kenton while displaying a very distinctive style of its own. Among the key members of the band at the time were trumpeter Ray Linn, trombonist Ollie Wilson, tenor saxophonist Lucky Thompson and pianist Dodo Marmarosa. This important music (taken from radio broadcasts) deserves to be reissued on CD. —*Scott Yanow*

Experiments in Big Band Jazz (1945) / Jan. 26, 1945-May 13, 1945 / Musicraft ✦✦✦✦
Although the Boyd Raeburn Orchestra appeared on earlier radio airchecks, transcriptions and a vocal date featuring Don Darcy, its Musicraft sides were its first

real studio recordings. The 1945 edition of the big band was swing-oriented and sometimes showed the influence of Count Basie. Trumpeter Dizzy Gillespie guests on "A Night in Tunisia" and "March of the Boyds" and the other key soloists include altoist Johnny Bothwell (a great lover of the sound of Johnny Hodges), tenor saxophonist Frankie Socolow, trumpeter Tommy Allison and (on "Boyd's Nest") trombonist Trummy Young. The arrangements (mostly by Eddie Finckel, George Williams and Johnny Mandel) are generally colorful, making this somewhat historic set of interest to swing and bop fans alike. —*Scott Yanow*

Rhythms by Raeburn / Jun. 19, 1945-Aug. 7, 1945 / Aircheck ✦✦✦✦
This interesting LP features radio appearances by the Boyd Raeburn Orchestra taken from five occasions dating from a seven-week period. Highlights include "A Night in Tunisia," "Boyd Meets Girl," "The Hep Boyd," "Bagdad" and an advanced arrangement behind singer David Allyn on "Who Started Love." Unfortunately, the personnel is not listed, but it includes trumpeter Tommy Allison, trombonist Trummy Young on the June 19 session, either Johnny Bothwell or Hal McKusick on altos and tenor saxophonist Frankie Socolow. The music is often quite intriguing; this was an orchestra that really took chances. —*Scott Yanow*

Where You At / Jul. 1945-May 26, 1948 / Hep ✦✦✦✦✦
For this collector's LP from the English Hep label, the innovative Boyd Raeburn Orchestra is heard on five separate occasions during its prime periods. The music (mostly arranged by George Handy, Eddie Finckle or Johnny Richards) is quite adventurous with plenty of surprising moments. The personnel changes drastically from date to date; the key soloists include pianist Dodo Marmarosa, trombonist Britt Woodman, trumpeter Ray Linn, Harry Klee (taking a rare early flute solo on "Caravan"), clarinetist Buddy DeFranco, tenorman Frank Socolow and vocalists David Allyn and Ginnie Powell. This is a particularly strong all-round set that displays the uniqueness of the remarkable but short-lived ensemble. —*Scott Yanow*

● **Jewells** / Oct. 15, 1945-Sep. 19, 1949 / Savoy ✦✦✦✦
Boyd Raeburn, who played bass saxophone in the sections of his big bands, was never much of a musician but during 1945-47 he led one of the most exciting, advanced and unpredictable of all the big bands around. Raeburn was open to the ideas of his arrangers, and George Handy (during 1945-46) and Johnny Richards (1946-47) certainly challenged his musicians. Raeburn's music sometimes even made Stan Kenton's sound conservative in comparison. This two-LP set (which is long overdue to be reissued on CD) has Raeburn's studio recordings and is highlighted by such memorable tunes as "Tonsillectomy," "Dalvatore Sally," "Boyd Meets Stravinsky," a remarkable satire (with countless key changes) of "Over the Rainbow" and "Hep Boyd's." Of particular interest are some of the vocals by Ginnie Powell and David Allyn (particularly "Temptation" and "Body and Soul") because the "background" is so busy and dissonant as to make it quite a struggle for them to sing the songs straight. In addition to featuring the 1946 Raeburn Orchestra (with four selections apiece from 1945 and 1947), this two-fer concludes with David Allyn singing four numbers in 1949 with Johnny Richards' Orchestra. Fascinating and quite unique music. —*Scott Yanow*

☆ **Jubilee Broadcasts: 1946** / Dec. 29, 1945-Apr. 1946 / Hep ✦✦✦✦✦
Boyd Raeburn was not much of a musician and, although he played bass sax in his mid-'40s orchestra, he never soloed and could barely be heard in the ensembles. However, the jazz world owes him a debt of gratitude because he not only allowed but encouraged such advanced arrangers as Ed Finckel, Johnny Richards and particularly George Handy to let their imaginations run wild and not be concerned about selling records or pleasing dancers. Ironically Raeburn's earlier bands were quite conservative but by 1944 he started changing directions. At a time when the swing era was ending and jazz orchestras were breaking up, his big band was soon playing some of the most adventurous music around although it would involve quite a struggle to survive (which he lost by the end of the 1940s). This Hep CD features 22 selections from 1945-46 that were performed on radio broadcasts. The Boyd Raeburn Orchestra is captured at the height of its powers with such soloists as trumpeter Ray Linn, trombonist Ollie Wilson, the great tenor Lucky Thompson and pianist Dodo Marmarosa getting their share of solo space. A dozen of the charts are George Handy's, including "Tonsillectomy," bizarre renditions of "Temptation" and "Body and Soul" and a four-part suite. Other highlights include a guest appearance by Dizzy Gillespie on "A Night in Tunisia," Mel Tormé and the Mel-Tones being featured on "That's Where I Came In," a performance by Ray Linn's septet on "Caravan" that has an early flute solo by Harry Klee and two versions of "Boyd Meets Stravinsky." This is an essential set both for bebop collectors (although the harmonies are often beyond bop) and jazz historians. Boyd Raeburn's music still sounds exciting decades later. —*Scott Yanow*

Memphis in June / Dec. 1945-Feb. 5, 1947 / Hep ✦✦✦✦✦
The Boyd Raeburn Orchestra was one of the most consistently interesting and unpredictable big bands of 1945-47, but because its music was beyond bebop and

that played by Stan Kenton, it was just too modernistic to survive for long. This particular LP has some rare and unusual material related to the Raeburn legacy. There are four selections from December 1945 by the full orchestra with a vocal apiece from Ginnie Powell and David Allyn and a remake of George Handy's classic "Tonsillectomy." Most unusual are four songs from early 1946 by a unit comprising alto/flute, oboe, English horn, bass clarinet, baritone, French horn, two guitars, two basses, drums and pianist Erroll Garner. Two of the four songs feature David Allyn ballad vocals, but it is "C Jam Blues" and "Caravan" that are of greatest interest; Tom Talbert contributed all four arrangements. The second side of the album has five numbers from February 1947 arranged by Johnny Richards. Ginnie Powell takes two vocals on these advanced charts and clarinetist Buddy DeFranco is well featured on "Sheharazade." This stimulating music (among the last recorded performances by the Boyd Raeburn Orchestra before it finally broke up) is well worth searching for. —*Scott Yanow*

Hep Boyds / 1945-Dec. 1947 / Golden Era ✦✦✦
For this collectors' LP, two editions of the Boyd Raeburn Orchestra are featured. There are eight numbers from mid-1945 (three with vocals by Ginny Powell and/or David Allyn) that find the Raeburn big band entering its prime period. Tenorman Frankie Socolow, altoist Johnny Bothwell, trombonist Trummy Young and trumpeter Tommy Allison are the key soloists, and highlights include "March of the Boyds," "Hep Boyds" and "Where You At." The other half of this album is from the Raeburn Orchestra when it was past its prime, in December 1947. By then several former Woody Herman and Stan Kenton sidemen were in the band (including trumpeter Pete Candoli, trombonist Milt Bernhardt and tenorman Jimmy Giuffre) along with clarinetist Buddy DeFranco. The latter date is among the final recordings of Raeburn's 1940s orchestras, and is not without interest although this album as a whole is more for completists than for general collectors. —*Scott Yanow*

Dance Spectacular / 1956 / Columbia ✦✦✦
After his band broke up permanently in 1948, Boyd Raeburn did not lead any record dates until 1956-57 when he cut three albums worth of material for Columbia. However, these last recordings featured studio groups and the arrangements were no longer radical but performed primarily as background for dancing. Ginnie Powell has a few vocals, some with a group called "the Classmates." Otherwise the big band (not identified on this obscure album) sticks to swing standards such as "A String of Pearls," "Elmer's Tune" and "You Stepped out of a Dream." Among the sidemen are trumpeters Charlie Shavers and Buck Clayton, tenor saxophonist Frank Socolow, pianist Nat Pierce and bassist Oscar Pettiford but little significant occurs on this commercial if historically interesting set. —*Scott Yanow*

Doug Raney

b. Aug. 29, 1956
Guitar / Cool

The son of legendary guitarist Jimmy Raney, Doug has understandably been heavily influenced by his father. He's an impressive soloist, and utilizes almost identical full tones, crisp chording and fluid voicings. He made his first recording with his father and Al Haig in the mid-'70s, then did duo dates with his dad in the late '70s. Raney recorded for Steeple Chase in the '70s and '80s, and Criss Cross in the '80s. He's recorded with Chet Baker and Bernt Rosengren, and played in Horace Parlan's band. Raney has a couple of sessions available on CD. —*Ron Wynn*

Meeting the Tenors / Apr. 29, 1983 / Criss Cross ✦✦✦✦

Blue and White / Apr. 29, 1984 / Steeple Chase ✦✦✦✦

Lazy Bird / Nov. 1, 1984 / Steeple Chase ✦✦✦✦✦

● **The Doug Raney Quintet** / Aug. 1988 / Steeple Chase ✦✦✦✦✦

Jimmy Raney

b. Aug. 20, 1927, Louisville, KY, **d.** May 10, 1995, Louisville, KY
Guitar / Cool

Jimmy Raney was the definitive cool jazz guitarist, a fluid bop soloist with a quiet sound who had a great deal of inner fire. He worked with local groups in Chicago before spending nine months with Woody Herman in 1948. From then on he was in the major leagues, having associations with Al Haig, Buddy DeFranco, Artie Shaw and Terry Gibbs. His work with Stan Getz (1951-52) was historic as the pair made for a classic musical partnership. Raney was also very much at home in the Red Norvo Trio (1953-54) before spending six years primarily working in a supper club with pianist Jimmy Lyon (1954-60). After playing with Getz during 1962-63, he returned to Louisville and was outside of music until resurfacing in the early '70s. During the 1970s Raney recorded often for Xanadu. He worked frequently with his son Doug Raney (who has a very similar sound on guitar) and was less active in the late '80s and '90s up until his 1995 death. —*Scott Yanow*

Visits Paris, Vol. 1 / Feb. 6, 1954 / Vogue ✦✦✦✦✦

Too Marvelous for Words / Feb. 10, 1954 / Biograph ✦✦✦✦
Intimate, tasteful mid-'50s recordings from guitarist Jimmy Raney. His delicate, fluid voicings were also featured during this period with the Red Norvo trio, and Raney's solos are carefully paced and developed, marked by understated technique and a light, expressive sound. —*Ron Wynn*

Jimmy Raney: A / May 28, 1954-Feb. 18, 1955 / Original Jazz Classics ✦✦✦✦✦

★ **Live in Tokyo** / Apr. 12, 1976+Apr. 14, 1976 / Xanadu ✦✦✦✦✦
This album features the great guitarist Jimmy Raney in a trio with bassist Sam Jones and drummer Leroy Williams, all regulars for the Xanadu label in the 1970s. The boppish performances (which Raney considered among his very best) are subtle with lots of interplay between the players. High points include "Anthropology," "A Burning Cherokee" and Raney's unaccompanied playing on "Stella by Starlight." —*Scott Yanow*

Duets / Apr. 21, 1979 / Steeple Chase ✦✦✦✦

Raney (1981) / Feb. 27, 1981 / Criss Cross ✦✦✦✦✦
This was the first release by Criss Cross, one of the top bop-based labels in Europe. The CD reissue adds six alternate takes to the original seven-song program. The cool-toned guitarist Jimmy Raney is teamed with his son Doug (who has a very similar style on guitar) along with bassist Jesper Lundgaard and drummer Eric Ineke. Together they perform one original and six standards in light but forcefully swinging style. The interplay between the two guitarists is a major plus. —*Scott Yanow*

The Master / Feb. 6, 1983 / Criss Cross ✦✦✦✦
A nice mid-'80s session with the relaxed, fluid guitar of Jimmy Raney playing such standards as "The Song Is You" and "Tangerine." He's supported with style by pianist Kirk Lightsey, who emerges as the date's other dominant solo voice. The other musicians, bassist Jesper Lundgaard and drummer Eddie Gladden, are complementary figures and do their jobs competently. —*Ron Wynn*

Nelson Rangell

b. Denver, CO
Alto Saxophone, Flute, Piccolo / Instrumental Pop, Crossover Jazz

Nelson Rangell has primarily played pop-jazz throughout his career, although he did a credible job playing some soulful alto with the straightahead GRP Big Band. The records he cut for GRP in the early '90s made him into a popular contemporary jazz attraction in the David Sanborn tradition.

A native of Denver, Colorado, Nelson Rangell learned how to play flute at the age of 15, and within six months he was studying music at the Interlochen Arts Academy. Shortly afterward, he learned the saxophone, and in 1979, he won *Downbeat's* Best High School Jazz Soloist competition. Following his graduation from high school, he attended the New England Conservatory of Music in Boston; this time he won the *Downbeat* contest on the college level. In 1984, Rangell moved to New York. He spent three years in New York playing clubs and working as a sideman, not only on jazz sessions, but on jingles and pop records.

Rangell finally began his solo career in 1987, releasing *To Begin Again* on the Gaia label. Two years later, he moved to GRP, where he released *Playing for Keeps*. His second album became a major contemporary jazz hit, and with each subsequent release, his popularity grew. His next four albums—*Nelson Rangell* (1990), *In Every Moment* (1992), *Truest Heart* (1993), *Yes Then Yes* (1994)—were all popular on the contemporary jazz charts. In addition to recording his solo albums, Rangell was involved in the GRP All-Star Big Band, playing both in the studio and on the road. *Destiny*, an album that found Rangell incorporating hip-hop rhythms into his sound, was released in 1994. It was followed in 1997 by *Turning Night into Day*. —*Scott Yanow & Stephen Thomas Erlewine*

Playing for Keeps / 1989 / GRP ✦✦✦

Nelson Rangell / 1990 / GRP ✦✦✦✦

In Every Moment / 1992 / GRP ✦✦
This CD features the leader's R&B alto, soprano (on which he sounds like a Kenny G. clone) and flute on a variety of forgettable material, all of it funky, poppish and produced by the Rippingtons' Russ Freeman. Rangell is certainly capable of much better than this by-the-book crossover music, which is strictly recommended for unimaginative dancers. —*Scott Yanow*

Yes Then Yes / 1994 / GRP ✦✦
Nelson Rangell plays with plenty of energy throughout his R&Bish set and sounds fine on flute and piccolo during two tracks, but his alto playing can barely be told apart from David Sanborn; the lack of individuality can be a serious problem, even in instrumental pop music. Essentially this is a set of background dance music that stays quite predictable and obvious. —*Scott Yanow*

● **Destiny** / Nov. 1994-Jan. 1995 / GRP ✦✦✦✦✦
This is one of Nelson Rangell's strongest recordings to date. Although he is rightfully known for playing poppish jazz (crossover), Rangell really stretches himself on parts of this disc, taking a couple of impressive workouts on flute and featuring his alto and soprano in several different settings including a few intimate songs. This CD is not only recommended to Rangell's fans but to more purist listeners who wrote him off years ago. —*Scott Yanow*

Turning Night into Day / 1997 / GRP ✦✦✦

Kenny Rankin

Vocals, Guitar / Pop, Standards, Traditional Pop, Adult Contemporary
Although he has spent most of his career as a pop singer, Kenny Rankin in the mid-'90s started emphasizing veteran standards in his performances and using jazz accompaniment. He is an unusual jazz singer, sticking to the lyrics of songs but improvising and constantly altering the notes.

In 1967, Rankin released his first album *Mind Dusters*, which featured the soft-rock hit "Peaceful." Over the course of the early '70s, Rankin slowly built up a following with a steady stream of records and performances that balanced originals, new songs and standards. As the decade drew to a close, he began to return to his singer-songwriter roots, particularly on *After the Roses*, his 1980 debut for Atlantic Records. He continued to perform during the '80s, but he only recorded sporadically. In 1991, he recorded a pair of albums, *Hiding in Myself* and *Because of You*, for two separate labels. Three years later, he signed with Private Music and released *Professional Dreamer*, an album that found him concentrating on standards. That record was followed in 1997 by *Here in My Heart.* —*Scott Yanow & Stephen Thomas Erlewine*

● **Professional Dreamer** / 1994 / Private Music ✦✦✦✦✦
Kenny Rankin sings like Chet Baker would have if Baker had had a voice. His tone is high (Rankin's speaking voice is actually fairly low) and he has a subtle cool style. It is a bit of a surprise but Rankin (whose previous output has been in pop music) is actually a fine jazz singer. He always sticks to the lyrics when performing veteran standards (there is no scatting) but changes many of the notes, even during the melody statements, and he is definitely improvising. Rankin's concept is strange ("At Last" and "The Very Thought of You" are radically changed) but successful and he has a strong and likable voice. An all-star acoustic trio (consisting of pianist Mike Wofford, bassist Brian Bromberg and drummer Roy McCurdy) backs the singer on most of the tracks, and Tom Scott (on tenor and alto) and trombonist Bill Watrous add melodic bop solos to three songs apiece. "It Had to Be You" is taken as a romping duet with pianist Alan Broadbent, and the remarkable singer Sue Raney interacts with Rankin on "I've Got a Crush on You." This surprising CD is highly recommended. —*Scott Yanow*

Enrico Rava

b. Aug. 20, 1943, Trieste, Italy
Trumpet, Fluegelhorn / Avant-Garde
One of Italy's finest jazz trumpeters, Enrico Rava has been recording stimulating music for 25 years. He started on trombone before taking up the trumpet and fluegelhorn. Rava was with Gato Barbieri in 1964, played with Steve Lacy during 1965-68 in several countries and spent much of 1969-72 with Roswell Rudd's groups. By 1975 he had a band with John Abercrombie and was soon recording for ECM. Other than stints with Gil Evans (1982) and Cecil Taylor (1984), he has generally been a bandleader ever since. Rava often plays quite free but, due to his mellow tone, his music is fairly accessible. He has releases available on ECM and Soul Note. —*Scott Yanow*

● **The Pilgrim and the Stars** / Jun. 1975 / ECM ✦✦✦✦✦
The trumpet of Enrico Rava perfectly fits into the ECM sound. He never gets all that heated, has a healthy respect for the value of space and recalls Miles Davis a bit in spots. Joined by a sparse trio (guitarist John Abercrombie, bassist Palle Danielsson and drummer Jon Christensen), Rava explores seven of his moody originals and creates thoughtful and introspective music. —*Scott Yanow*

The Plot / Aug. 1976 / ECM ✦✦✦✦
Italian trumpeter with quartet. Original ideas and compositions. With guitarist John Abercrombie. —*Michael G. Nastos*

Quartet / Mar. 1978 / ECM ✦✦✦✦

Rava String Band / Apr. 11, 1984-Apr. 12, 1984 / Soul Note ✦✦✦
This release ranges from moments of reflective, ambient serenity to periods with more intense activity, although there's seldom any real instrumental ardor or passion exhibited. Trumpeter Enrico Rava's glorious tone and Nana Vasconcelos' percussive dexterity on berimbau and gongs are the closest anyone gets to displaying some fire, but all the participants are expert musicians and nicely demonstrate their proficiency. This finely crafted mood music seems more up ECM's alley than

Soul Note's, but Rava and company showed that they could play the same game to perfection. —*Ron Wynn*

Secrets / Jul. 1986 / Soul Note ✦✦✦✦

Italian Ballads / Mar. 2, 1996-Mar. 4, 1996 / Music Masters ✦✦✦

Lou Rawls

b. Dec. 11, 1935, Chicago, IL
Vocals / Soul, R&B, Pop Rock, Philly Soul
When Chicago-born Lou Rawls croons a soulful love song, his deep-hued pipes rumble with simmering passion. Rawls did the usual gospel apprenticeship before breaking out on a landmark jazz album with pianist Les McCann's trio for Capitol that launched his secular career. But it took Rawls a while to establish himself as a soul artist—perhaps he was perceived as a little too sophisticated and jazzy (although his uncredited responses on Sam Cooke's "Bring It on Home to Me" certainly proved he could wail). "Love Is a Hurtin' Thing" instantly changed that notion when it topped the R&B charts in 1966, and the unyielding "Dead End Street" and "Your Good Thing (Is About to End)" perpetuated his success.

After memorably delivering Bobby Hebb's powerful "A Natural Man" in 1971, Rawls joined forces with Philadelphia producers Kenny Gamble and Leon Huff in 1976, emerging with the silky "You'll Never Find Another Love like Mine," another gigantic R&B and pop smash tailor-made for nattily sweeping across the classiest disco dance floors. The disco era's long gone now, but Rawls maintains elegantly. He's still as cool as cool can be. —*Bill Dahl*

● **Stormy Monday** / Feb. 5, 1962+Feb. 12, 1962 / Capitol ✦✦✦✦✦
Lou Rawls has had a long and commercially successful career mostly singing soul, R&B and pop music. Originally a gospel singer, Rawls' first album as a leader (reissued on CD) features him performing soulful standards backed by the Les McCann Trio. Few of the songs have exactly been underrecorded through the years but they sound fresh and lively when sung by Rawls; highlights include "Stormy Monday," "In the Evening" and "I'd Rather Drink Muddy Water." Pianist McCann gets a generous amount of solo space and the reissue has three "bonus cuts" that were being released for the first time. This is still Lou Rawls' definitive recording in the jazz idiom, cut before he went on to more lucrative areas. —*Scott Yanow*

Black and Blue / Oct. 1, 1962-Nov. 1, 1962 / Capitol ✦✦✦
Super blues and jazzy soul by Lou Rawls from an early period on Capitol. He hadn't yet found the hit formula, but was cutting some superb singles. His voice had a resonance and strength developed for years on the gospel trail, and also during his work backing Sam Cooke. Even though he didn't get any hits, it's well worth the cost if you can find this album. —*Ron Wynn*

Tobacco Road / Jul. 29, 1963-Aug. 20, 1963 / Capitol ✦✦✦
His third album for Capitol had a good version of the title track, and tried to mix blues, soul, and R&B. Rawls sang in a strong, rousing manner, turning in both outstanding ballads and good uptempo tunes, but the company wasn't able to promote any song enough for the album to even get on the charts. —*Ron Wynn*

For You My Love / Oct. 27, 1964-Nov. 27, 1968 / Capitol ✦✦
This reissue CD has highlights from two earlier albums. Singer Lou Rawls is featured in 1964 with a big band arranged by Benny Carter and in 1968 while backed by Benny Golson arrangements. It is a pity that neither Carter nor Golson were playing much at the time, because their horns are very much missed. Rawls alternates superior standards with period soul/pop material such as "If I Had My Life to Live Over," "Whispering Grass" and "I Love You Yes I Do." Needless to say, the earlier material (including "Gee Baby, Ain't I Good to You," "Just Squeeze Me" and a previously unissued "That's Your Red Wagon") is better but overall this set is a rather mixed bag, making one wish that Rawls had chosen to stick to jazz and blues. —*Scott Yanow*

Live! / Jan. 31, 1966-Feb. 1, 1966 / Capitol ✦✦✦
Riding high on the success of his mid-'70s soul and R&B dates, Philadelphia International issued this live recording featuring Rawls doing the straight blues, jazzy ballads and pre-rock standards he normally reserved for clubs and concerts. There were none of the big radio hits here; instead, Rawls covered such songs as "Six Cold Feet of Ground," "Blues for a Four String Guitar," and "Everyday I Have the Blues." It also didn't stay on the charts very long, and Gamble and Huff got back to commercial basics the next time out. Still, it's one of his finest and most representative albums. —*Ron Wynn*

At Last / Jun. 1989 / Blue Note ✦✦✦
He's never deserted either blues or jazz, but Lou Rawls hasn't always found a receptive audience for these styles at notoriously conservative major labels. That wasn't the case on this 1989 album, on which Rawls performed straightahead jazz and pre-rock pop or blues, and was backed by an all-star lineup including Ray Charles, Cornell Dupree, Steve Khan, Richard Tee and Dianne Reeves. His voice

had an exuberance and fervor that spoke volumes about how happy he was in the setting. —*Ron Wynn*

Ballads / 1989-1992 / Capitol ✦✦✦

Lou Rawls' soulful voice and romantic style are well featured on this sampler CD, which draws its music from three of his Blue Note albums from 1989-92. The bluesy ballads find Rawls in fine form, and there are brief contributions from tenors Stanley Turrentine, David "Fathead" Newman and Joe Lovano, altoist Hank Crawford, and (during a memorable "At Last") fellow singer Dianne Reeves. Rawls' true fans will want the complete CDs, but this is an okay sampler of his later work. Other highlights include "I Wonder Where Our Love Has Gone," "Good Morning Blues," "This Bitter Earth" and "Oh What a Nite." —*Scott Yanow*

It's Supposed to Be Fun / 1990 / Blue Note ✦✦

Alfred Lion would not have been pleased to have this CD on the Blue Note label he founded. Lion rarely recorded vocalists (Sheila Jordan was one of the very few to lead her own session), and he would never have considered coming out with a soft soul-pop date like this 1990 session. The music is closer to lightweight country than to jazz and, although there are some notable cameos (by altoists Hank Crawford, Bobby Watts and Dick Oatts, the tenors of Eddie Harris, and Rick Margitza, trumpeter Jack Walrath and trombonist Steve Turre), Rawls' so-so vocals and the weak material sink the effort. —*Scott Yanow*

Portrait of the Blues / Apr. 13, 1992-Oct. 3, 1992 / Capitol ✦✦✦

The Las Vegas lounge act of Lou Rawls over the last two decades may blemish some critics' view of him as a blues interpreter. However, this album holds the potential to put such thoughts to rest. From Willie Dixon's "I Just Want to Make Love to You" to Big Joe Turner's "Chains of Love," in his low baritone, Rawls gives the blues an authentically sophisticated turn. Joe Williams, Cornell Dupree and other stellar roots musicians give their all on the set. A highlight is Rawls' calypso styled rendition of "A Lover's Question" with Phoebe Snow. However, for the most part, this is a polished set of blues standards, light enough to please Rawls' pop crowd, but genuine enough to attract some blues fans. —*Bil Carpenter*

Real Group

f. 1986
Group, Vocals / Bop

The Real Group is an a cappella quintet from Stockholm, Sweden, consisting of three men and two women. Inspired by Bobby McFerrin, the unit brilliantly performs bop, vocalese and a few originals on their Town Crier debut, leading Jon Hendricks himself to say "I wish I was in this group!" —*Scott Yanow*

Debut / Mar. 1987 / Edenroth ✦✦✦✦

The first recording by Swedish a cappella quintet the Real Group finds them quickly hitting their stride. Eight of the 13 selections are jazz standards; the band clearly has fun on the early rock 'n' roll of "Who Put the Bomp," and there are four obscurities and group originals. The sound of the singers (three males and two females) is very appealing, and they swing their way through very likable renditions of such numbers as "All of Me," "Joy Spring," "Blues for Alice" and "As Time Goes By." This private release is worth searching for. —*Scott Yanow*

● Unreal! / 1991-1994 / Town Crier ✦✦✦✦✦

The Real Group is a three-male two-female Swedish acappella quintet that, on the basis of its debut recording, ranks near the top of its field. Their CD for Town Crier is highlighted by Neal Hefti's "Flight of the Foobirds," "Walkin'," a heated "I've Found a New Baby" and "It Don't Mean a Thing." Although the ballads (including "A Child Is Born" and "Body and Soul") are sometimes a bit too respectful, this disc continually holds on to one's interest. In addition to the jazz standards, there are also a few originals (of which "A Cappella in Acapulco" is most memorable), adaptations of two Swedish folk songs and a version of The Beatles' "Come Together." This release is worth searching for. —*Scott Yanow*

Live in Stockholm / 1996 / Town Crier ✦✦✦✦✦

The Real Group, an a cappella quintet from Sweden, seems poised to reach the top. Comprising three males and two females, the vocal group performs their renditions of a folk song, "Strawberry Fields Forever," and ten jazz standards on this continually interesting and enjoyable CD. Among the highlights are "Splanky," "Good Bait," "Night and Day" and "I've Found a New Baby." Although each singer proves to be a fine soloist, the ensembles by this highly appealing group are most notable; they can easily outswing most of their competition. Highly recommended. —*Scott Yanow*

Sonny Red (Sylvester Kyner)

b. Dec. 17, 1932, Detroit, MI, d. Mar. 20, 1981, Detroit, MI
Alto Saxophone / Hard Bop

Sonny Red was a good but not great altoist who was somewhat lost in the shuffle in the 1960s and '70s. He worked in Detroit with Barry Harris (1949-52), in 1954

temporarily switched to tenor while with Frank Rosolino and later that year joined Art Blakey briefly. In 1957 with his arrival in New York he gained some recognition, recording with Curtis Fuller and Paul Quinichette in addition to having several dates as a leader (1958-62) for Savoy, Blue Note and particularly Jazzland. Despite some freelancing and recording with Clifford Jordan, Pony Poindexter, Donald Byrd, Kenny Dorham and Yusef Lateef among others in the 1960s, Red was in obscurity by the 1970s. —*Scott Yanow*

● Out of the Blue / Dec. 5, 1959+Jan. 23, 1960 / Blue Note ✦✦✦✦✦

Sonny Red, a fine altoist inspired by Charlie Parker and Jackie McLean, never really made it in jazz and some of his recordings are rather uninspired. However, that does not hold true for his Blue Note album, which has been reissued on this 1996 CD along with five previously unissued selections. Red, who is joined by pianist Wynton Kelly, either Sam Jones or Paul Chambers on bass and either Roy Brooks or Jimmy Cobb on drums, never sounded better on records. He performs mostly little-known standards (along with six of his originals) and displays a fair amount of originality and a great deal of potential that was never really fulfilled. Recommended. —*Scott Yanow*

Images / Jul. 1962 / Original Jazz Classics ✦✦✦✦

The leader, Sonny Red Kyner (alto), never really became the individual strong player that his playing hinted he might develop into. Basically he was in the Charlie Parker-Jackie McLean tradition, and the material here had that spirit, but little punch. Others involved were Grant Green (guitar), Barry Harris (piano), George Tucker, (bass), Lex Humphries or Jimmy Cobb (drums). Trumpeter Blue Mitchell was also featured on three cuts. —*Bob Rusch, Cadence*

Freddie Redd

b. May 29, 1928, New York, NY
Piano, Composer / Hard Bop

A classic bop pianist and a composer of haunting melodies, Freddie Redd has had an episodic career, with high points followed by periods in which he maintained a low profile. After a period in the Army (1946-49), Redd worked with drummer Johnny Mills and then in New York played with Tiny Grimes (with whom he recorded), Cootie Williams, Oscar Pettiford and the Jive Bombers. Redd, who appeared with both jazz and early R&B groups, recorded his debut as a leader for Prestige in 1955 (reissued in the OJC series), appeared on dates led by Gene Ammons and Art Farmer, and toured Sweden in 1956 with Ernestine Anderson and Rolf Ericson, cutting an obscure trio set in Sweden for the Metronome label. When he returned to the US, Redd settled for a time in San Francisco, where he worked as the house pianist at Bop City and recorded for Riverside. He found his greatest fame when he wrote the music for the play *The Connection*. He acted and played in the landmark show in New York, London and Paris, was in the film, and recorded the music for Blue Note, the first of his three sessions for the label (all of which were reissued on a Mosaic limited-edition box set as two-CD sets). Unfortunately, there were no encore writing assignments, and Redd soon moved to Europe, where he performed regularly but became quite obscure in the US. In 1974, he moved to Los Angeles, but despite worthy sessions for Interplay (1977), Uptown (1985), Triloka (1988) and Milestone (1990), Freddie Redd remains an underrated great, still playing in his prime without gaining much recognition. —*Scott Yanow*

San Francisco Suite for Jazz Trio / Oct. 2, 1957 / Original Jazz Classics ✦✦✦✦

This early recording by pianist Freddie Redd (a straight CD reissue of the original Riverside LP) features Redd's trio of the time, with bassist George Tucker and drummer All Dreares. The CD reissue is highlighted by the 13-minute title piece, a suite that in its five melodies depicts the jazz life in San Francisco during the era. Redd shows potential both in his writing and his boppish playing. The remainder of the fine set has the group's interpretations of three other Redd originals and a trio of standards. An excellent effort. —*Scott Yanow*

The Music from "The Connection" / Feb. 15, 1960 / Blue Note ✦✦✦✦✦

Freddie Redd composed the music for Jack Gelber's *The Connection*, a gritty play about musician junkies. Gelber had originally thought that the play would feature real musicians—who would also double as actors in minor roles—improvising on blues and jazz standards in the tradition of Charlie Parker, but Redd convinced him to use an original score. The two weaved Redd's original compositions into the score, making it an integral part of the play, but the music holds up superbly on its own. Using the direction "in the tradition of Charlie Parker" as a starting point, the pianist wrote seven pieces of straightahead bop, wide open for improvisations, and then assembled a sterling quartet featuring himself, alto saxophonist Jackie McLean, bassist Michael Mattos and drummer Larry Ritchie. The end result was a set of dynamic straightahead bop. While both Redd and McLean show signs of their influences—the pianist blends Monk and Powell, while the saxophonist has built off of Bird's twisting lines—they have developed their own voices, which gives the driving, bluesy bop on *The Connection* an edge. McLean's full, robust tone often dominates, but he never overshadows Redd's complex, intricate playing, and both musicians, as well as Mattos and Ritchie, effortlessly keep up with the changes from hard-hitting, uptempo bop numbers to lyrical, reflective ballads. Musically, *The Connection* might not offer anything unexpected, but whenever straightahead bop is done this well, it should be celebrated. —*Stephen Thomas Erlewine*

★ **The Complete Blue Note Freddie Redd** / Feb. 15, 1960-Jan. 17, 1961 / Mosaic ✦✦✦✦✦
Available in a box set as either three LPs or two CDs, this limited-edition release has all of the music recorded at pianist Freddie Redd's three Blue Note sessions. In addition to the selections originally included on the LPs *Music from the Connection* and *Shades of Redd*, there is a completely unissued date that adds to the fairly slim Freddie Redd discography. Altoist Jackie McLean (who is on all three sets) and tenor saxophonist Tina Brooks (a key soloist on two) co-star with the pianist; trumpeter Benny Bailey is also heard from on the later date. The music comprises mostly Redd's originals (including seven songs written for the stage play *The Connection*) and fits into the style of the mainstream hard bop of the day although with a few personal touches. Straightahead fans and Blue Note collectors can consider this set to be essential. —*Scott Yanow*

☆ **Shades of Redd** / Aug. 13, 1960 / Blue Note ✦✦✦✦✦
Quintet with Tina Brooks on tenor sax and Jackie McLean on alto sax plays all Redd originals with flair and bluesy poignancy. —*Michael G. Nastos*

Straight Ahead! / Dec. 3, 1977 / Interplay ✦✦✦

Extemporaneous / Aug. 14, 1978-Sep. 23, 1978 / Interplay ✦✦✦✦
This album from Interplay gave Freddie Redd a rare opportunity to record unaccompanied solos. He interprets eight of his own somewhat obscure compositions with swing, taste and enough variety to hold on to one's attention. Redd has long been underrated and this is one of his better recordings of the past 25 years. —*Scott Yanow*

Lonely City / Jan. 18, 1985-Jan. 19, 1985 / Uptown ✦✦✦✦
Pianist Freddie Redd's first recording in seven years is quite intriguing. Redd is matched with seven diverse players (tenor saxophonist Clifford Jordan, altoist C Sharpe, baritonist Gerry Cappuccio, trumpeter Don Sickler, bassist George Duvivier and drummer Ben Riley) on six of his compositions, most of which are little known. The music is high-quality hard bop, and the fresh material inspires the musicians. Recommended. —*Scott Yanow*

Live at the Studio Grill / May 19, 1988+May 26, 1988 / Triloka ✦✦✦✦✦
Due to his timeless style and relatively few recordings, Freddie Redd is a legend. A fine bop pianist who was an associate of his idols Bud Powell and Thelonious Monk, Redd (62 at the time of this set) will probably always be best known for his work on the play *The Connection*. Although maintaining a low profile, Redd had been playing continuously through the decades. One listen to his unaccompanied rendition of Powell's "I'll Keep Loving You," his very memorable original "I'm Gonna Be Happy" and his magical version of "I'll Remember April" makes it obvious that Redd is an unrecognized giant. Bassist Al McKibbon and drummer Billy Higgins offer short solos and sympathetic support on this highly recommended trio set, which also has fine versions of "I'll Remember April," "'Round Midnight" and "All the Things You Are." —*Scott Yanow*

Everybody Loves a Winner / Oct. 9, 1990+Oct. 10, 1990 / Milestone ✦✦✦✦✦
Pianist Freddie Redd has not recorded all that much during his 45-year career, but most of his records have been special events. This particular set has eight of Redd's tightly arranged compositions being performed by a fine sextet that also features tenor saxophonist Teddy Edwards, altoist Curtis Peagler and trombonist Phil Ranelin. —*Scott Yanow*

Dewey Redman (Walter Dewey Redman)

b. May 17, 1931, Fort Worth, TX
Tenor Saxophone / Post-Bop, Free Jazz
One of the great avant-garde tenors, Dewey Redman has never received anywhere near the acclaim that his son Joshua Redman gained in the 1990s even though Dewey is much more of an innovative player. He began on clarinet when he was 13 and played in his high school marching band, a group that also included Ornette Coleman, Charles Moffett and Prince Lasha. Redman was a public school teacher during 1956-59 but, after getting his master's degree in education from North Texas State, he moved to San Francisco where he freelanced as a musician for seven years; Pharoah Sanders was among his sidemen. All of this was a prelude to his impressive association with the Ornette Coleman Quartet (1967-74) during which Redman's tenor playing was a perfect match for Ornette's alto. Redman could play as free as the leader but his appealing tone made the music seem a little more accessible. He also worked with Charlie Haden's Liberation Music Orchestra and was an important part of Keith Jarrett's greatest group, his quintet

of the mid-'70s. Redman guested on Pat Metheny's notable *80/81* album and teamed up with Don Cherry, Charlie Haden and Ed Blackwell in the Ornette Coleman reunion band called Old and New Dreams. Despite all of this activity and plenty of recordings (including occasional ones as a leader), Dewey Redman has yet to be fully recognized for his innovative talents. —*Scott Yanow*

Look for the Black Star / Jan. 4, 1966 / Freedom ✦✦✦✦✦
Although always a bit under recognized and overshadowed by his contemporaries, tenor saxophonist Dewey Redman has long been one of the giants of the avant-garde and free bop. This early recording finds Redman discovering his own individual voice on five of his frequently emotional originals. Assisted by pianist Jym Young, bassist Donald Raphael Gareet and drummer Eddie Moore, this San Francisco date is quite adventurous and holds one's interest throughout. —*Scott Yanow*

Tarik / Oct. 1, 1969 / Affinity ✦✦✦

The Ear of the Behearer / Jun. 8, 1973-Jun. 9, 1973 / Impulse! ✦✦✦✦

Coincide / Sep. 9, 1974-Sep. 10, 1974 / Impulse! ✦✦✦

Musics / Oct. 17, 1978-Oct. 19, 1978 / Galaxy ✦✦✦✦✦
This is one of tenor saxophonist Dewey Redman's more accessible sessions. With the assistance of pianist Fred Simmons, bassist Mark Helias and drummer Eddie Moore, Redman is heard on the lyrical ballad "Alone Again (Naturally)," a bossa nova, jamming over parade rhythms and performing originals that sometimes are advanced bop. The music is excellent although not as explorative as most of Redman's other recordings. —*Scott Yanow*

Redman and Blackwell in Willisau / Aug. 31, 1980 / Black Saint ✦✦✦

● **The Struggle Continues** / Jan. 1982 / ECM ✦✦✦✦✦
His best shows great teamwork from bassist Mark Helias, drummer Ed Blackwell and pianist Charles Eubanks. It's a record to make you say "wow." "Turn over Baby" is a good boogie and "Joie de Vivre" is one of Redman's best vehicles for improv. —*Michael G. Nastos*

Living on the Edge / Sep. 13, 1989-Sep. 14, 1989 / Black Saint ✦✦✦✦✦
The great tenor Dewey Redman has always been a versatile player and he really gets a chance to show off his individuality on this set, whether it is some freebop à la early Ornette Coleman, "Mirror Windows" (which is an explosion of sound and pure energy), the soulful "Blues for J.A.M.—Part 1," a free and speechlike tenor-piano duet with Geri Allen on "As One" and a boppish "Lazy Bird." On "If I Should Lose You," Redman has a rare chance to play some conventional but cliché-free alto. With bassist Cameron Brown and drummer Eddie Moore forming a solid team, this is an easily recommended set of inside/outside music. —*Scott Yanow*

In London / Oct. 1996 / Palmetto ✦✦✦✦✦
Accompanied by pianist Rita Marcotulli, bassist Cameron Brown and drummer Matt Wilson, veteran tenor saxophonist Dewey Redman puts on a well-rounded program. On "I Should Care," "The Very Thought of You" (a tribute to Dexter Gordon) and the bossa nova "Portrait in Black and White," he shows that, although his roots are in avant-garde jazz, Redman is quite capable of caressing a melody. In contrast, his renditions of "I-Pimp," "Tu-inns" and "Eleven" emphasize freer improvising and plenty of fire. In both contexts, Dewey Redman emerges as an underrated giant. —*Scott Yanow*

Don Redman

b. Jul. 29, 1900, Piedmont, WV, d. Nov. 30, 1964, New York, NY
Clarinet, Alto Saxophone, Leader, Composer, Arranger, Vocals / Classic Jazz, Swing
The first great arranger in jazz history, Don Redman essentially invented the jazz-oriented big band with innovative arrangements that left room for solo improvisations.

After graduating from college at the age of 20 with a music degree, Redman played for a year with Billy Paige's Broadway Syncopators and then met up with Fletcher Henderson. Redman became Henderson's chief arranger (although Fletcher was often later on mistakenly given credit for the innovative charts) in addition to playing clarinet, alto and (on at least one occasion) oboe. Redman, whose largely spoken vocals were charming, recorded the first ever scat vocal on "My Papa Doesn't Two Time" in early 1924, predating the style of Louis Armstrong. Although his early arrangements were futuristic, they could be a bit stiff and it was not until Armstrong joined Henderson's Orchestra that Redman (learning from the brilliant cornetist) began to really swing in his writing; "Sugar Foot Stomp" and "The Stampede" are two of his many classic charts.

It was a shock to Fletcher Henderson when Redman was persuaded in 1927 by Jean Goldkette to direct McKinney's Cotton Pickers. Redman soon turned the previously unknown group into a strong competitor of Henderson's, composing such future standards as "Gee Baby, Ain't I Good to You" and "Cherry." He sang more, emphasized his alto over his more primitive sounding clarinet (guesting on some famous recordings with Louis Armstrong's Savoy Ballroom Five in 1928) and made a strong series of memorable records. In 1931 Redman put together his own big band that lasted (if not prospered) up until 1941. After that he freelanced as an arranger for the remainder of the swing era, led an all-star orchestra in 1946 that became the first band to visit postwar Europe and eventually became Pearl Bailey's musical director. Although he recorded a few sessions in the late '50s, Don Redman's main significance is for his influential work of the 1920s and '30s. —*Scott Yanow*

Shakin' the African / Sep. 24, 1931-Sep. 19, 1932 / Hep ✦✦✦✦
Although the pair of Don Redman Hep LPs have since been superseded by the Classics CDs, the inclusion of liner notes and a few alternate takes might make this release superior in some collector's minds. The first of two Redman LPs covers the pre-swing big band's first five sessions, featuring either Red Allen or Sidney DeParis on trumpets, the underrated (and now forgotten) tenor of Robert Carroll, and several vocalists including Halran Lattimore and the cheerful leader. Of the 16 numbers on this fine LP from Scotland, the most memorable tracks include "Chant of the Weed," "I Heard," "How'm I Doin'," "Hot and Anxious" and "I Got Rhythm." —*Scott Yanow*

● **1931-1933** / Sep. 24, 1931-Feb. 2, 1933 / Classics ✦✦✦✦✦
The first of three Don Redman Classics CDs consists of his orchestra's earliest sessions. Although Redman's big band never hit it as big as his former employers (Fletcher Henderson and McKinney's Cotton Pickers), it was an impressive outfit thanks to the leader's advanced arrangements. Among the key sidemen on these performances are trumpeters Red Allen (who is on the first two sessions) and Sidney DeParis, tenor saxophonist Robert Carroll and pianist Horace Henderson. Highlights include "Chant of the Weed" (Redman's atmospheric theme song), "I Heard," "How'm I Doin'," and "Hot and Anxious." The main Don Redman CD to get. —*Scott Yanow*

Doin' the New Lowdown / Sep. 16, 1932-Apr. 26, 1933 / Hep ✦✦✦✦
The second of two Don Redman LPs released by the Scottish Hep label has two alternate takes not included on the Classics CDs. Altoist/vocalist/arranger Don Redman led a fine big band during this era, even if they never really hit it big. Such numbers as "Doin' What I Please," "Nagasaki," and "Sophisticated Lady" are memorable, while the two-part "Doin' the New Lowdown" features such guests as tap dancer Bill "Bojangles" Robinson, Cab Calloway and the Mills Brothers. Since there are vocals on all but one selection (the best are the leader's good-natured half-spoken refrains), the talented orchestra is not always showcased as much as one wishes, but the music overall is quite enjoyable. —*Scott Yanow*

1933-1936 / Feb. 2, 1933-May 7, 1936 / Classics ✦✦✦✦✦
The great arranger Don Redman made Fletcher Henderson's Orchestra in the mid-1920s the first real swing band, but during the swing era itself, Redman was little known to the general public. His big band (heard here on the second of three "complete" Classics CDs) failed to really catch on, although it stayed together throughout the 1930s. After recording a bunch of sessions in 1933, Redman's orchestra only cut two sides in January 1934 and then none until May 1936. There are vocals on 22 of the 25 selections on this CD; of the three instrumentals, this version of "Christopher Columbus" might not be by Redman. The leader's charming vocals are fine, but the nine by Harlan Lattimore are of lesser interest, and Chick Bullock dominates a six-song session. There are some good solos along the way, particularly by trumpeter Sidney DeParis, trombonists Benny Morton and Claude Jones and the forgotten tenor Robert Carroll, but this CD is primarily for completists. —*Scott Yanow*

1936-1939 / May 7, 1936-Mar. 23, 1939 / Classics ✦✦✦✦✦
The third in the series of Don Redman Classics CDs finds the innovative arranger adjusting to the swing era. His big band is heard on sessions cut for ARC in 1936 ("Bugle Call Rag" is excellent), Variety in 1937 (including a previously unreleased "Swingin' with the Fat Man"), and Bluebird during 1938-39 (including "I Got Ya," "Down Home Rag" and "Milenberg Joys"). A lot of interesting names passed through the band during this era, including trumpeter Sidney DeParis, trombonist Quentin Jackson and singer Laurel Watson, and there is some pleasing music despite a fair amount of vocals. This series ended before Redman's last two big band sessions, but those have often been made available by RCA/Bluebird. The first CD in Classics' Redman series is the most essential. —*Scott Yanow*

For Europeans Only / Sep. 15, 1946 / Steeple Chase ✦✦✦
The music on this CD reissue is taken from the first visit by an American band to Denmark after World War II. Arranger/singer/altoist Don Redman, who was undertaking his last significant contribution to jazz, led an all-star big band that included such notable stars as trumpeter/vocalist Peanuts Holland, trombonist Quentin Jackson, Tyree Glenn on vibes and trombone, pianist Billy Taylor and the great tenor Don Byas. In fact, Byas enjoyed Europe so much during the tour that he made it his permanent home, only returning to the US once briefly decades

later. Byas is the star of several of the numbers (particularly "How High the Moon" and "Laura"), but many of the other sidemen also get some solo space. The music is essentially late-period swing with hints of bop in places, including the Tadd Dameron piece "For Europeans Only." Unfortunately, the recording quality of the privately made acetates is not always the greatest, although the sound and balance is a lot better on the CD than on the earlier LP. Important historic music that has some strong moments. —*Scott Yanow*

Joshua Redman

b. Feb. 1, 1969, Berkeley, CA
Tenor Saxophone / Post-Bop, Hard Bop
Every few years it seems as if the jazz media goes out of its way to hype one young artist, overpraising him to such an extent that it is easy to tear him down when the next season arrives. In the early '90s Joshua Redman briefly became a media darling, but in his case he largely deserved the attention. A talented bop-based tenorman, Redman (who will probably never be an innovator) is a throwback to the styles of Red Holloway and Gene Ammons but also has an inquisitive spirit and can play intriguing music when inspired.
The son of the great tenor saxophonist Dewey Redman, Joshua graduated from Harvard and (after debating about whether to become a doctor) he seemed headed towards studying law at Yale. However, Redman came in first place at the 1991 Thelonious Monk competition, landed a recording contract with Warner Bros. and was soon on the cover of most jazz magazines. Pat Metheny was a guest on one of his albums (the Redman-Metheny interplay during their engagements was quite memorable) and, although Redman has had success constantly touring with his own group, it is a pity that his apprentice period as a sideman was so brief. In 1996 Joshua Redman recorded and briefly toured with Chick Corea's "Tribute to Bud Powell" sextet. —*Scott Yanow*

Joshua Redman / 1993 / Warner Brothers ✦✦✦✦

★ **Wish** / 1993 / Warner Brothers ✦✦✦✦✦
Joshua Redman may be the person to unite warring sects, since he is neither a committed neobop conservative nor a jazz/hip-hopper or "acid" player. He is one of the few Young Lions that has made great music from day one. Redman's soaring tone, intelligently constructed solos, control, and ability to play riveting uptempo, midtempo, or slow works has justifiably made him a sensation. When the lineup includes Pat Metheny offering marvelous solos on electric and acoustic, and Charlie Haden and Billy Higgins being their customary masterful selves on bass and drums, you have the kind of great, uncompromising jazz work you seldom get from a major label in the 1990s. —*Ron Wynn*

Blues for Pat / 1994 / Jazz Door ✦✦✦✦
In 1994, tenor saxophonist Joshua Redman really broke through to become a major jazz star. After recording *Wish* (which used guitarist Pat Metheny as a star sideman), Redman went on a tour with Metheny, bassist Christian McBride and drummer Billy Higgins. This live CD from the European Jazz Door label is of dubious origin (and is probably a bootleg), but musically is quite excellent. The recording quality is listenable and the playing by the four all-stars is fiery and stimulating. In particular, the interplay between Redman and Metheny brings out the best in both players, and their rendition of "St. Thomas" is really blazing. Worth searching for. —*Scott Yanow*

Mood Swing / 1994 / Warner Brothers ✦✦✦✦✦

Spirit of the Moment: Live at the Village Vanguard / Aug. 29, 1995 / Warner Brothers ✦✦✦✦✦
This double-CD gives one a definitive look at how the much-acclaimed tenor saxophonist Joshua Redman sounded in the mid-'90s. Joined by pianist Peter Martin, bassist Christopher Thomas and drummer Brian Blade, Redman stretches from Gene Ammons (who is saluted on "Jig-a-Jug") to late-period John Coltrane, showing off both his wide range and his lyricism. Redman is heard at his best on the four-minute cadenza that opens "St. Thomas," digging into "My One and Only Love" and playing almost outside on "Lyric." Of the 14 songs, nine are his originals and, although Redman was not at this point an innovator, he was well on his way to forming his own personal style. Recommended. —*Scott Yanow*

Freedom in the Groove / Apr. 10, 1996-Apr. 13, 1996 / Warner Brothers ✦✦✦✦
Joshua Redman's fifth recording for Warner Bros. certainly has its moments, as the talented tenor shows off his versatility. "Hide and Seek" pays tribute (maybe not intentionally) to Eddie Harris; "Home Fries" is a happy swinger; the humorous "Can't Dance" drops four beats each funky chorus; and, on part of "Invocation," Redman (switching to alto) hints strongly at Eric Dolphy during the freer spots. The interplay between Redman, the soulful guitarist Peter Bernstein, and the alert rhythm section (pianist Peter Martin, bassist Christopher Thomas and drummer Brian Blade) are consistently impressive. Unfortunately, the leader's soprano playing falls way short; his erratic intonation (particularly on "Pantomine" and "One

Shining Soul") is far from appealing. That reservation aside, Joshua Redman shows that his fame has not slowed his development—*Scott Yanow*

Dizzy Reece (Alphonso Son Reece)

b. Jan. 5, 1931, Kingston, Jamaica
Trumpet / Hard Bop

Dizzy Reece is a fine hard-bop trumpeter who has been overshadowed by the innovators of the style. He started on trumpet when he was 14 and moved to Europe in 1949. It was while he was based in England (1954-59) that he achieved some recognition through a series of recordings with top English musicians plus a 1958 date with Donald Byrd. He moved to New York in 1959 but, after a few notable recordings and a bit of publicity, Reece seemed to largely fade away despite remaining active. He was with the Dizzy Gillespie's Orchestra in 1968 and the Paris Reunion Band in 1985. —*Scott Yanow*

Blues in Trinity / Aug. 24, 1958 / Blue Note ✦✦✦✦✦

As Dizzy Reece's first album for Blue Note, *Blues in Trinity* goes a long way to establish the trumpeter's signature sound. Reece doesn't take chances stylistically—he prefers to stay within the confines of hard bop. Nevertheless, he has a bold, forceful sound that simply burns with passion. Even on slower numbers, there's a fire to his playing that keeps *Blues in Trinity* from being predictable. What makes the high quality of the album even more impressive are the recording circumstances. The English-based Reece was playing in Paris at the time, and he assembled a sextet featuring the vacationing British musicians Tubby Hayes (tenor saxophone) and Terry Shannon (piano), visiting American stars Donald Byrd (trumpet) and Art Taylor (drums), and Canadian bassist Lloyd Thompson, who was playing in Paris with Zoot Sims. Although the band was thrown together, there's a definite spark to this combo, which interacts as if it had been playing together for a long time. Throughout it all, Reece steals the show with his robust playing, and that's why *Blues in Trinity* rises above the level of standard-issue hard bop and becomes something special. —*Stephen Thomas Erlewine*

Star Bright / Nov. 9, 1959 / Blue Note ✦✦✦✦✦

Soundin' Off / May 12, 1960 / Blue Note ✦✦✦✦

● **Asia Minor** / Mar. 13, 1962 / Original Jazz Classics ✦✦✦✦✦

This is one of trumpeter Dizzy Reece's finest recordings, a well-planned sextet date (reissued on CD) with baritonist Cecil Payne, Joe Farrell on tenor and flute, pianist Hank Jones, bassist Ron Carter and drummer Charlie Persip that is on the level of a Blue Note album. Reece (who contributed three diverse originals) performs mostly minor-toned songs that seem to really inspire the musicians. The solos tend to be concise but quite meaningful and overall this hard bop but occasionally surprising session is quite memorable. Strange that Reece would not get another opportunity to lead a record date until 1970. —*Scott Yanow*

Manhattan Project / Jan. 17, 1978 / Bee Hive ✦✦✦✦

Blowin' Away / Jun. 9, 1978 / Interplay ✦✦✦

Eric Reed

b. 1970, Philadelphia, PA
Piano / Post-Bop

A superior pianist who is growing in stature year by year, Eric Reed began playing piano when he was two, and in his childhood often performed in his father's church. He started classical lessons when he was seven, moved with his family to Los Angeles when he was 11 and first met Wynton Marsalis when he was 14, impressing the trumpeter. Reed played in L.A. with John Clayton and the Gerald Wilson Orchestra, toured with Marsalis when he was 18, worked with Freddie Hubbard and Joe Henderson, and in the early '90s became a regular member of Wynton Marsalis' group, replacing Marcus Roberts. Eric Reed has recorded with Marsalis and led a few of his own sessions for Candid, MoJazz and Impulse. —*Scott Yanow*

Soldier's Hymn / Nov. 7, 1990 / Candid ✦✦✦✦

Youthful pianist Eric Reed, who at the time of this recording was debuting as Marcus Roberts' replacement in the Wynton Marsalis band, plays carefully and sometimes tentatively on his first release as a leader. It's a trio affair, and although Reed doesn't throw many challenges toward bassist Dwayne Burno or drummer Gregory Hutchinson, he's certainly a solid player with the potential to become a great one. —*Ron Wynn*

● **It's All Right to Swing** / Apr. 5, 1993+Apr. 6, 1993 / MoJazz ✦✦✦✦✦

The Swing and I / Aug. 9, 1994-Aug. 11, 1994 / MoJazz ✦✦✦

West Coast Jazz Summit / Oct. 29, 1995 / Mons ✦✦✦✦

Calling the gathering for this CD a "summit" might be overstating the case a bit. The Los Angeles-based quartet (tenor saxophonist Ralph Moore, pianist Eric Reed, bassist Bob Hurst and drummer Jeff Hamilton) may not all play together on a reg-

ular basis, but their paths have crossed many times. For this set, they perform ten veteran standards, including "Pick Yourself Up," "Old Folks," "Golden Earrings," "Caravan" and "Tequila." Moore and Reed take many fine solos, and the music, although not containing any real surprises, is satisfying and swinging. —*Scott Yanow*

Musicale / Mar. 10, 1996+Apr. 19, 1996 / GRP ✦✦✦✦✦

It is easy to be fooled initially by pianist Eric Reed's latest recording. He starts off the set with an effective tribute to Art Blakey and sometimes takes solos that are influenced by McCoy Tyner's chord voicings, but the music on a whole is actually fresh and fairly original, rather than just a copy of the Blue Note sound. Except for the final two numbers (pieces by James Leary and Wessell Anderson), all of the music was composed by Reed, and these range from somber ballads and solid swing to the upbeat church feel of "Baby Sis" (which has a heated wah-wah solo from guest trombonist Wycliffe Gordon). Half of the selections are trio numbers for Reed with bassist Ben Wolfe and drummer Gregory Hutchinson, while the remainder of the set has a two-horn quintet (except for altoist Wessell Anderson's ballad feature on "Upper Wess Side"). Anderson and trumpeter Nicholas Payton (who sounds more like Freddie Hubbard every day) make for a potent team, particularly when they solo together on "Pete and Repete." Although the three "Scandal" pieces, which are brief fragments of the same number, are a bit frivolous and certainly inconclusive, the remainder of the program serves as a strong example of modern mainstream jazz. Eric Reed continues to grow as an improviser and composer with each recording. —*Scott Yanow*

Pure Imagination / Jul. 28, 1997-Jul. 29, 1997 / Impulse! ✦✦✦

Pure Imagination finds pianist Eric Reed offering fresh arrangements of traditional pop songs from classic Broadway and Hollywood productions. Supported by bassist Reginald Veal and drummer Gregory Hutchinson, Reed offers tasteful, inventive versions of such songs as "Maria," "Hello, Young Lovers," "42nd Street," "Send in the Clowns," "Nice Work If You Can Get It" and "I Got Rhythm." It's a clever, engaging record that only confirms that Reed is a singular pianist. —*Leo Stanley*

Waymon Reed

b. Jan. 10, 1940, Fayetteville, NC, **d.** Nov. 25, 1983, Nashville, TN
Trumpet, Fluegelhorn / Hard Bop

A journeyman jazz trumpeter, Reed was a reliable bop-oriented soloist. After attending the Eastman School of Music and gaining experience playing with R&B groups and with Ira Sullivan in Miami, Reed was a member of James Brown's group during 1965-69 and then was with Count Basie (1969-73). Short stints with the Frank Foster and Thad Jones–Mel Lewis big bands preceded another tour of duty with Basie (1977-78). Reed was married for a time to Sarah Vaughan and he worked with her during much of 1978-80 before their marriage broke up and he was stricken with cancer. —*Scott Yanow*

46th & 8th / May 25, 1977 / Artists House ✦✦✦✦

Trumpeter Waymon Reed was considered a reliable bop-influenced soloist and a fine section player in big bands. This was his only opportunity to lead a record date and the results are pleasingly straightahead. Reed is heard on one original (the title cut, which is a blues) and four standards along with tenor saxophonist Jimmy Foster, pianist Tommy Flanagan, bassist Keter Betts and drummer Bobby Durham. Nothing surprising occurs but Reed (particularly on a warm version of the ballad "But Beautiful") is in fine form. —*Scott Yanow*

Dianne Reeves

b. 1956, Detroit, MI
Vocals / Hard Bop, R&B, Pop, Vocal Jazz, Traditional Pop Standards, Vocal Pop

Dianne Reeves has thus far had a rather confusing and career. Blessed with a very attractive voice and the ability to be the premiere jazz singer of this era, Reeves seems reluctant to stick to jazz. Her recordings are often rather schizophrenic affairs, rarely reaching the heights of her exciting live performances. Reeves sang (and recorded) with her high school band and was encouraged by Clark Terry, performing with him while a college student at the University of Colorado. She did session work in Los Angeles starting in 1976, toured with Sergio Mendes (1981) and Harry Belafonte (1984) and first started recording as a solo artist in 1982, soon becoming a familiar name on the festival circuit. Finally in 1994 after shifting back and forth between jazz, pop and African music, Reeves started to commit herself more to jazz, recording the first of several strong jazz sets for Blue Note. It is not yet too late for the singer to fulfill her enormous potential. —*Scott Yanow*

The Palo Alto Sessions / 1981-1985 / Blue Note ✦✦✦

This disc reissues Reeves' entire 1982 LP, *Welcome to My Love*, plus three tracks from 1985's *For Every Heart* and one selection from her days as a vocalist with the band Caldera. It contains the first recorded version of her classic "Better Days," and one of the best renditions of the overworked standard "My Funny Valentine" as you're likely to hear. On *Welcome*, Reeves was exploring the jazz/R&B territory she would claim as her own a decade later. "For Every Heart" was much more commercial, but the three cuts chosen here are worthwhile, especially a duet with Jon Lucien, "Separate Vacations." —*Frank Federico*

Better Days / 1987 / Blue Note ✦✦✦

Title track was a huge hit. Fluctuates from R&B to jazz. —*Ron Wynn*

I Remember / Apr. 27, 1988–Sep. 11, 1990 / Blue Note ✦✦✦✦

Never Too Far / 1990 / EMI ✦✦✦

Quiet After the Storm / 1994 / Blue Note ✦✦✦✦✦

Dianne Reeves, who has always had a beautiful voice and the potential for greatness in jazz, has conducted a rather directionless career, performing many concerts filled with spontaneity while at the same time recording erratic albums that usually feature both veteran jazz ballads and newer material that is closer to pop and folk music. There are some strong jazz moments on this CD. "Comes Love" has an inventive arrangement that uses a riff from the Miles Davis version of "'Round Midnight" and a familiar rhythmic phrase from "Star Eyes" in surprising ways. "Detour Ahead" is fine and "The Benediction" ("Country Preacher" with Reeves' lyrics) is a sincere tribute to Cannonball Adderley (who makes a brief appearance on soprano via sampling), but on some of the other pieces Reeves wanders far away from jazz. She sings a couple of folk songs with guitarist Dori Caymmi, introduces the heartwarming if poppish original "Nine" and performs a very straight version of Joni Mitchell's "When Morning Comes" that makes the song sound like a Broadway show tune. Perhaps Dianne Reeves' eventual niche will be as a jazz-influenced folk-pop singer; someday she should probably make up her mind. —*Scott Yanow*

Art and Survival / 1993 / EMI America ✦✦✦

Versatility has gotten vocalist Dianne Reeves in trouble. Those who feel she could be a great jazz singer want her to stick to scat singing and interpreting show tunes; others who enjoyed the light fusion and urban contemporary hits prefer that she look toward the future. Reeves does a little of both on her this set. *Art and Survival* includes her most hard-hitting message songs to date. The only problem is that Reeves' voice doesn't lend itself to shouts or expressing defiance; she sounds strained on "Endangered Species" and seems more like she's presenting a diatribe than expounding on a theme. Overall, *Art and Survival* is neither '90s revisited bop nor overtly commercial Quiet Storm fodder. Dianne Reeves is really seeking a middle ground between her two audiences, and if everything here doesn't work, at least she keeps forging ahead. —*Ron Wynn*

● **The Grand Encounter** / Apr. 4, 1996–Apr. 9, 1996 / Blue Note ✦✦✦✦✦

This CD could have been titled "Finally!" Dianne Reeves has long had the potential to be the top female jazz singer but so many of her previous recordings were erratic as she skipped back and forth between idioms without committing herself. However, after years of flirting with jazz and being seemingly undecided whether she would rather be a pop star, she at last came out with a full jazz album in 1996 and it is a gem. The supporting cast on the ten selections (which feature different personnel on each cut) is remarkable and everyone gets a chance to play: trumpeters Clark Terry and Harry "Sweets" Edison, altoists Phil Woods and Bobby Watson, tenorman James Moody, trombonist Al Grey, harmonica great Toots Thielemans (on "Besame Mucho"), pianist Kenny Barron, bassist Rodney Whittaker and drummer Herlin Riley. In addition, Joe Williams shares the vocal spotlight on "Let Me Love You" and a touching version of "Tenderly," Germaine Bazzle sings along with Reeves on "Side by Side" and a rendition of Charlie Ventura's "Ha!" has a vocal group consisting of Reeves, Bazzle, Terry, Moody and the young Kimberly Longstreth. Other highlights include Nat Adderley's "Old Country," "Some Other Spring" and "Cherokee." Despite the heavy "competition," the leader emerges as the star of the set due to her beautiful voice and highly expressive singing. This highly recommended CD is the Dianne Reeves release to get. —*Scott Yanow*

That Day . . . / 1997 / Blue Note ✦✦✦✦

After two solid jazz recordings, this effort by Dianne Reeves finds her returning a bit to her eclectic ways. She sounds joyous and swinging on "Exactly like You," making one wonder why she still spends so much time singing R&B and pop. Other highlights include the sexy and saucy "That Day," a spacey version of "Blue Prelude," and the folkish "The Twelfth of Never," but there are also several less interesting numbers that are only worthwhile due to Reeves' attractive voice. The singer is assisted by a small group that includes pianist Mulgrew Miller and drummer Terri Lyne Carrington. —*Scott Yanow*

Reuben Reeves

b. Oct. 25, 1905, Evansville, IN, **d.** Sep. 1975, New York, NY
Trumpet / Classic Jazz

At one point in the late '20s, Reuben "Red" Reeves was one of the more exciting trumpeters in jazz although his star soon faded. After playing locally in the Midwest, he moved to New York in 1924. The following year Reeves relocated to Chicago and in 1926 he became a member of Erskine Tate's Orchestra. He recorded with Fess Williams and worked with Dave Peyton during 1928-30 but most importantly led a series of record dates in 1929 with his Tributaries and his River Boys; sidemen included his brother Gerald Reeves on trombone and the great clarinetist Omer Simeon. Reuben Reeves had a wild extroverted style that was a little bit like Roy Eldridge would develop a few years later. Reeves was with Cab Calloway's Orchestra during 1931-32 and then in 1933 returned to Chicago and organized his River Boys for one final session. He toured with his River Boys during 1933-35, freelanced for a few years, served with the Army during World War II (leading an Army band) and then joined Harry Dial's Bluesicians in 1946. His last few years were largely spent outside of music. An RST CD has all of Reuben Reeves' recordings as a leader. —*Scott Yanow*

● **Reuben 'River' Reeves and His River Boys** / May 22, 1929–Dec. 14, 1933 / RST ✦✦✦✦✦

Rufus Reid

b. Feb. 10, 1944, Atlanta, GA
Bass / Post-Bop

A prolific bassist who's seemingly always in the recording studio, Rufus Reid appears on countless hard bop, bebop, swing, and even some pop sessions. His restrained, yet emphatic and pungent tone, time, harmonic sensiblity and discernible, if understated, swing are welcome on any session. Trumpet was Reid's first love, but he switched to bass while in the Air Force. He played with Buddy Montgomery in Sacramento, then studied music in Seattle and Chicago in the late '60s and early '70s. Reid worked in Chicago with Sonny Stitt, James Moody, Milt Jackson, Curtis Fuller and Dizzy Gillespie, and recorded with Kenny Dorham, Dexter Gordon, Lee Konitz and Howard McGhee in 1970. He toured internationally several times with the Bobby Hutcherson-Harold Land quintet, Freddie Hubbard, Nancy Wilson, Eddie Harris and Gordon through the '70s. Reid moved to New York in 1976, playing and recording with a quartet co-led by Thad Jones and Mel Lewis, and taught at William Patterson College in Wayne, New Jersey, starting in 1979. He recorded with Konitz, Ricky Ford, Jack DeJohnette's Special Edition with Kenny Burrell, with a quintet co-led by Frank Wess and Art Farmer, and in duos with Kenny Burrell and Harold Danko in the 1980s. Reid also did sessions with Art Farmer and Jimmy Heath. He has co-led a group with drummer Akira Tana since the late '80s that is called TanaReid. As a leader, Rufus Reid has cut sets for Theresa, Sunnyside and Concord. —*Ron Wynn*

Perpetual Stroll / Jan. 27, 1980 / Theresa ✦✦✦✦

Bassist Rufus Reid, pianist Kirk Lightsey and drummer Eddie Gladden (all three of whom worked together for awhile as Dexter Gordon's rhythm section) are in fine form on this trio set. Reid contributed two of the songs, and Lightsey brought one to the date. In addition the musicians play a rapid version of Herbie Hancock's "One Finger Snap" while Oscar Pettiford's classic "Tricrotism" becomes a solo bass feature for Reid. Since all three musicians have tended to be underrated through the years, this recording serves as a excellent showcase for their often overlooked talents. —*Scott Yanow*

Seven Minds / Nov. 25, 1984 / Sunnyside ✦✦✦✦✦

Premier bassist Reid with pianist Jim McNeely and drummer Teri Lyne Carrington. Extraordinary playing, approaching telepathic. —*Michael G. Nastos*

Corridor to the Limits / Mar. 5, 1989 / Sunnyside ✦✦✦

A teacher at William Patterson College throughout the 1980s, bassist Rufus Reid, his trio (which includes pianist Rob Schneiderman and drummer Victor Lewis) and guest tenor Harold Land can be heard on this CD playing at a concert for the student body. With the exception of Oscar Pettiford's "Swinging 'till the Girls Come Home," all of the songs are somewhat obscure including compositions by Harold Danko, Wayne Shorter, Take 6, Geoff Keezer, Thad Jones and Reid. The pacing is a bit odd, starting off with three straight ballads (six of the ten selections are somewhat introspective) and there are no real crowd pleasers on the date. Land contributed the scalar piece "Short Subject" and shows that his tenor playing has grown through the years. Rufus Reid takes nearly as much solo space as Schneiderman and Land, displaying a beautiful tone and creative ideas. The music is at times a bit dry but rewards repeated listenings. —*Scott Yanow*

● **Yours and Mine** / Sep. 1990 / Concord Jazz ✦✦✦✦✦

Rufus Reid (b) and Akira Tana (d). Effective session with strong help from Young Lions Ralph Moore (ts), Jesse Davis (as). Released in 1991. —*Ron Wynn*

Doublebass Delights / Nov. 5, 1996 / Double-Time ✦✦✦

Django Reinhardt (Jean Baptiste Reinhardt)

b. Jan. 23, 1910, Liverchies, Belgium, d. May 16, 1953, Fontainebleau, France
Guitar / Swing

Django Reinhardt was the first hugely influential jazz figure to emerge from Europe—and he remains the most influential European to this day, with possible competition from Joe Zawinul, George Shearing, John McLaughlin, his old cohort Stephane Grappelli and a bare handful of others. A free-spirited gypsy, Reinhardt wasn't the most reliable person in the world, frequently wandering off into the countryside on a whim. Yet Reinhardt came up with a unique way of propelling the humble acoustic guitar into the front line of a jazz combo in the days before amplification became widespread. He would spin joyous, arcing, marvelously inflected solos above the thrumming base of two rhythm guitars and a bass, with Grappelli's elegantly gliding violin serving as the perfect foil. His harmonic concepts were startling for their time—making a direct impression upon Charlie Christian and Les Paul, among others—and he was an energizing rhythm guitarist behind Grappelli, pushing their groups into a higher gear. Not only did Reinhardt put his stamp upon jazz, his string-band music also had an impact upon the parallel development of Western swing, which eventually fed into the wellspring of what is now called country music. Although he could not read music, with Grappelli and on his own, Reinhardt composed several winsome, highly original tunes like "Daphne," "Nuages" and "Manoir de mes reves," as well as mad swingers like "Minor Swing" and the ode to his record label of the '30s, "Stomping at Decca." As the late Ralph Gleason said about Django's recordings, "They were European and they were French and they were still jazz."

A violinist first and a guitarist later, Jean Baptiste "Django" Reinhardt grew up in a gypsy camp near Paris where he absorbed the gypsy strain into his music. A disastrous caravan fire in 1928 badly burned his left hand, depriving him of the use of the fourth and fifth fingers, but the resourceful Reinhardt figured out a novel fingering system to get around the problem that probably accounts for some of the originality of his style. According to one story, during his recovery period, Reinhardt was introduced to American jazz when he found a 78 rpm disc of Louis Armstrong's "Dallas Blues" at an Orleans flea market. He then resumed his career playing in Parisian cafes until one day in 1934 when Hot Club chief Pierre Nourry proposed the idea of an all-string band to Reinhardt and Grappelli. Thus was born the Quintet of the Hot Club of France, which quickly became an international draw thanks to a long, splendid series of Ultraphone, Decca and HMV recordings.

The outbreak of war in 1939 broke up the Quintet, with Grappelli remaining in London where the group was playing and Reinhardt returning to France. During the war years, he led a big band, another quintet with clarinetist Hubert Rostaing in place of Grappelli, and after the liberation of Paris, recorded with such visiting American jazzmen as Mel Powell, Peanuts Hucko and Ray McKinley. In 1946, Reinhardt took up the electric guitar and toured America as a soloist with the Duke Ellington band but his appearances were poorly received. Some of his recordings on electric guitar late in his life are bop escapades where his playing sounds frantic and jagged, a world apart from the jubilant swing of old. However, , starting in Jan. 1946, Reinhardt and Grappelli held several sporadic reunions where the bop influences are more subtly integrated into the old, still-fizzing swing format. In the 1950s, Reinhardt became more reclusive, remaining in Europe, playing and recording now and then until his death from a stroke in 1953. His Hot Club recordings from the '30s are his most irresistible legacy; their spirit and sound can be felt in current groups like Holland's Rosenberg Trio. —*Richard S. Ginell*

☆ **Djangologie/USA, Vols. 1-7** / Mar. 15, 1928-Oct. 1, 1940 / Swing ✦✦✦✦✦

This seven-LP box set, made available domestically by DRG, mostly features the remarkable guitarist Django Reinhardt with the Quintet of the Hot Club of France during 1936-39, showing that not only could Europeans play swinging jazz as far back as the 1930s but they could be pacesetters and innovators too. Violinist Stephane Grappelli also stars throughout this set, which includes appearances with bands led by Benny Carter, Coleman Hawkins, Rex Stewart, harmonica wizard Larry Adler, trumpeter Philippe Brun, trumpeter Bill Coleman, violinist Eddie South and trombonist Dicky Wells along with many performances by the Quintet. The first album is in some ways the most interesting, because it features Django as a sideman with a wide variety of French groups including two very early appearances on banjo. A book included in the box has a complete discography of Django Reinhardt's career. Highly recommended, it's superior to the CD reissues of some of this material. —*Scott Yanow*

The Versatile Giant / Aug. 1934-Feb. 10, 1951 / Inner City ✦✦✦✦✦

This hard-to-find LP contains a variety of collectors items that nearly span guitarist Django Reinhardt's entire career. He is heard on three very early recordings (two with violinist Stephane Grappelli), playing four songs taken from his erratic

1946 tour with Duke Ellington (Ellington's orchestra unfortunately is very much in the background), on a few rarities with his 1947 sextet and in 1951 performing two numbers recorded live at the Club Saint Germain in Paris. Reinhardt collectors will have to be patient searching for this one. —*Scott Yanow*

Django Reinhardt (1935) / 1935 / GNP ✦✦✦✦

Of the dozen selections on this LP, six feature the Quintet of the Hot Club of France, either tenor saxophonist Alix Combelle or multi-instrumentalist Frank "Big Boy" Goudie (heard on trumpet, tenor and clarinet) sit in on four other numbers and two songs find guitarist Django Reinhardt and violinist Stephane Grappelli welcoming three trumpeters and a trombonist to the Quintet. Highlights include "Djangology," "Smoke Rings," "Cloudsof" and "The Sheik of Araby." All of the GNP Django LPs are recommended and they generally do not duplicate other reissue series. —*Scott Yanow*

Parisian Swing / Apr. 1935-Aug. 25, 1939 / GNP ✦✦✦✦

Over a period of time, GNP/Crescendo released seven LPs featuring guitarist Django Reinhardt, violinist Stephane Grappelli and The Quintet of the Hot Club of France. This particular set has four titles from 1935 and the remainder from 1938-39. Of the latter, four songs actually find Reinhardt and Grappelli playing duets (Stephane is on piano on three of those cuts). High points of this enjoyable LP include "Undecided," "Djangology," "Nocturne" and "I've Got My Love to Keep Me Warm." —*Scott Yanow*

Django '35-'39 / Sep. 30, 1935-Mar. 21, 1939 / GNP ✦✦✦✦

Although it would have been preferable for GNP/Crescendo in their seven LPs of Django Reinhardt recordings to reissue his music in strict chronological order, each of these sets are well worth acquiring. Guitarist Reinhardt and violinist Stephane Grappelli are in superb form on the 14 selections that comprise this particular LP, performances taken from four different recording sessions. Such numbers as "Limehouse Blues," "I Found a New Baby," "It Don't Mean a Thing" and "Swing '39" are among the highlights of this consistently swinging set. —*Scott Yanow*

Nuages / May 4, 1936-Dec. 13, 1940 / Arkadia Jazz ✦✦✦

The fledgling Arkadia Jazz label's first historical project, a musical bullseye, hitting Django Reinhardt's most fabled period right down the center. There are plenty of samples of the vintage Hot Club of France Quintet at its peak—with Stephane Grappelli, brother Joseph on guitar and Louis Vola on bass—as well as a few selections outside the Quintet with Bill Coleman, Dicky Wells and the Benny Carter Orchestra. Rather than organizing the set chronologically, Arkadia has chosen to lead with a few Django compositions played by the Quintet ("Nuages," "Minor Swing" "Swing Guitars"), followed by a lot of killer Quintet renditions of popular tunes and concluding with the non-Quintet tracks. While Arkadia diligently gives recording dates, it is cagier about the sources of these tracks. However, apparently almost all of them have been issued and reissued before; for example, a cluster of five hot tracks from 1937 clearly comes from the HMV/EMI archives. Arkadia claims two "newly discovered" performances from 1937 featuring Carter and Coleman Hawkins (with Grappelli on piano)—a sedate "Out of Nowhere" and a jumping "Sweet Georgia Brown" where Django only plays rhythm. Arkadia has actually done a better job of remastering these tracks than a lot of the major labels' attempts at "cleaning up" shellac 78s for CDs; the variable yet decent sound is usually bright and forward with little distortion, though the bass could be stronger. As a single-disc introduction to an ingratiating group of great musicians, this release is very competitive. —*Richard S. Ginell*

☆ **Djangology** / May 4, 1936-Mar. 10, 1948 / EMI ✦✦✦✦✦

This massive ten-CD set of Django Reinhardt's recordings covers some of the same ground as the earlier 20-LP *Djangology* EMI series, duplicating the music on *Vols. 2-15* along with three tracks from the first LP and ten from *Vol. 16*. However, there are 34 additional selections that were formerly overlooked (on some of those songs Reinhardt only plays a minor role). This essential box contains 243 performances taken from a 12-year period, tracing Reinhardt's career from his performances with the Quintet of the Hot Club of France (which co-starred violinist Stephane Grappelli) through the war years (with the guitarist heard in a wide variety of settings) and the formation of his postwar quintet with clarinetist Hubert Rostaing before concluding with a reunion with Grappelli. Recommended to all serious Django Reinhardt collectors. —*Scott Yanow*

Django Reinhardt & Stephane Grappelli / Jan. 31, 1938-Feb. 1, 1946 / GNP Crescendo ✦✦✦✦✦

Of the seven LPs of Django Reinhardt's recordings reissued by GNP/Crescendo, this is the most consistently exciting set. Guitarist Django Reinhardt and violinist Stephane Grappelli are heard teaming up in their 1938-39 quintet and on a reunion session in 1946. They are in particularly superb form on "Honeysuckle Rose," "Liza," "Nuages" and "Sweet Georgia Brown"; actually all 14 performances are quite rewarding. —*Scott Yanow*

Vol. 3 / Mar. 14, 1938-May 17, 1939 / JSP ✦✦✦✦
This CD from the English label JSP will fill some major gaps even for veteran Django Reinhardt collectors—the 24 selections (which include five alternate takes) are among the rarest in Django's discography. The remarkable guitarist is teamed with violinist Stephane Grappelli and the Quintet of the Hot Club of France for consistently exciting and heated swing performances. Highlights include "Swing from Paris," "Swing '39," "Tea for Two" and "My Melancholy Baby." —*Scott Yanow*

Paris 1945 / 1945 / Columbia ✦✦✦✦
This French Columbia LP will be difficult to find but contains a variety of valuable music from postwar Paris. Guitarist Django Reinhardt is heard jamming on four selections with an American sextet that also features trumpeter Bernie Privin, Peanuts Hucko on tenor and pianist Mel Powell. Hucko (on clarinet) is featured on four other songs in a trio and Powell gets a few unaccompanied piano solos including "Hommage a Fats Waller" and "Hommage a Debussy." High-quality late-swing music that has not been reissued in recent times. —*Scott Yanow*

Swing Guitar / Oct. 26, 1945-Mar. 1946 / Jass ✦✦✦✦
In late 1945 the great guitarist Django Reinhardt had an opportunity to broadcast regularly with the ATC (Air Transport Command) Orchestra, a big band filled with talented but now-forgotten American servicemen. Reinhardt is the main soloist throughout, whether with the full orchestra or with small groups out of the band; he also takes "Improvisation No. 6" unaccompanied. In addition, the ATC band is heard on six selections without the guitarist. All in all this is a surprising and consistently interesting release. —*Scott Yanow*

Brussels and Paris / Mar. 21, 1947-Apr. 8, 1953 / DRG ✦✦✦✦✦
Even collectors with dozens of Django Reinhardt records may not have the formerly rare performances included on this 1996 reissue CD. The great Reinhardt is heard throughout on electric (rather than acoustic) guitar and he shows that during his last years he was one of the top bop-based guitarists in the world. Reinhardt is teamed with clarinetist Hubert Rostaing in a 1947 quintet for nine songs but it is the other 16 selections (his final recordings) that are of greatest interest. Reinhardt during 1951-53 was joined with such top young French modernists as trumpeters Bernard Hullin and Roger Guerin, altoist Hubert Fol, pianists Raymond Fol and Martial Solal and bassist Pierre Michelot. Django Reinhardt shows that, although he maintained a low profile in the early '50s, he was still the top jazz guitarist in the world. Highly recommended. —*Scott Yanow*

★ **Peche a La Mouche** / Apr. 16, 1947-Mar. 10, 1953 / Verve ✦✦✦✦✦
Legend has it that guitarist Django Reinhardt was at his absolute peak in the 1930s during his recordings with violinist Stephane Grappelli and that when he switched from acoustic to electric guitar after World War II, he lost a bit of his musical personality. Wrong on both counts. This double CD documents his Blue Star recordings of 1947 and 1953 and Reinhardt (on electric guitar) takes inventive boppish solos that put him at the top of the list of jazz guitarists who were active during the era. Most of the earlier tracks feature Reinhardt in the Quintet of the Hot Club of France with clarinetist Hubert Rostaing but it is the eight later selections in which he is backed by a standard rhythm section that are most interesting. These well-recorded performances hint at what Django Reinhardt might have accomplished in the 1950s had he lived longer. Highly recommended. —*Scott Yanow*

Legendary Django / Sep. 7, 1947-Nov. 8, 1947 / GNP ✦✦✦
This GNP/Crescendo LP (which lists neither dates nor personnel) is drawn from several session from 1947, a year when guitarist Django Reinhardt recorded quite a bit. He is heard with violinist Stephane Grappelli on four standards (including interesting remakes of "Tiger Rag" and "Dinah") and with quintets featuring either Hubert Rostaing or Gerald Leveque on clarinets. This is one of seven Reinhardt albums put out by GNP/Crescendo and all are recommended. —*Scott Yanow*

The Immortal Django Reinhardt / Sep. 7, 1947-Nov. 21, 1947 / GNP ✦✦✦
On this GNP/Crescendo LP (one of seven Django Reinhardt albums the label has released), the guitarist is featured in two settings. He joins violinist Stephane Grappelli for a 1947 reunion that swings fairly well and is also heard with his quintet (featuring clarinetist Hubert Rostaing) for ten other numbers from the same period. The recording dates are unfortunately not listed in the liner notes but the music (which shows the influence of bop) is timeless. —*Scott Yanow*

Django Reinhardt/Sidney Bechet—Deux Geants Du Jazz / 1947-Jun. 26, 1957 / Vogue ✦✦✦
Despite the title, unfortunately, guitarist Django Reinhardt and soprano saxophonist Sidney Bechet do not actually play together. Instead they are heard on alternating tracks. Reinhardt's performances (taken from radio broadcasts) feature him in 1947 with his Quintet (starring clarinetist Maurice Meurnier) and are fine but it is the Bechet selections (that originated from a variety of sources between 1952-57) that are most exciting, particularly "Roses of Picardy," "Down by the Old Stream"

and his hit "Petite Fleur." It's worth picking up as an introduction to these two classic jazzmen. —*Scott Yanow*

● **Djangology 49** / Jan. 1949-Feb. 1949 / Bluebird ✦✦✦✦✦
In 1949, guitarist Django Reinhardt and violinist Stephane Grappelli met up in Italy, playing several engagements with Italian rhythm sections and recording an extensive series of songs. This Bluebird CD contains 20 of the best performances and, even if the rhythm section is fairly irrelevant, Django and Grappelli constantly challenge each other to play at their most creative. These recordings do not duplicate the ones reissued by EMI. —*Scott Yanow*

At Club St. Germain / Feb. 1951 / Honeysuckle Rose ✦✦✦✦
This collector's LP contains music privately recorded at two live engagements in 1951 that feature the great guitarist Django Reinhardt just two years before his death. Performing with a quintet and a sextet that also includes altoist Hubert Fol and sometimes trumpeter Bernard Hulin, Reinhardt is in fine form on the mixture of standards and originals, playing in a boppish style that shows that he was continuing to evolve. —*Scott Yanow*

Emily Remler

b. Sep. 18, 1957, New York, NY, **d.** May 4, 1990, Sydney, Australia
Guitar / Hard Bop
Emily Remler's death at age 32 from a heart attack (certainly not helped by her frequent use of heroin) was a shock to the jazz world, and a sad waste. She was just beginning to emerge from the Wes Montgomery influence and develop her own voice. Remler began playing guitar when she was ten, attended Berklee (1976-79) and recorded as a leader for the first time in 1980. She played with the L.A. version of the show *Sophisticated Ladies* (1981-82) and in 1985 had a duo with Larry Coryell but otherwise mostly worked as a leader with her own small groups. After recording bop-oriented dates for Concord, she had a "contemporary set for Justice and toured with David Benoit before her sudden death. —*Scott Yanow*

Firefly / Apr. 1981 / Concord Jazz ✦✦✦✦

Retrospective, Vol. 1: Standards / 1981-1988 / Concord Jazz ✦✦✦
Good overview. —*Ron Wynn*

Retrospective, Vol. 2 / 1981-1988 / Concord Jazz ✦✦✦

● **Take Two** / Jun. 1982 / Concord Jazz ✦✦✦✦✦

Transitions / Oct. 1983 / Concord Jazz ✦✦✦✦✦

Catwalk / Aug. 1984 / Concord Jazz ✦✦✦✦✦
Guitarist Emily Remler's fourth and Concord recording makes one regret even more her premature death at age 32. While her earlier dates were very much in the bop mainstream, this one (in a quartet with trumpeter John D'Earth, bassist Eddie Gomez and drummer Bob Moses) finds her looking ahead and partly finding her own voice on her seven diverse originals. Although she never became an innovator, Remler certainly had a lot to offer the jazz world and this fairly adventurous effort was one of the finest recordings of her short career. —*Scott Yanow*

East to Wes / May 1988 / Concord Jazz ✦✦✦✦
The late guitarist's last CD to be released before her premature death is her finest effort. Emily Remler's fluid technique brightens such seldom heard numbers as Clifford Brown's "Daahoud" and her simplified arrangement of Claude Thornhill's lovely "Snowfall," as well as more relaxed tunes like "Sweet Georgia Fame." The polished rhythm section includes the masterful pianist Hank Jones, bassist Buster Williams, and drummer Marvin "Smitty" Smith. Highly recommended. —*Ken Dryden*

This Is Me / 1990 / Justice ✦✦✦
Emily Remler's first—and tragically, her last—excursion into electric jazz-pop indicates that she could have become a strong force in that area had she not died. Though Remler's Concord recordings earned her a great deal of respect in hard bop circles, she felt limited creatively and was quite anxious to experiment in the electric realm. On her final session, *This Is Me,* the guitarist incorporates pop and rock elements on her own terms—maintaining her musical integrity and avoiding radio-oriented smooth jazz drivel altogether. What remains constant is the warm and lyrical nature of her playing. While the influence of Wes Montgomery and Herb Ellis remains, some of these pieces indicate that she was paying close attention to Pat Metheny. —*Alex Henderson*

Revolutionary Ensemble

f. 1971, **db.** 1977
Group / Avant-Garde
One of the most radical jazz groups of 1971-77, the Revolutionary Ensemble comprised violinist Leroy Jenkins, bassist Sirone and drummer Frank Clayton (who was replaced by Jerome Cooper in September 1971). Their music emphasized

group improvisations, made strong use of space and "miscellaneous instruments" (following in the tradition of the AACM and the Art Ensemble of Chicago) and was quite original, if not accessible. The group recorded for ESP, India Navigation, Horizon and Enja before disbanding. —*Scott Yanow*

Manhattan Cycles / Dec. 31, 1972 / India Navigation ✦✦✦✦

Vietnam / 1972 / ESP ✦✦✦✦

★ **The People's Republic** / Dec. 4, 1975-Dec. 6, 1975 / A&M ✦✦✦✦✦
Definitive statement from the all-time best avant-garde band (next to the Art Ensemble). Open-minded listeners only. This album is a must-buy. —*Michael G. Nastos*

Mel Rhyne

b. Oct. 12, 1936, Indianapolis, MN
Organ / Hard Bop, Groove
Organist Melvin Rhyne's greatest fame is his participation on four Wes Montgomery Riverside sessions (including Wes' first and last album for the label). Fortunately, Rhyne survived long enough after some lean years to return to the major-league jazz scene and record some CDs of his own. Born in Indianapolis, Rhyne (a largely self-taught pianist) was an important part of the city's jazz scene. He played with the then-unknown Roland Kirk during 1955-56 and soon switched to organ. He also had opportunities to back a series of blues (including T-Bone Walker and B.B. King) and R&B artists. Rhyne was part of Montgomery's group for most of 1959-64. In 1969, he moved to Madison, Wisconsin, and four years later he relocated to Milwaukee, where he remained active if obscure for the next two decades. In 1990 he emerged, recording with Herb Ellis and Brian Lynch. Mel Rhyne has since recorded two excellent sets for Criss Cross, including a quartet session that has Joshua Redman as his sideman, and shown that he is an excellent soul-jazz and hard bop soloist in his own right. —*Scott Yanow*

Organizing / Mar. 31, 1960 / Jazzland ✦✦✦✦
With Johnny Griffin on tenor sax and Blue Mitchell on trumpet. —*Michael G. Nastos*

The Legend / Dec. 30, 1991 / Criss Cross ✦✦✦✦

● **Boss Organ** / Jan. 6, 1993 / Criss Cross ✦✦✦✦✦
Mel Rhyne, best known for his association in the 1960s with Wes Montgomery, re-emerged with this Criss Cross CD as one of the finest jazz organists around. He is matched with guitarist Peter Bernstein, drummer Kenny Washington and the young tenor great Joshua Redman for a set of good-natured and often hard-swinging performances. In addition to superior versions of "All God's Chillun Got Rhythm" and "Jeannine," the quartet explores lesser-known songs such as Hubert Laws' "Shades of Light," Stevie Wonder's "You and I" and Mel Tormé's "Born to Be Blue." The music is consistently stimulating and swinging. —*Scott Yanow*

Mel's Spell / Dec. 22, 1994-Dec. 9, 1995 / Criss Cross ✦✦✦✦

Stick to the Kick / 1997 / Criss Cross ✦✦✦✦

Buddy Rich (Bernard Rich)

b. Sep. 30, 1917, New York, NY, **d.** Apr. 2, 1987, Los Angeles, CA
Drums, Leader / Bop, Swing
When it came to technique, speed, power and the ability to put together incredible drum solos, Buddy Rich lived up to the billing of "the world's greatest drummer." Although some other drummers were more innovative, in reality none were in his league even during the early days. Buddy Rich started playing drums in vaudeville as "Traps, the Drum Wonder" when he was only 18 months old; he was completely self-taught. Rich performed in vaudeville throughout his childhood and developed into a decent singer and a fine tap dancer. But drumming was his purpose in life and by 1938 he had discovered jazz and was playing with Joe Marsala's combo. Rich was soon propelling Bunny Berigan's Orchestra; he spent most of 1939 with Artie Shaw (at a time when the clarinetist had the most popular band in swing) and then from 1939-45 (except for a stint in the military) he was making history with Tommy Dorsey. During this era it became obvious that Buddy Rich was the king of drummers, easily dethroning his friend Gene Krupa. Rich had a boppish band during 1945-47 that did not catch on, toured with Jazz at the Philharmonic, recorded with a countless number of all-stars in the 1950s for Verve (including Charlie Parker, Lester Young, Art Tatum and Lionel Hampton) and worked with Les Brown, Charlie Ventura, Tommy Dorsey (1954-55) and Harry James (off and on during 1953-66). A heart attack in 1959 only slowed him down briefly and, although he contemplated becoming a full-time vocalist, Rich never gave up the drums.

In 1966 Buddy Rich beat the odds and put together a successful big band that would be his main outlet for his final 20 years. His heart began giving him trouble starting in 1983 but Rich never gave his music less than 100% and was still push-

ing himself at the end. A perfectionist who expected the same from his sidemen (some of whom he treated cruelly), Buddy Rich is definitively documented in Mel Tormé's book *Traps, the Drum Wonder*. His incredible playing can be viewed on several readily available videotapes although surprisingly few of his later big-band albums have been made available yet on CD. —*Scott Yanow*

And His Legendary '47-'48 Orchestra / Oct. 1946-Sep. 1948 / Hep ✦✦✦✦

This One's for Basie / Aug. 24, 1956-Aug. 25, 1956 / Verve ✦✦✦✦✦
Drummer Buddy Rich put together an interesting 11-piece group for this tribute to Count Basie. The only Basie alumnus present is trumpeter Harry "Sweets" Edison but the other soloists (trombonist Frank Rosolino and Bob Enevoldsen, Bob Cooper on tenor and pianist Jimmy Rowles) easily fit into the setting. Marty Paich contributed the arrangements, there are plenty of drum solos and the music, if not all that memorable, can easily be enjoyed by straightahead jazz fans. —*Scott Yanow*

Rich Versus Roach / Apr. 1959 / Mercury ✦✦✦
The idea probably looked good on paper. Why not combine Buddy Rich's Quintet of 1959 (which consisted of altoist Phil Woods, trombonist Willie Dennis, pianist John Bunch and bassist Phil Leshin) with Max Roach's band of the time (consisting of trumpeter Tommy Turrentine, tenor saxophonist Stanley Turrentine, trombonist Julian Priester and bassist Bobby Boswell)? This CD reissues all of the music (including four "new" alternate takes) but the excess of drum solos and the relative brevity of space given to the horns results in a great deal of sameness from track to track. An unexpected bore. —*Scott Yanow*

Swingin' New Big Band / Sep. 29, 1966-Oct. 10, 1966 / Pacific Jazz ✦✦✦✦✦
The year 1966 was a most illogical time for anyone to try forming a new big band but Buddy Rich beat the odds. This CD reissues the first album by the Buddy Rich Orchestra, augmenting the original LP program with nine previously unissued performances from the same sessions. The arrangements (eight by Oliver Nelson along with charts by Bill Holman, Phil Wilson, Jay Corre, Don Rader and others) swing, put the emphasis on the ensembles, and primarily feature Corre's tenor although trumpeter Bobby Shew, altoist Pete Yellin, pianist John Bunch and guitarist Barry Zweig are also heard from. Most of the songs did not stay in the drummer's repertoire long (other than Bill Reddie's adaptation of "West Side Story" and "Sister Sadie") and in fact only three members of the 17-piece orchestra would still be working for Rich a year later. An enjoyable and somewhat historic set. —*Scott Yanow*

The Best of Buddy Rich: The Pacific Jazz Years / 1966-1970 / Blue Note ✦✦✦
The Best of Buddy Rich: The Pacific Jazz Years features ten tracks culled from Rich's explosive years at Pacific Jazz. There are eight near-standards—including "Groovin' Hard," "Love for Sale," "Mercy, Mercy, Mercy" and "Greensleeves"—as well as two previously unreleased cuts: a live version of "Apples" recorded at the Chez Club in LA and an alternate take of "Diabolus." Although the compilation isn't definitive, it remains a good sampling of a short period of Rich's long, prolific career. —*Stephen Thomas Erlewine*

Big Swing Face / Feb. 22, 1967-Mar. 10, 1967 / Pacific Jazz ✦✦✦✦
This CD not only reissues the second recording by the Buddy Rich Big Band but doubles the program with nine previously unissued performances from the same engagement at the Chez Club in Hollywood. Rich's orchestra was in its early prime, displaying a very impressive ensemble sound, charts by Bill Holman, Shorty Rogers, Bob Florence, Bill Potts and others, and such soloists as altoist Ernie Watts (a newcomer), trumpeter Bobby Shew, Jay Corre on tenor and the remarkable drummer-leader. Even with the presence of "Norwegian Wood" and "The Beat Goes On" (the latter features Rich's teenage daughter Cathy on a vocal), this is very much a swinging set. Rich has some outstanding solos and lots of drum breaks but does not hog the spotlight; he was justifiably proud of his band. —*Scott Yanow*

The New One / Jun. 15, 1967-Nov. 30, 1967 / Pacific Jazz ✦✦✦✦

● **Mercy, Mercy** / Jul. 10, 1968 / World Pacific ✦✦✦✦✦
This CD reissue brings back the finest all-round recording by Buddy Rich's big band. The original version of "Channel 1 Suite" is a classic and contains tenor saxophonist Don Menza's most memorable solo, plus a couple of brilliant improvisations from the explosive drummer/leader. Another highlight is an inventive Phil Wilson arrangement of "Mercy, Mercy, Mercy," and even "Alfie" (a melodic feature for altoist Art Pepper) and "Ode to Billie Joe" come across well. In addition to the original LP program, three selections were released for the first time on this CD. "Chelsea Bridge" is particularly significant, because it showcases Pepper, who was making a brief (and unsuccessful) comeback seven years before he finally returned to the scene. This spirited and often-exciting set is a real gem and is essential. —*Scott Yanow*

Buddy & Soul / Jan. 3, 1969-Jun. 22, 1969 / Pausa ✦✦✦✦

Keep the Customer Satisfied / Feb. 1970 / Liberty ✦✦✦

Different Drummer / Jul. 14, 1971-Jul. 16, 1971 / RCA ✦✦✦✦

● **Time Being** / Aug. 13, 1971-Aug. 10, 1972 / Bluebird ✦✦✦✦✦

Rich in London / Dec. 6, 1971-Dec. 8, 1971 / RCA ✦✦✦✦✦

The Roar of '74 / Oct. 1973 / Groove Merchant ✦✦✦✦
Mid-'70s big-band tracks featuring the Buddy Rich Orchestra doing a mixture of straight swing, pop, rock, and even a little soul-jazz and blues on this set. It was originally issued on the now-defunct Groove Merchant label, and included some high-voltage Rich drum solos as well. —*Ron Wynn*

Transition / 1974 / Groove Merchant ✦✦✦
This LP has two separate sessions that perhaps was supposed to bridge the gap between the past and the present; in this case the past definitely wins. On four songs (three swing standards plus Lionel Hampton's "Ham Hock Blues") drummer Buddy Rich has fun jamming with vibraphonist Hampton, pianist Teddy Wilson, tenor saxophonist Zoot Sims and bassist George Duvivier. Nothing all that significant occurs but these versions of "Avalon," "Airmail Special" and "Ring Dem Bells" are fun. However, the second session, which has Rich and Hampton playing two forgettable funk originals with a larger group featuring Sal Nistico on tenor, guitarist Jack Wilkins and Joe Romano's soprano, is much less interesting, making this album definitely a mixed bag. —*Scott Yanow*

Buddy Rich Plays and Plays and Plays / Feb. 2, 1977 / RCA ✦✦✦✦

Lionel Hampton Presents Buddy Rich / Jul. 1977 / Who's Who ✦✦✦✦
One in the series of albums Hampton produced and issued on the Who's Who label in the '70s, this one featured Buddy Rich's late-'70s orchestra. It was a well-polished, cohesive group, although it lacked dynamic soloists other than tenor saxophonist Steve Marcus. Still, Rich drove them hard and provided his own excitement with powerhouse drumming. —*Ron Wynn*

Class of '78 / Oct. 1977 / Gryphon ✦✦✦✦
A mostly uptempo, driving session that's marred only by its extremely short playing time, less than a half hour. But it was more in a jazz/swing vein than many other '70s Rich sessions, and included a sensational treatment of "Birdland," plus plenty of torrid tenor sax solos by Steve Marcus. —*Ron Wynn*

Live at King Street Café / Apr. 3, 1985 / Cafe ✦✦✦✦

Johnny Richards (John Cascales)

b. Nov. 2, 1911, Querétaro, Mexico, **d.** Oct. 7, 1968, New York, NY
Arranger, Leader / Progressive Jazz
Johnny Richards was one of the more progressive-minded arrangers of the 1950s and '60s, turning out big, heavily orchestrated scores with sometimes unabashed use of dissonance and a good feel for Latin rhythms. His music has been called "provocatively colorful," though in the case of his notoriously portentous "Prologue" for the ego-tripping Stan Kenton, simply the word "provocative" says it all. Richards grew up in Schenectady, New York, learning piano, violin, banjo and trumpet; his mother was a concert pianist who had studied with Paderewski. He started writing film scores, first in London in 1932-33 and then in Hollywood for the remainder of the decade as Victor Young's assistant at Paramount, while studying composition with Arnold Schoenberg. From 1940 to 1945, he led a big band and then returned to Los Angeles to arrange for Charlie Barnet and Boyd Raeburn. He also arranged a string album for Dizzy Gillespie in 1950, along with recording dates with Sarah Vaughan, Helen Merrill and Sonny Stitt. His most famous association was with Kenton, with whom he started arranging in 1952; Kenton's album *Cuban Fire!* is an outstandingly flamboyant example of Richards' work. Richards continued to lead his own orchestras in 1956-60 and 1964-65, recording for Capitol, Coral, Roulette and Bethlehem, and co-wrote one of Frank Sinatra's signature songs, "Young at Heart." —*Richard S. Ginell*

● **Something Else Again** / 1956 / Bethlehem ✦✦

Aijalon / Aug. 1956 / Discovery ✦✦✦✦✦

Something Else by Johnny Richards / Aug. 1956 / Discovery ✦✦✦✦

Wide Range /June 27, 1957-July 11, 1957 / Creative World ✦✦✦

Je Vous Adore / Apr. 28, 1958-Apr. 29, 1958 / Discovery ✦✦✦✦

Walk Softly / Run Wild / May 12, 1959-Jun. 9, 1959 / Coral ✦✦

My Fair Lady / Oct. 4, 1964 / Roulette ✦✦✦

Aqui se Habla Espanol / Dec. 1966 / Roulette ✦✦✦

Jerome Richardson (Jerome C. Richardson)

b. Nov. 15, 1920, Sealy, TX
Tenor Saxophone, Flute, Soprano Saxophone, Alto Saxophone / Cool, Hard Bop
Jerome Richardson was always a talented jazz improviser coming out of the bop tradition, displaying individuality on each of his reeds. But because he has spent most of his career as a studio musician, he has often maintained a low profile in the jazz world. Richardson started on alto when he was eight, was playing in public by the time he was 14, and later attended San Francisco State College. The years 1942-45 was spent in the military, often working in a dance band led by Marshall Royal. He picked up experience playing with the bands of Lionel Hampton (1949-51) and Earl Hines (1952-53) before moving to New York. Richardson freelanced throughout the 1950s, gigging with Lucky Millinder, Cootie Williams, Oscar Pettiford, Chico Hamilton, Gerry Mulligan and Gerald Wilson, among others. He toured Europe with Quincy Jones' ill-fated "Free and Easy" Orchestra during 1959-60 and was the lead altoist and soprano with the Thad Jones/Mel Lewis Orchestra from 1965-70. After he moved to Hollywood in 1971, Richardson primarily worked as a studio musician, often for Quincy Jones, although he has resurfaced as a jazz player on an occasional basis. Jerome Richardson led a pair of sessions for New Jazz in 1958-59 (during which he plays flute, flute and baritone) that have been reissued in the Original Jazz Classics series, and was on many sessions in the 1950s, including dates with Kenny Burrell. Further dates were made as a leader for United Artists (1962) and Verve (1967) (by then he was also playing soprano); the latter features his original tune "Groove Merchant." —*Scott Yanow*

● **Midnight Oil** / Oct. 10, 1958 / Original Jazz Classics ✦✦✦✦✦
Flutist Jerome Richardson (who switches to tenor on one of the five selections on this CD reissue) has long been underrated and has had relatively few opportunities to lead his own record dates—only four up to the present time, of which *Midnight Oil* was the first. The music (three of Richardson's originals, Artie Shaw's "Lyric," and the standard "Caravan") is performed in swinging fashion by Richardson, trombonist Jimmy Cleveland (the unusual flute-trombone blend heard on three of the songs is quite pleasing), pianist Hank Jones, guitarist Kenny Burrell, bassist Joe Benjamin and drummer Charlie Persip. This set offers cool-toned bop that, although brief in playing time (just over 35 minutes), is enjoyable. —*Scott Yanow*

Roamin' with Richardson / Oct. 21, 1959 / Original Jazz Classics ✦✦✦✦
Jerome Richardson has long been one of the most versatile of jazzmen, able to get a personal sound and to swing on flute, tenor, alto, soprano and baritone. For his quartet date with pianist Richard Wyands (who at this point often sounded like Red Garland), bassist George Tucker and drummer Charlie Persip, Richardson plays baritone on three songs (in a deep tone a little reminiscent of Pepper Adams and Leo Parker), two on tenor and one on flute. The CD reissue (the second of only four sessions that the reedman has had as a leader) finds Richardson in excellent form, swinging through three group originals, "I Never Knew," "Poinciana" and a strong version (on baritone) of Duke Ellington's "Warm Valley." —*Scott Yanow*

Groove Merchant / Oct. 13, 1967+Oct. 17, 1967 / Verve ✦✦✦

Jazz Station Runaway / Jun. 1996-Feb. 1997 / TCB ✦✦✦✦✦

Dannie Richmond (Charles D. Richmond)

b. Dec. 15, 1935, New York, NY, **d.** Mar. 15, 1988, New York, NY
Drums / Post-Bop
Closely associated with Charles Mingus, Dannie Richmond was on most of his sessions from 1955-78, showing impressive versatility. Richmond and Mingus made for a very potent team, shifting rhythms, tempos and grooves together, hinting at New Orleans jazz now and then while sometimes playing very freely. Richmond was originally a tenor saxophonist who as a teenager played R&B, touring with Paul Williams. He took up the drums in 1955 and six months later joined Charles Mingus when he proved that he could play at very fast tempos. During Mingus' off periods, Richmond freelanced with Chet Baker, the group Mark-Almond, Joe Cocker and even Elton John. After Mingus' death, Richmond played with Mingus Dynasty and then became a member of the George Adams-Don Pullen Quartet (1980-85), occasionally leading his own groups. —*Scott Yanow*

In Jazz for the Culture Set / 1965 / Impulse! ✦✦✦✦
With pianist Jaki Byard and harmonicist Toots Thielemans. Andy Warhol soup-can cover art. Great record. —*Michael G. Nastos*

Ode to Mingus / Nov. 23, 1979-Nov. 24, 1979 / Soul Note ✦✦✦✦✦
A super tribute to his longtime employer and musical comrade. The set should have made the jazz world notice Bill Saxton on tenor sax. —*Ron Wynn*

Plays Charles Mingus / Aug. 16, 1980 / Timeless ✦✦✦✦
Drummer Dannie Richmond had a rare opportunity to lead a group for this album, subtitled "The Last Mingus Band." He heads what was the final Charles Mingus combo, a quintet with tenor saxophonist Ricky Ford, trumpeter Jack Walrath, pianist Bob Neloms and bassist Cameron Brown (the latter in Mingus' place). Together they perform spirited versions of five Charles Mingus' compositions along with Sy Johnson's "Wee." Everyone is in fine form and, although one misses Mingus, the music has its exciting moments. —*Scott Yanow*

● **Quintet** / Sep. 24, 1980 / Gatemouth ✦✦✦✦✦
Mingus drummer with bandmates trumpeter Jack Walrath, saxophonist Ricky Ford. Great twenty-one-and-a-half-minute version of "Cumbia & Jazz Fusion." —*Michael G. Nastos*

Gentleman's Agreement / Jan. 11, 1983-Jan. 12, 1983 / Soul Note ✦✦✦
Sizzling cuts, with old pros Jimmy Knepper on trombone and Hugh Lawson on piano taking care of business. —*Ron Wynn*

Dionysius / May 30, 1983 / Red ✦✦✦✦
An album played by ex-Mingusites, this is one side originals and one side of Charles Mingus' music. Features Jack Walrath (tpt), Ricky Ford (ts), Bob Neloms (p), and Cameron Brown (b). —*Michael G. Nastos*

Larry Ridley

b. Sep. 3, 1937, Indianapolis, IN
Bass / Hard Bop
An excellent accompanist and a thoughtful soloist, Larry Ridley has appeared on a countless number of sessions as a sideman. He studied at Indiana University and the Lenox School of Jazz. After gigging in his hometown with Freddie Hubbard, James Spaulding and Wes Montgomery, Ridley relocated to New York, where he has been active ever since. Among his more significant musical associations in the 1960s were with Slide Hampton, Max Roach, Red Garland, Art Farmer, Jackie McLean, Sonny Rollins, Horace Silver, Lee Morgan and George Wein's Newport All-Stars (1969). Thelonious Monk's regular bassist during 1970-73, Ridley became involved in jazz education, heading the jazz program and music department at Rutgers. He worked with Philly Joe Jones' Dameronia (1981-1985) and has been active up until the present time. Larry Ridley only recorded an obscure Strata East LP as a leader (1975), but he has been a valuable sideman on many dates. —*Scott Yanow*

Ben Riley

b. Jul. 17, 1933, Savannah, GA
Drums / Hard Bop
An excellent drummer whose strong support has helped a variety of advanced bop sessions, Ben Riley is best-known for his association with Thelonious Monk's Quartet even though he was only a member for three years. Prior to playing with Monk, Riley performed with many combos including those led by Randy Weston, Sonny Stitt, Stan Getz, Junior Mance, Kenny Burrell, Eddie "Lockjaw" Davis-Johnny Griffin (1960-62), Ahmad Jamal, Billy Taylor and Ray Bryant. His well-documented stint with Monk (1964-67) was followed by associations with Alice Coltrane (on and off during 1968-75), the New York Quartet (throughout the 1970s and '80s), Ron Carter (1975-77), Jim Hall (1981) and the group Sphere. In addition, Riley has toured extensively with Abdullah Ibrahim. —*Scott Yanow*

The Rippingtons

f. 1987
Group / Instrumental Pop, Crossover Jazz
One of the most popular groups in what is loosely termed "contemporary jazz," the Rippingtons were formed (and have been led ever since) by guitarist/keyboardist Russ Freeman (no relation to the veteran West Coast bop pianist of the same name). Freeman (b. Feb. 11, 1960 in Nashville) studied at Cal Arts and UCLA, and recorded *Nocturnal Playground* as a leader in 1985 for the Brainchild label, a one-man project. In 1987, he was approached to record for the Japanese Alfa label and came up with the Rippingtons name for the all-star group he used on the disc (*Moonlighting*), an ensemble featuring David Benoit, Kenny G. and Brandon Fields. Their album was released domestically by Passport and became a hit. Freeman soon formed a regular touring band (usually including saxophonist Jeff Kashiwa, bassist Kim Stone, drummer Tony Morales and percussionist Steve Reid), cut a second disc for Passport and the group has since recorded regularly for GRP. Russ Freeman writes all of the music for the Rippingtons, much of which falls in the pop/R&B genre. —*Scott Yanow*

Moonlighting / 1987 / GRP ✦✦✦
This debut album features Kenny G. on saxophone. —*Paul Kohler*

● **Best of the Rippingtons** / 1987-1993 / GRP ✦✦✦
From the mid-1980s to late 1990s, keyboardist Russ Freeman's band the Rippingtons was a consistent favorite on what were called "contemporary jazz" stations, although most of their material was actually bland instrumental pop with jazz overtones. Released in late 1997, *The Best of the Rippingtons* draws on eight of their GRP albums and illustrates the mindless nature of their work for the high-profile label. Light, sleep-inducing tunes like "Vienna" and "Principles of Desire" are nothing more than elevator music, while even upbeat numbers such as "Tourist in Paradise" and the previously unreleased "Garden of Babylon" sound like the

themes from prime-time television programs. Either way, this collection is boring and forgettable by both jazz and pop standards. —*Alex Henderson*

Kilimanjaro / Apr. 1988 / GRP ✦✦✦

Tourist in Paradise / May 1989 / GRP ✦✦✦

Welcome to the St. James' Club / 1990 / GRP ✦✦✦

Curves Ahead / Aug. 1991 / GRP ✦✦

Weekend in Monaco / Aug. 1992 / GRP ✦✦

● **Live in L.A.** / Sep. 1992 / GRP ✦✦✦✦✦
In September of 1992, on two separate nights and in two separate venues, the Rippingtons played and recorded this album before a live audience. Russ Freeman is the driving force on electric, acoustic and classical guitars as well as guitar synthesizer. He is backed by the core members of the group: Tony Morales, drums, Jeff Kashiwa, saxophone, Mark Portmann, keyboards, Steve Reid, percussion, and Kim Stone, bass. The band is augmented by a solid horn section of alto saxophone, trumpet and trombone. To add to the evenings' excitement and pleasure, special guest artists David Benoit and Carl Anderson joined the proceedings . . . —*MusD*

Black Diamond / 1997 / Windham Hill ✦✦✦

Lee Ritenour

b. Nov. 1, 1952, Hollywood, CA
Guitar / Instrumental Pop, Crossover Jazz
Lee Ritenour has long been the perfect studio musician, one who can melt into the background without making any impact. While he possesses impresive technique, Ritenour has mostly played instrumental pop throughout his career, sometimes with a Brazilian flavor. His few jazz efforts have found him essentially imitating Wes Montgomery, but despite that he has been consistently popular since the mid-'70s. After touring with Sergio Mendes' Brasil '77 in 1973, Ritenour became a very busy studio guitarist in Los Angeles, taking time off for occasional tours with his groups and in the mid-'90s with Bob James in Fourplay. He has recorded many albums as a leader, most recently for GRP. —*Scott Yanow*

First Course / 1976 / Epic ✦✦

Gentle Thoughts / May 1977 / JVC ✦✦✦

Sugarloaf Express / Sep. 1977 / JVC ✦✦✦

Captain Fingers / 1977 / Epic ✦✦

Captain's Journey / 1978 / Elektra ✦✦✦
Guitarist Lee Ritenour had just switched from Epic to Elektra when he cut *Captain's Journey* in 1978. It was a follow-up to the successful crossover work *Captain Fingers* and used a similar strategy: tight, hook-laden arrangements, polished production, and minimal solo space. What individual things it has are dominated by Ritenour, a supremely talented guitarist who doesn't display that much of it with these arrangements. —*Ron Wynn*

Rio / Aug. 1979-Sep. 1979 / GRP ✦✦✦✦

Feel the Night / 1979 / Elektra ✦✦

On the Line / Mar. 1983 / GRP ✦✦

Banded Together / 1984 / Elektra ✦✦

Earth Run / Apr. 1986 / GRP ✦✦

Portrait / Jan. 1987 / GRP ✦✦✦

The Best of Lee Ritenour / 1981-1987 / Epic ✦✦
The Best of Lee Ritenour selects eight highlights from the records the guitarist made for Epic in the '80s. It's a nice sampler, featuring such songs as "Sun Song," "Little Bit of This Land and a Little Bit of That," "Fly by Night" and "Isn't She Lovely," which give a good sense of what his stint at the label was like. It's not definitive, but it makes for a good sampler for the curious. —*Stephen Thomas Erlewine*

Festival / May 1988 / GRP ✦✦✦

Color Rit / Mar. 1989 / GRP ✦✦✦

Stolen Moments / 1990 / GRP ✦✦✦✦

Wes Bound / Sep. 1992-Oct. 1992 / GRP ✦✦✦✦
Lee Ritenour, a superior studio guitarist, has recorded very few jazz albums throughout his career, preferring to play melodic pop and light funk. On the rare occasions when he has had an urge to perform jazz, Ritenour has been more than happy to show off the influence of Wes Montgomery; therefore, this tribute is a logical move, even if the results are not all that exciting. Ritenour mostly plays pieces from the latter (and more commercial) half of Montgomery's career, along with four of his own originals that are sort of in the tradition. He also hedges his bet a little by throwing in a Bob Marley reggae tune. For jazz listeners who wish to sample some Lee Ritenour, this is one of his better recordings, but why purchase

Wes Bound when there are so many more significant Wes Montgomery albums currently in print? —*Scott Yanow*

● **Larry & Lee** / Jun. 1994-Jan. 1995 / GRP ✦✦✦✦

Larry Carlton and Lee Ritenour have had parallel careers but this CD is their first joint meeting on records. The two guitarists complement each other well and there are hints of Wes Montgomery along with a tribute to Joe Pass ("Remembering J.P."), but the songs (all of them their originals) are little more than rhythmic grooves most of the time with the usual fadeouts. The consistently lightweight music is reasonably pleasing but never too stimulating. —*Scott Yanow*

Alive in L.A. / Jul. 1, 1997 / GRP ✦✦✦✦

Although often quite derivative (Lee Ritenour's love for Wes Montgomery is all too obvious at times), this is one of the studio guitarist's finest jazz recordings. Recorded live, Ritenour performs straightahead tunes and light funk with a sextet also including Bill Evans on tenor and soprano (he too should work on developing a more original sound), keyboardist Alan Pasqua, bassist Melvin Davis, drummer Sonny Emory and second keyboardist Barnaby Finch. With such numbers as "A Little Bumpin'," "Wes Bound" and "4 on 6," the Wes connection is obviously intentional and heartfelt; it is good to hear Rit stretching out for a change and not being so concerned about potential airplay. —*Scott Yanow*

Ray Rivera

Guitar, Guiro / Swing, Bop

The life of rhythm guitarist, singer, songwriter and composer Ray Rivera is a textbook example of the American story of how hard work plus determination equals success. Rivera grew up in an orphanage on Long Island and a foster home in the Bronx. As a teenager, he began to hang out in the clubs in Harlem, where jazz was being played all the time. He had started taking guitar lessons in his early teens and began his recording career in the 1950s.

Rivera's songs have been recorded by Hank Jones, Billy Taylor, Cal Tjader, Joe Williams, Pucho and the Latin Soul Brothers, Claus Ogerman, Gale Garnett, Donald Byrd, the Ramsey Lewis Trio, Enzo Stuarti and others. Rivera has sung, recorded or performed with a who's-who of jazz musicians, among them, Jones, Ogerman, Dr. Billy Taylor, Milt Hinton, Roy Haynes, Donald Byrd, Art Mooney, and Deodato among others. One of his best-known songs, "You Been Talkin' 'Bout Me Baby," was recorded by Janis Joplin's San Francisco-based backing band, Big Brother and the Holding Company, and became a smash hit in 1968, via that group's album, *Cheap Thrills*. It also became a hit for the Ramsey Lewis Trio, who sold over a million copies of the song. Rivera has recorded with Donald Byrd, Taylor, Art Mooney and Irving Fields.

Rivera began his recording career in the 1950s for Webb Records, followed by singles for MGM and Decca. He's recorded more than a dozen albums under his own name. They include *Light 'n' Easy* for Rivelli Records and *Ain't That Good News* for Merry-Go-Round Records in the late '60s. In the early '70s, he recorded *Latin Workout* for Mercury, arranged by Claus Ogerman, and *The Now Sound of the Ray Rivera Orchestra* (MGM Records), as well as *A Touch of Latin* for Hindsight Records. His 1980 album called *Let Me Hear Some Jazz,* for Insight Records, was nominated for a Grammy award. While some of Rivera's old vinyl is now out of print, fortunately some of the sides are seeing the light of day on compact disc. His most recent recording is a 1991 release, *Nightwind,* for Studio West, with Dr. Billy Taylor as guest pianist. Jazz film buffs will be interested to know that Rivera appears in the film *The Cotton Club* as guitarist in the Cab Calloway Orchestra. —*Richard Skelly*

Nightwind / Nov. 5, 1990 / Studio West ✦✦✦

This CD differs from the previous four Studio West releases in that the music was new at the time rather than being drawn from 1962 radio transcriptions. Of the seven musicians on the date, only pianist Billy Taylor is well known. Ray Rivera plays rhythm guitar, has a couple of personable vocals (best on "I'm Confessin'") and whistles a bit. Lou Caputo (on tenor, alto and flute) and bass trombonist Jack Jeffers are (along with Taylor) the main soloists on these bop-flavored selections. All but two of the dozen numbers are group originals with Rivera responsible for eight, many of which are actually based on the chord changes of more familiar songs. The music consistently swings, the ensembles are colorful and bop fans will enjoy this effort from these little-known veterans. —*Scott Yanow*

Sam Rivers

b. Sep. 25, 1923, El Reno, OK

Tenor Saxophone, Flute, Soprano Saxophone / Avant-Garde, Post-Bop

Although often overlooked, Sam Rivers has long been one of the most original voices of the avant-garde, equally skilled on tenor, soprano and flute. Music ran in his family—his grandfather published a book of hymns and black folk songs in 1882, his mother played piano and his father sang with the Fisk Jubilee Singers. Rivers' musical interests, however, were in a different direction. He started on

piano when he was five and then learned violin, alto, soprano and finely tenor. He played regularly in Boston from 1947 when he went to the Boston Conservatory and during 1955-57 he was freelancing in Florida. By 1958 Rivers was back in Boston with the Herb Pomeroy big band and in the early '60s he was leading a band that backed R&B and blues singers (including a tour with T-Bone Walker). Rivers, who by then had become very interested in the music of Cecil Taylor and Ornette Coleman, was still fairly obscure as a Boston legend.

In 1964 Tony Williams (who had played with Rivers when he was a young teenager) recommended him for the tenor opening with Miles Davis' Quintet. Although Rivers' playing was too advanced for Davis at the time, he did last through a tour of Japan that was recorded. Rivers made a few records for Blue Note before becoming a member of Cecil Taylor's Unit during 1968-73. With his wife Bea, he opened Studio Rivbea as a jazz loft in New York in 1971 and became involved in teaching in addition to presenting concerts. Other than a late-'80s association with Dizzy Gillespie (where he good-naturedly played bebop and even took an occasional scat vocal), Sam Rivers has mostly been a leader during the past 25 years in a wide variety of settings. In the late 1990s, he has been active in Florida, forming his own record label and acting as the inspiration and teacher for a jazz youth movement. —*Scott Yanow*

Fuschia Swing Song / Dec. 11, 1964 / Blue Note ✦✦✦✦

For Sam Rivers' debut, *Fuchsia Swing Song,* the tenor saxophonist lined up a fine quartet featuring pianist Jaki Byard, bassist Ron Carter and drummer Tony Williams and pursued a refreshing, unpredictable spin on the avant-garde. Rivers has a hard bop foundation, but he incorporated Coltrane and Coleman's developments into his music, resulting in an adventurous and quite rewarding debut. His original compositions aren't always memorable, but his playing is always startling, as is the interaction between Carter, Williams and Byard. Rivers would take his music further into uncharted territory within just a few months, but *Fuchsia Swing Song* remains a fresh debut. —*Stephen Thomas Erlewine*

The Complete Blue Note Sam Rivers Sessions / Dec. 11, 1964-Mar. 17, 1967 / Mosaic ✦✦✦✦

This three-CD limited-edition box set from Mosaic features the underrated avant-gardist Sam Rivers (who plays tenor, soprano and flute) on his four Blue Note albums as a leader: *Fuschia Swing Song* (a quartet date with pianist Jaki Byard, bassist Ron Carter and drummer Tony Williams), *Contours* (which features trumpeter Freddie Hubbard, pianist Herbie Hancock, Carter and drummer Joe Chambers), *A New Conception* (which has pianist Hal Galper leading the rhythm section) and *Involution* (a sextet outing with altoist James Spaulding, trumpeter Donald Byrd and trombonist Julian Priester), plus three previously unreleased selections. The earliest set shows off Rivers' roots, *A New Conception* has his adventurous (yet often tasteful) renditions of standards, and *Involution* (a 1967 set not released until 1977) has the most advanced music. A perfectly done reissue. —*Scott Yanow*

★ **Contours** / May 21, 1965 / Blue Note ✦✦✦✦

On *Contours,* his second Blue Note album, tenor saxophonist Sam Rivers fully embraced the avant-garde, but presented it in a way that wouldn't be upsetting or confusing to hard bop loyalists. Rivers leads a quintet featuring trumpeter Freddie Hubbard, pianist Herbie Hancock, bassist Ron Carter and drummer Joe Chambers through a set of originals that walk a fine line between probing, contemplative post-bop and densely dissonant avant-jazz. Each musician is able to play the extremes equally well while being sensitive to the subtleties in compositions. Rarely is *Contours* anything less than enthralling, and it remains one of the high-water marks of the mid-'60s avant-garde movement. —*Stephen Thomas Erlewine*

☆ **Involution** / Mar. 7, 1966-Mar. 17, 1967 / Blue Note ✦✦✦✦

This double LP, which came out in 1975, contains two superior (and previously unissued) sessions that feature the great tenor saxophonist Sam Rivers. Actually one of the dates was originally led by pianist Andrew Hill who performs in a quartet with Rivers, bassist Walter Booker and drummer J.C. Moses. While that set has six of Hill's provocative originals, the other album (which teams Rivers with altoist James Spaulding, trumpeter Donald Byrd, trombonist Julian Priester, bassist Cecil McBee and drummer Steve Ellington) features six of the tenor's compositions. These very adventurous performances (some of Blue Note's finest avant-garde dates) are often intense and always adventurous. The music on the stimulating two-fer deserves to be reissued eventually on CD for this ranks with Sam Rivers' most significant recordings. —*Scott Yanow*

A New Conception / Oct. 11, 1966 / Blue Note ✦✦✦

The title of *A New Conception* refers to Sam Rivers' ingenious interpretations of standards on this record. Rivers treats the songs—such familiar items as "When I Fall in Love," "I'll Never Smile Again," "That's All," "What a Difference a Day Makes" and "Secret Love"—with respect, but he doesn't treat them as museum pieces. He knows that if the songs are to remain fresh, they need to be heard in different ways, and he skillfully opens up each composition to contemporary avant-garde techniques. Rivers and his supporting trio of pianist Hal Galper, bassist Herbert Lewis and drummer Steve Ellington gradually ease each number into more adventurous territory, slowly shifting into exploratory instrumental sections, slyly varying the melodic themes, or adding shaded dissonant textures. It's challenging music that remains accessible, since it reconfigures familiar items in new, intriguing ways. The sheer skill in Rivers' arrangements once again confirms his large, unfortunately underappreciated, talent. —*Stephen Thomas Erlewine*

Dimensions and Extensions / Mar. 17, 1967 / Blue Note ✦✦✦✦✦
Ambitious, atonal, challenging—all are accurate descriptions of *Dimensions and Extensions,* Sam Rivers' fourth album for Blue Note. Rivers remains grounded in hard bop structure, working with a sextet featuring Donald Byrd (trumpet), James Spaulding (alto saxophone, flute), Julian Priester (trombone), Cecil McBee (bass) and Steve Ellington (drums), but he explodes the boundaries of the form with difficult, dissonant compositions. With his unique, mercurial tone and edgy solos, he keeps pushing the sextet in different directions. It's intense, cerebral music, but since it has distinct themes and strong rhythms, the forays into free jazz, dissonant harmonies and unpredictable tonal textures are actually quite accessible. Rivers simply burns on each track, whether playing tenor, soprano or flute. Byrd doesn't display the wild imagination of Rivers, yet he keeps the pace with alternately languid and biting solos. Similarly, the remaining musicians each make a lasting impression with their individual time in the spotlight. With music as risky at this, it's forgivable that it occasionally meanders (especially on the slower numbers), but overall, *Dimensions and Extensions* offers more proof that Sam Rivers was one of the early giants of the avant-garde. —*Stephen Thomas Erlewine*

Hues / Feb. 13, 1971-Nov. 10, 1973 / Impulse! ✦✦✦

Streams: Live at Montreux / Jul. 6, 1973 / Impulse! ✦✦✦✦✦
Streams featured Sam Rivers as the lead voice on the album-long "Streams," a lengthy multisectioned free improvisation recorded at the Montreux Jazz Festival. With support from the brilliant bassist Cecil McBee and subtle drumming from the pre-disco Norman Connors, Rivers took a powerful solo on tenor, sung through his flute, rambled a bit on piano and concluded with a strong dosage of his soprano. *Streams* remains one of Sam Rivers' strongest recordings. —*Scott Yanow*

Crystals / 1974 / Impulse! ✦✦✦✦✦
Creative orchestra music. Out of this world. —*Michael G. Nastos*

Sizzle / 1975 / Impulse! ✦✦✦✦
Trio with Barry Altschul (d) and Dave Holland (b). Funky with electric touches. Fierce. —*Michael G. Nastos*

☆ **Sam Rivers/Dave Holland, Vol. 1** / Feb. 18, 1976 / Improvising Artists ✦✦✦✦✦
The first of two CD reissues that bring back a daylong duet session by Sam Rivers and bassist Dave Holland consists of two lengthy improvisations featuring Rivers on soprano and tenor; volume two features him playing flute and piano. Rivers' adventurous solos and interplay with the virtuosic Holland make this CD of interest to listeners with open ears towards the avant-garde, despite the LP-length playing time. —*Scott Yanow*

Sam Rivers/Dave Holland, Vol. 2 / Feb. 18, 1976 / Improvising Artists ✦✦✦
When Sam Rivers met up with bassist Dave Holland for a set of duets, he decided to record two LPs and play a different instrument on each of the side-long pieces. While Rivers performs on tenor and soprano during the first volume, the second recording finds him playing "Ripples" on flute and switching to piano for "Deluge"; both performances are over 23 minutes long. Since tenor is easily Rivers' strongest ax, this set (which has now been reissued on CD) is of somewhat limited interest yet is generally successful. The flute piece has several different sections that keep both the musicians and listeners interested, while Rivers' piano feature is quite intense; he leaves few notes unplayed. Still, the first volume should be acquired. —*Scott Yanow*

The Quest / Mar. 12, 1976-Mar. 13, 1976 / Red ✦✦✦✦

Paragon / Apr. 18, 1977 / Fluid ✦✦✦

Waves / Aug. 1978 / Tomato ✦✦✦✦✦
An explosive late-'70s set with underrated composer, multi-instrumentalist, and arranger Sam Rivers leading a strong quartet. While bassist and cellist Dave Holland and percussionist Thurman Barker merged to form a strong, challenging rhythm section, Rivers and Joe Daley, playing tuba and baritone horn, worked together to create instrumental dialogues in sequence. Their array of contrasting voicings, with Rivers on tenor and soprano sax and flute, makes for compelling listening. —*Ron Wynn*

Contrasts / Dec. 1979 / ECM ✦✦✦✦

Colours / Sep. 13, 1982 / Black Saint ✦✦✦✦
Stomping, swinging arrangements. Exuberant 11-piece orchestra supervised and spurred by Rivers. —*Ron Wynn*

Freddie Roach

b. May 11, 1931, New York, NY
Organ / Soul-Jazz

One of the more underrated soul-jazz organists of the '60s, Freddie Roach recorded a series of seven albums for Blue Note and Prestige. While his contemporaries played hard-driving, bluesy soul-jazz, Roach's was more textured and shaded. He was capable of blistering leads, but he was more interested in dynamics, harmonics and tonal color. As his career progressed, he became more interested in funky grooves, but his knack for tasteful, shaded solos and support never subsided.

Freddie Roach was born in the Bronx borough of New York City on May 11, 1931. His mother was a church organist, and many of his relatives on his maternal side were also musical. Roach grew up in several cities as a child, living with a variety of relatives. At the age of eight, he was living with his aunt in White Plains, New York, when he began playing the pipe organ. Over the next few years, he taught himself how to play the organ and piano, eventually studying at the Newark Conservatory for one term. In his late teens, he began playing professionally, joining Grachan Moncur's group the Strollers. At the age of 20, he joined the Marine Corps and stayed for two years, playing in the band. Following his discharge in 1953, Roach returned to Canada, settling in Canada for a short while before returning to the New York area. He soon hit the road, playing piano and organ with Chris Columbus, Cootie Williams and Lou Donaldson.

By the end of the decade, he had decided to concentrate on organ. He settled in Newark, New Jersey, where he regularly played with his own band and as a solo act. He often jammed at the Club 83 with musicians like Kenny Dorham, Cannonball Adderley and Jackie McLean. But the key musical association for Roach was tenor saxophonist Ike Quebec, who asked the organist to join his band. Roach played on the sessions that became Quebec's Blue Note albums *Heavy Soul* and *It Might as Well Be Spring.* His playing on the two records impressed Blue Note president Alfred Lion, who offered Roach his own contract in 1962. That year, Roach recorded his debut set *Down to Earth,* supported by guitarist Kenny Burrell, tenor saxophonist Percy France and drummer Clarence Johnston.

Over the next two years, Roach recorded four more albums for Blue Note. In 1963, he made *Mo' Greens Please,* which also featured Burrell and Johnston, and *Good Move,* where he was supported by tenor saxophonist Hank Mobley, trumpeter Blue Mitchell and guitarist Eddie Wright. The following year, he cut *Brown Sugar* with tenor saxophonist Joe Henderson, Wright and Johnston. In October 1964, he recorded his final Blue Note album, *All That's Good,* a bizarre variation on his signature soul-jazz that boasted a vocal choir. He left the label the following year, reappearing in 1966 on Prestige. His first album for his new label was *The Soul Book,* a funkier effort than any of his Blue Note recordings. Two albums, *Mocha Motion* and *My People (Soul People),* followed in 1967. None of his Prestige records were particularly successful, and he never recorded again. Over the next three decades, Roach emerged as a cult figure of sorts, appealing to soul-jazz fans who became introduced to the genre through acid jazz. —*Stephen Thomas Erlewine*

● **Down to Earth** / Aug. 23, 1962 / Blue Note ✦✦✦✦✦
Freddie Roach differentiated himself from the legions of soul-jazz organists on his debut album, *Down to Earth.* Many jazz organists played the instrument down and dirty, and while there's funk in Roach's playing, his style is ultimately lighter than many of his peers, with clean, concise solos and chords. His backing trio—guitarist Kenny Burrell, tenor saxophonist Percy France, drummer Clarence Johnston—follow his lead, providing supple instrumental backdrops that never lose sight of the groove. Furthermore, Burrell and France both have their chance to shine, contributing some nicely understated solos. Nevertheless, *Down to Earth* remains Roach's show—he wrote five of the six songs and his organ is at center stage on each number. The legato blues of "De Bug" is a terrific showcase for Roach's elegantly funky style, while the sprightlier "Ahm Miz" proves that he can get gritty if he so chooses. But the signature of *Down to Earth* is Roach's tasteful bluesy grooves, which prove to be just as entertaining as the hotter styles of his Blue Note peers Jimmy Smith and John Patton. —*Stephen Thomas Erlewine*

Mo' Greens Please / Jan. 21, 1963 / Blue Note ✦✦✦

Good Move / Nov. 29, 1963 / Blue Note ✦✦✦✦
Laidback and loosely swinging, *Good Move* captures organist Freddie Roach near the peak of his form. Roach never leans too heavily on his instrument, preferring a calmer, tasteful attack, yet he is never boring because he has a strong sense of groove. He keeps things moving on slower numbers like Erroll Garner's "Pastel" and Gershwin's "It Ain't Necessarily So," but the true highlights are on originals like "Wine, Wine, Wine" and "On Our Way Up," where the bluesy structures and fluid rhythms give Roach a chance to stretch out. Throughout the record, he is capably supported by guitarist Eddie Wright and drummer Clarence Johnston, as

well as trumpeter Blue Mitchell and tenor saxophonist Hank Mobley, who both contribute fine solos. —*Stephen Thomas Erlewine*

Brown Sugar / Mar. 18, 1964-Mar. 19, 1964 / Blue Note ♦♦♦♦♦

Brown Sugar marks a turning point for Freddie Roach: it's the moment he decided to get dirty, funky and soulful. Previously, he had plenty of funk in his playing, but he was tasteful, at times a little bit too tasteful. On *Brown Sugar,* he simply burns. The album is devoted to blues, R&B and soul, with the title track, the lone original on the album, functioning as a rallying cry of sorts. Roach is hotter than ever, but he never overplays or overloads the organ—whether it's slow blues or smoking R&B, he gets deep into the groove and works it hard, without neglecting to contribute compelling solos. And if you're looking for compelling solos, tenor saxophonist Joe Henderson proves that he as exceptional with R&B and soul-jazz as he is with hard bop. Clarence Johnston, Roach's longtime drummer, provides stable support and guitarist Eddie Wright has his moments as well, helping make *Brown Sugar* the standout item in Roach's catalog. —*Stephen Thomas Erlewine*

All That's Good / Oct. 16, 1964 / Blue Note ♦♦

On his final album for Blue Note, Freddie Roach decided to step outside—way outside—the tasteful soul-jazz that had become his trademark. Roach decided to make a concept album, one that captured the sound and vibe of what he calls "Soultown," or what critics like to call "Black culture." Those terms would suggest that *All That's Good* is a gritty, funky collection of blues vamps and soul, but that's not the case at all. Supported by a trio of lesser-lights—guitarist Calvin Newborn, drummer Clarence Johnston and tenor saxophonist Conrad Lester—Roach never hits upon a groove, choosing to create a series of bizarre, hazy textures. That atmosphere is catapulted into the realms of the surreal by vocalists Phyllis Smith, Willie Tate, and Marvin Robinson, whose wordless, floating singing sounds spectral—the intent may have been to mimic a gospel choir, but the effect is that of a pack of banshees wailing in the background. The structures of the songs may follow traditional paths, but the eerie voices make the music surprisingly unsettling, which certainly wasn't Roach's intent. He may have been trying to make an epic portrait of contemporary Black culture, but he's undone by his off-kilter arrangements (Harlan Howard's familiar "Busted" is nearly unrecognizable) and pedestrian, unmemorable songwriting. It's likely that if the songs were delivered as straightahead soul-jazz, they wouldn't have made much impact, so, in a weird way, it's almost fortunate that Roach attempted something grand, because *All That's Good* sounds like no other Blue Note record of the early '60s. —*Stephen Thomas Erlewine*

The Soul Book / Jun. 13, 1966 / Prestige ♦♦♦♦

Mocha Motion! / Jan. 5, 1967 / Prestige ♦♦♦

My People (Soul People) / Jun. 22, 1967+Jun. 29, 1967 / Prestige ♦♦♦

Max Roach

b. Jan. 10, 1924, New Land, NC

Drums, Leader / Bop, Hard Bop, Avant-Garde, Post Bop

In a profession star-crossed by early deaths—especially the bebop division—Max Roach at this writing is a shining survivor, one of the last living giants from the birth of bebop. He and Kenny Clarke instigated a revolution in jazz drumming that persists to this day; instead of the swing approach of spelling out the pulse with the bass drum, Roach shifted the emphasis to the ride cymbal. The result was a lighter, far more flexible texture, giving drummers more freedom to explore the possibilities of their drum kits and drop random "bombs" on the snare drum, while allowing bop virtuosos on the front lines to play at faster speeds. To this base, Roach added sterling qualities of his own—a ferocious drive, the ability to play a solo with a definite storyline, mixing up pitches and timbres, the deft use of silence, the dexterity to use the brushes as brilliantly as the sticks. He would use cymbals as gongs and play mesmerizing solos on the tom-toms, creating atmosphere as well as keeping the groove pushing forward.

But Roach didn't stop there, unlike other jazz pioneers who changed the world when they were young yet became set in their ways as they grew older. He has always had the curiosity and the willingness to grow as a musician and as a man, moving beyond bop into new compositional structures, unusual instrument lineups, unusual time signatures, atonality, music for Broadway musicals, television, film and the symphony hall, even working with a rapper well ahead of the jazz/hip-hop merger. An outspoken man, he became a fervent supporter of civil rights and racial equality, and that no doubt hurt his career at various junctures. At one point in his militant period in 1961, he disrupted a Miles Davis/Gil Evans concert in Carnegie Hall by marching to the edge of the stage holding a "Freedom Now" placard protesting the Africa Relief Foundation (for which the event was a benefit). When Miles' autobiography came out in 1989, Roach decried the book's inaccuracies, even going so far as to suggest that Miles was getting senile (despite the bumpy patches, their friendship nevertheless lasted until Miles' death). Roach has

also received a MacArthur Foundation "genius" grant; as an articulate lecturer on jazz, he has taught at the Lenox School of Jazz and has been a professor of music at the University of Massachusetts, Amherst.

Roach's mother was a gospel singer, and that early exposure in the church had a lasting effect on his musical direction. He started playing the drums at age ten and undertook formal musical studies at the Manhattan School of Music. By the time he was 18, Roach was already immersed in proto-bop jam sessions at Minton's Playhouse and Monroe's Uptown House (where he was the house drummer) with Charlie Parker and Dizzy Gillespie, listening to Kenny Clarke and absorbing his influence. He made his recorded debut in 1943 with the progressive-minded Coleman Hawkins on the Apollo label, and played with Benny Carter's orchestra in California and Gillespie's quintet, as well as briefly with Duke Ellington in 1944. By 1945, Roach was red-hot in jazz circles, and he joined Parker's group that year for the first of a series of sporadic periods (1945, 1947-49, 1951-53). He participated in many of bop's seminal recordings (including Parker's incendiary "Ko-Ko" of 1945 and Miles' *Birth of the Cool* recordings of 1949-50), although he would not lead his own studio session until 1953. Even then, Roach would not be forced into a narrow box;/ he also played with R&B/jazz star Louis Jordan and Dixieland's Henry "Red" Allen. With Charles Mingus, Roach co-founded Debut Records in 1952, though he was on the road too often to do much minding of the store. But Roach later said that Debut gave his career a springboard—and indeed, Debut released his first session as a leader, as well as the memorable Massey Hall concert in which Roach played with Parker, Gillespie, Mingus and Bud Powell.

In 1954, not long after recording with Howard Rumsey's Lighthouse All-Stars, Roach formed a quintet in Los Angeles to take out on the road at the suggestion of Gene Norman. This group included one Clifford Brown, who had been recommended to Roach by Dizzy several years before. The Brown/Roach Quintet made a stack of essential recordings for EmArcy that virtually defined the hard bop of the '50s, and though Brown's death in a 1956 auto accident absolutely devastated Roach, he kept the quintet together with Kenny Dorham and Sonny Rollins as the lead horns. For the remainder of the '50s, he would continue to use major talents like Booker Little, George Coleman and Hank Mobley in his small groups, dropping the piano entirely now and then.

Heavily affected by the burgeoning civil rights movement and his relationship with activist singer Abbey Lincoln (to whom he would be married from 1962 to 1970), Roach recorded the *We Insist: Freedom Now Suite,* a seven-part collaboration with Oscar Brown, Jr., in 1960, and he would continue to write works that used solo and choral voices. Throughout the 1960s, Roach was a committed political crusader, and that, along with the general slump of interest in jazz, reduced his musical visibility, although he continued to record sporadically for Impulse! and Atlantic. In 1970, Roach took another flyer and formed M'Boom, a ten-piece percussion ensemble that borrowed languages and timbres from classical contemporary music and still performs now and then. Now interested in the avant-garde, Roach recorded with the likes of Anthony Braxton, Archie Shepp and Cecil Taylor in the late 1970s, though the results were mostly issued on erratically distributed foreign labels. In the 1980s, he began to experiment with a double quartet (with Odean Pope, Cecil Bridgewater and Tyrone Brown)—his regular jazz quartet combined with the partly improvising Uptown String Quartet (which includes his daughter Maxine on viola).

The late '80s and '90s found Roach unveiling special projects like a double-CD duo concert with a sadly faded Dizzy Gillespie, the much more successful *To the Max!,* which combined several of Roach's assorted groups and idioms, and a huge, uneven concerto for drum soloist and symphony orchestra, "Festival Journey." Thus, Roach has been outside the consciousness of most jazz historians since the 1960s, as he refuses to be bound and secured into some tight little niche of history—and that makes him a rare, unclassifiable, treasurable breed of cat. —*Richard S. Ginell*

The Max Roach Quartet, Featuring Hank Mobley / Apr. 10, 1953-Apr. 21, 1953 / Original Jazz Classics ♦♦♦

Drummer Max Roach's first studio session as a leader falls stylewise between bop and hard bop. The earlier set, which has four group originals played by a septet that also includes trumpeter Idrees Sulieman, trombonist Leon Comegys, altoist Gigi Gryce, Hank Mobley on tenor, pianist Walter Davis, Jr., and bassist Frank Skeete, was the recording debut for both Mobley and Davis. The other session (two standards, two originals by Roach including his solo "Drum Conversation," Mobley's "Kismet" and Charlie Parker's "Chi Chi") features the same rhythm section, with Mobley as the only horn. The music is enjoyable although not as essential as the great drummer's later dates. This CD reissue adds "Drum Conversation Part 2" to the original LP program. —*Scott Yanow*

Standard Time / Aug. 14, 1954-May 14, 1959 / EmArcy ♦♦♦

This is the type of reissue that frustrates collectors. The double-LP (which came out in 1984) has two lengthy selections (a very fast version of "Move" and "What Is

This Thing Called Love") from a familiar but exciting jam session featuring the trumpets of Clifford Brown, Maynard Ferguson and Clark Terry. In addition there are five selections from Roach's groups featuring such top players as trumpeters Kenny Dorham, Booker Little and Tommy Turrentine and tenors Sonny Rollins, George Coleman and Stanley Turrentine, among others. However, the real reason to get this set is that there are also five previously unreleased selections; an alternate take of "The Blues Walk" with Clifford Brown has reappeared on CD, but the other four performances ("Love Letters," "Minor Trouble," "It Don't Mean a Thing" and "Tune Up") have not. All have Kenny Dorham and three also feature Sonny Rollins. Completists will be forced to duplicate some numbers in order to get all of Max Roach's important EmArcy recordings. —*Scott Yanow*

Max Roach Plus Four / Oct. 12, 1956 / EmArcy ♦♦♦♦♦
After the tragic deaths of trumpeter Clifford Brown and pianist Richie Powell in a car accident a few months earlier, drummer Max Roach regrouped with trumpeter Kenny Dorham and pianist Ray Bryant filling in the unfillable holes; tenor great Sonny Rollins and bassist George Morrow remained from the earlier band. This EmArcy CD finds Roach taking plenty of solo space including almost all of "Dr. Free-zee" and the climaxes of "Just One of Those Things" and "Woody 'n You." The horns have plenty of good spots and other highlights of this worthy set includes George Russell's "Ezz-thetic" and a warm rendition of "Body and Soul." —*Scott Yanow*

Jazz in 3/4 Time / Mar. 18, 1957-Mar. 21, 1957 / Mercury ♦♦♦♦
The post-Clifford Brown quintet that drummer Max Roach led tends to get overlooked, but it actually ranked up there with the Jazz Messengers and the Horace Silver Quintet in the late '50s. With tenor saxophonist Sonny Rollins becoming a stronger soloist month-by-month (he was arguably the top tenor in jazz at the time) and veteran trumpeter Kenny Dorham in prime form, Roach was able to stretch himself; the obscure pianist Billy Wallace and bassist George Morrow completed the group. On this LP, Roach explores six songs in waltz time, an innovation for the period (predating Dave Brubeck's recording of "Take Five" by two years). Roach contributed two originals and the group played 3/4 versions of three standards, but it was Rollins' "Valse Hot" (which clocks in on this EmArcy album at 14:15) that was the hit of the date. These excellent performances show that jazz does not always have to be in 4/4 time in order to swing. —*Scott Yanow*

Max Roach 4 Plays Charlie Parker / Dec. 23, 1957 / Mercury ♦♦♦♦
The music on this CD finds drummer Max Roach for the first time dropping the piano out of his quintet and performing with a pianoless quartet. With the departure of Sonny Rollins (who is replaced on three songs apiece by either Hank Mobley or George Coleman), Roach's group (which also featured trumpeter Kenny Dorham and either George Morrow or Nelson Boyd on bass) was temporarily without any major innovators (outside of the leader). So it was perfectly fitting that Roach would look backwards and perform six of Charlie Parker's compositions. Highlighted by "Yardbird Suite," "Confirmation" and "Ko Ko," this set is generally fine although the lack of a piano is really felt on some of this material. —*Scott Yanow*

Percussion Discussion / 1957-Jan. 4, 1958 / Chess ♦♦♦♦
This double-LP from Chess combines together unrelated sessions led by drummer Max Roach and Art Blakey, both of which were originally made for the Cadet label. Blakey features the 1957 version of his Jazz Messengers (which includes altoist Jackie McLean, trumpeter Bill Hardman, pianist Sam Dockery and bassist Spanky DeBrest) on a pair of Duke Jordan songs (including "Flight to Jordan"), a selection apiece from Blakey and altoist Gigi Gryce and a brief four-song "Gershwin Medley." The Roach selections are most significant for featuring a young pianist named Ramsey Lewis in a straightahead setting; the other musicians are trumpeter Kenny Dorham, Hank Mobley on tenor and bassist George Morrow, and the music is dominated by group originals. Overall, neither of the two sets are essential or overly innovative, but they helped to define what hard bop sounded like in the late '50s and will be savored by straightahead jazz fans. —*Scott Yanow*

Max Roach Plus Four on the Chicago Scene / Jun. 1958 / EmArcy ♦♦♦♦
Drummer Max Roach's abilities as a talent scout have often been overlooked through the years, but quite a few musicians (from Hank Mobley and Clifford Brown to Stanley Turrentine and Odeon Pope) have benefitted greatly from their association with Roach. An ill-fated trumpeter who the drummer helped introduce was Booker Little, who made his recording debut at the age of 20 on this excellent LP. With George Coleman on tenor, pianist Eddie Baker and bassist Bob Cranshaw also in the quintet, this album might be brief (only around 31 minutes) but it has plenty of fine playing. Little's feature on "My Old Flame" is a high point, Coleman sounds fine on "Stompin' at the Savoy," the uptempo blues "Memo to Maurice" and "Stella by Starlight" are both quite enjoyable, and Roach has several typically well-constructed solos. Recommended, as are all the mostly hard-to-find Roach-Little sessions. —*Scott Yanow*

Max Roach Plus Four at Newport / Jul. 6, 1958 / EmArcy ♦♦♦♦
The main reason to search for this out-of-print LP is for the playing of the great, if short-lived, trumpeter Booker Little, who was the first on his instrument to emerge from the shadow of Clifford Brown and start to develop his own voice. With tenor saxophonist George Coleman, Ray Draper on tuba, bassist Art Davis and the drummer/leader (then 33 but already considered a giant for over a decade), the quintet performs six consistently enjoyable and hard-swinging numbers; highlights include "Night in Tunisia," "Tune-Up," Little's "Minor Mode" and "Love for Sale." —*Scott Yanow*

Deeds, Not Words / Sep. 4, 1958 / Original Jazz Classics ♦♦♦♦♦
This CD reissue of a Max Roach Riverside date is notable for featuring the great young trumpeter Booker Little and for utilizing Ray Draper's tuba as a melody instrument; tenor saxophonist George Coleman and bassist Art Davis complete the excellent quintet. Highlights include "It's You or No One," "You Stepped out of a Dream" and Roach's unaccompanied drum piece "Conversation." This is fine music from a group that was trying to stretch itself beyond hard bop. —*Scott Yanow*

The Many Sides of Max / Oct. 1959 / Mercury ♦♦♦
This album (although listed in some discographies as 1959) was probably recorded in 1961. A reunion of Max Roach's sidemen, it features a particularly strong group comprising the great trumpeter Booker Little, George Coleman on tenor, trombonist Julian Priester, pianist Ray Bryant and bassist Bob Boswell. Among the many high points of this LP (which was reissued on a Trip album but is not yet on CD) include Roach's tympani work on "Tympanalli," "Bemsha Swing" and "There's No You," but all seven selections on the admittedly brief album (around 31 minutes) are worth hearing. —*Scott Yanow*

Long As You're Living / Feb. 5, 1960 / Enja ♦♦♦
The most obscure group that drummer Max Roach led actually recorded four albums in 1960; a quintet with tenor saxophonist Stanley Turrentine (then a complete unknown), his brother Tommy on trumpet, trombonist Julian Priester and bassist Bobby Boswell. Strange that this Enja release is the only one of their recordings thus far to appear on CD. Although the playing of the Turrentines is not at the same innovative level as Roach's prior group with Booker Little and George Coleman, they come up with consistently fresh statements during the well-rounded set and the tenorman was already instantly recognizable. Highlights include a couple of Roach drum features, two Kenny Dorham compositions ("Lotus Blossom," "The Villa") and "Night in Tunisia." —*Scott Yanow*

★ **Freedom Now Suite** / Aug. 31, 1960+Sep. 6, 1960 / Columbia ♦♦♦♦♦
This is a classic. At a time when the civil rights movement was starting to heat up, drummer Max Roach performed and recorded a seven-part suite dealing with Black history (particularly slavery) and racism. "Driva' Man" has a powerful statement by veteran tenor Coleman Hawkins and there is valuable solo space elsewhere for trumpeter Booker Little and trombonist Julian Priester, but it is the overall performance of Abbey Lincoln that is most notable. Formerly a nightclub singer, Lincoln really came into her own under Roach's tutelage and she is a strong force throughout this intense set. On "Tryptich: Prayer/Protest/Peace," Lincoln is heard in duets with the drummer and her wrenching screams of rage are quite memorable. This timeless protest record is a gem. —*Scott Yanow*

★ **Percussion Bitter Sweet** / Aug. 1961 / Impulse! ♦♦♦♦♦
This CD reissue brings back a classic album, one of the finest of drummer Max Roach's very productive career. The illustrious sidemen (trumpeter Booker Little; trombonist Julian Priester; Eric Dolphy on alto, bass clarinet and flute; tenorman Clifford Jordan, pianist Mal Waldron; and bassist Art Davis in addition to some guest percussionists) all have opportunitites to make strong contributions and Dolphy's pleading alto solo on "Mendacity" is particularly memorable. Abbey Lincoln has two emotional and very effective vocals, but it is the overall sound of the ensembles and the political nature of the music that make this set (along with Roach's *Freedom Now Suite*) quite unique in jazz history. —*Scott Yanow*

It's Time / Feb. 15, 1962-Feb. 27, 1962 / Impulse! ♦♦♦♦
This Max Roach date had been out of print for around 30 years when it was finally reissued on CD by Impulse in 1996. An unusual set, this outing featured the drummer's all-star sextet (which consisted of trumpeter Richard Williams, tenor saxophonist Clifford Jordan, trombonist Julian Priester, pianist Mal Waldron and bassist Art Davis) joined by a vocal choir conducted by Coleridge Perkinson and orchestrated by Roach (who contributed all six originals). Unlike most other collaborations, the choir was not overly gospel-oriented and was utilized as a jazz ensemble. Each of the horns has a feature or two and singer Abbey Lincoln stars on "Lonesome Lover." But despite the sincerity of this effort, there are times when one wishes the choir would leave altogether and let the quintet really stretch out. —*Scott Yanow*

Speak Brother Speak / Oct. 4, 1962 / Original Jazz Classics ✦✦✦✦
This reissue CD of a live set originally put out on Debut has two very lengthy tracks (the 25-minute "Speak, Brother, Speak" and the twenty-two-and-a-half minute "A Variation") featuring solos by tenor saxophonist Clifford Jordan, pianist Mal Waldron, bassist Eddie Khan and drummer Max Roach (who wrote both of the pieces). The music is somewhere between hard bop and the avant-garde and the musicians really push each other, although the results are not quite essential. Clifford Jordan fans in particular will find this to be an interesting set. —*Scott Yanow*

The Max Roach Trio, Featuring the Legendary Hasaan / Dec. 4, 1964+Dec. 7, 1964 / Atlantic ✦✦✦✦✦
Pianist Hasaan Ibn Ali only made one recording in his life, this trio set with drummer Max Roach and bassist Art Davis. A very advanced player whose style fell somewhere between Thelonious Monk and Cecil Taylor (with hints of Herbie Nichols), Hasaan actually had a rather original sound. His performances of his seven originals on this set (a straight CD reissue of a long out-of-print LP) are intense, somewhat virtuosic and rhythmic, yet often melodic in a quirky way. This is a classic of its kind and it is fortunate that it was made, but it is a tragedy that Hasaan would not record again and that he would soon sink back into obscurity. —*Scott Yanow*

Drums Unlimited / Oct. 14, 1965-Apr. 25, 1966 / Atlantic ✦✦✦✦
Other than a trio set with the legendary pianist Hasaan Ibn Ali, this set was Max Roach's only recording as a leader during 1963-67. Three of the six numbers ("Nommo," "St. Louis Blues" and "In the Red") find Roach heading a group that includes trumpeter Freddie Hubbard, altoist James Spaulding, pianist Ronnie Mathews, bassist Jymie Merritt and, on "St. Louis Blues," Roland Alexander on soprano. Their music is essentially advanced hard-bop with a generous amount of space taken up by Roach's drum solos. The other three selections ("The Drum Also Waltzes," "Drums Unlimited" and "For Big Sid") are unaccompanied features for Max Roach and because of the melodic and logically planned nature of his improvisations, they continually hold on to one's attention. —*Scott Yanow*

Force: Sweet Mao—Suid Africa '76 / Jul. 1976 / BASF ✦✦✦✦
Duets with Archie Shepp (sax). Extended pieces from two virtuosos. Quintessential. —*Michael G. Nastos*

The Loadstar / Jul. 27, 1977 / Horo ✦✦✦✦
Quartet two-fer (one piece per album) with Billy Harper (ts), Cecil Bridgewater (tpt), Reggie Workman (b). This is powerful music. —*Michael G. Nastos*

Birth and Rebirth / Sep. 1978 / Black Saint ✦✦✦✦✦
The first of drummer Max Roach's two duet sets with multireedist Anthony Braxton consists of seven fairly free improvisations that they created in the studio. Each of the selections (particularly "Birth", which builds gradually in intensity to a ferocious level; the waltz time of "Magic and Music" ;the atmospheric "Tropical Forest" and "Softshoe") have their own plot and purpose. Braxton (who performs on alto, soprano, sopranino and clarinet) and Roach continually inspire each other, which is probably why they would record a second set the following year. Stimulating avant-garde music. —*Scott Yanow*

Pictures in a Frame / Sep. 10, 1979-Sep. 17, 1979 / Soul Note ✦✦✦✦
Although drummer Max Roach has been engaged in many special projects during the past 20 years, his main group has been his regular quartet. On this Soul Note LP from 1979, trumpeter Cecil Bridgewater, Odean Pope (on tenor, flute and oboe) and bassist Calvin Hill (who would later be succeeded by Tyrone Brown) join Roach for concise interpretations of eight group originals (everyone contributes at least one song) along with Clifford Jordan's "Japanese Dream." Although the group would continue to grow and evolve, it was already a fairly impressive unit by 1979. As usual with Max Roach's bands, this group filled the gap between hard bop and the avant-garde. —*Scott Yanow*

☆ **One in Two, Two in One** / Aug. 31, 1979 / Hat Hut ✦✦✦✦✦
The second of two duet albums by drummer Max Roach and multireedist Anthony Braxton was recorded live and released on this two-LP set; this is the more interesting of the two projects since it is a nearly 78-minute continual improvisation. Braxton gets to stretch out on alto, soprano, sopranino, contra bass clarinet (which really gets a monstrous sound), clarinet and flute. With Roach pushing Braxton, the results are quite adventurous, yet full of joy. Followers of avant-garde jazz can consider this set to be essential. —*Scott Yanow*

Historic Concerts / Dec. 15, 1979 / Soul Note ✦✦✦✦
Drummer Max Roach met up with the intense avant-garde pianist Cecil Taylor for a 1979 concert that resulted in this double CD. After Roach and Taylor play separate five-minute solos (Taylor's is surprisingly melodic and bluesy), they interact during a two-part 78-minute encounter that finds Roach not shy to occasionally take control. The passionate music is quite atonal but coherent with Taylor dis-

playing an impressive amount of energy and the two masters (who had not rehearsed or ever played together before) communicating fairly well. This set is weakened a bit by a 17-minute radio interview that includes excerpts from the concert one just heard, although some of the anecdotes are interesting. No revelations really occur in the music, but it certainly holds one's interest. —*Scott Yanow*

Chattahoochee Red / 1981 / Columbia ✦✦✦✦
For this quartet outing, Max Roach performs seven group originals plus tributes to Clifford Brown ("I Remember Clifford"), Thelonious Monk ("'Round Midnight") and John Coltrane ("Giant Steps"). Roach's regular band (with trumpeter Cecil Bridgewater, Odean Pope on tenor, flute and oboe, bassist Calvin Hill and on "Wefe," guest pianist Walter Bishop, Jr.) is in excellent form on this spirited outing; pity that this LP has been out of print for quite some time. —*Scott Yanow*

In the Light / Jul. 1982 / Soul Note ✦✦✦
An early-'80s date with drummer Max Roach's regular quartet. There was talk that Roach was starting to run out of steam during this period, but his drumming doesn't lack energy or pace. True, some of the compositions weren't as good as in the past, but the quartet's earnest ensemble lines and solos compensated for any weaknesses in material. —*Ron Wynn*

Scott Free / May 31, 1984 / Soul Note ✦✦✦✦✦
This strong set from the Max Roach Quartet (one of the finest regular bands of the 1980s) finds the group performing a 40-minute version of trumpeter Cecil Bridgewater's "Scott Free." Because the piece has plenty of solo space (two lengthy improvisations apiece for Bridgewater, tenor saxophonist Odean Pope, bassist Tyrone Brown and drummer Roach, with a medium-tempo section, a rapid segment and some free interludes), there is more variety on this lengthy work than one might expect. This is excellent music, easily recommended as an example of the underrated but consistently brilliant Max Roach Quartet. —*Scott Yanow*

It's Christmas Again / Jun. 2, 1984-Jun. 26, 1984 / Soul Note ✦
Poetry and jazz rarely mix, with jazz generally delegated to the background. That is the case with this disappointing set which finds the poems of Bruce McMarion Wright accompanied by rather anonymous blues playing from Max Roach's quartet. One of the two lengthy tracks also has playing from guests altoist Lee Konitz and clarinetist Tony Scott but they are subservient to the routine storytelling. —*Scott Yanow*

Survivors / Oct. 19, 1984-Oct. 21, 1984/ Soul Note ✦✦✦✦
Drummer Max Roach kept his string of excellent small combo sessions alive with this mid-'80s effort. Trumpeter Cecil Bridgewater and tenor saxophonist Odean Pope were the ideal players for Roach's taut, clipped, and mostly uptempo pieces. They were both solid soloists, and also were able to execute difficult chord changes or switch tempos quickly. Max Roach also played with his customary drive and expressiveness. —*Ron Wynn*

Easy Winners / Jan. 1985 / Soul Note ✦✦✦✦✦
The Max Roach Double Quartet, which combined the drummer's regular group (comprising trumpeter Cecil Bridgewater, tenor saxophonist Odean Pope and electric bassist Tyrone Brown) with the Uptown String Quartet, was a perfect match, and its few recordings are all quite enjoyable and occasionally wondrous. In addition to a transcription of Scott Joplin's "Easy Winners" for the strings, this superior release has colorfully arranged versions of works by Bridgewater ("Birds Says"), Pope ("Sis") and Roach ("A Little Booker"). The wide variety of colors and the consistently-strong improvisations make this a highly recommended set of stirring music. —*Scott Yanow*

Bright Moments / Oct. 1, 1986-Oct. 2, 1986 / Soul Note ✦✦✦✦✦
The combination of drummer Max Roach's regular group (which includes trumpeter Cecil Bridgewater, tenor saxophonist Odean Pope and electric bassist Tyrone Brown) with the Uptown String Quartet to form his Double Quartet works extremely well. Because the strings get to improvise and are not restricted to the background, the interplay between the two groups is a special highlight of this particularly strong outing. In addition to works by Pope and Brown (the latter contributed "Tribute to Duke and Mingus"), the Double Quartet interprets Steve Turre's "Double Delight," Randy Weston's "Hi Fly" and Roland Kirk's happy "Bright Moments." A frequently exquisite yet adventurous album, highly recommended. —*Scott Yanow*

Max & Dizzy: Paris 1989 / Mar. 23, 1989 / A&M ✦✦
This double-CD set is a big mistake. Teaming drummer Max Roach and trumpeter Dizzy Gillespie together as a duo might have worked had it taken place 20 years earlier when Dizzy was still in his musical prime. However, the immortal players did not even discuss what they were going to play beforehand and the result is a series of rambling sketches, essentially a long drum solo with occasional trumpet interludes that are full of clams. The closing thirty-two-and-a-half-minute "Interview" also wanders and could have been cut in half. —*Scott Yanow*

☆ **To the Max** / Sep. 15, 1990-Jun. 25, 1991 / Blue Moon ✦✦✦✦
Max Roach is heard in a variety of settings on this colorful and varied double CD. The three-part "Ghost Dance" features the innovative drummer with a vocal choir and his percussion group, M'Boom. M'Boom also pops up on two other selections, the Max Roach Quartet (with trumpeter Cecil Bridgewater, Odean Pope on tenor and electric bassist Tyrone Brown) has four features, Roach takes two unaccompanied drum solos and the Quartet joins up with The Uptown String Quartet to form Roach's Double Quartet on a 21-minute version of "A Little Booker." The music, which crosses quite a few boundaries, is consistently fascinating and forms a definitive portrait of the ageless drummer's wide musical interests in the early '90s. —*Scott Yanow*

Max Roach with The New Orchestra of Boston and the So What Brass Quintet / Dec. 2, 1993+Oct. 5, 1995 / Blue Note ✦✦
Max Roach has long been one of the most adventurous and stimulating improvisers in music. For this unusual CD, the drummer is featured on the 50-minute "Festival Journey," an episodic and sometimes dramatic piece by Fred Tillis that falls closer to the realm of Western classical music than to jazz. Roach is the only soloist and he frequently interacts with the orchestra, but after repeated listenings no real revelations occur. The music is interesting but not too memorable. Roach's 12-minute "Ghost Dance," performed by a brass quintet along with the leader, is more colorful. Steve Turre takes a fine trombone solo and, although also a little classical-oriented, the theme sticks more in one's mind and the ensembles have their exciting moments. But overall this CD is recommended mostly to Max Roach completists. —*Scott Yanow*

George Robert

b. 1960
Alto Saxophone / Hard Bop, Swing, Big Band
One of the finest jazz musicians born in Switzerland, altoist George Robert has long considered his main influences to be Charlie Parker and Phil Woods. He started on piano when he was eight and clarinet at ten, playing with a family band that included his four brothers. Robert switched permanently to alto as a teenager. In 1980, he moved to the US to study at Berklee, settling in New York in 1985. Robert recorded his first album that year (for his GPR label), and in 1987, formed a quintet that he co-led with trumpeter Tom Harrell on and off through 1992. George Robert, who has toured with Clark Terry, has recorded many albums as a leader for Contemporary, TCB, Mons and Jazz Focus. —*Scott Yanow*

Sun Dance / 1987 / Contemporary ✦✦✦✦
Although altoist George Robert is the leader and plays quite well, it is for the participation of trumpeter Tom Harrell that this LP (not yet reissued on CD) is most notable. Harrell is actually much more boppish than usual, probably due to Robert's inspiration; the leader is most influenced by Phil Woods. With young pianist Dado Moroni, bassist Reggie Johnson and drummer Bill Goodwin all fine in support, the quintet performs four Robert and two Harrell originals that build upon the tradition of hard-swinging and thoughtful improvising. —*Scott Yanow*

● **Tribute** / Jun. 3, 1994 / Jazz Focus ✦✦✦✦✦

David Thomas Roberts

b. Jan. 16, 1955
Composer, Piano / Ragtime
David Thomas Roberts is one of the top ragtime composers of the post-1970 period. His best rags approach the level of a Scott Joplin piece; among his best-known works are "Roberto Clemente," "Pinelands Memoir" and "New Orleans Streets." Although he performs occasionally at ragtime festivals and composes for chamber orchestras, it is for his thoughtful and melodic folk rags that David Thomas Roberts is most significant. He has recorded for several labels, including Euphonic, Stomp Off, Piano Mania, and an early Jelly Roll Morton set for Mardi Gras. —*Scott Yanow*

Music for a Pretty Baby / Mar. 1978 / Mardi Gras ✦✦✦✦
An Album of Early Folk Rags / Jun. 29, 1981+Jul. 2, 1981 / Stomp Off ✦✦✦✦
The Amazon Rag and Other Rags / Jun. 29, 1981-Jul. 22, 1983 / Stomp Off ✦✦✦✦
Through the Bottomlands / 1981-1983 / Stomp Off ✦✦✦✦✦
Pinelands Memoir and Other Rags / 1982-1983 / Euphonic ✦✦✦✦✦
● **15 Ragtime Compositions** / Oct. 9, 1992-Oct. 15, 1992 / Piano Mania ✦✦✦✦✦

Hank Roberts

b. 1955
Cello / Avant-Garde
One of the finest jazz cellists of the past decade, Hank Roberts can always be counted upon to add adventure, color and unpredictability to any session. Roberts

started on the cello when he was ten and also played trombone and guitar in high school, performing in local funk bands. After a year at Indiana State University and a short period at Berklee, Roberts had a day job (which he finally quit in 1988) while playing cello at every opportunity. His most important associations have been with Tim Berne, as co-leader of the trio Miniature (with Berne and Joey Baron), a string trio called Arcado (which also included Mark Feldman and Mark Dresser), and Bill Frisell's band, until the mid-'90s. Roberts has recorded for CBS (with Tim Berne), JMT (with Miniature, Arcado and his own group), and Verve (as a leader). —*Scott Yanow*

● **Black Pastels** / Nov. 1987-Dec. 1987 / JMT ✦✦✦✦✦
Birds of Prey / Jan. 1990-Feb. 1990 / JMT ✦✦✦✦
Miniature / Jul. 1, 1991 / JMT ✦✦✦
Little Motor People / Dec. 1992 / JMT ✦✦✦✦

Howard Roberts (Howard Mancel Roberts)

b. Oct. 2, 1929, Phoenix, AZ, **d.** Jun. 28, 1992, Seattle, WA
Guitar / Cool
Howard Roberts was a talented guitarist on the level of a Barney Kessel or Herb Ellis who spent most of his career playing commercial music in the studios. Shortly after he moved to Los Angeles in 1950, Roberts was firmly established in the studios although on occasion he recorded jazz (most notably twice for Verve during 1956-59, a Concord session from 1977 and one for Discovery in 1979); however, most of his other output (particularly for Capitol in the 1960s) is of lesser interest. The co-founder of the Guitar Institute of Technology in Hollywood, Roberts was an enthusiastic and talented educator and wrote a regular instructional column for *Guitar Player*. —*Scott Yanow*

Mr. Roberts Plays Guitar / Oct. 22, 1956-Jan. 17, 1957 / Verve ✦✦✦✦✦
H.R. Is a Dirty Guitar Player / Jun. 3, 1963-Jun. 16, 1963 / Capitol ✦✦✦
● **The Real Howard Roberts** / Aug. 26, 1977 / Concord Jazz ✦✦✦✦✦
Turning to Spring / Nov. 6, 1979 / Discovery ✦✦✦

Luckey Roberts (Charles Luckeyeth Roberts)

b. Aug. 7, 1887, Philadelphia, PA, **d.** Feb. 5, 1968, New York, NY
Piano / Stride
Luckey Roberts was considered one of the all-time great stride pianists but unfortunately he left very few records behind, and none from his early years. Roberts actually pre-dated stride, publishing "Pork and Beans" and "Junk Man Rag" as early as 1913. He spent most of his career leading society bands and writing for musical comedies; his "Ripples of the Nile" became a hit for Glenn Miller in 1941 as "Moonlight Cocktail." Although much of his career was actually at the fringe of jazz, Roberts showed on his 1946 record session (which resulted in six stunning solos) and a couple of dates in 1958 that he deserved his legendary status. —*Scott Yanow*

★ **Luckey Roberts & Ralph Sutton** / May 21, 1946-Jun. 11, 1952 / Solo Art ✦✦✦✦✦
Luckey Roberts, considered one of the big three of 1920s stride piano (along with James P. Johnson and Fats Waller), was by far the most obscure of the trio, running a successful society band for decades but leading only three record sessions during his long career. This Solo Art CD brings back the six songs from his earliest (1946) date and is quite impressive. Roberts' virtuosity and total command of the piano is remarkable and he really tears into his originals which include "Ripples of the Nile" (turned by Glenn Miller into the pop hit "Moonlight Cocktail"), "Pork & Beans" and "Music Box Rag." Also on this valuable CD are pianist Ralph Sutton's four performances (plus an alternate take) from his debut as a leader in 1949 and eight exciting stride-filled duets with drummer George Wettling from 1952. While Sutton shows the influences of Bob Zurke and Joe Sullivan on the earlier titles, by 1952 he had found his own voice within the classic idiom. A highly recommended disc. —*Scott Yanow*

Happy Go Lucky / 1958 / Period ✦✦✦
Luckey Roberts and Willie The Lion Smith / Mar. 8, 1958 / Good Time Jazz ✦✦✦✦✦
Despite his talents as a pioneering stride pianist, Luckey Roberts only led three recording sessions in his long career. The second date (which comprises half of this CD reissue) ranks up there with his earlier Solo Art set. Roberts performs six originals on this release, none of which (including "Nothin'," "Inner Space" and "Outer Space") are particularly known, although trad jazz pianists would be well advised to explore these pieces. The second half of the release features the equally distinctive Willie "The Lion" Smith on six piano solos of his own, including five originals (highlighted by "Relaxin'" and "Concentratin'") and the standard "Between the Devil and the Deep Blue Sea." Wonderful and classic music. —*Scott Yanow*

Marcus Roberts

b. Sep. 7, 1963, Jacksonville, FL
Piano / Post-Bop, Hard Bop, Stride

Marcus Roberts is a very talented—if very raw—young musician, whose good fortune it was to capture the attention and goodwill of the all-powerful Wynton Marsalis. Roberts is one of the generation of young African-American jazz musicians who seems bent on forging the future by reinventing the past; his infatuation with older forms renders his music a pastiche of obsolete styles. Roberts is a gifted mimic, though his adoption of his idols' surface mannerisms does not penetrate to the essence of their art.

Roberts is without sight; he attended a school for the blind near his childhood home of Jacksonville, FL. He began playing piano in his youth, and studied the instrument at Florida State University in the mid-'80s. Roberts replaced Kenny Kirkland as Marsalis' pianist in 1985. He recorded as a sideman with the trumpeter through the rest of the decade and into the '90s, while at the same time making records under his own name for Columbia. Roberts became Marsalis' *aide de camp* at Jazz at Lincoln Center, writing and arranging extensively for the house big band, and participating in most of the cultural center's activities variously as a composer, performer, or teacher. Roberts is an outspoken proponent of jazz traditionalism; he has little patience for styles of jazz that lie outside the narrow parameters set down by his mentors. His lack of interest in expanding jazz's creative possibilities causes his music to have a hermetic quality, which is unfortunate, because one gets the feeling by listening to his recent compositions that, were Roberts to broaden his horizons a bit, he might be capable of doing excellent work. —*Chris Kelsey*

The Truth Is Spoken Here / Jul. 26, 1988-Jul. 27, 1988 / Novus ✦✦✦✦
Stirring, strong piano. —*Ron Wynn*

Deep in the Shed / Aug. 9, 1989-Dec. 10, 1989 / Novus ✦✦✦
Pianist Marcus Roberts' second album as a leader is plagued by an excess of seriousness and an overly high if noble sense of purpose that made one wonder if writer Stanley Crouch was starting to influence Roberts. The music is often so dry and sober as to be lacking the joy of life. The six Roberts originals, although referred to by Crouch in the liner notes as blues, have the feeling rather than the 12-bar structure of the blues and are generally quite melancholy. Roberts utilizes several of Wynton Marsalis' sidemen including the trumpeter himself (under the pseudonym of E. Dankworth) and the expert wa-wa trombone of Wycliffe Gordon, who gives the date a much needed dose of humor. Marcus Roberts also plays quite well but one wishes he had lightened up a bit. —*Scott Yanow*

Alone with Three Giants / Jun. 3, 1990-Sep. 22, 1990 / Novus ✦✦✦✦✦
Fifteen tracks of solo piano from young, blind pianist from Jacksonville, FL. Repertoire of Monk, Ellington, and Jelly Roll Morton. Fares best on the Monk, and there are five of them. —*Michael G. Nastos*

Prayer for Peace / Jun. 5, 1991-Jun. 7, 1991 / Novus ✦✦✦
This Marcus Roberts solo piano CD features Christmas-related material, all performed in a relaxed manner. Two originals ("Christmas Blues" and "Prayer for Peace") are joined by 11 familiar Yuletide favorites. Roberts rarely wanders far from the melody and his lefthand stride work, although impressive, never really cuts loose. The pleasant recital is overly respectful and thoughtful, and it would have benefited from the inclusion of a few stomps (such as "Jingle Bells"). —*Scott Yanow*

● **As Serenity Approaches** / Jun. 1991-Nov. 1991 / Novus ✦✦✦✦✦
Every one of pianist Marcus Roberts' recordings thus far are recommended. This outing has 11 impressive solo performances and eight duets with trumpeters Scotty Barnhart, Nicholas Payton and Wynton Marsalis (the latter on a fun version of Jelly Roll Morton's "King Porter Stomp"), Todd Williams on clarinet and tenor and trombonist Ronald Westray in addition to two meetings with fellow pianist Ellis Marsalis. This music finds Roberts using techniques of the past (especially stride and old-time breaks) in both his new originals and revivals of classic tunes. However, he never resorts to mere copying and feels free to update elements of the music or to throw in eccentric ideas. There is a great deal for listeners to investigate on this thoroughly fascinating recital. —*Scott Yanow*

If I Could Be with You / 1993 / Novus ✦✦✦✦

Gershwin for Lovers / 1994 / Columbia ✦✦✦

Plays Ellington / 1995 / Novus ✦✦✦✦

Portraits in Blue / Jun. 2, 1995-Jul. 13, 1995 / Sony ✦✦✦✦

Time and Circumstance / Mar. 4, 1996-Mar. 6, 1996 / Columbia ✦✦✦✦
Pianist Marcus Roberts and his fine trio (with bassist David Grossman and drummer Jason Marsalis) perform a 14-song original suite on this CD that traces the ups and downs of a longterm love affair. Marsalis, who is one of the more versatile of today's pianists, plays quite modern throughout the date while always swinging.

The music is sometimes dramatic, at other times wistful or introspective, but rarely loses one's interest. It is doubtful if any of the themes will catch on as future standards (none of the melodies are all that memorable) but taken as a whole this is a thought-provoking and enjoyable set. —*Scott Yanow*

Blues for the New Millennium /1997 / Columbia ✦✦✦✦✦
This intriguing release features pianist Marcus Roberts and a dozen of his originals played by a variety of young musicians in groups as large as 11 pieces. The compositions (other than Robert Johnson's "Cross Road Blues" and Jelly Roll Morton's "Jungle Blues") are all by the pianist, as are the arrangements. In general, the original tunes themselves are not all that memorable (none of the melodies are destined to catch on), but the charts are quite colorful and often make the ensembles sound like a distortion of early-1930s Duke Ellington (with some McCoy Tyner-like piano here and there from Roberts). There are plenty of excellent solos from the band (which includes trumpeter Marcus Printup, trombonist Ronald Westley and altoist Sherman Irby) during the episodic music, and the CD rewards repeated listenings. An intriguing set. —*Scott Yanow*

Ikey Robinson

b. Jul. 28, 1904, Dublin, VA, **d.** Oct. 25, 1990, Chicago, IL
Banjo, Guitar, Vocals / Classic Jazz

Ikey Robinson was an excellent banjoist and singer who was versatile enough to record both jazz and blues from the late '20s into the late '30s. Unfortunately, he spent long periods off records after the swing era, leading to him being less known than he should be. After working locally, Robinson moved to Chicago in 1926, playing and recording with Jelly Roll Morton, Clarence Williams and (most importantly) Jabbo Smith during 1928-29. He led his own recording sessions in 1929, 1931, 1933 and 1935 (all have been reissued on a CD from the Austrian label RST). Robinson played with Wilbur Sweatman, Noble Sissle, Carroll Dickerson and Erskine Tate in the 1930s, recorded with Clarence Williams and led small groups from the 1940s on. In the early '60s he was with Franz Jackson and in the 1970s (when he was rediscovered) he had an opportunity to tour Europe and be reunited with Jabbo Smith. —*Scott Yanow*

● **"Banjo" Ikey Robinson** / Jan. 4, 1929-May 19, 1937 / RST ✦✦✦✦✦
It would not be an understatement to call this CD definitive of Ikey Robinson's work since it includes every selection (except for two songs that have Half Pint Jaxon vocals) ever led by the banjoist/vocalist. The diversity is impressive, for Robinson is heard (on "Got Butter on It" and "Ready Hokum") with a hot group featuring cornetist Jabbo Smith, singing the blues, performing with the Hokum Trio and the Pods of Pepper (both good-time bands), backing singer Charlie Slocum and heading his own Windy City Five (a fine swing group) in 1935; he even plays clarinet on one song. This consistently enjoyable Austrian import is well worth searching for. —*Scott Yanow*

Jim Robinson (Nathan Robinson)

b. Dec. 25, 1892, Deer Range, LA, **d.** May 4, 1976, New Orleans, LA
Trombone / New Orleans Jazz

Jim Robinson was a very reliable New Orleans trombonist who was much more consistent than most of the musicians he performed with, never seeming to have an off day. A jazz pioneer, Robinson played guitar as a child and started playing trombone in 1917 while stationed in France during World War I; he was already 24. He started working in New Orleans in 1919 with Kid Rena, the Golden Leaf Band and the Tuxedo Band. In 1923, Robinson became part of the Morgan band, which, under Sam Morgan's leadership, had a recording session in 1927. He was a fixture in New Orleans for decades, playing with many local groups while working days in the 1930s as a longshoreman. Robinson was part of Kid Rena's 1940 recording session and joined Bunk Johnson's band in 1942, meeting up with George Lewis. He returned to New Orleans with Lewis in 1946 and was a part of Lewis' popular band during the 1950s and '60s, touring the world and recording extensively. He was the top musician in the Preservation Hall Jazz Band in the 1970s, staying active until his death at age 83. Jim Robinson recorded as a leader for AM (1944), Riverside (1961), Atlantic, Pearl, Jazz Crusade, and finally Smoky Mary (Jan. 1976). —*Scott Yanow*

● **New Orleans: The Living Legends—Jim Robinson Plays Spirituals and Blues** / Jan. 30, 1961/ Original Jazz Classics ✦✦✦✦✦

Orphy Robinson

b. Oct. 13, 1960, London, England
Vibes / Post-Bop

Orphy Robinson was one of the many young British jazz musicians who was discovered by Americans in the mid-'80s. Inspired originally by Roy Ayers, Robinson played funk, pop and avant-garde music before joining Courtney Pine's Jazz Warriors. An open-minded player who has worked with Pine's small group, Andy Sheppard and his own band, Robinson has recorded for Blue Note but not really had a breakthrough in the US yet; his style is quite eclectic. —*Scott Yanow*

● **When Tomorrow Comes** / Oct. 11, 1991-Oct. 13, 1991 / Blue Note ✦✦✦✦
English vibraphonist Orphy Robinson's Blue Note CD features original compositions that use repetition, funky rhythms and long vamps a great deal but lack any particularly memorable melodies. The solos by Robinson and his rhythm section are fine and the inclusion of Tunde Jegede's kora and cello (the former sounds like an upper register guitar) add color to the ensembles, but the music makes no lasting impression. —*Scott Yanow*

The Vibes Describes / 1994 / Blue Note ✦
This effort from English vibraphonist Orphy Robinson is appallingly dull, the type of recording that Alfred Lion would never have allowed to be released on his label. Most of the ten pieces feature a lazy funk bass, background long tones from the synthesizer and Robinson's speedy but directionless vibes on top. The musicianship is good but the material is instantly forgettable. When Leroy Osbourne on one song sings about the need of "making a change," one wonders if he means adding a chord change to uplift the monotonous vamp. —*Scott Yanow*

Perry Robinson

b. Sep. 17, 1938, New York, NY
Clarinet / Avant-Garde, Free Jazz
Throughout his career Perry Robinson has sought to do the near-impossible: establish himself as an avant-garde leader on an instrument still closely associated with the swing era. After extensive formal study (including the Lenox School of Jazz in 1959), Robinson played with such advanced musicians as Paul Bley, Archie Shepp and Bill Dixon. He was with Roswell Rudd's quintet in 1968, appeared on several works by the Jazz Composers' Orchestra and in 1972 worked with Gunter Hampel. In a change of pace, Robinson was with Dave Brubeck's Two Generations of Brubeck band in 1973 but he has continued recording and performing avant-garde jazz up to the present time. —*Scott Yanow*

● **Funk Dumpling** / 1962 / Savoy ✦✦✦✦✦
Perry Robinson / 1965 / ESP ✦✦✦
Kundalini / Feb. 2, 1978+Feb. 9, 1978 / Improvising Artists ✦✦✦
Clarinetist Perry Robinson is heard at his best on "Shenandoah," an original duet with Badal Roy on tablas that finds Robinson looking backwards towards the New Orleans clarinet tradition while also playing quite adventurous. A second duo, "Kundalini," is more Indian-oriented while the lengthy "Always Backwards," a trio with Roy and percussionist Nana Vasconcelos, wanders a bit but is generally colorful. This CD reissue has less than 33 minutes of music, which keeps it from being essential, but it is one of the few Perry Robinson sets currently available. —*Scott Yanow*

The Traveler / 1978 / Chiaroscuro ✦✦✦✦

Reginald R. Robinson

b. 1973, Chicago, IL
Piano / Ragtime
As a young Black man who plays ragtime piano, Reginald Robinson certainly stands out in his generation. In addition he has composed dozens of rags. He started on piano at 13 and dropped out of school the following year to devote himself to his music, memorizing rags by ear because he had not yet learned to read music! Robinson began serious lessons the following year and gradually gained a reputation. Reginald Robinson has thus far recorded two solo piano albums for Delmark, the first cut when he was 20. All but three of the 41 songs he has recorded are his own and they fit squarely into the classic rag tradition. —*Scott Yanow*

Strongman / 1993 / Delmark ✦✦✦✦✦
Robinson demonstrates his mastery of ragtime and his own voice on the 22 tunes that comprise his Delmark debut. Whether you're a rag fan or not, hearing Robinson deconstruct, rework and smoothly conclude "Maple Leaf Rag," "Spring Rag" and "The Original Slow Drag" is impressive. He's also accomplished at boogie-woogie, blues and even straight jazz, but uses these only in bits and pieces as stylistic relief, along with incorporating bits and pieces of familiar pop tunes into his rags. What's more amazing is that only Scott Joplin's "Maple Leaf Rag" is a cover; the other 21 numbers are Robinson originals, and he's nailed the vintage style without turning the songs into museum pieces. —*Ron Wynn*

● **Sounds in Silhouette** / 1994 / Delmark ✦✦✦✦✦
Ragtime, which had largely died with Scott Joplin in 1917, did not begin a renaissance until Marvin Hamlisch used some of Joplin's compositions as the basis for his soundtrack to *The Sting* in 1973. Reginald R. Robinson, who coincidentally was

born in 1973, quickly emerged not only as one of ragtime's top practioners of the mid-'90s but (along with David Thomas Roberts) as its top contemporary composer. On his second Delmark release he performs 19 selections including Scott Joplin's "Peacherine Rag," a medley of turn-of-the-century pieces by Charles Johnson and 17 of his own compositions. Robinson does not feel the need to "update" ragtime but he does infuse it with many fresh new melodies and his enthusiasm. He also plays a bit of boogie and stride on this set but, since improvising is not his main forte, the emphasis fortunately is on extending the legacy of Scott Joplin. Ragtime fans should go out of their way to discover Robinson's music. —*Scott Yanow*

Spike Robinson

b. Jan. 16, 1930, Kenosha, WI
Tenor Saxophone / Cool
Spike Robinson in the mid-'90s is just about the last major tenor stylist who plays in the Four Brothers cool-toned style popularized by Stan Getz, Zoot Sims and Al Cohn. The remarkable part is that Robinson seemed to emerge fully formed in 1981 when he was already past 50. Originally he started on alto when he was 12 and, after being in the military, in 1950 Spike played with some of England's top bop musicians, recording with them. However, after he returned to the US, Robinson got a degree in engineering and had a day job in Colorado for the next 30 years, just gigging on a part-time basis in local clubs on tenor. When he began playing music full-time in 1981, Robinson initially created a bit of a sensation. Spike Robinson has continued swinging (often sounding close to Stan Getz) up to the present day and he has recorded many excellent sets for Discovery, Capri, Concord and particularly Hep. —*Scott Yanow*

At Chester's, Vol. 1 / Jul. 1984 / Hep ✦✦✦✦
At Chester's, Vol. 2 / Jul. 26, 1984 / Hep ✦✦✦✦
Spring Can Really Hang You Up the Most / Jul. 17, 1985 / Capri ✦✦✦✦
Spike Robinson's sessions are usually pleasant, casually swinging, and musically proficient, and this quartet outing isn't any different. Robinson explores ballads, mid-tempo standards, and originals with a steady, big tone and full sound. He doesn't try anything too intricate, sticking close to the melody and then adding some embellishments and slight alterations. The backing group featuring Ted Beament, Peter Ind, and Bill Eyden follow the same formula. —*Ron Wynn*

It's a Wonderful World / Jul. 21, 1986 / Capri ✦✦✦✦
Tenor saxophonist Spike Robinson has had many visits to England throughout his career, including time spent as a member of London's Club 11 in the early 1950s. This Capri LP (not yet out on CD) finds Robinson back in England recording with veteran trombonist Roy Williams and a fine British rhythm section (pianist Ted Beament, bassist Paul Bridge and drummer Allan Ganley). The music is predictably excellent (Spike has long been very consistent), containing swinging renditions of such standards as "Have You Met Miss Jones," "The Man I Love" and "Indian Summer." —*Scott Yanow*

London Reprise / Aug. 9, 1984 / Capri ✦✦✦✦✦
Spike Robinson's return to the jazz scene in the early '80s after 34 years as an engineer (during which he only worked part-time as a musician) was a welcome event. His cool tone (very much in the "Four Brothers" tradition of Stan Getz and Zoot Sims) was fully formed, and he could swing as hard as any of the younger players. For this Capri set, Robinson is teamed with guitarist Martin Taylor, bassist Dave Green and drummer Spike Wells for mostly concise renditions of eight veteran standards; only Horace Silver's "Opus De Funk" was written after the swing era. Pleasing music that has not yet been reissued on CD. —*Scott Yanow*

● **Plays Harry Warren** / Dec. 18, 1981-Aug. 18, 1993 / Hep ✦✦✦✦✦
This CD reissues tenor saxophonist Spike Robinson's 1981 Discovery LP of the same name and adds six additional selections recorded in 1993. The Discovery date was recorded when Robinson was already 51 and returning to jazz after a 30-year absence from full-time activity. The cool-toned tenor (heard with pianist Victor Feldman, bassist Ray Brown and drummer John Guerin) proved to be very much in his prime, a new type of young lion who brought back the Four Brothers sound. The 1993 selections with pianist Pete Jolly, bassist John Leitham and drummer Paul Kreibich are on the same high level. Since the underrated Harry Warren was one of the top songwriters of the 1930s and '40s, Robinson had plenty to choose from on this tribute set. His high-quality repertoire includes "This Heart of Mine," "There Will Never Be Another You," "Serenade in Blue", "Lulu's Back in Town" and even "Chattanooga Choo Choo." A highly recommended and swinging program. —*Scott Yanow*

In Town / Oct. 1986 / Hep ✦✦✦✦

Henry B. Meets Alvin G. Once in a Wild / Apr. 1988 / Capri ✦✦✦✦✦

After working as an engineer for 34 years, Spike Robinson finally became a full-time musician late in 1985. This outing with fellow tenor Al Cohn and a rhythm section comprising pianist Richard Wyands, bassist Steve La Spina and drummer Akira Tana finds Robinson holding his own with his better-known sidemen. The two tenors had similar but complementary styles (Cohn's tone at this point in time was deeper and darker than Spike's), and their interplay and occasional tradeoffs are delightful. In addition to some standards, they perform Miles Davis' "Sippin' at Bells," Bob Brookmeyer's "Rustic Hop" and Johnny Mandel's "Low Life" on this easily recommended LP. —*Scott Yanow*

Odd Couple / Aug. 11, 1988 / Capri ✦✦✦✦

Since keyboardist Rob Mullins in the late 1980s was best known for his poppish crossover recordings and Spike Robinson is a bop/swing player in the Four Brothers tradition, this matchup (which also includes bassist Fred Hamilton and drummer Jill Fredericksen) might at first seem a bit odd. However, all of the musicians were based in Denver at the time; Mullins had gigged with Robinson, and he was flexible enough to play standards. Spike sounds typically fine on such tunes as "In Love, In Vain," "Melancholy Baby," "Street of Dreams" and "I Love You." Although Mullins does double on synthesizer, he fits in quite well. —*Scott Yanow*

Just a Bit O' Blues, Vol. 1 / Sep. 19, 1988 / Capri ✦✦✦

On the first of two CDs, tenor saxophonist Spike Robinson teams up with trumpeter Harry "Sweets" Edison, pianist Ross Tompkins, bassist Monty Budwig and drummer Paul Humphrey. It is not too surprising that Robinson (whose tone often recalls Zoot Sims) works well with swing legend Edison. Although the title piece is a blues, the repertoire primarily comprises swing standards, with some heat generated on such tunes as "The One I Love," "Autumn Leaves" and "Slow Boat to China." —*Scott Yanow*

Just a Bit O' Blues, Vol. 2 / Sep. 21, 1988 / Capri ✦✦✦

This second of two CDs once again teams together the hard-swinging but cool-toned tenor of Spike Robinson with veteran trumpeter Harry "Sweets" Edison. Accompanied by pianist Ross Tompkins, bassist Monty Budwig and drummer Paul Humphrey, the two complementary horn soloists are in fine form on a variety of standards and blues. The music always swings and, even if no surprises occur, the chemistry makes this set (along with its first volume) worth picking up. —*Scott Yanow*

Three for the Road / Jul. 1989 / Hep ✦✦✦✦✦

Stairway to the Stars / Oct. 1990 / Hep ✦✦✦

Real Corker / 1991 / Capri ✦✦✦✦

Reminiscin / Dec. 12, 1991-Dec. 15, 1991 / Capri ✦✦✦✦✦

Tenor saxophonist Spike Robinson sounds quite comfortable performing his "Blues for Sooz" and seven standards with a pianoless rhythm section. Guitarist Mundell Lowe, bassist Monty Budwig and drummer Jake Hanna were all veterans who, like Spike, knew how to swing hard even at a quiet volume and a relaxed tempo. Robinson's warm tone sounds quite appealing on such numbers as "Dancing in the Dark," "Yours Is My Heart Alone" and "My Silent Love." Recommended. —*Scott Yanow*

Gershwin Collection / Dec. 7, 1995 / Hep ✦✦✦✦

The mellow-toned tenor Spike Robinson performs ten veteran George Gershwin songs on this release from the Scottish Hep label. Four selections find Spike accompanied by a 12-piece string section, while the other six numbers are by his British quartet with pianist Brian Lemon, bassist Len Skeat and drummer Allan Ganley. While the majority of the tunes are taken as slow ballads, there are also cooking versions of "Lady Be Good" and "I've Got Rhythm." Straight-ahead jazz collectors will find virtually every Spike Robinson recording worth acquiring. —*Scott Yanow*

Betty Roche (Mary Elizabeth Roche)

b. Jan. 9, 1920, Wilmington, DE

Vocals / Standards, Traditional Pop

Betty Roche had an oddly episodic career with its high points being two separate moments with Duke Ellington's Orchestra. She sang and recorded with the Savoy Sultans (1941-42) and had short stints with Hot Lips Page and Lester Young. Roche had the misfortune of being with Duke Ellington in 1943, a year when the recording strike kept all bands off records. However, at Duke's premiere Carnegie Hall concert she sang the celebrated "Blues" section of his "Black, Brown and Beige Suite"; four decades later this was finally released by Prestige. After a period with Earl Hines, Roche spent time outside of music but she rejoined Ellington in 1952 and recorded a classic version of "Take the 'A' Train" that was later adopted by Ray Nance. She recorded three solo albums during 1956-61 but then went back into obscurity, having made her brief mark on jazz history. —*Scott Yanow*

Take the 'A' Train / Mar. 1956 / Bethlehem ✦✦✦✦✦

This CD (put out by Evidence) brings back singer Betty Roche's definitive session. Although she had sung briefly with Duke Ellington on two occasions in 1943 and the early '50s, fame had eluded Roche. After this album she would record two more records (available in the Original Jazz Classics series) over the next few years and then disappear back into obscurity. Assisted by vibraphonist Eddie Costa, trumpeter Conte Candoli, pianist Donn Trenner, bassist Whitey Mitchell and drummer Davey Williams, Roche is heard at her best on this set of standards. Highlights include a remake of "Take the 'A' Train" (she had previously recorded a classic version with Ellington), "Something to Live For," "Route 66" and "September in the Rain." Two additional versions of "Go Away Blues" round out the excellent release. —*Scott Yanow*

Singin' & Swingin' / Jun. 1960 / Original Jazz Classics ✦✦✦✦✦

★ **Lightly and Politely** / Jan. 24, 1961 / Original Jazz Classics ✦✦✦✦✦

It is ironic that what is arguably singer Betty Roche's finest all-around recording was also her last. For this session, which has been reissued in the **OJC** series on CD, Roche (backed by pianist Jimmy Neeley, guitarist Wally Richardson, bassist Michel Mulia and drummer Rudy Lawless) improvises constantly and uplifts a variety of superior standards including "Someone to Watch over Me," "Polka Dots and Moonbeams," "I Had the Craziest Dream" and three songs by her former boss Duke Ellington. It's recommended, particularly to jazz fans not aware of Betty Roche's musical talents. —*Scott Yanow*

Claudio Roditi

b. May 28, 1946, Rio de Janeiro, Brazil

Trumpet, Fluegelhorn / Latin Jazz, Hard Bop

A superior if sometimes overlooked trumpeter (the Kenny Dorham of the 1990s), Claudio Roditi is a frequently exciting hard bop-oriented player. He came to the US to study at Berklee (1970-71) and gigged around the Boston area until moving to New York in 1976. Roditi played with Charlie Rouse and Herbie Mann, and most importantly in the early '80s he started working regularly with Paquito D'Rivera. The reliable trumpeter has been on many straightahead recording sessions since, in addition to being a member of Dizzy Gillespie's United Nation Orchestra. Roditi has recorded as a leader for Green Street (an obscure date in 1984), Uptown, Candid and most recently Reservoir. —*Scott Yanow*

Claudio / 1985 / Uptown ✦✦✦✦

The quintet showcases this straightahead trumpeter from Brazil on six standards played with bop flavor (Dorham, Stiff, and J.J. Johnson wrote three.) Slide Hampton plays trombone. This is a good, upbeat band. —*Michael G. Nastos*

Gemini Man / Mar. 7, 1988-Mar. 22, 1988 / Milestone ✦✦✦✦

Slow Fire / 1989 / Milestone ✦✦✦

Two of Swords / Sep. 24, 1990-Sep. 25, 1990 / Candid ✦✦✦✦

A solid, although conservative in arrangements and direction, release by trumpeter Claudio Roditi. His pungent melodies and clipped, striking solos are among the disc's positive points. Another is a good crop of supporting musicians, including Edward Simon, Jay Ashby, Duke Fonseca, and Danilo Perez. —*Ron Wynn*

● **Milestones** / Nov. 13, 1990-Nov. 14, 1990 / Candid ✦✦✦✦✦

There aren't many trumpeters around more animated and energetic than Claudio Roditi. His searing solos and equally fiery accompaniment have been featured in several bands, and he takes center stage on *Milestones*. Besides his solos, the disc has some first-rate songs and an even better group. Alto saxophonist Paquito D'Rivera, pianist Kenny Barron, bassist Ray Drummond, and drummer Ben Riley would constitute a great band by themselves, and are no less playing with Roditi. —*Ron Wynn*

Free Wheelin': the Music of Lee Morgan / Jul. 29, 1994 / Reservoir ✦✦✦✦✦

Samba: Manhattan Style / May 12, 1995-May 13, 1995 / Reservoir ✦✦✦✦

Metropole Orchestra / Feb. 20, 1996 / Mons ✦✦✦

The talented trumpeter is backed by the 51-piece Metropole Orchestra for this enjoyable session. Although the strings occasionally give it an easy-listening flavor, Roditi's strong solos and director Rob Pronk's arrangements overcome this reservation. "Speak Low" is underscored with swirling strings beneath Roditi's soaring horn. His take of "On the Trail" owes a clear debt to Clark Terry's landmark recording, as well as his legendary humor. Roditi's chops on both fluegelhorn and trumpet compare favorably to Terry as well. —*Ken Dryden*

Red Rodney (Robert Chudnick)

b. Sep. 27, 1927, Philadelphia, PA, **d.** May 27, 1994, Boynton Beach, FL

Trumpet, Fluegelhorn / Bop, Hard Bop

Red Rodney's comeback in the late '70s was quite inspiring and found the veteran bebop trumpeter playing even better than he had during his legendary period with Charlie Parker. He started his professional career by performing with Jerry Wald's orchestra when he was 15 and he passed through a lot of big bands including those of Jimmy Dorsey (during which Rodney closely emulated his early idol Harry James), Elliot Lawrence, Georgie Auld, Benny Goodman and Les Brown. He totally changed his style after hearing Dizzy Gillespie and Charlie Parker, becoming one of the brighter young voices in bebop. Rodney made strong contributions to the bands of Gene Krupa (1946), Claude Thornhill and Woody Herman's Second Herd (1948-49). Off and on during 1949-51, Rodney was a regular member of the Charlie Parker Quintet, playing brilliantly at Bird's recorded Carnegie Hall Concert of 1949. But drugs cut short that association and Rodney spent most of the 1950s in and out of jail. After he kicked heroin, almost as damaging to his jazz chops was a long period playing for shows in Las Vegas. When he returned to New York in 1972, it took Rodney several years to regain his former form. However, he hooked up with multi-instrumentalist Ira Sullivan in 1980 and the musical partnership benefitted both of the veterans; Sullivan's inquisitive style inspired Rodney to play post-bop music (rather than continually stick to bop) and sometimes their quintet (which also featured Garry Dial) sounded like the Ornette Coleman Quartet! After Sullivan went back to Florida a few years later, Rodney continued leading his own quintet, which in later years featured the talented young saxophonist Chris Potter. Red Rodney, who was portrayed quite sympathetically in the Clint Eastwood film *Bird* (during which he played his own solos), stands as proof that for the most open-minded veterans there is life beyond bop. —*Scott Yanow*

Modern Music from Chicago / Jun. 20, 1955 / Original Jazz Classics ✦✦✦✦

The Red Arrow / Nov. 22, 1957-Nov. 24, 1957 / Onyx ✦✦✦✦✦
With Ira Sullivan (tpt/sax) and Tommy Flanagan Trio. Historic early meeting between Rodney and Sullivan. Two by Rodney, one by bassist Oscar Pettiford, three standards. —*Michael G. Nastos*

Red Rodney Returns / 1959 / Argo ✦✦✦

Bird Lives! / Jul. 9, 1973 / Muse ✦✦✦
Quintet with Roy Brooks (d), Charles McPherson (as), Barry Harris (p), Sam Jones (b). Three Bird compositions, Monk's rousing "52nd St. Theme," "'Round Midnight," and one standard. —*Michael G. Nastos*

Superbop / Mar. 26, 1974 / Muse ✦✦✦✦

Red Tornado / Sep. 30, 1975+Oct. 2, 1975 / Muse ✦✦✦✦
Nicely played mid-'70s bop, one in a series that marked the return of trumpeter Red Rodney to the jazz scene after a lengthy absence. His solos are solidly executed, and ensemble interaction, production, and arrangements are conservative, but well done. —*Ron Wynn*

Red, White & Blues / May 11, 1976-May 12, 1976 / Muse ✦✦✦
Plenty of straight bop and blues, plus some ballads and standards from trumpeter Red Rodney. This one features some aggressive, energized solos on bop and uptempo pieces, plus nice interpretations on the slower material. —*Ron Wynn*

Home Free / Dec. 19, 1977 / Muse ✦✦✦✦
Good, consistently-played mainstream fare by trumpeter Red Rodney. This 1977 date was one among many he did for the Muse label that followed the same pattern. They minimized the length and extent of Rodney's solos, had him doing anthems and unexacting originals, and got the best takes of him and his group, smoothly executing the hard bop and mainstream formulas. —*Ron Wynn*

The Three R's / Mar. 13, 1979-Mar. 14, 1979 / Muse ✦✦✦✦✦

Hi Jinx (At the Vanguard) / May 5, 1980-Jul. 5, 1980 / Muse ✦✦✦✦

Live at the Village Vanguard / May 8, 1980-Jul. 7, 1980 / Muse ✦✦✦✦✦
With Ira Sullivan (tpt/sax) and quintet. Three Jack Walrath originals, three standouts. This is one of the most together jazz bands of the '80s. A perfect vehicle for both of them to blow. Sullivan plays saxs, flute, and fluegelhorn. —*Michael G. Nastos*

Night and Day / Jun. 15, 1981-Jun. 16, 1981 / Muse ✦✦✦✦✦

Spirit Within / Sep. 21, 1981-Sep. 24, 1981 / Elektra ✦✦✦✦✦

Sprint / Nov. 3, 1982-Nov. 4, 1982 / Elektra ✦✦✦✦✦

● **Alive in New York** /May 8, 1980-Jul. 5, 1980/ Muse ✦✦✦✦✦

No Turn on Red / Aug. 10, 1986-Aug. 11, 1986 / Denon ✦✦✦✦

Red Giant / Apr. 1988 / Steeple Chase ✦✦✦

One for Bird / Jul. 1988 / Steeple Chase ✦✦✦

Red Snapper / Jul. 1988 / Steeple Chase ✦✦✦

Red Alert! / Oct. 1990-Nov. 1990 / Continuum ✦✦✦

Then and Now / May 13, 1992+May 15, 1992 / Chesky ✦✦✦✦

Shorty Rogers (Milton M. Rajonsky)

b. Apr. 14, 1924, Great Barrington, MA, **d.** Nov. 7, 1994, Van Nuys, CA
Trumpet, Arranger, Leader / Cool

A fine middle-register trumpeter whose style seemed to practically define "cool jazz," Shorty Rogers was actually more significant for his arranging, both in jazz and in the movie studios. After gaining early experience with Will Bradley and Red Norvo and serving in the military, Rogers rose to fame as a member of Woody Herman's First and Second Herds (1945-46 and 1947-49), and somehow managed to bring some swing to the Stan Kenton Innovations Orchestra (1950-51), clearly enjoying writing for the stratospheric flights of Maynard Ferguson. After that association ran its course, Rogers settled in Los Angeles where he led his Giants (which ranged from a quintet to a nonet and a big band) on a series of rewarding West Coast jazz-styled recordings and wrote for the studios, helping greatly to bring jazz into the movies; his scores for *The Wild One* and *The Man with the Golden Arm* are particularly memorable. After 1962, Rogers stuck almost exclusively to writing for television and films but in 1982 he began a comeback in jazz. Rogers reorganized and headed the Lighthouse All-Stars and, although his own playing was not quite as strong as previously, he remained a welcome presence both in clubs and recordings. —*Scott Yanow*

Jazz Origin: Shorty Rogers/Stan Kenton/June Christy / Feb. 5, 1950-Oct. 8, 1951 / Pausa ✦✦✦✦
This valuable out-of-print Pausa LP puts the focus on Shorty Rogers the arranger. Five of his best charts for Stan Kenton (dating from 1950-51) are here (including "Jolly Rogers", "Art Pepper" and "'Round Robin") as are three selections written for a June Christy recording session. This album concludes with the six numbers that Rogers recorded on his own debut as a leader. For the latter he utilized an octet, which (with its inclusion of a French horn and tuba) is reminiscent of Miles Davis' "Birth of the Cool" nonet. Altoist Art Pepper, tenorman Jimmy Giuffre and the leader on trumpet all have excellent solos on such tunes as "Popo," "Four Mothers" and Pepper's feature "Over The Rainbow." Fortunately most of this music has since been reissued on CD. —*Scott Yanow*

☆ **The Complete Atlantic and EMI Jazz Recordings** / Oct. 8, 1951-Mar. 30, 1956 / Mosaic ✦✦✦✦✦
This four-CD limited-edition box set from Mosaic (which was also made available as six LPs) features all of the recordings that trumpeter-arranger Shorty Rogers made for the Atlantic and EMI labels. Six titles from 1951 find Rogers leading an octet based on Miles Davis' "Birth of the Cool" nonet and featuring solos from altoist Art Pepper, the tenor of Jimmy Giuffre and pianist Hampton Hawes. Rogers also heads a quintet with altoist Bud Shank in 1954, a quintet with Giuffre (tripling on clarinet, tenor and baritone) in 1955 and some slightly larger groups (with such sidemen as the Candoli Brothers, trumpeter Harry "Sweets" Edison, altoists Herb Geller and Shank, pianists Lou Levy and Pete Jolly and drummer Shelly Manne among others. Although West Coast jazz has received a bad rap by East Coast writers through the years, Rogers shows that his recordings actually contained plenty of fire and swing, looking back towards the swing era and ahead simultaneously. Among the many highlights of this essential set are "Popo," "Lotus Bud," "Not Really the Blues," "Trickleydidlier," "Martians Go Home," "Martians Come Back," "March of the Martians" and "Martians Stay Home." —*Scott Yanow*

Popo and Art Pepper / Dec. 27, 1951 / Xanadu ✦✦✦✦
The recording quality is not the greatest on this 1980 LP but the very early session by the Lighthouse All-Stars is both historic and quite listenable. Trumpeter Shorty Rogers teams up with altoist Art Pepper, pianist Frank Patchen, bassist Howard Rumsey and drummer Shelly Manne for his own "Popo" (a blues that was Shorty's theme song) plus nine jazz standards including "Lullaby in Rhythm," "Robbins Nest," "Scrapple from the Apple" and "Cherokee." This is one of Pepper's best early showcases and it is for his playing that the album is most highly recommended. —*Scott Yanow*

Shorty Rogers and His Giants, Vol. 2 / Nov. 19, 1952-Sep. 14, 1954 / RCA ✦✦✦✦
Most but not all of the music on this French RCA LP has since been reissued on CD. Rarest are two somewhat humorous titles ("Blockbuster" and "Dynamite") that find trumpeter Shorty Rogers (under the pseudonym of "Boots Brown") playing simplistic rhythm and blues with an all-star West Coast group that also includes baritonist Gerry Mulligan and the honking tenor of Jimmy Giuffre among his personnel. Also on the album are three titles from Rogers' score for the Hollywood movie *The Wild One* and a pair of sessions from 1954 that find him leading slightly larger (nine and eleven pieces) versions than usual of his "Giants." An interesting, diverse and well-rounded album of swinging West Coast jazz. —*Scott Yanow*

Big Band, Vol. 1 / 1953 / Time Is ✦✦✦✦
Trumpeter Shorty Rogers is best-known for his arrangements and for leading a series of small combos in the 1950s under the titles of his "Giants." This privately

recorded CD is a bit unusual in that Rogers is heard at the head of a short-lived 15-piece jazz orchestra. Among the sidemen are the high-note trumpeter Maynard Ferguson, valve trombonist Bob Enevoldsen, altoist Herb Geller, Bill Perkins and Jack Montrose on tenors and pianist Lorraine Geller. Rogers contributed five originals to the 13-song program (including a long version of his theme "Popo") and all the arrangements. This is excellent music that is reasonably well-recorded and was previously unissued before this 1991 CD came out. —*Scott Yanow*

● **Short Stops** / Jan. 12, 1953-Mar. 3, 1954 / Bluebird ✦✦✦✦✦
This double LP offers listeners a strong introduction to the trumpet playing and arrangements of Shorty Rogers but unfortunately it has gone out of print and was the first and last in its series. The 32 selections feature six different groups headed by Rogers during 1953-54, ranging from an octet to a big band, and all of the bands feature sidemen who essentially formed the who's who of West Coast jazz. Among the other soloists are altoist Art Pepper, tenors Bill Holman, Bill Perkins, Zoot Sims, Bob Cooper and Jimmy Giuffre, trumpeter Harry "Sweets" Edison, pianist Hampton Hawes and altoists Herb Geller and Bud Shank among others. The majority of the selections are Rogers' originals; there is music from the Marlon Brando film *The Wild One* and a Count Basie tribute set. Swinging and surprisingly fiery "cool jazz" that deserves to be reissued on CD in full. —*Scott Yanow*

Shorty Rogers and His Giants, Vol. 3 / Mar. 25, 1953-Jul. 2, 1956 / RCA ✦✦✦✦
This LP splits its material between 1953 and 1956, featuring trumpeter Shorty Rogers heading a pair of overlapping big bands. All dozen selections are Rogers' originals; best known are "Coop De Graas" (featuring the French horn of John Graas), "Infinity Promenade" and "Sweetheart of Sigmund Freud." Joined by some of the top West Coast players of the era, Rogers is heard in top form, making one wish that all of this material had been reissued in chronological order on CD. —*Scott Yanow*

Collaboration / Mar. 30, 1954-Sep. 14, 1954 / RCA ✦✦✦
For this slightly unusual LP (which has not yet been reissued on CD), Shorty Rogers and Andre Previn split the arranging chores in a somewhat competitive fashion. Rogers arranges a standard, which is followed by a Previn original based on the same chord structure. This procedure is followed until the halfway point of the date when they reverse roles. As performed by a nonet featuring Rogers' trumpet, Previn's piano, altoist Bud Shank, Bob Cooper on tenor, baritonist Jimmy Giuffre, trombonist Milt Bernhart and a rhythm section, the result is a dead heat with some fine swinging solos on tunes (and variations) of such songs as "It's DeLovely," "You Stepped out of a Dream" and "You Do Something to Me." This will be a difficult album to locate. —*Scott Yanow*

Shorty Rogers Plays Richard Rogers / Jan. 30, 1957-Feb. 3, 1957 / Fresh Sound ✦✦✦✦

Portrait of Shorty / Jul. 15, 1957+Aug. 11, 1957 / RCA ✦✦✦

Gigi in Jazz / Jan. 27, 1958+Jan. 30, 1958 / RCA ✦✦✦

Swings / Dec. 9, 1958-Feb. 10, 1959 / Bluebird ✦✦✦✦
Although it is difficult to know it from the scanty and overly breezy liner notes, this CD reissues the Shorty Rogers record *Chance Are, It Swings* plus five of the 11 numbers from a set titled *The Wizard of Oz and Other Harold Arlen Songs;* all of *The Wizard of Oz* songs have been skipped over. Rogers, who provided the arrangements, heads several all-star big bands and such top players as trumpeters Conte Candoli and Don Fagerquist, trombonists Bob Enevoldsen and Frank Rosolino, altoist Bud Shank, tenors Bob Cooper, Bill Holman and Richie Kamuca and clarinetist Jimmy Giuffre all make strong contributions. Fine swinging music by the continually underrated Shorty Rogers. —*Scott Yanow*

The Wizard of Oz and Other Harold Arlen Songs / Feb. 3, 1959-Feb. 10, 1959 / RCA ✦✦✦✦
All of trumpeter/arranger Shorty Rogers' recordings from the 1950s (which were quite influential on both arrangers and cool-toned soloists) are well worth searching for. Unfortunately, many are out of print, including half of this excellent LP; the second side has been reissued on the Bluebird CD *Swings*. On the first side, Rogers and his orchestra (which includes such fine soloists as Jimmy Giuffre on clarinet and tenor, valve trombonist Bob Enevoldsen, altoists Bud Shank and Herb Geller, guitarist Barney Kessel and pianist Pete Jolly) perform five familiar songs from *Oz,* plus "The Jitterbug," which did not make it into the final cut. This date is rounded out by fresh versions of five of Arlen's most famous songs, including "Get Happy," "Blues in the Night" and "That Old Black Magic." Wonderful music. —*Scott Yanow*

The Fourth Dimension in Sound / Nov. 10, 1961 / Warner Brothers ✦✦✦
As was true of many records from the early 1960s, the emphasis on this out-of-print LP (especially in the lengthy liner notes) is on the stereophonic sound rather than the music. Rogers (sticking to fluegelhorn) leads a group that includes three reeds, trombonist Ken Shroyer, vibraphonist Emil Richards, pianist Pete Jolly, bassist Red Mitchell or Joe Mondragon on bass and drummer Shelly Manne. The

music is better than the liner notes (which spend most of their time describing the sound) lets on but is not all that significant, emphasizing swing standards along with an occasional Latin novelty. —*Scott Yanow*

The Shorty Rogers Quintet / 1962 / Studio West ✦✦✦
The first of four CDs taken from radio transcriptions used in the show "The Navy Swings" features trumpeter/fluegelhornist Shorty Rogers playing with two versions of his quintets in 1962, just prior to him greatly de-emphasizing his playing in favor of full-time writing for the studios. The 13 selections generally clock in around three minutes so the cool bop performances are quite concise. Jeri Southern has three warm vocals and Rogers shares the front line with either Harold Land or Gary Lefebvre on tenors. The results are not quite essential but will be enjoyed by Shorty's fans; highlights include "Paul's Pal," "Martian's Go Home," "Popo" and two versions of "What Is This Thing Called Love." —*Scott Yanow*

Return to Rio / Jun. 12, 1962-Jun. 14, 1962 / Discovery ✦✦
Fluegelhornist Shorty Rogers' next-to-last jazz date before becoming a full-time studio arranger for 20 years is quite forgettable. Rogers utilizes seven horns, a rhythm section and five percussionists in an attempt to cash in on the bossa nova fad. The 11 selections are generally quite concise (only one exceeds four minutes by more than a few seconds) and total up to less than 33 minutes. The emphasis is on ensembles with occasional statements from Rogers but surprisingly little happens. The overall results are pleasant but a bit of a disappointment. —*Scott Yanow*

Jazz Waltz / Dec. 1962 / Discovery ✦✦✦
This is a big band (28 different players at one time or another) of all-stars too numerous to mention. Songs are by Shorty and Duke Ellington, and there are four other standards. —*Michael G. Nastos*

Yesterday, Today and Forever / Jun. 1983 / Concord Jazz ✦✦✦✦✦
Other than an album cut for the Japanese Atlas album the previous month, this was trumpeter Shorty Rogers' first jazz record in 20 years; he had worked in the interim as a full time studio arranger. Rogers is in fairly good form on the quintet date although occasionally overshadowed by altoist Bud Shank (who doubles on flute). The rhythm section (pianist George Cables, bassist Bob Magnusson and drummer Roy McCurdy) is excellent, the repertoire (highlighted by "Budo," Tiny Kahn's "TNT," "Wagon Wheels" and Shorty's "Have You Hugged a Martian Today") is full of vehicles for swinging improvisations and the musicians sound fairly inspired. Recommended. —*Scott Yanow*

Back Again / Feb. 5, 1984+Aug. 5, 1984 / Choice ✦✦✦✦
Recorded early in Shorty Rogers' comeback after 20 years of writing exclusively for the studios, this Choice release (put out by Bainbridge) features fluegelhornist Shorty Rogers and altoist Bud Shank with Vic Lewis' 18-piece big band. Highlights of the somewhat obscure but swinging set include the four-part "Bud Shank" (composed by Shorty Rogers) and Bill Holman's "Shorty." An excellent outing for all concerned. —*Scott Yanow*

America the Beautiful / Aug. 4, 1991-Aug. 5, 1991 / Candid ✦✦✦✦✦
The 1991 version of the Lighthouse All-Stars gave trumpeter Shorty Rogers and altoist Bud Shank top billing. For this Candid CD, Rogers supplied eight of the selections (including "Less Is More," "Lotus Bud," "Fun" and "Here's That Old Martian Again") and the band also stretched out on Bud Powell's "Un Poco Loco" and a Rogers' arrangement of "America the Beautiful." This was one of the final records for both Shorty and the great tenor Bob Cooper and overall it is a typically swinging, witty and beautiful effort. Also in fine form are trumpeter Conte Candoli, Bill Perkins (on baritone, tenor and soprano), pianist Pete Jolly, bassist Monty Budwig and drummer Larence Marable. —*Scott Yanow*

Adrian Rollini

b. Jun. 28, 1904, New York, NY, **d.** May 15, 1956, Homestead, FL
Bass Saxophone, Vibes / Classic Jazz

Adrian Rollini was the greatest bass saxophonist of all time, one of the first jazz vibraphonists, and a talented multi-instrumentalist who could make music on such novelty instruments as the "hot fountain pen" (a miniature clarinet with a saxophone mouthpiece) and a "goofus." The older brother of tenor saxophonist Arthur Rollini, he played piano and xylophone as a youth, performing Chopin at the Waldorf Astoria when he was four. After joining the California Ramblers in 1922, Rollini ws encouraged to learn the potentially cumbersome bass sax; it only took him a week. An important member of the California Ramblers, Rollini made many records with the studio group and also with his "Goofus Five." A participant on Bix Beiderbecke and Frankie Trumbauer recordings in 1927, Rollini also cut sides with Red Nichols and Joe Venuti. He spent two years (from the latter part of 1927 through 1929) in London performing with Fred Elizalde. After his return to New York, Rollini worked in the studios, leading many record dates from 1933-40; in 1934, he opened his own club, Adrian's Tap Room, and began to emphasize his vibes playing. A decent but not outstanding vibraphonist, Rollini continued working with small groups in various hotels during the 1940s and into the '50s (recording a Mercury LP on vibes in the early '50s), settling finally in Florida. —*Scott Yanow*

Swing Low / Oct. 23, 1934-Jan. 7, 1938 / Affinity ✦✦✦✦

● **Adrian Rollini, His Quintet, His Trio** / Jan. 18, 1938-May 7, 1940 / Tax ✦✦✦✦✦

Sonny Rollins (Theodore Walter [Newk] Rollins)

b. Sep. 7, 1930, New York, NY

Tenor Saxophone, Composer / Bop, Hard Bop, Post-Bop

Sonny Rollins has for over 40 years been one of the true jazz giants, ranking up there with Coleman Hawkins, Lester Young and John Coltrane as one of the all time great tenor saxophonists. He started on piano, took up the alto and then permanently switched to tenor in 1946. After making his recording debut with Babs Gonzales in 1949, Rollins made a major impact on dates with J.J. Johnson and Bud Powell the same year; the latter session also matched him with Fats Navarro. Rollins' abilities were obvious to the jazz world from the start and he started recording with Miles Davis in 1951 and with Thelonious Monk two years later. After a period out of music, Rollins joined the Max Roach-Clifford Brown Quintet in late 1955, continuing after Brownie's death until 1957. From then on he was always a leader.

Sonny Rollins' series of brilliant recordings for Prestige, Blue Note, Contemporary and Riverside in the 1950s found him in peak form and he was acclaimed the top tenor saxophonist of the time, at least until John Coltrane rose to prominence. Therefore Rollins' decision to drop out of music from 1959-61 shocked the jazz world. When he came back in 1961 with a quartet featuring Jim Hall, his style was largely unchanged but he soon became a much freer player who was well aware of Ornette Coleman's innovations; he even used Ornette's cornetist Don Cherry for a time. Although his playing was a bit more eccentric than previously, Rollins was a major force until 1968, when he again decided to retire.

Upon his return in 1971, Sonny Rollins was more open to the influence of R&B rhythms and pop music and his recordings since then have not always been essential (often using sidemen not up to his level) but Rollins remains a very vital soloist. His skill at turning unlikely material into jazz, his unaccompanied flights and his rhythmic freedom and tonal distortions have kept Sonny Rollins one of the masters of jazz into the mid-'90s. He has literally dozens of superior recordings currently available. —*Scott Yanow*

☆ **The Complete Prestige Recordings** / May 26, 1949-Dec. 7, 1956 / Prestige ✦✦✦✦✦

This seven-CD box set lives up to its title, reissuing in chronological order all of tenor saxophonist Sonny Rollins' recordings for Prestige. Dating mostly from 1951-56, these valuable performances find Rollins developing from a promising player to a potential giant; many of his best recordings would take place a year or two after this program ends. In addition to his own sessions, Rollins is featured with trombonist J.J. Johnson, on four dates with Miles Davis and on sessions led by Thelonious Monk and trumpeter Art Farmer. Among the other musicians participating are trumpeters Kenny Dorham and Clifford Brown, pianists John Lewis, Kenny Drew, Horace Silver, Elmo Hope, Ray Bryant, Red Garland and Tommy Flanagan, drummers Max Roach, Roy Haynes, Art Blakey and Philly Joe Jones, the Modern Jazz Quartet, Julius Watkins on French horn, altoist Jackie McLean and even Charlie Parker. Among the many highlights are the original versions of Rollins' compositions "Airegin," "Oleo," "Doxy," "St. Thomas" and "Blue 7" and his one recorded meeting with John Coltrane ("Tenor Madness"). Essential music that is treated as it should be. The attractive booklet is a major plus too. —*Scott Yanow*

Sonny Rollins with the Modern Jazz Quartet / Jan. 17, 1951-Oct. 7, 1953 / Prestige ✦✦✦✦

This CD reissue has tenor saxophonist Sonny Rollins' first recording sessions as a leader. The initial selection, "I Know," was recorded at the tail end of a Miles Davis date and it finds Davis switching to piano to back Rollins' solo on the "Confirmation" chord changes. Eight selections showcase Rollins with the rhythm section of pianist Kenny Drew, bassist Percy Heath and drummer Art Blakey, mixing together standards and originals and also somehow making worthwhile music out of "Shadrack." The Modern Jazz Quartet (vibraphonist Milt Jackson, pianist John Lewis, bassist Percy Heath and drummer Kenny Clarke) is actually only on four numbers (despite the release's title) including "Almost like Being in Love" and Rollins' original "No Moe." The program overall shows that, even in his formative stage, Rollins was near the top of his field. —*Scott Yanow*

Moving Out / Aug. 18, 1954-Oct. 25, 1954 / Original Jazz Classics ✦✦✦✦

Work Time / Dec. 2, 1955 / Original Jazz Classics ✦✦✦✦

For this LP-length CD reissue, tenor great Sonny Rollins plays five songs (including the unlikely "There's No Business like Show Business") in a quartet with pianist Ray Bryant, bassist George Morrow and his then-current employer drummer

Max Roach. Rollins was an original stylist from the start and in late 1955 he was ready to take his place among the greats. The enjoyable outing (which is included in Rollins' huge Prestige box set) may not be essential but it is a strong effort. —*Scott Yanow*

Sonny Rollins Plus Four / Mar. 22, 1956 / Original Jazz Classics ✦✦✦✦✦

In 1956 Sonny Rollins used the Clifford Brown-Max Roach Quintet (of which he was a member) as his sidemen for this Prestige set. The high points of this particularly strong hard bop set include "Valse Hot" (an early jazz waltz), a rapid rendition of "I Feel a Song Coming On" and Rollins' classic "Pent-Up House." Trumpeter Brown (heard on one of his final sessions) is in excellent form as is the strong rhythm section and the young tenor-leader himself. This excellent music is also included as part of Rollins' seven-CD box set for Prestige. —*Scott Yanow*

Tenor Madness / May 24, 1956 / Original Jazz Classics ✦✦✦✦✦

This CD (whose contents have since been reissued many times) is highlighted by the one meeting on records between Sonny Rollins and John Coltrane, an exciting battle on "Tenor Madness." Otherwise this is a more conventional but no less worthy Rollins quartet session with him turning such odd material as "My Reverie" and "The Most Beautiful Girl in the World" into creative jazz. —*Scott Yanow*

Plays for Bird / Oct. 5, 1956 / Original Jazz Classics ✦✦✦

Sonny Rollins, heard in his early prime, performs "I've Grown Accustomed to Your Face," "Kids Know" and a seven-song "Bird Medley" on this CD reissue of a Prestige LP. Actually Rollins is only on four of the tunes in the medley and not all of the songs have a close connection with Charlie Parker. Featured in a quintet with trumpeter Kenny Dorham, pianist Wade Legge, bassist George Morrow and drummer Max Roach, Rollins is in fine form although the hard bop music falls slightly short of being essential. —*Scott Yanow*

Sonny Boy / Oct. 5, 1956 / Original Jazz Classics ✦✦✦

The music on this former LP was the last of tenor saxophonist Sonny Rollins' Prestige dates to appear on CD. Actually the release is a bit odd because it reissues four of the six numbers from the previously released CD *Tour de Force* (OJC 095), replacing "My Ideal" and "Two Different Worlds" (the latter an Earl Coleman vocal) with "The House I Live In" from an earlier session that resulted in the *Plays for Bird* album; usually the Original Jazz Classics series avoids such duplication. *Tour de Force* is a more logical purchase although the music on this CD does feature the immortal tenor saxophonist in fine form with a quartet comprising pianist Kenny Drew, bassist George Morrow and drummer Max Roach (other than the earlier selection that also has trumpeter Kenny Dorham). A bit of a discographical mess. —*Scott Yanow*

Tour de Force / Dec. 7, 1956 / Original Jazz Classics ✦✦✦✦

A better purchase than *Sonny Boy* (OJC 348), which has four of this set's six numbers plus "The House I Live In" from an earlier date. None of the Sonny Rollins' originals (which include "B. Swift," "B. Quick" and "Ee-Ah") on this release caught on. With pianist Kenny Drew, bassist George Morrow and drummer Max Roach completing the quartet, Rollins is in consistently creative form during this prime period but the overall set is not as classic as most of the tenor's other recordings from the 1950s. —*Scott Yanow*

Sonny Rollins, Vol. 1 / Dec. 16, 1956 / Blue Note ✦✦✦✦

Compared to Sonny Rollins' other classics of this era, this Blue Note LP usually gets lost in the shuffle but the music is actually quite good. The trumpeter is teamed with trumpeter Donald Byrd, pianist Wynton Kelly, bassist Gene Ramey and drummer Max Roach for four of his originals (none of which caught on) and an interesting transformation of "How Are Things in Glocca Morra?" —*Scott Yanow*

The Complete Blue Note Recordings / Dec. 16, 1956-Nov. 3, 1957 / Blue Note ✦✦✦✦✦

The Complete Blue Note Records is a five-disc box set that contains everything Sonny Rollins recorded for the label between 1956 and 1957. Each disc has been previously released individually—this set simply collects *Sonny Rollins, Vols. 1 & 2, Newk's Time* and *A Night at the Village Vanguard, Vols. 1 & 2* in one slipcase, with no new remastering. For anyone intending to replace their Rollins Blue Note collection, or wishing to acquire all of this music at the same time, this set is essential, but anyone that already owns the individual discs needn't bother with this set. —*Stephen Thomas Erlewine*

★ **Way out West** / Mar. 7, 1957 / Original Jazz Classics ✦✦✦✦✦

This timeless recording established Sonny Rollins as jazz's top tenor saxophonist (at least until John Coltrane surpassed him the following year). Joined by bassist Ray Brown and drummer Shelly Manne, Rollins is heard at one of his peaks on such pieces as "I'm an Old Cowhand," his own "Way out West," "There Is No Greater Love" and "Come, Gone" (a fast stomp based on "After You've Gone"). The William Claxton photo of Rollins wearing Western gear (and holding his tenor) in the desert is also a classic. —*Scott Yanow*

Alternate Takes / Mar. 7, 1957-Oct. 22, 1958 / Contemporary ✦✦✦✦✦
This LP contains alternate versions of selections from two famous Sonny Rollins albums: *Way out West* and *Sonny Rollins and the Contemporary Leaders*. These "new" renditions of "I'm an Old Cowhand," "Come, Gone," "Way out West" "The Song Is You," "You" and "I've Found a New Baby" (released for the first time in mid-'80s) hold their own against the classic versions. Rollins is heard with bassist Ray Brown and drummer Shelly Manne on the first session and is joined by a four-piece rhythm section (including pianist Hampton Hawes and guitarist Barney Kessel) on the later date. In any case, the music is often hard-swinging and is frequently superb. —*Scott Yanow*

Sonny Rollins, Vol. 2 / Apr. 14, 1957 / Blue Note ✦✦✦
Compared to his Prestige, Riverside and Contemporary recordings of the 1950s, some of Rollins' appearances on Blue Note seemed anticlimactic but none should be overlooked. This unusual LP mostly has Rollins in an all-star quintet with trombonist J.J. Johnson, pianist Horace Silver, bassist Paul Chambers and drummer Art Blakey, but Thelonious Monk sits in on his ballad "Reflections," and on "Misterioso" both Silver and Monk get to take contrasting solos. Of the other selections, Rollins' two originals ("Why Don't I" and "Wail March") are worth reviving and he finds something new to say on "Poor Butterfly" and an uptempo "You Stepped out of a Dream." —*Scott Yanow*

The Sound of Sonny / Jun. 11, 1957-Jun. 19, 1957 / Original Jazz Classics ✦✦✦✦✦
Tenor saxophonist Sonny Rollins, who was in one of his prime periods at the time, takes "It Could Happen to You" as an unaccompanied solo, performs six numbers (including the rather unlikely "Toot, Toot, Tootsie" and an intense "Just in Time") with pianist Sonny Clark, bassist Percy Heath and drummer Roy Haynes, and improvises the "Funky Hotel Blues" (which made its debut on a sampler) with Clark, Haynes and bassist Paul Chambers. This is an excellent if not quite essential release from the masterful tenorman. —*Scott Yanow*

Newk's Time / Sep. 22, 1957 / Blue Note ✦✦✦✦
This fairly conventional but frequently exciting quartet session finds Sonny Rollins in top form on material ranging from "Tune Up" and "The Surrey with the Fringe on Top" to his own "Blues for Philly Joe." With pianist Wynton Kelly, bassist Doug Watkins and drummer Philly Joe Jones, Rollins shows on the CD that even his less-acclaimed sessions from this era are brilliant. —*Scott Yanow*

☆ **A Night at the Village Vanguard** / Nov. 3, 1957 / Blue Note ✦✦✦✦✦
This CD is often magical. Sonny Rollins, one of jazz's great tenors, is heard at his peak with a pair of pianoless trios (either Wilbur Ware or Donald Bailey on bass and Elvin Jones or Pete La Roca on drums) stretching out on particularly creative versions of "Old Devil Moon," "Softly as in a Morning Sunrise," "Sonnymoon for Two" and "A Night in Tunisia" among others. Not only did Rollins have a very distinctive sound but his use of time, his sly wit and his boppish but unpredictable style were completely his own by 1957. —*Scott Yanow*

☆ **A Night at the Village Vanguard, Vol. 1** / Nov. 3, 1957 / Blue Note ✦✦✦✦✦
One of two incendiary live dates from Vanguard in the late '50s. The pianoless trio steps forth and claims its fame. —*Ron Wynn*

☆ **A Night at the Village Vanguard, Vol. 2** / Nov. 3, 1957 / Blue Note ✦✦✦✦✦
An excellent follow to a legendary album. —*Ron Wynn*

More from the Vanguard / Nov. 3, 1957 / Blue Note ✦✦✦✦✦
This double LP added ten more performances to Sonny Rollins' famous night at the Village Vanguard, and the music is at the same level as the original set. With bassist Wilbur Ware and drummer Elvin Jones (on one song bassist Donald Bailey and drummer Pete La Roca take their place), Rollins was inspired to come up with some of his best extended improvisations, sticking to standards but making fresh and unpredictable statements. —*Scott Yanow*

Sonny Rollins [Everest] / Nov. 4, 1957 / Everest ✦✦✦
The material included on this budget LP has been bouncing around for years, turning up on many records. The great tenor Sonny Rollins is heard in a quintet with trombonist Jimmy Cleveland in 1957 performing his "Sonnymoon for Two," the ballad "Like Someone in Love" and strangely enough the "Theme from Tchaikovsky's Symphony Pathetique." In addition cornetist Thad Jones performs two of his originals ("Lust for Life" and "I Got It Thad") and a ballad medley with a variety of modern swing players, many from Count Basie's Orchestra. Nowhere on this set does it mention that Rollins is absent on half of the selections and that he never does play with Thad Jones (who is simply listed as "Guest Artist"). The music is better than the crummy packaging. —*Scott Yanow*

Freedom Suite / Feb. 11, 1958+Mar. 7, 1958 / Original Jazz Classics ✦✦✦✦
Tenor saxophonist Sonny Rollins' last Riverside album has been reissued on this Original Jazz Classics CD. Jamming in a pianoless trio with bassist Oscar Pettiford and drummer Max Roach, Rollins is very creative, stretching out on his lengthy "Freedom Suite," clearly enjoying investigating the obscure Noel Coward melody "Someday I'll Find You," turning the showtune "Till There Was You" into jazz and

finding beauty in "Shadow Waltz" and "Will You Still Be Mine." A near-masterpiece. —*Scott Yanow*

Brass & Trio / Jul. 10, 1958 / Verve ✦✦✦✦✦
In 1958 Sonny Rollins split an LP between two very different settings. On four selections he is backed by a big band arranged by Ernie Wilkins (Rollins' appearances with big bands have been quite rare through the years) including Gershwin's "Who Cares?" The flip side showcases the great tenor in a trio with bassist Henry Grimes and drummer Charles Wright including "Manhattan," one of the very few jazz versions of "If You Were the Only Girl in the World" and a brilliant unaccompanied performance of a song often associated with his idol Coleman Hawkins, "Body and Soul." Rollins excels in both of these settings, making this an easily recommended set. —*Scott Yanow*

Sonny Rollins and the Contemporary Leaders / Oct. 20, 1958-Oct. 22, 1958 / Original Jazz Classics ✦✦✦✦✦
The last of the classic Sonny Rollins albums prior to his unexpected three-year retirement features the great tenor with pianist Hampton Hawes, guitarist Barney Kessell bassist Leroy Vinnegar and drummer Shelly Manne (all bandleaders for Contemporary Records during this era) on an unusual but inspired list of standards. Rollins creates explorative and often witty improvisations on such songs as "Rock-A-Bye Your Baby with a Dixie Melody," "You," "In the Chapel in the Moonlight" and roaring versions of "I've Found a New Baby" and "The Song Is You." Great music. —*Scott Yanow*

In Stockholm (1959) / Mar. 4, 1959 / Dragon ✦✦✦✦
This radio broadcast is taken from one of Sonny Rollins' final concerts before going into an unexpected three-year retirement. Joined by bassist Henry Grimes and drummer Pete La Roca, Rollins explores seven songs that he had previously recorded including "St. Thomas," "There Will Never Be Another You," "Oleo" and "Paul's Pal." The music is quite enjoyable and sometimes fairly adventurous, making one very sorry that Rollins decided to drop out of music altogether during some key years. —*Scott Yanow*

Aix-En-Provence / Mar. 11, 1959 / Royal Jazz ✦✦✦
This broadcast from a French concert was Sonny Rollins' last recording before his surprising retirement; he would not resurface until late 1961. Along with John Coltrane, Rollins was the most important tenor saxophonist of the period; during the trio set on this CD with bassist Henry Grimes and drummer Kenny Clarke, Rollins really stretches out on "Woody 'n You," "But Not for Me" and "Lady Bird"; the individual selections range in time from 15:50 to 18:35. Although not as essential as his studio recordings of the period, this decently recorded concert performance will be savored by Sonny Rollins collectors. —*Scott Yanow*

● **The Bridge** / Jan. 30, 1962-Feb. 14, 1962 / Bluebird ✦✦✦✦✦
The music on this 1996 CD has been reissued many times including in the Bluebird series. Tenor saxophonist Sonny Rollins' first recording after ending a surprising three-year retirement found the great saxophonist sounding very similar to how he had played in 1959 although he would soon start investigating freer forms. In a pianoless quartet with guitarist Jim Hall, bassist Bob Cranshaw and drummer Ben Riley, Rollins explores four standards (including "Without a Song" and "God Bless the Child") plus two fiery originals (highlighted by the title cut). The interplay between Rollins and Hall is consistently impressive, making this CD a near-classic and a very successful comeback. —*Scott Yanow*

Alternatives / May 14, 1962-Apr. 14, 1964 / Bluebird ✦✦✦✦✦
Sonny Rollins' RCA recordings of 1962-64 found him really stretching out his style, listening to and learning from Ornette Coleman without losing his own musical personality. This CD, in addition to two numbers with bassist Bob Cranshaw and the congos of Candido ("Jungoso" and "Bluesongo") that were originally on the album *What's New*, has four selections from *Now's the Time* along with four very different alternate takes. For example, the original version of "52nd Street Theme" was four minutes long but the alternate is 14. The personnel also differs much of the time with cornetist Thad Jones and pianist Herbie Hancock making appearances, but the emphasis is on the exciting improvisations of Rollins, one of the great tenorsaxophonists of all time. —*Scott Yanow*

The Complete RCA Victor Recordings / Jan. 30, 1962-Jul. 9, 1964 / RCA ✦✦✦✦✦
This six-CD set has all of tenor saxophonist Sonny Rollins' recordings for RCA, including the complete contents of *The Bridge, What's New, Our Man in Jazz, Sonny Meets Hawk, Now's the Time* and *The Standard Sonny Rollins*, the three selections originally included in the sampler *3 for Jazz*, and 11 alternate takes only previously released on the French album *The Alternative Rollins*. Less known than Rollins' earlier Prestige and Riverside records and slightly later Impulse albums, his output for RCA was recorded right after the great tenor came back from an extended sabbatical. The music on *The Bridge* (which co-stars guitarist Jim Hall) is the most famous of these dates. Rollins became increasingly interested in the avant-garde during the era, and he used two of Ornette Coleman's sidemen

(trumpeter Don Cherry and drummer Billy Higgins) in his group for a period. On *Sonny Meets Hawk*, Rollins challenged his idol Coleman Hawkins by playing as outside as possible (Hawkins responded well). Other musicians heard on the recordings include bassists Bob Cranshaw, Ron Carter and Henry Grimes, drummers Ben Riley and Mickey Roker, pianists Paul Bley and Herbie Hancock and (on a couple of numbers) cornetist Thad Jones. However, Rollins is the main star throughout the adventurous and sometimes eccentric performances, coming up with many remarkable ideas, often rollicking with a pianoless rhythm section and in two cases taking duets with the congas of Candido. Serious Sonny Rollins collectors will have to have this valuable set, although since most of the selections have also been reissued on individual CDs, more casual jazz fans may be satisfied with one or two of the smaller reissues. —*Scott Yanow*

On the Outside / Jul. 27, 1962-Feb. 20, 1963 / Bluebird ✦✦✦✦✦
A very interesting CD of material from Sonny Rollins. It reissues the complete *Our Man in Jazz* (three lengthy performances including a 25-minute version of "Oleo") along with three briefer selections previously on a sampler. These are among Rollins' most avant-garde improvisations; he seems inspired by trumpeter Don Cherry's presence (although Cherry clearly could not keep up with the great tenor). Rollins really digs into "Oleo" and the 15-minute "Doxy" and plays some remarkable music. —*Scott Yanow*

All the Things You Are / Jul. 15, 1963-Jul. 2, 1964 / Bluebird ✦✦✦✦
Half of this CD contains the famous session on which Sonny Rollins teamed up with his idol, the great tenor Coleman Hawkins. Actually the competitive Rollins did everything he could during these performances to throw Hawk off with plenty of sound explorations and free playing but Hawkins keeps from getting lost and battles Rollins to a tie; pianist Paul Bley plays well, too. The remainder of this CD (three selections apiece from the former LPs *Now's the Time* and *The Standard Sonny Rollins*) is more conventional but has its moments of interest. The young Herbie Hancock is on piano for all of these tracks and guitarist Jim Hall helps on "Trav'lin Light." Rollins' RCA recordings of the 1960s are all worth picking up even though they are currently being reissued in piecemeal fashion. —*Scott Yanow*

Stuttgart (1963) / Nov. 1963 / Jazz Anthology ✦✦✦
Sonny Rollins and his 1963 quartet (with trumpeter Don Cherry, bassist Henry Grimes and drummer Billy Higgins) play very long versions of "Green Dolphin Street" (18 minutes) and "Sonnymoon for Two" (over 22 minutes) with some of the improvising being very free. The solos generally hold one's interest (Rollins' always do) but the so-so recording quality and some aimless sections lower this LP's rating a little. It's still worth picking up. —*Scott Yanow*

Sonny Rollins & Co. 1964 / Jan. 24, 1964-Jul. 9, 1964 / Bluebird ✦✦✦✦
This CD from the Bluebird reissue series fills a lot of gaps in Sonny Rollins' discography. The 13 selections are taken from six different sessions from 1964. The personnel changes from date to date with either Ron Carter or Bob Cranshaw on bass and Roy McCurdy or Mickey Roker on drums along with pianist Herbie Hancock (on five songs) and guitarist Jim Hall on three others. Some of the music is actually alternate takes and, in contrast to a rambling 16-minute version of "Now's the Time," a few of the briefer songs (seven are under 31 minutes) shut down prematurely. However, the great tenor's improvisations are consistently fascinating as he reconciles his avant-garde flights to the standards he is performing; "Autumn Nocturne" is a high point. —*Scott Yanow*

There Will Never Be Another You / Jun. 17, 1965 / Impulse! ✦✦
This LP features Sonny Rollins and a quintet (pianist Tommy Flanagan, bassist Bob Cranshaw and both Billy Higgins and Mickey Roker on drums) playing an outdoor concert in the rain. Rollins was in a strolling mood and he wanders all over the stage, which means that he is off-mike much of the time. His playing on these five standards (which includes a 16-minute version of the title tune) is fine but the erratic recording quality makes this one of the lesser Rollins albums. —*Scott Yanow*

Sonny Rollins on Impulse! / Jul. 8, 1965 / Impulse! ✦✦✦✦
The first of three studio albums that tenor saxophonist Sonny Rollins recorded for Impulse contains the joyous calypso "Hold 'Em Joe" and four unusual versions of standards in which the rhythms he plays are more important than the actual melodies. Joined by pianist Ray Bryant, bassist Walter Booker and drummer Mickey Roker, Rollins sounds quite distinctive on this brief but enjoyable set. This enjoyable outing (which has among its highlights eccentric versions of "Blue Room" and "Three Little Words") was reissued on CD in 1997. —*Scott Yanow*

Alfie / Jan. 26, 1966 / Impulse! ✦✦✦✦✦
Sonny Rollins compositions for the film *Alfie* (which benefited greatly from Oliver Nelson's arrangements) are heard on this CD as played by Rollins and a ten-piece band. The music easily stands by itself without the movie and Rollins is in fine form on these generally memorable themes, particularly "On Impulse" and "Alfie's

Theme." This superlative effort was most recently reissued on an Impulse CD in 1997. —*Scott Yanow*

☆ **East Broadway Rundown** / May 9, 1966 / Impulse! ✦✦✦✦✦
Sonny Rollins' last recording before taking another long retirement (this time six years) is a real gem, one of his top albums of the 1960s. This CD includes the 20-minute title cut (which has some rather free moments but always remains quite coherent), the tenor's memorable original "Blessing in Disguise" and his glorious ballad statement on "We Kiss in a Shadow." Trumpeter Freddie Hubbard helps out on "East Broadway Run Down," but otherwise this excellent set showcases Rollins in a trio with bassist Jimmy Garrison and drummer Elvin Jones. —*Scott Yanow*

Next Album / Jul. 1972 / Original Jazz Classics ✦✦✦✦✦
Sonny Rollins first album after ending his six-year retirement is a particularly strong effort. The high point is a ten-minute version of "Skylark" that has a long unaccompanied section by the great tenor. Other memorable selections include "The Everywhere Calypso" and "Playing in the Yard." Rollins plays soprano on "Poinciana" and is heard using electronics (George Cables' electric piano) for the first time but this music is not all that different from what he was playing prior to his retirement. —*Scott Yanow*

Horn Culture / Jun. 1973-Jul. 1973 / Original Jazz Classics ✦✦✦
This decent effort from Sonny Rollins finds the classic tenorsaxophonist at his best on "Good Morning Heartache" and "God Bless the Child" although some of his own originals seem a touch lightweight. His backup band (which includes keyboardist Walter Davis, Jr., and guitarist Masuo) is supportive but somewhat anonymous. Nothing too essential occurs but the music is generally enjoyable. —*Scott Yanow*

The Cutting Edge / Jul. 6, 1974 / Original Jazz Classics ✦✦✦✦
Sonny Rollins' 1974 appearance at the Montreux Jazz Festival was warmly received. Joined by his usual band of the period (pianist Stanley Cowell, guitarist Masuo, electric bassist Bob Cranshaw, drummer David Lee and percussionist Mtume), Rollins manages to turn such unlikely material as "To a Wild Rose" and "A House Is Not a Home" into jazz. The world's only jazz bagpipe player (Rufus Harley) makes his presence felt on "Swing Low, Sweet Chariot." —*Scott Yanow*

Nucleus / Sep. 2, 1975-Sep. 5, 1975 / Original Jazz Classics ✦✦✦
It has long been a disappointment to many longtime followers that Rollins' recordings of the 1970s and '80s were generally not at the same level as his earlier sessions. *Nucleus* is a case in point. This funky date (which also includes trombonist Raul DeSouza, Bennie Maupin on reeds and keyboardist George Duke) has its moments (including an updated version of "My Reverie") but falls far short of hinting at any new innovations —*Scott Yanow*

The Way I Feel / Aug. 1976-Oct. 1976 / Original Jazz Classics ✦✦
One of Sonny Rollins' lesser sets of the 1970s, this CD reissue matches his tenor (which often sounds as dirty as an R&B stylist) with the dated electric keyboards of Patrice Rushen, guitarist Lee Ritenour, either Alex Blake or Charles Meeks on bass, drummer Billy Cobham and percussionist Bill Summers. There are some moments of interest (mostly due to Rollins' sound and his melodic playing) but none of the seven "contemporary" songs managed to catch on. —*Scott Yanow*

Easy Living / Aug. 3, 1977-Aug. 6, 1977 / Original Jazz Classics ✦✦✦✦
One of Sonny Rollins' better recordings of the 1970s, this spirited Milestone set (reissued on CD in the Original Jazz Classics series) finds the veteran tenor adopting a thicker and raunchier R&Bish tone. Although sticking close to the melody, he really tears into Stevie Wonder's "Isn't She Lovely" and finds interesting new variations to play on "My One and Only Love" (on soprano) and "Easy Living." The fine backup group includes keyboardist George Duke and drummer Tony Williams. —*Scott Yanow*

Don't Stop the Carnival / Apr. 13, 1978-Apr. 15, 1978 / Milestone ✦✦✦
This set (recorded live over a three-day period at the Great American Music Hall in San Francisco in 1978) finds the great tenor Sonny Rollins welcoming trumpeter Donald Byrd to half of the selections; Byrd was beginning his comeback but sounds rusty and is only in so-so form. The four-piece rhythm section includes drummer Tony Williams and these versions of "Don't Stop the Carnival" and "Autumn Nocturne" are memorable but most of the rest of the set, although spirited, is a bit lightweight; when was the last time anyone performed "Camel," "President Hayes" or "Sais"? —*Scott Yanow*

Silver City: A Celebration of 25 Years on Milestone / Jul. 1972-Oct. 7, 1995 / Milestone ✦✦✦✦
Sonny Rollins' Milestone period, which resulted in 20 separate recordings from 1972-96, has been much maligned by dissatisfied jazz critics who feel the great tenor's later output has not been on the same level as his earlier work. Although there have been a few inconsistent sets during the time, the best of Rollins' records from those years ranks with his finest of all time. This two-CD set has 19 selections taken from 13 of the albums, mixing together diverse originals with classic

versions of "Autumn Nocturne," "Duke of Iron," "Cabin in the Sky," "Tennessee Waltz," and a rendition of "Skylark" that has a long melodic cadenza by Rollins. A fine sampler of Rollins' later years with superior liner notes by Chip Stern, although collectors will want to get many of these complete sets (virtually all of which are currently available on CD). —*Scott Yanow*

Milestone Jazzstars in Concert / Sep. 1978-Oct. 1978 / Milestone ✦✦✦✦
In 1978 a tour was set up that would feature three of the top jazz stars of Milestone Records (tenor saxophonist Sonny Rollins, pianist McCoy Tyner and bassist Ron Carter) in a quartet with drummer Al Foster. The resulting recording has many strong moments including Rollins' unaccompanied solo on "Continuum," his duet with Tyner on "In a Sentimental Mood," Tyner's showcases on "A Little Pianissimo" and "Alone Together" (the latter a duet with Carter) and the bassist's lengthy reworking of "Willow Weep for Me." The quartet pieces generally work well too, with these compatible but very individual stylists blending together much better than one might expect. —*Scott Yanow*

Don't Ask / May 15, 1979-May 18, 1979 / Original Jazz Classics ✦✦✦
The main reasons to acquire this release are for the Sonny Rollins-Larry Coryell duets on "The File" and particularly "My Ideal." Less worthwhile is a song given the hideous title of "Disco Monk" and Rollins' attempt to forge a personality on the lyricon on "Tai Chi." A bit erratic, this LP is still worth acquiring for its stronger moments. —*Scott Yanow*

Love at First Sight / May 9, 1980-May 12, 1980 / Original Jazz Classics ✦✦✦
Sonny Rollins has an all-star backup band on this 1980 release: keyboardist George Duke, bassist Stanley Clarke, drummer Al Foster and on some selections percussionist Bill Summers. The music ranges from "The Very Thought of You" and a remake of "Strode Rode" to some more lightweight group originals. Decent music but nothing that memorable occurs. —*Scott Yanow*

No Problem / Dec. 9, 1981-Dec. 15, 1981 / Milestone ✦✦✦
An average effort from the great tenor saxophonist Sonny Rollins, *No Problem* also features guitarist Bobby Broom, vibraphonist Bobby Hutcherson, electric bassist Bob Cranshaw and drummer Tony Williams. Rollins is in generally fine form but none of the compositions are all that inspiring and for these fine players this session sounds too safe and routine. —*Scott Yanow*

Reel Life / Aug. 17, 1982-Aug. 22, 1982 / Milestone ✦✦
As is often the case on Sonny Rollins' recordings of the '80s, he sounds best on a ballad (in this case Billy Strayhorn's "My Little Brown Book") yet often coasts on his own originals. The backup band (guitarists Bobby Broom and Yoshiaki Masuo, electric bassist Bob Cranshaw and drummer Jack DeJohnette) does little to uplift this decent but somewhat forgettable effort. —*Scott Yanow*

Sunny Days, Starry Nights / Jan. 23, 1984-Jan. 27, 1984 / Milestone ✦✦✦
By 1984 it was a common complaint that Sonny Rollins' live appearances were much more exciting than his studio recordings. Although none of the latter were throwaways (and virtually all of the Milestone sessions have their moments of interest), few were real gems. *Sunny Days, Starry Nights* as usual finds the great tenor at his best on the two ballads ("I'm Old Fashioned" and Noel Coward's "I'll See You Again") while the other four originals have been largely forgotten. His backup crew features tromonist Clifton Anderson and keyboardist Mark Soskin. —*Scott Yanow*

The Solo Album / Jul. 19, 1985 / Milestone ✦
One of the few complete duds of Sonny Rollins' career, this rambling live session is a major disappointment. His unaccompanied explorations (which in the past usually clocked in at around three minutes) gave one the impression that he would be heard best in a solo setting where he could fly freely without having to be concerned about his accompanists. Perhaps that is true, but for this concert he apparently planned nothing in advance, resulting in 56 minutes of wandering around, throwing in occasional song quotes but managing to not play anything of real value. In other words, it sounds as if Rollins were merely warming up, playing whatever came into his mind without any thought of developing a coherent statement. —*Scott Yanow*

G-Man / Aug. 16, 1986 / Milestone ✦✦✦✦
The soundtrack to the performance film *Saxophone Colossus* features long Sonny Rollins tenor solos on "G-Man" and "Don't Stop the Carnival" and a briefer one during "Kim." Joined by his usual quintet of the era (trombonist Clifton Anderson, pianist Mark Soskin, electric bassist Bob Cranshaw and drummer Marvin "Smitty" Smith), Rollins is in good form, saying little that is new but delivering passionate messages with his typical spirit; the video is worth getting too. —*Scott Yanow*

Dancing in the Dark / Sep. 15, 1987-Sep. 25, 1987 / Milestone ✦✦✦
The better-than-usual repertoire (including the calypso "Duke or Iron," "Dancing in the Dark" and the Warren & Dubin number "I'll String Along with You") makes this outing by Sonny Rollins' usual band (with trombonist Clifton Anderson, keyboardist Mark Soskin, electric bassist Jerome Harris and drummer Marvin

"Smitty" Smith) one of the more interesting Rollins albums of recent times. Although not up to the level of his best live performances, this studio album is quite enjoyable and gives one a clear idea as to how Sonny Rollins sounded in the 1980s. —*Scott Yanow*

Falling in Love with Jazz / Jun. 3, 1989-Sep. 9, 1989 / Milestone ✦✦✦
This average effort from Sonny Rollins and his regular sextet is most notable for two numbers ("For All We Know" and "I Should Care") that find Branford Marsalis joining Rollins in a quintet with pianist Tommy Flanagan. Unfortunately Marsalis makes the fatal error of trying to imitate Rollins (instead of playing in his own musical personality) and he gets slaughtered. Much better are Rollins' romps on "Tennessee Waltz" and "Falling in Love with Love." —*Scott Yanow*

Here's to the People / Aug. 10, 1991-Aug. 27, 1991 / Milestone ✦✦✦
Sonny Rollins' usual sextet (with trombonist Clifton Anderson, pianist Mark Soskin, guitarist Jerome Harris, electric bassist Bob Cranshaw and drummer Steve Jordan) welcomes guest drummers Jack DeJohnette and Al Foster and, most importantly, trumpeter Roy Hargrove on two selections. Hargrove sounds fine on "I Wish I Knew" and "Young Roy" while Rollins is in good form on such songs as "Why Was I Born," "Someone to Watch over Me" and "Long Ago and Far Away." Nothing very innovative occurs but the music is quite pleasing. —*Scott Yanow*

Old Flames / 1993 / Milestone ✦✦✦✦
Sonny Rollins mostly sticks to standard ballads on this excellent CD, which finds him joined by trombonist Clifton Anderson, pianist Tommy Flanagan, bassist Bob Cranshaw, drummer Jack DeJohnette and, on two selections, a five-piece brass choir arranged by Jimmy Heath. Comfortable and occasionally passionate music by one of the classic tenor saxophonists. —*Scott Yanow*

Sonny Rollins Plus Three / 1996 / Milestone ✦✦✦✦✦
Ever since Sonny Rollins signed with Milestone in the mid-1970s, critics who prefer his earlier work have complained that Rollins' sidemen are not worthy of him. For this superb effort, detractors have nothing to complain about, because the immortal tenor is joined by either Tommy Flanagan or Stephen Scott on piano, his longtime electric bassist Bob Cranshaw and either Al Foster or Jack DeJohnette on drums. Rollins is in wonderful form, stretching out on two basic originals and five standards including "What a Difference a Day Made," "Cabin in the Sky" and "I've Never Been in Love Before." Building his rhythmic improvisations off of the songs' strong melodies (returning to the themes often), Rollins sounds quite exuberant. This studio set captures the excitement of a Sonny Rollins concert and is highly recommended. —*Scott Yanow*

Wallace Roney

b. May 25, 1960, Philadelphia, PA
Trumpet / Post-Bop, Hard Bop
Listening to Wallace Roney can be a frustrating experience because, despite his obvious technical skills, virtually all of his solos sound like an imitation of Miles Davis circa 1965-70. It is not that he is copying phrases so much as his sound, phrasing and approach are nearly identical; now that Roney is in his late-30s, one wonders if he is ever going to develop his own voice.
Roney joined Abdullah Ibrahim's Big Band in 1979 and was with Art Blakey's Jazz Messengers in 1981 (subbing for Wynton Marsalis when he was touring with Herbie Hancock). Since that time he has spent a long period with the Tony Williams Quintet, assisted Miles Davis at the 1991 Montreux Jazz Festival (in which Davis revisited for one last time the arrangements of Gil Evans), played as a substitute Miles in both Gerry Mulligan's Rebirth of the Cool and Herbie Hancock's Tribute to Miles Davis quintet, and recorded steadily as a leader. His own records tend to be modal-based and they all contain strong (if derivative) trumpet playing. —*Scott Yanow*

Verses / Feb. 19, 1987 / Muse ✦✦✦✦
Aggressive, attacking material with fiery exchanges between Gary Thomas (reeds) and Roney. Top front line of young talent, Roney and Gary Thomas. —*Ron Wynn*

Intuition / Jan. 6, 1988 / Muse ✦✦✦✦✦
This is a stirring set from one of the best "young lion" trumpeters. Very dynamic hard-bop line with superior alto and tenor sax by Kenny Garret (as/ts) and Gary Thomas (ts). —*Ron Wynn*

The Standard Bearer / Mar. 3, 1989 / Muse ✦✦✦✦
To say that Wallace Roney (30 at the time of this Muse CD) resembles mid-'60s Miles Davis in his playing is the same as stating that Sonny Stitt sounded a little like Charlie Parker. That objection aside, Roney's *The Standard Bearer* (dedicated to Woody Shaw) is excellent. The leader is in fine form on six familiar standards and "Loose" has Roney successfully holding one's interest while backed by just drummer Cindy Blackman and percussionist Steve Berrios. Tenor saxophonist Gary Thomas (who does have a very original sound) is fiery during his four appearances and the rhythm section (which also includes pianist Mulgrew Miller

and bassist Charnett Moffett) is quite superior. Creative frameworks and inspired solos keep this recording from being just a bop revival session. In fact, except for Roney's sound, everything about the music is quite fresh. —*Scott Yanow*

Obsession / Sep. 7, 1990 / Muse ✦✦✦✦
The latest from this trumpet whiz boasts excellent songs supplied by both Roney and pianist Donald Brown. —*Ron Wynn*

Seth Air / Sep. 28, 1991 / Muse ✦✦✦✦✦
Trumpeter Wallace Roney, 31 at the time of this recording, has yet to escape from the shadow of Miles Davis. However, he is one of the stronger brassmen in jazz of the 1990s and plays quite well on this set, which includes three numbers by younger brother Antoine Roney (who is heard on this CD on tenor), two from Roney's pianist Jacky Terrasson and three odd standards: "People," Gershwin's "Gone" and Burt Bacharach's "Wives & Lovers." The music is straightahead but occasionally as unpredictable as the repertoire. —*Scott Yanow*

● **Crunchin'** / Jul. 30, 1993 / Muse ✦✦✦✦✦
Trumpeter Wallace Roney sounds poignant and fabulous throughout the eight tracks on his latest release. His lines on "What's New" and "You Stepped out of a Dream" are full and gorgeous, while his soloing on "Woody 'n You" and "Time After Time" has warmth, intensity and edge. Alto saxophonist Antonio Hart chimes in with equal facility and spark, while Geri Allen shows that she is just as outstanding as an accompanist on standards and hard bop as in trios or as a leader. —*Ron Wynn*

Misterios / 1994 / Warner Brothers ✦✦✦✦
Trumpeter Wallace Roney avoids the standard repertoire altogether on this CD, playing pieces by Pat Metheny, the Beatles, Egberto Gismonti, Jaco Pastorius and even Dolly Parton among others but, try as hard as he may, he still sounds like Miles Davis every time he hits a long tone or plays a double-time passage. Backed by a small orchestra that mostly interprets Gil Goldstein arrangements, Roney is the main soloist throughout this interesting ballad-dominated set. —*Scott Yanow*

The Wallace Roney Quintet / Feb. 20, 1995-Feb. 22, 1995 / Warner Brothers ✦✦✦✦

Village / 1997 / Warner Brothers ✦✦✦
This is really two albums in one, with a clear line of demarcation between two concepts. Roney says that he wanted to "incorporate African rhythms with a *Nefertiti* approach" on the whole CD, but *Nefertiti* easily overwhelms, even obliterates, the African element up until track six ("Village"), where Steve Berrios' percussion and Robert Irving III's synthesizers kick in. Now the music becomes more interesting, sometimes following the direction of Herbie Hancock's Mwandishi Sextet—and the last four tracks are appropriately linked to one another by Berrios' interludes. The best track, "EBO," has a great theme, an amalgam of *Kind of Blue*, *Filles de Kilimanjaro* and Gil Evans, with Chick Corea's Fender Rhodes electric piano complementing Geri Allen's acoustic piano. You guessed it; by now, the boo birds have been out again accusing Roney of being a Miles imitator. But the means are justified here, because Roney creates thoughtful music within his post-Miles idiom and, like his late idol, tries to stretch himself. Besides, there was a good reason for revisiting the past this time; the death of Roney's former employer and bandmate Tony Williams in 1997 made this album, though recorded over three months earlier, a memorial—unnervingly so in the way Roney and drummer Lenny White follow the Williams rhythmic method in Cole Porter's "I Love You." Also, Pharoah Sanders puts in a pair of (for him) rather safe cameo appearances. —*Richard S. Ginell*

Wally Rose (Walter L. Rose)

b. Oct. 2, 1913, Oakland, CA, **d.** Jan. 12, 1997, Walnut Creek, CA
Piano / Ragtime, Dixieland
Wally Rose's most famous recording was "Black and White Rag," cut with the Yerba Buena Jazz Band in 1941, one of the first ragtime recordings and quite influential in launching a mini-ragtime revival. An important player in the San Francisco jazz scene of the 1940s and 50s, Wally Rose was with Lu Watters' Yerba Buena Jazz Band during its entire existence (1939-50) and then worked with Bob Scobey (1951) and Turk Murphy (1952-54) before having a career mostly as a solo pianist. He recorded as a leader for Jazz Man (1941-42), Good Time Jazz (several sets including a 1958 LP), Columbia, and a solo date for Stomp Off in 1982 (his first recording as a leader in 24 years). Wally Rose was an inspirational figure to young Dixielanders up until his death in early 1997. —*Scott Yanow*

● **Ragtime Classics** / Oct. 15, 1958-Oct. 20, 1958 / Good Time Jazz ✦✦✦✦
Wally Rose was a pioneer in reviving ragtime. This CD is a full-length set of rags performed by the pianist's trio (with bassist Morty Corb and drummer Nick Fatool). Rose plays the rags with spirit, taste and a bit of subtle improvisation although the rhythm section tends to be a bit metronomic (Nick Fatool sounds as

if he is working hard to combat his apparent boredom). In addition to intepreting five Scott Joplin rags and a pair of Jelly Roll Morton tunes, Rose runs through pieces by Joseph Lamb, James Scott, Tom Turpin, Paul Pratt and Henry Lodge. His performances are miles above the faddish "honky tonkers" of the period. Although this would have been a better recital if it consisted of unaccompanied piano solos, Wally Rose's music should delight ragtime and classic jazz collectors. —*Scott Yanow*

Michele Rosewoman

b. 1953, Oakland, CA
Piano / Avant-Garde
A stirring and adventurous pianist with a sound of her own, Michele Rosewoman came from a very musical northern California family. She started playing piano at age six and as a teenager studied with pianist Ed Kelly. After working extensively locally, Rosewoman moved to New York in 1977. Since then she has played and recorded with many advanced players, including Oliver Lake, Billy Bang, Greg Osby and the members of M-Base, among many others. Most important have been her own projects. Well trained in Cuban percussion and African music, Rosewoman has led the versatile big band New Yor-Uba (unfortunately thus far unrecorded) on an occasional basis since the mid-1980s, as well as her quintet Quintessence. Michele Rosewoman has thus far led stimulating sessions for Soul Note, Enja, Evidence and Blue Note. She has developed into one of the unsung leaders of the jazz avant-garde of the 1990s while remaining connected to the tradition. —*Scott Yanow*

The Source / Dec. 1984 / Soul Note ✦✦✦

Quintessence / Jan. 27, 1987-Jan. 28, 1987 / Enja ✦✦✦✦✦
Pianist Michele Rosewoman makes a strong showing on this 1987 release, leading a group with alto saxophonist Steve Coleman, alto and soprano saxophonist Greg Osby, bassist Anthony Cox, and drummer Terri Lyne Carrington. The material is mainly originals, and mixed Afro-Latin, hard bop, and animated arrangements with some free influences. —*Ron Wynn*

● **Contrast High** / Jul. 1988 / Enja ✦✦✦✦✦
With Quintessence. Pianist with intriguing compositions. —*Michael G. Nastos*

Occasion to Rise / Sep. 13, 1990-Sep. 15, 1990 / Evidence ✦✦✦✦
Pianist Michele Rosewoman shows tremendous rhythmic drive, fine harmonic skills, and outstanding phrasing and playing throughout the ten cuts on this 1990 set. With drummer Ralph Peterson briskly outlining the rhythmic direction and bassist Rufus Reid proving the link between his piercing rhythms and Rosewoman's energetic playing, this is not polite or casual piano fare. It is fiery, sometimes slashing ("The Sweet Eye of Hurricane Sally") and sometimes sentimental ("Prelude to a Kiss" and "We Are"). —*Ron Wynn*

Spirit / Jul. 9, 1994 / Blue Note ✦✦✦✦✦
Although she takes two effective vocals on this release (the catchy "For Agauyu," which finds her singing some African dialect, and "Spirit," a gospel ballad by Maurice White), it is for her versatile and consistently explorative piano that Michele Rosewoman deserves to be much better known. Although she sounds at times a little like Herbie Hancock (purposely on his "Dolphin Dance") and shows the influence of McCoy Tyner, Rosewoman is quite successful in moving the modern mainstream forward; there are occasional hints of Cecil Taylor also to be heard in her playing. Actually, by the mid-1990s (on her sixth recording as a leader), Michele Rosewoman sounded quite original. On "Passion Dance Blues," she shows how to be both soulful and adventurous simultaneously; she completely reworks "When Sunny Gets Blue" while keeping the melody close by, and her five compositions (which are sometimes more accessible than expected due to her utilization of rhythms) are full of unpredictable twists. This trio set (with bassist Kenny Davis and drummer Gene Jackson) is one of Michele Rosewoman's strongest outings so far. —*Scott Yanow*

Renee Rosnes

b. 1962, Regina, Saskatchewan, Canada
Piano / Hard Bop, Post-Bop
Renee Rosnes, who plays in an advanced and flexible hard bop style, seems on the brink of great success. A native of Canada, she began piano lessons at age three and violin when she was five. She worked throughout Canada, performing on CBC Jazz Radio Canada shows, gigging with her trio regularly at a hotel and playing on the S.S. Rotterdam Cruise Liner. Rosnes moved to New York in 1985 and has played and/or recorded with a wide variety of artists including Joe Henderson, Wayne Shorter, J.J. Johnson, Jon Faddis, James Moody, the group Out of the Blue, Gary Thomas and Robin Eubanks. In addition, Renee Rosnes has recorded several excellent sessions for Blue Note as a leader. —*Scott Yanow*

Renee Rosnes / Apr. 18, 1988-Feb. 4, 1989 / Blue Note ◆◆◆◆
The music on pianist Renee Rosnes' self-titled debut as a leader features her in several settings. "Diana," a moody ballad, is a relatively uneventful soprano-synthesizer duet with Wayne Shorter that was performed during a concert in Copenhagen. Three quartet tracks feature the tenor of Ralph Bowen, who demonstrates how Shorter used to sound (circa 1964-65); the McCoy Tyner-inspired piano of the leader fits in perfectly. Two other selections find Branford Marsalis on either soprano or tenor, faring best on the latter instrument during Thelonious Monk's "Bright Mississippi." A boppish trio version of Cole Porter's "Everything I Love" is the strongest performance by Renee while "Fleur-de-lis" is a wandering but generally intriguing acoustic duet with Herbie Hancock. Overall, this CD was a good starting point for Renee Rosnes, who was 28 at the time. —*Scott Yanow*

For the Moment / Feb. 15, 1990-Feb. 16, 1990 / Blue Note ◆◆◆◆◆
It was a measure of pianist Renee Rosnes' self-confidence that she could invite the great Joe Henderson to be a sideman on her second date as a leader. And it was an indication of her rapidly emerging talent that Rosnes was not at all overshadowed by the tenor master. Using McCoy Tyner as a foundation, Renee Rosnes had already created her own style within the modal mainstream. With the assistance of Henderson, Steve Wilson on soprano and alto (for four of the eight selections) and a topnotch rhythm section, Rosnes performs four of her originals along with an exuberant version of Thelonious Monk's "Four in One" and three obscurities. A fine effort. —*Scott Yanow*

● **Without Words** / Jan. 8, 1992-Jan. 9, 1992 / Blue Note ◆◆◆◆◆

Ancestors / Oct. 9, 1995-Oct. 10, 1995 / Blue Note ◆◆◆
Renee Rosnes, who left her native Canada to settle in New York and play with Joe Henderson, Jon Faddis and her own groups, is an excellent pianist inspired by early Herbie Hancock and McCoy Tyner. She heads a top New York sextet on this CD that includes the potentially great trumpeter Nicholas Payton (here showing a strong Freddie Hubbard influence), bassist Peter Washington, drummer Al Foster and percussionist Don Alias. However, the musician who makes the biggest impression on the date is Chris Potter, mostly on tenor but also contributing some effective soprano, bass clarinet and alto flute. Potter, who by the mid-'90s already had his own sound on each of his instruments, gained his earliest recognition playing with Red Rodney's quintet in the 1980s but has since developed into a major postbop stylist with an explorative and colorful style. It is for his playing on these selections (five of which are challenging Rosnes originals) that *Ancestors* is chiefly recommended. —*Scott Yanow*

As We Are Now / Mar. 12, 1997-Mar. 12, 1997 / Blue Note ◆◆◆◆
As We Are Now is another wonderful session from pianist Renee Rosnes, finding her nativgating a challenging set of six original compositions and three covers. Rosnes is supported by drummer Jack DeJohnette, bassist Christian McBride and saxophonist Chris Potter, an impressive lineup that allows Rosnes to stretch her limits. *As We Are Now* finds the limits of hard bop and pushes it further, resulting in an adventurous, rewarding listen. —*Leo Stanley*

Frank Rosolino

b. Aug. 20, 1926, Detroit, MI, **d.** Nov. 26, 1978, Los Angeles, CA
Trombone / Bop
The horrible way that Frank Rosolino's life ended (killing himself after shooting his two sons) has largely overshadowed his earlier musical accomplishments. One of the top trombonists of the 1950s, Rosolino's fluid and often-humorous style put him near the top of his field for awhile.

He was a guitarist when he was ten but switched to trombone as a teenager. After serving in the military, Rosolino played with the big bands of Bob Chester, Glen Gray, Gene Krupa (1948-49), Tony Pastor, Herbie Fields and Georgie Auld. However, all of those experiences were just preludes to his high-profile association with Stan Kenton (1952-54), which gave him fame. Rosolino recorded frequently in Los Angeles as a member of the Lighthouse All-Stars (1954-60), a freelancer and as a studio musician. His song "Blue Daniel" became a jazz standard and Rosolino was a popular attraction as a brilliant trombonist and a comical singer. He was with Supersax for a period in the 1970s. Rosolino's shocking death was a surprise to even his closest associates. —*Scott Yanow*

Frankly Speaking / May 4, 1955-May 5, 1955 / Affinity ◆◆◆◆◆
Perhaps his greatest album as a leader. Immaculate trombone solos. —*Ron Wynn*

● **Frank Rosolino Quartet** / Jun. 1957 / V.S.O.P. ◆◆◆◆◆
This matchup works out quite well. Trombonist Frank Rosolino and tenor saxophonist Richie Kamuca make for a potent front line and are accompanied quite ably by pianist Vince Guaraldi, bassist Monty Budwig and drummer Stan Levey. This 1957 studio session, originally put out on the long-defunct Mode label, has been reissued on CD by V.S.O.P. and is well worth picking up. Rosolino contrib-

utes three originals, Bill Holman arranged some of the ensembles and the solos are consistently enjoyable and swinging. —*Scott Yanow*

Free for All / Dec. 22, 1958 / Original Jazz Classics ◆◆◆◆
This CD reissue expands upon the original eight-song program by adding three alternate takes. The fine bop trombonist Frank Rosolino teams up with tenor saxophonist Harold Land and a West Coast rhythm section (pianist Victor Feldman, bassist Leroy Vinnegar and drummer Stan Levey) for a set of standards and melodic group originals. Originally cut for Specialty, the formerly rare session has its strong moments although it is not really all that essential, but fans of Rosolino and Land will want to get it. —*Scott Yanow*

Thinking About You / Apr. 21, 1976-Apr. 23, 1976 / Sackville ◆◆◆
Recorded live at Bourbon Street in Toronto with Ed Bickert (g), Don Thompson (b), and Terry Clarke (d), this album includes four long standards. With room to stretch, the whole band is up to the task. This is on the mellow side. —*Michael G. Nastos*

Annie Ross (Annabelle [Née Short] Lynch)

b. Jul. 25, 1930, Surrey, England
Vocals / Vocalese, Bop
Annie Ross moved with her aunt, singer Ella Logan, to Los Angeles at the age of three, where she became a juvenile film actress, starting on the *Our Gang* series at five. As a teenager, she moved to New York to study acting, then back to England, where she became a nightclub and band singer. She returned to the US and gained attention in 1952 for her song "Twisted," a "vocalese" setting of humorous lyrics to what had been a saxophone solo by Wardell Gray. Also quite famous were her versions of "Farmer's Market" and "Jackie." She visited Europe with Lionel Hampton's big band in 1953, staying for a few years. In 1958, Ross teamed with Dave Lambert and Jon Hendricks in the vocalese trio Lambert, Hendricks & Ross, and they toured and recorded successfully, their best-known album being their first, *Sing a Song of Basie*. Ross left the trio in 1962 and settled in England, continuing to sing and work as an actress. She returned again to the US in 1985. In 1993, she had a featured role in the Robert Altman film *Short Cuts*, and she sang most of the songs on the soundtrack album. —*William Ruhlmann*

Skylark / Aug. 27, 1956-Aug. 28, 1956 / DRG ◆◆◆◆
This little-known set (reissued on CD) from 1956 features singer Annie Ross four years after she originally recorded "Twisted" but a year before the formation of Lambert, Hendricks & Ross. Based in London at the time, Ross avoids scatting and vocalese in favor of conventional swinging and jazz-oriented interpretations of standards. Backed tastefully by pianist Tony Crombie, clarinetist Bob Burns, guitarist Roy Plummer and bassist Lennie Rush, Annie Ross shows that she could have been a successful solo artist if she had not met up with Dave Lambert and Jon Hendricks; at times she almost sounds like Susannah McCorkle. —*Scott Yanow*

★ **Annie Ross Sings a Song of Mulligan** / Feb. 11, 1958-Sep. 25, 1958 / Pacific Jam ◆◆◆◆◆
Singer Annie Ross' first solo album after joining Lambert, Hendricks and Ross finds her at the peak of her powers. Ross is joined by two versions of the Gerry Mulligan Quartet with either Chet Baker or Art Farmer on trumpet, Bill Crow or Henry Grimes on bass and drummer Dave Bailey. For this CD reissue, there are also five previously unissued selections and one that was originally on a sampler. Annie Ross is at her best (and most appealing) on "I've Grown Accustomed to Your Face," "Give Me the Simple Life," "How About You" and "The Lady's in Love with You," but all 16 selections are quite rewarding and her interplay with baritonist Mulligan is consistently memorable. This CD plus its follow-up *A Gasser* are both essential. —*Scott Yanow*

Gypsy / 1959 / World Pacific ◆◆◆
This CD reissue brings back one of Annie Ross' most obscure albums of the 1950s. Recorded at a time when the singer was just starting to get known for her work with Lambert, Hendricks & Ross, the set is a swinging but largely straight rendition of the score from the play *Gypsy*. The all-star backup band mostly functions as an ensemble during the Buddy Bregman arrangements (although altoist Herb Geller and trombonist Frank Rosolino have short spots on "All I Needis a Boy"), taking "Overture" as an instrumental that introduces some of the main melodies. Ross is in excellent form, performing a memorable version of the score's one real hit, "Everything's Coming Up Roses," and somehow sounding serious on "Let Me Entertain You." Still, this release is mostly recommended to fans of show tunes and Annie Ross completists. —*Scott Yanow*

Gasser! / Feb. 1959-Mar. 1959/ World Pacific ◆◆◆◆◆
Most of this CD reissue contains one of singer Annie Ross' finest sessions away from the premiere jazz vocal group Lambert, Hendricks & Ross. She is joined by either Zoot Sims or (on two numbers) Bill Perkins on tenor, pianist Russ Freeman,

Billy Bean or Jim Hall on guitar, bassist Monty Budwig and Mel Lewis or Frankie Capp on drums. Ross' renditions of such tunes as "I'm Nobody's Baby," "Invitation to the Blues," "I Didn't Know About You" and "You Took Advantage of Me" are highlights. Also on this set are five instrumentals taken from samplers that showcase the talents of Zoot Sims and Russ Freeman. Recommended. —*Scott Yanow*

Annie Ross Sings a Handful of Songs / Jul. 26, 1963-Jul. 1, 1964 / Fresh Sound ✦✦✦✦

By 1963, Annie Ross had permanently moved back to England and had started working more as an actress than as a singer. This interesting set (reissued by DCC as an audiophile CD) features Ross backed by an orchestra arranged and conducted by Johnnie Spence. The obvious high point is one of the darkest and scariest versions of "Love for Sale" ever recorded; Ross' desperate-sounding rendition is haunting. Otherwise, she performs a variety of standards in lightly swinging fashion, not scatting or using vocalese but instead working on interpreting the lyrics. Other highlights include "All of You," "Nature Boy," "Like Someone in Love" and "Limehouse Blues." This worthy set was also put out on CD by the Fresh Sound label. —*Scott Yanow*

Short Cuts / 1993 / Imago ✦✦✦✦✦

In the movie *Short Cuts*, Annie Ross, a jazz singer (formerly of Lambert, Hendricks & Ross), plays a jazz singer, and Lori Singer, who can play cello, plays her cello-playing daughter. This soundtrack album of "music from and inspired by the film" alternates songs by Ross, many of which appear in the film, with classical music performances by Singer, alone and with a quartet. Although they sound like old jazz standards, most of the Ross songs are newly written pieces, with her singing, playing, and songwriting collaborators including a who's who of rockers—Bono and The Edge of U2, Terry Adams of NRBQ, Doc Pomus and Dr. John (who contribute four compositions), Elvis Costello, Iggy Pop, and Michael Stipe of R.E.M. All of them subsume their usual tendencies to fit into the smoky, late-night ambience of the approach. And Ross, her voice full of knowledge beyond even the sophisticated lyrics, dominates the proceedings. The result is a brilliant album that works well with or without the movie it was constructed to accompany. —*William Ruhlmann*

Music is Forever / Dec. 1995 / DRG ✦✦✦✦

Annie Ross' first album in much too long is a look back at some of her best-known songs from the perspective of a still sassy 65-year-old. Accompanied by a top-flight jazz band including Mike Renzi on piano (Tommy Flanagan sits in on two tracks), Joe Beck on guitar, Peter Washington on bass, Louis Hayes on drums, Frank Wess on tenor and flute, and Al Grey on trombone, Ross revisits her famous vocalese lyrics of the '50s, "Twisted," "Jackie," and "Farmer's Market," plus jazz tunes and standards like "It Had to Be You" and "It Never Entered My Mind." Her range has narrowed, and her readings are as much spoken as sung, but her phrasing remains precise, and these recordings are musical acting performances by a veteran capable of ringing every nuance from them while continuing to swing. —*William Ruhlmann*

Charlie Rouse

b. Apr. 6, 1924, Washington, DC, d. Nov. 30, 1988, Seattle, WA
Tenor Saxophone / Hard Bop
Possessor of a distinctive tone and a fluid bop-oriented style, Charlie Rouse was in Thelonious Monk's Quartet for over a decade (1959-70) and, although somewhat taken for granted, was an important ingredient in Monk's music. Rouse was always a modern player and he worked with Billy Eckstine's orchestra (1944) and the first Dizzy Gillespie big band (1945), making his recording debut with Tadd Dameron in 1947. Rouse popped up in a lot of important groups including Duke Ellington's Orchestra (1949-50), Count Basie's octet (1950), on sessions with Clifford Brown in 1953 and with Oscar Pettiford's sextet (1955). He co-led the Jazz Modes with Julius Watkins (1956-59) and then joined Monk for a decade of extensive touring and recordings. In the 1970s he recorded a few albums as a leader and in 1979 he became a member of Sphere. Charlie Rouse's unique sound began to finally get some recognition during the 1980s. He participated on Carmen McRae's classic *Carmen Sings Monk* album and his last recording was at a Monk tribute concert. —*Scott Yanow*

Les Jazz Modes / Jun. 1956-Dec. 4, 1956 / Biograph ✦✦✦✦✦

For a short time during 1956-58, tenor saxophonist Charlie Rouse and Julius Watkins (the wizard of the jazz French horn) teamed up to form a regular quintet that they named Les Jazz Modes. Their first three (and best) records have been reissued on this two-CD set. In addition to the co-leaders, the group featured pianist Gildo Mahones, a variety of bassists and drummers, guest appearances by Chino Pozo on congas (not Chano Pozo as listed on the back cover) and (on five numbers) the out-of-place classical soprano voice of Eileen Gilbert. In general the music is hard bop of the period but it does give one a good chance to hear Watkins really

stretching out. The tenor-French horn front line does sound a bit unusual but they blend together quite nicely on the ensembles. This reissue is well worth investigating. —*Scott Yanow*

The Chase Is On / Aug. 29, 1957+Sep. 8, 1957 / Bethlehem ✦✦✦

This relaxed set matches together the very different tenor tones of Charlie Rouse and Paul Quinichette with a fine rhythm section (Wynton Kelly or Hank Jones on piano, bassist Wendell Marshall and drummer Ed Thigpen). The music includes a few forgotten songs of the era (including "You're Cheating Yourself," "Tender Trap" and Carmen McRae's "Last Time for Love") and has competent if generally polite playing from the tenors. However, the boppish music (which contains no real surprises) is enjoyable overall. —*Scott Yanow*

Takin' Care of Business / May 11, 1960 / Original Jazz Classics ✦✦✦✦✦

Quintet with Blue Mitchell (tpt) and the Walter Bishop (p) Trio plays two numbers penned by Randy Weston, one apiece by Kenny Drew and Rouse, and two standards. This is a supremely confident group that plays strong music in a somewhat cool mood. —*Michael G. Nastos*

Unsung Hero / Dec. 20, 1960-Jul. 13, 1961 / Epic ✦✦✦✦✦

Tenor saxophonist Charlie Rouse, who would spend all of the 1960s as a member of Thelonious Monk's Quartet, had relatively few opportunities to lead his own sessions. This CD reissue has an LP and a half's worth of material that the instantly recognizable tenor cut for Epic. Well versed in the swing/bop tradition and a veteran of both the Duke Ellington and Dizzy Gillespie orchestras, Rouse plays thoughtful solos with a pair of conventional rhythm sections on this album (which includes either Billy Gardner or Gildo Mahones on piano, Peck Morrison or Reggie Workman on bass and Dave Bailey or Art Taylor on drums), sticking mostly to standards and avoiding Monk tunes (which he performed on a nightly basis anyway). A fine example of Charlie Rouse's playing outside of the world of Thelonious Monk. —*Scott Yanow*

● **Two is One** / 1974 / Strata East ✦✦✦✦✦

Surprising set. Animated Rouse solos and a Latin flavor. —*Ron Wynn*

Cinnamon Flower / 1976 / Rykodisc ✦✦✦

Moment's Notice / Oct. 20, 1977 / Storyville ✦✦✦✦

This quartet features pianist Hugh Lawson, bassist Bob Cranshaw, and drummer Ben Riley. —*Michael G. Nastos*

The Upper Manhattan Jazz Society / 1981 / Enja ✦✦✦

A fine early-'80s album with tenor saxophonist Charlie Rouse leading a group featuring bassist Buster Williams, pianist Al Dailey, trumpeter Benny Bailey, and drummer Keith Copeland. This contains some of Rouse's strongest post-Monk playing and compositions. —*Ron Wynn*

Social Call / Jan. 21, 1984-Jan. 22, 1984 / Uptown ✦✦✦✦

This studio session with Red Rodney and the Albert Dailey Trio consisted of all post-bop standards save Rouse's "Little Chico." Arrangements were by Don Sickler. —*Michael G. Nastos*

Epistrophy / Oct. 10, 1988 / Landmark ✦✦✦✦✦

ROVA

f. 1977
Group / Avant-Garde, Free Jazz
The most advanced of the saxophone quartets, ROVA (consisting of Jon Raskin, Larry Ochs, Andrew Voigt and Bruce Ackley) was formed in 1977. Since then this adventurous unit has recorded extensively for many labels (including Metalanguage, Moers, Ictus, New Albion, Sound Aspects, Hat Art and Black Saint), visited Europe and the Soviet Union (the latter twice) and put out sets of Steve Lacy and Anthony Braxton tunes in addition to many originals. In 1988 Steve Adams took Voigt's place. —*Scott Yanow*

Cinema Rovate / Jul. 25, 1978+Aug. 2, 1978 / Metalanguage ✦✦✦✦✦

This debut album of open-ended compositions was a response to the groups' perceived lack of discipline in contemporary free jazz. —*Myles Boisen*

Daredevils / Mar. 11, 1979 / Metalanguage ✦✦✦

An early collaboration with guitarist Henry Kaiser. —*Myles Boisen*

This, This, This / Aug. 7, 1979-Aug. 24, 1979 / Moers ✦✦✦✦

Invisible Frames / May 15, 1980-Oct. 4, 1981 / Fore ✦✦✦

As Was / Apr. 1981 / Metalanguage ✦✦✦✦

Saxophone Diplomacy / Jun. 1983 / Hat Art ✦✦✦✦✦

The least-heralded saxophone ensemble on the scene, but ROVA's music is just as emphatic and frenetic as the World Sax Quartet's, even if no one is a compositional match for David Murray or Hamiett Bluiett. They make dynamic, hard-hitting, free-wheeling music that never degenerates into chaos. —*Ron Wynn*

Favorite Street / Nov. 15, 1983-Nov. 17, 1983 / Black Saint ✦✦✦✦
ROVA plays (and deconstructs) the music of saxophonist Steve Lacy—a triumph of structural improv and a personal favorite. —*Myles Boisen*

The Crowd / Jun. 20, 1985-Jun. 23, 1985 / Hat Art ✦✦✦✦✦

Beat Kennel / Apr. 1987 / Black Saint ✦✦✦✦
A late-'80s session with the ROVA sax quartet. The lineup at this time included Jon Raskin, Larry Ochs, Andrew Voigt, and Bruce Ackley. They did mostly originals in an energized, explosive manner. —*Ron Wynn*

Electric Rags II / Sep. 1989 / New Albion ✦✦✦

● **This Time We Are Both** / Nov. 1989 / New Albion ✦✦✦✦
Recorded during their second tour of the Soviet Union, these six performances by ROVA (Larry Ochs on tenor and sopranino, Bruce Ackley on soprano, Steve Adams on alto and sopranino, and baritonist Jon Raskin) are consistently exciting and inventive. In general, the four masterful saxophonists start off with fairly accessible and rhythmic patterns before venturing into loose but controlled freedom. The sound explorations cover a great deal of emotional ground and usually change or conclude shortly after reaching their optimal length; there is no self-indulgent screaming or aimless wandering. One of ROVA's finest recordings. —*Scott Yanow*

☆ **The Aggregate** / Dec. 1991 / Sound Aspects ✦✦✦✦✦
This superb live set with Anthony Braxton (sax) as a fifth member was one of the last recordings with Voight. —*Myles Boisen*

Long on Logic / Dec. 1991 / Sound Aspects ✦✦✦✦
With music by ROVA, Henry Kaiser (g), and Fred Frith, this was an outgrowth of a successful local concert series. It's one of the few sax quartet albums that utilizes studio and sampling technology as an artistic tool. —*Myles Boisen*

John Coltrane's Ascension / Dec. 6, 1995 / Black Saint ✦✦✦✦✦
In 1965, John Coltrane led a famous screamfest, a nearly 40-minute jam called "Ascension," which was essentially a free improvisation (except for a loose melody and some frameworks that were played at spontaneous moments); the performances had wild free-form solos that were divided by even more intense group improvising. This 1995 live recording is not so much a recreation as much as a re-investigation of the original concept. The members of the avant-garde saxophone quartet ROVA (altoists Jon Raskin and Steve Adams, tenors Larry Ochs and Bruce Ackley) are joined by Glenn Spearman also on tenor, trumpeters Dave Douglas and Raphe Malik, pianist Chris Brown, bassists George Cremaschi and Lisle Ellis, and drummer Donald Robinson. The CD opens with a seven-minute version of John Coltrane's "Welcome" featuring Larry Ochs with the rhythm section, but unfortunately Ochs does not have 'Trane's warmth in his playing. The new "Ascension," which is one second short of 50 minutes long, follows the original's format. Of the solos, Spearman and Malik have the most creative statements, although all seven horn players (plus the rhythm section) make the most of their individual spots. But it is the raging ensembles that are most memorable. Don't look for any mellow moments on this date. —*Scott Yanow*

Jimmy Rowles

b. Aug. 19, 1918, Spokane, WA, **d.** May 28, 1996, Los Angeles, CA
Piano / Bop, Swing

Long known for his expertise in coming up with the perfect chord for the perfect situation, the subtle Jimmy Rowles was in demand for decades as an accompanist while being underrated as a soloist. After playing in local groups in Seattle, Rowles moved to Los Angeles in 1940 and worked with Slim Gaillard, Lester Young, Benny Goodman and Woody Herman. After serving in the military he returned to Herman (in time to play with the first Herd), recorded with Benny Goodman and also had stints with Les Brown and Tommy Dorsey. Working as a studio musician, Rowles appeared in a countless number of settings in the 1950s and '60s but was best known for his playing behind Billie Holiday and Peggy Lee. In 1973 he moved to New York where he recorded more extensively in jazz situations (including duets with Stan Getz), but after touring with Ella Fitzgerald during 1981-83 he returned to California. His song "The Peacocks" became a standard, and Rowles recorded for many labels throughout his career including with his daughter, fluegelhornist Stacy Rowles. —*Scott Yanow*

Weather in a Jazz Vane / 1958 / V.S.O.P. ✦✦✦
The focus is on Jimmy Rowles' piano throughout this relaxed and well-rounded LP reissue of an Andex session. Rowles is joined by trumpeter Lee Katzman, valve trombonist Bob Envoldsen, Bill Holman on tenor, altoist Herb Geller, bassist Monty Budwig and drummer Mel Lewis for renditions of nine superior standards, all of which have references to seasons, weather or the sun in their titles. Highlights include "With the Wind and the Rain in Your Hair," "When the Sun Comes Out," "Some Other Spring" and Rowles' spontaneous vocal (his first on record) on "Too Hot for Words." —*Scott Yanow*

Let's Get Acquainted with Jazz (For People Who Hate Jazz) / Jun. 20, 1958 / V.S.O.P. ✦✦✦
The drawing on the cover and the liner notes, such as they are, is rather silly, but the music on this brief, but enjoyable, CD reissue features some fine playing from a variety of top West Coast-based musicians. Pianist Jimmy Rowles is the leader and is assisted by guitarist Barney Kessel, bassist Red Mitchell, drummer Mel Lewis, sometimes vibraphonist Larry Bunker and either tenor saxophonist Harold Land or trumpeter Pete Candoli. They perform six standards, "The Blues" and three obscurities that one assumes are Rowles originals. Tasteful and lightly swinging music. —*Scott Yanow*

Our Delight / 1968 / V.S.O.P. ✦✦✦✦
Recorded in 1968 but not released for the initial time until this 1997 CD, this set of live but private recordings feature pianist Jimmy Rowles with either Max Bennett or Chuck Berghofer on bass and Nick Martinis or Larry Bunker on drums. The very spontaneous and relaxed music finds Rowles often quoting other songs and playing a wide repertoire. The music ranges from "You're Driving Me Crazy" and "Our Delight" to "America the Beautiful," "Moon of Manakoora" and "Lulu's Back in Town," plus songs by Freddie Hubbard and Wayne Shorter. Although not essential, the set does feature Rowles during an era (1961-69) when he did not lead a single studio session. —*Scott Yanow*

The Special Magic of Jimmy Rowles / Apr. 7, 1974 / Halcyon ✦✦✦✦
This album includes duets with Rusty Gilder on bass. Solo, Rowles shows he can do it alone, and with Gilder, sparks occasionally fly. Mostly, this is laidback. They play lots of Duke Ellington. There is a good version of Carl Perkin's "Grooveyard." —*Michael G. Nastos*

Grandpaws / Mar. 1976 / Choice ✦✦✦✦
The trio for this pianist includes Buster Williams on bass and Billy Hart on drums. They play two by Rowles, the others are standards. They do an exquisite medley of "Lush Life/A Train/I Hadn't Anyone 'till You/Margie/Chicago/Desert Fire." Rowles shows his ballad skills best. —*Michael G. Nastos*

We Could Make Such Beautiful Music Together / Apr. 1978 / Xanadu ✦✦✦✦
Solo, trio, and quartet performances by pianist Jimmy Rowles from the late '70s. These were originally issued on the Xanadu label, then reissued on CD in 1989 for EPM. Rowles plays with bassists Sam Jones or George Mraz, drummers Leroy Williams or Freddie Waits, and trumpeter Sam Noto. His prickly, sometimes humorous and sometimes poignant piano playing provides the disc's high points. —*Ron Wynn*

Isfahan / May 1978 / Sonet ✦✦✦

Paws That Refresh / Sep. 1980 / Choice ✦✦✦
Nice, casually swinging set by pianist Jimmy Rowles. Rowles plays in an easy, relaxed manner with a pace that's neither hurried nor slow; he doesn't offer waves of notes or blistering rhythms, yet crams more ideas into his solos than many players who take more time and rip off barrages of chords and fancy phrases. —*Ron Wynn*

With the Red Mitchell Trio / Mar. 18, 1985-Mar. 19, 1985 / Contemporary ✦✦✦✦
With Red Mitchell. Excellent date; splendid Rowles trio material. —*Ron Wynn*

Jimmy Rowles, Vol. 2 / 1985 / Contemporary ✦✦✦✦
Rowles, Red Mitchell (b), Rowles' daughter Stacey, and Colin Bailey (d). —*Ron Wynn*

Looking Back / Jun. 8, 1988 / Delos ✦✦✦
This CD is filled with the type of music one would expect from pianist Jimmy Rowles and his daughter Stacy Rowles: tasteful and melodic renditions of standards. Stacy, who gives "Looking Back" an effective vocal, is a warm-toned and lyrical fluegelhornist and is featured in a quartet with her father, bassist Eric Von Essen and drummer Donald Bailey. However, the music is too safe and predictable, making one wish that a fire had been lit under the soloists. Jimmy Rowles' reworking of "Take the 'A' Train" is the closest that this uneventful session comes to the sound of surprise. Otherwise, little memorable or special occurs. —*Scott Yanow*

Trio / Aug. 11, 1988-Aug. 12, 1988 / Capri ✦✦✦✦

● **Plus 2, Plus 3, Plus 4** / Dec. 16, 1988-Dec. 20, 1988 / JVC ✦✦✦✦✦
This CD reissue's title refers to the fact that pianist Jimmy Rowles appears with a drumless trio (including guitarist Larry Koonse and bassist Eric Von Essen) on four numbers, with a quartet on three songs (drummer Ralph Penland is added) and a quintet (with the addition of cornetist Bill Berry) on four other pieces. The music throughout is mellow and quiet with Rowles' chordal style very much the dominant force; he also takes half-spoken vocals on "I Never Loved Anyone" and "I've Grown Accustomed to Her Face." Only "I Wished on the Moon," "Sweet Lorraine" and the closing blues move above a medium-slow pace. —*Scott Yanow*

Stacy Rowles

b. Sep. 11, 1955
Trumpet, Fluegelhorn, Vocals / Bop, Swing
A mellow-toned fluegelhornist who emphasizes ballads, Stacy Rowles (the daughter of pianist Jimmy Rowles) has recorded for Concord and Delos and become a fixture in the L.A. area with her work in the group Jazz Birds. —*Scott Yanow*

● **Tell It like It Is** / Mar. 1984 / Concord Jazz ✦✦✦✦
On trumpeter Stacy Rowles' only album as a leader to date, she teams up with her father (veteran pianist Jimmy Rowles) for a set of generally exquisite music. With the assistance of Herman Riley on tenor and flute, bassist Chuck Berghofer and drummer Donald Bailey, the two Rowles play a variety of lyrical material including a moving duet on "Lotus Blossom." Stacy, who has emphasized ballads throughout her career, is in fine form on this set although one wonders when she will get around to recording an encore. —*Scott Yanow*

Marshall Royal

b. May 12, 1912, Sapulpa, OK, d. May 9, 1995, Los Angeles, CA
Alto Saxophone, Clarinet / Swing
For close to 20 years—from the early '50s until 1970—the characteristic sax sound of Count Basie's big band was topped by the clear, vibrating lead alto of Marshall Royal. Royal was, by all accounts, a competent swing-based soloist, but his strength was first and foremost as a team player. Royal's style became the prototype for swinging a sax section; his slightly behind-the-beat phrasing, pronounced vibrato, and aggressive leadership influenced a subsequent generation of ensemble players.

As a child, Royal learned to play violin, guitar, and various reed instruments; trumpeter Ernie Royal was his brother. He began performing in public at the age of 13. Royal spent much of the '30s with Les Hite's band; he also recorded with Art Tatum around that time. Royal joined Lionel Hampton's band in 1940, staying two years. During the war, Royal served in a Navy band. In 1946, he played with Eddie Heywood before moving to Los Angeles. Royal worked in the studios for a time, and then, in 1951, he joined the septet Count Basie had formed following the demise of his big band. Basie reorganized the big band the next year, with Royal ensconced as lead altoist and music director—dual roles he would occupy until 1970. After leaving Basie, Royal settled for good in Los Angeles. Royal played and recorded with Bill Berry's big band and the Frankie Capp-Nat Pierce Juggernaut. In 1977, he recorded as a soloist with Dave Frishberg, and in 1978 with Warren Vache. In the late '70s and early '80s, Royal recorded with a band he co-led with Snooky Young, as well as under his own name. Royal kept busy during the '80s; among his activities was a 1982 record date with Ella Fitzgerald and a 1987 Concord Jazz Festival Basie tribute led by Gene Harris. Royal stayed in touch with his ex-Basie colleagues as well, recording with the big bands of Ernie Wilkins and Frank Wess in 1990. —*Chris Kelsey*

● **First Chair** / Dec. 1978 / Concord Jazz ✦✦✦✦
Other than six isolated titles from 1951-53, an obscure Everest LP in 1960, and a date co-led with Snooky Young for Concord, this album was altoist Marshall Royal's debut as a leader. Although he had been playing with major bands since the 1930s (including 20 years with Count Basie), Royal had always been thought of as a dependable sideman and a first altoist in big bands rather than a leader. For the first of his two Concord dates (neither of which have yet been reissued on CD), Royal is joined by the underrated guitarist Cal Collins, pianist Nat Pierce, bassist Monty Budwig and drummer Jake Hanna. In addition to a Royal blues line ("Jump"), the quintet performs seven veteran standards, only one of which (Neal Hefti's "Li'l Darlin'") was from the Count Basie band book. Royal was long overdue to be showcased in this setting, as he shows on likable interpretations of such numbers as "I've Got the World on a String," "Jitterbug Waltz" and "My Ideal." —*Scott Yanow*

Royal Blue / Mar. 1980 / Concord Jazz ✦✦✦✦
Altoist Marshall Royal's second and final Concord recording as a leader is the equal of his first. With the assistance of pianist Monty Alexander, guitarist Cal Collins, bassist Ray Brown and drummer Jimmie Smith, Royal digs into a variety of swing standards (including "Mean to Me," "Avalon" and "I Got It Bad") and two of his basic originals. Throughout the date, Royal shows that in the 1980s, he was one of the few more significant survivors of the swing alto tradition. This fine release is worth picking up, but has not yet been reissued on CD. —*Scott Yanow*

Gonzalo Rubalcaba

b. May 27, 1963, Havana, Cuba
Piano / Post-Bop, Afro-Cuban Jazz, Latin Jazz
Only in recent times has Gonzalo Rubalcaba, one of the great Cuban jazz musicians, been able to freely travel in the US. He studied classical piano from 1971-83,

toured France and Africa with the Orquesta Aragon in 1983 and formed the Grupo Proyecto in 1985, touring Europe frequently. In 1986 he met Charlie Haden, who sang his praises and helped arrange his appearances at the Montreal and Montreux festivals. By 1990 Gonzalo Rubalcaba had been discovered by the jazz world and his records began to be released on Blue Note. An advanced improviser with a dense style, Rubalcaba has unlimited potential. —*Scott Yanow*

Mi Gran Pasion / Jul. 1987 / Messidor ✦✦✦✦✦
Cuba's most celebrated musical prodigy, Rubalcaba is presently busy becoming a major jazz pianist, having expanded his activities well outside Cuba. This album, recorded in Germany with a Cuban band, is a masterpiece: his salute to danzon, the music Rubalcaba's father (Guillermo Rubalcaba) still plays in Havana. Modernist, and at the same time an elegant essay on how to play this most decorous of musical forms. —*Ned Sublette*

Giraldilla / 1989 / Messidor ✦✦✦
Rubalcaba's follow-up to *Mi Gran Pasion* couldn't have been more unlike its predecessor. Musicians from a country where the phones don't work are set down in a high-tech German studio. It's strident, sprawling, and brilliant. World music? This is it. Dissonant counterpoint worthy of an Austrian, percussion that only a Cuban could play—and the excitement of a young world-class pianist still learning to control his power. —*Ned Sublette*

Live in Havana / Jun. 1989 / Messidor ✦✦✦✦
Many consider Rubalcaba the next dominant Afro-Latin pianist, while others criticize what they see as too much flash and not enough substance. There's plenty of fire on this live session, and also some impressive, percussive solos from a keyboard dynamo. —*Ron Wynn*

Discovery: Live at Montreux / Jul. 15, 1990 / Blue Note ✦✦✦✦✦

★ **The Blessing** / May 12, 1991-May 15, 1991 / Blue Note ✦✦✦✦✦
The virtuosic Cuban pianist Gonzalo Rubalcaba's first recording to be issued in the US is still one of his best. With strong accompaniment from bassist Charlie Haden (one of his early champions) and drummer Jack DeJohnette, Rubalcaba is in frequently exciting form throughout these performances. Highlights include an outstanding investigation of "Besame Mucho," "Giant Steps," Ornette Coleman's beautiful "The Blessing" and an unusual treatment given Bill Evans' "Blue in Green." —*Scott Yanow*

Images: Live at Mt.Fuji / Aug. 24, 1991-Aug. 25, 1991 / Blue Note ✦✦✦✦
A powerhouse live session from dynamic Cuban pianist Gonzalo Rubalcaba. It was recorded live for Blue Note, and is a trio date with bassist John Patitucci and drummer Jack DeJohnette. Patitucci, normally heard in either a fusion or an instrumental pop setting, shows his facility and versatilty as he smoothly adjusts to Rubalcaba's upbeat, unorthodox style and meshes with DeJohnette. —*Ron Wynn*

Suite 4 Y 20 / May 7, 1992-May 12, 1992 / Blue Note ✦✦✦✦
Recorded in Spain, this excellent set by the remarkable Cuban pianist Gonzalo Rubalcaba features his working group (trumpeter Reynaldo Melian, electric bassist Felipe Cabrera and drummer Julio Barreto) along with guest bassist Charlie Haden on four songs. The repertoire includes several pieces by Cuban composers, five of Rubalcaba's originals, "Perfidia," "Love Letters," Haden's "Our Spanish Love Song" and the Beatles' "Here, There and Everywhere." Gonzalo Rubalcaba shows maturity and self-restraint throughout much of this disc, performing a well-rounded set of advanced music. —*Scott Yanow*

Rapsodia / Nov. 15, 1992-Nov. 21, 1992 / Blue Note ✦✦✦✦✦
Pianist Gonzalo Rubalcaba has such impressive technique that he has the potential of completely overwhelming any song he plays, but he shows admirable restraint throughout much of this quartet date. Influenced to a degree by Chick Corea and Herbie Hancock, Rubalcaba still shows a fresh personality when he utilizes an electric keyboard on a few of the selections. His quartet (which includes trumpeter Reynaldo Melian, bassist Felipe Cabrera and drummer Julio Barreto), in addition to fine support, offers a contrasting solo voice in its virtuosic trumpeter. This is a well-rounded set of complex but fairly accessible music. —*Scott Yanow*

Imagine / May 14, 1993-Jun. 24, 1994 / Blue Note ✦✦✦✦✦
Gonzalo Rubalcaba, a Cuban jazz treasure, is heard on his CD from three separate occasions. Although Howard Mandel's odd liner notes make it sound like most of the music originated from Rubalcaba's 1993 New York concert at Alice Tully Hall (he even refers to a duet Rubalcaba had with singer Dianne Reeves as if it were included on this release), only the searching version of "First Song" with bassist Charlie Haden and drummer Jack DeJohnette is actually from that appearance. "Imagine" and "Circuito II" (both taken solo) were recorded in a Hollywood studio a year later and the remaining four songs (three with a Cuban quartet) are taken from a 1994 Westwood concert. Rubalcaba has limitless technique and (even with its touches of Herbie Hancock and Chick Corea) a sound of his own. His lyrical rendition of "Imagine" is a highlight as is the eccentric "Contagio" and a melan-

choly exploration of "Perfidia." Of Rubalcaba's sidemen, electric bassist Felipe Cabrera offer a very active accompaniment that recalls Jaco Pastorius, drummer Julio Barreto is fine in support and trumpeter Reynaldo Melian is a virtuoso with a rather cold sound. All in all, this is a fine all-round set by Gonzalo Rubalcaba that is full of complex ideas and subtle surprises.—*Scott Yanow*

Diz / Dec. 14, 1993-Dec. 15, 1993 / Blue Note ◆◆◆◆

Although one might assume that having the title of "Diz" means that this set would be a tribute to Dizzy Gillespie, only four of the nine selections were actually associated with the great trumpeter; the other numbers range from Bird and Bud Powell to Benny Golson and Charles Mingus ("Smooch"). Gonzalo Rubalcaba makes each of the jazz standards his own by reharmonizing the chord structures, playing in his own dense style and coming up with fresh new statements rather than just recreating bebop. He is quite lyrical and somber on the ballads, makes "Donna Lee" unrecognizable and (with the assistance of bassist Ron Carter and drummer Julio Barreto) modernizes all of the potential warhorses. This is a very interesting workout.—*Scott Yanow*

Vanessa Rubin

b. , Cleveland, OH
Vocals / Standards

An appealing singer who does not improvise much, Vanessa Rubin has recorded several fine albums for Novus. She studied classical music but switched to jazz early on. Rubin sang with and managed the Blackshaw Brothers (an organ quartet from Cleveland). After working with several groups locally (and recording with the Cleveland Jazz All-Stars) in 1982, Rubin moved to New York. She worked with Pharoah Sanders, Frank Foster's Loud Minority and the big bands of Mercer Ellington and Lionel Hampton and studied with Barry Harris in addition to teaching in the NYC public school system. In 1992 she signed with Novus and all of her releases thus far have been quite enjoyable (showing continual growth) including a fine tribute to Carmen McRae.—*Scott Yanow*

Soul Eyes / 1991 / Novus ◆◆◆◆

Vanessa Rubin at the time of her Novus debut had been a high-school English teacher for seven years. This CD was a good start for her singing career although the results are a little mixed. Rubin displays an attractive voice (sounding great when holding long notes), but at this point in time ballads were not her strong point (on "When We Were One" she recalls Barbra Streisand). In addition, producer Onaje Allan Gumbs cannot resist gumming up the works in a few places with phony strings from his keyboards; he funks up what may be the initial vocal version of Mal Waldron's classic "Soul Eyes" along with a slower-than-usual "Giant Steps." On the plus side, Rubin's workout on a flag-waving "I've Got the World on a String" is enjoyable, the backup crew (which includes pianist Kirk Lightsey, trumpeter Eddie Allen and saxophonist Roger Byam) get occasional solos and the singer does a fine tribute to Sarah Vaughan on "Tenderly." This was a worthwhile debut but Vanessa Rubin's best work would be in the future.—*Scott Yanow*

● **Pastiche** / 1993 / Novus ◆◆◆◆◆

Throughout this well-planned date, Vanessa Rubin sounds like an able successor to the more jazz-oriented sides of Nancy Wilson, Lorez Alexandria and Ernestine Anderson. Rubin's soulful voice and subtle variations blend in well with the solos of the various horns even if she is not really an improviser herself. Assisted by a fine rhythm section and such sidemen as trumpeters E.J. Allen and Cecil Bridgewater, trombonist Steve Turre and (on one song) tenorman Houston Person, Rubin expertly interprets the lyrics with both honest emotion and swing, occasionally scatting in unison or in counterpoint with the horns. This disc offers a good example of her talents.—*Scott Yanow*

I'm Glad There Is You / May 1994 / Novus ◆◆◆◆

This Vanessa Rubin release is a tribute to Carmen McRae. Although she cites McRae as a major influence, Rubin actually does not sound much like her and leans as much towards middle-of-the-road music as jazz. Also, not all of these songs are really identified with McRae (most notably "Send in the Clowns," which was largely owned by Sarah Vaughan). The ballad-dominated set does have a reasonable amount of variety, Rubin gets off some fine scatting on "Yardbird Suite" and she introduces an excellent original in "No Strings Attached." A variety of guests (including Grover Washington, Jr., Frank Foster, Antonio Hart, Cecil Bridgewater, Kenny Burrell and Monty Alexander) only appear on one or two songs apiece and do not make that much of an impression. However, Vanessa Rubin's attractive voice is strong enough to carry the music and this release is a step forward for her.—*Scott Yanow*

Vanessa Rubin Sings / 1995 / Novus ◆◆◆

Vanessa Rubin has a lovely voice but rarely wanders much from the melody. Since many of the songs that she performs on this Novus CD have already been done definitively dozens of times by others (such as "Our Love Is Here to Stay," "My

Ship," "Morning" and even "Being Green"), the value of the release is not as high as it should be. Rubin does contribute new lyrics to Wayne Shrter's "Speak No Evil" (renamed "All for One"), her singing is heartfelt on "His Eye Is on the Sparrow" and Steve Turre's four appearances (on trombone and conch shells) are a major asset. But why revive "Black Coffee" (another song that has already been done perfectly) with its self-pitying attitude and dated references to cigarettes?—*Scott Yanow*

New Horizons / Jul. 15, 1997 / RCA ◆◆

For this release, Vanessa Rubin mostly discards jazz in favor of somewhat mundane R&B. She does bring a jazz sensibility to most of the songs (particularly the ballads), but in general the material is lightweight (even "Here's That Rainy Day" is watered down), and there is little to distinguish the date from dozens of others in the crossover idiom. Other than a few short spots from trumpeter Cecil Bridgewater, the backup band (a rhythm quartet) sounds fairly anonymous. Pass.—*Scott Yanow*

Ellyn Rucker

b. Jul. 29, 1937, Des Moines, IA
Piano, Vocals / Bop, Hard Bop

A talented bop-based pianist and a highly appealing and sensuous singer, Ellyn Rucker has long been a fixture in the Denver area. Although she started playing piano when she was eight, discovered jazz at 13 and studied classical piano at Drake University, she did not decide to become a full-time musician until 1979. Rucker has toured Europe several times (with and without Spike Robinson), recorded several albums for Capri, has a full-length video on Leisure Jazz and performed at many festivals. Perhaps if Ellyn Rucker had taken up music full-time 20 years earlier or lived in a larger area than Denver she would be a bigger name. However, her talent has long been in the major leagues and her recordings are all quite appealing and powerful.—*Scott Yanow*

Ellyn / Sep. 2, 1987-Sep. 3, 1987 / Capri ◆◆◆

Ellyn Rucker is a strong enough pianist that she does not really need to sing, and she is a talented enough vocalist that she would be a popular attraction if she did not play a note of music. The Denver-based pianist-vocalist is equally skilled in both areas as shown on this Capri set, her debut as a leader. With the assistance of tenor saxophonist Pete Christlieb, bassist John Clayton and drummer Jeff Hamilton, Rucker's sensuous voice and Bill Evans-influenced piano make for a perfect combination on such tunes as "In Your Own Sweet Way," "One Morning in May," "'Round Midnight" and "The Night Has a Thousand Eyes." A special bonus is a three-song "Solo Medley."—*Scott Yanow*

● **This Heart of Mine** / Aug. 18, 1988-Aug. 19, 1988 / Capri ◆◆◆◆◆

Pianist-vocalist Ellyn Rucker's second Capri release (a trio outing with bassist Red Mitchell and drummer Marvin "Smitty" Smith) is even better than her first. A particularly strong pianist soloist who is also the perfect accompanist for her softtoned vocals, Rucker has long fallen into the "underrated category" due to her decision to live in Denver. However, as she shows throughout this CD, she is a world-class performer and deserves to be much better-known.—*Scott Yanow*

Nice Work! / Jan. 18, 1989-Jan. 19, 1989 / Capri ◆◆◆◆◆

Although she shares the billing on this session with tenor saxophonist Spike Robinson, this is very much an Ellyn Rucker album. A bop-based pianist so talented that she really does not have to sing, and a highly appealing jazz vocalist who would be quite notable if she did not play an instrument, Ellyn Rucker has long deserved to be famous in the jazz world. Based in Denver, Rucker combines her two skills at a level that has not been heard since Nat "King" Cole; when she accompanies her vocals, the piano playing is so stimulating that one would swear that there were two people involved. Spike Robinson, one of the last practitioners of the Four Brothers cool-toned Lester Young sound, is in excellent form and has swinging solos on most of the 11 standards. But it is for the playing and singing of Ellyn Rucker (heard at her best on such songs as "El Cajon," "Nobody Else but Me," "You Took Advantage of Me" and "As Long as I Live") that this CD (released in 1995 and also featuring the late bassist Monty Budwig and drummer Ralph Penland) is most highly recommended.—*Scott Yanow*

Thoughts of You / Feb. 24, 1992-Feb. 26, 1992 / Capri ◆◆◆

Roswell Rudd

b. Nov. 17, 1935, Sharon, CT
Trombone / Free Jazz, Avant-Garde

One of the pioneer trombonists in free jazz, Roswell Rudd was heard at his best in the mid-'60s matching wits with Archie Shepp. He studied French horn from age 11 and during 1954-59 played Dixieland trombone with a variety of groups including Eli's Chosen Six (with whom he recorded). After recording with Cecil Taylor in 1960 and working (but not recording) with Herbie Nichols, Rudd teamed up with another former Dixielander, Steve Lacy, to have a quartet that exclusively played the music of Thelonious Monk. He was with Bill Dixon in 1962 and then was a member of the New York Art Quartet with John Tchicai in 1964. The period 1965-67 was spent mostly with Archie Shepp although Rudd also recorded a couple albums of his own. He played with Robin Kenyatta in 1968 and Charlie Haden's Liberation Music Orchestra in 1969; there were also recordings with Gato Barbieri, Beaver Harris, Lonnie Liston Smith, the Jazz Composers' Orchestra, Enrico Rava, Misha Mengelberg and more as a leader. Rudd taught at Bard College and the University of Maine but by the 1990s was playing in obscurity for a time in the Catskills. However, during the past few years Roswell Rudd has resumed recording again, still sounding in prime form. —*Scott Yanow*

Everywhere / Sep. 1966 / Impulse! ✦✦✦✦✦

Numatik Swing Band / Jul. 6, 1973 / JCOA ✦✦✦✦
With the Jazz Composers Orchestra. —*Michael G. Nastos*

● **Flexible Flyer** / Mar. 1974 / Freedom ✦✦✦✦✦
Date for creative trombonist who fell in the cracks when Ray Anderson arrived. A solid album, with Sheila Jordan (v). —*Michael G. Nastos*

Inside Job / May 21, 1976 / Freedom ✦✦✦
Solid quintet date w/ intense Dave Burrell on piano. —*Ron Wynn*

The Unheard Herbie Nichols, Vol. 1 / Nov. 19, 1996-Nov. 20, 1996 / CIMP ✦✦✦✦
Although he was a major composer who wrote over 200 pieces, pianist Herbie Nichols never had an opportunity to document most of his work, orchestrate any of his pieces for a group larger than a trio, or even to work regularly playing his music. When he passed away in 1963 at the age of 44, he was unknown except to a very small group of fans and musicians, one of whom was trombonist Roswell Rudd. On this 1996 set, Rudd debuts seven Nichols compositions that were never previously recorded. The trombonist performs in an unusual trio with guitarist Greg Millar and drummer John Bacon, Jr. (who doubles on vibes). Five of the pieces (which range in length from the nearly 16 minute "Jamaica" to "Valse Macabre," which clocks in at 1:37) feature the entire group, and although the structures are quite tricky, the music (even when it is in waltz time) generally swings in its own fashion. The final two numbers ("One Twilight" and "Passing Thought") are taken as unaccompanied trombone solos and find Rudd putting plenty of feeling into his interpretations of his fallen friend's music. Overall, this is an intriguing set of "new" music. —*Scott Yanow*

Pete Rugolo (Peter Rugolo)

b. Dec. 25, 1915, San Piero, Sicily
Arranger, Leader / Progressive Jazz

Pete Rugolo was one of the most prolific arrangers for Stan Kenton's 1945-1949 orchestras, following through on the leader's swashbuckling example to help shape the band's exciting, blasting style. Brought to the US at age five, Rugolo grew up in Santa Rosa, CA, and became a student of Darius Milhaud at Mills College in Oakland. After a stint with the Army, he submitted an arrangement to Kenton and then settled in with the band, turning out a series of "Artistry in . . ." compositions (Bass, Percussion, Bolero, Boogie), as well as some of the earliest, most startling pieces for the Innovations in Modern Music Orchestra. However, Rugolo soon gravitated toward pop, landing a position as music director of Capitol Records in 1949, where he cranked out arrangements—some of which bordered on easy-listening treacle—for June Christy, Nat "King" Cole, Harry Belafonte (in his brief pop period), the Four Freshmen and others. In 1957, he became music director of Mercury Records, making a number of albums for that label, and briefly led a big band in 1954. From the '50s onward, Rugolo moved into Hollywood, scoring TV series like "The Fugitive and Run for Your Life" and several films. Consequently, his importance to jazz lessened as the years passed. —*Richard S. Ginell*

● **Adventures in Rhythm** / Apr. 28, 1954-Jun. 21, 1954 / Columbia ✦✦✦✦✦
Pete Rugolo's early recordings as a leader after leaving Stan Kenton's Orchestra are quite rewarding and innovative in their own way yet have been long underrated and out of print. This LP finds Rugolo leading all-star groups filled with such top West Coast jazz stars as trumpeters Pete Candoli, Shorty Rogers and Maynard Ferguson, trombonists Milt Bernhardt and Herbie Harper, Bob Cooper on tenor and oboe, altoist Bud Shank, baritonists Jimmy Giuffre and Bob Gordon, pianist Claude Williamson, guitarist Laurindo Almeido and drummer Shelly Manne. On such numbers as "Mixin' the Blues," "Rugolo Meets Shearing," "Jingle Bells Mambo" and "King Porter Stomp," Pete Rugolo's arrangements are full of surprises while leaving space for his sidemen's short solos. Well worth searching for. —*Scott Yanow*

Hilton Ruiz

b. May 29, 1952, New York, NY
Piano / Bop, Latin Jazz, Afro-Cuban Jazz

One of the finest pianists in Afro-Cuban jazz, Hilton Ruiz is also an expert bop player. A child prodigy who appeared at Carnegie Recital Hall when he was eight, Ruiz gigged with Latin bands as a teenager and gained early experience playing with Joe Newman, Frank Foster, Freddie Hubbard. He studied with Mary Lou Williams and had an important association with Rahsaan Roland Kirk (1973-77). After touring with George Coleman (1978-79) he recorded with Charles Mingus, Betty Carter, Archie Shepp, Clark Terry and Chico Freeman among others. Hilton Ruiz has mostly led his own groups since the early '80s and fortunately he has recorded quite a few rewarding discs. —*Scott Yanow*

Piano Man / Jul. 10, 1975 / Steeple Chase ✦✦✦✦s

Excitation / Feb. 7, 1977 / Steeple Chase ✦✦✦

New York Hilton / Feb. 8, 1977 / Steeple Chase ✦✦✦✦

Steppin' into Beauty / Feb. 7, 1977-Feb. 8, 1977/ Steeple Chase ✦✦✦✦✦

Cross Currents / Nov. 1984 / Vintage Jazz ✦✦✦✦✦
These trio and quintet performances helped cement Ruiz's status in the Afro-Latin and jazz communities. —*Ron Wynn*

Something Grand / Oct. 14, 1986-Oct. 15, 1986 / Novus ✦✦✦✦
Fine Afro-Latin jazz excursion by this solid pianist. Sensational trombone by Steve Turre. Sam Rivers (sax) is also in the ensemble. —*Ron Wynn*

● **El Camino [The Road]** / Jun. 1988 / Novus ✦✦✦✦✦
An ambitious, often dazzling set from '86 with pianist Hilton Ruiz. He's heading an outstanding band that includes some great players who seldom ever recorded on major label sessions. Trombonist Dick Griffin, saxophonist Sam Rivers, and guitarist Rodney Jones are dynamite, while trumpeter Lew Soloff and Ruiz are dependable and entertaining during their solos and more explosive in their exchanges with Griffin, Rivers, and Jones. —*Ron Wynn*

Strut / Nov. 30, 1988+Dec. 1, 1988 / Novus ✦✦✦✦✦
Pianist Hilton Ruiz mixes together elements of salsa, R&B, funk and jazz but, instead of his music becoming some type of hybrid, the result is a very danceable variety of jazz that is both accessible and challenging. Ruiz, whose main influence is McCoy Tyner, gathered together a very interesting assortment of players for *Strut*. Trumpeter Lew Soloff contributes some high notes and leads the horn riffing, trombonist Dick Griffin's extroverted trombone is witty in its short spots, Sam Rivers (mostly on tenor) and percussionist Mongo Santamaria add their sounds to the brew and guitarist Rodney Jones is second only to Ruiz in taking solo honors. It is particularly rewarding to hear a Latin remake of "The Sidewinder" and many of the other good-natured melodies are catchy. *Strut* should be able to win over both jazz fans and those listeners who claim to not understand or be able to appreciate creative music. —*Scott Yanow*

Doin' It Right / Nov. 9, 1989-Nov. 11, 1989 / Novus ✦✦✦
This is a mostly straightahead jazz date by pianist Hilton Ruiz that achieves some variety by alternating the instrumentation. The pianist/leader adds percussionist Daniel Ponce to some numbers (such as "Doin' It Right") for some Latin-jazz, jams with his trio (which also includes bassist Jimmy Rowser and drummer Steve Berrios) and pays tribute to both Thelonious Monk and Bud Powell. Don Cherry sits in on his muted trumpet for the ballad "Misty Moods" and the minor-keyed "Scottish Blues" but his solos wander and his intonation is shaky. Much better is Ruiz's unaccompanied exploration of "I Didn't Know What Time It Was" and a quartet version of his original "The Blessing." Other than Cherry's appearances, this is a satisfying modern mainstream set. —*Scott Yanow*

A Moment's Notice / Feb. 25, 1991-Mar. 12, 1991 / Novus ✦✦✦✦✦
This CD is a success on all levels. For this Latin jazz date, the rhythm section's power and energy constantly inspire the horn soloists. Tenor saxophonist George Coleman is in top form, altoist Kenny Garrett gets in his licks and flutist Dave Valentin, whose playing was often a bit watered down on his own GRP releases, takes what may be his finest recorded solo on "Cuchi Cuchi." Not to be overlooked is Ruiz's McCoy Tyner-inspired piano, which fuels the rhythm section and really pushes the horns. Ruiz wisely chose nine superior songs to perform, including several rarely heard in this type of setting ("Una Mas," "Like Someone in Love," "Naima" and "Moment's Notice"). Highly recommended. —*Scott Yanow*

Manhattan Mambo / Apr. 28, 1992 / Telarc ✦✦✦✦
Pianist Hilton Ruiz is heard with a superior group of musicians adept at playing both bebop and Latin-jazz. With a front line of trumpeter Charlie Sepulveda, David Sanchez on tenor and trombonist Papo Vazquez in addition to four percussionists, Ruiz's nonet displays plenty of fire on a set of originals, Perez Prado's "Mambo Numero Cinco" and John Coltrane's "Impressions." —*Scott Yanow*

Live at Birdland / Jun. 24, 1992-Jun. 25, 1992 / Candid ✦✦✦✦

Heroes / Nov. 8, 1993-Nov. 9, 1993 / Telarc ✦✦✦

Hands on Percussion / 1994-1995 / Tropijazz ✦✦✦✦

Pianist Hilton Ruiz has had a very successful career in both jazz and Latin music. On this Tropijazz release, he combines the two styles to form a very likable brand of Latin jazz. Ruiz utilizes such sidemen as Tito Puente (playing vibes or timbales on three songs), flutist Dave Valentin, tenor saxophonist David Sanchez, trumpeter Charlie Sepulveda, trombonist Papo Vasquez, bassist Andy Gonzalez and three notable percussionists (Giovanni Hidalgo, Ignacio Berroa and Steve Berrios) for Latinized versions of four jazz standards and five group originals (including three by Ruiz). The music is quite catchy, danceable and reasonably challenging. Recommended to fans of Latin-jazz. —*Scott Yanow*

Rhythm in the House / 1976 / RMM ✦✦✦✦

On *Rhythm in the House,* Hilton Ruiz decided to spice up traditional Latin jazz with contemporary dance, soul and disco music. The result is a kinetic, entertaining record that proves Latin jazz is not a static form. Ruiz has enlisted a stellar supporting group, featuring Tito Puente, Richie Flores and bassist Ruben Rodriguez, among others. He wrote or co-wrote and provided arrangements for all eight songs on the album, and while not every song has a memorable melody, it's all infectious Latin dance music that proves Ruiz' versatility. —*Stephen Thomas Erlewine*

Howard Rumsey

b. Nov. 7, 1917, Brawley, CA
Bass / Cool, Bop, Latin Jazz

Although a good enough bassist to play with Stan Kenton's big band, Howard Rumsey was best known as the organizer of the Lighthouse All-Stars and manager of the Lighthouse. Originally a drummer, Rumsey switched to bass while at college. He played with Vido Musso in the late '30s and when Stan Kenton formed his first band in 1941, Rumsey became its bassist. A year later he started freelancing in the Los Angeles area. In 1949 Rumsey brought jazz into the Lighthouse in Hermosa Beach, CA. Within a few years the jam sessions featured some of the top jazz-oriented studio players in the area and the bassist was heading "the Lighthouse All-Stars," which recorded frequently for Contemporary in the 1950s, starring such players as Shorty Rogers, Jimmy Giuffre, Bob Cooper, Bud Shank and Bill Perkins. In the 1960s Rumsey quit playing to devote full-time to running the Lighthouse and, after he sold the establishment, for a time he ran the nearby club Concerts by the Sea. —*Scott Yanow*

Patrice Rushen

b. Sep. 30, 1954, Los Angeles, CA
Keyboards, Vocals / Crossover Jazz, R&B, Soul

Patrice Rushen has long had the potential to be a top jazz keyboardist, but she has thus far mostly stuck to more commercial areas. She started on classical piano lessons when she was three, developed quickly, and as a teenager was already creating a stir in jazz circles. Rushen gained experience in the mid-1970s playing with Abbey Lincoln, Gerald Wilson, Donald Byrd, Benny Golson, Jean-Luc Ponty, Stanley Turrentine and most notably Sonny Rollins (1976). But her solo career (which started in 1974) has been mostly pure pop/R&B and often emphasized her more mundane singing. There have been exceptions along the way, most notably in guest spots and her occasional work with drummer Ndugu Chancler and tenor saxophonist Ernie Watts as the quartet called the Meeting (which recorded one CD in the mid-'90s for Silva Screen). But in general, Patrice Rushen's career from the jazz standpoint has been rather disappointing, particularly considering her obvious talents. —*Scott Yanow*

Prelusion / 1974 / Prestige ✦✦✦

Those who only knew Patrice Rushen from her big hit crossover tracks might be surprised by this 1974 debut. She was a slashing, expressive pianist on these cuts, spearheading a band that included tenor sax veteran Joe Henderson. While it was mostly an electric rather than acoustic set, Rushen showed a capability for improvising that hasn't been equaled since she switched to more profitable Urban Contemporary and light jazz material. —*Ron Wynn*

Before the Dawn / 1975 / Prestige ✦✦✦

Before she found the charts and crossover success, keyboardist Patrice Rushen demonstrated her facility with conventional hard bop and straight mainstream material. Her accompaniment was clean and brisk and her solos were well played and constructed, if not always the most harmonically challenging. This was her best straight jazz release, and among her last. —*Ron Wynn*

Patrice / 1977 / Elektra ✦✦

Shout It Out / 1976 / Prestige ✦✦✦

Pizzaazz / 1980 / Elektra ✦✦

Posh / 1979 / Elektra ✦✦

Straight from the Heart / 1982 / Rhino ✦✦✦

Straight from the Heart is Patrice Rushen's most successful fusion of R&B and jazz. The album doesn't delve too deeply into either R&B and fusion; instead, it charts a light, mellow and soulful middle ground. And the approach was successful: Three of the songs—"Forget Me Nots," "Breakout!," "I Was Tired of Being Alone (Glad I Got Cha)"—were R&B hits, while "Number One" was nominated for a Grammy. Rhino's 1996 reissue of *Straight from the Heart* includes single edits and 12-inch remixes of the album's singles. —*Stephen Thomas Erlewine*

Now / 1984 / Elektra ✦✦

● **The Meeting** / 1990 / GRP ✦✦✦✦

The selections on this diverse CD (a collaboration featuring keyboardist Patrice Rushen, saxophonist Ernie Watts, bassist Alphonso Johnson and drummer Ndugu Chancler) alternate between soulful jazz, inventive R&B, a bit of funk and ballads. Watts is in top form, and Rushen (who recalls Chick Corea on "Tango" and Herbie Hancock in other spots) shows that she can still play with creativity. A few of the tracks are throwaways, especially "Elements of Mystery" and "Virgin," but overall, the set is a pleasant surprise and is recommended to listeners who enjoy R&B-oriented jazz. —*Scott Yanow*

Signature / 1997 / Discovery ✦✦

After making R&B singing her number-one priority for 20 years, Patrice Rushen shocked the music world in 1997 by recording *Signature,* her first instrumental album since 1977's *Shout It Out.* Rushen showed a lot of promise as a jazz instrumentalist when she was recording for Fantasy in the mid-1970s, but when she hit big as an R&B star, it seemed doubtful that she'd ever record another jazz album under her own name. A mixed bag, this jazz/urban contemporary/pop release isn't the improvisatory gem Rushen would be quite capable of delivering, but the keyboardist/pianist does have some nice spots on the funky "Oneness" (a duet with drummer Ndugu Chancelor), the congenial "Wise Ol' Souls" and the intellectual post-bop piece "L'esprit De Joie." Some of the more commercial material, however, is fairly lightweight. "Days Gone By" is outright elevator music, and Rushen's covers of Sade's "Sweetest Taboo" and the Stylistics' "Hurry Up This Way Again" show little imagination. While it was nice to have Rushen back in an instrumental setting, one wishes she would spend less time catering to radio and more time demonstrating how strong a soloist she can be. Jazz fans would be better off with one of her early albums on Fantasy, such as *Prelusion* or *Before the Dawn.* —*Alex Henderson*

● **Haven't You Heard: The Best of Patrice Rushen** / Elektra/Rhino ✦✦✦✦

Nearly every one of Patrice Rushen's R&B hits—including the Top 10 singles "Haven't You Heard," "Forget Me Nots," "Feels So Real (Won't Let Go)," and "Watch Out"—are featured on the single-disc anthology *Haven't You Heard: The Best of Patrice Rushen.* With the exception of "Watch Out," her only Top 40 hit for Arista Records, the material is entirely drawn from Rushen's heyday at Elektra Records, when she was fusing jazz with R&B and pop. The songs on *Haven't You Heard* represent the highwater mark of her fusions, which makes the compilation both an excellent introduction and a comprehensive career retrospective. —*Stephen Thomas Erlewine*

Jimmy Rushing

b. Aug. 26, 1903, Oklahoma City, OK, **d.** Jun. 8, 1972, New York, NY
Vocals / Swing, Blues Jazz, East Coast Blues, Jump Blues

He was known as "Mister Five-by-Five"—an affectionate reference to his height and girth—a blues shouter who defined and then transcended the form. The owner of a booming voice that radiated sheer joy in whatever material he sang, Jimmy Rushing could swing with anyone and dominate even the loudest of big bands. Rushing achieved his greatest fame in front of the Count Basie band from 1935 to 1950, yet unlike many band singers closely associated with one organization, he was able to carry on afterwards with a series of solo recordings that further enhanced his reputation as a first-class jazz singer.

Raised in a musical family, learning violin, piano and music theory in his youth, Rushing began performing in nightspots after a move to California in the mid-1920s. He joined Walter Page's Blue Devils in 1927, then toured with Bennie Moten from 1929 until the leader's death in 1935, going over to Basie when the latter picked up the pieces of the Moten band. The unquenchably swinging Basie rhythm section was a perfect match for Rushing, making their earliest showing together on a 1936 recording of "Boogie Woogie" that stamped not only Rushing's presence onto the national scene but also that of Lester Young. Rushing's recordings with Basie are scattered liberally throughout several reissues on Decca, Columbia and RCA. While with Basie, he also appeared in several film shorts and features.

After the Basie ensemble broke up in 1950, a victim of hard times for big bands, Rushing briefly retired, then formed his own septet. He started a series of solo albums for Vanguard in the mid-1950s, then turned in several distinguished recordings for Columbia in league with such luminaries as Dave Brubeck, Coleman Hawkins and Benny Goodman, the latter of whom he appeared with at the Brussels World's Fair in 1958 as immortalized in "Brussels Blues." He also recorded with Basie alumni such as Buck Clayton and Jo Jones, as well as with the Duke Ellington band on *Jazz Party*. He appeared on TV in *The Sound of Jazz* in 1957, was featured in Jon Hendricks' *The Evolution of the Blues*, and also had a singing and acting role in the 1969 film *The Learning Tree*. —*Richard S. Ginell*

● **The Essential Jimmy Rushing** / Dec. 1, 1954-Mar. 5, 1957 / Vanguard ✦✦✦✦
This single CD reissues an earlier Jimmy Rushing two-LP set, leaving off two cuts due to lack of space. Jimmy Rushing, who may very well have been the definitive male big band singer, sticks mostly to blues and Kansas City swing on the release and is backed by a variety of top swing all-stars including most notably tenor saxophonist Buddy Tate, trumpeter Emmett Berry and trombonists Lawrence Brown and Vic Dickenson. The sidemen receive plenty of space for concise solos, particularly pianists Pete Johnson and Sammy Price. The performances (plus the 11 other songs that are awaiting reissue someday) are among the most rewarding of Jimmy Rushing's post-Basie career and are full of joy and timeless swing. —*Scott Yanow*

Mr. Five by Five / Nov. 7, 1956-Jul. 13, 1960 / Columbia ✦✦✦✦
From 1956-60, veteran swing/blues singer Jimmy Rushing recorded six albums for Columbia. Most of the sets have not yet been reissued on CD, so this two-LP sampler from 1980 (which inexcusably does not give the recording dates) is still worth picking up by listeners lucky enough to run across it. Rushing is featured in eight different settings on 30 selections, including with all-star groups featuring trumpeter Buck Clayton, tenors Coleman Hawkins and Buddy Tate, trombonist Dickie Wells and pianist Ray Bryant. In addition, there are numbers with the Dave Brubeck Quartet, the Benny Goodman big band, and (on four previously unreleased songs) fellow singer Helen Humes and tenor saxophonist Ben Webster. Throughout the high-quality program, Rushing is heard in prime form, making one wonder why so much of this swinging material has not been brought back yet. —*Scott Yanow*

Rushing Lullabies / Feb. 20, 1958-Jun. 19, 1959 / Columbia ✦✦✦✦
Although named after a former LP, this CD actually contains the complete contents of two albums (the other one was called *Little Jimmy Rushing and the Big Brass*) plus a brief previously unreleased number. Known for his renditions of swing-oriented blues, but also quite effective on ballads and jumping standards, the great singer is featured with a big band (which has solo space for many musicians, including tenors Buddy Tate and Coleman Hawkins, trumpeter Buck Clayton, and trombonist Dicky Wells) and a sextet with Tate, organist Sir Charles Thompson and pianist Ray Bryant. These were two of Rushing's better sets from the 1950s, and he is heard throughout the mostly veteran tunes in top form. Highlights include "I'm Coming Virginia," "Mister Five by Five," "When You're Smiling," "Good Rockin' Tonight" and "Russian Lullaby." —*Scott Yanow*

Everyday I Have the Blues / Feb. 9, 1967-Feb. 10, 1967 / Bluesway ✦✦✦✦✦

Bluesway Sessions / Feb. 9, 1967-1968 / Charly ✦✦✦✦
Singer Jimmy Rushing's two albums for Bluesway have been reissued in full on this British double-LP from 1986. Although recorded near the end of Rushing's life, he still sounds strong on the set of blues, ballads and swinging material. The first album finds Rushing joined by the Oliver Nelson Orchestra (which includes fluegelhornist Clark Terry and trombonist Dicky Wells), while the other has a septet that includes Wells, tenor saxophonist Buddy Tate and pianist Dave Frishberg, plus a slightly funky studio rhythm section. Both combinations work well, and Rushing shows plenty of spirit throughout the performances. —*Scott Yanow*

Gee, Baby, Ain't I Good to You / Oct. 30, 1967 / Master Jazz ✦✦
This is a decent session that, considering the lineup, does not live up to its potential. At what was essentially a jazz party held in a recording studio, the musicians (trumpeter Buck Clayton, trombonist Dickie Wells, tenor saxophonist Julian Dash, pianist Sir Charles Thompson, bassist Gene Ramey and drummer Jo Jones) are all veterans of the famous series of Buck Clayton jam sessions held in the 1950s and, along with singer Jimmy Rushing, the majority are alumni of the Count Basie Orchestra. The problem is that their rendition of the blues and swing standards are often quite loose, there are a generous amount of missteps and, although Clayton is heroic under the circumstances (this was one of his final recordings before ill health caused his retirement), most of the musicians would have benefited from running through the songs an additional time. It's recommended only to completists. —*Scott Yanow*

Who Was It Sang That Song / Oct. 30, 1967 / Master Jazz ✦✦✦
Recorded the same day as the music released on the Master Jazz album *Gee Baby, Ain't I Good to You*, this is the superior of the two recordings. This CD reissue not only has the original five songs from the LP, but also previously unreleased versions of "Deed I Do," Sir Charles Thompson's "Almost Home" and "Moten Stomp." The classic swing singer Jimmy Rushing is joined by six veterans, including three fellow Basieites: trumpeter Buck Clayton (near the end of his playing career), trombonist Dickie Wells and drummer Jo Jones, plus Julian Dash on tenor, bassist Gene Ramey and pianist Thompson. They jam enthusiastically, if predictably so loose versions of jazz standards including "Baby Won't You Please Come Home," a blues medley, and "All of Me." —*Scott Yanow*

The You and Me That Used to Be / Oct. 1971 / Bluebird ✦✦✦✦✦
On this straight CD reissue of Jimmy Rushing's final recording sessions, the singer is in spirited form despite being little more than a year from his death. On the ten swing standards and a lone blues ("Fine and Mellow"), Rushing is joined by pianist Dave Frishberg (also responsible for the arrangements), bassist Milt Hinton, and drummer Mel Lewis, plus either Ray Nance on cornet and violin and tenor saxophonist Zoot Sims, or Budd Johnson (on soprano) and Al Cohn (on tenor). Touching renditions of "I Surrender Dear" and "More Than You Know" find Rushing backed only by Frishberg's very able piano. This recommended CD is proof that "Mr. Five by Five" (whose career spanned more than 40 years) went out on top. —*Scott Yanow*

George Russell

b. Jun. 23, 1923, Cincinnati, OH
Arranger, Composer, Leader, Piano / Avant-Garde, Post-Bop
While George Russell has been very active as a free-thinking composer, arranger and bandleader, his biggest effect upon jazz has been that of the quieter role of theorist. His great contribution, apparently the first by a jazz musician to general music theory, was a book with the intimidating title *The Lydian Chromatic Concept of Tonal Organization*, where he concocted a concept of playing jazz based on scales rather than chord changes. Published in 1953, Russell's theories directly paved the way for the modal revolutions of Miles Davis and John Coltrane—and Russell even took credit for the theory behind Michael Jackson's huge hit "Wanna Be Startin' Somethin,'" which uses the Lydian scale (no, he didn't ask for royalties). Russell's stylistic reach in his own compositions eventually became omnivorous, embracing bop, gospel, blues, rock, funk, contemporary classical elements, electronic music and African rhythms in his recent, ambitious extended works—most apparent in his large-scale 1983 suite for an enlarged big band, *The African Game*. Like his colleague Gil Evans, Russell never stopped growing, but his work is not nearly as well known that that of Evans, being more difficult to grasp and, in any case, not as well documented by US record labels.

Russell's first instrument was the drums, which he played in the Boy Scout Drum and Bugle Corps and at local clubs when he was in high school. At 19, he was hospitalized with tuberculosis, but he used the enforced inactivity to learn the craft of arranging from a fellow patient. Once back on his feet, he played with Benny Carter, but after being replaced on drums by Max Roach, Russell began to zero in on composing and arranging. He moved to New York to join the crowd of young firebrands who gathered in the Gil Evans "salon," and he was actually invited to play drums in Charlie Parker's band. But once again, he fell ill, finding himself in a Bronx hospital for 16 months (1945-46), where he began to formulate the ideas for the Lydian Concept. Upon his recovery, Russell leaped into the embryonic fusion of bebop and Afro-Cuban rhythms by writing "Cubana Be" and "Cubana Bop," which the Dizzy Gillespie big band recorded in 1947. He contributed arrangements to Claude Thornhill and Artie Shaw in the late 1940s and wrote the first (and not the last) speculatory scenario of a meeting between Charlie Parker and Igor Stravinsky, "A Bird in Igor's Yard," recorded by Buddy De Franco.

While working on his Lydian theories, Russell dropped out of active music making for awhile, working at a sales counter in Macy's when his book was published. But when he resumed composing in 1956, he had established himself as an influential force in jazz. Russell's connection with Gunther Schuller resulted in the commission of *All About Rosie* for the 1957 Brandeis University jazz festival, and he also taught at the Lenox School of Jazz that Schuller co-founded. He formed a rehearsal sextet in the mid-1950s that became known as the George Russell Smalltet, with Art Farmer, Bill Evans, Hal McCusick, Barry Galbraith and various drummers and bassists. Their 1956 recording *Jazz Workshop* (RCA Victor) became a landmark of its time, and Russell continued to record intriguing LPs for Decca in the late 1950s and Riverside in the early 1960s. Another key album from this period, *Ezz-thetics*, featured two important progressive players, Eric Dolphy and Don Ellis.

Finding the American jazz scene too confining for his music, Russell left for Europe in 1963, living in Sweden for five years. From his new base, he toured Scandinavia with a new sextet of European players and received numerous commissions—including a ballet based on *Othello*, a mass, and an orchestral suite

Electronic Sonata for Souls Loved by Nature. Upon his return to the US in 1969, he joined the faculty of the New England Conservatory of Music, where Schuller had started a jazz department, and this gave him a secure base from which to tour occasionally with his own groups. Russell stopped composing from 1972 to 1978 in order to finish a second volume on the Lydian Chromatic Concept. He led a 19-piece big band at the Village Vanguard for six weeks in 1978, played the Newport Jazz Festival when it was based in New York City, and made tours of Italy, the US West Coast and England in the 1980s. Among his most imposing commissions of the last decade or so have been *An American Trilogy* and the monumental three-hour work *Time Line* for symphony orchestra, jazz ensembles, rock groups, choir and dancers. In addition to *The African Game* and *So What* on Blue Note, Russell made several recordings for Soul Note in the 1970s and '80s. —*Richard S. Ginell*

● **Jazz Workshop** / Mar. 31, 1956-Dec. 21, 1956 / Bluebird ◆◆◆◆◆
Arranger/composer George Russell's debut release as a leader (reissued on CD in 1987) is full of surprising writing that swings and yet is quite original and unpredictable. Russell gathered together some of his favorite musicians of the era (trumpeter Art Farmer, Hal McKusick on alto and flute, the young pianist Bill Evans, guitarist Barry Galbraith, either Milt Hinton or Teddy Kotick on bass, and either Joe Harris, Paul Motian or Osie Johnson on drums) to perform 12 of his originals, including "Ezz-thetic" (easily the best-known piece) and "Concerto for Billy the Kid," a feature for Evans. The reissue adds two "new" alternate takes to the intriguing program. Well worth exploring. —*Scott Yanow*

☆ **New York, N.Y./Jazz in the Space Age** / Sep. 12, 1958-Aug. 1, 1960 / MCA ◆◆◆◆◆
George Russell's second and third recording projects as a leader are considered classics, and they were combined on this mid-'70s double LP; neither are currently available on CD. A very original arranger/composer, Russell utilizes larger groups than usual for these sessions to perform his adventurous works. Best known is the narration by Jon Hendricks on "Manhattan" (which also includes among its soloists John Coltrane); other important players on the dates include valve trombonist Bob Brookmeyer, pianists Bill Evans and Paul Bley, trumpeter Art Farmer, tenor saxophonist Benny Golson, drummer Max Roach and Russell himself on tuned drums. The unique music is more difficult to describe than to enjoy, and these two sets remain among the more accessible of George Russell's many innovative projects. —*Scott Yanow*

Jazz in the Space Age / May 1960 / Decca ◆◆◆◆

George Russell at the Five Spot / Sep. 20, 1960 / Decca ◆◆◆◆

Stratusphunk / Oct. 18, 1960 / Original Jazz Classics ◆◆◆◆
From 1960-62, arranger/composer George Russell recorded six albums with his working combo that found him contributing "arranger's piano." The two Decca dates are very scarce, but the four Riversides have fortunately been reissued on CD in the Original Jazz Classics series. For this particular date, Russell is joined by five students at the School of Jazz in Lenox: trumpeter Al Kiger, trombonist Dave Baker (who in the future would become an important jazz educator), tenor saxophonist Dave Young, bassist Chuck Israels and drummer Joe Hunt. Surprisingly, only three of the six selections are Russell originals ("Bent Eagle" was an early effort by Carla Bley), but the leader's influence can be felt in all of the adventurous and slightly unusual yet swinging music. —*Scott Yanow*

★ **Ezz-Thetics** / May 8, 1961 / Original Jazz Classics ◆◆◆◆◆
This is a true classic. Composer/pianist George Russell gathered together a very versatile group of talents (trumpeter Don Ellis, trombonist Dave Baker, Eric Dolphy on alto and bass clarinet, tenor saxophonist Steve Swallow and drummer Joe Hunt) to explore three of his originals, "'Round Midnight" (which is given an extraordinary treatment by Dolphy), Miles Davis' "Nardis" and David Baker's "Honesty." The music is post-bop and although using ideas from avant-garde jazz, it does not fall into any simple category. The improvising is at a very high level and the frameworks (which include free and stoptime sections) really inspire the players. Highly recommended. —*Scott Yanow*

The Stratus Seekers / Jan. 31, 1962 / Original Jazz Classics ◆◆◆◆◆
In 1962, the George Russell Septet included both obscure names (altoist John Pierce, tenor saxophonist Paul Plummer and drummer Joe Hunt, who would later work with Bill Evans) and future stars (trumpeter Don Ellis, trombonist Dave Baker, who would become a significant jazz educator, and bassist Steve Swallow). The six selections (plus a "new" alternate) heard on the CD reissue are highlighted by "Blues in Orbit" (later recorded by Gil Evans) and the title cut; two other numbers were written by the sidemen. It is particularly interesting to hear the young Ellis in this setting. The music has its own logic and is difficult to classify, and deserves further attention by jazz historians and analysts. —*Scott Yanow*

The Outer View / Aug. 27, 1962 / Original Jazz Classics ◆◆◆◆◆
Composer George Russell's early-'60s Riverside recordings are among his most accessible. For this set (the CD reissue adds an alternate take of the title cut to the

original program), Russell and his very impressive sextet (which comprises trumpeter Don Ellis, trombonist Garnett Brown, Paul Plummer on tenor, bassist Steve Swallow and drummer Pete La Roca) are challenged by the complex material; even Charlie Parker's blues "Au Privave" is transformed into something new. It is particularly interesting to hear Don Ellis this early in his career. The most famous selection, a very haunting version of "You Are My Sunshine," was singer Sheila Jordan's debut on records. —*Scott Yanow*

At Beethoven Hall / Aug. 31, 1965 / Saba ◆◆◆◆
This intriguing double LP (the music has not yet been reissued on CD) was innovative composer George Russell's first recording after breaking up his young combo of the early '60s. Recorded in Germany at a concert, Russell (who plays fairly basic piano) is joined by cornetist Don Cherry, trumpeter Bertil Lovgren, trombonist Brian Trentham, tenor saxophonist Ray Pitts, bassist Cameron Brown and drummer Albert "Tootie" Heath for explorations of several lengthy pieces and a remake of "You Are My Sunshine." Most unusual is a suite dedicated to Russell's Lydian concept that includes abstract versions of "Bags' Groove," "Confirmation" and "'Round Midnight." —*Scott Yanow*

Othello Ballet Suite and Electronic Sonata No.1 / Nov. 3, 1967-Oct. 1, 1968 / Flying Dutchman ◆◆◆
An uneven but compelling work by George Russell that combines jazz, classical, and Shakespeare. The results range from magnificent to chaotic; there's a large band that includes mostly obscure foreign musicians. It was one of the first times that Norway's Jan Garbarek appeared playing tenor sax on a major label. This has been reissued on CD. —*Ron Wynn*

Electronic Sonata: 1968 / Apr. 28, 1969 / Soul Note ◆◆◆
The performances on this CD are much more interesting from the historical standpoint than they are musically. George Russell's "Electronic Sonata" has two parts and 14 "events" that often mix together acoustic instruments with electronics; the net result is colorful, adventurous and somewhat inconclusive. However, the sextet features future ECM stars Jan Garbarek (on tenor) and guitarist Terje Rypdal in addition to trumpeter Manfred Schoof, bassist Red Mitchell, drummer John Christensen and the composer on piano. The music does reward repeated listenings but it falls short of being essential. —*Scott Yanow*

Listen to the Silence / Jun. 1971 / Concept ◆◆◆◆

Vertical Form 6 / Mar. 10, 1977 / Soul Note ◆◆◆◆
A magnificent and critically acclaimed large band recording with arrangements by George Russell, who also conducted. His compositions, with their intricate, unpredictable, and keenly structured pace, textures, and layers, are expertly played by an international orchestra. This '77 release was unfortunately poorly distributed in America, since it was on a foreign label. —*Ron Wynn*

Electronic Sonata for Souls Loved by Nature 1980 / May 9, 1980-Jun. 10, 1980 / Strata East ◆◆◆◆◆

American Time Spiral / Jun. 9, 1980-Jun. 10, 1980 / Soul Note ◆◆◆

African Game / Jun. 18, 1983 / Blue Note ◆◆

Hal Russell

b. 1926, Detroit, MI, **d.** 1992, Chicago, IL
Leader, Drums, Tenor Saxophone, Trumpet, Soprano Saxophone / Avant-Garde
An important figure in the Chicago avant-garde of the 1980s, Hal Russell was a multi-instrumentalist with a strong sense of history and an effective sense of humor. He started playing drums when he was four, gigged locally in Chicago, and majored in trumpet at the University of Illinois. Russell toured one summer with Woody Herman (with whom he made his debut recording), and also had short stints with the big bands of Boyd Raeburn and Claude Thornhill. Freelancing in Chicago in the 1950s, Russell showed flexibility by performing with the who's who of jazz who happened to be passing through town, including Duke Ellington, Benny Goodman and John Coltrane. He became a session player and then in 1959 joined tenor saxophonist Joe Daley's adventurous trio; they recorded at the 1963 Newport Jazz Festival. Russell mostly freelanced in obscurity during the next decade until he formed the NRG Ensemble in the late 1970s. He started playing tenor in 1979, regained his trumpet chops, and wrote many extended works for the band. Hal Russell recorded with the NRG Ensemble for Nessa (1981-82) and Principally Jazz (1984), and at the end of his life made several sets for ECM (1990-92), including his final CD, ironically called *The Hal Russell Story.* —*Scott Yanow*

NRG Ensemble / May 11, 1981 / Nessa ◆◆◆◆◆

Eftsoons / Aug. 21, 1981 / Nessa ◆◆◆◆

Conserving NRG / Mar. 15, 1984-Mar. 16, 1984 / Principally Jazz ◆◆◆◆◆
Hal Russell, a Chicago legend, switches between tenor, cornet, vibes and drums on this fascinating avant-garde session. Together with saxophonist Chuck Burdelik, Brian Sandstrom (who plays trumpet, guitar and bass), bassist Curt Bley and

drummer Steve Hunt, Russell explores seven diverse and consistently colorful group originals that are more accessible than expected. This highly expressive music (which has plenty of variety) is worth checking out although this small label release will be difficult to locate. —*Scott Yanow*

The Finnish/Swiss Tour / Nov. 1990 / ECM ✦✦✦

Naked Colours / Dec. 17, 1991 / Silkheart ✦✦✦✦

● **Hal's Bells** / May 1992 / ECM ✦✦✦✦✦

Luis Russell

b. Aug. 6, 1902, Careening Clay, Panama, **d.** Dec. 11, 1963, New York, NY
Piano, Leader, Arranger / Classic Jazz, Swing

Luis Russell led one of the great early big bands, an orchestra that during 1929-31 could hold its own with nearly all of its competitors. Unfortunately, his period in the spotlight was fairly brief and ironically Russell fell into obscurity just as the big-band era really took hold. Russell studied guitar, violin and piano in his native Panama. After winning $3000 in a lottery, he moved with his mother and sister to the US where he began to make a living as a pianist in New Orleans. In 1925 Russell moved to Chicago to join Doc Cook's Orchestra and then became the pianist in King Oliver's band. He was with Oliver when the cornetist relocated to New York before leading his own band at the Nest Club in 1927. Russell had recorded seven songs at two sessions as a leader in 1926 with his Hot Six and Heebie Jeebie Stompers. By 1929 his ten-piece band (which included several former Oliver sidemen) boasted four major soloists in trumpeter Red Allen, trombonist J.C. Higginbotham, altoist Charlie Holmes and clarinetist Albert Nicholas; the other trumpeter, Bill Coleman, ended up leaving because of the lack of solo space! In addition, Russell, a decent but not particularly distinctive pianist, was part of one of the top rhythm sections of the era along with guitarist Will Johnson, the powerful bassist Pops Foster and drummer Paul Barbarin. During the next couple of years Luis Russell's band recorded a couple dozen sides that (thanks to the leader's arrangements) combined the solos and drive of New Orleans jazz with the riffs and ensembles of swing; some of these performances are now considered classics. The band also backed Louis Armstrong on a few of his early orchestra recordings. But after a few commercial sides in 1931, Luis Russell only had one more opportunity to record his band (a so-so session in 1934) before Louis Armstrong took it over altogether in 1935. For eight years the nucleus of Russell's orchestra primarily functioned as background for the great trumpeter/vocalist, a role that robbed it of its personality and significance. From 1943-48 Russell led a new band that played the Savoy and made a few obscure recordings for Apollo before quietly breaking up. He spent his last 15 years, before dying of cancer in 1963, largely outside of music, running at first a candy shop and then a toy store. Fortunately most of Russell's early recordings have been made available on CD by European labels. —*Scott Yanow*

The Luis Russell Collection (1926-1934) / Mar. 10, 1926-Aug. 8, 1934 / Collector's Classics ✦✦✦✦✦
Bandleader Luis Russell's most successful recordings were during 1929-30 when his brilliant orchestra featured such soloists as trumpeter Red Allen, trombonist J.C. Higginbotham, clarinetist Albert Nicholas and altoist Charlie Holmes along with what was arguably (thanks to bassist Pops Foster and drummer Paul Barbarin) the top rhythm section of the period. This CD from Collector's Classics (which is made available through Storyville) only has one session from the prime period (two songs plus a previously unissued version of "The Way He Loves Is Just Too Bad") but has all of Russell's earlier and slightly later recordings. Best are the initial two sessions, six titles plus an alternate take that feature hot jazz in 1926 from such fine players as George Mitchell or Bob Shoffner on cornet, Kid Ory or Preston Jackson on trombone, Nicholas or Darnell Howard on clarinet, pianist Russell and Johnny St. Cyr on banjo. However, the most impressive soloist is clarinetist Barney Bigard, who sticks exclusively to tenor and stakes out his claim as the number two tenor player (behind Coleman Hawkins) of the period. In addition three rare sessions from 1930-31 hint at the band's former greatness (trumpeter Red Allen stars but there are also some indifferent vocals) and this CD closes with the six titles from Russell's 1934 date (highlighted by Rex Stewart's dynamic cornet on "Ol' Man River"). Collectors will want this one. —*Scott Yanow*

★ **Luis Russell and His Louisiana Swing Orchestra** / Nov. 17, 1926-Aug. 8, 1934 / Columbia ✦✦✦✦✦
Pianist Luis Russell led one of the finest jazz bands between 1929-31, a unit that featured such talented soloists as trumpeter Red Allen, trombonist J.C. Higginbotham, altoist Charlie Holmes and clarinetist Albert Nicholas in addition to one of the top rhythm sections of the era (with bassist Pops Foster and drummer Paul Barbarin). This two-LP set includes almost all of their recordings (leaving out just three lesser sessions) and has very enjoyable (and frequently exciting) music that serves as a transition between New Orleans jazz and swing. In addition there are

two earlier dates (including one with Nicholas, trumpeter Bob Shoffner and Barney Bigard who ranks as one of the top tenor players of the era) and Russell's complete session of 1934, which features cornetist Rex Stewart. There are a few minor mistakes in the personnel listing and the dates are not included, but otherwise this is a definitive release of a somewhat forgotten classic band. —*Scott Yanow*

Pee Wee Russell (Charles Ellsworth Russell)

b. Mar. 27, 1906, St. Louis, MO, **d.** Feb. 15, 1969, Alexandria, VA
Clarinet / Dixieland

Pee Wee Russell, although never a virtuoso, was one of the giants of jazz. A highly expressive and unpredictable clarinetist, Russell was usually grouped in Dixieland-type groups throughout his career but his advanced and spontaneous solos (which often sounded as if he were thinking aloud) defied classification. A professional by the time he was 15, Pee Wee Russell played in Texas with Peck Kelley's group (meeting Jack Teagarden) and then in 1925 he was in St. Louis jamming with Bix Beiderbecke. Russell moved to New York in 1927 and gained some attention for his playing with Red Nichols' Five Pennies. Russell freelanced during the era, making some notable records with Billy Banks in 1932 that matched him with Red Allen. He played clarinet and tenor with Louis Prima during 1935-37, appearing on many records and enjoying the association. After leaving Prima, he started working with Eddie Condon's freewheeling groups and would remain in Condon's orbit on and off for the next 30 years. Pee Wee's recordings with Condon in 1938 made him a star in the trad Chicago jazz world. Russell was featured (but often the butt of jokes) on Condon's Town Hall Concerts. Heavy drinking almost killed him in 1950 but Pee Wee Russell made an unlikely comeback and became more assertive in running his career. He started leading his own groups (which were more swing- than Dixieland-oriented), was a star on the 1957 television special "The Sound of Jazz" and by the early '60s was playing in a pianoless quartet with valve trombonist Marshall Brown whose repertoire included tunes by John Coltrane and Ornette Coleman; he even sat in with Thelonious Monk at the 1963 Newport Jazz Festival and took up abstract painting. But after the death of his wife in 1967, Pee Wee Russell accelerated his drinking and went quickly downhill, passing away less than two years later. —*Scott Yanow*

Giants of Jazz / Aug. 15, 1927-Nov. 12, 1962 / Time-Life ✦✦✦✦✦
This three-LP box set is regrettably out of print, for it serves as a fine introduction to the unique clarinetist Pee Wee Russell. The 40 selections included here span a 35-year period and are highlighted by early sides with Red Nichols, many encounters with Eddie Condon's bands (including some real classic performances), a few numbers from Russell's mid-'30s association with Louis Prima and later recordings with his own pickup groups. Along with an excellent booklet, this box is an excellent tribute to a truly individual stylist. —*Scott Yanow*

A Chronological Remembrance / Sep. 6, 1927-Sep. 4, 1965 / IAJRC ✦✦✦✦✦
IAJRC, the superb collector's label, issued this single LP, full of rare studio recordings and concert performances from a wide assortment of groups, all of them featuring the distinctive clarinet of Pee Wee Russell. Whether heard with the Charleston Chasers in 1927, with Red McKenzie, Louis Prima, Bobby Hackett, Teddy Wilson or "in concert" with Eddie Condon, Russell is in fine form. An extra bonus is an ad-lib blues from the 1964 Monterey Jazz Festival shared with baritonist Gerry Mulligan. —*Scott Yanow*

Jazz Original / Jan. 17, 1938-Sep. 30, 1944 / Commodore ✦✦✦✦
Clarinetist Pee Wee Russell was certainly an original, squawking his way quite expressively in an unpredictable fashion, carving out his own distinctive voice. This 1997 CD is meant to augment the two-CD set called *The Commodore Story;* it includes some alternate takes whose master versions are on the former release or on another CD altogether, enough to drive completists and collectors crazy. This practice does not take into account listeners with a limited budget who do not want merely to have the alternates, and those specialists who want to be able to find certain recordings quickly. Russell is heard on this single CD on some performances with Eddie Condon's all-star groups of 1938-42, one selection apiece (both alternates) with Muggsy Spanier and Wild Bill Davison, during the four titles he cut with "The Three Deuces" (a trio with pianist Joe Sullivan and drummer Zutty Singleton) in 1941, and (best of all) on eight of the nine performances with his own "Hot Four" of 1944 (a group with pianist Jess Stacy, bassist Sid Weiss and drummer George Wettling). The programming is a bit ill-considered, but the music is often classic, with Russell and such top Chicago jazz all-stars as those mentioned, plus cornetist Bobby Hackett, tenor saxophonist Bud Freeman, trombonist Jack Teagarden and trumpeter Max Kaminsky in spirited form. —*Scott Yanow*

★ **Jack Teagarden / Pee Wee Russell** / Aug. 31, 1938-Dec. 15, 1940 / Original Jazz Classics ✦✦✦✦✦
This classic set reissues a couple of important sessions that were made for the H.R.S. label and later acquired by Riverside. The great trombonist Jack Teagarden is heard in 1940 with an octet dominated by Duke Ellington sidemen (including

cornetist Rex Stewart, clarinetist Barney Bigard and tenor saxophonist Ben Webster). Recorded during a period when Teagarden was struggling with his big band, it was a rare treat for him to stretch out with a combo and the results (which include a superior version of "St. James Infirmary") are memorable. In addition, clarinetist Pee Wee Russell is heard with an all-star octet of his own that co-stars trumpeter Max Kaminsky, trombonist Dicky Wells and pianist James P. Johnson in 1938; the final two numbers feature the unique trio of Russell, Johnson and drummer Zutty Singleton. The musicians seem quite inspired and both trad and swing fans are advised to get this excellent reissue. —*Scott Yanow*

The Pied Piper of Jazz / Sep. 30, 1944 / Commodore ♦♦♦♦♦
Now here's some cooking music. I'd recommend this record just for the seven trio tracks; the added quartet tracks are a good bonus, but clearly of a more common cloth, though Pee Wee Russell was never really common—as in average. Surprisingly, to me, these sessions were rather overlooked by annotations of Russell's music, but then again Zutty Singleton (drums) and Joe Sullivan (piano) are often overlooked in favor of derivative or lesser talent. Sullivan was a great two-fisted pianist, and Singleton, along with Baby Dodds, a great stylist and father of traditional jazz whose influence could probably be traced right up to Ed Blackwell through Gene Krupa and Art Blakey. And it was absolutely fitting that he be the drummer on this trio date, because with Singleton at the drums you really never need a bass. On this record one gets to hear some prime playing from the clarinetist, but pay attention to the rhythm, particularly Sullivan and Singleton. —*Bob Rusch, Cadence*

The Individualism of Pee Wee Russell / Jan. 27, 1952 / Savoy ♦♦♦♦
In December 1950, Russell nearly died from the effects of years of excessive drinking and limited eating. By the time of the Boston engagement that resulted in this double LP, he was 90% recovered. Leading a strong sextet that boasted fine solos from trombonist Eph Resnick and the great young trumpeter Ruby Braff, Russell performs mostly veteran, Dixieland standards during these extended workouts, avoiding cliches and playing his typically unique ideas with spirit and enthusiasm. —*Scott Yanow*

Clarinet Strut / Jan. 27, 1952-Feb. 19, 1958 / Drive Archive ♦♦♦
The unique clarinetist Pee Wee Russell is heard on this CD at two separate key points in his career. Five selections are taken from his first recordings after recovering from a near fatal illness in 1951. Russell jams in better-than-expected form with a sextet that includes the great young cornetist Ruby Braff. The other eight numbers date from 1958 when Russell was beginning to escape from the confines of Dixieland and playing more modern swing-oriented standards. Pianist Nat Pierce contributed the arrangements for a septet that also features Braff, tenor saxophonist Bud Freeman and trombonist Vic Dickenson. The music is uniformly excellent although virtually all of the performances from these two sessions are available in more complete form elsewhere. —*Scott Yanow*

We're in the Money / 1953-Oct. 2, 1954 / Black Lion ♦♦♦♦♦
His unique clarinet style is featured on this CD with two overlapping groups, both of which include trombonist Vic Dickenson and pianist George Wein. One band has Russell matching wits with the brilliant trumpet of Wild Bill Davison while the other date showcases the more mellow horn of Doc Cheatham, heard in a rare solo spot in the mid-'50s. This music mostly avoids the old warhorses and features superior swing standards by some of the top Condonites. —*Scott Yanow*

Over the Rainbow / Feb. 18, 1958-Feb. 19, 1958 / Xanadu ♦♦♦♦
With the exception of a 1965 version of "I'm in the Market for You," which has a few notes at its close by cornetist Bobby Hackett, this LP finds Russell (normally heard in Dixieland bands) showcased as the only horn. The other selections (taken from two sessions in 1958) feature him and one of two rhythm sections playing some of his favorite songs, including "I Would Do Anything for You," "I'd Climb the Highest Mountain" and "If I Had You." Russell, always a modern player although usually confined to more traditional settings, is really heard at his most lyrical throughout this very interesting set. Three of these performances are also included on *Portrait of Pee Wee.* —*Scott Yanow*

A Portrait of Pee Wee / Feb. 18, 1958-Feb. 19, 1958 / Dunhill ♦♦♦
Issued originally on Counterpoint and reissued many times since by budget labels like Everest, this CD version has superior sound. From 1958, this set matches the great clarinetist Pee Wee Pussell with an all-star horn section (trumpeter Ruby Braff, trombonist Vic Dickenson and tenor saxophonist Bud Freeman) on a program of swing standards along with "Pee Wee Blues." Russell, a bit weary of playing Dixieland by this time, was starting to look towards more modern eras of music, although in reality his own playing was always beyond categorization. —*Scott Yanow*

Salute to Newport / Feb. 23, 1959-Oct. 12, 1962 / ABC/Impulse! ♦♦♦♦
This out-of-print double LP reissues Pee Wee Russell's 1959 Dot album with trumpeter Buck Clayton, trombonist Vic Dickenson and veteran tenor Bud Freeman

along with a particularly hot session from Impulse by George Wein's Newport All-Stars (which also includes Freeman along with cornetist Ruby Braff and trombonist Marshall Brown) from 1962. The earlier record is fine but the Newport All-Stars (whose exciting performance is highlighted by such tunes as "At the Jazz Band Ball," Freeman's feature on "Crazy Rhythm" and Russell's "The Bends Blues") is the reason to search for this set. —*Scott Yanow*

Memorial Album / Mar. 29, 1960 / Prestige ♦♦♦♦
Teaming together trumpeter Buck Clayton with clarinetist Pee Wee Russell in 1960 was a logical move. Both of these individual stylists had been stuck often in Dixieland settings in the 1950s, yet they were really highly distinctive swing soloists. Joined by a modern rhythm section led by pianist Tommy Flanagan, Clayton and Russell are in top form on six fine standards, making one wish that they had teamed up in this type of setting more often. —*Scott Yanow*

Jazz Reunion / Feb. 23, 1961-Mar. 8, 1961 / Candid ♦♦♦♦♦
The reunion that took place in this 1961 session was between Russell and tenor-great Coleman Hawkins; they had first recorded one of the songs, ("If I Could Be with You") back in 1929. Both Hawk and Russell had remained modern soloists and on this unusual but very satisfying date (which also features trumpeter Emmett Berry and trombonist Bob Brookmeyer) they explore such numers as a pair of Ellington classics ("All Too Soon" and "What Am I Here For?"), two Russell originals, and even the boppish "Tin Tin Deo." —*Scott Yanow*

New Groove / Nov. 12, 1962-Nov. 26, 1962 / Columbia ♦♦♦♦♦

Gumbo / 1964 / Honey Dew ♦♦♦
The second of two LPs taken from a pickup date in 1964, this album finds Russell jamming Dixieland standards with some local musicians from New England; trumpeter Tony Tomasso and trombonist Porky Cohen keep up with Russell on this upbeat if somewhat predictable session. —*Scott Yanow*

Hot Licorice / 1964 / Honey Dew ♦♦♦
In 1964, the clarinet great was caught live jamming through some Dixieland standards with a pickup group of New England musicians. Only trombonist Porky Cohen (who later played with Roomful of Blues) is slightly known, although trumpeter Tony Tomasso acquits himself well on this decent outing. Russell fans will want to search for this now-rare LP, the first of two Honeydews from this gig. —*Scott Yanow*

☆ **Ask Me Now!** / 1965 / Impulse! ♦♦♦♦♦
After a lifetime spent playing unusual and unpredictable clarinet solos in Dixieland settings, Russell late in life broke out of the stereotype and played in more modern settings. This Impulse LP (begging to be reissued on CD) has his clarinet placed in a pianoless quartet with valve-trombonist Marshall Brown, playing tunes by John Coltrane, Thelonious Monk, and Ornette Coleman, along with some classic ballads. It is a remarkable and very lyrical date that briefly rejuvenated the career of this veteran individualist. —*Scott Yanow*

The Spirit of '67 / Feb. 14, 1967-Feb. 15, 1967 / Impulse! ♦♦♦♦
Pee Wee Russell's final recording found the veteran clarinetist joined by a big band arranged by Oliver Nelson. The tunes range from the recent "The Shadow of Your Smile" to such classics from Pee Wee's career as "Love Is Just Around the Corner," "Pee Wee's Blues" and "Ja-Da." In general, the charts are colorful and complement Russell well during what would be his swan song. —*Scott Yanow*

College Concert of Pee Wee Russell and Henry Red / Apr. 17, 1966 / Impulse! ♦♦♦♦
Although trumpeter Red Allen (heard in his final recording) and Russell had recorded back in 1932, their paths only crossed on an infrequent basis through the years. For this LP, the two veteran modernists (who spent much of their careers in Dixieland settings) are joined by a young rhythm-section pianist Steve Kuhn, bassist Charlie Haden and drummer Marty Morell). The music is generally relaxed with an emphasis on blues and a fine feature for Allen on "Body and Soul." —*Scott Yanow*

Paul Rutherford

b. Feb. 29, 1940, Liverpool, England
Trombone / Avant-Garde

An experimental, unpredictable player who also has a good sense of humor, trombonist Paul Rutherford has worked in many seminal free bands since the '60s. He started on saxophone in the mid-'50s, then switched to trombone and played that instrument in Royal Air Force bands from 1958 to 1963. He met John Stevens and Trevor Watts in the RAF, and they co-formed the Spontaneous Music Ensemble in 1965. Rutherford studied days at the Guildhall School of Music in London and played free sessions at night during the mid- and late '60s. He began working regularly with Mike Westbrook in 1967, and formed his own group Iskra 1903 with Derek Bailey and Barry Guy in the early '70s. Rutherford also played with the London Jazz Composers Orchestra, Globe Unity Orchestra and Tony Oxley septet, as well as Evan Parker and Paul Lovens. He began developing an unusual trombone language in the mid-'70s, mixing electronics, vocal effects, traditional jazz devices and intriguing sounds and voicings. Rutherford issued some compelling solo sessions in the '70s, then formed a new edition of Iskra 1903 with Guy and Phil Wachsmann in the '80s. He also continued working with The London Jazz Composers Orchestra, played in the Free Jazz Quartet and recorded duos with George Haslam. —*Ron Wynn*

● **Gentle Harm of the Bourgeoisie** / Jul. 2, 1974-Dec. 17, 1974 / Emanem ✦✦✦✦
Recording of solo trombone. One of the most revered avant-garde statements. —*Michael G. Nastos*

Ali Ryerson

b. 1952, New York, NY
Flute / Hard Bop
A fine bop-oriented flutist, Ali Ryerson is the daughter of guitarist Art Ryerson. She started on flute at age eight and had extensive classical training, graduating from Hart College. However, Ryerson developed a strong interest in jazz and has maintained a versatile career, playing both classical and jazz. Ryerson spent three years freelancing in Belgium and then became a top studio player in New York. She performed with Art Farmer, Lou Donaldson, Maxine Sullivan and Stephane Grappelli among others and has recorded two sets as a leader for Bob Thiele's Red Baron label and several excellent sets for Concord. —*Scott Yanow*

Blue Flute / Dec. 9, 1991 / Red Baron ✦✦✦

I'll Be Back / Jul. 28, 1993 / Red Baron ✦✦✦✦
It is a testament to flutist Ali Ryerson that on her second release she is not overshadowed by her all-star rhythm section (pianist Kenny Barron, bassist Cecil McBee and drummer Danny Gottlieb) and that her sidemen sound happy to be playing with her. The music on this CD ranges from Bobby Jaspar's blues "Bobby's Minor" to a memorable version of Horace Silver's "Peace" and an emotional "That's All." Nothing that innovative occurs, but Ryerson's very pleasing flute sounds perfectly at home in this modern mainstream setting. Recommended for straightahead jazz fans. —*Scott Yanow*

Portraits in Silver / Sep. 12, 1994-Sep. 13, 1994 / Concord Jazz ✦✦✦✦

● **In Her Own Sweet Way** / Sep. 18, 1995-Sep. 19, 1995 / Concord Jazz ✦✦✦✦✦

Brasil: Quiet Devotion / 1997 / Concord Jazz ✦✦✦

Terje Rypdal

b. Aug. 23, 1947, Oslo, Norway
Guitar / Avant-Garde, Fusion, Post-Bop
Terje Rypdal has long had an unusual style, mixing together elements more commonly found in new age and rock than in jazz; yet he is also an adventurous improviser. Associated with the ECM label since the early '70s, Rypdal's playing is definitely an acquired taste, using space and dense sounds in an unusual manner. Classically trained as a pianist, Rypdal was largely self-taught on guitar and originally most influenced by Jimi Hendrix. He attended Oslo University, where he was taught the Lydian chromatic concept of tonal organization by its author, George Russell. Rypdal played with Russell for a time and started an association with Jan Garbarek in the late '60s. He formed the group Odyssey in 1972 and has led vari-

ous small groups during the past two decades. An important guitarist and composer in Norway, Terje Rypdal has gained a cult following in the US. He has recorded steadily for ECM since 1972 (using such sidemen at times as Garbarek, pianist Bobo Stenson, trumpeter Palle Mikkelborg, bassist Miroslav Vitous, drummer Jack DeJohnette and cellist David Darling). His two earlier sessions (for the Karusell label in 1968 and a notable 1969 Baden-Baden concert put out by MPS) are more difficult to find. —*Scott Yanow*

Waves / Aug. 1973-Sep. 1977 / ECM ✦✦✦✦
This contains some of Rypdal's jazziest music—"Per Ulv" even verges on bebop, despite its chattering rhythm box—alongside the more characteristic free-fall rhapsodies. —*Michael P. Dawson*

Whenever I Seem to be Far Away / 1974 / ECM ✦✦

● **Works** / 1974-1981 / ECM ✦✦✦✦✦
An excellent sampler of Rypdal's music, it includes two cuts from his superb (but currently unavailable) early-'70s albums. —*Michael P. Dawson*

Odyssey / Aug. 1975 / ECM ✦✦✦✦✦
A magnificent effort that combines crushingly powerful rock/jazz ("Over Bierkerot" is a killer) with long, brooding electric ruminations, it was originally a double album; one track has been left off the CD. —*Michael P. Dawson*

After the Rain / Aug. 1976 / ECM ✦✦

Rypdal, Vitous, DeJohnette / Jun. 1978 / Polygram ✦✦✦
Recorded with Miroslav Vitous and Jack DeJohnette, Rypdal gets spacy but muscular support from two of the superstars of '70s jazz on this 1978 session. —*Michael P. Dawson*

Descendre / Mar. 1979 / ECM ✦✦✦✦
The unusual trio form of guitar, trumpet, and drums makes for some gorgeous floating sounds. —*Michael P. Dawson*

To Be Continued / Jan. 1981 / ECM ✦✦✦

Eos / May 1983 / ECM ✦✦✦
Probably Rypdal's most experimental release, it's a set of heavily electronic duets with cellist David Darling. —*Michael P. Dawson*

Chaser / May 1985 / ECM ✦✦✦✦
This 1985 release finds Rypdal working in a hard-hitting power-trio format with his new group, the Chasers. —*Michael P. Dawson*

Blue / Nov. 1986 / ECM ✦✦✦✦
The second album with the rock-oriented Chasers adds keyboards to the mixture. —*Michael P. Dawson*

The Singles Collection / Aug. 1988 / ECM ✦✦✦✦
The title is a joke: this is actually the third album by the Chasers. Inspirational song title: "There Is a Hot Lady in My Bedroom and I Need a Drink." —*Michael P. Dawson*

Undisonus / 1990 / ECM ✦✦✦
None of Rypdal's haunting guitar here: this is an album of his purely orchestral compositions. —*Michael P. Dawson*

Skywards / Feb. 1996 / ECM ✦✦✦

Eddie Safranski

b. Dec. 25, 1918, Pittsburgh, PA, **d.** Jan. 10, 1974, Los Angeles, CA

Bass / Bop

Eddie Safranski was best known for his gig as the bass anchor of the most popular of Stan Kenton's big bands (1945-48). The owner of a solid, clear, precisely articulated tone and a sure command of the swing and bop idioms, Safranski was also lucky enough to have been the beneficiary of terrific recording quality from Kenton's engineers at Capitol Records; his bass registered far more cleanly and powerfully than many of those who recorded for rival companies. Having studied violin as a child, Safranski took up the double bass in high school, playing with Hal McIntyre from 1941 to 1945 and Miff Mole in 1945 before joining Kenton. His success with Stan enabled him to make some records as a leader for Savoy and Atlantic; after leaving Kenton, he worked with Charlie Barnet's bop big band in 1948-49 and moved to New York to seek work in radio and television studios. While there, he also played with Benny Goodman in 1951-52 and caught on as a staff musician with NBC. From the late '60s until his death, he ran workshops and master classes for a double bass manufacturer and played swing and bop with various combos in the Los Angeles area. Among his many Kenton records, some of the best examples of Safranski can be savored on "Artistry in Bolero," "Painted Rhythm," "Concerto to End All Concertos" and a showcase written for him by Pete Rugolo, "Safranski (Artistry in Bass)." —*Richard S. Ginell*

Johnny St. Cyr

b. Apr. 17, 1890, New Orleans, LA, **d.** Jun. 17, 1966, Los Angeles, CA

Banjo, Guitar / New Orleans Jazz

A fine rhythmic banjoist and guitarist, Johnny St. Cyr was a New Orleans pioneer who was greatly in demand in the 1920s. Self-taught, St. Cyr had his own trio as far back as 1905. He played in New Orleans with A.J. Piron, the Superior, Olympia and Tuxedo bands and with Kid Ory (when King Oliver was the cornetist) in addition to Fate Marable's riverboat band. After moving to Chicago in 1923, St. Cyr made his place in history by recording with King Oliver, Jelly Roll Morton and Louis Armstrong (as a key member of Armstrong's Hot Five and Hot Seven) while performing nightly with Doc Cook's Dreamland Orchestra. In 1930 he returned to New Orleans where he made his living outside of music but still played with local groups (including with Paul Barbarin and Alphonse Picou). In 1955 St. Cyr moved to Los Angeles and returned to music fulltime, leading the Young Men from New Orleans at Disneyland from 1961 until his death in 1966. —*Scott Yanow*

Johnny St. Cyr/Paul Barbarin / May 13, 1954+Aug. 31, 1956 / GHB ✦✦✦✦✦

Guitarist-banjoist Johnny St. Cyr, best known for his many recordings with Louis Armstrong's Hot Five and Seven during 1925-27, only led one recording session during his long career. The first half of this LP has that entire date, featuring a sextet also including trumpeter Thomas Jefferson, trombonist Joe Avery, clarinetist Willie Humphrey, pianist Jeanette Kimball and drummer Paul Barbarin. Jefferson, who takes spirited vocals on "Bill Bailey," "Bye and Bye" and "Darktown Strutters Ball," is the main star; Sister Elizabeth Eustis has a guest vocal on "We Shall Walk Through The Streets of the City." The second half of the album features an overlapping group headed by Paul Bararin in 1956 and including Humphrey, Kimball, trumpeter Alvin Alcorn, trombonist Jim Robinson and banjoist Lawrence Marrero. Their four selections are fairly long, particularly an exciting rendition of "It's a Long Way to Tipperary." An easily recommended set for New Orleans jazz fans. —*Scott Yanow*

Dan St. Marseille

b. Jun. 1, 1962, Sudbury, Ontario, Canada

Tenor Saxophone / Bop, Cool, Hard Bop

A fine cool-toned tenor saxophonist, Dan St. Marseille came from a musical family in which his father sang opera, his great-uncle played clarinet, and his grandfather was a violinist. St. Marseille grew up in El Toro, CA, and since the late 1980s has been a steady fixture in the Los Angeles and Orange County areas. He founded

and has run Resurgent Music, a label that has not only documented his own music since 1992, but has released other top Los Angeles-based jazz players. —*Scott Yanow*

Long Ago and Far Away / Aug. 12, 1992-Mar. 17, 1993 / Resurgent ✦✦✦✦

Tenor saxophonist Dan St. Marseille's debut as a leader is a tribute to Chet Baker. Marseille has a soft tone that works well with his swinging style, and his rhythm section (pianist Cecilia Coleman, bassist Ernie Nunez and drummer Denny Dennis) is excellent, but it is trumpeter Larry Gillespie (who takes vocals that sound eerily close to Baker, certainly an acquired taste) who is most responsible for the project's success. With only a couple of exceptions (most notably the leader's "Phillippe Sleep"), the music is largely from Baker's repertoire, including a nine-minute, six-tune medley. Altoist Gary Foster sits in quite effectively on an "April Medley" comprising "I'll Remember April" and Lennie Tristano's "April." —*Scott Yanow*

Contour / Dec. 9, 1993-Dec. 10, 1993 / Resurgent ✦✦✦✦

● **Retrospection** / May 23, 1995 / Resurgent ✦✦✦✦✦

The cool-toned but hard-swinging tenor saxophonist Dan St. Marseille has a perfectly suitable band on this release, a pianoless quintet also including guitarist Ron Eschete, bassist Benjamin May, drummer Denny Dennis and percussionist Poncho Sanchez. St. Marseille explores seven standards and three obscurities (including his title cut), creating fresh bop-oriented statements on such numbers as "Blue Skies," "After You've Gone" and "Like Someone 70sin Love." Recommended. —*Scott Yanow*

Sal Salvador

b. Nov. 21, 1925, Monson, MA

Guitar / Bop, Cool

A versatile guitarist and recent head of the guitar department at the University of Bridgeport, Sal Salvador has been a capable soloist and accompanist since the late '40s. His single string style, shaped by his early interest in the music of Charlie Christian, has been augmented by extensive studies of guitar technique. Salvador's years of research, playing and analysis eventually led to his writing guitar methodology books, among them *Sal Salvador's Chord Method for Guitar* and *Sal Salvador's Single String Studies for Guitar* in the '50s and '60s. He became interested in jazz during his teens, and began playing professionally in Springfield, MA, in 1945. He worked with Terry Gibbs and Mundell Lowe in New York at the end of the '40s, then joined Stan Kenton's orchestra in 1952. Salvador worked with Kenton until the end of 1953, and appeared on the *New Concepts of Artistry in Rhythm* album. He led bebop bands featuring Eddie Costa and Phil Woods. Salvador was featured in the film *Jazz on a Summer's Day* and headed a big band in the late '50s and early '60s. He worked in a guitar duo with Alan Hanlon in the early '70s, and began recording again as a leader later in the decade. He reformed his big band in the '80s and was named to his position at the University of Bridgeport. Salvador has led recordings through the years for Blue Note (1953), Capitol, Bethlehem, Decca, Jazz Unlimited, Dauntless (1963), Bee Hive, GP, and Stash. —*Ron Wynn*

Starfingers / Mar. 24, 1978 / Bee Hive ✦✦✦✦

After years of low-profile teaching and playing, guitarist Sal Salvador started to re-emerge on a more national basis in 1978. He is teamed up for this project with five fellow veterans (trombonist Eddie Bert, baritonist Nick Brignola, pianist Derek Smith, bassist Sam Jones and drummer Mel Lewis) for four standards (including "Nica's Dream" and "Don't Get Around Much Anymore") and two of his originals (highlighted by "Blue Gnu's Blues"). An excellent modern bop album. —*Scott Yanow*

Juicy Lucy / Sep. 5, 1978 / Bee Hive ✦✦✦✦

Guitarist Sal Salvador's second Bee Hive album of 1978 puts the focus on his playing in a quartet with pianist Billy Taylor, bassist Art Davis and drummer Joe Morello. The well-conceived set has swinging versions of two of Salvador's originals, Taylor's "Daddy-O" and three standards. "Tune for Two" (an intense Salvador-

Morello duet) and the medium-tempo blues "Northern Lights" are highlights of the enjoyable set. —*Scott Yanow*

Parallelogram / 1978 / GRP ✦✦✦

Guitarist Sal Salvador, who had not recorded as a leader since 1963, recorded much more frequently starting in 1978. This obscure LP matches the bop-based guitarist in a fairly modern setting with keyboardist Neil Slater, bassist Rick Petrone and drummer Joe Corsello. The repertoire includes a few standards (such as "There Will Never Be Another You" and "I'm Old Fashioned") plus three of Salvador's originals and a few obscurities. Although the results are not as essential as Salvador's later Stash recordings, the music is worthwhile. —*Scott Yanow*

In Our Own Sweet Way / Nov. 1982 / Stash ✦✦✦✦

The first of guitarist Sal Salvador's three Stash albums is as much a showcase for Nick Brignola (who takes colorful solos on baritone, soprano and alto) as it is for the leader. With pianist Don Friedman, bassist Gary Mazzaroppi and drummer Butch Miles all making strong contributions, this is an excellent straightahead date highlighted by "I'm Afraid the Masquerade Is Over," "Blue Monk" and a twelve-and-a-half minute version of Dave Brubeck's "In Your Own Sweet Way." —*Scott Yanow*

World's Greatest Jazz Standards / Nov. 1983 / Stash ✦✦✦

These 11 songs might not be the world's greatest jazz standards but they are certainly all familiar songs. Veteran guitarist Sal Salvador, along with vibraphonist Paul Johnson, bassist Gary Mazzaroppi and drummer Butch Miles, give the warhorses fairly straightforward treatments and there are few surprises, with all but one of the performances being between three and five minutes. The music is pleasing but somewhat predictable. —*Scott Yanow*

● Plays Gerry Mulligan / Nov. 1984 / Stash ✦✦✦✦✦

Gerry Mulligan, in addition to being one of the top jazz baritonists ever, was a major if underrated composer. On this set, guitarist Sal Salvador, in groups ranging from a sextet to a quartet, interprets eight of Mulligan's better songs, including "Bernie's Tune," "Song for Strayhorn," "Walkin' Shoes" and "Line for Lyons." With fine playing from the supporting cast (trumpeter Randy Brecker, baritonist Nick Brignola, vibraphonist Paul Johnson, bassist Gary Mazzaroppi and drummer Butch Miles), Salvador is heard in top form throughout the consistently inspired and swinging effort. Highly recommended. —*Scott Yanow*

Sal Salvador and Crystal Image / 1989 / Stash ✦✦✦✦✦

Guitarist Sal Salvador started his two-guitar quartet Crystal Image with the idea of reviving the group he had had with Mundell Lowe in the early '50s. This CD adds another element to the music, the voice of Barbara Oakes which is often used as if it were a third guitar. With guitarist Mike Giordano, bassist Phil Bowler and drummer Greg Burrows completing the group, the arrangements of Salvador and Hank Levy on these complex originals and a few standards (plus Chick Corea's "Got a Match?") give Crystal Image its own fresh group sound. Worth investigating. —*Scott Yanow*

The Way of the Wind / 1994 / JazzMania ✦✦✦✦
Lorinda's Kitchen / Jun. 18, 1995-Jun. 24, 1995 / JazzMania ✦✦✦✦
Second Time Around / Aug. 20, 1996 / Westside ✦✦✦

Sergio Salvatore

b. Mar. 3, 1981, Ringwood, NJ

Piano / Post-Bop

Sergio Salvatore certainly qualifies as a prodigy, having recorded two albums for GRP by the time he was 13. His father is a music teacher while his mother is a singer. Sergio began taking serious piano lessons at age four and amazingly enough his first two recordings give no hint as to his youth. Salvatore, who is influenced by Keith Jarrett and Chick Corea among others, held his own with the all-star casts (which include Dave Samuels, Bob Mintzer, Randy Brecker and even Corea), quite an impressive start to what should be a lengthy career. —*Scott Yanow*

Sergio Salvatore / 1993 / GRP ✦✦✦✦✦

The youngest of the "Young Lions," pianist Sergio Salvatore was 11 at the time of this recording. However one quickly forgets his age for he plays with surprising maturity, starting off his debut with a thoughtful unaccompanied version of "Like Someone in Love" that sounds like Keith Jarrett in spots; other selections hint more at Chick Corea. Salvatore has good technique but it's his self-restraint on the ballads that is most impressive. The selections (seven of the pianist's originals plus three standards) are both funky and straightahead, and there are solos from vibraphonist Dave Samuels and (on three cuts) Bob Mintzer on tenor, but the remarkable Sergio Salvatore is the main reason to acquire this disc. —*Scott Yanow*

● Tune Up / 1994 / GRP ✦✦✦✦✦

Pianist Sergio Salvatore was only 13 at the time of this recording, his second release. But, despite his extreme youth, one forgets Salvatore's age by the third song. He certainly gets the star treatment on the date, playing quartets with Gary Burton, interacting with the Brecker Brothers and even duetting with Chick Corea on "Sea Journey." But Salvatore somehow manages to keep up with his illustrious sidemen, and the fairly complex music (which includes three of his impressive originals) rewards repeated listenings. It will be very interesting to see how Sergio Salvatore sounds ten years from now. —*Scott Yanow*

Point of Presence / 1994 / N2K ✦✦✦
Always a Beginning / Jan. 15, 1996-Jan. 17, 1996 / Concord Jazz ✦✦✦✦

Joe Sample

b. Feb. 1, 1939, Houston, TX

Piano, Keyboards / Hard Bop, Soul Jazz, Crossover Jazz, Fusion

One of the many jazzmen who started out playing hard bop but went electric during the Fusion Era, Joe Sample was, in the late 1950s, a founding member of the Jazz Crusaders along with trombonist Wayne Henderson, tenor saxman Wilton Felder and drummer Stix Hooper. The Crusaders' debt to Art Blakey's Jazz Messengers was hard to miss—except that the L.A.-based unit had no trumpeter and became known for its unique tenor/trombone front line. Sample, a hard-swinging player who could handle chordal and modal/scalar improvisation equally well, stuck to the acoustic piano during the Crusaders' early years—but would place greater emphasis on electric keyboards when the band turned to jazz/funk in the early '70s and dropped "Jazz" from its name. Though he'd recorded as a trio pianist on 1969's obscure *Fancy Dance*, 1978's *Rainbow Seeker* was often described as his first album as a leader. In contrast to the gritty music the Crusaders became known for, Sample's own albums on MCA and later, Warner Bros., have generally favored a very lyrical and introspective jazz/pop approach. —*Alex Henderson*

Fancy Dance / Apr. 20, 1969 / Gazell ✦✦✦✦

This LP (a reissue of a project for Sonet) was pianist Joe Sample's first solo set, although he was already well-known for his nine high-profile years with the Jazz Crusaders. Teamed with bassist Red Mitchell and drummer J.C. Moses, Sample plays mostly adventurous straightahead jazz on his date. There are some funky moments (particularly on the two blues), but all six of his originals have their challenging moments and Sample is heard stretching himself way beyond the predictable. —*Scott Yanow*

The Three / Nov. 28, 1975 / Inner City ✦✦✦✦

This Japanese East Wind LP (which was made available domestically on the now-defunct Inner City label) features pianist Joe Sample, bassist Ray Brown and drummer Shelly Manne exploring five jazz standards plus Sample's "Funky Blues" in purely straightahead fashion. One of Joe Sample's finest sessions as a leader, this obscure outing is highlighted by his renditions of Oliver Nelson's "Yearnin'," "On Green Dolphin Street" and "Manha Do Carnaval." —*Scott Yanow*

Swing Street Cafe / Nov. 29, 1978-Nov. 30, 1978 / MCA ✦✦✦✦

This album is one of keyboardist Joe Sample's more interesting solo dates. He pays tribute to vintage R&B with performances of such soulful tunes as "Hallelujah, I Love Her So," "Rockhouse," "C.C. Rider" and "After Hours." Assisted by guitarist David T. Walker, bassist James Jamerson, drummer Earl Palmer and several horn players (including tenor saxophonist Herman Riley and fluegelhornist Al Aarons), Sample sounds quite distinctive on electric piano and performs music that is both accessible and creative within the idiom. —*Scott Yanow*

● Carmel / 1978 / MCA ✦✦✦✦✦

The very best of Joe Sample's crossover efforts of the 1970s and '80s, this melodic session features Sample's acoustic piano in the forefront on seven catchy numbers. The backup group includes guitarist Dean Parks, bassist Abraham Laboriel, drummer Stix Hooper, percussionist Paulinho Da Costa and (on "Midnight & Mist") a guest flute solo by Hubert Laws. —*Scott Yanow*

Rainbow Seeker / 1978 / MCA ✦✦✦✦✦
Collection / 1978-1985 / GRP ✦✦✦

Because of the success he's enjoyed in the pop and R&B markets, critics have tended to dismiss Joe Sample's albums as a leader. But in fact, the keyboardist/pianist's work has often been imaginative and quite soulful. Despite the inclusion of a few throwaways—including the aimless "Woman, You're Driving Me Mad"—*Collection* isn't a bad introduction to his MCA Records output of the late '70s and early to mid-'80s. His playing is warm and intimate on "Carmel," "Sunrise," "Fly with the Wings of Love" and other poetic jazz-pop gems included on this 1991 compilation. The CD's greatest emphasis is on songs from *Rainbow Seeker* and *Carmel*, which is appropriate given that they are Joe Sample's strongest albums. —*Alex Henderson*

Voices in the Rain / 1980 / MCA ✦✦✦

There is a fair amount of variety on this reasonably enjoyable but not essential release from keyboardist Joe Sample. Most of the tunes fall into the area of funky crossover with strong melodies, danceable rhythms and few chances taken. Flora Purim takes the vocal on "Shadows" and is joined by two other singers for the spirited "Burnin' Up the Carnival." The acoustic "Sonata in Solitude" has violinist L. Subramaniam, guitarist John Collins and bassist Ray Brown, but that is a one-time departure on what is basically a commercial set geared for radio airplay. —*Scott Yanow*

The Hunter / 1982 / MCA ✦✦✦

Roles / 1983 / MCA ✦✦

Spellbound / 1989 / Warner Brothers ✦✦✦

Ashes to Ashes / 1990 / Warner Brothers ✦✦✦

Joe Sample's recordings throughout much of his career have been consistent and quite interchangeable. Backed by a semi-metronomic if usually grooving rhythm section, Sample's acoustic piano on this Warner Bros. CD is almost always in the lead, playing easy-listening pop-jazz; nothing memorable or unique occurs. The lightweight melodies are quite easy to take (serving as excellent background music) but it is a pity that Joe Sample has often seemed satisfied to stay at this unimaginative level, emulating Ramsey Lewis. —*Scott Yanow*

Invitation / 1993 / Warner Brothers ✦✦✦✦

Did You Feel That? / 1994 / Warner Brothers ✦✦✦✦✦

Fans of the Crusaders of the early '70s will want this set. Joe Sample utilizes a Fender Rhodes keyboard much of the time, and a two-horn front line (with trumpeter Oscar Brashear and tenorman Joel Peskin) is reminiscent of his former group; even guitarist Arthur Adams returns. This is intelligent and lightly funky soulful jazz-oriented dance music that is very enjoyable. —*Scott Yanow*

Old Places, Old Faces / 1995 / Warner Brothers ✦✦✦

Pianist Joe Sample's Warner Bros. session mostly features relaxed acoustic music. Sample emphasizes his original melodies during his improvisations and is backed quite ably by bassist Jay Anderson, drummer Ralph Penland and an occasional percussionist. Most notable is that tenor saxophonist Charles Lloyd guests on three tracks, playing in his usual mellow version of John Coltrane. But in general this is a relaxing trio set, not overly memorable but quite pleasing. —*Scott Yanow*

Sample This / 1997 / Warner Brothers ✦✦✦✦

In case anyone has forgotten how ingratiating and prolific Joe Sample the songwriter has been, the master of elegant funk re-records 14 of them here. And it is a cooler, more reflective light in which Sample and producer George Duke see his old tunes in the 1990s: with relaxed, uncomplicated, to-the-point acoustic piano leads; a mildly percolating beat; and a veneer-thin garnish of electronics. It is both safe and risky to revisit the past—safe because one is surrounded by comfortable material and risky because artists seldom recapture all of the old spark. Alas, more often than not, the latter applies to Sample's attempt to go home again, though the good tunes remain good tunes. Some of the songs go back to the Crusaders; "Free as the Wind" especially lacks the energy of the original, but "Put It Where You Wanted," thanks in part to Sample's use of a funky old Wurlitzer electric piano, has a nice groove. Finally, just for fun, Sample slips in a jaunty solo benediction courtesy of Jelly Roll Morton, "Shreveport Stomp." —*Richard S. Ginell*

Edgar Sampson

b. Aug. 31, 1907, New York, NY, **d.** Jan. 16, 1973, Englewood, NJ

Arranger, Composer, Alto Saxophone, Violin / Swing

However long and varied Edgar Sampson's career was, he became a jazz immortal solely on the brilliant contributions he made for a few short years as a member of the Chick Webb band. Sampson songs like "Stompin' at the Savoy" and "Don't Be That Way" still evoke the cozy yet swinging ambience of the big-band era like few others, and he was also responsible for "Blue Lou," "Lullaby in Rhythm," "Blue Minor," and "If Dreams Come True." Sampson started playing the violin at age 6, following that up with alto sax study while in high school. He began working professionally as a teenager in a violin/piano duo with Joe Coleman in 1924 and spent a season with Duke Ellington at the Kentucky Club in 1925. He worked his way through several bands, including those of Bingie Madison, Billy Fowler, Arthur Gibbs (at the Savoy Ballroom), Charlie Johnson, Alex Jackson, Fletcher Henderson and Rex Stewart, until he landed a spot in the Webb band in 1933. There, Sampson made his reputation as an arranger and composer, and after he left in July 1936, he had become an in-demand freelance arranger for Benny Goodman (who made huge hits of some of his tunes), Artie Shaw, Red Norvo, Teddy Hill, Teddy Wilson and Webb himself. After Webb's death in 1939, Sampson briefly served as musical director for Ella Fitzgerald when she took over the band. He played alto and baritone sax for Al Sears in 1943, and then led his own band in

New York (1949-51). By the late '40s, Sampson had become interested in Latin music, arranging for Marcellino Guerra, Tito Puente and Tito Rodriguez through the '50s; later in the decade, he started leading small groups. He recorded only one album under his own name in 1956, *Swing Softly, Sweet Sampson* (Coral). Sampson became inactive in the late '60s when illness forced him to have a leg amputated. —*Richard S. Ginell*

Sampson Swings Again / Apr. 2, 1956-Apr. 4, 1956 / MCA ✦✦✦✦

Other than two titles in 1939 that were features for the Three Swingsters, arranger Edgar Sampson (who composed such swing-era hits as "Don't Be That Way," "Blue Lou," "Lullaby in Rhythm," "If Dreams Come True" and "Stompin' at the Savoy") only led one recording session in his entire career and was completely unknown to the general public. This budget LP from the later period of MCA's Jazz Heritage series (which has versions of the five aforementioned songs) only contains ten of the 12 selections from Sampson's lone date (a total of just 30 minutes of music). Edgar Sampson leads a big band that features concise solos from trumpeters Charlie Shavers and Jimmy Nottingham, trombonists Tyree Glenn and Lou McGarity and tenor saxophonist Boomie Richman. Even in its inexcusably truncated state, this swing-oriented LP is worth searching for. —*Scott Yanow*

Dave Samuels

b. Oct. 9, 1948, Waukegan, IL

Vibes, Marimbas / Post-Bop, Crossover Jazz

A talented vibraphonist and marimba player, Dave Samuels has gained his greatest fame for his many years with Spyro Gyra. He started on his first instrument, the drums, when he was six, but by the time he attended Boston University (from which he graduated with a psychology degree), he was studying mallet instruments. Samuels attended the Berklee School of Music, where one of his teachers was Gary Burton, and soon became an educator himself. Samuels had the opportunity to work with Pat Metheny and John Scofield while in Boston, and then in 1974, he toured and recorded with Gerry Mulligan. Other early experiences included working with the group Timepiece, Frank Zappa, and Double Image, where he interacted with fellow vibraphonist Don Friedman from 1977-80. Samuels began his association with Spyro Gyra in 1979 by guesting on their recordings; finally, in 1986, he became a member and the one soloist with the band that jazz critics went out of their way to praise. Unfortunately, his own records through the years, particularly from the mid-1980s on for MCA and GRP, have tended to be commercial and a bit disappointing. However, after leaving Spyro Gyra in the mid-1990s, Samuels has done some impressive work with the Caribbean Jazz Project. Sticking mostly to marimba with the band (which he co-leads with steel drummer Andy Narrell and altoist/clarinetist Paquito D'Rivera), Dave Samuels is at his best during their very likable concerts. —*Scott Yanow*

● **Double Image** / Jun. 1977 / Enja ✦✦✦✦✦

Ten Degrees North / 1989 / MCA ✦✦

When jazz reviewers wrote about Spyro Gyra in the past, they nearly always had something good to say about vibraphonist Dave Samuels, implying that if he would go out on his own, creative music would occur. This CD is proof to the contrary—easy-listening music that is very predictable, with light funk rhythms that are upbeat but instantly forgettable. Samuels does play well throughout, with "Footpath" being an impressive unaccompanied feature. However, despite the presence of guitarist Steve Khan, bassist John Patitucci and guest clarinetist Eddie Daniels, the rest of this set falls into the soothing and vacuous world of airplay jazz. —*Scott Yanow*

Natural Selection / 1991 / GRP ✦✦✦✦

Dave Samuels' release offers music that is often more pleasant than it is challenging, but Samuels has an original voice on the marimbas and vibes, the groove tunes are generally quite enjoyable (particularly the calypso "Cara Linda" and the tricky "Knots"), and the leader's solos are uniformly strong. With the help of the Yellowjackets' rhythm section (keyboardist Russell Ferrante, electric bassist Jimmy Haslip and drummer William Kennedy) and some guests, this pop-jazz effort is reasonably satisfying and one of Dave Samuels' best solo sets. —*Scott Yanow*

Del Sol / 1992 / GRP ✦✦✦

Vibraphonist Dave Samuels plays quite well on this CD but he is often overshadowed by his sidemen, especially pianist Danilo Perez, flutist Dave Valentin, guitarist Jorge Strunz and (on two numbers) steel drummer Andy Narell. The easy-listening music is pleasing and, due to the utilization of several groupings of players, there is a certain amount of variety. However the lack of any memorable melodies and real climaxes in the improvisations mean that this recording falls into the lightweight pop-jazz vein. A decent effort that could have been stronger. —*Scott Yanow*

David Sanborn

b. Jul. 30, 1945, Tampa, FL

Alto Saxophone / Crossover Jazz, Soul Jazz

David Sanborn has been the most influential saxophonist on pop, R&B and crossover players of the past 20 years. Most of his recordings have been in the dance music/R&B vein although Sanborn is a capable jazz player. His greatest contributions to music have been his passionate sound (with its crying and squealing high notes) and his emotional interpretations of melodies which generally uplift any record he is on. Unlike his countless number of imitators, Sanborn is immediately recognizable within two notes. While growing up in St. Louis, Sanborn played with many Chicago blues greats (including Albert King) and became a skilled alto saxophonist despite battling polio in his youth. After important stints with Paul Butterfield (he played with the Butterfield Blues Band at Woodstock), Gil Evans, Stevie Wonder, David Bowie and the Brecker Brothers, Sanborn began recording as a leader in the mid-'70s and he racked up a string of pop successes. Over the years he has worked with many pop players but he has made his biggest impact leading his own danceable bands. Occasionally Sanborn throws the music world a curve—his eccentric but rewarding *Another Hand,* a guest stint with avant-gardist Tim Berne on a 1993 album featuring the compositions of Julius Hemphill and a set of ballads (*Pearls*) on which he is accompanied by a string orchestra arranged by Johnny Mandel. For a couple years in the early '90s, Sanborn was the host of the syndicated television series *Night Music* which had a very eclectic lineup of musicians (from Sonny Rollins and Sun Ra to James Taylor and heavy metal players), most of whom were given the unique opportunity to play together. It displayed David Sanborn's wide interest and musical curiosity even if many of his own recordings remain quite predictable. *—Scott Yanow*

Taking Off / 1975 / Warner Brothers ✦✦✦

Altoist David Sanborn has long been one of the leaders of what could be called rhythm & jazz (R&B-oriented jazz). His debut for Warner Brothers was a major commercial success and helped make him into a major name. The music is fairly commercial but certainly danceable and melodic. Even at that point in time, Sanborn's alto cries were immediately recognizable. The Brecker Brothers, guitarist Steve Khan and Howard Johnson on baritone and tuba are prominent in support. *—Scott Yanow*

The Best of David Sanborn / 1975-1987 / Warner Brothers ✦✦✦✦✦

During the 13 years he spent recording for Warner Bros., David Sanborn had more than his share of artistic triumphs, but at times, wasted his considerable talents on radio-friendly schlock. Containing more pluses than minuses, *The Best of David Sanborn* paints an honest picture of his jazz/R&B/pop work for that label. Sanborn's distinctive alto is a joy on both rugged, gritty jazz/R&B like "Slam" and "Anything You Want" and such lyrical and heartfelt ballads as "Rain on Christmas," "A Tear for Crystal" and "Lisa." Meanwhile, a mindless, note-for-note cover of Gladys Knight & the Pips' "Neither One of Us" exemplifies Sanborn at his radio-friendly worst. But despite the inclusion of a few stinkers, this 16-song CD isn't a bad introduction to his Warner Bros. output. *—Alex Henderson*

Sanborn / 1976 / Warner Brothers ✦✦✦

This album is one of David Sanborn's better early recordings. Although the record is perhaps best known for the altoist's version of Paul Simon's "I Do It for Your Love," Sanborn's playing on some of the other cuts (most notably "Mamacita" and "7th Avenue") finds him really stretching within the R&B/crossover genre. Only "Smile" (which has some mundane vocalizing) is a minus, and it is more than compensated for by Sanborn's passionate improvising elsewhere. *—Scott Yanow*

Love Songs / 1976-1988 / Warner Brothers ✦✦✦

This single CD is an okay sampler taken from altoist David Sanborn's many Warner Bros. records. The emphasis is on ballads although Sanborn does infuse some of the songs with his usual brand of R&Bish passion. However his many fans will prefer to get his complete sessions, and more general collectors would probably want to hear Sanborn in more heated settings, so this CD is of only limited interest. *—Scott Yanow*

Promise Me the Moon / Dec. 1977 / Warner Brothers ✦✦

Heart to Heart / Jan. 1978 / Warner Brothers ✦✦✦✦

By the time of his third album, altoist David Sanborn's popularity and influence was growing month by month. Most of these numbers feature Sanborn with an enlarged rhythm section (with such studio vets as guitarists Hugh McCracken and David Spinozza, Don Grolnick or Richard Tee on keyboards, vibraphonist Mike Mainieri, bassist Herb Bushler and drummer Steve Gadd). However, "Short Visit" is something special, for Sanborn was joined by what was mostly the Gil Evans Orchestra; Evans even wrote the chart. Otherwise, this is a typical Sanborn release with plenty of danceable rhythms and the focus on his passionate alto. *—Scott Yanow*

Hideaway / 1979 / Warner Brothers ✦✦✦✦

● **Voyeur** / 1980 / Warner Brothers ✦✦✦✦✦

This 1980 recording is an excellent example of David Sanborn's music. The highly influential altoist is joined by familiar studio veterans (including guitarist Hiram Bullock and drummer Steve Gadd) with bassist/composer Marcus Miller being a key figure in creating the funky rhythms and colorful backgrounds. Miller, who shared the writing chores with Sanborn, not only contributed his powerful bass but backed the altoist during a duet version of "Just for You" on piano. Easily recommended to fans of R&B-ish jazz. *—Scott Yanow*

As We Speak / 1981 / Warner Brothers ✦✦✦

It was about this time in his career that one sensed David Sanborn getting a bit tired of the formula he was using on his records. However, his great popularity kept him from changing direction much. The highly influential altoist as usual blows his heart out over a lot of funky rhythms, but surprisingly, he switches to his less notable soprano on four of the nine tunes. Bassist Marcus Miller is a key force in the background, leading the expanded rhythm sections through some pop-oriented material that is appealing but not too substantial. *—Scott Yanow*

Backstreet / 1982 / Warner Brothers ✦✦✦

Straight to the Heart / 1984 / Warner Brothers ✦✦✦✦✦

With bassist Marcus Miller acting as producer and some memorable tunes being performed (most notably "Hideaway" and "Straight to the Heart"), this is one of altoist David Sanborn's better R&B-ish recordings. Joined by keyboardist Don Grolnick, guitarist Hiram Bullock, bassist Miller, drummer Buddy Williams and various guest musicians, Sanborn sounds fairly inspired and is in top form. *—Scott Yanow*

A Change of Heart / 1987 / Warner Brothers ✦✦✦

This is a fairly typical 1980s outing by the popular R&B-ish altoist David Sanborn. The main difference from the past is that the music often uses synthesizers and electronic rhythms to a greater degree than previously, but Sanborn's distinctive crying sound was still very much intact. The music is produced by Marcus Miller ("Chicago Song" and "Imogene"), Michael Colina, Ronnie Foster or Philippe Saisse; each of the producers plays keyboards and is responsible for the backgrounds behind the leader. Funky and danceable but no real surprises occur. *—Scott Yanow*

Close-Up / 1988 / Reprise ✦✦✦

This set is very much a collaboration between altoist David Sanborn and Marcus Miller, who serves as producer, bassist and frequently the lead keyboardist. With the exception of Randy Newman's "Same Girl" and "You Are Everything," all of the music was written or co-composed by Sanborn and Miller. Some selections utilize such additional players as guitarist Hiram Bullock, keyboardist Ricky Peterson and drummer Vinnie Colaiuta. In general, the music fits the formula well, offering Sanborn's emotional sax backed by then-modern electronics and funky rhythms, all of it designed for maximum radio airplay. Sanborn's recording is worthier than most of the output by his many imitators, but one senses that even he knew he could do much better. *—Scott Yanow*

Concerto / 1990 / Warner Brothers ✦

This CD, which features the usually distinctive alto of David Sanborn with the National Philharmonic Orchestra, seemed like a logical matchup, but something went wrong. Composer/producer/conductor Michael Kamen contributed the 27-minute "Concerto for Sanborn and Orchestra" and some shorter pieces, but the music sounds very much like a soundtrack. Rather than conjuring up images, it seems incomplete, without a picture or a plot. Worse yet, the often-bombastic orchestra seems to inspire Sanborn to play in a curiously soulless tone, almost as if he were trying to be "legit" rather than himself. Kamen's string writing also weighs down the session, making this a remarkably dull listening experience and a major disappointment. *—Scott Yanow*

Another Hand / 1991 / Elektra ✦✦✦✦

When David Sanborn debuted on Elektra with *Another Hand* after a 13-year stay at Warner Bros., the altoist swore off formulaic, radio-oriented muzak and vowed to make artistic considerations his main priority. There's nothing shallow or contrived about the album, an exploratory, heartfelt effort generally defined by his introspective, soul-searching improvisations. Sanborn tends to be reflective rather than extroverted—an exception being the soul-jazz gem "Hobbies." Instead of avoiding complexity as some of his more commercial recordings did, *Another Hand* often thrives on it. The album's main flaw lies in the fact that too often the sidemen tend to serve as a backdrop for Sanborn instead of being active soloists. But given the depth and overall excellence of Sanborn's playing, one tends to overlook that shortcoming. *—Alex Henderson*

Upfront / 1992 / Elektra ✦✦✦✦

Directly following his adventurous *Another Hand,* some listeners were disappointed with the fact that David Sanborn did not permanently switch from R&B/crossover to creative jazz. However, this CD is generally quite appealing and takes some chances within its genre. Although bassist Marcus Miller is once again an important collaborator, the emphasis is on "real" instruments, most notably the organ of Ricky Peterson; other musicians in the backup groups include John Purcell on various reeds, trumpeter Randy Brecker, drummer Steve Jordan and guest Eric Clapton, who takes a guitar solo on "Full House." The most unusual selection is the final cut, a version of Ornette Coleman's "Ramblin'" that finds Sanborn, Miller, Peterson and Jordan joined by the avant-garde trumpeter Herb Robertson. Overall, this is an above-average effort from the highly influential altoist. —*Scott Yanow*

Hearsay / 1994 / Elektra ✦✦✦

Pearls / Mar. 28, 1995 / Elektra ✦✦✦✦✦

David Sanborn is joined on this CD by an orchestra arranged by Johnny Mandel for a set of music dominated by melodic versions of standards. Sanborn does not get all that far away from the themes (which include "Try a Little Tenderness," "Smoke Gets in Your Eyes," "For All We Know," "This Masquerade" and a very emotional "Everything Must Change" in addition to a few newer songs) but his sound is so soulful and full of passion that he does not really need to improvise much to make his point. It's a fine change of pace for the highly influential altoist. —*Scott Yanow*

Songs from the Night Before / 1996 / Elektra ✦✦✦✦

David Sanborn's distinctive alto is all over this set, caressing the melodies and playing short soulful solos in typical fashion. Joined by an electronic quartet that features prominent work by Ricky Peterson on keyboards (including bass and drum programming), plus a horn section, Sanborn gives humanity and honest feeling to what could have been an anonymous effort. In addition to the many originals, the influential altoist plays tasteful versions of Wayne Shorter's "Infant Eyes" and Eddie Harris' catchy "Listen Here." —*Scott Yanow*

David Sanchez

b. 1968, Guaynabo, Puerto Rico

Tenor Saxophone / Post-Bop, Latin Jazz

David Sanchez took up the conga when he was eight and started playing tenor at age 12. He graduated from a performing arts high school in 1986, spent a year studying psychology and then moved to New York City in 1988, having decided to become a musician. Sanchez attended Rutgers University, studying with Kenny Barron, Ted Dunbar and John Purcell. After a period freelancing in New York with many top Latin players (including Paquito D'Rivera and Claudio Roditi), Sanchez joined Dizzy Gillespie's United Nation Orchestra in 1990, also getting the opportunity to play with Dizzy's small group. Since then he has toured with the Philip Morris SuperBand, recorded with Slide Hampton's Jazz Masters, Charlie Sepulveda, Kenny Drew, Jr., Ryan Kisor, Danilo Perez, Rachel Z and Hilton Ruiz (among others) and headed his own sessions for Columbia. David Sanchez is an up-and-coming tenor player whose music mixes together Afro-Cuban rhythms with advanced bebop on releases like 1994's *Sketches of Dreams* and 1996's *Street Scenes*. —*Scott Yanow*

● **Sketches of Dreams** / Dec. 7, 1994-Dec. 9, 1994 / Columbia ✦✦✦✦

David Sanchez, who has an appealing tone on the tenor (at times hinting at Joe Henderson and Stanley Turrentine), matches well with trumpeter Roy Hargrove and the creative Latin percussionists during the first two numbers. However at that point Hargrove disappears (only popping up on "Sketches of Dreams") and the percussionists are often de-emphasized in favor of more straightahead music; three numbers are played with just a standard rhythm section. Pianists David Kikoski and Danilo Perez both have plenty of solo space with Perez's complex yet accessible style sometimes coming close at times to stealing honors. But Sanchez's warm sound (which is quite appealing on the ballad "Tu y Mi Cancion" and a tender "It's Easy to Remember") eventually emerges as the main star. Perhaps in the future he should do a full Latin album or an entire set of ballads. This sampler CD (which includes two outings on soprano) is a good example of his talents. —*Scott Yanow*

Street Scenes / Feb. 12, 1996-Mar. 1, 1996 / Columbia ✦✦✦✦✦

David Sanchez shows off his versatility and talented improvising style throughout this diverse and well-conceived set. Ranging from bop (making Thelonious Monk's "Four in One" sound easy) to music in the same area that Joshua Redman is exploring to moments that almost sound like Steve Coleman's M-Base, Sanchez is in consistently creative form. The equally talented pianist Danilo Perez helps out on most cuts, a few selections have added percussion, and there are guest spots for altoist Kenny Garrett (who trades off with Sanchez on a fiery "The Elements") and singer Cassandra Wilson (who sticks to a haunting background on "Los Cronopios"), but the focus is mostly on the leader, who plays some lyrical soprano on two numbers. David Sanchez, who is improving and evolving year by year, has the potential to become a major force in jazz. —*Scott Yanow*

Poncho Sanchez

b. Oct. 30, 1951, Laredo, TX

Leader, Percussion / Latin Jazz

Ever since he led his first record date in 1982, Poncho Sanchez has headed one of the most popular and influential Latin-jazz bands around. The youngest of 11 children, Sanchez taught himself to play guitar, flute, drums and timbales before settling on the congas. After a period playing with local bands, he joined Cal Tjader's band in 1975 and was an important part of Tjader's pace-setting group until his idol's death in 1982. Shortly after, he formed his own band and has since recorded on a regular basis for Concord Picante. Sanchez's group is very active, playing in clubs, concerts and festivals on a regular basis. —*Scott Yanow*

Poncho / Jan. 10, 1979 / Discovery ✦✦✦✦

A fine 1979 date matching percussionist Poncho Sanchez with pianist and bandleader Clare Fischer, who also did the arrangements and conducted the band. This was among the last things the two did together, because Sanchez soon left and formed his own band. Excellent arrangements, plus some exciting ensemble work and good solos. —*Ron Wynn*

Straight Ahead / Mar. 12, 1980 / Discovery ✦✦✦✦

Another collaboration between pianist/bandleader Clare Fischer and conga player Poncho Sanchez. This one was tailored more towards mainstream jazz than Afro-Latin and Latin material, although it also included some effective Latin songs. The Fischer and Sanchez collaboration lasted into the early '80s and was mutually beneficial. —*Ron Wynn*

Sonando / 1982 / Concord Picante ✦✦✦

Good, sometimes entrancing Afro-Latin jazz and salsa by a consistently effective conguero and bandleader. Sanchez is just a notch below Mongo Santamaria and Ray Barretto as a pure percussionist, while his bands are never spectacular but always energetic and entertaining. —*Ron Wynn*

Baila Mi Gente: Salsa! / Aug. 20, 1982-Mar. 8, 1995 / Concord Picante ✦✦✦

Although instrumental Latin jazz is Poncho Sanchez's forte, the L.A. percussionist usually included one or two salsa tunes with vocals on his Concord albums of the 1980s and 1990s. Focusing primarily on Sanchez's salsa recordings, this excellent 1996 compilation spans 1982-1995 and draws on eight of his Concord albums. Sanchez is best known for his work as a percussionist, but the fact that he's far from a bad singer is evident on his infectious original "Baila Mi Gente" and versions of Eddie Palmieri's "Cuidate Compai" and the classic "Co Co My My." One of the disc's best-known tracks is "Sonando," a catchy cha-cha based on Ray Barretto's major hit "Cocinando." The exuberant "Este Son" would have been a better choice than "Soul Sauce"—not because Sanchez's Cal Tjader-influenced take on that Dizzy Gillespie/Chano Pozo classic isn't enjoyable, but because "Este Son" is a better example of outright salsa. But despite that shortcoming, this is a highly rewarding CD that makes us wish Sanchez recorded salsa (as opposed to Latin jazz) a lot more. —*Alex Henderson*

Bien Sabroso / Nov. 1983 / Concord Picante ✦✦✦✦

An average set for Poncho Sanchez and his Afro-Cuban jazz octet. Despite the presence of trumpeter Steve Huffsteter and valve trombonist Mark Levine in the front line (along with the tenor of Dick Mitchell), there are not that many memorable horn solos on the nine selections (mostly group originals and obscurities, except for Kenny Dorham's "Una Mas"). There is some heated playing by the three-piece percussion section, which includes Sanchez on conga, and plenty of good spirits, so Poncho Sanchez's fans will find this CD reissue enjoyable. But his most significant recordings would be in the future. —*Scott Yanow*

El Conguero / May 1985 / Concord Picante ✦✦✦✦

By 1985, Poncho Sanchez's Latin-jazz band had found its niche. This CD from the fine conga player finds his octet in excellent form on originals, obscurities, an unusual Latinized "Shiny Stockings," and "Tin Tin Deo." A couple songs have group vocals, but the emphasis is on the group's heated rhythms and the fine solos of Dick Mitchell (on alto and tenor) and trumpeter Sal Cracchiolo. —*Scott Yanow*

★ **Papa Gato** / Oct. 1986 / Concord Picante ✦✦✦✦✦

Percussionist Poncho Sanchez has long led one of the top Latin-jazz groups, succeeding his former boss, the late Cal Tjader. On this enjoyable release, Sanchez features plenty of solos from Justo Almario (on alto, tenor and flute), trumpeter Sal Cracchiolo and trombonist Art Velasco, and the three percussionists have many opportunities to romp. The jazz content is fairly high with such songs as "Jumpin' with Symphony Sid," "Senor Blues" and "Manteca" alternating with group originals. A fine introduction to the accessible Latin jazz of Poncho Sanchez. —*Scott Yanow*

Fuerte / Nov. 1987 / Concord Picante ✦✦✦✦✦

Features an octet with standout pianist/composer Charlie Otwell, who wrote the title track and two other cookers. Saxophonist Ken Goldberg wrote two others.

Because of these two, this stands as a prime Sanchez album, aside from the group's hot playing. —*Michael G. Nastos*

La Familia / Nov. 1988 / Concord Picante ✦✦✦✦

Chile con Soul / Nov. 1989 / Concord Picante ✦✦✦✦✦

Cambios / Oct. 15, 1990-Oct. 17, 1990 / Concord Picante ✦✦✦✦
Poncho Sanchez's many recordings for Concord Picante, going back to 1982, are quite consistent. Boppish solos mix in with an emphasis on Latin percussion to create high-quality, accessible Latin jazz. This particular CD is another delightful and infectious effort highlighted by a group vocal on "El Sabroson," melodic improvisations and the three exciting percussionists. Trombonist Art Velasco (featured on "In a Sentimental Mood") is powerful on "Pique" and emerges as the top soloist of the program, along with pianist David Torres (who is the musical director). Trumpeter Freddie Hubbard makes three guest appearances, but these are disappointments—he is average on "Yesterdays" and "Sky Dive" and cracks an excess of notes on "My Foolish Heart." Otherwise, this is a rewarding and typically infectious Poncho Sanchez set. —*Scott Yanow*

A Night at Kimball's East / Dec. 8, 1990 / Concord Picante ✦✦✦
This concert performance (which is also available on video) features spirited Latin-jazz from Poncho Sanchez's octet. There are some strong contributions from trumpeter Sal Cracchiolo, trombonist Art Velasco and saxophonist Gene Burkert along with the percussionists. The excessive amount of group vocals and the often-routine (if infectious) material keep this set from being essential but Sanchez's many fans should enjoy it. —*Scott Yanow*

El Mejor / Apr. 18, 1992-Apr. 19, 1992 / Concord Picante ✦✦✦✦
A 1992 session with bandleader Poncho Sanchez spearheading his group through his latest collection of Afro-Latin jams, originals, and the occasional standard. The band includes the dynamic Justo Almario, who provides some welcome intensity, plus Sanchez's driving, steady rhythms. —*Ron Wynn*

Para Todos / Oct. 25, 1993-Oct. 26, 1993 / Concord Picante ✦✦✦✦✦
Everyone plays flawlessly, and Sanchez's conga work provides an array of expertly placed accents, multiple rhythms and support. The songs are uniformly excellent, and Sanchez's group smoothly handles standards, hard bop and Afro-Latin numbers. —*Ron Wynn*

Soul Sauce: Memories of Cal Tjader / Mar. 7, 1995-Mar. 8, 1995 / Concord Picante ✦✦✦✦✦

Conga Blue / Nov. 13, 1995-Nov. 14, 1995 / Concord Picante ✦✦✦✦
Conga player Poncho Sanchez has been one of the leaders in Latin jazz for a decade. This outstanding studio recording delivers the excitement with the addition of special guest Mongo Santamaria on "Watermelon Man" and several originals. Great solos by trumpeter Stan Martin and baritone saxophonist Scott Martin add spice to the lively percussion of Sanchez and his group. —*Ken Dryden*

Freedom Sound / Mar. 3, 1997-Mar. 5, 1997 / Concord Picante ✦✦✦✦
Latin jazz's hardest-working conguero invites two of the original Jazz Crusaders, tenor Wilton Felder and trombonist Wayne Henderson, on board to graft their sound and a few old JC numbers onto his classic salsa ensemble. The results are not entirely lodged in Sanchez's camp—the title track leans toward a 6/8 jazz feeling, and "MJ's Funk" is a more or less straightahead blues, both butting horns with Sanchez's domineering congas—while "Scratch" has a cool Latin funk feeling and some spiffy solo trade-offs near the end. But Felder and Henderson appear together only on three of the 11 cuts and Felder on one other, so this is only a partial tribute album at most. When the two Jazz Crusaders are not around, Sanchez's regular reedman Scott Martin, trombonist Alex Henderson, and trumpeter Sal Cracchiolo fill the breach quite capably. And should the faithful become restless, there is pure Poncho salsa on "Prestame Tu Corazon" and "(Baila El) Suave Cha" to infectiously prop up guest "annotator" Bill Cosby's droll warning, "If this is your first Poncho Sanchez album, I advise you to get another job." —*Richard S. Ginell*

Pharoah Sanders (Farrell Sanders)

b. Oct. 13, 1940, Little Rock, AR
Tenor Saxophone / Free Jazz, Avant-Garde, Hard Bob
Pharoah Sanders has had a rather unique career. He came to fame when he made the John Coltrane Quartet a Quintet, taking ferocious, emotional and atonal solos that started where Coltrane's left off. After Coltrane's death, for a period Sanders came close to making the avant-garde popular as his alternately intense and peaceful solos proved to be a perfect team with singer Leon Thomas ("The Creator Has a Master Plan"). Unfortunately most of Sanders' output since the late '70s has been quite derivative of Coltrane's hard-bop-oriented music circa 1959, years before Sanders joined 'Trane. After graduating high school, Pharoah Sanders freelanced in San Francisco. He moved to New York in 1962, struggled in obscurity for two years, then made his recording debut on ESP. He came to the attention of

John Coltrane and from mid-1965 until 'Trane's death in 1967 he was usually a part of Coltrane's controversial group with his role being largely to create violent sound explorations. Sanders' most rewarding recordings took place during the late '60s/early '70s for Impulse with and without Leon Thomas. However by the mid-'70s his sessions had become predictable and Sanders' career never seemed to regain its earlier momentum. Pharoah Sanders' decision in the early '80s to explore standards melodically pleased the bebop purists but resulted in many of his followers being disappointed by the absence of his own musical personality. Since that time Sanders (now a legend) has largely continued in that direction although occasionally (such as on drummer Franklin Kiermyer's very intense Evidence CD) the real Pharoah Sanders shows up and reminds the jazz world of his significance! —*Scott Yanow*

● **Pharoah's First** / 1964 / ESP ✦✦✦✦✦
Pharoah Sanders' debut as a leader has been reissued on this ESP CD. Sanders, who is joined by trumpeter Stan Foster, pianist Jane Getz, bassist William Bennett and drummer Marvin Pattillo, sounds remarkably like John Coltrane on "Seven by Seven"; he had not found his own musical personality yet. "Bethera" is a bit more distinctive and overall this historic set should greatly interest fans of both Coltrane and Sanders. —*Scott Yanow*

Tauhid / Nov. 15, 1966 / Impulse! ✦✦
This was Pharoah Sanders' first recording on Impulse as a leader but it is a surprisingly weak effort. It takes quite awhile for the 16-minute "Upper Egypt and Lower Egypt" to get going. That piece sets a spiritual mood but Sanders does not really play tenor until the music had already been meandering for 12 minutes. The mercifully brief "Japan" mostly focuses on the leader's off-key chant-like singing, so virtually the only interesting performance is a long medley that spotlights guitarist Sonny Sharrock. This CD can safely be skipped by all but Pharoah Sanders completists. —*Scott Yanow*

Izipho Zam / Jan. 14, 1969 / Strata East ✦✦✦✦
Wild, crazy, and frenzied. Sanders and Sonny Sharrock (g) explore. —*Ron Wynn*

★ **Karma** / Feb. 14, 1969-Oct. 20, 1969 / Impulse! ✦✦✦✦✦
Karma was a real rarity, an avant-garde "hit." One could almost call it "free jazz for the masses." Pharoah Sanders, who in 1966 would have easily won a poll for "least likely to succeed commercially," by 1969 was out on his own featuring his Jekyll-and-Hyde tenor (alternately peaceful and screaming) over rhythmic vamps. With Leon Thomas singing and yodelling, the 33-minute atmospheric "The Creator Has a Master Plan" caught on and received quite a bit of airplay on jazz stations at the time. —*Scott Yanow*

Jewels of Thought / Oct. 20, 1969 / Impulse! ✦✦✦✦✦
The follow-up to Pharoah Sanders' surprisingly popular *Karma*, this LP consists of the 15-minute "Hum-Allah-Hum-Allah-Hum Allah" (featuring singer Leon Thomas) and the two-part 28-minute "Sun in Aquarius." In addition to Sanders (who is in intense form) and Thomas, the group includes pianist Lonnie Liston Smith, bassists Richard Davis and Cecil McBee and drummers Idris Muhammad and Roy Haynes. This passionate music is long overdue to be reissued on CD. —*Scott Yanow*

Deaf Dumb Blind / Jul. 1, 1970 / Impulse! ✦✦✦
The supporting cast is particularly strong on this Pharoah Sanders LP (trumpeter Woody Shaw, altoist Gary Bartz, pianist Lonnie Liston Smith, bassist Cecil McBee, drummer Clifford Jarvis and two percussionists) but unfortunately Pharoah Sanders does not play any of his passionate tenor. Instead he sticks to soprano, which keeps this album from being essential. However the side-long versions of "Summun, Bukmun, Umyun" and "Let Us Go into the House of the Lord" certainly have plenty of atmosphere and passion. —*Scott Yanow*

Thembi / Nov. 25, 1970+Jan. 12, 1971 / Impulse! ✦✦✦✦
The music on this Impulse LP is taken from two different sessions. Pharoah Sanders (on tenor, soprano, alto flute and percussion) is teamed with violinist Michael White on the first date, while the second has drummer Roy Haynes and four African percussionists; in addition keyboardist Lonnie Liston Smith and bassist Cecil McBee are on both sets. Although the performances are fairly concise (only two numbers are over seven minutes), Sanders has plenty of typically fiery spots and certainly gets his message of musical freedom across. —*Scott Yanow*

Black Unity / Dec. 8, 1971 / Impulse! ✦✦✦
This CD consists only of the thirty-seven-and-a-half-minute "Black Unity." The piece starts out logically for its first ten minutes, building from a drone and a simple rhythmic melody up to an intense Pharoah Sanders tenor solo. But its final 20 or so minutes ramble on endlessly, with a lot of aimless and purposeless playing from the oversized rhythm section (which includes pianist Joe Bonner, both Cecil McBee and Stanley Clarke on basses and the two drummers Norman Connors and Billy Hart). Very little happens of any real substance, making the CD reissue a disappointment. —*Scott Yanow*

Live at the East / 1971 / Impulse! ✦✦✦✦✦
By 1971 Pharoah Sanders' playing essentially alternated between two moods: fero-cious and peaceful. This live LP (whose contents have not yet been reissued on CD) gives one a good example of how the passionate tenor sounded in clubs during the early '70s. Sanders is joined by an impressive group of players: trumpeter Marvin "Hannibal" Peterson, flutist Carlos Garnett, Harold Vick on tenor, pianist Joe Bon-ner, the basses of Stanley Clarke and Cecil McBee, drummers Norman Connors and Billy Hart and percussionist Lawrence Killian. On the 20-minute "Healing Song," the lengthy "Memories of J.W. Coltrane" and the two-part "Lumkili," Pharoah Sanders is heard in top form. —*Scott Yanow*

Village of the Pharoahs / Dec. 8, 1971-Sep. 14, 1973 / Impulse! ✦✦✦
This LP is one of tenor saxophonist Pharoah Sanders' lesser efforts. Sanders actu-ally only plays tenor on one song ("Went Like It Came"), otherwise jamming on soprano and taking some spirited vocals. Very much a hodge-podge collection with performances taken from three different settings, best is Sanders' heartfelt "Memo-ries of Lee Morgan." But there are many more significant Pharoah Sanders records than this one. —*Scott Yanow*

Elevation / Sep. 7, 1973-Sep. 13, 1973 / Impulse! ✦✦✦

Journey to the One / 1980 / Evidence ✦✦✦✦✦
Formerly a Theresa double LP, this single CD contains all ten of Pharoah Sanders' performances from the sessions. As usual, Sanders shifts between spiritual peace and violent outbursts in his tenor solos. The backup group changes from track to track but often includes pianist John Hicks, bassist Ray Drummond and drummer Idris Muhammad. Sanders really recalls his former boss John Coltrane on "After the Rain" (taken as a duet with pianist Joe Bonner) and a romantic "Easy to Remember"; other high points include "You've Got to Have Freedom" (which has Bobby McFerrin as one of the background singers) and the exotic "Kazuko" on which Sanders is accompanied by kato, harmonium and wind chimes. —*Scott Yanow*

● **Rejoice** / 1981 / Evidence ✦✦✦✦✦
Originally a two-LP set on Theresa, this single CD (which contains all of the music) features Pharoah Sanders in excellent form in 1981. Sanders sounds much more mellow than he had a decade earlier, often improvising in a style similar to late-'50s John Coltrane, particularly on "When Lights Are Low," "Moments Notice" and "Central Park West." The personnel changes on many of the selections and includes such top players as pianists Joe Bonner and John Hicks, bassist Art Davis, drum-mers Elvin Jones and Billy Higgins, vibraphonist Bobby Hutcherson, trombonist Steve Turre, trumpeter Danny Moore, a harpist and (on "Origin" and "Central Park West") five vocalists. The music always holds on to one's interest, making this one of Sanders' better later recordings. —*Scott Yanow*

Heart Is a Melody / Jan. 23, 1982 / Evidence ✦✦✦
This Evidence CD is a reissue of a Theresa LP, adding two songs ("Naima" and "Rise 'n' Shine) to the original program. Pharoah Sanders is heard at his best on a 22-minute version of "Ole" where the tenor really gets a chance to stretch out. His "vocal" on "Goin' to Africa" is spirited but otherwise most of his solos are very much in the tradition of John Coltrane. There are some fiery moments but few sur-prises on this date chiefly recommended to Sanders' fans. —*Scott Yanow*

Live / Nov. 19, 1982-Nov. 20, 1982 / Theresa ✦✦✦✦
This Theresa LP (not yet reissued on CD) features Pharoah Sanders playing some no-nonsense tenor in a quartet with pianist John Hicks, bassist Walter Booker and drummer Idris Muhammad. Sanders performs "It's Easy to Remember" (in a style very reminiscent of early-'60s John Coltrane), an original blues and two of his com-positions including the passionate "You've Got to Have Freedom." The musician-ship is at a high level and, although Sanders does not shriek as much as one might hope (the Tranish influence was particularly strong during this relatively mellow period), he is in fine form. —*Scott Yanow*

Shukuru / 1985 / Evidence ✦✦✦
Pharoah Sanders and singer Leon Thomas had a reunion on this Theresa LP on two of the numbers (most notably "Sun Song") and, although the magic of "The Creator Has a Master Plan" is not recaptured, the music is still enjoyable. The other four numbers are instrumentals featuring Sanders' tenor with keyboardist William Henderson, bassist Ray Drummond and drummer Idris Muhammad. Sanders does a close impression of late-'50s John Coltrane on "Body and Soul" and "Too Young to Go Steady" and shows a bit more heat on the other two numbers. But fans of his most passionate dates are advised to get a sampling of the earlier Impulse record-ings instead. —*Scott Yanow*

Oh Lord, Let Me Do No Wrong / Jul. 13, 1987 / Doctor Jazz ✦✦✦✦
This 1987 release features tenor saxophonist Pharoah Sanders with either Donald Smith or William Henderson on keyboards, bassist Tarik Shah and drummer Greg Banoy. Sanders mostly plays in a derivative late-'50s John Coltrane style on "Equi-nox," "Polka Dots and Moonbeams" and "Clear Out of This World" while welcom-

ing vocalist Leon Thomas to the three other songs. Few surprises occur but the music should please Sanders' late-period fans. —*Scott Yanow*

A Prayer Before Dawn / Sep. 1987 / Evidence ✦✦✦
For this Theresa LP, on most of the selections Pharoah Sanders (on tenor) duets with the keyboards of William Henderson; the emphasis is on ballads. Pianist John Hicks guests on "After the Rain" while "Midnight at Yoshi's" also adds Alvin Queen on drums and a couple of musicians on Indian instruments. The music overall is spiritual and peaceful with just a bit of heat. —*Scott Yanow*

Crescent with Love / Oct. 19, 1992-Oct. 20, 1992 / Evidence ✦✦✦✦
This two-CD set from the Evidence label features tenor saxophonist Pharoah Sand-ers accompanied by a supportive rhythm section (pianist William Henderson, bass-ist Charles Fambrough and drummer Sherman Ferguson). Although there are some passionate moments, this is actually one of his mellower sessions and he explores such songs as "Misty," "In a Sentimental Mood," "Too Young to Go Steady," "Body and Soul," "Naima" and "After the Rain" in a ballad style not that different than John Coltrane's of the early '60s. There are some heated moments on some of the other selections (such as "Wise One" and "Crescent") but Sanders' trademark screeches are at a minimum this time around. —*Scott Yanow*

● **Message from Home** / 1996 / Verve ✦✦✦✦
The world music-minded producer Bill Laswell gets a hold of Pharoah Sanders here and lo, the sleeping volcano erupts with one of his most fulfilling albums in many a year. *Message from Home* is rooted in, but not exclusively devoted to, Afri-can idioms, as the overpowering hip-hop groove of "Our Roots (Began in Africa)" points out. But the record really develops into something special when Sanders pits his mighty tenor sound against the pan-African beats, like the ecstatically joy-ful rhythms of "Tomoki" and the poised, percolating fusion of American country & western drums and Nigerian juju guitar riffs on "Country Mile." In addition, "Nozi-pho" is a concentrated dose of the old Pharoah, heavily spiritual and painfully pas-sionate, with a generous supply of the tenor player's famous screeching rhetoric, and kora virtuoso Foday Musa Suso shows up on "Kumba" with a touch of village Gambian music. This resurrection will quicken the pulse of many an old Pharoah fan. —*Richard S. Ginell*

Randy Sandke

b. 1949, Chicago, IL
Trumpet / Classic Jazz, Mainstream Jazz, Swing
Since his emergence in the mid-'80s, Randy Sandke has been one of the top swing-oriented trumpeters in jazz. His older brother Jordan (himself a fine trum-peter) introduced Randy to the many styles of jazz. In 1968 he formed a rock band with Michael Brecker that featured a horn section and they played at the Notre Dame Jazz Festival. However Sandke had to turn down the opportunity to join Janis Joplin's band due to a hernia in his throat. Although an operation corrected the problem, Sandke's loss of confidence resulted in him deciding to take up the guitar and he worked in New York as a guitarist for the next decade. Finally he was persuaded to take up the trumpet again and Sandke spent five years with Vince Giordano's Nighthawks, worked regularly with Bob Wilber and he was a part of Benny Goodman's last band during 1985-86. Since that time Sandke has worked and recorded with Buck Clayton, Michael Brecker, the Newport All-Stars, Jon Hendricks, Ralph Sutton, Kenny Davern, Benny Carter, Dizzy Gillespie, the World's Greatest Jazz Band, Mel Tormé and Joe Williams among many others, touring Europe over 20 times. In addition he has recorded several impressive albums as a leader for Jazzology and Concord. —*Scott Yanow*

New York Stories / May 30, 1985 / Stash ✦✦✦✦
This is a surprisingly modern date for the mainstream trumpeter Randy Sandke. Teamed up with tenor saxophonist Michael Brecker, trombonist Joel Helleny, pia-nist Jim McNeely, bassist John Goldsby and drummer Kenny Washington, Sandke is in excellent form on eight of his unusual originals, including one ("Elegy for Albert") which also uses some strings. In addition to his fine playing, Randy Sandke's extensive liner notes (which tell the story behind each of his composi-tions) are quite colorful. This LP has been reissued as part of the Stash CD *The Sandke Brothers. —Scott Yanow*

The Sandke Brothers / May 30, 1985-Jun. 12, 1985 / Stash ✦✦✦✦

Stampede / Dec. 4, 1990+Dec. 6, 1990 / Jazzology ✦✦✦✦✦
Randy Sandke meets up with other mostly young New York-based classic jazz musicians on this delightful CD (clarinetist Ken Peplowski, trombonist Dan Bar-rett, pianist Ray Kennedy, drummer Dave Ratacjzak, either Linc Milliman on tuba or bass saxophonist Scott Robinson, plus veteran guitarist Marty Grosz). Together they revive 15 songs from the 1920s, some well-known but most quite obscure. Rather than merely recreating past records, Sandke contributed fresh arrange-ments for the septet, and the results are quite lively and creative within the bound-aries of 1920s jazz. Among the highlights are "Stampede," "Palesteena," Bix

Beiderbecke's "Candlelights," "Irish Black Bottom" and "Grandpa's Spells." —*Scott Yanow*

Wild Cats / Jul. 9, 1992+Jul. 13, 1992 / Jazzology ✦✦✦✦✦

The second recording by trumpeter Randy Sandke's New Yorkers is the equal of their first (*Stampede*). Joined by clarinetist Ken Peplowski, trombonist Dan Barrett, pianist Mark Shane, guitarist James Chirillo, bassist Jack Lesberg and drummer Dave Ratajczak, Sandke performs 11 songs from the 1920s given fresh arrangements. Obscurities alternate with jazz standards and the highlights include "Wild Cat," "Shim-Me-Sha-Wabble," "Japanese Sandman" and "Stomp Off, Let's Go." Highly enjoyable hot jazz. —*Scott Yanow*

● **I Hear Music** / Feb. 1993 / Concord Jazz ✦✦✦✦✦

Get Happy / Sep. 1993 / Concord Jazz ✦✦✦✦

Chase / Aug. 3, 1994-Aug. 4, 1994 / Concord Jazz ✦✦✦✦

Because Randy Sandke is best known as a swing trumpeter, this CD (which features such highly individual modernists as the outrageous trombonist Ray Anderson, tenor great Michael Brecker, altoist Chris Potter and multi-instrumentalist Scott Robinson who is heard on the selections in which he appears sticking to tenor) is a bit of a surprise. As it turns out Sandke had gone to school with Anderson and Brecker and is a much more flexible trumpeter than one might have thought. Joined by a talented rhythm section comprising pianist Ted Rosenthal, bassist John Goldsby and drummer Marvin "Smitty" Smith, Sandke leads his unusual group through a variety of material ranging from a version of "Lullaby of Broadway" that often simulates a traffic jam, a cooking "Jordu" and four of his originals to the Bix Beiderbecke-associated "Oh Miss Hannah." This set is full of surprises (check out the baroque beginning of "Jordu") and there is plenty of space for each of Sandke's sidemen. Despite all of the potential competition, it is to his credit that Randy Sandke is not all overshadowed on his stimulating set from Concord. —*Scott Yanow*

Arturo Sandoval

b. Nov. 6, 1949, Artemisa, Cuba

Trumpet, Fluegelhorn, Timbales / Bop, Afro-Cuban Jazz, Latin Jazz

A blazing, technically flawless trumpeter from Cuba, Arturo Sandoval has been dazzling audiences all over the world with his supercharged tone and bop-flavored flurries way up in the trumpet's highest register. In slower numbers, he sports a golden, mellow tone on the fluegelhorn, marked with a sure, subtle sense of swing. Apparently he is capable of playing anything, proving it more than once by tackling classical repertoire as well as jazz in the same concert, and he has enough curiosity to search far beyond his Cubop base for repertory. Yet he often lets his desire to please the crowd with high-note displays get in the way of musical values, and he has yet to make a great record that can stand with those trumpet giants that have preceded him.

The son of an auto mechanic, Sandoval took up the classical trumpet at 12 and was enrolled in the Cuban National School of the Arts at 15, studying with a Russian classical trumpeter. Early in the 1970s, he became one of the founding members of the Orquesta Cubana de Musica Moderna, which by 1973 had evolved into the Afro-Cuban, rock-influenced band Irakere. Sandoval met his idol Dizzy Gillespie in 1977, who promptly became a mentor and colleague, playing with Sandoval in concerts in Europe and Cuba and later featuring him in the United Nation Orchestra. After recording an album with David Amram, *Havana/New York*, and a couple of high-profile Irakere albums on Columbia, Sandoval left the group in 1981 to tour with his own band and record in Cuba. Occasionally, the Castro government would allow Sandoval to appear in various international jazz festivals and with orchestras like the BBC Symphony and Leningrad Philharmonic. Though he chafed under a regime that restricted his touring, Sandoval bided his time until he could get his wife and son out of Cuba, and only then, in July 1990 during a long European tour, did he defect at the American Embassy in Rome, settling in Florida. Signing with GRP, Sandoval's first American album, appropriately titled *Flight to Freedom*, demonstrated his versatility in several idioms, and he toured with his own high-energy Afro-Cuban group in the 1990s. —*Richard S. Ginell*

Tumbaito / 1986 / Messidor ✦✦✦✦

This early solo effort (made available on CD by Messidor) by trumpeter Arturo Sandoval was recorded in Madrid, Spain, a few years before his defection from Cuba. Sandoval really lets loose on the six selections (five originals plus "A Night in Tunisia"), showing off his tremendous technique and his ability to play rapid lines. The high-powered music (which also features pianist Hilario Duran and guitarist Jorge Chicoy) may turn some listeners off due to its ferocity and lack of space, but one cannot help but be impressed by Sandoval's talents. —*Scott Yanow*

★ **Straight Ahead** / Aug. 1988 / Ronnie Scotts Jazz House ✦✦✦✦✦

With his remarkable range and phenomenal technique, Arturo Sandoval is one of the world's great trumpeters; he can do virtually anything he wants on his instrument. Some detractors have claimed that he has too much technique (is such a thing possible?) and that his recordings thus far for GRP are a bit erratic. The latter criticism cannot be applied to this 1988 release. Sandoval is heard with a standard quartet comprising the great pianist Chucho Valdes (the leader of Irakere), bassist Ron Matthewson and drummer Martin Drew. Recorded in England before Sandoval broke ties with Cuba, Arturo is in near-miraculous form on some blues, a lyrical "My Funny Valentine" and a few basic originals. Just listen to him tear through "Blue Monk," playing in the low register with the speed of an Al Hirt before jumping into the stratosphere like Maynard Ferguson. This CD serves as an excellent introduction for the bop lover to the very talented Arturo Sandoval. —*Scott Yanow*

Flight to Freedom / 1991 / GRP ✦✦✦✦

In July 1990 after playing trumpet in his native Cuba for 28 of his 41 years, Arturo Sandoval had the opportunity to defect from Cuba along with his family. A brilliant virtuoso, Sandoval finally was able to play whatever music he wanted without having to satisfy a dictator and his potential was enormous. On his American debut, Sandoval mostly performs boppish jazz (other than the dull "Marianela") with slight touches of rock and spiced with Latin percussion. The trumpeter shows restraint on the ballads (including a tasty "Body and Soul") and displays plenty of fire on the often-funky uptempo romps, not overdoing the effortless high notes. With the assistance of the high-powered tenor of Ed Calle, the versatile guitarist Rene Luis Toledo and a variety of talented sidemen (including guest Chick Corea on three songs), Arturo Sandoval's long-overdue debut is well rounded, exciting and highlighted by a fast rendition of Dizzy Gillespie's "Tanga." —*Scott Yanow*

I Remember Clifford / 1992 / GRP ✦✦✦✦✦

Due to the straightahead nature of the music on this CD, plus trumpeter Arturo Sandoval's self-restraint, the release has thus far been most jazz purists' favorite among the trumpeter's releases. Sandoval, who is joined by pianist Kenny Kirkland, bassist Charnett Moffett, drummer Kenny Washington and either Ernie Watts, David Sanchez or Ed Calle on tenor, pays tribute to the great Clifford Brown by performing ten selections previously recorded by Brown, plus his original "I Left This Space for You." The emphasis is on bebop (no Latin or Cuban rhythms on this date) with the highlights including "Daahoud," "Joy Spring," "Cherokee" and an emotional "I Remember Clifford." —*Scott Yanow*

Danzon (Dance On) / Oct. 10, 1993-Nov. 24, 1993 / GRP ✦✦✦✦

Trumpeter Arturo Sandoval comes close on *Danzon* to cutting the Afro-Cuban masterpiece everyone's awaited since his glorious sound first surfaced. From the animated solos on "Africa," "Tres Palabras," and "Conjunto" to the flowing, crisply articulated lines on "Groovin' High," Sandoval plays with imagination, verve and flair, displaying a more original and distinctive concept than on any of his GRP albums to date. He's joined by many top Latin musicians, plus special guest ringers like Vikki Carr, Bill Cosby, and Gloria Estefan, but there's no pandering or stylistic compromises to integrate them into the proceedings. For those who've longed for Sandoval to cut loose, here's the evidence that justifies his reputation. —*Ron Wynn*

Dreams Come True / 1993 / GRP ✦✦✦✦

This is one of trumpeter Arturo Sandoval's more restrained sessions but he cuts loose effectively in some spots. Accompanied by one of two orchestras arranged and conducted by Michel Legrand on most of the selections, Sandoval displays his warm tone and infuses songs such as "Little Sunflower," "Once upon a Summertime" and "To Diz with Love" with lots of feeling; his duet with Legrand on Dizzy Gillespie's "Con Alma" is touching. The ten-minute "Dahomey Dance" (which also has solos from tenor saxophonist Ernie Watts and trombonist Bill Watrous) and a hyper "Giant Steps" are among the many highlights of this recommended disc. —*Scott Yanow*

Arturo Sandoval and the Latin Train / 1995 / GRP ✦✦✦✦✦

Swingin' / Jan. 6, 1996-Jan. 9, 1996 / GRP ✦✦✦✦✦

It seems remarkable that Arturo Sandoval never seems to win any jazz polls for few trumpeters can come close to equaling his technique, jazz chops and warm sound. On this advanced hard-bop date, the music is strictly straightahead without any Latin rhythms. Sandoval matches wits quite successfully with clarinetist Eddie Daniels on two songs, tenor great Michael Brecker on three (including a memorable rendition of "Moment's Notice") and veteran fluegelhornist Clark Terry on a joyous "Mack the Knife." In addition, Sandoval pays tribute to Woody Shaw, John Coltrane and Dizzy Gillespie. Other highlights include the moody "Streets of Desire" (on which Sandoval plays piano), the racehorse tempo of "Real McBop" (which has an impossible but impeccably played melody chorus) and Arturo's humorous use of the plunger mute on "It Never Gets Old." All in all, this is one of Arturo Sandoval's finest recordings to date. —*Scott Yanow*

Mongo Santamaria

b. Apr. 7, 1922, Jesus Maria, Havana, Cuba
Percussion, Leader / Latin Jazz, Afro-Cuban Jazz, Salsa

A Mongo Santamaria concert is a mesmerizing spectacle for both eyes and ears, and even in his 70s, this seemingly ageless Cuban percussionist/bandleader could energize packed behemoth arenas such as the Hollywood Bowl. A master conguero, Santamaria at his best creates an incantory spell rooted in Cuban religious rituals, quietly seating himself before his congas and soloing with total command over the rhythmic spaces between the beats while his band pumps out an endless vamp (a potent example on records is the hypnotic "Mazacote" available on *Afro-Roots* (Prestige)). He has been hugely influential as a leader, running durable bands that combine the traditional charanga with jazz-oriented brass, wind and piano solos, featuring such future notables as Chick Corea and Hubert Laws. He also reached out into R&B, rock and electric jazz at times in his long career. No Cuban percussionist, with the possible exception of Santana's Armando Peraza (and let's not count Desi Arnaz!), has reached more listeners than Mongo.

Ramon "Mongo" Santamaria originally took up the violin but then switched to drums before dropping out of school to become a professional musician. A performer at the Tropicana Club in Havana, Mongo traveled to Mexico City with a dance team in 1948 and then moved to New York City in 1950, where he made his American debut with Perez Prado and spent six years trading percussive barrages with Tito Puente and performing and recording with Cal Tjader (1957-60). Mongo's first significant recordings in America were made in 1958 for Fantasy; his second Fantasy album *Mongo* (1959) contained a composition called "Afro-Blue" which quickly became a Latin-jazz standard, taken up by John Coltrane, Dizzy Gillespie and others.

Santamaria's breakthrough into the mass market may have come as a result of a bad night at a Cuban nightclub in the Bronx in 1962. As the story goes, only three people showed up in the audience, so the musicians held a bull session in which the substitute pianist for the gig, Herbie Hancock, demonstrated his new blues tune, "Watermelon Man." Everyone gradually joined in, the number became a part of Mongo's repertoire, and when producer Orrin Keepnews heard it, he rushed the band into a studio and recorded a single that leaped to the No. 10 slot on the pop charts in 1963.

The success of Santamaria's cross-pollenization of jazz, R&B and Latin music on "Watermelon Man" and a string of Battle and Riverside albums led to a high-profile contract with Columbia that resulted in a wave of hot, danceable albums between 1965 and 1970. With a brighter, brassy sound propelled by trumpeter Marty Sheller's driving charts, often covering hits of the day, the Santamaria band perfectly reflected the mood of the go-go '60s, and Mongo continued to mix genres into the '70s. Since then, Santamaria has returned to his Afro-Cuban base, recording for Vaya in the early '70s, teaming with Gillespie and Toots Thielemans for a live gig at Montreux for Pablo in 1980, recording several albums for Concord Picante (1987-90), a sole effort for Chesky in 1993 and a return to the Fantasy fold via its Milestone subsidiary in 1995. —*Richard S. Ginell*

Afro-Roots / Dec. 1958-May 1959 / Prestige ✦✦✦✦✦
Mongo Santamaria made a pair of superb Latin jazz albums for Fantasy in the late '50s. These were subsequently reissued on a two-record set on vinyl in the '70s, then repackaged again for CD. The disc contains the full albums *Yambu* and *Mongo*, each one brilliant. —*Ron Wynn*

★ **Mongo's Greatest Hits** / 1958-1963 / Fantasy ✦✦✦✦✦
This is an excellent single-disc sampler of what Mongo was like before "Watermelon Man" catapulted him into the charts. Some of the Fantasy tracks sound like they were just off the boat from Havana, a bit primitive in contrast to the brassy Mongo of the mid- to late '60s, but they have overwhelming charm. The revered "Afro-Blue" can be heard in its original, spooky, stripped-down form, and it would be hard for anyone to resist the voodoo spell that the ten-minute-plus "Mazacote" conveys. Included among the world-class percussionists on this record, besides Mongo himself, are Willie Bobo and Armando Peraza. The CD version adds four tracks, including "Watermelon Man" from the Battle/Riverside period and an alternate take of "Para Ti." —*Richard S. Ginell*

Sabroso / May 1959 / Original Jazz Classics ✦✦✦✦
1987 reissue of a wonderful album with Willie Bobo (per) and Pete Escovedo. —*Ron Wynn*

Our Man in Havana / 1959 / Fantasy ✦✦✦
Our man, of course, is Mongo (or was, in early 1960). And what a lineup this one boasts, including the great tres player Nino Rivera (wonderful solos on "Miss Patti Cha Cha") and a couple of the finest lucumi-oriented singers ever, Mercedita Valdes and Carlos Embales, plus a raft of other fine players (great flutist) identified irritatingly only by first names. —*John Storm Roberts, Original Music*

At the Black Hawk / 1962 / Fantasy ✦✦✦✦✦
Applying their famous two-fer philosophy to the digital era, Fantasy combines *Mighty Mongo* and *Viva Mongo!* on a single CD, showcasing two somewhat different slants on Mongo Santamaria's music during a period of exploration. *Mighty Mongo* leans more to Mongo's jazz side without sacrificing his Afro-Cuban rhythmic base, while *Viva Mongo* has a more distinctly ethnic Cuban sound with Rudy Calzado's solo vocals and the band's group chanting, Rolando Lozano's wooden flute riding playfully above the ensemble, and the traditional Cuban use of string counterlines. On *Mighty Mongo*, "Descarga at the Black Hawk" sets an especially tasty groove, with some timbales/congas/cymbals action on an extended vamp. Lozano shines in an extended flute solo on "Bacoso" before a scorcher of a percussion battle develops, while composer/pianist Joao Donato also doubles on trombone on "Sabor." *Viva Mongo's* highlights include "Las Guajiras," a relaxed spellbinder at a guajira tempo; "Merengue Changa," a stupefying merger of two different rhythmic feelings; and the appropriately titled "Mambo Terrifico." Jose "Chombo" Silva, the Cuban Stan Getz worshipper who also evokes Coleman Hawkins on occasion, careens pleasingly on both albums. Of the two, *Viva Mongo* is perhaps the more vital record, but it's a close call; both are vibrant expressions of Mongo's art. —*Richard S. Ginell*

★ **Skins** / Jul. 9, 1962-1964 / Milestone ✦✦✦✦✦
This CD (originally *So Mongo* and *Mongo Explodes* on Riverside) includes many compositions by trumpeter Marty Sheller. Guests include Hubert Laws, Chick Corea, and Jimmy Cobb. Every track is vital. —*Michael G. Nastos*

Watermelon Man / Dec. 17, 1962+Sep. 2, 1963 / Milestone ✦✦✦✦
Herbie Hancock's "Watermelon Man" was a gigantic hit for Mongo Santamaria in 1962, doing for him in the '60s what Perez Prado's big mambo hits did for him in the '50s. Naturally, then, the follow-up LP to the single is devoted to 12 airplay-length tracks loaded with bright, swinging Latin cha-chas and mambo rhythms mixed with blues, soul and jazz, presumably suitable for twisting the night away. Rodgers Grant's piano supplies a good deal of the harmonic foundation of jazz, with the help of an occasional jazz solo from saxes Pat Patrick and Bobby Capers, while Marty Sheller's commanding party-time trumpet rides above the thundering congas of Mongo. In this setting, even the venerable "The Peanut Vendor" is brought right up to date. —*Richard S. Ginell*

Mongo at the Village Gate / Sep. 2, 1963 / Original Jazz Classics ✦✦✦✦✦
This is a nonet with Pat Patrick, Bobby Capers, Marty Sheller and Chihuahua Martinez—a Latin, jazz, and soul combo. MC'd by Symphony Sid, it is startlingly fresh for its era. It still sounds fresh. —*Michael G. Nastos*

La Bamba / 1964 / Columbia ✦✦✦✦
One good hit deserves a remake, so Columbia had Mongo Santamaria redo his breakthrough record "Watermelon Man" on his second LP for the label. Indeed, it is this brighter, better-recorded version that we generally hear on the radio nowadays instead of the Battle original. Even better, though, are "Fatback" and the wildly swinging workout on "La Bamba" that kicks off the album, to which you can imagine the foxy blonde model on the cover dancing the boogaloo. Marty Sheller's charging arrangements and trumpet are in the driver's seat of this sports car with the Mongo engine, and Hubert Laws has a ball in his flute and tenor sax solos. Few records embodied the go-go spirit of the '60s as well as this Latin-jazz album. —*Richard S. Ginell*

Stone Soul / Nov. 1969 / Columbia ✦✦✦✦✦
By now, Mongo Santamaria was basically tied to the formula of translating pop and soul hits of the day—"See Saw," "Love Child," "Little Green Apples," etc.—into his Latin soul jazz idiom, but he and his band perform with so much energy and pizzazz that the music seems anything but routine. Way up front on most of these tunes is featured soloist Sonny Fortune, wailing in a blatantly exciting R&B mode on alto sax. Marty Sheller does most of the hyped-up charts, but the best one may be the sensuous cha-cha treatment of "Where We Are" by pianist Rodgers Grant. Mongo even got a Top 40 hit (No. 32) out of his flaming treatment of the Temptations' "Cloud Nine"—and he gets to work up a fine sweat on his "Hitchcock Railway" solo. A great match of a hot-tempered Latin band and commercial considerations. —*Richard S. Ginell*

Working on a Groovy Thing / 1969 / Columbia ✦✦✦
The Mongo Santamaria/Columbia formula of Top 40 tunes retrofitted with an Afro-Cuban boogaloo beat gets another hyperactive workout here. The title tune, "Spinning Wheel," "Proud Mary," "My Cherie Amour" and "Get Back" are among the choices here, with Sonny Fortune occasionally scorching the earth on alto sax (and probably on flute), Joe Farrell turning up on tenor, and ever-versatile Bernard "Pretty" Purdie stoking the fires alongside Mongo. Yet the band is finally beginning to show some audible weariness with the whole operation—for which one cannot blame them. —*Richard S. Ginell*

Sofrito, 5 on the Color Side / 1976 / Vaya ✦✦✦

A much-sought-after 1976 release, it links Mongo's once groundbreaking Latin-jazz funk to the somewhat spacy jazz-fusion of the era. The jazz names aren't really "names," the heavies being Pretty Purdie, Gaugua Rivera, and arranger Marty Sheller. But the absence of stars may be one reason for the very cohesive effect of the whole affair. The sound is very much of its time, but in no way dated. —*John Storm Roberts*

Red Hot / 1979 / Columbia ✦✦

In reaching for another shot at the big time, Mongo Santamaria sold much of the heart out of his music by turning himself over to producer Bob James, his arranger Jay Chattaway, and the fading disco fad. The result is a near disaster, an overproduced, overdubbed, rhythmically overbearing affair, staffed largely by James and his family of New York session players (including the Brecker Brothers, Eric Gale, and Steve Gadd) with only a handful of Mongo's sidemen, polished to a slick fare-thee-well. "You Better Believe It" is the sole Marty Sheller-arranged track; despite the Anglo-sounding chorus, the Guajiro groove conquers the production. Mongo alumni Hubert Laws has some nice moments in the Brazil-flavored "Sambita," but when you hear "Watermelon Man" redone to a horrible disco beat . . . goodbye. —*Richard S. Ginell*

Summertime / Jul. 19, 1980 / Original Jazz Classics ✦✦

Soy Yo / 1987 / Concord Picante ✦✦✦✦✦

On his first Concord album (now on CD), Mongo Santamaria remains anchored to his Afro-Cuban base but is more than willing to acknowledge the 1980s world around him. Just like the 1960s, you would say. With longtime conductor Marty Sheller at the controls, Mongo's band ventures twice into Top Fortyland, covering Anita Baker's "Sweet Love" in a Latin funk manner and finding a perfect candidate for easygoing guajira swing in Sade's "Smooth Operator." Mongo also pays a convincing visit to the Brazilian samba on the title track, and "Salazar" is an ambitious, tense Sheller workout that flits unpredictably in and out of Brazilian rhythms, but not without plenty of complex Cuban drumming from Mongo and his four percussionists. As a one-off bonus, pianist Charlie Palmieri (in one of his last recordings) and trumpeter Piro Rodriguez make galvanizing guest appearances on "Mayeya." —*Richard S. Ginell*

Afro Blue: Picante Collection / Apr. 6, 1987-Mar. 9, 1990 / Concord Picante ✦✦✦✦

In assembling its own "Mongo's Greatest Hits" entry, Concord Picante had only a slim catalog of four albums, a narrow time frame, and one of Mongo's less incendiary phases to choose from. But they stuck with a purist concept, avoiding pop covers and experiments, targeting Mongo's vintage standards and numbers that conjure some of the old Afro-Cuban heat, and they came up with a nice overview of the Picante years. Whenever possible, we get authentic guajiras, mambos and guarachas, as well as the charanga-band sound that harkens back to Mongo's recordings of the 1950s—all now in gleaming modern sound. Some of the highlights: the hypnotic Cuban voodoo-like incantation of "La Tumba," stimulating live renditions of "Manteca" and "Afro Blue," and pianist Charlie Palmieri's valedictory appearance with Mongo on "Mayeya." While this wouldn't qualify as the basic Mongo collection, you will still find it vastly entertaining. —*Richard S. Ginell*

Soca Me Nice / May 1988 / Concord Picante ✦✦✦✦

Another good date with his '80s band, though more Afro-Cuban jazz than Soca. —*Ron Wynn*

Ole Ola / 1989 / Concord Picante ✦✦✦

Veteran percussionist Mongo Santamaria emphasizes the easy-listening side of Latin jazz on this Concord Picante CD. Only two of the band originals include vocals with the title cut being a bit poppish and "La Tumba" having more typical rhythmic group chanting. The majority of the instrumentals are rather concise (four to six minutes apiece) ballads. Stars of Mongo's 1989 octet are altoist Bobby Porcelli (who has an appealing tone and is best featured on "Who's Got the Bread" and "Mother Jones"), pianist Bob Quaranta (mostly in the background but sounding like a young Herbie Hancock on "Now Is Forever") and the warm trumpet of Ray Vega. Overall this is a pleasant if lightweight outing. —*Scott Yanow*

Live at Jazz Alley / Mar. 1990 / Concord Picante ✦✦✦✦✦

This is as close to Latin purist Mongo as we have heard in recent years, an eight-piece salsa band—including several members of the 1997 Tito Puente ensemble, like trumpeter Ray Vega, altoist Bobby Porcelli and tenorman Mitch Frohman—playing a brace of Mongo classics and Latin-jazz pieces live before a hushed crowd in Seattle's Jazz Alley. There are no pop covers, one electric instrument (a bass), lots of extended jazz solos (Porcelli and Frohman really burn on the pioneering Afro-Cuban classic "Manteca"), and an unusual (for Mongo) emphasis on the timbales on many tracks, which shoves the rhythms closer to the salsified Puente manner. However, tracks like "Juan Jose," "Home" and "Bonita" do have the smooth Mongo cha-cha and guajira grooves, and elsewhere, Mongo lifts himself

out of the background often enough to deliver some stirring polyrhythmic conga salvos. For a specific jolt from Mongo's own past, there is "Para Ti" and ten-and-a-half stimulating minutes of "Afro Blue." Though the general electricity level of the gig could be higher, Mongo's ageless spirit triumphs again. —*Richard S. Ginell*

Mambo Mongo / Mar. 30, 1992-Mar. 31, 1992 / Chesky ✦✦✦

Mongo Returns / Jun. 28, 1995-Jun. 29, 1995 / Milestone ✦✦✦✦

Mongo returns—to the Fantasy label group, not the scene, from which he had never been missing in action. Yet in another sense, it is a return to the basic Mongo Santamaria Afro-Cuban-rooted sound and concept—with a few contemporary elements—that the ageless leader had been employing ever since he stopped trying to chase after hits. Marty Sheller continues to turn out the charts; in addition to three of his own tunes, he gratefully revives two unusual overlooked '70s gems, Stevie Wonder's "You've Got It Bad, Girl" and Marvin Gaye's "When Did You Stop Loving Me, When Did I Stop Loving You" in his old boogaloo manner. The then-current edition of Mongo's large ensemble sounds sharp, at home with the Latin beat, up-to-date electronic instruments and occasional skipping bass line, and Mongo thunders away with his usual polyrhythmic vigor. All we miss is the extra snap and ebullient fire that Mongo's band had when it was right in tune with popular culture, but that's not a deterrent toward having a good time with this disc. —*Richard S. Ginell*

Saheb Sarbib

b. 1944

Bass / Avant-Garde

Raised in Europe, bassist Saheb Sarbib came to New York around 1977-78 and although he has received little publicity since, he has recorded several notable records as a leader of both a big band and a quartet; Sarbib's albums have come out on the Cadence and Soul Note labels. Although a fine bassist, Sarbib's main significance thus far has been as an underrated but important avant-garde bandleader. —*Scott Yanow*

Ufo! Live on Tour / Mar. 1, 1979-Mar. 21, 1979 / Cadence ✦✦✦✦✦

This is a superior free-jazz session. Bassist Saheb Sarbib (who also plays some piano and the exotic-sounding shenai) contributed four originals which are performed in a quartet with altoists Mark Whitecage and Daunik Lazro plus drummer Martin Bues. The lengthy performances (which each clock in between 12 and thirteen-and-a-half minutes) are full of fire and excitement and yet have plenty of variety. Well worth exploring by open-eared listeners. —*Scott Yanow*

● **Live at the Public Theater** / Oct. 17, 1980 / Cadence ✦✦✦✦✦

Although often overlooked, bassist Saheb Sarbib is a strong innovator on his instrument and a bandleader with inventive ideas. On the first of his two big-band albums for Cadence, Sarbib heads an unusual 22-piece group consisting of three trumpeters, three trombonists, three sopranos, three tenors, three altoists, a baritonist, two guitarists, an electric bassist, a drummer, a percussionist and his own acoustic bass. The four movements of "Concerto for Rahsaan" (which lasts over thirty-four-and-a-half minutes) plus "Daybreak" (which is dedicated to Charles Mingus) are both memorable. The latter piece has a haunting trumpet solo by Jack Walrath while "Rahsaan" includes some solo space (both individually and as part of "dialogues") for most of the horn players. The inside/outside performances (which feature both avant-gardists and more conventional players) are quite colorful and stimulating. Highly recommended. —*Scott Yanow*

Aisha / Jul. 1981-Aug. 1981 / Cadence ✦✦✦✦✦

The second of bassist Saheb Sarbib's two big-band albums for Cadence features six of his originals, including pieces dedicated to Steve Lacy, Albert Ayler and John Lennon, plus the 17-minute, four-movement "Aisha." Sarbib's unusual orchestra (consisting of three trumpeters, two trombones, three sopranos, three altos, three tenors, one baritone, two guitars, electric bass, drums, percussion and the leader's bass) is quite adventurous without losing sight of its roots. Among the better-known sidemen are trumpeters Ahmed Abdullah and Roy Campbell, altoists Mark Whitecage and Jemeel Moondoc and guest tenor Frank Wright. The consistently exciting music serves as proof that there is life for creative big bands after the end of the swing era and apart from the stage band movement. Recommended. —*Scott Yanow*

Seasons / Nov. 5, 1981 / Soul Note ✦✦✦✦

Although Saheb Sarbib switches between bass and piano and contributed all but one of the eight selections heard on this disc (every piece but Ornette Coleman's "Round Trip"), this live set is most notable for the saxophone solos of Mel Ellison (on alto, soprano and tenor) and altoist Mark Whitecage. With the support of drummer Paul Motian, Sarbib lays down a solid foundation for the adventurous horns. The music is quite coherent but often free, making for a stimulating listen. —*Scott Yanow*

Jancin' at Jazzmania / 1982 / JazzMania ✦✦✦✦✦

It Couldn't Happen Without You / Jan. 1984-Feb. 1984 / Soul Note ✦✦✦✦

Gray Sargent

Guitar / Swing

Guitarist Gray Sargent, based in New England, has worked with Illinois Jacquet, Ruby Braff and George Wein's Newport All-Stars but gained national recognition for his recordings with Dave McKenna and Scott Hamilton. A talented swing/bop player, Sargent's 1993 Concord release *Shades of Gray* was his debut as a leader. —*Scott Yanow*

● **Shades of Gray** / Feb. 1993 / Concord Jazz ✦✦✦✦✦
Throughout this enjoyable set, guitarist Gray Sargent is the epitome of cool, unhurried and relaxed no matter what the tempo. Sargent is accompanied by bassist Marshall Wood and drummer Ray Mosca and, on half of the set, the great pianist Dave McKenna. The music falls between swing and bop, sounding both spontaneous and fully under control. Sargent, who has a very appealing sound, uplifts each of the standards and some of them (particularly the ones with McKenna) swing quite hard. —*Scott Yanow*

Carl Saunders

b. Aug. 1943, Las Vegas, NV

Trumpet / Bop, Cool

A superior bop trumpeter inspired by Don Fagerquist, Carl Saunders has long been one of the top jazz soloists based in Los Angeles, but has recorded far too infrequently to gain the fame he deserves. As a teenager, he played with Stan Kenton (1960) and his uncle Bobby Sherwood (Dave Pell is also an uncle). Saunders picked up experience touring with Benny Goodman, Charlie Barnet, Harry James, Buddy Rich, and Maynard Ferguson (1967), and played regularly in show bands in Las Vegas until moving to Los Angeles in 1984. Since then, Saunders has worked in the studios, performed with the new Dave Pell Octet, popped up in many local big bands, and finally, in 1995, recorded a CD of his own for the small S&L label. —*Scott Yanow*

● **Out of the Blue** / Jul. 3, 1995-Jul. 4, 1995 / S&L ✦✦✦✦
This CD could have been titled "It's About Time!" It is hard to believe that trumpeter Carl Saunders, a fixture in Los Angeles since he moved from Las Vegas in 1984, had never before led his own record date. A superb bop-based improviser whether featured in big bands, with the Dave Pell Octet or in smaller combos, Saunders has long been in demand for jazz sessions. For this release he is showcased in a quartet with pianist Roger Kellaway, bassist Buster Williams and drummer Santo Savino; two numbers add the tenor of Jerry Pinter and trombonist Andy Martin. Saunders gets the opportunity to stretch out on four standards, five originals (either by him or Scott Tibbs) and, best of all, an unusual and exciting version of Chopin's "Minute Waltz." Varying romps with ballads and showing off not only his creative ideas but his warm tone, Carl Saunders' maiden effort as a leader is quite impressive and highly recommended. —*Scott Yanow*

Alex Schlippenbach (Alexander von Schlippenbach)

b. Apr. 7, 1938, Berlin, Germany

Piano / Avant-Garde

One of Europe's premier free-jazz bandleaders and pianist, Alexander von Schlippenbach's music mixes free and contemporary classical elements, with his slashing solos often the link between the two in his compositions. Schlippenbach formed the Globe Unity Orchestra in 1966 to perform the piece "Globe Unity," which had been commissioned by the Berliner Jazztage. He remained involved with the orchestra into the '80s, with the exception of one period from 1971 to 1972. Schlippenbach began taking lessons at eight, and studied at the Staatliche Hochschule for Musik in Cologne with composers Bernd Alois Zimmermann and Rudolf Petzold. He played with Gunther Hampel in 1963 and was in Manfred Schoof's quintet from 1964 to 1967. Schlippenbach began heading various bands after 1967, among them a 1970 trio with Evan Parker and Paul Lovens, and a duo with drummer/vocalist Sven-Ake Johansson which they co-formed in 1976. Schlippenbach has also given many solo performances. He's recorded for the FMP, Japo, Saba, and Po Torch labels, both as a leader and with the Globe Unity Orchestra. These CDs can be obtained through diligent searches and mail order. —*Ron Wynn*

● **Globe Unity** / 1966 / Saba ✦✦✦✦✦

Anticlockwise / Jul. 1984 / FMP ✦✦✦

Maria Schneider

b. Nov. 27, 1960, Windom, MN

Composer, Arranger, Leader, Piano / Avant-Garde, Post-Bop

In the late-'90s, Maria Schneider is widely thought of as a potentially great arranger who is following in the footsteps of Gil Evans (her main inspiration),

George Russell and Bob Brookmeyer. After extensive musical study, Schneider moved to New York in 1985 and from 1985-88 was an assistant to Gil Evans. She has since conducted her music with a variety of European radio orchestras, written for the Mel Lewis big band and received many commissions. Schneider's highly original music often falls between avant-garde jazz and modern classical. —*Scott Yanow*

● **Evanescence** / Sep. 1992 / Enja ✦✦✦✦✦
Maria Schneider's debut as a leader is quite impressive. Her complex arrangements of her nine originals are most influenced by Gil Evans and Bob Brookmeyer although her own musical personality shines through. There are strong solos from tenors Rick Margitza and Rich Perry, trumpeter Tim Hagan, altoist Tim Ries and particularly pianist Kenny Werner, but it is the moody ensembles that most stick in one's mind. Schneider's arrangements are often dense, a bit esoteric and thought-provoking; this music may need several listens for one to grasp all that is going on. —*Scott Yanow*

Coming About / Nov. 9, 1995-Nov. 10, 1995 / Enja ✦✦✦✦
Composer/arranger Maria Schneider and her 18-piece orchestra perform a variety of advanced and difficult music on this CD. The centerpiece of the set is her three-part "Scenes from Childhood" which deals with fear, confusion and grudging acceptance; do not look here for any childlike melodies or playfulness. In addition the big band plays a reworked version of "Giant Steps," the "Love Theme from *Spartacus*," the Spanish-flavored "El Viento" (which is slightly reminiscent of Gil Evans' writing for *Sketches of Spain*) and "Waxwings." There are strong solos from trumpeters Greg Gisbert and Tim Hagans, Rich Perry and Rick Margitza on tenors and baritonist Scott Robinson among others but it is the sound of the full ensemble that is most memorable about this rather heavy and melancholy set. —*Scott Yanow*

Rob Schneiderman

b. Jun. 21, 1957, Boston, MA

Piano / Hard Bop, Post-Bop

A fine advanced straightahead pianist, Rob Schneiderman has recorded several stimulating sets for Reservoir. He grew up in San Diego and at age 16 was playing in clubs. Before moving to New York in 1982, Schneiderman picked up valuable experience playing with Charles McPherson and Eddie Harris. Since arriving in New York, the pianist has worked with many top musicians, including Zoot Sims, James Moody, Art Farmer, Chet Baker, Slide Hampton and J.J. Johnson. In addition to his own solo records, Schneiderman has toured and recorded as part of the Tana Reid band. —*Scott Yanow*

New Outlook / Jan. 5, 1988 / Reservoir ✦✦✦✦

Smooth Sailing / Feb. 28, 1990 / Reservoir ✦✦✦✦

Radio Waves / May 9, 1991 / Reservoir ✦✦✦✦✦
Pianist Rob Schneiderman and a top-notch sextet (with trumpeter Brian Lynch, Ralph Moore on tenor, baritonist Gary Smulyan, bassist Todd Coolman and drummer Jeff Hirshfield) perform seven of the leader's swinging but unpredictable originals and two standards ("Blue Moon" and "There's a Small Hotel"). The strong musicianship, obvious enthusiasm and creative improvisations make this a recommended set for adventurous straightahead jazz fans. —*Scott Yanow*

● **Standards** / Aug. 26, 1992 / Reservoir ✦✦✦✦

Dark Blue / May 17, 1994 / Reservoir ✦✦✦✦

Keepin' in the Groove / Jan. 9, 1996 / Reservoir ✦✦✦✦

Dancing in the Dark / May 28, 1997 / Reservoir ✦✦✦✦

David Schnitter

b. Mar. 19, 1948, Newark, NJ

Tenor Saxophone / Hard Bop

An excellent hard-bop tenor saxophonist most influenced by Dexter Gordon, David Schnitter's rise in the jazz world in the 1970s preceded the Young Lions; unfortunately, he has maintained a much lower profile during the past 15 years. After starting on clarinet, Schnitter permanently switched to tenor when he was 15. He played locally, moved to New York, gigged with Ted Dunbar and then was a member of Art Blakey's Jazz Messengers from 1974-79. He worked with Freddie Hubbard from 1979-81 and had associations with Frank Foster, Charles Earland and Groove Holmes. David Schnitter sounded fine on numerous records with Blakey and as a leader for Muse during 1976-81, but not enough has been heard from him since. —*Scott Yanow*

Invitation / 1976 / Muse ✦✦✦✦✦
Recording debut from East Coast tenor saxophonist. Top-notch. —*Michael G. Nastos*

Goliath / Oct. 29, 1977 / Muse ✦✦✦✦

David Schnitter's second of four Muse albums as a leader features the underrated hard-bop tenor with a fine rhythm section consisting of the obscure keyboardist Hubert Eaves, bassist Cecil McBee and drummer Eddie Moore; the then-unknown trumpeter Claudio Roditi has guest appearances on two of the five selections. Eaves, Schnitter and Roditi contributed an original apiece which fit in quite nicely with an easy-swinging "My Funny Valentine" and the hotter "Night and Day." Fine straightahead music, but, as with all of David Schnitter's Muse recordings, this one has yet to be reissued on CD. —Scott Yanow

Thundering / Sep. 13, 1978 / Muse ✦✦✦✦

● **Glowing** / Dec. 1981 / Muse ✦✦✦✦✦

Tenor saxophonist David Schnitter's fourth and final LP in his string of Muse releases would serve as a perfect introduction to his playing, except that it is out of print. The hard-bop stylist is heard teamed with trumpeter Claudio Roditi, pianist Albert Dailey, bassist Mark Helias and drummer Ed Blackwell. Despite the presence of the more adventurous Helias and Blackwell, the treatments of four veteran standards (including "Where or When" and "I'll Remember April") plus Schnitter's "Ellipsis" are conventional and hard-swinging. The brief "If I Loved You," which has a vocal by Schnitter in which he is joined by a completely different five-piece rhythm section, is a leftover track from the previous 1978 album *Thundering*. All in all, this is an enjoyable set of modern, straightahead music. —Scott Yanow

Loren Schoenberg

b. 1958, Fair Lawn, NJ
Tenor Saxophone / Swing

Loren Schoenberg took piano lessons from the age of four and early on he became a jazz historian, working at the New York Jazz Museum. In 1974 he began playing tenor and within two years was playing professionally. Schoenberg worked with a variety of swing greats (including Benny Goodman) and started leading a regular big band in 1980. Since then the increasingly distinctive soloist (and prolific liner note writer) has recorded a series of excellent swing-oriented records for Aviva and Music Masters, both with his big band and with a combo. —Scott Yanow

That's the Way It Goes / Jul. 19, 1984-Jul. 20, 1984 / Aviva ✦✦✦✦

Tenor saxophonist Loren Schoenberg's recording debut (he was 26 at the time) is quite impressive. Four songs feature his swing tenor in a quintet with pianist Dick Katz, guitarist Howard Alden, bassist Phil Flanigan and drummer Mel Lewis; Barbara Lea takes a vocal on "Keepin' Myself for You." The other six selections on this LP feature Schoenberg's notable big band playing new arrangements by Benny Carter and Buck Clayton, plus classics by Fletcher Henderson ("Wrappin' It Up") and Eddie Sauter (Alec Wilder's "That's the Way It Goes"). Barbara Lea sings "I Got It Bad," and the soloists besides Schoenberg include trumpeters John Eckert and Dick Sudhalter and clarinetist Ken Peplowski. Enjoyable music that deserves to be reissued on CD. —Scott Yanow

● **Time Waits for No One** / 1987 / Music Masters ✦✦✦✦✦

Tenor saxophonist Loren Schoenberg led a part-time swing orchestra throughout the 1980s. This definitive set finds his big band playing an arrangement apiece from Benny Carter ("Symphony in Riffs"), Buck Clayton, Eddie Sauter, Duke Ellington (a remake of "Harmony in Harlem"), Gil Evans, Jimmy Mundy, Gary McFarland, Horace Henderson, Bob Brookmeyer and Eddie Durham (his classic rendition of "Blue Room"); in addition, Schoenberg is featured with the rhythm section on "I Cover the Waterfront" and Pete Rugolo's "Overtime." Among the many concise soloists heard from the excellent big band are trumpeter Dick Sudhalter and John Eckert, trombonist Matt Finders, clarinetist Ken Peplowski and pianist Dick Katz. This is a creative outing that avoids the usual nostalgia trappings associated with some swing-oriented big bands. —Scott Yanow

Solid Ground / Aug. 8, 1988-Aug. 9, 1988 / Music Masters ✦✦✦✦

The third record by the Loren Schoenberg Jazz Orchestra finds the band mostly exploring superior obscurities, along with a few underplayed standards. On such memorable tunes as "Midriff," "Coquette," "Only Trust Your Heart" and "I Double Dare You," the swinging big band gets to show off its diversity. The talented singer Barbara Lea has three vocals, and such soloists are featured as tenorman Schoenberg, trombonists Eddie Bert and Matt Finders, pianist Dick Katz, guitarist Howard Alden, and trumpeters John Eckert, Dick Sudhalter and Randy Brecker. All of the recordings by this underrated orchestra are easily recommended and quite enjoyable. —Scott Yanow

Just A-Settin' and A-Rockin' / Sep. 6, 1989+Sep. 7, 1989 / Music Masters ✦✦✦✦✦

S'posin' / Jun. 21, 1990-Jun. 22, 1990 / Music Masters ✦✦✦✦✦

Manhattan Work Song / Apr. 21, 1992-Apr. 22, 1992 / Jazz Heritage ✦✦✦✦✦

Loren Schoenberg's Jazz Orchestra (which has been around for over a decade) is a top-notch modern swing band with a fresh repertoire, mostly new arrangements

and a lot of colorful soloists who are able to make the most of their short spots. This CD, their fifth recording, is one of their most rewarding. Such arrangers as Schoenberg, Mark Lopeman, James Chirillo, John Carisi (his last work, a new version of his advanced "Springville"), Bill Finegan, Nat Pierce and Benny Carter contributed charts. Four lesser-known Ellington pieces are among the high points while solo-wise Schoenberg's full-toned tenor often takes honors although there are also features for baritonist Danny Bank and Ken Peplowski. It would be nice to hear the musicians get more opportunities to stretch out beyond the usual three- to five-minute time limit but this is a satisfying effort. —Scott Yanow

Gunther Schuller

b. Nov. 11, 1925, Jackson Heights, NY
Arranger, Composer, French Horn / Ragtime, Third Stream

Gunther Schuller is probably the greatest friend jazz has ever had from the classical world. A jazz devotee from the beginning, he has been the most outspoken advocate of a fusion between elements of European classical music and jazz, inventing the term "Third Stream" at a 1957 Brandeis University lecture to describe it. Although Third Stream music had been around in some form since the beginning of the century, it was Schuller who crystallized the idea, and thanks to alliances with such jazz figures as John Lewis, George Russell, Charles Mingus and Jimmy Giuffre, he actively encouraged new works in that form. Schuller's own compositions often include jazz elements, though usually far more abstractly integrated into his own 12-tone music than the works of the jazz musicians he has encouraged. As a conductor, Schuller inadvertently helped touch off a popular ragtime fad in the 1970s with his spirited performances of Scott Joplin, and he has participated in some key jazz recordings as a French horn player. He has also been a tireless mover and shaker for jazz studies programs in universities, which have had a profound and controversial effect on the direction of the music in the last third of the 20th century.

Ironically, in view of his efforts to bring jazz into academia and the concert hall, Schuller is entirely self-taught as a composer. As befitting the son of a violinist with the New York Philharmonic, he did study theory, flute, and French horn privately, but his progress on the latter was so swift that he began playing professionally with the American Ballet Theatre in 1943, and held down first-desk positions with the Cincinnati Symphony (1943-45) and the Metropolitan Opera (1945-59). He first attracted notice on the jazz side of the fence by playing French horn on four tracks of Miles Davis' seminal *Birth of the Cool* sessions in 1950, also appearing in Gil Evans' orchestra on Miles' *Porgy and Bess*. As his enthusiasm for mergers of both of his worlds grew during the 1950s, Schuller founded the Jazz and Classical Music Society with John Lewis in 1955, which presented concerts of music written by both classical and jazz composers. One of the outcroppings from this society was a Columbia recording, *Music for Brass*, which contained various compositions by Schuller, Lewis, Giuffre and J.J. Johnson as performed by musicians from across the spectrum like Miles Davis, Schuller himself, and New York Philharmonic conductor Dimitri Mitropoulos.

In conjunction with his famous Brandeis lecture, Schuller started a jazz festival there in 1957, commissioning works from Russell, Mingus, and Giuffre. He continued to turn out Third Stream compositions like "Transformation" (1957), "Concertino for Jazz Quartet and Orchestra" (1959), "Conversations for the Double Quartet of the Modern Jazz Quartet and Beaux Arts String Quartet" (heard on the MJQ's *Third Stream* album), and "Variants on a Theme of Thelonious Monk" (1960). He and Lewis founded the Lenox School of Jazz Summer School and presented the first jazz concert ever held at Lenox's hitherto solidly classical bastion, Tanglewood, in 1963.

Having given up the French horn in 1962, Schuller merely narrowed his multipronged activities down to conducting, composing, teaching and writing. 1967 found Schuller becoming the president of the New England Conservatory of Music in Boston, where he promptly established a jazz department that became the first to offer a four-year B.A. degree in jazz. Schuller also started the New England Conservatory Jazz Repertory Orchestra and Ragtime Ensemble, and he soon became immersed in transcribing the works of Duke Ellington and Jelly Roll Morton and performing period arrangements of Scott Joplin rags. The latter activity resulted in *The Red Back Book* (Angel), which became a runaway hit album in 1973, reawakening interest in the rags of Joplin and touching off their use in the popular movie *The Sting*. Schuller's involvement in the ragtime revival reached its apogee in 1975, when he conducted the first (and thus far, only) recording of Joplin's opera *Treemonisha* (Deutsche Grammophon) with the Houston Grand Opera, and Schuller and the NEC Ragtime Ensemble would tour well into the next decade.

In recent years, Schuller reconstructed, edited and conducted the posthumous premiere of Mingus' *Epitaph* at Lincoln Center in 1989, while modestly not claiming to have said the last word on this huge, chaotic work. In the classical sphere, his symphonic piece *Of Reminiscences and Reflections* won the Pulitzer Prize for music in 1994. He also found the time to write two massive, erudite tomes on jazz,

Early Jazz: Its Roots and Musical Development (1968) and *The Swing Era: The Development of Jazz 1930-1945* (1989), which chronicle and analyze the music in unprecedentedly thorough detail. He is currently working on Vol. 3, which will take readers from bebop to the present. —*Richard S. Ginell*

John Lewis Presents Jazz Abstractions / Dec. 19, 1960-Dec. 20, 1960 / Atlantic ✦✦✦✦

★ **Art of Scott Joplin** / Dec. 15, 1973-Jan. 4, 1974 / GM ✦✦✦✦✦
Shortly before *The Sting* turned ragtime into a bit of a fad in the mid-1970s, Gunther Schuller conducted the New England Ragtime Ensemble (formerly a classical ensemble) through a dozen Scott Joplin pieces that had been orchestrated 70 years earlier for the legendary Red Back Book. This wonderful CD reissue features the group (comprising trumpet, trombone, flute/piccolo, clarinet, tuba, piano, bass, drums and a string quartet with occasional guests on oboe, clarinet, bassoon and French horn) on very colorful versions of such numbers as "Elite Syncopations," "Wall Street Rag" (one of four pieces actually arranged by Schuller), "Solace," "Euphonic Sounds" and "Gladiolus Rag." The arrangements bring out fresh colors in Joplin's music and demonstrate that ragtime was not the exclusive domain of solo pianists. This delightful and important set is highly recommended. —*Scott Yanow*

● **Jumpin' in the Future** / Mar. 26, 1988-May 1, 1988 / GM ✦✦✦✦✦
George Schuller, drummer and one of the founders of the Boston jazz orchestra Orange Then Blue, ran across some of his father's older unrecorded arrangements, obtained a grant to preserve the pieces on disc and then surprised his father, Gunther Schuller, with news of his discovery. Both Schullers worked with Orange Then Blue to rehearse the difficult charts and they have documented some important works on this CD, all but two of which predate the elder Schuller's first ventures into Third Stream music. The earliest composition, "Jumpin' in the Future" (from 1947), is possibly the first atonal jazz work, heavily influenced by contemporary classical music but still using jazz phrasing and a lightly swinging rhythm section. While Schuller's rendition of "When the Saints Go Marching In" is really a wholly written-out classical fantasy based on the first four notes of that standard, several other arrangements ("Blue Moon," "Anthropology" and "Yesterdays") are heavily influenced by Gil Evans' work with Claude Thornhill although all are a step closer to classical music than Evans' work of the time. "Summertime" also seems reminiscent of Gil Evans but actually dates from 1949, nine years before Evans recorded his famous version with Miles Davis. "Night Music," originally a 1961 feature for Eric Dolphy, has Howard Johnson doing an extraordinary imitation of Dolphy on bass clarinet. The concluding work (1966's "Teardrop") is a bit dry with its five movements seeking to portray the five senses. It is a pity that Gunther Schuller's adventurous charts were not recorded when they were originally composed for they might have strongly influenced the orchestral music of the 1960s; they still sound quite fresh and exciting. Highly recommended. —*Scott Yanow*

The Art of the Rag / Jan. 3, 1989-Jan. 4, 1989 / GM ✦✦✦✦✦
Fifteen years after the New England Ragtime Ensemble's initial recording, Gunther Schuller brought the group back into the studios to perform a well-rounded set of ragtime-oriented music. The ensemble (consisting of up to five brass, flute, oboe, clarinet, bassoon, a string quartet and a four-piece rhythm section) interprets classic ragtime (including "Maple Leaf Rag"), pieces associated with Jim Europe and Eubie Blake, a bit of 1920s jazz (a couple of Jelly Roll Morton tunes), novelty ragtime (Zez Confrey's "Dizzy Fingers") and five much later, "modern" rags. The memorable program concludes with "Castle House Rag," which features a rare ragtime drum solo. Recommended. —*Scott Yanow*

Diane Schuur

b. 1953, Seattle, WA
Vocals, Piano / Standards, Pop
Diane Schuur, who has often been on the periphery of jazz, has the potential to be an important jazz singer although she still includes a large dose of pop tunes in her repertoire. Early in her career she had the tendency to screech in her upper register but with maturity that flaw has largely disappeared and she has become a very impressive singer. Blinded at birth due to a hospital accident, Schuur (who would later be nicknamed "Deedles") imitated singers as a child. She had her first gig at a Holiday Inn when just ten and originally sang country music. The turning point in her career occurred when she sang "Amazing Grace" at the 1979 Monterey Jazz Festival, greatly impressing Stan Getz. After Getz featured her singing at a televised concert from the White House in 1982, Schuur was signed to GRP and began recording regularly. Although her 1987 collaboration with the Count Basie Orchestra was a high point, Diane Schuur's recordings tend to be a mixed success from the jazz standpoint; hopefully her best work is still in the future. —*Scott Yanow*

Deedles / 1985 / GRP ✦✦✦
Schuur Thing / 1985 / GRP ✦✦✦
Timeless / 1986 / GRP ✦✦✦✦
Diane Schuur has always enjoyed singing standards, but *Timeless*, her third recording, was her first full-length set to be continually interesting to jazz listeners. With arrangements by Billy May, Johnny Mandel, Patrick Williams and Jeremy Lubbock, Schuur is backed by a large string orchestra and a big band. Among the guest soloists are tenor saxophonist Stan Getz (on "How Long Has This Been Going On" and "A Time for Love"), trombonist Bill Watrous, vibraphonist Larry Bunker and trumpeter Warren Luening. Schuur, who does not play any piano on the album, sounds in excellent voice, particularly during the two Getz tracks and on such tunes as "Easy to Love," "How About Me" and "Please Send Me Someone to Love." —*Scott Yanow*

Diane Schuur & the Count Basie Orchestra / 1987 / GRP ✦✦✦✦✦
This CD features a logical combination: singer Diane Schuur with the Count Basie big band. In what would be longtime rhythm guitarist Freddie Green's final performance, Schuur and the Basie ghost band (under the direction of Frank Foster) perform material that includes her standards (such as "Deedles' Blues" and "Climbing Higher Mountains"), Dave Brubeck's "Travelin' Blues" and the Joe Williams-associated "Everyday I Have the Blues." Unfortunately, the Basie band is mostly used in accompaniment without any significant solos, but Schuur sounds quite comfortable in this format and her voice is in prime form. —*Scott Yanow*

Talkin' 'Bout You / 1988 / GRP ✦✦✦
Pure Schuur / 1991 / GRP ✦✦✦
In Tribute / 1992 / GRP ✦✦✦✦
On this well-intentioned set, Diane Schuur sings 13 standards that she individually dedicated to 12 singers: Billie Holiday (who is saluted with two songs), Helen Morgan, Anita O'Day, Sarah Vaughan, Carmen McRae, Ella Fitzgerald, Libby Holman, Peggy Lee, Dinah Washington, Ivie Anderson, Nancy Wilson and Mabel Mercer. In most cases, the arrangements for the huge string orchestra (contributed by Billy May, Johnny Mandel, Jeremy Lubbock, Clare Fischer or Alan Broadbent) weigh down the music a bit, and none of Schuur's renditions quite reach the heights of her role models. Still, Diane Schuur's voice is quite attractive, and taken on its own merit, this sincere CD (which has an informative 40-page booklet) is generally enjoyable. —*Scott Yanow*

● **Love Songs** / 1993 / GRP ✦✦✦✦✦
The jazz content on this CD from singer Diane Schuur is rather slight but this is actually one of her finest recordings. Schuur (who has a lovely voice) sings straightforward versions of ten veteran ballads while accompanied by one of two string orchestras. Tom Scott on reeds and trumpeter Jack Sheldon have short spots but this is very much Schuur's show. She really excels in the restrained setting, making this a superior middle-of-the-road pop recording. —*Scott Yanow*

Heart to Heart / 1994 / GRP ✦✦
B.B. King's recent recordings have been thoroughly professional, occasionally engaging albums that showcase his still striking vocal skills and add infrequent examples of his fabulous guitar skills. This one includes a partner in the stylish pop-jazz singer Dianne Schuur (she actually gets first billing, but this is really King's LP). King's guitar solos are expertly articulated but restrained, while Schuur is also careful not to oversing or allow any excesses to ruin their chemistry. Indeed, they seem so attuned and in sync that there is little tension or edge to the performances. They're well done and enjoyable, but this CD sounds more like a recital between old friends than a genuine exchange or dialogue. —*Ron Wynn*

Love Walked In / 1995 / GRP ✦✦✦✦
This set of ten concise standards (which totals in at around 36 minutes) finds Diane Schuur singing in prime form. The interpretations are straightforward, without much improvising, although Schuur is quite soulful, showing the influence of late-period Dinah Washington (whose hit "Blue Gardenia" she revives). The excess of Schuur's early years is gone, and in its place is a warm, contented voice that sounds best on such ballads as "Say It Isn't So" and "How Deep Is the Ocean," as well as the swingers "Love Walked In" and "You're a Sweetheart." There are occasional short solos for trumpeter Jack Sheldon, trombonist Andy Martin and the tenor of Pete Christlieb, but this is very much Schuur's show. A fine effort. —*Scott Yanow*

Blues for Schuur / 1997 / GRP ✦✦✦✦
Diane Schuur is in prime voice throughout this swinging date. Backed by an 11-piece group arranged by Greg Adams, Schuur emphasizes the blues feeling on a variety of mostly older but fresh material, including "Stormy Monday," "Save Your Love for Me," "When Did You Leave Heaven" and four Charles Brown songs. There are occasional solos from the backup crew (most notably guitarist David T. Walker and an uncredited altoist on "Save Your Love for Me" that might be Gary Herbig),

but the emphasis is on Schuur's voice. An infectious outing from the talented singer. —*Scott Yanow*

Bob Scobey

b. Dec. 9, 1916, Tucumcari, NM, d. Jun. 12, 1963, Montreal, Canada
Trumpet, Leader / Dixieland

Throughout his prime years, Bob Scobey was one of the more popular trumpeters in Dixieland. After many low-profile jobs in dance bands in the 1930s, in 1938 Scobey met trumpeter Lu Watters. As a member of Watter's Yerba Buena Jazz Band in San Francisco during 1940-49 (with much of 1942-46 spent in the military), Scobey participated in one of the most influential bands of the Dixieland revival movement. In 1949 he left to form his own Frisco Jazz Band, recording frequently (most notably for Good Time Jazz) and often featuring Clancy Hayes or appearing with Lizzie Miles. In 1959 Scobey opened his Club Bourbon Street in Chicago but four years later he died at the age of 46 from cancer. Many of Bob Scobey's Good Time Jazz dates have been reissued on CD and they still contain stirring and joyful music. —*Scott Yanow*

● **Bob Scobey's Frisco Band, Vol. 1** / Apr. 29, 1950-Nov. 6, 1951 / Good Time Jazz ♦♦♦♦♦
This rather brief CD (just 35 minutes, a straight reissue of an LP) gives listeners a good example of the playing of trumpeter Bob Scobey. Taken from his earliest period as a bandleader, these Dixieland performances also feature trombonist Jack Buck, either Darnell Howard, Albert Nicholas or George Probert on clarinet, pianists Burt Bales or Wally Rose and banjoist Clancy Hayes who also takes a few vocals. Excellent good-time music. —*Scott Yanow*

The Scobey Story, Vol. 2 / Apr. 12, 1952-Nov. 10, 1953 / Good Time Jazz ♦♦♦♦♦
The second of two CDs (both clock in around 35 minutes and are reissues of original LPs) continues the documentation of trumpeter Bob Scobey's earliest performances as a bandleader. With trombonist Jack Buck, clarinetist George Propert, pianist Wally Rose, bassist Dick Lammi and drummer Fred Higuera, Scobey had a hot and enjoyable band. In Clancy Hayes, the trumpeter was fortunate to have a major attraction who played banjo, set the standard for singing in this format, and contributed a minor hit in "Huggin' & A-Chalkin'" which is heard here in its original version. Other high points include "Big Butter and Egg Man," "Silver Dollar," "Ace in the Hole" and "Hindustan." —*Scott Yanow*

Bob Scobey's Frisco Band / Jan. 17, 1955-Jan. 21, 1955 / Good Time Jazz ♦♦♦♦♦
Trumpeter Bob Scobey's Dixieland bands in the 1950s were fairly consistent. This CD reissue brings back one of Scobey's better dates. After a weak start on a somewhat square version of "Battle Hymn of the Republic," the remainder of the program mixes together Dixieland standards (including "Sweet Georgia Brown" and "Bill Bailey") with a few obscurities ("Parsons, Kansas Blues" and "Friendless Blues"). Co-starring with Scobey is one of the top trad jazz singers, Clancy Hayes, who is far superior to most "musician vocalists." Also well featured are clarinetist Bill Napier and trombonist Jack Buck —*Scott Yanow*

Scobey and Clancy / Jul. 6, 1955-Jul. 7, 1955 / Good Time Jazz ♦♦♦♦♦
Trumpeter Bob Scobey and singer/banjoist Clancy Hayes always made for a delightful team. Clancy takes seven vocals on this CD reissue, and Scobey's fiery trumpet gets plenty of solo space. The latter's band (which also features trombonist Jack Buck and clarinetist Bill Napier) is quite musical and Dixieland-ish without playing clichés. The interesting repertoire (which includes such numbers as "When the Midnight Choo-Choo Leaves for Alabam," "At the Devil's Ball" and "I Want to Go Back to Michigan," along with some more familiar standards) is also an added plus on this enjoyable set. —*Scott Yanow*

Direct from San Francisco / Mar. 13, 1956-Mar. 15, 1956 / Good Time Jazz ♦♦♦♦
This is an enjoyable date of Dixieland, emphasizing familiar warhorses. Trumpeter Bob Scobey is in his usual consistent form and is assisted in the front line by trombonist Jack Buck and clarinetist Bill Napier. Banjoist Clancy Hayes has six excellent vocals (particularly "Curse of an Aching Heart" and "Travelin' Shoes"), and the spirit and high musicianship overcome the familiar repertoire. —*Scott Yanow*

Bob Scobey, Vol. 1 / 1956-Nov. 1960 / Jazzology ♦♦♦♦
This 1996 CD has all of the contents from trumpeter Bob Scobey's first release on the Jansco label and six of the ten cuts from his final recording session, an album originally out on the obscure Ragtime label. The earlier set is of particular interest due to the occasional vocals of Clancy Hayes and Lizzie Miles, plus plenty of heated ensembles and fine solo work from Scobey, clarinetist Bill Napier and trombonist Bob Short. Highlights include "My Honey's Loving Arms," "I Can't Give You Anything but Love," "I'll See You in C.U.B.A." and "Panama Rag." The later session also finds Scobey in fine form, and even if trombonist Richard Nelson is sometimes a bit corny (particularly on his feature "Basin Street Blues"), the band shows plenty of spirit. Scobey consistently led rewarding Dixieland bands in the 1950s, and this CD is an excellent look of his work. —*Scott Yanow*

Swingin' on the Golden Gate / Jan. 21, 1957-Jan. 22, 1957 / RCA ♦♦♦♦
Trumpeter Bob Scobey used an expanded version of his Frisco Jazz Band for this fine effort, last available as a now out-of-print LP. Matty Matlock's arrangements for the six horns (including three trombones), four-piece rhythm section and banjoist Clancy Hayes (who takes five vocals) are colorful and swinging. Some of the song choices are a bit off the wall (including "It Happened in Sun Valley," "Wabash Cannonball" and the recent "Let's Dance the Ragtime Darlin'"), but this brand of Dixieland avoids corn in favor of sincere swinging. In addition to Scobey (who is in fine form), the supporting cast has such strong players as trumpeter Dick Cathcart, clarinetist Matlock and pianist Ralph Sutton. —*Scott Yanow*

College "Classics" / Dec. 12, 1957-Dec. 14, 1957 / RCA ♦♦♦♦
While Bob Scobey's recordings for Good Time Jazz are all available on CD, his RCA and Verve recordings (which are generally of the same quality) have been difficult to find for many years. This fine LP is a bit unusual in that the tunes were mostly favorites on college campuses in the 1920s, including "I've Been Working on the Railroad," "Let Me Call You Sweetheart," "Put on Your Old Grey Bonnet," "Wedding Bells Are Breaking Up That Old Gang of Mine," etc. Scobey's Frisco Jazz Band (an eight-piece band with two trombones) was a no-name outfit in 1957 except for the leader and Clancy Hayes who, in addition to his banjo playing, sings every song with spirit and good feeling. —*Scott Yanow*

Raid the Juke Box / Jan. 19, 1958-Jan. 20, 1958 / Good Time Jazz ♦♦♦
Bob Scobey and his Dixielandish Frisco Band attempted to get hip on this project (which has been reissued on CD) by playing a set of then-current pop tunes. Some of the songs (particularly the jazz standards "Yellow Dog Blues," "Blueberry Hill," "C.C. Rider" and "Singing the Blues") were obvious ringers, but these versions of "All Shook Up," "Love Letters in the Sand," "Tammy" and "Bye Bye Love" were certainly unique in their own way. Clancy Hayes sings six songs (mostly the jazz tunes) and fortunately did not attempt "Tammy." An interesting but far from essential effort. —*Scott Yanow*

Rompin' and Stompin' / Jun. 2, 1958-Jul. 9, 1959 / RCA ♦♦♦♦
Trumpeter Bob Scobey still had a spirited Dixieland group in 1959, but the addition of pianist Art Hodes for this date clearly uplifted the band. Scobey performs six songs associated with Jelly Roll Morton (including "The Pearls," "Kansas City Stomp" and "The Chant"), plus six other songs dating mostly from the 1920s. A strictly instrumental date (although Clancy Hayes helps out the rhythm section on banjo), clarinetist Brian Shanley, trombonist Jim Beebe and the tuba of Rich Matteson are strong assets, along with Hodes and Scobey. Well worth searching for by Dixieland collectors. —*Scott Yanow*

John Scofield

b. Dec. 26, 1951, Dayton, OH
Guitar, Leader / Post-Bop

One of the "big three" of current jazz guitarists (along with Pat Metheny and Bill Frisell), Scofield's influence has been growing in recent years. Possessor of a very distinctive rock-oriented sound that is often a bit distorted, Scofield is a masterful jazz improviser whose music generally falls somewhere between post-bop, fusion and soul-jazz. He started on guitar while at high school in Connecticut and from 1970-73 Scofield studied at Berklee and played in the Boston area. After recording with Gerry Mulligan and Chet Baker at Carnegie Hall, Scofield was a member of the Billy Cobham-George Duke band for two years. In 1977 he recorded with Charles Mingus and later joined the Gary Burton quartet and Dave Liebman's quintet. His own early sessions as a leader were funk-oriented. During 1982-85 Scofield toured the world and recorded with Miles Davis. Since that time he has led his own groups, played with Bass Desires and recorded frquently as a leader for Gramavision and Blue Note, using such major players as Charlie Haden, Jack DeJohnette, Joe Lovano and Eddie Harris. —*Scott Yanow*

East Meets West / Aug. 1977 / Black Hawk ♦♦♦

John Scofield Live / Nov. 4, 1977 / Enja ♦♦♦♦

Rough House / Nov. 27, 1978 / Enja ♦♦♦
This early outing (reissued on CD) finds guitarist John Scofield playing advanced post-bop jazz with pianist Hal Galper (who here sounds strongly influenced by McCoy Tyner), bassist Stafford James and drummer Adam Nussbaum. They perform five Scofield originals and Galper's "Triple Play." Although this was not the usual setting for Sco, his tone is immediately recognizable and his adventurous solos will be of interest to his many fans. —*Scott Yanow*

Who's Who? / 1979-Aug. 1980 / Novus ♦♦♦
This CD reissue features guitarist John Scofield (who was then 27) searching for his own sound. Four of the selections from the original LP have Scofield backed by a light funky quartet while two other pieces feature him with three notable jazzmen: saxophonist Dave Liebman, bassist Eddie Gomez and drummer Billy Hart. The problem with this date is that Scofield is a much stronger guitarist than

he is a composer, and none of his complex melodies are all that memorable. The CD is rounded off by four tunes originally on Scofield's *Bar Talk* LP but the same criticsm applies despite the excellent trio (with bassist Steve Swallow and drummer Adam Nussbaum) and the stronger jazz orientation. This set is recommended mostly for John Scofield completists; other listeners are advised to pick up his more recent releases instead. —*Scott Yanow*

Shinola / Dec. 12, 1981-Dec. 13, 1981 / Enja ++++
Shortly before Miles Davis' group, guitarist John Scofield recorded this passionate trio set with electric bassist Steve Swallow and drummer Adam Nussbaum. Much of Sco's playing here is quite rockish although he does show off his jazz chops on Jackie McLean's "Dr. Jackle." The frequently intense music (which has been reissued on CD), which is not as essential as many of the guitarist's later sets, has plenty of fiery moments. —*Scott Yanow*

Out like a Light / Dec. 14, 1981 / Enja ++++
Fine trio date from 1981, with guitarist John Scofield stretching out in multiple directions and showing his facility with the swing style, mainstream, and jazz-rock genres. Besides his fluid, inventive solos, Scofield works well with bassist Steve Swallow, who approaches his instrument like a second guitar, and drummer Adam Nussbaum. —*Ron Wynn*

Electric Outlet / Apr. 1984-May 1984 / Gramavision +++
Slo Sco: The Best of Ballads / 1984-1989 / Gramavision +++
Still Warm / Jun. 1986 / Gramavision +++
Blue Matter / Sep. 1986 / Gramavision ++++
Pick Hits Live / Oct. 7, 1987 / Gramavision ++++
Loud Jazz / Dec. 1987 / Gramavision +++
Flat Out / Dec. 1988 / Gramavision ++++

Time on My Hands / Nov. 19, 1989-Nov. 21, 1989 / Blue Note +++++
John Scofield's airy and instantly recognizable guitar is featured in a sparse quartet on this Blue Note CD. He performs 11 of his quirky compositions which, although occasionally hinting at Charles Mingus or Ornette Coleman, are true originals with new chord changes and sly unpredictable melodies. Bassist Charlie Haden and drummer Jack DeJohnette, both experts at utilizing space as part of the music, fit in perfectly with Scofield and display fire and swing in the appropriate spots. Joe Lovano's tenor also has its own sound and his stimulating solos consistently inspire Scofield. Recommended. —*Scott Yanow*

The Best of John Scofield / Nov. 19, 1989-Jun. 1995 / Blue Note ++++
All of the highlights of Scofield's work from his late 1980s-early 1990s tenure on Blue Note is included in this collection, which features cameos from Pat Metheny and Bill Frisell. Also included is material from *Hand Jive*, Scofield's collaboration with Eddie Harris, and an unreleased take on Wayne Shorter's "Tom Thumb." —*Jason Ankeny*

Meant to Be / Dec. 1990 / Blue Note +++++
Meant to Be features guitarist John Scofield's 1990 pianoless quartet on 11 of his compositions. During the best selections (such as "Big Fun" and "Mr. Coleman to You") one can hear the influence of not just the original Ornette Coleman Quartet but the Keith Jarrett/Dewey Redman Quintet. Joe Lovano's increasingly original tenor sound (mixing together John Coltrane, Dewey Redman and even Eddie Harris on this set) works well with Scofield, and the tight but loose rhythm section (bassist Marc Johnson and drummer Bill Stewart). "Eisenhower" (a slightly tongue-in-cheek, boppish romp) and "Some Nerve" (which uses New Orleans parade rhythms) are also memorable performances. The colorful and enjoyable set is modern mainstream music of the 1990s, stretching ahead while holding on to the roots of hard bop, funk and fusion. —*Scott Yanow*

Grace Under Pressure / Dec. 1991 / Blue Note +++++
Guitarist John Scofield leads a top-notch group on this 1991 session. It's a pianoless band, with Scofield's nimble guitar lines contrasted by those of second guitarist Bill Frisell. They team with trombonist Jim Pugh, bassist Charlie Haden, and drummer Joey Baron, plus Randy Brecker on fluegelhorn and John Clark on French horn. —*Ron Wynn*

What We Do / May 1992 / Capitol +++++
★ **Hand Jive** / Oct. 1993 / Blue Note +++++
Guitarist John Scofield and tenor saxophonist Eddie Harris make a very complementary team on this upbeat set of funky jazz for both have immediately identifiable sounds and adventurous spirits. Along with a fine rhythm section that includes Larry Goldings on piano and organ, Scofield and Harris interact joyfully on ten of the guitarist's originals. —*Scott Yanow*

Groove Elation / 1995 / Blue Note +++++
John Scofield has continued to grow and evolve year-by-year. This 1995 set is quite blues-oriented, sometimes boppish and fairly laidback, almost sounding like a

Jimmy Smith or Groove Holmes date from the 1960s. Larry Goldings (who doubles occasionally on piano) is almost as significant in the ensembles as the leader/guitarist and has become the most important arrival on organ since Joey De Francesco and Barbara Dennerlein. Many of the tunes (all Scofield originals) use parade-like rhythms propelled by Idris Muhammad and Dennis Irwin (particularly the eccentric "Peculiar" and "Groove Elation") and the interplay between the two lead voices is quite appealing. Scofield is quite unselfish as far as taking solo space goes (he clearly enjoys the light funky grooves set by Goldings) and the results are quite appealing. —*Scott Yanow*

Quiet / Apr. 3, 1996-Apr. 6, 1996 / Verve +++
A Go Go / 1997 / Verve +++++
Out once again to stretch his considerable funk chops, Scofield returns joyously to the groove in tandem with a young hard-swinging band out of time, Medeski, Martin and Wood. With their hip-hop grooves and retro keyboards—the funky old Wurlitzer electric piano, Hohner clavinet and organ—MMW's testament on the Gospel-derived-from-James Brown comes on like a custom-tailored engine behind Scofield's jagged guitar. In his deceptively offhand way, Scofield locks right into the grooves, matching John Medeski's shafts of keyboards, Chris Wood's popping bass and Billy Martin's crazy rhythms with unpredictable accents and musical sidetrips. They really bear down on the home stretch of "Boozer"—the groove is at its most irresistible here—and they also change the pace a bit with a mood piece like "Kubrick." Scofield's tunes are often very catchy, occasionally reminding us that he has been listening to a lot of records by the Meters (dig "Jeep on 35"). This is one of the most viscerally enjoyable releases of 1998; in other words, this group gets *down*. —*Richard S. Ginell*

Hazel Scott

b. Jun. 11, 1920, Port of Spain, Trinidad, West Ind, **d.** Oct. 2, 1981, New York, NY
Piano / Swing, Cool
Though she didn't call it Third Stream, and it wasn't associated with the genre, Hazel Scott was a musician who found a successful way to blend jazz and classical influences. Scott took classical selections and improvised on them, a practice dating back to the ragtime era. Such numbers as "Hungarian Rhapsody No. 2" (Liszt) backed by "Valse in D Flat Major, Op. 64 No. 1" (Chopin) were audience favorites, even if some critics suggested they smacked of gimmickry (which sometimes they did). Scott was also a good bebop soloist, nice ballad interpreter, fair blues player and underrated vocalist. Her nightclub act was often more appealing than her albums, where the absence of mitigating circumstances like an audience and club setting resulted in her compositions getting more scrutiny than they could stand. Scott studied classical piano at Juilliard from the age of eight, while also playing jazz in clubs. She became an attraction at downtown and uptown branches of Cafe Society in the late '30s and early '40s. Scott had her own radio show in 1936, appeared on Broadway in 1938, and was in five films during the '40s, among them *Rhapsody in Blue*. She wrote such songs as "Love Comes Softly" and "Nightmare Blues." Scott later had her own television show and was married to Adam Clayton Powell, Jr. Their highly visible, high-profile relationship degenerated under the heat of a nationwide obsession with Powell's activities, influence and behavior, finally ending in divorce. Scott recorded for Decca, Signature, Tioch and Columbia, but made her finest jazz album for Charles Mingus' Debut label, *Relaxed Piano Moods*, in 1955. Mingus and Max Roach joined Scott on this session. It's her only date currently available on CD. —*Ron Wynn and Michael G. Nastos*

● **Late Show** / 1952 / Capitol +++++
Relaxed Piano Moods / Jan. 21, 1955 / Original Jazz Classics +++++
Definitive piano trio with Charles Mingus (b) and Max Roach (d). A must-buy. —*Michael G. Nastos*

Raymond Scott (Harry Warnow)

b. Sep. 10, 1910, New York, NY, **d.** Feb. 8, 1994, North Hills, CA
Composer, Arranger, Leader, Piano / Novelty, Swing
Raymond Scott was a quirky figure on the periphery of jazz, best known for a combo that turned out a series of nifty instrumentals with oddball titles like "Dinner Music for a Pack of Hungry Cannibals" and "Reckless Night on Board an Ocean Liner." Born Harry Warnow (his stage name came from the Manhattan phone book), Scott was hired by CBS as a staff pianist in 1931 and started his series of recordings with the Raymond Scott Quintette (which originally included Bunny Berigan) in 1937. Though these pieces have jazz phrasings and a degree of swing, not one note is improvised. Moreover, nothing was written down; a ruthless perfectionist, Scott taught his musicians each part by rote and rehearsed them endlessly. In 1938, upon being named music director of CBS, Scott expanded the Quintette into a big band, whose music lacked the antic humor of the Quintette. Scott deserves credit for forming the first racially integrated network studio

orchestra at CBS in 1942, which included Coleman Hawkins, Ben Webster, Charlie Shavers and Cozy Cole, among others. He also conducted the Your Hit Parade band in the 1950s and invented several electronic instruments bearing such strange names as the Karloff and the Clavivox. But Scott's immortality rests on the fact that Warner Bros. licensed his tunes in 1941, using them in hundreds of cartoons that have delighted millions. —*Richard S. Ginell*

● **Powerhouse, Vol. 1** / Mar. 11, 1935-Nov. 11, 1939 / Stash ✦✦✦✦✦

Between 1937-39 composer-pianist Raymond Scott and his six-piece "Quintette" recorded 24 originals that were most notable for their hilarious titles, somewhat bizarre but somehow logical arrangements and tight ensembles. To Scott's surprise, the group caught on for awhile and such numbers as "Powerhouse" and "The Toy Trumpet" became hits. This CD gathers together tapes from Scott's own library of radio broadcasts and rehearsals, all of it previously unissued and two of the performances predating the formation of the Quintette. Certainly occupying their own unique niche, the colorful arrangements somehow fit the titles (which include "Dinner Music for a Pack of Hungry Cannibals," "New Year's Eve in a Haunted House," "Oil Gusher," "Reckless Night on Board an Ocean Liner" and "Bumpy Weather over Newark!") and one can understand why Carl Stalling was inspired to utilize many of these pieces in Warner Bros. cartoons. —*Scott Yanow*

● **The Music of Raymond Scott: Reckless Nights & Turkish Twilights** / Feb. 20, 1937-Jun. 17, 1940 / Columbia ✦✦✦✦✦

The name may not be immediately familiar, but the music itself certainly is: to anyone weaned on the legendary Warner Bros. cartoons of the 1940s and 1950s, Raymond Scott's deliriously inventive freak-jazz is the soundtrack of childhood, with each and every note capable of conjuring up indelible images of such immortal characters as Bugs Bunny, Porky Pig and Daffy Duck. The WB connection is both Scott's greatest legacy and his greatest curse, however; he never composed a note specifically for cartoons, and his most memorable and distinctive melodies were actually co-opted for animated use by Warner's brilliant music director, Carl Stalling. *Reckless Nights and Turkish Twilights*, then, restores Scott's work to its original, stand-alone setting, confirming his cult reputation as one of the most innovative and original musical thinkers of his era. Even free of cartoon mayhem, his music is remarkably visual and colorful, perfectly evocative of such surreal titles as "Dinner Music for a Pack of Hungry Cannibals" and "War Dance for Wooden Indians"; probably the best-known cut here is the opening "Powerhouse," a uniquely mechanized piece used in any number of cartoons and television commercials and a perfect summation of Scott's intricate arrangements, complex shifting rhythms and formal lunacy. Recommended for listeners ages eight to 80. —*Jason Ankeny*

Shirley Scott

b. Mar. 14, 1934, Philadelphia, PA

Organ / Hard Bop, Soul-Jazz, Groove

An admirer of the seminal Jimmy Smith, Shirley Scott has been one of the organ's most appealing representatives since the late 1950s. Scott, a very melodic and accessible player, started out on piano and played trumpet in high school before taking up the Hammond B-3 and enjoying national recognition in the late '50s with her superb Prestige dates with tenor sax great Eddie "Lockjaw" Davis. Especially popular was their 1958 hit "In the Kitchen." Her reputation was cemented during the '60s on several superb, soulful organ/soul jazz dates where she demonstrated an aggressive, highly rhythmic attack blending intricate bebop harmonies with bluesy melodies and a gospel influence, punctuating everything with great use of the bass pedals. Scott married soul-jazz tenor man Stanley Turrentine, with whom she often recorded in the '60s. The Scott/Turrentine union lasted until the early '70s, and their musical collaborations in the '60s were among the finest in the field. Scott wasn't as visible the following decade, when the popularity of organ combos decreased and labels were more interested in fusion and pop-jazz (though she did record some albums for Chess/Cadet and Strata East). But organists regained their popularity in the late '80s, which found her recording for Muse. Though known primarily for her organ playing, Scott is also a superb pianist—in the 1990s, she has played piano exclusively on some trio recordings for Candid, and embraced the instrument consistently in Philly jazz venues. —*Alex Henderson and Ron Wynn*

Great Scott! / May 27, 1958 / Prestige ✦✦✦

Shirley's Sounds / May 27, 1958 / Prestige ✦✦✦

From the 1958 recording with Scott, George Duvivier on bass and Arthur Edgehill on drums. Includes a version of "Cherokee." —*AMG*

Workin' / May 27, 1958-Mar. 24, 1960 / Prestige ✦✦✦

One of several trio and/or combo works that organist Shirley Scott recorded for Prestige in the late '50s and early '60s. Her swirling, driving lines, intense bass

pedal support, and bluesy fervor were ideal for the soul jazz format, and this is a typical example. —*Ron Wynn*

Shirley Scott Trio / May 27, 1958-Apr. 8, 1960 / Moodsville ✦✦✦

A trio recording with Scott, George Tucker on bass, and Earl Coleman (vcl). —*Michael Erlewine*

Scottie Plays the Duke / Apr. 24, 1959 / Prestige ✦✦✦

The Shirley Scott Trio with George Duvivier on bass and Arthur Edgehill on drums. This is a collection of Ellington tunes including "In a Sentimental Mood." —*Michael Erlewine*

Soul Searching / Dec. 4, 1959 / Prestige ✦✦✦

Shirley Scott with Wendell Marshall on bass and Arthur Edgehill on drums. Includes title tune and "Boss." —*AMG*

Stompin' / Apr. 8, 1960-Mar. 24, 1961 / Prestige ✦✦✦

Mucho, Mucho / Jun. 23, 1960 / Prestige ✦✦✦

An early date with Gene Casey (p), Bill Ellington (b), Manny Ramos (timb), Phil Diaz (bgo), and Juan Amalbert (cga). —*Michael Erlewine*

Soul Sisters / Jun. 23, 1960 / Prestige ✦✦✦

With Lem Winchester on vibes, George Duvivier on bass, and Arthur Edgehill on drums. A dauntless, swinging affair. —*Ron Wynn*

Like Cozy / Sep. 27, 1960 / Moodsville ✦✦

Her standard trio with George Duvivier on bass and Arthur Edgehill on drums. —*AMG*

Satin Doll / Mar. 7, 1961 / Prestige ✦✦✦

With George Tucker on bass and Jack Simpkins on drums. A bit more prim, though Scott still burns. —*Ron Wynn*

Hip Soul / Jun. 2, 1961 / Prestige ✦✦✦✦✦

Here is Stanley Turrentine recording under the name Stan Turner. Slashing, aptly titled. —*Ron Wynn*

Blue Seven / Aug. 22, 1961 / Prestige ✦✦✦

A quintet with Roy Brooks (d), Oliver Nelson (ts) and Joe Newman (tpt) plays one Scott original, the title song by Sonny Rollins, and an excellent "Wagon Wheels." —*Michael G. Nastos*

Hip Twist / Nov. 17, 1961 / Prestige ✦✦✦

Scott with Stanley Turrentine (sax), George Tucker (b), and Otis Finch (d). Any Turrentine/Scott albums are worth hearing, even with a title like this one. —*Michael Erlewine*

Shirley Scott Plays Horace Silver / Nov. 17, 1961 / Prestige ✦✦✦✦✦

Just what it says. The queen of the Hammond organ (along with Henry Grimes (b) and Otis Finch (d)) plays compositions by the funk-master himself, Horace Silver. Included are "Senor Blues" and "The Preacher." —*Michael Erlewine*

☆ **Sweet Soul** / Dec. 5, 1962 / Prestige ✦✦✦✦✦

Reissued from the "Happy Talk" session this features Earl May on bass and Roy Brooks on drums. It includes a nice "Jitterbug Waltz." All are standards. —*Michael G. Nastos*

★ **Soul Shoutin'** / Jan. 10, 1963+Oct. 15, 1963 / Prestige ✦✦✦✦✦

Organist Shirley Scott and her then-husband tenor great Stanley Turrentine always made potent music together. This CD, which combines together the former Prestige LPs *The Soul Is Willing* and *Soul Shoutin'*, finds "Mr. T." at his early peak, playing some intense yet always soulful solos on such pieces as Sy Oliver's "Yes Indeed," "Secret Love" and his memorable originals "The Soul Is Willing" and "Deep Down Soul." Scott, who found her own niche within the dominant Jimmy Smith style, swings hard throughout the set and (together with drummer Crassella Oliphant and either Major Holley or Earl May on bass) the lead voices play with such consistent enthusiasm that one would think these were club performances. Highly recommended. —*Scott Yanow*

☆ **For Members Only/Great Scott** / Aug. 22, 1963-May 20, 1964 / Impulse! ✦✦✦✦✦

During the 1960s, Shirley Scott's Impulse albums were often split between big band selections (with orchestras arranged by Oliver Nelson) and trio performances. This CD reissue from 1989 includes all of the contents from two of Scott's better Impulse albums, *Great Scott* and *For Members Only*. In general the eight trio numbers are the most rewarding performances on the disc since the material is fairly superior while the big-band tracks emphasize then-current show and movie tunes. Overall this generous CD gives one a good overview of Shirley Scott's playing talents. —*Scott Yanow*

Blue Flames / Mar. 31, 1964 / Original Jazz Classics ✦✦✦✦

All of the many collaborations between organist Shirley Scott and tenor saxophonist Stanley Turrentine in the 1960s resulted in high-quality soul jazz, groovin' music that was boppish enough to interest jazz listeners and basic enough for a wider audience. This CD reissue has the duo (joined by bassist Bob Cranshaw and

Music Map

Alto Saxophone

Pioneers
Benny Krueger (1920-21, recorded with Original Dixieland Jazz Band)
Don Redman (recorded with Fletcher Henderson starting in 1921)
Jimmy Dorsey (1926, first recorded with Red Nichols)

Most Significant Altoists of the Swing Era
Johnny Hodges • Benny Carter • Willie Smith

Other Top Swing Altoists
Charlie Holmes (1929-31, with Luis Russell)
Hilton Jefferson
Pete Brown
Tab Smith
Don Stovall
Russell Procope (with John Kirby Sextet)
Woody Herman

Superior Section Players
Toots Mondello (1934–35 and 1939-40, with Benny Goodman)
Earle Warren (1937-45, with Count Basie)
Marshall Royal (1951-70, with Count Basie)

Early R&B Stars
Louis Jordan • Earl Bostic

Creator of Bop
Charlie Parker

Other Important Bop-Based Altoists
Sonny Stitt	Sonny Criss
Charlie Mariano	Herb Geller
Gigi Gryce	Lou Donaldson
Phil Woods	Richie Cole
Cannonball Adderley	Charles McPherson

Cool Jazz Innovators
Lee Konitz • Art Pepper • Paul Desmond

Hard Bop to Modern Mainstream
Jackie McLean	Sonny Red
Oliver Nelson	James Spaulding
Gary Bartz	Bud Shank
Frank Morgan	Bobby Watson
Paquito D'Rivera	Kenny Garrett
Antonio Hart	Vincent Herring

Free Jazz/Avant-Garde Innovators
Ornette Coleman • Eric Dolphy • Anthony Braxton

Other Top Avant-Garde Altoists
Jimmy Lyons (with Cecil Taylor 1960-86)
Ken McIntyre
Marion Brown
John Tchicai (later switched to tenor)
Roscoe Mitchell (founder of Art Ensemble of Chicago)
Joseph Jarman (founder of Art Ensemble of Chicago)
Sonny Simmons
Henry Threadgill
Julins Hemphill
Marshall Allen (1951-93 with Sun Ra)
Oliver Lake
Arthur Blythe
John Zorn
Tim Berne

Free Funk Players
Steve Coleman • Greg Osby

Crossover
Hank Crawford
David Sanborn
Sadao Watanabe
Marc Russo (of the Yellowjackets)

Best 96-Year-Old Altoist
Benny Waters

---

drummer Otis "Candy" Finch) performing a pair of Scott originals, Benny Golson's "Five Spot After Dark," Sonny Rollins' obscure "Grand Street" and the veteran standard "Flamingo." The only fault of this CD reissue is its brief length, just 32 minutes. *—Scott Yanow*

● **Queen of the Organ** / Sep. 23, 1964 / Impulse! ✦✦✦✦✦
This CD reissue brings back all of the music previously put out on the two-LP set *The Great Live Sessions* with the exception of one number ("Shirley's Shuffle") left out due to lack of space; with over 70 minutes of music, one cannot complain too much about the omission. Overall, this is a fairly definitive live set featuring organist Shirley Scott, tenor saxophonist Stanley Turrentine, bassist Bob Cranshaw and drummer Otis "Candy" Finch, one of the great soul-jazz combos of the 1960s. In addition to a swinging "Just in Time" and Duke Ellington's "Squeeze Me, But

Please Don't Tease Me," the set mostly features obscurities and originals, plus a surprisingly effective version of the Beatles' "Can't Buy Me Love." The musicians sound quite heated and consistently inspired. Highly recommended. *—Scott Yanow*

Roll 'em / Apr. 15, 1966-Apr. 19, 1966 / Impulse! ✦✦✦
Organist Shirley Scott focuses on swing-era tunes throughout this enjoyable CD reissue. Four songs showcase her organ accompanied by a 17-piece big band arranged by Oliver Nelson while the remaining six numbers find her jamming with a trio that also includes either George Duvivier or Richard Davis on bass and Grady Tate or Ed Shaughnessy on drums. Although nothing all that unexpected occurs, it is fun to hear an organ performing such numbers as "For Dancers Only," "Little Brown Jug" and "Stompin' at the Savoy." *—Scott Yanow*

Soul Duo / Aug. 19, 1966+Aug. 22, 1966 / Impulse! ✦✦✦✦
This is one of organist Shirley Scott's lesser-known Impulse LPs (not yet reissued on CD), a quartet outing with fluegelhornist Clark Terry, drummer Mickey Roker and either George Duvivier or Bob Cranshaw on bass. Together they perform four Scott originals, a pair of C.T.'s compositions, the swinging "Until I Met You" and the standard "Heat Wave." Although not playing with the force that Stanley Turrentine exhibited while jamming with the organist, Clark Terry adds humor and a wistfulness to the date that easily compensates. —Scott Yanow

On a Clear Day / 1966 / Impulse! ✦✦✦✦
Most of organist Shirley Scott's records in the 1960s featured her husband, tenor saxophonist Stanley Turrentine, so this trio effort (not yet reissued on CD) with bassist Ron Carter and drummer Jimmy Cobb was a change of pace. As usual, Scott features an off-the-wall tune ("What the World Needs Now Is Love") in her repertoire, along with standards (including "On a Clear Day" and selections by Henry Mancini, Antonio Carlos Jobim and Irving Berlin) and a couple of basic originals. The music grooves and Scott shows that she did not need a competing horn in order to come up with soulful and swinging ideas. —Scott Yanow

Girl Talk / 1967 / Impulse! ✦✦✦
Soul Song / Sep. 9, 1968 / Atlantic ✦✦
Organist Shirley Scott's first of three Atlantic LPs (all are very difficult to find these days) was her last recording with her husband, tenor saxophonist Stanley Turrentine, who would soon gain great fame along with a divorce. Although Scott plays well enough and the supporting cast (which includes guitarist Eric Gale) is funky, the material is quite erratic, including Ray Stevens' "Mr. Businessman," "Like a Lover" (which has a rare vocal by the organist) and "Blowin' in the Wind." This collector's item has its interesting moments, but it is one of Shirley Scott's less significant dates. —Scott Yanow

Shirley Scott and the Soul Saxes / Jul. 9, 1969 / Atlantic ✦✦✦✦
Steamy workout with Scott, Hank Crawford (as), King Curtis (ts), and David Newman (ts). —Ron Wynn

One for Me / Nov. 1974 / Strata East ✦✦✦✦✦
The record is a beauty with Harold Vick, perhaps the most suited and sensitive horn player Ms. Scott has worked with . . . [a] thoroughly enjoyable album of bop stream music, and while it is nothing overly heavy or deep, it's thoughtfully and sensitively produced and of its kind an almost perfect album. —Bob Rusch, Cadence

Oasis / Aug. 28, 1989 / Muse ✦✦✦✦✦
A sophisticated bop outing. Some nice mid-sized band music here. —Michael Erlewine

Blues Everywhere / Nov. 23, 1991 / Candid ✦✦✦✦
Trio session with Scott and Arthur Harper (b) and Mickey Roker (d). The twist is that Scott is playing acoustic piano throughout. It's not the usual sound, but she can play that thing. —Michael Erlewine

Stephen Scott

b. 1969
Piano / Hard Bop, Post-Bop
Another in the latter-day parade of tradition-respecting Young Lions, Stephen Scott brings a formidable technique, some of Ahmad Jamal's locked-groove obsessions, and elements of Wynton Kelly, Bud Powell and McCoy Tyner to his work. However, Scott may be on the verge of expanding beyond his neo-bop base; his most recent album, *The Beautiful Thing*, has pronounced Latin and soul-jazz tendencies on some tracks. He started piano at the age of five and progressed rapidly to the point where he was taking private lessons at Juilliard at 12. Although grounded in classical music, he was also exposed to reggae and salsa on the radio, but wasn't introduced to jazz until his high school years (he gives saxophonist Justin Robinson the credit for that). By the age of 18, Scott was playing in the band of singer/talent scout Betty Carter, and soon began performing or recording with the likes of the Harper Brothers, Wynton Marsalis, Bobby Watson and Bobby Hutcherson. Since 1991, Scott has turned out a steady supply of mainstream albums for Verve, using mixtures of fellow Young Lions and esteemed veterans like Joe Henderson, Ron Carter and Elvin Jones as sidemen, and he also played on Henderson's 1991 commercial breakthrough, *Lush Life*. —Richard S. Ginell

Something to Consider / Jan. 30, 1991-Mar. 18, 1991 / Verve ✦✦✦✦
Young Lion roars out of the box with impressive piano debut, aided by both old stars like Joe Henderson (sax) and fellow brats like Roy Hargrove (tpt). —Ron Wynn

Aminah's Dream / Oct. 8, 1992-Oct. 9, 1992 / Verve ✦✦✦✦✦
One of the most promising of the "Young Lions," pianist Stephen Scott has a versatile style that can range from McCoy Tyner to Wynton Kelly without resorting to

mere copying. On his second release as a leader, Scott holds his own during six trio performances with bassist Ron Carter and drummer Elvin Jones. The other four selections add four nonsoloing horns playing harmonies behind Scott's piano. With eight of the ten songs being his originals, this is a fine all-around showcase for the talented Stephen Scott. —Scott Yanow

● **Renaissance** / Aug. 1, 1994-Aug. 2, 1994 / Verve ✦✦✦✦✦
Beautiful Thing / Mar. 13, 1996-Mar. 15, 1996 / Verve ✦✦✦✦✦

Tom Scott

b. May 19, 1948, Los Angeles, CA
Tenor Saxophone, Alto Saxophone, Flute / Instrumental Pop, Crossover Jazz, Fusion
Since he was a teenager Tom Scott has been consistent, a talented multireedist with little or no interest in playing creative jazz. His mother was a pianist and father a composer. Scott early on became a studio musician and arranger. Able to play most reeds with little difficulty, Scott performed with the Don Ellis and Oliver Nelson bands and his L.A. Express became one of the most successful pop-jazz groups of the 1970s. Associations with Joni Mitchell, Carole King and George Harrison were just a few of his successful assignments in the pop world and, although his 1992 GRP release *Born Again* was surprisingly inventive, it was a one-time departure from crossover. —Scott Yanow

Tom Scott & LA Express / Aug. 1973-Sept. 1973 / Ode ✦✦✦✦
Most of Tom Scott's GRP albums of the '80s and '90s have been shallow, formulaic releases offering little evidence of the saxman's improvisatory skills. But most of his earlier recordings of the 1970s were appealing jazz/funk/R&B efforts that, although commercial and highly accessible, demonstrated his capabilities as a soloist. If the version of Scott's L.A. Express band heard on this album (reissued on CD in 1996) brings to mind the Crusaders, it's because two of its members, keyboardist Joe Sample and guitarist Larry Carlton, were also Crusaders members. Although the Express was never in a class with that band, it was a likable unit defined by its cohesiveness, warmth and spontaneity. As slick as the Express was, it took risks. It's hard to imagine Scott providing a funk-drenched version of John Coltrane's "Dahomey's Dance" as he does here—or incorporating Middle Eastern influences as he does on "King Cobra"—on his calculated GRP recordings of the '90s. Solid jazz-funk like "L.A. Expression" and "Nunya" is well worth hearing. And "Spindrift," though congenial and mellow, is far more substantial than the "muzak" he would later inundate us with. —Alex Henderson

Tom Cat / 1974 / Ode ✦✦✦✦
Despite the absence of Joe Sample and Larry Carlton, Scott's L.A. Express remains very Crusaders-influenced on *Tom Cat*—a highly accessible jazz/funk/R&B date that, as commercial as it is, leaves room for inspired blowing courtesy of both the leader and sidemen like electric guitarist Robben Ford and keyboardist Larry Nash. Sweaty, hardhitting jazz-funk is the rule on such down-home grooves as "Good Evening Mr. & Mrs. America and All the Ships" and "Day Way," which allow the players to let loose, blow and say what needs to be said. "Love Poem" is a pleasant, likable piece of delicate mood music (but not "muzak"!) that features wordless vocals by pop/folk singer Joni Mitchell and has a slightly Flora Purim-ish appeal. Unfortunately, a CD as good as *Tom Cat* serves as a reminder of how dreadfully unimaginative most of Scott's GRP albums would be. —Alex Henderson

New York Connection / Aug. 25, 1975-Aug. 29, 1975 / Ode ✦✦✦
For *New York Connection*, Scott left his L.A. Express in California and ventured to the Big Apple to join forces with keyboardists Bob James and Richard Tee, guitarist Richard Tee, drummer Steve Gadd and others who—like the saxman—had decent jazz chops, but devoted much of their time to R&B/soul session work. While Scott was never in a class with Stanley Turrentine, Grover Washington, Jr., or David "Fathead" Newman, gritty, down-home smokers like "Midtown Rush," "Dirty Old Man" and "Look Out for Number Seven" provide additional evidence that he was indeed a capable, enjoyable soloist who, at the time, played from the heart. Though softer pieces such as "Time and Love" and the CD's title song make for a sort of disco-ish "easy listening," they're far more substantial than the rubbish that was to come. —Alex Henderson

Blow It Out / 1976 / Epic ✦✦
Blow It Out was among Tom Scott's bestselling albums of the 1970s, but it was also among his weakest of the decade. The spontaneity and grit that defined his work with the L.A. Express is sorely missing on the album, a session plagued by excessive producing and arranging, bland material and appalling lack of improvisation. Scott's sax is consistently smothered by cliched, Bob James-ish arrangements. Fans of '70s cop shows may want to hear "Gotcha (Theme from 'Starsky & Hutch')," but on the whole, Scott's pop and R&B melodies are as schlocky as they are forgettable. Making a rare and unsuccessful attempt to sing on the R&B-pop number "Down to Your Soul"—which sounds like fifth-rate Steely Dan—Scott

unveils a voice that's thin at best. Unquestionably, an L.A. Express date like *Tom Cat* would be a much better investment. —*Alex Henderson*

Apple Juice / Jan. 15, 1981-Jan. 17, 1981 / Columbia ✦✦✦

Desire / Jul. 23, 1982-Jul. 24, 1982 / Elektra ✦✦

Target / Jul. 23, 1983-Jul. 24, 1983 / Atlantic ✦✦✦

Night Creatures / Aug. 22, 1984-Oct. 17, 1984 / GRP ✦

Granted that this Tom Scott CD (as with many of his) is not really a jazz set but, even when rating this music as R&B or funk, its lack of originality is appalling. Four songs are dominated by anonymous vocalists (Phil Perry and Philip Ingram, who are among the dozen or so singers, are capable of much better) and the other tracks misuse electronic percussion. Scott mostly sticks to passionate but mundane melodies that he could play in his sleep. Even in pop music individuality is a must and there is really nothing to distinguish this strictly-for-the-money release. —*Scott Yanow*

One Night/One Day / 1986 / Soundwings ✦✦✦

Streamlines / Jul. 1987 / GRP ✦✦

Flashpoint / 1988 / GRP ✦✦

Them Changes / 1990 / GRP ✦✦

Keep This Love Alive / 1991 / GRP ✦✦

A shamelessly contrived effort, *Keep This Love Alive* is, for the most part, yet another tremendous waste of Tom Scott's talents. There are a few enjoyable moments here, including guest Dianne Schurr's sensuous vocal on "Whenever You Dream of Me" and Scott's gritty jazz-funk blowing on "Mis Thang." But on the whole, this CD is a throwaway by both jazz and pop standards. R&B-pop singer Brenda Russell is anything but memorable on the bloodless adult-contemporary song "If You're Not the One for Me," and most of the instrumentals would sound boring and lackluster even in a dentist's office. Throwing creativity to the wind, Scott leaves no doubt that his only concern is commercial radio airplay. The saxman recorded more than his share of stinkers for GRP in the 1980s and '90s, and *Keep This Love Alive* is at the top of the list. —*Alex Henderson*

● **Born Again** / 1992 / GRP ✦✦✦✦✦

Longtime session and studio saxophonist Tom Scott surprised many inside and outside the jazz community in 1992 when he made this non-fusion, mainstream and straightahead session. It showed he could still play strong, undiluted tenor sax solos, and also fit in with a group that included such distinguished players as pianist Kenny Kirkland, trumpeter Randy Brecker, and trombonist George Bohannon. Bassist John Patitucci and drummer Will Kennedy were the fusion stars who rounded out the date. —*Ron Wynn*

Reed My Lips / 1993 / GRP ✦✦

Saxophonist Tom Scott sticks to R&Bish pop music on his release with electronic rhythms, two throwaway vocal tracks and cliches dominating an utterly forgettable program. The presence of Grover Washington, Jr., on the title track is largely wasted and Scott succeeds in hiding his individuality on this strictly-for-the-money release. At best, these performances can function as routine background music. —*Scott Yanow*

Bluestreak / 1996 / GRP ✦✦✦✦

Although Tom Scott recorded one throwaway after another in the 1980s and '90s, he's still quite capable of recording a decent album—which he proved on his 1992 straightahead date *Born Again* and his 1996 reunion with the L.A. Express, *Bluestreak*. Spontaneity and inspired blowing are the rules this time. Instead of pandering to smooth jazz radio, Scott lets loose and plays from the heart for a change. The Angelino (who's heard on tenor & soprano sax and flute) avoids smothering this very 1970s-sounding jazz/R&B/pop date with production and gives ample solo space to both himself and such Express alumni as Joe Sample (electric keyboards) and Robben Ford (electric guitar). A forgettable version of Marvin Gaye's "Got to Give It Up" never really takes off, but that's the only really disappointing song on *Bluestreak*—an album that was long overdue. —*Alex Henderson*

Tony Scott

b. Jun. 17, 1921, Morristown, NJ

Clarinet / Cool, Post-Bop, New Age

Since leaving New York in 1959, Tony Scott (a top bebop-oriented clarinetist) has been an eager world traveler who enjoys exploring the folk music of other countries. Unfortunately, his post-1959 recordings have been few, far between, difficult-to-locate and sometimes erratic but Scott was an unheralded pioneer in both world music and new age.

Tony Scott attended Juilliard during 1940-42, played at Minton's Playhouse and then after three years in the military he became one of the few clarinetists to play bop. His cool tone (heard at its best on a 1950 Sarah Vaughan session that also

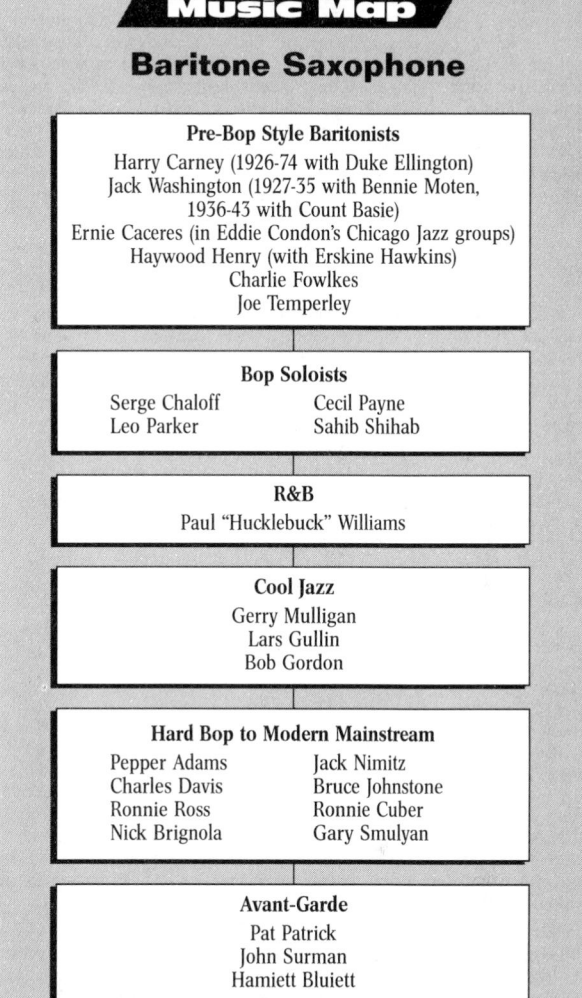

Music Map

Baritone Saxophone

Pre-Bop Style Baritonists
Harry Carney (1926-74 with Duke Ellington)
Jack Washington (1927-35 with Bennie Moten,
1936-43 with Count Basie)
Ernie Caceres (in Eddie Condon's Chicago Jazz groups)
Haywood Henry (with Erskine Hawkins)
Charlie Fowlkes
Joe Temperley

Bop Soloists
Serge Chaloff   Cecil Payne
Leo Parker   Sahib Shihab

R&B
Paul "Hucklebuck" Williams

Cool Jazz
Gerry Mulligan
Lars Gullin
Bob Gordon

Hard Bop to Modern Mainstream
Pepper Adams   Jack Nimitz
Charles Davis   Bruce Johnstone
Ronnie Ross   Ronnie Cuber
Nick Brignola   Gary Smulyan

Avant-Garde
Pat Patrick
John Surman
Hamiett Bluiett

includes Miles Davis) stood out from the more hard-driving playing of Buddy DeFranco. Scott worked with a wide variety of major players (including Ben Webster, Trummy Young, Earl Bostic, Charlie Ventura, Claude Thornhill, Buddy Rich and Billie Holiday), led his own record dates (among his sidemen were Dizzy Gillespie and a young Bill Evans) which ranged from bop and cool to free improvisations (all are currently difficult to locate) and ranked with DeFranco at the top of his field.

Unfortunately the clarinet was not exactly a popular instrument in the 1950s (as opposed to during the swing era) and Tony Scott remained an obscure name outside of jazz circles. In 1959 he gave up on the US and began extensive tours of the Far East. He played Eastern classical music, recorded meditation music for Verve and, other than some brief visits to the US, has lived in Italy since the 1970s where he has sometimes experimented with electronics. —*Scott Yanow*

The Touch of Tony Scott / Jul. 2, 1956+Jul. 3, 1956 / Victor ✦✦✦✦

This rare set features the cool-toned clarinetist Tony Scott with a big band on five numbers, heading a ten-piece band for three others and jamming with a quartet that also features the young pianist Bill Evans on the four remaining songs. The songs range from swing standards and the tongue-in-cheek "Rock Me But Don't Roll Me" to "Aeolian Drinking Song" and an original titled "Vanilla Frosting on a Beef Pie." Musically, the performances are fairly modern for the period while never failing to swing. This LP is well worth searching for, as are most of Tony Scott's recordings of the 1950s. —*Scott Yanow*

The Complete Tony Scott / Dec. 11, 1956-Feb. 6, 1957 / Victor ✦✦✦✦✦

The Modern Art of Jazz / 1957 / Seeco ◆◆◆◆

This obscure LP features the talented but somewhat forgotten clarinetist Tony Scott (whose cool approach contrasted with Buddy DeFranco's more hyper style) doubling on baritone. In addition to trumpeter Clark Terry and baritonist Sahib Shihab, Scott featured some young talent he was greatly impressed with: trombonist Jimmy Knepper, pianist Bill Evans, bassist Henry Grimes (who alternates with veteran Milt Hinton) and drummer Paul Motian. Most of the songs (including Scott's "Blues for 3 Horns") are either standards or based on familiar chord changes, but Bill Evans' "Five" was introduced during the date. This worthy album will be a difficult one to locate. —*Scott Yanow*

I'll Remember / Aug. 1, 1959+Aug. 9, 1959 / Muse ◆◆◆◆

The follow-up to clarinetist Tony Scott's *Golden Moments* (both of which were released for the first time on Muse albums of the mid-1980s) uses the same group (a quartet with pianist Bill Evans, bassist Jimmy Garrison and drummer Pete La Roca) and almost reaches the same heights. Scott was one of the finest clarinetists of the late 1950s before deciding to become a sketchily documented world traveler. This live date has lengthy versions of "Stella by Starlight," "I'll Remember April," "A Night in Tunisia" and the blues "Garrison's Raiders." The boppish music hints at future developments and both this album and *Golden Moments* (which gets the edge) are highly recommended. —*Scott Yanow*

Sung Heroes / Oct. 28, 1959-Oct. 29, 1959 / Sunnyside ◆◆

This melancholy date (released for the first time in 1986) was clarinetist Tony Scott's last before heading for Europe. He was mourning the deaths of many of his heroes, and among his pieces are "Misery (to Lady Day)," "Rememberance of Art Tatum" and "Requiem for Hot Lips Page." On three selections Scott is backed by the classic Bill Evans Trio (with bassist Scott LaFaro and drummer Paul Motian); the Tatum piece ironically does not have any pianist, and two selections are duets with Evans. In addition, Scott plays baritone and guitar on one tune apiece and duets with guitarist Juan Sastre on the final number. But, even with the strong playing, the downbeat nature of the material makes this album of only historical interest. —*Scott Yanow*

● **Golden Moments** / 1959 / Muse ◆◆◆◆◆

Tony Scott was one of the major jazz clarinetists of the 1950s, but his decision to become a world traveller in 1960 has resulted in him becoming rather obscure. This valuable Muse release features the clarinetist in top form on an original blues and four standards (including 12-minute versions of "Walkin'" and "Melancholy Baby") in a quartet that also includes the up-and-coming pianist Bill Evans (who had just left Miles Davis' Sextet), bassist Jimmy Garrison and drummer Pete La Roca. The bop-oriented improvisations hold one's interest and make one wish that Scott had stayed in New York throughout the '60s; he had much more to say. —*Scott Yanow*

Music for Zen Meditation (And Other Joys) / Feb. 1964 / Verve ◆◆◆

This elegant, contemplative set of pieces was conceived during one of the jazz artist's trips to Japan when Scott had the opportunity to record with a shakuhachi flutist and a koto player. Though ears unaccustomed to oriental styles might assume it's a performance of traditional Japanese music, the album is actually a set of finely wrought improvisations merging Eastern and Western sensibilities. —*Linda Kohanov*

Clarinet Album / May 16, 1994 / Philology ◆◆◆

Clarinetist Tony Scott, who was 73 at the time, plays mostly ballads on this standards date with an Italian rhythm section of pianist Massimo Farao, bassist Aldo Zunino and drummer Guilio Capiozzo. Scott still mostly retains his cool-toned clarinet sound, but his intonation is erratic in spots, particularly on a 15-minute version of "Speak Low" that should have been re-recorded. One admires the spontaneity, but the overall results, which are generally quite relaxed (including such songs as "My Funny Valentine," "Easy Living" and "I Can't Get Started"), are just OK, but not an important milestone. One wishes that Tony Scott, one of the top jazz clarinetists of the 1950s and one who has spent most of his post-1960 years overseas, had done much more with his musical talents through the years. —*Scott Yanow*

Al Sears

b. Feb. 21, 1910, Macomb, IL, **d.** Mar. 23, 1990, New York, NY

Tenor Saxophone / Early R&B Jazz, Swing, Groove

It is ironic that tenor saxophonist Al Sears' one hit, "Castle Rock," was recorded under Johnny Hodges' name (the altoist is virtually absent on the record!), denying Sears his one chance at fame. Sears had actually had his first important job in 1928 replacing Hodges with the Chick Webb band. However despite associations with Elmer Snowden (1931-2), Andy Kirk (1941-42), Lionel Hampton (1943-4) and with his own groups (most of 1933-41), it was not until Sears joined Duke Ellington's Orchestra in 1944 that he began to get much attention. His distinctive tone,

R&Bish phrasing and ability to build up exciting solos made him one of Ellington's most colorful soloists during the next five years although his period was overshadowed by both his predecessor (Ben Webster) and his successor (Paul Gonsalves). Among Sears' many recordings with Ellington are notable versions of "I Ain't Got Nothing but the Blues" and a 1945 remake of "It Don't Mean a Thing." Sears worked with Johnny Hodges' group during 1951-52, recorded a variety of R&B-oriented material in the 1950s and cut two excellent albums for Swingville in 1960 before going into semi-retirement. —*Scott Yanow*

● **Swing's the Thing** / Nov. 29, 1960 / Swingville ◆◆◆◆◆

Al Sears had the misfortune of having his one hit "Castle Rock" released under the leadership of Johnny Hodges, cheating him of his one chance at fame. A fine swing-based tenor who could stomp and honk with the best of them (although he rarely screamed), Sears had relatively few opportunities to record as a leader and this CD (which reissues a 1960 LP) was one of his last. Sears (along with pianist Don Abney, guitarist Wally Richardson, bassist Wendell Marshall and drummer Joe Marshall) sticks to basic originals, blues and standards and is in top form on these swinging and generally accessible performances. —*Scott Yanow*

Don Sebesky

b. Dec. 10, 1937, Perth Amboy, NJ

Arranger, Trombone / Hard Bop, Crossover Jazz, Instrumental Pop

Don Sebesky is best known as house arranger for many of producer Creed Taylor's Verve, A&M and CTI productions—the man whose orchestral backgrounds helped make artists like Wes Montgomery, Paul Desmond, Freddie Hubbard and George Benson acceptable to audiences outside jazz. He has taken critical heat for this, but Sebesky's arrangements have usually been among the classiest in his field, reflecting a solid knowledge of the orchestra, drawing variously from big-band jazz, rock, ethnic music, classical music of all eras and even the avant-garde for ideas. He once cited Bartok as his favorite composer but one also hears lots of Stravinsky in his work.

Sebesky started out professionally as a trombonist while still at the Manhattan School of Music, working with Kai Winding, Claude Thornhill, the Tommy Dorsey Band led by Warren Covington, Maynard Ferguson and Stan Kenton. In 1960, he gave up the trombone to concentrate upon arranging and conducting, eventually receiving the breakthrough assignment of Montgomery's *Bumpin'* album (1965). Some of the most attractive examples of his work for jazz headliners include *Bumpin',* Benson's *The Shape of Things to Come,* Desmond's *From the Hot Afternoon,* and Hubbard's *First Light.* He began to step out into the spotlight with the release of his all-star *Giant Box,* which was followed by sporadic further releases on CTI and GNP/Crescendo. He has also written classical works and a book, *The Contemporary Arranger* (Port Washington, NY, 1975). —*Richard S. Ginell*

Don Sebesky and the Jazz-Rock Syndrome / Jan. 19, 1968-Jun. 1968 / Verve ◆◆◆

● **Giant Box** / Apr. 1973-May 1973 / Columbia ◆◆◆◆◆

This may have been Creed Taylor's most ambitious single project. As the cash was flowing in the wake of Deodato's massive "2001" hit, Taylor rounded up almost every headliner on CTI's roster, had house-arranger Don Sebesky write big-thinking charts for them, and gave Sebesky top billing and two LPs of space. Two decades later, the lineup reads almost like a gathering of the gods—Freddie Hubbard, Randy Brecker, Hubert Laws, Paul Desmond, Joe Farrell, Grover Washington, Jr., Milt Jackson, George Benson, Bob James, Ron Carter, Jack DeJohnette, Billy Cobham, Airto Moreira, Jackie Cain and Roy Kral, all on one album. Thankfully the music making lives up to the billing. Everything that gave CTI its distinctive sound and identity is here—the classical adaptations (Stravinsky's *Firebird* is merged shotgun-style with John McLaughlin's "Birds of Fire"), elaborate orchestrations and structuring, pop-tune covers, plenty of room for the star soloists to stretch out in a combo format. The stars all come out to shine; Desmond sounds especially inspired in a shimmering "Song to a Seagull" and Hubbard and Washington burn furiously on the appropriately titled "Free as a Bird." And Sebesky was given a flyer to experiment; hence the wild extended swarms of freeform strings on "Firebird" and Laws' fancy Echoplexed winds on "Fly." The two original LPs were gathered in a classical-style box, complete with a booklet of photos and an interview with Sebesky, but the austere CBS CD reissue condenses everything onto a generic single disc. However less ostentatious, *Giant Box* still ranks as a sensational coup and a reminder of how potent CTI was at its peak. —*Richard S. Ginell*

The Rape of El Morro / Apr. 1975-May 1975 / CTI ◆◆◆

Three Works for Jazz Soloists and Symphony Orchestra / Jul. 1979 / Gryphon ◆◆◆

Interesting, if uneven, work that blends symphonic and jazz concepts in a quasi-Third Stream fashion. This was conceived by Don Sebesky, who's achieved more fame for his productions and arrangements with CTI in the '70s and A&M in the late '60s. The solo sections don't fully mesh with the structured ones, but Sebesky deserves credit for trying something different. —Ron Wynn

Moving Lines / Nov. 1984 / Columbia ✦✦✦

Full Cycle / 1984 / GNP ✦✦✦✦

From the familiar jacket design, you would swear that this LP was a souvenir from Creed Taylor's late-'60s tenure at A&M, but no, Taylor is nowhere to be found—the year is 1984, and the label is Crescendo. What is significant are the subtle changes that have crept into Don Sebesky's sound. Here he takes five jazz standards and one should-be standard (Freddie Hubbard's "Intrepid Fox"), assembles a big band, selects and mixes colors freely instead of piling on blocks of trumpets, saxes and trombones, and adds an electric rhythm section. The results don't scream at you; they are shaded, meticulously balanced, ultimately a mellow mutation of Sebesky's CTI work, and in the cases of "Waltz for Debby" and "All Blues," bordering on the sound and ethos of Gil Evans. Sebesky's supporting cast isn't nearly as starry as those on his CTI projects but you do hear Jon Faddis on trumpet and fluegelhorn, the still-little-known Eddie Daniels on reeds, and Sebesky himself on electric piano. And the charts are not easy; the winds and brasses have their hands full switching instruments within each selection. While this is not on CD yet, the LP and cassette versions remain in print at this date. —Richard S. Ginell

Cathy Segal-Garcia

b. May 28, 1953, Boston, MA

Vocals / Bop, Post-Bop

One of the top jazz singers based in Los Angeles in the 1990s, Cathy Segal-Garcia has a beautiful voice and is an adventurous improviser, even when interpreting a well-known standard. After singing on the East Coast from the age of 12, she moved to L.A. in 1976, recorded CDs for her CSG label and the Japanese Koyo Sounds company and has performed often in Japan and Europe. —Scott Yanow

Point of View / 1985 / CSG ✦✦✦✦

This early recording from singer Cathy Segal-Garcia has some strong originals ("When You Wish upon a Star" is the only standard), excellent singing from Segal-Garcia (who has grown a great deal since then) and backup by both acoustic and electric musicians including keyboardist Russell Ferrante, pianist Rick Helzer and many other Los Angeles-based musicians. Highlights include "Mr. Hall" (dedicated to guitarist Jim Hall), "Diane" and "Everything's Down to Earth." A fine early set from Cathy Segal-Garcia, who deserves to record much more often. —Scott Yanow

● **Song of the Heart** / Sep. 1992 / Koyo Sounds ✦✦✦✦✦

Despite her obvious talents as a highly expressive and chance-taking jazz vocalist, Cathy Segal-Garcia's first two recordings were made for obscure labels. This particular CD, which was released by the Japanese Koyo Sounds label, features Segal-Garcia with pianist Phillip Jones, bassist Marc Johnson and drummer Peter Erskine. Highlights include the singer's lyrics to "Mr. Hall" and Chick Corea's "Bud Powell" along with her renditions of "Some Other Time," "September in the Rain" and "A Sleeping Bee." —Scott Yanow

Mitch Seidman

b. 1953, Albany, NY

Guitar / Hard Bop, Post-Bop

A fine guitarist with a few releases on the Brownstone label, Mitch Seidman started off playing with rock bands in Albany, NY. He moved to Boston in 1973 to attend Berklee and, other than six years in New York, has been based in Boston ever since. He considers Jim Hall, Jimmy Raney and Tal Farlow to be his main influences and has played with many musicians through the years, including Harold Vick, Ted Brown, George Garzone and Herb Pomeroy. Seidman's 1995 release *Ants in a Trance* utilizes the unusual instrumentation of guitar, bass, bass clarinet and viola. —Scott Yanow

● **Fretware** / Jun. 20, 1994-Jun. 21, 1994 / Brownstone ✦✦✦✦✦

Mitch Seidman has remained somewhat obscure despite over 20 years of professional experience, mostly in Boston. An excellent guitarist most influenced by Jim Hall and Jimmy Raney, on this CD he is heard in a trio with bassist Harvie Swartz and drummer Alan Dawson and, with the addition of Charlie Kohlhase on baritone and alto and Leonard Hochman on tenor and bass clarinet, in quartet/quintets. This well-paced set has plenty of memorable selections including strong versions of Duke Ellington's "Going Up," "It Could Happen to You" and the intriguing calypso "Dyani." The interplay between Seidman, Swartz and Dawson is consistently impressive, making this forward-thinking bop set well worth checking out. —Scott Yanow

Ants in a Trance / Jun. 1995-Oct. 1995 / Brownstone ✦✦✦✦

For his second Brownstone release, the quiet but inwardly intense guitarist Mitch Seidman explores mostly originals and obscurities with an unusual chamber quartet also featuring bassist Harvie Swartz, bass clarinetist Leonard Hochman and the

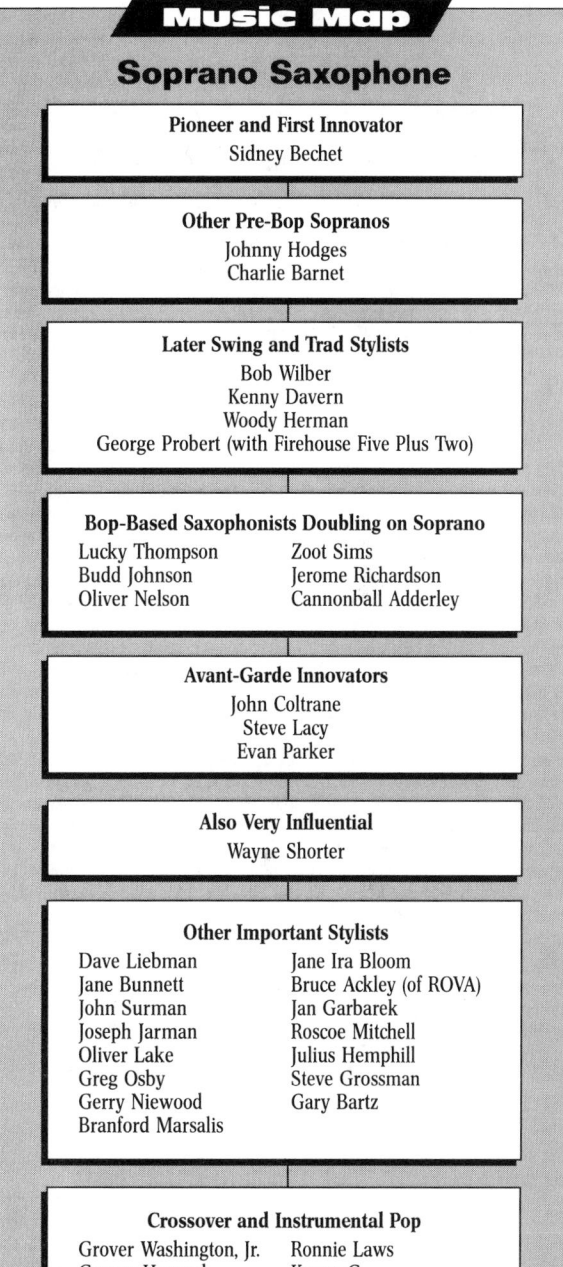

Music Map

Soprano Saxophone

Pioneer and First Innovator
Sidney Bechet

Other Pre-Bop Sopranos
Johnny Hodges
Charlie Barnet

Later Swing and Trad Stylists
Bob Wilber
Kenny Davern
Woody Herman
George Probert (with Firehouse Five Plus Two)

Bop-Based Saxophonists Doubling on Soprano
Lucky Thompson   Zoot Sims
Budd Johnson   Jerome Richardson
Oliver Nelson   Cannonball Adderley

Avant-Garde Innovators
John Coltrane
Steve Lacy
Evan Parker

Also Very Influential
Wayne Shorter

Other Important Stylists
Dave Liebman   Jane Ira Bloom
Jane Bunnett   Bruce Ackley (of ROVA)
John Surman   Jan Garbarek
Joseph Jarman   Roscoe Mitchell
Oliver Lake   Julius Hemphill
Greg Osby   Steve Grossman
Gerry Niewood   Gary Bartz
Branford Marsalis

Crossover and Instrumental Pop
Grover Washington, Jr.   Ronnie Laws
George Howard   Kenny G.
Bill Evans

viola of Ella Lou Weber. The interplay between Seidman and Swartz in particular is consistently impressive while the colors provided by Hochman and Weber are a major plus. The band (in a variety of settings) plays four of the guitarist's diverse originals plus tunes by Thelonious Monk ("Bye-Ya"), Jimmy Giuffre, Attila Zoller, Dave Brubeck ("In Your Own Sweet Way"), bassist Bob Nieske, Joe Zawinul (his forgotten gem "Midnight Mood") and Charlie Kohlhase in addition to the full group's "Boulevard of Broken Strings." The music ranges from the introspective to performances emphasizing the subtle wit of the players; in general every note counts. —Scott Yanow

Ingrid Sertso

Vocals / Post-Bop, Avant-Garde

Through her work with such avant-jazz musicians as Don Cherry and Karl Berger, Ingrid Sertso established herself as a captivating, adventurous vocalist, capable of blending jazz, African, South American and other worldbeat influences into a distinctive, hypnotic sound.

Although Sertso didn't become well-known until the release of *Dance with It* in 1994, she spent over 20 years honing her art. During the late '60s, she lived in Europe, leading her own trios and performing with the likes of Eric Dolphy, Don Cherry, Steve Lacy, Karl Berger and Leo Wright; she also worked as a music teacher at several institutions in Europe. In 1972, she became a permanent resident of the US and she released her first album, *We Are You*, on Calig Records. Over the next few years she taught, while she performed in North America and Europe with the likes of Cherry, Ed Blackwell, Lee Konitz, Sam Rivers, Jimmy Giuffre, Bob Moses, Dave Holland, Perry Robinson and Jumma Santos. In 1974, she released *Kalaparush* on Trio Records in Japan. It was followed in 1975 by *Peace Church Concerts* on India Navigation/CMC Records.

In 1975, Sertso became a faculty member at the Naropa Institute in Boulder, CO. She stayed there through 1975 and 1976, before moving to the Banff Centre of Fine Arts in Calgary, Canada. She had two residencies at Banff before moving to the Creative Music Studio in Woodstock, NY, where she became the co-director. While working at the Creative Music Studio, she began singing in the Art of Improvisation with Berger and David Inzenon. In 1979, she toured major European cities as a solo artist, supported by the Woodstock Workshop Orchestra. She also released an album on MPS Records that year.

During the early '80s, Sertso remained a co-director at the Creative Music Studio, while continuing to record and perform with a variety of musicians, including such mainstays as Don Cherry and Karl Berger, as well as Paulo Moura, Nana Vasconcelos, Steve Gorn, Dan Brubeck and Mike Richmond. In 1984, she performed with the Music Universe Orchestra at the Kool Festival in New York and released a duet album, *Changing the Time*, with Berger on Horo Records in Italy. She also toured Europe twice during this time and she also toured West Africa with Olatunji and Aiyb Dieng.

Sertso's career picked up momentum during the latter half of the '90s. She held a series of concerts and workshops in Rio de Janeiro, Brazil, and she regularly toured the US on the club and festival circuit. Sertso also toured Europe twice and sang solo vocals on Berger's orchestral ballet, *The Bird*. She was one of the co-leaders of Rhythm Changes, who released the *Jazzdance* album on ITM Records. During these five years, she also performed and recorded with a variety of artists, including Pauline Oliveros, Lee Konitz, Frank Luther, Anthony Cox, Leroy Jenkins, Jimmy Cobber, Linda Montano and Karl Berger.

In 1990, Sertso catapulted back into the mainstream jazz spotlight through her version "Until the Rain Comes" on Don Cherry's *Multi Kulti* album. Shortly afterward, she began working on a new album, but she became sidetracked by collaborating with Karl Berger and guitarist Paul Koji Shigihara. The trio blended original compositions with Sertso's poetry, improvisations and interpretations of traditional tunes. Sertso also regularly performed poetry readings at the Tinker Street Cafe in Woodstock and the Knitting Factory in New York, and she also regularly played clubs along the Northeast coast. In 1994 she released her comeback album *Dance with It*, which earned positive reviews. —*Stephen Thomas Erlewine*

● **Dance with It** / 1994 / Enja ✦✦✦✦✦

Doc Severinsen

b. Jul. 7, 1927, Arlington, OR

Trumpet, Leader / Swing, Instrumental Pop, Big Band

Though faithful watchers of *The Tonight Show with Johnny Carson* and most of the '70s and beyond generation identify Doc Severinsen as a garish dresser and pseudo-hip bandleader with minimal ability, Severinsen has a substantial bebop heritage. He's also a much better trumpeter than he usually showed during his television years, gifted with great range and excellent timbre and tone. He was a soloist in Tommy Dorsey's big band in the late '40s and early '50s, and had brief stints with Charlie Barnet and Benny Goodman. Severinsen joined NBC in 1949, and 13 years later was assistant leader of the orchestra, with Skitch Henderson running the band. Henderson left in 1967 and Severinsen took over. He lasted until 1992, when Carson retired and Jay Leno brought in a new band. Though it seems like 43 years at one place, and 25 years heading a band would be a great run, there were rumors everyone, including Severinsen, got pushed rather than voluntarily left their post. He's led brass workshops for years, conducted the Phoenix Pops, played with other orchestras and led various groups, among them the unctuous Xebron. Severinsen took *Tonight Show* alumni around the nation on a farewell tour in 1993. —*Ron Wynn*

Facets / 1960 / Amherst ✦✦

For this effort, trumpeter Doc Severinsen, in one of his rare recordings away from a big-band format, teams up with the reeds of Ernie Watts, guitarist Lee Ritenour, a variety of studio musicians and a large string orchestra to perform crossover-oriented music. With arrangements contributed by producer Jeff Tyzik and Allen Vizzutti, even such songs as "My Funny Valentine," "Take the 'A' Train" and "Maiden Voyage" are transformed into rather routine, funky dance music. —*Scott Yanow*

Tonight Show Band with Doc Severinsen / Aug. 5, 1986+Aug. 7, 1986 / Amherst ✦✦✦✦

Nineteen years after Doc Severinsen took over leadership of the Tonight Show Band, he finally got the big band into the studio. A strong all-star unit featuring such fine players as trumpeters Snooky Young and Conte Candoli, altoist Tommy Newsom, tenors Pete Christlieb and Ernie Watts and pianist Ross Tompkins, the group should have had five records out by this time. Due to the somewhat predictable music (mostly remakes of swing-era standards), this program (highlighted by "King Porter Stomp," "One O'Clock Jump" and "Flying Home") is not as classic as one would hope. The music is reasonably enjoyable, but *Once More... With Feeling* is the definitive recording to get. —*Scott Yanow*

The Tonight Show Band, Vol. 2 / Aug. 5, 1986-Aug. 7, 1986 / Amherst ✦✦✦✦

The second of two long-overdue recordings by the Tonight Show Band has its moments, but its reliance on swing-era warhorses and the generally predictable arrangements (Bill Holman's reworkings of "The World Is Waiting for the Sunrise," "Take the 'A' Train" and "Serenade in Blue" are exceptions) are disappointments. However, there is some excellent solo space for trumpeters Doc Severinsen, Snooky Young and Conte Candoli, tenors Pete Christlieb and Ernie Watts and pianist Ross Tompkins and, since this legendary big band recorded so little (just three albums for Amherst), all are worth picking up. —*Scott Yanow*

● **Once More, With Feeling!** / 1991 / Amherst ✦✦✦✦✦

Of the Tonight Show Band's three Amherst CDs, this is the most highly recommended one. The repertoire is fresher than the songs featured on the two earlier releases and, in addition to the usual swing-era standards, such tunes as Tommy Newsom's "Three Shades of Blue" and Stevie Wonder's "Isn't She Lovely" are included. Guest appearances by trumpeter Wynton Marsalis ("Avalon") and singer Tony Bennett ("I Can't Get Started") add some variety, the arrangements (mostly by the innovative Bill Holman and Tommy Newsom) are generally colorful, and the band (featuring such soloists as trumpeters Doc Severinsen, Snooky Young and Conte Candoli, tenor saxophonist Pete Christlieb and pianist Ross Tompkins) sounds in prime form. Recommended. —*Scott Yanow*

Bud Shank (Clifford Everett Shank, Jr.)

b. May 27, 1926, Dayton, OH

Alto Saxophone, Flute / Cool, Hard Bop, Post Bop

Bud Shank began his career pigeonholed as a cool-schooler, but those who have listened to the altoist progress over the long haul know that he has become one of the hottest, most original players of the immediate post-Parker generation. Lumped in with the limpid-toned West Coast crowd in the '50s, Shank never ceased to evolve; in the '90s, he has more in common with Jackie McLean or Phil Woods than with Paul Desmond or Lee Konitz. Shank's keening, blithely melodic, and tonally expressive style is one of the more genuinely distinctive approaches to have grown out of the bebop idiom.

Shank attended the University of North Carolina from 1944-46. Early on, he played a variety of woodwinds, including flute, clarinet, and alto and tenor saxes; he began to concentrate on alto and flute in the late '40s. After college, Shank moved to California, where he studied with trumpeter/composer Shorty Rogers and played in the big bands of Charlie Barnet (1947-8) and Stan Kenton (1950-51). Shank made a name for himself in the '50s as a central member of the West Coast jazz scene. In addition to those named above, he played and recorded with bassist Howard Rumsey's Lighthouse All-Stars, tenor saxophonist Bob Cooper, and Brazilian guitarist Laurindo Almeido, among others. Shank made a series of albums as a leader for World Pacific in the late '50s and early '60s.

Shank ensconced himself in the L.A. studios during the '60s, emerging occasionally to record jazz and bossa nova albums with the likes of Chet Baker and Sergio Mendes. Shank's 1966 album with Baker, *Michelle*, was something of a popular success, reaching No. 56 on the charts. Film scores on which Shank can be heard include *The Thomas Crown Affair* and *The Barefoot Adventure*.

In the '70s, Shank formed the L.A. Four with Almeido, bassist Ray Brown, and, at various times, drummers Chuck Flores, Shelly Manne, and Jeff Hamilton. Shank had been one of the earliest jazz flutists, but in the mid-'80s, he dropped the instrument in order to concentrate on alto full-time. Over the last two decades, he has recorded small-group albums at a modestly steady pace for the Contemporary, Concord, and Candid labels. Shank's 1997 Milestone album, *By Request: Bud Shank Meets the Rhythm Section*, presents the altoist in top form, burning down

Music Map

Tenor Saxophone

Pioneer and First Innovative Tenor
Coleman Hawkins

1920s
Barney Bigard
Happy Caldwell

Second Innovative Tenor
Lester Young

Swing Era
Chu Berry	Ben Webster	Charlie Barnet
Gene Sedric	Herschel Evans	Buddy Tate
Dick Wilson	Budd Johnson	Benny Waters

Chicago Dixieland
Bud Freeman • Eddie Miller

1940s Stompers - Swing to R&B
Illinois Jacquet	Arnett Cobb
Flip Phillips	Don Byas
Ike Quebec	Georgie Auld
Eddie "Lockjaw" Davis	Al Sears
Charlie Ventura	Hal Singer
Willis "Gator" Jackson	Jimmy Forrest

1940s Los Angeles Bop
Dexter Gordon	Wardell Gray
Teddy Edwards	Lucky Thompson

Cool School
Stan Getz	Zoot Sims
Al Cohn	Herbie Steward
Brew Moore	Allan Eager
Jimmy Giuffre	Paul Quinichette
Buddy Collette	Bob Cooper
Bill Perkins	Richie Kamuca
Dave Pell	Jack Montrose
Frank Wess	Dick Hafer
Fraser MacPherson	Spike Robinson

1950s
Sonny Stitt	Gene Ammons	Paul Gonsalves
Frank Foster	James Moody	Benny Golson
Warne Marsh	J.R. Monterose	Johnny Griffin
Harold Land	Junior Cook	Hank Mobley
Jimmy Heath		

Third Innovative Tenor
Sonny Rollins

1960s
Yusef Lateef	Charlie Rouse	Booker Ervin
Clifford Jordan	Sal Nistico	George Coleman
Joe Henderson	Joe Farrell	Charles Lloyd

Versatile Genius
Rahsaan Roland Kirk

Fourth Innovator and Biggest Influence on Post-1960 Tenors
John Coltrane

Free Jazz/Avant-Garde
John Gilmore	Archie Shepp
Pharoah Sanders	Albert Ayler
Dewey Redman	Frank Wright
Roscoe Mitchell	Joseph Jarman
Sam Rivers	Charles Tyler
Fred Anderson	Dave Liebman
John Purcell	Von Freeman
Chico Freeman	George Adams
Evan Parker	Jan Garbarek
Willem Breuker	Peter Brotzmann
Vladimir Chekasin	Joe McPhee
David Murray	Charles Gayle
David S. Ware	

Modern Swing
Scott Hamilton • Ken Peplowski • Harry Allen

Soul Jazz to Crossover
Stanley Turrentine	David "Fathead" Newman
Eddie Harris	Houston Person
Wilton Felder	John Klemmer
Gato Barbieri	Tom Scott
Grover Washington, Jr.	

Most Influential Tenors of the Past 20 Years
Wayne Shorter • Mike Brecker

1980s-90s
Lew Tabackin	Don Menza
Pete Christlieb	Benny Wallace
Billy Harper	John Stubblefield
Odean Pope	Ricky Ford
Eddie Daniels	Steve Grossman
Billy Pierce	Ralph Moore
Joe Lovano	Branford Marsalis
David Sanchez	Edward Wilkerson
Bill Evans	Bob Mintzer
Bob Berg	Bob Malach
Javon Jackson	Jean Toussaint
Courtney Pine	Tommy Smith
Don Braden	Ralph Bowen
Todd Williams	Joshua Redman
James Carter	

the house with a band of relative youngsters which includes neo-bopper pianist   Cyrus Chestnut. —*Chris Kelsey*

Live at the Haig / 1956 / Bainbridge ✦✦✦✦✦
Altoist Bud Shank recorded frequently as a leader during 1954-69 for Richard Bock's Pacific Jazz and World Pacific labels, but very few of those diverse records (other than his collaborations with guitarist Laurindo Almeido) are currently available. An exception is this CD reissue (on Choice) of a live set by his 1956 group for the obscure Concept label. Recorded in early stereo by Gerry MacDonald, the Shank Quartet (with pianist Claude Williamson, bassist Don Prell and drummer Chuck Flores) was caught during a seven-month period when they worked regularly at the Haig in Los Angeles. They stretch out on Williamson's "Ambassador Blues" and a variety of standards, playing cool-toned bop and pushing themselves. Easily recommended to straightahead jazz fans. — *Scott Yanow*

Bud Shank and the Sax Section / Dec. 1966 / Pacific Jazz ✦✦✦
During an era when altoist Bud Shank was recording an extensive series of fairly commercial albums for World Pacific, this LP was better than most. Teamed with a saxophone section that included altoist Bill Perkins, both Rick Hardaway and Bob Cooper on tenors and baritonists Jack Nimitz and John Lowe plus guitarist Dennis Budimir, bassist Ray Brown and drummer Larry Bunker, Shank and his sidemen play rather concise versions of a dozen songs arranged by Bob Florence. One wishes that the saxes could have stretched out more on such tunes as "The Sidewinder," "On a Clear Day," "Take Five" and "Senor Blues," since none of the performances exceed three-and-a-half minutes, but overall, the music on this out-of-print LP is reasonably enjoyable within its limitations. — *Scott Yanow*

Sunshine Express / Jan. 1976 / Concord Jazz ✦✦✦
Recorded during a period when he was gradually returning to jazz from a studio career, Bud Shank (who was a member of the L.A. Four with Laurindo Almeido during the period) doubles on alto and flute on this set with trumpeter Bobby Shew, pianist Mike Wofford, bassist Fred Atwood and drummer Larry Bunker. With the exception of "Here's That Rainy Day," all of the music was composed by either Shank or Wofford, and even if none of the originals were all that memorable, the playing is excellent. — *Scott Yanow*

Heritage / Dec. 19, 1978 / Concord Jazz ✦✦✦✦
Some torrid, energetic alto sax solos by Bud Shank in the midst of a busy late-'70s stretch that saw him re-establish himself on alto after many years of playing mostly flute. He was working with what was his regular band at the time, with pianist Billy Mays providing both an occasional composition and some strong support as the second soloist. — *Ron Wynn*

Crystal Comments / Oct. 1979 / Concord Jazz ✦✦✦✦
Although Bud Shank has since given up the flute, his playing on the instrument was at its peak in the late 1970s. On this unusual trio set, he sticks to flute while joined by both pianist Bill Mays and Alan Broadbent on electric piano; the keyboardists switch instruments on "How Are Things in Glocca Morra." Despite the odd instrumentation, the music is essentially advanced hard bop, with the talented players exploring six standards including "Scrapple from the Apple," "Body and Soul" and "On Green Dolphin Street." An offbeat success that is a good companion to the classical-oriented Shank-Mays duets of *Explorations: 1980* recorded at the same sessions. — *Scott Yanow*

Explorations 1980 / 1980 / Concord Jazz ✦✦✦✦
This unusual set features Bud Shank (exclusively on flute) and pianist Bill Mays performing selections from Ravel, Debussy, Bach and Scriabin, in addition to Mays' five-part twenty-seven-and-a-half-minute "Suite for Flute and Piano." Despite the original sources, there is plenty of improvisation on the date, as Shank and Mays use the original melodies and chord changes as points of departure, treating the music with respect but also adding spontaneous adventure. The enjoyable set makes one regret that Shank has since given up the flute in favor of concentrating full-time on alto. — *Scott Yanow*

This Bud's for You / Nov. 14, 1984 / Muse ✦✦✦✦✦
Originally known as a cool-toned altoist and occasional flutist, Bud Shank's playing from this recording forward surprised many listeners. There was a forcefulness and a passion to his alto solos (he had given up the flute) that had not been heard that much from him previously. Assisted by pianist Kenny Barron, bassist Ron Carter and drummer Al Foster, Shank rips into five bop standards, his own "Cotton Blossom" and Walter Norris's "Space Maker" with plenty of intensity, stretching himself and inspiring his sidemen. Highly recommended. — *Scott Yanow*

California Concert / May 19, 1985 / Contemporary ✦✦✦✦
Altoist Bud Shank and fluegelhornist Shorty Rogers worked together on a fairly regular basis after Rogers returned to active playing in 1982. While Shank had advanced as an improviser (developing a wider range of expression and playing with more intensity than previously), Rogers' cool-toned style was largely unchanged. With pianist George Cables, bassist Monty Budwig and drummer Sherman Ferguson completing the quintet, Shank and Shorty perform three of Rogers'

originals plus inventive reworkings of four swing and bop standards arranged by the fluegelhornist. A fine outing. — *Scott Yanow*

● **That Old Feeling** / Feb. 17, 1986+Feb. 18, 1986 / Contemporary ✦✦✦✦✦
After many years of studio work and a period co-leading the L.A. Four, Bud Shank permanently put away his flute and started concentrating exclusively on alto. This modern bop set with pianist George Cables, bassist John Heard and drummer Tootie Heath finds Shank at his most passionate and creative, stretching out on jazz standards and an eccentric blues. He shows listeners just how much he has grown as an improviser since gaining his initial fame in the 1950s. — *Scott Yanow*

At Jazz Alley / Oct. 16, 1986-Oct. 18, 1986 / Contemporary ✦✦✦
Altoist Bud Shank celebrated his move to the Seattle area by utilizing two talented Seattle players (pianist Dave Peck and bassist Chuck Deardorf) plus drummer Jeff Hamilton for this fine live set. On a well-rounded program of originals, an obscurity and a couple of standards ("A Nightingale Sang in Berkeley Square" and "I Loves You Porgy"), Shank is in top form, really stretching himself on the frequently challenging material. A good example of Bud Shank's playing in the 1980s. — *Scott Yanow*

Serious Swingers / Dec. 2, 1986-Dec. 4, 1986 / Contemporary ✦✦✦
Altoist Bud Shank and tenor saxophonist Bill Perkins had last shared a record date back in 1954. Both had grown quite a bit as players during the decades since, and by the time of this CD, neither had soft or cool tones anymore. Assisted by pianist Alan Broadbent, bassist John Heard and drummer Sherman Ferguson, the co-leaders are in excellent form on six underplayed standards and three group originals. The music swings hard without being overly predictable; highlights include "Out of This World," "C.T.A." and "Remember." — *Scott Yanow*

Tomorrow's Rainbow / Sep. 2, 1988-Sep. 3, 1988 / Contemporary ✦✦✦

Plays Tales of the Pilot: The Music of David Peck / Dec. 2, 1989-Dec. 3, 1989 / Capri ✦✦✦
David Peck, a Seattle-based pianist, heads the group Syzygy, a quartet that also includes guitarists David Peterson, bassist Chuck Deardorf and drummer Dave Coleman. Altoist Bud Shank had Peck and Deardorf as regular members of his own unit for a few years before deciding to feature nine of the pianist's compositions (and his full group) during his Capri CD. Shank had become a much more passionate and distinctive altoist since his initial fame as a cool altoist in the 1950s and he is in typically fine form during this pleasing release. Peck's originals range from the gospelish "Why Tell Me Now" and the driving "Cedar and Billy" to the pretty "Waltz for Janet E." and the lyrical ballad "Bouquet of Fires." The music falls into the area of modern mainstream jazz but has enough variety for the set to stay stimulating all the way through. — *Scott Yanow*

Drifting Timelessly / 1990 / Capri ✦✦✦

The Doctor is In / Sep. 9, 1991-Sep. 10, 1991 / Candid ✦✦✦✦
Good 1991 session featuring the steady cool and bop-tinged alto sax solos of Bud Shank in a combo setting. He's backed by pianist Mike Wofford, bassist Bob Magnusson, and drummer Sherman Ferguson. They tackle familiar standards and a few originals, and make satisfying, if unchallenging, music. — *Ron Wynn*

I Told You So / Jun. 26, 1992-Jun. 27, 1992 / Candid ✦✦✦✦

Plays the Music of Bill Evans / Mar. 13, 1996-Mar. 14, 1996 / Fresh Sound ✦✦✦✦✦
Although they had parallel careers, altoist Bud Shank and pianist Bill Evans only met once—in 1980, when they played a concert opposite each other. Shank and Evans were supposed to record a duet album of the pianist's compositions for Pacific Jazz in the early 1960s, but even though Bud was sent the tunes they were to perform, the project never materialized. In recent times, the discovery of the music resulted in this memorable CD. Joined by what he calls his favorite rhythm section (pianist Mike Wofford, bassist Bob Magnusson and drummer Joe La Barbera), Shank performs eight of Evans' originals, plus Wofford's "Bill's Vane" and his own "Evanescent." The altoist has grown as a soloist through the decades, and the harmonically sophisticated and often complex music inspires him to consistently satisfying improvisations. Although Bill Evans was never that famous as a composer (other than his hit "Waltz for Debby," which is included here), his tricky and unpredictable originals are well worth exploring. Among the highlights of the set are "Peri's Scope," "Funkallero," "My Bells" and "No Cover, No Minimum." This easily recommended concept album works quite well, putting the focus on Bud Shank's continued excellence as a soloist and on the underrated compositional talents of Bill Evans. — *Scott Yanow*

Bud Shank Sextet Plays Harold Arlen / 1996 / Jimco ✦✦✦
Four veterans of the West Coast jazz scene of the 1950s (altoist Bud Shank, tenorman Bill Perkins who doubles on soprano, baritonist Jack Nimitz and trumpeter Conte Candoli) team up with bassist John Clayton and drummer Sherman Ferguson on the Jimco release *The Bud Shank Sextet Plays Harold Arlen*. At first glance

one might think that this is a jam session, but the performances by the pianoless sextet are quite special due to the inventive arrangements, six of which are by either Bill Holman or the late Marty Paich. Most of the songs (including "Blues in the Night," "Over the Rainbow," "Come Rain or Come Shine" and "Out of This World") have the potential to be overfamiliar but the charts (lots of written-out ensembles and development throughout the song rather than being merely repetitive) greatly uplift the music. Shank is the main improviser (he is in fiery form) but everyone gets their short spot on the worthy date. —*Scott Yanow*

By Request: Bud Shank Meets the Rhythm Section / 1997 / Milestone ✦✦✦
This CD undertook a torturous path from conception to completion; originating from a "fan request" list of tunes submitted by a Japanese jazz magazine, it passed through the hands of two bankrupt record labels before Fantasy got a hold of it. While one should be grateful that it came out at all, the results amount to a fairly routine bebop session, with pianist Cyrus Chestnut, bassist George Mraz and drummer Lewis Nash making up the conventional, if expert, rhythm section. The 70-year-old Shank is in a feisty mood, still enjoying himself long after his liberation from the L.A. studio scene. Yet his tone is often unpleasantly shrill in his alto's upper register, and his inventions careen about in a Parker-derived way without adding much insight to the collection of standards at hand. As interviewed in the booklet, Shank eagerly embraces what he calls the "classic format" of bop ("We all do it. And we do it because it works."). But as presented here, one is struck by how staid it all seems—the traditional order of the solos (horn, piano, bass), the trading of fours, the obligatory token bossa nova number, and all that. There has to be—and is—more to jazz than that. —*Richard S. Ginell*

Kendra Shank

b. Apr. 23, 1958, Woodland, CA
Vocals / Standards, Brazilian Jazz
An excellent jazz singer with a warm voice and a subtle improvising style, Kendra Shank's 1992 debut recording, *Afterglow*, is quite appealing, although she has continued to evolve as a vocalist since then. Growing up in San Diego as part of an artistic family, Kendra acted with her mother in plays from the age of five. She started playing guitar when she was 13 and was initially inspired by folk music. Kendra gained a degree in French literature from the University of Washington and started her career as a folk singer, until she discovered Billie Holiday's recordings. Gaining experience playing in France and studying with Jay Clayton in Seattle, she developed quickly. Kendra Shank (no relation to Bud) has since toured the West Coast as a member of the Bob Dorough Quartet and worked as a solo act in Seattle, France, Japan and New York. —*Scott Yanow*

Afterglow / Jul. 5, 1992-Jul. 6, 1992 / Mapleshade ✦✦✦✦
Singer Kendra Shank, who has a beautiful voice, has grown a lot since her debut CD, but her maiden effort is still worth checking out. In general, this set emphasizes slow ballads, and her voice is quite haunting on the more atmospheric pieces. Shank, who plays a bit of basic Brazilian guitar, is joined by a trio that includes pianist Larry Willis, plus (on two songs) guest altoist Gary Bartz. Other than "Devil May Care," the material is generally fairly obscure; Jobim's "Photograph," Billie Holiday's "Left Alone" and Shank's "Paris Bossa" are among the highlights. —*Scott Yanow*

Avery Sharpe

b. 1955
Bass / Post-Bop
An excellent bassist, Avery Sharpe is best known for his longtime association with McCoy Tyner's trio. He originally played piano (starting when he was eight) and accordion, switching to electric (and eventually acoustic) bass a few years later. At the University of Massachusetts, Sharpe had the opportunity to study with Reggie Workman, and he gigged with Wynton Marsalis and Pat Metheny. Sharpe first teamed up with McCoy Tyner in his early-'80s sextet and has been a member of the pianist's trio since 1984. In addition, Sharpe has led one session for Sunnyside (1988) and a pair of CDs for his JKNM label. —*Scott Yanow*

● **Unspoken Words** / Jan. 1988 / Sunnyside ✦✦✦✦
Extended Family / Feb. 1993 / JKNM ✦✦✦

Sonny Sharrock (Warren Harding Sharrock)

b. Aug. 27, 1940, Ossining, NY, **d.** May 25, 1994, Ossining, NY
Guitar / Avant-Garde, Free Jazz
Along with Derek Bailey (whose free-form explorations went in a different direction), Sonny Sharrock was the top avant-garde guitarist. His sonic explorations mixed together Jimi Hendrix with Pharoah Sanders and were often quite ferocious. From 1953-60 Sharrock was a singer in a doo wop group, then in 1960 he started playing guitar. He studied composition at Berklee in 1961 (although he

was thrown out of the guitar class!). Sharrock worked with Byard Lancaster (1966), was with Pharoah Sanders during 1967-68, participated (uncredited) on Miles Davis' *Jack Johnson* album and had his most high-profile job as a member of Herbie Mann's popular group where his adventurous guitar contrasted with Mann's flute and David Newman's soulful tenor. A long period of obscurity occurred after leaving Mann but by the 1980s Sharrock was being rediscovered, recording with Material in 1982 and Last Exit (a quartet with saxophonist Peter Brotzmann) later in the decade. 1991's *Ask the Ages* teamed Sharrock with Sanders, bassist Charnett Moffett and Elvin Jones. But just when he seemed on the brink of a potential commercial breakthrough, Sonny Sharrock died unexpectedly at the age of 53. —*Scott Yanow*

Paradise / 1975 / Atco ✦✦✦

Guitar / 1986 / Enemy ✦✦✦✦✦

Seize the Rainbow / May 1987 / Enemy ✦✦✦
After some years off the scene, the avant-garde guitarist Sonny Sharrock started to record regularly again in the mid-1980s. This album from Enemy has him joined by bassist Melvin Gibbs and both Abe Speller and Pheeroan AkLaff on drums for seven intense originals in which Sharrock shows off the wide range of sounds he could create on his instrument. An interesting set, but definitely for specialized tastes. —*Scott Yanow*

Live in New York / Aug. 1989 / Enemy ✦✦✦✦

Faith Moves / 1989 / CMP ✦✦✦✦
One would think that, considering his power and often violent attack, the last thing Sonny Sharrock needs in a duet session is another guitarist. Actually this CD, which matches Sharrock with Nicky Skopelitis (who also plays the Greek baglama, a Turkish sax, the Carol sitar, an Iranian tar and an electric bass) is a set of passionate music that is more melodic than expected but still full of Sharrock's avant-rock explorations and explosions. —*Scott Yanow*

Highlife / Oct. 1990 / Enemy ✦✦✦

★ **Ask the Ages** / 1991 / Axiom ✦✦✦✦✦
Sonny Sharrock was often thought of as the "Pharoah Sanders of the guitar," so it was quite fitting that one of his finest recordings is this matchup with Sanders, bassist Charnett Moffett and drummer Elvin Jones. This fiery outing was also very good for Sanders who, after many years of recording more lyrical material in the John Coltrane vein, returned to his prime early form with ferocious solos that match the intensity of Sharrock's. —*Scott Yanow*

Charlie Shavers

b. Aug. 3, 1917, New York, NY, **d.** Jul. 8, 1971, New York, NY
Trumpet / Swing
Charlie Shavers was one of the great trumpeters to emerge during the swing era, a virtuoso with an open-minded and extroverted style along with a strong sense of humor. He originally played piano and banjo before switching to trumpet and he developed very quickly. In 1935 he was with Tiny Bradshaw's band and two years later he joined Lucky Millinder's big band. Soon afterward he became a key member of John Kirby's Sextet where he showed his versatility by mostly playing crisp solos while muted. Shavers was in demand for recording sessions and participated on notable dates with New Orleans pioneers Johnny Dodds, Jimmy Noone and Sidney Bechet. He also had many opportunities to write arrangements for Kirby and had a major hit with his composition "Undecided." After leaving Kirby in 1944, Charlie Shavers worked for a year with Raymond Scott's CBS staff orchestra and then was an important part of Tommy Dorsey's Orchestra from 1945 until past TD's death in 1956. Although well featured, this association kept Shavers out of the spotlight of jazz but fortunately he did have occasional vacations in which he recorded with the Metronome All-Stars and toured with Jazz at the Philharmonic; at the latter's concerts in 1953 Shaver's trumpet battles with Roy Eldridge were quite exciting. After Dorsey's death, Shavers often led his own quartet although he came back to the ghost band from time to time. During the 1960s his range and technique gradually faded and Charlie Shavers died from throat cancer in 1971 at the age of 53. —*Scott Yanow*

We Dig Cole / 1957-1958 / Jass ✦✦✦✦
This overly brief LP (which has under 30 minutes of music) consists of swinging versions of eight Cole Porter songs as played by an all-star group of top studio musicians: trumpeter Charlie Shavers, tenor saxophonist Sam "The Man" Taylor, trombonist Urbie Green, clarinetist Sol Yaged, pianist Buddy Weed, guitarist Barry Galbraith, bassist Bob Haggart and drummer Cozy Cole. Larry Clinton's arrangements for the concise renditions of such songs as "Just One of Those Things," "Night and Day" and "What Is This Thing Called Love" leave plenty of room for short solos. Shavers emerges as the main star. —*Scott Yanow*

● **Like Charlie** / Oct. 1960-Nov. 1960 / Everest ✦✦✦✦✦

This LP may be a bit difficult to find, but it is one of swing trumpeter Charlie Shavers' finest as a leader. His playing on an uptempo "The Best Things in Life Are Free" is quite spectacular and, although the dozen performances are all under three minutes long, Shavers makes every emotional note count. Joined by pianist Ray Bryant, bassist Tommy Bryant and drummer Oliver Jackson, the trumpeter is heard throughout in colorful form. Well worth searching for. *—Scott Yanow*

Live from Chicago / May 1962 / Spotlite ✦✦✦✦

Trumpeter Charlie Shavers' sessions as a leader (as opposed to his high-profile sideman associations with John Kirby, Tommy Dorsey and Jazz at the Philharmonic) are generally lesser known and underrated. This live set from Chicago's London House with pianist Larry Novack, bassist Tommy Bryant and drummer Francis Bruce is the most easily available of Shaver's dates, and it finds the masterful trumpeter in excellent form. Highlights include "St. Louis Blues," "What Is This Thing Called Love," and "I Want a Little Girl." Recommended. *—Scott Yanow*

Charlie Shavers at Le Crazy Horse / Jun. 1964 / Everest ✦✦✦

Although only 47 at the time, this was (with the exception of two 1970 albums released on the Black & Blue label) trumpeter Charlie Shavers' last official record as a leader. Backed by an unidentified rhythm section, Shavers is in fine form on the ten songs but the extreme brevity of the LP (just 25 minutes of music!) makes it of lesser interest despite good versions of such tunes as "It Might as Well Be Spring," "Indiana" and "Lover." *—Scott Yanow*

Artie Shaw (Arthur Jacob Arshawsky)

b. May 23, 1910, New York, NY
Clarinet / Swing

One of jazz's finest clarinetists, Artie Shaw never seemed fully satisfied with his musical life, constantly breaking up successful bands and running away from success. While Count Basie and Duke Ellington were satisfied to lead just one orchestra during the swing era and Benny Goodman (due to illness) had two, Shaw led five, all of them distinctive and memorable. After growing up in New Haven, CT, and playing clarinet and alto locally, Shaw spent part of 1925 with Johnny Cavallaro's dance band and then played off and on with Austin Wylie's band in Cleveland during 1927-29 before joining Irving Aaronson's Commanders. After moving to New York, Shaw became a close associate of Willie "The Lion" Smith at jam sessions and by 1931 was a busy studio musician. He retired from music for the first time in 1934 in hopes of writing a book but when his money started running out, Shaw returned to New York. A major turning point occurred when he performed at an all-star big band concert at the Imperial Theatre in May 1936, surprising the audience by performing with a string quartet and a rhythm section. He used a similar concept in putting together his first orchestra, adding a Dixieland-type front line and a vocalist while retaining the strings. Despite some fine recordings, that particular band disbanded in early 1937 and then Shaw put together a more conventional big band. The surprise success of his 1938 recording of "Begin the Beguine" made the clarinetist into a superstar and his orchestra (which featured the tenor of Georgie Auld, vocals by Helen Forrest and Tony Pastor and, by 1939, Buddy Rich's drumming) into one of the most popular in the world. Billie Holiday was with the band for a few months although only one recording ("Any Old Time") resulted. Shaw found the pressure of the band business difficult to deal with and in November 1939 he suddenly left the bandstand and moved to Mexico for two months. When Shaw returned, his first session, one utilizing a large string section, resulted in another major hit "Frenesi"; it seemed that no matter what he did he could not escape from success! Shaw's third regular orchestra, which had a string section and such star soloists as trumpeter Billy Butterfield and pianist Johnny Guarnieri, was one of his finest, waxing perhaps the greatest version of "Stardust" along with the memorable "Concerto for Clarinet." The Gramercy Five, a small group out of the band (using Guarnieri on harpsichord), also scored with the million-selling "Summit Ridge Drive." Despite all this, Shaw broke up the orchestra in 1941, only to reform an even larger one later in the year. The latter group featured Hot Lips Page along with Auld and Guarnieri. After Pearl Harbor, Shaw enlisted and led a Navy band (unrecorded unfortunately) before getting a medical discharge in Feb. 1944. Later in the year his new orchestra featured Roy Eldridge, Dodo Marmarosa and Barney Kessel and found Shaw's own style becoming quite modern, almost boppish. But, with the end of the swing era, Shaw again broke up his band in early 1946 and was semi-retired for several years, playing classical music as much as jazz. His last attempt at a big band was a short-lived one, a boppish unit that lasted for a few months in 1949 and included Zoot Sims, Al Cohn and Don Fagerquist; its modern music was a commercial flop. After a few years of only limited musical activity, Shaw returned one last time, recording extensively with a version of the Gramercy Five that featured Tal Farlow or Joe Puma on guitar along with Hank Jones. Then in 1955 Artie Shaw permanently gave up the clarinet to pursue his dreams of being a writer. Although he served as

frontman (with Dick Johnson playing the clarinet solos) for a reorganized Artie Shaw orchestra in 1983, Shaw never played again. He received plenty of publicity for his six marriages (including to actresses Lana Turner, Ava Gardner and Evelyn Keyes) and for his odd autobiography *The Trouble with Cinderella* (which barely touches on the music business or his wives!) but the still outspoken Artie Shaw deserves to be best remembered as one of the truly great clarinetists. His RCA recordings, which were reissued in complete fashion in a perfectly done Bluebird LP series, have thus far only been made available in piecemeal fashion on CD. *—Scott Yanow*

One Night Stand with Artie Shaw at the Steel Pier / Apr. 8, 1936-Apr. 8, 1945 / Joyce ✦✦✦✦

Half of this LP from the collector's label Joyce features the 1941 Artie Shaw Orchestra during a broadcast which is highlighted by "Frenesi" and Hot Lips Page singing and playing on a Bill Challis arrangement of "Blues in the Night." Also included on this set are a few numbers from Shaw's orchestra in 1940 and two cuts from 1945 (featuring trumpeter Roy Eldridge on "Little Jazz"), but the most significant selection is the earliest: Artie Shaw's historic 1936 performance of "Interlude" (here mistitled "Blues in B Flat") with a string quartet. The acclaim received from the latter inspired the clarinetist to form his first big band. Overall this is a varied and continually interesting set. *—Scott Yanow*

The Best of the Big Bands / Jun. 11, 1936-Oct. 30, 1936 / Columbia ✦✦✦✦

Artie Shaw's first big band was quite unusual, originally comprising four horns, a string quartet and a four-piece rhythm section. This unimaginatively titled CD (whose chatty liner notes unfortunately do not include personnel and date information) has the first 16 recordings by this fine orchestra, featuring vocals by the forgettable Wesley Vaughn, Peg LaCentra and the young Tony Pastor but more importantly, successfully matching together the horns with the strings on such enjoyable numbers as "Japanese Sandman," "Sugar Foot Stomp" and "The Skeleton in the Closet." Pity that this potentially great orchestra did not catch on. *—Scott Yanow*

Artie Shaw and the Rhythmakers, Vol. 1 / Feb. 19, 1937-Apr. 29, 1937 / Swingdom ✦✦✦✦✦

During 1937-38, Artie Shaw and two of his orchestras participated in six marathon recording sessions in which they cut 127 selections for radio transcriptions. Swingdom, on a pair of two-LP sets and a four-LP box, has released these well-recorded performances in complete chronological order. The first two-fer is among the most interesting, for it captures the clarinetist's first orchestra (which, in addition to five horns and a four-piece rhythm section, featured a string quartet) a few days after its final regular recording session, and his second band shortly before its first record date; the only holdovers were Tony Pastor (on tenor and vocals), bassist Ben Ginsberg and Shaw himself. The first band deserved to succeed (it had a unique new sound of its own) but could not compete with the much more powerful ensembles of its competitors. The second orchestra, which a year later was a surprise sensation, was more conventional but no less musical. Artie Shaw collectors in particular will have to acquire this valuable series. *—Scott Yanow*

Artie Shaw and the Rhythmakers, Vol. 2 / Apr. 29, 1937-Jul. 13, 1937 / Swingdom ✦✦✦✦✦

This second of three LP sets taken from Artie Shaw's recordings made for radio transcriptions features his second orchestra in its very early days. In fact, the earlier of the two sessions included on this two-LP set was actually cut before that particular band even had a regular recording date. Although heard here a year or so before his orchestra hit it big with "Begin the Beguine," Shaw's band already had an easily recognizable sound at the time of these transcriptions. Singers Dorothy Howe and Peg LaCentra would not last, and surprisingly, Tony Pastor sticks to playing tenor, but otherwise the orchestra's style was quickly being formed. Artie Shaw fans should particularly enjoy hearing these rare sides for many of the selections were not otherwise recorded by the great clarinetist. *—Scott Yanow*

Artie Shaw and the Rhythmakers, Vols. 5-8 / Jul. 13, 1937-Feb. 15, 1938 / Swingdom ✦✦✦✦

During 1937-38, the somewhat unknown Artie Shaw Orchestra participated in six marathon recording sessions in which they cut 127 selections as radio transcriptions. A pair of two-LP sets were released by Marlor Productions in 1988, and they were followed by this appealing but out-of-print four-LP box, which has 63 of the songs. Shaw's clarinet was already quite recognizable (he would catch on later in 1938, when he recorded "Begin the Beguine"), and his orchestra was starting to come together. Tony Pastor doubled on tenor and vocals, while Louise Farrell sings one song and Anita Bradley is also heard on eight tunes; Helen Forrest would soon take over the female vocalist spot. Actually, the majority of the numbers are instrumentals, with Shaw as the main soloist, trumpeter John Best and Pastor getting some space (tenorman Georgie Auld was not yet in the band), and plenty of spirited yet clean ensembles. Although not essential, this set is quite historic, compares favorably to Artie Shaw's studio output of the period, and can be enjoyed by swing collectors. —*Scott Yanow*

The Complete Artie Shaw, Vol. 1: 1938-39 / Jul. 24, 1938-Jan. 23, 1939 / Bluebird ✦✦✦✦✦

The Artie Shaw success story really began in 1938 with his signing to Victor. Between then and 1945, Shaw would lead and break up four separate orchestras, but his artistic and commercial success would be consistently phenomenal. Fortunately, RCA, in its Bluebird series of two-LP sets, released every Shaw recording in its vaults on eight volumes; unfortunately, much of this music (outside of the better-known hits) has not yet appeared in coherent fashion on CD, so I would advise searching for (and treasuring) the LPs. The first volume finds Shaw debuting on Victor with his giant hit "Begin the Beguine" and continuing with such classics as "Back Bay Shuffle," "Any Old Time" (Billie Holiday's only recording with Shaw), his theme "Nightmare," "Softly, As in a Morning Sunrise," "If They Say" (featuring Helen Forrest's vocal) and "Carioca," among many others. It is no wonder that by 1939 Artie Shaw led the most popular big band in jazz and popular music. —*Scott Yanow*

● Begin the Beguine [Bluebird/RCA] / Jul. 24, 1938-Jul. 23, 1941 / Bluebird ✦✦✦✦✦

Since Artie Shaw's Victor recordings have not been reissued in full on CD, this sampler serves as a fine place for swing beginners to start. Featured are many of the more popular recordings of his second and third orchestras including the title cut, "Frenesi," "Star Dust" and "Summit Ridge Drive," giving one a good idea as to why Artie Shaw was so popular and still remains highly rated as a clarinetist today, decades after his retirement. —*Scott Yanow*

Greatest Hits [RCA] / Jul. 24, 1938-Nov. 12, 1941 / RCA Victor ✦✦✦

This CD is part of RCA's 1996 *Introduction to Jazz* series which mostly features swing-era recordings. For this CD clarinetist Artie Shaw is represented by 14 recordings from his second, third and fourth big bands. His "greatest hits" ("Begin the Beguine," "Frenesi" and the finest version ever of "Stardust") are here along with some lesser-known tracks and vocals by Helen Forrest and Billie Holiday. Surprisingly Shaw's Gramercy Five (which had a million-seller in "Summit Ridge Drive") is absent and not even mentioned in the breezy liner notes; there is also no personnel listing for the orchestra and the music is programmed somewhat randomly. This CD is okay for beginners if found at a budget price but there are more definitive Artie Shaw sets easily available. —*Scott Yanow*

Personal Best / Jul. 24, 1938-Jul. 19, 1945 / Bluebird ✦✦✦

This is a rather odd but intriguing collection of Artie Shaw recordings. Shaw himself picked out these performances as his personal favorites and they include both familiar studio recordings and lesser-known broadcasts. Most Shaw collectors will already have "Any Old Time," the magnificent "Concerto for Clarinet" and "Lover, Come Back to Me" but may not possess copies of the seven broadcast performances. This hodgepodge set is actually more highly recommended for the clarinetist's lengthy quotes in the liner notes than for the music; the broadcasts should be released in the future separately from the studio sides. —*Scott Yanow*

Radio Years, Vol. 1 / Nov. 25, 1938-Dec. 30, 1938 / Jazz Unlimited ✦✦✦

These two radio broadcasts feature the Artie Shaw Orchestra at the Hotel Lincoln in a period when the band was becoming more popular week by week. The recording quality is excellent on this 1994 CD, and Shaw's band (which features the clarinetist, tenors Georgie Auld and Tony Pastor, and occasional vocals by Pastor and Helen Forrest) is in fine form. The music is somewhat predictable (most of the selections were recorded commercially during the period) with no real revelations, so this CD is mostly recommended to Artie Shaw completists and his greatest fans. Among the hotter selections are "Sobbin' Blues," "The Old Stamping Ground" and two versions of "Copenhagen." —*Scott Yanow*

Traffic Jam / Dec. 14, 1938-May 30, 1939 / Natasha ✦✦✦✦

Of all of Artie Shaw's orchestras (not counting his Army band, he had six significant ones), his second was by far the most popular. During 1938-39, Shaw's ensemble was way ahead of the competition, dethroning Benny Goodman's orchestra and not fully surpassed by Glenn Miller until the clarinetist's sudden decision to flee to Mexico to escape the pressure. *Traffic Jam* contains lively radio performances from this era with many fine moments from Tony Pastor, tenor saxophonist Georgie Auld, singer Helen Forrest, a young but powerful Buddy Rich and the leader/clarinetist. An excellent sampling of Artie Shaw's most famous band. —*Scott Yanow*

22 Original Big Band Hits / 1938-1939 / Hindsight ✦✦✦✦

Hindsight specializes in reissuing radio broadcast performances and transcriptions from most of the main swing bands. This fine CD features Shaw's most famous orchestra, his 1938-39 band with tenor Georgie Auld, Tony Pastor, singer Helen Forrest and (in 1939) Buddy Rich. There is no version of "Begin the Beguine" (their

big hit) on this CD but there are many superior examples of the band's music with solos always differing from their studio records. —*Scott Yanow*

Complete Artie Shaw, Vol. 2 (1939) / Jan. 31, 1939-Jun. 22, 1939 / Bluebird ✦✦✦✦✦

The second of seven two-LP sets released by RCA Bluebird in the late '70s (still the best Artie Shaw series ever) traces his orchestra throughout 1939, the year they were the most popular in the land. Among the 32 studio sides are "Deep Purple," "One Night Stand" and "Traffic Jam." In addition to the leader/clarinetist, the main soloists include Georgie Auld on tenor, trumpeter Bernie Privin and pianist Bob Kitsis while Helen Forrest and Tony Pastor provide vocals on half of the songs. Shaw would lead stronger orchestras but this band remains the best loved. —*Scott Yanow*

Complete Artie Shaw, Vol. 7 (1939-1945) / Jun. 12, 1939-Aug. 2, 1945 / RCA ✦✦✦✦✦

The final volume in this definitive series of two-LP sets covers Artie Shaw's 1945 orchestra, a band that boasted the playing of trumpeter Roy Eldridge, pianist Dodo Marmarosa and guitarist Barney Kessel; all three joined Shaw and the rhythm section in his Gramercy Five also. The band often hints strongly at bop and has moments of excitement, but the end of the swing era brought its demise. All seven volumes in this series should be acquired if they can still be found. This one wraps up the series with a few earlier alternate takes. —*Scott Yanow*

Complete Artie Shaw, Vol. 3 (1939-1940) / Aug. 27, 1939-Sep. 3, 1940 / Bluebird ✦✦✦✦✦

The third of seven two-LP sets in Bluebird's definitive series consists of the last 18 recordings by Shaw's very popular 1939 orchestra (riding on the success of "Begin the Beguine"), his two orchestral sessions of 1940 (recorded after the clarinetist's return from his celebrated flight to Mexico) and three of the four selections performed by his new small group, the Gramercy Five, in September 1940. The 1939 orchestra (featuring Georgie Auld's tenor, Buddy Rich's drums and vocals from Helen Forrest and Tony Pastor) is at its best on "Lady Be Good" and "I Surrender Dear." Artie Shaw's first session after his return yielded his second biggest hit ("Freseni") and some fascinating classical-influenced pieces with a full string section. The initial Gramercy Five date included yet another major best seller in "Summit Ridge Drive." Shaw just could not avoid success at this time despite his best efforts. —*Scott Yanow*

Complete Artie Shaw, Vol. 4 (1940-1941) / Sep. 3, 1940-Mar. 20, 1941 / Bluebird ✦✦✦✦✦

Of the six main orchestras that Shaw formed and broke up during 1936-49 his third, the "Stardust" band, was arguably his greatest. He had a strong variety of soloists in trumpeter Billy Butterfield, trombonist Jack Jenney, tenor saxophonist Jerry Jerome and pianist Johnny Guarnieri, in addition to a string section. Such arrangers as William Grant Still, Lennie Hayton, Jerry Gray and Ray Conniff were employed and the writing was as creative as the solos, with the string section really uplifting the music instead of weighing it down. The results, as heard on this two-fer, include such classics as "Temptation," "Prelude in C Major," "Moonglow," "Love of My Life" and particularly "Concerto for Clarinet" and the best-ever version of "Stardust." As a bonus, this set also has five of the eight recordings made by Shaw's original Gramercy Five (with Johnny Guarnieri heard on harpsichord). —*Scott Yanow*

☆ The Complete Gramercy Five Sessions / Sep. 3, 1940-Aug. 2, 1945 / Bluebird ✦✦✦✦✦

Many swing big-band leaders featured small groups out of their orchestra as added attractions, particularly Benny Goodman, Tommy Dorsey with his Clambake Seven and Bob Crosby's Bobcats. In contrast, Artie Shaw recorded relatively few sides with his Gramercy Five. His original unit from 1940 found the great pianist Johnny Guarnieri playing harpsichord exclusively and matched Shaw's clarinet with trumpeter Billy Butterfield. Their early recordings include "My Blue Heaven," "Smoke Gets in Your Eyes" and a million-seller, "Summit Ridge Drive." The remainder of this CD is from 1945 and features Shaw, trumpeter Roy Eldridge and the two young modernists pianist Dodo Marmarosa (on piano!) and guitarist Barney Kessel. Shaw would lead a few other Gramercy Fives in the future, but these are his two most famous. The music is consistently brilliant with every note counting. —*Scott Yanow*

Artie Shaw at the Hollywood Palladium / Oct. 26, 1940-Sep. 6, 1941 / Hep ✦✦✦✦

Although there are many releases featuring radio broadcasts from Artie Shaw's very popular 1939 orchestra, relatively few exist from his next two bands, the outfits from 1940 and 1941. This particular LP shows just how creative the writing was for his string orchestras. Billy Butterfield, Hot Lips Page, Jack Jenney and Georgie Auld are among the many soloists and there is one rare small-group live version of "Dr. Livingstone I Presume." —*Scott Yanow*

Complete Artie Shaw, Vol. 5 (1941-1942) / Mar. 20, 1941-Jan. 20, 1942 / Bluebird ✦✦✦✦

Despite his success with his "Stardust" band, Shaw broke up the orchestra and took time off in early 1941. This fifth in a highly recommended (but increasingly hard-to-find) series of two-LP sets documents his activity during the remainder of 1941. The clarinetist led a very successful, if unusual, orchestral session with such guests as trumpeter Red Allen, trombonist J.C. Higginbotham, altoist Benny Carter and singer Lena Horne, and then later in the year formed his fourth big band. The new orchestra had an even larger string section than its predecessor and such alumni as trombonist Jack Jenney, Georgie Auld on tenor and pianist Johnny Guarnieri in addition to the great trumpeter/singer Hot Lips Page. Unfortunately Shaw impulsively broke it up shortly after Pearl Harbor but, as can be heard on this very enjoyable set, it also had a personality of its own. High points include "Blues in the Night," "Beyond the Blue Horizon" "St. James Infirmary Blues" and several classical-oriented pieces. Fascinating if relatively obscure recordings from another of Shaw's great orchestras. —*Scott Yanow*

Blues in the Night / Sep. 2, 1941-Jul. 26, 1945 / Bluebird ✦✦✦✦

While Bluebird in the late '70s released all of Shaw's recordings in chronological order on a series of two-LP sets, its CD reissues have thus far been samplers. *Blues in the Night* has ten selections from the 1941 string orchestra that featured trumpeter/singer Hot Lips Page in addition to 11 by the 1945 big band that showcased trumpeter Roy Eldridge. Filled with such memorable performances as "Blues in the Night," "St. James Infirmary," "Lady Day," "Little Jazz" and a classic Eddie Sauter arrangement of "Summertime," this excellent CD is recommended to those not already possessing the two-fers. —*Scott Yanow*

Complete Artie Shaw, Vol. 6 (1942-1945) / Jan. 21, 1942-Jul. 3, 1945 / Bluebird ✦✦✦✦✦

The sixth in a seven-volume set of two-fer LPs that reissue all of clarinetist Artie Shaw's recordings for Victor during 1938-45, after including the last session by his fourth orchestra, concentrates on his fifth big band, a modern swing outfit from 1944-45 that featured trumpeter Roy Eldridge, pianist Dodo Marmarosa and guitarist Barney Kessel among others. Quite a few of the arrangements are memorable; among the classics are Jimmy Mundy's "Lady Day," Eddie Sauter's "Summertime," Buster Harding's "Little Jazz" and Ray Coniff's "'S Wonderful." It is difficult to believe that, with one brief exception, this was Shaw's last regularly working big band. —*Scott Yanow*

The Indispensable Artie Shaw, Vols. 5 & 6 / Nov. 23, 1944-Aug. 1, 1945 / RCA ✦✦✦✦

This two-CD set, a straight reissue of the original French RCA two-LP release, has most of the highlights from clarinetist Artie Shaw's final year with the Victor label. Not a "complete" series but more of a "best of," the two-fer features exciting solos from the clarinetist/leader, trumpeter Roy Eldridge, guitarist Barney Kessel and pianist Dodo Marmarosa and the more memorable selections including "Lady Day," "'S Wonderful," "The Grabtown Grapple," "Little Jazz," "Summertime," "Love Walked In," "Dancing on the Ceiling" and "Scuttlebutt." The set is well worth picking up by collectors who do not already have the complete LP series of Artie Shaw recordings reissued in the late '70s. —*Scott Yanow*

Spotlight on Artie Shaw: 1945 / Sep. 12, 1945-Sep. 26, 1945 / Joyce ✦✦✦

This collector's LP contains three rare broadcasts from September 1945 by Shaw's fifth big band, a unit featuring trumpeter Roy Eldridge. Three performances by Shaw's Gramercy Five and two vocals from Imogene Lynn add variety to this fine set, recorded shortly before the clarinetist gave up the big-band business altogether. —*Scott Yanow*

Mixed Bag / Sep. 1945-Feb. 1954 / Music Masters ✦✦✦

Most of the music reissued on this Music Masters CD has been out many times before. There are four titles from clarinetist Artie Shaw's 1945 big band (which include a couple of solos from the fiery trumpeter Roy Eldridge) and 14 songs recorded with studio orchestras in 1946. Of the latter, several feature the vocals of Mel Tormé and his Mel-Tones including a minor hit version of "What Is This Thing Called Love." Most of the arrangements from these dates (which were originally issued by Musicraft) are closer to dance music than jazz and the string sections play pretty rather than swing. Shaw has a few fine moments but the results are not too essential. The final number is a leftover from Shaw's other Music Master CDs, a rendition of "Sunny Side Up" by his 1954 Gramercy Five, the group that the clarinetist led just prior to retiring permanently from music. —*Scott Yanow*

With Strings / Nov. 14, 1945-Jun. 19, 1946 / Musicraft ✦✦✦

By the end of 1945, Shaw was ready to leave the big-band business and become semiretired musically. He recorded his fifth big band (which by this time no longer had trumpeter Roy Eldridge) and then broke it up. This Musicraft LP, the first of two, features Shaw with his modern swing band of 1945 (Ray Linn takes the trumpet solos) and then on some less significant dance sides from 1946. A young Mel

Tormé sings two numbers, his Mel-Tones romp on "I Got the Sun in the Morning" and the clarinetist himself is in generally good form, but one senses by the later sessions that his heart was not always in the music anymore. —*Scott Yanow*

Irresistible Swing / Nov. 14, 1945-Jun. 25, 1946 / Drive Archive ✦✦✦

The music on this budget CD is taken from clarinetist Artie Shaw's studio recordings for Musicraft. It has been reissued in more complete form elsewhere but, if found at a low price, this set is worth picking up. "The Hornet" and "The Glider" feature Shaw's 1945 Orchestra (his last major big band) playing a pair of swinging Buster Harding arrangements; there are also a pair of vocal features for Hal Stevens. The remainder of the set showcases Shaw with a studio orchestra that includes strings. The music ranges from first-class dance charts to showcases for Mel Tormé and the Mel-Tones, most notably their hit version of "What Is This Thing Called Love." —*Scott Yanow*

For You, for Me, Forever / Apr. 30, 1946-Oct. 18, 1946 / Musicraft ✦✦✦

On the second of two LPs of Shaw's recordings for Musicraft, the great clarinetist is heard with studio musicians playing superior standards and obscurities in 1946. Mel Tormé and/or his Mel-Tones are actually the stars on nine of these 15 selections, including a spirited "What Is This Thing Called Love?" The clarinetist plays well enough but often sounds as if his heart was not really in the music; at this point it was just a day's work for him. —*Scott Yanow*

Later Artie Shaw, Vol. 1 / May 31, 1949-Apr. 4, 1950 / Ajazz ✦✦✦✦

Shaw's recordings of 1949-52 remain his rarest, last issued on this collector's LP series. Having largely given up the band business by mid-1946, the clarinetist came out of semiretirement in 1949 to lead his sixth and final regularly working orchestra, but that modern bop group was a quick flop and left few recordings. *Vol. 1* (out of seven) in the *Later Artie Shaw* series has a wide variety of recordings, including two with a studio orchestra, a pair of intriguing items in which the clarinetist fronts a quartet consisting of cello, piano, bass and drums, six titles with his short-lived orchestra and two with a new Gramercy Five (featuring vocalist Mary Ann McCall and trumpeter Don Fagerquist). Although Shaw's career had become directionless, his playing remained in its prime. This "lost" music deserves to be reissued on CD. —*Scott Yanow*

Pied Piper / Dec. 1949 / First Heard ✦✦✦✦

In 1949 Shaw put together what would be his last regularly working orchestra, a modern outfit featuring such younger players as trumpeter Don Fagerquist, the tenors of Al Cohn and Zoot Sims, pianist Dodo Marmarosa and guitarist Jimmy Raney. Striking a balance between his earlier swing hits and the new bop music, Artie Shaw's new orchestra had a great deal of potential and seemed like a perfect outlet for his always-modern playing. But it stood little chance in 1949 when the big-band era was gone and his older fans wanted Shaw to put on a nostalgic show. The orchestra flopped commercially. This LP of live performances shows that the music of his last big band was excellent, swinging and well worth remembering. —*Scott Yanow*

● **1949** / 1949 / Music Masters ✦✦✦✦✦

In 1949 the swing era was already in the past and the public's enthusiasm for bebop was quickly receding. No matter, Artie Shaw decided that it was time to put together a modern big band. The venture only lasted three months, but the largely forgotten music that it performed was quite rewarding. This Musicmasters CD consists of private recordings of the barely documented orchestra, valuable performances that feature the always-modern clarinetist with an outfit that included trumpeter Don Fagerquist, a great saxophone section with the tenors of Al Cohn and Zoot Sims and guitarist Jimmy Raney. It is a real pleasure to hear Artie Shaw stretching out in this setting and a real pity that this band could not have lasted. —*Scott Yanow*

Later Artie Shaw, Vol. 2 / Apr. 4, 1950-Jul. 19, 1950 / Ajazz ✦✦✦✦

With the collapse of his short-lived bop big band in early 1950, Shaw went back into semiretirement. His recordings, heard on this LP (the second in a valuable seven-volume series), finds him with studio groups ranging from a standard big band to ballads with string sections and two jazz performances with a new Gramercy Five (this time featuring Lee Castle's trumpet and Don Lanphere's tenor). Most of these performances, however, have Shaw merely backing up commercial vocalists including Dick Haymes, Don Cherry (no relation to the trumpeter) and the Chelsea Three. —*Scott Yanow*

Later Artie Shaw, Vol. 3 / Sep. 14, 1950-Jul. 2, 1953 / Ajazz ✦✦✦✦

The third volume in this seven-LP series by the collector's label (a subsidiary of Joyce) has some real rarities, taken from a period of time when Shaw was barely active in music. He is heard with studio big bands on such songs as "Jingle Bells," "White Christmas" and "In the Still of the Night," backing singer Trudy Richards and with two versions of the Gramercy Five (but somewhat confined to accompanying vocals by June Hutton and Connie Boswell). True Artie Shaw collectors will have to get this intriguing set but more general listeners are advised to acquire his earlier recordings instead. —Scott Yanow

Later Artie Shaw, Vol. 4 / Jul. 2, 1953-Feb. 1954 / Ajazz ✦✦✦✦
The fourth in a seven-LP series documenting Artie Shaw's little-known "later" recordings has six selections featuring the clarinetist with a studio orchestra and strings, and seven more rewarding performances with his final Gramercy Five, a sextet featuring pianist Hank Jones, guitarist Tal Farlow and vibraphonist Joe Roland. Shaw had listened closely to bebop and had subtly modernized his style; now he was fully prepared to stretch out with younger players. Most of this material has not been reissued on CD. —Scott Yanow

Later Artie Shaw, Vol. 5 / Feb. 1954 / Ajazz ✦✦✦
The fifth of seven LPs in this collector's series of recordings from the post-swing era features seven lengthy performances from the clarinetist's last Gramercy Five, a boppish unit with guitarist Tal Farlow, pianist Hank Jones and vibraphonist Joe Roland that served as a perfect outlet for Shaw's creativity. It is a real shame that he did not have the will power to keep similar groups in existence for the remainder of the decade, instead choosing to quit altogether the following year. —Scott Yanow

Later Artie Shaw, Vol. 6 / Feb. 1954 / Ajazz ✦✦✦✦
The sixth in a valuable seven-LP series put out by the collector's label Ajazz focuses on Shaw's final working band, a version of the Gramercy Five that also boasts solos by pianist Hank Jones, guitarist Tal Farlow and vibraphonist Joe Roland. On such songs as "Besame Mucho," "The Grabtown Grapple," "Stop and Go Mambo" and "Love of My Life," Artie Shaw shows that he never did decline and that there was no musical reason (except his own boredom) why he chose to quit playing clarinet entirely shortly after this band broke up. All of the entries in this series are worth searching for. —Scott Yanow

★ **The Last Recordings, Vol. 1: Rare and Unreleased** / Feb. 1954-Jun. 1954 / Music Masters ✦✦✦✦✦
The first of two double-CD sets contains a healthy share of the recordings the clarinetist made with his final Gramercy Five, a unit that included pianist Hank Jones, either Tal Farlow or Joe Puma on guitar and usually Joe Roland's vibes. Unlike his longtime competitor Benny Goodman, Shaw felt perfectly comfortable with younger modernists. In fact his own clarinet playing had evolved through the years and sometimes he hints strongly at Buddy DeFranco without losing his own musical personality during these 20 performances. This is very rewarding music that makes one especially regret that Artie Shaw chose to give up the clarinet after this band ran its course. —Scott Yanow

More Last Recordings / Feb. 1954-Jun. 1954 / Music Masters ✦✦✦✦✦
The second two-CD set of recordings by Shaw's final Gramercy Five is comparable to the first. He would give up his clarinet permanently shortly after this band broke up, but the musical evidence shows that he was still very much in his prime and growing as an improviser, making his retirement a tragedy for jazz. With pianist Hank Jones, vibraphonist Joe Roland and guitarist Tal Farlow contributing strong solos and inspiration for Shaw, this cool bop music (which even has updated performances of "Begin the Beguine," "Frenesi" and "Stardust" that owe surprisingly little to the original hit versions) is quite enjoyable and creative. —Scott Yanow

Later Artie Shaw, Vol. 7 / Jun. 1954-Nov. 21, 1955 / Ajazz ✦✦✦✦
The seventh and final volume in this valuable LP series completes the Artie Shaw story only 19 years after his first recording session as a leader. There are five lengthy performances with his final Gramercy Five in June 1954 (featuring solos from pianist Hank Jones and guitarist Joe Puma) and three final performances with a string orchestra in November 1955. Shaw then became one of the very few major jazz figures to retire at his prime, a major loss to the music. This LP does show that he pretty much went out on top, still sounding quite modern. —Scott Yanow

Marlena Shaw

b. Sep. 22, 1942, New Rochelle, NY
Vocals / Blues Jazz, Ballads, Pop Jazz, Soul Jazz, Mainstream Jazz, R&B, Soul
Marlena Shaw is among the most versatile and charismatic jazz vocalists on the scene today. Her performances are marked by an artful blend of pop standards and straightahead jazz tunes. Her extroverted stage presence gives her an edge over other vocalists, and clearly, singing live before an audience is where she feels most comfortable.

After her uncle Jimmy Burgess introduced her to the recordings of Dizzy Gillespie and Miles Davis, she caught the jazz bug and purchased records by Al Hibbler, a vocalist who had a big influence on her singing style. When she was ten she performed at Harlem's Apollo Theater, and despite the enthusiastic reception she received in front of one of the world's toughest audiences, her mother refused

to let her go on the road with her uncle, a trumpet player. Shaw attended the State Teachers' College in Potsdam, NY, but later dropped out. For some time in 1963 she worked around New England with a trio led by Howard McGhee. By the mid-'60s she was performing regularly for audiences in the Catskills, Playboy clubs and other New York area clubs. In 1966, she recorded "Mercy, Mercy, Mercy" for Cadet Records, and the single sold very well for an unknown singer. The single's success, a rare vocal version of the tune, prompted executives at Cadet to encourage her to record a whole album for the label in 1967. The diversity of styles, including blues, jazz and pop standards, is reflected in the album's title, *Out of Different Bags*. Through her accountant, she was brought to the attention of bandleader Count Basie, and she ended up singing with the Basie band for four years.

In 1972, after leaving the Basie Orchestra, Shaw was the first female vocalist signed to Blue Note Records, and she toured for a while with the late Sammy Davis, Jr. Shaw recorded five albums and several singles for Blue Note, and critics likened her singing style to Dinah Washington and Sarah Vaughan. Her more recent albums include *Live at Vine Street* for PolyGram/Verve and *Love Is in Flight* in 1993 and 1994. Shaw's latest album, *Dangerous*, (1996) is her first for the Concord Jazz label. —Richard Skelly

The Best of Marlena Shaw: Blue Note Years / 1972-1976 / Blue Note ✦✦✦✦
Marlena Shaw is a middle-of-the-road R&B singer who sometimes gets associated with jazz. During 1972-76 she recorded four albums for Blue Note from which this sampler CD draws its material. Shaw certainly shows off her versatility, playing a prostitute in "Street Walkin' Woman" which is followed immediately by some gospel on "Be for Real!" A soulful singer who rarely sings a song very straight, Shaw is heard in prime form in these R&Bish settings, interpreting material from Eugene McDaniels ("Feel Like Making Love"), Bob Dorough ("But for Now"), Bernard Ighner, Marvin Gaye and Horace Silver among others. —Scott Yanow

Live at Montreux / Jul. 5, 1973 / Blue Note ✦✦
This Blue Note CD reissue is a rarity in its own way for it features the R&Bish singer Marlena Shaw in a more spontaneous setting than usual with a trio led by pianist George Gaffney at the 1973 Montreux Jazz Festival. It is not too surprising that Shaw found her greatest successes in pop/soul music for the stylized way that she bends nearly every note and overplays the lyrics (not much subtlety here) fits that idiom quite well. She does her best on Annie Ross' "Twisted" but sounds much more comfortable shouting out over R&B vamps, making this recording of limited interest from the jazz standpoint. —Scott Yanow

● **It Is Love** / 1986 / Verve ✦✦✦✦

Dangerous / Feb. 12, 1996-Feb. 13, 1996 / Concord Jazz ✦✦✦✦
After neglecting jazz in favor of more financially lucrative soul, funk and disco in the late '70s and much of the '80s, Marlena Shaw has returned to jazz with often rewarding results in the '90s. A sassy, big-voiced diva full of vitality, humor and soul, Shaw lets us know how much she missed jazz on very enthusiastic interpretations of chestnuts ranging from Benny Golson's "Whisper Not" (on which she embraces Leonard Feather's seldom-heard lyrics) to the pop standards "The Nearness of You" and "Out of This World." A most pleasant surprise is Shaw's duet with promising singer Kevin Mahogany on the Stylistics' "You Make Me Feel Brand New," a Philadelphia soul/pop ballad they successfully turn into swingin', mid-tempo jazz. —Alex Henderson

Woody Shaw

b. Dec. 24, 1944, Laurinburg, NC, d. May 10, 1989, New York, NY
Trumpet, Fluegelhorn / Hard Bop, Post-Bop
Woody Shaw was one of the top trumpeters of the 1970s and '80s, a major soloist influenced by Freddie Hubbard but more advanced harmonically who bridged the gap between hard bop and the avant-garde. Unfortunately he never broke through to greater stardom (due partly to "personal problems" and failing eyesight) and his premature death from injuries incurred after being hit by a train was a major loss. Woody Shaw grew up in Newark, NJ, where his father was a member of the Diamond Jubilee Singers. After starting on bugle, he switched to the trumpet when he was 11. Shaw left town for a tour with Rufus Jones when he was 18 and then joined Willie Bobo at a time when Bobo's band included Chick Corea. Shaw played and recorded with Eric Dolphy and, after being invited by Dolphy, travelled to Paris in 1964 just a little too late to join the late saxophonist's band. After a period in Europe playing with (among others) Bud Powell and Johnny Griffin, Shaw spent periods in the groups of Horace Silver (1965-66), Max Roach (1968-69) and Art Blakey (1973) in addition to making many recordings (some as a sideman for Blue Note) with such players as Jackie McLean, Andrew Hill and McCoy Tyner. Other than playing with Dexter Gordon in 1976, Shaw was primarily a leader from this point on, recording for Columbia (important sessions reissued in a Mosaic box set), Red, Enja, Elektra, Muse and Timeless plus two Blue Note dates co-led with Freddie Hubbard. But overshadowed throughout his career by Hub-

bard, Miles Davis, Dizzy Gillespie and later on Wynton Marsalis, Woody Shaw would never find much fame or fortune. —*Scott Yanow*

Last of the Line / Dec. 1965-Nov. 1975 / 32 Jazz ✦✦✦✦
All of the music from two Woody Shaw Muse albums (*Cassandranite* and *Love Dance*) and one selection from a 1971 date led by drummer Joe Chambers ("Medina") are reissued on this 1997 two-CD set. Trumpeter Shaw is heard near the beginning of his career on the former session, a 1965 outing with tenor saxophonist Joe Henderson and two different rhythm sections (featuring either Larry Young or Herbie Hancock on piano). Although more influenced by Freddie Hubbard at that time than he would be, Shaw's harmonically advanced style was already quite recognizable. The *Love Dance* set (from 1975) has the trumpeter joined by other forward-thinking players, including altoist Rene McLean, Billy Harper on tenor and pianist Joe Bonner. The emphasis throughout is on original material, and the music is modal-oriented while looking towards the avant-garde. A logical pairing of advanced music by one of the great jazz trumpeters. —*Scott Yanow*

Blackstone Legacy / Dec. 8, 1970-Dec. 9, 1970 / Contemporary ✦✦✦✦✦
This double LP (not yet reissued on CD) was trumpeter Woody Shaw's long-overdue official debut on record as a leader (although an earlier set would eventually surface on Muse). The young all-star septet (Shaw, Gary Bartz on alto and soprano, Bennie Maupin on tenor, bass clarinet and flute, keyboardist George Cables, both Ron Carter and Clint Houston on basses and drummer Lenny White) performs four of Shaw's originals, plus two by Cables. Despite the length of some of the numbers (only one of which is under ten-and-a-half minutes), the adventurous but quite coherent renditions always hold on to one's interest. Woody Shaw shows throughout why he was one of the pacesetters of the trumpet throughout the 1970s. —*Scott Yanow*

Song of Songs / Sep. 15, 1972+Sep. 18, 1972 / Original Jazz Classics ✦✦✦✦
This CD reissue would be recommended if only for trumpeter Woody Shaw's autobiographical liner notes which definitively sum up both this recording and his career up to 1972. Four of Shaw's originals are interpreted by a sextet also including Emanuel Boyd on flute and tenor, keyboardist George Cables, bassist Henry Franklin, drummer Woodrow Theus II, tenorman Ramon Morris (on two songs) and Bennie Maupin on tenor for "The Goat and the Archer." The music falls between hard bop, modal musings and the avant-garde. Although possessing a tone similar to Freddie Hubbard's, Woody Shaw was a more advanced player and his solos throughout the date are both original and consistently exciting. —*Scott Yanow*

The Moontrane / Dec. 11, 1974+Dec. 18, 1974 / Muse ✦✦✦✦✦
Although he never received the notoriety of Freddie Hubbard or (at the time) Chuck Mangione, Woody Shaw was one of the leading trumpeters of the 1970s. This CD reissue brings back a strong date by one of Shaw's finest units, a band including Azar Lawrence on tenor and soprano, the up-and-coming trombonist Steve Turre, keyboardist Onaje Allen Gumbs, either Buster Williams or Cecil McBee on bass, drummer Victor Lewis, Tony Waters on congas and percussionist Guilherme Franco. Although none of the group originals (best known is the leader's "Moontrane") caught on, the adventurous music still sounds stimulating more than two decades later. Recommended. —*Scott Yanow*

Little Red's Fantasy / Jun. 29, 1976 / Muse ✦✦✦✦✦
Woody Shaw was one of the great trumpeters of the 1970s. Although influenced soundwise by Freddie Hubbard, Shaw's more advanced improvisations on his modal originals were quite original and fiery. This Muse set has three of his compositions (including "In Case You Haven't Heard") and a song apiece from pianist Ronnie Mathews and bassist Stafford James; altoist Frank Strozier and drummer Eddie Moore complete the quintet. The varied originals give the musicians strong foundations for their freewheeling and spontaneous solos, making this one of Woody Shaw's better recordings. —*Scott Yanow*

Woody Shaw Concert Ensemble at the Berliner Jazztage / Nov. 6, 1976 / Muse ✦✦✦✦✦
The Woody Shaw Quintet (featuring the trumpeter/leader, altoist Rene McLean, pianist Ronnie Mathews, bassist Stafford James and drummer Louis Hayes) were joined by tenor saxophonist Frank Foster and trombonist Slide Hampton for this frequently exciting and often quite advanced Berlin concert. The obscure originals are given lengthy treatment (Joe Chambers' "Hello to the Wind" is nearly 17 minutes long) and yet there are no slow moments. The solos are uniformly creative and often quite explorative. —*Scott Yanow*

The Iron Men / Apr. 6, 1977+Apr. 13, 1977 / Muse ✦✦✦✦
This is a particularly interesting set by Woody Shaw (not yet reissued on CD) because it teams the trumpeter with the great avant-gardist Anthony Braxton and such forward-thinking players as altoist Arthur Blythe, pianist Muhal Richard Abrams, bassist Cecil McBee and drummer Joe Chambers. Highlights are versions of Eric Dolphy's "Iron Man" and Fats Waller's "Jitterbug Waltz" that are based on renditions Shaw had recorded with Dolphy back in 1963; the latter has Braxton playing clarinet. A couple of brief free improvisations by the trio of Shaw, Abrams and McBee in addition to Andrew Hill's "Symmetry" and the trumpeter's "Song of Songs" round out this continually intriguing and adventurous program. —*Scott Yanow*

★ **Rosewood** / Dec. 15, 1977-Dec. 19, 1977 / CBS ✦✦✦✦✦
This album, Woody Shaw's first for a major label, has been reissued as part of his Mosaic box set. Shaw, one of the top trumpeters of the late '60s and throughout the next decade, is heard with a sextet (either Joe Henderson or Carter Jefferson on tenor, pianist Onaje Allan Gumbs, bassist Clint Houston and drummer Victor Lewis) on two numbers and with a "concert ensemble" (which reaches as many as 14 pieces) on the other four selections. Shaw is in top form throughout, particularly on "Rosewood," "Rahsaan's Run" and "Theme for Maxine." This modal music ranks with his best work, making the Mosaic box particularly essential. —*Scott Yanow*

☆ **The Complete CBS Studio Recordings of Woody Shaw** / Dec. 15, 1977-Mar. 17, 1981 / Mosaic ✦✦✦✦✦
Between late 1977 and early 1981 trumpeter Woody Shaw recorded four albums for Columbia. This Mosaic three-CD set reissues those LPs plus one previously unissued selection. Shaw was one of the great hard-bop trumpeters, able to improvise comfortably and with creativity over difficult modal progressions and, although he had a sound that was similar to Freddie Hubbard's, he was a more advanced soloist. These performances feature him in a variety of settings ranging from a 15-piece group to a quintet. The strong supporting cast includes such fine players as tenors Joe Henderson and Carter Jefferson, altoists Gary Bartz and James Spaulding, trombonists Steve Turre and Curtis Fuller, and pianists Mulgrew Miller, Larry Willis, George Cables and Onaje Allan Gumbs. Shaw wrote the majority of the compositions but also jams on a couple of standards. This important reissue finds him at the peak of his powers. —*Scott Yanow*

Stepping Stones / Aug. 5, 1978-Aug. 6, 1978 / Columbia ✦✦✦✦
While trumpeter Woody Shaw's four studio recordings for Columbia have been reissued on CD as part of a Mosaic box set, this live session remains out of print and a bit obscure. Shaw, Carter Jefferson (doubling on tenor and soprano), pianist Onaje Allan Gumbs, bassist Clint Houston and drummer Victor Lewis stretch out on four eight-to-eleven minute group originals. The advanced hard bop gives each of the musicians plenty of space in which to express themselves, and Woody Shaw in particular is heard in prime form. —*Scott Yanow*

Woody III / 1978 / Columbia ✦✦✦✦✦
This superb LP has only been thus far reissued on CD as part of a Mosaic limited-edition three-CD box set, not counting "Escape Velocity" (a leftover track from Woody Shaw's previous live set *Stepping Stones*) which has yet to appear on CD. Woody Shaw, one of the finest trumpeters of the 1970s and '80s, heads a 12-piece group on the first half of the program ("Woody I," "Woody II" and "Woody III") that features such sidemen as tenor saxophonist Carter Jefferson, trombonists Steve Turre and Curtis Fuller, altoist James Spaulding and pianist Onaje Allan Gumbs. The flip side of the LP has a pair of other Shaw originals ("To Kill a Brick" and "Organ Grinder") plus bassist Clint Houston's "Escape Velocity." For the latter performances, Shaw (who doubles on fluegelhorn and cornet for the date) is showcased with groups ranging from a quartet to a sextet. Throughout, he is in peak form, and the strong compositions (along with some adventurous solos) make this one of Woody Shaw's most essential recordings. —*Scott Yanow*

United / 1981 / Columbia ✦✦✦✦
Of Woody Shaw's five Columbia albums (the four studio dates have been reissued on CD as a Mosaic box set), this LP is the one that sounds most like a blowing session. The trumpeter and his regular band of the period (with trombonist Steve Turre, pianist Mulgrew Miller, bassist Stafford James and drummer Tony Reedus) welcome guest altoist Gary Bartz to two of the six selections. In addition to selections by Shaw, Miller and Wayne Shorter, "What Is This Thing Called Love" and "The Greene Street Caper" (the latter an "original" closely based on "On Green Dolphin Street") are performed on this fairly straightahead and accessible yet adventurous date. Worth searching for. —*Scott Yanow*

Master of the Art / Feb. 25, 1982 / Elektra ✦✦✦✦
Recorded at the same live session that resulted in *Night Music*, this LP features trumpeter Woody Shaw's excellent quintet of the 1980s, a group also including trombonist Steve Turre, pianist Mulgrew Miller, bassist Stafford James and drummer Tony Reedus, plus guest vibraphonist Bobby Hutcherson. Still very much in prime form at the time, Shaw performs Walter Davis Jr.'s "400 Years Ago Tomorrow," Thelonious Monk's "Misterioso," the standard "Diane" and one of his best-known originals "Sweet Love of Mine." In addition, the album concludes with a brief interview during which the trumpeter mostly talks about the recording. This

excellent outing will be difficult to find but is worth searching for, as is *Night Music*. —*Scott Yanow*

Night Music / Feb. 25, 1982 / Elektra ♦♦♦♦
This out-of-print Elektra LP features the great trumpeter Woody Shaw with one of his final regular groups, a quintet with trombonist Steve Turre, pianist Mulgrew Miller, bassist Stafford James, drummer Tony Reedus and guest vibraphonist Bobby Hutcherson. Recorded at the same session that resulted in Shaw's prior Elektra release *Master of the Art*, the set features three uptempo pieces and a slightly slower "All the Things You Are." There are plenty of fine solos from the principals on this enjoyable if not quite essential outing. —*Scott Yanow*

Time Is Right / Jan. 1, 1983 / Red ♦♦♦♦♦
Although the quintet featured on this CD reissue from the Italian Red label was one of trumpeter Woody Shaw's finest, it failed to make much of an impact before breaking up. Teamed with trombonist Steve Turre, pianist Mulgrew Miller, bassist Stafford James and drummer Tony Reedus for an Italian concert, Shaw stretches out on two of his originals plus "You and the Night and the Music" and "We'll Be Together Again"; all four of the numbers clock in between 10-12 minutes apiece. High-quality advanced hard bop. —*Scott Yanow*

Setting Standards / Dec. 1, 1983 / Muse ♦♦♦♦
This Muse release (which is overdue to be reissued on CD) finds the brilliant trumpeter Woody Shaw in fine form. Heard for the only time in his career on a full set with just a rhythm trio (pianist Cedar Walton, bassist Buster Williams and drummer Victor Jones), the focus is very much on Shaw's attractive sound and his creative improvising skills. He performs four standards (including "There Is No Greater Love" and "What's New"), plus his own "Spiderman Blues" and Walton's "When Love Is New." The music is reasonably accessible and swinging yet imaginative in a subtle way. Recommended. —*Scott Yanow*

Woody Shaw with the Tone Jansa Quartet / Apr. 1985 / Timeless ♦♦♦
By 1985, trumpeter Woody Shaw's health and eyesight were starting to decline, but he still played well. This obscure effort for the Dutch Timeless label matches Shaw with four little-known Europeans (Tone Jansa on tenor, soprano and flute, pianist Renato Chicco, bassist Peter Herbert and drummer Dragan Gajic) on six of Jansa's originals. The music is tricky yet usually swinging and is worth investigating, even if it is not all that essential. —*Scott Yanow*

Bemsha Swing / Feb. 26, 1986-Feb. 27, 1986 / Blue Note ♦♦♦♦

● **Solid** / Mar. 1986 / Muse ♦♦♦♦♦
This CD serves as a perfect introduction to the memorable but always underrated trumpeter Woody Shaw, who tragically only had three years left to live. Sticking to jazz standards (including "There Will Never Be Another You," a ten-minute rendition of "It Might As Well Be Spring" and a surprisingly effective uptempo romp through "The Woody Woodpecker Song"), Shaw is heard in a quartet with pianist Kenny Barron, bassist Neil Swainson and drummer Victor Jones, leading a quintet on two numbers with the up-and-coming altoist Kenny Garrett and welcoming guest guitarist Peter Leitch to a sextet rendition of Sonny Rollins' "Solid." A gem. —*Scott Yanow*

In My Own Sweet Way / Feb. 7, 1987 / In & Out ♦♦♦♦♦
Although trumpeter Woody Shaw never really broke through to gain the recognition he deserved, he also never recorded an unworthy album. This late-period set for the German In & Out label (recorded only two years before his death) features Shaw with the Austrian drummer Alex Deutsch and a couple of talented Canadians: pianist Fred Henke and bassist Neil Swainson. They perform three standards (including Dave Brubeck's "In Your Own Sweet Way" and "Estate"), plus a pair of group originals and Theresa Trainello's "Just a Ballad for Woody." Excellent advanced hard bop. —*Scott Yanow*

Imagination / Jun. 24, 1987 / Muse ♦♦♦♦
Trumpeter Woody Shaw's final album as a leader (cut less than two years before his passing) is surprisingly upbeat. Although his health became shaky, Shaw never declined as a player, as he shows throughout the spirited quintet outing with his longtime trombonist Steve Turre, pianist Kirk Lightsey, bassist Ray Drummond and drummer Carl Allen. Other than Turre's "Steve's Blues," all of the pieces are veteran standards (including "If I Were a Bell," "Imagination" and "You and the Night and the Music"), yet they sound quite fresh and contain more than their share of subtle surprises. Recommended. —*Scott Yanow*

George Shearing

b. Aug. 13, 1919, London, England
Piano, Leader / Bop, Cool, Latin Jazz
For a long stretch of time in the 1950s and early 1960s, George Shearing had one of the most popular jazz combos on the planet—so much so that, in the usual jazz tradition of distrusting popular success, he tends to be underappreciated. Shearing's main claim to fame was the invention of a unique quintet sound, derived

from a combination of piano, vibraphone, electric guitar, bass and drums. Within this context, Shearing would play in a style he called "locked hands," which he picked up and refined from Milt Buckner's early-'40s work with the Lionel Hampton band, as well as Glenn Miller's sax section and the King Cole Trio. Stating the melody on the piano with closely knit, harmonized block chords, with the vibes and guitar tripling the melody in unison, Shearing sold tons of records for MGM and Capitol in his heyday.

The wild success of this urbane sound obscures Shearing's other great contribution during this time, for he was also a pioneer of exciting, small-combo Afro-Cuban jazz in the 1950s. Indeed, Cal Tjader first caught the Latin jazz bug while playing with Shearing, and the English bandleader also employed such esteemed congueros as Mongo Santamaria, Willie Bobo and Armando Peraza. As a composer, Shearing is best known for the imperishable, uniquely constructed bop standard "Lullaby of Birdland," as well as "Conception" and "Consternation." His solo style, though all his own, reflects the influences of the great boogie-woogie pianists and classical players, as well as those of Fats Waller, Earl Hines, Teddy Wilson, Erroll Garner, Art Tatum and Bud Powell—and fellow pianists have long admired his light, refined touch. He has also been known to play accordion and sing in a modest voice on occasion.

Shearing, who was born blind, began playing the piano at the age of three, receiving some music training at the Linden Lodge School for the Blind in London as a teenager but picking up the jazz influence from Teddy Wilson and Fats Waller 78s. In the late 1930s, he started playing professionally with the Ambrose dance band and made his first recordings in 1937 under the aegis of fellow Brit Leonard Feather. He became a star in Britain, performing for the BBC, playing a key role in the self-exiled Stephane Grappelli's London-based groups of the early 1940s, winning seven consecutive *Melody Maker* polls before emigrating in New York City in 1947 at the prompting of Feather. Once there, Shearing quickly absorbed bebop into his bloodstream, replacing Garner in the Oscar Pettiford Trio and leading a quartet in tandem with Buddy DeFranco. In 1949, he formed the first and most famous of his quintets, which included Marjorie Hyams on vibes (thus striking an important blow for emerging female jazz instrumentalists), Chuck Wayne on guitar, John Levy on bass and Denzil Best on drums. Recording briefly first for Discovery, then Savoy, Shearing settled into lucrative associations with MGM (1950-55) and Capitol (1955-69), the latter for which he made albums with Nancy Wilson, Peggy Lee and Nat Cole. He also made a lone album for Jazzland with the Montgomery Brothers (including Wes Montgomery) in 1961 and began playing concert dates with symphony orchestras.

After leaving Capitol, Shearing began to phase out his by-now-predictable quintet, finally breaking it up in 1978. He started his own label Sheba—which lasted for a few years into the early '70s—and made some trio recordings for MPS later in the decade. In the '70s, his profile had been lowered considerably, but upon signing with Concord in 1979, Shearing found himself enjoying a renaissance in all kinds of situations. He made a number of acclaimed albums with Mel Tormé, raising the singer's profile in the process, and recorded with the likes of Ernestine Anderson, Jim Hall, Marian McPartland, Hank Jones and classical French horn player Barry Tuckwell. He also recorded a number of solo piano albums where his full palette of influences come into play. He continued to play beautifully in several formats after signing with Telarc in 1992, extending what had become one of the longest, most prolific recording careers in jazz history. —*Richard S. Ginell*

The London Years 1939-1943 / Mar. 2, 1939-Dec. 21, 1943 / Hep ♦♦♦♦♦
Most of pianist George Shearing's earliest recordings are included on this enjoyable swing-oriented CD. During the war years, when he was in his early 20s, Shearing was most influenced by Teddy Wilson, Earl Hines and Art Tatum but even at that early stage, he was developing his own musical personality. A virtuoso from the start, Shearing is in consistently brilliant form on these standards, originals, and a few interesting boogie-woogie stomps. Of the 25 selections, 22 are piano solos, two are duets with drummer Carlo Krahmer, and one song ("Squeezin' the Blues") is a rare outing for Shearing on accordion; his backup group consists of Krahmer and Leonard Feather on piano. Highly recommended. —*Scott Yanow*

So Rare / Feb. 12, 1947-Jan. 31, 1949 / Savoy ♦♦♦♦
This excellent LP is a must for George Shearing fans for it has the pianist's first recordings cut in the US (eight trio sides from 1947 with either Gene Ramey or Curly Russell on bass and Cozy Cole or Denzil Best on drums) and his earliest quintet sides, eight numbers cut for the Discovery label in early 1949. Less than three weeks later Shearing's quintet would hit it big on their first MGM session with "September in the Rain." The Discovery date, which has the same personnel (vibraphonist Margie Hyams, guitarist Chuck Wayne, bassist John Levy and drummer Denzil Best), is quite appealing and the real birth of this classic group. Two songs ("Cherokee" and "Four Bars Short") are rare examples of Shearing playing jazz accordion. This album is recommended; hopefully Savoy will get around to reissuing the valuable material on CD eventually. —*Scott Yanow*

Jazz Masters 57 / Feb. 17, 1949-Mar. 26, 1954 / Verve ✦✦✦✦

All of the CDs in this extensive Verve reissue series (this is really the 57th set) are samplers designed to give listeners some of the highlights of the artist's career. The 16 titles on the album are taken from pianist George Shearing's period on MGM, the early years of his famed piano-vibes-guitar-bass-drums quintet. Highlights include the original version of his greatest hit "Lullaby of Birdland" plus "September in the Rain," "East of the Sun," "Jumpin' with Symphony Sid," "How High the Moon" and "I'll Remember April." To annoy completists, a previously unheard alternate take of "I Wished on the Moon" is included. Among the sidemen are vibraphonists Marjorie Hyams, Joe Roland and Cal Tjader and guitarists Chuck Wayne, Dick Garcia and Toots Thielemans. There is plenty of classic music on this CD; hopefully it will someday be released complete and in chronological order. —*Scott Yanow*

Lullaby of Birdland / Feb. 17, 1949-Mar. 28, 1954 / Verve ✦✦✦✦✦

This double LP from 1986, although not "complete," does a fine job of summing up the MGM recordings of the George Shearing Quintet. The popular group is heard at its best on such songs as "September in the Rain," "East of the Sun," "Conception," "Tenderly," "Pick Yourself Up" and the original version of "Lullaby of Birdland." With such sidemen as Marjorie Hyams, Don Elliott, Joe Roland, Cal Tjader or George Devins on vibes, and Chuck Wayne, Dick Evans or Toots Thielemans on guitar (and assistance on the final three of the 28 selections by either Candido or Armando Peraza on bongos), Shearing's groups were quite exciting during this era, showing stronger solo strength than they would in the 1960s although the pianist/leader was clearly the main star. This definitive collection will hopefully resurface on CD eventually. —*Scott Yanow*

George Shearing Goes Hollywood / Dec. 12, 1949-Apr. 15, 1953 / Lion ✦✦✦

A dozen of the George Shearing Quintet's recordings from the 1949-53 period (when the pianist was with the MGM label) were reissued on this late-'50s LP. Although all of the songs were originally debuted in Hollywood films, they were actually recorded by Shearing at a variety of sessions over a three-year period. Unfortunately the personnel is not given on the otherwise attractive album and even Teddi King's vocal on "It's Easy to Remember" goes uncredited. However the music is excellent with the many highlights including "I'll Remember April," "Pick Yourself Up," "They All Laughed" and "Love Is Just Around the Corner." A good sampling of music that deserves to be reissued complete and in chronological order on CD. —*Scott Yanow*

The Shearing Spell / 1955 / Capitol ✦✦✦✦

This was the first recording that George Shearing and his Quintet made for Capitol, an association that lasted up until 1969 and would result in quite a few enjoyable but now long-out-of-print LPs that have not been reissued since. At the time Shearing's popular group consisted of the leader/pianist, vibraphonist Johnny Rae, guitarist Toots Thielemans, bassist Al McKibbon, drummer Bill Clark and on some selections Armando Peraza and Willie Bobo on percussion. Their easy-listening brand of bop-based music is heard at its best on this LP on "Autumn in New York," "Out of This World," "Moonray" and "Cuban Fantasy." —*Scott Yanow*

Latin Escapade / Nov. 25, 1956 / Capitol ✦✦✦

George Shearing's popular Quintet (with vibraphonist Emil Richards, guitarist Toots Thielemans, bassist Al McKibbon and drummer Percy Brice) is joined by the congas of Armando Peraza for a variety of melodic and rhythmic pieces. Highlights of this easy-listening but enjoyable LP include "Perfidia," "Mambo with Me," "Old Devil Moon," "Cuban Love Song" and even "Poodle Mambo." —*Scott Yanow*

Shearing Piano / Nov. 1956-Sep. 1957 / Capitol ✦✦

This Capitol LP is a bit unusual for it features George Shearing (who always played with his Quintet during this period) performing a set of solo piano. Actually the results are a bit disappointing for Shearing mostly sticks to dreamy versions of ballads with the results generally closer to mood music than jazz. The music is pleasing for what it is but it could have been much more considering Shearing's technique and improvising skills. —*Scott Yanow*

The Complete Capitol Live Recordings / Mar. 8, 1958-Jul. 6, 1963 / Mosaic ✦✦✦✦✦

Pianist George Shearing, whose vibes-guitar-piano-bass-drums quintet was one of the most popular in jazz throughout the 1950s and '60s, seemed to have had a dual career while signed to Capitol. While his studio recordings often found his quintet augmented by strings, voices, brass and/or Latin percussion in performances closer to mood music (or even muzak) than jazz, his live engagements were definitely in the cool/bop vein. This Mosaic five-CD limited-edition box set brings back his five in-concert recordings, two of which are now double in length thanks to the inclusion of 13 previously unissued selections. There is more variety than expected to this program with the full quintet featured on most numbers but space also set aside for showcases by the trio, Shearing's solo piano and his regular "guest" Armando Peraza on congas. Although the sidemen include such fine players as

vibraphonist Gary Burton, Emil Richards and Warren Chiasson, guitarists Toots Thielemans (who plays harmonica on "Caravan"), Dick Garcia, John Gray and Ron Anthony, bassists Al McKibbon, Ralph Pena, Bill Yancey and Gene Cherico and drummers Percy Brice and Vernel Fournier, Shearing is the star throughout. His funny comments to the audience have also been included and the result is a classy show filled with accessible but surprisingly inventive bop-based music. —*Scott Yanow*

Latin Lace / Mar. 1958 / Capitol ✦✦✦

The second of pianist George Shearing's full-length Latin albums once again finds his quintet (with vibraphonist Emil Richards, guitarist Toots Thielemans, bassist Al McKibbon and drummer Percy Brice) being joined by the exciting congas of Armando Peraza. Most of the easy-listening melodies are from south of the border, but even the ones that aren't (such as "The Story of Love," "The Moon Was Yellow" and "It's Not for Me to Say") are given a Latinized treatment. This is nice (if rather safe) music but the LP is long out of print. —*Scott Yanow*

Latin Affair / Dec. 1958 / Capitol ✦✦✦

Pianist George Shearing's third Latin LP for Capitol is similar to his first two. Although the personnel in his popular Quintet had changed a bit (this album has vibraphonist Warren Chasen, guitarist Toots Thielemans, bassist Carl Pruitt and drummer Roy Haynes), Shearing and his guest Armando Peraza on congas remain the main soloists. The music on their melodic set includes South American melodies and swing standards; in both cases the easy-listening music is Latinized yet still influenced by bop. This enjoyable LP will be difficult to find. —*Scott Yanow*

Satin Brass / Oct. 1959 / Capitol ✦✦✦

The George Shearing Quintet (comprising piano, vibes, guitar, bass and drums) is joined by four trumpets, four trombones, two French horns and a tuba for a dozen easy-listening performances on this Capitol LP. The pianist/leader arranged the majority of the selections which include a few standards and several obscurities. Although the instrumentation might lead one to believe that this LP will contain shouting performances, actually the playing is often quite mellow and restrained with the Quintet very much in the lead throughout. Nice music but not too essential. —*Scott Yanow*

San Francisco Scene / Apr. 28, 1960 / Capitol ✦✦✦✦

George Shearing's best Capitol recordings of this period were his live Quintet performances, all of which have been reissued in a definitive Mosaic five-CD box set. This live LP (which was also reissued by the Pausa label as a 1986 album) features the pianist/leader, vibraphonist Warren Chasen, guitarist Dick Garcia, bassist Ralph Pena and drummer Vernell Fournier (with guest Armando Peraza on congas during a few tracks including a Latinized remake of "Lullaby of Birdland") all in top form. Highlights include "The Be-Bop Irishman," "Jumpin' with Symphony Sid" and "Cocktails for Two." —*Scott Yanow*

George Shearing and the Montgomery Brothers / Oct. 9, 1961 / Original Jazz Classics ✦✦✦✦

Pianist George Shearing meets up with guitarist Wes, vibraphonist Buddy and bassist Monk Montgomery on this enjoyable if slightly lightweight outing. The performances are a bit too concise at times but the CD reissue does add three extra takes to the original 11-song program and has some fine soloing by the principals. Highlights include "Love Walked In," "Love for Sale" and "The Lamp Is Low." —*Scott Yanow*

Mood Latino / 1961 / Capitol ✦✦✦

During his Capitol years, pianist George Shearing recorded several Latin-flavored albums which generally found his popular piano-vibes-guitar-bass-drums Quintet augmented by the congas of Armando Peraza. For this particular album not only is Peraza added to the group but so are a couple of other percussionists and an unidentified flutist. The Quintet sound is still quite dominant during the rhythmic easy-listening set with the music ranging from "Blue Moon" and "You and the Night and the Music" to "Jackie's Mambo" and "Say 'Si Si'." The performances on this LP have not yet been reissued on CD. —*Scott Yanow*

Jazz Moments / Jun. 20, 1962-Jun. 21, 1962 / Blue Note ✦✦✦✦

This fairly rare LP freed pianist George Shearing from the confines of his popular Quintet and showcases him in a trio with Ahmad Jamal's former sidemen (bassist Israel Crosby and drummer Vernel Fournier). Crosby, heard in his final recording, is in excellent form during these performances and receives some rare opportunities to solo. The main star as usual is the pianist, whose style was perfectly suited to the material heard on this album. Highlights include "Makin' Whoopee," "Like Someone in Love," "Symphony," "When Sunny Gets Blue" and "It Could Happen to You." This date, which was reissued on LP by Pausa in 1985, is worth searching for. —*Scott Yanow*

Jazz Concert / Feb. 15, 1963 / Capitol ✦✦✦✦

This is one of five live albums by the George Shearing Quintet that was reissued on CD in a box set by the Mosaic label. The LP has six fine performances by

Shearing's group in 1963; the vibraphonist is a young Gary Burton. The most memorable tracks include "Walkin'," "Love Walked In" and a nearly 12-minute rendition of "Love Is Just Around the Corner." Although the group always had a dominant easy-listening sound, a lot of hard-swinging often took place beneath the surface, particularly during their live sets. —*Scott Yanow*

Rare Form / Jul. 5, 1963-Jul. 6, 1963 / Capitol ✦✦✦
George Shearing and his 1963 quintet (which includes Gary Burton on vibes) are heard on a variety of spirited live performances throughout this LP. Most of the selections (highlighted by "The Sweetest Sounds," Bud Powell's "Hallucinations," "They All Laughed" and "I'll Never Smile Again") clock in around three minutes apiece although "Bop, Look and Listen" stretches out to over eight minutes. This is the fifth of five live performances by the Shearing Quintet to be reissued as part of a definitive Mosaic CD box set. —*Scott Yanow*

As Requested / 1972 / Sheba ✦✦✦
After pianist George Shearing's longtime association with Capitol ended in 1969, he formed his own Sheba label and started to gradually de-emphasize his quintet. On the fifth of Sheba's seven LPs (none of which have been reissued on CD yet), the George Shearing Quintet (with the exception of a specially assembled group gathered for an MPS record in 1974) is heard on records for the final time. The music is typically easy-listening with three- to five-minute versions of such songs as "I'll Never Smile Again," "Over the Rainbow," "Moon Ray" and current pop songs "Close to You" and "We've Only Just Begun" among others. With vibraphonist Charlie Shoemake and guitarist Ron Anthony in the group, the Quintet was not without interest, but it was clearly running out of gas. —*Scott Yanow*

My Ship / Jun. 25, 1974 / Polydor ✦✦✦✦
This solo piano set by George Shearing (which has been reissued on CD through Polygram) is quite eccentric and unpredictable. Freed from the constraints of his popular Quintet, Shearing lets his imagination loose on songs ranging from "My Ship," "Happy Days Are Here Again," "The Entertainer" (which is turned into jazz after a rag beginning), "Londonberry Air," and unfortunately "Send in the Clowns," on which he makes the mistake of singing. Some of the classical allusions are a bit too cute, but Shearing's wit and charm eventually win one over. —*Scott Yanow*

Light Airy and Swinging / Jul. 23, 1974-Jul. 24, 1974 / MPS ✦✦✦✦
George Shearing, after over two decades as leader of his popular Quintet, was largely taken for granted as a pianist. His trio recordings for MPS in the mid-'70s did a lot to salvage and restore his former reputation as a virtuoso and a distinctive player. On this trio set with bassist Andy Simpkins and drummer Stix Hooper, Shearing fully investigates a variety of superior standards, particularly "Speak Low," Johnny Mandel's "Emily" and "Beautiful Friendship" which are given the most extensive explorations of the eight songs; only "Love Walked In" is a holdover from the quintet days. This enjoyable LP is long overdue to be reissued on CD. —*Scott Yanow*

The Reunion / Apr. 11, 1976 / Pausa ✦✦✦✦✦
A wonderful duo release from 1976 with pianist George Shearing collaborating with violinist Stephane Grappelli. Shearing's sessions are usually more introspective and light than upbeat and hot, but Grappelli's soaring, exuberant violin solos seem to put a charge into Shearing, who responds with some of his hottest playing in many years. —*Ron Wynn*

Getting in the Swing of Things / Sep. 19, 1979-Sep. 21, 1979 / Pausa ✦✦✦✦
This particular George Shearing Trio (with guitarist Louis Stewart and bassist Niels Pedersen) recorded three albums for MPS during 1977-79 and provided an excellent outlet for the brilliant pianist just prior to his association with the Concord label. The Pausa reissue LP has the trio's renditions of five standards and four obscure originals including two ("Consternation" and "G & G") by Shearing. His renditions of "Don't Get Around Much Anymore" and "This Can't Be Love" are most memorable among these generally swinging tracks. —*Scott Yanow*

● **Blues Alley and Jazz** / Oct. 1979 / Concord Jazz ✦✦✦✦✦
Pianist George Shearing started a productive ten-year association with the Concord label with this live set, a duo outing matching him with the brilliant bassist Brian Torff. Their performances are virtuosic, intuitive, full of sly wit and always swinging; it is surprising that Torff did not become more famous. The close interaction between the two masterful musicians on such numbers as Billy Taylor's "One for the Woofer," "The Masquerade Is Over" and a humorous "Lazy River" are quite impressive as is Shearing's surprisingly effective vocal on "This Couldn't Be the Real Thing." This CD is recommended. —*Scott Yanow*

Two for the Road / Jun. 1980 / Concord Jazz ✦✦✦✦✦
For this ballad-oriented set, singer Carmen McRae is accompanied during a duet performance by pianist George Shearing. "Ghost of a Chance," "More Than You Know," "Ghost of Yesterday" and "What Is There to Say" are fairly memorable, although the lack of tempo variation (only "Gentleman Friend" is uptempo) makes the set fall short of classic status. —*Scott Yanow*

On a Clear Day / Aug. 1980 / Concord Jazz ✦✦✦✦✦
George Shearing's second Concord album, a set of duets with bassist Brian Torff like the previous *Blues Alley Jazz*, is the equal of the first. The close communication between the duo, and their ability to think fast and react to each other immediately, makes it possible for them to uplift such songs as "Love for Sale," "On a Clear Day," "Lullaby of Birdland" and even "Happy Days Are Here Again." Brilliant music. —*Scott Yanow*

Alone Together / Mar. 1981 / Concord Jazz ✦✦✦
Pianists George Shearing and Marian McPartland, both originally from England, teamed up for this polite but swinging affair. In addition to an original apiece and a collaboration, the duo is heard on seven standards and the results are quite tasteful, as one would expect from these fine players. Few surprises occur but the results are pleasing. —*Scott Yanow*

First Edition / Sep. 1981 / Concord Jazz ✦✦✦✦
This tasteful set matches together pianist George Shearing and guitarist Jim Hall in a program of duets. The fresh material (two originals apiece by Shearing and Hall, the obscure "I See Nothing to Laugh About" and just three standards challenge the pair and their quiet and subtle styles match together well. The pianist's tributes to Antonio Carlos Jobim and Tommy Flanagan are among the more memorable pieces in this interesting and somewhat unexpected musical collaboration. —*Scott Yanow*

Top Drawer / Mar. 1983 / Concord Jazz ✦✦✦✦✦
A year after their first meeting on record, pianist George Shearing and singer Mel Tormé (this time with Don Thompson on bass) had an equally successful joint recording. The material is often a bit offbeat (including the obscure swing song "Shine on Your Shoes," "How Do You Say Auf Wiedersehen" and the early bop vocal "What's This") but there are also inventive remakes of "Stardust" and "Hi Fly" along with two instrumentals: "Oleo" and a Shearing piano solo on "Away in the Manger." Obviously this CD is full of surprises; all of the Tormé-Shearing Concord sessions (which bring out the best in both of the principals) are well worth acquiring. —*Scott Yanow*

Live at the Cafe Carlyle / Jan. 1984 / Concord Jazz ✦✦✦✦
Don Thompson spent several years as George Shearing's bassist and this album is his best recording with the veteran pianist. Thompson, who plays second piano on Herbie Hancock's "Tell Me a Bedtime Story," jams with strong intuition and consistent swing, easily picking up on Shearing's musical directions during such songs as "Pent Up House," "The Shadow of Your Smile," "Cheryl" and a couple of originals. Shearing, who takes "I Cover the Waterfront" as a piano solo, had his career rejuvenated during his years on Concord through stimulating musical encounters such as this one. Fine music. —*Scott Yanow*

An Elegant Evening / May 1985 / Concord Jazz ✦✦✦
This collaboration by pianist George Shearing and vocalist Mel Tormé differs from most of their others in that the performances are duets (rather than with bass and occasional drums) and the repertoire sticks exclusively to ballads. With the exception of the closing "You're Driving Me Crazy" (which is taken at a medium bounce), all of the tunes are performed at slow tempos. The lack of variety and the use of some songs from outside of jazz (including "Last Night When We Were Young" and "Brigg Fair") lower the value of this CD to jazz listeners, who are advised to get the other Tormé-Shearing sets first, but Shearing does play well, and Tormé displays some beautiful long tones. —*Scott Yanow*

Grand Piano / May 1985 / Concord Jazz ✦✦✦
George Shearing recorded frequently while on Concord but this was his first full-length session of unaccompanied solos for the label. Most of the ten selections are interpreted as ballads (Shearing takes an effective vocal on his original "Imitations") but he does cook a bit on "Nobody Else but Me" and "Easy to Love." However the emphasis is on slow thoughtful tempos and introspective improvising. —*Scott Yanow*

Plays Music of Cole Porter / Jan. 1986 / Concord Jazz ✦✦✦
Released as part of Concord's Concerto subsidiary, this unusual release matches together pianist George Shearing with the classical French horn player Barry Tuckwell for a set of 11 Cole Porter songs. Five selections use a full string section, two are performed with a quartet and four others are duets by Shearing and Tuckwell. In general Tuckwell does not improvise but Shearing's arrangements give a jazz feel to all of the performances and make the music accessible (if not really essential) to both classical and jazz listeners. —*Scott Yanow*

More Grand Piano / Oct. 1986 / Concord Jazz ✦✦✦✦
This was a very spontaneous session. For his second solo piano date for Concord, George Shearing picked out ten songs while he was at the studio and, without any real prior planning, simply played. The results are consistently enjoyable as Shearing performs some of his favorite songs. A few of the tunes (such as "You Don't Know What Love Is" and "East of the Sun") had long been part of his repertoire but

some of the other songs (such as "My Silent Love," an unusual reworking of "Change Partners" and "Dream") are full of surprises. An excellent outing. —*Scott Yanow*

Breakin' Out / May 1987 / Concord Jazz ✦✦✦✦
Most of George Shearing's recordings for Concord feature the pianist with his regular duo or trio. This release is different for the great pianist is matched up with bassist Ray Brown (who he had first played with in 1948) and drummer Marvin "Smitty" Smith. The nine songs they perform include four by Duke Ellington, Leonard Feather's "Twelve Tone Blues," Bud Powell's exciting "Hallucinations," two standards and Shearing's own down-home "Break Out the Blues." The music is as rewarding and swinging as one would expect from this lineup. —*Scott Yanow*

Dexterity / Nov. 1987 / Concord Jazz ✦✦✦✦✦
For his first tour of Japan in 24 years, pianist George Shearing worked for the initial time with bassist Neil Swainson who soon afterward became a regular member of his duo. This Concord CD features Shearing and Swainson performing a variety of material including Charlie Parker's "Dexterity," "You Must Believe in Spring," a traditional Japanese melody and a couple of ballads. In addition, singer Ernestine Anderson sits in with the group on "As Long As I Live" and a typically soulful "Please Send Me Someone to Love" before the duo concludes the show (recorded at the second annual Fujitsu-Concord Jazz Festival) with a five-song Duke Ellington medley. A well-rounded and consistently enjoyable program. —*Scott Yanow*

The Spirit of 1776 / Mar. 1988 / Concord Jazz ✦✦✦✦
George Shearing and Hank Jones have always been very well-rounded pianists fully capable of playing unaccompanied solos. Their unique matchup as a two-piano duo on this Concord release works surprisingly well for the two pianists manage to stay out of each other's way and the ensembles are not overcrowded. The pianist's tackle colorful material including "Angel Eyes," Thelonious Monk's "I Mean You," an original apiece, Mary Lou Williams' "Lonely Moments," "Star Eyes" and "Confirmation," and the results are swinging and tasteful. This somewhat obscure Concord CD is worth investigating. —*Scott Yanow*

Perfect Match / May 1988 / Concord Jazz ✦✦✦✦
Pianist George Shearing and singer Ernestine Anderson (who had teamed up briefly at the 1987 Fujitsu-Concord Jazz Festival) collaborated on this full-length Concord release. With strong assistance from bassist Neil Swainson and drummer Jeff Hamilton, Shearing and Anderson mostly stick to standards and their versions uplift the veteran songs. "Body and Soul" is taken as a vocal-piano duet while "The Best Thing for You" is given an instrumental treatment. Other highlights include Anderson's vocals on "I'll Take Romance," a heartfelt "I Remember Clifford," "On the Sunny Side of the Street" and "Some Other Time." An excellent outing for all concerned. —*Scott Yanow*

George Shearing in Dixieland / Feb. 1989 / Concord Jazz ✦✦
This promising effort is a major disappointment. Pianist George Shearing planned to revisit his roots in Dixieland and swing but he hedged his bets. Despite having an impressive septet with such players as cornetist Warren Vache, Ken Peplowski on tenor, trombonist George Masso and clarinetist Kenny Davern, Shearing wrote out most of the ensembles, taking away from the spontaneity and potential excitement of the music. Despite the interesting repertoire (ranging from "Truckin'," "Honeysuckle Rose" and "Jazz Me Blues" to "Take Five," "Desafinado" and even a Dixiefied "Lullaby of Birdland"), this date falls far short of its potential. —*Scott Yanow*

Piano / May 1989 / Concord Jazz ✦✦✦
This relaxed solo set features the great pianist George Shearing playing 14 songs; some of them (such as Mel Tormé's "Daisy," "Thinking of You," "Miss Invisible" and two of Shearing's originals) are quite obscure. The emphasis is on slower tempos and relaxed improvising but Shearing's distinctive solos and subtle creativity hold on to one's interest throughout. A tasteful set. —*Scott Yanow*

I Hear a Rhapsody: Live at the Blue Note / Feb. 27, 1992-Feb. 29, 1992 / Telarc ✦✦✦✦✦
This excellent trio set by George Shearing with bassist Neil Swainson and drummer Grady Tate finds the veteran pianist still in prime form. The repertoire mostly consists of challenging material and tunes not overplayed by Shearing throughout the years. The musical communication between the players on such tunes as "Bird Feathers," "The End of a Love Affair," "The Duke," "The Masquerade Is Over" and an original apiece by Shearing and Swainson is very impressive and the pianist's solos are typically distinctive. This CD (Shearing's debut on the Telarc label) is a fine example of George Shearing's still-viable playing as he neared his mid-70s. —*Scott Yanow*

Walkin'-Live at the Blue Note / Feb. 27, 1992-Feb. 29, 1992 / Telarc ✦✦✦✦✦
Shearing is often in joyous form on the uptempo tracks of this well-paced trio date. Highlights include such bop classics as "That's Earl, Brother," Bud Powell's "Celia"

and "Subconscious Lee" along with a couple of familiar blues. In contrast the ballads are generally rather melancholy affairs with the pianist wringing as much emotion as possible out of each note. Neil Swainson contributes fluid bass solos and alert accompaniment while Grady Tate plays supportive drums. Shearing (in his early 70s at the time of this recording) is heard near his creative peak throughout this consistently enjoyable live set. —*Scott Yanow*

How Beautiful Is Night / Sep. 1992 / Telarc ✦✦
George Shearing recorded many mood albums with strings during the 1950s (at the same time as his more jazz-oriented Quintet albums) and this CD is a throwback to that era. Robert Farnon's writing for the 29-piece string orchestra is unremittingly pretty and filled with overblown drama. Many of the selections come across as sickly sweet with "Lady Be Good" (which is turned into a saccharine waltz) being the low point. Shearing plays well enough and four of the selections bring back the sound of his famous quintet, but it is not enough to save this misfire. —*Scott Yanow*

That Shearing Sound / Feb. 14, 1994-Feb. 16, 1994 / Telarc ✦✦✦✦
This was pianist George Shearing's first recording in a piano-vibes-guitar-bass-drums quintet since he broke up his original group in 1978 after 30 years of steady work; Shearing sounds surprisingly inspired throughout. With guitarist Louis Stewart, vibraphonist Steve Nelson, bassist Neil Swainson and drummer Dennis Mackrel, Shearing explores such vintage Quintet standards as "East of the Sun" and "I'll Never Smile Again" along with two Horace Silver compositions, a pair of his own songs ("Conception" and his biggest hit "Lullaby of Birdland") and a variety of other suitable material. The music ranges from easy-listening to hard-driving bebop. The sound of the George Shearing Quintet remains as appealing as ever. —*Scott Yanow*

Jack Sheldon

b. Nov. 30, 1931, Jacksonville, FL
Trumpet, Vocals / Bop
One of the great jokesters in jazz (whose spontaneous monologues are as hilarious as they are tasteless), Jack Sheldon's personality has sometimes overshadowed his excellent trumpet playing and effective vocals. Sheldon started playing professionally at age 13. He moved to Los Angeles in 1947, joined the Air Force and played in military bands. After his discharge, Sheldon became a popular figure on the West Coast, playing and recording with many top musicians including Jimmy Giuffre, Herb Geller, Wardell Gray, Stan Kenton, Benny Goodman, Curtis Counce and Art Pepper. He worked as an actor in the 1960s (including starring in the short-lived television series *Run Buddy Run*), was seen nightly on *The Merv Griffin Show* and in the 1970s and '80s he performed with Benny Goodman, Bill Berry's big band, in the studios and with his own groups. Into the mid-'90s Jack Sheldon (who often uses a big band arranged by Tom Kubis) remains quite active in the Los Angeles area, recording regularly for Concord and his Butterfly label. —*Scott Yanow*

Jack Sheldon and His All Star Band / Jul. 19, 1957-Sep. 5, 1957 / GNP ✦✦✦✦
Although the liner notes to this album state that these two sessions were Jack Sheldon's first as a leader, he actually led two full sets for Jazz West during 1954 and 1956, plus three titles for Pacific Jazz in '55. However, this was the initial album to gain wide recognition and helped to introduce the L.A.-based trumpeter's talents to the East Coast. Five selections feature Sheldon with a ten-piece band arranged by Lennie Niehaus and some have spots for valve trombonist Stu Williamson, pianist Pete Jolly and baritonist Billy Root. The later session features the writing of Paul Moer and such fine soloists as trumpeter Chet Baker (in a rare sideman outing for another trumpeter), altoists Art Pepper and Herb Geller, tenorman Harold Land and valve trombonist Williamson. High-quality and consistently swinging West Coast jazz. —*Scott Yanow*

Jack Sheldon Presents the Entertainers / Mar. 1964+Mar. 1, 1965 / V.S.O.P. ✦✦✦
The recording quality of the two concerts that comprise this CD is far from optimal, but there is enough good music and nutty humor to make it worth acquiring. Trumpeter Jack Sheldon has four vocals, including "Born to Lose," which has a mostly humorous monologue; trombonist Frank Rosolino scats and yodels briefly on a speedy "Pennies from Heaven"; Johnny Mercer drops by to sing "Charade" and an original blues about the band; all three take their turns on "How Long, How Long Blues"; and there are four instrumentals that also feature guitarist Howard Roberts. None of the boppish music is all that essential, and there are some overly loose moments, but the high spirits of the date (which also includes bassist Joe Mondragon, either Shelly Manne or Stan Levey on drums and rhythm guitarist Jack Marshall) generally overcomes the recording quality. —*Scott Yanow*

Angel Wings / Feb. 21, 1980-Feb. 22, 1980 / Atlas ✦✦✦
Other than a set for Bill Berry's Beez label, this obscure instrumental Japanese LP was trumpeter Jack Sheldon's first as a leader since 1969. Mostly of interest due to

the pairing of Sheldon with altoist Art Pepper, the Los Angeles date (with pianist Milcho Leviev, bassist Tony Dumas and drummer Carl Burnette) finds the group mostly sticking to jazz standards (including Gigi Gryce's "Minority," which is mistakenly attributed to Pepper). Few fireworks occur, although the musicians play well, particularly on Pepper's "Angel Wings," "Jack's Blues" and "Broadway." —*Scott Yanow*

Playin' It Straight / Nov. 13, 1980-Nov. 14, 1980 / Real Time ✦✦✦✦
This very well recorded LP (which is out of print) helped end a shortage of albums by trumpeter Jack Sheldon. He is heard with top musicians taken from the *Tonight Show* band (tenor Pete Christlieb, altoist Tommy Newsom, pianist Alan Broadbent, guitarist Mundell Lowe, bassist Joel DiBartolo and drummer Ed Shaughnessy) performing Don Menza's "Playing It Straight," the jam tune "Steeple Chase" and six familiar standards. Sheldon, who sticks here exclusively to playing trumpet, sounds perfectly at home in the boppish setting, and all of the musicians solo with plenty of spirit and swing. —*Scott Yanow*

● **Stand By for Jack Sheldon** / Mar. 1983 / Concord Jazz ✦✦✦✦✦
This is one of Jack Sheldon's better recordings. His trumpet solos (accompanied by pianist Ross Tompkins, bassist Ray Brown and drummer Jake Hanna) are consistently excellent and his five vocals, although not containing the humor one generally hears in his live performances, are also well done. The ten standards and ballads are given swinging and melodic treatment, making this a fine all-round showcase for Sheldon. —*Scott Yanow*

Playing for Change / May 24, 1986-May 25, 1986 / Uptown ✦✦✦✦

Hollywood Heroes / Sep. 1987 / Concord Jazz ✦✦✦✦✦
This is the Jack Sheldon record to get. Sheldon, who is assisted by a swinging four-piece rhythm section comprising guitarist Doug MacDonald, pianist Ray Sherman, bassist Dave Stone and drummer Gene Estes, is in jubilant form, whether playing colorful trumpet solos or taking humorous vocals. The seven standards (which include memorable versions of "The Joint Is Jumpin'," "Rosetta" and "I Thought About You" along with a touching rendition of "Poor Butterfly") serve as perfect outlets for Sheldon's brand of witty swing. Highly recommended. —*Scott Yanow*

On My Own / Sep. 12, 1991 / Concord Jazz ✦✦✦✦✦
Frequently during the 1990s, trumpeter/vocalist Jack Sheldon and pianist Ross Tompkins appeared as a duo in Los Angeles-area clubs. Their duet CD is most notable for Sheldon's singing, which was in prime form during the period. The emphasis is on ballad renditions of swing standards, although there are a few hotter numbers. Highlights include "This Love of Mine," "Blues in the Night," "How About You," a "New York Medley" and "Laughing on the Outside." —*Scott Yanow*

Sings / Sep. 1, 1992 / Butterfly ✦✦✦

Jack Is Back! / 1995 / Butterfly ✦✦
The title of this CD for the tiny Butterfly label makes little sense, for trumpeter-vocalist Jack Sheldon had not previously retired or disappeared. The date finds Sheldon joined by his big band (with arrangements provided by Tom Kubis) but the personnel listing does not bother to give each individual's instruments. Actually, the leader is the dominant force on each of the selections, but, with the exception of his "There's No Fool like an Old Fool" and "Too Blue," the repertoire is a bit tired and predictable; dredging up "New York, New York" was not too necessary, and the "comedy" by Merv Griffin and Pat McCormick on "How About You" is fairly weak. Sheldon does play and sing well in spots, but more thought should have gone into making this so-so effort something special. —*Scott Yanow*

Archie Shepp

b. May 24, 1937, Fort Lauderdale, FL

Tenor Saxophone, Soprano Saxophone / Avant-Garde, Free Jazz, Hard Bop
Archie Shepp has been at various times a feared firebrand and radical, soulful throwback and contemplative veteran. He was viewed in the '60s as perhaps the most articulate and disturbing member of the free generation, a published playwright willing to speak on the record in unsparing, explicit fashion about social injustice and the anger and rage he felt. His tenor sax solos were searing, harsh and unrelenting, played with a vivid intensity. But in the '70s, Shepp employed a fatback/swing-based R&B approach, and in the '80s he mixed straight bebop, ballads and blues pieces displaying little of the fury and fire from his earlier days. Shepp studied dramatic literature at Goddard College, earning his degree in 1959. He played alto sax in dance bands and sought theatrical work in New York. But Shepp switched to tenor, playing in several free-jazz bands. He worked with Cecil Taylor, co-led groups with Bill Dixon and played in the New York Contemporary Five with Don Cherry and John Tchicai. He led his own bands in the mid-'60s with Roswell Rudd, Bobby Hutcherson, Beaver Harris and Grachan Moncur III. His Impulse albums included poetry readings and quotes from James Baldwin and Malcolm X. Shepp's releases sought to paint an aural picture of African-American life, and included compositions based on incidents like Attica or folk sayings. He

also produced plays in New York, among them "The Communist" in 1965, and "Lady Day: A Musical Tragedy" in 1972 with trumpeter/composer Cal Massey. But starting in the late '60s, the rhetoric was toned down and the anger began to disappear from Shepp's albums. He substituted a more celebratory, and at times reflective, attitude. Shepp turned to academia in the late '60s, teaching at SUNY in Buffalo, then the University of Massachusetts. He was named an associate professor there in 1978. Shepp toured and recorded extensively in Europe during the '80s, cutting some fine albums with Horace Parlan, Niels-Henning Orsted Pedersen and Jasper van't Hof. He has recorded extensively for Impulse, Byg, Arista/Freedom, Phonogram, Steeple Chase, Denon, Enja, EPM and Soul Note among others over the years. Unfortunately his tone declined from the mid-1980s on (his highly original sound was his most important contribution to jazz) and Archie Shepp is a less significant figure in the 1990s than one might hope. —*Ron Wynn and Scott Yanow*

Archie Shepp—Bill Dixon Quartet / Oct. 1962 / Savoy ✦✦✦✦

The New York Contemporary Five / Nov. 11, 1963 / Storyville ✦✦✦✦✦
This historically significant CD has ten of the 11 selections recorded by the New York Contemporary Five (and originally issued on two separate LPs) on November 11, 1963. The short-lived group, which consists of cornetist Don Cherry, altoist John Tchicai, Archie Shepp on tenor, bassist Don Moore and drummer J.C. Moses, was avant-garde for the period, influenced most by Ornette Coleman's Quartet; the participation of Coleman's cornetist certainly helped. However Tchicai (although sometimes hinting at Coleman) had a different approach than Ornette Coleman and it was obvious that Shepp had already developed his own original voice and was the group's most passionate soloist. Together this very interesting quintet (which would soon break up) performs pieces by Ornette Coleman, Thelonious Monk (short melodic renditions of "Monk's Mood" and "Crepuscule with Nellie"), Bill Dixon, Tchicai, Shepp and Cherry. —*Scott Yanow*

Archie Shepp in Europe / Nov. 15, 1963 / Delmark ✦✦✦✦✦
The New York Contemporary Five was a co-op that in 1963 featured such up-and-coming talent as tenor saxophonist Archie Shepp (who had previously been with Cecil Taylor), altoist John Tchicai, cornetist Don Cherry (well-known due to his association with Ornette Coleman), bassist Don Moore and drummer J.C. Moses. Their music was a bridge between the innovations of Ornette Coleman's Quartet and the avant-garde explosion of 1965. The performances of originals by Cherry, Coleman, Shepp and Tchicai, in addition to Thelonious Monk's "Crepuscule with Nellie," are not flawless but are generally quite fascinating as these young talents did what they could to break through the "rules" of bebop and create new music and sounds. A historic set. —*Scott Yanow*

The House I Live In / Nov. 21, 1963 / Steeple Chase ✦✦✦✦
This is a fascinating release. Tenor saxophonist Archie Shepp would not burst upon the US avant-garde scene until 1964-65 but here he is featured at a Danish concert with the great cool-bop baritonist Lars Gullin and a top-notch straightahead rhythm section (pianist Tete Montoliu, bassist Niels Pedersen and drummer Alex Riel). The quintet stretches out on four lengthy standards (including "Sweet Georgia Brown" and a 19-minute rendition of "You Stepped Out of a Dream") and it is particularly interesting to hear the reactions of the other musicians to Shepp's rather free flights; at a couple of points Gullin tries to copy him. An important historical release. —*Scott Yanow*

★ **Four for Trane** / Aug. 10, 1964 / Impulse! ✦✦✦✦✦
Tenor saxophonist Archie Shepp's debut for Impulse is a classic. This LP (reissued on an Impulse CD in 1997) features the avant-garde innovator playing four of John Coltrane's compositions, including "Cousin Mary" and "Naima," along with his own "Rufus." To his great credit, Shepp never sounded like Coltrane—his raspy tone was much closer to a free version of Ben Webster—and he is heard in top form on this studio date with a sextet also including fluegelhornist Alan Shorter, trombonist Roswell Rudd, altoist John Tchicai, bassist Reggie Workman and drummer Charles Moffett. Shepp's interpretations of the Coltrane tunes are quite fresh and original. Highly recommended to open-eared listeners. —*Scott Yanow*

Fire Music / Feb. 16, 1965+Mar. 28, 1965 / Impulse! ✦✦✦✦
This particular early Archie Shepp recording (reissued on CD) has its strong moments, although it is a bit erratic. Four selections utilize an advanced sextet. Of these songs, "Hambone" has overly repetitive and rather monotonous riffing by the horns behind the soloists, and Shepp's bizarre exploration of "The Girl from Ipanema" gets tedious, but the episodic "Los Olvidaos" is quite colorful, and the tenorman sounds fine on a spacey rendition of "Prelude to a Kiss." "Malcolm, Malcolm-Semper Malcolm" has Shepp reading a brief poem for the fallen Malcolm X before he jams effectively on tenor in a trio with bassist David Izenzon and drummer J.C. Moses. The CD is rounded out by a "bonus" cut not on the original LP—a live version of "Hambone" that is much more interesting than the earlier rendition. Overall, this set, even with its faults, is recommended. —*Scott Yanow*

● **On This Night** / Mar. 9, 1965+Aug. 12, 1965 / Impulse! ◆◆◆◆◆
Tenor saxophonist Archie Shepp made his mark early in his career and reached heights that he had trouble attaining later on. This Impulse reissue gathers together all of Shepp's recordings from two dates, some of which were originally scattered on a variety of LPs. Highlights include the three very different versions of the explosive "The Chased," a reworking of "In a Sentimental Mood" and "The Original Mr. Sonny Boy Williamson." Shepp's quintet also features vibraphonist Bobby Hutcherson who is heard early in his career. This passionate music is not for the fainthearted. —*Scott Yanow*

Live in San Francisco / Feb. 19, 1966 / Impulse! ◆◆◆◆
This out-of-print Impulse LP features the fiery tenor Archie Shepp with his regularly working group of the period, a quintet also featuring trombonist Roswell Rudd, drummer Beaver Harris and both Donald Garrett and Lewis Worrell on basses. Although two pieces (Shepp's workout on piano on the ballad "Sylvia" and his recitation on "The Wedding") are departures, the quintet sounds particularly strong on Herbie Nichols' "The Lady Sings the Blues" and "Wherever June Bugs Go" while Shepp's ballad statement on "In a Sentimental Mood" is both reverential and eccentric. —*Scott Yanow*

Three for a Quarter, One for a Dime / Feb. 19, 1966 / Impulse! ◆◆◆◆◆
This is an LP long overdue to be reissued on CD. Archie Shepp's main contributions to jazz were an adventurous spirit and the introduction of a forceful, raspy sound that, even with its debt to Ben Webster, was quite original—unlike many of his contemporaries in the avant-garde, he owed nothing to John Coltrane. Shepp and his regular quintet of 1966, which also includes trombonist Roswell Rudd, drummer Beaver Harris, and bassists Donald Garrett and Lewis Worrell, really stretch out on this live blowout, playing continuously for nearly 33 minutes. There is some solo space for his sidemen, but Shepp dominates the performance, and his emotional style and endurance are in peak form. Intense and rewarding music. —*Scott Yanow*

Mama Too Tight / Aug. 1966 / Impulse! ◆◆◆◆◆
Tenor saxophonist Archie Shepp's Impulse recordings are among the most rewarding of his career. This LP matches his raspy, explorative tenor with trumpeter Tommy Turrentine, trombonists Roswell Rudd and Grachan Moncur, clarinetist Perry Robinson, Howard Johnson on tuba, bassist Charlie Haden and drummer Beaver Harris. Although three of the four songs (including the nearly 19-minute "A Portrait of Robert Thompson," which uses a section of "Prelude to a Kiss") are eulogies for fallen heroes, the music goes through a wide variety of emotions, makes strong use of the blues, and is both adventurous and often surprisingly accessible. —*Scott Yanow*

The Magic of Ju-Ju / Apr. 26, 1967 / Impulse! ◆◆◆◆◆
For this Impulse LP (not yet reissued on CD), innovative avant-garde tenor Archie Shepp is well featured on his four originals, including the eighteen-and-a-half minute side-long title cut. Assisted by the trumpets of Martin Banks and Michael Zwerin, bassist Reggie Workman and five drummer/percussionists (Beaver Harris, Norman Connors, Ed Blackwell, Frank Charles and Dennis Charles), Shepp is heard in peak form throughout the album, hinting at the past while often playing with great intensity. —*Scott Yanow*

☆ **Live at the Donaueschingen Music Festival** / Oct. 21, 1967 / MPS ◆◆◆◆◆
This is an exciting album. The important tenor Archie Shepp and his 1967 group—with both Roswell Rudd and Grachan Moncur on trombones, bassist Jimmy Garrison and drummer Beaver Harris—romp through the continuous forty-three-and-a-half-minute "One for the Trane" before an enthusiastic audience at a German music festival. Although he improvises very freely and with great intensity, Shepp surprised the crowd by suddenly bursting into a spaced-out version of "The Shadow of Your Smile" near the end of this memorable performance. On the whole, this very spirited set represents avant-garde jazz at its peak and Archie Shepp at his finest. —*Scott Yanow*

The Way Ahead / Jan. 29, 1968 / Impulse! ◆◆◆◆

Live at the Pan-African Festival / Jul. 29, 1969-Jul. 30, 1969 / Affinity ◆◆◆◆
Archie Shepp probably led more BYG recordings than anyone else. The first of his BYG's has been reissued as *Live at the Pan African Festival*. The Pan African Festival in Algiers served as a great realization of art and culture for many of the participants and on this recording we hear Shepp, Clifford Thornton, and Grachan Moncur III in an impromptu jam ("Brotherhood at Ketcha") with various native Algerian percussionists and "horn" men ... Any study of Shepp makes listening to all of his BYG recordings essential. —*Bob Rusch, Cadence*

Yasmina: A Black Woman / Aug. 12, 1969 / Affinity ◆◆◆◆
There is some intriguing music on this out-of-print Affinity LP. Tenor saxophonist Archie Shepp met up with members of the Chicago avant-garde school for the first time, including Art Ensemble of Chicago members Lester Bowie, Roscoe Mitchell and Malachi Favors, on the lengthy "Yasmina," a track that also includes drum-

mers Philly Joe Jones, Art Taylor and Sunny Murray. On "Sonny's Back," there is an unlikely tenor tear-off between Shepp and Hank Mobley, while "Body and Soul" gives Shepp a showcase opportunity. Although this set is not essential, it is unique enough to be recommended to avant-garde collectors fortunate enough to find it. —*Scott Yanow*

Poem for Malcolm / Aug. 14, 1969 / Affinity ◆◆◆
This LP from the English Affinity LP is a mixed bag. Best is "Rain Forest" on which tenor saxophonist Archie Shepp, in a collaboration with trombonist Granchar Moncur III, pianist Vince Benedetti, bassist Malachi Favors and drummer Philly Joe Jones performs some stirring free jazz; the interplay between Shepp and Jones is particularly exciting. On a four-and-a-half-minute "Oleo," Shepp "battles" some bebop with fellow tenor Hank Mobley but the other two tracks, a workout for the leader's erratic soprano on "Mama Rose" and his emotional recitation on "Poem for Malcolm," are much less interesting, making this a less-than-essential release despite "Rain Forest." —*Scott Yanow*

Blase / Aug. 16, 1969 / Charly ◆◆◆

Black Gypsy / Nov. 9, 1969 / Prestige ◆◆◆

Archie Shepp & Philly Joe Jones / Nov. 1969-Dec. 1969 / Fantasy ◆◆
This intriguing LP does not live up to its potential. Three generations of jazzmen were involved in this 1969 project, with veteran drummer Philly Joe Jones and the great avant-garde tenor Archie Shepp meeting up with two of the top "new jazz" players (altoist Anthony Braxton and violinist Leroy Jenkins). Unfortunately, both of the side-long pieces have recitations, the performances are overly long, and there is quite a bit of rambling. This is a lesser effort that has been long out-of-print. —*Scott Yanow*

Live at Antibes / Jul. 18, 1970 / BYG ◆◆◆

Things Have Got to Change / May 17, 1971 / Impulse! ◆◆◆

Attica Blues / Jan. 24, 1972-Jan. 26, 1972 / Impulse! ◆◆◆

The Cry of My People / Sep. 25, 1972-Sep. 27, 1972 / ABC/Impulse! ◆◆◆

Coral Rock / Oct. 1973 / Prestige ◆◆◆

There's a Trumpet in My Soul / Apr. 12, 1975 / Freedom ◆◆◆
Raspy avant-garde tenor saxophonist Archie Shepp (who unfortunately also plays some soprano on this date) is the lead voice in a group that sometimes grows to 13 pieces, including four brass players, two keyboards and two percussionists, on this reissue. Two vocals and a poem recitation weigh down the music a bit, although Shepp gets in some good licks. The overall results are not essential, but Archie Shepp was still in his musical prime at the time. —*Scott Yanow*

Montreux, Vol. 1 / Jul. 18, 1975 / Freedom ◆◆◆◆
The first of two CDs that resulted from the great tenor Archie Shepp's appearance at the 1975 Montreux Jazz Festival features the important avant-garde player in a quintet with trombonist Charles Greenlee, pianist Dave Burrell, bassist Cameron Brown and drummer Beaver Harris. Shepp, who was nearing the end of his free-jazz period (soon he would be exploring hymns and traditional melodies) puts a lot of emotion into "Lush Life" and sounds fine on originals by Burrell and Greenlee in addition to his own "U-jamsa." A worthy effort. —*Scott Yanow*

Montreux, Vol. 2 / Jul. 18, 1975 / Arista/Freedom ◆◆◆◆◆
Tenor saxophonist Archie Shepp was at a turning point of sorts in 1975. He was near the end of his free jazz phase and would soon be exploring melodies from both the jazz tradition and the early 20th century; in addition his tone would begin to decline within a decade. However that is not in evidence during this fairly rousing live appearance at the Montreux Jazz Festival with his quintet (which also includes trombonist Charles Greenlee, pianist Dave Burrell, bassist Cameron Brown and drummer Beaver Harris). This second of two CDs is the better of the pair and a good outing for Archie Shepp. —*Scott Yanow*

A Sea of Faces / Aug. 4, 1975-Aug. 5, 1975 / Black Saint ◆◆◆

Steam / May 14, 1976 / Enja ◆◆◆◆
This colorful live LP features Archie Shepp on tenor, and a bit of his more basic piano, playing three lengthy compositions (Duke Ellington's "Solitude," Cal Massey's "A Message from Trane" and Shepp's own "Steam") in a sparse trio with bassist Cameron Brown and drummer Beaver Harris. The avant-garde innovator Shepp still sounds fairly strong at what was for him a fairly late period, displaying his distinctive raspy tone and what were for him some typically emotional ideas. —*Scott Yanow*

The Rising Sun Collection / Apr. 12, 1977 / Just a Memory ◆◆◆
This 1994 CD released for the first time a live set from 1977 by tenor saxophonist Archie Shepp from the Rising Sun Celebrity Jazz Club in Montreal. Shepp starts quite strong with his original "Ujaama" and a forceful statement on "Sonny's Back" (balancing the jazz tradition with his own distinctive raspy sound and avant-garde explorations). His outings on soprano are quite a bit weaker despite the presence

of a fine rhythm section (pianist Dave Burrell, bassist Cameron Brown and drummer Charlie Persip) but, after a few uneven tracks, Shepp finishes with memorable versions of Burrell's "Crucificado" and Charlie Parker's "Confirmation." The good outweighs the bad, making this CD one that Archie Shepp fans will want. —*Scott Yanow*

Goin' Back Home / Apr. 25, 1977 / Steeple Chase ✦✦✦✦✦
Archie Shepp's two duet albums with pianist Horace Parlan on Steeple Chase (the other one is 1980s *Trouble in Mind*) both find the innovative avant-garde tenor in relaxed and melodic form, respectfully interpreting music of the 1920s and before. *Goin' Home* features Shepp (who doubles on soprano) and Parlan playing tasteful versions of nine ancient black folk melodies including "Swing Low, Sweet Chariot," "Nobody Knows the Troubles I've Seen" and "Deep River." Those listeners only familiar with Shepp's earlier *Fire Music* will find these compelling performances to be a revelation. —*Scott Yanow*

Ballads for Trane / May 7, 1977 / Denon ✦✦✦✦
Day Dream / Jun. 3, 1977 / Denon ✦✦✦✦
On Green Dolphin Street / Nov. 28, 1977 / Denon ✦✦✦
Duet with Dollar Brand / Jun. 5, 1978 / Denon ✦✦✦✦
Live in Tokyo / Jun. 6, 1978 / Denon ✦✦✦
Trouble in Mind / Feb. 6, 1980 / Steeple Chase ✦✦✦✦✦
The second set of duets by Archie Shepp (doubling on tenor and soprano) and pianist Horace Parlan (the earlier Steeple Chase set is *Goin' Home*) features the duo on a dozen blues-oriented pieces from the 1920s, two of which were released for the first time on this CD reissue. It is particularly interesting to hear Shepp, best known for his ferocious free-jazz performances of the mid- to late '60s, adjusting his sound and giving such songs as "Trouble in Mind," Earl Hines' "Blues in Thirds" and "St. James Infirmary" tasteful and respectful yet emotional treatment. Recommended. —*Scott Yanow*

Looking at Bird / Feb. 7, 1980 / Steeple Chase ✦✦✦✦✦
Avant-garde tenor saxophonist Archie Shepp created a stir in 1977 when he recorded a set of hymns and folk melodies in melodic duets with pianist Horace Parlan. On February 6, 1980, he reunited with Parlan for a set of blues associated with Bessie Smith, and the following day, as a sort of sequel, Shepp played eight songs associated with Charlie Parker in collaboration with bassist Niels-Henning Orsted Pedersen. Although never a bebopper, Shepp does surprisingly well on such tunes as "Moose the Mooche," "Ornithology," "Yardbird Suite" and "Confirmation," even if he makes the mistake of doubling on his erratic soprano during a few numbers. Archie Shepp pays tribute to Bird not by copying him, but by being creative and playing Parker's repertoire in his own sound. Recommended. —*Scott Yanow*

I Know About the Life / Feb. 11, 1981 / Sackville ✦✦✦✦
By the time tenor saxophonist Archie Shepp recorded this Sackville date, which has been reissued on CD, he had shifted his focus from free-form improvisations to exploring standards. Joined by pianist Ken Werner, bassist Santi Debriano and drummer John Betsch, Shepp stretches out on "Giant Steps," "'Round Midnight" and "Well You Needn't," in addition to his own "I Know About the Life." Shepp's sound was not as strong as it had been previously and would continue to get more erratic as the decade progressed, but he comes up with consistently inventive ideas, showing listeners that he did indeed know how to "play changes." A worthy effort. —*Scott Yanow*

Mama Rose / Feb. 5, 1982 / Steeple Chase ✦✦✦
Soul Song / Dec. 1, 1982 / Enja ✦✦
This is one of Archie Shepp's more erratic sets. On the fifteen-and-a-half-minute "Mama Rose," the great tenor (who is joined by pianist Ken Werner, bassist Santi DeBriano and drummer Marvin "Smitty" Smith) unfortunately plays his out-of-tune soprano and takes an eccentric vocal. Additionally, Werner's brief "Soul Song" tends to wander without much direction. Much better is the eighteen-and-a-half-minute "Geechee," a lengthy workout for Shepp's emotional tone, but due to this release's weak first half, it can be safely passed by. —*Scott Yanow*

The Good Life / 1984 / Varrick ✦✦
Archie Shepp's most rewarding recordings were mostly in the 1960s, when he was at his most fiery and innovative, and in the '70s, when he began exploring older standards and his tone was still in its prime. By the 1980s, Shepp was recording too frequently, spending more time than he should on his generally out-of-tune soprano and taking an excess of shouting vocals; worst of all, his tenor playing was losing some of its power. On this quartet session with pianist Kenny Werner, bassist Avery Sharpe and drummer Marvin "Smitty" Smith, Shepp plays three bop standards as best he can, although the recording quality has an exaggerated echo, then makes the mistake of singing "The Good Life" and plays his unfortunate soprano on two originals. An erratic and lesser effort. —*Scott Yanow*

California Meeting / May 22, 1985 / Soul Note ✦✦✦
Archie Shepp recordings in the 1980s are hit and miss; this is one of the more interesting ones. Shepp does make the mistake of playing soprano on "A Night in Tunisia" (his abilities on that instrument pale next to his tenor) and having a guest singer (Royal Blue) brought out of the audience to sing "St. James Infirmary." But Shepp's tenor playing is excellent on a roaring "Giant Steps" and the ballad "My Romance," and his sidemen (pianist George Cables, bassist Herbie Lewis and drummer Eddie Marshall) are flexible and versatile enough for the diverse music. Not essential but this CD is worth picking up by Archie Shepp's fans. —*Scott Yanow*

Little Red Moon / Dec. 11, 1985-Dec. 13, 1985 / Soul Note ✦
By 1985 Archie Shepp's tone on tenor had declined quite a bit from just a few years earlier. This should have been a strong set, for the sidemen (trumpeter Enrico Rava, keyboardist Siegfried Kessler, bassist Wilbur Little and drummer Clifford Jarvis) are excellent and the repertoire is both diverse and challenging. However Shepp fouls up "Naima" by playing his out-of-tune soprano, talks and sings on the 18-minute "Little Red Moon" more than he plays tenor and his sax sounds quite sloppy on "Whisper Not" and "Sweet Georgia Brown." Despite some good moments from the supporting cast, this is one to skip. —*Scott Yanow*

The Fifth of May / May 7, 1987-May 8, 1987 / Optimism ✦✦✦
This is an unusual CD with Archie Shepp mostly playing tenor but also contributing a couple of vocals and a bit of soprano, and performing duets with the keyboards and synthesizer of Jasper Van't Hof. The music (originals by Shepp or Van't Hof, along with John Coltrane's "Naima") ranges from danceable tracks and mood pieces to explorative works and generally holds one's interest. A good couple of days for Archie Shepp, who could be quite erratic in the 1980s. —*Scott Yanow*

In Memory Of / Mar. 13, 1988-Mar. 14, 1988 / Optimism ✦✦
This is one of the odder releases of the 1980s. For the first and only time, trumpeter Chet Baker and tenor saxophonist Archie Shepp teamed up for a pair of concerts in a quintet which also included pianist Horace Parlan, bassist Herman Wright and drummer Clifford Jarvis. The fact that Shepp is an emotional avant-gardist and Baker a cool-toned lyrical trumpeter and that both have radically different singing styles (they take a vocal apiece) results in the obvious: these two individualists do not blend together very well. Other than Shepp's "Dedication to Bessie Smith's Blues," the repertoire is all standards. Baker plays pretty, while Shepp sounds sloppy and heavy. This CD is definitely a historical curiosity, but does not need to be listened to more than once. —*Scott Yanow*

Swing Low / Sep. 27, 1991-Sep. 28, 1991 / Plainisphare ✦✦✦✦
Tenor saxophonist Archie Shepp and pianist Horace Parlan had teamed up for a series of well-received Steeple Chase studio duet albums that found the former avant-garde tenor exploring melodic and emotional renditions of traditional folk songs and blues. For this fairly rare Plainisphare CD, Shepp (who plays effective alto on two of the eight songs) is once again matched with Parlan although this time in a club. They mix together such tunes as "Swing Low, Sweet Chariot," "See See Rider" and "Go Down Moses" with a couple of standards ("Embraceable You" and Duke Ellington's "I Didn't Know About You") and Parlan's original "Billie's Bossa." Although Shepp's three vocals are an acquired taste, this set features some of his finest playing of the 1990s. —*Scott Yanow*

Andy Sheppard

b. Jan. 20, 1957, Warminster, Wilshire, England
Tenor Saxophone, Soprano Saxophone, Flute / Post-Bop, Crossover Jazz
One of the more intriguing and versatile British musicians, Andy Sheppard has on occasion made a big impression in the US. He did not start playing music until he was 19 and planning to go to art college; a listen to John Coltrane's recordings changed the direction of his life. Within three weeks Sheppard was playing in public but quite a few years of scuffling followed as he learned his craft and developed his own sound. In 1986 Andy Sheppard won a jazz competition and was signed to the Antilles label which served as his breakthrough. Among his activities since then has been work with Gil Evans in France (1987), George Russell and Carla Bley. Although he has led his own group, Sheppard's highest profile thus far has been his involvement in a trio recording (*Songs with Legs*) with Carla Bley and Steve Swallow. —*Scott Yanow*

Andy Sheppard / 1988 / Antilles ✦✦✦✦
Young British star, with Randy Brecker (tpt) making guest appearance. —*Ron Wynn*

● **Soft on the Inside** / Nov. 6, 1989-Nov. 9, 1989 / Antilles ✦✦✦✦✦
This Andy Sheppard CD was dedicated to Gil Evans, Carla Bley and George Russell and, like those three, Sheppard does not use his fellow horn playiers in conventional brass and reed sections but as individual players. The ensembles tend to be crowded but loosely organized with the horn riffs often stealing the spotlight

from the soloists. Sheppard wrote and arranged the four lengthy tracks and his 15-piece group (which includes two keyboards, cello and two drummers) has among its stars vibraphonist Orphy Robinson, cellist Ernst Reijseger, trombonist Gary Valente, trumpeter Claude Deppa and the leader's tenor. Although there is nothing too radical about the colorful music, this fine effort shows that there is still life to be found in big-band jazz. —*Scott Yanow*

Introductions in the Dark / 1989 / Antilles ✦✦✦✦

Contemporary date. Yes, there are synthesizers galore and relatively simple rhythms. Still, Sheppard's sax solos are meaty and cleverly executed, despite an occasional indulgence for post-Coltrane theatrics. —*Ron Wynn*

In Co-Motion / Feb. 1991 / Antilles ✦✦✦

British jazz-rock pianist Andy Sheppard leads a combo with Claude Deppa, Steve Lodder, Sylvan Richardson, Jr., and Dave Addams. They run through everything from rock and reggae to straightahead jazz and fusion, playing it with style and energy, although the solos sometimes lack ideas. —*Ron Wynn*

Rhythm Method / May 21, 1993-Jun. 12, 1993 / Blue Note ✦✦✦

Andy Sheppard, a fine tenor and soprano saxophonist, is heard here on an above-average fusion date. While Sheppard's solos are good enough, his rhythm section is somewhat anonymous and the six originals (all but one being over nine minutes long) do little other than set up grooves for Sheppard's fairly basic improvisations. Not a bad release but not all that memorable either. —*Scott Yanow*

Songs with Legs / 1995 / BMG ✦✦✦

Daryl Sherman

b. Woonsocket, RI

Vocals / Swing

Jazz vocalist Daryl Sherman first surfaced in 1988 as part of the group Mr. Tram Associates, lending her singing as well as her piano skills to the album *Getting Some Fun Out of Life*. In 1990, she issued her solo debut *I've Got My Fingers Crossed: A Celebration of Jimmy McHugh*. In 1996 she teamed with vibraphonist John Cocuzzi for *Celebrating Mildred Bailey and Red Norvo*, as well as releasing the solo *Look What I Found*. —*Jason Ankeny*

I've Got My Fingers Crossed: A Celebration Of . . . / Aug. 1989-May 1990 / Audiophile ✦✦✦✦

Look What I Found / Jun. 22, 1995-Jul. 12, 1995 / Arbors ✦✦✦✦✦

Daryl Sherman's relaxed and straightforward approach to singing, paying attention to the meaning of the lyrics but always swinging, is quite winning. Whether being lyrical on "Any Old Time" or saucy on "Knock Me a Kiss," Sherman is in delightful form throughout this set, and she contributes two fine originals, "Simple as That" and the humorous (if sad) "Something Brazilian." A major asset to the CD are the arrangements of Dan Barrett, which utilize his trombone, trumpeter Randy Sandke, four reeds (Jerry Dodgion, Ken Peplowski, Scott Robinson and Chuck Wilson) and a fine rhythm section (guitarist Bucky Pizzarelli, pianist John Bunch, bassist Boots Maleson and drummer Klaus Suonsaari) quite colorfully. The reeds all double and sometimes triple (Scott Robinson's bass clarinet is quite atmospheric), and a variety of instrumentation is used: "Any Old Time" is taken as a Sherman duet with Pizzarelli, "Many a New Day" finds the singer accompanied only by bassist Maleson, "Things Are Looking Up" (one of a few numbers on which Daryl herself plays piano) is taken solo, and she forms an appealing duo with Barrett on "Why Do I Love You." All of the horn players have their spots and, most importantly, Daryl Sherman is perfectly suited for the material. Recommended. —*Scott Yanow*

● **Celebrating Mildred Bailey and Red Norvo** / Apr. 21, 1996-Apr. 22, 1996 / Audiophile ✦✦✦✦✦

The talented swing singer Daryl Sherman and vibraphonist John Cocuzzi pay tribute to Mildred Bailey and Red Norvo on this very enjoyable CD. Sherman does a superlative job of emulating "The Rockin' Chair Lady" without needing to change her own basic approach much on some of Bailey's greatest hits, plus a few obscurities. "Georgia on My Mind" and "Rockin' Chair" are effectively combined in a medley, the spirit of Bailey's saucy rendition of "Squeeze Me" is recreated, "It's So Peaceful in the Country" is wistful, and "I've Got My Love to Keep Me Warm" really swings. Cocuzzi (whose sound is somewhere between Norvo and Lionel Hampton) takes some fine solos, but the spectacular trumpeter Randy Sandke (reminding one of both Bunny Berigan and Charlie Shavers) steals the show every time he appears. Trombonist Randy Reinhart and clarinetist Bobby Gordon also fare well, and both "The Man I Love" (which has a memorable Sandke-Reinhart trade-off) and "Wrap Your Troubles in Dreams" are taken as instrumentals. But it is Daryl Sherman's wonderful singing that makes this a particularly memorable outing. —*Scott Yanow*

Bobby Shew (Robert Joratz)

b. Mar. 4, 1941, Albuquerque, NM

Trumpet, Fluegelhorn / Hard Bop

A very valuable trumpeter, Bobby Shew has the rare dual ability of being able to play lead in big bands and star as a soloist in combos. His style is out of the hard-bop tradition. Shew, who became an important jazz educator, was ironically mostly self-taught. He worked with Woody Herman (1965), Buddy Rich (1966-67) and then for a long stretch in Las Vegas show bands. In 1973, Shew settled in Los Angeles and worked in the studios, but found time to play jazz, most notably with the Toshiko Akiyoshi-Lew Tabackin big band. Louie Bellson has used him on many occasions over the past 25 years, and Shew has often been in demand for big-band work with Buddy Rich, Don Menza, and the Capp/Pierce Juggernaut. Starting in the 1980s, he has appeared more often with smaller groups. Bobby Shew has recorded as a leader for Inner City, Sutra, Jazzhounds, Atlas, Delos, Pausa, Mo Pro, Mons, Double-Time and MAMA. —*Scott Yanow*

Telepathy / Mar. 4, 1978+Apr. 16, 1978 / Jazz Hounds ✦✦✦✦

Trumpeter Bobby Shew's debut as a leader (he was already 37) is a fine duet set with pianist Bill Mays. The recording was quite spontaneous, for a planned quintet album had been cancelled at the last minute due to scheduling conflicts, and studio time was suddenly available. Shew and Mays selected six standards (including "It Might as Well Be Spring," "Poor Butterfly" and "Indian Summer") that they performed without much discussion, and the duo also created a pair of free improvisations that are quite coherent and have a momentum of their own. This out-of-print LP is worth searching for. —*Scott Yanow*

Outstanding in His Field / Dec. 18, 1978-Jul. 3, 1979 / Inner City ✦✦✦

The album photo on this obscure LP from the defunct Inner City label has trumpeter Bobby Shew and his sidemen "out standing in his field" like farmers. Shew teamed up with tenor saxophonist Gordon Brisker, keyboardist Bill Mays, bassist Bob Magnusson and drummer Dick Berk for group originals (five by Shew and one from Mays) that fall into the genre of advanced hard bop. Most memorable are the ballad "Blue" (which was dedicated to trumpeter Blue Mitchell) and "The Red Snapper." —*Scott Yanow*

Class Reunion / 1980 / Sutra ✦✦✦✦

Play Song / May 20, 1981-May 21, 1981 / Jazzhounds ✦✦✦✦✦

Trumpeter Bobby Shew and some of his favorite Los Angeles-based players of the early 1980s (tenor saxophonist Gordon Brisker, keyboardist Bill Mays, bassist Bob Magnusson, drummer Dick Berk and percussionist David Levine) perform five group originals, plus Clifford Brown's "La Rue," on this spirited modern mainstream Jazz Hounds LP, which is unfortunately long out of print. "Surprise Samba" is a highlight. —*Scott Yanow*

Shewhorn / Jun. 1982-Jul. 1983 / Pausa ✦✦✦✦

On this out-of-print LP from the obsolete Pausa label, the versatile Bobby Shew (who is able to play first trumpet parts as well as boppish solos) performs with a fine sextet of Los Angeles jazzmen: Gordon Brisker on tenor and flute, trombonist Bill Reichenbach, either Butch Lacy or Bill Mays on piano, bassist Bob Magnusson and drummer Billy Mintz. None of the originals (by Shew, Magnusson, Claudio Roditi and Bengt Hallberg) would catch on, but the advanced straightahead music should interest hard-bop collectors. —*Scott Yanow*

Breakfast Wine / Sep. 1983 / Pausa ✦✦✦✦✦

For this obscure effort, trumpeter Bobby Shew and drummer Sherman Ferguson team up with two young talents who were fairly unknown at the time: pianist Makoto Ozone and bassist John Patitucci. In addition to the title cut, Lyle Mays' tasteful "Waltz for Bill Evans" and Ozone's "Shew-In," the quartet performs three standards. Throughout, Shew is heard in top form, and the interplay between his horn and Ozone is quite appealing. It is a pity that this valuable record (as with too many of Bobby Shew's recordings) will be difficult to find. —*Scott Yanow*

Trumpets No End / Oct. 1983 / Delos ✦✦✦✦✦

This LP contains an exciting set of music. Trumpeters Bobby Shew and Chuck Findley (who are accompanied by pianist Art Resnick, bassist John Patitucci and drummer Sherman Ferguson) are both complementary and competitive on such songs as Clifford Brown's "Brownie Speaks," "Stompin' at the Savoy" and Carl Saunders' "Will Do-Won't Do." The superior and spirited bop-oriented music deserves to be made more widely available. —*Scott Yanow*

Round Midnight / Dec. 17, 1984-Dec. 19, 1984 / Mo Pro ✦✦✦✦✦

In the 1980s, the Cincinnati label Mopro recorded several valuable, swinging bop-oriented sessions, including this one. The talented Bobby Shew (heard on trumpet, fluegelhorn and his own Shewhorn) performs seven standards with pianist Steve Schmidt, bassist Lynn Seaton and drummer John Von Ohlen. Highlights include "If I Should Lose You," "Straight, No Chaser" and "I'll Close My Eyes." Shew's warm tone and creative ideas make this an LP worth searching for by straightahead jazz fans. —*Scott Yanow*

Playing with Fire / Sep. 17, 1986 / MAMA ✦✦✦✦

Metropole Orchestra / Dec. 16, 1986+Nov. 24, 1988 / Mons ✦✦✦✦

Tribute to the Masters / Mar. 19, 1995-Mar. 20, 1995 / Double-Time ✦✦✦✦

Trumpeter Bobby Shew, a long underrated but talented bop-oriented trumpeter, helped to launch the new Double-Time label with this fine release. Shew teams up with saxophonist Jamey Aebersold (world renowned for his series of play-along instructional recordings) in a quintet with pianist Steve Schmidt, bassist Tyrone Wheeler and drummer Ed Soph for a set of music paying tribute to a variety of jazz composers (Horace Silver, Benny Golson, Thelonious Monk, Dave Brubeck, Charlie Parker, Clifford Brown, Duke Ellington, Hank Mobley and Dizzy Gillespie). Nothing all that surprising occurs (the standards are given conventional and respectful treatment) but the solos are of a consistently high level and the music always swings. Bop fans will enjoy this CD. —*Scott Yanow*

● **Heavyweights** / Sep. 20, 1995-Sep. 21, 1995 / MAMA ✦✦✦✦✦

Trumpeter Bobby Shew had been wanting to make an album with the underrecorded trombonist Carl Fontana for 25 years when he finally had the opportunity in 1995. Using swinging arrangements by the recently deceased Herbie Phillips, Shew and Fontana (who are assisted by pianist George Cables, bassist Bob Magnusson and drummer Joe La Barbera) perform a bop-oriented program comprising nine jazz standards. The interplay between the two very fluent horns is consistently delightful, and the highlights include "The Night Has a Thousand Eyes," "My Romance," "The Girl from Ipanema" and "While My Lady Sleeps." Recommended for straightahead jazz fans. —*Scott Yanow*

Sahib Shihab (Edmund Gregory)

b. Jun. 23, 1925, Savannah, GA, d. Oct. 24, 1989, Tennessee

Baritone Saxophone, Alto Saxophone, Soprano Saxophone, Flute / Bop, Hard Bop

Besides being one of the first jazz musicians to convert to Islam and change his name (1947), Sahib Shihab was also one of the earliest boppers to use the flute. But he was also a fluent soloist on the alto, as well as the baritone, sax, the latter being the instrument with which he became most frequently associated. Shihab first worked professionally with the Luther Henderson band at the age of 13 while still studying with Elmer Snowden. At 16, he attended the Boston Conservatory (1941-42) and later worked as the lead alto in the 1944-45 Fletcher Henderson band, billed as Eddie Gregory. After his religious conversion, he fell in with the early bop movement, recording several now-famous sides on alto with Thelonious Monk for Blue Note in 1947 and 1951, and playing with Art Blakey in 1949-50 and the Tadd Dameron band in 1949. Following some empty patches where he had to work odd jobs for a living, Shihab played with Dizzy Gillespie in 1951-52, Illinois Jacquet in 1952-55, and the Oscar Pettiford big band in 1957. After arriving in Europe with Quincy Jones' big band in 1959-60, he remained there until 1986 (mostly in Copenhagen), except for a long Los Angeles interlude (1973-76). While on the Continent, he played in the Clarke-Boland big band for nearly a decade (1963-1972); he can be heard applying advanced vocal effects to his attractive flute work on the superb *Clarke-Boland Big Band* LP (Atlantic, 1963). He recorded only a handful of albums as a leader over the decades for Savoy, Argo, Atlantic and Chess; a 1963 live date in Copenhagen is available on Black Lion. —*Richard S. Ginell*

● **All Star Sextets** / Jun. 6, 1957-Sep. 7, 1957 / Savoy ✦✦✦✦✦

Conversations / Oct. 3, 1963 / Black Lion ✦✦✦✦✦

Because he spent so much of his career living in Europe, Sahib Shihab is primarily known for being a baritonist in the bop era. As this very interesting CD shows, he was also quite original on the alto, soprano and flute and by the early 1960s was open to the influence of the avant-garde without losing his own musical personality. Shihab, who is teamed on this live Copenhagen session with fluegelhornist Allan Botchinsky, guitarist Ole Molin, drummer Alex Riel and the 17-year-old bassist Niels Henning Orsted Pedersen, performs "Someday My Prince Will Come," "Charade" and a lengthy version of "Billy Boy" along with five originals including the three-part "Conversations." This surprising music is well worth several listens and shows that Shihab was a much more diverse player than is usually thought. —*Scott Yanow*

Summer Dawn / May 8, 1964-May 9, 1964 / Chess ✦✦✦

Sentiments / Mar. 1971 / Storyville ✦✦✦

Matthew Shipp

b. Dec. 7, 1960, Wilmington, DE

Piano / Avant-Garde

A complex player with a sound of his own, Matthew Shipp has created a stir in the

jazz avant-garde within a relatively short period of time. Shipp studied at the University of Delaware and the New England Conservatory of Music; although very interested in 20th century classical music, he decided to become an improvising musician, working for a time with saxophonist David Ware. He made his recording debut on a duet record with altoist Rob Brown and has recorded as a leader for Quinton, Silkeart, Brinkman, No More, 213 and Hat Art, often working closely with bassist William Parker. —*Scott Yanow*

Points / Jan. 14, 1990-Mar. 18, 1990 / Silkheart ✦✦✦

Prism / Mar. 26, 1993 / Brinkman ✦✦✦✦

Zo / Aug. 5, 1994 / Thirsty Ear ✦✦✦

● **Critical Mass** / Sep. 23, 1994 / 213 Records ✦✦✦✦

Circular Temple / Aug. 8, 1995 / Warner Brothers ✦✦✦

Symbol Systems / Nov. 22, 1995 / No More ✦✦✦✦✦

By the Law of Music / Aug. 5, 1996 / Hat Art ✦✦✦

This CD gives listeners an interesting, if often wandering, set of fairly free music by pianist Matthew Shipp (who wrote 12 of the 13 numbers), violinist Mat Maneri and bassist William Parker. Shipp's thoughtful approach and inventive use of melody holds one's interest throughout. The concluding piece, Duke Ellington's "Solitude," makes one wish that this trio had also performed other abstract interpretations of standards. —*Scott Yanow*

Duo with Roscoe Mitchell / Oct. 8, 1996 / Thirsty Ear ✦✦✦✦

The adventurous yet usually thoughtful pianist Matthew Shipp meets up with Roscoe Mitchell (doubling on alto and soprano) for 11 generally concise free improvisations. The unpredictable music moves logically, contains a fair share of variety and a good use of space, and covers a wide range of emotions. It is particularly rewarding to hear Mitchell stretching out in this type of sparse setting. —*Scott Yanow*

Flow of X / 1997 / Thirsty Ear ✦✦✦

Thesis / 1997 / Hatology ✦✦✦✦

Charlie Shoemake

b. Jul. 27, 1937, Houston, TX

Vibes / Bop, Hard Bop

Vibraphonist and bandleader Charlie Shoemake initially played with Charles Lloyd, Art Pepper, and Howard Rumsey's Lighthouse All-Stars, among others. He later worked as a studio musician with Quincy Jones, Lalo Schifrin, and played with George Shearing. —*Michael Erlewine*

Sunstroke / Aug. 5, 1978 / Muse ✦✦✦✦

Blue Shoe / Jul. 21, 1979 / Muse ✦✦✦✦✦

Record dates by the boppish vibraphonist Charlie Shoemake are relatively infrequent but always rewarding. This Muse LP teams Shoemake with the high-powered tenor of Pete Christlieb, pianist Kenny Barron, bassist Mark Helias and drummer Ben Riley for six obscure and often complex but swinging pieces, three by the leader. Sandi Shoemake takes a sweet vocal on "The Dream," and Christlieb competes with Shoemake for solo honors throughout the stimulating set. —*Scott Yanow*

Sometime Yesterday / Jul. 1980-Mar. 1984 / Discovery ✦✦✦

Away from the Crowd / Jul. 1980-Sep. 25, 1981 / Discovery ✦✦✦✦

Cross Roads / Sep. 24, 1982 / Discovery ✦✦✦✦

Charlie Shoemake Sextet Plays the Music of David Raksin / May 30, 1983 / Discovery ✦✦✦

Incandescent / Aug. 3, 1984 / Discovery ✦✦✦

Collaboration / Jan. 5, 1985 / Pausa ✦✦✦✦✦

Satin Nights / Sep. 3, 1986 / Black Hawk ✦✦✦✦

Stand-Up Guys / Mar. 7, 1988-Mar. 8, 1988 / Chase Music ✦✦✦✦✦

● **Strollin'** / 1991 / Chase Music ✦✦✦✦✦

A 1991 session with saxophonist Charlie Shoemake heading both guest stars and the Bill Holman Orchestra. It's textbook West Coast cool and swing, with Shoemake, pianist Billy Childs, saxophonist Pete Christlieb, and guitarist Ron Eschete, among others, taking solo honors. —*Ron Wynn*

Travis Shook

b. 1969, Oroville, CA

Piano / Post-Bop

Travis Shook's career got off to a fast start although it has stalled somewhat since then. He started on piano at seven, spent some time playing heavy metal guitar and then came back to the piano. While at William Paterson College in New Jersey, he had the chance to play with such musicians as Benny Golson and Branford Marsalis. Shook won several contests (most notably the 1991 Great American Jazz Piano Competition at the Jacksonville Jazz Festival) and in 1993 he made his recording debut on his self-titled Columbia CD in a quartet that included Tony Williams and Bunky Green. His future musical directions should be worth watching. —*Scott Yanow*

● **Travis Shook** / 1993 / Columbia ✦✦✦✦✦

Travis Shook's debut as a leader features four standards and four lesser-known pieces and finds the 22-year-old pianist displaying very impressive technique and (almost as importantly) plenty of self-restraint. His style shows slight echoes of McCoy Tyner and Herbie Hancock but also builds and releases tension in a colorful fashion reminiscent of Ahmad Jamal. Shook acquits himself well in the trio outing with bassist Ira Coleman and drummer Tony Williams and even maintains the spotlight during the two intense appearances by veteran altoist Bunky Green. Shook's solo version of "My Foolish Heart" is a high point. —*Scott Yanow*

Wayne Shorter

b. Aug. 25, 1933, Newark, NJ

Tenor Saxophone, Soprano Saxophone, Composer / Hard Bop, Fusion, Post-Bop

Though some will argue about whether Wayne Shorter's primary impact on jazz has been as a composer or as a saxophonist, hardly anyone will dispute his overall importance as one of jazz's leading figures over a long span of time. Though indebted to a great extent to John Coltrane, with whom he practiced in the mid-'50s while still an undergraduate, Shorter eventually developed his own more succinct manner on tenor sax, retaining the tough tone quality and intensity and, in later years, adding an element of funk. On soprano, Shorter is almost another player entirely, his lovely tone shining like a light beam, his sensibilities attuned more to lyrical thoughts, his choice of notes becoming more spare as his career unfolded. Shorter's influence as a player, stemming mainly from his achievements in the 1960s and '70s, has been tremendous upon the neo-bop brigade who emerged in the early '80s, most notably Branford Marsalis. As a composer, he is best known for carefully conceived, complex, long-limbed, endlessly winding tunes, many of which have become jazz standards yet have spawned few imitators.

Shorter started on the clarinet at 16 but switched to tenor sax before entering New York University in 1952. After graduating with a BME in 1956, he played with Horace Silver for a short time until he was drafted into the Army for two years. Once out of the service, he joined Maynard Ferguson's band, meeting Ferguson's pianist Joe Zawinul in the process. The following year (1959), Shorter joined Art Blakey's Jazz Messengers, where he remained until 1963, eventually becoming the band's music director. During the Blakey period, Shorter also made his debut on records as a leader, cutting several albums for Chicago's Vee-Jay label. After a few prior attempts to hire him away from Blakey, Miles Davis finally convinced Shorter to join his Quintet in September 1964, thus completing the lineup of a group whose biggest impact would leap-frog a generation into the '80s.

Staying with Miles until 1970, Shorter became at times the band's most prolific composer, contributing tunes like "E.S.P.," "Pinocchio," "Nefertiti," "Sanctuary," "Footprints," "Fall" and the signature description of Miles, "Prince of Darkness." While playing through Miles' transition from loose post-bop acoustic jazz into electronic jazz-rock, Shorter also took up the soprano in late 1968, an instrument which turned out to be more suited to riding above the new electronic timbres than the tenor. As a prolific solo artist for Blue Note during this period, Shorter expanded his palette from hard bop almost into the atonal avant-garde, with fascinating excursions into jazz-rock territory toward the turn of the decade.

In November 1970, Shorter teamed up with old cohort Joe Zawinul and Miroslav Vitous to form Weather Report, where after a fierce start, Shorter's playing grew mellower, pithier, more consciously melodic, and gradually more subservient to Zawinul's concepts. By now, he was playing mostly on soprano, though the tenor would re-emerge more toward the end of WR's run. Shorter's solo ambitions were mostly on hold during the WR days, resulting in but one atypical solo album, *Native Dancer*, an attractive side trip into Brazilian-American tropicalismo in tandem with Milton Nascimento. Shorter also revisited the past in the late '70s by touring with Freddie Hubbard and ex-Miles sidemen Herbie Hancock, Ron Carter and Tony Williams as V.S.O.P.

Shorter finally left Weather Report in 1985, but promptly went into a creative slump from which he has yet to fully recover. Still committed to electronics and fusion, his recorded compositions from this point became more predictable and labored, saddled with leaden rhythm sections and overly complicated arrangements. After three routine Columbia albums during 1986-88, he lapsed into silence, finally emerging in 1995 with *High Life*, a somewhat more engaging collaboration with keyboardist Rachel Z. In concert, he has fielded an erratic series of bands, which could be incoherent one year (1995), and lean and fit the next (1996).

Throughout the difficult decade, though, Shorter continued to play well, even brilliantly at times—and he lived up to his high reputation when touring with Carlos Santana's Latin jazz-rock alumni band in 1988 and with Wallace Roney and the V.S.O.P. rhythm section in the "A Tribute to Miles" band in 1992. Given his long track record, Shorter's every record and appearance are still eagerly awaited by fans in the hope that he will thrill them again. —*Richard S. Ginell*

Introducing Wayne Shorter / Nov. 10, 1959 / Vee-Jay ✦✦✦✦

Also known as *Blues à la Carte*, this Vee-Jay LP has tenor saxophonist Wayne Shorter's first session as a leader and it shows that, even at this early stage, Shorter was far along towards developing his own sound. Teamed up with trumpeter Lee Morgan, pianist Wynton Kelly, bassist Paul Chambers and drummer Jimmy Cobb, the six selections (five of which are Shorter originals) capture the young tenor shortly after he joined Art Blakey's Jazz Messengers. The music is essentially hard bop and, although none of these Shorter tunes caught on, the music is quite enjoyable. A special treat is the one standard of the date, a swinging version of "Mack the Knife." The Vee-Jay date has unfortunately not yet been reissued on CD. —*Scott Yanow*

Second Genesis / Oct. 11, 1960 / Vee-Jay ✦✦✦✦

The second of tenor saxophonist Wayne Shorter's three Vee-Jay LP's (only the third one has been reissued on CD thus far), this album has five of Shorter's quirky originals plus the obscure "Ruby & The Pearl" (from a 1950s movie) and a pair of standards. Joined by a particularly strong rhythm section (pianist Cedar Walton, bassist Bob Cranshaw and drummer Art Blakey), Shorter sounds quite distinctive on the advanced hard-bop material. Pity that this fine early record is currently difficult to find. —*Scott Yanow*

Wayning Moments Plus / 1962 / Vee-Jay ✦✦✦✦

Wayne Shorter's third and final recording for Vee-Jay is reissued on this CD which augments the original eight songs with seven additional alternate takes. Shorter already had an original sound by this time and, with a young and fiery Freddie Hubbard joining him in the front line and a fine rhythm section (pianist Eddie Higgins, bassist Jymie Merritt and drummer Marshall Thompson), the young tenor is heard in his early prime. There are some fine chance-taking solos on this hard-bop date; "Black Orpheus," "Moon of Manakoora" and "All or Nothing at All" are among the highlights. —*Scott Yanow*

Night Dreamer / Apr. 29, 1964 / Blue Note ✦✦✦✦✦

Tenor saxophonist Wayne Shorter's Blue Note debut found him well prepared to enter the big time. With an impressive quintet that includes trumpeter Lee Morgan, pianist McCoy Tyner, bassist Reggie Workman and drummer Elvin Jones, Shorter performed a well-rounded program consisting of five of his originals (this CD reissue adds an alternate take of "Virgo") plus an adaptation of an "Oriental Folk Song." Whether it be the brooding title cut, the Coltranish ballad "Virgo" or the jams on "Black Nile" and "Charcoal Blues," this is a memorable set of high-quality and still fresh music. —*Scott Yanow*

Jazz Profile / Apr. 29, 1964-Aug. 26, 1970 / Blue Note ✦✦✦

Blue Note's *Jazz Profile* series is designed for neophytes and beginners curious about a certain musician. Collectors and diehard fans will have everything on this collection, and while they may quibble with the selections, *Jazz Profile* provides a succinct, helpful introduction to Wayne Shorter's Blue Note recordings for novices. —*Stephen Thomas Erlewine*

★ **JuJu** / Aug. 3, 1964 / Blue Note ✦✦✦✦✦

On this CD reissue, which adds "new" takes of "JuJu" and "House of Jade" to the original six-song LP program, tenor saxophonist Wayne Shorter has an opportunity to play with two then-current members of the John Coltrane Quartet (pianist McCoy Tyner and drummer Elvin Jones) and an alumnus (bassist Reggie Workman). There are times during these performances that Shorter recalls 'Trane but his brooding sound, relaxed approach and his ability to compose quirky originals set him apart even then. Of the repertoire on this quartet date, none were destined to become standards although "Yes or No," "Twelve More Bars to Go" and "JuJu" were all somewhat memorable. With the rhythm section sounding quite advanced if not as passionate as they usually played with Coltrane, Shorter has the perfect accompaniment for his melancholy and introverted flights. This CD is a fine example of his early work. —*Scott Yanow*

★ **Speak No Evil** / Dec. 24, 1964 / Blue Note ✦✦✦✦✦

This CD reissue brings back one of the classic Wayne Shorter albums. The highly original tenor, who had joined Miles Davis' Quintet a few months earlier, utilizes pianist Herbie Hancock and bassist Ron Carter from the group along with trumpeter Freddie Hubbard and drummer Elvin Jones. The masterful players help introduce six of Shorter's unusual originals including "Fee-Fi-Fo-Fum," "Speak No Evil" and "Infant Eyes." The music is often quite complex but also memorable and the style falls between advanced hard-bop/modal jazz and the avant-garde. Well worth numerous listens. —*Scott Yanow*

The Soothsayer / Mar. 4, 1965 / Blue Note ✦✦✦✦✦

It seems odd that this set was originally not released until the late 1970s for the music holds its own with tenor saxophonist Wayne Shorter's best albums of the 1960s. The CD reissue (from 1990) adds an alternate take of "Angola" to the six-song program. All but the adaptation of Jean Sibelius' "Valse Triste" were Shorter originals with "Lady Day" being perhaps the best known. The utilization of an impressive sextet (which includes altoist James Spaulding, trumpeter Freddie Hubbard, pianist McCoy Tyner, bassist Ron Carter and drummer Tony Williams) gave Wayne Shorter the rare opportunity to write for three horns. This is stimulating and thought-provoking music that was way beyond the usual hard bop of the period. —*Scott Yanow*

Et Cetera / Jun. 14, 1965 / Blue Note ✦✦✦✦✦

It is strange that this classic Blue Note album was not released for the first time until 1980 for it finds tenor saxophonist Wayne Shorter in prime form, his four originals (along with Gil Evans' "Barracudas") are quite inventive and the rhythm section (pianist Herbie Hancock, bassist Cecil McBee and drummer Joe Chambers) is state of the art for 1965. These challenging performances find the musicians really listening closely to each other and pushing themselves. Although advanced, the music should not be labelled "avant-garde" or "free jazz" as much as just simply being called "original." —*Scott Yanow*

The All Seeing Eye / Oct. 15, 1965 / Blue Note ✦✦✦✦✦

With such titles as "The All Seeing Eye," "Genesis," "Chaos," "Face of the Deep" and "Mephistopheles," it is clear from the start that the music on this CD reissue is not basic bop and blues. Wayne Shorter (who composed four of the five originals) picked an all-star cast (trumpeter Freddie Hubbard, altoist James Spaulding, trombonist Grachan Moncur III, pianist Herbie Hancock, bassist Ron Carter and drummer Joe Chambers along with brother Alan Shorter on fluegelhorn for the final song) to perform and interpret the dramatic selections and their brand of controlled freedom has plenty of subtle surprises. This is stimulating music that still sounds fresh over three decades later. —*Scott Yanow*

☆ Adam's Apple / Feb. 24, 1966 / Blue Note ✦✦✦✦✦

This Wayne Shorter quartet session (with pianist Herbie Hancock, bassist Reggie Workman and drummer Joe Chambers) is perhaps most notable for the introduction of Shorter's famous blues "Footprints," recorded a few months before Miles Davis' renowned version. In addition to Jimmy Rowles' "502 Blues," the CD reissue has four other Shorter originals including "Adam's Apple" and "El Gaucho." Wayne Shorter was at the peak of his creativity during this period and all of his Blue Note albums from the 1960s are well worth acquiring by adventurous listeners. —*Scott Yanow*

Schizophrenia / Mar. 20, 1967 / Blue Note ✦✦✦✦✦

Wayne Shorter was at the peak of his creative powers when he recorded *Schizophrenia* in the spring of 1967. Assembling a sextet that featured two of his Miles Davis bandmates (pianist Herbie Hancock and bassist Ron Carter), trombonist Curtis Fuller, alto saxophonist/flutist James Spaulding and drummer Joe Chambers, Shorter found a band that was capable of conveying his musical "schizophrenia," which means that this is a band that can play straight just as well as they can stretch the limits of jazz. At their best, they do this simultaneously, as they do on the opener "Tom Thumb." The beat and theme of the song are straightforward, but the musical interplay and solos take chances that result in unpredictable music. And "unpredictable" is the operative phrase for this set of edgy post-bop. Shorter's compositions (as well as Spaulding's lone contribution, "Kryptonite") have strong themes, but they lead into uncharted territory, constantly challenging the musicians and the listener. This music exists at the border between post-bop and free—it's grounded in post-bop, but it knows what is happening across the border. Within a few years, he would cross that line, but *Schizophrenia* crackles with the excitement of Shorter and his colleagues trying to balance the two extremes. —*Stephen Thomas Erlewine*

Super Nova / Aug. 29, 1969+Aug. 2, 1969 / Blue Note ✦✦✦✦

This CD reissue brings back an important transitional album for tenor saxophonist Wayne Shorter. Doubling on soprano (which he had recently begun playing), Shorter interprets five of his originals (including "Water Babies" which had been recorded previously by Miles Davis) and Antonio Carlos Jobim's "Dindi." He definitely used a forward-looking group of sidemen, for his "backup band" includes guitarists John McLaughlin and Sonny Sharrock, Walter Booker (normally a bassist) on classical guitar for "Dindi," bassist Miroslav Vitous, both Jack DeJohnette and Chick Corea (!) on drums and percussionist Airto; Maria Booker takes a vocal on the touching version of "Dindi." The influence of Miles Davis' early fusion period is felt throughout the music but there is nothing derivative about the often-surprising results. As with Wayne Shorter's best albums, this set rewards repeated listenings. —*Scott Yanow*

Moto Grosso Feio / Aug. 26, 1970 / One Way ✦✦✦

Recorded on the same day as the superior *Odyssey of Iska*, this loose session (Wayne Shorter's final one for the Blue Note label) is quite unusual. Although Shorter sticks to his customary tenor and soprano, pianist Chick Corea plays marimba, drums and percussion, bassist Ron Carter mostly performs on cello, electric guitarist John McLaughlin sticks to the 12-string guitar and bassist Dave Holland also plays acoustic guitar; drummer Michelin Prell rounds out the group. Not released until 1974 (and not yet reissued on CD), the music (which is influenced by early fusion) has its interesting moments although it often wanders. The group performs Milton Nascimento's "Vera Cruz" and four of Shorter's originals of which "Montezuma" is the best known. —*Scott Yanow*

Odyssey of Iska / Aug. 26, 1970 / Blue Note ✦✦✦

On Aug. 26, 1970, Wayne Shorter recorded two separate albums for Blue Note (the other one is *Moto Grosso Feio*), his final projects for the label. For this set, Shorter (doubling on tenor and soprano) utilizes a double rhythm section comprising vibraphonist Dave Friedman, guitarist Gene Bertoncini, both Ron Carter and Cecil McBee on basses, drummers Billy Hart and Alphonse Mouzon and percussionist Frank Cuomo. On the verge of joining Weather Report (referred to in the liner notes as "Weather Forecast"), it is not surprising that Shorter's originals include titles such as "Wind," "Storm" and "Calm." These moody works were never covered by other jazz players but they work quite well in this context, launching melancholy flights by Shorter. This LP (and its companion) have yet to be reissued on CD. —*Scott Yanow*

Native Dancer / Sep. 12, 1974 / Columbia ✦✦✦✦

Wayne Shorter surprised the jazz world with this exotic excursion into Brazilian music in 1975. Milton Nascimento, who accompanies Shorter, wrote five of the nine compositions on this album. Reminiscent of the best of the jazz-samba fusion recordings of Stan Getz, *Native Dancer* is every bit as lush and rich. This is an inspired recording of the first caliber and in a word: lovely. —*Michael Erlewine*

Atlantis / 1985 / Columbia ✦✦

When it was released in 1985, this set (reissued on CD) was Wayne Shorter's first solo album in nine years and it disappointed listeners who hoped he would return to the style of his Blue Note years. The music is quite difficult to describe since it contains some unpredictable funk rhythms, the feel of electronics (even though much of the music is actually acoustic) and decent (if typically eccentric) soprano and tenor solos from the leader. Although some of the tracks are catchy, none of the melodies are all that memorable (which is why they have not been covered through the years) and quite a few of the performances do not have definitive beginnings or endings. Overall this set is worth a listen but far from essential. —*Scott Yanow*

Phantom Navigator / 1986 / Columbia ✦✦

1987 release, not among his most daring. —*Ron Wynn*

Joy Ryder / 1988 / Columbia ✦✦

Wayne Shorter's occasional Columbia records of the 1980s are all disappointments. His compositions (there are seven on this out-of-print set) lacked the originality and quirkiness of his 1960s work and, although his sound was still very much intact, Shorter's improvisations tend to wander a bit aimlessly. On this album, Shorter (doubling on soprano and tenor) is joined by a basic trio (keyboardist Patrice Rushen, bassist Nathan East and drummer Terri Lyne Carrington) and such guest musicians as keyboardists Herbie Hancock and Geri Allen, bassist Darryl Jones and (on "Someplace Called Where") vocalist Dianne Reeves; it does not help. Skip this one and get Wayne Shorter's Blue Notes instead. —*Scott Yanow*

High Life / 1994-1995 / Verve ✦✦✦✦

Wayne Shorter's debut for Verve was his first release as a leader in quite a long time and his most rewarding recording since the prime years of Weather Report, 15 years before. Shorter and keyboardist Rachel Z. spent a year working on developing and orchestrating his ideas and the results are these nine originals. Although use was made of orchestral horns and strings, most of the backing in these often-dense ensembles is by a standard rhythm section (which includes Marcus Miller on electric bass and bass clarinet) and Rachel Z's synthesizers. The pieces set moods rather than state singable melodies, are not afraid to utilize electronic rhythms now and then in an unpredictable fashion, and are both intelligent and largely danceable. However Wayne Shorter's playing (not only on soprano and tenor but a bit on alto and baritone) is always distinctive and he sounds very much as if he is pushing himself. In fact his emotional statements and the complexity of the ensembles push this music way above virtually all of the so-called "contemporary jazz" (which is often merely a synonym for jazzy pop) into the idiom of creative music. It helps for listeners to have a liking for the sound of Weather Report (even though this group is not a copy) but even Shorter's older fans will find his playing here to be quite stimulating. —*Scott Yanow*

Don Sickler

Trumpet / Hard Bop

Trumpeter and arranger Don Sickler made his initial splash in 1983, debuting with the LP *The Music of Kenny Dorham;* however, he then spent the next dozen years out of the spotlight, focusing instead on backing and producing artists including Freddie Redd, Larry Coryell and Cindy Blackman. He also enjoyed a brief stint with Art Blakey and the Jazz Messengers. Perhaps Sickler's most productive extended collaboration was with drummer T.S. Monk, whom he met at the Thelonious Monk Institute; a founding member of the T.S. Monk Sextet, Sickler played on albums including 1991's *Take One* and 1993's *Changing of the Guard* before finally taking the reins and leading his own date, 1995's *Nightwatch.* He also served as an associate music professor and director of the University Jazz Orchestra at New York's Columbia University. *—Jason Ankeny*

● **Music of Kenny Dorham** / Nov. 12, 1983 / Uptown ♦♦♦♦♦

Nightwatch / Mar. 24, 1995 / Uptown ♦♦♦♦

Horace Silver

b. Sep. 2, 1928, Norwalk, CT

Piano, Composer, Leader / Hard Bop, Soul Jazz, Groove

From the perspective of the late '90s, it is clear that few jazz musicians have had a greater impact on the contemporary mainstream than Horace Silver. The hard-bop style that Silver pioneered in the '50s is now dominant, played not only by holdovers from an earlier generation, but also by fuzzy-cheeked musicians who had yet to be born when the music fell out of critical favor in the '60s and '70s.

Silver's earliest musical influence was the Cape Verdean folk music he heard from his Portuguese-born father. Later, after he had begun playing piano and saxophone as a high schooler, Silver came under the spell of blues singers and boogie-woogie pianists, as well as boppers like Thelonious Monk and Bud Powell. In 1950, Stan Getz played a concert in Hartford, CT, with a pickup rhythm section that included Silver, drummer Walter Bolden, and bassist Joe Calloway. So impressed was Getz, he hired the whole trio. Silver had been saving his money to move to New York anyway; his hiring by Getz sealed the deal. Silver worked with Getz for a year, then began to freelance around the city with such big-time players as Coleman Hawkins, Lester Young, and Oscar Pettiford. In 1952, he recorded with Lou Donaldson for the Blue Note label; this date led him to his first recordings as a leader. In 1953, he joined forces with Art Blakey to form a cooperative under their joint leadership. The band's first album, *Horace Silver and the Jazz Messengers*, was a milestone in the development of the genre that came to be known as hard bop. Many of the tunes penned by Silver for that record—"The Preacher," "Doodlin'," "Room 608"—became jazz classics. By 1956, Silver had left the Messengers to record on his own. The series of Blue Note albums that followed established Silver for all time as one of jazz's major composer/pianists. LPs like *Blowin' the Blues Away* and *Song for My Father* (both recorded by an ensemble which included Silver's longtime sidemen Blue Mitchell and Junior Cook) featured Silver's harmonically sophisticated and formally distinctive compositions for small jazz ensemble.

Silver's piano style—terse, imaginative, and utterly funky—became a model for subsequent mainstream pianists to emulate. Some of the most influential horn players of the '50s, '60s, and '70s first attained a measure of prominence with Silver—musicians like Donald Byrd, Woody Shaw, Joe Henderson, Benny Golson, and the Brecker brothers all played in Silver's band at a point early in their careers. Silver has even affected members of the avant-garde; Cecil Taylor confesses a Silver influence, and trumpeter Dave Douglas played briefly in a Silver combo.

Silver recorded exclusively for Blue Note until that label's eclipse in the late '70s, whereupon he started his own label, Silveto. Silver's '80s work was poorly distributed. During that time he began writing lyrics to his compositions; his work began to display a concern with music's metaphysical powers, as exemplified by album titles like *Music to Ease Your Disease* and *Spiritualizing Your Senses.* In the '90s, Silver abandoned his label venture and began recording for Columbia. With his re-emergence on a major label, Silver is once again receiving a measure of the attention his contribution deserves. Certainly, no one has ever contributed a larger and more vital body of original compositions to the jazz canon. *—Chris Kelsey*

The Trio Sides / Oct. 9, 1952-Mar. 25, 1968 / Blue Note ♦♦♦♦♦
This double LP includes all of Horace Silver's trio recordings for Blue Note including 14 selections from 1952-53 and nine other performances dating from 1956-68 when he normally recorded with his quintet. Silver, a highly individual composer and pianist whose funky style became very influential by the late '50s, is sometimes overlooked as a keyboard soloist so this hard-to-find set (which includes early versions of "Ecaroh" and "Opus de Funk") sheds new light on his versatile talents. Well worth searching for. *—Scott Yanow*

Jazz Profile / Oct. 9, 1952-Jan. 2, 1976 / Blue Note ♦♦♦♦
Jazz Profile compiles highlights from Horace Silver's recordings for Blue Note, drawing a rough portrait of his career. The compilation features both soul-jazz and hard-bop cuts, giving a good sense of Silver's depth and range. While there isn't anything here that will appeal to collectors, *Jazz Profile* does offer a nice introduction for curious listeners. *—Leo Stanley*

Horace Silver Trio, Vol. 1: Spotlight on Drums / Oct. 23, 1952 / Blue Note ♦♦♦♦
This CD reissue has pianist Horace Silver's first sessions as a leader, trios with drummer Art Blakey and either Gene Ramey, Curly Russell or Percy Heath on bass. Silver already had his funky style fairly well together by 1952 (two years after being discovered by Stan Getz), and the program is most notable for introducing his compositions "Ecaroh" and "Opus de Funk." In addition, there are two percussion features: a drum solo by Blakey on "Nothing but Soul" and "Message from Kenya," a duet by the drummer with the percussion and vocals of Sabu Martinez. *—Scott Yanow*

★ **Horace Silver and the Jazz Messengers** / Nov. 13, 1954-Feb. 6, 1955 / Blue Note ♦♦♦♦♦
A true classic, this CD found pianist Horace Silver and drummer Art Blakey co-leading the Jazz Messengers; Silver would leave a year later to form his own group. Also featuring trumpeter Kenny Dorham, Hank Mobley on tenor and bassist Doug Watkins, this set is most notable for the original versions of Silver's "The Preacher" and "Doodlin'," funky standards that helped launch hard bop and both the Jazz Messengers and Silver's quintet. Essential music. *—Scott Yanow*

Silver's Blue / Jul. 2, 1956-Jul. 17, 1956 / Portrait ♦♦♦♦
This LP documents the birth of the Horace Silver Quintet, recorded shortly after he left the Jazz Messengers along with some of the other original members. The seven selections (three of which are Silver compositions) feature either Joe Gordon or Donald Byrd on trumpet, tenor saxophonist Hank Mobley, bassist Doug Watkins and either Kenny Clarke or Art Taylor on drums. Although Silver's piano style was already largely formed, his group did not yet have the distinctive sound it would develop. However this hard-bop music is still quite enjoyable and very historical. *—Scott Yanow*

Six Pieces of Silver / Nov. 10, 1956 / Blue Note ♦♦♦♦♦
The first classic album by the Horace Silver Quintet, this CD is highlighted by "Senor Blues" (heard in three versions including a later vocal rendition by Bill Henderson) and "Cool Eyes." The early Silver quintet was essentially the Jazz Messengers of the year before (with trumpeter Donald Byrd, tenor saxophonist Hank Mobley and bassist Doug Watkins while drummer Louis Hayes was in Blakey's place) but already the band was starting to develop a sound of its own. "Senor Blues" officially put Horace Silver on the map. *—Scott Yanow*

Sterling Silver / Nov. 10, 1956-Jan. 28, 1964 / Blue Note ♦♦♦
This very interesting collector's LP comprises versions of "Senor Blues" and "Tippin'" that were originally part of a 45, along with seven previously unissued performances from a variety of sets by the Horace Silver Quintet (in addition to a trio rendition of "Que Pasa"). General collectors should get the pianist/composer's regular Blue Note releases first but Silver's longtime fans will find this fresh music fascinating and quite enjoyable. *—Scott Yanow*

The Stylings of Silver / May 8, 1957 / Blue Note ♦♦♦♦
The 1957 Horace Silver Quintet (featuring trumpeter Art Farmer and tenor saxophonist Hank Mobley) is in top form on this date, particularly on "My One and Only Love" and their famous version of "Home Cookin'." All of Silver's Blue Note quintet recordings are consistently superb and swinging and, although not essential, this is a very enjoyable set. *—Scott Yanow*

Further Explorations by the Horace Silver Quintet / Jan. 3, 1958 / Blue Note ♦♦♦♦
For a brief time, tenor saxophonist Clifford Jordan and trumpeter Art Farmer were the front line of the Horace Silver Quintet. This 1997 CD reissue finds the group (which also includes bassist Teddy Kotick and drummer Louis Hayes) performing five of Silver's lesser-known originals and the standard "Ill Wind." The lyrical Farmer and the up-and-coming Jordan have plenty of fine solos, as does the influential Silver, whose funky, witty style stood apart from the prevailing Bud Powell influence of the era. Although none of the newer songs caught on as standards, this set (which has plenty of mood and groove variation) holds together very well and still sounds fresh 40 years later. *—Scott Yanow*

☆ **Finger Poppin' with the Horace Silver Quintet** / Feb. 1, 1959 / Blue Note ♦♦♦♦♦
The first recording by the most famous version of the Horace Silver Quintet is also one of the high points of the pianist/composer's career. Among the more memorable tracks of this classic set are "Juicy Lucy" (the epitome of funky jazz), "Cookin' at the Continental" and "Come on Home" but all eight performances are superlative. With trumpeter Blue Mitchell, Junior Cook's tenor, bassist Eugene Taylor and

drummer Louis Hayes, Horace Silver had found the perfect forum for his piano and his highly accessible songs. Essential music. —Scott Yanow

Blowin' the Blues Away / Aug. 10, 1959 / Blue Note ♦♦♦♦♦
The second recording by the classic version of the Horace Silver Quintet (with trumpeter Blue Mitchell, tenor saxophonist Junior Cook, bassist Eugene Taylor and drummer Louis Hayes) introduced Silver's compositions "Sister Sadie" and "Peace" (both of which became jazz standards) in addition to the title track. No jazz library is complete without at least three or four Horace Silver albums. —Scott Yanow

Horace-Scope / Jul. 9, 1960 / Blue Note ♦♦♦♦♦
The most famous version of the Horace Silver Quintet lasted five years (1959-64) and resulted in six albums of which HoraceScope was the third. "Strollin'" is the best known of the new Silver compositions introduced on this set although his "Nica's Dream" (which was already a few years old) is the only standard. With trumpeter Blue Mitchell, tenor saxophonist Junior Cook, bassist Gene Taylor and his new drummer Roy Brooks, this was the perfect group for Horace Silver's music. —Scott Yanow

Doin' the Thing (At the Village Gate) / May 19, 1961-May 20, 1961 / Blue Note ♦♦♦♦♦
This live set (recorded at the Village Gate) finds pianist/composer Horace Silver and his most acclaimed quintet (the one with trumpeter Blue Mitchell, tenor saxophonist Junior Cook, bassist Gene Taylor and drummer Roy Brooks) stretching out on four selections, including his new song "Filthy McNasty." Two shorter performances were added to the CD version of this enjoyable and always funky hard-bop session. —Scott Yanow

The Tokyo Blues / Jul. 13, 1962-Jul. 14, 1962 / Blue Note ♦♦♦♦
Pianist Horace Silver had his most stable group during 1960-64 when his sidemen were trumpeter Blue Mitchell, tenor saxophonist Junior Cook, bassist Gene Taylor and drummer Roy Brooks. For this set (a straight CD reissue of the original LP), Joe Harris (listed as John Harris, Jr.) is in Brooks' place. The quintet performs four Silver originals (best known is the title cut) plus Ronnell Bright's obscure ballad "Cherry Blossom" which is well worth reviving. Although the four songs are dedicated to Japan and the Orient, there is nothing inherently Asian about the music; it is a typically funky Horace Silver hard-bop date, one of his many recommended Blue Note sets. —Scott Yanow

Silver's Serenade / Apr. 11, 1963-Apr. 12, 1963 / Blue Note ♦♦♦♦
The sixth and final recording session by the most famous of Horace Silver's quintets (the version with trumpeter Blue Mitchell and tenor saxophonist Junior Cook) did not introduce any new classic tunes ("Silver's Serenade" is the best known) but, as with the previous sets, the results are swinging, funky and quite creative within the idiom. All of Silver's Blue Note quintet recordings are quite enjoyable. —Scott Yanow

Horace Silver Live: 1964 / Jun. 6, 1964 / Emerald ♦♦♦♦
Released by Horace Silver's own label, this LP contains "new" versions of "Filthy McNasty," "The Tokyo Blues," "Senor Blues" and the lesser-known "Skinney Minnie," as played by his quintet with tenorman Joe Henderson and trumpeter Carmell Jones. These renditions make for an interesting comparison with the earlier versions cut by Silver with Junior Cook and Blue Mitchell and they are reasonably well recorded. Recommended. —Scott Yanow

★ Song for My Father / Oct. 26, 1964 / Blue Note ♦♦♦♦♦
Horace Silver's most famous album includes the memorable title cut, four of his other recent compositions (including "Calcutta Cutie" and "Lonely Woman") and Joe Henderson's "The Kicker." Although trumpeter Blue Mitchell and tenor saxophonist Junior Cook reunited for "Calcutta Cutie," the remainder of this classic set features Henderson's tenor and trumpeter Carmell Jones. Funky hard bop at its best, this is essential music for any jazz collection. —Scott Yanow

Re-Entry / Apr. 16, 1965+Feb. 1966 / 32 Jazz ♦♦♦♦
The Horace Silver Quintet was arguably one of the best jazz combos of the mid-'60s, and this live CD documents two editions through broadcasts from the Half Note in New York City. A long version of his hit "Song for My Father" gives the pianist and tenor saxophonist Joe Henderson a chance to explore this landmark work at length. "Que Pasa" has a percolating descending line followed by a rather understated Silver solo. One of the two takes of "African Queen" is somewhat marred by tape flutter, but both feature enjoyable trumpet solos by the late Woody Shaw. —Ken Dryden

Cape Verdean Blues / Oct. 1, 1965-Oct. 22, 1965 / Blue Note ♦♦♦♦♦
By late 1965 Horace Silver's Quintet featured trumpeter Woody Shaw and tenor saxophonist Joe Henderson and, on half of this set, the great trombonist J.J. Johnson sits in. "The Cape Verdean Blues," "Pretty Eyes" and Henderson's "Mo' Joe" are among the highlights of this high-quality set of funky hard bop by one of the pacesetting groups. —Scott Yanow

The Jody Grind / Nov. 2, 1966-Nov. 23, 1966 / Blue Note ♦♦♦♦
This excellent set finds Horace Silver fronting a particularly advanced edition of his quintet. This band featured trumpeter Woody Shaw, tenor saxophonist Tyrone Washington and, on half of the six tracks (all Silver compositions) the alto and flute of James Spaulding. "The Jody Grind" and "Dimples" are the closest any of these songs came to becoming standards but Silver fans will find much to enjoy here. —Scott Yanow

Serenade to a Soul Sister / Mar. 25, 1968-Mar. 25, 1968 / Blue Note ♦♦♦♦♦
One of the final classic albums by the Horace Silver Quintet, this set finds Silver using such sidemen as trumpeter Charles Tolliver, either Stanley Turrentine or Bennie Maupin on tenors and, on half of the tracks, the young drummer Billy Cobham. The six Silver compositions include "Psychedelic Sally" and "Serenade to a Soul Sister." This music is both timeless and very much of the period. —Scott Yanow

You Gotta Take a Little Love / Jan. 10, 1969 / Blue Note ♦♦♦♦
One of the final Horace Silver Quintet Blue Note albums, this somewhat forgotten LP, dedicated to "The Brotherhood of Men," is an instrumental set that introduced six new compositions by the pianist/leader (none of which caught on as standards) along with Bennie Maupin's "Lovely's Daughter." Maupin (on tenor and flute), trumpeter Randy Brecker, bassist John Williams and drummer Billy Cobham comprise Silver's excellent late-'60s hard-bop group. —Scott Yanow

That Healin' Feelin' / Apr. 8, 1970-Jun. 18, 1970 / Blue Note ♦♦♦

Total Response (Phase I) / 1970 / Blue Note ♦♦
When jazz critics complain about the decline of Blue Note in the late '60s and early '70s, Total Response is the kind of album they have in mind. A sprawling, incoherent and just plain weird mess of funk, fusion, soul-jazz, African spirituality and hippie mysticism, Total Response aims at the transcendent and stumbles upon its own ludicrous ambitions. Building from familiar, funky soul-jazz vamps, Silver wrote a set of nine songs that were designed to "bring a little more Health, Happiness, Love and Peace into your life." Appropriately, the album is filled with songs about the evils of the modern world ("Acid, Pot or Pills," "Big Business") and how self-awareness ("What Kind of Animal Am I?," "I'm Aware of the Animal Within Me") and open minds ("Won't You Open Up Your Senses," "Soul Searchin'," "I've Had Little Talk") can lead to spiritual peace and fulfillment ("Total Response"). All this may be true, but the way that it's said—laid-back, featureless fusion vamps with awkward lyrics by Silver ("Our water isn't pure/When fluoride we endure") that are wailed tunelessly by Salome and Andy Bey—is terribly clumsy and ridiculous. It wouldn't matter that there is "little jazz content" to the music if these fusions of soul, funk, jazz and poetry worked, but since they fail so miserably, the lack of improvisation and inspiration from Silver, saxophonist Harold Vick, trumpeter Cecil Bridgewater, guitarist Richie Resnicoff, bassist Rob Cranshaw and drummer Mickey Roker only emphasizes what a mess Total Response is. —Stephen Thomas Erlewine

Total Response (Phase II) / Nov. 15, 1970+Jan. 29, 1971 / Blue Note ♦♦

In Pursuit of the 27th Man / 1970+Nov. 10, 1972 / Blue Note ♦♦♦♦
This obscure Horace Silver LP features two separate sessions by the pianist/composer. On three selections he is joined by trumpeter Randy Brecker, tenor great Michael Brecker, Bob Cranshaw on electric bass and drummer Mickey Roker. The other four numbers feature vibraphonist David Friedman in a quartet with Silver, Cranshaw and Roker, a very unusual sound for a Horace Silver set. But no matter what the instrumentation, the style is pure Silver, hard-driving and melodic hard bop with a strong dose of funky soul. —Scott Yanow

All (Phase III) / Jan. 17, 1972+Feb. 14, 1972 / Blue Note ♦♦

Silver 'n Brass / Jan. 10, 1975+Jan. 17, 1975 / Blue Note ♦♦♦♦
The first of five LPs that feature Horace Silver's Quintet being augmented by other instrumentalists, this set finds trumpeter Tom Harrell, tenor saxophonist Bob Berg, either Ron Carter or Bob Cranshaw on bass and either Al Foster or Bernard Purdie on drums joined by five brass players and two reed specialists. Although there are tributes to Tadd Dameron ("Dameron's Dance") and Duke Ellington ("The Sophisticated Hippie"), the music is recognizably Silver—funky hard bop. —Scott Yanow

Silver 'n Wood / Nov. 7, 1975-Jan. 3, 1976 / Blue Note ♦♦♦
The second of five LPs that find Horace Silver's Quintet (which by 1976 featured trumpeter Tom Harrell and tenor saxophonist Bob Berg) augmented by a group of other players, this set has six reeds and two trombones, giving Silver more tone colors to work with than usual. The two side-long works ("The Tranquilizer Suite" and "The Process of Creation Suite") are not all that memorable but the music overall (helped out by strong solos) is typical Silver hard bop. —Scott Yanow

Silver 'n Voices / Sep. 24, 1976-Oct. 1, 1976 / Blue Note ♦♦
Horace Silver, a brilliant composer of funky melodies, was never that strong a lyricist despite his good intentions. For this set (following the Silver 'n' Brass and Sil-

ver 'n' Wood sessions), the pianist's quintet (featuring trumpeter Tom Harrell and tenorman Bob Berg) is joined by six voices under the direction of Alan Copeland. The self-help lyrics get a bit cloying and the voices simply weigh down the music but there are some good solos along the way. —*Scott Yanow*

Silver 'n Percussion / Nov. 12, 1977-Nov. 17, 1977 / Blue Note ✦✦✦

Following sessions that featured Horace Silver's Quintet being augmented respectively by brass, reeds and voices, percussion was the logical next step. Silver's 1977 band starred trumpeter Tom Harrell and tenor saxophonist Larry Schneider and on this record they are joined by one or two percussionists, and seven voices. The pianist/leader pays tribute to his African heritage and to the American Indians' spiritual beliefs in two separate side-long suites but, even with the "plot," the music has its funky moments. —*Scott Yanow*

Silver 'n Strings Play the Music of the Spheres / Nov. 3, 1978-Nov. 2, 1979 / Blue Note ✦✦

Horace Silver's final Blue Note record (after over 25 years on the label) is a double LP that augments his quintet (featuring fluegelhornist Tom Harrell and tenor saxophonist Larry Schneider) with 14 strings and a harp. In addition, there are four vocalists (including Gregory Hines) singing lyrics that reflect Silver's self-help and spiritual beliefs. He was never as strong a lyricist as he was a composer and pianist so the vocals weigh down the music a bit. The song titles probably kept a few of these pieces from becoming better known. Who ever heard of such songs as "Negative Patterns of the Subconscious," "Progress Through Dedication and Discipline" and "We Expect Positive Results"? —*Scott Yanow*

Spiritualizing the Senses / Jan. 19, 1983 / Silveto ✦✦✦

There's No Need to Struggle / Aug. 25, 1983-Sep. 1, 1983 / Silveto ✦✦✦

Continuity of Spirit / Mar. 25, 1985 / Silveto ✦✦

After the original Blue Note label eventually collapsed, pianist Horace Silver (who was with the company for over 25 years) formed his own private label, Silveto (using the Emerald subsidiary to issue older concert performances). The *Continuity of Spirit* finds Silver (along with the Los Angeles Modern String Orchestra, four woodwinds, fluegelhornist Carl Saunders and three vocalists) paying tribute to Duke Ellington, W.C. Handy and Scott Joplin. The idea of using disc jockey Chuck Niles as "the spirit of Duke Ellington" is fairly hokey and the original music owes little to Ellington, Handy or Joplin; everything is in Horace Silver's own style. But there are some swinging moments on this well-intentioned set. —*Scott Yanow*

Music to Ease Your Disease / Mar. 31, 1988 / Silveto ✦✦✦

Horace Silver has long been a believer in the self-help holistic movement and this has been reflected in the lyrics he has written during the past decade. Andy Bey interprets such songs on this LP as "What Is the Sinus-Minus," "The Respiratory Story" and the title cut, none of which seem destined to be covered by others. However there are plenty of strong instrumental moments from an all-star quintet that includes pianist Silver, fluegelhornist Clark Terry, tenor saxophonist Junior Cook, bassist Ray Drummond and drummer Billy Hart, and for that reason this is the strongest release on Silveto to date. —*Scott Yanow*

It's Got to Be Funky / Feb. 8, 1993+Feb. 9, 1993 / Columbia ✦✦✦✦

After a 13-year period in which he mostly recorded for his private Silveto label, pianist/composer Horace Silver was rediscovered by Columbia for this session. Rather than featuring a standard quintet as he did throughout his career, the funky pianist is heard with his trio, a six-piece brass ensemble and guest tenors Red Holloway, Eddie Harris and Branford Marsalis; Andy Bey contributes four vocals. All of the music (except for a remake of "Song for My Father") was new and served as proof that the master of jazz-funk had not lost his stuff. —*Scott Yanow*

Pencil Packin' Papa / 1994 / Columbia ✦✦✦✦

This CD's main assets are the many new compositions by Horace Silver and his colorful arrangements for the six-piece brass section. Although not enough is heard from the brass players on an individual basis (the greatly underrated trumpeter Oscar Brashear and trombonist George Bohanon get just one solo apiece), this is partly alleviated by the guest tenors. Red Holloway solos on seven songs while James Moody, Eddie Harris and Rickey Woodard each pop up twice. In addition, O.C. Smith does a fine job on his four vocals although Silver's abilities as a lyricist are still open to question. However his piano solos are typically exciting and inventive and Silver has obviously lost none of his enthusiasm even after four decades of music making. —*Scott Yanow*

Hard Bop Grandpop / Feb. 29, 1996-Mar. 1, 1996 / GRP ✦✦✦✦✦

Pianist Horace Silver's 1996 CD introduced ten new compositions and, although none of the originals will probably become standards, they are consistently catchy, full of the infectious Silver personality and very viable vehicles for improvisation. The instrumental set matches Silver with quite an all-star group comprising trumpeter Claudio Roditi, tenor saxophonist Michael Brecker (an alumnus), trombonist Steve Turre, baritonist Ronnie Cuber, bassist Ron Carter and drummer Lewis Nash.

Most of the selections feature solo space for one or two of the horn players (all get their spots), and the results live up to the great potential. One of Horace Silver's finest recordings in his post-Blue Note era. —*Scott Yanow*

A Prescription for the Blues / 1997 / GRP ✦✦✦

For this 1997 quintet set, pianist/composer Horace Silver has a reunion with a pair of his alumni (tenor saxophonist Michael Brecker and trumpeter Randy Brecker) and interacts with bassist Ron Carter and drummer Louis Hayes. None of Silver's nine recent originals (which include tributes to Lester Young, Martin Luther King, his two late brothers, and even cowboy movies) are destined to become standards, and the tenorman sounds a bit restrained, but the leader's piano solos are witty (with many humorous song quotes), swinging, typically funky and creative. —*Scott Yanow*

Omer Simeon

b. Jul. 21, 1902, New Orleans, LA, **d.** Sep. 17, 1959, New York, NY
Clarinet, Tenor Saxophone / New Orleans Jazz, Swing

Omer Simeon's career can easily be divided into three parts due to significant associations with Jelly Roll Morton, Earl Hines and Wilbur DeParis. Although born in New Orleans, Simeon ironically did not start to play clarinet until he moved with his family to Chicago in 1914. He took lessons from Lorenzo Tio, Jr., and soon afterward was working professionally. After playing with his brother, violinist Al Simeon's band, Omer spent four years (1923-27) with Charlie Elgar's Creole Orchestra. It was during this time that he met up with Jelly Roll Morton (he soon became Morton's favorite clarinetist) and recorded classic sides with him in 1926 and 1928; among the many gems were "Black Bottom Stomp," "The Chant," "Someday Sweetheart" (taking a reluctant solo on bass clarinet), "Doctor Jazz" and a trio rendition of the complex "Shreveport Stomp."

Simeon worked regularly with King Oliver in 1927 and with his successor Luis Russell the following year. After returning to Chicago, he was with Erskine Tate's Vendome Orchestra (1928-30) and then joined Earl Hines' big band in 1931, where during the next six years he was well featured on both clarinet and tenor, making many recordings with the great pianist. After leaving Hines, Simeon spent briefer periods in the big bands of Horace Henderson (1938), Walter Fuller (1940) and Coleman Hawkins. He was a member of the Jimmie Lunceford Orchestra from 1942 on, not only staying during the big band's declining years but remaining after Lunceford's death in 1947 during the three years that Ed Wilcox led the ghost orchestra; Simeon also recorded Dixieland with Kid Ory during 1944-45. Moving back to New York, Omer Simeon became the clarinetist with Wilbur DeParis' "New New Orleans Jazz" Band, touring and recording with the spirited ensemble up until his death in 1959. Although a highly rated clarinetist for 35 years and considered one of the most technically skilled of all New Orleans-born reed players, Omer Simeon's only opportunities to lead record sessions resulted in just two songs in 1929 and a Jazztone trio set in 1954. —*Scott Yanow*

Sonny Simmons (Huey Simmons)

b. Aug. 4, 1933, Sicily Island, LA
Alto Saxophone / Avant-Garde, Free Jazz

Altoist Sonny Simmons made a strong impression in the 1960s as one of the most promising avant-garde players. He grew up in Oakland, CA, started playing English horn and then at 16 took up the alto. Stints with Lowell Fulsom and Amos Milburn and some time spent playing bebop preceded Simmons finding his own sound in free jazz. In 1961 he spent some time with Charles Mingus and then in 1962 he formed a group with flutist Prince Lasha. After they recorded *The Cry*, Simmons moved to New York, recorded with Elvin Jones and Eric Dolphy and then in 1965 he returned to the Bay Area. Simmons met and married the powerful trumpeter Barbara Donald, recorded for ESP and the duo performed and recorded in several settings. However by the mid-'70s Simmons largely dropped out of music, the marriage broke up and the altoist was forgotten for nearly 20 years. In 1994 Sonny Simmons (who had apparently played on the streets and been scuffling) suddenly re-emerged in peak form and as adventurous as ever, recording a brilliant trio album (*Ancient Ritual*) for Qwest/Warner Bros that earned him long overdue recognition and launched the beginning of his second career. Simmons has since recorded an additional set for Qwest and a few dates for the CIMP label. —*Scott Yanow*

Staying on the Watch / Aug. 30, 1966 / ESP ✦✦✦✦

Altoist Sonny Simmons' debut as a leader is a typically stimulating and dense ESP blowout. Performing in a quintet with trumpeter Barbara Donald, the up-and-coming pianist John Hicks, bassist Teddy Smith and drummer Marvin Pattillo, Simmons stretches out on four colorful and mostly free-form originals. The intense set (which has been reissued on CD) still sounds quite advanced over three decades later. —*Scott Yanow*

Music from the Spheres / Dec. 1966 / ESP ✦✦✦✦

Sonny Simmons' second of two ESP sessions (both have been reissued on CD) is, if anything, even more powerful than his first. The altoist is joined by trumpeter Barbara Donald, pianist Michael Cohen, bassist Juney Booth, drummer James Zitro and, on "Dolphy's Days" (one of Simmons' four originals), tenor saxophonist Bert Wilson. The compositions are a bit stronger than on the first date (including "Zarak's Symphony" and "Balladia"), while the improvisations are just as intense; Donald deserves to be rated with Valaida Snow as the top female jazz trumpeter of all time. Unlike with most ESP dates (which tend to be overly brief), Simmons' albums have a reasonable amount of playing time. This recommended set clocks in at 47 minutes. —*Scott Yanow*

Manhattan Egos / Feb. 10, 1969 / Arhoolie ✦✦✦✦

During 1966-70 the avant-garde altoist Sonny Simmons recorded five albums as a leader. His third set, a memorable outing for Arhoolie, has yet to be reissued on CD and is probably the least known of the five. Simmons, his wife trumpeter Barbara Donald, bassist Juma and drummer Paul Smith make for a very potent combination on five originals by the leader (including "Coltrane in Paradise" and "Manhattan Egos"). On "Seven Dances of Salami," Voodoo Bembe is added on conga, Juma switches to conga and Simmons plays English horn; definitely an unusual trio. The music overall is avant-garde, often quite free and powerful. —*Scott Yanow*

Rumasuma / Jul. 31, 1969-Aug. 1, 1969 / Contemporary ✦✦✦✦

This is an LP long overdue to be reissued on CD. The masterful but underrated avant-garde altoist Sonny Simmons is featured with the powerful trumpeter Barbara Donald, pianist Mike Cohen, both Jerry Sealund and Bill Pickens on basses and drummer Billy Higgins during four of his originals. The compositions range from a structured piece and two fairly free-form numbers to "Reincarnation," which is based in an abstract way on a blues. Exciting and very creative music. —*Scott Yanow*

Burning Spirits / Nov. 24, 1970 / Contemporary ✦✦✦✦

A two-fer with Barbara Donald (tpt), Cecil McBee (b) and Richard Davis (d). —*Michael G. Nastos*

● Backwoods Suite / Jan. 1982 / West Wind ✦✦✦✦✦

Ancient Ritual / Dec. 7, 1992-Dec. 8, 1992 / Qwest ✦✦✦✦✦

When this CD was released in 1994, it should have resulted in altoist Sonny Simmons getting a comeback-of-the-year award. Playing in a sparse trio with bassist Charnett Moffett and his son Zarak Simmons on drums, the veteran saxophonist proved to not only be in prime form after many years off the scene, but just as fiery and adventurous as he had been in the 1960s. Simmons' eight originals (which include "Reincarnation," "Country Parson" and "Sundown in Egypt") have plenty of variety, but it is the frequently telepathic interplay between the three musicians during improvisations that makes this CD essential for open-minded listeners. —*Scott Yanow*

Transcendence / Apr. 9, 1996 / CIMP ✦✦✦✦

On this CD, the combination of instruments really should not work. The trio consists of altoist Sonny Simmons, Michael Marcus doubling on two horns made famous by Rahsaan Roland Kirk (stritch and manzello), and drummer Charles Moffett; there is no piano, guitar or bass. Both Marcus and Simmons also perform duet pieces with Moffett, while the leader is unaccompanied on "Geraldine's Dream." Somehow, the band usually sounds quite full during the spontaneous and adventurous but coherent jams. The musicians are not afraid of melody or rhythm, but they are also free to play as outside as they feel. An intriguing set. —*Scott Yanow*

Judgment Day / May 4, 1996 / CIMP ✦✦✦✦

As with altoist Sonny Simmons' previous CIMP release, this CD is unusual, but for different reasons. Simmons is once again joined by Michael Marcus (who this time doubles on manzello and C-melody sax) and drummer Charles Moffett, but also by bassist Steve Neil, whose presence makes the music seem slightly more conventional. However, Simmons decided to play the entire set on tenor, and he is surprisingly effective, still holding onto his quite individual musical personality. Marcus is showcased in a duet with Neil ("Monk Mania"), while "The Call for Old Sirius" was performed by the trio without Marcus. The six selections (four of which are quite lengthy) contain rather adventurous playing, but the communication between the musicians (including drummer Moffett, who is heard on one of his final recordings) is impressive. Recommended to open-eared listeners. —*Scott Yanow*

American Jungle / Apr. 8, 1997 / Qwest ✦✦✦✦

Altoist Sonny Simmons' second Warner Bros. release is not quite on the same level as his first. "Coltrane Story" and "My Favorite Things" are too close in style to John Coltrane (with pianist Travis Shook, bassist Reggie Workman and drummer Cindy Blackman closely emulating 'Trane's rhythm section), and even the other three numbers hint strongly at Coltrane. Simmons does play quite well throughout, and

this set helped consolidate his unlikely comeback. However, *Ancient Ritual* is the Sonny Simmons CD to get first. —*Scott Yanow*

Nina Simone

b. Feb. 21, 1933, Tryon, NC
Vocals, Piano / Standards

Of all the major singers of the late 20th century, Nina Simone is one of the hardest to classify. She's recorded extensively in the soul, jazz, and pop idioms, often over the course of the same album; she's also comfortable with blues, gospel, and Broadway. It's perhaps most accurate to label her as a "soul" singer in terms of emotion, rather than form. Like, say, Aretha Franklin, or Dusty Springfield, Simone is an eclectic, who brings soulful qualities to whatever material she interprets. These qualities are among her strongest virtues; paradoxically, they also may have kept her from attaining a truly mass audience. The same could be said of her stage persona; admired for her forthright honesty and individualism, she's also known for feisty feuding with audiences and promoters alike.

If Simone has a chip on her shoulder, it probably arose from the formidable obstacles she had to overcome to establish herself as a popular singer. Raised in a family of eight children, she originally harbored hopes of becoming a classical pianist, studying at New York's prestigious Juilliard School of Music—a rare position for an African-American woman in the 1950s. Needing to support herself while she studied, she generated income by working as an accompanist and giving piano lessons. Auditioning for a job as a pianist in an Atlantic City nightclub, she was told she had the spot if she would sing as well as play. Almost by accident, she began to carve a reputation as a singer of secular material, though her skills at the piano would serve her well throughout her career.

In the late '50s, Simone began recording for the small Bethlehem label (a subsidiary of the vastly important early R&B/rock 'n' roll King label). In 1959, her version of George Gershwin's "I Loves You Porgy" gave her a Top 20 hit—which would, amazingly, prove to be the only Top 40 entry of her career. Nina wouldn't need hit singles for survival, however, establishing herself not with the rock 'n' roll/R&B crowd, but with the adult/nightclub/album market. In the early '60s, she recorded no less than nine albums for the Candix label, about half of them live. These unveiled her as a performer of nearly unsurpassed eclecticism, encompassing everything from Ellingtonian jazz and Israeli folk songs to spirituals and movie themes.

Simone's best recorded work was issued on Philips during the mid-'60s. Here, as on Candix, she was arguably overexposed, issuing seven albums within a three-year period. These records can be breathtakingly erratic, moving from warm ballad interpretations of Jacques Brel and Billie Holiday and instrumental piano workouts to brassy pop and angry political statements in a heartbeat. There's a great deal of fine music to be found on these, however. Simone's moody-yet-elegant vocals are like no one else's, presenting a fiercely independent soul who harbors enormous (if somewhat hard-bitten) tenderness.

Like many African-American entertainers of the mid-'60s, Simone was deeply affected by the civil rights movement and burgeoning Black pride. Some (though by no means most) of her best material from this time addressed these concerns in a fashion more forthright than almost any other singer. "Old Jim Crow" and, more particularly, the classic "Mississippi Goddam" were especially notable self-penned efforts in this vein, making one wish that Nina had written more of her own material instead of turning to outside sources for most of her repertoire.

Not that this repertoire wasn't well chosen. Several of her covers from the mid-'60s, indeed, were classics: her revision of Weill-Brecht's "Pirate Jenny" to reflect the bitter elements of African-American experience, for instance, or her mournful interpretation of Brel's "Ne Me Quitte Pas." Other highlights were her versions of "Don't Let Me Be Misunderstood," covered by the Animals for a rock hit; "I Put a Spell on You," which influenced the vocal line on the Beatles' "Michelle"; and the buzzing, jazzy "See Line Woman."

Simone was not as well served by her tenure with RCA in the late '60s and early '70s, another prolific period which saw the release of nine albums. These explored a less eclectic range, with a considerably heavier pop-soul base to both the material and arrangements. One bona fide classic did come out of this period: "Young, Gifted & Black," written by Simone and Weldon Irvine, Jr., would be successfully covered by both Aretha Franklin and Donny Hathaway. She did have a couple of Top Five British hits in the late '60s with "Ain't Got No" (from the musical *Hair*) and a cover of the Bee Gees' "To Love Somebody," neither of which rank among her career highlights.

Simone fell on turbulent times in the 1970s, divorcing her husband/manager Andy Stroud, encountering serious financial problems, and becoming something of a nomad, settling at various points in Switzerland, Liberia, Barbados, France, and Britain. After leaving RCA, she recorded rarely, although she did make the critically well-received *Baltimore* in 1978 for the small CTI label. She had an unpredictable resurgence in 1987, when an early track, "My Baby Just Cares for

Me," became a big British hit after being used in a Chanel perfume television commercial. 1993's *A Single Woman* marked her return to an American major label, and her profile was also boosted when several of her songs were featured in the film *Point of No Return*. She published her biography, *I Put a Spell on You*, in 1991. —*Richie Unterberger*

Little Girl Blue / 1957 / Bethlehem ◆◆◆◆◆

Evidence's CD reissues Nina Simone's first recording which originally came out on Bethlehem. Backed by bassist Jimmy Bond and drummer Al "Tootie" Heath, Simone gives a variety of standards some rather emotional treatments, really disguising "Mood Indigo" and "Good Bait," turning "You'll Never Walk Alone" into a powerful spiritual and adding an odd shuffle beat to "My Baby Just Cares for Me." The latter would be a surprise hit for Simone upon its reissue decades later but it was this version of "I Loves You Porgy" that gave her her initial fame. Even at this early stage, Nina Simone was a very individual singer and pianist. Recommended. —*Scott Yanow*

☆ Nina at Town Hall / Sept. 12, 1959 / Colpix ◆◆◆◆◆

One of Nina Simone's finest recordings, this Colpix LP features the unique singer-pianist performing classic versions of "Black Is the Color of My True Love's Hair," "The Other Woman" and "Wild Is the Wind." With supportive work from bassist Jimmy Bond and drummer Al "Tootie" Heath, Simone also sounds fine on a few instrumentals. "Summertime" is performed twice, once as a vocal. From the start of her career, Nina Simone carved out her own unique niche, meshing together her classical piano technique with folk singing, civil rights protest lyrics and jazz. All of those elements are in evidence on this highly recommended set. —*Scott Yanow*

The Amazing Nina Simone / 1959 / Colpix ◆◆◆◆◆

There is a remarkable amount of variety on this LP, Nina Simone's second recording. Her repertoire ranges from a swinging "Stompin' at the Savoy" and an emotional "It Might as Well Be Spring" to an English folk ballad ("Tomorrow"), spirituals, an R&B song ("You've Been Gone Too Long") and the theme song from the movie *Middle of the Night*. Somehow Simone brings credibility to each of these very different songs. She does not play much piano (just cameos on two songs) and is backed by a subtle orchestra arranged by Bob Mersey that is effective accompanying her vocals. This long-out-of-print LP finds Nina Simone's voice in top form and with a few exceptions is generally jazz-oriented. —*Scott Yanow*

★ The Best of the Colpix Years / 1959-1963 / Roulette ◆◆◆◆◆

Nineteen tracks from her Colpix label recordings. Dating from 1959 to 1963, this mix of studio and live material is considerably more weighted toward jazz and standards by the likes of Ellington, Cole Porter, Rodgers & Hammerstein, and Irving Berlin than the more eclectic albums she would later cut in the '60s and '70s for Philips and RCA. The highlights are when she steps out of the soulful supper club style into more earthier settings, as on "House of the Rising Sun," "Forbidden Fruit," "Gin House Blues," "Work Song," and her own "Children Go When I Send You" (all of which she would considerably rework over the years). Includes three previously unreleased tracks in a traditional jazz style with minimal arrangements. Note: the version of "(I Loves You) Porgy," her sole Top 20 entry, is not her 1959 hit single, but a live 1960 version. —*Richie Unterberger*

Anthology: The Colpix Years / 1959-1964 / Rhino ◆◆◆◆◆

Simone recorded prolifically during her affiliation with Colpix in the late '50s and early '60s. This 40-song, two-CD set presents choice extracts from approximately ten albums worth of material. It isn't quite as impressive as what she recorded for Philips in the mid-'60s, sticking to a more pop- and light jazz-based approach, and not mining blues and soul nearly as heavily. She was also writing hardly any of her own tunes, and had yet to fully expound upon issues of black pride and social justice. These are ultimately minor quibbles; it's a fine set, in which Simone already demonstrates commanding vocals and a wide-ranging stylistic base that incorporates material by Duke Ellington, Rodgers & Hart, Billie Holiday, Nat Adderley, "House of the Rising Sun," and even a Hebrew tune. It also has three non-LP cuts, including the self-penned, African-tinged "Blackbird," and "Come on Back, Jack," an answer record to Ray Charles' "Hit the Road, Jack." By the way, this doesn't make the single-disc *Colpix Years* CD on Roulette totally redundant, as that release has half a dozen tracks which don't appear on this anthology. —*Richie Unterberger*

Nina Simone at the Village Gate / 1961 / Roulette ◆◆◆◆◆

Nina Simone has the rare ability of really being able to dig into material and bring out unexpected meaning in familiar lyrics. On "Just in Time" from this CD reissue, she gives one the impression that if she had not been found "Just in Time," she would have committed suicide. During "He Was Too Good to Me," Simone sounds absolutely stunned about the end of a love affair. "Brown Baby" is both hopeful and defiant in its call for freedom while "Zungo" is an African work song. Also from her 1961 trio performance at the Village Gate, Simone performs the overly serious "If He Changed My Name," the good-time gospel piece "Children Go Where

I Send You," a regretful rendition of "House of the Rising Sun" and an unpredictable instrumental version of "Bye Bye Blackbird." Nina Simone, who was always in a category by herself, is heard throughout in her early prime. —*Scott Yanow*

Broadway-Blues-Ballads / 1964 / Verve ◆◆◆

There's a lot more Broadway and a lot more ballads than blues on this, which ranks as one of her weaker mid-'60s albums. Almost half the record features Broadway tunes on the order of Cole Porter and Rodgers & Hammerstein; most of the rest was composed by Bennie Benjamin, author of her first-rate "Don't Let Me Be Misunderstood," which the Animals covered for a hit shortly afterwards (and which leads off this record). The other Benjamin tunes are modified uptown soul with string arrangements and backup vocals in the vein of "Don't Let Me Be Misunderstood," but aren't in the same league, although "How Can I?" is an engaging cha-cha. Besides "Don't Let Me Be Misunderstood," the album is most notable for the great "See Line Woman," a percolating call-and-response number that ranks as one of her best tracks. The CD reissue includes the strange bonus cut "The Monster," an odd attempt at a soul novelty tune. —*Richie Unterberger*

Nina Simone in Concert / 1964 / Philips ◆◆◆◆◆

This is probably the most personal album that Simone issued during her stay on Philips in the mid-'60s. On most of her studio sessions, she worked with orchestration that either enhanced her material tastefully or smothered her, and she tackled an astonishingly wide range of material that, while admirably eclectic, made for uneven listening. Here, the singer and pianist is backed by a spare, jazzy quartet, and some of the songs rank among her most socially conscious declarations of African-American pride: "Old Jim Crow," "Pirate Jenny," "Go Limp," and especially "Mississippi Goddam" were some of the most forthright musical reflections of the civil rights movement to be found at the time. In a more traditional vein, she also reprises her hit "I Loves You, Porgy," and the jazz ballad "Don't Smoke in Bed." This LP was combined with the 1965 album *I Put a Spell on You* on a CD reissue. —*Richie Unterberger*

Verve Jazz Masters, Vol. 58: Nina Simone Sings Nina / Mar. 21, 1964-1987 / Polygram ◆◆◆

The sequel to Nina Simone's *Verve Jazz Masters, Vol. 17*, *Verve Jazz Masters, Vol. 58: Nina Simone Sings Nina* features a selection of Simone's original songs, as well as her adaptations of jazz standards. Though jazz purists will find the sampler nature of this compilation a bit maddening, the compilation nevertheless is useful for casual fans and neophytes, hitting many of her best-known songs, inlcuding "Sugar in My Bowl" and "The Last Rose of Summer." —*Thom Owens*

Verve Jazz Masters 17: Nina Simone / 1964-1966 / Verve ◆◆◆

Simone's inclusion in Verve's "Jazz Masters" series is a bit suspect; there was a lot of jazz in Simone, true, but wasn't there quite a bit of pop and soul as well, not to mention some blues? Anyway, this is an excellent survey of her mid-'60s work, with 16 tracks spanning 1964 to 1966 that find Nina at her most versatile and assured. Quite a range is encompassed here: traditional folk ("Black Is the Color of My True Love's Hair"), R&B (her jazzy rendition of "I Put a Spell on You"), Jacques Brel ("Ne Me Quitte Pas"), Billie Holiday ("Strange Fruit"), the Gershwins ("I Loves You Porgy"), Rodgers/Hart ("Little Girl Blue"), and modern jazz (Nat Adderley's "Work Song"). Other highlights are the mesmerizing "See-Line Woman" and the original version of "Don't Let Me Be Misunderstood," which was a hit for the Animals shortly afterwards. On the two original compositions, "Four Women" and "Mississippi Goddam," Simone confronts racism in a head-on fashion rare for the time. Discographical details: the version of "Little Girl Blue" is a mono alternate take, and the recording of "My Baby Just Cares for Me" is not from the mid-'60s, but a 1987 live album. —*Richie Unterberger*

The Ultimate Nina Simone / Mar. 21, 1964-Aug. 1966 / Verve ◆◆◆

On this celebrity's choice tour through the Verve archives, singer Dianne Reeves comes up with a most interesting, idiosyncratic selection of the Philips recordings of Nina Simone, intuitively sequencing the tracks herself. Reeves zeroes in on the experimental side of Simone, celebrating her differences from Tin Pan Alley-oriented singers, even equivocating a bit on the term "jazz singer" in describing her style. Reeves mostly avoids standards like the plague, opting for unusual songs like the stark a cappella "Images," the chain-gang-styled "Be My Husband," the hypnotic, percussion-backed "Come Ye," or an example of Nina on piano only ("Blue on Purpose"). Besides being her congenitally feisty self, Simone is also caught displaying poignant moodiness on "The Other Woman," a live remake of her hit "I Loves You, Porgy," and "Don't Explain"—all sequenced together. Any adventurous listener coming to Nina Simone for the first time through this collection will definitely be tempted to explore some more of her output. —*Richard S. Ginell*

I Put a Spell on You / Jan. 1965 / Mercury ◆◆◆

One of her most pop-oriented albums, but also one of her best and most consistent. Most of the songs feature dramatic, swinging large-band orchestration, with the accent on the brass and strings. Simone didn't write any of the material, turning to popular European songsmiths Charles Aznavour, Jacques Brel, and Anthony Newley, her husband Andy Stroud and her guitarist Rudy Stevenson for bluesier fare. Really fine tunes and interpretations, on which Simone gives an edge to the potentially fey pop songs, taking a sudden (but not uncharacteristic) break for a straight jazz instrumental with "Blues on Purpose." The title track, a jazzy string ballad version of the Screamin' Jay Hawkins classic, gave the Beatles the inspiration for the phrasing on the bridge of "Michelle." This LP has been combined with the 1964 *In Concert* album on a CD reissue. —*Richie Unterberger*

Pastel Blues / May 19, 1965-May 20, 1965 / Mercury ♦♦♦

If this is blues, it's blues in the Billie Holiday sense, not the Muddy Waters one. This is one of Nina's more subdued mid-'60s LPs, putting the emphasis on her piano rather than band arrangements. It's rather slanted toward torch-blues ballads like "Strange Fruit," "Trouble in Mind," Billie Holiday's own composition "Tell Me More and More and Then Some," and "Nobody Knows You When You're Down and Out." Simone's then-husband, Andy Stroud, "wrote" "Be My Husband," an effective adaptation of a traditional blues chant. By far the most impressive track is her frantic ten-minute rendition of the traditional "Sinnerman," an explosive tour de force that dwarfs everything else on the album. *Pastel Blues* has been combined with the 1966 LP *Let It Out* onto a single-disc CD reissue. —*Richie Unterberger*

☆ High Priestess of Soul / 1966 / Philips ♦♦♦♦♦

Perhaps a bit more conscious of contemporary soul trends than her previous Philips albums, this is still very characteristic of her mid-'60s work in its eclectic mix of jazz, pop, soul, and some blues and gospel. Hal Mooney directs some large-band arrangements for the material on this LP without submerging Simone's essential strengths. The more serious and introspective material is more memorable than the good-natured pop selections here. The highlights are her energetic vocal rendition of the Oscar Brown/Nat Adderley composition "Work Song" and her spiritual composition "Come Ye," on which Simone's inspirational vocals are backed by nothing other than minimal percussion. —*Richie Unterberger*

Let It All Out / 1966 / Philips ♦♦♦

One of her more adult pop-oriented mid-'60s albums, with renditions of tunes by Duke Ellington ("Mood Indigo"), Billie Holiday ("Don't Explain"), Irving Berlin ("This Year's Kisses"), and Rodgers & Hart ("Little Girl Blue"). As ever, Simone ranges wide in her selection: Bob Dylan's "The Ballad of Hollis Brown," a swaggering adaptation of "Chauffeur Blues" (credited to her husband of the time, Andy Stroud), the gospel hymn "Nearer Blessed Lord," and Van McCoy's "For Myself." "Images" is an a cappella adaptation of a poem about the beauty of blackness by W. Cuney. All of Simone's Philips albums are solid, and this is no exception, while it isn't the best of them. This LP has been combined with the 1965 album *Pastel Blues* on a single-disc CD reissue. —*Richie Unterberger*

Wild Is the Wind / 1966 / Philips ♦♦♦

This album was apparently a bit of a pastiche of leftovers from sessions for her four previous albums on Philips. But you'd never guess from listening; the material is certainly as strong and consistent as it is on her other mid-'60s LPs. As is the case with most of her albums of the time, the selections are almost unnervingly diverse, ranging from jazz ballads to traditional folk tunes ("Black Is the Color of My True Love's Hair") to the near calypso of "Why Keep on Breaking My Heart" to the somber, almost chilling title track. Highlights are two outstanding pop-soul numbers written by the pre-disco Van McCoy ("Either Way I Lose," "Break Down and Let It All Out") and "Four Women," a string of searing vignettes about the hardships of four African-American women that ranks as one of Simone's finest compositions. This LP has been combined with the 1967 album *High Priestess of Soul* on one CD reissue. —*Richie Unterberger*

The Blues / Dec. 19, 1966-Jun. 24, 1971 / Novus ♦♦♦♦♦

Most of the music on this CD reissue dates from 1966-67, featuring the unique singer-pianist Nina Simone joined by a funky rhythm section (with Eric Gale and Rudy Stevenson on guitars and organist Ernest Hayes) in addition to Buddy Lucas on tenor and harmonica; a few of the other selections utilize a larger backup group. Simone is the star throughout the blues-based material, performing fresh and emotional versions of such songs as Lil Green's "In the Dark," "My Man's Gone Now," "Since I Fell for You" and "The House of the Rising Sun." Some of Simone's original songs deal frankly with love and sex while others protest racism and poverty. Stimulating and still-timely music. —*Scott Yanow*

The Essential Nina Simone, Vol. 2 / Jun. 21, 1967-Feb. 17, 1971 / RCA ♦♦

Simone's stint with RCA in the late '60s and early '70s was not her most fruitful. Whether of her own volition or RCA's, she pursued a more consciously pop/soul direction. While her vocal skills remained intact, the arrangements and material were not among her best. *Essential, Vol. 2* collects 16 tracks from 1967-71, many of them inappropriate pop or rock covers. "Here Comes the Sun" and "Just like a Woman" are great songs, but these are not great versions. "Angel of the Morning,"

"Everyone's Gone to the Moon," and "Cherish" aren't bad mainstream pop songs, but they will not be remembered as the best ones that Simone was given to sing. Simone herself wrote none of this material (except "Revolution"), and her considerable jazz inclinations are virtually absent. She's most effective when singing with nothing except a piano, as she does on "The Human Touch," "Another Spring," and "The Desperate Ones." —*Richie Unterberger*

The Essential Nina Simone / 1967-1972 / RCA ♦♦

Nina Simone has penned unforgettable protest material, covered jazz, folk, rock, and pop with equal flair, and created a body of work that's kept her popularity high. While this title is hardly accurate, since it only covers RCA material from 1967-1972, there's plenty of anthemic fare among the CD's 16 selections. These include "Mr. Bojangles," "To Be Young, Gifted, and Black," "Seems I'm Never Tired Lovin' You," and "Since I Fell for You." While the absence of "Baltimore," "I Wish I Knew How It Feels to Be Free," and "Here Comes the Sun" (to name only three) is sizable, and the weighting of this compilation toward well-known rock types (Bob Dylan, Randy Newman, Jimmy Webb, George Harrison, two Bee Gees cuts) debatable, there's still no way it can be dismissed. —*Ron Wynn*

A Single Woman / 1993 / Asylum ♦♦♦

Vocalist, composer and pianist Nina Simone returned from a lengthy self-imposed exile in 1993 with an autobiography and outstanding CD highlighting her still impressive singing and interpretative skills in an intriguing context, surrounded by strings and guitars. While the backdrops were lush and occasionally corny, Simone's deep, penetrating voice, careful pacing and dramatic delivery kept the songs from becoming sappy. While she's always been a great protest and political singer, Simone is also a superb romantic/love song stylist. Simone remains among America's premier performers, and this CD was a welcome addition to her sparkling legacy. —*Ron Wynn*

Zoot Sims (John Haley Sims)

b. Oct. 29, 1925, Inglewood, CA, **d.** Mar. 23, 1985, New York, NY
Tenor Saxophone / Bop, Cool

Throughout his career, Zoot Sims was famous for epitomizing the swinging musician, never playing an inappropriate phrase. He always sounded inspired, and although his style did not change much after the early 1950s, Zoot's enthusiasm and creativity never wavered.

Zoot's family was involved in vaudeville, and he played drums and clarinet as a youth. His older brother Ray Sims developed into a fine trombonist who sounded like Bill Harris. At age 13, Sims switched permanently to the tenor, and his initial inspiration was Lester Young, although he soon developed his own cool-toned sound. Sims was a professional by the age of 15, landing his first important job with Bobby Sherwood's Orchestra, and joined Benny Goodman's big band for the first time in 1943; he would be one of BG's favorite tenormen for the next 30 years. He recorded with Joe Bushkin in 1944, and even at that early stage, his style was largely set.

After a period in the Army, Sims was with Goodman from 1946-47. He gained his initial fame as one of Woody Herman's "Four Brothers" during his time with the Second Herd (1947-49). Zoot had brief stints with Buddy Rich's short-lived big band, Artie Shaw, Goodman (1950), Chubby Jackson and Elliot Lawrence. He toured and recorded with Stan Kenton (1953) and Gerry Mulligan (1954-56). Sims was also a star soloist with Mulligan's Concert Jazz Band of the early 1960s and visited the Soviet Union with Benny Goodman in 1962. A freelancer throughout most of his career, Sims often led his own combos or co-led bands with his friend Al Cohn; the two tenors had very similar sounds and styles. Zoot started doubling on soprano quite effectively in the 1970s. Through the years, he appeared in countless situations, and always seemed to come out ahead. Fortunately, Zoot Sims recorded frequently, leading sessions for Prestige, Metronome, Vogue, Dawn, Storyville, Argo, ABC-Paramount, Riverside, United Artists, Pacific Jazz, Bethlehem, Colpix, Impulse, Groove Merchant, Choice, Sonet, and a wonderful series for Pablo. —*Scott Yanow*

Quartets / Sep. 16, 1950+Aug. 14, 1951 / Original Jazz Classics ♦♦♦♦

This CD reissue features the great tenor saxophonist Zoot Sims (who was then 25) leading his first American recording dates. He is heard with two quartets, the team of pianist John Lewis, bassist Curly Russell and drummer Don Lamond and with pianist Harry Biss, bassist Clyde Lombardi and drummer Art Blakey. All but two numbers clock in around the three-minute mark: an over eight-minute alternate version of "Zoot Swings the Blues" and an 11-minute "East of the Sun." Sims is in fine form throughout these cool-toned but hard-swinging sets. —*Scott Yanow*

Zoot Sims in Paris / June 26, 1950+Nov. 18, 1953 / Vogue ♦♦♦♦♦

This reissue CD from Vogue (made available domestically through BMG) has all of the music that the constantly swinging tenor Zoot Sims recorded at two Paris sessions. He is heard on seven titles (plus six alternate takes) in 1950 with a quiet but firm quartet comprising pianist Gerald Wiggins, bassist Pierre Michelot and drummer Kenny Clarke; "Night and Day," "I Understand" and "Zoot and Zoot" are among the high points. The final six selections feature Sims with trombonist Frank Rosolino, pianist Henri Renaud, guitarist Jimmy Gourley, bassist Don Bagley and drummer Jean-Louis Viale for some cool bop in the same basic style as the earlier set. —*Scott Yanow*

One to Blow On / Jan. 11, 1956+Jan. 18, 1956 / Biograph ✦✦✦✦
This 1979 Biograph LP (seven of the eight numbers have since been reissued by the label on CD) features some exciting if "cool" performances by tenorman Zoot Sims and valve trombonist Bob Brookmeyer in a quintet with pianist John Williams, bassist Milt Hinton and drummer Gus Johnson. Highlights include "September in the Rain," "Them There Eyes" and several of Sims' fairly basic originals including the medium-tempo blues "One to Blow On." The LP is filled with swinging music that features some exciting jammed ensembles. —*Scott Yanow*

The Rare Dawn Sessions / Jan. 11, 1956-Aug. 10, 1956 / Biograph ✦✦✦
This CD is a bit of a disappointment, not for the music but for the packaging. During 1979-1980, Biograph came out with two Zoot Sims LPs (*One to Blow On* and *The Big Stampede*) that contained 16 selections in all. But this CD just has ten of the songs, seven of the eight tunes from the first album (why did they leave out "September in the Rain"?) and three of the eight numbers from the second date. The incomplete nature of this reissue series is a pity for the music is excellent. Sims' tenor fits in very well with the valve trombone of Bob Brookmeyer during the earlier quintet date and also blends nicely with the cool-toned trumpet of Jerry Lloyd on the final three numbers. The music is swinging with Sims already starting to show an original musical personality built out of the sound of Lester Young. But the CD is only recommended to those listeners unable to find the two earlier LPs. —*Scott Yanow*

● **Tonite's Music Today** / Jan. 31, 1956 / Black Lion ✦✦✦✦✦
Valve trombonist Bob Brookmeyer's musical partnerships in the 1950s with Stan Getz and especially Gerry Mulligan were celebrated but he also recorded three fine albums with tenor saxophonist Zoot Sims in 1956 that are quite enjoyable, feature colorful jammed ensembles and hard-swinging yet cool-toned solos that owe as much to the swing tradition as to the innovations of bebop. This Storyville CD finds Zoot and Brookmeyer accompanied by pianist Hank Jones, bassist Wyatt Reuther and drummer Gus Johnson. Highlights include "I Hear a Rhapsody," "Blue Skies" and Sims' first ever recorded vocal on a "Blues." This release is easily recommended as is its companion Storyville CD Morning Fun. —*Scott Yanow*

● **Morning Fun** / Feb. 1956 / Black Lion ✦✦✦✦✦
Although it claims on the back of this CD that the music was recorded in August 1956, discographies state February and that seems more logical since valve trombonist Bob Brookmeyer and tenor saxophonist Zoot Sims did not team up for a very long period (although three records resulted from their valuable collaboration). With assistance from pianist John Williams, bassist Bill Crow and drummer Jo Jones, Sims and Brookmeyer are in fine form on such selections as a rollicking "The King," "Lullaby of the Leaves," a brief two-song ballad medley and Brookmeyer's "Whooeeeee!" Sims takes a rare (and fairly effective) vocal on "I Can't Get Started." Recommended, as is the other Black Lion Zoot Sims CD from the same period, *Tonite's Music Today*. —*Scott Yanow*

The Big Stampede / Aug. 10, 1956-Sep. 1956 / Biograph ✦✦✦✦
This LP features tenor saxophonist Zoot Sims in a quintet with trumpeter Jerry Lloyd (a fine if somewhat forgotten cool-toned bopper), pianist John Williams, Bill Anthony or Knobby Totah on bass and drummer Gus Johnson. The band plays a rare version of Thelonious Monk's "Bye Ya" (one of the first by a non-Monk group), three standards and originals by Jerry Lloyd, John Williams and Al Cohn ("Jerry's Jaunt"). Although nothing all that surprising occurs, Sims blends in well with Lloyd and the solos by the principals are up to par. Straightahead jazz collectors will want this LP which has only been partly (three out of the eight songs) reissued on CD. —*Scott Yanow*

Zoot! / Dec. 13, 1956+Dec. 18, 1956 / Original Jazz Classics ✦✦✦
For a little while in the mid-'50s, Zoot Sims occasionally doubled on alto although he soon switched back exclusively to tenor where he had a stronger musical personality. On this CD reissue of a Riverside set from 1956, Sims plays alto on two of the seven tracks and works well with trumpeter Nick Travis. Actually pianist George Handy, who contributed four originals (two standards and drummer Osie Johnson's "Osmosis" complete the program) and did all of the arranging, comes across as the key supporting player; bassist Wilbur Ware and Johnson are fine in quiet support. Although Handy's arrangements are a bit modern, this is still a typically hard-swinging and melodic Zoot Sims date. —*Scott Yanow*

Zoot Sims Plays Four Altos / Jan. 11, 1957 / ABC/Paramount ✦✦
This brief LP (under 33 minutes) is a bit of a novelty since Zoot Sims, normally a tenor player, overdubbed his playing on four altos (with support from pianist John Williams, bassist Knobby Totah and drummer Gus Johnson). The obvious question

("Why?") is never answered and the music (arranged and composed by George Handy) is nothing that unique or special. Zoot Sims completists will want to get these obscure but swinging solos but this experimental date was ultimately rather pointless. —*Scott Yanow*

The Four Brothers: Together Again / Feb. 11, 1957 / RCA ✦✦✦✦✦
The original "Four Brothers" as heard in the 1947-48 Woody Herman Orchestra were tenors Stan Getz, Zoot Sims and Herbie Steward and baritonist Serge Chaloff. In 1948 Al Cohn replaced Steward. In 1957 for this "reunion" session Getz was not available so instead Sims, Steward, Cohn and Chaloff were contacted. Accompanied by a rhythm section that includes pianist Elliott Lawrence, they naturally revived "Four Brothers" but otherwise mostly played newer songs by Gerry Mulligan, Manny Albam (who provided the date's arrangements), Lawrence, Cohn and Sims. Due to his bad health, Chaloff did not play many of the ensemble passages (Charlie O' Kane filled in) but he did take all of the solos; this would be his final recording. The music overall on this CD reissue is quite enjoyable and Sims, Cohn and Steward show how much they had grown during the previous decade. —*Scott Yanow*

Happy Over There / 1957-1958 / Jass ✦✦✦
There is less than a half-hour of music on this date and the liner graphics are dumb but there are some fine moments to be heard from the boppish players. Pianist Elliott Lawrence actually organized the date (which was not released until this LP came out in 1987) and Bill Elton wrote the colorful arrangements. In addition to tenor saxophonist Zoot Sims, the other musicians include Al Cohn (sticking to baritone), trumpeter Nick Travis, trombonist Jimmy Cleveland, bassist Milt Hinton and drummer Osie Johnson. Together they perform eight of Hoagy Carmichael's best-known compositions including "Skylark," "The Nearness of You," "Georgia on My Mind" and "Stardust." The playing is fine although, due to the set's brevity, this LP is only recommended to those listeners who can find it at a budget price. —*Scott Yanow*

Down Home / Jul. 1960 / Bethlehem ✦✦✦✦
Tenor saxophonist Zoot Sims recorded on a regular basis as a leader for most of 45 years, and virtually all of his many sessions are worth acquiring. Sims' Bethlehem date also gives one a look at the great pianist Dave McKenna in his early days, along with bassist George Tucker and drummer Danny Richmond. Sims mostly explores standards from the swing era (including a rare version of "Bill Bailey") on this enjoyable and consistently swinging set. —*Scott Yanow*

Either Way / Feb. 1961 / Evidence ✦✦✦✦
This formerly obscure set (reissued on CD by Evidence) matches together the always complementary (and sometimes identical-sounding) tenors of Zoot Sims and Al Cohn. A special treat to the spirited quintet date (with Mose Allison on piano, bassist Bill Crow and drummer Gus Johnson) are the three excellent vocals from the long-forgotten singer Cecil "Kid Haffey" Collier. Based on his swinging version of "Nagasaki" and fine renditions of "Sweet Lorraine" and "I Like It like That," he certainly did not deserve his obscurity. It is fun to hear Sims and Cohn work with a vocalist, jamming behind him and launching into their solos. The five instrumentals, which include the riffing "P-Town," the only ballad of the date ("Autumn Leaves") and the heated blues "Morning Fun," are excellent too, making this a set well worth picking up. —*Scott Yanow*

Two Jims and Zoot / May 1964 / Mainstream ✦✦✦
This slightly unusual date features tenor saxophonist Zoot Sims interacting with two guitarists (Jimmy Raney and Jim Hall) while given subtle support by bassist Steve Swallow and drummer Osie Johnson. Although the eight selections (none of which caught on as standards) had all been written recently and sometimes display the influence of bossa nova, the quiet performances could pass for 1954 rather than 1964. The cool-toned improvisations and boppish playing have a timeless quality about them although for the time period aspects of this music already sounded a bit old-fashioned. —*Scott Yanow*

Suitably Zoot / Oct. 29, 1965+Nov. 26, 1965 / Pumpkin ✦✦✦✦
It is strange to think that Zoot Sims, who made many records in the 1950s and the '70s, only had one studio date as a leader between 1964-1971 (not counting this Pumpkin LP). On this album Zoot Sims is teamed with fellow tenors Al Cohn and Richie Kamuca (along with pianist Dave Frishberg, bassist Tommy Potter and drummer Mel Lewis) for lengthy versions of "Tickle Toe" and "Broadway"; Cohn takes solo honors. In addition Sims has a reunion with valve trombonist Bob Brookmeyer (they had played together regularly during part of 1956) and (with fine work from pianist Roger Kellaway, bassist Bill Crow and drummer Dave Bailey) their versions of "On the Alamo" and "The King" are hard-swinging and enjoyable. This collector's LP (whose music has not yet been reissued on CD) is highly recommended for Zoot Sims and bebop fans. —*Scott Yanow*

Nirvana / 1972 / GM ✦✦✦✦

Zoot at Ease / May 1973-Aug. 1973 / Mobile Fidelity ✦✦✦✦
This Mobile Fidelity audiophile CD reissues a long-out-of-print and rare Zoot Sims set originally made for the defunct Famous Door label. Accompanied by pianist Hank Jones, bassist Milt Hinton and either Louie Bellson or Grady Tate on drums, Zoot (who doubles on tenor and soprano) is in typically swinging form. In addition to a few standards, Sims explores some obscurities (including "Alabamy Home" and "In the Middle of a Kiss") and even turns the theme of "Rosemary's Baby" into jazz. A slightly above-average set from a saxophonist who always sounded inspired. —*Scott Yanow*

Zoot Sims Party / Apr. 1974 / Choice ✦✦✦✦
Just prior to starting his longtime association with Norman Granz's Pablo label, Zoot Sims recorded this relaxed set for Choice. Sims, who switches between tenor and soprano, swings lightly with pianist Jimmy Rowles, bassist Bob Cranshaw and drummer Mickey Roker on six standards, three of which ("Fred," "Restless" and "Dream Dancing") are somewhat obscure. The results are tasteful, informal and typically swinging. —*Scott Yanow*

☆ **Zoot Sims and the Gershwin Brothers** / Jun. 6, 1975 / Original Jazz Classics ✦✦✦✦✦
Along with his album with Count Basie (*Basie and Zoot*) during the same period, this is one of Sims' most exciting recordings of his career. Greatly assisted by pianist Oscar Peterson, guitarist Joe Pass, bassist George Mraz and drummer Grady Tate, he explores ten songs written by George and Ira Gershwin. Somehow the magic was definitely present and, whether it be stomps such as "The Man I Love," "Lady Be Good" and "I Got Rhythm" or warm ballads (including "I've Got a Crush on You" and "Embraceable You"), Zoot Sims is heard at the peak of his powers. A true gem that has been reissued on CD. —*Scott Yanow*

Zoot Plays Soprano / Jan. 8, 1976-Jan. 9, 1976 / Pablo ✦✦✦✦✦
Zoot Sims, known throughout his career as a hard-swinging tenor saxophonist, started doubling successfully on soprano in 1973 and managed to become one of the best by simply playing in his own musical personality. This particular LP (not yet available on CD) was his only full-length set on soprano but it is a rewarding one. Assisted by pianist Ray Bryant, bassist George Mraz and drummer Grady Tate, Sims is in top form on such songs as "Someday Sweetheart," "Wrap Your Troubles in Dreams," "Ghost of a Chance" and two of his originals. A delightful set of swinging jazz, it's a surprise success. —*Scott Yanow*

Zoot Sims with Bucky Pizzarelli / Aug. 1976 / Classic Jazz ✦✦✦
Tenor saxophonist Zoot Sims and guitarist Bucky Pizzarelli perform eight highly enjoyable duets although, at under 32 minutes, this album is overly brief. However what is here is excellent with the highlights including "What Is This Thing Called Love," "Take Ten" and "There Will Never Be Another You." This music has not yet been reissued on CD. —*Scott Yanow*

Hawthorne Nights / Sep. 20, 1976-Sep. 21, 1976 / Original Jazz Classics ✦✦✦✦
Unlike most of his Pablo sessions, this Zoot Sims CD is not a quartet outing but an opportunity for his tenor to be showcased while joined by a nine-piece group that includes six horns (three reeds among them). Bill Holman's inventive arrangements are a large part as to why the date is successful but Sims' playing on the five standards, two Holman pieces and his own "Dark Cloud" should not be overlooked. Fortunately there is also some solo space saved for the talented sidemen (which include Oscar Brashear and Snooky Young on trumpets, trombonist Frank Rosolino and the woodwinds and reeds of Jerome Richardson, Richie Kamuca and Bill Hood). A well-rounded set of swinging jazz. —*Scott Yanow*

If I'm Lucky / Oct. 27, 1977-Oct. 28, 1977 / Original Jazz Classics ✦✦✦✦
Tenor saxophonist Zoot Sims recorded quite a few albums with pianist Jimmy Rowles during his Pablo years; all are recommended. Rowles assisted Sims in coming up with obscurities to interpret, and this CD reissue is highlighted by such little-performed songs as "If I'm Lucky," "Shadow Waltz," "Gypsy Sweetheart" and "I Wonder Where Our Love Has Gone." The lead voices are backed ably by bassist George Mraz and drummer Mousey Alexander on this enjoyable straightahead date. —*Scott Yanow*

For Lady Day / Apr. 10, 1978-Apr. 11, 1978 / Pablo ✦✦✦✦✦
It is strange that this album was not released until the CD came out in 1990 for tenor saxophonist Zoot Sims and pianist Jimmy Rowles' tribute to Billie Holiday is melodic, tasteful and largely memorable. Together with bassist George Mraz and drummer Jackie Williams back in 1978, they perform 11 songs associated with Billie Holiday including quite a few that would have been lost in obscurity if Lady Day had not uplifted them with her recordings. Highlights include "Easy Living," "Some Other Spring," "I Cried for You," "Body and Soul" and "You're My Thrill." A lyrical and heartfelt tribute. —*Scott Yanow*

Live in Copenhagen / Aug. 24, 1978 / Storyville ✦✦✦✦
This delightful and solidly swinging club date was first released on this 1995 CD. The great tenor Zoot Sims is assisted by pianist Kenny Drew, bassist Niels Peder-

sen and drummer Ed Thigpen; the music is as enjoyable as one would expect. Sims, who switches to soprano on "The Very Thought of You," never seems to have played an uninspired chorus. Highlights include "Groovin' High," "All the Things You Are" and "It's All Right with Me." Recommended. —*Scott Yanow*

Warm Tenor / Sep. 18, 1978-Sep. 19, 1978 / Pablo ✦✦✦✦
The Pablo label was a perfect home for Zoot Sims during the second half of the 1970s for the cool-toned tenor always sounded at his best in informal settings with small groups where he had the opportunity to stretch out. This quartet set with pianist Jimmy Rowles, bassist George Mraz and drummer Mousey Alexander (which has been reissued on CD) gives Zoot a chance to interpret a variety of mostly underplayed standards along with a duet with Mraz on an ad-lib "Blues for Louise." Highlights include "Old Devil Moon," "You Go to My Head," "Blue Prelude" and "You're My Thrill." —*Scott Yanow*

Just Friends / Dec. 18, 1978-Dec. 20, 1978 / Original Jazz Classics ✦✦✦
Although from different generations, tenor saxophonist Zoot Sims and trumpeter Harry "Sweets" Edison both always liked to swing, making their successful collaboration on this CD reissue not much of a surprise. With assistance from pianist Roger Kellaway, bassist John Heard and drummer Jimmie Smith, the two veterans jam on seven standards and Edison's "A Little Tutu." The results are predictable but colorful and inventive within the boundaries of the idiom. —*Scott Yanow*

Passion Flower / Aug. 14, 1979-May 13, 1980 / Pablo ✦✦✦✦
Benny Carter provided the arrangements for the 16-piece band that accompanies the great tenor Zoot Sims on this set of Duke Ellington songs. The LP is highlighted by "In a Mellow Tone," "I Got It Bad," "Passion Flower" and "Bojangles," but all nine selections are enjoyable and Sims is in top form. In fact it can easily be argued that Zoot Sims never made an indifferent or unswinging album, so it is not much of a surprise that this date is quite successful and should greatly appeal to straightahead jazz fans. —*Scott Yanow*

The Swinger / Dec. 10, 1979-Dec. 11, 1979 / Pablo ✦✦✦✦
This Pablo LP gave tenor saxophonist Zoot Sims a rare opportunity to record with his brother Ray, a spirited trombonist who was greatly influenced by Bill Harris. Together they join forces with pianist Jimmy Rowles and one of two rhythm sections (John Heard or Michael Moore on bass and Shelly Manne or John Clay on drums) for a set of standards, obscurities (including Andy Kirk's "Now I Lay Me Down to Dream of You" and Al Cohn's "Danielle") and Zoot's "Mr. J.R. Blues." The Sims brothers (who should have collaborated more often) blend together quite well and the music often swings quite hard; other highlights include "The Jeep Is Jumping" and "She's Funny That Way." —*Scott Yanow*

I Wish I Were Twins / Jul. 6, 1981 / Pablo ✦✦✦✦
Zoot Sims (doubling on tenor and soprano) teams up once again with pianist Jimmy Rowles; this time bassist Frank Tate and drummer Akira Tana are the supporting cast. Rowles is a master not only at accompanying soloists (he always seems to come up with the perfect chord) but in picking up superior obscurities to perform. In addition to "Georgia on My Mind" and "The Touch of Your Lips," this LP contains such tunes as "I Wish I Were Twins," "Changes" and Johnny Mercer's "You Go Your Way"; Sims contributed "The Fish Horn" to feature his soprano. A fine swinging date filled with thoughtful improvisations. —*Scott Yanow*

Blues for Two / Mar. 6, 1982+Jun. 23, 1982 / Original Jazz Classics ✦✦✦✦✦
Although guitarist Joe Pass recorded many unaccompanied solo albums, he made relatively few dates as part of a duo. This CD reissue of a session with tenor saxophonist Joe Pass works quite well because Zoot Sims was a natural swinger who did not need a full rhythm section to push him. His playing on the selections (mainly standards including "Dindi," "Poor Butterfly," "Pennies from Heaven" and "I Hadn't Anyone till You") is as heated and lyrical as usual. Pass also warms up quickly to the situation (Sims must have been easy to accompany) and takes many fine solos of his own. The pair collaborated on the opening "Blues for 2" and "Takeoff" which wraps up the highly enjoyable set. —*Scott Yanow*

Innocent Years / Mar. 9, 1982 / Pablo ✦✦✦
For this Pablo album, the great tenor Zoot Sims (who doubles on soprano) interprets five pretty melodies plus his own "Pomme au Four" with a quartet comprising pianist Richard Wyands, bassist Frank Tate and drummer Akira Tana. All of the selections are highlights so they are worth mentioning: "I Hear a Rhapsody," "Over the Rainbow" (which Sims plays for nearly 11 minutes), "The Very Thought of You," "If You Were Mine" and "Indian Summer." This ballad-oriented set is successful both as background music and for close listening. —*Scott Yanow*

Zoot Case / Jun. 8, 1982 / Sonet ✦✦✦✦✦
During a 30-year period the very complementary tenors Zoot Sims and Al Cohn teamed up on an irregular but always consistently satisfying basis. This club date from Stockholm, one of their final joint recordings, features the pair backed by pianist Claes Croona, bassist Palle Danielsson and drummer Petur Ostlund. Both Zoot and Cohn sound quite inspired and they really push each other on "Exactly like

You," "After You've Gone" (which features Sims on soprano) and even a surprisingly heated version of "The Girl from Ipanema." Al Cohn's tone had deepened during the years and, although they sounded nearly identical in the 1950s, it is quite easy to tell the two tenors apart during this encounter. The CD (available through the Swedish Sonet label) is highly recommended for fans of the saxophonists and for bop collectors in general. —*Scott Yanow*

On the Korner / Mar. 20, 1983 / Pablo ♦♦♦♦♦

Just two years and three days away from his death at age 59, the great tenor Zoot Sims is heard in prime form on this live session from San Francisco's legendary club Keystone Korner. The music was not initially released until this 1994 CD but it was worth the wait. The hard-swinging tenor (who plays equally effective soprano on Duke Ellington's "Tonight I Shall Sleep" and "Pennies from Heaven") is ably supported by the fine pianist Frank Collett, bassist Monty Budwig and drummer Shelly Manne. Sims plays his usual repertoire from the period (including "I Hear a Rhapsody," "If You Could See Me Now" and "Dream Dancing") but, although he had previously recorded virtually all of these selections, the "new" versions are well worth hearing. This late date gives one a definitive look into Zoot Sims' playing of his last decade, when he interpreted standards in a timeless style that had grown but not really changed since the 1950s. Recommended. —*Scott Yanow*

Suddenly It's Spring / May 26, 1983 / Original Jazz Classics ♦♦♦♦

This CD reissue of one of tenor saxophonist Zoot Sims' final recordings adds a version of "Emaline" to the original program. Pianist Jimmy Rowles often co-stars on the date (with bassist George Mraz and drummer Akira Tana offering solid support). The lyrical repertoire emphasizes ballads and pretty melodies with the high points including such offbeat material as Woody Guthrie's "So Long," Sims' "Brahms...I Think," "In the Middle of a Kiss" and the more familiar "Never Let Me Go" and "Suddenly It's Spring." The melodic performances are quite warm, romantic and enjoyable, fine examples of subtle creativity. —*Scott Yanow*

Quietly There: Zoot Sims Plays Johnny Mandel / Mar. 20, 1984-Mar. 21, 1984 / Pablo ♦♦♦♦

For his final Pablo session and next-to-last recording (just a year before his death), tenor saxophonist Zoot Sims shows that, on record at least, he never did decline. With tasteful accompaniment provided by pianist Mike Wofford, bassist Chuck Berghofer, drummer Nick Ceroli and Victor Feldman on percussion, the great tenor performs seven of Johnny Mandel's compositions. The emphasis is on ballads but, other than "A Time for Love" and "Emily," the material is somewhat obscure and therefore quite fresh. A special highlight is a song that Mandel wrote for Sims that is aptly titled "Zoot." Overall this is a tasteful and typically swinging session that finds Zoot Sims exiting on top while still in his musical prime. —*Scott Yanow*

In a Sentimental Mood / Nov. 21, 1984 / Sonet ♦♦♦♦

Frank Sinatra

b. Dec. 12, 1915, Hoboken, NJ, **d.** May 14, 1998, Los Angeles, CA
Vocals / Swing, Pop, Show Tunes, Soft Rock, Traditional Pop, Ballads
Though Frank Sinatra's reputation as celebrity, icon, bad boy, and possibly the greatest singer of American popular songs of the century are paramount to the general public, he has always been valued highly in the jazz community, especially among musicians. Though not a jazz singer per se, he was a child of the big-band era, incubated with an ability to swing in a relaxed, ingratiating way in all kinds of material. Whenever he had the chance, Sinatra would credit Billie Holiday as a primary influence on his vocal style—even recording a tribute song called "Lady Day" in 1970—and he learned circular breathing at the feet of trombonist Tommy Dorsey. Particularly from the mid-1950s into the mid-1960s, Sinatra would use expert jazzmen prominently in his recording orchestras, as well as arrangers who cut their teeth in the big-band era. He was at his freest and loosest when paired with a great big band like that of Count Basie, where he would bend to the rhythm, embroider the melody, and stray from the tune to the point where non-jazz-oriented aficionados of singing would become disoriented. Indeed, the theory has been advanced that during the '60s, flinging himself head-on against the rock 'n' roll tide of the time, Sinatra was actually able to revive the big-band era in terms of mass popularity, record sales, concert receipts, and media exposure—although this time, the orientation was in favor of the singer rather than the band. Had he chosen to explore it more, Sinatra could have also been the most important bossa nova singer of his time; even so, the two albums he did make with Antonio Carlos Jobim display an uncanny emotional affinity for the idiom. Other than Brazilian music, though, Sinatra stayed away from developments in jazz beyond swing (unless one counts a quirk like his notorious "do-be-do-be-do" scatting at the close of "Strangers in the Night").

The son of an ex-boxer and a domineering, ambitious mother, Sinatra quit school early in order to begin his musical career, winning the Major Bowes Amateur Hour radio contest at 19 as a member of the Hoboken Four. Shortly after leaving Benny Goodman to form his own big band, Harry James hired Sinatra as a featured singer in 1939, and graciously relinquished him to Tommy Dorsey the following year. Backed by the vocal group the Pied Pipers, Sinatra's star rose to the point where in 1942, he broke out of the Dorsey ranks with four solo sides on his own. The wild, orgiastic reaction that Sinatra aroused during the war years announced the rise of the solo singer act in pop music, a development that would help send the big bands reeling. Though Sinatra was known mostly for his smooth, straightforward ballads during what are now known as the Columbia years (1943-52), occasionally his primary arranger Axel Stordahl and others like George Siravo would cook up a big-band chart for him. He also recorded "Sweet Lorraine" with the Metronome All-Stars (including Nat Cole and members of the Dorsey and Ellington bands) in 1946 and other intimately jazzy sides with the small combos of Page Cavanaugh, Phil Moore and Tony Mottola.

Upon moving to the Capitol label in 1953, many of Sinatra's recordings took on a tougher, more swinging, jazz-driven edge, with first Nelson Riddle and then, more vehemently, Billy May contributing sophisticated extensions of big-band-era techniques. The apex of the Riddle recordings is *Songs for Swingin' Lovers* (1955-56), where Sinatra rides confidently along with the swing of the band; May's charts for *Come Fly with Me* (1957) and *Come Swing with Me* (1958) push the swing envelope even farther and harder. The move to Sinatra's own label Reprise in 1961 found the singer working with other jazz-grounded arrangers like Johnny Mandel, Neal Hefti and Quincy Jones, as well as May and Riddle. In addition to *Sinatra and Swingin' Brass*, Hefti wrote the charts for Sinatra's initial studio encounter with Basie, *Sinatra/Basie*, while Jones did the follow-up, *It Might as Well Be Swing*, and conducted the live album with Basie, *Sinatra at the Sands*. A bit late for the bossa nova boom, Sinatra started working with Jobim in 1967 and again in 1969—the latter session did not come out in its entirety until 1995—and 1967 also saw a one-time-only summit meeting with Duke Ellington's orchestra.

Following a short "retirement" (1971-73), a darker-toned Sinatra usually worked live in tandem with a big band sometimes augmented by strings, playing the vintage and occasionally new arrangements whose creators the singer almost always credited by name. The Woody Herman band played the old charts on Sinatra's live album *The Main Event*, and for Sinatra's last ungimmicked studio album, *L.A. Is My Lady*, Quincy Jones assembled an all-star band full of famous jazzers like George Benson, Randy and Michael Brecker, and Lionel Hampton. Sinatra kept on singing into his late 70s, well after the point when his voice had lost its luster and elasticity. All that was left was his exquisite control over phrasing stemming largely from jazz influences—and in many cases, that was enough. He retired unofficially, possibly for good, in 1995 after experiencing memory lapses in performances, but with his reputation as the master of American popular song unassailably intact. —*Richard S. Ginell*

● Sinatra / 1931-1979 / Warner Brothers ♦♦♦♦

This is the two-disc soundtrack to a 1992 television mini-series about the life of Frank Sinatra. There is no musical scoring, and there are no rerecordings. Rather, this is a collection of 30 songs recorded between 1931 and 1979, most by Sinatra, although Bing Crosby, Benny Goodman, and Billie Holiday also make appearances. What is notable about the set is that it is the only album to combine tracks from Sinatra's recordings on Columbia, RCA Victor, Capitol, and Reprise, and thus the only one offering the breadth of his work over a period of 40 years. Of course, it remains a sampler, and there's far more great Sinatra material, but the unique circumstances make this an excellent compilation for the beginner. —*William Ruhlmann*

☆ The Song Is You / Feb. 1, 1940-Jul. 2, 1942 / RCA ♦♦♦♦♦

This very attractive five-CD box set has every studio recording that Frank Sinatra recorded with Tommy Dorsey's Orchestra plus a full disc of mostly unreleased radio broadcasts. Since Sinatra has never really been a jazz singer and most of the selections are ballads, jazz listeners may not consider this box essential but Frank Sinatra fans will not need to be told of its existence twice. Sinatra's first session as a leader (from early 1942) is also included (along with a large and colorful booklet), giving listeners a very definitive look into his early days. —*Scott Yanow*

Greatest Hits / Feb. 1, 1940-Aug. 6, 1942 / RCA Victor ♦♦♦

For this entry in RCA Victor's *Beginner's Guide to Jazz* series, 15 selections featuring Frank Sinatra with Tommy Dorsey's Orchestra are reissued. All are available in more complete series but, despite the somewhat random programming (which is far from chronological) and the omission of a personnel list, this is a fine introductory set. Sinatra is heard (sometimes with the Pied Pipers) on such famous recordings as "I'll Never Smile Again," "The One I Love," "Polka Dots and Moonbeams," "Without a Song" and "Once in a While." —*Scott Yanow*

The V-Discs: Columbia Years: 1943-45 / 1943-1945 / Columbia ♦♦♦

Sinatra's earliest wartime recordings are finally collected on this lovingly assembled two-disc set, which is essential for his serious fans. Sinatra's style isn't as smooth as his recordings with Tommy Dorsey or his Captiol records, but his developing style is very exciting in its own right. —*Stephen Thomas Erlewine*

☆ **The Best of the Columbia Years: 1943-1952** / 1943-1952 / Columbia ◆◆◆◆

A four-disc distillation of the mammoth 12-disc box *The Columbia Years (1943-1952): The Complete Recordings*, *The Best of the Columbia Years 1943-52* provides everything most listeners need to know about Frank Sinatra's early career. Nearly all of his classic performances of the era are included in these 100 tracks, which are sequenced chronologically. Completists will need the 12-disc set, but *The Best of the Columbia Years* will satisfy the needs of most fans. —*Stephen Thomas Erlewine*

The Columbia Years (1943-1952): The Complete Recordings / 1943-1952 / Columbia ◆◆◆◆◆

For serious students of popular singing, this 12-disc box set is indispensable. During his early years at Columbia, Sinatra defined what popular singing was, and these 285 songs show why he was so revolutionary. For many, 12 discs is too much music, but for collectors, the set is essential. —*Stephen Thomas Erlewine*

★ **Portrait of Sinatra: Columbia Classics** / 1943-1952 / Sony ◆◆◆◆◆

Portrait of Sinatra: Columbia Classics is a double-disc, 36-track collection that features Sinatra's biggest hits from his Columbia years, including "Someone to Watch over Me," "The House I Live In," "All or Nothing at All" and "Stormy Weather." Although the compilation contains eight unreleased cuts that will appeal only to collectors, it remains the best and most affordable overview of Sinatra's early years. —*Stephen Thomas Erlewine*

☆ **Songs for Young Lovers/Swing Easy** / Nov. 5, 1953-Apr. 19, 1954 / Capitol ◆◆◆◆

Combining Frank Sinatra's first two 10-inch albums for Capitol, the compact disc *Songs for Young Lovers/Swing Easy* not only contains some of the best music Sinatra recorded, it captures a turning point in popular music. *Songs for Young Lovers* was the first album Frank Sinatra recorded for Capitol, as well as his first collaboration with Nelson Riddle. It was also one of the first—arguably the very first—concept album. Sinatra, Riddle, and producer Voyle Gilmore decided that the new album format should be a special event, featuring a number of songs that are arranged around a specific theme; in addition, the new format was capable of producing a more detailed sound, which gave Riddle more freedom in his arrangements and orchestrations. *Songs for Young Lovers* is a perfect example of this. Supported by a small orchestra, Sinatra and Riddle create an intimate, romantic atmosphere on the record, breathing new life to standards like "My Funny Valentine," "They Can't Take That Away from Me," "I Get a Kick Out of You," and "A Foggy Day." Sinatra sounds revived. No longer does he have to sing the lightweight pop drivel that was forced on him during his latter days at Columbia—he is given weighty songs, and he tears into them. There is a breezy confidence to his singing, as he inhabits each song as if he were living the emotions. Riddle's arrangements are light but jazzy and are more complex than they intially appear. Sinatra and Riddle expanded this approach on his second Capitol album, *Swing Easy!* As the title implies, the record concentrates on uptempo swingers. Again, the songs were all standards—"Just One of Those Things," "Wrap Your Troubles in Dreams," "All of Me"—that benefitted from the new thematic setting, the new arrangements and, of course, Sinatra's increasingly playful and textured vocals. Sinatra plays around with the melodies without leaving them behind, delivering each line with precision. It ranks as one of his most jazzy performances, as well as one of his most fun and carefree records. —*Stephen Thomas Erlewine*

The Best of the Capitol Years: Selections from "The Capitol Years" Box Set / Apr. 30, 1953-Apr. 13, 1960 / Capitol ◆◆◆◆◆

The Best of the Capitol Years is an effective distillation of the 3-disc set, *The Capitol Years*. Featuring singles and album tracks, the disc contains a fair number of highlights from one of Sinatra's most creative periods. Although the albums really are more effective as individual works—and, therefore, straight singles compilations would be ideal—*The Best of the Capitol Years* gives a good introduction to this pivotal phase of Sinatra's career. —*Stephen Thomas Erlewine*

Complete Capitol Singles Collection / Apr. 2, 1953-Sep. 12, 1961 / Capitol ◆◆◆◆◆

The Complete Capitol Singles Collection is exactly what it says it is—all of Frank Sinatra's singles for Captiol Records, both the A-sides and B-sides, as well as duets with artists like Jo Stafford, June Hutton, and the Nuggets, presented in chronological order. Although the majority of these tracks have been collected on other compilations, this four-disc box set is the first time all of the singles have been collected on one set. It also represents the first time many of these tracks—over 20—have appeared on disc and quite a few haven't been reissued since their original release. Arguably, Sinatra was at his creative peak during his tenure at Capitol and while he did release carefully considered albums, his singles—which never

appeared on the albums—were just as electrifying and satisfying as the full-length LPs. In other words, it's an essential set. —*Stephen Thomas Erlewine*

Sinatra 80th: All the Best / 1953-1961 / Capitol ◆◆◆◆◆

Released to coincide with Frank Sinatra's 80th birthday, *Sinatra 80th—All the Best* is a double-disc set that draws from his classic Capitol concept albums, as well as singles from the '50s and a couple of rarities, which aren't particularly compelling. The main strength of the package is as an introduction, since it recaps most of his essential recordings of the '50s and gives a sense of his accomplishments. Nevertheless, the set is only a teaser, since most of Sinatra's Capitol records—both the original albums and single compilations—are better-sequenced and more rewarding. —*Stephen Thomas Erlewine*

☆ **In the Wee Small Hours** / Mar. 1, 1954-Mar. 4, 1955 / Capitol ◆◆◆◆

Expanding on the concept of *Songs for Young Lovers*, *In the Wee Small Hours* was a collection of ballads arranged by Nelson Riddle. The first 12-inch album recorded by Sinatra, *Wee Small Hours* was more focused and concentrated than his two earlier concept records. It's a blue, melancholy album, built around a spare rhythm section featuring a rhythm guitar, celesta, and Bill Miller's piano, with gently aching strings added every once and a while. Within that melancholy mood, is one of Sinatra's most jazz-oriented performances—he restructures the melody and Miller's playing is bold throughout the record. Where *Songs for Young Lovers* emphasized the romantic aspects of the songs, Sinatra sounds like a lonely, broken man on *In the Wee Small Hours*. Beginning with the newly-written title song, the singer goes through a series of standards that are lonely and desolate. In many ways, the album is a personal reflection of the heartbreak of his doomed love affair with actress Ava Gardner, and the standards that he sings form their own story when collected together. Sinatra's voice had deepened and worn to the point were his delivery seems ravished and heartfelt, as if he were living the songs. —*Stephen Thomas Erlewine*

★ **Songs for Swingin' Lovers!** / Oct. 17, 1955-Jan. 16, 1956 / Capitol ◆◆◆◆◆

After the ballad-heavy *In the Wee Small Hours*, Frank Sinatra and Nelson Riddle returned to uptempo, swing material with *Songs for Swingin' Lovers*, arguably the vocalist's greatest swing set. Like Sinatra's previous Capitol albums, *Songs for Swingin' Lovers* consists of reinterpreted pop standards, ranging from the ten-year old "You Make Me Feel So Young" to the 20-year old "Pennies from Heaven" and "I've Got You Under My Skin." Sinatra is supremely confident throughout the album, singing with authority and joy. That joy is replicated in Riddle's arrangements, which manage to rethink these standards in fresh yet reverent ways. Working with a core rhythm section and a full string orchestra, Riddle writes scores that are surprisingly subtle. "I've Got You Under My Skin," with its breathtaking middle section, is a perfect example of how Sinatra works with the band. Both swing hard, stretching out the rhythms and melodies but never losing sight of the original song. *Songs for Swingin' Lovers* never loses momentum. The great songs keep coming and the performances are all stellar, resulting in one of Sinatra's true classics. —*Stephen Thomas Erlewine*

☆ **Come Fly with Me** / Oct. 1, 1957-Oct. 8, 1957 / Capitol ◆◆◆◆◆

Constructed around a light-hearted travel theme, *Come Fly with Me*, Frank Sinatra's first project with arranger Billy May is a breezy change of pace from the somber *Where Are You*. From the first swinging notes of Sammy Cahn and Jimmy Van Heusen's "Come Fly with Me"—which is written at Sinatra's request—it's clear that the music on the collection is intended to be fun. Over the course of the album, Sinatra and May travel around the world in song, performing standards like "Moonlight in Vermont" and "April in Paris," as well as humorous tunes like "Isle of Capri" and "On the Road to Mandalay." May's signature bold, brassy arrangements give these songs a playful, carefree, nearly sarcastic feel, but never is the approach less than affectionate. In fact, *Come Fly with Me* is filled with varying moods and textures, as it moves from boisterous swing numbers to romantic ballads, and hitting any number of emotions in between. There may be greater albums in Sinatra's catalog, but few are quite as fun as *Come Fly with Me*. —*Stephen Thomas Erlewine*

Close to You / 1957 / Capitol ◆◆◆◆

Close to You is one of Frank Sinatra's most gentle and intimate albums, and that is due in no small part to the Hollywood String Quartet, which forms the core of the album's instrumental support. It also was one of the most difficult to record, taking eight months and five different sessions. Certainly, it is one of the most unusual and special of Sinatra's albums, featuring subdued and detailed performances that accentuate both the romantic longing and understated humor of the numbers, which are mainly torch songs. With the Quartet's support, the album comes closer to sounding like a classical album, like a pop variation on chamber music. Where the intimacy of *In the Wee Small Hours* sounded confessional and heart-broken, *Close to You* has a delicate, lovely quality; it may not be seductive, but it is charming and romantic. —*Stephen Thomas Erlewine*

☆ **A Swingin' Affair!** / 1957 / Capitol ✦✦✦✦

In some ways, *A Swingin' Affair* is *Songs for Swingin' Lovers!, Pt. 2*, following the same formula of Sinatra's hit album of the previous year. Beneath the surface, there are enough variations on *A Swingin' Affair* to make it a distinctive, and equally enjoyable listen. The most noticeable difference between the two records is their basic approach. Where *Songs for Swingin' Lovers!* swung hard but managed to stay rather light, *A Swingin' Affair* is a forceful, brassy album—it exudes a self-assured, confident aura. It is a hard, jazzy album. However, the attack is more brash. *—Stephen Thomas Erlewine*

☆ **Where Are You** / 1957 / Capitol ✦✦✦✦✦

Following the hard-driving *A Swingin' Affair*, Frank Sinatra released another all-ballads record, *Where Are You?* The album was the first he recorded at Capitol without Nelson Riddle, as well as the first he recorded in stereo. Where Nelson Riddle's downbeat albums are stately and sullen, Jenkins favors lush, melancholy arrangements played by large, string-dominated orchestras. Jenkins' arrangements suggested classical textures, although the tempos alluded to Billie Holiday's ballad style. *Where Are You?* primarily consists of torch songs, including "The Night We Called It a Day," "I Cover the Waterfront," and "Lonely Town." Throughout the record, Sinatra blends with Jenkins' sumptuous strings, making his voice sound rich, relaxed and regretful. It doesn't have the stark despair of *In the Wee Small Hours*, but its luxurious sadness makes *Where Are You?* a majestic experience of its own. *—Stephen Thomas Erlewine*

☆ **Only the Lonely** / May 25, 1958-Sep. 11, 1958 / Capitol ✦✦✦✦✦

Originally, Frank Sinatra had planned to record *Only the Lonely* with Gordon Jenkins, who had arranged his previous all-ballads album, *Where Are You?* Jenkins was unavailable at the time of the sessions, which led Sinatra back to his original arranger at Capitol, Nelson Riddle. The result is arguably his greatest ballads album. *Only the Lonely* follows the same formula as his previous down albums, but the tone is considerably bleaker and more desperate. Riddle used a larger orchestra for the album than he had in the past, which lent the album a stately, nearly classical atmosphere. At its core, however, the album is a set of brooding saloon songs, highlighted by two of Sinatra's tour de forces—"Angel Eyes" and "One for My Baby." Sinatra never forces emotion out of the lyric, he lets everything flow naturally, with grace. It's a heartbreaking record, the ideal late-night album. *—Stephen Thomas Erlewine*

☆ **Come Dance with Me!** / Dec. 9, 1958-Dec. 23, 1958 / Capitol ✦✦✦✦✦

Working with Billy May again, Frank Sinatra recorded his hardest swing album ever with *Come Dance with Me!* Driven by an intensely swinging horn section, the album has a fair share of slower numbers, but the songs that make the biggest impression are the uptempo cuts. With May's charts wildly careening all over the place, Sinatra relies on his macho swagger; as a result, *Come Dance with Me!* is an intoxicating rush of invigorating dance songs. *—Stephen Thomas Erlewine*

Live in Australia, 1959 / Mar. 31, 1959+Apr. 1, 1959 / Blue Note ✦✦✦✦

In 1959, Frank Sinatra sang two concerts in Australia with the accompaniment of a sextet including his longtime pianist Bill Miller and vibraphonist Red Norvo's group. The show begins with Norvo playing an instrumental version of "Perdido" ("Between the Devil and the Deep Blue Sea," which is referred to in the song listing and Will Friedwald's liner notes, is actually not included on this 1997 CD). Otherwise, this is very much Sinatra's show, as he performs current hits and swing standards. He has the closest interplay with Norvo on the closing "Night and Day"; other highlights include "I Get a Kick Out of You," "I've Got You Under My Skin," a typically swinging "The Lady Is a Tramp" and "One for My Baby." A local big band appears out of nowhere to help out on the final three numbers. Although few revelations occur (and some of Sinatra's talking and use of various synonyms for women get tiring), this was a good setting for his voice. *—Scott Yanow*

No One Cares / 1959 / Capitol ✦✦✦✦✦

Frank Sinatra's second set of torch songs recorded with Gordon Jenkins, *No One Cares* was nearly as good as its predecessor, *Where Are You?* Expanding the melancholy tone of the duo's previous collaboration, *No One Cares* consists of nothing but brooding, lonely songs. Jenkins gives the songs a subtly tragic treatment, and Sinatra responds with a wrenching performance. It lacks the grandiose melancholy of *Only the Lonely*, nor is it as lush as *Where Are You?*, but in its slow, bluesy tempos and heartbreaking little flourishes, it is every bit moving. *—Stephen Thomas Erlewine*

Sinatra's Swingin' Session!!! / Aug. 22, 1960-Sep. 1, 1960 / Capitol ✦✦✦✦✦

Sinatra's Swingin' Session is a fast, driving album, the speediest and hardest swing collection Frank Sinatra ever recorded. The majority of the album is a re-recording of six of the eight songs from his first LP, *Sing and Dance with Frank Sinatra*, as rearranged by Nelson Riddle. Sinatra performed the songs twice as fast as expected; consequently, it's one of his jazziest swing sets, with the musicians spitting out energetic, forceful solos and providing tough, gutsy support. Not only do the uptempo numbers speed by, the ballads are sprightly. It doesn't have the brassy verve of *A Swingin' Affair*, but *Sinatra's Swingin' Session* does have a confident, swaggering flavor of its own that makes it nearly as enjoyable. *—Stephen Thomas Erlewine*

☆ **Nice 'n' Easy** / 1960 / Capitol ✦✦✦✦✦

Breaking slightly from his pattern of a swing album following the release of ballads set, Frank Sinatra followed *No One Cares* with *Nice 'n' Easy*, a breezy collection of midtempo numbers arranged by Nelson Riddle. Not only is it the lightest set that he recorded for Capitol, it is the one with the loosest theme. Sinatra selected a collection of songs he had sang early in his career, having Riddle rearrange the tunes with warm, cheery textures. Unlike his previous ballads albums, *Nice 'n' Easy* doesn't have a touch of brooding sorrow—it rolls along steadily, charming everyone in its path. *—Stephen Thomas Erlewine*

Ring a Ding Ding / Dec. 19, 1960-Dec. 21, 1960 / Reprise ✦✦✦

Ring a Ding Ding, Frank Sinatra's first album for his own record label, broke somewhat from the strict concepts of his Capitol Records; in the process, it set a kind of template for the rest of his '60s Reprise albums. Instead of following a theme, the record captures the atmosphere of Sinatra in 1961—a time when he was running the Rat Pack, so it's no coincidence that the album is named after one of his favorite phrases of the era. The title track was written especially for Sinatra by Sammy Cahn and Jimmy Van Heusen. And that song reflects the brassy, swaggering feeling of the record—even the ballads are arrogant and self-confident. *—Stephen Thomas Erlewine*

★ **The Very Best of Frank Sinatra [Warner Bros.]** / Dec. 19, 1960-Sep. 19, 1979 / Reprise ✦✦✦✦✦

The Very Best of Frank Sinatra is a simple double-disc collection of 40 Sinatra classics from his Reprise Recordings. For casual fans wanting something more than the single-disc *The Very Good Years* but don't want the four-disc *The Reprise Collection*, *The Very Best of Frank Sinatra* is ideal, since it contains all of the true essentials he recorded during the '60s and '70s, including "Summer Wind," "Strangers in the Night," "My Way," "It Was a Very Good Year" and "Theme from New York, New York." *—Stephen Thomas Erlewine*

The Complete Reprise Studio Recordings / Dec. 19, 1960-Dec. 18, 1979 / Warner Brothers ✦✦✦✦✦

Encased in a small, leather-bound trunk and comprising a grand total of 20 discs, Frank Sinatra's *The Complete Reprise Studio Recordings* is easily the most lavish box set ever assembled. In addition to the 20 compact discs, the set comes with a hardcover book containing insightful essays by respected Sinatra scholars like Will Friedwald; the only drawback to the book is every photograph, including the reproduced album covers, is in color-tinted black and white. Nevertheless, the main attraction of *The Complete Reprise Studio Recordings* is the music. Sinatra founded Reprise Records in 1961, and he continued to record for his label over the next two decades, completing nearly 500 songs. Every recording, including several previously unreleased tracks and a handful of cuts that have never appeared on compact disc, that Sinatra made for Reprise is included in the set. By and large, the recordings are sequenced according to session order; the only exceptions are concept albums like *September of My Years* or the *Future* section of the triple album *Trilogy*. (Strangely, the song cycle *Watertown*, which tells a story with its songs, is presented out of order.) Frequently, the sequencing of the original studio albums is more effective than the set's strict chronological presentation, but that's not to say there aren't immense rewards in any one of these long discs. Throughout the 20-disc set, Sinatra comes to grips with rock and contemporary pop music, eventually recording material from songwriters like Jimmy Webb, George Harrison, Neil Diamond, and Billy Joel, as well as occasionally performing arrangements that had more in common with soft rock and easy-listening pop than swinging big bands or the lush orchestrations of Nelson Riddle and Gordon Jenkins. While the quality of his voice does decline during the two decades documented on the box set, much of the music is compelling; although they might not match the consistently brilliant efforts on Columbia and Capitol, the Reprise recordings are rich in variety and drama. The chronological sequencing is effective in portraying Sinatra's evolution, even if the presentation is a bit academic and intimidating for some listeners. Then again, the casual fan isn't going to spend five hundred dollars on a box set. For listeners willing to spend that much money, *The Complete Reprise Studio Recordings* will be endlessly enjoyable and fascinating. *—Stephen Thomas Erlewine*

Come Swing with Me / Mar. 20, 1961-Mar. 22, 1961 / Capitol ✦✦✦

Arranged by Billy May, *Come Swing with Me* was Frank Sinatra's final swing session for Capitol Records. The album falls somewhere between the carefree *Come Fly with Me* and the hard-swinging *Come Dance with Me*, borrowing elements of the humor of *Fly* and the intense, driving rhythms of *Dance*. Recorded without strings or saxes, the brass-heavy sound of the album was noticeable, but it wasn't nearly as distinctive as the ping-ponging, stereo effects of the album. With its extreme stereo separation, *Come Swing With Me* has a bizarre, off-kilter feel that is accentuated by Sinatra's restless vocals. At the time of recording the album, Sinatra was also recording *I Remember Tommy* for Reprise and his affections were with his new label. That doesn't mean he sounds careless on *Come Swing with Me*—in fact, his intense, speedy energy gives the album an edge that distinguishes the record. The album might not be as special as his two previous May collaborations, but it does have enough genuine gems to make it necessary. —*Stephen Thomas Erlewine*

I Remember Tommy / May 1, 1961-May 3, 1963 / Reprise ◆◆◆

As the title suggests, *I Remember Tommy* is an affectionate tribute to Tommy Dorsey, the legendary bandleader who helped elevate Frank Sinatra to stardom. Arranged by Sy Oliver, who also gained attention through Dorsey, the album contains a number of songs that were part of the Sinatra/Dorsey repertoire, given slightly new readings. Though the intentions were good, the new versions pale in comparison to the originals. Nevertheless, there are a handful of gems included on the record, making it worthwhile for dedicated Sinatra aficionados. —*Stephen Thomas Erlewine*

Sinatra Swings [Swing Along with Me] / May 18, 1961-May 23, 1961 / Reprise ◆◆◆

Recorded with Billy May, *Sinatra Swings* was Frank Sinatra's first straight swing album for Reprise Records. In terms of content and approach, the record is remarkably similar to his final Capitol swing effort, *Come Swing with Me*. In fact, Capitol thought the album, originally titled *Swing Along with Me*, was so close in its sound and title that they sued Sinatra. The record label won the suit and the singer had to change the name of his Reprise album to *Sinatra Swings*. Of course, that didn't change the actual content of the record. Even though the tone was similar, there were some differences from *Come Swing with Me*—the ballads have strings, there are saxophones on the record, and the material is more lighthearted on *Sinatra Swings*, much like the songs on *Come Fly with Me*. The restored sense of humor makes *Sinatra Swings* preferable to *Come Swing with Me*, even if it doesn't have the concentrated precision of the first two Sinatra/May sets. —*Stephen Thomas Erlewine*

Point of No Return / Nov. 11, 1961-Nov. 12, 1961 / Capitol ◆◆◆

At the time he recorded his final Capitol album, *Point of No Return*, Frank Sinatra was no longer interested in giving his record label first-rate material, preferring to save that for his new label, Reprise. However, someone persuaded the singer to make the album a special occasion by reuniting with Axel Stordahl, the arranger/conductor who helped Sinatra rise to stardom in the '40s; he also arranged the vocalist's first Capitol session, so his presence gave a nice sense of closure to the Capitol era. Even though the Voice gave a more heartfelt, dedicated performance than expected, the project was rushed along, necessitating the use of a ghost-arranger, Heinie Beau, for several tracks. *Point of No Return* remains a touching farewell, consisting of moving renditions of standards like "September Song," "There Will Never Be Another You," "I'll Remember April," and "These Foolish Things," with only three charts being replications of their previous work ("I'll Be Seeing You," "September Song," "These Foolish Things"). Sinatra would never sing these standards with such detailed, ornate orchestrations and, as such, the album has a feeling of an elegy. [The compact disc edition includes the first Sinatra/Stordahl sessions for Capitol.] —*Stephen Thomas Erlewine*

Sinatra and Strings / Nov. 20, 1961-Nov. 22, 1961 / Reprise ◆◆◆

Sinatra and Strings, Frank Sinatra's first album with arranger Don Costa, is an exquisite, romantic collection of ballads and is one of his most sensual records. Costa has given the songs—which consist entirely of standards [the CD version added two newer songs]—exceedingly lush, heavily orchestrated arrangements that sound like updated, contemporary versions of Axel Stordahl's ornate charts. Sinatra responds with smooth, nuanced yet powerful vocals that make these traditional songs sound fresh. The pair take some chances with their arrangements—"Stardust" never reaches the chorus, for instance—but *Sinatra and Strings* remains a definitive ballads album, complete with impassioned readings and endlessly rich, detailed arrangements. —*Stephen Thomas Erlewine*

Frank Sinatra's Greatest Hits! / 1961-1968 / Reprise ◆◆◆◆◆

Frank Sinatra's Greatest Hits concentrates on the Chairman of the Board's pop hits from the mid- and late '60s, several of which were single-only releases or only available on movie soundtracks. Appropriately, it begins with his biggest solo hit of the '60s, "Strangers in the Night," and then vascillates between adult contemporary pop songs and ballads. Much of the production has dated, with its guitars, reverb, and arrangements bearing all the hallmarks of '60s pop. While some of the songs rank among Sinatra's finest moments, particularly "Summer Wind" and "It Was a Very Good Year," most of these songs are guilty pleasures. They might not have the emotional resonance of his finest ballad and swing albums, but fluff like the Nancy Sinatra duet "Somethin' Stupid," the fuzz guitar-tinged "The World We

Knew (Over and Over)" and the bluesy "This Town" are enjoyable as pop singles. As such, *Frank Sinatra's Greatest Hits* isn't a good introduction to his music, as it isn't even a representative chronicle of his '60s Reprise recordings. Instead, it's a fun and effective portrait of Sinatra as he was in the late '60s, illustrating how he was struggling to come to terms with contemporary pop music. —*Stephen Thomas Erlewine*

The Reprise Collection / 1961-1975 / Reprise ◆◆◆◆◆

Like *The Capitol Years*, the four-disc box set *The Reprise Collection* was released to celebrate Frank Sinatra's 75th anniversary. However, it works as a better sampler than the Capitol set, partially because Sinatra released so many albums on Reprise that it is necessary to have an introduction to such a large body of work. Also, his Reprise records, while still being concept albums, were more inconsistent and therefore easier to anthologize. Many highlights, as well as most of his biggest hits from the era, are included on *The Reprise Collection*, along with a handful of rarities that are nearly as enjoyable. It's a dynamite collection and proves that the '60s and '70s were a surprisingly diverse, rewarding time for Sinatra. —*Stephen Thomas Erlewine*

★ **Sinatra Reprise: The Very Good Years** / 1961-1975 / Reprise ◆◆◆◆◆

Sinatra Reprise: The Very Good Years is an excellent single-disc retrospective of Sinatra's career at Reprise, including most of his signature songs from the '60s, '70s, and '80s. Hits like "My Way," "That's Life," "Summer Wind," "Strangers in the Night," "It Was a Very Good Year" and "New York, New York" are present, as are songs that were never singles but were extremely popular, like "Luck Be a Lady," "Fly Me to the Moon," "Love and Marriage," and "The Way You Look Tonight." For many casual fans, this disc captures the essence of Sinatra as an icon and provides a perfect introduction to the singer. —*Stephen Thomas Erlewine*

All Alone / Jan. 15, 1962-Jan. 17, 1962 / Reprise ◆◆◆

Originally, *All Alone* was going to called *Come Waltz with Me*. Though the title and the accompanying specially written title song were dropped before the album's release, the record remained a stately collection of waltzes, arranged and conducted by Gordon Jenkins. Out of all the arrangers Sinatra regularly worked with, Jenkins had the most overt classical influences in his writing, making him the perfect choice for the project. Nevertheless, *All Alone* is an uneven album, even as it is one of the most intriguing records Sinatra recorded. Divided between standards and relatively recent tunes, the most distinctive element of the album is the rich, neo-classical arrangements by Jenkins. Sinatra doesn't strictly follow Jenkins' intentions. Instead of playing close to the vest, he wrenches the emotions out of the songs. Most of the time, the results are quite moving, especially on the opening and closing Irving Berlin ballads, "All Alone" and "The Song Is Ended." When the results aren't quite as successful, they are still interesting and the elegant, ruminative music makes *All Alone* a necessary listen for dedicated Sinatra fans. —*Stephen Thomas Erlewine*

Sinatra and Swingin' Brass / Feb. 21, 1962-Apr. 11, 1962 / Reprise ◆◆◆

Sinatra and Swingin' Brass, a collection of brash, bold uptempo numbers, followed the all-ballads effort, *Sinatra & Strings*. Again working with Billy May, Sinatra turned in a robust, energetic performance, which was infectious even when his voice was showing signs of wear—he was suffering from a cold during the sessions. The record captures the spirit of the Rat Pack era nearly as well as *Ring a Ding Ding*. —*Stephen Thomas Erlewine*

Sinatra Sings Great Songs from Great Britain / Jun. 12, 1962-Jun. 14, 1962 / Warner Brothers ◆◆

Sinatra Sings Great Songs from Great Britain is one of the oddest albums in Sinatra's catalog. Recorded in the summer of 1962 and available only in the UK for a number of years, the album consists of songs by British composers, performed with British musicians, and recorded in Britain, while Sinatra was on tour. As it happened, Sinatra was tired and worn out during the sessions and arranger/conductor Robert Farnon had written a set of charts that were ambitious, lush, ornate, and sweeping. Although the arrangements are provocative—occasionally they are more interesting than the actual songs—Sinatra was simply not in good shape for the sessions, which is clear by his thin, straining singing. As such, *Great Songs from Great Britain* isn't much more than a curiosity. —*Stephen Thomas Erlewine*

At Villa Venice, Chicago, Live 1962, Vol. 1 / Nov. 1962 / Jazz Hour ◆◆◆

The appearance of Frank Sinatra, Dean Martin, and Sammy Davis, Jr., at the Villa Venice nightclub outside Chicago during the week after Thanksgiving, 1962, was both a historic and a notorious event. It was notorious because the performers reportedly appeared for a nominal fee at the behest of a Mafia kingpin. It was historic for the obvious reason: the triple bill brought together the primary members of the Sinatra Ratpack in one of their few recorded encounters. On this first volume, they perform separately, each doing about 15 minutes. Martin, introduced "directly from the bar," acts the drunk so effectively, notably in an opening medley of "When You're Smiling" and "The Lady Is a Tramp" with special comic lyrics, that he could only have achieved the performance sober. Sinatra combines expert singing with brutal humor, including an attack on columnist Dorothy Kilgallen. Davis plays it a little straighter, though he too punctuates his performance with comic asides and endures a few from his compatriots, who start to take over at the end of his set. (In the second volume, the show becomes a three-way free-for-all.) The result is a fascinating glimpse into nightclub performing of the era. —*William Ruhlmann*

At Villa Venice, Chicago, Live 1962, Vol. 2 / Nov. 1962 / Jazz Hour ✦✦✦✦✦
On this second volume, Frank Sinatra, Dean Martin and Sammy Davis Jr. perform together, trading impersonations, songs (with severely altered lyrics), and jokes. Certainly, this is not the place to hear definitive versions of these songs. But it is a hilarious show and a great example of nightclub entertaining. —*William Ruhlmann*

Sinatra & Sextet: Live in Paris / 1962 / Reprise ✦✦✦✦✦
If you've cringed at the quality of recent Sinatra projects, this 1962 session will remind you of his glorious past. The 26 cuts include many Sinatra signature pieces ("I've Got You Under My Skin," "The Second Time Around," "Night and Day," "Moonlight in Vermont") with backing from an intimate small band that provides lush, supportive frameworks around which Sinatra can build and create his inimitable charm. The session also shows Sinatra at his most loutish, with some crude (even for the time) commentary during the beginning of "One for My Baby," and borderline racist cracks at the end of "Ol' Man River" and the start of "The Lady Is a Tramp." But Sinatra's vocal excellence often overcame his idiocy and bad manners, and it does on this fine set. —*Ron Wynn*

Sinatra / Basie / 1962 / Reprise ✦✦✦
The pairing of Frank Sinatra and Count Basie always promised more rewards than it actually yielded. *Sinatra/Basie* was the first of their three collaborations and it is the most successful studio album they recorded as a pair. Sinatra isn't in particularly fine voice, nor does Basie shine, but the two come up with enough fine moments to make it worthwhile for devoted listeners. —*Stephen Thomas Erlewine*

The Concert Sinatra / Feb. 18, 1963-Feb. 21, 1963 / Reprise ✦✦✦
The Concert Sinatra is one of Frank Sinatra's best records of the early '60s, an album that successfully rearranges a selection of show tunes, primarily those composed by Richard Rodgers, for the concert stage. Nelson Riddle arranged and conducted one of the largest orchestras that had ever supported Frank Sinatra and his work is light and delicate. Despite the large number of musicians, the music is never overbearing—instead, it is grand and sweeping, providing appropriately epic settings for songs like "Lost in the Stars," "You'll Never Walk Alone," and the stunning "Soliloquy." Sinatra is given the opportunity to demonstrate his full emotional range, from the melodrama of "Ol' Man River" to the tender romanticism of "Bewitched," which helps make *The Concert Sinatra* one of his most fulfilling albums of the era. —*Stephen Thomas Erlewine*

Sinatra's Sinatra / Apr. 29, 1963-Apr. 30, 1963 / Reprise ✦✦✦
In the early '60s, Columbia and Capitol were issuing collections of Frank Sinatra's biggest hits, which tended to sell quite well. *Sinatra's Sinatra* was the singer's attempt to get a piece of that action for his new record label, Reprise. Arranged and conducted by Nelson Riddle, the album is a collection of re-recorded versions of 12 of his favorite songs, including two new charts ("Nancy" and "Oh What It Seemed to Be"). Some of his biggest hits and most famous songs are included in his picks, including "I've Got You Under My Skin" and "Young At Heart," and while many of the performances are quite enjoyable, they tend to pale in direct comparison to the originals. Nevertheless, *Sinatra's Sinatra* is successful on its own terms—it's entertaining, if inconsequential. —*Stephen Thomas Erlewine*

Softly, As I Leave You / Jul. 31, 1963-Oct. 4, 1964 / Reprise ✦✦✦
Softly, As I Leave You was Frank Sinatra's first tentative attempt to come to terms with the rock 'n' roll revolution, even if it was hardly a rock 'n' roll album. In fact, it wasn't much of an album to begin with. The highlight of the record was the hit title song, which featured a subdued but forceful steady backbeat. The rhythm itself was indicative of Sinatra's effort to accept the new popular music. Arranged by Ernie Freeman, "Softly, As I Leave You," "Then Suddenly Love," and "Available" are definitely stabs at incorporating rock 'n' roll into Sinatra's middle-of-the-road pop, featuring drum kits, backing vocals, and keyboards. As pop singles, they were well constructed and deservedly successful. The rest of the album is pieced together from leftovers from various early '60s sessions, giving the record a decidedly uneven tone. Some of the songs work well as individual moments, particularly the Nelson Riddle-arranged "Emily," but the varying tone is too distracting to make the album a satisfying listen. —*Stephen Thomas Erlewine*

Sings Days of Wine and Roses, Moon River & Other Academy Award Winners / Jan. 27, 1964-Jan. 28, 1964 / Reprise ✦✦✦
Featuring a selection of Oscar-winning standards, ranging from 1934's "The Continental" to 1962's "Days of Wine and Roses," *Academy Award Winners* is a profes-

sional and stylish album, but it only yields a handful of true gems. That isn't the fault of either Frank Sinatra or arranger/conductor Nelson Riddle. Although their performances aren't quite as distinguished as their past collaborations, they are nevertheless highly enjoyable. Sinatra is charming and lively, even if he doesn't demonstrate the full range of his technique on each track, while Riddle's charts are light and entertaining. The main problem with the record is how it plays as a series of individual moments, not as a cohesive collection. Granted, some of the moments are first-rate—"The Way You Look Tonight" is one of Sinatra's classic performances, and "Three Coins in the Fountain" and "All the Way" are nearly as good—but the moments never form a whole, which makes the album an occasionally frustrating listen. —*Stephen Thomas Erlewine*

It Might as Well Be Swing / Dec. 1964 / Reprise ✦✦✦
Frank Sinatra and Count Basie's second collaboration, *It Might as Well Be Swing*, was a more structured, swing-oriented set than *Sinatra-Basie* and in many ways the superior album. The album consists of recently written songs, arranged as if they were swing numbers. The results work splendidly, not just because arranger/conductor Quincy Jones found the core of each of the songs, but because Basie and his band were flexible. Adding a string section to their core band, Basie plays a more standard swing than he did on *Sinatra-Basie*, but that doesn't mean *It Might as Well Be Swing* is devoid of jazz. Both Basie and Sinatra manage to play with the melodies and the beat, even though the album never loses sight of its purpose as a swing album. However, what makes *It Might As Well Be Swing* more successful is the consistently high level of the performances. On their previous collaboration, both Sinatra and Basie sounded a bit worn out but throughout this record they play with energy and vigor. —*Stephen Thomas Erlewine*

☆ **September of My Years** / Apr. 13, 1965-May 27, 1965 / Reprise ✦✦✦✦
September of My Years is one of Frank Sinatra's triumphs of the '60s, an album that consolidated his strengths while moving him into new territory, primarily in terms of tone. More than the double-disc set *A Man and His Music*—which was released a year after this album—*September of My Years* captures how Sinatra was at the time of his 50th birthday. Gordon Jenkins rich, stately and melancholy arrangements give the album an appropriate reflective atmosphere. Most of the songs are new or relatively recent numbers; every cut fits into a loose theme of aging, reflection and regret. Sinatra, however, doesn't seem stuck in his ways—though the songs are rooted in traditional pop, they touch on folk and contemporary pop. As such, the album offered a perfect summary, as well as suggesting future routes for the singer. —*Stephen Thomas Erlewine*

Moonlight Sinatra / Nov. 29, 1965-Nov. 30, 1965 / Reprise ✦✦✦
Driven by a set of lush, sparkling Nelson Riddle arrangements, *Moonlight Sinatra* is a low-key, charming collection. Although the basic concept is somewhat nebulous—all of the songs have the word "moon" in the title—Riddle wrote a series of charts that suggest a warm, lovely evening with a variety of tones and moods, from light Latin rhythms to sweet ballads. While the album is a minor entry in Sinatra's catalog, it is nevertheless an enjoyable, romantic listen. Half of the songs on *Moonlight Sinatra* were originally associated with Sinatra's idol Bing Crosby, making the album somewhat of a loose tribute. —*Stephen Thomas Erlewine*

A Man and His Music / Dec. 1965 / Reprise ✦✦✦
Released around his 50th birthday, *A Man and His Music* is an ambitious double-album set that provides a brief history of Frank Sinatra's career. Though the concept sounds quite promising in theory, the execution is somewhat lacking. Instead of using the original recordings—which were made for RCA, Columbia, and Capitol, not his then-current label, Reprise—Sinatra re-recorded the majority of the album's songs. That in itself isn't bad. Many of the new versions are quite enjoyable, with lively, inspired vocals. However, there is also an intrusive narration from Sinatra that runs throughout the album. Although it does offer some amusing anecdotes and gives a sense of his long, complex history, the narration prevents the album from being a consistently engaging listen. —*Stephen Thomas Erlewine*

My Kind of Broadway / 1965 / Reprise ✦✦✦
Pieced together from a variety of sessions and soundtracks, *My Kind of Broadway* is an uneven record, featuring a handful of gems among a bunch of competent, but undistinguished, peformances. Most of the songs—from "Luck Be a Lady" and "Hello, Dolly!" to "I'll Only Miss Her When I Think of Her," "They Can't Take That Away from Me," "Yesterdays," and "Nice Work If You Can Get It"—are classics, but the arrangements and performances frequently are nothing more than competent. When Sinatra delivers, as he does on the show-stopper "Luck Be a Lady," the results are fairly spectacular, but the majority of the album is merely pleasant. —*Stephen Thomas Erlewine*

Greatest Hits, Vol. 2 / 1965-1972 / Reprise ✦✦✦
Much like its predecessor, *Frank Sinatra's Greatest Hits, Vol. 2* is more effective as a portrait of Sinatra at a particular stage in his career than as a comprehensive collection. Like *Greatest Hits*, the album mainly consists of pop hits and songs pulled

from movie soundtracks, adding in a pair of pop-rock hits for good measure. Although "My Way" became Sinatra's signature song of the '70s and '80s—primarily because his spectacular performance rescues the cliched song—none of these tracks were particularly big hits; several of the cuts are album tracks, while the highest-charting single was "Cycles," which peaked at No. 23. While the 11 tracks might not all be hits, they are fairly representative of the sound of Sinatra's music in the late '60s. There's a couple of forgotten gems, particularly the wonderfully moving "What's Now Is Now" and a gorgeous arrangement of George Harrison's "Something," but there is also more dross than the previous *Greatest Hits* collection. Even with a handful of mediocre tracks, *Greatest Hits, Vol. 2* remains an enjoyable sampler, containing several classic Sinatra performances ("My Way," "The September of My Years"). —*Stephen Thomas Erlewine*

Strangers in the Night / Apr. 11, 1966-May 16, 1966 / Reprise ✦✦✦
Strangers in the Night marked Frank Sinatra's return to the top of the pop charts in the mid-'60s and it consolidated the comeback he started in 1965. Although he later claimed he disliked the title track, the album was an inventive, rich effort from Sinatra, one that established him as a still-viable star to a wide, mainstream audience without losing the core of his sound. Combining pop hits ("Downtown," "On a Clear Day (You Can See Forever)," "Call Me") with show tunes and standards, the album creates a delicate but comfortable balance between big-band and pop instrumentation. Using strings, horns, and an organ, Riddle constructed an easy, deceptively swinging sound that appealed to both Sinatra's dedicated fans and pop radio. And Sinatra's singing is relaxed, confident, and surprisingly jazzy, as he plays with the melody "The Most Beautiful Girl in the World" and delivers a knockout punch with the assured, breathtaking "Summer Wind." Although he would not record another album with Riddle again, Sinatra would expand the approach of *Strangers in the Night* for the rest of the decade. —*Stephen Thomas Erlewine*

Sinatra at the Sands / Apr. 1966 / Reprise ✦✦✦✦
In many ways, *Sinatra at the Sands* is the definitive portrait of Frank Sinatra in the '60s. Recorded in April of 1966, *At the Sands* is the first commercially released live Frank Sinatra album, recorded at a relaxed Las Vegas club show. For these dates at the Sands, Sinatra worked with Count Basie and his Orchestra, which was conducted by Quincy Jones. Like any of his concerts, the material was fairly predictable, with his standard show numbers punctuated by some nice surprises. Throughout the show, Sinatra is in fine voice, turning in a particularly affecting version of "Angel Eyes." He is also in fine humor, constantly joking with the audience and the band, as well as delivering an entertaining, if rambling, monologue halfway through the album. Some of the humor has dated poorly, appearing insensitive, but that sentiment cannot be applied to the music. Basie and the orchestra are swinging and dynamic, inspiring a textured, dramatic and thoroughly enjoyable performance from Sinatra. —*Stephen Thomas Erlewine*

That's Life / Oct. 18, 1966-Nov. 18, 1966 / Reprise ✦✦✦
Following the across-the-boards success of *Strangers in the Night*, *That's Life* continued Frank Sinatra's streak of commercially successful albums. Adding mainstream pop music techniques to his repertoire of show tunes, *That's Life* made contemporary pop concessions while satisfying Sinatra's own taste for weightier, more respected material. Although it was a pop-oriented record, Sinatra had not begun to rely on rock-influenced productions; instead, arranger/conductor Ernie Freeman contributed charts that alternated between bluesy, brassy swingers and mildy schmaltzy string arrangements, supported by an overbearing backing chorus. While the title track was the hardest blues Sinatra ever attempted, that approach wasn't attempted for the entire album. A few tracks—particularly a rearrangement of the New Vaudeville Band's campy "Winchester Cathedral" and the static version of "The Impossible Dream"—fall flat, but the album works when Sinatra is either tearing into the song (like "That's Life") or coaxing life out of mid-level ballads like "You're Gonna Hear from You" —*Stephen Thomas Erlewine*

Francis Albert Sinatra and Antonio Carlos Jobim / Jan. 30, 1967-Feb. 1, 1967 / Reprise ✦✦✦✦✦
By 1967, bossa nova had become quite popular within jazz and traditional pop audiences, yet Frank Sinatra hadn't attempted any Brazil-influenced material. Sinatra decided to record a full-fledged bossa nova album with the genre's leading composer, Antonio Carlos Jobim. Arranged by Claus Ogerman and featuring Jobim on guitar and backing vocals, *Francis Albert Sinatra and Antonio Carlos Jobim* concentrated on Jobim's originals, adding three American classics—"Baubles, Bangles and Beads," "Change Partners," and "I Concentrate on You"—that were rearranged to suit bossa nova conventions. The result was a subdued, quiet album that used the Latin rhythms as a foundation, not as a focal point. Supported by a relaxed, sympathetic arrangement of muted brass, simmering percussion, soft strings, and Jobim's lilting guitar, Sinatra turns in an especially noteworthy performance—he has never sounded so subtle, underplaying every line he delivers and showcasing vocal techniques that he never had displayed before. *Francis Albert*

Sinatra and Antonio Carlos Jobim doesn't reveal its pleasures immediately; the album is too textured and understated to be fully appreciated within one listen. After a few plays, the album begins to slowly work its way underneath a listener's skin and it emerges as one of his most rewarding albums of the '60s. —*Stephen Thomas Erlewine*

Francis A. Sinatra & Edward K. Ellington / Dec. 12, 1967 / Reprise ✦✦✦✦✦
The much-anticipated collaboration between Frank Sinatra and Duke Ellington, *Francis A. & Edward K.* didn't quite match its high expectations. At the time of recording, the Ellington band was no longer at its peak and Sinatra was concentrating on contemporary pop material, not standards. For the album, it was decided that the record would be a mixture of standards and new material; as it happened, only one Ellington number, "I Like the Sunrise," was included. Due to a mild cold, Sinatra was not at his best during the sessions and his performance is consequently uneven on the record, varying between robust, expressive performances and thin singing. Similarly, Ellington and his band are hot and cold, occasionally turning in inspired performances and just as frequently walking through the numbers. That doesn't mean there is nothing to recommend on *Francis A. & Edward K.* On the contrary, the best moments on the album fulfill all of the duo's promise. All eight songs are slow numbers, which brings out Sinatra's romantic side. "Indian Summer" is a particular standout, with a sensual vocal and a breathtaking solo from saxophonist Johnny Hodges. Much of the material on the album doesn't gel quite as well, but devoted Sinatra and Ellington fans will find enough to treasure on the record to make it a worthwhile listen. —*Stephen Thomas Erlewine*

Frank Sinatra and the World We Knew / 1967 / Reprise ✦✦
More of a singles collection than a proper album, *The World We Knew* illustrates just how heavily Frank Sinatra was courting the pop charts of the late '60s. Much of the material on the record is given a rock-oriented pop production, complete with fuzz guitars, reverb, folky acoustic guitars, wailing harmonicas, drum kits, organs, and brass and string charts that punctuate the songs rather than provide the driving force. Indeed, many of the songs recall the music Nancy Sinatra was making at the time, which the presence of the hit father-daughter duet "Somethin' Stupid" emphasizes. But the songs that Sinatra tackles with a variety of arrangers—everyone from Nancy's hitmaker Lee Hazlewood, Billy Strange, Ernie Freeman, and H.B. Barnum to Don Costas, Gordon Jenkins, and Claus Ogerman—are more ambitious than most middle-of-the-road, adult-oriented soft rock of the late '60s. "The World We Knew" has an odd, deep winding melody supported by the toughest approximated rock arrangement Sinatra ever used. Similarly, "This Town" is quite bluesy, with pounding brass and harmonica. Even the least successful pop numbers have something enjoyable as far as '60s pop-craftmanship is concerned—"Don't Sleep in the Subway" may be burdened by a histrionic female backing chorus, but the rest of the track is well layered and as well constructed as the Petula Clark original. Sinatra doesn't sound engaged with all of the material—"Some Enchanted Evening," with Barnum's ridiculously bombastic arrangement and a tossed-off vocal from the singer, is easily one of the worst versions of the tune recorded—but he generally turns in a fine performance throughout the record. However, there is one true gem on *The World We Knew*. Buried midway through the album, Johnny Mercer's ballad "Drinking Again" is given an exceptional treatment, with Sinatra squeezing out every nuance in the lyric; the song ranks as one of the best he recorded in the late '60s. —*Stephen Thomas Erlewine*

Cycles / Nov. 12, 1968-Nov. 14, 1968 / Reprise ✦✦
Cycles was Frank Sinatra's first fully fledged pop-rock-oriented album, concentrating on a more orchestrated variation on the popular folk-rock of the late '60s. The foundation of the arrangements on *Cycles* are guitars, bass, and drum kits, all played gently and unobtrusively; the strings are layered on top of the pop rhythm section. Appropriately, Sinatra sang a variety of material associated with folk-rock, particularly Joni Mitchell's "Both Sides Now" and Glen Campbell's "Gentle on My Mind' and "By the Time I Get to Phoenix." Sinatra responds to the softer material by phasing out most of the edginess in his phrasing. He doesn't sing with the nuanced textures of his Jobim albums—he is simply restrained. That doesn't result in an embarrassing album, yet *Cycles* isn't the successful rock and traditional pop fusion that it might've been. Some of the material isn't well-suited for Sinatra—neither "Little Green Apples" nor "Pretty Colors" sounds convincing—but the main problem is with Don Costa's arrangements and production. There simply isn't enough variety to sustain interest throughout the course of the short, ten-song album. Certain sections work well, particularly the Glen Campbell numbers, but there isn't anything distinctive about the record, which makes it one of the weakest albums Sinatra ever released. —*Stephen Thomas Erlewine*

My Way / Feb. 13, 1969-Feb. 24, 1969 / Reprise ✦✦✦
Although it follows the same patterns and approach as *Cycles*, *My Way* is a stronger album, with a better, more varied selection of material and a more focused, gutsy performance from Sinatra. Built around the hit single "My Way," the album again alternates between rock covers ("Yesterday," "Hallelujah, I Love Her So," "For

Once in My LIfe," "Didn't We," "Mrs. Robinson"), a couple of adapted French songs, and a handful of standards. This time out, Don Costa has written more engaging charts than the previous *Cycles*. The Beatles' "Yesterday" is given an affecting, melancholy treatment that brings out the best in Sinatra, as does the new arrangment of "All My Tomorrows" which is lush and aching. If Sinatra doesn't quite pull off the R&B of "Hallelujah, I Love Her So," he does sing the light Latin stylings of "A Day in the Life of a Fool" beautifully and he has fun with Paul Simon's "Mrs. Robinson," changing the lyrics dramtically so they become a tongue-in-cheek, swinging hipster tribute. For that matter, most of the record is successful in creating a middle ground between the traditional pop Sinatra loves and the contemporary pop-rock that dominated the charts in the late '60s. *My Way* doesn't have the macho swagger of his prime Rat Pack records, but its reflective, knowing arrangements show that Sinatra could come to terms with rock 'n' roll at some level. —*Stephen Thomas Erlewine*

A Man Alone & Other Songs of Rod McKuen / Mar. 19, 1969-Mar. 21, 1969 / Reprise ♦♦

After making a successful mainstream, contemporary pop album with *My Way*, Frank Sinatra branched out with *A Man Alone*, subtitled *The Words & Music of McKuen*. Unlike most poets, Rod McKuen was extremely popular and successful, selling over a million copies of his books in the late '60s. After meeting at a party, the singer decided to record an entire album of the poet's verse and music. McKuen wrote a selection of new songs and poems for Sinatra; that material became *A Man Alone*. McKuen's musical contributions amount to tone poems more than songs. Six of the pieces are actual songs, with the remaining tracks being spokenword pieces with instrumental backdrops, including one number that is half-sung, half-spoken without any instrumental accompaniment at all. Certainly, with all this emphasis on words, *A Man Alone* was intended to be a serious statement, but much of it comes off as embarrassing posturing. McKuen's compositions are lyrically slight and musically insubstantial, but what saves *A Man Alone* from being a total failure is the conviction of Sinatra's performance, as well as Don Costa's skillful arrangements. Although he's not able to recite the poetry convincingly, Sinatra's singing is textured and passionate, drawing more emotion from the lyrics than are actually there. Similarly, Costa's charts are lush without being sentimental and very sympathetic to Sinatra's vocals, easily masking the compositional weakness. Sinatra and Costa pull so much out of so little on *A Man Alone*, it makes the listener wish they applied their talents and ambitions to a similar, but more substantial set of songs. As it stands, the album is an intriguing listen, but ultimately a failure. —*Stephen Thomas Erlewine*

Watertown / Jul. 14, 1969-Jul. 17, 1969 / Reprise ♦♦♦

Watertown is Frank Sinatra's most ambitious concept album, as well as his most difficult record. Not only does it tell a full-fledged story, it is his most explicit attempt at rock-oriented pop. Since the main composer of *Watertown* is Bob Gaudio, the author of the Four Seasons' hits "Can't Take My Eyes Off of You," "Walk like a Man," and "Big Girls Don't Cry," that doesn't come as a surprise. With Jake Holmes, Gaudio created a song cycle concerning a middle-aged, small-town man whose wife had left him with the kids. Constructed as a series of brief lyrical snapshots that read like letters or soliloquies, the culminating effect of the songs is an atmosphere of loneliness, but it is a loneliness without much hope or romance—it is the sound of a broken man. Producer Charles Calello arranged musical backdrops that conveyed the despair of the lyrics. Weaving together prominent electric guitars, keyboards, drum kits, and light strings, Calello uses pop-rock instrumentations and production techniques, but that doesn't prevent Sinatra from warming to the material. In fact, he turns in a wonderful performance, drawing out every emotion from the lyrics, giving the album's character depth. —*Stephen Thomas Erlewine*

Sinatra & Company / 1969-1971 / Reprise ♦♦♦

In 1969, Frank Sinatra recorded a second album with Antonio Carlos Jobim. For unknown reasons, Reprise decided not to release *Sinatra-Jobim*, but seven of the ten songs intended for the record did appear on the first side of 1971's *Sinatra & Company*. The selections from *Sinatra-Jobim* have a decidedly different flavor than the material on *Francis Albert Sinatra and Antonio Carlos Jobim*, largely due to the charts of arranger Eumir Deodato. Where Claus Ogerman's arrangements were quite subdued and understated, Deodato's charts are looser and more relaxed; consequently, the music is lighter, more immediate, and arguably more fun. Sinatra responds to the arrangements with more forceful singing than on the previous Jobim collaboration, but his phrasing is still more nuanced than even his soft pop-rock-oriented material. Nevertheless, that subtle phrasing carries over into the second side of *Sinatra & Company*, a collection of pop-oriented tracks. Although the music on the second half of the album is neither as adventurous nor as compelling as that on the first, it is still highly entertaining. The seven songs were arranged by Don Costas, who keeps the material shiny and commerically oriented. In the case of "Close to You," "Leaving on a Jet Plane," "I Will Drink the Wine," "Bein' Green," and "Sunrise in the Morning," that isn't bad—this is material that demands to be delivered in slick, polished arrangements. Under Costas' direction, these songs are given arrangements that feature both strings and gentle folkrock underpinnings, particularly strummed acoustic guitars. Taken on its own terms, the second half of *Sinatra & Company* ranks as some of his best soft-rock-influenced material of the late '60s, even if it doesn't sit comfortably with the excellent bossa nova that comprises the first side of the record. —*Stephen Thomas Erlewine*

Ol' Blue Eyes Is Back / Jun. 4, 1973-Aug. 20, 1973 / Reprise ♦♦

Frank Sinatra returned from his brief retirement in 1973 with the appropriately titled *Ol' Blue Eyes Is Back*. Released amidst a whirlwind of publicity, the album was a commercial success, earning a gold album and nearly climbing its way into the Top Ten, but it wasn't a return to form. Produced by Don Costa, the album doesn't follow the sound of Sinatra's last handful of albums (*Sinatra & Company, Watertown, A Man Alone, My Way*), jettisoning recent pop hits for selections by upcoming songwriters, particularly Joe Raposo, as well as several current film and Broadway numbers. Much of the material is unmemorable, featuring slight melodies and cliched, underdeveloped lyrics. The noticeable exceptions are "Send in the Clowns" and the moving "There Used to Be a Ballpark," both featuring sublime, subtle arrangements from Gordon Jenkins and outstanding singing by Sinatra. However, Jenkins' arrangements are undercut by the lethargic, uneventful production by Costa. Not that Jenkins' arrangements are all perfect—on "Noah," one of the worst songs Sinatra ever recorded, his writing actually accentuates the banality of Raposo's tune. Much of the material is indicative of the lack of songwriting ingenuity in the early '70s; straddling the line between rock-inflected pop and traditionalist pop, most of the songs wind up making a small impression, if they make one at all. Apart from "Send in the Clowns" and "There Used to Be a Ballpark," there's little on *Ol' Blue Eyes Is Back* that's rewarding, and Sinatra recorded better versions of both of those songs. —*Stephen Thomas Erlewine*

Some Nice Things I've Missed / Dec. 10, 1973-May 21, 1974 / Reprise ♦♦

After returning to the spotlight with *Ol' Blue Eyes Is Back*, Frank Sinatra continued his comeback with *Some Nice Things I've Missed*. As the title suggests, the bulk of the album consists of songs that became popular during Sinatra's brief retirement, including hits by Stevie Wonder, Neil Diamond, Jim Croce, Bread, and Tony Orlando & Dawn; the two tracks that weren't hits, "I'm Gonna Make It All the Way" and "Satisfy Me One More Time," were written by Floyd Huddleston, best known for contributing several songs to Disney cartoons. By and large, the material is adapted for big bands, with a couple of tracks featuring slight contemporary touches, like folky acoustic guitar. The majority of the album is arranged and produced by Don Costa, who must bear some of the blame for the failure of the record. Most of the songs he had to work with were too simple to withstand substantial orchestration and rearrangement, but Costa's charts are overwhelmingly trite and unimaginative, underscoring how unsuited the material is for Sinatra. With the exception of the breezily swinging "You Are the Sunshine of My Life," the arrangements are forced and awkward, trying to inject swing where there isn't any in "Sweet Caroline" and "Bad, Bad Leroy Brown." Although they occasionally border on muzak, the slower numbers are more effective, with "What Are You Doing the Rest of Your Life?" leading the way among Costa's efforts, but none of his numbers equal Gordon Jenkins' subtle arrangements of "The Summer Knows" and "If," which nevertheless aren't among his most memorable work. Even though the music doesn't provide a good foundation for Sinatra, the vocalist doesn't make an effort to save the material. Throughout the album, he sounds bored, even irritated, with the songs. There are a couple of exceptions to the rule—he brings some life to "You Are the Sunshine of My Life," "What Are You Doing the Rest of Your Life," "The Summer Knows," "You Turned My World Around"—but Sinatra sounds disinterested in the project, as if he can't wait to leave the studio. And given the insipidness of "I'm Gonna Make It All the Way," "Satisfy Me One More Time," and "Tie a Yellow Ribbon Round the Old Oak Tree," who could blame him? —*Stephen Thomas Erlewine*

The Main Event—Live / Oct. 1974 / Reprise ♦♦

Following the release of *Some Nice Things I've Missed*, Frank Sinatra embarked on a six-concert tour of the East Coast in October of 1974, working with Woody Herman and the Young Thundering Herd, which was conducted by Bill Miller, Sinatra's longtime pianist. Dubbed *The Main Event*, the tour culminated with a televised concert from Madison Square Garden on October 13, 1974. Later in the year, an accompanying record, also called *The Main Event*, was released. Subtitled "Live from Madison Square Garden," the album isn't an exact document of the concert. Instead, it's a compilation, taken from various shows from *The Main Event* tour; on two occasions, "I Get a Kick Out of You" and "Let Me Try Again," two performances are spliced together. Even if it constructs a concert—which the good majority of live albums from the '70s tended to do—*The Main Event* is a delight, full of inspired performances. While there are a couple of contemporary numbers thrown in ("Bad, Bad Leroy Brown," "You Are the Sunshine of My Life"), the majority of the songs are standards, from "The Lady Is a Tramp" to "I've Got You Under My Skin." Both Sinatra and Herman's Herd are lively, spurring each other on to consistently strong performances. Sinatra's singing might be a little too loose for some tastes, as he injects lyrical asides, impressions, and jokes throughout the record, as well as occasionally changing the lyrics by making them a little more "hip." Nevertheless, his singing cannot be faulted. Not only does he sound fine on his trademark numbers, particularly a lovely piano duet on "Angel Eyes," but he brings the contemporary material to life, which he failed to do in the studio. Even with all of its pleasures, *The Main Event* remains a minor entry in Sinatra's canon—dedicated fans will certainly find more to cherish here than the casual listener—but it remains one of his most enjoyable records of the '70s. —*Stephen Thomas Erlewine*

Trilogy / Sep. 17, 1979-Dec. 18, 1979 / Reprise ✦✦
By the time the triple-record set *Trilogy* was released, Frank Sinatra had become somewhat of a recluse from the recording studio. For six years, the Chairman of the Board had spent as little time as possible in the studio, preferring to tour. He had recorded some tracks, with a few of the cuts appearing on singles, but he hadn't made an album since 1974's disappointing *Some Nice Things I've Missed*. *Trilogy* was an audacious, ambitious way to stage a comeback. Each of the album's three records are conceived as an individual work, with the first covering "The Past," the second "The Present," and the third "The Future." Each record was arranged by one of Sinatra's major collaborators—Billy May ("The Past"), Don Costa ("The Present"), and Gordon Jenkins ("The Future"). The concept was intended to tie together the diverse strands of Sinatra's music, sum up his career while pointing towards his future. As a concept, *Trilogy* certainly has its flaws, as does some of the music on the lengthy set. However, the best moments are triumphant, proving that the Voice was still vital in his fourth decade of recording. "The Past" is easily the best record on the album. For the first time since the early '60s, Sinatra recorded a record of standards ("The Song Is You," "It Had to Be You," "All of You"), which is the material best suited for his talents. "The Present" isn't quite as accomplished. Featuring a selection of material from the post-rock era, the record concentrates on pop hits like "Love Me Tender," "Something," "Song Sung Blue," "MacArthur Park," and "Just the Way You Are." Some of the material is mediocre, but Don Costa's arrangements are lovely, as is Sinatra's singing. Together, they make mid-level songs like "Theme from New York, New York" into anthems. However good the first two records are, "The Future" is an unqualified mess. Written by Jenkins, the songs on "The Future" are ambitious, experimental, and self-referential—in fact, it's more of a free-form suite than a set of songs. Most of the record is devoid of melody and while the arrangements and orchestration are certainly interesting, they're not very effective. Singing cliched, trite lyrics about peace, space travel, and his past, Sinatra sounds lost in the murky atmospheric music of "The Future." It might be an anticlimatic way to end an otherwise enjoyable set, but "The Future" doesn't ruin the pleasures of *Trilogy*, it just puts them into greater perspective. —*Stephen Thomas Erlewine*

She Shot Me Down / 1981 / Reprise ✦✦✦
She Shot Me Down is Frank Sinatra's last great album, a dark, brooding record of saloon songs delivered with an understated authority by Sinatra. Arranged and conducted by Gordon Jenkins and produced by Don Costa, the record largely consists of contemporary material, including five that were basically tailored for Sinatra. It's a dense, moody record that works spectacularly—Sinatra's vocals are more alive and rich in detail than on *Trilogy*, and the concept is more concise and well executed. *She Shot Me Down* might not consist of the classic saloon songs, but it has that feeling more than any of his other albums. —*Stephen Thomas Erlewine*

Sinatra 80th—Live in Concert / 1981-1986 / Capitol ✦✦
Culled from a number of different live performances recorded during the '80s (as well as an awkward outtake from the *Duets* sessions: a version of "My Way" recorded with Luciano Pavarotti), *80th Live* is a surprisingly good document of Frank Sinatra in the final stages of his career. By the time this material was recorded, Sinatra's voice had eroded somewhat, as his range had decreased and his voice had become reedier. Nevertheless, his singing was still impressive, as he re-interprets many of his classics in a new light, bringing a fresh emotional slant to many of the songs. Not all of the performances are comparable to some of his previously recorded versions, but all of the songs offer definitive proof that Sinatra was still capable of producing fine music in his 70s. —*Stephen Thomas Erlewine*

L.A. Is My Lady / May 17, 1984 / Qwest ✦✦
Frank Sinatra's final studio album of the '80s—arguably the last true original album Sinatra recorded—was an uneven but surprisingly enjoyable set that tried to adapt the singer's style to contemporary pop standards. Under the direction of arranger/producer Quincy Jones, the album incorporated more synthesizers and slick production techniques than any previous Sinatra album but the result usually doesn't sound forced, especially on the hit title song. When the album does fail, it is

because Jones' overly ambitious and commercial production—such as the insistent dance beat of "How Do You Keep the Music Playing"—prevents the song from taking root. Nevertheless, everyone involved, from Sinatra and Jones to the band themselves, sounds like they're having fun and that sense of joy effortlessly translates to the listener. —*Stephen Thomas Erlewine*

Duets / 1993 / Capitol ✦
As a marketing concept, Frank Sinatra's comeback album *Duets* was a complete success. A collection of Sinatra standards produced by Phil Ramone, the record wasn't a duets album in the conventional sense—Sinatra never recorded in the studio with his partners. Instead, the other singers recorded their tracks separately, sometimes in different studios, and the two tracks were pasted together to create the illusion of a duet. Certainly, this recording method prevented any spontaneous interaction between the singers, and it also limited the emotional impact of the songs. Since neither vocalist could construct an effective single performance, sustaining a mood throughout the course of the song, each singer sounds restrained. In the case of several duet partners, including Bono and Barbara Streisand, this means they rely on camp as a way of making their performance interesting. Sinatra, meanwhile, is oblivious to all of the vocal grandstanding on the part of his duet partners, simply because he recorded his track well in advance of their contributions. The result is a mess. Not only do the vocalists never mesh, the orchestrations are ham-fisted and overblown, relying more on bombast than showmanship. Furthermore, Sinatra's performance is uneven; occasionally, his voice is remarkable, but just as often, it is thin and worn. Nevertheless, *Duets* was a gigantic hit, selling over two million copies and becoming Sinatra's single most commercially successful record. None of its commercial success had anything to do with the album's artistic merit—the album is easily the worst Sinatra released during his lengthy career. Instead, *Duets* rose to No. 2 on the pop charts because of its masterful marketing strategy. The album was promoted as a piece of nostalgia, primarily to baby boomers but also to Generation X as a piece of kitsch. Both approaches ignore the emotional core of Sinatra's music, which is evident on only one track—"One for My Baby," which was essentially a solo performance introduced by an instrumental from saxophonist Kenny G. Perhaps if *Duets* remained true to the essence of Sinatra's music, it would have been more effective, but as it stands, the album is only admirable as a piece of product, not a piece of music. —*Stephen Thomas Erlewine*

Duets II / 1994 / Capitol ✦✦
Following the multi-platinum success of *Duets*, Capitol Records assembled *Duets II*, a sequel that followed the blueprint of its predecessor to the letter. Assembled from leftover tracks from the first album, *Duets II* is a somewhat more consistent album than the original. Lacking the superstar names of the first (Tony Bennett, Julio Iglesias, Kenny G., Barbara Streisand, Bono, Aretha Franklin), the artist roster on the sequel generally consists of either faded stars (Neil Diamond, Willie Nelson, Gladys Knight) or mid-level singers (Luis Miguel, Lorrie Morgan) that are popular within their genre, but fail to command the attention of the general public. However, there are standouts like Lena Horne and Carlos Jobim, that help lift *Duets II* to a higher level than *Duets*. But that's a minor distinction, actually. The nature of the electronic duet prohibits the album from having any sort of emotional resonance, even on tracks that feature strong vocals by Sinatra or his partner. It might be nice to hear Horne and Sinatra together on "Embraceable You," but the song doesn't rise above anything more than a technical marvel. The real tragedy is, their performance hints that the album could have been so much more. —*Stephen Thomas Erlewine*

Hal "Cornbread" Singer

b. Oct. 8, 1919, Tulsa, OK
Tenor Saxophone / Swing, Early R&B Jazz, Groove, Jazz Blues
Equally at home blowing scorching R&B or tasty jazz, Hal "Cornbread" Singer has played and recorded both over a career spanning more than half a century. Singer picked up his early experience as a hornman with various Southwestern territory bands, including the outfits of Ernie Fields, Lloyd Hunter, and Nat Towles. He made it to Kansas City in 1939, working with pianist Jay McShann (whose sax section also included Charlie Parker) before venturing to New York in 1941 and playing with Hot Lips Page, Earl Bostic, Don Byas, and Roy Eldridge (with whom he first recorded in 1944). After the close of the war, Singer signed on with Lucky Millinder's orchestra.

Singer had just fulfilled his life's ambition—a chair in Duke Ellington's prestigious reed section—in 1948 when a honking R&B instrumental called "Cornbread" that he'd recently waxed for Savoy as a leader began to take off. That presented a wrenching dilemma for the young saxist, but in the end, his decision to go out on his own paid off—"Cornbread" paced the R&B charts for four weeks and gave him his enduring nickname. Another of his Savoy instrumentals, "Beef Stew," also cracked the R&B lists.

Singer recorded rocking R&B workouts for Savoy into 1956 (the cuisine motif resulting in helpings of "Neck Bones," "Rice and Red Beans," and "Hot Bread"), working with sidemen including pianists Wynton Kelly and George Rhodes, guitarist Mickey Baker, bassist Walter Page, and drummer Panama Francis. One of his last dates for the firm produced the torrid "Rock 'n' Roll," which may have featured Singer as singer as well as saxist!

By the late '50s, Singer had abandoned rock 'n' roll for a life as a jazz saxist. He recorded for Prestige in a more restrained manner in 1959 and stayed in that general groove. Singer relocated to Paris in 1965, winning over European audiences with his hearty blowing and engaging in quite a bit of session work with visiting blues and jazz luminaries. The old R&B fire flared up temporarily in 1990, when he cut *Royal Blue* for Black Top with boogie piano specialist Al Copley. —*Bill Dahl*

● **Rent Party** / Jun. 1948-May 3, 1956 / Savoy ◆◆◆◆◆
Tenor saxophonist Hal Singer, who had a surprise hit with "Cornbread" which led to him leaving Duke Ellington's Orchestra shortly after joining it (he had temporarily become more popular than Ellington), was a honker if not a screamer. His 16 R&Bish sides that are reissued on this CD are full of spirited and joyfully repetitious tenor. Most of the chord changes are related to "Flying Home" or the blues although Singer did sneak in a couple of ballads ("Indian Love Call" and "Easy Living"). Singer did not have any future hits that would quite equal "Cornbread" (a one-note blues that is the leadoff cut) but he remained a popular attraction on the R&B circuit for a decade. These jump sides (which also include such memorable numbers as "Hot Rod" and "Rock 'n' Roll") might be a bit lightweight compared to the bop music of the time but they are quite fun. This is Hal Singer's definitive set. —*Scott Yanow*

Blue Stompin' / Feb. 20, 1959 / Prestige ◆◆◆◆◆
This is a fun set of heated swing with early R&B overtones. The title cut is a real romp, with tenor saxophonist Hal Singer and trumpeter Charlie Shavers not only constructing exciting solos but riffing behind each other. With the exception of the standard "With a Song in My Heart," Singer and Shavers wrote the remainder of the repertoire, and with the assistance of a particularly strong rhythm section (pianist Ray Bryant, bassist Wendell Marshall and drummer Osie Johnson), there are many fine moments on this enjoyable set. Recommended. —*Scott Yanow*

Royal Blue / May 1989 / Black Top ◆◆◆
There's no way that this collaboration between the veteran saxist and boogie piano specialist Al Copley could equal the searing power of Singer's late-'40s/early-'50s sides for Savoy; a few too many years had passed for Singer to play in the same searing fashion. But his jazzy riffs and Copley's keyboard antics are enjoyable enough in their own right. —*Bill Dahl*

Noble Sissle

b. Jul. 10, 1889, Indianapolis, IN, **d.** Dec. 17, 1975, Tampa, FL
Vocals, Leader / Classic Jazz, Pop
Noble Sissle was one of the nation's premier composers and bandleaders, particularly in the early days of American popular song and theatre. He worked in a band with Eubie Blake in Baltimore as early as 1915; Luckey Roberts sometimes played piano. The Sissle/Blake team scored an early hit with "It's All Your Fault," which Sophie Tucker performed in her act. Sissle later teamed with James Europe from 1916 until his death in 1919. They co-wrote and produced with Blake the historic shows *Shuffle Along* and *Chocolate Dandies*. Sissle recorded over 30 vocals during the early and mid-'20s, many times accompanied by Blake. Sissle and Blake appeared as a duo in some pioneering sound film shorts in the early 1920s that can be considered the first jazz on film.

Sissle led several bands and visited Europe often; his traveling ways led to a split with Blake, who preferred staying in America. Sissle's circle of friends also included Cole Porter and Fred Waring, while the Prince of Wales was guest drummer at one of his concerts in 1930. When Sissle returned to America, he was featured on a broadcast from the Park Central Hotel in 1931, effectively breaking that establishment's color barrier. Lena Horne sang with his band in the mid-'30s; Nat King Cole was reportedly among the cast of *Shuffle Along* of 1933, which didn't enjoy the success of its predecessor. Sissle's band included Buster Bailey, Tommy Ladnier and Sidney Bechet. His orchestra was a featured attraction at Billy Rose's Diamond Horseshoe club from 1938 to 1950, except for USO tours during World War II. Sissle succeeded Bill "Bojangles" Robinson as honorary mayor of Harlem in 1950, and played at Eisenhower's inaugural in 1953. He was WMGM's first Black disc jockey in 1960, ran his own publishing company and owned a club. But repeated muggings led him to close it and retire to Florida to spend time with his son. The book *Reminiscing with Sissle and Blake* in 1973 detailed his varied experiences. Sissle's music is featured on import CDs and anthologies of early stage, show and popular music. —*Ron Wynn*

Sissle & Blake: Early Rare Recordings, Vol. 2 / Feb. 1920-1933 / Eubie Blake Music ◆◆◆◆
The second (and now-rarer) of two LPs featuring vocalist Noble Sissle and pianist Eubie Blake has plenty of variety. The first side starts with Blake playing "Baltimore Buzz," "Ma!" and a 1933 medley (released here for the first time) of "Oh Me! Oh My!" and "Say It with Music" as piano solos. "Sweet Lady" finds Blake accompanying the unfortunate singer Irving Kaufman and backing Alberta Hunter on 1922's "I'm Going Away Just to Wear You Off My Mind," and there is a 1931 dance-band version of "My Blue Days Blew Over." The second half of the program has four duets by the Sissle-Blake team that were only previously out in England; there is a previously unreleased duet from 1926 and also a couple of 1920 selections featuring Sissle with an orchestra. Overall, although the performances are not programmed in strictly chronological order, this is a strong sampling of the historically significant music of Sissle and Blake. —*Scott Yanow*

● **Sissle & Blake: Early Rare Recordings, Vol. 1** / Sep. 1920-Feb. 1927 / Stash ◆◆◆◆
During 1920-27, the songwriting team of Noble Sissle and Eubie Blake recorded a series of interesting if soon dated vocal-piano duets. The 14 selections on this Stash LP (which were originally released on Eubie Blake's label in the mid-1980s, along with a second volume) has some of the better early Sissle-Blake performances. Highlights include "Love Will Find a Way," "I'm Craving for That Kind of Love" and "Bandanna Days," plus an instrumental orchestral version of "Baltimore Buzz" from 1921. Historic and generally listenable music. —*Scott Yanow*

Noble Sisle and His Sizzling Syncopators / Jan. 24, 1931-Mar. 11, 1936 / Fat Cat Jazz ◆◆◆◆
Noble Sissle, a notable songwriter and a personable singer, was one of the few bandleaders wise enough to give the great soprano saxophonist Sidney Bechet regular employment during the early years of the Depression. All of the music from four of his big-band sessions (two from 1931 plus one apiece from 1934 and 1936) is included on this valuable but long-out-of-print LP. Bechet's later dates with Sissle (from 1937-38) have been made more readily available by Columbia and Decca. Bechet has some solo space on most of the selections on this LP, most notably during two versions of "Loveless Love," "Basement Blues," "Roll On, Mississippi, Roll On" and "Polka Dot Rag." In addition to vocals by Sissle and Billy Banks, Lena Horne is heard on her recording debut, and there are some spots on the 1931 dates for trumpeter Tommy Ladnier. Although not as essential as Bechet's later recordings, this set is a collectors' item. —*Scott Yanow*

Harry Skoler

b. 1956, Syracuse, NY
Clarinet / Swing
Clarinetist Harry Skoler followed firmly in the tradition of his idol Benny Goodman, resurrecting the classic music of the swing era for appreciative contemporary audiences. Born in Syracuse, NY, in 1956, Skoler was introduced to Goodman's music while still a teen; announcing his intentions to become a professional jazz clarinetist, in the years to follow he also added saxophone, flute, and piano to his repertoire before graduating from Berklee College of Music in 1978. A three-year period in Nashville followed, during which time he performed with jazz groups, taught privately, and first entered the recording studio; becoming intrigued with architecture, Skoler then decided to study design at Syracuse University, but while in New York returned to music by participating in local jam sessions. His commitment to jazz renewed, he subsequently enrolled at New England Conservatory, where he studied under Jimmy Giuffre and graduated in 1986 with a master's degree in jazz studies. With a quartet comprising vibraphonist/pianist Ed Saindon, bassist Roger Kimball and drummer Tom Gilmore, in 1995 Skoler issued his debut LP, *Conversations in the Language of Jazz; Reflections on the Art of Swing* appeared a year later. —*Jason Ankeny*

Conversations in the Language of Jazz / Nov. 21, 1994-Jan. 6, 1995 / Brownstone ◆◆◆◆
It is not surprising listening to this CD to find out that Benny Goodman has long been Harry Skoler's idol for his interplay with vibraphonist Ed Saindon (three songs are clarinet-vibes duets) and the inclusion of such songs as "Stompin' at the Savoy," "Memories of You" and "Sweet Lorraine" (among others) point directly at BG. On the other hand, Skoler's quartet (with bassist Roger Kimball and drummer Tim Gilmore) does not include a piano (except on two pieces when Saindon or Skoler switch instruments) and a few of the selections are more modern; also Ed Saindon looks much more towards Gary Burton as a role model than to Lionel Hampton. In any case, this enjoyable set offers listeners melodic swing-based music played at a high level. —*Scott Yanow*

● **Reflections on Art of Swing** / Aug. 12, 1996 / Brownstone ◆◆◆◆◆
Harry Skoler's original inspiration was Benny Goodman, so it was only fitting that he would record a tribute CD to BG. Sticking to clarinet except for a lone appear-

ance on tenor ("Undecided"), Skoler teams up with vibraphonist Ed Saindon, bassist Roger Kimball and drummer Tim Gilmore in a pianoless quartet to play 11 songs associated with the King of Swing, plus his originals "Benny" and "Reflections on the Art of Swing." Some of the tunes (such as "After You've Gone" and "What Can I Say After I Say I'm Sorry") are played in a fashion similar to the Goodman small-group recordings, but in general, Skoler (who actually sounds closer to Buddy DeFranco than Benny) displays his own musical personality within the genre of swing. Recommended. —*Scott Yanow*

Carol Sloane

b. 1937, Providence, RI
Vocals / Bop, Standards
Singer Carol Sloane started singing professionally when she was 14 and at 18 she toured Germany in a musical comedy. She was with the Les and Larry Elgart orchestra during 1958-60 and, after appearing at a jazz festival in 1960, she was heard by Jon Hendricks who later sent for her to sub for Annie Ross with Lambert, Hendricks and Ross. Sloane made a big impression at the 1961 Newport Jazz Festival and soon cut two records for Columbia. Unfortunately her career never got going and, except for a live set from 1964 released on Honey Dew, Sloane would not record again until 1977, working as a secretary in North Carolina and singing just now and then locally. However in the mid-'70s she became more active again, caught on in Japan (where she began to record frequently) and her career finally got on more solid footing. Sloane's releases for Audiophile, Choice, Progressive, Contemporary and most recently Concord feature a mature bop-based singer with a sound of her own. —*Scott Yanow*

● **Out of the Blue** / Nov. 27, 1961-Jan. 27, 1962 / Columbia ♦♦♦♦♦
Carol Sloane, who made a strong impression with her performance at the 1961 Newport Jazz Festival, shortly after recorded her first album (originally on Columbia) which has been reissued on this Koch CD along with a previously unreleased "April in My Heart" and Sloane's 45 version of "I Want You to Be the First to Know." At the time her voice sounded a little like Ella Fitzgerald's in spots but Sloane's own personality frequently pops through. She mostly sticks to ballads along with an occasional swinger on this set, and the only partly identified band is mostly confined to a quiet supporting role by arrangers Bill Finegan and Bob Brookmeyer. After recording a second album for Columbia, Sloane would slip into obscurity until her rediscovery (at first by the Japanese) in the late '70s but, as this reissue shows, Carol Sloane was a highly appealing singer from the start. —*Scott Yanow*

Carol Sloane Live at 30th Street / 1962 / Columbia ♦♦♦

Sophisticated Lady / Oct. 16, 1977 / Audiophile ♦♦♦♦
After recording an impressive set for Columbia in 1961, a lesser-known album in 1962, and a live date in 1964 that came out many years later, Carol Sloane did not lead another record session until this 1977 effort, which was made originally for the Japanese Trio label and released domestically by Audiophile. Sloane, who spent years working outside of music as a secretary, was finally rediscovered, first by the Japanese (the majority of her recordings in the 1970s and '80s were for Japanese labels). This particular set finds Sloane (who is joined by pianist Roland Hanna, bassist George Mraz and drummer Richie Pratt) performing 11 of Duke Ellington's more familiar songs, plus two versions of Billy Strayhorn's "Take the 'A' Train." Despite virtually all of the tunes (which include such warhorses as "Satin Doll," "It Don't Mean a Thing," "Sophisticated Lady" and "Mood Indigo") having been recorded a countless number of times through the decades, Carol Sloane's beautiful voice and strong sense of swing make the material seem fresher than expected. —*Scott Yanow*

Cotton Tail / Nov. 12, 1978 / Choice ♦♦♦♦♦
Classy late '70s session by vocalist Carol Sloane. She sings sophisticated ballads, reworks standards, and does pre-rock pop, all of it in a polished, entertaining manner. —*Ron Wynn*

Carol Sings / Oct. 28, 1979-Oct. 29, 1979 / Progressive ♦♦♦♦♦
Originally released by Progressive, this Carol Sloane album is quite definitive. After 15 years of neglect, the appealing jazz singer began to emerge on records again in 1977. On her effort, Sloane performs ten superior songs, which range from swing standards such as "Cheek to Cheek" and "Prelude to a Kiss" to lesser-known numbers such as a pair of Johnny Mercer-Jimmy Rowles collaborations ("Morning Star" and "Frasier the Sensuous Lion"), Norris Turney's "Checkered Hat" and "An Older Man Is like an Elegant Wine." The singer is ably assisted by pianist Rowles (who also arranged the tunes), tenor saxophonist Frank Wess, altoist Norris Turney (who guests on his composition), bassist George Mraz and drummer Joe La Barbera. Recommended. —*Scott Yanow*

As Time Goes By / Aug. 29, 1982 / Eastwind ♦♦♦♦
An early '80s session highlighted by the clean, confident vocals of Carol Sloane. Although she's more jazz-influenced than anything, her understated delivery and

surprising range give her renditions of prerock standards and pop flavor, depth, and character. —*Ron Wynn*

Love You Madly / Oct. 6, 1988-Oct. 28, 1988 / Contemporary ♦♦♦♦♦
Carol Sloane has long been one of jazz's more underrated singers. On her Contemporary CD, Sloane holds her own with some illustrious sidemen (fluegelhornist Art Farmer, tenor saxophonist Clifford Jordan, guitarist Kenny Burrell, pianist Kenny Barron, bassist Rufus Reid and drummer Akira Tana); her two duets with Burrell ("I Wish I'd Met You" and "For All We Know") are among the high points, along with "Love You Madly," "That Old Devil Called Love" and "Getting Some Fun Out of Life." This is a strong effort that finds Carol Sloane in prime form. —*Scott Yanow*

The Real Thing / May 24, 1990-May 25, 1990 / Contemporary ♦♦♦♦♦

Heart's Desire / Sep. 25, 1991-Sep. 27, 1991 / Concord Jazz ♦♦♦♦
Singer Carol Sloane's debut for Concord features her swinging and putting the proper amount of emotion into lyrics of both familiar and obscure songs. Accompanied by pianist Stefan Scaggiari, bassist John Lockwood and drummer Colin Bailey, Sloane is heard in fine form on a program ranging from "Secret Love" and "Them There Eyes" to Dave Frishberg's "Heart's Desire" and a pair of songs co-written by Chan Parker. —*Scott Yanow*

Sweet & Slow / Apr. 19, 1993-Apr. 21, 1993 / Concord Jazz ♦♦♦♦

When I Look in Your Eyes / Jun. 16, 1994-Jun. 17, 1994 / Concord Jazz ♦♦♦♦

The Songs Carmen Sang / Mar. 21, 1995-Mar. 22, 1995 / Concord Jazz ♦♦♦♦♦

The Songs Sinatra Sang / Mar. 4, 1996-Mar. 5, 1996 / Concord Jazz ♦♦♦

Songs Ella & Louis Sang / 1997 / Concord Jazz ♦♦♦♦
This release both is—and in a sense, isn't—a tribute to the mighty and lovable Ella Fitzgerald and Louis Armstrong. As far as the repertoire goes, of course, these songs were associated with Ella and Louis in their separate and joint projects. But Carol Sloane and Clark Terry are definitely not imitators of anybody; it is their inimitable styles, mannerisms, lyrical bents and distinctive senses of humor that make this disc happen. Clark's slippery trumpet slides and bounces over the notes in a completely different manner than Armstrong, and he displays just as much personality in doing so. We also hear much more of Clark's actual singing than usual (as opposed to his Mumbles act on "Stompin' at the Savoy"), breezy and full of jive. Carol Sloane is closer to Shirley Horn in soft-focused tone than she is to Ella, and she makes a fine dusky-voiced foil for Terry's talking horn obligatos. With only the backing of a piano trio, this is as relaxed and ingratiating a set in its own way as the first Ella/Louis albums on Verve were, evoking the atmosphere, if not the actual sound, of a 1950s Norman Granz production. —*Richard S. Ginell*

Bessie Smith

b. Apr. 15, 1894, Chattanooga, TN, **d.** Sep. 26, 1937, Clarksdale, MS
Vocals / Classic Jazz, Classic Female Blues, Traditional Jazz
The first major blues and jazz singer on record and one of the most powerful of all time, Bessie Smith rightly earned the title of "The Empress of the Blues." Even on her first records in 1923, her passionate voice overcame the primitive recording quality of the day and still communicates easily to today's listeners (which is not true of any other singer from that early period). At a time when the blues were in and most vocalists (particularly vaudevillians) were being dubbed "blues singers," Bessie Smith simply had no competition.

Back in 1912, Bessie Smith sang in the same show as Ma Rainey who took her under her wing and coached her. Although Rainey would achieve a measure of fame throughout her career, she was soon surpassed by her protégé. In 1920 Bessie had her own show in Atlantic City and in 1923 she moved to New York. She was soon signed by Columbia and her first recording (Alberta Hunter's "Downhearted Blues") made her famous. Bessie worked and recorded steadily throughout the decade, using many top musicians as sidemen on sessions including Louis Armstrong, Joe Smith (her favorite cornetist), James P. Johnson and Charlie Green. Her summer tent show Harlem Frolics was a big success during 1925-27 and Mississippi Days in 1928 kept the momentum going.

However by 1929 the blues were out-of-fashion and Bessie Smith's career was declining despite being at the peak of her powers (and still only 35!). She appeared in *St. Louis Blues* that year (a low-budget movie short that contains the only footage of her) but her hit recording of "Nobody Knows You When You're Down and Out" predicted her leaner Depression years. Although she was dropped by Columbia in 1931 and made her final recordings on a four-song session in 1933, Bessie Smith kept on working. She played the Apollo in 1935 and substituted for Billie Holiday in the show *Stars over Broadway*. The chances are very good that she would have made a comeback, starting with a Carnegie Hall appearance at John Hammond's upcoming "From Spirituals to Swing" concert, but she was killed in a car crash in Missouri. Columbia has reissued all of her recordings, first in five two-LP sets and more recently on five two-CD boxes that also contain her five alternate takes, the soundtrack of *St. Louis Blues* and an interview with her niece Ruby Smith. "The Empress of the Blues," based on her recordings, will never have to abdicate her throne! —*Scott Yanow*

☆ **The Complete Recordings, Vol. 1** / Feb. 16, 1923-Apr. 8, 1924 / Columbia/Legacy ◆◆◆◆◆

In the 1970s Bessie Smith's recordings were reissued on five double LPs. Her CD reissue series also has five volumes (the first four are double-CD sets) with the main difference being that the final volume includes all of her rare alternate takes (which were bypassed on LP). The first set (which, as with all of the CD volumes, is housed in an oversize box that includes an informative booklet) contains her first 38 recordings. During this early era, Bessie Smith had no competitors on record and she was one of the few vocalists who could overcome the primitive recording techniques; her power really comes through. Her very first recording (Alberta Hunter's "Down Hearted Blues") was a big hit and is one of the highlights of this set along with "'Tain't Nobody's Bizness If I Do" (two decades before Billie Holiday), "Jail-House Blues" and "Ticket Agent, Ease Your Window Down." Smith's accompaniment is nothing that special (usually just a pianist and maybe a weak horn or two) but she dominates the music anyway, even on two vocal duets with her rival Clara Smith. All of these volumes reward close listenings and are full of timeless recordings. —*Scott Yanow*

● **The Essential Bessie Smith** / Apr. 11, 1923-Nov. 24, 1933 / Columbia/Legacy ◆◆◆◆◆

Although there are a multitude of box sets chronicling Bessie's entire recorded career, this two-disc, 36-song set sweats it down to the bare essentials in quite an effective manner. Bessie could sing it all, from the lowdown moan of "St. Louis Blues" and "Nobody Knows You When You're Down and Out" to her torch treatment of the jazz standard "After You've Gone" to the downright salaciousness of "Need a Little Sugar in My Bowl." Covering a time span from her first recordings in 1923 to her final session in 1933, this is the perfect entry-level set to go with. Utilizing the latest in remastering technology, these recordings have never sounded quite this clear and full, and the selection—collecting her best-known sides and collaborations with jazz giants like Louis Armstrong, Coleman Hawkins and Benny Goodman—is first rate. If you've never experienced the genius of Bessie Smith, pick this one up and prepare yourself to be devastated. —*Cub Koda*

★ **The Collection** / 1923-1933 / Columbia ◆◆◆◆◆

While there's no denying the importance and quality of Columbia/Legacy's *Complete Recordings* series, nine discs may seem a bit intimidating to the newcomer. *Collection*, a mid-priced, 16-track collection which spans most of Smith's career, ultimately does a better service to the casual listener with a limited budget. This is probably the best introduction—undoubtedly many will seek out the more comprehensive packages afterwards. —*Chris Woodstra*

★ **The Complete Recordings, Vol. 2 (1924-1925)** / Apr. 8, 1924-Nov. 18, 1925 / Columbia/Legacy ◆◆◆◆◆

Bessie Smith, even on the evidence of her earliest recordings, well deserved the title "Empress of the Blues" for in the 1920s there was no one in her league for emotional intensity, honest blues feeling and power. The second of five volumes (the first four are two-CD sets) finds her accompaniment improving rapidly with such sympathetic sidemen as trombonist Charlie Green, cornetist Joe Smith and clarinetist Buster Bailey often helping her out. However they are overshadowed by Louis Armstrong whose two sessions with Smith (nine songs in all) fall into the time period of this second set; particularly classic are their versions of "St. Louis Blues," "Careless Love Blues" and "I Ain't Goin' to Play Second Fiddle." Other gems on this essential set include "Cake Walkin' Babies from Home," "The Yellow Dog Blues" and "At the Christmas Ball." —*Scott Yanow*

Complete Recordings, Vol. 5: The Final Chapter / May 6, 1925-Nov. 24, 1933 / Sony/Legacy ◆◆◆◆◆

Bessie Smith cut 160 sides for the Columbia and OKeh labels between 1923 and 1933, and the four previous two-CD/cassette box sets of her complete recordings released in the 1990s covered 154 of them, which introduces the question, what can a fifth two-CD/cassette boxed set contain in addition to the remaining six cuts? First, there are five previously unreleased alternate takes; second, there is the 15-minute low-fi soundtrack to the two-reel short *St. Louis Blues,* which constitutes the only film of Smith; and third, taking up all of the second CD/cassette, there are 72 minutes of interview tapes of Ruby Smith, Bessie Smith's niece, who traveled as part of her show. The box contains a "Parental Advisory—Explicit Lyrics" warning because of the nature of Ruby Smith's reminiscences. You won't learn much about Bessie Smith's music from her niece's remarks, but you will learn a lot about her sexual preferences. —*William Ruhlmann*

The Complete Recordings, Vol. 3 / Nov. 20, 1925-Feb. 16, 1928 / Columbia/Legacy ◆◆◆◆◆

On the third of five volumes (the first four are double-CD box sets) that reissue all of her recordings, the great Bessie Smith is greatly assisted on some of the 39 selections by a few of her favorite sidemen: cornetist Joe Smith, trombonist Charlie Green and clarinetist Buster Bailey. But the most important of her occasional musicians was pianist James P. Johnson who makes his first appearance in 1927 and can be heard on four duets with Bessie including the monumental "Back Water Blues." Other highlights of this highly recommended set (all five volumes are essential) include "After You've Gone," "Muddy Water," "There'll Be a Hot Time in the Old Town Tonight," "Trombone Cholly," "Send Me to the 'Lectric Chair" and "Mean Old Bedbug Blues." The power and intensity of Bessie Smith's recordings should be considered required listening; even 70 years later they still communicate. —*Scott Yanow*

The Complete Recordings, Vol. 4 / Feb. 21, 1928-Jun. 11, 1931 / Columbia/Legacy ◆◆◆◆◆

The fourth of five volumes (the first four are two-CD sets) that reissue all of Bessie Smith's recordings traces her career from a period when her popularity was at its height down to just six songs away from the halt of her recording career. But although her commercial fortunes might have slipped, Bessie Smith never declined and these later recordings are consistently powerful. The two-part "Empty Bed Blues" and "Nobody Knows You When You're down and Out" (hers is the original version) are true classics and none of the other 40 songs (including the double-entendre "Kitchen Man") are throwaways. With strong accompaniment during some performances by trombonist Charlie Green, guitarist Eddie Lang, Clarence Williams' band and on ten songs (eight of which are duets) the masterful pianist James P. Johnson, this volume (as with the others) is quite essential. —*Scott Yanow*

Buster Smith (Henry Smith)

b. Aug. 24, 1904, Ennis, TX, d. Aug. 10, 1991, Dallas, TX
Alto Saxophone / Swing
A talented alto saxophonist and an arranger/composer who probably wrote "One O'Clock Jump" (although Count Basie received the credit), Buster Smith's contributions to jazz are difficult to assess because he was underrecorded throughout his career. Charlie Parker often acknowledged Smith's influence on his tone, and the few early recordings of the older altoist do show some similarity (although Bird's style would become much more advanced); Parker played in Smith's band in 1937.

Buster Smith was a fixture in Kansas City for the bulk of his most significant years. He was with Walter Page's Blue Devils from 1925-33 (the band only made two recordings) and Bennie Moten's Orchestra during its last period (1933-35), and co-led the Barons of Rhythm with Count Basie. Unfortunately, he chose not to accompany Basie to New York. When Smith finally went East, he contributed arrangements to several orchestras (including those led by Gene Krupa, Count Basie and Benny Carter) and had short stints with Don Redman, Hot Lips Page, Eddie Durham and Snub Mosley. Buster Smith returned first to Kansas City and then finally to Texas for the remainder of his life. He recorded one very obscure (and long-out-of-print) Atlantic album in 1959. —*Scott Yanow*

● **The Legendary Buster Smith** / Jun. 17, 1959 / Atlantic ◆◆◆◆◆

Carrie Smith

b. Aug. 25, 1941, Fort Gaines, GA
Vocals / Blues, Swing
A blues belter in the classic tradition, Carrie Smith was born August 25, 1941, in Fort Gaines, GA. Despite making her debut at the 1957 Newport Jazz Festival while a member of a New Jersey church choir, she did not truly emerge on the jazz circuit until the early 1970s, in the company of Big "Tiny" Little. In November of 1974, Smith's riveting performance as Bessie Smith (no relation) in Dick Hyman's Carnegie Hall production of *Satchmo Remembered* brought her fame throughout the international musical community. Soon she began touring as a solo act, and in a short time began recording as well; still, despite subsequent performances in conjunction with the New York Jazz Repertory Orchestra, Tyree Glenn and the World's Greatest Jazz Band, Smith remained little more than a cult figure in the US, proving better received in Europe. While rooted firmly in the blues and gospel, she was a singer of considerable range and depth, as recordings like 1976's *Do Your Duty* and the following year's *When You're Down and Out* prove; despite never earning significant success, she remained an active figure both on stage and in the studio through the 1990s. —*Jason Ankeny*

Do Your Duty / Jul. 26, 1976 / Classic Jazz ◆◆◆

Nice updated set of classic blues done in a strutting, assertive fashion by Carrie Smith. Smith, also a good singer in a jazzy vein, was among the few surviving female vocalists capable of doing authentic bawdy blues, and she shows how it's done throughout this date. —*Ron Wynn*

● **Confessin' the Blues** / Jul. 26, 1976-Jul. 19, 1977 / Evidence ✦✦✦✦✦

This CD reissues not only Carrie Smith's original hard-to-find *Black & Blue* LP but six selections from two other sessions including three previously unissued alternate takes. Smith, who was coming into her own during this period, is in top form on a variety of vintage material ranging from Bessie Smith songs in the 1920s to the '50s Ruth Brown hit "Mama He Treats Your Daughter Mean" and Big Bill Broonzy's "When I've Been Drinkin'." It is interesting to hear some of the altered lyrics which have been changed to reflect a female rather than a male singing; "I Want a Little Boy" is the most obvious example. Most selections find Smith backed by a quartet that includes tenor saxophonist George Kelly and pianist Ram Ramirez while a few of the added tracks have short spots for trumpeter Doc Cheatham and trombonist Vic Dickenson. This is one of the best Carrie Smith CDs currently available. —*Scott Yanow*

Fine and Mellow / Nov. 1976 / Audiophile ✦✦✦

Carrie Smith / Nov. 15, 1978-Nov. 16, 1978 / West 54 ✦✦✦✦

Derek Smith

b. Aug. 17, 1931, London, England
Piano / Swing

A jazz pianist noted for his versatility and elegance, Derek Smith was born August 17, 1931, in London, England. After taking up the piano in early childhood, he began his professional career at the age of just 14, and by the early 1950s was a staple on the UK jazz scene, regularly performing with the likes of Kenny Graham, John Dankworth and Kenny Baker. In the mid-1950s Smith relocated to New York City, where he became a session musician in much demand by studio orchestras and other recording units; he also continued pursuing his jazz aspirations in the company of Benny Goodman and Connie Kay. Smith continued moving back and forth from studio work to live jazz dates for years to come, and at the end of the 1960s added to his workload piano duties in Doc Severinsen's *Tonight Show* orchestra. In the 1970s he reunited frequently with Goodman, and in 1978 finally led his own recording date, *Love for Sale. The Man I Love* followed later that same year, and in the decades to come, Smith's presence on the jazz landscape increased considerably—in addition to solo performances, he also regularly played in a trio with Milt Hinton and Bobby Rosengarden. —*Jason Ankeny*

● **Derek Smith Trio, Plays Jerome Kern** / Mar. 27, 1980 / Progressive ✦✦✦✦✦

Hal Smith

b. Jul. 30, 1953, Indianapolis, IN
Drums / Classic Jazz

A drummer with strong inclinations towards traditional jazz performance, Hal Smith was born in Indianapolis, Indiana, on July 30, 1953. Taking up drums at the age of ten—among his teachers was the great Jake Hanna—he made his professional debut in 1978, and in the years to follow served with the likes of the Dukes of Dixieland and the Grand Dominion Jazz Band. Smith also led groups including the Frisco Syncopaters and the Down Home Jazz Band, and regularly collaborated with Butch Thompson and Bobby Gordon. Among his recording dates are 1994's *California Here I Come*, 1995's *Swing, Brother, Swing* and 1996's *Bourbon Street Memories;* Smith is also a respected jazz journalist, contributing countless articles to publications including *Jazz Rambler, Mississippi Rag* and *West Coast Rag.* —*Jason Ankeny*

Califoria Here I Come / Aug. 10, 1994 / Jazzology ✦✦✦✦

● **Swing, Brother, Swing** / Jan. 9, 1995-Jan. 10, 1995 / Jazzology ✦✦✦✦✦

This is a particularly likable release featuring a hot quintet mostly playing standards from the 1930s. Drummer Hal Smith primarily sticks to a supportive role behind the Benny Goodman-inspired clarinet of Tim Laughlin, rhythm guitarist Rebecca Kilgore (whose eight laidback yet swinging vocals are a consistent delight), pianist Chris Dawson and bassist Marty Eggers. This is difficult music not to enjoy, with the more memorable selections including "With Plenty of Money and You," "Swing, Brother, Swing," "You" and "If Dreams Come True." Recommended. —*Scott Yanow*

Bourbon Street Memories /Sept. 13, 1995 / GHB ✦✦✦✦

Jabbo Smith (Cladys Smith)

b. Dec. 24, 1908, Pembroke, GA, d. Jan. 16, 1991, New York, NY
Trumpet / Classic Jazz

Jabbo Smith had one of the oddest careers in jazz history. A brilliant trumpeter, Jabbo had accomplished virtually all of his most significant work by the time he turned 21 yet lived to be 82. He learned to play trumpet at the legendary Jenkins Orphanage in Charleston and by the time he was 16 Jabbo showed great promise. During 1925-28 he was with Charlie Johnson's Paradise Ten, a top New York jazz group that made some classic recordings. Jabbo was on a recording session with

Duke Ellington in 1927 (resulting in a memorable version of "Black and Tan Fantasy") and played in the show *Keep Shufflin'* with James P. Johnson and Fats Waller. The high points of Smith's career were his 1929 recordings with his Rhythm Aces. These superb performances feature Jabbo Smith playing with daring, creativity and a bit of recklessness, displaying an exciting style that hints at Roy Eldridge (who would not burst upon the scene for another six years). But although Jabbo Smith at the time was considered a close competitor of Louis Armstrong, he had hit his peak. His unreliability, excessive drinking and unprofessional attitude resulted in lost jobs, missed opportunities and a steep decline. After playing with one of Claude Hopkins' lesser orchestras during 1936-38, Smith settled in Milwaukee and became a part-time player. Decades passed and when he was rediscovered in the 1970s (when he was picked to perform in the musical show *One Mo' Time*), he was a weak player, a mere shadow of what he could have been. —*Scott Yanow*

★ **Complete 1929-1938 Sessions** / Jan. 29, 1929-Aug. 22, 1929 / Epm Musique ✦✦✦✦✦

Jabbo Smith had a strange career, recording classics when he was 18-20 but essentially a has-been by the time he turned 21. The fiery trumpeter's greatest recordings were the 19 selections he cut with his Rhythm Aces, and they are all on this 1996 CD, along with a previously unreleased "Weird and Blue" and two hot numbers cut with Ikey Robinson's pickup group. Despite this reissue's title, all of the numbers are from 1929, Jabbo Smith's greatest year. His exciting (and sometimes reckless) trumpet solos are quite memorable on such tunes as "Jazz Battle," "Ace of Rhythms," "Decatur Street Tutti" and "Band Box Stomp." In addition, Smith was a fine jazz vocalist (best on "As Time Gets Better"), takes a decent trombone solo on "Lina Blues" and is assisted by such talented sidemen as clarinetist Omer Simeon, pianist Cassino Simpson and banjoist Ikey Robinson. Essential music for classic jazz and 1920s collectors. —*Scott Yanow*

★ **Jabbo Smith 1929-1938** / Jan 29, 1929-Feb. 1, 1938 / Challenge ✦✦✦✦✦

Although only 20 years old, trumpeter Jabbo Smith cut virtually all of his finest recordings in 1929, when he was touted as a competitor to Louis Armstrong. Smith's 19 sides with his Rhythm Aces (all of which are on this essential CD) are some of the most exciting recordings of the era. Often teamed in a quintet with Omer Simeon (on clarinet and alto), pianist Cassino Simpson, banjoist Ikey Robinson and the tuba of Hayes Alvis (subs appear on a few numbers), Jabbo's reckless and explorative trumpet flights are often thrilling. Highlights include "Jazz Battle," "Till Times Get Better," "Ace of Rhythm" and "Band Box Stomp," but all of the performances (including Smith's trombone solo on "Lina Blues" and his occasional and effective vocals) are well worth hearing. The CD concludes with Jabbo Smith's four-song 1938 session, which is disappointingly tame. Strange as it seems, Smith was past his prime by 1930 when he was only 21. Except for some early sideman appearances and forgettable efforts in later years (plus one previously unissued Rhythm Ace side from 1929 that was unearthed in the mid-1990s by the Retrieval label), this CD essentially contains Jabbo Smith's entire legacy, although he would live until 1991. —*Scott Yanow*

Hidden Treasure, Vol. 1 / Jun. 3, 1961-Oct. 15, 1961 / Jazz Art ✦✦

In 1983 a pair of albums were released that consist of selections performed at two rehearsals in 1961 by trumpeter Jabbo Smith. These excerpts, which have erratic recording quality, would not be of much interest except that they were Smith's only recordings from the 1939-77 period. Jabbo, who was a brilliant player in 1929, had drifted away from music by the 1940s, but was urged by the young sidemen heard on these LPs to try a comeback. Smith sounds better on the dates than he would in 1978, but was clearly rusty and not at the level of his earlier days. Actually his sidemen (which include the Pee Wee Russell-influenced clarinetist Frank Chase, bass saxophonist John Dengler and rhythm guitarist Marty Grosz) often take solo honors on the swing and classic jazz standards, which include more than their share of clams and hesitant moments from the leader. The two albums overall are mostly for jazz historians. —*Scott Yanow*

Hidden Treasure, Vol. 2 / Jun. 3, 1961-Oct. 15, 1961 / Jazz Art ✦✦

The second of two LPs taken from a pair of 1961 rehearsals is notable for briefly ending the silence of trumpeter Jabbo Smith, who had not recorded since 1938 and would not officially record again until the mid-1970s. However, the music (which was released for the first time in 1983) finds an out-of-practice Jabbo only hinting at his earlier greatness. The sidemen include clarinetist Frank Chase, rhythm guitarist Marty Grosz (who was fairly obscure at the time), and bass saxophonist John Dengler. Of historical interest is that Jabbo Smith doubles on trombone during two of the numbers, but the overall music is a bit rough, sounding very much like a rehearsal. —*Scott Yanow*

Jabbo! / Dec. 12, 1978 / Memories ✦✦

40 years after his last studio recordings as a leader, the way-over-the-hill trumpeter Jabbo Smith (who was ready to turn 70) began to attempt a long-overdue come-

back. Jabbo tries his best on this set with the New Orleans Joymakers, a trad jazz quintet that includes clarinetist Orange Kellin, trombonist Waldren "Frog" Joseph, pianist Lars Edegran, bassist Frank Fields and drummer John Robichaux, but it was much too late for him to regain his former trumpet chops. Jabbo sings a few of the songs to compensate, but the set, which does include such numbers as "Climax Rag," "Panama," "Original Dixieland One Step" and a pair of Jabbo's originals ("Absolutely" and "Love"), was an example of too little, too late. *—Scott Yanow*

Jimmy Smith

b. Dec. 8, 1925, Norristown, PA
Organ / Soul Jazz, Hard Bop, Groove
Though he never received any exaggerated title like the king of soul jazz, Jimmy Smith certainly ruled the Hammond organ in the '50s and '60s. He revolutionized the instrument, showing it could be creatively used in a jazz context and popularized in the process. His Blue Note sessions from 1956 to 1963 were extremely influential and are highly recommended. Smith turned the organ into almost an ensemble itself. He provided walking bass lines with his feet, left hand chordal accompaniment, solo lines in the right and a booming, funky presence that punctuated every song, particulary the uptempo cuts. Smith turned the fusion of R&B, blues and gospel influences into a jubilant, attractive sound that many others immediately absorbed before following in his footsteps. Smith initially learned piano, both from his parents and on his own. He attended the Hamilton School of Music in 1948, and Ornstein School of Music in 1949 and 1950 in Philadelphia. Smith began playing the Hammond in 1951, and soon earned a great reputation that followed him to New York, where he debuted at the Cafe Bohemia. A Birdland date and 1957 Newport Jazz Festival appearance launched Smith's career. He toured extensively through the '60s and '70s. His Blue Note recordings included superb collaborations with Kenny Burrell, Lee Morgan, Lou Donaldson, Tina Brooks, Jackie McLean, Ike Quebec and Stanley Turrentine among others. He also did several trio recordings, some which were a little bogged down by the excess length of some selections. Smith scored more hit albums on Verve from 1963 to 1972, many of them featuring big bands and using fine arrangements from Oliver Nelson. These included the excellent *Walk on the Wild Side*. But Verve went to the well once too often seeking crossover albums, loading down Smith's late '60s album with hack rock covers. His '70s output was quite spotty, though Smith didn't stop touring, visiting Israel and Europe in 1974 and 1975. He and his wife opened a club in Los Angeles in the mid-'70s. Smith resumed touring in the early '80s, returning to New York in 1982 and 1983. He resigned with Blue Note in 1985, and has done more representative dates for them and Milestone in the '90s. *—Ron Wynn and Bob Porter*

A New Sound, a New Star: Jimmy Smith at the Organ, Vol. 1-2 / Feb. 13, 1956+Feb. 18, 1956 / Capitol ✦✦✦✦✦
The emergence of Jimmy Smith in 1956 was quite noteworthy—here was an organist who could play his instrument with the facility of a Charlie Parker and yet could also dig into a lowdown blues. Smith's first three LPs (*At the Organ, Vols. 1-3*) are reissued in full on this double CD, along with four previously unreleased cuts and one selection ("I Can't Give You Anything But Love") only out earlier as a single. Although Smith's basic sound was slightly different than it would become (in fact, on the opening "The Way You Look Tonight," he often sounds like his main predecessor, Wild Bill Davis), he clearly had something new and fresh to offer. It is on the uptempo burners (such as "Lady Be Good" and "The Champ") that Jimmy Smith immediately showed the jazz world that he had no competitors. Even four decades later, he remains the dominant force on virtually all organists. Teamed with guitarist Thornel Schwartz and either Ray Perry (for the first nine numbers) or Donald Bailey on drums, Smith (who had only taken up the organ three years earlier) is well featured on 28 spirited selections. A historic set. *—Scott Yanow*

A New Star, a New Sound: Jimmy Smith at the Organ, Vol. 1 / Feb. 13, 1956+Feb. 18, 1956 / Blue Note ✦✦✦✦✦
The debut of Jimmy Smith on records (he was already 30) was a major event, for he introduced a completely new and very influential style on the organ, one that virtually changed the way the instrument was played. This LP features the already-recognizable organist in a trio with guitarist Thornel Schwartz and Bay Perry on drums. Highlights of this very impressive debut include "The Way You Look Tonight," "Lady Be Good" and Horace Silver's "The Preacher." [Volume 1 and Volume 2 were packaged together and issued by Blue Note in 1997]. *—Scott Yanow*

Jazz Profile / Feb. 18, 1956-Jan. 31, 1963 / Blue Note ✦✦✦✦
Jazz Profile compiles highlights from Jimmy Smith's recordings for Blue Note, drawing a rough portrait of his career. The compilation not only concentrates on Smith's hard-swinging soul-jazz and funk, but there's also more reflective numbers, giving a good sense of his depth and range. While there isn't anything here that will appeal to collectors, *Jazz Profile* does offer a nice introduction for curious listeners. *—Leo Stanley*

Greatest Hits, Vol. 1 / Mar. 27, 1956-Feb. 8, 1963 / Blue Note ✦✦✦✦✦
This double LP, even with its clichéd title, is a real gem. It contains eight of the greatest performances recorded by organist Jimmy Smith during his important period with Blue Note. "The Champ" from his second recording features Smith taking around 50 choruses on a blazing blues, and it set a standard that has still not been surpassed. Also included on this valuable two-fer (some of the material has since been reissued on CD) are "All Day Long," a 20-minute "The Sermon," "Midnight Special," "When Johnny Comes Marching Home," "Can Heat," "Flamingo" and "Prayer Meetin." In the supporting cast are trumpeter Lee Morgan, altoist Lou Donaldson, Tina Brooks and Stanley Turrentine on tenors, guitarists Kenny Burrell, Thornel Schwartz and Quentin Warren, and drummers Art Blakey and Donald Bailey. This set serves as a perfect introduction to Jimmy Smith's early years and has lots of hard-swinging and soulful jams. *—Scott Yanow*

Incredible Jimmy Smith at Club Baby Grand, Vol. 1 / Aug. 1, 1956 / Blue Note ✦✦✦

Incredible Jimmy Smith at Club Baby Grand, Vol. 2 / Aug. 1, 1956 / Blue Note ✦✦✦

The Sounds of Jimmy Smith / Feb. 11, 1957 / Blue Note ✦✦✦✦
This LP, which has been included as part of a Mosaic Jimmy Smith three-CD box set, features the organist taking a pair of rare unaccompanied solos on "All the Things You Are" and a fairly free "The Fight" and jamming several songs ("Zing Went the Strings of My Heart," "Somebody Loves Me" and "Blue Moon") with his trio. Art Blakey fills in for drummer Donald Bailey on "Zing" while guitarist Eddie McFadden is heard throughout the three selections. Excellent straightahead jazz from the innovative organist. *—Scott Yanow*

A Date with Jimmy Smith, Vol. 1 / Feb. 11, 1957-Feb. 12, 1957 / Blue Note ✦✦✦✦
After cutting five albums with his trio, organist Jimmy Smith on Feb. 11, 1957, recorded with trumpeter Donald Byrd, altoist Lou Donaldson and tenor saxophonist Hank Mobley in a sextet that also included guitarist Eddie McFadden and drummer Art Blakey. Among the five songs recorded that day, two (lengthy versions of "Falling in Love with Love" and "Funk's Oats") are included on this LP along with a shorter trio rendition of "How High the Moon" from two days later with McFadden and drummer Donald Bailey in a trio. All of this music has been reissued by Mosaic on a definitive CD box set. *—Scott Yanow*

A Date with Jimmy Smith, Vol. 2 / Feb. 11, 1957-Feb. 12, 1957 / Blue Note ✦✦✦✦
This LP is one of five that has been reissued by Mosaic in a three-CD box set. For the jam session date altoist Lou Donaldson has a duet with organist Jimmy Smith on "I'm Getting Sentimental over You," and together they match up forces in a sextet with trumpeter Donald Byrd, Hank Mobley on tenor, guitarist Eddie McFadden and drummer Art Blakey, playing lengthy versions of Mobley's "Groovy Date" and Duke Ellington's "I Let a Song Go Out of My Heart." All of the Jimmy Smith jam sessions are easily recommended to fans of straightahead jazz; get the Mosaic box. *—Scott Yanow*

☆ **The Complete February 1957 Jimmy Smith Blue Note Sessions** / Feb. 11, 1957-Feb. 13, 1957 / Mosaic ✦✦✦✦✦
It would not be an overstatement to say that organist Jimmy Smith was busy during Feb. 11-13, 1957, for he recorded enough material for these three CDs, 21 often-lengthy performances that originally appeared on five LPs plus three others that had been previously unissued. Smith is not only heard early in his career with his regular trio but in a sextet with trumpeter Donald Byrd, altoist Lou Donaldson, tenor saxophonist Hank Mobley and drummer Art Blakey, in duets with Donaldson and with a quartet that also stars guitarist Kenny Burrell. These jam sessions feature plenty of exciting solos over fairly common chord changes and, despite the heavy competition, Jimmy Smith (who is still the king of the jazz organ) is the dominant force. Recommended. *—Scott Yanow*

Jimmy Smith at the Organ, Vol. 1: All Day Long / Feb. 12, 1957 / Blue Note ✦✦✦✦
There is a fair amount of variety on this jam session LP. Organist Jimmy Smith plays "Summertime" in duet with altoist Lou Donaldson, and with guitarist Kenny Burrell and drummer Art Blakey completing the all-star quartet, performs swinging versions of "Yardbird Suite," "There's a Small Hotel" and Burrell's "All Day Long." The music (which has been reissued on CD in a Mosaic box set) will be enjoyed by bop fans even though nothing all that essential occurs. *—Scott Yanow*

Jimmy Smith at the Organ, Vol. 2 / Feb. 13, 1957 / Blue Note ✦✦✦✦
Five LPs of material (including this one) that were recorded by organist Jimmy Smith within a three-day period have been reissued on CD by Mosaic. But listeners who do not have that set and run across any of the albums would not go wrong by picking them up. This interesting record features Smith in a duet (titled "The Duel") with drummer Art Blakey, jamming with his trio (which includes guitarist Eddie McFadden and drummer Donald Bailey) on "Buns a Plenty" and "Plum Nellie," and interacting with guitarist Kenny Burrell, drummer Blakey and altoist Lou

Donaldson on "Billie's Bounce." Excellent bop-oriented jam sessions. —*Scott Yanow*

Plays Pretty Just for You / May 8, 1957 / Blue Note ✦✦✦

Jimmy Smith Trio + LD / Jul. 4, 1957 / Blue Note ✦✦✦
Theoretically, the pairing of Jimmy Smith and Lou Donaldson is a smart idea. Both musicians were instrumental in the development of soul-jazz and were recognized as among the leaders of their genre. Instead of catching fire, however, *Jimmy Smith Trio + LD* falls flat. There are a few moments that fulfill the duo's potential—both Smith and Donaldson trade hot lines on "Star Eyes"—but in general, the session is bland but pleasant, offering nothing truly memorable. —*Stephen Thomas Erlewine*

House Party / Aug. 25, 1957 / Blue Note ✦✦✦✦✦
Music from two different sessions are included on this enjoyable LP. All of organist Jimmy Smith's jam sessions are worth acquiring although several (such as this one) have been long out of print. Lengthy versions of "Au Privave" and "Just Friends" and more concise renditions of "Lover Man" and "Blues After All" match Smith with quite a variety of all-stars: trumpeter Lee Morgan, trombonist Curtis Fuller, Lou Donaldson or George Coleman on altos, Tina Brooks on tenor, guitarists Kenny Burrell or Eddie McFadden and Art Blakey or Donald Bailey on drums. Everyone plays up to par and the passionate solos (and Smith's heated background riffing) keep the proceedings continually exciting. —*Scott Yanow*

Confirmation / Aug. 25, 1957+Feb. 25, 1958 / Blue Note ✦✦✦✦
Organist Jimmy Smith led a series of exciting jam sessions for Blue Note from 1957-60, including the three selections heard on this LP. These performances were not released for the first time until 1979, but their quality is as strong as Smith's other output from the era. "Confirmation" matches Smith with altoist Lou Donaldson, tenor saxophonist Tina Brooks, trumpeter Lee Morgan, guitarist Kenny Burrell and drummer Art Blakey, while a 15-minute rendition of "What Is This Thing Called Love" and a 20-minute "Cherokee" have Morgan, Burrell, Blakey, trombonist Curtis Fuller and George Coleman on alto. The heated solos are quite enjoyable, and the organist keeps the momentum constantly flowing throughout this infectious set. —*Scott Yanow*

Standards / Aug. 25, 1957-May 24, 1959 / Blue Note ✦✦✦
Standards is a 12-track collection that is culled from the sessions that resulted in the *House Party* and *Home Cookin'* albums, both of which featured Jimmy Smith in a trio with guitarist Kenny Burrell and drummer Donald Bailey. All of the songs are familiar standards along the lines of "Bye Bye Blackbird," "I'm Just a Lucky So and So," "September Song," "Mood Indigo" and "It Might As Well Be Spring," and seven of the tracks are previously unreleased. Throughout the album, the trio is relaxed and laidback, resulting in a warm, inviting collection of standards. It's among Smith's mellowest recordings, and it's all the better for it. —*Stephen Thomas Erlewine*

Groovin' at Small's Paradise, Vols. 1 & 2 / Nov. 14, 1957+Nov. 18, 1957 / Blue Note ✦✦✦✦✦

Lonesome Road / Nov. 20, 1957 / Blue Note ✦✦✦✦
Jimmy Smith recorded for Blue Note so frequently during the late '50s that many of his sessions remained unreleased for years. The music that comprises *Lonesome Road* sat in the vaults for years, until the Japanese division of Blue Note released the album in the '80s. Since Smith had so many albums on the market, it's understandable that Blue Note wanted to limit the number of records they released from him, but the music on *Lonesome Road* is almost as fine as that on *The Sermon* or *Groovin' at Small's Paradise*. Smith, guitarist Eddie McFadden and drummer Donald Bailey play a selection of eight standards, but the songs don't sound stale; they sound fresh and alive. A few of the ballads are a little slow and treacly, but many of the numbers cook, with a couple of the songs featuring Smith at his hottest. It doesn't have the mastery he would later demonstrate on *Back at the Chicken Shack*, nor is it quite as consistent as *The Sermon*, but *Lonesome Road* is worthwhile for any fan of Smith. —*Stephen Thomas Erlewine*

☆ **The Sermon** / Feb. 25, 1958 / Blue Note ✦✦✦✦✦
This CD reissue has two of the three selections (the 20-minute "The Sermon" and "Flamingo") from the original LP, adding five additional selections that are related. With such soloists as trumpeter Lee Morgan, trombonist Curtis Fuller, altoist Lou Donaldson, Tina Brooks on tenor, either Eddie McFadden or Kenny Burrell on guitar and Art Blakey or Donald Bailey on drums, the straightahead music is as good as one would expect (with the lengthy title cut being the obvious high point), and the CD overall offers listeners a strong dose of Jimmy Smith's Blue Note period. —*Scott Yanow*

Softly as a Summer Breeze / Feb. 26, 1958 / Blue Note ✦✦✦✦

☆ **Cool Blues** / Apr. 7, 1958 / Blue Note ✦✦✦✦✦
This CD should greatly interest all Jimmy Smith collectors, including those who already have the original LP. In addition to four excellent selections (quintets with

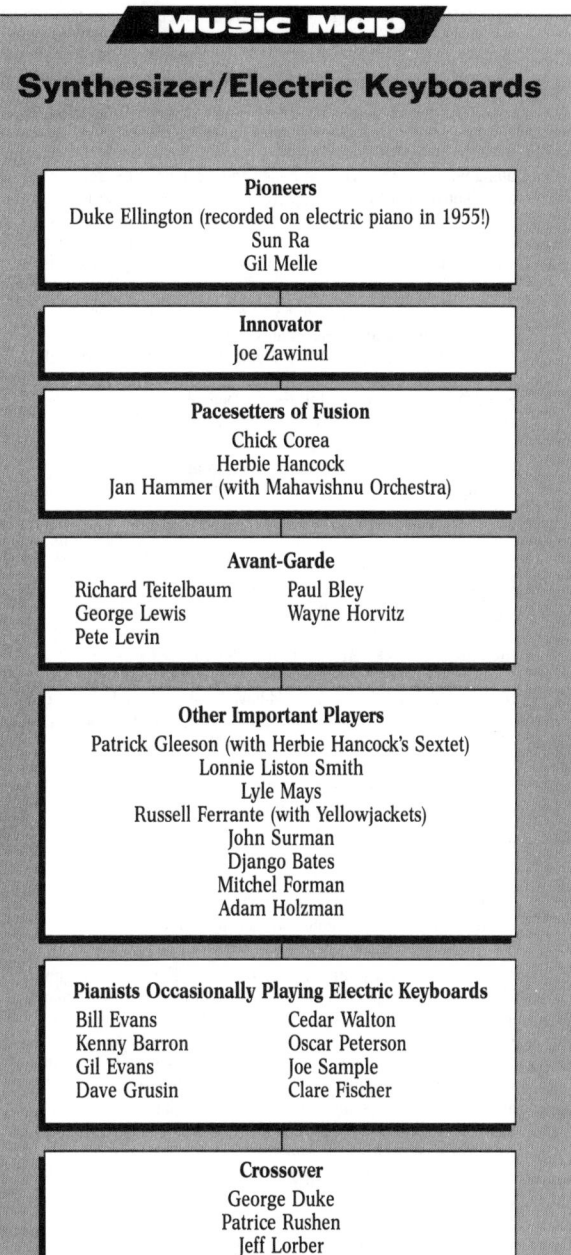

Music Map

Synthesizer/Electric Keyboards

Pioneers
Duke Ellington (recorded on electric piano in 1955!)
Sun Ra
Gil Melle

Innovator
Joe Zawinul

Pacesetters of Fusion
Chick Corea
Herbie Hancock
Jan Hammer (with Mahavishnu Orchestra)

Avant-Garde
Richard Teitelbaum	Paul Bley
George Lewis	Wayne Horvitz
Pete Levin	

Other Important Players
Patrick Gleeson (with Herbie Hancock's Sextet)
Lonnie Liston Smith
Lyle Mays
Russell Ferrante (with Yellowjackets)
John Surman
Django Bates
Mitchel Forman
Adam Holzman

Pianists Occasionally Playing Electric Keyboards
Bill Evans	Cedar Walton
Kenny Barron	Oscar Peterson
Gil Evans	Joe Sample
Dave Grusin	Clare Fischer

Crossover
George Duke
Patrice Rushen
Jeff Lorber
Bob James

altoist Lou Donaldson, Tina Brooks on tenor, guitarist Eddie McFadden, either Art Blakey or Donald Bailey on drums and the organist/leader), there are three previously unissued numbers from the same gig, featuring the quartet of Donaldson, Smith, McFadden and Bailey. The repertoire is filled with blues and bop standards and the soloing is at a consistently high and hard-swinging level. Jimmy Smith fans will be pleased. —*Scott Yanow*

On the Sunny Side / Jul. 15, 1958 / Blue Note ✦✦✦✦
Organist Jimmy Smith recorded quite a bit of material for Blue Note during 1956-63. This 1981 LP released for the first time eight selections cut during four sessions in the late '50s. In all cases, Smith is joined by guitarist Kenny Burrell and drummer Donald Bailey; Stanley Turrentine makes the group a quartet on "The Sunny Side of the Street" while his fellow tenor Percy France does the same on his origi-

nal "Apostrophe." All of the songs (other than the latter) are standards and the tunes generally clock in around a concise five minutes. The results are predictably swinging and highlights include "On the Sunny Side," "Since I Fell for You," "Bye Bye Blackbird" and "I'm Just a Lucky So and So." Excellent music. —*Scott Yanow*

Home Cookin' / Jul. 17, 1958-Jun. 16, 1959 / Blue Note ✦✦✦✦
Organist Jimmy Smith and guitarist Kenny Burrell always had a close musical relationship, making each of their joint recordings quite special. This LP features the pair along with drummer Donald Bailey and (on four of the seven songs) the obscure but talented tenor saxophonist Percy France. The emphasis is on blues and basic material including versions of "See See Rider," Ray Charles' "I Got a Woman" and several group originals, and as usual, the performances are swinging and soulful. The CD reissue adds five "new" performances to the original seven. —*Scott Yanow*

☆ **Crazy! Baby** / Jan. 4, 1960 / Blue Note ✦✦✦✦✦
Unlike most of the Jimmy Smith recordings from the era, this CD reissue (which adds "If I Should Lose You" and "When Lights Are Low" to the original LP program) features organist Jimmy Smith's regular group (rather than an all-star band). With guitarist Quentin Warren and drummer Donald Bailey completing the trio, Smith is heard in peak form on swinging and soulful versions of such tunes as "When Johnny Comes Marching Home," "Makin' Whoopee," "Sonnymoon for Two" and "Mack the Knife." Despite claims and some strong challenges by others, there has never been a jazz organist on the level of Jimmy Smith. —*Scott Yanow*

Open House/Plain Talk / Mar. 22, 1960 / Blue Note ✦✦✦✦✦
A two-fer with two classic Smith albums, "Open House" and "Plain Talk," on one CD. Recorded in Hackensack, NJ. Studio session featuring Blue Mitchell (tpt), Ike Quebec (ts) and Jackie McClean (as). This is essentially a jam session without Smith's regular sidemen. More mainstream than most, but very nice tracks—fast and slow. This is an excellent album. —*Michael Erlewine*

★ **Back at the Chicken Shack** / Apr. 25, 1960 / Blue Note ✦✦✦✦✦
This may be the quintessential funky soul-jazz album. Period. I know of no better single recording and this is the one I would have to take to that desert island when I go. The term "all star" was coined for this group. Jimmy Smith is as hot as he gets and so is Stanley Turrentine on tenor sax. Just hot! Kenny Burrell is in top form too and Donald Bailey keeps the beat tight. Every jazz fan should hear it and every groove fan must own it. Also see the Smith album *Midnight Special*, which was recorded at the same session. —*Michael Erlewine*

☆ **Midnight Special** / Apr. 25, 1960 / Blue Note ✦✦✦✦✦
Recorded in Englewood Cliffs, NJ. Small Group. This was recorded at the same session as "Back at the Chicken Shack," and it is also as fine—that is: magical! This is a must-have for jazz organ fans. With Stanley Turrentine (ts) and Kenny Burrell (g). Every collector of groove music should have a copy. —*Michael Erlewine*

Prayer Meetin' / Jun. 13, 1960+Feb. 8, 1963 / Blue Note ✦✦✦✦✦
Prayer Meetin' was organist Jimmy Smith's final Blue Note recording until 1986. On this CD reissue two earlier selections featuring Smith, tenor saxophonist Stanley Turrentine, guitarist Quentin Warren, bassist Sam Jones (the only time on Blue Note that Smith used a bassist) and drummer Donald Bailey jam on versions of "Lonesome Road" and the original "Smith Walk"; both selections went unreleased until popping up on a 1984 Japanese CD. The bulk of this set is from February 8, 1963, featuring the same personnel without Jones. Highlights include the title cut, a soulful version of "When the Saints Go Marching In" and the Gene Ammons blues "Red Top." Excellent music. —*Scott Yanow*

Jimmy Smith Plays Fats Waller / Jan. 23, 1962 / Blue Note ✦✦✦✦
Although Fats Waller was the first jazz organist, he mostly played piano throughout his career. Organist Jimmy Smith's tribute to Waller is not imitative at all, but a good excuse to interpret seven jazz standards associated with Fats. With assistance from his regular trio—guitarist Quentin Warren and drummer Donald Bailey—Smith plays such unlikely numbers as "Everybody Loves My Baby," "I've Found a New Baby" and Waller's two biggest hits ("Ain't Misbehavin'" and "Honeysuckle Rose") with soul and swing. An enjoyable outing. —*Scott Yanow*

☆ **Bashin': The Unpredictable Jimmy Smith** / Mar. 26, 1962+Mar. 28, 1962 / Verve ✦✦✦✦✦
Although still a regular Blue Note artist (he would make four more albums for the company within the next year), *Bashin'* was organist Jimmy Smith's debut for Verve, a label that he would record extensively for during 1963-72. On the first half of the program (reissued in full on this CD), Smith was for the first time joined by a big band. Oliver Nelson provided the arrangements, trumpeter Joe Newman and altoist Phil Woods have a solo apiece and "Walk on the Wild Side" became Smith's biggest hit up to that point. The final three numbers feature Smith's regular trio with guitarist Quentin Warren and drummer Donald Bailey swinging with soul as usual. The historical set (a bit of a turning point for Jimmy Smith's career) has its strong moments although it is not all that essential. —*Scott Yanow*

Walk on the Wild Side: The Best of the Verve Years / 1962-1973 / Verve ✦✦✦✦
Smith recorded most of his most popular sides for Verve, and this double CD contains 25 tracks taken from his recordings for the label between 1962 and 1973, in both small-combo and big-band settings. There are a few Jimmy Smith compilations out there, and this isn't necessarily the best; anthologies which focus on his early and mid-'60s prime might be better values overall. It does have his most famous performances—"Walk on the Wild Side," "Got My Mojo Workin'," and a couple of his great duets with guitarist Wes Montgomery. It's a decent enough pickup if you just want one or two Smith albums for your library, though not so definitive that it's worth getting if you already have some Smith compilations that cover the Verve era. —*Richie Unterberger*

I'm Movin On / Jan. 31, 1963 / Blue Note ✦✦✦
This CD reissue of a formerly rare date has a perfectly suitable title for it is the first of four albums that organist Jimmy Smith made within an eight-day period for Blue Note before permanently leaving the label for Verve. Although notable for matching Smith with guitarist Grant Green in what would be their only joint recording (drummer Donald Bailey completes the trio), the music is fairly typical of a Jimmy Smith session with the repertoire including blues, a couple of standards and ballads. The solos are well played but nothing too surprising occurs (except perhaps for the sappiness of "What Kind of Fool Am I"); the original LP program is expanded by the inclusion of two other selections from the same date. —*Scott Yanow*

Bucket! / Feb. 1, 1963 / Blue Note ✦✦✦

Rockin' the Boat / Feb. 2, 1963 / Blue Note ✦✦✦✦
Organist Jimmy Smith's next-to-last LP for Blue Note after a very extensive seven-year period is up to his usual level. With altoist Lou Donaldson joining Smith's regular group (which included guitarist Quentin Warren and drummer Donald Bailey), the quartet swings with soul on such numbers as "When My Dream Boat Comes Home," "Can Heat," "Please Send Me Someone to Love" and "Just a Closer Walk with Thee." With the exception of the closing ballad, "Trust in Me," all seven of the selections are closely related to the blues. This is fine music well deserving of being reissued on CD someday. —*Scott Yanow*

Hobo Flats / Mar. 15, 1963+Mar. 20, 1963 / Verve ✦✦✦

Talkin' Verve: Roots of Acid Jazz / Mar. 20, 1963-Sep. 11, 1972 / Verve ✦✦✦✦
Designed to appeal to hip-hop and acid jazz fans, not jazz purists, *Talkin' Verve: The Roots of Acid Jazz* collects 14 tracks Jimmy Smith cut for Verve during the late '60s. Comprising pop covers and funky workouts, the music is "jazzy," not jazz—there's little improvisation on the record, but there is a lot of hot vamping, with Smith creating dense, funky chord clusters and bluesy leads. It's music that is devoted to the groove, and while a few of these cuts fall flat—"Ode to Billlie Joe" has no funk in it, no matter how hard you try—but for the most part *Talkin' Verve* is soulful fun. Not much of this sounds like acid jazz, especially since the rhythms are a little stiff, but it's enjoyable lite-funk, and it's more palatable in the compilation than it is on their original albums. —*Stephen Thomas Erlewine*

Live at the Village Gate / May 31, 1963 / Metro ✦✦✦✦

Any Number Can Win / Jul. 10, 1963-Jul. 29, 1963 / Verve ✦✦✦

Jazz 'Round Midnight / 1963-1972 / Blue Note ✦✦✦
Another of those Verve compilations that focus on a specific mood or aspect of repertoire, in order to maximize the mileage from back catalog. This focuses on Jimmy's ballads and slow groovers with an afterhours atmosphere. Given Smith's immense discography (at one time it seemed like he was on the album-a-month plan), it's really not a bad way for novices to acquaint themselves with more of his material, though this compilation doesn't have the pumping uptempo chuggers for which he's most renowned. The ten songs span 1963 to 1972 (all but one were recorded prior to 1967), and feature top-notch sidemen like Wes Montgomery, Kenny Burrell, and Grady Tate. —*Richie Unterberger*

Who's Afraid of Virginia Woolf? / Jan. 20, 1964-Apr. 27, 1964 / Verve ✦✦✦

The Cat / Apr. 27, 1964-Apr. 29, 1964 / Verve ✦✦✦✦
Compared to his earlier Blue Note recordings, organist Jimmy Smith's outings for Verve are not as strong from a jazz standpoint. Certainly his renditions of the "Theme from *Joy House*," "The Cat" and the "Main Title from *The Carpetbaggers*" are not all that significant. However, this CD has some tasteful arrangements for the big band by Lalo Schifrin, and some good playing by the great organist on a variety of other blues-oriented material. Also the combination of organ with a big band is sometimes quite appealing, making this CD worth picking up despite its commercial tracks. —*Scott Yanow*

Monster / Jan. 19, 1965-Jan. 20, 1965 / Verve ✦✦
Due to the material, which includes the two-part "Goldfinger," and the themes from *Bewitched*, *The Munsters* and *The Man with the Golden Arm*, this is one of organist Jimmy Smith's lesser recordings. The LP does have some reasonably

inventive arrangements for the accompanying big band by Oliver Nelson and some spirited organ playing, but overall is a rather forgettable and overproduced effort. —*Scott Yanow*

And His Trio / May 28, 1965 / RTE ♦♦♦
Jimmy Smith has been a very dominant influence on jazz organists since his arrival on the scene in 1956. This previously unreleased concert appearance by his trio (released on a double CD in 1996) is a fairly typical Jimmy Smith program from the mid-'60s. Although such songs as "Who's Afraid of Virginia Woolf," "Goldfinger" and "Walk on the Wild Side" may make this appear to be a commercial set, Smith turns much of the music into either long one-chord vamps or blues. Guitarist Quentin Warren does not get much solo space and drummer Billy Hart plays a supporting role so this is very much Smith's show. He hotdogs it a bit, sometimes holds on to a note for an eternity and continually shows off his technique but Smith also swings up a storm and demonstrates why over three decades later he is still the king of organists. —*Scott Yanow*

Organ Grinder Swing / Jun. 14, 1965-Jun. 15, 1965 / Verve ♦♦♦♦
Most of organist Jimmy Smith's recordings for Verve during the mid- to late '60s were with big bands, making this trio outing with guitarist Kenny Burrell and drummer Grady Tate a special treat. This CD reissue is a throwback to Smith's Blue Note sets (which had concluded two years earlier) and gives the organists the opportunity to stretch out on three blues and three standards. This release shows that, even with all of his commercial success during the period, Jimmy Smith was always a masterful jazz player. —*Scott Yanow*

Got My Mojo Workin'/Hoochie Cooche Man / Dec. 16, 1965-Jul. 1966 / Verve ♦♦♦♦
After leading a series of notable jam sessions for Blue Note, organist Jimmy Smith signed a lucrative contract with Verve in 1962. Throughout the remainder of the decade, he recorded songs that ranged from treasures to trash, turning most of the music into bluesy vamps. On this CD, a reissue of the LPs *Got My Mojo Workin'* and *Hoochie Cooche Man*, Smith's repertoire ranges from Billy Strayhorn's "Johnny Come Lately" and Oliver Nelson's "Blues and the Abstract Truth" to "I'm Your Hoochie Coochie Man" and "I Can't Get No Satisfaction." In most cases, Smith's versions bear little resemblance to the original recordings. The earlier set has Smith featured with both a quartet and an octet arranged by Oliver Nelson. The remainder of the CD is a big band with Nelson's charts making the orchestra as exuberant as Smith's solos. Overall, the CD is not as essential as Jimmy Smith's better Blue Note dates, but is a worthwhile acquisition for fans of the jazz organ due to his enthusiasm and his ability to uplift the material. —*Scott Yanow*

Peter and the Wolf / May 11, 1966-May 12, 1966 / Verve ♦♦♦♦♦
Of all of organist Jimmy Smith's big-band albums recorded for Verve, this is one of the most imaginative ones. Oliver Nelson arranged a variety of themes from Prokofiev's *Peter & the Wolf* into a swinging suite featuring the great organist Jimmy Smith. Although there is no verbal narrative on this LP, Nelson's liner notes tell the story (which can actually be followed through the music) and Smith pays respect to the original melodies while making strong statements of his own. A classic of its kind but long out of print. —*Scott Yanow*

☆ The Dynamic Duo / Sep. 21, 1966+Sep. 28, 1966 / Verve ♦♦♦♦♦
This CD—a straight reissue of the original LP—is a classic. Organist Jimmy Smith and guitarist Wes Montgomery, both the main pacesetters on their instruments at the time, make for a perfect team on quartet renditions (with drummer Grady Tate and percussionist Ray Barretto) of "James and Wes" and "Baby, It's Cold Outside." However, it is the three numbers with a big band arranged by Oliver Nelson (particularly "Night Train" and a very memorable version of "Down by the Riverside") that really stick in one's mind. Although it is unfortunate that the Smith-Wes collaboration was short-lived (just one other album), it is miraculous that they did find each other and created this brilliant music. —*Scott Yanow*

Further Adventures of Jimmy and Wes / Sep. 21, 1966-Sep. 28, 1966 / Verve ♦♦♦♦♦
Organist Wes Montgomery and guitarist Wes Montgomery did all of their recordings together during several sessions in September 1966, but despite the relatively low quantity, the results were consistently memorable. This CD, a follow-up to *The Dynamic Duo*, has one selection ("Milestones") in which the two lead voices are joined by Oliver Nelson's big band and several numbers (including the pop hits "King of the Road" and "Call Me") with a quartet that also includes drummer Grady Tate and percussionist Ray Barretto. Although not reaching the heights of the other set, this CD has more than its share of exciting solos from the immortal co-leaders. —*Scott Yanow*

Respect / Jun. 2, 1967+Jun. 14, 1967 / Verve ♦♦
Organist Jimmy Smith, joined by one of two guitar/bass/drums rhythm sections, mostly sticks to then-current R&B hits on this out-of-print LP. He does what he can with "Mercy, Mercy, Mercy," a brief "Respect" and "Funky Broadway" while con-

tributing his own blues "T-Bone Steak." The 31-minute set has its moments but no real surprises, swinging funkily throughout. —*Scott Yanow*

Stay Loose / Jan. 1968 / Verve ♦♦

Livin' It Up / May 13, 1968-May 14, 1968 / Verve ♦♦

The Boss / Nov. 20, 1968 / Verve ♦♦♦
Recorded at Paschal's La Carousel, Atlanta, GA. Lots of fine solos. George Benson (g) does best soul-jazz work since McDuff days. —*Ron Wynn*

Groove Drops / Oct. 1969 / Verve ♦♦♦

Root Down / Feb. 8, 1972 / Verve ♦♦

Bluesmith / Sep. 11, 1972 / Verve ♦♦♦♦♦
It is ironic that one of Jimmy Smith's best Verve releases would be his next-to-last for the label. This surprisingly freewheeling but relaxed jam session also features Teddy Edwards on tenor, guitarist Ray Crawford, bassist Leroy Vinnegar, drummer Donald Dean and the congas of Victor Pantoja. Together they perform five of Smith's fairly basic originals and Harvey Siders' "Mournin' Wes," a tribute for Wes Montgomery. Fine straightahead music that deserves to be reissued again. —*Scott Yanow*

Portuguese Soul / Feb. 8, 1973-Feb. 9, 1973 / Verve ♦♦
Recorded in NYC. Big band. Smith with large orchestra under the direction of Thad Jones. —*Michael Erlewine*

I'm Gonna Git Myself Together / 1973 / MGM ♦♦

Other Side of Jimmy Smith / 1973 / MGM ♦♦♦
Another big-band outing by Smith. W/ Johnny Pate and orchestra. —*Michael Erlewine*

It's Necessary / Jul. 6, 1977-Jul. 7, 1977 / Mercury ♦♦♦
Although he still won popularity polls and remained a household name in the jazz world, the end of organist Jimmy Smith's long period with Verve in 1972 kept him in relative obscurity until he re-emerged on the Elektra Musician label in 1982. This live album, recorded at Smith's short-lived North Hollywood supper club, finds the great organist and his quartet (with guitarist Ray Crawford) welcoming such guests as tenors Teddy Edwards and Harold Land and trumpeter Blue Mitchell. The material is decent ("Red Top" and "Sometimes I'm Happy" are stronger than the recent originals) and the recording quality is decent, if not state of the art. Superior to his other, more commercial sets of the period, this reasonably enjoyable LP does not measure up to the excitement level of Smith's earlier, classic Blue Note sessions, but is worth picking up by his fans. —*Scott Yanow*

The Cat Strikes Again / Jul. 1980 / LaserLight ♦♦♦
Recorded in Hollywood. Big band. W/ Lalo Schifrin and orchestra. —*Michael Erlewine*

All the Way Live / Aug. 29, 1981 / Milestone ♦♦♦♦
Strange as it seems, organist Jimmy Smith and tenor saxophonist Eddie Harris only played together once. Their recorded collaboration at San Francisco's Keystone Korner in 1981 was released for the first time by Milestone on *All the Way Live*. Harris (who utilizes an electrified tenor) and Smith (along with drummer Kenny Dixon) jam a couple of blues, the funky "8 Counts for Rita" (which has some audience participation) and three familiar standards. The recording quality is not state-of-the-art but is certainly listenable and the high level of the playing overcomes any technical deficiencies. Essentially a hard-bop stylist, Eddie Harris' brilliance and originality are sometimes hidden under his innovative use of electronics but he has long had his own sound while Jimmy Smith is the originator of his very influential style. Highlights of the date include "Autumn Leaves," "A Child Is Born" and "Old Folks" and this live set easily surpasses Smith and Harris' studio recordings of the time period. —*Scott Yanow*

Off the Top / Jun. 7, 1982 / Elektra ♦♦♦♦
It had been nine years since organist Jimmy Smith recorded for a major label when Bruce Lundvall approached him to make an album for Elektra Musician. Smith plays some unusual material (including Lionel Richie's "Endless Love" and the "Theme from *M.A.S.H.*") on this LP but swings everything and has a particularly strong supporting cast—guitarist George Benson, Stanley Turrentine on tenor, bassist Ron Carter and drummer Grady Tate. A fine comeback date. —*Scott Yanow*

Keep On Comin' / Sep. 3, 1983 / Elektra ♦♦♦♦
Organist Jimmy Smith's second of two LPs for the Elektra Musician label is unusual in a couple of respects. He had never played organ with tenor saxophonist Johnny Griffin before and on one piece, "Piano Solo Medley," Smith has a very rare feature on piano. Otherwise the music, which comprises recent originals by Smith, Griffin and guitarist Kenny Burrell who with drummer Mike Baker completes the quartet, is in the soulfully swinging vein that one associates with the great organist. —*Scott Yanow*

Go for Whatcha' Know / Jan. 2, 1986 / Blue Note ✦✦✦✦
23 years after leaving the label, organist Jimmy Smith returned to the Blue Note label. In addition to signing up two of his old associates who had been with him on many classic Blue Note albums of the past (guitarist Kenny Burrell and tenor saxophonist Stanley Turrentine), Smith uses such fine players as guest pianist Monty Alexander (on two songs), bassist Buster Williams and drummer Grady Tate (who takes a warm ballad vocal on "She's out of My Life"). "Fungii Mama" and "Go for Whatcha Know" are the highlights of this enjoyable LP. —*Scott Yanow*

Prime Time / 1989 / Milestone ✦✦✦✦✦
For this Milestone release, organist Jimmy Smith utilized some of the top veterans then residing in Los Angeles, many of whom had been long underrated. With sidemen that include Curtis Peagler on tenor and alto, tenors Herman Riley and Rickey Woodard, either Phil Upchurch or Terry Evans on guitar, bassist Andy Simpkins, Michael Baker or Frank Wilson on drums and Barbara Morrison (who takes a vocal on "Farther on up the Road"), this is a particularly strong band. The fresh material (only "C Jam Blues" and "Honky Tonk" are standards) and spirited solos make this an easily recommended set of swinging jazz. —*Scott Yanow*

Fourmost / Nov. 16, 1990-Nov. 17, 1990 / Milestone ✦✦✦✦✦
Organist Jimmy Smith has a reunion on this CD with his 30 plus-year associates tenor saxophonist Stanley Turrentine and guitarist Kenny Burrell along with drummer Grady Tate. Together they play spirited and creative versions of standards and blues. The high points include "Midnight Special," a swinging "Main Stem," Tate's warm vocal on "My Funny Valentine" and a lengthy rendition of "Quiet Nights." Suffice it to say that this all-star date reaches its potential and is easily recommended to fans of straightahead jazz. —*Scott Yanow*

The Master / Dec. 24, 1993-Dec. 25, 1993 / Blue Note ✦✦✦
Organist Jimmy Smith, in a trio with guitarist Kenny Burrell and drummer Jimmie Smith (no relation) performs six diverse blues and three familiar standards. Although the music is somewhat predictable, it swings hard and is often rollicking. Burrell sounds inspired and Smith, who largely originated this idiom, shows that he is still an enthusiastic and masterful player. —*Scott Yanow*

Master 2 / Dec. 24, 1993-Dec. 25, 1993 / Blue Note ✦✦✦
The second of two CDs coming from the same two days of sessions in Japan, this set once again matches organist Jimmy Smith with drummer Jimmie Smith (no relation) and guitarist Kenny Burrell. Actually, other than occasional spots for Burrell, the focus is entirely on the organist, who is heard in top form, showing off both his technique and his melodic creativity. The better of the two releases, this hard bop-oriented performance features the trio on five veteran standards plus T-Bone Walker's "Stormy Monday." Highlights include "My Romance" and a swinging "Mack the Knife." —*Scott Yanow*

Sum Serious Blues / 1993 / Milestone ✦✦✦
Organist Jimmy Smith performs a spirited set of blues-based material (only "You've Changed" is a change of pace) with a dozen of his Los Angeles-based friends including trumpeter Oscar Brashear, the underrated tenor Herman Riley (who is best among the supporting cast), guitarist Philip Upchurch and singers Marlena Shaw and Bernard Ighner who have two vocals apiece. Nothing that surprising occurs other than Smith's surprisingly effective vocal on "Hurry Change, If You're Comin'," but the swinging music, which was arranged by Johnny Pate, should please Jimmy Smith's fans. —*Scott Yanow*

Damn! / Jan. 24, 1995-Jan. 25, 1995 / Verve ✦✦✦✦

Angel Eyes: Ballads & Slow Jams / Jan. 25, 1995+Jan. 26, 1995 / Verve ✦✦✦
A follow-up to the mostly heated performances of *Damn!*, this CD features organist Jimmy Smith sticking to ballads and slower material. There is a sextet rendition of "Stolen Moments" (with both Roy Hargrove and Nicholas Payton on trumpets), duets with both trumpeters, bassist Christian McBride and guitarist Mark Whitfield, a trio, a quartet, and solo organ renditions of "Bess, Oh Where's My Bess" and "What a Wonderful World." Despite the constant changing of instrumentation, the results (although pleasant) are uneventful and somewhat predictable. Good for late-night background music rather than for close listening. —*Scott Yanow*

Johnny "Hammond" Smith

b. Dec. 16, 1933, Louisville, KY, d. Jun. 4, 1997, Chicago, IL
Organ / Soul Jazz, Hard Bop, Groove
Johnny (Robert) "Hammond" Smith was born on December 16, 1933, in Louisville, KY. From a musical family, he learned piano early on. Bud Powell and Art Tatum were his idols. Originally a pianist based in Cleveland, after hearing Wild Bill Davis he switched to the organ. Also known as Johnny Hammond, Smith worked for a period in the late '50s as Nancy Wilson's accompanist but had spent most of his career as a leader, recording a series of enjoyable soul-jazz albums for Prestige during 1959-1970. Although he also utilized synthesizers in the 1970s, Smith in the 1980s and '90s (before being struck down by cancer) stuck exclusively to the

organ in a timeless style unchanged from three decades before. Johnny "Hammond" Smith was one of the many organists to come to prominence in the 1960s who was greatly influenced by Jimmy Smith. —*Michael Erlewine & Scott Yanow*

● **That Good Feelin'** / Sep. 11, 1959-Nov. 4, 1959 / Prestige ✦✦✦✦✦
Organist Johnny "Hammond" Smith's first two albums as a leader are reissued in full on this single CD. Joined throughout by guitarist Thornel Schwartz, bassist George Tucker and drummer Leo Stevens, Smith displays a wide range of sounds, plenty of grease and the ability to jam like Erroll Garner in spots. His repertoire is wider than expected, with just five originals among the 14 numbers and plenty of bop and swing standards included in addition to the expected groovin' blues. This CD offers an excellent example of the organist's talents. —*Scott Yanow*

Talk That Talk / Apr. 22, 1960 / Prestige ✦✦✦✦

Look Out! / Jan. 22, 1962 / New Jazz ✦✦✦

Johnny Hammond Cooks with Gator Tail / Jun. 12, 1962 / Prestige ✦✦✦

Black Coffee / Nov. 8, 1962 / Milestone ✦✦✦✦✦
Two of organist Johnny "Hammond" Smith's earliest gems (*Black Coffee* and *Mr. Wonderful*) are reissued in full on this single CD. Although influenced by Jimmy Smith, this particular organist was also a strong grooving player, able to play both blues and more complicated chord changes. He is showcased with a quartet that includes tenor saxophonist Seldon Powell and guitarist Eddie McFadden, and in a quintet with McFadden, tenorman Houston Person and trumpeter Sonny Williams; in both cases Leo Stevens is on drums. The material (which includes eight colorful originals, "I Remember Clifford," "Body and Soul" and "He's a Real Gone Guy" among the 15 numbers) has a fair amount of variety, and Johnny "Hammond" Smith is heard at his best throughout this reissue. —*Scott Yanow*

The Stinger / May 7, 1965 / Prestige ✦✦✦✦
Organist Johnny "Hammond" Smith is a decent soul-jazz player. He plays in short, swirling bursts and uses the bass pedals in a pounding, aggressive manner. These are primarily uptempo and funky jam numbers, particularly the title track. —*Ron Wynn*

● **Legends of Acid Jazz** / May 19, 1969+Dec. 22, 1969 / Prestige ✦✦✦✦✦
Out of all the soul-jazz organ players, only one was so thoroughly funked out that he personally adopted the name of his favorite keyboard, the B-3: Johnny "Hammond" Smith. While not as important in the development of jazz styles as other keyboard players such as Jimmy Smith, "Hammond" displayed an earthy, swinging talent worth listening to. *Legends of Acid Jazz: Johnny "Hammond" Smith* compiles under a single cover two albums Smith recorded in 1969, *Soul Talk* and *Black Feeling* (complete with the liner notes from both original issues). On *Legends*, Smith gets down in the heady company of, among others, tenor saxophonist Rusty Bryant, funky drummer Bernard Purdie and guitarist Wally Richardson; Richardson here pays tribute to his bandmates with his compositions "Purdie Dirty" and "Johnny Hammond Boogaloo." *Legends* includes the pop covers "When Sunny Gets Blue" and "This Guy's in Love with You," opens with the original version of Smith's hit "Soul Talk," and concludes with the updated version he later recorded for *Black Feeling*. Not groundbreaking, but solid and a funky good time. —*Chris Slawecki*

Wild Horses Rock Steady / 1971 / Kudu ✦✦✦

Johnny Smith

b. Jun. 25, 1922, Birmingham, AL
Guitar / Cool, Classical
Guitarist Johnny Smith will always be best remembered for his 1952 hit recording of "Moonlight in Vermont," a mellow ballad that also features Stan Getz. Smith, whose chordal-oriented style is self-taught, originally played trumpet, violin and viola before switching to guitar. A studio musician from 1947 on, Smith's impressive technique and quiet sound made him in great demand even before "Moonlight" and, although he never had another hit, he was a popular attraction throughout the 1950s. After moving to Colorado in the 1960s he opened a music store, taught and maintained a lower profile, occasionally recording in New York. —*Scott Yanow*

★ **Moonlight in Vermont** / Mar. 11, 1952-Aug. 1953 / Roulette ✦✦✦✦✦
All of guitarist Johnny Smith's most important recordings are on this definitive CD reissue. The talented guitarist (who always featured a very attractive tone and a relaxed style) had a major hit with "Moonlight in Vermont" thanks in large part to tenor saxophonist Stan Getz (who is heard on seven of the selections), and Smith was quite popular during the first half of the 1950s. This CD has all of the guitarist's 1952-53 recordings except for three cuts (two done with organist Joe Mooney) and has a previously unreleased alternate take of "Jaguar." With such sidemen as Getz or fellow tenors Zoot Sims and Paul Quinichette and a solid rhythm section,

Smith brings melodic beauty to a variety of standards, including "Where or When," "My Funny Valentine," "Tenderly" and "Cherokee." Recommended. —*Scott Yanow*

Leo Smith

b. Dec. 18, 1941, Leland, MS
Trumpet / Avant-Garde, Free Jazz
A consistently adventurous trumpeter who has stuck to playing avant-garde jazz throughout his career, Leo Smith's dry, introverted style (which makes extensive use of space) is a strong contrast to the more jubilant flights of Lester Bowie. Smith originally played drums, mellophone and French horn before settling on trumpet. He gained early experience performing in R&B groups and played in an Army band while serving in the military. By 1967, Leo Smith was a member of Chicago's AACM. He soon helped to found the Creative Construction Company, an innovative trio with violinist Leroy Jenkins and multi-instrumentalist Anthony Braxton that toured Europe in the late 1960s. Smith, who was involved in making the documentary film *See the Music* in 1970, formed the New Dalta Ahkri in New Haven, CT, an influential if underdocumented band that at times included Henry Threadgill, Anthony Davis and Oliver Lake. Smith studied ethnomusicology in the mid-'70s at Wesleyan, played with Braxton in 1976 and recorded with Derek Bailey's Company; he has freelanced with his own diverse groups during the past 20 years. After becoming a Rastafarian in the 1980s, he changed his name to Wadada Leo Smith. He has been teaching at Cal Arts since 1993. Leo Smith, who founded the Kabell label in 1971, has also recorded for Freedom, Moers, ECM, Nesssa, FMP, Black Saint, Nessa and Sackville in settings ranging from unaccompanied solos to a big band. —*Scott Yanow*

Mass on the World / May 1978 / Moers ✦✦✦✦

Budding of a Rose / Jun. 1979 / Moers ✦✦✦✦

Touch the Earth / Nov. 1979 / FMP ✦✦✦

Go in Numbers / Jan. 19, 1980 / Black Saint ✦✦✦✦✦

Spirit Catcher / Nov. 1980 / Nessa ✦✦✦✦
The dry and often esoteric trumpeter Leo Smith is featured with his quintet (consisting of Dwight Andrews on tenor, clarinet and flute, vibraphonist Bobby Naughton, bassist Wes Brown and drummer Pheeroan AkLaff) on the 19-minute "Images" and the colorful "Spirit Catcher." "The Burning of Stones" (dedicated to Anthony Braxton) has Smith's trumpet joined by three harpists for some unusual music. Throughout the LP the performances are unpredictable, and it's frequently difficult to know where the arrangement ends and the improvising begins. This is thought-provoking music that grows in interest with each listen. —*Scott Yanow*

● **Rastafari** / Jun. 12, 1983 / Sackville ✦✦✦✦✦
Few of trumpeter Leo Smith's recordings are readily available, making this introspective but very interesting collaboration with soprano saxophonist Bill Smith, violinist David Prentice, bassist David Lee and vibraphonist Larry Potter an important release. The playing by these adventurous musicians is advanced and quite free on the four group originals, and all five players share equally in the creation of these fresh explorations. —*Scott Yanow*

Lonnie Liston Smith

b. Dec. 28, 1940, Richmond, VA
Keyboards, Piano / Fusion, Post-Bop, Crossover Jazz
Pianist Lonnie Liston Smith underwent a great stylistic change during the '70s. At one point he was working with Pharoah Sanders and Gato Barbieri providing keyboard interludes for their highly charged, explosive settings. Then Smith played with Miles Davis, plugging into electric funk. When he formed the Cosmic Echoes with his brother Donald, things were radically different. Smith presented low-key arrangements, with Donald singing pseudo-mystic laments and pontifications, with minimal improvisation and solo space. But these albums put Lonnie Liston Smith on the fusion and crossover map; he enjoyed great sales for a string of releases in this pattern that continued through the '80s and into the '90s. He established himself as one of the more popular acts on the Black upper middle class professional circuit, playing college campuses and appearing in several cites with heavy African-American populations and high profile urban contemporary radio stations. Prior to this, Lonnie Liston Smith had graduated in music education from Morgan State in 1961, then moved to New York. He has played with Betty Carter, Rahsaan Roland Kirk, Art Blakey, Joe Williams and Sanders. Smith has recorded as a leader for Flying Dutchman, Doctor Jazz and Signature. He has several sessions available on CD. —*Ron Wynn*

Astral Travelling / 1973 / Flying Dutchman ✦✦✦✦

Golden Dreams / 1973-1976 / Bluebird ✦✦✦✦✦
This CD reissue has all ten selections from keyboardist Lonnie Liston's Smith album *Reflections of a Golden Dream*, plus four of the six cuts from his 1973 debut

as a leader. The performances are essentially high-quality mood music, funky and a bit fusion-oriented, yet with moments of creativity. The personnel differs on most selections, with such supporting players as (on the 1973 set) bassist Cecil McBee and guitarist Joe Beck and in 1976 Donald Smith on flute and vocals, the reeds of David Hubbard and some background singers. A good introduction to Lonnie Liston Smith's early recordings. —*Scott Yanow*

Cosmic Funk / 1974 / Flying Dutchman ✦✦✦

Expansions / 1974 / Flying Dutchman ✦✦✦✦✦
The best of his post-Pharoah Sanders releases. —*Ron Wynn*

● **Reflections of a Golden Dream** / Sep. 1976 / RCA ✦✦✦✦✦

Renaissance / 1977 / RCA ✦✦✦

Loveland / 1978 / Columbia ✦✦✦

Dreams of Tomorrow / 1979 / Doctor Jazz ✦✦

Visions of a New World / 1980 / Flying Dutchman ✦✦✦

Love Goddess / 1983 / Startrak ✦✦✦
At his best, Lonnie Liston Smith has been a wealth of imagination and creativity—a fact that makes so much of the often calculated *Love Goddess* difficult to listen to. Sometimes engaging and sometimes outright worthless, this erratic CD ranges from radio-oriented "muzak" to strong post-bop jazz. Smith excels as an acoustic trio pianist on very lyrical and warm interpretations of Kenny Dorham's "Blue Bossa," Miles Davis' "Blue in Green" and Thad Jones' "A Child Is Born." Much of the CD, however, contains shamelessly formulaic and contrived pop/R&B/jazz that throws artistic integrity to the wind and is concerned only with commercial radio airplay—the worst offender being a boring and cynical note-for-note cover of Anita Baker's "Giving You the Best That I Got." For consistently excellent listening, a much wiser investment would be *Astral Traveling, Expansions* or the acoustic trio gem *Make Someone Happy.* —*Alex Henderson*

Rejuvenation / Feb. 26, 1985-Feb. 27, 1985 / Doctor Jazz ✦✦✦
Keyboardist Lonnie Liston Smith, who had been a key member of Pharoah Sanders' band, always has a healthy dose of spirituality in his music. On this LP for Doctor Jazz, Smith (who alternates between electric and acoustic piano) is joined by Robert Zantay on a dated-sounding lyricon, soprano saxophonist Premik and a rhythm section including the great bassist Cecil McBee. None of the leader's six originals are all that memorable, and the moody performances are actually most successful as superior background music. —*Scott Yanow*

Make Someone Happy / 1989 / Doctor Jazz ✦✦✦
For this refreshing change of pace, Lonnie Liston Smith (best known for his atmospheric mood music) sticks exclusively to acoustic piano and plays mostly standards in a trio with bassist Cecil McBee and drummer Al Foster. One of Smith's very few straightahead dates, this LP (which is highlighted by his versions of "Close Your Eyes," "Speak Low" and "Duke's Place") is worth searching for as a strong example of Lonnie Liston Smith's acoustic playing. —*Scott Yanow*

Magic Lady / 1991 / Startrak ✦✦
For the most part, Lonnie Liston Smith's creativity is wasted on *Magic Lady*, an R&B/pop/jazz CD that usually ignores artistic considerations in its quest for commercial radio airplay. Some of the R&B cuts, including "Colour My Love," and "Let's Spend the Night," are enjoyable enough, but hardly remarkable. *Magic Lady* definitely contains some outright stinkers—such as a soulless note-for-note cover of Brenda Russell's adult contemporary hit "Get Here." Revisiting his very pretty and enchanting "Quiet Moments" (originally recorded on 1978's *Loveland*), Smith demonstrates what charismatic a soloist he can be. But on the whole, he doesn't give himself nearly enough room to stretch out and improvise. Of all the albums Smith has recorded, *Magic Lady* is his weakest and most disappointing. —*Alex Henderson*

Dr. Lonnie Smith

Organ / Hard Bop, Soul Jazz, Groove
Organist Lonnie Smith has often been confused with keyboardist/pianist Lonnie Liston Smith—and, in fact, more than a few retailers have wrongly assumed that they're one and the same. In the mid-1960s, the Hammond hero earned recognition for his membership in George Benson's classic quartet before going on to play with Lou Donaldson (contributing some memorable solos to the alto saxman's hit 1967 album *Alligator Boogaloo*) and recording enjoyable dates of his own for Blue Note. For all their accessibility and commercial appeal, funk-influenced Smith sessions like 1968's *Think* and 1970s *Drives* showed that he could be quite imaginative. Smith, who later entered academia and became Dr. Lonnie Smith, remained an inspired representative of soul-jazz and did some solid work with Donaldson in the '90s. —*Alex Henderson*

Finger Lickin' Good / Mar. 10, 1966-May 22, 1967 / Columbia ✦✦✦✦

● **Think** / Jul. 23, 1968 / Blue Note ◆◆◆◆◆

Organist Lonnie Smith's second recording as a leader and first of two for Blue Note is one of his strongest dates. Teamed up with trumpeter Lee Morgan, tenor saxophonist David Newman, guitarist Melvin Sparks, drummer Marion Booker, Jr., and three percussionists, Smith performs R&B-ish material in a soul-jazz vein. With Morgan and Newman playing stimulating solos and the leader keeping the performances grooving, the music is both accessible and challenging. This CD reissue is well worth picking up. —*Scott Yanow*

Turning Point / Jan. 3, 1969 / Blue Note ◆◆◆

Most Blue Note soul-jazz albums from the late '60s went one of three ways: it either was a straightahead commercial session, a slightly psychedelic outing or a funky workout with a vague Black-power theme. Lonnie Smith had followed the latter path with *Think*, the predecessor to *Turning Point*, and there are still remnants of that style on this session, particularly in the opening cover of Don Covay's "See Saw." Nevertheless, *Turning Point* is a more adventurous affair than *Think*, finding Smith—as well as trumpeter Lee Morgan, trombonist Julian Priester, guitarist Melvin Sparks, tenor saxophonist Bennie Maupin and drummer Leo Morris—exploring territory that isn't quite free, but certainly more "out there" than the average soul-jazz session. In particular, Smith's originals "Slow High" and "Turning Point" reach the outer edges of the style, playing with dissonance, complex melodies and expansive sound structures. Despite all these free flourishes, *Turning Point* remains a soul-jazz record and it has all the trappings of its era—the take on "Eleanor Rigby" finds the group approximating psychedelia. While the more adventurous elements of *Turning Point* make for an intriguing listen, the album isn't quite as enjoyable as the harder grooving sessions or the spacier soul-jazz records from the same era. Nevertheless, it's a worthwhile listen. —*Stephen Thomas Erlewine*

Move Your Hand / Aug. 9, 1969 / Blue Note ◆◆◆◆

Organist Lonnie Smith led a small combo—featuring guitarist Larry McGee, tenor saxist Rudy Jones, bari saxist Ronnie Cuber, and drummer Sylvester Goshay—through a set that alternated originals with two pop covers, the Coasters' "Charlie Brown" and Donovan's "Sunshine Superman." Throughout, the band works a relaxed, bluesy and, above all, funky rhythm; they abandon improvisation and melody for a steady groove, so much that the hooks of the two pop hits aren't recognizable until a few minutes into the track. No one player stands out, but *Move Your Hand* is thoroughly enjoyable, primarily because the group never lets their momentum sag throughout the session. Though the sound of the record might be somewhat dated, the essential funk of the album remains vital. —*Stephen Thomas Erlewine*

Drives / Jan. 2, 1970 / Blue Note ◆

The declining days of Blue Note brought out many blatant attempts to make hit records at the sacrifice of the music. Organist Lonnie Smith has always been a fine player and his quintet on this date includes baritonist Ronnie Cuber but the material is quite crummy. An unsuccessful search for humor on "Seven Steps to Heaven," the odd vocal sounds heard on "Psychedelic Pi," Smith's vocal on "Twenty Five Miles" and an attempt to uplift "Spinning Wheel" are strong reasons to skip this CD reissue altogether. —*Scott Yanow*

Live at Club Mozambique / May 21, 1970 / Blue Note ◆◆◆◆◆

Recorded on May 21, 1970, at Detroit's Club Mozambique, this was shelved and remained unreleased until it was retrieved for CD issue in 1995. It's odd that Blue Note decided to sit on it for so long, because it ranks as one of Lonnie's better sets. The band, featuring George Benson on guitar, is relaxed and funky without being in your face about it, and unlike much soul-jazz of the time, most of the material is original, Smith having penned six of the eight numbers. Although the riffs often owe a lot to James Brown, this is definitely at least as much jazz as soul, with Lonnie taking a rare vocal turn on "Peace of Mind." —*Richie Unterberger*

Mama Wailer / Jul. 14, 1971-Jul. 15, 1971 / Kudu ◆◆◆◆

This out-of-print LP has some fine soul-jazz by organist Lonnie Smith (who plays clavinet on the title track). The four selections include a soulful version of Carole King's "I Feel the Earth Move" and a side-long "Stand," which is highlighted by an early tenor solo by Grover Washington, Jr. Others in the supporting cast include tenors Marvin Cabell and Dave Hubbard, trumpeter Danny Moore, bassist Ron Carter and drummer Billy Cobham. —*Scott Yanow*

When the Night Is Right! / 1975-1979 / Chiaroscuro ◆◆◆

This obscure LP features organist Lonnie Smith (no relation to Lonnie Liston Smith) backed by a big band on three numbers from 1976 and 1979 and on two selections ("Apex" and "Impressions") in 1975 with a quartet including tenor saxophonist Joe Lovano (at the beginning of his career) and guitarist George Benson. The music ranges between soul-jazz and hard bop and holds one's interest, although this album will be a difficult one to locate. —*Scott Yanow*

Afro Blue / Jul. 17, 1993 / Music Masters ◆◆◆◆◆

After a long hiatus from the record shelves, the turbaned Dr. Lonnie Smith—along with guitarist John Abercrombie and drummer Marvin "Smitty" Smith—sets his sights upon John Coltrane, turning in five 'Trane tunes plus Mongo Santamaria's "Afro-Blue" and a grooving Smith tribute, "Traces of Trane." The propulsive title track is mostly dominated by Abercrombie, while "Impressions" continues the driving pace as Lonnie sprays Hammond B-3 organ notes all over the place with constant brief call-and-response dialogues with himself. Another highlight is one of the two breathers, the aptly named "Lonnie's Lament," which has a nice haunting lilt. Carelessly left off the label and booklet copy—but embedded in your CD anyway—is any mention of a 12-minute workout on "Greensleeves" in the push-pull, modal Coltrane manner, with a strong hint of Jimmy Smith. Abercrombie usually plays in his veiled, out-of-tempo manner, while "Smitty" is a volatile, hyperkinetic workhorse most of the time, offering a complex individualistic challenge to the Elvin Jones standard. —*Richard S. Ginell*

Foxy Lady: Tribute to Hendrix / Mar. 19, 1994 / Music Masters ◆◆◆

The resurrection of Lonnie Smith continues with this exciting mini-survey of the Jimi Hendrix legacy. This time, the material allows Smith's crackling, tightly knit collaborators, John Abercrombie and Marvin "Smitty" Smith, to run a bit wild—indeed, Abercrombie's tone and attack take on a Hendrix-like cast on the title track—while Lonnie mostly remains in the same cool soul-jazz frame of mind, an excellent foil. The most ambitious track, "Castles Made of Sand," takes on a military rhythm before breaking out into Smitty's everywhere-at-once drum patterns, cooking at a fine boil through its twenty-three-and-a-half-minute length before breaking into a suitably chaotic rendition of "The Star Spangled Banner" toward the end. On the latter, Abercrombie has a ball pouring on the sarcasm, and Lonnie bounces around the organ. "Third Stone from the Sun" moves at a casual, loping pace before Abercrombie and Smitty go into their guitar- and drum-slinger modes. Finally, there is a bit of fantasy in Lonnie's "Jimi Meets Miles"—a musical event that nearly happened—with Abercrombie doing a laconic Hendrix impression over a propulsive rhythm that recalls Miles' *Bitches Brew* period. —*Richard S. Ginell*

Purple Haze: A Tribute to Jimi Hendrix / Nov. 7, 1995 / Music Masters ◆◆

In the early '70s, Lonnie Smith's recordings frequently exhibited a debt to Jimi Hendrix's groundbreaking fusions, but he waited until 1994 to release *Foxy Lady*, a full-fledged tribute to the innovative guitarist. *Foxy Lady* was so successful, Smith decided to make another Hendrix album, again with John Abercrombie and Marvin "Smitty" Smith. *Purple Haze* is as entertaining as *Foxy Lady*—it's truly remarkable to hear how these blues-rockers can open up into soul-jazz numbers tinged with free-jazz influences—and confirms not only Hendrix's composing talents, but also Smith's vision. —*Leo Stanley*

Louis Smith (Edward Louis Smith)

b. May 20, 1931, Memphis, TN
Trumpet / Hard Bop

Louis Smith was a talented, but underrecorded, straightahead bop trumpeter who led two dates in the '50s before retiring to teach at the University of Michigan and the nearby Ann Arbor Public School system. For most of his career, he remained a teacher, making a brief comeback in the late '70s before returning to education. It wasn't until the mid-'90s that he began a recording career in earnest, turning out a series of albums for the Steeple Chase label.

A native of Memphis, TN, Louis Smith began playing trumpet as a teenager. He graduated high school with a scholarship to Tennessee State University, where he studied music and became a member of the Tennessee State Collegians. Following his college graduation, Smith did a little graduate work at Tennessee before transferring to the University of Michigan, where he studied with professor Clifford Lillya. At Michigan, he had opportunities to play with traveling musicians, including Miles Davis and Dizzy Gillespie.

In January 1954, Smith was drafted into the Army, spending a little over a year and a half in his tour of duty. Once he left the Army in late 1955, he began teaching at the Booker T. Washington High School in Atlanta, GA. While teaching at Booker T. Washington, Smith continued playing bop and hard bop in clubs, and was able to jam with Cannonball Adderley, Kenny Dorham, Donald Byrd, Lou Donaldson, Zoot Sims and Philly Joe Jones, among many others. In 1956, he made his recording debut as a sideman on Kenny Burrell's *Swingin'*. A year later, he had the opportunity to lead his own recording session for Tom Wilson's Boston-based label, Transition. He assembled a quintet featuring Cannonball Adderley (who performed under the pseudonym Buckshot La Funke), bassist Doug Watkins, drummer Art Taylor and pianists Duke Jordan and Tommy Flanagan, who alternated on the date. Transition went out of business before the label had the chance to release the record. Blue Note chief Alfred Lion purchased all the Transition masters and signed Smith to an exclusive contract, releasing the session as *Here Comes Louis Smith*. During 1958, the trumpeter played on two Blue Note sessions—Kenny Burrell's *Blue Lights* and Booker Little's *Booker Little 4 and Max Roach*—in addition to leading the date that became *Smithville*.

That brief burst of activity turned out to be his only recording dates for 20 years. Smith moved back to the Ann Arbor, MI area, where he taught at the University of Michigan and public schools. Between 1978 and 1979, he cut a pair of albums—*Just Friends* and *Prancis'*—before returning to teaching. A decade later, Smith began his recording career in earnest. After playing on Mickey Turner's *Sweet Lotus Lips* in 1989, he signed with Steeple Chase and recorded *Ballads for Lulu* in 1990. He didn't return to the studio for another four years, but he did record two albums—*Silvering* and *Strike up the Band*—in 1994. *The Very Thought of You* appeared in 1995. A year later, Smith recorded *I Waited for You,* which was followed by *There Goes My Heart* in 1997. —*Stephen Thomas Erlewine*

● **Here Comes Louis Smith** / Feb. 4, 1957+Feb. 9, 1957 / Blue Note ✦✦✦✦✦
Louis Smith had a brilliant debut on this Blue Note album, his first of two before becoming a full-time teacher. The opener (Duke Pearson's "Tribute to Brownie") was a perfect piece for Smith to interpret since his style was heavily influenced by Clifford Brown (who had died the previous year). He is also in excellent form on four of his basic originals and takes a particularly memorable solo on a haunting rendition of "Stardust." Altoist Cannonball Adderley (who used the pseudonym of Buckshot La Funke on this set, a name later used by Branford Marsalis), Duke Jordan or Tommy Flanagan on piano, bassist Doug Watkins and drummer Art Taylor make for a potent supporting cast but the focus is mostly on the criminally obscure Louis Smith. After cutting his second Blue Note set and switching to teaching, Smith would not record again as a leader until 1978. All bop and 1950s jazz fans are strongly advised to pick up this CD reissue before it disappears. —*Scott Yanow*

Smithville / Mar. 30, 1958 / Blue Note ✦✦✦✦
Like his debut, *Smithville* is another set of thoroughly winning straightahead bop from the underappreciated trumpeter Louis Smith. Stylistically, there are no surprises here—this is mainstream bop and hard bop, comprising original and contemporary bop numbers, as well as standards ("There'll Never Be Another You," "Embraceable You")—but since the music is performed so well, it doesn't matter. There is genuine passion to this music, not only from Smith, but also from pianist Sonny Clark, tenor saxophonist Charlie Rouse, bassist Paul Chambers and drummer Art Taylor. It's a first-rate hard-bop set that deserves wider distribution than it has received. —*Stephen Thomas Erlewine*

Just Friends / Mar. 19, 1978 / Steeple Chase ✦✦✦✦✦
Great date for master trumpeter with Memphis friends, including George Coleman on tenor sax. —*Michael G. Nastos*

Prancis' /Apr. 13, 1979 / Steeple Chase ✦✦✦

Mamie Smith

b. May 26, 1883, Cincinnati, OH, **d.** Aug. 16, 1946, New York, NY
Vocals / Classic Female Blues
Though technically not a blues performer, Mamie Smith notched her place in American music as the first Black female singer to record a vocal blues. That record was "Crazy Blues" (rec. Aug. 10, 1920), which sold a million copies in its first six months and made record labels aware of the huge potential market for "race records," thus paving the way for Bessie Smith (no relation) and other blues and jazz performers. An entertainer who sported a powerful, penetrating, feminine voice with belting vaudeville qualities, as opposed to blues inflections, Smith toured as a dancer with Tutt-Whitney's Smart Set Company in her early teens and sang in Harlem clubs before World War I. Apparently, Smith's pioneering recording session was an accident, since she was filling in for Sophie Tucker, but the success of the record made her wealthy.

Soon thereafter, Smith began touring and recording with a band called the Jazz Hounds, which featured such jazz notables as Coleman Hawkins, Bubber Miley, Johnny Dunn, etc., and she toured with the bands of Andy Kirk and Fats Pichon in the 1930s. She also appeared in several films, including *Paradise in Harlem* late in her life (1939). She recorded several sides for OKeh during her heyday; one unissued take of "My Sportin' Man" is included on Columbia's *Roots n' Blues Retrospective 1925-1950* box set. In the 1980s, all of her recordings were reissued on LP by the imported Document label. —*Richard S. Ginell*

★ **Complete Recorded Works, Vol. 1** / Feb. 14, 1920-Feb. 22, 1921 / Document ✦✦✦✦✦
This first volume of a five-volume import set of her complete recordings features her earliest and best sides, including the classic "Crazy Blues." —*Cub Koda*

Complete Recorded Works, Vol. 2 (1921-1922) / May 1921-Oct. 12, 1921 / Document ✦✦✦✦✦

Complete Recorded Works, Vol. 3 / Feb. 14, 1922-Sep. 6, 1922 / Document ✦✦✦✦✦

Complete Recorded Works, Vol. 4 / Dec. 6, 1922-Sep. 1924 / Document ✦✦✦✦✦

Complete Recorded Works, Vol. 5 / Sep. 1924-1942 / Document ✦✦✦✦✦

Marvin "Smitty" Smith

b. Jun. 24, 1961, Waukegan, IL
Drums / Post-Bop, Hard Bop
A prolific, constantly-in-demand drummer whose sensitive, yet authoritative playing has been heard on dozens of '80s and '90s sessions, Marvin "Smitty" Smith seems to live in the studio. A onetime Berklee student, he played with Jon Hendricks' band in New York during the early '80s, then worked with John Hicks, Bobby Watson, and Slide Hampton. Smith later recorded with Archie Shepp, then with a quintet co-led by Frank Wess and Frank Foster. He did sessions with Hamiett Bluiett, Kevin Eubanks and David Murray, as well as playing with Ray Brown, Dave Holland, Ron Carter, Hank Jones and the Jazztet. Smith made his recording debut as a leader in 1987, and also recorded that year with Sonny Rollins, and toured with Sting. Since then, Smith's been constantly featured on sessions, often paired with Ray Drummond. He has several Concord dates available and can also be heard on a countless number of releases by other musicians, ranging in style from bop and mainstream to M-Base and post-bop. —*Ron Wynn*

Keeper of the Drums / Mar. 1987 / Concord Jazz ✦✦✦✦
Drummer Marvin "Smitty" Smith, widely regarded among jazz's premier percussionists and accompanists, got his chance in the spotlight when he made his debut as a leader for Concord. This 1987 session was a brilliant first effort, with Smith heading a wonderful four-horn octet. The group included alto and soprano saxophonist Steve Coleman, tenor saxophonist Ralph Moore, trombonist Robin Eubanks and trumpeter Wallace Roney. The eight songs were not lengthy (none much longer than six minutes), but were structured to allow maximum individual identity and collective performances. It was the perfect blend of traditional setting and contemporary insights, which has been lacking in so much 1990s jazz material. —*Ron Wynn*

The Road Less Traveled / Feb. 1989 / Concord Jazz ✦✦✦✦✦
Despite the presence of an all-star personnel (which includes trumpeter Wallace Roney, trombonist Robin Eubanks, Ralph Moore on tenor, altoist Steve Coleman and pianist James Williams), the focus on *The Road Less Traveled* is on drummer Marvin "Smitty" Smith's originals. The music ranges from a couple of tunes in the Jazz Messengers tradition and a tribute to Benny Golson ("Concerto in BG") that features Eubanks' fluid trombone to the brooding ballad "Wish You Were Here" (which is heard in two similar parts). Smith's music stays in the modern mainstream but manages to sound fairly original most of the time, all of his sidemen have spots to be featured and this fine CD was a strong step forward for the significant drummer-composer. —*Scott Yanow*

● **Carryin' On** / 1993 / Concord Jazz ✦✦✦✦✦

Paul Smith

b. Apr. 17, 1922, San Diego, CA
Piano / Bop, Cool, Swing, Traditional Pop
Paul Smith is a brilliant pianist with technique on the level of an Oscar Peterson but a musician who never really dedicated himself to jazz. After playing early on with Johnny Richards in 1941 and spending a couple years in the military, he worked with Les Paul (1946-47) and Tommy Dorsey (1947-49) before moving to Los Angeles and becoming a studio musician. Smith has recorded frequently both with his trios and as a soloist. In addition to recording with Dizzy Gillespie, Anita O'Day, Buddy DeFranco, Louie Bellson, Steve Allen, Louie Bellson and Stan Kenton (among others) he toured with Ella Fitzgerald off and on during 1956-78. —*Scott Yanow*

● **Fine, Sweet and Tasty** / Nov. 13, 1953 / Tampa ✦✦✦✦✦
This CD reissue of a set originally cut for Tampa is a pleasant surprise. Pianist Paul Smith, who sometimes overwhelms music with his technique, pays tribute to the Nat King Cole Trio on several of the numbers. The presence of guitarist Tony Rizzi (playing in a Charlie Christian vein) is a major asset, while bassist Sam Cheifetz and drummer Irv Cottler are excellent in support. The original program is augmented by five extra alternate takes. Highlights include the delightful "Fine, Sweet & Tasty," "Crazy Rhythm" and "Got a Penny." Overall, this swinging affair is one of the most enjoyable of all of Paul Smith's many recordings. —*Scott Yanow*

Alpha Touch / 1976-1977 / Outstanding ✦✦✦✦
Good, although very conservative, mainstream jazz from pianist Paul Smith. Smith's style blends stride and boogie influences with bop voicings and is especially effective on mid-tempo tunes and ballads. —*Ron Wynn*

Art Tatum Touch, Vol. 1 / 1976-1977 / Outstanding ✦✦✦✦
It would be easy to dismiss this record as no more than easy listening, if it were not for the honesty and the heavy influences of Teddy Wilson and Art Tatum combined with Smith's own individual, rather elegant style. —*Bob Rusch, Cadence*

The Ballad Touch / 1976-1977 / Outstanding ✦✦✦
The title proclaims the set's strengths and weaknesses. Pianist Paul Smith is a fine interpreter and soloist, and his stylish playing and carefully developed statements are mostly impressive. But the menu is so heavily tilted toward ballads, with each performed at the same pace, that the session sometimes sounds a bit detached. —*Ron Wynn*

The Master Touch / 1976-1977 / Outstanding ✦✦✦✦
Outstanding solos from pianist Paul Smith, whose albums progressively became more spirited during the '70s and '80s. While his swing and stride roots can clearly be detected, Smith's willingness to try different styles and his looser, more unpredictable playing brings some unexpected tension and excitement to this collection. —*Ron Wynn*

Heavy Jazz, Vol. 1 / 1977 / Outstanding ✦✦✦✦
One of an extensive series of LPs that pianist Paul Smith recorded for the modestly titled Outstanding record label, this trio set with bassist Ray Brown and drummer Louis Bellson lives up to the company's name. Smith, who has always had very impressive technique, romps through seven familiar standards (including "Lover," "Pick Yourself Up," "I Got Rhythm" and "What Is This Thing Called Love") in a style not all that different from Oscar Peterson's. Although there are few surprises on this outing, the music should please straightahead jazz fans. —*Scott Yanow*

At Home / Dec. 1983 / Outstanding ✦✦✦✦
Pianist Paul Smith had a rare opportunity to record this trio LP at home on his own piano. Joined by bassist Wilfred Middlebrooks and drummer Frankie Capp, Smith plays energetic versions of six straightahead standards including "Cheek to Cheek," "Wave," "Cherokee" and an inventive treatment of "The Girl from Ipanema." —*Scott Yanow*

Paul Smith Plays Steve Allen / 1984 / Pausa ✦✦✦
Paul Smith frequently plays piano for Steve Allen (both on stage and on records). A brilliant technician, Smith tries his best on this out-of-print LP to uplift a dozen obscure Allen compositions, but unfortunately, none of the songs have caught on or are particularly memorable. This is overall a lesser effort despite Smith's swinging style. —*Scott Yanow*

Stuff Smith (Hezekiah Leroy Gordon Smith)

b. Aug. 14, 1909, Portsmouth, OH, d. Sep. 25, 1967, Munich, Germany
Violin / Swing
Stuff Smith was one of the big three of pre-bop violinists along with Joe Venuti and Stephane Grappelli. Many of his fans said that he could outswing all of his competitors and certainly Stuff was a major force on the bandstand. Smith, who cited Louis Armstrong as his main influence, studied music with his father and played with the family band as a child. His first major job and recordings were with Alphonse Trent's territory band in the 1920s but it was not until 1936 that he had his breakthrough. Leading a quintet at the Onyx Club with trumpeter Jonah Jones, Smith's comedy vocals and hard-swinging approach made the group a hit on 52nd Street for several years; his novelty "Tse a Muggin'" became a hit. Smith worked regularly with his trios in the 1940s but was in danger of being forgotten in the '50s when Norman Granz recorded him fairly extensively for Verve; Stuff also participated in Nat King Cole's After Midnight sessions for Capitol. The violinist moved to Copenhagen in 1965 and was active until his death two years later. —*Scott Yanow*

☆ **Stuff Smith (1936-1939)** / Feb. 11, 1936-Dec. 1939 / Classics ✦✦✦✦✦
This delightful CD has the first 24 titles ever led by violinist Stuff Smith, virtually all of Smith's prewar recordings and the complete output of the violinist's Onyx Club Boys (other than four songs from 1940). With trumpeter Jonah Jones and sometimes drummer Cozy Cole the stars of the supporting cast, this was one of the top swing combos of the era. Smith's hard-swinging violin, his enthusiastic vocals and his interplay with Jones made this a particularly hot unit. In addition to the hit "Tse a Muggin'," highlights of the disc include "I Hope Gabriel Likes My Music," "After You've Gone," "You'se a Viper," "Old Joe's Hittin' the Jug," "Twilight in Turkey" and the classic "Here Comes the Man with the Jive." Highly recommended. —*Scott Yanow*

The Stuff Smith Trio: 1943 / Nov. 17, 1943 / Progressive ✦✦✦✦
Violinist Stuff Smith is heard in top form on this set of radio transcriptions from 1943, a time when a musicians' strike kept Smith and others off records. Joined by pianist Jimmy Jones (who has plenty of solo space) and bassist John Levy, Smith performs ten songs and, in addition to the accepted versions, there are four alternate takes and three brief incomplete versions. Highlights include "Humoresque,"

three versions of "Minuet in Swing" and a pair of hot renditions of "Bugle Call Rag." Throughout Stuff Smith is heard in prime form, showing how hard a violin can be swung. —*Scott Yanow*

Stuff Smith-Dizzy Gillespie-Oscar Peterson / Jan. 21, 1957-Apr. 17, 1957 / Verve ✦✦✦✦✦
The great swing violinist Stuff Smith had not recorded as a leader since 1945 when producer Norman Granz got him to make three albums for Verve during a three-month period. Smith, who was still very much in his prime, recorded 11 selections (one previously unissued) with pianist Carl Perkins, either Red Callender or Curtis Counce on bass and Oscar Bradley or Frank Butler on drums (*Have Violin Will Swing*), jammed nine numbers (three released for the first time here) with the Oscar Peterson Trio (for the album titled *Stuff Smith*), and on five tunes teamed up with trumpeter Dizzy Gillespie and a rhythm section (*Dizzy Gillespie-Stuff Smith*); all are reissued in full on this generous two-CD set from 1994. In each of the settings, the violinist excels, making this an easily recommended and very satisfying release. —*Scott Yanow*

● **Live at the Montmartre** / Mar. 18, 1965 / Storyville ✦✦✦✦✦
Although he passed away in 1967, violinist Stuff Smith (who moved to Europe in 1965) did a fair amount of recording during his final two years. His CD reissue has an exciting concert from Copenhagen's Montmartre featuring Smith with pianist Kenny Drew, bassist Niels Pedersen and drummer Alex Riel. Stuff Smith never did decline, as he shows on hard-swinging versions of such songs as his "Skip It," "Take the 'A' Train," "Bugle Blues" and "Mack the Knife." —*Scott Yanow*

Swingin' Stuff / Mar. 23, 1965 / Storyville ✦✦✦✦✦
Recorded five days after a similar performance at the Montmartre in Copenhagen by the same personnel (violinist Stuff Smith, pianist Kenny Drew, bassist Niels Pedersen and drummer Alex Riel), Stuff and his quartet are once again heard in top form. Four of the nine songs are repeated from the earlier date, but unfortunately, the music on this LP is currently out of print. On such tunes as "Bugle Blues," "Mack the Knife," "One O'Clock Jump" and "Take the 'A' Train," Stuff Smith shows that he was as hard-swinging an improviser as any horn player and that at the age of 55 he had not run out of gas yet. —*Scott Yanow*

Hot Violins / Mar. 1965-Feb. 18, 1967 / Storyville ✦✦✦✦
Violinist Stuff Smith is heard on this CD during three different dates from his later years when he lived in Copenhagen. Best are four hard-swinging collaborations with fellow violinist Svend Asmussen, including a charming version of "Lady Be Good" that has both of the fiddlers singing. In addition, Smith performs two of his originals in 1967 with the Kenny Drew Trio (seven months before his death) and matches up with violinist Paul Olsen (who sounds a bit like Stuff) on four numbers, including a riff-filled "One O'Clock Jump." An excellent and well-recorded release by the exciting swing violinist Stuff Smith. —*Scott Yanow*

Stuff Smith [Everest] / Jun. 22, 1965 / Everest ✦✦✦✦
This budget LP release has music originally released by the French Barclay label. The chatty liner notes say nothing about the personnel (both Stuff Smith and Stephane Grappelli are on violins, with pianist Rene Urtreger, bassist Michel Gaudry and drummer Michel Delaporte) or the recording date, but the music is often exciting. Stuff and Stephane had collaborated eight years earlier, and they participated in Duke Ellington's "Violin Session" in the mid-'60s. Smith has "Skip It" as his feature, Grappelli is the only violinist on "Willow Weep for Me" and Stuff takes two vocals. The most memorable selections of the swinging set are "How High the Moon" and "This Can't Be Love." Worth searching for. —*Scott Yanow*

Tab Smith

b. Jan. 11, 1909, Kingston, NC, d. Aug. 17, 1971, St. Louis, MO
Alto Saxophone / Swing, Early R&B Jazz, Jump Blues
Tab Smith's career can easily be divided into two. One of the finest altoists to emerge during the swing era, Smith became a popular attraction in the R&B world of the 1950s due to his record "Because of You." After early experience playing in territory bands during the 1930s, Tab Smith played and recorded with Lucky Millinder's Orchestra (1936-38) and then freelanced with various swing all-stars in New York. He had opportunities to solo with Count Basie's band (1940-42) before returning to Millinder (1942-44) and took honors on a recording of "On the Sunny Side of the Street" with a stunning cadenza that followed statements by Coleman Hawkins, Don Byas and Harry Carney. After leaving Millinder, Smith led his own sessions which became increasingly R&B-oriented (he never became involved with bop). His string of recordings for United in the 1950s (which are being reissued by Delmark on CD) made him a fairly major name for a time even though he had a relatively mellow sound and avoided honking. In the early '60s Tab Smith retired to St. Louis and later became involved in selling real estate. —*Scott Yanow*

● **Jump Time** / Aug. 28, 1951-Feb. 26, 1952 / Delmark ✦✦✦✦

Altoist Tab Smith, who first gained recognition with Count Basie's Orchestra in the mid-'40s, became an unexpected R&B star in the early '50s, thanks in large part to his hit version of "Because of You." Between 1951-57, Smith recorded 90 songs for the United Record Company of which only 48 were issued. Delmark, in their CD reissue series, plans to come out with all of the music in chronological order. This first release has the initial 20 (including the hit) and Tab Smith sounds fine on the sweet ballads, blues and concise jump tunes; the backup crew includes trumpeter Sonny Cohn, tenor Leon Washington and either Lavern Dillon or Teddy Brannon on piano. —*Scott Yanow*

Ace High / Feb. 26, 1952-Apr. 23, 1953 / Delmark ✦✦✦

During 1951-57, Tab Smith recorded extensively for the United label, and although he was initially popular (due to the hit record "Because of You"), nearly half of the 90 titles he cut went unissued. Delmark in their Tab Smith CD series plans to eventually come out with all of the performances. Their second Tab Smith release has 20 selections, including five songs being released for the first time. Smith, a former swing stylist who was best known in the R&B market during the 1950s, was not a honker like many others in the genre, and his mixture of relatively gentle stomps and ballads is appealing. The distinctive altoist (who takes four vocals) is often joined by Sonny Cohn (mistakenly listed as "Sammy Cohn") or Irving Woods on trumpet and Leon Washington or Charlie Wright on tenor, along with a rocking rhythm section, on four complete sessions from 1952-53. Fun if not essential music. —*Scott Yanow*

● **Top 'n' Bottom** / Nov. 17, 1953-Aug. 26, 1954 / Delmark ✦✦✦

The third CD volume of altoist Tab Smith's United recordings features 21 selections, 14 of which had never been released before. The music ranges from Johnny Hodges-type small-group stomping swing and R&B-ish jump sides to sentimental ballads and a few vocal numbers (featuring unidentified singers). Among the personnel are trumpeter Irving Woods, pianist Teddy Brannon and drummer Walter Johnson. Accessible and fairly creative jazz, conservative for the early '50s but still quite enjoyable. —*Scott Yanow*

Tommy Smith

b. Apr. 27, 1967, Edinburgh, Scotland

Tenor Saxophone / Post-Bop, Hard Bop

A saxophonist who's recorded several albums for Blue Note, Smith is regarded as one of their up-and-coming stars. His debut was more in a fusion vein, while his second release featured his renditions of standards. —*Ron Wynn*

Forward Motion: The Berklee Tapes / Nov. 1984 / Hep ✦✦✦

Step by Step / Sep. 7, 1988-Sep. 8, 1988 / Blue Note ✦✦✦

1989 release that signals emergence of Smith as potentially fine soloist. —*Ron Wynn*

Peeping Tom / Jan. 9, 1990-Jan. 13, 1991 / Blue Note ✦✦✦✦

In the early '90s tenor saxophonist Tommy Smith based his style on John Coltrane (circa 1964-65) but he placed his solos in more contemporary settings and his own individuality was gradually emerging. Certainly Smith's introduction to "The New Road," played on the WX7, sounds unlike anyone else. He cooks on "Slip of the Tongue," does well on the introspective ballad "Follow Your Heart" and thinks fast on his feet during the title cut. Some of the original music on this CD is a bit dry and guitarist Paul Stacey (who is quite intense on "The New Road") should have had more opportunities to stretch out. But plenty of chances are taken overall and this early effort by Tommy Smith (with a quintet also including pianist Jason Rebello) is generally memorable. —*Scott Yanow*

● **Standards** / Jan. 1991 / Blue Note ✦✦✦✦✦

Essentially a hard-bop traditionalist but possessing a sound of his own, tenor saxophonist Tommy Smith (only 24 at the time of this CD) gives fresh if not startlingly innovative perspectives to some standards on the date plus he introduces a few new blowing tunes of his own including a superior ballad "Julia." In contrast to the fire often shown by the young tenor great, pianist Niels Lan Doky reins in his own formidable technique and is primarily in a relaxed and laidback mood. Bassist Mick Hutton and drummer Ian Froman are fine in support but the focus is mostly on Tommy Smith who is one of the most promising of the musicians in his age group. Highlights include a one-chorus version of "You've Changed," the contrast between a relatively light-hearted "Star Eyes" and a dead serious (and often Tranish) "Night and Day" and the interesting variations that he creates on a slow version of "My Old Flame." Recommended. —*Scott Yanow*

Misty Morning & No Time / Dec. 19, 1994+Dec. 1994 / Linn ✦✦✦

Beasts of Scotland / Feb. 25, 1996-Feb. 26, 1996 / Linn ✦✦✦

Willie "The Lion" Smith

b. Nov. 25, 1897, Goshen, NY, **d.** Apr. 18, 1973, New York, NY

Piano, Composer / Stride, Classic Jazz, Piano Blues

Willie "The Lion" Smith in the 1920s was considered one of the big three of stride piano (along with James P. Johnson and Fats Waller) even though he made almost no recordings until the mid-'30s. His mother was an organist and pianist and Smith started playing piano when he was six. He earned a living playing piano as a teenager, gained his nickname "The Lion" for his heroism in World War I and after his discharge he became one of the star attractions at Harlem's nightly rent parties. Although he toured with Mamie Smith (and played on her pioneering 1920 blues record "Crazy Blues"), Smith mostly freelanced throughout his life. He was an influence on the young Duke Ellington (who would later write "Portrait of the Lion") and most younger New York-based pianists of the 1920s and '30s. Although he was a braggart and (with his cigar and trademark derby hat) appeared to be a rough character, Smith was actually more colorful than menacing and a very sophisticated pianist with a light touch. His recordings with his Cubs (starting in 1935) and particularly his 1939 piano solos for Commodore (highlighted by "Echoes of Spring") cemented his place in history. Because he remained very active into the early '70s (writing his memoirs *Music on My Mind* in 1965), for quite a few decades Willie "The Lion" Smith was considered a living link to the glory days of early jazz. —*Scott Yanow*

● **Willie "The Lion" Smith 1925-1937** / Nov. 5, 1925-Sep. 15, 1937 / Classics ✦✦✦✦✦

Willie "The Lion" Smith, one of stride piano's Big Three of the 1920s (along with James P. Johnson and Fats Waller), recorded a lot less than his two friends. In fact, with the exception of two selections apiece with the Gulf Coast Seven in 1925 (which features trombonist Jimmy Harrison and clarinetist Buster Bailey) and 1927's Georgia Strutters (starring singer Perry Bradford, Harrison and cornetist Jabbo Smith), along with the rare and originally unreleased 1934 solo piano showcase "Finger Buster," this CD does not get started until 1935. Smith's Decca recordings of 1935 and 1937 were formerly quite obscure, showcasing his piano with three different versions of "His Cubs." The Lion is heard with a Clarence Williams-type quartet which includes cornetist Ed Allen and clarinetist Cecil Scott; matched up with trumpeter Dave Nelson and clarinetist Buster Bailey in a septet; and temporarily heading an early version of the John Kirby Sextet on a session dominated by drummer O'Neil Spencer's vocals. Highlights of this historic and enjoyable CD include "Santa Claus Blues," "Keep Your Temper," "Blues, Why Don't You Let Me Alone" and the earliest recording of the Lion's most famous composition, "Echo of Spring." —*Scott Yanow*

Willie "The Lion" Smith 1937-1938 / Sep. 15, 1937-Nov. 30, 1938 / Classics ✦✦

The second Classics CD in their Willie "The Lion" Smith series is surprisingly weak. Of the 25 selections, 21 actually feature the dated organ of Milt Herth. Smith's presence in the trio (with drummer-vocalist O'Neil Spencer) fails to uplift the music (Herth's wheezing organ mostly drowns him out) although guitarist Teddy Bunn helps a bit on the last seven numbers. Easily the best selections on the CD are two songs performed by Willie "The Lion" Smith and His Cubs (a septet with trumpeter Frankie Newton and clarinetist Buster Bailey) and a pair of duets with drummer Spencer on Smith's own "Passionette" and "Morning Air." But the preceding and following volumes in this program are much more valuable. —*Scott Yanow*

The Original 14 Plus Two / Nov. 30, 1938+Jan. 10, 1939 / Commodore ✦✦✦✦✦

This 1981 LP, released through Columbia, has the high points of Willie "The Lion" Smith's career. On Jan. 10, 1939, he recorded 14 piano solos including eight of his own impressionistic compositions. These include such classics as "Echoes of Spring," "Passionette," "Morning Air" and the rambunctious "Finger Buster" and find the pianist at the top of his form. Also on this LP are his versions of six standards along with two numbers ("Three Keyboards" and "The Lion and the Lamb") from a slightly earlier session in which he plays with drummer George Wettling and fellow pianists Joe Bushkin and Jess Stacy. This is essential music which has fortunately been reissued on CD by the European Classics series. —*Scott Yanow*

☆ **Willie "The Lion" Smith 1938-1940** / Nov. 30, 1938-Feb. 17, 1940 / Classics ✦✦✦✦✦

This is the one Willie "The Lion" Smith CD to get. The bulk of the release features Smith on 14 piano solos from Jan. 10, 1939, performing six standards and eight of his finest compositions. Although Smith (with his derby hat and cigar) could look quite tough, he was actually a sensitive player whose chord structures were very original and impressionistic. On such numbers as "Echoes of Spring" (his most famous work), "Passionette," "Rippling Waters" and "Morning Air," Smith was at his most expressive. In addition, this CD has a couple of collaborations with fellow pianists Joe Bushkin and Jess Stacy and a four-song 1940 swing/Dixieland 1940 session with an octet featuring trumpeter Sidney DeParis. Because of the classic piano solos, this memorable set is quite essential. —Scott Yanow

Willie "The Lion" Smith / Dec. 1, 1949-Dec. 24, 1949 / GNP ✦✦✦
On this album, Willie "The Lion" Smith is featured either as a piano soloist, in duets with drummer Wallace Bishop or in a quartet with Bishop, trumpeter Buck Clayton and clarinetist Claude Luter. Eight of the 12 selections were also included on a similarly titled Inner City LP although four were not. While the Inner City set is preferable (it has 16 cuts), the GNP LP will probably be a little easier to find. The Lion is in particularly fine form on "Relaxin'," "Contrary Motions," "Portrait of the Duke" and "La Madelon." —Scott Yanow

● **Willie the Lion Smith** / Dec. 1, 1949-Jan. 29, 1950 / Inner City ✦✦✦✦
This out-of-print LP has some of the highlights of pianist Willie "The Lion" Smith's four recording sessions recorded in Paris for the Vogue label during 1949-50. For the fine all-round showcase, the Lion is heard performing six originals in duet with drummer Wallace Bishop (including "Echoes of Spring," "Portrait of the Duke" and "Contrary Motion"), playing six romping piano solos (including his rendition of James P. Johnson's "Carolina Shout") and jamming three standards and a blues in a Dixieland quartet with trumpeter Buck Clayton, clarinetist Cladue Luter and drummer Bishop. The performances overlap with a similar GNP/Crescendo LP but this is the better buy although both sets will be difficult to find. —Scott Yanow

The Lion of the Piano / 1951 / Commodore ✦✦✦

☆ **The Legend of Willie Smith** / Aug. 21, 1957+Sep. 19, 1957 / Grand Award ✦✦✦✦✦
Impossible to find, wonderful release. —Ron Wynn

Echoes of Spring / Dec. 17, 1965 / Milan ✦✦✦
On this CD pianist Willie "The Lion" Smith is featured during a solo concert from France. The recording quality is just ok and Smith's performance (which combines his piano with a few unfortunate vocals and a little reminiscing) was typical for the period but his piano playing is generally fairly strong. He performs four of his originals (including "Echoes of Spring" and "Zig Zag"), a few standards, a James P. Johnson medley, a medley of songs associated with some of his favorite pianists, Chopin's "Polonaise" and even "La Marseillaise." Although not quite essential, there are enough colorful moments on this set to make the date recommended to Willie "The Lion" Smith collectors. —Scott Yanow

Pork and Beans / Nov. 8, 1966 / Black Lion ✦✦✦✦
One of the last of the major stride pianists, Willie "The Lion" Smith pays tribute to some of his contemporaries during this solo studio set. Smith performs four numbers by Luckey Roberts, three by Eubie Blake, two apiece from Fats Waller and George Gershwin and four veteran standards. Smith was in the last part of his musical prime and is still quite strong on this spirited and definitive late-period program, infusing his hot stride with impressionistic ideas. —Scott Yanow

Duets / Feb. 20, 1967 / Sackville ✦✦✦
To relieve the workload late in his career, Willie "The Lion" Smith often hired fellow pianist Don Ewell to join him for duets. On this Sackville session, Smith and Ewell romp on a variety of superior swing standards including "I've Found a New Baby," "I Would Do Anything for You," "Everybody Loves My Baby" and "You Took Advantage of Me." Although not as significant as other individual sets of Smith and Ewell, the combination works well, making this date easily recommended to fans of stride piano. —Scott Yanow

Memoirs of Willie the Lion Smith / Apr. 25, 1968-Apr. 28, 1968 / RCA ✦✦✦✦
This double LP is the equivalent of Jelly Roll Morton's Library of Congress recordings. The legendary Willie "The Lion" Smith reminisces about his colorful life, plays some piano and warbles out some vocals. Particularly interesting are his stories of the early days, his medleys of songs associated with Eubie Blake, James P. Johnson, Fats Waller and Duke Ellington, and his performances of eight of his own compositions, some of which are quite obscure. Not everything works and some of the talking rambles on a bit, but overall this is a fascinating historical document that has many interesting moments. —Scott Yanow

Relaxin' / 1970-1971 / Chiaroscuro ✦✦✦✦
For this Chiaroscuro LP (not yet reissued on CD), veteran stride pianist Willie "The Lion" Smith is heard in the studio in 1970 and live at a club in 1971, in both cases usually accompanied by drummer Dude Brown. The well-rounded program mostly sticks to veteran standards (including "I've Found a New Baby," "Nagasaki" and "Keeping Out of Mischief Now") plus "Chopin Variations" and three versions of "Relaxing" which Smith was using as a theme song. This fine outing (one of the Lion's last) is worth searching for. —Scott Yanow

Willie the Lion and His Washington Cubs / Feb. 20, 1971 / Fat Cat Jazz ✦✦✦✦
Willie "The Lion" Smith passed away in 1973 but this live jam session set shows that two years before his death he still retained most of his power. Teamed up with Australian trumpeter Tony Newstead, clarinetist Tommy Gwaltney, bassist Van

Perry and drummer Skip Tomlinson, Smith runs through ten veteran warhorses and brings a great deal of joy to such songs as "Ain't She Sweet," "Louisiana," "Darktown Strutters Ball" (which has one of Fat Cat McRee's two vocals) and "Love Is Just Around the Corner." This hard-to-find Fat Cat LP can easily be enjoyed by Dixieland and Willie "The Lion" Smith collectors. —Scott Yanow

Willie Smith

b. Nov. 25, 1910, Charleston, SC, d. Mar. 7, 1967, Los Angeles, CA
Alto Saxophone, Clarinet, Vocals / Swing

In the 1930s, Willie Smith ranked third among alto saxophonists, just behind Johnny Hodges and Benny Carter. He had a distinctive sound and a swinging style that was a major asset to Jimmy Lunceford's Orchestra. Smith also contributed occasional vocals ("Rhythm Is Our Business" was his best-known recording) and some effective clarinet solos during the era, in addition to writing some fine arrangements for Lunceford.

Willie Smith started on clarinet, gained a chemistry degree at Fisk University, and then became Lunceford's altoist in 1929. A superb lead player and the strongest soloist in the ensemble-oriented orchestra, Smith was one of the stars in the big band up until 1942. At that point, underpaid by Lunceford and weary of non-stop traveling, he departed. After a year with Charlie Spivak and a year in the Navy, Smith joined Harry James' big band, where he was paid properly and greatly appreciated. Well featured with James, Smith stayed for seven years the first time, before joining Duke Ellington in 1951 (as part of "the great James robbery"). After helping Ellington make up for the departure of Johnny Hodges, Smith spent time with Billy May's Orchestra at the time the arranger's big band was catching on, before returning to James in 1954, where he stayed for another decade. He took occasional time off for work with Norman Granz's Jazz at the Philharmonic, and was featured on some of Granz's Verve jam session records, including 1953's Apple Jam. After largely retiring, Willie Smith recorded his only full-length album for GNP Crescendo (1965) and recorded with Charlie Barnet before passing away from cancer. —Scott Yanow

The Best of Willie Smith / Aug. 13, 1965-Aug. 16, 1965 / GNP Crescendo ✦✦✦✦
Although Willie Smith was one of the finest altoists of the swing era and led a few sessions during 1945-47, this GNP set was his only full-length LP as a leader; it has yet to be reissued on CD. Cut two years before his death, the album finds Smith still in top form, performing two basic originals ("Never on Friday" and "Willie's Blues"), a couple of ballads and a few swing standards including "Uptown Blues." Four tunes match Willie Smith with pianist Johnny Guarnieri, Tommy Gumina on accordion, guitarist Irving Ashby, bassist Paul Ruhland and drummer Stan Levey, while the remaining three songs have Smith leading a quintet consisting of tenor saxophonist Bill Perkins, pianist Jimmy Rowles, bassist Max Bennett and drummer Stan Levey. In both settings, Willie Smith is heard at his best. —Scott Yanow

Valaida Snow

b. Jun. 2, 1903, Chattanooga, TN, d. May 30, 1956, New York, NY
Trumpet, Vocals / Swing

If fate had not seemingly conspired against her, Valaida Snow might well be counted among the greatest entertainers of the early 20th century; instead, she remains little known outside of an avid cult following, a gifted blues vocalist and multi-instrumentalist also noted for her skills as an arranger. Born June 2, 1903, in Chattanooga, TN (although other sources have stated otherwise), Snow was the product of a musical family; her mother, a music teacher, taught Valaida and her sisters Lavaida and Alvaida to play a wide variety of instruments, among them cello, bass, mandolin, violin, clarinet, saxophone and accordion. The girls also sang and danced, but when Valaida turned professional at the age of 15, she began focusing on vocals and trumpet, and by 1924 she was already a featured performer in the Noble Sissle/Eubie Blake musical In Bamville (a.k.a. The Chocolate Dandies).

By the age of 22, Snow was headlining Barron Wilkins' Harlem cabaret show, and throughout the remaining years of the 1920s, she toured relentlessly, appearing throughout the US in conjunction with the Will Mastin Trio and performing in London and Paris in the musical Blackbirds. In 1926 she toured the Far East, and in 1928 headlined Chicago's Sunset Cafe, where her energetic performances won the admiration of Louis Armstrong, as well as Earl Hines, who soon became her lover. By the early 1930s, Snow was starring in the Sissle/Blake revue Rhapsody in Black, and its success helped bring her to Hollywood, where alongside then-husband Ananais Berry she appeared in a number of films. By all rights Snow should have been a major superstar, but as a Black performer she was subject to considerable racism; worse still, as a woman, she was an outsider even within the jazz community—her perfect pitch, gifts for arranging and brilliant trumpeting did not help her cause, but only made her that much more of a curiosity.

After headlining the Apollo Theatre, Snow travelled back to Europe for more film work and live dates during the late 1930s; however, in 1941, while in Nazi-occupied Copenhagen, she was captured by German forces and interned in a concentration camp in Wester-Faengle. Eighteen months later, she was freed as an exchange prisoner and allowed to return to New York; tragically, Snow never fully recovered from the ordeal—scarred psychologically as well as physically, she attempted to return to performing, but the spark was clearly gone, so much so that when Hines saw her appear live in 1943 he reportedly did not even recognize her. Following her marriage to manager Earle Edwards, she continued to work in spite of her personal suffering, but after playing the Palace Theater in New York on May 30, 1956, she died of a massive cerebral hemorrhage. Valaida Snow was 52 years old. —*Jason Ankeny*

Swing Is The Thing / Jan. 18, 1935-Jul. 14, 1937 / Swing ✦✦✦✦✦

Hot Snow / Sep. 8, 1936-Jan. 1950 / Rosetta ✦✦✦✦

Elmer Snowden

b. Oct. 9, 1900, Baltimore, MD, **d.** May 14, 1973, Philadelphia, PA
Banjo, Guitar / Classic Jazz

A fine banjo player, Elmer Snowden was the original leader of the Washingtonians, a group that would become the Duke Ellington Orchestra; a dispute over money in the mid-'20s soon found him "at liberty." Snowden had met Ellington in 1919 and before that he had worked with Eubie Blake in Baltimore. He was quite active in the 1920s as a businessman, agent and musician, running several bands and recording occasionally. But although he worked steadily in the 1930s, '40s and '50s, he was essentially a minor figure during those years. In 1963 Snowden moved to California to teach at Berkeley, toured Europe with George Wein in 1967 and made a few final recordings. —*Scott Yanow*

Elmer Snowden / Dec. 1924-Aug. 3, 1963 / IAJRC ✦✦✦✦

This collector's LP features banjoist Elmer Snowden in a variety of settings from 1924, 1927, 1929, 1932, 1934 and 1963. Snowden is heard as a sideman with Booker's Dixie Jazz Band, the Roy Williams Orchestra (which was really Snowden's group of 1927), the Musical Stevedores, the Jungle Town Stompers, Jasper Davis, Snowden's Small's Paradise Orchestra in 1932 (taken from a short film soundtrack), the Sepia Serenaders and in 1963 on a broadcast with a trio. Among the key sidemen are cornetists Bubber Miley and Rex Stewart, trumpeter Louis Metcalf, altoist Charlie Holmes, pianist Cliff Jackson and clarinetist Darnell Howard. Although Snowden mostly functions in the background with an occasional solo, the music should be of great interest, particularly to 1920s collectors. There is a strong sampling of hot classic jazz on this IAJRC album. —*Scott Yanow*

● **Harlem Banjo** / Dec. 9, 1960 / Original Jazz Classics ✦✦✦✦✦

Banjoist Elmer Snowden only led two albums in the LP era, and this OJC CD reissue is his best showcase. Snowden, who is joined by pianist Cliff Jackson, bassist Tommy Bryant and drummer Jimmy Crawford, is the lead voice throughout the dozen standards, all of which date from the 1920s or '30s. Snowden's banjo style is a lost art, and this is his definitive recording. —*Scott Yanow*

Soft Winds

f. 1946, db. 1950
Group / Bop, Swing

Guitarist Herb Ellis, pianist Lou Carter and bassist John Frigo were all members of the Jimmy Dorsey Orchestra when in 1946 they decided to form a trio and go out on their own as the Soft Winds. Reminiscent, but not derivative, of the Nat King Cole and Page Cavanaugh Trios, the Soft Winds stayed together until 1950. Best known for jointly composing "Detour Ahead" and "I Told Ya I Love Ya, Now Get Out," the band struggled for a few years before breaking up. The 16 selections that they recorded for Majestic and Mercury in 1947 and 1949 have unfortunately never been reissued, but in 1995, Carter easily persuaded producer Hank O'Neil to release 13 previously unknown vintage acetate recordings that he had of the band. The Soft Winds had a reunion that was recorded that year by O'Neil's Chiaroscuro label, with Carter (who had had a long, if low-profile, career), Frigo (now a violinist), Ellis (still in his prime) and bassist Keter Betts all in fine form. —*Scott Yanow*

● **Then & Now** / 1947-Nov. 9, 1995 / Chiaroscuro ✦✦✦✦✦

The Soft Winds, a trio consisting of pianist Lou Carter, guitarist Herb Ellis and bassist Johnny Frigo, were originally members of the Jimmy Dorsey Orchestra. From 1946-50, they struggled along as an independent group, recording 16 selections for Majestic and Mercury that have yet to be reissued, as well as writing two hits ("Detour Ahead" and "I Told Ya I Love Ya, Now Get Out"), before breaking up. They had a reunion during the 1995 Floating Jazz Festival, and with Frigo on violin and Keter Betts on bass, they proved that the musical magic was still very much there. This two-CD set consists of previously unreleased radio transcriptions by the

Soft Winds from 1947-48 and 11 songs from their 1995 reunion. In addition, there is an informative and entertaining 16-minute "Jazz Speak," in which the three musicians talk colorfully and with humor about the group's history. This highly recommended set shows that the Soft Winds had developed their own sound out of the instrumentation of the Nat King Cole Trio, with Lou Carter's powerful, versatile and creative playing being the biggest revelation. Now, if only some label would reissue the Soft Winds' original studio sides too. —*Scott Yanow*

Martial Solal

b. Aug. 23, 1927, Algiers, North Africa
Piano / Post-Bop

One of the finest European jazz pianists of all time, Martial Solal (a unique stylist) has never received as much recognition in the US as he deserves. Born in Algiers to French parents, Solal has been based in Paris since the late '40s. Although a modernist, he was flexible enough to record an album with Sidney Bechet in 1957 and make other records with Django Reinhardt, Don Byas and Lucky Thompson. Solal has been primarily heard with his own trios through the years although he has recorded several notable albums with Lee Konitz. —*Scott Yanow*

In Concert / May 3, 1963 / Liberty ✦✦✦✦

It is a pity that the music on this LP will be difficult to find, for it offers listeners a strong example of the talents of pianist Martial Solal. Joined by bassist Guy Pedersen and drummer Daniel Humair, Solal performs six of his originals plus the jazz standard "Jordu," swinging in an unpredictable and adventurous manner. —*Scott Yanow*

Movability / Apr. 26, 1976 / MPS ✦✦✦✦

Few of French pianist Martial Solal's recordings as a leader have been made available in the US through the years. This set, originally cut for MPS and then released domestically on a 1981 Pausa LP, will be difficult to find, but is worth the search. The stimulating pianist is heard in a set of duets with bassist Niels Henning Orsted-Pedersen, performing five standards, two of his originals and Pedersen's "Afternoons Sentiment." Although essentially straightahead, the music is quite spontaneous and full of surprises. —*Scott Yanow*

● **Four Keys** / May 1979 / Pausa ✦✦✦✦✦

An all-star quartet (pianist Martial Solal, altoist Lee Konitz, guitarist John Scofield and bassist Niels Pedersen) explores seven diverse Solal originals that range from chamberlike pieces to fairly free group improvising. The results are often exciting if cool in both tone and volume. Thoughtful yet unpredictable music. —*Scott Yanow*

Lew Soloff

b. Jan. 20, 1944, New York, NY
Trumpet, Fluegelhorn / Post-Bop, Hard Bop

A brilliant high-note trumpeter long in great demand for big bands and session work, Lew Soloff is also a distinctive soloist and an expert with the plunger mute. After studying at Juilliard he freelanced in New York with Maynard Ferguson, Joe Henderson and Clark Terry among others and then was a part of Blood, Sweat & Tears during 1968-73. Soloff was closely associated with Gil Evans from 1973 on, and also played with George Gruntz's Concert Jazz Band, the Manhattan Jazz Quintet and Carla Bley; he was also teamed with the colorful trombonist Ray Anderson on several often-humorous recordings. —*Scott Yanow*

Yesterdays / Sep. 15, 1986-Sep. 16, 1986 / Pro Arte ✦✦✦

A stunning album of fusion-treated jazz standards, it includes several original compositions by Soloff and features Mike Stern (g), Charnett Moffett (b), and Elvin Jones (d). Mike Stern's guitar work is featured prominently throughout. —*Paul Kohler*

But Beautiful / Jun. 29, 1987-Jun. 30, 1987 / Evidence ✦✦✦✦

Lew Soloff's brilliant technique has often been utilized to hit the high notes in adventurous big bands, but he is also a very talented soloist. This quartet set with pianist Kenny Kirkland, bassist Richard Davis and drummer Elvin Jones (a reissue of a CD cut for the King label and first released domestically by Projazz as *Speak Low*) is sometimes a little more laidback than expected, but has its fiery moments. Soloff shows off his warm tone on the ballads (such as "But Beautiful") and swings hard on such numbers as "Speak Low," Charles Mingus' "Reincarnation of a Lovebird" and his own "Duty Blues." There are relatively few Lew Soloff albums available (and none thus far have been made for American labels), so this enjoyable CD is easily recommended. —*Scott Yanow*

● **Speak Low** / Jun. 29, 1987-Jun. 30, 1987 / Pro Arte ✦✦✦✦✦

Veteran NYC studio trumpeter steps out. —*Michael G. Nastos*

Soprano Summit

f. 1972, db. 1979

Group / Classic Jazz, Swing

The 1970s, an era best known in jazz as the "fusion years," seemed like a very unlikely time to form a classic jazz/mainstream group. At Dick Gibson's annual Colorado Jazz Party in 1972, Bob Wilber and Kenny Davern so enjoyed playing together during one song that within a short time Soprano Summit was formed. Wilber and Davern both doubled on sopranos and clarinets and were originally joined by pianist Dick Hyman, guitarist Bucky Pizzarelli, bassist George Duvivier and drummer Bobby Rosengarden, cutting their first two sets for the World Jazz label. By 1976, when the group really hit its stride, Wilber and Davern were teaming up with acoustic guitarist/vocalist Marty Grosz and a variety of bassists and drummers. The band featured passionate versions of pre-bop standards and obscurities, and the interplay between the co-leaders was often quite intense and consistently exciting. Before their breakup in 1979, Soprano Summit had recorded gems for Chiaroscuro, Jazzology, Concord and Fat Cat Jazz, in addition to a third album for World Jazz. In 1986, Davern (who was now exclusively playing clarinet) and Wilbur had an informal get-together, and they have played together on an occasional basis since, making recordings as Soprano Reunion (with the original rhythm section (with Milt Hinton filling in for the late Duvivier) in 1990 and 1992. The Chiaroscuro and Concord sets have since been reissued on CD and are highly recommended. —*Scott Yanow*

Soprano Summit I / Dec. 17, 1973-Dec. 22, 1973 / World Jazz ✦✦✦✦

The debut album by Soprano Summit features co-leaders Bob Wilber and Kenny Davern doubling on sopranos and clarinets while accompanied by pianist Dick Hyman, guitarist Bucky Pizzarelli, either George Duvivier or Milt Hinton on bass, and drummer Bobby Rosengarden. The music is often quite heated, particularly on the numbers associated with Sidney Bechet. The style falls between hot swing and Dixieland with the interplay between the reeds being a constant delight. —*Scott Yanow*

Soprano Summit II / May 5, 1974+Dec. 9, 1977 / World Jazz ✦✦✦✦

The second and final Soprano Summit record for World Jazz features Kenny Davern and Bob Wilber doubling on clarinets and sopranos, pianist Dick Hyman, guitarist Bucky Pizzarelli, bassist Milt Hinton and either Tommy Benford or Bobby Rosengarden on drums. This hard-to-find LP is mostly fairly ragtime-oriented (with two pieces from Scott Joplin and works by George Gershwin, Jelly Roll Morton and Willie "The Lion" Smith plus three by Wilber) but it also has its exciting and spontaneous moments. All of the Soprano Summit recordings are well worth acquiring. —*Scott Yanow*

● **Soprano Summit** / Feb. 29, 1976-Sep. 12, 1977 / Chiaroscuro ✦✦✦✦✦

During the mid-'70s, an era when interest in pre-bop jazz was near its lowest, Soprano Summit was formed and somehow flourished. Co-led by Kenny Davern (on soprano, clarinet and C-melody sax) and Bob Wilber (tripling on soprano, clarinet and alto), the group offered strong swing-based solos, a colorful repertoire and, best of all, exciting ensembles. This two-CD set features the 1976-77 edition of Soprano Summit with Marty Grosz's acoustic guitar and banjo acting as a third important voice while bassist George Duvivier and either Bobby Rosengarden and Fred Stoll on drums offer suitable support. Reissued are two complete LPs and in addition there are five previously unreleased selections from a live performance along with a 13-minute "Jazzspeak" during which Marty Grosz talks (with humor) about the history of the important group. Some of the many highlights of this essential set include "Grenadilla Stomp," "Ole Miss," "When Day Is Done," "Crazy Rhythm" and two versions of "Nagasaki." —*Scott Yanow*

At the Big Horn Jazzfest / May 30, 1976-May 31, 1976 / Jazzology ✦✦✦✦

This little-known live session was Soprano Summit's earliest recording as a pianoless quintet featuring guitarist-singer Marty Grosz. Although five of the eight selections appeared on either their first or third record, these renditions are quite a bit different and (if anything) even hotter. Co-leaders Bob Wilber and Kenny Davern (doubling on clarinet and soprano) have always made for a mutually inspiring team and, with Grosz, bassist Milt Hinton and drummer Fred Stoll completing the group, the results are fairly memorable. Highlights include "Swing Parade," "A Porter's Love Song to a Chambermaid," "Ole Miss" and "Swing That Music." —*Scott Yanow*

★ **In Concert** / Jul. 30, 1976 / Concord Jazz ✦✦✦✦✦

For several years in the 1970s, Bob Wilber and Kenny Davern teamed up to co-lead Soprano Summit, a group that featured the pair doubling on clarinets and sopranos. Their appearance at the 1976 Concord Jazz Festival found the group at its peak. With Marty Grosz contributing some perfectly suitable chordal acoustic guitar and vocals, and bassist Ray Brown and drummer Jake Hanna keeping the music moving, Wilber and Davern constantly challenge each other on such hot

numbers as "Stompy Jones," "Doin' the New Lowdown" and "Swing That Music." This exciting set is highly recommended. —*Scott Yanow*

Soprano Summit / Nov. 7, 1976 / Storyville ✦✦✦✦

Soprano Summit was one of the hottest mainstream bands of the 1970s, a potentially explosive unit co-starring Bob Wilber and Kenny Davern on sopranos and clarinets. Their repertoire included both classics from the 1920s and '30s and newer originals in a freewheeling style, but there was no need for strict re-creations; the musicians simply played like themselves. The second edition of Soprano Summit also featured the great acoustic guitarist and Fats Waller-inspired vocalist Marty Grosz. For this Storyville CD (featuring a European concert not initially released until 1996), the trio is joined quite ably by bassist Eddie de Haas and drummer Bob Cousins. The Grosz vocals and the interplay between the two reeds result in exciting versions of 11 songs, including "Stompy Jones," "How Can You Face Me," "Meet Me Tonight in Dreamland," and Wilber's "Grenadilla Stomp." Recommended. —*Scott Yanow*

Live at Concord / Aug. 5, 1977 / Concord Jazz ✦✦✦✦

Soprano Summit was one of the hottest mainstream groups of the 1970s, a unit co-led by Bob Wilber and Kenny Davern who on clarinets and sopranos really pushed and battled each other. For their appearance at the 1977 Concord Jazz Festival, the two heated reeds are joined by guitarist Marty Grosz (who sings in a Fats Waller-influenced style on "How Can You Face Me" and "The Panic Is On"), bassist Monty Budwig and drummer Jake Hanna. An unusual ballad medley features Wilber, Grosz and Davern on obscure originals of their own but the main sparks are reserved for stirring versions of "Strike Up the Band" and "Panama." Highly recommended for fans of pre-bop jazz. —*Scott Yanow*

Summit Reunion / May 30, 1990-May 31, 1990 / Chiaroscuro ✦✦✦✦

Summit Reunion 1992 / Oct. 27, 1992-Oct. 28, 1992 / Chiaroscuro ✦✦✦✦✦

After breaking up in the late 1970s, Soprano Summit did not regroup until 1990. This CD, the second of the group's later career, features the original version of Soprano Summit (with clarinetist Kenny Davern, Bob Wilber on clarinet, soprano and alto, pianist Dick Hyman, guitarist Bucky Pizzarelli, bassist Milt Hinton and drummer Bobby Rosengarden) performing on the SS *Norway* during the 1992 Floating Jazz Festival. The old magic was still very much present and the interplay between Wilber and Davern (who bring out the best in each other) is quite exciting. Tenor saxophonist Flip Phillips sits in and helps out on three of the ten selections. High points include "Lady Be Good," "Chinatown" and a lengthy rendition of "Apex Blues" that builds and builds. Recommended. —*Scott Yanow*

Jazz im Amerika Haus, Vol. 5 / Sep. 24, 1994 / Nagel-Heyer ✦✦✦✦✦

The fifth CD of mainstream jazz recorded at Hamburg's America House, this exciting session reunites the co-leaders of Soprano Summit, clarinetist Kenny Davern and Bob Wilber (who doubles on soprano and clarinet). Assisted by guitarist Dave Cliff, bassist Dave Green and drummer Bobby Worth, Davern and Wilber romp on such pieces as "Lady Be Good," "If Dreams Come True," "Comes Love" and "A Porter's Love Song to a Chambermaid." Whenever the two reeds get together, the results are explosive and hard-swinging; this highly recommended CD from the German Nagel-Heyer label is no exception. —*Scott Yanow*

Yellow Dog Blues / Mar. 14, 1995 / Chiaroscuro ✦✦✦✦✦

Although only a part-time affair in the 1990s, Soprano Summit (now often called Summit Reunion because it uses the same six musicians who appeared on the band's initial recording in 1973) remains one of the hottest groups in jazz. The interplay between Bob Wilber (usually on soprano) and clarinetist Kenny Davern is full of joy, the rhythm section would be difficult to improve upon and the ensembles are consistently memorable and often quite exciting. For this 1995 session, the sextet mostly brings new life to a variety of Dixieland warhorses (including "Darktown Strutters Ball," "Hindustan" and a lengthy "Somebody Stole My Gal") although Irving Berlin's "I'll See You in C-U-B-A" is a bit obscure and the folk song "Darling Nelly Gray" has not been recorded much in a jazz setting since Louis Armstrong teamed up with the Mills Brothers in the late 1930s. All of the musicians have opportunities to solo; Bucky Pizzarelli contributes some chordal guitar displays, Milt Hinton plays a few percussive bass solos, Bobby Rosengarden takes some drum breaks on "Somebody Stole My Gal" and Dick Hyman constructs some typically wondrous improvisations in the swing tradition. But the emphasis is on Wilber and Davern and they sound as complementary and competitive as ever. Recommended. —*Scott Yanow*

Eddie South

b. Nov. 27, 1904, Louisiana, MO, **d.** Apr. 25, 1962, Chicago, IL

Violin / Swing

One of the top violinists of the pre-bop era, Eddie South was a brilliant technician who, were it not for the universal racism of the time, would probably have been a top classical violinist. A child prodigy, South graduated from the Chicago Music

College. Since classical positions were not open to Black violinists in the 1920s, South learned to play jazz (helped out by Darnell Howard). In the early to mid-1920s, he worked in Chicago with Jimmy Wade's Syncopators, Charles Elgar and Erskine Tate. South's 1928 visit to Europe (where he studied at the Paris Conservatoire) made a deep impression on the violinist, particularly his visit to Budapest; later on, he would often utilize gypsy melodies as a basis for jazz improvising. In 1931, South returned to Chicago, where his regular band included the young bassist Milt Hinton. In 1937, he visited Paris and had the opportunity to record with Django Reinhardt and Stephane Grappelli. However, South never really had a major breakthrough commercially in his career. He did work on radio and television but spent most of his life in relative obscurity, gigging in New York, Los Angeles and especially Chicago. Eddie South's early recordings (covering 1927-41) have been reissued on a pair of Classics CDs. In later years he recorded for Chess and Mercury, and also made a final set released by Trip. *—Scott Yanow*

Eddie South 1923-1937 / Dec. 1923-Nov. 23, 1937 / Classics ✦✦✦✦
Eddie South was one of the top jazz violinists of the 1920s, '30s and '40s, but made fewer recordings than one would expect. This CD starts out with a rare 1923 performance ("Someday Sweetheart") in which South is heard with Wade's Moulin Rouge Orchestra. The remainder of the reissue has all of South's dates as a leader during 1927-37. The early numbers with his Alabamians are quite obscure and sometimes a little odd, including versions of "The Voice of the Southland," "By the Waters of Minnetonka," "Two Guitars" and "Hejre Kati." During the era (1927-31), the violinist sought to combine his roots in classical music with folk music and jazz. By 1933 (six swinging numbers that are among the first recordings of bassist Milt Hinton), South was swinging as much as Joe Venuti and the up-and-coming Stephane Grappelli. The final eight selections are from 1937, when South was visiting Paris, and they include notable collaborations with guitarist Django Reinhardt and Grappelli and, on "Lady Be Good," the third violin of Michel Warlop. Lots of timeless swing is featured throughout the first of Eddie South's two Classics CDs, both of which are highly recommended. *—Scott Yanow*

● **Eddie South 1937-1941** / Nov. 25, 1937-Mar. 12, 1941 / Classics ✦✦✦✦
On the second of two Classics CDs that have all of Eddie South's pre-war recordings as a leader, the great violinist is heard playing two selections with a quartet in Paris that includes guitarist Django Reinhardt and fellow violinist Stephane Grappelli, heading his own groups in 1938, 1940 and 1941, and on four numbers in which he led the backup band (which used John Kirby's front line) for pop singer Ginny Simms. The music ranges from swinging standards to true obscurities, giving listeners a strong sampling of Eddie South's unusual style; most of the performances were formerly quite rare. *—Scott Yanow*

South Side Jazz / 1947-Dec. 31, 1953 / Chess ✦✦✦
Although violinist Eddie South receives first billing on this long-out-of-print LP, he is featured on just six of the 16 numbers. South's lone session for Chess has him playing sentimental ballads and some fine swing in a Chicago sextet that also includes tenor saxophonist Eddie Johnson and vibraphonist Bill Thompson. Also on this LP (which has an overview of early Chess jazz recordings) are features for the booting tenor of Eddie Johnson, Lonnie Simmons on both organ and his overdubbed tenor, the Nat King Cole-inspired pianist/vocalist Prince Cooper, and bands led by drummer Red Saunders and tenor saxophonist Dave Young. The spirited music is enjoyable, if not all that essential. *—Scott Yanow*

The Distinguished Violin of Eddie South / Jul. 14, 1958-Jul. 15, 1958 / Mercury ✦✦✦✦
This little-known LP has what were probably Eddie South's final recordings. Although only 53 at the time, the talented violinist would pass away less than four years later. South, who is accompanied by either Ed Higgins or James Todd on piano, rhythm guitarist John Gray, bassist Johnnie Pate and sometimes drummer Al Duncan, shows off his versatility throughout the continually interesting set. In addition to a couple of jazz standards and his own swinging "Fiddle Ditty," South performs three Pate originals, his Hungarian theme song "Hejre Kati," "Nobody Knows the Trouble I've Seen," and pieces dedicated to classical violinist Fritz Kreisler and some Gypsy fiddlers. *—Scott Yanow*

Muggsy Spanier (Francis Joseph Spanier)

b. Nov. 9, 1906, Chicago, IL, **d.** Feb. 12, 1967, Sausalito, CA
Cornet / Dixieland

Muggsy Spanier was a predictable but forceful cornetist who rarely strayed far from the melody. Perfectly at home in Dixieland ensembles, Spanier was also an emotional soloist (equally influenced by King Oliver and Louis Armstrong) who was an expert at using the plunger mute. He started on cornet when he was 13, played with Elmer Schoebel's band in 1921 and first recorded in 1924. Spanier was a fixture in Chicago throughout the decade (appearing on several important early records) before joining Ted Lewis in 1929. Although Lewis was essentially a corny showman, Spanier's solos gave his band some validity during the next seven

years. After a stint with Ben Pollack's orchestra (1936-38), Spanier became seriously ill and was hospitalized for three months. After he recovered, the cornetist formed his famous eight-piece "Ragtime Band" and recorded 16 Dixieland performances for Bluebird (later dubbed "the Great 16") that virtually defined the music of the Dixieland revival movement. But because his group actually preceded the revival by a couple years, it soon had to break up due to lack of work! Muggsy joined Bob Crosby for a time, had his own short-lived big band, freelanced with Dixieland bands in New York and starting in 1950 he gradually relocated to the West Coast. During 1957-59 Spanier worked with Earl Hines' band and he continued playing up until his retirement in 1964, touring Europe in 1960 and always retaining his popularity in the Dixieland world. *—Scott Yanow*

★ **Muggsy Spanier (1924-1928)** / Feb. 25, 1924-Apr. 5, 1928 / Retrieval ✦✦✦✦✦
This is the type of definitive "complete" release that American labels always seem to leave up to the Europeans to do correctly. The English LP reissues all seven selections by the Bucktown Five, the two numbers from the Stomp Six, Charles Pierce's seven 1928 titles and two titles from the Jungle Kings. The somewhat generic group names mask the fact that these performances include solos from such greats as cornetist Muggsy Spanier, clarinetists Volly de Faut and Frankie Teschemacher, and pianist Joe Sullivan. These early recordings find Spanier gradually developing his own style; his solos on "Why Can't It Be Poor Little Me" and "Nobody's Sweetheart" are classics. 1920s collectors can consider this set to be essential. *—Scott Yanow*

Muggsy Spanier (1931+1939) / Mar. 1931-Dec. 12, 1939 / BBC ✦✦✦
Reissues of super 30s dates with Spanier and Fats Waller (p), Benny Goodman (cl), and Joe Bushkin (p). *—Ron Wynn*

★ **The Ragtime Band Sessions** / Jul. 7, 1939-Dec. 12, 1939 / Bluebird ✦✦✦✦✦
During four sessions in 1939 cornetist Muggsy Spanier performed definitive versions of 16 Dixieland standards that, due to the joy of the music and its huge influence on the future revival movement, would later be dubbed "The Great 16." This CD, which adds eight alternate takes, could have been subtitled "The Great 24." Spanier and his octet (which includes trombonist George Brunis, clarinetist Rod Cless, usually pianist Joe Bushkin and several different tenors) roar their way through such songs as "Big Butter and Egg Man," "That Da Da Strain," "I Wish I Could Shimmy like My Sister Kate," "Dinah" and "Mandy, Make Up Your Mind." Classic music. *—Scott Yanow*

Ragtime Jazz / 1940+1957 / Olympic ✦✦✦
The music on this budget LP is much better than the packaging, which does not give the complete personnel. The bulk of the album consists of seven of the eight titles that cornetist Muggsy Spanier recorded with a quartet also including soprano saxophonist Sidney Bechet, guitarist Carmen Mastren and bassist Wellman Braud (leaving out "If I Could Be with You"). The interplay between Spanier and Bechet on these longer-than-usual performances (clocking in around four minutes apiece instead of three) is quite memorable; highlights include "China Boy," "That's a Plenty" and "Sweet Sue." In addition, there are a pair of typical numbers by Spanier's 1957 Dixieland band, a sextet with trombonist Bill Johnson, clarinetist Joe Barufaldi and pianist Red Richards. Hopefully, all of this music will be reissued more coherently on CD. *—Scott Yanow*

Little David Play Your Harp / Dec. 20, 1941-Jan. 17, 1942 / Jazz Archives ✦✦✦✦
Muggsy Spanier's short-lived orchestra recorded just seven selections in the studios during 1942 before disbanding, but fortunately this 1976 LP preserves a full album of the big band's radio performances. The cornetist's group was a bit reminiscent of Bob Crosby's and had among its soloists trombonist Vernon Brown, tenor saxophonist Nick Caiazza, pianist Dave Bowman and (on its last three numbers) clarinetist Irving Fazola. This collector's LP (which is highlighted by "Chicago," "At the Jazz Band Ball," "Sunday" and "Columbia the Gem of the Ocean") is highly recommended to swing and Dixieland collectors. *—Scott Yanow*

Muggsy Spanier [Everybody's] / Oct. 17, 1944+Oct. 22, 1945 / Everybody's ✦✦✦✦
This LP contains Dixieland performances originally recorded as V-Discs by cornetist Muggsy Spanier. The two all-star jams also feature solos from trombonist Lou McGarity, clarinetists Pee Wee Russell and Peanuts Hucko, tenors Boomie Richman and Bud Freeman, and pianists Jess Stacy and Dave Bowman. The music is fairly straightforward with few surprises but plenty of heat generated from these masterful players. *—Scott Yanow*

Muggsy Spanier / Mar. 1, 1945-Mar. 2, 1945 / Storyville ✦✦✦✦✦
Many of cornetist Muggsy Spanier's hottest recordings were made during 1944-45. This LP (whose contents are long overdue to be reissued on CD) features the basic but exciting soloist at his best with groups also including Miff Mole or Lou McGarity on trombone, clarinetist Pee Wee Russell, baritonist Ernie Caceres, pianist Gene Schroeder and several overlapping rhythm sections. The 13 jazz standards (which include "Original Dixieland One Step," "I'm Sorry I Made You Cry," "Bugle Call

Rag" and "Fidgety Feet") plus Spanier's "Feather Brain Blues" are all given heated treatment, which should greatly please Dixieland fans. —*Scott Yanow*

Muggsy Spanier and His Dixieland Band / Mar. 27, 1950 / Mercury ✦✦✦

This LP is a cut above most of Muggsy Spanier's recordings of the 1950s due to a surprisingly fresh repertoire, which includes such songs as "Dixie Flyer," "Home," "Caution Blues," "Alabama Jubilee" and "Lazy Piano Man." The otherwise admirable (if hard-to-find) release inexcusably does not give the recording dates and personnel. The cornetist/leader is joined by either George Brunis, Henry Graves or Ralph Hutchinson on trombone, clarinetist Darnell Howard, pianist Floyd Bean, bassist Truck Parham and either Sid Catlett, Don Chester or Barrett Deems on drums; Buddy Charles takes the vocal on "Sunday." The concise performances (all but "Sunday" are under three minutes) successfully pack a great deal of heat into a brief space of time. —*Scott Yanow*

Relaxin' at the Touro / 1952 / Jazzology ✦✦✦✦

These radio transcriptions made for World are very brief renditions of fairly predictable Dixieland. Cornetist Muggsy Spanier and his regular touring band of the early '50s (with trombonist Ralph Hutchinson, clarinetist Darnell Howard, pianist Floyd Bean, bassist Truck Parham and drummer Barrett Deems) put as much spirit as they can into the warhorses, but since only one number clocks in at over 2:15, the music rarely has much time to get beyond the melodies. Strictly for Muggsy Spanier completists. —*Scott Yanow*

Rare Custom 45's / Apr. 1956 / IAJRC ✦✦✦✦

In 1956 cornetist Muggsy Spanier and a variety of other available trad jazz musicians in Chicago cut a series of 45s for the jukeboxes of Buzz Seeburg. Only a few of the 18 titles on this LP from the collectors' IAJRC label actually came out at the time. Spanier is featured with trombonist George Brunis, clarinetist Peanuts Hucko or Charlie Spero, pianist Floyd Bean and a rhythm section, jamming through brief versions of a variety of Dixieland standards. The music is frequently joyous and swinging, even if does not contain any real surprises. —*Scott Yanow*

Hot Horn / Mar. 2, 1945+1957 / Storyville ✦✦✦

The first 12 selections on this generous 16-song LP feature cornetist Muggsy Spanier's band of 1957 in what was his next-to-last full album as a leader. Spanier's spirited but predictable band (which includes trombonist Ralph Hutchinson, clarinetist Phil Gomez, pianist Red Richards, bassist Truck Parham and drummer George Wettling) performs such warhorses as "The Saints," "Tin Roof Blues," "Darktown Strutters Ball" and "Ja Da." The LP concludes with four titles left over from 1945 that had not been included with the batch reissued on the previous self-titled Muggsy Spanier LP (Storyville 4020). Those tracks find Spanier joined by trombonist Lou McGarity and clarinetist Pee Wee Russell and are on a higher level. —*Scott Yanow*

Columbia, the Gem of the Ocean / Jun. 13, 1962-Jun. 14, 1962 / Mobile Fidelity ✦✦✦✦✦

Cornetist Muggsy Spanier's final recording as a leader is a real gem. During 1941-43 he had led a fine big band similar to Bob Crosby's Bobcats that recorded seven selections before breaking up. Twenty years later, a new big band was put together for a record released by the Ava label that was later reissued on CD by Mobile Fidelity. Spanier and the 15-piece group are heard performing nine Dean Kincaide arrangements from the old band's book (only "Chicago" had been recorded commercially), plus a new chart by Harry Betts of "Midnight in Moscow." Although his health was starting to fail, Spanier sounds in top form during this set, with a band also featuring solos by trombonist Moe Schneider, clarinetist Matty Matlock and tenor saxophonist Eddie Miller. This final act in the Muggsy Spanier story is highly recommended. —*Scott Yanow*

James Spaulding

b. Jul. 30, 1937, Indianapolis, IN

Alto Saxophone, Flute / Post-Bop, Hard Bop

A superior alto saxophonist and flutist who can shift from bop and hard bop to very adventurous flights, James Spaulding gained his greatest recognition while a member of Freddie Hubbard's Quintet in the mid-1960s. He studied at the Chicago Cosmopolitan School of Music and then gigged and recorded regularly with Sun Ra during 1957-61. During the 1960s, Spaulding (who worked with Max Roach and Randy Weston) was in demand not only by Hubbard, but for Blue Note recordings by Joe Henderson, Wayne Shorter, Stanley Turrentine and Larry Young, among others. He had stints during the next couple of decades with a wide variety of top artists, including Charles Tolliver, Bobby Hutcherson, David Murray and (for a brief period) the World Saxophone Quartet, but is still vastly underrated. James Spaulding has recorded as a leader for Storyville (a Duke Ellington tribute set in 1976) and several dates for Muse (1988-93). —*Scott Yanow*

James Spaulding Plays the Legacy of Duke Ellington / Dec. 1, 1976-Dec. 2, 1976 / Storyville ✦✦✦

Despite being a top altoist and flutist since at least the mid-'60s, when he played with Freddie Hubbard's band, James Spaulding did not get his recording debut as a leader until this 1976 LP. Spaulding, on various flutes, piccolo, soprano and alto, performs eight songs associated with Duke Ellington, including "Take the 'A' Train" (a Billy Strayhorn composition mistakenly co-credited in the liners to Duke), "Come Sunday," an impressive flute showcase on "Sophisticated Lady" and "It Don't Mean a Thing." Spaulding is joined by pianist Cedar Walton, a young Steve Nelson on vibes, bassist Sam Jones, drummer Billy Higgins and percussionist Mtume. The most unusual aspect of this set is that Avery Brooks (who has a deep baritone that Ellington might have liked) sings four of the eight songs. A sincere tribute. —*Scott Yanow*

★ Brilliant Corners / Nov. 25, 1988 / Muse ✦✦✦✦✦

James Spaulding is a very distinctive altoist and flutist whose inside/outside playing can cover anything from bop to freer improvisations. On what was surprisingly only his third recording as a leader, Spaulding is heard at the peak of his powers, leading a quartet/quintet also including pianist Mulgrew Miller, bassist Ron Carter, drummer Kenny Washington and (on half of the selections) trumpeter Wallace Roney. They perform six Thelonious Monk tunes (including the complex title cut, the lyrical "Ask Me Now" and "Little Rootie Tootie") plus Bud Powell's "Down with It" and Miles Davis' "Little Willie Leaps." Spaulding takes four songs apiece on alto and flute, and this is his definitive recording. —*Scott Yanow*

Songs of Courage / Oct. 1991 / Muse ✦✦✦✦

Blues Nexus / Aug. 8, 1993 / Muse ✦✦✦✦

● Smile of the Snake / Dec. 3, 1996-Dec. 4, 1996 / High Note ✦✦✦✦✦

Special EFX

f. 1982, db. 1995

Group / World Fusion, Crossover Jazz

Combining Latin and African rhythms with the light textures of MOR jazz, Special EFX emerged as one of the most prominent world fusion groups of their era. Formed in New York in 1982, Special EFX was essentially a duo comprising guitarist Chieli Minucci and Hungarian-born drummer/percussionist George Jinda; debuting in 1985 with the album *Modern Manners*, they often recruited other musicians to help flesh out their state-of-the-art sound, among them Dave Grusin, Omar Hakim and McCoy Tyner. Long favoring an accessible and slick jazz-pop sound, the duo significantly altered their identity with 1990s *Just like Magic*, adopting a more acoustic texture and exchanging Jinda's electronic percussion for what he dubbed "wooden world music." After 1995's *Body Language*, Minucci and Jinda split, with the latter continuing to work under the Special EFX name; in early 1997, however, tragedy struck when Jinda—having recently completed the album *Here to Stay*—suffered a massive stroke, subsequently lapsing into a coma. As of this writing, he remains unable to speak or walk. —*Jason Ankeny*

Mystique / 1987 / GRP ✦✦✦

● Special EFX Collection / 1987-1992 / GRP ✦✦✦✦

Double Feature / 1988 / GRP ✦✦

Just like Magic / 1990 / GRP ✦✦✦

Peace of the World / 1991 / GRP ✦✦✦

Global Village / 1992 / GRP ✦✦

The duo of guitarist Chieli Minucci and percussionist George Jinda were co-leaders of Special EFX for many years. Generally their collaborations have been closer to folk and world music than to jazz. On this CD the many sidemen help take the music into other directions, especially towards lightweight jazz, soft funk and even pop. But, despite the participation of keyboardist Kenny Werner, bassist Gerald Veasley and saxophonist Bob Mintzer on some numbers, the music is never exciting and rarely at all memorable. A disappointment. —*Scott Yanow*

Play / Oct. 1992-Dec. 1992 / JVC ✦✦✦

Catwalk / 1994 / JVC ✦✦✦

Body Language / Apr. 1995-Jun. 1995 / JVC ✦✦✦✦

Here to Stay / 1996 / JVC ✦✦✦

The musicianship is excellent on this CD, but the music itself leaves a little to be desired. The originals, all but one co-written by leader/percussionist George Jinda and Szakcsi, all clock in between 4:46 and 5:27, so radio airplay was obviously the main goal of the program. The lack of any memorable melodies or meaningful improvising makes this mostly pleasant affair a rather forgettable effort, despite some good Wes Montgomery-type guitar solos from Mark Whitfield, Chuck Loeb and Ben Butler. —*Scott Yanow*

Sphere

f. 1982, **db.** 1988
Group / Hard Bop
On the very day that Thelonious Monk died (Feb. 17, 1982), the Monk tribute group Sphere—comprising Monk's longtime tenor saxophonist Charlie Rouse, pianist Kenny Barron, bassist Buster Williams and Monk's former drummer Ben Riley—recorded an album of Monk tunes. Although Sphere started out as a tribute band, it also performed originals and jazz standards during its existence. The quartet recorded for Elektra Musician, Red and Verve (including a set of Charlie Parker tunes) before disbanding after Rouse's death on Nov. 30, 1988. —*Scott Yanow*

● **Four in One** / Feb. 17, 1982 / Elektra ✦✦✦✦✦
Tremendous tribute effort, outstanding versions of Monk classics. Topflight Monk repertory effort. CD has two bonus cuts. —*Ron Wynn*

Flight Path / 1983 / Elektra ✦✦✦✦
On Tour / Nov. 1985 / Red ✦✦✦✦✦
Sphere was one of the great repertory groups to emerge in the '80s. Longtime Thelonious Monk associate saxophonist Charlie Rouse teamed with bassist Buster Williams and drummer Ben Riley to perform Monk's material, with pianist Kenny Barron capably handling the keyboard duties. The group cut this album live in the mid-'80s and were recorded by the Red label. It was the only time this fine quartet was caught in a live setting during their tenure. —*Ron Wynn*

Live at Umbria Jazz / Jul. 14, 1986 / Red ✦✦✦✦

Bird Songs / Mar. 12, 1988 / Verve ✦✦✦✦✦
1988 lineup of all-star players Kenny Barron (p), Charlie Rouse (ts), Buster Williams (b), and Ben Riley (d) play only Charlie Parker tunes, except for the lengthy and brilliant "I Didn't Know What Time It Was." —*Michael G. Nastos*

Four for All / Mar. 2, 1987 / Verve ✦✦✦✦

Victoria Spivey

b. Oct. 15, 1906, Houston, TX, **d.** Oct. 3, 1976, New York, NY
Vocals, Piano / Classic Female Blues, Acoustic Chicago Blues
Victoria Spivey was one of the more influential blues women simply because she was around long enough to influence legions of younger women and men who rediscovered blues music in the mid-1960s US blues revival brought about by British blues bands as well as their American counterparts, like Paul Butterfield and Elvin Bishop. Spivey could do it all: she wrote songs, sang them well, and accompanied herself on piano and organ, and occasionally ukulele.

Spivey began her recording career at age 19 and came from the same rough-and-tumble clubs in Houston and Dallas that produced Sippie Wallace. In 1918, she left home to work as a pianist at the Lincoln Theater in Dallas. In the early 1920s, she played in gambling parlors, gay hangouts and whorehouses in Galveston and Houston with Blind Lemon Jefferson. Among Spivey's many influences was Ida Cox, herself a sassy blues woman, and taking her cue from Cox, Spivey wrote and recorded tunes like "TB Blues," "Dope Head Blues" and "Organ Grinder Blues" in the 1920s. Spivey's other influences included Robert Calvin, Sara Martin and Bessie Smith. Like so many other women blues singers who had their heyday in the 1920s and '30s, Spivey wasn't afraid to sing sexually suggestive lyrics, and this turned out to be a blessing nearly 40 years later in the sexual revolution of the 1960s and early '70s.

She recorded her first song, "Black Snake Blues," for the OKeh label in 1926, and then worked as a songwriter at a music publishing company in St. Louis in the late 1920s. In the 1930s, Spivey recorded for the Victor, Vocalion, Decca and OKeh labels, and moved to New York City, working as a featured performer in a number of African-American musical revues, including the "Hellzapoppin' Revue." In the 1930s, she recorded and spent time on the road with Louis Armstrong's various bands. By the 1950s, Spivey had left show business and sang only in church. But in forming her own Spivey Records label in 1962, she found new life in her old career. Her first release on her own label featured Bob Dylan as an accompanist. As the folk revival began to take hold in the early 1960s, Spivey found herself an in-demand performer on the folk-blues festival circuit. She also performed frequently in nightclubs around New York City. Unlike others from her generation, Spivey continued her recording career until well into the 1970s, performing at the Ann Arbor Blues and Jazz Festival in 1973 with Roosevelt Sykes. Throughout the 1960s and 1970s, she had an influence on musicians as varied as Dylan, Sparky Rucker, Ralph Rush, Carrie Smith, Edith Johnson and Bonnie Raitt.

Spivey's many albums for Spivey and other labels include the excellent *Songs We Taught Your Mother* (1962), which also includes contributions from Alberta Hunter and Lucille Hegamin, *Idle Hours* (1961), *The Queen and Her Knights* (1965) and *The Victoria Spivey Recorded Legacy of the Blues* (1970).

In 1970, Spivey was awarded a "BMI Commendation of Excellence" from the music publishing organization for her long and outstanding contributions to many worlds of music. After entering Beekman Downtown Hospital with an internal hemorrhage, she died a short while later in 1976. Spivey is buried in Hempstead, NY. —*Richard Skelly*

Recorded Legacy of the Blues / Apr. 27, 1927-Mar. 12, 1937 / Spivey ✦✦✦✦
Victoria Spivey started her own Spivey label in 1961 and ran it successfully for 15 years. This album is the only Spivey release to reissue some of her earlier vintage material. The 14 selections (which give discographical details, although they are not programmed in chronological order) feature the classic blues singer on sessions from 1927-29, 1931 and 1936-37 using such sidemen as guitarists Lonnie Johnson and Tampa Red and trumpeters Louis Armstrong (on "How Do You Do It That Way"), King Oliver, Red Allen and Lee Collins; some of the versions are rare alternate takes. Although it is a pity that all of Spivey's early recordings were not put out by her label, this is a valuable collection. —*Scott Yanow*

And Her Blues, Vol. 2 / Jun. 10, 1961-Jun. 4, 1972 / Spivey ✦✦✦
Victoria Spivey, a classic blues singer of the 1920s, started her own Spivey label in 1961 and kept it going for 15 years. This LP, released posthumously, has three solo performances from 1961 (on which the singer plays either piano or ukulele), a trio rendition of "The Rising Sun" from 1962 with clarinetist Eddie Barefield, four numbers from 1972 in small combos and a loose three-song live performance from 1963 with a guitarist and a kazoo player. Although not essential, the music on this set is enjoyable and should be of interest to jazz historians. —*Scott Yanow*

● **Woman Blues!** / Sep. 1961 / Original Blues Classics ✦✦✦✦✦
Shortly before she formed her own Spivey label, veteran classic blues singer Victoria Spivey made a fine duo album (reissued on CD in the Original Blues Classic series) with guitarist/vocalist Lonnie Johnson whom she had last recorded with back in 1929. Spivey, 55 at the time, is also heard playing piano, and she takes four of the ten selections as solo performances. All of the compositions are hers, including "Christmas Without Santa Claus," "I'm a Red Hot Mama," "Grow Old Together" and "I Got Men All Over This Town." Recommended as a strong example of Victoria Spivey's later work. —*Scott Yanow*

And Her Blues / Feb. 12, 1962 / Spivey ✦✦✦✦✦
Victoria Spivey's first full-length set for her Spivey label is one of her best. Joined by Eddie Barefield (on alto and clarinet) and drummer Pat Wilson, Spivey mostly plays piano, but also has two songs apiece on organ and ukulele. Her singing voice was still in fine form, and she performs a dozen of her own blues (most recently written at the time), including "Grant Spivey," "From Broadway to 7th Avenue," "Cool Papa" and "Buddy Tate." —*Scott Yanow*

A Basket of Blues / Feb. 21, 1962-Aug. 16, 1962 / Spivey ✦✦✦✦
This LP, the first release from the Spivey label, has quite a grab bag of performers. Victoria Spivey and Hannah Sylvester (her only recordings after 1923) take four vocals apiece, while Lucille Hegamin has three (her all classic blues veterans of the 1920s); the backup band includes tenor saxophonist Buddy Tate (who is featured on the lone instrumental "Swingin' Away"), Eddie Barefield on alto and clarinet, pianist Sadik Hakim and (on one song) trumpeter Dick Vance. With the exception of the instrumental and the standard "He May Be Your Man," all of the music was composed by Victoria Spivey. An interesting if increasingly difficult-to-find blues set. —*Scott Yanow*

Three Kings and the Queen / Mar. 14, 1962-1963 / Spivey ✦✦✦
This sampler features pianist Roosevelt Sykes, guitarists Lonnie Johnson and Big Joe Williams, and pianist Victoria Spivey on four vocal selections apiece. With the exception of the closing "Thirteen Hours" (which has Spivey joining Sykes for a piano duet) and a pair of Joe Williams tracks (which utilize the then-unknown harmonica player Bob Dylan), all of the performances are unaccompanied. Although each of the blues greats have recorded more classic performances elsewhere, this obscure LP from the Spivey label has its colorful moments. —*Scott Yanow*

Spivey's Blues Parade / 1963-1965 / Spivey ✦✦✦
This LP is a grab bag of previously unreleased numbers recorded for the Spivey label and put together as a blues revue. There are many all-stars involved, plus fine supporting players including Sippie Wallace (heard on a remake of her hit "I'm a Mighty Tight Woman"), Sonny Boy Williamson, Lonnie Johnson, guitarists John Hammond, Benny Jefferson and Johnny Shines, pianists Sunnyland Slim and Little Brother Montgomery, altoist Eddie Barefield, trumpeter Dick Vance, singers Pat Blackman, Carolina Rose, Nita Washington, Little Sonny Parker and Delsey McKay, harmonica players Bill Dicey, Sugar Blue and Walter "Shakey" Horton, comedian Billy Mitchell and Victoria Spivey herself. Nothing essential occurs, but taken as a whole, it makes for an entertaining show. —*Scott Yanow*

The Queen and Her Knights / Apr. 12, 1965 / Spivey ✦✦✦
Victoria Spivey had an unlikely comeback in the 1960s, emerging from a long period off the blues scene to record frequently and run her own successful Spivey

label. Although known as a classic blues singer, she was flexible enough to record country-blues too, and to hold her own in collaborations with other famous performers. This little-known LP features such immortal bluesmen as guitarist Lonnie Johnson, pianist Little Brother Montgomery, and pianist Memphis Slim, along with guest drummer Sonny Greer. Spivey takes most of the vocals, Montgomery has two, Johnson and Slim are featured on one selection apiece, and Spivey also has vocal duets with Slim ("I'm a Tigress") and Johnson ("Somebody's Got to Go"). Spirited if not quite essential music. —*Scott Yanow*

Spyro Gyra

f. 1974, Buffalo, NY

Group / Crossover Jazz, Fusion

Founded in 1974 by altoist Jay Beckenstein, Spyro Gyra has consistently been one of the commercially successfully pop-jazz groups of the past 20 years. Although originally a studio group, the band became a full-time venture in 1979 and has been touring ever since. Critics love to attack this band's lightweight and rarely changing music, which combines R&B and elements of pop and Caribbean music with jazz, but its live performances are often stimulating—unlike many of its records, which emphasize the danceable melodies at the expense of improvising.

The roots of Spyro Gyra lay in Buffalo, NY, in the early '70s. Beckenstein and his longtime friend, keyboardist Jeremy Wall, had been leading a group with a revolving membership; every one of the many members in the band were loosely involved in the local jazz and rock scenes. Around 1974, the group was beginning to gel and cultivate a following. A club owner who wanted to advertise an upcoming appearance by the band asked Beckenstein for the group's name. The saxophonist told him "Spirogira," a word he learned in a college biology course. The owner misspelled the word as Spyro Gyra, and the band fell into place, featuring Beckentsen, Wall, electric guitarist Chet Catallo, bassist David Wolford, drummer Eli Konikoff and percussionist Gerardo Velez. Not long afterward, the group added keyboardist Tom Schuman.

Spyro Gyra independently funded and recorded their debut album, releasing the record on the local independent label Amherst in 1976. The record slowly became a success and Amherst sold the rights to the band to Infinity Records, a division of MCA. *Morning Dance*, their first album for Infinity, was released in 1979. The record became a huge hit, spawning a Top 40 single with "Morning Dance" and going platinum. In wake of the record's success, Wall retired from live performance, leaving Schuman as the group's main keyboardist; Wall stayed with the band as an assistant producer and occasional composer.

Morning Dance firmly placed Spyro Gyra as one of the most popular artists in contemporary jazz, and throughout the '80s, their popularity continued growing. Their albums were consistent best-sellers, and their concerts often sold out. In 1983, vibraphonist/marimba player Dave Samuels—who had played on several of the group's albums—became a full-fledged member of the band. Over the course of the '80s, the membership of Spyro Gyra fluctuated, but Beckenstein and Schuman remained at its core, keeping the group's signature sound intact.

In 1990, MCA's jazz roster was absorbed by GRP, so Spyro Gyra switched labels, releasing *Fast Forward*, their first album for GRP, later that year. In 1993, Samuels left the touring band, but he continued to play in the studio. By the late '90s, the band featured Beckenstein, Schuman, Julios Fernandez, Joel Rosenblatt and Scott Ambush. —*Scott Yanow & Stephen Thomas Erlewine*

Spyro Gyra / 1976 / MCA ◆◆◆

Collection / 1978-1990 / GRP ◆◆

Over the years, Spyro Gyra's music has ranged from inspired and boldly creative to bloodless and unimaginative—a fact this 1991 retrospective makes abundantly clear. The band is at its risk-taking best on the haunting, Spanish-influenced "Old San Juan," the passionate, Afro-Cuban-flavored "Para Ti Latino" and the driving jazz-rock scorcher "Breakout," but disappoints bitterly on such forgettable, radio-oriented "muzak" as "Catching the Sun" and the Kenny G.-ish "The Unknown Soldier." Exciting one minute and dull the next, this CD illustrates that while leader Jay Beckenstein could have taken his band to great artistic heights, he held it back artistically by so often resorting to formula. —*Alex Henderson*

Morning Dance / MCA ◆◆◆◆

Catching the Sun / 1980 / MCA ◆◆◆◆

One among many similar-sounding but highly popular albums by premier fusion ensemble Spyro Gyra. The group's songs usually contained catchy melodies, prominent backbeats, and some room for improvisational expression, although it was limited and required quick bursts rather than expansive statements. They were and still are near the top in the light jazz and fusion field. —*Ron Wynn*

Carnival / 1980 / MCA ◆◆◆◆

Freetime /1981 / MCA ◆◆◆

Incognito / 1982 / MCA ◆◆◆◆◆

● **Access All Areas** / Nov. 17, 1983+Nov. 19, 1983 / MCA ◆◆◆◆◆

An excellent live double album, it includes live versions of songs from early albums. —*Paul Kohler*

City Kids / 1983 / MCA ◆◆◆◆

Alternating Currents / 1985 / MCA ◆◆◆◆

Featured is great songwriting and playing, and nice work by keyboardist Tom Schuman. —*Paul Kohler*

Breakout / 1986 / MCA ◆◆◆◆◆

An album with more mid-tempo jazz-style tunes and nice arrangements, it features Julio Fernandez and synth programming by Eddie Jobson. —*Paul Kohler*

Stories without Words / 1987 / MCA ◆◆◆

A nice mix of jazz, with tenor and soprano sax melodies that really sing. —*Paul Kohler*

Rites of Summer / 1988 / MCA ◆◆◆

Point of View / 1989 / MCA ◆◆

Fast Forward / 1990 / GRP ◆◆

Three Wishes / 1992 / GRP ◆◆◆

Dreams Beyond Control / 1993 / GRP ◆◆◆◆◆

Spyro Gyra mostly sticks to their formula of danceable melodic music on this GRP release but there are a few temporary departures. The harmonica of the talented Howard Levy is used prominently on "Breakfast at Igor's," two different horn sections pop up on a few songs and there are a pair of throwaway pop vocals from Alex Ligertwood. However, longtime Spyro Gyra fans have little to fear for the solos of saxophonist Jay Beckenstein and vibraphonist Dave Samuels are predictably pleasant, the light funk rhythms push the ensembles and the band's sound remains distinctive, familiar and comfortable. —*Scott Yanow*

Love & Other Obsessions / 1995 / GRP ◆◆

This recording has a couple of changes from Spyro Gyra's usual formula with vibraphonist Dave Samuels no longer a regular member of the popular group (although he does guest on a few tracks) and R&B vocalists being utilized on a few of the selections, dominating two of them. Neither of these alterations have affected the group's sound or approach much. Jay Beckenstein (on alto and soprano) is still the lead voice, the danceable funk rhythms are as mindless as ever and the 11 selections (which clock in between 4:32 and 5:52) are clearly designed for radio airplay. One would think that Beckenstein would have been bored with this automatic pilot music years ago. —*Scott Yanow*

Heart of the Night / 1996 / GRP ◆◆

Road Scholars / 1997 / GRP ◆◆◆◆

As boring and formula-driven as Spyro Gyra has often been in the studio, the band's live shows of the 1980s and 1990s could be just the opposite—exciting, loose and spontaneous. This stems from the fact that on stage, Spyro wasn't catering to commercial radio's rigid formats, and was much more inclined to take risks, improvise and gamble with inspiration. Undeniably Spyro's best release of the 1990s, *Road Scholars* documents its 1997 tour and finds saxman/leader Jay Beckenstein, keyboardist Tom Schuman, guitarist Julio Fernandez and others in generally good form. Spyro sounds inspired rather than calculated on familar material like "Morning Dance" and "Shaker Song," and meaty solos are the rule. *Road Scholars'* only studio offering is "Best Friends," a routine, pedestrian number with a Najee-meets-George Howard flavor. But on the whole, the release of this CD proved to be a pleasant surprise. —*Alex Henderson*

20/20 / 1997 / GRP ◆◆◆

Artistically, Spyro Gyra hit an all-time low in the mid-1990s. The use of outside arrangers and pop vocalists had proven detrimental, and the band was sounding even more formulaic than usual on banal albums like 1995's *Love and Other Obsessions*. More self-contained and devoid of adult contemporary singing, *20/20* is a slight improvement. Though Spyro still sounds contrived and is hardly challenging, a few of the songs are somewhat likable, including the moody "The Unwritten Letter" and the angular "Rockaway to Sunset." Dave Samuels, once a full-time member, makes a guest appearance on the salsa-influenced "South American Sojourn" and the Brazilian-ish "Dark-Eyed Lady"—both of which, although pleasant enough, aren't nearly as interesting as the music he'd been creating in the Caribbean Jazz Project. And, not surprisingly, fluffy "elevator muzak" such as "Together" sounds like it was designed for only one purpose: radio airplay. —*Alex Henderson*

Jess Stacy

b. Aug. 11, 1904, Bird's Point, MO, **d.** Jan. 5, 1994, Los Angeles, CA

Piano / Swing

One of the great swing pianists, Jess Stacy's greatest moment of fame was an unexpected one, when during the latter part of "Sing, Sing, Sing" at Benny Goodman's historic 1938 Carnegie Hall Concert, the clarinetist motioned to Stacy to take a solo (which he never had previously on that song). The pianist constructed a remarkable impressionistic improvisation that stole solo honors and was fortunately documented (and released for the first time in 1950). A mostly self-taught player who performed on riverboats during the early '20s, Stacy was part of the fertile Chicago jazz scene of the 1920s with his style being influenced by both Earl Hines and Bix Beiderbecke. Still obscure when he joined Goodman's big band in 1935, the pianist soon became well-known as one of BG's top sidemen, working with him through 1939 and on and off during the next five years. Stacy also spent time with the bands of Bob Crosby, Horace Heidt and Tommy Dorsey, recorded with Eddie Condon, did some solo recordings of his own (starting in 1935), had a short-lived marriage to singer Lee Wiley and tried twice to lead big bands of his own. He became fairly obscure after moving to California in 1947 (mostly playing in piano bars) and in 1963 Stacy retired from music altogether, only to return briefly on a few special occasions (and for two Chiaroscuro recordings) over the next 20 years. —*Scott Yanow*

● **Jess Stacy 1935-1939** / Nov. 16, 1935-Nov. 30, 1939 / Classics ✦✦✦✦✦

Pianist Jess Stacy did not lead that many recording sessions during the swing era since he spent long periods playing with the big bands of Benny Goodman and Bob Crosby. This excellent CD contains his 21 selections as a leader from a four-year period. Stacy's three numbers from 1935 include a solo Bix Beiderbecke medley and two songs with bassist Israel Crosby and drummer Gene Krupa. In addition this set has Stacy's eight piano solos for Commodore, a duet with Bud Freeman on tenor ("She's Funny That Way") and eight very rare performances (plus an alternate take) cut for Varsity in 1939 that also feature trumpeter Billy Butterfield, tenor saxophonist Eddie Miller and either clarinetist Hank d'Amico or Irving Fazola in an octet. This CD contains more than its share of gems. —*Scott Yanow*

Piano Solos / Nov. 16, 1935-Mar. 3, 1956 / Swaggie ✦✦✦✦✦

1935-1956. Includes a nice cross-section of influential, fine Stacy cuts. —*Ron Wynn*

Jess Stacy and Friends / Apr. 30, 1938-Nov. 25, 1944 / Commodore ✦✦✦✦✦

Pianist Jess Stacy's Commodore recordings are reissued in full on this single CD. Stacy is heard during 1938-39 playing solos (Bix Beiderbecke's "Candlelights," "You're Driving Me Crazy" and five of his originals), performing a duo version of "She's Funny That Way" with tenor saxophonist Bud Freeman, accompanying his wife, singer Lee Wiley (along with cornetist Muggsy Spanier), on memorable versions of "Down to Steamboat Tennessee" and "Sugar," and performing six numbers (four standards and two originals) with drummer Specs Powell in 1944. Although not quite essential (certainly not the false starts!), collectors will find the step-by-step recreation of the session to be quite intriguing, for Jess Stacy was a strong improviser. The final versions of the standards (only "Jumpin' with Jess" and "Blue Notion" are originals) are near-classic, with the pianist heard in prime form. —*Scott Yanow*

Blue Notion / Oct. 6, 1944 / Jazzology ✦✦✦✦

On October 6, 1944, pianist Jess Stacy (along with bassist Bob Casey and drummer George Wettling) recorded extensively in the studio for the World Broadcasting Systems, making transcriptions to be played on the radio. This Jazzology LP has literally all of the music performed that day: 11 different songs with ten issued versions, three unissued renditions, four incomplete performances and seven false starts. Although not quite essential (certainly not the false starts!), collectors will find the step-by-step recreation of the session to be quite intriguing, for Jess Stacy was a strong improviser. The final versions of the standards (only "Jumpin' with Jess" and "Blue Notion" are originals) are near-classic, with the pianist heard in prime form. —*Scott Yanow*

Stacy 'n' Sutton /Apr. 10 1951-Jun. 3, 1953 / Affinity ✦✦✦✦

Two different classic pianists are featured on this LP from the British Affinity label. Jess Stacy is heard with a quartet in 1951 that also includes rhythm guitarist George Van Eps, bassist Morty Corb and drummer Nick Fatool, performing eight veteran swing standards. The great stride pianist Ralph Sutton, who had recorded his first solo sides just four years earlier, plays eight duets with drummer Cliff Leeman from 1953. The fresher material (which includes pieces associated with Fats Waller, Willie "The Lion" Smith, Bob Zurke and James P. Johnson) gives Sutton the edge over Stacy, but all of the music on the unrelated sessions is quite enjoyable and worthy of eventual reissue on CD. —*Scott Yanow*

A Tribute to Benny Goodman / Apr. 15, 1954-Oct. 6, 1955 / Atlantic ✦✦✦✦

This album was one of pianist Jess Stacy's last (he would soon drift into semi-retirement), even though he was only 50 at the time and lived until 1994. Stacy leads a reunion of swing veterans (most of whom had formerly been with Benny Goodman) in a nonet including trumpeter Ziggy Elman (on one of his last signifi-

cant sessions) and either Vido Musso or Babe Russin on tenor. In addition, Stacy is showcased on four trio numbers. With few exceptions ("Gee Baby Ain't I Good to You" and "Blues for Otis Ferguson"), the music is all taken from the repertoire of Benny Goodman's swing band, including "King Porter Stomp," "When Buddha Smiles," "Roll 'Em," "Don't Be That Way" and a brief "Sing, Sing, Sing." Easily recommended to swing collectors. —*Scott Yanow*

Stacy Still Swings / Jul. 5, 1974-Jul. 20, 1977 / Chiaroscuro ✦✦✦✦

At the time he recorded this music (which has been reissued on CD), pianist Jess Stacy had been retired from music for 14 years and had just returned to the spotlight briefly for a Carnegie Hall concert. On what would be his next-to-last record as a leader, Stacy concentrates mostly on relaxed tempos, playing in a piano style virtually unchanged from his early years. Stacy performs a set of standards plus five originals. A special bonus (in addition to the four previously unreleased tracks, which are highlighted by a sparkling "Riverboat Shuffle") is the inclusion of a lengthy and fascinating essay by Whitney Balliett that covers virtually the pianist's entire life. —*Scott Yanow*

Stacy's Still Swingin' / 1977 / Chiaroscuro ✦✦✦✦

Not to be confused with the previous album *Stacy Still Swings*, this solo LP was Jess Stacy's final recording (other than an appearance on Marian McPartland's *Piano Jazz* radio show); he had been semi-retired already for nearly 20 years. Stacy's absence from the jazz scene was quite unfortunate, for the veteran pianist still had plenty of life in his playing, as he shows throughout the well-rounded set. Highlights include "Stacy's Still Swinging," "100 Years from Today," "After You've Gone" and "What Is There to Say." —*Scott Yanow*

Terell Stafford

b. , Downingtown, PA

Trumpet / Hard Bop, Post-Bop

At this point, trumpeter Terell Stafford is best known for his five years touring and recording with Bobby Watson's quintet Horizon. Stafford, who graduated from the University of Maryland, has been the director of bands at Cheyney University since 1992. In addition to Watson, he has played with Herbie Mann, Shirley Scott and Kenny Barron, among others. Terell Stafford made his recording debut as a leader for Candid in 1995 and shows strong potential for the future. —*Scott Yanow*

● **Terrell Stafford** / Mar. 8, 1995-Mar. 9, 1995 / Candid ✦✦✦✦

Centripetal Force / Oct. 14, 1996-Oct. 15, 1996 / Candid ✦✦✦✦✦

Marvin Stamm

b. May 23, 1939, Memphis, TN

Trumpet, Fluegelhorn / Hard Bop

An excellent bop-based trumpeter and a busy session player during much of his career, Marvin Stamm has long been a flexible player. He started on trumpet when he was 12 and later studied at North Texas State University. Stamm was with Stan Kenton's Mellophonium Orchestra during 1961-63 (getting occasional solos) and played with Woody Herman during 1965-66. He gained some recognition for his playing with the Thad Jones/Mel Lewis Orchestra (1966-72) but spent much of his time during the next two decades in the studios. Stamm, who performed with Benny Goodman during 1974-75 and toured with George Gruntz's Concert Jazz Band in 1987, has in recent years concentrated much more on jazz playing and his Music Masters releases are good examples of his talents. —*Scott Yanow*

Machinations / Apr. 16, 1968-Apr. 24, 1968 / Verve ✦✦✦

Trumpeter Marvin Stamm's debut as a leader (he would not head another date until 1983) is an adventurous set in which he is backed by a big band arranged and conducted by Johnny Carisi. Six of the nine compositions are Carisi's; the others are Al Kooper's "Flute Thing," Rodgers and Hammerstein's "March of the Siamese Children" and the pop hit "Sunny." While the 29-year-old Stamm is the main soloist, there are also spots for guitarist Joe Beck, pianist Dick Hyman, trombonist Urbie Green, and Mortie Lewis on tenor and flute. This underrated and generally overlooked LP deserves to be reissued on CD. —*Scott Yanow*

Stampede / 1983 / Palo Alto ✦✦✦

Bop Boy / Jan. 5, 1990-Jan. 6, 1990 / Music Masters ✦✦✦✦✦

On this CD, trumpeter Marvin Stamm gathered together some notable players (tenor saxophonist Bob Mintzer, pianist Phil Markowitz, bassist Lincoln Goines and drummer Terry Clarke) for post-bop explorations of five Mintzer tunes, one song apiece by Markowitz, Kenny Wheeler and Lars Jansson, plus two standards ("My Ship" and "Lover Man"). Stamm and Mintzer make for a compatible and mutually inspiring team, and the results should please collectors of advanced straightahead jazz. —*Scott Yanow*

● **Mystery Man** / Sep. 3, 1992-Sep. 4, 1992 / Music Masters ✦✦✦✦✦

Trumpeter Marvin Stamm, rather than drag out the usual bebop standards, mostly introduces new material on his CD. Four songs are played by Berg's quartet with pianist Bill Charlap, bassist Mike Richmond and drummer Terry Clarke, six add Bob Mintzer's tenor, and of those songs three find Bob Malach (on tenor and soprano) making the band a sextet. Because Stamm paid as much attention to varying tempos and moods as he did to changing the instrumentation, this set holds one's interest throughout, swinging hard in a modern fashion. —*Scott Yanow*

State Street Ramblers

f. 1928, db. 1931

Group / Classic Jazz

The name "State Street Ramblers" was used for four different overlapping groups that recorded in 1928 and 1931. The first session features clarinetist Johnny Dodds but most of the other performances (which include such musicians as cornetist Natty Dominique, pianist Jimmy Blythe, trombonist Roy Palmer, clarinetist Darnell Howard and either W.E. Burton or Alfred Bell on kazoo and vocals) were more primitive. These good-time sessions are quite spirited and fun; all of their recordings are available on a pair of RST CDs. —*Scott Yanow*

● **State Street Ramblers, Vol. 1** / Aug. 12, 1927-Mar. 19, 1931 / RST ✦✦✦✦

The Austrian RST label has on two CDs reissued the complete output of the State Street Ramblers, a primitive but very spirited series of groups that recorded during 1927-28 and 1931 under that name. The first set has three selections that feature clarinetist Johnny Dodds and cornetist Natty Dominique in a quartet, Natty is showcased on six other erratic numbers (his solo on "Tack It Down" is hilariously bad), there is a sextet with alto, clarinet and the humorous vocal interjections of W.E. Burton and, for the final selections, three exciting numbers in which trombonist Roy Palmer dominates. Although not essential, fans of early jazz will want these occasionally riotous performances. —*Scott Yanow*

● **State Street Ramblers, Vol. 2** / Mar. 19, 1931-Apr. 3, 1936 / RST ✦✦✦✦✦

On the second of two CDs put out by the Austrian RST label, there is a very generous amount (26 songs) of enjoyable vintage music. Nine numbers feature the 1931 version of the State Street Ramblers which matched together the great percussive trombonist Roy Palmer with Darnell Howard (who doubles on alto and clarinet) and has plenty of spirit and drive. In addition there are 13 songs from the Memphis Nighthawks in 1932 and four by the 1936 Chicago Rhythm Kings; both groups are similar in style and also have plenty of space for Roy Palmer's unique playing. A special treat is a previously unreleased trombone-piano duet "The Trombone Slide." Heartily recommended to collectors of the era. —*Scott Yanow*

Statesmen of Jazz

f. 1994

Group / Classic Jazz

This remarkable group, put together in 1994 by the American Federation of Jazz Societies, features veteran jazz players, all of whom are at least 65 yet are still in their musical prime. Their one recording hints at the band's potential. Most notable among the personnel are 87-year-old violinist Claude Williams and Benny Waters who, at age 93, proved to still be a powerful altoist. —*Scott Yanow*

● **Statesmen of Jazz** / Dec. 20, 1994 / AFJS ✦✦✦✦✦

This is a rather historic recording, for it finds altoist Benny Waters, the oldest active jazz musician at a month shy of 93, in surprisingly fiery form; his feature on "Blue Waters" is easily the high point. The other members of the Statesmen of Jazz (a group sponsored by the American Federation of Jazz Societies) are all senior citizens too: violinist Claude Williams (86), fluegelhornist Clark Terry (74), trumpeter Joe Wilder (72), trombonist Al Grey (69), tenor saxophonist Buddy Tate (79), pianist Jane Jarvis (79), bassist Milt Hinton (84) and drummer Panama Francis (76). Although Tate was a little past his prime and Wilder a bit erratic due to recent dental surgery, this is a particularly infectious date of well-played swing. Waters, Williams and Terry take solo honors. Recommended. —*Scott Yanow*

Dakota Staton (Aliyah Rabia)

b. Jun. 3, 1932, Pittsburgh, PA

Vocals / Standards, Traditional Pop, Vocal Jazz

Dakota Staton gained a strong reputation as a soulful jazz singer early in her career, and although she has never broken through to become a truly major name, she has retained her popularity for several decades. Staton studied voice at the Filion School of Music in Pittsburgh. Her performance at a jam session in Harlem led to her signing with Capitol in 1954 and winning Downbeat's New Star award the following year. Staton's 1957 recording of "The Late Late Show" became her biggest hit. Although she never duplicated that song's commercial success, Staton

recorded steadily for Capitol through 1961 (including an album with George Shearing) and made worthwhile recordings for United Artists (1963-64), Groove Merchant (1973-74) and in the 1990s for Muse. Her timeless style remains largely unchanged from 40 years ago. —*Scott Yanow*

● **The Late, Late Show** / Feb. 28, 1957+Mar. 2, 1957 / Capitol ✦✦✦✦✦

Singer Dakota Staton's first full-length album was one of her best. She had a hit with "The Late, Late Show" and performed memorable versions of "Broadway," "A Foggy Day," "What Do You See in Her," "My Funny Valentine" and "Mooney." Backed by a largely unidentified orchestra arranged by Van Alexander (with Hank Jones on piano), Staton sounds both youthful and mature, displaying a highly appealing voice on a near-classic set. This LP is long overdue to be reissued on CD. —*Scott Yanow*

● **Dakota Staton** / Feb. 7, 1990-Feb. 8, 1990 / Muse ✦✦✦✦✦

Although Dakota Staton recorded extensively from 1954-61 for Capitol and 1963-64 for United Artists, her earlier recordings are almost all out of print and difficult to find. This 1991 CD finds the singer still in prime form, assisted on most tracks by tenor saxophonist Houston Person, pianist Bross Townsend, bassist Fred Hunter and drummer Paula Hampton. Staton performs a wide variety of music ranging from swing standards ("Mean to Me" and "Body and Soul") and blues to more current material ("The Thrill Is Gone" and "This Bitter Earth"). No matter what the source, Staton gives each of the tunes soul, swing, the proper amount of emotion, and a bluesy feeling. Recommended. —*Scott Yanow*

Darling Please Save Your Love / Oct. 3, 1991 / Muse ✦✦✦✦

Isn't This a Lovely Day / Dec. 23, 1992 / Muse ✦✦✦✦

Lou Stein (Louis Stein)

b. Apr. 22, 1922, Philadelphia, PA

Piano / Bop, Swing

Although a swing-oriented pianist, Lou Stein has always been able to fit comfortably in Dixieland, bop and commercial settings. His first major association was with Ray McKinley's band in 1942. While in the service Stein played domestically with Glenn Miller's Army Air Force Band although he did not go overseas. He gained recognition for his work with Charlie Ventura (1946-47) and for his most famous composition "East of Suez." After that period ended, Stein became a studio musician but found time to perform and record with the Lawson-Haggart band, Benny Goodman, Sarah Vaughan, the Sauter-Finegan orchestra, Louie Bellson, Red Allen, Coleman Hawkins and Lester Young in addition to recording a few albums as a leader. In later years he played with Joe Venuti (1969-72), Flip Phillips and recorded his own 1994 album for Pullen. —*Scott Yanow*

Tribute to Tatum / 1976 / Chiaroscuro ✦✦✦✦✦

This LP finds Lou Stein doing the impossible (and certainly improbable): duplicating note for note a dozen Art Tatum solos. Stein mostly stuck to Tatum's 1930s recordings (when Art was at the peak of his creativity); among the Tatum solos that he brought back to life are "Elegy," "Begin the Beguine," "Humoresque" and "The Man I Love" (wisely leaving out the much-too-incredible rendition of "Tiger Rag"). Lou Stein worked several years on perfecting these improvisations, and this Chiaroscuro album is quite unique in its own way. —*Scott Yanow*

Stompin' 'Em Down / 1978 / Chiaroscuro ✦✦✦✦

Lou Stein & Friends / 1980 / World Jazz ✦✦✦✦

The versatile pianist Lou Stein teams up with bassist Milt Hinton, drummer Connie Kay and (on four songs apiece) guitarist Bucky Pizzarelli and clarinetist Kenny Davern for a set of swing standards. The performers are concise (only "Honeysuckle Rose" exceeds four minutes) and relaxed, but there is plenty of variety in tempos and moods. Other than "Honeysuckle Rose," the highlights of the out-of-print LP include a tender "I'll Be Seeing You," "A Foggy Day," "What Is This Thing Called Love" and "Let's Face the Music and Dance." —*Scott Yanow*

Temple of the Gods / 1980 / Chiaroscuro ✦✦✦

The most significant aspect to this quartet outing by pianist Lou Stein is that he performs six of his own originals; only "East of Suez" is particularly well-known (the others are more recent). Stein, who doubles on electric piano during the date, plays much more modern and contemporary than one might expect. While bassist Frank Gravitz and drummer Bobby Rosengarden provide fine backing, tenor saxophonist Al Klink (an alumnus of Glenn Miller's Orchestra) has a rare opportunity to stretch out. Pity that this worthwhile LP is long out of print. —*Scott Yanow*

Live at the Dome / Jan. 17, 1981 / Dreamstreet ✦✦✦✦

For this fine trio LP with bassist Bob Haggart and drummer Butch Miles cut for the now-defunct Dreamstreet label, pianist Lou Stein performs five standards (including "Who Cares" and "Take the 'A' Train") and three of his little-known but worthy originals. The music is adventurous and unpredictable in spots, but also swings hard on the romps and sensitively for the ballads. Lou Stein has always deserved much greater recognition for his talents and versatility than he has received. —*Scott Yanow*

Solo / Jan. 28, 1984-Jan. 29, 1984 / Audiophile ✦✦✦✦
This excellent outing (thus far not reissued on CD) features the underrated but talented pianist Lou Stein on a solo set. Among the high points of Stein's diverse recital are the Dixieland standard "Hindustan," "Yesterdays," his "greatest hit" "East of Suez," Bix Beiderbecke's "In a Mist" and the very advanced "Skyscraper." Well worth checking out. —*Scott Yanow*

● **Go Daddy!** / 1994 / Pullen Music ✦✦✦✦✦
Pianist Lou Stein's first record as a leader in quite a few years is an excellent all-around showcase both for his solo and trio playing (with bassists Jeff Fuller or Brian Torff and drummers Joe Cucuzzo or Todd Strait) and for his composing; in addition to ten standards, there are six Stein originals on this fine CD. Although his daughter Elise Stein gets nearly equal billing, she only sings on about a third of the set, leaving the spotlight firmly on the veteran and still very viable pianist. Highlights include "Lullaby of the Leaves," "Deed I Do," "Here's That Rainy Day" and Stein's "greatest hit, "East of Suez." A fine outing. —*Scott Yanow*

Steps Ahead

f. 1979
Group / Fusion, Post-Bop
Originally called Steps when it was formed in 1979 by vibraphonist Mike Mainieri, this group at various times has included tenor saxophonist Michael Brecker, keyboardists Don Grolnick, Elaine Elias and Rachel Z, guitarist Mike Stern, bassists Eddie Gomez and Darryl Jones and drummers Peter Erskine and Steve Smith among others. Its music combines advanced jazz, R&B, rock and fusion and is frequently exciting. Steps Ahead was most active during 1979-86 although it still existed on a part-time basis in the mid-'90s. —*Scott Yanow*

Step by Step / Dec. 8, 1980-Dec. 10, 1980 / Denon ✦✦✦✦
This killer group consists of Michael Brecker (ts), Steve Gadd (d), Eddie Gomez (b) Don Grolnick (p), and Mike Mainieri (vibes). One of three releases available from Japan only, this excellent recording was recorded in the studio under the name Steps. —*Paul Kohler*

Smokin' in the Pit: Live! / Dec. 14, 1980-Dec. 16, 1980 / Denon ✦✦✦✦✦

Paradox / 1982 / Denon ✦✦✦✦

Steps Ahead / Jul. 1983 / Elektra ✦✦✦✦

● **Modern Times** / Jan. 1984-Feb. 1984 / Elektra ✦✦✦✦✦

Magnetic / 1985-1986 / Elektra ✦✦✦
The last Steps Ahead recording to feature Michael Brecker, this album finds the band exploring the use of electronic instruments and synthesis. Michael Brecker's use of the Akai E.W.I. (electronic wind instrument) is astonishing. —*Paul Kohler*

Live in Tokyo 1986 / Jul. 30, 1986 / NYC ✦✦
This Steps Ahead concert (which has long been available on laser disc) has both good and bad points. Michael Brecker's virtuosic tenor solos show a great deal of passion and creativity within the genre. Also Mike Maineri's vibes are an attractive part of the ensemble sound, making the R&Bish unit sound like Spyro Gyra with guts. Unfortunately the rhythm section (which consists of guitarist Mike Stern, bassist Darryl Jones and drummer Steve Smith) is never subtle, the rhythms are bombastic and the electronics (including at one point a drum machine) are excessive. The solos might be fiery but the unimaginative backup makes this potentially super band often sound run of the mill and monotonous. There are much better Steps Ahead concerts to preserve than this one. —*Scott Yanow*

N.Y.C. / 1989 / Intuition ✦✦✦
Decent fusion, jazz-rock, and instrumental pop from the East Coast band whose personnel has fluctuated over the years. This edition didn't include Brecker and instead revolved around vibist and keyboardist Mike Manieri. The band played the usual pop and fusion compositions with its usual competence. —*Ron Wynn*

Yin-Yang / 1992 / NYC ✦✦✦✦

Vibe / 1994 / NYC ✦✦✦✦

Leni Stern

b. Germany
Guitar / Post-Bop
Leni Stern, who has thus far received more recognition for her composing than for her guitar playing, has managed to carve out her own musical personality despite being married to fellow guitarist Mike Stern (a potential dominant influence). She began classical piano lessons when she was six but was much more inspired a few years later when she discovered a guitar in the attic and taught herself to play jazz. Stern's early years were actually spent as an actress in her native Germany,

featured on a national television show. However she took a summer off in 1977 to enroll at Berklee, and she never returned to acting. Stern lived in Boston until 1980, moved to New York and has worked steadily in clubs ever since, recording for Passport (now defunct), Enja and Lipstick. —*Scott Yanow*

Clairvoyant / Dec. 16, 1985-Dec. 17, 1985 / Passport ✦✦✦✦
Leni Stern's debut as a leader is most notable for two guitar duets ("Someday My Prince Will Come" and "Stella by Starlight") with her teacher, Bill Frisell. The duets act as a change of pace on a moody program otherwise comprising six Stern originals and featuring the two guitars, tenor saxophonist Bob Berg, pianist Larry Willis, bassist Harvie Swartz and drummer Paul Motian. A fine set of post-bop music that served as a good start to Leni Stern's solo career. —*Scott Yanow*

The Next Day / 1987 / Passport ✦✦✦
Leni Stern's second album as a leader (cut for the defunct Passport label and now a bit of a collector's item) features the guitarist/composer using four of the same five sidemen as she had on her debut, *Clairvoyant:* tenor saxophonist Bob Berg, pianist Larry Willis, bassist Harvie Swartz and drummer Paul Motian. Hiram Bullock adds his rhythm guitar to one piece. The absence of guitarist Bill Frisell (an important ingredient on the previous record) leaves a bit of a gap, since Leni Stern was at this point more distinctive as a composer (contributing all of the eight pieces except "Blue Monk") than she was as a guitarist. —*Scott Yanow*

Secrets / Sep. 24, 1988-Oct. 1, 1988 / Enja ✦✦✦✦
Leni Stern utilizes such impressive sidemen as fellow guitarist Wayne Krantz, tenor saxophonist Bob Berg, Lincoln Goines or Harvie Swartz on bass and drummer Dennis Chambers on eight selections, all but one being her originals. The music ranges from a three-guitar jam on "Groundhog" (which adds blues guitarist Dave Tronzo) to a song dedicated to Jaco Pastorius ("Who Loves You") and the melancholy strut "Maybe." Overall this set of music holds one's interest even if Stern was at this point a stronger composer than guitarist. —*Scott Yanow*

● **Closer to the Light** / Dec. 1989 / Enja ✦✦✦✦✦
Leni Stern had grown considerably as a soloist by the time she recorded her fourth album, *Closer to the Light*. The jazz/pop-rock guitarist already had a very recognizable sound—light, lyrical and definitely Pat Metheny-influenced, yet distinctively her own. But with *Light*, her improvising sounded more confident and assured. Stern's sympathetic company includes David Sanborn (alto sax), Paul Socolow (bass), Dennis Chambers (drums) and fellow guitarist Wayne Krantz (with whom she has often joined forces). Stern and Krantz seem an unlikely combination—in contrast to her subtlety and softness, Krantz can be very muscular and has made the mistake of overpowering her at times. But that's never a problem on this generally relaxed date, which offers additional proof of Stern's thoughtfulness as a composer. —*Alex Henderson*

Ten Songs / Oct. 1991 / Lipstick ✦✦✦✦

Like One / 1993 / Lipstick ✦✦✦
It isn't elitism that makes many in the jazz hardcore shudder whenever the word "fusion" is mentioned; it is the attempt to define any and everything instrumental as jazz, regardless of sound, structure, intent and content. Guitarist Leni Stern clearly has improvisational skills, and there are certainly songs on his current session designed in a jazz context. But neither Sting's "Every Breath You Take" nor Joni Mitchell's "Court and Spark" qualify; these are clearly pop covers, done with little or no jazz sensibility. Other songs reveal Stern's penchant for light, finely played voicings and bluesy chords, and includes some fervent blowing from tenor saxophonist Bob Malach. There is a lot on this session that is entertaining and commendable; just don't call the Sting cover jazz. —*Ron Wynn*

Words / Dec. 10, 1994-Feb. 9, 1995 / Lipstick ✦✦✦✦

Mike Stern

b. Jan. 10, 1953, Boston, MA
Guitar / Fusion, Post-Bop
A rocking, experimental guitarist who rose to fame playing in a pair of Miles Davis' bands, Mike Stern's a competent bebop and hard-bop player, but excellent fusion and jazz-rock musician. He's provided some wondrous riffs, blistering lines, complex voicings and dynamite phrases doing fusion, playing with much more force and vigor than on more conventional jazz. Stern attended Berklee in the early '70s, where he studied with Pat Metheny and Mick Goodrick. Metheny recommended him for a vacancy with Blood, Sweat and Tears, and Stern played with them two years. He later worked with Billy Cobham, then joined Davis' band in 1981. Stern stayed with him two years, then played with Jaco Pastorius' group "Word of Mouth." Stern made his recording debut as a leader in 1985; He later toured with Davis again, played with Steps Ahead, and worked in bands led by Mike Brecker and Harvie Swartz. Stern has recorded as a leader for Atlantic in the '80s and '90s. He has several sessions available as a leader. —*Ron Wynn and Michael G. Nastos*

Upside Downside / Mar. 1986-Apr. 1986 / Atlantic ✦✦✦

Time in Place / Dec. 1987 / Atlantic ✦✦✦✦
With Michael Brecker (sax) and Bob Berg (ts). "Gossip" a good opening track. —*Michael G. Nastos*

Jigsaw / Feb. 1989 / Atlantic ✦✦✦✦
High-powered jazz-rock with the emphasis on rock. —*Michael G. Nastos*

Odds or Evens / 1991 / Atlantic ✦✦✦✦
This is a powerhouse date of high-powered fusion, mixing together the sound of rock with the musicianship and improvising of jazz. With the assistance of tenor saxophonist Bob Berg, keyboardist Jim Beard and a rhythm section, guitarist Stern jams through a set of originals that serve as jumping-off devices for fairly long solos. The musicians really stretch themselves within the idiom and even the quieter numbers are full of intensity. —*Scott Yanow*

● **Standards (and Other Songs)** / 1992 / Atlantic ✦✦✦✦✦
Guitarist Mike Stern, best known for playing rock-oriented fusion and in more commercial settings, surprised many listeners by recording an album dominated by standards. Actually there are three originals included among the 11 pieces but Stern also digs into such songs as "Like Someone in Love," "Moment's Notice," Chick Corea's "Windows" and "Straight, No Chaser." Among Stern's sidemen on this fairly straightahead but adventurous set are trumpeter Randy Brecker, Bob Berg on tenor, and keyboardist Gil Goldstein. This little-known release is well worth acquiring before it inevitably goes out of print. —*Scott Yanow*

Is What It Is / 1993 / Atlantic ✦✦✦✦
Mike Stern is one of the more creative fusion guitarists, playing with the power of rock but often taking sophisticated improvisations. On this passionate set (which consists of nine of his originals), Stern is joined by the keyboards of Jim Beard, bassist Will Lee, Dennis Chambers or Ben Perowsky on drums and (on three songs apiece) the tenors of Michael Brecker and Bob Malach. Overall this is one of Mike Stern's better recordings. —*Scott Yanow*

Between the Lines / Feb. 27, 1996 / Atlantic ✦✦✦✦

Give and Take / 1997 / Atlantic ✦✦✦
This is a relatively straightahead set by the distinctive guitarist Mike Stern, whose airy sound seems quite fresh in this context. Stern performs three standards ("I Love You," "Giant Steps" and "Oleo"), Jimi Hendrix's "Who Knows," and six originals, mostly in a trio with bassist John Patitucci and drummer Jack DeJohnette. Percussionist Don Alias helps out on a few tracks; pianist Gil Goldstein is on two, and tenor great Michael Brecker nearly steals the show with three high-powered solos. Actually, the biggest surprise is "That's What You Think," a straightahead blues that has a very credible alto solo from guest David Sanborn. All in all, an excellent outing. —*Scott Yanow*

Bill Stewart

b. 1967, Des Moines, IA
Drums / Post-Bop
Drummer Bill Stewart, best known for his association with John Scofield, had a very impressive recording debut as a leader with *Snide Remarks* in 1995, a date featuring Scofield and Joe Lovano. Stewart first started on drums when he was seven and from an early age he listened steadily to jazz. At William Patterson College during 1986-88, Stewart studied with Dave Samuels, Harold Mabern, Rufus Reid and Joe Lovano. He made his first recording with tenorman Scott Kreitzer, cut a pair of best-selling albums with Maceo Parker, freelanced a bit and then spent five years with Scofield's band. *Telepathy* appeared in 1997. —*Scott Yanow*

Snide Remarks / Feb. 21, 1995-Feb. 22, 1995 / Blue Note ✦✦✦✦
Drummer Bill Stewart, formerly with John Scofield, composed all nine selections on his Blue Note disc. Rhythmically they are generally quite tricky with "Fred and Ginger" in 5/4 time and "7.5" not named after an earthquake but the fact that each chorus is 72 bars long (or in 30/4 time). The weak point to this music is that Stewart, though expert at setting moods (which range from hyper to melancholy), is not a gifted melodist; certainly none of the themes on this set could be considered memorable. However it is the strong musicianship and solowork (particularly by the great tenor Joe Lovano and trumpeter Eddie Henderson) that make this a worthy set. Stewart's quirky modern mainstream structures really challenge the players and they prove up to the task. —*Scott Yanow*

Telepathy / Mar. 11, 1997 / Blue Note ✦✦✦✦✦
Drummer Bill Stewart (best known for having formerly been a regular member of John Scofield's group) has been developing into a notable bandleader and composer himself. In fact, seven of the nine numbers on this CD are his (they are joined by Jackie McLean's "Little Melonae" and an eccentric version of Thelonious Monk's "Rhythm-A-Ning"), and the interesting and unusual structures clearly inspire Stewart's sidemen to some of their best playing. Steve Wilson (on alto and

soprano), tenor saxophonist Seamus Blake, pianist Bill Carrothers and bassist Larry Grenadier are all up-and-coming players, and someday this CD may be looked upon as an all-star group. The post-bop solos and occasional surprises make the stimulating set easily recommended. —*Scott Yanow*

Bob Stewart

b. Feb. 3, 1945, Sioux Falls, SD
Tuba / Post-Bop, Bop
A virtuoso tuba player, Bob Stewart's solos explore its full range and show its ability to serve as both a lead and support instrument within the jazz ensemble. He rivals Howard Johnson in terms of demonstrating depth, facility and imagination on tuba. Stewart began playing trumpet at ten, and studied trumpet and tuba at the Philadelphia College of the Performing Arts. He taught in the public school system in Pennsylvania, then later played in a traditional jazz band at a Philadelphia club. Stewart moved to New York in the late '60s, and joined the tuba ensemble Substructure. He played with Carla Bley, Frank Foster's Loud Minority, and the orchestras of Sam Rivers and Gil Evans in the late '60s. Stewart was a featured member of Arthur Blythe's mid-'70s band that recorded for Columbia, and also worked with the Globe Unity Orchestra, Charles Mingus and McCoy Tyner. Stewart played with David Murray's big band, Lester Bowie's Brass Fantasy and Henry Threadgill's orchestra in the '80s and into the '90s in addition to performing with Howard Johnson's all-tuba group Gravity. —*Ron Wynn*

● **First Line** / Nov. 1987 / JMT ✦✦✦✦✦

Goin' Home / Dec. 1988 / JMT ✦✦✦✦✦
The second recording by tuba player Bob Stewart's First Line Band is even better than the first. In 1988, Stewart's group also included trumpeter James Zoller, trombonist Steve Turre, guitarist Jerome Harris and either Buddy Williams or Ed Blackwell on drums; trumpeter Earl Gardner and John Clark on French horn have guest spots on this CD. The music ranges from the straightforward swing of Don Cherry's "Art Deco" and a good-humored "Sweet Georgia Brown" to a 12-minute exploration of Billy Harper's "Priestess" and originals by Stewart, Olu Dara and Kelvyn Bell. Stimulating and often-surprising music that is generally more accessible than one might expect. —*Scott Yanow*

Rex Stewart (William Stewart, Jr.)

b. Feb. 22, 1907, Philadelphia, PA, **d.** Sep. 7, 1967, Los Angeles, CA
Cornet / Dixieland, Swing
Rex Stewart achieved his greatest glory in a subsidiary role, playing cornet 11 years in the Duke Ellington Orchestra. His famous "talking" style, and half-valve effects were exploited brilliantly by countless Ellington pieces containing perfect passages tailored to showcase Stewart's sound. He played in a forceful, gripping manner that reflected the influence of Louis Armstrong, Bubber Miley and Bix Beiderbecke, whose solos he once reproduced on record. Stewart played on Potomac riverboats before moving to Philadelphia. He went to New York in 1921. Stewart worked with Elmer Snowden in 1925, then joined Fletcher Henderson a year later. But he felt his talents were not at the necessary level and departed Henderson's band, joining his brother Horace's band at Wilberforce College. Stewart returned in 1928. He remained five years and contributed many memorable solos. There was also a brief period in McKinney's Cotton Pickers in 1931, a stint heading his own band, and another short stay with Luis Russell before Stewart joined the Ellington Orchestra in 1934. He was a star throughout his tenure, co-writing classics "Boy Meets Horn" and "Morning Glory." He also supervised many outside recording sessions using Ellingtonians. After leaving, Stewart led various combos and performed throughout Europe and Australia on an extensive Jazz at the Philharmonic tour from 1947-1951. He lectured at the Paris Conservatory in 1948. Stewart settled in New Jersey to run a farm in the early '50s. He was semi-retired, but found new success in the media. He worked in local radio and television, while leading a band part-time in Boston. Stewart led the Fletcher Henderson reunion band in 1957 and 1958, and recorded with them. He played at Eddie Condon's club in 1958 and 1959, then moved to the West Coast. Stewart again worked as a disc jockey and became a critic. While he published many excellent pieces, a collection containing many of his best reviews came out posthumously, *Jazz Masters of the Thirties*. There's also a Stewart autobiography available. —*Ron Wynn*

Rex Stewart and the Ellingtonians / Jul. 23, 1940-1946 / Original Jazz Classics
✦✦✦✦✦
This CD reissue has the music from three unrelated sessions. Most valuable are four titles from 1940 that clock in around four minutes (rather than three) apiece and match cornetist Rex Stewart with fellow Ellingtonians (trombonist Lawrence Brown, clarinetist Barney Bigard and Duke's former bassist Wellman Braud) in addition to pianist Billy Kyle, guitarist Brick Fleagle and drummer Dave Tough. Their versions of "Bugle Call Rag" and "Diga Diga Doo" are quite exciting. There are also four titles (all Stewart originals) from 1946 that showcase the cornetist in

a quartet with pianist Kyle, bassist John Levy and drummer Cozy Cole. Ironically, the last two songs (also from 1946) are from a session without Rex that was led by pianist Jimmy Jones and included some more of Duke's men (past and present): trombonist Brown, altoist Otto Hardwick, baritonist Harry Carney and bassist Billy Taylor (in addition to trumpeter Joe Thomas, Ted Nash on tenor and drummer Shelly Manne). Overall, the music (small-group swing) is quite enjoyable, and these underrated titles are well worth picking up by mainstream collectors. — *Scott Yanow*

And His Dixielanders—Boston 1953 / Jun. 1953 / Jazz Anthology ◆◆◆◆
Although a major alumnus of Duke Ellington's Orchestra, by the 1950s cornetist Rex Stewart was often playing Dixieland nightly in clubs. This English LP (a reissue of a live Jazztone session) is particularly intriguing, for in addition to the fine front line (which also includes trombonist Fernando Arbello, clarinetist Albert Nicholas and baritonist John Dengler), the pianist is Herbie Nichols, who is most notable for his modern compositions and trio recordings. In this setting (which also includes bassist John Field and Jelly Roll Morton's former drummer Tommy Benford), Nichols plays fairly conventional Dixieland, as does Stewart. Highlights include "That's a Plenty," "Original Dixieland One Step" and "Wolverine Blues." — *Scott Yanow*

Irrepressible Rex Stewart / 1954 / Jazzology ◆◆◆
Cornetist Rex Stewart's music is always fun and full of good humor. In the 1950s he often popped up in Dixieland settings, as can be heard on this 1954 LP. Stewart is teamed with either Bob Jenney (Jack's brother) or Fred Waring, Jr., on trombone and John Dengler (who, despite being pictured on baritone, plays clarinet exclusively here) in a sextet. Other than the fairly basic "Rex's Blues," the repertoire comprises Dixieland warhorses (such as "Royal Garden Blues," "Tiger Rag" and "When the Saints Go Marching In"), and few surprises occur, but Stewart's chance-taking solos are often a bit exciting. — *Scott Yanow*

● **The Big Reunion** / Nov. 1957-Dec. 2, 1957 / Fresh Sound ◆◆◆◆◆
In 1957 cornetist Rex Stewart gathered together a large group dominated by Fletcher Henderson alumni and the result is this excellent tribute. Not every selection was from Henderson's book but the four main jams ("Sugar Foot Stomp," "Honeysuckle Rose," "Wrappin' It Up" and "King Porter Stomp") both revisit past glories and, with the fresh solos of Coleman Hawkins, Ben Webster, Buster Bailey, J.C. Higginbotham, Dickie Wells and Stewart among others, create some new history. — *Scott Yanow*

Rendezvous with Rex / Jan. 28, 1958+Jan. 31, 1958 / Felsted ◆◆◆◆
This interesting and well-rounded LP has two separate sessions originally cut for the Felsted label. Cornetist Rex Stewart is fiery on the first date, jamming on a trio of his worthy but obscure originals (when was the last time anyone played "Tillie's Twist" or "Tell Me More?") with trombonist George Stevenson, Haywood Henry (on clarinet and baritone), tenorman George Kelly, either Willie "The Lion" Smith or Dick Cary on piano, bassist Leonard Gaskin and drummer Arthur Trappier; Stewart takes a pleasant vocal on "My Kind of Gal." The three numbers from the later date have moody arrangements by Cary (who doubles on trumpet) and find Stewart in a septet with Hilton Jefferson (heard on clarinet and alto), clarinetist Garvin Bushell (whose bassoon work makes the date most memorable), guitarist Everett Barksdale, bassist Joe Benjamin and drummer Mickey Sheen. Superior music that will hopefully resurface on CD someday. — *Scott Yanow*

Porgy and Bess Revisited / 1958 / Warner Brothers ◆◆◆◆◆
This Swing LP, put out domestically by DRG in the 1980s, has rather unusual versions of 11 songs from *Porgy & Bess*. The two lead characters are played instrumentally by swing all-stars. Cornetist Rex Stewart portrays Sportin' Life, trumpeter Cootie Williams (who emerges as the main star) is Porgy, altoist Hilton Jefferson is Bess and trombonist Lawrence Brown is both Serena and Clara. Somehow it all works. Jim Timmens' arrangements for the big band keep the momentum going, making this a surprisingly successful effort. — *Scott Yanow*

Redhead / Feb. 1959 / Design ◆◆
In the late '50s, many jazz musicians were persuaded by record labels to record their interpretations of songs taken from the scores of Broadway shows. The play *Redhead* is long forgotten, as are virtually all of the songs from the show (other than maybe "My Girl Is Just Enough Woman for Me"). Cornetist Rex Stewart's quintet (which includes guitarist Bucky Pizzarelli, bassist Leonard Gaskin, drummer Mousey Alexander and either pianist John Bunch or Joe Venuto on marimba) does its best, but these numbers (which include "Uncle Sam Rag," "Erbie Fitch's Dilemma" and "Pick-Pocket Tango") are largely beyond help. This obscure album is for Rex Stewart completists. — *Scott Yanow*

The Happy Jazz of Rex Stewart / Mar. 18, 1960 / Prestige ◆◆◆◆◆
Other than a pair of European albums in 1966, this set was cornetist Rex Stewart's last full-length LP; in fact, it was reissued by Prestige as *The Rex Stewart Memorial*

Album. Stewart's technique and range had shrunk a bit by 1960, but his sense of humor and ability to make colorful tonal variations were still very much intact. This is a particularly fun set with Stewart doubling on kazoo and taking three good-time vocals, John Dengler switching between bass sax, washboard and kazoo, Wilbert Kirk heard on harmonica, and the rhythm section consisting of just two guitarists (Jerome Darr and Chauncey Westbrook) and drummer Charles Lampkin. The music is full of good spirits and memorable moments, with the highlights including "Rasputin" (a classic jam), "Please Don't Talk About Me When I'm Gone," "San," "I Would Do Most Anything For You" and "Nagasaki." Highly recommended and well worth searching for. — *Scott Yanow*

Just for Kicks / 1960 / Grand Award ◆◆◆
Cornetist Rex Stewart sounds typically colorful on this generally relaxed easy-listening swing date. Joined by studio musicians (pianist Moe Wechsler, guitarist Al Caiola, Joe Venuto on marimba, bassist Milt Hinton and drummer Don Lamond), Stewart plays melodic versions of a dozen swing standards. A few heated moments and Rex's witty approach to improvising keep the music on this obscure LP from being overly predictable. — *Scott Yanow*

Robert Stewart

b. Oakland, CA
Tenor Saxophone / Post-Bop
One of the most impressive hard-bop tenor saxophonists to emerge during the 1990s, Oakland, CA, native Robert Stewart did not take even take up the instrument until the age of 17; however, he so completely immersed himself in the music of Coleman Hawkins, Ben Webster, Sonny Rollins and John Coltrane—as well as the work of his own personal mentor, Pharoah Sanders—that he quickly developed his own muscular tone. After debuting in 1994 with *Judgement*, Stewart returned a year later with *In the Gutta*. — *Jason Ankeny*

● **Judgement** / 1994 / World Stage ◆◆◆◆◆
On a set of six straightahead originals and two standards, tenor saxophonist Robert Stewart sounds remarkably laidback and relaxed, particularly when one considers that this was his recording debut. Even on the uptempo tunes, Stewart is often content to emphasize his warm tone and hold long notes, taking his time to get his message across. Assisted by Eric Reed (who on this CD often emulates McCoy Tyner), bassist Mark Shelby and drummer Billy Higgins, this is a pleasing modern mainstream effort from the L.A.-based tenor. — *Scott Yanow*

In the Gutta / Aug. 12, 1995 / Warner Brothers ◆◆◆◆◆
Tenor saxophonist Robert Stewart's debut for Qwest is a bluish outing with a trio (organist Larry Bradford, guitarist Ralph Byrd and drummer Ranzel Merritt). He plays some really lowdown tenor with plenty of tonal distortions, growls, honks and an occasional scream; Stewart's well-titled "Get Out!" is a high point. The tenor's forceful solos (which generally avoid much doubletiming) are quite effective on such pieces as "Honky Tonk," "Green Onions," a medium-tempo "Misty" and some fairly basic originals. Stewart has a few shouting vocals and there is plenty of space for solos from Bradford and Byrd but it the leader's tenor that is most memorable. Although in some ways a throwback to the organ groups of the 1960s, this groovin' effort also sounds very much up-to-date. A highly enjoyable and easily recommended set of accessible yet dynamic music. — *Scott Yanow*

Slam Stewart (Leroy Elliot Stewart)

b. Sep. 21, 1914, Englewood, NJ, **d.** Dec. 10, 1987, Binghamton, NY
Bass / Swing
Slam Stewart was a superior swing-oriented bassist whose ability to bow the bass and hum an octave apart made him famous in the jazz world. He had thought of the idea while studying at Boston Conservatory when he heard Ray Perry singing along with his violin. In 1936 Stewart was with Peanuts Holland's group and the following year he started playing regularly with guitarist/singer/comedian Slim Gaillard in a group logically dubbed "Slim and Slam." "Flat Foot Floogie" became a huge hit and kept the group working through the early '40s. After leaving Gaillard, Stewart was in great demand. He played with Art Tatum's trio, was featured on records with the Benny Goodman Sextet, Red Norvo (a famous session with Charlie Parker and Dizzy Gillespie) and Lester Young (a classic rendition of "Sometimes I'm Happy"), and led his own group which for a period featured the up-and-coming pianist Erroll Garner. Stewart performed a couple of stunning duets with tenor saxophonist Don Byas at a 1945 Town Hall concert and later worked with Billy Taylor, Roy Eldridge, Bucky Pizzarelli, the Newport All-Stars and a countless number of other jazz greats. He even recorded two albums with bassist Major Holley (who also bowed and hummed but in unison). Up until the end, Slam Stewart occupied his own unique niche in jazz. — *Scott Yanow*

Two Big Mice / Jul. 14, 1977 / Black & Blue ◆◆◆◆

Dialogue / 1978 / Stash ✦✦✦✦

The music on this LP, which has been reissued on CD, features duets by bassist Slam Stewart and guitarist Bucky Pizzarelli. It is not surprising considering who is playing that the results are swinging, tasteful (thanks largely to Pizzarelli) and witty (due to Stewart's humming along with his bowed solos). In addition to some swing standards, the duo plays Peter Appleyard's "Slam Bow," a couple of Erroll Garner tunes, Leon Russell's "This Masquerade" and an ad-lib blues. —*Scott Yanow*

● **Shut Yo' Mouth!** / Dec. 6, 1981 / Delos ✦✦✦✦

With Major Holley. Two great bassists get together for a good time. Highly recommended. —*Michael G. Nastos*

The Cats Are Swingin' / Nov. 25, 1987+Dec. 20, 1987 / Sertoma ✦✦✦✦

For this album, bassist Slam Stewart planned a wide-ranging program that (with the exception of "Flat Foot Floogie") would consist of lesser-known material, including two songs by his wife Claire Stewart. Mostly recorded 16 days before Slam's death, the date features vibraphonist Peter Appleyard, pianist Richard Wyands, guitarist Bucky Pizzarelli, drummer Sherri Maricle, trombonist Kent McGarity and tenorman Al Hamme providing swinging playing and melodic solos. The project was nearly completed when Stewart became sick. Bassist Major Holley filled in on a few later bass tracks and guitarist John Pizzarelli helped out with a vocal on "Sertoma." The results are a fine close to Slam Stewart's productive career. —*Scott Yanow*

Sonny Stitt (Edward Stitt)

b. Feb. 2, 1924, Boston, MA, **d.** Jul. 22, 1982, Washington, DC

Tenor Saxophone, Alto Saxophone / Bop, Groove

Charlie Parker has had many admirers and his influence can be detected in numerous styles, but few have been as avid a disciple as Sonny Sitt. There was almost note-for-note imitation in several early Stitt solos, and the closeness remained until Stitt began de-emphasizing the alto in favor of the tenor, on which he artfully combined the influences of Parker and Lester Young. Stitt gradually developed his own sound and style, though he was never far from Parker on any alto solo. A wonderful blues and ballad player whose approach was one of the influences on John Coltrane, Stitt could rip through an uptempo bebop stanza, then turn around and play a shivering, captivating ballad. He was an alto saxophonist in Tiny Bradshaw's band during the early '40s, then joined Billy Eckstine's seminal big band in 1945, playing alongside other emerging bebop stars like Gene Ammons and Dexter Gordon. Stitt later played in Dizzy Gillespie's big band and sextet. He began on tenor and baritone in 1949, and at times was in a two-tenor unit with Ammons. He recorded with Bud Powell and J.J. Johnson for Prestige in 1949, then did several albums on Prestige, Argo and Verve in the '50s and '60s. Stitt led many combos in the '50s, and rejoined Gillespie for a short period in the late '50s. After a brief stint with Miles Davis in 1960, he reunited with Ammons and for a while was in a three-tenor lineup with James Moody. During the '60s, Stitt also recorded for Atlantic, cutting the transcendent *Stitt Plays Bird* that finally addressed the Parker question in epic fashion. He continued heading bands, though he joined the Giants of Jazz in the early '70s. This group included Gillespie, Art Blakey, Kai Winding, Thelonious Monk and Al McKibbon. Stitt did more sessions in the '70s for Cobblestone, Muse and others, among them another definitive date, *Tune Up*. He continued playing and recording in the early '80s, recording for Muse, Sonet and Who's Who in Jazz. He suffered a heart attack and died in 1982. —*Ron Wynn and Bob Porter*

Sonny Stitt with Bud Powell and J.J. Johnson / Oct. 17, 1949-Jan. 26, 1950 / Original Jazz Classics ✦✦✦✦✦

This superb CD reissues the complete output of three classic bop sessions including five "new" alternate takes. Sonny Stitt (who plays tenor throughout) is heard in a quintet with trombonist J.J. Johnson, pianist John Lewis, bassist Nelson Boyd and drummer Max Roach (playing three Johnson compositions and the original version of John Lewis' "Afternoon in Paris") and in a quartet with the great pianist Bud Powell, bassist Curly Russell and Max Roach. The latter two sessions are highlighted by rapid versions of "All God's Chillun Got Rhythm," "Strike Up the Band" and "Fine and Dandy." Highly recommended music. —*Scott Yanow*

Prestige First Sessions, Vol. 2 / Feb. 17, 1950-Aug. 14, 1951 / Prestige ✦✦✦✦✦

Sonny Stitt is heard in his early prime throughout this CD, sticking to tenor on all but two of the 24 selections. Few could play bebop with Stitt's sincerity, quick reflexes and large vocabulary. He swings hard throughout the performances, most of which feature him as the only soloist. Three dull vocals aside (by the forgotten Teddy Williams and Larry Townsend), this gap-filling CD is highly recommended to fans of classic bebop. —*Scott Yanow*

Kaleidoscope / Oct. 8, 1950-Feb. 25, 1952 / Original Jazz Classics ✦✦✦✦✦

Some of Sonny Stitt's better early sessions are collected together on this excellent CD. Stitt (switching between tenor, alto and on two numbers baritone) is heard with a variety of small groups ranging from quartets to an octet with three trumpeters and is the main star throughout these boppish performances. Highlights include "Cherokee," "Liza," "This Can't Be Love" and "Stitt's It." Recommended. —*Scott Yanow*

Symphony Hall Swing / Nov. 20, 1952 / Savoy ✦✦✦

This collector's LP contains the complete Sonny Stitt quartet session of Nov. 20, 1952 (four songs plus four alternate takes featuring Stitt on tenor with the obscure pianist Fletcher Peck, bassist John Simmons and drummer Jo Jones) and a quartet of "new" alternates from a 1956 Stitt date on which Sonny plays alto while joined by pianist Dolo Coker, bassist Edgar Willis and drummer Kenny Dennis. Nothing all that unusual occurs but bop fans should enjoy these hard-swinging straightahead performances. —*Scott Yanow*

At the Hi-Hat / Feb. 11, 1954 / Roulette ✦✦✦✦

Sonny Stitt is in excellent form on this Roulette CD. Recorded live at a Boston club, Stitt uses a local rhythm section (pianist Dean Earl, bassist Bernie Griggs and drummer Marquis Foster) as he jams on a variety of standards. Stitt mostly switches between alto and tenor, but on "Tri-Horn Blues" he takes solos not only on both of those saxes, but also on his rarely heard baritone. Overall, this CD gives one a good all-around sampling of early Sonny Stitt. —*Scott Yanow*

Live at the High Hat, Vol. 2 / Feb. 11, 1954 / Roulette ✦✦✦✦

The music on this 1996 CD was previously unissued. Sonny Stitt spent most of his career touring as a single, picking up rhythm sections wherever he appeared. On February 11, 1954, he was booked at the Hi-Hat in Boston and the local sidemen he came up with (pianist Dean Earl, bassist Bernie Griggs and drummer Marquis Foster) were competent but undistinguished. However that did not matter much for they were able to state basic chord changes, allowing Stitt to stretch out on standards and his riffing originals. Most unusual about this typical bebop jam is that in addition to his alto and tenor, Stitt triples on baritone (an instrument he otherwise only utilized on two songs for a Prestige date during this period). Stitt often switches horns during the brief piano spots and in fact on a 12-minute version of "One O' Clock Jump" he takes solos on tenor, alto and baritone. Although his flights and constant doubletime passages could be predictable, Sonny Stitt's huge mental storage of ideas, song quotes and personal licks is impressive and his fans will certainly enjoy this reasonably well-recorded set. —*Scott Yanow*

Verve Jazz Masters 50 / 1956-1961 / Verve ✦✦✦✦

Though Sonny Stitt recorded a lot, there are large gaps of material that have yet to be adequately documented on CD, particularly the Verves. Thus the *Jazz Masters* series rises again to the occasion, selecting from a dozen different Verve sources, including collaborative albums with Gene Ammons and Oscar Peterson and guest shots on records by Dizzy Gillespie and the so-called Modern Jazz Sextet. From this vantage point of his career, the old line about Stitt being a clone of Charlie Parker doesn't hold water, for despite an occasional Bird-like flurry, Stitt had his own harmonic ideas and somewhat mellower tone on alto and an even more individual majestic concept on tenor. The CD captures him in a quintessentially Verve series of diverse settings, with straightahead quartets, sextets, a lush Ralph Burns orchestra session, an off-center Jimmy Giuffre arrangement of "Laura," and mano-a-mano summit meetings, the most stimulating being a cooking 10-minute jam with Peterson and Roy Eldridge ("The String"). Sonny even duels with himself—on alto and tenor—on "Sonny's Tune." All told, an excellent introduction to Stitt in his prime. —*Richard S. Ginell*

● **Sits in with the Oscar Peterson Trio** / Oct. 10, 1957+May 18, 1959 / Verve ✦✦✦✦✦

This CD combines together a complete session that Sonny Stitt (doubling on alto and tenor) did with the 1959 Oscar Peterson Trio (which includes the pianist/leader, bassist Ray Brown and drummer Ed Thigpen) and three titles from 1957 with Peterson, Brown, guitarist Herb Ellis and drummer Stan Levey. The music very much has the feel of a jam session and, other than a themeless blues, all of the songs are veteran standards. Highlights of this fine effort include "I Can't Give You Anything but Love," "The Gypsy," "Scrapple from the Apple," "Easy Does It" and "I Remember You." Lots of cooking music. —*Scott Yanow*

Only the Blues / Oct. 11, 1957 / Verve ✦✦✦

This 1997 CD releases all of the music recorded by Sonny Stitt (who stuck to alto for the date) on Oct. 11, 1957. The original four songs teamed Stitt with trumpeter Roy Eldridge, pianist Oscar Peterson, guitarist Herb Ellis, bassist Ray Brown and drummer Stan Levey. Although three of the songs were blues, the most exciting number is ironically the opener, an "I Got Rhythm" run-through on a Stitt original "The String" that is note for note the same as his "Eternal Triangle." The two horns are quite combative and inspire each other. Not only is Stitt heard on a pair of standards without Eldridge from the same day, but there are 22 minutes of "I Know That You Know" consisting of three full versions, a false start, five breakdowns, an incomplete version and seven attempts at a coda. The latter serves as proof that more can be less, for there was little reason to release more than one or two versions of the song. —*Scott Yanow* ✦✦✦

Sonny Stitt / 1958 / MCA/Chess ✦✦✦

Sonny Stitt recorded extensively throughout his career, so frequently that he often could not remember his sessions a year later. This informal session, cut in Chicago in 1958, is one that Stitt apparently forgot about, which is why the personnel (probably a local rhythm section that might include pianist Barry Harris) has never been definitely identified. Stitt, doubling on alto and tenor, plays some songs with unfamiliar titles but all of the chord changes of the originals (half of them blues) are fairly basic. He is in above-average form, making this CD reissue of interest to bebop collectors. —*Scott Yanow*

Boss Tenors / Aug. 27, 1961 / Verve ✦✦✦✦✦

Stitt Meets Brother Jack / Feb. 16, 1962 / Original Jazz Classics ✦✦✦✦

Sonny Stitt (who sticks on this CD reissue to tenor) meets up with organist Brother Jack McDuff (along with guitarist Eddie Diehl, drummer Art Taylor and Ray Barretto on congas) for a spirited outing. Two standards ("All of Me" and "Time After Time") are performed with a variety of blues-based originals and the music always swings in a soulful boppish way. Worth picking up although not essential. —*Scott Yanow*

Soul Classics / Feb. 16, 1962-Feb. 15, 1972 / Original Jazz Classics ✦✦

This CD is a sampler of Sonny Stitt's Prestige recordings. Stitt (mostly heard here on tenor) is accompanied by organists (Brother Jack McDuff, Don Patterson or Gene Ludwig) on all but one selection but unfortunately half of the performances find him utilizing an electrified Varitone sax that watered down his sound and buried his individuality. This set can be safely passed by. —*Scott Yanow*

Boss Tenors in Orbit / Feb. 1962 / Verve ✦✦✦✦

Sonny Stitt and the Top Brass / Jul. 16, 1962-Jul. 17, 1962 / Atlantic ✦✦✦✦✦

This LP (reissued in Atlantic's *Jazzlore* series) features altoist Sonny Stitt accompanied by a nonet playing arrangements by either Tadd Dameron or Jimmy Mundy. The charts give this Stitt album more variety than usual and the superior material (which includes "On a Misty Night," "Poinciana" and Sonny's "Hey Pam") challenges the saxophonist to play at his best; trumpeter Blue Mitchell also has a couple of spots. Recommended. —*Scott Yanow*

Autumn in New York / 1962-Oct. 18, 1967 / Black Lion ✦✦✦

This Black Lion CD combines together four selections from a quintet session featuring altoist Sonny Stitt, trumpeter Howard McGhee, pianist Walter Bishop, bassist Tommy Potter and drummer Kenny Clarke (three boppish blues and a Stitt feature on "Lover Man") with four selections showcasing Stitt with unknown accompaniment from a 1962 date at Birdland. The saxophonist recorded so many sessions that it is not necesssary to acquire them all to get a good sampling of his playing (particularly since his style was virtually unchanged after the mid-'50s), but the CD has its heated moments. —*Scott Yanow*

● Stitt Plays Bird / Jan. 29, 1963 / Atlantic ✦✦✦✦✦

Sonny Stitt forged his own approach to playing bebop out of the sound and style of Charlie Parker, so this tribute album (reissued through Rhino on CD) was a very logical project. With fine support from guitarist Jim Hall, pianist John Lewis, bassist Richard Davis and drummer Connie Kay, Stitt performs ten Charlie Parker compositions, plus Jay McShann's "Hootie Blues"; these renditions of "Now's the Time" and "Yardbird Suite" were previously unreleased. Stitt, who mastered bebop and could play hot licks in his sleep, is in top form on such numbers as "Constellation," "Confirmation" and "Ko-Ko," making this an essential item for straightahead jazz fans (although the prolific altoist would record eight other albums in 1963 alone). —*Scott Yanow*

Salt and Pepper / Sep. 5, 1963 / GRP/Impulse! ✦✦✦✦✦

This 72-minute CD starts off with one of the underrated gems of the 1960s, an exciting matchup by tenors Sonny Stitt and Paul Gonsalves. Other than the brief throwaway "Theme from Lord of the Flies" (producer Bob Thiele's idea), this is very much a jam session set, with "Salt and Pepper" being a heated medium-tempo blues and the two competitive tenors stretching out on "S'posin'" and a lengthy "Perdido." Actually, the most memorable selection from the date is the one on which Stitt switches to alto, "Stardust." His beautiful playing behind Gonsalves' warm melody statement raises the session to the classic level. Also included on this consistently exciting CD is a Sonny Stitt quartet set originally titled *Now*. Although Stitt (doubling on alto and tenor) recorded scores of quartet sessions, he sounds particularly inspired here, especially on such offbeat material as "Estralita," the Dixieland standard "Please Don't Talk About Me When I'm Gone" and "My Mother's Eyes." Highly recommended to bebop and straightahead jazz fans. —*Scott Yanow*

Night Letter / Sep. 17, 1963+Oct. 27, 1969 / Prestige ✦✦✦✦

Two of Sonny Stitt's rarer Prestige LP's are combined together and reissued in full on this single CD. He jams on three standards and three basic originals (four on tenor and two on alto) in 1963 with organist Jack McDuff, bassist Leonard Gaskin and drummer Herbie Lovelle; "Sunday" and "Love Nest" are standouts. The later date finds Stitt on an electrified tenor (called the Varitone) which he often used in the late 1960s. His distinctive tone mostly survives and he is in excellent form on boppish tunes and originals playing with a quartet that also includes organist Gene Ludwig, the young guitarist Pat Martino and drummer Randy Gelispie. Stitt recorded many records in his career so this CD is not quite essential but his fans should enjoy the above-average effort. —*Scott Yanow*

● Soul People / Aug. 25, 1964-1966 / Prestige ✦✦✦✦✦

There are dozens of Sonny Stitt records available at any particular time; this CD reissue is one of the better ones. Mostly sticking to tenor, Stitt battles fellow tenor Booker Ervin with assistance from the fine organist Don Patterson and drummer Billy James on five selections and a ballad medley from 1964. Because both Stitt and Ervin always had very individual sounds, their trade-offs are quite exciting and end up a draw. Among the "bonus" cuts of this CD are a feature for Patterson with a trio in 1966 ("There Will Never Be Another You") and a collaboration between Stitt, Patterson, James and guitarist Grant Green on a 1966 version of "Tune Up." Enjoyable and generally hard-swinging music. —*Scott Yanow*

Sonny Stitt . . . Pow! / Sep. 10, 1965 / Prestige ✦✦✦✦

Altoist Sonny Stitt and trombonist Benny Green make for a potent team on this spirited quintet set. With the exception of the lone standard "I Want to Be Happy," all of the material is obscure. However, the two distinctive horns (along with pianist Kirk Lightsey, bassist Herman Wright and drummer Roy Brooks) have little difficulty essaying these bop pieces, blues and ballads, and their personable styles match well together. This LP has been out of print for quite awhile, so grab it if you see it. —*Scott Yanow*

Stardust / Jul. 28, 1966-Jul. 30, 1966 / Roulette ✦✦

On this Roulette LP, Sonny Stitt became the first musician to record on the Varitone sax, an electrified saxophone that allowed him to play octaves and to manipulate his sound a bit. Unfortunately the result was that Stitt (who used the instrument on and off for the next five years) lost much of his musical individuality when playing the generic sounding horn, and his fast doubletime runs could sound a bit silly and muddled. For this album, Stitt plays a dozen songs (mostly standards), is assisted by tenor saxophonist Illinois Jacquet on two pieces and welcomes a variety of accompanying musicians including trombonist J.J. Johnson, pianist Ellis Larkins and organist Ernie Hayes. But the net results (thanks to the Varitone) are no big deal. —*Scott Yanow*

Sonny Stitt and the Giants / Oct. 18, 1967 / Jazz Man ✦✦✦

This enjoyable LP features an all-star quintet at a session cut while in Zurich. Altoist Sonny Stitt and trumpeter Howard McGhee match together well and the rhythm section (pianist Walter Bishop, Jr., bassist Tommy Potter and drummer Kenny Clarke) is state of the art for bop of the period. Three blues feature the full group while "Lover Man," "Satin Doll" and "Don't Blame Me" are showcases for Stitt, the trio and McGhee, respectively; the latter two tracks have not yet been reissued on CD. —*Scott Yanow*

Made for Each Other / Jul. 13, 1968 / Delmark ✦✦

Sonny Stitt's regular group of the period (which included organist Don Patterson and drummer Billy James) plays a wide variety of material on this LP, ranging from "The Very Thought of You" and two versions of "Funny" to "Blues for J.J." and some then-current pop tunes. Unfortunately the set is from the period when Stitt often used a Varitone electronic attachment on his alto and tenor which gave him a much more generic sound, lowering the quality of this music despite some strong improvisations. It is an okay set that could have been better. —*Scott Yanow*

Legends of Acid Jazz / Jan. 4, 1971+Jul. 9, 1971 / Prestige ✦✦✦

This CD reissues the complete contents of two former LP's by saxophonist Sonny Stitt: *Turn It On* and *Black Vibrations*. These are rather unusual entries in Stitt's huge discography in that Sonny often sounds like a guest performer on his own sessions rather than the leader. During the earlier date, Stitt uses an electrical device (a Varitone) on his tenor that waters down his tone a bit. With organist Leon Spencer, guitarist Melvin Sparks and drummer Idris Muhammad setting down unrelenting grooves on most of the five numbers (including the 11-minute title cut), Stitt only seems to be making cameo appearances although trumpeter Virgil Jones gets in a few good solos on three of the numbers. The later date (which also has some good Jones trumpet) finds Stitt playing acoustically and switching to alto on two of the six jams, but once again it is the nonstop chugging of Sparks, Muhammad and either Leon Spencer or guest organist Don Patterson that fuels the fire. It is silly to call these soul jazz outings "acid jazz" since Sonny Stitt's solos are essentially bebop, but the grooves are danceable and funky. —*Scott Yanow*

★ **Endgame Brilliance: Constellation & Tune-Up** / Feb. 8, 1972+Jun. 27, 1972 / 32 Jazz ◆◆◆◆◆

Although the "endgame" part of this CD's title is not quite accurate (the sets from 1972 were made a decade before Sonny Stitt's passing), the "brilliance" definitely fits. Two of the prolific saxophonist's most exciting sessions ever were his Muse albums *Constellation* and *Tune-Up*. This essential single CD reissues the complete contents of both dates. Strangely enough, *Constellation* is listed in this set as having been recorded June 27, 1971 (it is actually from 1972) and thus cut earlier, so it takes up the first (rather than the second) half of this CD. On both dates, Stitt (doubling on tenor and alto) is joined by the superb bop pianist Barry Harris and bassist Sam Jones with either Roy Brooks or Alan Dawson on drums. Stitt, who recorded many quartet sets through the years, was very inspired on both of these occasions. His renditions of "Constellation," "Webb City," "Just Friends" and "Groovin' High" in particular are quite memorable. The high point is a nine-and-a-half-minute version of "I Got Rhythm" that features the classic saxophonist first taking a long solo on tenor and then following it up with an equally stunning flight on alto. A master of the bebop vocabulary, the competitive Sonny Stitt would have deserved fame if he had only recorded these two sessions and not bothered with the other 150 albums he led. This CD is essential for all bebop collections. —*Scott Yanow*

Goin' Down Slow / Feb. 15, 1972 / Prestige ◆◆◆◆◆

Sonny Stitt was in one of his prime periods during the early '70s and this LP finds him in particularly creative form. Best is the 14-minute "Miss Ann, Lisa, Sue and Sadie" which features Stitt, trumpeter Thad Jones, guitarist Billy Butler and pianist Hank Jones soloing over a small string section; Jones' arrangement is quite memorable. Although the other four selections are not quite at the same level, Stitt is in top form throughout this inventive date. —*Scott Yanow*

So Doggone Good / Sep. 13, 1972 / Prestige ◆◆◆

Despite its bragging title, this LP is decent but not essential. Sonny Stitt, who during the same period was recording classics for Cobblestone/Muse, is in above-average form for this set although the material (four fairly basic originals and two ballads) is not quite up to par. Stitt (switching between alto and tenor) is ably accompanied by pianist Hampton Hawes, bassist Reggie Johnson and drummer Lenny McBrowne) and the jam session-style music is reasonably enjoyable although recommended primarily for his greatest fans. —*Scott Yanow*

Sonny Stitt/12! / Dec. 12, 1972 / Muse ◆◆◆◆◆

Sonny Stitt was in prime form in the early '70s when he recorded two classics: *Tune Up* and *Constellation*. *12!* from a year later tends to get overlooked but this LP is also one of the saxophonist's most rewarding recordings. Assisted by pianist Barry Harris, bassist Sam Jones and drummer Louis Hayes, Stitt (switching between alto and tenor) is in superb form on five standards and two blues; highlights include "I Got It Bad," "Every Tub" and "Our Delight." This LP is worth searching for. —*Scott Yanow*

The Champ / Apr. 18, 1973 / Muse ◆◆◆

Sonny Stitt was in great form in the early '70s and the rhythm section on this release (which has been reissued on CD) is excellent: pianist Duke Jordan, bassist Sam Jones and drummer Roy Brooks. The problem is that trumpeter Joe Newman is not quite up to par and Stitt constantly cuts his own solos short to make room for Newman. While there are some good spots for Stitt's tenor and alto, his truncated improvisations are ultimately frustrating, especially compared to his classic recordings from the era. Get *Tune Up* instead. —*Scott Yanow*

Mellow / Feb. 14, 1975 / Muse ◆◆◆◆

Jimmy Heath (switching between tenor, soprano and flute) holds his own with Sonny Stitt (who as usual double on tenor and alto) for this quintet set with pianist Barry Harris, bassist Richard Davis and drummer Roy Haynes. Stitt sounds fairly relaxed throughout, Heath is a strong and contrasting foil and the repertoire (five mostly underplayed standards plus Stitt's "A Cute One") is fairly fresh. A good session of 1970s bop. —*Scott Yanow*

In Walked Sonny / May 16, 1975 / Sonet ◆◆◆◆◆

Stitt joined Art Blakey's Jazz Messengers for this hard-swinging LP, and he fits quite comfortably with the quintet (which includes the leader/drummer, trumpeter Bill Hardman, Dave Schnitter on tenor, pianist Walter Davis, Jr., and bassist Chin Suzuki). In addition to the title cut (a Sonny Stitt original), Stitt is in top form on "Blues March," "It Might as Well Be Spring," Freddie Hubbard's "Birdlike" and "I Can't Get Started"; he sits out on Davis' "Ronnie's a Dynamite Lady." The members of the Messengers sound inspired by Stitt's presence and everyone is in fine form on this excellent hard-bop session. —*Scott Yanow*

My Buddy: Stitt Plays for Gene Ammons / Jul. 2, 1975 / Muse ◆◆◆◆

Upon the death of his close friend, fellow tenor Gene Ammons, Sonny Stitt recorded this fine tribute album. In addition to an emotional version of the title cut and an original blues, Stitt (mostly on tenor) performs four songs that Ammons

used to play including "Red Top" and "Exactly like You." With fine assistance from pianist Barry Harris, bassist Sam Jones and drummer Leroy Williams, this is a high-quality bop set. —*Scott Yanow*

Forecast: Sonny & Red / Nov. 1975 / Catalyst ◆◆◆◆◆

Sonny Stitt and Red Holloway make a perfect team on this exciting jam session record which has not yet been reissued on CD. Stitt sticks here to tenor while Holloway alternates between tenor and alto. With fine backup by pianist Art Hillery, bassist Larry Gales and drummer Clarence Johnston, Sonny and Red share a ballad medley and battle it out on the title cut, "The Way You Look Tonight," "Lester Leaps In," "Just Friends" and "All God's Chillun Got Rhythm." Holloway was able to keep up with the combative Stitt and the fireworks are well worth savoring. —*Scott Yanow*

Blues for Duke / Dec. 3, 1975-Dec. 4, 1975 / Muse ◆◆◆

Sonny Stitt (on tenor exclusively except for an alto feature on "I Got It Bad") pays tribute to the recently departed Duke Ellington with renditions of five songs associated with Ellington, plus Stitt's title cut. The rhythm section (pianist Barry Harris, bassist Sam Jones and drummer Billy Higgins) is excellent, and although the results are somewhat predictable (with "C Jam Blues" and "Perdido" being the high points), the music on this LP can be enjoyed by bop fans. —*Scott Yanow*

Dumpy Mama / 1975 / Flying Dutchman ◆◆◆

Although Sonny Stitt (sticking to tenor except on "It Might as Well Be Spring" where he plays alto) teams up with a variety of musicians on this LP who he had rarely played with previously (including tenor saxophonist Pee Wee Ellis, altoist Frank Strozier, pianist Mike Wofford, bassist Brian Torff and drummer Shelly Manne), he plays in his usual bebop style. In addition to his alto feature there is a duet with Wofford on a sensitive "Danny Boy for Ben," the funky title cut (penned by Oliver Nelson) and boppish renditions of "Just Friends" and Stitt's original, "Jason." The playing is up to par if not overly memorable; this LP's music has yet to be reissued on CD. —*Scott Yanow*

Stomp Off Let's Go / 1976 / Flying Dutchman ◆◆◆

It would have been intriguing to hear bop altoist and tenor saxophonist Sonny Stitt play the title cut (an obscurity from the 1920s whose use as the album's name is actually irrelevant) but instead he performs the "Theme from *Black Orpheus*," "Duke's Place," "Perdido" and "Little Suede Shoes." Actually the most interesting aspect to this date (which also utilizes Frank Owens on keyboards, guitarist Bucky Pizzarelli, Richard Davis on electric bass, drummer Louie Bellson and percussionist Leopoldo Fleming) is that the two high-note trumpeters Jon Faddis and Lew Soloff are also in the front line and have a fair amount of solo space. Otherwise this is an average although enjoyable Sonny Stitt bop date. —*Scott Yanow*

Moonlight in Vermont / Nov. 23, 1977 / Denon ◆◆◆

Sonny Stitt, doubling on alto and tenor, is in fine form on this quartet session (a Japanese import CD) with either Barry Harris or Walter Davis on piano, bassist Reggie Workman and drummer Tony Williams. The repertoire (bop standards, blues and ballads) is fairly typical and nothing too unusual occurs, but fans of straightahead jazz in general and Sonny Stitt in particular will be satisfied with this above-average effort, highlighted by "It Might as Well Be Spring" and "Constellation." —*Scott Yanow*

I Remember Bird / 1977 / Catalyst ◆◆◆◆

The title refers to the Leonard Feather composition rather than a complete set of Charlie Parker songs. Sonny Stitt, who spent his entire career playing in a style built on Bird's, is in good form during this quintet date which features him on both alto and tenor. With trombonist Frank Rosolino, pianist Dolo Coker, bassist Allen Jackson and drummer Clarence Johnston, Stitt stretches out on the title tune, his own blues "Streamlined Stanley," three standards, Rosolino's "Waltz for Diane" and the traditional hymn "Yes Jesus Loves Me." This good bop date is long out of print. —*Scott Yanow*

Sonny Stitt with Strings / 1977 / Catalyst ◆◆◆

Sonny Stitt (on alto and tenor) is joined by a fine rhythm section featuring pianist Gildo Mahones and an eight-piece string section arranged by Bill Finegan for seven familiar Duke Ellington songs. No real surprises occur although the string charts are a cut above the usual. Stitt is at his most melodic and really romps on a few of these pieces, most notably "Cottontail." —*Scott Yanow*

Sonny Stitt Meets Sadik Hakim / Apr. 25, 1978 / Progressive ◆◆◆

Sadik Hakim (whose original name was Argonne Thornton) played with a few notable names from the bop era (including Charlie Parker), has long been a somewhat obscure pianist. His "meeting" with Sonny Stitt (who splits his time here evenly between alto and tenor) on this Progressive CD is about as high a profile as he ever had. With bassist Buster Williams and drummer J.R. Mitchell completing the quartet, Stitt is in his usual fine form on five veteran standards, a pair of blues-based originals and Stevie Wonder's "You Are the Sunshine of My Life." The music is not essential but has its heated moments; recommended for bop fans. —*Scott Yanow*

Sonny's Back / Apr. 7, 1980+Jul. 14, 1980 / Muse ✦✦✦✦
Sonny Stitt (sticking to tenor on all but one alto feature) uses one of his favorite rhythm sections on this Muse LP (pianist Barry Harris, bassist George Duvivier and drummer Leroy Williams) and for three of the seven selections he welcomes the much younger tenor Ricky Ford; their trade-offs are quite interesting and end up being a dead heat. Stitt is in fine form throughout this excellent set which consists of four standards, two Stitt originals and a remake of Charlie Parker's "Constellation." —*Scott Yanow*

In Style / Mar. 18, 1981 / Muse ✦✦✦✦
Sonny Stitt (heard on both alto and tenor) is in excellent form for this CD reissue, yet another quartet date; he led over 100 sessions through the years. With pianist Barry Harris, bassist George Duvivier and drummer Jimmy Cobb inspiring him, Stitt is creative within the boundaries of bebop on such songs as "Just You, Just Me," "Is You Is or Is You Ain't My Baby," "Yesterdays" and a pair of his basic originals which he titled "Western Style" and "Eastern Style." —*Scott Yanow*

Just in Case You Forgot How Bad He Really Was / Sep. 1981 / 32 Jazz ✦✦✦✦

The Bubba's Sessions with Eddie "Lockjaw" Davis & Harry "Sweets" Edison / Nov. 11, 1981 / Who's Who in Jazz ✦✦✦✦
The second of two Who's Who LPs recorded during a club appearance by Sonny Stitt (who doubles here on alto and tenor) has guest appearances by tenor saxophonist Eddie "Lockjaw" Davis and trumpeter Harry "Sweets" Edison in addition to fine backup work from pianist Eddie Higgins, bassist Donn Mast and drummer Duffy Jackson. This may look like a budget album but the playing (particularly by Stitt) on the blues, standards and ballads is top notch. Until the music is reissued on CD, this LP and the complementary set *Sonny, Sweets & Jaws* are collector's items. —*Scott Yanow*

Sonny, Sweets and Jaws / Nov. 11, 1981 / Who's Who in Jazz ✦✦✦
Taped at a club in Ft. Lauderdale, FL, this LP features Sonny Stitt (on alto and tenor) in a strong front line with trumpeter Harry "Sweets" Edison and tenor great Eddie "Lockjaw" Davis. With steady support from pianist Eddie Higgins, bassist Donn Mast and drummer Duffy Jackson, the three horns get to stretch out on Davis' "The Chef" and five fairly basic standards. These spontaneous performances contain plenty of exciting moments and this album from the small Who's Who label is worth picking up. —*Scott Yanow*

Battle of the Saxes / Dec. 1981 / AIM ✦✦✦✦
This Australian import is a real rarity for it teams together Sonny Stitt (mostly playing tenor) and altoist Richie Cole (along with pianist Jack Wilson, bassist Ed Gaston and drummer Allan Turnbull) for the first and only time. Stitt and Cole inspire each other on the seven boppish selections and, even if little surprising occurs, the heated exchanges make this CD worth searching for. —*Scott Yanow*

Last Stitt Sessions, Vols. 1 & 2 / Jun. 8, 1982-Jun. 9, 1982 / Muse ✦✦✦✦✦
It is difficult to believe after listening to this two-CD set that Sonny Stitt only had six weeks left in his life; he already had cancer but did not know it. Switching between tenor and alto, Stitt on the first disc is heard in top form with pianist Junior Mance, bassist George Duvivier and drummer Jimmy Cobb while the second CD (recorded the following day) adds trumpeter Bill Hardman and has Walter Davis in Mance's place. As was typical of Stitt's career, the music throughout is high-quality bebop with the saxophonist stretching out creatively over common chord changes. This double CD (a straight reissue of two single LPs) shows that Sonny Stitt went out on top. —*Scott Yanow*

Billy Strayhorn

b. Nov. 29, 1915, Dayton, OH, d. May 31, 1967, New York, NY
Piano, Composer, Arranger / Swing
An extravagantly gifted composer, arranger and pianist—some considered him a genius—Billy Strayhorn toiled throughout most of his maturity in the gaudy shadow of his employer, collaborator and friend, Duke Ellington. Only in the last decade has Strayhorn's profile been lifted to a level approaching that of Ellington, where diligent searching of the Strayhorn archives (mainly by David Hajdu, author of the excellent Strayhorn bio *Lush Life*) revealed that Strayhorn's contribution to the Ellington legacy was far more extensive and complex than once thought. There are several instances where Strayhorn compositions were registered as Ellington/Strayhorn pieces ("Day Dream," "Something to Live For"), where collaborations between the two were listed only under Duke's name ("Satin Doll," "Sugar Hill Penthouse," "C-Jam Blues"), where Strayhorn pieces were copyrighted under Ellington's name or no name at all. Even tunes that were listed as Strayhorn's alone have suffered; the proverbial man on the street is likely to tell you that "Take the 'A' Train"—perhaps Strayhorn's most famous tune—is a Duke Ellington song.

Still, among musicians and jazz fans, Strayhorn is renowned for acknowledged classics like "Lotus Blossom," "Lush Life," "Rain Check," "A Flower Is a Lovesome Thing" and "Mid-Riff." While tailored for the Ellington idiom, Strayhorn's pieces often have their own bittersweet flavor, and his larger works have coherent, classically influenced designs quite apart from those of Ellington. Strayhorn was alternately content with and frustrated by his second-fiddle status, and he was also one of the few openly gay figures in jazz, which probably added more stress to his life.

Classical music was Strayhorn's first and lifelong musical love. He started out as a child prodigy, gravitating to Victrolas as a child, working odd jobs in order to buy a used upright piano while in grade school. He studied harmony and piano in high school, writing the music for a professional musical, *Fantastic Rhythm*, at 19. But the realities of a Black man trying to make it in the then-lily-white classical world, plus exposure to pianists like Art Tatum and Teddy Wilson, led Strayhorn toward jazz; he gigged around Pittsburgh with a combo called the Mad Hatters. Through a friend of a friend, Strayhorn gained an introduction to Duke Ellington when the latter's band stopped in Pittsburgh in 1938. After hearing Strayhorn play, Ellington immediately gave him an assignment, and in January 1939, Strayhorn moved to New York to join Ellington as an arranger, composer, occasional pianist and collaborator without so much as any kind of contract or verbal agreement. "I don't have any position for you," Ellington allegedly said. "You'll do whatever you feel like doing."

A 1940-41 dispute with ASCAP that kept Ellington's compositions off the radio gave Strayhorn his big chance to contribute several tunes to the Ellington bandbook, among them "After All," "Chelsea Bridge," "Johnny Come Lately" and "Passion Flower." Over the years, Strayhorn would collaborate (and be given credit) with Ellington in many of his large-scale suites, like *Such Sweet Thunder, A Drum Is a Woman, The Perfume Suite* and *The Far East Suite*, as well as musicals like *Jump for Joy* and *Saturday Laughter* and the score for the film *Anatomy of a Murder*. Beginning in the 1950s, Strayhorn also took on some projects on his own away from Ellington, including a few solo albums, revues for a New York society called the Copasetics, theatre collaborations with Luther Henderson, and songs for his friend Lena Horne. In 1964, Strayhorn was diagnosed with cancer of the esophagus, aggravated by years of smoking and drinking, and he submitted his last composition, "Blood Count," to the Ellington band while in the hospital. Shortly after Strayhorn's death in May 1967, Ellington recorded one of his finest albums and the best introduction to Strayhorn's work, *And His Mother Called Him Bill* (RCA), in memory of his friend. —*Richard S. Ginell*

Billy Strayhorn/Johnny Dankworth / Dec. 28, 1958+1961 / Roulette ✦✦✦
This double LP has two unrelated sessions. Although Billy Strayhorn allegedly led the first date, the Duke Ellington Orchestra is heard playing their usual repertoire with only one Strayhorn composition ("Passion Flower"), and it sounds as if Duke himself is on piano; this set was probably released under Strayhorn's name for contractual purposes. The main star is altoist Johnny Hodges, on such tunes as "Things Ain't What They Used to Be," "Jeep's Blues" and "All of Me." Also heard from is Harry Carney (featured on "Sophisticated Lady"), trumpeter Shorty Baker and violinist Ray Nance, among others. The second half of the two-fer has the 1961 Johnny Dankworth big band, a much less distinctive group despite the presence of tenorman Danny Moss and trumpeter Dickie Hawdon. The music (mixing together Dankworth originals with a couple of Cannonball Adderley tunes, "When My Sugar Walks Down the Street" and even "The Avengers Theme") should please straightahead big-band collectors. —*Scott Yanow*

Cue for Saxophone / Apr. 14, 1959 / London ✦✦✦✦
Composer/arranger/pianist Billy Strayhorn led surprisingly few sessions throughout his career, and this was only his second full-length album. Actually, the main star is altoist Johnny Hodges (who goes here under the pseudonym of "Cue Porter"), while Strayhorn (who plays piano on the seven songs) only co-wrote two basic tunes ("Cue's Blue Now" and "Watch Your Cue") with Hodges and played a fairly minor role. Also in the septet are three fellow Ellingtonians (trumpeter Shorty Baker, trombonist Quentin Jackson and clarinetist Russell Procope), along with bassist Al Hall and drummer Oliver Jackson. The results are a fine mainstream session (which has been reissued on this CD) with highlights including "Gone with the Wind," the ten-minute "Cue's Blue Now" and "Rose Room." —*Scott Yanow*

The Peaceful Side / May 1961 / United Artists ✦✦✦✦
This is a little-known and rather melancholy set, virtually Billy Strayhorn's only recording away from the world of Duke Ellington. The focus is totally on Strayhorn's piano throughout his interpretations of ten of his compositions (including "Lush Life," "Take the 'A' Train" and "Something to Live For"). Three selections have the Paris Blue Notes adding sparse wordless vocals, two other numbers add some quiet playing by the Paris String Quartet, and bassist Michel Goudret is on five of the ten selections (including one apiece with the strings and the voices). "Strange Feeling" and "Chelsea Bridge" are taken as unaccompanied piano solos.

Of the ten songs, only "Just A-Sittin' and A-Rockin'" hints at happiness; otherwise, Strayhorn's melodic and concise playing is quite somber, peaceful in volume but filled with inner tension. —*Scott Yanow*

● **Lush Life** / Jan. 14, 1964-Aug. 14, 1965 / Red Baron ✦✦✦✦✦
Although not initially released until 1992, 25 years after composer Billy Strayhorn's death, this is his definitive CD. Strayhorn is heard singing "Lush Life" while backed by the Duke Ellington Orchestra in 1964 (his voice is not strong but his phrasing is quite sincere), jamming on piano with fluegelhornist Clark Terry and Bob Wilbur (on clarinet and soprano) in a quintet, backing singer Ozzie Bailey and taking a pair of piano solos ("Love Came" and "Baby Clementine"). These are very valuable and intriguing recordings, shedding some new light on a nearly invisible genius. —*Scott Yanow*

Frank Strazzeri

b. Apr. 24, 1930, Rochester, NY
Piano / Hard Bop
A solid pianist long based in the Los Angeles area, Frank Strazzeri has been in demand for straightahead sessions for decades. Although he originally started playing tenor and clarinet when he was 12, Strazzeri soon switched to piano. After studying at the Eastman School, he became the house pianist at a jazz club in Rochester in 1952, where he was able to accompany top jazz artists (including Roy Eldridge and Billie Holiday). In 1954, Strazzeri moved to New Orleans, where he played Dixieland with Sharkey Bonano and Al Hirt. That, however, was just a temporary departure, for he was always a bop-based player. Strazzeri worked with Charlie Ventura (1957-58) and Woody Herman (1959) before settling permanently in Los Angeles in 1960. He became a studio musician, appeared on many sessions and worked with the who's who of West Coast jazz. Strazzeri had opportunities to tour with Joe Williams and Maynard Ferguson and was with Les Brown's big band from 1971-74. Among his other musical associations have been Terry Gibbs, Herb Ellis, the Lighthouse All-Stars, Art Pepper, Bud Shank, Cal Tjader, Louie Bellson and Chet Baker, among many others, in addition to working with his own trios. As a leader, Strazzeri has headed sessions for Revelation, Glendale, Sea Breeze, Catalyst, Discovery and Fresh Sound. —*Scott Yanow*

View from Within / Jan. 6, 1973 / Creative World ✦✦✦
A more demonstrative, ambitious album than normal for pianist Frank Strazzeri. Perhaps being on an independent label gave him more freedom, or maybe he wanted to show that he's capable of going beyond the conventional. Whatever the reasons, his playing has more twists and turns, fire, edge, and spirit than any of his other releases. —*Ron Wynn*

Frames / 1975 / Glendale ✦✦✦
Some pleasant, occasionally arresting playing by pianist Frank Strazzeri, a longtime journeyman jazz musician. He's not an innovator, a spectacular soloist, or a great composer or arranger. He simply plays in a restrained, competent manner, whether it's a classic or his own unassuming originals. —*Ron Wynn*

Relaxin' / Jul. 28, 1980 / Sea Breeze ✦✦✦✦✦
Frank Strazzeri's first full set of piano solos was performed quite spontaneously, and the whole album came together in just two hours. The emphasis is on relaxed tempos, although there is a fair amount of variety in repertoire (which ranges from "As Long as I Live" and "Keepin' Out of Mischief Now" to "Star Eyes," Alec Wilder's "The Winter of My Discontent" and even "Send in the Clowns"). Although one may think of Frank Strazzeri as primarily a bebop pianist, he shows that he can also play swing and has a strong left hand. This LP is worth searching for. —*Scott Yanow*

Kat Dancin' / Apr. 2, 1985 / Discovery ✦✦✦

I Remember You / Jan. 31, 1989 / Fresh Sound ✦✦✦

Little Giant / Nov. 1989 / Fresh Sound ✦✦✦

The Very Thought of You / 1990 / Discovery ✦✦✦

Frank's Blues / 1992 / Night Life ✦✦✦✦
A 1992 release with pianist Frank Strazzeri playing his own and other composers' blues pieces, doing them nicely, with a modicum of passion and energy. He's assisted by a quintet of mostly faceless players, flute and saxophonist Sam Most excepted. —*Ron Wynn*

● **Wood Winds West** / Feb. 29, 1992 / Jazz Mark ✦✦✦✦✦
Pianist Frank Strazzeri, who composed seven of the eleven pieces on this CD and arranged all of the music, put together an impressive group of West Coast all-stars in 1992 that included tenor saxophonist Bob Cooper, baritonist Jack Nimitz, Bill Perkins on soprano, alto and flutes, bassist Dave Stone and drummer Paul Kreibich. The colorful charts swing, make inventive use of the three saxophonists (who play a total of eight reeds) and are both unpredictable and logical. This underrated disc is easily recommended. —*Scott Yanow*

Somebody Loves Me / Feb. 15, 1994-Feb. 16, 1994 / Fresh Sound ✦✦✦✦✦

String Trio of New York

f. 1979
Group / Avant-Garde, Post-Bop
The String Trio of New York has long been one of the more accessible avant-garde jazz units, not afraid to use melodies and swing even during its more advanced group improvisations. Formed in 1979, the band originally consisted of violinist Billy Bang, guitarist James Emery and bassist John Lindberg. In the late 1980s Bang departed and was replaced by Charles Burnham, and then in 1993 Regina Carter became the group's regular violinist. The trio has recorded rewarding sets for Black Saint, ITM (an obscure effort with singer Jay Clayton), Stash and Arabesque. —*Scott Yanow*

First String / Jun. 1979 / Black Saint ✦✦✦✦
This set was the debut of the String Trio of New York, an innovative yet generally accessible unit originally comprising violinist Billy Bang, guitarist James Emery and bassist John Lindberg. Each of the musicians contributed one lengthy composition apiece (including two with the intriguing titles of "Catharsis in Real Time" and "Subway Ride with Giuseppi Logan"), and the music expertly blends composition with improvisation. This music (free at times but always going in a logical direction) grows in interest with each listen. —*Scott Yanow*

Area Code 212 / Nov. 25, 1980-Nov. 26, 1980 / Black Saint ✦✦✦✦✦

Common Goal / Nov. 12, 1981-Nov. 13, 1981 / Black Saint ✦✦✦✦

Rebirth of a Feeling / Nov. 25, 1983-Nov. 26, 1983 / Black Saint ✦✦✦✦✦
The String Trio of New York's strongest lineup was arguably the edition that included violinist Billy Bang, guitarist James Emery and bassist John Lindberg. That unit was at its best here; the threesome played adventurous unison lines and offered wide-ranging solos. The best example of their interactive/reactive mode was the 14-minute "Utility Grey," with its array of textures, colors, moods and voicings. Emery wrote two selections, Bang a pair, and Lindberg the finale, but this was a unified effort. The String Trio of New York ranks as a premier outside group of the 1970s and '80s. —*Ron Wynn*

Natural Balance / 1986 / Black Saint ✦✦✦✦✦
This was the fifth and final recording by the original edition of the String Trio of New York before violinist Billy Bang departed. Comprising Bang, guitarist James Emery and bassist John Lindberg, the original String Trio and its descendants sought to combine fairly free soloing with involved and multi-thematic compositions. The six group originals on this set (most memorable is Emery's rollicking "Texas Koto Blues") cover a great deal of ground and range from the accessible to the esoteric. An excellent outing. —*Scott Yanow*

As Tears Go By / Dec. 1987 / ITM ✦✦✦

Ascendant / Jun. 24, 1990+Jun. 25, 1990 / Stash ✦✦✦✦

Time Never Lies / Jun. 24, 1990-Jun. 25, 1990 / Vintage Jazz ✦✦✦✦

● **Intermobility** / Jul. 1, 1992-Jul. 2, 1992 / Arabesque ✦✦✦✦✦
The 1992 edition of the String Trio of New York consisted of original members James Emery on guitar and bassist John Lindberg plus the great violinist Regina Carter. In addition to two originals apiece by Emery and Lindberg and one by Carter, the unique inside/outside group performs Wayne Shorter's "Ju-Ju," Ornette Coleman's "Peace," Eric Dolphy's "17 West," Thelonious Monk's "Ruby My Dear," Herbie Nichols' rarely played "House Party Starting" and a bop medley on this well-rounded CD. Due to the diversity of material, the adventurous improvisations and the high musicianship, this release serves as a perfect introduction to the music of the String Trio of New York. —*Scott Yanow*

Octagon / Nov. 5, 1992-Nov. 6, 1992 / Black Saint ✦✦✦✦✦

Blues . . . ? / Oct. 6, 1993-Oct. 6, 1993 / Black Saint ✦✦✦✦
The String Trio of New York, which since 1991 has consisted of violinist Regina Carter, guitarist James Emery and bassist John Lindberg (the latter two were founding members in 1979), is often classified as an avant-garde group due to its unusual instrumentation and chance-taking improvisations. However this Black Saint release is among their most accessible. Although not all of the nine performances are blues (Duke Ellington's obscure "I'm Afraid" is a ballad and calling "Hurry Up and Wait" a reggae blues is stretching the point a bit), all of the selections are given blues feeling. In addition to five diverse originals (including an eccentric country blues "Bellyachin' Blues"), the group performs the Ellington piece (which was apparently never recorded by Duke), Lee Morgan's "Speedball," a mournful version of "Freddie Freeloader" and a six-song Charlie Parker blues suite which purposely slows down and speeds up in spots to jarring effect. With the exception of the latter (which ends inconclusively), this is a successful effort, well worth seeking out by adventurous listeners. —*Scott Yanow*

With Anthony Davis / Nov. 20, 1996 / Music & Arts ✦✦✦✦

For an ensemble associated with the avant-garde, this album of familiar Ellington, Monk, and Mingus tunes is a bit of a departure. The group is particularly adept at handling the staccato rhythms and odd phrasing of the three Monk songs here, including a lovely version of "Ruby, My Dear." Given the brooding intellectualism of some of Davis' past work, his casually swinging piano work is somewhat of a surprise. The lone original piece, a specially commissioned composition by Davis, is a slowly developing blues of sorts that never really takes off. But for its outstanding musicianship and highly original takes on some classic material, this album is strongly recommended. —*Joel Roberts*

Frank Strozier

b. Jun. 13, 1937, Memphis, TN
Alto Saxophone / Hard Bop

A talented alto saxophonist who never became very famous, Frank Strozier has long been a top-notch hard-bop stylist whose intense sound recalls (but is not derivative of) Jackie McLean. One of many excellent jazzmen who grew up in Memphis, Strozier played with other Memphis musicians even after he moved to Chicago in 1954 (including Harold Mabern, Booker Little and George Coleman). He recorded with the MJT + 3 from 1959-60 and led sessions for Vee-Jay during the same period. After moving to New York, Strozier was briefly with the Miles Davis Quintet in 1963 (between Hank Mobley and George Coleman), gigged with Roy Haynes, and then relocated to Los Angeles. During his L.A. years, he worked with Chet Baker, Shelly Manne, and most notably the Don Ellis big band (with whom he took a memorable solo on "K.C. Blues" from Ellis' *Autumn* album). He returned to New York in 1971, working with the Jazz Contemporaries, the New York Jazz Repertory Company and Horace Parlan, among others, but not gaining the recognition he deserved. Frustrated with his lack of work, Strozier for a time reappeared as a pianist but little resulted from that. As a leader, Frank Strozier's Vee-Jay recordings (with a great deal of added material) have been reissued on CD; his Jazzland dates from 1961-62 remain out of print, and he also led sessions for Trident (1972) and Steeple Chase (1976-77). —*Scott Yanow*

● **Fantastic Frank Strozier, Plus** / Dec. 9, 1959-Feb. 3, 1960 / Vee-Jay ✦✦✦✦✦

Altoist Frank Strozier's first session as a leader has been reissued on this Vee-Jay CD with the original six selections joined by five additional and previously unreleased performances, only one of which is actually an alternate take. The altoist's quintet consists of Miles Davis' rhythm section of the time (pianist Wynton Kelly, bassist Paul Chambers and drummer Jimmy Cobb) along with the late great trumpeter Booker Little. The music, mostly comprising Strozier originals, is advanced hard bop and the music is both enjoyable and (due to Little's presence) somewhat historic. —*Scott Yanow*

Cool, Calm and Collected / Oct. 13, 1960 / Vee-Jay ✦✦✦✦

This advanced hard-bop session from 1960 was previously unreleased until it appeared on a Vee-Jay CD in 1994. Altoist Frank Strozier is heard with a Chicago-based trio comprising pianist Billy Wallace, bassist Bill Lee and drummer Vernel Fournier. The CD really gives listeners two records in one because of the seven songs, all but one are heard in two versions and two of the pieces are heard three times. Strozier is in fine form, the obscure Billy Wallace (mistakenly called Wallace Williams in the liner notes) plays some fiery solos and the performances are satisfying. Still, due to the duplicate titles, one might not want to consume the whole program in one sitting. —*Scott Yanow*

Long Night / Sep. 12, 1961 / Jazzland ✦✦✦✦

Driving bop, it features George Coleman (ts). —*David Szatmary*

March of the Siamese Children / Mar. 28, 1962 / Jazzland ✦✦✦✦✦

This outstanding session was recorded with Harold Mabern (p). —*David Szatmary*

Remember Me / Nov. 10, 1976 / Steeple Chase ✦✦✦✦

Despite being a talented altoist, Frank Strozier had not led a record date in 15 years when he headed this session (which was released domestically by Inner City). Teamed with fluegelhornist Danny Moore, Howard Johnson on tuba, pianist Harold Mabern, bassist Lisle Atkinson and drummer Michael Carvin, Strozier (who plays flute on one piece) shows that he was still in prime form in the mid-'70s. He performs five of his originals, a piece by Atkinson and Cole Porter's "Get Out of Town." The music, which falls between hard bop and post-bop, holds one's interest throughout, making one regret that this LP is long out of print and that Strozier has received few additional opportunities to lead his own dates. —*Scott Yanow*

What's Goin' Out / Nov. 5, 1977 / Steeple Chase ✦✦✦

John Stubblefield

b. Feb. 4, 1945, Little Rock, AR
Tenor Saxophone, Soprano Saxophone / Post-Bop

Long a talented tenor saxophonist able to fit into a wide variety of advanced settings, John Stubblefield's strong abilities have often been taken for granted. He moved to Chicago as a young player, joined the AACM, studied with Muhal Richard Abrams and made his recording debut in 1968 with Joseph Jarman. Stubblefield relocated to New York in 1971 where during that decade he worked with the Collective Black Artists' big band, Mary Lou Williams, Charles Mingus, the Thad Jones-Mel Lewis Orchestra, Tito Puente, Anthony Braxton, Abdullah Ibrahim, Miles Davis (1973), McCoy Tyner, Gil Evans, and Lester Bowie, among others. Stubblefield, who often worked as a jazz educator and with the famed Jazzmobile, sometimes appears with the Mingus Big Band. He has recorded as a leader for Storyville (1976), Sutra, Soul Note and Enja. —*Scott Yanow*

Prelude / Dec. 8, 1976-Dec. 9, 1976 / Storyville ✦✦✦✦

Tenor saxophonist John Stubblefield (who switches to soprano for one selection) explores six group originals with trumpeter Cecil Bridgewater, pianist Onaje Allen Gumbs, bassist Cecil McBee, drummer Joe Chambers and percussionist Mtume. For his debut as a leader, Stubblefield and the other musicians play what could be called free-bop, a style falling between the modern mainstream and the avant-garde, with fine results. Little unpredictable occurs but this is a good effort. —*Scott Yanow*

● **Bushman Song** / Apr. 22, 1986-Apr. 23, 1986 / Enja ✦✦✦✦✦

Countin' on the Blues / May 27, 1987-May 28, 1987 / Enja ✦✦✦

Confessin' / Sep. 18, 1994-Sep. 21, 1994 / Soul Note ✦✦✦✦

L. Subramaniam (Lakshiminarayana Subramaniam)

b. Jul. 23, 1947, Madras, India
Violin / World Fusion

A gifted South Indian counterpart of Jean-Luc Ponty on the electric violin and endlessly curious about all kinds of music, Subramaniam has been a pioneer in exploring intelligent fusions between European classical music, American jazz, rock and South Indian music. His father, a master Indian violinist, and mother, who played the Indian vina, were his first musical influences, and after abandoning a career in medicine, he formed a violin trio with his two brothers while still in India. He toured America and Europe with Ravi Shankar and ex-Beatle George Harrison in 1974, made his first fusion album in Copenhagen Garland and wrote material for Stu Goldberg and Larry Coryell in 1978. He settled in the Los Angeles area in the late '70s in order to earn a doctorate in Western music at California Institute of the Arts, where he also taught South Indian music. He led a group with Coryell, George Duke and Tom Scott in the 1980s and recorded several fascinating LPs for Milestone—including an LP with Stephane Grappelli—that fused classical music, electric and acoustic jazz, and South Indian music. Subramaniam has also written works for classical orchestras; his *Violin Concerto* juxtaposes naive Hollywood-ish Romantic music with South Indian instruments and structures. —*Richard S. Ginell*

Garland / Apr. 1978 / Storyville ✦✦✦

Fantasy without Limits / Sep. 26, 1979-Sep. 27, 1979 / Trend ✦✦✦✦

Nice East vs. West concept featuring the great Indian violinist L. Subramaniam with the great bop alto saxophonist Frank Morgan. They make an effective team, and the two sensibilities converge for an interesting but sometimes uneven dialogue. —*Ron Wynn*

Blossom / 1981 / MCA ✦✦✦

L. Subramaniam is an accomplished Indian violinist with an open mind towards fusion and jazz. On this somewhat obscure LP from a short-lived MCA subsidiary run by the Crusaders, Subramaniam is joined on various tracks by keyboardists Herbie Hancock, Stu Goldberg, George Cables and Ronnie Foster, guitarist Larry Coryell and some top studio players. Altoist John Handy (who has long been an exponent of combining Western and Eastern music) has a solo on "Roots." This is an interesting set, but it will be hard to find. —*Scott Yanow*

Spanish Wave / 1983 / Milestone ✦✦✦✦

The first of violinist L. Subramaniam's string of Milestone recordings (and one of the ones that have been reissued on CD), this fusion-oriented set has strong doses of world music. In addition to the leader, the key players include Tom Scott on lyricon, soprano and flute, and guitarists Jorge Strunz and Larry Coryell; other guests include keyboardist George Duke and bassist Stanley Clarke. The music is atmospheric, challenging and often quite accessible, certainly falling into a unique niche. —*Scott Yanow*

Indian Express / 1984 / Milestone ✦✦✦✦

L. Subramaniam's second of four Milestone recordings finds him not only playing violin but the brand-new violin synthesizer, viola and a mini-harp called the svarmandal. With the strong influence of Indian classical music, folk songs and fusion, L. Subramaniam welcomes such top open-minded musicians as guitarist Jorge Strunz, bassist Stanley Clarke, drummer Stix Hooper, keyboardist John Beasley and flutist Hubert Laws (who doubles on piccolo) to a consistently surprising and generally stimulating session of atmospheric and sometimes haunting music. —*Scott Yanow*

● **Conversations** / 1984 / Milestone ✦✦✦✦✦

Although fellow violinist Stephane Grappelli is billed as co-leader, this is very much L. Subramaniam's date. All eight compositions (except for Grappelli's solo piano rendition of his "Tribute to Mani") are by Subramaniam, and the music (which utilizes electronics, modern rhythms and the influence of Mani's Indian heritage) is quite unusual for a Grappelli session. Altoist Frank Morgan helps out on "Memories," and other sidemen include such notables as keyboardist Joe Sample and guitarist Jorge Strunz. The contrast between the two surprisingly complementary violinists is a strong reason to acquire this CD. —*Scott Yanow*

Mani and Co. / 1986 / Milestone ✦✦✦✦✦

As with the best jazz musicians, violinist L. Subramaniam has carved out his own unique area of music. Originally an Indian classical musician, Subramaniam developed into an expert improviser who combined together several jazz styles (including fusion and straightahead) with the strong influence of his homeland's heritage. On his fourth and thusfar final Milestone recording, Subramaniam plays seven originals, varying the personnel on each number. Among his guests are trumpeter Maynard Ferguson, Bud Shank on alto and flute, guitarist Larry Coryell, keyboardist Mark Massey and drummer Tony Williams. —*Scott Yanow*

Dick Sudhalter

b. Dec. 28, 1938, Boston, MA
Cornet / Swing, Classic Jazz

Dick Sudhalter has had an unusual dual career as a superior trad-oriented cornetist and as a jazz journalist. The crowning achievement of his latter career was the co-authorship (with Philip Evans and William Dean-Myatt) of the superb Bix Beiderbecke biography *Bix: Man and Legend*. Less known is that Sudhalter has long been a fine improviser himself. He grew up in Boston and played in England in the 1960s (organizing the New Paul Whiteman Orchestra). Since returning to the US Sudhalter has freelanced on the classic jazz scene, played with the New York Jazz Repertory Company and the Classic Jazz Quartet and recorded for several labels including Audiophile and Challenge. —*Scott Yanow*

Get Out and Get Under the Moon / Jul. 11, 1989-Aug. 8, 1989 / Stomp Off ✦✦✦✦

Trumpeters Dick Sudhalter and Connie Jones team up during most of this Stomp Off release. While Jones often sounds close to Bobby Hackett, Sudhalter has a touch more of Bix in his style. Rather than a trumpet battle, this is a relaxed collaboration between very complementary musicians. On a set long on charm and comfort, Jones has a fine feature on Willard Robison's "Ol' Pigeon-Toed Joad," while Sudhalter takes three duets with the versatile pianist Keith Ingham. Clarinetist Joe Muranyi (doing a great imitation of Pee Wheman Russell on "Singin' the Blues") and trombonist Bobby Pring make a few brief appearances, but the emphasis is on the lyrical interplay of the two trumpeters. —*Scott Yanow*

● **After Awhile** / May 30, 1994-Jun. 7, 1994 / Jazz Challenge ✦✦✦✦✦

Dick Sudhalter, best known as one of the three writers responsible for one of the great jazz biographies (*Bix—Man and Legend*), is also a fine trumpeter who has the influence of Bix Beiderbecke fairly well-buried in his own lyrical style. Sudhalter had lived in England during the 1965-75 period, making this get-together (subtitled "& His London Friends") a musical reunion. Sudhalter and 13 other musicians are heard together in different combinations caressing a set of high-quality swing standards. With Keith Nichols (doubling on piano and trombone), altoist John R.T. Davies and trombonists Roy Williams and Jim Shepherd emerging as the top soloists in the supporting cast, Sudhalter sounds quite inspired. Whether it be "Dream a Little Dream of Me," "Tea for Two," "The Blue Room" or "Rose of Washington Square," this is a delightful and very melodic set. —*Scott Yanow*

With Pleasure / Dec. 1, 1995 / Audiophile ✦✦✦

Idrees Sulieman

b. Aug. 7, 1923, St. Petersburg, FL
Trumpet, Fluegelhorn / Bop

A top bebop trumpeter with a wide range, Idrees Sulieman's decision to move to Scandinavia in 1961 has cut into his potential fame but resulted in steady work on the Continent. He studied at Boston Conservatory and gained early experience playing with the Carolina Cotton Pickers and the wartime Earl Hines Orchestra

(1943-44). Sulieman was closely associated with Mary Lou Williams for a time; he also worked with Thelonious Monk in 1947 and had stints with Cab Calloway, Count Basie and Lionel Hampton. Sulieman recorded with Coleman Hawkins (1957) and gigged with Randy Weston (1958-59) in addition to popping up in many other situations. He went to Europe in 1961 to tour with Oscar Dennard and then settled in Stockholm, moving to Copenhagen in 1964. A major soloist with the Kenny Clarke-Francy Boland Big Band from the mid-'60s through 1973, Sulieman has frequently worked with radio orchestras. His recordings as a leader have been for Swedish Columbia (1964) and Steeple Chase (1976 and 1985). —*Scott Yanow*

Now Is the Time / Feb. 16, 1976-Feb. 17, 1976 / Steeple Chase ✦✦✦✦

● **Bird's Grass** / Dec. 10, 1976 / Steeple Chase ✦✦✦✦✦

Prior to 1976, the talented bop-oriented trumpeter Idrees Sulieman had only led one record date (back in 1964). On this superior set, Sulieman is teamed in Copenhagen with tenor saxophonist Per Goldschmidt, pianist Horace Parlan, bassist Niels Pedersen and drummer Kenny Clarke. They perform a pair of straightahead originals, Michel Legrand's "The Summer Knows" and a pair of bop standards ("Wee" and "Billie's Bounce"). Excellent music with plenty of colorful solos. —*Scott Yanow*

Groovin' / Aug. 2, 1985 / Steeple Chase ✦✦✦✦

Nine years after his last Steeple Chase set, the underrated trumpeter Idrees Sulieman reunited with Per Goldschmidt (who doubles on tenor and baritone) and pianist Horace Parlan for another fine straightahead date. With bassist Mads Vinding and drummer Billy Hart completing the quintet, the talented players stretch out on "Groovin' High," a couple of obscurities and three group originals. Five days short of his 62nd birthday, Idrees Sulieman was still in fine form for this record. —*Scott Yanow*

Ira Sullivan

b. May 1, 1931, Washington, DC
Trumpet, Tenor Saxophone, Flute, Soprano Saxophone, Alto Saxophone / Bop, Post-Bop

Ira Sullivan, who is equally skilled on trumpet and a variety of reeds, is one of the great talents in jazz. But due to his desire to be away from the spotlight, his contributions have often been overlooked. His father taught him the trumpet and his mother the saxophone. Sullivan was a key part of the Chicago jazz scene of the 1950s, jamming with visiting all-stars and in 1956 spending some time with Art Blakey's Jazz Messengers. He settled in Florida in the early '60s and, although he has been active locally, he only emerges on the national jazz scene on an irregular basis. His most notable association during the past 20 years was with Red Rodney in a brilliant (and fortunately well recorded) quintet that also included pianist Garry Dial. Sullivan has retained an open-minded approach to music and has never been afraid to try new things. Virtually all of his recordings offer some surprises. —*Scott Yanow*

Nicky's Tune / Dec. 24, 1958 / Delmark ✦✦✦✦

The talented Ira Sullivan has led relatively few sessions throughout his career considering his skills. This CD brings back his second full album as a leader, adding the previously unissued "Mock and Roll Blues" (a stomping tune) to the original five-song program. Sullivan, who sticks here exclusively to trumpet, is joined by the obscure tenor Nicky Hill, pianist Jodie Christian, bassist Victor Sproles and drummer Wilbur Campbell. The music (two standards and four originals) is essentially straightahead bop and generally swings quite hard. —*Scott Yanow*

Blue Stroll / Jul. 26, 1959 / Delmark ✦✦✦✦✦

Ira Sullivan was an important force on the Chicago jazz scene during the 1950s, up until he moved to Florida in 1962. He led relatively few dates during the era, all of which are recommended. For this Delmark LP (reissued in 1988), Sullivan teams up with tenor saxophonist Johnny Griffin, pianist Jodie Christian, bassist Victor Sproles and drummer Wilbur Campbell for three group originals and the ballad "My Old Flame." Most interesting is the 17-minute "Bluzinbee," which finds Sullivan taking solos on baritone, trumpet, peck horn and alto while Griffin switches between alto, tenor and baritone. —*Scott Yanow*

Ira Sullivan Quintet: Blue Stroll / Jul. 26, 1959 / Delmark ✦✦✦✦✦

In Chicago with Johnny Griffin (sax) and Jodie Christian (p). Excellent. —*Michael G. Nastos*

Bird Lives! / Mar. 12, 1962 / Vee-Jay ✦✦✦✦

Ira Sullivan's quintet played at a Charlie Parker Memorial concert in Chicago on Mar. 12, 1962, and the results (six selections) were originally released on a single LP. The release of this double CD greatly expanded the program. The multi-instrumentalist Ira Sullivan sticks to trumpet and fluegelhorn throughout, the legendary tenor Nicky Hill (who made very few recordings) has a rare chance to stretch out on record (combining touches of Coltrane and Booker Ervin with a full tone of his own) and it is interesting to hear some hints of the then-current free jazz movement (particularly in the playing of bassist Don Garrett). Overall, a fine bop set. —Scott Yanow

Horizons / Mar 2, 1967 / Discovery ✦✦✦

Ira Sullivan's first recording in five years (which was originally released on Atlantic) features him switching between soprano, tenor, trumpet and fluegelhorn with a quintet consisting of some obscure Florida players: pianist Dolphe Castellano, trombonist Lon Norman, bassist William Fry and drummer Jose Cigno. The relaxed and thought-provoking performances of tunes ranging from "Norwegian Wood" and "Everything Happens to Me" to group originals display a solid group sound and Sullivan's interest in integrating freer music and ideas into his playing. —Scott Yanow

Ira Sullivan / Dec. 9, 1975-Mar. 9, 1976 / A&M ✦✦✦

Ira Sullivan has long been a remarkable multi-instrumentalist with a personal sound on each of his horns. On this A&M release, Sullivan mostly sticks to soprano and flute although he plays trumpet briefly on "Old Hundredth" and stretches out on tenor during a lengthy medley of his "Slighty Arched" and the standard "Spring Can Really Hang You Up the Most." His supporting cast includes the talented guitarist Joe Diorio and on one selection an unknown bassist named Jaco (here misspelled Joco) Pastorius. The generally thoughtful music is not as exciting as some of Sullivan's other sessions (particularly the later ones with Red Rodney) but has its strong moments. —Scott Yanow

Multimedia / Dec. 5, 1977-Sep. 21, 1978 / Galaxy ✦✦✦✦

One of two Ira Sullivan recordings for Galaxy (the other is Peace). On four of the five selections the multi-instrumentalist (who on the album plays tenor, alto flute, flute, soprano and trumpet) performs with guitarist Joe Diori in a quintet also including bassist John Heard, drummer Billy Higgins and percussionist Kenneth Nash; on the slightly earlier "Strut," Sullivan is joined by just Nash and bassist Monte Budwig. Among the highlights of the fairly straightforward program are a swinging "Anthropology," "Painted Ladies (A Confiscated Bolero)" and "Autumn Leaves." A fine effort. —Scott Yanow

Ira Sullivan / Dec. 11, 1977-Dec. 20, 1977 / Flying Fish ✦✦✦✦

The talented multi-instrumentalist Ira Sullivan made a rare return to Chicago for this set, performing with bassist Jodie Christian, guitarist Simon Salz, bassist Dan Shapera and drummer Wilbur Campbell. Switching between trumpet, fluegelhorn, soprano and flute, Sullivan performs a couple of originals and four standards including the bop classic "That's Earl, Brother." This is a more straightahead than usual program of music by the adventurous improviser. —Scott Yanow

Peace / Sep. 20, 1978+Sep. 21, 1978 / Galaxy ✦✦✦✦

The remarkable Ira Sullivan (who on this album plays trumpet, fluegelhorn, flute, alto flute, soprano and tenor with equal skill) teams up with the underrated guitarist Joe Diorio, bassist John Heard, drummer Billy Higgins and percussionist Kenneth Nash for a diverse program of music. Ranging from "I Get a Kick Out of You" and a tolerable version of "Send in the Clowns" to Diorio's "Gong" and Horace Silver's "Peace," Sullivan and Diorio contribute many intriguing solos. —Scott Yanow

● **The Incredible** / Jun. 1980 / Stash ✦✦✦✦✦

The title of this LP is not hype, for Ira Sullivan throughout the date shows off his impressive improvising skills on trumpet, fluegelhorn, alto, tenor and flute, sometimes overdubbing (mostly for melody statements). Joined by pianist Hank Jones, bassist Eddie Gomez and drummer Duffy Jackson, Sullivan plays several straightahead standards (including "Our Delight," "Bernie's Tune" and "Satin Doll") along with some newer pieces. He displays both his mastery of bop and of more advanced (and freer) ideas. A fairly definitive session by the underrated Ira Sullivan. —Scott Yanow

Ira Sullivan Does It All / Sep. 14, 1981 / Muse ✦✦✦✦✦

Most of the recordings by the early-'80s Red Rodney-Ira Sullivan Quintet were issued under Rodney's name, but this outing for Muse was an exception. With pianist Garry Dial, bassist Jay Anderson and drummer Steve Bagby completing the unit, this was a mighty group that consistently inspired Rodney to play music more advanced than bebop. Sullivan, who switches between soprano, alto and fluegelhorn, matched well with Rodney. They perform five fairly concise pieces (including "The More I See You" and "Amazing Grace"), plus lengthy renditions of John Coltrane's "Central Park West" and Herbie Hancock's "Dolphin Dance"; the latter two pieces add the effective bassoon of Mike Rabinowitz (the first fulltime jazz bassoonist). Recommended. —Scott Yanow

Strings Attached / Jan. 1982-Mar. 1983 / Pausa ✦✦✦

Ira Sullivan has recorded much less throughout his career than his talent deserves, partly because he has spent many years living in Florida. This obscure LP features Sullivan on trumpet, fluegelhorn and flute joined by saxophonist John Alexander, a rhythm section and a string quartet. Sullivan and the younger players perform six group originals that emphasize the lyrical side of the great multi-instrumental-

ist and effectively blend together the strings (of which viola player Debbie Spring is best-known) with the jazz ensemble. —Scott Yanow

Joe Sullivan (Joseph Michael Sullivan)

b. Nov. 4, 1906, Chicago, IL, **d.** Oct. 13, 1971, San Francisco, CA
Piano / Dixieland, Swing

One of the great Earl Hines disciples (along with Jess Stacy), Joe Sullivan's style was perfect for the freewheeling jazz of Eddie Condon's bands. Sullivan graduated from the Chicago Conservatory and was an important contributor to the Chicago jazz scene of the 1920s. He was in New York during the next decade and his solo recordings include an original ("Little Rock Getaway") that would become a standard. In 1936 Sullivan joined Bob Crosby's band but turberculosis put him in the hospital for ten months and Bob Zurke replaced him (having a hit with "Little Rock Getaway!"). However Sullivan recovered, led his own record dates and was involved in a lot of jam sessions with the Condon gang in the 1940s. By the 1950s he was largely forgotten, playing solo in San Francisco and drinking much more than he should. Despite an occasional recording and a successful appearance at the Teagarden family reunion at the 1963 Monterey Jazz Festival, Sullivan's prime years were long gone by the time he passed away. —Scott Yanow

★ **1933-1941** / Sep. 26, 1933-Mar. 28, 1941 / Classics ✦✦✦✦✦

All of pianist Joe Sullivan's early recordings as a leader are on this definitive CD. Sullivan is heard on a dozen solo performances from 1933, 1935 and 1941 (including the two earliest versions of his hit "Little Rock Getaway" along with memorable renditions of "My Little Pride and Joy" and "Honeysuckle Rose"), four selections with "the Three Deuces" (a trio with clarinetist Pee Wee Russell and drummer Zutty Singleton) and eight numbers with an octet featuring the underrated trumpeter Ed Anderson, trombonist Benny Morton, clarinetist Edmond Hall and vocals by Big Joe Turner (who manages to turn "I Can't Give You Anything but Love" into a blues) and Helen Ward. This French import is essential for fans of the great stride pianist. —Scott Yanow

Piano / 1944-1946 / Folkways ✦✦✦✦

This collector's LP features the great stride pianist Joe Sullivan in a variety of settings. He takes eight selections as unaccompanied solos (including "Begin the Beguine," "The Way You Look Tonight," "Keepin' Out of Mischief Now" and "Fidgety Feet"), jams two numbers with soprano saxophonist Sidney Bechet in a quartet, plays "St. Louis Blues" with a sextet headed by trumpeter Yank Lawson and backs singer Stella Brooks on "Rabbit Foot Blues." Sullivan is heard in prime form throughout, and this music (which will hopefully be reissued on CD) should interest Dixieland and swing collectors. —Scott Yanow

New Solos by an Old Master / Aug. 1951 / Riverside ✦✦✦✦

Pianist Joe Sullivan, although only 44 at the time, was already slipping into obscurity when he recorded these nine solo and three trio performances (with bassist Dave Lario and drummer Smoky Stover). Still in fine form, Sullivan romps through six of his originals (including "My Little Pride and Joy," "Gin Mill Blues" and his famous "Little Rock Getaway") and six standards (highlighted by "That's a Plenty" and "Honeysuckle Rose"), but this LP has not been available in far too many years and has thus far been overlooked by the Original Jazz Classics series. —Scott Yanow

Joe Sullivan / Apr. 29, 1963-Nov. 11, 1963 / Pumpkin ✦✦✦

Alcoholism and a lack of business sense resulted in the talented stride pianist Joe Sullivan being obscure for his last 20 years (he died in 1971). Richard Hadlock taped Sullivan playing piano solos at the Trident club in San Francisco during 1963, and they were released on this 1983 Pumpkin LP; these are the only recordings of Sullivan as a leader after 1955. In general, the pianist (even with a few minor missteps) is heard in good form, playing his usual repertoire of veteran swing tunes and songs associated with Fats Waller (along with his own "My Little Pride and Joy"). Because he was still only 57 at the time, it is a shame that this album (plus his appearance with Jack Teagarden at the 1963 Monterey Jazz Festival) was essentially the end of Joe Sullivan's career. Worth searching for. —Scott Yanow

Maxine Sullivan (Marietta Williams)

b. May 13, 1911, Homestead, PA, **d.** Apr. 7, 1987, New York, NY
Vocals / Swing, Standards

A subtle and lightly swinging jazz singer, Maxine Sullivan's delivery was very likable, and she did justice to all of the lyrics she sang during her long career. After moving to New York, Sullivan sang during intermissions at the Onyx Club and was discovered by pianist Claude Thornhill. Thornhill recorded her with a sympathetic septet singing a couple of standards and two Scottish folk songs performed in swinging fashion—"Annie Laurie" and "Loch Lomond." The latter became a big hit and Sullivan's signature song for the rest of her career.

Future sessions found her singing vintage folk tunes such as "Darling Nellie Gray," "I Dream of Jeanie," "Drink to Me Only With Thine Eyes" and "If I Had a Ribbon Bow." Even if lightning did not strike twice, she was now a popular attraction. She appeared briefly in the movie "Going Places" opposite Louis Armstrong and in the Broadway show *Swingin' the Dream*. From 1940-42, Sullivan often sang with her husband, bassist John Kirby's Sextet, a perfect outlet for her cool sound. She starred for two years on a radio series, *Flow Gently Sweet Rhythm;* she had a reasonably successful solo career, and then in the mid-1950s (similar to Alberta Hunter) became a trained nurse. In 1968, the singer began making a comeback, performing at festivals and even playing a little bit of valve trombone and fluegelhorn. Now married to pianist Cliff Jackson, Sullivan (whose style and appealing voice were unchanged from earlier years) sometimes appeared with the World's Greatest Jazz Band, and she recorded frequently. During her later period, she often sang with mainstream jazz groups, including Scott Hamilton's. Quite fittingly, the last song that she ever recorded in concert was the same as her first record, "Loch Lomond."

Maxine Sullivan's earliest recordings are available on a Classics CD. A Tono LP has some of her mid-period recordings, and from 1969 on, she recorded for Monmouth Evergreen (reissued on Audiophile), Fat Cat Jazz, Riff, Kenneth, Stash, Atlantic and Concord. —*Scott Yanow*

● **1937-1938** / 1937 / Classics ◆◆◆
The basic and pleasing vocals of Maxine Sullivan are quite enjoyable. This CD has her first 23 recordings, including three songs originally released under pianist Claude Thornhill's name; Thornhill (who helped discover the singer) is on all of the selections. The original version of "Loch Lomond" is among the highlights and became a huge hit, leading to Sullivan's lightly swinging renditions of other folk songs such as "Darling Nellie Gray" and "Dark Eyes." Joined by such fine musicians as trumpeters Manny Klein, Frank Newton, Charlie Shavers and Bobby Hackett (all of whom are heard from briefly), along with the future members of the John Kirby Sextet, Maxine Sullivan is heard throughout in her early prime (she was 26-27 years old during this period). Recommended. —*Scott Yanow*

The Biggest Little Band in the Land / Oct. 10, 1940-Jan. 20, 1941 / Circle ◆◆◆◆
This CD contains music recorded for the Lang-Worth Transcriptions by the John Kirby Sextet plus singer Maxine Sullivan. Actually Sullivan is only on five of the 18 songs, singing in her typically light and straightforward manner. The other selections feature the unique sextet (trumpeter Charlie Shavers, clarinetist Buster Bailey, altoist Russell Procope, pianist Billy Kyle, bassist John Kirby and drummer O'Neil Spencer) performing a program heavy on adaptations of classical themes and novel melodies. Shavers in particular comes across well and the set should please Kirby's fans. —*Scott Yanow*

Loch Lomond / 1940-1941 / Circle ◆◆◆◆
Singer Maxine Sullivan gets top billing on this CD reissue, and she has delightful vocals on 11 of the selections, but there are also 15 instrumentals by the "backup group," the John Kirby Sextet, as Sullivan was married to the bassist/leader at the time. In addition to the title cut (a remake of her biggest hit), she is in fine form on a variety of folk-oriented songs, including two versions of "If I Had a Ribbon Bow." However, it is the sextet features that are of greatest interest. The classic early cool jazz group (bassist Kirby, trumpeter Charlie Shavers, clarinetist Buster Bailey, altoist Russell Procope, pianist Billy Kyle and drummer Cozy Cole, who had replaced O'Neil Spencer) romps through such unlikely but swinging tunes as "Humoresque," "Haydn Gets Hip," "Bounce of the Sugar Plum Fairy" and "Amapola." These selections were originally recorded as radio transcriptions for the Lang-Worth service, and they are important additions to the discographies of both Kirby and Sullivan. —*Scott Yanow*

1944-1948 / Nov. 24, 1944-1948 / Tono ◆◆◆◆
Vocalist Maxine Sullivan, who had a hit with "Loch Lomond," recorded some other popular numbers in the late '30s and worked with John Kirby's Orchestra, making 18 obscure recordings during 1944-48 for the Bacon/Davis, International and Apollo labels. Sixteen selections (all but two songs that were included on an earlier Onyx album) are on this attractive collector's LP. The straightforward singer is heard backed by a quintet plus strings led by bassist Cedric Wallace, "The New Friends of Rhythm" (a different string group), Larry Johnson's Orchestra and, best of all, swinging on six numbers with pianist Ellis Larkins' trio. Despite the lack of sales at the time, Sullivan is heard in prime form throughout such numbers as "Skylark," "Legalize My Name," "Restless" and remakes of "If I Had a Ribbon Bow" and "Loch Lomond." Even with the high quality of these enjoyable recordings, Maxine Sullivan (who would find her sophisticated swing approach to be a bit out of fashion) would not record (other than two numbers in 1953) again until 1955. —*Scott Yanow*

● **Tribute to Andy Razaf** / Aug. 30, 1956 / DCC ◆◆◆◆◆
Maxine Sullivan always had a cheerful and subtly swinging style. This formerly rare release (originally on the Period label) finds her interpreting a dozen numbers that have the lyrics of Andy Razaf including such classics as "Keeping out of Mischief Now," "Stompin' at the Savoy," "Honeysuckle Rose," "Memories of You" and "Ain't Misbehavin'." Joined by a sextet reminiscent of John Kirby's group of 15 years earlier (and featuring such Kirby alumni as trumpeter Charlie Shavers and clarinetist Buster Bailey), Sullivan is in top form on this delightful session. —*Scott Yanow*

Manassas Jazz Festival / May 29, 1966 / Jazzology ◆◆◆◆
Maxine Sullivan was semi-retired and had not recorded for a decade when she appeared at the first annual Manassas Jazz Festival in 1966. Although she gets first billing, Sullivan is only on 40 percent of the album, but the singer manages to steal honors often. Accompanied by a quartet including clarinetist Tom Gwaltney and pianist Marian McPartland, she performs "Surprise Party," her old hit "If I Had a Ribbon Bow," "I Thought About You," "Loch Lomond" and "I'm Coming Virginia." Sullivan's husband, the great stride pianist Cliff Jackson, gets to romp on "Ain't Misbehavin'," "Honeysuckle Rose" and "Carolina Shout," in addition to accompanying Fat Cat McRee's vocal on "Tishomingo Blues." The second half of the album mostly features the guitar and vocals of Doc Souchon, sometimes joined by rhythm guitarist Steve Jordan. Overall, this little-known LP is both historic and enjoyable, particularly for classic jazz collectors. —*Scott Yanow*

Close As Pages in a Book / Jun. 11, 1969+Jun. 13, 1969 / Monmouth ◆◆◆◆◆
After a period off the music scene during which she worked as a nurse, Maxine Sullivan (who had not recorded a full album since 1956) really started her successful comeback with this strong effort. Originally made for Monmouth-Evergreen and later reissued on Audiophile, the set features the subtle and lightly swinging singer sharing the spotlight with Bob Wilber (who doubles on clarinet and soprano in addition to providing the arrangements), pianist Bernie Leighton, bassist George Duvivier and drummer Gus Johnson. Sullivan performs remakes of "Loch Lomond" and "Gone With the Wind" and also sings ten high-quality swing-era tunes, including most memorably "As Long as I Live," "Darn That Dream" and "Close as Pages in a Book." At 58, Maxine Sullivan (who was still in her musical prime) shows that she still had a long way to go. —*Scott Yanow*

Sullivan Shakespeare, Hyman / Jun. 15, 1971-Jun. 22, 1971 / Monmouth ◆◆◆
This CD reissues one of the stranger jazz recordings. Pianist Dick Hyman wrote the music for a dozen sonnets by William Shakespeare, songs that had appeared in some of Shakespeare's comedies. Classical baritonist Earl Wrightson originally recorded the pieces, and a few years later, Maxine Sullivan made this jazz version for Monmouth-Evergreen. Her performances (with Hyman, trumpeter Rusty Dedrick, guitarist Bucky Pizzarelli, bassist Milt Hinton and drummer Don Lamond) were rather brief, so for the Audiophile reissue, Hyman recorded additional solo renditions of most of the selections. Overall, Sullivan's vocals get a bit hard to take, due to the antiquated lyrics (although her voice sounds fine), and none of Hyman's melodies are all that memorable, even though a couple of his later solos display some heat. A historical curiosity, but little more. —*Scott Yanow*

Maxine / Oct. 12, 1975 / Audiophile ◆◆◆◆
In 1975 veteran singer Maxine Sullivan was touring Europe with the World's Greatest Jazz Band. She took time off to record with the Dutch band of drummer Ted Easton, a fine trad group. The pianoless sextet (which features solos from trumpeter Bob Wulffers, trombonist Henk Van Muyen and Frits Kaatee on clarinet and tenor) inspires Sullivan to some of her best singing of the period. Highlights of the 1982 LP include "The Lady's in Love With You," "I Cover the Waterfront," "I've Got the World on a String" and "As Long as I Live." —*Scott Yanow*

Maxine Sullivan [Riff] / Oct. 12, 1975 / Riff ◆◆◆◆
A solid date with Ted Easton's sextet. —*Michael G. Nastos*

We Just Couldn't Say Goodbye / Feb. 6, 1978 / Audiophile ◆◆◆◆
Two former LPs are combined on this single CD. The subtle but always swinging singer Maxine Sullivan is heard on a very pleasing 1983 session in which she is joined by trumpeter Doc Cheatham (who sounds quite lyrical), the underrated clarinetist Herb Hall, pianist Red Richards, bassist Ike Isaacs and drummer Tom Martin. But good as that date is, it is the first half of this CD that is most memorable. Sullivan sounds exuberant while being inspired by the great cornetist Ernie Carson, Spencer Clark on baritone, pianist Art Hodes, bassist Johnny Haynes and drummer Martin. Carson takes many heated solos; Hodes is often rollicking, and Sullivan's voice is heard throughout in prime form—she even takes a valve trombone solo on one song. Highlights include definitive versions of "We Just Couldn't say Goodbye," "Someday Sweetheart," "That Old Feeling" and "Between the Devil and the Deep Blue Sea." In addition, there is a previously unreleased version of "It's the Talk of the Town" from Feb. 8, 1978, a very spontaneous performance with

Hodes' band during an otherwise instrumental session. Highly recommended. —*Scott Yanow*

With Ike Isaacs Trio / Feb. 10, 1978 / Audiophile ◆◆◆
Stalwart 1979 session with Ike Isaacs trio. —*Ron Wynn*

Good Morning, Life! / Nov. 13, 1983-Nov. 14, 1983 / Audiophile ◆◆◆
Although 72 and less than four years away from her death, Maxine Sullivan's singing voice and lightly swinging style were still in prime form in 1983. Joined by a light quartet that includes pianist Loonis McGlohon and Phil Thompson on flute and clarinet, Sullivan interprets McGlohon's title tune, various standards (including "I Thought About You," "Small Fry" and "It Could Happen to You") plus a couple of Fats Waller tunes and surprisingly hard-swinging versions of "Ridin' High" and "This Can't Be Love." —*Scott Yanow*

It Was Great Fun / 1983 / Audiophile ◆◆◆◆◆
Solid vocals, nice arrangements. —*Ron Wynn*

On Tour With the Allegheny Jazz Quartet / Mar. 11, 1984-Mar. 15, 1984 / Jump ◆◆◆◆
For this fun LP, taken from a five-day tour, the Allegheny Jazz Quartet (consisting of pianist Keith Ingham, clarinetist Bob Reitmeier, bassist Lynn Seaton and drummer John Von Ohlen) are featured on three instrumentals (including "Rosetta" and "Jubilee"), Ingham and Reitmeier take the vocal on "Back in Your Own Backyard," and veteran swing singer Maxine Sullivan is featured on six of the ten numbers (including "As Long as I Live," "I Thought About You" and "We Just Couldn't Say Goodbye"). Enjoyable music. —*Scott Yanow*

Great Songs from the Cotton Club by Harold Arlen, Ted Koehler / Nov. 1984 / Milan ◆◆◆◆
On this fine set, 73-year-old singer Maxine Sullivan performs 16 songs composed by Harold Arlen and lyricist Ted Koehler between 1931-34 for the Cotton Club shows. With backing by pianist Keith Ingham's groups (which include Phil Bodner on reeds, a few guest appearances by tenor Al Klink and the great acoustic guitarist Marty Grosz), Sullivan brings out the beauty of the tunes. Many hits resulted from the Arlen-Koehler partnership, and the highlights of the program include "Happy as the Day Is Long," "As Long as I Live," "Between the Devil and the Deep Blue Sea," "Stormy Weather" and "I've Got the World on a String," along with a few obscurities. —*Scott Yanow*

Songs from the Cotton Club / 1984 / Mobile Fidelity ◆◆◆◆◆
Vocalist Maxine Sullivan sings the classic blues, jazz, and stomp tunes that were in vogue at the legendary Cotton Club in Harlem during the '20s, '30s, and '40s. Although well along in her career by this point ('84), she still had a hearty, animated voice and dynamic delivery and put enough punch in her versions to make these ancient tunes both authentic and contemporary. —*Ron Wynn*

Uptown / Jan. 1985 / Concord Jazz ◆◆◆◆
The first of her two Concord CDs, this set features veteran singer Maxine Sullivan performing ten of her favorite songs, all of which originated from the swing era or before. Sullivan sounds quite happy to be joined by tenor saxophonist Scott Hamilton's very complementary quintet (which also includes guitarist Chris Flory and pianist John Bunch). The best among the familiar songs are Maxine's renditions of "I Thought About You," "Wrap Your Troubles in Dreams," "By Myself" and "I Got a Right to Sing the Blues." —*Scott Yanow*

The Lady's in Love with You / May 15, 1985-Jun. 4, 1985 / Stash ◆◆◆◆
On this project, Maxine Sullivan (already a top jazz vocalist for 48 years) sings tasteful versions of 16 songs written by the underrated but very talented composer Burton Lane. Best known among the tunes (which feature Sullivan accompanied by pianist Keith Ingham and such fine players as trumpeter Glenn Zottola, Phil Bodner on clarinet and alto, and guitarist Marty Grosz) are "The Lady's in Love with You," "Everything I Have Is Yours," "On a Clear Day" and "I Hear Music," but even the obscurities are superior. —*Scott Yanow*

☆ **Sings the Music of Burton Lane** / May 15, 1985-Jun. 4, 1985 / Mobile Fidelity ◆◆◆◆◆
1986 release. Sullivan makes excellent tribute work. —*Ron Wynn*

Together / Jun. 1986-Jan. 1987 / Atlantic ◆◆◆◆
For her final studio album (the last cuts were recorded just three months before her death), the classic swing singer Maxine Sullivan interpreted 16 songs by Jule Styne dating from 1926's "Sunday" to 1983's "Killing Time." Sullivan's voice was still strong at the end of her career, and her interpretations of such numbers as "Just in Time," "It's Been a Long, Long Time," "I Don't Want to Walk Without You" and "I've Heard That Song Before" uplift the lyrics and make the tunes sound fresh and new. A fine close to a productive career. —*Scott Yanow*

Swingin' Sweet / Sep. 1986 / Concord Jazz ◆◆◆◆◆
Maxine Sullivan's final concert (although she would record part of her Jule Styne tribute studio album for Atlantic a few months later) is an excellent retrospective

of her career. Joined by tenor saxophonist Scott Hamilton's quintet (with pianist John Bunch and guitarist Chris Flory), Sullivan performs for the final time some of her favorite numbers, including nostalgic and near-classic renditions of "As Long as I Live," "I Got a Right to Sing the Blues," "A Hundred Years from Today" and "You're Driving Me Crazy." Ironically, the final song that Maxine Sullivan sang was also the same tune that she had used to start her recording career back in 1937, "Loch Lomond." Recommended. —*Scott Yanow*

Supersax

f. 1972
Group / Bop

In 1972 Med Flory and Buddy Clark formed a five-sax nonet (usually including a trumpeter) dedicated to playing the harmonized solos of Charlie Parker. Their recordings for Capitol, MPS and Columbia (unlike their live performances) did not contain any individual saxophone solos and found the sax section playing note-for-note Bird improvisations (including the roller coaster "Ko Ko") with impressive precision. Clark left the band in 1975 but Flory has continued the group on a part-time basis up to the present time, sometimes using the L.A. Voices. Among the top sidemen through the years have been Bill Perkins, Warne Marsh, Jay Migliori, Jack Nimitz, Lanny Morgan, trumpeter Conte Candoli and trombonist Carl Fontana. —*Scott Yanow*

● **Supersax Plays Bird** / 1972-1973 / Capitol ◆◆◆◆◆
Supersax's debut recording is still their best. The unusual group, which plays Charlie Parker solos harmonized for a five-piece saxophone section but with no individual sax solos (at least not on record; live they always did stretch out), found its own niche. With Conte Candoli as the trumpet soloist and a rhythm section comprising pianist Ronnell Bright, bassist Buddy Clark (who along with altoist Med Flory was the original co-leader) and drummer Jake Hanna, on this LP Supersax brought back quite a few of Bird's classic solos including "Just Friends," "Parker's Mood," "Lady Be Good," "Hot House" and most notably the rapid "Ko-Ko." This essential release is long overdue to be reissued on CD. —*Scott Yanow*

Salt Peanuts / 1973 / Pausa ◆◆◆◆◆
Supersax's second LP is almost the equal of their first. The five-piece sax section (who play harmonized versions of Charlie Parker solos) is joined by either trumpeter Conte Candoli or trombonist Carl Fontana and rhythm sections including either Walter Bishop, Ronnell Bright or Lou Levy on piano. Highlights include Parker's famous solos on "Yardbird Suite," "Groovin' High," "Embraceable You," "Confirmation" and "Salt Peanuts," although it was not such a good idea to recreate Bird's hesitant playing on "Lover Man." —*Scott Yanow*

Supersax Plays Bird with Strings / Oct. 1974 / Capitol ◆◆◆◆
Supersax's third and final LP for Capitol (none of which have yet been reissued on CD) finds the five saxes joined by a large string section on some of the selections so as to pay tribute to Charlie Parker's recordings with strings. Trumpeter Conte Candoli, trombonist Frank Rosolino and pianist Lou Levy have some solo space, and among the Bird solos that are recreated are "April in Paris," "Ornithology," "Cool Blues" and "I Didn't Know What Time It Was." But after this third recording, it was becoming clear that Supersax was running out of material and that the concept had largely run its course; pity that the group never did record a live album so the saxophonists could take individual solos. Instead, Supersax would soon become a part-time group. —*Scott Yanow*

Chasin' the Bird / 1977 / Verve ◆◆◆◆
For their fourth album, Supersax continued its practice of recreating recorded Charlie Parker solos harmonized for a full saxophone section. What was different this time around was that with one exception, all of the solos were taken from concerts rather than studio dates. The result is that the ensembles sound fresher (since Bird's live improvisations are generally not that well known) and longer. Trumpeters Blue Mitchell and Conte Candoli, trombonist Frank Rosolino and pianist Lou Levy get solo space, and highlights include "Shaw Nuff," "Drifting on a Reed," "Dizzy Atmosphere" and a six-minute rendition of "Night in Tunisia." —*Scott Yanow*

Dynamite / Apr. 24, 1978-Apr. 28, 1978 / MPS ◆◆◆◆◆
Supersax's fifth album is a departure from their earlier efforts. Rather than just having the five-piece saxophone section playing Charlie Parker solos, on this LP they perform three songs by Bud Powell (including "Tempus Fugit" and "Parisian Thoroughfare"), "Gloomy Sunday," Jobim's "Wave" and a pair of Med Flory originals in addition to two Bird numbers. The arrangements by leader Flory (Bill Holman wrote the chart for "Gloomy Sunday") are in the style of Charlie Parker, but the concept seems a bit pointless in this setting. Trumpeter Conte Candoli, trombonist Frank Rosolino and pianist Lou Levy get some solo space, while the saxophonists primarily stick to ensembles as usual. —*Scott Yanow*

Supersax & L.A. Voices, Vol. 2 / 1984 / Columbia ✦✦✦

On the second of three LPs matching Supersax (five saxophonists, trumpeter Conte Candoli and a rhythm section) with the five singers of L.A. Voices (which include Sue Raney on lead and leader-altoist Med Flory as one of the vocalists), only three of the nine pieces were actually recorded by Charlie Parker ("Just Friends," "They Can't Take That Away from Me" and "Bloomdido"), while the other sax choruses were written by the versatile Med Flory. The music (which includes "He Ain't Got Rhythm," "Speak Low" and "As Time Goes By") is interesting and spirited, but not too essential. —*Scott Yanow*

Supersax and L.A. Voices: Straighten Up and Fly Right / 1986 / Columbia ✦✦✦

For the third and final Columbia LP by Supersax and the L.A. Voices, the five saxes, five voices (which include Sue Raney and Supersax leader Med Flory), rhythm section (with pianist Lou Levy) and trumpeter Conte Candoli perform four songs recorded by Charlie Parker, John Coltrane's solo on "Someday My Prince Will Come," and Flory's arrangements on "Straighten Up and Fly Right" and three of the leader's originals (including one called "Super Sax"). The music is fun and swinging, but not as significant as Supersax's three Capitol recordings. —*Scott Yanow*

Stone Bird / 1989 / Columbia ✦✦✦

With the release of Clint Eastwood's film *Bird*, Supersax got together for their first instrumental recording (without the L.A. Voices) in ten years. They returned to their original concept, using Charlie Parker's original recorded solos (reharmonized for five saxophones) as melodies and featuring solos by trumpeter Conte Candoli and pianist Lou Levy (but none by the individual saxophonists). Several of the numbers had been recorded previously, but these renditions still sound fresh. Most memorable are "Scrapple from the Apple," "Salt Peanuts," "K.C. Blues" and "Confirmation." —*Scott Yanow*

John Surman (John Douglas Surman)

b. Aug. 30, 1944, Tavistock, England

Baritone Saxophone, Keyboards, Bass Clarinet, Soprano Saxophone / Post-Bop

The atmospheric sounds that John Surman creates on his horns have been a major asset to the ECM label ever since the late 1970s. One of England's top jazz players of the past 30 years, Surman is particularly strong on the baritone. Surman played in jazz workshops while still in high school. He studied at the London College of Music and London University Institute of Education in the mid-'60s. Surman played with Alexis Korner, worked with Mike Westbrook until the late '60s, and recorded with him until the mid-'70s. He was voted best soloist at the 1968 Montreux Festival while heading his band. Surman worked with Graham Collier, Mike Gibbs, Dave Holland, Chris McGregor and John McLaughlin in the '60s and toured Europe with the Kenny Clarke/Francy Boland big band in 1970. Surman toured and recorded with Barre Phillips and Stu Martin in the late '60s and early '70s, and again in the late '70s, adding Albert Mangelsdorff to the group. They called themselves the Trio, then Mumps. Surman played with Mike Osborne and Alan Skidmore in the sax trio SOS in the mid-'70s. He also collaborated with the Carolyn Carlson dance company at the Paris Opera through the mid- and late '70s. Surman recorded with Stan Tracey and Karin Krog, while working with Miroslav Vitous and Azimuth. He led the Brass Project in the early '80s and played in Collier's big band and Gil Evans' British orchestra. Surman toured with Evans again in the late '80s. He began recording as a leader for Pye in the early '70s, and did sessions for Ogun and ECM. Surman continued recording in the '80s, mostly for ECM. He worked with Terje Rypdal, Jack DeJohnette, Pierre Favre, Bengt Hallberg, Archie Shepp, Warne Marsh and Red Mitchell among others. Surman has made many recordings for ECM, spanning from free form to mood music, and he remains one of the label's most consistently stimulating artists. —*Ron Wynn*

Westering Home / 1972 / Island ✦✦✦✦

Solo work from multifaceted creative saxophonist —*Michael G. Nastos*

Upon Reflection / May 1979 / ECM ✦✦✦✦✦

John Surman's debut as a leader for ECM is an atmospheric solo set that utilizes overdubbing (although leaving space for unaccompanied solo sections). Surman performs eight of his moody and often-introspective originals, playing soprano, baritone, bass clarinet and synthesizer. Fortunately there is enough variety in this generally quiet music to hold one's interest. —*Scott Yanow*

The Amazing Adventures of Simon Simon / Jan. 1981 / ECM ✦✦✦

John Surman (on baritone, soprano, bass clarinet and synthesizer) meets up with drummer Jack DeJohnette (who also plays congas and electric piano) for this typically introspective and spacy ECM set. Surman's playing (especially on baritone and bass clarinet) during nine group originals is worth hearing, but this is not one of his more essential outings. —*Scott Yanow*

Such Winters of Memory / Dec. 1982 / ECM ✦✦✦

With vocalist Karin Krog and percussionist Pierre Favre. —*Michael G. Nastos*

Withholding Pattern / Dec. 1984 / ECM ✦✦✦✦

A saxophone workout from 1985 by outstanding British player John Surman. While solo sax can be extremely tiring, Surman mixes enough elements of rock, free, blues, and hard bop to keep the songs varied. His aggressive style, especially on baritone, keeps the energy level high. —*Ron Wynn*

● **Private City** / Dec. 1987 / ECM ✦✦✦✦✦

John Surman's sixth ECM release (and third in which he was the only musician) features his playing on baritone, soprano, bass clarinet, recorders and synthesizer. None of Surman's recordings are without interest, for he puts a surprising amount of intensity and color into his introspective and often sparse explorations. Two of his eight originals on this set were originally written for the ballet *Private City*. —*Scott Yanow*

Brass Project / Apr. 1992 / ECM ✦✦✦✦✦

For this ECM project, John Surman (who plays soprano, baritone, clarinet, bass clarinet and piano) and conductor John Warren wrote a full set of original music for Surman's reeds, a seven-piece brass section and a rhythm section to interpret. This episodic set has its share of sound explorations but also contains swinging sections and an impressive amount of excitement. The colorful solos (mostly by Surman) and the unpredictable writing make this a highly recommended disc. —*Scott Yanow*

Stranger than Fiction / Dec. 1993 / ECM ✦✦✦✦

John Surman's thoughtful solos (which take their time and make a liberal use of space) have long made him the perfect ECM artist. On his quartet set with pianist John Taylor, bassist Chris Laurence and drummer John Marshall, Surman mostly sticks to soprano although there are some short spots for his baritone and bass clarinet. Surman always sounds relaxed, even on the more heated originals. It's an interesting set of generally introverted music. —*Scott Yanow*

Nordic Quartet / Aug. 1994 / ECM ✦✦

This ECM CD is only a mixed success. John Surman is the lead voice most of the way and his playing (particularly on baritone and bass clarinet) is typically atmospheric and emotional. However, singer Karin Krog (who is on around half of the songs) only makes an impression on the closing "Wild Bird"; otherwise her long tones sound out of place. Pianist Vigleik Storaas is mostly used in an accompanying role while guitarist Terje Rypdal's feedback-dominated tone is primarily utilized for color. The group never really meshes their disparate voices together and few of the spacey (and sometimes meandering) group originals other than "Wild Bird" are at all memorable. All of the principals have sounded better elsewhere. —*Scott Yanow*

Ralph Sutton

b. Nov. 4, 1922, Hamburg, MO

Piano / Stride

Ralph Sutton is the greatest stride pianist to emerge since World War II with his only close competitors being the late Dick Wellstood and the very versatile Dick Hyman. Nearly alone in his generation, Sutton has kept alive the piano styles of Fats Waller and James P. Johnson, not as mere museum pieces but as devices for exciting improvisations. Although sticking within the boundaries of his predecessors, Sutton has infused the music with his own personality; few can match his powerful left hand. Ralph Sutton played with Jack Teagarden's big band briefly in 1942 before serving in the Army. After World War II he appeared regularly on Rudi Blesh's *This Is Jazz* radio show and spent eight years as the intermission pianist at Eddie Condon's club, recording frequently. He spent time playing in San Francisco, worked for Bob Scobey, moved to Aspen in the mid-'60s and became an original member of the world's Greatest Jazz Band with Yank Lawson, Bob Haggart and Bud Freeman. In the 1970s he recorded many exciting but now out-of-print albums for the Chaz label and since then has cut albums for quite a few labels. Sutton has kept a busy schedule through the mid-'90s, playing at jazz parties and festivals. Although he would have received much greater fame if he had been born 20 years earlier and come to maturity during the 1930s rather than the 1950s, Ralph Sutton has earned his place among the top classic jazz pianists of all time. —*Scott Yanow*

Ralph Sutton / Mar. 1950 / Commodore ✦✦✦✦✦

Sutton is one of the last great stride pianists, whose style directly reflects the Fats Waller and James P. Johnson influence. This early-'50s date offers marvelous stride solos and rollicking rhythms and was among the best releases in this vein done during the decade. —*Ron Wynn*

Live at Club Hangover, San Francisco / Aug. 7, 1954+Aug. 14, 1954 / Jazz Archives ✦✦✦✦✦

This LP contains a particularly exciting recording. The great stride pianist Ralph Sutton is teamed with the underrated but talented Dixieland trumpeter Clyde Hurley (a former soloist in Glenn Miller's Orchestra), bassist Walter Page and drummer

Charlie Lodice on two radio broadcasts from the Club Hangover in San Francisco. The great majority of the nine standards are uptempo, and the ensemble work and interplay between Hurley and Sutton is quite passionate and explosive. These versions of "I Found a New Baby," "Honeysuckle Rose," "St. Louis Blues" and "Love Is Just Around the Corner" should excite all trad jazz fans. —*Scott Yanow*

Jazz at the Olympics / Dec. 1959 / Omega ✦✦✦
Pianist Ralph Sutton's first recording as a leader in five years, and one of only three he made during 1955-67, was recorded at Squaw Valley before the 1960 Winter Olympics. The obscure trumpeter Ernie Figueroa fares well on the quartet date with bassist Vernon Alley and drummer Joe Dodge, but it is Sutton who is consistently the main star. Quite a few of the song titles have something to do with the weather (including "Winter Wonderland," "Button Up Your Overcoat" and "I've Got My Love to Keep Me Warm"), but all have viable chord changes for Sutton to romp over. This little-known LP is worth searching for. —*Scott Yanow*

With Ruby Braff, Vol. 1 / Feb. 28, 1968 / Storyville ✦✦✦✦✦
With the exception of a version of "On the Sunny Side of the Street" that had come out earlier on a collector's LP, all of the music on this 1996 CD was previously unreleased. Pianist Ralph Sutton's wife Sunnie ran a club in Aspen, CO, during the latter half of the 1960s called Sunnie's Rendezvous, which often featured small hot jazz groups. This set features the great stride pianist Ralph Sutton with the equally talented cornetist Ruby Braff, bassist Milt Hinton and drummer Mousie Alexander. They perform a dozen jazz standards, all of which were at least 30 years old at the time. The fresh variations give such tunes as "Rosetta," "Limehouse Blues," "Liza" and "Shine" fiery solos and exciting ensembles that make this a set easily recommended to fans of these masterful players. —*Scott Yanow*

Live at Sunnie's Rendezvous, Vol. 1 / Feb. 10, 1969-Feb. 14, 1969 / Storyville ✦✦✦✦
Released for the first time on this 1997 CD, this set features pianist Ralph Sutton leading a trio that also includes bassist Al Hall and drummer Cliff Leeman on his own "Dog Ass Blues," Willard Robison's "Think Well of Me," and nine familiar standards. Even though he played and recorded such numbers as "I've Found a New Baby," "I'm Crazy 'Bout My Baby," James P. Johnson's "Snowy Morning Blues" and "I Got Rhythm" countless times, the brilliant stride pianist always found something new to say, and the results are frequently exciting. —*Scott Yanow*

Piano Solos / Nov. 13, 1975 / Sackville ✦✦✦✦
After too few records (none since 1969), the great stride pianist Ralph Sutton recorded much more frequently, starting with five albums in 1975. This excellent solo set features Sutton playing a medley of Willard Robison songs along with numbers associated with Willie "The Lion" Smith, Bob Zurke, Bix Beiderbecke ("In the Dark"), Meade Lux Lewis and Fats Waller. Among the high points (in addition to the Robison medley) are "Echoes of Spring," "Honky Tonk Train Blues" and "Viper's Drag." —*Scott Yanow*

Off the Cuff / Apr. 17, 1976 / Audiophile ✦✦✦✦
Other than two numbers ("I've Found a New Baby" and "Memories of You") that feature an uncredited Koos Van Der Sluis on bass and drummer Ted Easton, all of the music on this excellent LP (a 1982 reissue of a date cut for the Dutch Riff label) comprises piano solos by the brilliant stride pianist Ralph Sutton. There are no real surprises in the repertoire (which includes such standbys as Willie "The Lion" Smith's "Echoes of Spring," "I Found a New Baby," "Viper's Drag" and "Dinah"), but neither is there a loss of enthusiasm or an excess of predictability. Sutton remains the best in his field and all of his recordings (particularly the solo sessions) are easily recommended. —*Scott Yanow*

The Ralph Sutton Quartet / May 24, 1977-May 25, 1977 / Storyville ✦✦✦✦
Ralph Sutton, one of the great stride pianists of the past four decades, is in excellent form on this European set. Joined on some selections by guitarist Lars Blach, bassist Hugo Rasmussen and drummer Svend Erik Norregard, Sutton takes two of the 12 songs unaccompanied) romps through a program of veteran standards that is highlighted by "Thou Swell" and "Jeepers Creepers." The 1995 CD reissue augments the original LP program with three alternate takes and a 13th selection: a duet version of "Old Fashioned Love" with bassist Rasmussen. —*Scott Yanow*

Ralph Sutton & Ruby Braff Duet / 1979 / Chaz Jazz ✦✦✦✦✦
Although it had long been true that the great stride pianist Ralph Sutton had not recorded enough throughout the early part of his career, that certainly was not true during 1979-81. For the Chaz label, Sutton was featured on no less than 12 LPs within the two-year period. Unfortunately, with the exception of his piano duets with Jay McShann, the music has been out of print since the mid-1980s. On this particular album, the first of two matchups with cornetist Ruby Braff, Sutton and Braff are showcased on a dozen duets. In addition to the usual stomps (including "Between the Devil and the Deep Blue Sea," "Royal Garden Blues" and "Dinah"),

the duo performs three Willard Robison songs. Braff's lyrical, subtle playing brings out the versatility in Sutton's accompaniment, making this a highly enjoyable (if rare) outing. —*Scott Yanow*

Ralph Sutton & Ruby Braff Quartet / 1979 / Chaz Jazz ✦✦✦✦
The second of two Chaz Jazz LPs featuring pianist Ralph Sutton and cornetist Ruby Braff is a quartet date with bassist Jack Lesberg and drummer Gus Johnson. They perform a dozen swing and Dixieland standards with creativity and plenty of surprising moments. Highlights include "Shoe Shine Boy," "Sweethearts on Parade," "Big Butter and Egg Man," and a heated "I'm Crazy 'Bout My Baby." Several of the songs are taken slower than usual, revealing some inner beauty that is usually hidden. Worth searching for, as are all of the hard-to-find Chaz albums. —*Scott Yanow*

Ralph Sutton & Kenny Davern, Vol. 1 / 1980 / Chaz Jazz ✦✦✦✦
The first of two Chaz Jazz LPs featuring pianist Ralph Sutton in a trio with clarinetist Kenny Davern and drummer Gus Johnson has plenty of delightful and hard-swinging moments that should greatly interest trad jazz fans lucky enough to find this long-out-of-print album. Sutton is typically powerful, Davern sounds in prime form and Johnson adds color and drive to the ensembles; both Davern ("Take Me to That Land of Jazz") and Johnson ("Sweet Lorraine") also take rare and fairly harmless vocals. High points of the date include "That's a Plenty," "My Honey's Lovin' Arms" and "I Would Do Most Anything for You." —*Scott Yanow*

Ralph Sutton & Kenny Davern, Vol. 2 / 1980 / Chaz Jazz ✦✦✦✦
The second of two trio albums by pianist Ralph Sutton, clarinetist Kenny Davern and drummer Gus Johnson (Sutton's powerful left hand means there is no need for a string bass) is one of a dozen LPs the pianist made for the now-defunct Chaz Jazz label during 1979-81. The masterful classic jazz musicians stretch out on six standards (highlighted by "St. Louis Blues," "A Porter's Love Song to a Chambermaid" and "Old Fashioned Love"), and Sutton takes one of his infrequent vocals on a brief version of "'Tain't Nobody's Business." Well worth searching for, as are all of the obscure Chaz Jazz releases. —*Scott Yanow*

The Other Side of Ralph Sutton / 1980 / Chaz Jazz ✦✦✦✦✦
Although Ralph Sutton recorded quite a few LPs for Chaz Jazz during 1979-81, this was his only full set of unaccompanied piano solos for the label. With the exception of the closing "Honeysuckle Rose," Sutton sticks to songs that he had always liked but had not had the opportunity to record previously, many of which are obscurities. In the program are a pair of Stan Wrightsman tunes ("Cattin' on the Keys" and "Stanley's Waltz") and six of Fats Waller's lesser-known originals (including "Say Yes," "Bond Street," "I'm Always in the Mood for You" and "When Gabriel Blows His Horn"). This will be a difficult LP to find; hopefully Sutton's valuable Chaz Jazz releases will be reissued on CD someday. —*Scott Yanow*

Big Noise from Wayzata / Jul. 15, 1981 / Chaz Jazz ✦✦✦✦
Pianist Ralph Sutton teams up with clarinetist Peanuts Hucko, bassist Jack Lesberg and drummer Cliff Leeman on this live set from Wayzata, MN. One of a dozen hard-to-find Chaz Jazz LPs featuring Sutton, this outing has the all-star quartet stretching out on fairly lengthy renditions (between 6:41 and 9:41 apiece) of five veteran standards. Although Sutton and company have certainly played these songs ("Honeysuckle Rose," "Memories of You," "The World Is Waiting for the Sunrise," "Ain't Misbehavin'" and "I've Got Rhythm") countless times, the enthusiastic interpretations contain their share of surprises and exciting moments. —*Scott Yanow*

Live at Hanratty's / Mar. 1981 / Chaz Jazz ✦✦✦
A typically enjoyable outing by pianist Ralph Sutton, this club date features him in a set of duets with bassist Jack Lesberg. Sutton romps through six standards (including "I'm Gonna Sit Right Down and Write Myself a Letter," "Honeysuckle Rose" and "Rosetta") and puts sincere emotion and some surprises into a three-song Duke Ellington ballad medley. This fun Chaz Jazz LP, as with the 11 others featuring the great stride pianist, will be hard to find, since only the two albums Sutton made with fellow pianist Jay McShann have been thus far reissued on CD. —*Scott Yanow*

The Ralph Sutton and the Jazzband / 1981 / Chaz Jazz ✦✦✦✦✦
Although the great stride pianist Ralph Sutton recorded 12 LPs for the now-defunct Chaz Jazz label during 1979-81, this set was his only one with a group larger than a quartet. The mighty Sutton is joined by some rather notable all-stars: cornetist Ruby Braff, trombonist George Masso, clarinetist Kenny Davern, tenor saxophonist Bud Freeman, bassist Milt Hinton and drummer Gus Johnson. They really stretch out on four Dixieland standards ("Struttin' with Some Barbecue," "Keeping Out of Mischief Now," "Ain't Misbehavin'" and "Muskrat Ramble"), all of which are at least nine minutes long ("Keeping Out of Mischief Now" is over 13). All of the musicians play up to their usual levels and seem to inspire each other; Sutton pushes the players to come up with fresh and consistently heated ideas. —*Scott Yanow*

We've Got Rhythm / 1981 / Chaz Jazz ✦✦✦✦✦
One of several LPs that the now-obsolete Chaz Jazz label recorded at Hanratty's in New York is an explosive duo outing by the great stride pianist Ralph Sutton and tenor saxophonist Eddie Miller. The usually mellow Miller is really pushed by Sutton into playing some of his most fiery solos so as not to be completely buried. The combination works quite well, particularly on passionate versions of "I Got Rhythm," "Three Little Words," "Lady Be Good," and an especially memorable "Everybody Loves My Baby." Miller gets to show off his luscious tone on the slower pieces (such as "I've Got a Crush on You" and his "Lazy Mood"), but it is the hotter numbers that make this a classic collaboration. —*Scott Yanow*

☆ **At Cafe Des Copains** / Jun. 1, 1983-Jan. 28, 1987 / Sackville ✦✦✦✦
Ralph Sutton is such a consistent pianist that virtually all of his releases are recommended. At the top of his admittedly small field (stride piano has become an almost extinct art form), Sutton always seems to sound inspired no matter how many times he has performed a particular number. This superior solo CD features Sutton live at Toronto's Cafe Des Copains, recorded live for radio during performances in 1983, 1984, 1985 and 1987. The stride pianist's style, which was fully formed by the mid-1950s, did not change during the era, so there is a strong unity to the music (as if it had all been played the same day). Highlights include "Laugh Clown Laugh," "You Can Depend on Me," "Somebody Stole My Gal" and "Christopher Columbus." —*Scott Yanow*

Partners in Crime / Aug. 25, 1983 / Sackville ✦✦✦✦
Through the years, the great stride pianist Ralph Sutton has recorded a surprising number of albums in quartets with trumpeters. For this CD, he teams quite successfully with the talented Australian trumpeter Bob Barnard, bassist Milt Hinton and drummer Len Barnard for a wide-ranging set of swing tunes, most of which are not performed that often. In addition to Bob Barnard's "West End Avenue Blues," the group is heard at its best on "Swing That Music," Hoagy Carmichael's "One Morning in May," "It's Wonderful" and "How Can You Face Me," but all ten selections are rewarding and swinging. Recommended. —*Scott Yanow*

More Ralph Sutton at Cafe Des Copains / Jan. 27, 1988+Jan. 25, 1989 / Sackville ✦✦✦✦
The second of two solo piano CDs by Ralph Sutton taken from performances at Toronto's Cafe Des Copains is the equal of the first. Sutton, who has had no close competitors among stride pianists since the late 1940s other than Dick Wellstood and Dick Hyman, romps through such songs as "Dinah," "Believe It Beloved" and "Baby Brown," in addition to performing a few ballads and a four-song Duke Ellington medley. A typically strong and spirited outing by an underrated master. —*Scott Yanow*

● **Last of the Whorehouse Piano Players** / Mar. 27, 1989-Mar. 28, 1989 / Chiaroscuro ✦✦✦✦✦
Not to be confused with the CD reissue of the same name (Chiaroscuro 206) recorded in 1979, this reunion encounter by pianists Ralph Sutton and Jay McShann (in a quartet with bassist Milt Hinton and drummer Gus Johnson) is up to the same level of the original dates, with plenty of heated moments on songs such as "Old Fashioned Love," "Sweet Georgia Brown," "Cherry" and "I've Found a New Baby." While Sutton is the definitive stride pianist of the past half-century, McShann (who also takes a couple of vocals) finds space to infuse the music with a strong dose of blues and Kansas City swing. A seven-minute "Jazzspeak" wraps up the enjoyable outing with some reminiscing about the sessions. —*Scott Yanow*

Easy Street / May 17, 1991 / Sackville ✦✦✦✦
During a 1991 tour of Australia, the great stride pianist Ralph Sutton teamed up with the talented cornetist Bob Barnard and drummer Len Barnard. There are a pair of duets apiece by Sutton with just one Barnard at a time and the pianist takes Fats Waller's "Handful of Keys" unaccompanied in addition to performing eight trio numbers. Sutton mixes together obscurities (such as J. Russell Robinson's "Mary Lou" and "June Night") and more familiar but superior numbers such as "Please Don't Talk About Me When I'm Gone," "Wolverine Blues" and "China Boy." Bob Barnard sounds in particularly inspired form, making this a delightful set that classic jazz fans will certainly enjoy. —*Scott Yanow*

Sunday Session / Dec. 6, 1992 / Sackville ✦✦✦✦
The great stride pianist Ralph Sutton teams up with bassist Milt Hinton and drummer Butch Miles for a spirited concert from Baden, Switzerland. All 14 selections (13 standards plus Fats Waller's "Clothes Line Ballet") had been recorded by Sutton previously but he plays with such enthusiasm and virtuosity that it sounds like he just discovered the joy of such tunes as "Sunday," "Dinah," "Three Little Words" and "All of Me"! This is an exciting and very enjoyable set. —*Scott Yanow*

Live at Maybeck Recital Hall, Vol. 30 / Aug. 1993 / Concord Jazz ✦✦✦✦
Ralph Sutton finally had his turn to perform in the famed Maybeck solo piano series in 1993. The top stride pianist still active in the 1990s, Sutton performs some of his specialties (including "Honeysuckle Rose," "Dinah" and "After You've

Gone") and pays tribute to Bix Beiderbecke (performing two of his numbers), Fats Waller and Willie "The Lion" Smith ("Echo of Spring"). This recital is as joyful and as hard-swinging as one would hope. —*Scott Yanow*

Svenska Hotkvintetten

f. 1934, db. 1942
Group / Swing
This little-known Swedish band (its name translated to English is the Swedish Hot Quintet) was closely modeled after the Quintet of the Hot Club of France. With violinist Emil Iwring and guitarists Sven Stiberg (single-string) and Folke Eriskberg (chordal) taking solos, this group was one of the hottest in existence during 1939-41. However its recordings rarely circulated outside of Sweden and, until the issue of a 1993 Dragon CD, it was one of the great unknown bands in jazz history! —*Scott Yanow*

● **Swedish Hot** / Apr. 1939-May 1941 / Dragon ✦✦✦✦
Here is a group no one has heard of. Starting in 1939 and continuing up through 1941, the Svenska Hotkvintetten was an all-string swing quintet closely inspired by Django Reinhardt and Stephane Grappelli. Prior to the release of most of their recordings on this CD, none of the group's performances had ever been available outside of Sweden. Violinist Emil Iwring was almost Grappelli's equal at the time while Sven Stiberg and Folke Eriksberg split the solo work; a third acoustic guitarist and a bassist completed the group. This CD from the Swedish Dragon label is quite generous with 27 selections, most of it falling into the category of hot swing. This is one that all collectors of prebop jazz should want to acquire. —*Scott Yanow*

Neil Swainson

b. Nov. 15, 1955, Victoria, B.C., Canada
Bass / Bop, Hard Bop
Neil Swainson worked for two years in Victoria with Paul Horn. He played with Woody Shaw frequently in the 1980s and also gigged with James Moody, George Coleman and Zoot Sims. A member of Moe Koffman's quintet during 1978-82, Swainson gained his greatest fame when he started working with George Shearing in 1988, an association that has continued into the late '90s. The reliable bassist has also recorded with Jay McShann, Ed Bickert and Rob McConnell among others. —*Scott Yanow*

● **49th Parallel** / May 1987 / Concord Jazz ✦✦✦✦
Bassist Neil Swainson is better known as an accompanist (most notably with George Shearing) than as a bandleader, and this was his first opportunity to head his own recording date. Swainson was able to secure the services of both trumpeter Woody Shaw (on his final studio session just two years before his death) and tenor saxophonist Joe Henderson, in addition to a couple of Toronto-based musicians: pianist Gary Williamson and drummer Jerry Fuller. Swainson, who has long had impressive technique and a beautiful tone, performs five of his originals, plus Henderson's "Homestretch." Overall this is an underrated, high-quality advanced hard-bop date worth exploring. —*Scott Yanow*

Steve Swallow

b. Oct. 4, 1940, Fair Lawn, NJ
Bass / Post-Bop
Steve Swallow has long been many jazz critics' favorite electric bassist for, rather than playing his instrument in a rock-oriented manner, Swallow emphasizes the high notes and approaches the electric bass to an extent as if it were a guitar. He originally started on piano and trumpet before settling on the acoustic bass as a teenager. Swallow joined the Paul Bley trio in 1960 and with Bley was a part of an avant-garde version of the Jimmy Giuffre 3 during 1960-62. Swallow recorded with George Russell and was a member of Art Farmer's quartet (1962-65), Stan Getz's band (1965-67) and an important edition of Gary Burton's quartet (1967-70). The latter group (starting with the addition of guitarist Larry Coryell) was actually one of the first fusion groups and it was during that time that Swallow began playing electric bass; within a few years he stopped playing acoustic altogether. Swallow spent a few years in the early '70s living in Northern California during which he mostly played locally. Since the late '70s he has been closely associated with Carla Bley's groups although he occasionally works on other projects (including a reunion of the Jimmy Giuffre 3). Steve Swallow has also proved to be a talented composer with "Eiderdown," "Falling Grace," "General Mojo's Well Laid Plan" and "Hotel Hello" being among his better-known pieces. —*Scott Yanow*

Home / Sep. 1979 / ECM ✦✦✦
Interesting concept with poetry from Robert Creeley. —*Ron Wynn*

Carla / 1986-1987 / ECM ✦✦✦
This is a sextet with a three-piece string ensemble playing eight cuts with a progressive focus. All are originals by Steve Swallow. —*Michael G. Nastos*

- **Swallow** / Sep. 1991-Nov. 1991 / ECM ◆◆◆◆◆
  All nine cuts were written by this premier electric bass guitarist and performed by a sextet with guests Gary Burton (vib) and John Scofield (g). —*Michael G. Nastos*

  Real Book / Dec. 1993 / ECM ◆◆◆◆

- **Deconstructed** / Dec. 1996 / ECM ◆◆◆◆◆
  This CD by electric bassist Steve Swallow is a major surprise, for his ten originals are essentially bebop, often using chord changes that sound familiar; for example, the opening "Running in the Family" uses the chords of "Basin Street Blues." The song titles tend to be humorous if inscrutable (including "Another Fine Mess," "I Think My Wife Is a Hat," and "Name That Tune"), but the spirited playing is quite serious. Tenor saxophonist Chris Potter (on his way to becoming one of the greats) and trumpeter Ryan Kisor have plenty of solo space, guitarist Mick Goodrick makes his presence felt, and drummer Adam Nussbaum offers stimulating support. This rare straightahead outing by Steve Swallow sounds fresh, lively and creative, and it is one of his most rewarding recordings as a leader. —*Scott Yanow*

Harvie Swartz

b. Dec. 6, 1948, Chelsea, MA
Bass / Post-Bop
A superior and flexible bassist able to contribute to a wide variety of advanced settings, Harvie Swartz is perhaps best known for his series of duet recordings and performances with singer Sheila Jordan. Originally a pianist, he started playing bass fairly late (in 1967, when he was already 19) but developed quickly. After attending Berklee, he performed in the Boston area with Al Cohn & Zoot Sims, Mose Allison, and Chris Connor, among others. After moving to New York in 1972, Swartz worked with Jackie & Roy, Jackie Paris, Thad Jones, Gil Evans, Lee Konitz, Barry Miles' Silverlight (1974-76), David Friedman, Double Image, Dave Matthews' big band, Steve Kuhn (1977-81), Paul Motian and countless other top musicians. Harvie Swartz has headed several of his own groups, including Urban Earth (which recorded for Gramavision); he has also led dates for Blue Moon and Novus and recorded often with Sheila Jordan. —*Scott Yanow*

Underneath It All / Mar. 1, 1980-Mar. 2, 1980 / Gramavision ◆◆◆◆◆
This bassist's debut album is with Ben Aranov on piano and John D'Earth on trumpet. This is challenging music, approaching fusion. All selections are Swartz's originals. —*Michael G. Nastos*

Urban Earth / Feb. 1985 / Gramavision ◆◆◆◆

Smart Moves / Feb. 1986 / Gramavision ◆◆◆◆◆
A fine, unjustly overlooked 1986 combo session with bassist Harvie Swartz stepping from behind the bandstand to take a leadership role. But while it's listed as his group, the key soloists are alto saxophonist Charlie Mariano and tenor saxophonist John Stubblefield, a superb one-two punch. Guitarist Mike Stern, pianist Ben Aranov, and drummer Victor Lewis mesh with Swartz, and percussionist Mino Cinelu adds some Afro-Latin flavoring and colors. —*Ron Wynn*

Full Moon Dancer / May 17, 1989-May 22, 1989 / Blue Moon ◆◆◆

- **In a Different Light** / Feb. 8, 1990-May 3, 1990 / Blue Moon ◆◆◆◆◆
  This is a very interesting set, for bassist Harvie Swartz had the opportunity to play with five of his favorite guitarists. There are lengthy workouts with guitarist Mike Stern and drummer Winard Harper on "Alone Together," "Softly as in a Morning Sunrise" and "Sunny Moon for Two" that find Stern in particularly exciting form. Two songs match Swartz with guitarist Mick Goodrick and drummer Leon Parker (who was making his recording debut), and on a third song guitarist Leni Stern makes the trio a quartet. In addition Swartz plays two duets with John Scofield ("Gone with the Wind" and "Nardis") and one with Gene Bertoncini ("Embraceable You"). Everything works, making this one of Harvie Swartz's best recordings to date. —*Scott Yanow*

Arrival / Sep. 5, 1991-Sep. 7, 1991 / Novus ◆◆◆◆

Gabor Szabo

b. Mar. 8, 1936, Budapest, Hungary, d. Feb. 26, 1982, Budapest, Hungary
Guitar / Post-Bop, Crossover Jazz
Gabor Szabo was one of the most original guitarists to emerge in the 1960s, mixing his Hungarian folk music heritage with a deep love of jazz and crafting a distinctive, largely self-taught sound. Inspired by a Roy Rogers cowboy movie, Szabo began playing guitar when he was 14 and often played in dinner clubs and covert jam sessions while still living in Budapest. He escaped from his country at age 20 on the eve of the Communist uprising and eventually made his way to America, settling with his family in California. He attended Berklee College (1958-60) and in 1961 joined Chico Hamilton's innovative quintet featuring Charles Lloyd. Urged by Hamilton, Szabo crafted a most distinctive sound, as agile on intricate, nearly-free runs as he was able to sound inspired during melodic passages. Szabo left the

Hamilton group in 1965 to leave his mark on the pop-jazz of the Gary McFarland quintet and the energy music of Charles Lloyd's fiery and underrated quartet featuring Ron Carter and Tony Williams. Szabo initiated a solo career in 1966, recording the exceptional album *Spellbinder*, which yielded many inspired moments and "Gypsy Queen," the song Santana turned into a huge hit in 1970. Szabo formed an innovative quintet (1967-69) featuring the brilliant, classically trained guitarist Jimmy Stewart and recorded many notable albums during the late 1960s. The emergence of rock music (especially George Harrison, Eric Clapton and Jimi Hendrix) found Szabo successfully experimenting with feedback and less successfully (but innovative at the time) with more commercially oriented forms of jazz. During the 1970s, Szabo regularly performed along the West Coast, hypnotizing audiences with his enchanting, spellbinding style. But from 1970, he was locked into a commercial groove—even though records like *Mizrab* occasionally revealed the success of his jazz, pop, Gypsy, Indian and Asian fusions. Szabo had revisited his homeland several times during the 1970s, finding opportunities to perform brilliantly with native talents. He was hospitalized during his final visit and died in 1982—just short of his 46th birthday. —*Douglas Payne*

Gypsy '66 / Nov. 1965 / Impulse! ◆◆◆◆
Guitarist Gabor Szabo's debut as a leader (after an important stint with the Chico Hamilton Quintet) is surprisingly successful. The reason this LP is a bit of a surprise is that the repertoire (in addition to two originals apiece by the leader and Gary McFarland) has a few unlikely songs by the Beatles ("Yesterday" and "If I Fell") and Burt Bacharach (including "Walk on By"). Usually jazz adaptations of rock songs in the 1960s are lightweight, but Szabo's original sound, the unusual instrumentation (two or three guitars, Sadao Watanabe on flute, Gary McFarland on marimba, bass, drums and percussion) and McFarland's clever arrangements uplift the music. The playing time at 35 minutes is a bit brief, and this LP will be difficult to find, but the performances are better than expected. —*Scott Yanow*

Memorabilia / Nov. 1965-1970 / MCA/Impulse! ◆◆◆
This sampler LP (put out in 1982) inexcusably does not list personnel or recording dates. Its eight selections are drawn from six albums (four on Impulse and two from Blue Thumb), and the set gives listeners some of the more interesting highlights of guitarist Gabor Szabo's career, including fine versions of "Caravan," "Breezin'," "What Is This Thing Called Love" and the "Love Theme from Spartacus." However, at 32 minutes, the album is quite brief, and more serious collectors will prefer to search for Szabo's original Impulse albums instead. —*Scott Yanow*

Spellbinder / May 6, 1966 / Impulse! ◆◆◆◆◆
Gabor Szabo's second LP as a leader, even with the inclusion of a couple of dated pop tunes ("It Was a Very Good Year" and "Bang Bang, My Baby Shot Me Down"), is one of the Hungarian guitarist's better recordings. Szabo is heard in a sparse quintet with bassist Ron Carter, drummer Chico Hamilton and both Victor Pantoja and Willie Bobo on Latin percussion. Among the highlights are "Spellbinder," "Gypsy Queen" and "My Foolish Heart." One to search for. —*Scott Yanow*

Simpatico / May 18, 1966-May 20, 1966 / Impulse! ◆◆
With Gary McFarland. A hastily conceived pop-rock album that finds Szabo and McFarland amateurishly singing, humming and whistling through a set of short, catchy Beatlesque tunes. A collection of poppish originals and rock covers, *Simpatico* would be much better without the vocals. The recording quality is terrible too. —*Douglas Payne*

Jazz Raga / Aug. 4, 1966+Aug. 17, 1966 / Impulse! ◆◆
Guitarist Gabor Szabo always had an open mind towards various forms of rock and pop music. For this out-of-print LP, not only does he play guitar, but he overdubbed sitar on all but one of the numbers. With originals that include "Mizrab," "Search for Nirvana," "Krishna," and "Ravi," the influence of Indian music is quite strong, and this must be the only album to have versions of both "Caravan" and the Rolling Stones' "Paint It Black." Szabo, who is joined by bassist Johnny Gregg, drummer Bernard Purdie and sometimes guitarist Bob Bushnell, emphasizes trance-like songs, but despite (or maybe because of) his attempts to be "with it," the music is somewhat dated today. —*Scott Yanow*

- **The Sorcerer** / Apr. 14, 1967-Apr. 15, 1967 / GRP/Impulse! ◆◆◆◆◆
  Gabor Szabo's quintet featuring Jimmy Stewart was one of the guitarist's very best units. Live performances like this, recorded at Boston's Jazz Workshop, capture some of the excitement the group stirred in 1967-68. Included in the 1997 CD reissue are three excellent tracks ("Los Matadoros," "People" and "Corcovado") recorded at the same concert, which originally appeared on *More Sorcery*. The playing seems inspired and the interplay within the group is something to behold—even when performing lightweight tunes like "The Beat Goes On." —*Douglas Payne*

More Sorcery / Apr. 14, 1967-Sep. 17, 1967 / Impulse! ◆◆◆◆◆
In 1967, guitarist Gabor Szabo had his finest working group, a quintet with the very complementary fellow guitarist Jimmy Stewart, bassist Louis Kabok, either

Marty Morrell or Bill Goodwin on drums and percussionist Hal Gordon. A live album, *Sorcery* (which has been reissued on CD) features this band at its best. *More Sorcery* has three selections taken from the same engagement at Boston's Jazz Workshop, plus three numbers from that year's Monterey Jazz Festival. Szabo, in addition to surprisingly successful versions of "People" and the Beatles' "Lucy in the Sky with Diamonds," performs a brief version of "Corcovado" and three of his better originals. This excellent LP is well worth searching for. —*Scott Yanow*

Light My Fire / Aug. 11, 1967+Sep. 14, 1967 / Impulse! ✦✦
With Bob Thiele. An inane attempt to marry rock hits to the big band sound. Sid Feller arranges tunes like the Doors' "Light My Fire" and the Byrds' "Eight Miles High" as though they were to be used in a cartoon. Tom Scott wails occasionally in Coltrane mode and Szabo periodically cranks out some substantial blues solos. —*Douglas Payne*

Wind, Sky and Diamonds / Sep. 12, 1967-Sep. 14, 1967 / Impulse! ✦✦
Wind, Sky and Diamonds celebrates much of what was important to the guitarist—the new world of rock music, the lure of California and the hope and inspiration of the "Summer of Love." But, at best, it's an ill-conceived jazz-rock concoction. Talent like Howard Roberts, Dennis Budimer, Herb Ellis, Mike Melvoin, Victor Feldman and Emil Richards is negligible here and subjugated to terrible vocalists, corny arrangements and occasional hints of Szabo's unique playing. Contains a stirring, heartfelt version of "Guantanamera" but little more. —*Douglas Payne*

Bacchanal / Feb. 9, 1968 / Skye ✦✦✦✦
After recording four albums for Impulse in 1967, the distinctive guitarist Gabor Szabo cut three records for the Skye label in 1968, of which this LP is the strongest. Szabo's regular group of the era is heard on record for the last time: guitarist Jimmy Stewart, bassist Louis Kabok, drummer Jim Keltner and percussionist Hal Gordon. With the exception of two Szabo originals, the material comprises current pop tunes including two songs by Donovan, "Love Is Blue," "The Look of Love" and "Theme from the Valley of the Dolls." Despite what should have been a complete lack of potential, the Hungarian guitarist uplifts the material and mostly turns the pieces into worthwhile jazz. —*Scott Yanow*

Dreams / Aug. 6, 1968-Aug. 9, 1968 / Skye ✦✦✦
Here, Gabor Szabo ambitiously pairs his outstanding quintet (featuring Jimmy Stewart) with Gary McFarland's subtle string and horn arrangements in a collection of originals, pop covers and classical reinterpretations. The result is a sort of accessible third-stream music. Szabo has many fine moments, and provides nice spaces for the beautiful guitar solos of Jimmy Stewart. —*Douglas Payne*

Gabor Szabo 1969 / Jan. 20, 1969-Jan. 24, 1969 / Skye ✦✦
The guitarist performs covers of chart-toppers like "Both Sides Now," "Michael From Mountains," "In My Life" and one that became part of his repertoire, "Stormy." Also includes Szabo's moody "Somewhere I Belong." Not available on CD. —*Douglas Payne*

Magical Connection / 1970 / Blue Thumb ✦✦✦
Consciously more percussive—and more commercial—Szabo's newly formed sextet was clearly up to the challenges of combining rock with jazz. More an instrumental-pop confection, *Magical Connection* doesn't quite live up to its promise. But even as Szabo covers pop hits by Lulu, Crosby, Stills & Nash and John Sebastian, he often plays with great wit and solos with energetic dexterity. Not available on CD. —*Douglas Payne*

High Contrast / 1970 / Blue Thumb ✦✦✦✦✦
An unusually successful pairing of Gabor Szabo with R&B legend Bobby Womack. Szabo digs deep into a soulful groove, inspired by Womack's silky-smooth originals. *High Contrast* features "Breezin'," the Womack tune written especially for Szabo, which George Benson parlayed into a huge hit in 1976, and several tunes Womack popularized in the film *Across 110th Street*. —*Douglas Payne*

Small World / Aug. 12, 1972-Aug. 13, 1972 / Four Leaf Clover ✦✦✦✦✦
An unusual and fascinating entry in Gabor Szabo's discography, *Small World* is a gem of Szabo's fine musicianship and one of the guitarist's more notable achievements. Recording in Sweden with Swedish studio musicians including guitarist Janne Schaffer, Szabo seems inspired and covers the spectrum: the energetic electric jazz of "Foothill Patrol," his own beautiful take on the otherwise corny "People" and a tremendous solo version of Rodrigo's "Concerto de Aranjuez." *Small World* is Gabor Szabo at his very best. Not available on CD. —*Douglas Payne*

Mizrab / Dec. 1972 / CTI ✦✦✦
Gabor Szabo, who always had an original sound on the guitar (displaying his Hungarian heritage), is backed by a string section, horns and a rhythm section (including bassist Ron Carter and either Billy Cobham or Jack DeJohnette on drums) on

this Bob James production. For the program which has not yet been reissued on CD, Szabo performs two originals, a pair of pop tunes and an adaptation of a Shostakovich classical concerto. The music is well played but not particularly memorable. —*Scott Yanow*

Gabor Szabo Live / 1972-1973 / Blue Thumb ✦✦✦
Features Szabo where he shone brightest—live. Good performances of reliable staples: "People," "Stormy" and, of course, "Spellbinder." "Sombrero Sam" features a brief, welcome reunion with Charles Lloyd. Not available on CD. —*Douglas Payne*

Rambler / Sep. 1973 / CTI ✦✦✦
Although this LP is a CTI production, guitarist Gabor Szabo is well featured in a conventional quartet (without strings, horns or "sweetening") that also includes the electric piano of Mike Wofford, bassist Wolfgang Melz and drummer Bobby Morin; Bob James sits in on some cuts on keyboards. For what would be Szabo's last significant recording, the Hungarian guitarist performs an obscurity and five of bassist Melz's originals, including "Rambler," "It's So Hard to Say Goodbye" and "Reinhardt." Although the individual melodies are not that memorable (none caught on), Gabor Szabo's distinctive sound and logical improvisations make this an album worth searching for. —*Scott Yanow*

Macho / Apr. 1975 / Salvation ✦✦✦
Here, producer, arranger and pianist Bob James helps Gabor Szabo wed elements of his heritage (Liszt's "Hungarian Rhapsody No.2") with interests in Latin ("Macho"), ballad ("Time") and groove ("Transylvania Boogie") music. Although *Macho* is clearly calculated to sell, tasty elements of Szabo's talents are heard to good effect here. —*Douglas Payne*

Faces / 1976 / Mercury ✦✦✦
The iconoclastic guitarist's final American record suffers producer Wayne Henderson's dated disco tendencies. But by the time the needle finds side two, some genuinely beautiful performances emerge ("Alicia," "The Last Song" and "Estate"), proving Szabo had not lost his ability to sustain a potent, hypnotic interest. Not available on CD. —*Douglas Payne*

Nightflight / 1976 / Mercury ✦✦
Disco hitmeister Bunny Seigler pairs the unique sound of Gabor Szabo here with a soulless group of Philadelphia studio musicians for a senseless exploration of money-making music. The guitarist is reduced to apathetic singing ("Keep Smiling") and comping furiously over repetitive dance riffs ("Baby Rattle Snake"). Of note, however, are the guitarist's Latin-esque "Concorde (Nightflight)" and the interesting "Theme for Gabor." Not available on CD. —*Douglas Payne*

Femme Fatale / 1978 / Pepita International ✦✦
Released in 1981 on a small Hungarian label, this 1978 session recorded in Hollywood is the guitarist's final record. "Out of the Night" interestingly pairs him with pianist Chick Corea. But the remainder of the record is a standard late-'70s fusion date without Corea, highlighted by the Return to Forever intrigue of "A Thousand Times." Not available on CD. —*Douglas Payne*

Belsta River / Jan. 6, 1978-Jan. 7, 1978 / Four Leaf Clover ✦✦✦✦✦
Exciting electric-jazz record made in Sweden with a good European sextet featuring Janne Schaffer. Not available on CD. —*Douglas Payne*

Szakcsi

b. Budapest, Hungary
Piano, Keyboards / Post-Bop
Although he achieved recognition for his work in new age, pianist Szakcsi surprised many listeners with his inventive 1994 GRP release *Straight Ahead* which found him leading a trio/quartet through a set of acoustic jazz originals. Szakcsi enrolled in the Budapest Secondary School of Music at the age of 12 and had originally planned to be a jazz pianist. In his 20s he played in Europe with Art Farmer, Charlie Mariano and Slide Hampton. Szakcsi eventually became an instrumental pop star but on his GRP date he showed that possibly there is life after new age! —*Scott Yanow*

● **Straight Ahead** / 1993 / GRP ✦✦✦✦✦
Pianist Szakcsi found his initial fame playing new age but this GRP CD shows that he was careful not to lose his jazz chops. In a trio with bassist Jay Leonhardt and drummer Marvin "Smitty" Smith (Tim Warfield guests on tenor during two songs), Szakcsi really challenged himself on this date, not only finding something fresh to say on "Body and Soul" and tackling Thelonious Monk's "Brilliant Corners" but coming up with eight new songs, many of them hard-driving and all quite straightahead. The excellent release shows that, at least for some of its practioners, there is life after new age. —*Scott Yanow*

Lew Tabackin

b. May 26, 1940, Philadelphia, PA

Tenor Saxophone, Flute / Hard Bop

Lew Tabackin is one of the few jazz musicians who has been able to develop completely different musical personalities on two instruments. As a tenor saxophonist, he is a hard-driving, tough-toned player reminiscent of Sonny Rollins, Don Byas, and sometimes, tone-wise, Ben Webster. But as a flutist, he sounds like a highly expressive master of Asian classical music. Whether heard as the main soloist with his wife Toshiko Akiyoshi's Jazz Orchestra or jamming with a small group, Tabackin has been a masterful player for the past 30 years.

Tabackin studied at the Philadelphia Conservatory from 1958-62 as a flute major. After serving in the Army and moving to New York in 1965, he worked with Maynard Ferguson, the Thad Jones-Mel Lewis Orchestra, Joe Henderson, Elvin Jones, and the Tonight Show Band, among others. From 1968-69, he was a main soloist with the Danish Radio Orchestra. After marrying Toshiko Akiyoshi, he toured Japan with her (1970-71). When they moved to Los Angeles in 1972, they formed her orchestra, which, thanks to Akiyoshi's arrangements and Tabackin's solo talents, became one of the top jazz big bands. In 1982, they relocated to New York, where the orchestra has continued on a part-time basis. Lew Tabackin has since played in many different small groups, remaining a brilliant improviser. He has recorded as a leader on an occasional basis through the years, most notably for Inner City (1974-77), Ascent (1979) and Concord (starting in 1989). —*Scott Yanow*

Tabackin / Dec. 19, 1974 / Inner City ◆◆◆

Recorded in Japan with bass and drums only, this album includes four standards and one apiece from leader, Toshiko Akiyoshi, and Sir Roland Hanna. —*Michael G. Nastos*

Dual Nature / Aug. 31, 1976+Sep. 3, 1976 / Inner City ◆◆◆◆◆

Lew Tabackin's two musical personalities (as a thick-toned tenor and an Eastern-influenced flutist) are well displayed on this excellent (but out-of-print) LP. Side one has him on flute for two obscurities and the standard "Out of This World" while side two finds Tabackin romping on tenor for his "Russian Lullaby," "My Ideal" and his "No Dues Blues." In both cases Tabackin is ably accompanied by pianist Don Friedman, bassist Bob Daugherty and drummer Shelly Manne. A superior showcase for the talented Lew Tabackin. —*Scott Yanow*

Tenor Gladness / Oct. 13, 1976-Oct. 14, 1976 / Inner City ◆◆◆◆◆

The two complementary but distinctive tenors Lew Tabackin and Warne Marsh stretch out on four jams in a quartet with bassist John Heard and drummer Larry Bunker. In addition, Tabackin is heard unaccompanied on "New-Ance," while Marsh has a ballad feature on "Easy"; the unidentified pianist on this track is most certainly Toshiko Akiyoshi. It is a pity that this enjoyable music was last out on this out-of-print LP from the defunct Inner City label, for it finds both Marsh and Tabackin in competitive and creative form. —*Scott Yanow*

Rites of Pan / Sep. 1977 / Inner City ◆◆◆◆

As one might guess from the title of this somewhat forgotten LP, Lew Tabackin sticks exclusively to flute (leaving his tenor home) for the performances. Joined by pianist Toshiko Akiyoshi, drummer Shelly Manne and either John Heard or Bob Daugherty on bass, Tabackin consistently shows that he is not only at the top of his field but one of the most original jazz flutists of all time. Highlights include the title cut (a flute-drums duet), an alto flute workout on "Speak Low," a rapid "Be-Bop" and Fats Waller's "Jitterbug Waltz." —*Scott Yanow*

Black and Tan Fantasy / Aug. 1979 / Ascent ◆◆◆◆◆

Put out on Toshiko Akiyoshi's Ascent label, this very obscure LP finds Lew Tabackin in superb form. Accompanied by bassist John Heard and drummer Billy Higgins, Tabackin plays flute on two originals (the fairly free "Flute Flite" and "Falling Petal") and tenor on the five other pieces. Actually Tabackin's tenor makes the bigger impression on this date, really ripping into Thelonious Monk's "I Mean You," "You've Changed" and "After You've Gone." Well worth searching for, hopefully Akiyoshi will someday reissue this exciting music on CD. —*Scott Yanow*

● **Desert Lady** / Dec. 1989 / Concord Jazz ◆◆◆◆◆

The great tenor saxophonist and flutist Lew Tabackin is joined by pianist Hank Jones, bassist Dave Holland and drummer Victor Lewis on this well-rounded program. The Concord CD has many highlights including "Hot House," Duke Ellington's "Serenade to Sweden," Tabackin's "A Bit Byas'd" and "You Leave Me Breathless"; the leader's tenor in particular is in top form. Highly recommended to fans of straightahead jazz, this release gives one a strong sampling of Lew Tabackin's talents. —*Scott Yanow*

I'll Be Seeing You / Apr. 16, 1992-Apr. 17, 1992 / Concord Jazz ◆◆◆◆◆

Lew Tabackin, whose extroverted tone on tenor (influenced most by Don Byas and Ben Webster) contrasts with the Eastern sound that he gets on flute, is teamed quite successfully with pianist Benny Green, bassist Peter Washington and drummer Lewis Nash on this Concord CD. The repertoire, mostly lesser-known standards like John Coltrane's "Wise One" and Thelonious Monk's "In Walked Bud," is well-treated by these masterful musicians. —*Scott Yanow*

What a Little Moonlight Can Do / Apr. 4, 1994-Apr. 5, 1994 / Concord Jazz ◆◆◆◆

Live at Vartan Jazz / Sep. 8, 1994-Sep. 10, 1994 / Vartan Jazz ◆◆◆◆

Tenority / Jun. 11, 1996-Jun. 12, 1996 / Concord Jazz ◆◆◆

Richard Tabnik

Alto Saxophone / Post-Bop, Free Jazz

Tabnik is a lyrically inclined altoist, affected greatly by the method and music of the late pianist/composer/educator Lennie Tristano. He played his first jazz gigs in the Providence, R.I. band of guitarist Tom Brown. From 1970-72, Tabnik studied with Tristano's chief acolyte, Lee Konitz. He played lead alto in Frank Foster's Big Band at the State University of New York at Buffalo from 1975-79. During that time, he also played in the federally funded big band of Allen Tinney. From 1979 to 1983, he studied under the eminent saxophone teacher Joe Allard; concurrently, he began to study with pianist Connie Crothers, who would become his greatest influence. With Crothers, Tabnik recorded *Duo Dimension* in 1987. In the early '90s, Tabnik recorded several times, both as a solo saxophonist and in bands that included drummer Carol Tristano, Lennie's daughter. Other Tabnik associates have included bassists Calvin Hill and Cameron Brown, guitarist Andy Fite, and tenor saxophonist Lenny Popkin. —*Chris Kelsey*

Solo Journey / Sep. 14, 1990 / New Artists ◆◆◆

In the Moment / Oct. 1992 / New Artists ◆◆◆◆◆

● **Life at the Cove** / Nov. 13, 1992 / New Artists ◆◆◆◆◆

The legacy of Lennie Tristano lives on in musicians whom he probably never met. The late pianist-teacher believed strongly in chordal improvisation with long lines and odd accents from the soloists, quiet rhythm sections restricted to timekeeping and the use of common chord changes that are disguised by the substitution of new melodies and song titles. Altoist Richard Tabnik, whose unusual tone and intonation will take some getting used to, does not sound like Lee Konitz (Tristano's most significant student) but follows some of the same principles championed by Tristano. Guitarist Andy Fite offers a fine second voice while bassist Calvin Hill and drummer Roger Mancuso fulfill their roles as timekeepers. All seven songs on this CD are "originals" that are usually based on earlier standards. For example "Reach" is really "All of Me," "Souliloquy" is a spacey "Body and Soul," "Timescapes" has similarities to "I'll Remember April," "Dearest" is "These Foolish Things," etc. Overall Tabnik offers stimulating music that is worth the struggle to meet halfway. But why no liner notes? —*Scott Yanow*

Jamaaladeen Tacuma

b. Jun. 11, 1956, Hempstead, NY

Bass / Free Funk

Since his emergence with Ornette Coleman's Prime Time in the mid-'70s, Jamaaladeen Tacuma has been one of the top electric bassists in a style of music that could be called "free funk." Growing up in Philadelphia, Tacuma (who before he converted to Islam was known as Rudy McDaniel) played with Charles Earland. Only 19 when he joined Ornette in 1975, his ability to combine funky rhythms with free jazz helped give Prime Time its distinctive (if overcrowded) sound. Tacuma's own solo career has been a bit erratic, alternating great moments with throwaway tracks. He also has played with a wide variety of advanced musicians (including James "Blood" Ulmer, Olu Dara, Julius Hemphill and David Murray) but has yet to fulfill his great potential. —*Scott Yanow*

● **Show Stopper** / 1982-1983 / Gramavision ✦✦✦✦✦
Electric bassist Jamaaladeen Tacuma's debut as a leader is still his best recording to date. A brilliant free funk player who excels in laying down some eccentric funk in overcrowded ensembles, Tacuma is heard in six different settings on this album. His own group (a quintet with altoist James Watkins and guitarist Rick Iannacone) plays four noisy numbers, he takes "Tacuma Song" as an unaccompanied bass feature, he is backed by the Ebony String Quartet, a harp, and pianist Anthony Davis on "The Bird of Paradise," he is accompanied by four percussionists on "From the Land of Sand" and he has a couple of jams featuring altoist Julius Hemphill, cornetist Olu Dara and guitarist James "Blood" Ulmer. Stimulating and unpredictable music. —*Scott Yanow*

Renaissance Man / 1983-1984 / Gramavision ✦✦✦✦
Jamaaladeen Tacuma's second free funk effort for Gramavision is almost the equal of his first (*Show Stopper*). Once again the first four songs feature his regular band (a quintet with guitarist Rick Iannacone and altoist James Watkins) while the second half of the program showcases his electric bass in diverse groups. "Dancing in Your Head" has some of the members of Ornette Coleman's Prime Time (including the innovative altoist); Tacuma often played with Ornette during this period. The lengthy "The Battle of Images" features Tacuma with the Ebony String Quartet and a percussionist, "There He Stood" has the leader joined by percussionists and a poet. Best is "Sparkle," a jam with tenor saxophonist David Murray and guitarist Venone Reid. Although a bit of a mixed bag, this set should appeal to listeners open to both the avant-garde and eccentric funk. —*Scott Yanow*

So Tranquilizin' / Sep. 1984-Jan. 1985 / Gramavision ✦✦

Music World / 1986 / Gramavision ✦✦✦
The virtuoso electric bassist Jamaaladeen Tacuma performs eight selections on his third Gramavision release in six different settings. The use of electronics by his sidemen is sometimes quite dominant and weakens the music a bit, making much of it sound both dense and dated. Some of the selections are intriguing, particularly singer Leon Thomas on an odd remake of "The Creator Has a Master Plan." Among the many obscure sidemen are the fiery fusion guitarist Kazumi Watanabe, percussionist Jerry Gonzalez (unfortunately only on one song) and Odean Pope on soprano and oboe. The overall results are interesting but not all that memorable. —*Scott Yanow*

Jukebox / Sep. 1987+Feb. 1988 / Gramavision ✦✦✦✦
One of the top graduates of Ornette Coleman's Prime Time, electric bassist Jamaaladeen Tacuma features his own free funk group Spectacle on this noisy and generally interesting album, his fourth for Gramavision. With Byard Lancaster on tenor, alto, flute and bird calls (!), keyboardist Alan Sukennik, guitarist Ronnie Drayton and drummer Dennis Alston (plus a couple of guest musicians), the emphasis is on Tacuma's heavy bass lines and the crowded ensembles; two songs (a solo piece and a duet with Alston's drums) are showcases for the leader. —*Scott Yanow*

Boss of the Bass / 1993 / Gramavision ✦✦

Sound Symphony / Jul. 29, 1994 / Moers ✦✦✦

Night of Chamber Music / Nov. 15, 1994 / Moers ✦✦✦✦

Intense / May 30, 1995 / ITM ✦✦✦

Gemini-Gemini / Aug. 1, 1995 / ITM ✦✦✦

Journey Into Gemini Territory / Nov. 12, 1996 / ITM ✦✦✦

Aki Takase

b. Jan. 26, 1948, Osaka, Japan
Piano, Koto / Post-Bop, Free Jazz
While remaining steeped in the musical traditions of her native Japan, pianist and composer Aki Takase emerged as one of the most versatile figures in contemporary jazz, her work running the gamut from conventional structures and harmonies to complete abstraction. Born in Osaka on January 26, 1948, and raised in Tokyo, she received her first piano lessons at the age of three, going on to study at Tohogakuen Music University. Influenced by the work of Ornette Coleman, John Coltrane and Charles Mingus, Takase soon turned to improvisation, and in 1971 was regularly performing professionally; by the age of 25, she was already leading her own groups. In 1978, she first travelled to the US, and later recorded with Dave Liebman; in 1981 she also journeyed to Europe, where she and her trio

played the Berlin Jazz Festival. By 1982, Takase was regularly in the studio, leading such dates as *A.B.C.* and *Perdido;* in New York, she recorded with artists including Sheila Jordan, Cecil McBee and Bob Moses, and also delivered a much-acclaimed performance at the East-West Festival in Nuremburg. From 1988 to 1994, Takase regularly played in a duo with Maria Joao and maintained her busy festival schedule; during the mid-1990s, she also toured with Coltrane alumni Rashed Ali and Reggie Workman, founded a septet comprising other Japanese musicians, composed for a string quartet, and continued to work as a solo performer (at times playing the koto, a traditional Chinese 17-string zither). —*Jason Ankeny*

● **A.B.C.** / May 20, 1982-May 24, 1982 / Eastwind ✦✦✦✦

Perdido / Jun. 19, 1982 / Enja ✦✦✦

Shima Shoka / Jul. 10, 1990+Jul. 11, 1990 / Enja ✦✦✦

Close Up of Japan / Jun. 1, 1992+Jun. 2, 1992 / Enja ✦✦

Clapping Music / Jun. 5, 1993+Jun. 6, 1993 / Enja ✦✦✦✦
Pianist Takase, bassist Workman and drummer Murray unite to perform compositions by Monk and Mingus on this 1996 release. —*Jason Ankeny*

Play Ballads of Duke Ellington / Jun. 20, 1995 / Tutu ✦✦✦

Oriental Express / Jul. 15, 1997 / Enja ✦✦✦

Take 6

f. 1985
Vocal Group / Free Funk, Urban, Black Gospel, A Capella, Bop, Soul
With its roots in gospel, doo wop, and sophisticated jazz-influenced singing groups of mid-century America like the Hi-Los, the a cappella vocal group Take 6 is both a throwback to an earlier, more genteel era of American music and a precursor for a number of black male pop groups of the '90s (most notably Boyz II Men). Its members include David Thomas, Alvin Chea, Cedric Dent, Mark Kibble, Claude V. McKnight III and Joey Kibble (who replaced Mervyn Warren). McKnight and Mark Kibble caught the a cappella bug at Alabama's Oakwood College in the early '80s, forming a vocal group that solidified into Take 6 when singer/arranger Warren joined up in 1985. They signed a pact with the Reunion label in 1988, recording arrangements of Negro spirituals and newly composed material on their first album, *Doo Be Doo Wop Bop!* They were quickly picked up by Warner Bros.' Reprise label, for whom they started making smooth yet vocally adventuresome albums that defy pigeonholing other than the all-purpose a cappella label. Take 6 has also recorded Christmas carols, toured with Al Jarreau, appeared on Quincy Jones' all-star *Back on the Block* album, and on *Join the Band* (1994) used instrumental backing for the first time. However, 1996's *Brothers* album indicated a turn toward commercial, sound-alike soul music that threatens to rob Take 6 of its unique identity. —*Richard S. Ginell*

Doo Be Doo Wop Bop! / 1988 / Reprise ✦✦✦✦

● **Take 6** / 1988 / Reprise ✦✦✦✦✦
Six Nashville gospel vocalists whose collective exchanges and massed harmonies make this an unusual, often spectacular release. Their approach more closely echoes classic jubilee than the more common quartet gospel. *Take 6* may yet put some Golden Age fervor back into '80s gospel. — *Ron Wynn, Rock & Roll Disc.*

So Much 2 Say / 1990 / Reprise ✦✦✦✦

Join the Band / 1994 / Reprise ✦✦✦
On their first collection of new material in four years, the group branches out with instrumental backing throughout for the first time, with appearances by Ray Charles, Stevie Wonder, Queen Latifah and a host of stellar sidemen. —*Thom Granger*

Brothers / 1996 / Reprise ✦
When Take 6 first became prominent, they were a unique and virtuosic a cappella sextet that emphasized swinging renditions of religious originals. However, the group has since made several inferior recording projects in which their individuality is greatly watered down. On this very mundane effort (most of which is pure R&B), the lyrics are generally secular, the arrangements are very predictable, and the singers are joined by electronic rhythms, horns and other unnecessary musicians. Nothing about the performances sound spontaneous, distinctive or original. Someone has been giving Take 6 some bad advice. —*Scott Yanow*

Thomas Talbert

b. Aug. 4, 1924, Crystal Bay, MN
Arranger, Leader, Composer, Piano / Bop, Post-Bop
Thomas Talbert has been one of the finest arrangers of the past half-century but remains quite underrated due to the relatively few recordings he has made as a leader. He was inspired to become an arranger while hearing the big bands of the

swing era on the radio. He developed his piano-playing skills and in high school organized bands to try out his arrangements. After a period in the military (1943-45), Talbert moved to California and on and off during 1946-49 he led an advanced orchestra that struggled unsuccessfully to survive; fortunately many of their rare recordings from this era (and quite a few previously unreleased) have come out on a Sea Breeze CD. Talbert spent part of 1947 touring with Anita O'Day and in 1950 he moved to New York. As a freelance writer he arranged for Claude Thornhill, Tony Pastor, Johnny Smith, Oscar Pettiford and Don Elliott among others. In the mid-'50s Talbert recorded an album featuring singer Patty McGovern (*Wednesday's Child*) and a classic of his own (*Bix Duke Fats*); both have been recently reissued on CD. From the mid-'60s until the early '70s Talbert lived in the Midwest, working with a 12-piece band. In 1975 he relocated to Los Angeles where he has written for the L.A. studios and led a part-time orchestra plus a septet, recording several sets for Sea Breeze. —*Scott Yanow*

★ **Tom Talbert Jazz Orchestra 1946-1949** / Jun. 25, 1946-Nov. 1949 / Sea Breeze ✦✦✦✦✦

Tom Talbert has long been a fixture in Los Angeles, writing arrangements, recording albums and occasionally appearing with his big band in local clubs. He is known for recording one classic set in the 1950s (*Bix Fats Duke*, which has been reissued by the Modern Concepts label) but even veteran collectors can be forgiven for not being familiar with the historic recordings that are on his Sea Breeze CD since the majority of these valuable performances were previously unissued. Talbert led an orchestra in Los Angeles during the 1946-50 period that was (thanks to his advanced writing) as modern as the big bands of Stan Kenton and Boyd Raeburn without copying either. The first four numbers on this CD feature trumpeter Frank Beach and tenor saxophonist Babe Russin as the chief soloists and "Flight of the Vout Bug" (which is actually from a session led by Lyle Griffin) showcases pianist Dodo Marmarosa and the tenor of Lucky Thompson. However it is the charts from 1949 that are of greatest interest, for among Talbert's sidemen are altoist Art Pepper, Jack Montrose on tenor and pianist Claude Williamson. The music, with its cool-toned reeds, powerful brass, advanced harmonies and solid swing, still sounds fresh and enthusiastic, and the occasional vocals are well done. Artistically this orchestra was quite successful, but the band business was collapsing at the time and, when Stan Kenton reformed his orchestra in 1950, Tom Talbert broke up his group and went back to writing full-time. Fans of modern big bands should be quite excited by the long-overdue release of this exciting and historic music on Sea Breeze. Highly recommended. —*Scott Yanow*

★ **Bix Duke Fats Interpreted by Thomas Talbert** / 1956 / Sea Breeze ✦✦✦✦✦

This is a classic album which has fortunately been reissued on CD by Ken Poston's Modern Concepts label (and most recently by Sea Breeze). Talbert, best-known at the time as a freelance arranger who had worked for Stan Kenton, recorded three separate sessions devoted to reworkings of originals by Fats Waller, Bix Beiderbecke and Duke Ellington; in addition he performed his own "Green Night & Orange Bright." These fresh charts cast new light on such songs as "In a Mist," "Prelude to a Kiss" and "Keepin' Out of Mischief Now" and feature such lyrical soloists as trumpeter Joe Wilder, trombonists Eddie Bert and Jimmy Cleveland and altoist Herb Geller. The colorful ensembles in particular make this a memorable set. —*Scott Yanow*

Louisiana Suite / Oct. 3, 1977-Oct. 5, 1977 / Sea Breeze ✦✦✦✦

Arranger Thomas Talbert had not recorded as a leader in over 20 years when he had a rare opportunity to document his California band. Half of the music on this Sea Breeze CD is the five-song "Louisiana Suite," which pays tribute to aspects of the state but does not hint at New Orleans jazz. Talbert also performs six of his shorter originals; his 14-piece band consists of four woodwinds, a French horn, four trumpets, two trombones and a rhythm section. Among the key soloists are trumpeters Bob Summers and Steve Huffsteter, tenorman Bob Hardaway and guitarist Joe Diorio. The results should easily please fans of modern big bands, and it does seem strange that Thomas Talbert's next record would not be cut for another decade. —*Scott Yanow*

Things as They Are / Aug. 11, 1987-Aug. 12, 1987 / Sea Breeze ✦✦✦✦

This CD, arranger Tom Talbert's first as a leader in ten years, differs from his other sets in that it is a small group date (although it does utilize his complex charts). The sextet (which includes trumpeter Bob Summers, trombonist Andy Martin, altoist Dick Mitchell, baritonist Lee Callet, bassist John Leitham, drummer Jeff Hamilton and occasionally Talbert's piano) performs eight of the leader's originals plus four standards ("Hello, Dolly," "Don't Get Around Much Anymore," "Lulu's Back in Town" and "Cute"). Although one misses the big band, Talbert's unusual harmonies and logical arrangements make this a CD certainly worth acquiring. —*Scott Yanow*

The Warm Cafe / Oct. 10, 1991-Jun. 2, 1992 / Modern Concepts ✦✦✦✦✦

For this CD (which has been reissued on the Sea Breeze label), arranger-composer Thomas Talbert's big band performs eight of the leader's originals plus fresh interpretations of Django Reinhardt's "Manoir De Mes Reves," "What Is This Thing Called Love" and Fats Waller's "Ain't Misbehavin." Of Talbert's pieces (some of which date back to the 1950s), "Someone's Rocking My Blues," "Flirtation" and "Swing Will Be on Time" are most memorable. This CD gives listeners a strong example of Talbert's writing style for his 14-piece band during recent times and also features some fine solos from trumpeters Steve Huffsteter and Bob Summers, altoist Lee Callet, Don Shelton on clarinet and alto, Bob Efford on tenor and trombonist Andy Martin. Recommended. —*Scott Yanow*

Duke's Domain / May 18, 1993-May 19, 1993 / Sea Breeze ✦✦✦✦✦

● **This Is Living!** / Jul. 1, 1997-Jul. 2, 1997 / Pipe Dream ✦✦✦✦✦

Arranger Tom Talbert ventured to New York for this superior big band date. He utilized four of the musicians who had been on his classic *Bix Fats Duke* album of 1956 (trumpeter Joe Wilder, trombonist Eddie Bert, clarinetist Aaron Sachs and the baritone, bass clarinet and clarinet of Danny Bank), and there are some similarities in style to the earlier set. Talbert utilized ten brass (including two French horns), four woodwinds and a pianoless rhythm section for four of his originals and such standards as "Django," "Blame It on My Youth," Willie "The Lion" Smith's "Echo of Spring" and "Our Delight." Many of the musicians get space for concise solos (including altoist Dick Oatts, tenorman Loren Schoenberg and guitarist Howard Alden), but Joe Wilder's lyrical playing consistently steals the show, along with Talbert's colorful arrangements. A gem. —*Scott Yanow*

Horace Tapscott

b. Apr. 6, 1934, Houston, TX
Piano, Leader / Avant-Garde, Post-Bop

Horace Tapscott has long been Los Angeles' top undiscovered legend, a brilliant pianist who has thus far only recorded for the tiniest (and most obscure) of labels. A powerful player perfectly able to interpret bop but heard at his best playing his own rhythmic originals with his quartet, Tapscott has had an original style for 30 years but his music is surprisingly accessible even at its most passionate. He moved with his family to Los Angeles in 1945 and was originally a trombonist; Tapscott caught the tail end of the legendary Central Avenue Scene (his early associates included Eric Dolphy and Don Cherry) and played with Gerald Wilson's Orchestra during 1950-51. While in the Air Force (1953-57) he took up the piano, which was fortunate because after touring with Lionel Hampton (1959-61), an automobile accident forced him to give up the trombone. Tapscott returned to Los Angeles in 1961, formed the Pan-Afrikan Peoples Arkestra and has been a major part of the local jazz community ever since. Among his most famous sidemen have been altoist Arthur Blythe and tenor saxophonist Azar Lawrence. Tapscott wrote the arrangements for the late-'60s Sonny Criss album *Sonny's Dream* and shared a Flying Dutchman album (reissued on CD by Novus as *West Coast Hot*) with the John Carter/Bobby Bradford Quartet. Otherwise his recordings have been made for Nimbus along with a pair of live sessions for Hat Art and one release for Arabesque. Tapscott's longtime quartet with saxophonist Michael Sessions, bassist Roberto Miranda and drummer Fritz Wise remains undocumented. —*Scott Yanow*

Songs of the Unsung / Feb. 18, 1978 / Interplay ✦✦✦✦

Horace Tapscott has long been one of Los Angeles' great jazz legends but the pianist has not been documented that thoroughly throughout his productive career. Other than a big band set from the same period, this solo piano LP was his first full-length recording. On what was a slightly more conservative set than most of his dates, Tapscott performs just two of his originals (including "Mary on Sunday") plus selections by Samuel Browne, Cal Massey ("Bakai"), Lester Robertson, Jesse Sharps, Elmo Hope and Billy Strayhorn ("Lush Life"). A fine outing that, if it were in print, could serve as a fairly accessible introduction to the masterful pianist. —*Scott Yanow*

The Call / Apr. 8, 1978 / Nimbus ✦✦✦✦

The second LP by Horace Tapscott's Pan-Afrikan Peoples Arkestra (a 16-piece trumpet-less big band) has four lengthy selections; three originals by band members plus Cal Massey's "Nakatini Suite." Best-known among the sidemen are veteran Red Callender (doubling on tuba and bass) and the powerful altoist Michael Session. Many of the other players (including the pianist-leader) have some space to stretch out, and the ensembles (with their unusual voicings and free spots) are quite colorful. —*Scott Yanow*

Flight 17 / 1978 / Nimbus ✦✦✦✦

Other than half an album cut in 1969 for Flying Dutchman (which was shared with the John Carter/Bobby Bradford group), this release was pianist Horace Tapscott's recording debut as a leader. Tapscott's Pan-Afrikan Peoples Arkestra (consisting of two pianos, six reeds, two trombones, Red Callender on tuba, a cello, two basses, a drummer and a percussionist) had an unusual sound and made three records during 1978-79. The band performs five group originals; surprisingly none were written by the leader. While there are some individual solos (particularly by Tapscott), it is the dense and frequently exciting ensembles that are most notable in this avant-garde but rhythmic music. —*Scott Yanow*

Live at the I.U.C.C. / Feb. 1979-Jun. 1979 / Nimbus ✦✦✦✦
Pianist-composer Horace Tapscott has made relatively few recordings considering his originality and obvious talents. Throughout the 1960s and '70s he led the U.G.M.A.A. Foundation (Union of God's Musicians & Artists Ascension), a big band that fell somewhere between post bop and the avant-garde. This double-LP is one of the group's few recordings and it actually features four different versions of the ensemble. Most of the sidemen are now obscure except for altoist Michael Session, Red Callender on tuba and bassist Roberto Miranda, but the music is quite dynamic and generally exciting. Worth searching for. —*Scott Yanow*

At the Crossroads / 1980 / Nimbus ✦✦✦
For this fairly rare LP, pianist Horace Tapscott and drummer Everett Brown, Jr., play four fairly free duets. Because Tapscott has always had a very impressive technique and a melodic style, the encounters hold one's interest throughout and build up logically. Tapscott's very original style is always fascinating to hear and this adventurous set is one of his better dates. —*Scott Yanow*

Live at Lobero / Nov. 12, 1981 / Nimbus ✦✦✦✦✦
Pianist Horace Tapscott is always at his best when he is leading a trio. This rare outing features Tapscott with his longtime bassist Roberto Miranda and drummer Sonship on three extended performances including Tapscott's colorful "Sketches Of Drunken Mary" and a 21-minute version of "The Dark Tree." Hopefully this valuable LP will someday be reissued on CD for Tapscott has made too few recordings during his long career. —*Scott Yanow*

Dial "B" for Barbara / 1981 / Nimbus ✦✦✦✦✦
The best of pianist Horace Tapscott's recordings for the tiny Nimbus label is this 1981 LP which features him in a sextet with trumpeter Reggie Bullen, altoist Gary Bias, tenor saxophonist Sabir Matteen, bassist Roberto Miranda and drummer Everett Brown, Jr. The group stretches out on a couple of Tapscott's originals plus a 19-minute version of Linda Hill's "Dem Folks." Although the music could be called avant-garde, its use of rhythms and repetition keep the results from being forbidding and the performances have a momentum of their own. —*Scott Yanow*

The Tapscott Sessions, Vol. 1 / Jun. 1982 / Nimbus ✦✦✦✦✦
Horace Tapscott has been one of the top "unknown" jazz pianists in the Los Angeles area since the 1960s, recording far too few sessions, which has led to him being continually overlooked by jazz fans from outside L.A. During 1982-84 he recorded seven solo piano albums for the tiny Nimbus label, but unfortunately they tend to be slight disappointments. Tapscott is actually best in a trio/quartet where he can work off of other fiery soloists. Playing unaccompanied solos, his improvisations often wander and ramble a bit. This first volume has three Tapscott originals (best is "This Is for Benny"), a couple of obscurities and his version of the standard "Alone Together." Interesting but not essential music. —*Scott Yanow*

The Tapscott Sessions, Vol. 2 / Nov. 1982 / Nimbus ✦✦✦✦
The second of Horace Tapscott's seven solo piano dates for Nimbus is one of the better ones, consisting of a nearly half-hour exploration of his "Struggle X" along with a 9-minute obscurity ("Many Nights Ago"). Tapscott has always had a strikingly original sound that, despite occasional hints at other pianists, is quite distinctive, falling between advanced hard bop and the avant-garde. Although best-heard in small groups rather than solo, this adventurous set is worth picking up. —*Scott Yanow*

The Tapscott Sessions, Vol. 3 / Mar. 1983 / Nimbus ✦✦✦
Horace Tapscott performs five of his obscure originals on the third of seven solo piano LPs in his Nimbus series. Although not without interest, Tapscott's solos in this series tend to be inconclusive with rambling moments and not as much excitement as his trio and quartet performances. Still, there is relatively little of the masterful pianist-composer's work on record and this album does have five of his lesser-known originals. —*Scott Yanow*

The Tapscott Sessions, Vol. 4 / Sep. 1982 / Nimbus ✦✦✦✦
The main purposes of this seven-LP set of piano solos were to document Horace Tapscott's playing and to introduce obscure compositions, the majority being his own. Tapscott tends to sound more fiery and focused when playing with a medium-size group, so these releases are not quite essential. However this date does have six worthy originals plus a song apiece by Louis Spears and his former band member Arthur Blythe ("As of Yet"). —*Scott Yanow*

The Tapscott Sessions, Vol. 5 / Jan. 1984 / Nimbus ✦✦✦
For the fifth of Horace Tapscott's seven solo piano LP's for Nimbus, he explores five of his most obscure originals; when was the last time anyone played "Stringeurisms," "I'll Have One When It's Over" or "Hy-Pockets' Swan Song"? Tap-

scott's playing throughout the series is generally not as exciting as his ensemble work but there is relatively little of the highly original pianist on record, so connoisseurs of adventurous jazz may very well want to pick up these interesting (if not essential) releases. —*Scott Yanow*

The Tapscott Sessions, Vol. 6 / Oct. 1983 / Nimbus ✦✦✦
Horace Tapscott sought in his seven-LP series of piano solos to both document his own playing and a variety of little-known compositions, many by himself. On this particular release Tapscott digs into three of his tunes (including the 13-minute "Ancestral Echoes") plus a trio of obscurities, best-known of which is Roy Porter's "Jessica." As is true with the other entries in this program, nothing all that essential occurs although the music is not without interest. —*Scott Yanow*

The Tapscott Sessions, Vol. 7 / Feb. 1983 / Nimbus ✦✦✦✦
One of the strongest of Horace Tapscott's seven solo piano albums for Nimbus, this session features the distinctive (if generally overlooked) stylist (who actually sounds best in trios or quartets) performing five of his originals (including "Sonnet of Butterfly McQueen") plus Thelonious Monk's "'Round Midnight" and Charles Tolliver's catchy "On the Nile." —*Scott Yanow*

● **The Dark Tree, Vol. 1** / Dec. 14, 1989-Dec. 17, 1989 / Hat Art ✦✦✦✦✦
Pianist Horace Tapscott has long been Los Angeles' great undiscovered legend. A very original stylist capable of playing bop, free jazz or anything in between, Tapscott does not sound like anyone else. Unfortunately he has made few recordings through the years and thus far none with his regular working band of the past decade, but his two Hat Art CDs partly fill the gap. Tapscott was teamed during a stint at Catalina's in Hollywood with clarinetist John Carter, bassist Cecil McBee and drummer Andrew Cyrille. The lengthy renditions they give three of the pianist's compositions (along with trombonist Thurman Green's "One for Lately") allows listeners outside of L.A. a rare opportunity to hear Tapscott stretching out on records; his playing and that of the all-stars is near peak form. —*Scott Yanow*

The Dark Tree, Vol. 2 / Dec. 14, 1989-Dec. 17, 1989 / Hat Art ✦✦✦✦✦
Pianist Horace Tapscott, a greatly under-recognized but very original pianist, is showcased even more on this set than on the first volume, for clarinetist John Carter is only on two of the five selections (four of which are Tapscott originals). With bassist Cecil McBee and drummer Andrew Cyrille propelling the all-star group, Tapscott's percussive yet generally melodic style is well-featured. But why doesn't some label record his regular working group? —*Scott Yanow*

Buddy Tate (George Holmes Tate)

b. Feb. 22, 1913, Sherman, TX
Tenor Saxophone, Clarinet / Swing, Groove
One of the more individual tenors to emerge from the swing era, the distinctive Buddy Tate came to fame as Herschel Evans' replacement with Count Basie's Orchestra. Earlier he had picked up valuable experience playing with Terrence Holder (1930-33), Count Basie's original Kansas City band (1934), Andy Kirk (1934-35) and Nat Towles (1935-39). With Basie a second time during 1939-48, Tate held his own with such major tenors as Lester Young, Don Byas, Illinois Jacquet, Lucky Thompson and Paul Gonsalves. After a period freelancing with the likes of Hot Lips Page, Lucky Millinder and Jimmy Rushing (1950-52), Tate led his own crowd-pleasing group for 21 years (1953-74) at Harlem's Celebrity Club. During this period Tate also took time out to record in a variety of settings (including with Buck Clayton and Milt Buckner), and he was one of the stars of John Hammond's Spirituals to Swing concert of 1967. Tate has kept busy since the Celebrity Club association ended, recording frequently, co-leading a band with Paul Quinichette in 1975, playing and recording in Canada with Jay McShann and Jim Galloway, visiting Europe many times and performing at jazz parties; he was also a favorite sideman of Benny Goodman's in the late '70s. Although age had taken its toll, in the mid-'90s Buddy Tate played and recorded with both Lionel Hampton and the Statesmen of Jazz. —*Scott Yanow*

Swinging Like Tate / Feb. 12, 1958+Feb. 26, 1958 / London ✦✦✦
For this CD reissue, which brings back material originally recorded by Stanley Dance for the Felsted label, veteran swing tenor Buddy Tate is heard at the head of two different groups for three obscure songs apiece. The first half has Tate leading his Celebrity Club Orchestra, a four-horn octet that lacked any big names but worked regularly throughout the era. For the second half, Tate is teamed with some of the Count Basie alumni including trumpeter Buck Clayton, trombonist Dicky Wells, altoist Earle Warren and drummer Jo Jones. The music overall is fine mainstream jazz of the 1950s that is easily recommended to straightahead jazz fans although little unexpected or all that memorable occurs. —*Scott Yanow*

Groovin' with Buddy Tate / Dec. 18, 1959-Feb. 17, 1961 / Prestige ✦✦✦✦

Tate-A-Tate / Oct. 18, 1960 / Original Jazz Classics ✦✦✦✦✦
This LP reissue of a Storyville set (which has not yet been put out on CD) matches the distinctive tenor Buddy Tate with trumpeter Clark Terry and a fine rhythm sec-

tion (pianist Tommy Flanagan, bassist Larry Gales and drummer Art Taylor). The swinging unit performs three C.T. originals, Tate's "No. 20 Ladbroke Square" and two standards ("Take the 'A' Train" and "All Too Soon"). The music is enjoyable and practically defines mainstream jazz of the era. —*Scott Yanow*

Unbroken / Jun. 30, 1970-Jul. 1, 1970 / Pausa ✦✦✦✦

Starting in 1952 and continuing into the early 1970s, tenor saxophonist Buddy Tate worked regularly at the Celebrity Club in Harlem with his septet/octet, which he logically called the Celebrity Club Orchestra. Tate and his group made relatively few recordings, which makes this set (cut for MPS and last available domestically as a Pausa LP) quite valuable. In addition to Tate, the group features trumpeter Dud Bascomb (who was with Erskine Hawkins' Orchestra during the swing era), pianist Nat Pierce, bassist Eddie Jones, and such lesser-known players as trombonist Eli Robinson, Ben Richardson (on clarinet, alto and baritone) and drummer George Reed. The unit performs six veteran swing standards (including "Undecided," "Airmail Special" and "Tuxedo Junction") and a couple of basic originals. The enjoyable music swings hard, making one wish that this fine session were reissued on CD. —*Scott Yanow*

Buddy Tate and His Buddies / Jun. 1, 1973 / Chiaroscuro ✦✦✦

Jam sessions featuring swing veterans were not that common an occurrence on record during the early '70s, making Hank O'Neal's Chiaroscuro label both ahead of and behind the times. This CD reissue is most notable for having pianist Mary Lou Williams (who rarely was invited to this type of freewheeling session) as one of the key soloists. Also heard from are the tenors of Buddy Tate and Illinois Jacquet and the aging but still exciting trumpeter Roy Eldridge; the backup players are rhythm guitarist Steve Jordan, bassist Milt Hinton and drummer Gus Johnson. Together they jam three group originals, Buck Clayton's "Rockaway" and the standard "Sunday." Although falling short of being a classic, this infectious and consistently swinging music is worth picking up. —*Scott Yanow*

Swinging Scorpio / Jul. 3, 1974 / Black Lion ✦✦✦✦

Although Buck Clayton was no longer playing trumpet by 1974 due to health problems, he was still writing swinging compositions. On this CD reissue, tenor saxophonist Buddy Tate and trumpeter Humphrey Lyttelton (both of whom double on clarinet) perform eight of Buck's tunes in an English septet also including altoist Bruce Turner, Kathleen Stobart (on tenor and baritone), pianist Mick Pyne, bassist Dave Green and drummer Tony Mann. The material (and many of the sidemen) may be obscure, but the music is fairly enjoyable; Clayton's arranged ensembles are an added plus. —*Scott Yanow*

The Texas Twister / Feb. 21, 1975 / New World ✦✦✦✦✦

The music on this New World release (originally put out by Master Jazz) is very much in the vein of Count Basie. Buddy Tate (playing tenor and clarinet in addition to taking a few of Jimmy Rushing-style vocals) is joined by fellow tenor Paul Quinichette (making one of his few recordings of the 1970s), pianist Cliff Smalls (an underrated swing player), bassist Major Holley and drummer Jackie Williams. Other than the opening original "The Texas Twister" and Tate's ballad feature on "Talk of the Town," all of the music is from the Basie book including "Chicago," "Boogie Woogie" and "Topsy." All of the musicians (most of whom were not making too many recordings in the mid-1970s) sound somewhat inspired and are in fine form. —*Scott Yanow*

Jive at Five / Jul. 23, 1975 / Storyville ✦✦✦✦

During an era when mainstream jam sessions were fairly rare and fusion reigned, Storyville documented an all-star group mostly comprising swing era veterans. Tenor saxophonist Buddy Tate, trombonist Vic Dickenson and trumpeter Doc Cheatham (who was 70 at the time and just beginning to emerge as a soloist) make for a potent front line, pianist Johnny Guarnieri is heard in prime form and bassist George Duvivier and drummer Oliver Jackson are typically tasteful in support. Two alternate takes were added to the original seven-song program for this CD reissue and there are features for Dickenson (who sings and plays his own "Constantly"), Cheatham ("I've Got a Right to Sing the Blues") and Tate ("There Goes My Heart"). However it is the four group jams that are most exciting. Easily recommended to mainstream jazz fans. —*Scott Yanow*

Tate a Tete at La Fontaine, Copenhagen / Sep. 23, 1975-Sep. 24, 1975 / Storyville ✦✦✦✦

Tenor saxophonist Buddy Tate meets up with pianist Tete Montoliu on this enjoyable blowing date. Other than "Buddy's Blues" (which has a Tate vocal), all of the songs are swing standards with "In a Mellow Tone" clocking in at seventeen-and-a-half minutes. Violinist Finn Ziegler makes worthwhile guest appearances on two of the five selections and the group is completed by bassist Bo Stief and drummer Svend Erik Norregard. Easily recommended for swing fans, this album finds Buddy Tate still very much in prime form. —*Scott Yanow*

Meets Dollar Brand / Aug. 25, 1977 / Chiaroscuro ✦✦✦✦

This CD reissue has an unusual matchup that works fairly well. Although veteran swing tenor Buddy Tate plays Abdullah Ibrahim's vamp tune "Goduka Mfundi," in most cases it is the pianist (at the time known as Dollar Brand) who goes the extra distance to make Tate comfortable. Ibrahim's other original for the quartet (which also includes bassist Cecil McBee and drummer Roy Brooks) is a blues; otherwise the repertoire comprises swing standards such as "Poor Butterfly" and "Just You, Just Me." Ibrahim plays quite sparsely and sometimes drops out altogether behind Tate. The tenor (who is in top form) easily emerges as the solo star. The CD adds two previously unissued trio numbers without Tate ("Shrimp Boats" and "Django") from the same day that give Ibrahim more of a chance to shine. Worth investigating. —*Scott Yanow*

Sherman Shuffle / Jan. 29, 1978 / Sackville ✦✦✦✦✦

Tenor saxophonist Buddy Tate and Bob Wilber (mostly on alto) make for a potent team on this consistently swinging quartet date with bassist Sam Jones and drummer Leroy Williams. Tate has one appearance apiece on baritone and clarinet (the latter for Wilber's exquisite "Curtains of the Night") while Bob Wilber also plays a bit of soprano and clarinet. A superior repertoire; the variety of lead voices and consistently strong solos make this a set worth picking up. —*Scott Yanow*

Buddy Tate Quartet / Jul. 16, 1978 / Sackville ✦✦✦✦

With the assistance of a fine Canadian rhythm section (pianist Wray Downes, bassist Dave Young and drummer Pete Magadini), veteran tenor saxophonist Buddy Tate is in fine form on seven standards. All of the songs but "June Night" are so well-known that they could be called "warhorses," yet Tate sounds consistently enthusiastic and creative within the swing idiom. Highlights include "June Night," "Bye Bye Blackbird" and "I'll Remember April." —*Scott Yanow*

★ Hard Blowin' / Aug. 25, 1978-Aug. 26, 1978 / Muse ✦✦✦✦✦

Muse has released at least six albums of material recorded at Sandy's Jazz Revival in Massachusetts during a week in 1978. This is veteran tenor Buddy Tate's most rewarding album from the engagement and a fine all-around showcase. Accompanied by pianist Ray Bryant, bassist George Duvivier and drummer Alan Dawson, Tate stretches out on four familiar standards and shows listeners that he really had one of the more distinctive tenor sounds of the swing era. Recommended. —*Scott Yanow*

Live at Sandy's / Aug. 25, 1978-Aug. 26, 1978 / Muse ✦✦✦✦✦

One of the six Muse albums recorded at Sandy's Jazz Revival in Massachusetts during an engagement in 1978, this is essentially tenor veteran Buddy Tate's set, although altoist Eddie "Cleanhead" Vinson and tenor Arnett Cobb join in on the closing blues "She's Got It." Tate is in fine form on the other four songs, which include an outing on clarinet for "Blue Creek," a warm version of the ballad "Candy" and two lengthy jams with pianist Ray Bryant, bassist George Duvivier and drummer Alan Dawson. Consistently swinging music and one of the better Buddy Tate recordings currently available. —*Scott Yanow*

Great Buddy Tate / Mar. 1981 / Concord Jazz ✦✦✦✦✦

This is a particularly well-rounded set that does indeed show off Buddy Tate's greatness. Tate is heard on his customary tenor plus clarinet (on "Softly As in a Morning Sunrise") and his rarely heard baritone (on "Bernie's Tune"). Tate's notable sidemen include cornetist Warren Vache, pianist Hank Jones, bassist Milt Hinton and either Mel Lewis or Jackie Williams on drums; on "I Realize Now" Buddy's son Paul Tate takes a fine vocal. Other highlights include "On Green Dolphin Street," "At Sundown" and "Shiny Stockings." This Concord release gives one a fine example of Buddy Tate's musical talents from the later part of his long career. —*Scott Yanow*

Ballad Artistry of Buddy Tate / Jun. 12, 1981-Jun. 13, 1981 / Sackville ✦✦✦

The veteran swing tenor Buddy Tate mostly sticks fairly close to the melody throughout these ten ballads, three of which were released for the first time on the CD reissue. The music is enjoyable enough if a bit restrained and guitarist Ed Bickert (who is heard along with bassist Don Thompson and drummer Terry Clarke) often shares solo honors on this tasteful affair. —*Scott Yanow*

Just Jazz / Apr. 28, 1984 / Reservoir ✦✦✦✦

Tenor saxophonist Buddy Tate (who also contributes a bit of clarinet) blends in perfectly with trombonist Al Grey on this swinging quintet session. With pianist Richard Wyands, bassist Major Holley and drummer Al Harewood completing the group, Tate and Grey perform an original apiece and four veteran standards; the CD reissue adds two alternate takes. Both Tate and Grey were in their late prime at the time and the high points include Grey's title cut, "Straight Up and Fly Right," "Topsy" and "Tangerine." —*Scott Yanow*

After Dark / 1985-Jan. 22, 1986 / Progressive ✦✦✦✦✦

Both tenor saxophonist Buddy Tate and trumpeter Harry "Sweets" Edison were still in near-prime form at the time these two sessions (reissued on a Progressive CD) were recorded. Tate is well showcased on both dates, quintet outings with

Edison or (for four of the dozen selections) trombonist Roy Williams and European rhythm sections led by drummer Ted Easton. The repertoire sticks to swing standards and emphasizes ballads, but still contains some fiery moments. Highlights include "I Cried for You," "September in the Rain," "Dream" and "I Cover the Waterfront." One of Tate's best late-period recordings. —*Scott Yanow*

Grady Tate

b. Jan. 14, 1932, Durham, NC
Drums, Vocals / Hard Bop, Soul Jazz

Grady Tate is renowned as a session drummer extraordinaire, an expert in the use of the rim shot for syncopation purposes, prized for his driving, pushing or subtle coaxing of the beat. Yet he has also displayed a warm, flexible, rhythmically agile baritone voice, which, in a reversal of the usual commercial situation, is less well-known than his drumming. He began singing at age four, impressing local Durham church and school audiences, but quit temporarily when his voice broke at age 12. Self-taught as a drummer at first, he picked up the fundamentals of jazz drumming during his hitch in the Air Force (1951-55), and arranger Bill Berry made some vocal charts for him there. Upon his discharge, he returned to Durham to study psychology, literature and theater at North Carolina College before moving to Washington, D.C. in 1959 to teach high school and take up a musical career with Wild Bill Davis. A move to New York City in 1963 led to a gig with the Quincy Jones big band, and soon he caught on as a recording session drummer. His most famous records as an accompanist were made under the aegis of producer Creed Taylor, for whom he became the house drummer of choice. Tate played on many of Wes Montgomery's and Jimmy Smith's most popular recordings, as well as some by Nat Adderley, Stan Getz, Tony Bennett, Kenny Burrell, Ella Fitzgerald, Benny Goodman, Roland Kirk, Count Basie, Oscar Peterson, Duke Ellington, J.J. Johnson and Kai Winding, among countless other artists. Arranger Gary McFarland thought enough of Tate's singing voice to record a number of vocal albums for his short-lived Skye label, yet despite further vocal sessions for Buddah, Janus, Impulse and a host of Japanese labels, Tate's profile as a singer has not been as high as it could have been. He returned to the American recording scene with 1991's excellent, vocal-only album for Milestone, *TNT*, where drummer Dennis Mackrel uses many patterns that he learned from Tate. —*Richard S. Ginell*

TNT / 1991 / Milestone ✦✦✦✦

● **Body & Soul** / Oct. 27, 1992-Nov. 2, 1992 / Milestone ✦✦✦✦

Art Tatum

b. Oct. 13, 1909, Toledo, OH, **d.** Nov. 5, 1956, Los Angeles, CA
Piano / Swing

Art Tatum was among the most extraordinary of all jazz musicians, a pianist with wondrous technique who could not only play ridiculously rapid lines with both hands (his 1933 solo version of "Tiger Rag" sounds as if there were three pianists jamming together!) but was harmonically 30 years ahead of his time; all pianists have to deal to a certain extent with Tatum's innovations in order to be taken seriously. Able to play stride, swing and boogie-woogie with a speed and complexity that could only previously be imagined, Tatum's quick reflexes and boundless imagination kept his improvisations filled with fresh (and sometimes futuristic) ideas that put him way ahead of his contemporaries.

Born nearly blind, Tatum gained some formal piano training at the Toledo School of Music but was largely self-taught. Although influenced a bit by Fats Waller and the semi-classical pianists of the 1920s, there is really no explanation for where Tatum gained his inspiration and ideas from. He first played professionally in Toledo in the mid-'20s and had a radio show during 1929-30. In 1932 Tatum traveled with singer Adelaide Hall to New York and made his recording debut accompanying Hall (as one of two pianists!). But for those who had never heard him in person, it was his solos of 1933 (including "Tiger Rag") that announced the arrival of a truly major talent. In the 1930s Tatum spent periods working in Cleveland, Chicago, New York, Los Angeles and (in 1938) England. Although he led a popular trio with guitarist Tiny Grimes (later Everett Barksdale) and bassist Slam Stewart in the mid-'40s, Tatum spent most of his life as a solo pianist who could always scare the competition. Some observers criticized him for having too much technique (is such a thing possible?), working out and then keeping the same arrangements for particular songs and for using too many notes, but those minor reservations pale when compared to Tatum's reworkings of such tunes as "Yesterdays," "Begin the Beguine" and even "Humoresque." Although he was not a composer, Tatum's rearrangements of standards made even warhorses sound like new compositions.

Tatum, who recorded for Decca throughout the 1930s and Capitol in the late '40s, starred at the Esquire Metropolitan Opera House concert of 1944 and appeared briefly in his only film in 1947, *The Fabulous Dorseys* (leading a jam session on a heated blues). He recorded extensively for Norman Granz near the end

of his life in the 1950s, both solo and with all-star groups; all of the music has been reissued by Pablo on a seven-CD and a six-CD box set. Art Tatum's premature death from uremia has not resulted in any loss of fame, for Art Tatum's recordings still have the ability to scare modern pianists! —*Scott Yanow*

Masters of Jazz, Vol. 8 / Aug. 1932-Jan. 1946 / Storyville ✦✦✦✦
The Swedish label Storyville's *Masters of Jazz* series released a dozen volumes of mostly rare music by swing-era greats. Tatum's set primarily comprises selections cut in 1935 for radio airplay, giving listeners a chance to hear the young genius perform some songs that he never recorded otherwise. In addition, there are two selections from 1945-46, along with his earliest recording: a broadcast version of "Tiger Rag." —*Scott Yanow*

☆ **Piano Starts Here** / Mar. 21, 1933+1949 / Columbia/Legacy ✦✦✦✦✦
There are many Art Tatum records currently available, but this is the one to pull out to amaze friends, particularly with Tatum's wondrous version of "Tiger Rag," during which he sounds like three pianists jamming together. This CD consists of Tatum's first studio session as a leader (which resulted in "Tea for Two," "St. Louis Blues," "Tiger Rag" and "Sophisticated Lady") and a remarkable solo concert performance from the spring of 1949. While "Tiger Rag" dwarfs everything else, the live set is highlighted by a very adventurous, yet seemingly effortless exploration of "Yesterdays," a ridiculously rapid "I Know That You Know," and the hard-cooking "Tatum Pole Boogie." This is an essential set of miraculous music that cannot be praised highly enough. —*Scott Yanow*

● **1932-1934** / Mar. 1933-Oct. 1934 / Classics ✦✦✦✦✦
This comprehensive CD contains Art Tatum's very first recording (a broadcast version of "Tiger Rag") four selections in which he accompanies singer Adelaide Hall (along with a second pianist) and then his first 20 solo sides. To call his virtuosic piano style remarkable would be a major understatement; he has to be heard to be believed. His studio version of "Tiger Rag" may very well be his most incredible recording; he sounds like three pianists at once. —*Scott Yanow*

Pure Genius / Feb. 27, 1934-1945 / Atlantis ✦✦✦✦
This English LP contains some rare solo performances that Tatum fans will want to get. A Cleveland broadcast from 1934 (less than a year after his initial recordings) features Tatum performing some rare material (particularly "Young & Healthy" and "Morning, Noon & Night"); he is also heard in duet with bassist Junior Raglin (1945's "The Man I Love") and on an extensive solo broadcast from the same year. Art Tatum was an amazing pianist and no jazz collection is complete without a few of his recordings. —*Scott Yanow*

1934-1940 / Oct. 1934-Jul. 26, 1940 / Classics ✦✦✦✦✦
The second CD in Classics' Art Tatum series features the remarkable pianist as a soloist for many gems recorded for Decca and with a sextet on four numbers. Although alternate takes are bypassed, making the Decca CDs preferable, the set is overflowing with classics. Highlights include Tatum's interpretations of "Chloe," "The Sheik of Araby," "Elegie," "Humoresque," "Get Happy" and "Begin the Beguine." —*Scott Yanow*

☆ **Classic Piano Solos (1934-39)** / 1934-1939 / Decca ✦✦✦✦✦
This excellent CD reissues all of Tatum's early Decca piano solos cut at three sessions in 1934 and one in 1937. He was decades ahead of his contemporaries not only in technique but in harmonic ideas. Highlights of this very impressive set include "Emaline," "After You've Gone, "The Shout," two versions of "Liza" and "The Sheik of Araby." —*Scott Yanow*

I Got Rhythm: Art Tatum, Vol. 3 (1935-44) / Dec. 21, 1935-Jan. 5, 1944 / Decca ✦✦✦✦✦
This third Decca CD wraps up GRP's Art Tatum reissue series. There are two piano solos ("Tea For Two" and "Deep Purple"), an obscure 1935 version of "Take Me Back to My Boots and Saddle" with an unidentified group, the full session (including two alternate takes) by Art Tatum's "Swingsters" in 1937, two instrumentals from 1940 with a sextet with trumpeter Joe Thomas and clarinetist Edmond Hall and ten performances by Tatum's famous 1944 trio with guitarist Tiny Grimes and bassist Slam Stewart. Tatum's playing throughout is typically miraculous and this CD offers ample proof that he could play with other musicians, providing they were flexible and strong themselves. Highly recommended. —*Scott Yanow*

Standard Transcriptions / Dec. 1935-1943 / Music & Arts ✦✦✦✦✦
On this double-CD there are 61 solo piano performances by Art Tatum, the majority of which are quite wondrous. Recorded as radio transcriptions, Tatum is featured in 1935, 1938, 1939 and 1943. The earlier tunes are particularly startling as Tatum really rips into such numbers as "After You've Gone," "Tiger Rag," "I Would Do Anything for You" and his own "The Shout." His advanced harmonies (some of which have still not been surpassed), remarkable speed and incredible technique will amaze most listeners; at times he actually sounds like three pianists. Highly recommended. —*Scott Yanow*

Standards / 1938-1939 / Black Lion ✦✦✦✦
This Black Lion CD features brilliant piano solos originally cut as noncommercial radio transcriptions during 1938-39. Duplicating part of Tatum's Music & Arts double CD, *Standards* features a great deal of magic from the remarkable virtuoso. —*Scott Yanow*

Solos (1940) / Feb. 22, 1940-Jul. 26, 1940 / Decca ✦✦✦✦✦
MCA's short-lived Decca CD-reissue program put out this gem, all of Tatum's piano solos from 1940, including two versions of the previously unknown "Sweet Emalina, My Gal." Some of the routines on these standards were a bit familiar by now (this "Tiger Rag" pales next to his 1933 version) but are no less exciting and still sound seemingly impossible to play. —*Scott Yanow*

God Is in the House / Nov. 11, 1940-Sep. 16, 1941 / Onyx ✦✦✦✦
A real historical curiosity, this out-of-print LP features Tatum playing in nightclubs and in an apartment sometimes with a bassist. Privately recorded (and not of digital quality), the music is still utterly fascinating, particularly a pair of jams with trumpeter Frankie Newton and bassist Ebbenezer Paul and two surprise blues vocals by Tatum himself. —*Scott Yanow*

The Remarkable Art of Tatum / Jan. 5, 1944 / Audiophile ✦✦✦✦
After years of appearing almost exclusively as a piano soloist, Tatum formed a trio in the mid-'40s with guitarist Tiny Grimes and bassist Slam Stewart. Fortunately Grimes and Stewart were quick thinkers and witty improvisers, for they needed all of their creativity in order to keep up with the astounding pianist. All 11 of the performances (including one alternate take) they cut for World Broadcasting transcriptions are included on this rather brief (under 27 minutes) LP. Their magical interplay was consistently memorable. —*Scott Yanow*

The V-Discs / Jan. 18, 1944-Jan. 21, 1946 / Black Lion ✦✦✦✦
This Black Lion CD mostly features the phenomenal Tatum playing solo during 1945-46, really digging into a variety of standards. A rare version of "Sweet Lorraine" (with bassist Oscar Pettiford and drummer Sid Catlett in 1944) and two numbers with his 1945 trio (featuring guitarist Tiny Grimes and bassist Slam Stewart) round out this excellent CD. —*Scott Yanow*

In Private / 1949 / Jazz Chronicles ✦✦✦
This collector's LP features the amazing Tatum playing solo piano at a private party. Although the recording quality is not flawless, his melodic interpretations of 11 standards are typically virtuosic and fascinating; he was always well worth hearing. —*Scott Yanow*

● **The Complete Capitol Recordings, Vol. 1** / Jul. 13, 1949-Dec. 20, 1952 / Capitol ✦✦✦✦✦
Tatum recorded 20 piano solos in 1949 and eight selections with his 1952 trio (which included guitarist Everett Barksdale and bassist Slam Stewart) for Capitol. Ten solos and four trios are included on each of the two CDs in this "complete" series; he can be heard here at the height of his powers. (He never did decline, creating miraculous variations of standards that still amaze today's pianists.) —*Scott Yanow*

● **The Complete Capitol Recordings, Vol. 2** / Sep. 29, 1949-Dec. 20, 1952 / Capitol ✦✦✦✦✦
On the second of two CDs, Art Tatum is heard playing solo in 1949 on ten standards and interacting with his 1952 trio (which included guitarist Everett Barksdale and bassist Slam Stewart) during four numbers. Tatum always had the ability to amaze fellow pianists (not to mention fans) and there are plenty of remarkable moments in this fine set. —*Scott Yanow*

The Complete Capitol Recordings / 1949-1952 / Blue Note ✦✦✦✦✦
Previously released as two separate volumes, *The Complete Capitol Recordings of Art Tatum* is a two-disc collection that presents everything the pianist recorded for Capitol Records in chronological order. —*Leo Stanley*

Art Tatum at His Piano, Vol. 1 / 1950 / GNP ✦✦✦
On the first of two LPs featuring Tatum live at the Crescendo Club in 1950, the great pianist interprets a dozen standards in familiar but impressive fashion. His routines on some tunes became set pieces but still were quite remarkable as evidenced by this fine performance. —*Scott Yanow*

Art Tatum at His Piano, Vol. 2 / 1950 / GNP ✦✦✦
The second of two LPs taken from a 1950 Los Angeles concert, Tatum performs concise melodic variations on another dozen standards. Although not his most adventurous set, he was definitely in fine form that day. —*Scott Yanow*

20th Century Piano Genius / Apr. 16, 1950+Jul. 3, 1956 / Verve ✦✦✦✦
This double CD was taped at a private party in 1956, featuring the amazing Art Tatum on solo piano. Tatum, who died the following year, never did decline, and he is in prime form throughout this highly enjoyable and frequently exciting set of

standards. There are no real romps à la "Tiger Rag," but the 27 performances contain plenty of remarkable moments. —*Scott Yanow*

The Complete Pablo Solo Masterpieces / Dec. 28, 1953-Jan. 19, 1955 / Pablo ✦✦✦✦
During four marathon recording sessions in 1953-55, Norman Granz recorded Art Tatum playing 119 standards, enough music for a dozen LPs. The results have been recently reissued separately on eight CDs and on this very full seven-CD box set. Frankly, Tatum did no real advance preparation for this massive project, sticking mostly to concise melodic variations of standards, some of them virtual set pieces formed over the past two decades. Since there are few uptempo performances, the music in this series has a certain sameness after awhile but, heard in small doses, it is quite enjoyable. A special bonus on this box (and not on the individual volumes) are four numbers taken from a 1956 Hollywood Bowl concert. —*Scott Yanow*

The Tatum Solo Masterpieces, Vol. 1 / Dec. 28, 1953-Jan. 19, 1955 / Pablo ✦✦✦✦
The first of eight CDs reissuing the 119 piano solo performances that Art Tatum recorded for Norman Granz during four marathon record sessions has its moments, although in general this series lacks the excitement of Tatum's earliest recordings. The pianist interprets such standards on this first volume as "Body and Soul," "It's Only a Paper Moon" and "Willow Weep for Me." —*Scott Yanow*

The Art Tatum Solo Masterpieces, Vol. 2 / Dec. 28, 1953-Jan. 19, 1955 / Pablo ✦✦✦✦
The second of eight CDs in this series of solo performances taken from four marathon record sessions has among its highlights "Elegy," "This Can't Be Love" and "Tea for Two," but in general this series lacks the excitement of Tatum's earliest recordings. Excellent but somewhat predictable performances by the classic virtuoso. —*Scott Yanow*

The Art Tatum Solo Masterpieces, Vol. 3 / Dec. 28, 1953-Jan. 19, 1955 / Pablo ✦✦✦✦
The third of eight CDs in the Norman Granz series of Tatum piano solos is highlighted by "Yesterdays," "Prisoner of Love" and "Begin the Beguine" among others. He did little prior preparation for the four marathon sessions that resulted in a dozen LPs (now reissued as eight CDs), so this series lacks the excitement and adventure of his earliest recordings, although it is still enjoyable in its own right. —*Scott Yanow*

The Art Tatum Solo Masterpieces, Vol. 4 / Dec. 28, 1953-Jan. 19, 1955 / Pablo ✦✦✦✦
On the fourth volume in this eight-CD series, Tatum sounds at his best on "Ill Wind" and "The Man I Love." Taken from the 119 piano solos he cut for Norman Granz in four lengthy recording sessions during 1953-55, these performances are concise, relaxed, and surprisingly predictable, if virtuosic. —*Scott Yanow*

The Art Tatum Solo Masterpieces, Vol. 5 / Dec. 29, 1953-Jan. 19, 1955 / Pablo ✦✦✦✦
The fifth volume of this eight-CD series features Tatum interpreting 15 of the 119 standards he recorded during four marathon solo recording sessions for Norman Granz. He sounds typically wondrous in spots even though there are few surprises throughout this generally relaxed set. —*Scott Yanow*

The Art Tatum Solo Masterpieces, Vol. 6 / Dec. 28, 1953-Jan. 19, 1955 / Pablo ✦✦✦✦
Volume Six of this eight-CD series features Tatum interpreting such standards as "Night and Day," "Cherokee," "Happy Feet" and "Someone to Watch Over Me" with taste and melodic creativity. There are no real barnburners or new revelations on this generally relaxed set, but the music should please Tatum's fans. —*Scott Yanow*

The Art Tatum Solo Masterpieces, Vol. 7 / Dec. 28, 1953-Jan. 19, 1955 / Pablo ✦✦✦✦
The next-to-last volume in this eight-CD series features interpretations of a variety of standards, including "Moon Song," "Japanese Sandman," "Moonlight on the Ganges" and even "Mighty like a Rose." Taken from the 119 numbers that Tatum recorded for Norman Granz during four marathon sessions, the music is pleasing, if at times a bit too relaxed for those who would like to hear the virtuoso really tear into these pieces. —*Scott Yanow*

The Art Tatum Solo Masterpieces, Vol. 8 / Dec. 29, 1953-Jan. 19, 1955 / Pablo ✦✦✦✦
The final volume of this eight-CD (and originally 12-LP) series is similar to the first seven in that Tatum melodically improvises on a variety of standards, in this case such tunes as "She's Funny That Way," "I Won't Dance," "Begin the Beguine" and "Humoresque." Few revelations occur (most of the interpretations are in the same relaxed medium tempo) but the music is typically well-played and generally quite enjoyable. —*Scott Yanow*

☆ **The Complete Pablo Group Masterpieces** / Jun. 25, 1954-Sep. 11, 1956 / Pablo ✦✦✦✦✦

Tatum spent most of his career as a solo pianist; in fact it was often said that he was such an unpredictable virtuoso that it would be difficult for other musicians to play with him. Producer Norman Granz sought to prove that that theory was false, so between 1954 and 1956 he extensively recorded Tatum with a variety of other classic jazzmen, resulting originally in nine LPs of material that is now available separately as eight CDs and on this very full six-CD box set. In contrast to the massive solo Tatum sessions that Granz also recorded during this period, the group sides have plenty of variety and exciting moments, which is not too surprising when one considers that Tatum was teamed in a trio with altoist Benny Carter and drummer Louie Bellson; with trumpeter Roy Eldridge, clarinetist Buddy DeFranco and tenor saxophonist Hen Webster in separate quartets; in an explosive trio with vibraphonist Lionel Hampton and drummer Buddy Rich; with a sextet including Hampton, Rich and trumpeter Harry "Sweets" Edison; and on a standard trio session. — *Scott Yanow*

The Tatum Group Masterpieces, Vol. 1 / Jun. 25, 1954 / Pablo ✦✦✦✦

During 1954-56 Norman Granz recorded the remarkable pianist Art Tatum with a variety of classic jazz masters, resulting in quite a bit of musical magic. This first of eight volumes finds Tatum matching wits with the classy alto of Benny Carter and drummer Louie Bellson—the results are both tasteful and frequently hardswinging. — *Scott Yanow*

The Tatum Group Masterpieces, Vol. 2 / Mar. 23, 1955-Mar. 29, 1955 / Pablo ✦✦✦✦

The second of eight CDs teaming the amazing pianist with a variety of his contemporaries finds Tatum sharing the stage with trumpeter Roy Eldridge, bassist John Simmons and drummer Alvin Stoller. Eldridge, normally a very combative player, knows better than to directly challenge Tatum and instead is surprisingly restrained and muted on this enjoyable set of swing standards. — *Scott Yanow*

The Tatum Group Masterpieces, Vol. 3 / Aug. 1, 1955 / Pablo ✦✦✦✦✦

The third of eight CDs matching the great pianist with a variety of classic jazzmen is the first of two that finds him in a trio with vibraphonist Lionel Hampton and drummer Buddy Rich; no weak spots in that group. Much of this music really burns. — *Scott Yanow*

The Tatum Group Masterpieces, Vol. 4 / Aug. 1, 1955 / Pablo ✦✦✦✦✦

The fourth of eight CDs featuring the pianist interacting with some of his most notable musical contemporaries is the second to match his virtuosity with that of vibraphonist Lionel Hampton and drummer Buddy Rich. The three immortals really challenge each other during this frequently heated jam session. — *Scott Yanow*

The Tatum Group Masterpieces, Vol. 5 / Sep. 7, 1955 / Pablo ✦✦✦✦

The fifth of eight CDs in this recommended series (which is also available complete as a six-CD box set) features the largest band in this program, a sextet with Tatum, vibraphonist Lionel Hampton, trumpeter Harry "Sweets" Edison, guitarist Barney Kessel, bassist Red Callender and drummer Buddy Rich. Their treatment of blues and standards is as exciting as one would expect from this all-star lineup. — *Scott Yanow*

The Tatum Group Masterpieces, Vol. 6 / Jan. 27, 1956 / Pablo ✦✦✦✦

For this CD, the sixth volume of Art Tatum's eight group recordings for Norman Granz in the 1950s, the remarkable pianist is teamed with bassist Red Callender and drummer Jo Jones. Due to the presence of his sidemen, Tatum is slightly restricted as far as changing keys and tempos at will, but his playing is still often stunning. Highlights of the trio performances include "Just One of Those Things," "Blue Lou" and "I'll Never Be the Same" and "More than You Know." This music (along with the other seven volumes) is also available as part of the massive six-CD set *The Complete Pablo Group Masterpieces*. — *Scott Yanow*

The Tatum Group Masterpieces, Vol. 7 / Feb. 6, 1956 / Pablo ✦✦✦✦✦

The seventh of eight CDs in this valuable series matches the remarkable pianist in a quartet with clarinetist Buddy DeFranco. DeFranco, no slouch himself, directly challenges Tatum and their uptempo romps are often quite wondrous. — *Scott Yanow*

The Tatum Group Masterpieces, Vol. 8 / Sep. 11, 1956 / Pablo ✦✦✦✦✦

The final volume in this very worthy series is a comparatively relaxed affair, a quartet set with tenor saxophonist Ben Webster. Webster lets Tatum fill the background with an infinite number of notes while emphasizing his warm tenor tone in the forefront on a variety of melodic ballads and standards. The combination works very well. — *Scott Yanow*

Art Taylor

b. Apr. 6, 1929, New York, NY, **d.** Feb. 6, 1995
Drums / Bop, Hard Bop

One of the great drummers of the 1950s, Art Taylor was on a countless number of hard bop and jam session-styled sessions. His first important gig was with Howard McGhee in 1948 and this was followed by associations with Coleman Hawkins (1950-51), Buddy DeFranco (1952), Bud Powell (1953 and 1955-57) and George Wallington (1954-56). Taylor seemed to live in Prestige's studios during the second half of the 1950s although he found time to lead his Wailers, visit Europe with Donald Byrd in 1958, gig and record with Miles Davis and play with Thelonious Monk (including his acclaimed Town Hall concert) in 1959. In 1963 Taylor moved to Europe, where he spent most of the next 20 years (mostly living in France and Belgium) playing with Europeans and such Americans as Dexter Gordon and Johnny Griffin. He interviewed scores of his colleagues and collected many of the insightful discussions in his very readable book *Notes and Tones* (which was re-released in 1993). After returning to the US, Taylor resumed his freelancing and in the early '90s he organized a new version of the Wailers which, during its short existence prior to his death, temporarily filled the gap left by the end of the Jazz Messengers. — *Scott Yanow*

● **Taylor's Wailers** / Feb. 25, 1956-Mar. 22, 1957 / Original Jazz Classics ✦✦✦✦✦

Five of the six selections on this CD reissue feature drummer Art Taylor in an all-star sextet of mostly young players comprising trumpeter Donald Byrd, altoist Jackie McLean, tenor Charlie Rouse, pianist Ray Bryant and bassist Wendell Marshall. Among the high points of the 1957 hard bop date are the original version of Bryant's popular "Cubano Chant" and strong renditions of two Thelonious Monk tunes ("Off Minor" and "Well, You Needn't") cut just prior to the pianist/composer's discovery by the jazz public. Bryant is the most mature of the soloists, but the three horn players were already starting to develop their own highly individual sounds. The remaining track (a version of Jimmy Heath's "C.T.A.") is played by the quartet of Taylor, tenor saxophonist John Coltrane, pianist Red Garland and bassist Paul Chambers, and is a leftover (although a good one) from another session. — *Scott Yanow*

Taylor's Tenors / Jun. 3, 1959 / Original Jazz Classics ✦✦✦✦

Drummer Art Taylor heads a quintet for a fine jam-session-flavored session featuring the tenors of Charlie Rouse (about the time he joined Thelonious Monk's Quartet) and Frank Foster (then with Count Basie), along with pianist Walter Davis and bassist Sam Jones. The repertoire on this CD reissue, originally recorded for Prestige's New Jazz subsidiary, includes two Monk tunes that are ideal for jamming ("Rhythm-Aning" and "Straight, No Chaser"), Jackie McLean's "Fidel" (which is given a memorable performance) and originals by Rouse, Davis and Taylor. All in all, this is a loose and enjoyable hard bop date. — *Scott Yanow*

Art Taylor's Delight / Aug. 6, 1960 / Blue Note ✦✦✦✦

Drummer Art Taylor was on many sessions as a sideman in the 1950s, but he only led three albums during the period and this was his only one for Blue Note. Heading a quintet/sextet also including the underrated bop trumpeter Dave Burns, the up-and-coming tenorman Stanley Turrentine, pianist Wynton Kelly, bassist Paul Chambers and (on three of the six songs) Potato Valdez on conga, Taylor performs a pair of Kenny Dorham tunes plus a song apiece by John Coltrane (the obscure "Syeeda's Song Flute"), Thelonious Monk, Denzil Best and his own calypso "Cookoo and Fungi." This well-rounded hard bop date was last available as a reissue LP in 1985. — *Scott Yanow*

Mr. A.T. / 1991 / Enja ✦✦✦✦✦

Drummer Art Taylor, who spent many years in Europe, re-emerged as an important bandleader with this Enja CD. Taylor's group (called "Taylor's Wailers") features four Young Lions: the fine tenor Willie Williams, altoist Abraham Burton (most heavily influenced by his teacher Jackie McLean), pianist Marc Cary and bassist Tyler Mitchell, in addition to the drummer/leader. On a variety of tunes from the 1950s and '60s (highlighted by "Hi-Fly," "Soul Eyes" and "Gingerbread Boy") the musicians play some high-quality modern hard bop. Enjoyable music. — *Scott Yanow*

Billy Taylor

b. Jul. 24, 1921, Greenville, NC
Piano / Bop, Hard Bop, Swing

Billy Taylor has been such an articulate spokesman for jazz, and his profiles on CBS' *Sunday Morning* television program (where he has been a regular since 1981) are so successful at introducing jazz to a wider audience, that sometimes one can forget how talented a pianist he has been for the past half-century. While not an innovator, Taylor has been flexible enough to play swing, bop and more advanced styles while always retaining his own musical personality. After graduating from Virginia State College in 1942, he moved to New York and played with such major musicians as Ben Webster, Eddie South, Stuff Smith (with whom he recorded in 1944) and Slam Stewart among others. In 1951 he was the house pianist at Birdland and soon afterward Taylor formed his first of many trios. He helped found the Jazzmobile in 1965, in 1969 he became the first Black band director for a network television series (*The David Frost Show*), and in 1975 he earned his doctorate at the University of Massachusetts and he both founded and served as director for the popular radio program *Jazz Alive*. But despite his activities in jazz education, Taylor has rarely gone long between performances and recordings, always keeping his bop-based style consistently swinging and fresh. —*Scott Yanow*

Billy Taylor Trio / Nov. 18, 1952-Dec. 29, 1953 / Prestige ◆◆◆◆
Two albums by pianist Billy Taylor are combined on this single CD reissue. With fine backing from bassist Earl May and drummer Charlie Smith, Taylor is tasteful, swinging and creative within the boundaries of bop and swing on this early set, among his first dates as a leader and excellent examples of his already individual style. —*Scott Yanow*

Cross Section / May 7, 1953+Jul. 30, 1954 / Original Jazz Classics ◆◆◆◆◆
For this CD reissue, pianist Billy Taylor is featured on eight songs with his trio of 1954 (which included bassist Earl May and drummer Percy Brice); the four originals (which alternate with standards) were all dedicated to disc jockeys of the time. The trio was fairly tight with Taylor in the lead and, although boppish, it also looked back towards the swing era. The remaining four numbers match Taylor and May with what was dubbed "Machito's Rhythm Section": Charlie Smith on conga, Joe Mangual on bongos, Uba Nieto playing timbales and Machito himself on maracas. The four mambos are ideal both for listening and for dance music. An enjoyable set. —*Scott Yanow*

With Candido / Sep. 7, 1954 / Original Jazz Classics ◆◆◆◆
This Prestige release (which has been reissued on CD) helped to introduce Candido to a jazz audience. Candido's conga and bongos fit in comfortably with pianist Billy Taylor's trio (which also includes bassist Earl May and drummer Percy Brice). Together they perform four of Taylor's boppish originals ("Bit of Bedlam" is straight from Bud Powell), "Love for Sale" and the highly appealing "Mambo Inn." Both Taylor and Candido have plenty of solo space and even if this CD is quite brief (under 32 minutes), the music is consistently delightful. —*Scott Yanow*

● **My Fair Lady Loves Jazz** / Jan. 8, 1957-Feb. 5, 1957 / Impulse ◆◆◆◆◆
Recorded at a time when *My Fair Lady* was a big Broadway hit (but a few years before it became a film), this CD reissue brings back one of the very best jazz interpretations of the classic score. The focus throughout is on the Billy Taylor trio (which included bassist Earl May and drummer Ed Thigpen) but Quincy Jones' arrangements for the seven horns are quite memorable. There is room for short solos from such players as trumpeter Ernie Royal, trombonist Jimmy Cleveland, altoist Anthony Ortega and baritonist Gerry Mulligan, and their presence clearly inspires pianist Taylor to some of his finest playing. Highly recommended. —*Scott Yanow*

Billy Taylor with Four Flutes / Jul. 20, 1959 / Original Jazz Classics ◆◆◆◆
In the 1950s, pianist Billy Taylor was best known for his work with his trios. For this Riverside set (reissued on CD in the *OJC* series) Taylor tried something different, writing arrangements for four flutists (including Frank Wess, Herbie Mann and Jerome Richardson), his rhythm section and the congas of Chino Pozo. The flutists get their opportunities to solo and the music (which includes "The Song Is Ended," "St. Thomas," "Oh Lady Be Good," "How About You" and four of Taylor's originals) is essentially bop but the unusual instrumentation gives the set its own personality. Enjoyable music that certainly stands out from the crowd. —*Scott Yanow*

I Wish I Knew How It Would Feel to Be Free / 1967 / Tower ◆◆◆◆
The title cut of this LP, a Billy Taylor composition, was a big seller for Solomon Burke during the era; Taylor's rendition is the first instrumental version. Teamed with bassist Ben Tucker and drummer Grady Tate, the pianist also performs Clare Fischer's two biggest hits ("Pensativa" and "Morning"), the pop tune "Sunny" and a few lesser-known numbers from the period. This out-of-print record gives one a good all-round showcase of Billy Taylor's playing. —*Scott Yanow*

Sleeping Bee / Apr. 1969 / Pausa ◆◆◆◆
Billy Taylor and his 1969 trio (which includes bassist Ben Tucker and drummer Grady Tate) perform four of Taylor's originals, Errol Garner's "La Petite Mambo," Oscar Brown, Jr.'s "Brother Where Are You" and two standards on this MPS set, which was last available as a Pausa LP. The enjoyable music swings and fits perfectly into the jazz mainstream of the era. —*Scott Yanow*

OK Billy / 1970 / Bell ◆◆◆◆
This album is a real obscurity. Pianist Billy Taylor was the leader of the 11-piece band that played nightly on *The David Frost Show*. For their one recording (which is long out of print), the orchestra performs the show's theme ("By George") and

mostly sticks to originals either by Taylor or band members. The most notable players in the ensemble are trumpeter Jimmy Owens, Frank Wess (on alto and flute), electric bassist Bob Cranshaw and drummer Bobby Thomas, in addition to the leader. A historical curiosity that is worth picking up. —*Scott Yanow*

Jazz Alive / Jun. 21, 1977 / Monmouth Evergreen ◆◆◆
Although the first side of this out-of-print LP has a three-song Billy Taylor original titled "Suite for Jazz Piano and Orchestra," it is actually performed by Taylor's trio (with bassist Victor Gaskin and drummer Freddie Watts) without an orchestra. The second half of the live performance (originally broadcast on the *Jazz Alive* radio series) consists of a six-song "Echoes of Ellington" that revisits several of Duke's more familiar compositions including "In a Mellotone," "Caravan" and "Satin Doll." Taylor plays well throughout the 48-minute LP, but little all that memorable or unusual occurs, making this a slightly above-average effort. —*Scott Yanow*

☆ **Live at Storyville** / Dec. 2, 1977-Dec. 3, 1977 / West 54 ◆◆◆◆◆
Recorded in New York City with drummer Grady Tate and bassist Victor Gaskin, this album includes classic standards and three Taylor originals including "I Wish I Knew . . ." It ranges from modern to bop to ballads. This is standard virtuosity from Taylor—you expect nothing less. —*Michael G. Nastos*

Where've You Been / Dec. 1980 / Concord Jazz ◆◆◆◆
This Concord release is most notable for featuring the obscure but talented violinist Joe Kennedy, who spent the bulk of his career teaching music in the Richmond, VA area. Teamed with pianist Billy Taylor, bassist Victor Gaskin and drummer Keith Copeland, Kennedy is the lead voice on many of the eight straightahead Taylor originals, and he plays at the peak of his powers; it is a real pity that he did not record more during his career. —*Scott Yanow*

You Tempt Me / Jun. 24, 1985 / Taylor Made ◆◆◆◆◆
In 1989 pianist Billy Taylor, who was between record contracts, started his own "Taylor-Made" label to document his own music. On this excellent set with his trio (which also includes bassist Victor Gaskin and drummer Curtis Boyd), Taylor starts off with a slower-than-usual rendition of "Take the 'A' Train," performs two originals and then concludes the program with five selections from his jazz suite "Let Us Make a Joyful Noise." Several of the latter pieces could stand on their own if played separately, for they are excellent vehicles for chordal improvisation. The CD overall finds Billy Taylor in top form. —*Scott Yanow*

White Nights and Jazz in Leningrad / Jun. 13, 1988-Jun. 14, 1988 / Taylor Made ◆◆◆◆◆
For this well-rounded set, the debut release from his Taylor-Made label, pianist Billy Taylor and his trio (with bassist Victor Gaskin and drummer Bobby Thomas) are featured performing live from Leningrad in the Soviet Union. The music is typically straightahead and surprisingly only one of the nine numbers ("C-A-G") is a Taylor original. Highlights include a pair of Clare Fischer's better-known songs ("Pensativa" and "Morning"), "Secret Love," Wes Montgomery's "Jingles" and a touching version of "A Child Is Born." One of the better Billy Taylor CDs currently available. —*Scott Yanow*

Solo / Aug. 1, 1988-Aug. 2, 1988 / Taylor Made ◆◆◆◆◆
Other than a pair of obscure albums from 1956, this was Billy Taylor's first solo piano recording. Released by his Taylor-Made label, the music on this CD is consistently colorful. On the opener "All the Things You Are," Taylor plays the first three choruses quite successfully with just his left hand. Other highlights of this straightahead set include the pianist's "A Bit of Bedlam" (one of seven originals among the 13 songs), "More than You Know," "For Undine" and "Billy's Beat." Well worth checking out. —*Scott Yanow*

Dr. T / 1993 / GRP ◆◆◆◆
For Billy Taylor's GRP release, his longtime trio with bassist Victor Gaskin and drummer Bobby Thomas is joined by baritonist Gerry Mulligan on three of the ten numbers (including "Line for Lyons"). The first five selections are jazz standards (best are "I'll Remember April," "Line for Lyons" and "Cubano Chant") while the last five include two Taylor originals, the ballad "Who Can I Turn To," Oscar Peterson's obscure "Laurentide Waltz" and Mulligan's "Rico Apollo," which is surprisingly performed without the composer. Excellent music. —*Scott Yanow*

It's a Matter of Pride / 1993 / GRP ◆◆◆◆◆
This is a particularly well-constructed session by pianist Billy Taylor, who is featured in a combo with bassist Christian McBride, drummer Marvin "Smitty" Smith, the congas of Ray Mantilla and, on three songs, tenor saxophonist Stanley Turrentine; Grady Tate also contributes two warm ballad vocals. All nine songs were composed by Taylor (including three pieces taken from a more extended work in tribute to Martin Luther King), and the results are melodic, boppish and swinging. —*Scott Yanow*

Homage / Oct. 10, 1994-Oct. 11, 1994 / GRP ◆◆◆◆
Billy Taylor's GRP release comprises two of the pianist's suites (which are actually a series of songs) along with a pair of shorter pieces. "Homage" pays tribute to

some of Taylor's earlier heroes including violinists Eddie South and Stuff Smith, bassists Slam Stewart and Oscar Pettiford, drummers Sid Catlett and Jo Jones, and pianist Art Tatum. None of those musicians are actually imitated, but the three-part work does feature excellent interplay between Taylor's trio (with bassist Chip Jackson and drummer Steve Johns) and The Turtle Island String Quartet. One misses the strings a bit during the ten-part "Step into My Dream," an episodic work that portrays a walk through Harlem and is designed to be performed in conjunction with the David Parsons Dance Company. Most of the music is straightahead in a boppish vein, although there is a stride piece, a calypso, a free-form section and even a rap that, although typically obnoxious, is more listenable than usual. Taylor plays quite well throughout the program, concluding the set with a jazz waltz and an encore ("One for Fun") with Turtle Island. Although not essential, there are enough bright moments on the stimulating set to make this a recommended release. —*Scott Yanow*

Music Keeps Us Young / Aug. 6, 1996-Aug. 8, 1996 / Arkadia ◆◆◆◆
It is extremely difficult to believe that Billy Taylor was 76 at the time of this frequently lively recording. For the trio set with bassist Chip Jackson and drummer Steve Johnson, Taylor performs five originals and six jazz standards with creativity and swing. The repertoire (which has among its highlights "Wouldn't It Be Loverly," a ten-and-a-half-minute exploration of "Body and Soul," "Naima," Freddie Hubbard's "Up Jumped Spring," and the pianist's most famous composition, "I Wish I Knew How It Would Feel to Be Free") is generally boppish, spontaneous and quite accessible, mixing together medium-tempo romps with ballads. Although always a bit underrated as a pianist, the seemingly ageless Taylor had by 1996 been recording for over 52 years! —*Scott Yanow*

Cecil Taylor

b. Mar. 15, 1929, New York, NY
Piano, Leader / Avant-Garde, Free Jazz
Soon after he first emerged in the mid-'50s, pianist Cecil Taylor was the most advanced improviser in jazz; four decades later he is still the most radical. Although in his early days he used some standards as vehicles for improvisation, since the early '60s Taylor has stuck exclusively to originals. To simplify describing his style, one could say that Taylor's intense atonal percussive approach involves playing the piano as if it were a set of drums. He generally emphasizes dense clusters of sound played with remarkable technique and endurance, often during marathon performances. Suffice it to say that Cecil Taylor's music is not for everyone.

Taylor started piano lessons from the age of six and attended the New York College of Music and the New England Conservatory. Taylor's early influences included Duke Ellington and Dave Brubeck, but from the start he sounded original. Early gigs included work with groups led by Johnny Hodges and Hot Lips Page but, after forming his quartet in the mid-'50s (which originally included Steve Lacy on soprano, bassist Buell Neidlinger and drummer Dennis Charles), Taylor was never a sideman again. The group played at the Five Spot Cafe in 1956 for six weeks and performed at the 1957 Newport Jazz Festival (which was recorded by Verve) but, despite occasional records, work was scarce. In 1960 Taylor recorded extensively for Candid under Neidlinger's name (by then the quartet featured Archie Shepp on tenor) and the following year he sometimes substituted in the play *The Connection*. By 1962 Taylor's quartet featured his longtime associate Jimmy Lyons on alto and drummer Sunny Murray. He spent six months in Europe (Albert Ayler worked with Taylor's group for a time although no recordings resulted) but upon his return to the US, Taylor did not work again for almost a year. Even with the rise of free jazz, his music was considered too advanced. In 1964 Taylor was one of the founders of the Jazz Composer's Guild and in 1968 he was featured on a record by the Jazz Composer's Orchestra. In the mid-'60s Taylor recorded two very advanced sets for Blue Note, but it was generally a lean decade.

Things greatly improved starting in the 1970s. Taylor taught for a time at the University of Wisconsin in Madison, at Antioch College and Glassboro State College. He recorded more frequently with his Unit and European tours became common. After being awarded a Guggenheim Fellowship in 1973, the pianist's financial difficulties were eased a bit; he even performed at the White House (during Jimmy Carter's administration) in 1979. A piano duet concert with Mary Lou Williams was a fiasco, but a collaboration with drummer Max Roach was quite successful. Taylor started incorporating some of his eccentric poetry into his performances and, unlike most musicians, he has not mellowed with age! The death of Jimmy Lyons in 1986 was a major blow, but Cecil Taylor has remained quite active up until the present day, never compromising his musical vision. His forbidding music is still decades ahead of its time. —*Scott Yanow*

In Transition / Dec. 10, 1955+Apr. 15, 1959 / Blue Note ◆◆◆◆
This double-LP from 1975 reissues all of the music from the two early Cecil Taylor records *Jazz Advance* and *Love for Sale;* the latter has not yet appeared on CD. When this set was more readily available, it served as the perfect introduction to

Taylor's forbidding music for, in addition to his originals, there are four songs by Cole Porter and one apiece from Thelonious Monk ("Bemsha Swing"), Duke Ellington ("Azure") and Gus Arnheim ("Sweet and Lovely"), allowing one to hear traces of the pianist's roots. While the first half of the two-fer matches Taylor with bassist Buell Neidlinger, drummer Dennis Charles and (on two of the seven songs) soprano saxophonist Steve Lacy, the later date (which includes the previously unissued "Carol/Three Points") finds Taylor leading a group comprisingcomprising Neidlinger (the liners inaccurately state Chris White), drummer Rudy Collins and (on three of the six pieces) trumpeter Ted Curson and tenor saxophonist Bill Barron. These sessions were the genesis of Cecil Taylor's unique music. —*Scott Yanow*

Jazz Advance / Dec. 10, 1955 / Blue Note ◆◆◆◆◆
This CD reissues Cecil Taylor's very first recording session. Although the album states that it is from Sept. 1956, all previous discographies state Dec. 10, 1955. Even at this early stage, the 26-year-old pianist was extremely advanced in his playing. One can hear Taylor's roots in Duke Ellington and Thelonious Monk, but his comping and chord voicings were already far ahead of most of his contemporaries. He takes "You'd Be So Nice to Come Home To" solo, has four trio numbers with bassist Buell Neidlinger and drummer Dennis Charles and, on C.T.'s "Charge 'Em Blues" and "Song," soprano saxophonist Steve Lacy makes the group a quartet. This is utterly fascinating music that hints strongly at what was to come. —*Scott Yanow*

Looking Ahead / Jun. 9, 1958 / Original Jazz Classics ◆◆◆◆
Due to the occasionally quiet ensembles, this CD reissue is one of the more accessible Cecil Taylor records despite the use of atonality in much of the music. Taylor, vibraphonist Earl Griffith, bassist Buell Neidlinger and drummer Dennis Charles explore six of Taylor's originals including "Wallering" (written in tribute to but not in the style of Fats Waller) and the explosive "Excursion on a Wobbly Rail." —*Scott Yanow*

Coltrane Time / Oct. 13, 1958 / United Artists ◆◆◆
This is a matchup that should have worked but was only a limited success. For the only joint recording ever of pianist Cecil Taylor and tenor saxophonist John Coltrane, trumpeter Ted Curson was scheduled to join the quintet but was unavailable; his replacement, Kenny Dorham, was much less sympathetic to Taylor's dissonant comping and constantly voiced disapproval. The tension can be felt on the four performances (two standards and a pair of blues), particularly when Dorham is playing. This unintentionally fascinating encounter has often been reissued under Coltrane's name (including as a Blue Note CD), but it was originally Taylor's date. —*Scott Yanow*

Love for Sale / Apr. 15, 1959 / United Artists ◆◆◆◆
The avant-garde pianist Cecil Taylor recorded relatively little during his formative years (1955-59), just five sessions, counting an appearance at the 1957 Newport Jazz Festival. On this out-of-print set (last available in the mid-'70s as part of a Blue Note two-LP set), Taylor plays three rather adventurous interpretations of Cole Porter songs ("Get Out of Town," "I Love Paris" and "Love for Sale") with a trio that includes bassist Buell Neidlinger and drummer Rudy Collins, and two originals that also include trumpeter Ted Curson and tenor saxophonist Bill Barron. The music is generally atonal but more accessible than Taylor's intense explorations of a few years later. —*Scott Yanow*

☆ **Complete Candid Recordings of Cecil Taylor** / Oct. 12, 1960-Jan. 10, 1961 / Mosaic ◆◆◆◆◆
This limited-edition set, originally available as either a four-CD or a six-LP set, includes all of pianist Cecil Taylor's recordings (including those originally under the leadership of bassist Buell Neidlinger) for the short-lived Candid label. There are four sessions in all, mostly featuring the quartet of Taylor, Neidlinger, tenor saxophonist Archie Shepp (making his recording debut) and drummer Dennis Charles; Sunny Murray replaces Charles on two cuts. Twelve of these twenty performances (which include many alternate takes) were previously unissued, six are trios without Shepp and there are a pair of Shepp-Neidlinger duets. The music is quite advanced for the period and, although the emotional tenor's sound was not mature yet, he generally works well with the very adventurous pianist. However, the music performed on Jan. 10, 1961, is the most memorable because the quartet (with Billy Higgins in Charles' place) is joined by soprano saxophonist Steve Lacy, baritonist Charles Davis, trombonist Roswell Rudd and trumpeter Clark Terry; the latter had never heard Taylor before and was apparently quite amazed. This unique group performs two versions apiece of "Things Ain't What They Used to Be" and "Jumpin' Punkins" and it is particularly interesting to hear Taylor playing behind the other soloists. The date is rounded out by a pair of trio numbers featuring Taylor, Neidlinger and Higgins. Some of the music has since been reissued on CD but not all of the alternate takes. For adventurous listeners, this box is essential. —*Scott Yanow*

Jumpin' Punkins / Jan. 9, 1961-Jan. 10, 1961 / Candid ✦✦✦✦
This single CD has some of the music formerly released on a limited-edition Cecil Taylor Mosaic box set. The two most intriguing performances are versions of Mercer Ellington's "Jumpin' Punkins" and "Things Ain't What They Used to Be," which feature the avant-garde pianist with trumpeter Clark Terry, trombonist Roswell Rudd, soprano saxophonist Steve Lacy, baritonist Charles Davis, tenor Archie Shepp, bassist Buell Neidlinger and drummer Billy Higgins. Taylor's jarring comping behind the other soloists is quite interesting and somehow works. "O.P." and "I Forgot" feature Taylor with Neidlinger, drummer Dennis Charles and (on the latter song) the young Archie Shepp. A good sampler of Cecil Taylor's marathon Candid sessions. —*Scott Yanow*

New York City R&B / Jan. 9, 1961-Jan. 10, 1961 / Candid ✦✦✦✦
The contents of this rather brief CD, originally released under bassist Buell Neidlinger's name, have since been reissued in the Cecil Taylor/Buell Neidlinger Mosaic box set. Two selections feature a trio with pianist Taylor, bassist Neidlinger and drummer Billy Higgins, and one performance adds the young tenor Archie Shepp (and has Dennis Charles in Higgins' place). This music is quite advanced for the period although more accessible to the average listener than Taylor's later recordings; at least one can hear (even in abstract form) his connection to the bebop tradition and to Duke Ellington. Speaking of the latter, the most intriguing selection is a version of "Things Ain't What They Used to Be" that not only has Taylor, Neidlinger, Higgins and Shepp, but Steve Lacy on soprano, baritonist Charles Davis, trombonist Roswell Rudd and trumpeter Clark Terry, making for a very interesting mixture of styles. —*Scott Yanow*

Nefertiti, the Beautiful One Has Come / Nov. 23, 1962 / Freedom ✦✦✦✦✦
This double-LP is the only recording that exists of Cecil Taylor and his group (other than two songs on the bootleg Ingo label) during 1962-65. Taylor's new altoist Jimmy Lyons (who occasionally hints at Charlie Parker) and the first truly "free" drummer Sonny Murray join the avant-garde pianist in some stunning trio performances recorded live at the Cafe Montmartre in Copenhagen. With the exception of an interesting version of "What's New" (which finds Lyons showing off his roots), the music comprises Taylor originals and is atonal and full of power. Surprisingly this stirring (and rather historical) music has not yet been reissued on CD. —*Scott Yanow*

★ **Unit Structures** / May 19, 1966 / Blue Note ✦✦✦✦✦
After several years off records, pianist Cecil Taylor finally had an opportunity to document his music of the mid-'60s on two Blue Note albums (the other one was *Conquistador*). Taylor's high-energy atonalism fit in well with the free jazz of the period, but he was actually leading the way rather than being part of a movement. In fact this septet outing with trumpeter Eddie Gale, altoist Jimmy Lyons, Ken McIntyre (alternating between alto, oboe and bass clarinet), both Henry Grimes and Alan Silva on basses, and drummer Andrew Cyrille is quite stunning and very intense. In fact it could be safely argued that no jazz music of the era approached the ferocity and intensity of Cecil Taylor's. —*Scott Yanow*

Conquistador / Oct. 6, 1966 / Blue Note ✦✦✦✦✦
For the second of Cecil Taylor's two Blue Note albums (following *Unit Structures*), the innovative pianist utilized a sextet comprising trumpeter Bill Dixon, altoist Jimmy Lyons, both Henry Grimes and Alan Silva on basses and drummer Andrew Cyrille. During the two lengthy pieces, Lyons' passionate solos contrast with Dixon's quieter ruminations while the music in general is unremittingly intense. Both of the Taylor Blue Notes are quite historic and near-classics but, despite this important documentation, Cecil Taylor (other than a pair of Paris concerts) would not appear on records again until 1973. —*Scott Yanow*

Student Studies / Nov. 30, 1966 / Affinity ✦✦✦✦✦
The music on this two-record set was recorded in concert in Paris. As usual, the whole was much larger than the parts and I found there was enough inspired listening here to easily recommend the music. *Student Studies* tells some good tales and is full of the Taylor dynamics; at the same time it is quite accessible. —*Bob Rusch*

Great Paris Concert / Jul. 29, 1969 / Prestige ✦✦✦✦
This three-LP set is a real blowout. Pianist Cecil Taylor, altoist Jimmy Lyons, Sam Rivers on tenor and soprano, and drummer Andrew Cyrille (there is no bass but it couldn't have been heard anyway) perform a 90-minute work followed by a 20-minute encore. The music is unrelentingly intense and Taylor does not let up for a moment. His fans are advised to pick up this major release, but those listeners new to Taylor's music should investigate his solo piano works first. —*Scott Yanow*

☆ **Great Concert of Cecil Taylor** / Jul. 29, 1969 / Prestige ✦✦✦✦✦
Boxed set with Taylor in searing live concert alongside Sam Rivers (sax) and Jimmy Lyons (as). Three discs of amazing playing. —*Ron Wynn*

Indent / Mar. 11, 1973 / Freedom ✦✦✦✦✦
After nearly 20 years of critical neglect and hostility, pianist Cecil Taylor finally began to gain some approval in 1973. This solo concert, originally put out by Taylor on his own short-lived Unit Core label, gained wider recognition when Arista Freedom released it in 1977. On three lengthy improvisations, Taylor is quite stunning in his control of the piano, his wide range of percussive sound and his endurance. As is often true of Cecil Taylor's music, this recital is not for the faint of heart, but those with open ears will find it rewarding and certainly stimulating. —*Scott Yanow*

★ **Silent Tongues** / Jul. 2, 1974 / Freedom ✦✦✦✦✦
This is a classic Cecil Taylor solo concert, performed at the 1974 Montreux Jazz Festival. Taylor plays his five-movement work "Silent Tongues" along with a couple of brief encores. To simplify in explaining what he was doing at this point of time, it can be said that Taylor essentially plays the piano like a drum set, creating percussive and thunderous sounds that are other worldly and full of an impressive amount of energy and atonal ideas. Many listeners will find these performances to be quite difficult, but it is worth the struggle to open up one's perceptions as to what music can be. —*Scott Yanow*

Dark Unto Themselves / Jun. 18, 1976 / Enja ✦✦✦✦✦
This CD reissue has a continuous 61-minute performance by pianist Cecil Taylor and his 1976 quintet (which also includes such fiery players as trumpeter Raphe Malik, his longtime altoist Jimmy Lyons, tenor saxophonist David Ware and drummer Marc Edwards). There is a quick theme along with brief transitions that form the composition "Streams and Chorus of Seed," but the bulk of the passionate performance is taken up by spontaneous and intense solos. Listeners with very open ears and longtime fans of Cecil Taylor can consider this explosive performance to be essential. —*Scott Yanow*

Air Above Mountains (Buildings Within) / Aug. 20, 1976 / Enja ✦✦✦✦
This Cecil Taylor solo concert features the radical pianist at a performance in Austria playing continuously for 51 minutes. Except for some brief moments, his music is quite intense, percussive, crowded and overflowing with passion. Taylor's longtime fans will find much to marvel at while newcomers to his music are advised instead to check out his earlier (and less dissonant) sessions from the 1950s first. —*Scott Yanow*

★ **The Cecil Taylor Unit** / Apr. 3, 1978-Apr. 6, 1978 / New World ✦✦✦✦✦
A sextet, this is as close to as definitive an ensemble as Taylor has launched. With Jimmy Lyons (sax), Raphe Malik (tpt), Ramsey Ameen (violin), Sirone (b), and R. Shannon Jackson (d). This runs 60 minutes on vinyl, including a 30-minute "Holiday en Masque." —*Michael G. Nastos*

Three Phasis / Apr. 1978 / New World ✦✦✦✦
The follow-up to *Unit*, this is one long piece of improv over two sides (57:12) with the same sextet. —*Michael G. Nastos*

One Too Many Salty Swifty and Not Goodbye / Jun. 4, 1978 / Hat Hut ✦✦✦✦✦
With one of his greatest groups in a powerful performance, this was the Unit at its peak. —*Michael G. Nastos*

It Is in the Brewing Luminous / Feb. 8, 1980-Feb. 9, 1980 / Hat Art ✦✦✦✦✦
Originally released as a double LP and then reissued as a single CD, this continuous 71-minute live performance from 1980 features pianist Cecil Taylor with a particularly intriguing sextet comprising his longtime altoist Jimmy Lyons, violinist Ramsey Ameen on bass and cello and both Jerome Cooper and Sunny Murray on drums. Not too surprisingly, the playing is quite intense and dense with only a few moments of lyricism popping through. Taylor sounds very much like a human dynamo while Lyons' solos are full of fragile beauty. This is brilliant music that will not sound "safe" or "easy listening" even a century from now. —*Scott Yanow*

Fly! Fly! Fly! Fly! Fly! / Sep. 14, 1980 / MPS ✦✦✦✦
This solo album by Cecil Taylor is a little unusual in that he performs eight originals, some of which are quite concise; "T (Beautiful Young'n)" is only 53 seconds long. That is not to imply that the pianist's music had suddenly mellowed with age, but his lyricism is emphasized a bit more than usual and he sometimes sounds quite relaxed (without compromising his music). Worth searching for. —*Scott Yanow*

Garden Pt. 1 / Nov. 1981 / Hat Art ✦✦✦✦✦

Garden Pt. 2 / Nov. 1981 / Hat Art ✦✦✦✦✦

Winged Serpent (Sliding Quadrants) / Oct. 22, 1984-Oct. 24, 1984 / Soul Note ✦✦✦✦✦
Utilizing what was called an "Orchestra of Two Continents," pianist Cecil Taylor has a larger orchestra than usual for this Soul Note release. The 11-piece group is filled with brilliant and adventurous players: trumpeters Enrico Rava and Tomasz Stanko, altoist Jimmy Lyons, tenors Frank Wright and John Tchicai, baritonist

Gunter Hampel, bassoonist Karen Borca, bassist William Parker and both Rashied Bakr and Andre Martinez on drums. On the four Taylor originals, the colorful ensembles are quite dense, although there is room for individual solos and heroics. Not too surprisingly Cecil Taylor is very much in control of the music. Incidentally this was probably Jimmy Lyons' last record with Taylor; he passed away in 1986. —*Scott Yanow*

For Olim / Apr. 9, 1986 / Soul Note ✦✦✦✦✦
One of Cecil Taylor's most satisfying solo concerts, this date features the always uncompromising and adventurous pianist exploring eight of his compositions, including a few that are quite brief (two are under two minutes). The difficult but lyrical live set rewards repeated listenings. —*Scott Yanow*

Olu Iwa / Apr. 1986 / Soul Note ✦✦✦✦✦
This session presented Taylor working alternately with a large group and intimate unit, recording two pieces on April 12. The opening 48-minute dialogue included the high-register wailing of tenor saxophonists Peter Brotzmann and Frank Wright and Taylor's undulating answering lines and sprawling solos. The second piece was a bit shorter (27 minutes), but no less ambitious, with shifting moods, themes and tempos. As usual, Taylor's music wasn't for the squeamish or those who desire nicely ordered, predictable material. It required intense concentration and attention from both performers and audience. —*Ron Wynn*

Alms/Tiergarten [Spree] / 1989 / FMP ✦✦✦
Two CDs from a large set with extensive booklet describing the pieces in detail with analyses, the workshop sessions that led to the final concert, with pictures galore. This set is interesting primarily to hear European musicians interpret Taylor's kinesthetic directing . . . mostly an intense density of "free playing" (actually following specific internalized instructions and images) with almost everyone going on different gestures at once, with slow unison melodies emerging from the environment. The most interesting series is "Weight—Breath—Sounding Trees." —*Blue Gene Tyranny*

Martin Taylor

b. 1956, Scotland
Guitar / Swing, Cool, Bop
Since the death of Joe Pass in 1994, Martin Taylor has become one of the most highly regarded guitarists in jazz. He was given his first guitar by his father, Buck Taylor. Although he was inspired at first by Django Reinhardt, it was piano players like Art Tatum that drew his attention and helped him practice to develop his phenomenal solo technique. In the late 1970s, Stephane Grappelli invited him to play in a series of concerts in France. The violinist was so impressed that he used Taylor often on tours and a variety of recording dates. Beginning in 1990, Taylor began recording a number of acclaimed CDs for the UK label Linn, distributed as Honest/Linn in the US, and also did an excellent duet date with David Grisman for the mandolin player's Acoustic Disc label. All that is missing from Taylor's current roster of recordings is a live date, though an excellent concert video is available. —*Ken Dryden*

● **Skye Boat** / Jul. 1981 / Concord Jazz ✦✦✦✦✦

Sarabanda / Jun. 23, 1987-Jun. 26, 1987 / Gaia ✦✦✦✦✦

Don't Fret / Sep. 1990 / Linn ✦✦✦

Change of Heart / Jun. 1991 / Linn ✦✦✦

Spirit of Django / Jun. 27, 1994-Aug. 1994 / Linn ✦✦✦✦

Portraits / Jul. 26, 1995-Dec. 12, 1995 / Linn ✦✦✦✦
Taylor's fifth release for Linn combines solo recordings along with a few duets with Nashville legend Chet Atkins and a pair of overdubbed duets. Taylor's fluid, unaccompanied playing makes him the most obvious heir to the legacy of Joe Pass. All of Martin Taylor's recordings for the Scottish label Linn are strongly recommended. —*Ken Dryden*

Sam "The Man" Taylor (Samuel L. Taylor)

b. Jul. 12, 1916, Lexington, TN
Tenor Saxophone / Blues Jazz, Groove, Jump Blues, R&B, Soul Jazz
A certified honking sax legend, Sam "The Man" Taylor's non-stop drive and power worked perfectly in swing, blues and R&B sessions. He had a huge tone, perfect timing and sense of drama, as well as relentless energy and spirit. Taylor began working with Scatman Crothers and the Sunset Royal Orchestra in the late '30s. He played with Cootie Williams and Lucky Millinder in the early '40s, then worked six years with Cab Calloway. Taylor toured South America and the Caribbean during his tenure with Calloway. Then Taylor became the saxophonist of choice for many R&B dates through the '50s, recording with Ray Charles, Buddy Johnson, Louis Jordan, and Big Joe Turner among others. He also did sessions with Ella Fitzgerald and Sy Oliver. During the '60s, Taylor led his own bands and

recorded in a quintet called The Blues Chasers. He currently has one session available on CD recorded in the late '50s with Charlie Shavers and Urbie Green. —*Ron Wynn*

Music with the Big Beat / 1955 / MGM ✦✦✦

Blue Mist / 1957 / MGM ✦✦✦✦

More Blue Mist / 1957-1958 / MGM ✦✦✦✦

Jazz for Commuters / Oct. 15, 1958+Oct. 22, 1958 / Metrojazz ✦✦✦

● **The Bad and the Beautiful** / Feb. 20, 1962 / Prestige ✦✦✦✦

It's a Blue World / 1962-1963 / Decca ✦✦✦

Misty Mood / 1962-1963 / Decca ✦✦✦

John Tchicai (John Martin Tchicai)

b. Apr. 28, 1936, Copenhagen, Denmark
Tenor Saxophone, Alto Saxophone / Avant-Garde, Free Jazz
John Tchicai will probably always be remembered for his alto playing on John Coltrane's monumental *Ascension* recording, but he's actually spent most of his life in Europe playing tenor sax. His style during the free period had a dry tone and featured a staccato attack; his later material has had a fuller, more soulful and earthy sound. Tchicai began playing violin at age ten, then clarinet and alto sax at 16. He studied saxophone three years at the Royal Conservatory in Copenhagen. Tchicai met Archie Shepp at a festival in Helsinki in 1962. That same year he made his recording debut in Warsaw leading a quintet. Tchicai moved to New York in 1963. He played with Shepp and Don Cherry in The New York Contemporary Five, and with Roswell Rudd and Milford Graves in The New York Art Quartet in 1964 and 1965. Both bands toured Europe and recorded. Tchicai also recorded with the Jazz Composers Guild and with Shepp, John Coltrane and Albert Ayler. He returned to Denmark in 1966, and led the workshop ensemble Cadentia nova danica from 1967 to 1971, performing with them in London in 1968. Tchicai cut back on his playing and began teaching full-time in 1972, then resumed active playing in 1977. He joined Pierre Dorge's New Jungle Orchestra in 1982 on tenor and has also played in recent times with Six Winds (a saxophone sextet with Cecil Taylor) and with various San Francisco-based ensembles. He settled in Northern California and in 1994 appeared at the Monterey Jazz Festival, still playing in an advanced but relatively thoughtful style. —*Ron Wynn and Scott Yanow*

John Tchicai Solo Plus Albert Mangelsdorff / Feb. 16, 1977 / FMP ✦✦✦✦

● **Real Tchicai** / Mar. 23, 1977 / Steeple Chase ✦✦✦✦✦

Darktown Highlights / Mar. 29, 1977 / Storyville ✦✦✦

John Tchicai and the Strange Brothers / Oct. 9, 1977 / FMP ✦✦✦✦

Ball at Louisiana Museum of Modern Art / Nov. 11, 1981 / Steeple Chase ✦✦✦

Timo's Message / Feb. 7, 1984 / Black Saint ✦✦✦✦✦

Put Up the Fight / Nov. 1987 / Storyville ✦✦✦✦

Grandpa's Spells / Mar. 28, 1992-Mar. 29, 1992 / Storyville ✦✦✦
Tenor saxophonist John Tchicai (doubling on bass clarinet), pianist Misha Mengelberg, bassist Peter Danstrup and drummer Gilbert Matthews are featured on this very diverse avant-garde set. The music ranges from nearly free explorations and interaction with prerecorded tapes to mellower pieces and even abstract renditions of two Jelly Roll Morton tunes (of which "Cannonball Blues" is the better one). Mengelberg has long been versatile, and Tchicai has his own sound, incorporating elements of Ornette Coleman and John Coltrane, so this is a rather intriguing, if not quite essential, CD. —*Scott Yanow*

Love Is Touching / 1995 / B&W ✦✦

Jack Teagarden (Weldon Leo Teagarden)

b. Aug. 29, 1905, Vernon, TX, d. Jan. 15, 1964, New Orleans, LA
Trombone, Vocals, Leader / Dixieland, Swing
One of the classic giants of jazz, Jack Teagarden was not only the top pre-bop trombonist (playing his instrument with the ease of a trumpeter) but one of the best jazz singers, too. He was such a fine musician that younger brother Charlie (an excellent trumpeter) was always overshadowed. Jack started on piano at age five (his mother Helen was a ragtime pianist), switched to baritone horn and finally took up trombone when he was ten. Teagarden worked in the Southwest in a variety of territory bands (most notably with the legendary pianist Peck Kelley) and then caused a sensation when he came to New York in 1928. His daring solos with Ben Pollack caused Glenn Miller to de-emphasize his own playing with the band and during the late-'20s/early Depression era "Mr. T." recorded frequently with many groups including units headed by Roger Wolfe Kahn, Eddie Condon, Red Nichols and Louis Armstrong ("Knockin' a Jug"); his versions of "Basin Street Blues" and "Beale Street Blues" (songs that would remain in his repertoire for the

remainder of his career) were definitive. Teagarden, who was greatly admired by Tommy Dorsey, would have been a logical candidate for fame in the swing era, but he made a strategic error. In late 1933, when it looked as if jazz would never catch on commercially, he signed a five-year contract with Paul Whiteman. Although Whiteman's Orchestra did feature Teagarden now and then (and he had a brief period in 1936 playing with a small group from the band, the Three T's, with his brother Charlie and Frankie Trumbauer), the contract effectively kept Teagarden from going out on his own and becoming a star. It certainly prevented him from leading what would eventually became the Bob Crosby Orchestra.

In 1939 Jack Teagarden was finally "free," and he soon put together a big band that would last until 1946. However, it was rather late to be organizing a new orchestra (the competition was fierce) and, although there were some good musical moments, none of the sidemen became famous, the arrangements lacked their own musical personality, and by the time the group broke up, Teagarden was facing bankruptcy. The trombonist, however, was still a big name (he had fared quite well in the 1940 Bing Crosby film *The Birth of the Blues*) and he had many friends. Crosby helped Teagarden straighten out his financial problems and from 1947-51 he was a star sideman with Louis Armstrong's All-Stars; their collaborations on "Rocking Chair" are classic. After leaving Armstrong, Teagarden was a leader of a steadily working sextet throughout the remainder of his career, playing Dixieland with such talented musicians as brother Charlie, trumpeters Jimmy McPartland, Don Goldie and Max Kaminsky and (during a 1957 European tour) pianist Earl Hines. Teagarden toured the Far East during 1958-59, teamed up one last time with Eddie Condon for a television show/recording session in 1961 and had a heartwarming (and fortunately recorded) musical reunion with Charlie, sister-pianist Norma and his mother at the 1963 Monterey Jazz Festival. He died from a heart attack four months later and has yet to be replaced. —*Scott Yanow*

★ **The Indispensable** / Mar. 14, 1928-Jul. 8, 1957 / RCA ✦✦✦✦✦
Much more complete than the Bluebird CD, this two-CD set has trombonist Jack Teagarden featured with Roger Wolfe Kahn's orchestra (two takes of "She's a Great, Great Girl"), Eddie Condon's Hot Shots, the Mound City Blue Blowers, eight numbers with Ben Pollack, his better recordings with Paul Whiteman's Orchestra and a complete session under his own leadership in 1947, in addition to three numbers with Bud Freeman in 1957. This set is highly recommended to those who can locate it. —*Scott Yanow*

● **That's a Serious Thing** / Mar. 14, 1928-Jul. 8, 1957 / Bluebird ✦✦✦✦✦
This readily available Bluebird CD gives one an excellent overview of the talents of trombonist/singer Jack Teagarden. "Mr. T." is featured with Eddie Condon on a pair of classic 1929 selections and also with Roger Wolfe Kahn's orchestra ("She's a Great Great Girl"), Ben Pollack, the Mound City Blue Blowers, Fats Waller, Benny Goodman, Paul Whiteman, the Three T's, the Metronome All-Stars, Louis Armstrong (the exciting "Jack-Armstrong Blues") and with Bud Freeman, in addition to a version of "St. Louis Blues" with Teagarden's group in 1947. Quite a few of these performances are famous and, although this is not a "complete" set, the consistent high quality of these recordings makes this CD highly recommended to all. —*Scott Yanow*

King of the Blues Trombone / Nov. 27, 1928-Jul. 23, 1940 / Epic ✦✦✦✦✦
This deluxe three-LP set (which will hopefully be reissued on CD eventually) features the great trombonist and vocalist Jack Teagarden in a variety of settings. These often-rare recordings showcase Teagarden as a sideman with Jimmy McHugh's Bostonians, Mills Merry Makers, the Whoopee Makers, Jack Pettis, Goody and His Good Timers, Joe Venuti, Ben Pollack, Benny Goodman, Frankie Trumbauer and Teagarden's own band; the supporting cast includes Goodman, Jimmy McPartland, Artie Shaw, Jimmy Dorsey, Bud Freeman, Fats Waller and many other classic jazz artists. If you are fortunate enough to run across this collection, don't let it out of your sight. —*Scott Yanow*

1930-1934 / Oct. 1, 1930-Mar. 2, 1934 / Classics ✦✦✦✦✦
This Classics CD has the first 23 titles ever issued under the leadership of trombonist Jack Teagarden. Many of these selections were formerly rare, particularly the earlier titles on Domino, Banner and Crown. Best is the session that co-starred pianist/vocalist Fats Waller and, while some of the titles are a bit commercial, Teagarden's playing (and that of his better sidemen) uplift the music; "A Hundred Years from Today" is a classic. —*Scott Yanow*

Jack & Charlie Teagarden & Franklin Trumbauer / Jan. 12, 1934-Jun. 15, 1936 / Teagarden ✦✦✦✦✦
Trombonist Jack Teagarden spent some of the prime years of the swing era tied to Paul Whiteman's Orchestra because in 1934 he signed a five-year contract. If he had not made that decision, Teagarden might very well have ended up as the leader of the Bob Crosby Orchestra. While with Whiteman, Teagarden was given the opportunity to record with a small group from the big band, one that was called "The Three T's" because of the participation of his brother Charlie Teagar-

den on trumpet and the great C-melody saxophonist Frankie Trumbauer. All of their recordings (most of which were issued under Trumbauer's name) are on this enjoyable CD, which also includes a few solos from clarinetist Artie Shaw and two Teagarden features with Whiteman. The music, essentially small-group swing, has plenty of solo space for the principals and there are many memorable selections. Highly recommended. —*Scott Yanow*

Featuring Jack Teagarden / Aug. 24, 1934-Dec. 8, 1938 / MCA ✦✦✦✦
This collector's LP from British MCA has some rarities from the swing era featuring the great trombonist Jack Teagarden as a sideman. Teagarden is heard on a couple of novelties sung by Johnny Mercer, in an all-star band headed by bass saxophonist Adrian Rollini (which includes clarinetist Benny Goodman), on four songs apiece accompanying singers Dick Robertson and the underrated Teddy Grace, and on six obscure recordings with Paul Whiteman's Orchestra and "Swing Wing" in 1938. Also heard on most of the latter tunes is the singing group the Modernaires. The Whiteman and Mercer performances in particular are rare, although the other 12 numbers (there are 20 on this generous LP) have been reissued on CD. —*Scott Yanow*

1934-1939 / Sep. 18, 1934-Jul. 19, 1939 / Classics ✦✦✦✦✦
The second of three Jack Teagarden Classics CDs contains all of his recordings as a leader during this pivotal period. There are three titles from 1934 with a pickup group also including clarinetist Benny Goodman and Frankie Trumbauer on C-melody sax. But the bulk of this CD is taken up by the first 21 studio performances by Jack Teagarden's ill-fated big band in 1939. The trombonist/leader is easily the most interesting soloist and his vocals are a joy while those of Linda Keene are okay. Teagarden's swing band did not have its own identity but its recordings are generally enjoyable. —*Scott Yanow*

On the Air / Jan. 12, 1936-Dec. 28, 1938 / Sandy Hook ✦✦✦
Trombonist Jack Teagarden spent most of the 1934-38 period buried in Paul Whiteman's Orchestra but Whiteman was wise enough to feature "Mr. T" from time to time. This Sandy Hook LP contains 16 rare performances, all radio airchecks from 1936 and 1938 that put the emphasis on Teagarden's trombone and vocals. Quite a few of the songs are then-current pop tunes but Teagarden's playing is of a consistent high quality and there are many enjoyable moments. —*Scott Yanow*

Jack Teagarden's Big Eight / Pee Wee Russell's Rhythmakers / Aug. 31, 1938-Dec. 15, 1940 / Riverside ✦✦✦✦✦
Two unrelated small-group sessions from the swing era that were originally recorded for the H.R.S. (Hot Record Society) label are reissued in full on this enjoyable CD. Trombonist Jack Teagarden takes a vacation from his big band to play with an all-star octet that also includes cornetist Rex Stewart, clarinetist Barney Bigard and tenor saxophonist Ben Webster. Teagarden sings "St. James Infirmary" and is quite fluent on "Shine." The other set has the unique clarinetist Pee Wee Russell and a different octet (which includes trumpeter Max Kaminsky, trombonist Dicky Wells, tenor saxophonist Al Gold and pianist James P. Johnson) romping on a blues and three Dixieland standards; in addition Russell, Johnson and drummer Zutty Singleton stretch out on "I Found a New Baby" and "Everybody Loves My Baby." Easily recommended to classic jazz fans. —*Scott Yanow*

Birth of a Band / Jan. 31, 1939-Nov. 1939 / Giants of Jazz ✦✦✦✦
This Giants of Jazz LP is a must for Jack Teagarden collectors due to its historic value. First Teagarden is heard on a radio broadcast with Benny Goodman's Orchestra in which it is announced that he has formed his own big band after five years with Paul Whiteman. Teagarden jams with BG on "Basin Street Blues," shares the vocal with Johnny Mercer on "Two Sleepy People" and plays a spirited "Roll 'Em" with the Goodman Orchestra and guest pianist Pete Johnson. The remainder of this album contains the earliest existing broadcast by Teagarden's big band. The trombonist's sidemen are enthusiastic and they swing hard on most of the selections. Although the band's potential was never realized, they sound full of spirit and power on this excellent set. —*Scott Yanow*

Sincerely Jack Teagarden / Apr. 14, 1939-Jun. 23, 1939 / IAJRC ✦✦✦✦
The collector's label IAJRC reissued 16 of the first 18 selections recorded by the Jack Teagarden Orchestra on this well-conceived LP. With such sidemen as first trumpeter Charlie Spivak, baritonist Ernie Caceres and rhythm guitarist Allan Reuss, the trombonist had a solid foundation for his big band. The orchestra in the long run never caught on (although it lasted seven years) and caused Teagarden many financial headaches, but that cannot be told from these enthusiastic early recordings. Teagarden has vocals on nine of the tracks, Linda Keene is heard from on three and Jean Arnold sings two, so the emphasis is on dance music rather than jazz, but these historic recordings have their memorable moments. —*Scott Yanow*

Rompin' and Stompin' / May 1939-Aug. 1944 / Swing Era ✦✦✦

The Jack Teagarden Orchestra never really caught on during the swing era and eventually the trombonist/leader went bankrupt. However, as these studio recordings show, the band was not without interest. Teagarden was easily the most interesting soloist in what was really a no-name outfit, but the 16 performances (the majority from 1942 and 1944) are full of swing, spirit and strong moments. Kitty Kallen has the vocal on "Swing Without Words" and the leader gets two chances to sing, but the emphasis on this LP is, as the title suggests, on "Rompin' and Stompin'." —*Scott Yanow*

1939-1940 / Aug. 23, 1939-Feb. 1940 / Classics ✦✦✦✦

The third in Classics' *Complete* Jack Teagarden series traces the trombonist's big-band recordings during his Columbia period. There were no great soloists among Teagarden's sidemen and some of these tunes (particularly the nine with Kitty Kallen vocals) are throwaways, but Teagarden's own singing on six songs (including "Beale Street Blues" and "If I Could Be with You") and distinctive trombone give listeners strong reasons to acquire this entry in the worthy series. Other highlights include "Peg of My Heart," "Wolverine Blues," "Swinging' on the Teagarden Gate" and "The Blues." —*Scott Yanow*

Varsity Drags / Feb. 19, 1940-Jul. 1940 / Savoy ✦✦✦

Savoy's reissue of Jack Teagarden's 16 recordings for Varsity with his big band is perfectly done but the music is streaky. When one eliminates the pop vocals of Kitty Kallen, Marianne Dunne and David Allyn, all that is left are five selections: four worthy vocals by the leader and just one instrumental ("The Blues"). Overall the music on this set is decent but generally more commercial than one would hope for a Jack Teagarden recording. —*Scott Yanow*

It's Time for Tea / Jan. 31, 1941-Jun. 1941 / Jass ✦✦✦✦

This is the first of two CDs put out by Jass that reissue all of the Standard Transcriptions recorded by Jack Teagarden's big band for radio airplay. These recordings are generally quite superior to his studio sides of the period. Although the trombonist did not have a great big band, his solos and those of trumpeter Pokey Carriere hold one's interest. A young David Allyn, Lynn Clark and Mr. T. himself have the vocals, but half of the selections are swinging instrumentals. —*Scott Yanow*

1941-1943 / Jan. 31, 1941-Nov. 16, 1943 / Classics ✦✦✦✦

The fifth Classics CD to reissue all of trombonist/vocalist Jack Teagarden's early recordings as a leader has more than its share of gems. A dozen selections feature his 1941 big band, and unlike earlier sessions, there are no indifferent vocals or unnecessary pop baggage. Teagarden is heard in prime form on "Chicks Is Wonderful" (which strangely enough is an instrumental), "A Hundred Years From Today" and "Nobody Knows the Trouble I've Seen." There are also two selections that Teagarden performed in the movie *Birth of the Blues* with Bing Crosby: the classic title cut (sung by Crosby) and "The Waiter and the Porter and the Upstairs Maid" which finds Teagarden, Bing and Mary Martin all interacting in cheerful form. The last seven numbers on this highly enjoyable CD feature Teagarden jamming with the Capitol International Jazzmen in 1943. Teagarden takes three vocals (including "Stars Fell on Alabama") and is well showcased on a previously unissued "Mighty Lak' a Rose." In addition, tenor saxophonist Dave Matthews takes his greatest solo on "In My Solitude"; Billy May takes his hottest trumpet solos throughout the date; pianist Joe Sullivan is a strong asset; and the clarinet spot is taken by either Jimmie Noone or Heinie Beau. "I'm Sorry I Made You Cry" and "'Deed I Do" are both quite hot. Recommended. —*Scott Yanow*

Has Anybody Here Seen Jackson? / Oct. 1941-Aug. 22, 1944 / Jass ✦✦✦✦

Jack Teagarden's Standard Transcriptions are reissued on this CD and the previous *It's Time for Tea*. Teagarden made few studio recordings with his ill-fated big band during this period and, even with the seven commercial vocals by David Allyn and Kitty Kallen, this music is superior to what was generally available to the public from the trombonist's orchestra at the time. Teagarden and his somewhat obscure sidemen are in consistently fine form on the varied material; pity that the big band never really caught on. —*Scott Yanow*

Big "T" & The Condon Gang / Dec. 2, 1944-Dec. 16, 1944 / Pumpkin ✦✦✦✦✦

Although trombonist Jack Teagarden is listed as the main star, in reality the music on this LP is taken from two of Eddie Condon's famous Town Hall concerts. Teagarden, taking a well-deserved vacation from his struggling big band, is consistently inspired by the presence of such all-stars as trumpeters Max Kaminsky, Bobby Hackett, Billy Butterfield and Wingy Manone, clarinetist Pee Wee Russell, baritonist Ernie Caceres and, on "Christmas at Carnegie," the great soprano Sidney Bechet. The music is freewheeling Chicago jazz with vocals from the trombonist, Lee Wiley and, on the lengthy "Big T & Wingy Blues," both Teagarden and Manone. Classic performances. —*Scott Yanow*

With His Sextet and Eddie Condon's Chicagoans / Jun. 1947-Oct. 30, 1961 / Pumpkin ✦✦✦✦

Trombonist Jack Teagarden is heard in two very different but equally rewarding settings on this worthy LP. He performs eight numbers with his short-lived sextet in 1947, shortly before he became a regular member of Louis Armstrong's All-Stars. Along with trumpeter Max Kaminsky and clarinetist Peanuts Hucko, Mr. T. is heard in top form on eight standards including several Hoagy Carmichael compositions. In addition, he participates in a reunion of Eddie Condon's Chicagoans in Oct. 1961 even though he was not an original member. Teagarden is heard along with cornetist Jimmy McPartland, clarinetist Pee Wee Russell, tenor saxophonist Bud Freeman, pianist Joe Sullivan, guitarist Eddie Condon, bassist Bob Haggart and drummer Gene Krupa on six selections taken from their appearance on *The Today Show*. The music is essentially spirited Dixieland with McPartland contributing some surprisingly advanced solos. —*Scott Yanow*

Club Hangover Broadcasts with Jackie Coon / Apr. 3, 1954-Apr. 24, 1954 / Arbors ✦✦✦✦

This double-CD from Arbors contains four half-hour broadcasts by the Jack Teagarden sextet during its stay at the Club Hangover in San Francisco. At the time the trombonist's band featured trumpeter Jackie Coon, the obscure but talented clarinetist Jay St. John, Jack's sister Norma Teagarden on piano, bassist Kas Malone and drummer Ray Bauduc. Because of some odd regulations, Jack Teagarden was not allowed to sing at these engagements (because otherwise the music would be classified as "entertainment" and the club-owner would be subject to an additional tax) so the performances are strictly instrumentals. In addition to the band numbers, on each broadcast the intermission pianist had a chance to play one number; Lil Armstrong and Don Ewell are both heard from twice. Although the talking by the announcer is a bit annoying at times (he knew nothing about jazz), the Dixieland music is generally quite spirited if predictable and the three horns all get in their fair share of heated solos on the familiar warhorses. —*Scott Yanow*

Meet Me Where They Play the Blues / Nov. 1954 / Bethlehem ✦✦✦

For this LP, trombonist Jack Teagarden is heard with three different groups on a dozen titles recorded in Nov. 1954. Although the supporting cast on various selections includes trumpeter Jimmy McPartland, clarinetists Edmond Hall and Kenny Davern, and Dick Cary, Norma Teagarden and Leonard Feather on pianos, Teagarden is the main star throughout. His trombone playing was still in prime form and his vocals give spirit to the music. High points of this enjoyable Dixieland set include "Original Dixieland One Step," "Blue Funk," "Eccentric" and "Milenburg Joys." —*Scott Yanow*

The Complete Capitol Fifties Jack Teagarden Sessions / Oct. 18, 1955-Apr. 14, 1958 / Mosaic ✦✦✦✦✦

Jack Teagarden was the top jazz trombonist to emerge before World War II. While his most innovative days were in the late 1920s and '30s, he remained a viable and highly enjoyable jazzman (and a popular attraction on the Dixieland circuit) up until his death in 1964. In the 1950s, he recorded six albums for Capitol, and they are reissued in full (plus some alternate takes and a "new" version of "St. James Infirmary") on Mosaic's four-CD box set. Teagarden is heard on two hot Dixieland dates (*Coast Concert* and *Jazz Ultimate*) with cornetist Bobby Hackett and either Matty Matlock or Peanuts Hucko on clarinet. An outing by his own working group (Big Ts Dixieland Band) is a surprising disappointment, for the sextet is hamstrung by dully arranged ensembles instead of getting a chance to really stretch out. However, Teagarden's three albums with larger groups are all better than expected. *This Is Teagarden* revisits some older material, *Swing Low, Sweet Spiritual* (even with the dumb background singers) is generally successful, and the instrumental mood record *Shades of Night* has some beautiful trombone playing on the ballads. Although Teagarden was no longer a pacesetter in the 1950s, he is heard throughout in prime form. Dixieland collectors can consider this box to be essential. —*Scott Yanow*

Jack Teagarden Sextet / May 3, 1958 / Pumpkin ✦✦✦✦

Trombonist Jack Teagarden led one of his finest regular bands in 1958. With cornetist Dick Oakley, clarinetist Jerry Fuller and pianist Don Ewell co-starring in the sextet, Teagarden had strong sidemen who knew how to sound individual in the Dixieland format. This broadcast (live from Cleveland) finds Teagarden and his band running through its usual repertoire, somehow sounding inspired while playing such warhorses as "Basin Street Blues" and "Muskrat Ramble." —*Scott Yanow*

Jack Teagarden and His All Stars / May 1958 / Jazzology ✦✦✦✦✦

Taken from the same period (but not duplicating the music) of Jack Teagarden's Pumpkin LP, this Jazzology CD finds the trombonist leading one of his strongest groups, a band that also features many fine solos from cornetist Dick Oakley, clarinetist Jerry Fuller and pianist Don Ewell. Even on such tunes as "Someday You'll

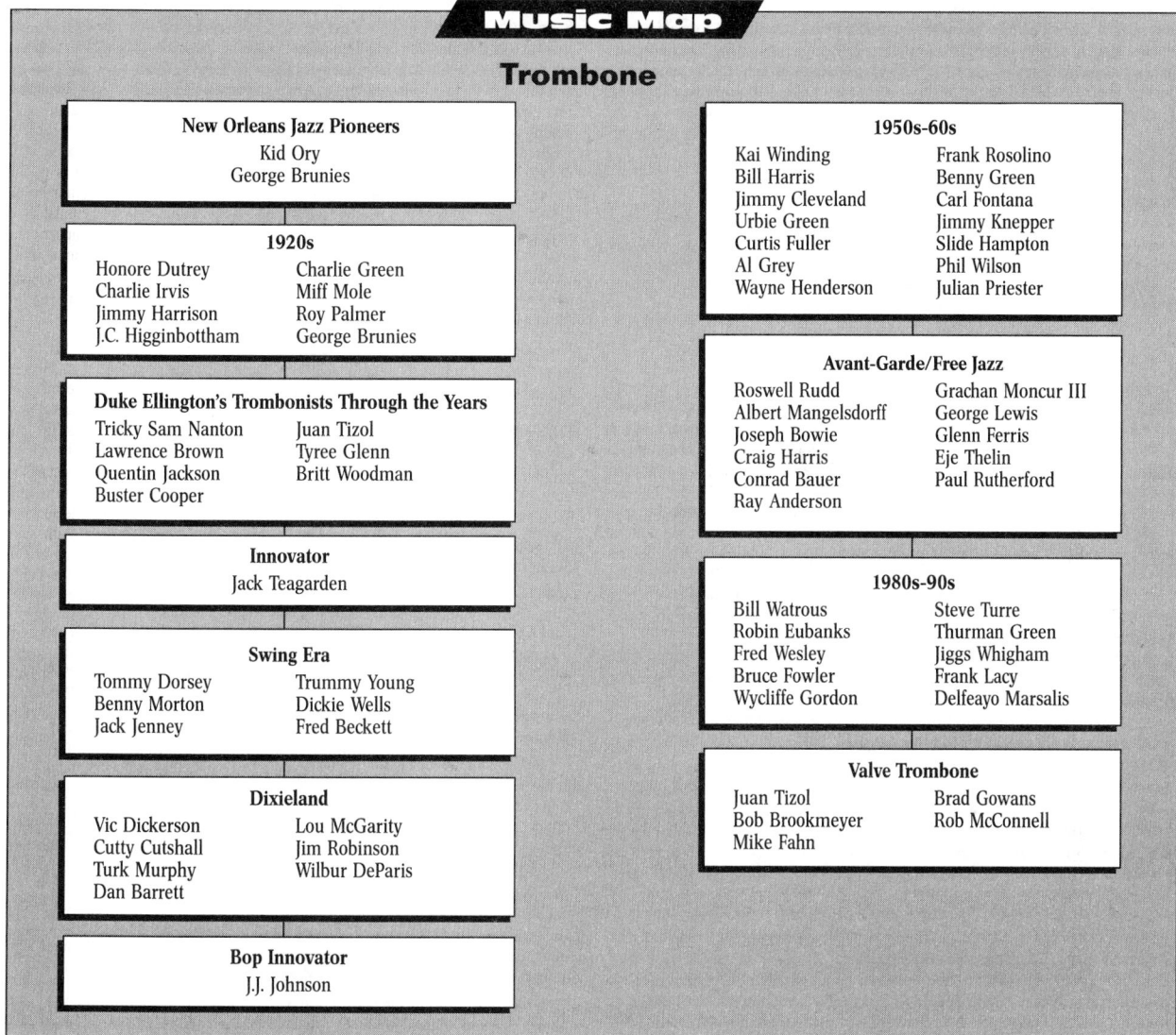

Music Map
Trombone

New Orleans Jazz Pioneers
Kid Ory
George Brunies

1920s

Honore Dutrey	Charlie Green
Charlie Irvis	Miff Mole
Jimmy Harrison	Roy Palmer
J.C. Higginbottham	George Brunies

Duke Ellington's Trombonists Through the Years

Tricky Sam Nanton	Juan Tizol
Lawrence Brown	Tyree Glenn
Quentin Jackson	Britt Woodman
Buster Cooper	

Innovator
Jack Teagarden

Swing Era

Tommy Dorsey	Trummy Young
Benny Morton	Dickie Wells
Jack Jenney	Fred Beckett

Dixieland

Vic Dickerson	Lou McGarity
Cutty Cutshall	Jim Robinson
Turk Murphy	Wilbur DeParis
Dan Barrett	

Bop Innovator
J.J. Johnson

1950s-60s

Kai Winding	Frank Rosolino
Bill Harris	Benny Green
Jimmy Cleveland	Carl Fontana
Urbie Green	Jimmy Knepper
Curtis Fuller	Slide Hampton
Al Grey	Phil Wilson
Wayne Henderson	Julian Priester

Avant-Garde/Free Jazz

Roswell Rudd	Grachan Moncur III
Albert Mangelsdorff	George Lewis
Joseph Bowie	Glenn Ferris
Craig Harris	Eje Thelin
Conrad Bauer	Paul Rutherford
Ray Anderson	

1980s-90s

Bill Watrous	Steve Turre
Robin Eubanks	Thurman Green
Fred Wesley	Jiggs Whigham
Bruce Fowler	Frank Lacy
Wycliffe Gordon	Delfeayo Marsalis

Valve Trombone

Juan Tizol	Brad Gowans
Bob Brookmeyer	Rob McConnell
Mike Fahn	

Be Sorry," "High Society" and "When the Saints Go Marching In," this very enjoyable sextet is able to play with enthusiasm and creativity, coming up with something fresh to say on songs the musicians had performed a countless number of times. —*Scott Yanow*

On Okinawa / Jan. 21, 1959 / IAJRC ✦✦✦✦
Recorded in Okinawa, Japan, during an Asian tour, the music on this set is pure Dixieland. The great trombonist Jack Teagarden, heading a sextet with trumpeter Max Kaminsky, clarinetist Jerry Fuller and pianist Don Ewell, performs lively versions of nine Dixieland standards plus a blues. Everyone plays up to par and comes up with spirited statements on the familiar repertoire. —*Scott Yanow*

Hundred Years from Today / Sep. 20, 1963-Sep. 21, 1963 / Memphis Archives ✦✦✦✦✦
Jack Teagarden's final recording, performed less than four months before his death, finds the trombonist/vocalist in particularly high spirits at the Monterey Jazz Festival. Mr. T. was reunited not only with his brother (trumpeter Charlie) and sister (pianist Norma), but his mother, who performs a couple of ragtime piano solos. The strong supporting cast, in addition to the many Teagardens, features clarinetist Pee Wee Russell, baritonist Gerry Mulligan and pianist Joe Sullivan. The two sets included on this historical CD are filled with blues, standards and Dixieland, the results of Jack Teagarden's two sets at Monterey. This important and enjoyable music is proof that the great trombonist went out on top. —*Scott Yanow*

Joe Temperley

b. Sep. 20, 1929, Fife, Scotland
Baritone Saxophone / Swing

Baritonist Joe Temperley is the perfect musician to fill in for Harry Carney during recreations of Duke Ellington's music, a role that has often overshadowed his own fine voice. Temperley actually started on the alto and recorded on tenor with English bands led by Harry Parry (1949), Jack Parnell, Tony Crombie and Tommy Whittle. He stuck to baritone during a long association with Humphrey Lyttelton's popular band (1958-65). In 1965 Temperley moved to New York, working with a variety of big bands (including Woody Herman, Buddy Rich, Thad Jones-Mel Lewis and Clark Terry). In 1974 he became the first replacement for Harry Carney with the Mercer Ellington Orchestra and has since then freelanced with the who's who of jazz including (starting in 1990) the Lincoln Center Jazz Orchestra under the direction of Wynton Marsalis. Temperley has several fine albums out as a leader, most notably for the Scottish Hep label. —*Scott Yanow*

Nightingale / Apr. 1991 / Hep ✦✦✦✦✦

★ **Concerto for Joe** / Sep. 22, 1993+Jul. 8, 1994 / Hep ✦✦✦✦✦
Joe Temperley's thick-toned baritone and swing-oriented style is heard at its best on this CD, his definitive release. Temperley's huge sound sometimes makes it seem as if he is playing a bass sax rather than a baritone, yet his fluidity is on the

level of an altoist. He performs seven selections (including four Duke Ellington songs) with a talented quartet headed by pianist Brian Lemon, and a six-song suite by the late trumpeter Jimmy Deuchar with an 11-piece group; the latter also features fine solos from altoist Peter King and trumpeter Gerard Presencer. The swinging music is all straightahead with appealing chord changes serving as an inspiration for the underrated baritonist. Recommended. —*Scott Yanow*

Jacky Terrasson

b. Nov. 27, 1966, Berlin, Germany
Piano / Post-Bop
By the mid-'90s, pianist Jacky Terrasson was being hailed as one of the bright Young Lions on the traditional jazz scene. His feathery keyboard touch is coupled with a lot of power and passion, a complete understanding of the blues and improvisation, and Terrasson is also a gifted arranger, putting his own personal stamp on well-known tunes. He's been one of the jazz world's most talked about piano player/composers since he captured everyone's attention when he won the Thelonius Monk Competition in 1993.

Born in Berlin to a French mother and an American father, Terrasson's distinctive piano style reflects his old and new influences. In his youth, he spent years studying and listening to recordings by Bud Powell, Bill Evans and Thelonius Monk. He began playing piano at age five, and his parents were always playing classical music on the stereo. He began listening intently to Billie Holiday and Miles Davis records that belonged to his mother when he was 11, and at that point, he was hooked on playing jazz piano.

He studied jazz at the Berklee College of Music in Boston with many other new traditionalists as classmates, including people like Danilo Perez. After graduation, he spent a year jamming at clubs in Chicago and New York before hooking up with ensembles led by his mentors, including Arthur Taylor and Betty Carter. At a recording session, Terrasson met Carter. The vocalist told him she needed a pianist to begin a tour the next day, and he accepted, spending nearly a year on the road with her.

Among many other sessions, Terrasson performed on Jimmy Scott's 1996 release, *Heaven,* for Warner Bros. He also did arranging for that record. Terrasson continues to perform around the world as leader of his own trio, and has made several European and Japanese tours. He's one of the most sought-after sidemen in jazz, constantly in demand for touring jazz bands and recording dates. —*Richard Skelly*

Jacky Terrasson / 1994 / Blue Note ✦✦✦✦
Jacky Terrasson delights in turning standards inside out. On his CD he gives odd rhythms to "I Love Paris," purposely speeds up and slows down the tempo on "Bye Bye Blackbird," takes "I Fall in Love Too Easily" very slow, and shows a grasp of dynamics worthy of Ahmad Jamal. It is fortunate that bassist Ugonna Okegwo and drummer Leon Parker are very alert (or perhaps well-rehearsed), because to the uninitiated listener these eccentric and rather quirky performances are often quite unpredictable and occasionally jarring. Well worth checking out. —*Scott Yanow*

● **Reach** / Feb. 20, 1996 / Blue Note ✦✦✦✦✦
The talented young pianist Jacky Terrasson and his trio (with bassist Ugonna Okegwo and drummer Leon Parker) find something new to say on a few standards (including a rare uptempo version of "For Sentimental Reasons") and introduce five of Terrasson's originals. Although he does not have an original style yet, Terrasson displays a great deal of potential for the future. Highlights include "I Should Care," "Just One of Those Things" and a medley of his "Reach" with "Smoke Gets in Your Eyes." —*Scott Yanow*

Rendezvous / Jan. 4, 1997-Apr. 4, 1997 / Blue Note ✦✦✦✦
For this notable set, pianist Jacky Terrasson teams up with the smoky, chance-taking vocalist Cassandra Wilson, either Lonnie Plaxico or Kenny Davis on bass and percussionist Mino Cinelu. The music is quite impressionistic and atmospheric. Terrasson and Wilson stick to standards, but their renditions of such songs as "Old Devil Moon," "My Ship," "Tea for Two" and even "Tennessee Waltz" are quite haunting and floating, slightly disturbing and occasionally sensuous. Terrasson, who takes "Autumn Leaves" and "Chicago 1987" (the one non-standard) as solo pieces, was on his way to forming his own style, while Wilson had certainly found her niche. An intriguing matchup. —*Scott Yanow*

Clark Terry

b. Dec. 14, 1920, St. Louis, MO
Fluegelhorn, Vocals / Bop, Swing
Possessor of the happiest sound in jazz, fluegelhornist Clark Terry always plays music that is exuberant, swinging and fun. A brilliant (and very distinctive) soloist, C.T. gained fame for his "Mumbles" vocals (which started as a satire of the less intelligible ancient blues singers) and is also an enthusiastic educator. He gained early experience playing trumpet in the viable St. Louis jazz scene of the early '40s

(where he was an inspiration for Miles Davis) and, after performing in a Navy band during World War II, he gained a strong reputation playing with the big band of Charlie Barnet (1947-48), the orchestra and small groups of Count Basie (1948-51) and particularly with Duke Ellington (1951-59). Terry, a versatile swing/bop soloist who started specializing on fluegelhorn in the mid-'50s, had many features with Ellington (including "Perdido") and started leading his own record dates during that era. He visited Europe with Harold Arlen's unsuccessful *The Free & Easy* show of 1959-60 as part of Quincy Jones' Orchestra and then joined the staff of NBC, where he was a regular member of the Tonight Show Orchestra. He recorded regularly in the 1960s including a classic set with the Oscar Peterson Trio and several dates with the quintet he co-led with valve trombonist Bob Brookmeyer. Throughout the 1970s, '80s and '90s C.T. has remained a major force, recording and performing in a wide variety of settings including at the head of his short-lived big band in the mid-'70s, with all-star groups for Pablo and as a guest artist who can be expected to provide happiness in every note he plays. —*Scott Yanow*

Clark Terry / Jan. 3, 1955-Jan. 4, 1955 / EmArcy ✦✦✦✦
With the exception of three songs cut as V-Discs in 1947, this set contains fluegelhornist Clark Terry's first recordings as a leader. Joined by trombonist Jimmy Cleveland, baritonist Cecil Payne, pianist Horace Silver, Oscar Pettiford on cello, bassist Wendell Marshall and drummer Art Blakey, C.T. performs eight obscure songs that are arranged quite expertly by Quincy Jones. Terry sounds much more influenced by Dizzy Gillespie than he would in just a couple of years, but his good-humored musical personality and control of his horn was already obvious. With Pettiford offering occasional cello solos (in addition to playing second bass) and Cleveland in top form, this is a highly recommended set. —*Scott Yanow*

Serenade to a Bus Seat / Apr. 1957 / Original Jazz Classics ✦✦✦✦
This CD reissue matches together trumpeter Clark Terry (before he switched to fluegelhorn) with tenor saxophonist Johnny Griffin, pianist Wynton Kelly, bassist Paul Chambers and drummer Philly Joe Jones. Most notable about the music is that Terry wrote five of the eight selections (including the colorful title cut, which pays tribute to life on the road with Duke Ellington); the other numbers are "Donna Lee," a pretty version of "Stardust" and a slightly Latinized "That Old Black Magic." Terry and Griffin were a potent team, making one regret that they did not record together much through the years. This set contains excellent straightahead jazz performed with plenty of spirit. —*Scott Yanow*

Duke with a Difference / Jul. 29, 1957+Sep. 6, 1957 / Original Jazz Classics ✦✦✦✦✦
For this CD reissue of a Riverside set, trumpeter Clark Terry and some of the top Ellington sidemen of the period (trombonist Britt Woodman, altoist Johnny Hodges, tenor saxophonist Paul Gonsalves, Tyree Glenn on vibes, bassist Jimmy Woode and drummer Sam Woodyard) perform eight songs associated with Duke, but with fresh arrangements. There is plenty of solo space for C.T., Gonsalves and Hodges, and the arrangements by Terry and Mercer Ellington cast a new light on some of the warhorses; highlights include "C-Jam Blues," "Cottontail," "Mood Indigo" and "Come Sunday." —*Scott Yanow*

In Orbit / May 1958 / Original Jazz Classics ✦✦✦✦✦
One of Thelonious Monk's rare appearances as a sideman is on this quartet set led by fluegelhornist Clark Terry. With bassist Sam Jones and drummer Philly Joe Jones, Terry and pianist Monk perform a set that surprisingly has only one Thelonious Monk song ("Let's Cool One"). Among the high points of this spirited, boppish date are C.T.'s "Globetrotter," "One Foot in the Gutter" and "Zip Co-Ed." —*Scott Yanow*

Top and Bottom Brass / Feb. 24, 1959-Feb. 26, 1959 / Original Jazz Classics ✦✦✦✦
This lesser-known Clark Terry session (reissued on CD in the *OJC* series) has an unusual lineup, with the fluegelhornist joined by Don Butterfield on tuba, pianist Jimmy Jones, bassist Sam Jones and drummer Art Taylor. Butterfield has nearly as much solo space as C.T. (and is given a prominent role in the ensembles) while Jimmy Jones' chordal solos are somewhat eccentric. Terry is in fine form on a variety of blues, originals and obscurities along with the interesting versions of "My Heart Belongs to Daddy" and "A Sunday Kind of Love," but the results overall are not all that significant. —*Scott Yanow*

Paris (1960) / Jan. 1960-Feb. 1960 / Swing ✦✦✦✦
This is a slightly unusual album recorded by fluegelhornist Clark Terry while in Europe performing with the Harold Arlen Show *Free and Easy.* Terry is featured with a sextet that includes Eric Dixon on flute and tenor, Elek Bacsik on guitar and Kenny Clarke on drums on three numbers (highlighted by Duke Jordan's "No Problem"); four other songs feature trombonist Quentin Jackson in Dixon's place; and Terry performs five of pianist Martial Solal's originals written for the Belgian film *Si Le Vent Te Fait Peur* with a French septet that includes the composer.

Although this LP, which benefits from lengthy liner notes by Dan Morgenstern, is not essential, it is worth picking up, if it can be found. —*Scott Yanow*

★ **Color Changes** / Nov. 19, 1960 / Candid ✦✦✦✦

This is one of fluegelhornist Clark Terry's finest albums. Terry had complete control over the music and, rather than have the usual jam session, he utilized an octet and arrangements by Yusef Lateef, Budd Johnson and Al Cohn. The lineup of musicians (C.T., trombonist Jimmy Knepper, Julius Watkins on French horn, Yusef Lateef on tenor, flute, oboe and English horn, Seldon Powell doubling on tenor and flute, pianist Tommy Flanagan, bassist Joe Benjamin and drummer Ed Shaughnessy) lives up to its potential, and the charts make good use of the sounds of these very individual stylists. The material, which consists of originals by Terry, Duke Jordan, Lateef and Bob Wilber, is both rare and fresh, and the interpretations always swing. Highly recommended. —*Scott Yanow*

Mellow Moods / Jul. 21, 1961-May 15, 1962 / Prestige ✦✦✦✦

This CD combines together two former LPs by fluegelhornist Clark Terry: *Everything's Mellow* and *All American*. Since those two sessions were cut for the Moodsville label (where all of the sets were supposed to emphasize quiet ballads) and the second date has songs from a forgotten musical, this CD would not seem to have much potential. However Terry is highly expressive on the former date (a quartet outing with pianist Junior Mance, bassist Joe Benjamin and drummer Charlie Persip) and does not stick only to ballads, throwing in some blues and obscure melodies. As for the *All American* score, Oliver Nelson was enlisted to write arrangements for Terry's septet (which comprises Budd Johnson on tenor, trombonist Lester Robertson, baritonist George Barrow, pianist Eddie Costa in one of his final recordings, bassist Art Davis and drummer Ed Shaughnessy) and, except for a couple of purposely corny moments, the music is greatly uplifted; in fact a few of the songs deserve to be revived. C.T. and Budd are in great form throughout. This surprising CD is recommended. —*Scott Yanow*

Clark Terry & Bob Brookmeyer / 1962 / Verve ✦✦✦

This obscure LP in 1973 released previously unknown performances from the Clark Terry–Bob Brookmeyer quintet, a very likable unit of the period. Terry's fluegelhorn and Brookmeyer's valve trombone blended together very well, they both had hard-swinging but witty styles, and their ensemble work was frequently exciting. With the fine support of pianist Eddie Costa (in one of his last sessions), bassist Joe Benjamin and drummer Osie Johnson, C.T. and Brookmeyer perform two originals, "Things Ain't What They Used to Be" and "Stolen Moments"; the four renditions clock in between eight-and-a-half and 12 minutes. Excellent music but this album will be difficult to find. —*Scott Yanow*

Tread Ye Lightly / 1963 / Cameo ✦✦✦✦✦

This is one of Clark Terry's finest records of the 1960s, but has yet to be reissued on CD. Possessor of the happiest sound in jazz, the fluegelhornist is particularly exuberant on "Georgia on My Mind," "Misty" and "Lilies of the Field." The colorful supporting cast includes Seldon Powell on tenor, baritone and flute, Buddy Lucas doubling on harmonica and tenor, Major Holley (who sings along with some of his solos) on bass and the mysterious "Homer Fields" on piano, who is actually Ray Bryant. Well worth searching for. —*Scott Yanow*

The Happy Horns of Clark Terry / Mar. 13, 1964 / GRP/Impulse! ✦✦✦✦✦

This all-star CD has plenty of memorable moments. Fluegelhornist Clark Terry teams up with altoist Phil Woods (who doubles on clarinet), tenor great Ben Webster, pianist Roger Kellaway, bassist Milt Hinton and drummer Walter Perkins for a varied program that includes a rollicking version of "Rockin' in Rhythm," Bix Beiderbecke's "In a Mist," a Duke Ellington medley and "Return to Swahili," which is mostly a fluegelhorn-drums duet. The lively music is quite enjoyable. —*Scott Yanow*

Live 1964 / May 8, 1964 / Emerald ✦✦✦

This LP from Horace Silver's Emerald label released for the first time in 1987 this particular live set from fluegelhornist Clark Terry. The 1964 quartet session (which also includes pianist Michael Abene, bassist Jimmy Gannon and drummer John Forte) finds Terry in typically joyful form playing his usual repertoire of the period: "Straight, No Chaser," "Stardust," "Perdido," "Misty," "Haig and Haig" and a twelve-and-a-half-minute version of "In a Mellow Tone." While the backup group is supportive without showing much of a personality, Terry makes it obvious from the first note who he is. C.T.'s fans will enjoy this one. —*Scott Yanow*

Quintet / Nov. 23, 1964-Nov. 24, 1964 / Mainstream ✦✦✦

Fluegelhornist Clark Terry and valve trombonist Bob Brookmeyer made for a very complementary pair in their mid-'60s quintet. Both had distinctive but similar sounds, impressive technique, the ability to swing anything and plenty of wit. On this Mainstream LP with pianist Roger Kellaway, bassist Bill Crow and drummer Dave Bailey, C.T. and Brookmeyer explore such songs as Herbie Hancock's "Blindman, Blindman," Charlie Parker's "Hymn," Thelonious Monk's "Straight, No Chaser" and a variety of originals. Unfortunately, all ten selections clock in at

around three minutes, so there is no real stretching out, but what is here is excellent. —*Scott Yanow*

☆ **Oscar Peterson Trio with Clark Terry** / 1964 / Mercury ✦✦✦✦✦

The Oscar Peterson Trio, with bassist Ray Brown and drummer Ed Thigpen, welcomed fluegelhornist Clark Terry to this very memorable studio session. Whether on "Brotherhood of Man," "Mack the Knife" or "They Didn't Believe Me," all of the players are mutually inspired, and the results are not only joyful, but explosively exuberant. However, this album (reissued on CD) will be best remembered for Clark Terry's introduction of his unique vocal style on "Mumbles" and "Incoherent Blues"; those spontaneous performances still sound funny. A gem. —*Scott Yanow*

Spanish Rice / Jul. 18, 1966-Jul. 20, 1966 / Impulse! ✦✦✦

Although Clark Terry (on fluegelhorn and occasional vocal) is the main star of this LP, arranger Chico O'Farrill is most responsible for the band's unusual sound. Utilizing an instrumentation of four trumpets, two guitars, bass, drums and four Latin percussionists, O'Farrill explores some veteran melodies (including "Peanut Vendor," "Mexican Hat Dance" and "Tin Tin Deo"), along with some newer pieces. The performances ("Joonji" is the longest at three-and-a-half minutes) are all quite concise and would have benefited from some more extended playing and perhaps an occasional solo by trumpeters Snooky Young, Joe Newman and Ernie Royal, but the overall results are quite joyful, and C.T. is in typically swinging form. —*Scott Yanow*

At the Montreux Jazz Festival / Jun. 22, 1969 / Polydor ✦✦✦✦

An impressive big band (mostly comprising Europeans) was put together by arranger Ernie Wilkins to back fluegelhornist Clark Terry at his 1969 appearance at the Montreux Jazz Festival. While Terry (who sings the humorous "Mumbling in the Alps") is the main soloist, there are also spots for Wilkins on tenor (well featured on "All Too Soon"), vibraphonist Dave Pike, guitarist Louis Stewart and some lesser-known players. This out-of-print LP will be a difficult one to find. —*Scott Yanow*

Live at the Wichita Jazz Festival / Apr. 21, 1974 / Vanguard ✦✦✦✦

Clark Terry led a short-lived big band in the mid-1970s and it is that 18-piece orchestra that is showcased on this set from the 1974 Wichita Jazz Festival. With arrangements by Ernie Wilkins, Phil Woods, Jimmy Heath and Allan Foust, the emphasis during this CD reissue is on swinging in a beboppish fashion. However C.T. kept an open mind, and his performance also has versions of Kenny Dorham's "Una Mas" and Wayne Shorter's "Nefertiti" along with some more basic material. In addition to the fluegelhornist-leader (who takes a trademark vocal on "Mumbles" and good-humoredly announces the songs), such soloists as altoist Phil Woods, tenorman Jimmy Heath and pianist Duke Jordan are among the more important voices. This is an easily recommended CD for straightahead jazz fans. —*Scott Yanow*

Big Bad Band Live at Buddy's Place / 1976 / Vanguard ✦✦✦✦

The Clark Terry big band has always been a part-time venture, which is a real pity, for the fluegelhornist sounds quite natural in front of a jazz orchestra. This out-of-print Vanguard LP contains a live date by the swinging outfit in 1976. Ernie Wilkins' arrangements give the band its own personality, and there is some solo space for Wilkins' tenor, altoist Chris Woods and pianist Ronnie Mathews, among others, although C.T. is the main star. The lesser-known material, which includes four Wilkins originals and Jimmy Heath's "Gap Sealer," is an added plus, but this album will be difficult to locate until it is eventually (and rightfully) reissued on CD. —*Scott Yanow*

Live at the Jazz House / 1976 / Pausa ✦✦✦✦

Although the backup trio, pianist Scott Bradford, drummer Hartwig Bartz and bassist Larry "Gailes" (probably Gales) is fairly anonymous, fluegelhornist Clark Terry is in typically exuberant form, performing five standards, a German folk song and his own "Jazzhouse Blues." The lengthy versions of "Perdido," "On the Trail," "Wham" and "Take the 'A' Train" all find C.T. in prime form, coming up with plenty of creative ideas on songs that he had already performed a countless number of times. This Pausa LP contains music originally put out on the MPS label. —*Scott Yanow*

The Globetrotter / 1977 / Vanguard ✦✦✦✦

For this sextet/septet session, fluegelhornist Clark Terry mostly drew his personnel from the big band that he occasionally fronted during the mid-'70s. Of special interest is getting a chance to hear tenor saxophonist Ernie Wilkins (better-known as an arranger) stretching out as a soloist; C.T.'s other sidemen include pianist Ronnie Mathews, bassist Victor Sproeles and drummer Ed Soph, with guest spots for pianist Walter Bishop and guitarist Roland Prince. The repertoire is particularly strong with classic ballads such as "Misty" and "Autumn Leaves" alternating with Terry's three colorful originals: "One Foot in the Gutter," "Zip Co-Ed" and "Globetrotter." This excellent LP is long overdue to be reissued on CD. —*Scott Yanow*

Swiss Radio Days, Vol. 8: Lucerne 1978 / Dec. 16, 1978 / TCB ✦✦✦✦

Ain't Misbehavin' / Mar. 15, 1979-Mar. 16, 1979 / Pablo ✦✦✦✦
This served as a sprightly showcase for tunes either written or associated with Fats Waller. Outstanding in his role as front-line mate was the underappreciated alto saxophonist Chris Woods. Clark Terry's unforced humor was evident throughout this session. —*Bob Rusch*

Live in Chicago, Vol. 1 / 1979 / Monad ✦✦✦✦
The great fluegelhornist Clark Terry teams up with Ernie Wilkins (doubling on alto and tenor), pianist Marty Harris, bassist Victor Sproles and drummer Ed Saple for the first of two CDs taken from a performance at Ratso's in Chicago. The music (released for the first time on this 1995 CD) is reasonably well-recorded, and C.T. is in top form. The quintet, which gives Wilkins a rare opportunity to really stretch out, performs five songs long in Terry's repertoire, including "Secret Love," "On the Trail" and his own "One Foot in the Gutter." Terry's enthusiastic playing excites the crowd, and both CDs are easily recommended to his fans. —*Scott Yanow*

Live in Chicago, Vol. 2 / 1979 / Monad ✦✦✦✦
The second of two CDs taken from a performance by fluegelhornist Clark Terry's 1976 quintet has plenty of fine playing by the leader and Ernie Wilkins (on tenor and alto) during lengthy versions of "Canadian Sunset" and "Autumn Leaves." Terry also exuberantly sings "I Want a Little Girl" and is in hilarious form ad-libbing lyrics to the blues "Chitlin' Woman." Only an overly long "Mumbles" is a bit of a minus. But in general straightahead jazz collectors will be interested in this surprisingly well-recorded outing. —*Scott Yanow*

Memories of Duke / Mar. 11, 1980 / Original Jazz Classics ✦✦✦✦
Fluegelhornist Clark Terry and a strong quartet (pianist Jack Wilson, guitarist Joe Pass, bassist Ray Brown and drummer Frank Severino) perform nine songs associated with Duke Ellington, including seven of Ellington's compositions, plus a tune apiece from Billy Strayhorn ("Passion Flower") and Mercer Ellington ("Things Ain't What They Used to Be"). Terry knows these songs, which include "Cottontail," "Come Sunday" and "Sophisticated Lady" backwards, but he infuses each of his renditions with enthusiasm and melodic creativity. Recommended. —*Scott Yanow*

Yes, the Blues / Jan. 19, 1981 / Pablo ✦✦✦✦✦
This blues-oriented Pablo LP has an ideal matchup: fluegelhornist Clark Terry and altoist Eddie "Cleanhead" Vinson. Both musicians take a good-humored vocal apiece, but the emphasis is on their playing. The complementary stylists, backed by pianist Art Hillery, bassist John Heard and drummer Roy McCurdy, work together very well on their originals, plus "Swingin' the Blues," and create some memorable, if fairly basic, music straddling the boundaries between swing, bop and early R&B. —*Scott Yanow*

To Duke and Basie / Jan. 28, 1986 / Enja ✦✦✦✦✦
Fluegelhornist Clark Terry and bassist Red Mitchell play a full program of duets, with most of the music being associated with either Count Basie or Duke Ellington. Actually, the most remembered selection of the date is C.T.'s humorous "Hey Mr. Mumbles, What Did You Say?," which has a call-and-response vocal by the two masterful musicians. Overall, this is a particularly delightful set, with plenty of wit displayed along with the hard swinging. —*Scott Yanow*

Metropole Orchestra / May 1988+May 1994 / Mons ✦✦✦
The music on this Mons CD is taken from two different occasions on which fluegelhornist Clark Terry is accompanied by the Metropole orchestra, a large string big band from Holland. Rob Pronk and Lex Jasper provided the arrangements, but C.T. mostly performs his usual repertoire. The music swings despite the large number of musicians and the focus is almost entirely on Terry, who sounds as joyful as usual. —*Scott Yanow*

Portraits / Dec. 16, 1988 / Chesky ✦✦✦✦✦
Fluegelhornist Clark Terry recorded quite frequently in the 1980s, and his consistency was very impressive. Terry's good humor, joyful and immediately distinctive sound, and creative, bop-oriented ideas combined to form a very accessible style. This Chesky CD finds C.T. joined by pianist Don Friedman, bassist Victor Gaskin and drummer Lewis Nash for a variety of superior standards and Terry's lone original, "Finger Filibuster." The songs all pay tribute to various trumpeters, and some, such as "Pennies from Heaven," "Little Jazz" and "I Don't Wanna Be Kissed," were not performed by the fluegelhornist all that often; the resulting music is fresher than usual and often quite inspired. Recommended. —*Scott Yanow*

☆ **The Clark Terry Spacemen** / Feb. 13, 1989 / Chiaroscuro ✦✦✦✦✦
This underrated Chiaroscuro CD is a joy from start to finish. Fluegelhornist Clark Terry is teamed with an unusually talented group of all-stars (trumpeter Virgil Jones, trombonists Al Grey and Britt Woodman, altoist Phil Woods, tenor Red Holloway, baritonist Haywood Henry, pianist John Campbell, bassist Marcus McLaurine and drummer Butch Ballard), which is filled with distinctive and colorful swing stylists. The standards and riff tunes give all of the horn players solo space, and it is a particular joy to hear Britt Woodman and Haywood Henry (the latter

near the end of his life) getting some feature spots. Highlights include "Swinging the Blues," "For Dancers Only" and "Just Squeeze Me." After 55 minutes of music Clark Terry is heard on the 19-minute "Jazzspeak," verbally telling informative stories about his lengthy career, some of which are quite humorous. Highly recommended. —*Scott Yanow*

Having Fun / Apr. 11, 1990-Apr. 12, 1990 / Delos ✦✦✦✦
The title of this CD definitely fits not only its music but Clark Terry's career. The colorful fluegelhornist is teamed with Red Holloway doubling on tenor and alto, bassist Major Holley (who sings along with his bass in his solos), pianist Jon Campbell and drummer Lewis Nash. Since C.T., Holloway and Holley were all humorists, the music is not only swinging, but quite enthusiastic. With titles like "Mumbles," "Meet the Flintstones," "The Snapper" and "Mule's Soft Claw," the humor isn't unexpected. An excellent and consistently swinging date. —*Scott Yanow*

Live from the Village Gate / Nov. 19, 1990-Nov. 20, 1990 / Chesky ✦✦✦✦
Fluegelhornist Clark Terry, three weeks shy of his 70th birthday at the time of this live performance, sounds very much at the peak of his powers throughout the date. Teamed up with old friend Jimmy Heath, who doubles on tenor and soprano, pianist Don Friedman, bassist Marcus McLauren and drummer Kenny Washington (altoist Paquito D'Rivera guests on "Silly Samba"), C.T. performs eight little-known originals. The tunes are all fairly basic, but they inspire these talented musicians to some of their best playing. The hard-swinging music, which includes a trumpet-drums duet on "Brushes & Brass" and some singing from the audience on "Hey Mr. Mumbles," is quite enjoyable, among the most accessible type of jazz. —*Scott Yanow*

Second Set / Nov. 19, 1990-Nov. 20, 1990 / Chesky ✦✦✦✦
Clark Terry has made so many fine records in the 1990s that virtually all of them are recommended; this Chesky CD is no exception. A quintet date with tenor saxophonist Jimmy Heath, pianist Don Friedman, bassist Marcus McLauren and drummer Kenny Washington, Terry plays a variety of original tunes based on the blues and other fairly common chord changes. The good-humored music (which includes such song titles as "One Foot in the Gutter," "Serenade to a Bus Seat" and "Ode to a Fluegelhorn") is quite enjoyable, highlighted by Terry's "Mumbles" vocal on "Juonji," a few creative sing-alongs and lots of exciting fluegelhorn playing. This fine set is rounded off by ten minutes of storytelling by Terry that covers Count Basie, Duke Ellington, jazz education, Dizzy Gillespie and Miles Davis. —*Scott Yanow*

What a Wonderful World: For Louis / Feb. 1, 1993 / Red Baron ✦✦✦✦✦
72-year-old Clark Terry is in exuberant form throughout this very enjoyable disc. On "Duke's Place" he constructs a frequently hilarious monologue about a fictional dive, extolling its virtues (mostly food and women) for quite some time without losing momentum or stumbling even once despite the obvious spontaneity. The other selections (tributes to Duke Ellington and Louis Armstrong) have many spirited solos from Terry on fluegelhorn and wah-wah trombonist Al Grey. The rhythm section is solid and swinging; violinist Lesa Terry (Clark's cousin) is an asset on two numbers. Even if Bob Thiele makes out like a bandit (he is credited with "writing" five of the nine songs, and he and Glenn Osser are listed as co-composers of "For Louis and Duke," a themeless blues), the high spirits and colorful playing of C.T. and Grey make this disc into a delightful hour of joyous music. —*Scott Yanow*

Shades of Blues / May 13, 1994 / Challenge ✦✦✦✦
Clark Terry at 74 teams up with the veteran wah-wah trombone of Al Grey, pianist Charles Fox and bassist Marcus McLaurine to interpret 11 blues on this highly enjoyable release. Still very much in his musical prime, fluegelhornist Terry has one of the happiest sounds in jazz, and he gives a surprising amount of variety to the otherwise similar material. Terry's humorous vocal on "Whispering the Blues," his quick tradeoffs between his two horns (the fluegelhorn and a muted trumpet) on "Cool Vibes" and his interplay with Al Grey make this an easily recommended CD. —*Scott Yanow*

Remember the Time / Aug. 29, 1994-Aug. 30, 1994 / Mons ✦✦✦✦
The ageless Clark Terry (who although 74 at the time of this recording could pass musically for 44) is teamed up on this CD from the German Mons label with the warm-toned trombonist Mark Nightingale, the talented bopster George Robert on alto, pianist Dado Moroni, bassist Ray Brown and drummer Jeff Hamilton. With the exception of two standards (which are mistakenly credited to Terry) and a throwaway version of a Michael Jackson tune, all of the songs are group originals that utilize fairly basic chord changes that are ideal for swinging. Terry's exuberant fluegelhorn is in prime form (he sounds particularly beautiful on "Gypsy" and "The Story of Love" while taking "Gwen" as a duet with bassist Brown) and he has a typically humorous vocal on "Hot Sauce." It's an enjoyable outing. —*Scott Yanow*

With Pee Wee Claybrook & Swing Fever / Jan. 1995 / D'Note ✦✦✦

Trumpeter Clark Terry and tenor saxophonist Pee Wee Claybrook were important players in the St. Louis swing scene of the early '40s. After they were both drafted and played together for a period in The Great Lakes Naval Training Station Band, they went their separate ways in 1944. While C.T. would eventually become famous, Claybrook settled in San Francisco, spent time playing with Earl "Fatha" Hines and had a day job. A member of Swing Fever for ten years, Pee Wee Claybrook was 82 at the time it was suggested that he have a reunion with Terry, and this recording for D' Note is the result. In addition to Claybrook, Swing Fever consists of Howard Dudune on alto, clarinet and tenor, trombonist Bryan Gould, guitarist Jim Putman, bassist Dean Reilly and drummer Harold Jones. With the exception of Louis Jordan's "Lemonade" (which gives Gould an opportunity to sing the blues) and Duke Ellington's "Serenade to Sweden," all ten selections on this session are famous swing standards. C.T. and Gould trade scat vocals on an eccentric version of "Straighten up and Fly Right," Claybrook shows the influence of Johnny Hodges in his wailing solos (although his Buddy Tate-flavored sound is much heavier), Terry is up to his usual exuberant level and there are plenty of fine spots for the versatile reeds of Dudune and trombonist Gould. In addition, the sparse pianoless rhythm section gives this material a lighter feel than expected. A fun date, easily recommended. —*Scott Yanow*

Frank Teschemacher

b. Mar. 13, 1906, Kansas City, MO, **d.** Feb. 29, 1932, Chicago, IL
Clarinet, Alto Saxophone / Classic Jazz

One of the early jazz legends, Frank Teschemacher was an exciting if erratic clarinetist and altoist who was an important participant in the Chicago jazz scene of the 1920s. A member of the fabled Austin High School Gang of young Chicago jazz musicians, Teschemacher started recording in 1927 (with the McKenzie-Condon Chicagoans) although observers of the period have stated that his records were not as strong as his live performances. A fine musician whose solos are a little reminiscent of his contemporary, Pee Wee Russell, Teschemacher recorded in Chicago with a variety of overlapping pickup groups in 1927, spent 1928 in New York (where he played with Ben Pollack, Sam Lanin and Red Nichols) and then returned to Chicago. His life was cut short by a tragic automobile accident, making one wonder how Tesch (a good all-round musician) would have fared in the swing era. All 34 of his recordings plus six others that he might be on are included on a perfectly done Time/Life three-LP box set. —*Scott Yanow*

★ **Frank Teschemacher** / Dec. 9, 1927-Jan. 13, 1932 / Time-Life ✦✦✦✦✦

This perfectly done three-LP set from the Time/Life *Giants of Jazz* series differs from their other releases in that, instead of being a sampler, it contains every possible recording by its subject, the ill-fated clarinetist and altoist Frankie Teschemacher. Although not a virtuoso and occasionally a bit erratic on records, Teschemacher was a consistently exciting performer who always pushed himself. He is heard on the four groundbreaking recordings of McKenzie and Condon's Chicagoans and with Charles Pierce, the Chicago Rhythm Kings, the Jungle Kings, Miff Mole's Little Molers, Eddie Condon, the Dorsey Brothers, the Big Aces, Wingy Manone, Ted Lewis, Elmer Schoebel, the Cellar Boys and on one lone title ("Jazz Me Blues") issued under his own name. Among the other sidemen are cornetists Jimmy McPartland, Red Nichols, Wingy Manone and Muggsy Spanier, Bud Freeman and Mezz Mezzrow on tenors, pianists Joe Sullivan and Art Hodes and drummers Gene Krupa and George Wettling. In addition to the 34 known recordings where he is obviously present, this set has six other titles (from Lennie Hayton, the Original Wolverines and Howard Thomas' Orchestra) that Tesch might possibly have been on (although it is doubtful). The 48-page booklet is quite definitive, making this very attractive out-of-print set (which can still be found, often at budget prices) essential for collectors of early jazz. —*Scott Yanow*

Toots Thielemans (Jean Baptiste Thielemans)

b. Apr. 29, 1922, Brussels, Belgium
Harmonica, Guitar / Bop, Swing, Brazilian Jazz, Latin Jazz

Although preceded by Larry Adler (who has actually spent much of his career playing popular and classical music), Toots Thielemans virtually introduced the chromatic harmonica as a jazz instrument. In fact, ever since the mid-'50s he has had no close competitors. Toots simply plays the harmonica with the dexterity of a saxophonist, and has even successfully traded off with the likes of Oscar Peterson.

Toots Thielemans' first instrument was the accordion, which he started when he was three. Although he started playing the harmonica when he was 17, Thielemans' original reputation was made as a guitarist who was influenced by Django Reinhardt. Very much open to bop, Thielemans played in American GI clubs in Europe, visited the US for the first time in 1947 and shared the bandstand with Charlie Parker at the Paris Jazz Festival of 1949. He toured Europe as a guitarist with the Benny Goodman Sextet in 1950 and the following year moved to the US.

During 1953-59 Toots was a member of the George Shearing quintet (mostly as a guitarist) and has freelanced ever since. He first recorded his big hit "Bluesette" (which featured his expert whistling and guitar) in 1961, and ever since has been greatly in demand (particularly for his harmonica and his whistling) on pop records (including many dates with Quincy Jones) and as a jazz soloist. Toots' two-volume *Brasil Project* was popular in the 1990s and found him smoothly interacting on harmonica with top Brazilian musicians. —*Scott Yanow*

Verve Jazz Masters 59 / Mar. 12, 1953-Apr. 4, 1991 / Verve ✦✦✦

Toots Thielemans' *Verve Jazz Masters, Vol. 59* is a 16-track compilation featuring a good cross-section of the harmonica player's finest moments for Verve Records, including collaborations with Bob James, Milt Jackson, George Shearing, Hubert Laws and Freddie Hubbard. Featuring classic tracks like "Hummin'," "Body and Soul" and "Nocturne," the compilation is useful for neophytes who want a sampling of Toots' sound, though more dedicated fans will find it incomplete and useless, simply because it was designed for the casual listener. —*Thom Owens*

The Sound / 1955 / Columbia ✦✦✦✦

Although Toots Thielemans (originally best-known as a guitarist) had recorded on harmonica as early as 1950 and had led several sessions in Europe (and six obscure titles for MGM during 1952-53), this Columbia LP was his first full-length American release and it really showcases his remarkable harmonica playing. Toots was immediately and (accurately) called "amazing" by most listeners, for he played the harmonica with the fluidity and speed of a saxophone. The dozen selections on this out-of-print release feature Thielemans in three separate settings: backed by a trombone quartet, a four-piece reed section, or interacting with the Ray Bryant trio. Sticking mostly to swing-era standards, Thielemans showed the audience what he could really do and took his first major step towards being recognized as a masterful jazz improviser. —*Scott Yanow*

Man Bites Harmonica / Dec. 30, 1957+Jan. 7, 1958 / Original Jazz Classics ✦✦✦✦✦

Although he plays guitar exclusively on two of the eight selections included on this CD reissue, it is Toots Thielemans' harmonica playing that is most unique. He holds his own on a hard bop blowing date with baritonist Pepper Adams, pianist Kenny Drew, bassist Wilbur Ware and drummer Art Taylor, jamming on such songs as "East of the Sun," "Struttin' with Some Barbecue" and "Isn't It Romantic." Even four decades later, no jazz harmonica player has dethroned the great Toots. —*Scott Yanow*

The Soul of Toots Thielemans / Oct. 1959-Nov. 1959 / Doctor Jazz ✦✦✦✦

This somewhat obscure date by the great jazz harmonica player Toots Thielemans also features the leader playing some fine guitar (most notably on "Lonesome Road") and taking one of his first whistling solos on "Brother John." With pianist Ray Bryant, bassist Tom Bryant and drummer Oliver Jackson completing the quartet, Thielemans is in excellent form introducing two of his originals and jamming such tunes as "You Are My Sunshine," "Nuages" and "Confirmation." The music on this enjoyable 1986 Doctor Jazz reissue LP of a Signature session is currently out of print. —*Scott Yanow*

Toots and Svend / Nov. 22, 1972-Nov. 23, 1972 / Sonet ✦✦✦

The great harmonica player Toots Thielemans teams up on this 1972 date with the talented veteran swing violinist Svend Asmussen, but the results are less interesting than one might hope. Backed by a rather anonymous-sounding rhythm section comprising Kjell Ohman's organ and electric piano, electric bassist Stefan Brolund and/or acoustic bassist Red Mitchell and drummer Ed Thigpen, Svend and Toots play fine but the material is rather erratic. Perhaps Thielemans had been in the studios too long at this point, but the somewhat commercial A&M LP (which was originally released in Europe on Sonet) is generally quite forgettable. Any album featuring a song titled "Mr. Nashville" can be considered ominous. —*Scott Yanow*

Live / Apr. 4, 1974 / Polydor ✦✦✦✦

Originally recorded for the Dutch Polydor label and then released domestically by the now defunct Inner City company, this fine session allowed Toots Thielemans to become free of the commercial studios and jam with an obscure but talented European rhythm section. Thielemans, who mostly plays harmonica on the sextet date with guitarist Joop Scholten and keyboardist Rob Franken, has fun jamming on six of his originals (including his famous "Bluesette") plus a couple of movie themes, European tunes and "There Is No Greater Love." An excellent effort that would be followed by two other *Live* albums with a similar group. —*Scott Yanow*

● **Images** / Sep. 16, 1974 / Candid ✦✦✦✦✦

Live, Vol. 2 / Apr. 10, 1975 / Polydor ✦✦✦✦✦

It is a pity that this session cut for Dutch Polydor was last available in the US on an LP by the obselete Inner City label, for it features harmonica great Toots Thielemans in prime form. Accompanied by guitarist Wim Overgaauw, keyboardist Rob Franken, bassist Niels Pederson and drummer Bruno Castelucci, Thielemans performs a varied but consistently superior program that ranges from "Tenor Madness" and "Bye Bye Blackbird" to a couple of early Duke Ellington tunes ("The Mooche" and the rarely performed "Black Beauty"), Paul Simon's "I Do It for Your Love," Joanne Brackeen's "Images" and Kid Ory's "Muskrat Ramble." Well worth searching for. —*Scott Yanow*

Live in the Netherlands / Jul. 13, 1980 / Original Jazz Classics ✦✦✦✦✦
This memorable Pablo CD, Thielemans' only album as a leader for Norman Granz's label (although he made several notable appearances as a sideman), features the great jazz harmonica player in a sparse trio with guitarist Joe Pass and bassist Niels Pedersen. The four main numbers ("Blues in the Closet," "Thriving from a Riff," "Autumn Leaves" and "Someday My Prince Will Come") are pure bebop and Thielemans' solo guitar rendition of "The Mooche" is also a highlight. —*Scott Yanow*

Autumn Leaves / May 1984 / Soul Note ✦✦✦
Do Not Leave Me / Jun. 19, 1986 / Stash ✦✦✦✦✦
Though associated with bebop and studio work, the remarkable harmonica player Toots Thielemans has always been a very flexible player. Accompanied by a modern rhythm section comprising pianist Fred Hersch, bassist Marc Johnson and drummer Joey Baron, Thielemans performs the romantic "Do Not Leave Me," a 19-minute exploration of "Blue and Green" and "All Blues," a concise "Stardust," "Autumn Leaves," Ivan Lins' "Velas" and Toots' biggest hit, "Bluesette," which features the enthusiastic audience whistling along. More than a decade later, this joyful set still sounds fresh; fortunately the music is readily available on CD. —*Scott Yanow*

● **Only Trust Your Heart** / Apr. 1988-May 1988 / Concord Jazz ✦✦✦✦✦
Although the liner notes claim that this Concord release was Toots Thielemans' first recording as a leader in more than a dozen years, somehow the harmonica great's 14 European dates (not to mention sets released by Stash and Pablo) were overlooked. In any case, this is a fairly definitive session by the harmonica virtuoso, who is joined by pianist Fred Hersch, either Marc Johnson or Harvie Swartz on bass and drummer Joey Baron. The material is filled with challenging and generally underplayed standards (including Wayne Shorter's "Speak No Evil," Thad Jones' "Three and One," Benny Carter's lyrical "Only Trust Your Heart" and Thelonious Monk's "Little Rootie Tootie") plus two fine Hersch originals. Ranging from hard bop to Brazilian music and post bop, this is a consistently enjoyable and highly recommended outing. —*Scott Yanow*

Footprints / Dec. 19, 1989-Dec. 20, 1989 / EmArcy ✦✦✦✦
For My Lady / 1991 / EmArcy ✦✦✦✦
The emphasis is on ballads for harmonica player Toots Thielemans' outing with the Shirley Horn Trio. Horn, in addition to contributing some tastefully supportive piano and occasional solos, takes a vocal on "Someone to Watch Over Me." Toots sounds quite relaxed performing 11 standards (only "Blues in the Closet" generates much heat) plus his original "For My Lady" with such comfortable backing. —*Scott Yanow*

The Brasil Project / 1992 / Private Music ✦✦✦✦
This popular set matches the brilliant harmonica player Toots Thielemans with such top Brazilian performers as Ivan Lins, Djavan, Oscar Castro-Neves, Dori Caymmi, Ricardo Silveira, Joao Bosco, Gilberto Gil, Milton Nascimento, Caetano Veloso, Luis Bonfa, Edu Lobo and Elaine Elias, in addition to bassist Brian Bromberg, keyboardist Mike Lang, trumpeter Mark Isham and Dave Grusin. Thielemans is often in a supportive role behind the many soothing Brazilian singers and performers. The atmospheric date surprisingly does not have any Jobim songs, instead emphasizing lesser-known tunes (other than Toots' greatest hit "Bluesette"). Easily recommended to fans of Brazilian pop and jazz, this CD was soon followed by a second (and equally rewarding) set featuring many of the same performers. —*Scott Yanow*

The Brasil Project, Vol. 2 / 1993 / Private Music ✦✦✦✦
Guitarist, harmonica player, and whistler Toots Thielemans' follow-up to the critically acclaimed *Brasil Project* doesn't stray far from its predecessor's path. There are 13 nice Afro-Latin selections with Thielemans backing such top Brazilian vocalists as Milton Nascimento, Gilberto Gil, Ivan Lins, Caetano Veloso, and Dori Caymmi, among others, and guitarists Oscar Castro-Nieves and Lee Ritenour assisting Thielemans with delicate shadings and accompaniment. —*Ron Wynn*

East Coast West Coast / 1994 / Private Music ✦✦
For this set, harmonica great Toots Thielemans recorded with separate all-star lineups in New York and Los Angeles. When one considers that such musicians as trumpeter Terence Blanchard, tenor saxophonist Joshua Redman, violinist Jerry Goodman and Ernie Watts on tenor are heard from, this should have been a classic album. The problem is that, for whatever reason, every performance is overly brief. Other than two of the ballads, none of the selections exceed five minutes, and Thielemans' sidemen are restricted to very brief solos. Imagine playing

"Groovin' High" with Blanchard and Redman and having the horns only solo for one chorus apiece. Thielemans is in fine form, as usual, and it is a pleasant surprise to hear Goodman (most famous for his association with the Mahavishnu Orchestra) sounding like a combination of Stephane Grappelli and Papa John Creach during his two appearances. But to have Blanchard's inspired outburst at the beginning of "In Walked Bud" cut off after one chorus is quite frustrating, making this set a missed opportunity. —*Scott Yanow*

Ed Thigpen

b. Dec. 28, 1930, Chicago, IL
Drums / Hard Bop

A tasteful and subtle drummer who is a master with brushes, Ed Thigpen is still most famous for his longtime membership with the Oscar Peterson Trio. The son of Ben Thigpen (who played drums with Andy Kirk's Orchestra throughout the 1930s), Ed gained early experience playing with Cootie Williams from 1951-52. After a period in the Army, he worked with Dinah Washington (1954), Lennie Tristano, Johnny Hodges, Bud Powell and Billy Taylor's Trio (1956-59). Thigpen replaced guitarist Herb Ellis with Peterson's group in 1959, staying with the masterful pianist through 1965 and appearing on dozens of records. His quiet yet swinging style perfectly supported Peterson and bassist Ray Brown. After leaving Peterson, Thigpen spent two periods touring the world with Ella Fitzgerald during 1966-72. He settled in Copenhagen in 1972, worked as a teacher, wrote several instructional books, and has since continued playing with the who's who of jazz as a freelancer. As an occasional leader, Ed Thigpen has recorded dates for Verve (an obscurity from 1966), GNP Crescendo, Reckless, Timeless and Justin Time. —*Scott Yanow*

Easy Flight / Nov. 13, 1989-Jan. 28, 1990 / Reckless ✦✦✦✦
Drummer Ed Thigpen will always be best-known for his long stint with the Oscar Peterson Trio. For this rare CD put out by the Dutch Reckless label, Thigpen heads a quartet also including the Peterson-inspired pianist Johnny O'Neal, guitarist Tony Purrone and bassist Marlene Rosenberg. With the exception of O'Neal's "Tropical Breeze" and Thigpen's "Easy Flight," the 11 songs are all familiar standards that serve as fine vehicles for the solos of O'Neal and Purrone; Thigpen is mostly content to accompany his younger sidemen. Thigpen's date is easily recommended to straightahead jazz collectors lucky enough to find this CD. —*Scott Yanow*

Young Men and Old / Nov. 20, 1990-Nov. 21, 1990 / Timeless ✦✦✦✦
● **Mr. Taste** / Apr. 11, 1991-Jul. 19, 1991 / Justin Time ✦✦✦✦
This is a fine CD from drummer Ed Thigpen, who has led relatively few sessions throughout his career. Heading a trio also including guitarist Tony Purrone and bassist Mads Vinding, Thigpen is generous in allocating solo space and, even though he contributed three of the compositions, the focus is mostly on his sidemen. The boppish music includes both standards (such as "Dewey Square," "A Child Is Born" and "'Round Midnight") and obscurities, including two pieces by the cool-toned and swinging Purrone. An easily overlooked but rewarding straightahead set. —*Scott Yanow*

Gary Thomas

b. Jun. 10, 1961, Baltimore, MD
Tenor Saxophone, Flute / Avant-Garde, Post-Bop, Free Funk

As with altoists Steve Coleman and Greg Osby, Gary Thomas has developed his own fresh approach to improvisation, avoiding bop clichés and taking solos that are consistently full of surprising twists and turns. Lots of chances are taken and, even if not everything works (the use of rap on one of his JMT albums is unfortunate), Gary Thomas' music would never be called predictable! In the late '80s Thomas gigged with both Miles Davis and Jack DeJohnette's Special Edition. He has also recorded frequently with Greg Osby, Michele Rosewoman and Wallace Roney in addition to leading his own sessions. —*Scott Yanow*

The Seventh Quadrant / Apr. 3, 1987-Apr. 4, 1987 / Enja ✦✦✦
Code Violations / Jul. 20, 1988-Jul. 25, 1988 / Enja ✦✦✦✦✦
Tenor saxophonist Gary Thomas has always had a lot of musical courage. Although the rhythm section he uses on this set (which includes Paul Bollenback on guitar synth, keyboardist Tim Murphy, Anthony Cox or Geoff Harper on bass and Steve Williams or Dennis Chambers on drums) is quite funky, the funk rhythms are very unpredictable and constantly changing. Over the crowded backgrounds, Thomas (who doubles on flute) plays quite freely in a style reminiscent but not derivative of the concepts of Steve Coleman and Greg Osby. The 11 originals included on this Enja CD (Thomas' second session as a leader) are consistently disturbing and stimulating, with solos full of dissonance and unexpected moments. —*Scott Yanow*

● **By Any Means Necessary** / May 1989 / JMT ✦✦✦✦✦

The M-Base concept, which never caught on in a big way but did influence the playing of a dozen or so top jazz improvisers, is heard in its prime on this Gary Thomas release. The tenor saxophonist (doubling on flute) meets up with the fiery altoist Greg Osby, keyboardist Geri Allen, keyboardist Tim Murphy, bassist Anthony Cox, drummer Dennis Chambers, percussionist Nana Vasconcelos and on some selections guitarists John Scofield and Mick Goodrick. The music features dense ensembles, simultaneous improvisations, eccentric funk rhythms and rhythmic but very dissonant horn solos that have a logic of their own. One can think of this noisy date as being an updated extension of Ornette Coleman's Prime Time, and it is recommended to open-minded listeners who think that nothing new has been played in jazz since the mid-'70s. —*Scott Yanow*

While the Gate Is Open / Nov. 2, 1989-Nov. 10, 1989 / JMT ✦✦✦✦

After having avoided standards during his first few recordings, tenor saxophonist Gary Thomas surprised his followers with this CD, which contains such jazz themes as "Star Eyes," "The Song Is You," "On the Trail" and "Epistrophy." With assistance on some selections by guitarist Kevin Eubanks, keyboardist Renee Rosnes, Dave Holland or Anthony Cox on bass and drummer Dennis Chambers, Thomas gives the eight tunes fresh treatments and as usual avoids all clichés (and the logic of bop) in his explorative improvisations. —*Scott Yanow*

The Kold Kage / Mar. 1991-Jun. 1991 / JMT ✦✦✦✦

Till We Have Faces / May 8, 1992-May 14, 1992 / JMT ✦✦✦✦✦

Exile's Gate / May 19, 1993-May 23, 1993 / JMT ✦✦✦

Joe Thomas

b. Jun. 19, 1909, Uniontown, PA, **d.** Aug. 3, 1986, Kansas City, MO
Tenor Saxophone / Swing, Jump Blues

Joe Thomas will always be best-known as the tenor soloist with Jimmy Lunceford's Orchestra. He was originally an altoist playing with Horace Henderson, but switched to tenor when he joined Stuff Smith's group. As a star with Lunceford from 1933 until the leader's death in 1947, Thomas had many short but often-memorable solos and took several vocals. After Lunceford's unexpected death, Thomas and pianist Ed Wilcox ran the ghost band for a year. Later Thomas on his own recorded a variety of R&B-oriented sides, left music in the mid-'50s to run his father's undertaking business and from the 1960s on returned to performing on a part-time basis, cutting a session in 1982 for Uptown. He is not to be confused with the fine swing trumpeter Joe Thomas. —*Scott Yanow*

Raw Meat / Apr. 3, 1979-Apr. 4, 1979 / Uptown ✦✦✦

Veteran swing tenor saxophonist Joe Thomas finally had an opportunity to lead his first record session in 1979 when he was already 69. Only musically active on an occasional basis since the mid-'50s, Thomas still sounded pretty good at this point, featured in a quartet with pianist Jimmy Rowles, bassist Walter Booker and drummer Akira Tana. Both Thomas and Rowles take vocals and Joe's large tenor sound was still mostly under control. The emphasis is mostly on relaxed material with six swing-era standards (including "Exactly like You," "Body and Soul" and "Charmaine") joined by Thomas' "Dog Food" (mistitled "Raw Meat") and Rowles' "The Lady in the Corner." A historic and enjoyable set that launched the Uptown label. —*Scott Yanow*

● **Blowin' in from K.C.** / Dec. 9, 1982-Dec. 10, 1982 / Uptown ✦✦✦✦✦

In the early '50s, tenor saxophonist Joe Thomas (most famous for playing with Jimmy Lunceford) led a flexible septet that performed early R&B, swing and fairly modern jazz. Thirty years later, using Don Sickler's transcriptions, Thomas had a reunion with three of his surviving sidemen (trumpeter Johnny Grimes, trombonist Dicky Harris and bassist George Duvivier) and using pianist Jay McShann, baritonist Haywood Henry and either Oliver Jackson or Jackie Williams on drums to fill in for the no longer active (and in some cases deceased) players. There are several exciting selections on this date including "Raw Meat," "Tearing Hall," the Kenton-influenced "Star Mist," "Jumpin' Joe" and "Backstage at the Apollo"; Thomas sings "If I Could Be with You." This very rewarding Uptown LP (Joe Thomas' last recording) is a near-classic. —*Scott Yanow*

Leon Thomas (Amos Leone Thomas, Jr.)

b. Oct. 4, 1937, East St. Louis, IL
Vocals / Post-Bop

Leon Thomas' moment of fame occurred when he recorded "The Creator Has a Master Plan" with Pharoah Sanders in 1969. His eccentric yodelling worked well with Sanders' emotional tenor, making the performance an unexpected avant-garde "hit." Thomas studied music at Tennessee State and in 1959 moved to New York. After some work with Randy Weston and Mary Lou Williams, Thomas was the regular singer with the Count Basie Orchestra during much of 1961-65, but few recordings (none significant) occurred. He worked often with Pharoah Sand-

ers during 1969-72, recorded a set with Oliver Nelson and Johnny Hodges and made a few recordings on his own, but Thomas (who changed his first name to Leon in 1976) has yet to fulfill his potential. —*Scott Yanow*

● **Spirits Known and Unknown** / Oct. 21, 1969-Oct. 22, 1969 / Flying Dutchman ✦✦✦✦✦

Facets / Oct. 21, 1969-1972 / Flying Dutchman ✦✦✦✦✦

This fine 1973 sampler LP features performances by singer Leon Thomas originally on three previous sets. Three numbers (including "Song for My Father" and a short remake of "The Creator Has a Master Plan") are taken from a 1969 album with the mysterious "Little Rock" (a pseudonym for Pharoah Sanders) on tenor. A trio of numbers feature Thomas with an R&Bish band arranged by Pee Wee Ellis (originally issued as part of *Blues and the Soulful Truth*) and the remaining selections ("Disillusion Blues," the downbeat "Welcome to New York" and "Duke's Place") are from the vocalist's memorable meeting with altoist Johnny Hodges and Oliver Nelson's Orchestra. Throughout, Leon Thomas (a somewhat unique singer whose career has been rather aimless since this period) is heard in prime form. —*Scott Yanow*

In Berlin / Nov. 6, 1970 / Flying Dutchman ✦✦✦✦✦

Blues and the Soulful Truth / 1972 / Flying Dutchman ✦✦✦✦✦

This is Thomas' best studio album. Contains many of his best numbers. —*Michael G. Nastos*

Full Circle / 1973 / Flying Dutchman ✦✦✦

Precious Energy / Mar. 6, 1987-Mar. 7, 1987 / Mapleshade ✦✦✦✦

Leon Thomas and Gary Bartz are two tremendously gifted artists who have had problems with direction and taste. Thomas' seminal works with Pharoah Sanders, Lonnie Liston Smith, Santana, and others in the '70s weren't matched by some things he did in the early '80s, while Bartz's tough combo dates also weren't equaled by some pop-oriented recordings he cut later. The two have since gone back to their strengths and made an excellent team on the 1987 session *Precious Energy*. Although he doesn't try the ambitious yodeling and special effects he did with Sanders, Thomas does demonstrate the creamy sound and full force of earlier years, while Bartz's solos are once more fluid, strong, and expansive. —*Ron Wynn*

Leon Thomas Blues Band / 1988 / Portrait ✦✦✦✦✦

Butch Thompson (Richard Enos Thompson)

b. Nov. 28, 1943, Marine, MN
Piano, Clarinet / Stride, Classic Jazz

One of the top pre-bop pianists to be active during the past 30 years, Butch Thompson's piano playing stretches from Jelly Roll Morton and James P. Johnson to swing; he is also an excellent (if occasional) New Orleans-style clarinetist. In 1962 he joined the Hall Brothers New Orleans Jazz Band in Minneapolis, an association that lasted over 20 years. Thompson has led his own trio since the mid-'60s and during 1974-86 he appeared regularly on Garrison Keillor's very popular radio series *A Prairie Home Companion*. Thompson has recorded extensively for many labels including Center, Jazzology, GHB, Stomp Off and Daring. —*Scott Yanow*

Butch Thompson Plays Jelly Roll Morton Solos / 1968 / Biograph ✦✦✦

For his recording debut, 24-year-old pianist Butch Thompson performs a dozen selections associated with Jelly Roll Morton, including a couple ("Tiger Rag" and Scott Joplin's "Original Rags') not actually composed by Morton but performed during his Library of Congress sessions. Thompson, who has long been considered one of the top interpreters of Morton's music, already had his technique and sound down at this early stage, and his solo recital (reissued on CD) is excellent. Highlights include "King Porter Stomp," "Tiger Rag," "Pep" and "The Crave." —*Scott Yanow*

Butch Thompson Plays Jelly Roll Morton, Vol. 2 / 1974 / Biograph ✦✦✦✦

Live from St. Paul / May 9, 1981-Aug. 1, 1981 / Prairie Home Companion ✦✦✦✦

The Butch Thompson Trio (consisting of the pianist-leader, bassist Bill Evans and drummer Red Maddock) were an important ingredient in the success of the popular radio series *Prairie Home Companion*. The group (with occasional guest guitarist Tom Lieberman and on "Lady Be Good" cornetist Charlie Devore) are featured throughout this 1981 LP, mostly playing stride-filled versions of standards including "China Boy," "The Pearls," "I'll Dance at Your Wedding" and Scott Joplin's "The Easy Winners." An original blues by drummer Maddock (who takes a vocal) and Garrison Keillor's "Clouds of Joy" wrap up this enjoyable if hard-to-find set. —*Scott Yanow*

A' Solas / Feb. 2, 1982-Apr. 28, 1982 / Stomp Off ✦✦✦✦

The talented classic jazz pianist Butch Thompson is heard on this Stomp Off LP playing 14 diverse solos. In addition to six Jelly Roll Morton compositions (including his *Library of Congress* interpretation of "Maple Leaf Rag" which is here retitled "Maple Leaf Stomp"), Thompson plays tunes by King Oliver, Leroy Carr,

Armand Piron, a few standards and his own "Ecuadorian Memories" and "A' Solas." A strong effort. —*Scott Yanow*

If You Don't Shake / Mar. 6, 1984+Mar. 8, 1984 / Stomp Off ✦✦✦✦

Hal Smith has been one of the top classic jazz drummers of the past decade (revitalizing the Chicago jazz tradition), while Butch Thompson is one of the most impressive pianists of pre-swing music. Their set of duets is dedicated to the music of the infamous New Orleans red-light district Storyville. Since Jelly Roll Morton was a frequent resident, four of his songs are here plus tunes by Kid Ory, Bunk Johnson ("King Bolden's Tune"), Clarence Williams, Little Brother Montgomery, Dink Johnson and even Zez Confrey ("Stumbling") among others. Whether most of these songs were actually performed in Storyville is debatable but the style (melodic, rhythmic, and influenced by ragtime yet bluesish) fits the album's theme. Delightful music by two of the best. —*Scott Yanow*

● **Milenberg Joys** / Mar. 8, 1984-Dec. 5, 1984 / Stomp Off ✦✦✦✦✦

Subtitled "Echoes from Storyville, Vol. 2," this follow-up album to pianist Butch Thompson's *If You Don't Shake* (a set of duets with drummer Hal Smith) has three fine leftover tracks from the latter session plus nine enjoyable trios with cornetist Charlie DeVore. Only four of the dozen selections can be considered classics and this particularly strong set revives such forgotten tunes as "Bedelia," Clarence Williams' "Brown Skin, Who You For," "Rag Bag Rag" and "Home in Pasadena." DeVore's melodic yet sometimes heated cornet is a major asset, as is Smith's colorful drumming. As for pianist Thompson, he has been near the top of his field since the 1970s. Highly recommended. —*Scott Yanow*

Butch Thompson and His Boys in Chicago / Apr. 28, 1985 / Jazzology ✦✦✦✦✦

A jam-session feel pervades this fine 1920s jazz set. Pianist Butch Thompson is the leader of the septet, but does not dominate the proceedings, liberally featuring the adventurous clarinet of Frank Chase, cornetist Charlie DeVore and altoist John Otto; guitarist John Meilahn, bassist Bill Evans and drummer Hal Smith complete the spirited band. For a change of pace, Thompson performs ten standards including such Dixieland warhorses as "Sweethearts on Parade," "You Took Advantage of Me" and "At the Jazz Band Ball." Due to the high level of musicianship and colorful soloists, this fun album is a standout. —*Scott Yanow*

Direct from the Ballroom of the Shattuck Hotel / May 5, 1985 / Stomp Off ✦✦✦✦

Pianist Butch Thompson meets up with a variety of top players (many from Northern California) on this loose but coherent live session. The music mostly comprises underplayed standards from the 1920s and '30s (including "Mandy, Make Up Your Mind," "I'm Checkin' Out Goombye" and "You're Lucky to Me") plus a few original blues. The personnel often changes from song-to-song and the talented players include the extroverted cornetist Leon Oakley, Richard Hadlock on soprano and alto, trombonist Bob Mielke, Thompson on both piano and clarinet, Ray Skjelbred also on piano (he takes his own "Clark and Addison" as a solo feature and takes part in a piano duet with Thompson on "Wonderful Life Blues"), bassist Mike Duffy and drummer Hal Smith; Barbara Lashley helps out with a couple of vocals. Other highlights are "A Monday Date" (which features Thompson's piano with a trio), "Blue Reed Blues," "A Shine on Your Shoes" and "Song of the Wanderer." Easily recommended to classic jazz and Dixieland fans. —*Scott Yanow*

Thompson's King Oliver Centennial Band / Jul. 13, 1988 / GHB ✦✦✦✦✦

Thompson has succeeded in creating a band that effectively celebrates the spirit of Oliver's Creole Jazz Band without indulging in note-for-note imitation. —*Bruce Raeburn*

New Orleans Joys 88's / Mar. 1, 1989-Mar. 3, 1989 / Daring ✦✦✦✦

The first of three piano solo CDs recorded during a three-day period by Butch Thompson pays tribute to the legacy of New Orleans jazz, in particular Jelly Roll Morton. Thompson, a masterful interpreter of prebop music, brings back the spirit of Morton on fresh interpretations of 11 of his compositions plus Dink Johnson's "Stomp de Lowdown" and a pair of orignals ("Ecuadorean Memories" and "Dink's Blues"). Fans of early jazz piano will certainly enjoy this set and its two follow-ups *Chicago Breakdown* and *Good Old New York*. —*Scott Yanow*

Chicago Breakdown 88's / Mar. 1, 1989-Mar. 3, 1989 / Daring ✦✦✦✦

There is a great deal of stylistic overlapping between the three solo projects that Butch Thompson recorded in early March 1989; the others are *New Orleans Joys* and *Good Old New York*. While the former focused mostly on Jelly Roll Morton, his Chicago tribute has six additional Morton tunes (including "King Porter Stomp" and "Fickle Fay Creep"), plus numbers by Dink Johnson, Leroy Carr, W.C. Handy ("Beale Street Blues"), King Oliver, Clarence Williams and Little Brother Montgomery; Thompson also remakes his own "A' Solas." It is a pity that Butch Thompson did not investigate the Chicago pianists (such as Earl Hines and Joe Sullivan) more on this CD, which would have given it more of a distinctive personality, but the music is certainly well played and will be enjoyed by 1920s jazz collectors. —*Scott Yanow*

Good Old New York 88's / Mar. 1, 1989-Mar. 3, 1989 / Daring ✦✦✦

While the first two CDs in this three-volume series (all recorded within a three-day period) paid tribute to Jelly Roll Morton in his New Orleans and Chicago periods (*New Orleans Joys* and *Chicago Breakdown*), this set of unaccompanied piano solos by the talented Butch Thompson has works by Eubie Blake, Willie "The Lion" Smith, James P. Johnson and Fats Waller plus the title cut (the lone Morton song). Thompson's New Orleans-influenced stride style revitalizes such songs as "Charleston Rag," "Echo of Spring," "Handful of Keys" and "Snowy Mornin' Blues." All three of the solo projects, while not essential, are excellent examples of Thompson's joyous playing. —*Scott Yanow*

The Butch Thompson Trio Plays Favorites / Mar. 16, 1992-Mar. 17, 1992 / Solo Art ✦✦✦✦✦

Pianist Butch Thompson has been quite consistent in his recording career, sticking to his vision of creatively interpreting pre swing New Orleans and Chicago jazz within the tradition. While most of his sets feature some obscurities, this CD with his trio (which also includes bassist Robbie Schlosser and the colorful drummer Hal Smith) sticks to warhorses but never sounds tired, overly predictable or without enthusiasm. Thompson, who overdubbed his effective clarinet on four of the 18 songs, manages to uplift such tunes as "The Charleston," "Darktown Strutters Ball," "Sweet Georgia Brown," "Tiger Rag" and "Honeysuckle Rose" without resorting to Dixieland clichés. The music therefore is both accessible and inventive, highly recommended. —*Scott Yanow*

Butch & Doc / Apr. 1994 / Daring ✦✦✦✦✦

Pianist Butch Thompson was clearly thrilled to get the chance to record a set of duets with trumpeter Doc Cheatham, who at the time was two months shy of turning 89. Cheatham, who still played with remarkable confidence for one at that advanced age (hitting some reasonable high notes), also takes a few charming vocals. Thompson proves to be an expert accompanist and his solos work well with Cheatham's style. Together they perform 11 familiar standards plus producer Mason Daring's "Too Much." Highlights include "After You've Gone," "Rosetta," "If Dreams Come True" and "I've Got a Crush on You." Delightful music. —*Scott Yanow*

Lincoln Avenue Blues / Jul. 28, 1996-Jul. 29, 1996 / Daring ✦✦✦✦✦

Butch Thompson is best-known for his interpretations of Jelly Roll Morton's music, so it is quite interesting to hear this solo tribute to Jimmy Yancey. Yancey, one of the first boogie-woogie players, had a lyrical and melodic style that was as close to blues as to jazz. Thompson recaptures Yancey's very subtle and sometimes gentle style on a variety of material; he even ends abruptly on E flat on "Jimmy's Preserve" as Yancey did on every song he recorded. This is a relaxed, bluish and soulful session (with a variety of 1920s standards alternating with Yancey songs) that could have used a stomp or two for variety but is overall quite pleasing. —*Scott Yanow*

Lucky Thompson

b. Jun. 16, 1924, Columbia, SC

Tenor Saxophone, Soprano Saxophone / Bop, Hard Bop

Lucky Thompson was one of the great tenors to emerge during the 1940s and one of the first "modern" soprano saxophonists (taking up the instrument prior to John Coltrane and around the same time as Steve Lacy), but he was always a bit overshadowed by more spectacular players. After some local gigs he moved to New York in the early '40s, playing briefly with Lionel Hampton and Don Redman in 1943 and Billy Eckstine and Lucky Millinder in 1944. During 1944-45 he gained some attention with Count Basie (where Thompson had succeeded his main influence, Don Byas). Although his large tone looked towards the swing era, Thompson's advanced improvising fit in well with bop players. He settled on the West Coast after leaving Basie, was hired as "insurance" by Dizzy Gillespie in case Charlie Parker did not show up (he recorded with both) and cut many sessions (his solo on "Just One More Chance" was a personal favorite) during his stay in Los Angeles, performing with Boyd Raeburn and the short-lived Stars of Swing. In 1947 Lucky moved to Detroit and the following year he returned to New York. He led a band regularly at the Savoy during 1951-53 and in 1954 starred on Miles Davis' famous *Walkin'* session. In 1956 Thompson was a top soloist with Stan Kenton (appearing on *Cuban Fire*) and during the next two years he cut many sessions both as a leader and as a sideman. He lived in France during two periods (1957-62 and 1968-71), started doubling on soprano and taught at Dartmouth during 1973-74. And then it all stopped. Lucky Thompson completely dropped out of the music business (despite still being in his musical prime) and, other than a few rumors, has not been heard from since; a major loss to jazz. —*Scott Yanow*

Test Pilot / Dec. 26, 1944-1950 / Swingtime ✦✦✦✦

Tenor saxophonist Lucky Thompson recorded many songs in the mid- to late '40s, particularly during the 1945-47 period when he was based in Los Angeles. This out-of-print European LP is filled with rarities; only three titles with Dinah Washington have been reissued much. Otherwise Thompson is heard in an unusual quartet (also including violinist Stuff Smith, pianist Erroll Garner and drummer George Wettling) playing the two part "Test Pilot," backing singer Estelle Edson on a practically unknown session led by rhythm guitarist Freddie Green (and featuring the young singer Sylvia Syms), jamming in Fletcher Henderson's final group (in 1950) and heading two forgotten sessions of his own. Originally released on such labels as Selmer, Black & White, Duke, Apollo (the Dinah Washington sides), Excelsior, Star Dust and Triumph, the music (which fills in the transition between swing and bop) is as valuable as it is obscure. —*Scott Yanow*

The Beginning Years / Nov. 1945-Jul. 7, 1947 / IAJRC ✦✦✦✦✦

The first CD put out by the collectors IAJRC label was a big success, a collection of some of tenor saxophonist Lucky Thompson's West Coast recordings. Thompson cut an enormous amount of sides while in Los Angeles during 1945-47, and some of the cream is on this CD. The skilled tenor (whose transitional style fell between swing and bop) is featured with ten different recording groups (many quite obscure), and among the other musicians are trumpeter Karl George, trombonist J.J. Johnson, clarinetist Rudy Rutherford, altoist Marshall Royal, pianists Bill Doggett and Dodo Marmarosa, bassists Oscar Pettiford and Charles Mingus, drummer Shadow Wilson, singers David Allyn and Ernie Andrews and the Mills Blue Rhythm Band. All of the 23 selections (which are of a consistently high quality) were formerly quite rare, making this CD a must for bop collectors. —*Scott Yanow*

Lucky Thompson and Gigi Gryce in Paris / Sep. 28, 1953-Apr. 17, 1956 / Vogue ✦✦✦✦

Tenor saxophonist Lucky Thompson recorded enough material as a leader during the first half of 1956 (mostly in Paris) to fill up 12 LPs. This CD has music from two of his rarer sessions, featuring Thompson playing 12 songs (ten of which are his originals) with a French octet that includes pianist Martial Solal and some fine sidemen; these sessions were last available as the Xanadu LP *Brown Rose*. Thompson's warm tenor is well showcased at a variety of tempos during the high-quality music. None of the songs caught on, but the performances are quite enjoyable. In addition, this CD reissue features altoist Gigi Gryce on six numbers cut in France in 1953 when he was touring with Lionel Hampton's Orchestra; those selections are from the same sessions that resulted in classic recordings by trumpeter Clifford Brown, although Brownie (who appears on one of these numbers) is not heard from here. The CD concludes with two selections from the same period featuring the young trumpeter Art Farmer in a sextet/septet with trombonist Jimmy Cleveland and altoist Anthony Ortega. Although not essential, this reissue is easily recommended to collectors of 1950s straightahead jazz. —*Scott Yanow*

☆ **Tricotism** / Jan. 24, 1956-Dec. 12, 1956 / GRP ✦✦✦✦✦

Thompson created a host of spectacular improvisations on the 16 songs on this wonderful CD reissue. It comprises two 1956 sessions; one featured Thompson heading a trio backed by bassist Oscar Pettiford and guitarist Skeeter Best, and the other has him heading either a quartet or quintet that included the great trombonist Jimmy Cleveland. Cleveland's smooth, superbly articulated phrases and statements rank alongside Thompson's gliding lines in their brilliance, and pianist Hank Jones (on three cuts) also sparkles with some marvelous solos. But Lucky Thompson is the star on this date; his elegant, yet robust and exuberant playing demonstrated again what a loss his voluntary departure from the scene constitutes. —*Ron Wynn*

Paris 1956, Vol. 1 / Feb. 22, 1956-Apr. 20, 1956 / Swing ✦✦✦✦

Lucky Thompson recorded quite a bit during his visit to France in 1956; fortunately most of the music has been reissued at one time or another. For this 1985 LP, the classic tenor is heard on side one mostly with a quintet comprising trumpeter Emmett Berry, pianist Henri Renaud, bassist Benoit Quersin and drummer Dave Pochonet. Berry has "Blues dor Frank" as a feature while Thompson is joined by just bass and drums on "Thin Ice." Side two has Thompson accompanied by a top-notch rhythm section that includes pianist Martial Solal and on three of the six numbers he is joined by fellow tenor Guy Lafitte. The emphasis throughout (except for a two-song ballad medley on side one) is on Thompson's originals which are fresh and swinging. Worth searching for. —*Scott Yanow*

Lucky Thompson / Mar. 2, 1956+Mar. 14, 1956 / Inner City ✦✦✦✦✦

This excellent but out-of-print Inner City release of material originally cut for Vogue features the great Lucky Thompson exploring a dozen standards in France with the assistance of vibraphonist Michel Hausser, pianist Martial Solal, guitarist Jean Pierre Sasson, either Pierre Michelot or Benoit Querson on bass and drummer Gerard Pochonet. A superior blowing session, Thompson makes such veteran

songs as "I Can't Give You Anything but Love," "I Cover the Waterfront," "Undecided" and "Indian Summer" sound quite fresh, alive and swinging. —*Scott Yanow*

Brown Rose / Mar. 27, 1956+Apr. 17, 1956 / Xanadu ✦✦✦✦

Taken from Lucky Thompson's very prolific period in France, this LP has a dozen selections (mostly the tenor's originals) cut at two recording sessions with a French octet. The music has since been reissued by RCA in their Vogue series, so is fortunately readily available. None of the songs became standards but Thompson is heard throughout in prime form and his backup group (which includes pianist Martial Solal) is excellent. —*Scott Yanow*

Lord Am I Ever Gonna Know / 1961 / Candid ✦✦✦✦

With the exception of one selection ("Lord, Lord, Am I Ever Gonna Know"), all of the music from this rare performance went unreleased until this 1997 CD. Thompson (who doubles evenly here on tenor and soprano) is joined by pianist Martial Solal, bassist Peter Trunk and drummer Kenny Clarke for the Paris date. The formerly lost, LP-length tapes find Thompson in prime form playing his relaxed originals. Most unusual is "Choose Your Own," which features Lucky playing unaccompanied solos, on both tenor and soprano. The CD actually opens with a spoken monologue by Thompson from March 20, 1968, describing some of his philosophy and telling the public to ignore hype and decide for themselves what music is best. Unfortunately, he would soon become so disillusioned with the music business that he would drop out altogether by the 1970s, a major loss to jazz. This fairly straightahead date is a valuable addition to Lucky Thompson's discography. —*Scott Yanow*

Happy Days / Mar. 8, 1963+Feb. 16, 1965 / Prestige ✦✦✦✦

This CD has the full contents of two of Lucky Thompson's LPs. The earlier session, since it was originally released on the Prestige subsidiary Moodsville, emphasizes ballads, as Thompson interprets eight Jerome Kern melodies (none of the obvious ones) plus his own moody original "No More." One of the first "modern" jazz musicians to start doubling on soprano (actually predating John Coltrane), Lucky Thompson displays a light but forceful tone on both soprano and tenor; his versions of "Look for the Silver Lining," "Who" and "They Didn't Believe Me" are particularly memorable. The second date was a six-song tribute to a new singer of the period, Barbra Streisand. Other than "People" (this version is harmless enough) and Thompson's "Safari," the other tunes are veteran standards, including "Happy Days Are Here Again" and a rare medium-tempo rendition of "As Time Goes By." Overall, this CD is full of excellent music by the always underrated Lucky Thompson. —*Scott Yanow*

● **Lucky Strikes** / Sep. 15, 1964 / Original Jazz Classics ✦✦✦✦✦

This CD reissue serves as a perfect introduction to the talents of the underrated saxophonist Lucky Thompson. Heard on four songs apiece on tenor and soprano (he was one of the first bop-oriented soprano players), Thompson plays two standards and six originals in a quartet with pianist Hank Jones, bassist Richard Davis and drummer Connie Kay. The playing time on this straight reissue of an earlier LP is a bit brief (just over 38 minutes), but the quality is quite high. Thompson's soprano solos in particular are quite memorable. —*Scott Yanow*

Lucky Meets Tommy / 1965 / Fresh Sound ✦✦✦✦

There are far too few Lucky Thompson records; in part because the legendary sax player had a reputation for being "difficult." These rare 1965 sessions with the great Tommy Flanagan on piano (on all but three tracks) produced 70 minutes of relaxed jazz that is a superb introduction to Thompson's tenor stylings—out of Coleman Hawkins and Don Byas—and his soft, airy sound on the soprano. —*Les Line*

Body and Soul / May 1, 1970-May 2, 1970 / Nessa ✦✦✦✦✦

Lucky Thompson, alternating between tenor and soprano, performs five originals and five standards on this well-rounded quartet set with pianist Tete Montoliu, bassist Eric Peter and drummer Peer Wyboris. Recorded in Spain (where it was originally released on a Spanish label before being put out by Nessa in 1978), these recordings find Thompson at the peak of his powers, just a few years before he permanently left jazz, robbing the music of a major voice. Highlights of this Nessa LP include "Blue 'n' Boogie," "What's New," "When Sunny Gets Blue," "I Got It Bad" and "Soul Carnival." —*Scott Yanow*

Goodbye Yesterday / 1972 / Groove Merchant ✦✦✦

During what would be the final part of his active career, Lucky Thompson recorded two records for Groove Merchant during 1972-73. On his debut for the label, Thompson switches between tenor and soprano while joined by keyboardist Cedar Walton, bassist Larry Ridley and drummer Billy Higgins. Thompson contributed all seven compositions (none of which are all that memorable) and, although he plays well enough (he never declined on records), this out-of-print LP is one of his lesser efforts. —*Scott Yanow*

I Offer You / 1973 / Groove Merchant ✦✦✦✦

After he stopped teaching in 1974, Lucky Thompson permanently dropped out of music and has been not heard from in the two decades since. On what would be his final album, Thompson (along with keyboardist Cedar Walton, bassist Sam Jones and drummer Louis Hayes) performs five mostly straightahead originals, "The Moment of Truth" and the standard "Cherokee." Thompson, switching between tenor and soprano, was still very much in his musical prime at the time of this out-of-print LP, but apparently soon became sick of the whole music business, a major loss to jazz. He plays quite well throughout the rare set. —*Scott Yanow*

Malachi Thompson

Trumpet / Avant-Garde

An excellent if underrated trumpeter, Malachi Thompson has played in free settings and recorded abstract tributes to jazz's possible founder, Buddy Bolden. Thompson grew up in Chicago, and after hearing Count Basie's Orchestra at a concert when he was 11, he persuaded his parents to get him a trumpet. By 1969, Thompson was a member of the AACM and working in diverse settings ranging from free jazz to R&B. After gaining a college degree at Governor's State University, he moved to New York in 1974. As a freelancer, Thompson worked with the Sam Wooding big band, Sam Rivers, Joe Henderson, Kalaparusha McIntyre, Jackie McLean, David Murray, and many others. He was a co-leader of Brass Proud (1975-80), an important part of Lester Bowie's Hot Trumpeter Repertory Company, and later on a member of Brass Fantasy. Thompson spent periods of time living in New York, Washington, D.C., and Vienna, Austria. Although knocked out of action for a few years by lymphoma in the late '80s, he survived the bout. In the 1990s, Thompson has headed the Freebop Band and Africa Brass, having relocated back to Chicago. An adventurous player with a strong sense of jazz's history, Malachi Thompson has led recording sessions for RA (1972 and 1981) and regularly for Delmark since the mid-1980s. —*Scott Yanow*

The Seventh Son / May 1972 / RA ✦✦

Trumpeter Malachi Thompson combines some of the innovations of the avant-garde along with dated electronics on this erratic but interesting LP. Thompson gets in a few good solos although most of his supporting cast is much more anonymous. This low-budget release has good intentions even if the results are mixed. —*Scott Yanow*

Spirit / 1983 / Delmark ✦✦✦✦

This is a varied advanced jazz set by trumpeter Malachi Thompson. Joined by tenor saxophonist Carter Jefferson, pianist Albert Dailey (in one of his final recordings) and a solid rhythm section, Thompson performs music that he accurately calls "Freebop." In addition to "I Remember Clifford," the strong band plays five originals that cover a lot of different moods; Leon Thomas ("No More Hard Times") and Arnae Burton take a vocal apiece that add to the set's variety. Worth exploring. —*Scott Yanow*

The Jaz Life / Jun. 30, 1991 / Delmark ✦✦✦✦

● **Lift Every Voice** / Aug. 24, 1992-Aug. 25, 1992 / Delmark ✦✦✦✦✦

Trumpeter Malachi Thompson merges hard bop, free, African rhythms and gospel stylings on this release. *Lift Every Voice* is reminiscent of what drummer Max Roach did with his regular band in collaboration with the J.C. White gospel singers in the 1970s (his album was also called *Lift Every Voice*), but Thompson has added some intriguing personnel and rhythmic elements. He uses four trumpets and trombonists, plus a bassist, drummer, two percussionists and eight singers on the title track. Thompson's ringing solos, crisp lines, declarative themes and bursts are also backed by his Freebop band. Thompson deserves high praise not just for trying something different, but succeeding. —*Ron Wynn*

New Standards / Apr. 20, 1993-Apr. 22, 1993 / Delmark ✦✦✦✦

47th Street / Apr. 20, 1993-Sep. 14, 1996 / Delmark ✦✦✦✦

Sir Charles Thompson

b. Mar. 12, 1918, Springfield, OH
Piano, Organ / Bop, Swing

The elegantly nicknamed Sir Charles was one of the few musicians associated with swing who was able to make a graceful, wholehearted transition to bop at the time the revolution was happening. His piano style is light-fingered and spare in a witty, inventive, Basie-descended bop manner, and he was able to adapt it effectively to the organ. Thompson's first instrument was the violin, but the piano beckoned when he was a teenager, and he started working with territory bands in the Midwest in the late 1930s. He briefly joined Lionel Hampton in 1940, but left in order to work with small groups and contribute arrangements to the Basie, Hampton, Fletcher Henderson, Jimmy Dorsey and other bands. While working in New York's 52nd St. clubs during World War II, he began to pick up on the begin-

nings of bop. In 1944-45, Thompson played in the Coleman Hawkins/Howard McGhee band, journeying to Hollywood with them to record several terrific swing/bop sides for Capitol (now on Hollywood Stampede) and also his lively tune "Ladies' Lullaby" for Asch. So thoroughly had Thompson absorbed the language and ethos of bop that he was able to write one of the quintessential classics of the idiom, "Robbins Nest," which became a hit for Sir Charles' next employer, Illinois Jacquet, and inspired a haunting, pathbreaking Gil Evans arrangement for Claude Thornhill in 1947.

Thompson recorded a number of small group albums for Vanguard in the 1950s, two more for Columbia in 1959 and 1960, and appeared as a sideman for Buck Clayton and Jimmy Rushing, but spent much of the '50s freelancing as an organist. He toured the US, Canada and Puerto Rico in the 1960s leading small groups, as well as Europe with Clayton. Following a bout of ill health, he returned to action in 1975. His early bop sides for Apollo, including some with Hawkins and Charlie Parker, are available on a Delmark reissue, *Takin' Off.* —*Richard S. Ginell*

● **Takin' Off** / Sep. 4, 1945-Dec. 29, 1947 / Delmark ✦✦✦✦✦

Pianist Sir Charles Thompson's first three sessions as a leader (all originally cut for Apollo) are reissued in full on this valuable Delmark CD. Actually, as good as Thompson plays (his main influence was always Count Basie), it is not surprising that he is often overshadowed by his all-star sidemen. The first date (four titles) finds him heading a septet that also includes altoist Charlie Parker, trumpeter Buck Clayton and tenor saxophonist Dexter Gordon. Thompson is also featured in a septet with trumpeter Joe Newman and baritonist Leo Parker that resulted in four songs and three alternate takes plus a ten-piece group with both Newman and Taft Jordan on trumpets and altoist Pete Brown; this CD not only has the original two titles from the latter date but two previously unissued songs and a pair of alternates. With the exception of Charlie Parker and Dexter Gordon, the music is generally swing-oriented with basic originals and concise (but colorful) solos. Highly recommended. —*Scott Yanow*

Sir Charles Thompson and the Swing Organ / 1960 / Columbia ✦✦✦

Pianist Sir Charles Thompson made his debut on organ for this out-of-print Columbia LP. Teamed with clarinetist Rudy Rutherford, tenorman Percy France, bassist Aaron Bell and drummer J.C. Heard, Thompson displays a light pre-Jimmy Smith touch on a set of swing standards and his originals. On some of the songs, Thompson plays piano with one hand and organ with the other, but it is the organ that is generally emphasized. Pleasing music but not that essential. —*Scott Yanow*

Portrait of a Piano / Mar. 18, 1984 / Sackville ✦✦✦✦

This Sackville release has pianist Sir Charles Thompson's first recordings in six years and his most recent to date. 66 at the time, Thompson had been playing solo piano in small bars for years, so he sounds quite comfortable performing these 11 unaccompanied solos. Other than his famous "Robbins Nest," two of his other originals and Bill Butler's "Portrait of a Piano," Thompson mostly sticks to swing standards. The results are generally quite relaxed and lightly swinging, with highlights including "Ain't Misbehavin'," "Happy Boogie" and a lyrical rendition of "Spring Can Really Hang You Up the Most." —*Scott Yanow*

Claude Thornhill

b. Aug. 10, 1909, Terre Haute, IN, d. Jul. 1, 1965, New York, NY
Arranger, Piano, Leader / Swing, Cool

Although some of his recordings were on the periphery of jazz and his orchestra was at its most popular in the early '40s, Claude Thornhill's main importance to jazz was the influence that his arrangements and orchestra's sound had on cool jazz of the late '40s. After studying at a music conservatory and playing piano in bands based in the Midwest, Thornhill worked for Paul Whiteman and Benny Goodman in 1934 and for Ray Noble's American band of 1935-36 (for whom he also arranged). He appeared on some Billie Holiday records, and his arrangement of "Loch Lomond" was a big hit for Maxine Sullivan. Although he recorded as a leader in 1937, it was in 1940 that Thornhill put together his own orchestra. The band, featuring long tones played by horns that de-emphasized vibrato, had an unusual sound that sometimes accompanied the leader's tinkling piano. The instrumentation included two French horns and a tuba; sometimes all six of the reeds played clarinets in unison. Although classified by some as a sweet rather than swing band (since the group played a lot of ballads), with the addition in 1941 of Gil Evans as one of the arrangers, the recordings of Thornhill's orchestra attracted a lot of attention in the jazz world. After a period in the military (1942-45), Thornhill put together a new orchestra, retaining the services of Gil Evans (and sometimes using Gerry Mulligan charts as well) and featuring such soloists as altoist Lee Konitz, clarinetist Danny Polo and trumpeter Red Rodney. Some of Evans' boppish arrangements for the group were classic, and the Miles Davis Nonet of 1948 was based on many of the cool-toned principles of the Thornhill big band. However by then the pianist's glory days were over. He continued leading bands on a part-time basis up until his death, but Claude Thornhill was largely neglected and forgotten during his final 15 years. —*Scott Yanow*

● **Tapestries** / Jun. 14, 1937-Dec. 17, 1947 / Affinity ✦✦✦✦✦

This double-LP is the best Claude Thornhill collection thus far, since little of his music has yet appeared on CD. After his theme song (the haunting "Snowfall") and a 1937 recording of "Stop! You're Breaking My Heart" with singer Maxine Sullivan, Thornhill's 1941-42 and 1946-47 orchestras are well featured on this set. There is an emphasis on Gil Evans' classic arrangements, and the 32 selections do give one a well-rounded picture of how unique and versatile the Thornhill ensemble was during its prime years. Highlights include "Portrait of a Guinea Farm," "Autumn Nocturne," "There's a Small Hotel," "A Sunday Kind of Love," two versions of "Thrivin' on a Riff," "Robbins Nest," "Donna Lee" and "Yardbird Suite." This definitive set deserves to be reissued in full on CD. —*Scott Yanow*

The Best of the Big Bands / Mar. 10, 1941-Dec. 17, 1947 / Columbia Special Products ✦✦✦

Most of the 16 selections on this Claude Thornhill CD are quite memorable, but the lack of recording dates and a personnel listing are inexcusable. The programming, which skips around between the 1941-42 and 1946-47 Thornhill orchestras rather than proceeding chronologically, is also rather random. Still, with so few of Thornhill's recordings on CD, this disc is worth picking up. Highlights include "Snowfall," "Sunday Kind of Love," "There's a Small Hotel," "Anthropology" and "Buster's Last Stand." —*Scott Yanow*

The Memorable Claude Thornhill / Mar. 10, 1941-Dec. 17, 1947 / Columbia ✦✦✦✦

Although only containing 20 selections, this out-of-print two-LP set (which unfortunately does not give a personnel listing or the recording dates, although the music is programmed largely in chronological order) gives one a good retrospective of the music of Claude Thornhill's Orchestra. There is one error: "Donna Lee" is absent and in its place is a quartet track featuring the leader on piano. Otherwise the high points include "Snowfall," "Portrait of a Guinea Farm," "There's a Small Hotel," "Anthropology" and "Robbins Nest." Among the key soloists are clarinetists Irving Fazola and Danny Polo, altoist Lee Konitz and trumpeter Red Rodney. —*Scott Yanow*

Claude Thornhill & His Orchestra (1941+1947) / Jul. 8, 1941-Jun. 18, 1947 / Circle ✦✦✦

The 1941 and 1947 Claude Thornhill orchestras are featured on this LP of radio transcriptions. The emphasis is on dance music ("Sorta Kinda" is the only Gil Evans arrangement) with vocals by Dick Harding, Fran Warren and Buddy Hughes. Eight of the twelve selections are from 1941 and include "Snowfall," "Le Papillon" and "Rustle of Spring"; the 1947 band is in good form on "Sorta Kinda." But this release overall is not too essential. —*Scott Yanow*

On Stage 1946-1947 / 1946-1947 / Monmouth Evergreen ✦✦✦✦

This valuable LP (which has not yet been reissued on CD) has live performances by Claude Thornhill's finest orchestra, the band he led during 1946-47. With vocals by Fran Warren and Buddy Hughes and charts contributed by Gil Evans, Bill Borden (who produced the album), Charlie Naylor and Thornhill, the dozen selections give one a good picture of how the Thornhill Orchestra often sounded. This version of "La Paloma" is nearly six minutes long, while the other selections are much more concise. Highlights include "La Paloma," "Arab Dance," "I Get the Blues When It Rains," "Sorta Kinda" and "Early Autumn." —*Scott Yanow*

In Disco Order, Vol. 8 / Sep. 4, 1947-Nov. 7, 1947 / Ajazz ✦✦✦✦

The Joyce label in the 1970s reissued on LPs the complete output of various swing bands. *Vol. 8* in their Claude Thornhill series covers a two-month period. There are eight big-band tracks including six Gil Evans arrangements (such as "Sorta Kinda," "Robbins Nest" and "Donna Lee") and featuring such top players as trumpeter Red Rodney, clarinetist Danny Polo, altoist Lee Konitz and the tenor of Mickey Folus. The final six selections are quite rare, quartet numbers performed by pianist Thornhill (who had a unique style), guitarist Barry Galbraith, bassist Joe Shulman and drummer Bill Exner. Until this music is reissued in full on CD, the hard-to-find Joyce series is worth searching for. —*Scott Yanow*

The Uncollected Claude Thornhill & His Orchestra / 1947 / Hindsight ✦✦✦✦

The 1947 Claude Thornhill Orchestra is well featured on this excellent Hindsight LP, which contains previously unreleased radio transcriptions. At the time trumpeter Red Rodney, clarinetist Danny Polo, altoist Lee Konitz and tenor saxophonist Mickey Folus were in the big band along with two French horns and the tuba of Bill Barber. With arrangements provided by Thornhill, Gil Evans and Gerry Mulligan among others, the 16-track program (which includes a three-song ballad medley) contains many memorable selections including "Robbins Nest," "'Deed I Do," "Donna Lee," "Polka Dots and Moonbeams" and "Anthropology." Recommended. —*Scott Yanow*

● **1948 Transcription Performance** / Apr. 1948-Oct. 1948 / Hep ✦✦✦✦✦

This CD has the only existing performances of the Claude Thornhill Orchestra from 1948, a year when a recording strike kept most bands off of records. With many charts by Gil Evans or Gerry Mulligan, the Thornhill big band was often quite bop-oriented and featured fine solos from clarinetist Danny Polo, altoist Lee Konitz and the tenor of Mickey Folus; a few numbers also include Brew Moore on tenor, baritonist Gerry Mulligan and trumpeter Gene Roland. In addition there are some vocals from the Snowflakes (a vocal quintet) and Joe Derise. The highly enjoyable and somewhat historical CD is easily recommended to bop collectors and listeners who are interested in the later Claude Thornhill Orchestra. —*Scott Yanow*

In Disco Order, Vol. 10 / Jan. 5, 1949-Jun. 9, 1949 / Ajazz ✦✦✦

The tenth LP in Joyce/Ajaz's Claude Thornhill series finds the bandleader after Gil Evans and Lee Konitz departed playing some more conservative and commercial music than he had earlier. A remake of "Autumn Nocturne" is a near classic and it is interesting to hear these later versions of "Where or When," "There's a Small Hotel" and Thornhill's theme "Snowfall." But although such sidemen pass through the band as trumpeter Gene Roland, clarinetist Tony Scott and altoist Hal McKusick, the music overall (which has quite a few vocals by the Snowflakes, Art Brown, Russ McIntyre and Nancy Clayton) is rarely all that memorable. —*Scott Yanow*

In Disco Order, Vol. 11 / Nov. 1, 1949-Apr. 10, 1950 / Ajazz ✦✦

The eleventh LP in a 1970s Claude Thornhill collector's series put out by Ajaz/Joyce continues the chronological reissuance of the bandleader's recordings, covering part of his later period. Actually by late 1949, Thornhill had largely abandoned his earlier innovations (there was only one French horn in the group and the tuba was gone), discarding bebop in favor of revivalist swing and pop tunes. Certainly few listeners will remember such Russ McIntyre vocals as "Iowa Indian Fight Song" and "In the Garden of Forget-Me-Nots." Best are the six Gershwin songs recorded during the Jan. 17, 1950 session, but overall this album is of more historical than musical interest. —*Scott Yanow*

Henry Threadgill

b. Feb. 15, 1944, Chicago, IL

Alto Saxophone, Flute, Composer / Avant-Garde

Although his music can be somewhat forbidding, Henry Threadgill has been one of the most respected members of the avant-garde for the past 20 years. As an altoist and flutist, he has long had an original tone, but it is his work as an innovative composer that is most impressive. He played percussion in marching bands while a child, learned baritone and clarinet in high school, studied at the American Conservatory of Music and played gospel music for traveling evangelists. In 1962-63 Threadgill was a part of Richard Abrams' Experimental Band and he became a member of the AACM. After a period in the Army, he worked in the house band at a Chicago blues club and recorded with Abrams. In 1971 Threadgill first teamed up with Steve McCall and Fred Hopkins in a trio and in 1975 the group became known as Air. Threadgill recorded and performed extensively with Air (and its successor New Air) and later led several unique ensembles including X75 (which had four bassists), his Sextett and Very Very Circus. His signing to Sony in 1994 was a big surprise, for Threadgill's compositions and improvisations are far from accessible; happily his Sony recordings show no sign of being watered-down. —*Scott Yanow*

X-75, Vol. 1 / Jan. 13, 1979 / Novus ✦✦✦

Four bassists predominate (Hopkins, Rufus Reid, Smith, and Leonard Jones) in this pre-sextet recording. Amina Myers (p) and Joseph Jarmen (reeds) also show. Unrestrained freedom and beauty. —*Michael G. Nastos*

When Was That? / 1982 / About Time ✦✦✦✦✦

The title track is a riot on record. Some extraordinary improvising and spontaneous combustion going on here. Landmark recording. —*Michael G. Nastos*

Just the Facts and Pass the Bucket / 1983 / About Time ✦✦✦✦✦

Sextet (actually seven pieces). Dynamite open-ended compositions, especially the surly "Black Blues" and the determined "Man Called Trinity Deliverance." Features Olu Dara, Pheeroan AkLaff, John Betsch and bassist Fred Hopkins. All pungently original material. —*Michael G. Nastos*

Subject to Change / Dec. 1984 / About Time ✦✦✦

Both blistering ensemble work and dynamic solos. —*Ron Wynn*

You Know the Number / Oct. 12, 1986-Oct. 13, 1986 / Novus ✦✦✦✦

New members include Frank Lacy, Rasul Siddik, and Reggie Nicholson. Retains a two-drummer backline. "Those Who Eat Cookies" is a hot one. —*Michael G. Nastos*

Easily Slip into Another World / Sep. 20, 1987 / Novus ✦✦✦✦

● **Rag, Bush and All** / Dec. 1988 / Novus ◆◆◆◆

This CD from altoist Henry Threadgill is a perfect mixture of improvisation and composition, hanging onto devices of the past while creating new music. Some of the ensembles (which match Threadgill with trumpeter Ted Daniels, bass trombonist Bill Lowe, cellist Diedre Murray, bassist Fred Hopkins and both Newman Baker and Reggie Nicholson on drums) recall Ornette Coleman's Free Jazz with the cello-bass interplay inspired by the one-time team of Scott LaFaro and Charlie Haden. The organized horn parts and the riffs behind the lead voices are quite original and sometimes more interesting than the solos themselves. Of the four songs, "Off The Rag" at first dispenses with the melody quickly, but the theme constantly pops up in surprising places. "The Devil" is highlighted by Murray's doubletime cello runs behind Threadgill's alto while "Gift" contrasts colorful percussion with solemn long tones from the ensemble. "Sweet Holy Rag" has several sections including a pretty classical-like melody, a danceable rumba, a drum feature and a fairly violent trumpet solo. However, the more one describes this music, the more seems to be left out. Highly recommended to open-eared listeners. —*Scott Yanow*

Spirit of Nuff...Nuff / Nov. 19, 1990-Nov. 21, 1990 / Black Saint ◆◆◆

Song out of My Trees / Aug. 1993 / Black Saint ◆◆◆

Even longtime Threadgill fans may be surprised at the direction and content on his most recent session. The five tunes include three pieces where Threadgill is absent, and one ("Over The River Club") is a nine-minute-plus opus dominated by three guitars colliding, intersecting, and dueling. The title track showcases Threadgill's blues and gospel roots, with some wonderful organ by Amina Claudine Myers. Only "Crea" and "Gateway" are similar to past Threadgill works, with "Crea" featuring the unusual sound of Ted Daniel on hunting horns. Even a champion of the unorthodox like Threadgill may have some people scratching their heads after they hear this, but it's a signal that he'll never settle for doing what's expected. —*Ron Wynn*

Too Much Sugar for a Dime / 1993 / Axiom ◆◆◆◆

Imagine writing for an instrumentation of two electric guitars, two tubas, French horn, drums and Henry Threadgill's alto. Threadgill was up to the challenge and his four avant-garde originals utilize the odd combination of tones to great advantage. Two additional songs feature Threadgill, just one tuba, drums, a few exotic instruments and three strings to create some particularly unusual music. It's for the open-eared listener only. —*Scott Yanow*

Carry the Day / 1994 / Columbia ◆◆◆◆◆

It seems that every five years or so Columbia signs a token avant-garde musician. Arthur Blythe and Tim Berne emerged from their experiences as major-label artists relatively unscathed and, on evidence of Henry Threadgill's somewhat forbidding Columbia debut, it would not be surprising if the altoist survived his stint with his priorities straight. There is certainly nothing commercial or watered down about this CD. The music ranges from "Come Carry the Day" (which builds from a group chart to some very dense ensembles) and Threadgill's Dolphyish alto on "Between Orchids," to a couple of very odd vocals and the intense group improv "Jenkins Boys." The group sound (with its accordions, tubas and Mark Taylor's French horn) is attractive in its own way even if the originals do little more than set mysterious moods. This unique music takes several listens to absorb, and even then it still might be somewhat incomprehensible. At 37 minutes, it is all over too soon. —*Scott Yanow*

Where's Your Cup / Aug. 1996 / Columbia ◆◆◆◆

The Three Sounds

f. 1957, **db.** 1970

Group / Soul Jazz, Groove, Hard Bop

The Three Sounds were one of the most popular artists on Blue Note Records during the late '50s and '60s, thanks to their nimble, swinging, blues-inflected mainstream jazz. Since their records sounded interchangeable and their warm, friendly jazz was instantly accessible, many critics dismissed the group at the time as lounge-jazz, but in the '90s, critical consensus agreed that the group's leader, pianist Gene Harris, was an accomplished, unique stylist whose very ease of playing disguised his technical skill. Similarly, his colleagues, bassist Andrew Simpkins and drummer Bill Dowdy, were a deft, capable rhythm section that kept the group in an appealing, bluesy groove. That groove was so appealing that the Three Sounds maintained a large fan following into the late '60s. During the group's prime period—from their 1958 debut for Blue Note to the departure of Dowdy in 1967—the Three Sounds cut an enormous number of records. Many records hit the shelves, while others stayed in the vaults, to be issued at a later date. Throughout it all, the trio's sound remained essentially the same, with no real dip in quality until the group began to splinter in the late '60s.

Gene Harris was at the center of the Three Sounds throughout its entire existence. A native of Benton Harbor, MI, he began playing piano as a child, performing in public at the age of six. He soon became distracted by boxing and sports, but he continued to perform music, occasionally in a trio with drummer Bill Dowdy. After they graduated from high school in 1951, both Harris and Dowdy joined the Army and were assigned to different units. However, both men were discharged in 1954, and after they left the Army, they began pursuing different musical careers. Harris played with a variety of bands throughout the South and Midwest, while Dowdy moved to Chicago and played with a number of blues and jazz bands. Two years later, both musicians happened to settle in South Bend, IN, and decided to form a band called the Four Sounds with bassist Andrew Simpkins and a tenor saxophonist. After running through a number of tenor saxophonists unsuccessfully, the three musicians decided to jettison the horn from their group and become the Three Sounds. For the next two years, the group played regularly at Midwest venues, particularly in Ohio. They played as a trio, also supporting such soloists as Lester Young and Sonny Stitt. During this time, Horace Silver became a fan of the group and recommended them to Alfred Lion, the head of Blue Note. Despite the good word, the group remained unsigned. They toured with Stitt and relocated to Washington, D.C., where they worked as a trio and as a rhythm section for touring soloists; during this time, they played with such musicians as Miles Davis and Kenny Burrell. In the fall of 1958, they moved to New York to work with Stitt. Shortly after they moved to the city, they signed to Blue Note, in addition to supporting Nat Adderley on a Riverside session.

The Three Sounds cut their first album for Blue Note in September of 1958. That record, *Introducing the Three Sounds*, became an unexpected success among record buyers, and the group's live performances earned fans like Horace Silver, Sonny Stitt, Miles Davis and Cannonball Adderley, even if critics tended to dismiss the group. In particular, a *Down Beat* reviewer panned the album, but that didn't stop the public from buying the record, which soon became one of the most popular jazz records of its years. Blue Note had the band re-enter the studio in February of 1959 to cut their second album, *Bottoms Up*. It was the third of a total of 17 sessions at Rudy Van Gelder's studio (*Introducing* had taken two sessions to complete). At one point, Harris estimated that the group has released 35 albums worth of material, with many left in the vaults. During their first stint at Blue Note, they released the following, in addition to *Introducing* and *Bottoms Up*: *Good Deal, Feelin' Good, Moods, Here We Come, It Just Got to Be, Hey There!, Out of This World,* and *Black Orchid*. The Three Sounds also supported such Blue Note artists as Stanley Turrentine and Lou Donaldson on several recording dates.

The Three Sounds continued successfully on Blue Note until 1962, when they switched labels shortly after recording *Black Orchid*. They cut one album, *Blue Genes*, for Verve, then moved to Mercury, where they made three records between December 1962 and 1964. Later in 1964, the trio signed to Limelight, where they made three records. In October of 1966, the group returned to Blue Note and recorded *Vibrations*. Shortly after the sessions, drummer Bill Dowdy left the group and was replaced by Donald Bailey, who made his first recorded appearance with the group on 1967's *Live at the Lighthouse*. That album was followed in 1968 by *Coldwater Flat*, an album that found the trio augmenting their sound with a string section. By the time the group returned to the studio in September 1968 to cut *Elegant Soul*, Bailey was replaced by Carl Burnett. *Elegant Soul* continued the pattern of smooth, string-heavy productions, as did 1969's *Soul Symphony*. By the time the group made *Soul Symphony*, bassist Andrew Simpkins had left the trio and was replaced by Henry Franklin.

Soul Symphony, for most intents and purposes, was the last record the Three Sounds made. They continued to perform live, and one of those concerts is documented on *Live at the It Club*, a 1970 show which was released in 1995. Later in 1970, Monk Montgomery replaced Franklin, but this version of the Three Sounds never recorded. Instead, Harris embarked on a solo career in 1971, releasing *Gene Harris & the Three Sounds*, which also featured Burnett and electric bassist Luther Hughes, along with a number of session men. From that point on, Harris concentrated on his solo career, recording for Blue Note over the next six years. Once his contract expired, Harris retired to Boise, ID, where he worked as a musical director at a hotel. Eventually, he returned to music after bassist Ray Brown convinced the pianist to play on an album for Pablo. Harris resumed his solo career in 1985, signing with Concord Jazz. His new albums, combined with CD reissues of classic Three Sounds dates, prompted a positive critical re-evaluation of his music, and he maintained a strong reputation into the late '90s. —*Stephen Thomas Erlewine*

★ **Introducing the Three Sounds** / Sep. 16, 1958+Sep. 18, 1958 / Blue Note ◆◆◆◆◆

What's remarkable about *Introducing the Three Sounds* is how the trio's lightly swinging sound arrived fully intact. From the basis of this album, it sounds as if pianist Gene Harris, bassist Andrew Simpkins and drummer William Dowdy have been playing together for years. There's empathetic, nearly intuitive interplay between the three musicians, and Harris' deft style already sounds mature and entirely distinctive. There's no question that this music is easy to listen to, but dismissing it because of that would be wrong—there's genuine style in their light touch and in Harris' bluesy compositions. The Three Sounds never really deviated from the sound they established on *Introducing,* but that's one of the things that is so remarkable—they were fully formed on their very first album. Even if it was a peak, it wasn't the only peak in their career. They would often match the heights of this album, but this debut remains a shining jewel in their catalog, and the way to become acquainted with their sound. [The CD reissue of *Introducing the Three Sounds* contains the five outtakes plus the alternate take of "Goin' Home" that originally comprised the Japanese album, *Introducing the Three Sounds, Vol. 2.*] —*Stephen Thomas Erlewine*

Introducing the Three Sounds, Vol. 2 / Sep. 16, 1958+Sep. 18, 1958 / Blue Note ✦✦✦✦✦

During the '70s, the Japanese division of Blue Note began issuing previously unreleased sessions that had sat in the vaults for decades. Most of these records comprised entirely unheard sessions. Others, like *Introducing the Three Sounds, Vol. 2,* comprised outtakes and alternate takes from beloved Blue Note albums. *Vol. 2* contains five songs that were recorded during the *Introducing* sessions but remained unreleased, as well as an alternate take of "Goin' Home." Stylistically, this music is identical to the initial release (or any other Three Sounds album, for that matter), and it should please any fan of the trio, but there's little reason to seek this record out, since all of the material was released as bonus tracks on the CD reissue of *Introducing the Three Sounds.* —*Stephen Thomas Erlewine*

● **The Best of the Three Sounds** / 1958-1970 / Blue Note ✦✦✦✦✦

The Best of the Three Sounds is a good overview of the trio's original stint at Blue Note. A handful of songs on this 13-song collection date from their late-'60s return to the label, when they played everything a little funkier than they did in their earlier days, but the bulk of the disc comprises their classic late-'50s and early-'60s records. Since all of the Three Sounds' albums sound quite similar and are of a consistently high quality, a novice could pick up any album and have a satisfactory introduction, but this nevertheless does a good job of picking up highlights like "Bobby," "Willow Weep for Me," "On Green Dolphin Street," "Poinciana," "Stompin' at the Savoy" and "At Last." It's a nice introduction to one of the most consistently entertaining and accessible artists on Blue Note's roster. —*Stephen Thomas Erlewine*

Bottoms Up / Feb. 11, 1959 / Blue Note ✦✦✦✦

The second record by the Three Sounds (which, like too many of their recordings, has yet to be reissued on CD in the US) features the increasingly popular group in prime form. Pianist Gene Harris, bassist Andy Simpkins and drummer Bill Dowdy are in top form performing their brand of funky jazz, which left plenty of room for inventive solos along with the percolating grooves. On this set, the trio plays seven standards (including "Besame Mucho," "Love Walked In" and "I Could Write a Book"), plus the original "Jinne Lou." Well worth searching for. —*Scott Yanow*

Good Deal / May 20, 1959 / Blue Note ✦✦✦

Good Deal is a typically fine record from the Three Sounds, who were beginning to hit their stride when this session was recorded in May of 1959. Like most of their records, it's laidback—even when the group works a swinging tempo, there's a sense of ease that keeps the mood friendly, relaxed and mellow. Balancing standards like "Satin Doll," "Soft Winds" and "That's All" with bop ("Robbins Nest"), calypso ("St. Thomas") and originals, the Three Sounds cover a lot of stylistic territory, putting their distinctive stamp on each song. It's very accessible, pleasant soul-jazz and mainstream hard bop, but Gene Harris' masterful technique means that *Good Deal* rewards close listening as well. —*Stephen Thomas Erlewine*

Standards / Oct. 10, 1959-Jun. 28, 1962 / Blue Note ✦✦✦✦

Released in 1998, *Standards* comprises 12 previously unreleased recordings the Three Sounds made on several different sessions in 1959 and 1962. All of the songs are familiar—"Makin' Whoopee," "Cry Me a River," "Witchcraft," "Stay as Sweet As You Are," "The Best Things in Life Are Free," "Red Sails in the Sunset," "Good Night Ladies"—and are given the familiar Three Sounds treatment, and the results are typically tasteful and delightful. —*Stephen Thomas Erlewine*

Feelin' Good / Jun. 28, 1960 / Blue Note ✦✦✦✦✦

An appropriate title for an utterly charming set from the Three Sounds. The trio works familiar territory on *Feelin' Good,* playing a set of swinging hard bop and classy soul-jazz, but there's a definite spark in the air. Working from a diverse set of standards, originals, contemporary jazz and blues, the Three Sounds created a cheerful, uptempo record. Its very ease is deceptive—the music is so accessible and entertaining, it's easy to overlook the sheer musical mastery of the group, which performs at something of a peak on this record. Gene Harris sounds better than ever, turning in an elegant interpretation of "It Could Happen to You," but he's just as able to inject "When I Fall in Love" with unexpectedly vigorous swing and

make Monk's "Straight, No Chaser" a foot-tapping, danceable delight. Bassist Andrew Simpkins and drummer Bill Dowdy follow Harris with graceful, imperceptible ease. It captures the Three Sounds at a peak, which means *Feelin' Good* is an excellent example of early soul-jazz. —*Stephen Thomas Erlewine*

Moods / Jun. 28, 1960 / Blue Note ✦✦✦✦

The Three Sounds open their signature sound a bit on the romantic *Moods.* They retain the same light touch that made their early albums so enjoyable, but they add more textures to the mix. Light Latin rhythms permeate *Moods,* from the inventive reworking of Cole Porter's "Love for Sale" to Harris' original "Tammy's Breeze." Like its predecessor, *Feelin' Good,* this record has a bluesy, soulful streak to its personality, as evidenced by the mellow take on "On Green Dolphin Street," the hep swing of "Loose Walk" and the infectious cover of Ellington's "I'm Beginning to See the Light." Occasionally, the Three Sounds play it a little too cool—while the slow, relaxed "Things Ain't What They Used to Be" manages to be engaging, "Li'l Darlin'" slows down to a crawl—but on the whole, *Moods* is an endearing collection of appealing mainstream jazz. —*Stephen Thomas Erlewine*

Here We Come / Dec. 13, 1960-Dec. 14, 1960 / Blue Note ✦✦✦

Here We Come is a typically classy and entertaining collection from the Three Sounds. The group stretches out on these pop standards and Gene Harris originals a little more than normal, which gives the pianist an opportunity to flaunt his underrated chops. Stylistically, nothing has changed—this is still light, deftly swinging mainstream jazz—but with songs like "Summertime" and "Our Love Is Here to Stay," *Here We Come* has a bit of a romantic feeling, which is certainly welcome. Of course, that's balanced by the jumping title track and "Poinciana," among others, but overall the album has a warm, relaxed vibe that makes the romanticism particularly welcoming. —*Stephen Thomas Erlewine*

It Just Got to Be / Dec. 13, 1960-Dec. 14, 1960 / Blue Note ✦✦✦

The material that comprises *It Just Got to Be* was recorded during the same sessions as *Here We Come,* and like that album, this record has its share of romantic standards, including "Stella By Starlight" and "The Nearness of You." *It Just Got to Be* also captures the Three Sounds in the mood to stretch out and improvise a little (ironically, two of the three original compositions are the shortest songs on the album). The performances throughout the record are predictably swinging and enjoyable, even if they find the trio taking no stylistic chances. That lack of adventure doesn't matter, though—the Three Sounds excel at making unpretentious, unabashedly enjoyable mainstream jazz, and there's something endearing about their ability to produce a body of work of consistently high quality. —*Stephen Thomas Erlewine*

Hey There! / Aug. 13, 1961 / Blue Note ✦✦✦

Hey There! finds the Three Sounds keeping themselves slightly in check, turning in snappy, concise versions of jazz and pop standards, as well as jumping originals from Gene Harris. The shorter song lengths mean that the trio emphasizes melody even more than usual, but that's hardly a bad thing. Each Three Sounds record thrives on laidback swing and deft melodic flourishes. By bringing these elements to the forefront, they highlight their accessibility, but that results in a thoroughly enjoyable record. Their technical prowess is better heard on records where they stretch out a bit more, but *Hey There!* is another artist record from the most consistently entertaining artist on Blue Note's roster. —*Stephen Thomas Erlewine*

Babe's Blues / Aug. 31, 1961-Mar. 8, 1962 / Blue Note ✦✦✦✦✦

The accessible and enjoyable material on this Blue Note album was not released for the first time until 1986. The popular Three Sounds (pianist Gene Harris, bassist Andy Simpkins and drummer Bill Dowdy) perform mostly standards on the album, infusing their swinging music with funk, soul and sincere feeling. Highlights include Randy Weston's "Babe's Blues," "Work Song" and "Shiny Stockings." —*Scott Yanow*

Out of This World / Feb. 4, 1962-Feb. 8, 1962 / Blue Note ✦✦✦✦

Out of This World relies less on originals than before, concentrating on standards that sound startlingly fresh. It's the loose, flexible groove that's the key. Simpkins and Dowdy keep things on track, while Gene Harris plays—he can be nimble, he can pound, but he keeps the music flowing at a nice, easy pace. He has a good sense of the groove, and he stays within the groove even as he plays a lot of notes; it's truly an indivdual style. Despite the R&B-flavored arrangements on "Girl of My Dreams" and the swinging, gospel-inflected "Sanctified Sue," *Out of This World* is a particularly light and breezy record from the Three Sounds. They're just as comfortable stretching out with the groove as they are with keeping things short, simple and concise—either way, it's thoroughly enjoyable music. But no matter how easy the group is to enjoy, they have true style, as Harris' bluesy flourishes and the rhythm section's supple support illustrate. It's hard to sound this light and easy, and the Three Sounds pull it off with grace. —*Stephen Thomas Erlewine*

Music Map

Trumpet (including cornetists)

Pioneer
Buddy Bolden (formed first band in 1895)

Early New Orleans "Kings"
Freddie Keppard	Manuel Perez
Buddy Petit	Chris Kelly
King Oliver	

1920-25
Nick LaRocca	Paul Mares
Phil Napoleon	Johnny Dunn
Joe Smith	

Biggest Influence and Most Important Innovator
Louis Armstrong

1926-30
Bix Beiderbecke	Red Nichols
Tommy Ladnier	George Mitchell
Jabbo Smith	Bob Shoffner
Leonard Davis	Lee Collins
Bobby Stark	Ed Allen
Red Allen	Natty Dominique
Reuben "River" Reeves	

The Ellington Trumpet Tradition
Bubber Miley	Louis Metcalf
Arthur Whetsol	Freddie Jenkins
Cootie Williams	Rex Stewart
Ray Nance	Cat Anderson
Taft Jordan	Al Killian
Shorty Baker	Clark Terry
Willie Cook	Bill Berry
Barry Lee Hall	

Swing Era
Roy Eldridge	Bunny Berigan
Charlie Shavers	Hot Lips Page
Buck Clayton	Shad Collins
Emmett Berry	Harry James
Ziggy Elman	Erskine Hawkins
Dud Bascomb	Bill Coleman
Valaida Snow	Nat Gonella
Phillippe Brun	Herman Autrey
Benny Carter	Jonah Jones
Frankie Newton	Sy Oliver
Snooky Young	Harry "Sweets" Edison

Bebop Innovator
Dizzy Gillespie

Bop Era
Joe Guy	Freddie Webster
Sonny Berman	Howard McGhee
Fats Navarro	

Innovator in Cool, Hard Bop, Modal, Avant-Garde and Fusion!
Miles Davis

New Orleans Jazz to Dixieland and Mainstream
Jimmy McPartland	Muggsy Spanier
Louis Prima	Sidney DeParis
Wingy Manone	Yank Lawson
Billy Butterfield	Bobby Hackett
Max Kaminsky	Wild Bill Davison
Johnny Windhurst	Lu Watters
Charlie Teagarden	Bob Scobey
Bunk Johnson	Mutt Carey
Pete Daily	Ken Colyer
Humphrey Lyttelton	Alex Welsh
Johnny Wiggs	Doc Evans
Sharkey Bonano	Punch Miller
Thomas Jefferson	Andrew Blakeney
Teddy Buckner	Dick Cathcart
Al Hirt	Kenny Ball
Ruby Braff	Warren Vache
Glenn Zottola	Tom Pletcher
Bent Persson	Dick Sudhaltar
Randy Sandke	Peter Ecklund
Jim Cullum, Jr.	
Alvin Alcorn (with Kid Ory)	
Danny Alguire (with Firehouse Five Plus Two)	
Frank Assunto (with Dukes of Dixieland)	

1950s
Shorty Rogers	Conte Candoli
Chet Baker	Jon Eardley
Don Fagerquist	Tony Fruscella
Art Farmer	Red Rodney
Idrees Sulieman	Joe Newman
Thad Jones	Joe Wilder
Ray Copeland	Joe Gordon

–Continued on next page–

Music Map

Trumpet (including cornetists)
—continued

Hard Bop

Clifford Brown	Lee Morgan
Freddie Hubbard	Woody Shaw
Bill Hardman	Donald Byrd
Blue Mitchell	Kenny Dorham
Sam Noto	Nat Adderley
Tommy Turrentine	Carmell Jones
Johnny Coles	Oscar Brashear
Tom Harrell	Franco Ambrosetti
Dusko Goykovic	Tim Hagans
Valery Ponomarev	Claudio Roditi
Michael Mossman	Brian Lynch

Avant-Garde

Booker Little	Don Ellis
Don Cherry	Bill Dixon
Donald Ayler	Lester Bowie
Bobby Bradford	Leo Smith
Barbara Donald	Kenny Wheeler
Baikida Carroll	Olu Dara
Hugh Ragin	Enrico Rava
Herb Robertson	Tomasz Stanko
Manfred Schoof	Dave Douglas
Malachi Thompson	Ahmed Abdullah
Hannibal Marvin Peterson	Paul Smoker

Greatest 90-Year-Old Trumpeter
Doc Cheatham

Young Lions

Wynton Marsalis	Terence Blanchard
Roy Hargrove	Wallace Roney
Philip Harper	Marlon Jordan
Ryan Kisor	Nicholas Payton

Other Fine Trumpeters of the 1980s-90s

Marcus Belgrave	Randy Brecker
Ted Curson	Cecil Bridgewater
Rolf Ericson	Jon Faddis
Maynard Ferguson	Jerry Gonzalez
Eddie Henderson	Terumasa Hino
Steve Huffstetter	Tiger Okoshi
Chuck Mangione	James Morrison
Bobby Shew	Arturo Sandoval
Jack Sheldon	Don Sickler
Lew Soloff	Marvin Stamm
Ira Sullivan	Byron Stripling
Charles Tolliver	Jack Walrath
Marcus Printup	Ingrid Jensen

Black Orchid / Mar. 7, 1962-Mar. 8, 1962 / Blue Note ✦✦✦✦
Between 1958 and 1962, the Three Sounds were one of the most prolific artists on Blue Note, recording over ten albums worth of material during those four years. During all that time, the group never changed their style much, concentrating on lightly swinging, lightly soulful mainstream jazz that balanced jazz and pop standards with bluesy originals. As time progressed, they veered closer to soul-jazz, but each of their records sounded quite similiar and were equally satisfying. *Black Orchid*, their last album for Blue Note in the early '60s (they would rejoin the label in another four years), was no exception to the rule. It displays their knack for deftly swinging uptempo numbers, light blues and sensitive standards. If anything, it swings a little harder and is a little more soulful than some of its predecessors. Again, the very fact that the music is instantly enjoyable and accessible makes some jazz critics write the Three Sounds off, but Gene Harris, Andrew Simpkins and Bill Dowdy are genuine stylists with prodigious technique. It's difficult to make music this consistently enjoyable, and the Three Sounds illustrate that they have the knack once again on *Black Orchid*. —*Stephen Thomas Erlewine*

Blue Genes / Oct. 13, 1962 / Verve ✦✦✦

Jazz on Broadway / Dec. 14, 1962-Dec. 15, 1962 / Mercury ✦✦✦

Some Like It Modern / Jul. 17, 1963-Jul. 18, 1963 / Mercury ✦✦✦

Live at the Living Room / 1964 / Mercury ✦✦✦
The Three Sounds (pianist Gene Harris, bassist Andy Simpkins and drummer Bill Dowdy) were quite popular in the early to mid-1960s and recorded many albums, but surprisingly few have been reissued on CD yet. This Mercury LP finds the trio mostly sticking to bluesy material, plus a couple of Oscar Peterson tunes ("Blues for Big Scotia" and the joyous "Hymn to Freedom"). Whether it be "Glory of Love," "Willow Weep for Me" or even "Mississippi Mud," every song sounds a bit like the blues on this hard-to-find set. —*Scott Yanow*

Three Moods / 1964 / Limelight ✦✦

Beautiful Friendship / 1965 / Limelight ✦✦

Today's Sounds / 1966 / Limelight ✦✦✦

Vibrations / 1966 / Blue Note ✦✦✦
The Three Sounds' return to Blue Note wasn't a celebrated event—no exact date even exists for these sessions, although in all likelihood it was recorded somewhere in October 1966. Even if the event was poorly documented, it was fairly important for the label, because it signaled that they were backing away from the adventurous hard bop and free jazz they had been recording, and were considering concentrating on the commercially oriented, mainstream soul-jazz the Three Sounds pioneered. Since *Vibrations* was recorded in 1966, not 1959, there were differences in the trio's approach. Pianist Gene Harris tried organ on a few tracks, and the group tackled contemporary R&B hits ("Let's Go Get Stoned," "Fever," "Yeh Yeh") as well as MOR pop ("It Was a Very Good Year"). The subtle tweaking makes no real difference in the group's sound, since on previous records they took the same approach (only without an organ), but *Vibrations* doesn't make the first rank of Three Sounds records because the performances are a little stiff, and the infrequent organ sounds a little awkward. There are certainly plenty of good things here—and there are more good than bad things—but *Vibrations* primarily offers the kind of pleasures that are only meaningful to dedicated fans. —*Stephen Thomas Erlewine*

Live at the Lighthouse / Jul. 1967 / Blue Note ✦✦✦✦
Shortly after the *Vibrations* sessions, the Three Sounds had their first major personnel shakeup when William Dowdy left the group. Donald Bailey replaced the drummer, and the group played a number of live dates over the course of 1967. During that summer, their concerts at the famed Los Angeles venue the Lighthouse were recorded and released as *Live at the Lighthouse*. The selection of nine Three Sounds staples gives the group a chance to stretch out and prove that they could survive without Dowdy. Not only do they prove that they can carry on without him, they flourish. The music on *Live at the Lighthouse* is hotter than some of their studio recordings, pulsating with energy and good feelings, demonstrating

that they had worked out the problems that hampered *Vibrations*. It's their finest set since *Black Orchid*. —*Stephen Thomas Erlewine*

Coldwater Flat / Apr. 11, 1968 / Blue Note ✦✦✦
Live at the Lighthouse captured the Three Sounds at their jazziest, but *Coldwater Flat*, the first studio session pianist Gene Harris and bassist Andrew Simpkins recorded with new drummer Donald Bailey, takes a different path. For this date, the group decided to emphasize its pop side, recording the record with the lush Oliver Nelson Orchestra and choosing to cover such pop hits as "The Look of Love," "Last Train to Clarksville" and, inexplicably, the theme to "Star Trek." One of the primary attractions of the Three Sounds' sound was its simplicity and their ability to find so much variation within the trio format. That magic is somewhat lost within the orchestra, which tends to overwhelm the trio. More than anything, that is what prevents *Coldwater Flat* from ranking among the group's finest efforts, but the glossy production has its appealing moments as well, and the record does function well as pleasant background music, even if it veers too close to easy listening to be true jazz. —*Stephen Thomas Erlewine*

Elegant Soul / Sep. 19, 1968-Sep. 20, 1968 / Blue Note ✦✦
Elegant Soul continues the pattern the Three Sounds began on *Coldwater Flat*, finding the trio moving away from mainstream jazz and closer to easy-listening pop. Once again, the trio is augmented with strings, this time conducted by Monk Higgins. This time around, the strings aren't quite as obtrusive as before, but the songs, which are divided between originals and covers of hits like "Harper Valley PTA," aren't as memorable or melodic as those on *Coldwater Flat*. Still, *Elegant Soul* has its moments, particularly in the ease of the trio's playing—listening to their interaction, you'd never know that Carl Burnett had just replaced drummer Donald Bailey, who only appeared on two of the group's albums. For longtime fans, the pop aspirations make it a frustrating record, but for listeners looking for a smooth, easy-listening pop-jazz album, *Elegant Soul* isn't a bad choice. —*Stephen Thomas Erlewine*

Soul Symphony / Sep. 1969 / Blue Note ✦✦
Soul Symphony, for most intents and purposes, is a Gene Harris solo album, even though it's credited to the Three Sounds. Two of the trio's founding members, drummer Bill Dowdy and bassist Andrew Simpkins, had left the group by the time this session was recorded in September 1969. Instead of starting a solo career, Harris hired bassist Henry Franklin and drummer Carl Burnett as replacements, and embarked on his most ambitious project to date. As the title of *Soul Symphony* suggests, the album is a song cycle about soul and urban life. At their core, the Three Sounds sound funkier than ever before, and that's funky according to the contemporary late '60s definition, since the elastic beats suggest the influence of Sly Stone and James Brown. But those funky rhythms are drowned out by an overbearing orchestra and bizarrely schlocky vocal arrangements. Evidently, the strings and chorus were added because the record was a "symphony," but their presence makes all of the proceedings sound awkward and not at all like the Three Sounds. After listening to this record, it's no surprise that Harris folded the trio after this session to pursue a solo career. —*Stephen Thomas Erlewine*

Live at the "It Club" / 1970 / Blue Note ✦✦✦
Recorded in 1970 but not released until 1996, *Live at the "It Club"* shows the Three Sounds pulling out funky, gritty rhythms out of their basic bluesy hard-bop sound. The group's funky influences are most noticeable in the rhythm section of drummer Carl Burnette and bassist Henry Franklin, who had been playing with Harris for only a short time when this set was recorded. The rhythm section pushes Harris, making the music loose and swinging—the groove matters more than anything on the album. Occasionally, the energy of the Three Sounds lags, but *Live at the "It Club"* is an enjoyable piece of grooving soul-jazz. —*Stephen Thomas Erlewine*

Bobby Timmons

b. Dec. 19, 1935, Philadelphia, PA, **d.** Mar. 1, 1974, New York, NY
Piano, Composer / Hard Bop, Soul Jazz, Groove
Bobby Timmons became so famous for the gospel and funky blues clichés in his solos and compositions that his skills as a Bud Powell-inspired bebop player have been long forgotten. After emerging from the Philadelphia jazz scene, Timmons worked with Kenny Dorham (1956), Chet Baker, Sonny Stitt and the Maynard Ferguson Big Band. He was partly responsible for the commercial success of both Art Blakey's Jazz Messengers and Cannonball Adderley's Quintet. For Blakey (who he was with during 1958-59), Timmons wrote the classic "Moanin'" and, after joining Adderley in 1959, his song "This Here" (followed later by "Dat Dere") became a big hit; it is little wonder that Adderley was distressed when Timmons in 1960 decided to return to the Jazz Messengers. "Dat Dere" particularly caught on when Oscar Brown, Jr. wrote and recorded lyrics that colorfully depicted his curious son. Timmons, who was already recording as a leader for Riverside, soon formed his own trio but was never able to gain the commercial success that his former bosses

enjoyed. Stereotyped as a funky pianist (although an influence on many players including Les McCann, Ramsey Lewis and much later on Benny Green), Timmons' career gradually declined. He continued working until his death at age 38 from cirrhosis of the liver. —*Scott Yanow*

★ **This Here Is Bobby Timmons** / Jan. 13, 1960-Jan. 14, 1960 / Original Jazz Classics ✦✦✦✦✦
This is a classic Riverside set that has been reissued on CD in the Original Jazz Classics series. Pianist Bobby Timmons by early 1960 had already had successful stints with Art Blakey (where he contributed "Moanin'") and Cannonball Adderley (writing "This Here" and "Dat Dere"). For his first recording as a leader, Timmons (whose "funky" style was beginning to become very influential) performs those three hits along with his own "Joy Ride" and five standards in a trio with bassist Sam Jones and drummer Jimmy Cobb. Always more than just a soul jazz pianist, Timmons (who effectively takes "Lush Life" unaccompanied) became a bit stereotyped later in his career, but at this early stage was at the peak of his creativity. Essential music. —*Scott Yanow*

Soul Time / Aug. 12, 1960+Aug. 17, 1960 / Original Jazz Classics ✦✦✦✦✦
Pianist Bobby Timmons, best known for his sanctified and funky playing and composing, is mostly heard in a straightahead vein on this CD reissue of a Riverside session. Timmons' four originals ("So Tired" is most memorable) alternate with three standards and are interpreted by a quartet with trumpeter Blue Mitchell, bassist Sam Jones and drummer Art Blakey. The swinging music is well-played, making this a good example of Bobby Timmons playing in a boppish (as opposed to funky) setting. —*Scott Yanow*

● **Moanin'** / Aug. 12, 1960-Sep. 10, 1963 / Milestone ✦✦✦✦✦
Compilation of five different albums 1960-1963. Great collection and collectable. —*Michael G. Nastos*

Easy Does It / Mar. 13, 1961 / Original Jazz Classics ✦✦✦✦
Pianist Bobby Timmons, who became famous for his funky originals and soulful playing, mostly sticks to more bop-oriented jazz on this trio set with bassist Sam Jones and drummer Jimmy Cobb. He provides three originals (none of which really caught on) and is in excellent form on the five standards with highlights including "Old Devil Moon," "I Thought About You" and "Groovin' High." The Riverside CD reissue shows that Timmons was a bit more versatile than his stereotype; in any case the music is excellent. —*Scott Yanow*

In Person / Oct. 1, 1961 / Original Jazz Classics ✦✦✦✦
For this excellent live set (recorded at the Village Vanguard), pianist Bobby Timmons, bassist Ron Carter and drummer Albert "Tootie" Heath perform a couple of the pianist's originals ("So Tired" and "Popsy") along with some standards. The funky bop-oriented music is quite enjoyable and was very popular during the early '60s. The CD reissue adds previously unreleased versions of "They Didn't Believe Me" and "Dat Dere" to the original program. Easily recommended. —*Scott Yanow*

Born to Be Blue / Sep. 1963 / Original Jazz Classics ✦✦✦✦
Throughout his career, Bobby Timmons was typecast as a soulful and blues-oriented pianist due to his hits ("Moanin'," "This Here" and "Dat Dere"). But as he shows on this 1963 trio date (with either Sam Jones or Ron Carter on bass and drummer Connie Kay), Timmons was actually a well-rounded player when inspired. The repertoire on his CD ranges from bop to spirituals, from three diverse originals to "Born to Be Blue." This is excellent music but unfortunately Timmons would not grow much musically after this period. His CD is worth picking up. —*Scott Yanow*

From the Bottom / 1964 / Riverside ✦✦✦
Pianist Bobby Timmons final recording for Riverside (cut right before the label went broke) was not released for the first time until this 1970 LP and has been out of print ever since. Bobby Timmons, a highly influential funk pianist, is in generally excellent form. Most of the songs feature his trio with bassist Sam Jones and drummer Jimmy Cobb, but a ballad medley of "You're Blase" and "Bewitched" finds Timmons unaccompanied, and he surprisingly switches to organ on his old hit "Moanin'" (his only recorded appearance ever on that instrument) and vibes on "Quiet Nights" and "Someone to Watch over Me." This fine effort is long overdue to be reissued on CD. —*Scott Yanow*

Live at the Connecticut Jazz Party / 1964 / Chiaroscuro ✦✦✦
This somewhat obscure live recording, which has appeared on Chiaroscuro and Early Bird LPs but not yet on CD, features pianist Bobby Timmons, altoist Sonny Red, bassist Sam Jones and drummer Mickey Roker really stretching out on five standards including a 12-minute rendition of "Here's That Rainy Day" and a nearly 12-minute "Now's the Time." The playing has plenty of spirit although the recording quality is not state-of-the-art, making this an LP more for Bobby Timmons and Sonny Red completists than for general collectors. —*Scott Yanow*

Workin' Out / Oct. 21, 1964+Jan. 20, 1966 / Prestige ✦✦✦✦✦
This CD reissues the contents of two of pianist Bobby Timmons' most advanced recordings of the 1960s. For an example of how the popular pianist had continued to evolve after his early funk hits, listen to his often-bitonal solo on "Bags' Groove" from 1964. That session features Timmons in a quartet with vibraphonist Johnny Lytle, bassist Keter Betts and drummer William "Peppy" Hinnant, and is filled with subtle surprises. The second recording is even more interesting, for Timmons is teamed with tenor saxophonist Wayne Shorter, bassist Ron Carter and drummer Jimmy Cobb in 1966. The immediately recognizable Shorter in particular plays very well (this version of his "Tom Thumb" is its earliest recording) and the very modern playing of Carter pushes Timmons to really stretch himself. Both of these generally overlooked sessions (even Shorter's best fans may not know about his collaboration with Timmons) were formerly rare and are quite adventurous, making this a highly recommended acquisition that falls somewhere between hard bop and the early avant-garde. —*Scott Yanow*

The Soul Man / Jan. 20, 1966 / Prestige ✦✦✦
With Wayne Shorter on tenor sax. Plenty of funk, blues, and soul-jazz, plus great piano. —*Ron Wynn*

Soul Food / Sep. 30, 1966+Oct. 14, 1966 / Prestige ✦✦✦
Ron Carter on bass and Wayne Shorter on sax. —*Michael Erlewine*

Cal Tjader

b. Jul. 16, 1925, St. Louis, MO, **d.** May 5, 1982, Manila, Philippines
Vibes, Leader / Cool, Latin Jazz, Afro-Cuban Jazz, Post-Bop
Cal Tjader was undoubtedly the most famous non-Latino leader of Latin jazz bands, an extraordinary distinction. From the 1950s until his death, he was practically the point man between the worlds of Latin jazz and mainstream bop; his light, rhythmic, joyous vibraphone manner could comfortably embrace both styles. His numerous recordings for Fantasy and Verve and long-standing presence in the San Francisco Bay Area eventually had a profound influence upon Carlos Santana, and thus Latin rock. He also played drums and bongos, the latter most notably on the George Shearing Quintet's puckishly titled "Rap Your Troubles in Drums," and would occasionally sit in on piano as well.

Tjader studied music and education at San Francisco State College before hooking up with fellow Bay Area resident Dave Brubeck as the drummer in the Brubeck Trio from 1949 to 1951. He then worked with Alvino Rey, led his own group, and in 1953, joined George Shearing's then-hugely-popular quintet as a vibraphonist and percussionist. It was in Shearing's band that Tjader's love affair with Latin music began, ignited by Shearing's bassist Al McKibbon, nurtured by contact with Willie Bobo, Mongo Santamaria and Armando Peraza, and galvanized by the '50s mambo craze. When he left Shearing the following year, Tjader promptly formed his own band that emphasized the Latin element yet also played mainstream jazz. Bobo and Santamaria eventually joined Tjader's band as sidemen and Vince Guaraldi served for awhile as pianist and contributor to the bandbook ("Ginza," "Thinking of You, MJQ"). Tjader recorded a long series of mostly Latin jazz albums for Fantasy from the mid-'50s through the early '60s, switching to Verve in 1961, where under Creed Taylor's aegis, he expanded his stylistic palette and was teamed with artists like Lalo Schifrin, Anita O'Day, Kenny Burrell and Donald Byrd. Along the way, Tjader managed to score a minor hit in 1965 with "Soul Sauce," a reworking of Dizzy Gillespie/Chano Pozo's "Guachi Guaro" which Tjader had previously cut for Fantasy. Tjader returned to Fantasy in the 1970s, then moved over to the new Concord Picante label in 1979, where he remained until his death. —*Richard S. Ginell*

Los Ritmos Calientes / May 6, 1954-Oct. 11, 1957 / Fantasy ✦✦✦
Vibraphonist Cal Tjader's 1950s recordings for Fantasy did a great deal to popularize Latin jazz and solidify its innovations. This CD has the complete contents of the two LPs *Ritmo Caliente* and *Mas Ritmo Caliente*. With such fine sidemen as flutist Jerome Richardson, pianists Richard Wyands, Eddie Cano, Manuel Duran and Vince Guaraldi, bassists Al McKibbon, Bobby Rodriguez and Eugene Wright, and quite a few percussionists (most notably Armando Peraza and, on three songs, Mongo Santamaria and Willie Bobo), the fusion of bop and Latin music results in some exciting playing. In addition to group originals, tunes such as Ray Bryant's "Cubano Chant," "Mambo Inn," "Bernie's Tune," "Perdido" and even "Big Noise From Winnetka" receive lively treatment. —*Scott Yanow*

Tjader Plays Mambo / Aug. 1954-Sep. 1954 / Original Jazz Classics ✦✦✦✦
Having finished his tenure with George Shearing in 1954, a thoroughly Latin-inoculated Cal Tjader took off on his own, recording several short slices of infectious Latin jazz, from which a dozen were selected for this album. Many of the selections are standards retrofitted with percolating Latin rhythms, cut and shaped to fit the old three-minute limit of 45 or 78 RPM singles. Tjader's crystalline vibes are teamed with a San Francisco Latin percussion section that lays down the grooves crisply and succinctly, with an occasional emulation of the more laidback Shear-

ing Latin sound ("East of the Sun"). Elsewhere, Cal experiments with a hot four-man trumpet section on four of the tracks, the best of which is a rhumba version of "Fascinating Rhythm." The earliest Tjader-led recording of "Guachi Guaro" (later known as "Soul Sauce") is also included here. These seminal tracks helped launch the Cal Tjader Latin jazz style, and they still sound fresher than many other such historical landmarks. —*Richard S. Ginell*

Tjader Plays Tjazz / Dec. 4, 1954 / Fantasy ✦✦✦✦✦
In a change of pace, for this out-of-print LP vibraphonist Cal Tjader recorded cool-toned bop without a Latin rhythm section. Half of the ten songs (mostly jazz standards) feature Tjader switching to drums (his original instrument) in a quartet also including the obscure trombonist Bob Collins, guitarist Eddie Duran and bassist Al McKibbon. Tjader is back on vibes for the quintet selections with tenor saxophonist Brew Moore, pianist Sonny Clark, bassist Eugene Wright and drummer Bobby White. He sounds right at home in both formats and the swinging quintet numbers in particular are a good reason to search for this valuable album, which hopefully will be reissued on CD eventually. —*Scott Yanow*

Latin Kick / Nov. 1956 / Original Jazz Classics ✦✦✦✦
Cal Tjader's era-defining mixture of Afro-Cuban rhythms and mainstream jazz solos undergoes a bit of a horizontal expansion in these 1956 sessions. The tracks are often longer than on previous albums, finally taking advantage of the logistics of the LP, and as a result, both the Latin and jazz elements benefit. Tenor saxophonist Brew Moore gets extended chances to blow in an easy-grooving Getz-like manner on several tracks, and on "I Love Paris," Luis Miranda (congas) and Bayardo Velarde (timbales) engage in some spirited percussion battles over the vamping of the brothers Duran (Manuel on piano and Carlos on bass). Everything cooks in a bright yet disciplined manner, and Tjader's elliptical, swinging vibes preside genially over the ensemble. —*Richard S. Ginell*

★ **Black Orchid** / 1956-1959 / Original Jazz Classics ✦✦✦✦
This CD has all of the music originally on the two LPs *Cal Tjader Goes Latin* and *The Cal Tjader Quintet*. Since each album had two sessions apiece, the CD does a fine job of giving one a sampling of the influential vibraphonist's popular Latin jazz groups of the era. Among the key sideman are flutist Paul Horn, Jose "Chombo" Silva on tenor, pianists Lonnie Hewitt, Vince Guaraldi and Manuel Duran, and Mongo Santamaria and Willie Bobo on percussion. The music (a mixture of Latinized standards and newer originals) is quite appealing, showing why this infectious blending of bop with Latin rhythms has always been one of the most accessible styles of jazz. —*Scott Yanow*

Jazz at the Blackhawk / Jan. 20, 1957 / Original Jazz Classics ✦✦✦✦
Latin jazz collectors note: the title emphatically is *Jazz at the Blackhawk*, and even the most determined listener will not find an iota of Cal Tjader's explorations of Latin rhythms here. In its place, we get a sturdy set of bop-flavored workouts by Tjader's expert quartet, recorded live in San Francisco's famous long-defunct nightspot. Tjader himself often sounds like Milt Jackson as he handles the mallets fluidly through a set of standards, a pair of originals by himself and his wife, and—appropriately enough—a witty Baroque-like tune by his pianist Vince Guaraldi called "Thinking of You, MJQ." Eugene "The Senator" Wright (bass) and Al Torre (piano) make up the bop rhythm section, and as long as you know what you're getting, a good time can be had. —*Richard S. Ginell*

The Cal Tjader-Stan Getz Sextet / Feb. 8, 1958 / Original Jazz Classics ✦✦✦✦✦
An amazing ad-hoc session, thrown together in a San Francisco studio with now-legendary personnel from two different groups. The lineup says it all—a meeting of the Latin jazz maestro and the future champion of Brazilian jazz, plus, from Tjader's group, Vince Guaraldi on piano and guitarist Eddie Duran, and from Getz's band, the then-unknown teenager Scott LaFaro on bass and Billy Higgins on drums. A moment for the history books is an 11-minute workout on Guaraldi's pentatonic souvenir of Tokyo, "Ginza Samba," where the fast-samba theme finds Getz blowing to a Brazilian rhythm four years before "Desafinado." The jamming, though, is in a straightahead bebop groove where Getz's eloquence unfolds with almost unearthly ease. The rest of the album alternates between lyric ballads and solid, though non-Latin, swinging where Tjader, Guaraldi and Duran graft onto the great Getz rhythm section like they've been playing together for decades (check out the funky combustion on "Crow's Nest"). Collectors' note: when Getz became a bossa nova star, this album was reissued in 1963 as *Stan Getz with Cal Tjader* with a different set of liner notes and remains available on LP and cassette in this form. —*Richard S. Ginell*

Cal Tjader's Latin Concert / Sep. 1958 / Original Jazz Classics ✦✦✦✦✦
This CD reissue gives one a fairly good sampling of vibraphonist Cal Tjader's influential Latin-jazz of the 1950s. With pianist Vince Guaraldi, bassist Al McKibbon, Willie Bobo on timbales and drums and the congas of Mongo Santamaria, Tjader's impressive unit performs four of his catchy originals and two by Santam-

aria in addition to Latinized versions of "The Continental" and Ray Bryant's "Cubano Chant." This highly rhythmic music is difficult to dislike. — *Scott Yanow*

★ **Monterey Concerts** / Apr. 20, 1959 / Prestige ✦✦✦✦✦

This CD (which reissues all of the music from the two LP's *Concert by the Sea* and *Vol. 2*) is the definitive early Cal Tjader album and one of the high points of his career. For a Carmel concert that was considered a preview concert for the 1959 Monterey Jazz Festival, Tjader was teamed up with flutist and altoist Paul Horn, pianist Lonnie Hewitt, bassist Al McKibbon, Willie Bobo (on drums and timbales) and percussionist Mongo Santamaria. Their renditions of Latinized jazz tunes along with a few Latin originals practically define the idiom. Highlights include "Doxy," one of the earliest versions of Santamaria's "Afro Blue" (predating John Coltrane's famous rendition by four years), "Let Me or Leave Me" and "A Night in Tunisia." Essential music for everyone's Latin-jazz collection. — *Scott Yanow*

☆ **Night at the Blackhawk** / 1959 / Original Jazz Classics ✦✦✦✦✦

Recording during a long holiday season gig at San Francisco's Blackhawk club, Tjader patched together a superb program split between straightahead jazz and Afro-Cuban workouts. At the time, Tjader had both Willie Bobo and Mongo Santamaria in his rhythm section; Bobo handles the trap drums during the bop numbers, while the Latin tunes find Willie and Mongo creating even more heat on the timbales and congas. Pianist Vince Guaraldi swings like a madman on "A Night in Tunisia" (though the piano is out of tune), comping and soloing elsewhere with his usual light-hearted assurance, if not the individuality that he would later bring to his own music. For this gig, Tjader adds the Cuban tenor saxophonist Jose "Chombo" Silva, who strikes the right husky Ike Quebec tone in "Blue and Sentimental" and elsewhere had been clearly listening to lots of Stan Getz. The Blackhawk was breaking in some excellent new stereo recording equipment at the time of this gig; hence the clear, sharp sound. This album is still in print on LP and cassette, but a CD issue ought to be placed in the pipeline. — *Richard S. Ginell*

West Side Story / Nov. 1960 / Fantasy ✦✦✦

This out-of-print LP is a real obscurity. During a period when there were many jazz versions of scores from films and plays, vibraphonist Cal Tjader and arranger Clare Fischer teamed up for a dozen themes from the show including "Maria," "America," "Tonight" and "I Feel Pretty." Fischer (who plays piano on the album) utilized a large string orchestra along with Tjader's Afro-Cuban group, but overall the music is a touch bland and not as adventurous as one might hope. — *Scott Yanow*

Latino / 1960 / Fantasy ✦✦✦✦✦

Vibraphonist Cal Tjader is heard leading five different groups throughout this CD, but the identities of the flutists, bassists and pianists are less important than knowing that Tjader, Willie Bobo (on drums and timbales) and the great conga player Mongo Santamaria are on every selection. The music really cooks with torrid percussion, inspired ensembles and occasional solos from the sidemen (who sometimes include pianists Lonnie Hewitt or Vince Guaraldi, bassist Al McKibbon and flutist Paul Horn). Highlights include Latinized versions of "Key Largo" and "September Song," "A Night in Tunisia," "The Continental" and a definitive version of Santamaria's "Afro Blue." This is Latin-jazz at its finest. — *Scott Yanow*

Concert on the Campus / 1960 / Original Jazz Classics ✦✦✦✦

Vibraphonist Cal Tjader expertly balances between cool jazz and Latin music on this fine live concert, reissued as an LP (but not yet a CD) in the Original Jazz Classics series. Utilizing two soon-to-be-famous percussionists (Willie Bobo and Mongo Santamaria) plus pianist Lonnie Hewitt and bassist Eddie Coleman, Tjader is in top form throughout the spirited set. Highlights include "Cuban Fantasy" (which has an exciting Bobo timbale solo), "Love for Sale" and "S.S. Groove." — *Scott Yanow*

Jazz Round Midnight / Aug. 28, 1961-Sep. 19, 1967 / Verve ✦✦

Jazz Round Midnight is a pleasant 16-track sampler of some of the most laid back and mellow tracks Cal Tjader recorded for Verve. Although there are some wonderful songs on the compilation, it is only useful for beginners, since the cut-and-paste nature of the collection will infuriate purists and serious jazz listeners. However, for neophytes, it's a nice introduction, even if it is a little bit too low-key. — *Stephen Thomas Erlewine*

Talkin' Verve: Roots of Acid Jazz / Aug. 28, 1961-Sep. 19, 1967 / Verve ✦✦✦

In apparent response to the sampling of old Latin jazz records by hip-hop artists, Verve raided its Cal Tjader archive to come up with this fiercely grooving collection drawn from nine of his Verve albums. For all of producer Creed Taylor's '60s penchant for fashioning two- to four-minute cuts aimed at airplay, he allowed Tjader's groups considerable room to stretch out on several of the tracks included here, particularly on the live "Los Bandidos" and the hypnotic collaboration with pianist Eddie Palmieri, "Picadillo." More importantly, Tjader's records with Taylor were more varied in texture than his earlier discs, venturing now and then from

his solid Afro-Cuban base into Brazilian rhythms, soul, big-band backings, and '60s pop touches. Among the best cuts included here are "Sambo Do Sueno"—which has a killer bossa/Afro-Cuban rhythm stoked by Grady Tate, Armando Peraza and Ray Barretto working in terrific symmetry—Peraza's fast, hard-swinging "Maramoor Mambo," and Horace Silver's "Tokyo Blues," as spearheaded by Lalo Schifrin's driving big band. — *Richard S. Ginell*

Several Shades of Jade/Breeze from the East / Apr. 23, 1963-Nov. 26, 1963 / Verve ✦✦✦✦

Prodded by producer Creed Taylor, Cal Tjader turned momentarily away from pure Latin jazz to explore some polystylistic fusions of East and West on a pair of 1963 Verve albums. The first, *Several Shades of Jade*, finds Tjader in the intriguing company of Lalo Schifrin, who provides some searching, delicate, challenging, and yes, grooving compositions and arrangements with an emphasis on Oriental scales and things, but who also is eager to mix in other idioms, including Tjader's beloved Latin jazz. One is, as usual, often reminded of Schifrin's film music cues, but that is a sign of a strong sonic personality—it's Schifrin, not any old film composer, that we recognize, and Tjader solos fluidly and colorfully over the Argentinian's shifting big-band backdrops. CD annotator Paul de Barros pans *Breeze from the East* in unusually brutal terms—give Verve credit; they didn't flinch—but really, it's not half as bad as advertised, though some of the tourist-view Orientalisms and thwacking mid-'60s electric guitars remind one of a Peter Sellers comedy set in Hong Kong. Besides, when left some room on these AM airplay-length tracks, Cal plays as splendidly as ever. Obviously, this is not going to be a basic Cal Tjader album, but aficionados will want to hear him in these unusual, sometimes bizarre settings. — *Richard S. Ginell*

Compact Jazz / Jan. 28, 1963-Feb. 11, 1966 / Verve ✦✦✦

This Cal Tjader anthology from 1989 isn't as thoroughgoing as *Talkin' Verve*, as it only draws from three of his Verve albums, with the lion's share (ten of the twelve tracks, five apiece) coming from 1963's *Sona Libre* and 1966's *Soul Burst*. Nor does it quite reflect the diversity of the recordings that Cal made with then-Verve producer Creed Taylor. Nevertheless, you do get some sizzle in these selections, which include such burners as "Samba Do Sueno," the tough Cuban-style drumming of "Descarga Cubana," the easygoing guajira "Soul Burst," and the spare, subtle groove of "It Didn't End." Throughout, it is instructive to hear pianists Chick Corea and Clare Fischer, who would go on to establish two distinctly different reputations fairly far away from salsa, comping away quite competently in a Latin rhythm section (though Chick may have the upper hand in the swing department). — *Richard S. Ginell*

Soul Sauce / Nov. 19, 1964-Nov. 20, 1964 / Verve ✦✦✦✦✦

One of Tjader's most influential '60s releases with Willie Bobo, Donald Byrd and Kenny Burrell. — *Ron Wynn*

El Sonid Nuevo (The New Soul Sound) / May 24, 1966-May 26, 1966 / Verve ✦✦✦

This Verve CD reissues the popular collaboration between vibraphonist Cal Tjader and pianist Eddie Palmieri (who provided the arrangements) titled *El Sonido Nuevo*, along with six other songs taken from a pair of Tjader's other Verve albums. Despite the claims of greatness expressed in the liners ("a landmark in the history of Latin jazz"), much of the music is actually quite lightweight although enjoyable enough, and the easy-listening melodies and accessible rhythms hold on to one's interest. Despite the changing personnel, Tjader is generally the lead voice, and he is in fine form even if the overall results are not all that memorable or unique. — *Scott Yanow*

Plugs In / Feb. 20, 1969-Feb. 21, 1969 / DCC ✦✦✦

The mostly obscure material (other than "Nica's Dream"), the audiophile reissue CD's title, and the time period may make one think that this is an overtly commercial release from vibraphonist Cal Tjader. But, although he utilizes the electric piano of Al Zulaica and electric bassist Jim McCabe (in addition to Armando Peraza and John Rae on percussion), Cal Tjader's music on the "Live at the Lighthouse" sessions is actually not all that different from his usual infectious brand of Latin jazz. The ensembles swing; there are plenty of heated rhythms, and the melodies are embraced with enthusiasm. The brief playing time (33 minutes) is a minus, and few surprises occur, but the music is enjoyable. — *Scott Yanow*

Primo / 1970 / Original Jazz Classics ✦✦✦✦

This CD brings back one of Cal Tjader's best late-period recordings and finds the vibraphonist adapting his 1950s Latin jazz concept to the 1970s without losing any vitality. Tjader is joined by four horns, the legendary keyboardist Charlie Palmieri, electric bassist Bobby Rodriguez, and six percussionists; Tito Puente (who plays timbales on Mario Bauza's "Tanga") and Palmieri provided the heated arrangements. A previously unreleased alternate take of "Bang Bang" is added to the CD reissue. Highly recommended to collectors of Latin jazz. — *Scott Yanow*

Descarga / 1971-1972 / Fantasy ✦✦✦
Descarga is a merger of two albums recorded near the beginning of the Seventies—the fascinating studio session *Agua Dulce* and the self-explanatory *Live at the Funky Quarters*. Having not yet lost his yen for adventure from the Verve days, Tjader neatly integrates Al Zulaica's Rhodes electric piano, electronic effects, and occasionally horns and voices into a bedrock Latin format, and the combination works even at its most outlandish. Two of the reasons why *Agua Dulce* stays on track are the solid Latin percussion team of Pete and Coke Escovedo and Michael Smithe, and Tjader's rippling, to-the-point, easily adaptable vibraphone manner, which hadn't changed a whit over the years. The title track, "Agua Dulce" ("Cool-Ade"), is a lot of fun, with its electronic bubbling and straight Latin grooves, and Cal even tackles the Rolling Stones' "Gimme Shelter," adding pink noise and spacy obligatos from an early Moog synthesizer. Much of the live portion of the CD—recorded at a San Diego nightclub in 1972—has a sound tied even more closely to its time, with Zulaica's electric piano, John Heard's bass and Dick Berk's drums often creating textures that evoke the jazz-rock era. Smithe's congas merely add punctuation, except when Tjader himself joins in on percussion, thus creating some Latin action. Nevertheless, this live gig is quite enjoyable and energetic, sprinkled with new material and updated Tjader standards like "Cubano Chant," "Manteca" and "Soul Sauce III" (same old "Guachi Guaro"). On the CD release, "Theme" was deleted for lack of space, though the seventy-eight-and-a-half-minute disc remains generously packed. —*Richard S. Ginell*

Tambu / Sep. 18, 1973-Sep. 20, 1973 / Original Jazz Classics ✦✦✦
Still trying to stay in tune with the '70s, Cal Tjader joins forces with another refugee from another time, guitarist Charlie Byrd, for an album of contemporary Brazilian-flavored jazz. The alliance is forged mostly on Byrd's terms, with bossa nova, samba and percussive displays from Brazil's interior dominating the grooves. This time, after proving very adaptable to previous experiments, Tjader seems to be out in the cold in these settings, and he lays out a lot more often than usual on this album. Byrd rides along in his gentle, prickly-toned manner on acoustic and electric guitars, and the rhythm section shifts personnel and instruments from track to track. Yet oddly enough, this is still a musically rich feast. Electric pianist Mike Wolff's "Samba de Oneida" is a marvelously propulsive samba, and "Tereza My Love," one of Antonio Carlos Jobim's most attractive sleepers, is given a lovely rendition. The title track, written by Airto Moreira, is given an authentic, rambunctious Airto-style treatment, very much up-to-date, but Cal doesn't sound totally comfortable with the rhythm on vibes, spending most of his time on timbales. Even though this isn't prime Tjader, the overall quality of the music makes it a winner. —*Richard S. Ginell*

Amazonas / Jun. 1975 / Original Jazz Classics ✦✦✦
Cal Tjader's Brazilian explorations continue and actually deepen with this release, as he joins forces with a host of progressive young Brazilian musicians, all overseen by producer Airto Moreira. By now, Tjader had figured out how to fit into the blend, doing so by losing himself in the complex mix of Afro-Brazilian rhythms, American funk and 1970s-era electronics, integrating his own identity for the sake of the ensemble. Indeed, Tjader actually appears on marimba on tracks like Joao Donato's "Amazonas" and his collaboration with Hermeto Pascoal, "Mindoro," his playing taking on a more brittle edge as a result. Tjader's Southern Hemisphere cohorts include such emerging luminaries as keyboardist Egberto Gismonti, percussionist Robertinho Silva, the sometimes wild flutist Hermeto Pascoal and on one track, the superb trombonist Raul de Souza. The intricate arrangements are in the hands of George Duke, and so are the funky, occasionally spaced-out keyboard sounds (albeit under the contractually dictated pseudonym "Dawilli Gonga"). CD buyers get a welcome bonus, an extended, impassioned outtake of "Cahuenga." —*Richard S. Ginell*

Grace Cathedral Concert / May 22, 1976 / Fantasy ✦✦✦
Unlike Vince Guaraldi's Grace Cathedral concert, vibraphonist Cal Tjader's was not a religious event. In fact, this quintet outing (which includes Lonnie Hewitt on electric piano and the young Poncho Sanchez on congas) is a fairly typical concert for the era, despite the location. As it turned out, Tjader was a replacement for Guaraldi, who had originally been scheduled but had recently passed away. The vibist's Latin Jazz group performs the leader's "I Showed Them," Milt Jackson's swinging "Bluesology," a medley from "Black Orpheus" and "Body and Soul." —*Scott Yanow*

Here and There / Sep. 1976-Jun. 18, 1977 / Fantasy ✦✦✦
This single CD reissues all of the music from vibraphonist Cal Tjader's *Guarabe* LP plus five of the six tracks from *Here*. During this period, the influential Latin-jazz pioneer was leading a hornless quintet/sextet that included Clare Fischer's electric piano as a key part of the band's sound. With guitarist Bob Redfield, bassist Rob Fisher, drummer Pete Riso, the talented (but at the time obscure) percussionist Poncho Sanchez and (on the first half of the reissue) Carmelo Garcia on timbales keeping the proceedings heated, Tjader's group livens up such numbers

as "This Masquerade," "Morning" and even the pop tune "If." An enjoyable if not essential release. —*Scott Yanow*

Breathe Easy / Sep. 1977 / Galaxy ✦✦✦
Vibraphonist Cal Tjader had a chance to display his jazz roots on this straightahead quintet set (which has not yet been reissued on CD). Tjader stretches out in conventional fashion on six familiar standards (including "Tangerine," "The Way You Look Tonight" and "Just Friends") with the obscure trumpeter Allan Smith, pianist Hank Jones, bassist Monty Budwig and drummer Shelly Manne. The interpretations overall are relaxed, tasteful and swinging but somewhat uneventful and without any real surprises. —*Scott Yanow*

La Onda Va Bien / Jul. 1979 / Concord Picante ✦✦✦
It was only fitting that vibraphonist Cal Tjader launched the Concord Picante label with this release, for Tjader did a great deal to popularize Latin-jazz. This was not his strongest effort (the solos of Tjader and flutist Roger Glenn are not all that substantial) but the drumming of Vince Lateano and the percussion of Poncho Sanchez keep the momentum flowing on these likable performances. —*Scott Yanow*

Gozame! Pero Ya / Jun. 1980 / Concord Picante ✦✦✦✦
Vibraphonist Cal Tjader was one of the major forces in Latin-jazz from the mid-'50s until his death in 1982. His final band was most notable for including Poncho Sanchez on congas; Sanchez would in his own way keep Tjader's legacy alive in future years. This fine effort features Cal Tjader's 1980, sextet which also includes keyboardist Mark Levine, flutist Roger Glenn, bassist Rob Fisher and drummer Vince Lateano; guitarist Mundell Lowe is a guest on three jazz ballads including the obscure Gerry Mulligan-Mel Tormé tune "This Couldn't Be the Real Thing." Other highlights are "Bye Bye Blues," "Roger's Samba" and "Will You Still Be Mine." —*Scott Yanow*

The Shining Sea / Mar. 1981 / Concord Picante ✦✦✦✦
Beautiful playing by Hank Jones (p), more straight jazz than Latin. —*Ron Wynn*

A Fuego Vivo / Aug. 1981 / Concord Picante ✦✦✦✦
For one of his final albums, vibraphonist Cal Tjader leads a septet that includes keyboardist Mark Levine, future bandleader Poncho Sanchez on congas and guest altoist-flutist Gary Foster. The Latinized versions of "The Continental" and "Naima" are most memorable, but all of the other selections also have their infectious moments. Typically high-quality Latin-jazz from Cal Tjader, one of the idiom's most important pacesetters. —*Scott Yanow*

Good Vibes / 1981 / Concord Jazz ✦✦✦
This CD reissue brings back one of vibraphonist Cal Tjader's final recordings. The Latin jazz pacesetter is in typically fine form, alternating rhythmic pieces with some standards and taking "Doxy" in straightforward fashion without the percussionists. Tjader's final regular group featured pianist Mark Levine, bassist Rob Fisher, Vince Lateano on drums and timbales, future bandleader Poncho Sanchez on congas and either flutist Roger Glenn or Gary Foster on flute, soprano and alto. Playing time is just 43 minutes (since this is a straight reissue of the original LP), but the quality is high, with the better tracks including "Guachi Guaro," "Speak Low," "Broadway" and "Doxy." —*Scott Yanow*

Heat Wave / Jan. 1982 / Concord Jazz ✦✦✦✦
Vibraphonist Cal Tjader's final album (he passed away four months later) found his band mostly accompanying singer Carmen McRae. The potentially exciting combination does not really come off that well. The musicians (Tjader, a rhythm section, two percussionists including Poncho Sanchez, and a pair of trombonists) had little to do. McRae sounds OK in the Latin setting, but does not uplift the diverse material (which includes "Besame Mucho," "Evil Ways," "Do Nothing Till You Hear from Me," "Speak Low" and two Stevie Wonder songs), and the effort overall is somewhat forgettable and disappointing. —*Scott Yanow*

Charles Tolliver

b. Mar. 6, 1942, Jacksonville, FL
Trumpet / Hard Bop, Post-Bop
In the early '70s Charles Tolliver was one of the brightest young trumpeters in jazz. He studied at Howard University and then moved to New York in 1964, playing and recording with Jackie McLean. Tolliver was on quite a few excellent advanced hard bop records in the mid-'60s, played with Gerald Wilson's Orchestra in Los Angeles (1966-67) and was a member of Max Roach's group at the same time (1967-69) as the compatible Gary Bartz. In 1969 Tolliver formed a quartet called Music Inc. that often featured pianist Stanley Cowell and was on a few occasions expanded to a big band. Tolliver and Cowell founded the Strata East label in 1971, which released many fine records in the 1970s. Although it was an era when there was a serious shortage of talented young trumpeters (prior to the rise of Wynton Marsalis), Tolliver after the mid-'70s maintained a low profile. Charles Tolliver, whose fat tone was influenced by Freddie Hubbard and whose ideas display

bits of John Coltrane, has recorded as a leader for Impulse (two songs from a 1965 concert), Black Lion, Enja and Strata East, most recently in 1988. —*Scott Yanow*

Paper Man / Jul. 2, 1968 / Black Lion ✦✦✦✦✦
Also released by the Freedom label, this was trumpeter Charles Tolliver's full-length album as a leader. One of the top brassmen to emerge during the era (although he never quite lived up to his potential), Tolliver had the fat tone of a Freddie Hubbard, the adventurous spirit of Woody Shaw and a somewhat original conception of his own that bridged the gap between hard bop and the avant-garde. He performs six of his originals with pianist Herbie Hancock, bassist Ron Carter, drummer Joe Chambers and (on three of the selections) altoist Gary Bartz. This explorative and stirring music is well worth investigating. —*Scott Yanow*

★ **The Ringer** / Jun. 2, 1969 / Freedom ✦✦✦✦✦
This is the Charles Tolliver record to get, although it may be hard to find. The masterful trumpeter, in a quartet with pianist Stanley Cowell, bassist Steve Novosel and drummer Jimmy Hopps, plays five of his strongest compositions. Highlights include the powerful "On the Nile," "The Ringer" and "Spur," but each of the numbers has its memorable moments. Tolliver is heard at the peak of his creative powers; it is strange that he never received the fame and recognition that he deserved. —*Scott Yanow*

Live at Slugs / May 1, 1970 / Strata East ✦✦✦✦✦
Strata East recordings are quite difficult to acquire, which is unfortunate considering their high quality. Charles Tolliver was one of the great trumpeters to emerge during the late '60s, yet has always been vastly underrated. On this quartet set with pianist Stanley Cowell, bassist Cecil McBee and drummer Jimmy Hopps, Tolliver has a real chance to stretch out. The 17-minute "Orientale" is particularly memorable. The music straddles the boundary between advanced hard bop and the avant-garde and rewards repeated listenings. —*Scott Yanow*

Music, Inc. Big Band / Nov. 11, 1971 / Strata East ✦✦✦✦✦
This first document of the progressive big band features 17 pieces, including the famous works "Ruthie's Heart," "On the Nile" and "Departure." —*Michael G. Nastos*

Grand Max / Aug. 9, 1972 / Black Lion ✦✦✦✦✦
Originally released by Strata East as *Live at the Loosdrecht Jazz Festival*, this CD reissue features the great but very underrated trumpeter Charles Tolliver in a quartet with pianist John Hicks, bassist Reggie Workman and drummer Alvin Queen. The group performs three of the leader's songs plus Cowell's "Prayer for Peace" and Neal Hefti's "Repetition"; the lengthy renditions clock in between 11 and 17 minutes apiece. Tolliver's music (which holds on to one's attention throughout the live set) has its connections to the bebop tradition but also forges ahead and can be quite passionate. Recommended. —*Scott Yanow*

Live in Tokyo / Dec. 7, 1973 / Strata East ✦✦✦✦

Impact / Jan. 17, 1975 / Strata East ✦✦✦✦✦
Trumpeter Charles Tolliver plays so well throughout this large group recording that it seems quite odd that (other than a Japanese date in 1977) his next record would be in 1988. Tolliver utilizes an all-star 14-horn big band, eight strings and a talented rhythm section on six of his compositions, all of which he also arranged. In addition to the leader, such soloists are heard from as altoists James Spaulding and Charles McPherson, tenors George Coleman and Harold Vick and pianist Stanley Cowell, for a particularly strong program of advanced big-band jazz. But when is this rare LP going to be reissued on CD? —*Scott Yanow*

Live in Berlin at the Quasimodo, Vol. 1 / Jul. 21, 1988-Jul. 22, 1988 / Strata East ✦✦✦✦
The talented, if underrecorded and underrecognized trumpeter Charles Tolliver is well showcased on this quartet date. Assisted by pianist Alain Jean-Marie, bassist Ugonna Okegwo and drummer Ralph Van Duncan, Tolliver shows that he is still in prime form, stretching out during lengthy renditions of four of his originals including "On the Nile." The music is modern modal jazz, and Tolliver's tone and adventurous style perfectly fit the idiom. This excellent CD is the first of two volumes. —*Scott Yanow*

Ross Tompkins

b. May 13, 1938, Detroit, MI
Piano / Swing, Bop, Cool
Best known to the public for his onetime regular gig with Doc Severinsen's *Tonight Show* band, Tompkins is a versatile, swinging pianist with a do-everything technique who is much in demand on the Los Angeles jazz scene. After studying at the New England Conservatory, he moved to New York, recording with Kai Winding and playing at times with Eric Dolphy (1964), Wes Montgomery (1966), the Bob Brookmeyer/Clark Terry quintet (1966) and Benny Goodman (1968). He also played with Bobby Hackett from 1965 to 1970 and the Al Cohn/Zoot Sims quintet (1968-72). Tompkins moved to Los Angeles in 1971, where he played with

the Louie Bellson big bands and joined the *Tonight Show* band, remaining until Johnny Carson left the show in 1992. His most frequent appearances on records were as a leader and sideman for Concord Jazz in the 1970s, including a gig with Joe Venuti, *Live at Concord '77,* and a session with Red Norvo, *Red and Ross.* —*Richard S. Ginell*

● **Scrimshaw** / Jul. 1976 / Concord Jazz ✦✦✦✦✦
Tompkins plays solo piano in this album of all standards. It features elegant classicism in a jazz framework. The worth of this is that we finally get to hear the voice normally submerged in the big-band context. This is a fine representation of Tompkins' worth. —*Michael G. Nastos*

Live at Concord (1977) / Aug. 5, 1977 / Concord Jazz ✦✦✦✦✦
From the summer of 1977 (one year before his death), this was violinist Joe Venuti's final recording session. Pianist/leader Ross Tompkins, bassist Ray Brown and drummer Jake Hanna first interpret "Softly As in a Morning Sunrise" and then welcome tenor saxophonist Scott Hamilton (then 23) for a warm version of "I Got It Bad". Soon, Venuti makes the group a quintet, and they romp on a lively rendition of "I Want to Be Happy". After a few more standards, Venuti and Ray Brown duet on "Dark Eyes," a great vehicle for the classic violinist to end his career. Recommended. —*Scott Yanow*

Lost in the Stars / 1977 / Concord Jazz ✦✦✦

Ross Tompkins and Good Friends / 1978 / Concord Jazz ✦✦✦

Festival Time / Aug. 1979 / Concord Jazz ✦✦✦
Recorded with all-stars Ray Brown (b), Cal Collins (g), Jake Hanna (d), Marshall Royal (as), and Snooky Young (tpt) at the Concord Jazz Festival. This is mostly early-period jazz with one Tompkins original, "Pavilion Blues." —*Michael G. Nastos*

Mel Tormé

b. Sep. 13, 1925, Chicago, IL
Vocals, Drums / Bop, Swing, Show Tunes, Traditional Pop, Ballads, Vocal Jazz
Mel Tormé is a genuine Renaissance man—one of the top jazz singers of the last third of the century but also a superb writer, a good arranger, a more-than-competent drummer, a songwriter with a number of standards to his credit, a versatile actor, and a most engaging raconteur. Known in his youth as the "Velvet Fog" for his high, murky, sustained vocals, Tormé gradually developed into a first-class jazz baritone with great scatting ability, superb control and a sophisticated way with ballads. Indeed, his voice actually grew stronger and more flexible in his later years, shedding old mannerisms and developing an ever-more-powerful sense of swing. Though Tormé notes that it takes him an agonizingly long time to write them, his arrangements for orchestra and big band are sonorous and intelligently conceived. Furthermore, Tormé is probably as fine a writer as he is a singer; his autobiography *It Wasn't All Velvet,* his memoir of Judy Garland *The Other Side of the Rainbow* and his biography of his friend Buddy Rich *Traps, The Drum Wonder,* are compulsively readable, chatty, and full of insight.

He started very early—singing in Chicago's Blackhawk club at the age of four, acting professionally at nine, publishing his first tune at 15, joining the Chico Marx band as a wise-cracking singer, vocal arranger and drummer at 16. At 19, he assured himself of immortality by co-writing "The Christmas Song," which in the wake of Nat King Cole's 1946 hit record has become an imperishable holiday standard. In the 1940s, Tormé began recording for Decca, Musicraft and Capitol, backed by his own vocal group the Mel-Tones, the Artie Shaw band, the Page Cavanaugh Trio and various studio orchestras. Amidst several parallel careers in show business and literature, he continued to refine his vocal abilities through the decades. Although Tormé's star dimmed somewhat in the 1960s when rock overwhelmed the music business, a series of fine, uncompromising albums for Concord Jazz from 1982 onward boosted his reputation in the jazz world—and the mass media caught on thanks to exposure on the hit TV series *Night Court,* where he played himself. Tormé continued to sing in top form into the mid-1990s, but a stroke suffered in August 1996 while recording a tribute album to Ella Fitzgerald has silenced him as of this writing. —*Richard S. Ginell*

The Mel Tormé Collection / 1944-Sep. 18, 1985 / Rhino ✦✦✦✦✦
Up until he suffered a stroke at age 70 in 1996, singer Mel Tormé continued to improve with age and seemed to have inexhaustible energy. This four-CD set from Rhino does a fine job of covering Tormé's pre-Concord output, although the omission of Tormé's Concord work of 1986-95 is unfortunate, for that catalog contains many of Tormé's most exciting recordings. In general the earlier selections (some of which were with his vocal group the Mel-Tones) feature Tormé on hip (for the period) swing tunes and ballads. By the time he cut the sessions included on this set from 1954, the singer was quite mature and sounding very much like himself. The small group dates of the 1950s are generally much more rewarding than some of the slower numbers in which Tormé is accompanied by string orchestras,

and the 1956-60 collaborations with the Marty Paich Dek-tette are classic. But once the 1960s hit, Tormé's career (at least on records) started to quickly decline. Although disc four (which covers 1962-85) does its best to focus on Tormé's better recordings of the period, a few of the tracks (such as "Strangers in the Night," "A Day in the Life of Bonnie and Clyde" and "Yesterday When I Was Young") are fairly sappy. Things greatly improve once the singer reaches the year 1975, and there are enough high points throughout the set to justify its purchase by Tormé's many fans. Three previously unreleased selections (best is "Walkin' Shoes" with Shorty Rogers in 1962) are a plus, and the colorful 84-page booklet is quite definitive. —*Scott Yanow*

A Foggy Day / 1945-1947 / Musicraft ✦✦✦

There's No One But You / 1945-1947 / Musicraft ✦✦✦

It Happened in Monterey / 1946 / Musicraft ✦✦✦✦
Brilliant harmonies, arrangements with the Mel-Tones. —*Ron Wynn*

Spotlight on Great Gentlemen of Song / Jan. 17, 1949-Oct. 4, 1951 / Capitol ✦✦✦✦
This very interesting CD gives listeners a cross section of Mel Tormé's Capitol recordings. Caught fairly early in his career, Tormé's voice was already quite recognizable and appealing. Ballads alternate with occasional romps, including several arranged by Frank DeVol in 1949 that are surprisingly boppish; Pete Rugolo, Nelson Riddle and Sonny Burke take care of the other charts. Highlights of the 18 cuts (four of which were previously unreleased) include a wild "Oh, You Beautiful Doll," "Stompin' at the Savoy," "Blue Moon," a spirited "Sonny Boy" and "You're a Heavenly Thing" (which finds Mel Tormé playing piano in a quartet with guitarist Mary Osborne). —*Scott Yanow*

Easy to Remember / 1953+1963 / Glendale ✦✦✦
This brief Hindsight CD (under 36 minutes) alternates Mel Tormé performances from 1953 with those from 1963; the backing personnel is not known in both cases. The previously unreleased material mostly emphasizes ballads, and only three of the 16 selections are over 21 minutes. Tormé sounds fine, sticking primarily to the melody, but since he has continued to grow through the years (the singer's later Concord recordings find him at his peak) this nice middle-of-the-road set is not essential for anyone but true Mel Tormé fanatics. —*Scott Yanow*

In Hollywood / Dec. 15, 1954 / GRP/Decca ✦✦✦✦
This is an intriguing CD containing 20 performances (seven previously unissued) from one night in the life of Mel Tormé. Recorded live at the Crescendo in Hollywood, Tormé not only sings, but also plays piano with a quartet comprising clarinetist/pianist Al Pellegrini, bassist James Dupre and drummer Richard Shanahan. Although not quite as strong a jazz singer as he would become, Tormé is consistently swinging on a well-rounded set highlighted by "That Old Black Magic," "My Shining Hour," "The Christmas Song," "Moonlight in Vermont," "Bernie's Tune," "Mountain Greenery" and "Get Happy." —*Scott Yanow*

★ **Tormé Touch** / Jan. 1956 / Bethlehem ✦✦✦✦✦
This Bethlehem LP (last reissued in 1978 and originally known as *Lulu's Back in Town*) is a classic. Singer Mel Tormé was matched for the first time with arranger Marty Paich's ten piece group, which was called The Dek-tette. Among the sidemen are trumpeters Pete Candoli and Don Fagerquist, valve trombonist Bob Enevoldsen, Bud Shank on alto and flute and either Bob Cooper or Jack Montrose on tenors; in addition Paich uses both a French horn and a tuba. The arranged ensembles and cool-toned soloists match perfectly with Tormé's warm voice, and there are many high points to this essential date. In particular "Lulu's Back in Town," "When the Sun Comes Out," "Fascinatin' Rhythm," "The Lady Is a Tramp" and "Lullaby of Birdland" are standouts, but all dozen selections are excellent. This is one of Mel Tormé's finest records of the 1950s. —*Scott Yanow*

Prelude to a Kiss / Nov. 1957 / Simitar ✦✦✦
Originally issued in 1957, *Prelude to a Kiss* was a concept LP built around a brief fling between our hero Mel Tormé and a woman whose voice is heard in short dialogue segments preceding each song. The songs follow the theme of each conversation and gradually build on that theme, from the innocent affection and naiveté of "I'm Getting Sentimental Over You" and "I Can't Believe That You're in Love with Me," to head-over-heels romance on "I've Got the World on a String" and "I Surrender Dear." Tormé is in possibly the best voice of his career, effortlessly breezy and refined (a tone which suits the theme perfectly). The only quibble with the original LP was that the spoken parts soon became tiresome, but after countless reissues and repackaging, Simitar Records issued *Prelude to a Kiss* on CD with separate track markers, which makes it possible to program the dialogue parts out of the LP. —*John Bush*

Back in Town / Apr. 23, 1959-Aug. 10, 1959 / Verve ✦✦✦✦✦
Mel Tormé had artistic—if not commercial—success with his vocal group the Mel-Tones in the mid-'40s. After its breakup in 1946, when Tormé was persuaded to go solo, the Mel-Tones were occasionally regrouped by Tormé for special projects.

These 1959 dates, which have been reissued in full on a Verve CD, were the group's final recordings, and they make for an interesting comparison with their earlier sessions. In addition to remakes of their two hits, "What Is This Thing Called Love" and "It Happened in Monterey," the arrangements (mostly by Marty Paich) have many quotes from jazz songs and are heavily influenced by Count Basie's Orchestra of the 1950s. The Mel-Tones, which at the time also included Sue Allen, Ginny O'Connor, Bernie Parke and Tom Kenny, swing throughout and sing attractive harmonies without really improvising. However, the concise solos of Art Pepper on both alto and tenor and trumpeter Jack Sheldon work well with the singers, making this a recommended set to fans of jazz vocal groups, of which the relatively short-lived Mel-Tones ranked near the top. —*Scott Yanow*

☆ **Mel Tormé Swings Shubert Alley** / Jan. 21, 1960-Feb. 11, 1960 / Verve ✦✦✦✦✦

Swingin' on the Moon / Aug. 3, 1960-Aug. 5, 1960 / Verve ✦✦✦
Swingin' on the Moon marks a bridge between Mel Tormé's excellent jazzy outings of the 1950s and the generally pop-oriented, novelty recordings of the '60s. Recorded over three days in August 1960, the album contains few standards, substituting instead lesser numbers that all contain the word "moon" in the title (including Tormé's own title song, which opens the set). Though he is in fine voice and the arrangements by Russ Garcia are solid, Tormé just can't come to grips with the lesser material, and the album is quite forgettable. It was released on Verve, which made it a jazz LP in theory, but *Swingin' on the Moon* can be consigned to the section of pop history that includes novelty "theme" albums arranged around a usually simple subject. This album should not be confused with the LaserLight collection titled *Swinging on the Moon*. —*John Bush*

I Dig the Duke, I Dig the Count / Dec. 12, 1960+Feb. 2, 1961 / Verve ✦✦✦✦✦

That's All / 1965 / Sony Special Products ✦✦✦
This 1997 CD reissues Mel Tormé's 1965 album *That's All*, ten songs only previously out as singles, and two unreleased titles. Tormé sings beautifully throughout the set, but there are a few problems. The arrangements (mostly by Robert Mersey and also including a few charts from Dick Hazard, Mort Garson and Pat Williams) are essentially unimaginative middle-of-the-road pop, with an orchestra and occasional strings and background singers greatly weighing down the proceedings. The 24 selections (all ballads) are mostly taken at slow tempos and were clearly geared for radio airplay, clocking in around the three-minute mark, which means that Tormé's improvising is held to a minimum. So if the melody is not strong, the singer was not given a chance to improve it, and if the tune was excellent, Mel's straightforward version added nothing to the song's legacy. At best, this CD makes for a pleasant listen, but get Mel Tormé's Concord releases instead. —*Scott Yanow*

Round Midnight: A Retrospective (1956-1962) / 1956-1962 / Stash ✦✦✦✦
This is a highly recommended set for Mel Tormé fans. The singer is heard on radio transcriptions (released for the first time in 1985) that compare favorably with his studio recordings of the period. Four selections are with the Marty Paich Dek-tette of 1956-57, while the other ten numbers (including instrumental versions of "Sugar Loaf" and "Marie") feature Tormé accompanied by a nonet headed by trumpeter Shorty Rogers. With such songs as "When the Sun Comes Out," "The Lady Is a Tramp," "The Surrey with the Fringe on Top," a "Porgy and Bess Medley" and two versions (with different arrangements) of "Lulu's Back in Town," this is a delightful set of cool but swinging jazz. —*Scott Yanow*

Right Now! / Jan. 28, 1966-Nov. 17, 1967 / Columbia/Legacy ✦✦
When Mel Tormé signed with Columbia in the mid-'60s, the jazz singer was talked into recording current pop tunes. The resulting music is so bad as to be laughable. This CD reissue sought to take advantage of the brief lounge music fad of the late '90s, but even fans of that idiom will find Tormé's treatments of a variety of teenager songs (he was over 40 at the time) to be quite awkward and embarrassing. Imagine hearing Mel Tormé trying to sound hip on "Walk on By," "If I Had a Hammer," "Strangers in the Night," "Secret Agent Man," "Molly Marlene" (which is about a go-go girl) and "Dominique's Discotheque," all of which have dated pop rhythms and background singers. One of the obvious low points of his career. —*Scott Yanow*

London Sessions / 1977 / DCC ✦✦✦
Mel Tormé had recorded relatively few rewarding albums in the decade before this set, originally put out by Gryphon before being reissued on CD by DCC Jazz. However, his voice had improved with time, his range had widened, and he had become an even stronger jazz singer than before. Since Tormé is joined here by the largely anonymous Chris Gunning Orchestra, with guest altoist Phil Woods, on a set of generally "contemporary" pop songs (including "All in Love Is Fair," "New York State of Mind," "Send in the Clowns" and "The First Time Ever I Saw Your Face"), this set is not too essential. However, Tormé's professionalism and ability to swing makes this an interesting outing anyway, and launched his "comeback." —*Scott Yanow*

Together Again: For the First Time / Jan. 1978 / Century ◆◆◆◆

Mel Tormé and Buddy Rich had been friends for decades prior to finally getting around to recording together. Although largely a Tormé vocal record, the Buddy Rich Orchestra, with guest altoist Phil Woods, is in top form, and the drummer/leader has several solos. Most memorable is Tormé's tribute to Ella Fitzgerald on "Lady Be Good" and a remarkable tour-de-force on "Blues in the Night." This enjoyable and somewhat historic LP, put out by Gryphon, deserves to be reissued on CD. —*Scott Yanow*

Live at Marty's / 1981 / Finesse ◆◆◆◆◆

Encore at Marty's, New York / Mar. 27, 1982 / DCC ◆◆◆◆

This CD reissues a full set of music from Mel Tormé with his 1982 trio: pianist Mike Renzi, bassist Jay Leonhart and drummer Donny Osborne. No editing took place except for the excision of some chatter, yet the music is consistently rewarding. Tormé, who was already 56, was amazingly just entering his musical prime. His well-paced set mixes together older songs (highlighted by a Fred Astaire medley) with some newer but worthy pieces (including the debut of Tormé's own "I'm Gonna Miss You"), alternating scat-filled romps with lyrical ballad interpretations. Throughout it all Tormé succeeds at everything he tries, with a humorous rendition of "I Like to Recognize the Tune" and some heated scatting on "Day In, Day Out" being among the memorable moments. This CD reissue of an album originally put out on the Flair label is recommended. —*Scott Yanow*

An Evening at Charlie's / Oct. 1983 / Concord Jazz ◆◆◆◆◆

Mel Tormé and pianist George Shearing had recorded together twice for Concord prior to this live set; both dates (*An Evening with George Shearing and Mel Tormé* and *Top Drawer*) gave Shearing top billing. For their third outing, the dynamic duo are up to their usual high level, with assistance from bassist Don Thompson and drummer Donny Osborne. Among the high points are "Nice's Dream," "Love Is Just Around the Corner" and a medley of "Just One of Those Things" and "On Green Dolphin Street." —*Scott Yanow*

My Night to Dream: The Ballads Collection / 1983-1996 / Concord Jazz ◆◆◆

★ **Mel Tormé, Rob McConnell and the Boss Brass** / May 1986 / Concord Jazz ◆◆◆◆◆

This was a very logical matchup that came out as well on record as it looked on paper. Valve trombonist/arranger Rob McConnell has long led one of the top mainstream jazz big bands, while Mel Tormé blossomed into one of the truly great jazz singers in the 1980s. McConnell's charts suited Tormé perfectly, and the result is this consistently enjoyable and swinging album. The singer is quite enthusiastic and in top form on "Just Friends," a touching "September Song," "Don'cha Go 'Way Mad," "A House Is Not a Home," "The Song Is You," a whimsical "Cow Cow Boogie," a "Stars" medley and an exciting six-song Duke Ellington medley. Highly recommended. —*Scott Yanow*

A Vintage Year / Aug. 1987 / Concord Jazz ◆◆◆◆◆

Singer Mel Tormé and pianist George Shearing make a perfect team, bringing out the best in each other. With the assistance of bassist John Leitham and drummer Donny Osborne, the swinging, witty duo perform a variety of standards, including Noel Coward's "Someday I'll Find You," "The Way You Look Tonight" and "Anyone Can Whistle," and a couple of medleys highlighted by a humorous six-song "New York, New York Medley." All of the Tormé/Shearing collaborations are quite enjoyable and highly recommended as some of their best work of the 1980s. —*Scott Yanow*

Reunion / Aug. 1988 / Concord Jazz ◆◆◆◆◆

In the 1950s, Mel Tormé recorded several memorable LPs on which he was joined by arranger Marty Paich and his Dek-tette (an all-star ten-piece band). For this long-overdue reunion, Paich utilized an 11-piece outfit (not counting two percussionists), adding a second trombone and a baritone to the original instrumentation while dropping the French horn. The results are quite enjoyable, with Tormé, remarkably still improving with age, in peak form on such songs as "Sweet Georgia Brown," "More than You Know," and several medleys, including one of bossa nova tunes and a combination of "For Whom the Bell Tolls" and Chick Corea's "Spain." The singer even attempts a couple of Steely Dan tunes with less success, since they are not that flexible; and Tormé seems to be in good spirits throughout this enjoyable set. —*Scott Yanow*

In Concert in Tokyo / Dec. 11, 1988 / Concord Jazz ◆◆◆◆◆

Mel Tormé and arranger Marty Paich (leading his ten-piece "Dek-tette") recorded several classic albums in the late '50s. On Reunion earlier in 1988 they had an enjoyable collaboration, and this live set was a follow-up. In general these in-concert performances are livelier, with Tormé sounding quite exuberant at times. Highlights include "Just in Time," "When the Sun Comes Out," "The Carioca," "The Christmas Song" and an instrumental version of "Cotton Tail" featuring clarinetist Ken Peplowski and Tormé on drums. A joyful outing. —*Scott Yanow*

Night at the Concord Pavilion / Aug. 1990 / Concord Jazz ◆◆◆◆◆

This spontaneous set finds Mel Tormé in typically fine form. The first seven selections, which find Tormé backed by pianist John Campbell, bassist Bob Maize and drummer Donny Osborne, have three medleys, including three songs having "Sing" in their title and a definitive eight-theme "Guys and Dolls Medley." As if that were not enough, Tormé is joined at this concert from the 1990 Concord Jazz Festival by the all-star Frank Wess-Harry Edison Orchestra for "Down for Double" and rollicking renditions of "You're Driving Me Crazy" and "Sent for You Yesterday and Here You Come Today." Mel Tormé fans will have to get this delightful session. —*Scott Yanow*

Mel and George Do WWII / Sep. 2, 1990-Sep. 3, 1990 / Concord Jazz ◆◆◆◆◆

All of the Mel Tormé-George Shearing collaborations are well worth acquiring, for the singer and the pianist constantly inspire each other. For this live concert, Tormé and Shearing perform a variety of songs popular during World War II. Shearing and bassist Neil Swainson duet on "Lilt Marlene" and "I've Heard That Song Before"; Shearing takes "I Know Why and So Do You" unaccompanied; and the duo is joined by drummer Donny Osborne and Tormé for a wide-ranging and consistently enjoyable set. Although "This Is the Army Mister Jones" is a bit dated, a four-song Duke Ellington medley, "I Could Write a Book" and a touching "We Mustn't Say Goodbye" are memorable. Recommended. —*Scott Yanow*

☆ **Fujitsu-Concord Festival (1990)** / Nov. 11, 1990 / Concord Jazz ◆◆◆◆◆

In 1990, a few months prior to this CD, Mel Tormé recorded a set with his trio at the Concord Jazz Festival, which climaxed with three songs with the Frank Wess-Harry Edison Orchestra. This particular CD is similar and just as enjoyable. With the assistance of pianist John Campbell, bassist Bob Maize and drummer Donny Osborne, Tormé is swinging on "Shine on Your Shoes" and a medley of "Don't cha Go 'Way Mad" and "Come to Baby Do." But it is his remarkable ballad renditions of "Star Dust" (during which Frank Wess sits in on tenor) and a definitive "A Nightingale Sang in Berkeley Square" that are most memorable; no other vocalist can hold notes so long. This time, the big band is led only by Wess, and in addition to vocal versions of "You're Driving Me Crazy" and "Sent for You Yesterday," Tormé happily sits in on drums for "Swingin' the Blues," which has a trumpet solo by Joe Newman. Virtually everything Mel Tormé has recorded for Concord is quite rewarding; this is one of his best all-around sets. —*Scott Yanow*

Nothing Without You / Mar. 12, 1991-Mar. 13, 1991 / Concord Jazz ◆◆

Mel Tormé is in typically fine form on this Concord set; the problem is his musical partner Cleo Laine. Although often classified as a jazz singer, Laine, who has a tremendous range and a lovely voice, seems incapable of improvising. Backed by a 12-piece group led by Laine's husband John Dankworth, the duo perform a variety of mostly superior standards, but nothing unexpected happens—except for a somewhat disastrous "Two Tune Medley." On the latter, Tormé and Laine sing 20 songs, generally two at a time, in less than five minutes; it is quite annoying. Otherwise, Tormé, who seems to have enjoyed the date, is weighed down and restricted by Cleo Laine's nonswinging style. Skip this one. —*Scott Yanow*

The Great American Songbook: Live at Michael's Pub / Oct. 1992 / Telarc ◆◆◆◆

Mel Tormé, 67 at the time of this recording, proves to still be very much in his musical prime. His range remains impressive, his creative abilities have grown through the years, and his breath control is remarkable; as proof Tormé holds some very long notes at the conclusion of some of the ballads. This live set finds Tormé backed by what he dubbed "the Great American Songbook Orchestra," his usual trio plus a dozen horns. The band gets "Ya Gotta Try" as an instrumental and Tormé sits in on drums on "Rockin' in Rhythm," but otherwise the orchestra sticks to its anonymous role in the background. The singer wrote ten of the 15 arrangements and programmed plenty of variety in moods and tempos for his voice, including a seven-song Duke Ellington mini-set. His masterful interpretation of "Stardust" is a high point. Recommended. —*Scott Yanow*

Sing Sing Sing / Nov. 1992 / Concord Jazz ◆◆◆◆

Although 14 minutes of this CD is a specific "Tribute to Benny Goodman," actually the entire release is at least an indirect homage to the King of Swing. Tormé and his trio (pianist John Colianni, bassist John Leitham and drummer Donny Osborne) are joined by clarinetist Ken Peplowski and vibraphonist Peter Appleyard (who are very reminiscent of Goodman and Lionel Hampton), and the emphasis is on swing-era standards. Tormé is in typically fine form on such tunes as "It's All Right with Me," "These Foolish Things," "Three Little Words" and the closing "Ev'ry Time We Say Goodbye." The singer even has some additional fun during this live in Japan concert by switching to drums for a rousing "Sing, Sing, Sing" that climaxes the Goodman medley. —*Scott Yanow*

A Tribute to Bing Crosby / May 12, 1994-May 17, 1994 / Concord Jazz ◆◆◆

As with most singers of his generation, Mel Tormé's early idol was Bing Crosby. On this set he is backed by 20 strings, his regular rhythm section (pianist John

Colianni, bassist John Leitham and drummer Donny Osborne) and three guests: guitarist Howard Alden, Ken Peplowski (on clarinet and tenor) and trumpeter Randy Sandke. Unfortunately the string arrangements (mostly by Bob Krogstad, Alan Broadbent and Angela Morley) weigh the music down, and Tormé is content to stick almost exclusively to slow ballads. Crosby introduced a countless number of standards, but Tormé mostly takes the songs fairly straight, swinging and improvising in only selected spots. His voice sounds consistently beautiful, but the lack of mood variation and the heavy strings keep the music from reaching the heights of Mel Tormé's other Concord recordings. —*Scott Yanow*

Velvet & Brass / Jul. 5, 1995-Jul. 6, 1995 / Concord Jazz ✦✦✦✦
Mel Tormé is in excellent voice for this matchup with Rob McConnell's Boss Brass, but somehow there is not as much musical magic as one might expect. With the exception of "My Sweetie Went Away" and "On the Swing Shift," none of the songs are exactly little-known, there are more ballads and less swingers than is optimal, and although there are a few short solos, the Boss Brass sounds surprisingly anonymous in this setting. The CD, although not without interest, does not quite live up to its great potential. —*Scott Yanow*

An Evening with Mel Tormé / Jul. 23, 1996 / Concord Jazz ✦✦✦
This was singer Mel Tormé's last recording before he was stricken with a serious stroke. Remarkably, Tormé had gradually improved both as a singer and as a jazz improviser all throughout his sixties (his voice was in phenomenal shape), and he is heard on this live set, filmed for a television special, in peak form despite being 70. Joined by his regular trio (pianist Mike Renzi, bassist John Leitham and drummer Donny Osborne), Tormé performs a typical swing-oriented program which includes a Benny Goodman medley, a memorable rendition of "A Nightingale Sang in Berkeley Square" (he could hold notes on ballads endlessly without wavering), a heated "Pick Yourself Up," and a tribute to Ella Fitzgerald on "Lady Be Good," among other numbers. Ironically, Tormé concluded what may be his final recording with a touching rendition of "Ev'ry Time We Say Goodbye." —*Scott Yanow*

Nestor Torres

b. Puerto Rico
Flute / Crossover Jazz, World Fusion, Latin Jazz
Jazz flutist Nestor Torres was born and raised in Puerto Rico, where he was inspired by people like Cal Tjader, Dave Brubeck and Tito Puente. He began studying flute at age 12. Torres' father, a talented musician, bought him a drum set when he was five. His playing incorporates a smorgasbord of Latin-jazz, pop, straightahead jazz and classical styles. After high school, he moved to New York with dreams of finding work with a profusion of Latin jazz bands. After realizing his skills as a flutist needed more honing, he enrolled in Berklee College of Music and the New England Conservatory of Music. He also studied with John Wummers at the Mannes School of Music. In 1977, he graduated and returned to New York City, heady with his new diploma. He sat in with his mentors like Puente and Eddie Palmieri, but also worked with a variety of lesser-known charanga (traditional Cuban) groups. In New York, Torres recorded three solo albums that were praised in the underground but not commercially successful.

In 1981, he hooked up with a Latin act called Hansel and Raul and moved to Miami, where he's been based ever since. Torres was immediately accepted into the city's vibrant salsa scene, and he's spent much of his time since then lecturing and performing on the college circuit in south Florida, as well as performing regularly at festivals and clubs in and around Miami. In 1989, Torres signed a multi-album contract with PolyGram Records and released his first album for Verve/Forecast, *Morning Ride*, in 1990. It climbed to the top of the contemporary jazz charts to become a Top Ten bestseller. Later that year, he had an accident in a celebrity boat race in Miami, crushing his upper body and damaging his powerful lungs. Then 34, he began a long recovery process before releasing *Dance of the Phoenix* in August 1991, finding strength by practicing Nichiren Shoshu Buddhism. Torres' brilliant debut is an exotic mix of styles that takes the listener through American, Brazilian and Afro-Cuban jazz. In 1994, Torres recorded *Burning Whispers* for Sony Latin Jazz, a newly formed label. Despite his boating accident injuries, Torres continues to record and perform. —*Richard Skelly*

● **Morning Ride** / 1989 / Verve/Forecast ✦✦✦✦
Taut piano from Herbie Hancock; otherwise nice, although a bit restrained. —*Ron Wynn*

Dance of the Phoenix / 1990 / Verve/Forecast ✦✦
This release features the leader's flute on some lightweight poppish and classical themes. With the exception of a token standard ("Solar") which shows that Torres is capable of better, this set is so nicely inoffensive that it will offend anyone who takes the time to listen closely. The music rarely even develops beyond the simple melodies and is quite forgettable. —*Scott Yanow*

Burning Whispers / 1994 / Sony Discos ✦✦✦
Talk to Me / 1996 / Sony International ✦✦✦

Jean Toussaint

b. Jul. 27, 1960, St. Thomas, Virgin Islands
Tenor Saxophone / Hard Bop
Thus far Jean Toussaint's claim to fame is his period (1982-86) with Art Blakey's Jazz Messengers. After playing calypso locally in St. Thomas, he attended the Berklee College of Music, toured with an R&B band in 1979 and formed a quintet with Wallace Roney. He was with Blakey during the same period as Terence Blanchard and Donald Harrison. After leaving the Jazz Messengers Toussaint began teaching in London and ever since has been based in London, mostly playing with English musicians although also gigging with Wynton Marsalis, McCoy Tyner and the Gil Evans Orchestra. Influenced by Wayne Shorter and Joe Henderson, Jean Toussaint's potential so far outweighs his accomplishments. —*Scott Yanow*

● **Life I Want** / 1996 / New Note ✦✦✦✦✦
Nazaire Who's Blues / 1996 / Jazz House ✦✦✦

Ralph Towner

b. Mar. 1, 1940, Chehalis, WA
Guitar / Post-Bop, Folk-Jazz
One of the founders of Oregon, Ralph Towner is one of the few modern jazz musicians to specialize in acoustic guitar. His playing often stretches beyond the boundaries of conventional jazz into world music, and is quite distinctive. He started playing piano when he was three and trumpet at five, performing in a dance band when he was 13. Towner studied classical guitar in Vienna and played with classical chamber groups in the mid-'60s. After moving to New York in 1969, Towner worked with Jimmy Garrison, Jeremy Steig and Paul Winter's Winter Consort (1970-71). In the latter group Towner first met up with Collin Walcott, Glen Moore and Paul McCandless, and in 1971 they broke away to form Oregon, a highly versatile group that ranges from jazz and free improvisations to folk music. Towner (who guested with Weather Report in 1971 and played with Gary Burton a bit during 1974-75) has performed and recorded with Oregon extensively since its formation in addition to recording as a leader and with many other artists on the ECM label. —*Scott Yanow*

Trios / Solos / Nov. 27, 1972-Nov. 28, 1972 / ECM ✦✦✦✦
Diary / Apr. 4, 1973-Apr. 5, 1973 / ECM ✦✦✦✦✦
Solstice / Dec. 1974 / ECM ✦✦✦✦✦
Not only sounds wonderful, it has Jan Garbarek (ts). —*Ron Wynn*

Works / 1974-1982 / ECM ✦✦✦
A great, great guitarist whose songs at worst are overly sentimental, at best hypnotic. This collection sums up some of his finer moments, but he's probably best experienced in actual sessions. —*Ron Wynn*

Sounds and Shadows / Feb. 1977 / ECM ✦✦✦✦
Old Friends, New Friends / Jul. 1979 / ECM ✦✦✦✦✦
Excellent group work with trumpeter Kenny Wheeler. —*Michael G. Nastos*

● **Solo Concert** / Oct. 1979 / ECM ✦✦✦✦✦
This very well-recorded album features Ralph Towner playing 12-string and classical guitar on "Nardis," two pieces by John Abercrombie and four of his own originals. The interpretations are typically sensitive, thoughtful and often introspective, but also show off Towner's impressive technique. —*Scott Yanow*

Blue Sun / Dec. 1982 / ECM ✦✦✦
Slide Show / May 1985 / ECM ✦✦✦
City of Eyes / Jan. 1988-Nov. 1988 / ECM ✦✦✦✦
Open Letter / Jul. 1991+Feb. 1992 / ECM ✦✦✦
Lost and Found / May 1995 / ECM ✦✦✦✦✦
The main surprise on this CD from acoustic guitarist Ralph Towner is that a few of the songs really cook. The 14 group originals (plus "Mon Enfant") vary the instrumentation from solo guitar by Towner and duets to a full quartet with the reeds of Denney Goodhew, bassist Marc Johnson and drummer Jon Christensen. Of the highlights, "Summer's End" has a memorable and rather pretty Towner melody, "Soft Landing" is both spaced and lyrical, and "Flying Cows" gets moving and shows some wit in spots. The overall session is introspective with some classical-oriented pieces and quiet sound explorations but the inclusion of a few swinging numbers gives this session just the right amount of variety. Johnson has plenty of bass solos, Goodhew (on four different reeds) is a major asset and drummer Christensen mostly plays quietly. The results are not essential but are certainly worthwhile. —*Scott Yanow*

Ana / 1997 / ECM ✦✦✦

Ana relies more on classical music than Ralph Towner's previous albums. While Towner isn't entirely successful in melding classical, jazz and new age—he frequently meanders—several sections of *Ana* are as lovely and hypnotic as anything else in his catalog. —*Stephen Thomas Erlewine*

Travelin' Light

f. 1991

Group / Swing

Formed in 1991, Travelin' Light is co-led by Frank Vignola (doubling on banjo and acoustic guitar) and the fluent tuba player Sam Pilafian. With occasional guest stars (including Ken Peplowski), Travelin' Light recorded several swinging and often-witty sets for Concord and Telarc. —*Scott Yanow*

Christmas with Travelin' Light / Jul. 15, 1992 / Telarc ✦✦✦✦

This is a melodic and often entertaining set of Christmas-related songs as performed by Travelin' Light (Sam Pilafian on tuba and Frank Vignola doubling on guitar and banjo) with several guests: clarinetist Ken Peplowski, guitarist Don Keiling, drummer Joe Ascione and percussionist Andy Kubiezewski. The interpretations range from Dixieland to folk, with a nutty version of "The Twelve Days of Christmas" thrown in as a surprise. —*Scott Yanow*

● **Makin' Whoopee: Travelin' Light** / Jul. 15, 1992 / Telarc ✦✦✦✦✦

Cookin' with Frank & Sam / Jan. 5, 1995-Jan. 6, 1995 / Concord Jazz ✦✦✦

Lennie Tristano

b. Mar. 19, 1919, Chicago, IL, d. Nov. 18, 1978, New York, NY

Piano, Leader / Cool

The history of jazz is written as a recounting of the lives of its most famous (and presumably, most influential) artists. Reality is not so simple, however. Certainly the most important of the music's innovators are those whose names are known by all—Armstrong, Parker, Young, Coltrane. Unfortunately, the jazz critic's tendency to inflate the major figures' status often comes at the expense of other musicians' reputations—men and women who have made significant, even essential, contributions of their own are, for whatever reason, overlooked in the mad rush to canonize a select few. Lennie Tristano is one of those who have not yet received their critical due. In the mid-'40s, the Chicago-born pianist arrived on the scene with a concept that genuinely expanded the prevailing bop aesthetic. Tristano brought to the music of Charlie Parker and Bud Powell a harmonic language that adapted the practices of contemporary classical music; his use of polytonal effects in tunes like "Out on a Limb" was almost Stravinsky-esque, and his extensive use of counterpoint was (whether or not he was conscious of it at the time) in keeping with the trends being set in mid-century art music. Until relatively recently, it had seldom been acknowledged that Tristano had been the first to perform and record a type of music that came to be called "free jazz." In 1949—almost a decade before the making of Ornette Coleman's first records—Tristano's group (which included Lee Konitz, Warne Marsh, and Billy Bauer) cut the first recorded example of freely improvised music in the history of jazz. The two cuts, "Intuition" and "Digression," were created spontaneously, without any pre-ordained reference to time, tonality, or melody. The resultant work was an outgrowth of Tristano's preoccupation with feeling and spontaneity in the creation of music. It influenced, among others, Charles Mingus, whose earliest records sound eerily similar to those of Tristano in terms of style and compositional technique. Mingus came by the influence honestly; he studied with the pianist for a period in the early '50s, as did many other well-known jazz musicians, such as Sal Mosca, Phil Woods, and the aforementioned Konitz and Marsh.

Tristano was stricken permanently blind as an infant. He first studied music with his mother, an avocational pianist and opera singer. From 1928-38, he attended a school for the blind in Chicago, where he learned music theory and developed proficiency on several wind instruments. Later, he attended Chicago's American Conservatory of Music, from which he received a bachelor's degree in 1943. During his early years as a professional performer and teacher, Tristano worked in and around Chicago, achieving his first measure of critical attention and attracting his first important students, Konitz and composer/arranger Bill Russo.

In 1946, Tristano moved to New York, where he made something of a big splash, performing with many of the leading musicians of the day, including Dizzy Gillespie and Charlie Parker. The influential critic Barry Ulanov took an extreme liking to Tristano's music and championed his work in the pages of *Metronome* magazine; Tristano was named the publication's Musician of the Year for 1947. Tenor saxophonist Warne Marsh began studies with Tristano in 1948, and when Bauer and Konitz came back aboard, he had the core of his great sextet. In 1949—with the addition of bassist Arnold Fishkin and alternating drummers Harold Granowsky and Denzil Best—Tristano, Bauer, Konitz and Marsh recorded

what was to become the basis of the band's collective legacy, the Capitol album *Crosscurrents*. The Capitol sessions spawned many of Tristano's best-known works, including the title track, and of course, the freely improvised cuts "Digression" and "Intuition" (these latter recorded without a drummer). The recordings synthesized the Tristano approach: long, rhythmically and harmonically elaborate melodies were played over a smooth, almost uninflected swing time maintained by the bassist and drummer. Counterpoint, which had been mostly abandoned by post-New Orleans/Chicago players, made a comeback in Tristano's music. Tristano's written lines were a great deal more involved than the already complex melodies typical of bebop; he subdivided and multiplied the beat in odd groupings, and his harmonies did not always behave in a manner consistent with functional tonality. The complexity of his constructs demanded that his rhythm section provide little more than a solid foundation. Tristano's bassists and drummers were not expected to interact in the manner of a bop rhythm section, but to support the music's melodic and harmonic substance. Such restraint lent Tristano's music an emotionally detached air, which to this day has been used by unsympathetic critics as a sledgehammer to pound him.

In 1951, Tristano founded a school of jazz in New York, the first of its kind. Its faculty consisted of many of his most prominent students, including Konitz, Bauer, Marsh, and pianist Sal Mosca. His public performances became fewer and farther between; for the rest of his life, Tristano was to concentrate on teaching, mostly to the exclusion of everything else. He shut down his school in 1956, and began teaching out of his home on Long Island. Thereafter he would play occasionally at the Half Note in New York City. Recordings became scarce. He made two albums for Atlantic, *Lennie Tristano* and *The New Tristano*. A compilation of odds and ends entitled *Descent into the Maelstrom* was released on Inner City; its title track documents Tristano's experiments in multitrack recording of the piano. He toured Europe in 1965; his last public performance in the US was in 1968.

Until his death in 1978, Tristano continued to teach. A later generation of his adherents continues to work and thrive in New York to this day. Musicians like pianist Connie Crothers, saxophonists Lennie Popkin and Richard Tabnik, and drummer Carol Tristano—the pianist's daughter—carry on his work into the next century. —*Chris Kelsey*

Lost Session / May 1945-1946 / Phontastic ✦✦✦

This LP contains some real rarities. Side one has four selections and three alternates taken from a previously unknown session in which pianist Lennie Tristano teams up with the talented but now forgotten tenor Emmett Carls and several members of Woody Herman's Orchestra (trumpeter Shorty Rogers, trombonist Earl Swope, bassist Chubby Jackson and drummer Don Lamond). Although Tristano was not as well-known as the others at the time, his unique playing really influences the sound of the ensembles. The flip side has four early and formerly rare piano solos plus a pair of trio outings with guitarist Billy Bauer and bassist Leonard Gaskin. Tristano collectors will have to acquire this European LP to fill some gaps in the pianist's relatively slim discography. —*Scott Yanow*

Live at Birdland (1949) / 1945-1949 / Jazz ✦✦✦✦

The Jazz label has made available several previously unknown Lennie Tristano sessions. The bulk of this LP features the pianist with tenor saxophonist Warne Marsh, guitarist Billy Bauer, bassist Arnold Fishkin and drummer Jeff Morton, performing five selections that utilize common chord changes. Tristano and Marsh in particular are in creative form. The final four numbers must rank as among Lennie Tristano's earliest recordings, for those unaccompanied solos were cut in 1945. Even at that early date, the pianist had his very unique style together. Although not as boppish as his playing would become, the basic principles are in place with long melodic lines and constant improvising being emphasized. —*Scott Yanow*

Rarest Trio / Quartet Sessions (1946-1947) / 1946-Dec. 31, 1947 / Raretone ✦✦✦✦✦

This collector's LP (from an Italian label) lives up to its name. These are among the rarest studio recordings of the remarkable pianist/teacher Lennie Tristano. He is heard on a dozen trio performances with guitarist Billy Bauer, and either Leonard Gaskin John Levy or John LaPorta (who was avant-garde for his time) joins Lennie for four explorative quartet pieces. The music is utterly fascinating overall and shows that Tristano was already well past bebop, which was considered a revolutionary music itself at the time. —*Scott Yanow*

☆ **The Complete Lennie Tristano on Keynote** / Oct. 8, 1946-Oct. 23, 1947 / Mercury ✦✦✦✦✦

★ **Intuition** / Mar. 4, 1949-Oct. 11, 1956 / Capitol ✦✦✦✦✦

This CD brings back a formerly rare set by Warne Marsh, plus seven classic performances that serve as the high point of Lennie Tristano's career. Oddly enough, the Tristano date is programmed second. First is a full-length album that matches Warne Marsh with the cooler but complementary tone of fellow tenor Ted Brown (plus pianist Robbie Ball, bassist George Tucker and drummer Jeff Morton). The original eight selections are joined by four alternate takes recorded in mono. Marsh and Brown blend together well, Ball has several creative solos, and most of the "originals" are based closely on familiar standards. However, the main reason to acquire this CD is for the seven remarkable Tristano tracks, which feature his finest group (consisting of the pianist/leader, altoist Lee Konitz, Marsh on tenor, guitarist Billy Bauer, bassist Arnold Fishkin and either Harold Granowsky or Denzil Best on drums). Tristano's music was unique and even more advanced than most bop of the late '40s. While he confined the rhythm section to very quiet timekeeping, the vibrato-less horns and Tristano himself played very long melodic lines, constantly improvising. The stunning unisons performed by Konitz and Marsh (particularly on "Wow") still sound remarkable today, as does the interplay of the two horns on "Sax of a Kind." "Intuition" and "Digression" were the first recorded free improvisations in jazz, but are quite coherent due to the musicians' familiarity with each other. Due to the Lennie Tristano performances, this CD reissue (which has over 75 minutes of music) is essential for all jazz collections. —*Scott Yanow*

Wow / 1950 / Jazz ◆◆◆◆
As is true of the Jazz label's CDs, there are no liner notes on this release and the total time falls into the range of an LP, but this is a rare live performance by pianist Lennie Tristano's finest group. The identities of the bassist and drummer (who are both relegated to quiet timekeeping) are unknown, but the other musicians are quite distinctive. With altoist Lee Konitz, tenor saxophonist Warne Marsh and guitarist Billy Bauer contributing their voices, Tristano explores a variety of common chord changes, a brief fugue by Bach and his remarkable title cut. Well worth acquiring. —*Scott Yanow*

Live in Toronto (1952) / Jul. 17, 1952 / Jazz ◆◆◆◆
By 1952, pianist Lennie Tristano was starting to withdraw from public performances, spending most of his time teaching. This formerly unknown recording matches him with four of his best students: altoist Lee Konitz, tenor saxophonist Warne Marsh, bassist Peter Ind and drummer Al Levitt. Together they explore six common chord changes, five of them given new titles. Although not essential, this music is quite enjoyable and a good example of Lennie Tristano's unique approach to jazz improvisation. —*Scott Yanow*

Descent into the Maelstrom / 1952-1966 / Inner City ◆◆◆◆◆
This hard-to-find LP starts off with the utterly unique title cut. On this completely atonal track (which predates Cecil Taylor by a few years), Lennie Tristano overdubbed several pianos and created picturesque and extremely intense music. The remainder of this album mostly comprises leftovers and rehearsal tracks which, considering Tristano's slim discography, is quite welcome. The pianist is heard solo in 1961 and 1965, in a trio with bassist Peter Ind and drummer Roy Haynes in 1952 and (in what might be his last recordings) performing a pair of originals with bassist Sonny Dallas and drummer Nick Stabulas in 1966. Tristano fans can consider this important release to be essential. —*Scott Yanow*

**The Complete Atlantic Recordings of Lennie Tristano, Lee Konitz & Warne
  Marsh** / Jun. 11, 1954-1961 / Mosaic ◆◆◆◆◆
Pianist Lennie Tristano was an early inspiration and a major influence on the playing of altoist Lee Konitz and tenor saxophonist Warne Marsh. Their very notable and highly original Capitol recordings of 1949—with the quiet metronomic rhythm section, advanced melodic improvising and reharmonizations—stood apart from the typical bop of the period. By 1955, when the earliest performances on this limited-edition 1997 six-CD set were recorded, the trio was not working together very often; in fact, Tristano was mostly functioning as a teacher, only surfacing for occasional records and club dates. Despite the title of the box, Tristano, Konitz and Marsh never all appeared on the same Atlantic record. However, their individual projects and collaborations during the era were of consistently high quality. Included on the set are a live quartet date with Konitz and Tristano, a couple of the pianist's solo and trio sessions (including a few controversial items where he overdubbed and even sped up piano parts), several Konitz quartet sets (with such sidemen as pianists Sal Mosca and Jimmy Rowles and guitarist Billy Bauer), a Marsh trio/quartet album, and a stimulating meeting between Konitz and Marsh (with Mosca and Bauer) in a sextet. Four of the performances were previously unreleased, and one of the Konitz albums was formerly only available in Japan. Although the inventive music often utilizes familiar chord changes, there are plenty of surprises in the cool-toned solos, and this is well worth acquiring by bop collectors. —*Scott Yanow*

Lennie Tristano Quartet / Jun. 11, 1955 / Atlantic ◆◆◆◆◆
These are previously unreleased performances from the Sing Song Room date. Here pianist Tristano presented his music in more refined terms with alto saxophonist Lee Konitz's interplay both in the Tristano tradition and on his own personal terms. This was a set of excellent vintage that remains remarkably stimulating. —*Bob Rusch*

☆ **Requiem** / Jun. 11, 1955-1961 / Atlantic ◆◆◆◆◆
This two-LP set reissues the complete contents of pianist Lennie Tristano's two Atlantic studio albums, which were originally titled *Lennie Tristano* and *The New Tristano*. The first album was considered very controversial, for on four selections Tristano overdubbed several pianos and altered the tape, speeding up and slowing down the individual tracks. The results are quite listenable but received a lot of negative comments at the time. The remainder of the first album matches Tristano with altoist Lee Konitz, bassist Gene Ramey and drummer Art Taylor and, although more conventional, are quite individual; the quartet takes apart and evaluates five standards. The second album features Tristano's solo piano (without any overdubbing) in 1961, years after he had stopped performing regularly in public. He has rarely played better than on these originals, making this set quite essential for all serious jazz collections. —*Scott Yanow*

New York Improvisations / 1955-1956 / Elektra ◆◆◆◆
By the mid-'50s pianist Lennie Tristano was pretty much a recluse, enthusiastically teaching his approach to jazz but rarely performing in public. This album has nine of his improvisations that were performed in his studio with the assistance of bassist Peter Ind and drummer Tom Weyburn. Tristano was one of the most talented jazz pianists in history, so practically every recording of his is worth savoring, especially considering that there are relatively few. These spontaneous solos (over common chord patterns) are no exception. —*Scott Yanow*

Continuity / Oct. 1958+Jun. 1964 / Jazz ◆◆◆◆
These valuable recordings document the great pianist Lennie Tristano during his later years, when public appearances were rare and recordings only an infrequent event. Tristano is heard playing at the Half Note on two separate occasions. Warne Marsh is on tenor, altoist Lee Konitz is a major asset to the selections from 1964, and the rhythm sections include either Henry Grimes or Sonny Dallas on bass and Paul Motian or Nick Stabulas on drums. The recording quality is decent if not admirable, but it is the music (six explorations of common chord changes and a 50-second "Everything Happens to Me") that is wonderful. Tristano, Marsh and Konitz constantly create new melody lines and make highly original music. —*Scott Yanow*

Note to Note / 1964-Mar. 12, 1993 / Jazz ◆◆
This LP-length CD contains five improvisations by pianist Lennie Tristano and bassist Sonny Dallas on "originals" based closely on common chord patterns and melodies. It was Tristano's wish that drums be added to these tapes at a later date, so his daughter Carol Tristano overdubbed her rather basic timekeeping in 1993. Tristano collectors and completists will be interested in acquiring this CD, but in reality the music is just average and nothing all that surprising occurs. —*Scott Yanow*

Lennie Tristano Memorial Concert / Jan. 28, 1979-Jan. 29, 1980 / Jazz ◆◆◆
After his death, pianist/teacher Lennie Tristano was paid tribute to at a lavish Town Hall concert. This five-LP set has all of the music, plus a seven-minute drum solo recorded by Max Roach a year later. Many of Tristano's top students (although not Lee Konitz) are heard from, including pianists Liz Gorrill, Lloyd Lifton, Virg Dzurinko, Sal Mosca and Connie Crothers, the solo guitar of Larry Meyer, unaccompanied flute performances by both Fran Canisius and Nomi Rosen, and six a cappella vocals from Lynn Anderson. Lennie Tristano was worshipped as a guru by some of these players (which sometimes results in overly precious performances) but in general the music is fairly rewarding. Not too surprisingly tenor saxophonist Warne Marsh (with a pianoless trio) and singer Sheila Jordan emerge as the solo stars. —*Scott Yanow*

Bobby Troup

b. Oct. 18, 1918, Harrisburg, PA
Piano, Vocals, Lyricist / Swing, Middle-Of-The-Road Pop
Bobby Troup is not strictly a jazz performer, but he has made several important contributions to the music. As a composer he has written "Daddy," "Snooty Little Cutie," "Baby, Baby All the Time" and the major hit "Route 66." Troup has long been a fine pianist (having a regular jazz trio in the 1950s), a personable singer (although some of his early records were overly mannered) and an actor, and during 1956-58 he moderated a legendary television series (*Stars of Jazz*) that featured a who's who of jazz players. He also produced some best-selling records for his wife, Julie London. —*Scott Yanow*

Bobby / Aug. 1953-May 1954 / Capitol ◆◆

Bobby Troup Sings Johnny Mercer / Jan. 28, 1955 / Bethlehem ◆◆◆◆◆

● **The Feeling of Jazz** / Sep. 17, 1955-Jun. 23, 1967 / Star Line ◆◆◆◆◆
Bobby Troup has long been a multitalented individual. This Star Line CD, which contains previously unissued performances from several settings, features Troup singing and playing a variety of high-quality songs, many of which he wrote. Highlights include Troup's lyrics to "Walkin' Shoes" and his hits "Daddy," "The

Three Bears," "Girl Talk" and "Route 66" along with some cheerful novelties and standards. Singing in a style that is both gentle and forceful (and somehow hip for the period without sounding dated today), Bobby Troup is in excellent form throughout this definitive release. —*Scott Yanow*

Bobby Swings Tenderly / 1957 / Mode ◆◆◆
This is one of pianist/vocalist/composer Bobby Troup's few (and possibly only) all-instrumental dates. Accompanied by cool-toned horns (valve trombonist Bob Enevoldsen, trumpeter Stu Williamson, tenor saxophonist Ted Nash and baritonist Ronnie Lang) along with bassist Buddy Clark and drummer Mel Lewis, Troup explores eight familiar standards plus his own "I See Your Bass Before Me." The easy-listening music that is heard on this V.S.O.P. LP (not yet out on CD) is fine if not overly stimulating. The emphasis is on ballads and mellow playing. —*Scott Yanow*

Frankie Trumbauer

b. May 30, 1901, Carbondale, IL, d. Jun. 11, 1956, Kansas City, MO
C-Melody Saxophone / Traditional Jazz, Classic Jazz, Dixieland
The preeminent white saxophonist of the 1920s, Frankie Trumbauer was a major influence on jazz performers of all colors—at his peak, his supreme standing on the C-melody sax was comparable to the kind of dominance later enjoyed by Charlie Parker on alto. Born May 30, 1901, in Carbondale, IL, Trumbauer—often called "Tram" by his contemporaries—was playing with Chicago's Benson Orchestra when he was spotted by Bix Beiderbecke and quickly recruited to join the legendary cornetist in Jean Goldkette's orchestra. Soon Tram had climbed to the position of Goldkette's musical director, earning notoriety for the impeccable technique of his light-toned solos; he cut some of the definitive records of the era with Beiderbecke, "Singin' the Blues" among them, and by 1927, the two were reunited in Paul Whiteman's orchestra. Trumbauer remained with Whiteman until 1932, returning in 1933 for a five-year stint. In 1936, he took command of the Three T's, a small group out of the Whiteman band that featured the Teagarden brothers; in 1938, he moved on to lead a big band of his own. With the onset of World War II, Trumbauer was assigned to the Civil Aeronautics Authority. After World War II, other than a few obscure recordings in 1946, Trumbauer permanently retired from music, working as a pilot. —*Jason Ankeny*

● **Tram 1** / June 14, 1923-May 22, 1929 / The Old Masters ◆◆◆◆
Frankie Trumbauer has received unfair treatment in some jazz history books. A brilliant C-melody saxophonist, Tram was overshadowed by his good friend, cornetist Bix Beiderbecke; many forget that some of Bix's greatest solos were taken on records actually led by Trumbauer. Fortunately, the collector's TOM label has reissued on three CDs not only all of Trumbauer's dates as a leader through 1934 that do not include Beiderbecke, but also Tram's features with Paul Whiteman, plus some other notable appearances as a sideman. The first volume is the most significant, featuring Tram as early as 1923 (on "I Never Miss the Sunshine" with the Benson Orchestra of Chicago) along with dates made with the Mound City Blue Blowers, the Cotton Pickers, Ray Miller's Orchestra, Red Nichols (including "Make My Cot Where the Cot-Cot-Cotton Grows"), Whiteman, the Mason-Dixon Orchestra, and Trumbauer's own recording group. The historic high point is provided on one of two previously unreleased numbers by vocalist Bee Palmer. During "Singin' the Blues," she sings some vocalese (based on the solos of Bix and Tram two years earlier), predating all other vocalese records by over 15 years. —*Scott Yanow*

Tram 2 / Sep. 18, 1929-Sep. 8, 1930 / The Old Masters ◆◆◆◆◆
The second of three TOM CDs that put the focus on the great C-melody saxophonist Frankie Trumbauer includes his features with Paul Whiteman's Orchestra and his own sessions as a leader during a 12-month period. Cornetist Bix Beiderbecke had departed by then, but Tram is in prime form. He shares the spotlight with cornetist Andy Secrest, violinist Joe Venuti and guitarist Eddie Lang; among the singers, Bing Crosby and Mildred Bailey make appearances. The music ranges from pre-swing jazz to high-quality dance music. Highlights include "Nobody's Sweetheart," "Manhattan Rag," "Runnin' Ragged," "Happy Feet" and "Get Happy." Highly recommended to 1920s collectors, as are the other two CDs in this rewarding series. —*Scott Yanow*

Tram 3 / Apr. 10, 1931-Feb. 23, 1934 / The Old Masters ◆◆◆◆
Due to an excess of routine appearances by a vocal group called "the King's Jesters," this CD is not quite as essential to early jazz collectors as the first two in this series, but it is worth picking up. C-melody saxophonist Frankie Trumbauer finally received his due in TOM's series, which reissued not only all of his early sessions as a leader (other than the very familiar selections with cornetist Bix Beiderbecke), but his features with Paul Whiteman's Orchestra and other groups. Despite all of the vocals, Trumbauer has plenty of solo space on these cuts from 1931-32, plus five from 1934. Bing Crosby drops by for "Love Me Tonight" and "Some of These Days," a young Johnny Mercer is excellent on "Sizzling One-Step Medley," and the

later tracks find trombonist-singer Jack Teagarden as Tram's co-star (including two versions of "China Boy"). —*Scott Yanow*

Tuck & Patti

f. 1981
Group / Folk, Crossover Jazz, Standards
Over a career of jazz, R&B and crossover recordings, husband-and-wife duo Tuck & Patti produce a remarkable amount of music, especially considering that the duo rely on the textures of only guitar and voice. Tuck Andress was born in Oklahoma and studied classical guitar at Stanford University before traveling to Las Vegas to audition for a show band in 1980; also there was Patti Cathcart, a San Francisco native who was classically trained in the Bay Area. The two hit it off immediately, and began to perform as a duo around California beginning in 1981. They were married in 1983, but resisted recording contracts so they could cement their unique sound. Finally, in 1987, Tuck & Patti signed to Windham Hill Jazz, recording albums for the label in 1988 (*Tears of Joy*), 1989 (*Love Warriors*) and 1991 (*Dream*). Tuck Andress also released several solo albums for Windham Hill, and the duo signed to Epic in 1995. Tuck & Patti's first album for Epic, *Learning How to Fly*, alternated Cathcart originals with several covers of contemporary standards. —*John Bush*

● **Tears of Joy** / 1988 / Windham Hill ◆◆◆◆◆
● **The Best of Tuck & Patti** / 1988-1991 / Windham Hill ◆◆◆◆◆
Love Warriors / 1989 / Windham Hill ◆◆◆◆◆
Reckless Precision / 1990 / Windham Hill ◆◆◆◆
Guitarist Tuck Andress of Tuck & Patti went off on his own temporarily to record this CD, a solo electric guitar outing utilizing no overdubbing and just a bit of editing on "Grooves of Joy." Jazz standards literally alternate with newer material (except "Louie, Louie," three of which are Tuck's compositions. Not too surprisingly, Tuck's guitar playing is quite self-sufficient, a group unto itself. He is respectful on the standards (which include "Over the Rainbow," "Body and Soul" and "Manha de Carnaval") and a bit more adventurous on the other material. Tuck's style at times hints a little at Stanley Jordan (although without the tapping) and Joe Pass (on "Stella by Starlight") but he is original enough to be distinctive. Other than the overlong and episodic "Grooves of Joy," every track is quite rewarding. —*Scott Yanow*

Dream / 1991 / Windham Hill ◆◆◆◆
The third effort from this duo has a mix of originals (three tunes by Patti) and fine versions of songs by Stevie Wonder, Bernstein/Sondheim, Jimmy Cliff, J.B. Lenoir and jazz artist Horace Silver among others. As usual, all you'll hear is Tuck's guitar and Patti's voice, two splendid instruments exploring their fullest potential. —*Backroads Music/Heartbeats*

Learning How to Fly / 1995 / Epic ◆◆◆

Big Joe Turner

b. May 18, 1911, Kansas City, MO, d. Nov. 24, 1985, Inglewood, CA
Vocals / Swing, Jump Blues, R&B, Rock 'n' Roll
The premier blues shouter of the postwar era, Big Joe Turner's roar could rattle the very foundation of any gin joint he sang within—and that's without a microphone. Turner was a resilient figure in the history of blues—he effortlessly spanned boogie-woogie, jump blues, even the first wave of rock 'n' roll, enjoying great success in each genre.

Turner, whose powerful physique certainly matched his vocal might, was a product of the swinging, wide-open Kansas City scene. Even in his teens, the big-boned Turner looked entirely mature enough to gain entry to various K.C. niteries. He ended up simultaneously tending bar and singing the blues before hooking up with boogie piano master Pete Johnson during the early '30s. Theirs was a partnership that would endure for 13 years.

The pair initially traveled to New York at John Hammond's behest in 1936. On December 23, 1938, they appeared on the fabled Spirituals to Swing concert at Carnegie Hall on a bill with Big Bill Broonzy, Sonny Terry, the Golden Gate Quartet, and Count Basie. Big Joe and Johnson performed "Low Down Dog" and "It's All Right, Baby" on the historic show, kicking off a boogie-woogie craze that landed them a long-running slot at the Cafe Society (along with piano giants Meade Lux Lewis and Albert Ammons).

As 1938 came to a close, Turner and Johnson waxed the thundering "Roll 'Em Pete" for Vocalion. It was a thrilling up-tempo number anchored by Johnson's crashing 88s, and Turner would re-record it many times over the decades. Turner and Johnson waxed their seminal blues "Cherry Red" the next year for Vocalion with trumpeter Hot Lips Page and a full combo in support. In 1940, the massive shouter moved over to Decca and cut "Piney Brown Blues" with Johnson rippling the ivories. But not all of Turner's Decca sides teamed him with Johnson; Willie

"The Lion" Smith accompanied him on the mournful "Careless Love," while Freddie Slack's Trio provided backing for "Rocks in My Bed" in 1941.

Turner ventured out to the West Coast during the war years, building quite a following while ensconced on the L.A. circuit. In 1945, he signed on with National Records and cut some fine small combo platters under Herb Abramson's supervision. Turner remained with National through 1947, belting an exuberant "My Gal's a Jockey" that became his first national R&B smash. Contracts didn't stop him from waxing an incredibly risqué two-part "Around the Clock" for the aptly named Stag imprint (as Big Vernon!) in 1947. There were also solid sessions for Aladdin that year that included a wild vocal duel with one of Turner's principal rivals, Wynonie Harris, on the ribald two-part "Battle of the Blues."

Few West Coast indie labels of the late '40s didn't boast at least one or two Turner titles in their catalogs. The shouter bounced from RPM to Down Beat/Swing Time to MGM (all those dates were anchored by Johnson's piano) to Texas-based Freedom (which moved some of their masters to Specialty) to Imperial in 1950 (his New Orleans backing crew there included a young Fats Domino on piano). But apart from the 1950 Freedom 78, "Still in the Dark," none of Big Joe's records were selling particularly well. When Atlantic Records bosses Abramson and Ahmet Ertegun fortuitously dropped by the Apollo Theater to check out Count Basie's band one day, they discovered that Turner had temporarily replaced Jimmy Rushing as the Basie band's front man, and he was having a tough go of it. Atlantic picked up his spirits by picking up his recording contract, and Big Joe Turner's heyday was about to commence.

At Turner's first Atlantic date in April of 1951, he imparted a gorgeously world-weary reading to the moving blues ballad "Chains of Love" (co-penned by Ertegun and pianist Harry Van Walls) that restored him to the uppermost reaches of the R&B charts. From there, the hits came in droves: "Chill Is On," "Sweet Sixteen" (yeah, the same downbeat blues B.B. King's usually associated with; Turner did it first), and "Don't You Cry" were all done in New York, and all hit big.

Big Joe Turner had no problem whatsoever adapting his prodigious pipes to whatever regional setting he was in. In 1953, he cut his first R&B chart-topper, the storming rocker "Honey Hush" (later covered by Johnny Burnette and Jerry Lee Lewis), in New Orleans, with trombonist Pluma Davis and tenor saxman Lee Allen in rip-roaring support. Before the year was through, he stopped off in Chicago to record with slide guitarist Elmore James' considerably rougher-edged combo and hit again with the salacious "T.V. Mama."

Prolific Atlantic house writer Jesse Stone was the source of Turner's biggest smash of all, "Shake, Rattle and Roll," which proved his second chart-topper in 1954. With the Atlantic braintrust reportedly chiming in on the chorus behind Turner's rumbling lead, the song sported enough pop possibilities to merit a considerably cleaned-up cover by Bill Haley & the Comets (and a subsequent version by Elvis Presley that came a lot closer to the original leering intent).

Suddenly, at the age of 43, Big Joe Turner was a rock star. His jumping follow-ups—"Well All Right," "Flip Flop and Fly," "Hide and Seek," "Morning, Noon and Night," "The Chicken and the Hawk"—all mined the same goodtime groove as "Shake, Rattle and Roll," with crisp backing from New York's top session aces and typically superb production by Ertegun and Jerry Wexler.

Turner turned up on a couple episodes of the groundbreaking TV program *Showtime at the Apollo* during the mid-'50s, commanding center stage with a joyous rendition of "Shake, Rattle and Roll" in front of saxman Paul "Hucklebuck" Williams' band. Nor was the silver screen immune to his considerable charms: Turner mimed a couple of numbers in the 1957 film *Shake Rattle & Rock* (Fats Domino and Mike "Mannix" Connors also starred in the flick).

Updating the pre-war number "Corrine Corrina" was an inspired notion that provided Turner with another massive seller in 1956. But after the two-sided hit "Rock a While"/"Lipstick Powder and Paint" later that year, his Atlantic output swiftly faded from commercial acceptance. Atlantic's recording strategy wisely involved recording Turner in a jazzier setting for the adult-oriented album market; to that end, a Kansas City-styled set (with his former partner Johnson at the piano stool) was laid down in 1956 and remains a linchpin of his legacy.

Turner stayed on at Atlantic into 1959, but nobody bought his violin-enriched remake of "Chains of Love" (on the other hand, a revival of "Honey Hush" with King Curtis blowing a scorching sax break from the same session was a gem in its own right). The '60s didn't produce too much of lasting substance for the shouter—he actually cut an album with longtime admirer Haley and his latest batch of Comets in Mexico City in 1966!

But by the tail end of the decade, Big Joe Turner's essential contributions to blues history were beginning to receive proper recognition; he cut LPs for BluesWay and Blues Time. During the '70s and '80s, Turner recorded prolifically for Norman Granz's jazz-oriented Pablo label. These were super-relaxed impromptu sessions that often paired the allegedly illiterate shouter with various jazz luminaries in what amounted to loosely run jam sessions. Turner contentedly roared the familiar lyrics of one or another of his hits, then sat back while some-

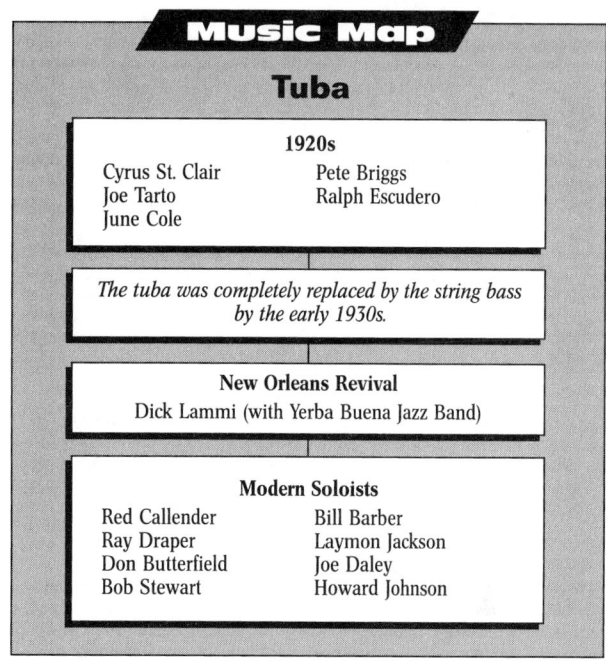

Music Map

Tuba

1920s

Cyrus St. Clair	Pete Briggs
Joe Tarto	Ralph Escudero
June Cole	

The tuba was completely replaced by the string bass by the early 1930s.

New Orleans Revival

Dick Lammi (with Yerba Buena Jazz Band)

Modern Soloists

Red Callender	Bill Barber
Ray Draper	Laymon Jackson
Don Butterfield	Joe Daley
Bob Stewart	Howard Johnson

body took a lengthy solo. Other notable album projects included a 1983 collaboration with Roomful of Blues, *Blues Train,* for Muse. Although health problems and the size of his humongous frame forced him to sit down during his latter-day performances, Turner continued to tour until shortly before his death in 1985. They called him the Boss of the Blues, and the appellation was truly a fitting one: when Big Joe Turner shouted a lyric, you were definitely at his beck and call. *—Bill Dahl*

☆ **Big, Bad & Blue: The Big Joe Turner Anthology** / Dec. 30, 1938-Jan. 26, 1983 / Rhino ♦♦♦♦♦

Rhino has done a stellar job of cross-licensing to present an exhaustive three-disc, 62-track compilation that traces the booming jump blues belter's recording career from its Kansas City-bred beginnings with pianist Pete Johnson in 1938 through the postwar years with the National, Aladdin, Down Beat, and Freedom labels and on into his R&B heyday on Atlantic from 1951 to 1959. Of course, all the great prototypical rockers are aboard—"Honey Hush," "Shake, Rattle and Roll," "Flip Flop and Fly," Corrine Corrina"—and the set closes with three far more recent entries that are the weakest tracks on the entire anthology. The sheer power of Big Joe's pipes was overwhelming, his combos cooked mercilessly, and this set is one to get. *—Bill Dahl*

I've Been to Kansas City / Nov. 11, 1940-Jul. 17, 1941 / Decca ♦♦♦♦♦

This excellent 1990 CD reissues singer Big Joe Turner's first eight recordings for Decca and the six songs (plus two alternate takes) that he made with the remarkable pianist Art Tatum. Turner is joined by trumpeter Hot Lips Page and a top Kansas City group (including pianist Pete Johnson) for "Piney Brown Blues," has four surprisingly effective duets with the sophisticated pianist Willie "The Lion" Smith, and is backed by pianist Sammy Price's trio for three of the four numbers that he recorded on July 17, 1941. The Tatum sides (highlighted by the classic "Wee Baby Blues" and "Corrine, Corrina") also feature trumpeter Joe Thomas and (on two songs) clarinetist Edmond Hall prominently in the backup group. Just 29 and 30 during this time, Turner already sounded quite mature and powerful. *—Scott Yanow*

☆ **Complete 1940-1944** / Nov. 11, 1940-Nov. 13, 1944 / Official ♦♦♦♦♦

Big Joe Turner's 25 Decca recordings are all included on this excellent set. The music is consistently exciting and finds the blues singer in prime form. His accompaniment is quite varied and always colorful, with such pianists as Art Tatum, Pete Johnson, Willie "The Lion" Smith (a perfect match), Sam Price and the surprisingly effective Freddie Slack all getting their spots. Turner had a remarkably long and commercially successful career considering that he never changed his basic approach; he just never went out of style. *—Scott Yanow*

Every Day in the Week / Sep. 8, 1941-Apr. 13, 1967 / GRP/Decca ♦♦♦♦♦

Most of the material on this grab bag dates from early- and mid-'40s sessions for Decca. Rather muted and jazzy in feel, they're made more interesting or tedious, depending on your perspective, by the inclusion of many alternate takes (some previously unissued). As these are grouped together one after another, it can make tough listening for the general fan, although Turner completists will appreciate the attention to detail. Rounding out the collection are four 1963-64 tracks which awkwardly update Turner's R&B with modern soul and pop touches, and a track from a 1967 Bluesway LP. —*Richie Unterberger*

Have No Fear, Big Joe Turner Is Here / Feb. 2, 1945-Nov. 29, 1947 / Savoy ◆◆◆◆
Producer Herb Abramson's first encounters with Big Joe Turner weren't at Atlantic, but for the National logo, where Turner paused from 1945 to 1947 and cut the 26 swinging numbers on this collection. For once, the CD format limits the amount of selections rather than enlarging it; the original two-LP version of this package boasted a few more cuts. Pete Johnson returns to run the 88s on the first seven numbers (including a two-part cover of Saunders King's "S.K. Blues"), and familiar names like saxman Wild Bill Moore and drummer Red Saunders also turn up. "Sally Zu-Zazz," "I Got Love for Sale," and "My Gal's a Jockey" capture the peerless shouter at his ribald best. —*Bill Dahl*

Tell Me Pretty Baby / Nov. 1947-1949 / Arhoolie ◆◆◆◆
Lusty, romping jump blues and boogies from 1947-1949 that teams Big Joe Turner with his longtime piano partner Pete Johnson and a coterie of solid L.A. sessioneers. The two dozen entries include party rockers like "Wine-O-Baby Boogie," "Christmas Date Boogie," "I Don't Dig It," and an incredibly raunchy two-part "Around the Clock Blues" (where Turner spends his time in a by-the-hour sexual tryst). —*Bill Dahl*

Rhythm & Blues Years / Apr. 17, 1951-Sep. 29, 1959 / Atlantic ◆◆◆◆◆
Picks up the rest of the 1950s Atlantic Records motherlode. The Chicago-cut double-entendre gem "TV Mama" (with Elmore James on guitar), the lighthearted rockers "Rock a While," "Morning Noon & Night," and "Lipstick, Powder & Paint," and a rip-snorting remake of Turner's classic "Roll 'Em Pete," here titled "(We're Gonna) Jump for Joy," that in its own way rivals the original (King Curtis' blistering sax solo doesn't hurt), are among the many highlights on the 28-song collection. —*Bill Dahl*

★ **Big Joe Turner's Greatest Hits** / Apr. 19, 1951-Jan. 22, 1958 / Atlantic ◆◆◆◆
The best single-disc collection available of Turner's seminal 1950s Atlantic sides (21 sides in all). Most of the essential stuff is here—the world-weary blues ballads "Chains of Love" and "Sweet Sixteen," the rockers "Shake, Rattle and Roll," "Flip Flop and Fly," and "Boogie Woogie Country Girl," and a lusty "Well All Right" that rates with Turner's best jump blues outings ever. —*Bill Dahl*

★ **Very Best of Big Joe Turner** / 1951-1959 / Rhino ◆◆◆◆◆
The Very Best of Big Joe Turner is an excellent 16-track collection that features his biggest hits from 1951-1959, including "Chains of Love," "Sweet Sixteen," "Honey Hush," "TV Mama," "Shake, Rattle and Roll," "Well All Right," "Flip Flop and Fly," "Hide and Seek," "The Chicken and the Hawk (Up, Up and Away)," "Boogie Woogie Country Girl," "Corrine Corrina" and "Midnight Special Train." All of his best-known songs in their hit versions are available on this concise, affordable disc, which makes for an ideal introduction to this legendary R&B vocalist. —*Stephen Thomas Erlewine*

☆ **Boss of the Blues** / Mar. 6, 1956-Mar. 7, 1956 / Atlantic ◆◆◆◆◆
During an era when Big Joe Turner recordings were often surprise hits with rock 'n' roll fans (particularly "Shake, Rattle and Roll"), he occasionally recorded no-nonsense blues-oriented jazz dates too. This reissue album matched Turner for one of the last times with the veteran boogie-woogie pianist Pete Johnson and also includes a variety of top swing players: trumpeter Joe Newman, trombonist Lawrence Brown, altoist Pete Brown, tenor saxophonist Frank Wess, guitarist Freddie Green, bassist Walter Page and drummer Cliff Leeman. It is not surprising, considering the number of Basieites on the date, that the band often sounds like a Count Basie combo. Turner is in top form on remakes of some of his early tunes (including "Cherry Red," "Roll 'Em Pete" and "Wee Baby Blues"), a few traditional blues and a couple of swing standards. This music should appeal to many listeners. —*Scott Yanow*

Big Joe Rides Again / Mar. 7, 1956-Sep. 10, 1959 / Atlantic ◆◆◆◆
With the exception of one selection ("Pennies from Heaven") left over from his 1956 record *The Boss of the Blue*, the music on this album was all recorded in September 1959. Veteran blues singer Big Joe Turner returns to his roots, belting out blues and early standards while accompanied by an octet arranged by Ernie Wilkins. Among the key sidemen are the great tenor Coleman Hawkins, trombonist Vic Dickenson, trumpeter Paul Ricard and altoist Jerome Richardson; and the highlights include "Nobody in Mind," "Rebecca" and "Don't You Make Me High." An excellent outing for Turner, whose boisterous style would be largely unchanged over his half-century career. —*Scott Yanow*

Singing the Blues / Dec. 1967 / Mobile Fidelity ◆◆◆
Big Joe Turner made relatively few recordings during 1960-66, but things started to look up in 1967 when he began recording for Bluesway. His initial Bluesway set has been reissued as a Mobile Fidelity audiophile CD. Backed by some top studio players of the era (Buddy Lucas on tenor and harmonica along with a four-piece rhythm section), the 56-year old classic blues singer shows that he was still in prime form. Nothing too surprising occurs other than the fact that the ten songs are all Turner's originals. Best-known are the two vintage hits "Roll 'Em Pete" and "Cherry Red," while some of the newer tunes are more forgettable although still delivered with spirit. —*Scott Yanow*

Bosses of the Blues, Vol. 1 / Aug. 18, 1969-Aug. 19, 1969 / RCA/Bluebird ◆◆◆◆
Two Bluesway albums recorded on consecutive days are reissued in full on this single CD. Big Joe Turner sings eight numbers while T-Bone Walker stretches out on seven; both mix together remakes of earlier hits with some newer material. While Turner is accompanied by an orchestra, Walker is joined by a crack studio group with some space allocated to the young tenor Tom Scott. Although not essential, this CD finds the two bluesmen in excellent form; pity that they did not record together. —*Scott Yanow*

Texas Style / Apr. 26, 1971 / Evidence ◆◆◆
This somewhat obscure Black & Blue session (reissued by Evidence on CD) features the great blues singer Big Joe Turner a year before he hooked up with the Pablo label. Turner is backed by a particularly colorful and supportive trio comprising pianist Milt Buckner (the master of block chords), bassist Slam Stewart (who takes a few of his trademark solos in which he sings along with his bowed bass) and veteran swing drummer Jo Jones. Turner was still in his prime at the time and, even if his material was not too adventurous, the music (which includes a few newer bluish originals plus such standbys as "Cherry Red" and "'Tain't Nobody's Bizness If I Do") is performed with enthusiasm and solid swing. —*Scott Yanow*

Flip, Flop & Fly / Apr. 17, 1972+Apr. 24, 1972 / Pablo ◆◆◆◆◆
Big Joe Turner's first of many recordings for Pablo was not initially released until 1989. In the spring of 1972 the 60-year-old blues singer toured Europe with the Count Basie Orchestra, and this CD has music from two concerts. Turner's repertoire offered few surprises at that late date (he mostly performs remakes of earlier hits) but his interplay with the Basie big band makes this set somewhat special. Among the soloists heard from are tenors Eddie "Lockjaw" Davis and Jimmy Forrest, trumpeter Pete Minger, altoist Curtis Peagler and trombonist Al Grey along with Basie himself. This is easily recommended to Big Joe Turner fans and a rare opportunity for him to be heard fronting a solid big band. —*Scott Yanow*

Life Ain't Easy / Jun. 3, 1974 / Original Jazz Classics ◆◆◆
Big Joe Turner's Pablo recordings of 1974-84 tended to be loose and sometimes a bit sloppy (with some overlong performances) but they were always full of spirit. On this particular CD, Turner's classic singing is matched with a mostly all-star crew including trumpeter Roy Eldridge, trombonist Al Grey, tenor saxophonist Lee Allen, bassist Ray Brown and drummer Earl Palmer (along with guitarist Thomas Gadson and Jimmy Robins on piano and organ). Turner performs Woody Guthrie's "So Long" and five of his recent originals; Eldridge and Grey's occasional competitive solos uplift the music. —*Scott Yanow*

The Trumpet Kings Meet Joe Turner / Sep. 19, 1974 / Original Jazz Classics ◆◆◆◆
This album has a most unusual session. Veteran blues singer Joe Turner and his usual rhythm section of the mid-'70s (which includes guitarist Pee Wee Crayton) are joined by four notable trumpeters: Dizzy Gillespie, Roy Eldridge, Harry "Sweets" Edison and Clark Terry. On three blues (including the 15-minute "I Know You Love Me Baby") and "Tain't Nobody's Bizness If I Do," the group stretches out with each of the trumpeters getting ample solo space. It is not a classic outing (a little more planning and better material might have helped) but it is colorful and unique enough to be easily recommended to straightahead jazz and blues fans. —*Scott Yanow*

In the Evening / Oct. 1977 / Original Jazz Classics ◆◆◆◆
Many of Big Joe Turner's Pablo recordings matched him with big names, but this workout finds him jubilant and in top form singing with some lesser-known musicians (altoist Bob Smith, Herman Bennett on second guitar, pianist J.D. Nicholson, bassist Winston McGregor, drummer Charles Randall and the only "name" of the date, guitarist Pee Wee Crayton). The solos of Smith (who sounds like a mixture of Tab Smith and Johnny Hodges) and Crayton are consistently excellent, and Big Joe turns everything into blues, including such unlikely material as "Sweet Lorraine" and "Pennies from Heaven." This CD reissue gives listeners a good example of what it was like to catch the great blues singer during a club date with a pickup band. —*Scott Yanow*

Joe Turner (Joseph H. Turner)

b. Nov. 3, 1907, Baltimore, MD, **d.** Jul. 21, 1990, Montreuil, France
Piano / Blues Jazz, New York Blues, West Coast Blues, Stride, Boogie-Woogie
Though endlessly confused with the singer Big Joe Turner, pianist Joe Turner came from a completely different direction, following the James P. Johnson/Fats Waller stride tradition, armed with a superb technique and a fine sense of swing. He started to learn the piano from his mother at age five and began to make a name for himself in Harlem as a teenager shortly after his move to New York in 1925. He was an accompanist to Adelaide Hall in a duo with first Alex Hill and then Francis Carter, the latter with whom he and Hall toured Europe in 1931. He remained in Europe through 1939 when war broke out, upon which he returned to the US to work as a single. After playing with Sy Oliver's army band in 1944-45 and Rex Stewart in 1946, Turner returned to the Continent, residing in Hungary in 1948 and then Switzerland from 1949 to 1962. He settled in Paris in 1962 in a residency at La Calvados, continued to play engagements elsewhere in Europe and occasionally the US and eventually survived to became the last major active stride pianist of his era. Among the few albums of his in print is a 1984 project with Knocky Parker and his Houserockers on Southland (beware: the Schwann catalogue mistakenly includes some Big Joe Turner albums in the Joe Turner listing). —*Richard S. Ginell*

● **Stride by Stride** / Dec. 6, 1960 / Solo Art ◆◆◆◆◆

Another Epoch: Stride Piano / Feb. 6, 1976 / Pablo ◆◆◆◆◆

Effervescent / May 29, 1976 / Classic Jazz ◆◆◆◆

Norris Turney

b. Sep. 8, 1921, Wilmington, OH
Alto Saxophone / Swing
One of the last great Ellingtonians, Norris Turney was the first flute soloist that the Duke Ellington Orchestra ever had. He was also a lyrical altoist influenced by Johnny Hodges and (when called for) an excellent tenor saxophonist too. He started his musical career playing in the Midwest with territory bands like the Jeter-Pillars Orchestra; he was also briefly with Tiny Bradshaw in Chicago and then relocated to New York. Turney was part of the Billy Eckstine Orchestra from 1945-46, but fame would elude him for many years. He soon returned to Ohio and mostly played with local groups. In 1967, Turney toured with Ray Charles, but it was not until his period with Ellington (1969-73) that his talents were fully recognized. Since that time he has been a member of the Savoy Sultans, the Newport All-Stars, various pit orchestras and any situation where his versatility and swinging style can be most appreciated. As a leader, Norris Turney led dates during 1975-78 for Master Jazz, the tiny Harlem label, Black & Blue, and in 1993 for Mapleshade. —*Scott Yanow*

● **Big, Sweet 'n Blue** / Apr. 5, 1993-Mar. 6, 1993 / Mapleshade ◆◆◆◆◆
Since there are not that many alumni of Duke Ellington's Orchestra still active, it is surprising that altoist Norris Turney (who was with Ellington from 1969-73 and eventually replaced the unreplaceable Johnny Hodges) has not been recorded all that extensively during the 20 years since. In fact his Mapleshade debut is the 72-year-old's first session at the head of a quartet, and the music's obvious success is even more impressive when one realizes that Turney had never played with the other musicians (pianist Larry Willis, bassist Walter Booker and drummer Jimmy Cobb) before. Norris Turney is a melodic swing player with a large tone and, since the rhythm section is quite supportive and sympathetic, these renditions of blues, ballads and standards (including his own "Checkered Hat" and three Ellington/Strayhorn pieces) came together rather quickly. Highlights include the lengthy "Blues for Edward," "Blood Count" and "Come Sunday." —*Scott Yanow*

Steve Turre

b. Sep. 12, 1948, Omaha, NE
Trombone, Conch Shell / Bop, Latin Jazz, Hard Bop
One of the finest trombonists of the 1980s and '90s, Steve Turre also introduced the conch shells to jazz. After a brief period on violin he switched to trombone when he was ten. Turre worked locally from age 13, played with Rahsaan Roland Kirk off and on from 1968, recorded with Santana in 1970 and in 1972 toured with Ray Charles. Turre had many diverse musical experiences in the 1970s, including tours with Art Blakey's Jazz Messengers and the Thad Jones/Mel Lewis Orchestra (both in 1973), an opportunity to play trombone and electric bass regularly with Chico Hamilton (1974-76) and recording dates with Woody Shaw and Rahsaan Roland Kirk. Kirk inspired Turre to play exotic shells, and his ability to get a wide range of clear tones is quite impressive. Since that time Turre toured with McCoy Tyner, Dexter Gordon, Slide Hampton, Poncho Sanchez, Hilton Ruiz and Tito Puente among others. In 1987 he joined Dizzy Gillespie's United Nations Orchestra and he has also played regularly with Lester Bowie's Brass Fantasy, the Lead-

ers and the Timeless All-Stars. Turre performed with his Sanctified Shells (a group featuring four trombonists doubling on shells, trumpeter E.J. Allen, bass, drums and several percussionists) at the 1995 Monterey Jazz Festival and has recorded as a leader for Stash, Antilles and Verve. —*Scott Yanow*

Viewpoint / Feb. 7, 1987-Feb. 8, 1987 / Stash ◆◆◆◆
Steve Turre covers a lot of styles on his debut as a leader; from tributes to Kid Ory and Duke Ellington to bop, a bit of free form, and Latin jazz. The trombonist proves that he is comfortable in all of those idioms, making this a rather impressive set. His supporting cast consists of pianist Mulgrew Miller, bassist Peter Washington, drummer Idris Muhammad, occasionally cellist Akua Dixon, extra percussion and (on the Dixielandish piece) clarinetist Haywood Henry, trumpeter Jon Faddis and the tuba of Bob Stewart. Everything works. —*Scott Yanow*

Fire and Ice / Feb. 5, 1988-Feb. 6, 1988 / Stash ◆◆◆◆◆
Steve Turre is one of the most versatile and talented trombonists to emerge during the past 15 years. For his second Stash recording, Turre (who also plays his conch shells on two of the ten songs) utilizes a superb rhythm section (pianist Cedar Walton, bassist Buster Williams and drummer Billy Higgins) plus a jazz string quartet (Quartette Indigo) on six of the selections. The music ranges from standards (including "When Lights Are Low," Monk's "Well You Needn't" and "Mood Indigo") to some memorable originals and one complex piece played by the strings alone. Stimulating music with more than its share of variety. —*Scott Yanow*

Right There / Mar. 30, 1991-Apr. 10, 1991 / Antilles ◆◆◆◆

Sanctified Shells / Jan. 31, 1992-May 11, 1992 / Antilles ◆◆◆◆◆

● **Rhythm Within** / 1995 / Verve ◆◆◆◆◆
Trombonist Steve Turre obviously put a lot of work into this CD, for each of the nine selections has its own purpose and the personnel changes on every cut. Turre doubles on the conch shells and on a few numbers utilizes a "shell choir"; in addition there are often three percussionists, other notable trombonists (including Britt Woodman, Frank Lacy and Robin Eubanks) and such guest soloists as trumpeter Jon Faddis, tenor saxophonist Pharoah Sanders and pianist Herbie Hancock. With highlights including "Funky-T," Yusef Lateef's "Morning," "Since I Fell for You" (a Woodman feature) and "All Blues," this is a particularly memorable and well-conceived set, one of Turre's best. —*Scott Yanow*

● **Steve Turre** / 1996 / Verve ◆◆◆◆◆
No wonder Steve Turre merely used his name as the title of this tour de force, for it is a supremely ambitious, self-defining project that covers an enormous amount of ground and means on one small disc. With his trombone and signature conch shells as a base, Turre expands his reach to embrace the Western Hemisphere—particularly Cuba and Brazil—arranging, composing, inviting stellar guests to chip in, and ending up with a beautiful, swinging record that can't be mistaken for anyone else's. One gets a powerful dose of Turre's unique sound world on the fascinating opening track "In a Sentimental Mood," done bossa nova style with a conch shell solo that sounds like late-period Dizzy Gillespie and a smoky Cassandra Wilson vocal. There are ample layers of Turre's multitracked conch shell harmonies, the sweetest ensemble sound this side of Lombardo and one that is used as a genuinely musical ingredient, not a gimmick. Turre is secure enough to feature the majestic sound of J.J. Johnson, who plays magnificently on the lengthy tone poem "The Emperor"—whose title undoubtedly refers to the elder trombone giant—and on "Steve's Blues." Afro-Cuban music plays a major role here, as Mongo Santamaria's veteran chartmeister Marty Sheller arranges "Ayer Lo Vi Llorar" for the 81-year-old Queen of Boleros, Graciela Perez—and then Mongo himself duels with the madly comping McCoy Tyner on, of course, "Mongo 'n' McCoy." The booklet notes (by Turre himself) are an exhaustive play-by-play of what was clearly an exhausting project, yet the final product has much of the exuberance of a spontaneous jam session. —*Richard S. Ginell*

Stanley Turrentine

b. Apr. 5, 1934, Pittsburgh, PA
Tenor Saxophone / Soul Jazz, Hard Bop, Groove
While highly regarded in soul jazz circles, Stanley Turrentine is one of the finest tenor saxophonists in any style in modern times. He excels at uptempo compositions, in jam sessions, interpretating standards, playing the blues or on ballads. His rich, booming and huge tone, with its strong swing influence, is one of the most striking of any tenor stylist, and during the '70s and '80s made otherwise horrendous mood music worth enduring.

To give you an idea where Turrentine is coming from: Early on, he toured with the R&B band of Lowell Fulson (1950-1951) whose featured pianist at the time was a young Ray Charles. From 1953-1954 he worked with Earl Bostic (perhaps the greatest R&B sax player of all time), where he replaced John Coltrane. He also worked and cut his first albums with Max Roach (1959-1960). Turrentine started recording as a leader on Blue Note in 1959 and 1960, while also participating in some landmark Jimmy Smith sessions such as *Midnight Special, Back at the Chicken Shack* and *Prayer Meetin'.*

His decade-plus association with Shirley Scott was both professional and personal, as they were married most of the time they were also playing together. They frequently recorded, with the featured leader's name often depending on the session's label affiliation. When they divorced and split musically in the early '70s, Turrentine became a crossover star on CTI. Several of his CTI, Fantasy, Elektra and Blue Note albums in the '70s and '80s made the charts. Though their jazz content became proportionally lower, Turrentine's playing remained consistently superb. He returned to straightahead and soul jazz in the '80s, cutting more albums for Fantasy and Elektra, then returning to Blue Note. He's currently on the Musicmasters label. Almost anything Turrentine's recorded, even albums with Stevie Wonder cover songs, are worth hearing for his solos. Many of his classic dates, as well as recent material, is available on CD.

Turrentine is an original, a one-of-a-kind. He does not fit neatly into ordinary jazz categories. What makes Turrentine great is his deep love of the roots of jazz—blues and groove music. He never abandoned these roots to join the more cerebral set of jazz soloists. His recording partnership with Jimmy Smith has given us some of the finest funk groove music of all time, a high-water mark for both artists. This man likes to groove and play funky music! He won't be tamed! —*Bob Porter, Michael Erlewine, and Ron Wynn*

Stan the Man Turrentine / 1959-1960 / Bainbridge ♦♦♦
His earliest album with Turrentine on sax, Sonny Clark or Tommy Flanagan on piano, George Duvivier on bass, and Max Roach on drums. This tends to be uptempo and mainstream. It lacks the distinctive Turrentine sound that later albums show. —*Michael Erlewine*

Look Out / Jun. 18, 1960 / Blue Note ♦♦♦♦♦
With Horace Parlan (p), George Tucker (b), and Al Harewood (d). —*Ron Wynn*

Blue Hour / Dec. 16, 1960 / Blue Note ♦♦♦♦♦
With the Three Sounds —Gene Harris (p), Andrew Simpkinds (b), and William Dowdy (d). A small group setting. This is a beautiful album of relaxed, bluesy sound. —*Michael Erlewine*

Comin' Your Way / Jan. 20, 1961 / Blue Note ♦♦♦♦
With Tommy Turrentine (tp), Horace Parlan (p) George Tucker (b), and Al Harewood (d). Horace Parlan at his bluesy best. —*Ron Wynn*

Up at Minton's / Feb. 23, 1961 / Blue Note ♦♦♦♦
Here is Turrentine with the groove master Grant Green on guitar together at New York's Minton's Playhouse for a live recording. This is very early Green, not long after he relocated to New York from St. Louis. The rhythm section is the trio known as Us Three—Horace Parlan (p), George Tucker (b), and Al Harewood (d). This is available as a 2-CD set from Blue Note and should grace every Turrentine or Green fan's shelves. Although not as funky as he would get, this is wonderful easy-paced listening. Plenty of bluesy soulful music. —*Michael Erlewine*

Up at Minton's, Vol. 2 / Feb. 23, 1961 / Blue Note ♦♦♦♦♦

Dearly Beloved / Jun. 8, 1961 / Blue Note ♦♦♦♦
A trio recording from Blue Note has Turrentine with Shirley Scott on Hammond organ and Roy Brooks on drums. This is the first recording with Turrentine and Scott, who would work together for ten years, later becoming married. —*Michael Erlewine*

Z.T.'s Blues / Sep. 13, 1961 / Blue Note ♦♦♦♦♦
An all-star lineup has Turrentine with Grant Green on guitar and Tommy Flanagan on piano. The rhythm section has Paul Chambers on bass and Art Taylor on drums. Green and Turrentine made few albums together, but the combination is a natural—the two greatest groove masters, bar none. Flanagan seldom appears in this type of setting and his playing is very tasteful. A studio recording by Rudy Van Gelder at Englewood Cliffs, NJ. If you can find a copy of this, it is a keeper. —*Michael Erlewine*

Ballads / 1961-1992 / Blue Note ♦♦♦
Although he's a monster tenor soloist on funky, exuberant, bluesy soul-jazz, Stanley Turrentine is even more awesome on ballads. His rich, steamy sound, full tone, and ability to pace and develop moods is ideal for show tunes and sentimental love songs. This nine-track set begins with Turrentine nicely caressing the melody and turning in a standout treatment on "Willow Weep For Me," continuing through tearjerkers ("Since I Fell For You") and blues anthems ("God Bless The Child"), and closing with Thad Jones' beautiful "A Child Is Born." Turrentine is matched with numerous premier players, and pianist McCoy Tyner, guitarist Jimmy Smith, and even Turrentine's brother Tommy (trumpet) gently support and complement the main soloist. One of the best Blue Note special discs, featuring moving, frequently hypnotic playing from a true tenor great. —*Ron Wynn*

★ **That's Where It's At** / Jan. 2, 1962 / Blue Note ♦♦♦♦♦
A Blue Note release with Les McCann on piano, Herbie Lewis on bass, and Otis Finch on drums. Small group format. Excellent (and exciting) soul-jazz session with Turrentine blowing hot. —*Ron Wynn & Michael Erlewine*

Jubilee Shout / Oct. 18, 1962 / Blue Note ♦♦♦♦
Featuring Turrentine with Sonny Clark on piano and Kenny Burrell on guitar. Also including Tommy Turrentine (tp), Butch Warren (b), and Al Harewood (d). Here is classic funky soul-jazz groove, three up-tempo, three slow. Sonny Clark (p) soars, Turrentine red-hot. —*Ron Wynn & Michael Erlewine*

Never Let Me Go / Jan. 18, 1963+Feb. 13, 1963 / Blue Note ♦♦♦
An early Blue Note album with the Stanley Turrentine Quintet: Turrentine, Shirley Scott (organ), Major Holley (b), Al Harewood (d), and Ray Barretto (cga). —*Michael Erlewine*

A Chip off the Old Block / Oct. 21, 1963 / Blue Note ♦♦♦♦
On Blue Note with Turrentine, Blue Mitchell (tp), Shirley Scott (organ), Earl May (b), and Al Harewood (d). Bluesy with tunes like "Midnight Blue" and "Blues in Hoss' Flat." —*Michael Erlewine*

Hustlin' / Jan. 24, 1964 / Blue Note ♦♦♦
A classic small group with Turrentine on tenor sax, Shirley Scott on the Hammond organ, and Kenny Burrell on guitar. The rhythm section has Bob Cranshaw on bass and Otis Finch on drums. Includes a version of "Goin' Home." —*Michael Erlewine*

In Memory Of / Jun. 3, 1964 / Blue Note ♦♦♦♦♦
The group includes Herbie Hancock (p), Blue Mitchell (tp), Curtis Fuller (tb), Bob Cranshaw (b), and Otis Finch (d). This has not yet been reissued by Blue Note. —*Michael Erlewine*

★ **Let It Go** / Sep. 21, 1964+Apr. 15, 1966 / Impulse! ♦♦♦♦♦
This is vital Turrentine with Shirley Scott on Hammond organ, Ron Carter on bass, and Mack Simpkins on drums. This album includes some additional tracks that were originally released on the Shirley Scott album *Everybody Loves a Lover.* Recorded in Englewood Cliffs, NJ. Husband and wife team Turrentine and Shirley Scott (organ) produce one classic soul-jazz groove album. —*Michael Erlewine*

Joyride / Apr. 14, 1965 / Blue Note ♦♦♦♦♦
Recorded at Englewood Cliffs, NJ, with a very large group that includes all kinds of horns plus Herbie Hancock (p) and Kenny Burrell (g). Arranged by Oliver Nelson. Throbbing tenor solos, with big-band backing. —*Ron Wynn*

Rough 'n Tumble / Jul. 1, 1966 / Blue Note ♦♦♦♦
A somewhat larger group (eight pieces) with Grant Green (g), Blue Mitchell (tp), James Spaulding (as), Pepper Adams (bar), and McCoy Tyner on piano. Recorded at NYC. One of his most popular, tightest soul-jazz releases. —*Ron Wynn*

Easy Walker / Jul. 8, 1966-May 23, 1969 / Blue Note ♦♦♦♦
Easy Walker is a fairly standard but highly enjoyable small-group soul-jazz session from Stanley Turrentine. Backed by a rhythm section of pianist McCoy Tyner, drummer Mickey Roker and bassist Bob Cranshaw, Turrentine turns in a number of rich, round and full-bodied leads which are perfectly complemented by Tyner's strutting, sympathetic piano. Largely divided between mid-tempo grooves and slow blues, with a couple of pop covers like "What the World Needs Now Is Love," thrown in, *Easy Walker* doesn't offer much challenging material, but it does let the musicians work a good groove, and occasionally showcase their improvisational skills, making it a good, relaxing soul-jazz session. The 1997 CD reissue features four bonus tracks that were recorded with drummer Billy Cobham and bassist Gene Taylor, along with Tyner; the highlight of these is a breezy version of Antonio Carlos Jobim's "Wave." —*Stephen Thomas Erlewine*

The Spoiler / Sep. 22, 1966 / Blue Note ♦♦♦♦♦
Other than a few short spots, Stanley Turrentine is the only significant soloist on this CD reissue, which features a diverse program including "When the Sun Comes Out," "Maybe September," "You're Gonna Hear from Me" and a previously unreleased rendition of Max Roach's jazz waltz "Lonesome Lover." Although he is accompanied by an all-star group that includes trumpeter Blue Mitchell, altoist James Spaulding, baritonist Pepper Adams and pianist McCoy Tyner, Turrentine's sidemen could almost have been anonymous studio players, for the tenor is the dominant voice throughout. It is surprising that Pearson did not make more extensive use of the other musicians' unique talents, particularly Tyner. However, despite some potentially indifferent material, Turrentine is in fine form throughout the date, even finding something to say on "Sunny." "La Fiesta" (no relation to the later Chick Corea tune) is the high point of a largely enjoyable set. —*Scott Yanow*

New Time Shuffle / Feb. 17, 1967+Jun. 23, 1967 / Blue Note ♦♦♦
A large-group album for Blue Note. —*Michael Erlewine*

Ain't No Way / May 10, 1968 / Blue Note ✦✦✦
Turrentine in small-group format. The cast includes Shirley Scott on the Hammond organ, McCoy Tyner on piano, Jimmy Ponder on guitar, Bob Cranshaw on bass, and Ray Lucas on drums. Substitute Gene Taylor (b) and Billy Cobham (d) for some cuts. —*Michael Erlewine*

Common Touch! / Aug. 30, 1968 / Blue Note ✦✦✦
This CD reissue brings back an easy-listening set in which tenor saxophonist Stanley Turrentine teams up with his then-wife, organist Shirley Scott, in what was probably their last joint recording. The original LP program is joined by "Ain't No Way" from a slightly earlier date with similar personnel. Even on "Blowin' in the Wind," Turrentine's soulful solos uplift the material, while Scott offers light accompaniment and some gospellish ideas of her own; guitarist Jimmy Ponder also has some spots on the quintet date. Although not essential (no one seems to sweat much and none of the tempos are above a slow-medium pace), this lazy date has its pleasurable moments. —*Scott Yanow*

Look of Love / Sep. 29, 1968-Oct. 6, 1968 / Blue Note ✦✦✦✦
Larger group setting that was recorded at Englewood Cliffs, NJ. Both romantic and lusty, nice sessions. —*Ron Wynn*

Always Something There / Oct. 14, 1968+Oct. 28, 1968 / Blue Note ✦✦
Large group session recorded by Van Gelder. Includes renditions of "Light My Fire" and "Hey Jude." —*Michael Erlewine*

Another Story / Mar. 3, 1969 / Blue Note ✦✦✦✦

Sugar / Nov. 1970 / CTI ✦✦✦✦✦

The Sugar Man / Feb. 1971-Apr. 1971 / CTI ✦✦✦✦

Cherry / May 17, 1972 / CTI ✦✦✦✦

Don't Mess with Mister T. / Jun. 7, 1973 / CTI ✦✦✦✦✦

Pieces of Dreams / May 30, 1974-May 31, 1974 / Original Jazz Classics ✦✦
Tenor saxophonist Stanley Turrentine's recording of Michel Legrand's "Pieces of Dreams" is quite memorable and made the song into a standard. There are two versions of that song on this CD reissue, but unfortunately, the other six numbers and the two added alternate takes are all quite commercial. Turrentine's tenor is joined by electric keyboards, up to three guitarists, a few background vocalists, and strings, all arranged by Gene Page. None of the other then-recent material is up to the level of "Pieces of Dreams," making this a disc that can be safely passed by. —*Scott Yanow*

The Best of Mr. T / 1974-1980 / Fantasy ✦✦✦
Selection of tunes from Turrentine's '70s output from *Everybody Come on Out, The Man with the Sad Face, West Side Highway, Pieces of Dreams, Nightwings, Have You Ever Seen the Rain,* and *Use the Stairs.* —*Michael Erlewine*

In the Pocket / Jan. 1975 / Fantasy ✦

Have You Ever Seen the Rain / Jul. 1975 / Fantasy ✦✦

Everybody Come on Out / Mar. 1976 / Fantasy ✦

The Man with the Sad Face / Aug. 25, 1976-Sep. 28, 1976 / Bainbridge ✦✦✦

Nightwings / Jun. 1977+Jul. 1977 / Fantasy ✦✦

West Side Highway / Jun. 1977+Jul. 1977 / Fantasy ✦✦

What About You! / Jun. 1978+Jul. 1978 / Fantasy ✦✦

Betcha / May 1979-Jun. 1979 / Elektra ✦✦

Tender Togetherness / Apr. 1981 / Elektra ✦✦

Straight Ahead / Nov. 24, 1984 / Blue Note ✦✦✦
Recorded at Power Play Studios, Long Island City, NY. Smaller group. Turrentine with George Benson (g), Jimmy Smith (organ), Ron Carter (b), and Jimmy Madison (d). On two cuts, also Jimmy Ponder (g), and Les McCann (p). Great combination of musicians as on earlier cookers, but time has passed—it does not come off. Pleasant enough, but lacks high spots. —*Michael Erlewine*

Wonderland / Dec. 1986 / Blue Note ✦✦✦✦

La Place / 1989 / Blue Note ✦✦✦

More than a Mood / 1992 / Music Masters ✦✦✦✦
For this quartet date with pianist Cedar Walton, bassist Ron Carter and drummer Billy Higgins (trumpeter Freddie Hubbard sits in on two numbers), Turrentine is in top form on a variety of standards plus Tommy Turrentine's "Thomasville" and Rahsaan Roland Kirk's "Spirits up Above." A fine session. —*Scott Yanow*

If I Could / May 10, 1993-May 12, 1993 / Music Masters ✦✦✦✦
This session from tenor saxophonist Stanley Turrentine often sounds like a CTI recording from the 1970s, although Creed Taylor had nothing to do with it. Backed by Don Sebesky's arrangements and assisted by a strong rhythm section and Hubert Laws' flute, Turrentine's solos are stronger than the melodies and he generally overcomes the unimaginative use of strings on the ballads. Mr. T. is in fine

form and he makes the most of each selection (particularly on the two blues "June Bug" and "A Luta Continua") while Laws comes across as much more creative than he does on most of his own recordings. Recommended. —*Scott Yanow*

Time / 1995 / Music Masters ✦✦✦

Tommy Turrentine

b. Apr. 12, 1928, Pittsburgh, PA
Trumpet / Hard Bop
Stanley Turrentine's older brother, Tommy had a parallel career for awhile. His most significant early gigs were with Benny Carter (1946), Earl Bostic (1952-55) and Charles Mingus (1956) in addition to big band work with Billy Eckstine, Dizzy Gillespie and Count Basie. Turrentine received some recognition playing next to his brother during a well-documented stint with Max Roach (1959-60). In the early '60s he recorded his lone session as a leader (for Time) and appeared on dates led by Horace Parlan, Jackie McLean, Sonny Clark, Lou Donaldson and Stanley Turrentine before retiring from music and falling into obscurity. Tommy Turrentine was a fine hard bop-oriented trumpeter who had the talent to go much further. —*Scott Yanow*

● **Tommy Turrentine** / Jan. 19, 1960 / Bainbridge ✦✦✦✦✦
When he recorded this album, his lone date as a leader, trumpeter Tommy Turrentine (who was a member of Max Roach's group along with his brother, the soon-to-be famous tenor Stanley Turrentine) seemed to have a potentially great future. Unfortunately ill health would eventually force his retirement. Turrentine's set for Time (which has been reissued on CD by Bainbridge) actually features the musicians of Roach's quintet (including brother Stanley, trombonist Julian Priester, bassist Bob Boswell and Roach himself) plus pianist Horace Parlan. The trumpeter contributed five of the seven songs (which are joined by Horace Parlan's "Blues for J.P." and Bud Powell's "Webb City") on this fine straightahead hard bop set. All of the musicians play up-to-par and the results are swinging and fit securely into the modern mainstream of the time. —*Scott Yanow*

Turtle Island String Quartet

f. 1985
Group / Post-Bop, Bop, Third Stream
While the Kronos Quartet cracked open the field of jazz for the once-exclusively-classical string quartet, the Turtle Island String Quartet is the first whose members can actually improvise, thus giving the foursome much credibility in the jazz world. Their repertoire extends from bebop standards like "A Night in Tunisia" to Third Stream material to rock 'n' roll treatments of Robert Johnson's Delta blues ("Crossroads"), throwing in bluegrass, South Indian ragas, and any other influences that they can latch onto—all without the crutch of a rhythm section.
Violinist/cofounder Darol Anger spent nine years (1975-84) as a founding member of the David Grisman Quintet, which helped to open up the possibilities of jazz improvisation for stringed instruments. Just before leaving Grisman, Anger played with violinist David Balakrishnan in a four-violin group called Saheeb. Soon thereafter, the two recorded an album with jazz violinist Matt Glaser—and together with cellist Mark Summer of the Winnipeg Symphony, Anger and Balakrishnan founded the TISQ in 1985. The viola chair has been a revolving door throughout much of the group's history, filled respectively by Irene Sazer, Katrina Wreede and Danny Seidenberg. Balakrishnan in turn was replaced in 1993 by Tracy Silverman. Their first self-titled album for Windham Hill Jazz—released in 1988—led to several more on that label, including the soundtrack for the film *Spider Dreams*. In 1993, the TISQ and the Billy Taylor Trio performed Taylor's *Homage*, one of the more gracefully balanced classical/jazz fusions around, in concert. —*Richard S. Ginell*

● **Windham Hill Essential Series** / 1988-1995 / Windham Hill ✦✦✦✦✦
Turtle Island String Quartet's *Windham Hill Essential Series* is a fine overview of the group's recordings for the label, culling the highlights from each of their albums to provide a definitive introduction to the contemporary instrumental quartet. —*Stephen Thomas Erlewine*

Metropolis / 1989 / Windham Hill ✦✦✦✦

Skylife / Oct. 1990 / Windham Hill ✦✦✦✦✦
The Turtle Island String Quartet's music spans many idioms, from the blues and bluegrass to country, classical and Indian music, with the improvisation and swing of jazz always being in the forefront. Their music, although obviously well-rehearsed, is quite spontaneous in spots and consistently takes chances. Each of the string players (violinists David Balakrishnan and Darol Anger, Katrina Wreede on viola and cellist Mark Summer) contributed compositions to this CD, which also includes a rockish version of Robert Johnson's "Crossroads" and Chick Corea's delightful "Senor Mouse." A stimulating session of surprising string music. —*Scott Yanow*

Shock to the System / 1990 / Windham Hill ✦✦✦

On the Town / 1991 / Windham Hill ✦✦✦✦✦

This CD is simply delightful. Unlike the Kronos Quartet, the members of Turtle Island (violinists Darol Anger and David Balakrishnan, Katrina Wreede on viola and cellist Mark Summer) all improvise; on this collection of swing standards, the effect is often as if one had four Stephane Grappellis. The inventive arrangements really showcase the group's power and creativity. The Billy Taylor trio helps out on "Love for Sale," "Angel Eyes" and "A Smooth One," another trio joins up on "Cheek to Cheek," and there are a couple of guests. But, as shown on a hard-driving version of "Lady Be Good," the Turtle Island String Quartet is quite capable of creating swinging jazz by itself. A gem. —*Scott Yanow*

Spider Dreams / 1992 / Windham Hill ✦✦✦

Who Do We Think We Are? / 1994 / Windham Hill ✦✦✦✦✦

Turtle Island String Quartet is funked up, cooled down, turned asunder, "rhythmatized" jazz played by a string quartet that goes way beyond the intellectual restrictions placed on the string quartet. Turtle Island String Quartet blows away any staid notions about the violin and cello on Thelonius Monk's "Who Do You Think We Are?," the album's title cut and the piece that sets the stage for musical acrobatics. Even Jimi Hendrix's "Gypsy Eyes" is fair game for the group's new musical tricks. —*MusD*

By the Fireside / May 1995 / Windham Hill ✦✦✦

On their Christmas album, *By the Fireside*, The Turtle Island String Quartet interprets a number of classical pieces that fit the mood of the season, as well as recording several carols and contributing several of their own songs. Featuring a guest vocal from Garrison Keillor, *By the Fireside* is designed to please their fans and it should, even if it won't win them any new fans. —*Stephen Thomas Erlewine*

Turtle Island String Quartet / 1998 / Windham Hill ✦✦✦✦

29th Street Saxophone Quartet

f. 1982

Group / Hard Bop, Post Bop

Formed in 1982 and comprising altoists Bobby Watson and Ed Jackson, Rich Rothenberg on tenor and baritonist Jim Hartog, the 29th Street Saxophone Quartet is hard bop's answer to the World Saxophone Quartet. Actually within the straightahead tradition, this part-time unit (which has recorded several sets for Red and Antilles) is fairly adventurous. —*Scott Yanow*

Pointilistic Groove / Nov. 19, 1983-Nov. 25, 1983 / Osmosis ✦✦✦✦

Watch Your Step / 1985 / Antilles ✦✦✦✦✦

The second release (following an obscure set for Osmosis in 1983) by this underrated saxophone ensemble has one original apiece from three of the players (altoist Ed Jackson, tenor saxophonist Rich Rothenberg and baritonist Jim Hartog) and two from the group's best-known player, altoist Bobby Watson. The Twenty-Ninth Street Sax Quartet, on this album from Watson's small label New Note, offers an alternative to the freer a cappella sax playing of the World Saxophone Quartet and Rova, but is also adventurous in its own way. Highlights include the spirited "K.C.Q.," "Watch Your Step" (which is a good feature for all of the players) and the somewhat scary "Hotel de Funk." —*Scott Yanow*

● **The Real Deal** / Jan. 14, 1987 / Antilles ✦✦✦✦✦

The 29th Street Saxophone Quartet (which consists of Bobby Watson and Ed Jackson on altos, Rich Rothenberg on tenor and baritonist Jim Hartog) is much more conservative in style than the other main a cappella sax groups (the World Saxophone Quartet and Rova), but although based in the hard bop tradition, it does have its free and explorative moments. Highlights of this generally stimulating CD include Thelonious Monk's "I Mean You," Bud Powell's "Un Poco Loco," Charlie Parker's "Confirmation" and Watson's "Wheel Within a Wheel." —*Scott Yanow*

Live / Jul. 1988 / Red ✦✦✦✦✦

Underground / 1991 / Antilles ✦✦✦✦

Your Move / 1992 / Antilles ✦✦✦

Milano New York Bridge / Nov. 1992-Dec. 6, 1993 / Red ✦✦✦✦

Charles Tyler

b. Jul. 20, 1941, Cadiz, KY, **d.** Jun. 27, 1992, Toulon, France

Baritone Saxophone, Alto Saxophone / Free Jazz, Avant-Garde

One of the unsung baritonists in jazz, Charles Tyler had huge tones on both of his instruments and played with a great deal of fire, usually in fairly free settings. After studying piano and drums in Indianapolis, Tyler switched to clarinet, alto and finally baritone. Tyler had met Albert Ayler at age 14, and after moving to Cleveland in 1960, he had opportunities to jam with Ayler; in fact, when Tyler moved to New York in 1965, it was specifically to play with the innovative saxo-

phonist. Soon he was part of Ayler's group, recording *Bells* and *Spirits Rejoice,* and led two sessions of his own for ESP (1966-67). Tyler studied with David Baker at Indiana University (1967-68) before he spent a four-year period teaching and playing with adventurous musicians in Los Angeles, including Arthur Blythe, Bobby Bradford and David Murray. He moved back to New York in 1973, where he freelanced, doing stints with Cecil Taylor, Dewey Redman and Billy Bang (1981-82). Despite his talents, Charles Tyler never became a major name, but he did lead rewarding albums for Ak-Ba (1974), Nessa, Adelphi, Sonet, Storyville and Silkheart. —*Scott Yanow*

Charles Tyler Ensemble / Feb. 4, 1966 / ESP ✦✦✦

Altoist Charles Tyler's recording debut as a leader (and first of two ESP CDs) has some heated playing on his four avant-garde originals but only a total of 29 minutes of music. Tyler, who is joined by Charles Moffett on orchestra vibes, cellist Joel Friedman, bassist Henry Grimes and drummer Ronald Shannon Jackson, blows up a storm as usual. Of historic value, this set is specifically for free jazz collectors. —*Scott Yanow*

Eastern Man Alone / Jan. 2, 1967 / ESP ✦✦✦✦✦

Charles Tyler's second session as a leader (it would be seven years before he would have a third chance) has much more playing time than his first effort (48 minutes as opposed to 29) and more of an avant-garde concept. The altoist is the lead voice in a quartet comprising cellist David Baker and both Brent McKesson and Kent Brinkley on basses, coming up with eccentric melodies and sound explorations on four of his originals. This is a worthy effort that is innovative in its own way although not recommended to listeners who feel that bebop is "modern jazz." —*Scott Yanow*

Saga of the Outlaws / May 20, 1976 / Nessa ✦✦✦✦✦

Other than a couple of obscure ESP dates and two albums for the tiny Ak-Ba label, Charles Tyler was largely undocumented on records before this blowout, one of his strongest recordings. The avant-garde altoist performs the 37-minute "Saga Out of the Outlaws" (which is supposed to depict musically a tale of the Old West) with trumpeter Earl Cross, both John Ore and Ronnie Boykins on bass and drummer Steve Reid. Whatever the "plot," the music is quite stirring and features the adventurous Tyler at his best. —*Scott Yanow*

Sixty Minute Man / Mar. 1979 / Adelphi ✦✦✦✦✦

★ **Definite, Vol. 1** / Oct. 20, 1981-Oct. 21, 1981 / Storyville ✦✦✦✦✦

For the first of two albums taken from an engagement in Stockholm, Charles Tyler (playing two songs apiece on alto and baritone) teams up with trumpeter Earl Cross, bassist Kevin Ross and drummer Steve Reid for some heated freebop. The expressive solos and explorative nature of the music hold one's interest throughout. —*Scott Yanow*

Definite / Oct. 20, 1981-Oct. 21, 1981 / Storyville ✦✦✦✦✦

This is the second of two albums that document a Charles Tyler club gig in Stockholm. Splitting his time between alto and baritone, Tyler (in a quartet with trumpeter Earl Cross, bassist Kevin Ross and drummer Steve Reid) has a real chance to stretch out on these five freebop originals. The compositions are strong, but it is the spirited and fairly free improvisations that make both of these volumes an excellent purchase for listeners with ears open toward the jazz avant-garde. —*Scott Yanow*

Autumn in Paris / Jun. 2, 1988 / Silkheart ✦✦✦✦

McCoy Tyner (Alfred McCoy Tyner)

b. Dec. 11, 1938, Philadelphia, PA

Piano / Post-Bop

It is to McCoy Tyner's great credit that his career after John Coltrane has been far from anti-climatic. Along with Bill Evans, Tyner has been the most influential pianist in jazz of the past 40 years with his chord voicings being adopted and utilized by virtually every younger pianist. A powerful virtuoso and a true original (compare his playing in the early '60s with anyone else from the time!), Tyner (like Thelonious Monk) has not altered his style all that much from his early days but he has continued to grow and become even stronger.

McCoy Tyner grew up in Philadelphia where Bud Powell and Richie Powell were neighbors. As a teenager he gigged locally and met John Coltrane. He made his recording debut with the Art Farmer-Benny Golson Jazztet but after six months left the group to join Coltrane in what (with bassist Jimmy Garrison and drummer Elvin Jones) would become the classic quartet. Few other pianists of the period had both the power and the complementary open-minded style to inspire Coltrane, but Tyner was never overshadowed by the innovative saxophonist. During the Coltrane years (1960-65), the pianist also led his own record dates for Impulse.

After leaving Coltrane, McCoy Tyner struggled for a period, working as a sideman (with Ike and Tina Turner!) and leading his own small groups; his recordings were consistently stimulating even during the lean years. After he signed with Milestone in 1972, Tyner began to finally be recognized as one of the greats, and he has never been short of work since. Although there have been occasional departures (such as a 1978 all-star quartet tour with Sonny Rollins and duo recordings with Stephane Grappelli), Tyner has mostly played with his own groups during the past 25 years, which have ranged from a quartet with Azar Lawrence and a big band to his current trio. —*Scott Yanow*

Inception/Nights of Ballads and Blues / Jan. 10, 1962+Apr. 3, 1963 / MCA/Impulse! ◆◆◆◆◆

Pianist McCoy Tyner's first and third albums as a leader have been reissued on this single CD from 1988, one of the best in the short-lived MCA series of Impulse sets (before GRP took over the project). Featured with two different trios (consisting of either Art Davis or Steve Davis on bass and Elvin Jones or Lex Humphries on drums), Tyner sounds more conservative and straightahead than on his live sessions with John Coltrane during the era. However his unique style is very much in evidence (almost fully formed at this early stage) and he introduces five fine originals (including "Inception" and "Effendi") and also performs fresh versions of nine standards, highlighted by "Speak Low," "We'll Be Together Again," "Star Eyes" and "Days of Wine and Roses." In 1997 the *Inception* session was reissued by Impulse as a separate CD, but obviously this two-for-the-price-of-one set (put out in 1988) is the better buy. —*Scott Yanow*

Reaching Fourth / Nov. 14, 1962 / Impulse! ◆◆◆◆◆

Pianist McCoy Tyner's second set as a leader is excellent. Featured in a trio with bassist Henry Grimes and drummer Roy Haynes, Tyner performs two of his originals ("Reaching Fourth" and "Blues Back") plus three standards and "Theme For Ernie." One of the two most original and influential pianists to fully emerge in the 1960s (along with Bill Evans), McCoy Tyner's unique chord voicings and ease at playing creatively over vamps pushed the evolution of jazz piano forward quite a bit. This outing, although not as intense as his work with the John Coltrane Quartet, is generally memorable and still sounds quite viable 35 years later. —*Scott Yanow*

Today and Tomorrow / Jun. 4, 1963 / GRP/Impulse! ◆◆◆◆

The great pianist McCoy Tyner teams up with trumpeter Thad Jones, altoist Frank Strozier, tenor saxophonist John Gilmore (on vacation from Sun Ra), bassist Butch Warren and drummer Elvin Jones on the first three selections of this reissue CD; it is a pity that the potentially exciting group did not have more of an opportunity to play together, for these three numbers are excellent. For the remainder of the set (three numbers from the original LP plus three others taken from samplers), Tyner is showcased in a trio primarily on standards with bassist Jimmy Garrison and drummer Albert "Tootie" Heath. Virtually all of McCoy Tyner's recordings are easily recommended, and this CD has more variety than most of his Impulses. —*Scott Yanow*

Live at Newport / Jul. 5, 1963 / Impulse! ◆◆◆◆◆

McCoy Tyner Plays Ellington / Dec. 2, 1964-Dec. 8, 1964 / GRP/Impulse! ◆◆◆◆

This is an interesting project (reissued on CD) that works quite well. The already distinctive pianist McCoy Tyner utilized bassist Jimmy Garrison, drummer Elvin Jones and two Latin percussionists to interpret a full set of Duke Ellington songs (although "Caravan" was actually composed by Juan Tizol). For this CD the original seven tunes are joined by a "new" alternate take of "Gypsy Without a Song" and previously unreleased renditions of "It Don't Mean a Thing" and "I Got It Bad." In addition to some well-known standards, Tyner debuted an unrecorded Ellington piece, "Searchin'," and revived "Mr. Gentle & Mr. Cool." This is an excellent outing that displays both Tyner's debt to the jazz tradition and his increasingly original style. This fine set was reissued on CD by Impulse in 1997. —*Scott Yanow*

The Real McCoy / Apr. 21, 1967 / Blue Note ◆◆◆◆◆

Two-and-a-half years after his last recording as a leader for Impulse, pianist McCoy Tyner emerged to start a period on Blue Note that would result in seven albums. Having left John Coltrane's Quartet in late 1965, Tyner was entering a period of struggle, although artistically his playing grew quite a bit in the late 1960s. For this release, the pianist is teamed with tenor saxophonist Joe Henderson, bassist Ron Carter and drummer Elvin Jones for five of his originals. Highlights of the easily recommended CD reissue include "Passion Dance," "Four By Five" and "Blues on the Corner." —*Scott Yanow*

Jazz Profile / Apr. 21, 1967-Nov. 27, 1989 / Blue Note ◆◆◆◆

Jazz Profile compiles highlights from McCoy Tyner's recordings for Blue Note, drawing a rounded portrait of his career. The compilation features both hard bop and free jazzcuts, giving a good sense of Tyner's depth and range. —*Leo Stanley*

● Tender Moments / Dec. 1, 1967 / Blue Note ◆◆◆◆◆

On this excellent set (reissued on CD by Blue Note), McCoy Tyner had the opportunity for the first time to head a larger group. His nonet is an all-star aggregation comprising trumpeter Lee Morgan, trombonist Julian Priester, altoist James Spaul-

ding, Bennie Maupin on tenor, the French horn of Bob Northern, Howard Johnson on tuba, bassist Herbie Lewis and drummer Joe Chambers in addition to the pianist-leader. Tyner debuted six of his originals and, although none became standards (perhaps the best-known are "The High Priest" and "All My Yesterdays"), the music is quite colorful and advanced for the period. Well worth investigating. —*Scott Yanow*

Time for Tyner / May 17, 1968 / Blue Note ◆◆◆◆

This CD reissue draws its music from two separate concerts nearly a year apart but utilizing the same personnel: pianist McCoy Tyner, vibraphonist Bobby Hutcherson, bassist Herbie Lewis and drummer Freddie Waits. Although three numbers were performed at a John Coltrane Memorial Concert, they are all Tyner originals; the pianist and Hutcherson blend together quite well and both are experts at coming up with inventive ideas over modal vamps. The other three selections are veteran standards. "I Didn't Know What Time It Was" is taken by the full quartet, Hutcherson sits out on "Surrey with the Fringe on Top" and a rhapsodic "I've Grown Accustomed to Your Face" is a piano solo. A fine all-round showcase for McCoy Tyner in the late 1960s. —*Scott Yanow*

● Expansions / Aug. 23, 1968 / Blue Note ◆◆◆◆◆

Of pianist McCoy Tyner's seven Blue Note albums of the 1967-70 period, *Expansions* is the most definitive. Tyner's group (comprising trumpeter Woody Shaw, altoist Gary Bartz, tenor saxophonist Wayne Shorter, Ron Carter on cello, bassist Herbie Lewis and drummer Freddie Waits) is particularly strong, the compositions (four Tyner originals plus Calvin Massey's "I Thought I'd Let You Know") are challenging and the musicians seem quite inspired by each other's presence. The stimulating music falls between advanced hard bop and the avant-garde, pushing and pulling at the boundaries of modern mainstream jazz. —*Scott Yanow*

Cosmos / Apr. 4, 1969-Jul. 21, 1970 / Blue Note ◆◆◆◆

The music on this double-LP was unreleased when the two-fer came out in 1976 and has yet to be reissued on CD, but that had more to do with the decline of Blue Note in the late 1960s than with the quality of the performances, which are consistently high. In fact the impressive variety makes this a release well worth bidding on. The innovative pianist McCoy Tyner performs two numbers with his 1969 trio (comprising bassist Herbie Lewis and drummer Freddie Waits); three other songs add Harold Vick's soprano, the reeds of Al Gibbons and a string quartet; while the three remaining pieces feature the trio with altoist Gary Bartz, flutist Hubert Laws and the oboe of Andrew White. All of the compositions (best-known is "Song For My Lady") are Tyner originals and the music is consistently intriguing. —*Scott Yanow*

Extensions / Feb. 9, 1970 / Blue Note ◆◆◆◆◆

This CD has an interesting combination of players. It may be the only recording to include both pianist McCoy Tyner and his successor with the John Coltrane Quartet and Alice Coltrane (who adds atmosphere with her harp). This set also matches the young altoist Gary Bartz with Wayne Shorter (doubling on tenor and soprano), whom he succeeded in Miles Davis' group, and has reunions between Shorter and bassist Ron Carter and by Tyner and drummer Elvin Jones. The all-star sextet stretches out on lengthy renditions of four of Tyner's modal originals and there is strong solo space for the leader and the two saxophonists. Wayne Shorter in particular is often quite intense. Stimulating music. —*Scott Yanow*

Asante / Sep. 10, 1970 / Blue Note ◆◆◆◆

The final McCoy Tyner Blue Note album found the innovative pianist during a lowpoint in his career. His records were not selling that well, his mentor John Coltrane had passed away three years earlier, and it was not obvious that Tyner would be able to continue struggling successfully to make a living out of music. Fortunately his fortunes would soon rise when he signed with Milestone in 1972 and the critics began to rediscover him. *Asante* is a bit unusual, for the emphasis is on group interplay rather than individual solos. The four originals feature Tyner with altoist Andrew White, guitarist Ted Dunbar, bassist Buster Williams, drummer Billy Hart, Mtume on congas and two spots for the voice of Songai. Worth investigating. —*Scott Yanow*

☆ Sahara / Jan. 1972 / Original Jazz Classics ◆◆◆◆◆

Pianist McCoy Tyner had three longtime associations with record labels: Impulse (1962-64), Blue Note (1967-70) and Milestone (1972-81). *Sahara* was his debut for Milestone, a quartet outing with altoist Sonny Fortune (who also plays soprano and flute), bassist Calvin Hill and drummer Alphonze Mouzon. This CD reissue is highlighted by the twenty-three-and-a-half minute title cut, which finds Tyner making a rare (and brief) appearance on flute and his piano solo feature "A Prayer For My Family." —*Scott Yanow*

Song for My Lady / Sep. 6, 1972+Nov. 27, 1972 / Original Jazz Classics ◆◆◆◆

It was during his years with Milestone (1972-81) that McCoy Tyner finally received recognition for his highly original and influential piano style. In general Tyner's Milestone records (most of which had their own personality) featured plenty of diversity and a strong purpose. This 1972 CD reissue is highlighted by "The Night Has a Thousand Eyes," "A Silent Tear" (a piano solo) and the title cut. Two of the five selections showcase Tyner in a quartet with the reeds of Sonny Fortune, bassist Calvin Hill and drummer Alphonse Mouzon while "Native Song" and "Essence" add fluegelhornist Charles Tolliver, violinist Michael White and the percussion of Mtume. Recommended. —*Scott Yanow*

★ **Echoes of a Friend** / Nov. 11, 1972 / Original Jazz Classics ◆◆◆◆◆
An obvious classic, this piano solo record (reissued on CD in the OJC series) features McCoy Tyner paying tribute to John Coltrane. Tyner not only plays three of Coltrane's songs ("Naima," "Promise" and "My Favorite Things") but two of his originals (a lengthy "The Discovery" and "Folks") which display how much the pianist had grown since leaving the saxophonist's group in late 1965. Few McCoy Tyner records are not easily recommended, but this one even ranks above most. —*Scott Yanow*

Song of the New World / Apr. 6, 1973-Apr. 9, 1973 / Original Jazz Classics ◆◆◆◆
This set gave pianist McCoy Tyner his first opportunity to write music for a larger group that included brass, flutes, and on two of the five songs, a string section. The powerful pianist is in fine form and the main soloist throughout (although there are spots for trumpeter Virgil Jones and the flute of Sonny Fortune). Most memorable is the title cut and a reworking of "Afro Blue." —*Scott Yanow*

★ **Enlightenment** / Jul. 7, 1973 / Milestone ◆◆◆◆◆
This is one of the great McCoy Tyner recordings. The powerful, percussive and highly influential pianist sounds quite inspired throughout his appearance at the 1973 Montreux Jazz Festival. Azar Lawrence (on tenor and soprano) is also quite noteworthy (why didn't he ever become famous?) and there is plenty of interplay with bassist Juney Booth and drummer Alphonse Mouzon. But Tyner is the main star, whether it be on his three-part "Enlightenment Suite," "Presence," "Nebula" or the 25-minute "Walk Spirit, Talk Spirit." —*Scott Yanow*

Sama Layuca / Mar. 26, 1974-Mar. 28, 1974 / Milestone ◆◆◆◆◆
Pianist McCoy Tyner is heard at the height of his powers throughout this rewarding set. He contributed all five compositions and has a colorful and diverse group of major players at his disposal to interpret them: vibraphonist Bobby Hutcherson, altoist Gary Bartz, Azar Lawrence on tenor and soprano, John Stubblefield doubling on oboe and flute, bassist Buster Williams, drummer Billy Hart and both Mtume and Guilherme Franco on percussion. The results (which include a brief Tyner-Hutcherson duet on "Above the Rainbow") are quite rewarding and serve as a strong example of McCoy Tyner's music. —*Scott Yanow*

Atlantis / Aug. 31, 1974-Sep. 1, 1974 / Milestone ◆◆◆◆◆
This single CD reissues all of the music from a former two-LP set. Pianist McCoy Tyner's 1974 quintet consisted of the talented youngster Azar Lawrence on tenor and soprano (who strangely enough never became more famous than he was at the time), bassist Joony Booth, drummer Wilby Fletcher and percussionist Guilherme Franco. As is accurately stated in the new liner notes by Neil Tesser, *Atlantis* was the final recording from Tyner's last band to be based on the music of his former boss John Coltrane. While Lawrence (who was only 20 at the time) derived his style partly from aspects of Coltrane and the rhythm section is fiery, McCoy Tyner creates some very powerful and highly original solos, really tearing into some of the more extended pieces. Recorded live at San Francisco's legendary Keystone Korner, this set has four of Tyner's modal originals played by the full group, a rendition of "My One and Only Love" performed by the leader, Lawrence and Franco as a trio, and a solo piano version of "In a Sentimental Mood." Essential music that still sounds fresh and adventurous. —*Scott Yanow*

Trident / Feb. 18, 1975-Feb. 19, 1975 / Original Jazz Classics ◆◆◆◆◆
Pianist McCoy Tyner's first full-length trio album since 1964 was one of his most popular. Accompanied by bassist Ron Carter and Elvin Jones, Tyner (who uses harpsichord and/or celeste for flavoring on three of the six pieces) shows why he was considered the most influential acoustic pianist of the era (before Bill Evans began to surpass him in that category). Whether it be Jobim's "Once I Loved," "Impressions," "Ruby, My Dear" or Tyner's three powerful originals, this set finds Tyner in peak form. —*Scott Yanow*

Fly with the Wind / Jan. 19, 1976-Jan. 21, 1976 / Original Jazz Classics ◆◆◆◆
One of the most difficult aspects for producer Orrin Keepnews of recording pianist McCoy Tyner so frequently in the 1970s was coming up with new ideas and settings for each record. *Fly with the Wind* gave Tyner a rare opportunity to write for strings. Joined by bassist Ron Carter, drummer Billy Cobham, flutist Hubert Laws, piccolo, oboe, harp, six violins, two violas and two cellos, Tyner performed four of his originals (including the title cut) plus the standard "You Stepped Out of a Dream." This CD reissue has plenty of memorable moments and is a surprising but logical success; Tyner's orchestral piano blended with the strings very well. —*Scott Yanow*

Focal Point / Aug. 4, 1976-Aug. 7, 1976 / Milestone ◆◆◆◆
In an attempt to avoid sameness, most of pianist McCoy Tyner's Milestone records of the 1970s used different instrumentation from each other. On this CD reissue, Tyner and his 1976 trio (with bassist Charles Fambrough and drummer Eric Gravatt) are joined by a trio of talented reed players (Gary Bartz, Joe Ford and Ron Bridgewater) and percussionist Guilherme Franco for three of Tyner's originals; in addition Ford is the only horn on his feature "Theme For Nana," and "Parody" is a Tyner-Gravatt duet. Because virtually all of McCoy Tyner's records are superior examples of modal-oriented jazz, this gem is merely an above-average effort. —*Scott Yanow*

☆ **Supertrios** / Apr. 9, 1977-Apr. 12, 1977 / Milestone ◆◆◆◆◆
This album features the great pianist McCoy Tyner with two separate trios, either bassist Ron Carter and drummer Tony Williams or bassist Eddie Gomez and drummer Jack DeJohnette. The former session, which has a Tyner/Williams duet on "I Mean You" and a collaboration between Tyner and Tyner on "Prelude to a Kiss," is the more interesting of the two, with the pianist interacting with Miles Davis' former rhythm section on six high-quality songs. But the Gomez-DeJohnette date (which includes four Tyner compositions plus "Stella by Starlight" and "Lush Life") also has its classic moments. Throughout, the percussive and highly influential pianist sounds inspired by the opportunity to create music with his peers. Recommended. —*Scott Yanow*

Inner Voices / Sep. 1, 1977-Sep. 8, 1977 / Milestone ◆◆◆
Not yet reissued on CD, this project by the powerful pianist McCoy Tyner is a bit unusual in that he is featured with an all-star rhythm section (guitarist Earl Klugh, bassist Ron Carter and either Jack DeJohnette or Eric Gravatt on drums), a horn section (which includes a few solos for trumpeter Jon Faddis, tenor saxophonist Alex Foster and trombonist Charles Stephens, and seven voices. Tyner was responsible not only for the five originals but the arrangements too. In reality the voices were not needed (they stick out as a bit of a frivolity) but Tyner plays as strong as usual; he has yet to record an uninspired solo. —*Scott Yanow*

The Greeting / Mar. 17, 1978-Mar. 18, 1978 / Milestone ◆◆◆◆
One of the better McCoy Tyner Milestone records not yet reissued on CD, this live set from San Francisco features the masterful pianist playing solo on "Naima" and leading a strong sextet (with George Adams on tenor, flute and soprano, Joe Ford on alto and flute, bassist Charles Fambrough, drummer Sonship and percussionist Guilherme Franco) for four of his originals. There are remakes (quite different from the originals) of "Fly With The Wind" and "The Greeting" and two newer pieces including the atmospheric "Hand in Hand." An excellent example of McCoy Tyner's playing in the 1970s. —*Scott Yanow*

Passion Dance / Jul. 28, 1978 / Milestone ◆◆◆◆
Recorded live in Tokyo, the great pianist McCoy Tyner performs three of his best originals ("Passion Dance," "Search For Peace" and "Song of the New World") plus two John Coltrane songs ("Moment's Notice" and "The Promise"). He takes three selections unaccompanied while "Moment's Notice" and "Song of the New World" are with a trio including bassist Ron Carter and drummer Tony Williams. This LP (long overdue to be reissued on CD) has plenty of fiery and passionate music. All of Tyner's Milestone records of the 1970s are recommended, and this is one of the better ones. —*Scott Yanow*

Together / Aug. 31, 1978-Sep. 3, 1978 / Milestone ◆◆◆◆
During his years on Milestone, McCoy Tyner had the opportunity to record in a variety of settings with many of his favorite players. For this LP (not yet reissued on CD), the innovative pianist is featured with quite an all-star crew: trumpeter Freddie Hubbard, flutist Hubert Laws, Bennie Maupin on tenor and bass clarinet, vibraphonist Bobby Hutcherson, Stanley Clarke (in a rare appearance at the time on acoustic bass), drummer Jack DeJohnette and percussionist Bill Summers. In addition to a pair of Tyner's originals, songs were contributed by Laws, DeJohnette, Hutcherson and Hubbard ("One of Another Kind"). The music is essentially high-quality advanced modal hard bop and each of the sidemen get their opportunities to be showcased. —*Scott Yanow*

Horizon / Apr. 24, 1979-Apr. 25, 1979 / Milestone ◆◆◆◆
Pianist McCoy Tyner's many recordings for Milestone are all easily recommended although a surprisingly large number of them have not yet been reissued on CD, including this one. Tyner's septet (which includes violinist John Blake, the reeds of Joe Ford and George Adams, bassist Charles Fambrough, drummer Al Foster and percussionist Guilherme Franco) performs two originals apiece by Tyner and Blake; the pianist is also heard with the rhythm trio on Fambrough's "One For Honor." None of the compositions had much life beyond this recording, but they serve as fine vehicles for inventive improvisations. —*Scott Yanow*

4 X 4 / Mar. 3, 1980-May 29, 1980 / Milestone ◆◆◆◆◆
This set matches the McCoy Tyner Trio (which includes bassist Cecil McBee and drummer Al Foster) with four different guests. Altoist Arthur Blythe and vibra-

phonist Bobby Hutcherson fare best, but both trumpeter Freddie Hubbard and guitarist John Abercrombie also have their strong moments. In addition to four Tyner compositions, there is one song apiece from McBee, Abercrombie and Hutcherson in addition to four jazz standards. This collection is a fine all-around showcase for the brilliant pianist even if no new ground is broken. —*Scott Yanow*

13th House / 1981 / Milestone ♦♦♦♦

After a decade of consistent recordings for Milestone, pianist McCoy Tyner ended his association with the label with this big band set. On originals by Tyner, Frank Foster and Jimmy Heath, such soloists are heard from as Hubert Laws (on flute and piccolo), tenor saxophonist Ricky Ford, trombonist Slide Hampton, bassist Ron Carter, trumpeters Oscar Brashear and Charles Sullivan, and Joe Ford on soprano; everyone wanted to play with McCoy Tyner! The powerful music lives up to its potential, making one wish that Fantasy will eventually reissue this LP. —*Scott Yanow*

La Leyenda de La Hora / 1982 / Columbia ♦♦♦♦

This relative obscurity is better than average. The great pianist is heard with an all-star nonet that includes Hubert Laws on flute, vibraphonist Bobby Hutcherson, altoist Paquito D'Rivera, Chico Freeman on tenor and trumpeter Marcus Belgrave plus a seven-piece string section. The music (five Tyner originals) is highly rhythmic and generally quite stimulating. A strong effort. —*Scott Yanow*

Looking Out / 1982 / Columbia ♦♦♦

Pianist McCoy Tyner's second of two Columbia LP's was a bit of a misfire. A surprisingly commercial effort with the vocals of Phyllis Hyman and unnecessary contributions by guitarist Carlos Santana and (on "I'll Be Around") the synthesizer of Denzil Miller along with unidentified strings and horns, the music is quite forgettable. Tyner plays well and with as much passion as usual, but one can clearly sense that not all of the musicians were recording the music at the same time, for they rarely react to each other's presence. One of the great pianist's weaker efforts. —*Scott Yanow*

Dimensions / Oct. 1983 / Elektra ♦♦♦♦

On this long out-of-print LP from the defunct Elektra Musician label, pianist McCoy Tyner is featured in one of his strongest groups, a quintet with altoist Gary Bartz, violinist John Blake, bassist John Lee and drummer Wilby Fletcher. A transitional set between Tyner's adventurous Milestone albums and his current repertoire (which falls in the tradition but still sounds quite original), this album has two standards ("Prelude to a Kiss" and "Just in Time"), Bartz's tribute to Thelonious Monk ("Uncle Bubba") and one original apiece by Tyner, Blake and Lee. Excellent music. —*Scott Yanow*

It's About Time / Apr. 6, 1985-Apr. 7, 1985 / Blue Note ♦♦♦

Pianist McCoy Tyner's matchup with veteran altoist Jackie McLean is reasonably enjoyable but less memorable than one might expect. Actually McLean is only on four of the six selections and trumpeter Jon Faddis (who appears on two cuts) sometimes even steals the spotlight. Tyner and McLean are accompanied by either Ron Carter or Marcus Miller on bass, drummer Al Foster and sometimes percussionist Steve Thornton. The pianist wrote five of the six selections (including "You Taught My Heart to Sing") but none of the musicians sounds all that inspired. —*Scott Yanow*

Double Trios / Jun. 7, 1986-Jun. 9, 1986 / Denon ♦♦♦♦♦

This little-known CD features the masterful pianist McCoy Tyner with two different trios: his regular group of the period (which includes bassist Avery Sharpe and drummer Louis Hayes) and a unit with electric bassist Marcus Miller and drummer Jeff "Tain" Watts. Percussionist Steve Thornton pops up with both groups. In addition to three Tyner originals and Miller's "Sudan," it is particularly interesting to hear the pianist's reworkings of "Lil' Darlin'," "Satin Doll," "Lover Man" and Thelonious Monk's "Rhythm-A-Ning," transforming them into modal masterpieces. —*Scott Yanow*

Bon Voyage / Jun. 1987 / Timeless ♦♦♦♦

Blues for Coltrane / Jul. 9, 1987 / MCA/Impulse! ♦♦♦♦

This is a rather unusual and interesting CD. Pianist McCoy Tyner has recorded many tributes to his former boss John Coltrane but in this particular situation he often plays a back seat to the tenors of Pharoah Sanders and/or David Murray. Murray and Sanders actually only meet up on Murray's "Trane" (with plenty of fireworks); otherwise these are quartet performances with bassist Cecil McBee and drummer Roy Haynes, and in one case ("Lazy Bird") a trio showcase for Tyner. Pharoah often sounds close to Coltrane while Murray as usual resembles no one but himself. In addition to "Trane," other highlights include "Naima," "The Promise" and "I Want to Talk About You." —*Scott Yanow*

Live at Musicians Exchange Cafe / Jul. 1987 / Who's Who in Jazz ♦♦♦

Revelations / Oct. 25, 1988-Oct. 27, 1988 / Blue Note ♦♦♦♦

On McCoy Tyner's first solo piano album in 16 years, the remarkable stylist really digs into six standards (including "Yesterdays," "In a Mellow Tone" and "Don't Blame Me") and four of his originals (highlighted by "You Taught My Heart to Sing"). Although somewhat typecast as John Coltrane's fiery pianist, Tyner at times on this record sounds romantic and in other spots hints a bit at Art Tatum. This is a rather special project from one of the finest jazz pianists of the past 35 years. —*Scott Yanow*

Uptown/Downtown / Nov. 25, 1988-Nov. 26, 1988 / Milestone ♦♦♦♦♦

The debut recording from McCoy Tyner's big band features the pianist's all-star 15-piece unit romping through five of his originals (including "Blues For Basie") plus Steve Turre's "Lotus Flower." With such fine soloists as tenors Junior Cook and Ricky Ford, trumpeter Kamau Adilifu, trombonist Steve Turre and the leader, the ensemble (which includes John Clark's French horn and the tuba of Howard Johnson) had quickly gained its own sound and the results are quite memorable and frequently exciting. Recommended. —*Scott Yanow*

☆ Live at Sweet Basil / May 19, 1989-May 20, 1989 / Evidence ♦♦♦♦♦

This double CD (originally recorded for King in 1989) finds the great pianist McCoy Tyner stretching out with bassist Avery Sharpe and drummer Aaron Scott on five standards, a pair of songs apiece by John Coltrane and Thelonious Monk, and two of his own originals. Tyner has continued to grow in density and power through the years and by this time possessed a technique nearly on the level of an Art Tatum; his version of "Yesterdays," although different, somehow recalls Tatum. With other high points including "Monk's Dream," "Don't Blame Me" and "Just in Time," this two-fer gives one a definitive look at McCoy Tyner in the late '80s. —*Scott Yanow*

Things Ain't What They Used to Be / Nov. 2, 1989 / Blue Note ♦♦♦♦

For this Blue Note project, pianist McCoy Tyner is heard solo on eight numbers and also has two duets with tenor saxophonist George Adams and three with guitarist John Scofield; Tyner dominates throughout. A standards-oriented set (there are only four songs by the leader including "Blues on the Corner" and the near-standard "Song For My Lady"), but the pianist makes every melody sound like a fresh original through his distinctive chord voicings and harmonies. This is a strong effort by one of the best. —*Scott Yanow*

Just Feelin' / 1991 / Palo Alto ♦♦♦♦

Pianist McCoy Tyner's first recording with his long-time bassist Avery Sharpe, this trio set with drummer Louis Hayes is somewhat obscure due to the Palo Alto label subsequently becoming obsolete. The music however deserved a far better fate, for this is a particularly strong set. Tyner performs two of his more basic originals (the title cut and "Blues For Basie") along with Sharpe's "Berliner" and four melodic standards. The project served as the real beginning of Tyner's current conservative but still lively music in which his formerly avant-garde style became very much a part of the jazz tradition. Worth searching for. —*Scott Yanow*

Autumn Mood / Feb. 11, 1991-Feb. 12, 1991 / Delta ♦♦♦

Soliloquy / Feb. 19, 1991-Feb. 21, 1991 / Blue Note ♦♦♦♦

This is a particularly well-rounded McCoy Tyner solo set. The masterful pianist performs four Coltrane tunes (including "After The Rain" and two versions of "Crescent"), five of his own originals (highlighted by "Tribute to Lady Day" and "Effendi"), Bud Powell's classic "Bouncin' With Bud," Dexter Gordon's "Tivoli" and three veteran standards. McCoy Tyner always sounds in prime form and these diverse songs bring out the best in his passionate style. Highly recommended. —*Scott Yanow*

Remembering John / Feb. 1991 / Enja ♦♦♦♦

For this tribute to John Coltrane (which he performs with bassist Avery Sharpe and drummer Aaron Scott), pianist McCoy Tyner performs some offbeat material including 'Trane pieces that preceded his stay with the classic quartet (such as "Giant Steps") plus a few unrelated standards (including "In Walked Bud" and "Good Morning Heartache"). Six of the nine selections were composed by Coltrane and, although this was his umpteenth 'Trane tribute, McCoy Tyner still sounds enthusiastic and adventurous performing the timeless music. —*Scott Yanow*

New York Reunion / Apr. 3, 1991-Apr. 4, 1991 / Chesky ♦♦♦♦♦

Pianist McCoy Tyner and tenor saxophonist Joe Henderson had not recorded together in over two decades when they finally met up for this Chesky CD. With strong assistance from bassist Ron Carter and drummer Al Foster, Tyner and Henderson make for a perfect team on four originals by group members (including the tenor's classic "Recorda Me") and four superior standards. The advanced hard bop music is as rewarding as one would expect. —*Scott Yanow*

44th Street Suite / May 11, 1991 / Red Baron ♦♦♦

Although tenor saxophonist David Murray and altoist Arthur Blythe are listed in the personnel along with pianist McCoy Tyner, bassist Ron Carter and drummer Aaron Scott, the two horns only meet up on three of the six selections; otherwise

Blythe is featured as the lone saxophone with the quartet. On what is in reality a bit of a jam session, the musicians romp through John Coltrane's "Bessie's Blues," Duke Ellington's obscure "Blue Piano," Tyner's "Not for Beginners" and the standard "Falling in Love With Love" while Blythe leads the quartet through the two-part "44th Street Suite," which starts out quite free before becoming a blues. Little all that memorable occurs, considering the players involved (a little more planning would have worked wonders) but the music does have its exciting moments. —*Scott Yanow*

The Turning Point / Nov. 19, 1991-Nov. 20, 1991 / Verve ♦♦♦♦♦
This recording may not have been an actual "turning point" in pianist McCoy Tyner's productive career, but its success gave momentum to his big band. Although only a part-time affair, Tyner's orchestra (seven brass, four reeds and a four-piece rhythm section) is considered one of the major jazz big bands of the 1990s, a perfect outlet for the leader's percussive and modal-oriented piano. With arrangements by Tyner, Dennis Mackrel, Slide Hampton, Steve Turre and Howard Johnson, many of these performances are quite powerful. It is a pity though that the liners do not identify the soloists, since there are several that are quite colorful. Recommended. —*Scott Yanow*

Journey / May 24, 1993-May 27, 1993 / Verve ♦♦♦♦
While this isn't among Tyner's greatest recordings, it's still a rigorous, often exciting big-band date. The repertoire includes familiar Tyner compositions "Peresina" and "Blues on the Corner," originals from trombonist Steve Turre ("Juanita") and bassist Avery Sharpe ("January in Brazil"), plus other numbers by Angel Rangelov, Dennis Mackrel and the interesting "You Taught My Heart to Sing," co-written by Tyner and legendary Broadway lyricist/tunesmith Sammy Cahn. Although Tyner doesn't play with the ferocity or unpredictable edge that's characterized his finest sessions, he solos crisply, easily moving through hard bop, Afro-Latin and even swing-oriented big band settings. There's a comfortable feel, but not a staid one. —*Ron Wynn*

Manhattan Moods / Dec. 3, 1993-Dec. 4, 1993 / Blue Note ♦♦♦♦
Pianist McCoy Tyner and vibraphonist Bobby Hutcherson (who doubles on marimba during this set) had recorded together previously on several occasions but never for a full set as a duet. It is not too surprising that they blend together

quite well, for both remain advanced improvisers who are tied to the hard bop/modal tradition. They perform two originals apiece plus five standards including "Blue Monk," "I Loves You Porgy" and Mal Waldron's "Soul Eyes." A pleasing effort full of subtle creativity. —*Scott Yanow*

Prelude and Sonata / Nov. 26, 1994-Nov. 27, 1994 / Milestone ♦♦♦♦
Infinity / Apr. 12, 1995-Apr. 14, 1995 / Impulse! ♦♦♦♦♦
It seems only fitting that the initial new release on the latest revival of the Impulse label features McCoy Tyner and Michael Brecker. When Impulse started out in 1960, John Coltrane and Tyner were the first artists to be signed, and when Impulse was briefly brought back by MCA in the 1980s, two of its most important albums were recordings by Brecker. There are not a lot of surprises on this quartet matchup (with bassist Avery Sharpe and drummer Aaron Scott) except perhaps for how well Tyner and Brecker mesh together. The music is somewhat similar to a set by the pianist's regular trio, with a solo piece ("Blues Stride"), a generous amount of Tyner originals and colorful versions of Thelonious Monk's "I Mean You" and "Good Morning Heartache," but Brecker's presence and consistently powerful playing does inspire Tyner and his sidemen. For a strong example as to why today's saxophonists have such a high opinion of Michael Brecker, his roaring statement on the extended "Impressions" will suffice. Highly recommended. —*Scott Yanow*

What the World Needs Now: The Music of Burt Bacharach / Mar. 51, 1996-May 6, 1996 / GRP ♦
McCoy Tyner, one of the most vital of all jazz pianists, performs nine songs written by the superior pop composer Burt Bacharach. Since the tunes selected include "Close to You," "A House Is Not a Home," "Alfie" and "The Look of Love," this project had potential. Unfortunately, the Tyner trio (with bassist Christian McBride and drummer Lewis Nash) is accompanied by a huge string section and an orchestra given mostly surprisingly sappy and overly lush arrangements by John Clayton (who is capable of much better). The pianist treats each melody as if it were precious, and the overall results are rather schlocky. Compare this lightweight version of "A House Is Not a Home" to Jackie McLean's intense exploration or Tyner's "Alfie" to Sonny Rollins' examples of how the pianist's project is an unimaginative misfire. A major disappointment. —*Scott Yanow*

James Blood Ulmer

b. Feb. 2, 1942, St. Matthews, SC
Guitar, Vocals / Free Funk, Avant-Garde, Crossover Jazz
One of the most individual and intense jazz guitarists, James "Blood" Ulmer has been a controversial figure ever since he started playing with Ornette Coleman. As a child he sang with the Southern Sons (a gospel group) but it was as a guitarist that he began performing professionally in 1959 in Pittsburgh. He spent a few years playing funky jazz with organ groups and during 1967-71 was based in Detroit. In 1971 Ulmer moved to New York, where he worked regularly at Minton's Playhouse and played briefly with Art Blakey, Paul Bley, Larry Young and Joe Henderson. The turning point of his career came in 1974 when he studied with Ornette Coleman; soon he would be in Ornette's free funk band Prime Time. By the time he made his debut as a leader for Artist's House, Ulmer had a style that mixed together the power and sound of rock with Coleman's harmolodics and free-form approach. He recorded with Arthur Blythe, was in groups called Phalanx and the Music Revelation Ensemble and led his own rather abstract bands. Ulmer's recordings have been inconsistent and erratic, both primitive and futuristic while often being quite noisy; an acquired taste! —*Scott Yanow*

★ **Tales of Captain Black** / Dec. 5, 1978 / Artists House ♦♦♦♦♦

Are You Glad to Be in America? / Jan. 17, 1980 / Rough Trade ♦♦♦♦♦

Freelancing / 1981 / Columbia ♦♦♦♦
Studio session. Also mind expanding. —*Michael G. Nastos*

Blues Preacher / Sep. 1992-Nov. 1992 / DIW/Columbia ♦♦
This effort from controversial guitarist James "Blood" Ulmer sticks to a harsh blues-rock groove with many of the one-chord vamps sounding like they are leftovers from John Lee Hooker's repertoire. There are no harmolodics (and little jazz) to be heard on the CD, and this rather primitive music is to be recommended only to fans of Ulmer's shouting vocals. —*Scott Yanow*

Odyssey / Mar. 1993-May 1993 / Columbia ♦♦♦
Odyssey is one of James Blood Ulmer's most adventerous and complex releases. Drawing equally from jazz, free-form noise, funk, and punk, *Odyssey* is dense with musical themes and sonic textures. Though the compositions often require some work in order to understand what Ulmer is trying to say, there is no mistaking that his guitar playing is bold and innovative, slamming together seemingly disparate and unagreeable genres and creating something gnarled, urban and new. It's one of his defining records. —*Leo Stanley*

Uptown String Quartet

f. 1985
Group / Post-Bop
The Uptown String Quartet really began as part of the Max Roach Double Quartet. Their 1985 joint recording had John Williams and Cecelia Hobbs on violins, Maxine Roach (Max's daughter) on viola and cellist Eileen Folson. By 1986 the string quartet had its name and the personnel of violinists Diana Monroe and Lesa Terry, Maxine Roach and cellist Zela Terry. By the time they debuted in 1989 on record as a separate entity of their own, Monroe, Lesa Terry and Roach were joined by Eileen Folson; the personnel has remained the same up to now. One of the very first string quartets to improvise (they were preceded by Turtle Island), the group's repertoire on their two releases (for Philips and Blue Moon) ranges from bop standards and traditional folk songs to new advanced originals. —*Scott Yanow*

Max Roach Presents . . . / Apr. 19, 1989-Apr. 22, 1989 / Philips ♦♦♦♦
The Uptown String Quartet was originally part of Max Roach's Double Quartet before having its own life. Comprising violinists Diane Monroe and Lesa Terry, Maxine Roach on viola and cellist Eileen Folson, the group ranks as the second major improvising string quartet ever, after Turtle Island. On this consistently enjoyable and often-surprising CD, the band plays a wide range of music including several ancient folk songs, John Carisi's "Jelly Roll Rag," Oscar Pettiford's classic "Tricotism," Scott Joplin's "Easy Winners" and some modern originals by Max

Roach, Odean Pope, Fred Tillis and Cecil Bridgewater. Listeners who have a resistance to hearing violins play jazz are well advised to check out this colorful effort. —*Scott Yanow*

● **Just Wait a Minute!** / Aug. 1991 / Blue Moon ♦♦♦♦♦
This is a fine all-around session for the chamber jazz quartet, which consisted at the time of violinists Lesa Terry and Diane Monroe, Maxine Roach on viola and cellist Eileen Folson. The wide range of material includes pieces by Benny Golson ("Along Came Betty" and "Blues March"), Charlie Parker, Gershwin, Jimmy Heath, Don Cherry, several group originals and even a song by James Brown (a humorous "I Feel Good"). Along with Turtle Island, Uptown (which is active on a more part-time basis) has ranked in the 1990s at the top of its admittedly very small field of improvising string quartets. This diverse yet unified CD gives listeners a strong example of the group's music. —*Scott Yanow*

Michal Urbaniak

b. Jan. 22, 1943, Warsaw, Poland
Violin, Tenor Saxophone / Avant-Garde, Fusion
Once Poland's most promising import in the jazz-rock 1970s, Michal Urbaniak's chief value in retrospect was as a fellow traveler of Jean-Luc Ponty, a fluid advocate of the electric violin, the lower-pitched violectra, and the lyricon (the first popular, if now largely underutilized, wind synthesizer). Like many Eastern European jazzmen, he would incorporate elements of Polish folk music into his jazz pursuits, and his other heroes range from the inevitable Miles Davis to Polish classicist Witold Lutoslawski. His electric violin was often filtered with a gauze of electronic modifying devices, and on occasion, he could come up with an attractively memorable composition like "Satin Lady."

Urbaniak began playing the violin at age six, followed by studies on the soprano and then tenor saxophones. His interests in jazz developed chronologically from Dixieland to swing to bop as he grew up, and he studied at the Academy of Music in Warsaw while working in various Polish jazz bands and playing classical violin. In 1965, he formed his own band in Scandinavia with singer Urszula Dudziak (later his wife), returning to Poland in 1969 to found Constellation, which included pianist Adam Makowicz. Having won a scholarship to the Berklee School upon being voted Best Soloist at the 1971 Montreux Jazz Festival, Urbaniak made the US his home in 1973. He soon formed a popular jazz-rock group called Fusion, recording for Columbia and Arista in a Mahavishnu Orchestra/Ponty fashion, with Dudziak adding darting, slippery scat vocals. This group lasted until 1977, and Urbaniak's profile would never be as high again, although he performed with Larry Coryell in 1982-83, led the new electric group Urbanator in the 1990s, and has performed and recorded in other styles ranging from bop to free jazz. —*Richard S. Ginell*

Super Constellation / 1973 / Columbia ♦♦

Fusion / 1975 / Columbia ♦♦♦♦

Body English / Dec. 1976 / Arista ♦♦♦

Urbaniak / Aug. 1977 / Inner City ♦♦♦♦♦

Music for Violin and Jazz Quartet / Dec. 17, 1980-Dec. 18, 1980 / JAM ♦♦♦♦

My One and Only Love / Jul. 1981 / Steeple Chase ♦♦♦♦

● **Take Good Care of My Heart** / Aug. 21, 1984 / Steeple Chase ♦♦♦♦♦

Cinemode / 1988 / Rykodisc ♦♦♦♦
Polish violinist and saxophonist Michal Urbaniak was a fresh voice on the horizon when he arrived here in the early '70s and began recording. Unfortunately, Urbaniak's once-vital sound was quickly absorbed into the trendy fabric of fusion, and his music was diluted to the point where it was indistinguished and empty. This 1988 solo set, with Urbaniak free from commercial pressures and considerations, ranks as his most accomplished, intriguing release. He plays violin, saxes, and keyboards, and his solos are fierce, extensive, and joyous. —*Ron Wynn*

Songbird / Oct. 1990 / Steeple Chase ♦♦♦

Manhattan Man / 1992 / Milan ✦✦

One never knows what to expect from violinist Michal Urbaniak, who has recorded bop, free jazz, funk and junk throughout his career with equal enthusiasm. Unfortunately, funk and junk are the main course on this CD, particularly during its first half. An odd collection, the set features plenty of electronic percussion and aimless grooves along with a few worthwhile moments. Urbaniak is overdubbed on strings, keyboards and saxophones but buries most of his guests under the mechanical percussion, including harmonica great Toots Thielemans on "Manhattan Man" and an otherwise acoustic trio featuring pianist Herbie Hancock on "Paris Groove." An odd record. —*Scott Yanow*

Friday Night at the Village Vanguard / Dec. 14, 1994 / Storyville ✦✦✦

Violinist Urbaniak performs "Stella By Starlight," "Stardust" and four originals on this 1985 live recording from the Village Vanguard. Reissued on CD, the set finds Urbaniak joined by pianist Mike Gerber, bassist Ron Carter and drummer Lenny White. Although the leader's violin is electrified and sometimes a bit distorted (à la Jean-Luc Ponty), this is essentially an acoustic set. However, the versions of the two standards (both over 11 minutes) seem stretched out with little excitement occurring, while Urbaniak's more concise compositions are just not all that memorable. An OK but largely forgettable effort. —*Scott Yanow*

Phil Urso

b. Oct. 2, 1925, Jersey City, NJ
Tenor Saxophone / Cool

Subtlety and restraint defined the playing of Phil Urso, a member of the 1950s "Cool School" who owed a strong artistic debt to Lester Young but never came

across as a clone of "the Prez." Urso started out on clarinet, but the tenor sax became his primary instrument after he studied it in high school. Though not all that well known, Urso was a solid and expressive jazzman who played with Woody Herman, Jimmy Dorsey, Miles Davis, Terry Gibbs, Oscar Pettiford, and others in the 1950s. In 1954, he co-led a quintet with trombonist Bob Brookmeyer that recorded for Savoy, but Urso's best-known association came in 1955 and 1956, when he was a sideman for Chet Baker. Urso was prominently featured on some of the trumpeter's Pacific Jazz recordings of 1956, which make one wish he'd become more visible instead of less so. But after the '50s, very little was heard about Urso on a national level, although he did remain active in the jazz scene of his adopted home of Denver well into the 1990s. —*Alex Henderson*

● **Philosophy of Urso** / Apr. 14, 1953-Feb. 18, 1954 / Savoy ✦✦✦✦✦

Sentimental Journey / Mar. 27, 1956 / Regent ✦✦✦

Taking Sides / Apr. 27, 1986+May 28, 1986 / Spinnster ✦✦✦✦✦

The cool-toned tenor Phil Urso is best-known for his stint with Chet Baker in the mid-'50s. He led a few sessions during 1953-58, but this rare 1986 LP was his first as a leader in 28 years. Urso is teamed with fellow tenor Allen Eager (another lost legend), the underrated trumpeter Pete Minger, pianist Eddie Higgins, bassist Don Coffman and drummer Steve Bagby for a set of bebop-oriented music. The sextet performs four jazz standards (including "The Night Has a Thousand Eyes" and Tadd Dameron's "Sid's Delight") plus two of Urso's originals, and each of the musicians plays up to their potential. This LP is a real collector's item and should greatly interest bop collectors. —*Scott Yanow*

Warren Vache

b. Feb. 21, 1951, Rahway, NJ

Cornet, Fluegelhorn / Dixieland, Swing

Several years before Wynton Marsalis gained headlines for helping to revive hard bop, Warren Vache (along with Scott Hamilton) was among the few young jazz musicians who were reviving small-group swing. Vache, who always had a beautiful tone and a chance-taking style, is the son of a fine bassist (Warren Vache, Sr.) and the brother of clarinetist Allen Vache. He studied music with Pee Wee Erwin, gained early experience playing with Benny Goodman, Vic Dickenson and Bob Wilber, and has been a leader since the mid-'70s. Often teamed in his early years with tenorman Scott Hamilton, Vache has recorded regularly for Concord since the late '70s (and more recently Muse) and has been a regular at jazz parties and swing-oriented festivals ever since. —*Scott Yanow*

Jersey Jazz at Midnight / Dec. 31, 1975 / New Jersey Jazz Society ♦♦♦

First Time Out / Nov. 22, 1976+Dec. 6, 1976 / Monmouth ♦♦♦♦♦
With the exception of a privately issued record, this album (not yet reissued on CD) features cornetist Warren Vache's debut as a leader on record. The music is quite impressive for Vache (at 25) is showcased on five numbers backed only by guitarist Bucky Pizzarelli, and he displays both a lovely tone and a creative imagination within the boundaries of small group swing (even on Clifford Brown's "Joy Spring"). The second side of the LP is more Dixieland-oriented, for Vache is teamed with soprano saxophonist Kenny Davern, both Pizzarelli and Wayne Wright on guitars, bassist Michael Moore and drummer Connie Kay. "Oh Baby" and "All of Me" in particular are quite heated. Well worth searching for. —*Scott Yanow*

Blues Walk / Nov. 1977 / Dreamstreet ♦♦♦♦♦
This Dreamstreet LP was the initial release from the short-lived label. Cornetist Warren Vache was matched with tenor saxophonist Scott Hamilton for one of the first times and they both represented an unexpected youth movement that helped to revitalize small-group swing. With guitarist Bucky Pizzarelli, pianist John Bunch, bassist Michael Moore and drummer Butch Miles providing stimulating backup, Vache and Hamilton make for a perfect team on such standards as "Blues Walk" (mistakenly credited to Vache), the leader's "Sissiboo" (based on "I Got Rhythm"), "Blue Bossa" and "The Walker." Heated originals alternate with advanced ballads (including "A Child Is Born" and "I Remember Clifford") during this historic but out-of-print session. —*Scott Yanow*

Jillian / Nov. 1978 / Concord Jazz ♦♦♦♦
The emphasis is on Warren Vache's pretty tone during this fine swing date, his debut as a leader for Concord. Alternating between cornet and fluegelhorn, Vache teams up with guitarist Cal Collins ("Love Locked Out" is a guitar-fluegelhorn duet), bassist Phil Flanigan, drummer Jake Hanna and occasionally altoist Marshall Royal and pianist Nat Pierce. In addition to the title cut (his original), Vache performs nine superior standards, sounding quite lyrical on such songs as "It's All Right with Me," "Taking a Chance on Love," "More Than You Know" and "Too Close for Comfort." Recommended. —*Scott Yanow*

● **Polished Brass** / Apr. 1979 / Concord Jazz ♦♦♦♦♦
Cornetist Warren Vache has never made an uninspired record, and all of his releases (particularly for Concord) are easily recommended to fans of lyrical straightahead jazz. On this particularly strong effort, Vache is joined by guitarist Cal Collins (a few songs are cornet-guitar duets), bassist Michael Moore and drummer Jake Hanna. Other than John Bunch's "It's Love in the Spring," all of the songs are veteran standards. Highlights include "I Hadn't Anyone Till You," "My Melancholy Baby," "Ida" and "If We Never Meet Again." —*Scott Yanow*

Iridescence / Jan. 1981 / Concord Jazz ♦♦♦♦♦
For this Concord effort (all of which are recommended), cornetist Warren Vache teams up with pianist Hank Jones, bassist George Duvivier and drummer Alan Dawson for a typically strong set of swinging jazz. Vache's beautiful tone and creative ideas uplift such songs as "Softly As in a Morning Sunrise," "Sweet and Slow," "The Song Is You," "The More I See You" and Jones' "Iridescence." —*Scott Yanow*

Midtown Jazz / Feb. 1982 / Concord Jazz ♦♦♦♦
Cornetist Warren Vache is well showcased in an intimate trio with pianist John Bunch and bassist Phil Flanigan on this lyrical date. Although essentially a swing/mainstream stylist, Vache's repertoire on the set ranges from "Out of Nowhere" and "We'll Be Together Again" to Bud Powell's "Tempus Fugit" (which he had never heard before) and an unusual version of Thelonious Monk's "Rhythm-A-Ning." An excellent set of melodic music that favorably showcases Vache's beautiful tone. —*Scott Yanow*

Easy Going / Dec. 1986 / Concord Jazz ♦♦♦♦♦
On this well-rounded set, cornetist Warren Vache is featured in a sextet also including trombonist Dan Barrett (who blends very well with Vache), guitarist Howard Alden, the unknown pianist John Harkins, bassist Jack Lesberg and drummer Chuck Riggs. The arrangements really uplift the music and the repertoire has many unusual items including "Little Girl," Bobby Hackett's "Michelle," Carroll Coates' "London By Night," "Moon Song" and the underrated Dixieland tune "Mandy Make Up Your Mind." This is one of Warren Vache's better Concord albums although in reality all are recommended. —*Scott Yanow*

Warm Evenings / Jun. 1989 / Concord Jazz ♦♦♦♦
For what would be Warren Vache's final Concord recording as a leader before he switched labels to Muse, the cornetist is showcased while backed by the Beaux-Arts String Quartet and a rhythm section led by pianist Ben Aronov. The string arrangements of Jack Gale are excellent and perfectly set up Vache's beautiful tone. The emphasis is on slower tempos and long melody statements with the highlights including "With the Wind and the Rain in Your Hair," "You Go to My Head," "He Loves and She Loves," "A Flower Is a Lovesome Thing" and "Day Dream." —*Scott Yanow*

Horn of Plenty / Sep. 8, 1993+Oct. 5, 1993 / Muse ♦♦♦♦♦
Warren Vache is in excellent form throughout this interesting set. The cornetist duets with guitarist Joe Puma on his "Bix Fix" and with bassist Michael Moore on "Buddy Bolden's Blues." Several songs match him with trombonist Joel Helleny and tenor saxophonist Houston Person (most notably "Eternal Triangle," "Struttin' With Some Barbecue," "All Blues" and "Joy Spring") and a few numbers showcase him with a quartet. Throughout, Vache is heard at the top of his game, adding a swing sensibility to music ranging from Dixieland to hard bop. Recommended. —*Scott Yanow*

Jazz Im Amerika Haus, Vol. 2 / Jun. 25, 1994 / Nagel-Heyer ♦♦♦♦
The second in a series of CDs from the German Nagel-Heyer label that features performances recorded at Hamburg's Amerika Haus puts the spotlight on cornetist Warren Vache. Notable for being one of the few recorded matchups of Vache with his brother, clarinetist Allan Vache, this set also has a fine British rhythm section comprising pianist Brian Lemon, guitarist Dave Cliff, bassist Dave Green and drummer Allan Ganley. Allan Vache is a bit erratic in spots but Warren is in good form on such tunes as "My Shining Hour," "Poor Butterfly," Billy Strayhorn's "Isfahan" and "Cherokee." —*Scott Yanow*

Bebo Valdes

b. 1918, Quivican, Cuba

Piano / Afro-Cuban Jazz, Latin Jazz

A top-notch pianist/composer/arranger, Bebo Valdes (father of pianist Chucho Valdes) was the musical director of nightclub shows at the Tropicana in Havana by 1948. Very active in the 1950s, Valdes was considered one of the giants of Cuban music, arranging many recordings, composing mambos and organizing Afro-Cuban jazz jam sessions. He defected from Cuba in 1960 and by 1963 had settled in Stockholm. In 1994, after 34 years off records, he cut *Bebo Rides Again* for the Messidor label, not only playing piano but composing eight numbers and arranging 11 songs in the 36 hours before the first session; he was 76 at the time! —*Scott Yanow*

★ **Bebo Rides Again** / Nov. 1994 / Messidor ✦✦✦✦✦

This CD is both historic and quite exciting. Bebo Valdes (father of Chucho, the leader of Irakere) was one of the giants of Cuban jazz and popular music until he fled the country in 1960. Amazingly enough he had not recorded since, despite living peacefully in Sweden. This recording is also significant in that it is one of the first times that Cuban exiles had recorded with Cubans still living under Castro (guitarist Carlos Emilio Morales and percussionist Amadito Valdes). Paquito D'Rivera (who organized this set) deserves a lot of credit for its success, but Bebo Valdes is the real star. He composed eight new selections in the 36 hours before the recordings began, although he was 76 years old at the time. Although Valdes claimed that with the lack of sleep and excess of writing (he also arranged ten of the 11 songs) his fingers felt a bit stiff, he plays quite well throughout the very enjoyable music. The final results are full of strong melodies, stirring rhythms, exciting ensembles and lots of variety. The instrumentation differs on each track with plenty of solo space for D'Rivera (on both alto and clarinet), trombonist Juan-Pablo Torres (who takes "Veinte Anos" as a duet with Valdes), trumpeter Diego Urcola and the pianist. The percussionists work together quite well behind the lead voices and every selection is well worth hearing. This is one of the finest Afro-Cuban jazz recordings of recent times. Highly recommended. — *Scott Yanow*

Chucho Valdes

b. Oct. 9, 1941, Quivican, Cuba
Piano / Afro-Cuban Jazz, Latin Jazz
The son of the noted musician Bebo Valdes, Chucho began playing piano when he was three, and by the time he was 16 he was leading his own group. In 1960 his father defected from Cuba, but Chucho stayed behind. In 1967 he formed the Orquesta Cubana de Musica Moderna and in 1973 he founded Irakere, the top Cuban jazz orchestra; among its original members were Arturo Sandoval and Paquito D'Rivera. Valdes has been Irakere's musical director almost from the start and has recorded with the full band, in small groups and as an impressive solo pianist. He remains one of the top jazz musicians living in Cuba. — *Scott Yanow*

Lucumbi: Piano Solo / Nov. 15, 1986 / Messidor ✦✦✦✦

This is the first solo piano recording by this masterful Cuban musician. Co-founder and musical leader of the legendary Cuban band, Irakere, Valdes creates improvisations that revolve around the rhythms of the African "bata" drum. He has forged a unique style of solo piano that blends Cuban montunos with the jazz traditions of Duke Ellington, Art Tatum, and Keith Jarrett. Though his command of jazz style and technique is evident, Valdes maintains an undeniable Cuban passion in his playing, particularly in color and rhythmic emphasis. — *Roundup newsletter*

● **Solo Piano** / Sep. 1991 / Blue Note ✦✦✦✦✦

The leader and founder of Irakere, Chucho Valdes is also a brilliant pianist who may be on the same level as Gonzalo Rubalcaba. He has a very impressive classical technique and is able to hint at such players as McCoy Tyner, Lennie Tristano and Cecil Taylor without watering down his Cuban heritage. This dazzling set covers a lot of ground, with highlights including "Blue Yes" (which is based on the chords of Charlie Parker's "Confirmation"), a sensitive Bill Evans tribute and several nearly free explosions. Despite the CD's title, the final two of the ten selections add bass, drums and percussion and feature Valdes closely interacting with and pushing his sidemen. Highly recommended. — *Scott Yanow*

Grandes De La Musica Cubana, Vol. 1 / Aug. 28, 1995 / Import ✦✦✦✦

Afrocubanismo / Nov. 15, 1996 / Bembe ✦✦✦

Pianissimo / 1997 / International Music ✦✦✦

Dave Valentin

b. 1954, New York, NY
Flute / Latin Jazz, Crossover Jazz
Dave Valentin, who has recorded over 15 albums for GRP, combines together the influence of pop, R&B and Brazilian music with Latin-jazz to create a slick and accessible form of crossover jazz. At age nine, Valentin enjoyed playing bongos and congas. He gigged at Latin clubs in New York from age 12, and it was not until he was 18 that he seriously started studying flute. Valentin's teacher Hubert Laws suggested that he not double on saxophone because of his attractive sound on the flute. In 1977 he made his recording debut with Ricardo Marrero's group, and he was also on a Noel Pointer album. Discovered by Dave Grusin and Larry Rosen, Valentin was the first artist signed to GRP, and he has been a popular attraction ever since. — *Scott Yanow*

Legends / 1979 / GRP ✦✦✦

Mind Time / 1987 / GRP ✦✦✦

Earl Klugh plays nicely, as does Valentin, on this session. — *Ron Wynn*

Live at the Blue Note / May 31, 1988-Jun. 1, 1988 / GRP ✦✦✦✦✦

Two Amigos / 1990 / GRP ✦✦✦✦✦

With Herbie Mann. — *Ron Wynn*

Musical Portraits / 1991 / GRP ✦✦✦

Joined by his usual sidemen of the period (a rhythm section led by pianist Bill O'Connell), flutist Dave Valentin is the main soloist on an appealing if not particularly unique program of Latin-tinged and generally funky jazz. When he stretches out, as on "Firecracker," Valentin shows that he could become one of the best jazz flutists, but thus far he has not quite lived up to his potential. Still, this is, overall, a pleasing effort. — *Scott Yanow*

Red Sun / 1992 / GRP ✦✦✦✦

This was flutist Dave Valentin's 15th release for GRP and, as with his previous ones, it features impeccable musicianship, subtle funk grooves, some heated Latin rhythms and rather lightweight melodies. Despite some passionate moments, the music always sounds a bit controlled, never exceeding prescribed time limits or emotional boundaries. There are some strong moments of interest on this relatively pleasing CD, particularly a restrained melodic statement by trumpeter Arturo Sandoval on "We'll Be Together Again" and a groovin' version of "With a Little Help from My Friends." — *Scott Yanow*

● **Tropic Heat** / 1993 / GRP ✦✦✦✦✦

Flutist Dave Valentin's 16th album for GRP is one of his best. His regular group (a quartet with pianist Bill O'Connell, bassist Lincoln Goines and drummer Robbie Ameen) is augmented by two percussionists and an excellent seven-member horn section that consists of the reeds of Dick Oatts, Mario Rivera and David Sanchez, trombonist Angel "Papo" Vasquez and three trumpeters including Charlie Sepulveda. All of the horns get their opportunities to solo, and the result is a particularly strong Latin jazz session. Valentin continues to grow as a player and he cuts loose on several of these tracks. — *Scott Yanow*

George Van Eps

b. Aug. 7, 1913, Plainfield, NJ
Guitar / Swing
George Van Eps is a quiet legend among jazz guitarists, one who as far back as the 1930s pioneered a harmonically sophisticated chordal/lead style that was eclipsed in influence by the single-string idioms of Charlie Christian and Django Reinhardt. Yet Van Eps, like his brassy colleague Les Paul, also stands apart from them as an iconoclastic inventor, designing a seven-string guitar in the late 1930s that adds an extra bass string. Thus, Van Eps was able to play bass lines simultaneously with chords and lead solos, a jazz equivalent of fingerpicking country guitarists like Merle Travis and Chet Atkins. Van Eps puckishly referred to his style of playing as "lap piano," and his seven-string guitar has been adopted by a select few figures like Howard Alden and Bucky and John Pizzarelli.

Van Eps came from a talented musical family; his father Fred was a famous master of the ragtime banjo and a sound engineer, his mother played the piano, and he had three brothers, Bobby, Freddy and John, who were also professional musicians. Self-taught on the banjo, Van Eps began playing professionally at 11, and after falling under the influence of Eddie Lang two years later, he learned the guitar well enough to play alongside Lang for six months as a teenager. From there, Van Eps worked with Freddy Martin (1931-33), Benny Goodman (1934-35) and Ray Noble (1935-36) before moving to Hollywood to become a freelance musician, author of a how-to guitar book, and instrument designer. After returning to Noble in 1940-41, Van Eps worked in his father's recording lab for two years before returning to the freelance arena, where, among other things, he worked for Paul Weston and took part in the 1950s film and TV series *Pete Kelly's Blues*.

Van Eps only made a handful of recordings as a leader or unaccompanied soloist, including *Mellow Guitar* (Columbia, 1956) and *My Guitar, George Van Eps' Seven-String Guitar* and *Soliloquy* for Capitol in the late 1960s. A bout of serious illness in the early 1970s, plus a 1977 hand injury that resulted in three broken fingers, reduced his activities. However, Van Eps returned to the studio in 1991 for the first of three exquisite duo albums for Concord Jazz with his former student Howard Alden, mixing venerable standards with a few Van Eps originals, and he shared a solo guitar album with Johnny Smith in 1994. Even in his 80s, he remained an eloquent exponent of easygoing modern swing. — *Richard S. Ginell*

Mellow Guitar / Aug. 1, 1956-Aug. 15, 1956 / Corinthian ✦✦✦

My Guitar / 1965 / Capitol ✦✦✦

George Van Eps' Seven-String Guitar / Nov. 20, 1967-Nov. 22, 1967 / Capitol ✦✦✦

Soliloquy / 1968 / Capitol ✦✦✦

● **Hand-Crafted Swing** / Jun. 11, 1991-Jun. 12, 1991 / Concord Jazz ✦✦✦✦✦

Seven & Seven / Dec. 1992 / Concord Jazz ✦✦✦✦

Keepin' Time / Sep. 6, 1994-Sep. 7, 1994 / Concord Jazz ✦✦✦✦✦

Guitarists George Van Eps (a veteran of the 1930s) and Howard Alden (36 at the time of this recording) had made three prior CDs before cutting a fine quartet date with bassist Michael Moore and drummer Jake Hanna. The two guitarists can easily be told apart, for Van Eps (the inventor of the seven-string guitar) plays some of the most beautiful chords in the world, while Alden often contributes single-note solos. Highlights of the disc include Alden's two renditions of Van Eps songs ("The Chant" and "Kay's Fantasy"), Van Eps' two features and such swing standards as "Blue Skies," "How High The Moon," "I Cover The Waterfront" and a duet rendition of "More Than You Know." All of the music is quite relaxed (with nothing over a slow-medium pace) but has plenty of inner fire. —Scott Yanow

Tom Varner

b. Jun. 17, 1957, New Jersey
French Horn / Post-Bop

There have been few French horn soloists in jazz but, even if there had been dozens, chances are that Tom Varner would rank near the top. He started on piano at age ten and a few years later switched to French horn, discovering his predecessor Julius Watkins' recordings when he was 17. He graduated from New England Conservatory and in 1979 moved to New York. Since that time Varner has recorded several albums (mostly for Soul Note) as a leader and has worked with such players as Dave Liebman, Bobby Watson, George Gruntz (with his Concert Jazz Band), John Zorn, Steve Lacy, Lee Konitz and Bobby Previte. Varner has almost single-handedly made the difficult French horn a viable jazz instrument for the 1990s. —Scott Yanow

Tom Varner Quartet / Aug. 29, 1980 / Soul Note ✦✦✦✦✦

Tom Varner turned heads and opened eyes on the jazz scene in the early '80s. There weren't, and still aren't, many French horn players who improvise and play with the facility he demonstrated on this 1980 session. There were five tracks, two of them over ten minutes, and Varner displayed impressive speed and fire, playing with distinction while matching alto saxophonist Ed Jackson in range, control through every register, phrasing, and tonal quality. —Ron Wynn

Motion / Stillness / Mar. 19, 1982 / Soul Note ✦✦✦✦

● **Jazz French Horn** / Oct. 8, 1985-Oct. 9, 1985 / New Note ✦✦✦✦✦

There have only been a few jazz French horn players of note throughout history, although the instrument became a little more common in the 1980s and '90s. Tom Varner, on his third recording as a leader (following two obscure efforts for Soul Note), holds his own in a quintet with altoist Jim Snidero, pianist Kenny Barron, bassist Mike Richmond and drummer Victor Lewis. The emphasis is on boppish soloing over appealing sets of chord changes with the oddly titled "What Is This Thing Called First Strike Capability" based on a familiar tune and such fine songs as "Quasimodo," Bud Powell's "So Sorry Please" and "I Love You" receiving swinging treatment. A perfect introduction to both Tom Varner and the "jazz French horn." —Scott Yanow

Covert Action / Jan. 22, 1987-Jan. 23, 1987 / New Note ✦✦✦✦

The Mystery of Compassion / Mar. 5, 1992-Mar. 7, 1992 / Soul Note ✦✦✦✦✦

Martian Heartache / Mar. 5, 1996-Mar. 6, 1996 / Soul Note ✦✦✦

Johnny Varro

Piano / Swing

One of the top swing-oriented pianists since the 1950s, Johnny Varro has long been a fixture in the trad jazz circuit even if the greater jazz world does not seem to know that he exists. He considers his influences to be Jess Stacy, Teddy Wilson and Eddie Miller. Varro's first professional job was with Bobby Hackett. In 1957 he replaced Ralph Sutton as the intermission pianist at Eddie Condon's club and was associated with Condon throughout the first half of the 1960s. He worked with many top trad and swing players during that era before moving to Miami in 1964; in the late '70s he relocated to Southern California. The veteran pianist has kept up a busy schedule playing at clubs, jazz parties and festivals where his impeccable swing style is appreciated. In recent times Varro has made several recordings for Arbors. —Scott Yanow

Sittin' In / Oct. 8, 1985 / Too Cool ✦✦✦✦

Pianist Johnny Varro and Don Nelson (the latter on soprano sax and vocals) perform a set of duets on this enjoyable LP. In addition to six veteran swing standards, Nelson contributes five originals (and Varro one); the fresh material results in some inspired playing. Varro has long been one of the top swing pianists (most influenced by Teddy Wilson) and the more obscure Nelson has an attractive tone and a personable singing style. Even if all of the newer lyrics are

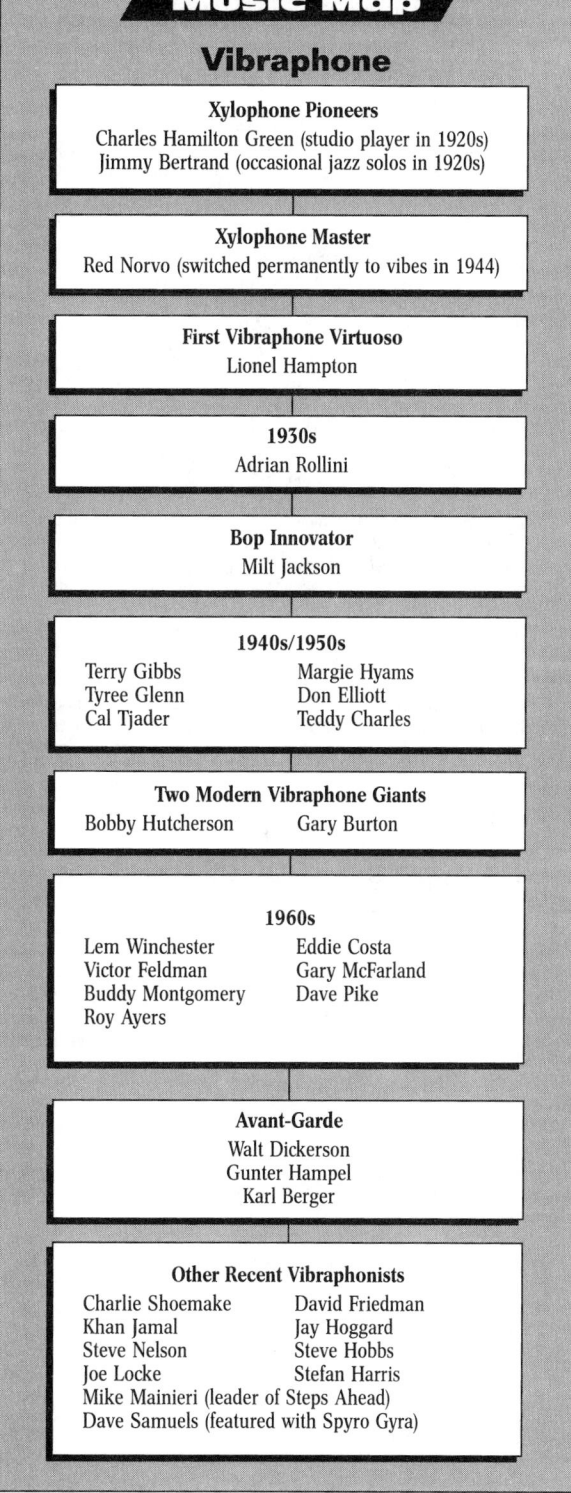

Music Map

Vibraphone

Xylophone Pioneers
Charles Hamilton Green (studio player in 1920s)
Jimmy Bertrand (occasional jazz solos in 1920s)

Xylophone Master
Red Norvo (switched permanently to vibes in 1944)

First Vibraphone Virtuoso
Lionel Hampton

1930s
Adrian Rollini

Bop Innovator
Milt Jackson

1940s/1950s
Terry Gibbs   Margie Hyams
Tyree Glenn   Don Elliott
Cal Tjader   Teddy Charles

Two Modern Vibraphone Giants
Bobby Hutcherson   Gary Burton

1960s
Lem Winchester   Eddie Costa
Victor Feldman   Gary McFarland
Buddy Montgomery   Dave Pike
Roy Ayers

Avant-Garde
Walt Dickerson
Gunter Hampel
Karl Berger

Other Recent Vibraphonists
Charlie Shoemake   David Friedman
Khan Jamal   Jay Hoggard
Steve Nelson   Steve Hobbs
Joe Locke   Stefan Harris
Mike Mainieri (leader of Steps Ahead)
Dave Samuels (featured with Spyro Gyra)

not necessarily classic, the performances are consistently excellent and swinging. —Scott Yanow

● **Everything I Love** / Sep. 8, 1992-Sep. 9, 1992 / Arbors ✦✦✦✦✦

Swing 7 / Jun. 28, 1994+Jun. 29, 1994 / Arbors ✦✦✦✦✦

Nana Vasconcelos

b. Aug. 2, 1944, Recife, Brazil
Percussion / World Fusion, Latin Jazz

Nana Vasconcelos is one of the cluster of endlessly inventive Brazilian percussionists who were changing the direction and sounds of Brazilian jazz in the postbossa nova 1970s. Vasconcelos is an especially inventive virtuoso of the berimbau, the weird yet expressive instrument shaped like an archer's bow, and he is also adept at the odd-numbered meters (5/4, 7/4) that were used frequently in the north of Brazil but not in the south.

As the son of a guitarist, Vasconcelos got his start in his father's band at age 12 playing bongos and maracas. Taking on a drum kit as part of his arsenal, he moved to Rio de Janeiro in the mid-1960s and caught on with the young Milton Nascimento, picking up several other Brazilian percussion instruments in the process. Gato Barbieri heard him and snatched him up for tours in Argentina, Europe and a US jaunt in 1971; Nana can be heard on a number of Gato's Flying Dutchman albums. Following the tour, he lived in Paris for two years, occasionally gigging with Don Cherry in Sweden. In 1976, he made a remarkable duo album with Brazilian guitarist/wood flute player Egberto Gismonti, *Danca Das Cabecas*, the first of several dates as a leader or sideman on the ECM label. He reunited with Cherry in 1978, and with Collin Walcott, formed Codona, a trio that played a fusion of music from four continents until Walcott's death in 1984. In the meantime, Vasconcelos joined the Pat Metheny Group from 1980 to 1983 as a "special guest," one who had the effect of re-routing Metheny's music in the general direction of Brazil. Since then, Vasconcelos has played on and off with Cherry, toured and recorded with Jan Garbarek, played on many recording sessions, and in 1995, formed an unusual duo with the Scottish classical percussionist Evelyn Glennie at the Bath International Music Festival. —*Richard S. Ginell*

★ **Saudades** / Mar. 1979 / ECM ✦✦✦✦✦

This 1979 recording is probably Afro-experimentalist Vasconcelos' finest. It presents his various facets—berimbau playing, intricate overlaid vocals, fine percussion, even gorgeous guitar—simply and almost overwhelmingly. This is one of those performances that remind one to never let natural dogmatism get too out of hand. —*John Storm Roberts*

Lester / Dec. 9, 1985-Dec. 10, 1985 / Soul Note ✦✦✦✦

Bush Dance / 1986 / Antilles ✦✦✦✦✦

Rain Dance / Oct. 1988 / Antilles ✦✦✦

Fragments: Modern Tradition / 1997 / Tzadik ✦✦✦

Sarah Vaughan

b. Mar. 27, 1924, Newark, NJ, **d.** Apr. 3, 1990, Los Angeles, CA
Vocals / Bop, Standards, Traditional Pop, Ballads

Possessor of one of the most wondrous voices of the 20th century, Sarah Vaughan ranked with Ella Fitzgerald and Billie Holiday in the very top echelon of female jazz singers. She often gave the impression that with her wide range, perfectly controlled vibrato, and wide expressive abilities, she could do anything she wanted with her voice. Although not all of her many recordings are essential (give Vaughan a weak song and she might strangle it to death), Sarah Vaughan's legacy as a performer and a recording artist will be very difficult to match in the future.

Vaughan sang in church as a child and had extensive piano lessons from 1931-39; she developed into a capable keyboardist. After she won an amateur contest at the Apollo Theatre, she was hired for the Earl Hines big band as a singer and second vocalist. Unfortunately, the musicians' recording strike kept her off record during this period (1943-44). When lifelong friend Billy Eckstine broke away to form his own orchestra, Vaughan joined him, making her recording debut. She loved being with Eckstine's orchestra, where she became influenced by a couple of his sidemen, Charlie Parker and Dizzy Gillespie, both of whom had also been with Hines during her stint. Vaughan was one of the first singers to fully incorporate bop phrasing into her singing, and to have the vocal chops to pull it off on the level of a Parker and Gillespie.

Other than a few months with John Kirby from 1945-46, Sarah Vaughan spent the remainder of her career as a solo star. Although she looked a bit awkward in 1945 (her first husband George Treadwell would greatly assist her with her appearance), there was no denying her incredible voice. She made several early sessions for Continental: a Dec. 31, 1944, date highlighted by her vocal version of "A Night in Tunisia," which was called "Interlude," and a May 25, 1945, session for that label that had Gillespie and Parker as sidemen. However, it was her 1946-48 selections for Musicraft (which included "If You Could See Me Now," "Tenderly" and "It's Magic") that found her rapidly gaining maturity and adding bop-oriented

phrasing to popular songs. Signed to Columbia, where she recorded during 1949-53, "Sassy" continued to build on her popularity. Although some of those sessions were quite commercial, eight classic selections cut with Jimmy Jones' band during May 18-19, 1950 (an octet including Miles Davis) showed that she could sing jazz with the best.

During the 1950s, Vaughan recorded middle-of-the-road pop material with orchestras for Mercury, and jazz dates (including a memorable collaboration with Clifford Brown) for the label's subsidiary, EmArcy. Later record label associations included Roulette (1960-64), Mercury (1963-67), and after a surprising four years off records, Mainstream (1971-74). Through the years, Vaughan's voice deepened a bit, but never lost its power, flexibility or range. She was a masterful scat singer and was able to outswing nearly everyone (except for Ella). Vaughan was with Norman Granz's Pablo label from 1977-82, and only during her last few years did her recording career falter a bit, with only two forgettable efforts after 1982. However, up until near the end, Vaughan remained a world traveler, singing and partying to all hours of the night with her miraculous voice staying in prime form. The majority of her recordings are currently available, including complete sets of the Mercury/EmArcy years, and Sarah Vaughan is as famous today as she was during her most active years. —*Scott Yanow*

Time After Time / Dec. 31, 1944-Dec. 29, 1947 / Drive Archive ✦✦✦

This CD skips around a lot but it gives one a decent overview of Sarah Vaughan during her first three years on records. Best are "East of the Sun" (from her first session as a leader), "September Song" (even if she was a bit too young to make its words fully believable), "The One I Love," her hit "Tenderly" and effective versions of "The Lord's Prayer" and "Motherless Child." Lots of variety on this disc. —*Scott Yanow*

Sarah Vaughan [Musica Jazz] / Dec. 31, 1944-Dec. 18, 1954 / Musica Jazz ✦✦✦✦

This hard-to-find Italian LP has some of the highlights of Sarah Vaughan's early years. Its main significance is that it has the four songs ("Singing Off," "Interlude," "No Smoke" and "East of the Sun") recorded at Vaughan's first session as a leader. Those rare titles have not been reissued in a long time and feature Dizzy Gillespie on trumpet, Georgie Auld on tenor and Leonard Feather on piano; "Interlude" is the first commercially recorded version of "A Night in Tunisia" and one of the very few vocal renditions. The remainder of this valuable LP features Sassy with Billy Eckstine's Orchestra, with Dizzy and Charlie Parker, singing with Tony Scott's septet and performing two titles apiece from 1946 (including "If You Could See Me Now"), 1949 and 1954 (the latter has trumpeter Clifford Brown on "Lullaby of Birdland"). —*Scott Yanow*

The Man I Love / Oct. 1, 1945-Apr. 8, 1948 / Musicraft ✦✦✦✦

This LP has 11 selections featuring the magnificent singer Sarah Vaughan during her period on Musicraft. On all but two of the selections (which mostly date from 1947) Sassy is backed by a commercial orchestra, but she excels on such songs as "Trouble Is a Man," "The Man I Love," "The One I Love" and "I Get a Kick out of You." In addition Vaughan is joined by a fine quartet on "Once in a While" while "Time and Again" (her very first record for the label, which served as her audition) is with violinist Stuff Smith. —*Scott Yanow*

The Divine Sarah / May 7, 1946-Oct. 10, 1947 / Mercury ✦✦✦✦✦

This Musicraft LP (which was released in 1980) has 14 titles from the early period of Sarah Vaughan. There are several classics here including "If You Could See Me Now," "You're Not the Kind" (the latter two songs have rare solos from trumpeter Freddie Webster), "Everything I Have Is Yours," "Body and Soul" and the earliest ever recording of "Tenderly" which was Vaughan's first hit. The last two performances, "The Lord's Prayer" and "Motherless Child," show just how powerful a singer (even beyond jazz) Sassy was from the start. Worth searching for. —*Scott Yanow*

One Night Stand: Town Hall Concert 1947 / Nov. 8, 1947 / Blue Note ✦✦✦✦

This 1997 CD has music from a previously unreleased Town Hall concert. The program is split between the Lester Young sextet and Sarah Vaughan, with the two principals only coming together on the final song, "I Cried for You." The recording quality is listenable, if not flawless, and it features the two giants at interesting points in their careers. Tenor great Lester Young sounds excellent on his seven features, but his backup group is sometimes a bit shaky, particularly during uncertain moments on "Just You, Just Me" and "Sunday"; bassist Rodney Richardson does not mesh well with the eccentric pianist Sadik Hakim. The young Roy Haynes is fine, although some of his "bombs" are overrecorded, while trumpeter Shorty McConnell comes across as a second-rate Howard McGhee, sincere but streaky. But the reason to acquire this CD is Sarah Vaughan, who at age 23 was already a marvel; what a voice! Very influenced by Dizzy Gillespie and Charlie Parker, Vaughan mostly lays way behind the beat during her ballad-oriented performances, swirling between notes like a first altoist and often settling on very unlikely (and boppish) notes. She gives the impression that she could do anything with her voice, and some of her flights (particularly on "Don't Blame Me," "I Cover the Waterfront" and "Mean to Me") border on the miraculous. —*Scott Yanow*

Columbia Years (1949-1953) / Jan. 20, 1949-Jan. 5, 1953 / Columbia ♦♦♦♦♦
This attractive double LP has the best 28 recordings that Sarah Vaughan cut for the Columbia label during 1949-53. On most of the selections (including memorable versions of "Black Coffee," "Just Friends," "I Cried for You," "Perdido" and "After Hours") the great singer is backed by fairly commercial orchestras. However, there are eight jazz selections from May 18-19, 1950, that match her beautiful voice with an all-star octet that includes trumpeter Miles Davis, Budd Johnson on tenor, trombonist Benny Green and clarinetist Tony Scott. Of the latter performances, her versions of "It Might as Well Be Spring," "Mean to Me," "Nice Work If You Can Get It" and "Ain't Misbehavin'" are true classics. Recommended. —*Scott Yanow*

In Hi-Fi / Dec. 21, 1949-Jan. 5, 1953 / Columbia/Legacy ♦♦♦♦♦
Most of Sarah Vaughan's Columbia recordings were on the commercial side, but not the memorable selections on this wonderful CD reissue. She recorded eight selections in 1950 with an octet that included trumpeter Miles Davis, trombonist Benny Green, the remarkably cool clarinetist Tony Scott and tenorman Budd Johnson. This CD adds alternate takes to seven of the numbers, increasing the discography of both Sassy and Miles. This version of "Ain't Misbehavin'" is a true classic (with memorable eight-bar solos by each of the four horns); "Mean to Me" and "Nice Work If You Can Get It" are gems, and the other performances are not far behind. In addition, Vaughan sings two versions of "The Nearness of You" in 1949; there is also a previously unknown recording of "It's All in the Mind," and three orchestra numbers from 1951 and 1953 wrap up the outstanding reissue. Sassy has rarely sounded better. Highly recommended. —*Scott Yanow*

16 Most Requested Songs / 1949-1953 / Columbia ♦♦♦
16 Most Requested Songs is a midline-priced collection that spotlights many of Sarah Vaughan's best-known and most popular performances for Columbia Records, including "Black Coffee," "Summertime," "The Nearness of You," "Goodnight My Love," "Come Rain or Come Shine," "Thinking of You," "Vanity," "Pinky," "Sinner or Saint," "My Tormented Heart" and "Spring Will Be a Little Late." Although it's far from a perfect retrospective of her career, it's still a nice sampler of familiar items, and it may satisfy the needs of some casual fans who only want the hits. —*Stephen Thomas Erlewine*

I'll Be Seeing You / 1949-1962 / Vintage Jazz Classics ♦♦♦♦
Shortly after Sarah Vaughan's death in 1990, this CD of previously unreleased live and radio performances was put out by Vintage Jazz Classics. The singer is heard in several different settings and excels in all of them. She sings two songs with a studio orchestra in 1949 (including Duke Ellington's "Tonight I Shall Sleep"), jams with her trio around 1961-62 (Woody Herman guests on clarinet for four songs), performs two short selections with Duke Ellington in 1951 and shares the vocal spotlight on "Love You Madly" with Nat King Cole and with Joe Williams on "Teach Me Tonight." Sassy's fans will want this very interesting release. —*Scott Yanow*

Perdido! Live (1953) / 1951-Apr. 21, 1953 / Natasha ♦♦♦♦
Most of this CD features Sarah Vaughan on radio broadcasts from Birdland during March and April 1953. She is in top form on the varied material (which is highlighted by "I Get a Kick out of You," "Tenderly" and "Perdido"), her trio is quite supportive and Dizzy Gillespie sits in on a few numbers, backing Sassy with respect. The CD concludes with a couple of fairly primitively recorded but impressive songs from a 1951 Apollo Theatre concert. Overall this release is quite valuable, for it features Vaughan in her early prime; her voice is quite beautiful throughout. —*Scott Yanow*

☆ **Complete Sarah Vaughan on Mercury, Vol. 1** / Feb. 10, 1954-Jun. 21, 1956 / Mercury ♦♦♦♦♦
Sarah Vaughan's years on Mercury (and its subsidiary EmArcy) feature inspired jazz performances, commercial recordings with string orchestras and big-band sides that fall in between jazz and middle-of-the-road pop music. All of her recordings for Mercury are on four impressive box sets that add up to 23 CDs. The first set (six CDs) is the best overall of the four, for it has a full set with her trio, the famous session with trumpeter Clifford Brown, a date with the Ernie Wilkins Orchestra (featuring altoist Cannonball Adderley) and a variety of orchestral sides. As with all of these sets, there are many previously unissued performances included too. More selective fans may want to get some of Sassy's individual packages instead (particularly the Clifford Brown date) but completists and true Sarah Vaughan fanatics will consider these four perfectly done sets to be essential. —*Scott Yanow*

The George Gershwin Songbook, Vol. 1 / Apr. 2, 1954-1957 / EmArcy ♦♦♦♦
With the exception of three songs recorded earlier, all of this set (the first of two CDs) dates from 1957 and finds the great Sarah Vaughan accompanied by her regular pianist Jimmy Jones plus a studio orchestra arranged by Hal Mooney. Since

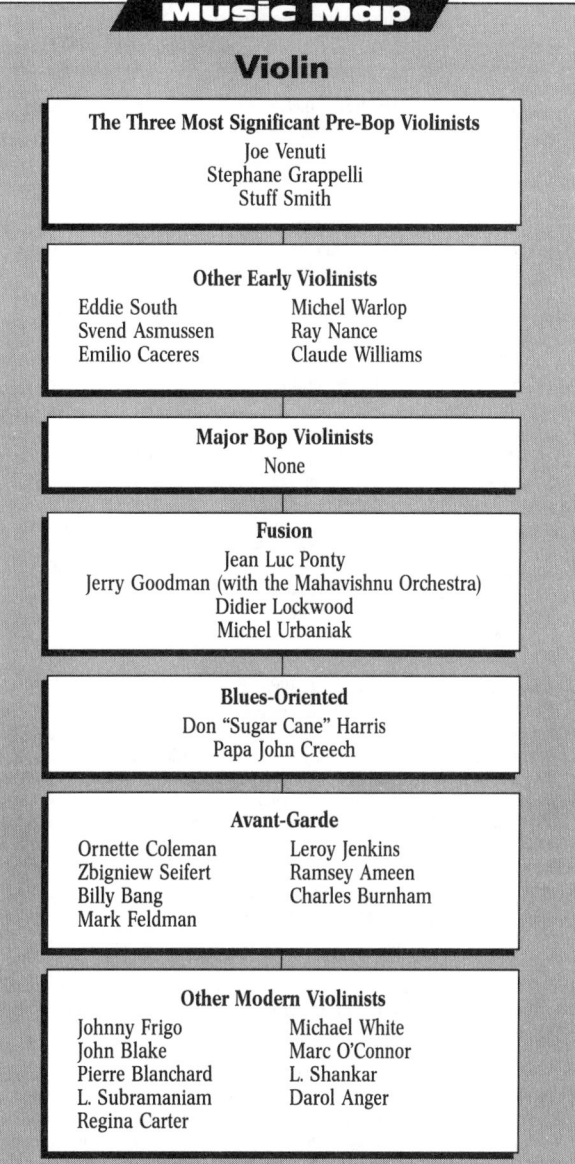

Music Map
Violin

The Three Most Significant Pre-Bop Violinists
Joe Venuti
Stephane Grappelli
Stuff Smith

Other Early Violinists
Eddie South   Michel Warlop
Svend Asmussen   Ray Nance
Emilio Caceres   Claude Williams

Major Bop Violinists
None

Fusion
Jean Luc Ponty
Jerry Goodman (with the Mahavishnu Orchestra)
Didier Lockwood
Michel Urbaniak

Blues-Oriented
Don "Sugar Cane" Harris
Papa John Creech

Avant-Garde
Ornette Coleman   Leroy Jenkins
Zbigniew Seifert   Ramsey Ameen
Billy Bang   Charles Burnham
Mark Feldman

Other Modern Violinists
Johnny Frigo   Michael White
John Blake   Marc O'Connor
Pierre Blanchard   L. Shankar
L. Subramaniam   Darol Anger
Regina Carter

these 15 selections are fairly concise (two to five minutes apiece), the emphasis is on the melody and the original lyrics without all that much improvising taking place. Sassy, who had a wondrous voice, is in excellent form on the superior material, making this CD a fine complement to Ella Fitzgerald's better-known *Gershwin Songbook*. —*Scott Yanow*

★ **Sarah Vaughan** / Dec. 18, 1954 / EmArcy ♦♦♦♦♦
This CD reissue features a classic (but unfortunately one-time only) collaboration between singer Sarah Vaughan and trumpeter Clifford Brown. In addition to Brownie, there is worthy solo space for flutist Herbie Mann and Paul Quinichette on tenor, who both fit in perfectly. Highlights include "Lullaby of Birdland," "He's My Guy," "You're Not the Kind" and "September Song." It is a special joy to hear Sarah Vaughan romping with her contemporaries in such a spontaneous yet coherent setting, swinging up a storm. All of the music on this CD is also included in *Vol. 1* of the box set titled *The Complete Sarah Vaughan on Mercury Vol. 1* (and also in a Clifford Brown box) but, for those listeners who just want a strong sampling of Sassy at her best, this is highly recommended. —*Scott Yanow*

● **In the Land of Hi-Fi** / Oct. 25, 1955-Oct. 27, 1955 / EmArcy ✦✦✦✦✦

This single CD (whose contents are also included in the box set *The Complete Sarah Vaughan on Mercury Vol. I*) has one of the great singer's best jazz dates for EmArcy. Accompanied by an all-star orchestra arranged by Ernie Wilkins and featuring altoist Cannonball Adderley (who was near the beginning of his career), Vaughan is in superior form during these concise (around three minutes apiece) performances, particularly on "Soon," "Cherokee," "I'll Never Smile Again" and "An Occasional Man." A strong session. —*Scott Yanow*

The George Gershwin Songbook, Vol. 2 / Oct. 26, 1955-Aug. 15, 1964 / EmArcy ✦✦✦✦

As with the first volume of this two-CD series, the majority of the selections date from 1957 and feature Sarah Vaughan (backed by an anonymous studio orchestra with pianist Jimmy Jones, arranged by Hal Mooney) doing straightforward and concise versions of George Gershwin classics. Vaughan, who is also heard on two other orchestral records (1955's "Maybe" and 1964's "Fascinatin' Rhythm") plus a rendition of "Embraceable You" with the Jimmy Jones Trio, is in typically expressive form. Highlights include "But Not For Me," "Someone to Watch Over Me," "The Man I Love," "I've Got a Crush on You" and "How Long Has This Been Going On." —*Scott Yanow*

Complete Sarah Vaughan on Mercury, Vol. 2: Sings Great American Songs (1956-1957) / Oct. 29, 1956-Jul. 12, 1957 / Mercury ✦✦✦✦✦

This five-CD box set, the second of four volumes that reissue all of Sarah Vaughan's recordings for Mercury and EmArcy (plus many previously unissued performances) contains her exploration of Gershwin songs, 13 vocal duets with her close friend Billy Eckstine and just five jazz numbers with her trio; all of the other selections feature Vaughan backed by large studio orchestras, usually led by Hal Mooney. Most of the material is a bit commercial (certainly the arrangements tend to be) but Sarah Vaughan generally uplifts the songs and overcomes her surroundings. Still, listeners strictly interested in her jazz performances are advised to get some of her single CD collections instead. —*Scott Yanow*

At Mister Kelly's / Aug. 6, 1957-Aug. 8, 1957 / EmArcy ✦✦✦✦✦

During an era when many of her studio recordings found Sarah Vaughan backed by large commercial orchestras, this live session reaffirmed her remarkable jazz talents. Accompanied by pianist Jimmy Jones, bassist Richard Davis and drummer Roy Haynes at a Chicago club, Sassy makes the standards sound as if they were written for her. High points include "September in the Rain," "Stairway to the Stars," "Honeysuckle Rose," "Poor Butterfly" and "Sometimes I'm Happy," but every selection is well worth hearing. Fortunately, this classic music has been reissued on CD. —*Scott Yanow*

The Complete Sarah Vaughan on Mercury, Vol. 3: Great Show on Stage (1954-1956) / Aug. 6, 1957-1959 / Mercury ✦✦✦✦✦

The third of four Sarah Vaughan Mercury box sets (this one has six CDs) traces her career during the last two and a half years of the 1950s. There are several very interesting sessions (expanded greatly by the inclusion of many previously unissued performances) on this box including 21 numbers from a gig at Mister Kelly's in Chicago with her trio (led by pianist Jimmy Jones), a meeting with the Count Basie Orchestra that resulted in the album *No Count Sarah*, and a live set with a septet (which includes cornetist Thad Jones and the tenor of Frank Wess) at the London House in Chicago. In addition, there are quite a few commercial sides with large orchestras (including some sessions arranged by Quincy Jones), so overall this box lets one hear the many sides of Sarah Vaughan; a special highlight is her first recorded version of "Misty." The reissue (and the other three volumes) is a must for Sarah Vaughan's greatest fans, although more general listeners may want to acquire one of the less expensive) single CDs instead. —*Scott Yanow*

No Count Sarah / Dec. 1958 / EmArcy ✦✦✦✦✦

Sarah Vaughan recorded in a variety of settings while with Mercury and EmArcy in the 1950s, but this particular matchup with the Count Basie Orchestra (pianist Ronnell Bright substitutes for the Count, thus the title) is pure jazz. During the classic encounter, Sassy fits in comfortably with the band, whether singing lyrics (such as "Darn That Dream," "Cheek to Cheek" or "Doodlin'") or scatting sensuously on "No Count Blues." The wit and constant swing (in addition to the spontaneous creativity), makes this one of the best of all Sarah Vaughan recordings. Highly recommended, either on this CD or as part of the six-CD set *The Complete Sarah Vaughan on Mercury, Vol. 3*. —*Scott Yanow*

The Singles Sessions / May 5, 1960-Feb. 1962 / Roulette ✦✦

During Sarah Vaughan's period with Roulette there were several attempts to come up with a hit record; none succeeded. This rather brief CD (around 35 minutes) has 14 songs, but despite some moments of interest (such as cover versions of "Don't Go to Strangers," "Love" and "Mama, He Treats Your Daughter Mean," the latter two being previously unissued), little memorable occurs. Although of some

interest to Sarah Vaughan completists, there are many more essential sets around than this one. —*Scott Yanow*

The Roulette Years / 1960-1964 / Roulette ✦✦✦

This CD contains 24 selections, so one cannot complain about its brevity, but it would have been preferable to have Sarah Vaughan's Roulette albums reissued in full (a few have been) rather than putting out this sampler. For the beginner there are many fine performances on the jazz-oriented set, with Sassy's accompaniment ranging from guitar-bass duets and the Count Basie Big Band to string orchestras. Exact recording dates are not given (which is rather inexcusable) but the music is consistently enjoyable with some of the high points being "Just in Time," "Have You Met Miss Jones," "Perdido," "'Round Midnight," "I'll Be Seeing You" and "Spring Can Really Hang You up the Most." —*Scott Yanow*

After Hours / Jun. 1961 / Roulette ✦✦✦✦

From 1961-62, Sarah Vaughan recorded two albums while accompanied by just guitar and bass. Her 1962 outing for the obscure Reactivation label (with guitarist Barney Kessel and bassist Joe Comfort) remains out of print, but her earlier set with guitarist Mundell Lowe and bassist George Duvivier, was finally reissued in 1997, along with one previously unreleased selection ("Through the Years") taken from a slightly exploratory session with the same players. Surprisingly, Lowe only has one solo, so the emphasis throughout is exclusively on Sassy's magnificent voice. The program mostly sticks to ballads, with a couple of exceptions (most notably "Great Day"), and is a quiet and intimate affair, with Vaughan more subtle than she sometimes was. Despite a lightweight version of "My Favorite Things" that will not remind listeners of John Coltrane, this is an excellent if brief set (34 minutes) with some fine jazz singing. —*Scott Yanow*

You're Mine, You / 1962 / Roulette ✦✦✦

This CD reissue finds Sarah Vaughan backed by big-band and string arrangements from Quincy Jones that could easily have been used for a Frank Sinatra date. Vaughan's voice is typically wondrous and sometimes a bit excessive on the ballads (some may find her slightly overblown version of "Maria" a bit difficult to sit through) but in top form on the more swinging numbers. In the repertoire are such tunes as "The Best Is Yet to Come," "The Second Time Around" and "Baubles, Bangles and Beads." More of a middle-of-the-road pop date than a creative jazz session (the personnel is not given), the set is not essential but should please those who love the sound of Sassy's remarkable voice. The final two "bonus" numbers ("One Mint Julep" and "Mama, He Treats Your Daughter Mean") were originally released as a single. —*Scott Yanow*

Star Eyes / 1962 / Roulette ✦✦✦

The great singer Sarah Vaughan is backed by an unknown studio orchestra on this set, which is directed and arranged by Marty Manning. The emphasis is on ballads (including "Star Eyes," "I'll Never Be the Same," "Do You Remember" and even "Call Me Irresponsible"). Although nothing all that memorable occurs, Sassy's voice is heard very much in its prime. Most of the selections on this LP have yet to be reissued on CD. —*Scott Yanow*

The Lonely Hours / Jan. 1963 / Roulette ✦✦✦

This LP, whose contents have been reissued on CD, features Sarah Vaughan accompanied by an orchestra arranged by Benny Carter. The dozen ballads that she performs are highlighted by "I'll Never Be the Same," "You're Driving Me Crazy," "What'll I Do," "Solitude" and "The Man I Love." It is a pity that altoist Carter does not play on this record (and that there is not much variety in tempos or moods), but overall it succeeds on its own terms. —*Scott Yanow*

Sarah Slightly Classical / May 1963-Jul. 1963 / Roulette ✦✦✦

Sarah Sings Soulfully / Jun. 6, 1963+1963 / Roulette ✦✦✦✦✦

Sarah Vaughan's final Roulette session before going back to Mercury was one of her best. Some of the tunes (such as "A Taste of Honey," "What Kind of Fool Am I" and "The Good Life") do not sound all that promising, but Sassy was near the peak of her powers during this era. Plus her renditions of "I Guess I'll Hang My Tears out to Dry," "Sermonette," "Gravy Waltz," "Moanin'," "'Round Midnight" and "Midnight Sun" are classics. Assisted by a sextet arranged by Gerald Wilson and including organist Ernie Freeman, trumpeter Carmell Jones and the tenor of Teddy Edwards, Vaughan is brilliant throughout this highly enjoyable CD reissue. —*Scott Yanow*

Sassy Swings the Tivoli / Jul. 18, 1963-Jul. 21, 1963 / Mercury ✦✦✦✦✦

After four years on Roulette, Sarah Vaughan returned to Mercury (her main label of the 1950s) with this wonderful live session, one of her very best of the 1960s. Joined by her rhythm section of the period (pianist Kirk Stuart, bassist Charles Williams and drummer Georges Hughes), Vaughan is quite expressive on such signature tunes as "Misty," "Sometimes I'm Happy," "Tenderly" and "I Cried For You." A gem. —*Scott Yanow*

Complete Sarah Vaughan on Mercury, Vol. 4, (1963-1967) / Jul. 19, 1963-Jan. 1967 / Mercury ✦✦✦✦

The fourth of four box sets reissuing every recording Sarah Vaughan made for the Mercury and EmArcy labels (including many previously unreleased performances) starts off (after four orchestra tracks) with its strongest selections, no less than 32 songs recorded during a live four-day engagement in Copenhagen during which the singer is accompanied by the Kirk Stuart Trio. Everything else on this six-CD set is somewhat anticlimactic in comparison, for Vaughan is otherwise hindered a bit by string orchestras, a big band and/or a choir. Better to get the live sessions (released as *Sassy Swings the Tivoli* in addition to a Japanese set by the same name that has extra material) instead, although lovers of Vaughan's voice will want to pick up this large reissue anyway. —*Scott Yanow*

Jazz Fest Masters / Jul. 1969 / Jazz Masters ✦✦✦✦

Sarah Vaughan made no studio recordings between Jan. 1967 and Nov. 1971, which makes her live performance from 1969 (first released on this 1992 CD) of historic interest. More importantly, the singer is in excellent form during these three different settings from the 1969 New Orleans Jazz Festival. She performs nine numbers with a quintet that includes fluegelhornist Clark Terry (who scats along with her on "Sometimes I'm Happy"); and the tenor of Zoot Sims and pianist Jaki Byard are accompanied by the University of Illinois Big Band on three Benny Carter arrangements and (during the most unusual track) collaborate with a Dixieland group and a gospel choir on "A Closer Walk With Thee." Overall, the recording quality is decent, and these lively performances add to the recorded legacy of the remarkable singer. —*Scott Yanow*

Time in My Life / Nov. 16, 1971-Nov. 20, 1971 / Mainstream ✦✦✦

With Michel Legrand / Apr. 17, 1972-Apr. 20, 1972 / Mainstream ✦✦✦

☆ **Complete: Live in Japan** / Sep. 24, 1973 / Mobile Fidelity ✦✦✦✦✦

This two-CD set contains all of the music that Sarah Vaughan recorded during her Tokyo concert for Mainstream. The 49-year-old singer is heard at the height of her powers, really digging into the standards and making magic out of such numbers as "Poor," "'Round Midnight," "Willow Weep," "My Funny Valentine," "Summertime" and "Bye Bye Blackbird." This two-fer (which finds Sassy accompanied by pianist Carl Schroeder, bassist John Gianelli and drummer Jimmy Cobb) gives one a definitive look at the brilliant (and sometimes miraculous) singer. —*Scott Yanow*

Send in the Clowns [Columbia/Legacy] / 1974 / Columbia/Legacy ✦

This CD reissue brings back one of Sarah Vaughan's worst recordings, a former LP made for Mainstream. The brilliant singer sticks mostly to dated pop tunes that even in the mid-'70s were somewhat obscure. Other than "Wave" (which she has done much better elsewhere), Jimmy Rowles' "Frasier the Sensuous Lion" (ditto) and "Send in the Clowns," the songs are long forgotten. The string arrangements (some by Michel Legrand) are insipid and Sassy's attempts to jazz up some of the inferior material are a dismal flop. Those listeners who are forced to hear this often-embarrasing date will be grateful that the entire program lasts less than 33 minutes. —*Scott Yanow*

I Love Brazil / Oct. 31, 1977-Nov. 7, 1977 / Pablo ✦✦✦

Sarah Vaughan's debut for the Pablo label is a bit of an acquired taste for the jazz fan. She is accompanied by a variety of Brazilian all-stars (including Milton Nascimento, Dori Caymmi and on two numbers Antonio Carlos Jobim himself) and Sassy (whose voice was still in tremendous form) fares quite well, but few of the performances are all that memorable and none of the dozen songs entered her permanent repertoire. This set is really more for fans of contemporary Brazilian music than for jazz collectors. —*Scott Yanow*

How Long Has This Been Going On? / Apr. 25, 1978 / Pablo ✦✦✦✦✦

This CD reissue features the great Sarah Vaughan in a typically spontaneous Norman Granz Pablo production with pianist Oscar Peterson, guitarist Joe Pass, bassist Ray Brown and drummer Louie Bellson. Sassy sounds wonderful stretching out on such songs as "Midnight Sun," "More than You Know," "Teach Me Tonight" and "Body and Soul," among others. All ten of the melodies are veteran standards that she knew backwards but still greeted with enthusiasm. A very good example of late-period Sarah Vaughan. —*Scott Yanow*

The Duke Ellington Songbook, Vol. 1 / Aug. 15, 1979-Sep. 13, 1979 / Pablo ✦✦✦✦✦

Sarah Vaughan interprets ten Duke Ellington-associated songs on the first of two sets; *Song Book Two* was recorded at the same two sessions as this CD reissue. Vaughan is accompanied by a variety of jazz all-stars including trumpeter Waymon Reed, trombonist J.J. Johnson and the tenors of Frank Foster, Frank Wess and Zoot Sims. Bill Byers contributed the arrangements for the larger band performances. The emphasis is on ballads with the highlights including "I'm Just a Lucky So and So," "I Didn't Know About You," "All Too Soon" and "Lush Life." Sassy's voice is in typically wondrous form throughout. —*Scott Yanow*

The Duke Ellington Songbook, Vol. 2 / Aug. 15, 1979-Sep. 13, 1979 / Pablo ✦✦✦✦✦

The second of two Pablo CDs featuring Sarah Vaughan interpreting Duke Ellington-associated material shows that the veteran singer never did decline. With assistance from trumpeter Waymon Reed, flutist Frank Wess, Eddie "Cleanhead" Vinson on alto and a surprise vocal, and several overlapping rhythm sections, Sassy sounds in top form throughout this date. Highlights include "I Ain't Got Nothing but the Blues," "Chelsea Bridge," "Rocks in My Bed," "I Got It Bad" and "Mood Indigo" but all 11 numbers are well worth hearing. Both of these well-conceived sets are easily recommended. —*Scott Yanow*

Send in the Clowns [Pablo] / Feb. 16, 1981-May 16, 1981 / Pablo ✦✦✦

Sarah Vaughan is accompanied by her regular rhythm section of the early '80s (pianist George Gaffney, bassist Andy Simpkins and drummer Harold Jones), guitarist Freddie Green, and the Count Basie horn sections on this enjoyable date, which has been reissued on CD. The arrangements by Sammy Nestico and Allyn Ferguson unfortunately do not leave much room for any of the Basie sidemen to solo, but Sassy is in superb form. She is at her best on "I Gotta Right to Sing the Blues," a remake of "If You Could See Me Now" and a rapid "When Your Lover Has Gone," although some listeners may enjoy her overly dramatic rendition of "Send in the Clowns." —*Scott Yanow*

Crazy and Mixed Up / Mar. 1, 1982+Mar. 2, 1982 / Pablo ✦✦✦✦✦

Sarah Vaughan had complete control over the production of this album (which would be her last small-group recording) and, even if the results are not all that unique, her voice is often in near-miraculous form. With fine backup work from pianist Roland Hanna, guitarist Joe Pass, bassist Andy Simpkins and drummer Harold Jones, Sassy sounds in prime form on such songs as "I Didn't Know What Time It Was," "Autumn Leaves," "The Island" and "You Are Too Beautiful." It is hard to believe, listening to her still-powerful voice on this CD reissue, that she had already been a recording artist for 48 years. —*Scott Yanow*

The Mystery of Man / Jun. 30, 1984 / Kokopelli ✦✦

This CD reissue brings back the music from an unusual project. Gene Lees was hired to translate the philosophical poems of Pope John II into English and match them to music. The project climaxed in a performance and recording by Sarah Vaughan, who was backed by a huge orchestra and chorus conducted by Lalo Schifrin. Unfortunately, despite the best efforts of everyone involved, the results often sound rather ponderous. The best pieces are the two original ones by Lees ("The Mystery of Man" and "Let It Live"), but otherwise this is a difficult set to sit through, not only from the jazz standpoint (the impressive all-stars who are in the orchestra are largely wasted) but musically; everything is too serious and a bit pompous. Skip. —*Scott Yanow*

Charlie Ventura

b. Dec. 2, 1916, Philadelphia, PA, **d.** Jan. 17, 1992, Pleasantville, NJ
Tenor Saxophone, Leader / Bop, Swing

Charlie Ventura was an extroverted and sometimes explosive tenor saxophonist whose solos could be tasteless but were rarely dull. He came to fame with the Gene Krupa big band (1942-43 and 1944-46) during which time he was often featured with Krupa in a trio; their wild rendition of "Dark Eyes" was a favorite. Ventura first recorded as a leader in 1945 and, after an attempt at leading a big band in 1946, he cut back to a highly successful septet that by 1949 featured trumpeter Conte Candoli, the vocal duo of Jackie and Roy (Roy Kral also played piano), trombonist Benny Green and the leader's tenor. During the bop fad of that year Ventura termed his music "Bop for the People." After that quickly ran its course, Ventura recorded with a dance band during 1949-50 and then he cut back to a quartet (sometimes doubling on baritone or bass sax), making occasional records and having some concert reunions with Krupa. After 1957 Ventura only made one further record as a leader (a 1977 date for Famous Door) but continued playing in his largely unchanged style into the 1980s. —*Scott Yanow*

Euphoria / Aug. 15, 1945-Oct. 1948 / Savoy ✦✦✦✦✦

Charlie Ventura, who rose to fame with Gene Krupa's Orchestra and Trio, was a fine tenor saxophonist who could get rather silly at times in his playing. There is little of the latter on this definitive two-LP set. Ventura is heard with a sextet in 1945 that co-stars trumpeter Buck Clayton, heads a fine quartet, tries to sound modern in a septet with trumpeter Charlie Shavers and trombonist Bill Harris, shares a front line with trombonist Kai Winding and jams with his septet in 1948. Some of the later selections with Jackie Cain and Roy Kral on the vocals are dated (check out their odd version of "I'm Forever Blowing Bubbles") as Ventura tried to get "with it" and take over the modern jazz movement with his "Bop for the People" music. However in general the music is quite rewarding and this two-fer gives one a strong look at his early dates as a leader. —*Scott Yanow*

Jumping with Charlie Ventura / Oct. 17, 1945-1948 / Trip ✦✦✦

This long out-of-print Trip LP features tenor saxophonist Charlie Ventura on 11 performances that were originally released on EmArcy, some of which have also been reissued by Savoy. Ventura's exuberant sound sometimes masked a creative swing style, although he also left his music open to the influence of bop. Ventura is heard on four big band numbers from 1946 and in combos with such sidemen as trumpeters Charlie Ventura and Buck Clayton, trombonists Bennie Green, Bill Harris and Kai Winding and pianist Lou Stein; in addition Buddy Stewart and Jackie & Roy take a few vocals. Due to the sampler nature of this set (all of Ventura's underrated music should be reissued complete and in chronological order), the album is not that essential. —*Scott Yanow*

Charlie Boy / Jan. 27, 1946-May 1946 / Phoenix ✦✦✦✦

On this hard-to-find collector's LP, the extroverted tenor saxophonist Charlie Ventura is heard on four sessions from 1946. Two dates team Ventura with swing clarinetist Barney Bigard while the other top sidemen include altoists Willie Smith and Charlie Kennedy, trumpeter Red Rodney (three years before he joined Charlie Parker), pianists Arnold Ross and Teddy Napoleon, guitarist Barney Kessel, bassist Red Callender and drummer Nick Fatool. The music is mostly small-group swing, although one can feel the influence of bebop in spots. These spirited performances (all recorded in Los Angeles) have once again become rare due to the cutout status of this recommended LP. —*Scott Yanow*

Charlie Ventura in Concert / May 9, 1949 / GNP ✦✦✦✦✦

● **Charlie Ventura in Concert** / May 9, 1949 / MCA/Decca ✦✦✦✦✦

Tenor saxophonist Charlie Ventura's 1949 concert at the Pasadena Civic Auditorium was fully recorded and documented in part by both Decca and GNP/Crescendo; both releases are completely different. The Decca half, made available on this CD by MCA, features Ventura with a septet that includes trumpeter Conte Candoli, trombonist Benny Green, altoist Boots Mussuli, pianist Roy Kral, bassist Kenny O'Brien, drummer Ed Shaugnessy and the vocals of Jackie Kain and Roy Kral. This was one of Ventura's finest groups, as can be heard on such numbers as "Euphoria," a bizarre "I'm Forever Blowing Bubbles," "How High The Moon" and Lou Stein's classic "East of Suez." In addition Candoli is featured on "Fine and Dandy," Ventura plays baritone on "If I Had You" and Green's humorous style is showcased on "Pennies from Heaven." This is a near-classic set that should greatly interest bop collectors; the GNP release is also quite rewarding. —*Scott Yanow*

Charlie Ventura Plays Hi Fi Jazz / 1956 / Tops ✦✦✦✦

By 1956 tenor saxophonist Charlie Ventura no longer had a regular band and was drifting into semi-retirement. In fact, other than an album for King the following year and a set for Famous Door in 1977, this LP was his final recording. Teamed with the then-unknown pianist Dave McKenna, guitarist Billy Bean, bassist Richard Davis (at the beginning of his career) and drummer Mousey Alexander, Ventura switches between tenor, alto, baritone and bass saxophones. The repertoire is filled with swing and Dixieland standards including such unlikely songs as "When the Saints Go Marching In," "Bill Bailey" and "Sweet Sue" (in addition to a remake of Ventura's old hit with Gene Krupa, "Dark Eyes"), but the interpretations are full of spirit and swing. Although it may not look too promising, this budget LP (which is long out of print but may be found at a cheap price) is actually well worth picking up. —*Scott Yanow*

Chazz / 1977 / Famous Door ✦✦✦✦

Joe Venuti (Giuseppi Venuti)

b. Sep. 16, 1903, Philadelphia, PA, d. Aug. 14, 1978, Seattle, WA
Violin / Classic Jazz, Swing, Dixieland

Although renowned as one of the world's great practical jokers (he once called a couple dozen bass players with an alleged gig and asked them to show up with their instruments at a busy corner so he could view the resulting chaos!), Joe Venuti's real importance to jazz is as improvised music's first great violinist. He was a boyhood friend of Eddie Lang (jazz's first great guitarist), and the duo teamed up in a countless number of settings during the second half of the 1920s, including recording influential duets. Venuti moved to New York in 1925, and immediately he and Lang were greatly in demand for jazz recordings, studio work and club appearances. Venuti seemed to play with every top White jazz musician during the segregated era, and in 1929 he and Lang joined Paul Whiteman's Orchestra, appearing in the film *The King of Jazz*.

Lang's premature death in 1933 was a major blow to Venuti, who gradually faded away from the spotlight. In 1935 after visiting Europe, the violinist formed a big band and, although it survived quite awhile and helped introduce both singer Kay Starr and drummer Barrett Deems, it was a minor-league orchestra that only recorded four songs (which Venuti characteristically titled "Flip," "Flop," "Something" and "Nothing!"). His brief stint in the military during World War II ended

the big band, and when he was discharged, Venuti stuck to studio work in Los Angeles. He was regularly featured on Bing Crosby's early-'50s radio show, but in reality the 1936-66 period was the Dark Ages for Venuti as he drifted into alcoholism and was largely forgotten by the jazz world.

However in 1967 Joe Venuti began a major comeback, playing at the peak of his powers at Dick Gibson's Colorado Jazz Party. His long-interrupted recording career resumed with many fine sessions (matching his violin with the likes of Zoot Sims, Earl Hines, Marian McPartland, George Barnes, Dave McKenna and Bucky Pizzarelli among others) and, despite his increasingly bad health, Venuti's final decade was a triumph. —*Scott Yanow*

Joe Venuti and Eddie Lang 1926-1930 / Sep. 29, 1926-Oct. 7, 1930 / Swaggie ✦✦✦✦✦

The first of two Swaggie LPs to document some of the classic performances of violinist Joe Venuti and guitarist Eddie Lang, this is filled with exciting performances that mostly do not duplicate the recordings on the Columbia two-LP set *Stringing the Blues*. Venuti and Lang (sometimes with the assistance of pianist Frank Signorelli) are heard on all of the takes that exist of "Black and Blue Bottom," "Stringing the Blues," "Doin' Things" and "Wild Cat." In addition, Venuti's Blue Four (with either Jimmy Dorsey on trumpet, clarinet, alto and baritone, C-melody saxophonist Frankie Trumbauer, bass-saxophonist Adrian Rollini or baritonist Pete Pumiglio) are heard on nine additional selections. The music is wonderful small-group New York jazz of the late '20s, played with high musicianship and plenty of spirit. —*Scott Yanow*

Joe Venuti and Eddie Lang (1926-1933) / Nov. 8, 1926-May 8, 1933 / ABC ✦✦✦

This somewhat random sampling of the recordings of violinist Joe Venuti and guitarist Eddie Lang contains a variety of gems but will at least partly duplicate most other Venuti collections from the era. Common selections alternate with rarities (such as Red McKenzie's "My Baby Came Home"). In addition to numbers from Venuti and Lang sessions, there are selections taken from dates led by Red Nichols, Frankie Trumbauer ("Krazy Kat," which also has a short solo from Bix Beiderbecke) and Lang. Robert Parker's inventive engineering gives these selections a slight echo and the feel of stereo; collectors vary as to their liking of his methods. —*Scott Yanow*

Violin Jazz 1927-1934 / Jun. 28, 1927-Sep. 20, 1934 / Yazoo ✦✦✦✦

This hodgepodge sampler contains 14 of violinist Joe Venuti's better recordings from the 1927-34 period, many of them also featuring guitarist Eddie Lang. The performances are mostly drawn from sessions by Venuti's Blue Four, with some of the soloists including Jimmy Dorsey (switching between clarinet, alto, trumpet and baritone), Frankie Trumbauer (on C-melody sax and bassoon), bass-saxophonist Adrian Rollini and, on "Sweet Lorraine," clarinetist Benny Goodman. The music is consistently exciting, although serious collectors will want to acquire releases from the more complete European series instead. —*Scott Yanow*

Big Bands of Joe Venuti, Vol. 1 / May 25, 1928-Sep. 6, 1930 / JSP ✦✦✦✦✦

In contrast to the hot small groups that violinist Joe Venuti led during the 1927-34 period, his big-band recordings were generally commercial with middle-of-the-road pop vocals, dance-band arrangements and melodic solos. Still, the two-volume JSP series contains a great deal of worthwhile music. The musicianship is top-notch, there are some good solo spots (particularly from Venuti and Jimmy Dorsey on clarinet and alto) and the music is pleasing if not too adventurous. 1920s collectors should pick up these two sets. —*Scott Yanow*

Big Bands of Joe Venuti, Vol. 2 / May 22, 1930-Oct. 13, 1933 / JSP ✦✦✦✦

There are many rarities on this dance-band album, the second of two LPs in JSP's valuable series. The music is not as essential as violinist Joe Venuti's small-group sides of the period, but there are some strong moments and the English JSP label wisely reissued everything. Five of these titles are from 1930, while the remaining 11 are from 1933. The personnel on the latter titles are mostly unknown but the musicianship is first rate. Overall this is not an essential acquisition but fans of the era will want to get this anyway. —*Scott Yanow*

Joe Venuti and Eddie Lang 1930-1933 / Nov. 12, 1930-Feb. 28, 1933 / Swaggie ✦✦✦✦✦

In Swaggie's second volume of small-group sides by violinist Joe Venuti and guitarist Eddie Lang, five sessions are reissued in full. The first ten titles match the pair with Jimmy Dorsey (who switches between clarinet, alto and baritone) on some delightful performances; composer Harold Arlen takes vocals on four of the numbers. In addition the Venuti-Lang All-Star Orchestra (with trumpeter Charlie Teagarden, trombonist Jack Teagarden and clarinetist Benny Goodman) performs classic versions of four standards ("Beale Street Blues," "After You've Gone," "Farewell Blues" and "Someday Sweetheart") and Venuti welcomes both Jimmy Dorsey and bass saxophonist Adrian Rollini to a particularly wild four-song session in 1933. Essential and timeless music. —*Scott Yanow*

Music Map

Vocalists—Male

First Important Jazz Singer and the Most Influential
Louis Armstrong

Pre-Bop Instrumentalists Who Also Sang
Don Redman (Took first recorded scat vocal in 1924)

Jack Teagarden	Fats Waller
Red Allen	Hot Lips Page
Wingy Manone	Louis Prima
Nat Gonella	Jelly Roll Morton
Woody Herman	Jay McShann
Nat King Cole	Danny Barker
Clancy Hayes	Louis Jordan
Cliff Edwards	

Middle-of-the-Road Pop Singers Who Have Influenced Jazz
Bing Crosby • Frank Sinatra

Kansas City Swing/Blues Tradition

Jimmy Rushing	Big Joe Turner
Jimmy Witherspoon	Big Miller
Joe Williams	Ernie Andrews
Bill Henderson	

Two Other Influential Swing Vocalists
Cab Calloway • Billy Eckstine

Jive Singers
Slim Gaillard • Leo Watson
Harry "The Hipster" Gibson

Bop and Vocalese

Dizzy Gillespie	Joe Carroll
Babs Gonzales	Jackie Paris
Eddie Jefferson	King Pleasure
Buddy Stewart	Dave Lambert
Jon Hendricks	

R&B
Ray Charles • Charles Brown • Al Jarreau

More Recent Instrumentalists Who Also Sing

Chet Baker	Clark Terry
Richard Boone	George Adams
Grady Tate	George Benson

1960s to the Present

Mel Tormé	Johnny Hartman
Earl Coleman	Bob Dorough
Oscar Brown, Jr.	Mose Allison
Leon Thomas	Mark Murphy
Dave Frishberg	Bobby McFerrin
Kevin Mahogany	Kurt Elling

☆ **Fiddlesticks** / Oct. 22, 1931-Jan. 25, 1939 / Conifer ◆◆◆◆◆
This CD combines together five complete sessions, some of violinist Joe Venuti's finest recordings from the 1930s. Venuti, guitarist Eddie Lang, trumpeter Charlie Teagarden, trombonist Jack Teagarden and clarinetist Benny Goodman team together for four classics ("Beale Street Blues," "After You've Gone," "Farewell Blues" and "Someday Sweetheart"), Jimmy Dorsey and Adrian Rollini constantly switch instruments on their wild meeting with Venuti and Lang, the violinist is heard on two obscure but worthy dates from 1935, and the only four recordings made by his unsuccessful big band (titled "Flip," "Flop," "Something" and "Nothing") wrap up this essential CD. Venuti would spend 30 years in obscurity (due partly to his alcoholism) but he is heard very much at the peak of his powers throughout this essential CD. —*Scott Yanow*

Pretty Trix / Dec. 26, 1934-Dec. 28, 1934 / IAJRC ◆◆◆◆
This very interesting CD from the collectors' IAJRC label contains previously unknown performances from late 1934. Violinist Joe Venuti is heard with a large studio group that sometimes features such musicians as trumpeter Louis Prima, xylophonist Red Norvo, trombonist Jerry Colonna (yes, the same person as the comedian), guitarist Frank Victor and Larry Binyon on tenor and flute. The music is essentially swing with a few elements of Dixieland and, although some of the performances (which were radio transcriptions) have their share of flubs (these were all first takes), the results on a whole are quite musical and swinging. —*Scott Yanow*

The Mad Fiddler from Philly / 1952-1953 / Shoestring ◆◆◆
Violinist Joe Venuti was in obscurity during the 1939-69 period, an alcoholic whose music was out of style and whose bands were filled mostly with minor leaguers. In the early '50s he renewed his friendship with Bing Crosby and for awhile became an important part of his radio show. Typically the pair would have some humorous dialogue and then Venuti would take a featured number. This Shoestring LP has a dozen of his performances (plus the preceding verbal banter),

filling in an important historical gap in the violinist's career. Worth searching for. —*Scott Yanow*

Joe Venuti in Milan / May 3, 1971 / Vanguard ◆◆◆◆
Violinist Joe Venuti's comeback after 30 years of obscurity began in earnest in 1969. By 1971 and his visit to Italy, he was fully back on the scene and would record quite frequently during his final seven years. This LP matches Venuti with a group of Italians on spirited versions of standards. The slightly unusual instrumentation includes guitarist Lino Patruno, baritone, trombone and a rhythm section and works perfectly on the material. An enjoyable outing. —*Scott Yanow*

15 Jazz Classics / May 3, 1971-Sep. 14, 1974 / Omega ◆◆◆◆
This CD reissue, which does not give the recording dates, brings back material recorded by the immortal jazz violinist Joe Venuti during his visits to Italy in 1971 and 1974. The former material was out domestically on a Vanguard LP (along with a few other cuts), but the latter is more obscure. In both cases, the violinist teams up with a group assembled by guitarist Lino Patruno, which at times has several horns (including baritone and flute) and a swinging rhythm section. Although the Italian players are fine, Joe Venuti is the main star on such numbers as "After You've Gone," "Jazz Me Blues," "Clementine," "Indiana" and a five-song Gershwin medley. Swinging and sometimes heated music. —*Scott Yanow*

Joe and Zoot / Sep. 27, 1973 / Chiaroscuro ◆◆◆◆◆
This is a very exciting LP. The veteran violinist Joe Venuti really hit it off with tenor great Zoot Sims (who is also heard here on soprano) and the results were three very memorable albums. Their first recorded encounter finds the two principal voices joined by the stride piano master Dick Wellstood, bassist George Duvivier and drummer Cliff Leeman. They perform a variety of familiar and high-quality standards, including such romps as "I've Found a New Baby," "The Wild Cat," "It's the Girl" and "Lady Be Good." Wonderful and consistently hard-swinging music. —*Scott Yanow*

The Joe Venuti Blue Four / May 20, 1974 / Chiaroscuro ✦✦✦✦✦

The second of violinist Joe Venuti's three recordings with tenor saxophonist Zoot Sims (who is actually only on four of the 12 selections) also features the legendary bass-saxophonist Spencer Clark, either Dick Hyman or Dill Jones on piano, guitaist Bucky Pizzarelli, bassist Milt Hinton and drummer Cliff Leeman in different combinations. This Chiaroscuro album (along with the other Venuti-Sims sessions) is long overdue to be reissued on CD. —*Scott Yanow*

Jazz Violin / Sep. 13, 1974-Sep. 14, 1974 / Vanguard ✦✦✦✦

Violinist Joe Venuti's second recording with Italian guitarist Lino Patruno's group follows the initial one by three years. The standards (which include a Gershwin medley) are all quite familiar, but these versions are full of enthusiasm and interesting ideas. Venuti was in top form throughout his final period (1969-77) and seemed to enjoy interacting with the five other horns on this session, not yet reissued on CD. —*Scott Yanow*

Joe Venuti and Zoot Sims / Jul. 1975 / Chiaroscuro ✦✦✦✦✦

Violinist Joe Venuti's three recordings with tenorman Zoot Sims are all quite joyful and exciting. This Chiaroscuro LP matches the pair with pianist John Bunch, bassist Milt Hinton, drummer Bobby Rosengarden and, on "Don't Take Your Love from Me," trombonist Spiegel Wicox, who was then 73. The small-group swing performances have plenty of life and more often than not are hard-swinging. —*Scott Yanow*

Gems / Aug. 28, 1975 / Concord Jazz ✦✦✦✦✦

This matchup between violinist Joe Venuti and guitarist George Barnes works quite well. With fine accompaniment from rhythm guitarist Bob Gibbons, bassist Herb Mickman and drummer Jake Hanna, the lead voices are free to romp on the ten standards. There are many high points, including "I Want to Be Happy," "Oh Baby," "Hindustan" and "Lady Be Good." —*Scott Yanow*

Hot Sonatas / Oct. 1975 / Chiaroscuro ✦✦✦✦

This is an unusual and frequently exciting album of duets between the two great veterans Joe Venuti and Earl Hines; despite both being active for over a half-century, they had never played together before. The interplay between the violinist and the pianist is consistently unpredictable and they communicate quite well on these swing standards (three of which were composed by Hines long ago). This unique encounter deserves to be reissued on CD. —*Scott Yanow*

Venuti-Barnes Live (At the Concord Summer Festival) / Jul. 30, 1976 / Concord Jazz ✦✦✦✦

Violinist Joe Venuti and guitarist George Barnes (joined by pianist Ross Tompkins, bassist Ray Brown and drummer Jake Hanna) make for a very complementary team on this live session. Tompkins is featured on "Too Close for Comfort," Barnes is showcased on "I Can't Get Started," the ensemble romps on "Sweet Georgia Brown" and the full group plays a lengthy five-song Duke Ellington/Billy Strayhorn medley. Few surprises occur but there are enough fireworks to justify this album's acquisition, even by those who already own 20 Joe Venuti albums. —*Scott Yanow*

S'Wonderful: 4 Giants of Swing / 1976 / Flying Fish ✦✦✦✦

For this session, the veteran jazz violinist Joe Venuti is teamed with a top-notch group of country players including mandolinist Jethro Burns, Curley Chalker on steel guitar and guitarist Eldon Shamblin. The repertoire is strictly jazz and these diverse players (who are backed by a conventional rhythm section) find plenty of common ground on the veteran standards, most of them from the pens of Ellington or Gershwin. Venuti sounds inspired by the unusual setting. —*Scott Yanow*

Sliding By / Apr. 15, 1977 / Gazell ✦✦✦✦

Violinist Joe Venuti, 73 at the time of this recording and only a little more than a year away from his death, was in typically swinging form for this quintet set with Dick Hyman (who doubles on piano and organ), guitarist Bucky Pizzarelli, bassist Major Holley and drummer Cliff Leeman. In addition to the six standards, there are four lesser-known Venuti compositions performed by this fine group. The music alternates between romantic ballads and stomps such as "Sweet Georgia Brown" and "Clarinet Marmalade." —*Scott Yanow*

Alone at the Palace / Apr. 27, 1977-Apr. 28, 1977 / Chiaroscuro ✦✦✦✦✦

For one of violinist Joe Venuti's final recording sessions, he engages in a set of duets with the talented swing pianist Dave McKenna. The original LP had a dozen performances and the reissue CD adds seven more. In addition to the usual standards, there are several Dixieland tunes (including three versions of "At the Jazz Band Ball") and four Venuti originals. McKenna (with his rolling basslines) was a perfect partner for the violinist, making this set one of the best of Venuti's later years. —*Scott Yanow*

Marlene Ver Planck

Vocals / Cabaret, Standards

A melodic singer with a beautiful voice and a surprisingly wide range, Marlene Ver Planck's singing swings while falling between jazz and cabaret. She recorded an excellent album for Savoy in 1955, spent much of the next 20 years as a studio singer, recorded with her husband (the excellent arranger Billy Ver Planck) on their own Mounted Records label in the 1960s (some of which have been reissued by Audiophile) and has recorded many fine albums for Audiophile since 1976 in settings ranging from a trio to a big band and a collaboration with the French group Saxomania. She is at the peak of her powers in the 1990s. —*Scott Yanow*

Every Breath I Take / Nov. 29, 1955 / Savoy ✦✦✦✦✦

Marlene Ver Planck's first recording (she is listed on the Savoy CD reissue as simply "Marlene" but fortunately does not sound like Marlene Dietrich) is a moody and wistful affair. Backed by the lyrical trumpet of Joe Wilder along with pianist Hank Jones, bassist Wendell Marshall, drummer Kenny Clarke and an uncredited Herbie Mann on flute, Ver Planck sounds typically beautiful on ten ballads; her talent was obvious even at this early stage. Highlights include "Some Other Time," "If I Love Again," "Deep in a Dream" and "You Leave Me Breathless." —*Scott Yanow*

A Breath of Fresh Air / 1968 / Audiophile ✦✦✦

The jazz content of this CD reissue is fairly light as singer Marlene Ver Planck (who as usual displays a beautiful voice with a wide range) is backed by rather commercial arrangements on a repertoire dominated by then-current show and movie tunes that often sound quite dated today. She certainly does her best (as can be heard on wordless versions of "Baby Elephant Walk" and "Mission Impossible"), but Ver Planck's later recordings are much more valuable from the jazz standpoint. —*Scott Yanow*

Loves Johnny Mercer / Sep. 1978+Aug. 2, 1988 / Audiophile ✦✦✦✦✦

Marlene Ver Planck is a perfect person to interpret the lyrics of Johnny Mercer because she has both a beautiful voice and a straightforward approach. The original LP had 16 selections and found the singer accompanied by pianist Tony Monte, guitarist Bucky Pizzarelli, bassist Milt Hinton and drummer Butch Miles in 1978. Ten years later, the same cast returned to record five additional songs to fill out the CD reissue. The performances are quite concise (only four of the 21 pieces are over three minutes) but each is long enough to get its point across. Highlights include "I Remember You," "Early Autumn," "Skylark," "Something's Gotta Give," "I Thought About You" and "Love's Got Me in a Lazy Mood." Recommended. —*Scott Yanow*

A New York Singer / 1980-Oct. 14, 1995 / Audiophile ✦✦✦

This CD mostly brings back a middle-of-the-road pop date featuring the beautiful voice of Marlene Ver Planck backed by a string orchestra arranged by Billy Ver Planck. The charts are sometimes overblown and more suited to Barbra Streisand than to Ella Fitzgerald, although Ver Planck generally carries it off. But the program (which includes "Go Away, Little Boy," "The Music That Makes Me Dance" and "Hopscotch") is not significant from a jazz standpoint. Much better are the five selections recorded especially for this reissue in 1995, for they swing a bit and match Ver Planck with a combo that often includes either trumpeter Joe Wilder or tenor saxophonist Phil Thompson. Ver Planck had continued growing as a singer during the intervening 15 years and the latter date finds her in fine form; pity that it could not have been paired with a jazz-oriented session. —*Scott Yanow*

Sings Alec Wilder / Mar. 10, 1986-Aug. 13, 1991 / Audiophile ✦✦✦✦✦

Alec Wilder wrote some of the most sophisticated and obscure songs. Best-known is "I'll Be Around," but most of his other compositions have been somewhat forgotten except by top cabaret singers. On this set, Marlene Ver Planck performs 20 of Wilder's best works (including the verses). Thirteen of the tunes were originally cut in 1986 but, for the CD reissue, seven more were recorded in 1991. Backed by pianist Loonis McGlohon, either Rick Petrone or Doug Burns on bass and Mel Lewis or Bill Stowe on drums (with Billy Ver Planck contributing the arrangements), Marlene Ver Planck sounds in prime form and gives each lyric the proper amount of sincere feeling and sensitivity. A highlight is "The Lady Sings the Blues," which Wilder wrote for Billie Holiday but which had not been previously recorded. —*Scott Yanow*

Pure and Natural / Jun. 1987-1992 / Audiophile ✦✦✦

A Quiet Storm / Dec. 1, 1989+Dec. 11, 1989 / Audiophile ✦✦✦✦

● **Meets Saxomania** / Jan. 29, 1993-Mar. 6, 1994 / Audiophile ✦✦✦✦✦

Marlene Ver Planck possesses one of the world's great voices; every note she hits is perfectly in tune. Despite this talent, she is a subtle improviser who goes out of her way to bring out the beauty of the lyrics she interprets. Occasionally she will throw in a high note (as if to remind listeners of her wide range), but it is all in the service of uplifting the song. Her husband/arranger Billy Ver Planck wrote colorful

Music Map

Vocalists - Female

1920s Classic Blues Singers
Mamie Smith (1920, first blues recording)
Ma Rainey
Bessie Smith ("Empress of the Blues")
Ida Cox
Bertha "Chippie" Hill
Sippie Wallace
Alberta Hunter

Pacesetters of the Late 1920s
Ethel Waters
Annette Hanshaw
Connie Boswell

The Definitive Swing Singer
Billie Holiday

Swing Era
Mildred Bailey	Ivie Anderson
Helen Ward	Helen Forrest
Lee Wiley	Helen Humes
Maxine Sullivan	

Two Major Innovators
Ella Fitzgerald
Sarah Vaughan

1940s-50s
Anita O'Day	June Christy
Dinah Washington	Peggy Lee
Helen Merrill	Chris Connor
Annie Ross	Betty Roche
Carmen McRae	

Avant-Garde
Betty Carter	Jeanne Lee
Patty Waters	Urszula Dudziak
Karin Krog	Jay Clayton
Norma Winstone	Maggie Nicols
Lauren Newton	Kate Hammett-Vaughan
Ann Dyer	

1960s to the Present
Abbey Lincoln	Sheila Jordan
Astrud Gilberto	Ernestine Anderson
Lorez Alexandria	Ruth Brown
Irene Kral	Etta Jones
Carol Sloane	Flora Purim
Janet Lawson	Dee Dee Bridgewater
Shirley Horn	Michele Hendricks
Dianne Reeves	Diane Schuur
Cassandra Wilson	Carmen Lundy
Vanessa Rubin	Nnenna Freelon
Banu Gibson	Roseanna Vitro
Diana Krall	Karrin Allyson
Patricia Barber	Holly Cole
Stephanie Haynes	Madeline Eastman
Kitty Margolis	Dominique Eade

charts on this CD for the French seven-piece four-reed unit called Saxomania to accompany her. He left plenty of room for solos and gave the ensembles the feel of a big band despite the absence of any brass instruments. Marlene Ver Planck is in peak form and even if a few of the newer songs ("Sooner or Later" from the *Dick Tracy* film and the overrated "Here's to Life") are not worthy of her, she is particularly delightful on "You Turned the Tables on Me," "Close Your Eyes," "Speak Low" and a quartet of Ellington and Strayhorn tunes. —*Scott Yanow*

Live! in London / Apr. 1993-May 1993 / Audiophile ✦✦✦✦
Marlene Ver Planck, a wonderful singer whose style falls somewhere between jazz and cabaret, is in fine form on this live CD. Ver Planck, although her improvisations are quite subtle, always swings and manages to find beauty in each song she interprets. This set has a wide variety of material that ranges from such classics as "Body and Soul" and "Let's Face the Music" to the potentially sticky "So in Love" and even a medley from "Doctor Doolittle." Backed by a solid if somewhat anonymous English rhythm section, Ver Planck (who is virtually the whole show) uplifts each song and surprises listeners with her occasional jumps into the stratosphere (her range is remarkable), although she mostly vocalizes in her warm middle register. Recommended. —*Scott Yanow*

You Gotta Have Heart: Marlene Sings Richard Adler / 1997 / Varese ✦✦✦✦

Harold Vick

b. Apr. 3, 1936, Rocky Mount, NC, **d.** Nov. 13, 1987, New York, NY
Tenor Saxophone / Soul Jazz, Hard Bop, Groove
An excellent thick-toned tenor, Harold Vick sounded quite at home in hard bop and soul jazz settings. His uncle, Prince Robinson (a reed player from the 1920s), gave him a clarinet when he was 13, and three years later Vick switched to tenor.

He rose to prominence playing with organ combos in the mid-'60s, recording and performing with Jack McDuff, Jimmy McGriff and Big John Patton among others. He started recording as a leader in 1966 and among his other associations were Jack DeJohnette's unusual group Compost (1972), Shirley Scott in the mid-'70s and Abbey Lincoln, with whom he recorded two Billie Holiday tributes for Enja just a short time before his death. —*Scott Yanow*

● **Steppin' Out** / May 27, 1963 / Blue Note ✦✦✦✦✦
This soul jazz outing by tenor saxophonist Harold Vick (his recording debut as a leader) casts him in a role that was often occupied by Stanley Turrentine. Vick, with a quintet that also includes trumpeter Blue Mitchell, guitarist Grant Green, organist John Patton and drummer Ben Dixon, performs four blues, a slightly trickier original (five of the six songs are his) plus the ballad "Laura" on this CD reissue. There are no real surprises but no disappointments either on what would be Harold Vick's only chance to lead a Blue Note date; at 27 he was already a fine player. —*Scott Yanow*

Commitment / Jun. 1966 / Muse ✦✦✦

Don't Look Back / Nov. 1974 / Strata East ✦✦✦

Leroy Vinnegar

b. Jul. 13, 1928, Indianapolis, IN
Bass / Cool
The owner of a swinging "walking bass" manner, comfortable in several idioms but not a prolific soloist, Leroy Vinnegar has had a couple of heydays—in the '50s and '60s as a busy freelance recording sideman, and as a member of Les McCann's most popular combo in 1969. As such, he played a major role in two of jazz's biggest hit albums, the trend-setting *My Fair Lady* set with Andre Previn and Shelly

Manne (1956) and the Eddie Harris/Les McCann soul-jazz manifesto *Swiss Movement* (1969).

A completely self-taught musician, Vinnegar "fooled around" with the piano but gravitated to the bass upon his first encounter. After turning pro at 20, he was the house bassist at Chicago's Beehive in 1952-53. Upon moving to Los Angeles in 1954, Vinnegar quickly settled in as the bass player of choice on records by Stan Getz, Shorty Rogers, Chet Baker, Shelly Manne and Serge Chaloff, among others. He also started recording as a leader in 1957, reeling off a pair of albums for Contemporary with the word "walks" appropriately inserted in each title. Starting in 1959, Vinnegar would work and tour frequently with Joe Castro and Teddy Edwards while continuing his freelance activities. In the early 1980s, he appeared on television as a member of the Dixieland-styled Panama Hats behind actor/banjoist George Segal. Although a bout of ill health caused him to move to Portland in the late '80s, Vinnegar remained an active player into the 1990s, and he returned to the recording scene as a leader in 1992 (on Contemporary again) with a CD entitled—what else?—*Walkin' the Basses*. —*Richard S. Ginell*

● **Leroy Walks!** / Jul. 15, 1957-Sep. 23, 1957 / Original Jazz Classics ✦✦✦✦✦
On this reissue CD of a Contemporary set (bassist Leroy Vinnegar's first as a leader), six of the seven songs have the word "walk," in their title including "Would You Like to Take a Walk," "Walkin' My Baby Back Home," "I'll Walk Alone" and Vinnegar's original "Walk On." Vinnegar actually does not take much solo space and generously features his talented sidemen: vibraphonist Victor Feldman, trumpeter Gerald Wilson, tenor saxophonist Teddy Edwards, pianist Carl Perkins and drummer Tony Bazley. A fine straightahead session. —*Scott Yanow*

Leroy Walks Again / Aug. 1, 1962+Mar. 5, 1963 / Original Jazz Classics ✦✦✦✦✦
The follow-up to Leroy Vinnegar's first Contemporary album, this CD reissue matches the excellent bassist (who is mostly content to back the other soloists) with trumpeter Freddy Hill, tenor saxophonist Teddy Edwards, Victor Feldman on piano and vibes and drummer Ron Jefferson for four of the seven selections; the other numbers also use Hill and Edwards along with pianist Mike Melvoin, vibraphonist Roy Ayers (at the beginning of his career) and drummer Milt Turner. The set (which has three originals by Vinnegar, Edwards' "Wheelin' and Dealin'," Don Nelson, Les McCann and Freddie Hubbard in addition to the one standard "I'll String Along with You") helps define the modern mainstream of the early '60s, when cool jazz was being replaced by hard bop. —*Scott Yanow*

Walkin' the Basses / Mar. 1992 / Contemporary ✦✦✦✦
Bassist Leroy Vinnegar was a familiar figure on the West Coast scene of the late '50s and early '60s and drew praises for his entertaining, yet musically sophisticated "walking" bass lines. Vinnegar has not lost his prowess, and this album features him heading a group with pianist Geoff Lee, drummer Mel Brown and percussionist Curtis Craft. While it is Vinnegar's date, he doesn't dominate, but sets the table. Vinnegar produced the session and arranged nine of the eleven songs, co-arranging a tenth with Lee. It isn't so much easy listening as nice, sophisticated material from four established pros who enjoy working with each other. —*Ron Wynn*

Integrity / May 14, 1995 / Jazz Focus ✦✦✦
Bassist Leroy Vinnegar, a fixture in Los Angeles from the 1950s on, has lived in Portland, OR, since the mid-'80s. Although he was mostly off records from 1977-92 and had a spell of bad health, he is in fine form throughout the 1995 concert documented on his fine release from Jazz Focus. Vinnegar and veteran drummer Mel Brown team up with a pair of excellent Portland-based players for a fine bop-oriented set. Tenorman Gary Harris (who switches to soprano on Freddie Hubbard's "Little Sunflower") is sometimes reminiscent of Harold Land with touches of Red Holloway (although he does a good job of hinting at Sonny Rollins on "Everywhere Calypso") while guitarist Dan Faehule is most influenced by Wes Montgomery and Herb Ellis. Both of the younger musicians show potential for the future. The repertoire is strictly standards and blues (except for Hampton Hawes' obscure "Me Ho") and highlights include the swinging "Blue 'n' Boogie," a tenor feature on "We'll Be Together Again" and the calypso. As usual Leroy Vinnegar is content to stick mostly to the background, holding the music together while inspiring the lead voices. Although few surprises occur, the music has plenty of spirit and will easily appeal to straightahead jazz fans. —*Scott Yanow*

Eddie "Cleanhead" Vinson

b. Dec. 18, 1917, Houston, TX, **d.** Jul. 2, 1988, Los Angeles, CA
Alto Saxophone, Vocals / Bop, Early R&B Jazz, Jump Blues, R&B Groove, West Coast Blues, New York Blues
An advanced stylist on alto saxophone who vacillated throughout his career between jump blues and jazz, bald-pated Eddie "Cleanhead" Vinson (he lost his hair early on after a botched bout with a lye-based hair-straightener) also possessed a playfully distinctive vocal delivery that stood him in good stead with blues fans.

Vinson first picked up a horn while attending high school in Houston. During the late '30s, he was a member of an incredible horn section in Milton Larkin's orchestra, sitting next to Arnett Cobb and Illinois Jacquet. After exiting Larkin's employ in 1941, Vinson picked up a few vocal tricks while on tour with bluesman Big Bill Broonzy. Vinson joined the Cootie Williams Orchestra from 1942 to 1945. His vocals on trumpeter Williams' renditions of "Cherry Red" and "Somebody's Got to Go" were in large part responsible for their wartime hit status.

Vinson struck out on his own in 1945, forming his own large band, signing with Mercury, and enjoying a double-sided smash in 1947 with his romping R&B chart-topper "Old Maid Boogie" and the song that would prove his signature number, "Kidney Stew Blues" (both songs featured Vinson's instantly identifiable vocals). A 1949-52 stint at King Records produced only one hit, the amusing sequel "Somebody Done Stole My Cherry Red," along with the classic blues "Person to Person" (later revived by another King artist, Little Willie John).

Vinson's jazz leanings were probably heightened during 1952-53, when his band included a young John Coltrane. Somewhere along about here, Vinson wrote two Miles Davis classics, "Tune Up" and "Four." Vinson steadfastly kept one foot in the blues camp and the other in jazz, waxing jumping R&B for Mercury (in 1954) and Bethlehem (1957), jazz for Riverside in 1961 (with Cannonball Adderley), and blues for Blues Time and ABC-BluesWay. A 1969 set for Black & Blue, cut in France with pianist Jay McShann and tenor saxophonist Hal Singer, beautifully recounted Vinson's blues shouting heyday (it's available on Delmark as *Kidney Stew Is Fine*). A much later set for Muse teamed him with the sympathetic little big band approach of Rhode Island-based Roomful of Blues. Vinson toured the States and Europe frequently prior to his death in 1988 of a heart attack. —*Bill Dahl*

● **Cherry Red Blues** / Aug. 10, 1949-Jul. 7, 1952 / King/Gusto ✦✦✦✦✦
Somehow, amidst all the CD reissues from the King Records vaults unleashed by Charly, Ace, Rhino, and King's current ownership, this versatile alto saxist has fallen through the cracks. Thus, this two-LP collection, boasting all but a handful of his jumping 1949-1952 outings for King, remains the best introduction to the Cleanheaded One's R&B output (along with the 1945-1947 sides he waxed for Mercury, which grace the seven-disc anthology *Blues, Boogie, & Bop: The 1940s Mercury Sessions*). —*Bill Dahl*

Back in Town / Sep. 1957 / Bethlehem ✦✦✦✦
Although he had achieved a certain amount of popularity in the late '40s with his blues vocals and boppish alto, Eddie "Cleanhead" Vinson's Bethlehem album was one of only two recordings he made as a leader between 1956-66. With arrangements by Ernie Wilkins, Manny Albam and Harry Tubbs, and his sidemen including several members (past and present) of the Count Basie Orchestra, the blues-oriented music (which gives Vinson a chance to sing such material as "It Ain't Necessarily So," "Is You Is or Is You Ain't My Baby" and "Caledonia") is quite enjoyable and really rocks; pity that this record did not catch on. —*Scott Yanow*

Eddie Cleanhead Vinson Sings / Sep. 1957 / Bethlehem ✦✦✦✦✦
One of only two albums that altoist/singer Eddie "Cleanhead" Vinson led during 1956-66, this infectious set finds him performing some of his best-known tunes. With assistance from a medium-size group that plays in a Count Basie groove (including such Basie-ites as trumpeter Joe Newman, trombonist Henry Coker, either Frank Foster or Paul Quinichette on tenor and pianist Nat Pierce), Cleanhead makes such songs as "Kidney Stew," "Caldonia," "Cherry Red," "Is You Is Or Is You Ain't My Baby" and "Hold It Right There" sound full of joy. This CD reissue adds three alternate takes that were originally recorded in stereo. A good sampling of the great Cleanhead. —*Scott Yanow*

Cleanhead & Cannonball / Sep. 19, 1961+Feb. 14, 1962 / Landmark ✦✦✦✦✦
During these two sessions, Eddie "Cleanhead" Vinson is joined by the Cannonball Adderley Quintet. Five of the ten selections were previously unissued altogether until this album came out in 1988. On Vinson's vocal numbers he is backed by altoist Cannonball Adderley, cornetist Nat Adderley, pianist Joe Zawinul, bassist Sam Jones and drummer Louis Hayes. Unfortunately on the instrumentals and the one vocal tune ("Kidney Stew") in which he plays, Vinson is the only altoist, as Cannonball sits out; it's a pity that the two very different stylists did not have a chance to trade off. Despite that missed opportunity, the music on this release is quite worthy, with Cleanhead in top form on such numbers as "Person to Person," "Just a Dream" and the three instrumentals. —*Scott Yanow*

Kidney Stew Is Fine / Mar. 28, 1969 / Delmark ✦✦✦✦✦
Although its programming has been juggled a bit and the CD has been given liner notes, this Delmark release is a straight reissue of the original LP. Clocking in at around 38 minutes, the relatively brief set is the only recording that exists of Vinson, pianist Jay McShann and guitarist T-Bone Walker playing together; the sextet is rounded out by the fine tenor Hal Singer, bassist Jackie Sampson and drummer Paul Gunther. Vinson, whether singing "Plese Send Me Somebody to Love," "Just a

Dream" and "Juice Head Baby" or taking boppish alto solos, is the main star throughout this album (originally on Black & Blue), a date that helped launch Vinson's commercial comeback. —*Scott Yanow*

You Can't Make Love Alone / Jun. 18, 1971 / Mega ✦✦✦

Eddie "Cleanhead" Vinson was in inspired form at the 1971 Montreux Jazz Festival. He stole the show when he sat in with Oliver Nelson's big band during their "Swiss Suite" and played a brilliant blues alto solo. The same day he recorded this Mega album but, due to its extreme brevity (under 24 minutes), perhaps this label should have changed its name to "Mini." Despite the low quantity, the quality of his performance (on which Vinson is joined by the guitars of Larry Coryell and Cornell Dupree, pianist Neal Creque, bassist Chuck Rainey and drummer Pretty Purdie) makes this album still worth acquiring, although preferably at a budget price. Vinson takes "Straight, No Chaser" as an instrumental and does a fine job of singing "Cleanhead Blues," "You Can't Make Love Alone," "I Had a Dream" and "Person to Person." —*Scott Yanow*

Jamming the Blues / Jul. 2, 1974 / Black Lion ✦✦✦✦

For this lesser-known outing (reissued on CD), the great altoist and blues singer Eddie "Cleanhead" Vinson is heard in fine form at the 1974 Montreux Jazz Festival. With fine support from a four-piece rhythm section that includes pianist Peter Wingfield and some solo space for tenor saxophonist Hal Singer, Vinson plays a few of his familiar but always welcome numbers ("Just a Dream," "Person to Person" and "Hold It Right There") plus "Laura" and some basic instrumental blues. An excellent outing from a performer who was claimed by both the jazz and blues worlds. —*Scott Yanow*

The Clean Machine / Feb. 22, 1978 / Muse ✦✦✦✦✦

What makes this album different from many of Eddie "Cleanhead" Vinson's is that four of the seven selections are taken as instrumentals. Vinson's alto playing has long been underrated due to his popularity as a blues singer, so this release gives one the opportunity to hear his bop-influenced solos at greater length. With the assistance of a strong rhythm section led by pianist Lloyd Glenn and some contributions from trumpeter Jerry Rusch and Rashid Ali on tenor, Vinson is in excellent form throughout this enjoyable set. —*Scott Yanow*

● **Hold It Right There!** / Aug. 25, 1978-Aug. 26, 1978 / Muse ✦✦✦✦✦

After years of neglect, Eddie "Cleanhead" Vinson was finally receiving long overdue recognition at the time of this live session—one of six albums recorded during a week at Sandy's Jazz Revival. Two of these albums featured tenors Arnett Cobb and Buddy Tate in lead roles. While Vinson has fine blues vocals on "Cherry Red" and "Hold It," it is his boppish alto solos on "Cherokee, "Now's the Time" and "Take the 'A' Train" (the latter also having spots for Cobb and Tate) that make this set recommended to blues and bop fans alike. —*Scott Yanow*

Live at Sandy's / Aug. 25, 1978-Aug. 26, 1978 / Muse ✦✦✦✦✦

Muse recorded six albums during one week at Sandy's Jazz Revival, a club in Beverly, MA; two of them (this one and *Hold It Right There*) feature the blues vocals and alto solos of Eddie "Cleanhead" Vinson. Some of the songs also have the tenors of Arnett Cobb and Buddy Tate in a supporting role, but this album is largely Vinson's show. Backed by a superb rhythm section (pianist Ray Bryant, bassist George Duvivier and drummer Alan Dawson), Vinson takes four fine vocals and plays many swinging alto solos, including one on "Tune Up," a song he wrote that has been mistakenly credited to Miles Davis for decades. —*Scott Yanow*

I Want a Little Girl / Feb. 10, 1981 / Original Jazz Classics ✦✦✦✦✦

Eddie "Cleanhead" Vinson, 64 at the time of this Pablo recording, is in superior form on the blues-oriented material. With Art Hillery (on piano and organ) and guitarist Cal Green leading the rhythm section, and trumpeter Martin Banks and the tenor of Rashid Ali offering contrasting solo voices, this is a particularly strong release. It is true that Vinson had sung such songs as "I Want a Little Girl," "Somebody's Got to Go," and "Stormy Monday" a countless number of times previously, but he still infuses these versions with enthusiasm and spirit, making this set a good example of Cleanhead's talents in his later years. —*Scott Yanow*

☆ **And Roomful of Blues** / Jan. 27, 1982 / Muse ✦✦✦✦✦

If there were justice in the world, Eddie "Cleanhead" Vinson would have been able to tour with this type of group throughout much of his career. Roomful of Blues, a popular five-horn nonet, has rarely sounded more exciting than on this musical meeting with the legendary singer/altoist. Vinson himself is exuberant on some of the selections, particularly "House of Joy," one of five instrumentals among the eight selections. Whether one calls it blues, bebop or early R&B, this accessible music is very enjoyable and deserves to be more widely heard. Among the supporting players, tenorman Greg Piccolo, trumpeter Bob Enos and guitarist Ronnie Earl (in one of his earliest recordings) win honors. —*Scott Yanow*

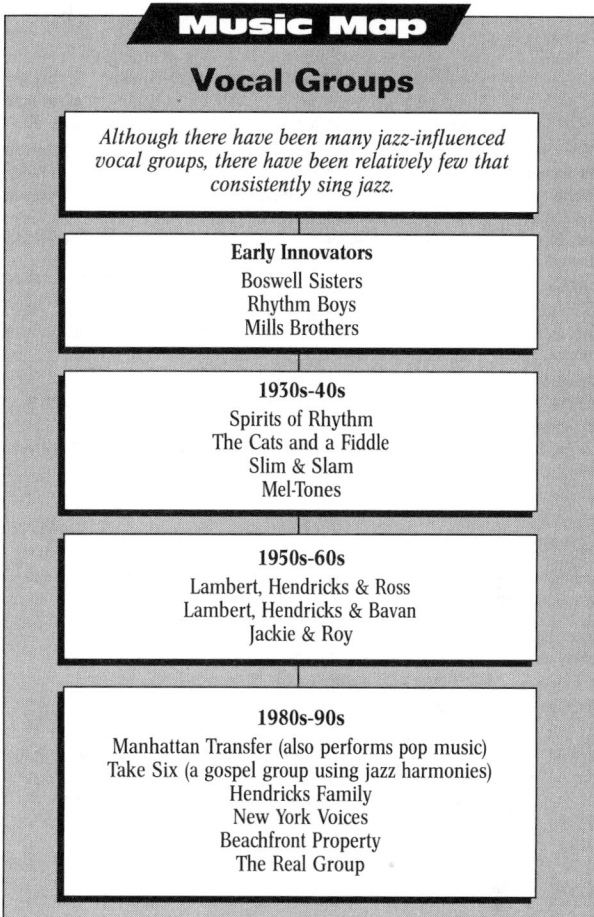

Music Map

Vocal Groups

Although there have been many jazz-influenced vocal groups, there have been relatively few that consistently sing jazz.

Early Innovators
Boswell Sisters
Rhythm Boys
Mills Brothers

1930s-40s
Spirits of Rhythm
The Cats and a Fiddle
Slim & Slam
Mel-Tones

1950s-60s
Lambert, Hendricks & Ross
Lambert, Hendricks & Bavan
Jackie & Roy

1980s-90s
Manhattan Transfer (also performs pop music)
Take Six (a gospel group using jazz harmonies)
Hendricks Family
New York Voices
Beachfront Property
The Real Group

Miroslav Vitous

b. Dec. 6, 1947, Prague, Czechoslovakia

Bass / Fusion, Post-Bop

Best known as one of the foremost young bassists in the jazz-rock movement of the late '60s and early '70s, Miroslav Vitous is one of Europe's most versatile imports, equally at home in mainstream idioms and even pop music. A sometime leader, his bass dances and skitters around an ensemble as a co-equal member of the front line, and he makes very creative use of the bow. He is influenced not only by bassists like Scott LaFaro, Ron Carter and Gary Peacock, but also by Czech folk music.

Vitous began his musical studies on the violin at age six, switching to piano from ages nine to fourteen before finally settling upon the bass. While studying at the Prague Conservatory, he played with a trio that included his brother Alan on drums and Jan Hammer—another future jazz-rock mover and shaker—on piano. After winning a scholarship to Berklee in 1966, he moved to New York the following year and wound up working with Art Farmer, Freddie Hubbard, Bob Brookmeyer, Clark Terry, and very briefly, Miles Davis.

Now one of the most highly touted prodigies in jazz, Vitous started playing in a recurring trio with Chick Corea and Roy Haynes on Corea's 1968 album *Now He Sings, Now He Sobs*. He then joined one of Herbie Mann's most popular groups from 1968 until 1970, with time out for a tour with Stan Getz; Mann produced his first album, a pioneering series of extended jazz-rock workouts called *Infinite Search* on the flutist's Embryo label. As a founding member of Weather Report, Vitous helped define the band's freewheeling initial stage, leaving the group in late 1973 as its music began to evolve into more structured forms. A move to Los Angeles in 1974 led to a year-long session of woodshedding in private with a new custom-made instrument, a double-necked guitar and bass. However, that experiment did not pan out, and he returned to the bass, leading sessions for Warner

Bros., Arista, and from 1979, a sporadic series of dates for ECM as a leader and in reunions of Corea's bop-to-free Trio Music group.

In the meantime, Vitous became immersed in academia, joining the faculty of the New England Conservatory in 1979 and becoming head of the jazz department in 1983. Although his profile isn't nearly as high as it was at the height of the jazz-rock era, he continued to play at jazz festivals and record into the 1990s. —*Richard S. Ginell*

★ **Mountain in the Clouds** / Oct. 8, 1969 / Atco ✦✦✦✦✦
A groundbreaking LP for fusioneers—pre–Weather Report—with John McLaughlin, Joe Henderson, Herbie Hancock, Jack DeJohnette, and Joe Chambers. All Vitous originals except "Freedom Jazz Dance," clocking in at 11 minutes. Originally "Infinite Search." —*Michael G. Nastos*

Miroslav / Dec. 1976-Jul. 1977 / Freedom ✦✦✦
1976-1977 sessions with Don Alias and Armen Halburian on percussion. Vitous overdubs bass and keyboards. A stunning musical trip through Afro-jazz texture music. "Tiger in the Rain" is absolutely captivating. —*Michael G. Nastos*

Guardian Angels / Nov. 9, 1978-Nov. 11, 1978 / Evidence ✦✦
This is a fusion date that mixes together Miroslav Vitous' acoustic bass with electric instruments including Kenny Kirkland's synthesizer and guitarist John Scofield. Some of the music grooves (such as "Off to Buffalo") while other tracks are episodic mood pieces. Actually most of the performances have an incomplete feel to them, with "Guardian Angels" wandering somewhat aimlessly, making this a CD recommended only to completists. —*Scott Yanow*

First Meeting / May 1979 / ECM ✦✦✦✦
Seven pieces written by Vitous. With John Surman (sax, b, cl), a very young Kenny Kirkland (p), and stellar Jon Christenson (d). This is very listenable music, rooted in freedom of expression. —*Michael G. Nastos*

Journey's End / Jul. 1982 / ECM ✦✦✦✦
Excellent in most facets, lacks individualistic character. —*Ron Wynn*

Emergence / Sep. 1985 / ECM ✦✦✦
Excellent bass playing, light on the jazz side. —*Ron Wynn*

Atmos / Feb. 1992 / ECM ✦✦✦
Bassist Miroslav Vitous and Jan Garbarek (on soprano and tenor) are featured throughout this ECM CD on a set of introspective duets. Garbarek does emit some passion on soprano and Vitous augments the music at times with some percussive sounds though by hitting his bass; once in awhile he also adds brief samples from what he calls "the Miroslav Vitous Symphony Orchestra Sound Library." But in general this is a stereotypical ECM date, recommended to fans of that genre. —*Scott Yanow*

Roseanna Vitro

b. 1951
Vocals / Bop, Standards
Although underrated, Roseanna Vitro's versatility, sense of swing and highly appealing voice have made her one of the most consistently interesting jazz singers of the 1990s. She started her career in Houston in the mid-'70s (originally singing blues and rock) where she had a two-year engagement at the Green Room while hosting a weekly live radio broadcast. Shortly after moving to New York in 1980 she worked with Lionel Hampton. Roseanna Vitro, who continually takes colorful chances in her singing, has recorded for the tiny Texas Rose Music and Skyline labels plus the Chase Music Group, Concord, and most recently Telarc. She deserves much greater recognition for her talents. —*Scott Yanow*

Listen Here / Oct. 4, 1982 / Texas Rose ✦✦✦✦
A straightahead date with the Kenny Barron (p) Trio, Arnett Cobb (sax), Bliss Rodriguez (p). Vitro proves her mettle on every tune, without fail. —*Michael G. Nastos*

A Quiet Place / 1987 / Skyline ✦✦
This album was singer Roseanna Vitro's second recording and unlike her first and the ones that would follow after she became better-known, much of the music borders on pop or "contemporary" jazz. Vitro co-wrote four of the nine numbers and, although she does a fine job with Chick Corea's "Times Lie," not much can be done with tunes by Lionel Richie and Patrice Rushen. Despite the presence of Eddie Daniels (mostly on tenor) and keyboardist Fred Hersch, this is a surprisingly forgettable effort by a talented singer. —*Scott Yanow*

Reaching for the Moon / 1991 / Chase Music ✦✦✦✦
A solid effort from a most expressive and emotional singer. Jazz, Brazilian, and pop-flavored music with pianist Ken Werner. She is one of the best. Highly recommended. —*Michael G. Nastos*

● **Softly** / 1993 / Concord Jazz ✦✦✦✦✦
Singer Roseanna Vitro is expert at interpreting lyrics and scats with a strong sense of adventure. Ballads predominate on her excellent Concord CD but there are also a few cookers (including a surprisingly rapid "I'm Through with Love"). The singer covers a wide variety of material (some of it of recent vintage) with a touching version of "So Many Stars" being a high point. Vitro is greatly assisted by a fine trio starring pianist Fred Hersch; the tenors of Tim Ries and George Coleman help out on some selections. This rewarding CD gives one a fine example of Roseanna Vitro's talents. —*Scott Yanow*

Passion Dance / Jul. 19, 1994-Jan. 1995 / Telarc ✦✦✦✦
One of the top jazz singers of the 1990s, Roseanna Vitro is a versatile vocalist who is not afraid to take chances. On her Telarc debut, the personnel changes on many of the ten selections with the stars among the sidemen including pianist Ken Werner (Vitro's musical director), altoist Gary Bartz, trumpeter Tim Hagans, bassist Christian McBride and drummer Elvin Jones. Among the high points of the diverse repertoire are an adventurous "Freedom Jazz Dance," "Out of This World," "Long as You're Livin'," McCoy Tyner's "Passion Dance" and "Strollin'" (an adaptation of Charles Mingus' "Nostalgia in Times Square"). The only number that does not work is an over-the-top rendition of "More than You Know" that is overly complex; simplicity would have been much more effective. Otherwise this is a superior set by a very appealing singer. —*Scott Yanow*

Catchin' Some Rays: The Music of Ray Charles / Mar. 26, 1997-Apr. 4, 1997 / Telarc ✦✦✦✦
Roseanna Vitro is a very talented and versatile singer, as she proves throughout this highly enjoyable set. Vitro performs 14 songs (including a pair of two-song medleys) associated with Ray Charles. Although jazz has long been only a small part of Charles' music, the tunes are transformed into swinging and soulful jazz by Vitro. The instrumentation changes throughout the date, but often features pianist Ken Werner (who duets with the singer on a medley of "You Don't Know Me" and "Ruby"), trumpeter Eddie Henderson, and tenorman David "Fathead" Newman, among others; some of the songs utilize a larger than usual band. Highlights include "Don't Let the Sun Catch You Cryin'," a swinging "One Mint Julep," "I Don't Need No Doctor" and "Lonely Avenue." Thankfully, Roseanna Vitro avoids many of Brother Ray's best-known hits (including "Georgia on My Mind") in favor of songs better suited to her style and to this setting. A continually interesting set. —*Scott Yanow*

Abdul Wadud

b. Apr. 30, 1947, Cleveland, OH
Cello / Avant-Garde
An outstanding cellist, Abdul Wadud has concentrated solely on the instrument since the age of nine, and never decided to double on bass. His plucking and bowed solos have been featured in jazz and symphonic/classical settings, and Wadud's easily the finest cellist to emerge from the '60s and '70s generation. He studied at Youngstown State and Oberlin in the late '60s and early '70s. He played in the Black Unity Trio at Oberlin and met Julius Hemphill; the two subsequently worked together well through the '80s. Wadud played in the New Jersey Symphony Orchestra in the '70s, and earned his master's degree in 1972. He played with Arthur Blythe for the first time in 1976, and has since maintained a working relationship with him. He also worked and recorded with Frank Lowe, George Lewis, Oliver Lake, Sam Rivers, Cecil Taylor, David Murray, Chico Freeman, Anthony Davis and James Newton in the '70s and '80s. Wadud, Newton and Davis were in both the octet Episteme and a trio from 1982 to 1984. Wadud recorded as a leader for Bishara and Gramavision in the '70s and '80s, and in a duo with Jenkins for Red in the '70s. —*Ron Wynn*

Harvey Wainapel

Tenor Saxophone, Soprano Saxophone, Alto Saxophone / Hard Bop, Post-Bop
A product of the San Francisco area, Harvey Wainapel established himself as one of the most promising and versatile jazz saxophonists of his generation; primarily known for his prowess on the soprano, he also proved a fine alto and tenor player. After receiving his early training at the Berklee College of Music in Boston, Wainapel spent the latter half of the 1970s in Europe, honing his craft in a variety of musical contexts, including a year as lead alto and featured soloist with the Frankfurt-based German Radio Big Band. Upon returning to the US, he toured with Ray Charles for ten months before settling in the Bay Area in 1982, subsequently performing with artists including McCoy Tyner, Joe Henderson, Johnny Coles and Billy Hart. Finally, in 1992, Wainapel released his first lead date, *At Home/On the Road;* three years later, he returned with *Ambrosia: The Music of Kenny Barron,* recorded in Europe with the Dutch national orchestra as well as a Brazilian octet. In 1996, he toured as a member of Joe Lovano's group. —*Jason Ankeny*

At Home/On the Road / May 1992-Jul. 1992 / JazzMission ♦♦♦
● **Ambrosia: the Music of Kenny Barron** / Dec. 1995-Jan. 1996 / A-Records ♦♦♦♦♦
Kenny Barron, who is widely recognized as one of the top modern mainstream jazz pianists, has never been thought of as a major composer, until now. Saxophonist Harvey Wainapel (who is most distinctive on soprano but also quite talented on tenor and alto), put together an ambitious program that pays tribute to Barron's underrated compositional talents. Five songs feature Wainapel backed by the Metropole Orchestra, a large string ensemble conducted by Rob Pronk. Jeff Beal's complex but colorful arrangements really challenge Wainapel to play at his best and he comes through. The final four numbers showcase Wainapel in a Latin group that co-stars keyboardist Marcos Silva and (on "Sambao") the accordion of Rich Kuhns. Wainapel does a bit of overdubbing on "If and When," trading off with himself on each of his three instruments. None of Kenny Barron's compositions (two of which received their debut on this CD) are close to being standards at this point, with "Ambrosia" and "Sambao" being perhaps the best known. The release of Harvey Wainapel's well-conceived project will hopefully result in Barron's writing ability and Wainapel's playing talents getting the recognition they deserve. Recommended. —*Scott Yanow*

Freddie Waits

b. Apr. 27, 1943, Jackson, MS, **d.** Nov. 18, 1989, New York, NY
Drums / Hard Bop
A versatile and well-respected drummer, Freddie Waits worked in many different situations throughout his career. He played flute early on, and even majored in

flute at Jackson Street College; however, he soon became a professional drummer. Some of his early gigs were for blues artists, including Memphis Slim and John Lee Hooker, and Waits also picked up experience performing soul music. He played with Jimmy Wilkins' orchestra in Detroit in 1962, was in Paul Winter's band from 1963-65, and worked in Los Angeles with Gerald Wilson's Orchestra before moving to New York in the mid-1960s. Some of Freddie Waits' more important musical associations were with Sonny Rollins (1966), Andrew Hill (1968-69), McCoy Tyner (1968-70), Max Roach (Waits was a founding member of M'Boom), the group Colloquium III, Bill Dixon and Cecil Taylor (1987). Unfortunately, he never led any record dates of his own. —*Scott Yanow*

Collin Walcott

b. Apr. 24, 1945, New York, NY, **d.** Nov. 8, 1984, Magdeburg, Germany
Percussion, Sitar, Tabla / World Fusion, Post-Bop
Collin Walcott was one of the first sitar players to play jazz. As a member of Oregon, Walcott's flexibility, interest in different cultures, and ability to play not only sitar but tabla and other percussion instruments made him a very valuable musician. Early on, he studied violin for two years and played both snare drum and tympani in school. Walcott also studied percussion at Indiana University and took sitar and tabla lessons with Ravi Shankar and Alla Rakha, respectively. After stints with Tony Scott (1967-69) and Tim Hardin, he became a member of the Paul Winter Consort in 1970. Walcott left the group with three other musicians (Ralph Towner, Paul McCandless and Glen Moore) in 1971 to form Oregon. In addition to recording and touring with Oregon, a unique folk/jazz group, Walcott recorded with Miles Davis in 1972 and was a member of Codona (a trio with Don Cherry and Nana Vasconcelos) that recorded for ECM. Tragically, Collin Walcott was killed in a traffic accident while on tour with Oregon in East Germany. He led three sessions for ECM and can be heard on the Codona and early Oregon recordings. —*Scott Yanow*

Cloud Dance / Mar. 1975 / ECM ♦♦♦♦
● **Works** / 1975-1984 / ECM ♦♦♦♦♦
A compilation of ECM work. —*Ron Wynn*

Grazing Dreams / Feb. 1977 / ECM ♦♦♦♦♦
With Don Cherry, John Abercrombie. Group music based around Walcott's sitar and tabla work. —*Michael G. Nastos*

Dawn Dance / Jan. 1981 / ECM ♦♦♦♦

Terry Waldo

b. 1944, Ironton, OH
Piano / Ragtime, Classic Jazz
One of the finest trad jazz pianists from the 1970s to the present and an interpreter who really brings new life to classic jazz and ragtime, Terry Waldo has often labored in near-anonymity, yet has recorded quite a few highly enjoyable records. He took three years of classical piano lessons starting at age six before discovering ragtime and Dixieland. He also learned to play trumpet, tuba, banjo, cello and bass to various degrees and led a group (the Fungus Five) on the Ted Mack Original Amateur Hour in 1962. In Ohio, Waldo played with Gene Mayl's Dixieland Rhythm Kings, spent time freelancing on various instruments in New Orleans and San Francisco, graduated from Ohio State and played tuba during his military service. He taught a history of jazz, blues and ragtime class at Denison University during 1971-78, hosted a series for National Public Radio called *This Is Ragtime* in 1972 and in 1976 wrote a definitive book on ragtime that used the same name. In the 1980s Waldo led the Gotham City Stompers, worked with the show *One Mo' Time,* toured with Leon Redbone and worked with Woody Allen. Terry Waldo has recorded for several labels including GHB (in 1969), Fat Cat Records, Stomp Off (with his Gutbucket Syncopators) and the Musical Heritage Society. —*Scott Yanow*

● **Feelin' Devilish** / Oct. 13, 1979-Oct. 14, 1979 / Stomp Off ♦♦♦♦
The Stomp Off label, which quickly became the premier record company in documenting classic jazz of the past 20 years, debuted with this lively and spirited out-

ing by Terry Waldo's Gutbucket Syncopators. The pianist-leader gathered together some of the best trad jazz players, most from the Midwest: trumpeter Roy Tate, trombonist Jim Snyder, Frank Powers on clarinet and tenor, banjoist Eddy Davis, Louise Anderson on tuba and drummer Hal Smith. Although there are five vocals (including two from Susan LaMarche) the emphasis is on colorful solos and exciting ensembles with such songs as "Dinah," "Milenberg Joys" and two versions of "Big Man from the South" being among the more memorable performances. —*Scott Yanow*

Wizard of the Keyboard / Jul. 22, 1980-Jul. 24, 1980 / Stomp Off ✦✦✦✦
The focus is on pianist Terry Waldo throughout this trio set with banjoist Eddy Davis and tuba player Vince Giordano. Waldo takes four of the dozen numbers as unaccompanied solos, sings four tunes (including "Don't Give Me No Goose for Christmas") and performs a set ranging from rags (including "Mississippi Rag," which was the first rag ever composed), his own "Proctology," "Charleston" and "Sailin' Down the Chesapeake Bay" to an obscurity by Jelly Roll Morton ("Exit Gloom") that might have been receiving its recording debut. Ragtime and pre-swing piano collectors will particularly enjoy this LP, the second one ever released by Stomp Off. —*Scott Yanow*

Ragtime Classics, Vol. 1 / Jul. 22, 1980-Jun. 24, 1983 / Musical Heritage Society ✦✦✦✦
The 20 selections included on this CD were all originally on one of three Stomp Off albums: *Waldo's Ragtime Orchestra, Spectacular Ragtime* and *Wizard of the Keyboard.* Pianist Terry Waldo performs with a couple of ragtime groups (which utilize both strings and horns in music that is mostly written down) plus four numbers with a trio also including banjo and tuba. The emphasis is on obscurities (with a few exceptions) from the ragtime era including "Knock Out Drops," "Eli Green's Cakewalk," "Slip Horn Stuff," "Yankee Bird March" and "Alkali Ike—A North Dakota Misunderstanding." Delightful music, easily recommended to early American music collectors who do not already have the Stomp Off LPs. —*Scott Yanow*

Ragtime Classics, Vol. 2 / Oct. 24, 1978-Jun. 24, 1983 / Musical Heritage Society ✦✦✦✦
The second of two Terry Waldo CDs released by the Musical Heritage Society in 1988 features the pianist in several different settings. With the exception of three numbers recorded at the same time as Waldo's 1987 *Footlight Variety* album but not put out in the Stomp Off set, all of the music has been previously released, although most of the LPs are now out of print. The title of this CD is slightly inaccurate since some of the music is classic jazz rather than ragtime, and many of the ragtime pieces are obscure rather than "classics." However the performances are consistently enjoyable. Waldo is heard with his ragtime orchestra, takes a couple of piano solos, jams with a couple of different trios and plays with a hot jazz combo. The bulk of the music was originally out on the Stomp Off albums *Smiles and Chuckles, Spectacular Ragtime, Wizard of the Keyboard, Waldo's Gutbucket Syncopators Present, Vamp 'Til Ready, Terry Waldo & The Gotham City Band* and the 1978 Dirty Shame release *Jazz Babies.* An excellent example of Waldo's playing and bandleading talents. —*Scott Yanow*

Smiles and Chuckles / Oct. 29, 1980 / Stomp Off ✦✦✦✦
Terry Waldo is a skilled pianist who was among the first musicians in the revival years to perform ragtime (which has been mostly been thought of as a piano music) with an orchestra. Other than some piano choruses, the music on this LP is orchestral ragtime, with each note taken from stock arrangements from the 1896-1920 era. Waldo is joined by two trumpets, one trombone, a string quartet, clarinet, flute/piccolo, tuba and drums on such forgotten but colorful numbers as "The Watermelon Trust," "That Mysterious Rag," "The Burning of Rome" (a descriptive march) and "Smiles and Chuckles." Worth searching for. —*Scott Yanow*

Waldo's Gutbucket Syncopators / Aug. 28, 1981-Aug. 29, 1981 / Stomp Off ✦✦✦✦✦
This is a fun group. Pianist Terry Waldo heads a spirited classic jazz septet (that includes trumpeter Roy Tate, clarinetist Frank Powers, trombonist Jim Snyder, Rod MacDonald on banjo and guitar, Louise Anderson on tuba and drummer Hal Smith) that also features some sassy vocals by Susan LaMarche. The band is creative within the boundaries of 1920s jazz, paying tribute to the past in spots but also coming up with fresh solos on some lesser-known material. This recommended Stomp Off LP is highlighted by Lil Hardin's "You're Next," "Hot Mustard," "Flat Foot," "Bozo" and "Down in Honky Tonk Town." —*Scott Yanow*

Spectacular Ragtime / Jun. 12, 1983+Jun. 24, 1983 / Stomp Off ✦✦✦✦
The second release by Terry Waldo's Ragtime Orchestra is the equal of the first. Although it is generally assumed that ragtime was a solo piano music, during the ragtime era many orchestras also performed the music. Waldo, who uses two trumpets, one trombone, clarinet, flute/piccolo, violin, cello, tuba, drums and his own piano on this LP (along with a few vocals by the flexible Susan LaMarche),

revives some colorful orchestrations from seven decades before, and the results are generally quite memorable. Highlights include "Some Sweet Day," "Slip Horn Stuff," "Slow and Easy," "Misery Rag," "Trombone Francois" and "The Hold Up Rag." —*Scott Yanow*

Terry Waldo & The Gotham City Band / Apr. 25, 1984+Dec. 6, 1984 / Stomp Off ✦✦✦✦✦
Pianist Terry Waldo teams up with some very impressive sidemen on this Stomp Off LP for a particularly strong program of classic jazz. With cornetist Peter Ecklund, Chuck Wilson (doubling on clarinet and alto), trombonist Dan Barrett, violinist Andy Stein, Howard Alden (on banjo and guitar), Vince Giordano (tripling on tuba, bass sax and string bass), drummer Arnie Kinsella and singer Susan LaMarche all making colorful contributions, Waldo explores such material from the 1920s and '30s as "Birmingham Bertha," Harry Reser's "Pickins," Bix Beiderbecke's "Candlelights," "Sugar Foot Strut," "Three Blind Mice" and "Forty-Second Street." This easily overlooked album (which has a bland cover) is well worth searching for. —*Scott Yanow*

Footlight Varieties / Jun. 23, 1985-Mar. 2, 1989 / Stomp Off ✦✦✦✦✦
This CD is a bit of a grab bag since its material was recorded at four different sessions from a four-year period. However with such talented soloists as cornetist Peter Ecklund, trombonist Dan Barrett, clarinetists Joe Muranyi and Ken Peplowski, guitarist Howard Alden and the leader/pianist, the mixture of complete obscurities and classic standards generally works quite well. There are vocals (of various quality) from Waldo, Muranyi, Susan LaMarche and even Leon Redbone, and highlights include "Good Old New York," "I Need Some Pettin," "Some Sweet Day" and "Exit Gloom." Fans of traditional and classic jazz will enjoy this one. —*Scott Yanow*

Mal Waldron

b. Aug. 16, 1926, New York, NY
Piano / Hard Bop, Post-Bop
A pianist with a brooding, rhythmic, introverted style, Mal Waldron's playing has long been flexible enough to fit into both hard bop and freer settings. Influenced by Thelonious Monk's use of space, Waldron has had his own distinctive chord voicings nearly from the start. Early on, Waldron played jazz on alto and classical music on piano, but he switched permanently to jazz piano while at Queens College. He freelanced around New York in the early '50s with Ike Quebec (for whom he made his recording debut), Big Nick Nicholas and a variety of R&B-ish groups. Waldron frequently worked with Charles Mingus from 1954-56 and was Billie Holiday's regular accompanist during her last two years (1957-59). Often hired by Prestige to supervise recording sessions, Waldron contributed many originals (including "Soul Eyes," which became a standard) and basic arrangements that prevented moving spontaneous dates from becoming overly loose jam sessions. He has mostly led his own groups since Holiday's death, although he was part of the Eric Dolphy Booker Little Quintet that was recorded extensively at the Five Spot in 1961, and also worked with Abbey Lincoln for a time during the era. He wrote three film scores (*The Cool World, Three Bedrooms in Manhattan* and *Sweet Love Bitter*) before moving permanently to Europe in 1965, settling in Munich in 1967. Waldron, who has occasionally returned to the US for visits, has long been a major force in the European jazz world. His album *Free at Last* was the first released by ECM, and his *Black Glory* was the fourth Enja album. Mal Waldron, who has frequently teamed up with Steve Lacy (often as a duet), has kept quite busy up to the present time, featuring a style that has evolved but is certainly traceable to his earliest record dates. Among the many labels that have documented his music have been Prestige, New Jazz, Bethlehem, Impulse, Musica, Affinity, ECM, Futura, Nippon Phonogram, Enja, Freedom, Black Lion, Horo, Teichiku, Hat Art, Palo Alto, Eastwind, Baybridge, Paddle Wheel, Muse, Free Lance, Soul Note, Plainisphere and Timeless. —*Scott Yanow*

● **One and Two** / Nov. 9, 1956-May 17, 1957 / Prestige ✦✦✦✦✦
Two of pianist Mal Waldron's first three albums as a leader (which are now available separately as CDs titled *Mal 1* and *Mal 2*) are combined on this two-LP set. Waldron is heard in a quintet with trumpeter Idrees Sulieman and altoist Gigi Gryce, leading a sextet with trumpeter Bill Hardman, altoist Jackie McLean and tenor saxophonist John Coltrane and with a different sextet that also stars Sulieman, Coltrane and altoist Sahib Shihab. Many of the Prestige sessions from the era were essentially jam sessions, but Waldron's dates were better organized and had more challenging material. Five of the pianist's originals are among the dozen selections on this two-fer, which also includes five standards and two obscurities. These hard bop performances are among Coltrane's lesser-known recordings and show that, even in his early days, Mal Waldron had his style. —*Scott Yanow*

Mal 3: Sounds / Jan. 31, 1958 / Original Jazz Classics ✦✦✦
This is an unusual set by pianist Mal Waldron. He utilizes a sextet with trumpeter Art Farmer, flutist Eric Dixon, cellist Calo Scott, bassist Julian Euell and drummer

Elvin Jones on three of his picturesque originals, and his wife Elaine Waldron contributes vocals to the wordless "Portrait of a Young Mother" and Harold Arlen's "For Every Man There's a Woman." The music is not essential but holds one's interest throughout the straight CD reissue of the original LP. —*Scott Yanow*

Mal / Four Trio / Sep. 26, 1958 / Original Jazz Classics ✦✦✦✦✦
It seems strange that this, pianist Mal Waldron's seventh session as a leader, was his first with a group as small as his trio. With the assistance of bassist Addison Farmer and drummer Kenny Dennis, Waldron performs four standards and three of his moody originals. His sometimes-brooding style was already quite recognizable and his inventive use of repetition was quite impressive. This CD reissue of the original LP gives listeners a definitive look at the early style of Mal Waldron. —*Scott Yanow*

Left Alone / Feb. 24, 1959 / Bethlehem ✦✦✦
This obscure CD reissue has the wrong date listed (it is from February 24, 1959, not November 1957) and fails to mention that altoist Jackie McLean sits in with pianist Mal Waldron's trio (which includes bassist Julian Euell and drummer Al Dreares) on the title cut, a number co-written by Waldron and Billie Holiday. Although Waldron dedicated the album to Lady Day and talks about her a bit on the last track in a short interview with vibraphonist Teddy Charles (which was recorded a bit later), he actually only performs one song from her repertoire: "You Don't Know What Love Is." Otherwise this rather brief CD has the title cut, two other typically brooding Waldron originals plus Sonny Rollins' "Airegin." McLean's emotional alto is such a strong asset on the title cut that one wishes he were on the rest of this worthwhile set. —*Scott Yanow*

Impressions / Mar. 20, 1959 / Original Jazz Classics ✦✦✦✦
This CD reissue brings back one of pianist Mal Waldron's lesser-known sessions from the 1950s. Teamed up in a trio with bassist Addison Farmer and drummer Al "Tootie" Heath, Waldron performs three originals from what he called his "Overseas Suite" along with a fine song by his wife ("All About Us") and three standards. Waldron's brooding Monk-influenced style is heard in its early prime on this excellent release. —*Scott Yanow*

The Quest / Jun. 27, 1961 / Original Jazz Classics ✦✦✦✦✦
Although often reissued under Eric Dolphy's name, this CD reissue gives the leadership back to pianist Mal Waldron. The seven originals not only feature altoist Dolphy (who makes a rare appearance on clarinet during "Warm Canto") but tenor saxophonist Booker Ervin, Ron Carter (on cello) and Waldron. With bassist Joe Benjamin and drummer Charlie Persip giving alert support, the complex music (which falls between hard bop and the avant-garde) is successfully interpreted. Worth checking out. —*Scott Yanow*

Free at Last / Nov. 24, 1969 / ECM ✦✦✦
The very first ECM release (which has been reissued on CD), this trio set features pianist Mal Waldron, bassist Isla Eckinger and drummer Clarence Becton improvising quite freely on five of Waldron's compositions plus "Willow Weep For Me." The music overall is not that memorable or unique but it does have its unpredictable moments and finds Waldron really stretching himself. —*Scott Yanow*

First Encounter / Mar. 8, 1971 / Catalyst ✦✦✦
Pianist Mal Waldron made many recordings (mostly in Europe) during 1969-72. This particular out-of-print LP was cut in Japan in a trio with bassist Gary Peacock and drummer Hiroshi Murakami. The long improvisations on the four originals (three by Waldron and one from Peacock) are melancholy, usually introverted and subtle. The interplay between Waldron and Peacock on the inside/outside music is the main asset to this obscure but generally rewarding session. —*Scott Yanow*

Plays the Blues / Jun. 29, 1971 / Enja ✦✦✦✦
Pianist Mal Waldron, with the assistance of bassist Jimmy Woode and drummer Pierre Favre, performs five blues-oriented pieces. The three Waldron and two Woode compositions generally have their own personalities (although none became standards) and serve as excellent showcases for Waldron's repetitive and percussive style. A fine effort. —*Scott Yanow*

Black Glory / Jun. 1971 / Enja ✦✦✦✦✦
This CD reissues one of the first Enja recordings, a trio outing for pianist Mal Waldron, bassist Jimmy Woode and drummer Pierre Favre. Waldron has continued to evolve through the decades while keeping his basic sound. A master at using repetition and brooding chords, Waldron is in excellent form on five of his originals plus Woode's brief "M.C.," playing with a knowledge of the avant-garde but still connected to the hard bop tradition. —*Scott Yanow*

Signals / Aug. 14, 1971 / Freedom ✦✦✦✦
One of two LPs by pianist Mal Waldron made available on the Freedom label in the mid-1970s when Arista was handling it, this set features a solo outing by Waldron that fully displays his continually evolving style. He had moved away from his earlier Thelonious Monk influence to an extent and developed his own brooding style which made expert use of repetition. Waldron's four originals give him

plenty of opportunity to stretch out; hopefully this intriguing set will be reissued on CD eventually. —*Scott Yanow*

Blues for Lady Day / Feb. 5, 1972 / Freedom ✦✦✦✦✦
Pianist Mal Waldron was Billie Holiday's final regular accompanist and has recorded several tributes to Lady Day through the years. This CD brings back a nine-song solo tribute that consists of eight songs associated with Holiday (including "Don't Blame Me," "You're My Thrill," "Strange Fruit" and "Mean to Me") plus Waldron's "Blues for Lady Day"; the emphasis is on thoughtful (and sometimes a bit downbeat) interpretations at ballad tempos. The reissue adds two lengthy and unrelated trio improvisations with bassist Henk Haverhoek and drummer Pierre Courbois ("A Little Bit of Miles" and "Here, There and Everywhere") that actually have nothing to do with Lady Day but do feature Mal Waldron coming up with some interesting and fresh ideas. —*Scott Yanow*

Up Popped the Devil / Dec. 28, 1973 / Enja ✦✦✦✦✦
Pianist Mal Waldron's music is characterized by a heavily brooding rhythmic quality, with the left hand usually carrying the theme at one repetitious tempo while the right hammers away in juxtaposition with a counter tempo (usually faster). Such was the case with "Up Popped the Devil," "Snake Out" and "Changachangachang," three very Waldronian pieces in both structure and execution, the latter deriving its melody from the whole-tone scale. Aside from Waldron, the record's strongest points were bassist Reggie Workman and drummer Billy Higgins, their work being sensitive and supportive throughout. —*Bob Rusch*

Hard Talk / May 4, 1974 / Enja ✦✦✦✦✦
This stimulating session (reissued on CD by Enja) features the masterful avant-garde cornetist Manfred Schoof (whose suprising jumps into the upper-register recall Kenny Wheeler), Steve Lacy on soprano, pianist Mal Waldron, bassist Isla Eckinger and drummer Allen Blairman. They explore four of Waldron's advanced pieces, and it is interesting to hear how Lacy's playing a couple decades ago (with its piercing high notes and very abstract combination of notes) differs from his present-day lyrical approach. Waldron's percussive style is a logical progression from his hard-bop playing of the 1950s, and the rhythm section is both alert and tight on these three romps and the ballad "Russian Melody." This is a strong live set that successfully combines together some distinctive musical personalities; Schoof often steals solo honors. —*Scott Yanow*

Moods / May 6, 1978+May 8, 1978 / Enja ✦✦✦✦
This double-LP features pianist Mal Waldron in two very different settings. On the first three songs (including the 20-minute side-long "Sieg Haile"), he performs three of his compositions in a sextet with cornetist Terumasa Hino, soprano saxophonist Steve Lacy, trombonist Hermann Breuer, bassist Cameron Brown and drummer Makaya Ntshoko. While that set has its share of fireworks, the remaining seven selections (six originals including his famous "Soul Eyes" plus the lone standard "I Thought About You") showcase Waldron as a sensitive solo pianist. This enjoyable and subtle music (which was also available at one time domestically on Inner City) gives one a well-rounded picture of Mal Waldron's talents in the late 1970s. —*Scott Yanow*

One Entrance, Many Exits / Jan. 4, 1982 / Palo Alto ✦✦✦✦✦
It is a pity that this album is long out of print for the combination of musicians works quite well. Pianist Mal Waldron has an inside/outside post bop style that matches perfectly with tenor saxophonist Joe Henderson, bassist David Friesen and drummer Billy Higgins. On five Waldron originals plus the standard "How Deep Is The Ocean," Henderson and the pianist are heard soloing in top form. Highlights include "Chazz Jazz" (dedicated to Charles Mingus), "Golden Golson" (which is purposely in the style of Benny Golson) and an ad-lib blues for the trio "Blues in 4 By 3." —*Scott Yanow*

Sempre Amore / Feb. 17, 1986 / Soul Note ✦✦✦✦
Pianist Mal Waldron and soprano saxophonist Steve Lacy have collaborated on many occasions (on an irregular basis) starting in the 1980s. Both masterful musicians are expatriates whose styles developed after they made their initial impact in the 1950s. On this likable set, they perform eight songs composed by Duke Ellington and/or Billy Strayhorn. Although adventurous in spots, their interpretations of such pieces as "Johnny Come Lately," "Prelude to a Kiss" and "Smada" are quite respectful and keep the strong melodies in mind. Recommended. —*Scott Yanow*

Update / Mar. 10, 1986 / Soul Note ✦✦✦✦✦
This solo set by pianist Mal Waldron serves as a perfect introduction to his unique style during the more recent part of his career. Waldron performs four standards (including "A Night in Tunisia" and "I Should Care") which show off his roots, but most significant are his lengthy "Free for C.T." and "Variations on a Theme by Cecil Taylor." It is always very interesting to hear musicians who started out in straightforward hard bop stretching themselves and playing quite freely. This recording rewards repeated listenings. —*Scott Yanow*

Left Alone '86 / Sep. 1, 1986 / Evidence ✦✦✦✦✦
Although he cannot maintain the same nonstop pace he had in the early '60s, Jackie McLean still plays magnificently. He demonstrates that repeatedly on this 1986 duo date with pianist Mal Waldron, whose lovely countermelodies, complementary solos, darting phrases, and supporting accompaniment proved a perfect contrast to McLean's forays. He is lyrical and engaging on some tracks; his explosive side emerges on others, where the McLean whose alto seemed ready to disintegrate on such sets as *Action* or *A Fickle Sonance* charges to the fore, hitting upper register home runs and ripping through the notes. It's good to know that McLean could still summon that drive. —*Ron Wynn*

Git Go: Live at the Village Vanguard / Sep. 16, 1986 / Soul Note ✦✦✦✦
Two spare Mal Waldron compositions act as the basis for lengthy compositions on this interesting set. With trumpeter Woody Shaw, tenor saxophonist Charlie Rouse, bassist Reggie Workman, drummer Ed Blackwell and the pianist-leader all having their opportunities to star, this advanced set has the feel of a high-quality jam session. —*Scott Yanow*

Crowd Scene / Jun. 10, 1989 / Soul Note ✦✦✦✦
For this quintet session, Mal Waldron contributed two somewhat episodic originals (titled "Crowd Scene" and "Yin and Yang") that are used as the basis for extended improvisations by altoist Sonny Fortune, tenor saxophonist Ricky Ford, bassist Reggie Workman, drummer Eddie Moore and the pianist/leader. Despite the obvious talents of these very individual players, there are some rambling moments on these lengthy performances, both of which clock in at over 25 minutes. Still, it is often fascinating to hear what the musicians come up with during these go-for-broke improvisations. —*Scott Yanow*

Where Are You? / 1989 / Soul Note ✦✦✦
Mal Waldron's mellow and sentimental side is tapped on this session recently issued by Soul Note. It's spotlighted on the unaccompanied second take of the title track, where Waldron's opening and major solo are played with a somber, introspective flair, as he slowly constructs his statement. There are elegant left-hand movements and answering right-hand rhythms, and his interpretation is ultimately satisfying and memorable. A less demonstrative, but still quite enjoyable, Mal Waldron date. —*Ron Wynn*

Bennie Wallace

b. Nov. 18, 1946, Chattanooga, TN
Tenor Saxophone / Post-Bop
Bennie Wallace has long had his own unique style, combining together the rapsy tone of Ben Webster with the frequent wide interval jumps of Eric Dolphy. He has an explorative style that soundwise looks back toward the swing era. Wallace started on clarinet when he was 12, and a few years later switched to tenor. He graduated from the University of Tennessee in 1968 and in 1971 moved to New York, where he debuted with Monty Alexander. Wallace gigged with Sheila Jordan, played with many avant-garde musicians, was in George Gruntz's Concert Jazz Band in 1979 and led his own trio/quartet on and off throughout the 1970s and '80s. He recorded frequently since 1985 for Enja, but his mid- to late '80s Blue Note recordings are more memorable, for they find him infusing his appealing sound with touches of New Orleans R&B and a healthy dose of humor. In recent times Wallace has been writing music for films, including *White Men Can't Jump.* —*Scott Yanow*

The Fourteen Bar Blues / Jan. 23, 1978 / Enja ✦✦✦✦
Tenor saxophonist Bennie Wallace's debut as a leader features the adventurous tenor in a trio with bassist Eddie Gomez and drummer Eddie Moore. This LP (long overdue to be reissued on CD) has six Wallace originals (including the title cut and "Yard 'n' Newk," which borrows aspects of Charlie Parker and Sonny Rollins) plus melodic interpretations of "Chelsea Bridge" and "Trinkle Tinkle" and a warm rendition of "Flamingo." Even at the near-start of his career, Bennie Wallace's sound, style and approach were fully formed. —*Scott Yanow*

Live at the Public Theater / May 26, 1978 / Enja ✦✦✦✦
Tenor saxophonist Bennie Wallace's second album as a leader, a pianoless date with bassist Eddie Gomez and drummer Dannie Richmond, is similar in style to his first. A few years later he would rediscover his Southern roots and add some R&Bish rhythms to his music, but at this point Wallace's accompaniment was sparse and sometimes bordered on the avant-garde. Wallace, whose huge tone (looking back toward Ben Webster) has always contrasted with his wide interval jumps and advanced improvising, stretches out on two originals, "In a Sentimental Mood" and "Blue Monk" during this stimulating session. —*Scott Yanow*

The Free Will / Jan. 31, 1980-Feb. 1, 1980 / Enja ✦✦✦✦

Plays Monk / Mar. 4, 1981-Mar. 5, 1981 / Enja ✦✦✦✦✦
Recorded a year before pianist/composer Thelonious Monk's death, this tribute by Bennie Wallace features the dynamic tenor in trios with bassist Eddie Gomez and

drummer Dannie Richmond, plus three quartets with the addition of trombonist Jimmy Knepper. Wallace's eccentric interval jumps and very expressive sound (along with his advanced harmonic knowledge) made him a natural to explore Monk's music, and he pours plenty of passion into these improvisations. In addition to seven of Monk's compositions, Wallace contributes his own "Prelude"; the CD reissue adds a second version of "'Round Midnight" to the original program. This colorful and chance-taking session can act as an introduction to both Bennie Wallace and Monk's music. —*Scott Yanow*

Sweeping Through the City / Mar. 1984-Apr. 1984 / Enja ✦✦✦✦
Tenor saxophonist Bennie Wallace's first six recordings as a leader (all for Enja during 1978-82) featured his large tone and advanced solos with sparse rhythm sections. *Sweeping Through The City* is a transitional record that looks toward his upcoming Blue Note dates. Wallace is teamed with the rambunctious trombonist Ray Anderson, guitarist John Scofield, bass, drums and the four-voice gospel group "The Wings of Song." Although the music looks toward the roots of black music, Wallace and Anderson's consistently wild solos keep the results from ever being predictable. Recommended. —*Scott Yanow*

★ **Twilight Time** / 1985 / Blue Note ✦✦✦✦✦
This Blue Note album is a classic. Although tenor saxophonist Bennie Wallace was originally thought of as an avant-gardist, his large tone (in the tradition of Ben Webster) and roots in Southern music always made him stand out from the crowd. On this inspired project, Wallace, trombonist Ray Anderson and guitarist John Scofield are well showcased in R&Bish and funky settings with such musicians as pianist Dr. John, Bob Cranshaw or Eddie Gomez on bass, Jack DeJohnette, Chris Parker or Bernard Purdie on drums and (during two numbers) blues guitar legend Stevie Ray Vaughan. To hear the lead voices rocking out on "Is It True What They Say About Dixie," "Tennessee Waltz" and "Trouble in Mind" is a unique experience, and Wallace's lively cadenza on "Twilight Time" steals the show. Highly recommended. —*Scott Yanow*

Brilliant Corners / Sep. 7, 1986-Sep. 8, 1986 / Denon ✦✦✦✦
A wonderful, overlooked 1986 session with the Japanese pianist Yosuke Yamashita. —*Ron Wynn*

The Art of the Saxophone / Feb. 7, 1987-Feb. 8, 1987 / Denon ✦✦✦✦✦
This is an ambitious project that works quite well. Tenor saxophonist Bennie Wallace, a flexible player able to range from swing to free jazz, clearly has fun matching wits on two or three songs apiece with guest tenors Harold Ashby, Jerry Bergonzi, Lew Tabackin and altoist Oliver Lake. Assisted by guitarist John Scofield, bassist Eddie Gomez and drummer Dannie Richmond on this Japanese import CD (which has been available domestically), Wallace is heard at his best battling Tabackin and Bergonzi, although he keeps up with the radical flights of Lake, too. In addition to "You Go to My Head," six Wallace originals and two Duke Ellington tunes are performed. Well worth searching for. —*Scott Yanow*

Bordertown / Jun. 1987 / Blue Note ✦✦✦✦✦
On a strong follow-up to his classic *Twilight Time*, tenor saxophonist Bennie Wallace continues in the same New Orleans R&Bish vein. The music includes funky originals and a few traditional numbers ("Stormy Weather" and "Carolina Moon") and features Wallace with trombonist Ray Anderson (on four of the eight tunes), pianist Dr. John, guitarist John Scofield, bassist Eddie Gomez and drummer Herlin Riley; guests include guitarist Mitch Watkins on two numbers. Although not quite reaching the heights of the earlier set, there is plenty of spirit displayed on this unusual and easily recommended set. —*Scott Yanow*

Old Songs / Jan. 18, 1993-Jan. 20, 1993 / Audio Quest ✦✦✦✦
Much of this date features Bennie Wallace's distinctive tenor in a pianoless trio with bassist Bill Hunington and drummer Alvin Queen. Although it could be said that Wallace combines the sound of Ben Webster with the interval jumps of Eric Dolphy (a very potent combination), he has had his own style for over a decade. These eight standards (along with an original blues "At Lulu White's") are taken at a variety of tempos, and Wallace really digs into these fertile chord changes after showing respect for the melodies. —*Scott Yanow*

Sippie Wallace (Beulah Thomas)

b. Nov. 1, 1898, Houston, TX, d. Nov. 1, 1986, Detroit, MI
Vocals / Blues, Classic Female Blues
A classic female blues singer from the '20s, Wallace kept performing and recording until her death. She was a major influence on a young Bonnie Raitt, who recorded several of Wallace's songs and performed live with her.

The daughter of a Baptist deacon, Sippie Wallace (born Beulah Thomas) was born and raised in Houston. As a child, she sang and played piano in church. Before she was in her teens, she began performing with her pianist brother, Hersal Thomas. By the time she was in her mid-teens, she had left Houston to pursue a musical career, singing in a number of tent shows and earning a dedicated fan base. In 1915, she moved to New Orleans with Hersal. Two years later, she married Matt Wallace.

In 1923, Sippie, Hersal, and their older brother George moved to Chicago, where Sippie became part of the city's jazz scene. By the end of the year, she had earned a contract with OKeh Records. Her first two songs for the label, "Shorty George" and "Up the Country Blues," were hits, and Sippie soon became a star. Throughout the '20s, she produced a series of singles that were nearly all hits. Wallace's OKeh recordings featured a number of celebrated jazz musicians, including Louis Armstrong, Eddie Heywood, King Oliver, and Clarence Williams; both Hersal and George Thomas performed on Sippie's records as well, in addition to supporting her at concerts. Between 1923 and 1927, she recorded over 40 songs for OKeh. Many of the songs were Wallace originals or co-written by Sippie and her brothers.

In 1926, Hersal Thomas died of food poisoning, but Sippie Wallace continued to perform and record. Within a few years, however, she stopped performing regularly. After her contract with OKeh was finished in the late '20s, she moved to Detroit in 1929. In the early '30s, Wallace stopped recording, only performing the occasional gig. In 1936, both George Thomas and Sippie's husband Matt died. Following their deaths, Sippie joined the Leland Baptist Church in Detroit, where she was an organist and vocalist; she stayed with the church for the next 40 years.

Between 1936 and 1966, Sippie Wallace was inactive on the blues scene–she only performed a handful of concerts and cut a few records. In 1966, she was lured out of retirement by her friend Victoria Spivey, who convinced Sippie to join the thriving blues and folk festival circuit. Wallace not only joined the circuit, she began recording again. Her first new album was a collection of duets with Spivey, appropriately titled *Sippie Wallace and Victoria Spivey*, which was recorded in 1966; the album wasn't released until 1970. Also in 1966, Wallace recorded *Sippie Wallace Sings the Blues* for Storyville, which featured support from musicians like Little Brother Montgomery and Roosevelt Sykes. The album was quite popular, as were Sippie's festival performances.

In 1970, Sippie Wallace suffered a stroke, but she was able to continue recording and performing, although not as frequently as she had before. In 1982, Bonnie Raitt–who had longed claimed Sippie as a major influence–helped Wallace land a contract with Atlantic Records. Raitt produced the resulting album, *Sippie*, which was released in 1983. *Sippie* won the WC Handy Award for best blues album of the year and was nominated for a Grammy. The album turned out to be Sippie Wallace's last recording–she died in 1986, when she was 88 years old. —*Stephen Thomas Erlewine & Cub Koda*

● **1923-1929** / Oct. 26, 1923-Feb. 7, 1929 / Document ✦✦✦✦✦
Sippie's earliest and best sides, including "I'm a Mighty Tight Woman." —*Cub Koda*

Fats Waller (Thomas Wright Waller)

b. May 21, 1904, New York, NY, **d.** Dec. 15, 1943, Kansas City, MO
Piano, Vocals, Composer, Organ / Stride, Classic Jazz, Swing, Traditional Jazz
Not only was Fats Waller one of the greatest pianists jazz has ever known, he was also one of its most exuberantly funny entertainers–and as so often happens, one facet tends to obscure the other. His extraordinarily light and flexible touch belied his ample physical girth; he could swing as hard as any pianist alive or dead in his classic James P. Johnson-derived stride manner, with a powerful left hand delivering the octaves and tenths in a tireless, rapid, seamless stream. Waller also pioneered the use of the pipe organ and Hammond organ in jazz–he called the pipe organ the "God box"–adapting his irresistible sense of swing to the pedals and a staccato right hand while making imaginative changes of the registration. As a composer and improviser, his melodic invention rarely flagged, and he contributed fistfuls of joyous yet paradoxically winsome songs like "Honeysuckle Rose," "Ain't Misbehavin,'" "Keepin' Out of Mischief Now," "Blue Turning Grey Over You" and the extraordinary "Jitterbug Waltz" to the jazz repertoire.

During his lifetime and afterward, though, Fats Waller was best known to the world for his outsized comic personality and sly vocals, where he would send up trashy tunes that Victor Records made him record with his nifty combo, Fats Waller and His Rhythm. Yet on virtually any of his records, whether the song is an evergreen standard or the most trite bit of doggerel that a Tin Pan Alley hack could serve up, you will hear a winning combination of good knockabout humor, foot-tapping rhythm and fantastic piano playing. Today, almost all of Fats Waller's studio recordings can be found on RCA's on-again-off-again series *The Complete Fats Waller*, which commenced on LPs in 1975 and was still in progress during the 1990s.

Thomas "Fats" Waller came from a Harlem household, where his father was a Baptist lay preacher and his mother played piano and organ. Waller took up the piano at age six, playing in a school orchestra led by Edgar Sampson (of Chick Webb fame). After his mother died when he was 14, Waller moved into the home

of pianist Russell Brooks, where he met and studied with James P. Johnson. Later, Waller also received classical lessons from Carl Bohm and the famous pianist Leopold Godowsky. After making his first record at age 18 for OKeh in 1922, "Birmingham Blues"/"Muscle Shoals Blues," he backed various blues singers and worked as house pianist and organist at rent parties and in movie theaters and clubs. He began to attract attention as a composer during the early and mid-1920s, forming a most fruitful alliance with lyricist Andy Razaf that resulted in three Broadway shows in the late '20s, *Keep Shufflin',* *Load of Coal,* and *Hot Chocolates*.

Waller started making records for Victor in 1926; his most significant early records for that label were a series of brilliant 1929 solo piano sides of his own compositions like "Handful of Keys" and "Smashing Thirds." After finally signing an exclusive Victor contract in 1934, he began the long-running, prolific series of records with his Rhythm, which won him great fame and produced several hits, including "Your Feet's Too Big," "The Joint Is Jumpin'" and "I'm Gonna Sit Right Down and Write Myself a Letter." He began to appear in films like *Hooray for Love* and *King of Burlesque* in 1935 while continuing regular appearances on radio that dated back to 1923. He toured Europe in 1938, made organ recordings in London for HMV and appeared on one of the first television broadcasts. He returned to London the following spring to record his most extensive composition, *London Suite*, for piano and percussion, and embark on an extensive continental tour (which, alas, was cancelled by fears of impending war with Germany). Well aware of the popularity of big bands in the '30s, Waller tried to form his own, but they were short-lived.

Into the 1940s, Waller's touring schedule of the US escalated, he contributed music to another musical, *Early to Bed*, the film appearances kept coming (including a memorable stretch of *Stormy Weather*, where he led an all-star band that included Benny Carter, Slam Stewart and Zutty Singleton), the recordings continued to flow, and he continued to eat and drink in extremely heavy quantities. Years of draining alimony squabbles plus overindulgence and, no doubt, frustration over not being taken more seriously as an artist, began to wear the pianist down. Finally, after becoming ill during a gig at the Zanzibar Room in Hollywood in Dec. 1943, Waller boarded the Santa Fe Chief train for the long trip back to New York. He never made it, dying of pneumonia aboard the train during a stop at Union Station in Kansas City.

While every clown longs to play Hamlet as per the cliché–and Waller did have so-called serious musical pretensions, longing to follow in George Gershwin's footsteps and compose concert music–it probably was not in the cards anyway due to the racial barriers of the first half of the 20th century. Besides, given the fact that Waller influenced a long line of pianists of and after his time, including Count Basie (who studied with Fats), Teddy Wilson, Art Tatum, Thelonious Monk, Dave Brubeck and countless others, his impact has been truly profound. —*Richard S. Ginell*

☆ **Piano Masterworks, Vol. 1** / Oct. 21, 1922-Sep. 24, 1929 / EPM ✦✦✦✦✦
Although he would become well-known in the '30s for his comic vocals and memorable personality, Fats Waller was always first and foremost a pianist. During the '20s he was purely an instrumentalist, one of the greatest and most powerful stride pianists of all time. This CD has all of Waller's early piano solos, including every one of the alternate takes (two versions of many titles and a very rare third take of "I've Got a Feeling I'm Falling"). With the exception of his initial two sides from 1922 and 1927's "Blue Black Bottom," all of these titles are from 1929, including the original version of "Ain't Misbehavin." —*Scott Yanow*

Fats Waller in London / Oct. 21, 1922-Jun. 13, 1939 / Disques Swing ✦✦✦✦
Other than Fats Waller's first two recorded piano solos (from 1922), this double LP concentrates on the recordings he made while in London during 1938-39. Doubling on piano and organ, Waller romps and sings with a fine English octet, takes six comparatively somber organ solos (featuring Black spirituals) and backs singer Adelaide Hall on a delightful version of "I Can't Give You Anything but Love." In addition, Waller (backed by drummer Max Lewin) performs one of his few long works, the six-part "London Suite." Excellent music with plenty of variety on this fine two-fer. —*Scott Yanow*

Giants of Jazz / Oct. 21, 1922-Jan. 23, 1943 / Time-Life ✦✦✦✦
Before the CD era, this three-LP box set was the definitive single Fats Waller collection. It hits most of the high points of the great pianist-vocalist-composer-organist-entertainer's career. Starting with his recording debut in 1922 (the piano solo "Muscle Shoals Blues") and continuing up until a 1943 version of "Honeysuckle Rose" taken from the soundtrack of *Stormy Weather*, all aspects of Waller's productive career are covered. He is heard on virtuosic piano solos, playing organ, sitting in with Fletcher Henderson's Orchestra ("Henderson Stomp"), backing singer Alberta Hunter, jamming with his "Buddies" in 1929, guesting with Ted Lewis and Jack Teagarden, and recording hits with his regular sextet of 1934-42. Although all of this music is now available on CD, the attractive and informative 56-page booklet is a good reason by itself to pick up this box. —*Scott Yanow*

Classic Jazz from Rare Piano Rolls / Mar. 1923-Jan. 1929 / Music Masters ◆◆◆
During 1922-27 Waller made 19 piano rolls, solos that could be reproduced by running marked paper through player pianos. Eleven of these are on this CD, along with a duet with his teacher James P. Johnson ("If I Could Be with You") and a version of Waller's "Ain't Misbehavin'" from 1929 by J. Lawrence Cook. Piano rolls always come a distant second to recorded piano solos, since the unchanging tempos and steady rhythms generally come across as mechanical. His piano rolls are as rollicking and swinging as it is possible to get, and this interesting CD gives listeners versions of several tunes that Waller never did record. —*Scott Yanow*

Fats at the Organ / 1923-1927 / ASV/Living Era ◆◆◆
This is a rather unusual LP, for it features Fats Waller's player-piano rolls (dating from 1923-27) being pumped through a pipe organ. The liner notes go into detail about the difficulties involved (for example the organ has 61 notes while the piano has 88), but the results are quite successful. Since Waller's piano solos tended to be much more jubilant and harder-swinging than his comparatively somber organ playing, it is fascinating to hear him suddenly romping on the organ. —*Scott Yanow*

☆ **Turn on the Heat: The Fats Waller Piano Solos** / Feb. 16, 1927-May 13, 1941 / Bluebird ◆◆◆◆◆
With the exception of a third take of "I've Got a Feeling I'm Falling" and his two earliest records from 1922, all of Fats Waller's recorded piano solos are on this superior double-CD set. Over half of these recordings are from 1929, but fortunately he also cut three sessions of piano solos after he became much more famous as a comedy personality with his Rhythm sides. Highlights include the virtuosic "Handful of Keys," the earliest version of "Ain't Misbehavin'," "Clothes Line Ballet," "I Ain't Got Nobody" and "Honeysuckle Rose." A special bonus is a pair of piano duets with Bennie Payne ("St. Louis Blues" and "After You've Gone"). Classic music. —*Scott Yanow*

☆ **Fats Waller and His Buddies** / May 20, 1927-Dec. 18, 1929 / Bluebird ◆◆◆◆◆
This CD has most of Fats Waller's best band recordings of the '20s, including eight selections by his "Buddies" (highlighted by "The Minor Drag" and "Harlem Fuss"), six (counting two alternate takes) from The Louisiana Sugar Babes (an odd quartet featuring Waller's organ and James P. Johnson's piano) and seven selections on which Waller sits in with cornetist Thomas Morris' Hot Babies in 1927. Surprisingly, other than his scat vocal on "Red Hot Dan," Fats Waller is heard strictly as a pianist, but his talents were so giant as an instrumentalist that one never minds. With trombonists Charlie Irvis and Jack Teagarden and trumpeters Red Allen and Jabbo Smith among the strong supporting cast, the one word for this superior CD is hot. —*Scott Yanow*

Greatest Hits / Mar. 1, 1929-Jan. 23, 1943 / RCA Victor ◆◆◆
Some of pianist-vocalist-composer Fats Waller's "greatest hits" are on this introductory sampler, but the packaging could certainly be better. The caricature on the cover shows Waller with a beard, the 14 selections are randomly programmed, some of the recording dates are inaccurate (this version of "Honeysuckle Rose" is from 1937 rather than 1941) and there is no personnel listing, an inexcusable omission in every CD in this well-intentioned but erratic series. There are some classic performances on Waller's CD including "Handful of Keys," the 1937 all-star rendition of "Honeysuckle Rose" (with uncredited appearances by Tommy Dorsey and Bunny Berigan!), "The Joint Is Jumpin'," and "Your Feet's Too Big," making this one of the better entries in this program. —*Scott Yanow*

Here 'Tis / Oct. 14, 1929-Dec. 1943 / Jazz Archives ◆◆◆◆
This long out-of-print LP is a real collector's item, featuring seven rare alternate takes and a few real Fats Waller oddities. Among the latter is an excerpt from the legendary production *Hot Chocolate* in 1929; Waller backs some of the dialogue. In addition, this LP has his final recordings, a broadcast from Los Angeles in Dec. 1943 with the pianist/singer performing "Your Feet's Too Big" and "Handful of Keys" one last time, just a short while before his premature death. This LP is well worth acquiring but will take a long search. —*Scott Yanow*

● **Breakin' the Ice: The Early Years, Part 1** / May 16, 1934-May 6, 1935 / Bluebird ◆◆◆◆◆
This two-CD set has the first 42 recordings of Fats Waller with his Rhythm. The brilliant stride pianist/vocalist/composer/personality became very popular due to these 1934-35 recordings, which feature either Herman Autrey or Bill Coleman on trumpet, Gene Sedric, Ben Whitted, Mezz Mezzrow or Rudy Powell on reeds, guitarist Al Casey and a rhythm section. All of Waller's Victor recordings have been reissued on CD, and this two-fer (which includes such memorable numbers as "A Porter's Love Song to a Chambermaid," "Serenade for a Wealthy Widow," "How Can You Face Me," "Honeysuckle Rose," "Believe It, Beloved," "I Ain't Got Nobody," "Oh Suzannah Dust Off That Old Pianna" and "You've Been Taking Lessons in Love") is a perfect place to start. —*Scott Yanow*

The Definitive Fats Waller, Vol. 2: Hallelujah / Mar. 11, 1935-Apr. 3, 1939 / Stash ◆◆◆◆◆
This second volume of rare Fats Waller items includes 24 selections performed at a marathon radio transcription session in 1935 (there were actually 31 pieces played, seven of which are on *Volume 1*). Waller is heard solo, singing and playing piano without the assistance of his sidemen, and he is in top form on a wide variety of material. This CD concludes with previously unreleased items from three different occasions: a 1936 solo broadcast from Bluefield, WV, two selections privately recorded in London in 1939, and Waller's appearance on *The George Jessel Show* during the same year. A superior release from the great stride pianist, vocalist, composer and personality. —*Scott Yanow*

The Definitive Fats Waller, Vol. 1: His Piano His Rhythm / Mar. 11, 1935-Aug. 7, 1939 / Stash ◆◆◆◆◆
In addition to his many studio recordings for Victor, the popular pianist/singer/composer Fats Waller recorded two extensive sessions of radio transcriptions which could be used to fill in time between radio shows. These have now been reissued in full on two CDs. The first volume finds Waller performing seven songs in 1935 (two duets with the reeds of Rudy Powell and five solos with some vocals) in addition to 23 performances from 1939 (17 with his Rhythm, an excerpt from an organ solo and three unaccompanied piano solos). Throughout, Waller, who never really needed an audience, is in exuberant form, playing material that was generally superior than the dog tunes he was often handed at recording sessions. A fun set. —*Scott Yanow*

I'm Gonna Sit Right Down: The Early Years, Part 2 / May 8, 1935-Feb. 1, 1936 / Bluebird ◆◆◆◆◆
The second in a series of five CD packages that reissue all of Fats Waller's Victor recordings with his Rhythm, this two-CD set traces the pianist/composer/vocalist/personality's career during a nine-month period. Among the sidemen are trumpeter Herman Autrey and either Rudy Powell or Gene Sedric on reeds; highlights include the hit version of "I'm Gonna Sit Right Down and Write Myself a Letter," a rambunctious "There'll Be Some Changes Made," "Truckin'," "Got a Bran' New Suit" and four performances from a big-band session. All of the Waller Victor recordings are full of joy and infectious swing. —*Scott Yanow*

Fractious Fingering: Early Years, Vol. 3 (1936) / Apr. 8, 1936-Nov. 29, 1936 / RCA ◆◆◆◆◆
With the release of this two-CD set in 1997, it became possible for the first time ever to easily acquire all of pianist/composer/vocalist Fats Waller's Rhythm recordings of 1934-43. They are available in their entirety on three double-disc and three triple-disc sets, 15 discs in all. The 41 selections on this set feature Waller with trumpeter Herman Autrey, Gene Sedric on clarinet and tenor, guitarist Al Casey, bassist Charles Turner and either Yank Porter or Slick Jones on drums. The rarest performance ("Stay") has Elizabeth Handy (W.C.'s daughter) joining Fats for a duet vocal, and there are also five alternate takes (all previously released) of various tunes. This hard-swinging music is quite enjoyable (especially in small doses), with the most memorable selections including "All My Life," "Christopher Columbus" (with its hilarious lyrics), "Black Raspberry Jam," "Fractious Fingering," two run-throughs of "The Curse of an Aching Heart," the jubilant "Floatin' Down to Cotton Town," and two classic versions of "Swingin' Them Jingle Bells." This music is impossible not to like, and, as is always true of Fats Waller, it is touched with genius. —*Scott Yanow*

Fats Waller and His Rhythm: The Middle Years, Part 1 (1936-1938) / Dec. 24, 1936-Apr. 12, 1938 / Bluebird ◆◆◆◆◆
Part of Bluebird's very admirable reissue of all of Fats Waller's 1934-42 Victor recordings, this three-CD set has the pianist-vocalist's 70 studio performances from a busy 16-month period. Most selections are with his sextet, which generally includes trumpeter Herman Autrey, Gene Sedric on clarinet and tenor, and guitarist Al Casey, plus there are eight songs with Waller's occasional big band in 1938. Among the many high points are "I'm Sorry I Made You Cry," "Nero," "Beat It Out," "The Joint Is Jumpin'" (the original hit record), "The Sheik of Araby" and instrumental versions of "Honeysuckle Rose" and "Blue, Turning Grey Over You." Highly recommended. —*Scott Yanow*

A Good Man Is Hard to Find: The Middle Years, Part 2 / Apr. 12, 1938-Jan. 12, 1940 / Bluebird ◆◆◆◆◆
Subtitled "The Middle Years, Part 2," this three-CD set contains all of pianist/vocalist Fats Waller's Victor recordings from a nearly two-year period, including all of the alternate takes. In fact, the first five selections (the only ones contained here from his short-lived big band) are all alternate takes to the selections that close "The Middle Years, Part 1." Otherwise these performances are by Waller's septet with either Herman Autrey or John Hamilton on trumpet and Gene Sedric (who doubled on tenor and clarinet); Chauncey Graham fills in for Sedric on one date. Waller's great popularity resulted in the large number of recordings from this era

(68 are on this set) and they range from hits ("Two Sleepy People," "Yacht Club Swing," an amazing version of "Hold Tight," "Your Feet's Too Big" and a new rendition of "Squeeze Me") and fresh originals and novelties to trash that Waller did his best (often through satirization) to uplift. Nearly every selection has a liberal dose of his classic piano, and taken as a whole these much-maligned recordings are quite listenable, enjoyable and historical. —*Scott Yanow*

Jugglin' Jive of Fats Waller and His Orchestra / Jul. 16, 1938-Oct. 18, 1938 / Sandy Hook ◆◆◆◆

This very enjoyable CD contains three radio broadcasts featuring Fats Waller and his Rhythm in 1938. Despite some dated chatter (and not-so-subtle racism) from a radio announcer, the music on these live performances is quite spirited, with Waller singing and playing heated stride piano with his sextet. While trumpeter Herman Autrey and Gene Sedric's reeds are major assets, Fats Waller is virtually the whole show, really driving his sidemen and stimulating both a memorable party atmosphere and creative swinging jazz. —*Scott Yanow*

Fine Arabian Stuff / Nov. 20, 1939 / Muse ◆◆◆

The music on this LP was all recorded in one day, and finds an unaccompanied Fats Waller dealing with a variety of folk songs and spirituals, much of them out of character with the stereotype of Waller as a happy-go-lucky, partying extrovert. He plays piano on the first six numbers while performing in a much more somber mood on organ for the last seven songs. Not essential music, but Fats Waller collectors will want this unusual set. —*Scott Yanow*

The Last Years (1940-1943) / Apr. 11, 1940-Jan. 23, 1943 / Bluebird ◆◆◆◆◆

Since all of the previous Fats Waller Rhythm reissue series start off in 1934 and get discontinued before reaching the '40s, this time around the newest program has started out with Waller's last recordings and is working its way backwards. This essential three-CD set contains the pianist/vocalist/composer's last 63 studio recordings. Some of the titles are quite laughable ("Little Curly Hair in a High Chair," "You're a Square from Delaware," "Abercrombie Had a Zombie" and "Come Down to Earth My Angel"), but Waller manages to either satirize or save virtually all of the somewhat dubious material. There are some out-and-out classics included on this set too, including "Fats Waller's Original E Flat Blues," "All That Meat and No Potatoes" and "The Jitterbug Waltz"; this wonderful set of spirited music concludes with "Ain't Misbehavin'" from the soundtrack of *Stormy Weather*. —*Scott Yanow*

Last Testament: 1943 / Sep. 23, 1943 / Drive Archive ◆◆◆◆◆

This CD contains most of pianist/vocalist Fats Waller's final recordings, V-Discs cut for servicemen overseas. These solo performances are priceless, for Waller is often hilarious (his reworking of "Two Sleepy People" is classic) yet still playing at his prime; "Hallelujah" has a particularly heated stride solo. Other highlights include "Ain't Misbehavin'," "You're Slightly Less than Wonderful," "This Is So Nice It Must Be Illegal" and "That's What the Birdie Sang to Me." In addition there is a song taken from the movie *Stormy Weather* ("That Ain't Right," which has Waller giving plenty of backtalk to Ada Brown's vocal) and a rare organ solo, "Bouncin' on a V-Disc." Less than three months later Fats Waller was dead; he definitely went out on top. Recommended. —*Scott Yanow*

George Wallington (Giacinto Figlia)

b. Oct. 27, 1924, Palmero, Sicily, Italy, d. Feb. 15, 1993, New York, NY
Piano / Bop

George Wallington was one of the first and best bop pianists, ranking up there with Al Haig, just below Bud Powell. He was also the composer of two bop standards that caught on for a time: "Lemon Drop" and "Godchild." Born in Sicily, Wallington and his family moved to the US in 1925. He arrived in New York in the early '40s and was a member of the first bop group to play on 52nd Street, Dizzy Gillespie's combo of 1943-44. After spending a year with Joe Marsala's band, Wallington played with the who's who of bop during 1946-52, including Charlie Parker, Serge Chaloff, Allan Eager, Kai Winding, Terry Gibbs, Brew Moore, Al Cohn, Gerry Mulligan, Zoot Sims and Red Rodney. He toured Europe with Lionel Hampton's ill-fated big band of 1953 and during 1954-60 he led groups in New York that included among their up-and-coming sidemen Donald Byrd and Jackie McLean (the latter succeeded by Phil Woods). Then in 1960 Wallington gave up on the music business altogether and retired to work in his family's air-conditioning company. Twenty-four years later he re-emerged, recording three albums of original material before time ran out. —*Scott Yanow*

The George Wallington Trio / Nov. 21, 1951 / Savoy ◆◆◆◆

● **The George Wallington Trios** / Sep. 4, 1952+May 25, 1953 / Original Jazz Classics ◆◆◆◆◆

Originally released as a pair of ten-inch Prestige albums, this CD reissue features the talented bop-oriented pianist George Wallington in trios with either Charles Mingus, Oscar Pettiford or Curly Russell on bass plus drummer Max Roach; gui-

tarist Chuck Wayne sits in on mandola on "Love Beat." The 15 songs include concise interpretations of ten of Wallington's originals, and it seems strange that latter-day jazz musicians have yet to really explore his inventive tunes. This is one of the best showcases ever of Wallington's playing and writing talents. —*Scott Yanow*

George Wallington Quintet Live at Cafe Bohemia / Sep. 9, 1955 / Original Jazz Classics ◆◆◆◆◆

This live set, although led by pianist George Wallington, is most significant for giving listeners early examples of the playing of trumpeter Donald Byrd and altoist Jackie McLean; bassist Paul Chambers and drummer Art Taylor complete the quintet. The music, although comprising mostly group originals (other than "Johnny One Note" and Oscar Pettiford's "Bohemia After Dark"), is essentially a bebop jam and it is particularly interesting to hear just how much McLean was influenced by Charlie Parker at this point (although his sound was already quickly recognizable). This was a solid if short-lived group, and their brand of hard bop will be enjoyed by straightahead jazz fans. The CD reissue adds a second version of "Minor March" to the original program. —*Scott Yanow*

Jazz for the Carriage Trade / Jan. 20, 1956 / Original Jazz Classics ◆◆◆◆

During 1956-57 trumpeter Donald Byrd and altoist Phil Woods (both important up-and-coming players) were regular members of pianist George Wallington's quintet. For this CD reissue, bassist Teddy Kotick and drummer Art Taylor complete the group on a program that includes three standards ("Our Delight," "Our Love Is Here to Stay" and "What's New"), a pair of Woods originals ("Together We Wail" and "But George") and Frank Foster's "Foster Dulles." The music falls between bebop and hard bop, with Woods sounding quite strong while Byrd comes across as a promising (but not yet mature) youngster. A fine example of this somewhat forgotten but talented group, easily recommended to bop collectors. —*Scott Yanow*

The New York Scene / Mar. 1, 1957 / Original Jazz Classics ◆◆◆◆◆

Before he retired from music in 1960, pianist George Wallington led a series of excellent bop-based quintet albums. For this particular CD (a reissue of a date originally put out by New Jazz), Wallington heads a group featuring altoist Phil Woods, trumpeter Donald Byrd, bassist Teddy Kotick and drummer Nick Stabulas. With the exception of the standard "Indian Summer," the repertoire is fairly obscure (with now-forgotten originals by Byrd, Woods and Mose Allison in addition to "Graduation Day") but of a consistent high quality. The emphasis is on hard-swinging, and this set should greatly please straightahead jazz fans. —*Scott Yanow*

Leonard Feather Presents / Jul. 1957-Sep. 1957 / V.S.O.P. ◆◆◆

The sessions on this LP reissue were originally organized by Leonard Feather to pay tribute to the bop era. The 11 selections (all dating from the mid- to late '40s) feature pianist George Wallington (who is actually the set's leader), altoist Phil Woods, either Idrees Sulieman or Thad Jones on trumpet, bassist Curley Russell and either Denzil Best or Art Taylor on drums. About the only surprise occurs on "Salt Peanuts," which has an off-key "vocal" from five-year-old Baird Parker, son of the late Charlie Parker. Otherwise the playing of Woods makes this a worthwhile session for bop fans. —*Scott Yanow*

Jazz at Hotchkiss / Nov. 14, 1957 / Savoy ◆◆◆◆

This LP-length CD reissue features pianist George Wallington and his 1957 quintet (which consists of trumpeter Donald Byrd, altoist Phil Woods, bassist Knobby Totah and drummer Nick Stabulas) stretching out on five numbers. The repertoire is highlighted by Bud Powell's "Dance of the Infidels" and Dizzy Gillespie's "Ow." Both Woods and Byrd (two up-and-coming players) are in excellent form, making this an enjoyable outing for bop fans. —*Scott Yanow*

Virtuoso / Jul. 5, 1984 / Interface ◆◆◆◆

After 24 years off the scene, pianist George Wallington surprised many who had forgotten him by recording this solo CD, the first of three. Although all ten of the selections are Wallington originals, his boppish style was largely unchanged from the 1950s, and some of the tunes are based on the chord changes of more common standards. However, the melodies are fresh, Wallington's improvisations are full of joyful swing, and the overall results (available as a Japanese import through Denon) are quite appealing. —*Scott Yanow*

The Pleasure of a Jazz Inspiration / Aug. 19, 1985 / V.S.O.P. ◆◆◆◆

Pianist George Wallington, who retired from jazz in 1960, returned in the mid-'80s and recorded three solo albums; he passed away in 1993. This CD, which contains eight originals (which are subtitled *A Jazz Tone Poem*), is not as adventurous as one might think. Actually a lot of the songs are based on fairly common chord changes. Wallington plays quite well (mixing in his dominant Bud Powell influence with touches of Teddy Wilson), making one regret that the important bop-based pianist took so many years off. At least his final efforts were impressive, and this CD offers some fine examples of his playing after his "comeback." —*Scott Yanow*

The Symphony of a Jazz Piano / 1985 / Denon ✦✦✦✦

The second of three George Wallington CDs made during his surprise comeback follows the pattern of the other two. It consists exclusively of his originals, most of which fall into the bop tradition, and Wallington playing unaccompanied solos. It is surprising that during his later years, the pianist never recorded with a trio or a group. This swinging Japanese import (available through Denon) is well worth searching for by bop collectors, for it shows that, even after all the time off, George Wallington had not lost a thing. —*Scott Yanow*

Winston Walls

b. Charleston, WV

Organ, Vocals / Soul Jazz, Hard Bop, Groove

Winston Walls was born in Charleston, WV, the son of well-known R&B pianist Harry Van Walls (with Joe Turner). At 15 Walls already knew some piano and had been playing in church and school for several years. He then learned drums from Frank Thompson and got a job playing drums for Bill "Honky Tonk" Doggett's band. He soon switched to organ and filled in on breaks for Doggett.

He acknowledges Jimmy Smith and Jack McDuff as major influences and has toured the country, playing with the Pointer Sisters, Sonny Stitt, Dionne Warwick, Al Green, Charlie Pride, Ike & Tina Turner, and Lou Donaldson.

His jazz organ also includes elements of R&B, rock, country and gospel. He once toured with Jimmy Smith, Groove Holmes, and Jack McDuff, but had never recorded a solo album. Then in 1993 he recorded a live session with fellow organist (and friend) Brother Jack McDuff which has been released on Schoolkids' Records. —*Michael Erlewine*

Boss of the B-3 / Oct. 25, 1993-Oct. 26, 1993 / Schoolkids ✦✦✦✦✦

Long overdue (like about 30 years!) debut album for Walls who is, as one reviewer put it, "the best organ player you never heard of." You can hear him now in live concert with long time friend and rival Jack McDuff. You guessed it. McDuff and Walls battle it out as in days of yore, note for note and screeching chord against chord. This is a classic jam battle with a few vocals thrown in for diversion. McDuff is bound to let Walls (after all these years) be heard, so he does not struggle too hard. Good funk fun. Live set means the balance is a little off, but who cares. —*Michael Erlewine*

Jack Walrath

b. May 5, 1946, Stuart, FL

Trumpet / Post-Bop

An often exciting, thoughtful trumpeter and good arranger, Jack Walrath has steadily gained attention and exposure through his contributions to outstanding sessions. Walrath began playing trumpet at nine, and studied at Berklee in the mid- and late '60s while working with other students and backing up R&B vocalists. He moved to the West Coast in 1969, and co-led the bands Change with Gary Peacock and Revival with Glenn Ferris. Walrath also toured a year with Ray Charles. Walrath relocated to New York in the early '70s and worked with Latin bands before playing with Charles Mingus from 1974 to 1979, an association that gave him a certain amount of recognition. Walrath contributed some arrangements and orchestrations to Mingus' final recordings. In the 1980s and '90s he led his own bands, toured Europe with Dannie Richmond and the British group Spirit Level, worked with Charlie Persip's Superband and Richard Abrams, and helped keep the music of Charles Mingus alive by playing with Mingus Dynasty. Jack Walrath has recorded as a leader for Gatemouth, Stash, Steeple Chase, Red, Muse, Spotlite, Blue Note and Mapleshade; he is still improving with age. —*Ron Wynn*

Demons in Pursuit / Aug. 21, 1979-Aug. 22, 1979 / Gatemouth ✦✦✦✦

Trumpeter Jack Walrath has long been best known for his important association with Charles Mingus. For his debut as a leader, Walrath mixed together a wide variety of different stylists, including Mingus' drummer Dannie Richmond, the harmonically advanced Jim McNeely on both piano and organ, the unique guitarist John Scofield and bassist Ray Drummond. Together they perform six of Walrath's quirky originals which, with titles such as "King Duke," "Ray Charles on Mars," "Spliptzill Rohenusi" and "Demons in Pursuit," lets one know that the music will not be all that predictable. Not everything works (the organ sounds dated) but overall this adventurous set is a successful effort. —*Scott Yanow*

Revenge of the Fat People / May 23, 1981 / Stash ✦✦✦✦

This Stash LP is a strong effort by the adventurous trumpeter Jack Walrath, who contributed four of the six compositions. Teamed up with tenor saxophonist Ricky Ford, pianist Michael Cochrane, bassist Cameron Brown and drummer Mike Clark, Walrath performs such numbers as the funky "Piggy Love," "Blues in the Guts," "Duke Ellington's Sound of Love" and "Beer!" The music is as colorful and as adventurous its the titles. —*Scott Yanow*

● **A Plea for Sanity** / Sep. 1982 / Stash ✦✦✦✦✦

This is one of the best showcases for Jack Walrath's trumpet playing. Well-featured in a trio with pianist Michael Cochrane and bassist Anthony Cox, Walrath plays five of his originals plus two by Cochrane. The music falls into the wide area of post-bop, more advanced than hard bop but not as free as most avant-garde music. Walrath, who has always had a gift for coming up with memorable songtitles (including on this LP "Li'l Stinker," "A Plea for Sanity" and "At Home in Rome"), gives each selection its own purpose, and his solos are full of spirit and consistent invention. Recommended. —*Scott Yanow*

At the Umbria Jazz Festival, Vol. 1 / Jul. 18, 1983 / Red ✦✦✦

On the first of two albums, trumpeter Jack Walrath (along with trombonist Glen Ferris, pianist Michael Cochrane, bassist Anthony Cox and drummer Mike Clark) stretches out on two of the leader's originals (including the nearly 27-minute "John Agar") and Cochrane's "Two in One." The playing is excellent, but little all that memorable actually occurs on this worthwhile but average post-bop set. —*Scott Yanow*

At the Umbria Jazz Festival, Vol. 2 / Jul. 18, 1983 / Red ✦✦✦✦

The second of two albums recorded by trumpeter Jack Walrath's quintet (with trombonist Glen Ferris, pianist Michael Cochrane, bassist Anthony Cox and drummer Mike Clark) is at the same level as the first. The music (long versions of four Walrath originals, including remakes of "A Plea for Sanity" and "Mucene the Genii") is well-played and adventurous, but does not stick in one's mind afterwards; in general it is easier to respect than to love, making this series of greater interest to Jack Walrath completists rather than more general listeners. —*Scott Yanow*

Wholly Trinity / Mar. 15, 1986+Apr. 1, 1986 / Muse ✦✦✦✦

This studio set is an excellent outing for trumpeter Jack Walrath, who is showcased in a trio with bassist Chip Jackson and drummer Jimmy Madison. Walrath's six originals all have their colorful moments, whether it be "(The Last Remake Of) I Can't Get Started" (which has solos based on the standard's melody rather than its chord changes), "Spherious" (based loosely on Thelonious Monk's interpretation of "Lulu's Back in Town"), the episodic "Baby, You Move Too Fast" and the group improvisation "Spontooneous." Stimulating and thought-provoking music. —*Scott Yanow*

Master of Suspense / Sep. 19, 1986 / Blue Note ✦✦✦✦✦

The biggest news of this CD by trumpeter Jack Walrath is that Willie Nelson sings and plays guitar on two numbers: "I'm Sending You a Big Bouquet of Roses" and "I'm So Lonesome I Could Cry." The other selections feature Walrath (who composed all but the two Nelson features) with a larger group than normal; a septet that includes altoist Kenny Garrett, tenor saxophonist Carter Jefferson, trombonist Steve Turre, pianist James Williams, bassist Anthony Cox and drummer Ronnie Burrage. As usual Walrath's music stretches the boundaries of hard bop without tossing away its roots. Among the more memorable titles are "Meat," "The Lord's Calypso" and "Monk on the Moon." —*Scott Yanow*

Neohippus / Aug. 19, 1988+Aug. 21, 1988 / Blue Note ✦✦✦✦✦

Trumpeter Jack Walrath's music by the mid-'80s tended to play off of the melodies of tunes and their moods rather than merely following chord changes and predictable patterns. Heading a sextet on this Blue Note CD that includes tenor saxophonist Carter Jefferson (who doubles on clarinet), guitarist John Abercrombie, pianist James Williams, bassist Anthony Cox and drummer Ronnie Burrage, Walrath performs such originals as the exciting "Village of the Darned," the somewhat scary "Fright Night," the impressionistic "England" and a remake of "Beer." Although somewhat overlooked, Jack Walrath is always well worth checking out, for he avoids the obvious and his music is full of surprises. —*Scott Yanow*

Gut Feelings / Sep. 10, 1990 / Muse ✦✦✦

Serious Hang / 1992 / Muse ✦✦✦✦

Jack Walrath and his Masters of Suspense turn to an idiom that was once among jazz's more popular, but in recent years has been almost ignored—funk/soul-jazz. Besides a decent remake of James Brown's "Get on the Good Foot," the group opens with "Anya and Liz on the Veranda" and also does Charles Mingus' "Better Get Hit in Your Soul." Walrath's trumpet and fluegelhorn solos are always intense and occasionally exciting; only the Brown remake falters, mainly because it was a textbook funk piece and doesn't translate well to a straight instrumental setting. Otherwise, the Masters of Suspense do a good job of displaying their soul-jazz chops. —*Ron Wynn*

Cedar Walton

b. Jan. 17, 1934, Dallas, TX

Piano / Hard Bop

One of the most valued of all hard bop accompanists, Walton is a versatile pianist whose funky touch and cogent melodic sense has graced the recordings of many of jazz's greatest players. He is also one of the music's more underrated composers; although he has always been a first-rate interpreter of standards, Walton wrote a number of excellent tunes ("Mosaic," "Ugetsu," and "Bolivia," to name a few) that found their way into Art Blakey's book during the pianist's early-'60s stint with the Jazz Messengers.

Walton was first taught piano by his mother. After attending the University of Denver, he moved to New York in 1955, ostensibly to play music. Instead, he was drafted into the Army. Stationed in Germany, Walton played with American musicians Leo Wright, Don Ellis, and Eddie Harris. After his discharge, Walton moved back to New York, where he began his career in earnest. From 1958-61, Walton played with Kenny Dorham, J.J. Johnson, and Art Farmer's Jazztet, among others. Walton joined Blakey in 1961, with whom he remained until '64. This was perhaps Blakey's most influential group, with Freddie Hubbard and Wayne Shorter. Walton served time as Abbey Lincoln's accompanist from 1965-66 and made records with Lee Morgan from 1966-68; from 1967-69, Walton served as a sideman on many Prestige albums as well. Walton played in a band with Hank Mobley in the early '70s and returned to Blakey for a 1973 tour of Japan. Walton's own band of the period was called Eastern Rebellion, and comprised a rotating cast that included saxophonists Clifford Jordan, George Coleman and Bob Berg, bassist Sam Jones and drummer Billy Higgins. In the '80s and '90s, Walton continued to lead his own fine bands, recording on the Muse, Evidence, and Steeple Chase labels. In addition to his many quantifiable accomplishments, Walton is less well known as the first pianist to record, in April 1959 with John Coltrane, the tenorist's daunting "Giant Steps"—unlike the unfortunate Tommy Flanagan a month later, Walton wasn't required to solo, though he does comp magnificently. —*Chris Kelsey*

Cedar! / Jul. 10, 1967 / Original Jazz Classics ✦✦✦✦✦
Pianist Cedar Walton's debut as a leader is quite impressive. This CD reissue (which includes a "new" rendition of "Take the 'A' Train") showcases Walton with bassist Leroy Vinnegar and drummer Billy Higgins on "My Ship," features a pair of quartet numbers with trumpeter Kenny Dorham, has tenor saxophonist Junior Cook in Dorham's place on two other pieces (including "Come Sunday") and uses a quintet on the two remaining selections. One of the top hard bop-based pianists to emerge during the 1960s, Walton also contributed four originals to his excellent set. —*Scott Yanow*

Plays Cedar Walton / Jul. 10, 1967-Jan. 14, 1969 / Original Jazz Classics ✦✦✦✦
1967-1969. 1988 reissue of Walton giving his own work a showcase. Host of great players, among them Kenny Dorham (tpt) and Clifford Jordan (ts). —*Ron Wynn*

Spectrum / May 24, 1968-Jan. 14, 1964 / Prestige ✦✦✦
Two of pianist Cedar Walton's lesser-known Prestige albums (*Spectrum* and *The Electric Boogaloo Song*) are combined on this single CD reissue. With strong assistance from trumpeter Blue Mitchell, tenor saxophonist Clifford Jordan and one of two rhythm sections (either Richard Davis or Bob Cranshaw on bass and Jack DeJohnette or Mickey Roker on drums), Walton performs six of his originals ("Ugetsu" is best-known while "The Electric Boogaloo Song" was an attempt at a hit), two standards, Clifford Jordan's "Impressions of Scandinavia" and Calvin Massey's "Lady Charlotte." The music, essentially advanced hard bop with a few odd twists, is well-played if not essential. —*Scott Yanow*

Soul Cycle / Jun. 25, 1969 / Original Jazz Classics ✦✦
Half of this Prestige set by Cedar Walton, which has been reissued on CD in the OJC series, is frankly commercial, with the pianist switching to electric keyboard; "My Cherie Amour" is a low point. However, there are a couple of acoustic trio features with bassist Reggie Workman and drummer Albert "Tootie" Heath, and some worthwhile if not particularly essential solos from James Moody on tenor and flute. Walton was trying to widen his audience a bit at the time—not a bad goal, except that he felt he had to water down his music on a few of these numbers. A mixed bag. —*Scott Yanow*

★ **Breakthrough** / Feb. 22, 1972 / Muse ✦✦✦✦✦
As strong as pianist Cedar Walton plays on his session, the main honors are taken by two of his sidemen. Tenor saxophonist Hank Mobley, whose career was about to go into a complete eclipse, is in brilliant form, showing how much he had grown since his earlier days. Baritonist Charles Davis, who too often through the years has been used as merely a section player, keeps up with Mobley and engages in a particularly memorable tradeoff on the lengthy title cut. Mobley is well-showcased on "Summertime," Davis switches successfully to soprano on "Early Morning Stroll" and Walton (with the trio) somehow turns the "Theme from *Love Story*" into jazz. Highly recommended. —*Scott Yanow*

A Night at Boomer's, Vol. 1 / Jan. 4, 1973 / Muse ✦✦✦✦✦
A Night at Boomer's, Vol. 2 / Jan. 4, 1973 / Muse ✦✦✦✦✦
The Pentagon / May 17, 1976 / Inner City ✦✦✦✦
Originally released by the Japanese East Wind label and made available briefly domestically on an LP from the defunct Inner City label, this quartet outing fea-

tures pianist Cedar Walton, the underrated tenor saxophonist Clifford Jordan, bassist Sam Jones and drummer Billy Higgins; Ray Mantilla adds his congas to three of the six selections. The group performs fresh versions of five jazz standards (including "Manteca," Kenny Dorham's "Una Mas" and Lester Young's "D.B. Blues") plus Jordan's "He Is a Hero." Superior to Walton's RCA recordings of the period and his upcoming output for Columbia, this obscure effort finds all of the musicians playing up to their usual level of creativity. —*Scott Yanow*

The Maestro / Dec. 15, 1980 / Muse ✦✦✦✦
The most notable aspect of this fine effort by the 1980 Cedar Walton Trio (which comprises the pianist-leader, tenor saxophonist Bob Berg, bassist Bob Williams and drummer Billy Higgins) is that Abbey Lincoln takes vocals on four of the eight selections. Lincoln (who is in top form) introduces two of her songs ("Not in Love" and "Castles") and also interprets "In a Sentimental Mood" and Walton's tribute to Duke Ellington, "The Maestro." Otherwise Walton's group plays a couple of common Thelonious Monk tunes, Jobim's "Sabia" and "On the Trail." A well-rounded and easily recommended set of advanced straightahead jazz. —*Scott Yanow*

Among Friends / Jul. 1982 / Evidence ✦✦✦✦
The music on this release was actually performed at San Francisco's Keystone Korner during a recorded engagement by the Bobby Hutcherson sextet. Pianist Cedar Walton opened each set with a few numbers, and he was playing so well that in 1990 it was decided to release his material as a separate CD. Walton performs three songs ("Ruby My Dear," "My Old Flame" and "I've Grown Accustomed to Her Face") solo, interprets four other pieces (three standards plus his own "Midnight Waltz") in a trio with bassist Buster Williams and drummer Billy Higgins, and Hutcherson himself makes the group a quartet on "My Foolish Heart." Excellent hard bop-based music from the talented pianist. —*Scott Yanow*

The Trio, Vol. 1 / Mar. 28, 1985 / Red ✦✦✦✦
There have been many Cedar Walton records put out through the years, and the three that he and his trio made during a Bologna concert in 1985 rank with his best. Joined by bassist David Williams and drummer Billy Higgins, Walton stretches out on four standards (highlighted by "My Ship") and a pair of originals ("Holy Land" and "Voices Deep Within Me") during this first volume; all are easily recommended to straightahead jazz collectors. —*Scott Yanow*

The Trio, Vol. 2 / Mar. 28, 1985 / Red ✦✦✦✦
The second of three albums recorded by pianist Cedar Walton, bassist David Williams and drummer Billy Higgins during a single concert in Bologna, Italy, is (like the other two) an excellent example of Walton's distinctive approach to hard bop. The trio stretches out on "Theme for Ernie," "For All We Know," Thelonious Monk's "Off Minor," Sonny Red's "Bluesville" and a couple of lesser-known Walton originals. —*Scott Yanow*

The Trio, Vol. 3 / Mar. 28, 1985 / Red ✦✦✦✦

Blues for Myself / Feb. 1986 / Red ✦✦✦✦✦
Cedar Walton's second set of unaccompanied solos (following his little-known Clean Cuts release *Piano Solos* by five years) features the talented veteran pianist exploring six standards (including "Without a Song" and "Just in Time") plus four of his originals. Although always a hard bop stylist, Walton was never just a one-handed pianist, and this superior release does not find him or listeners missing a bassist or drummer. Recommended. —*Scott Yanow*

Cedar Walton Plays / Sep. 29, 1986-Sep. 30, 1986 / Delos ✦✦✦✦
Pianist Cedar Walton heads a medium-size group on this 1986 Delos CD, a rhythm section with bassist Ron Carter and drummer Billy Higgins plus a five piece horn section: trumpeter Don Sickler, altoist Kenny Garrett, the obscure tenor Lou Orensteen, baritonist Charles Davis and trombonist Steve Turre. Unfortunately the horns mostly stick to ensemblework (except for an extended version of Benny Golson's "Out of the Past") but Walton and his trio are in top form on such numbers as Bud Powell's "Hallucinations," a lengthy rendition of Cole Porter's "So in Love," Nellie Lutcher's "He's a Real Gone Guy" and the leader's "Something in Common." —*Scott Yanow*

Art Blakey Legacy / Aug. 27, 1993-Aug. 28, 1993 / Evidence ✦✦✦

Composer / Jan. 9, 1996-Jan. 10, 1996 / Astor Place ✦✦✦✦✦
For Cedar Walton's debut on the Astor Place label, the widely respected veteran pianist contributed all nine selections. Although his "Bolivia" is a jazz standard, Walton is not normally thought of as a major composer. However, quite a few of his new pieces could possibly become standards in the future if jazz improvisers explore this disc. Of the more memorable originals, "Martha's Prize" has a light cheerful melody, "The Vision" gives Ralph Moore an opportunity to show just how distinctive he can sound on soprano, "Happiness" is a joyful hard bop tune a little reminiscent of "Little Rock Getaway" with a bridge added, "Underground Memoirs" (which has a particularly strong Walton solo) is a haunting ballad and "Theme For Jobim" swings with a strong bossa beat. The all-star lineup (trum-

peter Roy Hargrove, altoist Vincent Herring, Ralph Moore on tenor and soprano, bassist Christian McBride and drummer Vic Lewis) plays up to their potential, with Hargrove sometimes recalling Freddie Hubbard, Moore and Herring getting in their spots and the ensemble on a whole sometimes resembling the Jazz Messengers; due to the voicings, there are times when one would swear that a trombone was present. Highly recommended. — *Scott Yanow*

Carlos Ward

b. May 1, 1940, Ancon, Panama Canal Zone
Alto Saxophone, Tenor Saxophone, Flute / Post-Bop

A superior altoist whose bluesy sound is often more accessible than the music he plays, Carlos Ward is best known at this point as a valuable sideman. He grew up in Seattle, started on clarinet when he was 13, and while in the military studied at the Navy School of Music. He had opportunities to play music while stationed in Germany (including with Albert Mangelsdorff), where he heard Eric Dolphy, a major influence on his sound. After being discharged, Ward sat in regularly with John Coltrane during 'Trane's 1965 visit to Seattle, and after moving to New York, he also played with Coltrane's unrecorded octet. Ward freelanced in New York, performing with top "new jazz" artists including Sunny Murray, Don Cherry, Sam Rivers, Rashied Ali and Paul Motian. He joined the Jazz Composers' Orchestra, yet also was a part of B.T. Express, a big-selling funk group.

More important in the long run was his meeting pianist/composer Abdullah Ibrahim, with whom Ward has played off and on since 1973. Other important associations include membership in Don Cherry's mid-1980s bands, as well as filling in for the late Jimmy Lyons with the Cecil Taylor Unit in 1986. As a leader, Carlos Ward's only recording thus far is a quartet date with Woody Shaw for Leo (1988). — *Scott Yanow*

● **Lito** / Jul. 9, 1988 / Leo ✦✦✦✦

Live date at the North Sea Jazz Festival for saxophonist/flutist with quartet featuring trumpeter Woody Shaw. Extended work. Excellent. — *Michael G. Nastos*

David S. Ware

b. Nov. 7, 1949, Plainfield, NJ
Tenor Saxophone / Avant-Garde, Free Jazz

The critical buzz aroused by David S. Ware's work with Andrew Cyrille and Cecil Taylor in the '70s had, by the late '90s, turned into a consonant roar. New York's collective jazz press—always on the lookout for the music's next messiah—crowned Ware the "King of Free Jazz" on the basis of his energetic quartet albums from the mid-'90s. Ware's band (with Matthew Shipp on piano, William Parker on bass, and, variously, Susie Ibarra, Marc Edwards, or Whit Dickey on drums) became the decade's avant-garde supergroup by consensus. On closer listening, the unqualified praise received by the group seems merited mainly by its leader. Ware is indeed a splendid artist. His saxophone technique is total; unlike a good many free players, Ware does not base his style on any particular technical shortcoming or theoretical misunderstanding. His knowledge of functional harmony is above and beyond that of virtually any other free saxophonist. He's learned both the music and the horn up and down, inside and out, from the bottom up. In this respect, he's a true heir to Coltrane, who also based his free work on a comprehensive knowledge of his materials. Indeed, Ware's typical manner of performance—modal/free, rubato, high-energy collective improvisation—stems directly from *Meditations*-era Coltrane.

Ware's tenor sound is huge, centered, and multi-hued, all up and down its range. His facility is great, his imagination broad, and his expressive abilities immense. And no saxophonist now active plays with more unadulterated passion. Without question, he is a very, very fine, maybe even great, player. His band, however, while certainly capable, has not proved to be on his level. Shipp is an excellent, Cecil Taylor-cum-McCoy Tyner pianist, but his best work has come as a leader of his own trio. With Ware, he often seems at a loss as to what to say in the midst of the band's hyperkinetic collective improvisations—overwhelmed, or so it seems, by Ware's volcanic passion. Ware's finest, most complementary drummer has been Marc Edwards, a more roughly hewn and spontaneous player than the glib Ibarra and the coloristic Dickey. Of Ware's bandmates, only Parker is his equal as a creative presence. William Parker generates energy like no other bassist; a band with Parker on bass doesn't need a drummer, so powerful is his percussive drive.

Ware played alto, tenor and bari saxes in his teens. In the late '60s, he attended Berklee School of Music in Boston. There, he formed a band called Apogee, which played around Boston until 1973, when the band moved *en masse* to New York. In 1974, Ware performed in a large Cecil Taylor aggregation at Carnegie Hall. The mid-'70s found Ware a member of drummer Andrew Cyrille's group, in a trio with trumpeter Raphe Malik and on tour with Taylor. In 1977, he played in bop pianist Barry Harris' band; the two recorded a duo album that same year. Beginning in

the late '80s, he renewed his association with Cyrille, and played on the drummer's highly acclaimed Black Saint release, *Metamusicians' Stomp*. As a leader, Ware's recording career began in earnest with a pair of releases on the Silkheart label—1988's *Passage to Music* and 1990s *Great Bliss, Vol. 1*. In the early '90s, Ware began recording for the Japanese DIW label; that company's 1991 release, *Flight of i*, was distributed by Columbia, and remains in many ways the tenorist's most stunning work. The late '90s had Ware recording with his quartet for a number of independent companies, including most notably the alternative-rock (and now-defunct) Homestead label. — *Chris Kelsey*

Passage to Music / Apr. 4, 1988-Apr. 5, 1988 / Silkheart ✦✦✦✦

A fiery avant-garde tenor saxophonist, David Ware had recorded two early sets for Hat Hut and Palm during 1977-78; a decade later he had his third opportunity to lead a record session. Joined by bassist William Parker and drummer Marc Edwards, Ware performs five of his free jazz originals, mostly on tenor but also playing one song apiece on saxello and stritch. Not for the weak-of-heart, David Ware's searching improvisations reward repeated listenings by open-eared listeners. — *Scott Yanow*

Great Bliss, Vol. 1 / Jan. 1990 / Silkheart ✦✦✦✦

● **Flight of i** / Dec. 10, 1991+Dec. 11, 1991 / Columbia ✦✦✦✦✦

Third Ear Recitation / Oct. 14, 1992-Oct. 15, 1992 / DIW ✦✦✦✦

Wilbur Ware

b. Sep. 8, 1923, Chicago, IL, **d.** Sep. 9, 1979, Philadelphia, PA
Bass / Hard Bop

A creative bassist whose subtle and flexible style allowed him to feel comfortable in styles ranging from swing-based mainstream to fairly free, Wilbur Ware was at his best in advanced hard bop settings. He actually started on the banjo before switching to bass. Ware played with Roy Eldridge and Sonny Stitt as early as 1946, but did not come to prominence until the 1950s. He was a member of the house band at the Flame Lounge in Chicago, recorded with Johnny Griffin in 1954, joined the Jazz Messengers in 1956, was part of Thelonious Monk's legendary quartet with John Coltrane in 1957, made many recordings as a sideman for the Riverside label, and played with Sonny Rollins at the Village Vanguard. He was knocked out of action by illness during much of the 1963-68 period, but then became a bit more active during his last decade. He later worked with Archie Shepp, Elvin Jones, Blue Mitchell and Sun Ra. A harmonically advanced player who always swung, Wilbur Ware only led one recording session, a Riverside date from 1957 that has been reissued on CD in the Original Jazz Classics series. — *Scott Yanow*

● **Chicago Sound** / Oct. 16, 1957+Nov. 18, 1957 / Original Jazz Classics ✦✦✦✦✦

Bassist Wilbur Ware's only recording as a leader (which has been reissued on CD) mostly features Chicago musicians. Although Ware heads the set and contributed two originals, he does not dominate the music and delegated plenty of solo space to altoist John Jenkins (who also brought in two tunes), tenor saxophonist Johnny Griffin and pianist Junior Mance; Wilbur Campbell or Frank Dunlop on drums complete the group. This fine hard bop date (which also has versions of "Body and Soul," Stuff Smith's "Desert Sands," "Lullaby of the Leaves" and "The Man I Love") was a fine debut by Ware. It seems strange that in his remaining 20 plus years the bassist never led another album. — *Scott Yanow*

Butch Warren

b. Sep. 8, 1939, Washington, DC
Bass / Hard Bop

Throughout his career, Butch Warren was a bit of a throwback to an earlier era, when bassists stuck to walking behind soloists. Although a fairly modern player, Warren was only an occasional soloist and was at his best accompanying other musicians. His first professional job was playing in his father Edward Warren's group at age 14. Early on, the bassist worked locally in the Washington, D.C. area, most notably with Stuff Smith. In 1958, he moved to New York to play with Kenny Dorham at the Five Spot and stayed in town throughout most of his career. During the next six years, Warren was in great demand for club work and appeared on many recordings, particularly dates for the Blue Note label led by Joe Henderson, Jackie McLean, Stanley Turrentine, Donald Byrd, Herbie Hancock, Dexter Gordon, Sonny Clark and Dorham. He was a member of Thelonious Monk's Quartet from 1963-64 and then moved back to Washington, D.C., where he worked on a television show from 1965-66. After becoming seriously ill, Butch Warren largely dropped out of music, although he has played on a part-time basis (including with Richie Cole in 1975) during the past 25 years. Unfortunately, he never had an opportunity to lead his own record date. — *Scott Yanow*

Earle Warren

b. Jul. 1, 1914, Springfield, OH, **d.** 1995, Springfield, OH
Alto Saxophone / Swing

Earle Warren was Count Basie's longtime lead altoist and occasional pop ballad singer. He played piano, banjo and ukulele in a family band before taking up the saxophone, eventually settling on the alto. He led bands in the Midwest during part of the 1930s before joining Basie in 1937. Until the breakup of the band at the end of 1949, Warren was a strong presence in the saxophone section, even though he rarely was given a full solo. In later years he worked as manager for a variety of R&B acts, had opportunities to solo with Buck Clayton's groups, was featured in the 1970s film *Born to Swing* and headed the Countsmen starting in 1973. —*Scott Yanow*

● **The Count's Men** / Jul. 9, 1985 / Muse ✦✦✦✦

Three of Count Basie's alumni (altoist Earle Warren, trombonist Eddie Durham and bassist Jimmy Lewis) team together with pianist Don Coates and drummer Clarence "Tootsie" Bean for a set of music dominated by Count Basie-associated material. It is a particular pleasure to hear Warren and Durham at this late stage in their careers. It had been quite a while since Warren (who takes five vocals) had recorded as a singer, and Durham had been off records for a long time. Nothing that unusual occurs (one wishes that they had added a trumpeter, say, Harry "Sweets" Edison), but this historical set always swings. —*Scott Yanow*

Washboard Rhythm Kings

f. 1930, **db.** 1935
Group / Classic Jazz

The Washboard Rhythm Kings (which had different personnel on each session) played jubilant jazz that defied the soothing musical trend of the early Depression years, featuring a washboard player and usually a couple of horns along with spirited group vocals. The emphasis was on basic goodtime music that fell between Dixieland and swing. They debuted as the Alabama Washboard Stompers in 1930, became the Washboard Rhythm Kings in 1931 and by 1934-35 were known as the Georgia Washboard Stompers. Some of the personnel has never been identified, but among the known players are guitarist Teddy Bunn, trumpeters Taft Jordan and Valaida Snow, singer Leo Watson and such regulars as singer Jake Fenderson, Steve Washington on banjo and vocals, and Ben Smith on clarinet and alto. —*Scott Yanow*

Washboard Rhythm Kings: Walter Barnes Royal Creolians / Dec. 14, 1928-Oct. 5, 1932 / Harrison ✦✦✦✦

This collector's LP has eight selections by the Washboard Rhythm Kings (taken from two sessions) plus all seven titles that were recorded by the ill-fated Walter Barnes and his Royal Creolians; the latter band (a fine 12-piece hot jazz group) perished in a fire a few years later. The Washboard Rhythm Kings' performances (which feature trumpeter Valaida Snow among the three or four horns, plus vocals by Lavada Carter and banjoist Steve Washington) have since been reissued on CD, but the Barnes' titles are difficult to find, as is this valuable LP. —*Scott Yanow*

Washboard Rhythm Kings, Vol. 5 / Mar. 24, 1930-Jul. 19, 1935 / Collector's Classics ✦✦✦✦✦

The fifth CD in the Collector's Classics series on the Washboard Rhythm Kings stretches beyond the original boundaries. In fact, out of the 23 selections, only four (from a 1931 date) were actually recorded by the Washboard Rhythm Kings. The other groups (the Washboard Serenaders, the Scorpion Washboard Band, the Tramp Band and the Rhythm Kings) have similar instrumentation and sometimes overlapping personnel, including guitarist Teddy Bunn, pianist Clarence Profit and perhaps trumpeter Henry Red Allen on two cuts. This goodtime music often utilizes not just a washboard but a kazoo, heated rhythm sections and occasional horns and vocals, and does not really require close study in order to enjoy. Highlights include such numbers as "Kazoo Moan," "Washboards Get Together," "Nagasaki," "Dinah" and "You Rascal You." —*Scott Yanow*

● **Washboard Rhythm Kings, Vol. 1** / Apr. 2, 1931-Mar. 1, 1932 / Collector's Classics ✦✦✦✦✦

The Washboard Rhythm Kings (whose personnel changed from session to session) was an unusual group to be on records during the early part of the Depression, for it was a goodtime band usually featuring a washboard, spirited vocals, an occasional kazoo and a few horns. There were no major soloists in the group (guitarist Teddy Bunn, who is on ten of the 24 selections on this first volume, comes the closest) and they mostly covered current hits from other artists (including on this CD "Minnie the Moocher," "Walkin' My Baby Back Home," "You Rascal You," "I'm Crazy 'Bout My Baby," "Stardust" and "Georgia on My Mind"), but they were always a fun band to hear. This Swedish import CD has The Washboard Rhythm Kings' first two dozen recordings. —*Scott Yanow*

Washboard Rhythm Kings, Vol. 2 / Mar. 1, 1932-Nov. 23, 1932 / Collector's Classics ✦✦✦✦✦

Although the personnel of the Washboard Rhythm Kings changed a bit from session to session, the uninhibited swing, goodtime vocals and spirited ensembles were consistent features of their many recordings. The second CD in this series has four complete sessions from 1932. The sidemen include either Dave Riddick, Taft Jordan or Dave Page on trumpet, Jimmy Shine, Ben Smith and/or Carl Wade on reeds and such rhythm-section players as banjoist Steve Washington and drummer Leo Watson. Not all of the selections are classics but all are quite enjoyable, including "You Can Depend on Me," "Was That the Human Thing to Do," "Tiger Rag," "Somebody Stole Gabriel's Horn" and "Sloppy Drunk Blues." —*Scott Yanow*

Washboard Rhythm Kings, Vol. 3 / Oct. 5, 1932-Aug. 19, 1933 / Collector's Classics ✦✦✦✦✦

This CD contains three complete sessions by the prolific Washboard Rhythm Kings, originally cut for the Vocalion and Banner labels (the later recordings on Columbia and Bluebird are bypassed), including the group's last date. Three different overlapping groups are featured. The first six songs utilize several vocalists (including Lavaida Snow, Bella Benson and banjoist Steve Washington) along with fine trumpet work from Valaida Snow. The second date (which resulted in ten songs) has mostly unidentified personnel, other than Steve Washington, who takes vocals on all but one of the tunes, while the final session uses an expanded seven-piece horn section and has bassist George "Ghost" Howell's spirited vocals. The good time music (which features a washboard prominent in the ensembles) is hard-swinging and quite enjoyable. An early vocal version of "I'm Gettin' Sentimental Over You" is an oddity, while the highlights include "Sentimental Gentleman From Georgia," "I Would Do Anything for You," "Blue Drag," "Dog and Cat" and "Old Man Blues." —*Scott Yanow*

Washboard Rhythm Kings, Vol. 4 / Mar. 8, 1933-Sep. 12, 1933 / Collector's Classics ✦✦✦✦✦

This fourth CD from Collector's Classics (a subsidiary of Storyville) had three complete sessions from 1933 by three overlapping groups: the Washboard Rhythm Band, the Washboard Rhythm Kings and Williams' Washboard Band. The latter features vocals and trumpet playing by Taft Jordan (a future member of the Chick Webb and Duke Ellington orchestras) that are purposely near-copies of Louis Armstrong. Trumpeter Dave Page and singer Cal Clement take the vocals on the second date, while guitarist Ted Tinsley vocalizes on the final recordings. The goodtime music features five horns, piano, guitar, bass and washboard, with pianist Clarence Profit the best known of the sidemen. Highlights of the joyous set (which contrasts greatly with the Depression that was raging at the time) include "Hustlin' and Bustlin' for Baby," "Dinah," "Happy As the Day Is Long" and "Hot Nuts." —*Scott Yanow*

Dinah Washington (Ruth Lee Jones)

b. Aug. 29, 1924, Tuscaloosa, AL, **d.** Dec. 14, 1963, Detroit, MI
Vocals / Standards, Traditional Pop, Classic Female Blues, Ballads, Jump Blues, Pop

Dinah Washington was at once one of the most beloved and controversial singers of the mid-20th century—beloved to her fans, devotees and fellow singers; controversial to critics, who still accuse her of selling out her art to commerce and bad taste. Her principal sin, apparently, was to cultivate a distinctive vocal style that was at home in all kinds of music, be it R&B, blues, jazz, middle-of-the-road pop—and she probably would have made a fine gospel or country singer had she the time. Hers was a gritty, salty, high-pitched voice, marked by absolute clarity of diction and clipped, bluesy phrasing. Dinah's personal life was turbulent, with seven marriages behind her, and her interpretations showed it, for she displayed a tough, totally unsentimental, yet still gripping hold on the universal subject of lost love. She has had a huge influence on R&B and jazz singers who have followed in her wake, notably Nancy Wilson, Esther Phillips and Diane Schuur, and her music is abundantly available nowadays via the huge seven-volume series *The Complete Dinah Washington on Mercury*.

Born Ruth Lee Jones, she moved to Chicago at age three and was raised in a world of gospel, playing the piano and directing her church choir. At 15, after winning an amateur contest at the Regal Theatre, she began performing in nightclubs as a pianist and singer, opening at the Garrick Bar in 1942. Talent manager Joe Glaser heard her there and recommended her to Lionel Hampton, who asked her to join his band. Hampton says that it was he who gave Ruth Jones the name Dinah Washington, although other sources claim it was Glaser or the manager of the Garrick Bar. In any case, she stayed with Hampton from 1943 to 1946 and made her recording debut for Keynote at the end of 1943 in a blues session organized by Leonard Feather with a sextet drawn from the Hampton band. With Feather's "Evil Gal Blues" as her first hit, the records took off, and by the time she left Hampton to go solo, Washington was already an R&B headliner. Signing with the young Mercury label, Washington produced an enviable string of Top Ten hits on the R&B charts from 1948 to 1955, singing blues, standards, novelties, pop covers, even Hank Williams' "Cold, Cold Heart." She also recorded many straight jazz sessions with big bands and small combos, most memorably with Clifford Brown on *Dinah Jams* but also with Cannonball Adderley, Clark Terry, Ben Webster, Wynton Kelly, and the young Joe Zawinul (who was her regular accompanist for a couple of years).

In 1959, Washington made a sudden breakthrough into the mainstream pop market with "What a Diff'rence a Day Makes," a revival of a Dorsey Brothers hit set to a Latin American bolero tune. For the rest of her career, she would concentrate on singing ballads backed by lush orchestrations for Mercury and Roulette, a formula similar to that of another R&B-based singer at that time, Ray Charles, and one that drew plenty of fire from critics, even though her basic vocal approach had not changed one iota. Although her later records could be as banal as any easy-listening dross of the period, there are gems to be found, like Billie Holiday's "Don't Explain," which has a beautiful, bluesy Ernie Wilkins chart conducted by Quincy Jones. Struggling with a weight problem, Washington died of an accidental overdose of diet pills mixed with alcohol at the tragically early age of 39, still in peak voice, still singing the blues in an L.A. club only two weeks before the end. —*Richard S. Ginell*

The Best of the Blues / Dec. 29, 1943-Jun. 10, 1953 / Verve ◆◆◆

Slick Chick: R&B Years / Dec. 29, 1943-Nov. 17, 1954 / EmArcy ◆◆◆◆◆

This double LP has the cream of Dinah Washington's early recordings. She recorded extensively for Mercury and EmArcy, and all of the performances are available on multi-disc sets but, for those listeners who want just a sampling of Dinah Washington at her best, this two-fer is the one to get. All 16 of her R&B hits from 1949-54 are here, plus her very first recording session (which is highlighted by the original version of "Evil Gal Blues") and seven other selections. Whether backed by the Gerald Wilson Orchestra, Tab Smith, Cootie Williams, an all-star unit headed by drummer Jimmy Cobb or studio orchestras, she is in superb form. —*Scott Yanow*

Wise Woman Blues / 1943-Aug. 26, 1963 / Rosetta ◆◆◆◆

This Rosetta LP draws its material from three sources. Eight of the 15 recordings are from Dinah Washington's Apollo sessions of December 1945 (all of which are included on Delmark's CD). Six songs are taken from live performances with Lionel Hampton's orchestra during 1943-3 and "Do Nothing Till You Hear from Me" is a real rarity with Washington backed by Duke Ellington's Orchestra in 1963. The extensive liner notes (which have ten pictures of the singer from various stages of her career) are a major plus. —*Scott Yanow*

Mellow Mama / Dec. 10, 1945-Dec. 13, 1945 / Delmark ◆◆◆◆◆

Dinah Washington's first solo recordings (with the exception of a session supervised by Lionel Hampton in 1943) are included on this Delmark repackaging of her Apollo sides. Recorded in Los Angeles during a three-day period, the 12 selections feature the singer with a swinging jazz combo that has tenor saxophonist Lucky Thompson, trumpeter Karl George, vibraphonist Milt Jackson and bassist Charles Mingus among its eight members. The 21-year-old Washington was already quite distinctive at this early stage and easily handles the blues and jive material with color and humor. Recommended despite the brevity (34 minutes) of the CD. —*Scott Yanow*

★ **The Complete Dinah Washington on Mercury, Vol. 1 (1946-1949)** / Jan. 14, 1946-Sep. 27, 1949 / Mercury ◆◆◆◆◆

All of Dinah Washington's studio recordings from 1946-61 have been reissued in definitive fashion by Polygram on seven three CD sets. *Volume 1* finds the youthful singer (who was 21 on the earliest sessions) evolving from a little-known but already talented singer to a best-selling R&B artist. Ranging from jazz and spirited blues to middle-of-the-road ballads, this set (as with the others in the *Complete* series) includes both gems and duds, but fortunately the great majority fall into the former category. The backup groups include orchestras led by Gerald Wilson, Tab Smith, Cootie Williams, Chubby Jackson and Teddy Stewart, and there are a dozen strong numbers with just a rhythm section. The first five volumes in this series are highly recommended. —*Scott Yanow*

Verve Jazz Masters 19: Dinah Washington / Oct. 3, 1946-Oct. 6, 1959 / Verve ◆◆◆◆

Dinah Washington's *Verve Jazz Masters, Vol. 19* may not be a definitive overview of her time at the label, but it's nevertheless a good 16-track sampler, containing excellent versions of such songs as "What a Diff'rence a Day Makes," "Please Send Me Someone to Love," "Cold, Cold Heart," "This Can't Be Love," "A Foggy Day," "Pennies from Heaven," "Our Love Is Here to Stay" and "Unforgettable." —*Stephen Thomas Erlewine*

☆ **The Complete Dinah Washington on Mercury, Vol. 2 (1950-1952)** / Feb. 7, 1950-May 6, 1952 / Mercury ◆◆◆◆◆

Dinah Washington was a best-selling artist on the R&B charts during this period, but she was also a very versatile singer who could easily handle swinging jazz, schmaltzy ballads, blues and novelties with equal skill. The second of these seven three-CD sets in Mercury's *Complete* program mostly finds Washington being accompanied by studio orchestras although the Ravens join her on two numbers and drummer Jimmy Cobb heads a couple of jazz groups (including one with both Ben Webster and Wardell Gray on tenors). Not every selection is a classic but the quality level is quite high and the packaging is impeccable. Recommended. —*Scott Yanow*

☆ **Complete Dinah Washington on Mercury, Vol. 3 (1952-1954)** / 1952-Aug. 14, 1954 / Mercury ◆◆◆◆◆

Of the seven three-CD sets in Mercury's *Complete* series of Dinah Washington recordings, this is the most jazz-oriented one. The versatile singer participates in a very memorable jam session with an all-star group (featuring Clifford Brown, Maynard Ferguson and Clark Terry on trumpets!), meets up with Terry and tenor saxophonist Eddie Lockjaw Davis on another spontaneous date (highlighted by uptempo romps on "Bye Bye Blues" and "Blue Skies") and has several classic collaborations with the warm Lester Youngish tenor of Paul Quinichette. There are a few commercial sides with studio orchestras that are included (since they took place during the same period), but those are in the great minority on this essential volume. —*Scott Yanow*

Dinah Jams / Aug. 15, 1954 / EmArcy ◆◆◆◆◆

☆ **Complete Dinah Washington on Mercury, Vol. 4 (1954-1956)** / Nov. 2, 1954-Apr. 25, 1956 / Mercury ◆◆◆◆◆

The fourth of seven three-CD sets in Mercury's *Complete* series alternates between strong swinging jazz with the likes of trumpeter Clark Terry, tenor saxophonist Paul Quinichette, pianist Wynton Kelly and altoist Cannonball Adderley, and middle-of-the-road pop performances with studio orchestras. The third volume is the strongest in this series, but the first five sets all contain more than enough jazz to justify their purchase. *Vol. 4* really attests to Dinah Washington's versatility. —*Scott Yanow*

☆ **Complete Dinah Washington on Mercury, Vol. 5 (1956-1958)** / Jun. 25, 1956-Jul. 6, 1958 / Mercury ◆◆◆◆◆

Mercury has given the great singer Dinah Washington the complete treatment with seven three-CD sets that contain all of her recordings during the 1946-61 period, practically her entire career. *Vol. 5* is the final volume to be highly recommended, since it has her final jazz recordings. On many of these performances she is backed by orchestras led by Quincy Jones, Ernie Wilkins (including a tribute to Fats Waller) or Eddie Chamblee in arrangements that often leave room for short statements from some of the sidemen; one of the albums with Chamblee has a full set of songs associated with Bessie Smith. *Vol. 5* (which contains only a few commercial sides) concludes with her strong performance at the 1958 Newport Jazz Festival. —*Scott Yanow*

The Bessie Smith Songbook / Dec. 30, 1957-Jan. 20, 1958 / EmArcy ◆◆◆

It was only natural that the "Queen of the Blues" should record songs associated with the "Empress of the Blues." The performances by the septet/octet do not sound like the 1920s and the purposely ricky-tick drumming is insulting, but Dinah Washington sounds quite at home on this music. "Trombone Butter" (featuring trombonist Quentin Jackson in Charlie Green's role), "You've Been a Good Ole Wagon," "After You've Gone" and "Back Water Blues" are high points as she overcomes the cornball arrangements. —*Scott Yanow*

The Ultimate Dinah Washington / 1957-1961 / Verve ◆◆◆

Abbey Lincoln compiled *The Ultimate Dinah Washington*, a 16-track selection of her best-known songs that offers an excellent introduction to her Verve recordings. Although purists and collectors will have little use for this set, it suits the purposes of neophytes and curious listeners quite well. Among the highlights are "What a Diff'rence a Day Made," "Back Water Blues," "Cry Me a River," "I Wanna Be Loved," "Cold, Cold Heart," "Harbor Lights," "You Don't Know What Love Is," "I Won't Cry Anymore," "Unforgettable" and "This Bitter Earth." —*Stephen Thomas Erlewine*

What a Diff'rence a Day Makes! / Feb. 19, 1959-Aug. 1959 / Mercury ◆◆◆◆

Dinah Washington's career reached a turning point with this album. A very talented singer who could interpret jazz, blues, pop, novelties and religious songs with equal skill, Washington had an unexpected pop hit with her straightforward version of "What a Diff'rence a Day Makes." From then on she would only record with commercial studio orchestras and stick to middle-of-the-road pop music. This 1959 set is not as bad as what would follow, with such songs as "I Remember You," "I Thought About You," "Manhattan" and "A Sunday Kind of Love" all receiving tasteful melodic treatment (although no chances are taken) by Washington and an orchestra conducted and arranged by Belford Hendricks. —*Scott Yanow*

Complete Dinah Washington on Mercury, Vol. 6 (1958-1960) / Feb. 19, 1959-Nov. 12, 1960 / Mercury ♦♦

Up until 1959, Dinah Washington was able to excel in every musical setting that she found herself. A strong jazz/blues vocalist who had many R&B hits, Washington always sounded confident and soulful even when backed by insipid studio orchestras. However after her Feb. 19, 1959, recording of "What a Diff'rence a Day Makes" became a major hit and she gained fame, Dinah Washington stuck to safely commercial pop music. Even when she was singing superior songs during the 1959-63 period, Washington was always backed by large orchestras outfitted with extremely commercial charts better suited to country-pop stars. The sixth in Mercury's series of three-CD sets starts with the Feb. 19 session and covers 21 months in Dinah Washington's career. Most of the 73 performances are difficult to sit through. —*Scott Yanow*

Unforgettable / Aug. 1959-Jan. 15, 1961 / Mercury ♦♦

After her hit "What a Diff'rence a Day Makes" in 1959, Dinah Washington largely discarded her blues and jazz roots (at least on recordings) and played the role of a pop star. This CD (which has the original LP program of 12 songs joined by six others) finds Washington singing brief (mostly under three-minute) versions of standards in hopes of gaining another hit. The backing is strictly commercial and, although some may enjoy "This Bitter Earth," "The Song Is Ended" and "A Bad Case of the Blues," the music is consistently predictable and disappointingly forgettable. —*Scott Yanow*

Complete Dinah Washington on Mercury, Vol. 7 (1961) / 1961 / Mercury ♦♦

The seventh and final volume in Mercury's *Complete* series of Dinah Washington's recordings has impeccable packaging and largely inferior music, at least from the jazz standpoint. After recording a surprising hit version of "What a Diff'rence a Day Makes" in 1959, the singer stuck exclusively to middle-of-the-road pop music with large string orchestras on her recordings. This three-CD set (which contains Washington's final 67 recordings for Mercury plus a recently discovered alternate take from 1947) totally lacks surprises, suspense or spontaneity. For completists only, but get the first five volumes. —*Scott Yanow*

In Love / May 1962-Aug. 1962 / Roulette ♦♦

Dinah Washington's final four years of recordings (1959-63) were purely commercial. Even her mannerisms and phrasing leaned closer to middle-of-the-road pop than to her roots in jazz and blues. For this so-so Roulette CD, Washington interprets standards and current pop tunes in very predictable fashion. Everything has the impression of being planned in advance and the accompanying orchestra (arranged by Don Costa) is quite anonymous. Pass on this and get Dinah Washington's earlier jazz sides instead. —*Scott Yanow*

Back to the Blues / Jul. 5, 1962-Nov. 29, 1962 / Roulette ♦♦♦♦♦

Prior to her 1959 hit "What a Diff'rence a Day Makes," nearly every Dinah Washington recording (no matter what the style) was of interest to jazz listeners. However, after her unexpected success on the pop charts, most of Washington's sessions for Mercury and Roulette during the last four years of her life were quite commercial, with string arrangements better suited to country singers and Dinah nearly parodying herself with exaggerated gestures. Fortunately, this 1997 CD reissue brings back an exception, a blues-oriented collection that features Washington returning to her roots, backed by a jazz-oriented big band (although with occasional strings and background voices), in addition to the original program, there are previously unreleased versions of "No One Man" and "Me and My Gin." Eddie Chamblee and Illinois Jacquet have some tenor solos, guitarist Billy Butler is heard from and the trumpet soloist is probably Joe Newman. In general, this is a more successful date than Dinah Washington's earlier investigation of Bessie Smith material, since the backup band is more sympathetic and the talented singer is heard in prime form. Dinah Washington clearly had a real feeling for this bluesy material. —*Scott Yanow*

Jazz Profile, Vol. 5 / 1962-1963 / Blue Note ♦♦♦

This set is a bit out of place in this collector's series, for it is really a gap-filler, mostly comprising Dinah Washington recordings from her last two years that have not yet (with a few exceptions) been included in other CD reissues. Washington was at her best prior to 1959, but her later recordings are not without interest. Backed by an unidentified big band with occasional strings (why is no personnel given?), the music is superior to Dinah's later Mercury records and shows that she was still very much in her prime. Also obvious is how much of an influence she became on many black female singers that followed her. An excellent overview of her last period, recorded just prior to Washington's premature death, the 14 selections (highlighted by "The Blues Ain't Nothin'" and "I Wanna Be Around") are taken from six of her seven Roulette albums. —*Scott Yanow*

Dinah '63 / 1963 / Roulette ♦♦

It is fairly easy to evaluate Dinah Washington's recordings. Before 1959 virtually everything she recorded (even when in a commercial setting) is worth acquiring, but the opposite is true of the records from her final period (1959-63). As a pop artist, Washington was better than many but only a shadow of what she had been. Her pre-planned emotions and exaggerated mannerisms on her Roulette recordings (of which *Dinah '63* was one of her last) get tiring very fast. —*Scott Yanow*

Grover Washington, Jr.

b. Dec. 12, 1943, Buffalo, NY

Tenor Saxophone, Soprano Saxophone, Alto Saxophone / Soul Jazz, Crossover Jazz, Groove

One of the most popular saxophonists of all time (even his off records have impressive sales), Grover Washington, Jr., has long been the pacesetter in his field. His roots are in R&B and soul-jazz organ combos, but he also fares very well on the infrequent occasions when he plays straightahead jazz. A highly influential player, Washington has sometimes been blamed for the faults of his followers; Kenny G. largely based his soprano sound on Grover's tone. However, most of the time (except when relying on long hit medleys), Washington pushes himself with the spontaneity and chance-taking of a masterful jazz musician.

Grover Washington, Jr., whose father also played saxophone, started playing music when he was ten and within two years was working in clubs. He picked up experience touring with the Four Clefs from 1959-63 and freelancing during the next two years, before spending a couple years in the Army. He moved to Philadelphia in 1967, becoming closely identified with the city ever since, and worked with several organists including Charles Earland and Johnny Hammond Smith, recording as a sideman for the Prestige label. His biggest break occurred in 1971, when Hank Crawford could not make it to a recording date; Washington was picked as his replacement, and the result was *Inner City Blues*, a big seller. From then on he became a major name, particularly after recording 1975's *Mister Magic* and 1980s *Winelight;* the latter included the Bill Withers hit "Just the Two of Us."

Although some of his recordings since then find him coasting a bit, Washington usually stretches himself in concert, being almost overqualified for the R&B-ish music that he performs. He has developed his own personal voices on soprano, tenor, alto and even his infrequently used baritone. Grover Washington, Jr., has recorded as a leader for Kudu, Motown, Elektra and Columbia and has made notable guest appearances on dozens of records ranging from pop to straightforward jazz. —*Scott Yanow*

Inner City Blues / Sep. 1971 / Kudu ♦♦♦♦♦

Grover Washington, Jr.'s debut as a leader is a classic of its kind. Straddling the boundary between soul jazz and R&B-ish crossover, Washington on alto and tenor (under the direction of Creed Taylor and utilizing the arrangements of Bob James) puts plenty of feeling into his soulful versions of "Mercy Mercy Me," "Ain't No Sunshine," "Georgia on My Mind" and "I Loves You Porgy." It is obvious from listening to this music alone that he was destined to be a star. —*Scott Yanow*

All the King's Horses / May 19, 1972-Jun. 1972 / Kudu ♦♦♦♦

Grover Washington, Jr.'s second album as a leader once again utilizes Bob James arrangements for a string orchestra and a notable horn section. The backup group includes James' electric piano, organist Richard Tee and guitarist Eric Gale. Not as many high points are reached as on his debut but Washington is typically soulful on such numbers as "Where Is The Love," "Lean on Me" and "Lover Man," alternating quite effectively between tenor and alto. —*Scott Yanow*

Soul Box / Mar. 1973 / Kudu ♦♦♦♦

This deluxe two-LP box set features Grover Washington, Jr., in prime early form. As with many of his Kudu recordings, it is long overdue to be reissued on CD. Washington, who switches between tenor, alto and soprano (making his recording debut on the latter), puts a lot of emotion and soul into such songs as "You Are The Sunshine of My Life," a lengthy "Don't Explain" and a medley of "Easy Living" and "Ain't Nobody's Bizness If I Do." Backed by a large string, brass and woodwind orchestra arranged by Bob James, Grover Washington, Jr., even sounds strong on the weaker originals, and shows throughout why he is considered the pacesetter of R&B-ish jazz. —*Scott Yanow*

● **Mister Magic** / Nov. 1974 / MoJazz ♦♦♦♦♦

This is one of Grover Washington, Jr.'s best-loved recordings and considered a classic of R&B-ish jazz. All four songs (which include Billy Strayhorn's "Passion Flower") are quite enjoyable, but it is "Mister Magic" that really caught on as a major hit. Bob James provided the colorful if somewhat commercial arrangements, there are spots for guitarist Eric Gale, and Washington (mostly on tenor and soprano) is heard in particularly creative form. Highly recommended. —*Scott Yanow*

Feels So Good / May 1975+Jul. 1975 / Motown ♦♦♦

☆ **Winelight** / Jun. 1980 / Elektra ✦✦✦✦✦

Grover Washington, Jr., has long been one of the leaders in what could be called rhythm & jazz, essentially R&B-influenced jazz. *Winelight* is one of his finest albums, and not primarily because of the Bill Withers hit "Just the Two of Us." It is the five instrumentals that find Washington (on soprano, alto and tenor) really stretching out. If he had been only interested in sales, Washington's solos could have been half as long and he would have stuck closely to the melody. Instead he really pushes himself on some of these selections, particularly the title cut. A memorable set of high-quality and danceable soul jazz. —*Scott Yanow*

Come Morning / 1980 / Elektra ✦✦

Anthology [Elektra] / 1980-1984 / Elektra ✦✦✦

Anyone who's seen Grover Washington, Jr., live can attest to the fact that whether he's playing electric jazz/funk or going acoustic on Billy Strayhorn's music, the Philly resident is a masterful saxman who has as much technique as he does soul and charisma. However, the distinctive saxman's studio recordings (which range from outstanding to watered down) haven't always demonstrated just how commanding an improvisor he can be. *Anthology*, a 1985 CD focusing on his work for Elektra, contains more hits than misses. Well worth hearing are jazz/R&B/pop instrumentals like the congenial "East River Drive" and the seductive "Let It Flow" and the R&B numbers "The Best Is Yet to Come" (which boasts a heartfelt vocal by Patti LaBelle) and Washington's major hit with Bill Withers "Just the Two of Us." Unfortunately, Elektra made the mistake of including Washington's pointless version of reggae king Bob Marley's "Jammin'" (which is more of a pop cover than a genuine jazz interpretation), the insipid "Jet Stream" and the pleasant but not very memorable "In the Name of Love." —*Alex Henderson*

Inside Moves / Mar. 1984-Jun. 1984 / Elektra ✦✦

Although Grover Washington, Jr., (on alto, tenor, soprano and baritone) puts on his usual strong effort, the forgettable material (which included no hits) and the emphasis on vocals (particularly those of Jon Lucien, who is on five of the seven selections) makes this one of Washington's weaker efforts and the least essential of his four Elektra recordings. The background vocalists do not help much either. This was Grover Washington, Jr's only full-length album as a leader during the 1982-86 period but was not worth the effort. —*Scott Yanow*

Strawberry Moon / 1987 / Columbia ✦✦✦

Grover Washington, Jr's first album in three years (and debut for Columbia) did not yield any major hits but found him playing in prime form. Switching between his distinctive soprano, alto and tenor, Washington is joined by bassist-producer Marcus Miller, a large rhythm section and guest vocalists B.B. King ("Caught a Touch of Your Love") and Jean Carne (on two songs). Highlights include "Strawberry Moon," "The Look of Love," "Maddie's Blues" and "Summer Nights." —*Scott Yanow*

Then and Now / 1988 / Columbia ✦✦✦✦

This is one of Grover Washington, Jr's occasional strays away from R&B-oriented jazz to play in a more straightahead setting. Switching between soprano, alto and tenor, Grover is accompanied by either Tommy Flanagan or Herbie Hancock on piano during five of the eight selections, and he performs such numbers as Ron Carter's "Blues for D.P.," "Stolen Moments" and "Stella by Starlight" with swing and taste. Tenor saxophonist Igor Butman also helps out on three songs. Worth acquiring. —*Scott Yanow*

Time Out of Mind / 1989 / Columbia ✦✦✦

One of the most electrified of Grover Washington, Jr's albums, this Columbia set features the popular saxophonist (who plays soprano, alto and tenor) joined by oversized rhythm sections and plenty of keyboards on a variety of funky and danceable material. Not one of Washington's more essential releases (his Columbia records overall have not been that memorable), the pacesetter among R&Bish saxmen is actually in fine form; if only the material were better. —*Scott Yanow*

Next Exit / 1992 / Columbia ✦✦

The man who wrote the book on R&B/fusion returns with yet another set of what he does best. Washington's sax shares time with vocal tracks featuring the likes of Nancy Wilson, Lalah Hathaway and the Four Tops. A solid, if predictable, outing. —*Steve Aldrich*

All My Tomorrows / 1994 / Columbia ✦✦✦

Soulful Strut / 1996 / Columbia ✦✦✦

Kazumi Watanabe

b. Oct. 14, 1953, Tokyo, Japan
Guitar / Fusion

Kazumi Watanabe has for the past 15 years been one of the top guitarists in fusion, a rock-oriented player whose furious power does not mask a creative imagination. Watanabe studied guitar at Tokyo's Yamaha Music School, and he

was a recording artist while still a teenager. In 1979 he formed the group Kylyn and in 1983 he put together the Mobo band. Several of his recordings have been made available by Gramavision and they show that he ranks up with Al DiMeola (when he is electrified) and Scott Henderson among the pacesetters in the idiom. —*Scott Yanow*

Mermaid Boulevard / Dec. 17, 1977+Dec. 29, 1977 / Inner City ✦✦✦

To Chi Ka / Mar. 4, 1980-Mar. 26, 1980 / Denon ✦✦✦✦✦

A great album, it features Kenny Kirkland (k), Mike Manieri (vib) and Warren Bernhardt (p). —*Paul Kohler*

Mobo Splash / Aug. 1985 / Gramavision ✦✦✦✦✦

● **Spice of Life** / Oct. 1986-Nov. 1986 / Gramavision ✦✦✦✦✦

This album is a fusion-lover's dream. Bill Bruford (d) and Jeff Berlin (b) drive Watanabe. —*Paul Kohler*

Spice of Life Too / Feb. 1988-Mar. 1988 / Gramavision ✦✦✦✦✦

A continuation of *Spice of Life* with stronger compositions and a hint of softer tones, it's very nice! —*Paul Kohler*

Kilowatt / 1989 / Gramavision ✦✦✦

This release picks up where *Spice of Life Too* left off. Bunny Brunel's bass work shines. —*Paul Kohler*

Sadao Watanabe

b. Feb. 1, 1933, Utsunomiya, Japan
Alto Saxophone / Instrumental Pop, Bop

Sadao Watanabe has long had a split musical personality. He alternates excellent bebop dates with weak pop albums that pale next to the leaders of the idiom (such as Grover Washington, Jr., and David Sanborn). Watanabe learned clarinet and alto in high school and in the 1950s he moved to Tokyo, joining Toshiko Akiyoshi's bop-oriented group in 1953. When the pianist moved to the US in 1956, Watanabe took over the band. He attended Berklee during 1962-65 and had the opportunity to work with Gary McFarland, Chico Hamilton and Gabor Szabo. However Watanabe has remained mostly based in Japan throughout his career, where he is a major influence on younger players. He has recorded steadily through the years, most notably with Chick Corea in New York (1970) and with the Galaxy All-Stars (1978). Watanabe's bop records are inspired by Charlie Parker but his Brazilian-flavored pop dates are instantly forgettable. —*Scott Yanow*

Nabasada and Charlie / Jun. 27, 1967 / Catalyst ✦✦✦✦

An excellent date with fellow saxophonist Charlie Mariano. Standards played with verve. —*Michael G. Nastos*

● **Round Trip** / Jul. 15, 1974 / Vanguard ✦✦✦✦✦

Sadao Watanabe has been disappointing on more than a few occasions. In fact, some of his more commercial, radio-oriented efforts have been quite forgettable. But when he's playing from the heart instead of pandering to commercial radio, Watanabe can be captivating. An adventurous "inside/outside" post-bop date employing Chick Corea (acoustic and electric piano), Miroslav Vitous (upright bass) and Jack DeJohnette (drums), *Round Trip* is one of his finest accomplishments. There's nothing even remotely predictable about this CD, which ranges from the Celtic-influenced, Weather Report-ish "Pastoral" to the contemplative "Nostalgia" to the insistent, 20-minute "Round Trip: Going and Coming." Best known for his Charlie Parker-influenced alto playing, an especially inspired Watanabe sticks to the soprano sax and flute this time. —*Alex Henderson*

☆ **I'm Old Fashioned** / May 22, 1976 / Inner City ✦✦✦✦✦

Most of the recordings of Japanese altoist Sadao Watanabe that have been made available in the US through the years have been aimed at the so-called "contemporary" market. This one is one of the exceptions. Watanabe, joined by pianist Hank Jones, bassist Ron Carter and drummer Tony Williams, sticks to bebop. Three of the eight selections are Watanabe's, but the other five include two Billy Strayhorn tunes and three other standards. This LP features Sadao Watanabe at his best. —*Scott Yanow*

Bird of Paradise / May 4, 1977 / Elektra ✦✦✦✦✦

Altoist Sadao Watanabe is considered one of Japan's top jazzmen. Some of his recordings are quite commercial, but this particular one finds him paying tribute to Charlie Parker with what was called "the great jazz trio": pianist Hank Jones, bassist Ron Carter and drummer Tony Williams. The seven selections (four Bird compositions and three standards often played by Parker) are all given strong treatment by the quartet. Watanabe's true love is bebop and his solos here are very much in that tradition yet display a personality of his own. This LP will be difficult to find. —*Scott Yanow*

Parker's Mood / Jul. 13, 1985 / Elektra ✦✦✦✦✦

Close to his best, both on his merit and thanks to aid from James Williams (p) and Jeff Watts (d). —*Ron Wynn*

Go Straight Ahead 'n' Make a Left / 1997 / Verve ✦✦✦

Go Straight Ahead 'n' Make a Left actually sounds like its title—Watanabe takes straightahead bebop around a left corner, courtesy of funky rhythm arrangements piloted by his longtime keyboardist, Bernard Wright. Together, they illustrate that there are still some new variations on the saxophonist's modern-day Charlie Parker-styled bop improvisations. Occasionally, the music dips into dangerously smooth territory, but Watanabe's strong playing keeps things on course and makes the record a pleasurable listen. —*Stephen Thomas Erlewine*

Benny Waters

b. Jan. 23, 1902, Brighton, MD

Alto Saxophone, Tenor Saxophone, Clarinet / Classic Jazz, Swing

At the age of 96 in mid-1998, Benny Waters was not only the second oldest active jazz musician (to Eubie Blake, who made it to 100) but a powerful altoist who would be considered impressive if he were only 50. Waters' personal history covers virtually the entire history of recorded jazz although he never really became a major name. He worked with Charlie Miller from 1918-21, studied at the New England Conservatory and became a teacher; one of his students was Harry Carney! Waters played, arranged for and recorded with Charlie Johnson's Paradise Ten (1925-32) an underrated group that also for a time included Benny Carter and Jabbo Smith. Waters, who was primarily a tenor saxophonist and an occasional clarinetist during this period, was influenced to an extent by Coleman Hawkins, and he recorded with both Clarence Williams and King Oliver in the 1920s. Durng the next two decades Waters played in many groups, including those led by Fletcher Henderson (for a few months), Hot Lips Page, Claude Hopkins and Jimmie Lunceford. He led his own unit during part of the 1940s, played with Roy Milton's R&B band and in 1949 went to France with the Jimmy Archey Dixieland group. Waters settled in Paris, working steadily, although he was largely forgotten at home. By the 1980s he was visiting the US more frequently, and Waters is heard in brilliant form on a 1987 quartet set for Muse on which he plays tenor, alto and clarinet in addition to taking some effective vocals. A short time later he went blind and stuck exclusively to playing alto (on which he plays in a jump style reminiscent of Tab Smith that shows the occasional influence of John Coltrane!). The seemingly ageless Benny Waters has continued recording and performing with a remarkable amount of energy, touring with the Statesmen of Jazz in 1995 and creating some miraculous music. —*Scott Yanow*

Benny Waters & the Traditional Jazz Studio / Jan. 12, 1976+Jan. 14, 1976 / I Giganti Del Jazz ✦✦✦✦

The great veteran Benny Waters spent a long period living in Europe which led to him being largely forgotten in the US. This imported LP (which has liner notes in Italian) is part of a budget series that was made available domestically in the US and can still sometimes be found in second-hand stores. One of the label's stronger releases, this date features Benny Waters (then only in his mid-70s) on clarinet, tenor, alto, and an occasional vocal, and his rarely-played soprano in Prague, Czechoslovakia with an excellent classic jazz octet filled with local players. In addition to a few warhorses such as "Lady Be Good" and "Sweet Georgia Brown," the band performs three originals by Waters. The music is consistently hot with many exciting moments, making this very obscure album well worth picking up. —*Scott Yanow*

When You're Smiling / Aug. 28, 1980-Aug. 29, 1980 / Hep ✦✦✦✦✦

On the Sunny Side of the Street / Apr. 1981 / JSP ✦✦✦✦

★ **From Paradise (Small's) to Shangri-La** / Jun. 26, 1987 / Muse ✦✦✦✦✦

It was this CD that re-introduced the great Benny Waters to American jazz fans. Already 85 at the time, Waters plays with the energy and ideas of a 45-year-old. Most impressive on his thick-toned tenor, Waters also plays alto and clarinet in addition to taking energetic vocals on "Hit That Jive Jack" and "Romance Without Finance." Backed by a rhythm section led by pianist Don Coates, Waters is virtually the entire show on seven standards plus two of his originals ("Strollin' Along The Rhine" and "No Problem"). A swing stylist who kept his mind open not only toward bop but also John Coltrane, Waters sounds surprisingly modern on the stomps and ballads, making one wonder how he could be neglected for the previous 50 years. A highly recommended gem, this is Benny Waters' definitive recording. —*Scott Yanow*

Memories of the Twenties, Stomp Off / Sep. 22, 1988-Nov. 15, 1988 / Stomp Off ✦✦✦✦✦

This is a well-conceived set featuring one of the few veterans of the 1920s still active in the late 1980s. Benny Waters, 86 at the time, is heard with pianist Keith Nichols' Cotton Club Orchestra on seven selections, revisiting songs that he had recorded with (and sometimes arranged for) Charlie Johnson's Paradise Ten during 1927-29. Waters' tenor solos on such numbers as "Walk That Thing," "You Ain't The One" and "Hot Tempered Blues" is quite memorable. The other soloists from

the English band (including Nichols) are consistently excellent. The remaining seven performances feature Waters (who plays clarinet on "Gravier Street Blues") exploring six hot numbers from the 1920s with Keith Nichols Jazz Kings, an octet sometimes reminiscent of Clarence Williams. Although this Stomp Off album is not that well-known, it is a near-classic. —*Scott Yanow*

Swinging Again / May 4, 1993 / Jazzpoint ✦✦✦✦✦

Few people listening to this CD would guess that Benny Waters (heard exclusively on alto) was 91. Waters (a veteran of the 1920s) plays with such power and confidence throughout the standards and blues that he could pass for 51. With an excellent European rhythm section (pianist Thilo Wagner, bassist Jan Jankeje and drummer Gregor Beck) helping him out, the underrated but distinctive swing stylist is heard in top form, making this European import CD from Germany highly recommended. —*Scott Yanow*

Plays Songs of Love / Jul. 28, 1993 / Jazzpoint ✦✦✦✦✦

The remarkable Benny Waters (who sticks here exclusively to alto) was 91 at the time of this recording yet still displays a strong tone and creative ideas. Assisted by guitarist Vic Juris and three nearly ancient veterans (pianist Red Richards, bassist Johnny Williams, Jr., and drummer Jackie Williams), Waters performs ten standards that have love as their main topic (including "What Is This Thing Called Love," "When Your Lover Has Gone," "Always," "Taking a Chance on Love," etc.) but fortunately varies the tempos (not every selection is taken at a ballad pace) and comes up with fresh ideas on these songs. Along with his other Jazzpoint release from the same period (*Swinging Again*), this CD is recommended. —*Scott Yanow*

● **Birdland Birthday—Live at 95** / Jan. 23, 1997-Jan. 25, 1997 / Enja ✦✦✦✦✦

Altoist Benny Waters celebrated his 95th birthday with a recorded performance from Birdland in New York. Waters, whose energetic playing is a little reminiscent of Tab Smith in the 1950s and who could pass for a man in his 50s, performs five of his basic originals (including "Exactly Like Me," which is based on "Exactly Like You") and four standards with Mike LeDonne (mostly playing organ rather than piano), guitarist Howard Alden, bassist Earl May and drummer Ed Locke. Although LeDonne and Alden have plenty of solo space, Waters is the dominant voice, and whether scatting on "Everybody Loves My Baby," caressing "I'm in the Mood for Love," showing off his technique on "Callin' the Cats" or jamming on "Blues Amore," he sounds amazingly ageless. Recommended. —*Scott Yanow*

Ethel Waters

b. Oct. 31, 1896, Chester, PA, d. Sep. 1, 1977, Chatsworth, CA

Vocals / Classic Jazz, Swing, Traditional Pop, Classic Female Blues

Ethel Waters had a long and varied career and was one of the first true jazz singers to record. Defying racism with her talent and bravery, Waters became a stage and movie star in the 1930s and '40s without leaving the US. She grew up near Philadelphia and, unlike many of her contemporaries, developed a clear and easily understandable diction. Originally classified as a blues singer (and she could sing the blues almost on the level of a Bessie Smith), Waters' jazz-oriented recordings of 1921-28 swung before that term was even coined. A star early on at theaters and nightclubs, Waters introduced such songs as "Dinah," "Am I Blue" (in a 1929 movie) and "Stormy Weather." She made a smooth transition from a jazz singer of the 1920s to a pop music star of the '30s and she was a strong influence on many vocalists including Mildred Bailey, Lee Wiley and Connee Boswell. Waters spent the latter half of the 1930s touring with a group headed by her husband, trumpeter Eddie Mallory, and appeared on Broadway (*Mamba's Daughter* in 1939) and in the 1943 film *Cabin in the Sky;* in the latter she introduced "Taking a Chance on Love," "Good for Nothing Joe" and the title cut. In later years Waters was seen in nonmusical dramatic roles, and after 1960 she mostly confined her performances to religious work for the evangelist Billy Graham. The European Classics label has reissued all of Ethel Waters' prime recordings and they still sound fresh and lively today. —*Scott Yanow*

Ethel Waters 1921-1923 / Mar. 21, 1921-Mar. 1923 / Classics ✦✦✦✦✦

Ethel Waters was one of the few singers from the early '20s whose early recordings are still quite listenable. This CD from the Classics label has her first 22 sides (many previously rare, including five interesting instrumentals by Waters' band) and, although not on the same level as her performances from a few years later, the music is quite good for the time period. The sidemen are mostly obscure but include pianist Fletcher Henderson and cornetists Gus Aiken and Joe Smith, with the highlights being "The New York Glide," "Down Home Blues," "There'll Be Some Changes Made" and "Midnight Blues." —*Scott Yanow*

1923-1925 / Mar. 1923-Jul. 28, 1925 / Classics ✦✦✦✦✦

The European Classics label's Ethel Waters program completely wipes out all of the other Waters reissues, for it reissues all of her recordings from her prime years in chronological order. Since the singer was very consistent, there are very few duds and many gems in these sets. This particular CD traces Ethel Waters during a two-year period; both the recording quality and her accompaniment greatly improve during this time; cornetist Joe Smith is a standout and pianist Fats Waller is present on "Pleasure Mad" and "Back-Bitin' Mamma." Highlights includes "You Can't Do What My Last Man Did," "Sweet Georgia Brown," "Go Back Where You Stayed Last Night" and "Sympathetic Dan." —*Scott Yanow*

Ethel Waters' Greatest Years / Apr. 29, 1925-Mar. 30, 1934 / Columbia ✦✦✦✦✦

When this two-LP set was originally released, it was the definitive Ethel Waters reissue, although now it has been succeeded by Classics' more complete CD program. However this two-fer is still the best single package ever released of the singer. The first album (covering 1925-28) focuses on her jazz years and has particularly strong contributions from cornetist Joe Smith and pianist James P. Johnson among others; "Sweet Georgia Brown," "Go Back Where You Stayed Last Night," "You Can't Do What My Last Man Did," "Sweet Man," "I've Found a New Baby," "Sugar," "Guess Who's in Town" and "My Handy Man" all qualify as classics. The second album mostly dates from 1929-34 and finds Waters joined by studio orchestras on most tracks. The emphasis is on ballads and sweet melodies but Waters still excels, particularly on "Waiting at the End of the Road," "Porgy" and "A Hundred Years from Today." This set is highly recommended to listeners who do not have the Classics CDs. —*Scott Yanow*

★ **1925-1926** / Aug. 25, 1925-Jul. 29, 1926 / Classics ✦✦✦✦✦

This CD in the Classics Ethel Waters series contains plenty of gems, including "You Can't Do What My Last Man Did," the original version of "Dinah," "Shake That Thing," "I've Found a New Baby" (which had some memorable cornet playing from Joe Smith), "Sugar" and "Heebies Jeebies." on "Maybe Not at All" Ethel Waters does eerie imitations of both Bessie Smith and Clara Smith. She had few competitors as a jazz singer during this era, and the mostly intimate recordings (12 of the 23 tracks find her backed by just a pianist) feature Waters at her best. —*Scott Yanow*

Ethel Waters on Stage/Screen (1925-1940) / Oct. 20, 1925-Nov. 7, 1940 / Columbia ✦✦✦✦

This Columbia LP features Ethel Waters performing 16 songs that debuted in shows or movies. With the exception of "Dinah" (this 1925 version is the original one) and "I'm Coming Virginia," all of the music dates from the 1929-40 era when Waters was better known as a musical comedy star than as a jazz singer. However, although the backing is generally a bit commercial, her performances of such numbers as "You're Lucky to Me," "Stormy Weather," "Taking a Chance on Love" and "Cabin in the Sky" are consistently memorable and definitive. —*Scott Yanow*

☆ **1926-1929** / Sep. 14, 1926-May 14, 1929 / Classics ✦✦✦✦

Few female jazz singers were on Ethel Waters' level during this period, just Bessie Smith and Annette Hanshaw, and all three were quite different from each other. Waters has rarely sounded better than on the four numbers in which she is backed rather forcefully by pianist James P. Johnson (particularly "Guess Who's in Town" and "Do What You Did Last Night") but she is also in fine form on the other small-group sides. "I'm Coming Virginia," "Home," "Take Your Black Bottom Outside," "Someday Sweetheart" and "Am I Blue" (which she introduced) are among the many gems on this highly recommended entry in the Classics' complete series. —*Scott Yanow*

1929-1931 / Jun. 6, 1929-Jun. 16, 1931 / Classics ✦✦✦✦✦

During the period covered in this CD from Classics' Ethel Waters series, the singer was quickly developing into a top musical comedy and Broadway star. Although her backup was not as jazz-oriented as previously (despite the presence of such players as clarinetist Benny Goodman, trombonist Tommy Dorsey, Jimmy Dorsey on clarinet and alto and trumpeter Manny Klein), Waters' renditions of many of these future standards are definitive, particularly "True Blue Lou," "Waiting at the End of the Road," "Porgy," "You're Lucky to Me" and "When Your Lover Has Gone." Superior jazz-oriented singing from one of the very best. —*Scott Yanow*

1931-1934 / Aug. 10, 1931-Sep. 5, 1934 / Classics ✦✦✦✦✦

Ethel Waters was one of the very few Black performers who was able to keep working in music during the early years of the Depression; in fact her fame grew during the period covered by this excellent CD from Classics' Ethel Waters series. Among her backup musicians on these consistently excellent sides are violinist Joe Venuti, the Dorsey Brothers, trumpeter Bunny Berigan, trombonist Jack Teagarden, clarinetist Benny Goodman, members of the Chick Webb big band and the entire Duke Ellington orchestra (the latter on "I Can't Give You Anything but Love" and "Porgy"). High points include the Ellington tracks, "St. Louis Blues" (with the Cecil Mack Choir), the original version of "Stormy Weather," "A Hundred Years from Today" and a remake of "Dinah." Highly recommended, as are all of the Ethel Waters Classics discs. —*Scott Yanow*

Foremothers, Vol. 6 / Nov. 9, 1938-Aug. 15, 1939 / Rosetta ✦✦✦✦

This very attractive Rosetta LP (which has definitive liner notes and numerous pictures) includes all of singer Ethel Waters' 16 Bluebird recordings of 1938-39. She is accompanied by two different bands led by her husband (trumpeter Eddie Mallory) with Benny Carter on alto and clarinet and trombonist Tyree Glenn (doubling on vibes) among the sidemen. Waters was not a major part of the swing era, but her own career (on stage and in films) was booming around this period. Her voice is heard in its prime on a variety of period pieces that are highlighted by "Old Man Harlem," "Georgia on My Mind," "Jeepers Creepers" and "They Say." —*Scott Yanow*

Performing in Person: Highlights from Her Illustrious Career / 1957 / Monmouth Evergreen ✦✦✦

Ethel Waters is heard at the twilight of her career during this live performance. Recorded a decade after her last studio recordings, this was the singer's final non-religious album. Accompanied by pianist Reginald Beane, Waters revisits most of her hits ("Am I Blue," "Dinah," "Porgy," "Supper Time," "Stormy Weather" and a medley from "Cabin in the Sky") and shows that, even at this late stage, her voice was still quite expressive. This is an LP that her many fans will want to search for. —*Scott Yanow*

Patty Waters

Piano, Vocals / Free Jazz, Avant-Garde

Largely overlooked during her brief recording career in the mid-'60s, Patty Waters has come to be appreciated as a vocal innovator in not just jazz, but contemporary music as a whole. Much of her repertoire was given over to hushed piano solo ballads, in which her voice could fade to a whisper that was barely audible. What really attracted attention were her avant-garde outings, in which she stretched and permutated her voice with contorted shrieks and wails that could be downright blood-curdling. Producing an unsettling effect that is definitely not for everybody, Waters has to be acknowledged as a vocalist who has tested the limits of what the human voice is capable of, in a similar manner as fellow pioneers Joan LaBarbara and Yoko Ono.

Waters' early influences were the fairly conventional ones of Billie Holiday, Nancy Wilson, and Anita O'Day. After moving to New York in the early '60s, she was heard in a nightclub by Albert Ayler, who recommended her to the renowned experimental jazz label ESP. The first side of her 1965 debut (*Sings*) was given over entirely to self-composed solo piano miniatures, leaving listeners somewhat unprepared for the second side, which consisted solely of her 13-minute interpretation of "Black Is the Color of My True Love's Hair." Building into hair-raising screams and vocal improvisations, augmented by a small free jazz combo, it remains the performance for which she is most noted.

Waters, sadly, only recorded one more album, the live *College Tour*, just a few months later. A more determinedly avant-garde effort than her debut, it featured entirely different (and mostly self-composed) songs than her debut. Waters often eschewed words altogether for wordless moan-scats and wails, and opted for a fuller band backing, including appearances by pianists Ran Blake and Burton Greene. Aside from a subsequent appearance as a member of the Mazette Watts Ensemble on a 1968 LP, nothing else was heard from Waters on record until 1996. Her mystique was enhanced over the decades by the rarity of her two ESP discs, which have recently been reissued on CD in Germany. —*Richie Unterberger*

● **Patty Waters Sings** / Dec. 16, 1965 / ESP ✦✦✦✦✦

An album that could have just as well been titled *The Two Sides of Patty Waters*, divided between seven short, almost minimal whispery piano ballads and the 13-minute outburst of "Black Is the Color of My True Love's Hair," in which Waters unveils her arsenal of vocal improvisations. Building from haunting, barely audible moans to angst-ridden bleats, it is the performance that established her as a vocal innovator, albeit one that was too edgy for most listeners. —*Richie Unterberger*

College Tour / 1966 / ESP ✦✦✦✦✦

Although this live show was only recorded a few months after the *Sings* session, it's hardly extraneous, featuring entirely different material. It's also a considerably more aggressive and freer effort than her debut, as Waters challenges herself and the audience with avant-garde crescendos of peals and wordless, whispering moans, although she doesn't entirely neglect the more subdued and accessible features of her voice. —*Richie Unterberger*

Love Songs / Jan. 1996 / Jazz Focus ✦✦✦

Patty Waters' first recording in 30 years finds the former avant-garde singer sounding older, with a smaller range and a weaker voice, but still showing a great deal of honest emotion and intensity. Accompanied by the great pianist Jessica Williams (who effectively emulates a full band on her synth during "Mood Indigo"), Waters explores 11 standards, including two haunting versions of "Don't Explain." Most of her renditions are fairly straightforward, although quite eerie, and on "Nature Boy" she hints strongly at her past freer days. Other highlights include "I've Got a Crush on You," "Someone to Watch Over You," "Mean to Me," and the only song taken above a ballad pace, "Fine and Mellow." —*Scott Yanow*

Doug Watkins

b. Mar. 2, 1934, Detroit, MI, **d.** Feb. 5, 1962, Holbrook, AZ
Bass / Hard Bop

A very in-demand bassist for recording sessions (especially when Paul Chambers, his cousin by marriage, was not available), Doug Watkins was a basic soloist but a superb accompanist. After gaining experience as one of many very talented Detroit jazzmen in the local scene, touring with James Moody (1953) and playing with Barry Harris' Trio, Watkins settled in New York in 1954. He was a member of the original version of the Jazz Messengers from 1955-56, spent a year with the Horace Silver Quintet, and then freelanced with a who's who of hard bop, including Sonny Rollins, Jackie McLean, Donald Byrd, Lee Morgan, Gene Ammons, Art Farmer, Kenny Burrell, Phil Woods and Hank Mobley, among many others. He was Charles Mingus' choice to play bass in his 1961 group when Mingus was temporarily specializing on piano. Tragically, a car accident ended his life at age 27. Doug Watkins led a session apiece for Transition (1960) and New Jazz (1960), playing some cello on the latter. —*Scott Yanow*

Watkins at Large / Dec. 8, 1956 / Transition ✦✦✦✦

● **Soulnik** / May 17, 1960 / Original Jazz Classics ✦✦✦✦✦
Bassist Doug Watkins only led two recording sessions before his death in 1962, and this set (which was cut for New Jazz and reissued on CD in the OJC series) has sometimes appeared under Yusef Lateef's name. Watkins doubles on cello (an instrument he had reportedly only begun playing three days earlier) during the set with Lateef (who triples on tenor, flute and oboe), pianist Hugh Lawson, bassist Herman Wright and drummer Lex Humphries. The quintet performs three standards, Watkins' "Andre's Bag" and a couple of Lateef tunes. The use of oboe and cello on some numbers makes the date stand out a bit from the usual hard bop sessions of the period and straightahead jazz fans will want to get this CD. —*Scott Yanow*

Julius Watkins

b. Oct. 10, 1921, Detroit, MI, **d.** Apr. 4, 1977, Short Hills, NJ
French Horn / Hard Bop

Julius Watkins was virtually the father of the jazz French horn. He started playing French horn at the age of nine, although he worked with the Ernie Fields orchestra on trumpet (1943-46). In the late '40s he took some French horn solos on records by Kenny Clarke and Babs Gonzales and spent 1949 as a member of the Milt Buckner big band. After three years of study at the Manhattan School of Music, Watkins started appearing on small-group dates, including a pair of notable sessions led by Thelonious Monk in 1953-54. He co-led Les Jazz Modes with Charlie Rouse in 1956-59, toured with Quincy Jones' big band (1959-61) did plenty of studio work (including the Miles Davis-Gil Evans collaborations) and recorded with Charles Mingus (in 1965 and 1971), Freddie Hubbard, John Coltrane (the *Africa* sessions) and the Jazz Composer's Orchestra, among many others. —*Scott Yanow*

● **New Faces-New Sounds: Julius Watkins Sextet** / Aug. 1954 / Blue Note ✦✦✦✦✦

Bill Watrous

b. Jun. 8, 1939, Middletown, CT
Trombone, Leader / Bop

One of the finest bop-oriented trombonists of the past 30 years, Bill Watrous has had a low profile since moving to Los Angeles in the 1980s despite remaining quite active. Possessor of a beautiful tone and remarkable technique, Watrous has been constantly overlooked in jazz popularity polls of the past decade. His father was a trombonist and introduced Bill to music. He played in traditional jazz bands as a teenager and studied with Herbie Nichols while in the military. Watrous made his debut with Billy Butterfield and was one of the trombonists in Kai Winding's groups during 1962-67. He was a busy New York-based studio musician during the 1960s, working and recording with Quincy Jones, Maynard Ferguson, Johnny Richards and Woody Herman, playing in the television band for Merv Griffin's show (1965-68) and working on the staff of CBS (1967-69). After playing with the jazz-rock group Ten Wheel Drive in 1971, Watrous led his own big band (the Manhattan Wildlife Refuge) during 1973-77, recording two superb albums for Columbia. After moving to Los Angeles in the late '70s, Watrous continued working in the studios, appearing at jazz parties, playing in local clubs and leading an occasional big band. He has recorded as a leader for Columbia, Famous Door, Soundwings, GNP/Crescendo and with his late '90s big band for Double-Time. —*Scott Yanow*

Bone Straight Ahead / Dec. 15, 1972-Jan. 4, 1973 / Famous Door ✦✦✦✦

Manhattan Wildlife Refuge / May 1, 1974-May 3, 1974 / Columbia ✦✦✦✦✦
It is a pity that this LP and its follow-up *The Tiger of San Pedro* have been long out of print, for they are the only two recordings of trombonist Bill Watrous' impressive big band of the mid-1970s. Watrous, who takes an uncharacteristically crazy cadenza on "Fourth Floor Walk-Up," is in top form on such numbers as Chick Corea's "Spain," "Dichotomy" and "Zip City." Among his more notable sidemen are trumpeter Danny Stiles, guitarist Joe Beck and pianist Dick Hyman. Well worth searching for. —*Scott Yanow*

☆ **Tiger of San Pedro** / 1975 / Columbia ✦✦✦✦✦
Trombonist Bill Watrous' second and final big-band album for Columbia is the equal of his first. With such soloists as Watrous, trumpeter Danny Stiles and either Tom Garvin or Derek Smith on keyboards, this well-rounded set (which includes ballads, Latin pieces, the rockish "T.S., T.S." and some heated workouts) well deserves to be reissued on CD, along with the earlier *Manhattan Wildlife Refuge*. —*Scott Yanow*

I'll Play for You / May 19, 1980 / Famous Door ✦✦✦✦
The brilliant trombonist Bill Watrous led a string of excellent small group dates for the now-defunct Famous Door label during the late 1970s/early '80s. This set teams him with pianist Jim Cox, bassist Tom Childs, drummer Chad Wackerman and percussionist Dave Levine, but the emphasis is on the leader. Watrous performs four standards (most memorable are a rapid "Falling in Love With Love" and "Body & Soul") and two more recent tunes. A fine if obscure effort by an underrated trombonist. —*Scott Yanow*

Coronary Trombossa / Dec. 4, 1980-Dec. 8, 1980 / Famous Door ✦✦✦✦
The second of three Famous Door albums recorded by Bill Watrous with pianist Jim Cox, bassist Tom Childs, drummer Chad Wackerman and percussionist Dave Levine features the trombonist-leader performing five standards plus his own uptempo blues "Pig Farm." Watrous' beautiful tone is very much in evidence on "Blue and Sentimental" and "Goodbye" and his speed and dexterity are quite impressive on "Charmaine" and "No More Blues." One of Watrous' better Famous Door LPs; all are recommended if hard-to-find. —*Scott Yanow*

Bill Watrous in London / Mar. 1982 / Mole ✦✦✦✦
The virtuosic trombonist Bill Watrous was caught live for this little-known LP from the British Mole label. Assisted by pianist Brian Dee, bassist Len Skeat and drummer Martin Drew, Watrous stretches out on lengthy versions of "Straight, No Chaser," "When Your Lover Has Gone," the ballad "Diane" and "Falling in Love with Love"; the latter at nine-and-a-half minutes is the shortest performance. Watrous is in fine form and on the more rapid numbers ("Straight, No Chaser" and "Falling in Love with Love") he sounds surprisingly relaxed, even when playing doubletime runs. —*Scott Yanow*

Roarin' Back into New York, New York / Jul. 1982 / Famous Door ✦✦✦✦✦
Trombonist Bill Watrous is heard at the peak of his powers on this LP from the soon-to-be-obsolete Famous Door label. Joined by pianist Derek Smith, bassist Linc Milliman and drummer Ronnie Bedford, Watrous' technique on the rapid "7 Come 11" is outstanding, his tone on the ballads ("My Ideal" and "I've Got a Crush on You") is beautiful and he takes a near-classic solo on a lengthy "Serenade in Blue." Hopefully the Famous Door catalog (which contains six Watrous albums) will someday be reissued on CD. —*Scott Yanow*

Someplace Else / 1986 / Soundwings ✦✦✦
Bill Watrous recorded two albums for Soundwings during 1986-87, both of which showcased his trombone with orchestras arranged by Patrick Williams. On this diverse set, Watrous performs a few standards (including "There Is No Greater Love" and "Come Rain Or Come Shine") along with works inspired by classical music ("A Tribute to Debussy" and "Adieu Mon Petite Table" which is an aria made famous by Maria Callas). Watrous displays his pretty tone and impressive technique but, other than the repertoire, few surprises occur. —*Scott Yanow*

Reflections / 1987 / Soundwings ✦✦✦
Trombonist Bill Watrous is accompanied by a rhythm section, three trumpets and strings arranged by Patrick Williams on this obscure CD. The material is melodic but generally somewhat forgettable, and Watrous' decision to sing a bit is a mistake since he only has an average voice; his whistling, however, is outstanding. But overall this date (which is at its best during "Cinnamon and Clove," "Li'l Darlin'" and Michael Camilo's "Why Not") is merely average for the masterful trombonist. —*Scott Yanow*

● **Bone-Ified** / 1992 / GNP ✦✦✦✦
Considering his obvious talents, it is surprising that trombonist Bill Watrous has recorded relatively little through the years. This CD is one of his better efforts of the past 15 years, a quartet outing with pianist Shelly Berg, bassist Lou Fischer and either Randy Drake or Tom Cummings on drums. Although Watrous overdubbed some extra trombones on a few tracks and Berg added some synthesized

strings, the emphasis is on straightahead swinging by the basic quartet with the highlights including "Day In, Day Out," "Change Partners" and "A Hot One For Jason." —*Scott Yanow*

Time for Love / 1993 / GNP Crescendo ✦✦✦
Bill Watrous has long had one of the prettiest tones of any trombonist, especially in his impressive upper register. It is Watrous' beautiful sound that is emphasized during the nine Johnny Mandel compositions that comprise this CD. Watrous is accompanied by a big band, and on some selections a string section but, other than pianist Shelly Berg (who along with Sammy Nestico contributed all of the arrangements), the backup crew is never allowed to rise above its anonymous supportive role. Watrous tries to vary the program a little with the inclusion of some earlier (and hotter) Mandel pieces, such as the swinging "Low Life" and "Not Really the Blues," but otherwise this is a ballad showcase, highlighted by "Emily" and "The Shadow of Your Smile." —*Scott Yanow*

Space Available / Dec. 1996 / Double-Time ✦✦✦✦
In the mid-1970s, trombonist Bill Watrous led a couple of notable big band albums (both long out of print) for Columbia. Since relocating to the Los Angeles area in the '80s, Watrous has put together jazz orchestras on a part-time basis to play at local clubs. Finally, in 1997, a recording was released by the more recent version of the Bill Watrous Big Band. Featuring arrangements by Tom Kubis, Shelly Berg, Gordon Goodwin, Ken Kaplan and Frank Perowsky, the Double-Time set is largely straightahead but not exactly predictable. Most of the eight selections have their complex sections, but always swing. The warm-toned trombonist is the main soloist (fully showcased on "My Foolish Heart" and "My Romance"); powerhouse pianist Shelly Berg is the top supporting player, and other key voices include Gene Burkurt and Bill Liston on tenors, trumpeters Bob Summers and Steve Huffsteter, and altoist Sal Lozano. The music is as rewarding as one would expect, considering the caliber of these players, and is easily recommended to modern big-band fans. —*Scott Yanow*

Bobby Watson

b. Aug. 23, 1953, Lawrence, KS
Alto Saxophone, Leader / Post-Bop, Hard Bop
Bobby Watson has long been one of the top altoists in jazz, a flexible player able to play swing (he once recorded a tribute to Johnny Hodges), hard bop and free jazz. He started playing the alto when he was 13 and was soon arranging and composing for his school bands. After graduating from the University of Miami in 1975, Watson moved to New York, hitting the big time by joining (and soon becoming the musical director of) Art Blakey's Jazz Messengers during 1977-81, participating in what would be Wynton Marsalis' first recordings. In the 1980s Watson co-led groups with Curtis Lundy (with whom he formed the New Note label) and played with the George Coleman Octet, Charlie Persip's big band, Louis Hayes, Sam Rivers, Dameronia, the 29th Street Saxophone Quartet and the Savoy Sultans; quite a wide range of jazz styles! Watson also began leading his own regular bands in the mid-'80s and the following decade he headed a regular hard bop quintet known as Horizon. His many recordings (for Enja, Red, New Note, Blue Note, Evidence, Columbia and Kokopelli) are always stimulating and worth investigating. —*Scott Yanow*

E.T.A. / 1977 / Roulette ✦✦✦

Jewel / Apr. 1983 / Evidence ✦✦✦✦✦
Bobby Watson had not inked a major label recording pact and was not a finished improviser when he cut these songs in 1983. What he did not lack was intensity, passion, and drive, and those served him well. His solos and playing are spirited, and he builds and completes ideas impressively. Likewise, pianist Mulgrew Miller and vibist Steve Nelson were also growing young players and sometimes tried to cram too much into their solos. Drummer Marvin "Smitty" Smith, on the other hand, capably held things together rhythmically, along with bassist Curtis Lundy and percussionist Dom Um Romao. This was a pivotal session for Watson; he established his identity in the post-Blakey era and went on to become the star everyone felt he would be when they initially heard him in the Messengers. —*Ron Wynn*

Gumbo / Dec. 1983 / Evidence ✦✦✦✦✦
At the time of this recording, Watson was still building his reputation, playing in a group co-led by bassist Curtis Lundy. This was an outstanding band bolstered by the booming baritone sax of Hamiett Bluiett and featuring a strong rhythm section with pianist Mulgrew Miller and drummer Marvin "Smitty" Smith alongside Lundy. Special guest trumpeter Melton Mustafa provided sparkling lines and fiery solos, interacting smoothly with Watson and Bluiett in a solid front line. Watson has since recorded more impressively engineered and mastered dates, but few have been musically superior to this early-'80s session. —*Ron Wynn*

Advance / Aug. 8, 1984 / Enja ✦✦✦✦

Appointment in Milano / Feb. 5, 1985 / Red ✦✦✦✦✦
During 1983-86 altoist Bobby Watson recorded fairly regularly for the Italian Red label. On this album he is joined by an obscure but talented Italian rhythm section (pianist Piero Bassini, bassist Attilio Zanchi and drummer Giampiero Prina) called the Open Form Trio. Actually the high point of the date is Watson's unaccompanied solo on "If Bird Could See Me Now." Other memorable selections on the well-rounded set include "Watson's Blues," the ballad "Always Missing You" and the spirited "Funcalypso." Bobby Watson (who doubles on this album on soprano) at that point in time was combining advanced hard bop with some influences from the avant-garde, carving out his own style. Recommended. —*Scott Yanow*

Round Trip / Feb. 6, 1985 / Red ✦✦✦✦✦
Recorded the day after *Appointment in Milano* and with the same Italian trio (pianist Piero Bassini, bassist Attilio Zanchi and drummer Giampiero Prina), this quartet set by altoist Bobby Watson has plenty of variety. Watson performs an explorative version of Ornette Coleman's "Round Trip," a pair of sophisticated ballads ("Blue in Green" and the jazz waltz "Sweet Dreams"), fresh versions of two standards ("There Is No Greater Love" and a faster-than-usual rendition of Lee Morgan's "Ceora") and an original ("All the Things of Jo Maka") that is based on "All the Things You Are." Watson's music swings yet he was adapting elements of avant-garde innovations to his style; the results are quite stimulating. —*Scott Yanow*

Love Remains / Nov. 13, 1986 / Red ✦✦✦✦
Altoist Bobby Watson has always been a consistent improviser whose roots are in Art Blakey's Jazz Messengers but who is open to freer innovations. For this Red album, Watson is joined by pianist John Hicks, bassist Curtis Lundy and drummer Marvin "Smitty" Smith for five of his originals, one by his wife Pamela Watson and Curtis Lundy's "Sho Thang." With such titles as "The Mistery of Ebop," "Blues for Alto" and the title cut, the high-quality music is essentially advanced hard bop and gives Watson a good opportunity to stretch out on some challenging structures. —*Scott Yanow*

The Year of the Rabbit / Feb. 7, 1987 / New Note ✦✦✦✦✦
This CD is a surprise success, for it features the modern altoist Bobby Watson paying tribute to the great Johnny Hodges. Watson performs his own brief "Blues for Alto" plus nine ballads, blues and swing stomps associated with Hodges, using a group that mixes together his usual sidemen of the period (pianist Mulgrew Miller, bassist Curtis Lundy and drummer Kenny Washington), a few veterans (trumpeter Irv Stokes, trombonist Art Baron and guitarist Lawrence Lucie) and younger but compatible players (Bill Easley on tenor and clarinet plus baritonist Jim Hartog). Watson modifies his own style and, although not too closely imitative of Hodges, improvises close to his style. Highlights of the memorable set include "The Jeep Is Jumpin'," "Jeep's Blues," "Honey Bunny" and "Things Ain't What They Used to Be." —*Scott Yanow*

No Question About It / May 1, 1988 / Blue Note ✦✦✦✦✦
Altoist Bobby Watson's debut for the Blue Note label used his future group name Horizon but was actually more of a transition band recorded right before Horizon's personnel became stabilized. Most notable is the fact that Watson utilizes two up-and-coming players (trumpeter Roy Hargrove at the beginning of his career and trombonist Frank Lacy) in addition to a top-notch rhythm section comprising pianist John Hicks, bassist Curtis Lundy and either Kenny Washington or Victor Lewis on drums. Their repertoire on this disc is quite fresh (five of Watson's challenging originals, Pamela Watson's "And Then Again" and Billy Strayhorn's "Blood Count") and the advanced hard bop solos are full of spirit and unpredictable ideas. —*Scott Yanow*

The Inventor / Jun. 1989 / Blue Note ✦✦✦✦
Altoist Bobby Watson's group Horizon was starting to solidify at the time of this Blue Note recording. Most selections feature Watson with trumpeter Melton Mustafa, pianist Edward Simon, bassist Carroll Dashiell and drummer Victor Lewis; pianist Benny Green, up-and-coming tenor Willie Williams and percussionist Don Alias are guests on a few numbers. The band (playing in a hard bop style but without merely recreating the past) performs six Watson originals, two by Lewis plus one from Mustafa. The music swings hard but is never overly predictable; an easily recommended set. —*Scott Yanow*

Post-Motown Bop / Sep. 17, 1990-Sep. 18, 1990 / Blue Note ✦✦✦✦✦

● **Present Tense** / Dec. 9, 1991-Dec. 11, 1991 / Columbia ✦✦✦✦✦
After a period of time, Bobby Watson's Horizon became one of the top hard bop-oriented regular bands of the early '90s. Comprising the leader on alto and occasional soprano, trumpeter Terell Stafford, pianist Edward Simon, bassist Essiet Essiet and drummer Victor Lewis, Horizon performs "I Got It Bad," "Minority" and ten originals by group members including Watson's "Monk He See, Monk He Do." All of the talented young musicians (Watson himself was only 38 at the time) are

well-featured and heard throughout their definitive release in top form. — *Scott Yanow*

Tailor Made / Dec. 9, 1992-Dec. 11, 1992 / Columbia ✦✦✦✦

This CD was altoist Bobby Watson's first as the leader of a big band. He leads the orchestra through a dozen of his compositions, none of which they had performed together before meeting up in the studio. But due to the high caliber of the players, the music came together smoothly. In performances ranging from modern hard bop to Latin with subtle hints of freer styles of jazz, Watson is the main soloist (although there are a few short spots for trumpeter Terell Stafford), making the album a sort of "concerto for alto and orchestra." Even if the backup musicians have little opportunity to star, the music is consistently enjoyable and recommended to fans of modern mainstream jazz. — *Scott Yanow*

Midwest Shuffle / Oct. 22, 1993-Nov. 10, 1993 / Columbia ✦✦✦✦✦

This interesting live CD, which includes some rather frivolous but harmless onstage dialogue, features Bobby Watson's group Horizon. The quintet (comprising altoist Watson, trumpeter Terell Stafford, pianist Edward Simon, bassist Essiet Essiet and drummer Victor Lewis) was one of the finest hard bop units of the time and one of the few that played together with the same personnel on a regular basis. Highlights of their spirited set include the joyous "Blues of Hope," "Complex Dialogue," "Midwest Shuffle" and "Mable Is Able." — *Scott Yanow*

Urban Renewal / 1995 / Kokopelli ✦✦✦

After a long string of excellent jazz albums, including many with his modern hard bop group Horizon, Bobby Watson recorded this dud. On his debut for Kokopelli the masterful altoist went overtly commercial. The music has danceable rhythms that avoid being stimulating along with forgettable melodies (many of which sound like R&B clichés). Two songs have spoken word sections by Dejah and Victor Lewis that are barely listenable. Watson's own playing (which includes rare appearances on tenor and flute in addition to his usual alto and soprano) is a cut above the level of the usual crossover artists, but the music (most of which he wrote) is not worthy of him and he never climaxes his solos with the skill of a Grover Washington, Jr., or a David Sanborn. This is one to pass by. — *Scott Yanow*

Lu Watters (Lucious Watters)

b. Dec. 19, 1911, Santa Cruz, CA, d. Nov. 5, 1989, Santa Rosa, CA
Trumpet, Leader / Dixieland

It would be difficult to overestimate the importance of Lu Watters in the Dixieland revival movement. When he organized the two-trumpet Yerba Buena Jazz Band in late 1939, the New Orleans jazz of King Oliver and Jelly Roll Morton was not only considered old hat, but worthy of extinction. Over 55 years later there are a countless number of trad bands patterned after the two-beat Watters group, which like its predecessor, King Olivers' Creole Jazz Band, is now considered classic. Lu Watters formed his first jazz band in 1925, but he spent most of the 1930s playing in San Francisco in his own big band. By 1939 (at the height of the swing era) he had met fellow trumpeter Bob Scobey, trombonist Turk Murphy and pianist Wally Rose and was planning to bring back the music of the 1920s, which had been largely neglected for quite a few years. In December 1939 his new band started playing regularly at the Dawn Club, and by 1941 when they made their first recordings, the Yerba Buena Jazz Band was building up a large following in San Francisco. The records kept the band's legacy alive when some of their members were drafted; Watters spent 1942-45 in the Navy, leading a 20-piece band in Hawaii. In 1946 when the band regrouped at the Dawn Club on Annie Street, it was more successful than ever and its records from 1946-47 find the group at its height. In June 1947 the band's base of operations moved to Hambone Kelly's in El Cerrito. The eventual departure of Bob Scobey and Turk Murphy (who would soon lead important groups of their own) weakened the Yerba Buena Band slightly, but the vocals of its banjoist Clancy Hayes were a crowd-pleaser and the band remained a powerful force. However when business fell off in 1950, Lu Watters broke up the band at the end of the year (feeling that its time had passed) and retired from music to be a cook and a geologist. Watters said later that he could see the eventual commercialization of Dixieland coming. He continued following the music scene closely but did not pick up his trumpet again until 1963, when a utility company in Northern California announced plans to build a nuclear power plant on an earthquake fault. Watters appeared at a couple of protest rallies with Turk Murphy's band (playing as well as ever) and recorded one last record before permanently retiring; the power plant was never built! — *Scott Yanow*

☆ The Complete Good Time Jazz Recordings / Dec. 19, 1941-Aug. 16, 1947 / Good Time Jazz ✦✦✦✦✦

Lu Watters' Yerba Buena Jazz Band was one of the most influential Dixieland groups of all time. With Watters and Bob Scobey on trumpets, trombonist Turk Murphy, clarinetist Bob Helm, pianist Wally Rose, banjo, tuba (or bass) and drums, this band had a lot of power and enthusiasm. At a time when swing dominated jazz and bebop was ready to take over, Watters' successful extension of 1920s jazz

was a major force in fueling the Dixieland revival movement. This four-CD set has all of the group's studio recordings plus live broadcasts from 1946-47 and six rare performances by the wartime version of the YBJB featuring the talented but ill-fated trumpeter Benny Strickler. This reissue is absolutely essential for all traditional jazz fans and historians. The heated ensembles and joyous solos are great fun to hear. — *Scott Yanow*

Airshots from the Dawn Club 1941 / 1941-1946 / Homespun ✦✦✦✦

Even with the Good Time Jazz reissue (on a large CD box set) of all of the performances by Lu Watters' highly influential Yerba Buena Jazz Band, this set of radio performances is worth investigating. The LP has two selections from 1946 and nine from 1941; the latter are particularly valuable for they find Watters' group sounding much looser than on their studio recordings. With Watters and Bob Scobey on trumpets, trombonist Turk Murphy and clarinetist Ellis Horne (Bob Helm on the 1946 titles) pushing the two-beat ensembles, the Dixielandish music (which was quite unusual for the period) is quite enjoyable. High points include "Struttin' with Some Barbecue," "At the Jazz Band Ball," "Maple Leaf Rag" and two versions of "Shimme-Sha-Wabble." — *Scott Yanow*

Yerba Buena Days / Mar. 22, 1942-Dec. 7, 1949 / Dawn Club ✦✦✦✦

A variety of performances by Lu Watters' highly influential Yerba Buena Jazz Band (some of which are currently available elsewhere) are on this collector's LP. Four selections from trumpeter Benny Strickler's date with the wartime Yerba Buena Jazz Band and the alternate take of Wally Rose's 1942 hit version of "Black & White Rag" (which helped launch a mini-revival of ragtime) are on this album, as is an obscure version of "Maple Leaf Rag" by the full group in 1947 and four songs from a 1949 session. Side one of this LP actually has the most interesting music; nine selections from the band's 1947 appearance on Rudi Blesh's *This Is Jazz* radio show. Until all of the music is made available on CD, Dixieland fans who run across this LP are advised to pick it up. — *Scott Yanow*

Lu Watters' Yerba Buena Jazz Band / Dec. 7, 1949-Feb. 7, 1950 / Homespun ✦✦✦✦

The Homespun label has released several valuable LPs that document Lu Watters' later version of the Yerba Buena Jazz Band. Fellow trumpeter Bob Scobey and trombonist Turk Murphy had departed by 1949 to form their groups, but Watters still had a fine unit. Although he was now the only trumpeter (Scobey's absence robbed the band of part of its unique personality), trombonist Warren Smith, clarinetist Bob Helm and pianist Wally Rose were strong assets, as were the occasional vocals of banjoist Clancy Hayes. Dixieland fans are advised to search for all seven of the Homespun releases; this one is highlighted by "St. Louis Blues," "Ace in the Hole," "Alcoholic Blues" and "Down Home Rag." — *Scott Yanow*

Unissued Live Recordings from Hambone Kelly's, Vol. 2 / Dec. 7, 1949-Jul. 1950 / Homespun ✦✦✦✦

The music on this collector's LP, most of which was originally released on Verve, features the last version of Lu Watters' Yerba Buena Jazz Band before the trumpeter decided to retire. The sound of Watters' group had changed a little since the earlier days since he was no longer using two trumpets and banjoist Clancy Hayes was being featured on vocals, but one can definitely recognize the style of the influential Yerba Beuena Jazz Band. In addition to Watters and Hayes, the main stars are clarinetist Bob Helm, pianist Wally Rose and either Warren Smith or Don Noakes on trombone, but it is the ensemble sound and Hayes' vocals (the latter is heard at his best on a classic rendition of "Frankie and Johnny") that are most notable. — *Scott Yanow*

At Hambone Kelly's 1949-50 / Dec. 23, 1949-Mar. 3, 1950 / Merry Makers ✦✦✦✦

The later version of Lu Watters' Yerba Buena Jazz Band is featured on this enjoyable Dixieland CD. The music is taken from ten live performances at Hambone Kelly's and showcases Watters' octet, which comprises the leader's trumpet, clarinetist Bob Helm, trombonist Don Noakes, pianist Wally Rose, Clancy Hayes on banjo and vocals, second banjoist Pat Patton, the tuba of Dick Lammi and drummer Bill Dart. The recording quality is decent, the playing is quite spirited, and even though this group only had one trumpet (as opposed to two in Watters' more famous earlier band), the hard-driving rhythm and spirited ensembles sound very much in the tradition of the Yerba Buena Jazz Band. Recommended. — *Scott Yanow*

Unissued Live Recordings from Hambone Kelly's, Vol. 3 / 1949-1950 / Homespun ✦✦✦✦

Lu Watters is best-known for the two-trumpet version of his Yerba Buena Jazz Band that he led during 1941-42 and 1946-47. However his group of the late-1940s (which found the leader featured as the only trumpeter) was also excellent if underrated. On this LP (one of seven Watters albums put out by the collector's label Homespun), the band also features clarientist Bob Helm, trombonist Don Noakes (a good ensemble player), pianist Wally Rose and banjoist-vocalist Clancy Hayes; trombonist Turk Murphy makes a guest appearance on "Yellow Dog

Blues." Among the many fine Dixielandish performances are good versions of "Dusky Stevedore," "Sweethearts on Parade," "Clarinet Marmalade" and a surprisingly effective rendition of "Five Foot Two." —*Scott Yanow*

Unissued Live Recordings from Hambone Kelly's, Vol. 4 / 1949-1950 / Homespun ✦✦✦✦

This album from the collector's label Homespun is most notable for the memorable vocals of banjoist Clancy Hayes, especially on "Oh By Jingo, "Silver Dollar" and "Sailing Down Chesapeake Bay." Lu Watters had a fine group during 1949-50, although the trumpeter-leader (due to poor health) was forced to switch to washboard for several months; a few tunes on this LP find the band sounding fairly complete (with clarinetist Bob Helm in the lead) without the trumpet. This particular octet (which also featured trombonist Warren Smith and pianist Wally Rose) has been overshadowed through the years by the earlier two-trumpet version of the Yerba Buena Jazz Band, but it was actually an excellent unit. Other high points of this easily recommended album include "Copenhagen," "Ostrich Walk" and "Blues My Naughty Sweet Gives to Me." —*Scott Yanow*

The '50s Recordings, Vol. 2 / Jan. 31, 1950-Jul. 1950 / Dawn Club ✦✦✦✦

The second of two Dawn Club LPs that wrap up the later recordings of trumpeter Lu Watters and his Yerba Buena Jazz band feature the leader, either Don Noakes or Warren Smith on trombone, and clarinetist Bob Helm playing spirited Dixieland. Banjoist Clancy Hayes has five vocals—including definitive versions of "Frankie and Johnny," "My Little Bimbo" and "St. James Infirmary"—on this cheerful set, which also has excellent renditions of such tunes as "Maple Leaf Rag," "Irish Black Bottom" and "Royal Garden Blues." Most of this music was also reissued by the Homespun label. —*Scott Yanow*

Together Again / Jul. 28, 1963 / Merry Makers ✦✦✦✦✦

Trumpeter Lu Watters came out of his 12-year retirement to help lead a successful protest against a proposed nuclear power plant being built near the San Andreas Fault. After getting his "chops" back in shape, Watters appeared with Turk Murphy's band on three separate occasions and recorded a studio album for Fantasy before permanently quitting. This CD (the music was released for the first time in 1994) documents the second rally and is quite exciting. Watters and trombonist Turk Murphy are heard with a group also including cornetist Bob Neighbor, clarinetist Bob Helm, either Wally Rose or Pete Clute on piano, banjoist Dave Weirbach, Bob Short on tuba, drummer Thad Vandon and on some tracks bassist Squire Girsback. The music comprises Dixieland standards and songs from the repertoire of Lu Watters' Yerba Buena Jazz Band of the 1940s and is played with high musicianship, creativity and plenty of spirit. Well worth searching for, this set is essential for Dixieland fans. —*Scott Yanow*

Blues over Bodega / 1964 / Fantasy ✦✦✦✦

Nearly 14 years after he retired from music, trumpeter Lu Watters came out of retirement to musically protest the proposed building of a nuclear power plant on the San Andreas Fault. In addition to a few concerts with his former trombonist Turk Murphy, Watters recorded this lone Fantasy LP. After the nuclear project was shelved, Watters went back into permanent retirement. Surprisingly he is heard in prime form throughout this excellent set, leading a septet that also includes trombonist Bob Mielke, clarinetist Bob Helm and pianist Wally Rose through such numbers as "Some of These Days," "Emperor Norton's Hunch" and his new pieces "San Andreas Fault" and "Blues Over Bodega." Blues singer Barbara Dane helps out on a couple of songs and the results are so enjoyable that it seems remarkable that more than 30 years later this set has yet to be reissued by Fantasy. —*Scott Yanow*

Charlie Watts

b. Jul. 2, 1941, Islington, London, England

Drums / Rock, Bop

On first glance Charlie Watts would seem to be a funny choice to include in a jazz book, for he is the longtime drummer of the Rolling Stones. However jazz was Watts' first love and in the 1980s he toured worldwide with a huge big band that included many of England's top musicians (giving one a chance to hear Evan Parker play "Lester Leaps In!"). In 1991 he organized an excellent bop quintet (featuring altoist Peter King) that paid tribute to Charlie Parker, justifying Watts' place in any jazz history book. —*Scott Yanow*

Live at Fulham Town Hall / Mar. 23, 1986 / Columbia ✦✦✦✦✦

Charlie Watts, the Rolling Stones' longtime drummer, has his roots in jazz and always loved the music. In 1986 he financed a worldwide tour by an oversized orchestra comprising seven trumpeters, four trombones, three altoists, six tenors, a baritonist, a clarinetist, two vibraphonists, piano, two basses, cello and three drummers including the leader. Most of the musicians are English and they include among the bigger names altoist Peter King, the tenors of Evan Parker, Danny

Moss and Courtney Pine, trumpeters Harry Beckett and Jimmy Deuchar, trombonist Paul Rutherford, pianist Stan Tracey and Jack Bruce on cello. While "Moonglow" features the two vibes and "Scrapple from the Apple" focuses on the two bassists, the other swing-era numbers ("Stompin' at the Savoy," "Lester Leaps In," "Robbins Nest" and "Flying Home") have the full big band playing a bit ragged but with plenty of excitement; "Lester Leaps In" is a massive tenor battle. Although one wonders how much money the tour must have cost Watts, the music (which mixes together bop players with more avant-garde explorers) is well worth hearing. —*Scott Yanow*

From One Charlie / Feb. 26, 1991-Feb. 27, 1991 / Continuum ✦✦✦

This is a rather unusual package. Inside the box is a single CD, an illustrated childrens' book on Charlie Parker by Charlie Watts and a frameable photo of Bird. This expensive set does contain some excellent music on the CD, hot bop performances from a quintet featuring the great altoist Peter King and trumpeter Gerard Presencer in addition to Watts on drums, but unfortunately it is also rather brief (under 28 minutes). If there had been twice as much music this set would get a much higher rating, for the straightforward music is quite strong and the Bird tributes heartfelt. —*Scott Yanow*

● **Tribute to Charlie Parker With Strings** / Oct. 31, 1991-Nov. 1, 1991 / Continuum ✦✦✦✦✦

Charlie Watts, a charter member of the Rolling Stones and an okay jazz drummer, financed a few jazz projects during the 1980s and '90s. This particular set, a tribute to Charlie Parker that features a quintet, vocalist Bernard Fowler (who sings "Lover Man" and adds some narration about Parker's life), six strings, harp and oboe, has renditions of seven songs associated with Bird. Altoist Peter King is easily the solo star, trumpeter Gerard Presencer is decent but not on the same level and pianist Brian Lemon also gets in some spots; Watts stays in the background. This well-intentioned program is well worth acquiring and its highlights include versions of "Just Friends," "Dewey Square" and "Perdido." —*Scott Yanow*

Warm & Tender / 1993 / Continuum ✦✦✦✦

Long Ago and Far Away / 1996 / Pointblank ✦✦✦

Ernie Watts

b. Oct. 23, 1945, Norfolk, VA

Tenor Saxophone, Alto Saxophone / Post-Bop, Crossover Jazz, Instrumental Pop, Bossa Nova

Because he was involved in many commercial recording projects from the mid-'70s through the early '80s and on an occasional basis ever since, some observers wrote Ernie Watts off prematurely as a pop/R&B tenorman. Actually Watts' main hero has always been John Coltrane and his more recent work reveals him to be an intense and masterful jazz improviser who has developed his own sheets of sound approach along with a distinctive and soulful sound. After attending Berklee, he had an important stint with Buddy Rich's big band (1966-68) before moving to Los Angeles. Watts worked in the big bands of Oliver Nelson and Gerald Wilson, recorded with Jean-Luc Ponty in 1969 and became a staff musician for NBC, performing with the Tonight Show Band on a regular basis. His own records of the 1970s and early '80s were generally poppish (1982's *Chariots of Fire* was a big seller) and Watts played frequently with Lee Ritenour and Stanley Clarke in addition to recording with Cannonball Adderley (one of his idols) in 1972. However Ernie Watts' work became much more interesting from a jazz standpoint starting in the mid-'80s when he joined Charlie Haden's Quartet West and started recording no-nonsense quartet dates for JVC. Ernie Watts has developed into one of the most powerful of tenormen with complete control over his horn and the ability to bring intensity and passion (plus taste) to any musical situation. —*Scott Yanow*

Look in Your Heart / 1980 / Elektra ✦✦

Chariots of Fire / Oct. 19, 1981-Oct. 31, 1981 / Qwest ✦✦

Musician / 1985 / Qwest ✦✦

Sanctuary / 1986 / Qwest ✦✦

This Qwest project was a typical crossover project for Ernie Watts, who recorded a series of commercial sets for Elektra and Qwest. The rhythms are danceable, Watts displays attractive tones on tenor, alto and soprano, the supporting cast includes top L.A. studio musicians (who were used to sounding anonymous and playing funk clichés), Don Grusin contributes keyboards and electronic rhythms, among the many vocalists are Larry Williams and Phil Perry, and guitarist Lee Ritenour pops up on a few numbers. None of the music is at all memorable and the results (which sold fairly well) were dated within a year. Fortunately Ernie Watts would soon start recording more creative jazz and begin to realize his potential, which is largely wasted on this effort. —*Scott Yanow*

Ernie Watts Quartet / Dec. 14, 1987-Dec. 15, 1987 / JVC ✦✦✦✦✦

After years of being heard primarily in commercial settings, Ernie Watts finally had an opportunity to record exactly what he wanted as a leader on this JVC CD. Watts, in a quartet with pianist Pat Coil, bassist Joel DiBartolo and drummer Bob Leatherbarrow, features his Coltrane-influenced tenor and a bit of alto and soprano on some group originals and standards (including "My One and Only Love," "Skylark" and "Body and Soul"). One of his finest recordings to date. —*Scott Yanow*

World Class / 1988 / JVC ✦✦✦✦

Project: Activation Earth / 1989 / Amherst ✦✦

Jazz saxophonist Watts teams with the fusion band Gamalon with nice results! —*Paul Kohler*

Afoxe / 1991 / CTI ✦✦

● **Reaching Up** / Oct. 7, 1993-Oct. 8, 1993 / JVC ✦✦✦✦✦

For this quartet set with pianist Mulgrew Miller, bassist Charles Fambrough and drummer Jack DeJohnette, Ernie Watts definitely came to play. Virtually all of his solos are high-powered and even his ballad statements are filled with clusters of passionate notes. Trumpeter Arturo Sandval has two appearances and makes the music even more hyper. In addition, the rhythm section keeps the proceedings consistently stimulating. The main focus on these standards and originals is generally on Watts' tenor and, even though there isn't all that much variety, this CD is a strong example of his jazz talents. —*Scott Yanow*

Unity / Dec. 13, 1994-Dec. 14, 1994 / JVC ✦✦✦✦✦

The most unusual aspect to Ernie Watts' latest recording is that the great tenor is joined by a two-bass quartet. Eddie Gomez on acoustic and Steve Swallow on electric blend together quite well, are featured in a delightful version of Oscar Pettiford's "Tricotism" and (with pianist Geri Allen and drummer Jack DeJohnette) keep the accompaniment consistently stimulating. Ernie Watts is in top form throughout this fine modern mainstream date, playing with both passion and lyricism on a variety of standards and originals (which, in addition to four songs from the leader, include one apiece from DeJohnette and Swallow). There is just enough variety to keep the proceedings from ever getting predictable, making this one of Watts' finest sessions. —*Scott Yanow*

Long Road Home / May 8, 1996+May 9, 1996 / JVC ✦✦✦✦

Jeff "Tain" Watts

b. Jan. 20, 1960, Pittsburgh, PA
Drums / Post-Bop

Jeff "Tain" Watts came to fame as drummer with the early Wynton Marsalis band. He has been greatly in-demand ever since, playing and recording with such musicians as Geri Allen, Ricky Ford, Robin Eubanks, Betty Carter, McCoy Tyner, Gary Thomas and Branford Marsalis among others. He made his debut as a leader for the Sunnyside label in 1991 and joined the Tonight Show Band when Branford Marsalis became its director. Jeff Watts is both a virtuosic and a subtle drummer who is versatile enough to fit into many settings. —*Scott Yanow*

● **Megawatts** / Jul. 24, 1991+Jul. 25, 1991 / Sunnyside ✦✦✦✦

Weather Report

f. 1970, **db.** 1985
Group / Fusion

Weather Report started out as the jazz equivalent of what the rock world in 1970 was calling a "supergroup." But unlike most of the rock supergroups, this one not only kept going for a good 15 years, it more than lived up to its billing, practically defining the state of the jazz-rock art throughout almost all of its run. Weather Report also anticipated and contributed to the North American interest in world music rhythms and structures, prodded by keyboardist/co-founder Joe Zawinul. And WR, like many of jazz's great long-lived groups, proved to be an incubator for several future leaders who passed in and out of the band in a never-ending series of revolving-door personnel changes. The original members of the band were Zawinul, Wayne Shorter (saxophones), Miroslav Vitous (electric bass), Airto Moreira (percussion) and Alphonse Mouzon (drums), with only Zawinul and (until 1985) Shorter remaining in place throughout the band's lifespan. Zawinul, Shorter and Moreira all had experience playing in and influencing the studio and live electric bands of Miles Davis—and at first, WR was a direct extension of Miles' *In a Silent Way/Bitches Brew* period, with free-floating collective improvisation and interplay, combining elements of jazz, rock, funk, Latin and other ethnic musics. With the release of *Sweetnighter* in 1972, Zawinul's influence upon the band's direction began to deepen; the groove became more important, and structures were imposed upon the material (though the group continued its freewheeling interplay in live gigs). When the innovative bassist Jaco Pastorius replaced Alphonso Johnson in 1976, WR entered its most popular phase, with Pastorius

becoming a flamboyant third lead voice, Shorter's sax receding into more epigrammatic form, and Zawinul rediscovering his commercial touch and sharpening his electronic sophistication. The best-selling *Heavy Weather* album (1977) actually served up a hit song that became a jazz standard ("Birdland"), and with the entry of Peter Erskine on drums (1978), the group finally had a stable lineup for awhile. Contrary to accepted wisdom, the departures of Pastorius and Erskine in 1982 led to a recharging of WR's batteries; their replacements Victor Bailey (bass), Omar Hakim (drums), Jose Rossy and later, Mino Cinelu (percussion) were more amenable to Zawinul's deepening inclinations for Third World rhythms, sounds and textures. This edition of WR rattled off three more albums, including the outstanding *Procession*. But Shorter, who had gradually ceded nearly total artistic control to Zawinul, was getting restless; he took a leave of absence in 1985 and later that year, left WR for good. *This Is This* (1985), in which Erskine returns and Shorter plays only a limited role, was WR's swan song. Zawinul would tour in 1986 with a revamped version called Weather Update (a prelude to the keyboardist's own Zawinul Syndicate), and there was talk in 1996 about Zawinul and Shorter reuniting in the studio for a new edition of WR, but Zawinul later deflated the speculation. —*Richard S. Ginell*

★ **Weather Report** / Feb. 16, 1971-Mar. 17, 1971 / Columbia ✦✦✦✦✦

Here we have the free-floating, abstract beginnings of Weather Report, which would define the state of the electronic jazz/rock art from its first note almost to its last. Their first album is a direct extension of the Miles Davis *In a Silent Way/Bitches Brew* period, more fluid in sound and more volatile in interplay. Joe Zawinul ruminates in a delicate, liquid manner on Rhodes electric piano; at this early stage, he used a ring modulator to create weird synthesizer-like effects. Wayne Shorter's soprano sax shines like a beacon amidst the swirling ensemble work of co-founding bassist Miroslav Vitous, percussionist Airto Moreira and drummer Alphonse Mouzon. Zawinul's most memorable theme is "Orange Lady" (previously recorded, though uncredited, by Davis on *Big Fun*), while Shorter scores on "Tears" and "Eurydice." One of the most impressive debuts of all time by a jazz group. —*Richard S. Ginell*

I Sing the Body Electric / Nov. 1971-Jan. 13, 1972 / Columbia ✦✦✦✦✦

Like the weather itself, this band would assume a new shape with virtually every release—and this album, half recorded in the studio and half live in Tokyo, set the pattern of change. Exit Airto Moreira and Alphonse Mouzon; enter percussionist Dom Um Romao, drummer Eric Gravatt, and a slew of cameo guests like guitarist Ralph Towner, flutist Hubert Laws and others. The studio tracks are more biting, more ethnically diverse in influence, and more laden with electronic effects and grandiose structural complexities than before. The live material (heard in full on the import *Live in Tokyo*) is even fiercer and showcases for the first time some of the tremendous drive WR was capable of, though it doesn't give you much of an idea of its stream-of-consciousness nature. —*Richard S. Ginell*

This Is Jazz, Vol. 10 / 1971-1978 / Columbia/Legacy ✦✦✦✦

Because most diehard Weather Report enthusiasts already have everything included on this addition to Legacy/Sony's *This Is Jazz* series of compilations, the "best of" CD serves primarily as an introduction to the fusion innovators' breakthroughs of the 1970s. While hardly the last word on the band, *This Is Jazz* isn't a bad introduction at all. Naturally, the disc contains Weather's best-known piece, the infectious "Birdland." But equally captivating are the eerie yet funky "Mysterious Traveler," the intriguing "Man in the Green Shirt," the congenial "Young and Fine," the hauntingly abstract "The Moors" and the Asian-influenced "Black Market." Boasting improvisatory, risk-taking and imaginative gems full of blues feeling, *This Is Jazz 10* is jazz in the truest sense of the word. —*Alex Henderson*

Live in Tokyo / Jan. 13, 1972 / Columbia ✦✦✦✦✦

While side 2 of *I Sing the Body Electric* gives us heavily edited glimpses of Weather Report as heard live in Tokyo, this two-disc Japanese import contains entire group ensembles from that concert—and as such, it is a revelation. Now we can follow the wild stream-of-consciousness evolution of early Weather Report workouts, taking us into all kinds of stylistic territory from Joe Zawinul's lone acoustic piano to dissonant freeform and electronic explosions, with lots of adjustments of tempo and texture. The pulse of jazz is more evident in their work here than on the American albums, and the example of Miles Davis circa the Fillmore concerts directs the fierce interplay. In his subsequent recordings with WR and as a leader, Wayne Shorter would rarely equal the manic intensity he displayed in Tokyo. All of the music is encapsuled in five lengthy "medleys" of WR repertoire, three of which contain elongated versions of themes from WR's debut album. This would be the radical apogee of WR on records, though they could retain this level of fire in concert for years to come. —*Richard S. Ginell*

Sweetnighter / Feb. 3, 1973-Feb. 7, 1973 / Columbia ✦✦✦✦

Right from the start, a vastly different Weather Report emerges here, one that reflects co-leader Joe Zawinul's developing obsession with the groove. It is the groove that rules this mesmerizing album, leading off with the irresistible 3/4 marathon deceptively tagged as the "Boogie Woogie Waltz" and proceeding through a variety of Latin-grounded hipshakers. It is a record of discovery for Zawinul, who augments his Rhodes electric piano with a funky wah-wah pedal, unveils the ARP synthesizer as a melodic instrument and sound-effects device, and often coasts along on one chord. The once-fiery Wayne Shorter has been tamed, for he now contributes mostly sustained ethereal tunes on soprano sax, his tone sometimes doubled for a pleasing octave effect. The wane of freewheeling ensemble interplay is more than offset by the big increase in rhythmic push; bassist Miroslav Vitous, drummer Eric Gravatt, and percussionist Dom Um Romao are now cogs in one of jazz's great swinging machines. —*Richard S. Ginell*

Mysterious Traveller / 1973-1974 / Columbia ✦✦✦✦✦
Weather Report's fourth recording finds Wayne Shorter (on soprano and tenor) taking a lesser role as Joe Zawinul begins to really dominate the group's sound. Most selections also include bassist Alphonso Johnson and drummer Ishmael Wilburn, although the personnel shifts from track to track. "Nubian Sundance" adds several vocalists while "Blackthorn Rose" is a Shorter-Zawinul duet. Overall the music is fairly stimulating and sometimes adventurous; high-quality fusion from 1974. —*Scott Yanow*

Tale Spinnin' / 1975 / Columbia ✦✦✦✦
Weather Report's ever-changing lineup shifts again, with the somewhat heavier funk-oriented Leon "Ndugu" Chancler dropping into the drummer's chair and Alyrio Lima taking over the percussion table. As a result, *Tale Spinnin'* has a weightier feel than *Mysterious Traveller,* while continuing the latter's explorations in Latin-spiced electric jazz/funk. Zawinul's pioneering interest in what we now call world music is more in evidence with the African percussion, wordless vocals and sandy sound effects of "Badia," and his synthesizer sophistication is growing along with the available technology. Wayne Shorter's work on soprano sax is more animated than on the previous two albums and Alphonso Johnson puts his melodic bass more to the fore. While not quite as inventive as its two predecessors, this remains an absorbing extension of WR's mid-'70s direction. —*Richard S. Ginell*

Black Market / 1976 / Columbia ✦✦✦✦✦
The shifts in Weather Report's personnel come fast and furious now, with Narada Michael Walden and Chester Thompson as the drummers, Alex Acuna and Don Alias at the percussion table and Alphonso Johnson giving way to the mighty, martyred Jaco Pastorius. It is interesting to hear Pastorius expanding the bass role only incrementally over what the more funk-oriented Johnson was doing at this early point—that is, until "Barbary Coast," where suddenly Jaco leaps athletically forward into the spotlight. Joe Zawinul or just Zawinul, as he preferred to be billed—contributed all of side one's compositions, mostly Third World-flavored workouts except for "Cannon Ball," a touching tribute to his ex-boss Cannonball Adderley (who had died the year before). Shorter, Pastorius and Johnson split the remainder of the tracks, with Shorter now set in a long-limbed compositional mode for electric bands that would serve him into the 1990s. While it goes without saying that most Weather Report albums are transition albums, this diverse record is even more transient than most, paving the way for WR's most popular period while retaining the old sense of adventure. —*Richard S. Ginell*

☆ **Heavy Weather** / 1977 / Columbia ✦✦✦✦✦
Weather Report's biggest-selling album is that ideal thing, a popular and artistic success—and for the same reasons. For one thing, Joe Zawinul revealed an unexpectedly potent commercial streak for the first time since his Cannonball Adderley days, contributing what has become a perennial hit, "Birdland." Indeed "Birdland" is a remarkable bit of recordmaking, a unified, ever-developing piece of music that evokes, without in any way imitating, a joyous evening on 52nd St. with a big band. The other factor is the full emergence of Jaco Pastorius as a co-leader; his dancing, staccato bass lifting itself out of the bass range as a third melodic voice, completely dominating his own ingenious "Teen Town" (where he also plays drums!). By now, Zawinul has become WR's de facto commander in the studio; his colorful synthesizers dictate the textures, his conceptions are carefully planned, with little of the freewheeling improvisation of only five years before. Wayne Shorter's saxophones are now reticent, if always eloquent, beams of light in Zawinul's general scheme while Alex Acuna shifts ably over to the drums and Manolo Badrena handles the percussion. Released just as the jazz-rock movement began to run out of steam, this landmark album proved that there was plenty of creative life left in the idiom. —*Richard S. Ginell*

Mr. Gone / 1978 / Columbia ✦✦
On *Mr. Gone,* Weather Report becomes merely a cover name for a Joe Zawinul/ Jaco Pastorius jazz/rock/funk record production, with several guest drummers (Steve Gadd, Tony Williams, Peter Erskine), no resident percussionist, and Wayne Shorter as a still-potent solo saxophone threat. This album was denounced in its

time as a sellout, probably on the reputation of Jaco's pulsating "River People," which is as close as WR ever came to outright disco. But there is lots of diversity and adventure here, as the creative core of the band uses the latest electronics to push out the boundaries of sound while maintaining tight control over structure. "The Pursuit of the Woman with the Feathered Hat" is quintessential Zawinul; the Third World-centered groove is everything, no chord changes to impede this rush of layered electronics, percussion and voices. Shorter's spare "The Elders" flirts with the electronic avant-garde and he retrofits his Miles Davis-era "Pinocchio" in rapid-fire electro-acoustic garb. In other words, the multi-flavored WR stew continues to cook at a fine boil. —*Richard S. Ginell*

8:30 / Dec. 1979 / Columbia ✦✦✦✦✦
This double LP gives one a fine retrospective of Weather Report from the vantage point of 1979 with the first three sides being taken up with live performances. There are remakes of such memorable selections as "Black Market," "Teen Town," "A Remark You Made" and Weather Report's big hit "Birdland." Not everything works (Wayne Shorter's unaccompanied tenor solo on "Thanks for the Memory" is merely odd) and the new studio recordings on side four are not at the same level, but in general the music throughout this two-fer is quite rewarding. Keyboardist Joe Zawinul, Shorter, bassist Jaco Pastorius and drummer Peter Erskine are all in top form. —*Scott Yanow*

Night Passage / 1980 / Columbia ✦✦✦✦
All things being relative, this is Weather Report's straightahead album, where the elaborate production layers of the late-'70s gave way to sparer textures and more unadorned solo improvisation in the jazz tradition, electric instruments and all. The flaw of this album is the shortage of really memorable compositions; it is more of a vehicle for the virtuosic feats of what is considered by some to be the classic WR lineup—Joe Zawinul, Wayne Shorter, Jaco Pastorius, Robert Thomas, Jr., and Peter Erskine. For Erskine, this is his first full studio album and he amply demonstrates his terrific sense of forward drive, unique among the other superb drummers in WR annals. "Port of Entry" is a tour de force for Jaco, who knocks off several of those unbelievably slippery, pointed runs that have made him a posthumous legend. There is also a tremendously fun retro trip to Duke Ellington's "Rockin' in Rhythm," everybody swinging their heads and hands off. —*Richard S. Ginell*

Procession / Jun. 1983 / Columbia ✦✦✦✦
A new Weather Report lineup makes its debut here, with Victor Bailey filling Jaco Pastorius' shoes, Omar Hakim on drums, Jose Rossy on percussion, and Joe Zawinul now thoroughly in charge. But contrary to the conventional wisdom, which claims that WR went downhill after the departure of Pastorius/Erskine, the new lineup actually recharged WR's creative batteries; the material here is superior to that of the previous two albums at least. Bailey, while not Jaco's technical equal, is mobile enough to project through the texture, and Hakim has the versatility and swinging Third World rhythmic influences that must have appealed to Zawinul. "Procession" itself is a masterly Zawinul tone poem, with moody electronics and voices building to an emotional crescendo and ebbing away, a high point in WR's output. Even Wayne Shorter's sole composition "Plaza Real" is the most interesting tune he had come up with in a long time. The Manhattan Transfer, the champions of "Birdland," make a fascinating electronically distorted appearance on Zawinul's marvelous "Where the Moon Goes." This is an unjustly overlooked Weather Report treasure, hopefully due for CD reissue soon. —*Richard S. Ginell*

Domino Theory / 1983-1984 / Columbia ✦✦✦
Here's more proof that Weather Report actually became a more potent, life-affirming musical force after the departures of its best-known sidemen. Things begin on an oddly commercial note with a pop song, "Can It Be Done," sung by Carl Anderson, that actually lays out Weather Report's credo, searching for sounds never heard before. Then Joe Zawinul and company get down to business with the funky "D-Flat Waltz," marked by Omar Hakim's flamboyantly complex drumming. Zawinul's synthesizer textures become thicker and more flexible with the help of newly introduced digital instruments, and the funk element in general becomes more pronounced than on any record since *Tale Spinnin'.* Victor Bailey (bass), who spins his wheels on the title track, and Jose Rossy (percussion) remain on board (though Rossy left shortly thereafter) and Wayne Shorter's tenor sax has a rawer, tougher edge than it has had in awhile. Though not quite as triumphant as *Procession,* a triumph nonetheless. —*Richard S. Ginell*

Sportin' Life / 1984 / Columbia ✦✦
With de facto leader Joe Zawinul now even more set on a world music groove-oriented direction than ever, it is hard to place Weather Report even within the broad electric jazz—or fusion, if you must—category at this point. But forget labels; this is another superb WR album where the grooves percolate and thump along in an irresistible surge, rhythmic elements pouring in from the Caribbean, Africa, Mid-

dle East and the instrument designers at Yamaha, Korg, etc. There are more vocals than ever, mostly wordless chant by guests Carl Anderson, Bobby McFerrin and others, and there is a total departure in the form of an attractive folk-like song sung and played by the new percussionist/guitarist Mino Cinelu. Almost alone among synthesizer players, Zawinul took the trouble to learn how to swing on these instruments, and by *Sportin' Life*, he had become unstoppable. And Wayne Shorter? His beams of light are still around, as heard most hauntingly in a duet with Zawinul's synths on "The Face on the Barroom Floor." Yet Wayne's presence is just another color in Zawinul's multi-band palette, and as a result, their long partnership was coming to a close despite the still sky-high quality of their music. —*Richard S. Ginell*

This Is This! / 1985 / Columbia ✦✦

Chick Webb (William Henry Webb)

b. Feb. 10, 1909, Baltimore, MD, **d.** Jun. 16, 1939, Baltimore, MD
Drums, Leader / Swing, Big Band

Chick Webb represented the triumph of the human spirit in jazz and life. Hunchbacked, small in stature, almost a dwarf with a large face and broad shoulders, Webb fought off congenital tuberculosis of the spine in order to become one of the most competitive drummers and bandleaders of the big band era. Perched high upon a platform, he used custom-made pedals, goose-neck cymbal holders, a 28-inch bass drum and a wide variety of other percussion instruments to create thundering solos of a complexity and energy that paved the way for Buddy Rich (who studied Webb intensely) and Louie Bellson. Alas, Webb did not get a fair shake on records; Decca's primitive recording techniques could not adequately capture his spectacular technique and wide dynamic range. He could not read music, but that didn't stop him either, for he memorized each arrangement flawlessly. Although his band did not become as influential and revered in the long run as some of its contemporaries, it nevertheless was feared in its time in the battles of the bands in Harlem's Savoy Ballroom; a famous encounter with the high-flying Benny Goodman outfit at its peak (with Gene Krupa in the drummer's chair) left the latter band drained and defeated.

William Henry Webb bought his first set of drums with his earnings as a newsboy, and he began playing in bands on pleasure boats. After moving to New York in 1925, he led bands in various clubs before settling in for long regular runs at the Savoy beginning in 1931. Although Benny Carter and Johnny Hodges played with the band early on, the Webb band was oddly short on major soloists during its heyday from the mid-'30s onward; the young alto sax player Louis Jordan made the biggest impression after leaving the band. But the band made up for it with a crisp ensemble sound, Webb's disciplined, ferociously driving drum pyrotechnics, trumpeter Taft Jordan's impressions of Louis Armstrong, and most of all, a series of strong compositions and charts by Edgar Sampson ("Blue Lou" and "Stomping at the Savoy" among them). In 1935, Webb hired the teenaged Ella Fitzgerald after she won a talent contest at the Apollo Theatre, became her legal guardian, and rebuilt his band around the singer, who provided him with his biggest hit record, "A Tisket-A-Tasket," in 1938. The band's fame continued to grow, fueled by its reputation as a giant-killer in the Savoy battles and a continuous string of Decca 78s that featured such irresistible numbers as "T'aint What You Do (It's the Way That You Do It)" and the B-side of "Tasket," "Liza." But Webb's precarious health began to give way, and after a major operation in Johns Hopkins Hospital in Baltimore, he died (his last words reportedly were, "I'm sorry, I've got to go."). After Webb's death, Fitzgerald fronted the band until it finally broke up in 1942. —*Richard S. Ginell*

★ **Chick Webb (1929-1934)** / Jun. 14, 1929-Nov. 19, 1934 / Classics ✦✦✦✦✦
The perfect way to acquire drummer Chick Webb's recordings is to get his two Classics CDs, which contain all of his performances as a leader other than Ella Fitzgerald's features (which are in a separate Ella series), and a few numbers from Webb's final dates. On the first of the CDs, Webb leads a pickup band in 1929 (for "Dog Bottom" and "Jungle Mama"), an early orchestra in 1931 (highlighted by the first version ever of Benny Carter's "Blues in My Heart"), two numbers from 1933 and all of his classic swing sides of 1934. With arranger-altoist Edgar Sampson providing such compositions as "When Dreams Come True," "Don't Be That Way," "Blue Lou" and "Stompin' At The Savoy" (all of which would become better-known for their slightly later Benny Goodman recordings), trumpeter Taft Jordan taking some vocals purposely influenced by Louis Armstrong, Jordan, trombonist Sandy Williams and tenor saxophonist Elmer Williams coming up with consistently hot solos, and the drummer-leader driving the orchestra, this was one of the top jazz big bands of the era. Highly recommended, as is Classics' *1935-1938* Chick Webb volume. —*Scott Yanow*

Spinnin' the Web / Jun. 14, 1929-Feb. 17, 1939 / Decca ✦✦✦✦✦
Drummer Chick Webb led one of the finest swing bands of the 1930s, but ironically his orchestra is today best-remembered for backing singer Ella Fitzgerald in

her early days. This CD consists of 20 instrumentals (other than a Louis Bacon vocal on "Blues in My Heart" and Ward Pinkett's scatting on "Dog Bottom") and allows one to hear how strong a big band Webb's ensemble could be. Although one regrets that only one of the four recordings by Chick Webb's Little Chicks was included (this small group featured the pioneering jazz flutist Wayman Carver), there are many enjoyable performances on this single disc. Highlights include "Don't Be That Way," "Blue Lou," "Clap Hands! Here Comes Charlie," and "Liza." The soloists (including Taft Jordan and Bobby Stark on trumpets, trombonist Sandy Williams and Elmer Williams on tenor) are excellent, but it is the Edgar Sampson arrangements and the leader's drumming that really gave this band its own personality. —*Scott Yanow*

Immortal Chick Webb: Stompin' at the Savoy / Dec. 20, 1933-Mar. 17, 1936 / Columbia ✦✦✦✦
Although Chick Webb gets top billing on this LP, he is not present on five of the twelve selections; one features Ella Fitzgerald singing "My Melancholy Baby" with Teddy Wilson's Orchestra while trumpeter Taft Jordan (one of Webb's top sidemen) performs four songs with a small group that has Eddie Dougherty on drums. Webb's orchestra spent most of its short career signed to Decca, but the seven numbers from 1933-34 on this album do contain a fair number of gems, including its theme "Let's Get Together," "On the Sunny Side of the Street" (which features Jordan verbally imitating Louis Armstrong), "If Dreams Come True" and the original version of "Stompin' at the Savoy." Except for the Taft Jordan session, all of this music has since been reissued on CD. —*Scott Yanow*

☆ **Chick Webb (1935-1938)** / Jun. 12, 1935-May 3, 1938 / Classics ✦✦✦✦✦
To a large extent the Chick Webb big band is now chiefly remembered as the launching pad for Ella Fitzgerald, but during its peak years it was one of the top swing bands. This 25-song CD from the European Classics label reissues all of the band's recordings from a three-year period that did not feature Fitzgerald as a solo singer; she does make a brief appearance on "Wake up and Live." Although there are nine vocals on this set (including three from a young Louis Jordan), the emphasis is very much on the band's instrumental talents. Such soloists as trumpeters Taft Jordan and Bobby Stark, trombonist Sandy Williams, Elmer Williams and Ted McRae on tenors and altoist Edgar Sampson are heard while the drummer/leader propels the ensembles. A special highlight are the four numbers by Chick Webb's Little Chicks, an unusual quintet featuring the pioneering jazz flutist Wayman Carver and clarinetist Chauncey Haughton. This CD is highly recommended to swing fans. —*Scott Yanow*

Bronzeville Stomp / Feb. 19, 1936-Jan. 1939 / Jazz Archives ✦✦✦✦
Of the several LPs released in the 1970s that featured the Chick Webb Orchestra in live performances, this is the most rewarding release. "Liza" matches together trumpeter Roy Eldridge and drummer Webb on a radio show in 1938, and there is a very rare live version of "Stompin' At The Savoy" featuring Chick Webb's Little Chicks (a unique quintet with flutist Wayman Carver and clarinetist Chauncey Haughton that otherwise only recorded four songs). Otherwise the music showcases Webb's big band with three numbers from a 1937 live broadcast and a dozen well-recorded radio transcriptions from Feb. 1936; the latter are also available as a Circle release. With such soloists as trumpeters Taft Jordan and Bobby Stark, trombonist Sandy Williams and tenorman Teddy McRae (not to mention five vocals by a young Ella Fitzgerald), Chick Webb certainly had a mighty outfit. —*Scott Yanow*

Standing Tall / Feb. 10, 1939-May 4, 1939 / Drive Archive ✦✦✦
This Drive Archive CD features Chick Webb's Orchestra on two radio broadcasts performed shortly before the drummer passed away. Ella Fitzgerald takes vocals on six of the dozen selections, including a rollicking "Tain't What You Do," but it is the instrumentals that are of greatest interest, especially "Blue Room," "One O'Clock Jump" and "My Wild Irish Rose" (which has some exciting drum breaks from Webb). The recording quality of this music, formerly out as an Alamac LP, has been improved, and overall this CD, although not definitive, does give listeners a good idea of how the Chick Webb big band sounded live. —*Scott Yanow*

Eberhard Weber

b. Jan. 22, 1940, Stuttgart, Germany
Bass, Cello / World Fusion, Post-Bop

Though not strictly a jazz bassist and certainly one of the least flamboyant improvisers, Eberhard Weber is among Europe's finest bassists. His style doesn't embrace either a bluesy orientation or an animated, energetic approach. Weber's influences are primarily European, notably contemporary classical and new music. His technique of using contrasting ostinato patterns in different voices was taken from composer Steve Reich. He's also made innovations in bass design. Weber added an extra string to his electric bass at the top in the early '70s; this extended its range and gave it a deeper, more striking sound. He added yet another string above that in the late '70s. Weber once doubled on cello, but dropped it to concentrate on acoustic and electric bass. Weber's father taught him cello at six, and he began to play bass at 16. He worked in school orchestras, dance bands and local jazz groups. He met Wolfgang Dauner while participating in the Dusseldorf Amateur Jazz Festival in the early '60s; they worked together over the next eight years, both as a duo and in the group Et Cetera. Weber worked with Dave Pike in the early '70s, and co-led the band Spectrum with Volker Kriegel. His early '70s album *The Colours of Chloe* was one of ECM's most acclaimed. He formed the group Colours in 1974, and toured America in 1976, '78 and '79, heading it until 1981. Weber also played from the mid-'70s to the early '80s with The United Jazz and Rock Ensemble. During the '80s, Weber worked and recorded with Jan Garbarek, and also wrote film scores and gave solo concerts. He continued recording with ECM, both with his group and with other musicians such as Gary Burton. Weber has several ECM titles available on CD. —*Ron Wynn*

● **The Colours of Chloe** / Dec. 1973 / ECM ◆◆◆◆◆

Works / Dec. 1973-Jul. 1980 / ECM ◆◆◆◆◆

Yellow Fields / Sep. 1975 / ECM ◆◆◆◆

Following Morning / Aug. 1976 / ECM ◆◆◆

Silent Feet / Nov. 1977 / ECM ◆◆◆◆
In the late '70s and '80s, bassist Eberhard Weber's music epitomized the ECM sound. Emphasizing long tones, contrasting sound with silence and heading a quartet comprising Charlie Mariano on soprano and flute, keyboardist Rainer Bruninghaus and drummer John Marshall, Weber performs three stretched-out originals including the 17-minute "Seriously Deep." This music moves slowly and requires a lot of patience by the listener. —*Scott Yanow*

Fluid Rustle / Jan. 1979 / ECM ◆◆◆◆◆

Little Movements / Jul. 1980 / ECM ◆◆◆
Bassist Eberhard Weber's "Colours" is a quartet also including Rainer Bruninghaus on piano and synthesizer, Charlie Mariano on soprano and flutes, and drummer John Marshall. On their fairly typical ECM set, the generally introspective music develops slowly and the occasional fiery moments are outnumbered by the quiet spots. A close listen does reveal some fine playing, but most jazz collectors will probably think of this set as being superior background music. —*Scott Yanow*

Later That Evening / Mar. 1982 / ECM ◆◆◆◆◆
This is one of bassist Eberhard Weber's more stimulating ECM releases, due in part to his colorful sidemen: guitarist Bill Frisell, pianist Lyle Mays (in a rare vacation from Pat Metheny), Paul McCandless (switching between soprano, oboe, English horn and bass clarinet) and drummer Michael DiPasqua. The quintet plays four of Weber's originals (including the 16-minute "Death in the Car Wash") and, although the music is sometimes introspective and full of space, Frisell largely keeps the proceedings unpredictable and adds some fire and otherworldly sounds. —*Scott Yanow*

Chorus / Sep. 1984 / ECM ◆◆

Orchestra / May 1988-Aug. 1988 / ECM ◆◆

Pendulum / 1993 / ECM ◆◆◆◆◆
Although this is essentially a solo bass date, Eberhard Weber's use of overdubbing and an echo unit turns his bass into an orchestra of sorts. Since he is a strong composer, covering a wide span of moods during this set of melodic originals and avoiding the use of his effects as gimmickry, Weber creates an introverted but accessible program whose appeal should stretch beyond just lovers of bass solos. —*Scott Yanow*

Ben Webster

b. Mar. 27, 1909, Kansas City, MO, **d.** Sep. 20, 1973, Amsterdam, Netherlands
Tenor Saxophone / Swing, Traditional Pop
Ben Webster was considered one of the "big three" of swing tenors along with Coleman Hawkins (his main influence) and Lester Young. He had a tough, raspy and brutal tone on stomps (with his own distinctive growls), yet on ballads he would turn into a pussycat and play with warmth and sentiment. After violin lessons as a child, Webster learned how to play rudimentary piano (his neighbor Pete Johnson taught him to play blues). But after Budd Johnson showed him some basics on the saxophone, Webster played sax in the Young Family Band (which at the time included Lester Young). He had stints with Jap Allen and Blanche Calloway (making his recording debut with the latter) before joining Bennie Moten's Orchestra in time to be one of the stars on a classic session in 1932. Webster spent time with quite a few orchestras in the 1930s (including Andy Kirk, Fletcher Henderson in 1934, Benny Carter, Willie Bryant, Cab Calloway and the short-lived Teddy Wilson big band). In 1940 (after short stints in 1935 and 1936), Ben Webster became Duke Ellington's first major tenor soloist. During the next three years he was on many famous recordings including "Cotton Tail" (which in addition to his memorable solo had a saxophone ensemble arranged by Webster) and "All Too Soon." After leaving Ellington in 1943 (he would return for a time in 1948-49),

Webster worked on 52nd Street, recorded frequently as both a leader and a sideman, had short periods with Raymond Scott, John Kirby and Sid Catlett, and toured with Jazz at the Philharmonic during several seasons in the 1950s. Although his sound was considered out-of-style by that decade, Webster's work on ballads became quite popular, and Norman Granz recorded him on many memorable sessions. Webster recorded a classic set with Art Tatum and generally worked steadily, but in 1964 he moved permanently to Copenhagen where he played when he pleased during his last decade. Although not all that flexible, Webster could swing with the best and his tone was a later influence on such diverse players as Archie Shepp, Lew Tabackin, Scott Hamilton and Bennie Wallace. —*Scott Yanow*

Tribute to a Great Jazzman / Nov. 25, 1936-Feb. 19, 1945 / Jazz Archives ◆◆◆◆
This LP contains many very valuable live performances. The great tenor Ben Webster is heard on seven selections with Duke Ellington's Orchestra from the 1941-43 period, jamming with pianist Teddy Wilson's pickup septet on "I Got Rhythm" in 1936 (a band also including violinist Stuff Smith and trumpeter Jonah Jones), guesting with the Woody Herman All-Stars in 1945, sitting in with Mezz Mezzrow on "Lady Be Good" and performing four numbers with a little-known version of John Kirby's Sextet (featuring either Charlie Shavers or Hot Lips Page on trumpet, clarinetist Buster Bailey and the underrated altoist George Johnson). The recording quality is generally decent and there are many inspired solos on this strong collection of previously unknown material. —*Scott Yanow*

He Played It That Way / Apr. 4, 1943-Mar. 10, 1969 / IAJRC ◆◆◆◆◆
The collector's label IAJRC uncovered some real rarities for this LP. The great tenor Ben Webster is heard accompanying the vocals of Al Hibbler (with some Ellington sidemen) and Walter Brown; the latter also features pianist Jay McShann. "Hayfoot, Strawfoot" is a 1943 aircheck with Duke Ellington's Orchestra, Webster sits in with Raymond Scott's Orchestra for "Powerhouse" and is also showcased on two longer selections apiece with trumpeter Roy Eldridge in 1954 and both McShann and altoist Eddie "Cleanhead" Vinson in 1969. Overall the recording quality is good and the solos up to the high level one would expect. Ben Webster fans in particular are advised to search out this LP. —*Scott Yanow*

Alternate and Incomplete Takes / Feb. 8, 1944 / Circle ◆◆
Circle 41 (and Jazz Archives 35) has the master takes of the eight selections recorded on Feb. 8, 1944, by a quintet comprising tenor saxophonist Ben Webster, trumpeter Hot Lips Page, pianist Clyde Hart, bassist Charlie Drayton and drummer Denzil Best. Circle 42, in contrast, contains all nine of the alternate takes plus six false starts and one incomplete performance. Obviously this set will be of greatest interest to collectors rather than general listeners although there are some strong moments on the swing session. —*Scott Yanow*

Ben and the Boys / Feb. 8, 1944-May 3, 1958 / Jazz Archives ◆◆◆◆
This is the second of two Jazz Archives LPs that comprise rare Ben Webster performances. The first side has the eight selections recorded in 1944 by a hot quintet that stars the great tenor, trumpeter Hot Lips Page and pianist Clyde Hart; these strong swing sides were also reissued on the Circle label. The flip side has four oddities. Two other numbers are taken from a loose 1945 jam session and are of interest mainly because of the personnel, which includes pianist Duke Ellington, violinist Stuff Smith and both Don Byas and Dexter Gordon on tenors (along with Webster). Ben is also heard with an all-star group backing Woody Herman's vocal on "Somebody Loves Me" and jamming "Flying Home" in 1958 with trumpeter Buck Clayton; the latter is taken from a television show. There is a lot of exciting music on this unusual and diverse set. —*Scott Yanow*

The Complete Ben Webster on EmArcy (1951-1953) / Dec. 19, 1951-Apr. 7, 1953 / EmArcy ◆◆◆◆◆
The early '50s briefly found tenor saxophonist Ben Webster moving to Kansas City for awhile before settling in Los Angeles. He recorded in several different settings for EmArcy during this time (prior to signing with Norman Granz's Verve label) and all of the music (19 songs plus 14 alternate takes) was released on this valuable two-LP set. In addition to a set with an all-star sextet that includes altoist Benny Carter and trumpeter Maynard Ferguson and four numbers backed by Johnny Richard's septet, Webster is heard as a featured sideman with Jay McShann, Johnny Otis, Dinah Washington, Marshall Royal and even the Ravens. The tenorman, whose sound had continued to grow in emotional depth since leaving Duke Ellington, excels in all of these contexts, although the large number of alternate takes makes this two-fer of primary interest to collectors. —*Scott Yanow*

King of the Tenors / May 21, 1953+Dec. 8, 1953 / Verve ◆◆◆◆◆
Two sessions are combined on this reissue CD, both of which feature the very distinctive tenor of Ben Webster. Webster is heard with two versions of the Oscar Peterson Quartet plus (on six of the 11 numbers) trumpeter Harry "Sweets" Edison and altoist Benny Carter. The original LP had eight selections; the CD adds two alternate takes plus the previously unissued "Poutin." Webster is in fine form, with

the highlights including "Tenderly," "That's All," "Pennies from Heaven" and "Cotton Tail." —*Scott Yanow*

Music for Loving / May 28, 1954-Feb. 3, 1955 / Verve ✦✦✦✦
There is a great deal of music on this two-CD set. Tenor saxophonist Ben Webster is featured on two LPs' worth of performances while backed by a string section arranged by Ralph Burns; there are five previously unissued alternate takes, five quartet numbers (four with the Teddy Wilson trio) plus a full album showcasing baritonist Harry Carney (in one of only two dates that he had as a leader) with a string section. The emphasis throughout is naturally on ballads, but there are some exceptions and enough variety to hold one's interest. Webster and Carney both play beautifully. —*Scott Yanow*

The Soul of Ben Webster / Mar. 5, 1957-Jul. 1958 / Verve ✦✦✦✦✦
Although tenor saxophonist Ben Webster gets top billing, this two-CD set actually contains an LP apiece by Webster, trumpeter Harry "Sweets" Edison and altoist Johnny Hodges. Webster is on all of the recordings, but really only stars on the first date, a septet outing with trumpeter Art Farmer and fellow tenor Harold Ashby. The great tenor is at his best on a beautiful version of "Chelsea Bridge" and "When I Fall in Love." The Edison session is a sextet outing with Webster, the Oscar Peterson Trio and drummer Alvin Stoller mixing blues and swing standards; Edison's usually muted trumpet is quite effective. The final set puts the focus on altoist Hodges, who sounds beautiful on "Don't Take Your Love from Me," although the many blues performances also give solo space to trumpeter Roy Eldridge (literally explosive on "Honey Hill") and trombonist Vic Dickenson. A total of three previously unissued performances have been added to the program, and all three of these sessions had been long out of print; they add to the legacy of Norman Granz's Verve label, showing that many top swing all-stars were actually at their prime in the 1950s. Recommended. —*Scott Yanow*

★ **Soulville** / Oct. 15, 1957 / Verve ✦✦✦✦✦
The veteran tenor saxophonist Ben Webster met up with the Oscar Peterson trio on this CD. Other than two fairly basic originals, the great tenor is showcased on durable standards and the ballads in particular are quite memorable. Peterson, bassist Ray Brown, guitarist Herb Ellis and drummer Stan Levey are superior in support of the masterful saxophonist. —*Scott Yanow*

Tenor Giants / Oct. 16, 1957-Apr. 9, 1959 / Verve ✦✦✦✦✦
Coleman Hawkins was always Ben Webster's idol. They finally shared a record date on Oct. 16, 1957, and it was reissued as half of this two-LP set. With the backing of the Oscar Peterson Trio plus drummer Alvin Stoller, Webster and Hawk match wits and ideas on seven standards and two of Hawkins's originals. Webster was really no match for the elder tenor (and he knew it), particularly harmonically (Hawk was a master of chords), but he had the advantage of a huge emotional tone. Although Hawkins wins honors, it is not a runaway. The second album also features the two tenor greats plus the tenor of Budd Johnson, trumpeter Roy Eldridge and a four-piece rhythm section. Webster wrote three songs for the date (including tributes to Hawk and Budd) and there is a 20-minute version of "In a Mellow Tone" to wrap up the proceedings. The results are a dead heat except on "Time After Time" where Webster's beautiful sound is well-featured. Recommended, but it will take a search to locate this two-fer. —*Scott Yanow*

Ben Webster Meets Gerry Mulligan / Nov. 3, 1959 / Verve ✦✦✦✦✦
Ben Webster Meets Oscar Peterson / Nov. 6, 1959 / Verve ✦✦✦✦

Warm Moods / Jan. 18, 1960-Jan. 19, 1960 / Discovery ✦✦✦
The veteran tenor Ben Webster had a very warm tone on ballads that contrasted with the aggressive biting sound he used on faster material. For this 1960 set Webster is joined by a string quartet (arranged by Johnny Richards) and a rhythm section for his melodic interpretations of a dozen standards. Even when simply stating the melody, Webster brings out unexpected beauty in the songs. His tone has never been accurately duplicated and is the main reason to pick up this CD reissue. —*Scott Yanow*

At the Renaissance / Oct. 14, 1960 / Original Jazz Classics ✦✦✦✦
This live set features tenor great Ben Webster playing with pianist Jimmy Rowles, guitarist Jim Hall, bassist Red Mitchell and drummer Frank Butler in a club, and the music is consistently wonderful. Whether showing warmth and sentimentality on "Georgia on My Mind" and "Stardust" or growling and roaring on "Caravan" and "Ole Miss Blues," Webster (who was then somewhat taken for granted) is in superior and creative form. Recommended. —*Scott Yanow*

Ben and Sweets / Jun. 6, 1962+Jun. 7, 1962 / Columbia ✦✦✦
Tenor saxophonist Ben Webster and trumpeter Harry "Sweets" Edison, both veterans of the swing era (although associated with different orchestras), had long wanted to record a full album together. The results, a swinging quintet set with pianist Hank Jones, bassist George Duvivier and drummer Clarence Johnston, are quite rewarding. There are two ballad features for the tenor ("How Long Has This Been Going On" and a beautiful version of "My Romance") and one for Edison

("Embraceable You") along with three medium-tempo collaborations. Nothing unexpected occurs but the melodic music is quite enjoyable. —*Scott Yanow*

Soulmates / Sep. 20, 1963+Oct. 14, 1963 / Original Jazz Classics ✦✦✦✦

Live: Providence, Rhode Island, 1963 / Dec. 7, 1963 / Storyville ✦✦✦✦
Recorded shortly before he left the US to settle permanently in Europe, this live session features the great tenor saxophonist Ben Webster with a local trio consisting of the young pianist Michael Renzi, bassist Bob Petterutti and drummer Joe Veletri. The CD reissue (which adds a previously unissued version of "Tenderly" to the original program) has a typical set by Webster, who alternates stomps such as "Perdido" and "Wee Dot" with warm ballads. This release gives one an excellent example of Webster's work in the 1960s at a time when he was being overlooked in favor of younger and more adventurous tenors. —*Scott Yanow*

☆ **Meet You at the Fair** / Mar. 11, 1964-Nov. 10, 1964 / Impulse! ✦✦✦✦✦
Ben Webster's final American recording was one of his greatest. At 55, the tenor saxophonist was still very much in his prime but considered out of style in the US. He would soon permanently move to Europe where he was better appreciated. This CD has the nine selections originally included on the LP of the same name, a quartet set with either Hank Jones or Roger Kellaway on piano, bassist Richard Davis and drummer Osie Johnson. Webster's tone has rarely sounded more beautiful than on "Someone to Watch over Me" and "Our Love Is Here to Stay." In addition one song from the same session (but originally released on a sampler) and two tunes featuring Webster on an Oliver Nelson date (*More Blues and the Abstract Truth*) wrap up this definitive CD. —*Scott Yanow*

Stormy Weather / Jan. 30, 1965 / Black Lion ✦✦✦✦✦
Recorded around a month after the veteran tenor Ben Webster moved to Europe, this high-quality set with pianist Kenny Drew, bassist Neils Pederson and drummer Alex Riel features Webster stretching out on the traditional "Londonderry Air," two originals and seven familiar but fresh standards. Webster, although neglected in the US, was still in peak form in the mid-'60s as witness this and his other Black Lion CDs covering the period. —*Scott Yanow*

Gone with the Wind / Jan. 31, 1965 / Black Lion ✦✦✦✦✦
Recorded early in tenor saxophonist Ben Webster's long European period, this quartet set (reissued on a Black Lion CD) features Webster with pianist Kenny Drew, bassist Niels Pederson and drummer Alex Riel. The music is typical of the tenor's repertoire of the period, mostly swing standards with a few medium-tempo romps sandwiched by warm ballad statements. Highlights include "I'm Gonna Sit Right Down and Write Myself a Letter," "Sunday," "Gone with the Wind" and "Over the Rainbow." —*Scott Yanow*

In a Mellow Tone / May 14, 1965-May 15, 1965 / Jazz House ✦✦✦
Released for the first time in 1995, this live performance from tenor saxophonist Ben Webster was recorded early during his years in Europe. Webster, who is heard playing swing standards and blues with an English rhythm section (pianist Alan Branscombe, bassist Lennie Bush and drummer Jackie Dougan), is in fine form during his ten numbers although his solos are rather predictable, alternating stomps and ballads. The rhythm trio is competent but not at all distinctive. A short interview that concludes the CD gives one an opportunity to hear Webster's speaking voice, although once again nothing memorable or unusual occurs. This release, which is enjoyable enough, is strictly for Ben Webster completists. —*Scott Yanow*

There Is No Greater Love / Sep. 5, 1965 / Black Lion ✦✦✦✦
Ben Webster is reunited with pianist Kenny Drew, bassist Niels Pedersen and drummer Alex Riel for this fine studio recording. He had used the same sidemen earlier in the year at the Montmartre, resulting in two other Black Lion CDs. The emphasis here is on ballads and slower tempos for a very lyrical effort. Webster's tone sounds typically beautiful on the eight standards, highlighted by "Stardust," "There Is No Greater Love," "I Got It Bad" and "Autumn Leaves." —*Scott Yanow*

Black Lion Presents / Sep. 5, 1965-Apr. 27, 1967 / Black Lion ✦✦✦✦✦
This reissue is a box that simply houses three Ben Webster Black Lion releases, which are also readily available as single CDs. The veteran tenor saxophonist is showcased in a trio of settings from early in his European years. *There Is No Greater Love* is a ballad-oriented quartet date from 1965 with pianist Kenny Drew, bassist Niels Pedersen and drummer Alex Riel. *The Jeep Is Jumping* teams Webster with two other horns in a sextet that sounds very much like a Duke Ellington small group from the 1930s. The last album, *Ben Webster Meets Bill Coleman*, reunites Webster with the fine swing trumpeter Bill Coleman on record for the first time since 1946; both sound inspired. All self-respecting swing and mainstream fans who do not have these individual CDs are advised to get this very enjoyable box. —*Scott Yanow*

The Jeep Is Jumping / Sep. 13, 1965-Sep. 21, 1965 / Black Lion ✦✦✦✦
One of four Ben Webster Black Lion CDs from 1965, this is the only one on which he is matched with other horn players. The great tenor interacts engagingly with

trumpeter Arnved Meyer's mainstream quintet, with the resulting music sometimes a bit reminiscent of Duke Ellington's small-group recordings of the 1930s. In addition to his warm versions of "Nancy with the Laughing Face," "My Romance" and "Days of Wine and Roses," it is a pleasure to hear Webster romping on "Stompy Jones" and "The Jeep Is Jumping" over 20 years after he originally left Ellington's band. —*Scott Yanow*

Swingin' in London / Apr. 27, 1967 / Black Lion ◆◆◆◆
Tenor saxophonist Ben Webster, who had moved permanently to Europe in 1965, meets up with the veteran trumpeter Bill Coleman (a resident of Europe since the late '40s) for this upbeat swing session. In addition to three collaborations, they perform four standards, with Coleman having a feature on "But Not for Me" and taking a pair of vocals. The music is quite enjoyable and swinging, a good outing for all concerned. —*Scott Yanow*

Plays Ballads / Jul. 14, 1967-Nov. 22, 1971 / Storyville ◆◆◆◆
Ben Webster had a perfect tone for playing ballads, full of sentiment and emotion. On this Storyville release he caresses seven timeless melodies in a variety of settings, including trios with either Teddy Wilson, Ole Kock Hansen or Kenny Drew on piano, backing by the Danish Radio Big Band (on "Cry Me a River") or a version of "Greensleeves" with a string orchestra. Although largely forgotten in the US (he had moved to Europe in 1965), Ben Webster was still in fine form this late in his career. —*Scott Yanow*

Plays Duke Ellington / Jul. 14, 1967-Nov. 22, 1971 / Storyville ◆◆◆◆◆
Although he was only a member of Duke Ellington's Orchestra for three years, tenor saxophonist Ben Webster was linked with Duke Ellington throughout his career. This Storyville release features the great tenor playing nine songs associated with Ellington. The music is drawn from five separate sessions including trio gigs with pianists Kenny Drew and Teddy Wilson and three with The Danish Radio Band. The emphasis is on uptempo pieces such as "Perdido," "Rockin' in Rhythm" and "Stompy Jones"; a special highlight are the two very different versions of "Cottontail." —*Scott Yanow*

Ben Meets Don Byas / Feb. 1, 1968-Feb. 2, 1968 / Saba ◆◆◆◆

Masters of Jazz, Vol. 5 / 1968-Sep. 25, 1970 / Storyville ◆◆◆◆
This entry in Storyville's *Masters of Jazz* series (which does not duplicate his *Plays Duke Ellington* and *Plays Ballads* albums) alternates ballads and stomps to give listeners a well-rounded picture of Ben Webster during his last period. Webster is joined by trios led by pianists Kenny Drew and Teddy Wilson, interacts with a drumless piano-bass duo, plays with a Scandinavian quartet, romps with the Danish Radio Big Band on two numbers and is accompanied on "Going Home" and "Come Sunday" by a string orchestra. These Copenhagen recordings find the great tenor in consistently fine form. —*Scott Yanow*

At Work in Europe / May 26, 1969 / Prestige ◆◆◆◆
This double LP gives the veteran tenor saxophonist an opportunity to stretch out on five Ellington songs (plus his original "One for the Guv'nor") with a trio led by pianist Cees Slinger in addition to performing four fairly basic numbers ("The Preacher," "Straight, No Chaser," "Work Song" and "John Brown's Body") with an unusual quartet featuring both Kenny Drew and Frans Wieringa on pianos. Throughout Webster sounds quite relaxed, warm and swinging. He no longer had to prove himself and he clearly enjoyed himself on these performances. —*Scott Yanow*

No Fool, No Fun / Oct. 27, 1970 / Spotlite ◆◆
This unusual LP features the great tenorman Ben Webster at a rehearsal with the Denmark Radio Big Band and singers Matty Peters and Freddy Albeck. Webster often calls out instructions to the group and at various times sounds humorous, instructive and impatient. There is not a great amount of music on this set with its many breakdowns and interruptions, but Webster fans will find these candid and certainly spontaneous moments to be of interest. —*Scott Yanow*

Live at the Haarlemse Jazzclub / May 9, 1972 / Cat ◆◆◆
There are many CDs available from tenor saxophonist Ben Webster's period in Europe that were recorded live during club performances. Virtually all are worth hearing even though the veteran tenor's style was no longer evolving. This set, recorded in Holland with pianist Tete Montoliu and a pair of Dutch players, finds Webster playing six veteran standards including such standbys as "Sunday," "How Long Has This Been Going On" and "Perdido." The music is quite enjoyable and swinging if not all that essential. —*Scott Yanow*

Makin' Whoopee / Jun. 5, 1972 / Spotlite ◆◆◆◆◆
Due to the fresher than usual repertoire (which is highlighted by "Johnny Come Lately," "I Want a Little Girl" and two of his originals), this is one of Ben Webster's better recordings from his later years. Recorded just 15 months before his death, the veteran tenor is in excellent form. The French rhythm section (led by pianist Georges Arvanitas) is also excellent and the swinging music is given creative treatment. —*Scott Yanow*

Did You Call / Nov. 28, 1972 / Nessa ◆◆◆◆
The great tenor Ben Webster is in suprisingly solid form this late in his career for a quartet set. With the virtuosic pianist Tete Montoliu heading the rhythm section, Webster alternates standards with his riffing originals, showing that his memorable tone was still very much intact on what would be his final studio recording. —*Scott Yanow*

My Man / Jan. 1973-Apr. 1973 / Steeple Chase ◆◆◆
Just months before his death, the great tenor Ben Webster shows that even with an occasional shortness of breath, he never really declined musically. The six selections (five standards and his "Set Call") are all familiar (one wonders how many times Webster recorded "Sunday") but he still sounds enthusiastic and emotional. Joined by pianist Ole Kock Hansen, bassist Bo Stief and drummer Alex Riel for these appearances at the Montmartre in Copenhagen, Webster's warm ballad renditions and hard-driving romps are as always quite enjoyable to hear. —*Scott Yanow*

Freddy Webster

b. 1916, Cleveland, OH, **d.** Apr. 1, 1947, Chicago, IL
Trumpet / Bop
Evaluating the lyrical Freddy Webster (as with Freddie Keppard in the 1920s) can be a frustrating exercise due to his relatively few recordings. Miles Davis considered him a major influence and Dizzy Gillespie often praised his tone. After working with Earl Hines and Erskine Tate in 1938, Wesbter moved to New York, and in his short career he played with many top big bands including those led by Benny Carter, Eddie Durham (1940), Lucky Millinder, Jimmy Lunceford (1942-43) and Cab Calloway. He had a few memorable solos with Miss Rhapsody, Frankie Socolow and Sarah Vaughan ("You're Not the Kind") and can be heard on broadcasts with Lucky Millinder, but never led a session of his own. After playing with John Kirby's sextet, Dizzy Gillespie's big band and Sonny Stitt, drugs did him in at age 31. —*Scott Yanow*

George Wein

b. Oct. 3, 1925, Boston, MA
Piano / Dixieland, Mainstream Jazz
George Wein's main importance to jazz has been his work at organizing and booking festivals including Newport (which he helped found in 1954) and his own Storyville club in the 1950s. However Wein has long been a fine Earl Hines-inspired pianist (and an occasional vocalist), quite comfortable in swing and Dixieland-oriented settings. On an irregular basis since the 1950s he has toured and recorded with his Newport All-Stars, which has included cornetist Ruby Braff, clarinetist Pee Wee Russell and tenorman Bud Freeman; more recently Scott Hamilton on tenor and cornetist Warren Vache. —*Scott Yanow*

Wein, Women and Song / Apr. 11, 1955 / Atlantic ◆◆◆◆

The Magic Horn / May 27, 1956 / RCA ◆◆◆◆
This rather obscure LP was put together just prior to pianist George Wein leading this jazz band on a live television special called *The Magic Horn*. With the exception of the title cut, all of the numbers are veteran Dixieland standards. With an all-star lineup consisting of trumpeter Ruby Braff, trombonist Vic Dickenson, either Peanuts Hucko or Bill Stegmeyer on clarinet, baritonist Ernie Caceres, Wein, bassist Milt Hinton, drummer Buzzy Drootin and (for two guest shots) cornetist Jimmy McPartland (both McPartland and Braff wail away on "Dippermouth Blues"), it is of little surprise that the music is joyous and full of spirit. It is a pity that this fine session has been out of print for many years. —*Scott Yanow*

● **George Wein & The Newport All-Stars** / Oct. 12, 1962 / Impulse! ◆◆◆◆◆
Long overdue to be reissued by Impulse, this definitive set features one of the strongest versions of George Wein's Newport All-Stars: cornetist Ruby Braff, valve trombonist Marshall Brown, clarinetist Pee Wee Russell, tenor great Bud Freeman, bassist Bill Takas, drummer Marquis Foster and the leader-pianist. The repertoire includes several rousers (such as "At The Jazz Band Ball" and "Keepin' Out of Mischief Now") plus features for Russell ("The Bends Blues") and Freeman (an explosive "Crazy Rhythm"). Highly recommended for Dixieland and small-group swing fans. —*Scott Yanow*

George Wein Is Alive and Well in Mexico / Apr. 1967 / Columbia ◆◆◆◆◆
George Wein's Newport All-Stars in the 1960s featured a pair of great Eddie Condon alumnus (clarinetist Pee Wee Russell and tenor saxophonist Bud Freeman), a swinging rhythm section (the leader-pianist, bassist Jack Lesberg and drummer Don Lamond) and the highly expressive cornetist Ruby Braff. The music on this LP, taken from concerts in Mexico, are among Russell's last good recordings before his quick decline. The eight swing standards are all given inventive and spirited treatment and each of the musicians gets their chances to shine. Highly recom-

mended and worth searching for until Columbia gets around to reissuing this timeless music. —*Scott Yanow*

George Wein's Newport All-Stars / Feb. 26, 1969-Feb. 27, 1969 / Atlantic ✦✦✦✦

Unlike the earlier editions of the Newport All-Stars, the 1969 group leaned much more heavily toward swing and elements of bop than to Dixieland. In addition to pianist George Wein and cornetist Ruby Braff, the band heard on this Atlantic LP includes vibraphonist Red Norvo, both Tal Farlow and Barney Kessel on guitars, bassist Larry Ridley and drummer Don Lamond. Highlights include "In a Little Spanish Town," "Ja-Da," "My Melancholy Baby," "Exactly Like You" and even the pop tune "Sunny"; Braff's passion alone makes this a worthy release. —*Scott Yanow*

Tribute to Duke / Oct. 29, 1969 / MPS ✦✦✦✦

Although this LP is labeled as a tribute to Duke Ellington, only five of the ten songs have anything to do with Ellington. The personnel varies throughout the live concert with the great veteran Joe Venuti (in the early part of his successful comeback) being featured on the first three numbers (including "Sweet Georgia Brown" and "Undecided"), some unaccompanied guitar solos by Kenny Burrell and Barney Kessel, and a couple of ballad showcases for cornetist Ruby Braff. Also heard from are vibraphonist Red Norvo and the fine rhythm section led by pianist-leader George Wein. This is a strong mainstream set from an era when the swing-based music seemed to be in danger of becoming extinct. —*Scott Yanow*

The Newport Jazz Festival All-Stars / Apr. 1984 / Concord Jazz ✦✦✦✦✦

After a decade of inactivity, George Wein put together a new version of his New-port All-Stars in the early 1980s. Enlisting the young mainstream stars tenor saxo-phonist Scott Hamilton and cornetist Warren Vache, Wein's 1984 sextet also includes altoist Norris Turney (formerly with Duke Ellington), bassist Slam Stew-art, drummer Oliver Jackson and the leader on piano. This highly enjoyable dou-ble-LP (which has not yet been reissued on CD) features the group playing a dozen swing and Dixieland standards plus Wein's "Centennial Blues." Turney gets a chance to be showcased on some Ellington standards, Wein is excellent on "Rosetta," Hamilton comes up with a fresh statement on "Body and Soul" and there are plenty of spots for Stewart and Vache. Highly recommended. —*Scott Yanow*

European Tour / May 1987 / Concord Jazz ✦✦✦✦✦

This swinging Concord release teams together the young veterans Scott Hamilton (on tenor) and cornetist Warren Vache with former Ellingtonians Harold Ashby (also on tenor) and altoist Norris Turney as part of George Wein's 1987 Newport All-Stars. In addition to those four fine soloists, tenorman Al Cohn is a guest, bass-ist Slam Stewart (in what would be his final recording before his death a few months later) contributes some delightful wordless vocalizing in unison with his bowed bass, drummer Oliver Jackson is excellent in support and pianist Wein shows off his roots in Earl Hines. The group jams through seven swing standards including a 10 and-a-half minute version of "Love Me Or Leave Me." Easily recom-mended to mainstream collectors, this date lights plenty of sparks. —*Scott Yanow*

Swing That Music / Aug. 24, 1993-Aug. 25, 1993 / Columbia ✦✦✦

With a lineup comprising fluegelhornist Clark Terry, trumpeter Warren Vache, trombonist Al Grey, tenors Illinois Jacquet and Flip Phillips, guitarist Howard Alden, bassist Eddie Jones and drummer Kenny Washington, one would expect a lot of fireworks from the 1993 version of George Wein's Newport All-Stars. Unfor-tunately the music does not quite live up to one's expectations. Phillips and Jac-quet (two veterans of Jazz at the Philharmonic) never trade off, C.T. and Vache get in each other's way during ensembles and Grey's uptempo blues ("Open Wider Please") ends quite inconclusively. There are some exciting moments, such as Clark Terry's Mumbles vocal on "Tain't What You Do," a ballad medley ("Tears" and "Nuages") by the duo of Phillips and Alden and a passionate R&Bish alto solo by Jacquet on a blues. The music is full of good humor, but more planning would have made this enjoyable session into a great one. —*Scott Yanow*

Walt Weiskopf

b. 1959, Augusta, GA
Tenor Saxophone, Soprano Saxophone / Post-Bop

A potent tenor saxophonist and composer firmly in the tradition of John Coltrane and Sonny Rollins, Walt Weiskopf was born in Augusta, GA, and grew up in Syra-cuse, NY. Upon moving to New York City, he joined the Buddy Rich Big Band in 1981 at the age of 21; two years later, Weiskopf signed on with the Toshiko Akiy-oshi Jazz Orchestra, concurrently forming his own quartet with brother Joel on trumpet, Jay Anderson on bass and Jeff Hirshfeld on drums. His debut *Exact Sci-ence* appeared in 1989, followed a year later by *Mindwalking; Simplicity,* released in 1992, topped the European jazz charts for four weeks. After 1993's *A World Away,* Weiskopf for the first time departed from original compositions to record

1995's *Night Lights,* a collection of standards; 1997's *Song for My Mother,* however, returned his own material to the forefront. A graduate of the Eastman School of Music in Rochester, NY, Weiskopf and fellow Eastman alum Ramon Ricker teamed up in 1990 to write the books *Coltrane: A Player's Guide to His Harmony* and *The Augmented Scale in Jazz;* in 1994, Weiskopf also published *Intervalic Improvisa-tion,* a player's guide for broadening the scope of modern jazz improvisation. In 1996, he joined drummer Rick Hollander's quartet. —*Jason Ankeny*

Exact Science / 1989 / Iris ✦✦✦

Mindwalking / Jun. 1990-Sep. 1990 / Iris ✦✦✦

● Simplicity / Dec. 23, 1992 / Criss Cross ✦✦✦✦✦

A World Away / Dec. 21, 1993 / Criss Cross ✦✦✦✦

Night Lights / Oct. 14, 1995+Oct. 16, 1995 / Double-Time ✦✦✦✦

Walt Weiskopf performs seven standards and three originals on this quartet set with pianist Joel Weiskopf, bassist Drew Gress and drummer Steve Davis. Weiskopf, who has written an instructional book on John Coltrane's style, sounds too close for comfort to 'Trane on this otherwise enjoyable set. He is certainly a technically gifted player and his versions of such tunes as "You Go to My Head," "Moonlight on the Ganges," "Some Other Time" and "I Wish I Knew" are reason-ably adventurous, but Weiskopf should really work on developing his own musical personality. —*Scott Yanow*

Dicky Wells (William Wells)

b. Jun. 10, 1907, Centerville, TN, **d.** Nov. 12, 1985, New York, NY
Trombone / Swing

One of the more adventurous trombonists of the swing era, the distinctive Dicky Wells was somewhat innovative, playing his horn in a speechlike style filled with a great deal of color, humor and swing. Although he came to fame with Count Basie in 1938, Wells had been a major-league player for a decade before that. After mov-ing to New York in 1926 he recorded with Cecil Scott (to hilarious effect on "In a Corner") and Spike Hughes in addition to working with Fletcher Henderson, Benny Carter and Teddy Hill; during a European tour with Hill he recorded exten-sively. The Basie years (1938-45 and 1947-50) gave him some fame and his playing behind singer Jimmy Rushing was particularly memorable. His later years were somewhat anti-climatic, but there were engagements with Rushing, reunions with Basie sidemen, European tours with Buck Clayton, a stint (1961-63) with Ray Charles and occasional appearances (including on the classic TV special *The Sound of Jazz* in 1957). After about 1965 Wells' alcoholism and declining musi-cianship forced him to get a day job as a messenger, although he did write his memoirs (*The Night People*) and he came back for a final album in 1981. —*Scott Yanow*

● Dicky Wells in Paris, 1937 / Jul. 7, 1937+Jul. 12, 1937 / Prestige ✦✦✦✦✦

This LP (which is long overdue to be reissued on CD) has a dozen of the finest per-formances ever recorded by trombonist Dicky Wells. Wells, who is heard before he found fame with Count Basie's Orchestra, is featured on three numbers (including a memorable "Bugle Call Rag") with three trumpets (Bill Coleman, Shad Collins and Bill Dillard), guitarist Django Reinhardt and a pianoless rhythm section; three other songs use the same group with Coleman as the only trumpeter. In addition, Wells is heard with a septet and on versions of "Lady Be Good" and "Dicky Wells Blues" as the only horn in a quartet. Wells' humor, distinctive sound and ability to swing are all well showcased on these near-classic performances. —*Scott Yanow*

Bones for the King / Feb. 3, 1958-Feb. 4, 1958 / Affinity ✦✦✦

This Affinity LP draws its material from the short-lived Felsted label. Dicky Wells is heard in an unusual session with fellow trombonists Vic Dickenson, Benny Mor-ton and George Matthews on three songs that fail to live up to their potential; the inclusion of organist Skip Hall does not help and weighs down the ensembles. The other half of the set features Wells with some notable Basie alumni (including trumpeter Buck Clayton, clarinetist Rudy Rutherford and tenorman Buddy Tate) and fortunately on that occasion Skip Hall plays piano. There is some good swing-based music to be heard throughout this album but nothing essential occurs. —*Scott Yanow*

Lonesome Road / Apr. 8, 1981-Apr. 29, 1981 / Uptown ✦✦

This is a difficult LP to rate. Compared to the trombonist's best work, it is a weak effort, but considering that Dicky Wells (who had been in poor health) hadn't recorded for years and his extroverted personality still shines through (and he con-tinues taking wild chances), this is certainly a colorful album. Joined by pianist Dick Katz, either George Duvivier or Michael Moore on bass, drummer Oliver Jackson and on five of the nine songs, Buddy Tate on tenor and clarinet, Wells (on his final recording) mostly explores standards and blues with spirit, determination and swing. —*Scott Yanow*

Dick Wellstood

b. Nov. 25, 1927, Greenwich, CT, **d.** Jul. 24, 1987, Palo Alto, CA
Piano / Stride, Classic Jazz

One of the two great stride pianists (along with Ralph Sutton) to emerge during the 1940s when members of their generation were generally playing bebop, Wellstood kept an open mind toward later styles (he loved Monk) while sounding at his best playing classic jazz. A little more subtle than Sutton, Wellstood was also a powerful pianist who was a superb interpreter of the music of James P. Johnson and his contemporaries. He came to New York with Bob Wilber's Wildcats in 1946 and caught up in the trad jazz scene quickly. By 1947 he was playing with Sidney Bechet and in the 1950s he mostly worked with veteran players including trumpeters Roy Eldridge, Rex Stewart and Charlie Shavers and the Eddie Condon gang. He was in the intermission band at Condon's starting in 1956 and later was house pianist at the Metropole and Nick's. After a period with Gene Krupa's quartet, he toured with the World's Greatest Jazz Band. Wellstood remained active throughout his all-too-short life, playing solo concerts, performing at jazz parties and recording quite a few memorable albums. —*Scott Yanow*

Dick Wellstood Alone / Nov. 1970-Mar. 1971 / Solo Art ✦✦✦✦✦
Surprisingly this Jazzology album was only the second solo set ever recorded by the brilliant stride pianist Dick Wellstood. His repertoire on the date is offbeat, with not only tunes by Fats Waller, James P. Johnson and Scott Joplin ("Fig Leaf") but Zez Confrey's obscure "Poor Buttermilk," "Russian Rag" and two originals. This little-known album is easily recommended to followers of classic jazz. This 1997 CD adds four selections (including a three-song Duke Ellington medley) from 1975 to the original program. —*Scott Yanow*

★ **Dick Wellstood and His Famous Orchestra Featuring Kenny Davern** / Jul. 1973-1981 / Chiaroscuro ✦✦✦✦✦
This is the Dick Wellstood CD to get. Two former LPs (*Dick Wellstood and His Famous Orchestra Featuring Kenny Davern* and *The Blue Three at Hanratty's*) have been reissued in full on this single CD, which contains 78 minutes of music. The first eight selections (from 1973) feature Wellstood with soprano saxophonist Kenny Davern in a set of stirring duets while the final nine songs have a trio comprising Wellstood, Davern (sticking to clarinet) and drummer Bobby Rosengarden. Wellstood and Davern make a perfectly compatible team whether on surprising versions of Dixieland standards (such as "Original Dixieland One Step," "Tiger Rag" and "Indiana") or obscurities such as Eddie Condon's (not George Gershwin's) "Liza" and "Oh Peter"; the opening number is an original simply titled "Fast As a Bastard!" A highly recommended set of brilliant prebop hot jazz. —*Scott Yanow*

☆ **This Is the One . . . Dig!** / Oct. 12, 1975 / Solo Art ✦✦✦✦✦
This was the great pianist Dick Wellstood's personal favorite record and one can understand why. The music is very well recorded and Wellstood sounds quite inspired throughout the solo set. For the 1994 CD reissue, the original eight songs are joined by eight additional (and previously unreleased) performances and the quality stays consistently high. Wellstood, who had an open mind toward more modern styles of jazz while keeping his stride piano style undiluted, performs surprising versions of "You Are The Sunshine of My Life" and John Coltrane's "Giant Steps" in addition to some swing standards and classics associated with James P. Johnson, Fats Waller and Earl Hines. Among the high points are "Snowy Morning Blues," "If Dreams Come True," "Rosetta" and a piece based on a classical work ("Paganini's Thing"). This is an essential acquisition for classic jazz collectors. —*Scott Yanow*

Fats Waller Revisited / 1975 / Classic Jazz ✦✦✦✦
This is a long-forgotten but very worthy Fats Waller tribute performed by a septet led and arranged by pianist Dick Wellstood. With Zoot Sims on tenor, both Ed Polcer and John Bucher playing cornets, guitarist Al Casey (who was a regular member of Waller's bands 35 years earlier), bassist Major Holley, drummer Panama Francis, Wellstood and the seemingly ageless singer Jane Harvey, this is a particularly rewarding session. The group performs ten songs associated with Waller including "I'm Gonna Sit Right Down and Write Myself a Letter," "I Can't Give You Anything But Love," "Honeysuckle Rose" and "Ain't Misbehavin.'" The ensemble resembles one of Waller's bands, Wellstood had long assimilated Fats' musical language into his own distinctive style, and Jane Harvey sounds wonderful. Well worth searching for. —*Scott Yanow*

Take Me to the Land of Jazz / Jan. 2, 1978-Jan. 3, 1978 / Aviva ✦✦✦✦
The short-lived Aviva label was launched with this 1978 LP. Pianist Dick Wellstood and guitarist-vocalist Marty Grosz are the main stars (their musical partnership would soon result in the Classic Jazz Quartet) but the contributions of the underrated Sam Parkins (doubling on tenor and clarinet), bassist Mickey Galizio and drummer Tommy Benford (who used to play with Jelly Roll Morton) should not be overlooked either. This was one of the first albums to really give Grosz a strong

opportunity to sing in his witty Fats Waller-influenced style. Highlights include "Let Yourself Go," "Take Me to that Land of Jazz," James P. Johnson's "Snowy Morning Blues" (a piano solo feature for Wellstood), "I'd Do Anything for You" and two versions of "The Gold Digger's Song." It is a pity that all of the defunct Aviva label's recordings are currently difficult to find, for its swinging classic jazz is consistently enjoyable. —*Scott Yanow*

Live at Hanratty's / 1981 / Chaz Jazz ✦✦✦✦✦
It is ironic that this double-LP, one of pianist Dick Wellstood's finest recordings, has been out of print almost since its 1981 release by the short-lived Chaz Jazz label. Wellstood's lengthy solo recital finds him interpreting a particularly eclectic repertoire that includes "Jingle Bells," a medley of tunes associated with Cole Porter and Bessie Smith, Sidney Bechet's obscure "Quincy Street Stomp," his own "Cha Cha For Charlie" and Louis Armstrong's famous "Cornet Chop Suey" among others. Wellstood is heard at the top of his form throughout, making one wish that some enterprising record producer would lease or purchase the valuable Chaz Jazz catalog and reissue all of the valuable music. —*Scott Yanow*

I Wish I Were Twins / Mar. 3, 1983+Mar. 13, 1983 / Swingtime ✦✦✦✦✦
Dick Wellstood and Dick Hyman team up for a set of piano duos on this valuable German import LP. Wellstood ranked with Ralph Sutton as the top stride pianist to emerge since World War II, while Hyman has proven that he can play any style with the best. In addition to individual features (Hyman has "A Foggy Day" while Wellstood interprets Sidney Bechet's "Quincy Street Stomp"), they play eight often-stunning duos. High points include "The Sheik of Araby," "Somebody Stole My Gal," "Dinah," "I've Found a New Baby" and the title cut. Very exciting music. —*Scott Yanow*

Diane / Feb. 18, 1985-Feb. 19, 1985 / Swingtime ✦✦✦✦
Pianist Dick Wellstood never recorded an uninspired record, particularly solo. On this unaccompanied recital for the German Swingtime label (cut just two years before his early death), Wellstood plays a typically eclectic set of music that includes Fats Waller's "Keepin' Out of Mischief Now," Duke Ellington's "The Mooche," "Jingle Bells," the *Sesame Street* novelty "Rubber Dickie," James P. Johnson's "Willow Tree" and "The Entertainer." This LP is recommended to lucky listeners who can find the album. —*Scott Yanow*

Live at Cafe Des Copains / May 29, 1985 / Unisson ✦✦✦✦✦
For this live solo album from Toronto, pianist Dick Wellstood mostly plays remakes of songs he had recorded earlier (including "Jingle Bells," "The Entertainer" and "Rubber Duckie") plus a variety of veteran swing-era standards. Wellstood was one of the top stride pianists of the past 50 years (along with Ralph Sutton) yet had a strong musical curiosity that reached beyond early jazz, as can be heard in some of his improvisations. Excellent music. —*Scott Yanow*

Live at the Sticky Wicket / Nov. 9, 1986 / Arbors ✦✦✦✦✦

After You've Gone / Mar. 11, 1987 / Unisson ✦✦✦✦
Recorded just four months before his unexpected death at age 59, this live solo set from pianist Dick Wellstood is up to the quality of his best work. Wellstood reaches beyond his roots in stride piano to play such songs as "Here's That Rainy Day," "Pitter Panther Patter" and Thelonious Monk's "Bye-Ya" in addition to romping through such older pieces as Fats Waller's "The Joint Is Jumpin'," "Boots and Saddles" and "After You've Gone." The music is so strong in fact that it is difficult to realize that this was Dick Wellstood's final recording. —*Scott Yanow*

Kenny Werner

b. 1951, New York, NY
Piano / Post-Bop

A fascinating pianist/electronic keyboardist who is bound by few restrictions. An absolutely astounding trio pianist, he can back singers (notably Roseanna Vitro) with perfect empathy, and has done some interesting synthesizer programming. —*Michael G. Nastos*

Piano Music of (Bix Beiderbecke, Duke Ellington, George Gershwin, James P. Johnson) / 1977 / Finnakar ✦✦✦

Introducing the Trio / Mar. 6, 1989-Mar. 7, 1989 / Sunnyside ✦✦✦✦
Werner (p), Ratso Harris (b), Tommy Rainey (d). Contains four compositions by Werner, two by Harris, three standards. Nice tribute to Herbie Nichols. One of the finer trio dates of the last decade. —*Michael G. Nastos*

Uncovered Heart / Jan. 10, 1990-Jan. 11, 1990 / Sunnyside ✦✦✦✦
Kenny Werner's compositions on his CD are full of surprising turns and contrasting moods. Although none of his 12 complex originals on the date are destined to become standards, these complicated pieces serve as a strong challenge to the improvising talents of Werner's impressive group (which also includes trumpeter Randy Brecker, Joe Lovano on tenor and soprano, bassist Eddie Gomez, drummer John Riley and percussionist Edson Cafe Adasilva). The Keith Jarretish "Jacob" and

"Hi Sweetie" are brief piano features, while there are many strong solos on the other selections from Brecker and Lovano. Much of the music is rather somber and busy, with plenty of written ensembles and performances that may take a few listens to fully digest and appreciate. —*Scott Yanow*

Press Enter / Aug. 3, 1991-Aug. 4, 1991 / Sunnyside ◆◆◆◆

● **Live at Maybeck Recital Hall, Vol. 34** / Feb. 27, 1994 / Concord Jazz ◆◆◆◆◆

Live at Visiones / Aug. 29, 1995 / Concord Jazz ◆◆◆◆

Frank Wess

b. Jan. 4, 1922, Kansas City, MO
Flute, Alto Saxophone, Tenor Saxophone / Bop, Swing, Cool
One of the first major jazz flutists, Frank Wess has also been a top Lester Young-influenced tenorman, an expert first altoist, and an occasional composer/arranger—certainly a valuable man to have around. Early on he toured with Blanche Calloway, served in the military, and had stints with the Billy Eckstine Orchestra (1946), Eddie Heywood, Lucky Millinder and R&B star Bull Moose Jackson. That was all just a prelude to Wess' important period with Count Basie's big band, from 1953-64. His flute playing, so expertly utilized in Neal Hefti's arrangements, gave the Basie Orchestra a fresh new sound, and his cool-toned tenor contrasted well with the more passionate sound of fellow tenor Frank Foster; Wess also had opportunities to play alto with the classic big band. Since that time, Wess has freelanced in countless settings, playing with Clark Terry's big band, the New York Quartet (with Roland Hanna) during the second half of the 1970s, Dameronia (1981-85), and Toshiko Akiyoshi's big band, and has also had occasional reunions with Frank Foster. Frank Wess has led sessions for Commodore (1954), Savoy, Prestige, Moodsville, Pablo (with Foster), Progressive, Uptown, Concord and Town Crier. —*Scott Yanow*

Jazz for Playboys / Dec. 26, 1956+Jan. 5, 1957 / Savoy ◆◆◆◆
This CD reissue has three songs apiece from two similar sessions. One half of the set features Frank Wess (doubling on flute and tenor) accompanied by both Kenny Burrell and Freddy Green on guitars, bassist Eddie Jones and drummer Gus Johnson; the other three titles add trumpeter Joe Newman and have Ed Thigpen in Johnson's place. The music is essentially cool-toned swing/bop very much in a Count Basie vein, and is easily recommended to straightahead jazz fans despite the so-so packaging and LP-length playing time. —*Scott Yanow*

I Hear Ya' Talkin' / Dec. 8, 1959 / Savoy ◆◆◆◆
This lightly swinging session is very much in the Count Basie style of blues and swing. Frank Wess (switching between flute, tenor and alto) heads the septet but it is trumpeter Thad Jones (who wrote three of the five numbers) who often takes solo honors. Trombonist Curtis Fuller, baritonist Charlie Fowlkes and pianist Hank Jones are also heard from on this enjoyable session that for some obscure reason was not released until 1984. —*Scott Yanow*

Flute Juice / Apr. 8, 1981 / Progressive ◆◆◆◆◆
Frank Wess' first set as a leader in eight years finds the multireedist sticking to flute (his most distinctive ax) in a quintet with guitarist Chuck Wayne, pianist Tommy Flanagan, bassist George Mraz and drummer Ben Riley. The music is predictably excellent, lightly swinging and a bit more sophisticated than it might sound at first listen. Wess and his group perform four jazz standards (including "Love Come Back to Me" and "There Is No Greater Love") plus a couple of the leader's originals. —*Scott Yanow*

Two at the Top / Jun. 8, 1983-Jun. 9, 1983 / Uptown ◆◆◆◆◆
This Uptown LP is a bit unusual for Frank Wess because he left his flute at home and concentrated on his cool-toned tenor and alto. Wess is matched with fluegelhornist Johnny Coles (the co-leader), pianist Kenny Barron, bassist Reggie Johnson and drummer Kenny Washington on a variety of mostly little-played jazz pieces that are arranged by Don Sickler. Since altoist Gigi Gryce had recently passed away, the quintet performs two of his songs ("Nica's Tempo" and "Minority") plus a couple of Kenny Dorham obscurities ("Whistle Stop" and "An Oscar for Oscar"), "Stablemates," "Ill Wind," the little-known ballad "Morning Star" and Bud Powell's "Celia." The consistently strong material clearly inspired the players. The talented musicians are heard in top form throughout this inventive straightahead date. —*Scott Yanow*

Two for the Blues / Oct. 11, 1983-Oct. 12, 1983 / Original Jazz Classics ◆◆◆◆
The two veteran Count Basie tenors Frank Wess (who doubles here on alto) and Frank Foster co-led this 1983 Pablo session (which is sometimes also listed under Foster's name). With fine backup from pianist Kenny Barron, bassist Rufus Reid and drummer Marvin "Smitty" Smith, both Wess and Foster have opportunities to show how they have grown as musicians since the Basie days. While Wess has kept his cool tone, Foster was obviously influenced a bit by John Coltrane, so one should have little difficulty telling the two apart. In addition to some originals (three by Wess and one by Foster), Neal Hefti's title tune and a few ballads, the

quintet performs unusual uptempo versions of "Send in the Clowns" and "Spring Can Really Hang You Up the Most." Recommended. —*Scott Yanow*

Entre Nous / Nov. 11, 1990 / Concord Jazz ◆◆◆◆
During part of 1990 Frank Wess led a big band that not too suprisingly sounded very much like Count Basie's; Wess' 11 years with Basie plus the presence of many Basie alumni were two good reasons to continue the tradition. This live CD features plenty of enthusiastic playing on arrangements by Wess (who doubles on tenor and flute), Dennis Mackrel, Joe Newman (who sings "St. James Infirmary"), Pete Minger and Rick Wilkins. Among the main soloists are pianist Tee Carson (who closely emulates Basie), trumpeters Pete Minger, Snooky Young and Joe Newman, trombonist Art Baron, altoists Bill Ramsey and Curtis Peagler, guitarist Ted Dunbar, baritonist Babe Clark (showcased on "Lover") and Wess himself. Easily recommended to Count Basie fans, this valuable CD is the main existing documentation of the short-lived Frank Wess Orchestra. —*Scott Yanow*

Tryin' to Make My Blues Turn Green / Sep. 7, 1993-Sep. 8, 1993 / Concord Jazz ◆◆◆◆
Frank Wess has always been a steady, reliable swinger, able to play swaggering blues and soulful ballads with equal facility and hold his own on more challenging bop pieces. The 12 tracks on his release range from his own swing-tinged originals to the inevitable standards and fine reworkings of jazz pieces by Kenny Burrell and Horace Parlan. Highly professional, nicely played blues-swing material from an often overlooked, dependable improviser. —*Ron Wynn*

● **Going Wess** / Sep. 20, 1993-Sep. 21, 1993 / Town Crier ◆◆◆◆◆
This CD gave Frank Wess (doubling on tenor and flute) his first opportunity to record with an organ, and he is in top form on this trio outing with organist Bobby Forrester and drummer Clarence "Tootsie" Bean. Burners alternate with warm ballads and Wess (whether on his tough tenor or fluid flute) matches very well with Forrester's light pre-Jimmy Smith organ style. In fact, this session swings so naturally that it could have been recorded in 1958. The ten superior standards are all given very favorable treatment, making this a highly recommended outing. —*Scott Yanow*

Randy Weston

b. Apr. 6, 1926, New York, NY
Piano, Composer / Post-Bop, Hard Bop
Placing Randy Weston into narrow bop-derived categories only tells part of the story of this restless musician. Starting with the gospel of bop according to Thelonious Monk, Weston has gradually absorbed the letter and spirit of African and Caribbean rhythms and tunes, welding everything together into a searching, energizing, often celebratory blend. His piano work ranges across a profusion of styles from boogie-woogie through bop into dissonance, marked by a stabbing quality reminiscent of, but not totally indebted to, Monk.

Growing up in Brooklyn, Weston was surrounded by a rich musical community: he knew Max Roach, Cecil Payne and Duke Jordan; Eddie Heywood lived across the street; Wynton Kelly was a cousin. Most influential of all was Monk, who tutored Weston upon visits to his apartment. Weston began working professionally in R&B bands in the late 1940s before playing in the bebop outfits of Payne and Kenny Dorham. After signing with Riverside in 1954, Weston led his own trios and quartets and gained a prominent reputation as a composer, contributing jazz standards like "Hi-Fly" and "Little Niles" to the repertoire. He also met arranger Melba Liston, who has collaborated with Weston off and on into the 1990s. Weston's interest in his roots was stimulated by extended stays in Africa; he visited Nigeria in 1961 and 1963, lived in Morocco from 1968 to 1973 following a tour, and has remained fascinated with the music and spiritual values of the continent ever since. In the 1970s, Weston made recordings for Arista-Freedom, Polydor and CTI while maintaining a peripatetic touring existence—mostly in Europe—returning to Morocco in the mid-'80s.

However, starting in the late '80s, after a long recording drought, Weston's visibility in the US skyrocketed with an extraordinarily productive period in the studios for Antilles and Verve. Among his highly eclectic recording projects were a trilogy of "Portrait" albums depicting Ellington, Monk and himself, an ambitious two-CD work rooted in African music called *The Spirits of Our Ancestors*, a blues album, and a collaboration with the Master Gnawa Musicians of Morocco. Though he does tend now and then to recycle material written up to nearly half a century before, Weston in his 70s remains an unpredictable, unusually enterprising musician. —*Richard S. Ginell*

Zulu / Apr. 27, 1954-Sep. 10, 1956 / Milestone ◆◆◆◆
The early Randy Weston performances on this two-LP set have not yet resurfaced on CD. Pianist Weston is heard on two duets with bassist Sam Gill from his very first session ("In the Still of the Night" and "What Is This Thing Called Love"), six selections from a 1955 date with Gill and drummer Art Blakey, four piano solos from 1956 and an entire quartet session with baritonist Cecil Payne, bassist

Ahmed-Abdul Malik and drummer Wilbert Hogan. Even at that early stage, Weston sounds quite recognizable (he was 28-30 years old during these sessions), bringing his own original and often-percussive interpretations to a variety of standards plus four originals. One of the highlights is the original version of his "Little Niles." This two-fer is worth searching for, at least until these enjoyable and somewhat historic dates are reissued. —*Scott Yanow*

Get Happy / Aug. 29, 1955-Aug. 31, 1955 / Original Jazz Classics ✦✦✦✦

With These Hands / Mar. 14, 1956+Mar. 21, 1956 / Original Jazz Classics ✦✦✦✦
This CD reissues one of pianist Randy Weston's lesser-known sets. Weston, who already had a fairly distinctive style, mostly sticks to standards (which is quite unusual for him), including "The Man I Love," "This Can't Be Love" and "Do Nothing Till You Hear From Me." A quartet is featured that also includes baritonist Cecil Payne (who would be a longtime associate), bassist Ahmed Abdul-Malik and drummer Wilbert Hogan. However, the date does include two of Weston's originals and is actually highlighted by the debut of his famous "Little Niles." —*Scott Yanow*

Jazz á la Bohemia / Oct. 25, 1956 / Original Jazz Classics ✦✦✦✦✦
Randy Weston, who was more under Thelonious Monk's influence back in 1956 than he would be in the near future, is in top form during this live set. His quartet features the rarely heard but talented baritonist Cecil Payne, bassist Ahmed Abdul-Malik and drummer Al Dreares. High points of the straightahead set (which has been reissued on CD) include the calypso "Hold 'Em Joe" (recorded almost a decade before Sonny Rollins), "It's All Right with Me" (one of two trio tracks) and the lone Weston original on the date, the stimulating "Chessman's Delight." —*Scott Yanow*

How High the Moon / Nov. 21, 1956-Jan. 19, 1957 / Biograph ✦✦✦✦
This spirited LP (which has a jam session feel to it) features pianist Randy Weston for the first time with a group as large as a quintet. With assistance from trumpeter Ray Copeland, baritonist Cecil Payne (who switches to alto on "Well You Needn't"), bassist Ahmed-Abdul Malik and either Willie Jones or Wilbert Hogan on drums, Weston explores three of his originals, the calypso "Run Joe" and four jazz standards including a heated version of the title cut. This album (originally recorded for Dawn) does not deserve its obscurity. —*Scott Yanow*

Little Niles / Oct. 1958-Oct. 26, 1959 / United Artists ✦✦✦✦✦
This attractive two-LP set has selections drawn from three of pianist Randy Weston's most interesting sessions of the late '50s. Seven songs (taken from the original album *Little Niles*) feature Weston in a sextet with tenor saxophonist Johnny Griffin and either Ray Copeland or Idrees Sulieman on trumpet, while four other selections (drawn from *Destry Rides Again*) match the pianist with four trombonists. However it is the second disc (originally issued as *Live at the Five Spot*) that is of greatest interest, because Weston heads an all-star quintet (given Melba Liston's arrangements) that includes tenor saxophonist Coleman Hawkins and trumpeter Kenny Dorham. Overall the music is advanced bop with a strong nod toward African music. Well worth searching for. —*Scott Yanow*

★ **Uhuru Africa / Highlife** / Nov. 1960-Apr. 1963 / Roulette ✦✦✦✦✦
A couple of pianist Randy Weston's most significant albums are combined on this single CD. 1960s *Uhuru Afrika* is one of the finest (and earliest) combinations of African rhythms with advanced jazz, and it features Weston utilizing a 24-piece big band that includes 14 horns, one guitar, two bassists, three drummers and three percussionists; Martha Flowers and Brock Peters take vocals on "African Lady," the best-known of the four movements. Melba Liston was responsible for not only those charts but the *Highlife* session, which has Weston showcased in a stripped-down 12-piece ensemble. Highly recommended, these sessions are among the recorded high points of Randy Weston's productive career. —*Scott Yanow*

Berkshire Blues / Aug. 18, 1965+Oct. 14, 1965 / Black Lion ✦✦✦
This CD reissue can easily be divided into two. Pianist Randy Weston performs a dissonant version of "Three Blind Mice" along with a relatively slow "Perdido" and Duke Ellington's "Purple Gazelle" with bassist Bill Wood and drummer Lennie McBrowne. For the second half of the release (recorded two months earlier), Weston plays four of his own originals (including "Berkshire Blues" and "Sweet Meat") unaccompanied; none of the tunes would become standards. Throughout the set, Weston's solos hold on to one's interest, although the overall results are really not all that essential. —*Scott Yanow*

Monterey '66 / Sep. 18, 1966 / Verve ✦✦✦✦✦
Pianist Randy Weston's mid-1960s sextet was on the verge of breaking up after three years when they performed their "farewell" concert at the 1966 Monterey Jazz Festival. The performance was not released until it came out on this 1993 CD, but it was worth the wait. The group consists of trumpeter Ray Copeland, the great tenor Cecil Payne, Weston, bassist Bill Wood, drummer Lenny McBrowne and percussionist Big Black. Their well-received set consists of seven Weston compositions including "Little Niles," "Berkshire Blues," "Blues for Strayhorn" and "African

Cookbook." Ervin, Copeland and the leader all take consistently colorful and explorative solos that are full of power and creativity. A particularly strong effort. —*Scott Yanow*

Blue Moses / Mar. 1972-Apr. 1972 / CTI ✦✦✦
Randy Weston's most popular record, this LP (which he had mixed feelings about) features Weston not only on piano but electric keyboards. Backed by Don Sebesky arrangements and assisted by trumpeter Freddie Hubbard and tenor saxophonist Grover Washington, Jr., Weston plays quite well on four of his compositions; best-known are "Ganawa (Blue Moses)" and "Marrakesh Blues." The music retains the African feel of most of Weston's latter-day playing, but also has some commercial touches that do not hurt the performances. This rewarding date has not yet been reissued on CD. —*Scott Yanow*

Tanjah / May 21, 1973-May 22, 1973 / Verve ✦✦✦✦✦
Originally on the Polydor label, this lesser-known classic (reissued on CD) teams together pianist/composer Randy Weston and arranger Melba Liston (his musical soulmate) on seven of Weston's originals. The fairly large band is filled with distinctive soloists including trumpeter Jon Faddis (19 at the time), trombonist Al Grey, Billy Harper on tenor, altoist Norris Turney (heard on three versions of "Sweet Meat," two of which were previously unreleased) and several percussionists among others. The weak points are Weston's use of the Fender Rhodes on a few songs (it waters down his personality) and Candido's chanting during an otherwise exciting version of "Hi-Fly," but those are easily compensated for by the infectious calypso "Jamaican East" and Liston's inventive reworking of "Little Niles." Recommended. —*Scott Yanow*

Carnival / Jul. 5, 1974 / Freedom ✦✦✦✦✦
This CD reissue features pianist Randy Weston's performance at the 1974 Montreux Jazz Festival. Weston plays a very interesting solo "Tribute to Duke Ellington" that finds him quoting many of Duke's songs (Ellington had recently passed away). In addition he performs the joyous "Carnival" and a lengthy version of "Mystery of Love" with a quintet that also includes the intense tenor saxophonist Billy Harper, bassist William Allen, drummer Don Moye and percussionist Steve Berrios. This is an enjoyable and well-rounded set, easily recommended despite the LP length of the program. —*Scott Yanow*

Blues to Africa / Aug. 14, 1974 / Freedom ✦✦✦✦✦
This is a particularly strong solo performance by the unique pianist Randy Weston. He interprets eight of his originals, all of which are to an extent influenced by African music. Weston's percussive style has sometimes been compared to Thelonious Monk's (Monk is an influence) but he has long had his own original voice. After many group recordings, Weston started concentrating on solo playing in 1974 and this was the second of his five unaccompanied recitals of 1974-76, all for different labels. —*Scott Yanow*

African Nite / Sep. 21, 1975 / Inner City ✦✦✦✦
During 1974-76, Randy Weston recorded five solo piano albums. It was a natural move for him since, being quite percussive, he really did not need a drummer or even a bassist. This obscure LP (originally out on Owl and now long out of print) finds Weston performing eight of his originals (including "Little Niles") along with Dizzy Gillespie's "Con Alma." Many of the other songs were written during Weston's long stay in Morocco, where his music became even more African-oriented than previously. The playing is consistently exciting, but unfortunately this album is now quite rare. —*Scott Yanow*

Randy Weston / Jan. 28, 1976 / Pausa ✦✦✦
This solo recital by pianist Randy Weston is up to his usual musical standards, but the packaging of the Pausa LP, which does not list a recording date, the fact that this is a solo session, or even the songs on the back cover, is a bit appalling. Weston performs Benny Golson's "Out of the Past" and six of his originals, including "Monk Steps." None of Weston's songs on this date caught on as standards, but the typically percussive and melodic (if quirky) music is enjoyable. Hopefully this set will surface on CD. —*Scott Yanow*

Portraits of Monk / Jun. 3, 1989 / Verve ✦✦✦✦
The first of three albums recorded in a three-day period, this CD features pianist Randy Weston in a quartet with bassist Jamil Nasser, drummer Idris Muhammad and percussionist Eric Asante, interpreting seven of Thelonious Monk's songs. Since Monk was a major (but not dominant) influence on his style, Weston fully understands Thelonious' music without feeling compelled to closely copy his musical role model. Highlights include fresh versions of "Well You Needn't," "Misterioso" and a thirteen-and-a-half-minute rendition of "Functional." —*Scott Yanow*

Portraits of Duke Ellington / Jun. 4, 1989 / Verve ✦✦✦✦
On the second of three quartet recordings (with bassist Jamil Nasser, drummer Idris Muhammad and percussionist Eric Asante) recorded on three consecutive days, pianist Randy Wetson plays six Duke Ellington compositions. Other than "Caravan" and "C Jam Blues," the tunes are rarely performed ("Limbo Jazz" and

"Chromatic Love Affair" are far from standards), allowing Weston to construct inventive improvisations that do not borrow from the original recordings; even "Caravan" sounds fresh. All three of these releases (the others are a set of originals and a program of Thelonious Monk tunes) are easily recommended to Randy Weston's fans. —*Scott Yanow*

Self Portraits / Jun. 5, 1989 / Verve ✦✦✦✦

The Spirits of Our Ancestors / May 20, 1991-May 22, 1991 / Antilles ✦✦✦✦✦
Pianist Randy Weston and arranger Melba Liston had a musical reunion on this special double-CD, their first joint project since 1973's *Tanjah*. Liston's charts for the pianist's ten originals perfectly fit Weston's adventurous style and the twelve-piece group (which includes three percussionists) is filled with highly individual voices, including the tenors of Billy Harper and Dewey Redman. With trumpeter Dizzy Gillespie and tenor saxophonist Pharoah Sanders making guest appearances and Randy Weston heard at the peak of his powers, this is a highly recommended set. —*Scott Yanow*

Volcano Blues / Feb. 1993 / Antilles ✦✦✦✦✦
Pianist Randy Weston and trombonist/arranger Melba Liston have collaborated successfully for many years. This pairing was on a series of blues numbers, with Weston doubling as session producer and pianist while giving Liston almost total arranging control, except for three numbers. The results were an intriguing twist on standard 12-bar blues, as Weston's muscular piano led the way through rigorous performances of Count Basie's "Volcano" and his own "Blues For Strayhorn," "Sad Beauty Blues" and "In Memory Of." Liston's arrangements required disciplined solos, and Weston's steady hand generated impressive cohesion and interaction during the unison segments. A superb example of the African/African-American musical continuum. —*Ron Wynn*

Earth Birth / 1997 / Antilles ✦✦✦
Recorded in Montreal with 24 strings from the Montreal Symphony and two can't-miss jazz cohorts, bassist Christian McBride and drummer Billy Higgins, here we have another reunion between Weston and arranger Melba Liston in a collection of mostly early Weston tunes, some dating back to the early 1950s. The strings sound unearthly, as if they were recorded in a dead studio (the locale is the Ludget-Duvernay Hall of Montreal's Monument National), and even though Liston blends them with the piano in an integral manner, they respond stiffly; it's an uneasy, not terribly imaginative fusion. The most famous Weston tune "Hi-Fly" is completely retooled into a cocktail-hour ballad—it also features the most intricate string chart—and composer Weston enjoys poking around the tune's angles and corners. Coming after his exciting African experiments in the '90s, this CD, despite Weston's sharply etched solos, is a relatively minor nostalgic effort. —*Richard S. Ginell*

George Wettling

b. Nov. 28, 1907, Topeka, KS, **d.** Jun. 6, 1968, New York, NY
Drums / Dixieland
One of the great Dixieland drummers, George Wettling's ability to alertly change patterns behind each soloist usually inspired the other musicians to play their best. He was part of the Chicago jazz scene of the 1920s (where he moved with his family in 1921), and Baby Dodds was his main idol. Wettling, who recorded with Paul Mares in the mid-'30s, was still mostly an unknown when he came to New York in 1935, playing briefly with Jack Hylton's Orchestra. He did a fine job with Artie Shaw's 1936 big band, as well as the orchestras of Bunny Berigan (1937), Red Norvo, Paul Whiteman (1938-40) and Muggsy Spanier. However, his most rewarding work was done with small groups, notably his sessions in 1938 with a trio also including Bud Freeman and Jess Stacy; he also recorded with Jimmy McPartland, Wingy Manone and Eddie Condon. The Condon connection was most significant, for after stints with Joe Marsala and Ben Pollack, Wettling became a regular with Condon on his Town Hall broadcasts and at his club. Wettling's "day job" was as a staff musician at ABC (1943-52). He worked off and on with Condon to the end of his life and also gained some notoriety for his abilities as an artist (some of his work appeared on album jackets) and as an occasional jazz critic for *Downbeat* and *Playboy*. He played with virtually everyone in the Chicago jazz field, as well as Benny Goodman, Billie Holiday, Sidney Bechet and even Chico Marx. Although he did not lead bands on a regular basis for long (due to excessive alcohol consumption), George Wettling led excellent Dixieland dates for Decca (1940), Black & White (1944), Keynote, Stycon, Columbia (1951), JSP, Kapp and Stereocraft (1958). —*Scott Yanow*

● **Dixieland in Hi-Fi** / Mar. 2, 1951-Apr. 22, 1957 / Harmony ✦✦✦✦
George Wettling was always the perfect Dixieland drummer and was used as a sideman with many groups in the 1940s and '50s including those headed by Eddie Condon. This out-of-print LP has two four-song sessions headed by Wettling in 1951 plus a pair of numbers from 1957. The three overlapping groups (either sep-

tets or an octet) include such top Dixieland stars as trumpeters Wild Bill Davison and Max Kaminsky, trombonists Cutty Cutshall and Jimmy Archey, clarinetists Pee Wee Russell and Edmond Hall and pianists Ralph Sutton, Joe Sullivan and Dick Cary; an uncredited Bud Freeman is also featured on tenor during the two 1957 selections. Three fairly basic but obscure Wettling originals alternate with seven Dixieland warhorses (including "Runnin' Wild," "Indiana" and "After You've Gone") and the somewhat rare performances are quite enjoyable, making this LP one to search for. —*Scott Yanow*

Kirk Whalum

b. Memphis, TN
Tenor Saxophone / Instrumental Pop, Crossover Jazz
From the jazz standpoint, Kirk Whalum's career has thus far been a consistent disappointment. Although obviously a talented player, he has thus far been satisfied to make a good living by performing R&B and pop music while keeping well hidden any individuality that he might possess. Whalum debuted on record for Columbia in 1984 (on a Bob James record) and has been a popular attraction ever since. —*Scott Yanow*

Floppy Disk / 1985 / Columbia ✦✦

And You Know That! / 1988 / Columbia ✦✦✦
Light pop/fusion though Whalum's a very good player. —*Ron Wynn*

The Promise / 1989 / Columbia ✦✦✦

● **Cache** / 1993 / Columbia ✦✦✦✦

In This Life / 1995 / Columbia ✦✦✦

Colors (Colores/Couleurs) / 1997 / Warner Brothers ✦✦
Kirk Whalum's live performances in the 1980s and 1990s demonstrated that he had potential as a soul-jazz saxophonist, but his overproduced commercial albums were usually formula-driven disappointments that gave him little room to stretch out and put his improvisatory skills to work. Regrettably, *Colors* is no exception. Whalum shows how enjoyable a soloist he can be on the Brazilian-flavored "Escolhido (Chosen)," but most of the time, he sticks to a lightweight, unchallenging blend of pop, R&B and jazz that is short on substance and wastes his sizable chops. Especially weak is his version of the ballad "If Only for One Night"—this Luther Vandross hit could have been a sexy and alluring vehicle for jazz improvisation, but instead, he offers a note-for-note cover that is as unimaginative as it is bloodless. Whalum is capable of a lot more. —*Alex Henderson*

Kenny Wheeler

b. Jan. 14, 1930, Toronto, Canada
Trumpet, Fluegelhorn / Avant-Garde, Post-Bop
Kenny Wheeler has long been one of the most technically proficient of the avant-garde trumpeters. He started on cornet when he was 12, studied at the Toronto Conservatory and then in 1952 moved to England. He worked in many big bands during the next decade (including with John Dankworth during 1959-65) and became an excellent bop-based soloist. However by the mid-'60s his musical curiosity led him to freer forms of jazz and he did important work with John Stevens' Spontaneous Music Ensemble, Tony Oxley's sextet, the Mike Gibbs Orchestra, the Globe Unity Orchestra, Anthony Braxton (starting in 1972) and Azimuth. Wheeler has been a regular on ECM since the mid-'70s and during 1983-87 he was with the Dave Holland quintet. A thoughtful trumpeter with a wide range, Wheeler's playing is always stimulating yet generally introspective. —*Scott Yanow*

Windmill Tilter / Mar. 1968 / Fontana ✦✦✦✦

Song for Someone / 1973 / Incus ✦✦✦✦

● **Gnu High** / Jun. 1975 / ECM ✦✦✦✦✦
Trumpeter Kenny Wheeler's debut as a leader for ECM is a memorable quartet set with pianist Keith Jarrett (one of his best recordings as a sideman), bassist Dave Holland and drummer Jack DeJohnette. The group plays three of Wheeler's originals (including the 21-minute "Heyoke") and each of the musicians sound quite inspired. Wheeler's wide range, beautiful tone and searching style match particularly well with Jarrett's rhythmic and bluish accompaniment. Highly recommended. —*Scott Yanow*

1976 / Feb. 9, 1976-Feb. 10, 1976 / Just a Memory ✦✦✦✦
This CD reissues music that trumpeter Kenny Wheeler recorded for the Canadian Broadcasting Corp. (CBC) and has been forgotten since. Two aspects of the quintet date are unusual. Wheeler is heard for one of the few times in his career backed by an electric Fender Rhodes piano (played by Gary Williamson), and the music is much more straightahead than the avant-garde trumpeter usually plays. Not that his solos are predictable in any way, but Wheeler's sound and the feel of the group (which also includes tenor saxophonist Art Ellefson, bassist Dave Young and drummer Marty Morell) on the six group originals is oddly reminiscent of Freddie

Hubbard's music of a few years earlier. Although not essential, these formerly rare performances are worth hearing. *—Scott Yanow*

Deer Wan / Jul. 1977 / ECM ✦✦✦✦✦
Kenny Wheeler's beautiful sound on trumpet and his wide range are well-displayed on his four compositions, three of which are given performances over ten minutes long. With the assistance of ECM regulars Jan Garbarek (on tenor and soprano), guitarist John Abercrombie, bassist Dave Holland, drummer Jack DeJohnette and (on one song) guitarist Ralph Towner, Wheeler emphasizes lyricism and romantic moods on this fine set of original music. *—Scott Yanow*

Around 6 / Aug. 1979 / ECM ✦✦✦✦✦
Kenny Wheeler's third ECM album as a leader is most notable for teaming his trumpet with the innovative tenor and soprano of Evan Parker, a brilliant British avant-garde player who is often overlooked in the US. With fine playing from trombonist Eje Thelin, vibraphonist Tom Van Der Geld, bassist J.F. Jenny-Clark and drummer Edward Vesala, the sextet performs six Wheeler originals that combine together advanced swinging with fairly free explorations. Stimulating music. *—Scott Yanow*

Double, Double You / May 1983 / ECM ✦✦✦✦✦
Kenny Wheeler's string of ECM recordings are all quite rewarding, generally avoiding the ECM stereotype of introspective long tones and silence. A fiery but thoughtful trumpeter whose style can range from advanced swinging to sound explorations, Wheeler is joined on this excellent set by tenor saxophonist Michael Brecker, pianist John Taylor, bassist Dave Holland and drummer Jack DeJohnette. They perform a set of Wheeler's originals and each of the world class musicians has an opportunity to be featured. A generally memorable outing. *—Scott Yanow*

Welcome / Mar. 1986 / Soul Note ✦✦✦

Flutter By, Butterfly / May 26, 1987-May 27, 1987 / Soul Note ✦✦✦✦✦
Recorded at a time when trumpeter Kenny Wheeler was playing regularly in bassist Dave Holland's band, this quintet outing with Holland, Stan Sulzman (who switches between soprano, tenor and flute), pianist John Taylor and drummer Billy Elgart features six of Wheeler's originals, some of which were written quite a few years before. "Everybody's Song But My Own" and "Flutter By, Butterfly" are probably the most memorable of the compositions but each of the performances (which feature consistently rewarding solos) are worth hearing. *—Scott Yanow*

Music for Large and Small Ensembles / Jan. 1990 / ECM ✦✦✦✦✦

The Widow in the Window / Feb. 1990 / ECM ✦✦✦✦✦
Trumpeter Kenny Wheeler and his sidemen on this quintet CD (guitarist John Abercrombie, pianist John Taylor, bassist Dave Holland and drummer Peter Erskine) had all worked together previously in different settings. Their familiarity with each other's playing came in handy for the frequently intuitive session, which consists of explorations of six of Wheeler's complex but often-melodic originals (including "The Widow in the Window," "Hotel Le Hot" and the lengthy "Ana"). Kenny Wheeler's music occupies its own unique area between post bop and free jazz and virtually all of his recordings are recommended to adventurous listeners, including this one. *—Scott Yanow*

Angel Song / Feb. 1996 / ECM ✦✦
Considering the talent involved in this quartet set (trumpeter Kenny Wheeler, altoist Lee Konitz, guitarist Bill Frisell and bassist Dave Holland), the music on this CD is a bit of a disappointment. The nine Wheeler originals are moody, wandering and somewhat forgettable, the interplay between the trumpeter and Konitz fails to light any real sparks, and Frisell sounds surprisingly restrained and laidback. Although pleasant, this is not the superb collaboration that one would expect from innovative musicians of this caliber. *—Scott Yanow*

Touche / Jul. 19, 1996 / Justin Time ✦✦✦✦

Siren's Song / 1997 / Justin Time ✦✦✦✦

Arthur Whetsol

b. 1905, Punta Gorda, FL, **d.** Jan. 5, 1940, New York, NY
Trumpet / Classic Jazz, Swing
Arthur Whetsol, one of the original members in Duke Ellington's Washingtonians, had an attractive tone, impressive technique and a very lyrical style that set a standard for Ellington; in future years Harold "Shorty" Baker filled a similar role with Duke. A childhood friend of Ellington, Whetsol came to New York with Duke to join Elmer Snowden's group in 1923 but left a year later to study medicine at Howard University. He eventually returned to music and was a fixture in Duke's orchestra during 1928-36 until a brain disorder forced him to permanently retire. Featured prominently in Ellington's 1929 film short *Black and Tan*, Whetsol took many fine solos in the late '20s when his melodic style was a contrast to that of Bubber Miley and (a little later) Cootie Williams, most notably on "Mood Indigo,"

"Black and Tan Fantasy" and "Black Beauty"; his role became less prominent in the 1930s. *—Scott Yanow*

Brian White

Clarinet / Dixieland
Leader of the Magna Jazz Band in London since the mid-'50s, Brian White is a fine veteran clarinetist who (along with trumpeter Alan Gresty) was responsible for the rewarding tribute to Muggsy Spanier titled *Muggsy Remembered;* he has recorded several easily available and rewarding CDs for Jazzology. *—Scott Yanow*

Pleasure Mad / Apr. 24, 1982+Feb. 4, 1984 / Jazzology ✦✦✦✦
Clarinetist Brian White's Magna Jazz Band has been a popular Dixieland outfit in England since the mid-'50s. For this CD reissue, White is joined by trumpeter Ben Cohen, trombonist Geoff Cole, pianist Alan Thomas, Joe Becket or Gordon Davis on bass and drummer Ian Castle. The music is spirited and well-played with the highlights including "Yes Yes in Your Eyes," "1919 March," "Chattanooga Stomp," "Come Back Sweet Papa" and "I Double Dare You"; even "McKinley Morganfield" (an out-of-place tribute to Muddy Waters) is successful. Recommended to Dixieland fans. *—Scott Yanow*

★ **Muggsy Remembered** / 1986+Oct. 30, 1993 / Jazzology ✦✦✦✦✦
In 1939 cornetist Muggsy Spanier recorded 16 selections with his four-horn seven-piece Ragtime Band that helped define Dixieland. Unfortunately he was just a little early, for gigs soon became difficult to find, and he had to break up the group before the year ended. In 1986, the English clarinetist Brian White decided to feature cornetist Alan Gresty on a dozen of the 16 numbers at a recording session, because Gresty's sound and style (particularly when muted) uncannily resembled Muggsy Spanier's. This CD, which reissues that complete program, also has four additional tracks recorded in 1993. The music on a whole is quite enjoyable, hinting strongly at Spanier's band without actually copying any solos. Highlights include such numbers as "That Da Da Strain," "Lonesome Road," "Monday Date," "Relaxin' at the Touro" and "Sunday." The musicianship is excellent and the soloists (who also include trombonist Geoff Cole and the tenor of Goff Dubber) are consistently colorful and swinging. This is a highly recommended set for Dixieland fans. *—Scott Yanow*

C'est Magnifique / Nov. 14, 1992-Dec. 12, 1992 / Jazzology ✦✦✦✦✦
Clarinetist Brian White has led the Magna Jazz Band in his native England since 1954, but his group has made surprisingly few recordings through the years. The 1992 version of the Magna Jazz Band (as heard on this CD) is a strong Dixieland-oriented unit. White, a fluid clarinetist, is excellent in ensembles; cornetist Ben Cohen's clipped phrasing recalls the more ancient New Orleans trumpeters, but his choice of notes is influenced by Louis Armstrong; and trombonist Geoff Cole looks toward Kid Ory some of the time but overall simply sounds like himself. The emphasis throughout this CD is on obscurities, with just a few standards tossed in. Highlights include "Chicago Buzz," a pair of Sidney Bechet's best originals from the 1950s (the exuberant "The Fishseller" and "Dens Les Rues D'Antibes"), Duke Ellington's "Misty Morning," "Strut Miss Lizzie," and "No One Else But You." A Dixieland version of the title cut (a Cole Porter song from the show *Can Can*) wraps up the enjoyable effort. *—Scott Yanow*

Carla White

b. Oakland, CA
Vocals / Post-Bop, Bop
Although she has not recorded enough (and there are long gaps between some of her recordings), Carla White has been one of the better jazz singers of the past decade. Raised in New York, her original goal was to be an improvising jazz dancer. However in high school she started singing and became involved in acting. After spending two years at the Webber-Douglas Academy of Dramatic Art in London (1969-71) and some time traveling overseas, White studied with Lennie Tristano for four years and later with Warne Marsh. In the late '70s she started collaborating with trumpeter Manny Duran, co-leading a band and recording for Stash. An expert scat singer, White started concentrating more on interpreting lyrics by the time she recorded two albums for Milestone, and her 1991 Evidence set is one of her best to date. *—Scott Yanow*

Andruline / Mar. 21, 1983-Mar. 22, 1983 / Stash ✦✦✦✦
The delightful jazz singer Carla White made her debut on this boppish Stash LP. She shared co-leadership with trumpeter Manny Duran and they were joined by pianist Peter Madsen, bassist Ed Howard and drummer Taro Okamoto. White mostly sticks to scat singing on the four bop tunes ("Dig, "Lover Man," "Good Morning Heartache" and Fats Navarro's "Fat's Flats") and two group originals. Her interplay with Duran's trumpet in some of the ensembles is often exciting, making this a historic release that hopefully Stash will reissue on CD eventually. *—Scott Yanow*

Orient Express / Dec. 20, 1985-Apr. 27, 1986 / Milestone ✦✦✦✦
After sticking mostly to scatting on her recording debut (Stash's *Andruline*), Carla
White decided to emphasize her interpretative ability with lyrics during this
release, particularly on such songs as "Something to Live For," "The Man with the
Horn" (which has a guest appearance by trumpeter Manny Duran), "Detour
Ahead," "Snuggled on Your Shoulder" and her memorable ballad "Snowbound."
Fortunately White (who is accompanied by a fine rhythm section) did not com-
pletely neglect her impressive scatting abilities, especially on "Orient Express" and
"You'd Be So Nice to Come Home To." Since she was one of the top jazz singers to
emerge in the 1980s, it is a bit surprising that her two Milestone releases (of which
this is the first) have not yet been reissued on CD. —*Scott Yanow*

Mood Swings / Apr. 4, 1988-Apr. 6, 1988 / Milestone ✦✦✦✦✦
Carla White's third recording (and second for Milestone) features the highly
appealing jazz singer tackling a wide variety of superior songs including the
swing standard "If Dreams Come True," "You're My Thrill," "For Heaven's Sake,"
Bob Dorough's "Love Came on Stealthy Fingers" and Charlie Parker's lyrics on his
own "Yardbird Suite (What Price Love)." Tenor great Lew Tabackin guests on five
songs (one on flute) and guitarist Joshua Breakstone joins the supportive rhythm
section (pianist Peter Madsen, bassist Phil Bowler and drummer Tim Horner) for
four of the nine selections. Whether scatting or giving the proper amount of emotion to ballads, Carla White by 1988 had emerged as one of the top jazz singers
around. —*Scott Yanow*

● **Listen Here** / Sep. 4, 1991-Sep. 5, 1991 / Evidence ✦✦✦✦✦
Three years after the release of singer Carla White's previous Milestone album
(*Mood Swings*), she finally emerges with a new gem. True, her voice on *Listen
Here* sounds as if she has experienced a great deal of life in the meantime, but it
has lost none of its power, flexibility, optimism or sensuality. Joined by tenor
great Lew Tabackin and a strong rhythm section, White really stretches herself on the
diverse program, which ranges from wild scatting and long vamps to ballad interpretations that would do credit to Susannah McCorkle. Whether it be an eccentric
calypso duet with bassist Dean Jackson on "It's Only a Paper Moon," a touching
"Lotus Blossom" or an unusual vocal rendition of "Harlem Nocturne," Carla White
takes plenty of chances throughout this very satisfying release. Jazz needs more
singers like her. —*Scott Yanow*

Peter White

Keyboards, Guitar / Crossover Jazz, Fusion
A veteran session player from Al Kooper's band and several Basia albums, cross-
over/fusion guitarist/keyboard player Peter White became a leader with 1990s
Reveillez-Vous, on the Chase Music label. Signed to Sindrome the following year,
White released three albums for the label before moving on to Columbia by 1996.
His debut album for the label, *Caravan of Dreams*, continued his light acoustic
guitar texturing in a mainstream/electronic vein. —*John Bush*

Reveillez-Vous / Nov. 1989-Apr. 1990 / Chase Music ✦✦

Excusez-Moi / 1991 / Sindrome ✦✦

Promenade / Jan. 1993-Apr. 1993 / Sindrome ✦✦✦

Reflections / 1994 / Sindrome ✦✦✦

● **Caravan of Dreams** / 1996 / Columbia ✦✦✦
On this contemporary jazz release, guitarist Peter White (who doubles on keyboards) offers superior background music. White has a pretty sound on the acoustic guitar, which is backed by reasonably subtle electronic rhythms on a variety of
pleasant but forgettable melodies, many of which could serve as theme songs for
television shows. Other than their role in supporting the rhythms, White's sidemen
(which include saxophonist Boney James, guest guitarist Marc Antoine and on one
song fluegelhornist Rick Braun) merely provide colors to the ensembles. Nothing
at all that fiery or exciting occurs and every note sounds preplanned for maximum
radio airplay. —*Scott Yanow*

Paul Whiteman

b. Mar. 28, 1890, Denver, CO, **d.** Dec. 29, 1967, Doylestown, PA
Leader / Classic Jazz, Pop
Because press agents dubbed him "The King of Jazz" in the 1920s, Paul Whiteman
has always been considered a controversial figure in jazz history. Actually his
orchestra was the most popular during the era and at times (despite its size) it did
play very good jazz; perhaps "King of the Jazz Age" would have been a better title.
    Originally a classically trained violinist, Paul Whiteman led a large Navy band
during World War I and always had a strong interest in the popular music of the
day. In 1918 he organized his first dance band in San Francisco and, after short
periods in Los Angeles and Atlantic City, he settled in New York in 1920. His initial recordings ("Japanese Sandman" and "Whispering") were such big sellers that
Whiteman was soon a household name. His superior dance band used some of the

most technically skilled musicians of the era in a versatile show that included
everything from pop tunes and waltzes to semi-classical works and jazz. Trumpeter Henry Busse (featured on "Hot Lips" and "When Day Is Done") was Whiteman's main star during the 1921-26 period. Seeking to "make a lady out of jazz,"
Whiteman's symphonic jazz did not always swing, but at Aeolian Hall in 1924 he
introduced "Rhapsody in Blue" (with its composer George Gershwin on piano) in
what was called "An Experiment in Modern Music." Red Nichols and Tommy
Dorsey passed through the band, but it was in 1927 with the addition of Bix
Beiderbecke, Frankie Trumbauer and Bing Crosby (the latter originally featured as
part of a vocal trio called the Rhythm Boys) that Whiteman began to finally have
an important jazz band. Joe Venuti and Eddie Lang soon joined up and many of
Whiteman's recordings of 1927-30 (particularly the ones with Bill Challis arrangements) are among his finest.
    After Beiderbecke left the band in 1929 and Whiteman filmed the erratic but
fascinating movie *The King of Jazz* in 1930, the Depression forced the bandleader
to cut back on his personnel (which at one time included two pianos, tuba, bass
sax, string bass, banjo and guitar in its rhythm section!). Although his orchestra in
the 1930s at times featured Bunny Berigan, Trumbauer and both Jack and Charlie
Teagarden, Whiteman's music was considered old hat by the time of the swing era
and he essentially retired (except for special appearances) by the early '40s. Many
of his recordings (particularly those with Beiderbecke) have been reissued numerous times and are more rewarding than his detractors would lead one to believe.
In the 1970s Dick Sudhalter for a time organized and led "The New Paul Whiteman Orchestra" which recorded a couple of fine recreation records. —*Scott Yanow*

The King of Jazz / Aug. 9, 1920-Jun. 26, 1936 / ASV/Living Era ✦✦✦✦✦
Despite its title, the 1996 UK album *The King of Jazz* is not the soundtrack to Paul
Whiteman's 1930 film of the same name. Rather, with a subtitle reading "His
Greatest Recordings 1920-1936," it is a 75-minute, 18-track compilation drawn
from Whiteman's glory years, between his first recording session and the arrival of
the Swing Era. Though it leads off with "Whispering" and "Wang-Wang Blues," two
of Whiteman's biggest hits, it is not primarily a hits collection. Instead, it gathers
together recordings especially notable for the participants, including a version of
"Rhapsody in Blue" with George Gershwin on piano recreating the concert at
which Whiteman introduced the work, Paul Robeson singing "Ol' Man River,"
Mildred Bailey singing "When It's Sleepy Time Down South," and solos by such
jazz stars as Bix Beiderbecke (on "Changes"), Frank Trumbauer (on "The Bouncing Ball"), and Jack Teagarden (on "The Darktown Strutters' Ball," which also features his vocals). Bing Crosby's name turns up in the credits to five songs, but he is
usually part of the Rhythm Boys trio or an even larger chorus. The album concludes with an extended medley, "A Night with Paul Whiteman at the Biltmore,"
which includes excerpts from hits like "The Japanese Sandman" that are otherwise missing from the disc. —*William Ruhlmann*

● **Jazz à La King (1920-1936)** / Aug. 23, 1920-Jun. 2, 1936 / RCA ✦✦✦✦✦
This definitive two-LP set traces the recording career of bandleader Paul Whiteman, who was given the unfortunate title of "The King of Jazz." Whiteman did lead
the most popular jazz-influenced orchestra of the 1920s and his oversized ensemble sometimes played fine jazz. The orchestra was at its creative peak during 1927-
29 when cornetist Bix Beiderbecke was its top soloist, but since those performances are readily available elsewhere, Bix is only heard on three of the 33
recordings reissued on this very interesting two-fer. Starting with 1920s "Wang
Wang Blues" and "Whispering" and ending with the 1936 edition, which sometimes featured trombonist Jack Teagarden, many of the jazz high points of Whiteman's career are on the set, programmed in chronological order. Highlights
include "Hot Lips," "Charleston," "Milenberg Joys," "St. Louis Blues," "Whiteman
Stomp," "Sensation," "From Monday On," "G. Blues" and "Nobody's Sweetheart."
Thus far this release is superior to any Paul Whiteman collection reissued on CD.
—*Scott Yanow*

Paul Whiteman and His Orchestra with Bing Crosby / May 17, 1928-Oct. 18,
    1929 / Columbia ✦✦✦✦
Of the 16 selections included on this LP, only two or three are regularly reissued.
Paul Whiteman's large orchestra played first-class dance music with some spots
for brief jazz solos. The legendary cornetist Bix Beiderbecke is heard from on six
of the selections (not always the ones credited) but the main emphasis is on the
early vocals of Bing Crosby (who is heard from on all but one number) and the
distinctive ensembles. 1920s collectors will want to pick this album up due to the
rarity of some of the recordings. —*Scott Yanow*

The Complete Capitol Recordings / Jun. 5, 1942-Oct. 26, 1951 / Capitol ✦✦✦
Although he had been the most popular bandleader of the 1920s, by the '40s Paul
Whiteman was considered a bit of a has-been. This CD has his last significant
recordings. There are eight songs from June 1942 (with vocals by Martha Tilton,
Larry Neil, the Mellowaires, on "The Old Music Master" Johnny Mercer and Jack
Teagarden and for the most famous selection, "Trav'lin Light," Billie Holiday) that

find Whiteman doing his best to emulate Glenn Miller without outright copying him; a swinging "I've Found a New Baby" featuring pianist Buddy Weed is best. Two selections from 1945 really close the book on Whiteman: remakes of "San" (originally recorded with Bix Beiderbecke in 1928) and 1920s "Wang Wang Blues" (Whiteman's very first recording). The CD concludes with routine concert versions of "An American in Paris" and "Rhapsody in Blue" from 1951. Whiteman collectors and historians may find this set of interest but it pales next to his performances of the 1920s. —*Scott Yanow*

Mark Whitfield

b. 1967, Syosset, NY
Guitar / Soul Jazz, Hard Bop
A talented guitarist influenced by George Benson and versatile enough to play straightahead jazz or R&B, Mark Whitfield was originally a bassist. At 15 he switched to guitar and soon won a scholarship to Berklee. After graduating from Berklee in 1987 Whitfield temporarily moved to Brooklyn and appeared at many sessions. George Benson suggested he work for Jack McDuff and that association was a big break for Whitfield. He has since recorded as a leader for Warner Bros. and Verve and as a sideman with many players including Jimmy Smith, Nicholas Payton, Ray Brown and Courtney Pine. —*Scott Yanow*

The Marksman / 1990 / Warner Brothers ✦✦✦✦
Good young guitarist swings hard in the tradition. —*Michael G. Nastos*

Patrice / 1991 / Warner Brothers ✦✦✦✦

Mark Whitfield / 1993 / Warner Brothers ✦✦✦✦✦

● **True Blue** / 1994 / Verve ✦✦✦✦✦

7th Ave. Stroll / Jun. 16, 1995-Jun. 21, 1995 / Verve ✦✦✦✦✦

Forever Love / 1997 / Verve ✦✦✦✦
Mark Whitfield has long had an attractive tone, and his melodic style is in the forefront throughout this fairly varied date. Accompanied by a 21-piece string orchestra arranged by Dale Oehler, Whitfield and his quartet mostly stick to standards. Fortunately, tempos are varied (although there are a few sleepy ballads) and Diana Krall has guest vocals on "Some Other Time" and "Early Autumn." The strings generally do not add much, but Whitfield's inventive playing makes this a recommended set anyway. Highlights include "You Don't Know What Love Is," "My One and Only Love," an accompanied guitar feature on "I Want to Talk About You" and Whitfield's "Forever." —*Scott Yanow*

Weslia Whitfield

Vocals / Standards
One of today's foremost interpreters of popular standards, Weslia Whitfield won widespread acclaim for her elastic vocals, clarion pitch and impeccable phrasing. A native of the Los Angeles area, Whitfield took both voice and piano lessons as a child, later studying classical music in college and going on to sing in the chorus of the San Francisco Opera. However, the opera took away from her true love, the pop standards of her youth, and she frequently moonlighted in local piano bars; finally, during the mid-1970s, Whitfield began pursuing a cabaret career full-time, initially taking a job as a singing waitress. In 1977, she was the victim of a seemingly random street shooting that left her paralyzed from the waist down; after extensive therapy, she returned to music, and in 1981 began collaborating with pianist Michael Greensill, who five years later became her husband. Over time, Whitfield gradually moved away from her classical background toward jazz, her voice lowering from soprano to alto; she began recording extensively during the mid-1980s on her own Myoho label, later moving to Landmark with 1990s *Lucky to Be Me*. She subsequently jumped to the High Note label with 1997's *Teach Me Tonight*. —*Jason Ankeny*

Until the Real Thing Comes Along / Nov. 3, 1987-Nov. 5, 1987 / Myoho ✦✦✦✦

Nobody Else But Me / Nov. 7, 1988-Nov. 9, 1988 / Landmark ✦✦✦✦

● **Lucky to Be Me** / Nov. 9, 1989+Nov. 10, 1989 / Landmark ✦✦✦✦✦

Live in San Francisco / Apr. 23, 1991-Apr. 25, 1991 / Landmark ✦✦✦✦✦

Beautiful Love / Nov. 30, 1992-Dec. 1, 1992 / Cabaret ✦✦✦

Nice Work . . . / Dec. 11, 1994-Dec. 12, 1994 / Landmark ✦✦✦✦✦

My Shining Hour / Apr. 3, 1996-Apr. 5, 1996 / High Note ✦✦✦✦

Teach Me Tonight / Jan. 26, 1997+Jan. 28, 1997 / High Note ✦✦✦✦✦

Sebastian Whittaker

b. Sep. 12, 1966, Houston, TX
Drums / Hard Bop
A fine musician, Sebastian Whittaker models his drumming and bandleading after his idol Art Blakey. Blind since the age of one, Whittaker began playing drums

when he was three. After extensive musical study (he also took lessons on piano and composition), Whittaker resettled in Houston and has in recent times led a few dates for the Justice label. —*Scott Yanow*

First Outing / 1990 / Justice ✦✦✦✦
The first of three Justice releases led by drummer Sebastian Whittaker has eight originals by band members plus John Coltrane's "Impressions" but is very much in the style of Art Blakey's Jazz Messengers. None of the Texas-based musicians in Whittaker's septet (John Gordon and Shelly Carrol on tenors, trumpeter Dennis Dotson, trombonist James Lakey, pianist Stefan Karlsson, bassist David Craig and the drummer-leader) have become all that famous yet, but they play quite well throughout this swinging modern mainstream set. —*Scott Yanow*

● **Searchin' for the Truth** / 1991 / Justice ✦✦✦✦✦
Drummer Sebastian Whittaker's role model is Art Blakey, so it is little surprise that his series of recordings for Justice sound strongly influenced by Blue Note and the Jazz Messengers. However this sextet session emphasizes group originals and features particularly colorful soloists in trumpeter Barry Lee Hall (the last great graduate from Duke Ellington's Orchestra) and altoist Jesse Davis. Trombonist James Lakey, pianist Stefan Karlsson and bassist David Craig (holdovers from Whittaker's previous release) keep up with the better-known players and the result is high-quality hard bop. Recommended. —*Scott Yanow*

And the Creators / 1992 / Justice ✦✦✦✦✦
The word is out about drum sensation Sebastian Whittaker, and he justifies it on this sensational set. Whittaker takes the spotlight at the end of "Cherokee" for some whiplash licks and drumming, but otherwise provides steady, often explosive beats, support and rhythms. He's just as effective playing with subtlety or aggression; sometimes he's spurring on the soloists, and other times meshing behind them. He heads a superb trio that sounds like a revamped '90s version of Art Blakey's Jazz Messengers at times; then they'll switch modes and become a funky R&B horn section or blues-tinged gutbucket ensemble. This music has a vibrant quality, and shows that Sebastian Whittaker is ready to make his mark on the jazz and blues scene. —*Ron Wynn*

One for Bu!! / 1992 / Justice ✦✦✦✦✦
Drummer Sebastian Whittaker's Justice CD is an effective tribute to Art Blakey and his Jazz Messengers even though none of the sidemen in his septet (which includes trumpeter Barrie Lee Hall, altoist Jesse Davis and pianist Jacky Terrasson) actually played with Blakey and all but two standards are group originals. The swinging hard bop date has many concise but colorful solos from a wide variety of talented stylists and a few surprises. The melancholy "Present State of Mind" (which has some fine bowed bass from David Craig) gets away a bit from the Messengers tribute and the minor blues "Mopac at Midnight" ends up with a ragged Dixielandish section (with altoist Shelley Carroll switching to clarinet) that reminds one of the presence of trumpeter Hall, arguably the last great Ellingtonian. Strangely enough some of the tracks also have G.T. Hogan on drums but, due to the lack of liner notes, it is difficult to know which songs. In any case Sebastian Whittaker demonstrates throughout this CD that he deserves to be ranked as one of the more promising of the younger bandleaders. —*Scott Yanow*

Gerald Wiggins

b. May 12, 1922, New York, NY
Piano / Bop, Swing
Gerald Wiggins has long been a highly flexible pianist quite comfortable in swing or bop settings, but he is at his best when performing with his longtime trio, a group also including bassist Andy Simpkins and drummer Paul Humphrey. Wiggins' swinging and consistently witty style, typically filled with catchy riffs, is at times reminiscent of Erroll Garner and Art Tatum, but is generally quite distinctive.

"The Wig" started with piano lessons when he was four, switching from classical music to jazz as a teenager. He doubled on bass while attending the High School & Art and worked for a time in the early '40s as a piano accompanist for Stepin Fetchit. Wiggins played with Les Hite, and in 1943 toured with the big bands of Louis Armstrong and Benny Carter. While in the military (1944-46), he often played in local jazz clubs in Seattle. After his discharge, he settled permanently in the Los Angeles area. A popular accompanist for singers, Wiggins worked with Lena Horne (touring with her from 1950-51), Helen Humes, Ella Mae Morse, Eartha Kitt, Nat King Cole, Kay Starr, Lou Rawls, Ernie Andrews, Linda Hopkins, and Joe Williams, among others. Wiggins was also employed as a vocal coach at Hollywood film studios and had the opportunity to work with Marilyn Monroe.

In the Los Angeles area, Wiggins has led trios since the 1950s, becoming a consistent fixture in local clubs. In recent times, he has played piano with Frank Capp's Juggernaut and worked with fellow Concord artists like Scott Hamilton. Gerald Wiggins has led sessions through the years for Swing and Vogue (both in

1950), Ember, Crown, Tampa, Specialty, Motif, Mode, Challenge, Hi-Fi, Contemporary (1961), Black & Blue and, in the 1990s, Concord. His son J.J. Wiggins is a fine bassist. —*Scott Yanow*

Gerald Wiggins Trio / Oct. 1956 / V.S.O.P. ♦♦♦♦

Due to his skills as an accompanist and his work in Hollywood, Gerald Wiggins has always been a bit underrated, but the pianist has long had his own style within the swing/bop tradition. For this trio date (originally out on Tampa and reissued on LP by V.S.O.P.), Wig is teamed with bassist Joe Comfort and drummer Bill Douglas for a set of seven standards and two originals. The music swings with both subtlety and soul, and the overall results are quite enjoyable. Highlights include "Love for Sale," Duke Ellington's "I Don't Know What Kind of Blues I Got," "Surrey with the Fringe on Top" and "The Man That Got Away." —*Scott Yanow*

Around the World in 80 Days / 1956-1957 / Original Jazz Classics ♦♦♦

The problem with Victor Young's score to *Around the World in 80 Days* is that, other than the title song, none of the melodies were at all memorable. When was the last time anyone performed "Aouda," "Passepartout" or "The Royal Barge?" This CD reissue was made during a period when many Broadway show and film scores were being recorded in jazz settings but, although pianist Gerald Wiggins (along with bassist Eugene Wright and drummer Bill Douglass) does his best, the results (under a half-hour of music) are pleasant and swinging but predictably lightweight and not too substantial. —*Scott Yanow*

Reminiscin' with Wig / Feb. 1957 / Fresh Sound ♦♦♦

On this CD reissue, pianist Gerald Wiggins performs charming and sly versions of some unlikely material, including "Three O'Clock in the Morning," "Oh, You Beautiful Doll," "Ma, She's Making Eyes at Me" and "In My Merry Oldsmobile." The lightly swinging renditions (which also feature bassist Eugene Wright and drummer Bill Douglass) are enjoyable if not essential; the relatively brief program adds a previously unissued second version of "In My Merry Oldsmobile" to the original program. —*Scott Yanow*

The King and I / 1958 / Fresh Sound ♦♦♦

This CD reissue brings back a trio date originally cut for the obscure Challenge label and featuring pianist Gerald Wiggins, bassist Eugene Wright (shortly before he joined Dave Brubeck's Quartet) and drummer Bill Douglass. Together they perform eight selections from the show *The King and I*. Best-known of the Richard Rodgers melodies are "Getting to Know You," "We Kiss in a Shadow" and "Hello, Young Lovers," although the other five songs are superior too. Wiggins, showing hints of his roots in Erroll Garner and Art Tatum, performs an enjoyable if often easy-listening set of melodic improvisations that are pleasing, even if they contain few surprises. —*Scott Yanow*

Relax and Enjoy It / 1961 / Original Jazz Classics ♦♦♦♦♦

Wig Is Here / Mar. 25, 1974 / Classic Jazz ♦♦♦♦

This Black & Blue set (which has been reissued on CD with three additional selections) was pianist Gerald Wiggins' first recording session as a leader in 13 years even though he was quite active in the Los Angeles area during that time. Recorded in Paris with bassist Major Holley (who has a few solos on which he sings along with his bass) and drummer Ed Thigpen, Wig performs some standards (including "You Are the Sunshine of My Life," "Lover" and "There Is No Greater Love"), obscurities and a couple of originals. The music always swings and has plenty of subtle surprises; worth searching for. —*Scott Yanow*

● Live at Maybeck Recital Hall, Vol. 8 / Aug. 1990 / Concord Jazz ♦♦♦♦♦

Soulidarity / Aug. 23, 1995-Aug. 24, 1995 / Concord Jazz ♦♦♦♦♦

This spirited CD gives listeners a very good example of how pianist Gerry Wiggins was sounding in the mid-'90s. It is strange that it had been many years since his last trio album, for this was always the perfect setting for Wiggins. Joined by bassist Andy Simpkins and drummer Paul Humphrey, the pianist swings creatively on such numbers as "The Way You Look Tonight," "Some Other Spring," "Strip City," "What Is There to Say," "Lover" and even "Alexander's Ragtime Band." An inspired outing. —*Scott Yanow*

Bob Wilber

b. Mar. 15, 1928, New York, NY

Soprano Saxophone, Clarinet, Alto Saxophone / Classic Jazz, Mainstream Jazz

Throughout his long career Bob Wilber has done a lot to keep classic jazz alive. A bit misplaced (most jazz players of his generation were much more interested in bop and hard bop), Wilber (along with Kenny Davern, Ralph Sutton and Dick Wellstood) was one of the few in his age group to stick to prebop music. In high school he formed a band that included Wellstood and as a teenager he sat in at Jimmy Ryan's club in New York. Early on he became Sidney Bechet's protege and led his own young group the Wildcats (with whom he made his recording debut). The close association with the dominant Bechet led to a bit of a personality crisis in the 1950s as Wilber sought to find his own voice. He studied with Lennie

Tristano and formed The Six, a group that tried to modernize early jazz. When that ended, he played Dixieland with Eddie Condon and in 1957 joined Bobby Hackett's band for a year. Wilber freelanced throughout the 1960s, in 1968 became a founding member of the World's Greatest Jazz Band and in 1973 he formed Soprano Summit with Kenny Davern, one of the top swing-oriented groups of the decade. A few years later the band broke up and Wilber teamed up with his wife, singer Pug Horton, in Bechet Legacy (which also featured either Glenn Zottola or Randy Sandke on trumpet). In addition Bob Wilber has worked with the New York Jazz Repertory Company, released music on his own Bodeswell label, written the authentic soundtrack to the movie *The Cotton Club* (1984), led a band at Carnegie Hall to celebrate the 50th anniversary of Benny Goodman's famous concert (in 1988) and authored his frank memoirs *Music Was Not Enough*. Influenced on soprano, clarinet and alto by respectively Bechet, Goodman and Johnny Hodges, Wilber has long had his own sound on each of his instruments. He has recorded frequently through the years for many labels, most recently Arbors. —*Scott Yanow*

Bob Wilber and His Famous Jazz Band / Apr. 28, 1949+Jun. 8, 1949 / Jazzology ♦♦♦♦

This LP brings together two related sessions. Bob Wilber (doubling on clarinet and soprano), who had first recorded two years earlier with his youth group (the Wildcats), was 21 at the time and Sidney Bechet's protege. Wilber is teamed up with pianist Dick Wellstood and a variety of top veterans (trumpeter Henry Goodwin, trombonist Jimmy Archey, bassist Pops Foster and drummer Tommy Benford) for six selections (including "The Mooche," "The Saints" and "Limehouse Blues"), while on six others he welcomes a rather dominant guest, Bechet himself. "Box Car Shorty" has a vocal by calypso singer the Duke of Iron, Bechet talks a bit on "Love Me with a Feeling" and introduces his original "I'm Through, Goodbye." Timeless and somewhat offbeat New Orleans jazz. —*Scott Yanow*

The Music of Hoagy Carmichael / Jun. 1969 / Monmouth ♦♦♦♦♦

Bob Wilber, in his first record as a leader since 1960, pays tribute to composer Hoagy Carmichael by playing 14 of his originals, including such classics as "Riverboat Shuffle," "Georgia on My Mind," "Skylark," "Lazy River" and of course "Stardust." Wilber mostly utilized members of the World's Greatest Jazz Band (including tenor saxophonist Bud Freeman, trumpeter Yank Lawson and trombonist Lou McGarity) on this enjoyable date; singer Maxine Sullivan, who had just emerged from retirement, is an added bonus on five songs. This LP is well deserving of reissue on CD. —*Scott Yanow*

Bob Wilber & The Scott Hamilton Quartet / Jun. 30, 1977-Jul. 1, 1977 / Chiaroscuro ♦♦♦♦

On this CD reissue, Bob Wilber (who triples on clarinet, soprano and alto) meets up quite successfully with the relatively young swing stylist Scott Hamilton (heard near the beginning of his career) and the tenor's rhythm section of the period (guitarist Chris Flory, bassist Phil Flanagan and drummer Chuck Riggs). Together they perform melodic and swinging renditions of six of Wilber's originals along with six veteran standards; the logical arrangements help to set up the solos. Also included on the reissue is a seven-minute "Jazzspeak" in which Wilber remembers how the date came about. Easily recommended to mainstream and small-group swing fans. —*Scott Yanow*

In the Mood for Swing / May 30, 1979-May 31, 1979 / Phontastic ♦♦♦♦

This set is a tribute to the classic Lionel Hampton recordings of 1937-41. Bob Wilber's set has been reissued on CD by Phontastic. Vibraphonist Lars Erstrand (whose main influence was obviously Hampton) gets second billing and the other sidemen are also quite notable: altoist Norris Turney, trumpeter Jimmy Maxwell, the tenors of Al Klink and Frank Wess, pianist Hank Jones, guitarist Bucky Pizzarelli, bassist Michael Moore and drummer Connie Kay. Highlights include "I'm in the Mood for Swing," "Dinah," "Ring Dem Bells" and "The Sheik of Araby." Wilber triples on clarinet, alto and soprano and the music does not merely imitate the past but is creative within the boundaries of swing. —*Scott Yanow*

Dizzy Fingers / Aug. 24, 1980 / Bodeswell ♦♦♦♦

For the initial LP on his short-lived Bodeswell label, Bob Wilber sticks to clarinet and heads a tribute to Benny Goodman. The instrumentation (which utilizes the fine Swedish vibraphonist Lars Erstrand, pianist Mark Shane, guitarist Chris Flory, bassist Phil Flanagan and drummer Chuck Riggs) brings back the Benny Goodman Sextet. Pug Horton helps out with a pair of vocals, and the instrumental highlights include "Dizzy Fingers," "Airmail Special," "Jumpin' at the Woodside," "Royal Garden Blues," "The World Is Waiting for the Sunrise" and a rare small-group version of Mel Powell's "Clarinade." —*Scott Yanow*

Bob Wilber and the Bechet Legacy / Jan. 22, 1981 / Bodeswell ♦♦♦♦♦

Bob Wilber formed the Bechet Legacy in 1980 to pay tribute to his former teacher, the great soprano saxophonist Sidney Bechet. Wilber, who used to sound like Bechet on soprano and clarinet but has long since developed his own sound, heads a fine sextet also including trumpeter Glenn Zottola, pianist Mark Shane, guitarist Chris Flory, bassist Phil Flanigan and drummer Chuck Riggs on a set of tunes associated with Bechet. Pug Horton takes vocals on three songs (in the style of Eva Taylor) and the final two numbers ("Kansas City Man" and "China Boy") find Wilber and Zottola interacting with fire in a sparse quartet with Flory and Flanigan. The music on this LP has many highlights including "Down in Honky Tonk Town," "Roses of Picardy" and "Petite Fleur." It is quite fitting that the debut recording by Bechet Legacy was recorded live at a club called Bechet's. —*Scott Yanow*

Music of King Oliver / May 10, 1981 / GHB ✦✦✦✦

King Oliver's Creole Jazz Band was the top group on records in 1923, and it introduced not only the cornetist-leader but Louis Armstrong and clarinetist Johnny Dodds. In 1981 Bob Wilber sought to recreate the spirit and arrangements of the original band. Utilizing an octet with both Bob and Glenn Zottola on trumpets and trombonist Tom Artin, Wilber recorded 15 selections; Oliver cut 13 in 1923, "Wa Wa Wa" dates from slightly later and Wilber's "Lincoln Gardens Stomp" is in the style of the Creole Jazz Band. The ensembles (transcribed by Wilber and Mark Tucker) are pretty much note-for-note from the early records, although the soloists were free to depart in subtle ways. This is an interesting release that allows today's listeners to hear just how intricate the ensembles of King Oliver's band were back in the early 1920s. Although Wilber mentions in the liner notes that this was the first of three albums in the project, it is actually the only one to ever come out. —*Scott Yanow*

On the Road / Nov. 24, 1981 / Bodeswell ✦✦✦✦

Bob Wilber's Bechet Legacy group (which was most active in the early 1980s) successfully paid tribute to Wilber's early teacher Sidney Bechet. Wilber (on soprano and clarinet) brings back Bechet's spirit on this frequently exciting LP without copying the master. Trumpeter Glenn Zottola is a key member of the sextet and Pug Horton takes a few worthy vocals. High points of the date include "Lady Be Good," "Polka Dot Stomp," "Egyptian Fantasy," "Santa Claus Blues" and "Danse Le Rue D'Antibes." —*Scott Yanow*

Ode to Bechet / Aug. 5, 1982-Aug. 6, 1982 / Jazzology ✦✦✦✦✦

The 1982 version of Bob Wilber's Bechet Legacy (which consists of Wilber on soprano, trumpeter Glenn Zottola, pianist Mark Shane, guitarist Mike Peters, bassist Reggie Johnson, drummer Butch Miles and singer Pug Horton, who is heard on three songs) is joined by veteran trombonist Vic Dickenson for this spirited CD reissue from 1995. As expected, most of the songs are associated with Bechet (Wilber's original teacher), including "Margie," "I Can't Believe That You're in Love With Me," "The Mooche," "Shake It and Break It," and three Bechet originals, plus Wilber's "Ode to Bechet." Dickenson, who helps Horton out with the vocal of "I Get the Blues When It Rains," gets to show off both his sly wit and his subtle playing. Enjoyable music, recommended to trad jazz fans. —*Scott Yanow*

Reflections / Jun. 8, 1983+Jun. 10, 1983 / Bodeswell ✦✦✦

Bob Wilber, on alto and soprano, is accompanied by a rhythm section and strings on this pretty and melodic date. Wilber contributed the arrangements and three of the dozen ballads, but few surprises occur. He mostly pays tribute to the style (but not the sound) of Johnny Hodges with improvisations that stick close to the melodies of such songs as "Deep Purple," "In the Wee Small Hours" and "Body and Soul." This LP has been long out of print and works well as high-quality background music. —*Scott Yanow*

● **Bob Wilber & Bechet Legacy** / Jan. 29, 1984 / Challenge ✦✦✦✦✦

After the breakup of Soprano Summit in the early '80s, Bob Wilber formed a group dedicated to reviving the music of his teacher, Sidney Bechet. Wilber (who triples here on soprano, clarinet and alto) is heard with his intimate quartet (which also includes trumpeter Randy Sandke, guitarist Mike Peters and bassist John Goldsby) during a live performance on nine selections associated with Bechet. This CD (its contents were released for the first time in 1995) has plenty of passionate and heated swing, with the high points including "Down in Honky Tonk Town," "Promenade Aux Champs-Elysees," "China Boy" and "Lady Be Good." Quite enjoyable. —*Scott Yanow*

The Bob Wilber-Dick Wellstood Duet / Mar. 27, 1984-May 22, 1984 / Progressive ✦✦✦✦✦

Bob Wilber and pianist Dick Wellstood first played together on a regular basis back when they were teenagers in the late 1940s, but this LP was their first duet set. With Wilber doubling on clarinet and soprano, the music ranges from "Cornet Chop Suey" and "The Entertainer" to numbers by Fats Waller, James P. Johnson and Wilber's "Soulful Soliloquy." Heated moments alternate with more lyrical pieces, and both Wilber and Wellstood show off their versatility; the relatively complex "I've Got You Under My Skin" was no problem for these two masters. Recommended to fans of prebop jazz. —*Scott Yanow*

Nostalgia / Mar. 27, 1995-Mar. 28, 1995 / Arbors ✦✦✦

With a few exceptions, the emphasis is on slower tempos on this generally wistful and lyrical set. Bob Wilber (sticking to soprano) is assisted by the great stride pianist Ralph Sutton, guitarist Bucky Pizzarelli, bassist Bob Haggart and drummer Butch Miles for a variety of songs that he enjoys. Included are three classical themes, a few ancient standards (such as two versions of Willie "The Lion" Smith's "Echo of Spring," "Floatin' Down to Cotton Town" and "Roses of Picardy"), and some off-the-wall choices (including "Mexicali Rose" and "Sonny Boy"). A melodic, pleasant and usually lightly swinging program. —*Scott Yanow*

The Hamburg Concert / Oct. 22, 1995 / Nagel-Heyer ✦✦✦✦

Bob Wilber's Bechet Legacy has been a part-time group since 1980. Wilber (on soprano and clarinet) was always enthusiastic about paying tribute to his former teacher Sidney Bechet, and was able to interpret Bechet's music without directly imitating the great soprano saxophonist. For this live outing, Wilber is ably assisted by the talented trumpeter Randy Sandke, pianist Mark Shane, guitarist Dave Cliff, bassist Dave Green, drummer Butch Miles and (on a few numbers) singer Pug Horton. In addition to ten Bechet compositions, the group plays six songs that Bechet performed at one time or another. The solos are melodic and full of chance-taking, the ensembles are heated and the overall program is quite delightful and swinging. Highlights include "Down in Honky Tonk Town," "Egyptian Fantasy," "Maryland My Maryland" and "Dans Le Rue D'Antibes." —*Scott Yanow*

A Man and His Music / 1995 / Progressive ✦✦✦✦

The most unusual aspect of this Bob Wilber CD is that, in addition to his usual clarinet and sopranos (both curved and straight), he also plays a bit of alto and tenor. Wilber's tenor (heard on four of the 14 numbers) is a bit of a revelation, for his thick tone is reminiscent of Coleman Hawkins. Joined by pianist Mick Pyne, guitarist Dave Cliff, bassist Dave Green and drummer Bobby Worth, Wilber performs five originals, a couple of surprisingly modern pieces ("Django" and "Lazy Afternoon"), and seven swing standards. An excellent set of mainstream jazz. —*Scott Yanow*

At The March of Jazz '96 / Mar. 23, 1996 / Arbors ✦✦✦

Joe Wilder

b. Feb. 22, 1922, Colwyn, PA
Trumpet, Fluegelhorn / Swing

A versatile trumpeter sporting a beautiful tone quality, Joe Wilder's playing is full of character and the invaluable ability to tell a story with his horn—a trait he says was fueled by one of his "original inspirations," Benny Carter. Wilder was raised in Philadelphia, where his father led a band, making his debut on a local radio show spotlighting talented black children. His first professional job was with Les Hite in 1941, where he met Dizzy Gillespie in the trumpet section. He joined Lionel Hampton the following year and became co-bandmaster for a Marine band during World War II. Rejoining Hampton after the war, Wilder moved on to the Jimmie Lunceford, Lucky Millander, Sam Donahue and Herbie Fields bands while also playing in the pit orchestras for Broadway musicals (including three years with *Guys and Dolls*). He played with Count Basie for the first six months of 1954 and was a member of the music staff of ABC-TV from 1957 to 1973, taking time out to tour Russia with Benny Goodman and substitute with the New York Philharmonic. Upon leaving ABC in 1973, Wilder worked as a freelance studio musician. As a leader, Wilder recorded an album for Savoy in 1956 and two for Columbia in 1959; more recently, he appeared in memorably sly form on Benny Carter's *A Gentleman and His Music* (Concord) in 1985 and resurfaced in the 1990s with a pair of albums on the Evening Star label. —*Richard S. Ginell*

Wilder N' Wilder . . . / Jan. 19, 1956 / Savoy ✦✦✦✦✦

Joe Wilder has long had one of the most appealing tones of all trumpeters, and his lyrical style is well suited to lightly swinging jazz. On this CD reissue, Wilder is joined by pianist Hank Jones, bassist Wendell Marshall and drummer Kenny Clarke for five melodic standards (including a ten-minute version of "Cherokee"), Ozzie Cadena's "Sixbit Blues" and three previously unissued alternate takes. This is one of Savoy's better CD reissues and contains enjoyable and thoughtful music. —*Scott Yanow*

The Pretty Sound of Joe Wilder / Dec. 1, 1958+Dec. 31, 1958 / Columbia ✦✦✦✦

Jazz from "Peter Gunn" / Jan. 18, 1959 / Columbia ✦✦✦✦

● **Alone with Just My Dreams** / Aug. 6, 1991-Aug. 7, 1991 / Evening Star ✦✦✦✦✦

No Greater Love / Aug. 3, 1993-Aug. 4, 1993 / Evening Star ✦✦✦✦✦

Veteran trumpeter Joe Wilder is very much in his prime on this late-period CD, playing in a variety of settings with Seldon Powell (who doubles on tenor and flute), pianist Bobby Tucker, guitarist James Chirillo, bassist Milt Hinton and drummer Sherman Ferguson. Performing three of his originals, Tucker's "Thinking of Lady," Benny Carter's "The Courtship," and nine standards, the lyrical trumpeter is heard on several sextet numbers, a couple of trios with piano and guitar, and duets with both Tucker and Chirillo. Wilder's pretty sound, lyrical style and melodic approach are featured throughout in relaxed and frequently exquisite form. —*Scott Yanow*

Lee Wiley

b. Oct. 9, 1915, Fort Gibson, OK, d. Dec. 11, 1975, New York, NY
Vocals / Swing, Standards, Traditional Pop

Lee Wiley occupies her own place in jazz history. Although a cool-toned and sophisticated singer, her interpretations of superior standards were often quite sensuous and, even if she did not improvise much, she was a favorite of many musicians, particularly Eddie Condon. She came to New York in the early '30s and at age 17 was singing and recording with Leo Reisman's orchestra. She spent most of that decade singing with commercial radio orchestras (including Victor Young and Johnny Green) but eventually also appeared at clubs backed by small jazz groups, having a close relationship with Bunny Berigan. Starting in 1939 Lee Wiley became the first singer to devote an entire album to the music of one composer; her George Gershwin, Cole Porter, Harold Arlen and Rodgers & Hart sessions are considered classic and the high points of her career. Wiley married Jess Stacy in 1943, but after five years both their big band and marriage were history. She appeared at a few of Eddie Condon's Town Hall concerts, but from the late '40s on Wiley performed and recorded less frequently. After some sessions for Columbia during 1950-51, for Storyville in 1954 and Victor during 1956-57, all that remained was a final record for Monmouth-Evergreen in 1971. By then she was forgotten to all but veteran record collectors, but Lee Wiley had made her mark decades earlier. —*Scott Yanow*

Complete Young Lee Wiley (1931-37) / Jun. 30, 1931-Feb. 10, 1937 / Vintage Jazz ◆◆◆◆

The sensuous singer Lee Wiley is featured on 22 tracks on this CD, all of her appearances on record during 1931-37. Wiley sings three ballads with Leo Reisman's Orchestra in 1931-32 (trumpeter Bubber Miley takes a short solo on "Take It From Me"), several numbers (including four takes of "Let's Call It a Day") with the 1933 Dorsey Brothers Orchestra, her initial version of "A Hundred Years From Today," a few songs with Victor Young's Orchestra and Johnny Green, and her first solo recordings. This was Lee Wiley's "pop phase," which concluded a couple years before she became more closely associated with the jazz world. Although most of this material is not all that essential, it does give listeners a very complete picture of the vocalist in her earliest years and will be savored by Lee Wiley's fans. —*Scott Yanow*

Broadcasts and Rarities, Vol. 2 / Mar. 7, 1933-Apr. 4, 1952 / Jass ◆◆◆◆

This LP, the second of two, has a variety of odds and ends that feature vocalist Lee Wiley. The first four numbers (from her "pop" period) have since been reissued by Vintage Jazz Classics and are most notable for her version of "I Got a Right to Sing the Blues." There are a couple of aircheck performances from 1938 (including a five-song medley) and a 1948 version of "Stormy Weather." The second side of the album features Wiley in 1952 at a pair of jam sessions with a local Dixieland group in 1952; three songs add the trumpet of the great Red Allen. Throughout, Lee Wiley is in top form and these two albums (released in the late '80s) were important additions to her rather slim discography. —*Scott Yanow*

Broadcasts and Rarities / 1936-1959 / Jass ◆◆◆◆

The first of two Lee Wiley Jass LPs feature the legendary singer on radio broadcasts from 1936 and 1938, private acetates from the late 1930s, appearances on a 1950 radio show, four previously unknown duets with pianist Joe Bushkin (probably from the early 1960s) and two songs from a 1959 television show. In general the recording quality is better than expected (although some songs have surface noise) and Lee Wiley's singing sounds generally inspired. This is a valuable addition to Wiley's legacy. —*Scott Yanow*

Sings the Songs of Ira and George Gershwin and Cole Porter / Nov. 13, 1939-Apr. 1940 / Audiophile ◆◆◆◆◆

Lee Wiley was the first jazz singer to record a full album (eight songs in the '78' days) dedicated to the music of one composer; her "songbooks" preceded Ella Fitzgerald's by more than 15 years. The greatest recordings of her career were these four projects, the first two of which are on this Audiophile reissue. Wiley, who had an introverted and quietly straightforward yet sensuous (and somewhat smoldering) style, is heard singing eight songs apiece by the Gershwins and Cole Porter. Her accompaniment includes all-star groups headed by pianist Joe Bushkin and trumpeter Max Kaminsky (which include tenor saxophonist Bud Freeman, clarinetist Pee Wee Russell and on four songs Fats Waller), a quartet with Bushkin and trumpeter Bunny Berigan, and Paul Weston's Orchestra. Wiley's renditions of such songs as "How Long Has This Been Going On," "I've Got a Crush on You," "Someone to Watch Over Me," "Let's Do It" and "Easy to Love" are both memora-

ble and haunting. This reissue is a gem, as is the follow-up Audiophile release of Rodgers & Hart and Harold Arlen songs. —*Scott Yanow*

Sings the Songs of Rodgers and Hart & Harold Arlen / Feb. 1940-Apr. 1943 / Audiophile ◆◆◆◆◆

Lee Wiley pioneered the "songbook" concept, for which a singer exclusively interpreted the work of one composer. Her Gershwin and Cole Porter projects of 1939-40 were major successes, as is the music on this Audiophile reissue. In a fairly straight but strangely sensuous manner, Wiley sings eight songs apiece by Rodgers & Hart and Harold Arlen while backed by a variety of all-star players associated with Eddie Condon, including pianist Joe Bushkin, trumpeters Max Kaminsky, Billy Butterfield and Bobb Hackett, tenor saxophonist Bud Freeman, and Ernie Caceres on baritone and clarinet. Although many of these songs have been interpreted countless times since, few singers have reached the emotional peaks that Lee Wiley scaled in her versions of "A Ship Without a Sail," "Let's Fall in Love," "I've Got the World on a String," "Down With Love" and especially "Glad to Be Unhappy." This set (along with the previous one) belongs in every serious jazz collection. —*Scott Yanow*

Night in Manhattan / Dec. 12, 1950+Dec. 14, 1950 / Columbia ◆◆◆◆

This set was singer Lee Wiley's most successful recording of the postwar years. Wiley is joined on eight selections by the sensitive trumpeter Bobby Hackett, a small string section, a rhythm section led by pianist Joe Bushkin and sometimes two clarinets and an accordion; highlights include "A Woman's Intuition," "Sugar," "Manhattan" and "I've Got a Crush on You," although all eight songs are enjoyable. This set is rounded out by four numbers taken from a pair of slightly later Columbia albums (programs of the music of Vincent Youmans and Irving Berlin) that found Wiley backed by the two-piano team of Stan Freeman and Cy Walter; best is "More than You Know" and "How Deep Is The Ocean." It seems strange, considering the popularity of this particular collection, that Lee Wiley would gradually disappear from the active jazz scene. Well worth picking up. —*Scott Yanow*

The Carnegie Hall Concert / 1952+Jul. 5, 1972 / Audiophile ◆◆◆◆

Lee Wiley was a superior singer whose style fell between swing and cabaret. She gave straightforward interpretations of lyrics, yet also had a strong sense of swing. Discouraged by the music business, Wiley retired in 1958 when she was still in her prime. She made a brief return during 1971-72 when she recorded a final album and performed at the first Newport in New York Jazz Festival. The latter concert has been released for the first time on this Audiophile CD and is Wiley's final recording. Accompanied by cornetist Bobby Hackett, pianist Teddy Wilson, guitarist Bucky Pizzarelli, bassist George Duvivier and drummer Don Lamond, Lee Wiley sounds in surprisingly good form. Although her voice had deepened a little, she is quite recognizable and had not declined at all. Before a loving crowd (that sounds quite delighted to get the rare chance to see her), Wiley sings 11 songs. Best are "Indiana," "You're Lucky to Me," an emotional "Come Sunday" and "Sugar." Although she forgets the words at one point on "Manhattan" (a surprise request from George Wein), Lee Wiley does quite well and exits on top. The remainder of this CD comprises ten songs recorded at a rehearsal in 1952 with Wein himself on piano, bassist John Field and drummer Marquis Foster. The trumpeter is listed as Johnny Windhurst, but I would opt for Bobby Hackett. Although quite informal (and some of the renditions are under two minutes), this rehearsal is an important addition to the relatively slim discography of the charming Lee Wiley. —*Scott Yanow*

Duologue / Jul. 7, 1954 / Black Lion ◆◆◆◆

Although only 38 at the time of this recording and still in her musical prime, singer Lee Wiley was already thought of as a has-been, and was finding it increasingly difficult to locate work. Her sophisticated, gentle, yet sincere swing style was out of favor by the mid-'50s, but she still had something to say. This CD reissue features her haunting voice showcased on eight numbers with a quartet that includes trumpeter Ruby Braff, pianist Jimmy Jones, bassist Bill Pemberton and drummer Jo Jones; the best are "My Heart Stood Still," "My Funny Valentine" and especially memorable versions of "It Never Entered My Mind" and "Glad to Be Unhappy." Although pianist Ellis Larkins, who is heard on four unrelated unaccompanied solos, gets co-billing on the CD, he and Wiley never actually meet. —*Scott Yanow*

● As Time Goes By / Jun. 12, 1956-Jul. 25, 1957 / Bluebird ◆◆◆◆◆

Shortly before she slipped completely into obscurity, singer Lee Wiley recorded two albums for Victor. This Bluebird CD has ten of the twelve songs from *West of the Moon*, nine of the twelve originally on *A Touch of the Blues* and a rendition of "Stars Fell on Alabama" taken from a sampler album. Wiley, only 41 at the time of these last recordings, was essentially through with her career despite still being in prime form. Other than "Stars," Wiley is backed by big bands led by either arranger Ralph Burns or trumpeter Billy Butterfield and mostly performs swing standards including "You're a Sweetheart," "Can't Get Out of This Mood," "Ace in the Hole," "Between the Devil and the Deep Blue Sea" and her signature song "A Hundred Years from Today." An excellent introduction to the work of this unusual and greatly underrated singer. —*Scott Yanow*

Back Home Again / Sep. 30, 1971-Oct. 11, 1971 / Monmouth ✦✦✦
Fourteen years after her last record, singer Lee Wiley came back for one final studio recording. Although she does a good job on "Indiana" and "I'm Coming, Virginia" and the backup band (which includes trumpeter Rusty Dedrick, clarinetist Johnny Mince, trombonist Buddy Morrow and pianist Dick Hyman) is excellent, in general this is a disappointing LP. Wiley's voice was no longer in its prime and, although her distinctive phrasing was still intact, her earlier sessions are far superior while her final Carnegie Hall recording is much more emotional and historic. This album is only recommended to Lee Wiley completists. —*Scott Yanow*

Don Wilkerson

b. Jul. 1932, Moreauville, LA, d. Jul. 18, 1986, Houston, TX
Tenor Saxophone / Hard Bop, Soul Jazz, Modern Creative
Large-toned Texas tenorman Don Wilkerson was born in Louisiana in July of 1932, but was raised in Houston. Starting out on alto sax, Wilkerson was playing tenor with Amos Milburn by his late teens. He went on to play with Charles Brown and is perhaps most well-known for his various stints with Ray Charles. His solo on Charles' classic "I Got a Woman" remains an outstanding example of his work. A lovely ballad from *Texas Twister* is available on the Prestige CD *Texas Tenors*, produced by Bob Porter.

Cannonball Adderley produced an album with Wilkerson in 1960 on Riverside, called *The Texas Twister*. When Ray Charles expanded his group to the size of a big band, Wilkerson rejoined that group. At the invitation of Ike Quebec in 1962, Wilkerson made three excellent albums on Blue Note (all three with Grant Green as a sideman), *Elder Don*, *Preach Brother*, and *Shoutin',* in 1962 and 1963. He was, however, not very successful as a leader and spent his later years in Houston, where he died in 1986. —*Michael Erlewine*

The Texas Twister / May 19, 1960-May 20, 1960 / Riverside ✦✦✦✦

● **Elder Don** / May 3, 1962 / Blue Note ✦✦✦✦✦
Don Wilkerson's first Blue Note session, *Elder Don* (it was recorded before *Preach, Brother!,* but released afterward), is a highly enjoyable set of hard-swinging, bluesy soul-jazz and hard-bop. It's hardly a one-note collection—"Senorita Eula" swings with a Latin lilt, "Scrappy" is a hard-hitting R&B number, the lightly Cuban recasting of Bob Wills's Western Swing classic "San Antonio Rose" is fluid and infectious, "Lone Star Shuffle" and "Drawin' a Tip are wonderful blues shuffles, and the ballad "Poor Butterfly" has a graceful, lyrical quality—which is part of the reason why it's so impressive. Still, all of the credit for *Elder Don*'s success has to go to Wilkerson, whose vibrant, robust tone dominates the session, and since he's playing with the exceptional guitarist Grant Green and excellent drummer Willie Bobo, as well as pianist Johnny Acean and bassist Lloyd Trotman, that's no small accomplishment. In fact, records like this go a long way in proving that Wilkerson was one of the great underrated saxophonists of his time. —*Stephen Thomas Erlewine*

Preach, Brother! / Jun. 18, 1962 / Blue Note ✦✦✦✦
Recorded after *Elder Don* but released before that album, *Preach, Brother!* finds Don Wilkerson in top form, running through a set of hard-driving soul-jazz, R&B, swing, hard bop and blues. Supported by pianist Sonny Clark, guitarist Grant Green, bassist Butch Warren and drummer Billy Higgins, Wilkerson works up a hot groove on each of these six songs, which are mainly instrumental. His playing is vigorous and aggressive on the uptempo blues and shuffles, and surprisingly nimble on the ballads. Clark and Green match their leader with alternately forceful and sensitive accompaniment and solos, and the rhythm section keeps a steady, attractive groove. The result is another fine record that proves Wilkerson was one of the best, hardest-hitting soul-jazz saxophonists of the early '60s. —*Stephen Thomas Erlewine*

Shoutin' / Jul. 30, 1963 / Blue Note ✦✦✦✦✦
Don Wilkerson's final album, *Shoutin',* found him returning to the confines of a quartet, which actually liberated his playing. Without the competition provided from a trumpeter, Wilkerson has plenty of room to roam, and he needs it—he was one of the most forceful and full-bodied tenor saxophonists in soul-jazz during the '60s. Throughout *Shoutin',* he impresses with his ability to switch between rich, graceful ballads and hard-hitting, hard-driving blues and R&B. Fortunately, he's supported by an excellent trio—guitarist Grant Green, organist John Patton, drummer Ben Dixon—that can play it hard and play it soft with equal aplomb. And, like on *Preach, Brother!,* Green and Patton not only contribute fine accompaniment, but also terrific solos that keep things cooking. The original compositions (and most of the album comprises original material) may not be distinctive, but they do what they were intended to do: provide launching pads for hot grooves and kinetic interplay. All through *Preach, Brother!,* the quartet works soulful grooves with

invigorating dexterity, and the high quality of the music on this album, as well as Wilkerson's other three records, will make most soul-jazz fans regret that this was his last record. It will also make them treasure the albums all the more. —*Stephen Thomas Erlewine*

Ernie Wilkins

b. Jul. 20, 1922, St. Louis, MO
Arranger, Tenor Saxophone / Bop, Swing
A fine, slippery bop tenor sax player, and a creator of sharp-edged arrangements for bop and swing big bands who helped define the Count Basie Mk. II style of the 1950s, Ernie Wilkins had been a regular fixture on the American jazz scene until 1979, when he pulled up stakes and moved to Europe. He first learned piano and violin, then studied music at Wilberforce University before going into the Navy during the war. He caught on with the Earl Hines band in 1948 and worked around the St. Louis area before joining the Basie band in 1952. He remained in the Basie fold until 1955, but continued to freelance arrangements to the Count, as well as arrange for and perform with the Dizzy Gillespie band that toured the Middle East and South America in 1956. Also in 1956, he wrote three of the six movements of the exciting Wilkins/Manny Albam *The Drum Suite* (RCA Victor)—reputedly the first time anyone had tried to integrate four drummers into one band—and led big band albums under his own name for Savoy and Everest in the 1950s. He was the staff composer for the Harry James orchestra from 1958 to 1960 and served as musical director for albums by Nat Adderley, Sarah Vaughan, Buddy Rich, Oscar Peterson, and Dinah Washington, among others. In 1968, he joined Clark Terry's Big B-A-D Band, serving as a composer and music director, after which he assembled his own band and became head of A&R for the Mainstream label (1971-73). He would continue to provide Basie with arrangements and toured Europe with Terry in the late '70s, ultimately settling in Copenhagen in 1979, where he formed the Almost Big Band. Most of the recorded examples of Wilkins' work on sax are as a sideman with Basie and Terry. —*Richard S. Ginell*

Ernie Wilkins-Kenny Clarke Septet / May 30, 1955 / Savoy ✦✦✦✦✦
This CD reissue from the Japanese Denon label brings back a formerly rare Savoy set co-led by arranger Ernie Wilkins and drummer Kenny Clarke. The six basic originals by Wilkins and producer Ozzie Cadena leave plenty of room for the musicians to stretch out. Wilkins doubles on alto and tenor, George Barrow plays both tenor and baritone, Cecil Payne sticks to baritone, trombonist Eddie Bert is in top form and pianist Hank Jones and bassist Wendell Marshall are fine in supporting roles. Kenny Clarke, who has some drum breaks here and there, gets "Now's the Time" as an unaccompanied drum solo, taking five choruses. Overall this is an excellent outing for all concerned. —*Scott Yanow*

Here Comes the Swingin' Mr. Wilkins / Dec. 9, 1959-Jan. 11, 1960 / Everest ✦✦✦✦✦

The Big New Band of the '60s / Mar. 11, 1960-Apr. 28, 1960 / Everest ✦✦✦
Despite its title, the Ernie Wilkins Orchestra did not become "the big new band of the '60s," and this LP was its only recording. With such an all-star cast (including trumpeters Clark Terry and Charlie Shavers, tenors Zoot Sims and Yusef Lateef, vibraphonist Eddie Costa and guitarist Kenny Burrell) the big band would not have had much of a chance anyway in the 1960s. Wilkins' progressive but swinging arrangements for three of his originals and nine standards are enjoyable, but the brevity of the tracks (the longest one is three minutes) and the rather short solos are unfortunate. This LP falls a bit short of its great potential. —*Scott Yanow*

● **Ernie Wilkins & the Almost Big Band** / Oct. 30, 1980-Nov. 2, 1980 / Storyville ✦✦✦✦✦
After permanently moving to Copenhagen in 1979, the American arranger Ernie Wilkins formed his "Almost Big Band," a 13-piece orchestra that consisted of talented Europeans and a few Americans. For their first of four recordings, Wilkins (who arranged all eight selections) and his band perform two standards ("Hi-Fly" and "Sugar"), three of the leader's originals and three obscurities. Among the key soloists are tenors Jesper Thilo, Bent Jaedig and Wilkins, the up-and-coming trumpeter Tim Hagans, pianist Kenny Drew, baritonist Per Goldschmidt and drummer Ed Thigpen. This was an underrated and often-overlooked ensemble and their debut recording is easily recommended to big band collectors. —*Scott Yanow*

Montreux / Jul. 1983 / Steeple Chase ✦✦✦✦

On the Roll / Nov. 17, 1986-Nov. 18, 1986 / Steeple Chase ✦✦✦✦✦
The fourth and final recording by Ernie Wilkins' "Almost Big Band" (a 13-piece group including ten horns) features the leader's arrangements of five of his swinging compositions plus "Lover Man." Wilkins' pieces include several tributes ("Almost Basie," "Ode to Billy Strayhorn" and "A Little Bit of Duke") and among his better-known sidemen (all Europeans or American expatriates) are trombonist Richard Boone (who sings "B.P. Blues"), the tenors of Jesper Thilo and Bert Jaedig,

baritonist Per Goldschmidt, pianist Kenny Drew and drummer Ed Thigpen. Excellent swinging music. —*Scott Yanow*

Jack Wilkins

b. Jun. 3, 1944

Guitar / Hard Bop

A superior, slightly underrated improviser, Jack Wilkins has proven on his infrequent recordings as a leader that he ranks near the top. Wilkins, who studied with John Mehegan early on, learned vibes, piano and classical guitar, but has stuck to jazz guitar throughout his career. He gained a strong reputation during his long association with Buddy Rich. Since then, he has recorded as a sideman with Jack DeJohnette, Eddie Gomez, Phil Woods, Harvie Swartz and the Brecker Brothers, among others. But it is his own recordings for Mainstream, Music Masters, CTI and especially his pair of essential Chiaroscuro albums in 1977 (the single CD *Merge* reissued all of the music except one song) that allow one to hear what a talented player Jack Wilkins has always been. —*Scott Yanow*

Windows / 1973 / Mainstream ◆◆◆◆

● **Merge** / Feb. 1977+Oct. 31, 1977 / Chiaroscuro ◆◆◆◆◆

This CD reissues nine of the ten selections that were formerly out on two LPs: *The Jack Wilkins Quartet* and *You Can't Live Without It*. The only cut left off is a guitar-piano duet by leader Jack Wilkins and Jack DeJohnette. The earlier date features Wilkins, fluegelhornist Randy Brecker, bassist Eddie Gomez and Jack DeJohnette (on drums for all but one tune). Although they play three group originals, the most memorable performances are their versions of "Falling in Love with Love" and Chick Corea's "500 Miles High." The later session, which has Wilkins, Randy Brecker, Michael Brecker on tenor, pianist Phil Markowitz, bassist Jon Burr and drummer Al Foster, is more of a jam session. The sextet romps through lengthy versions of Tommy Flanagan's "Freight Train," "Invitation," "What Is This Thing Called Love" and the ballad "What's New," and there are many exciting solos. This very enjoyable CD is most highly recommended to listeners who think that the Brecker Brothers can only play funk. —*Scott Yanow*

Call Him Reckless / May 1989 / Music Masters ◆◆◆◆

Considering his talents, guitarist Jack Wilkins has not recorded many sessions as a leader. On this CD he plays an interesting variety of straightahead and post bop material (including three of his originals) in a pianoless trio with bassist Steve LaSpina and drummer Mike Clark. Wilkins' playing, based in bop but at times more adventurous, is fairly distinctive, and highlights of the date include "If I Were a Bell," Joe Henderson's "Isotope," Oliver Nelson's obscure "Butch and Butch" and Bill Evans' "B Minor Waltz." —*Scott Yanow*

Alien Army / Jun. 13, 1990-Jun. 15, 1990 / Music Masters ◆◆◆◆

Baby Face Willette

b. Sep. 11, 1933, New Orleans, LA

Organ / Soul Jazz, Hard Bop, Groove

"Baby Face" Willette was born on September 11, 1933, in New Orleans. The nickname "Baby Face" was due to his youthful appearance. He started playing piano at the age of four, mostly due to the influence of his uncle Fred Freeman, a pianist of some popularity in the 1920s. He is largely self-taught and never learned to read music. His father, a minister, and his mother, a missionary, had Willette playing church organ fairly early on. But his main instrument was to remain, for many years, the piano.

He started out professionally working with gospel and rhythm & blues groups in his late teens and was soon touring extensively in the US, Canada, and Cuba. He traveled almost non-stop for some 15 years, working with R&B groups like Big Jay McNeely, Johnny Otis, Joe Houston, Roy Brown, Guitar Slim, King Colax, and the Caravan Gospel singers.

While visiting Chicago, he became intrigued by the sounds the organ could produce after hearing several outstanding gospel organists (Herman Stevens and Mayfield Wood) demonstrate the range and power of the instrument. He was turned on to jazz around that time after listening to Charlie Parker records. Jazz became his main passion from that time forward. As for influences, he credits Jimmy Smith and Shirley Scott on the Hammond B-3 and jazz greats Thelonious Monk, Bud Powell, Erroll Garner and Oscar Peterson. There is not a lot of recorded Willette material available, with *Stop and Listen* being the album to hear. —*Michael Erlewine*

Face to Face / Jan. 30, 1961 / Blue Note ◆◆◆

Willette's first album, this is straightahead bluesy jazz rather than real groove music (even with Grant Green on the date), mostly due to the hard, bright sax of tenor player Fred Jackson, whose playing is in the style of Gene Ammons. All but one of the tunes ("Whatever Lola Wants") are by Willette. —*Michael Erlewine*

● **Stop and Listen** / May 22, 1961 / Blue Note ◆◆◆◆◆

This is an excellent bluesy groove album, a trio with guitarist Grant Green and Ben Dixon on drums. There are some Willette originals ("Jumpin' Jupiter" stands out), plus a very nice rendition of "Worksong" and the standards "Willow Weep for Me" and "At Last," which give Green a chance to stretch out and show his stuff. This is a very enjoyable album and worth seeking out. —*Michael Erlewine*

Mo-Roc / Mar. 27, 1964+Apr. 2, 1964 / Argo ◆◆◆

Behind the 8-Ball / Nov. 30, 1964 / Argo ◆◆◆

Buster Williams (Charles Anthony Williams)

b. Apr. 17, 1942, Camden, NJ

Bass / Post-Bop, Hard Bop

One of jazz's most valuable sidemen, Buster Williams has been able to flourish through many periods of changing fashions in jazz. Best known since the 1980s for his solid, dark tone and highly refined technique on the acoustic bass, the jazz-rock generation knew him as the mobile anchor of Herbie Hancock's exploratory "Mwandishi" Sextet from 1969 to 1973, doubling on acoustic and electric basses sometimes attached to electronic effects devices.

Williams learned both the double bass and the drums from his father, but having been enormously impressed by Oscar Pettiford's recordings, he ultimately decided to concentrate on the bass. After studying theory and composition at Philadelphia's Combs College of Music in 1959, Williams joined Jimmy Heath's unit the following year and played with Gene Ammons and Sonny Stitt in 1960 and 1961, as well as behind singers Dakota Staton (1961-62), Betty Carter (1962-63), Sarah Vaughan (1963) and Nancy Wilson (1964-68). The gig with Wilson prompted a move to Los Angeles, where the Jazz Crusaders used him on concert dates and recordings from 1967 to 1969, and he also played briefly with Miles Davis in 1967 and the Bobby Hutcherson/Harold Land quintet. Moving to New York in 1969, Williams joined Hancock's sextet, appearing on all of his Warner Bros. albums, as well as *The Prisoner* (Blue Note), *Sextant* (Columbia) and with trumpeter Eddie Henderson's spinoff group on Capricorn and Blue Note. Over a five-year period (1976-1981), Williams led numerous recording sessions for Muse, Denon and Buddah while continuing to freelance before, during and after that span. In the 1980s, he was a member of both the Timeless All-Stars and Sphere, writing a number of compositions for the latter. Among the musicians for whom he has played from the 1980s onward are Kenny Barron, Frank Morgan, Stanley Cowell, Steve Turre, Emily Remler and Larry Coryell. —*Richard S. Ginell*

Crystal Reflections / Aug. 30, 1976 / Muse ◆◆◆◆

Bassist Buster Williams had one of his few opportunities to lead a record session on this diverse set, which has been reissued on CD (with an alternate take of "I Dream Too Much" added to the original program). Of the six selections, Williams has a duet apiece with Kenny Barron (who plays electric piano), pianist Jimmy Rowles and vibraphonist Roy Ayers ("My Funny Valentine"). Two other numbers feature the quartet of Williams, Ayers, Barron and drummer Billy Hart, while the leader's original "Prism" has the quartet joined by singer Suzanne Klewan and percussionist Nobu Urushiyama. The music ranges from slightly commercial to introspective and hard swinging, and its variety (plus an opportunity to hear bassist Williams in the lead) is a good reason for post-bop jazz collectors to pick up this CD. —*Scott Yanow*

Tokudo / Jan. 7, 1978 / Denon ◆◆◆

Heartbeat / Mar. 28, 1978-Apr. 3, 1978 / Muse ◆◆◆◆

A diverse session of jazz touches by pop guests on the four originals by bassist Williams, one standard, and one by Jimmie Rowles. Includes Rowles (p), Kenny Barron (p), Ben Riley (d), and vocalist Suzanne Klewan, and strings from Pat and Gayle Dixon. —*Michael G. Nastos*

Dreams Come True / Sep. 1978-Oct. 1978 / Buddah ◆◆◆

With 12 strings and three "background" vocalists sometimes being utilized in keyboardist Onaje Allen Gumbs' arrangements, this effort by bassist Buster Williams is often overly commercial. However the guest spots by pianist Kenny Barron, altoist Hank Crawford, flutist Hubert Laws and trumpeter Eddie Henderson are generally worthwhile and the material (four group originals plus "Ain't Misbehavin'" and "Betcha By Golly, Wow") is stronger than expected. In any case, this long out-of-print album will be a difficult one to locate. —*Scott Yanow*

● **Something More** / May 8, 1989-May 9, 1989 / In & Out ◆◆◆◆

Clarence Williams

b. 1896, Plaquemine, LA, d. Nov. 6, 1965, New York, NY

Leader, Piano, Vocals, Composer / Classic Jazz, Blues

Clarence Williams' main importance to jazz was his ability to organize scores of hot jazz recording sessions in the 1920s and '30s, featuring a who's who of top young performers. Although he was quite spirited playing jug, Clarence Williams was only a decent pianist and a likable but limited vocalist. However, he was also a talented composer, writing or co-writing dozens of memorable songs like "Royal Garden Blues," "Everybody Loves My Baby," "West End Blues," "Sugar Blues," "Tain't Nobody's Bizness If I Do" and "Baby Won't You Please Come Home."

A superior businessman and an inventive hustler, Williams worked at all kinds of odd jobs in New Orleans, where he moved in 1906. He played piano in Storyville, always keeping aware of the latest hits from New York; he was a singer, dancer and emcee with a minstrel show, and ran his own cabaret. He also co-ran a small publishing company with Armand J. Piron and soon realized its potential. Williams moved at first to Chicago, where he ran a music store, and then to New York, where he had great success with his publishing house. He composed songs, put together all-star groups to record them, and was also involved in selling sheet music of his hits; each activity helped the others. Williams managed some artists on the side, including Bessie Smith (whom he helped get started) for a brief time. Starting in 1923, he was also an A&R man for OKeh Records, and frequently accompanied blues singers.

A fascinating figure and one of the most successful black businessmen of the era, Clarence Williams had a real ear for talent. Among the more notable classic jazz musicians who appeared on his records (many of which were issued as being by his Blue Five or Blue Seven) were soprano saxophonist Sidney Bechet, trumpeters Louis Armstrong, Joe Smith, Bubber Miley, Tommy Ladnier, Louis Metcalf, King Oliver, Red Allen and Ed Allen, trombonists Charles Irvis, Tricky Sam Nanton and Jimmy Harrison, clarinetists Buster Bailey and Cecil Scott, flutist Albert Socarras, tenors Coleman Hawkins and Benny Waters, Cyrus St. Clair on tuba, drummer/washboard player Floyd Casey, pianists James P. Johnson and Willie "The Lion" Smith, and Eva Taylor (whom he married in 1923) on vocals. Quite remarkably, all of Clarence Williams' recordings as a leader have been made available by the Classics label on 14 CDs.

At the height of his power in the early '30s, Clarence Williams' importance waned as the decade continued and swing took over. After 1937, he only appeared on one final session (two songs in 1941), concentrating on the business side of music. In 1943, he sold his company to Decca and became a shop owner in Harlem. Williams was seriously injured when hit by a taxi in 1956 and passed away in 1965. The 1976 bio-discography *Clarence Williams* by Tom Lord gives one an idea of his many accomplishments. —*Scott Yanow*

1921-1924 / Oct. 11, 1921-Nov. 6, 1924 / Classics ✦✦✦✦✦
Although this is not the most essential of the Clarence Williams CDs released in the complete Classics series, all of the releases are highly recommended to fans of early jazz. Many of these titles are quite rare and historical. First Williams is heard as a singer on five period numbers from 1921 ("The Dance They Call the Georgia Hunch" is the most memorable) and has a vocal duet with Daisy Martin on "Brown Skin (Who You For)". Williams also takes four piano solos and on most of the other titles features the great soprano saxophonist Sidney Bechet (heard in his earliest recordings); "Wild Cat Blues" and "Kansas City Man Blues" are classics. In addition Louis Armstrong joins the group on three numbers, two of which have vocals from Eva Taylor. —*Scott Yanow*

The Complete Sessions, Vol. 1 (1923-1926) / Jul. 30, 1923-Nov. 12, 1923 / Hot 'n' Sweet ✦✦✦
This imported CD has all of Clarence Williams' recordings from a three-and-a-half month period; not only The Blue Five performances but Williams' work with blues singers Sara Martin, Mamie Smith, Rosetta Crawford and Margaret Johnson in addition to his wife, Eva Taylor. Most valuable are the eight instrumentals, for they feature the great soprano saxophonist Sidney Bechet on his earliest recordings along with trumpeter Thomas Morris. Highlights include "Wild Cat Blues," "Kansas City Man Blues" and "Oh! Daddy Blues," although "I've Got the 'Yes We Have No Bananas' Blues" is amusing. The Classics reissues series bypasses the sometimes so-so blues singers. —*Scott Yanow*

The Complete Sessions, Vol. 2 (1923-1931) / Nov. 14, 1923-Mar. 4, 1925 / Hot 'n' Sweet ✦✦✦
The second Clarence Williams CD from the French Hot 'n' Sweet label not only has all of the performances by the pianist's Blue Five during a 16-month period (featuring Louis Armstrong and Sidney Bechet) but lesser-known sides backing blues singers Virginia Liston (on which Bechet allegedly plays guitar), Maureen Englin, Margaret Johnson, Sippie Wallace and Eva Taylor. Although it is nice to have those rarities, the selections that match Armstrong and Bechet (particularly the explosive "Cake Walkin' Babies from Home" and "Mandy Make up Your Mind" which has an odd sarrusophone solo from Bechet) are the most memorable performances, and those are also available on the Classics label. —*Scott Yanow*

1924-1926 / Dec. 17, 1924-Feb. 1926 / Classics ✦✦✦✦✦
The second CD in the Classics label's "complete" Clarence Williams series traces the pianist/bandleader's recordings during a 14-month period. The first six titles feature soprano great Sidney Bechet (who has a unique sarrusophone solo on

"Mandy Make up Your Mind") while the first 13 also have Louis Armstrong. The pairing of these two classic and competitive greats is at its zenith on a brilliant version of "Cake Walking Babies from Home"; Satch gets the edge. In addition there are notable contributions on these 23 performances by trombonist Charlie Irvis, tenor saxophonist Coleman Hawkins, cornetists Joe Smith, Bubber Miley and Ed Allen, clarinetist Buster Bailey and singer Eva Taylor among others. Williams' series of hot performances really epitomized small-group 1920s jazz, and every entry in this Classics series is highly recommended. Other highlights include "Coal Cart Blues," "Shake That Thing," "Dinah" (which features Hawkins on baritone), "I've Found a New Baby" and two versions of "Santa Claus Blues." —*Scott Yanow*

1926-1927 / Mar. 7, 1926-Jan. 29, 1927 / Classics ✦✦✦✦
The third CD in the Classics label's Clarence Williams program reissues all of the pianist/bandleader's dates from a ten-month period, 23 selections in all. Such groups as Joe Jordan's Ten Sharps and Flats (performing a memorable version of "Morocco Blues"), The Dixie Washboard Band, The Blue Grass Foot Warmers and Clarence Williams' Stompers (or Blue Seven or Jazz Kings or Washboard Four). Williams uses some of the top musicians of the era (including cornetists Bubber Miley, Tommy Ladnier and Ed Allen, trombonist Jimmy Harrison, clarinetist Buster Bailey, Coleman Hawkins on tenor, Cyrus St. Clair on tuba and Jasper Taylor on washboard among others) for the heated and freewheeling performances. Highlights include "Jackass Blues," "I Found a New Baby," "Senegalese Stomp" and a truly classic version of "Candy Lips" (which features two clarinets in hot pursuit). All of the CDs in this valuable series are highly recommended to classic jazz fans. —*Scott Yanow*

Clarence Williams (1927-1934) / Jan. 25, 1927-1933 / ABC ✦✦✦
Engineer Robert Parker is famous (or in some minds infamous) for remastering early jazz recordings and making them sound as if they were originally made for stereo. This CD from the Australian Broadcasting Corporation, made available domestically through DRG, has 16 performances by the bandleader and occasional pianist Clarence Williams. Most of the selections are quite enjoyable, but the programming, jumping back and forth over a seven-year period, is fairly random and lowers this sampler's value. Still, there are quite a few enjoyable tracks, including "Candy Lips," "You're Bound to Look like a Monkey When You Get Old," "Close Fit Blues" and "He Wouldn't Stop Doin' It," with many all-stars getting a chance to solo during the heated small-group jams. —*Scott Yanow*

1927 / Mar. 8, 1927-Sep. 23, 1927 / Classics ✦✦✦✦✦
Pianist/bandleader Clarence Williams was at the height of his productivity in 1927; the 22 numbers on this CD were recorded within a six-and-a-half-month period. With the exception of the Dixie Washboard Band, all of the performances were originally released under Clarence Williams' name, but the personnel and instrumentation often differ from session to session. The fourth in Classics' complete reissue of Williams' recordings features such top sidemen as cornetists Ed Allen and Louis Metcalf, trumpeter Red Allen (in what was probably his earliest recording), trombonist Charlie Irvis, clarinetist Buster Bailey and a variety of lesser-known players with some of the best performances being "Cushion Foot Stomp" (which is heard three different times), "Shooting the Pistol," "Baby, Won't You Please Come Home" and Williams' solo version of "When I March in April with May." Highly recommended to collectors of vintage jazz. —*Scott Yanow*

1927-1928 / Oct. 1927-Aug. 1, 1928 / Classics ✦✦✦✦✦
The fifth CD in Classics' "complete" Clarence Williams program (all are highly recommended to collectors of 1920s jazz) has 22 selections from 11 separate recording sessions, all of the pianist/bandleader's dates for a ten-month period. There are a pair of piano solos, two numbers in which Williams' vocals (including an eccentric "Farm Hand Papa") are backed by the great pianist James P. Johnson and band performances featuring cornetists Ed Allen and King Oliver, clarinetists Buster Bailey and Arville Harris, trombonist Ed Cuffee, Coleman Hawkins and Benny Waters on tenors, Cyrus St. Clair on tuba and the washboard of Floyd Casey. Highlights include "Jingles," "Church Street Sobbin' Blues," "Sweet Emmalina," and "Mountain City Blues." —*Scott Yanow*

Complete Recorded Works, Vol. 2 (1927-1932) / 1927 / Document ✦✦✦✦✦

1928-1929 / Aug. 1928-Jan. 1929 / Classics ✦✦✦✦✦
The sixth volume in the very valuable Classics Clarence Williams reissue program contains 22 numbers in its attractive CD, mostly from a four-month period. There is a lot of variety on these sessions, with many of the best tracks featuring both King Oliver and Ed Allen on cornets along with tenorman Benny Waters. There are also numbers by Clarence Williams' Washboard Five, his Novelty Four (a quartet with Oliver and guitarist Eddie Lang) and a larger orchestra. Throughout all of the selections there are spirited ensembles, heated but coherent solos and plenty of joy and swing. The high points include "Organ Grinder Blues," "Have You Ever Felt That Way," "Wildflower Rag," "Bozo," "Bimbo" and "Beau-Koo Jack" (which is closely based on the Louis Armstrong recording). —*Scott Yanow*

● **1929** / Jan. 1929-May 28, 1929 / Classics ✦✦✦✦

The seventh volume in the European Classics label's complete reissuance of bandleader Clarence Williams' very valuable recordings documents his music during a four-month period. Included are two Williams piano solos, his sessions leading the Barrelhouse Five Orchestra, Jazz Kings and the Memphis Jazzers, and quite a bit of superior small-group jazz. Among the sidemen are cornetist Ed Allen, trombonist Ed Cuffee, Arville Harris and Albert Socarras on reeds, banjoist Leroy Harris, pianist James P. Johnson (on two songs), the exuberant tuba of Cyrus St. Clair, Floyd Casey on drums and washboard and Williams himself on piano and occasional vocals. Highlights include "Endurance Stomp," "If You Like Me like I Like You," "Steamboat Days," "Baby, Won't You Please Come Home," "In Our Cottage of Love" and the original version of "Breeze." All of the CDs in this enjoyable series are easily recommended to 1920s collectors. —*Scott Yanow*

1929-1930 / Jun. 21, 1929-Apr. 23, 1930 / Classics ✦✦✦✦✦

The eighth CD in the European Classics series which is reissuing complete and in chronological order all of the recordings led by pianist/composer Clarence Williams, documents his activity from a ten-month period. During this era Williams varied his personnel and instrumentation from session to session, and the results are quite varied yet consistently hot. Williams' groups feature such sidemen as cornetist Ed Allen, trumpeter Charlie Gaines, the reeds of Arville Harris and Russell Procope, the enthusiastic tuba of Cyrus St. Clair, Floyd Casey on drums and washboard, two excellent vocals apiece by Margaret Webster (her "You've Got to Give Me Some" is a near-classic) and Eva Taylor and, on eight selections, the masterful pianist James P. Johnson. The high points are "How Could I Be Blue?" and "I've Found a New Baby," performances taken as piano duets by Johnson and Williams that include some humorous conversation. All of the CDs in this very valuable series are highly recommended to collectors of 1920s jazz. —*Scott Yanow*

1930-1931 / May 22, 1930-Feb. 19, 1931 / Classics ✦✦✦✦✦

This CD is the ninth in an extensive series that reissues all of the recordings led by pianist/composer Clarence Williams. Since Williams headed a wide variety of exciting small groups in the 1920s and '30s that utilized the playing of many top jazz players, all of the CDs are worth acquiring by collectors of classic jazz. The 22 selections on this particular CD range from novelty Williams solo performances to groups featuring trumpeters Red Allen and Ed Allen, Albert Socarras on several reeds (including flute), clarinetists Buster Bailey and Cecil Scott, Prince Robinson doubling on clarinet and tenor, pianist Herman Chittison, Ikey Robinson on banjo, the great tuba player Cyrus St. Clair, singer Eva Taylor, Floyd Casey on washboard, the Bingie Madison big band and Williams himself on vocals, piano and jug. Highlights of this spirited program include "You're Bound to Look like a Monkey When You Get Old," "High Society Blues," "Hot Lovin'," "Baby, Won't You Please Come Home" and four different versions of "Shout Sister Shout." —*Scott Yanow*

1933 / May 15, 1933-Sep. 1, 1933 / Classics ✦✦✦✦

The tenth CD in the Classics label's very valuable Clarence Williams series has its strong moments, although his band was starting to become somewhat predictable. Two titles feature clarinetist Albert Nicholas in a washboard-jug quintet, and six intriguing songs utilize both Herman Chittison and Willie "The Lion" Smith on piano (with Eva Taylor taking most of the vocals). But most of the other selections are by a quartet comprising pianist Williams, cornetist Ed Allen (a terrible singer, as he shows on two songs), clarinetist Cecil Scott and the washboard of Floyd Casey. The music is fine, but not quite as special as Williams' slightly earlier recordings with more diverse and versatile bands. Still, this is worth picking up for classic jazz collectors. —*Scott Yanow*

1933-1934 / Dec. 6, 1933-Jun. 28, 1934 / Classics ✦✦✦✦

The 11th CD in Classics series of recordings led by pianist-composer-singer Clarence Williams is actually one of the weaker ones due to Chick Bullock taking vocals on seven of the 23 numbers; the two contributions apiece by Dick Robertson and Little Buddy Farrior are not much better even if Williams' own verbal spots on six songs are reasonably enjoyable. With only three instrumentals, the results are less memorable than usual, although there are some strong moments contributed by cornetist Ed Allen, clarinetist Cecil Scott, pianist James P. Johnson (who is not featured enough) and guitarist Roy Smeck. Recommended mostly to completists. —*Scott Yanow*

1934 / Jul. 6, 1934-Aug. 22, 1934 / Classics ✦✦✦✦

1934-1937 / Sep. 11, 1934-Apr. 8, 1937 / Classics ✦✦✦✦

Classics' 13th Clarence Williams CD, although not quite on the same level as Williams' earlier sides, has some spirited performances. Cornetist Ed Allen, Cecil Scott (on clarinet and tenor) and clarinetist Buster Bailey (on the six selections from 1937) are the key soloists; most numbers have a washboard in the ensembles, and vocals are taken by Chick Bullock (forgettable in his three appearances), Eva Taylor, William Cooley and Williams himself. Classics deserves congratulations for persevering with this important series, for Clarence Williams led some of the hot-

test small group dates of the 1920s and '30s; all of the discs are recommended to pre-bop collectors. —*Scott Yanow*

1937-1941 / 1937 / Classics ✦✦✦

The 14th and final Clarence Williams Classics CD completes the complete reissuance of all of his recordings. By 1937, Williams' career was winding down, and his music was far overshadowed by the big swing orchestras. Although the first 15 selections on this CD are listed as being by "Clarence Williams' Swing Band," all but three numbers are spirituals that showcase the forgettable singing of William Cooley. The impressive group (which includes cornetist Ed Allen, clarinetist Buster Bailey, altoist Russell Procope and Cecil Scott on tenor and clarinet) has little to do, except on the instrumentals, and the overall results are a bit disappointing. Also on the CD are three selections from 1938 by an organ-piano-drums trio (two of the songs have vocals by Babe Matthews) that does not actually include Williams. Concluding the lesser release is a pair of performances from 1941 in which Eva Taylor and Clarence Williams are heard on vocals while joined by pianist James P. Johnson (Williams plays second piano), two guitars and bassist Wellman Braud. These final numbers (pity there were not more) hint at the earlier classic recordings and served as Clarence Williams' last hurrah. Completists will want this set. —*Scott Yanow*

Claude Williams

b. Feb. 22, 1908, Muskogee, OK

Violin, Guitar / Swing

Bad luck kept Claude Williams from ever gaining the fame he deserved, but late in his life he finally achieved some notoriety. Early on Williams worked with the family band of Oscar Pettiford, and in 1928 he joined Terrence Holder's territory band, a group that soon became Andy Kirk's 12 Clouds of Joy. The violinist made his recording debut with Kirk in 1929 but had departed before the band finally made it big in 1936. By then Williams (after a stint with Alphonso Trent) was playing rhythm guitar and occasional violin with Count Basie's Orchestra. Unfortunately producer John Hammond did not care for Williams' violin playing and shortly after the band had relocated to New York and was on the verge of making it, Hammond persuaded Basie to replace Williams; Freddie Green filled the spot for the next 50 years. Claude Williams returned to Kansas City and decades of obscurity, although he generally worked and had a stint with Roy Milton in the early '50s. However, starting in 1972 (due to his association with Jay McShann and some new recordings), Williams began to be discovered and tour more often. He recorded both as a leader and as a sideman and in 1994-45 played with the Statesmen of Jazz. A month younger than Stephane Grappelli, Claude Williams was still in his musical prime as he entered his late 80s. —*Scott Yanow*

Call for the Fiddler / Feb. 1976 / Steeple Chase ✦✦✦✦✦

Fiddler's Dream / Mar. 28, 1977+Mar. 31, 1977 / Classic Jazz ✦✦✦✦

Veteran swing violinist Claude Williams' second recording as a leader after decades of obscurity features him in prime form, doubling on guitar with a rhythm section that includes either Jay McShann and Andre Persiany on piano, bassist Gene Ramey and drummer Gus Johnson. Sixty-nine at the time and just getting started in his career, Williams performs three originals (including the title cut) and a variety of upbeat swing standards such as "C Jam Blues," "Sweet Georgia Brown" and "All of Me." The spirited violin solos are enough of a reason to search for this out-of-print LP. —*Scott Yanow*

Live at J's, Vol. 1 / Apr. 24, 1989+May 1, 1989 / Arhoolie ✦✦✦✦

Violinist Claude Williams, one of the last surviving links to the swing era, had important stints with the big bands of Andy Kirk and Count Basie that were just barely documented. Unjustly obscure for decades, he is in excellent form on a live quintet date with guitarist James Chirillo, pianist Ron Mathews, bassist Al McKibbon and either Akira Tana or Grady Tate on drums. Williams fiddles and occasionally sings on a variety of swing standards and blues, showing that in 1989 he still very much had it. This is the first of two CDs from this engagement. —*Scott Yanow*

Live at J's, Vol. 2 / Apr. 24, 1989+May 1, 1989 / Arhoolie ✦✦✦✦

On the second of two volumes, veteran swing violinist Claude Williams (81 at the time of this live recording) proves that he is still in top form. The repertoire is primarily swing standards and (with the assistance of guitarist James Chirillo, pianist Ron Mathews, bassist Al McKibbon and either Akira Tana or Grady Tate on drums), Williams is easily the main star of this swinging set. His violin solos are excellent (a little rougher in tone but near the level of a Stephane Grappelli) while his occasional vocals show plenty of personality. This is fine music that helps to put the focus on a much neglected swing stylist. —*Scott Yanow*

Swingtime in New York / Sep. 5, 1994 / Progressive ✦✦✦✦✦

Violinist Claude Williams, at the age of 86, shows that he is still in his musical prime during this quintet date with Bill Easley (who switches between tenor, clarinet and flute), pianist Sir Roland Hanna, bassist Earl May and drummer Joe Ascione. Williams was with both Andy Kirk and Count Basie shortly before they made it big, but has spent most of his long career in Kansas City in obscurity. Fortunately he has made several worthy recordings in his later years and this is one of his best, a well-rounded set ranging in repertoire from one of the first songs he ever learned ("You've Got to See Your Mama Ev'ry Night or You Can't See Mama at All") to Ellington, Monk ("Straight, No Chaser") and even Stevie Wonder ("You Are the Sunshine of My Life"). The emphasis is on swing and Claude Williams is heard near the peak of his powers. —*Scott Yanow*

● **King of Kansas City** / May 28, 1996-May 29, 1996 / Progressive ◆◆◆◆◆
Eighty-eight at the time of this date, the apparently ageless violinist Claude Williams plays a variety of swing standards with plenty of energy, an appealing tone, and creative ideas. He features some excellent players (all from Kansas City) in the supporting cast, including tenor saxophonist Kim Park (who steals the show on the opening "Lester Leaps In"), guitarist Rod Fleeman and singers Karrin Allyson and Lisa Henry (who are on two songs apiece). Williams, who sings "St. Louis Blues" and "Gee Baby, Ain't I Good to You," has rarely sounded better, and he is remarkably youthful throughout. —*Scott Yanow*

Cootie Williams (Charles Melvin Williams)

b. Jun. 24, 1910, Mobile, AL, **d.** Sep. 14, 1985, New York, NY
Trumpet / Swing, New York Blues, Jump Blues
Cootie Williams, one of the finest trumpeters of the 1930s, expanded upon the role originally formed by Bubber Miley with Duke Ellington's Orchestra. Renowned for his work with the plunger mute, Cootie was also a fine soloist when playing open. Starting as a teenager, Cootie Williams played with a variety of local bands in the South, coming to New York with Alonzo Ross' Syncopators. He played for a short time with the orchestras of Chick Webb and Fletcher Henderson (recording with the latter) before joining Duke Ellington as Miley's replacement in February 1929. He was a fixture with Duke's band during the next 11 years, not only recording many classics with Ellington (including "Echoes of Harlem" and "Concerto for Cootie") but leading some of his own sessions and recording with Lionel Hampton, Teddy Wilson and Billie Holiday in addition to being a guest at Benny Goodman's Carnegie Hall Concert in 1938. His decision to leave Ellington and join Goodman's Orchestra in 1940 was considered a major event in the jazz world. During his year with BG, Williams was well-featured with both the big band and Goodman's sextet. The following year he became a bandleader, heading his own orchestra, which at times in the 1940s featured such up-and-coming players as pianist Bud Powell, tenorman Eddie "Lockjaw" Davis, altoist-singer Eddie "Cleanhead" Vinson and even Charlie Parker. Although he had a hit (thanks to Willis Jackson's honking tenor) on "Gator," by 1948 Cootie had cut his group back to a sextet. Playing R&B-oriented music, he worked steadily at the Savoy, but by the 1950s was drifting into obscurity. However in 1962, after a 22-year absence, Cootie Williams rejoined Duke Ellington, staying even beyond Duke's death in 1974 as a featured soloist. By then his solos were much simpler and more primitive than earlier (gone was the Louis Armstrong-inspired bravado) but Cootie remained the master with the plunger mute. He was semi-retired during his final decade, taking a final solo in 1978 on a Teresa Brewer record, and posthumously serving as an inspiration for Wynton Marsalis' own plunger playing. —*Scott Yanow*

● **Echoes of Harlem** / Jan. 4, 1944-Aug. 22, 1944 / Affinity ◆◆◆◆◆
The little-known big band that trumpeter Cootie Williams led in 1944 had some rather notable sidemen: pianist Bud Powell (in his first recordings), altoist-vocalist Eddie "Cleanhead" Vinson and tenor saxophonist Eddie "Lockjaw" Davis. This superior English LP from Affinity has all 16 recordings by Williams from that year, eight songs apiece from his sextet and his big band. In addition to the other soloists, a young Pearl Bailey has two vocals and future R&B tenor star Sam "The Man" Taylor gets in a few licks. Among the many highlights of this historic program are "Echoes of Harlem," "Honeysuckle Rose," "Cherry Red Blues," "Blue Garden Blues" and the earliest recording ever of Thelonious Monk's "'Round Midnight." —*Scott Yanow*

Typhoon / Feb. 26, 1945-1950 / Swingtime ◆◆◆◆
After a pretty successful year in 1944, the Cootie Williams big band struggled for a period before breaking up in 1947. The veteran trumpeter (who had been a bandleader since leaving Benny Goodman in late 1941) is heard on this imported LP leading his orchestra on two titles from 1945 and the last eight recordings by his big band in 1947, along with a pair of small group sides from both 1947 and 1950. Although Cootie was always a swing stylist, his ensembles were open to the influences of both early R&B and bop. Ten of the 14 numbers on this LP have vocals (by either Tony Warren, Bob Merrell or Eddie Mack), but those are usually reasonably enjoyable. Highlights of the set are the more rambunctious R&B selections, especially "Typhoon," which features the screaming tenor of Weasel Parker. —*Scott Yanow*

The Big Challenge / Apr. 30, 1957+May 7, 1957 / Jazztone ◆◆◆◆◆
This CD reissue from the Spanish Fresh Sound label brings back a fun and unusual Jazztone session. Six distinctive and very different veterans were teamed together: trumpeter Cootie Williams, cornetist Rex Stewart, trombonists Lawrence Brown and J.C. Higginbotham, and the tenors of Coleman Hawkins and Bud Freeman. With pianist Hank Jones, guitarist Billy Bauer, bassist Milt Hinton and drummer Gus Johnson providing solid backup and Ernie Wilkins sketching out some arrangements, the unique matchups are very successful. Each of the musicians has an opportunity to be featured and the tradeoffs are quite memorable. A colorful gem. —*Scott Yanow*

James Williams

b. Mar. 8, 1951, Memphis, TN
Piano / Hard Bop, Mainstream Jazz
One of the most consistent and reliable pianists in what could be called modern mainstream jazz, James Williams has made many rewarding recordings through the years. He started playing piano when he was 13, primarily gospel and soul music at first (influences that can still be felt in his solos). He studied at Memphis State University and taught at Berklee during 1972-77. While based in Boston, Williams played regularly with such visiting all-stars as Woody Shaw, Art Farmer, Clark Terry and Joe Henderson. He came to fame during his period with Art Blakey's Jazz Messengers (1977-81) and since then has performed and recorded frequently with a wide variety of players including Sonny Stitt, Bobby Hutcherson, Tom Harrell, his own trios and the very interesting Contemporary Piano Ensemble. —*Scott Yanow*

Everything I Love / Apr. 1979 / Concord Jazz ◆◆◆◆
Other than a couple of records in 1977 for Zim and Red, this Concord release was pianist James Williams' recording debut as a leader. At the time he was halfway through his four-year stint with Art Blakey's Jazz Messengers and he uses two of Blakey's sidemen (tenor saxophonist Bill Pierce and bassist Dennis Hart) on the fine hard bop-oriented quartet program with drummer Billy Hart. Williams performs a couple of his originals plus six standards (including "That's All," "It Could Happen to You" and "Please Send Me Someone to Love") in swinging and creative fashion. —*Scott Yanow*

Images (of Things to Come) / Jun. 1980 / Concord Jazz ◆◆◆◆
Pianist James Williams' second of three Concord recordings once again uses two of his fellow sidemen with Art Blakey's Jazz Messengers (tenor saxophonist Bill Pierce and bassist Charles Fambrough) plus drummer Carl Burnette. He mixes together five standards (including an unaccompanied version of "You Go to My Head") with three of his better originals and the result is a high-quality set of modern hard bop. —*Scott Yanow*

Arioso Touch / Feb. 1982 / Concord Jazz ◆◆◆◆
Pianist James Williams' first recording as a leader after leaving Art Blakey's Jazz Messengers matches him with bassist Buster Williams and drummer Billy Higgins and looks toward the future. The all-star lineup predates the "Magical Trio" of 1987 and one of Williams' originals, "Phineas: The Living Legend" makes one think of the Contemporary Piano Ensemble, his four-piano band of the 1990s that constantly pays tribute to the great pianist Phineas Newborn. Throughout his trio set, Williams is heard in top form for the period, uplifting such standards as "You'd Be So Nice to Come Home To," Irving Berlin's "Remember" and "I Didn't Know About You" in addition to contributing three diverse originals. —*Scott Yanow*

● **Alter Ego** / Jul. 19, 1984+Jul. 20, 1984 / Sunnyside ◆◆◆◆◆
Pianist James Williams learned a great deal from his stint with Art Blakey's Jazz Messengers and, when he emerged from the group, he was perfectly qualified to be a bandleader. His Sunnyside session features such up-and-coming players as guitarist Kevin Eubanks, the reeds of Billy Pierce and Bill Easley, bassist Ray Drummond and drummer Tony Reedus on a set of original material. Five of the seven songs were composed by Williams, while the other two (including the memorable "Waltz for Monk") were contributed by Donald Brown. The frequently exciting music (high-quality modern hard bop) still sounds fresh. —*Scott Yanow*

Progress Report / May 22, 1985-May 24, 1985 / Sunnyside ◆◆◆◆◆
Progress Report featured three Art Blakey alumni: James Williams (keyboards), Billy Pierce (reeds) and guitarist Kevin Eubanks (a member of Blakey's short-lived 1980 big band). None of the six originals (half by the leader, one from Eubanks and a pair by Donald Brown, Williams' successor with Blakey) had memorable melodies, but all contained plenty of room for explorative chord-based improvisations. —*Scott Yanow*

Magical Trio 1 / Jun. 26, 1987 / EmArcy ◆◆◆◆◆
The first of three CDs headed by pianist James Williams that feature his *Magical Trio* (a recording group rather than a regular band), this strong outing matches the inventive hard bop stylist with bassist Ray Brown and his former employer, drum-

mer Art Blakey. They perform three of Williams' compositions (including "The Soulful Mr. Timmons"), one piece by Brown, Thad Jones' "Mean What You Say," three underplayed standards plus the trio's ad-lib "J's Jam Song." A high-quality modern mainstream outing. —*Scott Yanow*

Magical Trio 2 / Nov. 23, 1987-Nov. 24, 1987 / EmArcy ✦✦✦✦

The second of pianist James Williams' three *Magical Trio* releases features him interacting with bassist Ray Brown and drummer Elvin Jones on trio renditions of three of his originals (including "A Portrait of Elvin") plus four fresh standards. The spontaneous results are quite stimulating, and the matchup between these masterful musicians (who do not play together very often) on the straightahead set is quite successful. —*Scott Yanow*

Meet the Magical Trio / Sep. 2, 1988 / EmArcy ✦✦✦✦

While the first two *Magical Trio* sessions teamed pianist James Williams with classic veterans (bassist Ray Brown and either Art Blakey or Elvin Jones on drums), this outing matches him with a couple of talented younger musicians: bassist Charnett Moffett and drummer Jeff Watts. But, despite the change in personnel, the advanced straightahead music is not all that different from the earlier dates. Once again Williams contributes a few originals (four this time, including a remake of "Arioso") and uplifts some older tunes. Highlights include Thad Jones' "Fingers," John Coltrane's "Lazybird" and a solo medley of "Single Petal of a Rose" and "A Flower Is a Lovesome Thing." Easily recommended. —*Scott Yanow*

Meets the Saxophone Masters / Sep. 23, 1991 / DIW/Columbia ✦✦✦✦

Pianist James Williams picked three of the top tenor players of the 1990s (Joe Henderson, George Coleman and Billy Pierce) to participate in a jam session-type set. The sextet (with bassist James Genus and drummer Tony Reedus) performs six selections, all but one of which are over 9 minutes long. Each of the saxophonists have plenty of solo space and many chances to trade off. The material is generally fairly basic, with two blues, a runthrough on rhythm changes, the folk song "Calgary" and a pair of standards being performed. The tenors are quite aware of each other's presence, so the playing is of a consistently high quality even if no real explosions occur. An enjoyable set. —*Scott Yanow*

Talkin' Trash / Mar. 4, 1993 / DIW/Columbia ✦✦✦✦✦

Although pianist James Williams is the nominal leader of this CD and there is also room for many concise solos from Billy Pierce (mostly on tenor), vibraphonist Steve Nelson and the remarkable bassist Christian McBride, the star throughout is actually fluegelhornist Clark Terry. Seventy-two at the time but showing no sign of decline, Terry contributed three of the numbers, sings in his famous Mumbles voice on two humorous pieces (including a preacher routine on "The Orator") and plays quite well throughout. High points of this straightahead session include the boppish "Serenade to a Bus Seat," the uptempo blues "Chuckles" and Terry's spectacular solo on "Moonglow." —*Scott Yanow*

Jessica Williams

b. Mar. 17, 1948, Baltimore, MD
Piano / Bop, Post-Bop

Due to her being based in Northern California, Jessica Williams is a bit underrated but (on evidence of her recent sets for Jazz Focus and Hep) she is one of the top jazz pianists of the 1990s. Williams is a powerful virtuoso whose complete control of the keyboard, wit, solid sense of swing and the influence of Thelonious Monk have combined to make her a particularly notable player. She started taking piano lessons when she was four and was gigging as a teenager. Williams took extensive classical lessons but also gigged with Philly Joe Jones in Philadelphia before moving to San Francisco in 1977. She was the house pianist at Keystone Korner for a time and made a few interesting recordings (some as Jessica Jennifer Williams) during the period, sometimes utilizing electronics. Although she appeared on Charlie Rouse's final record and gigged steadily, Williams was largely off record (outside of her own private Quanta label) until re-emerging in the late '80s as a brilliant solo acoustic player. She is a giant whose many dates for Jazz Focus (five of its first ten releases feature Williams) and Hep are consistently brilliant. —*Scott Yanow*

Rivers of Memory / 1974 / Clean Cuts ✦✦✦✦

Portal of Antrim / 1976 / Adelphi ✦✦✦

Jessica Williams' first record as a leader features the 28-year-old pianist performing six unaccompanied solos, playing on piano, electric piano and organ during four cuts with bassist Mark Bradshaw and drummer Dave Tucker, and taking "Plath's Return" as an overdubbed solo on keyboards, keyboard bass and drums. With the exception of John Coltrane's "Transition," all of the compositions are Williams' originals and, although not yet a giant of the keyboard, her musical personality was already beginning to emerge. This out-of-print LP will be difficult to find. —*Scott Yanow*

Portraits / May 16, 1977 / Adelphi ✦✦✦✦

Jessica Williams' recording career can easily be divided into three parts. Her first four records (for Adelphi and its subsidiary Clean Cuts) feature the pianist searching for her own sound, a couple of transitional records from the 1980s show off her impressive growth and then, starting in the latter part of the decade, Williams was a major artist. *Portraits*, Jessica Williams' second recording, is the best all-round showcase from her first period. This out-of-print double-LP has eight solo piano improvisations on seven of Williams' themes (all dedicated to specific people) and the standard "My Romance." The playing is both adventurous and melodic, full of chance-taking yet with plenty of lyricism. Well worth a search. —*Scott Yanow*

Orgonomic Music / Jun. 1979 / Clean Cuts ✦✦✦✦

Pianist Jessica Williams' fourth recording finds her taking a giant step forward. Utilizing a septet that includes trumpeter Eddie Henderson, tenor saxophonist Jim Grantham, guitarist Henry Robinette, both Kim Stone and Richard Saunders on bass and drummer Dave Tucker, Williams is quite powerful on seven of her originals plus a reverential version of John Coltrane's "Dear Lord." This memorable effort is long overdue to be reissued on CD. —*Scott Yanow*

Nothin' But the Truth / Feb. 26, 1986 / Black Hawk ✦✦✦✦

By 1986 pianist Jessica Williams had largely developed her own style and sound. Influenced by Thelonious Monk but improvising with her own voice (and a rather phenomenal technique), Williams performs four of her originals, the standard "Stars Fell on Alabama" and two Monk tunes ("Ugly Beauty" and "'Round Midnight"). Jessica Williams' witty and consistently surprising playing on the trio set with bassist John Wiitala and drummer Bud Spangler is quite memorable and enjoyable but, due to Black Hawk going out of business, this LP is currently a bit of a collector's item. —*Scott Yanow*

And Then, There's This / Feb. 1, 1990 / Timeless ✦✦✦✦✦

This Timeless CD was pianist Jessica Williams' first really mature statement after several very impressive releases. Performing in a trio with bassist John Wiitala and drummer Kenny Wollesen, Williams displays a technique second to none, the influence of Thelonious Monk, an exciting chance-taking style and a strong wit. She plays six of her originals (including tributes to Herbie Nichols, Charlie Rouse and Sonny Rollins), a pair of Monk tunes, Irving Berlin's "All Alone" and George Gershwin's "Swanee"; Williams takes two of the songs as unaccompanied solos. Highly recommended. —*Scott Yanow*

Live at Maybeck Recital Hall, Vol. 21 / Feb. 16, 1992 / Concord Jazz ✦✦✦✦✦

One of the happiest events of the 1990s has been the emergence of Jessica Williams as one of the most talented pianists in jazz. Her Maybeck Recital Hall solo concert is as good a place as any to discover her abilities. She explores a variety of standards and four of her originals (along with Dave Brubeck's fairly obscure "Summer Song") with creativity and wit. Sometimes Williams shows off the influence of Thelonious Monk but she rarely stays predictable for long and her sense of humor is quite original. This is an impressive outing with her interpretations of "Why Do I Love You?," "I'm Confessin'" and "It's Easy to Remember" being among the highlights. —*Scott Yanow*

☆ Next Step / Apr. 6, 1993 / Hep ✦✦✦✦✦

Jessica Williams, although hardly a household name, is actually one of the finest jazz pianists of the 1990s and her Hep CD gives listeners ample proof. She does a brilliant imitation of Thelonious Monk on the first half of "Easter Parade" (before displaying her own strong musical personality), not only capturing Monk's unique chord patterns but his touch and his wit. Throughout the rest of her colorful solo set, Williams also hints at Art Tatum and Lennie Tristano and yet comes across as a true original. Her creative interpretations of such standards as "Taking a Chance on Love," "Like Someone in Love" and a medium-tempo "I Got It Bad" are quite memorable and full of more than their share of surprises, including some funny quotes from other songs. The polyrhythms on "Bongo's Waltz" are worthy of Dave Brubeck, whose tender "I Didn't Know Till You Told Me" Williams also revives. Highly recommended. —*Scott Yanow*

★ Arrival / Oct. 29, 1993 / Jazz Focus ✦✦✦✦✦

Jessica Williams is such an impressive pianist that Philip Barker originally started the Jazz Focus label primarily to record her. This solo outing (the debut of the label) is one of Williams' finest. She digs into a wide variety of material ranging from a traditional "Japanese Folk Song" and "The Creator Has a Master Plan" to compositions by Thelonious Monk, Dizzy Gillespie, Randy Weston and Duke Ellington ("Mood Indigo"). Having mastered the musical vocabulary of Monk, Williams is able to quote from Monk at will, but she uses his language to humorous effect (although respectfully) rather than allowing it to dominate her own individual style. "Lulu's Back in Town" and "Wrap Your Troubles in Dreams" are among the high points of this very stimulating (and often witty) outing. Highly recommended. —*Scott Yanow*

Momentum / Feb. 7, 1994 / Jazz Focus ✦✦✦✦

Cedar Walton on the back of this CD writes "Jessica has few peers on the jazz scene today" and, although she remains a bit underrated, the statement is quite true. This trio set with bassist Jeff Johnson and drummer Dick Berk has many exciting moments, with the pianist finding plenty of fresh ideas on such songs as "We Kiss in a Shadow," Thelonious Monk's "Shuffle Boil," "It's Easy to Remember" and "Autumn Leaves" in addition to four of her own originals. The music is quite unpredictable while remaining consistently exciting. Jessica Williams really is one of the best. —*Scott Yanow*

Song That I Heard / Mar. 2, 1994 / Hep ✦✦✦✦✦

Encounters / Sep. 10, 1994 / Jazz Focus ✦✦✦✦

Inventions / Jul. 17, 1995 / Jazz Focus ✦✦✦✦

Jessica Williams' long string of recordings for Jazz Focus are all recommended. This trio outing with bassist Jeff Johnson and drummer Dick Berk is a little unusual, for the pianist sticks exclusively to her own originals (except for her solo feature "T4 2," which is really "Tea for Two"). She covers quite a bit of ground, with "Clear Blue Lou," "Last Trane," the adventurous "Sputnik," "Toshiko" and "Blues R Us" being among the highlights; wit and swing are never absent. —*Scott Yanow*

Joy / Nov. 27, 1995+Jan. 30, 1996 / Jazz Focus ✦✦✦✦

Intuition / Dec. 15, 1995 / Jazz Focus ✦✦✦✦

For her set of unaccompanied solos, Jessica Williams mostly focuses on relaxed material, showing off her virtuosity and creative skills at slower tempos. Highlights include her interpretations of Rahsaan Roland Kirk's haunting but rarely performed "Black and Crazy Blues," Miles Davis' "Flamenco Sketches," four of her own originals (including "Holocaust Blues"), and two lesser-known Thelonious Monk tunes. Every Jessica Williams recording is well worth picking up. —*Scott Yanow*

Jessica's Blues / Oct. 23, 1996-Oct. 24, 1996 / Jazz Focus ✦✦✦✦✦

Victoria Concert / Nov. 11, 1996 / Jazz Focus ✦✦✦✦✦

Jessica Williams' virtuosity sometimes allows her to sound like two pianists at once (as one can hear during parts of this CD's opener, "I Want to Be Happy"), but she also knows how to use space and dynamics. On this live solo set, the pianist sometimes shows the influence of Thelonious Monk (in her witty stride), McCoy Tyner (as shown on "Mr. Syms"), and Oscar Peterson, while her lengthy trill on "Straight, No Chaser" is right from Earl Hines. But in reality, Jessica Williams has her own style, a wicked sense of humor (complete with unexpected song quotes), and seemingly the ability to play whatever pops into her mind. Among the many highlights of this continually intriguing and unpredictable program are "I Want to Be Happy," "Willow Weep for Me" (played in answer to a request), Jessica's three originals, and a fascinating 15-minute exploration of "Straight, No Chaser." Highly recommended. —*Scott Yanow*

Higher Standards / May 20, 1997 / Candid ✦✦✦✦✦

For this typically superb effort, the brilliant pianist Jessica Williams (with the assistance of bassist Dave Captein and drummer Mel Brown) digs into nine standards and comes up with fresh variations and consistently inventive ideas. Although a few of the songs (most notably "Mack the Knife," "A Night in Tunisia" and "East of the Sun") have been recorded many times, Williams comes up with original musical thoughts, full of wit and chance-taking, that make each of the selections sound new. Well worth acquiring. —*Scott Yanow*

Joe Williams (Joseph Goreed)

b. Dec. 12, 1918, Cordele, GA

Vocals / Blues, Swing, Standards, Traditional Pop

Joe Williams was possibly the last great big band singer, following in the tradition of Jimmy Rushing but carving out his own unique identity. Equally skilled on blues (including double entendre ad-libs), ballads and standards, Williams has always been a charming and consistently swinging performer. In the late '30s he performed regularly with Jimmie Noone, gigged with Coleman Hawkins and Lionel Hampton in the early '40s and toured with Andy Kirk during 1946-47. After stints with Red Saunders and Hot Lips Page and recordings with King Kolax (including a 1951 version of "Every Day I Have the Blues"), Williams joined Count Basie's Orchestra in 1954. During the next seven years he and Basie had a mutually satisfying relationship, both making each other more famous! His version of "Every Day" with Basie became his theme song while many other pieces (such as "Goin' to Chicago" and "Smack Dab in the Middle") became permanent parts of Williams' repertoire. After leaving Basie in 1961, the singer worked with the Harry Edison quintet for a couple of years and has freelanced as a leader ever since, having occasional reunions with the Basie band. His collaborations with Cannonball Adderley and George Shearing were successful, as was an album with the Thad

Jones/Mel Lewis Orchestra. Joe Williams has remained one of the most popular and talented singers in jazz. —*Scott Yanow*

Everyday I Have the Blues / 1951-Sep. 28, 1953 / Savoy ✦✦✦✦

From the Roulette catalog, this superior Joe Williams/Count Basie collaboration finds the singer concentrating on the blues with consistently excellent results. In addition to a remake of the title cut, Williams is heard at his best on the classic "Going to Chicago" and such numbers as "Just a Dream," "Cherry Red" and "Good Mornin' Blues." This LP is well worth searching for. —*Scott Yanow*

★ **Count Basie Swings** / **Joe Williams Sings** / Jul. 17, 1955-Jul. 26, 1955 / Verve ✦✦✦✦✦

This is the definitive Joe Williams record, cut shortly after joining Count Basie's orchestra. Included are his classic versions of "Every Day I Have the Blues," "The Comeback," "Alright, Okay, You Win,," "In the Evening," and "Teach Me Tonight." Williams' popularity was a major asset to Basie and getting to sing with that swinging big band on a nightly basis certainly did not harm the singer. This gem belongs in everyone's jazz collection. —*Scott Yanow*

The Best of Joe Williams: The Roulette, Solid State & Blue Note Years / 1957-1968 / Blue Note ✦✦✦✦✦

The Best of Joe Williams: The Roulette, Solid State & Blue Note Years is an excellent sampler of Williams' work for Roulette and Solid State, providing a terrific overview of Williams' early records. Most of these 18 tracks feature Williams with the Count Basie Orchestra; there are also several cuts with Jimmy Jones, Harry "Sweets" Edison, Horace Ott, Jimmy Mundy, the Thad Jones-Mel Lewis Orchestra and Lambert, Hendricks and Ross. For anyone wondering why Williams is considered one of the great blues and big band vocalists, this offers a reason why. —*Stephen Thomas Erlewine*

A Swingin' Night at Birdland / Jun. 1962 / Roulette ✦✦✦✦

In 1961, after six years as one of the main attractions of Count Basie's orchestra, Williams (with Basie's blessing) went out on his own. One of his first sessions was this live recording cut at Birdland with a strong quintet that featured trumpeter Harry "Sweets" Edison and Jimmy Forrest on tenor. Williams mostly sings standards and ballads, but also tosses in a few of his popular blues (including "Well Alright, Okay, You Win" and "Goin' to Chicago") during a well-rounded and thoroughly enjoyable set. —*Scott Yanow*

Me and the Blues / Jan. 2, 1963-Dec. 5, 1963 / RCA ✦✦✦✦✦

This CD is a straight reissue of the original LP, and features singer Joe Williams backed by a studio orchestra headed and arranged by Jimmy Jones. Williams mostly sticks to blues-oriented material but there is a surprising amount of mood variation on the dozen selections along with short solos by trumpeters Thad Jones and Clark Terry, altoist Phil Woods and Seldon Powell on tenor; Ben Webster has a guest spot on "Rocks in My Bed." Williams, heard at the peak of his powers, is at his best on "Me and the Blues," "Rocks in My Bed," "Work Song," and "Kansas City." —*Scott Yanow*

● **The Overwhelmin'** / Feb. 6, 1963-Jun. 18, 1965 / Bluebird ✦✦✦✦✦

A CD sampler taken from five former LPs, this fine CD features Joe Williams doing three songs from Duke Ellington's play *Jump for Joy*, five numbers at the 1963 Newport Jazz Festival (during which he is joined by trumpeters Clark Terry and Howard McGhee and tenor greats Coleman Hawkins, Zoot Sims and Ben Webster), four blues backed by an all-star jazz group and five ballads in front of an orchestra. Although it would be preferable to have each of the five original albums intact, this superb collection features Joe Williams on a wide variety of material, and he is heard close to his peak throughout. —*Scott Yanow*

Jump for Joy / Feb. 4, 1963-Mar. 13, 1963 / RCA ✦✦✦✦✦

After a remarkable six-year tenure, vocalist Joe Williams left Count Basie's orchestra for a solo career in 1961. He recorded the 12 tracks on this disc two years later (this is a '93 CD reissue), assisted by a crack band under the co-leadership of Jimmy Jones and Oliver Nelson. But unlike the Basie years, Williams' mellow, commanding voice clearly dominated at all times. Although none of these numbers are long, each one is superbly sung. Williams' diction, storytelling ability, pacing and delivery are consistently magnificent. Whether singing sweetly or fiercely, doing love songs or blues, uptempo or ballad cuts, Williams' treatments are memorable despite their brevity. —*Ron Wynn*

☆ **And the Thad Jones/Mel Lewis Orchestra** / Sep. 30, 1966 / Blue Note ✦✦✦✦

This CD reissues one of Joe Williams' finest recordings, Accompanied by the Thad Jones/Mel Lewis Orchestra, the singer is heard at the peak of his powers. The big band primarily functions as an ensemble (Snooky Young gets off some good blasts on "Nobody Knows the Way I Feel This Morning"), but the inventive Thad Jones arrangements insure that his illustrious sidemen have plenty to play. Many of the selections (half of which have been in the singer's repertoire ever since) are given definitive treatment on this set (particularly a humorous "Evil Man Blues," "Gee

Baby Ain't I Good to You?" and "Smack Dab in the Middle") and Williams scats at his best on "It Don't Mean a Thing." Get this one. —Scott Yanow

Live in Vegas / 1971 / Monad ✦✦✦✦
This previously unreleased set features Joe Williams at a late-night performance in Las Vegas. Very well-recorded, the music offers few surprises but finds the singer in prime form. Although the Count Basie Orchestra backs him on most selections, the personnel is not listed, there are no significant solos and Basie himself is probably not on most of the tracks. The breezy liner notes say that "John Young, pianist extraordinaire" sat in during "Midnight Medley" (four ballads and "Thou Swell") and "Going to Chicago"; is this the Chicago-based player of the early '60s? Highlights include an animated "Nobody Loves You When You're Down & Out" (during which Williams really tells a story with the words), "Going to Chicago" (on this version he sings all of the famous big-band riffs along with his regular vocal) and the joyous "Smack Dab in the Middle." This is an excellent recording, easily recommended to Joe Williams fans. —Scott Yanow

Joe Williams Live / Aug. 7, 1973 / Original Jazz Classics ✦✦✦✦
Joe Williams meets the Cannonball Adderley Septet on this rather interesting session. The expanded rhythm section (which includes keyboardist George Duke and both acoustic bassist Walter Booker and the electric bass of Carol Kaye) gives funky accompaniment to Williams while altoist Cannonball and cornetist Nat have some solo space. Actually the singer easily steals the show on a rather searing version of "Goin' to Chicago Blues," his own "Who She Do" and a few unusual songs, including Duke Ellington's "Heritage." —Scott Yanow

Prez Conference / 1979 / GNP ✦✦✦✦✦
Dave Pell's Prez Conference was to Lester Young what Supersax is to Charlie Parker. Pell's short-lived group featured harmonized Lester Young solos recreated by three tenors and a baritone; their matchup with singer Joe Williams is quite enjoyable. Since Young was in Count Basie's orchestra when Jimmy Rushing was the vocalist, Joe Williams has a rare opportunity to give his own interpretation to Rushing and Billie Holiday classics like "I May Be Wrong," "You Can Depend on Me," "If Dreams Come True" and "Easy Living." A delightful and swinging date. —Scott Yanow

Nothin' But the Blues / Nov. 16, 1983-Nov. 17, 1983 / Delos ✦✦✦✦
Sticking to blues, Joe Williams is in prime form on this special session. His backup crew includes such all-stars as tenor saxophonist Red Holloway, organist Brother Jack McDuff and (on alto and one lone vocal) the great Eddie "Cleanhead" Vinson. The many blues standards are familiar but these versions are lively and fresh. —Scott Yanow

I Just Wanna Sing / Jun. 29, 1985-Jun. 30, 1985 / Delos ✦✦✦✦
For this session, Joe Williams is backed by such master jazzmen as trumpeter Thad Jones, the contrasting tenors of Eddie "Lockjaw" Davis and Benny Golson and guitarist John Collins. The material varies from the dated humor of "It's Not Easy Being White" to classic versions of "Until I Met You" and "I Got It Bad." Joe Williams is in prime form and this is one of his better sessions from his later years. —Scott Yanow

Every Night: Live at Vine St. / May 7, 1987-May 8, 1987 / Verve ✦✦✦✦✦
The focus is entirely on Joe Williams (who is backed by a standard four-piece rhythm section) during this live session from Vine Street. Then 69, Williams had not lost a thing, and his voice has rarely sounded stronger. This version of "Every Day I Have the Blues" is transformed into Miles Davis' "All Blues," Williams revives Eubie Blake's "A Dollar for a Dime" and sounds wonderful on such songs as "Too Marvelous for Words," "I Want a Little Girl" and "Roll 'Em Pete." This is the best of Joe Williams' records from the '80s. —Scott Yanow

Ballad and Blues Master / May 7, 1987-May 8, 1987 / Verve ✦✦✦✦
Taken from the same sessions that had previously resulted in *Every Night*, the identical adjectives apply. Joe Williams is in superior form for this live date, putting a lot of feeling into such songs as "You Can Depend on Me," "When Sunny Gets Blue" and "Dinner for One Please, James." A closing blues medley is particularly enjoyable and the backup by a quartet that includes pianist Norman Simmons and guitarist Henry Johnson is tasteful and swinging. —Scott Yanow

In Good Company / Jan. 19, 1989-Jan. 21, 1989 / Verve ✦✦✦✦
A bit of a grab-bag, this CD finds Joe Williams joined by Supersax on two numbers, doing a pair of vocal duets with Marlena Shaw ("Is You Is or Is You Ain't My Baby") is excellent), teaming up with vocalist/pianist Shirley Horn for two ballads and being joined by the Norman Simmons Quartet for the remainder. Sticking mostly to standards, Joe Williams shows that at 70 he still had the magic. —Scott Yanow

Live at Orchestra Hall, Detroit / Nov. 20, 1992 / Telarc ✦✦✦✦
Joe Williams is so closely associated with the Count Basie Orchestra that it is difficult to believe that this Telarc CD was his first recording with jazz's great institution in over 30 years. Williams (in generally fine form despite an occasionally

raspy voice) performs a well-rounded set of blues, ballads and standards with the Frank Foster-led Basie orchestra, combining some of his older hits with a few newer songs such as Grady Tate's "A Little at a Time" and "My Baby Upsets Me." Foster's sidemen are mostly heard in an ensemble role with all of the instrumental solos being rather brief; there is little interaction with the vocalist. That fault aside, this is one of Joe Williams' better recordings of the past decade. —Scott Yanow

Here's to Life / Aug. 16, 1993-Aug. 18, 1993 / Telarc ✦✦
Joe Williams loves the string arrangements of Robert Farnon and the sappy ballad "Here's to Life," but in truth the charts border on muzak and the slow tempos on this Telarc CD have little variety. Reminiscent a bit of Nat King Cole's string sessions of the 1950s with Gordon Jenkins, there is little jazz content to this set. Williams is in particularly strong form, interpreting the ballads in dramatic and sensitive fashion, but, despite his charm, this is one of his lesser recordings. —Scott Yanow

Feel the Spirit / Sep. 20, 1994-Sep. 23, 1994 / Telarc ✦✦✦
Joe Williams had been wanting to record an album of spirituals since 1957 and this is it. The veteran singer gives a blues feeling and swing to the traditional pieces, which range from the rollicking title cut to "Go Down Moses," "I Couldn't Hear Nobody Pray" and "The Lord's Prayer." He is assisted by Marlena Shaw (a particularly effective partner on three of the numbers) and a five-piece chorus on four other songs. The backing usually features Patrice Rushen getting organ sounds out of her synthesizer. Despite the one-message content, the music has more variety than one might expect and Joe Williams acquits himself very well on this sincere and heartfelt effort. —Scott Yanow

Mary Lou Williams

b. May 8, 1910, Atlanta, GA, **d.** May 28, 1981, Durham, NC
Piano / Swing, Stride, Bop, Post-Bop

To say that Mary Lou Williams had a long and productive career is an understatement. Although for decades she was often called jazz's greatest female musician (and one has to admire what must have been a nonstop battle against sexism), she would have been considered a major artist no matter what her sex.

Just the fact that Williams and Duke Ellington were virtually the only stride pianists to modernize their style through the years would have been enough to guarantee her a place in jazz history books. Williams managed to always sound modern during a half-century career without forgetting her roots or how to play in the older styles.

Born Mary Elfrieda Scruggs (although she soon took the name of her stepfather and was known as Mary Lou Burley), she taught herself the piano by ear and was playing in public at the age of six. Growing up in Pittsburgh, Williams' life was always filled with music. When she was 13, she started working in vaudeville, and three years later married saxophonist John Williams. They moved to Memphis, and she made her debut on records with the Synco Jazzers. John soon joined Andy Kirk's Orchestra, which was based in Kansas City, in 1929. Mary Lou wrote arrangements for the band, filled in for an absent pianist on Kirk's first recording session, and eventually became a member of the orchestra herself. Her arrangements were largely responsible for the band's distinctive sound and eventual success. Williams was soon recognized as Kirk's top soloist, a stride pianist who impressed everyone (even Jelly Roll Morton). In addition, she wrote such songs such as "Roll 'Em" (a killer hit for Benny Goodman) and "What's Your Story Morning Glory" and contributed arrangements to other big bands, including those of Goodman, Earl Hines, and Tommy Dorsey.

Mary Lou Williams stayed with Kirk until 1942, by which time she had divorced John Williams and married trumpeter Harold "Shorty" Baker. She co-led a combo with Baker before he joined Duke Ellington. Williams did some writing for Duke (most notably her rearrangement of "Blue Skies" into a horn battle called "Trumpets No End") and played briefly with Benny Goodman's bebop group in 1948. She had gradually modernized her style, and by the early to mid-1940s was actively encouraging the young modernists who would lead the bebop revolution, including Thelonious Monk, Bud Powell, Tadd Dameron and Dizzy Gillespie. Williams' "Zodiac Suite" showed off some of her modern ideas, and her "In the Land of Oo-Bla-Dee" was a bebop fable recorded by Gillespie.

Williams lived in Europe from 1952-54 and then became very involved in the Catholic religion. She retired from music for a few years before appearing as a guest with Dizzy Gillespie's Orchestra at the 1957 Newport Jazz Festival. Williams returned to jazz and by the early '70s sounded more like a young modal player (clearly she was familiar with McCoy Tyner) than a survivor of the 1920s. Although she did not care for the avant-garde, she occasionally played quite freely, although a 1977 duo concert with Cecil Taylor was a complete fiasco. Williams wrote three masses and a cantata, was a star at Benny Goodman's 40th anniversary Carnegie Hall Concert in 1978, taught at Duke University, and often planned her later concerts as a history of jazz recital. By the time she passed away at the age of 71, she had a list of accomplishments that could have filled three lifetimes.

Mary Lou Williams recorded through the years as a leader for many labels, including Brunswick (a pair of piano solos in 1930), Decca (1938), Columbia, Savoy, extensively for Asch and Folkways during 1944-47, Victor, King (1949), Atlantic, Circle, Vogue, Prestige, Blue Star, Jazztone, her own Mary label (1970-74), Chiaroscuro, Steeple Chase and finally Pablo (1977-78). —*Scott Yanow*

☆ **1927-40** / Jan. 1927-Nov. 18, 1940 / Classics ✦✦✦✦✦
This CD features the great pianist Mary Lou Williams during her earliest period. She is heard in 1927 on six selections with the Synco Jazzers (a small group that included her then-husband John Williams on alto) and then on the first 19 selections ever recorded under her own name. Performed during the long period when she was the regular pianist with Andy Kirk's 12 Clouds of Joy, Williams is featured on two hot stride solos in 1930, leading trios in 1936 and 1938, playing "Little Joe from Chicago" unaccompanied in 1939 and heading septets in 1940; among her sidemen were trumpeter Harold "Shorty" Baker and the legendary tenor Dick Wilson. Many of the compositions were written by Williams including "Night Life," "New Froggy Bottom," "Mary's Special," and "Scratchin' the Gravel"; her version of Jelly Roll Morton's "The Pearls" is a high point. —*Scott Yanow*

First Ladies of Jazz / Jan. 26, 1940-Feb. 1954 / Savoy ✦✦✦✦✦
Three female pianists are well-showcased on this Muse-sponsored CD reissue of Savoy material. The great Mary Lou Williams leads a septet of musicians from Andy Kirk's Orchestra (including the legendary tenor Dick Wilson) on four numbers, the interesting but now somewhat forgotten pianist Jutta Hipp heads a quartet with tenor saxophonist Hans Koller and Beryl Booker is featured with a quartet that also includes Don Byas on tenor. The high-quality music overall ranges from swing to bop and these rarities are well worth hearing. —*Scott Yanow*

Roll 'Em / 1944 / Audiophile ✦✦✦
Pianist Mary Lou Williams, in a trio with bassist Al Lucas and drummer Jack "The Bear" Parker, is heard playing nine numbers for radio transcriptions on this LP. In addition to the regular takes, all of the music she performed that day is here including five false starts, five alternate takes and two incomplete versions. Because of the odd programming, it is a bit difficult to follow the evolution of some of these performances, but the finished results are generally quite good. Highlights include "Limehouse Blues," "Froggy Bottom" and "Roll 'Em." —*Scott Yanow*

Asch Recordings, 1944-1947 / Mar. 12, 1944-1947 / Smithsonian/Folkways ✦✦✦✦✦
Mary Lou Williams recorded exclusively for Asch during this period, and most of her performances are included on this two-LP boxed set. Williams' style was in a state of transition as she was gradually discarding stride piano and developing a much more boppish approach. She is heard here in a wide variety of settings ranging from piano solos to small groups and even a big band. Among her sidemen are trumpeters Frankie Newton, Dick Vance, Bill Coleman (who is well featured) and Kenny Dorham, clarinetist Edmund Hall, trombonist Vic Dickenson and tenors Don Byas and Coleman Hawkins. This very valuable set is well worth an extensive search and will hopefully be put out on CD eventually by Folkways. —*Scott Yanow*

Town Hall (1945): The Zodiac Suite / Dec. 31, 1945 / Smithsonian/Folkways ✦✦✦✦
Mary Lou Williams' *Zodiac Suite,* a 12-piece work with a different theme made for each of the signs of the zodiac (and keeping in mind the personalities of a few jazz musicians born during each period), was composed and first recorded in 1945. With the assistance of bassist Al Lucas and drummer Jack "The Bear" Parker, pianist Williams performs these moody and often-introspective (but occasionally playful) sketches in a forward-looking swing style. Five alternate takes have been added to the original program on this CD reissue which, although not quite essential, has its interesting moments. —*Scott Yanow*

The First Lady of the Piano / Jan. 23, 1953 / Inner City ✦✦✦✦
Mary Lou Williams, who had started her career as a stride pianist, was one of the few early jazz players who successfully made the transition to more modern styles. On this Inner City LP (drawn from recordings made for Vogue), Williams and her trio (with clarinetist Tony Scott sitting in on bongos) performs such standards as "'Round Midnight," Tadd Dameron's "Lady Bird" and Wild Bill Davis' "Titoros" in convincing fashion, very much in a bop vein. Excellent music. —*Scott Yanow*

A Keyboard History / Mar. 8, 1955+Mar. 10, 1955 / Jazztone ✦✦✦
This LP contains Mary Lou Williams' last recording sessions before she retired for a period to devote herself to the Catholic religion. A bit of a retrospective, Mary Lou Williams on this trio set with bassist Wendell Marshall and drummer Osie

Johnson plays some blues, stride and boogie-woogie along with "Taurus" from her *Zodiac Suite* and some more recent modern originals. This set will be very difficult to find. —*Scott Yanow*

Zoning / 1974 / Smithsonian/Folkways ✦✦✦✦
Mary Lou Williams emerged in the early '70s after a long period in which she worked in the Catholic church to resume her always-stimulating career as a jazz pianist. On this CD reissue, one of her finest recordings of her later years has been brought back and augmented by two previously unissued performances. Williams performs in duos and trios with bassist Bob Cranshaw and drummer Mickey Roker, uses Zita Carno on second piano during a couple of the more avant-garde pieces, and also performs some trios with bassist Milton Suggs and Tony Waters on congas. Rather than sounding like a veteran of the 1920s, Mary Lou Williams sounds 40 years younger, shows the influence of McCoy Tyner and hints at free jazz in spots. An often-surprising set of modern jazz. —*Scott Yanow*

Free Spirits / Jul. 8, 1975 / Steeple Chase ✦✦✦
Includes great trio cuts w/ Buster Williams (b) and Mickey Roker (d). —*Ron Wynn*

● **Live at the Cookery** / Nov. 1975 / Chiaroscuro ✦✦✦✦✦
This CD gives one a definitive look at the talented pianist Mary Lou Williams in her later years. In these duets with bassist Brian Torff, Williams essentially takes listeners on a trip through the history of jazz from hymns and blues to stride, swing, and bop (including "All Blues"). The CD reissue adds three fine performances to the original program. Recommended. —*Scott Yanow*

Embraced / Apr. 17, 1977 / Original Jazz Classics ✦
This encounter is a disaster. Mary Lou Williams, who always prided herself on being open-minded, arranged to perform a duo piano concert with the avant-garde master Cecil Taylor. She wanted them to go through her usual history-of-jazz program but neglected to gain Taylor's consent and, since he never compromises his atonal music, the lack of communication between the two players is laughable. While Williams tries to demonstrate blues, ragtime, stride and swing, Taylor plays in his usual dense and dissonant style on top of her. The result is a complete mess that is almost impossible to listen to. —*Scott Yanow*

My Mama Pinned a Rose on Me / Dec. 27, 1977 / Pablo ✦✦✦
In this studio set with bassist Buster Williams and the occasional vocals of Cynthia Tyson, pianist Mary Lou Williams performs a full set of original blues. A certain sameness is heard after awhile, but in general the music is quite stimulating, showing that Williams (even this late in her career) had not lost her power and authority at the keyboard. —*Scott Yanow*

Mary Lou Williams Solo Recital / Jul. 16, 1978 / Original Jazz Classics ✦✦✦✦
Mary Lou Williams' final recording (performed three years before her death) gives one a strong retrospective of her career. This solo concert at the 1978 Montreux Jazz Festival has a medley encompassing spirituals, ragtime, blues and swing. Other highlights include Williams' reworkings of "Tea for Two," "Honeysuckle Rose" and her two compositions "Little Joe from Chicago" and "What's Your Story Morning Glory." Recommended. —*Scott Yanow*

Richard Williams (Richard Gene Williams)

b. May 4, 1931, Galveston, TX, d. Nov. 5, 1985, New York, NY
Trumpet / Hard Bop
Richard Williams, although inspired by Fats Navarro, had developed his own sound (along with an impressive technique) on the trumpet by the 1960s and is best remembered for his occasional work with Charles Mingus. He was originally a tenor player, even gigging on the instrument with local bands. By the time he completed his time in the Air Force, Williams was a trumpeter, and he toured Europe with Lionel Hampton in 1956. He had off-and-on associations with many top players including Mingus (1959-64), Gigi Gryce, Quincy Jones, Roland Kirk, Eric Dolphy, Duke Ellington and the Thad Jones/Mel Lewis Orchestra (1966-69). He worked with Gil Evans, played in some Broadway musicals, gigged with Clark Terry's big band in the mid-'70s and performed with Mingus Dynasty in 1982, but never did gain much recognition. Williams' lone set as a leader (which was cut for Candid in 1960) is available on CD. —*Scott Yanow*

● **New Horn in Town** / Sep. 27, 1960 / Candid ✦✦✦✦✦
Considering how well trumpeter Richard Williams plays on this session, it is hard to believe that this was the only record he ever led. Best known for his association with Charles Mingus, Williams was a strong bop improviser with a wide range. For this album (which is split between standards and originals) Williams and his quintet (altoist Leo Wright, pianist Richard Wyands, bassist Reggie Workman and drummer Bobby Thomas) are in fine form performing a set of strong hard bop. —*Scott Yanow*

Tony Williams (Anthony Williams)

b. Dec. 12, 1945, Chicago, IL, **d.** Feb. 23, 1997, Daly City, CA

Drums / Post-Bop, Fusion, Hard Bop

Tony Williams' death in 1997 of a heart attack after routine gallbladder surgery was a major shock to the jazz world. Just 51, Williams (who could be a very loud drummer) seemed so youthful, healthy and ageless even though he had been a major drummer for nearly 35 years. The open style that he created while with the Miles Davis Quintet in the mid- to late '60s remains quite influential, and he had a long list of accomplishments during the past couple of decades.

Williams' father, a saxophonist, took his son out to clubs that gave him an opportunity to sit in; at 11 the youngster already showed potential. He took lessons from Alan Dawson and at 15 was appearing at Boston-area jam sessions. During 1959-60 Williams often played with Sam Rivers, and in December 1962 (when he was barely 17) the drummer moved to New York and played regularly with Jackie McLean. Within a few months he joined Miles Davis, where his ability to imply the beat while playing quite freely influenced and inspired the other musicians; together with Herbie Hancock and Ron Carter he was part of one of the great rhythm sections. Williams, who was 18 when he appeared on Eric Dolphy's classic *Out to Lunch* album, stayed with Davis into 1969, leading his own occasional sessions and becoming a household name in the jazz world. In addition to his interest in avant-garde jazz, Tony Williams was a fan of rock music, and when he left Miles he formed the fusion band Lifetime, a trio with Larry Young and John McLaughlin. After leading other versions of Lifetime (one of them starring Allan Holdsworth), Williams stuck to freelancing for a time, studied composition and toured with Herbie Hancock's V.S.O.P. band. By the mid-'80s he was heading his own all-star hard bop group, which featured Wallace Roney as a surrogate Miles Davis and a repertoire dominated by the drummer's originals (including the standard "Sister Cheryl"). After breaking up his longtime quintet in 1995, Williams gigged a bit with a trio, recorded a very interesting set of original music for the Ark 21 label and seemed to have a limitless future. His premature death makes one grateful that he started his career early and that he was extensively documented. —*Scott Yanow*

Life Time / Aug. 21, 1964-Aug. 24, 1964 / Blue Note ◆◆◆◆◆

Drummer Tony Williams' first recording as a leader (made when he was 18 and still billed as "Anthony Williams") gave him an opportunity to utilize an advanced group of musicians: tenor saxophonist Sam Rivers, vibraphonist Bobby Hutcherson, pianist Herbie Hancock and both Richard Davis and Gary Peacock on basses. Williams wrote all four of the pieces and has a different combination of players on each song. The freely improvised "Memory" features Hutcherson, Hancock and Williams in some colorful and at times spacey interplay, "Barb's Song to the Wizard" is a Hancock-Carter duet, "Tomorrow Afternoon" has Rivers, Peacock and Williams in a trio while all of the musicians (except Hutcherson) are on the side-long "2 Pieces of One." The unpredictable music holds one's interest; a very strong debut for the masterful drummer. —*Scott Yanow*

Spring / Aug. 12, 1965 / Blue Note ◆◆◆

Drummer Tony Williams' second recording as a leader (reissued on CD) is surprisingly avant-garde and forbidding. Tenor saxophonist Sam Rivers is on four of the five Williams originals, as is bassist Gary Peacock, while tenorman Wayne Shorter and pianist Herbie Hancock are on three apiece; "Echo" is an unaccompanied drum solo. Other than the closing "Tee" (nearly 10 minutes long), none of the drummer's tunes are particularly memorable, and, although the contrast between the distinctive tenors is interesting, the overall results are a bit forgettable. —*Scott Yanow*

☆ **Emergency!** / May 26, 1969+May 28, 1969 / Polydor ◆◆◆◆◆

Tony Williams' *Emergency* was one of the first and most influential albums in late-'60s fusion, a record that shattered the boundaries between jazz and rock. Working with guitarist John McLaughlin and organist Larry Young, Williams pushed into new territory, creating dense, adventurous, unpredictable soundscapes. With *Emergency,* Tony Williams helped create the foundation of the style and sound of fusion. It's a seminal release, originally released on two albums and now available on one CD. —*Leo Stanley*

● **Spectrum: The Anthology** / May 26, 1969-1972 / Verve ◆◆◆◆◆

Spectrum: Anthology is a double-disc, 25-track compilation that traces the evolution of Tony Williams' early '70s jazz-fusion combo, Lifetime. Over the course of their career, Lifetime featured a number of top jazz and rock players, including John McLaughlin, Ron Carter, Alan Holdsworth, Larry Young and Jack Bruce, with many of the musicians turning in edgy, exciting performances. In fact, *Spectrum* is a better way to get acquainted with Lifetime than the actual albums, since it condenses the cream of the crop down to one illuminating anthology. —*Leo Stanley*

Turn It Over / 1970 / Polydor ◆◆◆◆

The addition of former Cream bassist Jack Bruce to Tony Williams' Lifetime not only gave the fusion group a harder rock edge, but it helped push the band toward both bluesier and more adventurous territory. While the end result wasn't as consistently impressive as *Emergency!, Turn It Over* was still unpredictable, challenging music that helped establish Williams as an influential bandleader in his own right. —*Leo Stanley*

Ego / 1970 / Polydor ◆◆◆

The Old Bum's Rush / 1972 / Polydor ◆◆

The Collection / 1975-1976 / Columbia/Legacy ◆◆◆◆

This CD has all of the music from drummer Tony Williams' *Believe It* and *Million Dollar Legs* LPs. The best-known version of Williams' Lifetime is the trio he led during 1969-70 with guitarist John McLaughlin and organist Larry Young. There are times (particularly on the first half of this reissue) that this later edition of Lifetime approaches the power and creativity of the original group. Key among the sidemen is guitarist Allan Holdsworth, a very underrated and creative musician whose style falls between rock and jazz and who often improvises more like a keyboardist than a guitarist. Alan Pasqua on electric piano and bassist Tony Newton (who also takes a few forgettable vocals) complete the group; background brass and strings are added to some of the songs in the later date. Although not flawless (some of the music has dated), these long-overlooked performances are worth exploring by fusion collectors, especially for Holdsworth's fiery yet thoughtful solos. —*Scott Yanow*

Joy of Flying / 1978 / Columbia ◆◆◆◆

It would be an understatement to say that there was a fair amount of variety on this set. Drummer Tony Williams is heard in two duets with keyboardist Jan Hammer, with a quartet also including keyboardist Herbie Hancock, Tom Scott (who unfortunately sticks to lyricon) and bassist Stanley Clarke, and he welcomes rock guitarist Ronnie Montrose, keyboardist Brian Auger, guitarist George Benson, Hammer and tenorman Michael Brecker on other tracks. Much of this music is closer to R&B than to jazz, although there are many strong moments. But the most interesting selection is certainly "Morgan's Motion," which matches Williams with pianist Cecil Taylor in a powerful (and completely atonal) collaboration. —*Scott Yanow*

Foreign Intrigue / Jun. 18, 1985-Jun. 19, 1985 / Blue Note ◆◆◆◆

Williams had never led a straightahead recording session before and is a little higher in the mix than drummers usually rate. But despite the fact that he almost drowns out Bobby Hutcherson's vibes at times, Williams' playing is consistently colorful and would hold one's interest even if he were under-recorded. —*Scott Yanow*

Civilization / Nov. 24, 1986-Nov. 26, 1986 / Blue Note ◆◆◆◆

Although he had recorded the year before using trumpeter Wallace Roney and pianist Mulgrew Miller on *Foreign Intrigue*, *Civilization* was the debut record by drummer Tony Williams' hard bop quintet, a group also including Billy Pierce on tenor and soprano and bassist Charnett Moffett (who would later be succeeded by Ira Coleman). The leader's loud and forceful drumming forced the other soloists to use their maximum power, and his eight originals gave his sidemen challenging compositions to play. With Roney emulating Miles Davis as usual, Williams must have been pleased to have his former boss' sound at his disposal. Although none of the songs caught on as standards, this is an excellent effort. —*Scott Yanow*

Angel Street / Apr. 4, 1988-Apr. 6, 1988 / Blue Note ◆◆◆◆◆

All of the recordings by Tony Williams' hard bop quintet of the late '80s/early '90s are worth owning. Trumpeter Wallace Roney, Billy Pierce (on tenor and soprano) and pianist Mulgrew Miller offered consistently satisfying solos, bassist Charnett Moffett was excellent in support and the drummer-leader constantly pushed his sidemen; in concert his "support" could nearly drown out the soloists. For this 1988 studio session, Williams contributed nine originals including "Pee Wee" from his days with Miles Davis. The music is generally straightahead and full of passion. —*Scott Yanow*

Native Heart / Sep. 11, 1989-Sep. 13, 1989 / Blue Note ◆◆◆◆◆

Although a bit underrated, drummer Tony Williams' Quintet was one of the top hard bop units of the late '80s. Williams' originals (he contributed all seven of the compositions to this CD) gave his group a fresh repertoire, and his rather loud drumming really forced trumpeter Wallace Roney, Billy Pierce (on tenor and soprano), pianist Mulgrew Miller and the alternating bassists Ira Coleman (who would soon become the group's permanent member) and Bob Hurst to play with all of the energy and volume they could muster. This date is easily recommended to fans of the more adventurous side of straightahead jazz. —*Scott Yanow*

The Story of Neptune / Nov. 29, 1991-Dec. 1, 1991 / Blue Note ◆◆◆◆◆

The Tony Williams Quintet has two obvious assets that put it ahead of most acoustic jazz bands: Williams' powerful and consistently creative drumming and his compositional talents. On this group's fifth Blue Note recording, the drummer contributed the three-part "Neptune," essentially a feature for his drums, a more memorable original, "Crime Scene" and arrangements of three standards. —*Scott Yanow*

★ **Tokyo Live** / Mar. 2, 1992-Mar. 8, 1992 / Blue Note ✦✦✦✦
This live two-CD set, one of the last recordings by the Tony Williams Quintet before it disbanded, is a fine retrospective of the group's music. All but the Beatles' "Blackbird" are originals by the drummer/leader and the 11 lengthy performances (only two songs clock in at less than 9:51) give one a strong idea as to how the quintet sounded during a typical club performance. Trumpeter Wallace Roney and the versatile Bill Pierce (on tenor and soprano) have their spots, and pianist Mulgrew Miller is well featured on the thoughtful "Citadel," while bassist Ira Coleman is heard purely in a supportive role. There is never any doubt who the leader is, for Tony Williams dominates the ensembles, taking several five-minute drum solos and being quite prominent in the mix. —*Scott Yanow*

Wilderness / Dec. 1996 / Ark 21 ✦✦
One of drummer Tony Williams' final studio projects, this adventurous effort alternates selections by an all-star quintet (which includes tenor saxophonist Michael Brecker, guitarist Pat Metheny, pianist Herbie Hancock and bassist Stanley Clarke) with string orchestra tracks (usually using the rhythm section). Williams wrote most of the music (there is one song apiece from Metheny and Clarke), and despite the general unpredictability of the music (which ranges from melancholy to fiery), there is a surprising unity throughout the CD. Highlights include the pretty opener for strings "Wilderness Rising," a lyrical quintet number, "The Night You Were Born," the rockish freakout "China Moon" and the heated "Gambia"; only guitarist Lyle Workman's guest spot on his droning "Machu Picchu" is a minus. Otherwise, this is intriguing music that rewards repeated listenings, making one further appreciate the great loss suffered as a result of Tony Williams' premature death. —*Scott Yanow*

Claude Williamson

b. Nov. 18, 1926, Brattleboro, VT
Piano / Bop, Cool
A superior bop pianist influenced by Bud Powell, Claude Williamson has been busy playing on the West Coast since the 1950s. The older brother of trumpeter Stu Williamson, Claude started on piano when he was seven and had ten years of classical piano lessons, also studying at the New England Conservatory. Williamson's first major musical job was with Charlie Barnet's Orchestra in 1947. This was followed by stints with Red Norvo (1948), Barnet's bebop big band of 1949, and June Christy (1950-51). In the 1950s, Williamson worked regularly with Bud Shank, the Lighthouse All-Stars, with his own trios, and as a studio musician. He spent most of the 1960s and '70s in the studios, although he returned to jazz in the 1980s with his improvising style virtually unchanged. Claude Williamson, who has led sessions for Capitol (1954-55), Bethlehem, Criterion, Contract (1961-62), Sea Breeze (1977), Interplay, Discovery, Fresh Sound and a few Japanese labels, recorded a memorable tribute to Bud Powell set for V.S.O.P. in 1995. He currently plays regularly in the Los Angeles area. —*Scott Yanow*

Kenton Presents Jazz: Claude Williamson / Jun. 26, 1954-Jul. 29, 1954 / Capitol ✦✦✦✦

Key West / Dec. 14, 1955 / Capitol ✦✦✦✦

Claude Williamson / Jun. 27, 1956 / Bethlehem ✦✦✦✦

Round Midnight / Dec. 1956 / Bethlehem ✦✦✦
Claude Williamson was one of the better bebop-oriented pianists to be active during the 1950s. This trio set with bassist Red Mitchell and drummer Mel Lewis has been reissued on CD. With the exception of four-minute renditions of "Stella by Starlight" and Horace Silver's "Hippy," all of the numbers clock in around the three-minute mark. The repertoire (which includes such tunes as "Somebody Loves Me," "The Surrey with the Fringe on Top," "Just One of Those Things" and "The Song Is You") is typical for the time period and Williamson brings to the music his own approach to playing bop. The set is quite enjoyable and, even if the program (which is around 39 minutes) is a bit brief, it should appeal to straightahead jazz fans. —*Scott Yanow*

Theatre Party / 1962 / Fresh Sound ✦✦✦✦✦

★ **Hallucinations** / Feb. 28, 1995+Mar. 1, 1995 / V.S.O.P. ✦✦✦✦✦
For his V.S.O.P. release, veteran pianist Claude Williamson performs six Bud Powell compositions plus six other standards that the innovative bop pianist enjoyed playing. With the assistance of bassist Dave Carpenter and drummer Paul Kreibich, Williamson displays both the Powell influence and his own approach to bebop piano. The music always swings, has enough surprises to hold on to one's interest and shows that Claude Williamson (who has been somewhat underrated through the years) was still in prime form four decades after his initial recogni-

tion. Highlights of this easily recommended disc include "Hallucinations," "Bud's Bubble," "Parisian Thoroughfare" and "Bouncing with Bud." —*Scott Yanow*

Stu Williamson (Stuart Lee Williamson)

b. May 14, 1933, Brattleboro, VT, **d.** Oct. 1, 1991, Studio City, CA
Trumpet, Valve Trombone / Cool
The younger brother of pianist Claude Williamson, Stu Williamson was a fixture on West Coast jazz dates of the 1950s. He moved to Los Angeles in 1949 and spent periods playing with Stan Kenton (1951), Woody Herman (1952-53) and Kenton again (1954-55) in addition to shorter stints with Billy May and Charlie Barnet. The mellow-toned Williamson, best-known for his association with Shelly Manne (off and on during 1954-58), was on a countless number of sessions up until 1968 when he dropped out of the music scene. A drug addict, Stu Williamson spent most of his last two decades struggling outside of music. —*Scott Yanow*

● **Stu Williamson Plays** / Jan. 18, 1955-Jan. 16, 1956 / Fresh Sound ✦✦✦✦✦
Stu Williamson led relatively few sessions in his career and over half of them are on this excellent Fresh Sound CD. The cool-toned trumpeter is mostly heard in a quintet with altoist Charlie Mariano, pianist Claude Williamson (his brother), either Max Bennett or Leroy Vinnegar on bass and Stan Levey or Mel Lewis on drums. The remaining four songs (all Bill Holman compositions) feature a sextet with Holman on tenor, baritonist Jimmy Giuffre, Claude, Vinnegar and Lewis. The music swings lightly but firmly with excellent solos from all concerned, making this CD a prime example of West Coast jazz from the 1950s. Recommended. —*Scott Yanow*

Bert Wilson

Tenor Saxophone, Alto Saxophone, Soprano Saxophone / Avant-Garde, Free Jazz
Though renowned as one of the avant-garde's most creative improvising players, saxophonist Bert Wilson was little known to all but the most dedicated jazz buffs. A skilled and original performer equally at home on tenor, alto and soprano, he first emerged during the 1960s, appearing on records from the likes of Sonny Simmons and James Zitro; when Wilson finally began leading his own dates years later, most of his albums were released on his own FMO label, and as a result were never privy to the kind of wide distribution they deserved. Those issued on other, more high-profile labels, like 1986's *The Next Rebirth* and 1994's *Endless Fingers*, typically earned high marks from critics. —*Jason Ankeny*

The Next Rebirth / 1986 / Nine Winds ✦✦✦✦
One of the finest saxophonists of the avant-garde, Bert Wilson has mostly recorded for his own FMO label through the years. This Nine Winds LP was a welcome exception, giving the highly original improviser (heard here on tenor, alto and bass clarinet) a little more exposure than usual. He is featured on nine of his originals along with flutist Nancy Curtis (whose gentle sound complements Wilson well), pianist Allen Youngblood, bassist Chuck Metcalf, drummer Bob Meyer and percussionist Michael Olson. While fairly free in spots, the compositions each have their own personality, and some utilize swinging rhythms and chordal improvising. The highlight is the tenor/drums duet on "Speed of Light." —*Scott Yanow*

Live at the Zoo / Aug. 3, 1988 / Nine Winds ✦✦✦✦✦

Further Adventures in Jazz / Jan. 26, 1992-Jan. 27, 1992 / FMO Productinos ✦✦✦

● **Endless Fingers** / Jun. 6, 1994-Jul. 28, 1994 / Arabesque ✦✦✦✦✦
Bert Wilson, a survivor of the 1960s, has maintained a low profile through the decades but is still a major improviser. Most of his recordings for the past 15 years have been with his own FMO label, making this better-distributed effort for Arabesque probably the most available of all of his sets. Wilson, who switches between alto, tenor, bass clarinet and soprano, has an original sound on all of his instruments, inspired by the freer flights of Eric Dolphy and Ornette Coleman. Teamed up with the fine flutist Nancy Curtis, pianist Craig Hoyer, either Dan Schulte or Peter Vinikow on bass and drummer Bob Meyer, Wilson displays his versatility on originals that are generally straightahead but open to explorative solos; his bass clarinet cadenza on the opening "Endless Fingers" is particularly memorable. Two songs add the tenor of Chuck Stentz with "Onslaught" being a colorful and boppish tenor battle. A particularly impressive effort with inventive playing from all of the musicians, this adventurous but not inaccessible set of original music serves as a perfect introduction to the talented Bert Wilson. —*Scott Yanow*

Cassandra Wilson

b. Dec. 1955, Jackson, MS
Vocals / Standards, Free Funk, Country Blues, World Fusion, Avant-Garde
Although her recording career has been somewhat erratic, Cassandra Wilson is one of the top jazz singers of the 1990s, a vocalist blessed with a distinctive and flexible voice who is not afraid to take chances. She began playing piano and gui-

tar when she was nine and was working as a vocalist by the mid-'70s, singing a wide variety of material. Following a year in New Orleans, Wilson moved to New York in 1982 and began working with Dave Holland and Abbey Lincoln. After meeting Steve Coleman, she became the main vocalist with the M-Base collective. Although there was really no room for a singer in the overcrowded free funk ensembles, Wilson did as good a job of fitting in as was possible. She worked with New Air and recorded her first album as a leader in 1985. By her third record, a standards date, she was sounding quite a bit like Betty Carter. After a few more albums in which she mostly performed original and rather inferior material, Cassandra Wilson changed directions and performed an acoustic blues-oriented program for Blue Note called *Blue Light 'Til Dawn*. By going back in time, she had found herself, and Wilson has continued interpreting in fresh and creative ways vintage country blues and folk music up until the present day. During 1997 she toured as part of Wynton Marsalis' *Blood on the Fields* production. —*Scott Yanow*

Songbook / Mar. 1985-Aug. 1991 / JMT ✦✦✦✦

Point of View / Dec. 14, 1985-Dec. 15, 1985 / JMT ✦✦✦✦

Cassandra Wilson's debut as a leader features the chance-taking singer in a funky M-Base setting. The overcrowded ensembles (played by altoist Steve Coleman, trombonist Grachan Moncur III, guitarist Jean-Paul Bourelly, bassist Lonnie Plaxico and drummer Mark Johnson) did not leave much space for a singer but the flexible Wilson did her best to find a role for her voice and she sounds enthusiastic. In addition to group originals, the sextet performs "Blue in Green" (which has Wilson's lyrics) and "I Wished on the Moon." —*Scott Yanow*

Days Aweigh / May 1987 / JMT ✦✦✦

The formative years of singer Cassandra Wilson's career found her associated with the "M-Base" school of eccentric funk. On this set of advanced originals (which also has versions of "Let's Face the Music" and "Some Other Time"), Wilson is the lead voice in dense ensembles that include (on various cuts) cornetist Olu Dara, guitarist Jean-Paul Bourelly, trumpeter Graham Haynes and altoist Steve Coleman with a very active rhythm section. "Some Other Time" is a change of pace, a duet with pianist Rod Williams, but otherwise this is advanced free funk dance music. —*Scott Yanow*

Blue Skies / Feb. 1988 / JMT ✦✦✦✦✦

Primarily associated with the M-Base school of creative funk, Cassandra Wilson was having a difficult time finding a place for her vocals in the dense ensembles that usually dominate that music. *Blue Skies* was a real change of pace, a set of nine standards in which Wilson is backed by a creative but conventional trio (pianist Mulgrew Miller, bassist Lonnie Plaxico and drummer Terri Lyne Carrington). Her voice in this setting (and her improvising style) sounds very much like Betty Carter, but Wilson would develop much more individuality during the next few years. —*Scott Yanow*

Jumpworld / Jul. 1989-Aug. 1989 / JMT ✦✦✦

She Who Weeps / Oct. 1990-Dec. 1990 / JMT ✦✦

This is a transition set of sorts for Cassandra Wilson. Having had good notices for her *Blue Skies* album (which found her interpreting standards in a style similar to Betty Carter), Wilson performs "Chelsea Bridge" and "Body and Soul." Most of the other selections still use the free funk rhythms that were a carryover from the singer's association with Steve Coleman and the M-Base players although no horns are present this time around; just a three or four-piece rhythm section. Interesting but not overly memorable music. —*Scott Yanow*

Live / May 9, 1991 / JMT ✦✦

Singer Cassandra Wilson was still searching for her own style during the time of this live concert. Accompanied by keyboardist James Weidman, electric bassist Kevin Bruce Harris and drummer Mark Johnson, Wilson performs four of her originals (none of which are too memorable), Steve Coleman's "Desperate Move" and a couple of standards ("'Round Midnight" and "Body and Soul"). This forgettable (and somewhat boring) set is strictly for Cassandra Wilson completists; more general listeners are advised to get her more interesting mid-'90s recordings instead. —*Scott Yanow*

After the Beginning Again / Jul. 1991-Aug. 1991 / JMT ✦✦

Dance to the Drums Again / 1992 / DIW/Columbia ✦

It is obvious listening to this music in hindsight that vocalist Cassandra Wilson was at the crossroads of her career in 1992. She had spent several years often singing in a free funk M-Base setting, an idiom with little use for a vocalist. On this CD not only does she sound bored to death on her own unimaginative material but Wilson sings virtually everything in the same world-weary tone of voice. The rhythms are quite ponderous and annoying. Despite his best efforts, guitarist Jean-Paul Bourelly is unable to do much to uplift this fiasco. —*Scott Yanow*

★ **Blue Light Til Dawn** / 1993 / Blue Note ✦✦✦✦✦

Cassandra Wilson has steadfastly refused to be pigeonholed or confined to any stylistic formula. Her highly anticipated Blue Note debut may stir renewed controversy, as she is once again all over the place. She begins the set with her intriguing version of "You Don't Know What Love Is." Then she moves from two Robert Johnson covers ("Come On in My Kitchen" and "Hellhound on My Trail") to rock compositions from Van Morrison and Joni Mitchell, then to her own title track and blues cut "Redbone" and a piercing version of "I Can't Stand The Rain" that can hold up to comparisons with Ann Peebles' classic. She doesn't have Johnson's menacing quality (who does?), but does invoke an equally compelling air. Wilson has great timing, pacing and delivery and certainly has blues sensibility in her sound. —*Ron Wynn*

New Moon Daughter / 1995 / Blue Note ✦✦✦✦✦

Singer Cassandra Wilson, who has had a rather diverse career that has ranged from the free funk of M-Base to standards à la Betty Carter, has in recent times adopted a folk-oriented style a little reminiscent of Nina Simone. On this CD her repertoire ranges from U2 to Son House, from Hoagy Carmichael to Hank Williams ("I'm So Lonesome I Could Cry"); it is certainly the only album ever that contains both the Monkees' "Last Train to Clarksville" and "Strange Fruit." This CD is a surprise best-seller, for Wilson's voice actually sounds quite bored and emotionally detached. She deserves great credit for stretching herself but one has to dig deep to find any warmth in her overly cool approach. —*Scott Yanow*

Garland Wilson

b. Jun. 13, 1909, Martinsburgh, WV, **d.** May 31, 1954, Paris, France
Piano / Stride

A fine stride pianist, Garland Wilson spent much of his career in Europe, which led to him being underrated. After studying at Howard University, he came to New York in 1929 and played regularly in Harlem for the next three years, recording as a soloist starting in 1931. The following year he went to France as singer Nina Mae McKinney's accompanist and he played regularly overseas in both Great Britain and France, recording as a leader and with Nat Gonella. Due to World War II Wilson returned to the US in 1939 where he worked in nightclubs until going back to Paris in 1951. —*Scott Yanow*

● **1931-1938** / May 18, 1931-Mar. 9, 1938 / Classics ✦✦✦✦

With the exception of five songs cut in 1951, this CD has every recording from the sessions led by Garland Wilson. The excellent swing pianist (who was influenced a bit by Earl Hines) is at his best on slower to medium material, for on the faster performances his ideas run a bit thin. On two numbers, Wilson accompanies actress Nina Mae McKinney, and two others are spirited duets with violinist Michel Warlop; the remaining 20 selections are all piano solos. This formerly rare music should be enjoyed by fans of swing piano. —*Scott Yanow*

Gerald Wilson

b. Sep. 4, 1918, Shelby, MS
Arranger, Leader, Trumpet / Hard Bop, Traditional Pop, Big Band

From time to time, Gerald Wilson seems like one of Los Angeles' better-kept secrets, an unusually skillful, imaginative and charismatic bandleader who hasn't received his due outside the West Coast. His arrangements have distinctive, often complex voicings and harmonies, rooted in swing and bop, yet always forward-looking and energetic in tone. He likes to play around with structures, which contributes to the restless quality in much of his music—and being a bullfight aficionado, he was one of the first arrangers to make use of Spanish influences. He has been consistently able to attract top-rank musicians to his bands, who play with immaculate precision and brio for the flamboyantly gesticulating maestro.

Upon moving from Memphis to Detroit with his family in 1932, Wilson studied music in high school and played with the Plantation Music Orchestra before undergoing the formative experience of his life, working with the Jimmie Lunceford band from 1939 to 1942. Replacing Sy Oliver as arranger, conductor and trumpet soloist, Wilson learned his craft in the Lunceford band, after which he took off for Los Angeles to play with the bands of Les Hite, Benny Carter and Willie Smith. Wilson organized his first big band in 1944, which sported an intriguing blend of swing and bop and featured musicians like Melba Liston and Snooky Young. But it only lasted three years, and after playing for Count Basie and Dizzy Gillespie in 1947-48, Wilson quit the music business for a while to try his hand in the grocery trade. After a tentative return as a bandleader in 1952, it took awhile for Wilson to gradually ease his way back into jazz full-time; he even made appearances as a TV actor.

In 1961, after experimenting with a workshop band for four years, Wilson formed a new orchestra which made a string of successful albums for the Pacific Jazz label throughout the '60s, featuring soloists like Harold Land, Teddy Edwards, Bud Shank, Jack Wilson and Joe Pass. One tune that he wrote for the *Moment of*

Truth album, "Viva Tirado" (later reprised on *Live and Swinging*) became a surprise hit single for the Latin rock group El Chicano in 1970. He scored films and TV programs, worked as an arranger on recordings by singers such as Al Hibbler, Bobby Darin and Johnny Hartman, contributed arrangements to the Duke Ellington band, and wrote music for the Los Angeles Philharmonic. He also started a series of hugely entertaining and informative classes in jazz history at California State University, Northridge (then San Fernando Valley State College) in 1970, moving them to UCLA in 1992, and had his own radio program on Los Angeles' KBCA-FM from 1969 to 1976.

Wilson continued to lead big bands off and on through the 1980s and '90s, as well as running the orchestra for Redd Foxx's NBC shows and serving as one of the Los Angeles jazz scene's more revered elder statesmen. In 1995, he commemorated more than half a century as a leader by releasing *State Street Sweet*, a vigorous tribute to the durability of his work, and scoring a solid hit at the Playboy Jazz Festival. —*Richard S. Ginell*

Cruisin' with Gerald / 1945-1947 / Sounds of Swing ✦✦✦✦
Bandleader Gerald Wilson's Los Angeles recordings of 1945-49 are among the rarest of his career. Of the 38 selections that he recorded for such labels as Excelsior, Black & White, United Artists and Aladdin, 26 were instrumentals and 15 of those are on this collector's LP plus a vocal by Estelle Edson. Wilson used some of the top Los Angeles-based players of the era along with a few ringers; among his sidemen are trumpeters Snooky Young, Emmett Berry and Hobart Dotson, trombonists Melba Liston and Vic Dickenson, saxophonists Eddie "Lockjaw" Davis (on an early 1945 session) and Buddy Collette and pianist Jimmy Bunn. The music, mostly originals but also including versions of "Come Sunday," "One O'Clock Jump" and "Cruisin' with Cab," is often quite boppish. These little-known recordings are quite interesting and will hopefully be reissued on CD eventually. —*Scott Yanow*

You Better Believe It / Sep. 1961-Oct. 1961 / Pacific Jazz ✦✦✦✦

The Best of the Gerald Wilson Orchestra / Sep. 1961-1969 / Pacific Jazz ✦✦✦
This out-of-print LP (put out in 1978) gives one a fine sampling of the 1960s Pacific Jazz recordings of Gerald Wilson. Most of the bandleader-arranger's "greatest hits" are here including "Blues for Yna Yna," "Milestones," "Equinox" and "Viva Tirado"; those four songs were still part of Wilson's repertoire in the mid-'90s. Although it is preferable to acquire Wilson's complete big band albums, only a few have thus far been reissued on CD, making this an album worth picking up if it can be found. —*Scott Yanow*

● **Moment of Truth** / Sep. 1962 / Pacific Jazz ✦✦✦✦✦
Gerald Wilson's Pacific Jazz albums of the 1960s were arguably the most significant of his career. This CD reissues his second record of the period and has among its highlights the original version of "Viva Tirado" (a catchy number made into a surprise pop hit by El Chicano later in the decade) and a driving rendition of "Milestones"; the other seven songs (six of which are Wilson's originals) are also quite enjoyable. Among the more notable soloists are trumpeter Carmell Jones, both Teddy Edwards and Harold Land on tenors, guitarist Joe Pass and pianist Jack Wilson. Recommended. —*Scott Yanow*

Portraits / 1963 / Pacific Jazz ✦✦✦✦
This fine CD reissue of an earlier LP features the colorful Gerald Wilson Orchestra. Wilson's arrangements have always been distinctive, and his reworkings of "So What" and "'Round Midnight" (which are performed here along with five of the leader's lesser-known originals) are inventive. With such top L.A.-based players as trumpeter Carmell Jones, Teddy Edwards and Harold Land on tenors, guitarist Joe Pass and pianist Jack Wilson, this was a very impressive unit, although now somewhat underrated. —*Scott Yanow*

On Stage / Jan. 13, 1965+Mar. 16, 1965 / Pacific Jazz ✦✦✦✦
Arranger Gerald Wilson led one of the finest big bands of the 1960s. This out-of-print LP features the Los Angeles orchestra in top form although, since it is a studio album, its title is inaccurate. Trumpeter Bobby Bryant, tenors Teddy Edwards and Harold Land, altoist Anthony Ortega, guitarist Joe Pass and (on five of the nine cuts) the organ of Jack Wilson are the dominant solo voices, but it is the charts that give this orchestra its own personality. Highlights include "Who Can I Turn To," "Lighthouse Blues" and "Perdido." —*Scott Yanow*

Feelin' Kinda Blues / 1966 / Pacific Jazz ✦✦✦✦
This live CD reissue features the 1960s Gerald Wilson Orchestra in prime form. Surprisingly Wilson did not contribute any of the ten songs (which are highlighted by "When I'm Feeling Kinda Blue," "Freddie Freeloader," "Watermelon Man" and "Well, Son Shuffle"), but his arrangements make all of the pieces sound fresh and swinging. The main soloists are tenor saxophonist Teddy Edwards (who is featured on seven of the songs), trumpeters Bobby Bryant and Freddie Hill, guitarist Dennis Budimir and altoist Anthony Ortega. —*Scott Yanow*

The Golden Sword / 1966 / Discovery ✦✦✦✦✦
This sadly out-of-print LP (a Pacific Jazz release last put out by Discovery in 1984) has long been considered a classic. Bandleader-arranger Gerald Wilson has always been a great admirer of bullfighters and the powerful "Carlos" from this album became a permanent part of his repertoire. The other nine selections also pay tribute to aspects of Mexico and the soloists (which include trumpeters Jimmy Owens, Conte Candoli and Nat Meeks, Roy Ayers or Victor Feldman on vibes, guitarist Laurindo Almeido and the tenors of Harold Land and Teddy Edwards) seem quite inspired by the material. One of Gerald Wilson's most memorable albums. —*Scott Yanow*

California Soul / 1968 / Pacific Jazz ✦✦
Gerald Wilson's next-to-last Pacific Jazz release is one of his weakest due in large part to the commercial material. Certainly when one thinks of such songs as "Light My Fire," the "Lullaby from Rosemary's Baby," "Sunshine of Your Love" and "Down Here on the Ground," the Gerald Wilson big band is not the first group that comes to mind. Although such players as vibraphonist Bobby Hutcherson, tenor saxophonist Harold Land and trumpeter Bobby Bryant have short solos, the overall results are quite forgettable. It is doubtful if this LP will be reissued anytime in the near future. —*Scott Yanow*

Lomelin / Mar. 13, 1981-Mar. 14, 1981 / Discovery ✦✦✦✦
Arranger-bandleader Gerald Wilson's first recording in 12 years resulted in the first of his four albums for Albert Marx's Discovery/Trend labels. Wilson's arranging style was essentially the same as it had been in the 1960s and his large big band featured many alumni, plus some other younger L.A.-based jazzmen. *Lomelin* (the title cut is dedicated to a bullfighter) has six newly written Wilson originals including tributes to his son, Zubin Mehta ("Blues for Zubin") and Marx ("You Know"). The music is straightahead with plenty of solo space for such players as pianist Mike Wofford, trumpeter Oscar Brashear, guitarist Shuggie Otis and the tenors of Ernie Watts, Harold Land and Jerome Richardson. —*Scott Yanow*

Jessica / Nov. 29, 1982+Dec. 8, 1982 / Trend ✦✦✦✦✦
For these 1982 sessions, arranger Gerald Wilson and his big band perform three Duke Ellington compositions, "Blues, Bones and Bobby" (a feature for trumpeter Bobby Bryant), the title cut and one departure: a funky "Getaway" which was made famous by Earth, Wind & Fire. With tenor saxophonist Ernie Watts, pianist Gerald Wiggins, trumpeter Oscar Brashear, tenorman Harold Land and (on "Don't Get Around Much Anymore") trumpeter Snooky Young taking some significant solo space, this is a highly enjoyable and consistently swinging album. —*Scott Yanow*

Calafia / Nov. 29, 1984-Nov. 30, 1984 / Trend ✦✦✦✦

Jenna / Jun. 27, 1989-Jun. 28, 1989 / Discovery ✦✦✦✦✦
Gerald Wilson's fourth and final recording for Albert Marx's Discovery and Trend labels features him revisiting a couple of his 1960s charts ("Carlos" and "Blues for Yna Yna") and paying tribute on four songs to his period with Jimmy Lunceford ("Yarddog Mazurka," "48 Years Later," "Lunceford Special" and "Margie"). In addition, Wilson's big band plays a head arrangement of "Flying Home" and he debuts such pieces as "Jenna," "Back to the Roots" and "B-Bop and the Song." The soloists include trumpeters Oscar Brashear, Ron Barrows and Snooky Young, Carl Randall on tenor, altoists Danny House and Randall Willis, trombonist Thurman Green and Anthony Wilson (Gerald's son) on guitar among others. This CD is an excellent all-round showcase for both Gerald Wilson's arrangements and his superior big band. —*Scott Yanow*

State Street Sweet / 1994 / MAMA ✦✦✦✦✦
Bandleader/arranger Gerald Wilson's first recording in several years is a success. He revisits "Carlos" (featuring trumpeter Ron Barrows) and "Lighthouse Blues" and performs some newer originals including "State Street Sweet," "Lakeshore Drive" and "Jammin' in C." With such soloists as trumpeters Barrows, Bobby Shew, Tony Lujan and Snooky Young, altoist Randall Willis, tenors Louis Taylor, Plas Johnson (showcased on "Come Back to Sorrento") and Carl Randall, pianist Brian O'Rourke and guitarists Anthony Wilson and Eric Otis, this edition of the Gerald Wilson Orchestra is quite strong but it is the leader's colorful and distinctive arrangements that give the band its personality. Recommended. —*Scott Yanow*

Jack Wilson

b. Aug. 3, 1936, Chicago, IL
Piano / Soul Jazz, Hard Bop, Latin Jazz, Post-Bop, Cool, Soul
Jack Wilson was a talented, if understated, mainstream jazz pianist. Wilson's music had elements of hard bop, swing, cool jazz and soul-jazz, and it was all tied together by his tasteful playing.

Wilson was born in Chicago, but his family moved to Fort Wayne, IN, when he was seven years old. Two years later, Wilson began to learn piano. Between 1949 and 1954, he studied with Carl Atkinson at the Fort Wayne College of Music. During that time, he became infatuated with the George Sharing Quintet. He picked up the baritone saxophone, which he played in the high school band, and then began playing locally with a small combo he led. Just before his 15th birthday, he became the youngest member of the Fort Wayne Musicians Union. When he was 17, he played as a substitute in James Moody's band for a couple of weeks. Following his high school graduation, he attended the University of Indiana for a year and a half. At the school, he met Freddie Hubbard, Slide Hampton, Dave Baker and Jerry Coker.

Once he left college, he moved to Columbus, OH, where he worked with local musicians, including Nancy Wilson and Roland Kirk. After spending a year in Columbus, he moved to Atlantic City, where he led the house band at the Cotton Club. Dinah Washington passed through the club while Wilson worked there and invited him to join her band. He accepted the offer and spent a year performing with her, eventually moving to Chicago in 1958. A year later, he made his recording debut as a sideman for bassist Richard Davis. The same day he cut his first session, he was drafted into the Army. In the service, Wilson became the music director for the Third Army Area and played tenor saxophone in the Army band. Upon his discharge in 1961, he returned to Washington's band. After spending another year in her band, Wilson decided to settle in Hollywood, where he kept busy, playing with combos, supporting a number of singers—including Julie London, Sammy Davis, Jr., Sarah Vaughan, Eartha Kitt and Sonny & Cher—and working on film and telvision soundtracks, both as a sideman (playing both piano and organ) and composer.

In 1963, Wilson recorded his first session as a leader, *The Jack Wilson Quartet,* which was released on Atlantic. It was followed in 1964 by *Two Sides.* After cutting *Brazilian Mancini* for Vault in 1965, he moved to Blue Note in 1966, recording *Something Personal* in August of that year. It was the first of three albums for Blue Note—*Easterly Winds* followed in 1967, *Song for My Daughter* in 1968. After the release of *Song for My Daughter,* Wilson remained quiet for nearly ten years, apart from the occasional date supporting Esther Phillips. In the late '70s, he returned to action as a sideman and leader, recording four albums—*Innovations, Autumn Sunset, Margo's Theme, Corcovado*—for Discovery. He continued to gig as a sideman into the early '80s, playing with the likes of Lorez Alexandria, Tutti Camarata and Eddie Harris, before quietly disappearing from active duty again. —*Stephen Thomas Erlewine*

The Jack Wilson Quartet / Feb. 6, 1963 / Atlantic ✦✦✦✦

Two Sides / May 13, 1964 / Atlantic ✦✦✦✦
Trio with Leroy Vinnegar on bass and Philly Joe Jones on drums. Good swinging stuff from West Coast piano legend. —*Michael G. Nastos*

Brazilian Mancini / 1965 / Vault ✦✦✦

● **Something Personal** / Aug. 9, 1966-Aug. 10, 1966 / Blue Note ✦✦✦✦✦
On this CD reissue, pianist Jack Wilson's first of three albums for Blue Note, the emphasis is on his interaction with vibraphonist Roy Ayers. Some of the selections recall the Modern Jazz Quartet, while a few of the other songs look toward Herbie Hancock and Bobby Hutcherson. The other musicians on the date are bassist Ray Brown (who plays cello on two numbers that include Charles Williams, Jr., on bass) and drummer Varney Barlow. In two cases (Ornette Coleman's "The Sphinx" and Wilson's "Shosh"), complex melody statements are succeeded by disappointingly conventional chordal jams, but in general this album is an excellent showcase for the often-overlooked Jack Wilson. —*Scott Yanow*

Easterly Winds / Oct. 1967 / Blue Note ✦✦✦✦
Easterly Winds provides an excellent contrast to Jack Wilson's first Blue Note album, *Somethin' Personal.* Where his label debut was cool and romantic, *Easterly Winds* is a brassy, funky collection of soul-jazz and hard bop with instant appeal. Wilson keeps the tone fairly diverse, both in his originals and covers. After hitting hard with the funky opening pair "Do It" and "On Children" (both of which illustrate that he was familiar with contemporary soul), he quiets the mood with a nice version of Johnny Mandel's "A Time for Love." On the second half, he turns in soul-jazz ("Easterly Winds"), straight hard bop ("Frank's Tune") and the charmingly lyrical "Nirvanna." Throughout it all, Wilson is subtle and tasteful, allowing trumpeter Lee Morgan and alto saxophonist Jackie McLean their time in the spotlight; trombonist Garnett Brown has a couple of nice moments as well, while bassist Bob Cranshaw and Billy Higgins lend solid rhythmic support. It's another impressive, enjoyable effort from one of the most underrated pianists on Blue Note's '60s roster. —*Stephen Thomas Erlewine*

Song for My Daughter / Sep. 1968 / Blue Note ✦✦✦
On *Song for My Daughter,* his third record for Blue Note, Jack Wilson "changed with the times," to paraphrase one of the record's songs. Like many of his peers on the label, Wilson pursued a pop direction as the '60s drew to a close, which meant he covered pop hits like "Scarborough Fair/Canticle" and "Stormy," and that he recorded the album with a large band augmented by a string section. It is a testa-

ment to Wilson's strengths as a pianist that he doesn't get lost in this heavy-handed setting and manages to contribute some typically graceful moments, including the lovely title song. Nevertheless, the song selection is a little uneven, and there isn't much room for the band to improvise, which makes the album of marginal interest to serious jazz listeners. Audiences that aren't quite so concerned with such matters will find this an engaging pop-jazz album. Although the production has dated somewhat, it remains a pleasant artifact of its time, and fans of that sound should search for it. —*Stephen Thomas Erlewine*

Matt Wilson

Drums / Avant-Garde, Post-Bop
Flexible, subtle drummer Matt Wilson gained a strong reputation with his debut recording as a leader, a 1996 set for Palmetto that prominently features tenor saxophonist Dewey Redman. Wilson started playing drums in grade school; he studied at Wichita State University and spent time in the Midwest, both as a freelancer and as a teacher. In 1987, he moved to Boston, where he was soon playing with the Either/Orchestra and Charlie Kohlhase's Quintet. In 1992, Matt Wilson relocated to New York, where he has since played with Redman, Cecil McBee, Lee Konitz, Fred Hersch, Tim Hagans, Ingrid Jensen and others, appearing on a couple dozen records as a sideman. —*Scott Yanow*

● **As Wave Follows Wave** / Apr. 12, 1996 / Palmetto ✦✦✦✦✦
Drummer Matt Wilson teams up with three rather distinctive voices (tenor saxophonist Dewey Redman, bassist Cecil McBee and on three numbers organist Larry Goldings) for a very interesting set of music that combines together folk melodies, avant-garde improvising and a surprising amount of lyricism. As well as Wilson and McBee play, Redman is the runaway star. Whether stretching out on "Body and Soul" and "I Remember Lona" (the latter is based on "I Remember You") or giving a great deal of feeling to the traditional "Sweet Betsy From Pike" and a tribute to Don Cherry, the underrated tenor is heard in top form. The leader's three short unaccompanied features, Goldings' welcome appearances (pity that he is not on the whole record) and a piece featuring the musicians' voices add to the date's variety. This consistently surprising session is a gem that serves as a perfect introduction to the playing of Dewey Redman and the inventiveness of Matt Wilson. —*Scott Yanow*

Nancy Wilson

b. Feb. 20, 1937, Chillicothe, OH
Vocals / R&B, Pop, Standards, Traditional Pop
Nancy Wilson was among contemporary music's most stylish and sultry vocalists; while often crossing over into the pop and R&B markets—and even hosting her own television variety program—she remained best known as a jazz performer, renowned for her work alongside figures including Cannonball Adderley and George Shearing. Born February 20, 1937 in Chillicothe, OH, Wilson first attracted notice performing the club circuit in nearby Columbus; she quickly earned a growing reputation among jazz players and fans, and she was recording regularly by the late 1950s, eventually signing to Capitol and issuing LPs including 1959's *Like in Love* and *Nancy Wilson with Billy May's Orchestra.* Her dates with Shearing, including 1960s *The Swingin's Mutual,* solidified her standing as a talent on the rise, and her subsequent work with Adderley—arguably her finest recordings—further cemented her growing fame and reputation.

In the years to follow, however, Wilson often moved away from jazz, much to the chagrin of purists; she made numerous albums, many of them properly categorized as pop and R&B outings, and toured extensively, appearing with everyone from Nat King Cole and Sarah Vaughan to Ruth Brown and LaVern Baker. She even hosted her own Emmy-winning variety series for NBC, *The Nancy Wilson Show,* and was a frequent guest performer on other programs; hits of the period included "Tell Me the Truth," "How Glad I Am," "Peace of Mind," and "Now, I'm a Woman." Regardless of how far afield she traveled, Wilson always maintained her connections to the jazz world, and in the 1980s, she returned to the music with a vengeance, working closely with performers including Hank Jones, Art Farmer, Ramsey Lewis and Benny Golson. By the 1990s, she was a favorite among the "new adult contemporary" market, her style ideally suited to the format's penchant for lush, romantic ballads; she also hosted the *Jazz Profiles* series on National Public Radio. —*Jason Ankeny*

● **Swingin's Mutual** / Jun. 29, 1960-Jan. 7, 1961 / Capitol ✦✦✦✦
Singer Nancy Wilson has only made a few recordings throughout her career that are of any interest to jazz listeners. This CD reissue brings back her third album, an excellent collaboration with the George Shearing Quintet. Originally Wilson participated on six of the 12, selections but since five new tracks (with only one vocal) have been added, she is now on seven out of 17. Very much under the influence of Dinah Washington at this point, Nancy Wilson is generally good form, particularly on "The Nearness of You," "All Night Long" and "The Things We Did

Last Summer." As far as the instrumentals by pianist Shearing's Quintet go, "I Remember Clifford," "Evansville," "Blue Lou" and "Lullaby of Birdland" are most memorable, with short solos heard from vibraphonist Warren Chiasson and guitarist Dick Garcia. —*Scott Yanow*

Nancy Wilson & Cannonball Adderley / Sep. 1, 1962 / Capitol ✦✦✦✦✦

Lush Life / May 13, 1967-May 16, 1967 / Blue Note ✦✦✦

This CD does not belong in the Capitol Jazz reissue series, for it contains no jazz. Nancy Wilson's singing on the middle-of-the-road pop session from 1967 is consistently melodramatic, lacks subtlety, contains no improvisation and has enough preplanned cracks in her voice to irritate anyone; her version of "Lush Life" is a low point. The overblown string arrangements by Billy May and Oliver Nelson would have defeated most singers anyway, so this misfire does not deserve a second glance. —*Scott Yanow*

But Beautiful / 1969 / Capitol ✦✦✦✦

Nancy Wilson has been on the fringes of jazz throughout her career, mostly performing middle-of-the-road pop and R&B. Most of her albums were major productions, but this CD reissue is quite different. On a relaxed and tasteful program of ballads (including three previously unreleased numbers), Wilson sounds properly expressive and a bit influenced by Dinah Washington while backed by a flawless rhythm section comprising pianist Hank Jones, guitarist Gene Bertoncini, bassist Ron Carter and drummer Grady Tate. Her performances are straightforward, a little soulful and very mindful of the melody and the lyrics. There is little of jazz interest, but this is superior ballad singing and one of Nancy Wilson's finest recordings to date. —*Scott Yanow*

If I Had My Way / Jul. 15, 1997 / Sony ✦✦✦

The 1990s found Nancy Wilson appealing to what was called the "new adult contemporary" market, as well as the Black adult contemporary audience. The veteran singer wasn't embracing straightahead jazz (something she hadn't done a lot of anyway), although a few songs on *If I Had My Way* contain slightly jazzy touches. At 59, Wilson brings a relaxed confidence to "Loving You, Loving Me," "Hello Like Before" (a Bill Withers tune), "Anything For Your Love," and other pleasant pop and pop/R&B ballads that would work equally well on an Anita Baker album. In fact, one of the CD's producers, Michael Powell, has often worked with Baker. Wilson's appealing voice has held up well, and she demonstrates that she can still be charming on this collection of enjoyable mood music. —*Alex Henderson*

Reuben Wilson

b. Apr. 9, 1935, Mounds, OK

Organ, Keyboards / Soul Jazz, Hard Bop, R&B, Jazz Funk, Fusion

Reuben Wilson was one of many soul-jazz organists to emerge in the late '60s, but he was one of only a handful of new organists from that era to be signed to Blue Note. By that point in the label's history, most of their artists were concentrating on accessible soul-jazz, and while he occasionally strayed outside of the conventions of the genre, Wilson more or less followed their rule. Between 1968 and 1971, he recorded five sessions for the label. None of his records received much acknowledgment at the time, but they were later rediscovered by a new generation of soul-jazz fans, becoming collector's items within acid-jazz and soul-jazz revivalist circles.

Wilson began performing professionally in 1962. A native of Mounds, OK, he moved to Pasadena, CA, as a child, where he attended school with such future jazz musicians as Bobby Hutcherson and Herb Lewis. As a teenager, Wilson began to teach himself to play piano, but his attention was diverted by boxing. When he was 17, he moved to Los Angeles and married a nightclub singer, through whom he met a number of professional musicians. Associating with musicians convinced Wilson to return to music. Instead of pursuing the piano, he decided to take up the organ, and it wasn't long before he became a regular at the Caribbean club, where he played with drummer Eddie Williams, guitarist George Freeman and, eventually, Clifford Scott. He played the Los Angeles circuit for several years before deciding to try his luck in Las Vegas. That venture proved unsuccessful, so he moved back to Los Angeles, where he struck up a friendship with Richard "Groove" Holmes, an organist who would greatly influence his own style.

In December 1966, Wilson relocated to New York, where he formed the soul-jazz trio the Wildare Express with drummer Tommy Derrick. The Wildare Express lasted about six months, playing venues throughout the East Coast and Detroit, and then Wilson decided to concentrate on more complex variations of hard bop and soul-jazz. Eventually, such respected musicians as Grant Green, Roy Haynes and Sam Rivers began playing with Wilson. Around the same time, Blue Note offered the organist a contract based on a demo he had sent the label. *On Broadway*, Reuben Wilson's first album for Blue Note, was a quartet session featuring his old bandmate Derrick recorded in October of 1968. It was followed in March of 1969 by *Love Bug*, which featured contributions from trumpeter Lee Morgan

and guitarist Grant Green. His third album, *Blue Mode*, was cut in December 1969 and offered some of his hottest playing. With his fourth album, 1970s *A Groovy Situation*, Wilson moved in a commercial direction, much like many of his Blue Note peers. In July of 1971, he recorded *Set Us Free*, his final album for the label. Wilson's contract with Blue Note expired after *Set Us Free*, and he moved to Groove Merchant, where he released three albums—*Cisco Kid*, *Bad Stuff*, and *The Sweet Life*—during the mid-'70s. Throughout the decade, he also played on sessions by funk, soul and jazz artists, including a record by the Fatback Band. During the late '70s, he recorded sporadically, eventually retiring from music in the early '80s.

By the late '80s, Wilson's music had been rediscovered by a new generation, listeners who didn't dismiss his records as commercial fluff. Like several of his peers, his late-'60s and '70s records, through sampling, became cornerstones in the newly emerging acid-jazz and jazz-rap genres. Soon, his out-of-print records became collector's items, and his sampled licks were appearing on dance floors throughout England and parts of New York. Eventually, samples of his records were included on hit albums by A Tribe Called Quest, Us3, Brand New Heavies and Nas. In light of all this new attention, Wilson decided to return to performing, and he toured with Guru's Jazzamatazz revue in 1995. He also began writing new material and performing in new groups, including combos he led himself. In 1996, he signed to Hip Bop and released two albums, *Live at SOB's* and *Organ Donor*. The following year, he recorded *Organic Grooves* with Dr. Lonnie Smith and Doug Carn. —*Stephen Thomas Erlewine*

On Broadway / Oct. 4, 1968 / Blue Note ✦✦✦

On Broadway, Reuben Wilson's debut for Blue Note, is a little undistinguished, but it remains an enjoyable exercise in late-'60s soul-jazz. Like many of his peers on Blue Note, Wilson's soul-jazz displayed a familiarity with contemporary soul and R&B styles. Not only does he cover R&B hits like "On Broadway," "Baby I Love You" and "Ain't That Peculiar," but the interplay between Wilson, guitarist Malcolm Riddick and Tommy Derrick occasionally recalls Stax, Motown and uptown soul. The combo, which also features tenor saxophonist Trevor Lawrence, remains rooted in jazz, with the organist demonstrating a Jimmy Smith influence, but the jazz feeling is tempered by a desire to work a groove instead of improvising or attempting to reach new sonic territory. And *On Broadway* is a successful groove record, but in comparison to the two albums that followed, it's a little uneven. —*Stephen Thomas Erlewine*

Love Bug / Mar. 21, 1969+Oct. 31, 1969 / Blue Note ✦✦✦✦

Love Bug was an attempt to establish Reuben Wilson as an organist with either the vision of Larry Young or the fiery style of John Patton, and while it comes up short on both accounts, it nevertheless remains quite enjoyable. Working with an impressive backing band of guitarist Grant Green, trumpeter Lee Morgan, tenor saxophonist George Coleman and drummer Idris Muhammad, Wilson leads his band through a number of soul-jazz workouts, none of which ever really catch fire. Instead of working tight, funky grooves, the quintet tends to spiral off into vaguely experimental territory, which loses sight of the spirit of the song. Still, Green has a number of shining moments, as does Morgan and Coleman—in fact, they tend to overshadow Wilson, who nevertheless turns in a fine performance. Still, there are flashes on *Love Bug*, particularly on "Hot Rod" and the bonus track "Hold On, I'm Comin," that demonstrate the organist coming into his own. —*Stephen Thomas Erlewine*

● **Blue Mode** / Dec. 12, 1969 / Blue Note ✦✦✦✦✦

If *Love Bug* skirted the edges of free jazz and Black power, *Blue Mode* embraces soul-jazz and Memphis funk in no uncertain terms. Opening with the cinematic, stuttering "Bambu" and running through a set of relaxed, funky grooves, including covers of Eddie Floyd's "Knock on Wood" and Edwin Starr's "Twenty-Five Miles," *Blue Mode* isn't strictly a jazz album, but its gritty, jazzy vamps and urban soul-blues make it highly enjoyable. Reuben Wilson has a laid back, friendly style, and his supporting band—tenor saxophonist John Manning, guitarist Melvin Sparks and drummer Tommy Derrick—demonstrate a similarly warm sense of tone. While none of them break through with any improvisations that would satiate hardcore jazz purists, they know how to work a groove, and that's what makes *Blue Mode* a winner. —*Stephen Thomas Erlewine*

A Groovy Situation / Sep. 25, 1970 / Blue Note ✦✦✦

Much like its predecessor, *Blue Mode*, *A Groovy Situation* finds organist Reuben Wilson turning in a funky collection of R&B and pop covers. Supported by guitarist Eddie Diehl, alto saxophonist Earl Turbinton, and drummer Harold White, Wilson runs through familiar soul hits like "If You Let Me Make Love to You (Then Why Can't I Touch You)," "A Groovy Situation" and "Signed, Sealed, Delivered I'm Yours," plus the Turtles hit "Happy Together." With songs like this, there's no question that Wilson is going for a wide audience, and while these smooth, funky grooves will do nothing for jazz purists, it's an entertaining record, and some of the grooves are quite hot indeed. —*Stephen Thomas Erlewine*

Set Us Free / Jul. 23, 1971 / Blue Note ✦✦✦

On *Set Us Free*, his final album for Blue Note, Reuben Wilson decided to break down the borders of his funky soul-jazz and incorporate such flourishes as electric sitar, harps, congas and a dominant, overly arranged vocal choir. These embellishments tend to overshadow Wilson's fine playing, and they also mean that the group can never work up a real groove. Still, there are moments that work on the record, and there's a certain bizarre quality to these overstuffed arrangements that make it an entertaining artifact from the early '70s. —*Stephen Thomas Erlewine*

The Sweet Life / 1972 / Groove Merchant ✦✦✦

Cisco Kid / 1974 / Groove Merchant ✦✦✦

Organ Donor / 1996 / Jazzateria ✦✦✦✦

Teddy Wilson (Theodore Shaw Wilson)

b. Nov. 24, 1912, Austin, TX, **d.** Jul. 31, 1986, New Britain, CT
Piano / Swing

Teddy Wilson was the definitive swing pianist, a solid and impeccable soloist whose smooth and steady style was more accessible to the general public than Earl Hines or Art Tatum. He picked up early experience playing with Speed Webb in 1929 and appearing on some Louis Armstrong recordings in 1933. Discovered by John Hammond, Willie joined Benny Carter's band and recorded with the Chocolate Dandies later that year. In 1935 he began leading a series of classic small-group recordings with swing all-stars that on many occasions featured Billie Holiday. That was also the year that an informal jam session with Benny Goodman and Gene Krupa resulted in the formation of the Benny Goodman Trio (Lionel Hampton made the group a quartet the following year). Although he was a special added attraction rather than a regular member of the orchestra, Wilson's public appearances with Goodman broke important ground in the long struggle against segregation.

Between his own dates, many recordings with Benny Goodman's small groups and a series of piano solos, Teddy Wilson recorded a large number of gems during the second half of the 1930s. He left BG in 1939 to form his own big band but, despite some fine records, it folded in 1940. Wilson led a sextet at Cafe Society during 1940-44, taught music at Julliard during the summers of 1945-52, appeared on radio shows and recorded regularly with a trio, as a soloist and with pick-up groups in addition to having occasional reunions with Goodman. Teddy Wilson's style never changed and he played very similar in 1985 to how he sounded in 1935; no matter, the enthusiasm and solid sense of swing were present up until the end. —*Scott Yanow*

1934-1935 / May 1934-Dec. 1935 / Classics ✦✦✦✦✦

There have been several overlapping reissue programs covering the material in the Classics series, especially the many Teddy Wilson recordings in which the pianist accompanied Billie Holiday. This particular CD has Wilson's first five sessions as a leader. He is heard on four fairly rare piano solos from 1934 (a year before he became a member of the Benny Goodman Trio), six other solos from October 7 and November 22, 1935, and on two band dates that resulted in nine numbers (including seven Billie Holiday vocals); the sidemen include trumpeter Roy Eldridge, tenorman Ben Webster and (on three songs) clarinetist Benny Goodman. Lady Day's "What a Little Moonlight Can Do" and "I Wished on the Moon" are famous classics. —*Scott Yanow*

1935-1936 / Dec. 3, 1935-Aug. 24, 1936 / Classics ✦✦✦✦✦

The second CD in Classics' Teddy Wilson series features the definitive swing pianist on two piano solos and leading all-star groups. There are seven generally familiar Billie Holiday vocals (including classic renditions of "I Cried for You" and "These Foolish Things"), a pair from Ella Fitzgerald (her first recordings outside of the Chick Webb Orchestra), two rare ones from Helen Ward, a vocal by Roy Eldridge on a heated "Mary Had a Little Lamb" and seven instrumentals. The strong supporting cast includes such players as altoist Johnny Hodges, trumpeters Frankie Newton, Jonah Jones and Eldridge, trombonist Benny Morton, clarinetist Buster Bailey, tenorman Chu Berry and baritonist Harry Carney; Benny Goodman makes guest appearances on the two Helen Ward sides. Classic music, although most of it is also easily available elsewhere. —*Scott Yanow*

1936-1937 / Aug. 24, 1936-Mar. 31, 1937 / Classics ✦✦✦✦✦

Swing collectors may very well find the Teddy Wilson series on Classics to be a bit troubling for, although it logically reissues all of the great swing pianist's recordings as a leader in order (skipping the alternate takes), many of the sides (those featuring Billie Holiday) are also available on Columbia's complete Lady Day program. This particular CD not only has 16 Holiday vocals (including "The Way You Look Tonight," "Pennies from Heaven," a version of "I Can't Give You Anything but Love" in which she shows off the influence of Louis Armstrong, and four won-

derful titles from her first recorded meeting with tenor saxophonist Lester Young), but also three instrumentals and two rarities apiece from singers Red Harper and Midge Williams, which are sure to frustrate completists. —*Scott Yanow*

★ **And His All-Stars [Columbia]** / 1936-1940 / Columbia ✦✦✦✦✦

Pianist Teddy Wilson's most famous recordings of the 1930s as a leader are the ones in which he is joined by Billie Holiday, so it is a pleasure to have a double-LP dominated by the lesser-known—but often quite exciting—instrumentals performed by his all-star groups. Holiday is heard on six of these selections and Ella Fitzgerald on two others, but otherwise, the emphasis is on the hot soloing of such major swing stars as trumpeters Cootie Williams, Roy Eldridge, Jonah Jones, Frankie Newton, Buck Clayton, Harry James (heard at his best on "Just a Mood" and "Honeysuckle Rose") and Bill Coleman, clarinetists Benny Goodman, Buster Bailey and Pee Wee Russell, altoist Johnny Hodges, baritonist Harry Carney and the tenors of Ben Webster and Chu Berry among others. Until this music is reissued domestically on CD, this two-fer is well worth searching for. —*Scott Yanow*

1937 / Mar. 31, 1937-Aug. 29, 1937 / Classics ✦✦✦✦✦

For this Classics CD (one in a series of Teddy Wilson releases that reissue all of the pianist's early recordings as a leader), Billie Holiday is featured on nine of the titles including "I'll Get By," "Mean to Me," "Foolin' Myself" and "Easy Living"; all of those gems also feature tenor saxophonist Lester Young. Much rarer are three songs with singer Helen Ward, a vocal by Frances Hunt ("Big Apple"), three by the forgotten vocalist Boots Castle and five instrumentals. It is a pity that the selections without Holiday were not reissued separately, since the Lady Day performances are generally quite common. Such immortal sidemen are heard from as Young, trumpeters Cootie Williams, Harry James and Buck Clayton, altoist Johnny Hodges, baritonist Harry Carney and clarinetists Buster Bailey and Benny Goodman; this music is essential in one form or another. —*Scott Yanow*

1937-1938 / Sep. 5, 1937-Apr. 28, 1938 / Classics ✦✦✦✦✦

This Classics CD traces pianist Teddy Wilson's recordings during a seven-month period. He backs singer Billie Holiday on eight memorable performances (including "My Man," "Can't Help Lovin' Dat Man," "When You're Smiling" and "I Can't Believe That You're in Love with Me"), is showcased on a pair of piano solos, accompanies singer Sally Gooding on four songs that were not initially released until the 1980s, and is heard on four almost-as-rare numbers with vocalist Nan Wynn. Most significant among the occasional instrumentals are a few tunes (including the two part "Just a Mood" and "Honeysuckle Rose") that Wilson performs in an exquisite quartet with trumpeter Harry James, xylophonist Red Norvo and bassist John Simmons. Among the other sidemen heard on this valuable CD are trumpeters Buck Clayton, Hot Lips Page and Bobby Hackett, clarinetist Pee Wee Russell, the tenors of Chu Berry and Lester Young and altoist Tab Smith. —*Scott Yanow*

1938 / Apr. 28, 1938-Nov. 28, 1938 / Classics ✦✦✦✦

In addition to ten Billie Holiday vocals that are easily available elsewhere (best is "They Say"), this CD has some Wilson piano solos, a few rare Nan Wynn vocals and a band instrumental of "Jungle Love" with cornetist Bobby Hackett, clarinetist Pee Wee Russell and altoist Johnny Hodges. Excellent music, but the best tracks have been reissued many times, making this CD of less interest than most of the other Classics. —*Scott Yanow*

Teddy Wilson (1938-1941) / Jul. 29, 1938-Apr. 11, 1941 / Tax ✦✦✦✦✦

This Tax LP contains an excellent cross section of pianist Teddy Wilson's work from the late '30s/early '40s. Wilson is heard with an all-star septet that includes trumpeter Jonah Jones, altoist Benny Carter and tenor saxophonist Ben Webster backing four fine vocals from the forgotten but talented Nan Wynn, taking four piano solos in 1938-39, playing "Lady Be Good," accompanying three fine Helen Ward vocals with an octet in 1940, and jamming with a trio in 1941. Throughout these lesser-known performances, Wilson is heard at his prime, setting the standard for swing piano. —*Scott Yanow*

1939 / Jan. 27, 1939-Sep. 12, 1939 / Classics ✦✦✦✦✦

This CD has quite a bit of variety. Teddy Wilson is featured on four of his better piano solos, backs Billie Holiday on one session (which resulted in superior versions of "More than You Know" and "Sugar") and has some fine solo space for altoist Benny Carter and trumpeter Roy Eldridge) and is heard on 13 selections with his new (and unfortunately short-lived) big band. The Teddy Wilson Orchestra was impeccable, tasteful and swinging (just like its leader) but, despite the presence of such soloists as trumpeter Harold "Shorty" Baker and tenor saxophonist Ben Webster, it never really stood a chance in the competitive swing world of 1939; the orchestra would only record eight additional titles. However the music on this CD is quite enjoyable and not as common as most of the recordings reissued by the Classics label. —*Scott Yanow*

Teddy Wilson and His Big Band (1939-1940) / May 10, 1939-Jan. 18, 1940 / Tax ✦✦✦✦✦

Although he was one of the most popular and influential pianists of the swing era, Teddy Wilson (like Coleman Hawkins and Jack Teagarden) was unsuccessful at keeping a big band together. As with Hawkins and Teagarden, the reason Wilson's orchestra did not catch on is obvious when one hears its recordings; the band did not have a strong personality of its own or a purpose for its existence. This Tax LP contains 16 performances by this orchestra which, due to its strong soloists (including Wilson, trumpeter Shorty Baker and tenor saxophonist Ben Webster who is heard shortly before he joined Duke Ellington), high musicianship, and a few memorable performances (including a version of "In the Mood" much different than Glenn Miller's), is well worth searching for. —*Scott Yanow*

Solo Piano: Keystone Transcriptions 1939-1940 / 1939 / Storyville ✦✦✦✦

The release of this 1997 CD was a special event, for none of the 26 piano solos by Teddy Wilson had ever been released before. Made as radio transcriptions, the performances are all quite brief (none reach the three-minute mark) but are particularly valuable, as 12 of the selections are Wilson originals, the majority of which were never recorded again. The pianist also performs swinging versions of a variety of standards and was clearly in his early prime when cutting these highly enjoyable sides. —*Scott Yanow*

Teddy Wilson & His 1939 Big Band / 1939-Feb. 9, 1945 / Fanfare ✦✦✦

Despite its title, there is more to this LP than performances by Teddy Wilson's orchestra. The first side does contain a fine aircheck from 1939 by the big band with solos from trumpeter Shorty Baker and tenor saxophonist Ben Webster in addition to the pianist/leader, but the remainder of this album finds Wilson featured with studio groups on radio shows from 1944-45, some of which also include vibraphonist Red Norvo. Solid swing from one of jazz's greats. —*Scott Yanow*

B Flat Swing / 1944 / Jazz Archives ✦✦✦✦✦

One of pianist Teddy Wilson's lesser-known bands is the sextet he led during 1940-44, shortly after his orchestra broke up and before he cut back to a trio. This unit, well featured on this Jazz Archives LP, by 1944 featured trumpeter Emmett Berry, trombonist Benny Morton and clarinetist Edmond Hall, and played swinging versions of standards. The contents of this LP are taken from a session recorded for play on radio, and unlike the studio recordings of the era, many of these performances are over four minutes long. —*Scott Yanow*

Teddy Wilson Sextet: 1944, Vol. 2 / Jun. 15, 1944-Dec. 22, 1944 / Jazz Archives ✦✦✦✦

This Jazz Archives LP, a follow-up to *"B" Flat Swing,* features the great swing pianist Teddy Wilson in a variety of settings from the same time period. He is heard on four songs with the sextet that also performed on the latter LP, jamming with trumpeter Emmett Berry, trombonist Benny Morton and clarinetist Edmond Hall. However, seven other selections star either the fiery Roy Eldridge, the exciting Charlie Shavers or the great Cootie Williams on trumpet in Wilson's unit with vibraphonist Red Norvo, and "Sweet Lorraine" finds the pianist showcased as the lead voice with Paul Barron's radio orchestra. Timeless music. —*Scott Yanow*

Teddy Wilson All-Star Sessions / Dec. 18, 1944-Aug. 14, 1945 / Musicraft ✦✦✦✦

Teddy Wilson, the definitive swing pianist, led a variety of interesting groups during 1940-45 before he reverted to touring with trios. In late 1944, he began to record for Musicraft, and this LP contains the earliest of that series. Eight selections feature the exciting unit that he had with trumpeter Charlie Shavers and vibraphonist Red Norvo; two numbers also have vocals by Maxine Sullivan. The remainder of this LP (four songs plus three alternate takes from August 14, 1945) finds Wilson heading an all-star group with trumpeter Buck Clayton and tenor saxophonist Ben Webster. Throughout this highly enjoyable set are many fine examples of high-quality swing. —*Scott Yanow*

Isn't It Romantic / 1944-1946 / Musicraft ✦✦✦

Time After Time / 1945 / Musicraft ✦✦✦✦

The second in a series of four LPs that reissue the bulk of pianist Teddy Wilson's Musicraft recordings of the mid-'40s features the great swing pianist in four different settings. Wilson plays in an octet that also includes trumpeter Buck Clayton and tenor saxophonist Don Byas; in a quartet with the extroverted tenor of Charlie Ventura; with a quartet showcasing trumpeter Buck Clayton; and also heading a trio. In the early stage of her career, Sarah Vaughan is outstanding during her four appearances, particularly on "September Song" and "Don't Worry About Me." Despite the rise of bebop, Teddy Wilson's style remained unchanged, as he shows on such romps as "I Want to Be Happy," "Sheik of Araby" and "Chinatown My Chinatown." —*Scott Yanow*

Sunny Morning / 1946 / Musicraft ✦✦✦✦

The third of four LPs released by Discovery that document Teddy Wilson's recordings for Musicraft, this set contains a dozen of his piano solos from 1946 when he

was involved much more in teaching and performing on the radio than in making public appearances. These concise performances (all under three minutes) are melodic and swing lightly, showing why Wilson's influence reached beyond jazz and affected middle-of-the-road pianists such as Frankie Carle. —*Scott Yanow*

★ **Central Avenue Blues** / 1948 / Vintage Jazz ✦✦✦✦✦

Teddy Wilson was the definitive swing pianist, an influential stylist still best-known for his association with Benny Goodman; however Wilson had a long career after his years with Goodman. This CD mostly features him with his brilliant sextet of 1944-45, which also includes trumpeter Charlie Shavers and vibraphonist Red Norvo playing concise versions of swing standards. Much of this music had previously been issued but never as complete as on this worthy set. Also here are three Wilson performances from a V-Disc session that features trumpeter Joe Thomas and clarinetist Edmund Hall and two other numbers in which the pianist is backed by a radio orchestra. —*Scott Yanow*

The Complete Verve Recordings of the Teddy Wilson Trio / Dec. 16, 1952-1957 / Mosaic ✦✦✦✦

By 1952, Teddy Wilson's flawless swing style had already been fully formed for at least 17 years, and it would not change at all during the remaining three decades of his life. Wilson's performances were predictably excellent, but predictable nonetheless. This limited-edition five-CD set has all of the pianist's Verve trio recordings, which includes six-and-a-half former LPs (the half was an appearance at the 1957 Newport Jazz Festival), a set only released previously in Japan, and a live date that had never come out before. Wilson is teamed with bassists John Simmons, Aaron Bell, Arvell Shaw, Milt Hinton, Geme Ramey and Al Lucas and Buddy Rich, Denzil Best, J.C. Heard, Stick Evans, Jo Jones, Specs Powell, Roy Burnes and Bert Dahlander in the drum slot. A version of "Sweet Georgia Brown" from the Newport Festival adds baritonist Gerry Mulligan. No real surprises occur, and the music, although quite pleasing, is best heard in small doses. —*Scott Yanow*

"Gypsy" in Jazz / Sep. 3, 1959 / Columbia ✦✦✦

Pianist Teddy Wilson interprets a dozen songs from the musical *Gypsy* with his 1959 trio (bassist Arvell Shaw and drummer Bert Dahlender). None of these songs became standards ("Everything's Coming up Roses" and "Let Me Entertain You" came close), but it is interesting to hear Wilson get away from his usual swing repertoire and uplift this music with his sparkling style. This long out-of-print LP is difficult to find. —*Scott Yanow*

Live at Santa Tecla / 1964 / Classic Jazz ✦✦✦

For this Italian session, pianist Teddy Wilson is joined by bassist Lino Patruno and drummer Carlo Sola for a run-through on a variety of standards. A pair of Ellington two-song medleys, three songs from *Porgy and Bess* and the usual repertoire (including a fresh version of "After You've Gone") form a predictable but enjoyable set by the definitive swing pianist. —*Scott Yanow*

Air Mail Special / Jun. 1967 / Black Lion ✦✦✦✦

After several years of near-silence on records (only one album as a leader during 1960-66), Teddy Wilson recorded on a much more regular basis for the next 15 years. This Black Lion set (partly cut on the same day as the *Stomping at the Savoy* CD) matches the great swing pianist with a few of London's best (clarinetist Dave Shepherd, vibraphonist Ronnie Gleaves, bassist Peter Chapman and drummer Johnny Richardson) on a variety of superior standards. The music, if a bit predictable, is quite enjoyable. —*Scott Yanow*

Stomping at the Savoy / Jun. 18, 1967 / Black Lion ✦✦✦✦

Strange as it seems, Teddy Wilson only made one record as a leader during 1960-66. His playing had not declined in the slightest, but the veteran swing pianist's style was overlooked in favor of newer players and, although still a household name in the jazz world, he was somewhat neglected. In 1967, with this excellent CD and its companion, *Air Mail Special,* Wilson returned to a more regular recording schedule. Recorded in London, this studio session finds Wilson joined by some fine English musicians (including clarinetist Dave Shepherd and vibraphonist Ronnie Gleaves) for a spirited run-through of swing standards. Although the date on the CD says 1969, it is definitely 1967. —*Scott Yanow*

Masters of Jazz, Vol. 11 / Dec. 1968-Jun. 1980 / Storyville ✦✦✦✦✦

Storyville's *Masters of Jazz* series (which has since been reissued on CD) features swing stars playing material that has sometimes been released as part of other sets. In the case of Teddy Wilson, the two sessions that are included here are not on other releases. Wilson's swing piano style was unchanged through the years (at least since the mid-'30s) so these two dates (both recorded in Copenhagen) are equally rewarding, with fine backup from either Jesper Lundgaard or Niels Pedersen on bass and Ed Thigpen or Biarne Rostvold on drums. —*Scott Yanow*

In Europe 1968 / 1968 / Prestige ✦✦✦

This fine LP was only Teddy Wilson's second American record to be released since 1959; his swing piano was not "in style" during the 1960s although he was still very much in his prime. Joined by the young bassist Niels Pedersen and drummer Bjarne Rostvold, Wilson is in good form on some familar tunes including several (such as "My Silent Love," "Serenata" and "Serenade in Blue") that he did not play all that often. *—Scott Yanow*

Swingin' Piano / Apr. 14, 1970-Apr. 16, 1970 / Piccadilly ✦✦✦✦✦
One of pianist Teddy Wilson's lesser-known studio dates, this reissue of a set recorded in Stockholm for Sonet (neither recording dates nor personnel are listed on the LP) find him joined by a sextet that also includes clarinetist Ove Lind, vibraphonist Lars Erstrand and guitarist Rolf Berg. All 11 selections were composed by Swedish musicians, giving Wilson the opportunity to play fresh material. This set is worth searching for, even if it looks like a bootleg. *—Scott Yanow*

Meets Eiki Kitamura / Oct. 1970 / Storyville ✦✦✦
For this session recorded in Japan, the masterful swing pianist Teddy Wilson is teamed up with one of Japan's top musicians, the swing clarinetist Eiji Kitamura. Kitamura mixes together the influences of Benny Goodman and Buddy DeFranco on these ten swing standards. No real surprises occur on the LP, but the music, which also features vibraphonist Ichiro Masuda, can be enjoyed by swing fans. *—Scott Yanow*

☆ **With Billie in Mind** / May 1972 / Chiaroscuro ✦✦✦✦✦
The concept seemed so logical that it was surprising that no one else had thought of it earlier. Producer Hank O'Neal suggested to the veteran swing pianist Teddy Wilson that he record a set of Billie Holiday tunes since Lady Day had cut many of her greatest sides with Wilson in the 1930s. This solo CD, which was originally a 14-song LP, has been expanded with the release of six other solos cut at the same sessions. Wilson, who is in peak form, clearly enjoyed playing several tunes that he had not performed in years, and he is heard at the top of his game. Classic swing music. *—Scott Yanow*

And the Dutch Swing College Band / Nov. 15, 1972 / Everest ✦✦✦✦✦
For several decades, the Dutch Swing College Band was one of Europe's top regular groups, able to play both Dixieland and swing with equal skill. This LP contains some full band selections (including a Dixieland-ish "Riverboat Shuffle"), combo numbers with the band's two clarinetists, solos, and features pianist Teddy Wilson with the rhythm section. This celebratory occasion (thus far only available on LP) resulted in some highly enjoyable music that deserves to be reissued on CD. *—Scott Yanow*

Lionel Hampton Presents Teddy Wilson / 1973 / Who's Who in Jazz ✦✦✦✦
In the mid- to late '70s, vibraphonist Lionel Hampton had the opportunity to record with some of his favorite jazz musicians on his Who's Who label. For his reunion with pianist Teddy Wilson, Hamp also utilized the fine clarinetist Jerry Fuller, bassist George Duvivier, Sam Turner on congas and Teddy Wilson, Jr., on drums, making this the only time that father and son recorded together. The music is a bit predictable with eight veteran swing standards, but the enthusiasm of Hampton makes the results more exciting than one might expect. *—Scott Yanow*

Runnin' Wild / Jul. 4, 1973 / Black Lion ✦✦✦✦✦
Black Lion has reissued several Teddy Wilson sessions on CD, but this one is by far the most exciting. Recorded live at the 1973 Montreux Jazz Festival, Wilson plays some surprisingly extroverted solos, even starting "One O'Clock Jump" off with some torrid boogie-woogie. The majority of the standards are taken at faster than usual paces, with Wilson sounding very enthusiastic. Joined by bassist Kenny Baldock and drummer Johnny Richardson on eight of the nine selections, Wilson really inspires clarinetist Dave Shepherd during his four appearances to play what must have been some of the hottest solos of his career. This gem is highly recommended, showcasing the great swing pianist on a very good day. *—Scott Yanow*

Blues for Thomas Waller / Jan. 28, 1974+Jan. 31, 1974 / Black Lion ✦✦✦✦
Teddy Wilson, the definitive swing pianist, never really sounded like Fats Waller, although his style was complementary. This solo session finds him swinging his way through 11 of Waller's compositions, including two versions of "Honeysuckle Rose," along with two tributes—"Blues for Thomas Waller" and "Striding After Fats." Wilson's style was unchanged from 40 years earlier, but he still infused his solos with enthusiasm and melodic creativity, and this set is a fairly inspired effort. *—Scott Yanow*

Teddy Wilson in Tokyo / Dec. 1975 / Sackville ✦✦✦✦
The majority of pianist Teddy Wilson's recordings from his later period were recorded outside of the US and later released domestically. This solo set, issued by the Canadian Sackville label, finds the swing master melodically interpreting a dozen veteran standards, showing that his enthusiasm and creativity had not lessened, even on songs that he had already played regularly for more than 30 years. *—Scott Yanow*

And His All-Stars / Jun. 23, 1976-Jun. 24, 1976 / Chiaroscuro ✦✦✦
This CD reissues one of the last band dates headed by the impeccable swing pianist Teddy Wilson, who was usually featured with trios during the era. He per-

forms with an all-star sextet that also includes trumpeter Harry "Sweets" Edison, trombonist Vic Dickenson, Bob Wilber on clarinet and soprano, bassist Major Holley and drummer Oliver Jackson. Instead of jamming on the set of standards and obscurities (which includes such tunes as "Hallelujah," "Alice Blue Gown," "Just Friends" and "I'll Get By"), the musicians mostly play Bob Wilber's arrangements. Other than "Blues in D Flat," the performances are quite concise (most clock in around the three-minute mark) and some of the charts make the group sound like a dance band rather than a spontaneous jam. The music overall is less exciting than one would expect, but it has its moments and is quite pleasing. This CD adds a 7-minute "Jazzspeak" from August 11, 1995, that features Bob Wilber reminiscing about both Teddy Wilson and this session. *—Scott Yanow*

Three Little Words / Jul. 1976 / Classic Jazz ✦✦✦
Pianist Teddy Wilson's style had been unchanged for decades by the time he recorded this LP for Classic Jazz but, although his playing was somewhat predictable, it still sounded swinging and flawless. With bassist Milt Hinton and drummer Oliver Jackson, the great swing pianist performs versions of ten veteran standards with the high points including "Three Little Words," "Don't Be That Way," "My Heart Stood Still," "Where or When" and "Flyin' Home." Recommended for Teddy Wilson fans. *—Scott Yanow*

Revamps Rodgers & Hart / 1977 / Chiaroscuro ✦✦✦
This Chiaroscuro LP features the great swing pianist Teddy Wilson playing relaxed versions of 13 Rodgers & Hart compositions. Since virtually all of these songs were longtime standards, Wilson was quite familiar with most of them including such tunes as "Thou Swell," "You Took Advantage of Me," "Where or When" and "The Lady Is a Tramp." It is doubtful if either Richard Rodgers or Lorenz Hart would have objected to these respectful and lightly swinging renditions. *—Scott Yanow*

Cole Porter Classics / Nov. 3, 1977 / Black Lion ✦✦✦
The tasteful and lightly swinging pianist Teddy Wilson performs 11 well-known Cole Porter standards on this solo set. This generally relaxed session contains no new revelations (Wilson had solidified his swing style 40 years earlier) but should please Teddy Wilson's fans; it is always enjoyable to hear him play unaccompanied. *—Scott Yanow*

Lem Winchester

b. Mar. 19, 1928, Philadelphia, PA, **d.** Jan. 13, 1961, Indianapolis, IN
Vibes / Hard Bop
Lem Winchester had great potential as a vibraphonist, but it was all cut short by a tragic accident. Influenced by Milt Jackson but developing a sound of his own, Winchester actually played tenor, baritone and piano before choosing to stick exclusively to vibes. A police officer in Wilmington, DE, he made a big impression at the 1958 Newport Jazz Festival and was soon recording regularly with such major players as Oliver Nelson, Benny Golson and Tommy Flanagan. Winchester resigned from the police force in 1960 so as to be a musician full-time, but then on January 13, 1961, he unsuccessfully demonstrated a trick with a revolver! *—Scott Yanow*

Lem Winchester and the Ramsey Lewis Trio / Oct. 8, 1958 / Argo ✦✦✦✦
This out-of-print LP, Lem Winchester's first as a leader, matches his vibes with the early Ramsey Lewis trio on a tribute to the late trumpeter Clifford Brown. They perform two of Brownie's best compositions ("Joy Spring" and "Sandu"), four standards (including "Jordu"), the obscure "A Message from Boysie" and Winchester's "Where It Is." The little-known set (a good example of Ramsey Lewis' original piano style) is actually excellent and would be easily recommended to straightahead jazz fans if it could be found. *—Scott Yanow*

Winchester Special / Sep. 25, 1959 / Original Jazz Classics ✦✦✦✦✦
This excellent CD reissue features the ill-fated vibraphonist Lem Winchester teamed up with tenor saxophonist Benny Golson, pianist Tommy Flanagan, bassist Wendell Marshall and drummer Art Taylor for three standards, an obscurity and two of the leader's originals. The music falls between bop and hard bop with consistently swinging solos that are generally fairly inventive. This was one of Winchester's three recordings for the New Jazz label; all are easily recommended to straightahead jazz fans. *—Scott Yanow*

Lem's Beat / Apr. 19, 1960 / Original Jazz Classics ✦✦✦✦
Lem Winchester, an ill-fated vibraphonist who was influenced musically by Milt Jackson, teams up with tenor saxophonist Oliver Nelson, altoist Curtis Peagler and a fine rhythm section for a good straightahead date that has been reissued on CD. Nelson emerges as the most distinctive solo voice and, since he contributed three of the six songs, the tenorman's musical personality dominates this set. Winchester shows much potential that, due to his untimely death in early 1961, was never fulfilled. Good bop-based music. *—Scott Yanow*

● **Another Opus** / Jun. 4, 1960 / Original Jazz Classics ✦✦✦✦✦
Vibraphonist Lem Winchester died on Jan. 13, 1961, after an accident with a gun. Although he did not stick around long enough to carve out his own original voice (remaining influenced to a large degree by Milt Jackson), Winchester did record several worthy albums during his final couple of years. This set, which has been reissued on CD in the *OJC* series, was one of his last and best. Winchester, in a quintet with flutist Frank Wess, pianist Hank Jones, bassist Eddie Jones and drummer Gus Johnson, is in swinging and creative form on three of his originals, Oliver Nelson's "The Meetin'" and the standard "Like Someone in Love," A "bonus cut" from Oct. 14, 1960, finds Winchester playing "Lid Flippin'" with a quintet that features organist Johnny "Hammond" Smith. Overall this CD is one of Lem Winchester's definitive sets. —*Scott Yanow*

Lem Winchester with Feeling / Oct. 7, 1960 / Original Jazz Classics ✦✦✦
Winchester leads bassist George Duvivier, pianist Richard Wyands and drummer Roy Haynes on this passionate hard bop date featuring renditions of "Skylark," "My Romance" and "With a Song in My Heart." —*Jason Ankeny*

Kai Winding

b. May 18, 1922, Aarhus, Denmark, d. May 6, 1983, Yonkers, NY
Trombone / Bop
One of the finest trombonists to emerge from the bebop era, Kai Winding was always to an extent overshadowed by J.J. Johnson, although they co-led one of the most popular jazz groups of the mid-'50s. Born in Denmark, Winding immigrated to the US with his family when he was 12. He had short stints with the orchestras of Alvino Rey and Sonny Dunham and played in a service band in the Coast Guard for three years. Winding's first burst of fame occurred during his year with Stan Kenton's Orchestra (1946-47) during which his phrasing influenced and was adopted by the other trombonists, leading to a permanent change in the Kenton sound. He also participated in some early bop sessions, played with Tadd Dameron (1948-49) and was on one of the Miles Davis nonet's famous recording sessions. After playing with the big bands of Charlie Ventura and Benny Goodman, he formed a quintet with J.J. Johnson (1954-56); the two trombonists (who sounded nearly identical at the time) had occasional reunions after going their separate ways. Winding led a four-trombone septet off and on through the latter half of the 1950s and into the '60s, was music director for the Playboy clubs in New York and during 1971-72 worked with the Giants of Jazz (an all-star group with Dizzy Gillespie, Sonny Stitt and Thelonious Monk). Although he recorded frequently both as a leader and a sideman throughout his career, most of Winding's sessions are not currently available on CD. —*Scott Yanow*

★ **Kai Winding, Jay Jay Johnson and Bennie Green with Strings** / May 13, 1952+Dec. 3, 1954 / Original Jazz Classics ✦✦✦✦✦
Two unrelated session are combined on this CD reissue of an LP. Trombonist Bennie Green is heard on four ballads from 1952 while backed by a rhythm section and six strings. However the more significant selections are eight songs that for the first time matched together trombonists J.J. Johnson and Kai Winding in a quintet. The J.J. and Kai group would be quite popular during the next two years and, listening to the colorful and melodic versions of such tunes as "How Long Has This Been Going On," "Dinner for One" and "We'll Be Together Again," it is easy to see why. —*Scott Yanow*

The Swingin' States / Aug. 22, 1958-Aug. 29, 1958 / Columbia ✦✦✦
The gimmick of this out-of-print LP by trombonist Kai Winding is that all dozen songs have a state in their title including "Jersey Bounce," "Carry Me Back to Old Virginia," "California Here I Come" and "Oklahoma." Only "At Last Alaska" (named after the recently admitted 49th state) is an original. At the time Winding was leading a four-trombone septet (which included two bass trombones). Winding and fellow trombonist Frank Rehak along with pianist Hank Jones split up all of the solo space on the spirited if somewhat lightweight music. —*Scott Yanow*

The Incredible Kai Winding Trombones / Nov. 17, 1960-Dec. 13, 1960 / Impulse!
✦✦✦✦
After the J.J. Johnson-Kai Winding Quintet broke up in 1956, Kai Winding formed a four-trombone septet of his own that he led on a fairly regular basis through 1967. This long out-of-print Impulse LP was probably the group's best-known recording. Seven standards (including "Speak Low," "Doodlin'" and "Bye Bye Blackbird") and three of Winding's basic originals are played by the band, with solos allocated not only to Kai but pianists Ross Tompkins and Bill Evans along with guest conga player Olatunji. Fine straightahead music obviously most enjoyed by listeners who like the sound of trombones. —*Scott Yanow*

Kai Winding Solo / Jan. 23, 1963-Feb. 5, 1963 / Verve ✦✦✦✦
Trombonist Kai Winding is not featured here on unaccompanied solos despite the title of this album, but it does showcase his horn without the usual three or four trombones that he regularly used during the period. With support from pianist

Ross Tompkins, bassist Russell George, either Gus Johnson or Tommy Check on drums and guitarist Dick Garcia (on three of the 11 selections), this is one of Winding's best (and least commercial) recordings of the 1960s. The performances are concise (none exceed four minutes) and are highlighted by "How Are Things in Glocca Morro," "The Things We Did Last Summer" and "You've Changed." This LP is long overdue to be reissued on CD. —*Scott Yanow*

● **Lionel Hampton Presents Kai Winding** / Sep. 1, 1977 / Who's Who in Jazz
✦✦✦✦✦
Trombonist Kai Winding made relatively few quartet sessions throughout his career, but this was his fourth of the 1974-77 period. One of the few Who's Who LPs that did not have a guest appearance by vibraphonist Lionel Hampton, this outing by Winding features him in fine form with pianist Frank Strazzeri, bassist Kevin Brandon and drummer Ted Hawke. Together they perform one original apiece by Kai and Strazzeri plus six standards (highlighted by "Crazy She Calls Me," "Yardbird Suite" and "If I Didn't Care"). If this album were more widely available, it could serve as a strong introduction to Kai Winding's talents. —*Scott Yanow*

Giant Bones / Apr. 17, 1979 / Sonet ✦✦✦✦
Superior two-trombone set with Curtis Fuller (tb). —*Ron Wynn*

Paul Winter

b. Aug. 31, 1939, Altoona, PA
Soprano Saxophone, Alto Saxophone / World Fusion, Hard Bop
Winter first came to public prominence in 1961 as the winner of a collegiate jazz festival held at Notre Dame University; one of that event's judges, John Hammond, subsequently signed the group to a Columbia recording contract. In 1962, the band was sent on a State Department tour of Latin America. That venture planted the first seeds of change in Winter's concept. In 1967, he abandoned the traditional jazz format in favor of a lineup that featured non-Western instruments. The Paul Winter Consort, as the band was renamed, became one of the earliest exponents of world music, combining elements from various African, Asian, and South American cultures with jazz. Members of the Consort interested in extending the music's experimental component—guitarist Ralph Towner, oboist Paul McCandless, sitarist and percussionist Collin Walcott—broke away from Winter's leadership in the early '70s to form the group Oregon. Meanwhile, Winter became increasingly involved in activities with the Greenpeace organization, and worked toward a successful integration of music and nature. Winter recorded his attempts at communication with whales off the coast of California, and used the tapes as the foundation of his 1977 album, *Common Ground*. Since 1980, Winter has headed a non-profit group dedicated to increasing public awareness of music's relationship to spiritual and environmental health. He continues to perform in support of his organization, frequently in settings conducive to the production of (and interaction with) ambient sound, such as the Grand Canyon, or New York's Cathedral of St. John the Divine. —*Chris Kelsey*

Jazz Premiere: Washington / Dec. 1961 / Columbia ✦✦✦✦✦
This LP has altoist Paul Winter's second recording as a leader (it was preceded by a 1959 date for Offbeat). Featured is Winter's Sextet, which won a highly publicized Intercollegiate Jazz Festival, played at the White House and toured Latin America. Of the sidemen, best-known are pianist Warren Bernhardt, drummer Harold Jones and bassist Richard Evans; trumpeter Dick Whitsell and baritonist Les Rout remained obscure despite their talent. Most of the ten selections were composed by band members and Jimmy Heath's "The Thumper" comes the closest of any of the songs to being a standard. The music was forward-thinking for the time, essentially straightahead while being open to rhythms and folk melodies from other countries, although there is little hint here of the world music/new age direction that Paul Winter would head in future years. —*Scott Yanow*

Winter Consort's Road / 1969-1970 / A&M ✦✦✦✦✦
Paul Winter, a pioneer in playing world music and what would become new age, is a bit underrated as a talent scout. This version of his Winter Consort consists of cellist David Darling (a future ECM star) and four musicians who would soon break away to form Oregon: guitarist Ralph Towner, Paul McCandless (heard here on oboe and English horn), bassist Glen Moore and Colin Walcott on tabla and percussion. With what was arguably his finest group on this CD reissue, Paul Winter takes some fine spots on alto and soprano and leads the colorful folk-oriented ensembles. It is a pity he could not have kept this band together longer. —*Scott Yanow*

Icarus / 1973 / Epic ✦✦✦✦✦
This, a reissue of saxophonist Paul Winter's finest album, marks a transitional point in his career from jazz to his own brand of contemporary instrumental. But one can simply revel in the lovely melodies, the contemplative sounds, and the

tasteful production of George Martin, especially on the justly famous title track by Ralph Towner. —*William Ruhlmann*

★ **Common Ground** / 1977 / A&M ✦✦✦✦✦

This is a good example of Winter's nature-conscious music, as he has incorporated the sounds of birds, wolves, and humpback whales into his ensemble. It's surprising how close such wild animals come to playing pop music. —*William Ruhlmann*

Sun Singer / 1983 / Living Music ✦✦✦✦

On this striking example of Winter's lyricism, Paul Halley on keyboards and Glen Velez playing frame drum and percussion. —*Linda Kohanov*

Earthbeat / Mar. 1987 / Living Music ✦✦✦

Billed as the album of original music created by Americans and Russians together, this album features Halley, Velez, guitarist Oscar Castro-Neves, and cellist Eugene Friesen collaborating on some selections with the Dmitri Pokrovsky Singers, a vocal ensemble rooted in the tradition of Russian village music. Traditional music from throughout Russia is mixed with Winter's Brazilian-influenced sound. There are also some beautiful instrumentals and, true to Winter's style, some natural sounds, most notably the calls of the Alaskan tundra wolf and Russian loon. —*Linda Kohanov*

Earth: Voices of a Planet / 1990 / Living Music ✦✦✦

Winter regulars and some special guest artists have put together a musical journey that starts in North America and travels through Africa, Antarctica, South America, Australia, Asia, and Europe. Selections feature indigenous nature sounds and traditional influences from various regions. —*Linda Kohanov*

Canyon Lullaby / 1996 / Living Music ✦✦✦

Much is made in the liner notes of this recording about the lengths Winter and his compatriots went to to find just the perfect place in the Grand Canyon to record. For once, all the hyperbole is justified. The sound here is nothing short of breathtaking. Winter's saxophone reverberates off the canyon walls and has a truly transcendent sound and feeling. That said, the compositions—21 of them, lasting over an hour in total time—are as evanescent as the sound of Winter's saxophone fading into the rocks, and there's only so much solo saxophone one can take (Winter's bandmate Paul Halley adds organ on two cuts). Interesting and exhilarating in small doses, *Canyon Lullaby* can go beyond soothing to soporific if listened to in one sitting. —*Ross Boissoneau*

Jimmy Witherspoon

b. Aug. 8, 1923, Gurdon, AR, **d.** Sep. 18, 1997, Los Angeles, CA
Vocals / Jump Blues, Swing, Jazz Blues, Urban Blues, Texas Blues

One of the great blues singers of the post-World War II period, Jimmy Witherspoon was also versatile enough to fit comfortably into the jazz world. As a child he sang in a church choir, and made his debut recordings with Jay McShann for Philo and Mercury in 1945 and 1946. His own first recordings, using McShann's band, resulted in a No. 1 R&B hit in 1949 with "Ain't Nobody's Business Parts 1 & 2" on Supreme Records. Live performances of "No Rollin' Blues" and "Big Fine Girl" provided 'Spoon with two more hits in 1950. The mid-'50s were a lean time, with his style of shouting blues temporarily out of fashion; singles were tried for Federal, Chess, Atco, Vee-Jay, and others, with little success. Witherspoon's album *Live at the Monterey Jazz Festival* (HiFi Jazz) from 1959 lifted him back into the limelight. Partnerships with Ben Webster or Groove Holmes were recorded, and he toured Europe in 1961 with Buck Clayton, performing overseas many more times in the decades to follow; some memorable music resulted, but Witherspoon's best '60s album is *Evening Blues* (Prestige), which features T-Bone Walker on guitar and Clifford Scott on saxophone. Despite contracting throat cancer in the early '80s, Witherspoon remained active, a popular attraction until his death in 1997. —*Bob Porter & Scott Yanow*

Jimmy Witherspoon & Jay McShann / 1947-1949 / Black Lion ✦✦✦✦

Although Jimmy Witherspoon gets first billing on this CD reissue, he actually only has vocals on 11 of the 24 selections and is just present on three of the seven sessions; high points include two versions of his signature song "Ain't Nobody's Business." Pianist Jay McShann is the real leader of these Los Angeles recordings and the brand of music he performs mixes together swing, blues, slight touches of bebop and early R&B. Most of the songs are basic originals and there are spirited solos from many lesser-known horn players; only the young trumpeter Art Farmer, his brother, bassist Addison Farmer, and the popular studio tenor saxophonist Maxwell Davis are still remembered. In addition to Witherspoon (who is in excellent early form), Lois Booker, Maxine Reed and Crown Prince Waterford also take vocals. An easily recommended set of rarities from the later period of Kansas City jazz. —*Scott Yanow*

Ain't Nobody's Business / May 9, 1949-1950 / Drive Archives ✦✦✦✦

It is unfortunate that the recording dates and personnel are not given on this budget CD, for the performances (although not always that well-recorded) are excellent. Singer Jimmy Witherspoon is heard near the beginning of his career. Five songs (the third through the seventh) are taken from a Pasadena concert on May 9, 1949. Backed by pianist Gene Gilbeaux's quartet (with Donald Hill featured on alto), Witherspoon is in extroverted form entertaining the enthusiastic crowd; on "New Orleans Woman," a few unidentified horns honk away to the audience's enjoyment. Of the other five songs, two are from 1950 ("I Done Found Out" and "Fickle Woman") and have Witherspoon backed by a nonet including pianist Jay McShann and tenor saxophonist Maxwell Davis. "Good Jumpin'" is with the Buddy Floyd sextet in 1948, and two others are not listed in discographies. But details aside, the enjoyable music straddles the boundary between blues, early R&B and jazz. —*Scott Yanow*

Spoon So Easy: The Chess Years / Jun. 10, 1954-Aug. 15, 1956 / MCA/Chess ✦✦✦

By the mid-'50s it seemed that Jimmy Witherspoon's brand of Kansas City blues was going permanently out of style; Big Joe Turner was starting to turn toward rock 'n' roll, and many of the older singers were no longer recording. Witherspoon, who was only in his early 30s, was flexible enough to fit into different situations so the Chess label (best-known for its intense Chicago blues) took a chance on him. This CD contains most of Witherspoon's records for the Chess and Checker labels: five that were issued and nine that remained in the vaults until the release of this CD in 1990. Unfortunately Witherspoon did not have any hits during this era (his comeback would not really get going until his appearance at the 1959 Monterey Jazz Festival) but fortunately these records did survive. 'Spoon is actually heard in good form and, even if the personnel is mostly unidentified, he received suitable backup. Since all but three of Witherspoon's Chess recordings are on this CD (which clocks in around 39 minutes), one does wonder why it was not decided to make this a "complete" set. —*Scott Yanow*

Goin' to Kansas City Blues / Dec. 4, 1957-Dec. 5, 1957 / RCA ✦✦✦✦

A reunion of sorts with McShann, with whom Witherspoon had sung for four years in the late '40s. A relaxed, swinging set that bisects jazz and blues, it holds no great surprises, but 'Spoon fans will find this an enjoyable and accomplished record. About half of the material was penned by McShann or Witherspoon, including a remake of "Confessin' the Blues," and "Blue Monday Blues," Jimmy's adaptation of "Kansas City Blues." —*Richie Unterberger*

★ **The Spoon Concerts** / Oct. 2, 1959-Dec. 2 1959 / Fantasy ✦✦✦✦✦

This single-CD (which reissues all of the music from an earlier two-LP set) includes the high point of singer Jimmy Witherspoon's career. On October 2, 1959, he appeared at the Monterey Jazz Festival and created such a sensation that it caused his career to go through a renaissance. Heard at the peak of his powers, Witherspoon holds his own with a mighty group of veterans (trumpeter Roy Eldridge, both Ben Webster and Coleman Hawkins on tenors, clarinetist Woody Herman, pianist Earl Hines, bassist Vernon Alley and drummer Mel Lewis). Although the five-song set only lasted 25 minutes, Witherspoon's performance was the hit of the festival. The other half of this CD features Witherspoon romping through ten mostly-traditional blues songs two months later with Webster, baritonist Gerry Mulligan, pianist Jimmy Rowles, bassist Leroy Vinnegar and drummer Mel Lewis; the performance is equally exciting. Highly recommended, this CD is the one truly essential Jimmy Witherspoon release. —*Scott Yanow*

'Spoon & Groove / 1961 / Rykodisc ✦✦✦✦✦

This was originally released as *Groovin' & Spoonin'* on Olympic 7107. It's a decent if unremarkable set of blues-jazz, heavier on the blues, with organist Groove Holmes being Witherspoon's most important sideman on this date (which also features tenor saxophonist Teddy Edwards). Several of the numbers are shopworn standards like "Take This Hammer," "Key to the Highway," "Please Send Me Someone to Love," and "Since I Fell for You," though everything's performed with taste. If you're looking for Witherspoon blues-jazz with an organ groove, the 1963 album *Evenin' Blues* (1963) is more highly recommended, though *'Spoon & Groove* has no serious flaws. —*Richie Unterberger*

Olympia Concert / Apr. 22, 1961 / Inner City ✦✦✦✦

Recorded in Paris when he was touring with a group dominated by Count Basie alumni, this concert features singer Jimmy Witherspoon in prime form. His repertoire was fairly typical (highlighted by "See See Rider," "Roll 'Em Pete" and his biggest hit "'TAin't Nobody's Business"), but Witherspoon pours so much enthusiasm and soul into the music that he sounds as if he had recently discovered the songs. This sadly out-of-print LP also features some short solos and excellent support from 'Spoon's sidemen: trumpeters Buck Clayton and Emmett Berry, trombonist Dicky Wells, altoist Earl Warren, tenor saxophonist Buddy Tate, pianist Sir Charles Thompson, bassist Gene Ramey and drummer Oliver Jackson. Fortunately the band appeared on television in Europe and a Shanachie video (readily available) has been released of the Buck Clayton All-Stars. —*Scott Yanow*

Baby Baby Baby / May 6, 1963 / Original Blues Classics ✦✦✦

Veteran singer Jimmy Witherspoon is in good voice on this CD reissue, performing a dozen two- to four-minute songs that include such blues standards as Duke Ellington's "Rocks in My Bed," "Bad Bad Whiskey," "One Scotch, One Bourbon, One Beer" and "It's a Lonesome Old World." He is joined by a quintet featuring altoist Leo Wright and guitarist Kenny Burrell on the first eight numbers and a background septet (with trumpeter Bobby Bryant and Arthur Wright on harmonica) for the remainder of the set. The music is enjoyable if not classic and should please Witherspoon's many fans. —*Scott Yanow*

Evenin' Blues / Aug. 15, 1963 / Original Blues Classics ✦✦✦✦

A good relaxed (but not laidback) session, and one of his bluesier ones, with organ, Clifford Scott (who played on Bill Doggett's "Honky Tonk") on sax, and T-Bone Walker on guitar. Nothing too adventurous about the song selection, including well-traveled items like "Good Rockin' Tonight" and "Kansas City," but Witherspoon sings them with ingratiating soul, reaching his peaks on his cover of "Don't Let Go" (perhaps better than the hit version by Roy Hamilton) and the late-night ambience of the title track. The CD reissue adds previously unissued alternate takes of four of the songs. —*Richie Unterberger*

Blues Around the Clock / Nov. 5, 1963 / Original Blues Classics ✦✦✦

Veteran singer Jimmy Witherspoon (who bridges the gap between jazz and blues) mostly sticks to the latter on this spirited set. His backup group (organist Paul Griffin, guitarist Lord Westbrook, bassist Leonard Gaskin and drummer Herbie Lovelle) is fine in support, but the spotlight is almost entirely on Witherspoon throughout these ten concise performances, only one of which exceeds four minutes. Highlights include "No Rollin' Blues," "S.K. Blues" and "Around the Clock." Witherspoon is in fine voice and, even if nothing all that memorable occurs, the music is enjoyable. —*Scott Yanow*

Some of My Best Friends Are the Blues / Jun. 15, 1964 / Original Jazz Classics ✦✦✦✦

Jimmy Witherspoon is accompanied by a large orchestra arranged by Benny Golson for a set emphasizing slow tempos (even on "And the Angels Sing" and "Who's Sorry Now"), ballads and blues. Nothing all that memorable occurs, but the singer is in strong voice and his fans will want to pick up this interesting CD reissue. —*Scott Yanow*

Blues for Easy Livers / 1965-1966 / Original Jazz Classics ✦✦✦✦

Despite the title, this actually leans considerably further to the jazz side of Witherspoon's muse than the blues one, with backing by Pepper Adams on baritone sax, Roger Kellaway on piano, Bill Watrous on trombone, Richard Davis on bass, and Mel Lewis on drums. The songs, too, are much more in the jazz/pop vein than the blues/jazz one, heavy on standards by the likes of Johnny Mercer, the Gershwins, and Ellington. Witherspoon's one of the masters of closing-time bluesy jazz, and he doesn't let anyone down on that account on this relaxed (but not sleepy) session. —*Richie Unterberger*

Jimmy's Blues / Sep. 15, 1969 / MCA ✦✦✦✦

This out-of-print MCA album from 1983 reissued a fairly obscure session from singer Jimmy Witherspoon. Backed by a Los Angeles rhythm section that includes pianist Charles Brown (who unfortunately does not sing on this date) along with tenor saxophonist Red Holloway (who is not included in the personnel listing), Witherspoon sticks mostly to blues with tunes by Brownie McGhee, Art Hillery (who plays organ on one song), Buddy Scott and four of his own originals (including "You Can't Do a Thing When You're Drunk" and "Pillar to Post"). This set (originally titled *Hunh*) was cut for the Bluesway label. —*Scott Yanow*

Live / 1976 / MCA ✦✦✦

Jimmy Witherspoon sticks exclusively to the blues during this Los Angeles club date from 1976. Guitarist Robben Ford's fiery Chicago blues playing is consistently exciting and imaginative, often stealing the show from 'Spoon. This CD can easily be enjoyed by fans of both blues and swinging jazz. —*Scott Yanow*

Sings the Blues / May 25, 1980 / Muse ✦✦✦✦✦

The Savoy Sultans, as revived by drummer Panama Francis, was one of the hottest small-group swing bands of the late '70s/early '80s. Singer Jimmy Witherspoon fits right in with the group, emphasizing the Kansas City swing and blues side of his repertoire. With the Sultans (a nonet also including trumpeters Francis Williams and Irv Stokes, tenorman George Kelly and pianist Red Richards) inspiring him, Witherspoon revives some of the most memorable songs associated with Jimmy Rushing including "Sent for You Yesterday," "I Want a Little Girl" and "Boogie Woogie." This highly recommended set is one of Jimmy Witherspoon's best from his later years. —*Scott Yanow*

Patcha, Patcha, All Night Long / Apr. 11, 1985 / Pablo ✦✦✦

This wouldn't find a place in the cutting edge of either Turner or Witherspoon's catalog, but it's a decent enough 1985 session of Kansas City-type blues/jazz. Saxophonists Red Holloway and Lee Allen are the featured players in a band which bisects the swing and jump blues idioms, Witherspoon acquitting himself better than Turner (the latter of whom died later that year). —*Richie Unterberger*

Midnight Lady Called the Blues / Jan. 14, 1986 / Muse ✦✦✦

Singer Jimmy Witherspoon was starting to show his age by 1986, but he is in fairly strong form on these seven selections co-composed by Dr. John and Doc Pomus. With altoist Hank Crawford (who also wrote some of the arrangements) and tenor saxophonist David "Fathead" Newman contributing plenty of solos while pianist Dr. John leads the rhythm section, the spirited set has more than its share of interesting and exciting moments despite the obscurity of the material. —*Scott Yanow*

Rockin' L.A. / Oct. 24, 1988-Oct. 25, 1988 / Fantasy ✦✦✦✦

This CD finds Jimmy Witherspoon at age 65 on one of his last fairly strong records before his voice began to really shrink and fade. 'Spoon, assisted on this live set by tenor saxophonist Teddy Edwards, pianist Gerald Wiggins, bassist John Clayton and drummer Paul Humphrey, revives some of his hits, performs a pair of medleys and emphasizes swinging blues and ballads. Highlights include "Sweet Lotus Blossom" (a standard whose authorship should not have been credited to Witherspoon), "Stormy Monday" and "I Want a Little Girl." Easily recommended to Jimmy Witherspoon fans. —*Scott Yanow*

Mike Wofford

b. San Antonio, TX
Piano / Hard Bop

Despite leading a number of recording dates under his own name, pianist, composer and arranger Mike Wofford was better known as a consummate accompanist, lending his skills to the music of such giants as Ella Fitzgerald, Sarah Vaughan and Benny Carter. A native of San Antonio, TX, Wofford was raised in San Diego, CA and gained his earliest professional experience at the famed Lighthouse club in nearby Hermosa Beach. There he played with the likes of James Moody, and later enlisted with the bands of Shelly Manne and Shorty Rogers; over the decades to come, he also worked in the company of Zoot Sims, Joe Pass, Kenny Burrell, Barney Kessel, Harry "Sweets" Edison, Eddie "Cleanhead" Vinson, Bud Shank, and countless others. While already a respected figure in jazz circles on the strength of such solo dates as 1966's *Strawberry Wine* and the following year's *Summer Night*, Wofford's visibility was raised considerably in 1979 when he, longtime friend and drummer Roy McCurdy, and bassist Andy Simpkins were tapped to back Sarah Vaughan. Wofford remained with the legendary singer for about a year, at which time he exited to pursue other projects, among them several recordings of Jerome Kern standards. By 1988, he was regularly performing with Benny Carter, and a year later appeared on *All That Jazz*, the final studio recording from Ella Fitzgerald. After touring with Fitzgerald until her 1994 retirement, Wofford signed on with Kenny Rankin; on occasion, he also continued leading his own sessions. —*Jason Ankeny*

Mike Wofford Trio Plays Jerome Kern / Feb. 6, 1980 / Discovery ✦✦✦✦

Mike Wofford Quartet Plays Jerome Kern, Vol. 2 / Jul. 7, 1980 / Discovery ✦✦✦

● **Plays Jerome Kern, Vol. 3** / Jan. 5, 1981 / Discovery ✦✦✦✦✦

For his third of three investigations of Jerome Kern's music, pianist Mike Wofford (with the assistance of bassist Andy Simpkins and drummer Jim Plank) interprets nine of Kern's songs, four of which are little-known. Wofford reharmonized many of the tunes, in effect creating new compositions and coming up with surprising versions. This project overall resulted in some of Wofford's better recorded performances. Highlights of this album include "The Folks Who Live on the Hill," "I Won't Dance," "The Waltz in Swingtime" and "Go Little Boat." —*Scott Yanow*

Francis Wong

Tenor Saxophone / Post-Bop

Long involved in the reparations movement to compensate Japanese Americans put in prison camps during World War II, Francis Wong has been a major force on the Asian Improv label (which he co-founded in 1987 with Jon Jang), recording stimulating music both as a sideman and a leader. He has recorded with Jang, Fred Ho, Glenn Horiuchi, Mark Izu and with his own Great Wall Ensemble, being quite active in the San Francisco Bay area. —*Scott Yanow*

● **Ming** / Jul. 29, 1994 / Asian Improv ✦✦✦✦✦

On this CD tenor saxophonist Francis Wong sometimes plays with both the ferocity of an Albert Ayler and the thoughtfulness of Sonny Rollins. Although a few themes and specific moods are utilized, much of the music is quite free. It generally succeeds due to the close musical communication between Wong, pianist

Glenn Horiuchi and percussionist Elliot Kaves, even if Horiuchi's occasional vocal shouts are quite eccentric. Because Wong also plays a bit of flute and violin and Kaves uses a wide variety of percussion (including what is listed as "dishes, pots, pans, oven rack and kitchen sink"), even the rambling moments tend to hold one's interest. A rewarding disc. —*Scott Yanow*

Chicago Time Code / Sep. 6, 1994 / Asian Improv ✦✦✦

Pilgrimage / Nov. 18, 1994 / Music & Arts ✦✦✦✦

Anthony Wonsey

Piano / Post-Bop, Hard Bop

An adventurous yet flexible pianist with a potentially significant future, Anthony Wonsey started playing music when he was six. Wonsey studied first with his mother (a classical pianist) and then Zilner Randolph. After earning a full scholarship to Berklee, from which he graduated in 1994, Wonsey moved to Boston and played locally with Roy Hargrove and Antonio Hart, among others. While still at Berklee, Wonsey toured with Christopher Hollyday, Nnenna Freelon and Kenny Garrett. During the past few years, Anthony Wonsey has played regularly and recorded with the groups of Carl Allen and Nicholas Payton. His debut CD as a leader, *Anthonyology*, was recorded for the Japanese Alfa Jazz label and released domestically by Evidence. —*Scott Yanow*

● **Anthonyology** / 1995 / Evidence ✦✦✦✦

Another Perspective / Jun. 14, 1996+Jun. 15, 1996 / Evidence ✦✦✦✦✦
Throughout this fine trio outing with bassist Christian McBride and drummer Carl Allen, pianist Anthony Wonsey demonstrates his expertise in straightahead jazz. His very interesting repertoire includes four Bud Powell tunes, two originals, Nicholas Payton's "Herbie's Hands," Hank Jones' catchy "We're All Together" and a pair of standards. Wonsey sometimes sounds close to Powell, while at other times he lets his own musical personality shine through. Excellent music in the bop mainstream. —*Scott Yanow*

Rickey Woodard

b. 1956, Nashville, TN

Tenor Saxophone, Clarinet, Alto Saxophone / Hard Bop

Rickey Woodard picked up early experience playing in a family band. After attending Tennessee State University, Woodard joined Ray Charles in 1980. In 1988 he moved to Los Angeles and since then has recorded (both as a leader and as a sideman) for Concord Records, has led quartets and been a member of the Clayton/Hamilton Jazz Orchestra, the Juggernaut and the Cheathams in addition to making guest appearances. —*Scott Yanow*

California Cooking / Feb. 27, 1991 / Candid ✦✦✦✦✦
Tenor saxophonist Rickey Woodard's first CD as a leader is a swinging quartet set with pianist Dwight Dickerson, bassist Tony Dumas and drummer Harold Mason. Woodard, who plays alto on three of the ten selections, is heard at his best on such numbers as Hank Mobley's "This I Dig of You," "Jeannine" and Oscar Brashear's "Sashay." Uncomplicated bebop as played by an appealing, warm-toned soloist. —*Scott Yanow*

Night Mist / Oct. 22, 1991 / Fresh Sound ✦✦✦✦✦
Tenor saxophonist Rickey Woodard's many fans may be unaware of this particular CD. Recorded in 1991 for the Spanish Fresh Sound label, this somewhat obscure outing finds Woodard in top form heading a straightahead quartet comprising pianist Eric Reed, bassist Tony Dumas and drummer Roy McCurdy. Together the Los Angeles all-stars play a variety of standards plus Woodard's "Night Mist," the only song on which he switches to alto. The music consistently swings, features inventive solos within the boundaries of hard bop and is well-paced with the highlights including "Thou Swell," "Secret Love," "Billie's Bounce" and "My Shining Hour." Well worth searching for. —*Scott Yanow*

The Tokyo Express / Jun. 1992 / Candid ✦✦✦✦

● **Yazoo** / 1994 / Concord Jazz ✦✦✦✦✦

The Silver Strut / Aug. 29, 1995-Aug. 30, 1995 / Concord Jazz ✦✦✦✦

Britt Woodman

b. Jun. 4, 1920, Los Angeles, CA

Trombone / Swing

An extremely versatile trombone soloist, Britt Woodman led Duke Ellington's section in the '50s and was flexible enough to record with Charles Mingus and Miles Davis. Woodman had range, fire and the harmonic knowledge to handle sophisticated big band and swing dates, and Mingus' futuristic, challenging arrangements. Woodman and Mingus were boyhood friends as well as longtime musical associates. Woodman played with Phil Moore and Les Hite in the '30s, then with Boyd Raeburn and Eddie Heywood in the mid-'40s before joining Lionel Hampton in

1946. He studied music at Westlake College in Los Angeles from 1948 to 1950, then joined Ellington. Woodman replaced Lawrence Brown and remained with Ellington until 1960. In 1955 he also recorded in a band led by Miles Davis that included Mingus. Woodman worked in several Broadway shows in the '60s, and also recorded with Mingus on three sessions ranging from 1960 to 1963. He then returned to California in 1970, where he recorded, leading an octet, and played with the Akiyoshi-Tabackin, Capp-Pierce and Bill Berry bands. Woodman toured Japan twice with Benny Carter in the late '70s, then returned to New York in the '80s, where he played with swing and bebop bands. —*Ron Wynn*

Chris Woods

b. Dec. 25, 1925, Memphis, TN, d. Jul. 4, 1985, New York, NY

Alto Saxophone / Bop, Early R&B Jazz

A fine altoist who was influenced by both bop and R&B, Chris Woods first played in Memphis and then after moving to St. Louis he performed with the Jeter-Pillars Orchestra and with George Hudson in the 1950s. Woods also recorded as a leader during the era. Moving to New York in 1962, Woods played and recorded with Dizzy Gillespie and Clark Terry, worked with Sy Oliver (1970-73) and had a stint with Count Basie in 1983. He never became a major name, but was an excellent player. —*Scott Yanow*

● **Somebody Done Stole My Blues** / Jun. 4, 1952-Feb. 24, 1953 / Delmark ✦✦✦✦
Altoist Chris Woods only had one session as a leader before 1973. This album has all eight performances from that date for the United label (including two alternate takes), only two of which were originally issued; in addition, Woods is featured on four titles with Tommy Dean's Gloom Chasers. Although geared a bit toward the commercial R&B market, the music on this LP (which features a pair of sextets) is quite worthwhile, displaying Chris Woods' interest in both bop and the blues. Well worth checking out. —*Scott Yanow*

Modus Operandi / 1978 / Delmark ✦✦✦✦

Jimmy Woods

b. Oct. 29, 1934, St. Louis, MS

Alto Saxophone / Avant-Garde, Post-Bop

Not a great deal is known about Jimmy Woods, an explorative altoist who recorded two impressive albums for Contemporary during 1961-63 and then largely dropped out of the music scene. A passionate improviser, Woods joined Homer Carter's R&B band in 1951. After a period in the Air Force (1952-56) he worked in some other R&B bands with Roy Milton's. He played with Horace Tapscott in 1960, recorded with Joe Gordon the following year and spent a period playing with Gerald Wilson's big band and Chico Hamilton. However Jimmy Woods rarely made a living out of music, and has been little heard from since the mid-'60s. —*Scott Yanow*

● **Awakening** / Aug. 1962 / Original Jazz Classics ✦✦✦✦✦
Altoist Jimmy Woods, whose style fell between hard bop and the avant-garde, only recorded two albums as a leader; this CD reissue brings back his first. The backup musicians include Joe Gordon or Martin Banks on trumpet, Amos Trice or Dick Whittington on piano, Jimmy Bond or Gary Peacock on bass and drummer Milt Turner, but Woods is by far the most advanced musician. On six of his originals, an obscurity and "Love for Sale," Jimmy Woods' original sound and passionate chance-taking style make one wonder why he was never able to really make it; his music has not really dated. —*Scott Yanow*

Conflict / Mar. 25, 1963 / Contemporary ✦✦✦✦

Phil Woods

b. Nov. 2, 1931, Springfield, MA

Alto Saxophone, Leader, Clarinet / Bop, Hard Bop

One of the true masters of the bop vocabulary, Phil Woods has had his own sound since the mid-1950s and stuck to his musical guns throughout a remarkably productive career. There has never been a doubt that he is one of the top alto saxophonists alive, and he has lost neither his enthusiasm nor his creativity through the years.

Woods' first alto was left to him by an uncle, and he started playing seriously when he was 12. He gigged and studied locally until 1948, when he moved to New York. Woods studied with Lennie Tristano, at the Manhattan School of Music, and at Juilliard, where he majored in clarinet. He worked with Charlie Barnet (1954), Jimmy Raney (1955), George Wallington, the Dizzy Gillespie Orchestra, Buddy Rich (1958-59), Quincy Jones (1959-61) and Benny Goodman (for BG's famous 1962 tour of the Soviet Union), but has mostly headed his own groups since 1955, including co-leadership of a combo with fellow altoist Gene Quill in the '50s logically known as "Phil & Quill." Woods, who married the late Charlie Parker's former wife Chan in the 1950s (and became the stepfather to singer Kim Parker), was sometimes thought of as "the new Bird" due to his brilliance in bop settings, but he never really sounded like a copy of Parker.

Phil Woods popped up in a variety of settings in the 1960s—on Benny Carter's classic *Further Definitions* record, touring Europe with the short-lived Thelonious Monk Nonet, and appearing on studio dates like the soundtracks to *The Hustler* and *Blow Up*. Always interested in jazz education (although he believes that there is no better way to learn jazz than to gig and travel constantly), Woods taught at an arts camp in Pennsylvania in the summers of 1964-67. Discouraged with the jazz scene in the US, he moved to France in 1968. For the next few years, Woods led a very advanced group, The European Rhythm Machine, which leaned toward the avant-garde and included pianist George Gruntz. Their recordings still sound fresh and exciting today, although this venture would only be a detour in Woods' bebop life. In 1972, he returned to the US and tried unsuccessfully to lead an electronic group that featured keyboardist Pete Robinson.

In 1973, Woods formed a quintet with pianist Mike Melillo, bassist Steve Gilmore, drummer Bill Goodwin and guitarist Harry Leahey that had much greater success. Their recording *Live at the Showboat* officially launched the band which today, after a few personnel changes, still tours the world. After Leahey left in 1978, it was known as the Phil Woods Quartet until trumpeter Tom Harrell (1983-89) joined; his spot has since been assumed by trombonist Hal Crook (1989-92) and trumpeter Brian Lynch. Pianist Melillo went out on his own in 1980, and his successors have been Hal Galper (1980-90), Jim McNeely (1990-95) and Bill Charlap; Gilmore and Goodwin have been with Woods since the group's start. Not just a bebop repertory band, Woods' ensembles have developed their own repertoire, taken plenty of chances, and stretched themselves while sticking to his straightahead path.

Woods contributed the famous alto solo to Billy Joel's hit recording of "Just the Way You Are" and has been one of Michel Legrand's favorite artists, guesting with Legrand on an occasional basis; he has made dozens of rewarding recordings himself through the years. He debuted as a leader in 1954 and has since recorded for Prestige, Savoy, RCA, Mode, Epic, Candid (the brilliant *The Right of Swing* in 1961), Impulse, MGM, Verve, Embryo, Testament, Muse, Omnisound, Enja, Chesky and with his Quintet/Quartet for RCA, Gryphon, Adelphi, Clean Cuts, Sea Breeze (two sets adding Chris Swansen's inventive synthesizer to the band), Red, Antilles, Palo Alto, Black Hawk, Denon and quite extensively for Concord. An Italian label, Philology (which has some broadcasts and live performances from Woods' bands), is named after the popular and still brilliant altoist. —*Scott Yanow*

Early Quintets / Aug. 11, 1954+Mar. 3, 1959 / Original Jazz Classics ✦✦✦✦
A pair of formerly rare quintet sets featuring altoist Phil Woods are combined on this CD reissue from the *OJC* series. One session was actually led by guitarist Jimmy Raney in 1954 (and also includes trumpeter John Wilson, bassist Bill Crow and drummer Joe Morello) while the other group (with trumpeter Howard McGhee, bassist Teddy Kotick and drummer Roy Haynes) was headed by pianist Dick Hyman in 1959. Both bop-oriented dates have their moments, with the edge going to Hyman's session. —*Scott Yanow*

Pot Pie, with Jon Eardley / Oct. 12, 1954+Feb. 4, 1955 / Original Jazz Classics ✦✦✦✦✦
Phil Woods was only 22 at the time of this program (reissued on CD), but he was already an explosive and very talented bop-oriented altoist. This obscure set, one of his earliest recordings, has seven group originals, plus the lone standard "Mad About the Boy," and is full of excitement. Woods, trumpeter Jon Eardley, pianist George Syran, bassist Teddy Kotick and drummer Nick Stabulas all display both youthful energy and a strong knowledge of Charlie Parker's innovations, making this an essential, if little-known acquisition for bop collectors. —*Scott Yanow*

Bird Calls, Vol. 1 / Feb. 8, 1955+Nov. 14, 1957 / Savoy ✦✦✦✦
This enjoyable straightahead LP has two separate Savoy sessions featuring altoist Phil Woods. The first four titles (which also have pianist Hall Overton, bassist Teddy Kotick and drummer Nick Stabulas) are from a "Music Minus One" date. Woods takes boppish and consistently inventive solos on four standards (including "Pennies from Heaven" and "It's Only a Paper Moon"). The flip side finds Woods performing as a member of pianist George Wallington's Quintet (along with trumpeter Donald Byrd, bassist Knobby Totah and drummer Stabulas). The group performs three numbers including Bud Powell's "Dance of the Infidels" and a ten-and-a-half-minute version of "Ow." While Byrd is heard in the early stage of his career, Phil Woods already sounds quite mature and easily recognizable. —*Scott Yanow*

Woodlore / Nov. 25, 1955 / Original Jazz Classics ✦✦✦
Altoist Phil Woods' second recording as a leader has been reissued as a rather brief 33-minute CD. Accompanied by a quiet but swinging rhythm section (pianist John Williams, bassist Teddy Kotick and drummer Nick Stabulas), Woods swings hard on four standards (including "Slow Boat to China" and "Be My Love"), plus a pair of his originals: "Strollin' With Pam" and "Woodlore." The altoist displays plenty of

energy and a strong command of the bebop vocabulary, sounding quite enthusiastic. —*Scott Yanow*

Pairing Off / Jun. 15, 1956 / Original Jazz Classics ✦✦✦✦
The title of this excellent CD reissue comes from the fact that the featured septet consists of two altos (Phil Woods and Gene Quill) and two trumpets (Donald Byrd and Kenny Dorham) in addition to a rhythm section (pianist Tommy Flanagan, bassist Doug Watkins and drummer Philly Joe Jones). Of the pairings, Woods and Dorham were more distinctive in 1956, but both Quill and Byrd get in some good licks. The full group stretches out on four lengthy numbers: three Woods originals and the ballad "Suddenly It's Spring." —*Scott Yanow*

The Young Bloods / Nov. 2, 1956 / Original Jazz Classics ✦✦✦✦
For this early hard bop date, altoist Phil Woods and trumpeter Donald Byrd were co-leaders. In fact, the music had at one point earlier on been released with Byrd getting first billing. Since the spirited altoist contributed four of the six tunes (including "House of Chan" and "In Walked George") and consistently takes solo honors, it is only right that the date has finally been reissued on CD under Woods' name. With pianist Al Haig (who did not record that extensively during this period), bassist Teddy Kotick and drummer Charlie Persip offering stimulating accompaniment, this is an easily recommended release (despite its brief LP length) for straightahead jazz collectors. —*Scott Yanow*

Four Altos / Feb. 9, 1957 / Original Jazz Classics ✦✦✦
Even with Phil Woods standing out, the "four altos" on this jam session all sound fairly similar. Few listeners will be able to consistently pick out which solos are by Gene Quill and which by Sahib Shihab, Hal Stein or Woods, and unfortunately there are no real liner notes (except basic information) on this budget LP. The solos (and the backup of pianist Mal Waldron, bassist Tommy Potter and drummer Louis Hayes) are generally hard-swinging and well-played, but the strong influence of Charlie Parker makes all of the altoists sound alike. —*Scott Yanow*

Phil and Quill with Prestige / Mar. 29, 1957 / Original Jazz Classics ✦✦✦✦✦
Altoists Phil Woods and Gene Quill always made for a mutually inspiring team. Both of the similar-sounding musicians were competitive, influenced by (but not imitative of) Charlie Parker, and really knew bebop. This CD reissue (which adds two selections from the same session that were originally part of the sampler *Bird Feathers*) features the two altoists in top form on six of Woods' obscure originals, plus "Airegin" and "Solar." The rhythm section (pianist George Syran, bassist Teddy Kotick and drummer Nick Stabulas) is tasteful and quietly supportive. —*Scott Yanow*

Sugan / Jul. 19, 1957 / Original Jazz Classics ✦✦✦✦
This CD from Fantasy's Original Jazz Classics series is essentially a bebop jam session. The quintet (altoist Phil Woods, trumpeter Ray Copeland, pianist Red Garland, bassist Teddy Kotick and drummer Nick Stabulas) performs three Charlie Parker compositions and three originals by Woods, but the melodies are quickly discarded in favor of heated solos. Woods and the greatly underrated Copeland work together very well, and Garland is a major asset both as a soloist and as an accompanist to the horns. This little-known date is quite enjoyable. —*Scott Yanow*

Phil Talks with Quill / Sep. 11, 1957-Oct. 8, 1957 / Columbia ✦✦✦
Phil Woods and fellow altoist Gene Quill had similar styles at the time of this quintet recording, for which they are accompanied by pianist Bob Corwin, bassist Sonny Dallas and drummer Nick Stabulas. They jam enthusiastically on five bop standards and Woods' "Hymn for Kim." Although not really essential, bebop fans may want to search for this hard-to-find LP. —*Scott Yanow*

Warm Woods / Oct. 18, 1957+Nov. 8, 1957 / Portrait ✦✦✦
For this lyrical LP reissue from 1988, altoist Phil Woods (who is joined by pianist Bob Corwin, bassist Sonny Dallas and drummer Nick Stabulas) emphasizes ballads. He performs five standards (highlighted by "In Your Own Sweet Way," "I Love You" and "Like Someone in Love"), an obscurity and two of his originals (including "Waltz for a Lovely Wife"). A tasteful, swinging and boppish set, mostly played at slower tempos. —*Scott Yanow*

★ **Right of Swing** / Jan. 26, 1960 / Candid ✦✦✦✦✦
This Candid recording is such a major success that it is surprising that altoist Phil Woods has rarely recorded in this context. The all-star octet not only features the altoist/leader but trumpeter Benny Bailey, trombonist Curtis Fuller, baritonist Sahib Shihab, the innovative French horn player Julius Watkins (a major factor in this music), pianist Tommy Flanagan, bassist Buddy Catlett and drummer Osie Johnson. This set (reissued by Black Lion on CD) consists entirely of Woods' five-part "Rights of Swing" suite, which clocks in around 38 minutes. The colorful arrangements use the distinctive horns in inventive fashion, and the music (which leaves room for many concise solos) holds one's interest throughout. One of Phil Woods' finest recordings, it's a true gem. —*Scott Yanow*

The Birth of the ERM / Jun. 1968-Oct. 1968 / Philology ✦✦✦✦✦

At the Montreux Jazz Festival / Jun. 18, 1969-Jun. 22, 1969 / Verve ✦✦✦✦✦

Phil Woods' European Rhythm Machine, an adventurous unit that really challenged the altoist, was one of the most underrated groups of the 1968-70 period. This hard-to-find but exciting LP features Woods with pianist George Gruntz, bassist Henri Texier and drummer Daniel Humair on lengthy renditions of compositions by Gruntz, Carla Bley, Herbie Hancock ("Riot") and Leonard Feather (an emotional "I Remember Bird"). It is very good to hear Phil Woods playing post-bop and almost avant-garde music for a change, but it is a pity that all of the intriguing group's recordings are currently out of print. —*Scott Yanow*

At the Frankfurt Jazz Festival / Mar. 21, 1970 / Atlantic ✦✦✦✦✦

Altoist Phil Woods' European Rhythm Machine was the most adventurous group he ever led, bordering on the avant-garde at times. The 1970 version (which includes pianist Gordon Beck, bassist Henri Texier and drummer Daniel Humair) is showcased on this 1986 reissue performing two group originals, Victor Feldman's "Joshua" and "Freedom Jazz Dance." Beck's "The Meeting" is the briefest performance at 11 minutes, while the other three selections all clock in around 13 minutes. Woods' longtime bebop fans may not be that excited by these fairly free improvisations (although the musicians were clearly listening closely to each other), but the altoist's tone remained quite recognizable. Challenging and stimulating music. —*Scott Yanow*

New Phil Woods Quartet / 1973 / Testament ✦✦✦

When Phil Woods returned to the US after several years in Europe, he formed a quartet with keyboardist Pete Robinson, bassist Henry Franklin and drummer Brian Moffatt that utilized electronics. Ten months of rehearsal resulted in four nights at a club and then little else before the band broke up. This LP, recorded at rehearsals in 1973, was the group's only album. On a pair of Robinson's challenging originals, the standard "Yesterdays" and a medley of Wayne Shorter's "Nefertiti" and Herbie Hancock's "Riot," Woods and Robinson challenge each other. However, the electronics do sound a bit dated, and the band was only in what should have been the early stages of its development; it sometimes sounds a bit uncomfortable and never really had a chance to mature. —*Scott Yanow*

Musique Du Bois / Jan. 14, 1974 / 32 Jazz ✦✦✦✦✦

Images / Feb. 1975 / RCA ✦✦✦

For this orchestra date, Phil Woods is backed by strings, brass, woodwinds and a rhythm section arranged and conducted by Michel Legrand (who also contributed three pieces). Altoist Woods is showcased throughout on some then-current pop tunes (including "The Windmills of Your Mind," "A Song for You" and a nice version of "We've Only Just Begun"), plus Debussy's "Clair de Lune" and Legrand's lengthy "Images." The overall results are not as essential as Woods' typical combo dates, but the altoist's tone does sound quite passionate at times. —*Scott Yanow*

New Phil Woods Album / Oct. 1975-Dec. 1975 / RCA ✦✦✦

Phil Woods Quartet/Quintet 20th Anniversary Set / June 1, 1976-Aug. 3, 1992 / Mosaic ✦✦✦✦✦

Mosaic's limited-edition five-disc box *Phil Woods Quartet/Quintet 20th Anniversary Set* is a treasure trove for hardcore fans of the altoist. All the material on this set is previously unreleased; Woods has been saving this material for 20 years and decided to license the tapes to Mosaic to celebrate his band's twentieth anniversary. Much of this music is dynamic and exciting, and it will certainly be a welcome addition to the collection of any serious Woods fan. —*Leo Stanley*

Live from the Showboat / Nov. 1976 / RCA ✦✦✦✦

This CD reissue brings back most of the earliest recording session by what would become Phil Woods' quintet. Unfortunately, four selections (including the twenty-one-and-a-half-minute "Brazilian Affair") which were on the original two-LP set were left off of this release. Altoist Woods is joined by guitarist Harry Leahey, pianist Mike Melillo, bassist Steve Gilmore, drummer Bill Goodwin and percussionist Alyrio Lima for the live set. While Lima would soon depart and Leahey was only aboard for a second record, Gilmore and Goodwin spent over 20 years with Woods' group. Highlights of the high-quality modern bop date include "A Sleepin' Bee," "Bye Bye Baby" and a lengthy "Cheek to Cheek." But get the two-LP set if it can be found. —*Scott Yanow*

Song for Sisyphus / Nov. 9, 1977 / Gryphon ✦✦✦✦

This recording features an early version of altoist Phil Woods' Quintet, the second of two albums that includes guitarist Harry Leahey. With pianist Mike Melillo, bassist Steve Gilmore and drummer Bill Goodwin completing the group, the Woods band's sound and musical philosophy were very much in place. The great altoist performs a few boppish tunes, some group originals (two songs by Melillo) and a couple of ballads. Highlights of the lesser-known but worthy recording include "Nuages," "Change Partners" and a cooking version of "Shaw Nuff." —*Scott Yanow*

I Remember / Mar. 1978 / Gryphon ✦✦✦✦

Taking time off from his combo projects, altoist Phil Woods and his quartet (also including pianist Mike Melillo, bassist Steve Gilmore and drummer Bill Goodwin) teamed up with a British orchestra (which includes trumpeter Kenny Wheeler, keyboardist Gordon Beck and a string quartet) on this LP to pay tribute through Woods' compositions to eight musicians who had by 1978 passed on: Cannonball Adderley, Paul Desmond, Oscar Pettiford, Oliver Nelson, Charlie Parker, percussionist Willie Rodriguez, trombonist Willie Dennis and Gary McFarland. Although none of the selections became well known, the altoist is in typically inspired form, putting plenty of emotion and exuberance into these inventive pieces. Worth searching for. —*Scott Yanow*

More Live / May 23, 1978+May 26, 1979 / Mobile Fidelity ✦✦✦✦

A follow-up to *The Phil Woods Quartet Volume 1*, this set (recorded live in Austin, TX) has lengthy versions of "Milestones," Steve Swallow's underrated "Eidendown," Horace Silver's "Strollin'" and (from 1978) pianist Mike Melillo's "See, Hunt & Liddy"; all of the selections are at least ten minutes long. Woods, Melillo, bassist Steve Gilmore and drummer Bill Goodwin had by 1979 become one of the top regularly working bop-based acoustic jazz groups around. The leader's enthusiastic alto and the tight rhythm section made for a mutually inspiring combination, and virtually all of Woods' records since first forming his combo in 1976 are well worth acquiring. —*Scott Yanow*

Crazy Horse / Jul. 1979 / Sea Breeze ✦✦✦✦

The 1979 Phil Woods Quartet (which consists of the altoist/leader, pianist Mike Melillo, bassist Steve Gilmore and drummer Bill Goodwin) meets up with the colorful synthesizers of Chris Swansen on this little-known album. On four Swansen originals and four standards (including Bill Evans' "Time Remembered" and "Bloomdido"), acoustic and electric instruments mix together quite well. Swansen's keyboards make the boppish music sound unusual without slowing down the momentum. Worth investigating, as is the Woods-Swansen 1984 rematch *Piper at the Gates of Dawn*. —*Scott Yanow*

Phil Woods Quartet, Live, Vol. 1 / May 26, 1979 / Clean Cuts ✦✦✦✦

This CD is a straight reissue of the original *Clean Cuts* LP. The four selections (which are joined by a brief "Phil's Theme") are superior jazz standards: Charlie Parker's blues "Bloomdido," "Everything I Love," Benny Golson's "Along Came Betty" and Bud Powell's "Hallucinations." Altoist Phil Woods and his regular group (pianist Mike Melillo, bassist Steve Gilmore and drummer Bill Goodwin) are in typically inspired form, and the results are high-quality modern bop. —*Scott Yanow*

Phil Woods / Lew Tabackin / Dec. 10, 1980 / Omnisound ✦✦✦✦✦

This album has such a logical matchup, it's surprising that it has not happened since. Altoist Phil Woods and tenor saxophonist Lew Tabackin (along with pianist Jimmy Rowles, bassist Michael Moore and drummer Bill Goodwin) are quite explosive on "Limehouse Blues," display their ability to caress a ballad on a lengthy "Sweet and Lovely," and cook on Tadd Dameron's "Theme of No Repeat" and three Woods originals. "Petite Chanson" finds Tabackin switching to flute, while Woods brings out his clarinet. Everything on this hard-to-find LP works, making one hope that the music will eventually be reissued on CD. —*Scott Yanow*

Three for All / Jan. 6, 1981-Jan. 7, 1981 / Enja ✦✦✦✦✦

Birds of a Feather / Aug. 11, 1981-Aug. 12, 1981 / Antilles ✦✦✦✦✦

This 1981 album has pianist Hal Galper's first recording as a member of the Phil Woods Quartet (replacing the departed Mike Melillo), the regularly working group that also included the altoist/leader, bassist Steve Gilmore and drummer Bill Goodwin. Woods performs two of his stronger originals ("Petite Chanson" and "Goodbye Mr. Evans") in addition to four standards, which are highlighted by "Star Eyes" and "Nica's Dream." When it comes to modern bebop, few players of the post-1970 era have been in Phil Woods' class, and his solos on this album are consistently fiery and inventive. —*Scott Yanow*

Live from New York / Oct. 7, 1982 / Quicksilver ✦✦✦✦

In October 1982, the Phil Woods Quartet (comprising the leader on alto, pianist Hal Galper, bassist Steve Gilmore and drummer Bill Goodwin) performed two albums at the Village Vanguard on consecutive nights for two different labels (Palo Alto and Antilles). The former set, which was released a couple of years later to celebrate the 10th anniversary of the band, has mostly lengthy renditions of the five songs (only one of which is under nine minutes in length). Woods is particularly inspired on John Carisi's "Springsville," Bill Evans' "Very Early" and Bud Powell's memorable "Webb City." Virtually all of the many recordings by Woods' quartet and quintets are recommended to straightahead jazz fans, and this one is no exception. —*Scott Yanow*

At the Vanguard / Oct. 8, 1982 / Antilles ✦✦✦✦✦
Recorded the day after a similar album (*Live From New York*) was cut for Palo Alto, this fine effort by the Phil Woods Quartet (with pianist Hal Galper, bassist Steve Gilmore and drummer Bill Goodwin) features the great altoist performing his usual mix of superior and generally less-played standards, ballads and obscurities (including Red Mitchell's "It's Time to Emulate the Japanese") along with his original "Reet's Neet." The music is straightahead and boppish but not overly predictable. A burning version of "All Through The Night" and Woods' clarinet feature on "Nardis" are highlights. — *Scott Yanow*

Piper at the Gates of Dawn / 1984 / Rykodisc ✦✦✦✦
The second recorded matchup by altoist Phil Woods and Chris Swansen's synthesizers is the equal of the first. Once again, Woods' regular group (with pianist Hal Galper, bassist Steve Gilmore and drummer Bill Goodwin) interacts with the two co-leaders, although this time around an extra plus are the two vocals by Kim Parker (on "'Round Midnight" and "Piper's Mood"). The repertoire mixes together bop standards (including three Charlie Parker songs) with atmospheric originals by the co-leaders. This unlikely collaboration once again is successful, containing more than its share of surprising moments. — *Scott Yanow*

Heaven / Dec. 28, 1984-Dec. 29, 1984 / Black Hawk ✦✦✦✦
Other than an album for the Italian Red label the previous March, this out-of-print CD from the defunct Black Hawk label was the first to feature trumpeter Tom Harrell with the Phil Woods Quintet. At this point in time, bassist Steve Gilmore and drummer Bill Goodwin had been with the band since its beginning 12 years before, while pianist Hal Galper was a five-year veteran. The repertoire on the set is quite strong, with a pair of less-played Duke Ellington pieces (the beautiful "Heaven" and "Azure") being performed along with Dave Brubeck's "The Duke," Sam Rivers' "222," the standard "I'm Getting Sentimental Over You" and Harrell's "Occurrence." Phil Woods sounds quite inspired throughout the date by Harrell's presence, giving him another horn to work off of. Recommended. — *Scott Yanow*

Gratitude / Jun. 19, 1986 / Denon ✦✦✦✦
Rather than being merely a bebop revival band, the Phil Woods Quintet (particularly after trumpeter Tom Harrell joined the group) has often performed obscurities and group originals that extend rather than merely reinforce the bebop vocabulary. On this CD from the Japanese Denon label, Woods and his group (which also includes pianist Hal Galper, bassist Steve Gilmore and drummer Bill Goodwin) play pieces by Oliver Nelson ("111-44"), Bill Mays, Joe Roccisano, Joe Emley, Harrell and Galper with just one standard (the ballad "Serenade in Blue"). The results are swinging, inventive and high-quality modern bop-based music. — *Scott Yanow*

Bouquet / Nov. 1987 / Concord Jazz ✦✦✦✦✦
Phil Woods' combos of the 1970s, '80s and '90s have helped to keep the tradition of bop alive by adding to the music's repertoire and featuring creative solos within bop structures; high musicianship and stable personnel have also helped. Recorded live at the 1987 Fujitsu-Concord Jazz Festival in Tokyo, *Bouquet* is a well-balanced set consisting of five lengthy workouts for the altoist's 1987 quintet (which also includes trumpeter Tom Harrell, pianist Hal Galper, bassist Steve Gilmore and drummer Bill Goodwin). "Theme From Star Trek" is taken at a blazing tempo that is highlighted by a fiery and witty tradeoff of two-bar phrases by Woods and Harrell. The trumpeter's moody ballad "Bouquet" precedes Hal Galper's "Tune of the Unknown Samba," a Latin piece that finds the pianist taking solo honors. Woods' emotional "Mom" and a surprisingly brisk "Willow Weep For Me" (with the altoist hinting at Eric Dolphy) wrap up this fine CD, easily recommended to Phil Woods' fans. — *Scott Yanow*

● **Bop Stew** / Nov. 1987 / Concord Jazz ✦✦✦✦✦
Phil Woods is in particularly inventive form throughout this live set from the 1987 Fujitsu-Concord Jazz Festival. Joined by his longtime quintet (with trumpeter Tom Harrell, pianist Hal Galper, bassist Steve Gilmore and drummer Bill Goodwin), the altoist stretches out on five selections, including a clarinet feature on "Poor Butterfly," and two of his originals. Galper's "Bop Stew" (which quotes several bop-era songs) is a highlight. Virtually every Phil Woods recording is easily recommended to modern mainstream jazz fans (he is one of the most consistent of all jazzmen), but this one seems even a touch more inspired than usual. — *Scott Yanow*

Evolution / May 1988 / Concord Jazz ✦✦✦✦✦
This release is somewhat special, for the Phil Woods Quintet (consisting of the altoist/leader, trumpeter Tom Harrell, pianist Hal Galper, bassist Steve Gilmore and drummer Bill Goodwin) is joined by trombonist Hal Crook (who would take Harrell's place in the near future), baritonist Nick Brignola and tenor saxophonist Nelson Hill to form the "Phil Woods Little Big Band." Woods contributed five of the eight songs (which are played along with selections from Crook, Jerry Dodgion and Miles Davis) and, since the chatty liner notes make no mention of it, chances are that he also wrote the colorful arrangements. The consistently inventive horn

solos (which are often concise) and the telepathic communication by the rhythm section (which had been together for years) makes this a particularly notable release even among the dozens of excellent Phil Woods recordings. — *Scott Yanow*

Here's to My Lady / Dec. 20, 1988-Dec. 21, 1988 / Chesky ✦✦✦✦
Altoist Phil Woods took a rare vacation from playing with his regular group to collaborate with pianist Tommy Flanagan, bassist George Mraz and drummer Kenny Washington on this fine straightahead quartet date. The 13 selections are fairly concise (clocking in between 3-7 minutes apiece) and most of the material (other than "Canadian Sunset," "Yours Is My Heart Alone," "Blue and Sentimental" and Bill Evans' classic "Waltz for Debby") consists of either obscurities or recent originals. A special bonus is that Woods plays his appealing clarinet on three numbers. Highlights include "Charles Christopher" (a tribute to Charlie Parker), "Butter" and Hal Galper's "Just Us." — *Scott Yanow*

Flash / Apr. 1989 / Concord Jazz ✦✦✦✦

All Bird's Children / Jun. 1990 / Concord Jazz ✦✦✦✦✦
For this 1990 set by Phil Woods' Quintet, the altoist welcomed trombonist Hal Crook to his group, joining longtime members pianist Hal Galper, bassist Steve Gilmore and drummer Bill Goodwin. Galper's melancholy ballad "Gotham Serenade" and Crook's modal blues "Ixtlan" on this CD contrast with Woods' three originals: "All Bird's Children," the upbeat "My Man Benny" (for Benny Carter) and an enthusiastic "Ole Dude." The quintet's treatments of three standards (all arranged by Crook) practically disguise the tunes and a particular highlight is the group's version of Benny Carter's "Just a Mood," which pits Woods' clarinet with Crook's wah-wah trombone. A highly enjoyable outing. — *Scott Yanow*

Real Life / Sep. 27, 1990-Sep. 28, 1990 / Chesky ✦✦✦✦

Flowers for Hodges / 1991 / Concord Jazz ✦✦✦✦
Throughout this CD, altoist Phil Woods often pays tribute to the ballad (rather than the stomping blues) side of the great fellow altoist Johnny Hodges. The set of duets with pianist Jim McNeely includes several songs identified with Hodges, along with a few originals by Woods (who also plays soprano, clarinet and bass clarinet) and McNeely. One of the highlights is Woods' melodic soprano on "I Didn't Know About You," although his weak vocal on "Hodges" is a low point. Woods' clarinet and bass clarinet work (some of which is overdubbed) is pleasing, but most of the program naturally showcases his familiar alto. McNeely's harmonically advanced style is partly modified on the Hodges tunes, but he does display his own musical personality. A nice change of pace from Phil Woods' long series of quartet/quintet dates, *Flowers for Hodges* has more than its share of surprises and is well worth acquiring. — *Scott Yanow*

Our Monk / Nov. 21, 1994 / Philology ✦✦✦✦✦
This lively duo date with pianist Franco D'Andrea is a very enjoyable all-Monk affair. Woods was a part of several larger groups led by Thelonious Monk, and his effortless swing makes it clear why he was chosen. Another choice track is "I Mean You," highlighted by Woods' singing tone. D'Andrea isn't nearly as well known, but he justifies his presence with a clever tapestry of chords around Woods on "Well, You Needn't." Recommended. — *Ken Dryden*

Alto Summit / Jun. 4, 1995+Jun. 5, 1995 / Milestone ✦✦✦✦
This is a sizzling meeting of three fine alto saxophonists in a session co-produced by Vincent Herring and Carl Allen. Phil Woods is the acknowledged dean of the alto, and his smooth chops contrast with Herring's grittier tone on bop classics like "Blue Minor" and "Minority." The veteran creates a sensational mood on "Stars Fell on Alabama," while Herring matches him with a lovely take of "Autumn in New York." The talented youngster Antonio Hart delivers a compelling solo in his feature "God Bless the Child." All three saxophonists solo with gusto on Woods' "Song for Sass." The rhythm section includes Carl Allen on drums, Anthony Wonsey on piano, and Reuben Rogers on bass. — *Ken Dryden*

Mile High Jazz / Apr. 20, 1996 / Concord Jazz ✦✦✦✦
Altoist Phil Woods and his 1996 quintet (which includes trumpeter Brian Lynch, pianist Bill Charlap, bassist Steve Gilmore and drummer Bill Goodwin) jam on six lengthy numbers on this live performance from Denver. Highlights include the exciting uptempo "Blues For K.B.," George Wallington's classic "Godchild" and Benny Carter's relaxed "Walkin' Thing." With Lynch (who successfully keeps up with Woods) and Charlap contributing some fine solos, Phil Woods has come up with another highly recommended and creative combo date that keeps the spirit of bop alive while avoiding the clichés. — *Scott Yanow*

Astor & Elis / May 28, 1996-May 30, 1996 / Chesky ✦✦✦
Phil Woods can usually be counted on to record consistently explosive bop-oriented sets with his regular quintet, but *Astor & Elis* is quite different. The altoist dedicates the performance to the singer Elis Regina, the influential modern tango composer Astor Piazzolla and indirectly to Dizzy Gillespie. Joined by a sextet that includes the talented cellist Eric Friedlander, pianist Bill Charlap and Phil Markowitz on synthesizer, Woods alternates between playing alto on Brazilian-fla-

vored material and utilizing his clarinet for Piazzolla's music. The emphasis is generally on lyrical and heartfelt ballad statements with occasional heated passages; Dizzy's "Con Alma" is the only jazz standard on the set. This attractive music favorably shows off Woods' versatility. —*Scott Yanow*

Celebration / Jan. 21, 1997-Jan. 22, 1997 / Concord Jazz ✦✦✦✦

Altoist Phil Woods has recorded a countless number of records through the years, but few with a big band, and none previous to this release with an orchestra that he actually put together. Woods' quintet, which includes trumpeter Brian Lynch and pianist Bill Charlap, is expanded to 16 pieces for this release with such familiar associates as altoist Nelson Hill and trombonist Hal Crook (who is showcased on "Willow Weep for Me"). The altoist wrote most of the arrangements and contributed six of the nine compositions, including "Reet's Neet," "Goodbye Mr. Evans" and "All Bird's Children." The music is boppish but not overly predictable, and the charts are consistently colorful, making this an easily recommended set for straightahead jazz fans. —*Scott Yanow*

Reggie Workman

b. Jun. 26, 1937, Philadelphia, PA
Bass / Avant-Garde, Hard Bop
Reggie Workman has long been one of the most technically gifted of all bassists, a brilliant player whose versatile style fits into both hard bop and very avant-garde settings. He played piano, tuba and euphonium early on but settled on bass in the mid-'50s. After working regularly with Gigi Gryce (1958), Red Garland and Roy Haynes, he was a member of the John Coltrane Quartet for much of 1961, participating in several important recordings and even appearing with Coltrane and Eric Dolphy on a half-hour West German television show that is currently available on video (*The Coltrane Legacy*). After Jimmy Garrison took his place with Coltrane, Workman became a member of Art Blakey's Jazz Messengers (1962-64) and was in the groups of Yusef Lateef (1964-65), Herbie Mann and Thelonious Monk (1967). He recorded frequently in the 1960s (including many Blue Note dates and Archie Shepp's classic *Four for Trane*). Since that time Workman has been an educator, played with everyone from Max Roach and Art Farmer to Mal Waldron and David Murray, and in 1989 recorded with Marilyn Crispell and Jeanne Lee. —*Scott Yanow*

Synthesis / Jun. 15, 1986 / Leo ✦✦✦✦✦

Images: The Reggie Workman Ensemble in Concert / Jan. 31, 1989-Jul. 1989 / Music & Arts ✦✦✦✦

● **Cerebral Caverns** / Apr. 27, 1995-Apr. 28, 1995 / Postcards ✦✦✦✦✦

World Saxophone Quartet

f. 1977
Group / Avant-Garde
The World Saxophone Quartet has long been an innovative group, an a cappella saxophone group that originally consisted of altoists Julius Hemphill and Oliver Lake, David Murray on tenor and baritonist Hamiett Bluiett. Playing without a rhythm section, this band plays adventurous music that somehow always stays coherent; the baselines and rhythms provided by Bluiett help a great deal. In addition to their original music they have recorded tributes to Duke Ellington and 1960s R&B. However with Hemphill's departure in 1993 (replaced at times by Arthur Blythe, James Spaulding and Eric Person), the group has been weakened in recent years. —*Scott Yanow*

Point of No Return / Jun. 1977 / Moers ✦✦✦✦

The debut recording by the World Saxophone Quartet, which has been reissued on CD, is quite a screamfest. Although there are a few written-out passages that are quieter, this live set generally consists of intense and violent improvisations. The main piece, the 23-minute "Scared Sheetless," is essentially a series of unaccompanied solos by the saxmen (Oliver Lake on alto and soprano, altoist Julius Hemphill, tenor saxophonist David Murray and baritonist Hamiett Bluiett), and despite the obvious passion and the adoration of the audience, much of the playing is quite tedious. In future years, the WSQ would better temper their free solos with inventive writing, but this early set is fairly self-indulgent. —*Scott Yanow*

Steppin' With / Dec. 1978 / Black Saint ✦✦✦✦✦

The second recording by the World Saxophone Quartet (which follows by a year their Moers Music release *Point of No Return*) gives one a well-rounded look at this powerful group. Comprising altoist Julius Hemphill (who contributes four of the six group originals), altoist Oliver Lake, tenorman David Murray and baritonist Hamiet Bluiett, the explorative yet rhythmic group is heard in their early prime on this stimulating release. —*Scott Yanow*

W.S.Q. / Mar. 1980 / Black Saint ✦✦✦✦✦

There is plenty of variety to the third album by the unique World Saxophone Quartet. The music ranges from nearly free improvisations to the four-part "Suite

Music," which was almost completely written out. Rather than being a screamfest for the four innovative saxophonists (baritonist Hamiet Bluiett, altoists Julius Hemphill and Oliver Lake and tenor saxophonist David Murray, all of whom double on other reeds), this is a well constructed and sometimes surprisingly accessible (although always explorative) program. —*Scott Yanow*

Revue / Oct. 14, 1980 / Black Saint ✦✦✦✦✦

The World Saxophone Quartet always believed in putting on a show, although without watering down its adventurous music. The nine numbers on this set are generally concise (only two songs exceed six minutes) and consist of originals by all four saxophonists: altoist Julius Hemphill (who contributed four of the nine pieces), baritonist Hamiet Bluiett, altoist Oliver Lake and tenor saxophonist David Murray. Sometimes quite rhythmic (and almost danceable) despite not having a rhythm section, the WSQ used melodies and rhythm for their own purposes, creating unpredictable music that always holds one's attention. This release is a good example of their talents. —*Scott Yanow*

Prophet / 1980 / Black Saint ✦✦✦✦✦

Live in Zurich / Nov. 6, 1981 / Black Saint ✦✦✦✦✦

By 1981, after four years of existence, it was obvious that the most talented writer in the World Saxophone Quartet was altoist Julius Hemphill. This Black Saint release finds Hemphill contributing six of the eight pieces (the other two are by Hamiet Bluiett), including the hard-swinging "Bordertown," the colorful "Steppin'" and a vivid feature for David Murray's tenor on "My First Winter." A particularly strong release by a classic and innovative group. —*Scott Yanow*

Live at Brooklyn Academy of Music / Dec. 6, 1985-Dec. 7, 1985 / Black Saint ✦✦✦✦

The World Saxophone Quartet's first recording in four years found the group's power and adventurous nature unchanged. In existence on a part-time basis for eight years at this point, the band still sounded quite unique, making avant-garde explorations almost seem accessible at times and playing quite rhythmically in places even without the presence of a rhythm section. Altoists Julius Hemphill and Oliver Lake, tenor saxophonist David Murray and baritonist Hamiet Bluiett (all of whom double on other reeds) were individually quite innovative, but they were also able to blend together to form an unusual group sound. Of their six originals, it is as usual the three Hemphill contributions that are most memorable. —*Scott Yanow*

★ **Plays Duke Ellington** / Apr. 1986 / Elektra ✦✦✦✦✦

On their first six recordings, the World Saxophone Quartet (comprising altoists Oliver Lake and Julius Hemphill, tenor saxophonist David Murray and baritonist Hamiet Bluiett) stuck exclusively to group originals. This 1986 release was a major departure, for the innovative group performed fresh and generally unpredictable versions of five songs by Duke Ellington and two (including two renditions of "Take the 'A' Train") by Billy Strayhorn. Although the tunes (which include "Lush Life," "Sophisticated Lady" and "In a Sentimental Mood") are familiar, the interpretations are certainly unusual, showing respect for the original melodies and then coming up with new directions. This thought-provoking music that serves as the perfect introduction to the unique World Saxophone Quartet. —*Scott Yanow*

Dances and Ballads / Apr. 1987 / Elektra ✦✦✦✦

For this 1987 release, the World Saxophone Quartet performs ten group originals: three apiece by tenor saxophonist David Murray and altoist Oliver Lake and two by baritonist Hamiet Bluiett and altoist Julius Hemphill. Celebrating its tenth year as a part-time group at the time, the WSQ was not as radical as ROVA, but their mixture of melodies and abstraction, rhythms and adventure were still quite appealing and filled their own niche. This is an underrated release, recorded between their better-known *Plays Duke Ellington* and *Rhythm and Blues* CDs. —*Scott Yanow*

Rhythm & Blues / Nov. 1988 / Elektra ✦✦✦✦✦

With tunes such as "Let's Get It On," "(Sittin' On) The Dock of the Bay," "Try a Little Tenderness" and "Night Train" being included, this CD certainly qualifies as one of the most unusual of all the World Saxophone Quartet recordings. Far from being a sellout to commercialism, this set features the WSQ (altoists Julius Hemphill and Oliver Lake, tenor saxophonist David Murray and baritonist Hamiet Bluiett) meeting the six soul and R&B tunes (which are joined by three complementary originals) head on. The WSQ was always open to playing rhythmically and was not allergic to strong melodies while including solo and group improvisations that were quite advanced. The combination works quite well on this surprising success. —*Scott Yanow*

Metamorphosis / Apr. 1990 / Elektra ✦✦✦✦

Amazing mix of African rhythms, African-American harmonies and solos. Spectacular solos augmented by thrilling African percussion. —*Ron Wynn*

You Don't Know Me / 1992 / Elektra ✦✦✦✦

Moving Right Along / 1993 / Black Saint ✦✦✦✦✦
This title applies to the World Saxophone Quartet's personnel as well as its music. Charter residents David Murray, Oliver Lake and Hamiett Bluiett were joined by special guest James Spaulding on two tracks, making it a quintet, and throughout by new member Eric Person. Person's composition "Antithesis," like several other selections, represented a change in the group's approach. Instead of their hallmark collectively improvised unison passages, most numbers had one or two featured soloists, with the others operating as harmony/contrast players. The WSQ did its usual array of material, from bubbling R&B and funk-tempered numbers to hard bop and swing-oriented tunes, plus two stirring renditions of "Amazing Grace." —*Ron Wynn*

Breath of Life / 1995 / Elektra ✦✦✦

Takin' It 2 the Next Level / Jun. 10-12, 1996 / Justin Time ✦✦✦✦
It is obvious from the first notes that this is a very different outing by the World Saxophone Quartet—the band is backed by a rhythm section. The playing of keyboardist Donald Blackman, bassist Calvin Jones and drummer Ronnie Burrage actually adds to the music rather than taking away from the core band, for their funky rhythms are fairly unpredictable and adventurous in their own way. The WSQ (which at the time consisted of David Murray on tenor and bass clarinet, baritonist Hamiet Bluiett, altoist Oliver Lake and John Purcell on saxello and tenor) sounds inspired by the "new" setting, and their playing is as adventurous as ever. Mostly sticking to group originals, the expanded band explores many moods on such numbers as "Wiring," "Rio," "The Desegregation of Our Children" and "When Thee Monarchs Come to Town." —*Scott Yanow*

World's Greatest Jazz Band

f. 1968, db. 1978
Group / Dixieland
This all-star group was founded in 1968 by Dick Gibson at his sixth annual Jazz Party. Despite the impossibility of living up to its outrageous name, the band was indeed the finest in Dixieland/classic jazz. Co-led by Yank Lawson and Bob Haggart and also featuring Billy Butterfield, Bud Freeman, Bob Miller and Ralph Sutton, the WGJB originally alternated standards with Dixiefied versions of current pop tunes like "Mrs. Robinson" but its finest album (*Live* on Atlantic) sticks to hot jamming. After the personnel changed a bit (Eddie Miller and Dick Wellstood passed through the band) the group broke up in 1978, although reunions by Lawson and Haggart in later years sometimes revived the name. Their recordings for Project 3, Atlantic and their own World Jazz label are pretty much all worth getting. —*Scott Yanow*

Jazz in the Mountains / 1967-1969 / World Jazz ✦✦✦✦
This LP from the World Jazz label features what would become the World's Greatest Jazz Band in its early stages. During a set that includes jam session-type versions of five Dixieland warhorses and three veteran standards, a variety of top all-star trad players have a chance to stretch out. Pianist Ralph Sutton ("Viper's Drag"), trombonist Lou McGarity ("Tin Roof Blues"), clarinetist Peanuts Hucko ("Just a Closer Walk with Thee") and trumpeter Billy Butterfield ("Summertime") get individual features while the full band performs "Savoy Blues" and romping versions of "South Rampart Street Parade" and "After You've Gone." The other notable musicians on this set of live performances from the Elitch Gardens in Denver are trumpeter Yank Lawson, trombonists Cutty Cutshall and Carl Fontana, clarinetists Bob Wilber and Peanuts Hucko, tenor saxophonist Bud Freeman, bassist Bob Haggart and drummers Morey Feld and Gus Johnson. Easily recommended to Dixieland fans. —*Scott Yanow*

More Jazz in the Mountains / 1967-1969 / World Jazz ✦✦✦✦
The second LP taken from concerts performed at Denver's Elitch Gardens during 1967-69, the lineup of musicians here is similar to what would become by late-1968 the World's Greatest Jazz Band: trumpeters Billy Butterfield and Yank Lawson, clarinetists Bob Wilber and Peanuts Hucko, trombonists Cutty Cutshall (a month before his death in 1968), Carl Fontana and Lou McGarity, tenor great Bud Freeman, pianist Ralph Sutton, bassist Bob Haggart and drummers Morey Feld and Gus Johnson. The repertoire is typical Dixieland (with plenty of sparks on a lengthy version of "Royal Garden Blues") but the musicians sound quite inspired by each other's presence and the music is consistently exciting. Other highlights include a pair of features for trombonists McGarity and Cutshall ("Cherry" and "Beale Street Blues"), the interplay between trumpeters Lawson and Butterfield on "St. James Infirmary Blues" and an explosive rendition of "That's a Plenty." —*Scott Yanow*

World's Greatest Jazz Band of Yank Lawson and Bob Haggart / Dec. 10, 1968 / Project 3 ✦✦✦
Originally known as the Nine (and then Ten) Greats of Jazz and renamed by its sponsor Dick Gibson as the World's Greatest Jazz Band, the unit officially debuted

on this Project Three LP. The WGJB may not have been the greatest or most significant jazz group at the time but, when it came to playing hard-driving Chicago jazz, few other regular bands could compete. Its late-1968 lineup consisted of trumpeters Yank Lawson and Billy Butterfield, trombonists Lou McGarity and Carl Fontana, clarinetist-soprano Bob Wilber, tenor saxophonist Bud Freeman, banjoist Clancy Hayes (who would soon leave the group), pianist Ralph Sutton, bassist Bob Haggart and drummer Morey Feld. In its two projects for Project Three, it was decided to alternate the usual Dixieland standards with swinging renditions of current pop tunes, in hopes of enlarging the audience and perhaps further inspiring the musicians. Therefore this album finds the WGJB uplifting such unlikely tunes as "Sunny," "Up, Up and Away," "Ode to Billy Joe," "A Taste of Honey" and "Mrs. Robinson." Although those renditions are more tolerable than expected, the high points of this album predictably come during "Panama," "Limehouse Blues" and "Bugle Call Rag." —*Scott Yanow*

Extra! / Dec. 1968 / Project 3 ✦✦✦
In its first year, it was the goal of the World's Greatest Jazz Band (which consisted of trumpeters Yank Lawson and Billy Butterfield, trombonists Lou McGarity and Cutty Cutshall, Bob Wilber on clarinet and soprano, tenor saxophonist Bud Freeman, pianist Ralph Sutton, bassist Bob Haggart and drummer Gus Johnson, Jr.) to perform not only Dixieland standards but pop tunes of the day that were felt might very well turn out to be the standards of the future. Due to that philosophy, the WGJB's second record includes such tunes as "What the World Needs Now Is Love," "Windmills of Your Mind," "Do You Know the Way to San Jose," "Wichita Lineman," "The 59th Street Bridge Song," "Alfie" and "Love Is Blue." As it turns out, only "Alfie" came close to being accepted in the jazz world, and the most rewarding renditions on this out-of-print LP are of "I'm Prayin' Humble (What's New)," "Wolverine Blues," "Savoy Blues" and "South Rampart Street Parade." The World's Greatest Jazz Band's best recordings were in the future, when they would finally decide to stick with superior jazz tunes. —*Scott Yanow*

★ **Live** / Apr. 17, 1970-Apr. 18, 1970 / Atlantic ✦✦✦✦✦
This is the finest record ever recorded by the World's Greatest Jazz Band, an exciting Dixieland nonet consisting in 1970 of trumpeters Yank Lawson and Billy Butterfield, trombonists Vic Dickenson and Lou McGarity, Bob Wilber on clarinet and soprano, tenor saxophonist Bud Freeman, pianist Ralph Sutton, bassist Bob Haggart and drummer Gus Johnson. Reissued on CD with a previously unreleased version of "Just One of Those Things" (which features Freeman and Wilber), this live set has many high points: An explosive version of "That's a Plenty," Lawson's playing on "Five Point Blues," a rambunctious "My Honey's Lovin' Arms," heated trumpet solos on "Come Back Sweet Papa" and Dickenson's showcase on "Constantly." This gem is highly recommended, even for listeners who may not think they like Dixieland. —*Scott Yanow*

What's New / Dec. 16, 1970 / Atlantic ✦✦✦✦
This is one of the World's Greatest Jazz Band's better studio albums. The repertoire has standbys ("Bourbon Street Parade," "The Eel" and "What's New"), "Mercy Mercy Mercy" and some newer and lesser-known material. The all-star lineup (trumpeters Yank Lawson and Billy Butterfield, trombonists Vic Dickenson and Eddie Hubble, tenor saxophonist Bud Freeman, Bob Wilber on clarinet and soprano, pianist Ralph Sutton, bassist Bob Haggart and drummer Gus Johnson) is particularly strong and most of the players get features. Best are a Lawson-Haggart duet on "Smile," Freeman's "The Eel" and Butterfield's warm sound and lyrical style on "What's New." —*Scott Yanow*

Plays George Gershwin / Jun. 1, 1971-Jun. 3, 1971 / World Jazz ✦✦✦

Century Plaza / Jan. 17, 1972-Jan. 19, 1972 / World Jazz ✦✦✦
After two albums apiece for the Project 3 and Atlantic labels, the World's Greatest Jazz Band started their own record company where they would record ten LPs during 1972-77. The first release is a bit unusual in that it emphasizes new material. Bassist Bob Haggart contributed four songs, clarinetist Bob Wilber brought in three and the group also performs Leonard Feather's little-known "Heavy Hearted Blues" in addition to just two standards ("At Sundown" and "She's Funny That Way"). Although the all-star lineup (trumpeters Yank Lawson and Billy Butterfield, trombonists Vic Dickenson and Eddie Hubble, Bob Wilber on clarinet and soprano, tenorman Bud Freeman, pianist Ralph Sutton, bassist Bob Haggart and drummer Gus Johnson), few of the new songs are all that memorable. Recommended primarily to WGJB completists. —*Scott Yanow*

Hark the Herald Angels Swing / Sep. 5, 1972-Sep. 7, 1972 / World Jazz ✦✦✦✦
This is one of the happier Christmas jazz LPs ever released. Although barely 32 minutes, this outing by the World's Greatest Jazz Band is filled with delightful performances of Yuletide favorites including "Rudolph the Red Nosed Reindeer," "Joy to the World," "Jingle Bells" and "Winter Wonderland," showing that many Christmas songs lend themselves well to Dixieland. The hot music is performed by trumpeters Yank Lawson and Billy Butterfield, trombonists Vic Dickenson and

Eddie Hubble, Bob Wilber on clarinet and soprano, tenor saxophonist Bud Freeman, pianist Ralph Sutton, bassist Bob Haggart and drummer Gus Johnson. Recommended. —*Scott Yanow*

At Massey Hall / Dec. 4, 1972 / World Jazz ✦✦✦✦
One of the last recordings by the best version of the World's Greatest Jazz Band, this fun live concert mostly finds the ensemble sticking to Dixieland, displaying enthusiasm and hard-driving swing on such numbers as "Original Dixieland One Step," "I Want to Be Happy," "Fidgety Feet" and "South." Pianist Ralph Sutton has "California Here I Come" as his feature; cornetist Bobby Hackett appears throughout as a "guest artist," since former second trumpeter Billy Butterfield had left the group shortly beforehand; and the musicians (who also include trumpeter Yank Lawson, trombonists Eddie Hubble and Vic Dickenson, Bob Wilber on clarinet and soprano, tenor saxophonist Bud Freeman, bassist Bob Haggart and drummer Gus Johnson) play up to par. An excellent and occasionally exciting performance. —*Scott Yanow*

Plays Cole Porter / May 1975 / World Jazz ✦✦
By 1975 the World's Greatest Jazz Band was starting to decline. Its personnel had changed but was still impressive (trumpeters Yank Lawson and John Best, trombonists Carl Fontana and George Masso, tenor saxophonist Tommy Newsom, clarinetist Peanuts Hucko, pianist Ralph Sutton, bassist Bob Haggart and drummer Gus Johnson) despite Bob Wilber, Vic Dickenson and Bud Freeman having departed. But its *Songbook* series (which resulted in full sets of the music of Cole Porter, Rodgers & Hart, Duke Ellington and George Gershwin) was generally disappointingly tepid and over-arranged. There are some fine solos on the 12 Cole Porter tunes, but only two of the performances exceed three minutes in length (and just barely), and the arrangements would be better suited to a dance band than an all-star Dixieland group. —*Scott Yanow*

In Concert at the Lawrenceville School / 1975 / Flying Dutchman ✦✦✦✦
Although the World's Greatest Jazz Band was starting to decline and undergo a lot of turnover by the mid-'70s, this is a generally strong effort. With trumpeter Yank Lawson, trombonist Urbie Green, Bob Wilber on soprano, clarinetist Johnny Mince, pianist Hank Jones, guitarist Bucky Pizzarelli, bassist Bob Haggart and drummer Ronnie Traxler forming the lineup for this concert, the music is typically Dixieland-oriented. The hottest performances are "Indiana," "South Rampart Street Parade" and surprisingly "Birth of the Blues." There are also individual features for Mince ("The Man I Love"), Wilber ("Indian Summer"), Green ("Old Folks") and Haggart ("Big Noise From Winnetka"). A fine effort by a classic group during its later period. —*Scott Yanow*

Plays Rodgers and Hart / 1975 / World Jazz ✦✦✦

On Tour, Vol. 1 / Oct. 1975 / World Jazz ✦✦✦✦
1975 was the last strong year for the World's Greatest Jazz Band although its two *On Tour* albums found the group still in prime form. At the time the band consisted of Yank Lawson and Billy Butterfield (who had returned to the fold after a few years' absence) on trumpets, trombonists George Masso and Sonny Russo, clarinetist Peanuts Hucko, tenor saxophonist Al Klink, pianist Ralph Sutton, bassist Bob Haggart and drummer Bobby Rosengarden. An added treat on this LP is that Maxine Sullivan sings "Wrap Your Troubles in Dreams" and "Just One of Those Things." Other highlights of the fine Dixieland set include "Sheik of Araby," "St. Louis Blues," Klink's feature on "Stardust," "Mandy, Make Up Your Mind" and "Limehouse Blues"; even "The Saints" fares well. Worth searching for. —*Scott Yanow*

On Tour, Vol. 2 / Oct. 1975 / World Jazz ✦✦✦✦
The second of two LPs taken from a 1975 tour by the World's Greatest Jazz Band has several fine Dixieland performances, particularly "Stumbling," "Runnin' Wild" (a feature for clarinetist Peanuts Hucko), "Big Butter and Egg Man" and "Hindustan." Maxine Sullivan takes a couple of warm and lightly swinging vocals while the rest of the band (trumpeters Yank Lawson and Billy Butterfield, trombonists George Masso and Sonny Russo, tenorman Al Klink, pianist Ralph Sutton, bassist Bob Haggart and drummer Bobby Rosengarden) is heard on plenty of spirited solos and rousing ensembles. This album is recommended, as is the first volume. —*Scott Yanow*

World's Greatest Jazz Band of Bob Haggart & Yank Lawson / Oct. 20, 1985 / Timeless ✦✦✦✦
By 1985 the World's Greatest Jazz Band (which had last recorded in 1977) had been history for quite a few years. However under their original title, the former co-leaders (trumpeter Yank Lawson and bassist Bob Haggart) put together a talented octet for a European tour that also included clarinetist Abe Most, tenor saxophonist Eddie Miller, trombonist Bob Havens, pianist Lou Stein, guitarist Marty Grosz and drummer Nick Fatool. The liner notes to this album often confuse the composers with which musicians get featured (Abe Most did not write "I Can't Give You Anything but Love"), but the record is worth searching for by Dixieland

collectors. Although Yank Lawson and Eddie Miller were both 74 at the time, they emerge as the main stars and sound quite strong. Highlights include "At the Jazz Band Ball," "St. Louis Blues" and "Jazz Me Blues." —*Scott Yanow*

Frank Wright

b. Jul. 9, 1935, Grenada, MS, d. May 17, 1990, Germany
Tenor Saxophone / Avant-Garde, Free Jazz
Throughout his career Frank Wright always played free jazz with the emphasis on passionate sound explorations. Early on he was an electric bassist who played R&B. However upon meeting Albert Ayler he was inspired to switch to tenor and perform much more adventurous music. He moved to New York in the early '60s and played with many musicians including Larry Young, Sunny Murray and even briefly Cecil Taylor and John Coltrane. Wright recorded as a leader for ESP in 1967 and 1969 and then spent much of the rest of his career living and playing in Europe, touring with Cecil Taylor in the mid-'80s. —*Scott Yanow*

Frank Wright Trio / Nov. 11, 1965 / ESP ✦✦✦✦
All of tenor saxophonist Frank Wright's recordings can be considered a bit of a blowout. For his debut as a leader, Wright (who is joined by bassist Henry Grimes and drummer Tom Price) rips into three of his originals: "The Earth," "The Moon" and "Jerry." Due to the brevity of this CD reissue (34 minutes), his follow-up ESP date *Your Prayer* gets the edge, but both are easily recommended to open-eared listeners who enjoy hearing fiery sound explorations. —*Scott Yanow*

● **Your Prayer** / May 1967 / ESP ✦✦✦✦✦
For his second and final ESP date as a leader, the avant-garde tenor saxophonist Frank Wright teams up with four little-known players (altoist Arthur Jones, trumpeter Jacques Coursil, bassist Steve Tintweiss and drummer Muhammad Ali) for passionate explorations of four of his originals plus Jones' "The Lady." Rather intense at times, these emotional performances (which, unusual for an ESP date, clock in at over 50 minutes) still sound groundbreaking three decades later. One of Frank Wright's finest recordings. —*Scott Yanow*

Kevin, My Dear Son / Oct. 1978 / Chiaroscuro ✦✦✦✦

Stove Man, Love Is the Word / May 22, 1979 / Sandra ✦✦✦✦
Live at the Loft in Munich, Germany, with sextet. Rev. Wright is on the edge. This is an extension of Dolphy. Must have open ears. —*Michael G. Nastos*

Richard Wyands

b. Jul. 2, 1928, Oakland, CA
Piano / Hard Bop
A fine pianist whose chord voicings are a little reminiscent of Red Garland, Richard Wyands has spent most of his career as a sideman. He started working in local clubs when he was 16, graduated from San Francisco State College, and gained experience playing in the San Francisco Bay area. Wyands, who was a sideman on a few early dates for Fantasy, spent time accompanying Ella Fitzgerald (1956) and Carmen McRae. He moved to New York in 1958, where he played with Roy Haynes, Charles Mingus (1959), Gigi Gryce's quintet, Oliver Nelson, Etta Jones, Eddie "Lockjaw" Davis, and Gene Ammons, among others. Wyands was associated with Kenny Burrell, with whom he toured extensively during 1964-77, and has played with many other top musicians, including Freddie Hubbard, Zoot Sims, Frank Foster, the Illinois Jacquet Big Band, Benny Carter, Ernie Andrews, and Milt Hinton, among others. Richard Wyands has also headed his own trios, but has only had three sessions as a leader thus far, a 1978 date for Storyville and sessions for DIW (1992) and Criss Cross (1995). —*Scott Yanow*

● **Then, Here and Now** / Oct. 12, 1978 / Storyville ✦✦✦✦✦

Reunited / Jun. 15, 1995 / Criss Cross ✦✦✦✦

Get Out of Town / 1997 / Steeple Chase ✦✦✦✦

Albert Wynn

b. Jul. 29, 1907, New Orleans, LA, d. May 1973, Chicago, IL
Trombone / Classic Jazz, New Orleans Jazz
Albert Wynn was best known for his work in the 1920s, although he survived and continued playing into the mid-'60s. Wynn grew up in Chicago, where he was based throughout most of his life. Early in his career, Wynn played in the Bluebirds' Kids Band and toured with Ma Rainey. Wynn performed and recorded with Charlie Creath's Jazz-O-Maniacs in St. Louis (1927) and spent time in Europe (1928-32), working for 18 months with Sam Wooding. After returning to the US, he performed briefly with Sidney Bechet's New Orleans Feetwarmers (1932) and then worked in Chicago with Carroll Dickerson, Jesse Stone, Reuben "River" Reeves, Jimmie Noone, Richard M. Jones and the Earl Hines Orchestra. Wynn was part of Fletcher Henderson's Orchestra (1937-39), played with Jimmie Noone's short-lived big band, and in the 1940s performed with many local groups, includ-

ing bands featuring Baby Dodds and Lil Armstrong. He also owned a record store. A member of Franz Jackson's Original Jazz All-Stars (1956-60), Wynn had his last major job playing with the Gold Coast Jazz Band (1960-64). Albert Wynn recorded six songs as a leader during the 1926-28 period (among his sidemen were Barney Bigard on tenor and cornetist Punch Miller) and in 1961 led a set for Riverside and recorded an album with Lil Armstrong; both of the latter have since been reissued on CD. —*Scott Yanow*

● **Chicago: The Living Legends** / Sep. 5, 1961 / Original Jazz Classics ◆◆◆◆◆
Trombonist Albert Wynn, a veteran of the Chicago jazz scene of the 1920s, recorded six selections as a leader from 1926-28 and then headed no further sessions until he cut this full-length album in 1961 as part of Riverside's "Living Leg-

ends" series. Reissued on CD in the Original Jazz Classics program along with two additional cuts ("I Ain't Gonna Give Nobody None O' This Jelly Roll" and the alternate take of "How Long Blues") originally only on samplers, this is a particularly exuberant date. In addition to Wynn, the septet includes such alumni of the 1920s as clarinetist Darnell Howard, the obscure trumpeter Bill Martin, Bus Moten (Bennie's brother) and Blind John Davis alternating on piano, guitarist Mike McKendrick, bassist Robert Wilson and drummer Booker T. Washington. On a variety of Dixieland and swing standards (including "Ice Cream," "Someday Sweetheart," "Bourbon Street Parade" and "Nobody's Sweetheart"), these veterans show that they were still in their musical prime in 1961. The musicians, who were mostly in their mid-50s, were considered ancient at the time. —*Scott Yanow*

Yosuke Yamashita

b. Feb. 26, 1942, Tokyo, Japan
Piano / Avant-Garde, Free Jazz
One of the top Japanese jazz pianists, Yosuke Yamashita is a very adventurous and passionate improviser. After attending the Kunitachi Music University, Yamashita formed an avant-garde trio in 1969. Starting in 1974, Yamashita visited Europe most years. Since breaking up his trio in 1983, he has performed in a variety of settings ranging from a big band to solo. Most of Yamashita's recordings remain unavailable in the US. —*Scott Yanow*

Clay / Jun. 2, 1974 / Enja ◆◆◆◆

Chiasma / Jun. 6, 1975 / MPS ◆◆◆◆◆

Inner Space / Jun. 24, 1977 / Enja ◆◆◆◆

Tribute to Mal Waldron / Jun. 17, 1980+Jun. 18, 1980 / Enja ◆◆◆◆

Sakura (Cherry) / May 1, 1990-May 3, 1990 / Antilles ◆◆◆◆◆

● **Kurdish Dance** / 1993 / Antilles ◆◆◆◆

Dazzling Days / Mar. 22, 1994 / Antilles ◆◆◆◆

Asian Games / May 17, 1994 / Antilles ◆◆◆◆

Ways of Time / Dec. 12, 1995 / Antilles ◆◆◆◆

Jimmy Yancey

b. 1894, Chicago, IL, d. Sep. 17, 1951, Chicago, IL
Piano / Boogie-Woogie, Piano Blues
One of the pioneers of boogie-woogie piano, Jimmy Yancey was generally more subtle than the more famous Albert Ammons, Pete Johnson and Meade Lux Lewis, falling as much into the blues genre as in jazz. Yancey, who could romp as well as anyone, made many of his most memorable recordings at slower tempos. No matter what key he played in, Yancey ended every song in E flat, leading to some hilarious conclusions to some recordings. He worked in vaudeville as a singer and tap dancer starting at age six and in 1915 settled in Chicago as a pianist. But Yancey spent his last 26 years (from 1925 on) earning his living as a groundskeeper at Comiskey Park for the Chicago White Sox. He played part-time in local clubs and began recording in 1939, on a few occasions backing his wife, singer Mama Yancey. Jimmy Yancey never achieved the fame of his contemporaries, but he remained a major influence on all practioners in the genre. —*Scott Yanow*

★ **Complete Recorded Works, Vol. 1 (1939-1940)** / May 4, 1939+Oct. 25, 1939 / Document ◆◆◆◆◆
The first of three Document CDs that reissue all of pianist Jimmy Yancey's recordings (other than his final Atlantic session) is filled with classic performances. Yancey, a subtle boogie-woogie/blues pianist who was a major influence and inspiration on the better-known players of the 1930s, is featured on his first two solo sessions including "The Fives," "La Salle Street Breakdown," "South Side Stuff," "Yancey's Getaway," "Yancey Stomp" and "State Street Special." Highly recommended, as are the two following volumes in this valuable Document series. —*Scott Yanow*

☆ **Complete Recorded Works, Vol. 2 (1940-1943)** / Feb. 23, 1940-Dec. 1943 / Document ◆◆◆◆◆
On the second of three CDs that trace virtually his entire recording career, pianist Jimmy Yancey is showcased on a variety of solo tracks. Two numbers from February 1940 are highlighted by the classic "Bear Trap Blues." There are a couple of numbers made for the tiny Art Center Jazz Gems label, a four-song (plus two alternate takes) definitive set cut for Bluebird (which includes "Death Letter Blues" and "Yancey's Bugle Call") and nine songs (five previously unissued) from 1943; on one version of "How Long Blues," Mama Yancey sings while Jimmy switches to the spooky sounding harmonium. This set also has Jimmy Yancey's only four recorded vocals, which are quite effective even though his voice is limited. All three volumes in this series are highly recommended for the subtle pianist, who made expert use of space and ended every tune in E flat. —*Scott Yanow*

☆ **Complete Recorded Works, Vol. 3 (1943-1950)** / Dec. 1943-Dec. 23, 1950 / Document ◆◆◆◆◆
The third of three CDs tracing the recording career of the unique boogie-woogie pianist Jimmy Yancey, whose subtlety could often result in some dramatic music, completes his December 1943 session and also has his December 23, 1950 solo set; his final recordings from July 1951 are available on an Atlantic release. The 1943 titles, three of which were previously unreleased, include two with Mama Yancey vocals (on one Jimmy switches to harmonium) and are highlighted by "White Sox Stomp," "Yancey Special" and two versions of "Pallet on the Floor." After the six fine titles from 1950, this CD finishes off with the only four numbers that Jimmy's older brother, the more ragtime-oriented Alonzo Yancey, ever recorded. Although his style was different, on "Ecstatic Rag" Alonzo does sound a bit like Jimmy. All three of these Document CDs, plus the Atlantic set, are highly recommended and preferable to the piecemeal domestic Bluebird reissues. —*Scott Yanow*

Chicago Piano, Vol. 1 / Jul. 18, 1951 / Atlantic ◆◆◆◆
Jimmy Yancey was one of the pioneer boogie-woogie pianists but, unlike many of the other pacesetters, he had a gentle and thoughtful style that also crossed over into the blues. This Atlantic CD, a straight reissue of the 1972 LP, contains Yancey's final recordings, cut just eight weeks before his death from diabetes. The pianist is in fine form on these introspective and often emotional performances which, with the exception of Meade Lux Lewis' "Yancey Special" and the traditional "Make Me a Pallet on the Floor," comprise Yancey's originals. His wife Mama Yancey takes five memorable vocals on this memorable set of classic blues. —*Scott Yanow*

The Yellowjackets

f. 1981
Group / Post-Bop, Crossover Jazz, Fusion
Although sometimes grouped with Spyro Gyra, the Yellowjackets are actually one of the most creative regular groups in the "rhythm and jazz" genre. Founded in 1981 as an R&B-oriented band that starred guitarist Robben Ford, the group took a giant step forward when after Ford's departure, altoist Marc Russo took his place. With original members Russell Ferrante on keyboards and electric bassist Jimmy Haslip in addition to drummer William Kennedy, the band found its own R&Bish sound, sometimes playing original compositions that sounded like Joe Zawinul at his most melodic. In recent times Russo chose to go out on his own, and his replacement Bob Mintzer (on tenor and bass clarient), has added more jazz credibility to the group's music. Through the years the Yellowjackets have continued to evolve, sacrificing their popularity a bit by refusing to be overly predictable. They have recorded for Warner Brothers, MCA, GRP and Warner Bros. —*Scott Yanow*

Yellowjackets / 1981 / Warner Brothers ◆◆◆

Samurai Samba / 1984 / Warner Brothers ◆◆◆◆

Mirage a Trois / 1985 / Warner Brothers ◆◆◆◆

Shades / 1986 / MCA ◆◆◆◆

Four Corners / 1987 / MCA ◆◆◆◆◆

Politics / 1988 / MCA ◆◆◆◆◆
Politics features the appealing sax of Marc Russo and the compositions of Russell Ferrante. Unpretentious, melodic and memorable, it has fine studio sound. —*David Nelson McCarthy*

★ **The Spin** / 1989 / MCA ◆◆◆◆◆

Green House / 1990 / GRP ◆◆◆◆◆

Live Wires / Nov. 15, 1991-Nov. 16, 1991 / GRP ◆◆◆◆
This live set by the Yellowjackets (taped at the Roxy in Hollywood) has plenty of solo space for Bob Mintzer (on tenor, soprano, bass clarinet and EWI) and keyboardist Russell Ferrante (who takes a particularly colorful spot on "Homecoming") along with fine backup wrok by bassist Jimmy Haslip, drummer William Kennedy and percussionist Paulinho Da Costa. Although the back cover of the CD says "Featuring: Michael Franks, Take 6, Brenda Russell & Marilyn Scott," fortu-

nately Franks, Russell and Scott are only heard on one harmless selection ("The Dream") while Take 6 just pops by for the closer "The Revelation." The strength of the improvisations and of Ferrante's Joe Zawinul-like originals make this one of the Yellowjackets' stronger efforts. —*Scott Yanow*

Like a River / Apr. 1992 / GRP ✦✦✦✦

Other than the easy-listening pieces that appear near the beginning of the program, this is one of the Yellowjackets' strongest jazz dates. Bob Mintzer's creative reeds (switching between tenor, bass clarinet, soprano and the EWI) keep the music stimulating and keyboardist Russell Ferrante has come a long way as both an improviser (where he is most influenced by Herbie Hancock) and as the band's main composer. With bassist Jimmy Haslip and drummer William Kennedy in strong supporting roles, the ensemble plays intelligent funk grooves, some mood music and occasional sections of straightahead jamming. The inclusion of the Miles Davis-influenced trumpeter Tim Hagans on half of the selections adds variety to a particularly enjoyable set. —*Scott Yanow*

Run for Your Life / 1993 / GRP ✦✦✦✦✦

This is one of the Yellowjackets' most jazz-oriented sets. Roughly half of the music uses funky rhythms while the remainder is straightahead. "Jacket Town" sounds like it could have come from a good Eddie Harris record, Bob Mintzer's tenor is heard on a rapid run-through of rhythm changes on "Runferyerlife," keyboardist Russell Ferrante hints strongly at Chick Corea's acoustic playing on "Muhammed" and Mintzer's ballad "Sage" is memorable. This fine release is recommended both to the Yellowjackets' longtime fans and those listeners who mistakenly think that this popular group is a mundane fusion band. —*Scott Yanow*

Dreamland / 1994 / Warner Brothers ✦✦✦✦

Blue Hats / 1997 / Warner Brothers ✦✦✦✦

As they continue to evolve, the Yellowjackets have gradually gone from being an R&B-oriented fusion band to a more acoustic group that emphasizes fairly straightahead improvisations. Although this CD has nine originals by band members and some electronics are utilized (primarily by keyboardist Russell Ferrante for color), much of the music would satisfy even hard bop listeners. Bob Mintzer's many solos on tenor, soprano, bass clarinet and EWI are excellent, but it is the tightness of the rhythm section (which also includes bassist Jimmy Haslip and drummer William Kennedy) that continues to give the Yellowjackets its own original sound. —*Scott Yanow*

Dave Young

Bass / Bop

A jazz and classical acoustic bassist noted for his subtlety and versatility, Dave Young was raised in Winnipeg, Ontario, later relocating to Toronto in the hopes of pursuing a career in music. He first attracted notice in collaboration with guitarist Lenny Breau, whom he joined in 1961; exiting Breau's band a half-decade later, Young went on to perform and record with such renowned figures as Clark Terry, Zoot Sims, Moe Koffman, Nat Adderley and Oscar Peterson. After spending decades as the bass accompanist of choice for performers traveling through Toronto, Young led his first recording date, *Fables and Dreams*, in 1993; two years later, he recruited a group of pianists including the aforementioned Peterson, Mulgrew Miller, Tommy Flanagan and Renee Rosnes for the acclaimed *Two by Two*, the first in a series of bass and piano duets. —*Jason Ankeny*

Fables and Dreams / May 1993 / Justin Time ✦✦✦

This CD features a quiet quartet that is often filled with inner tension and low-volumed heat. Bassist Dave Young engages in close interplay with guitarist Rob Piltch (whose tone is sometimes reminiscent of the late Jimmy Raney's), Phil Dwyer contributes lyrical tenor solos and some moody piano (sometimes sounding a bit like McCoy Tyner on the latter instrument) while drummer Michel Lambert is fine in support. Five of the nine songs are originals by band members while the other pieces (including an abstract "All of Me" and a rather passionless version of Charles Mingus' "Fables of Faubus") almost sound like new compositions; the closing tenor-bowed bass duet on "Whims of Chambers" is most memorable. If the overall results on this session are not all that unique, the well-played set does serve as a good example of today's modern mainstream acoustic jazz and should satisfy most listeners. —*Scott Yanow*

● **Two by Two: The Complete Sessions** / Jan. 23, 1995-Jun. 19, 1995 / Justin Time ✦✦✦✦✦

Larry Young (Khalid Yasin Abdul Aziz)

b. Oct. 7, 1940, Newark, NJ, d. Mar. 30, 1978, New York, NY
Organ / Hard Bop, Post-Bop, Fusion, Groove, Soul Jazz

If Jimmy Smith was "the Charlie Parker of the organ," Larry Young was its John Coltrane. One of the great innovators of the mid- to late 1960s, Young fashioned a distinctive modal approach to the Hammond B-3 at a time when Smith's earthy,

blues-drenched soul-jazz style was the instrument's dominant voice. Initially, Young was very much a Smith admirer himself. After playing with various R&B bands in the 1950s and being featured as a sideman with tenor saxman Jimmy Forrest in 1960, Young debuted as a leader that year with *Testifying*, which, like his subsequent soul-jazz efforts for Prestige, *Young Blues* (1960) and *Groove Street*, (1962), left no doubt that Smith was his primary inspiration. But when Young went to Blue Note in 1964, he was well on his way to becoming a major innovator. Coltrane's post-bop influence asserted itself more and more in Young's playing and composing, and his work grew much more cerebral and exploratory. *Unity*, recorded in 1965, remains his best-known album. Quick to embrace fusion, Young played with Miles Davis in 1969, John McLaughlin in 1970 and Tony Williams' groundbreaking Lifetime in the early 1970s. Unfortunately, his work turned uneven and erratic as the '70s progressed. Young was only 38 when, in 1978, he checked into the hospital suffering from stomach pains, and died from untreated pneumonia. The Hammond hero's work for Blue Note (as both a leader and a sideman) was united for Mosaic's limited-edition six-CD box set *The Complete Blue Note Recordings*. —*Alex Henderson*

Testifying / Aug. 2, 1960 / Original Jazz Classics ✦✦✦

Organist Larry Young was 19 when he made this, his debut recording. Although he would become innovative later on, Young at this early stage was still influenced by Jimmy Smith even if he had a lighter tone; the fact that he used Smith's former guitarist, Thornel Schwartz, and a drummer whose name was coincidentally Jimmie Smith kept the connection strong. R&Bish tenor Joe Holiday helps out on two songs and the music (standards, blues and ballads) always swings. Easily recommended to fans of the jazz organ. —*Scott Yanow*

Young Blues / Sep. 30, 1960 / Original Jazz Classics ✦✦✦✦✦

Organist Larry Young's second recording (cut shortly before he turned 20) is the best from his early period before he completely shook off the influence of Jimmy Smith. With guitarist Thornel Schwartz in top form, and bassist Wendell Marshall and drummer Jimmie Smith excellent in support, Young swings hard on a few recent jazz originals, some blues and two standards ("Little White Lies" and "Nica's Dream"). Recommended as a good example of his pre-Blue Note work. —*Scott Yanow*

Groove Street / Feb. 27, 1962 / Original Jazz Classics ✦✦✦

Larry Young's third and final Prestige recording (reissued in the *OJC* series on CD) concludes his early period; he would next record as a leader two-and-a-half years later on Blue Note, by which time his style would be much more original. For his 1962 outing, Young is joined by the obscure tenor Bill Leslie, guitarist Thornel Schwartz and drummer Jimmie Smith for some original blues and two standards ("I Found a New Baby" and "Sweet Lorraine"). Nothing all that substantial occurs, but fans of Jimmy Smith will enjoy the similar style that Larry Young had at the time. —*Scott Yanow*

☆ **Complete Blue Note Recordings** / Sep. 11, 1964-Feb. 7, 1969 / Mosaic ✦✦✦✦✦

Larry Young, one of the most significant jazz organists to emerge after the rise of Jimmy Smith, is heard on this limited-edition six-CD set at the peak of his creativity [The set comprises the following original albums: Grant Green *Talkin' About*, Larry Young *Into Somethin',* Grant Green *Street of Dreams*, Grant Green *I Want to Hold Your Hand*, Larry Young *Unity*, Larry Young *of Love and Peace*, Larry Young *Contrasts*, Larry Young *Heaven on Earth*, Larry Young *Mother Ship*, Larry Young *40 Years of Jazz, The History of Blue Note* (box 4 Dutch), Larry Young *The World of Jazz Organ* (Japanese), Larry Young *The Blue Note 50th Anniversary Collection Volune Two: The Jazz Message*. Formerly available as nine LPs (three of which were actually under guitarist Grant Green's leadership), Young was still very much under Smith's influence on the first four sessions (which feature a trio with Green and drummer Elvin Jones plus guests Sam Rivers or Hank Mobley on tenor and vibraphonist Bobby Hutcherson). However, starting with the monumental *Unity* session (a quartet outing with Joe Henderson on tenor, trumpeter Woody Shaw and Elvin Jones), Young emerged as a very advanced and original stylist in his own right. The final four dates are generally fairly explorative and feature such notable sidemen as altoist James Spaulding and Byard Lancaster, guitarist George Benson and trumpeter Lee Morgan along with some forgotten local players. This definitive Larry Young set is highly recommended. —*Scott Yanow*

Into Somethin' / Nov. 12, 1964 / Blue Note ✦✦✦✦✦

Larry Young, who like most organists originally sounded close to Jimmy Smith, took a big step away from the organ's dominant influence on this adventurous and colorful set, which was his debut as a leader for Blue Note. Performing with a quartet also including tenor saxophonist Sam Rivers, guitarist Grant Green and drummer Elvin Jones, Young performs four of his originals plus Green's "Plaza De Toros." Other than the blues "Backup," the music is fairly complex, grooving in its own fashion and showing that Young was quite aware of John Coltrane's modal excursions. —*Scott Yanow*

The Art of Larry Young / 1964-1969 / Blue Note ◆◆◆◆
The Art of Larry Young is a seven-track collection that draws highlights from the organist's five years at Blue Note during the mid- to late '60s. During that time, Young established himself as one of the most adventurous organists in jazz, unafraid to break free from the confines of soul-jazz and tackle free jazz. While missing many fine tracks, this isn't a bad summary of his accomplishments, and since many of his Blue Note albums are hard to find—they've either been reissued in the expensive, limited-edition Mosaic box or limited-edition CDs—this compilation is even more valuable. —*Stephen Thomas Erlewine*

★ **Unity** / Nov. 10, 1965 / Blue Note ◆◆◆◆◆
This is a classic album, the finest of organist Larry Young's career. On this date (a quartet outing with trumpeter Woody Shaw, tenor saxophonist Joe Henderson and drummer Elvin Jones), Young emerged as the first original voice on the organ since Jimmy Smith. Young keeps up with his illustrious sidemen on three Shaw originals (best known is "The Moontrane"), Henderson's "If," "Monk's Dream" and the standard "Softly As in a Morning Sunrise." The performances grow in interest with each listen and find all of the musicians inspired by each other and by the high-quality material. A gem. —*Scott Yanow*

Of Love and Peace / Jul. 28, 1966 / Blue Note ◆◆◆◆◆
By 1966, Larry Young was playing music that fell between advanced hard bop/soul-jazz and the avant-garde. For this stimulating Blue Note date (which has been reissued as part of Young's Mosaic box set), the organist meets up with trumpeter Eddie Gale (who was playing with Cecil Taylor during this era), altoist/flutist James Spaulding and three obscure but fine sidemen: tenor saxophonist Herbert Morgan and both Wilson Moorman III and Jerry Thomas on drums. Two of the selections ("Of Love and Peace" and "Falaq") are essentially free improvisations that have a momentum and purpose of their own, moving forward coherently. In addition, Young and his group perform adventurous versions of "Pavanne" and "Seven Steps to Heaven." Very stimulating and intriguing music—this was one of Larry Young's best recordings. —*Scott Yanow*

Contrasts / Sep. 18, 1967 / Blue Note ◆◆◆◆
For this interesting set, organist Larry Young (the first musician on his instrument to really move beyond Jimmy Smith's soul-jazz into the avant-garde) mostly utilized lesser-known musicians from the Newark, NJ, area: Tyrone Washington and Herbert Morgan on tenors, fluegelhornist Hank White, guitarist Eddie Wright, drummer Eddie Gladden and Stacey Edwards on congas. "Major Affair" is an organ-drums duet, and Larry's wife Althea Young does a haunting version of "Wild Is the Wind," while the other four selections use all of the horns. The adventurous music is sometimes quite intense but also grooves in its own eccentric way, offering listeners a very fresh sound on organ. —*Scott Yanow*

Heaven on Earth / Feb. 9, 1968 / Blue Note ◆◆◆
Organist Larry Young, who really found his own sound back in 1965 with the classic *Unity* album, is deep in the funk on this later Blue Note album (which has been included in the Mosaic box set *The Complete Blue Note Recordings of Larry Young*). With altoist Byard Lancaster, tenor saxophonist Herbert Morgan, guitarist George Benson and drummer Eddie Gladden completing the quintet, there are some explorative solos but the less imaginative funk rhythms lower the content of the music somewhat. Young's wife Althea Young has an effective vocal on "My Funny Valentine," but overall this is a lesser effort. —*Scott Yanow*

Mother Ship / Feb. 7, 1969 / Blue Note ◆◆◆
Organist Larry Young's final Blue Note album was not released until 1980. Teamed up with tenor saxophonist Herbert Morgan, the great trumpeter Lee Morgan and drummer Eddie Gladden, Young performs five of his originals, which range from the funky "Street Scene" and the samba "Love Drops" to a spacy "Trip Merchant" and the complex "Visions." This highly original set does not deserve to be so obscure. —*Scott Yanow*

Lawrence of Newark / 1973 / Perception ◆◆

Fuel / 1975 / Arista ◆◆

Spaceball / 1975 / Arista ◆◆

Lester Young

b. Aug. 27, 1909, Woodville, MS, **d.** Mar. 15, 1959, New York, NY
Tenor Saxophone, Clarinet / Swing, Cool
Lester Young was one of the true jazz giants, a tenor saxophonist who came up with a completely different conception in which to play his horn, floating over barlines with a light tone rather than adopting Coleman Hawkins' then-dominant forceful approach. A non-conformist, Young (nicknamed "Pres" by Billie Holiday) had the ironic experience in the 1950s of hearing many young tenors try to sound exactly like him!

Although he spent his earliest days near New Orleans, Lester Young lived in Minneapolis by 1920, playing in a legendary family band. He studied violin, trum-

pet and drums, starting on alto at age 13. Because he refused to tour in the South, Young left home in 1927 and instead toured with Art Bronson's Bostonians, switching to tenor. He was back with the family band in 1929 and then freelanced for a few years, playing with Walter Page's Blue Devils (1930), Eddie Barefield in 1931, back with the Blue Devils during 1932-33, Bennie Moten and King Oliver (1933). He was with Count Basie for the first time in 1934 but left to replace Coleman Hawkins with Fletcher Henderson. Unfortunately it was expected that Young would try to emulate Hawk, and his laidback sound angered Henderson's sidemen, resulting in Young not lasting long. After a tour with Andy Kirk and a few brief jobs, Lester Young was back with Basie in 1936, just in time to star with the band as they headed East. Pres made history during his years with Basie, not only participating on Count's record dates but starring with Billie Holiday and Teddy Wilson on a series of classic small group sessions. In addition, on his rare recordings on clarinet with Basie and the Kansas City Six, Young displayed a very original cool sound that almost sounded like altoist Paul Desmond in the 1950s. After leaving Basie in 1940, Young's career became a bit aimless, not capitalizing on his fame in the jazz world. He co-led a low-profile band with his brother drummer Lee Young in Los Angeles until rejoining Basie in December 1943. Young had a happy nine months back with the band, recorded a memorable quartet session with bassist Slam Stewart and starred in the short film *Jammin' the Blues* before he was drafted. His experiences dealing with racism in the military were horrifying, affecting his mental state of mind for the remainder of his life.

Although many critics have written that Lester Young never sounded as good after getting out of the military, despite erratic health he actually was at his prime in the mid- to late '40s. He toured (and was well-paid by Norman Granz) with Jazz at the Philharmonic on-and-off through the '40s and '50s, made a wonderful series of recordings for Aladdin and worked steadily as a single. Young also adopted his style well to bebop (which he had helped pave the way for in the 1930s). But mentally he was suffering, building a wall between himself and the outside world and inventing his own colorful vocabulary. Although many of his recordings in the 1950s were excellent (showing a greater emotional depth than in his earlier days), Young was bothered by the fact that some of his White imitators were making much more money than he was. He drank huge amounts of liquor and nearly stopped eating, with predictable results. 1956's *Jazz Giants* album found him in peak form as did a well-documented engagement in Washington, D.C., with a quartet and a last reunion with Count Basie at the 1957 Newport Jazz Festival. But for the 1957 telecast *The Sound of Jazz* Young mostly played sitting down (although he stole the show with an emotional one-chorus blues solo played to Billie Holiday). After becoming ill in Paris in early 1959, Lester Young came home and essentially drank himself to death. Nearly 40 years after his death, Pres is still considered (along with Coleman Hawkins and John Coltrane) one of the three most important tenor saxophonists of all time. —*Scott Yanow*

★ **Kansas City Sessions** / Mar. 16, 1938-Mar. 27, 1944 / GRP/Commodore ◆◆◆◆◆
This is a CD overflowing with classic performances. The great Lester Young is heard with the 1938 version of the Kansas City Six, a group also including trumpeter Buck Clayton (in prime form), Eddie Durham on electric guitar (where he preceded Charlie Christian), the rhythm guitar of Freddie Green, bassist Walter Page and drummer Jo Jones. The four selections (all of which are joined by an alternate take apiece) are most notable for Young's switching to clarinet on some of the pieces. His clarinet solo on "I Want a Little Girl" sounds eerily like Paul Desmond's alto of 15 years later. These classic cool jazz performances have delightful interplay between the two horns. The second part of the reissue features the 1944 Kansas City Six, in which Young (sticking to tenor) and trumpeter Bill Coleman are joined by a three-piece rhythm section and trombonist Dickie Wells. Wells, who takes some very colorful and nearly riotous solos, rarely sounded better, and the four selections are highlighted by three equally rewarding versions of "I Got Rhythm" and two of "Three Little Words." The CD concludes with the four titles by 1938's Kansas City Five, which was essentially the early Kansas City Six without Young. Clayton is once again in top form, and Durham's guitar solos were among the first worthwhile examples of the electric guitar on record. This gem is highly recommended for all jazz collections. —*Scott Yanow*

★ **Lester Young and Charlie Christian** / 1939-Oct. 28, 1940 / Jazz Archives ◆◆◆◆
This LP from the collectors' label Jazz Archives starts out with rare radio appearances by the Count Basie Orchestra during 1939-40; star soloists include the great tenor saxophonist Lester Young, trumpeters Buck Clayton and Harry "Sweets" Edison and Basie himself. The Benny Goodman Sextet of 1939 (featuring Lionel Hampton and Charlie Christian, the pioneer of the electric guitar) is heard on three numbers and then comes five selections from a very special studio session. In late 1940 Benny Goodman was toying with the idea of breaking up his big band and touring with an octet comprising these all-stars: Clayton, Young, Basie, Christian, rhythm guitarist Freddie Green, bassist Walter Page and drummer Jo Jones. They actually got together for one recording date although the perfor-

mances were not released until decades later. The results, heard on the latter half of this LP, are as brilliant as one might hope. —*Scott Yanow*

Historical Prez / 1940-May 20, 1944 / Everybody's ◆◆◆◆◆
This superior LP fills two important gaps in the discography of tenor saxophonist Lester Young. After leaving Count Basie's Orchestra in 1940, Young led a band of his own with trumpeter Shad Collins and guitarist John Collins that, other than for a session backing singer Una Mae Carlisle, never recorded. This LP has broadcast versions of "Tickle Toe" and "Taxi War Dance" by this excellent group, along with "Benny's Bugle" from the otherwise unrecorded unit that Pres co-led with his brother, drummer Lee Young, in 1941 on the West Coast. The remainder of this set features Young during his second (and also otherwise unrecorded) stint with Basie's Orchestra in 1944. Other soloists with Basie include trumpeters Harry "Sweets" Edison and Joe Newman, trombonist Dickie Wells and Basie himself. Recommended. —*Scott Yanow*

☆ **The Complete Aladdin Sessions** / Jul. 15, 1942-Dec. 29, 1948 / Blue Note ◆◆◆◆◆
Although it has often been written that the cool-toned tenor saxophonist Lester Young's experiences with racism in the military during 1944-45 so scarred him that musically he never played at the same level as he had previously, the music on this essential two-CD reissue disproves that theory. It is true that his attitude toward life was affected and Young became somewhat self-destructive, but his postwar solos rank with the greatest work of his career. This two-fer, which has four selections from 1942 in which Young is heard in a trio with pianist Nat King Cole and bassist Red Callender and a rare 1945 session headed by singer Helen Humes (including a previously unknown instrumental "Riffin' Without Helen"), is mostly taken up with Lester Young's very enjoyable 1945-48 small-group dates. Highlights include "D.B. Blues," "Jumpin' with Symphony Sid" (which was a minor hit), "Sunday" and "New Lester Leaps In," among many others. Minor errors aside (trumpeter Snooky Young is left out of the personnel listing for the Humes date and Young's final Aladdin session is from 1948, not 1947), this is a well-conceived and brilliant set filled with exciting performances by one of the true greats of jazz. —*Scott Yanow*

★ **The Complete Lester Young on Keynote** / Dec. 28, 1943+Mar. 22, 1944 / Verve ◆◆◆◆◆
This CD has two classic sessions featuring the great tenor saxophonist Lester Young. He is heard with the Kansas City Seven, a small group taken from the Count Basie Orchestra (which he had recently rejoined) and consisting of trumpeter Buck Clayton, trombonist Dicky Wells, pianist Basie, guitarist Freddie Green, bassist Rodney Richardson and drummer Jo Jones. The full group plays three jump pieces (plus three alternate takes), but the high point of the session is Pres' romp with the rhythm section, trading off with Basie on "Lester Leaps Again." However, that date is actually overshadowed by the four numbers (plus four alternate takes) that Young performed with pianist Johnny Guarnieri, bassist Slam Stewart and drummer Sid Catlett on Dec. 28, 1943. "I Never Knew" and "Afternoon of a Basie-ite" are heated jams, and "Just You, Just Me" is definitive, but it is "Sometimes I'm Happy" (especially the originally released version) that is truly memorable. The charming Slam Stewart solo (singing along with his bass) is only surpassed by Pres' absolutely perfect improvisation, which has been quoted many times by later jazz musicians. Highly recommended. —*Scott Yanow*

Master Takes / Apr. 18, 1944-Jun. 28, 1949 / Savoy ◆◆◆◆◆
Lester Young recorded for Savoy three separate times in four different settings. On Apr. 18, 1944, he performed as part of the Count Basie Orchestra (although Basie himself was absent) for three numbers and then cut four more songs with a septet that included trumpeter Billy Butterfield and pianist Johnny Guarnieri. A few weeks later he was featured on four selections in front of the Count Basie rhythm section. Pres made his final Savoy appearance in 1949, fronting a young sextet that also included pianist Junior Mance and drummer Roy Haynes. All of those performances are included on this CD minus the many alternate takes, which can be heard (along with this entire program) on *The Complete Savoy Recordings*. —*Scott Yanow*

Pres: The Complete Savoy Recordings / Apr. 18, 1944-Jun. 28, 1949 / Savoy ◆◆◆◆
This set only has 15 selections but also 21 alternate takes. Most of the sessions date from 1944 when Lester Young was briefly back with Count Basie's Orchestra. He is heard with the Basie band (minus the pianist), in a septet with trumpeter Billy Butterfield and pianist Johnny Guarnieri and, best of all, on four titles ("Blue Lester," "Ghost of a Chance," "Indiana" and "Jump Lester Jump") with Basie and his rhythm section. The last part of the set finds Young in 1949 fronting a young sextet (which includes trumpeter Jesse Drakes, trombonist Jerry Elliot and pianist Junior Mance). Throughout, the cool-toned tenor is in excellent form. Pres collectors will have to get this set, although most listeners would be satisfied with *Master Takes*. —*Scott Yanow*

Jammin' with Lester / 1944-Jun. 3, 1946 / Jazz Archives ◆◆◆◆
This LP from the collectors' label Jazz Archives includes the soundtrack of the award-winning short film *Jammin' the Blues*, which in 1944 gave Lester Young, Harry "Sweets" Edison and Illinois Jacquet an opportunity to be seen as well as heard. Not only are the three songs from the film on this set, but also three other previously unheard performances from the same date that did not make it onto the screen. The second side of this enjoyable set features Young at a trio of different jam sessions: playing "Lady Be Good" with fellow tenors Coleman Hawkins and Illinois Jacquet, sharing the ballad "I Can't Get Started" with Hawk and trumpeter Buck Clayton, and romping on "Tea for Two" in a quintet with trumpeter Joe Guy. The music is frequently exciting and worth searching for. —*Scott Yanow*

Lester Swings / Dec. 1945-Mar. 8, 1951 / Verve ◆◆◆◆◆
Verve did such a fine job with their two-LP Lester Young sets of the late '70s that it is surprising that they have lagged behind in reissuing the material on CD. This two-fer is a real gem, featuring the Lester Young-Nat King Cole-Buddy Rich Trio in 1945, showcasing the great tenor with pianist Hank Jones, bassist Ray Brown and Buddy Rich in 1950, and matching Pres with pianist John Lewis and a pair of different rhythm sections during 1950-51. Young was in particularly top form for the matchup with Cole and Rich and, even if his cool brand of small-group swing was out of style by 1950, his tone had become extremely influential among younger players. Highly recommended. —*Scott Yanow*

● **Prez Conferences (1946-1958)** / Mar. 20, 1946-1958 / Jass ◆◆◆◆◆
The great tenor Lester Young is heard in a variety of different settings on this CD, chiefly taken from radio and television broadcasts. The best performances find Pres playing two songs with the Nat King Cole Trio and drummer Buddy Rich in 1946, jamming three standards with trumpeter Buck Clayton and fellow tenor Coleman Hawkins, sitting in with the Count Basie Orchestra in 1952, and performing three numbers with the Bill Potts Trio in 1956. Throughout this very interesting set, Lester Young is in excellent form, making this an excellent introductory CD for listeners not already familiar with Pres' music, and a bonus for collectors who will probably not already have most of these rare performances. —*Scott Yanow*

Carnegie Blues / May 27, 1946-Oct. 19, 1957 / Verve ◆◆◆
The great tenor saxophonist Lester Young toured with Norman Granz's traveling jam session Jazz at the Philharmonic during 1949-53 and occasionally afterwards. This in-concert LP contains three selections in which Young is backed by the Oscar Peterson Quartet in 1953, a pair of excerpts (all that survives) from jams in 1946, a ballad medley from 1957 (on which he plays "Polka Dots and Moonbeams") and, best yet, versions of "Tea for Two" (with trumpeter Joe Guy) and "Carnegie Blues" (which also features the trumpeter Buck Clayton and the tenors of Coleman Hawkins and Illinois Jacquet) in 1946. Although not essential music, this set is quite enjoyable and has its exciting moments. —*Scott Yanow*

Pres Lives! / Apr. 2, 1950 / Savoy ◆◆
Many of tenor saxophonist Lester Young's club performances of the early '50s were taped and came out on LPs posthumously (when he was not around to protest). In general they do little to help his legacy, for the crowd noises, distorted sound quality and sometimes routine solos are not up to the level of his studio sessions. This Savoy set, with an unknown rhythm section and the average trumpeter Jesse Drakes, falls into that general category, although Young himself takes some fine solos. Mostly recommended to Lester Young fanatics. —*Scott Yanow*

Pres Is Blue / 1950-May 2, 1952 / Charlie Parker ◆◆
This LP claims that it has "Unprecedented Hi Fidelity." The streaky sound quality of these bootleg live recordings makes a joke out of that statement. Taken from a few club appearances during 1950-52 and featuring tenor saxophonist Lester Young, trumpeter Jesse Drakes and either Kenny Drew, John Lewis or Wynton Kelly on piano, these six standards have seen better days. Young has a few swinging solos but the crowd noise gets fairly distracting at times. —*Scott Yanow*

Ultimate Lester Young / 1950-1958 / Verve ◆◆◆
Although serious fans and collectors will have little use for the disc, *Ultimate Lester Young* is a solid collection of 12 highlights from the saxophonist's Verve recordings as selected by Wayne Shorter. For the curious neophyte, the disc offers a good overview of Young's time at the label, featuring the saxophonist in a variety of different settings, including combos with Harry "Sweets" Edison, Oscar Peterson, Buddy Rich, Nat King Cole, Roy Eldridge and Count Basie. Certainly, the disc should be thought of as an introduction, not the final word, but on that level it works well. Among the featured numbers are "Sometimes I'm Happy," "Love You Madly," "In the Wee Small Hours of the Morning," "Blues for Big Scotia," "Mumbles" and "Chicago." —*Stephen Thomas Erlewine*

Masters of Jazz: Lester Young / May 19, 1951-Dec. 29, 1956 / Storyville ◆◆◆
This LP from the European Storyville label has some of tenor saxophonist Lester Young's better live performances from the 1950s. Trumpeter Jesse Drakes is on

about half of the set and the young pianist Horace Silver is heard on three songs from 1951. However the better performances are from 1956 with Young joined by the Bill Potts Trio and, on four songs, the fine trumpeter Idrees Sulieman. Although Young's health declined gradually throughout the 1950s, his playing (when his strength did not give out) was generally at a fairly high level, actually superior emotionally to his earlier recordings. This is an excellent set of rarities. —*Scott Yanow*

★ **With the Oscar Peterson Trio** / Aug. 4, 1952 / Verve ◆◆◆◆◆

Defying what has become conventional wisdom, tenor saxophonist Lester Young (when he was reasonably healthy) actually cut some of his greatest recordings in the 1950s. On this wonderful effort with pianist Oscar Peterson, guitarist Barney Kessel, bassist Ray Brown and drummer J.C. Heard, Pres performs definitive versions of "Just You Just Me" and "Tea for Two" and plays a string of concise but memorable ballad renditions: "On the Sunny Side of the Street," "Almost Like Being in Love," "I Can't Give You Anything but Love," "There Will Never Be Another You" and "Confessin'." The 1997 CD reissue augments the original dozen songs with a version of the good-humored "It Takes Two to Tango" (which feature Young's only recorded vocals) and has a rather unnecessary false start ("I Can't Get Started") along with some studio chatter. Essential music. —*Scott Yanow*

Mean to Me / Dec. 10, 1954-Dec. 1, 1955 / Verve ◆◆◆◆

This double LP consists of two separate studio sessions featuring tenor saxophonist Lester Young. The first set has his regular working group of the mid-'50s with trumpeter Jesse Drakes, pianist Gildo Mahones, bassist John Ore and drummer Connie Kay (just prior to him joining the Modern Jazz Quartet). Although that session is decent, the other half of this two-fer (which matches Young with fellow Basie veteran Harry "Sweets" Edison on trumpet, the Oscar Peterson Trio and Buddy Rich) is the reason to search for this valuable out-of-print set. —*Scott Yanow*

Pres and Sweets / Dec. 1, 1955 / Verve ◆◆◆◆◆

This CD reissue features a logical front line comprising tenor saxophonist Lester Young and trumpeter Harry "Sweets" Edison. With pianist Oscar Peterson, guitarist Herb Ellis, bassist Ray Brown and drummer Buddy Rich completing the sextet, it is not surprising that the music is quite swinging. Young was in good form that day, obviously happy to be having a reunion with his fellow Count Basie alumnus Sweets. On a variety of swing standards (highlighted by "Mean to Me," "Pennies From Heaven" and "One O'Clock Jump") plus "Bad Boy Blues," Pres and Sweets perform infectiously enjoyable music. —*Scott Yanow*

☆ **Pres and Teddy** / Jan. 13, 1956 / Verve ◆◆◆◆◆

Although it has been written much too often that Lester Young declined rapidly from the mid-'40s on, the truth is that when he was healthy, Young played at his very best during the 1950s, adding an emotional intensity to his sound that had not been present during the more carefree days of the '30s. This classic session, a reunion with pianist Teddy Wilson and drummer Jo Jones (bassist Gene Ramey completes the quartet), finds the great tenor in particularly expressive form. His rendition of "Prisoner of Love" is quite haunting, the version of "All of Me" is also memorable and all of the swing standards (which are joined by his original "Pres Returns") are well worth hearing. This date (which has been reissued on CD) was recorded the day after Young's other classic from his late-period, *Jazz Giants '56*. —*Scott Yanow*

☆ **The Jazz Giants '56** / Jan. 12, 1956 / Verve ◆◆◆◆◆

Even critics who feel (against the recorded evidence to the contrary) that little of tenor saxophonist Lester Young's postwar playing is at the level of his earlier performances make an exception for this session. Young was clearly inspired by the other musicians (trumpeter Roy Eldridge, trombonist Vic Dickenson, pianist Teddy Wilson, guitarist Freddie Green, bassist Gene Ramey and drummer Jo Jones), who together made for a very potent band of swing all-stars. The five songs on this LP include some memorable renditions of ballads and a fine version of "You Can Depend on Me," but it is the explosive joy of the fiery "Gigantic Blues" that takes honors. This set, a real gem, is highly recommended. —*Scott Yanow*

Prez in Europe / Oct. 1956-Jan. 2, 1957 / Onyx ◆◆◆

Although the veteran tenor saxophonist Lester Young was not in the best physical shape at the time of these club performances, he generally plays quite well throughout this LP. Five songs from Oct. 1956 find him in good form on some standards and blues with the assistance of pianist Horst Ornimert, bassist Al King and drummer Lex Humphries. The final two tracks are a pair of short fragments from Jan. 1957. Overall the recording quality is quite streaky but the music deserved to be released, although those just starting to investigate Lester Young's music should acquire his studio sessions first. —*Scott Yanow*

Lester Young in Washington, D.C., 1956, Vol. 1 / Dec. 3, 1956-Dec. 9, 1956 / Pablo ◆◆◆◆◆

In December 1956 the great tenor saxophonist had a gig in Washington, D.C., playing at a club with the house rhythm section, the Bill Potts Trio. This engagement would have been long forgotten except that all of the music from one of the nights was recorded and released decades later on four LPs. The recording quality is excellent (studio quality) and, most importantly, Lester Young was in superb form throughout the night. Although there is nothing that distinctive about the trio, they are quite competent and evidently pleased Pres. The first volume of this highly enjoyable series features fine versions of five standards, a blues and Pres' "D.B. Blues." —*Scott Yanow*

Lester Young in Washington, D.C., 1956, Vol. 2 / Dec. 3, 1956-Dec. 9, 1956 / Original Jazz Classics ◆◆◆◆◆

The second of four volumes documenting a particularly strong musical night in the life of the great tenor saxophonist Lester Young features Pres with a very competent trio (led by pianist Bill Potts) performing five standards and Young's two most famous compositions: "Lester Leaps In" and "Jumpin' with Symphony Sid." The recording quality is excellent on this fine showcase for the swinging and emotionally deep style that Young developed in his later years. —*Scott Yanow*

Lester Young in Washington, D.C., 1956, Vol. 3 / Dec. 3, 1956-Dec. 9, 1956 / Original Jazz Classics ◆◆◆◆◆

The third of four volumes, as with its counterparts, features the great tenor saxophonist Lester Young sounding contented and quite comfortable playing in the company of the excellent trio that pianist Bill Potts led in 1956. Pres is near peak form on two of his originals and four veteran standards, bringing new life to "Indiana" and "Just You, Just Me." Those jazz fans who mistakenly feel that Young's post-1944 work is not worth bothering with are advised to purchase at least one of these volumes for proof to the opposite. —*Scott Yanow*

Lester Young in Washington, D.C., 1956, Vol. 4 / Dec. 3, 1956-Dec. 9, 1956 / Original Jazz Classics ◆◆◆◆◆

The fourth of four sets, all presumably recorded the same night (the liners are a little vague on that matter, although this quartet definitely only played together that week), documents tenor saxophonist Lester Young in excellent form, only a little more than two years before his death, with a complementary trio led by pianist Bill Potts. All four sets are recommended, for Pres sounds quite enthusiastic, swings consistently, and comes up with creative ideas on standards and fairly basic originals. Superior postwar Lester Young. —*Scott Yanow*

Laughin' to Keep from Cryin' / Feb. 8, 1958 / Verve ◆◆◆◆

One of tenor saxophonist Lester Young's final studio sessions (he died a year later), this date apparently had a lot of difficulties, but the recorded results are excellent. Pres is joined by two great swing trumpeters (Roy Eldridge and Harry "Sweets" Edison) and a fine rhythm section for two standards, two originals and the ballad "Gypsy in My Soul." Young takes rare clarinet solos on two of the selections with his emotional statement on "They Can't Take That Away from Me" being one of the high points of his career. Recommended. —*Scott Yanow*

Lester Young in Paris / Mar. 4, 1959 / Verve ◆◆◆

Snooky Young

b. Feb. 3, 1919, Dayton, OH
Trumpet / Swing

A great surviving stylist of the trumpet, Eugene "Snooky" Young is the absolute master of the plunger mute, an instantly recognizable star with whomever he plays. He can make his horn speak, shout, growl and sigh with his mutes, while always swinging irresistibly. Yet Young has made his reputation almost entirely from within the bands who employ him, rarely stepping out on his own since leading his own band in his hometown of Dayton from 1947 to 1957.

Young took up the trumpet at the age of five and first began to make a name for himself as the lead trumpeter of the Jimmie Lunceford band from 1939 to 1942. He briefly joined Count Basie in 1942 and moved on to the bands of Lionel Hampton and Gerald Wilson before rejoining Basie from 1945 to 1947 and again from 1957 until 1962. Upon leaving Basie, Young became a studio trumpeter at NBC, was a founding member of the Thad Jones-Mel Lewis Orchestra in 1966, and was constantly in demand for all kinds of sessions (including a live, recorded New Year's Eve gig with the rock group the Band in 1971). While at NBC in New York, he was a member of the Tonight Show Orchestra, moving to Los Angeles with the show in 1972 and holding down his chair until 1992, when Johnny Carson's departure broke up the band. Young has been busy in the Los Angeles area ever since, appearing regularly as a lead trumpeter in several local big bands, sounding as sharp and witty as ever into his late 70s. The self-effacing Young has issued only three albums under his own name, and of these, only *Horn of Plenty* (Concord) features Young as the sole headliner. —*Richard S. Ginell*

Boys from Dayton / Aug. 26, 1971 / Master Jazz ✦✦✦

Although he had been a well-respected trumpeter for over 30 years by 1971, this was Snooky Young's first session as a leader. Actually the LP consists of two separate dates: one features Young with altoist Norris Turney, trombonist Booty Wood and a surprisingly R&Bish rhythm section (which is turned a bit loose on Pee Wee Ellis' "Hard Boiled Rock") that includes Richard Tee on piano and organ and guitarist Cornell Dupree, while the flip-side showcases Turney in 1975 with pianist Cliff Smalls, guitarist Billy Butler, bassist Al Hall and drummer Mickey Roker. The emphasis throughout is mostly on light swing and ballads, with the highlights including "Lil' Darlin'," "My Blue Heaven," Turney's "The Seventh Day" and "For All We Know." Nothing all that substantial occurs on this LP (which has yet to be reissued on CD) but it has its moments of interest. — *Scott Yanow*

Snooky & Marshall's Album / 1978 / Concord Jazz ✦✦✦✦

Veteran swing trumpeter Snooky Young's second session as a leader finds him co-leading the date with altoist Marshall Royal. Backed by a very supportive rhythm section (pianist Ross Tompkins, rhythm guitarist Freddie Green, bassist Ray Brown and drummer Louie Bellson), the attractive front line plays pleasing and melodic solos that occasionally get a little heated. Guest vocalist Scatman Crothers sings his "Mean Dog Blues," there are recent originals by Ray Brown and Tom Peterson along with a three-song ballad medley, and the sextet romps on "I Let a Song Go Out of My Heart," "Limehouse Blues" and "Should I." Subtle and tasteful music. — *Scott Yanow*

★ **Horn of Plenty** / Mar. 1979 / Concord Jazz ✦✦✦✦✦

One of only three recording sessions led by the talented trumpeter Snooky Young and his only one as the lone horn, this Concord set (which includes pianist Ross Tompkins, guitarist John Collins, bassist Ray Brown and drummer Jake Hanna) features Snooky on four standards, an original blues and three compositions by saxophonist Tom Peterson. The music is essentially modern mainstream, allowing the leader to show off his wide range and swinging style. — *Scott Yanow*

Trummy Young

b. Jan. 12, 1912, Savannah, GA, **d.** Sep. 10, 1984, San Jose, CA
Trombone / Swing, Dixieland

Trummy Young was one of the finest trombonists to emerge during the swing era and, even though he was never really a star or a bandleader himself, he did have one hit with his version of "Margie" which he played and sang with Jimmy Lunceford's Orchestra. Growing up in Washington, Young was originally a trumpeter, but by the time he debuted in 1928 he had switched to trombone. Extending the range and power of his instrument, Young was a major asset to Earl Hines' Orchestra during 1933-37 and really became a major influence in jazz while with Lunceford (1937-43). Young was a modern swing stylist with an open mind who fit in well with Charlie Parker and Dizzy Gillespie on a Clyde Hart-led session in 1945 and with Jazz at the Philharmonic. It was therefore a surprise when he joined the Louis Armstrong All-Stars in 1952 and stayed a dozen years. Trummy Young was a good foil for Armstrong (most memorably on their 1954 recording of "St. Louis Blues"), but he simplified his style due to his love for the trumpeter. In 1964 Young quit the road to settle in Hawaii, occasionally emerging for jazz parties and special appearances. — *Scott Yanow*

A Man and His Horn / 1975 / Flair ✦✦✦✦

Considering his talent, trombonist Trummy Young led surprisingly few sessions throughout his career. Some lesser-known outings during 1944-46 and five songs in 1955 were all that preceded this obscure 1975 LP (which was followed by a final effort in 1979). Heard in Hawaii where he settled after leaving Louis Armstrong in 1964, Young is backed by a trombone section on "Margie" and "Mood Indigo"; a few songs use strings, and background vocalists pop up harmlessly in a few instances. Young, who sings some of the tunes, still sounded in his musical prime in the mid-1970s. The program mixes together swing standards with songs written by Hawaiians, and throughout, Trummy Young is in typically joyful and highly expressive form. — *Scott Yanow*

Rachel Z

b. New York, NY

Keyboards / Post-Bop, Crossover Jazz

A keyboardist with great potential, Rachel Z worked closely with Wayne Shorter in 1995, arranging and soloing on his album and touring extensively with his group. Born and raised in Manhattan, Rachel Z had singing lessons when she was two and started studying piano at age seven. A summer session at Berklee College in 1979 gave her a strong interest in jazz. She studied with Joanne Brackeen, had a lesson with John Hicks, attended the New England Conservatory of Music (1980-84) and after graduation studied with Richie Beirach. She worked in the Boston area with a quartet that also included George Garzone and then moved to New York in 1988. In 1989 she toured with Najee and then joined Steps Ahead for a few years; leader/vibraphonist Mike Mainieri named her Rachel Z. Since that time she has recorded for Columbia and NYC, showing talent on both acoustic and electric keyboards. —*Scott Yanow*

● **Trust The Universe** / 1992 / Columbia ◆◆◆◆

Keyboardist Rachel Z divides her debut CD into "mainstream" and "contemporary" sections, but in reality she plays basically the same in both sessions, emphasizing her acoustic work in a style most influenced by Chick Corea, Herbie Hancock and occasionally Bill Evans. The music is usually soulful enough for the jazz lite listeners and contains just enough chance-taking for more serious jazz collectors. Nothing too unexpected occurs, but this enjoyable set has some fine solos from the leader and the contrasting saxophones of David Sanchez and David Mann. —*Scott Yanow*

Room of One's Own / 1996 / NYC ◆◆◆◆◆

Rachel Z, a talented young keyboardist, sticks to acoustic piano and varies the personnel and instrumentation from track-to-track on this interesting set. In addition to a woodwind section, such players as violinist Regina Carter, tenor saxophonist George Garzone, bassist Charnett Moffett and drummers Terri Lyne Carrington and Cindy Blackman are among the supporting cast. Rachel's ten originals (which are dedicated to various women ranging from her mother and a 17th-century painter to Billie Holiday and Joni Mitchell) cover a lot of moods with the emphasis on relaxed and thoughtful pieces. Although her own piano playing sometimes recalls Herbie Hancock and Chick Corea (along with touches of Bill Evans and Keith Jarrett), Rachel Z is gradually developing her own style. This is the type of record that needs to be heard several times to be fully appreciated, for Rachel Z's subtle playing and moody themes contain much of value beneath the surface. Well worth checking out. —*Scott Yanow*

Joe Zawinul

b. Jul. 7, 1932, Vienna, Austria

Piano, Keyboards, Leader / Soul Jazz, Fusion, Hard Bop, World Fusion

Joe Zawinul belongs in a category unto himself—a European from the heartland of the classical music tradition (Vienna) who learned to swing as freely as any American jazzer, and whose appetite for growth and change remains insatiable. Zawinul's curiosity and openness to all kinds of sounds made him one of the driving forces behind the electronic jazz-rock revolution of the late '60s and '70s—and later, he would be almost alone in exploring fusions between jazz-rock and ethnic music from all over the globe. He is one of a bare handful of synthesizer players who actually learned how to play the instrument, to make it an expressive, swinging part of his arsenal. Prior to the invention of the portable synthesizer, Zawinul's example helped bring the Wurlitzer and Fender-Rhodes electric pianos into the jazz mainstream. Zawinul also has become a significant composer, ranging (like his idol Duke Ellington) from soulful hit tunes to large-scale symphonic-jazz canvases. Yet despite his classical background, he now prefers to improvise compositions spontaneously onto tape, not writing them out on paper.

At six, Josef Erich Zawinul started to play the accordion in his native Austria, and studies in classical piano and composition at the Vienna Conservatory soon followed. His interest in jazz piano, initially influenced by George Shearing and Erroll Garner, led to jobs with Austrian saxophonist Hans Koller in 1952 and gigs with his own trio in France and Germany. He emigrated to the US in late 1958 after winning a scholarship to Berklee, yet after just one week in class, he left to join Maynard Ferguson's band for eight months, where Miles Davis first took notice of him. Following a brief stay with Slide Hampton, Zawinul became Dinah Washington's pianist from 1959 to 1961, and then spent a month with Harry "Sweets" Edison before Cannonball Adderley picked him to fill the piano chair in his Quintet. There Zawinul stayed and blossomed for nine years, contributing several compositions to the Adderley bandbook—among them the major pop hit "Mercy, Mercy, Mercy," "Walk Tall" and "Country Preacher"—and ultimately helping to steer the Adderley group into the electronic era. While with Adderley, Zawinul evolved from a hard bop pianist to a soul-jazz performer heavily steeped in the blues, and ultimately a jazz/rock explorer on the electric piano. Toward the end of his Adderley gig (1969-1970), he was right in the thick of the new jazz-rock scene, recording several pioneering records with Miles Davis, contributing the title tune of Davis' *In a Silent Way* album.

After recording a self-titled solo album, Zawinul left Adderley to form Weather Report with Wayne Shorter and Czech bassist Miroslav Vitous in November 1970. Weather Report gave the increasingly self-confident Zawinul a platform to evolve even further as his interest in propulsive grooves and music from Africa and the Middle East ignited and developed. He gradually dropped the electric piano in favor of a series of ever-more-sophisticated synthesizers, which he mastered to levels never thought possible by those who derided the instruments as sterile, unfeeling machines. Weather Report eventually became a popular group that appealed to audiences beyond jazz and progressive rock, thanks in no small part to Zawinul's hit song "Birdland."

When Zawinul and Shorter finally came to a parting of the ways in 1985, Zawinul started to tour all by himself, surrounded by keyboards and rhythm machines, but resurfaced the following year with a short-lived extension of Weather Report called Weather Update (which did not leave any recordings). Weather Update quickly evolved into another group, the Zawinul Syndicate, which over the span of a decade has been tilting increasingly toward groove-oriented world music influences. Zawinul has also shown renewed interest in his European roots, collaborating with fellow Viennese classical pianist Friedrich Gulda from 1987 to 1994, producing a full-blown classical-based symphony *Stories of the Danube* in 1993 and following the near-disastrous Malibu fires of 1994, moving from California to New York City in order to be closer to Europe.

Though he continues to explore new musical paths at an age when most jazzers are long set in their ways, Zawinul's influence upon jazz has waned in recent years due to the jazz mainstream's retreat from electronics back to acoustic post-bop. But Zawinul's uplifting, still-invigorating later music may make him a prophet again if global music infiltrates the jazz world. —*Richard S. Ginell*

And the Austrian All Stars 1954-1957 / Oct. 18, 1954-Mar. 21, 1957 / RST ◆◆◆◆

This Austrian import CD is a real historical curiosity, for it features pianist Joe Zawinul several years before he left his native Austria for the US and fame with Cannonball Adderley and later Weather Report. Zawinul is heard as the pianist in the Austrian All-Stars, a cool jazz group featuring altoist Hans Solomon and tenorman Karl Drewo (who sometimes recall Lee Konitz and Warne Marsh or Art Pepper with Jack Montrose); trumpeter Dick Murphy is on a few numbers, and three songs are trio features for the young pianist. Zawinul, who hints at Dave Brubeck and Lennie Tristano in spots, plays quite well but, even if he were not present, the music would be quite enjoyable. Highlights include "There's a Small Hotel," two versions of "Takin' a Chance on Love," "Beat" and a pre-Miles Davis version of "Dear Old Stockholm" (here listed under its original title "Ack Varmeland Du Skona"). —*Scott Yanow*

● **Rise & Fall of the Third Stream/Money in the Pocket** / 1965-Dec. 12, 1967 / Rhino ◆◆◆◆◆

Two of keyboardist Joe Zawinul's finest recordings as a leader were reissued on this single CD. *The Money in the Pocket* album from 1965 features Zawinul on acoustic piano in a sextet with trumpeter Blue Mitchell, tenor saxophonist Joe

Henderson and baritonist Pepper Adams playing superior hard bop highlighted by the funky title cut, "If" and Zawinul's feature on "My One and Only Love." The other session utilizes a string quartet, trumpeter Jimmy Owens and the tenor and arrangements of William Fischer. Its diverse music hints at fusion (Zawinul doubles on electric piano) and has many colorful moments. This gem of a CD is highly recommended. —*Scott Yanow*

Zawinul / Aug. 6, 1970-Aug. 12, 1970 / Atlantic ◆◆◆◆

Conceptually, sonically, this is really the first Weather Report album in all but name, confirming that Joe Zawinul was the primary creative engine behind the group from the beginning. It is also the link between WR and Miles Davis' keyboard-laden experiments on *In a Silent Way;* indeed, the tune "In a Silent Way" is redone in the more complex form in which Zawinul envisioned it, and Miles even contributes a brief, generous tribute to Joe on the liner. Two keyboardists—Zawinul and the formidable Herbie Hancock—form the underpinning of this stately, probing album, garnishing their work with the galactic sound effects of the Echoplex and ring modulator. Earl Turbinton provides the Wayne Shorter-like beams of light on the soprano sax, spelled by Wayne himself on "Double Image." The third founder of WR, Miroslav Vitous, checks in on bass, and hard-bopping trumpeter Woody Shaw proves to be perfectly adept at the jazz-rock game. Two short-lived standards of the jazz-rock era, the aforementioned "Double Image" and "Doctor Honoris Causa," are introduced here, yet it is mood pieces like "His Last Journey" and "Arrival in New York" that with the help of tape-speed manipulation, establish the lasting, murky, reflective ambience of this CD. —*Richard S. Ginell*

★ **Dialects** / Jun. 1986 / Columbia ◆◆◆◆◆

If Joe Zawinul was out to prove that he didn't need Weather Report anymore, he succeeded spectacularly in this virtual one-man show. Zawinul recorded many of the vocals (assisted now and then by Bobby McFerrin and a vocal trio) and all of the synthesizers and rhythm machine tracks himself in his Pasadena home studio, yet the results are anything but mechanical. Zawinul in fact achieves a rare thing; he manages to get his stacks of electronics to swing like mad in these pan-global grooves that pick up where WR was about to leave off. "Waiting for the Rain" generates a ribbon of tension and anticipation, while "Zeebop" is a noisy rush of pure adrenaline. And "Carnivalito" is a total gas, a percolating, outrageously joyous evocation of a carnival that would put the world's best percussion players out of business if Zawinul's swinging talent could be bottled and sold. This is an important, overlooked album because it proves that electronic instruments can reach your emotions and shake your body when played by someone who has bothered to learn how to master them. —*Richard S. Ginell*

The Immigrants / 1988 / Columbia ◆◆◆

Although Zawinul tried touring alone in the immediate wake of the breakup of Weather Report, he soon returned to a group format, first with Weather Update in 1986 and a couple of years later with the raffishly named Zawinul Syndicate. The multi-national Syndicate basically expands the Weather Report format into a sextet, with a rock guitar (Scott Henderson) replacing the sax, an extra percussionist on board to join WR's Alex Acuna, and more vocal support then ever—and if a Wayne Shorter-like melody line was needed, Zawinul would play it himself on his new Korg Pepe wind synthesizer. If anything, *The Immigrants* burrows even further into the world-music bloodstream than WR ever did, with vocals in Spanish and wordless syllables on top of Zawinul's one-chord Third World grooves. There is also a heavier pop emphasis (again nothing new for Zawinul), including a recomposition of "Mercy Mercy Mercy" called "No Mercy for Me," now an assertive paean to self-reliance that is soulfully sung by the Perri sisters. Some of the tunes and grooves fall short of Zawinul's irresistible best, but "King Hip" swaggers at a high level and "From Venice to Vienna"—another of Zawinul's nostalgic memoirs of Europe—lingers hauntingly at the album's close. —*Richard S. Ginell*

Black Water / 1989 / Columbia ◆◆◆

With a few changes in personnel, the Zawinul Syndicate continues to be Joe Zawinul's personal vehicle for pan-global fusions of jazz, Afro-Latin rhythms, rock and whatever world music he can lay his hands on. Again Zawinul keeps a configuration of vocalists on board, including his own gritty electronically processed voice, and he even dusts off his childhood accordion for a bit of Austrian local color on "Medicine Man." The leadoff track, a group remake of "Carnivalito" recorded live in Copenhagen, is, oddly enough, inferior to Zawinul's solo version—too cluttered. But with the South African freedom-fighting, percolating "Black Water," the Syndicate is back on track, empowered as always by Zawinul's unquenchable urge to swing right in the pocket. And far from being predictable in its format, the Syndicate takes considerable time out to do Thelonious Monk's "Monk's Mood" and "Little Rootie Tootie" in amazingly reverent, though electronic, fashion. One can, however, do without bassist Gerald Veasley's spoken admonition to Monk's critics that reeks of PC. —*Richard S. Ginell*

Lost Tribes / 1992 / Columbia ◆◆◆◆

Now reduced in size to a quintet (dropping the extra percussionist), Zawinul's Syndicate delivers its most overtly political album—or shall we say, its most anti-political album with its forget-our-differences, one-world tone poems. If *Lost Tribes* sounds more like a Weather Report album than its Syndicate predecessors, it may be because the CD is loaded with Zawinul's uncanny impersonations of Wayne Shorter on his Pepe synthesizer. Yet the album also cuts down on the pop and straight jazz strains of yore as it explores the sounds and grooves of world music, and Zawinul also resumes using introductory sound collages that produce effects not unlike twisting a short-wave radio dial. The record begins powerfully with the circulating, tense "Patriots"—depicting, oddly enough, the role of Black soldiers in the Persian Gulf War—and segues into the relaxed, swinging "South Africa," a celebratory sequel to "Black Water" with vocals by Perri. Bass player Gerald Veasley contributes a track called "San Sebastian" that comes very close to pure flamenco. This CD ranks above the other Syndicate Columbias because it is emotionally deeper; Zawinul allows himself to brood and ponder as well as party. —*Richard S. Ginell*

My People / 1992-1996 / Escapade ◆◆◆◆◆

If one must indulge in categories, *My People*, featuring the Zawinul Syndicate and a United Nations coterie of guests, probably belongs on the vast world music shelf, the links to so-called jazz now so tenuous as to be nearly, but not quite, invisible. On the percolating "Slivovitz Trail," "Orient Express," "Many Churches," and the Caribbean-tinged cleverly titled "In an Island Way," the music does suggest earlier versions of the Syndicate and Zawinul's nostalgic evocations of Wayne Shorter on the Korg Pepe reach back even further. Otherwise, Zawinul is looking entirely toward ethnic cultures for musical sustenance. The musical structures are linear, the rhythms full of intricacies welded to Zawinul's love affair with the groove, the synthesizer textures usually sparer than ever. There are vocals in several languages by Zawinul's longtime colleague Salif Keita (for whom Zawinul produced a great album in 1991), Syndicate percussionist Arto Tuncboyaciyan, a throat vocal specialist from South Siberia named Bolot, Thania Sanchez, Zawinul himself and several others. When translated, the lyrics speak of joy and unity among the cultures, and there isn't any doubt that Zawinul's bubbling music feeds the message of uplift. Hear it; you purists may be jiggling along in spite of yourselves. —*Richard S. Ginell*

Stories of the Danube / Nov. 1995-Feb. 1996 / Verve ◆◆◆

Billed as Joe Zawinul's First Symphony, this large-scale classical work may seem like a radical departure to the composer/keyboardist's jazz and pop fans, but it is really a logical expression of Zawinul's indestructible European roots. Moreover, it is not as alien to his jazz work as one might suppose; at times, one can hear trademark Zawinul ostinato lines in fleshed-out, orchestrated form, and rhythms and tunes of his jazz-rock days ("Doctor Honoris Causa," "Pharoah's Dance" "Unknown Soldier") turn up like old friends crashing a black-tie ceremony. The storyline of the work is a spinoff of Smetana's "The Moldau," tracing the path of a river from its springhead through Central Europe and the deep historical currents (the Ottoman Empire, Vienna's Golden Age, World War II, etc.) that its journey suggests. Zawinul's own keyboards appear most noticeably in the brooding Third Worldish introductions to the fourth and seventh movements, and the Czech State Philharmonic Orchestra, Brno under Caspar Richter handles the long symphonic writing smoothly. At 63 minutes, this piece is a real stretch—Zawinul is dealing with a Brucknerian timespan—and skillful orchestrator, composer and boundless eclectic that he is, he can't quite fill the huge tapestry consistently. Yet repeated listening reveals a coherent if loose overall structure and some emotional depth; if you work at it, the rewards will come. —*Richard S. Ginell*

Denny Zeitlin

b. Apr. 10, 1938, Chicago, IL

Piano / Post-Bop, Hard Bop

Denny Zeitlin, a fine Bill Evans-inspired pianist, has throughout his life had a dual career as a psychiatrist and as a pianist. He had extensive classical training but found time to play jazz, even while a medical student at Johns Hopkins University. In 1964 he recorded his first album and has since maintained his two careers in San Francisco, recording and performing colorful and usually unpredictable jazz on an occasional basis. —*Scott Yanow*

Cathexis / Feb. 19, 1964-Mar. 6, 1964 / Columbia ◆◆◆◆

Carnival / Oct. 28, 1964-Oct. 30, 1964 / Columbia ◆◆◆◆◆

Live at the Trident / Mar. 22, 1965-Mar. 24, 1965 / Columbia ◆◆◆◆◆
With Charlie Haden (b), Jerry Granelli (d). A great find. —*Michael G. Nastos*

Zeitgeist / Apr. 11, 1966-Mar. 18, 1967 / Columbia ◆◆◆◆
'60s trio recordings. Rare and wonderful. —*Michael G. Nastos*

Tidal Wave / Jan. 1981-Mar. 1983 / Quicksilver ✦✦✦✦
Because he earns his main living as a psychiatrist, pianist Denny Zeitlin has only recorded on an irregular basis since his initial emergence on the jazz scene in 1964. In fact, other than obscure efforts for the Double Helix and 1750 Arch labels in the 1970s, this LP was Zeitlin's first recording as a leader since 1967. Fortunately, the pianist had stayed in top musical form, as can be heard on a well-rounded set that consists of five Zeitlin compositions plus Billy Strayhorn's "Chelsea Bridge" and Charlie Parker's "Billie's Bounce." The latter song, taken as a piano solo, dates from 1981, while the remainder of the program (duets, trios and quartets with guitarist John Abercrombie, bassist Charlie Haden and drummer Peter Donald) has plenty of advanced but straightahead swinging. Worth searching for. —*Scott Yanow*

● **Time Remembers One Time Once** / Jul. 1981 / ECM ✦✦✦✦✦
Live date at Keystone Korner in San Francisco with bassist Charlie Haden. Extraordinary recording of compositions by Ornette Coleman, Coltrane, and the participants. —*Michael G. Nastos*

Homecoming / 1986 / Living Music ✦✦✦
Paul Winter's Living Music label mostly specialized in new age and meditation music, so this solo jazz piano set from Denny Zeitlin was a bit unusual for the company. Actually, Zeitlin mostly concentrated on quiet ballads during the date, playing ten of his originals (best-known is "Quiet Now") and showing off his lyrical rather than his swinging side. More mood variations would have uplifted the music, but the results are pleasing. —*Scott Yanow*

Trio / 1988 / Windham Hill ✦✦✦✦✦
Pianist Denny Zeitlin's first of two albums for Windham Hill Jazz shows off his roots in Bill Evans along with his own musical personality. Teamed up with bassist Joel DiBartolo and drummer Peter Donald, Zeitlin is in superior form on five of his originals, Charles Mingus' "Goodbye Porkpie Hat," "All The Things You Are," J.J. Johnson's "Lament" and Ornette Coleman's "Turnaround." An excellent all-around showcase for the part-time pianist who holds a day job as a psychiatrist. —*Scott Yanow*

In the Moment / 1988-1989 / Windham Hill ✦✦✦✦✦
This enjoyable effort, one of pianist Denny Zeitlin's infrequent recordings, has four trio selections recorded with bassist Joel DiBartolo and drummer Peter Donald (the other performances from the same sessions comprise Zeitlin's earlier Windham Hill release *Trio*) plus four 1989 duets with bassist David Friesen. Six Zeitlin originals are joined by Friesen's "Underlying," Ornette Coleman's obscure "Broadway Blues" and the standard "Blues in the Night." Harmonically advanced and thought-provoking yet mostly swinging music. —*Scott Yanow*

● **Live at Maybeck Recital Hall, Vol. 27** / Oct. 18, 1992 / Concord Jazz ✦✦✦✦✦
Although Denny Zeitlin, M.D., is probably a fine psychiatrist, it is the jazz world's loss that he is not a full-time musician. This live solo performance is one of his greatest triumphs, starting with his infectious opener, "Blues on the Side," which is far too complex to be compared to typical blues. He tackles John Coltrane's "Lazy Bird" at a furious tempo worthy of its composer. Zeitlin's refreshingly deliberate approach to "'Round Midnight" best captures its dark undertones. The pianist's lyrical side is also evident. "Sophisticated Lady" captures the essence of Duke Ellington's landmark work, while "Just Passing By" is a subtle original that conjures images of a brisk stroll at the beginning of autumn. Zeitlin then shifts into high gear for an intense medley of "What Is This Thing Called Love" and "Fifth House" to close with a flourish. —*Ken Dryden*

Attila Zoller (Attila Cornelius Zoller)

b. Jun. 13, 1927, Visegrad, Hungary, d. Jan. 25, 1998, Vermont
Guitar / Post-Bop
Due to being based in Europe and having an introverted style, guitarist Attila Zoller has always had an underground reputation. He took violin lessons from his father when he was four and trumpet at nine, but as a teenager after World War II he was playing guitar with jazz groups. Based in Vienna during 1948-54 and in Germany during 1954-59, Zoller worked with touring American jazzmen and such local players as Jutta Hipp and Hans Koller. Zoller came to the US in 1959 to study at the Lenox School of Jazz, played with Chico Hamilton (1960), was a member of Herbie Mann's group during 1962-65 and worked with Benny Goodman (1967), Lee Konitz (on an occasional basis since 1968) and later a duo with Jimmy Raney (1979-80). Fame has thus far eluded him but his many recordings (most of which are difficult to find) attest to Attila Zoller's talent. —*Scott Yanow*

Common Cause / May 6, 1979-Oct. 11, 1979 / Enja ✦✦✦✦✦
Most of Hungarian guitarist Attila Zoller's early recordings have not been made available in the US, but fortunately his two 1979 Enja releases were leased domestically through Inner City, allowing Americans an opportunity to hear Zoller's unique sound. Like his countrymate Gabor Szabo, Zoller (who has a much more intro-

verted style) uses aspects of his Hungarian folk heritage in his music while playing creative jazz. This quiet trio date with bassist Ron Carter and drummer Joe Chambers (comprising four Zoller originals plus a tune from tenorman Bobby Jones) is a good example of Zoller's subtle improvising style. —*Scott Yanow*

Conjunction / Oct. 11, 1979 / Enja ✦✦✦✦
This very interesting set features spontaneous solo guitar playing by Attila Zoller. The four free improvisations are generally melodic and lyrical but quite ad-lib, leading to some surprising twists and turns. This Enja LP (which was made available in the US for a while through the now-defunct Inner City label) is a bit brief (just 32 minutes), but the colorful and subtle music is well worth acquiring. —*Scott Yanow*

● **Memories of Pannonia** / Jun. 1986 / Enja ✦✦✦✦✦
The distinctive guitar sound of Attila Zoller is joined by two creative and very supportive sidemen (bassist Michael Formanek and drummer Daniel Humair) for a set of thought-provoking music. The three musicians often seem to speak as one during their interpretations of Don Friedman's "Circle Waltz" and originals by Zoller and Formanek. In addition Zoller plays a beautiful unaccompanied guitar solo on "Sophisticated Lady." Recommended. —*Scott Yanow*

Overcome / Nov. 1986 / Enja ✦✦✦

When It's Time / Oct. 1995 / Enja ✦✦✦

John Zorn

b. Sep. 12, 1953, New York, NY
Alto Saxophone / Avant-Garde, Free Jazz
It is possible to call John Zorn a "jazz" musician, but that would be much too limiting a description. While jazz feeling is present in a good deal of his work, and the idea of improvisation is vitally important to him, Zorn doesn't operate within any idiom's framework, drawing from just about any musical, cultural or noise source that a fellow who grew up in the TV and LP eras could experience. This eclecticism gone haywire can result in such wildly jump-cutting works as *Spillane*, whose plethora of diverse and incompatible styles makes for a listening experience akin to constantly punching the station buttons on a car radio. Zorn believes that the age of the composer as an "autonomous musical mind" had come to an end in the late 20th century; hence the collaborative nature of much of his work, both with active musicians and music and styles of the past. Like Mel Brooks, the zany film director, many of Zorn's works are tributes to certain musical touchstones of his—such as Ennio Morricone, Sonny Clark and Ornette Coleman—all filtered through his unpredictable hall of mirrors. While it would be foolhardy to single out a handful of dominant influences, Zorn's music seems very close in spirit to that of Warner Bros. cartoon composer Carl Stalling, both in its transformation of found material and manic, antic moods.

This calculating wild man started playing the piano as a child before taking up the guitar and flute at age ten. By the time he was 14, Zorn had discovered contemporary classical music and began composing; his college years in St. Louis brought about his introduction to avant-garde jazz, particularly that of Anthony Braxton. He dropped out of college, settled in lower Manhattan, and began working with free improvisers, rock bands, and tape, sometimes working duck and bird calls into his arsenal. After putting out releases on tiny domestic and poorly distributed import labels, Zorn signed with Elektra-Nonesuch in the mid-1980s, which increased his visibility considerably. Along the way, he has formed tribute bands to play the music of Coleman, Hank Mobley, Lee Morgan and others; featured musicians as diverse as Big John Patton, Tim Berne, Bill Frisell and the Kronos Quartet; and assembled a group called Masada that merges Coleman with Yiddish music. Jazz buffs should be directed to his Coleman tribute album *Spy Vs. Spy* (Nonesuch), which makes exciting, thrashing yet concise hashes of 17 Ornette tunes with a quintet. —*Richard S. Ginell*

Yankees / 1984 / Celluloid ✦✦✦✦
A collective improvisation by Derek Bailey, acoustic and electric guitars, George Lewis, trombone, John Zorn, alto and soprano saxes, clarinets, game calls. Subtle, droll, hilarious takes on the trivia of baseball sounds—Lewis speaks through the trombone "ball one, ball one . . . " there are snippets of a slipping and sliding version of "Take Me Out to the Ball Game," and so on. Sections are titled "City City City", "The Legend of Enos Slaughter", "Who's on First," followed by "On Golden Pond" . . . tongue-in-cheek tone poem of the flora and fauna, mosquitos etc. and "The Warning Track" . . . about a very tiny railroad system (?). —*"Blue" Gene Tyranny*

Big Gundown / Sep. 1984-Sep. 1985 / Elektra/Nonesuch ✦✦✦✦✦
On this intriguing concept album, altoist John Zorn (who also "sings" and plays harpsichord, game calls, piano and musical saw) utilizes an odd assortment of open-minded avant-garde players (with a couple of ringers) on nine themes originally written for Italian films by Ennio Morricone plus his own "Tre Nel 5000."

These often-radical interpretations (which Morricone endorsed) keep the melodies in mind while getting very adventurous. Among the musicians heard on the colorful and very eccentric set (which utilizes different personnel and instrumentation on each track) are guitarists Bill Frisell and Vernon Reid, percussionist Bobby Previte, keyboardist Anthony Coleman, altoist Tim Berne, pianist Wayne Horvitz, organist Big John Patton and even Toots Thielemans on harmonica and whistling among many others. There are certainly no dull moments on this often-riotous program. —*Scott Yanow*

Classic Guide to Strategy / 1985 / Lumina ✦✦✦
Solo woodwind improvisations with game calls, parts of saxes and clarinets. Eccentric, pure Zorn. —*"Blue" Gene Tyranny*

Cobra / Oct. 21, 1985+May 9, 1986 / Hat Art ✦✦✦
A studio and live performance recording with many of NYC's "downtown" improvisors: Anthony Coleman, Bill Frisell, Wayne Horvitz, Bob James, Guy Klucesvek, Arto Lindsay, Christian Marclay, Zeena Parkins, Bobby Previte, Elliott Sharp, Jim Staley, David Weinstein, J.A. Deane, and Carol Emanuel. —*"Blue" Gene Tyranny*

★ **Voodoo: The Music of Sonny Clark** / Nov. 25, 1985-Nov. 26, 1985 / Black Saint ✦✦✦✦✦
This unusual album is an unlikely success. Altoist John Zorn, who is best-known for his avant-garde flights and rather eccentric concept albums, here plays it fairly straight. He interprets seven compositions (all fairly obscure) by the somewhat forgotten hard bop pianist Sonny Clark including "Cool Struttin'," "Voodoo" and "Sonny's Crib." With alert support from pianist Wayne Horvitz, bassist Ray Drummond and drummer Bobby Previte, Zorn creates fairly boppish solos with occasional hints at more advanced improvising techniques. Worth checking out. —*Scott Yanow*

Classic Guide to Strategy, Vol. 2 / 1986 / Lumina ✦✦✦
More beautifully intense solo pieces with inflections like ancient Japanese music. Sections are named after various Japanese artists—Aoyama Michi, Enoken, Kazumi Shigeru, Kondo Toshinori, Yano Akiko, Togawa Jun and Mori Ikue. Cover art is calligraphy of the character for "water." —*"Blue" Gene Tyranny*

Spillane / Aug. 1986-Sep. 1987 / Elektra/Nonesuch ✦✦✦✦
An album of nice, dense, and foreboding concept work, with everything from shuffle guitar by Albert Collins to the Kronos Quartet. —*Ron Wynn*

☆ **News for Lulu** / Aug. 30, 1987 / Hat Hut ✦✦✦✦✦
This unusual set is an unlikely success. Avant-garde altoist John Zorn teams up with trombonist George Lewis and guitarist Bill Frisell to form a unique trio. Without the benefit of piano, bass or drums, they interpret the hard bop compositions of Kenny Dorham, Hank Mobley, Sonny Clark and Freddie Redd, generally not even the better-known ones. The performances are quite concise (Dorham's "Windmill" is covered in 40 seconds!), respectful to the melodies, and unpredictable. There are hints of the avant-garde here and there, but also plenty of swinging, bop-oriented solos and coherent ensembles. Very intriguing music that is highly recommended to a wide audience of jazz listeners. —*Scott Yanow*

Spy Vs. Spy: The Music of Ornette Coleman / Aug. 18, 1988-Aug. 19, 1988 / Elektra ✦✦✦✦✦
John Zorn teams up with fellow altoist Tim Berne, bassist Mark Dresser and both Joey Baron and Michael Vatcher on drums to perform 17 Ornette Coleman tunes that range chronologically from 1958's "Disguise" to four selections from 1987's *In*

All Languages. The performances are concise with all but four songs being under three minutes and seven under two, but the interpretations are unremittingly violent. The lack of variety in either mood or routine quickly wears one out. After about ten minutes, boredom sets in, although, when taken in short doses, the performances have the potential of shocking (or at least annoying) most listeners. —*Scott Yanow*

More News for Lulu / Jan. 18, 1989-Jan. 19, 1989 / Hat Art ✦✦✦✦
Another CD of wonderful trio improvisations with John Zorn, George Lewis and, this time, Bill Frisell. Odd, humorous, melodic, dramatic. —*"Blue" Gene Tyranny*

Naked City / 1989 / Elektra/Nonesuch ✦✦✦✦✦
The violent cover photo (which shows a man after he was shot dead) sets the stage for the rather passionate music on this John Zorn set. With guitarist Bill Frisell, keyboardist Wayne Horvitz, bassist Fred Frith, drummer Joey Baron and guest vocalist Yamatsuka Eye making intense contributions, altoist Zorn performs his unpredictable originals, abstract versions of some movie themes (including "A Shot in the Dark," "I Want to Live," "Chinatown" and "The James Bond Theme") plus Ornette Coleman's "Lonely Woman." The stimulating music rewards repeated listenings by more open-minded listeners. —*Scott Yanow*

John Zorn's Cobra Live at the Knitting Factory / 1992 / Knitting Factory ✦
Calling this set of performances bizarre would be an understatement. John Zorn inspired (through obscure game playing that is not explained anywhere on this CD) these 14 eccentric "tributes" to different types of cobras. Because many of the performances utilize samplers and voices (in addition to conventional instruments and miscellaneous devices), the wide range of sounds attained from the 87 musicians (heard in different combinations) is impressive if often quite unlistenable, ranging from humorous interludes to very obnoxious noise. For a few examples, "Cobra 4" has a man screaming over and over again, "Cobra 2" features a sound collage with a male opera singer repeating the same four notes continuously and "Cobra 5" has, among its many vocal noises, a man imitating a dog barking. There are some colorful segments, but in general, these self-indulgent performances would be much more interesting to see in person than to hear on record. Taken purely as a listening experience, one is surprised that this material has even been released. —*Scott Yanow*

John Zorn's Cobra: Tokyo Operations '94 / 1994 / Avant ✦✦✦✦
John Zorn's Cobra: Tokyo Operations '94 captures Zorn's most famous composition as performed by a group of traditional Japanese musicians led by Makigami Koichi. The group is augmented by a rock group— guitar, bass, drums—but it's the traditional Japanese instruments that make this a version of Cobra to remember. —*Stephen Thomas Erlewine*

Elegy / Oct. 1995 / Tzadik ✦✦✦
A mysterious, elegant, exotic tone poem built around Jean Genet's image relating flowers and prisoners. There are four parts entitled *Blue, Yellow, Pink* and *Black*. A constantly changing soundscape of images—sweet, tortured, folk ceremony, hellishly cosmic, dungeon sounds of chains and locks, breathing and much more—highlighted by silences. Brilliantly evocative. With Barbara Chaffe, alto and bass flutes, David Abel, viola, Scummy, guitar, David Shea, turntables, David Slusser, sound effects, William Winant, percussion, and Mike Patton, voice. —*"Blue" Gene Tyranny*

The 1930's Big Bands/ Dec. 11, 1930-Dec. 14, 1939 / Columbia ✦✦✦✦
This excellent sampler contains 16 big-band performances, many of them formerly rare. Such orchestras as Casa Loma (playing "San Sue Strut"), Claude Hopkins, Duke Ellington, Don Redman, Cab Calloway, Fletcher Henderson, Chick Webb, Teddy Hill, the Blue Rhythm Band, Erskine Hawkins, Red Norvo, Ben Pollack ("Jimtown Blues" which features Harry James), Earl Hines, Jimmie Lunceford, Count Basie and Benny Goodman are heard on a selection apiece, making this a set of great interest to swing collectors. —*Scott Yanow*

The 1930's: The Singers / 193 / Columbia ✦✦✦✦✦

The 1930's: The Small Combos / Apr. 4, 1930-Jul. 28, 1939 / Columbia ✦✦✦✦✦
Swing is the thing on this very enjoyable sampler which features 16 recordings by the same number of groups. Most of the combos are pickup bands but the quality of musicianship is so high that they sound like regularly working groups. Represented by a song apiece are Jack Purvis, the Chocolate Dandies, the Rhythmakers, Red Allen, Wingy Manone, Red Norvo, Jones-Smith Inc, Stuff Smith, Teddy Wilson, Roy Eldridge, Cootie Williams, the Gotham Stompers, Frankie Newton, Sidney Bechet, Chu Berry and John Kirby. Although one would prefer the complete sessions, this sampler serves as a perfect introduction to these brilliant players. —*Scott Yanow*

● **The 1940's Jazz: The Small Groups—New Directions** / Mar. 8, 1945-Nov. 3, 1947 / Columbia ✦✦✦✦✦

☆ **The 1940's Mercury Sessions** / Sep. 25, 1945-Oct. 27, 1951 / Mercury ✦✦✦✦
This seven-CD set is remarkable in several ways. The packaging is quite unique: the box is a plastic reproduction of a 1940s radio. Subtitled "Blues, Boogie & Bop," the music lives up to the billing, giving listeners the complete Mercury output of several top artists. There are 34 songs from pianist Albert Ammons (two featuring blues singer Sippie Wallace) which find Ammons turning everything (including "Red Sails in the Sunset," "Roses of Picardy" and "Margie") into boogie-woogie; a session with his son, tenor saxophonist Gene Ammons, is a high point. Singer Helen Humes is showcased on 16 stomps and ballads, pianist Jay McShann (often with vocalists Jimmy Witherspoon or Walter Brown) has 24 songs and Eddie "Cleanhead" Vinson (on alto and vocals) is heard in a variety of settings on 30 selections. In addition there are nine tunes featuring R&B pianist/singer Professor Longhair, four songs apiece from singers Julia Lee, Myra Taylor and cornetist Rex Stewart, 12 pieces from Buddy Rich's bebop big band and ten by trumpeter Cootie Williams, including the Willis "Gator" Jackson R&B hit "Gator Tail." As if that were not enough, the seventh disc has previously unreleased alternate takes from Ammons, Humes, McShann, Vinson, Cootie and two "new" numbers by pianist Mary Lou Williams. The 80-page booklet (with notes from several writers including Dan Morgenstern) is definitive. Since this is a limited-edition release, it should be acquired as soon as possible; there are literally dozens of musical highlights. —*Scott Yanow*

The 1940's: Bebop / 194 / Columbia ✦✦✦✦✦

The 1940's: The Big Bands / 194 / Columbia ✦✦✦✦✦

The 1940's: The Singers / Feb. 9, 1940-Dec. 21, 1949 / Columbia ✦✦✦
A variety of different singers (most from the swing era) are heard on this excellent collection. The music is enjoyable, if generally not all that essential, although Mildred Bailey's "I'm Nobody's Baby" (with its advanced Eddie Sauter arrangement and Roy Eldridge's futuristic trumpet solo) and Billie Holiday's "All of Me," Woody Herman's "Caldonia" and "Nat Meets June" from Nat King Cole and June Christy with the Metronome All-Stars are classics. Also heard from are Maxine Sullivan, Big Joe Turner, Jack Teagarden, Cab Calloway, Slim Gaillard, Anita O'Day, Jimmy Rushing, Peggy Lee, Roy Eldridge, Eddie "Cleanhead" Vinson, Hot Lips Page and Sarah Vaughan. —*Scott Yanow*

The 40's in Hollywood / Oct. 27, 1945-Jul. 6, 1946 / Jump ✦✦✦✦✦
This excellent LP reissues three four-song sessions from the 1945-46 era that feature Dixieland-style jazz as performed in Los Angeles by a variety of top-notch (if not overly famous) studio musicians. Yukl's Wabash Five (a septet) has the leader

on trombone, clarinetist Pate Legare and cornetist George Thow, Bob Anderson's Oshkosh Serenaders features Anderson's cornet, Joe Rushton on bass sax and clarinet and trombonist Warren Smith, and Mackey's Michigan Boulevard Gang has solos from trumpeter Mackey, trombonist Floyd O'Brien and clarinetist Matty Matlock. Forget the lack of major names; fans of this style of music would be well advised to pick up this increasingly rare LP. —*Scott Yanow*

The 1950's: The Singers / Feb. 1, 1950-Aug. 6, 1959 / Columbia ✦✦✦
A variety of jazz singers are represented on this fine collection including Lee Wiley, Louis Armstrong (the original version of "Mack the Knife"), Billie Holiday, Jimmy Rushing, Sarah Vaughan ("Mean to Me" with a small group that co-stars Miles Davis), Hot Lips Page, Dolores Hawkins, Joe Williams, Betty Roche (a classic version of "Take the 'A' Train" with Duke Ellington), Babs Gonzalez, Betty Carter, Lambert, Hendricks and Ross, and surprisingly enough, Johnny Mathis on a jazz-oriented version of "Easy to Love." It's a good well-rounded set. —*Scott Yanow*

The 1960's: The Singers / 196 / Columbia ✦✦✦✦✦

The 1960's: Trumpet Traditionalists / 196 / Columbia ✦✦✦

The 1986 Floating Jazz Festival / Oct. 15, 1986-Oct. 23, 1986 / Chiaroscuro ✦✦✦
This CD is a bit of a collector's item, a variety of interesting performances recorded during the S.S. Norway's Fourth Annual Jazz Cruise. The oddest selection is a long trumpet-drums duet by Dizzy Gillespie and Buddy Rich that is only partially successful. In addition to Joe Williams singing "I Want a Little Girl" with a big band and vibraphonist Gary Burton jamming with the Berklee Ensemble, such notables as Kenny Davern and Bob Wilber (who have a Soprano Summit reunion on "Moonglow"), violinist Svend Asmussen, pianist Mel Powell, fluegelhornist Clark Terry, trumpeter Warren Vache (jamming some Dixieland on "Jazz Me Blues") and (on "Flying Home") the tenors of Flip Phillips, Al Cohn, Buddy Tate and Scott Hamilton are heard from. Although a bit erratic, this CD has enough special moments to justify its acquisition. —*Scott Yanow*

25 Years of Prestige / Jan. 11, 1949-Jul. 26, 1970 / Prestige ✦✦✦✦✦
This is a two-LP set that really delighted collectors when it was released in 1974. To celebrate the 25th year of the Prestige label, unissued material, alternate takes and a few rarities were compiled for this two-fer. Starting out with the very first Prestige recording (Lee Konitz's "Progression"), the set is highlighted by performances featuring Stan Getz (with the similar-sounding tenors of Al Cohn, Allen Eager, Brew Moore and Zoot Sims), Fats Navarro, Wardell Gray, Miles Davis (the alternate take of "Blue Room"), King Pleasure, Thelonious Monk, John Coltrane (jamming "Blue Calypso" with a Mal Waldron group), Benny Golson, Gene Ammons, Dexter Gordon and Eric Dolphy among others. Much of this material has since appeared on CD but the attractive set is still worth acquiring. —*Scott Yanow*

50 Years of Jazz Guitar / Jul. 1921-Aug. 14, 1971 / Columbia ✦✦✦✦
Twenty-seven performances by guitarists are included in this well-rounded two-LP sampler. Sam Moore is heard in 1921 taking a solo on the octocorda and there are examples of the talents of Lonnie Johnson, Eddie Lang, King Nawahi (playing Hawaiian guitar in 1929), Bobby Leecan, Teddy Bunn, Coco Heimal, Dick McDonough, Carl Kress, Leon McAuliffe, Buddy Woods, Joe Sodja, Charlie Christian, Slim Gaillard, Memphis Minnie, Django Reinhardt, George Van Eps, Hank Garland, Kenny Burrell, Eddie Durham, Herb Ellis, George Benson, Charlie Byrd and even John McLaughlin. Obviously not every jazz guitarist is represented (Wes Montgomery is absent and there is only one fusion performance and no real avant-garde) but there are quite a few rarities on this two-fer, making this a set that collectors will want to look for. —*Scott Yanow*

52nd Street Swing / Sep. 11, 1934-Apr. 3, 1941 / GRP/Decca ✦✦✦✦✦
This fine CD includes performances from many of the most popular small jazz groups that played in New York's 52nd Street during the swing era. There are two hot numbers by the Delta Four (featuring trumpeter Roy Eldridge and clarinetist Joe Marsala), three from the good-time ensemble the Spirits of Rhythm, a trio from violinist Stuff Smith's Onyx Club Band (which co-starred trumpeter Jonah Jones, three others from John Kirby's sextet, four numbers by Leonard Feather's All-Star Jam Band (with altoists Benny Carter and Pete Brown, cornetist Bobby Hackett and

clarinetist Joe Marsala), three from trumpeter/vocalist Hot Lips Page and a pair of selections by pianist Sam Price's Texas Bluesicians including "Just Jivin' Around" which has a particularly rare solo from the great tenor Lester Young. Veteran collectors will have most of these performances in more complete fashion elsewhere but this is an excellent sampler for fans of small-group swing. —*Scott Yanow*

● **Afro-Cuban Jazz** / Dec. 1948-Mar. 24, 1954 / PolyGram ✦✦✦✦✦
This double LP (which was released in 1977) has some of the most important early Afro-Cuban and Latin-jazz recordings. Machito's Orchestra welcomes guests Charlie Parker, Flip Phillips and Buddy Rich to such selections as "Tanga," "Mango Mangue" and Chico O'Farrill's five-part "Afro-Cuban Suite." In addition O'Farrill's own exciting big band (using some of the same personnel as Machito) in 1951 plays some of his originals, and Dizzy Gillespie's 1954 orchestra performs O'Farrill's four-part "Manteca Suite." The music (which belongs in all serious jazz collections) overall is quite exciting and historic; much of it has not yet been reissued on CD. —*Scott Yanow*

All Star Swing Groups / Mar. 13, 1944-Jan. 31, 1946 / Savoy ✦✦✦✦✦
This double LP from 1977 (when Arista was reissuing recordings from the valuable Savoy catalog) has more than its share of gems. Drummer Cozy Cole's three 1944 sessions have overlapping personnel (including trumpeters Lamar Wright or Emmett Berry, trombonist Ray Coniff, the tenors of Ben Webster, Budd Johnson and Coleman Hawkins and pianist Johnny Guarnieri). Those classic musicians all get their solo space and play up to par with some exciting moments. In addition pianist Pete Johnson leads two bands that feature some great playing from trumpeter Hot Lips Page (who is quite memorable on the two versions of "Page Mr. Trumpet"), either J.C. Higginbotham or Clyde Bernhardt on trombone, clarinetist Albert Nicholas, Ben Webster or Budd Johnson on tenor, the underrated altoist Don Stovall, and on a few numbers, singer Etta Jones. The influence of the emerging bebop music is not felt at all on these highly enjoyable swing performances. Most of this music has not yet been reissued in coherent form on CD. —*Scott Yanow*

All the Things You Are: The Jerome Kern Songbook / Dec. 1952-Feb. 7, 1968 / Verve ✦✦✦
The legacy of composer Jerome Kern is celebrated on this hodgepodge release which collects 16 performances of his songs by a variety of singers: Ella Fitzgerald, Arthur Prysock, Helen Merrill, Sarah Vaughan, Joe Williams, Jackie and Roy, Ernestine Anderson, Fred Astaire, Billie Holiday, Bing Crosby and three by Margaret Whiting. None of the music is particularly rare and the emphasis overall is on straight versions of the lyrics and Kern's melodies. This release is more for the general listener than for any serious collector. —*Scott Yanow*

Almost Forgotten / Jun. 15, 1955-Dec. 10, 1962 / Columbia ✦✦✦✦✦
This LP (released by Columbia in 1983) contains eight previously "lost" recordings that were released for the first time. Many all-stars appear and there are some historic performances. Drummer Dave Bailey leads a sextet in 1960 also featuring trumpeter Clark Terry, trombonist Curtis Fuller and Junior Cook on tenor. Terry interacts with the great tenor Coleman Hawkins on a 1962 version of "Ain't Misbehavin'," altoist Pony Poindexter performs an alternate take of his "Lanyop" in 1962 with five other saxophonists including Eric Dolphy, and Wes Montgomery is heard on "Love for Sale" in 1955, four years before his discovery. Side two of this LP has trumpeter Johnny Coles leading a quartet with pianist Randy Weston, trombonist Slide Hampton at the head of an 11-piece group, the English tenor Tubby Hayes in a quintet with Clark Terry, and a combo matching trombonist J.J. Johnson and cornetist Nat Adderley in 1958. The bop-oriented music is consistently rewarding, making this an album well worth searching for. —*Scott Yanow*

Alto Summit / Jun. 2, 1968-Jun. 3, 1968 / Saba ✦✦✦
For this brainchild of Joachim Berendt, four top altoists (Lee Konitz, Pony Poindexter, Phil Woods and Leo Wright) team up with a fine rhythm section led by pianist Steve Kuhn to explore mostly originals. There are two quintets but otherwise all of the performances are by the full septet. A four-song ballad medley goes well until the ending when all of the saxophonists solo together quite chaotically to unintentionally hilarious effect. Much better is "Lee's Tribute to Bach and Bird," which goes from a Bach piece to Charlie Parker's solo on "Honeysuckle Rose." —*Scott Yanow*

Amarcord Nino Rota / May 1982 / Hannibal ✦✦✦
This tribute to the music of film composer Nino Rota was the first of Hal Willner's unusual multiartist projects and one of his more jazz-oriented ones. Such musicians as pianist Jaki Byard, vibraphonist Dave Samuels, guitarist Bill Frisell, soprano saxophonist Steve Lacy, trumpeter Wynton Marsalis, and bands headed by Carla Bley, Muhal Richard Abrams and David Amram are heard on these eccentric but very musical adaptations of Rota's themes from Fellini movies. —*Scott Yanow*

Americans in Europe / Jan. 3, 1960 / GRP/Impulse! ✦✦✦
On Jan. 3, 1963 producer-writer Joachim Berendt organized a concert in Germany featuring some of the top American jazzmen who were then residing in Europe. Originally released as 13 songs on two LPs, eight of the performances have been

reissued on this single CD; left out are five of the seven numbers from *Vol. 1* (three with clarinetist Albert Nicholas and one apiece with bluesmen Champion Jack Dupree and Curtis Jones). The CD contains a pair of fine features for tenor saxophonist Don Byas (including a lengthy workout on "All the Things You Are"), ballad showcases for trumpeter Idrees Sulieman ("I Can't Get Started") and pianist Bud Powell ("'Round Midnight"), two numbers by a trio consisting of guitarist Jimmy Gourley, organist Lou Bennett and drummer Kenny Clarke, and a pair of Bill Smith originals featuring the clarinetist in a quintet with altoist Herb Geller and guitarist Gourley. A fine bop-oriented set of music by a variety of mostly underrated players. —*Scott Yanow*

Anthology of Big Band Swing (1930-1955) / Jan. 14, 1931-Aug. 1955 / GRP ✦✦✦✦
This two-CD set is an unusually successful sampler. Although there are a few hits among the 40 selections, many obscurities are also included, and not all of the big bands represented are major names, such as Tiny Bradshaw, Noble Sissle, Spud Murphy, Teddy Powell and Jan Savitt. The emphasis is very much on jazz, and this worthy reissue is overflowing with forgotten classics. The music is programmed in chronological order, so one can experience the evolution of big bands from Duke Ellington, Fletcher Henderson and Luis Russell to postwar recordings from Artie Shaw, Tommy Dorsey and Benny Goodman. —*Scott Yanow*

Art Deco: Sophisticated Ladies / Apr. 5, 1929-Dec. 17, 1940 / Columbia/Legacy ✦✦✦✦✦
This is a very rewarding two-CD sampler that introduces listeners to a wide variety of singers who were active in the 1930s, ranging from jazz vocalists (Annette Hanshaw, Ethel Waters, Connie Boswell, the Boswell Sisters, Lee Wiley, Helen Ward, Ella Logan, Maxine Sullivan and Mildred Bailey) to cabaret and pop artists of the time (Ruth Etting, Helen Morgan, Greta Keller, Frances Langford, Alice Faye, Nan Wynn and Ginny Simms). This set has more than its share of rarities (including some previously unissued alternate takes) and there are many rewarding performances. The set is recommended to anyone with an interest in the singing stylists who rose to prominence between Bessie Smith and Billie Holiday. —*Scott Yanow*

Art Deco: The Crooners / Sep. 1926-Oct. 6, 1941 / Columbia/Legacy ✦✦✦✦✦
A wide span of styles is represented on this two-CD salute to the male singers of the 1930s, the "crooners." Some of the vocalists are quite enjoyable to hear while a few are very dated, but overall the 49 performances contain more than their share of highlights. There are selections featuring Willard Robison, Gene Austin, Seger Ellis, Smith Ballew, the completely forgotten Lew Bray, Bing Crosby, Harlan Lattimore, Russ Columbo, Red McKenzie, Cliff Edwards (who is heard on eight songs), Pinky Tomlin, Chick Bullock, Jack Teagarden, Harold Arlen ("You're a Builder-Upper"), Buddy Clark, Eddy Howard (a rare jazz session with an all-star group that includes trumpeter Bill Coleman, pianist Teddy Wilson and guitarist Charlie Christian), Frank Sinatra (with Harry James) and Dick Haymes. This set acts as a perfect introduction to these mostly very talented singers. —*Scott Yanow*

The Art of the Duo, Vol. 1 / Enja ✦✦✦
This is an unusual CD, nine duets taken from nine previous Enja releases. The music varies from modern hard bop to world music with six of the performances having bass and/or piano, two featuring drums and just one (a matchup between trombonist Albert Mangelsdorff and altoist Lee Konitz) with two horns; unfortunately the recording dates are not given for any of this material. Such notables as pianist Abdullah Ibrahim, tenor saxophonist Joe Henderson (who duets with bassist Wayne Darling), tenors John Tchicai and Jim Pepper, singer Karin Krog (performing a haunting version of "'Round Midnight" and Joe Lovano (on soprano duetting with drummer Ed Blackwell) are heard from on a program dominated by originals. This interesting music serves well as an introduction to these fine artists. —*Scott Yanow*

At the Jazz Band Ball: Chicago/New York Dixieland / Feb. 8, 1929-Jul. 19, 1939 / Bluebird ✦✦✦✦✦
This 1988 CD contains what was originally called "the Great 16," the four 1939 recording sessions (16 songs in all) by cornetist Muggsy Spanier's hot Ragtime Band. All of that music (plus eight alternate takes) was reissued on CD by Bluebird in 1994 but this CD also contains two selections from Eddie Condon in 1929 and four songs from Bud Freeman's Summa Cum Laude Orchestra in 1939. For those listeners who do not need his alternates, this is a highly recommended set with plenty of exciting and heated Chicago jazz. —*Scott Yanow*

Atlantic Jazz Keyboards / Rhino ✦✦✦✦✦
Rhino's various artists/sampler series focuses on keyboards on this release, with cuts from 13 players. The opening track features Jimmy Yancey's sparkling boogie piano, and continues through several styles from Erroll Garner's flashy solos through Thelonious Monk's amazing bop improvisations, John Lewis' sedate, sophisticated phrases, Lennie Tristano's intricate material, and bluesier fare from Ray Charles, Junior Mance, and Les McCann. Keith Jarrett and Chick Corea take

more adventurous directions, while the Mitchell-Ruff duo with drummer Charlie Smith falls somewhere in the center. The set's compositional variety and artist lineup is impressive; while none of these tracks qualify as rare or obscure, they show the wealth of keyboard talent once on the Atlantic roster. —*Ron Wynn*

Atlantic Jazz: Best of the '50s / 195 / Rhino ✦✦✦

Atlantic Jazz: Best of the '60s, Vol. 1 / 196 / Rhino ✦✦✦

Atlantic Jazz: Best of the '70s / 197 / Rhino ✦✦

During the 1970s, Atlantic eventually lost most of the acts that made it a power-house in the 1950s and '60s, while increasingly turning to formulaic commercial fare in an attempt at trendiness and survival. This 12-track anthology shows the perils of jazz life in the 1970s; there are top-caliber tunes by the duos of Gary Burton/Keith Jarrett and Les McCann/Eddie Harris, as well as Jimmy Scott's histrionic but ardently performed "Dedicated to You" and the Modern Jazz Quartet's stately "Blues in a Minor." But Atlantic really put its muscle behind such songs as Herbie Mann's "Push Push," Billy Cobham's "Funky Thide of Things" and Jean-Luc Ponty's "Molecules." They were pleasant, but were neither on the aesthetic cutting edge nor constructed with enough hooks to be pop smashes. —*Ron Wynn*

Atlantic Jazz: Classics / 194 / Rhino ✦✦✦✦

Released to celebrate Atlantic's 50th anniversary, *Atlantic Jazz: Classics* is a budget priced, 13-track collection that culls highlights from the Atlantic vaults. The collection spans the '40s to the '70s and features cuts by Ray Charles ("Sweet Sixteen Bars"), the Modern Jazz Quartet ("The Golden Striker"), Art Blakey & Thelonious Monk ("In Walked Bud"), David "Fathead" Newman ("Hard Times"), Charles Mingus ("Wednesday Night Prayer Meeting"), Ornette Coleman ("Ramblin'"), John Coltrane ("My Favorite Things"), Mose Allison ("Your Mind Is on Vacation"), Roland Kirk ("The Inflated Tear") and Les McCann & Eddie Harris ("Compared to What"). Although it isn't a comprehensive overview, the disc is nevertheless a sharp sampler showcasing the finest singers on Atlantic, making it a nice budget-priced introduction to the label for curious listeners on a budget. —*Stephen Thomas Erlewine*

Atlantic Jazz: Vocal Classics / 194 / Rhino ✦✦✦✦

Released to celebrate Atlantic's 50th anniversary, *Atlantic Jazz: Vocal Classics* is a budget-priced, 14-track collection that culls highlights from the Atlantic vaults. The collection spans from the '40s to the '70s and features cuts by Al Hibbler ("Trav'lin' Light"), Ray Charles ("Don't Let the Sun Catch You Cryin'"), Bobby Darin ("Easy Living"), Betty Carter ("Round Midnight"), Mel Tormé ("Broadway"), Esther Phillips ("Every Time We Say Goodbye"), Carmen McRae ("Day by Day"), Mose Allison ("Your Molecular Structure"), Aretha Franklin ("Crazy He Calls Me"), Jimmy Scott ("Exodus") and the Manhattan Transfer ("Birdland"). It's a solid sampler that indicates the richness of the label's roster, and for the curious or listeners on a budget, it's an introduction well worth its price. —*Stephen Thomas Erlewine*

A Bag of Sleepers, Vol. 1 / Oct. 28, 1927-Oct. 3, 1932 / Arcadia ✦✦✦✦✦

All three LPs in this series feature obscure jazz and hot dance bands from the 1927-32 period so these releases are highly recommended to collector's of early jazz who want to get beyond only hearing the most famous names. Hoagy Carmichael heads a group for three songs (including the earliest recorded version of "Star Dust" which is here taken as an uptempo instrumental) before the Emil Seidel, Johnny Burris and Howard Thomas Orchestras are featured. The Burris band would soon be reorganized as the Casa Loma Orchestra. —*Scott Yanow*

A Bag of Sleepers, Vol. 2 / Sep. 15, 1927-Aug. 12, 1930 / Arcadia ✦✦✦

The second of three LPs in Arcadia's series of obscure but hot jazz and dance bands from the late '20s has recordings by groups even veteran collectors will most likely be unfamiliar with: Henry Lange's Orchestra, Clarie Hull's Boys, the original Atlanta Footwarmers, Hal Frazer's Georgians, Ruby Green's Manhattan Madcaps, Lew Weimer's Black and Gold Aces, Art Payne's Orchestra, Bob McGowan's Orchestra, Tommy Meyers' Gang, Ducky Yountz's Orchestra, Dick Coy's Racketeers and Dexter's Pennsylvanians. The music from these territory bands (most of whom were recorded in the Midwest) ranges from melodic jazz to hot dance arrangements and this set has more than its share of interesting moments. —*Scott Yanow*

A Bag of Sleepers, Vol. 3 / Jul. 19, 1927-Dec. 8, 1930 / Arcadia ✦✦✦✦✦

On the third of three LPs put out by Arcadia, there are two surprisingly hot numbers from an early edition of Lawrence Welk's Orchestra ("Spiked Beer" and "Doin' the New Lowdown") and jazz-oriented performances from a variety of obscure late-'20s groups including Bernie Schultz's Crescent Orchestra, the Cotton Pickers, Berlyn Baylor, Dick Kent, Joe Ward, Roy Wilson and Jack Davies' Kentuckians. None of the sidemen (except trumpeter Jack Purvis) went on to much, but this music should delight fans of the era. —*Scott Yanow*

Barrelhouse Boogie / May 7, 1936-Jun. 17, 1941 / Bluebird ✦✦✦✦✦

The four most important boogie-woogie pianists are all represented on this enjoyable CD. Meade Lux Lewis performs a 1936 remake of his classic "Honky Tonk Train Blues" and accompanies himself on "Whistlin' Blues"; the subtle Jimmy Yancey plays ten solos from 1939-40; and Pete Johnson and Albert Ammons (with

drummer James Hoskins) jam on nine duets from 1940-41. Although there are more complete reissues of the pianists' work available from European labels, this Bluebird set gives listeners a strong sampling of boogie-woogie during its prime years. —*Scott Yanow*

Battle of Tenor Saxes / Jul. 17, 1945-May 27, 1951 / IAJRC ✦✦✦

There is no actual tenor battle on this valuable IAJRC LP but a dozen different bop-based tenors are heard on 16 studio selections, some of which were formerly rare. On side one (which is titled "The Big Sound") Coleman Hawkins, Ben Webster, Gene Ammons, Ike Quebec, Paul Gonsavles and Illinois Jacquet (Quebec and Jacquet twice) are heard, while side two ("The Cool School") features Lester Young, Dexter Gordon, Allen Eager, Warne Marsh, James Moody and Wardell Gray; Young and Marsh pop up twice. Although this is very much a sampler (which unfortunately leaves out Teddy Edwards, Stan Getz and Zoot Sims), all of the diverse tenors play quite well; it is recommended to fans of the bop era. —*Scott Yanow*

The Be Bop Era / Feb. 27, 1946-Feb. 6, 1950 / RCA ✦✦✦✦✦

This LP gives listeners a strong cross-section of the better bop recordings that were made for Victor during 1946-50. Much of the material has since been reissued on CD but, taken as a whole, this is a fairly definitive set of the era. Coleman Hawkins lets his fellow tenor Allen Eager stretch out on "Allen's Alley," Illinois Jacquet romps on "Mutton Leg," Lucky Thompson plays "Boppin' the Blues," drummer Kenny Clarke leads an advanced nonet (with trumpeter Fats Navarro, saxophonist Sonny Stitt and pianist Bud Powell) on four numbers (including two by Thelonious Monk), Charlie Ventura's "Bop for the People" band jams on "Ha," Count Basie's 1950 sextet performs "Rat Race" and Dizzy Gillespie's big band plays five of its lesser-known songs. In addition the Metronome All-Stars of 1949 (with altoist Charlie Parker, pianist Lennie Tristano and the remarkable trumpet trio of Dizzy Gillespie, Miles Davis and Fats Navarro) perform "Overtime" (during which the three trumpeters trade off) and "Victory Ball." —*Scott Yanow*

The Bebop Boys / Aug. 23, 1946-Oct. 9, 1953 / Arista ✦✦✦✦✦

This double LP is from the era when Arista (under the guidance of producers Bob Porter and Steve Backer) was doing a superlative job of reissuing music from the Savoy catalog. The emphasis is very much on bop with eight different groups heard from. The all-star quintet of trumpeter Kenny Dorham, altoist Sonny Stitt, pianist Bud Powell, bassist Al Hall and either Wally Bishop or Kenny Clarke on drums performs eight heated numbers from 1946; there is a session led by bassist Ray Brown that has Dizzy Gillespie and Milt Jackson among the sidemen, and Gil Fuller has a rare opportunity to lead his own date. In addition vocalists Kenny Hagood, Babs Gonzales and Eddie Jefferson (the latter's "Body and Soul" and "The Birdland Story" are among the high points of this two-fer) are heard from. This highly recommended and historic package concludes with a pair of dates headed by baritonist Leo Parker that also feature trumpeter Joe Newman, trombonist J.J. Johnson and the young tenor-great Dexter Gordon. Until Savoy's timeless recordings are reissued in more coherent form on CD, these Arista sets are worth a lengthy search. —*Scott Yanow*

Bebop Revisited, Vol. 1 / 1945 / Xanadu ✦✦✦✦✦

The first of six LPs put out by the Xanadu label that reissues important but generally obscure bop sessions from the 1945-55 period has three very enjoyable dates. Tenor-great Dexter Gordon is teamed with trombonist Melba Liston in a 1947 quintet (they perform two versions apiece of two songs), trumpeter Fats Navarro joins tenor saxophonist Don Lanphere in a backup group behind singer Earl Coleman (the sextet does get to play two takes of the instrumental "Move") and bassist Chubby Jackson leads a heated sextet that features trumpeter Conte Candoli, Frank Socolow on tenor and vibraphonist Terry Gibbs. There are many exciting moments on this LP; bop collectors will want the whole series. —*Scott Yanow*

Bebop Revisited, Vol. 2 / Jan. 9, 1945-Jun. 8, 1946 / Xanadu ✦✦✦✦✦

The second of six Xanadu LPs to reissue obscure bop sessions from the mid-'40s to mid-'50s has four interesting dates from very early in the bebop era. Bassist Oscar Pettiford leads a large band for four selections, three of which feature the so-so singer Rubberlegs Williams. However trumpeter Dizzy Gillespie's presence in this Jan. 1945 session gives it great historic value. In addition there are four selections apiece from groups led by trombonists Kai Winding (with a no-name septet) and J.J. Johnson (with a variety of Count Basie sidemen including tenorman Buddy Tate) and a quintet set by vibraphonist Terry Gibbs with clarinetist Aaron Sachs. This is historic and enjoyable music. —*Scott Yanow*

Bebop Revisited, Vol. 3 / Apr. 27, 1951-Dec. 29, 1953 / Xanadu ✦✦✦✦✦

On the third of six Xanadu LPs that reissue little-known early bop sessions, there are more than its share of highlights. Trombonist Kai Winding heads a quintet with tenor saxophonist Warne Marsh and pianist Billy Taylor; two of the four selections have fine vocals from the forgotten Melvin Moore. Trumpeter Tony Fruscella had one of his few opportunities to lead a session in 1952 and his septet (with altoist Herb Geller and Phil Urso on tenor) is in excellent form on four numbers. The most memorable set is the one led by Sam Most (doubling on clarinet and flute) which also features trumpeter Doug Mettome, trombonist Urbie Green and Bob Dorough on piano. Most, one of the pioneers of the jazz flute, actually plays clarinet (which he rarely touched in later years) on five of the seven selections, showing off some virtuoso chops on "Notes to You" (a tribute to Benny Goodman). This LP (and the five others in the valuable series) is essential for bop collectors who want to expand their knowledge beyond the most famous recordings. —*Scott Yanow*

Bebop Revisited, Vol. 4 / Dec. 2, 1948-Aug. 13, 1950 / Xanadu ◆◆◆◆◆

For the fourth LP volume of six in a series, the focus is once again on early and obscure bebop sessions. tenor saxophonist James Moody leads a pair of sextets; the one from 1948 features the vocals of Babs Gonzales along with trumpeter Dave Burns and trombonist Bennie Green on such numbers as "Honeysuckle Bop!" and "A Lesson in Bopology," while the group from 1950 was recorded in France with trumpeter Ernie Royal (who gets a rare opportunity to stretch out). This LP is rounded out by a completely forgotten date led by trombonist Bennie Green that also features the tenor of Budd Johnson. Although the album on a whole is not essential, bop fans will want it. —*Scott Yanow*

Bebop Revisited, Vol. 5 / Apr. 17, 1957+Aug. 21, 1964 / Xanadu ◆◆◆◆◆

Unlike the other volumes in this six-LP series, *Vol. 5* does not feature music from the early bop years. As it turns out the music is very much in the bop vein even though recorded a decade later. Trumpeter Conte Candoli and tenor saxophonist Richie Kamuca really stretch out with a quintet on "Allen's Alley" and "Counting" in 1957; the two songs clock in at over 24 minutes. In addition a quartet set by trumpet-great Kenny Dorham with pianist Barry Harris from 1964 was released for the first time on this 1985 LP and it finds Dorham in top form playing before a teenaged audience at a school. It's easily recommended (along with the other albums in this very valuable series) to bop collectors. —*Scott Yanow*

Bebop Revisited, Vol. 6 / May 2, 1945-Dec. 8, 1952 / Xanadu ◆◆◆◆◆

The sixth and final LP released by Xanadu in this valuable series from the mid-'80s has four rare bop sessions. The first set, a three-song date led by tenor saxophonist Frankie Socolow, feature the rarely recorded (and legendary) trumpeter Freddy Webster and pianist Bud Powell in one of his earliest recordings. Although their playing is worth the price of this LP, there are also excellent performances by tenor saxophonist John Hardee (in a quartet), the fiery tenor Eddie "Lockjaw" Davis (during his early uninhibited R&B days) and Lester Young-soundalike Paul Quinichette in 1952. Bop collectors will want all six of the consistently exciting LPs in this series. —*Scott Yanow*

● Bebop in Britain / Jan. 13, 1948-Apr. 13, 1953 / Esquire ◆◆◆◆◆

England was not often thought of as a haven for bebop but once the records of Charlie Parker and Dizzy Gillespie started becoming common in 1947, many of the top swing players began to modernize their styles and record. This very interesting four-CD set contains many of the most significant English bop recordings, starring such important players as tenor saxophonist Ronnie Scott, Johnny Dankworth (on alto and clarinet), trumpeter Jimmy Deuchar, pianist Tommy Pollard and bandleaders Tito Burns and Vic Lewis among others. Even bop fanatics will probably not already own many of these rare recordings which, once they hit their stride, hold their own with their American counterparts. —*Scott Yanow*

★ The Best of Blue Note, Vols. 1 & 2 / Blue Note ◆◆◆◆◆

Japanese import. An incredible (just the best!) collection of the very best cuts from the Blue Note label. A perfect introduction to hard-bop and soul-jazz, if you can find it. —*Michael Erlewine*

Best of Smooth Jazz / Warner Brothers ◆◆◆◆

One could imagine this extremely radio-friendly grab-bag as the sole "jazz" album on the shelf of a casual Wal-Mart shopper who bought it on an impulse. Indeed, it will give the harried consumer-on-the-go an hour or so of easy-listening jazz, chosen with some care from a 21-year span of Warner Bros. recordings and ranging from the most recycled Fuzak cliches to borderline R&B and genuine, if always relaxed, stretches of musically satisfying electric jazz. The list of artists is a reasonably good representation of who was hot in crossover music from the '70s through the '90s: George Benson, Randy Crawford, George Duke, Fourplay, Michael Franks, Bob James, Boney James, Al Jarreau, Earl Klugh, Joe Sample, David Sanborn and the Yellowjackets. Furthermore, almost every track is fairly representative of each musician's work for Warner (and earlier outfits like Bob James' Tappan Zee label)—and some, like Benson's "Breezin'," James' "Angela (Theme from *Taxi*)," and Sample's "Hippies on a Corner," are particularly pleasing choices. —*Richard S. Ginell*

The Best of the Jazz Pianos / 1957-1969 / Denon ◆◆◆

One of five CDs in Denon's series, this release has some interesting if hard-to-trace material. Bill Evans performs two numbers with his classic 1961 trio (which includes bassist Scott LaFaro and drummer Paul Motian), Bud Powell plays two lengthy songs with a quintet that features trumpeter Clark Terry in 1957, Teddy

Wilson's trio runs through a pair of standards, Thelonious Monk and a quintet with Charlie Rouse on tenor and trumpeter Thad Jones play a version of "Light Blue" that is supposedly from a European tour in 1958 (doubtful) and Chick Corea is heard on the out-of-place and rather spacey "Sundance," a lengthy improvisation with a group of modernists in 1969. It's a mixed bag. —*Scott Yanow*

The Best of the Jazz Saxophones / 1958-1980 / Denon ◆◆◆

As with the other entries in this Denon series (which also include CDs devoted to big bands, pianos, singers and trumpets), the origin of the material on this set is difficult to trace. Stan Getz performs two numbers while in France during 1958-59, Gerry Mulligan and his quartet play "Jeru" in 1958, and the baritonist jams with tenorman Bud Freeman and trumpeter Ruby Braff on "Rose Room" from the same year. In addition, Zoot Sims leads a quartet in 1974 for two numbers, altoist Hank Crawford and Eddie Daniels (on tenor) team up in 1980, Eddie Lockjaw Davis jams in 1961, Sonny Stitt plays "My Little Suede Shoes" in 1972 and the tenors of Coleman Hawkins, Stan Getz and Don Byas team up for a rousing 1958 version of "Indiana." In general this is one of the most rewarding releases in the Denon series but the lack of any additional information (or liner notes) makes it a recommended set only if located at a budget price. —*Scott Yanow*

The Best of the Jazz Singers / 1954-1974 / Denon ◆◆◆

Only five singers appear on this sampler (part of a five-CD Denon series also including sets devoted to big bands, piano, saxophones and trumpets) but they are five of the best. Ella Fitgerald and her trio in 1959 perform eight numbers (including "Air Mail Special"), Sarah Vaughan does a song apiece from 1954 and 1960, Carmen McRae is caught during 1972-73, Ruth Brown sings "Fine Brown Frame" with the assistance of the Thad Jones/Mel Lewis Orchestra and Dakota Staton in 1974 sings two numbers. There is nothing too essential on this set but, if seen at a budget price, it is worth picking up. —*Scott Yanow*

The Best of the Jazz Trumpets / 1958-1976 / Denon ◆◆◆

One of five best-of CDs put out by Denon (along with collections featuring big bands, singers, saxophonists and pianists), this sampler features Chet Baker and Donald Byrd on one selection apiece from 1958, Dizzy Gillespie performing "Kush" in 1976, Freddie Hubbard on 1970's "Blues for Duane," three short numbers from Louis Armstrong in 1959, Maynard Ferguson's 1965 "Got the Spirit" and an unusual version of "The Theme" that features Thad Jones, Howard McGhee and Kenny Dorham. There is nothing all that essential on this release (some of whose material comes from the Groove Merchant catalog) but it does have its strong moments. —*Scott Yanow*

Big Band Hit Parade / Aug. 3, 1988 / Telarc ◆◆◆

This CD is a bit of an oddity but largely a success. A group of all-star jazzmen (trumpeter Doc Severinsen, trombonist Buddy Morrow, clarinetist Eddie Daniels, baritonist Gerry Mulligan, pianist Dave Brubeck, bassist Ray Brown and drummer Ed Shaughnessy) along with the great singer Cab Calloway team up with Erich Kunzel's Cincinnati Pops Big Band Orchestra to perform hits of the swing era; never mind that only Calloway was from that period. The arrangements (mostly by Jeff Tyzik and Tommy Newsom) for the string orchestra are not re-creations of the past but fresh and sometimes surprising reworkings of such songs as "One O'Clock Jump," "You Made Me Love You," "In the Mood" and "Artistry in Rhythm." Calloway gets to revisit "St. James Infirmary" and the episodic almost suite-like version of "When the Saints Go Marching In" is a near-classic. —*Scott Yanow*

Big Band Jazz: Tulsa to Harlem / Nov. 29, 1949-Jun. 30, 1953 / Delmark ◆◆◆

This Delmark LP has music from three different big bands. Cab Calloway's Orchestra is heard in 1950 shortly before their breakup on four titles dominated by the leader's vocals (although the tenors of Sam "The Man" Taylor and Ike Quebec have brief spots). Duke Ellington clarinetist Jimmy Hamilton switches to tenor and heads a big band on two okay numbers (including "Tattooed Bride") from 1953. On the flip side the obscure Ernie Fields big band performs seven songs that are R&B-oriented; in the personnel are future Ellington members trombonist Booty Wood and altoist Geezil Minerve. This is an interesting set for collectors but general listeners can pass on this one. —*Scott Yanow*

Big Band Renaissance / Apr. 30, 1941-Jan. 1, 1991 / Smithsonian ◆◆◆◆◆

This five-CD set traces the development of the big band in jazz from the end of the swing era up until the 1990s. Fifty-eight different orchestras are heard from, generally in one selection apiece although there are some exceptions (most notably Duke Ellington). The music is divided into four categories (Road Bands, Part-Time Bands, Studio Bands and Avant-Garde Bands) but many groups really fall into overlapping genres. The set's greatest fault is that the recordings (which range from Ted Heath to Sun Ra) have not been programmed in strict chronological order which, more than any other method, would have best shown off the music's evolution. However there are many rarities included on this set, the 88-page booklet is quite informative, and fans of modern jazz big bands will find much to savor. —*Scott Yanow*

The Big Beat / Sep. 4, 1958-Feb. 20, 1964 / Milestone ✦✦✦
This CD reissue brings back all of the music of the double LP of the same name except for Max Roach's version of "You Stepped out of a Dream." The sampler features four different drummer-led units in performances that are available on other Fantasy CDs. Art Blakey's 1962-64 Jazz Messengers (with trumpeter Freddie Hubbard, trombonist Curtis Fuller and tenor saxophonist Wayne Shorter) performs "Caravan," "The High Priest" and a brief "The Theme"; Max Roach's 1958 Quintet (with trumpeter Booker Little and George Coleman on tenor) plays three selections including Roach's drum solo "Conversation"; Elvin Jones meets up with his two brothers (cornetist Thad and pianist Hank) on some sextet sides; and Philly Joe Jones heads two all-star groups which include such top musicians as trumpeters Lee Morgan and Blue Mitchell and flutist Herbie Mann. Because the performances are available elsewhere, this CD is not all that essential but it does serve as a good example of the talents of the four major drummers. —*Scott Yanow*

Billie, Ella, Lena, Sarah / Jul. 2, 1935-May 19, 1950 / Columbia ✦✦✦
This is a straight CD reissue of the original LP with four recordings apiece from Billie Holiday and Sarah Vaughan and two from Lena Horne and Ella Fitgerald. All of the performances are available elsewhere and this CD is rather brief in playing time (just 36 minutes, less than half of its capacity). The music is generally excellent with Lady Day heard during 1935-39, Fitzgerald's two songs are from a 1936 session with Teddy Wilson's Orchestra and Lena Horne also is backed by Wilson in 1941. However Sarah Vaughan takes honors: she is heard in prime form in 1950 on "Nice Work If You Can Get It," "East of the Sun," "Goodnight My Love" and a classic version of "Ain't Misbehavin'"; her all-star backup group includes Miles Davis. —*Scott Yanow*

Bird Feathers / Mar. 29, 1957-Dec. 27, 1957 / Original Jazz Classics ✦✦✦
Five different altoists are featured in three different quintets on this CD reissue. Meant to show off the influence of Charlie Parker on the younger players, these performances are (with the exception of Hal McKusick's "Interim") all bop standards. Phil Woods and Gene Quill team up for "Solar" and "Airegin," Jackie McLean meets John Jenkins on "Bird Feathers" and the three remaining selections ("Interim," "Don't Worry 'Bout Me" and "Con Alma") feature McKusick with trombonist Billy Byers. Although full sessions did result from some of the dates, these particular selections were first issued in this format. It's recommended for fans of 1950s bop. —*Scott Yanow*

★ **Birdland All Stars at Carnegie Hall** / Sep. 25, 1954-Dec. 1, 1954 / Roulette ✦✦✦✦✦
There is a great deal of worthy and often historic music on this double CD. Most of the performances are taken from a Sept. 25, 1954 Carnegie Hall concert. Count Basie's Orchestra is in superb form on their seven selections; tenors Frank Foster and Frank Wess, in particular, blow up a storm. Billie Holiday (backed by the Basie band and pianist Carl Drinkard) is a bit out of it on her six numbers, sometimes getting remarkably far behind the beat. Charlie Parker, in a quartet with pianist John Lewis, bassist Percy Heath and drummer Kenny Clarke, is also a bit sub-par on his two numbers, but Lester Young, having a rare reunion with the Basie orchestra, is wonderful on an emotional "Pennies from Heaven" and a cookin' "Jumpin' at the Woodside." The second half of the concert features Sarah Vaughan (backed at first by the Basie band and then by her trio) in wondrous form on a jazz-oriented set. She has rarely sounded better. This set concludes with the Basie band live at Birdland on Dec. 1, 1954 welcoming Stan Getz to sit in on five enjoyable numbers. —*Scott Yanow*

Birdology / Jun. 7, 1989 / Verve ✦✦✦
An all-star group (consisting of trumpeter Don Sickler, altoist Jackie McLean, tenor saxophonist Johnny Griffin, baritonist Cecil Payne, pianist Duke Jordan, bassist Ron Carter and drummer Roy Haynes) is heard performing five Charlie Parker compositions and McLean's "Bird Lives" at a Paris concert on this enjoyable CD. McLean in particular is in superior form and Sickler's transcriptions (which sometimes feature the group playing excerpts from Charlie Parker and Duke Jordan recorded solos) uplifts the set above the level of a jam session. —*Scott Yanow*

● **Birth of Cool, Vol. 2** / Jan. 23, 1951-Jan. 31, 1953 / Blue Note ✦✦✦✦✦
Although its title might lead some to believe that this CD contains more "Birth of the Cool" recordings from Miles Davis, it actually consists of West Coast jazz performances that were influenced by those records. Trumpeter/arranger Shorty Rogers leads an octet that also features altoist Art Pepper and Jimmy Giuffre on tenor for six numbers; that date launched what became Shorty Rogers and his Giants. There are also eight performances by Gerry Mulligan's tentet (featuring trumpeter Chet Baker) and two selections from the 1951 Metronome All-Stars, an 11-piece unit that includes altoist Lee Konitz, Stan Getz on tenor, pianist George Shearing and Miles Davis himself. The music overall is both historically significant and quite enjoyable, making this a highly recommended set. —*Scott Yanow*

The Birth of the Third Stream / Jun. 14, 1956-Jun. 18, 1957 / Columbia/Legacy ✦✦✦✦
In the mid-'50s Gunther Schuller came up with the term "Third Stream" to describe the musical experiments of the time that sought to combine together jazz and classical music. This CD has all of the contents from the earlier LP *The Birth of the Third Stream* and four of the six pieces (leaving out two advanced classical pieces) from *Modern Jazz Concert*. Those two albums were among the first and most publiciziered of the Third Stream recordings. Strangely enough the orchestra utilized is essentially a large brass band with plenty of trumpets, trombones, French horns and baritone horns but at the most only a few woodwinds and no violins, violas or cellos at all. The most famous of the works are two that featured Miles Davis and preceded *Miles Ahead* ("Three Little Feelings" and "Poem for Brass") and George Russell's "All About Rosie" (which puts the focus on pianist Bill Evans). The other selections include Charles Mingus' "Revelations" and two compositions apiece by Jimmy Giuffre and Gunther Schuller. Although the short-lived Third Stream movement would be less influential than expected and would soon be overshadowed by free jazz, the music is still quite intriguing to hear four decades later. —*Scott Yanow*

Black & White & Reeds All Over / Mar. 4, 1944-Sep. 1, 1944 / Pickwick ✦✦✦✦✦
One of six Pickwick CDs drawn from the Black & White catalog, this release has four complete sessions from 1944 that feature clarinetists in small groups. Rod Cless is heard with trumpeter Sterling Bose, the great pianist James P. Johnson and bassist Pops Foster, the obscure Bingie Madison plays tenor and clarinet with pianist Hank Duncan, the erratic Mezz Mezzrow interacts with pianist Gene Schroeder and drummer George Wettling, and Pee Wee Russell takes solo honors with a group also including pianist Cliff Jackson. All of the releases in this short-lived series are recommended to collectors of '40s small-group jazz. —*Scott Yanow*

Black Legends of Jazz / Apr. 20, 1926-Mar. ??, 1959 / GRP/Decca ✦✦
This is a rather self-indulgent and ultimately pointless reissue, although it does contain some timeless music. Thirty-eight jazz greats (all Black) are featured on 39 selections (Louis Armstrong gets two songs) that are programmed in alphabetical order according to the artist's name. Although professing to represent a full spectrum of jazz history, the great majority of the numbers feature swing stylists since the music is (with four exceptions) restricted to performances originally cut for the Decca label. There are some underrated classics (such as Coleman Hawkins' 1958 remake of "Body and Soul," Carmen McRae's "Something to Live For" and Hot Lips Page's "I Won't Be Here Long") but many of these songs (such as Nat King Cole's "Sweet Lorraine," Duke Ellington's "Mood Indigo" and Billie Holiday's "Good Morning Heartache," etc.) certainly did not need to be reissued again. And using Count Basie's original version of "One O'Clock Jump" as an example of Lester Young's playing is absurd. Skip. —*Scott Yanow*

Black Lion at Montreux / Jul. 4, 1973 / Black Lion ✦✦✦
This all-star concert from the 1973 Montreux Jazz Festival features a variety of top swing-oriented players. A septet with trumpeter Freddy Randall, trombonist Dave Hewitt, clarinetist Dave Shepherd and tenor saxophonist Danny Moss performs "I Surrender Dear" and trumpeter Bil Coleman and Guy Lafitte on tenor romp on a lengthy version of "I Want a Little Girl" and "I Know That You Know." The second side of the LP has the great pianist Teddy Wilson teaming up with clarinetist Shepherd for "Poor Butterfly," violinist Stephane Grappelli jamming "All God's Chillun Got Rhythm," guitarist Barney Kessel featured on "Old Devil Moon" and the duo of Grappelli and Kessel digging into "Tea for Two." This is an enjoyable and consistent program of fine straightahead swing music. —*Scott Yanow*

Blue Break Beats, Vol. 1 / Jun. 17, 1964-Jun. 8, 1973 / Blue Note ✦✦✦✦✦
Blue Note released the two volume *Blue Break Beats* compilation in the early '90s. The music on *Blue Break Beats* dates from the late '60s and early '70s, when a large portion of Blue Note's soul-jazz artists began experimenting with funk and rock, creating dense electric fusions that concentrated on rhythm, not improvisation. None of this music has ever received much critical praise from jazz purists, but in the late '80s and early '90s, scores of hip-hop and dance DJs discovered these old records and began sampling the original tracks to use in new rap and dance songs. By the early '90s, this jazz/rap/funk fusion had become hip and profitable, which led Blue Note to assemble the *Blue Break Beats* compilations. All of the tracks on the two discs are rare tracks from out-of-print late '60s and early '70s albums, featuring multi-layered percussion, organs, and guitars. Every song on the two discs—which are sold seperately—is hot, with a deep funky groove, and there are no dull spots on the albums. Though it's designed to appeal to fans of contemporary funk and rap, fans of rock-influenced soul-jazz will find *Blue Break Beats* a necessary purchase. —*Stephen Thomas Erlewine*

Blue Break Beats, Vol. 2 / 1966 / Blue Note ✦✦✦✦

Blue Break Beats, Vol. 3 / 1966 / Blue Note ✦✦✦
Blue Note's *Blue Break Beats* series spotlights songs from their vaults that have

been sampled for various hip-hop and techno tracks. As a result, it's been one of their most popular and entertaining series of the '90s, and for good reason—this funky soul-jazz lends itself to compilations much easier than bop, since the groove is the only thing that matters. Unfortunately, the compilers of *Vol. 3* don't always keep that in mind. Much of the collection is weighed down with vocal cuts like Shirley Bassey's "Light My Fire" and Jackie McLean's "Soul," which intercuts nearly free bop with beat poetry. While these are interesting in their own right, they stop the momentum of the disc cold. However, the remainder of *Blue Break Beats, Vol. 3* is on par with its two predecessors, featuring funky soul-jazz from the likes of Cannonball Adderley and Lou Donaldson. These are the tracks that can be sampled effectively, and they make for excellent listening in their own right. —*Stephen Thomas Erlewine*

Blue Guitar / Feb. 5, 1941-Nov. 1989 / Blue Note ✦✦✦
This sampler contains music by 17 guitarists who recorded for Blue Note. Four (including Charlie Christian's acoustic feature on "Jammin' in Four" and the rare "Jimmy's Blues" by Jimmy Shirley) songs are from Blue Note's early days, seven are from its prime bop and hard bop years and the remaining six (ranging from Earl Klugh to Al DiMeola) are of more recent vintage. The CD gives one a good introduction to these talented players although this release is not too essential. —*Scott Yanow*

Blue Note Rare Grooves / Jan. 9, 1967-May 19, 1971 / Blue Note ✦✦✦✦✦
Balancing previously unreleased tracks with obscure gems from out-of-print albums, *Blue Note Rare Grooves* is an excellent collection of extremely funky soul-jazz. All of the tracks were recorded between 1967 and 1971, with the majority dating between 1968 and 1969. Though some of the tracks on the disc have been featured on other Blue Note collections, none of the albums they were pulled from are easily available, which makes *Blue Note Rare Grooves* all the more valuable. A good cross-section of artists—featuring John Patton, Richard "Groove" Holmes, Larry Young, Stanley Turrentine, Jack McDuff, Jimmy McGriff, Donald Byrd, Candido, Reuben Wilson, and several others—are included and every single track has a raw, intoxicating groove. *Blue Note Rare Grooves* may not be for jazz purists, but for listeners looking for a first-rate jazz-funk sampler, it's essential. —*Stephen Thomas Erlewine*

Blue Piano, Vol. 1 / Jan. 6, 1939-Nov. 23, 1953 / Blue Note ✦✦✦
On this sampler there are 14 performances by a variety of pianists from the first 15 years of Blue Note Records. Few of the recordings are particularly rare but the CD does give one a fine sampling of boogie-woogie (Albert Ammons, Meade Lux Lewis and Pete Johnson), swing and stride (Earl Hines, James P. Johnson, Nat Cole, Art Tatum and Art Hodes) and bop (Bud Powell, Lennie Tristano, Thelonious Monk, Wynton Kelly, Al Haig and Horace Silver). The music is consistently excellent with none of the groups being larger than a quartet. —*Scott Yanow*

Blue Piano, Vol. 2 / Aug. 1, 1955- 199 / Blue Note ✦✦✦
The second of two CDs containing a sampling of the many great pianists who recorded for Blue Note and its related labels, this program has performances from a dozen masters (Duke Ellington, Herbie Nichols, Cecil Taylor, Sonny Clark, Bill Evans, Herbie Hancock, Chick Corea, Michel Petruccianni, Benny Green, McCoy Tyner, Don Pullen and Andrew Hill). With three recordings from the 1950s, four dating from the '60s and five from 1987-90, after Blue Note's rebirth. Overall these two sets gives one a strong (if not really complete) sampling into the music of some of the great jazz pianists. —*Scott Yanow*

Blue Series: Female Vocals / Jan. 1945-Feb. 1990 / Blue Note ✦✦✦
Eighteen different female vocalists are heard on one selection apiece during this CD reissue. Some of the material is rarer than others but there are quite a few worthy tracks from the likes of Anita O'Day, Billie Holiday ("Detour Ahead"), Kay Starr, Abbey Lincoln (during her earliest recording session), Annie Ross, Peggy Lee, Sheila Jordan, Sarah Vaughan, Carmen McRae and even Rachelle Ferrell. It's a good introduction to these diverse stylists. —*Scott Yanow*

Blue Series: Male Vocals / Jun. 12, 1942-Jan. 1989 / Blue Note ✦✦✦
The first of two CDs from Blue Note has vocals from 19 different male vocalists including Louis Armstrong and Bing Crosby (collaborating on "Now You Has Jazz"), Nat King Cole, Charles Brown, a previously unreleased item from Mel Torme, Chet Baker, Mark Murphy, King Pleasure, Jon Hendricks, Joe Williams, Tony Bennett (how did he get here?) and Billy Eckstein. The emphasis is very much on the swing and bop stylists and, once one eliminates Lou Rawls' 1989 outing, all of the music is from 1942-62. —*Scott Yanow*

Blues, Boogie, and Bop: The Best of the 1940's Mercury Sessions / Verve ✦✦✦✦✦
If the exquisitely packaged—the box is shaped like an old-time radio—limited-edition *The 1940s Mercury Sessions* is too extravagantly priced or simply unobtainable, this single-disc sampler is the next best thing. For all of the diverse backgrounds and destinations of Mercury's artists, the music on this CD has a distinct

identity, conjuring a forgotten time when swing and bop mixed easily with emerging rhythm & blues in bite-sized, under-three-minute slices suitable for every jukebox in every juke joint in the land. The CD leads off with a sampling of the supercharged Albert Ammons piano boogie sessions with a tight little rhythm section (there are more madly swinging choices than these, but you'll get the idea). We hear a pair of Helen Humes blues cuts with loose Buck Clayton-led backup groups, a neat Jay McShann sextet with vintage blues shouting by Jimmy Witherspoon, Eddie "Cleanhead" Vinson's exuberantly bright blues vocals and alto sax, Professor Longhair's early blues-drenched incarnation as plain old Roy Byrd, and Cootie Williams leading a hot jump sextet with tenor Willis Jackson blowin' his fool head off. Only the ornery Buddy Rich defies the Mercury jump-blues sound with two unrepentant sides of big-band swing. Above all, this is a most entertaining souvenir of a time when jazz was still a form of popular music. —*Richard S. Ginell*

The Bop Session / May 19, 1975-May 20, 1975 / Sonet ✦✦✦
This LP matches together trumpeter Dizzy Gillespie and Sonny Stitt (on alto and tenor) with an all-star rhythm section (John Lewis or Hank Jones on piano, bassist Percy Heath and drummer Max Roach) for six classic bop standards. Gillespie was near the end of his prime but is in generally good form while Stitt typically eats the material (songs such as "Confirmation," "Groovin' High" and "All the Things You Are") with no difficulty. Bop fans should enjoy this date despite the lack of surprises. —*Scott Yanow*

British Dance Bands / Feb. 12, 1926-Dec. 13, 1935 / ABC ✦✦✦
This entry from the Robert Parker collection comprises 16 selections from as many British big bands. Some of the performances are more jazz-oriented than others (particularly Fred Elizalde's "Singapore Sorrows," the Arcadian Dance Orchestra's version of "'Leven Thirty Saturday Night" and Billy Cotton's "Somebody Stole My Gal") while most of the remainder is more commercial although usually using a reasonably swinging rhythm section. Even veteran collectors will not have had all of these formerly rare tracks, which on a whole give one a good idea as to how the English were coping musically during the Depression. —*Scott Yanow*

CTI Records: The Birth of Groove / Jul. 13, 1971-Mar. 1976 / Sony ✦✦✦✦
CTI Records: The Birth of Groove is a budget-priced, ten-track sampler that was designed to promote Sony's 1997 reissue of the CTI catalog. During the '70s, CTI was one of the leading fusion and jazz-rock labels, boasting a roster full of big names like Stanley Turrentine, George Benson, Milt Jackson, Esther Philips and Deodato. All of those musicians, plus several others, are showcased on *Birth of Groove*, which offers an excellent portrait of the smooth, laidback, vaguely funky jazz that was the label's trademark. For the curious, it's a neat way to become acquainted with the label. —*Stephen Thomas Erlewine*

☆ **California Concert** / Jul. 18, 1971 / CBS ✦✦✦✦✦
This double LP (whose contents are long overdue to appear on CD) is a classic. For a concert held at the Hollywood Palladium in 1971, Creed Taylor gathered together most of his top stars and demonstrated why CTI was one of the most significant labels of the era. On lengthy renditions of "Fire and Rain," "Red Clay," "Sugar," "Blues West" and "Leaving West," the all-star lineup (trumpeter Freddie Hubbard, tenor saxophonist Stanley Turrentine, altoist Hank Crawford, flutist Hubert Laws, guitarist George Benson, keyboardist Johnny Hammond, bassist Ron Carter, drummer Billy Cobham and percussionist Airto) is in inspired form, particularly Hubbard and Turrentine. This wonderful music belongs in every serious jazz collection. —*Scott Yanow*

Capitol Jazz Sings the Gershwin Songbook / Jul. 23, 1946-May ??, 1976 / Blue Note ✦✦✦
The music of George Gershwin (and in most cases the lyrics of Ira Gershwin) is interpreted by 16 fine singers on a sampler CD taken from sessions currently owned by Capitol and its related labels. The music jumps around chronologically and is not programmed with all that much coherence but the music is consistently enjoyable with such notable vocalists as Nat King Cole, Carmen McRae, Chet Baker, Annie Ross, Sarah Vaughan, Mel Torme, Peggy Lee, Johnny Hartman and Nina Simone ("Summertime"). With one exception, all of the music is from the 1946-63 period. —*Scott Yanow*

The Caribbean Jazz Project / Heads Up ✦✦✦✦✦
This was the debut release by the Caribbean Jazz Project, a colorful co-op project that combines the very different but complementary styles of Paquito D'Rivera (doubling on alto and clarinet), Dave Samuels (on marimba and vibes) and the brilliant steel drummer Andy Narell. Backed by a four-piece rhythm section, the accessible group sticks mostly to catchy group originals that range from Latin jazz to Caribbean music. The likable results are melodic and not overly predictable. This CD gives listeners an excellent example of the group's sound. —*Scott Yanow*

Celebration of Duke / Sep. 12, 1979-May 13, 1980 / Pablo ✦✦✦✦✦
Although Sarah Vaughan gets top billing on this set, she takes vocals on just two of the ten songs. Four different groupings of Pablo's all-star musicians are heard from

during a tribute to Duke Ellington, and there are many moments. Guitarist Joe Pass, vibraphonist Milt Jackson, bassist Ray Brown and drummer Mickey Roker make for a potent quartet on three songs; fluegelhornist Clark Terry heads a quintet; Zoot Sims is featured on his lyrical soprano during memorable versions of "Rockin' in Rhythm" and the beautiful "Tonight I Shall Sleep"; and Sassy (backed by just pianist Mike Wofford and guitarist Joe Pass) comes up with fresh interpretations of "I Ain't Got Nothin' but the Blues" and "Everything but You." This is a well-rounded and enjoyable set with plenty of variety. —*Scott Yanow*

Chartbusters! / Jan. 3, 1995-Jan. 4, 1995 / NYC ◆◆◆

For this unusual CD, eight songs from the prime years of Blue Note (compositions by Horace Silver, Hank Mobley, Bobby Timmons, Sonny Clark, Kenny Dorham, Freddie Hubbard, McCoy Tyner and the standard "If Ever I Would Leave You") are revisited. What is different from the original versions are not the styles of the solos, but the instrumentation. Although tenor saxophonist Craig Handy is on six of the songs (two of which find trombonist Papo Vazquez blending with Handy to create a Jazz Crusaders feel), the dominant forces are organist Lonnie Smith (who, with drummer Lenny White, is on every selection) and a variety of guitarists. There are no trumpeters, and it is the guitarists (either John Scofield, David Fiuczynski or Hiram Bullock) who make it obvious that these recordings are not from 1965; they generally take solo honors, particularly Scofield. Organist Smith avoids getting into the cliched boogaloo rhythm that he often played on his Blue Note recordings of the late '60s, and the overall music is quite satisfying and swinging in its own way. —*Scott Yanow*

● Chicago Jazz Summit / Jun. 22, 1986 / Atlantic ◆◆◆◆◆

Traditional jazz fans can consider this set to be essential for in reality it was the last Eddie Condon record (even though Condon had passed away several years earlier). While Vince Giordano's Nighthawks (a group including the then-unknown clarinetist Ken Peplowski and trumpeter Randy Sandke) act as the "house band," such classic jazz veterans as trumpeters Wild Bill Davison, Yank Lawson, Max Kaminsky and Jimmy McPartland (the latter two making their final recordings), the tenors of Eddie Miller and Franz Jackson, clarinetists Clarence Hutchenrider, Frank Chase and Kenny Davern, trombonist George Masso, guitarist Ikey Robinson, pianists Art Hodes, Marian McPartland and George Wein, bassists Truck Parham and Milt Hinton and drummer Barrett Deems all have their moments. This historic and spirited set of Dixieland standards could have been titled "We're All Together Again for the Last Time." —*Scott Yanow*

Chicago Style / Apr. 18, 1932-Jan. 14, 1942 / Jazz Archives ◆◆◆

This LP launched the Jazz Archives label, a company whose releases of early jazz put an emphasis on alternate takes and unusual performances. This excellent album has eight exciting performances by The Rhythmakers, most of which match together trumpeter Henry Red Allen and clarinetist Pee Wee Russell in 1932; their four versions of "Oh! Peter" are classic. In addition there are selections from Eddie Condon's groups in 1938 and 1940 (featuring trombonist Jack Teagarden, trumpeter Marty Marsala, clarinetist Russell and pianist Fats Waller), a Joe Sullivan piano solo and a version of "Honeysuckle Rose" that was the high point of Fats Waller's erratic 1942 Carnegie Hall concert. This album is worth searching for by prebop fans. Fortunately many of the Jazz Archives releases have been reissued on CD by a European label using the same name. —*Scott Yanow*

● Chicago in the Twenties / Sep. 16, 1926-Oct. 4, 1928 / Arcadia ◆◆◆◆◆

In the mid-to-late '70s the Arcadia label came out with a variety of significant compilations of '20s jazz and dance music, much of it formerly rare. This particular LP has all of the recordings from Elgar's Creole Orchestra (four titles plus two alternate takes), the four numbers recorded by Carroll Dickerson's Savoy Orchestra (including two with Louis Armstrong in 1928) and four songs from Sammy Stewart's Orchestra. On the whole, these performances show that there were plenty of big bands active in the jazz years before the swing era. Elgar's "Nightmare" (heard in two versions) is quite eerie, the Dickerson sides are classics and Stewart's band holds its own. It's recommended to 1920s collectors. —*Scott Yanow*

Chicago in the Twenties, Vol. 2 / Sep. 1924-1932 / Arcadia ◆◆◆

The second of two LPs put out by Arcadia in this series has a set of true obscurities. Elmer Kaiser's Ballroom Orchestra from 1924 plays "Monkey Business," the modestly titled "Super Syncopators" jams on four songs, Charley Straight's Orchestra is excellent on two numbers, Husk O'Hare's Footwarmers, the Midnight Serenaders, Bill Haid's Cubs and the Manhattan Entertainers are all heard from and there are previously unknown versions of "China Boy" and "Nobody's Sweetheart" taken from a 1932 jam session that might include pianist Jess Stacy. This set is not essential but fans of early jazz will find it quite interesting. —*Scott Yanow*

Chicago: The Living Legends / Original Blues Classics ◆◆◆

Alberta Hunter, one of the classic blues women, began her professional career in Chicago in 1912; by 1957, she had dropped out of show business to become a practical nurse. Hunter was, however, coaxed out of retirement to record this heartfelt

---

reunion with veteran Chicago pianist Lovie Austin. Ten tracks are here, including "St. Louis Blues," "Moanin' Low," and "Sweet Georgia Brown." —*Roundup Newsletter*

Christmas Jubilee / Aug. 8, 1945-1953 / Vintage Jazz Classics ◆◆◆

This enjoyable collector's CD contains two complete Christmas radio shows (one from 1947 and the other one performed in 1945, on August 8), a brief Frank Sinatra Christmas program and a couple of miscellaneous items. Such performers as Count Basie's Orchestra, the Delta Rhythm Boys, Lena Horne, Bing Crosby (singing "Gotta Be This or That"), Duke Ellington, Art Tatum, Louis Armstrong, the Nat King Cole Trio, Kay Starr and Les Brown make notable appearances. Overall, the results are an interesting variety of mid-'40s music that will be enjoyed by fans of the swing era. —*Scott Yanow*

☆ Classic Capitol Jazz Sessions / Jun. 5, 1942-Dec. 11, 1953 / Mosaic ◆◆◆◆◆

Even for the Mosaic label, this limited-edition 12-CD box set is miraculous. Unlike most of their other efforts, this is not a "complete" set, although each of the 65 sessions covered is complete. A collection of mostly formerly rare sessions made for Capitol during its first 11 years, the music ranges from Dixieland in the Bob Crosby Bobcats manner to some swing-oriented big bands and a touch of bop. The quantity (245 selections) and the high quality are both remarkable. Included are exciting sessions by Paul Whiteman, Eddie Miller, Nappy Lamare, Ray Bauduc, Marvin Ash, Wingy Manone, Johnny Mercer, Scatman Crothers, Deane Kincaide, Armand Hug, Frankie Trumbauer (his last recordings), Pud Brown, Bud Freeman, Zutty Singleton, Bobby Hackett, Sid Catlett, Al Casey, the Capitol Jazzmen, Jack Teagarden, Anita O'Day, Ten Cats and a Mouse, the Benny Carter big band, Jess Stacy, Joe Sullivan, Mel Powell, the exciting and very underrated Cootie Williams Orchestra, Murray McEachern, Rex Stewart, Sonny Greer, Louie Bellson, Carl Kress, Kay Starr, Red Norvo and Stan Hasselgard. A remarkable and highly enjoyable set which contains many previously unreleased recordings. —*Scott Yanow*

● Classic Tenors / Dec. 8, 1943-Dec. 23, 1943 / Doctor Jazz ◆◆◆◆◆

"Classic" is an accurate description of the music on this LP. The great tenor Coleman Hawkins is heard in peak form on a quartet set with pianist Eddie Heywood, bassist Oscar Pettiford and drummer Shelly Manne, particularly during a brilliant version of "The Man I Love." Hawk is almost as creative on a septet date with trumpeter Bill Coleman and pianist Ellis Larkins, roaring on "Hawkins' Barrel House" and "Stumpy." The other four selections feature the equally great tenor Lester Young, interacting with trumpeter Bill Coleman and trombonist Dickie Wells. "I Got Rhythm" finds Prez at his best and Wells' high-note work on "I'm Fer It Too" is both humorous and memorable. This classic set has since been reissued on CD. —*Scott Yanow*

Classic Tenors, Vol. 2 / Dec. 18, 1943-Dec. 1950 / Doctor Jazz ◆◆◆

Some of the music on this LP duplicates the Doctor Jazz album titled *The Big Three* (the two Coleman Hawkins and Lester Young selections), but it is completely different from the first volume of *Classic Tenors*. Hawkins is heard on an obscure two-song set with a quintet featuring pianist Ellis Larkins ("Lover Come Back to Me" and "Blues Changes"), while Lester Young plays the alternate versions of "Hello Babe" and "I'm Fer It Too" in a septet with trumpeter Bill Coleman and trombonist Dickie Wells. Julian Dash (best known as a sideman with Erskine Hawkins' Orchestra) heads a combo for four rare titles from 1950, while Edie "Lockjaw" Davis is heard during one of his earliest sessions (from May 1946) interpreting four heated songs, including one ("Lockjaw") that gave him his nickname. The music on this album might not be in the "classic" category, but the four different approaches to playing swing tenor are interesting to compare. —*Scott Yanow*

Colorado Jazz Party / Sep. 5, 1971-Sep. 6, 1971 / MPS ◆◆◆◆◆

It is surprising that the music on this double LP has not been reissued yet on CD for there are many exciting performances. Taken from Dick Gibson's 1971 Colorado Jazz Party, there are mini-sets from four separate groups. Trumpeters Clark Terry and Harry "Sweets" Edison lead a six-horn nonet (which includes Zoot Sims' tenor) for spirited versions of "On the Trail" and "The Hymn." Terry gets a chance to stretch out with tenor saxophonist Flip Phillips in a quintet while a similar-sized group showcases the underrated trombonist Carl Fontana and James Moody on tenor. Finally there is a four-trombone septet (with Fontana, Kai Winding, Urbie Green and an effective Trummy Young) performing long versions of "Undecided" and "Lover, Come Back to Me." Fans of straightahead jazz who run across this twofer will not need to be told twice to get it. —*Scott Yanow*

☆ Complete Blue Note Recordings of Hall/Johnson/DeParis/Dickenson / Feb. 5, 1941-Jun. 24, 1952 / Mosaic ◆◆◆◆◆

To say that this limited-edition six-LP Mosaic box is overflowing with classics is an understatement. Included are a variety of small-group sessions (with overlapping personnel) from the early days of Blue Note, The Edmond Hall Celeste Quartet has five songs that are the only examples that exist of Charlie Christian playing acoustic guitar; clarinetist Hall, Meade Lux Lewis (on celeste) and bassist Israel Crosby complete the unique group. The king of stride piano, James P. Johnson, is heard on eight solos and other combos are led by Johnson, Hall (who heads four groups in all), trumpeter Sidney DeParis and trombonist Vic Dickenson (heard in a 1952 quartet with organist Bill Doggett). Among the other key soloists are vibraphonist Red Norvo, pianist Teddy Wilson, tenor great Ben Webster, baritonist Harry Carney, clarinetist Omer Simeon and trombonist Benny Morton. More important than the all-star personnel is the fact that the musicians are consistently inspired and the performances (ranging from Dixieland to advanced swing) are well-planned, yet spontaneous. The accompanying 26-page booklet is a major plus too. Essential music; get this box while you can. —*Scott Yanow*

★ **Complete Commodore Jazz Recordings, Vol. 1** / Apr. 1929-Dec. 21, 1943 / Mosaic ✦✦✦✦✦

The punchline for this 23-LP limited-edition box set is in its title, *Vol. 1*. On a total of 66 albums, Mosaic has reissued the entire jazz output of Milt Gabler's Commodore label, one of the most important jazz record companies of all time. There is an incredible amount of music included on this first set (the most essential of the three). After five early titles that Commodore acquired from other labels (featuring Cow Cow Davenport, Fletcher Henderson and Django Reinhardt), one hears the birth of Commodore with the exciting Jan. 17, 1938 outing by Eddie Condon. In addition to a lot more of Condon's freewheeling sessions (much of his best work was for Commodore), there are dates led by Bud Freeman, the Kansas City Five and Six (with Lester Young), Teddy Wilson, Jess Stacy, Chu Berry, Willie "The Lion" Smith, Billie Holiday, Stuff Smith, Jelly Roll Morton, Jack Teagarden, Art Hodes, Joe Marsala, Joe Bushkin, Coleman Hawkins, Lee Wiley, Pee Wee Russell, Bunk Johnson, Mel Powell (with Benny Goodman), Wild Bill Davison, George Brunis and Edmond Hall. There are many previously unissued performances (not just alternate takes) and literally dozens of classics. Fans of Chicago jazz and small-group swing should bid as much as necessary to acquire this out-of-print box (along with the other two volumes). —*Scott Yanow*

☆ **Complete Commodore Jazz Recordings, Vol. 2** / Feb. 5, 1944-Mar. 16, 1945 / Mosaic ✦✦✦✦✦

The second of three "volumes" put out by Mosaic that reissues the entire Commodore catalog is, like the first, a 23-LP set; all of the music in this massive box was recorded within 13 months. The limited-edition series is a must (although it will be quite difficult to locate) for collectors of Chicago jazz and small-group swing— it is literally overflowing with classics. The first box is the most essential but *Vol. II* is pretty close with recording sessions led by Sidney and Wilbur DeParis, Albert Ammons, Eddie Heywood, Hot Lips Page, Sid Catlett, Billie Holiday, the Kansas City Six with Lester Young, George Zack, Muggsy Spanier, Miff Mole, Joe Bushkin, Max Kaminsky, Edmond Hall, George Wettling, Bobby Hackett, Hot Lips Page, Pee Wee Russell, Red McKenzie, Jess Stacy, Jack Teagarden and Wild Bill Davison. In addition to the usual performances (many of which were previously hard-to-find), there are quite a few previously unissued alternate takes and some selections (including an entire Joe Bushkin Trio date) that were never out before. This set (if it can be found) will be expensive but worth it. —*Scott Yanow*

☆ **Complete Commodore Jazz Recordings, Vol. 3** / Jul. 12, 1938-Jul. 9, 1957 / Mosaic ✦✦✦✦

The third and final Mosaic box set that reissues all of the valuable recordings from Milt Gabler's Commodore label is the smallest of these reissues, a mere 20-LP set. All three of the volumes (which total 66 albums) are wonderful but since they were originally limited-edition releases (just 2500 copies apiece) and have gone out-of-print, they will be difficult to locate and expensive to acquire; buy them anyway if you have any interest in small-group swing and Chicago dixieland. *Vol. III* starts out with some recently discovered alternate takes by Bud Freeman, Chu Berry, Bunk Johnson and Billie Holiday from 1938-44, before concentrating mostly on the 1945-46 period. There are sessions led by Red Norvo, Bill Coleman, Gene Krupa, Stuff Smith, Teddy Wilson and the duo of Don Byas and Slam Stewart (all of those are from a legendary 1945 Town Hall concert) plus dates headed by George Zack, Jonah Jones, Wild Bill Davison, Eddie Edwards, George Brunis and Mel Powell; in addition there are later sets by Bob Wilber, Ralph Sutton, Sidney Bechet, Johnny Wiggs, Willie "The Lion" Smith, Frank Wess and Peck Kelley. One exhausts superlatives when discussing this remarkable project. —*Scott Yanow*

★ **The Complete Keynote Collection** / Mar. 14, 1941-May 23, 1947 / Polygram ✦✦✦✦✦

This is an incredible set, a 21-LP box that has all of the jazz recordings ever made for Harry Lim's Keynote label. Much of this music has been reissued in piecemeal fashion on CD by Polygram but this is the way to get it, complete and in chronological order with all of the alternate takes. Lim had impeccable taste and recorded Chicago jazz, small-group swing and bop by many of the top musicians of the period; all but the first session (George Hartman Dixieland sides from 1941) are from Dec. 1943 to May 1947. This box has dates by Lester Young, Dinah Washington, Roy Eldridge, Coleman Hawkins, Cozy Cole, the Kansas City Seven, Charlie

Shavers with Earl Hines, Benny Morton, Rex Stewart, the Keynoters, Pete Brown, Red Norvo, bassist Billy Taylor, Jonah Jones, George Wettling, Chubby Jackson, Barney Bigard, Bill Harris, Willie Smith, Corky Corcoran, Milt Hinton, J.C. Heard, Irving Fazola, Bud Freeman, Ted Nash, Babe Russin, Manny Klein, Herbie Haymer, Clyde Hurley, Arnold Ross, Juan Tizol, Benny Carter, Marie Bryant, Bernie Leighton, Ann Hathaway, Joe Thomas, George Barnes, Lennie Tristano, Danny Hurd, Dave Lambert and Buddy Stewart, Gene Sedric, Neal Hefti and Red Rodney, and that is only the leaders. There is so much music (334 performances including 115 that were not previously released) that in addition to the 21 LPs included is a 45 with an extra Lennie Tristano song. This box will be very difficult to locate but fans of small-group swing and historic jazz should get it at any price. —*Scott Yanow*

● **The Complete Master Jazz Piano Series** / Mar. 11, 1969-Jan. 9, 1974 / Mosaic ✦✦✦✦✦

During a five-year period the Master Jazz label recorded 11 swing-based pianists in solo settings. Although the label went under later in the decade, the recordings were treasured by collectors. Mosaic, on this four-CD set, brought back all of the music from the original five-volume *Master Jazz Piano* series, adding two unissued selections and a full album released separately of Ram Ramirez's playing. In addition to Ramirez (who is heard on 13 numbers), there are 13 performances by Earl Hines, four apiece from Claude Hopkins, Cliff Jackson, Keith Dunham, Sonny White, Teddy Wilson, Cliff Smalls and the obscure Gloria Hearn, eight by Jay McShann and two from Sir Charles Thompson. Most of these pianists (other than Hines and Wilson) rarely recorded during this period in their careers, making this box very important both musically and historically. —*Scott Yanow*

Concert in Argentina / Nov. 1974 / Jazz Alliance ✦✦✦

Although this double LP has been reissued by the Jazz Alliance label on CD, the LP version is preferable because it contains more performances. Pianists Marian McPartland, Teddy Wilson, Ellis Larkins and Earl Hines all play about 20 minutes apiece during a swing-oriented solo set. McPartland (whose performance is highlighted by a Duke Ellington medley), Wilson (who plays a couple of Gershwin medley), and Larkins (sticking as usual to quiet ballads) are all in fine form but it was wise to put Hines on last as he cuts everyone with his chancetaking set. —*Scott Yanow*

Concord Jazz Festival: Live 1990 / Aug. 18, 1990 / Concord Jazz ✦✦✦

The first of three CDs taken from the 1990 Concord Jazz Festival features three trombonists (Rob McConnell, Al Grey and Benny Powell), trumpeter Harry "Sweets" Edison and a fine rhythm section (guitairst Ed Bickert, pianist Gene Harris, bassist Neil Swainson and drummer Alan Dawson) playing straightahead jazz. Edison, Powell, Harris, Grey and Bickert have individual features, the full group plays "Cottontail" and the trombonists (without Edison) get to stretch out on "Undecided." Nothing too surprising occurs but the good-humored music (Grey's "St. James Infirmary" is a high point) is fun and swinging. —*Scott Yanow*

Concord Jazz Festival: Live 1990, Second Set / Aug. 18, 1990 / Concord Jazz ✦✦✦

The second of three Concord CDs documenting this 1990 festival matches four veteran horn soloists (Frank Wess on tenor and flute, altoist Marshal Royal, Rick Wilkins on tenor and fluegelhornist Pete Minger) with a fine rhythm section (pianist Gerry Wiggins, bassist Lynn Seaton and drummer Harold Jones) for a variety of jazz standards. Wess, Royal and Minger each have features (Royal's outing on "Don't Get Around Much Anymore" is a high point), Seaton sings "Just Squeeze Me" in humorous fashion and the full group jams on "The Blues Walk" and "Broadway." Few surprises occur but fans of straightahead jazz should enjoy this music. —*Scott Yanow*

Concord Jazz Festival: Live 1990, Third Set / Aug. 18, 1990 / Concord Jazz ✦✦✦✦

Although there is no official leader on the CD, this is really an Ernestine Anderson date. Pianist Gene Harris and his quartet (with guitarist Ed Bickert, bassist Lynn Seaton and drummer Harold Jones) romp through Oscar Pettiford's "Blues in the Closet" and then the singer takes over for the final six numbers; Frank Wess guests on tenor during "I Should Care" and altoist Marshall Royal is heard from on "Skylark." Ernestine Anderson is in top form during her well-rounded set with highlights including the lengthy "I Should Care," a swinging "There Is No Greater Love," "On My Own" and a definitive 15-minute version of "Never Make Your Move Too Soon." —*Scott Yanow*

Cool Whalin' / 1948-1970 / Spotlite ✦✦✦✦✦

Six different bop-oriented vocalists are heard on rare recordings on this LP, an English import from Spotlite, Joe Carroll performs "I Don't Want Love" and "Gambler's Blues" with a quartet led by trumpeter Howard McGhee in 1970, the forgotten Kenny "Pancho" Hagood sings four numbers with the Joe Sample Trio in 1967 and Babs Gonzales jams two songs with his usual enthusiasm in 1952. Side two has what might be Eddie Jefferson's earliest recordings ("Bless My Soul" and

"Beautiful Memories" from 1948-49), Pancho Hagood and Earl Coleman are heard in 1948 and the obscure Frankie Passions sings "Especially to You" and "Nobody Knows" with a late '50s group that surprisingly includes pianist Thelonious Monk. This is an album that lovers of bop singing will have to get. —*Scott Yanow*

Cotton Club Stars / Feb. 9, 1927-Apr. 1945 / Stash ✦✦✦✦✦
This double LP pays tribute to the legacy of the Cotton Club on 30 mostly rare recordings by a wide variety of jazz-oriented performers. Taken more or less in chronological order, this collection has among its many highlights "I Found a New Baby" by Andy Preer's Cotton Club Orchestra from 1927, "A Night at the Cotton Club Medley" by Duke Ellington and selections by the Missourians, Bill Bojangles Robinson, Cab Calloway (including a Cotton Club radio broadcast from 1932), Harold Arlen, Buck and Bubbles, Ethel Waters, the Nicholas Brothers, Ella Fitzgerald, Lena Horne and Louis Armstrong with the Mills Brothers. Even veteran collectors will probably not have all of these performances, making this attractive two-fer from 1984 worth picking up. —*Scott Yanow*

Crime Jazz: Music in the First Degree / 1954 / Rhino ✦✦✦✦
Eighteen excerpts from movie and television soundtracks to crime drama, recorded between 1954 and 1964; in the few cases when these are not from the actual soundtrack itself, they're clearly inspired by the genre. Several notable composers (Elmer Bernstein, Henry Mancini, Count Basie, Leonard Bernstein, David Amram) and performers (Shorty Rogers, Stan Kenton, Quincy Jones) show up here with snazzy, tense works with feet in both the jazz and soundtrack idioms. Several of the tracks are classics of the style—the theme to the *Johnny Staccato* series, "Frankie Machine" from *The Man with the Golden Arm*, Shorty Rogers' *The Wild One* theme, Henry Mancini's "Peter Gunn" (done here by Quincy Jones), and Mancini's ominous main title music to the film noir classic *Touch of Evil*. It's slightly recommended over its companion volume, *Crime Jazz: Music in the Second Degree*, because it has a higher concentration of familiar classics. Each of the volumes, however, will appeal far more to the soundtrack specialist than the jazz fan—not that you can't be both at once. —*Richie Unterberger*

Crime Jazz: Music in the Second Degree / Rhino ✦✦✦✦
Numerous notable jazz musicians contributed to movie and television soundtracks of crime thrillers, and this well-annotated 18-song compilation gathers several of the more outstanding examples. It's not so much a jazz anthology, however, as it is an anthology of some of the more memorable and effective musical backgrounds from suspense films, albeit ones that happened to feature a jazzy flair and some notable players. Stan Kenton, Lalo Schifrin, Quincy Jones, Kai Winding, and Stan Getz are among the most recognizable contributors to the disc; Henry Mancini is not, it's fair to say, beloved by many jazz connoisseurs, but he often used jazzy flourishes in his soundtrack work. There are extracts from *West Side Story*, *77 Sunset Strip*, *Touch of Evil*, *The Asphalt Jungle*, and *Mickey One*, though many of the other sources will be familiar only to film noir buffs. It's still a decent collection for those who like ominous, jazz-influenced soundtracks of this vintage, characterized by the anxious crescendos, prattling bongos, and elongated brass bursts that underpinned many an action scene. —*Richie Unterberger*

Danish Jazz in the 50's, Vol. 1 / Jun. 25, 1956-Mar. 10, 1957 / Olufsen ✦✦✦
While Sweden became known for its talented cool jazz performers during the 1950s, Denmark's interesting scene of the period has long been neglected. On the first of two Olufsen LPs to document the era, there are broadcasts by groups led by musicians unfamiliar to most Americans: tenor saxophonist Max Bruel, trumpeter Jorgen Ryg, pianists Otto Francker and Bertrand Bech and big bands headed by Peter Rasmussen and Ib Glindemann. Along with a few originals, the players perform bop and swing standards with subtle creativity and a surprising amount of individuality. The two LPs are worth checking out by bop fans who think they have heard everything. —*Scott Yanow*

Danish Jazz in the 50's, Vol. 2 / Mar. 10, 1957-May 30, 1959 / Olufsen ✦✦✦
The second of two Olufsen LPs shows off some of the top jazz talents to be found in Denmark during the 1950s. These radio broadcasts feature the Ib Glindemann big band on eight selections along with combos headed by vibraphonist Louis Hjulmand, pianist Paul Godske and tenor saxophonist Frank Jensen. No household names appear (pianist Bent Axen and trumpeter Allan Botchinsky are the best-known in the US) but the music is generally quite rewarding, emphasizing bop and swing standards. —*Scott Yanow*

● **The Debut Records Story** / 1952 / Debut ✦✦✦✦✦
The Debut label was a gutsy project, launched by Charles Mingus, his wife Celia, Max Roach and girlfriend Margo Ferraci as an end-run around the record industry of the 1950s. It only lasted five years—1952-57—but Debut managed to record a galaxy of bop and progressive-minded jazzers of the time, and this four-CD box set is a great way to get a taste of almost all of the label's releases. For those who have already invested in the huge 12-CD Mingus Debut box, this one has lots of non-Mingus material its predecessor lacks. A handful of tracks pre-date the

label—mostly poorly recorded live snapshots of Charlie Parker—but the sound quality picks up considerably thereafter. We go through some quirky Mingus, or Roach-led sessions that simply reek of the hip early-'50s bop underground before sampling the famous 1953 Massey Hall concert with Bud Powell, Dizzy Gillespie, Parker, Mingus and Roach—the records that put Debut on the map. Some of the exciting four-trombone bop sessions with J.J. Johnson, Kai Winding, Bennie Green and Willie Dennis are here, as are three downcast excerpts from Miles Davis' sole Debut LP *Blue Moods*. Besides Roach, we hear trumpeters Kenny Dorham and Thad Jones, pianists Paul Bley and Alonzo Levister, trombonist Jimmy Knepper, singer Ada Moore, clarinetist Sam Most, and saxophonist John LaPorta in their debuts as leaders. In a curious jumping-of-the-gun, a description of some Teo Macero Quintet tracks is left in the booklet, even though Fantasy couldn't obtain the rights to the music. By and large, the set is dominated by first-rate bebop, with sprinklings of avant-garde experiments like some really odd, dissonant stuff from the Mingus Octet and Orchestra and LaPorta's offbeat group concepts. Ultimately, *The Debut Records Story* paints a compelling picture of a quirky yet courageously uncompromising label that catered to what amounted to a small dissident sect in a conformist decade. —*Richard S. Ginell*

Dr. Jazz Sampler / Dec. 20, 1951-May 25, 1952 / Storyville ✦✦✦
For seven months during 1951-52, announcer Aime Gauvin (as "Dr. Jazz") hosted a weekly half-hour radio show that spotlighted many of the Dixieland groups then performing nightly in New York clubs. Storyville has released quite a few CDs from these previously unissued broadcasts, focusing on individual bands. This sampler has 11 selections not included on the other sets, featuring bands headed by Eddie Condon, Wilbur DeParis, Buck Clayton, Bobby Hackett, Ralph Sutton, Red Allen, Pee Wee Erwin, Hot Lips Page and Jimmy Archey. The music is straightahead Dixieland including two versions of "Sweet Georgia Brown" and Buck Clayton's reworking of "Jingle Bells." With sidemen taken from the who's who of classic jazz, this CD gives one a fine sampler of the early-'50s Dixieland scene. —*Scott Yanow*

Dylan Jazz / 1967 / GNP Crescendo ✦✦
This is a most unusual record. Five studio musicians (including saxophonist Jim Horn and a then-unknown guitarist named Glenn Campbell) play jazz versions of ten Bob Dylan songs. This LP mostly finds the players sticking fairly close to the melodies (including such tunes as "Blowin' in the Wind," "Hey Mr. Tambourine Man" and "Like a Rolling Stone") in renditions that are generally under three minutes long. It's a very interesting novelty record. —*Scott Yanow*

Dynamic Duos: Memorable Meetings in Jazz / Dec. 12, 1938-Oct. 29, 1951 / Drive Archive ✦✦✦
This CD is essentially a sampler drawn from the many swing-era recordings reissued by the budget Drive Archive label. The sound quality ranges from decent to mediocre although the music (some tracks are more common than others) is generally worthwhile. There is one selection apiece from these teams: Billie Holiday/Stan Getz, Count Basie/Jimmy Rushing, Ella Fitzgerald/Chick Webb, Charlie Parker/Woody Herman (a live version of "Four Brothers"), Dizzy Gillespie/Charlie Parker, Sarah Vaughan/Dizzy Gillespie, Louis Armstrong/Fats Waller, Billie Holiday/Duke Ellington (although Duke actually only conducts the backup band), Lionel Hampton/Dinah Washington, Artie Shaw/Mel Tormé and Don Byas/Erroll Garner (a hot version of "One O'Clock Jump"). At only a little over a half-hour of music, it is fortunate that this CD is selling at an inexpensive price. —*Scott Yanow*

Early Black Swing: The Birth of Big Band Jazz: 1927-1934 / Apr. 27, 1927-Aug. 4, 1936 / Bluebird ✦✦✦
The music on this CD is quite historic but available in more complete fashion elsewhere. However listeners wishing to acquire an overview of early swing (mostly prior to the rise of Benny Goodman) could certainly do much worse than these 22 performances. Included are strong examples of the big band music of Fletcher Henderson, Duke Ellington, Bennie Moten, McKinney's Cotton Pickers, Earl Hines, Charlie Johnson's Paradise Ten, the Missourians, Red Allen, Jimmie Lunceford and Louis Armstrong. —*Scott Yanow*

East Coast Jive / Aug. 9, 1946-Dec. 17, 1947 / Delmark ✦✦✦
The music varies on this collection but nearly all of the 21 performances are fun. Taken from the Apollo catalog, the Delmark CD has rare selections from singers Babs Gonzales, Loumell Morgan, Artie Simms, Babe Wallace, the Four Blues and Ben Smith. Ranging from swing to bop with many of the singers being influenced by the style of the Nat King Cole Trio, this "jive music" may not be all that original but it is quite accessible and full of joy. —*Scott Yanow*

● **Echoes of the Thirties** / Jan. 4, 1930-Nov. 1, 1939 / Columbia ✦✦✦✦✦
This five-LP box set goes in chronological order from 1930-39 and amazingly enough nearly all of its 70 performances are rare. The music ranges from dance bands and swing to personalities and vocal groups, but the emphasis is largely on jazz with plenty of previously unreleased recordings and alternate takes along

with some very obscure items. There are many highlights with everyone from the California Ramblers, Fletcher Henderson, Ruth Etting, Red Nichols and Bing Crosby to Phil Harris, the Four Blackbirds, Red Allen, Raymond Scott (with Jerry Colonna), Cab Calloway and Benny Goodman being heard. Collectors of music from the era will want to search for this box which was originally issued in 1977. —*Scott Yanow*

Esquire's All-American Hot Jazz Sessions / Jan. 10, 1946-Apr. 22, 1947 / Bluebird ✦✦✦✦✦
This exciting CD has 20 diverse performances that were originally produced by Leonard Feather for the Victor label during 1946-47. The first eight selections feature various versions of Esquire's All-American Award Winners and have some unique combinations of musicians. "Long Long Journey" was the first record to match Duke Ellington (who verbally introduces the song) with Louis Armstrong, and on "Snafu" Armstrong takes a surprisingly modern solo that hints at bebop. Trumpeter Charlie Shavers creates a remarkable improvisation on "The One That Got Away," altoist Johnny Hodges plays beautifully on "Gone with the Wind" and other key players include tenor saxophonist Don Byas, trumpeter Buck Clayton, trombonist J.J. Johnson and tenor saxophonist Coleman Hawkins. In addition, there are selections featuring trombonist Jack Teagarden ("Blues After Hours"), the 52nd Street All-Stars (with Shavers, Hawkins and tenorman Allan Eager), the tenor of Lucky Thompson (his rendition of "Just One More Chance" is a classic), trumpeter Neal Hefti (on the humorous and memorable "From Dixieland to Bop"), altoist Benny Carter, singer Mildred Bailey ("I Don't Wanna Miss Mississippi") and solo piano records by Art Tatum and Erroll Garner. The mid- to late '40s were a particularly rich period for jazz and this highly recommended CD is filled with gems. —*Scott Yanow*

● **Exciting Battle: JATP Stockholm '55** / Feb. 2, 1955 / Pablo ✦✦✦✦✦
This is one of the great JATP recordings. Norman Granz's traveling jam session was at its height whenever trumpeter Roy Eldridge and Dizzy Gillespie teamed up. The octet heard on this CD reissue also includes trombonist Bill Harris, tenorsaxophonist Flip Phillips, pianist Oscar Peterson, guitarist Herb Ellis, bassist Ray Brown and drummer Louie Bellson. They all play well on the jam "Birks" and a four-song ballad medley; "Ow" is a drum feature for Bellson. However it is the blues "Little David" that is quite classic for Oscar Peterson sets the groove with a masterful solo and then (after the other horns have their say) Roy Eldridge has one of the finest improvisations of his career. He builds up his solo ever so gradually and dramatically through chorus after chorus and, while the other players riff, Eldridge makes every sound fit, climaxing with some perfectly placed notes in the upper register. It is one of the great moments in recorded jazz history and enough of a reason to acquire this CD by itself. —*Scott Yanow*

☆ **The First Esquire All-American Jazz Concert** / Jan. 18, 1944 / Radiola ✦✦✦✦✦
This set has one of the great jazz concerts of all time, one that features the who's who of the jazz world of 1944. In 1943 *Esquire* magazine held the first Critics Poll and sponsored a concert featuring many of the winners (those in first or second place); the results are released on this two-fer in its entirety. The high point is a remarkable version of "I Got Rhythm" that has Louis Armstrong and Roy Eldridge on trumpets, trombonist Jack Teagarden, clarinetist Barney Bigard, Coleman Hawkins on tenor, xylophonist Red Norvo, pianist Art Tatum, guitarist Al Casey, bassist Oscar Pettiford and drummer Sid Catlett. In addition there are individual features and notable appearances by clarinetist Benny Goodman, Lionel Hampton on vibes and drums, pianists Teddy Wilson and Jess Stacy, bassist Sid Weiss, drummer Morey Feld (the latter three on "Rachel's Dream" with Benny Goodman) and vocals from Billie Holiday and Mildred Bailey. The recording quality of the performances (some of which were broadcast over the radio) is generally quite good and getting to hear Tatum backing Louis Armstrong and Coleman Hawkins' playing on "Basin Street Blues" are two of the many reasons to acquire this unique set. —*Scott Yanow*

Four French Horns / Apr. 14, 1957 / Savoy ✦✦✦
This is an unusual session. Accordionist Mat Mathews came up with the idea of utilizing four French horns as the leading voices on a jazz date so, with guitarist Joe Puma, bassist Milt Hinton and drummer Osie Johnson, Mathews welcomed the French horns of Julius Watkins, David Amram, Fred Klein and Tony Miranda. Watkins has the lion's share of the solo space on this CD reissue but all of the horns are heard from both as soloists and in the colorful (and sometimes imaginative) ensembles. This is a moody bop-oriented date that succeeds beyond its novelty value. —*Scott Yanow*

Fourtune / Dec. 5, 1980-Dec. 6, 1980 / Drive Archive ✦✦✦✦✦
Originally released on the RealTime label as a double LP, this CD (which contains 11 of the 14 selections) is quite notable for containing some brilliant playing by Ernie Watts (during a period when his own recordings were very commercial). Chick Corea (sticking to acoustic piano) is also in excellent form as are bassist

Andy Simpkins and drummer John Dentz (who was the actual leader). Although a few of the shorter numbers have their free moments, the high points are "My One and Only Love," "Night and Day," "Invitation," "Blues for John C.," "Bud Powell" and "Oleo," intense straightahead explorations that allow Watts and Corea opportunities to stretch out. —*Scott Yanow*

Friends in Need: 1991 Triangle Jazz Partyboys / Sep. 29, 1991 / Friends in Need ✦✦✦
Recorded as a fundraiser for Friends in Need, an organization working to provide health care equipment for people with serious diseases, this CD (released through Arbors) has some heated Dixieland and swing from a septet featuring trombonist Dan Barrett, trumpeter Randy Sandke, clarinetist Chuck Hedges, Rick Fay on tenor and soprano, and pianist Ralph Sutton; the final four of the 15 selections are by a sextet led by trumpeter Dick Gable. The music is quite joyous and easily recommended to fans of classic jazz. —*Scott Yanow*

★ **From Spirituals to Swing: Carnegie Hall Concerts, 1938-1939** / 1938-1939 / Vanguard ✦✦✦✦✦
During a pair of Carnegie Hall concerts in late 1938 and late 1939, producer John Hammond had an opportunity to present many of his favorite artists, tracing the evolution of music (as its title said) from spirituals to swing. This double CD is a reissue of the previous double LP and features quite a few historic performances. Featured in good form are the Benny Goodman Sextet (with vibraphonist Lionel Hampton and guitarist Charlie Christian), the Count Basie Orchestra with singer Helen Humes and guest Hot Lips Page (the latter is wonderful on "Blues with Lips"), the Kansas City Six (an all-star group with Lester Young, Buck Clayton and Charlie Christian), pianist James P. Johnson, the hot New Orleans Feetwarmers which features the soprano of Sidney Bechet, the Golden Gate Quartet, blues singer Ida Cox, the blues harmonica of Sonny Terry, Big Bill Broonzy, Mitchell's Christian Singers, singer Joe Turner with boogie-woogie pianists Pete Johnson, Meade Lux Lewis and Albert Ammons and a jam session version of "Lady Be Good" that includes many of these musicians. The recording quality is decent for the period and the music is generally quite timeless. It's an essential acquisition for all serious jazz collections. —*Scott Yanow*

From the Newport Jazz Festival: Tribute to Charlie Parker / Jul. 1964+Feb. 15, 1967 / Bluebird ✦✦✦✦✦
Although it is not apparent from the outside of this CD, these performances are actually taken from two separate occasions. Trumpeter Howard McGhee, trombonist J.J. Johnson, Sonny Stitt (sticking to tenor), pianist Harold Mabern, bassist Arthur Harper Jr. and drummer Max Roach are heard at the 1964 Newport Jazz Festival jamming on three songs in tribute to Charlie Parker: "Buzzy," "Now's the Time" and "Wee." In addition, the MC, Father Norman O'Connor, gets a few of the veterans to say a few words about Bird. The remainder of the CD features altoist Jackie McLean with his quartet at a studio session in 1967 performing searing ballad versions of "Embraceable You" and "Old Folks." A very interesting and well-rounded program, worth picking up. —*Scott Yanow*

Fujitsu-Concord 26th Jazz Festival / Aug. 12, 1994 / Concord Jazz ✦✦✦✦✦
Recorded at the 26th-annual Concord Jazz Festival, this two-CD set features music from three different performances. The first disc has a well-rounded set with guitarist Charlie Byrd, Hendrik Meurkens on harmonica, clarinetist Ken Peplowski and a fine rhythm section paying tribute to the music of Antonio Carlos Jobim. A group billed as "Seven Sensational Saxophones" is good but not all that sensational with four altos being featured on two songs, four tenors on two others and six of the saxes soloing on "Tryin' to Make My Blues Turn Green"; the horns are altoists Jesse Davis, Gary Foster, tenors Ken Peplowski, Chris Potter and Frank Wess, Bill Ramsay on alto and baritone and Rickey Woodard doubling on tenor and alto. The remainder of this two-fer has eight numbers from what was dubbed "the Gene Harris/Rob McConnell/Frank Wess Concord Jazz All-Star Big Band." The three leaders are the main soloists and Jeannie Cheatham takes a couple of spirited guest vocals. Overall, this set should easily please fans of Concord's usual mainstream output. —*Scott Yanow*

Fun on the Frets: Early Jazz Guitar / 1936-1949 / Yazoo ✦✦✦✦✦
This Yazoo LP has many rather rare acoustic guitar performances. Carl Kress, a great chordal player, is heard on ten duets with fellow guitarist Tony Mottola in 1941, a couple of hot numbers with Dick McDonough (1934's "Danzon" and "I've Got a Feeling You're Fooling" from 1936) and two 1939 solos. In addition the seven-string guitar pioneer George Van Eps is featured on four numbers with a trio from 1949. Those listeners who have only heard of Django Reinhardt and Charlie Christian among early guitarists are well-advised to search for this fascinating LP. —*Scott Yanow*

Gentle Duke: The Ellington Soloists Play Duke / Prestige ✦✦✦✦
Much like Fantasy's contemporary Jazz Giants series in concept but under different auspices, a brace of former Ellington sidemen are heard interpreting a dozen

of Duke's standards. The time frame of the recordings has shrunk to only a six-year period, and oddly, some of the leaders here were not Ellington alumni (their featured sidemen were). But as if to compensate, half of the tracks are making their CD debuts (a much higher percentage than the Jazz Giants series thus far), often originating from two of Prestige's more obscure holdings, the Moodsville and Swingville labels. Bud Freeman, Clark Terry, Taft Jordan, Ben Webster (with Joe Zawinul), Jimmy Forrest (with Oliver Nelson's big band), Betty Roche, Cootie Williams, Bill Harris and Buddy Tate are the leaders, with a Swingville All-Stars jam on "Things Ain't What They Used to Be" as a closer. Among one listener's choice cuts, Webster is eloquence personified on "Come Sunday" (an alternate take yet!) and as a counterpoint to Harris on "In a Mellotone." —*Richard S. Ginell*

★ **Giants of Funk Tenor Sax** / Prestige ✦✦✦✦✦
A great two-disc introduction to both honking-blues and funk (soul-jazz) tenor saxophone. Great for beginners, but should be in any collection. Over three hours of blues/funk greats like Arnett Cob, Eddie "Lockjaw" Davis, Sonny Stitt, Willis Jackson, Houston Person, Stanley Turrentine, Rusty Bryant, and Gene Ammons. A classic collection. —*Michael Erlewine*

Giants of Small Band Swing, Vol. 1 / 1946 / Riverside ✦✦✦
The first of two CDs reissuing material originally on the H.R.S. label has generally strong performances by a variety of small swing-oriented bands from 1946. The personnel overlaps in five groups headed by pianist Billy Kyle, altoist Russell Procope, trombonist Sandy Williams, pianist Jimmy Jones and trombonist Dicky Wells; the sidemen include such veteran greats as trumpeters Dick Vance, Harold Baker and Pee Wee Erwin, trombonist Trummy Young, clarinetist Buster Bailey, altoists Lem Davis and Tab Smith and the tenors of John Hardee and Budd Johnson. Although the music overall is not that essential (the bop recordings of the period are much more significant), there are some memorable performances on this well-conceived set. —*Scott Yanow*

Giants of Small Band Swing, Vol. 2 / Nov. 5, 1945-Jun. 3, 1946 / Riverside ✦✦✦
The second of two CDs put out in the *Original Jazz Classics* series that reissues material originally on the H.R.S. label, this volume has fine performances from bands led by three trombonists (Dicky Wells, Sandy Williams and J.C. Higginbotham) and trumpeter Joe Thomas; among the sidemen are Budd Johnson and Ted Nash on tenors, altoists Tab Smith, Lem Davis and Johnny Hodges, trumpeters Pee Wee Erwin and Sidney DeParis and baritonist Harry Carney. Although none of the recordings are classic and one can argue that the music is slightly behind the times, the solos are quite enjoyable and will be savored by small-group swing fans. —*Scott Yanow*

Giants of Traditional Jazz / Mar. 21, 1944-Aug. 21, 1952 / Savoy ✦✦✦✦
The emphasis is on Dixieland throughout this historical and very enjoyable two-LP set put out by Arista in 1980. The primitive trumpeter Mutt Carey is heard on his only two sessions as a leader performing some jazzy versions of ragtime along with a couple of veteran tunes; Carey's band includes trombonist Jimmy Archey, either Albert Nicholas or Edmond Hall on clarinet and Cliff Jackson or Hank Duncan on piano. English trumpeter Humphrey Littleton welcomes the great soprano Sidney Bechet to his septet ("Some of These Days" is a highlight), cornetists Bobby Hackett and Wild Bill Davison star on a few Dixieland standards, drummer Ben Pollack features trombonist Jack Teagarden on "Mightly Lak a Rose" and there are eight selections by Edmond Hall with a sextet that also stars trumpeter Ruby Braff and trombonist Vic Dickenson. Dixieland fans should bemoan the fact that most of this music has yet to be reissued on CD. —*Scott Yanow*

Giants of the Blues Tenor Sax / Nov. 7, 1958-Mar. 25, 1969 / Prestige ✦✦✦
This two-LP set (which has been reissued as part of a similarly titled three-CD set) has a dozen performances from a variety of great tenor saxophonists who recorded for Prestige during the period: Buddy Tate, Jimmy Forrest, Coleman Hawkins, Arnett Cobb, Eddie "Lockjaw" Davis, Hal Singer, Al Sears, Illinois Jacquet, King Curtis, Frank Foster and Jimmy Forrest. In addition to the later CD reissue, virtually all of the music is also available in its original context, making this two-fer far from essential, but it serves as a good introduction to these many bop-oriented and full-toned tenors. —*Scott Yanow*

Giants of the Blues Tenor Sax/Giants of the Funk Tenor Sax / Prestige ✦✦✦
If you can locate it, this 3-CD box from Prestige, is worth whatever it takes. What it is: 23 fat tracks—12 classic blues sax tracks and 11 more prime funk sax gems. The liner notes and selections are by Atlantic producer Bob Porter, who is *the* authority when it comes to blues in jazz—honkers, bar walkers, original funk, soul-jazz, whatever. This is your guide to some of the best of blues in jazz, not (mind you) jazz tinged with blues, but tunes that will scratch that blues itch plus some real ear-scorchin' rockers. —*Michael Erlewine*

The Golden Era of Swing / Apr. 7, 1936-Jun. 30, 1958 / Drive Archive ✦✦✦
This single CD from the budget reissue label Drive Archive has a dozen selections that are (with the exception of one song by Claude Thornhill) available on other

Drive sets. The emphasis is on dance band charts and there is a song apiece from Les Brown, Harry James, Les & Larry Elgart, Billie Holiday with Count Basie, Glenn Miller (a broadcast version of "In the Mood"), Ella Fitzgerald with Chick Webb, Duke Ellington, Woody Herman, Mel Tormé & the Mel-Tones with Artie Shaw ("What Is This Thing Called Love"), Thornhill, Stan Kenton and the Dorsey Brothers. The programming is somewhat random but general swing collectors may enjoy this sampler. —*Scott Yanow*

Good Time Jazz Story / 1949 / Good Time Jazz ✦✦✦✦✦
The Good Time Jazz label was formed in 1949 to record the Firehouse Five Plus Two and during its 20 years (particularly during 1949-59) it was one of the top Dixieland labels. It has been revived in the 1990s, most of its releases have been reissued on CD and there have even been a few new recordings. This four-CD box set is a definitive overview of the label. There is no previously unreleased material included but virtually every group that recorded for GTJ is represented: Jelly Roll Morton (1938 solos acquired years later), Burt Bales, Paul Lingle, Luckey Roberts, Willie "The Lion" Smith, Wally Rose, the Banjo Kings, Jesse Fuller, Bunk Johnson, Kid Ory, George Lewis, Johnny Wiggs, Eddie Pierson, Santo Pecora, Armand Hug, Sharkey Bonano, Paul Barbarin, Bill Matthews, George Girard, the Silver Leaf Jazz Band, Scott Black's Hot Horns, Lu Watters, Benny Strickler, Turk Murphy, Bob Scobey, the Bay City Jazz Band, Don Ewell, Clancy Hayes, Pete Daily, the Castle Jazz Band and the Firehouse Five Plus Two. Although completists will prefer to get the full sessions (except for some of the Banjo Kings titles, virtually all of the selections are available elsewhere on CD) but the very attractive 60-page booklet and the definitive nature of the box will make it a tempting purchase. —*Scott Yanow*

● **The Greatest Jazz Concert in the World** / Mar. 26, 1967+Jul. 1, 1967 / Pablo ✦✦✦✦✦
In addition to having a somewhat immodest title, this three-CD set was not actually one single concert but two. That reservation aside, the music on the reissue is often quite special. There is a jam session in the Jazz at the Philharmonic vein with fluegelhornist Clark Terry, altoist Benny Carter, the tenors of Zoot Sims and Paul Gonsalves and the Oscar Peterson Trio with the all-stars playing a ballad medley and heated run-throughs of a few familiar standards. In addition the Oscar Peterson Trio has a few features, an aging Coleman Hawkins does what he can on two numbers, Hawk teams up with altoists Benny Carter and Johnny Hodges on "C Jam Blues" and special guest T-Bone Walker sings and plays a couple of blues with assists from C.T., Gonsalves, Hodges and Peterson. But that's not all. The Duke Ellington Orchestra is in prime form performing a great deal of new material plus having guest spots for Sims (along with fellow tenors Gonsalves and Jimmy Hamilton on "Very Tenor"), Oscar Peterson (who gets to lead the band through a unique version of "Take the 'A' Train") and Carter; Johnny Hodges is also well-showcased. Ella Fitgerald completes the memorable set with her usual classy performance (accompanied by the Jimmy Jones Trio and sometimes the Ellington Orchestra), finishing the show with some hot scatting on "Cotton Tail." Maybe this really was "the Greatest Jazz Concert" after all. —*Scott Yanow*

Greenwich Village Jazz / Sep. 29, 1944-Jan. 5, 1945 / Pickwick ✦✦✦✦✦
One of six Pickwick CDs drawn from the mid-'40s Black & White catalog, this set has a lot of valuable swing and Dixieland-oriented performances. Clarinetist Barney Bigard leads two dates, one with trumpeter Joe Thomas and tenorman George Auld and the other one with Thomas, a tenor player by the same name and the great pianist Art Tatum. Pianist Willie "The Lion" Smith heads a spirited Dixieland set with trumpeter Max Kaminsky and clarinetist Rod Cless while pianist Cliff Jackson's Village Cats is a particularly impressive group with trumpeter Sidney DeParis, trombonist Wilbur DeParis, Gene Sedric on tenor and the unique Sidney Bechet on soprano. There is plenty of enjoyable music on this easily recommended set. —*Scott Yanow*

● **Greenwich Village Sound** / Nov. 29, 1944-Jan. 12, 1945 / Pickwick ✦✦✦✦✦
Of the six Pickwick CD reissues drawn from the Black & White catalog of the mid-'40s, this one is the most valuable. Clarinetist Joe Marsala leads ten of the 14 performances. The first six songs feature his septet with trumpeter Joe Thomas and the brilliant jazz harpist Adele Girard, who fortunately has a fair amount of solo space. However, it is the other four selections that really grab one's attention, for the swing-oriented Marsala is matched with stride pianist Cliff Jackson and bebop innovator and trumpeter Dizzy Gillespie. On "My Melancholy Baby" all three of the stylists are heard in uncompromising fashion, first in individual solos and then (much too briefly) battling it out in a unique ensemble. This CD is rounded out by singer Etta Jones (backed by a Barney Bigard combo) interpreting four blues from Dinah Washington's repertoire. This is a highly recommended set. —*Scott Yanow*

A GRP Christmas Collection / 1988 / GRP ✦✦✦
Most of the notables on GRP's roster in 1988 participated in this pleasing Christmas CD. There is one selection apiece from guitarist Daryl Stuermer, Tom Scott, David Benoit, Diane Schuur, Dave Valentin, Lee Ritenour, Gary Burton, Yutaka,

Chick Corea's Elektric Band ("God Rest Ye Merry Gentlemen"), Szakcsi, Eddie Daniels, Mark Egan, Special EFX, Kevin Eubanks and Dave Grusin. This relaxed set will be enjoyed by fans of those artists. —*Scott Yanow*

GRP Super Live in Concert / Oct. 8, 1987 / GRP ✦✦✦
This double CD is most notable for its second half which has a strong outing from Chick Corea's Elektric Band, his pacesetting fusion band with guitarist Frank Gambale, altoist Eric Marienthal, bassist John Patitucci and drummer Dave Weckl. The first CD is of lesser interest since it contains three routine vocals by Diane Schuur and some dull R&B jams with guitarist Lee Ritenour, keyboardist Dave Grusin and saxophonist Tom Scott. This set is worth buying for Corea's contributions if seen at a budget price. —*Scott Yanow*

The Guitar Album / Aug. 14, 1971 / Columbia ✦✦✦✦
This double LP has a lot of interesting performances from a Town Hall concert that puts the emphasis on a variety of guitarists. Charlie Byrd, Joe Beck and Chuck Wayne are featured in trios, swing stylist Tiny Grimes has a rare opportunity to record, Bucky Pizzarelli and George Barnes team up for some delightful duets and John McLaughlin (who is a bit out of place) backs his wife Eve's vocal. This set is now a collector's item and is worth searching for. —*Scott Yanow*

● **The Guitarists** / 1927-Oct. 1, 1941 / Time Life ✦✦✦✦✦
Despite its title, this three-LP boxed set from Time Life focuses only on jazz guitarists up to and including Charlie Christian, but it does a definitive job. Eddie Lang (six songs including a duet with fellow guitarist Carl Kress), Django Reinhardt (six), Oscar Aleman (one), Charlie Christian (six, five including a duet with Lang), Bernard Addison (two), Teddy Bunn (three), Dick McDonough (two), Eddie Durham (two), Carmen Mastren (two), Carl Kress (two), George Van Eps (one) and Al Casey (two) are all featured in a wide variety of settings ranging from unaccompanied solos to large bands. The swing-oriented music is often classic, some of the performances are fairly rare and the 56-page booklet is excellent. This is one of the best of the Time Life jazz reissues but long out of print. —*Scott Yanow*

Halloween Stomp / May 21, 1929-1950 / Jass ✦✦✦✦✦
This collection of "spooky" performances is dominated by songs dealing with ghosts and monsters, everything from "Mysterious Mose" and "Got the Jitters" to "Zombie," "Skeleton in the Closet," "The Ghost of Smokey Joe" and "With Her Head Tucked Underneath Her Arm." Most of the music is from the swing era with such bands as those led by Red Nichols, Don Redman, Glen Gray, Louis Prima, Ozzie Nelson, Cab Calloway, Tommy Dorsey and even Rudy Vallee alternating with much more obscure groups. The producers at Jass have also "enhanced" the music by inserting odd sound effects between songs. This CD certainly qualifies as the definitive (and only) Halloween jazz album. —*Scott Yanow*

Happy Anniversary Charlie Brown / 1987 / GRP ✦✦✦
The 40th anniversary of the Charlie Brown comic strip is celebrated on this 1987 CD by performances of songs used on the cartoon series (most of which were originally composed by Vince Guaraldi). A variety of artists participated in the project including David Benoit, B.B. King (singing "Joe Cool"), Dave Grusin, Chick Corea ("The Great Pumpkin Waltz"), Joe Williams, Gerry Mulligan, Lee Ritenour, Patti Austin and even Kenny G. ("Breadline Blues") and Dave Brubeck ("Benjamin"). The results are pleasing if lightweight. —*Scott Yanow*

Highlights in Jazz / 1985 / Stash ✦✦✦
Jack Kleinsinger's series of concerts titled *Highlights in Jazz* gave New Yorkers an opportunity to see swing-oriented veteran all-stars in fresh settings. Performances from his 12th-anniversary concert comprise this interesting LP which has features for clarinetist Phil Bodner ("After You've Gone"), singer Carrie Smith, pianist Marty Napoleon, tenor saxophonist Loren Schoenberg and multi-instrumentalist Glenn Zottola. However it is trumpeter Doc Cheatham, who is heard on "Sweet Georgia Brown" and a delightful version of "You're Lucky to Me," who takes honors. —*Scott Yanow*

Hill & Dale Rarities / Oct. 2, 1924-Jun. 1, 1928 / IAJRC ✦✦✦
Thomas Edison was a genius but he did not care much for jazz. His Edison label did not record much jazz before the company folded in 1929; many of the more interesting examples are included on this IAJRC LP, The music ranges from jazz to dance music and blues with performances from the Charleston Seven (which includes cornetist Red Nichols and trombonist Miff Mole), singers Josie Miles, Rosa Henderson and Viola McCoy and such bands as those led by Ross Gorman, B.A. Rolfe and Joe Herlihy. Interesting music, it's worth checking out by '20s collectors. —*Scott Yanow*

★ **History of Classic Jazz** / May 1921-Dec. 1953 / Riverside ✦✦✦✦✦
This three-CD reissue of an earlier Riverside five-LP set gives listeners a perfect introduction to early jazz. The 60 selections are divided into ten categories: Backgrounds (including African music, a sermon and marching music), Ragtime (both piano rolls and solo recordings), Blues, New Orleans Style, Boogie Woogie, South Side Chicago, Chicago Style, Harlem, New York Style and New Orleans Revival.

The performances contain many highlights (nearly every selection is a gem) and, although emphasizing the 1920s, they do not neglect later developments in Dixieland. The informative booklet is also a major asset. It's a highly recommended acquisition even to collectors who may already have the majority of these recordings. —*Scott Yanow*

Homemade Jam, Vol. 1 / Nov. 19, 1935-Jul. 2, 1936 / World ✦✦✦✦✦
Virtually no English musician could make a living during the 1930s from playing exclusively jazz but fortunately quite a few had opportunities to record it. On the first of two LPs put out by the English World label (a subsidiary of EMI), there are 18 selections from 1935-36 featuring such interesting soloists as violinist Hugo Rignold, trumpeters Norman Payne and Duncan Whyte, trombonist Lew Davis, clarinetist Jack Miranda, tenorman Buddy Featherstonaugh and Freddy Gardner (who played clarinet, alto and baritone). The repertoire is primarily American swing standards and these now somewhat forgotten players acquit themselves quite well. Highly recommended to swing collectors. —*Scott Yanow*

Homemade Jam, Vol. 2 / Sep. 19, 1936-Jan. 24, 1938 / World ✦✦✦✦✦
The second of two LPs released by the British label World in the late '70s continues reissuing some of the best jazz recordings cut in England during the mid- to late '30s. This generous album has 20 selections (an hour of music) and features such strong soloists as Freddy Gardner (on clarinet, alto, tenor and baritone), trumpeter Duncan Whyte, trombonist George Chisholm and violinist Eric Siday among others. This rare music (primarily Dixieland and swing standards) is consistently enjoyable and full of surprises including a version of "Tiger Rag" featuring the violins of Eric Siday and Reg Leopold. Both of the valuable *Homemade Jam* sets are highly recommended to collectors of '30s jazz. —*Scott Yanow*

★ **Honkers & Bar Walkers, Vol. 1** / Oct. 1949-Sep. 7, 1953 / Delmark ✦✦✦✦✦
A blasting R&B sax-anthology consisting of early '50s tracks from the Regal and United labels. —*Michael G. Nastos*

● **Hot British Dance Bands** / Oct. 7, 1925-Jul. 8, 1937 / Timeless ✦✦✦✦✦
When one thinks of British music of the '30s, it is usually of polite society dance bands and sappy vocalists. This 22-song CD gives one a very different picture of the scene overseas. Twenty-two different bands (including those led by Fred Elizalde, Jack Hylton, Spike Hughes, Billy Cotton, Ray Noble and Ambrose) are represented by some of their hottest recordings. The music ranges from Dixieland-oriented tracks to sophisticated swing and, whether it be the Devonshire Restaurant Dance Band's rendition of "Sugar Foot Stomp," the Rhythm Maniacs' "That's a Plenty" or Ambrose's classic "Cotton Pickers' Congregation," this is an historic and very enjoyable reissue, made available by the Dutch Timeless label. Highly recommended to fans of swing who are tired of hearing the same familiar bands all the time. —*Scott Yanow*

Hot Jazz for Cool Nights / Sep. 12, 1990-Jun. 29, 1992 / Music Masters ✦✦✦
A cross-section of top musicians who have recorded for Music Masters are heard on these 14 Christmas-related songs, including Vincent Herring, Jim Hall, Loren Schoenberg, Marvin Stamm, Dave Brubeck ("We Three Kings"), Stanley Turrentine, Kenny Davern (jamming "Jingle Bells" in a duet with Howard Alden), the Vanguard Jazz Sextet, Benny Carter (playing "A Child Is Born" while backed by Hank Jones), Jack Wilkins, Eastern Rebellion, Dick Hyman (a solo "White Christmas"), Rebecca Parris and Louie Bellson. A joyous, swinging collection of Christmas jazz. —*Scott Yanow*

I Got No Kick Against Modern Jazz / 1995 / GRP ✦✦✦
The mainstream jazz community takes a crack at the Holy Grail with *I Got No Kick Against Modern Jazz—A GRP Artists' Celebration of the Songs of the Beatles*. It's hard to imagine anyone doing a worse job with this catalogue than country music managed last year with *America Salutes the Beatles*, but GRP's stable of jazz-pop-lite artists gives it the old college try. A solid 75% of the content you could quite easily drift through obliviously in your local elevator. When the life of the party is George Benson scat-*Breezin'* his way through "The Long and Winding Road," you know you're in for a hard day's night. Arturo Sandoval at least swings with enthusiasm through "Blackbird." Other suspects include Chick Corea, McCoy Tyner, Lee Ritenour, and Spyro Gyra. —*Roch Parisien*

I Like Jazz / 1926-Oct. 13, 1954 / Columbia ✦✦✦
Many listeners were introduced to jazz through this well-conceived sampler LP from the late '50s. The dozen selections range from the ragtime of Wally Rose and the blues of Bessie Smith through the various forms of Dixieland and swing. Oddly enough bop is bypassed but there is "Progressive Jazz" from Pete Rugolo and "Modern Jazz" from Dave Brubeck. A much more recent *I Like Jazz* Columbia set on CD has a completely different program that is much less memorable. —*Scott Yanow*

Impulse! Jazz: A 30 Year Celebration / GRP ✦✦✦✦
Shortly after MCA handed GRP its jazz holdings for safekeeping in 1990, this 2-CD Impulse! retrospective was compiled and packaged in a handsome, bound,

fold-out book. Although producer Michael Cuscuna was handed an impossible task of summing up an important label on two discs—especially one that allowed some of its artists to record tracks over half an hour in length—the box gives the newcomer a pretty good overview of some of the high spots of the catalogue. Of course there is much John Coltrane, though only one of the three tracks, "Afro-Blue," finds him in full cry (the others are collaborations with Duke Ellington and Johnny Hartman, classics both). We get Gil Evans from his emancipating *Out of the Cool* album, *the* classic Oliver Nelson tune "Stolen Moments," a great choice from the Keith Jarrett Quartet file ("Southern Smiles"), and good single-cut capsules of Charles Mingus, Yusef Lateef, Sonny Rollins and Chico Hamilton—the latter featuring another prolific Impulse! artist, Gabor Szabo. Lo and behold, even the avant garde is represented by Archie Shepp, Gato Barbieri, and the first thirteen-and-a-half minutes of Pharoah Sanders' epic "The Creator Has a Master Plan"—which is long enough to give you the idea. No Albert Ayler or late free Coltrane, but that may have been too much to expect. Lest we forget, Cuscuna also illuminates the traditional side of Impulse! by including tracks from Count Basie, Ben Webster and Coleman Hawkins with Ellington. Ironically, in his booklet notes, Cuscuna complains about the lack of information to consumers on the outside covers of the original Impulse! albums—and this box is guilty of exactly the same thing. Moreover, the CD labels and inside cover only list the titles of the tunes; you have to dig laboriously inside the booklet to find the artists. But there is definitely a lot of fine, even occasionally startling music to enjoy here, and newcomers may well be tempted to explore some of the more dangerous Impulse! albums. And veteran collectors who cringed at the horrible original LP pressings of these tracks will be really pleased with the marvelous unobstructed sound of these CDs. —*Richard S. Ginell*

In Performance at the Playboy Jazz Festival / Jun. 1982 / Elektra Musician ♦♦♦♦♦

The Playboy Jazz Festival was established as a yearly institution in Los Angeles in 1979. This double LP, the only recordings thus far to emanate from the marathon two-day festival, has some of the highlights from the 1982 edition. "Pieces of a Dream" (tackling "Take the 'A' Train" and "Pop Rock") are in above-average form and Grover Washington, Jr., pleases the crowd with "Winelight." Tenor-great Dexter Gordon (in a quintet with trumpeter Woody Shaw) performs a pair of fine numbers, Weather Report romps on "Volcano for Hire" and is joined by Manhattan Transfer for a smoldering version of "Birdland." The Art Farmer/Bennie Golson Quintet is fine on five numbers although Nancy Wilson (who guests) is out of place. This two-fer concludes with three performances from an all-star quartet comprising trumpeter Freddie Hubbard, pianist McCoy Tyner, bassist Ron Carter and drummer Elvin Jones. It is surprising that this well-rounded set has not yet been reissued on CD. —*Scott Yanow*

Introducing Verve Jazz Masters, Vol. 20 / Apr. 19, 1994 / Verve ♦♦♦

At least this pocket-sized, budget-priced trip through 22 years of jazz doesn't pretend to be a definitive primer on jazz. It is simply and purely a sampler from the first 19 issues of Verve's *Jazz Masters* series; in other words, a sampler of a sampler. There is some clever segueing; the opening track, Louis Armstrong's "Just One of Those Things" with Oscar Peterson, leads right into Peterson in all his high-speed fury with his trio in "Woody 'n' You." There are some predictable choices—the 328th reissue of Wes Montgomery's "Impressions," or the 1,243rd reissue of Getz/Gilberto/Jobim's "The Girl from Ipanema"—and as befitting the composition of the Verve archives, there is heavy emphasis (five out of 16 tracks) upon female singers. But the stylistic range is reasonably wide, or as reasonable as these archives would allow, even to the point of including an electric track, Chick Corea's "Captain Marvel" from 1972, and thanks to a bit of doubling or tripling up, every artist from the first 19 volumes except Stephane Grappelli is represented. Eventually, the *Jazz Masters* would come to its conclusion after 60 volumes, the last of which is yet another sampler. For jazz newcomers only, or impulse buyers who want a token jazz CD on their shelf. —*Richard S. Ginell*

Isn't It Romantic: Rodgers and Hart Songbook / 1950-Aug. 2, 1994 / Verve ♦♦♦

Fifteen selections taken from the valuable vaults of Verve have been reissued on this CD, which salutes the Rodgers & Hart songwriting team with a full set of instrumentals. The roster of artists is quite impressive: Shirley Horn, Stan Getz, Max Roach, Sonny Rollins, Coleman Hawkins with Ben Webster, Art Tatum, Bill Evans, Clifford Brown with Max Roach, J.J. Johnson, Erroll Garner, Charlie Parker, pianist Stephen Scott, Gerry Mulligan, Benny Carter with Ben Webster. All of the performances are currently available on other CDs so this release will only be of passing interest to serious collectors but it does give listeners a well-rounded overview of the important music recorded for Verve through the years. —*Scott Yanow*

Jam Session in Swingville / Apr. 14, 1961+May 19, 1961 / Prestige ♦♦♦

This single CD has all of the music reissued in the mid-'70s on a two-LP set. Although sometimes issued under the names of Coleman Hawkins and Pee Wee Russell, the two great jazzmen actually do not appear together. The music, which is

performed by two all-star groups with arrangements by either Jimmy Hamilton or Al Sears, is generally modern swing. Hawkins' band comprises trumpeter Joe Newman, trombonist J.C. Higginbottham, clarinetist Hamilton, altoist Hilton Jefferson and a four-piece rhythm section. Pianist Cliff Jackson plays "I Want to Be Happy," and clarinetist Russell's outfit also features trumpeter Joe Thomas, trombonist Vic Dickenson and both Al Sears and Buddy Tate on tenors. Nothing all that memorable or innovative occurs, but the performances are enjoyable. —*Scott Yanow*

The Jam Sessions / Jul. 13, 1977-Jul. 14, 1977 / Pablo ♦♦♦♦♦

Norman Granz and his Pablo label took over a large part of the 1977 Montreux Jazz Festival (as they had done in 1975) and there were quite a few albums released that documented his all-star groups caught live and in spontaneous form. This double LP (six of the nine selections have since been issued as a single CD with the same title) has performances not included on the other albums. A who's who of veteran jazz greats are heard from including trumpeters Dizzy Gillespie, Clark Terry, Jon Faddis and Roy Eldridge, tenors Eddie "Lockjaw" Davis, Zoot Sims and Ronnie Scott, altoist Benny Carter, trombonists Vic Dickenson and Al Grey, pianists Oscar Peterson, Count Basie and Monty Alexander, guitarist Joe Pass, bassists Niels Pedersen and Ray Brown, and drummers Bobby Durham and Jimmie Smith. The tunes they perform (in five overlapping groups) are generally fairly basic but the playing has its share of surprising moments and this two-fer gives one a strong overview of the Pablo label in the 1970s. —*Scott Yanow*

The Jam Sessions: Montreux '77 / 1977 / Original Jazz Classics ♦♦♦

This is a rare case where the CD reissue is inferior to the original LP. Put out in 1977 as a double LP that included nine performances from five different all-star groups playing at that year's Montreux Jazz Festival, this single CD just has six of the selections (the remaining tracks have been reissued as "bonus cuts" on other reissues). However what is here is excellent. There are bands headed by pianist Oscar Peterson, vibraphonist Milt Jackson with co-leader bassist Ray Brown, Dizzy Gillespie (teaming up with his protege Jon Faddis) and Count Basie (in addition to one called the Pablo All-Stars Jam; among the sidemen are trumpeters Clark Terry and Roy Eldridge, the tenors of Eddie "Lockjaw" Davis, Zoot Sims and Ronnie Scott, altoist Benny Carter, trombonists Vic Dickenson and Al Grey, guitarist Joe Pass and pianist Monty Alexander). There are lots of fine solos on these fairly basic tunes but get the original double LP if possible. —*Scott Yanow*

James Moody/Frank Foster in Paris / Jul. 13, 1951-Apr. 4, 1954 / Vogue ♦♦♦

On this Vogue CD there are three different sessions, none of which have been available domestically in many years. James Moody plays alto with a French quintet (which includes trumpeter Roger Guerin and pianist Raymond Fol) on six standards and two of his originals; "This Is Always" and "That's My Desire" are particularly memorable. Moody is also heard doubling on tenor and alto while backed by a string section on six French melodies. The emphasis in on ballads and there is little on that date to grab one's attention. This CD concludes with a 1954 hard-bop set from tenor Frank Foster in which he is backed by a quiet French trio led by pianist Henri Renaud. Overall this is a CD that bop collectors will want because unlike many of the Vogue reissues, this music did not appear on the American Inner City label in the 1970s. —*Scott Yanow*

Jazz 'Round Midnight: Great Sax / Dec. 8, 1953-Aug. 1967 / Verve ♦♦♦

The "Jazz 'Round Midnight" series is a Verve CD reissue program that consists of ballad samplers. This box has three CDs featuring baritonist Gerry Mulligan and the tenors of Ben Webster and Stan Getz; each of the CDs is also available individually. Getz and Webster (who have very different sounds) were both famous as memorable ballad interpreters, while Mulligan was also quite skilled in that area. Getz's set features the cool-toned tenor playing bossa nova, straightahead and advanced ballads. Webster mostly sticks to swing standards (including a meeting with fellow tenor Coleman Hawkins on "Prisoner of Love"), and Mulligan (who is heard in settings ranging from a pianoless quartet with Bob Brookmeyer to his Concert Jazz Band) performs mostly lesser-known material, including four of his originals; altoist Johnny Hodges and tenors Webster and Zoot Sims make appearances on Jeru's disc. But overall, most jazz listeners will prefer to get more complete reissues by these three masterful saxophonists. —*Scott Yanow*

The Jazz Age/New York in the Twenties / Feb. 11, 1927-Oct. 7, 1930 / Bluebird ♦♦♦♦♦

Although other releases cover this music in greater depth, this is an excellent CD filled with some classic (if generally overlooked) performances from the late '20s. Red and Miff's Stompers (a sextet/septet with cornetist Red Nichols, trombonist Miff Mole and either Jimmy Dorsey or Pee Wee Russell on clarinet) perform six complex and unpredictable numbers, the Ben Pollack Orchestra gives some future-greats (clarinetist Benny Goodman, cornetist Jimmy McPartland and trombonist Glenn Miller) a few early opportunities to solo, Phil Napoleon's Emperors from 1929 feature the Dorsey Brothers and violinist Joe Venuti, and Venuti stars on four numbers with his own groups. This enjoyable set gives proof (if it were needed) that '20s jazz was not all Dixieland. —*Scott Yanow*

Jazz Arranger, Vol. 1 (1928-1940) / 1928-1940 / Columbia ◆◆◆
A good overview of early jazz sides and the arrangers who made them work for such groups as the Dorseys, Cab Calloway, and Ellington. —*Ron Wynn*

Jazz Arranger, Vol. 2 (1946-1963) / 1945-1970 / Columbia ◆◆◆
A variety of odds and ends are tossed together in this sampler which inexcusably leaves off specific recording dates and personnel. Some of the selections (Neal Hefti's chart of "The Good Earth" for Woody Herman, Gerry Mulligan's "How High the Moon" for Gene Krupa and Oliver Nelson's "Trinkle Tinkle" for a Thelonious Monk big-band date) are common while some of the others (such as George Russell's "All About Rosie" and John Lewis' "Three Little Feelings") have otherwise been long out of print. Excellent music, dumb packaging. —*Scott Yanow*

● **Jazz Band Ball** / Dec. 24, 1947-May 5, 1951 / Good Time Jazz ◆◆◆◆◆
Four different New Orleans jazz bands are heard from on three or four selections apiece on this CD, a straight reissue of the original LP; none of the music is available elsewhere. Clarinetist George Lewis and his 1950 group (with Elmer Talbert on trumpet and the reliable trombonist Jim Robinson), Turk Murphy's 1947 band (recorded shortly after he left Lu Watters and featuring trumpeter Bob Scobey), trombonist Kid Ory's 1951 Creole Jazz Band (with trumpeter Teddy Buckner and clarinetist Joe Darensbourg) and the 1947 edition of trumpeter Pete Daily's Rhythm Kings are all in excellent form. This set offers listeners a good sampling of their work and, considering that Lewis, Murphy and Ory led three of the most popular traditional jazz bands of the 1950s (although each sounded quite different from each other), this CD is well worth picking up. —*Scott Yanow*

Jazz Classics in Digital Stereo, Vol. 1: New Orleans / Jul. 17, 1918-Sep. 12, 1934 / ABC ◆◆◆
As with the other CDs in the Robert Parker series, this release contains a variety of early jazz performances that have been enhanced to sound closer to stereo. The music is consistently enjoyable although programmed in an almost random fashion. There are selections from Jelly Roll Morton, King Oliver, Johnny Dodds, Louis Armstrong, Freddie Keppard, Oscar Celestin, the New Orleans Owls, Louis Dumaine's Jazzola Eight, the New Orleans Rhythm Kings, Red Allen, the Jones-Collins Astoria Hot Eight, Monk Hazel, and Sidney Bechet and the Original Dixieland Jazz Band. Virtually all of the music is currently available elsewhere but listeners not already familiar with 1920s jazz will find this CD of interest. —*Scott Yanow*

Jazz Classics in Digital Stereo, Vol. 2: Chicago / Sep. 17, 1926-Sep. 12, 1934 / ABC ◆◆◆
All of the CDs in the BBC Robert Parker series (which has been made available at times through different sources) contain remastered and sonically improved recordings from the early days of jazz. Unfortunately the 20 selections on this set are rather randomly programmed and, although this set has a few rare items (such as Richard M. Jones' "African Hunch," the Mound City Blue Blowers' "What Do I Care What Somebody Said," and Omer Simeon's "Beau Koo Jack"), there are also many familiar recordings (including Jelly Roll Morton's "Sidewalk Blues," Frankie Trumbauer's "Singin' the Blues" and Earl Hines' "Maple Leaf Rag") that are easily available elsewhere. It's a good acquisition for newcomers to early jazz. —*Scott Yanow*

Jazz Classics in Digital Stereo, Vol. 3: New York / May 29, 1925-Aug. 26, 1935 / ABC ◆◆◆
On the third of four CDs in the Robert Parker series that reissues a cross section of early jazz recordings from a regional area, the music ranges from the famous (Jelly Roll Morton, Fletcher Henderson, Bessie Smith and Duke Ellington) to the lesser known (Charlie Johnson's Paradise Ten, Lloyd Scott and Freddy Jenkins). Veteran collectors will prefer to skip this sampler and get the complete sessions elsewhere but listeners just beginning to explore early jazz should find these early recordings (which range from pre-swing to some heated jams) worth investigating. —*Scott Yanow*

Jazz Classics in Digital Stereo, Vol. 4: Hot Town / Feb. 27, 1927-Dec. 4, 1933 / ABC ◆◆◆
This CD sampler in the Robert Parker series mostly features territory bands from cities other than New York, Chicago and New Orleans. Other than a selection apiece from Jimmie Lunceford (1930's "In Dat Mornin'"), Duke Ellington, Andy Kirk and Benny Moten, all of the groups are quite obscure (such as those led by Alonzo Ross, Charley Williamson, Troy Floyd and Slatz Randall), making this release of greater than usual interest although unfortunately complete sessions are not reissued. Excellent music most highly recommended to listeners who want a general sampling of early rarities. —*Scott Yanow*

Jazz Fest Masters / 1969 / Scotti Bros. ◆◆◆
This is one of five CDs taken from the 1969 New Orleans Jazz Festival and released by Scott Bros. in 1992. The set consists of fine Dixieland from groups led

by trombonist Jim Robinson, trumpeter Johnny Wiggs, drummer Barry Martyn and trombonist Papa Bue; sidemen include clarinetist Louis Cottrell, drummer Zutty Singleton, Danny Barker on banjo and clarinetist Raymond Burke. There are plenty of heated moments from these similar but distinctive groups and the music is consistently joyful and swinging. —*Scott Yanow*

Jazz Fest Masters / 1969 / Scotti Bros. ◆◆◆
A lot of classic greats are heard on this CD, taken from the 1969 New Orleans Jazz Festival. Roy Eldridge performs four songs while backed by pianist Jaki Byard, bassist Richard Davis and drummer Alan Dawson; on "Perdido" fellow trumpeters Bobby Hackett and Clark Terry sit in. Dizzy Gillespie plays two obscure numbers with his quintet of the time (with James Moody on tenor and flute) while Buck Clayton heads an octet on "St. Louis Blues" that also includes Buddy (not Bunny as it says in the scanty liner notes) Tate and trombonist Dickie Wells. The performances are quite enjoyable, obscure and well-recorded. This CD is worth getting for Roy Eldridge's playing by itself. —*Scott Yanow*

Jazz Fusion, Vol. 1 / Rhino ◆◆◆
Rhino's two-volume *Jazz Fusion* overlooks the late '60s/early '70s beginnings of fusion in favor of late '70s and '80s fusion. By that time, the truly radical elements of fusion had been smoothed out, as *Jazz Fusion, Vol. 1* illustrates. Although it never gets as bland as the Yellowjackets or Spyro Gyra, these cuts by Herbie Hancock, Larry Coryell, Jean-Luc Ponty, Joe Zawinul and Chick Corea's Return to Forever simply aren't as adventurous as early fusion, including music made by those very artists. Still, that does mean that *Jazz Fusion* is a fairly accurate representation of the genre's latter incarnation, and for many jazz fans, these two volumes will function as a good primer. —*Stephen Thomas Erlewine*

Jazz Fusion, Vol. 2 / Rhino ◆◆◆
The presence of Miles Davis may suggest that *Jazz Fusion, Vol. 2* is a better listen than *Vol. 1*, but it suffers from the same flaws as its predecessor—it prefers the watered-down fusion of the late '70s to the wildly adventurous early fusion of the late '60s and early '70s. If anything, the set has less distinguishing characteristics than the first, featuring cuts by the Brecker Bros., art-rockers Brand X, and Southern rockers the Dixie Dregs. Tracks by Larry Carlton and Miles illustrate how fusion could be intriguing, but the inclusion of metal guitarist Ronnie Montrose is baffling and totally unforgivable. —*Stephen Thomas Erlewine*

Jazz Giants Plays Horace Silver / Jun. 16, 1954-Jan. 30, 1978 / Prestige ◆◆◆◆
Now here is a really enterprising subject for a songbook album—a composer who was not a Tin Pan Alley pop craftsman and whose output had not been anthologized until this release. True, Silver wrote fewer standards than, say, Porter or the Gershwins, and fewer jazz artists covered them, thus limiting Fantasy's choices (the zany Eddie Jefferson is heard on three of the 16 tracks, and his rendition of "The Preacher" is followed by another from Shirley Scott), yet this collection gives ample and valuable evidence of how underregarded Silver has been as a composer. Working within a hard-bop context garnished with gospel and the blues, Silver's tunes often achieve a winning combination of sophistication and earthiness, and they serve as fine launching pads for bop, soul and even Latin-oriented players. Besides variations of the well-known "Señor Blues," "Song for My Father," and "Sister Sadie," there are also sleepers like the haunting bossa nova styled "Moon Rays" of Vince Guaraldi and Bola Sete and the easy-strutting "Doodlin'" by the Barney Kessel/Ray Brown/Shelly Manne trio (both in their CD debuts). A plethora of soulful musicians from the Prestige, Riverside, Contemporary, Fantasy, and Galaxy archives lead the sessions, including Phineas Newborn, Wes Montgomery, Milt Jackson, Art Pepper, Tommy Flanagan, Richard "Groove" Holmes, Blue Mitchell and Jack McDuff, along with those mentioned before. Silver himself is to be found on only one track, backing Jackson on "Buhaina"—and that's understandable, given his long-standing ties to Blue Note through the timespan of this anthology. But this contractual quirk actually makes the collection even more of a significant tribute, showcasing a body of work that may prove to be as durable as that of the other great composer/pianist from this period, Thelonious Monk. —*Richard S. Ginell*

A Jazz Gumbo 1 / Apr. 18, 1993+Apr. 21, 1993 / Jazz Crusade ◆◆◆
For this very spirited CD, trombonist Big Bill Bissonnette utilized 18 musicians (mostly obscure names other than clarinetist/altoist Sammy Rimington) in a variety of settings. The music is a rambunctious and often erratic but always sincere variety of New Orleans jazz. Not everything works but listeners who enjoy classic jazz and do not mind tonal variations (not everyone is in tune at all times) will find the unusual set of interest. —*Scott Yanow*

Jazz Ltd., Vol. 1 / Feb. 1949-1951 / Delmark ◆◆◆◆◆
Starting in 1947 and continuing throughout the 1950s, Bill Reinhardt and his wife Ruth ran Jazz Ltd., a Chicago club that served as a haven for Dixieland. Reinhardt (a fine clarinetist) led the house band, a unit that invariably left a spot open for guest artists. This Delmark CD features the Jazz Ltd. group on 13 selections with such all-stars as soprano great Sidney Bechet, cornetist Muggsy Spanier, trumpeter

Doc Evans, trombonist Miff Mole and pianist Don Ewell; the disc is rounded off by an informative five-minute interview with the Reinhardt's from the 1960s. The freewheeling music is quite enjoyable; Dixieland fans are advised to pick up this exciting disc. —*Scott Yanow*

Jazz Masters: Verve at 50 / 1994 / Verve ◆◆◆

Verve Records celebrated the 50th anniversary of Norman Granz's first Jazz at the Philharmonic concert with an all-star get-together at Carnegie Hall. Different groups of top players from Verve's legacy (both past and present) had opportunities to perform and this CD has many of the highlights. Pianist Peter Delano plays "Tangerine" with a trio, Dee Dee Bridgewater sings "Shiny Stockings" with the Carnegie Hall Jazz Band, Hank Jones pays tribute to Art Tatum, Abbey Lincoln sings "I Must Have That Man," Joe Henderson meets up with Antonio Carlos Jobim (who made his final concert appearance) on "Desafinado," "Manteca" features trumpeter Roy Hargrove and trombonist Steve Turre, pianist Yosuke Yamashita pays tribute to Bud Powell, Betty Carter scats on "How High the Moon," Herbie Hancock and John McLaughlin play a restrained acoustic version of Bill Evans' "Turn out the Stars," Hargrove teams up with altoist Jackie McLean and guitarist Pat Metheny for "The Eternal Triangle," organist Jimmy Smith revisits Oliver Nelson's arrangement of "Down by the Riverside," Art Porter and Jeff Lorber play some crossover and J.J. Johnson contributes a few trombone solos. Not that many special moments occur (too many of the original Verve stars had long since passed away) but jazz historians and bop fans may want to get this one. —*Scott Yanow*

Jazz Piano / Apr. 1924-Jan. 1972 / Smithsonian ◆◆◆

This four-CD boxed set attempts to trace the history of jazz piano through 68 recordings by 42 pianists. Actually the avant garde is largely ignored (with no examples of the playing of Cecil Taylor, Paul Bley or Don Pullen) but otherwise the various acoustic styles are fairly well-covered, even with the absence of Ralph Sutton and Dick Wellstood. One can argue with the individual choices but the music is generally quite excellent. There are one or two selections from each of these players: Jelly Roll Morton, James P. Johnson, Willie "The Lion" Smith, Fats Waller, Earl Hines (who gets four songs), Teddy Wilson, Jimmy Yancey, Meade Lux Lewis, Pete Johnson, Avery Parrish, Count Basie, Billy Kyle, Mary Lou Williams, Art Tatum (five performances), Duke Ellington, Jess Stacy, Nat King Cole, Erroll Garner, Jimmy Jones, Bud Powell, Lennie Tristano, Dodo Marmarosa, Ellis Larkins, Dave McKenna, Al Haig, Oscar Peterson, Jimmy Rowles, Thelonious Monk, Phineas Newborn, Jr., Horace Silver, Martial Solal, Herbie Nichols, Hank Jones, Tommy Flanagan, John Lewis, Randy Weston, Ray Bryant, Bill Evans, McCoy Tyner, Chick Corea, Keith Jarrett and Herbie Hancock. —*Scott Yanow*

★ **Jazz Scene [Verve]** / Mar. 1946-Feb. 4, 1955 / Verve ◆◆◆◆◆

In 1949 producer Norman Granz released a remarkable album of 78s that consisted of a dozen selections (many of them specially recorded for the occasion) that perfectly summed up the modern jazz scene of the time. The deluxe set consisted of two Duke Ellington features for baritonist Harry Carney with strings, a pair of complex Neal Hefti arrangements, small-group sides by Lester Young, Charlie Parker, Bud Powell and altoist Willie Smith, Machito's "Tanga," major works by arrangers Ralph Burns and George Handy and, as the pièce-de-résistance, Coleman Hawkins' pioneering unaccompanied tenor solo "Picasso." Now all of this music has been reissued on a very attractive double-CD set that also contains five alternate takes plus three previously unknown Billy Strayhorn piano solos, further examples of Lester Young and Willie Smith, an obscure Hawkins session with J.J. Johnson from 1949, a few numbers from a forgotten Flip Phillips session and three selections by Ralph Burns in 1955, two of which feature explosive trumpet work from Roy Eldridge. The new packaging is magnificent with many Gjon Mili photographs of the top jazzmen of the era and extensive liner notes. This was one of the top reissues of 1994 and is essential for all serious historical jazz collections. —*Scott Yanow*

Jazz Sketches of Sondheim / 1995 / Sony ◆◆◆

With so few major composers still alive by the mid-'90s, it was logical that jazz musicians would try to expand their repertoire by exploring the works of non-jazz writers. None of Stephen Sondheim's compositions have thus far become jazz standards but that may change after the release of this CD. Three of the tracks unfortunately feature overdramatic Nancy Wilson and the R&Bish Peabo Bryson, but Holly Cole (on two numbers) fares much better. The most interesting moments are provided by the all-star musicians which include tenors Joshua Redman and Grover Washington, Jr., guitarist Jim Hall, pianist Herbie Hancock, Wayne Shorter on soprano and trumpeter Terence Blanchard, among others. Sondheim himself makes a guest appearance in a piano duet with Hancock on "They Ask Me Why I Believe in You." And best of all, there is no version here of "Send in the Clowns." This varied set has its memorable performances. —*Scott Yanow*

Jazz at Lincoln Center Presents: The Fire of the Fundamentals / Aug. 8, 1991-Feb. 14, 1993 / Columbia ◆◆◆

This CD, which actually features the Lincoln Center Jazz Orchestra on only two selections, has highlights from a variety of concerts held at Lincoln Center during 1991-93. A fine octet with clarinetist Michael White, trumpeter Wynton Marsalis and pianist Marcus Roberts do an effective re-interpretation of Jelly Roll Morton's "Jungle Blues," pianist Kenny Barron strides enthusiastically on a solo version of Thelonious Monk's "Trinkle Tinkle" and Jimmy Heath's soprano playing is showcased on "Ellington's Stray-Horn." Pianist/vocalist Jay McShann recreates "Hootie Blues," pianist Marcus Roberts romps through Monk's "Bolivar Blues" and then "Dahomey Dance" offers particularly strong solos from a septet with Marsalis and tenorman Todd Williams. Betty Carter sings a spacey version of "You're Mine You," Marcus Roberts returns for a solo rendition of Morton's "The Crave," Marsalis' Sextet interprets Miles Davis' moody "Flamenco Sketches" and vocalist Milt Grayson finishes the CD anti-climactically with the ballad "Multi Colored Blue." It's an interesting if not essential set with plenty of variety and many worthwhile performances. —*Scott Yanow*

● **Jazz at Santa Monica Civic '72** / Aug. 2, 1972 / Pablo ◆◆◆◆◆

The Pablo label (and Norman Granz's return as a full-time producer) was launched with this wonderful package, first released as a three-LP set and now available as a three-CD reissue. The 1972 concert was originally supposed to only feature the Count Basie Orchestra and Ella Fitzgerald but Granz surprised everyone by inviting some "guests": trumpeters Roy Eldridge and Harry "Sweets" Edison, the tenors of Stan Getz and Eddie "Lockjaw" Davis, pianist Oscar Peterson and bassist Ray Brown. Together with Basie-trombonist Al Grey they formed the Jazz at the Philharmonic All-Stars and play wonderfully on three jams (listen to Eldridge's break on "In a Mellow Tone") and a ballad medley. In addition there are four selections from Basie's band (featuring the tenor of Jimmy Forrest, trumpeter Pete Minger and altoist Curtis Peagler), a full set from Fitzgerald and a Peterson-Brown duet on "You Are My Sunshine." The high point of the concert however is the final song, a classic version of "C Jam Blues" which finds Fitzgerald trading off in very humorous fashion with Grey, Getz, Sweets, Lockjaw and Eldridge; each of the encounters has at least one remarkable moment. This gem is highly recommended. —*Scott Yanow*

Jazz at the Hollywood Bowl / Aug. 15, 1956 / Verve ◆◆◆◆◆

This double LP was the first jazz concert ever recorded at the Hollywood Bowl (and only the second one held at that L.A. institution). Although not an official Jazz at the Philharmonic concert, it has the same basic format and was also produced by Norman Granz. Trumpeters Roy Eldridge and Harry "Sweets" Edison, tenors Flip Phillips and Illinois Jacquet, the Oscar Peterson Trio and drummer Buddy Rich all jam on "Honeysuckle Rose" and "Jumpin' at the Woodside" and there is also a ballad medley and a drum solo by Rich. In addition the Oscar Peterson Trio plays two numbers, the remarkable pianist Art Tatum (in one of his final appearances) has four, Ella Fitzgerald sings six songs (including a scat-filled "Airmail Special") and collaborates with Louis Armstrong on two others. For the grand finale nearly everyone returns to the stage for "When the Saints Go Marching In" which Armstrong sings and largely narrates, cheerfully introducing all of the participants. This is a historic and very enjoyable release featuring more than its share of classic greats. —*Scott Yanow*

Jazz at the Pawnshop, Vol. 1 / 1976 / Proprius ◆◆◆◆

This is the first of four CD volumes that fully document a legendary engagement at the Pawnshop club in Stockholm, Sweden. Featured are Arne Domnerus (doubling on alto and clarinet), pianist Bengt Hallberg, vibraphonist Lars Erstrand, bassist Georg Riedel and drummer Egil Johansen. They mostly stick to swing standards, recalling the groups of Benny Goodman and Lionel Hampton. Highlights include a heated "Limehouse Blues," the African folk song "High Life," "Lady Be Good" and Coleman Hawkins' "Stuffy." All of the volumes in this series are well worth getting by straightahead jazz fans, particularly those not familiar with Arne Domnerus' excellent playing. —*Scott Yanow*

Jazz at the Pawnshop, Vol. 2 / 1976 / Proprius ◆◆◆◆

The second of four volumes that fully document a 1976 engagement at the Pawnshop Jazz Club in Stockholm, Sweden, this set differs from the others in that vibraphonist Lars Erstrand is not present. Arne Domnerus (on alto and clarinet) heads a quartet also featuring pianist Bengt Hallberg, bassist Georg Riedel and drummer Egil Johansen. Other than an African folk song (a second version of "High Life,") and a Swedish folk song, the repertoire is dominated by swing standards; highlights include a lengthy "In a Mellow Tone," "Poor Butterfly" and "Things Ain't What They Used to Be." —*Scott Yanow*

Jazz at the Pawnshop, Vol. 3 / 1976 / Proprius ◆◆◆◆

Taken entirely from the second of a legendary two-day engagement at Stockholm's Pawnshop club, this third of four CDs that fully document the gig puts the focus on vibraphonist Lars Erstrand who even gets top billing. Arne Domnerus on alto and clarinet co-stars and the rhythm section (pianist Bengt Hallberg, bassist Georg Riedel and drummer Egil Johansen) is also excellent. With the exception of a Charlie Parker blues ("Now's the Time"), the quintet sticks to swing and Dixieland standards and there are many swinging moments on such tunes as "In a Mellow Tone," "Take the 'A' Train" and "Struttin' with Some Barbeque." All of the volumes in this enjoyable series are worth picking up by straightahead jazz fans. — *Scott Yanow*

Jazz in L.A.: the 1940s / Sep. 1, 1941-1949 / KLON ◆◆◆◆◆
This CD, issued by radio station KLON in anticipation of presenting the Hollywood Jazz Festival (a major event that never occurred due to the L.A. riots), will be a tough one to find but is worth the search. Most of its material (all recorded in Los Angeles in the 1940s) is extremely rare. Its contents include a medley from the play "Jump for Joy" that features Duke Ellington, Herb Jeffries, Ivie Anderson and Joe Turner, a jam from a broadcast by the Lee and Lester Young band, live performances by Cee Pee Johnson's Orchestra, Benny Carter's big band, Dizzy Gillespie with Charlie Parker, the Nat King Cole Trio, Howard McGhee's Sextet and Boyd Raeburn's Orchestra plus mostly obscure studio sides by Lucky Thompson, the orchestras of Gerald Wilson, Earle Spencer and Lyle Griffin, Teddy Edwards, Dexter Gordon with Wardell Gray ("The Chase") and Charles Mingus (in 1949). The program traces the evolution of bop in Los Angeles and nearly every selection is quite successful. Historic music that deserves better distribution. — *Scott Yanow*

★ **Jazz in the Thirties** / Feb. 28, 1933-Dec. 13, 1935 / Disques Swing ◆◆◆◆◆
There is a great deal of remarkable music included on this two-hour two-CD set. Among the 40 selections (all dating from the early years of swing) are sessions led by violinist Joe Venuti, bass saxophonist Adrian Rollini, Benny Goodman (in an all-star group with trombonist Jack Teagarden), Bud Freeman, trumpeter Bunny Berigan, Gene Krupa and piano solos by Joe Sullivan and Jess Stacy. The recording sessions are all complete and the music is quite rewarding and often very exciting. It's highly recommended as is the companion set *Ridin' in Rhythm*. — *Scott Yanow*

Jazz the World Forgot, Vol. 1 / 1923-1931 / Yazoo ◆◆◆◆
The vintage music on this first of two CDs put out in 1996 by Yazoo is consistently enjoyable and heated. Unfortunately, the rather random selection of 23 selections by 23 bands, although full of hot obscurities, does not include complete sessions, is not programmed in chronological order, and (most inexcusably) does not give the personnel or exact dates. So what should have been an essential acquisition ends up being a worthwhile sampler that will force serious collectors to consult their discographies. But musically, there are quite a few memorable moments. Included on this CD are one selection apiece by Louis Dumaine's Jazzola Eight, Roy Johnson's Happy Pals, Mamie Smith, Sam Morgan, the Pickett-Parham Apollo Syncopators, Paul Tremaine's Aristocrats (the classic "Four-Four Rhythm"), Charlie Johnson, Bennie Moten, the Ross De Luxe Syncopators, Frenchy's String Band, Taylor's Dixie Serenaders, Jelly Roll Morton, Ben Tobier's California Cyclones, Fowler's Favorites, Oliver Naylor, George McClennon's Jazz Devils, Floyd Mills' Marylanders, Maynard Baird, King Oliver, Gowan's Rhapsody Makers, Sammie Lewis' Bamville Syncopators, the Hotentots and Frankie Franko. — *Scott Yanow*

Jazz the World Forgot, Vol. 2 / 1923-1930 / Yazoo ◆◆◆◆
The second of two CDs put out by Yazoo that have a variety of obscurities (plus a few better-known performances) from the 1920s, this set shares with the earlier volume the fault of not listing the full personnel and the exact recording dates. Musically, the program contains 23 selections from as many groups (this is not a release for completists) and covers a wide span of hot 1920s jazz, with one number apiece from J. Neal Montgomery, Sam Morgan, the Whoopee Makers, Andy Preer's Cotton Club Orchestra, George McClennon's Jazz Devils, Edna Winston, Louis Dumaine's Jazzola Eight, Clarence Williams (featuring Sidney Bechet on "Wild Cat Blues"), Dixon's Jazz Maniacs, the Ross De Luxe Syncopators, Paul Howard's Quality Serenaders, Bennie Moten, Bennett's Swamplanders, Phil Baxter, Thomas Morris' Seven Hot Babies, Johnny DeDroit, Lou Weimer, Reb Spikes' Majors and Minors, Charles Creath's Jazz-O-Maniacs, King Oliver, Slim Lamar, the Five Hot Chocolates and the New Orleans Owls. — *Scott Yanow*

Jazz: Classic Cuts from 80 Years of Jazz / 1918-Oct. 28, 1977 / BBC Music ◆◆◆
Britain's *BBC Music Magazine*, normally a classical magazine with maybe a couple of pages devoted to jazz, tried to reach for the impossible as part of its special Spring 1997 jazz issue—squeezing 80 years of recorded jazz onto a one-hour CD. Actually, the Brits did a creditable job—up to 1957, at least—hitting several essential targets while avoiding many obvious, overplayed pieces. The disc starts near the beginning of recorded time with the Original Dixieland Jass Band's "Clarinet Marmalade Blues," proceeds through three more so-called blues of the '20s by King Oliver, Louis Armstrong and his Hot Seven and Bix Beiderbecke. The swing era is represented by Benny Goodman's "King Porter Stomp," Duke Ellington's "Harlem Air Shaft" (a great unhackneyed choice) and, in an understandable tilt toward Europe, Django Reinhardt's "Nuages." Bebop gets Charlie Parker's "Klactoveesedstene" from the Dial sessions, and Dizzy Gillespie's Afro-Cuban-accented

big band in "Good Bait." The disc sums up the '50s with "Nights at the Turntable" from Gerry Mulligan and Chet Baker, the Miles Davis Quintet in "If I Were a Bell" (which conveniently gets Coltrane out of the way) and a debatable bit of late Billie Holiday, "Stars Fell on Alabama." So far, so good. But the next 40 years of jazz are compressed down to a mere two cuts—Wes Montgomery's "Impressions" with Wynton Kelly (1965) and Zoot Sims' "(I Wonder) Where Our Love Has Gone" (1977). Where's free jazz? Where's jazz-rock? Where are the neo-boppers? Is the BBC trying to imply that half of jazz's history isn't worth bothering with, or was it just a matter of not being able to license the right material? In any case, the remastering is quite good, often crediting European issues in the case of 78 RPM material, and the accompanying magazine contains several absorbing historical essays on jazz personalities and styles—which do a much better job covering the last few decades than the disc. The disc and magazine were made continuously available by mail from BBC Music after the issue left the newsstands. — *Richard S. Ginell*

Jazznost / 1989 / Mapleshade ◆◆◆
Jazz has long since ceased to be an exclusively American music; top-flight foreign musicians live in all corners of the world, so no one should be surprised that there are some in what used to be the Soviet Union. This 1989 affair linked the talents of gifted pianist Walter Davis, Jr., and exciting drummer Bobby Battle with expert Russian improvisers, the best of whom turns out to be saxophonist Igor Butman. They handle some songs ("Blue 'N Green") better than others ("Blue Monk"), but do everything with sufficient cohesion, showing that music remains the universal language. — *Ron Wynn*

★ **Jazzvisions: Latina Familia** / PolyGram ◆◆◆◆◆
Sheila Escovedo—better known as Sheila E.—was still cresting the peak of her Prince-sponsored pop career at the time this installment of Verve's Jazzvisions series was taped; hence the top billing over her father Pete Escovedo and the formidable Tito Puente. But Prince and his entourage stayed home, for this is strictly a cooking Latin jazz session, recorded live at Los Angeles' Wiltern Theatre. Nor is this a predictable salsa session, for the Escovedos, Puente and a large supporting cast mix up the medicine with an excursion into Brazil, tense progressive-minded jazz charts, David Yamasaki's jarring rock electric guitar, and some lyrical vibraphone from Tito. And naturally, there are some stirring three-way timbales battles between Tito, Sheila and Pete, augmented by Sheila's brother Juan on congas. This concert was available in five formats (LP, CD, cassette, laserdisc, VHS video). — *Richard S. Ginell*

The John Reid Collection 1940-1944 / Jun. 17, 1940-Jun. 24, 1944 / American Music ◆◆◆
This is a very unusual CD which will be of greatest interest to collectors of New Orleans jazz of the Bunk Johnson variety. A radio broadcast from 1944 features trumpeter Peter Bocage, and the clarinets of Big Eye Louis Nelson and Alphonse Picou in a septet. In addition there are two piano solos from Burnell Santiago, a "talking record" from 1944 (in which one can hear the voices of Sidney Bechet, Manuel Perez, Nelson, Picou and Santiago), a couple of unaccompanied Bechet solos, his "Message to Bunk" in which he urges the veteran trumpeter to come up north, and a 1940 performance by clarinetist George Bacquet in a small group; Bechet guests on one selection. This is a very historical (if "lo-fi") release that fills a few gaps in the story of the New Orleans jazz revival. — *Scott Yanow*

The Joy of Christmas Past / 1948-1968 / GRP ◆◆◆
The Christmas jazz recordings heard on this varied sampler CD are drawn from the catalogs of ABC-Paramount, Decca, Chess and Argo. Such artists as Louis Armstrong (how did "What a Wonderful World" become a Xmas song?), Les Brown, Mel Tormé, Ramsey Lewis, Peggy Lee, Kenny Burrell, Ahmad Jamal, Al Hibbler, Duke Ellington ("Silent NIght") and Gene Ammons are heard from and, even with the emphasis on ballads, this is a well-rounded set. — *Scott Yanow*

★ **Kings of the Ragtime Banjo** / 1900 / Yazoo ◆◆◆◆◆
Although many lazy banjoists through the decades (who are content to merely strum chords four to the bar) have hurt the reputation of their instrument, in the early days of recording two of the top instrumental stars were banjoists. This superior collector's LP features Vess Ossman on seven selections from the 1900-1910 period (including "Smoky Mokes" and "St. Louis Tickle") and Fred Eps (father of guitarist George Van Eps) on seven tunes from 1911-23 (including "Red Pepper Rag" and "Ragtime Oriole"). The virtuosity of the two legendary banjoists still sounds impressive many decades later and their recordings are among the finest of the prejazz period. Recommended. — *Scott Yanow*

Krupa & Rich / May 16, 1955+Nov. 1, 1955 / Verve ◆◆◆◆◆
Although drummers Gene Krupa and Buddy Rich are pictured together on this CD's cover, they actually only play together on one selection, a lengthy "Bernie's Tune." The first five performances (with two songs apiece for Rich and Krupa) also feature short solos from trumpeters Dizzy Gillespie and Roy Eldridge, tenors Flip Phillips and Illinois Jacquet and pianist Oscar Peterson; Rich is reasonably

restrained on his numbers but has his explosive moments. "Bernie's Tune" is far superior to the in-concert Rich/Krupa drum battles that were recorded at other times. The final two performances find Rich leading a different all-star group with consistently excellent solos from trumpeters Thad Jones and Joe Newman and tenors Ben Webster and Frank Wess. This swinging set (which contains formerly rare recordings) is easily recommended to fans of straightahead and bop-oriented jazz. —*Scott Yanow*

Last Night When We Were Young / 1994 / Classical Action ✦✦✦✦✦
Pianist Fred Hersch organized this jazz project, a fundraiser in the fight against AIDS. All 13 performances are ballads and some of them (most notably Jane Ira Bloom's rendition of "In the Wee Small Hours") are quite touching. In addition to Hersch and Bloom, such artists as altoist Bobby Watson, the late pianist Dave Catney, vibraphonist Gary Burton, Toots Thielemans on harmonica, vocalists Janis Siegel and Mark Murphy, pianist George Shearing and Phil Woods (heard here on clarinet) all get to make contributions. The mood is consistently melancholy but rarely downbeat, superior music recorded for a noble cause. —*Scott Yanow*

The Legendary Big Band Singers / Mar. 3, 1931-Jan. 24, 1951 / GRP/Decca ✦✦✦
Twenty-one different singers from the swing era are mostly heard backed by big bands on this interesting but not essential sampler. Generally the performances give one a good idea as to the vocalists' abilities (such as Cab Caloway's "Minnie the Moocher," Louis Armstrong's "Thanks a Million," Jimmy Rushing's "Sent for You Yesterday" and Sister Rosetta Tharpe's "Trouble in Mind") and some of the singers (particularly June Richmond, Bon Bon, and Ella Johnson who is heard on the original version of "Since I Fell for You") deserve the recognition. On the minus side, the decision not to list the personnel of the many orchestras may lead one to wonder who is playing various tenor, trumpet and piano solos, information that should have been provided. —*Scott Yanow*

Live at Newport 1960 / Jul. 1960 / Omega ✦✦✦
The music is predictable but pleasing on this consistent CD, recorded at the 1960 Newport Jazz Festival. Cannonball Adderley's Quintet (with trumpeter Nat Adderley) swings hard on "Work Song" and "Stay on It," Gerry Mulligan's Concert Jazz Band sounds fine on three songs (although this version of "Blueport" does not quite compare to Mulligan's classic matchup with fluegelhornist Clark Terry), the Oscar Peterson Trio jams two numbers and Dizzy Gillespie's three song miniset is highlighted by "Night in Tunisia." Nothing that unusual occurs in any of the performances but the playing is up-to-par and occasionally exciting. —*Scott Yanow*

Live at the Festival / 1970-1973 / Enja ✦✦✦
This very interesting CD contains four unrelated performances from three editions of Yugoslavia's Ljubljana Jazz Festival. The Bill Evans Trio (with bassist Eddie Gomez and a slightly out-of-place Tony Oxley on drums) plays "Nardis," "'Round Midnight" is explored by the duo of Karin Krog (who half-speaks her vocal) and bassist Arild Andersen, tenor saxophonist Archie Shepp and his quintet romp through the uptempo blues "Sonny's Back" in fairly straightahead if ragged fashion and, best of all, the 1970 Bobby Hutcherson-Harold Land quintet explores an original in 7/8; Land in particular is outstanding. This CD offers listeners four examples of the jazz modern mainstream of the early '70s. —*Scott Yanow*

The Lost Grooves / 1967-1970 / Blue Note ✦✦✦✦✦
Nine soul-jazz cuts from the Blue Note vaults from between 1967 and 1970, all previously unreleased, alternate takes, or (in one case) only released on a single, by major figures such as Grant Green, Lou Donaldson, Lonnie Smith, and John Patton. This doesn't really rate with the cream of the genre—all of the aforementioned artists have better work in the style available on their own full-length albums, and some of the cuts are fairly unremarkable adaptations of late '60s soul and pop hits. It's a good deal for the collector, though, offering over 70 minutes of material unavailable elsewhere. —*Richie Unterberger*

The Magnificent VII: Live at the Hilton / Dec. 6, 1992 / Arbors ✦✦✦✦
Arbors in the 1990s has become one of the top Dixieland labels around, generally focusing on all-star groups. This spirited set has an interesting cast of players: trumpeter Jon-Erik Kellso, trombonist Dan Barrett, clarinetist Chuck Hedges, Rick Fay on tenor and soprano, pianist Johnny Varro, bassist Bob Haggart and drummer Gene Estes. Together they romp through ten Dixieland and swing standards along with a lengthy "Blues for an Unknown Gypsy." Highlights include "Mandy, Make up Your Mind," "Sensation," and "Nobody's Sweetheart." Fans of these musicians and of traditional jazz in particular are advised to get this fine CD. —*Scott Yanow*

Masters of Jazz, Vol. 1: Traditional Classics / Rhino ✦✦✦
Masters of Jazz, Vol. 1: Traditional Classics is the first installment in Rhino's attempt to distill the history of jazz to a handful of discs. Of course, that means that it is designed with the neophyte in mind—scholars and jazz purists, who always disdain various artists collections and compilations in general, will find the cut and paste nature of the series overwhelmingly frustrating. However, if you are looking for an introduction to a genre as rich and complex as jazz, *Masters of Jazz* does a

fairly good job. *Masters of Jazz, Vol. 1: Traditional Classics* covers a number of standards that need to be known by any jazz fan, such as Fats Waller's "Honeysuckle Rose," Bessie Smith's "St. Louis Blues," Benny Goodman's "That's a Plenty," Duke Ellington's "Black and Tan Fantasie," and Louie Armstrong's "Struttin' with Some Barbecue." While the artists involved may have written or recorded songs that are equally classic—and several classic artists are nowhere to be seem—*Traditional Classics* remains an excellent overview of the early years of recorded jazz and the compositions and styles that provided the foundation of the entire genre. —*Leo Stanley*

Masters of Jazz, Vol. 2: Bebop's Greatest Hits / Rhino ✦✦✦
The second volume of Rhino's *Masters of Jazz* series concentrates on *Bebop's Greatest Hits,* drawing together many of the most important songs and performers from the subgenre's formative days. Featuring Charlie Parker, Dizzy Gillespie, Miles Davis, Thelonious Monk, Max Roach, Clifford Brown, Dexter Gordon, Bud Powell, and Lester Young among many others, *Bebop's Greatest Hits* hits all the main bases, making it a good introduction to the genre for neophytes. —*Stephen Thomas Erlewine*

Masters of Jazz, Vol. 3: Big Bands of the '30s & '40s / Rhino ✦✦✦
Big Bands of the '30s & '40s is the third installment in Rhino's *Masters of Jazz.* Featuring performances by the orchestras of Duke Ellington, Count Basie, Lionel Hampton, Dizzy Gillespie, Billy Eckstine, Benny Goodman, Erskine Hawkins, Jimmie Lunceford, Bennie Moten, Earl Hines and Jimmy Dorsey, the disc gives a good overview of the era when jazz was still one of the most popular musical genres in America. —*Stephen Thomas Erlewine*

Masters of Jazz, Vol. 4: Big Bands of the '50s & '60s / Rhino ✦✦✦
Big Bands of the '50s & '60s begins where the previous volume of Rhino's *Masters of Jazz* series left off, picking up the story of the big bands at the dawn of the '50s, when the genre was beginning to lose steam. Consequently, the 18 tracks on this collection don't all adhere to the formula that was written by the big bands documented on the previous disc. Instead, this compilation presents variations on the formula, whether its Jimmy Smith & Wes Montgomery playing with a large band as support, or the innovations of Charles Mingus' "Better Get Hit in Yo' Soul." Of course, the beginning of the disc features several standards, like Count Basie's "April in Paris" or Stan Kenton's "What's New?." But, of all the discs in the *Jazz Masters* series, *Big Bands of the '50s & '60s* has to stretch the most to make its case. It's to its credit that it does and, in the process, it provides the neophyte with a good basic knowledge of the music. —*Stephen Thomas Erlewine*

Masters of Jazz, Vol. 5: Female Vocal Classics / Mar. 23, 1937-Dec. 6, 1963 / Rhino ✦✦✦✦
Seventeen different female jazz singers are heard on 18 numbers (Ella Fitzgerald appears twice) on this worthwhile sampler. Many of the performances were quite popular and there are strong examples of the talents of Lena Horne ("Stormy Weather"), Mildred Bailey ("Rockin' Chair"), Billie Holiday, Anita O'Day ("Let Me Off Uptown"), Ella, Sarah Vaughan ("If You Could See Me Now"), Betty Roche ("Take the 'A' Train" with Duke Ellington), Annie Ross ("Twisted"), Peggy Lee, June Christy, Jeri Southern, Chris Connor, Gloria Lynne, Nancy Wilson, Etta Jones ("Don't Go to Strangers"), Nina Simone and Betty Carter. Worth picking up by listeners new to jazz who do not already own these classics. —*Scott Yanow*

Masters of Jazz, Vol. 6: Male Vocal Classics / Dec. 23, 1930-Mar. 3, 1969 / Rhino ✦✦✦✦
While *Vol. 5* of this valuable sampler series features female vocalists, this CD has one selection apiece from 18 male singers with more than its share of classic performances. The vocalists include Cab Calloway ("Some of These Days"), Louis Armstrong, Louis Prima, Dizzy Gillespie, Billy Eckstine, Nat King Cole ("Lush Life"), King Pleasure ("Moody's Mood for Love"), Chet Baker ("My Funny Valentine"), Jon Hendricks (a rare early version of "Cloudburst"), Joe Williams, Jackie Paris, Bill Henderson ("Senor Blues"), Oscar Brown Jr., Jack Teagarden, Mose Allison ("Your Mind Is on Vacation"), Mel Tormé, Johnny Hartman ("My One and Only Love") and Jimmy Scott. An excellent introduction to these unique performers. —*Scott Yanow*

Masters of Jazz, Vol. 7: Jazz Hit Singles / Oct. 12, 1949-Jun. 26, 1967 / Rhino ✦✦✦✦
Although one does not think of the 1950s and '60s as a period when jazz had a lot of "hits," occasionally a fluke recording would make the charts and catch on. Nineteen fairly popular cuts (although not "Take Five" or "Hello Dolly") from the 1949-67 period (all but the first two are from 1959-67) are included on this Rhino CD collection in their 45 single versions which were often expertly edited to be briefer than their LP counterpart. Such artists as James Moody (a version of "I'm in the Mood for Love" that was the basis for "Moody's Mood for Love"), Count Basie, Charles Mingus, the Jazztet ("Killer Joe"), Gene Ammons, John Coltrane (a greatly truncated version of "My Favorite Things"), Eddie Harris ("Exodus"), Herbie Mann,

Stan Getz ("Desafinado"), Jimmy Smith, Hank Crawford, Vince Guaraldi ("Cast Your Fate to Tthe Wind"), Jimmy McGriff, Mongo Santamaria, Donald Byrd, Horace Silver, Ramsey Lewis, Cannonball Adderley ("Mercy, Mercy, Mercy") and Wes Montgomery are all represented in this interesting sampler. —*Scott Yanow*

Masters of Regional Jazz / Feb. 1, 1935-Sep. 18, 1937 / Harrison ✦✦✦
With one exception (four numbers from a Clarence Williams led group from 1935 titled the Birmingham Serenaders) all of the music on this collectors' LP features bands from the South. The original Yellow Jackets (no relation to the Yellowjackets of the 1990s), Jimmy Luverte's Society Troubadours and Ted Mays' Band are long forgotten, but two numbers from the Carolina Cotton Pickers in 1937 are notable for being the recording debut of both trumpeter Cat Anderson and pianist Cliff Smalls. It's an interesting if now difficult-to-find LP that is recommended to specialists of the era. —*Scott Yanow*

Masters of Regional Jazz, Vol. 2 / Jan. 29, 1935+Aug. 14, 1935 / Harrison ✦✦✦
Even collectors of 1930s jazz will be unfamiliar with the two San Antonio-based groups heard on this collectors' LP: the KXYZ Novelty Band and Joe Kennedy's Rhythm Orchestra. Both groups are two-horn sextets that mostly stick to swing and Dixieland standards of the era; none of the sidemen succeeded in becoming famous later on. This is interesting and rare music that is unlikely to be reissued on CD anytime soon. —*Scott Yanow*

Masters of Regional Jazz, Vol. 3 / Jan. 2, 1931-Apr. 6, 1938 / Harrison ✦✦✦
Harrison's series of obscure and mostly unheard hot dance and jazz band recordings from the 1920s and '30s (which numbers around 25 LPs) includes three volumes in a miniseries of *Regional Jazz* recordings. Nine of the 16 recordings on this LP are by Boots and His Buddies, a spirited if sometimes out-of-tune San Antonio band; all of its music has since been reissued on CD. In addition there are five good numbers from the Original St. Louis Crackerjacks and a song apiece from Leon Rene's Orchestra and Williams' Purple Knights. The overall results are not too essential but collectors of the era's music who do not have the Boots sides elsewhere (and who can locate this hard-to-find album) may want to get the Harrison LP. —*Scott Yanow*

Masters of the Modern Piano / Apr. 25, 1955-Feb. 1, 1966 / Verve ✦✦✦✦✦
This excellent two-LP set (which draws its material from the vaults of Verve) has a strong cross-section of modern pianists covering a ten-year period. Bud Powell is heard on six numbers with bassist George Duvivier and drummer Art Taylor in 1955 and, although Powell was no longer in peak form, in general he plays well. There is also music from Mary Lou Williams (performing "The Zodiac Suite" and "Carioca" with the Dizzy Gillespie Orchestra), Paul Bley (three fairly free trios from 1961 with clarinetist Jimmy Giuffre and bassist Steve Swallow), Wynton Kelly (who plays "Blues on Purpose" in 1965) and two songs from the 1966 Bill Evans Trio. The most interesting selections however are the three numbers performed by the Cecil Taylor Quartet (with Steve Lacy on soprano, bassist Buell Neidlinger and drummer Dennis Charles) at the 1957 Newport Jazz Festival. It is fascinating to hear Taylor take apart Billy Strayhorn's "Johnny Come Lately," a blues and his own "Tune 2"; this is as accessible as Cecil Taylor ever got. Although some of the music on this two-fer has been reissued on CD, the attractive set is still recommended to those listeners who happen to run across it. —*Scott Yanow*

Mercury 40th Anniversary / Dec. 5, 1945-Mar. 27, 1965 / Mercury ✦✦✦✦✦
To celebrate its 40th birthday and revival, Mercury came up with this attractive and valuable four-LP box set which comprises material largely unreleased at the time. The performances (mostly from the 1950s) feature such greats as Erroll Garner, Arnett Cobb, Clark Terry, Dinah Washington, Paul Quinichette, Junior Mance, Paul Bley, Helen Merrill, Clifford Brown, John Williams, Herb Geller, Maynard Ferguson, Jimmy Cleveland, Cannonball Adderley, the Quincy Jones Orchestra, Billy Taylor, the Jazztet, Bob James (as an acoustic pianist in 1962) and Dizzy Gillespie. Some but not all of this material has resurfaced on CD and virtually all of the music is quite enjoyable. —*Scott Yanow*

The Mills Brothers—the Boswell Sisters—the Inkspots / 1935 / SMS ✦✦✦
This is a budget CD from England but, despite the very chintzy playing time (under 35 minutes) and the lack of liner notes, personnel listing or even recording dates, collectors will want it. There are four selections apiece from the Mills Brothers, the Boswell Sisters and the Inkspots and these rare items are presumably taken from radio shows. While the Boswell Sisters are heard late in their career (around 1935 as shown by the inclusion of "The Music Goes Round and Round") and the Mills Brothers are featured doing their classic imitations of instruments ("Caravan" is a gem), the Inkspots are showcased before they found their ballad style, when they were a hot group that was closely emulating the Mills Brothers; "Christopher Columbus" and "With Plenty of Money and You" is the type of jazz-oriented material that they did not perform after hitting it big. This is a set for the group's greatest fans; hopefully the enjoyable music will be reissued in a more coherent form someday. —*Scott Yanow*

Milton Jazz Concert 1963 / Apr. 26, 1963 / IAJRC ✦✦✦
Released on CD by the collector's label IAJRC, this concert features an all-star front line (cornetist Bobby Hackett, trombonist Vic Dickenson and clarinetist Edmond Hall) with a local rhythm section. Together they perform a blues, a ballad medley and ten hot Dixieland/swing standards (including "Struttin' with Some Barbecue," "Indiana," "Fidgety Feet" and "China Boy"). The recording quality is decent, all of the principals are in fine form and one can consider this to be a predecessor of the quintet that Hackett and Dickenson would co-lead at the tail-end of the decade. —*Scott Yanow*

Milton Jazz Concert 1964 / Apr. 24, 1964 / IAJRC ✦✦✦
For a concert put on in Milton, MA, (and released for the first time on this 1995 CD) several classic jazz veterans were teamed with some solid local musicians for a variety of Dixieland standards. Trumpeter Yank Lawson, trombonist Vic Dickenson, clarinetist Edmond Hall and pianist Dick Wellstood appear in a sextet for four songs (highlighted by Dickenson's witty growls on "Basin Street Blues" and a spirited "Hello Dolly") while trumpeter Buck Clayton stars on four other warhorses. High points of the CD are on the two numbers ("At the Jazz Band Ball" and "Struttin' with Some Barbecue") on which the two bands are combined; in both cases Yank and Buck get to trade off hot phrases. It's a worthy release by the collector's club IAJRC (International Association of Jazz Record Collectors). —*Scott Yanow*

☆ **Mod Jazz** / 1958 / Kent ✦✦✦✦✦
Taken from the vaults of the Prestige, Riverside, Battle, and Fantasy labels, this is one of the finest collections of vintage soul-jazz you're likely to come across. The 25 tracks span 1958 to 1971, and include good cuts from core proponents of the style, such as Brother Jack McDuff, Boogaloo "Joe" Jones, and Jimmy Witherspoon. What gives this compilation a leg up on some of the competition is its eclecticism: there are vocalists (Mose Allison), organists (Shirley Scott), Latin jazzers (Cal Tjader, Mongo Santamaria), and a few top jazz names not primarily associated with the genre (Eddie Jefferson, Otis Spann, Kenny Burrell, Sonny Stittt). To its credit, it's not stuffily purist either, making way for a bunch of nifty soul-jazz TV themes, a cover of "Evil Ways" by Cal Tjader, and no-names like Pat Bowie, the Merced Blue Notes, and Billy Hawks. It results in much more variety than most anthologies of the sort, without any drop in the groove factor. —*Richie Unterberger*

New Orleans 1924-1925 / Mar. 15, 1924-Jan. 23, 1925 / Rhapsody ✦✦✦
This interesting LP has the first jazz records ever made in New Orleans. OKeh Records conducted two field trips (one during March 15-16, 1924, and the other during Jan. 22-23, 1925) and the results were excellent recordings from Johnny DeDroit, two blues from singer Lola Bolden, disappointingly primitive performances by Fate Marable (his band's only two recordings), a pair of vaudevillian numbers from Billy & Mary Mack, one song apiece from Russ Papalia and the New Orleans Rhythm Kings and three fine numbers by Oscar Celestin's Original Tuxedo Jazz Orchestra. This worthy English import contains some music not yet reissued on CD. —*Scott Yanow*

● **New Orleans Collective** / Dec. 28, 1992 / Evidence ✦✦✦✦✦
Trumpeter Nicholas Payton is teamed up with Wessell Anderson (who doubles on sopranino and alto), pianist Peter Martin, bassist Christopher Thomas and drummer Brian Blade for an unusual set of music that shifts between hard bop and New Orleans jazz. While "Rhonda Mile" (which uses the chord changes to "Indiana") is pure bop, other selections combine the two idioms, and "Four or Five Times" (listed as an Anderson original but actually a standard from the 1920s) is strictly Dixieland. A high point is the 16-minute "He Was a Good Man, Oh Yes He Was" which musically depicts a New Orleans funeral. Throughout, Anderson (particularly on the sopranino which he plays like a clarinet) and Payton work together quite well in the exciting ensembles and show impressive knowlege of earlier forms of jazz while carving out their own individual voices. —*Scott Yanow*

New Orleans Jazz Giants: 1936-1940 / Jan. 15, 1936-Jun. 5, 1940 / JSP ✦✦✦✦✦
There are 26 recordings on this imported CD from the English JSP label. These interesting and often historical performances feature a variety of New Orleans veterans, particularly clarinetists Jimmie Noone and Johnny Dodds. Noone is heard on 14 performances including a session with trumpeter Guy Kelly and trombonist Preston Jackson, a particularly strong outing with trumpeter Charlie Shavers and altoist Pete Brown, and on two songs with a group that includes the erratic cornetist Natty Dominique. Dodds' final session uses the same Dominique group but his earlier sextet set with Shavers is much more rewarding. In addition there are two songs apiece from trumpeter Red Allen and drummer Zutty Singleton, both recorded the same day in 1940 with the identical personnel. In general the music is quite enjoyable and, Dominique excepted, the veterans and relative youngsters (Shavers was 20) play quite well. —*Scott Yanow*

New Orleans Trumpets / Nov. 1, 1950-May 16, 1954 / Storyville ✦✦✦
On ten LPs (and reissued as ten CDs), the European Storyville label came out with a variety of rare performances recorded in New Orleans during the 1950s. None of

the 13 selections on this particular volume were included in the other entries in this series. The focus is very much on trumpeters and there are selections featuring Ernie Cagnolatti, Alvin Alcorn, Lee Collins, Papa Celestin ("The Saints"), Percy Humphrey, Lee Collins, Johnny Wiggs (who gets two songs), George Hartman, the forgotten Johnny Bayersdorffer (who is unfortunately not in good shape), Sharkey Bonano and the ill-fated but talented George Girard. These mostly live and free-wheeling performances (a few are previously unreleased alternate takes) are generally quite rewarding and easily recommended to lovers of New Orleans jazz. —*Scott Yanow*

The New Wave in Jazz / Mar. 28, 1965 / Impulse ✦✦✦✦
On March 28, 1965 several of the top "New Thing" artists who were then recording for Impulse performed at a heated concert at the Village Gate that was fully documented. This CD reissue adds two selections to the original LP while dropping an Albert Ayler performance that will be included in an Ayler reissue in the future. There is plenty of fire on the release including a searing version of "Nature Boy" from the John Coltrane Quartet, a workout on "Hambone" by tenor saxophonist Archie Shepp's Septet and two numbers apiece from trumpeter Charles Tolliver (with altoist James Spaulding) and trombonist Grachan Moncur III (with a young Bobby Hutcherson on vibes). Some of the performances are free and ferocious while other tracks are on the advanced side of bop. Over 30 years later the music still sounds adventurous and full of life. —*Scott Yanow*

New York Horns / Sep. 1924-Oct. 19, 1928 / Hot 'N Sweet ✦✦✦
This European import CD has a variety of rare early performances. Cornetist Bubber Miley is heard in his pre-Duke Ellington period performing four odd duets with organist Arthur Ray (under the title of the Texas Blue Destroyers) and jamming with the interesting if erratic Kansas City Five. In addition there are three numbers from the Blue Rhythm Orchestra (a sextet with trombonist Jimmy Harrison and clarinetist Buster Bailey), three titles by the similar Gulf Coast Seven (although its 1928 selection includes several Ellingtonians), three songs from the Five Musical Blackbirds (a quintet with cornetist Thomas Morris) and, best of all, two hot numbers from the Roy Williams Band. Even for 1920s collectors this CD is not really essential but it does have its interesting moments. —*Scott Yanow*

New York Jazz in the Roaring Twenties / Apr. 16, 1926-Jan. 27, 1928 / Biograph ✦✦✦✦✦
This CD is subtitled "Tommy Dorsey—Red Nichols—Jimmy Dorsey" but in reality the Dorsey Brothers are only heard as sidemen. Included on the enjoyable set are four selections from Red & Miff's Stompers (co-led by cornetist Nichols and trombonist Miff Mole), seven selections by the California Ramblers, two featuring the obscure Joe Herlihy's Orchestra and one by Phil Napoleon. The music ranges from hot (if complicated) '20s jazz to some jazz-oriented dance music. An improvement on Biograph's LP of the same name (due to the inclusion of a couple of extra tracks), the performances on this CD (originally released by the Edison label) are longer than the usual recordings of the era, often over four (as opposed to three) minutes long. Fans of '20s jazz will want to get this one. —*Scott Yanow*

New York Stories / 1992 / Blue Note ✦✦✦✦✦
This interesting outing by an all-star group (guitarist Danny Gatton, altoist Bobby Watson, trumpeter Roy Hargrove, Joshua Redman on tenor, pianist Franck Amsallem, bassist Charles Fambrough and drummer Yuron Israel) is most notable for featuring the brilliant Gatton in a jazz setting. Together the septet, performs nine originals by group members and Gatton and Watson emerge as the main solo stars. Despite its somewhat generic name, this advanced hard bop date is quite memorable. —*Scott Yanow*

Newport Jazz Festival: Live / Jul. 7, 1956-Jul. 7, 1963 / Columbia ✦✦✦✦✦
At the time of the release of this 1982 double LP, all of its performances (which are taken from the 1956, 1958 and 1963 Newport Jazz Festival) were previously unissued. Quite a variety of musicians are featured and most of the music is quite enjoyable. Louis Armstrong pops up in three different settings, Rex Stewart leads an all-star group comprising Duke Ellington alumni and there are selections from Ellington himself, Ben Webster, Willie "The Lion" Smith, Jimmy Rushing, Benny Goodman, Teddy Wilson, Dave Brubeck, the Miles Davis Quintet with John Coltrane ("Bye Bye Blackbird"), Thelonious Monk, Sonny Stitt, Gerry Mulligan and three all-star groups that include the likes of Bud Freeman, Ruby Braff, Buck Clayton, Jack Teagarden, Pee Wee Russell, Lester Young and Coleman Hawkins. Since the music (with a few exceptions) has not yet been reissued on CD, this two-LP set (which will be hard to find) is quite valuable both musically and historically. —*Scott Yanow*

Nova Bossa: Red Hot on Verve / 1959-1996 / Verve ✦✦✦✦✦
In the hope that *Red Hot* and *Rio* would ignite interest in Brazilian music within the X-Generation, Verve simultaneously released a historical survey with similar cover art, similar noise interludes between tracks, and occasionally, the same tunes (do not be confused!). Although some of the same old stuff reissued a thousand

times before is here (the Getz/Gilberto "The Girl from Ipanema," the Getz/Byrd "Desafinado," et al), Verve also went through the trouble to unearth some unusual items. Among the prizes are a bizarre track by organist Walter Wanderley called "Bicho Do Mato," Edu Lobo's marvelous high-energy original version of his "Upa, Neguinho," and Sergio Mendes' folk-back-to-their-roots treatment of "After Sunrise." Commendably, half of the CD is devoted to songs by composers other than Antonio Carlos Jobim—worthy figures like Lobo, Jorge Ben, Baden Powell, Joao Gilberto, Caetano Veloso and Gilberto Gil. Not all bases are adequately covered—there is no tropicalismo beyond its late '60s infancy and there is nothing from a giant like Milton Nascimento. Still, this is one of those rare collections that will appeal to the newcomer and the connoisseur. —*Richard S. Ginell*

● **Obscure and Neglected Chicagoans** / 1925-Dec. 21, 1929 / IAJRC ✦✦✦✦✦
This CD from the International Association of Jazz Record Collectors (IAJRC) is one of their most exciting, particularly for collectors of 1920s jazz. Even fanatics of the era will probably not have the great majority of the 25 selections included on this very valuable disc. Released for the first time anywhere are two numbers from a demonstration record by Dud Mecum's Wolverines in 1925 that feature the remains of the group that launched the career of Bix Beiderbecke; it is miraculous that these well-recorded performances (starring the tenor of George Johnson) still exist. Also included on this set are six numbers from the Original Wolverines in 1927-28 with cornetist Jimmy McPartland, eleven selections by Ray Miller's hot dance orchestra from 1928-29 (some of which have cornet solos from Muggsy Spanier) and six songs from the totally forgotten but enjoyable band Thelma Terry and Her Boyfriends, a group that also includes a young Gene Krupa. Highly recommended to serious collectors of vintage jazz. —*Scott Yanow*

● **One Night with Blue Note Preserved** / Feb. 22, 1985 / Blue Note ✦✦✦✦✦
This four-LP set, whose material was also made available as single LPs and single CDs, not only extensively documented a historic concert that paid tribute to the Blue Note label's legacy but was the start of that important record company's comeback. *Vol. 1* features veterans Herbie Hancock on piano, trumpeter Freddie Hubbard, tenor saxophonist Joe Henderson, bassist Ron Carter, drummer Tony Williams and vibraphonist Bobby Hutcherson on remakes of "Canteloupe Island" and "Recorda Me" and a pair of Hutcherson pieces but flutist James Newton takes honors with his version of Eric Dolphy's "Hat and Beard." The second set features strong advanced hard bop music from an all-star quintet (pianist McCoy Tyner, altoist Jackie McLean, trumpeter Woody Shaw, bassist Cecil McBee and drummer Jack DeJohnette), a trio workout by tenor Bennie Wallace and a typically intense piano solo from Cecil Taylor. The third album has an Art Blakey reunion band playing "Moanin'," numbers featuring either tenor Stanley Turrentine or altoist Lou Donaldson with organist Jimmy Smith, guitarist Kenny Burrell and drummer Grady Tate, and two songs in which Grover Washington, Jr., (on soprano) plays with Burrell, Tate and bassist Reggie Workman. The final set has five numbers by Charles Lloyd (on tenor and flute at the beginning of a successful comeback), pianist Michel Petrucciani, bassist Cecil McBee and drummer Jack Dejohnette but saves the best for last, two amazing guitar solos from Stanley Jordan. Obviously this music on the whole is highly recommended for all jazz collections. —*Scott Yanow*

The Original Sound of "The Twenties" / Jul. 29, 1922-Aug. 9, 1932 / Columbia ✦✦✦✦✦
One of many valuable box sets released by Columbia in the mid-'60s, this particular three-LP reissue has 47 selections that range from jazz and dance music to pop vocals and piano solos. Paul Whiteman's Orchestra is well-represented and such major names of the 1920s as Duke Ellington, Bing Crosby, Joe Venuti, Louis Armstrong, Ted Lewis, Ruth Etting, Ethel Waters, Sophie Tucker, Rudy Vallee and Kate Smith are also heard from, in addition to lesser knowns such as Cass Hagan's Park Central Hotel Orchestra, Red McKenzie (a great version of "From Monday On"), Blossom Seely and Lee Morse. Although not quite essential, there are enough rarities on the set (in addition to a very attractive booklet) to make this box worth searching for. —*Scott Yanow*

The Original V-Disc Collection / Jun. 1943-Dec. 30, 1944 / Pickwick ✦✦✦✦✦
This two-CD set contains 40 selections taken from V-Discs, special recordings made specifically for servicemen abroad during World War II. Since a Musicians Union recording strike was taking place during the period, these performances are even more valuable than usual because they document musicians at a time when they were not on commercial records. Nearly all of the music was previously included in Time/Life's four-CD V-Disc set but those collectors who do not have that reissue will find the selections of great interest. Not all of the performances are jazz (Marian Anderson, Perry Como, Andre Kostelanetz, Josh White, Paul Robeson and Kay Kyser make appearances), but most are and the highlights are many: Hot Lips Page's "The Sheik of Araby," Pee Wee Russell's strange vocal on "Pee Wee Speaks," Louis Jordan's "Is You Is or Is You Ain't My Baby," Tony Pastor's alternate lyrics to "Makin' Whoopee," Johnny Long's "In a Shanty in Old Shantytown," a re-

creation of the Original Dixieland Jazz Band's version of "Tiger Rag," Woody Herman's early rendition of "Apple Honey" and Art Tatum's reworking of "Liza." —*Scott Yanow*

The Pablo All-Stars Jam: Montreux '77 / Jul. 14, 1977 / Original Jazz Classics ✦✦✦

This CD reissue expands upon the original Pablo LP by adding a fifth song ("Sweethearts on Parade") to the original fourtune program. This jam session differs from Pablo's other recordings in that it includes the great English tenor Ronnie Scott along with the regular all-star personnel (vibraphonist Milt Jackson, flugehornist Clark Terry, guitarist Joe Pass, pianist Oscar Peterson, bassist Niels Pedersen and drummer Bobby Durham). Everyone plays well on the standards but Terry takes honors with a beautiful statement on "God Bless the Child." —*Scott Yanow*

The Pete Johnson/Earl Hines/Teddy Bunn Blue Note Sessions / Jul. 29, 1939-Mar. 28, 1940 / Mosaic ✦✦✦✦✦

One of Mosaic's pet projects was the complete reissue of all of the Blue Note label's early prebop recordings. This single LP has three unrelated but enjoyable small-group sessions originally cut for Blue Note. Pete Johnson is heard on two piano solos and in a trio for four other songs with guitarist Ulysses Livingston and bassist Abe Bolar. Earl Hines takes a couple of typically miraculous piano solos ("The Father's Getaway" and "Reminiscing at Blue Note") and guitarist Teddy Bunn is featured unaccompanied on four cuts plus an alternate take, one of his very rare opportunities to lead a recording session. Although this set is now out of print, swing fans will want to go out of their way to find it if they do not have the music elsewhere. —*Scott Yanow*

A Piano Anthology / Apr. 20, 1926-Mar. 8, 1968 / GRP/Decca ✦✦✦

This CD contains selections from 20 pianists, all but two (Dodo Marmarosa and Bill Evans) who play in pre-bop styles. Taken mostly from the Decca catalog, the collection has many fine performances highlighted by Jelly Roll Morton's "The Pearls," Fats Waller and James P. Johnson playing together on Johnny Dunn's "What's the Use of Being Alone," Joe Sullivan's "Little Rock Getaway," an alternate take of Art Tatum's "Deep Purple" and rare performances from Frank Melrose, Billy Kyle, Clarence Profit and Ralph Sutton. Not essential but this reissue has plenty of enjoyable music for fans of swing piano. —*Scott Yanow*

Piano Players & Significant Others (Jazz in July Live at the 92nd Street Y) / Jul. 31, 1985-Jul. 20, 1988 / Music Masters ✦✦✦

This is a fun CD. The 13 performances are taken from Dick Hyman's Jazz in July series and, as the title implies, the emphasis is on the pianists which in this case include Hyman, Derek Smith, Jay McShann, Ralph Sutton, Dick Wellstood, Marian McPartland and Roger Kellaway. There are a pair of wonderful Ralph Sutton solos, duets by Hyman with Wellstood and Smith and a closing "Nagasaki" that finds Hyman, Sutton and Smith all battling it out on three pianos. In addition cornetist Ruby Braff is on two numbers and Carrie Smith sings "Fine and Mellow." Excellent swing-based music. —*Scott Yanow*

Piano Playhouse / Sep. 13, 1957 / V.S.O.P. ✦✦✦

The recordings on this LP were originally supposed to be released by the Mode label in the late '50s but the company went defunct before it could come out. Released for the first time by V.S.O.P. in 1986, these 16 selections (all recorded the same day) feature five different pianists (Carl Perkins, Jimmy Rowles, Paul Smith, Gerald Wiggins and Lou Levy) in fine form on three or four songs apiece. It is interesting to compare the players' similar but individual styles and to see how they adapt their bop-based approaches to the demands of playing solo. —*Scott Yanow*

Piano Singer's Blues / Nov. 15, 1926-Mar. 14, 1962 / Rosetta ✦✦✦

The hook for this typically attractive Rosetta LP is that the 16 selections all feature female singers accompanying themselves on piano. Many of the performances are a bit rare and such diverse artists as Georgia White, Gladys Bentley, Edith Johnson, Billie Pierce, Arizona Dranes, Fannie May Goosby, Cleo Brown, Hociel Thomas, Julia Lee, Bernice Edwards, Hazel Scott, Nellie Lutcher, Una Mae Carlisle, Victoria Spivey, Hadda Brooks and Lil Armstrong are all heard in fine form. Recommended to fans of classic jazz. —*Scott Yanow*

Piano Summit / Oct. 30, 1965 / Philology ✦✦✦

This must have been a very interesting concert to attend. On "Blues in D" bassist Niels Pedersen and drumer Alan Dawson accompany six pianists: Earl Hines, Teddy Wilson, John Lewis, Lennie Tristano, Bill Evans and Jaki Byard. In addition there are individual features for each of the pianists in a trio and Hines performs "All of Me" with Wilson and "Rosetta" with Byard. Released by an Italian label but available through mail order, this unique outing (which has some of Tristano's final concert performances) lives up to its potential. —*Scott Yanow*

Playboy's 40th Anniversary: Four Decades of Jazz 1953-1993 / Jul. 1953-1993 / Verve ✦✦✦

To celebrate the 40th anniversary of *Playboy* Magazine, this four-CD box set was compiled and released. The music is drawn from many catalogs (in addition to Verve) and is a sampler of some of the jazz styles from the 40-year period with the emphasis on greatest hits. From Charlie Parker's "Now's the Time," Errol Garner's "Misty," Dave Brubeck's "Take Five," John Coltrane's "Giant Steps," Astrud Gilberto's "The Girl from Ipanema," and Lee Morgan's "Sidewinder" to Donald Byrd's "Black Byrd," Grover Washington, Jr.'s "Mister Magic," Kenny G.'s "Songbird" and Bobby McFerrin's "Don't Worry, Be Happy," many famous numbers are included, although Dixieland, the avant-garde, and creative fusion are completely ignored. The general collector may want to pick up this set as an introduction to some of these jazz artists, but they should be warned that this reissue does not give listeners the entire picture of the jazz world. —*Scott Yanow*

Playing for Keeps / Jan. 4, 1992 / GM ✦✦✦

This CD matches together three under-recorded veterans: trumpeter Joe Wilder (69 at the time of the 1992 session), trombonist Britt Woodman and tenor saxophonist John LaPorta (the latter two were both 71). Although Wilder and Woodman both show their age at times, the trumpeter's tone remains one of the prettiest ones around while Woodman (wah-wahing his way through "Britt's Blues") often steals the show with his spirited solos. LaPorta, doubling between tenor and clarinet, was never a major stylist but his fairly complex playing still sounds quite viable. Guitarist Jack Wilkins (along with bassist Ed Schuller and drummer George Schuller) does a fine job but this set would have swung harder and been more versatile had a pianist been included. Even with a few adventurous pieces (most notably "While You Were Out"), the majority of the performances are straightforward renditions of standards. An interesting set, both musically and historically. —*Scott Yanow*

RCA Victor 80th Anniversary / 191 / RCA ✦✦✦✦✦

This is an attractive eight-CD set, whose discs are also available as eight separate releases, that could have been a great reissue but settled for being merely quite good. To celebrate the 80th anniversary of the first jazz recording, RCA released a disc apiece covering each of the past eight decades. In listening to the music straight through, one becomes aware of RCA's strengths and weaknesses as a jazz label. Victor was one of the most important jazz labels during the 1920s, '30s and '40s, catching on to bebop during the late (1946) but still documenting many classic recordings. By the 1950s, the label's attention was wandering elsewhere; it missed free jazz almost completely in the '60s, and in the last three decades has only had a few significant artists, mostly Young Lions whose output sounds conservative compared to the earlier masters. This reissue is particularly strong during the first three discs, and then for some reason (starting with disc four) commits a major error in departing from programming the music in strict chronological order (although each disc does stay within the ten-year period). Also, the selection of the performances is much better in the earlier decades (especially the 1917-29 set) than during the past two decades. There are many highlights throughout the large undertaking, with such artists as the Original Dixieland Jazz Band, Jelly Roll Morton, Fletcher Henderson, Duke Ellington, King Oliver, Louis Armstrong, Cab Calloway, Benny Goodman, Glenn Miller, Coleman Hawkins, Dizzy Gillespie, Benny Carter, Art Tatum, Charles Mingus, Red Allen, Bud Powell, Sonny Rollins, Buddy Rich, Gil Evans, the Brecker Brothers, Roy Hargrove, Marcus Roberts, Steve Coleman and Dominique Eade among the many represented. In addition, a "bonus" disc has two numbers by the ODJB (including for the second time "Livery Stable Blues") and a previously unreleased Mingus dramatic piece "A Colloquial Dream." If only some better planning had gone into the later discs. —*Scott Yanow*

● RCA Victor Jazz Workshop: The Arrangers / Mar. 3, 1956-Jul. 8, 1965 / Bluebird ✦✦✦✦✦

A lot of unusual music appears on this Bluebird CD. Altoist Hal McKusick (with arrangements contributed by George Russell and Gil Evans) performs five numbers (including a version of "Blues for Pablo" that was cut a year before Miles Davis' recording) with a variety of musicians including trumpeter Art Farmer and trombonist Jimmy Cleveland. Arranger John Carisi (heard here on trumpet) interprets seven previously unreleased numbers with an octet and trombonist Rod Levitt performs five of his arrangements with his own advanced octet. Although these performances would have little influence on future developments in jazz (the free jazz movement of the 1960s overshadowed the trend towards using elements of modern classical music in charts), the music still sounds quite fresh and unpredictable today. —*Scott Yanow*

● RCA Victor Jazz: The First Half-Century—The Twenties Through the Sixties / Mar. 25, 1918-Aug. 18, 1967 / Bluebird ✦✦✦✦✦

RCA has long had an up-and-down relationship with jazz and that is reflected in this very interesting five-CD boxed set drawn completely from their archives. Each disc focuses on a specific decade and the producers did an excellent job of picking representative recordings. The 1920s and '30s are covered particularly well (with

23 selections on each disc); virtually every major name is heard at their prime. The 1940s disc also contains many valuable recordings (although RCA had been slow to record bop), but by the '50s and '60s RCA was not in the forefront of discovering up-and-coming artists; there are only hints of the avant-garde and many of the giants (Miles Davis, John Coltrane and Thelonious Monk to name three) never made it into the label's studios. However, even in the later decades, a variety of great veterans and modernists did make significant recordings for the label and there is not a loser among the 96 recordings. Overall this reissue gives one a superb overview of RCA jazz activities through the years (from Coleman Hawkins' "Body and Soul" to Sonny Rollins' "The Bridge") and is recommended to jazz historians along with beginners starting to explore this classic music. —*Scott Yanow*

Rags to Rhythms / Jan. 24, 1906-Jul. 15, 1926 / Memphis Archives ◆◆◆
This is an interesting but odd reissue CD. The first 11 selections are mostly rarities from the ragtime era (1906-1913) including Jim Europe's Society Orchestra ("Down Home Rag"), three banjo showcases, two piano solos and a xylophone feature on "Dill Pickles Rag." However, the remaining seven recordings are from the 1920s and, although "Rag" appears in all of their titles, the music (by the likes of King Oliver, Jelly Roll Morton and the New Orleans Rhythm Kings) is actually early jazz and mostly available elsewhere. This project would have been more significant if it had stuck exclusively with pre-1915 material. —*Scott Yanow*

☆ **Ragtime** / 1900-Dec. 10, 1930 / RCA ◆◆◆◆◆
It is a pity that the music on this two-LP set has not yet been reissued in RCA's Jazz Tribune series for it contains are some of the finest recordings of the prejazz era. The 38 selections feature such top early artists and bands as banjoist Vess Ossman, John Phillip Sousa, Arthur Pryor, the Victor Dance Orchestra, banjoist Fred Van Eps, pianist Felix Arndt (playing his "Desecration Rag"), James Reese Europe, Conway's Band (on the classic "Hungarian Rag"), the Six Brown Brothers (a saxophone sextet in 1916) and Eubie Blake, concluding with a version of "Maple Leaf Rag" from 1930. A definitive survey into the ragtime era on records, among the selections are "Trombone Sneeze," "Saint Louis Rag," "Dill Pickles Rag," "At a Georgia Camp Meeting," "Alexander's Ragtime Band," "The Ragtime Drummer" (a drum feature in 1912!) and "Too Much Mustard." A gem. —*Scott Yanow*

Ragtime Piano Originals / Jun. 27, 1913-Jul. 6, 1929 / Smithsonian/Folkways ◆◆◆
During the 1970's, Folkways put out a series of hodge-podge ragtime collections that, although not complete and often lacking recording dates, made available a variety of very rare recordings. This particular LP has 16 examples of pianists performing their own works. Other than Rube Bloom, Arthur Schutt and Mike Bernard (and those players are no longer household names), the performers are quite obscure. However the performances (which often fall into the novelty ragtime genre) contain plenty of exciting moments and show off the musicians' technical skills. —*Scott Yanow*

The Rare Dawn Sessions / May 12, 1949-Sep. ??, 1956 / Biograph ◆◆◆
This CD reissue, which features four classic tenor saxophonists, brings back material released by Biograph on LPs in the 1980s. Stan Getz jams on four songs with a five-piece rhythm section that includes pianist Al Haig and guitarist Jimmy Raney in 1949, Wardell Gray uses a similar group on his two pieces, Paul Quinichette does his impressions of Lester Young on two songs in a quintet with trumpeter Gene Roland and pianist Nat Pierce, and Zoot Sims swings on six pieces with a quintet including trumpeter Jerry Lloyd. The music should satisfy straightahead jazz fans and, although no longer all that rare, it serves as a good introduction to the work of the four tenors. —*Scott Yanow*

The Real Kansas City / May 1925-Mar. 2, 1939 / Columbia/Legacy ◆◆◆
Put together to coincide with the release of Robert Altman's film *Kansas City*, this sampler traces the evolution of Kansas City jazz from 1925-39. Certainly recommended much more for general listeners than for completists, this CD has fine music (fortunately programmed in chronological order) from Bennie Moten, Jesse Stone, Julia Lee, George E. Lee's Novelty Singing Orchestra, Walter Page's Blue Devils, Fletcher Henderson, Andy Kirk, Don Albert, the Carolina Cotton Pickers, the Original Yellow Jackets, Harry James, Pete Johnson, Count Basie, Ernie Fields, Pete Johnson and Joe Turner, Mary Lou Williams, Harlan Leonard, Jay McShann, Horace Henderson and Billie Holiday. A fine introduction to the joyful swing music of Kansas City. —*Scott Yanow*

● **Recorded in New Orleans, Vol. 1** / Mar. 24, 1956-Apr. 28, 1956 / Good Time Jazz ◆◆◆◆◆
In 1956 the Good Time Jazz label traveled to New Orleans and recorded eight different regularly working bands for three songs apiece, releasing the results on two LPs; both volumes have been reissued on CD. The musicianship is quite high throughout this series and there are many fine soloists in addition to spirited ensembles. *Vol. 1* has music from trumpeter Sharkey Bonano's Kings of Dixieland (a sextet that includes a young Pete Fountain on clarinet) along with bands headed

by drummer Paul Barbarin, trombonist Bill Matthews and the late great trumpeter George Girard. It's recommended as is *Vol. 2*. —*Scott Yanow*

● **Recorded in New Orleans, Vol. 2** / Mar. 10, 1956-May 26, 1956 / Good Time Jazz ◆◆◆◆◆
The Good Time Jazz label in 1956 ventured to New Orleans and recorded eight working bands for three songs apiece, giving listeners a good overview of the then-contemporary New Orleans jazz scene. The two LPs that were released at the time have been reissued on CDs and both are highly recommended to fans of New Orleans jazz. *Vol. 2* has performances from bands led by cornetist Johnny Wiggs, trombonist Eddie Pierson and trombonist Santo Pecora in addition to pianist Armand Hug's trio. The high-quality music has impressive musicianship and plenty of spirit. —*Scott Yanow*

Red, White & Blues / Aug. 23, 1928-Nov. 26, 1961 / Rosetta ◆◆◆
The LPs released by Rosetta generally feature pre-bop female jazz vocalists dealing with a particular subject matter. The 15 performances on this set all have a city, state or some aspect of a town in its title. There are consistently strong performances from Billie Holiday, Ethel Waters, Lillian Glinn, Ivie Anderson, Victoria Spivey, Rosetta Howard, Mildred Bailey, Bessie Smith ("St. Louis Blues" from the film of the same name), Blue Lou Barker, Ella Fitzgerald, Helen Humes, Bertha "Chippie" Hill, Betty Roche (a rare broadcast version of "Take the 'A' Train" with Duke Ellington), Julia Lee, Lil Armstrong and Blossom Seeley. Although the LP is not really essential, the very appealing packaging and high-quality music makes it difficult to resist. —*Scott Yanow*

Riverboat Shuffle / 1926-1936 / Memphis Archives ◆◆◆
The 18 songs on this unusual sampler all have something to with the Mississippi River. With such titles as "Steamboat Bill," "Mississippi Mud," "River Stay Away from My Door" and "Floating down to Cotton Town," the plot of the CD is obvious. Some of the material is rare while other cuts are fairly common. Highlights include The Boswell Sisters' "Roll on, Mississippi, Roll On," Paul Whiteman's "Selections from *Showboat*," Paul Robeson singing "Ol' Man River" and two titles from Wingy Manone. —*Scott Yanow*

● **Riverside Records Story** / Jan. 25, 1955-Sep. 20, 1963 / Riverside ◆◆◆◆
The *Riverside Records Story* is essentially Orrin Keepnews' baby—and why not, for the grizzled jazz producer/journalist co-founded the label, ran it from day one in 1952 until it suddenly went bankrupt in 1964, and produced almost all of the original sessions. Riverside's current custodians at Fantasy had Keepnews select and sequence four CDs' worth of the label's output, which over the span of less than nine years made a big splash in the cloistered world of hard bop. Keepnews also writes a voluminous set of notes that settles old scores, crows about What Went Right, offers often self-deprecating analyses of What Went Wrong, and generally keeps the reader riveted to the pages. The box is loosely organized around four topics instead of the usual chronological rundown—indeed, the earliest track, Randy Weston's "Zulu," comes last—and Keepnews devotes lots of time to four major figures whose extensive recordings for Riverside form the cornerstones of their reputations—Cannonball Adderley, Bill Evans, Thelonious Monk and Wes Montgomery. There are some imaginative sequences that give the collection extra star power—like Monk performing his standards with Coleman Hawkins, John Coltrane, Gerry Mulligan and Clark Terry respectively—and there is a welcome touch of the bizarre, too, like Philly Joe Jones' hammy "Blues for Dracula." Moreover, gratefully defying some of his holier-than-thou pronouncements elsewhere, Keepnews does not shy away from his own ventures into the commercial sphere, including Wes with strings on "Tune Up," Charlie Byrd likewise on "Meditation," Mongo Santamaria's Top Ten hit "Watermelon Man," and some soul-jazz singles. The first two discs by and large are consistently strong, while some of the lesser tracks on the remaining discs may be there more to represent the artist than to thrill the listener. Riverside collectors will note that there are none of the leased early jazz tracks from Riverside's infancy, no unreleased tracks, and only two of the 53 selections have never been reissued by Fantasy. But the sound is mostly superb, everything coming from crisp new 1997 digital transfers from the original master tapes—and truthfully, they have never sounded better than they do here. —*Richard S. Ginell*

● **Saturday Night Swing Club** / Jun. 12, 1937 / Memphis Archives ◆◆◆◆◆
This double CD brings back an entire radio broadcast, the first anniversary show of the legendary *Saturday Night Swing Club*. The many performances are often classic, the recording quality is excellent (except for three songs by Django Reinhardt and Stephane Grappelli that were performed live in France and are very full of static) and even the announcing by Paul Douglas is lively. Such musicians as Duke Ellington, harpist Casper Reardon, vibraphonist Adrian Rollini, trumpeter Bunny Bergian, the Raymond Scott Quintet, the Casa Loma Orchestra, pianist Claude Thorhill, the Benny Goodman Trio and Quartet, the guitar duo of Carl Kress and Dick McDonough and an impressive house band are all in excellent

form. To use a cliché, it is almost like being there. One can truly feel the excitement of the swing era during this highly recommended release. — *Scott Yanow*

Sax Appeal / 1954-1956 / Vee-Jay ✦✦✦✦✦

The corny cover photo (a female model allegedly playing a saxophone), the hodge-podge nature of the program and the barely adequate liner notes mask the fact that this CD contains a great deal of interesting music. Most of the 24 performances (nine previously unissued) put the emphasis on its tenor soloists and the music falls somewhere between bop and early rhythm & blues. Included are complete sessions by Julian Dash, bassist David Shipp (whose sidemen include altoist Porter Kilbert and pianist Andrew Hill), keyboardist Tommy Dean (one of his songs features altoist Oliver Nelson), the great tenor Wardell Gray (the four numbers from his final session), honker Big Jay McNeely ("Big Jay's Hop"), Al Smith (featuring the tenor of Red Holloway), Arnett Cobb and Noble "Thin Man" Watts. Collectors in particular will want to pick up this very interesting set. — *Scott Yanow*

Small Band Jazz / Mar. 8, 1936-Jan. 10, 1943 / Fanfare ✦✦✦

The collector's label Fanfare released some very valuable LPs in the late '70s that contained radio aircheck performances. On this album the 1936 Red Norvo Octet (with trumpeter Stew Pletcher and tenor saxophonist Herbie Haymer) perform two songs, Miff Mole's Nicksieland Six jams on two of their own (including "Peg of My Heart") and Raymond Scott's Captivators (its personnel is unknown) is fine on four pieces. However, it is the music on side two that is most memorable—Bud Freeman's Summa Cum Laude Orchestra of 1940 is showcased. The tenor's all-star group features such fine soloists as trumpeter Max Kaminsky, valve trombonist Brad Gowans, clarinetist Pee Wee Russell and Freeman. Their broadcast includes hot swing, dance music and a three-song Bix Beiderbecke tribute. Traditional jazz historians will want this album, if they can find it. — *Scott Yanow*

Small Band Jazz, Vol. 2 / Feb. 11, 1940-Jan. 27, 1941 / Fanfare ✦✦✦✦

This LP has performances taken from some of the broadcasts of the Chamber Society of Lower Basin Street, a program that satirized the pretentiousness of some classical music shows while featuring notable jazz artists. On this album Jelly Roll Morton is heard during his last recorded appearance and there are spots for Charlie and Jack Teagarden, pianist Joe Sullivan, clarinetist Pee Wee Russell, cornetist Bobby Hackett, vibraphonist Lionel Hampton, soprano saxophonist Sidney Bechet (in exciting form), the Count Basie rhythm section, drummer Zutty Singleton and trumpeter Roy Eldridge. Most of the guests sat in with the fine house band led by trumpeter Hot Lips Levine and many of these performances are quite memorable. Highly recommended. — *Scott Yanow*

The Smithsonian Collection of Classic Jazz, Vols. 1-5 / Smithsonian ✦✦✦✦✦

The Smithsonian Collection of Classic Jazz is itself somewhat of a classic, referred to in many books, and used as the main learning source in at least one. If you don't know what you like in jazz and are looking for a well-put-together introduction, this set is a good bet. It starts with ragtime's Scott Joplin, and proceeds through Bessie Smith, Louis Armstrong, Art Tatum, Duke Ellington … all the way up to and including the free jazz of Ornette Coleman, and even the World Saxophone Quartet. Of course John Coltrane, Thelonious Monk, Miles Davis, and all the other big guns are there—even Horace Silver and Lennie Tristano. This five-CD set (94 tracks) contains classic cuts in most cases. This set is a great place to begin. — *Michael Erlewine*

Some Other Time: Tribute to Chet Baker / Apr. 17, 1989-Apr. 18, 1989 / Triloka ✦✦✦

Recorded a year after Chet Baker's death, this tribute album (which was organized by pianist Richie Beirach) features trumpeter Randy Brecker, tenor-great Michael Brecker, guitarist John Scofield, Beirach, bassist George Mraz and drummer Adam Nussbaum on material associated with Baker. Actually Beirach contributed five of the ten songs and, since Baker rarely if ever performed three of them, this session's purpose gets watered down a bit. However the solos are generally of high quality and the music of this modern mainstream session holds one's interest throughout. — *Scott Yanow*

Songposts, Vol. 1 / Mar. 14, 1987-Sep. 10, 1991 / Word of Mouth ✦✦✦

This CD sampler features a wide variety of adventurous singers. Most memorable are two duets by the great Sheila Jordan and bassist Harvie Swartz, Kate Hammett-Vaughan with Garbo's Haton "The Oft Repeated Dream" and Jeanne Lee's unaccompanied "Journey to Edaneres." Also included are performances by Georgia Ambros, Paula Owen, Jeannette Lambert, Irene Aebi (in duet with Steve Lacy's piano), Corry Sobol with bassist Dave Young, Jay Clayton with pianist Kirk Nurock, the Anne LeBaron Ensemble and David Drain. Although not everything works, this release from the Canadian label Word of Mouth gives listeners a taste of many different singers, some of whom are barely known in the US — *Scott Yanow*

☆ **The Sound of Chicago: Jazz Odyssey, Vol. 2** / Jun. 23, 1923-May 8, 1940 / Columbia ✦✦✦✦✦

The second of three three-LP box sets released by Columbia in their *Jazz Odyssey* series of the early '60s is as highly recommended (and as rare) as the New Orleans and Harlem sets. Among the many bands featured on the 48 selections are those of King Oliver, Jelly Roll Morton, Carroll Dickerson, Mckenzie and Condon's Chicagoans, Bud Freeman, a few blues singers, Jimmie Noone, Paul Mares, Earl Hines, Roy Eldridge and Horace Henderson. The attractive booklet (which is full of interesting information) is a strong asset, and although some of the music has since been reissued on CD, much of it hasn't. This set will be difficult to find so it should not be passed by; it serves as an excellent introduction to 1920s and early '30s jazz. — *Scott Yanow*

☆ **The Sound of Harlem** / Aug. 10, 1920-Apr. 1, 1942 / Columbia ✦✦✦✦✦

The third of three three-LP box sets released by Columbia in the early '60s in their *Jazz Odyssey* series, as with the New Orleans and Chicago samplers, contains some common selections but quite a few rarities among its 48 performances. In addition to such major names as Mamie Smith (her pioneering 1920 recording of "Crazy Blues"), James P. Johnson, Fletcher Henderson, Louis Armstrong, Ethel Waters, Fats Waller, Cab Calloway and Billie Holiday, there are numbers from Edith Wilson, Thomas Morris, Leroy Tibbs, Mattie Hite, Lena Wilson, Buck and Bubbles and the Hokum Trio. Most of the first two LPs stick to the 1920s and early '30s while the last one goes up to Cootie Williams' 1942 recording of "Epistrophy." Highly recommended although this set will be very difficult to find. — *Scott Yanow*

☆ **The Sound of New Orleans** / Jan. 24, 1917-Sep. 23, 1947 / Columbia ✦✦✦✦✦

The first of three three-LP box sets put out by Columbia in the early '60s in their *Jazz Odyssey* series is (as is true of the Chicago and Harlem entries) a perfect introduction to early jazz. The 48 selections range from the Original Dixieland Jazz Band ("Darktown Strutters' Ball," the first jazz record ever made) and Clarence Williams to Wingy Manone, Bunk Johnson, King Oliver, Louis Armstrong, Fate Marable, the New Orleans Rhythm Kings and all eight titles cut by Sam Morgan's Jazz Band. Most of the music is from the mid- to late '20s and many rarities are included along with just a few familiar items. The large and very informative booklet included in the box is a major plus too. — *Scott Yanow*

Spirituals to Swing [Columbia] / 1938-1939 / Columbia ✦✦✦

Although this John Hammond-produced concert was billed as the "30th Anniversary," it actually took place 28 years after his original Spirituals to Swing concert. Count Basie, Big Joe Turner and an obviously ill Pete Johnson were back from the earlier event. The two-LP set has spirituals (Marion Williams), blues (Big Mama Thornton and Turner), new stars (George Benson and John Handy) and a few swing all-stars (including trumpeter Buck Clayton, clarinetist Edmond Hall and tenor saxophonist Buddy Tate). The spirited program certainly holds one's interest, making this a two-fer worth acquiring. — *Scott Yanow*

● **Stars of Jazz, Vol. 1** / 1972 / Jazzology ✦✦✦✦✦

On the first of two CDs (and originally released on three LPs), pianist Art Hodes leads a particularly strong all-star group through a variety of familiar Dixieland standards. Presented to the audience in an informative and educational way, this music is often quite exciting, not a surprise when one considers the lineup: cornetist Wild Bill Davison (in peak form), trombonist Jim Beebe, clarinetist Barney Bigard, guitarist Eddie Condon, bassist Rail Wilson and drummer Hillard Brown. This CD would be worth getting if only to hear Davison's highly expressive (and sometimes sarcastic) playing on "Just a Closer Walk with Thee." Traditional jazz fans should consider the two volumes in this series to be essential. — *Scott Yanow*

● **Stars of Jazz, Vol. 2** / 1972 / Jazzology ✦✦✦✦✦

The second of two CDs taken from a single concert (which was originally released as three LPs) features pianist Art Hodes leading a brilliant Chicago-style jazz group (with cornetist Wild Bill Davison in top form, trombonist Jim Beebe, clarinetist Barney Bigard, guitarist Eddie Condon, bassist Rail Wilson and drummer Hillard Brown) on a variety of mostly familiar Dixieland and swing standards. Hodes presents the music in an entertaining and educational fashion for the audience and this concert is rounded out by a version of "Kansas City Blues" which was recorded before the concert, at the group's soundcheck. Both of the volumes in this short series are highly recommended, particularly for Davison's emotional and often-humorous solos. — *Scott Yanow*

Stars of the Apollo / Mar. 31, 1927-Jan. 7, 1965 / Columbia/Legacy ✦✦✦

This double CD is a straight reissue of the original double LP. Its 28 selections mostly focus on singers and bands from the swing era that performed at one time or another at the Apollo; all but eight of the numbers are from the 1927-42 period. High points of this hodgepodge collection include Bessie Smith's "Gimme a Pigfoot," the Mills Brothers' "Sweet Sue," Bill "Bojangles" Robinson's "Doin' the New Lowdown," Slim Gaillard's "Sploghm," Sarah Vaughan's "Ain't Misbehavin',"

Screamin' Jay Hawkins' remarkable "I Put a Spell on You" and Aretha Franklin's "Evil Gal Blues." —*Scott Yanow*

Straight, No Chaser / Blue Note ◆◆

Blue Note keeps the "concept" packages coming with this two-disc set presenting catalog tracks sampled by the hip-hop/jazz ensemble Us3. The 15 selections include dialogue snippets from Birdland's irrepressible Pee Wee Marquette and the great Art Blakey, with the other material divided between hard bop and soul-jazz, and Herbie Hancock, Horace Silver, and Donald Byrd getting two tracks each. John Patton, Reuben Wilson, Grant Green, Lou Donaldson, Thelonious Monk, Blakey, and Bobby Hutcherson are other featured artists. The songs are first-rate, but Blue Note could have also included the recording years of the tracks as an additional service to listeners, particularly those coming from rap with little knowledge of the label's accomplishments or legacy. —*Ron Wynn*

The Sullivan Years: Big Band All-Stars / Feb. 10, 1957-Jun. 4, 1967 / TVT ◆◆◆

The performances on this CD are taken from the soundtrack of several episodes of *The Ed Sullivan Show*. The orchestras of Harry James, Woody Herman, Lionel Hampton, Benny Goodman, Count Basie along with the Glenn Miller ghost band are heard from during a ten-year period. The music in general is quite predictable with Herman's "Apple Honey" and Goodman's "Sing Sing Sing" providing the best moments; when are videos from these programs going to become available? —*Scott Yanow*

● Sunset Swing / Mar. 1, 1945-Nov. 12, 1945 / Black Lion ◆◆◆◆

This CD contains 22 generally exciting performances from jazz's transitional years. While the music technically falls into the swing idiom, one can often hear the influence of bop (and even early rhythm & blues) creeping in. Nine different groups are heard from. Trumpeter Howard McGhee and tenor saxophonist Charlie Ventura head a sextet; the 16-year old pianist Andre Previn makes his recording debut on a trio version of "California Clipper" and joins trumpeter Buddy Childers; altoist Willie Smith and the tenor of Vido Musso in a sextet; McGhee, Willie Smith and tenor great Lucky Thompson join forces on another date; guitarist Les Paul is heard in a sextet with trumpeter Harry Edison; pianist Arnold Ross duets with bassist Red Callender, trumpeter Emmett Berry, trombonist Vic Dickenson and altoist Lem Davis swing in a sextet; and drummer Ray Bauduc leads an unidentified group. Recommended. —*Scott Yanow*

☆ Swing Street / Mar. 13, 1931-Oct. 28, 1947 / Columbia ◆◆◆◆◆

The many groups that appeared on 52nd Street during the 1930s and '40s are saluted on this magnificent four-LP set. There are a numerous amount of classics included among the 64 selections with music provided by Ella Logan and the Spirits of Rhythm, Eddie Condon, Stuff Smith, the Mound City Blue Blowers, Wingy Manone, Red Allen, Frank Froeba, Louis Prima, Frankie Newton, the Three Peppers, Fats Waller, Art Tatum, Teddy Wilson, Clarence Profit, Bunny Berigan, Joe Marsala, Midge Williams, Maxine Sullivan, John Kirby, Charlie Barnet, Mildred Bailey, Red Norvo, Slim Gaillard, Bud Freeman, Bobby Hackett, Billie Holiday, Pete Johnson, Will Bradley, Count Basie, Woody Herman, Hot Lips Page, Roy Eldridge, Coleman Hawkins, Noble Sissle and even Dizzy Gillespie—and that's only the bandleaders. Much of the music has resurfaced on CD but this set serves as a strong introduction to small-group swing and will be treasured by swing fans. —*Scott Yanow*

Swing That Music! / 1929-1956 / Smithsonian ◆◆◆◆

The Smithsonian's four-disc tribute to the swing/big band era, compiled by the late, great Martin Williams, offers as comprehensive a look at the genre as possible from a general perspective. Williams featured great and lightweight bands, highly popular vocalists like Bing Crosby and Frank Sinatra, dubious ones with large followings like Bob Eberly and Doris Day and underrated ones such as Al Hibbler and Helen Humes. Duke Ellington, Count Basie, Woody Herman and Benny Goodman are well-represented, but so are Harry James, Glenn Miller and Bob Crosby. The sound quality is first-rate and the liner notes are informative, and the material is nicely divided between familiar cuts and obscure tracks. The Smithsonian's sets are sometimes attacked for emphasizing one style over another or not representing each era of a genre; that cannot be leveled at this anthology. —*Ron Wynn*

● Swing Time! (1925-1955) / May 14, 1925-Feb. 15, 1955 / Columbia ◆◆◆◆

This three-CD box set does an excellent job of covering the big-band era through 66 recordings (by almost as many orchestras) owned by Columbia. The selections (programmed in chronological order), although emphasizing the 1934-45 era, also include 18 earlier and six later recordings. The 60 Columbia/OKeh sides, which include the real rarities, are spiced with six tracks (Tommy Dorsey's "Marie," Jimmy Dorsey's "Green Eyes," Glenn Miller's "In the Mood," Duke Ellington's "Take the 'A' Train," Bob Crosby's "South Rampart Street Parade," and Stan Kenton's "The Peanut Vendor") licensed from RCA, MCA etc., which cover some familiar bases for the benefit of beginners. The accompanying booklet is also excellent. —*Scott Yanow & Bruce Eder*

Swing Trumpet Kings / Jun. 3, 1956-Nov. 21, 1960 / PolyGram ◆◆◆◆◆

This double CD gathers together three former LPs that are unrelated except that they feature swing-era trumpeters in the 1950s. The most consistent date is the largely predictable *Harry Edison Swings Buck Clayton and Vice Versa*. The two complementary trumpeters Edison and Clayton are joined by tenorman Jimmy Forrest (in excellent form) and a supportive rhythm section. Despite the title, there are no Clayton originals on the date, although Edison does contribute four mostly blues-based tunes. The music (which includes two alternate takes and a ballad medley) swings and is as tasteful as one would expect. Taste is not the main quality one thinks of while hearing the inaccurately titled *Red Allen Plays King Oliver* (few of the songs have anything to do with Oliver). The frequently uptempo music is quite exciting, has its erratic moments, and is often on the verge of going out of control; check out the false ending to "Bill Bailey." Trumpeter Red Allen sounds like he had been playing a little too long for the loud and drunken Metropole audience, taking wild chances, while clarinetist Buster Bailey (who always had very impressive technique) sometimes comes across as a bit nuts. The music (which also has solo space for trombonist Herb Fleming and either Bob Hammer or Sammy Price on piano) is certainly full of spirit and adventure. Roy Eldridge tries his best on *Swing Goes Dixie*, playing melody lines and riffs to the Dixieland standards in the ensembles (some of which might have been written out), although his more modern solos do not always fit the music. The band (which includes trombonist Benny Morton, clarinetist Eddie Barefield and pianist Dick Wellstood) is excellent, and the repertoire (which is highlighted by "That's A Plenty" two versions of "Royal Garden Blues," "Jazz Me Blues" and "Bugle Call Rag") is certainly unique for an Eldridge date. Roy was in prime form during the era, and he shows the influence of early-'30s Louis Armstrong on some spectacular solos. This historic reissue is certainly worth picking up by Dixieland, swing and mainstream collectors, for all three of these sessions were formerly rare. —*Scott Yanow*

● Swingin' Britain: The Thirties / Feb. 1, 1935-Nov. 10, 1938 / Decca ◆◆◆◆◆

This double LP from British Decca will be difficult to find but it is worth the search for fans of swing music. The two-fer has 32 jazz-oriented recordings (most of them rare) by a variety of English groups: Danny Polo's Swing Stars, George Chisholm's Jive Five, the Embassy Rhythm Eight, Leonard Feather and Ye Old English Swynge Band, Lew Davis' Trombone Trio and Tiny Winters' Bogey Seven. Although the stereotype of British bands of the 1930s is of polite dance music, these performances show that the English had several very impressive swing stylists. Most notable, in addition to the American clarinetist Danny Polo (a bit of a ringer), are trumpeters Tommy McQuater, Max Goldberg and Dave Wilkins, trombonists George Chisholm and Lew Davis, Benny Winestone on clarinet and tenor and the tenors of Don Barrigo and Buddy Featherstonhaugh. This very worthy reissue is a collector's item. —*Scott Yanow*

Swingin' Jazz for Hipsters, Vol. 1 / Concord Jazz ◆◆

Would someone care to explain the point of this exercise? The bachelor pad cover art is supposed to represent some vague early '60s space age atmosphere, the CD label is designed to look like a 45 RPM record, and the brief liner note is right out of a vintage *Playboy* magazine ad. One can only surmise that Concord believes that the cynics in Generation X are ready to buy jazz if it is delivered in a trendy (as of the mid-1990s) lounge package. But how does that jibe with the selection of music, which skips blithely over two decades of the Concord back catalog without a single track from the period that they are trying to evoke? (In any case, Concord wasn't around at that time anyway.) The selections are covers of pop hits as old as "Honeysuckle Rose" and as recent as "Isn't She Lovely" and "The Lady Wants to Know"; the artists include Ray Brown, Jack McDuff, Mel Tormé, Stephane Grappelli, Hendrik Meurkens, Stefan Scaggiari, Tania Maria, Ruby Braff, Ron Eschete, Ernestine Anderson, Howard Roberts and Charlie Byrd. For a concept totally unrelated to content, which itself has no unifying thought behind it, this release takes the cake. —*Richard S. Ginell*

Swingin' Jazz for Hipsters, Vol. 2 / Concord Jazz ◆◆

Vol. 2 of this weird series is identical in concept to the baffling first installment. The packaging and come-on are the same, the wildly mismatched music is even more incongruous through time from "Frenesi" to the theme from the TV show *Frasier*—and for good measure, the Mel Tormé track "I'm Hip" makes raucous fun of the whole idea of "hipsters." For the record, the other artists this time include Jim Hall, Ken Peplowski, Charlie Byrd, Gary Burton, Frank Vignola, the Heath Brothers, Jack McDuff, Gerry Mulligan, Cal Tjader, Scott Hamilton, Monty Alexander, and George Shearing—and I defy any Generation X-er (to whom this CD is presumably aimed) to make any sense of that. At least the music is good, though its only value as a whole is as a random sampler of Concordiana. —*Richard S. Ginell*

Swinging Big Band Christmas / 194 / LaserLight ◆◆◆

This budget CD release from LaserLight does not give recording dates but the ten selections (totalling only around 36 minutes of music) mostly are from the 1940s.

Such performers as Claude Thornhill ("Snowfall"), Gene Krupa, Larry Clinton, Jack Teagarden, Bob Crosby, the Glenn Miller Army Air Force Orchestra (playing a Christmas medley), Les Brown and even Guy Lombardo are all heard in fine form. The results as a whole are a satisfying and rather atmospheric set of nostalgic Christmas jazz. —*Scott Yanow*

Tar Heel Jazz / Jun. 18, 1936-Aug. 4, 1937 / IAJRC ✦✦✦✦✦

This CD from the collector's label IAJRC contains the complete output of three obscure bands plus seven of the ten sides cut by the Hod Williams Orchestra. All of these sessions were recorded in the same building in Charlotte, NC, during 1936-37 and feature territory bands with their own strong and weak qualities. Jimmie Gunn's band is excellent on its three instrumentals but plagued by bad vocalists on the other three tracks. The Frankie and Johnny orchestra is more consistent and often often quite hot. The Hod Williams Orchestra took its inspiration (and to an extent its arrangememts) from the sophisticated swing style of The Hudson-DeLange Orchestra while the recordings of the Frankie Reynolds Orchestra are swinging if not particularly distinctive. 1930s collectors should consider this set of rare material to be essential. —*Scott Yanow*

The Territorial Bands / Oct. 14, 1927-Jun. 1931 / IAJRC ✦✦✦✦✦

This enjoyable LP puts the focus on five long-forgotten but talented territory bands of the late '20s and early '30s. All eight selections recorded by Curtis Mosby's Dix-ieland Blue Blowers (an excellent group from Los Angeles) fill up side one, while one of the two songs cut by Maynard Baird's Orchestra (a band from Knoxville, TN), three of the four sides performed by Red Perkins' Dixie Ramblers and both of the titles recorded by singer Victoria Spivey with Hunter's Serenaders (which, like Perkins, was from Omaha, NE) and Grant Moore's New Orleans Balack Devils (from Arkansas) are on the flip side. It is surprising that none of the sidemen became well-known because these are excellent bands with Mosby's being most memorable on titles such as "Whoop 'Em up Blues," "Tiger Stomp" and "Blue Blowers Blues." Recommended. —*Scott Yanow*

The Territories, Vol. 2 / 1927-Jun. 14, 1933 / Arcadia ✦✦✦✦✦

There is quite a variety of performances on this interesting LP, much of it quite valuable. It starts off with all of the recordings of the important Kansas City band George E. Lee's Novelty Singing Orchestra (two titles from 1927 and four from 1929) plus the two songs on which the band backs the vocals of its pianist, the legendary (and future star) Julia Lee ("He's Tall, Dark and Handsome" and "Won't You Come over to My House"). In addition there are four songs from the spirited if primitive Alex Jackson's Plantation Orchestra (their "Jackass Blues" is a classic), a number by Curtis Mosby's Dixieland Blue Blowers that is taken from a movie and the complete output (two songs) by the completely obscure Erwing Brothers Orchestra in 1933. Collectors of early jazz should consider this music (most of which has not yet been reissued on CD) to be essential. —*Scott Yanow*

The Territories, Vol. 3: The South / Oct. 6, 1926-Jul. 15, 1936 / Arcadia ✦✦✦

The third of three LPs put out by Arcadia in their mini-series has a variety of rare recordings cut in the South during the 1926-30 period. Eddie Heywood, Sr., (the father of the famous pianist) is heard on his only two band sides, Williamson's Beale Street Frolic Orchestra romps on four songs, the primitive Black Birds of Paradise struggle through "Muddy Water," the Triangle Harmony Boys do what they can on three songs, pianist Sammy Price's Four Quarters play "Blue Rhythm Stomp" (their only recording) and there is music by Ben Tobier's California Cyclones and Edgewater Crows; the latter from 1936. Interesting performances overall, most are highly recommended to connoisseurs of the era. —*Scott Yanow*

Texas Tenors / 1946-Aug. 11, 1969 / Prestige ✦✦✦✦✦

Thirteen carefully chosen tenor classics, selected by none other than blues/jazz/R&B expert and producer Bob Porter. The extensive liner notes alone (by Porter) are worth the price of the CD. Included are killer cuts from every major "Texas Tenor" player, from Illinois Jacquet on down to David "Fathead" Newman, and Arnett Cobb, Buddy Tate, Budd Johnson, Wild Bill Moore, Don Wilkerson, King Curtis, and Booker Ervin. Lesser-known tenor greats like Herschel Evans, Clifford Scott, Wilton Felder, Jessie Powell, and Russell Procope are also represented. Sidemen include Hammond organ greats Charles Kynard and Don Patterson, pianists Red Garland, Tommy Flanagan, Wynton Kelly, and Barry Harris, plus many others. The ballad "Where or When" by Don Wilkerson, in particular, is breathtaking in its beauty. This entire collection is outstanding. —*Michael Erlewine*

That Newport Jazz / Jul. 4, 1963+Jul. 6, 1963 / Columbia ✦✦✦✦✦

There is over an hour's worth of music on this generous LP, which features two different all-star groups at the 1963 Newport Jazz Festival. One band (with trumpeters Clark Terry and Howard McGhee, tenors Coleman Hawkins and Zoot Sims, pianist Joe Zawinul, bassist Wendell Marshall and drummer Roy Haynes) could be considered more boppish than the other (which has trumpeter Ruby Braff, trombonist Al Grey, tenor Bud Freeman, pianist George Wein, bassist Wendell Marshall and

drummer Haynes), but in reality, the groups overlap stylistically. The jam sessions (eight standards including ballad features for Hawkins and Terry and the original blues "Chasin' at Newport") are quite fun and generate plenty of heat. Historic and enjoyable music from quite a few classic greats. —*Scott Yanow*

That's the Way I Feel Now: Tribute to T. Monk / Oct. 1984 / A&M ✦✦✦

Two years after the death of pianist-composer Thelonious Monk, this very unusual and quite memorable double-LP tribute was put together. Producer Hal Willner's most successful project, the 23 interpretations of Monk originals all feature a different group of all-star players and stretch beyond jazz. Some of the performances are fairly straightforward while others are quite eccentric; certainly the crazy duet on "Four in One" by altoist Gary Windo and Todd Rundgren (on synthesizers and drum machines) and the version of "Shuffle Boil" featuring John Zorn on game calls (imitating the sound of ducks) are quite unique. There are many colorful moments throughout the project and the roster of musicians is remarkable: Bobby McFerrin with Bob Dorough, Peter Frampton, Joe Jackson, Steve Lacy, Dr. John, Gil Evans, Randy Weston, Roswell Rudd, Eugene Chadbourne and Shockabilly, the Fowler Brothers, NRBQ, Steve Khan, Carla Bley, Barry Harris, Was (Not Was) and many others. There is not a slow moment or uninteresting selection on this highly recommended set. —*Scott Yanow*

☆ Thesaurus of Classic Jazz / Sep. 1926-Feb. 6, 1930 / Columbia ✦✦✦✦✦

In the early '60s, Columbia started digging into its vaults and coming out with box sets of valuable music from the 1920s. This four-LP set has 13 selections from Miff Mole's Molers, a dozen by the Charleston Chasers, eight apiece from the Redheads and the Arkansas Travellers, two by the Dorsey Brothers, three from Frankie Trumbauer, one apiece from the Goofus Five and Joe Venuti and four featuring Eddie Lang's Orchestra. Overall this superior collection gives one a large sampling of the White small groups of the era with plenty of solos from cornetists Red Nichols and (on three songs) Bix Beiderbecke, trombonists Tommy Dorsey and Miff Mole, Jimmy Dorsey on clarinet and alto and clarinetist Pee Wee Russell among others. The accompanying booklet is quite informative too. Recommended, but this will be a hard set to find. —*Scott Yanow*

This Is Acid Jazz: After Hours / Feb. 16, 1957+Jun. 21, 1957 / Instinct ✦✦✦

This two-LP set combines a pair of leaderless jam session albums: *Olio* and *After Hours;* the latter set has since been reissued on CD in the OJC series. The overlapping personnel features trumpeter Thad Jones, Frank Wess on tenor and flute, either vibraphonist Teddy Charles or guitarist Kenny Burrell, pianist Mal Waldron, Doug Watkins or Paul Chambers on bass and Elvin Jones or Art Taylor on drums. Waldron contributed six of the ten originals, Charles brought in three and the band also interprets "Embraceable You." This straightahead collection finds these young musicians playing quite well and uplifting the dates above the level of just a routine jam session. —*Scott Yanow*

This Is Art Deco / Jan. 7, 1913-Jan. 1982 / Columbia ✦✦

What do Al Jolson, Gertrude Lawrence, Guy Lombardo, Mae West and Jack Lemmon have in common? Nothing, except that they each have one recording included on this rather pointless sampler. While the liner notes totally ignore the music and instead discuss the origin of Art Deco, the 20 selections (which are programmed in chronological order) start off with Bert Williams in 1913, feature a variety of showbiz singers, leave space for the Boswell Sisters, the Mills Brothers and Ethel Merman and advance finally to Alberta Hunter in 1982. None of the performances are rare and all can be acquired in more logical sets elsewhere. —*Scott Yanow*

This Is Jazz, Vol. 1 / Jan. 18, 1947-Mar. 1, 1947 / Jazzology ✦✦✦✦

For eight months in 1947, critic Rudi Blesh hosted a weekly live jazz radio show, "This Is Jazz." He sought to popularize classic New Orleans jazz by featuring an all-star group and explaining the music's history a bit. After years of only being available in piecemeal and often semi-underground fashion, the half-hour programs are being reissued on a series of Jazzology two-CD sets that contain four shows apiece. *Vol. 1* has Blesh's audition show on "For Your Approval" and then the first three "This Is Jazz" programs. The writer does have a tendency to talk a bit too much (particularly during the audition) and he is not always completely accurate, but his heart was in the right place. More important is the music. There are six songs on each show; heard regularly is cornetist Muggsy Spanier, clarinetist Albert Nicholas, trombonist George Brunis, either Luckey Roberts, Joe Sullivan or James P. Johnson on piano, Cyrus St. Clair (tuba and bass) or bassist Pops Foster, and drummer Baby Dodds. The first show has trumpeters Punch Miller and Max Kaminsky instead of Spanier, along with some very erratic Mezz Mezzrow clarinet. The vaudeville team of Coot Grant and Kid Socks Wilson and the great soprano Sidney Bechet guest on a program apiece. The music is solid Dixieland, and highlights include one of the very few versions of "Charleston" that its composer (James P. Johnson) ever recorded, several solos by the legendary (but barely documented) pianist Luckey Roberts, and many spirited ensembles. —*Scott Yanow*

This is Jazz Sampler / Jul. 19, 1929-1976 / Columbia/Legacy ✦✦

This hodge-podge sampler is actually a sampler of a sampler, taking its ten selections from some of the 20 earlier releases in the "This Is Jazz" series. There is one song apiece from Louis Armstrong ("Ain't Misbehavin'"), Duke Ellington, Count Basie, Billie Holiday, Dave Brubeck ("Blue Rondo à la Turk"), Sarah Vaughan, Stan Getz ("The Peacocks"), Weather Report, John McLaughlin and Wayne Shorter. All of this music is readily available elsewhere (not just in the earlier samplers), making the release a bit of a frivolity. — *Scott Yanow*

Tin Pan Alley Blues / May 4, 1916-Mar. ??, 1925 / Memphis Archives ✦✦✦

The Memphis Archives label has mixed together some fairly common blues performances with some real oddities, blues as performed by vaudevillian performers. In addition to the original Dixieland Jazz Band ("Home Again Blues"), Trixie Smith, Bessie Smith and Edith Wilson, there is Marie Cahill singing "The Dallas Blues" (from 1917), the very early "Homesickness Blues" from Nora Bayes in 1916 and even a rare example of Eddie Cantor singing blues. Obviously the music is not for everyone's taste but collectors of early American music will find this CD to be quite interesting. — *Scott Yanow*

Town Hall Jazz Concert 1945 / Jun. 9, 1945 / Atlantic ✦✦✦✦✦

There is nearly two hours of music on this double LP, all taken from a historic Town Hall concert. The swing-oriented performances (which have been reissued by Mosaic in their massive Commodore reissue series) are often quite exciting with strong appearances by such greats as vibraphonist Red Norvo, tenors Flip Phillips and Charlie Ventura, pianist Teddy Wilson, bassist Slam Stewart, tenor saxophonist Don Byas (who has a pair of classic duets with Stewart on "Indiana" and "I Got Rhythm"), trumpeter Bill Coleman, drummer Gene Krupa and violinist Stuff Smith. Although a couple of selections (particularly a 16-minute "In a Mellotone") go on a bit too long, there are plenty of memorable moments during this highly recommended set which deserves to be reissued in full on CD. — *Scott Yanow*

● **A Tribute to Carl Jefferson** / Nov. 14, 1992-May 29, 1996 / Concord Jazz ✦✦✦✦✦

Carl Jefferson, who passed away in 1995, made a very strong impact on the jazz world. After a successful career as a used car dealer, Jefferson founded the Concord Jazz Festival in 1969, was the main person responsible for the Concord Pavilion being built in 1975, and in the mid-'70s founded the Concord label, for whom he produced over 500 records that set the standard for mainstream jazz. On July 8, 1995, a marathon six-hour, five-set concert was performed in Jefferson's memory at the Concord Pavilion. Around 60 different major musicians participated (generally playing one or two songs apiece), and this four-CD set is the result. Although not every Concord artist was able to make it to the unique event (which they all played for free), the lineup is quite outstanding. Some of the highlights of the 40 selections taken from the event include Toshiko Akiyoshi's rendition of "Count Your Blessings," singer Eden Atwood backed by trumpeter Randy Sandke on "Centerpiece," Susannah McCorkle's "They Can't Take That Away from Me," Karrin Allyson romping through "Yardbird Suite," Rob McConnell's strutting version of "On The Sunny Side of the Street," cornetist Ruby Braff playing beautifully on "The Very Thought of You" and Rickey Woodard's "Tippin' the Jug." Acoustic guitarist Laurindo Almeida, in what would be his last recording (and next-to-last concert), is heard on four short pieces (including two with Charlie Byrd). Since there were many other Concord artists who wanted to pay tribute to Carl Jefferson, the package concludes with nine performances taped on other occasions, including a Ken Peplowski-Howard Alden duet on "It Had to be You" and appearances by Rosemary Clooney, Poncho Sanchez and Marian McPartland. The final number was the only previously issued selection, but it is quite fitting—Mel Tormé singing "Ev'ry Time We Say Goodbye." Highly recommended. — *Scott Yanow*

A Tribute to Duke / 1977 / Concord Jazz ✦✦✦

For this tribute to Duke Ellington, Rosemary Clooney (making her debut on Concord) and Tony Bennett take two vocals apiece, Woody Herman plays "In a Sentimental Mood" and Bing Crosby guests on "Don't Get Around Much Anymore." Actually the three instrumentals are most significant for the quintet (which includes pianist Nat Pierce, trumpeter Bill Berry, bassist Monty Budwig and drummer Jake Hanna) helped introduce the young tenor Scott Hamilton. The CD is a straight reissue of the original LP, a historic if not essential release. — *Scott Yanow*

A Tribute to Lee Morgan / Dec. 3, 1994-Dec. 4, 1994 / NYC ✦✦✦✦✦

Unlike many of the other recent tribute albums, this program of the music of the late trumpeter Lee Morgan casts his compositions in familiar surroundings not all that different from the original recordings. Trumpeter Eddie Henderson, who was influenced by Morgan but found his own voice, is a good choice for the lead role and his muted outing on the one non-Morgan piece, "You Don't Know What Love Is," is a strong feature. Tenorman Joe Lovano, who can sound like Joe Henderson at times and hints at the passion of Coltrane on the date's most advanced piece "Search for the New Land," has a strong personality of his own and matches well with Eddie Henderson. The solid rhythm section (pianist Cedar Walton, bassist

Peter Washington and drummer Billy Higgins) is a major asset while Grover Washington, Jr., makes a pair of guest appearances on soprano and shows once again that he can play swinging soulful jazz; pity that he never seems to play tenor in this type of setting. The eight Lee Morgan songs heard on this recommended CD are interpreted in the same basic hard bop style that the trumpeter spent most of his career playing, an idiom that serves as the modern jazz mainstream of today. Highlights include "Sidewinder," "Ceora," "Speedball" (which has some heated tradeoffs by the horns) and the infectious "Ca-Lee-So." — *Scott Yanow*

Tribute to Miles / 1992 / Qwest ✦✦✦

This Miles Davis tribute set brings back four-fifths of his second classic quintet with Wallace Roney the logical choice to fill in for the late trumpeter. Roney comes across as a sideman and is not as forceful here as one would have hoped. Wayne Shorter, Herbie Hancock, Ron Carter and Tony Williams had all grown with time and this reunion has Hancock and Williams taking on more prominent leadership roles than in the earlier days. With the exception of the drummer's "Elegy," all of the music ("So What," "RJ," "Little One," "Pinocchio," "Eighty One" and "All Blues") was regularly performed by the quintet back in the 1960s. In general this reunion is a success even if it contains no new revelations. It is particularly nice to hear Wayne Shorter in this setting again. — *Scott Yanow*

The Trumpet Summit Meets the Oscar Peterson Big 4 / Mar. 10, 1980 / OJC ✦✦✦✦

To call this CD (a reissue of a Pablo date) an all-star session would be an understatement. Joining pianist Oscar Peterson, guitarist Joe Pass, bassist Ray Brown and drummer Bobby Durham are three classic trumpeters: Dizzy Gillespie, Clark Terry and Freddie Hubbard. They clearly inspire each other (Gillespie flew in from the East Coast specifically for this date) and the music ("Daahoud," "Just Friends," the new blues "Chicken Wings" and a torrid version of "The Champ") has plenty of exciting moments. Other performances from the same date can be heard on *The Alternate Blues*, an LP overdue to be reissued on CD. — *Scott Yanow*

Trumpets in Modern Jazz / Feb. ??, 1981-Jun. ??, 1993 / Enja ✦✦✦

With the exception of an alternate take of Dusko Goykovich's "Adriatica," all of the dozen performances on this CD sampler are taken from previously released Enja albums. Of the trumpeters featured, Clark Terry, Woody Shaw (in a duet with drummer Roy Brooks) and the obscure Reiner Winterschladen are heard in cameos, Dizzy Gillespie is past his prime on 1989's "Kush" and Chet Baker plays a forgettable ballad "For Now." However Art Farmer, Benny Bailey, Goykovich, John D'Earth, Franco Ambrosetti and Jerry Gonzalez are in excellent form while young Nicholas Payton steals solo honors on "Body and Soul." Overall this CD gives one an interesting overview of a variety of trumpeters. — *Scott Yanow*

Unreleased Edison Laterals / Feb. 10, 1928-Apr. 6, 1929 / Diamond Cut Productions ✦✦✦

This CD contains 21 formerly rare performances originally recorded for the Edison label during 1928-29. The music covers a wide variety of styles from dance bands (including the California Ramblers) and pop vocalists to the New York Military Band; some titles were previously unreleased. Lovers of 1920s music (as opposed to jazz collectors) will enjoy this sampler the most. — *Scott Yanow*

Usa All-Stars in Berlin / Feb. 1955 / Jazz Band ✦✦✦

The Jazz at the Philharmonic All-Stars are featured on this enjoyable, if not quite essential CD imported from England. Trumpeters Dizzy Gillespie and Roy Eldridge, trombonist Bill Harris, tenor saxophonist Flip Phillips, pianist Oscar Peterson, guitarist Herb Ellis, bassist Ray Brown and drummer Louis Bellson stretch out on two fairly exciting jams and play a ballad medley. In addition, Bellson has a drum feature, the Oscar Peterson Trio romps through two songs, clarinetist Buddy DeFranco is showcased with Peterson on "Billie's Bounce," and Ella Fitzgerald sings the bright "Papa Loves Mambo" and scats throughout a brief "Perdido." — *Scott Yanow*

● **V-Disc: The Songs That Went to War** / Aug. 27, 1943-Jul. ??, 1948 / Time Life ✦✦✦✦

During World War II a strike by the Musicians Union kept professional players off records for a long period. To fill the gap, a special "V-Disc" program was instituted to provide new music for military personnel serving overseas. This attractive four-CD box set from Time-Life contains 79 performances by a wide variety of artists from the period. Most of the music is jazz but there are some numbers from pop performers; such notables as Benny Goodman, Woody Herman, San Kenton, Lionel Hampton, Glenn Miller, the Nat King Cole Trio, Muggsy Spanier, Hoagy Carmichael, Ella Fitzgerald, Roy Eldridge, Paul Robeson, Hot Lips Page, Marian Anderson, Jack Teagarden, Louis Armstrong, Bunk Johnson, Les Paul and even Ethel Merman make strong appearances. There is a lot of valuable music on this well-conceived reissue. — *Scott Yanow*

Violin Summit / Sep. 30, 1966 / Verve ✦✦✦✦✦

This album is a jazz collector's dream come true. Four of the greatest jazz violinists of all time (Stuff Smith, Stephane Grappelli, Svend Asmussen and Jean-Luc Ponty) met up one day in the recording studio and recorded these swing-oriented performances. Accompanied by pianist Kenny Drew, bassist Niels Pedersen and drummer Axel Riel, the fiddle players all take solos on "It Don't Mean a Thing" and are well-featured on the standards with "Pent up House" (which showcases Grappelli and Ponty) being a high point. This unique outing (which will hopefully be reissued on CD eventually) is highly recommended. — *Scott Yanow*

Warner Jams, Vol. 1 / Warner Brothers ✦✦✦

On this CD some of the top young jazz players from the Warner Brothers roster (trumpeter Wallace Roney, altoist Kenny Garrett, Joshua Redman on tenor, guitarist Peter Bernstein, organist Larry Goldings, pianist Brad Mehldau, bassist Clarence Seay and drummer Brian Blade) are featured both individually and collectively. There are five showcases (for the three horns and the two keyboards), three songs in which a different duo of horns gets to extensively trade off, and three looser numbers including an opening medium-up blues ("Blue Grass") that sounds like an outtake from a Jimmy Smith jam session. In general Kenny Garrett and Larry Goldings come across best. Garrett is the most advanced soloist on the date (sometimes hinting at the ideas of the M-Base players) while Goldings constantly pushes the horns in the ensembles and drives the rhythm section. Joshua Redman and Wallace Roney (the latter at his best on "Nature Boy") also have their strong moments. Although nothing all that innovative occurs during the hard bop-oriented performances, the straightahead music from these Young Lions is enjoyable and consistently swinging. — *Scott Yanow*

Weird Nightmare: Meditations on Mingus / Nov. 12, 1992 / Columbia ✦✦✦

On this installment of Hal Willner's series of tribute albums, Willner assembled a house band for his guests (including Keith Richards, Chuck D, Elvis Costello, Bill Frisell, Vernon Reid, Charlie Watts, Gary Lucas, Leonard Cohen, and Henry Rollins) to sit in with. *Weird Nightmare: Meditations on Mingus* is predictably uneven and wildly entertaining; it is a fitting tribute to the genius of Charles Mingus. — *AMG*

West Coast Jazz, Vol. 1 / Jun. 1922-Aug. 1931 / Arcadia ✦✦✦✦

The collector's label Arcadia found a niche by reissuing obscure recordings from territory bands of the 1920s and early '30s. On this LP, their first release, all of the music is by Los Angeles-based bands. Included are the two titles by Kid Ory's 1921 or 1922 band (which went by the odd title of "Spikes Seven Pods of Pepper Orchestra") along with various groups led by pianist Sonny Clay, Reb Spikes' Majors and Minors, the Dixie Serenaders and the excellent Curtis Mosby and his Dixieland Blue Blowers including the soundtrack of their appearance in the 1929 film *Hallelujah*. This historic music is easily recommended to collectors of 1920s jazz. — *Scott Yanow*

West Coast Jazz, Vol. 2 / Feb. 1925-1931 / Arcadia ✦✦✦

The second of two LPs by the Arcadia label to reissue obscure recordings from West Coast groups in the 1920s features bands from Hollywood and San Francisco. Included are long-forgotten performances by the Wilshire Dance Orchestra, Eddie Frazier's Plantation Orchestra, Carlyle Stevenson, Fred Elizade (his first two sides before moving to England), the Rhythm Makers, Tom Gerunovitch, Jack Danford's Ben Franklin Hotel Orchestra (which includes trumpeter Lu Watters in its personnel), Claude Sweeten's R.K. Olians and the Mezzanine Melodies. The hot dance music (often influenced by Red Nichols' Five Pennies) should delight 1920s collectors although this set is not too essential for more general listeners. — *Scott Yanow*

West Coast Jive / Aug. 2, 1945-Feb. 27, 1946 / Delmark ✦✦✦

This Delmark CD features music recorded in Los Angeles during 1945-46 that puts the focus on its colorful vocals yet is generally pretty jazz-oriented. Wynonie Harris shouts out three numbers, Duke Henderson is backed by such musicians as tenors Lucky Thompson and Wild Bill Moore in addition to bassist Charles Mingus, the barely documented Cee Pee Johnson Band is heard on six songs and there are features for the obscure Al "Stomp" Russell Trio and singer Frank Haywood. None of the music is really all that essential but these often jivey performances are quite accessible and fun. — *Scott Yanow*

What is Jazz / 1955 / Columbia ✦✦✦

This LP is a real collector's item. Leonard Bernstein talks about jazz and, with the assistance of vintage recordings and an all-star group assembled by trumpeter Buck Clayton, demonstrates various jazz styles. Most memorable are several examples of the standard "Sweet Sue" being played in different styles including a recording by the Miles Davis Quintet. Most of Bernstein's talking on this mid-'50s recording is surprisingly undated and collectors will find the album quite interesting. — *Scott Yanow*

World's Greatest Jazz Concert No. 1 / Feb. 22, 1947 / Jazzology ✦✦✦✦✦

With a title such as this one, it is impossible for the music to quite live up to the billing. However the performances (released for the first time on this Jazzology CD) are often quite special. On the first of two volumes (the second set was recorded at a different concert two months later), cornetist Wild Bill Davison, clarinetist Albert Nicholas and trombonist George Brunis (with the assistance of pianist Joe Sullivan, bassist Pops Foster and drummer Baby Dodds) form a very potent front line on three songs. Brunis and Davison also have individual features, veteran blues singer Bertha "Chippie" Hill takes a vocal, trumpeter Muggsy Spanier leads a group (with , Brunis, pianist Art Hodes and clarinetist Cecil Scott) on two songs and trumpeter-vocalist Hot Lips Page heads a hard-charging septet with clarinetist Tony Parenti. With all of those classic players, the music (not too surprisingly) is very enjoyable and spirited. Recommended. — *Scott Yanow*

World's Greatest Jazz Concert No. 2 / Apr. 26, 1947 / Jazzology ✦✦✦✦✦

The second of two CDs in this series was recorded two months after the earlier Jazzology release. This all-star concert is almost up to the level of the first. Trumpeter Muggsy Spanier, trombonist George Brunis and the great soprano saxophonist Sidney Bechet are heard on five spirited numbers, trombonist Jack Teagarden teams up in separate performances with Spanier and trumpeter Johnny Windhurst, Windhurst is heard with pianist Dick Wellstood in a quartet, Bechet has a couple of features, The Two Gospel Keys sing a couple of traditional numbers and finally Spanier, Windhurst, Brunis and clarinetist Bob Wilber team up for the closing "Dippermouth Blues." Dixieland and New Orleans jazz are urged to pick up both of these Jazzology sets. — *Scott Yanow*

Yes Sir, That's My Baby: The Songs of Walter Donaldson / ASV/Living Era ✦✦✦✦✦

Though not as much of a household name as such contemporaries as Irving Berlin, Walter Donaldson (1893-1947) was among the most successful composers on Tin Pan Alley from the end of World War I to the mid-1930s, when not a year went by that he didn't have a hit song. The biggest of those hits were "My Mammy," "Carolina In the Morning," "My Buddy," "Yes Sir, That's My Baby," "My Blue Heaven," and "Makin' Whoopee," but there were dozens more. *Yes Sir, That's My Baby: The Songs of Walter Donaldson* collects 26 Donaldson hits recorded between 1922 and 1944, many of them the original hit recordings made by Eddie Cantor, Al Jolson, Paul Whiteman, Ted Lewis, Gene Austin, Ruth Etting, Cliff "Ukulele Ike" Edwards, Maurice Chevalier, Louis Armstrong, the Boswell Sisters, the Mills Brothers, Billie Holiday, and Bing Crosby. For example, the version of "My Blue Heaven" (the most popular song in record history until "White Christmas" came along) is the hit version by Gene Austin from 1927, "That Certain Party" is the Ted Lewis original from 1925, and "Sleepy Head" is the Mills Brothers' 1934 recording. The album is not perfect—for one thing, there's no version at all of "My Buddy," and for another, the recordings of songs like "My Mammy" and "Yes Sir, That's My Baby," while performed by their popularizers, Jolson and Cantor, are '40s re-recordings, not the originals. But this extensive collection (running more than 76 minutes) is a major step in recognizing one of the most important songwriters of the interwar period, and for that it gets high marks. — *William Ruhlmann*

The Young Lions [1983] / Jun. 30, 1982 / Vee-Jay ✦✦✦✦✦

This two-LP set documents a very interesting and historic concert. While the term "Young Lions" later came to be applied to young hard bop-oriented soloists who were intent on playing swinging jazz, many of the 17 musicians heard during this concert came to be associated with the avant-garde. Performing in different combinations ranging from solo vibes to a version of "Nigerian Sunset" that includes everyone, the talented musicians (many of whom were only slightly known at the time) are trumpeter Wynton Marsalis (then just 21), vocalist Bobby McFerrin, the reeds of Paquito D'Rivera, John Purcell and Chico Freeman, trombonist Craig Harris, baritonist Hamiet Bluiett, flutist James Newton, guitarist Kevin Eubanks, violinist John Blake, vibraphonist Jay Hoggard, cellist Abdul Wadud, pianist Anthony Davis, bassists Avery Sharpe and Fred Hopkins, drummer Ronnie Burrage and percussionist Daniel Ponce. A strong highlight is "B 'N' W" which features the trio of McFerrin, Marsalis and Sharpe but quite a few of the selections are memorable. This two-fer, a near-classic, deserves to be reissued on CD. — *Scott Yanow*

Yule Struttin' / Oct. 27, 1953-Jul. 20, 1990 / Blue Note ✦✦✦

This CD has ten performances of Christmas songs from 1990 plus a few earlier recordings (Chet Baker's "Winter Wonderland," Count Basie's "Jingle Bells," Dexter Gordon's "Have Yourself a Merry Little Christmas" and Stanley Jordan's 1986 version of "Silent Night." With such top stars as Bobby Watson, Lou Rawls, Eliane Elias, Benny Green (who has two piano solos), Dianne Reeves, John Hart, John Scofield, Joey Calderazzo and Rick Margitza playing music not available elsewhere, this melodic CD is worth picking up. A particular highlight are two versions of "A Merrier Christmas," a previously unknown Thelonious Monk composition here performed separately by Benny Green and Dianne Reeves. — *Scott Yanow*

An Overview and Introduction to Jazz

Scott Yanow

Jazz, with its 100 plus years of history and countless number of significant names, can be a difficult music to explore, at least until one becomes addicted! Although there are few listeners who would equally appreciate all eras and styles of the music, its heritage, variety and depth are so vast that there are conversely few people who would not truly enjoy at least one or two of the styles if they were properly exposed. This essay will explore some of the more common questions asked about jazz and should give readers a friendly introduction to the music.

What is jazz? Through the decades many writers have attempted to answer this question but have generally fallen short by putting too many restrictions on what is and isn't jazz. Essentially jazz is music that puts an emphasis on improvisation and always has the feeling of the blues. Every other potential quality (swing, high musicianship, even whether the players are in-tune) is optional. What Dixieland, bebop, fusion and free jazz have in common are the constant opportunities for the musicians to constantly be creative and come up with new ideas; this is a major contrast to pop music where the players often try to duplicate a recording for a live audience. The blues feeling separates jazz from other styles (such as bluegrass, New Age and Indian ragas) that also use improvisation but are outside of jazz. Jazz can be a high-powered big band or a solo saxophonist playing long tones, it can be a singer interpreting a ballad, a rockish guitarist "freaking out" or a funky organ group. It can "borrow" its ideas from other types of music but as long as the musicians are trying their best to express themselves and are free to take the music in another direction if inspiration hits them, it is jazz.

How did jazz start? Unfortunately the answer to that question is not definitively known because the first jazz recordings (by the Original Dixieland Jazz Band in 1917) took place at least 20 years after jazz first began to be played. The theory I opt for is that jazz originated with New Orleans brass bands. Since the groups performed marches and popular songs of the 1880s and '90s during long parades and many of the musicians did not have formal musical education, after playing a melody several times, they would began to improvise variations, partly to relieve boredom and often for the pure fun of it. Since the first major name in jazz, cornetist Buddy Bolden, formed his original band in 1895, that year can serve as a useful starting point for jazz history even though one can only speculate what the music sounded like.

The evolution of jazz was originally quite slow (due to it being a regional music) until recordings in the 1920s began to speed up its progress. During a 50-year period the music evolved rapidly from the ensemble-oriented New Orleans jazz and Dixieland to swinging big bands, sophisticated bebop, several overlapping offshoots (cool jazz, hard bop, soul-jazz), avant-garde jazz (with free improvisations) and fusion which took some of the better elements from rock's most creative period. Since the mid-'70s, jazz's evolution has greatly slowed down even with the many new names taking the place of the elders. Where during the 1925-75 period, old styles were quickly discarded by modernists, during the past two decades various revival movements have resulted in virtually every jazz style being performed creatively (in addition to many recreations of past glories) and being kept alive.

Why isn't jazz more popular? Jazz was at the height of its popularity during the swing era when it was often utilized as dance music for teenagers. Unfortunately during the mid- to late '40s, an entertainment tax resulted in most nightclubs eliminating their dance floors. In addition, bop musicians (in trying to uplift the music above being mere entertainment) discouraged dancers. The result was that teenagers drifted away towards early R&B, pop ballad singers and eventually rock 'n' roll in the 1950s and Motown in the '60s. The ironic part is that most jazz (outside of the avant-garde) can be easily danced to; all it needs is a steady beat. The easiest way to immediately increase the audience would be to bring back dance floors, hire dance teachers and show listeners that not everyone has to sit down during performances! The acid jazz movement of the 1990s revived older soul-jazz records for dance clubs but unfortunately the music was often "dumbed down" by adding rather obvious funk rhythms, as if dancers could not figure out where the beat is!

Jazz has long been stuck between being an art form and entertainment, but there are advantages. Jazz festivals are generally much more fun than their equivalents in rock and classical. Jazz marathons have the party atmosphere of rock concerts but without the danger (few in the audience ever get arrested!) and it has the intelligence of a classical series but without the potential stuffiness.

A common question about jazz is "Where is it going?" The future of jazz is always unpredictable. In the late '50s when many jazz books came out, most commentators predicted that jazz and classical music would merge in the future; virtually no one predicted the rise of free jazz or fusion. Chances are that in the 21st century the current trend of mixing together different styles will continue and more sophisticated electronic instruments will be used creatively. Whether jazz will again catch on as America's popular music is not known but the potential is always there. Jazz, with its many styles, is diverse enough to appeal to anyone but it has long suffered from a lack of exposure. When the music is properly marketed (it takes more work than simpler forms of pop music), it shows a great deal of life; witness the surprise celebrity status of Joe Henderson and Joshua Redman, both of whom became famous without simplifying their music.

How does a beginner start to learn about jazz? Obviously purchasing this book is a good start! In exploring the great masters of the music, it is wise to begin with recordings from the six immortal giants who virtually invented large aspects of the music: Louis Armstrong, Duke Ellington, Charlie Parker, Dizzy Gillespie, Miles Davis and John Coltrane. From that point on, when one discovers what area of the music is most enjoyable, one can start exploring the music of these musicians' sidemen and contemporaries such as Jelly Roll Morton, Sidney Bechet, Bix Beiderbecke, Fats Waller, Bessie Smith, Benny Goodman, Coleman Hawkins, Lester Young, Art Tatum, Count Basie, Billie Holiday, Ella Fitzgerald, Bud Powell, Thelonious Monk, Gerry Mulligan, Dave Brubeck, Stan Getz, Lee Morgan, Cannonball Adderley, Sonny Rollins, Horace Silver, Jimmy Smith, Art Blakey, Bill Evans, Charles Mingus, Ornette Coleman, Cecil Taylor, Chick Corea, Weather Report, Wynton Marsalis, Keith Jarrett and Pat Metheny. The number of significant and colorful jazz musicians and singers is endless and learning about jazz can be a very enjoyable way to spend one's life!

A few tips for getting started. If one is coming to jazz through R&B or pop music, try some Grover Washington, Jr. and David Sanborn first and then progress to John Coltrane and Chick Corea. Listeners who enjoy the sound of rock should explore Weather Report, John Scofield, Jean-Luc Ponty and fusion-era Miles Davis before reaching Coltrane and Ornette Coleman. Classical fans can enter the jazz world through Bill Evans, the Miles Davis/Gil Evans recordings of the 1950s and the Modern Jazz Quartet. Enjoy current dance music with catchy melodies and funky rhythms? Try Lee Morgan's The Sidewinder, most Horace Silver albums and records by the Stanley Turrentine/Shirley Scott group of the 1960s. And everyone can benefit from getting a few Louis Armstrong records!

There are a countless number of ways to enter the jazz world. The key is to keep an open mind towards different styles (most of the more rewarding jazz recordings grow in interest with each listen) and not miss jazz altogether! One usually has to go a little out of their way to find the music, but it is well worth the search. — *Scott Yanow*

Fifteen Recommended Jazz Recordings to Start With:

Louis Armstrong, *Plays W.C. Handy* (Columbia—1997 version)

Benny Goodman, *Sing, Sing, Sing* (Bluebird)

Billie Holiday, *The Quintessential, Vol. 5* (Columbia)

Count Basie, *The Atomic Mr. Basie* (Roulette)

Duke Ellington, *Uptown* (Columbia)

Charlie Parker, *Yardbird Suite* (Rhino)

Dizzy Gillespie, *At Newport* (Verve)

Dave Brubeck, *Time Out* (Columbia)

Miles Davis, *Kind of Blue* (Columbia)

John Coltrane, *My Favorite Things* (Atlantic)

Stan Getz, *Getz/Gilberto* (Verve)

Wes Montgomery, *The Incredible Jazz Guitar* (Original Jazz Classics)

Lee Morgan, *The Sidewinder* (Blue Note)

Weather Report, *Heavy Weather* (Columbia)

Wynton Marsalis, *Blue Interlude* (Columbia)

Six Essential Jazz Books:

American Musicians II by Whitney Balliett (Oxford Univ. Press, 1997)

The Encyclopedia of Jazz by Leonard Feather (Da Capo Press, 1960)

Jazz Anecdotes by Bill Crow (Oxford Univ. Press, 1990)

The Jazz Life by Nat Hentoff (Da Capo Press, 1961)

The Jazz Scene by W. Royal Stokes (Oxford Univ. Press, 1991)

Jazz—The Rough Guide by Ian Carr, Digby Fairweather & Brian Priestley (Penguin Group, 1995)

A Brief History of Jazz

One of the major questions that will go forever unanswered is "How did jazz start?" The first jazz recording was in 1917, but the music existed in at least primitive forms for 20 years before that. Influenced by classical music, marches, spirituals, work songs, ragtime, blues and the popular music of the period, jazz was already a distinctive form of music by the time it was first documented.

The chances are that the earliest jazz was played by unschooled musicians in New Orleans marching bands. Music was a major part of life in New Orleans from at least the 1890s with brass bands hired to play at parades, funerals, parties and dances. It stands to reason that the musicians (who often did not read music) did not simply play the melodies continuously but came up with variations to keep the performances interesting.

Since cornetist Buddy Bolden (the first famous musician to be considered a jazz player) formed his band in 1895, one can use that year as a symbolic birthdate for jazz. During the next two decades the undocumented music progressed but probably at a slow pace. Bolden (whose worsening mental illness led to his being committed in 1906) was succeeded by Freddie Keppard as the top New Orleans cornetist and Keppard was eventually surpassed by King Oliver. Although some New Orleans musicians traveled up North, jazz remained strictly a regional music until the World War I years.

On Jan. 30, 1917 a White group immodestly called the Original Dixieland Jazz Band recorded "Darktown Strutters' Ball" and "Indiana" for Columbia. The often-riotous music was considered too radical to be released at the time, so on Feb. 26 the ODJB went to Victor and recorded "Livery Stable Blues" and "The Original Dixieland One Step." The latter performances were immediately released. "Livery Stable Blues" (which featured the horns imitating animals!) became a best-seller and jazz was discovered, sort of. Within a short period of time other groups were recorded playing in a similar all-ensemble style (the ODJB had virtually no solos). Jazz became a fad for a few years (as promoters rushed to make money off of the new music) and the Original Dixieland Jazz Band in 1919 was a sensation in London. However it would be a few years before Black jazz musicians were recorded, leading some observers a the time to the false conclusion that Whites (and the ODJB in particular) had invented the music! A backlash later on led to others feeling that only Blacks could play jazz and that all of the White players were poor imitations. Obviously both beliefs have been proven false many times since then.

In 1920 Mamie Smith recorded the first blues, "Crazy Blues," and the jazz fad was soon supplanted by a blues craze. However jazz continued to progress and the New Orleans Rhythm Kings (one of the first groups to feature short solos) in 1922 sounded a decade ahead of the ODJB. 1923 was a key year for jazz because during that year King Oliver's Creole Jazz Band (which had among its sidemen cornetist Louis Armstrong and clarinetist Johnny Dodds), blues singer Bessie Smith and pianist-composer Jelly Roll Morton all made their recording debuts. While King Oliver's band would be considered the definitive ensemble-oriented New Orleans group, Louis Armstrong would soon permanently change jazz.

In the early 1920s Chicago was the center of jazz. When Louis Armstrong joined Fletcher Henderson's big band in New York in 1924, he found that the Big Apple's musicians (although technically superior) often played with a staccato feeling and without much blues feeling. Armstrong, through his explosive, dramatic and swinging solos with Henderson, was extremely influential in changing the way that jazz musicians phrased and in opening up possibilities for improvisers. In fact it could be argued that Louis Armstrong was chiefly responsible (although it probably would have happened eventually) for jazz's emphasis shifting from collective improvisation to individual solos, setting the stage for the swing era.

The 1920s became known as the Jazz Age (although as much for its liberal social attitudes as for its music). Jazz began to greatly influence dance bands and even the most commercial outfits started having short solos and a syncopated rhythm section. Louis Armstrong's remarkable series of Hot Five and Hot Seven recordings

inspired other musicians to stretch themselves while his popularization of scat singing and a relaxed vocal phrasing influenced Bing Crosby (who in turn influenced everyone else!). Such players as cornetist Bix Beiderbecke (who had a cooler sound than Armstrong), pianist Jelly Roll Morton (both in solos and with his Red Hot Peppers), pianist James P. Johnson (the king of stride pianists), arranger-composer Duke Ellington and the up-and-coming tenor Coleman Hawkins became important forces in the jazz world.

By the latter half of the decade, larger jazz-based orchestras had become popular and the collective improvisation to be found in Dixieland was going out of style and restricted to smaller groups. When the Depression hit, it pushed Dixieland almost completely underground for a decade. The general public did not want to be reminded of the carefree days of the 1920s and instead for a few years preferred ballads and dance music. However when Benny Goodman suddenly became popular in 1935, the newer generation showed that they were interested in doing what they could to overlook the Depression by having a good time and dancing to hard-swinging orchestras. The 1935-46 period was accurately known as the big band era for the large orchestras dominated the pop music charts. During this decade jazz was a large part of popular music, not just an influence as it had been earlier. Glenn Miller and Artie Shaw had million sellers and Benny Goodman, Count Basie and Duke Ellington were household names and celebrities.

During those years jazz developed in several ways. New soloists (such as pianists Art Tatum and Teddy Wilson, tenor saxophonist Lester Young and trumpeters Roy Eldridge and Bunny Berigan) came up with alternative styles, big band arranging became more sophisticated, Dixieland was revived and rediscovered (Lu Watters' Yerba Buena Jazz Band was a major force) and jazz was celebrated for the first time as an important part of America. However this golden age of popularity would not last.

Due to jazz's continual evolution, it was perhaps inevitable that it would eventually advance far ahead of what the general public preferred in its popular music. In the early 1940s many of the younger musicians sought to move beyond swing music (which was bogging down in clichéd arrangements and novelties) and develop their own conception of playing. Altoist Charlie Parker and trumpeter Dizzy Gillespie were the main founders of the new music called bebop or bop but they were not alone and were soon joined by dozens of other musicians. Themes were often quickly discarded as the soloists indulged in more advanced chordal improvisations (leading some critics to ask, "Where's the melody?"), harmonies and rhythms became much more complicated and, most seriously of all, the music was performed less and less for dancers. A recording strike during 1942-44, a prohibitive entertainment tax (which closed many dance halls) and the growing popularity of pop singers doomed the big bands, and the elimination of dance floors at many clubs made jazz into a music strictly for listening. By being uplifted to the level of an art music, jazz was isolated from the pop music world and saw its audience shrink drastically as other simpler styles rushed in to fill the gap.

However its commercial decline did not slow down jazz's artistic growth. Bop, once considered a radical music (the recording strike stopped many listeners from hearing its gradual growth), became a large part of the jazz mainstream by the 1950s. Cool jazz (or West Coast jazz), which put a greater emphasis on softer tones and arrangements and was at its height in popularity in the mid-50s, and hard bop (which brought out more soulful elements of jazz that were sometimes discarded in bop) were outgrowths of bebop and had their fans. But it was with the rise of the avant-garde (sometimes called free jazz) that improvised music moved a giant step forward, leaving even more listeners behind!

When Ornette Coleman and his quartet were featured at the Five Spot in New York in 1959, many listeners who were just beginning to accept the music of Thelonious Monk were bewildered. Ornette and his sidemen quickly stated a theme in unison and then improvised very freely without using chords at all! During the same period John Coltrane, who had taken bop to its extreme with the endless number of chords he used in "Giant Steps," began to jam passionately over simple repetitive vamps. Pianist Cecil Taylor's percussive atonality owed as much to contemporary classical music as to earlier jazz stylists and Eric Dolphy's wide interval jumps were completely unpredictable. Avant-garde jazz had arrived!

By the mid-1960s free jazz was filled with high-energy improvisers who explored sounds as much as notes. Within a few years with the rise of the Art Ensemble of Chicago and Anthony Braxton, space was utilized much more liberally in the music and by the 1970s many avant-garde artists were spending much of their time integrating improvisations with complex compositions. The music was no longer continuously free form but musicians had complete freedom in their solos to create whatever sounds they felt fit. Although this music has been overshadowed by other styles since the 1970s, it is still a viable option for creative improvisers, and its innovations continue to indirectly influence the modern mainstream of jazz.

The 1970s are best remembered as the fusion era, when many jazz musicians integrated aspects of rock, R&B and pop into their music. Until the late '60s, the jazz and rock worlds had stayed pretty much separate but, with the rise of electric keyboards, a great deal of experimentation took place. Miles Davis, who was an innovator in bop, cool jazz, hard bop and his own brand of the avant-garde, became a pacesetter in fusion when he recorded *In a Silent Way* and *Bitches Brew*. Groups began to be formed that combined together the improvising and musicianship of jazz with the power and rhythms of rock; most notable were Return to Forever, Weather Report and the Mahavishnu Orchestra. By 1975 this movement began to run out of gas artistically but due to its moneymaking potential it has continued up to the present time, often in watered-down form as crossover or instrumental pop and given the inaccurate name of "contemporary jazz."

The history of jazz from 1920-75 was a constant rush forward with new styles considered out of date within five or ten years. In the 1980s it suddenly became acceptable to honor the past and to look back before bop for inspiration. While Dixieland had remained quite active as an underground music for decades (it was at its height of popularity in the 1950s), few in the jazz modern mainstream acknowledged its existence and importance before the '80s. Wynton Marsalis, who symbolized the decade, began as a trumpeter greatly inspired by the playing of Miles Davis of the mid-'60s. He eventually found his own sound by going back in time and exploring the music of the pre-bop masters, and the result was that (even when he played modern new music) Marsalis was able to come up with fresh approaches by borrowing and adapting ideas from the distant past.

Many of the young players that have followed Marsalis ignore fusion and even most of the innovations of the avant-garde to use hard bop as the basis for their music. It was a rather unusual development to have so many musicians in their twenties playing in a style that was at its prime before their birth, but by the 1990s many of these "Young Lions" were finally developing their own sounds and starting to build on the earlier innovations.

Nearly all styles of jazz are still active in the 1990s including Dixieland, classic jazz, mainstream (essentially small group swing), bop, hard bop, post-bop, the avant-garde and various forms of fusion. Very much an international music (some of the most stimulating sounds of recent times have come from Europe), the evolution of jazz has definitely slowed down during the past 20 years. At this point in time it is not apparent which direction jazz will go in the future (some cynics even think the music has essentially reached the end of its development), but one can bet that as long as recordings exist (along with the need for self-expression), jazz will survive.

Jazz Innovators

Scott Yanow

Throughout the history of jazz there have been literally thousands of talented improvisers and hundreds who have developed their own individual voices and approaches. There are six, however, whose accomplishments, originality, innovations and influence tower above the rest; each one of the six greatly altered the vocabulary of jazz and permanently changed the music:

Louis Armstrong (trumpet, vocals)
Duke Ellington (composer, arranger, bandleader, piano)
Charlie Parker (alto sax)
Dizzy Gillespie (trumpet)
Miles Davis (trumpet, bandleader)
John Coltrane (tenor sax, soprano sax)

Here is a list of the second level of jazz greats, artists whose music also greatly enhanced jazz. The categories are meant as a guide and do not necessarily sum up the musicians' entire careers:

New Orleans Jazz

Jelly Roll Morton (piano, composer)
King Oliver (cornet)
Red Allen (trumpet)
Kid Ory (trombone)
Johnny Dodds (clarinet)
Sidney Bechet (soprano, clarinet)

Classic Jazz

Bix Beiderbecke (cornet)
Jack Teagarden (trombone, vocals)
Pee Wee Russell (clarinet)
Bud Freeman (tenor)
James P. Johnson (piano)
Fats Waller (piano, composer, vocals)
Earl Hines (piano)
Joe Venuti (violin)

Bessie Smith (vocals)
Eddie Condon (bandleader)

Swing

Roy Eldridge (trumpet)
Bunny Berigan (trumpet)
Charlie Shavers (trumpet)
Clark Terry (fluegelhorn)
Benny Goodman (clarinet, bandleader)
Artie Shaw (clarinet, bandleader)
Coleman Hawkins (tenor)
Lester Young (tenor)
Ben Webster (tenor)
Johnny Hodges (alto)
Benny Carter (alto, arranger)
Harry Carney (baritone)
Art Tatum (piano)
Teddy Wilson (piano)
Count Basie (piano, bandleader)
Nat King Cole (piano, vocals)
Django Reinhardt (guitar)
Charlie Christian (guitar)
Lionel Hampton (vibes)
Stephane Grappelli (violin)
Jimmy Blanton (bass)
Gene Krupa (drums)
Buddy Rich (drums)
Louis Bellson (drums)
Billie Holiday (vocals)
Ella Fitzgerald (vocals)

Bop

Howard McGhee (trumpet)
Fats Navarro (trumpet)
J.J. Johnson (trombone)
Buddy DeFranco (clarinet)
Dexter Gordon (tenor)
Bud Powell (piano)
Thelonious Monk (piano, composer)
Oscar Peterson (piano)
Erroll Garner (piano)
Milt Jackson (vibes)
Joe Pass (guitar)
Oscar Pettiford (bass)
Max Roach (drums, bandleader)
Sarah Vaughan (vocals)
Lambert, Hendricks & Ross (vocal group)

Cool Jazz

Gerry Mulligan (baritone)
Lennie Tristano (piano, bandleader)

Hard Bop

Clifford Brown (trumpet)
Lee Morgan (trumpet)
Freddie Hubbard (trumpet)
Cannonball Adderley (alto)
Phil Woods (alto)
Art Pepper (alto)
Sonny Rollins (tenor)
Rahsaan Roland Kirk (tenor, stritch, manzello, flutes)
Wes Montgomery (guitar)
Horace Silver (piano, composer)
Jimmy Smith (organ)
Art Blakey (drums, bandleader)

Avant-Garde

Charles Mingus (bass, bandleader)
Eric Dolphy (alto, bass clarinet, flute)
Ornette Coleman (alto, composer)
Anthony Braxton (alto, composer)
Cecil Taylor (piano)

Post Bop

Woody Shaw (trumpet)
Jackie McLean (alto)
Joe Henderson (tenor)
Wayne Shorter (tenor, soprano, composer)
Bill Evans (piano)
McCoy Tyner (piano)
Elvin Jones (drums)
Tony Williams (drums)
Gil Evans (arranger)

Fusion

Chick Corea (piano, keyboards)
Herbie Hancock (piano, keyboards)
Joe Zawinul (keyboards)
Jaco Pastorius (electric bass)

Modern Mainstream/1990s Jazz

Wynton Marsalis (trumpet)
Eddie Daniels (clarinet, tenor)
Keith Jarrett (piano)
Pat Metheny (guitar)
John Scofield (guitar)
Bill Frisell (guitar)

Although this list could easily be twice as long, it is accurate to say that any representative jazz record collection should include at least some of the music recorded by each of these important stylists. — *Scott Yanow*

Jazz Singers

Scott Yanow

For decades the question has been asked: What is a jazz singer? Some listeners claim that a vocalist has to scat like a horn (what do they consider Billie Holiday?) while others say that simply swinging is enough (do they include Tony Bennett and Jack Jones?).

Here is the most logical definition. A jazz singer is a vocalist who brings his or her own interpretation to a song and improvises through words, sounds, notes and/or phrasing. The difference between a jazz and a pop singer (and the same can be said for musicians) is that a jazz vocalist is spontaneous in concert. The goal is not to duplicate a record (although arrangements and frameworks can be followed) but rather to express how one feels at the moment. Respect can be shown for the original lyrics and melody but, if one is only duplicating the written music, the chances are that the singer falls into the cabaret area.

Since the human voice was the first musical instrument and the earliest music had to be spontaneous, one can accurately surmise that the first musical sounds were made by a jazz singer! However it was in the 1920s that the first jazz vocalists were documented on record.

For simplicity sake, the history of male and female jazz singers are here discussed separately. Starting with the former, Louis Armstrong and Bing Crosby were the most important male jazz singers of the '20s but they were not the first. Cliff Edwards (known as Ukulele Ike), a talented performer who also played ukulele and kazoo, was a colorful jazz-oriented singer who led his first record dates in 1924. Although he became an alcoholic and a part-time actor used for comedy relief, Edwards made a brief comeback in the early 1940s as the voice of Jiminy Cricket in Pinocchio, singing "When You Wish Upon A Star." Another early singer was the versatile arranger-reed player Don Redman who took the first ever recorded scat vocal (substituting nonsense syllables for words) with Fletcher Henderson on 1924's "My Papa Doesn't Two-Time No Time."

Most male singers who were caught on record in the 1920s are difficult to listen to today. Notable primarily for their volume and ability to sing words clearly, the great majority come across as pompous and semi-classical. The early blues singers were exceptions but they had less of a connection to the jazz world than their female counterparts (such as Bessie Smith).

Louis Armstrong was the first major male jazz singer. Other than one early song with Fletcher Henderson, his initial vocals on record were in 1925-26 with his Hot

Five and they still sound fresh and lively today. Armstrong vocalized with the phrasing of a trumpeter, he consistently improvised and (starting with "Heebies Jeebies") he proved to be a masterful scat singer. Even when Satch was sticking close to the words, his phrasing was spontaneous and he altered both the notes and their timing to dramatic effect. Through the years his singing was such a huge influence on everyone from Bing Crosby and Billie Holiday to Ella Fitzgerald and Jon Hendricks that it would not be much of an exaggeration to say that he largely invented jazz singing.

Bing Crosby, a great admirer of Armstrong's, brought Louis' innovations into the world of pop music, first as part of the Rhythm Boys with the Paul Whiteman Orchestra and then as the premiere "crooner" of the 1930s. Crosby's baritone voice saved the world from the many "boy tenors" who were threatening to dominate music of the late 1920s. Other important pre-swing male singers included the always-exciting Cab Calloway, trombonist Jack Teagarden and pianist Fats Waller plus the Mills Brothers. While the Mills Brothers became famous in later years for their pop records, in the 1930s they brought the art of imitating instruments to an unparalleled level, often sounding like a five piece band when in fact the only "real" instrument that they used was an acoustic guitar.

During the swing era, female singers were much more common than male jazz vocalists (virtually every big band had the former) but there were some major stylists. From Kansas City came the two memorable blues singers Jimmy Rushing (with Count Basie's Orchestra) and Big Joe Turner, both of whom had long careers. Billy Eckstine made his debut with Earl Hines' band and Frank Sinatra (an inspiration to jazz vocalists although not an improvising jazz singer himself) became famous with Tommy Dorsey. A brilliant pianist, Nat King Cole's highly appealing singing would eventually draw him to the world of pop. Two other influential forces were the jivey Slim Gaillard (whose "Flat Foot Floogie" kept him going for 50 years) and the charismatic Louis Jordan who with his Tympani Five helped launch R&B.

With the rise of bebop in the mid-1940s, jazz and pop singing largely split apart. Scat singing became more complex as practiced by Babs Gonzales (with his Four Bips and a Bop), Joe Carroll and Dizzy Gillespie. Vocalese, the art of writing lyrics to fit recorded solos, was developed by Eddie Jefferson, popularized by King Pleasure (whose "Moody's Mood for Love" and "Parker's Mood" are classics) and brought to its highest level by Jon Hendricks in the 1950s as part of the definitive jazz vocal group (Lambert, Hendricks and Ross with Dave Lambert and Annie Ross). Manhattan Transfer in the 1980s and '90s, when they perform jazz, sometimes approaches the magic of L, H & Ross.

While Ray Charles mixed together gospel, soul and R&B with the spirit of jazz, and Jimmy Witherspoon, Ernie Andrews, Bill Henderson and Joe Williams fell into both the jazz and blues worlds, Chet Baker's boyish charm on ballads in the '50s made him a heartthrob for a period. Billy Eckstine's warm baritone voice would have made him a movie star were it not for the racism of the period; Blacks were not given romantic leads in the 1950s! Eckstine did influence a generation of ballad singers including Earl Coleman and Johnny Hartman (whose 1963 collaboration with John Coltrane is a classic).

Two of the most significant male jazz singers of the 1960s (and beyond) were both talented lyricists who sang ironic and socially conscious words: Oscar Brown Jr. and Mose Allison. However there were few important male singers in the avant-garde and fusion movements although Leon Thomas' yodelling with Pharoah Sanders made "The Creator Has A Master Plan" into a surprise hit. Mark Murphy and Bob Dorough had their niches and Dave Frishberg developed into a superb lyricist and composer but by the 1980s and into the 90s, there was a serious shortage of significant jazz singers under the age of 60. Dominating the era was the swinging and remarkable Mel Tormé (who until his stroke in 1996 was improving with age throughout his sixties) and the seemingly ageless Joe Williams. The talented Al Jarreau had shown great promise in the 1970s but then chose to spend his musical life in R&B. Bobby McFerrin, an incredible singer (check out the hard-to-find Elektra Musician LP The Voice for an unaccompanied concert), maintained a disappointingly low profile after having a major hit in 1988 with "Don't Worry, Be Happy." The gospel-jazz acapella group Take Six also were wandering away from jazz into pop music.

However in the mid-1990s two new voices emerged. While Kevin Mahogany is building his career on the tradition of Joe Williams, bop and standards, Kurt Elling is an extension of Mark Murphy who also takes wild chances, sometimes improvising words and stories. Both show great promise in keeping alive the legacy largely founded by Louis Armstrong seventy years before.

In contrast, there has never been a shortage of female singers. Starting with the classic blues singers in the 1920s (Mamie Smith began it all with "Crazy Blues" in 1920), females have largely graced bandstands as singers rather than musicians; that situation has only been gradually changing in the 1990s. The fact that so many females can sing at least at a mediocre level (and an average singer always seems to get more applause than any mere musician) has resulted in a great deal of unfair prejudice against the species in general through the decades. As is true of the male vocalists, the best female singers are the ones that have a real feel for the music rather than just a pleasant voice, and the greats always emerge eventually from the masses.

An incomplete history of female jazz singers can be described in four words: Bessie, Billie, Ella and Sassy. Bessie Smith, the Empress of the Blues, towered over the 1920s. After Mamie Smith started the blues craze, many female singers who had ties to the vaudeville stage, carnival shows or just had strong voices were rushed to the recording studios. Among the more memorable performers were Ma Rainey, Ida Cox and Alberta Hunter (who made a successful comeback in the late 1970s when she was in her '80s) but Bessie Smith outshone everyone. Her powerful voice overcame both the primitive recording facilities of 1923 and erratic musicians; her interpretations of timeless messages still communicate to today's listeners. Fortunately Columbia has made all of Smith's recordings available, most recently on five double-CD's.

Ethel Waters was Bessie Smith's closest competitor in the 1920s and she eventually surpassed Bessie. A versatile singer who started with the blues, Waters was one of the first Black performers who was permitted to interpret superior American popular songs; Irving Berlin even wrote several numbers specifically for her. Waters, who introduced such standards as "Dinah," "Am I Blue" and "Stormy Weather," also became a dramatic actress and a major influence on such slightly later singers as Lee Wiley.

Ruth Etting was probably the best-known female vocalist of the early 1930s and, although more of a pop singer than a jazz performer, her voice is still worth hearing. Annette Hanshaw was her counterpart in jazz and only her decision to retire when she was but 23 kept her from gaining worldwide fame for her very likable style. The Boswell Sisters also broke up early (in 1936 when all of the sisters got married) but during the seven previous years they set a very high standard for jazz vocal groups that was not reached until Lambert, Hendricks and Ross were formed two decades later. Connee Boswell continued a reasonably successful solo career but it is her early work with Martha and Vet Boswell that is most stirring.

Mildred Bailey was the first "girl singer" to perform regularly with a big band (Paul Whiteman's). She soon became a leader in her own right and during her marriage to xylophonist Red Norvo, co-led his orchestra. Her high voice appealed to many and she helped to popularize "Georgia On My Mind" and "Rockin' Chair."

During the swing era there were a countless number of female singers who straddled the boundary between jazz and pop music. Most were used by big bands to add glamour to the stage and they generally only had the opportunity to take one melody chorus per song. Among the better band singers were Helen Ward with Benny Goodman, Helen O'Connell with Jimmy Dorsey, Ivie Anderson with Duke Ellington and Helen Forrest who spent time with the bands of Goodman, Harry James and Artie Shaw.

However the mid- to late 1930s were most notable for the emergence of Billie Holiday and Ella Fitzgerald. Lady Day's behind the beat phrasing disturbed some clubowners and fans at first before they became used to her approach. Her phrasing was subtle (influenced initially by Louis Armstrong) and Holiday frequently altered melodies to fit her small range and her particular mood. She spent mostly undocumented periods with the orchestras of Count Basie and Artie Shaw but it was her small group recordings with all-star groups headed by pianist Teddy Wilson (and which by 1937 often teamed her with tenor saxophonist Lester Young) that initially made her famous. Lady Day's chaotic personal life and eventual heroin addiction ruined her life and career (during the 1950s her voice declined year-by-year) but her prime (1935-52) was filled with classic music that still inspires other singers for Billie Holiday often lived the words she sang.

Ella Fitzgerald had a major hit ("A-Tisket, A-Tasket") with Chick Webb's Orchestra in 1938 when she was only 20. Although quite popular from then on, she was often saddled in her early years with juvenile novelty tunes despite the fact that she was actually superior at that point on ballads. After becoming a solo artist in 1942, Ella developed quickly as a jazz singer and within a few years was a superb scat singer who was a witty ad-libber. Her beautiful voice allowed her to uplift virtually everything she sang and she was a major attraction throughout the 1940s, '50s, '60s, '70s, '80s and into the early '90s when bad health forced her retirement. Some observers have carped that Ella always sounded too happy (she absolutely loved singing) and that she did not put enough feeling into heavier songs such as "Love For Sale" and "Lush Life." However late in life, Ella once again became a superior ballad interpreter. The ironic part is that her upbringing was as tumultuous as Billie Holiday's, but to her singing was an escape from her beginnings. Certainly when it came to swinging and adding beauty to a song, she had few competitors.

Other top female singers from the swing era include Anita O'Day (who found her initial fame with Gene Krupa's band), Helen Humes (who came into her own after leaving Count Basie's band), the sophisticated Lee Wiley (the first singer to

record full sets of a specific composer's songbook), Maxine Sullivan and Peggy Lee (whose quiet style foreshadowed and inspired the cool-toned singers of the 1950s).

Late in the swing era, Dinah Washington and Sarah Vaughan made their first impact. Dinah Washington, after starting with Lionel Hampton, proved during the 1945-58 period that she could sing anything: jazz, blues, R&B, religious hymns and pop. Her distinctive and spirited voice made her a regular big seller. After having a giant hit in "What a Difference a Day Makes" in 1959, Washington stuck mostly to pop music during her last few years.

Sarah Vaughan, who first sang with the Earl Hines and Billy Eckstine Orchestras, had an incredible voice. From the mid-1940s until her death in 1990, Sassy was always one of the top jazz singers, even when she spent long periods off records. She understood bebop (recording with Charlie Parker and Dizzy Gillespie) and she had the technique to interpret any song that interested her; sometimes she would strangle to death weak material. If only Sassy had recorded with Ella!

Ella Fitzgerald and Sarah Vaughan dominated the postwar years but they were far from alone among female jazz singers. Anita O'Day's sly swinging style was an influence on June Christy, whose work with Stan Kenton in turn inspired other cool-toned singers. The 1950s and '60s found such vocalists maturing as Carmen McRae (who had a productive 40-year career), Helen Merrill, Chris Connor, Annie Ross (the female third of the innovative vocal group Lambert, Hendricks and Ross), Ernestine Anderson and Peggy Lee. Abbey Lincoln interpreted dramatic lyrics under the tutelage of Max Roach, Betty Carter stretched the boundaries of scat singing and a housewife named Astrud Gilberto cooed "The Girl From Ipanema."

Although initially tied to the bop tradition, Betty Carter could be considered among the first avant-garde jazz singers. Sheila Jordan (who is one of the few who can improvise intelligent words in rhyme) recorded infrequently but always memorably before becoming more active in the 1980s. Patty Waters recorded two atmospheric (and somewhat scary) records for ESP before slipping away; she re-emerged in the mid-1990s. Jeanne Lee, who debuted on a duet set with pianist Ran Blake, created some very explorative music in Europe, Flora Purim frequently hinted at greatness and Urszula Dudziak utilized electronic devices. However most female jazz singers have preferred to stick to standards.

With the passing of Ella and Sassy, there is not currently one single dominant female singer, but that is not from a lack of candidates. Veterans such as Shirley Horn (who mostly sticks to slow ballads), Ernestine Anderson, Etta Jones and Abbey Lincoln continued in the 1990s to make fine music. Dee Dee Bridgewater (based in France), Vanessa Rubin and Nnenna Freelon give consistently fresh viewpoints to standards. Kitty Margolis, Madeline Eastman, Roseanna Vitro and Karryn Allyson keep the spirit of bop alive, Diana Krall's Nat King Cole tribute delights many, Diane Schuur sounds at her best when a big band is blaring behind her, Banu Gibson is the finest of all the classic jazz singers and, when it comes to interpreting lyrics from the golden age of the American popular song, Susannah McCorkle is difficult to beat.

The biggest problem facing today's singers is the lack of new material that can be successfully turned into jazz; most pop songs of the 1980s and '90s are not easily transferable. Cassandra Wilson, who has gained a great deal of publicity in the mid-1990s after years spent performing complex M-Base funk, has found a fresh repertoire by combining together ancient country blues with odd pop songs and World Music. Dianne Reeves, who has the potential to be the pacesetter, has spent much of her career alternating between pop, R&B, World Music and jazz but in recent times her formerly erratic recordings have been as exciting as her wonderful live performances.

Whether Dianne Reeves or Kurt Elling will affect the future of jazz at the level of an Ella Fitzgerald or Mel Tormé is open to question, but one has few doubts about the health of creative singing as jazz continues in its second century. — *Scott Yanow*

Twenty-Two Essential Jazz Vocal Recordings

Louis Armstrong, *Vol. 6: St. Louis Blues* (Columbia)

The Mills Brothers, *Chronological, Vol. 1* (JSP)

Cab Calloway, *1932-1934* (Classics)

Jimmy Rushing, *The Essential* (Vanguard)

Joe Williams, *Count Basie Swings/Joe Williams Sings* (Verve)

King Pleasure Sings With Annie Ross (Original Jazz Classics)

Lambert, Hendricks And Ross, *The Hottest New Group In Jazz* (Columbia/Legacy)

Mose Allison, *I Don't Worry About A Thing* (Rhino/Atlantic)

Johnny Hartman, *And John Coltrane* (Impulse)

Mel Tormé, *Fujitsu-Concord Festival* (1990) (Concord Jazz)

Kurt Elling, *The Messenger* (Blue Note)

Bessie Smith, *The Complete Recordings Vol. 3* (Columbia/Legacy)

Ethel Waters, *1926-1929* (Classics)

Boswell Sisters, *Vol. 1* (Collector's Classics)

Billie Holiday, *The Complete Decca Recordings* (Decca)

Dinah Washington, *Dinah Jams* (EmArcy)

Ella Fitzgerald, *The Complete Ella in Berlin* (Verve)

Abbey Lincoln, *Straight Ahead* (Candid)

Sarah Vaughan, *Complete: Live in Japan* (Mobile Fidelity)

Banu Gibson, *You Don't Know My Mind* (Swing Out)

Susannah McCorkle, *I'll Take Romance* (Concord Jazz)

Dianne Reeves, *Quiet After the Storm* (Blue Note)

Eight Books About Jazz Singers

American Singers by Whitney Balliett (Oxford Univ. Press, 1988)

Jazz Singing by Will Friedwald (Charles Scribners & Sons, 1990)

Alberta Hunter by Frank Taylor & Gerald Cook (McGraw-Hill, 1987)

His Eye Is On The Sparrow by Ethel Waters & Charles Samuels (DaCapo Press, 1950)

Wishing On The Moon by Donald Clarke (Viking, 1994)

Ella Fitzgerald by Stuart Nicholson (Da Capo Press, 1993)

High Times, Hard Times by Anita O'Day & George Ellis (Berkley Publ, 1981)

Stormy Weather by Linda Dahl (Limelight Editions, 1984)

Ragtime

Scott Yanow

Ragtime developed parallel to jazz but, because in its purest form it is not improvised, ragtime is America's equivalent to classical music rather than an actual jazz style. Often interpreted by solo pianists, it was an influence on early jazz and performed in the legendary bordellos of Storyville, New Orleans' red light district. However ragtime's true home was in Sedalia, Missouri (and later St. Louis) where composer Scott Joplin resided. Tom Turpin was actually the first known composer of a rag ("Harlem Rag" which was written in 1892 and finally published in 1897), but the big three of ragtime were Joplin, James Scott and Joseph Lamb although there were many other lesser-known composers.

From the time that Scott Joplin's "Maple Leaf Rag" caught on in 1899 up until the beginning of World War I, ragtime was the main popular musical style of the US. Its song structure (with four themes usually played in this format: A-A-B-B-A-C-C-D-D) and syncopated rhythms formed a bridge between standard marching bands and the early jazz compositions of pianists Jelly Roll Morton and James P. Johnson. It was so popular for a time that songs having little to do with the style (such as Irving Berlin's "Alexander's Ragtime Band") went out of their way to be associated with ragtime. Because the recording industry was in its infancy (surprisingly few solo pianists recorded before the 1920s), ragtime's fame spread largely through the sales of sheet music during an era when all "respectable" homes owned a piano. Although now thought of as primarily as a vehicle for solo pianists, ragtime was also played by banjoists (Vess Ossman and Fred Van Eps made numerous early recordings), small groups and full orchestras. Even John Phillip Sousa was wise enough to include some ragtime in his shows and James Reese Europe (the first Black bandleader to record) arranged ragtime pieces that were performed by the famous dance team of Vernon and Irene Castle.

Scott Joplin had much bigger designs for the music but fell short of his goals. Being Black in the early part of the century was a definite disadvantage (he was much less known to the general public than the imitative Tin Pan Alley composers), and prejudice against ragtime in general (in comparison to European classical music) made his hope of producing a long run of his ragtime opera "Treemonisha" merely a dream. As it turned out, Joplin's death in 1917 effectively ended the ragtime era. The onset of World War I (which made the innocent music seem naive) and the rise of jazz soon caused classic ragtime to be forgotten. Although novelty ragtime was briefly in vogue in the 1920s (with virtuosic pianists trying to top each other by writing nearly impossible to play workouts) and Zez Confrey (its most successful composer) became a celebrity with such numbers as "Kitten on the Keys" and "Dizzy Fingers," ragtime was by 1930 largely extinct. "Maple Leaf Rag" did become a jazz standard and some New Orleans revival musicians used the name "ragtime" to describe their Dixieland or New Orleans-based music (including Muggsy Spanier and George Lewis) but it was considered both a novelty and a historic event in 1941 when pianist Wally Rose recorded "Black & White Rag." A mini-ragtime revival occurred after Rose's recording and, with the rise of Dixieland in the mid-'40s, ragtime pieces were sometimes performed although usually as vehicles for improvisation rather than being interpreted as written. The classic book *They All Played Ragtime* by Rudi Blesh and Harriet Janis (published in 1950) helped increase interest in the historic style. But during that decade the commercialization of Dixieland led to the cornball "honky-tonk" style (usually pre-

World War I pop tunes played on out-of-tune pianos) becoming a fad. Honky-tonk did more harm than good to ragtime and when the public became sick of honky-tonk, ragtime went back underground.

In 1970 Joshua Rifkin recorded the first of three ragtime albums. His fairly straight classical versions of Scott Joplin rags sold well and soon all of Joplin's compositions became available on sheet music, inspiring many up-and-coming pianists. In 1973 the release of the film *The Sting*, which liberally used Joplin's music (adapted by Marvin Hamlisch) in the soundtrack, made a surprise pop hit out of Joplin's "The Entertainer" and started a major ragtime revival that continues to an extent to this day. Eubie Blake, as the last living ragtime composer (he died in 1986 at the age of 100), became in great demand as a colorful entertainer, new composers (most notably David Thomas Roberts and Reginald Robinson) began to emerge, the veteran Max Morath (who was a lonely voice for ragtime in the 1960s) continued putting on educational programs and the Stomp Off label began documenting ragtime performances not only of solo pianists but of orchestras playing long-lost scores. Even Scott Joplin's *Treemonisha* was resurrected and staged.

Although it will certainly never become the main popular music in America again, ragtime (which was always more than a mere predecessor to jazz) has been accepted as an important part of this country's heritage. — *Scott Yanow*

Six Essential Ragtime Recordings:

Richard Zimmerman—Scott Joplin— *His Complete Works* (only available as a 5-LP set from Murray Hill)

William Albright, *The Complete Rags of Scott Joplin* (Music Masters)

William Albright, *Joplin: Marches, Waltzes & Rags* (Music Masters)

Eubie Blake, *The 86 Years of Eubie Blake* (Columbia)

Reginald Robinson, *Sounds in Silhouette* (Delmark)

Paragon Ragtime Orchestra, *On the Boardwalk* (Newport Classics)

Five Essential Books on Ragtime:

They All Played Ragtime by Rudi Blesh & Harriet Janis (Oak Publishers, 1950)

This Is Ragtime by Terry Waldo (Da Capo Press, 1976)

Scott Joplin by James Haskins & Kathleen Benson (Doubleday, 1978)

King of Ragtime by Edward A. Berlin (Oxford Univ. Press, 1994)

James Reese Europe—A Life in Ragtime by Reid Badger (Oxford Univ. Press, 1995)

Important Events

1892 - Tom Turpin composes the earliest-known rag ("Harlem Rag") although it is not published until 1897.

1895 - Scott Joplin's first two songs are published.

1897 - William Krell's "Mississippi Rag" is the first rag to appear in print.

1899 - Scott Joplin's "Maple Leaf Rag" is published and becomes ragtime's biggest seller, launching ragtime craze.

1902 - Scott Joplin writes "The Entertainer," "The Ragtime Dance" and "Elite Syncopations."

1904 - St. Louis World's Fair holds ragtime contest.

1906 - James Scott's "Frog Legs Rag" is his first to be published.

1907 - Joseph Lamb meets Scott Joplin and Joplin helps Lamb get his music published.

1911 - Scott Joplin completes his ragtime opera "Treemonisha." Irving Berlin has much better luck with his pop hit "Alexander's Ragtime Band."

1914 - Joplin writes his last two rags.

1917 - Scott Joplin dies and the classic ragtime era is officially over.

1921 - Zez Confrey records "Kitten on the Keys," the most famous composition from the brief novelty ragtime period.

1938 - James Scott dies in obscurity.

1941 - Wally Rose records "Black and White Rag." His ragtime features with the Yerba Buena Jazz Band start a mini-revival of interest in ragtime.

1950 - Rubi Blesh and Harriet Janis write their classic book *They All Played Ragtime*.

1955 - Johnny Maddox as "Crazy Otto" has hit as honky-tonk piano is at the height of its popularity.

1959 - Joseph Lamb records an album a year before his death.

1970 - Joshua Rifkin records the first of three albums of Scott Joplin rags.

1973 - The release of *The Sting*, which liberally used Scott Joplin's music in the soundtrack, starts a major ragtime revival which has lasted to an extent to the present day.

1986 - Eubie Blake, the last of the original ragtime pianist/composers, dies at age 100.

New Orleans Jazz (1895-1940)

Scott Yanow

Arguably the happiest of all forms of music is New Orleans jazz and its later descendant Dixieland. The sound of several horns all improvising together on fairly simple chord changes with definite roles for each instrument but a large amount of freedom cannot help but sound consistently joyful.

In New Orleans jazz, the emphasis is on ensembles rather than solos. The style overlaps with Dixieland and classic jazz; to confuse matters more, all three idioms have often been called "traditional jazz" while the charts of Billboard Magazine classify any style of jazz with a walking bass as "traditional!" New Orleans jazz usually features a trumpeter (or a cornetist) in the lead and not wandering far from the melody. The trombonist plays harmonies (occasional saxophonists have similar roles) while the clarinetist is free to supply countermelodies and fills around the brass. While the tuba player (or string bassist) emphasizes the first and third beats of the bar, the drummer amd the banjoist (or guitarist) accent the second and fourth and the pianist often pounds chords on all four beats. The most exciting New Orleans jazz groups are fairly dense during the ensembles (with so much going on that they resemble a three-ring circus) while remaining quite coherent and purposeful.

New Orleans jazz (and jazz itself) really began with the brass bands. In New Orleans (starting in the 19th century), brass bands were plentiful and hired for everything from weddings, parties and parades to funerals. Musicians who might be playing the same song for 15 or 20 minutes naturally chose to come up with fresh variations as they marched and the result was jazz. Influenced by church music and spirituals (some of which have been effectively turned into New Orleans jazz), blues singers (who generally performed solo, backing their vocals with their own guitar while performing on street corners), work songs, marches, ragtime and folk music of the 1800s, jazz began to have its own identity by 1895 when cornetist Buddy Bolden (the music's first legend) formed his earliest group. Bolden was the first New Orleans "King" among cornetists. In future years (after mental illness forced his retirement in 1906) he would be succeeded by Freddie Keppard and Joe "King" Oliver before Louis Armstrong permanently gained the distinction of the top New Orleans trumpeter.

Because there were no jazz recordings before the Original Dixieland Jazz Band in 1917 (and the first Black New Orleans group, Kid Ory's band, would not make any records until 1921 or 1922), one can only guess how the early New Orleans groups sounded. Some bands (such as Bolden's) emphasized the lowdown blues and fairly basic chord changes while other had more sophisticated (and sometimes classically-trained) musicians who played written-out arrangements based on ragtime and folk songs. Since New Orleans bands played at a wide variety of functions (from rundown bars and dances to more polite concerts) and parades were plentiful, versatile musicians with plenty of endurance were always in great demand!

New Orleans jazz would have remained just a regional force were it not for two factors: an exodus of musicians from the area starting around 1910 and the booming recording industry of the 1920s. Both trends resulted in the music receiving exposure outside of the South and influencing musicians everywhere.

The exodus began when New Orleans musicians, having outgrown the small pond, decided to explore the rest of the country. Some, like pianist Jelly Roll Morton, traveled throughout the South and spent time on the West Coast. Others eventually headed for Chicago. Years later the legend would be that the closing of New Orleans' red-light district Storyville in 1917 led to the city's musicians going "up the Mississippi" to Chicago but that is rather simplistic. Few other than solo pianists played in Storyville's bordellos, not all of the players went immediately to Chicago and New Orleans continued to have a viable (if reduced) music scene in the 1920s. However many of the city's top musicians did eventually end up for a period in Chicago where by the early '20s they were dominating the city's Black music world.

The first jazz band to ever record, the Original Dixieland Jazz Band, was a White group that was musically limited but frequently exciting. Their first record release, "Livery Stable Blues," featured the horns (led by cornetist Nick LaRocca) imitating animals and it became a sensation; the group also introduced such future Dixieland standards as "Tiger Rag," "Original Dixieland One Step," "Margie," "Indiana" and "At the Jazz Band Ball." The ODJB (which was fairly original for the time although certainly not the originators of jazz that LaRocca sometimes claimed they were), introduced jazz to many listeners and in 1919 during a pioneering tour they brought jazz to Europe for the first time. So strong was the group's initial impact that during 1919-21, the word "jazz" was being applied to nearly every new song and quite a few heated White bands did their best to play in the ODJB style.

The next big step forward (at least on records) was made by the New Orleans Rhythm Kings. In 1922 the group (featuring leader-cornetist Paul Mares, the gifted but ill-fated clarinetist Leon Rappolo and trombonist George Brunis) made recordings that sounded a decade ahead of the ODJB. They featured short solos, high musicianship and (unlike the ODJB) the horns were strong improvisers. Mares later modestly claimed that he got many of his ideas from another Chicago-based New Orleans import, King Oliver.

King Oliver's Creole Jazz Band, which recorded in 1923, was the finest of all the classic New Orleans jazz groups. Although they emphasized ensembles, the band also had influential soloists in cornetist Oliver, the great clarinetist Johnny Dodds and the young second cornetist, Louis Armstrong. Oliver had sent to New Orleans for Armstrong the previous year and the interplay between the two cornets gave the group an explosive power and spontaneity that amazed listeners.

Louis Armstrong has sometimes been called jazz's first truly significant soloist but actually he was preceded by Sidney Bechet. Bechet, a remarkable clarinetist and soprano saxophonist whose wide vibrato made him either loved or detested by listeners, was a virtuoso whose early tours of Europe (starting in 1919) gave him fame overseas although it reduced his initial impact at home. He would end up his life in the 1950s fairly unknown in the US but a national celebrity in France where he resided and played in his timeless style.

Another important early force was pianist-composer Jelly Roll Morton. Although Morton's tendency to brag (claiming to have invented jazz in 1902) has resulted in him being underrated by many, he was jazz's first important composer, a highly original pianist and an important bandleader in Chicago. His recordings with his Red Hot Peppers (particularly during 1926-28) had a perfect balance of worked-out ensembles, group improvising, brief solos and dynamics. Morton's compositions (which sometimes had three or four themes similar to ragtime) were a transition between ragtime and swing and in fact one of his earliest songs, "King Porter Stomp," became a standard among swing big bands in the 1930s during a period when Jelly Roll himself was completely forgotten.

The decision of Louis Armstrong to leave King Oliver's band in 1924 (in addition to a money dispute, his wife Lil Armstrong convinced Louis that he needed room to grow) ended the Creole Jazz Band and resulted in a major development. Armstrong moved to New York to join Fletcher Henderson's Orchestra. At the time New

---

Music Map

Significant Ragtime Players

Ragtime Composers from Classic Era

Scott Joplin
Joseph Lamb
James Scott
Tom Turpin
Eubie Blake

Transitional Composers from Ragtime to Early Jazz

Jelly Roll Morton
James P. Johnson

Early Ragtime Banjoists

Vess Ossman
Fred Van Eps

Drums

James I. Lent (recorded "The Ragtime Drummer" in 1904)

Recent Composers

David Thomas Roberts
Reginald Robinson

Ragtime Pianists from 1940s On

Wally Rose	Dick Hyman
Max Morath	Joshua Rifkin
Scott Kirby	David Thomas Roberts
Reginald Robinson	

Music Map

Significant Early New Orleans Jazz Players

Cornet/Trumpet

Buddy Bolden	Freddie Keppard
Manuel Perez	King Oliver
Louis Armstrong	Paul Mares
Oscar Celestin	Lee Collins
Punch Miller	Tommy Ladnier
Muggsy Spaniel	Wingy Manone
Louis Prima	Sidney DeParis
Red Allen	

Trombone

Kid Ory	George Brunies
Charlie Green	Roy Palmer
J.C. Higginbottham	

Clarinet

Sidney Bechet	Leon Rappolo
Johnny Dodds	Jimmy Noone
Buster Bailey	Albert Nicholas
Barnney Bigard	Omer Simeon

Soprano

Sidney Bechet

Banjo

Johnny St. Cyr

Piano

Jelly Roll Morton	Tony Jackson
Lil Harden	Luis Russell

Bass

Bill Johnson	Ed Garland
John Lindsay	Pops Foster

Drums

Tony Sbarbaro	Baby Dodds
Zutty Singleton	Paul Barbarin

Vocals

Louis Armstrong

bles of New Orleans jazz were gradually being replaced by written-out arrangements. With the 1929 stock market crash, New Orleans jazz largely went underground and such musicians as Oliver, Morton and Dodds stopped recording altogether while others had to adapt to the newer styles.

In New Orleans itself, such trumpet kings emerged as Manuel Perez, Buddy Petit and Chris Kelly but, other than occasional field trips to the South conducted by Victor, few recordings actually took place in New Orleans; in fact none of those three legendary trumpeters made any records. By the late '20s, jazz in New Orleans itself was being influenced by records made up North and was gradually evolving with the times and often losing its uniqueness.

The Depression years were a barren time for New Orleans jazz although the music was still being performed. New Orleans-styled trumpeters Wingy Manone and Louis Prima had success with combo recordings, Bob Crosby's big band featured Dixieland solos in a swing setting and Louis Armstrong was quite famous (although he was regularly touring with a big band and would not return to the New Orleans format until 1947). By the late '30s the jazz world was ready for a New Orleans revival.

The 1939 book *Jazzmen* summed up jazz history to that point and made readers aware of the existence of the thus far undocumented trumpeter Bunk Johnson who was languishing in retirement. With the rise in popularity of Dixieland (whether it be the Eddie Condon-associated groups or the San Francisco style jazz of Lu Watters' Yerba Buena Jazz Band which took Oliver's Creole Jazz Band as a direct model), jazz historians and fanatics started to descend on New Orleans in hopes of discovering some lost links to the past. Bunk Johnson, who had been a major figure in New Orleans during 1910-30, was given a new set of teeth along with a horn. Soon Bunk became the symbol of ancient New Orleans, he came up North and he began recording fairly frequently. His original band included clarinetist George Lewis and trombonist Jim Robinson and Johnson was proclaimed by his supporters to be playing "true jazz," unspoiled by the influence of swing. Actually Bunk, who soon became erratic due to his excessive drinking, was well aware of swing and enjoyed incorporating current pop tunes into his repertoire but his ensemble-oriented style had strong hints of the past and he enjoyed playing the role of a New Orleans trumpet king even if his playing was not consistently at that level.

While Bunk Johnson had a few years of glory before returning back into obscurity and other veterans were brought out of retirement, New Orleans jazz tended to be overshadowed by Dixieland during the 1945-60 period. George Lewis, who had also returned to New Orleans after a period, formed his own band by 1950 out of the nucleus of Bunk's group and became one of the most popular figures in the movement for the next 15 years. Another renowned group was led by trombonist Kid Ory who with either Teddy Buckner or Alvin Alcorn on trumpet perfectly balanced solo space with exciting ensembles. In the 1950s there were really two types of New Orleans jazz players, the more primitive (at least technically) stylists who played with sincerity, simplicity and spontaneity (such as Lewis and veteran trumpeter Oscar Celestin) and the slicker and usually younger Dixieland groups which were no less enjoyable (such as the Dukes of Dixieland); often there was a lot of overlapping between the two idioms.

While Dixieland faded in popularity in the US by the late '50s, New Orleans jazz received a major boost in the early '60s with the opening of Preservation Hall, which served as a homebase for the veteran players. Soon a Preservation Hall Jazz Band was formed to take the music worldwide and, although the group declined in later years, it did serve as a way to keep the music popular. Several small labels in the 60s (most notably George Buck's Jazzology and GHB companies and Big Bill Bissonnette's Jazz Crusade label) documented the music of such players as trumpeter Kid Thomas Valentine, altoist Captain John Handy, trombonist Jim Robinson, clarinetist George Lewis, Billie and De De Pierce, pianist Alton Purnell and the Preservation Hall Jazz Band among others.

With the passing of time, New Orleans jazz declined greatly by the 1970s. However it began to enjoy a bit of renaissance in the 1980s when Wynton Marsalis, who originally played hard bop and post bop, began to explore his roots. Marsalis paid tribute to Louis Armstrong, King Oliver and even Buddy Bolden in some of his projects and his example was followed at least on a part-time basis by other New Orleans modernists who enjoyed incorporating parade rhythms and some group improvising in their music. The rise of pianists Harry Connick Jr. and Marcus Roberts, trumpeters Nicholas Payton and Leroy Jones and the Dirty Dozen Brass Band (a modern brass band that combined their heritage with R&B) also helped to keep classic New Orleans jazz alive and fresh. In the 1990s New Orleans jazz is played at festivals, jazz parties, overseas and even in New Orleans itself. And it's still the happiest music on earth! — Scott Yanow

Ten Essential New Orleans Jazz Recordings:

Original Dixieland Jazz Band, *75th Anniversary* (Bluebird)

New Orleans Rhythm Kings, *And Jelly Roll Morton* (Milestone)

York musicians may have been technically advanced but they trailed behind the New Orleans players in blues feeling and ability to swing. Armstrong's virtuosity immediately impressed New Yorkers and by the time he returned to Chicago a year later, he was responsible for most top jazzmen virtually changing the way they phrased, used space and drama and developed their ideas.

It is somewhat ironic that Louis Armstrong has always symbolized New Orleans jazz for, starting with his first Hot Five recordings in late '25, he paved the end of the road for classic New Orleans jazz, starting the gradual transition towards swing. Armstrong was such a brilliant soloist that it seemed a waste for him to always be playing in ensembles. The early Hot Fives found him sharing the spotlight with trombonist Kid Ory (his former employer in the late teens) and clarinetist Johnny Dodds but by 1927 he was so far ahead of his contemporaries that he had pushed the music beyond New Orleans jazz.

Although many New Orleans players were recording (including trumpeters Red Allen, Jabbo Smith and King Oliver, trombonist Ory, clarinetists Dodds and Jimmie Noone and the groups of Jelly Roll Morton), by the late '20s the improvised ensem-

King Oliver, *Creole Jazz Band 1923-4* (Reservoir)

Jelly Roll Morton, *1926-1928* (Classics)

Louis Armstrong, *Hot Fives Vol. 1* (Columbia)

Johnny Dodds, *Blue Clarinet Stomp* (Bluebird)

Sidney Bechet, *Master Takes: Victor Sessions* (Bluebird)

Bunk Johnson, *Complete Deccas, Victors and V Discs* (Document)

George Lewis, *Hot Creole Jazz: 1953* (DCC)

Kid Ory, *Creole Jazz Band—1954* (Good Time Jazz)

Seven Essential Books on New Orleans Jazz:

In Search of Buddy Bolden by Donald Marquis (Da Capo Press, 1978)

Jazz Masters of New Orleans by Martin Williams (Da Capo Press, 1967)

Jazzmen by Frederic Ramsey & Charles Edward Smith (Harves/HBJ Books, 1939)

Mister Jelly Roll by Alan Lomax (Pantheon Books, 1950)

Sidney Bechet—Wizard of Jazz by John Chilton (Oxford Univ. Press, 1987)

Satchmo by Gary Giddins (Anchor Books, 1988)

The Jazz Crusade by Big Bill Bissonnette (Special Request Books, 1992)

Important Events

1895 - Buddy Bolden forms his first band.

1902 - Jelly Roll Morton, then just 12, starts playing piano in Storyville. Later he would claim that he invented jazz that year.

1906 - Buddy Bolden, suffering from mental illness, is committed to an institution. Freddie Keppard, Bolden's successor, stars with the Olympia Orchestra.

1908 - Bassist Bill Johnson travels to Los Angeles, introducing New Orleans Jazz to the West Coast.

1914 - Freddie Keppard leaves New Orleans to join the Original Creole Band.

1917 - The Original Dixieland Jazz Band make first jazz recordings. Jelly Roll Morton settles in Los Angeles. Storyville closes.

1918 - King Oliver moves to Chicago.

1919 - Sidney Bechet travels overseas with Will Marion Cook's Orchestra, introducing jazz to the European continent.

1922 - Kid Ory records two titles in Los Angeles.

The New Orleans Rhythm Kings make their first recordings.

King Oliver forms Creole Jazz Band.

1923 - King Oliver, Jelly Roll Morton, Johnny Dodds, Sidney Bechet and Louis Armstrong make their debuts on record.

1924 - Louis Armstrong stars with the Fletcher Henderson Orchestra, shows New York musicians how to swing. Muggsy Spanier makes recording debut. Fate Marable records his only session.

1925 - Louis Armstrong starts series of Hot Five recordings including "Cornet Chop Suey."

1926 - Jelly Roll Morton records with his Red Hot Peppers in Chicago. Freddie Keppard cuts his best recording. King Oliver records with his Dixie Syncopators.

1927 - Red Allen joins King Oliver's band. Louis Armstrong records with his Hot Seven.

1928 - Louis Armstrong teams up with Earl Hines, most notably for "West End Blues" and "Weatherbird."

Jimmy Noone records with his Apex Club Orchestra.

1929 - Louis Armstrong begins recording exclusively with big bands.

Luis Russell band makes finest recordings.

Red Allen leads first record dates.

New Orleans jazz goes underground as Depression hits.

1931 - The long forgotten Buddy Bolden dies.

1932 - Sidney Bechet records a session with his New Orleans Feetwarmers.

1933 - Freddie Keppard dies.

1935 - The Bob Crosby Orchestra is formed, features New Orleans-flavored jazz in a swing setting.

1938 - Jelly Roll Morton records extensively for the Library of Congress. King Oliver dies.

Johnny Dodds records for the first time since 1930.

1940 - Johnny Dodds dies. Louis Armstrong and Sidney Bechet team up on a record date.

1941 - Jelly Roll Morton dies as New Orleans revival starts to take off.

Classic Jazz (Jazz from the 1920s)

Scott Yanow

When one thinks of the 1920s as it is portrayed by the mass media, the images of Dixieland, college kids wearing raccoon coats, the Charleston, gangsters and speakeasies come quickly to mind. It was termed "The Jazz Age" by F. Scott Fitzgerald and was thought of nostalgically as a somewhat hedonistic era by later generations who had to live through the Depression and World War II.

Although there is some truth in the stereotypes, there was much more to the decade than is seen in movies depicting the era, and there was more to its jazz scene than Dixieland. The term "classic jazz" refers to music from the era and its later revivals and recreations, overlapping with New Orleans jazz and Dixieland but covering a wider area.

The 1920s were arguably the most important decade in the evolution of jazz. In 1920, jazz was largely unknown to the general public and those that knew of it often disapproved, considering it barbaric and even sinful compared to more sedate dance music, marches, ragtime and classical music. By 1930, even though it was still not taken all that seriously as an art form, jazz had become a permanent influence on popular music and it was danced to by a countless number of people who had never heard of Jelly Roll Morton or King Oliver.

The number of significant developments that occurred during the decade in jazz are remarkable. It was during the 1920s that important soloists first emerged in jazz, causing the music to develop beyond its brass band roots (where all of the musicians generally played at the same time) to a vehicle for creative virtuosoes. Musicians began to phrase differently, changing from a staccato approach to legato and not hitting every note right on the beat. Arrangers began to infuse dance band arrangements with the rhythm and phrasing of jazz, leaving room for soloists; even most of the more commercial orchestras featured a brief trumpet solo after the vocalist. The recording industry grew drastically, propelled by the change in the mid-1920s (mostly during 1925-27) from an acoustic to an electric process that greatly improved the technical quality of recordings. And perhaps most importantly, it was in the '20s that top Black jazz musicians began to record.

In 1920, jazz was primarily known to the general public as the colorful and primitive music of the Original Dixieland Jazz Band. The ODJB's sound dominated records of the 1917-21 period to the point where most groups (virtually all White) who attempted to record jazz sounded similar to them. While the ODJB was very important in helping to introduce listeners to jazz (including in England where they visited in 1919), it is not surprising that its music scared off some listeners. The group's initial recording "Livery Stable Blues" (a big hit) found the horn players imitating the whinnying, roars and cackles of barnyard animals and, beyond its novelty value, it was not comparable on any level to the typical playing of a classical violinist.

It was up to bandleader Paul Whiteman to make jazz accessible to the general public. Called "The King Of Jazz" by a press agent (which has led to his importance being underrated and ridiculed through the years), Whiteman could more properly be called "The King Of The Jazz Age." Starting with a million-selling 1920 recording of "Whispering," Whiteman's bands featured high musicianship and versatility. Its jazz content throughout the first half of the 1920s was not that strong but Whiteman always featured superior dance music and kept his ears open. In 1924 he persuaded George Gershwin to compose "Rhapsody In Blue" and his string section often played semi-classical works, an early predecessor of Third Stream music. In Henry Busse, Whiteman had a limited but appealing trumpeter whose hot choruses were generally just doubletime repetitions but had the feel of jazz; hit versions of "Hot Lips" and "When Day Is Done" were due to the excitement that Busse could generate. By the mid-'20s, Whiteman started signing up serious jazz players such as cornetist Red Nichols and trombonist Tommy Dorsey and in 1927, with the collapse of the Jean Goldkette Orchestra, he added such important musicians as cornetist Bix Beiderbecke, C-melody saxophonist Frankie Trumbauer, violinist Joe Venuti, guitarist Eddie Lang and the inventive arranger Bill Challis. When Bing Crosby joined as part of the Rhythm Boys, Whiteman during 1927-29 finally had a frequently great jazz orchestra. Other contemporary dance bands followed in his path.

While one thinks of the big band era as having begun in 1935 when Benny Goodman caught on, the 1920s were filled with preswing jazz orchestras. Shortly after Paul Whiteman began to become famous, pianist Fletcher Henderson formed his own big band and started to record on a frequent basis in 1923. Arranger Don Redman (credited with being the first to divide an orchestra musically into trumpet, trombone, saxophone and rhythm sections) wrote complex, experimental and futuristic charts for Henderson that put the orchestra at the top of its class by 1924. However it was the emergence of Louis Armstrong that made the Henderson big band into the first swinging jazz orchestra. At the time, the New York musicians were better technically than the New Orleans players who were based in Chicago, but it took Armstrong to introduce blues phrasing and swing to the East Coast.

Louis was an expert at constructing dramatic statements that expertly used space and he made each note count. By the time his year with Henderson was up, Armstrong's influence had permanently changed the band and the New York jazz scene.

New York had heard the blues before. In fact in 1920 Mamie Smith recorded "Crazy Blues" and her record started a blues craze that lasted a few years. Suddenly the word "blues" was tacked on to the titles of many songs and scores of vaudevillian-oriented female singers began to record. Although some (including Alberta Hunter and Ethel Waters) were quite talented, it was not until Bessie Smith recorded Hunter's "Downhearted Blues" in 1923 that listeners began to know the difference between a singer performing a blues and a real blues singer. Throughout the 1920s, many "classic blues singers" would pop up on records but the one who made the biggest impact was Bessie Smith (rightfully called "The Empress Of The Blues"); even when faced with very primitive recording facilities and weak sidemen, Bessie (who recorded until 1933) overpowered the surroundings and created performances that still communicate to today's listeners.

It was when the blues craze was at its height that jazz began to emerge more fully on record. During 1921-22 trumpeter Phil Napoleon started recording frequently in New York with small bands that were more creative and swinging than the ODJB; the Original Memphis Five was the best known (and most prolific) of these recording groups. In Los Angeles trombonist Kid Ory in 1921 with the Seven Pods Of Pepper Orchestra (his usual band with cornetist Mutt Carey) recorded two instrumentals that were the first documentation of a Black New Orleans group. During 1922-23 the New Orleans Rhythm Kings (with clarinetist Leon Rappollo) showed that not all the early jazz pioneers were Black and then in 1923 King Oliver's Creole Jazz Band (an octet with both Oliver and Louis Armstrong on cornets, clarinetist Johnny Dodds and drummer Baby Dodds) proved to be the finest of the early New Orleans jazz bands to make it on record. A few years later pianist-composer Jelly Roll Morton with his Red Hot Peppers perfectly blended together arrangements and creative frameworks with concise solos.

However classic New Orleans jazz was soon overshadowed by the rise of the great soloists. James P. Johnson, called "the father of the stride piano," was a brilliant pianist whose complex left-hand patterns ("striding" up and down between bass notes and chords) inspired youngsters such as Fats Waller and often scared away his potential competitors. His first recorded piano solos were in 1921 and even now few listeners probably realize that this multi-faceted talent composed "Charleston." Sidney Bechet, a masterful soprano saxophonist and clarinetist, recorded some virtuosic sides during 1923-24 although his extensive stays in Europe cut back on his impact in the US. Cornetist Bix Beiderbecke, who had a beautiful cool tone and a harmonically advanced style, recorded solos with the Wolverines (a fine Midwest jazz band) in 1924 that were full of subtlety and unexpected moments. Symbolic of the "jazz age," Beiderbecke became the top White jazz player of the decade yet was unknown to the general public. He was the star sideman with the short-lived Jean Goldkette Orchestra, recorded many brilliant solos in 1927 with recording groups headed by Frankie Trumbauer and was featured in occasional spots with Paul Whiteman's Orchestra during 1927-29 before alcoholism caused his rapid decline and death in 1931. His death at age 28 made him a jazz martyr and a legend.

But it was Louis Armstrong who, although a New Orleans player, really helped end the New Orleans era and pave the way towards swing. He was just too skilled a soloist to be confined to ensembles. After leaving Fletcher Henderson and returning to Chicago in 1925, he worked nightly with big bands and recorded a series of classics with his Hot Five and Hot Sevens. His 1925-27 records generally also included clarinetist Johnny Dodds (arguably the top clarinetist of the era) and trombonist Kid Ory who at first were nearly equals until Armstrong's rapid growth made him the dominant force. Armstrong's 1928 records with pianist Earl Hines (one of his few matches in rhythmic daring) are among the most advanced of Louis' career and his playing on the flawless "West End Blues" (with its memorable opening cadenza) was his personal favorite recording.

Even without Louis Armstrong, it seemed only a matter of time before soloists would become more important. The muffled sound of acoustic recordings were giving way to their much more lifelike electric counterparts by 1925-26 and jazz stars were destined to emerge. Dixieland was evolving from New Orleans jazz and the number of distinctive players that were inspired by the New Orleans Rhythm Kings, King Oliver, Bix and Armstrong were increasing yearly. While Armstrong and Beiderbecke were the pacesetters among cornetists and trumpeters, there were also such up-and-coming brassmen as Jabbo Smith (who in 1929 at the age of 19 showed tremendous potential that he never lived up to), Red Allen (the last major New Orleans trumpeter of the era), Jimmy McPartland and Red Nichols (a Bix-inspired player who was very important during the era as the leader of many jazz-oriented record sessions in New York, often under the name of his Five Pennies). The trombone evolved from the percussive and guttural playing of Kid Ory and the wide interval jumps of the unique Miff Mole (who often teamed up with

Nichols to create unpredictable music) to the more influential Jimmy Harrison and Jack Teagarden. The New Orleans clarinetists (chiefly Johnny Dodds and Jimmie Noone) ruled during the decade but the young Benny Goodman was showing great promise with drummer Ben Pollack's fine big band. The saxophone, considered a novelty instrument and a poor replacement for a trombone at the beginning of the decade, worked perfectly in dance orchestras and some important voices emerged including on tenor Coleman Hawkins and Bud Freeman, both Johnny Hodges and Benny Carter on alto, Frankie Trumbauer on the C-melody sax (which soon became nearly extinct), bass saxophonist Adrian Rollini and baritonist Harry Carney.

As far the rhythm section went, James P. Johnson's followers and contemporaries at nightly jam sessions included Fats Waller, Willie "The Lion" Smith, Earl Hines (in Chicago) and the young Duke Ellington. Banjos and tubas by the late 1920s gave way to more flexible rhythm guitars and string basses. Eddie Lang occasionally had brief guitar solos (often teaming up with the immortal violinist Joe Venuti) and bassist Steve Brown drove ensembles in the mid-1920s, their instruments were largely confined to a supportive role. The same was true of drummers who, until Gene Krupa in 1927, were not even allowed to record with a bass drum or a full set due to fears that it would overpower the recording balance. Baby Dodds, thought of as one of the era's top drummers, generally recorded with just a cymbal, woodblocks and a snare drum! It was not until the late 1920s that one can hear how a drummer really sounded.

While instrumentalists evolved quickly during the 1920s, vocalists lagged behind. Other than the female classic blues singers and the male blues performers (who were in a different musical world than players of jazz and dance music), very few vocalists on record were worth hearing before 1925. Singers were hired for their volume and ability to enunciate words, and many sounded like rejects from opera who were lowering themselves to sing pop music. An exception was Cliff Edwards (known as Ukulele Ike) but it was once again Louis Armstrong who introduced swing to singing. In addition to popularizing scat singing (substituting nonsense syllables for lyrics), Armstrong phrased his vocals like a trumpeter and virtually changed the world of pop singing. Bing Crosby, who was in Paul Whiteman's band at the time, learned from Louis' example and his rise saved the world from the pompous baritones and boy tenors who appeared on far too many jazz-oriented records through the late 1920s.

By the end of the '20s, jazz was a major part of popular music and Duke Ellington's innovations with his Cotton Club Orchestra were leading the way towards the future. Jazz, although hardly considered respectable by the middle class, was being utilized at least to a small degree by nearly every commercial dance orchestra and it was the vocabulary of talented musicians at after-hours jam sessions who indulged in freewheeling Dixieland-oriented solos and of territory bands from outside the major metropolitan areas. In addition, the spontaneity of jazz by 1927 had become the soundtrack of the freewheeling 1920s.

With the onset of the Depression and the development of swing, the classic jazz era came to a close. Dixieland went underground and then re-emerged full force in the 1940s as did New Orleans jazz. Enthusiasts from later decades often tried their best to bring back the spirit and sound of classic jazz circa 1925-33 but it is a difficult task both because the recording quality has improved so much since then, and because most later musicians phrase in a more modern fashion. There have been exceptions along the way, particularly since the Stomp Off label began to extensively document the traditional jazz scene in the 1980s, but it is a tricky balancing act to recreate the excitement and joy of the early recordings and particularly to play with creativity (rather than merely copying the original records) while sticking within the older boundaries. Fortunately many (but not all) of the classic recordings are readily available on CD and, with the proliferation of so many Dixieland and trad jazz festivals, the music lives on in different forms. — *Scott Yanow*

Eleven Essential Classic Jazz Recordings

The Original Memphis Five, *Collection, Vol. 1* (Collector's Classics)

Fletcher Henderson, *1927* (Classics)

Louis Armstrong, (Classics)

Louis Armstrong, Vol. 4: Louis Armstrong And Earl Hines (Columbia)

Bix Beiderbecke, *Volume 1: Singin' The Blues* (Columbia)

Bix Beiderbecke and Paul Whiteman, *Bix Lives* (Bluebird)

James P. Johnson, *Snowy Morning Blues* (GRP/Decca)

Fats Waller, *Fats And his Buddies* (Bluebird)

Jabbo Smith, *1929-1938* (Retrieval)

Red Allen, *1929-1933* (Classics)

Benny Goodman and Red Nichols, *BG & Big Tea In NYC* (GRP/Decca)

Duke Ellington, *Okeh Ellington* (Columbia)

Five Essential Books About the Classic Jazz Era

Music Map

Significant Classic Jazz Players

Louis Armstrong - cornet/trumpet, vocals
Bix Beiderbecke - cornet
Jelly Roll Morton - piano, composer
Johnny Dodds - clarinet
James P. Johnson - piano
Duke Ellington - bandleader, composer,
arranger, piano
Bessie Smith - vocals

Other Significant Players in 1920s

Alto Saxophone
Jimmy Dorsey

Banjo
Johnny St. Cyr

Bass
Steve Brown
Wellman Braud
Pops Foster

Bass Saxophone
Adrian Rollini

Clarinet

Leon Rappolo	Sidney Bechet
Jimmy Noone	Frankie Teschemacher
Omer Simeon	Benny Goodman
Jimmy Dorsey	

Cornet/Trumpet

King Oliver	Bubber Miley
Phil Napoleon	Red Nichols
Jabbo Smith	Red Allen

Drums
Tony Sbarbaro
Baby Dodds
Vic Berton
Zutty Singleton

Guitar
Eddie Lang
Lonnie Johnson

Piano
Fats Waller
Earl Hines

Soprano Saxophone
Sidney Bechet

Tenor Saxophone
Coleman Hawkins
Bud Freeman

Trombone
Kid Ory
Miff Mole
Jimmy Harrison
Tricky Sam Nanton
Jack Teagarden

Violin
Joe Venuti

Vocals - Male
Bing Crosby
Jack Teagarden

Vocals - Female
Ethel Waters
Annette Hanshaw
Boswell Sisters

Big Bands
Paul Whiteman
Fletcher Henderson
Duke Ellington
McKinney's Cotton Pickers

Early Jazz by Gunther Schuller (Oxford Univ. Press, 1968)

Bix—Man And Legend by Richard Sudhalter, Philip Evans and William Dean Myatt (Schirmer Books, 1974)

Jazz Masters Of The Twenties by Richard Hadlock (Da Capo Press, 1965)

Voices Of The Jazz Age by Chip Deffaa (Univ. Of Illinois press, 1990)

Ellington—The Early Years by Mark Tucker (Univ. Of Illinois Press, 1991)

Important Events

1917 - The Original Dixieland Jazz Band (ODJB) cuts the first jazz recordings. "Livery Stable Blues" is a best-seller.

1919 - The ODJB visits England and is a big sensation.

1920 - Mamie Smith records the first blues record, "Crazy Blues."

1922 - Kid Ory's band records in Los Angeles, under the name of "Spikes' Seven Pods of Pepper Orchestra!"
The New Orleans Rhythm Kings debuts on record.

1923 - King Oliver's Creole Jazz Band (with Louis Armstrong and Johnny Dodds) is the band of the year, playing nightly in Chicago.

Bessie Smith and Sidney Bechet make their first recordings.

1924 - Bix Beiderbecke records with the Wolverines.
Louis Armstrong joins Fletcher Henderson's Orchestra.
Paul Whiteman seeks to "make a lady out of jazz" and presents a watered-down version at Aeolian Hall.

1925 - Louis Armstrong's classic series of Hot Five recordings begins.

1926 - Jelly Roll Morton records his first Hot Peppers sessions.

1927 - Duke Ellington wins a regular gig at the Cotton Club.
Bix Beiderbecke, during his finest period, splits the year between the orchestras of Jean Goldkette and Paul Whiteman.

1928 - Louis Armstrong records "West End Blues" and "Weather Bird Rag"; the latter as a duet with Earl Hines.

1929 - Cootie Williams replaces Bubber Miley with Duke Ellington. Jabbo Smith records with his Rhythm Aces.

1930 - Paul Whiteman's Orchestra films *The King of Jazz*.

1931 - King Oliver's last recordings.
Bix Beiderbecke dies.

Jazz/Blues Crossover

Richie Unterberger

The blues and jazz both draw from a wellspring of similar roots in African-American popular music and culture. The paths of each genre have diverged widely since the beginning of the 1900s, but before 1950, the styles were often deeply intertwined with each other. It's a marriage that will endure to some degree as long as blues and jazz are around; even today, contemporary jazz acts throw in plenty of bluesy quotes, and many musicians boast service in both jazz bands and R&B/blues outfits. Many festivals spotlight both blues and jazz artists, the most famous of them being the annual New Orleans Jazz & Blues festival. Not many current artists, however, could be said to straddle the blues/jazz fence to such an extent that they could be classified as members of either camp.

The distinctions were much blurrier in the early 1900s, when both blues and jazz had yet to fully form their identities. The influence of ragtime music and barrelhouse piano styles were strong formative elements of each. W.C. Handy, the Father of the Blues, led brass bands whose instrumentation and arrangements were likely more akin to jazz. The first artists to record the blues were women singers, but these were the blues more in song structure and vocal phrasing than in the jazz/pop arrangements, which employed jazz greats such as Louis Armstrong and Coleman Hawkins. (The significance of the classic female blues singers is detailed in a separate piece.) Much later, in the 1950s, traditional jazz bandleader Chris Barber would play a key role in exposing the blues in his native Britain by featuring bluesmen as part of his shows, often imported from the States.

The most active period of cross-fertilization between blues and jazz may have been the 1930s and 1940s, when swing and big band styles were at their peak, and when the blues was moving toward a fuller and more citified sound. Jazz was still often played in dance halls, and needed some singers and song structures to help maintain its accessibility. Blues was moving toward a more sophisticated sound that would soon encompass full bands and electricity. Each form had much to learn from the other.

Several of the early big bands featured vocalists that not only borrowed from the blues in their songs and phrasing, but in turn influenced the evolution of other bluesmen. Jimmy Rushing, in his work with Count Basie, may have been the first notable blues-based singer to front a big band with a precursor to the "shouting" style. This was developed to its fullest shortly afterwards by singers with Kansas City-based swing bands, including Big Joe Turner, Jimmy Witherspoon, and Walter Brown.

Brown and Witherspoon both sang with the band of pianist Jay McShann, the bandleader with whom Charlie Parker first recorded. McShann is one of the artists most likely to be found in either the blues or jazz section of fine record stores; Turner and Witherspoon, throughout their career, moved with ease between the jazz and R&B worlds, sometimes changing their focus to fit the requirements of the gig or the record date. Eddie "Cleanhead" Vinson, who doubled on vocals and saxophone, was another performer who would be hard to tie to either style; he could not only sing the blues, but could play bop jazz as well, and led a band including John Coltrane in the late '40s, long before Coltrane made his mark on the jazz world.

Besides the "shouters," the main tributary of blues feeding into jazz was found in the boogie-woogie pianists of the late '30s and early '40s. Taking some cues from blues styles that had been developed in barrelhouses, Albert Ammons, Pete Johnson, and Meade Lux Lewis were the most instrumental figures in introducing boogie-woogie to jazz. The famed Spirituals To Swing concerts in New York City's Carnegie Hall in the late 1930s found the marriage between the idioms at their peak, featuring pioneers like Ammons, Johnson, Lewis, and Turner on the same stage; Robert Johnson, interestingly, was also planned to be included in the events, but had died before he could be contacted.

Jazz greats would often use bluesy riffs and signatures in their work; the Rhino collection *Blues Masters, Vol. 13: New York City Blues* contains some good illustrations. The wild sax solo of Illinois Jacquet in Lionel Hampton's "Flying Home" rates as a leading forerunner of R&B, particularly the "honking" style of sax associated with the form. The shouters, honkers, and boogie-woogie would coalesce in the 1940s into jump blues, which in some senses was the ultimate jazz-blues fusion. As pioneered by Louis Jordan, Roy Milton, and many others starting in the mid1940s (again, detailed in a separate piece), jump blues took the above factors and added a raw power and playful pop elements (particularly in the vocals) to the equation, while maintaining a rhythmic base and instrumentation quite close to swing jazz in some ways.

Jump blues wasn't solely composed of the above elements. The introduction of the electric guitar had far-reaching effects on pop music that nobody could have guessed in 1940, when a jazzman, Charlie Christian, established himself as the first virtuoso of the instrument. Christian can't be considered a blues/jazz artist (though examples of bluesy playing can be heard in his scant body of recorded

work), but there's no question that he was a huge influence on the jump blues guitarists, particularly T-Bone Walker, one of the key figures of both jump blues and West Coast blues. Walker's single-string solos owed so much to jazz, as played by Christian on guitar and other jazzers on other instruments, that a case can be made for classifying Walker as a blues/jazzman as well, though his songs and roots were very much in the blues camp.

On the whole, the end of the jump blues phenomenon spelled an end to the intense interchange between blues and jazz. Jazz was evolving into be-bop and beyond; jump blues fed into R&B and rock 'n' roll. Chuck Berry's "Maybellene" may owe a little to jazz, for example, but the distance between Chuck Berry and, say, a mid-'50s jazz artist like Clifford Brown is a lot further than the distance between Louis Jordan and Lionel Hampton. Jazz bands were less oriented toward the dance halls now, and less apt to employ singers for that purpose, although some (such as Joe Williams, not to be confused with Big Joe Williams the country blues singer) kept the flame of old-school Jimmy Rushing-type vocals alive.

It's interesting to note, though, that quite a few major jazzmen were schooled in blues/R&B bands, or recorded sessions with them to help pay the rent, from Coltrane and Coleman on down. There was some movement in the other direction as well; guitarist Mickey Baker originally had his heart set on being a jazz musician, but instead became one of the best blues influenced rock 'n' roll guitarists of all time—partly, again, as a result of being repeatedly called upon to play R&B sessions. Earl Bostic, who played in Lionel Hampton's band in the 1940s, found his true calling as an R&B saxophonist. Two respected jazz players, saxophonists David "Fathead" Newman and Hank Crawford, had bluesy leanings that would come in handy when they worked as sidemen on some of Ray Charles' bluesiest recordings. But even here, the relationship between blues and jazz grows increasingly tangential.

The blues-jazz link had another fling in the '60s, albeit in a somewhat distant form, in the work of several keyboardists. Organists Jack McDuff, Jimmy McGriff, Jimmy Smith, and John Patton, nowadays recognized as pioneers of "soul-jazz," often drew upon blues styles and material; one of Smith's biggest set pieces, for instance, was a cover of "I've Got My Mojo Working." Jazz pianist/vocalist Mose Allison (who began recording in the late 1950s) had a distinctive bluesy hipster style, both on originals like "Young Man's Blues" and "Parchman Farm," and covers of songs by Willie Dixon and Sonny Boy Williamson; he'd prove to be an unexpected influence on British groups like the Who, Yardbirds, and John Mayall, all of whom covered Allison songs. In Britain itself, Georgie Fame took up a blues/jazz style similar to Allison's, though with much more of a pop/R&B base.

Fifteen Recommended Albums:

Various Artists, *Blues Masters Vol. 11: Classic Blues Women* (Rhino)

Various Artists, *Blues Masters, Vol. 13: New York City Blues* (Rhino)

Jimmy Rushing, *The Essential Jimmy Rushing* (Vanguard)

Big Joe Turner, *Complete 1940-1944* (Official)

Jimmy Witherspoon & Jay McShann, *Jimmy Witherspoon & Jay McShann* (DA)

Albert Ammons, *King of Boogie (1939-1949)* (Blues Classics)

Meade Lux Lewis, *1939-1954* (Story of Blues)

Various Artists, *Blues Masters Vol. 5: Jump Blues Classics* (Rhino)

Various Artists, *Blues Masters Vol. 14: More Jump Blues* (Rhino)

Louis Jordan, *The Best of Louis Jordan* (MCA)

T-Bone Walker, *The Complete Capitol/Black & White Recordings* (Capitol)

Mose Allison, *Greatest Hits* (Prestige)

Ray Charles, *Blues & Jazz* (Rhino)

Various Artists, *Blue Funk: The History of the Hammond Organ* (Blue Note)

Eddie "Cleanhead" Vinson, *And Roomful of Blues* (Muse)

Classic Female Blues Singers

Richie Unterberger

The image of the blues as a man hunched over his acoustic guitar in the Mississippi Delta—or, alternately, hunched over his electric axe or harmonica as he moans into a microphone at a sweaty club—is so ingrained in the collective consciousness that it comes as a shock to many to learn that the first blues stars were women. Indeed, women dominated the recorded blues field in the 1920s, the first decade in which a market for blues records existed. Except for the very most famous of these singers, these pioneers are largely forgotten today, having been retroactively surpassed in popularity by some Southern bluesmen who only recorded a precious handful of sides in the '20s and '30s. But these women were the performers who first took the blues to a national audience.

The popularity of the early blueswomen was intimately tied to the birth of the recording industry itself. There were many kinds of nascent blues on the rise in the early 20th century-Delta guitarists, yes, but also songsters, jug bands, and dance bands that employed elements of jazz, blues, and pop. And there was the vaudeville stage circuit, which frequently featured women singers. Presenting productions that toured widely, the musicians involved couldn't helped but be exposed to blues forms, if they hadn't been already.

It so happened that female-sung blues, with a prominent vaudeville-jazz-pop flavor, was the first kind of blues to be recorded for the popular audience. There are many possible reasons for this. Perhaps the record companies felt that other styles of blues were too raw to market. Or they may have been largely unaware of more rural and Southern blues styles. The female vaudevillian blues singers had a jazzier and more urban sound that commercial companies may have been more likely to encounter and stamp with approval.

What's far more certain is that "Crazy Blues," recorded by Mamie Smith in 1920, was the first commercial recording of what came to be recognized as the blues. By the standards of the day, the record was a phenomenal success, selling 75,000 copies within the first month—in an era, it must be remembered, when much of the US population, and an even higher percentage of the US African-American population, didn't own a record player. It set off an immediate storm of records in the same vein, by Smith and numerous other women.

But to today's listener, "Crazy Blues" hardly sounds like a blues at all. It sounds more like vaudeville, with a bit of the blues creeping into the edges of the vocal delivery and the song structure. The more judgemental might find that it resembles the music found in contemporary Broadway productions that offer a nostalgic facsimile of pre-Depression Black theater. The song has to be taken in the context of its era, however. It was the first time anything with some allegiance to the blues form had been recorded—and the industry quickly found that such productions were being bought not just by Blacks, but by all Americans.

Mamie Smith's success opened the floodgates for numerous blueswomen to record in the 1920s, often on the OKeh and Paramount labels. Ida Cox, Sippie Wallace, Victoria Spivey, Lucille Bogan, Ethel Waters, and Alberta Hunter are some of the most famous; there were many others. The best of them were Ma Rainey and Bessie Smith, both of whom had rawer, more emotional qualities that gives their recordings a feel more akin to what later listeners expect of the blues.

Today, the early recordings by the "classic" female blues singers, as they have sometimes been labeled, sound as much or more like jazz as blues. The vocalists were usually accompanied by small jazz combos, often featuring piano, cornet, and other horn instruments. The guitar, the instrument associated with the blues more than any other, was frequently absent, and usually secondary when it was used. Lots of early jazz stars, in fact, can be heard on the early blueswomen's records, including Louis Armstrong, King Oliver, Duke Ellington, and Coleman Hawkins.

Yet the music *is* identifiable as blues, primarily via the vocal phrasing and the widespread use of the 12-bar song structures that are among the blues' most immediate trademarks. And it was not a form that thrived in isolation from the other styles of blues that were emerging throughout America. As top blues scholar Samuel Charters writes in his liner notes to *Blues Masters Volume 11: Classic Blues Women,* "Even the men living in the South and playing the blues for themselves and their neighbors learned many of their songs from the records that made their way down to local music stores or came through the post office from the mail-order blues companies in Chicago. If they didn't learn the songs themselves, they learned the form and the style of what the record companies thought of as the blues.

"So when the companies sent scouts to find new artists in the South, what they found were the same three or four ways of putting blues verses together. After the sweeping success of the first recordings by women blues artists, the 12-bar harmonic form on the records had become so ubiquitous that even the Delta players who only fingered a single chord on their guitars managed to suggest all the usual chord changes with their singing."

The blues could also be heard in the singers' frank discussions of topics like sex, infidelity, and money and drink problems, often with a palpable hurt. These were offered with a female perspective that has never been as widespread in the blues since, as the music came to be dominated by male performers after the Depression. Listeners from all eras can cut through the often scratchy recordings to find the seeds of the blues, and much modern pop music, in their depiction of hard times, and the struggle and endurance necessary to survive them. It's not all bleakness—the celebratory tunes could have a frank bawdiness, particularly when dealing with sexual double entendres, that would probably generate warning stickers if they were being purchased by today's teenagers.

The onset of the Depression meant hard times for the record business, as it did for every other industry. The craze for female blues singers, which may have already peaked in the mid'20s, was over, and not just because of artistic trends. Record labels in general were recording less sides. And they weren't eager to devote a lot of resources to the "race" market, populated as it was by the poorest Americans. These African American listeners would have even less purchasing power in the 1930s, as the Depression lowered their already low standard of living.

But it wasn't just economic factors that heralded the demise of the classic women blues singers. Urban African-American music was becoming more uptempo and elaborate. The swing and big band sound came to fruition in the 1930s, making the staider accompaniment common to many '20s female blues recordings sound tame in comparison. And the vaudeville/theatrical circuit that supported the singers was crumbling, threatening their livelihood just years after they enjoyed positively unimaginable wealth (by the standards of African-Americans of the '20s). Many were unable to make records or, after a few years, even perform; the tale of Mamie Smith, who died penniless in 1946, is unfortunately not unique. Bessie Smith and Ma Rainey would themselves be dead by 1940.

It may be that many of the women who would have been blues singers had they started in the 1920s ended up as jazz ones. Jazz as a whole proved much more fruitful for women singers fronting a band than blues would in the ensuing decades. Billie Holiday, acclaimed by many as one of the finest singers of any kind in the 20th century, certainly owed a great deal to the female blues vocalists of the '20s. Several of her earlier sides in particular could just as well be classified as blues as jazz. The blues feel remained prominent in many if not most of the major female jazz singers, from Dinah Washington to Cassandra Wilson.

The original female blues stars of the '20s didn't always disappear entirely. Alberta Hunter, for instance, if anything became more popular after the 1920s, and made an unexpectedly successful comeback as a senior citizen in the 1970s and 1980s, after about 25 years of retirement. Ethel Waters expanded into jazz, and then into movies, getting an Academy Award nominiation for Best Supporting Actress for a 1949 film. Victoria Spivey, returning to active recording in the 1960s, started her own label; Bob Dylan made his first appearance on an official recording for the company, playing harmonica on a Big Joe Williams session.

The blues revival of the 1960s, however, largely passed the classic female blues singers by, though Sippie Wallace did record an album with the Jim Kweskin Jug Band. The vocalists were a considerable influence on pioneering '60s rock singers Janis Joplin and Tracy Nelson (who recorded an entire album of Ma Rainey and Bessie Smith songs in her folkie days), thereby influencing rock performers who had never heard the originals. In any case, the styles that the early women blues singers brought to record had by then infiltrated all of blues, rock, soul, and pop, to be heard in almost everyone from Aretha Franklin on down.

Ten Recommended Albums:

Various Artists, *Blues Masters, Vol. 11: Classic Blues Women* (Rhino)

Bessie Smith, *The Collection* (CBS)

Ma Rainey, *Ma Rainey* (Milestone)

Sippie Wallace, *1923-29* (Alligator)

Victoria Spivey, *1926-31* (Document)

Mamie Smith, *In Chronological Order, Vol. 1* (Document)

Lucille Bogan, *1923-35* (Story of Blues)

Alberta Hunter, *Young Alberta Hunter* (Vintage Jazz)

Ethel Waters, *Jazzin' Babies' Blues, 1921-1927* (Biograph)

Various Artists, *Women's Railroad Blues: Sorry But I Can't Take You* (Rosetta)

Piano Blues

Richie Unterberger

The piano hasn't occupied as prominent a place in the blues as the guitar; in terms of blues virtuosos of recent decades, there may even be more harmonica players than keyboard specialists. The piano will certainly always have a place in the blues combo for both its rhythmic and melodic qualities, despite the hysterical predictions of some observers that the synthesizer will soon make it obsolete. Many of blues' finest singers and songwriters have been piano players; blues piano has also played a big part in influencing the directions of jazz, rock, and soul music.

Blues piano styles have much of their origins in the rough and tumble barrelhouses and railroad/lumber camps of the late 1800s and early 1900s. Here pianists had to develop a rhythmic, aggressive sound to be heard above the crowd, and to keep pace with the rowdy atmopshere. It's no accident that some of the early blues piano greats are noted for a "barrelhouse" style.

In some respects, early piano players may have been at a disadvantage when competing with guitarists and other instrumentalists. The acoustic guitar (or, say, the harmonica) is extremely portable, a big plus for musicians working the road in the days when private automobile travel was a lot less common. It might not have been as much as a drawback as one may think, though. Most settlements had entertainment establishments with house pianos; if residents or travelers could prove their skills, they were often welcome to have at it.

There's little question that considerably more blues guitarists were recorded than blues pianists in the early days of the phonograph. Blues scholars justifiably bewail the loss of important chapters in blues history because of the preferences of the companies responsible for recording blues in the 1920s and 1930s. Many pianists hardly recorded at all, and are now only represented on obscure import blues compilations. Many, no doubt, never had the opportunity to record at all.

Blues pianists, however, began to be recorded shortly after the first appearance of the blues itself on record. Some of the most significant early ones were Cow Cow Davenport, Roosevelt Sykes, and Clarence "Pine Top" Smith. Smith's "Pine Top's Boogie Woogie," from 1929, is generally credited as introducing the term "boogie-woogie" into widespread use.

The boogie-woogie piano style is characterized by a 12-bar blues structure and constantly repeating rhythmic patterns of the left hand, while the right hand plays the melodies and improvisations. It quickly caught on not just in blues, but in popular music as a whole; millions of people who couldn't tell you diddley squat about Robert Johnson know exactly what a boogie-woogie is. Boogie-woogie patterns would become a foundation of jazz in the 1930s and 1940s, jump blues in the 1940s and 1950s, and early R&B/rock 'n' roll in the 1950s.

Records by blues pianists in the 1930s, however, didn't necessarily showcase their instrumental skills. As Mike Rowe notes in *The Blackwell Guide to the Blues,* "There had been a subtle change in the market for piano blues. Those pianists, such as Leroy Carr, Walter Davis, and even Roosevelt Sykes, who had lasted out the Depression were popular for their songs and singing; that they played piano was incidental. While the sawmill pianists played for dancers and had to survive on pianistic prowess, the blues pianist of the urban 1930s had to achieve success as a singer or songwriter. Piano blues had been taken out of the lumber camps and whorehouses and into the homes of an increasingly sophisticated urban audience.

"This accent on the content of the song meant that pianists had little encouragement to stretch themselves, and Davis or Peetie Wheatstraw, for example, could make recording after recording using the same introduction and tempo, which tended to mask their abilities as pianists. Boogie-woogie had become integrated into blues accompaniments, and ragtime was all but eliminated. There was a smoother, more regular sound to the 1930s piano blues, and although a few field trips by Bluebird, Decca, and ARC preserved some regional styles, and the iconoclastic Texas piano in particular, it was the cities such as Chicago and St. Louis that provided the bulk of the artists."

Key figures in the urbanization of blues piano—really, in the urbanization of the blues as a whole—would include Big Maceo Merriweather, Champion Jack Dupree, Sunnyland Slim, and Jimmy Yancey. Boogie-woogie was certainly a big element in swing and big band jazz, and several blues-based boogie-woogie pianists, such as Meade Lux Lewis, Albert Ammons, and Pete Johnson, fed into the jazz tributary with work that straddled the line between the two genres. A Carnegie Hall appearance in 1938 featuring all three of the aforementioned boogie-woogie specialists did much to popularize and legitimize the style.

When the blues started to electrify in Chicago and elsewhere during the 1940s and 1950s, the guitar and harmonica assumed more prominence than the piano. This wasn't true on the West Coast, however, were jump blues reigned supreme between the mid-'40s and mid-'50s. Jump blues' blend of blues and jazz ingredients made it a natural for pianists, and some of jump blues' greatest performers were keyboardist/singers. Amos Milburn, Floyd Dixon, and Camille Howard were some of the best; their achievements are described in greater depth in the jump blues essay. Several other West Coast blues pianists made their mark with a more ballad-inclined, gospel-influenced R&B style, including Charles Brown, Percy Mayfield, Cecil Gant (a great boogie-woogie player as well), and, (on his earliest sides) Ray Charles. The blues/jazz piano connection would be kept alive, to a much subtler degree, via the work of blues-and boogie-influenced soul/jazz organists/pianists of the '60s and '70s, such as Jimmy Smith, Big John Patton, and Jimmy McGriff.

There was still room for a piano in the classic-style Chicago electric blues lineup, as Otis Spann proved during his lengthy stint with Muddy Waters. It took a while for Spann to emerge from Waters' shadow, but recordings on his own established him as a worthy artist in his own right, and perhaps the finest of the post-World War II piano players. Other players of note on the Chicago blues scene were Memphis Slim, Little Johnny Jones (whose two fisted work as a member of Elmore James' Broomdusters made the absence of a rhythm guitar in that band totally unnoticeable), Roosevelt Sykes, Eddie Boyd, Willie Mabon, and Johnnie Johnson, who's probably more famous for his contributions to rock 'n' roll, as the pianist featured on many of Chuck Berry's classic sides.

Piano players as stars or singers, rather than side musicians, have been much thinner on the ground in the last few decades than they were 50-60 years ago. Louisiana was something of a pocket of blues and blues-influenced pianists; Professor Longhair, James Booker, and Katie Webster (all of whom have ties of varying strength to the region) developed some of the funkiest and most idiosyncratic styles to be found in the whole blues piano idiom. Memphis Slim and Pinetop Perkins, among others, kept old-school blues piano styles alive with frequent touring well past the 1960s. Keyboards are still a staple of many a blues band, and will

probably remain so. But the day may have passed when piano players exerted as fundamental an influence on the direction of the blues as they did in the heyday of boogie-woogie and barrelhouse.

Sixteen Recommended Albums:

Cow Cow Davenport, *Alabama Strut* (Magpie)
Roosevelt Sykes, *Roosevelt Sykes (1929-41)* (Story of Blues)
Leroy Carr, *Naptown Blues* (Yazoo)
Albert Ammons, *King of Boogie Woogie (1939-1949)* (Blues Classics)
Meade Lux Lewis, *Complete Blue Note Recordings* (Mosaic)
Jimmy Yancey, *Vol. 1 (1939-40)* (Document)
Big Maceo, *King of Chicago Blues Piano, Vol. 1 & 2* (Arhoolie)
Amos Milburn, *Down the Road Apiece: The Best of Amos Milburn* (EMI)
Floyd Dixon, *Marshall Texas Is My Home* (Specialty)
Camille Howard, *Vol. 1: Rock Me Daddy* (Specialty)
Cecil Gant, *Rock the Boogie* (Krazy Kat)
Sunnyland Slim, *Sunnyland Slim* (Flyright)
Otis Spann, *Otis Spann Is the Blues* (Candid)
Professor Longhair, *Fess: Professor Longhair Anthology* (Rhino)
James Booker, *New Orleans Piano Wizard: Live!* (Rounder)
Memphis Slim, *Rockin' the Blues* (Charly)

Swing And The Big Band Era

Scott Yanow

There was a time when teenagers and young adults danced to jazz-oriented bands, when jazz orchestra dominated the pop charts and when influential clarinetists were household names. During 1935-46, the swing era, such musicians as clarinetists Benny Goodman, Artie Shaw and Jimmy Dorsey, trombonists Glenn Miller and Tommy Dorsey, trumpeter Harry James, pianist Count Basie, vibraphonist Lionel Hampton, drummer Gene Krupa and the unclassifiable Duke Ellington were not only leaders of very popular big bands but international celebrities.

Although swing music really caught on with the masses with the emergence of Benny Goodman in 1935, the style had already existed for more than a decade. Jazz in its earliest forms had emphasized spontaneous melodic improvisation but, as larger dance bands became popular in the 1920s and started utilizing more than three or four horns, it became necessary for arrangements to be written so the music would be organized and coherent. So instead of jammed ensembles, a much larger percentage of the music than previously was written out by arrangers. Prior to 1924, big bands (including Paul Whiteman's, which had a huge hit back in 1920 with "Whispering") tended to play arrangements that largely stuck to the melodies, offered few surprises and lacked the spontaneity and excitement of the best soloists.

In 1924, young cornet star Louis Armstrong joined the Fletcher Henderson Orchestra. His legato phrasing, dramatic use of space and sense of swing greatly impressed and influenced Henderson's chief arranger Don Redman, and one can trace the birth of swing to this collaboration. Redman's post-Armstrong arrangements were light years ahead of his pre-Armstrong work and his writing became a very influential force on big bands as did his work for McKinney's Cotton Pickers which he joined upon leaving Henderson in 1927.

Other important big bands of the decade included Bennie Moten's Kansas City Orchestra (the vestiges of which in the mid-1930s would become Count Basie's), Jean Goldkette's in 1927 (which had notable arrangements by Bill Challis and solos by cornetist Bix Beiderbecke and the C-melody sax of Frankie Trumbauer), the Ben Pollack band (an early training ground for Benny Goodman, Glenn Miller and trombonist Jack Teagarden) and Paul Whiteman's, which by 1927 had finally become a major jazz orchestra. However at this point in time arrangements were often more advanced than the soloists who looked back towards New Orleans jazz for inspiration.

The most significant big band of the late 1920s and one that succeeded Fletcher Henderson's as the pacesetter was Duke Ellington's. A masterful bandleader-pianist, Ellington was even equally talented as an arranger-composer. His ability to write arrangemnets specifically for certain soloists (emphasizing their strengths and making a virtue out of their limitations) resulted in an incredible quantity of high-quality music from the time of his first recordings in 1925 up until his death in 1974.

With the Wall Street crash of 1929 and the rise of the Depression, one would expect that big bands would have become less viable economically, but ironically the opposite occurred. While jazz itself dropped in popularity in favor of soothing ballads, radio (a free form of entertainment) and the popularization of dance halls (a fairly inexpensive way to escape from economic woes) resulted in a growing demand for dance bands. In addition to the many commercial orchestras that

Music Map

Significant Swing Players

Trumpet

Louis Armstrong	Roy Eldridge
Bunny Berigan	Charlie Shavers
Hot Lips Page	Buck Clayton
Harry "Sweets" Edison	Harry James
Ziggy Elman	Cootie Williams
Rex Stewart	Ray Nance
Taft Jordan	Erskine Hawkins
Bill Coleman	Jonah Jones
Frankie Newton	Yank Lawson
Billy Butterfield	Bobby Hackett

Trombone

Jack Teagarden	Tommy Dorsey
Dickie Wells	Trummy Young
Tricky Sam Nanton	Lawrence Brown
Jack Jenney	

Clarinet

Benny Goodman	Artie Shaw
Jimmy Dorsey	Woody Herman
Barney Bigard	Edmond Hall

Tenor

Coleman Hawkins	Lester Young
Chu Berry	Ben Webster
Charlie Barnet	Herschel Evans
Buddy Tate	Dick Wilson
Georgie Auld	Illinois Jacquet
Flip Phillips	Don Byas

Alto

Johnny Hodges	Benny Carter
Willie Smith	Jimmy Dorsey
Woody Herman	Tab Smith

Baritone

Harry Carney

Piano

Art Tatum	Fats Waller
Earl Hines	Teddy Wilson
Duke Ellington	Mary Lou Williams
Joe Sullivan	Jess Stacy
Count Basie	Billy Kyle
Johnny Guarnieri	Mel Powell
Nat King Cole	Jay McShann

Vibes

Lionel Hampton
Red Norvo

Violin

Stephane Grappelli
Stuff Smith

Guitar

Django Reinhardt	Charlie Christian
Carl Kress	Dick McDonough
Freddie Green	Al Casey
Oscar Moore	Tiny Grimes

Bass

Walter Page	Israel Crosby
John Kirby	Milt Hinton
Bob Haggart	Slam Stewart
Jimmy Blanton	

Drums

Gene Krupa	Chick Webb
Jo Jones	Dave Tough
Big Sid Catlett	Cozy Cole
Buddy Rich	

Male Vocalists

Louis Armstrong	Cab Calloway
Jimmy Rushing	Big Joe Turner
Jack Teagarden	Fats Waller
Hot Lips Page	Wingy Manone
Louis Prima	Billy Eckstine
Nat King Cole	

Female Vocalists

Billie Holiday	Ella Fitzgerald
Ethel Waters	Mildred Bailey
Ivie Anderson	Helen Ward
Helen Forrest	Helen Humes
Maxine Sullivan	

Arrangers

Duke Ellington	Don Redman
Fletcher Henderson	Benny Carter
Sy Oliver	Edgar Sampson
Mary Lou Williams	Horace Henderson
Jimmy Mundy	Glenn Miller
Eddie Sauter	

Significant Big Bands of the Swing Era

Duke Ellington	Benny Goodman
Count Basie	Glenn Miller
Fletcher Henderson	Bennie Moten
McKinney's Cotton Pickers	Earl Hines
Luis Russell	Casa Loma Orchestra
Cab Calloway	Jimmy Lunceford
Chick Webb	Andy Kirk
Tommy Dorsey	Jimmy Dorsey
Artie Shaw	Charlie Barnet
Bob Crosby	Harry James
Erskine Hawkins	Jay McShann
Gene Krupa	Lionel Hampton
Stan Kenton	Woody Herman

largely stuck to straight renditions of melodies, such new jazz bands emerged as those led by Cab Calloway (whose energetic singing style and regular broadcasts from the Cotton Club made him one of the most famous Black entertainers of the Depression years), drummer Chick Webb, arranger Jimmy Lunceford, Earl Hines' outfit from Chicago and the various groups headed by Louis Armstrong. Most significant was the rise of the Casa Loma Orchestra, a band able to play both excitable romps (with many arranged choruses by Gene Gifford) and dreamy ballads which set the standard for the future groups.

Although the word "swing" was used on an irregular basis from the mid-1920s on and a 1932 Duke Ellington hit was titled "It Don't Mean A Thing If It Ain't Got That Swing," 1935 was the year that the style really caught on with the masses. Benny Goodman, a 26-year old clarinetist, had led his newly-formed big band as one of three groups featured on the "Let's Dance" radio series. When that engagement ended, he was persuaded to take a cross-country tour. The road trip had its ups and some disastrous downs before the band reached California. At Oakland the group was well received but BG was quite surprised when on Aug. 21, 1935 at the Palomar Ballroom in Los Angeles teenagers in the overflowing crowd exploded with joy. Goodman and his associates did not realize the great popularity that the "Let's Dance" radio shows had had on the West Coast. Word spread quickly about the "new" swing music and the return trip was full of excitement including a long stay in Chicago and some sensational and record breaking runs at theatres in New York. Swing had arrived and the fallout spread all across the country. Within months, many new big bands had been formed and the swing industry soon became huge.

During 1935-42, swing was the popular music of the time and new stars seemed to emerge on a weekly basis. Benny Goodman's first hit record "King Porter Stomp" (which Fletcher Henderson had actually recorded back in 1927 and its composer Jelly Roll Morton way back in 1923) had a memorable trumpet solo by Bunny Berigan in 1935. Berigan was also responsible for adding a great deal of fire to two recordings ("Marie" and "Song Of India") that made Tommy Dorsey famous in 1937. Berigan had a hit that year on his own ("I Can't Get Started") but failed as a bandleader himself due to alcoholism.

The emergence of Count Basie's big band from Kansas City in late-1936 helped redefine both the role of the rhythm section in jazz and the joy of swinging while Glenn Miller in 1939 mixed together a very appealing blend of swing, pop ballads and novelties to become the most popular big band of all (and a soundtrack for a full generation). Other successful big bands of the mid- to late 1930s included Artie Shaw (whose 1938 hit record of "Begin The Beguine" made him a strong challenger to Goodman and Dorsey), Bob Crosby (infusing swing with elements of Dixieland), Will Bradley (whose record of "Beat Me Daddy, Eight To The Bar" started a heated boogie-woogie fad), Charlie Barnet and the surviving orchestras of Ellington, Lunceford, Calloway, Webb and Henderson among dozens of others.

During the swing era, the musicianship of the average musician rose greatly as soloists (whose individual contributions contrasted with the full ensembles of the big bands) became stars and the music gradually evolved. Louis Armstrong's trumpet playing inspired such major stylists as Berigan, Roy Eldridge and Harry James, the most influential trombonists were Tommy Dorsey and Jack Teagarden, Benny Goodman was rightfully crowned the "King Of Swing" while Artie Shaw was a close second on clarinet, the thick-toned tenor of Coleman Hawkins, formerly challenged by Chu Berry and Ben Webster, was matched by the cool sound of Lester Young and the key altoists were Johnny Hodges (from Duke Ellington's Orchestra) and Benny Carter (himself a major arranger). While guitarists and bassist were confined to rhythmic support, Gene Krupa (first in Goodman's band and then with his own orchestra) pushed the drums to the forefront; Chick Webb and Jo Jones were other drum giants. On piano the masters of stride (James P. Johnson and Fats Waller) were joined by the lighter playing of Teddy Wilson and the pure virtuosity of Art Tatum. And among the arrangers (whose contributions were often overlooked) were such important writers as Edgar Sampson (who composed "Stompin' At The Savoy"), Fletcher Henderson, Eddie Sauter, Benny Carter, Sy Oliver (with Jimmy Lunceford and Tommy Dorsey), Bill Finegan and Jimmy Mundy.

While big bands reigned supreme during the 1935-42 era, many of the top jazz musicians also had opportunities (in after-hours jam sessions, as part of combos taken from big bands such as the integrated Benny Goodman Trio and Quartet or in nightclubs) to play in smaller groups. 52nd Street in New York, which had many clubs in close proximity to each other, offered nightly jazz festivals and similar scenes were repeated in other cities. Combos led by John Kirby (his innovative sextet), Fats Waller, trumpeters Wingy Manone and Louis Prima worked regularly and in Paris the Quintet of the Hot Club Of France (starring guitarist Django Reinhardt and violinist Stephane Grappelli) held their own against all Americans.

Plus there were the singers. Nearly every big band had both female and male vocalists who were featured for a chorus or two on records and in performance, helping to sell both the orchestra and individual songs. In the jazz field Louis Armstrong and Billie Holiday (with her behind-the-beat phrasing) were quite influen-

tial, Bing Crosby dominated pop music and among the more notable singers to emerge from swing bands were Ella Fitzgerald (Chick Webb), Sarah Vaughan (Earl Hines), Jimmy Rushing (Count Basie), Frank Sinatra (Harry James and Tommy Dorsey) and Doris Day (Les Brown). Their roles however were secondary at the time to the big band itself, a situation that would reverse itself by the mid-1940s.

Two of the high points of the swing era were certainly Benny Goodman's Jan. 16, 1938 Carnegie Hall Concert (which found the King of Swing at the height of his power) and Duke Ellington's first Carnegie Hall concert in 1943 (when he introduced the 50-minute "Black, Brown & Beige Suite"); fortunately both epic events were recorded. As the 1940s began, the future of swing looked secure and virtually everyone had jumped on the bandwagon, but there were many warning clouds.

The biggest problem was the beginning of World War II and its aftermath. When the United States entered the war, many swing musicians were drafted (Glenn Miller and Artie Shaw were among many who entered the service) and it became more difficult (with gas rationing) for orchestras to travel. In addition during 1942-44, a disastrous recording strike by the Musicians Union (a second one took place in 1948) resulted in singers (who were not in the union) getting the upper hand as bands were kept out of recording studios. The New Orleans jazz revival was underway (and starting to offer competition) while some of the more adventurous musicians, who felt confined having only short solos in swing orchestras, were moving towards creating bebop which, despite its great influence, never caught on with the general public.

The end of World War II in 1945 should have resulted in the renaissance of swing. Harry James' Orchestra was still hugely popular and musicians were recording again. However the jazz world was undergoing a bit of a civil war, with young musicians leaning towards bop, older ones playing Dixieland and more expensive big bands stuck in between. With the rise of the pop singer, many clubs preferring to hire combos and a ruinous entertainment tax discouraging establishments from having dance floors, the swing era was doomed and in 1946 many of the big bands broke up. The bigger names struggled on but by 1950 Duke Ellington was one of the very few leading an important fulltime jazz orchestra.

For decades after the swing era ended, one of the most asked questions has been "Are the big bands coming back?" Although there have been big bands since that time (Ellington, a successful second Count Basie orchestra formed in the early 1950s, Woody Herman, Stan Kenton, Buddy Rich and a countless number of stage bands), most have been either nostalgic ghost bands (such as the still-touring Glenn Miller Orchestra) or more modern part-time jazz groups headed by arrangers. A few bands in the 1950s (Ray Anthony, Billy May, the Sauter-Finegan Orchestra) had pop hits, but they were rare exceptions.

But although the swing big bands have not survived, swing music is still quite viable. In the 1950s critic Stanley Dance coined the phrase "mainstream" to describe the music played by swing veterans such as trumpeter Buck Clayton in small groups. 20 years later the "modern swing" movement (covered in the Mainstream essay) was launched by tenor saxophonist Scott Hamilton and trumpeter Warren Vache and in the 1990s there are quite a few musicians playing swing standards who are much too young to have played with the original big bands. So although the big bands never came back, swing still lives! — Scott Yanow

Twenty Essential Recordings

Fletcher Henderson, *A Study In Frustration* (Columbia)

Louis Armstrong, *Collection Vol. 5: Louis In New York* (Columbia)

Cab Calloway, *1930-1931* (Classics)

Jimmy Lunceford, *Stomp It Off* (GRP/Decca)

Benny Goodman, *The Birth Of Swing* (Bluebird)

Benny Goodman, *Carnegie Hall Jazz Concert* (Columbia)

Bunny Berigan, *The Pied Piper* (Bluebird)

Duke Ellington, *The Blanton-Webster Band* (Bluebird)

Count Basie, *The Complete Decca Recordings* (GRP/Decca)

Artie Shaw, *Begin The Beguine* (Bluebird)

Glenn Miller, *The Popular Recordings* (Bluebird)

Tommy Dorsey, *Yes, Indeed!* (Bluebird)

Harry James, *Best Of Big Bands* (Columbia)

Gene Krupa, *Uptown* (Columbia)

Woody Herman, *Blues On Parade* (GRP/Decca)

Earl Hines, *Piano Man* (Bluebird)

Charlie Barnet, *Drop Me Off In Harlem* (GRP/Decca)

Benny Carter, *All Of Me* (Bluebird)

Art Tatum, *Classic Piano Solos 1934-39* (GRP/Decca)

Three Great Swing Saxophonists (Bluebird)

Ten Essential Books On Swing

The Big Bands by George T. Simon (Collier Books, 1974)

Bunny Berigan by Robert Dupuis (Louisiana Univ. Press, 1993)

Drummin' Men by Burt Korall (Schirmer Books, 1990)

Duke Ellington—Beyond Category by John Edward Hasse (Simon & Schuster, 1993)

The Duke Ellington Reader by Mark Tucker (Oxford Univ. Press, 1993)

Jazz Masters Of The Thirties by Rex Stewart (Da Capo Press, 1972)

Glenn Miller by George T. Simon (Da Capo Press, 1974)

The Swing Era by Gunther Schuller (Oxford Univ. Press, 1989)

Swing Swing Swing by Ross Firestone (W.W. Norton, 1993)

The World Of Swing by Stanley Dance (Da Capo Press, 1974)

Important Events

1923 - Don Redman, the first important jazz arranger, becomes a regular member of the Fletcher Henderson Orchestra.

Duke Ellington visits New York for the initial time with little success.

Bennie Moten's Kansas City Orchestra makes debut on records.

1924 - Fletcher Henderson's big band (featuring Louis Armstrong) begins its long-time residency at the Roseland Ballroom.

1927 - Don Redman leaves Fletcher Henderson to become leader of McKinney's Cotton Pickers.

Duke Ellington wins regular job at the Cotton Club.

1928 - Johnny Hodges joins Duke Ellington's Orchestra.

Earl Hines first plays with his big band at the Grand Terrace in Chicago.

1929 - The influential Casa Loma Orchestra makes its first recordings.

Count Basie joins Bennie Moten's Orchestra.

Louis Armstrong begins recording regularly with big bands.

1930 - Cab Calloway takes over the Missourians and begins playing at the Cotton Club.

1931 - Don Redman forms his own big band.

1932 - Duke Ellington with Ivie Anderson records "It Don't Mean a Thing If It Ain't Got That Swing."

1933 - Duke Ellington's Orchestra visits Europe.

Art Tatum makes his debut on records.

Billie Holiday records her first two songs.

1934 - Coleman Hawkins leaves Fletcher Henderon's Orchestra after a decade, moves to Europe.

Jimmy Lunceford makes his first important recordings. Benny Goodman's orchestra begins appearing on the "Let's Dance" radio show.

Chick Webb records "Stompin' at the Savoy." Ella Fitzgerald joins band.

Fats Waller's extensive series of recordings with his Rhythm start.

1935 - Benny Goodman's Orchestra becomes a surprise sensation, launching the swing era.

Fletcher Henderson breaks up band, contributes arrangements to Benny Goodman.

Bennie Moten dies.

Count Basie soon forms own orchestra.

Billie Holiday starts recording with Teddy Wilson.

Tommy and Jimmy Dorsey have a public argument, break up Dorsey Brothers Orchestra and form their own separate big bands.

1936 - Woody Herman takes over the remains of the Isham Jones Orchestra and forms his first big band.

Fletcher Henderson's new orchestra has a hit in "Christopher Columbus" but his group would break up three years later.

Count Basie is discovered by John Hammond over the radio.

Lester Young makes his debut on records.

Artie Shaw puts together his first orchestra, but it flops.

Andy Kirk's Twelve Clouds of Joy become popular.

1937 - Tommy Dorsey records "Marie" and "Song of India" featuring trumpeter Bunny Berigan.

Berigan forms his own big band, records "I Can't Get Started."

Count Basie's Orchestra makes its first recordings.

Chu Berry joins Cab Calloway.

Glenn Miller forms an orchestra that quickly fails.

1938 - Benny Goodman has a historic concert at Carnegie Hall.

Gene Krupa soon leaves Goodman to form his own big band.

Artie Shaw has a major hit with "Begin the Beguine."

John Kirby's Sextet debuts on record.

1939 - Arranger Sy Oliver quits Jimmy Lunceford's Orchestra to join Tommy Dorsey.

Charlie Barnet's band catches on.

Artie Shaw, at the height of his popularity, breaks up his orchestra and flees to Mexico.

Harry James leaves Benny Goodman to form his own big band.

Glenn Miller's Orchestra becomes the most popular in the world.

Jimmy Blanton and Ben Webster join Duke Ellington.

Chick Webb dies; Ella Fitzgerald takes over band.

Coleman Hawkins, back from Europe after five years, records "Body and Soul."

Charlie Christian joins Benny Goodman.

1940 - Artie Shaw returns to U.S. and has major hit in "Frenesi."

Cootie Williams leaves Duke Ellington and joins Benny Goodman for a year.

Lester Young quits the Count Basie Orchestra.

1941 - Charlie Parker records with the Jay McShann big band.

Gene Krupa has several hits with Anita O'Day and Roy Eldridge.

Stan Kenton forms his first orchestra.

Chu Berry dies.

1942 - Glenn Miller and Artie Shaw break up their big bands to enlist in the military.

A disastrous recording strike starts the beginning of the end of the big band era.

Harry James' Orchestra succeeds Glenn Miller's as the most popular.

Bunny Berigan, Fats Waller, Jimmy Blanton and Charlie Christian die.

Lionel Hampton records "Flying Home."

1943 - Duke Ellington's Orchestra has debut at Carnegie Hall, introducing "Black, Brown & Beige."

1944 - Willie Smith, formerly with Jimmy Lunceford, joins Harry James.

Woody Herman's Orchestra becomes known as the Herd.

Glenn Miller dies.

1945 - Harry James ("It's Been a Long Long Time") and Les Brown ("Sentimental Journey") have major hits but the big bands are being replaced in popularity by vocalists.

1946 - Benny Goodman, Woody Herman, Harry James, Tommy Dorsey and Jack Teagarden are among many who break up their big bands.

1947 - Jimmy Lunceford dies.

Louis Armstrong breaks up orchestra, forms All-Stars.

Bop (R)evolution

Scott Yanow

In 1940 the jazz world was divided into two overlapping camps: swing (primarily big bands with occasional combos) and the gradually growing New Orleans jazz revival. Some of the younger musicians who worked in swing orchestras wanted not only opportunities to stretch out but sought to move the music ahead and develop their own original styles. Feeling that swing had largely got into a rut with an abundance of cliched riffing and predictable solos, young modernists gathered together at jam sessions (most notably at Minton's Playhouse and Monroe's Uptown House in New York City) and experimented with more advanced chords and chancetaking improvising. By 1945 the jazz world was permanently altered with the sudden emergence of bebop. To returning World War II veterans and jazz fans from outside of New York who were accustomed to Glenn Miller and Benny Goodman, bop seemed to appear fully formed in 1945. The recording strike of 1942-44 had kept most musicians off records for up to two years so most listeners had few opportunities to hear the music develop, and when it suddenly appeared, it appeared be to a radical and revolutionary departure with its rapid tempoes, eccentric rhythms and very advanced harmonies. In reality it was a logical evolutionary step beyond swing.

The bop musicians considered such veteran players as trumpeter Roy Eldridge, tenors Coleman Hawkins and Lester Young, the Count Basie rhythm section and pianist Art Tatum as their role models and heroes but, rather than imitate their idols, they sought to change jazz from a dance music to an art form. The results were rather divisive at a time when jazz would have benefited from being unified against pop music, but in time bebop became the foundation of modern jazz.

Bop differed from swing in many respects, most notably in the use of the piano. While classic jazz and swing pianists kept the beat with striding from their left hand (alternating between bass notes and chords) while the right played melodic variations) bop pianists (led by the brilliant Bud Powell) had a much sparser use for their left hand, occasionally stating chords while the right played speedy horn-like solos; this approach has since been adopted for virtually all modern jazz styles. The timekeeping function was taken over by bassists who, despite the emergence of Jimmy Blanton (the short-lived innovator with Duke Ellington) and Oscar Pettiford, continued playing strictly four-to-the-bar behind soloists. Drummers no longer felt compelled to keep the beat with their bass drum and their accompaniment became much more unpredictable, playing colorful accents while no longer functioning as much like a metronome.

As for the horn players, their solos became much less tied to the melody and more to the chord structure. Chordal improvisation allowed soloists to discard melodies and try to make up their own themes while still using the structure of the song. Many of the "originals" put together during the bop era actually used chord patterns from swing standards but had different melodies; for example "Groovin' High" was really "Whispering" in disguise, "Donna Lee" was a complex "Indiana" and "Anthropology" was one of many songs that "borrowed" its chords from "I Got Rhythm."

Three giants dominated the bop era (1945-49) and changed jazz forever: Charlie Parker, Dizzy Gillespie and Bud Powell. Altoist Charlie "Bird" Parker, who gained valuable early experience with pianist Jay McShann's Kansas City big band, permanently altered the vocabulary of jazz and his phrases were soon echoed by a countless number of musicians on all instruments. Able to play perfectly coherent solos at a blinding speed, Bird was not only a very explorative improviser but a topnotch blues player too. He only lived to be 34 (passing away in 1955) due to a ruinous heroin addiction and far too much alcohol, but during his ten years in the spotlight Bird recorded many gems for the Savoy, Dial and Verve labels, introduced both trumpeter Miles Davis and drummer Max Roach in his quintet and consistently amazed his fellow musicians.

Trumpeter John Birks "Dizzy" Gillespie first gained some fame while playing with Cab Calloway's band during 1939-41 where Calloway often accused Dizzy of playing "Chinese music" for coming up with so many notes that sounded wrong. Actually Gillespie was always among the most harmonically advanced of all soloists, and he had the ability to play an obviously "wrong" note, hold on to it and make it seem logical. In addition to his miraculous collaborations with Parker, Gillespie led the most significant bop big band during 1946-49, lived to the age of 75 (thereby evolving from a former revolutionary to an elder statesman), recorded for over 50 years and was an enthusiastic teacher who urged other horn players (including Miles Davis) to learn the piano in order to fully understand chords. Gillespie was also a humorous entertainer who helped demystify bop and make it seem more accessible.

Bud Powell was a tragic figure through no fault of his own. Beaten on the head by racist police in 1944, he suffered from mental illness throughout the remainder of his tortured life. Despite his problems, Powell recorded many gems during 1947-51 (especially for Blue Note) and on an occasional basis in his erratic later years, virtually changing the way that the piano is played in jazz.

In addition to developing innovative styles, Bird, Diz and Bud were all gifted virtuosos who ranked with the greatest ever on their instruments. They of course were not alone in developing bop. At Minton's and Monroe's, such important players as pianist-composer Thelonious Monk (whose highly personal and complex music always stood apart from the boppers), drummer Kenny Clarke (who first shifted the drum's timekeeping role from the bass drum to the much lighter-sounding cymbals) and guitarist Charlie Christian (from Benny Goodman's band) stretched out on common chord changes, pushing their brand of jazz music beyond swing. Other musicians who were major forces during the prime bop years included trumpeters Howard McGhee and Fats Navarro, trombonist J.J. Johnson, clarinetist Buddy DeFranco, altoist Sonny Stitt, tenors Dexter Gordon, Wardell Gray, Teddy Edwards and Gene Ammons, pianists Al Haig and Dodo Marmarosa, bassist Oscar Pettiford, drummers Max Roach and Art Blakey and arranger-composer Tadd Dameron.

The 1940-44 period can be thought of as bop's incubation period before it was discovered. In 1943 both Gillespie and Parker (on tenor) became members of the Earl Hines orchestra, an important interim big band that unfortunately (due to the recording strike) never recorded. Also in the group were singers Billy Eckstine and Sarah Vaughan. The following year Eckstine formed his own big band, taking Gillespie, Parker (back on alto) and Vaughan along with him. The Billy Eckstine Orchestra of 1944-47 was the first bop big band and before Eckstine broke up the group, most of the who's who of modern jazz had played with him including trumpeters Navarro and Miles Davis, tenors Gordon and Ammons, altoist Stitt and

drummer Blakey. Also important in the shrinking big band field were Woody Herman (whose first Herd featured tenor saxophonist Flip Phillips and trombonist Bill Harris while his second Herd helped lead the way towards cool jazz) and the unique Stan Kenton who like Monk created a musical world of his own.

Although Gillespie had participated on a pair of Coleman Hawkins sessions in 1944 that may now consider the first bop recordings (others can argue for the Cootie Williams Orchestra's 1942 version of Monk's "Epistrophy"), in 1945 bop really exploded on the scene with the first joint Parker/Gillespie records. Many swing veterans spoke out against the music (including Louis Armstrong and Tommy Dorsey) while listeners tried to figure it out. With the decline of swing, by 1947 bop was beginning to be accepted and during 1948-49 the major record labels did their best to turn bebop into a new fad. Benny Goodman, Ziggy Elman ("Boppin' With Zig"), Charlie Barnet, Lionel Hampton, Gene Krupa and even Frank Sinatra ("Bop Goes My Heart") recorded variations of bop in the hope of starting a new bandwagon to replace swing as America's popular music. Unfortunately the attempt failed (the ballad-oriented pop singers had already taken over) and by 1950 the bop movement seemed to collapse.

Actually bop never really stood a chance of succeeding as pop music, largely because the musicians (and a new and unfortunate entertainment tax) discouraged listeners from dancing to it. One of the main reasons that swing caught on in 1935 was that, even at its most frantic, it was designed for dancers. Bop can be danced to (one can always dance in halftime!) but not when dance floors are unavailable and the music is being portrayed in the mass media as some type of exotic nonsense. During the bop years Dizzy Gillespie's physical appearance (with "bop glasses," a goatee and a beret) gained more publicity than Charlie Parker's playing. In 1949 it was bop this and bop that, to the extent that by the following year nearly everyone was tired of the word bop!

Fortunately bebop survived the 1940s. Some of its practitioners evolved and became involved in cool jazz and hard bop in the 1950s, others (due to the heroin epidemic during the period) did not last long. Quite a few (such as Gillespie and Sonny Stitt) had long careers sticking to their original vision and were joined by younger players such as altoists Phil Woods and Richie Cole. Ironically by 1960 when free jazz was starting to be noticed and some of the veterans were speaking out against Ornette Coleman, bebop was considered conservative and traditional!

— Scott Yanow

Ten Essential Bop Recordings

Charlie Parker, *Yardbird Suite* (Rhino)

Various Artists, *Charlie Parker & Stars Of Modern Jazz At Carnegie Hall* (Jass)

Dizzy Gillespie, *Complete RCA Victor Recordings* (Bluebird)

Billy Eckstine, *Mister B And The Band* (Savoy)

Bud Powell, *Complete Blue Note And Roost Recordings* (Blue Note)

Coleman Hawkins, *Hollywood Stampede* (Capitol)

Fats Navarro And Tadd Dameron (Blue Note)

Thelonious Monk, *Complete Blue Note Recordings* (Blue Note)

Dexter Gordon, *The Chase* (Stash)

Sonny Stitt, *Tune Up* (Muse)

Five Essential Books About Bop

Bird by Robert Reisner (Da Capo Press, 1962)

Celebrating Bird by Gary Giddins (Beechtree Books, 1987)

Jazz Masters Of The Forties by Ira Gitler (Da Capo Press, 1966)

Swing To Bop by Ira Gitler (Oxford Univ. Press, 1985)

To Be Or Not To Bop by Dizzy Gillespie & Al Fraser (Doubleday, 1979)

Important Events

1937 - Dizzy Gillespie makes initial recordings with Teddy Hill.

1939 - Gillespie joins Cab Calloway's Orchestra.

Charlie Parker visits New York for the first time.

1940 - Dizzy Gillespie and Charlie Parker meet.

Parker makes first recordings with Jay McShann.

1941 - Late night jam sessions at Minton's Playhouse and Monroe's Uptown House feature Thelonious Monk and Kenny Clarke in the house bands with frequent guests Charlie Christian, Charlie Parker and Dizzy Gillespie among others.

1942 - Gillespie plays bop solo with Lucky Millinder on "Little John Special."

1943 - Earl Hines' big band features both Parker (on tenor) and Gillespie, but recording strike keeps association from being documented.

Gillespie co-leads early bop group with Oscar Pettiford.

1944 - Billy Eckstine forms bebop big band that for a time includes Charlie Parker and Dizzy Gillespie.

Music Map

Significant Bebop Players

Charlie Parker - alto
Dizzy Gillespie trumpet
Bud Powell - piano
Thelonious Monk - piano, composer
J.J. Johnson - trombone
Max Roach - drums
Tadd Dameron - composer, arranger

Other Significant Players of Classic Bop

Alto Saxophone

Sonny Criss	Sonny Stitt
Phil Woods	Lou Donaldson
Richie Cole	Charles McPherson

Bass

Oscar Pettiford
Charles Mingus
Ray Brown
Percy Heath

Clarinet

Buddy DeFranco

Drums

Kenny Clarke
Art Blakey
Roy Haynes

Guitar

Charlie Christian	Barney Kessel
Tal Farlow	Herb Ellis
Kenny Burrell	Joe Pass

Percussion

Chano Pozo

Piano

Al Haig	Dodo Marmarosa
Duke Jordan	John Lewis
Barry Harris	

Tenor Saxophone

Don Byas	Dexter Gordon
Wardell Gray	Teddy Edwards
Gene Ammons	Sonny Stitt

Trombone

Kai Winding
Jimmy Cleveland

Trumpet

Howard McGhee
Fats Navarro
Jon Faddis

Vibes

Milt Jackson
Terry Gibbs

Vocals - Male

Dave Lambert	Eddie Jefferson
King Pleasure	Jon Hendricks

Vocals - Female

Ella Fitzgerald	Sarah Vaughan
Anita O'Day	Annie Ross

Big Bands

Billy Eckstine
Dizzy Gillespie
Woody Herman's First Two Herds
Stan Kenton

Coleman Hawkins leads earliest bop record date; group features Gillespie.

Charlie Parker heard on Tiny Grimes combo session.

Thelonious Monk composes "'Round Midnight" which is recorded by Cootie Williams orchestra with Bud Powell on piano.

1945 - Charlie Parker and Dizzy Gillespie make many recordings that stun the jazz world.

Howard McGhee (traveling with Coleman Hawkins) helps bring bebop to Los Angeles.

Gillespie leads his first big band but it fails.

Bird and Diz make trip to West Coast.

J.J. Johnson is with Count Basie's orchestra.

1946 - Dizzy Gillespie forms his second big band which is much more successful than the first.

Parker spends half year at Camarillo State Hospital.

J.J. Johnson's first recordings as a leader are so fluent that some suspect he is playing valve trombone!

Fats Navarro leaves Billy Eckstine's orchestra and starts recording many classic small group sides.

1947 - Gillespie adds innovative conga player Chano Pozo to big band.

Parker returns to New York and puts together his strongest regular quintet, a group featuring Miles Davis and Max Roach.

Thelonious Monk makes first sessions for Blue Note.

Billy Eckstine reluctantly breaks up his big band.

Bud Powell cuts his first trio sides.

Dexter Gordon and Wardell Gray record "The Chase."

1948 - Second recording strike keeps most artists off records but Charlie Parker still records "Parker's Mood."

1949 - Bop is everywhere; even Benny Goodman, Gene Krupa and Charlie Barnet record it.

Dizzy Gillespie signs with Capitol as larger record companies seek to make a fad out of bop.

Charlie Parker records with strings.

All-Star bop concert at Carnegie Hall on Christmas Day.

1950 - Bebop "fad" ends abruptly.

Fats Navarro dies.

Dizzy Gillespie breaks up big band.

Post 1950 - Despite pronouncements of bop's "death," the once radical music becomes part of the jazz mainstream, greatly influencing all future styles and surviving in many forms up to the present day.

Chicago Jazz and the Dixieland Revival

Scott Yanow

Dixieland has long been one of jazz's most popular styles but musicians often shy away from the idiom's name. Because "Dixieland" suffers from a bad image problem due to it being associated with the commercial (and often amateurish and corny) product pushed by record labels in the 1950s to fans who often could not tell the difference, musicians who play in the style often prefer to be called "traditional" or "classic jazz" players. The stereotype of a Dixieland band is of middle-aged White amateurs wearing straw hats and dated clothes while strumming banjos, blowing incompetently into tubas and singing "When The Saints Go Marching In" at right-wing political rallies!

However Dixieland, like the much maligned fusion, is an honorable style when played with sincerity and creativity and its name is here to stay. A typical Dixieland band comprises a trumpet or cornet (which functions as the lead voice and keeps the melody nearby), trombone (harmonizing with the trumpet), a clarinet weaving in and out of the ensembles, piano, string bass or tuba, drums and sometimes guitar or banjo. Occasionally a tenor is added. Dixieland differs from New Orleans jazz in that its repertoire is generally more predictable, the musicianship is more consistent and less erratic (some New Orleans players have had shaky intonation) and, even though it features heated ensembles, there is generally much more space for solos. A typical song will have one or two ensembles, solos for clarinet, trombone, trumpet and piano, two closing ensembles, a four-bar break for the drums and a final four bars for the full group. However in recent times the more inventive bands have used more unpredictable frameworks.

Dixieland overlaps with New Orleans jazz, which is logical because it grew out of the music of the New Orleans pioneers such as Buddy Bolden (who led the city's leading brass band during 1895-1906), cornetist Freddie Keppard, clarinetist (and later soprano saxophonist) Sidney Bechet, trombonist Kid Ory, cornetist Joe "King" Oliver and pianist-composer Jelly Roll Morton. The first New Orleans jazz band to record, the Original Dixieland Jazz Band, introduced quite a few songs that would become Dixieland standards including "Tiger Rag" (which Morton claimed to have written), "Indiana," "Darktown Strutters' Ball," "At The Jazz Band Ball," "Fidgety Feet" and "Original Dixieland One Step." But despite its name, the ODJB mostly played ensembles and was closer to New Orleans jazz than to Dixieland. An important transition band between New Orleans jazz and Dixieland was the New Orleans Rhythm Kings, the pacesetting group which recorded during 1922-23, introduced "Tin Roof Blues," "Farewell Blues," "Panama" and "That's A Plenty," and in clarinetist Leon Rappolo had the first important horn soloist on record.

1923 was the breakthrough year for both styles of music for it found Sidney Bechet making his recording debut on some dazzling numbers with Clarence Williams' Blue Five, and it brought to record King Oliver's Creole Jazz Band. The latter was the perfect New Orleans jazz band since its performances were full of exciting ensembles played by such colorful musicians as both King Oliver and the young Louis Armstrong on cornets, clarinetist Johnny Dodds and drummer Baby Dodds. In the audience quite often at the Lincoln Gardens in Chicago were a group of fans from a local high school who would become known as the Austin High School Gang. Inspired to take up instruments, such players as cornetist Jimmy McPartland, tenor saxophonist Bud Freeman, clarinetist Frankie Teschemacher, drummer Gene Krupa and banjoist (later guitarist) Eddie Condon at first tried to emulate Oliver's band and then searched for sounds of their own.

The rise of Louis Armstrong during 1924-25 inspired the young Dixielanders as did the beautiful cornet sound (and advanced playing) of Bix Beiderbecke with the Wolverines. With Eddie Condon as the ad-hoc group's leader, the Chicagoans recorded four selections in 1927 and soon headed for New York. Although "Chicago jazz" failed to catch on during a period when the public preferred large dance orchestras, their recordings gained a strong underground reputation and would be one of many inspirations on the Dixieland revival of the 1940s.

Besides the Chicagoans, many other players participated in Dixieland-oriented sessions during the mid- to late 1920s including trumpeters Muggsy Spanier and Wingy Manone, the up-and-coming trombonist Jack Teagarden, clarinetist Pee Wee Russell, pianists Fats Waller and Joe Sullivan among many others.

With the Wall Street crash of 1929, the freewheeling and happy jazz represented by Dixieland went largely undercover for the next few years. The music was never extinct but it was thought of as "old hat" by fans of swing music in the mid-1930s and as a bit chaotic by listeners who preferred melodic dance bands. However musicians on their off hours from swing bands often enjoyed playing the more spontaneous style at late-night jam sessions.

Prior to 1938, Dixieland could be heard on records by Wingy Manone, Louis Prima, Fats Waller and in Tommy Dorsey's Clambake Seven, a small group taken from his orchestra. Bob Crosby's big band was one of the few to use the feel of Dixieland and his Bobcats from the orchestra featured such top hot players as trumpeters Yank Lawson and Billy Butterfield, clarinetist Irving Fazola, tenorman Eddie

Miller and pianist Bob Zurke. When Milt Gabler founded his Commodore label in 1938, his first session featured an all-star group of Dixielanders put together by Eddie Condon. But when Muggsy Spanier recorded "The Great 16" with his exciting octet in 1939, he was unable to find steady work for his group and had to disband. It was just a couple years too early, both ahead of and behind the times!

Dixieland began its revival period during 1940-41. In San Francisco, trumpeter Lu Watters founded the Yerba Buena Jazz Band, an octet whose two-trumpet lead was based on King Oliver but which soon developed its own repertoire and sound. Its 1941 recordings (sometimes called San Francisco Jazz) were quite influential on the entire Dixieland jazz movement and, after a couple years off due to military service, the band regrouped and had its glory years during 1946-47. Among its alumni were such future bandleaders as trumpeter Bob Scobey (who recorded frequently in the 1950s) and trombonist Turk Murphy (a major force into the 1980s) plus the superior singer-banjoist Clancy Hayes and pianist Wally Rose. Many bands have been formed since that time that seek to recreate the excitement of Watters' group.

The early to mid-1940s also found several veteran New Orleans players (most notably Bunk Johnson and George Lewis) being rediscovered and reviving New Orleans jazz; highlights from that movement are covered in the style's essay. Also brought back to record was trombonist Kid Ory, a veteran of the 1920s whose bands during 1944-60 featured strong trumpeters (most notably a past-his-prime but still viable Mutt Carey, Teddy Buckner, Alvin Alcorn and even briefly Red Allen), high musicianship and a fine mixture of stirring ensembles and colorful solos.

Eddie Condon, although just a decent rhythm guitarist, was a major force in the Dixieland and Chicago jazz revival. An expert at gathering together complementary (but diverse) stylists, at picking tunes and tempos and at making wisecracks, Condon was a major propagandist for the music. His Town Hall Concerts, which were broadcast weekly during 1944-45, found him during a half-hour show featuring not only an oversized Dixieland band (usually including three trumpets and two clarinets) but many guest stars and often vocalists Red McKenzie and Lee Wiley; somehow no one got shortchanged. Condon regularly led a group at Nick's in the 1940s until opening his own club Condon's which lasted under his leadership for a couple decades. Among his many important sidemen through the years were trumpeters/cornetists Wild Bill Davison (an emotional player who was the perfect Dixieland lead voice), Bobby Hackett, Max Kaminsky and Billy Butterfield, trombonists Jack Teagarden (usually a special guest), Brad Gowans, Benny Morton, Lou McGarity, Cutty Cutshall and Miff Mole, clarinetists Pee Wee Russell, Edmond Hall, Joe Marsala and Bob Wilber, tenor saxophonist Bud Freeman, baritonist Ernie Caceres, pianists Joe Sullivan, Joe Bushkin, Jess Stacy, Gene Schroeder, Dick Cary and Art Hodes, several bassists and drummers Dave Tough and George Wettling among others. Even during the music's slow periods, Condon was successful in keeping the style alive.

With the rise of bebop in the mid-1940s and the decline of swing, many of the top swing soloists spent some time playing Dixieland (including trumpeters Buck Clayton, Rex Stewart and Roy Eldridge). In fact, even with all of the other jazz developments, Dixieland was the most popular jazz style during 1945-60. Louis Armstrong broke up his big band in 1947 and spent the rest of his career leading a Dixieland-oriented sextet, his All-Stars. The Good Time Jazz label exclusively recorded traditional jazz including Kid Ory's band and the popular Firehouse Five Plus Two. Wilbur DeParis put together his "New New Orleans Jazz Band," cornetist Red Nichols (an important recording leader in the 1920s) jammed nightly with his Five Pennies, in New Orleans trumpeter Al Hirt and clarinetist Pete Fountain became major attractions and the Dukes Of Dixieland's many records for Audio Fidelity were steady sellers.

The record companies took notice of these developments and in the 1950s (with the development of the LP) they flooded the market with cheaply produced and rather unimaginative Dixieland records which often had cornball covers that did not bother identifying the musicians. A purposely corny satire by trombonist Pee Wee Hunt of "12th Street Rag" (which most listeners took seriously) became a major hit and Dixieland in general became a fad. After World War II, Dixieland also caught on overseas. Graeme Bell's many records for Swaggie in Australia helped created a classic jazz scene down under, Sidney Bechet moved to France where he was considered a national celebrity and England, lagging a few years behind, soon had clubs filled with fans eager to see bands playing what was called "skiffle" or "trad." Trumpeter Kenny Ball (who in the early 1960s had a major hit with "Midnight In Moscow"), trombonist Chris Barber and clarinetist Monty Sunshine became famous celebrities.

By the late 1950s in the US, the Dixieland fad was running out of steam. Rock and roll soon buried all competitors although Louis Armstrong in 1964 with "Hello Dolly" showed that Dixieland still retained its potential appeal. New Orleans jazz was revitalized a bit in the 1960s with the opening of Preservation Hall but in general the music slipped back underground, enjoyed by a core of fans

Music Map

Significant Dixieland Revival Players

Louis Armstrong- trumpet, vocals
Eddie Condon- bandleader
Jack Teagarden - trombone, vocals
Lu Watters - trumpet, bandleader
Kid Ory - trombone, bandleader

Other Significant Dixieland Players
Alto Saxophone
Captain John Handy

Baritone Saxophone
Ernie Caceres

Bass
Pops Foster
Bob Haggart

Bass Saxophone
Joe Rushton

Clarinet

Pee Wee Russell	Barney Bigard
Edmond Hall	George Lewis
Peanuts Hucko	Matty Matlock
Pete Fountain	Bob Wilber
Kenny Davern	Ken Peplowski

Drums
Baby Dodds
George Wettling
Nick Fatool
Ray Bauduc
Paul Barbarin

Guitar
Danny Barker
Marty Grosz
Howard Alden

Piano

Earl Hines	Joe Sullivan
Jess Stacy	Art Hodes
Wally Rose	Ralph Sutton
Dick Wellstood	Dick Hyman
Dave McKenna	James Dapogny
Judy Carmichael	

Tenor Saxophone
Bud Freeman
Eddie Miller

Trombone

George Brunies	Trummy Young
Vic Dickenson	Lou McGarity
Jim Robinson	Turk Murphy
Wilbur DeParis	Dan Barrett

Trumpet

Red Allen	Hot Lips Page
Wingy Manone	Sidney DeParis
Louis Prima	Yank Lawson
Billy Butterfield	Muggsy Spaniel
Bobby Hackett	Max Kaminsky
Jimmy McPartland	Wild Bill Davison
Bob Scobey	Red Nichols
Ruby Braff	Warren Vache
Peter Ecklund	Jim Cullum, Jr.
Doc Cheatham	

Vocals - Male

Red Allen	Wingy Manone
Louis Prima	Jelly Roll Morton
Clancy Haynes	Danny Barker
Marty Grosz	

Vocals - Female

Lee Wiley	Alberta Hunter
Lizzie Miles	Banu Gibson

but no longer noticed much by the general public. There were exceptions, such as the World's Greatest Jazz Band (a group co-led by Yank Lawson and bassist Bob Haggart) and Soprano Summit (a two-reed quintet/sextet with Bob Wilber and Kenny Davern doubling on clarinets and sopranos) but those were fairly rare.

However Dixieland (along with New Orleans and Classic Jazz) never died altogether and it has made a gradual comeback since the 1970s. The Stomp Off label in the 1980s and '90s released several hundred records that documented (and showed the depth and viability) of the current traditional jazz scene. George Buck's GHB and Jazzology labels also continued its important work that began in 1949, the new Arbors company featured many inventive sessions and even Good Time Jazz (which had been dormant since 1969) made a limited comeback. The formation of the huge Sacramento Jazz Jubilee helped spark an interest in Dixieland jazz festivals to the point where now it is possible to go to such events nearly every weekend of the year. In addition more expensive jazz parties often have a healthy dose of Dixieland along with mainstream and bop.

While the older greats have gradually passed on (pianist Ralph Sutton and clarinetists Bob Wilber and Kenny Davern are among the few current survivors from the 1940s and '50s), Wynton Marsalis and some other young players (such as Nicholas Payton) celebrate the New Orleans heritage in their more modern music, often incorporating New Orleans parade rhythms and a bit of collective improvisa-

tion. Both in the US and in Europe, there are currently a countless number of exciting groups playing in the idiom. Two of the best are trumpeter Jim Cullum's band from San Antonio (which is featured regularly on the creative radio series Riverwalk, Live From The Landing) and singer Banu Gibson's New Orleans Hot Jazz (whose wide repertoire stretches into small-group swing).

Even if the mass media and the general public never get around to noticing it, Dixieland continues in the late 1990s to be a major musical force. — *Scott Yanow*

Fifteen Essential Dixieland and Chicago Jazz Records

Various Artists, *Obscure And Neglected Chicagoans* (IAJRC)
Bob Crosby, *South Rampart Street Parade* (GRP/Decca)
Eddie Condon, *Dixieland All-Stars* (GRP/Decca)
Eddie Condon, *Town Hall Concerts Vol. 2* (Jazzology)
Wild Bill Davison, *The Commodore Master Takes* (Commodore)
Lu Watters, *Vol. 1: Dawn Club Favorites* (Good Time Jazz)
Turk Murphy, *Jazz Band Favorites* (Good Time Jazz)
Bob Scobey, *Scobey & Clancy* (Good Time Jazz)
Recorded In New Orleans, Vols. 1+2 (Good Time Jazz)
Louis Armstrong, *Plays W.C. Handy* (Columbia—1997 version)

Jack Teagarden, *And His All-Stars* (Jazzology)

Dukes Of Dixieland, *At Disneyland* (Columbia, a classic but not yet on CD)

World's Greatest Jazz Band, *Live* (Atlantic)

Soprano Summit (Concord)

Jim Cullum, *Hooray For Hoagy* (Audiophile)

Eight Essential Books About Dixieland and Classic Jazz

Really The Blues by Mezz Mezzrow & Bernard Wolf (Doubleday, 1946)

We Called It Music by Eddie Condon & Thomas Sugrue (Da Capo Press, 1947)

Pee Wee Russell by Robert Hilbert (Oxford Univ. Press, 1993)

Hot Man by Art Hodes & Chadwick Hansen (Univ. Of Illinois Press, 1992)

Jazz Band by Max Kaminsky & V.E. Hughes (Da Capo Press, 1963)

The Great Jazz Revival by Jim Goggin & Pete Clute (Ewald Publ, 1994)

Music Was Not Enough by Bob Wilber & Derek Webster (Oxford Univ. Press, 1987)

Traditionalists & Revivalists In Jazz by Chip Deffaa (Scarecrow Press, 1993)

Important Events

1929 - Freewheeling Dixieland goes out of style.

Louis Armstrong begins recording with big bands.

1932 - Sidney Bechet gets a single recording session with his New Orleans Feetwarmers.

1934 - Wingy Manone and Louis Prima both start recording frequently as singing Dixieland trumpeter bandleaders.

Fats Waller and His Rhythm began their popular series of Bluebird records.

1935 - Tommy Dorsey starts extensive series of good-natured Dixieland recordings with his Clambake Seven.

1937 - Bob Crosby's Dixieland-oriented swing big band and his Bobcats begin to become popular.

1938 - Jelly Roll Morton records extensively for the Library of Congress but his attempt at a comeback (which ended with his death in 1941) is largely unsuccessful.

Eddie Condon records several classics for the new Commodore label.

1939 - Cornetist Muggsy Spanier records "The Great 16" with his Ragtime Band. Despite the major influence of this music on future Dixieland bands, Spanier's group cannot get a regular job and soon break up.

1940 - Sidney Bechet records for Bluebird.

1941 - The Dixieland revival really gets going full force with the first recordings of Lu Watters Yerba Buena Jazz Band.

1942 - Bunk Johnson emerges from retirement to make an unlikely comeback.

1943 - Wild Bill Davison records the definitive version of "That's a Plenty" for Commodore.

1944 - Kid Ory, who had spent the 1930s running a chicken farm, comes out of retirement and forms his Creole Jazz Band.

Eddie Condon's Town Hall Concerts feature all-star integrated jazz groups broadcasting over the radio on a weekly basis.

1945 - Mezz Mezzrow launches his King Jazz label.

1946 - Louis Armstrong stars in the fictional but entertaining movie *New Orleans.*

1947 - Louis Armstrong breaks up his big band and forms his All-Stars with Jack Teagarden and Barney Bigard.

Turk Murphy and Bob Scobey leave the Yerba Buena Jazz Band and soon form their own successful groups.

Rudi Blesh's hosts the legendary *This Is Jazz* radio series.

1949 - Firehouse Five Plus Two makes first recordings, helps launch Good Time Jazz label.

Sidney Bechet moves to France and soon becomes national hero.

Eddie Condon's Floor Show, a pioneering half-hour jam session series, is televised each week.

1950 - George Lewis' band begins to record and soon starts touring the world.

Lu Watters breaks up the Yerba Buena Jazz Band and retires.

1955 - Wilbur DeParis and his "New New Orleans Jazz Band" make their first recording for Atlantic.

1958 - *The Five Pennies,* a hit movie, features Danny Kaye in the fictional role of Red Nichols along with Louis Armstrong; Nichols himself plays on the soundtrack.

1959 - Pete Fountain, featured Dixieland clarinetist with the *Lawrence Welk Show,* leaves the series and begins his own lucrative career.

1961 - Kenny Ball has big hit with "Midnight in Moscow." Preservation Hall opens in New Orleans.

Dukes of Dixieland sign with Columbia where they will make their finest recordings.

1964 - "Hello Dolly" becomes a huge hit for Louis Armstrong.

Lu Watters returns to music briefly (sounding in fine form on his one recording) before retiring again.

1968 - Yank Lawson and Bob Haggart team up to form "The World's Greatest Jazz Band."

1971- Louis Armstrong dies.

1974 - The first Sacramento Dixieland Jubilee is held and the huge annual event attests to the continuing artistic (if not commercial) health of Dixieland.

1979 - Stomp Off label is formed and extensively documents the classic jazz scene of the 1980s and '90s.

Mainstream Jazz

Scott Yanow

When the swing era ended during 1945-46, sidemen from the big bands seemed to have only two choices: To alter their style and try to learn bebop or switch to playing Dixieland warhorses. The evolution of jazz had raced by so fast that it seemed to pass many swing stylists by when they were still very much in their prime. Some of the musicians suffered from identity problems including trumpeter Roy Eldridge. Always a fierce competitor and proud of being a very modern musician, Eldridge was surpassed by Dizzy Gillespie (who considered Roy to be his main influence) and, compared to Dizzy, he sounded a decade behind the times. Eldridge went to France in 1950 on tour with Benny Goodman, was appreciated by European audiences and soon regained his self-confidence. He realized that being the most "modern" musician was not as important as being true to oneself and sticking to one's own style.

In the mid-'50s jazz critic Stanley Dance coined the phrase "mainstream" to describe the music played by swing veterans who managed to avoid both bop and Dixieland. Among the musicians who fit into this area were alumni of the Count Basie and Duke Ellington Orchestras, the surviving swing greats and some younger players. Since mainstream is a continuation of the swing style minus the big bands, World War II nostalgia and pop elements, it is difficult to state when it originated. Small group swing of the 1930s and '40s generally qualifies, especially performances by such major players as tenors Coleman Hawkins, Lester Young and Ben Webster, trumpeters Roy Eldridge, Charlie Shavers, Buck Clayton and Harry "Sweets" Edison, altoists Benny Carter and Johnny Hodges, vibraphonist Lionel Hampton, pianists Teddy Wilson and Count Basie, drummers Jo Jones and Gene Krupa among others. Happily all of these musicians were quite active in the 1950s and were part of a mini-movement simply by choosing to be themselves.

In 1944 producer Norman Granz put together his first organized jam session which was called Jazz at the Philharmonic. During the next 13 years he would have annual tours in the US (and later on Europe) with JATP, featuring top swing and bop soloists battling it out on medium-tempo blues and fairly basic chord changes in addition to having ballad medleys and individual features. Although some critics harped about the staged tenor and trumpet battles (accusing musicians of playing to the audiences which were often rambunctious), much of the music was indeed quite exciting. Granz, an early civil rights crusader, featured integrated bands, paid his musicians well and helped revive (and sometimes keep alive) many careers. Among the stars of JATP through the years were trumpeters Eldridge, Shavers, Gillespie, Clayton and Edison, trombonists J.J. Johnson and Bill Harris, tenors Hawkins, Young, Illinois Jacquet (who took a famous screaming solo during the initial 1944 concert), Flip Phillips (who became identified with "Perido"), Ben Webster and Stan Getz, altoists Charlie Parker, Benny Carter and Willie Smith, the Oscar Peterson Trio, drummers Buddy Rich and Louie Bellson and singer Ella Fitzgerald.

Granz fortunately recorded many of the concerts and also caught most of his stars in the studios for his Norgran and Clef labels, eventually consolidating all of his sessions on Verve. During an era when jazz was polarized between modern and trad, Norman Granz had the courage of his convictions, recorded his favorite jazz musicians no matter what the style and documented many classic encounters for posterity.

By the early 1950s many of the swing players who were not under Granz's protective wing drifted into R&B sessions as sidemen (a few of the tenors emulted the honking of Illinois Jacquet) or Dixieland. Even Buck Clayton, whose middle-of-the-road swing style epitomizes mainstream, spent time in Dixieland bands. A few years later he recorded the first of the famous Buck Clayton Jam Sessions for

Columbia, classic sets that have been made available in full on a limited-edition Mosaic box set but have mostly otherwise not yet appeared on CD. In addition, longtime swing propagandist and producer John Hammond organized a series of worthy Basie-oriented dates for Vanguard headed by Clayton, trombonist Vic Dickenson, singer Jimmy Rushing, pianist Sir Charles Thompson, trumpeter Ruby Braff and some of his other favorites.

The rise of West Coast jazz in the early 1950s led to modern jazz re-evaluating some of the elements of swing including the light feel of Count Basie's rhythm sections and the cool tone of Lester Young's tenor. Throughout the 1950s there were many examples of cool meeting swing in mainstream settings; baritonist Gerry Mulligan for one was always eager to record with his elders and made successful sets with Johnny Hodges and Ben Webster. In other cases swing veterans teamed up together while using younger rhythm sections. Coleman Hawkins and Roy Eldridge frequently co-led a quintet and were happy to use the versatile pianist Ray Bryant.

In the 1960s much of mainstream jazz seemed to disappear. The swing veterans continued to age and their numbers greatly decreased. Rock took the audience away, the avant-garde gained the headlines, hard bop and soul-jazz became the new mainstream and Norman Granz sold Verve. With the rise of fusion in the late '60s, mainstream seemed to be dying altogether along with its originators.

But in the mid-1970s mainstream began its slow comeback. Soprano Summit (co-led by Bob Wilber and Kenny Davern who doubled on clarinets and sopranos) and the Ruby Braff-George Barnes Quartet helped to keep the music alive and both groups were popular for a time. Tenor saxophonist Scott Hamilton and cornetist Warren Vache, talented players in their early '20s, were the first significant members of their generation to play mainstream and, due to their obvious abilities, they inspired other musicians. While Hank O'Neal's Chiaroscuro label had been largely alone in the early 1970s at documenting this style, Norman Granz returning to active recording by starting Pablo (documenting old favorites Ella, Eldridge, Gillespie, Edison, Oscar Peterson and Basie along with guitarist Joe Pass, vibraphonist Milt Jackson, tenors Zoot Sims and Eddie "Lockjaw" Davis and fluegelhornist Clark Terry among others) and Concord (which ended up being the most important mainstream jazz label) was founded by Carl Jefferson.

In the 1980s such young talents as trombonist Dan Barrett, guitarist Howard Alden and Ken Peplowski (on clarinet and tenor) joined forces (sometimes with Vache and/or Hamilton) with some veterans (including pianists Dave McKenna and Dick Hyman) and a full-fledged "modern swing" movement was underway. Although Granz eventually retired again (and Pablo became much less active), the Chiaroscuro label made a comeback, Concord has continued a busy schedule and other record companies (some from Europe plus Arbors from Florida) went out of their way to document the music. Up to the present time mainstream (sometimes overlapping with Dixieland and bop) seems quite healthy. In addition to making many records, the mainstream players of the 1990s appear often at jazz parties, at festivals (particularly in Europe) and in clubs, being creative within the swing tradition without worrying about breaking down new boundaries or making the best seller charts.-Scott Yanow

Eighteen Essential Mainstream Jazz Records

Jazz At The Philharmonic, *The First Concert* (Verve)

Benny Carter, *3, 4, 5: The Verve Small Group Sessions* (Verve)

Buck Clayton, *The Essential* (Vanguard)

Lester Young, *The Jazz Giants '56* (Verve)

Ben Webster, *Soulville* (Verve)

Clark Terry, *Duke With A Difference* (Original Jazz Classics)

Coleman Hawkins, *Alive!* (Verve)

Harry "Sweets" Edison, *Jawbreakers* (Original Jazz Classics)

Johnny Hodges, *Everybody Knows* (GRP/Impulse)

Zoot Sims And The Gershwin Brothers (Original Jazz Classics)

Roy Eldridge, *Montreux 1977* (Original Jazz Classics)

Ruby Braff, *A Sailboat In The Moonlight* (Concord Jazz)

Scott Hamilton, *Major League* (Concord Jazz)

Warren Vache, *Midtown Jazz* (Concord Jazz)

Dan Barrett, *Strictly Instrumental* (Concord Jazz)

Howard Alden, *The ABQ Salutes Buck Clayton* (Concord Jazz)

Ken Peplowski, *Steppin' With Peps* (Concord Jazz)

Dave McKenna, *The Keyman* (Concord Jazz)

Four Essential Books About Mainstream Jazz

The World Of Count Basie by Stanley Dance (Charles Scribner's Sons, 1980)

A Lester Young Reader by Lewis Porter (Smithsonian Institntuion Press, 1991)

In The Mainstream by Chip Deffaa (Scarecrow Press, 1992)

Swing Legacy by Chip Deffaa (Scarecrow Press, 1989)

Early Rhythm & Blues

Richie Unterberger

When rhythm & blues began in the mid-'40s, it didn't even have a name. When the term caught on, though, it caught on in a big way. Right up until the present day, R&B has come to refer to the entire world of Black popular music, although it's mostly identified as R&B—rather than rap, soul, or urban contemporary—by specialized audiences and music industry insiders, not general fans.

In its earliest form, rhythm & blues was among the most important precursors of rock 'n' roll, if not THE most important. Early rock 'n' roll is basically R&B blended with country & western and pop influences. R&B wasn't only a crucial bridge between blues and rock 'n' roll, but between blues and soul, R&B's longest-lived and most important offshoot.

The blues, of course, was a big part of rhythm and blues, but jazz was nearly as important. The earliest rhythm & blues artists emerged from the big-band and swing-jazz era. Before World War II, jazz, much more so than today, was a dance-oriented music, often featuring vocalists. Around World War II, many major jazz players began developing bebop and cool jazz, a decidedly less danceable (though equally worthy) style; economic factors, as well as the draft and wartime restrictions on travel, made big bands less viable. Audiences, especially the rapidly growing metropolitan African-American communities, still wanted dance music. The musicians accomodated them by playing louder, more electric instruments, and accentuating riffs, boogies, and vocals.

The first popular style of rhythm & blues is often referred to as "jump" blues. From jazz, jump blues took its horn-driven lineup and swing rhythms; from blues, it took its general riffs and chord structures. Cab Calloway was perhaps the most important precursor of the style, but in jump blues, the vocals were harsher, the rhythms faster. The instrumentation was different, too; the pianos pounded harder, and, most important, the saxes didn't just blow, but honked and squealed.

The most important and popular jump blues star was Louis Jordan, whose records, unusually for the era, enjoyed success with both Black and White audiences; he was a particularly big influence on Chuck Berry. Many of the early jump blues performers emerged from Los Angeles, where a large Black community had been growing during the Depression and the war; most other big cities had jump blues stars of their own by the end of the 1940s. Independent labels such as L.A.'s Specialty and Alladin jump-started their success with the jump blues sound, filling a demand that the majors were basically unaware of. Joe Liggins, Tiny Bradshaw (the original performer of "The Train Kept A-Rollin'"), Amos Milburn, Camille Howard—all are largely forgotten by record collectors, but all had huge R&B successes in the jump blues style, and ranked among the most popular Black musicians of their time.

Jump blues itself came in several different styles. There were the vocalists that came to be known as the "shouters," adding energy, soul, and gospel to the more restrained brand of big-band singing. Big Joe Turner, who got his start with Kansas City jazz bands, was the most legendary link between the eras, shifting into the R&B era with ease, and even scoring some early rock 'n' roll hits. Wynonie Harris, Roy Brown, Roy Milton, and Nappy Brown were a few of the most popular "shouters" of the late '40s and early '50s, although they aren't nearly as well remembered by history as Turner. There were also showmen, usually saxophonists, whose appeal was primarily instrumental: Big Jay McNeely, Illinois Jacquet, and Joe Houston, with strong roots in jazz, drove dance crowds crazy with their acrobatic honking. And there were smoother, more urbane singers, like Charles Brown, Percy Mayfield, and Cecil Gant, who were as adept at ballads as uptempo material.

By the time the '50s started, "race" music, as it was known within the industry, had been renamed the more appropriate "rhythm & blues" by Billboard magazine staff-member Jerry Wexler. As an A&R man at Atlantic Records, Wexler helped shape jump blues into something with more appeal to pop listeners and teenagers. The recordings by early Atlantic stars like Ruth Brown, LaVern Baker, the first incarnation of the Drifters, and Chuck Willis (who actually began at the Okeh label) retained a strong jump blues flavor, but their rhythms, riffs, and lyrics point more clearly toward rock 'n' roll. Indeed, Baker and Willis managed to enjoy some success in the early rock 'n' roll era with material that was tailored toward a younger audience. As rock 'n' roll began to emerge in the early and mid-'50s, several distinct branches of R&B had developed that would each exert a large influence on popular music in their own rights: doo wop groups, electric blues, and New Orleans rhythm & blues. All of these sub-genres are examined in greater depth in this book in essays of their own, and all would prove to have a greater and more lasting impact on rock 'n' roll than the earlier, jazzier forms of R&B.

Still, there were quite a few performers who survived through the 1950s, and sometimes thrived, recording music that could not be called anything but R&B. Ike Turner, Ivory Joe Hunter, Faye Adams, Wynona Carr, Big Mama Thornton, Big Maybelle—none of these were straight blues artists, but their music wasn't rock 'n' roll either. Blues singers like Bobby "Blue" Bland, Junior Parker, and Little Milton bridged electric blues and soul, but they couldn't be pigeonholed as straight rock 'n' roll singers. Occasionally R&B performers like Johnny Otis, Screamin' Jay Hawkins, and Wilbert Harrison crossed over to the rock 'n' roll audience with their most hook-savvy songs; Harrison's "Kansas City" is largely jump blues with a shuffle beat, at least until it gets to the searing electric guitar break.

Several 1950s singers began as more or less straight R&B performers, but added an earthier, more pronounced gospel and church influence than had ever been heard before. Today, we recognize the greatest of these vocalists—Ray Charles, James Brown, Jackie Wilson, Little Willie John, Johnny Ace, Jessie Belvin, and Clyde McPhatter—as the forefathers of soul. Some of them, like Charles and Brown, would indeed become soul superstars in the '60s. Others, like McPhatter and John, were unable to make the transition, due to a combination of inability to grow with the times and personal problems that proved insurmountable. R&B, though it has changed greatly since its birth, remains a crucial part of rock, soul, and rap, just below or very much above the surface.

For all of its monumental significance, and the vast critical acclaim it has belatedly received, early R&B recordings can be tough to swallow in large lumps for the neophyte. The R&B performers and labels of the '40s and '50s were concerned with entertaining, not establishing diverse artistic oeuvres, and the similar chord patterns and arrangements can be wearing on a compact disc rather than a juke box or dance floor, which is where the songs were often played in their heyday. Those investigating the genre in-depth for the first time are advised to start with some general various artist samplers, and move on from there according to their degrees of interest.

Recommended Recordings (omitting doo wop, electric blues, New Orleans R&B, or soul collections):

Various Artists, *Blues Masters, Volume 5: Jump Blues Classics* (Rhino). The best jump blues introduction, with key cuts by Joe Turner, Wynonie Harris, Roy Brown, Tiny Bradshaw, Jay McNeely, Big Mama Thornton, Ruth Brown, and others.

Various Artists, *Blues Masters, Volume 14: More Jump Blues* (Rhino). Up to the same level as Jump Blues Classics, with tracks by Louis Jordan, LaVern Baker, Big Maybelle, Faye Adams, and many more.

Big Joe Turner, *Big, Bad & Blue: The Big Joe Turner Anthology* (Rhino). As mammoth as the man himself, this three-disc set encompasses several decades, reflecting R&B's evolution from the days of big-band jazz through rock 'n' roll. Too extensive for the casual fan; as alternatives, there are other Turner anthologies that focus on specific phases of his career.

Louis Jordan, *The Best of Louis Jordan* (MCA). Jordan recorded a great deal of material in the 1940s and 1950s, and no collection satisfactorily encompasses all of his classics; this one is the best.

Various Artists, *Atlantic Rhythm & Blues Vol. 1-4* (Atlantic). The most important label in the development of modern R&B, this is part of a seven-volume series that goes up to 1974. There's a whole box set of them if you want to go whole hog, but the first four cover 1947-1962, before R&B had been fully renamed rock and soul.

Various Artists, *Specialty Story* (Specialty). At five discs, this is too much for non-specialists, if you'll pardon the pun. But it does offer a comprhensive survey of one of early R&B and rock 'n' roll's most important labels, with tracks by such greats as Joe Liggins, Percy Mayfield, Roy Milton, and Lloyd Price, up through early rock stars like Little Richard and Larry Williams.

Ruth Brown, *Rockin' in Rhythm: The Best of Ruth Brown* (Rhino). The singer on whom much of Atlantic's early fortune was built, this disc contains her most popular 1950s sides.

LaVern Baker, *Soul on Fire: The Best of LaVern Baker* (Rhino). One of the most important singers to lead the transition from R&B to rock 'n' roll.

The Drifters, *Let the Boogie-Woogie Roll: Greatest Hits (1953-1958)* (Atlantic). The first lineup of the Drifters, featuring Clyde McPhatter, could be called a doo wop group as well, but also had strong early R&B/jump blues influences.

Ike Turner, *I Like Ike: The Best of Ike Turner* (Rhino). Before joining Tina, Ike was an important talent scout, sideman, and bandleader. This collection of odds'n'ends is mostly from the 1950s, and often walks the edge between R&B and electric blues.

Ray Charles, *Birth of Soul* (Rhino). Aptly titled three-disc box of Charles' work for Atlantic in the 1950s.

Johnny Otis, *The Capitol Years* (Capitol). An enormously popular figure in R&B as a bandleader, musician, and talent scout, Otis crossed over to success in the rock market in the late '50s by adding a Bo Diddley beat. Although Otis himself preferred straight R&B, this collection of late-'50s sides is his best.

Little Willie John, *Fever: The Best of Little Willie* John (Rhino). One of R&B's most versatile vocalists, and a huge influence on James Brown.

Clyde McPhatter, *Deep Sea Ball: The Best of Clyde McPhatter* (Rhino). His biggest hits for Atlantic in the late '50s, after he left the Drifters.

James Brown, *Roots of a Revolution* (PolyGram). A double-CD retrospective of 1956-1964 recordings, bringing us from hardcore R&B to the verge of the birth of funk.

Jump Blues

Richie Unterberger & Cub Koda

The currents of jazz and blues may have run closer together in the 1940s than they did in any other decade. One of the biggest offshoots of this cross-breeding was jump blues, a form that thrived in the late 1940s and early 1950s in particular. With its rhythmic swing, boisterous vocalists, and oft-lighthearted songs about partying, drinking, and jiving, it hasn't lent itself as extensively to critical analysis as styles like rural Delta guitarists or electric Chicago blues. During the decade or so when it thrived, however, it laid much of the groundwork for what became known as rhythm and blues, and thus by extension rock 'n' roll.

The roots of jump blues, like many popular styles that became widespread in the middle of the 20th century, can be traced to larger trends of social modernization. In the 1940s, the large big bands of the 1930s scaled back into smaller combos, partially because of economic considerations (particularly during World War II) that made supporting a large ensemble difficult. There were still plenty of African-American patrons for dance halls, however, who wanted a sound that was both danceable and loud. This led many swing bands to place a greater emphasis on honking saxophones and hard-driving vocalists who could be heard over the din, often categorized after the event as "honkers and shouters."

There were many notable forerunners of the jump blues sound to be heard in the jazz community of the 1930s. Pianists like Meade Lux Lewis, Albert Ammons, and Jimmy Yancey devised boogiewoogie patterns; singers like Slim Gaillard and Cab Calloway sang hipster lyrics (sometimes dubbed "jive") with links to both blues and pop traditions. The midwestern cities of Kansas City and St. Louis acted as incubators for the jump blues scene, with their heritage of hot swing bands with vocalists that were open to the influence of the blues.

As Peter Grendysa writes in his liner notes to Rhino's *Blues Masters, Vol. 5: Jump Blues Classics*, "The antiphonal (call-and-response) characteristic of African music so evident in country blues and gospel was adapted by jump blues, often with the voice of the saxophone played against the vocalist, who shouted rather than sang the lyrics. The saxophone was played with athletic power and exuberance; the saxman squeezing out honks, bleats, and squeals to the delight of the crowds and the dismay of traditional jazz fans. Strong backbeats were provided by the drummer's snares and rim shots on the second and fourth beats of every bar and reinforced by the bass player marking every beat."

Some of the first performers to sing in a readily identifiable "jump blues" style were very grounded in the jazz world. Big Joe Turner, one of the few performers to bridge the jazz, R&B, and rock 'n' roll eras, had been singing jazz since the late 1930s, even appearing at the famed Spirituals to Swing concert in 1938 at New York's Carnegie Hall. Turner may be more responsible than anyone else for founding the "shouting" school of R&B singing, emphasizing smooth but commanding vocal presence. Based (like Turner) in Kansas City, bandleader Jay McShann may be most famous for cultivating the talents of the young Charlie Parker, but he also did his part to create jump blues by employing Walter Brown, another of the earliest shouters.

The most influential architect of jump blues, however-indeed, one of the more significant figures in 20th century American music—was alto saxophonist and singer Louis Jordan. After serving in Chick Webb's band in the 1930s, he formed his own outfit, the Tympany Five. In the mid- and late-1940s, he ran off an astonishing series of R&B hits that set much of the tone for the jump blues genre, especially the fast, danceable rhythms and the joking, novelty-tinged lyrics—traits that did not pass unnoticed by Chuck Berry. Jordan was also a rock 'n' roll forefather in that he was one of the first R&B performers to make significant inroads into the pop and White audiences.

Jump blues really began exploding commercially after World War II, as America got set to relax and party after years of contributing to the war effort, as jazz headed off in directions less conducive to dancing, and as large numbers of African-Americans moved from the country to the city, taking some of the country blues tradition with them. The West Coast, particularly Los Angeles, was a hotbed of jump blues/proto-R&B. There was a large Black community (many recent arrivals), and large numbers of small combo bands looking to survive the transition from big bands to earthier small ones. And there were new independent labels cropping up—Specialty, Modern, Aladdin, Swingtime—that saw a niche for Black popular music that was being ignored by the majors.

Los Angeles in particular was a breeding ground for the saxophonists that would become known as the honkers—musicians who got a grainy, squealing tone and summon frenetic bursts of notes on the uptempo tunes. They were often great showmen in concert as well, playing on their backs sometimes to whip the crowds into more frenzy. Illinois Jacquet had set a model of sorts for the style on his classic soloing on Lionel Hampton's huge hit "Flying Home" and his work on the live Norman Granz Jazz At The Philharmonic recordings song which introduced a few elements that would become widespread in R&B and rock 'n' roll. Big Jay McNeely, Joe Houston, and Chuck Higgins were some of the most noteworthy saxophonists of the style, sometimes doing without vocals entirely, the sheer bravado of their solos being enough to build their studio tracks around.

The West Coast favored an urbane brand of jump blues that owed much to jazz. Electric guitar pioneer T-Bone Walker is usually thought of as a bluesman, but certainly his 1940s recordings—which are usually pegged as his best and most influential—incorporated a lot from jazz and jump blues. Though not a bluesman per se, Nat King Cole in his early days would approach a jump blues mood, and traces of his suave charm can be found in many 1940s jump blues sides.

Several West Coast bandleaders had a lot of success in the late 1940s with a sort of polished grit. On Specialty Records alone, there was Joe Liggins, his brother Jimmy, and Roy Milton. Milton, though only a hazily remembered figure, was a huge star in his day, landing well over a dozen singles in the R&B Top Ten in the late 1940s and early 1950s. His pianist, Camille Howard, was a notable recording artist in her own right, and a premier example of a jazz-boogie performer who seemed to have gotten dragged into the R&B world more by happenstance and the forces of historical change than anything else. Johnny Otis would organize a lot of L.A. talent as a bandleader, vocalist, talent scout, promoter, label owner, and general all-around champion of the scene.

The boogie-woogie-derived structure of much jump blues lent itself well to pianists, and several of the best jump blues singers also excelled at the keyboards. Prominent among them was Amos Milburn, who could handle both Charles Brown-ish ballads and rowdy songs about drinking and Floyd Dixon, famous as the originator of "Hey Bartender," served to the masses decades later via the Blues Brothers. For those who liked their jump blues a bit rougher, there were the preeminent shouters, Roy Brown and Wynonie Harris. Both of them had big R&B hits with "Good Rockin' Tonight," and both were influences upon Elvis Presley, who would make the tune his second Sun single. Jump blues also had more room for female participation than many other blues sub-genres, with Camille Howard and Wynona Carr both scoring substantial successes for Specialty, and R&B-based singers like Big Maybelle and Big Mama Thornton recording singles heavily indebted to the style.

There were an enormous number of jump blues records cut between 1945 and 1955, and a brief survey of some of the most famous pianists, bandleaders, saxophonists, shouters, and women singers still leaves out a great many names that are treasured by blues and R&B fans. Just to scratch the surface, you could mention shouter Nappy Brown, Tiny Bradshaw (who did the original version of "The Train Kept A-Rollin'"), Red Prysock, Bullmoose Jackson, the pre-Atlantic recordings of Ray Charles, and Billy Wright (the last of whom was Little Richard's chief early inspiration). The Savoy label alone recorded enough singers, briefly and extensively, to generate numerous various artist compilations.

Yet by the mid-'50s, the jump blues style was definitely on the wane. It was a story that has repeated itself numerous times throughout the history of pop—a whole school of stylists, seemingly at its peak, was swept aside by a horde of younger and rawer upstarts. It wasn't just a few Elvis Presleys and Little Richards, though—it was the whole tidal wave of rock 'n' roll.

Certainly the dividing line between jump blues and R&B is a very fine one. A transitional figure like Jackie Brenston, for instance, could fall into either camp. Early sides by Atlantic R&B artists like Ruth Brown and LaVerne Baker sometimes owed a lot to jump blues and the same could be said of early rock instrumentalists like Bill Doggett. And many early doo-wop sides have a lot of jump blues in them—listen to Drifters tracks like "Fools Fall In Love" or "Such a Night" for the evidence. But the hard fact was that R&B, and its close relation rock 'n' roll, had dropped much of the jazz and boogie woogie so prominent in jump blues. The most raucous sounds of its saxophones were retained, but there was progressively more emphasis on electric guitars, group vocals, and younger performers with a greater appeal to teenagers.

By 1956, most of the jump blues stars were scuffling for survival. Some adapted to the rock 'n' roll era with some success, most notably Joe Turner and Johnny Otis; others tried to adapt to rock 'n' roll trends unsuccessfully, like Roy Brown and even Louis Jordan. There were a few, like Turner and Jimmy Witherspoon, who could slide back into the jazz world if they wished, having never strayed far from it in the first place. Sometimes an old star would surface unexpectedly like Amos Milburn, who had a surprise tenure with Motown in the early 1960s.

Unless you're a devoted collector or scholar, it can seem as though most jump blues greats have vanished into a black hole of history. Perhaps that's because the form bridged blues, jazz, R&B, and pop, without quite fitting into any of the forms comfortably. Another factor is the general absence of hot guitar solos, a general touchstone for most modern fans connecting with older forms of blues.

Jump blues, however, is blues at its most fun—a call to arms not to bewail tribulations or reflect upon the abyss, but to let loose, wail, and party. In the bargain, it was probably *the* most important foundation for what became known in the 1950s as R&B, and gave us much of the rhythm and humor that we take for granted in contemporary rock, blues, and soul.

Twelve Recommended Albums:

Various Artists, *Blues Masters Vol. 5: Jump Blues Classics* (Rhino)
Various Artists, *Blues Masters Vol. 14: More Jump Blues* (Rhino)
Big Joe Turner, *Big, Bad & Blue: The Joe Turner Anthology* (Rhino)
Louis Jordan, *The Best of Louis Jordan* (MCA)
Roy Milton, *Roy Milton & His Solid Senders* (Specialty)
T-Bone Walker, *The Complete Capitol Black & White Recordings* (Capitol)
Amos Milburn, *Down the Road Apiece: The Best of Amos Milburn* (EMI)
Joe Houston, *Cornbread and Cabbage Greens* (Specialty)
Floyd Dixon, *Marshall Texas is My Home* (Specialty)
Roy Brown, *Good Rocking Tonight: The Best of Roy Brown* (Rhino)
Wynonie Harris, *Bloodshot Eyes: The Best of Wynonie Harris* (Rhino)
Various Artists, *The Original Johnny Otis Show* (Savoy)

Cool

Scott Yanow

Cool (or West Coast) jazz came into prominence in the early 1950s but has often been criticized or overlooked by jazz historians, particularly New Yorkcentric writers who feel that every significant jazz style after 1930 was born in New York. In fact Joe Goldberg's otherwise admirable book Jazz Masters Of The '50s, outside of a chapter on Paul Desmond, treats West Coast jazz as if it did not exist!

Cool jazz was a natural evolution from bop but differed from previous styles in that it was a conservative reaction to a fairly radical music rather than an obvious move forward. In the late 1940s, young jazz musicians faced a dilemma. How could anyone play saxophone at the level of a Charlie Parker or trumpet in as complex a style as Dizzy Gillespie (who was not successfully copied until Jon Faddis emerged over 30 years later)? Bird and Diz had originated and completely mastered the bebop style, to the point where they were untoppable in their own field and most of their followers could hope for nothing better than to be considered top imitators. Bebop in its most classic form featured rapid romps, virtuosic solos and fresh harmonies. Although exciting to hear, it often scared away audiences accustomed to swing who preferred more relaxed and danceable music. It needed to grow and develop more variety.

The jazz scene has always contrasted the hot with the cool. In the 1920s cornetist Bix Beiderbecke's lyrical style contrasted with the more explosive flights of Louis Armstrong, the following decade Teddy Wilson's gentle stride playing became influential with pianists unable to duplicate Fats Waller's powerful solos, and John Kirby's Sextet became popular utilizing both soft tones with inventive arrangements. Lester Young, whose relaxed tenor style eventually surpassed the more intense Coleman Hawkins in influence among younger players, always seemed to epitomize "cool," both in his thoughtful playing and his quietly hip personality. He became the unwitting father figure of cool jazz.

When Charlie Parker put together his strongest regular band in 1947, he chose Miles Davis as his trumpeter. Davis, 20 at the time, realized that he could not duplicate on his horn what his idol Dizzy Gillespie played so he developed his own sparser approach. Miles made every note count, stuck to the middle register and played in a quiet style that contrasted with Parker's explosive improvisations. The chemistry worked quite well.

Within the next year, Davis befriended arranger-composer Gil Evans who wrote regularly for the Claude Thornhill Orchestra. Pianist Thornhill's big band was quite unusual in that it utilized a couple of French horns and a tuba as melody instruments, avoided vibrato and had a dreamy ensemble sound. The combination of swing, ballads and bop (particularly in Evans's charts) made this a memorable unit that would serve as an inspiration for the cool jazz movement.

When Miles Davis had the opportunity to lead his first record dates outside of the world of Charlie Parker, he headed a nonet featuring cool-toned soloists (including altoist Lee Konitz and baritonist Gerry Mulligan) and placed an emphasis on arrangements (by Evans, Mulligan, John Lewis, Johnny Carisi and Davis). The band (which was later dubbed "The Birth Of The Cool Nonet") only played in public during a two-week gig (as an intermission group for Count Basie at the Royal Roost in 1948) and recorded a dozen titles for Capitol during 1949-50 but its impact was felt for a decade.

Another important and influential early cool jazz group was the sextet headed by pianist Lennie Tristano. A sort of guru to his sidemen (who were also his students), Tristano believed in long melodic lines, an absence of vibrato, advanced chordal improvisation (which used thinly disguised themes based on familiar chord changes) and having his bassist and drummer restrict themselves to quiet timekeeping. With altoist Lee Konitz, tenor saxophonist Warne Marsh and guitarist Billy Bauer, Tristano cut some of his most important recordings in 1949. The well-rehearsed (and often-miraculous) unisons by his saxophonists, their unusual tones and some unpredictable accents made this music sound quite unique. In addition Tristano (on "Intuition" and "Digression") performed two of the very first free improvisations on record.

During 1947-48 Woody Herman's Second Herd, the "Four Brothers" band (named after Jimmy Giuffre's famous original), featured three young tenors (Stan Getz, Zoot Sims and Herbie Steward who was later replaced by Al Cohn) playing in styles similar to Lester Young. Stan Getz's hit record of "Early Autumn" with Herman helped to popularize the cool tenor sound, his playing on a 1952 session by guitarist Johnny Smith made "Moonlight In Vermont" into a best-seller and Getz's beautiful tone became known as "The Sound."

One would never call Stan Kenton's often-bombastic and dramatic music "cool," but many of his sidemen ironically made major contributions to the music. Howard Rumsey, Kenton's original bassist, in 1949 persuaded the owner of a small Hermosa Beach club called the Lighthouse to start featuring jazz. The nightly jam sessions would eventually lead to the formation of the Lighthouse All-Stars. As many of the former Kenton and Herman sidemen settled in Los Angeles with hopes of landing work in the film and television studios, a nucleus started playing regularly at the Lighthouse and at other local clubs. Among the more significant players were trumpeter-arranger Shorty Rogers (who became an important force in writing jazz-flavored scores for films), drummer Shelly Manne, tenors Bob Cooper and Bill Perkins, altoist Bud Shank, Jimmy Giuffre (tripling on tenor, clarinet and baritone), trombonist Frank Rosolino and trumpeter Conte Candoli among many others. While Rumsey's Lighthouse All-Stars were a fixture throughout the 1950s, Shorty Rogers soon left to form his Giants and Shelly Manne too headed his own swinging quintet.

Some of the main criticisms that West Coast Jazz has had through the years is that the music was "bloodless" (due to its emphasis on subtlety), conservative (since some groups used tight arrangements and its sound was more introverted) and even that it was too "white". Racism did play an indirect part because the studios, even with some early attempts at integration, were largely segregated, leading to more White musicians settling in the area than Blacks. While the important Black clubs on Central Avenue (L.A.'s equivalent to New York's 52nd Street) have been largely neglected in jazz history books (their heyday was in the 1940s), West Coast jazz did gain quite a bit of publicity during the first half of the '50s, leading to some resentment by New York-based writers along with musicians who felt shut out by the system. There were Black participants in the movement including pianist Hampton Hawes, multi-reedist Buddy Collette (a pioneer on the flute) and even drummer Max Roach (before he formed his quintet with trumpeter Clifford Brown). But, racial politics aside, the music does hold up quite well.

Cool jazz really took off when baritonist Gerry Mulligan started playing nightly at the Haig in 1952 with a pianoless quartet that also featured trumpeter Chet Baker. Mulligan, a pianist himself, was never against piano players but he enjoyed the extra freedom that having such an intimate group allowed him; he loved to play harmonies behind Baker's (and later on valve trombonist Bob Brookmeyer's) solos. The quartet's hit version of "My Funny Valentine" made both Mulligan and Baker famous.

Pianist Dave Brubeck, who had led an experimental third-stream octet during 1946-49 and a trio during 1949-51, found phenomenal success when he teamed up with the cool-toned altoist Paul Desmond in a quartet. When the group was booked at college campuses, it reached a new audience who otherwise might have become attached to R&B or early rock and roll. Brubeck, who loved to indulge in polytonal and polyrhythmic flights, was often criticized by conservative critics who felt that all jazz pianists should sound like Bud Powell, but his powerful chord voicings were quite distinctive and served as the perfect foil for the witty and inventive Desmond. While the Dave Brubeck Quartet is most famous for "Take Five" (from their million-selling album Time Out), they were actually famous by the mid-1950s; in fact Brubeck appeared on the cover of Time Magazine as early as 1954!

The West Coast jazz movement benefitted greatly by the development of the LP, which allowed the musicians to stretch out beyond the former three-minute time limit. Lester Koenig's Contemporary label (based in Los Angeles) recorded such groups as those led by Shorty Rogers, Shelly Manne, altoist Art Pepper and pianist

Hampton Hawes, the Pacific Jazz label documented Gerry Mulligan and Chet Baker, and in time the major labels caught on.

By the mid-1950s, cool jazz was at the height of its popularity. Although not based on the West Coast, the Modern Jazz Quartet (with vibraphonist Milt Jackson, pianist John Lewis, bassist Percy Heath and drummer Connie Kay) and the George Shearing Quintet played music that could be considered "cool" bop. The Dave Pell Octet, with its quiet but hard-swinging solos and a colorful mixture of arranged and jammed ensembles, perfectly symbolized the West Coast sound while the Shelly Manne Trio (with pianist Andre Previn) started a trend by recording jazz interpretations of the music of the Broadway show My Fair Lady. Drummer Chico Hamilton, formerly with Gerry Mulligan, formed his first quintet in 1955 which, in addition to reeds (played by Buddy Collette), guitar, bass and drums, inventively utilized a cellist (Fred Katz); later editions of the popular group had either Paul Horn or Eric Dolphy in Collette's spot. It became one of the leading groups in chamber jazz, the movement to blend aspects of classical music with jazz.

However by the late-1950s, the music had largely run its course. Hard bop, a more overtly exciting style of jazz which added a stronger blues and gospel element, was taking over the modern mainstream while the free jazz of Ornette Coleman (who ironically was at the time based in Los Angeles) was starting to emerge; plus rock and roll was making inroads into the audience. A few too many watered-down and overarranged West Coast jazz albums made the music easy to write off and by 1960 cool jazz was no longer a pacesetting style.

Most of the main players in West Coast jazz had long and productive careers. Gerry Mulligan, who put together another superior pianoless quartet in 1958 with trumpeter Art Farmer, led what could be considered the definitive cool jazz big band in the early 1960s, his Concert Jazz band. Although he took many years off in the 1960s and '70s when he worked fulltime as a writer in the studios, Shorty Rogers reformed the Lighthouse All-Stars with Bud Shank, Bob Cooper, Bill Perkins and Conte Candoli for a few years in the 1990s. Dave Brubeck has never lost his popularity, Art Pepper continued to evolve and Chet Baker became a legendary cult figure. And as for Miles Davis and Gil Evans who had helped to start the whole thing, by the time West Coast Jazz was becoming popular, they had moved on to other projects.

Because it in ways served as a resting place chronologically between the innovations of bop of the 1940s and avant-garde jazz of the '60s, the main legacy of West Coast jazz can be heard in the countless number of enjoyable recordings that were made during the 1950s. — *Scott Yanow*

Fourteen Essential Cool Jazz Recordings

Claude Thornhill, *Best Of The Big Bands* (Columbia)

Miles Davis, *Birth Of The Cool* (Capitol)

Lennie Tristano and Warne Marsh, *Intuition* (Capitol)

Stan Getz, *Roost Quartets* (Roulette)

Gerry Mulligan, *In Paris Vol. 1* (Vogue)

Chet Baker, *Quartet* (Pacific Jazz)

Gerry Mulligan/Paul Desmond Quartet (Verve)

Lighthouse All-Stars, *Sunday Jazz A La Lighthouse* (Original Jazz Classics)

Lighthouse All-Stars, *Volume 6* (Original Jazz Classics)

Shorty Rogers, *Short Stops* (Bluebird)

Shelly Manne, *Vol. 1: The West Coast Sound* (Original Jazz Classics)

Shelly Manne, *My Fair Lady* (Original Jazz Classics)

Dave Brubeck, *Jazz Goes To College* (Columbia)

Modern Jazz Quartet, *Django* (Original Jazz Classics)

Important Events

1936 - Lester Young makes recording debut with a small group out of Count Basie's band, introducing to the jazz world a new softer sound for the tenor.

1938 - John Kirby forms his cool-toned swing sextet.

1942 - Claude Thornhill adds two French horns to his big band.

One of his main arrangers is Gil Evans.

1945 - Miles Davis makes his recording debut.

1946 - Lennie Tristano cuts his first records.

1947 - Miles Davis joins the Charlie Parker Quintet.

Woody Herman forms his Second Herd, an orchestra that features Stan Getz, Zoot Sims and Herbie Steward (later Al Cohn) on tenors and baritonist Serge Chaloff playing Jimmy Giuffre's "Four Brothers."

1948 - Miles Davis forms a nonet whose twelve very influential Capitol recordings of 1949-50 are later billed as "The Birth of the Cool." Despite the par-

Music Map

Significant Cool Players

Lester Young - tenor
Miles Davis - trumpet
Lennie Tristano - piano
Shorty Rogers - trumpet, arranger
Shelly Manne - drums, leader
Gerry Mulligan - baritone, arranger
Chet Baker - trumpet
Dave Brubeck - piano
Paul Desmond - alto
Stan Getz - tenor
Art Pepper - alto
Lee Konitz - alto
Gil Evans - arranger

Other Significant Cool Players

Alto Saxophone
Bud Shank

Baritone Sax
Lars Gullin

Bass

Red Callender   Percy Heath
Red Mitchell   Monty Budwig
Leroy Vinnegar

Clarinet
Jimmy Giuffre
Tony Scott

Drums
Chico Hamilton
Connie Kay
Stan Levey

Flute
Frank Wess
Bud Shank
Buddy Collette

Guitar
Billy Bauer
Jimmy Raney
Johnny Smith
Jim Hall

Piano

John Lewis   Russ Freeman
Claude Williamson   Pete Jolly
Lou Levy

Tenor

Zoot Sims   Al Cohn
Jimmy Giuffre   Bob Cooper
Bill Perkins   Richie Kamuca
Jack Montrose

Trombone
Frank Rosolino
Bob Brookmeyer
Carl Fontana

Trumpet
Conte Candoli
Jon Eardley
Don Fagerquist

Vocals - Female
June Christy
Chris Connor
Helen Merrill

Big Bands
Claude Thornhill
Woody Herman's Second Herd

Groups
Miles Davis Birth of the Cool Nonet
Lennie Tristano Sextet
Dave Brubeck Quartet
Modern Jazz Quartet
Lighthouse All-Stars
Shorty Rogers & His Giants
Shelly Manne & His Men
The Dave Pell Octet
Jimmy Giuffre 3
Chico Hamilton Quintet

---

ticipation of Lee Konitz, Gerry Mulligan, John Lewis and Gil Evans, this band was only able to secure one gig!

Dave Brubeck plays concerts with an octet.

1949 - Lennie Tristano records with his sextet, a group featuring altoist Lee Konitz and tenor saxophonist Warne Marsh.

Tenors Stan Getz, Zoot Sims, Al Cohn, Allan Eager and Brew Moore record four songs together; it is impossible to tell any of the cool-toned players apart!

1950 - The Dave Brubeck Trio is popular on the West Coast.

1951 - Shorty Rogers' first recordings as a leader utilizes an octet similar in style to Miles Davis' famous nonet.

Dave Brubeck forms his quartet with altoist Paul Desmond.

Many former Stan Kenton and Woody Herman sidemen settle in Los Angeles to work in the studios.

1952 - First recordings by the Modern Jazz Quartet.

Gerry Mulligan and Chet Baker team up in a very popular pianoless quartet.

Miles Davis' recordings show a direct turn away from cool jazz toward what would be hard bop.

Howard Rumsey's Lighthouse All-Stars is featured on the first of a series of records that would last until 1957.

1953 - Shorty Rogers settles in Los Angeles and has a busy and influential studio and recording career (both playing and arranging) throughout the remainder of the decade.

Chet Baker forms his own quartet with pianist Russ Freeman.

Shelly Manne begins a long series of recordings for Contemporary.

The Dave Pell Octet debuts on record.

1954 - Bob Brookmeyer tours with Gerry Mulligan's Quartet.

1955 - The Chico Hamilton Quintet (with cellist Fred Katz and flutist Buddy Collette) is formed.

Connie Kay replaces Kenny Clarke as drummer with the Modern Jazz Quartet.

1956 - The Shelly Manne Trio's recording of songs from "My Fair Lady" (featuring pianist Andre Previn) becomes a major hit.

1957 - West successfully meets East as altoist Art Pepper records a classic album with members of the Miles Davis Quintet titled *Art Pepper Meets the Rhythm Section*.

1958 - The Jimmy Giuffre 3 consists of the leader's clarinet, valve trombonist Bob Brookmeyer and guitarist Jim Hall.

1959 - The Dave Brubeck Quartet records "Take Five."

1960 - Gerry Mulligan forms his Concert Jazz Band.

1961 - The Jimmy Giuffre 3 becomes avant-garde. Dave Pell's Octet make their last recordings of the era.

Chico Hamilton drops the cello from his quintet so as to get a harder sound.

West Coast Jazz is essentially extinct as a separate style although it would remain an influence.

Hard Bop

Scott Yanow

Hard bop, like cool jazz and soul-jazz, started out as a subsidiary of another style of music, in this case bop. With the rise of bop in the mid- to late '40s, the chord structures, rhythms and improvising in jazz had become much more complex. Although its pacesetters were masterful virtuosoes, many of the followers sacrificed feeling for precision, emotion for speed. Charlie Parker and Dizzy Gillespie were nearly impossible musical role models and they certainly could not be topped at the music they had originated.

When cool jazz emerged in the late '40s, some of the qualities of swing that had been de-emphasized (arrangements, a use of space and more of an emphasis on tone) were restored to jazz. However other young musicians wanted to utilize a wider range of emotions than was to be found in cool jazz, and they sought to infuse jazz with elements of spiritual and gospel music (ie: soul). Hard bop gradually developed and by the mid-'50s it had become the new modern mainstream.

Although based in bop, hard bop had a few differences. Tempoes could be just as blazing but the melodies were generally simpler, the musicians (particularly the saxophonists and pianists) tended to be familiar with (and open to the influence of) rhythm & blues and the bass players (rather than always being stuck in the role of a metronome) were beginning to gain a little more freedom and solo space. Due to the soulful nature of some of the solos and the occasionally catchy rhythms, hard bop was nicknamed "funk" for a time. By the early '60s soul-jazz (which relied more on a groove) had developed out of hard bop although the two styles frequently overlapped. As the '60s evolved, hard bop players started to incorporate aspects of both modal music (staying on one chord for longer periods of time) and avant-garde into their music.

The beginning of hard bop on record is difficult to determine since its development from bop was a gradual process. A good starting point is Miles Davis' Blue Note sessions of 1952-54; Davis seemed to be at the start of a half-dozen styles! His Blue Note sides featured such important young hard bop stylists as altoist Jackie McLean (whose sound was much different than the cooler-toned Paul Desmond and Lee Konitz), tenor saxophonist Sonny Rollins (a hard bop extension of Coleman Hawkins), trombonist J.J. Johnson, the highly influential pianist Horace Silver and drummer Art Blakey.

Another important series of recordings were made by the Max Roach/Clifford Brown Quintet of 1954-56, a unit that featured either Harold Land or Sonny Rollins on tenor. While Dizzy Gillespie and Miles Davis were important influences on other trumpeters, Clifford Brown took his main inspiration from Fats Navarro (who partly derived his style from Howard McGhee), a short-lived and fiery bop player whose warm tone and logical ideas were easier for brassmen to follow than Gillespie's angular flights. Brownie, before his tragic death in a car accident at age 25 in 1956, became jazz's brightest new trumpeter and his huge influence on other trumpeters (and the entire hard bop movement in general) continues to this day. Since his time, Lee Morgan, Freddie Hubbard and Woody Shaw to a large extent based their early styles on Clifford's.

With the gradual decline of West Coast Jazz during the mid- to late '50s, hard bop essentially took over. A whole generation of top young modernists developed

in the wake of the innovations of Parker and Gillespie, eager to develop their own voices. The development of the LP in the late '40s had made recordings not only lengthier (individual songs could now reach 20 minutes rather than the previous three) but much more numerous. While many labels opted for inexpensive jam sessions, Blue Note (under the direction of Alfred Lion and Francis Wolff) paid musicians for rehearsals and encouraged the inclusion of new material. Their numerous releases were not only consistently high-quality (particularly during 1952-67) but classy.

There were many top musicians involved in hard bop, but few were more important than drummer-leader Art Blakey. The co-founder of the Jazz Messengers in 1955 with Horace Silver, Blakey retained the group's name after Silver went out on his own. Throughout a 35-year period, Blakey was a masterful talent scout (perhaps even surpassing Fletcher Henderson in earlier years and Miles Davis). The passionate drummer pushed his musicians to play themselves rather than copy their role models and to come up with original compositions. Here is a partial list of the young talent that benefitted from their periods as members of the Jazz Messengers: tenors Benny Golson, Hank Mobley, Johnny Griffin, Wayne Shorter, Billy Harper, Bill Pierce and Javon Jackson, altoists Jackie McLean, Bobby Watson, Branford Marsalis and Donald Harrison, pianists Bobby Timmons, Walter Davis Jr., Cedar Walton, John Hicks, Keith Jarrett, James Williams, Donald Brown, Mulgrew Miller, Benny Green and Geoff Keezer, bassists Doug Watkins, Reggie Workman and Charles Fambrough, trombonists Curtis Fuller and Robin Eubanks and trumpeters Kenny Dorham, Donald Byrd, Bill Hardman, Lee Morgan, Freddie Hubbard, Chuck Mangione, Woody Shaw, Valeri Ponomarev, Wynton Marsalis, Wallace Roney, Terence Blanchard, Phillip Harper and Brian Lynch!

In addition to the Jazz Messengers, other significant hard bop groups included the Horace Silver Quintet (particularly when it featured trumpeter Blue Mitchell and the tenor of Junior Cook), the Jazztet (with trumpeter Art Farmer and Benny Golson on tenor) and the Cannonball Adderley Quintet (which crossed over into soul-jazz).

Even though the avant-garde began to garner most of the headlines by the early '60s, hard bop was quantity-wise the most dominant jazz style of 1955-68. In general the pacesetters were trumpeters Clifford Brown, Lee Morgan (who had a major hit in the mid-'60s with "The Sidewinder") and Freddie Hubbard, trombonists J.J. Johnson and Curtis Fuller, tenors Sonny Rollins and Hank Mobley (although John Coltrane's influence was felt by the late '50s), altoists Phil Woods, Jackie McLean and Cannonball Adderley, guitarists Kenny Burrell, Grant Green and Wes Montgomery, organist Jimmy Smith and pianists Horace Silver and Bobby Timmons. As the 1960s progressed, such new players as tenors Joe Henderson and Stanley Turrentine and trumpeter Woody Shaw emerged to give the music some fresh blood.

But by the mid- to late '60s hard bop was running out of gas. With the sale of Blue Note to Liberty and eventually United Artists, the style (and jazz in general) gradually lost its most significant label. Soul jazz, which was becoming more commercial, took part of hard bop's audience and many of the musicians were looking elsewhere towards the emerging fusion movement, the avant-garde or more commercial sounds. The rise of commercial rock and the consolidation of most of the independent record labels caused hard bop to have a much lower profile in the 1970s as it was overshadowed by other trends.

However hard bop never died and in the 1980s it served as the inspiration for the Young Lions movement. Wynton Marsalis and many of the other later graduates of Art Blakey's Jazz Messengers used hard bop (along with the post bop music of Miles Davis' mid-60s quintet) as a starting point for their own careers. With so many young players being signed to major labels (at least for brief periods), hard bop suddenly returned full force to the extent where detractors complained that the new musicians were merely recycling the past. Although that was true to an extent, the top members of the Young Lions eventually developed their own musical vision without forgetting their straightahead roots.

In the 1990s, hard bop is the modern mainstream music of the era. Sometimes called "traditional" or merely "mainstream," this style of music still seems to offer improvisers endless possibilities and is the foundation of modern acoustic jazz. — *Scott Yanow*

Seventeen Essential Hard Bop Recordings:

Miles Davis, *Vol. 1* (Blue Note)

Clifford Brown/Max Roach, *At Basin Street* (EmArcy)

Sonny Rollins, *A Night at the Village Vanguard* (Blue Note)

Horace Silver, *And the Jazz Messengers* (Blue Note)

Art Blakey, *Moanin'* (Blue Note)

Art Farmer/Benny Golson, *Meet the Jazztet* (Chess)

Jackie McLean, *Bluesnik* (Blue Note)

Hank Mobley, *Workout* (Blue Note)

Music Map

Significant Hard Bop Players

Regular Working Groups
Art Blakey's Jazz Messengers
Horace Silver Quintet
The Jazztet
Clifford Brown-Max Roach Quintet
Cannonball Adderley Quintet
The Three Sounds

Trumpet
Miles Davis	Clifford Brown
Art Farmer	Lee Morgan
Freddie Hubbard	Woody Shaw
Donald Byrd	Blue Mitchell
Kenny Dorham	Nat Adderley

Trombone
J.J. Johnson	Kai Winding
Jimmy Cleveland	Curtis Fuller
Jimmy Knepper	Julian Priester

Alto Saxophone
Cannonball Adderley	Jackie McLean
Oliver Nelson	James Spaulding
Gary Bartz	

Tenor Saxophone
Sonny Rollins	Benny Golson
Johnny Griffin	Harold Land
Junior Cook	Hank Mobley
Jimmy Heath	Yusef Lateef
Clifford Jordan	Joe Henderson
George Coleman	Stanley Turrentine
Eddie Harris	Houston Person

Baritone Saxophone
Pepper Adams

–Continued next column–

Piano
Horace Silver	Red Garland
Wynton Kelly	Bobby Timmons
Les McCann	Gene Harris
Mal Waldron	Randy Weston
Phineas Newborn	Kenny Drew
Walter Bishop, Jr.	Walter Davis

Organ
Jimmy Smith	Charles Earland
Groove Holmes	Jack McDuff
Jimmy McGriff	Lonnie Smith
Johnny Hammond Smith	

Guitar
Wes Montgomery
Grant Green
Kenny Burrell

Bass
Paul Chambers	Doug Watkins
Sam Jones	Wilbur Ware
Richard Davis	Ron Carter
Buster Williams	

Drums
Max Roach	Art Blakey
Philly Joe Jones	Art Taylor
Jimmy Cobb	Louis Hayes
Roy Brooks	Grady Tate
Roy Haynes	

Composers & Arrangers
Horace Silver	Benny Golson
Bobby Timmons	Sonny Rollins
Kenny Dorham	Thad Jones
Randy Weston	Melba Liston
Oliver Nelson	Duke Pearson
Wayne Shorter	

Freddie Hubbard, *Ready for Freddie* (Blue Note)

Donald Byrd, *Chant* (Blue Note)

Wes Montgomery, *Full House* (Original Jazz Classics)

Lee Morgan, *The Sidewinder* (Blue Note)

Joe Henderson, *Page One* (Blue Note)

Grant Green, *Idle Moments* (Blue Note)

Cannonball Adderley, *Dizzy's Business* (Milestone)

Horace Silver, *Song for My Father* (Blue Note)

Art Blakey, *Straight Ahead* (Concord Jazz)

Important Events

1949 - The young Sonny Rollins records with J.J. Johnson.

1950 - Horace Silver is discovered by Stan Getz in Boston.

1951 - Miles Davis records his first hard bop records with Sonny Rollins and Jackie McLean.

1954 - Clifford Brown and Max Roach form their quintet.

Miles Davis records "Walkin."

J.J. Johnson and Kai Winding team up for a two-trombone quintet.

1955 - Cannonball Adderley sits in with Oscar Pettiford's group at the Cafe Bohemia and becomes "new Bird."

Art Blakey and Horace Silver form the Jazz Messengers.

1956 - Horace Silver leaves the Jazz Messengers to form his own quintet; records "Senor Blues."

Jimmy Smith makes his first recordings and is an immediate sensation.

Sonny Rollins and John Coltrane have a battle on "Tenor Madness."

Clifford Brown dies.

Lee Morgan makes his debut as a leader.

1957 - Jimmy Smith records ten albums for Blue Note, including five in a three-day period!

1958 - Booker Little joins Max Roach's pianoless quartet.

The Jazz Messengers introduce "Moanin'" and "Blues March."

Wes Montgomery records his first full-length album.

Gene Harris and the Three Sounds start to catch on.

1959 - Bobby Timmons' "This Here" is major hit for Cannonball Adderley.

Jackie McLean's *Jackie's Bag* is the first hard bop album to show influence of the avant-garde.

Wayne Shorter joins the Jazz Messengers.

Sonny Rollins retires for three years.

Blue Mitchell joins the Horace Silver Quintet.

1960 - Max Roach's quintet includes both Stanley and Tommy Turrentine.

Wes Montgomery records *The Incredible Jazz Guitar*.

Les McCann makes his first of many albums for Pacific Jazz.

The Jazztet debuts and introduces "Killer Joe."

Freddie Hubbard leads his first record date, *Open Sesame*.

1961 - Eddie Harris records "Exodus."

Oliver Nelson records classic album *Blues and the Abstract Truth*.

Lee Morgan leaves the Jazz Messengers and is succeeded by Freddie Hubbard.

Grant Green records five albums as a leader for Blue Note.

1962 - The Jazztet breaks up.

1963 - Lee Morgan records "The Sidewinder."

1964 - Horace Silver records "Song for My Father."

Freddie Hubbard leads quintet featuring James Spaulding.

1965 - Wes Montgomery switches to pop music with "Goin' Out of My Head."

Lee Morgan introduces "Ceora."

1966 - "Mercy, Mercy, Mercy" is a hit for Cannonball Adderley who moves away from playing hard bop.

1967 - Blue Note is sold to Liberty. The classic hard bop era begins to end.

Jackie McLean makes his final Blue Note album.

Eddie Harris records "Listen Here."

1968 - Wes Montgomery dies.

1970 - Woody Shaw records *Blackstone Legacy* and tries his best to keep hard bop alive in the 1970s.

Freddie Hubbard records *Red Clay* and *Straight Life* for CTI but soon switches to pop music.

1972 - Lee Morgan is killed.

1978 - Horace Silver, the final jazz artist on Blue Note, finally leaves the label.

Soul Jazz

Scott Yanow

The most popular jazz style of the 1960s was not bebop, hard bop or free jazz; it was the much-maligned soul-jazz idiom. While many young jazz musicians were attempting to redefine jazz as an "art form" suitable for concert halls, soul-jazz thrived in small Black bars and clubs. Largely ignored by the jazz media during the era (but not by record buyers), soul-jazz has still yet to be properly discussed in a full-length book or to gain the respect that it deserves.

Soul jazz differs from bebop and hard bop in that the emphasis is on the rhythmic groove. Although soloists follow the chords as in bop, the basslines (often played by an organist if not a string bassist) dance rather than stick strictly to a four-to-the bar walking pattern. The musicians build their accompaniment around the bassline and, although there are often strong melodies, it is the catchiness of the groove and the amount of heat generated by the soloists that determine whether the performance is successful. Since the goal is to be as catchy and as rhythmic as possible, it is little surprise that soul-jazz has usually had a large audience and been one of the most accessible of jazz styles.

When bebop emerged in the mid-1940s, a valid criticism was that its players sometimes sacrificed feeling in favor of virtuosity and speed. In the 1950s cool jazz generally slowed down the tempoes and smoothed out some of bop's rougher edges but it took hard bop to add a wider range of emotions to straightahead jazz. Soul jazz was an outgrowth of hard bop and one can trace its roots to pianist Horace Silver. Although also a fine hard bop-based player, Silver had his own style from as early as when he was discovered by Stan Getz in 1950. By 1954 he was recording with Miles Davis (sounding quite unlike the dominant pianist of the era Bud Powell) and the following year Silver co-founded the Jazz Messengers with Art Blakey. Horace Silver, who started leading his own quintet in 1956, has the main talent of all soul-jazz players: the ability to turn every song into the blues.

Silver's prominence as a pianist, a popular bandleader and a major composer largely launched the soul-jazz movement. Other pianists followed in his wake

including Bobby Timmons (who starred with Blakey and Cannonball Adderley before leading his own trios), Junior Mance, Les McCann, Gene Harris (with his Three Sounds) and Ramsey Lewis. These funky stylists were not shy to infuse jazz with gospel, blues and soul influences and each became popular stylists. Their playing also affected the mainstream of jazz so that other pianists (such as Oscar Peterson and Herbie Hancock) felt free to play funky when the spirit moved them.

The next major event in soul-jazz history was the discovery of organist Jimmy Smith in 1956. Although there had been jazz organ players in earlier times (including Fats Waller in the 1920s, Milt Buckner, Bill Doggett, Wild Bill Davis and occasionally Count Basie), the organ was thought of as a novelty instrument until Jimmy Smith emerged. Over four decades later Smith remains his instrument's dominant force. His Blue Note recordings of 1956-63 (which were often jam sessions with top soloists) found Smith not only holding his own with other players but being the consistent star. Although Jimmy Smith has been called "the Charlie Parker of the organ" since he was its first modern soloist and he is capable of playing bop standards, it is Smith's mastery of the blues and his melding together of bop's sophistication with the feeling of the blues that makes him most significant.

By the late 1950s organ combos started becoming common, usually utilizing a tenor saxophonist, guitarist, drummer and an occasional bassist (at least on records). The repertoire of such bands tended to have blues at several tempos, soulful ballads and some well-known melodic standards. Smith's all-encompassing influence resulted in most organists sounding like a close relative but the best ones also displayed their own soulful approach. Among the top organists of the 1960s were Brother Jack McDuff (who played with Willis Jackson before launching his own bands), Shirley Scott (who had powerful bands with first Eddie "Lockjaw" Davis and then her husband Stanley Turrentine on tenors), Jimmy McGriff, Charles Earland, Richard "Groove" Holmes," Big John Patton, Johnny Hammond Smith, Don Patterson and Lonnie Smith among others. Only Larry Young, who explored modal and avant-garde jazz after the mid-1960s, managed to eventually escape from Smith's influence.

While organists were usually the bandleaders, they were not the only colorful soloists. Among the guitarists were the great Grant Green, George Benson (who first played with Jack McDuff), the young Pat Martino, the underrated Boogaloo Joe Jones and such part-time soul-jazz players as Wes Montgomery and Kenny Burrell.

Many of the tenor saxophonists who appeared with soul-jazz groups had experience both in jazz and early R&B where emotion (and the ability to honk) were highly valued. Stanley Turrentine, whose every note drips soul (and whose unchanging sound through the decades is surprisingly flexible), was always the perfect soul-jazz tenor but he was far from alone. Willis "Gator" Jackson, Eddie "Lockjaw" Davis, David "Fathead" Newman, Gene "Jug" Ammons (great nicknames!), Houston Person, Jimmy Forrest, King Curtis (best-known for his R&B and pop recordings), Red Holloway and Eddie Harris (whose "Listen Here" was a soul-jazz hit) were only a few of the thick-toned saxophonists who helped to keep the idiom alive and creative. All of the above (plus Hank Crawford, the definitive soul-jazz altoist) inspired such later R&B-influenced stars as Grover Washington Jr. (who picked up early experience playing with organ groups) and David Sanborn.

Soul jazz, although not well publicized by the jazz press, was very well documented on recordings from the late 1950s up until the early '70s. With such a large roster of viable players and a core of dedicated fans, why did soul-jazz start to drop in popularity during the latter half of the 1960s? The competition had become a lot stronger with the rise of rock and the emergence of fusion. Electric keyboards were much easier to move around than organs and some of the top soul-jazz organists in the 1970s switched to the lighter instruments although few were able to retain their own musical personality on the Fender Rhodes. Motown had made inroads with the Black audience and when disco in the mid-1970s became the main dance music, soul-jazz was greatly eclipsed and seemed to disappear.

However the tide turned by the mid-1980s. The young Joey DeFrancesco emerged as the first important new jazz organist in a decade, playing in a style nearly identical to Jimmy Smith. The surviving organists gradually reappeared on records, playing in an unchanged style and showing that they had lost none of their soul or fire. In addition, with the rise of acid jazz in the 1990s there has been a great demand for the reissuance of groove-oriented soul-jazz organ records of the 1960s and many of the earlier sessions are once again available, leading to the rediscovery of such veterans as Baby Face Willette, Mel Rhyne and Big John Patton in addition to the still powerful Jimmy Smith.

Now that all styles of jazz are able to co-exist, soul-jazz has a bright future as one of the more likable areas of creative music. — <I>*Scott Yanow*

Twenty Essential Recordings

Horace Silver, *Finger Poppin'* (Blue Note)

Cannonball Adderley, *Live In San Francisco* (Original Jazz Classics)

Bobby Timmons, *This Here Is Bobby Timmons* (Original Jazz Classics)

Music Map

Soul Jazz

Hard Bop

Clifford Brown • Lee Morgan • Freddie Hubbard • Cannonball Adderley • Phil Woods • Art Pepper • Sonny Rollins • Rahsaan Roland Kirk • Wes Montgomery • Jimmy Smith • Art Blakey

Father of Soul Jazz

Horace Silver

Key Soul Jazz Pianists

Bobby Timmons • Junior Mance • Les McCann • Gene Harris • Ramsey Lewis

Jimmy Smith

"The Charlie Parker of the Organ." The first modern organist, his discovery in 1956 established the organ as a vital jazz element.

Top Soul Jazz Guitarists of the 1960s

Grant Green • George Benson • Pat Martino • Boogaloo Joe Jones • Wes Montgomery • Kenny Burrell

Top Soul Organists of the 1960s

Brother Jack McDuff • Shirley Scott • Jimmy McGriff • Charles Earland • Richard "Groove" Holmes • Big John Patton • Johnny "Hammond" Smith • Don Patterson • Lonnie Smith • Larry Young

Top Soul Jazz Saxophonists of the 1960s

Stanley Turrentine • Willis "Gator" Jackson • Eddie "Lockjaw" Davis • David "Fathead" Newman • Gene "Jug" Ammons • Houston Person • Jimmy Forrest • King Curtis • Red Holloway • Eddie Harris • Hank Crawford

Developments of the 1980s and 1990s

Joey DeFranceso emerges during the mid-'80s as the first important new jazz organist in a decade • With rise of acid jazz in the '90s, there is great demand for the reissuance of groove-oriented soul jazz records of the '60s, leading to the rediscovery of Baby Face Willets, Mel Rhyne, Big John Patton and Jimmy Smith

Les McCann, *Swiss Movement* (Rhino/Atlantic)
Gene Harris, *Brotherhood* (Concord Jazz)
Jimmy Smith, *House Party* (Blue Note)
Jimmy Smith, *Midnight Special* (Blue Note)
Jimmy Smith, *Back at the Chicken Shack* (Blue Note)
Jack McDuff, *Live!* (Prestige)
Shirley Scott, *Soul Shoutin'* (Prestige)
Jimmy McGriff, *Right Turn On Blues* (Telarc)
Charles Earland, *Black Talk* (Original Jazz Classics)
Richard "Groove" Holmes, *Soul Message* (Original Jazz Classics)

Grant Green, *Grantstand* (Blue Note)
Grant Green, *Idle Moments* (Blue Note)
George Benson, *The New Boss Guitar* (Original Jazz Classics)
Willis Jackson, *Please Mr. Jackson* (Original Jazz Classics)
Gene Ammons, *Brother Jack Meets The Boss* (Original Jazz Classics)
Stanley Turrentine, *Let It Go* (Blue Note)
Eddie Harris, *The Electrifying Eddie Harris* (Atlantic)
Houston Person, *Stolen Sweets* (Muse)
Hank Crawford, *Soul Survivors* (Milestone)

Brazilian Jazz (Bossa Nova)

Richard S. Ginell

A fresh breeze of warm South American air blew through American jazz in the early 1960s, the seductive blend of Brazilian rhythms, American cool jazz, and advanced European classical harmony that became known as bossa nova. The term roughly means "new wave" in Portuguese—and at the time, it was a viable alternative for an American jazz scene that had become polarized between the hard boppers and the emerging avant-garde, trapped in a repertoire of venerable standards, and marginalized in a mass culture dominated by easy listening and rock 'n' roll.

The classic bossa nova rhythm, a soft yet propulsively ticking, regular stream of eighth notes with irregular accents, developed as an outgrowth of the Brazilian samba, a series of wild rhythmic patterns rooted in African music which used any percussion instruments that one could lay hands upon even sticks on tin cans. The bossa nova pioneers took the samba and stripped it down, taking out the noise and complexities, lowering the volume but leaving the hypnotic accents. To that, they added a distinctive loping rhythm from an acoustic guitar, lovely gliding melodies and lyrics (in Portuguese or English) that often conjured an aching, yearning feeling that the Brazilians call saudade, and sophisticated harmonies derived from Debussy and Ravel that resolved in ways that were beyond the reach of Tin Pan Alley. Ultimately, bossa nova opened the door to other emerging influences from Brazil and most significantly, established a new body of great songs for everyone in jazz to draw upon.

Prior to bossa nova, Brazilian music to Americans usually meant cliches like Carmen Miranda with a basket of fruit on her head or an occasional catchy samba hit like Ary Barroso's "Brazil" or Peggy Lee's "Manana." Conversely, by the 1950s, a few open-eared Brazilians were listening seriously to American jazz, particularly the West Coast cool variety as preached by the likes of Chet Baker, Gerry Mulligan and Shorty Rogers. By 1953, Brazilian guitarist Laurindo Almeida was groping toward a bossa nova rhythm on parts of some early albums with American saxophonist Bud Shank and those records also found their way to Brazil. A young singer named Joao Gilberto pushed the envelope further by playing his guitar with a distinctive rhythm that would become the basis of the new hybrid, and a composer-turned-record company employee named Antonio Carlos Jobim was writing unusual new songs with advanced harmonies. In 1958, Gilberto scored a big hit in Brazil with one of Jobim's songs "Chega de Saudade" (backed by Gilberto's own "Bim Bom"), which effectively launched the movement in Brazil. Also Jobim and Luiz Bonfa wrote incidental music to a play called Black Orpheus which was made into a 1959 film that swept the world, introducing enduring songs like "Manha de Carnaval" and "Samba de Orfeo." On the soundtrack, one can hear the agitated street samba rhythms being converted into the cooler bossa nova.

Bossa nova's North American breakthrough had to wait until 1962 when guitarist Charlie Byrd, fresh from a State Department tour of South America, persuaded Stan Getz to record an album of bossa novas, Jazz Samba, with him. "Desafinado," a song from the album that was placed on the the B-side of a single, suddenly took off and became a hit, catapulting Getz into pop stardom and focusing attention upon its composer, Jobim. The timing was right, and bossa nova became the object of a gold rush, with record companies falling all over each other issuing records with the words "bossa nova" on them. Gene Ammons, Dave Brubeck, Herbie Mann, Eddie Harris, Quincy Jones, Jon Hendricks, Stan Kenton, George Shearing, even Miles Davis were among many jazz artists who made bossa nova albums—most of which, contrary to received wisdom, hold up pretty well today (not so the obvious pop cash-ins like Eydie Gorme's "Blame It On The Bossa Nova" or Elvis Presley's "Bossa Nova Baby" which only use the name, not the style). A whole gaggle of Brazilian musicians were flown to New York for the first North American bossa nova concert at Carnegie Hall Nov. 22, 1962; the event was a sonic fiasco but it left a mark on the American scene.

The bossa nova fad seemed to have faded from the mass culture by 1964 but Getz, Jobim, Joao Gilberto and his wife Astrud proved the doomsayers wrong that year by scoring a massive pop hit with Jobim's "The Girl From Ipanema." Producer Creed Taylor, who shepherded Jazz Samba, proved to be a staunch champion of Brazilian music, producing several superb albums of Brazilian or Brazilian-tinged music by Getz, Jobim, Paul Desmond, Walter Wanderley, the Tamba 4 and the young Milton Nascimento for Verve and/or A&M, while getting his other jazz artists to record Brazilian tunes. Sergio Mendes, a jazz pianist from Brazil, came up with a new sexy blend of bossa nova and pop female vocals that produced several hits for his Brasil '66 group. When Frank Sinatra finally recorded with Jobim in 1967, that put an official seal of approval upon Jobim's stature—and a whole crop of superb Brazilian composers like Edu Lobo, Jorge Ben, Baden Powell, Joao Donato and Dori Caymmi flourished in Jobim's wake.

Yet in the '70s, bossa nova went into a long American eclipse, hastened by overexposure of a few choice songs and the decline of the audience for acoustic jazz.

The focus of Brazilian influences on jazz shifted from the coast of Brazil to the interior as percussionists like Airto Moreira started to bring exotic instruments and complex folk-based rhythms to the music of Miles Davis, Weather Report, Santana (in the band's jazz period), the first edition of Return To Forever and then his own. In Brazil, an eclectic movement called tropicalismo took hold, with Nascimento in the forefront, where jazz began to take a back seat to rock as the main American influence. Wayne Shorter's collaboration with Nascimento Native Dancer , the electrified Brazilian jazz-funk of Azymuth, and George Duke's A Brazilian Love Affair made some impact during the lean years.

By the mid-1980s, though, a second, less commercial yet more enduring and eclectic Brazilian wave started up, spurred by the world music boom and propelling jazz-influenced Brazilians like Djavan and Ivan Lins into prominence. Jobim started touring again, and his stature gradually rose to a level comparable to that of the Gershwins; several tribute and sampler albums of his music were issued after his death in 1994 . Nowadays, concerts of Brazilian jazz regularly draw large crowds, and Brazilian music has become so much a part of jazz that every other mainstream set that you encounter at a club or hall will likely include at least one bossa nova. And as 1996's highly stimulating Red Hot + Rio project indicates, today's younger musicians have the capacity to interact with older Brazilian music and make it grow into something new. — *Richard S. Ginell*

Ten recommended Brazilian jazz albums

Laurindo Almeida and Bud Shank, *Brazilliance, Vol. 1* (World Pacific)

Original Soundtrack, *Black Orpheus* (Verve)

Antonio Carlos Jobim, *The Man From Ipanema* (Verve, 3-CD set)

Stan Getz w. Charlie Byrd, Joao & Astrud Gilberto, etc., *The Bossa Nova Years* (Verve, 4-CD set)

Charlie Byrd, *Bossa Nova Pelos Passaros* (OJC/Riverside)

Paul Desmond, *From The Hot Afternoon* (A&M)

Wayne Shorter and Milton Nascimento, *Native Dancer* (Columbia)

Airto Moreira, *The Best Of Airto* (Columbia)

Djavan, *Bird Of Paradise* (Columbia)

Various Artists, *Red Hot + Rio* (Antilles)

Important Events

1954 - Laurindo Almeida and Bud Shank team up for two Pacific Jazz recordings that hint strongly at bossa nova years before the term was coined.

1958 - Joao Gilberto records Antonio Carlos Jobim's "Chega De Saudade" in Brazil.

1959 - The film *Black Orpheus* features an exciting score by Antonio Carlos Jobim and Luiz Bonfa.

1960 - Joao Gilberto and Antonio Carlos Jobim record the little-known Capitol album *Samba De Uma Note So*.

1962 - Stan Getz and Charlie Byrd team up for *Jazz Samba* which features the hit "Desafinado" and really launches the bossa nova movement.

Herbie Mann records in Brazil with Baden Powell, Sergio Mendes and Antonio Carlos Jobim.

1963 - Bossa-nova has become a fad in danger of quickly dying out but then *Getz/Gilberto* (featuring Stan Getz, Antonio Carlos Jobim, Joao Gilberto and, on the major hit "The Girl from Ipanema," Astrud Gilberto) is recorded and immediately recognized as a classic.

Laurindo Almeida records with the Modern Jazz Quartet

1964 - Joao Gilberto records with Stan Getz at Carnegie Hall.

Stan Getz and Astrud Gilberto perform "The Girl from Ipanema" in the movie *Get Yourself a College Girl* but Getz soon turns away from bossa nova.

1965 - Astrud Gilberto records her definitive albums.

Bossa-Nova, no longer a fad, becomes a permanent part of American popular music.

Latin Jazz

Richard S. Ginell

As it is in European classical music—and American popular music, for that matter—the Latin influence in jazz has usually been treated as an exotic spice somewhat removed from the mainstream, and thus not taken very seriously. Yet Latin jazz has been one of jazz's more durable idioms over the last half century, never quite going out of fashion precisely because it offers such a different and exciting alternative to the mainstream.

Basically Latin jazz is a merger of Latin American dance rhythms and jazz improvisation, often with a heavy emphasis on maintaining a constant, revolving, hypnotic groove. Although the rhythms are often based upon a regular stream of eighth notes, what gives Latin jazz its kick is where the accents on the notes are placed—often on unpredictable beats. Unlike most jazz forms which are content only to use a trap drum kit for percussion, Latin jazz employs a wide variety of percussion instruments like conga drums, bongo drums, timbales, claves, cowbells and maracas. The classic Latin jazz combo often consists of eight players—a three-horn front line (a trumpet, trombone and sax, for example), piano, bass, and three Latin percussionists capable of providing the power of a big band, the freedom of a small group, and the added drive of all that dueling percussion. And while Latin jazz is usually irresistibly danceable—another reason why some pundits don't take it seriously—it is also capable of forming the underpinning for extended concert works.

The Latin strain in jazz dates back almost to the beginning of the century; the second section of W.C. Handy's "St. Louis Blues" is based on a straight tango rhythm, as are parts of piano rags like Scott Joplin's and Louis Chauvin's "Helio-trope Bouquet" and the Pastime Rags Nos. 3 and 5 of Artie Matthews. Jelly Roll Morton made use of Latin rhythms in the '20s, as did Duke Ellington in the '30s under the influence of his Puerto Rican valve trombonist Juan Tizol ("Caravan"). In Cuba around 1938, Cachao created the mambo, which would become the rhythmic base for the Latin jazz explosion to follow.

However the fusion of Latin rhythms with jazz did not become a full-blown force until just after World War II—no doubt helped by the wave of giddy high spir-its following the Allied victory. Cuban-born Mario Bauza installed an intoxicating mixture of jazz arrangements and solos and Afro-Cuban rhythms into his brother-in-law Machito's Afro-Cuban band, starting in 1941. Bauza also served as a catalyst for Dizzy Gillespie's interest in Latin rhythms, introducing him to the electrifying Cuban percussionist Chano Pozo. By adding Pozo to his bebop big band in 1947, Gillespie became an American Latin jazz pioneer, running off a string of Latin jazz standards ("Manteca," "Tin Tin Deo," the opening bars of "A Night In Tunisia"), and he would continue to explore Afro-Cuban rhythms for the rest of his life. Also Stan Kenton recorded "The Peanut Vendor" that year with guitarist Laurindo Almeida and bongo player Jack Costanzo (who would soon join Nat Cole's trio in 1949), and Kenton would reinforce long-standing Latin ties on such later albums as Cuban Fire! and Viva Kenton.

By the 1950s, hot Latin jazz bands led by Machito, Tito Puente, Perez Prado and Chico O'Farrill had become very popular, sparked by waves of Latin dance crazes such as the mambo and cha-cha-cha (one also cannot underestimate the impact of exposure to Cuban rhythms that Desi Arnaz gave American TV audiences on I Love Lucy). The calypso craze of 1956-57 directly affected jazz musicians like Sonny Rollins, who added calypso tunes and rhythms to his repertoire. Cuban musicians continued to flock to America while they could, and White jazz combo leaders like Cal Tjader, George Shearing and Herbie Mann began to concentrate upon Afro-Cuban rhythms. But new Cuban influences were cut off when Fidel Castro came to power in Havana and banned emigration.

By adding streaks of American R&B influences, Mongo Santamaria eventually scored a huge hit with "Watermelon Man" in 1962, and his band became a hot attraction by transforming Top 40 tunes from the rock/soul charts into blazing Afro-Cuban workouts. By now, the conga drum had become a fixture within many combos and on commercial jazz recording dates, with session congueros like Willie Bobo, Ray Barretto and Candido in constant demand. Several records by jazz or Latin jazz artists with Latin rhythms dented the charts in the open-minded '60s, among them Barretto's "El Watusi," Eddie Harris' "Listen Here," and Wes Montgomery's "Tequila." In the avant-garde, John Coltrane experimented with Afro-Latin percussion on "Kulu Se Mama" and Gato Barbieri brought Argentine rhythms into his passionate music. In 1969, the dominant rock idiom received a depth charge of Latin jazz influences from the thundering band of Carlos Santana, who cut his teeth on Latin jazz records and in turn, would inspire young rock listeners to investigate Latin music.

The 1970s brought a new umbrella word to describe the classic Machito/Puente variety of Latin jazz, "salsa"—a term which dates back to the 1930s but probably began to achieve some currency with the success of Cal Tjader's "Soul Sauce" in 1965. In the meantime, leaders like Santamaria and Barretto were toying with American funk and rock influences, and Santana himself pushed further into jazz from his Latin rock base. Chucho Valdes' eclectic modern group Irakere burst briefly out of Cuba in 1978 but its impact has since been hampered by political red tape—and two of its stars, the versatile Arturo Sandoval and bop-minded Paquito D'Rivera defected in the 1980s.

These days, most of the surviving masters of Latin jazz, along with younger leaders like Poncho Sanchez, have become pretty much set in older styles; the Con-cord Picante label has been faithfully documenting many of them since 1979. Yet their live and studio performances remain bright and vital, defying the potentially paralyzing effects of repetition, and young bop-oriented players like Gonzalo Rubalcaba and Danilo Perez still bring the heat and rhythms of Latin music to

Music Map
Significant Latin Jazz Players

Bandleaders

Machito	Tito Puente
Cal Tjader	Mongo Santamaria
Poncho Sanchez	Chuco Valdes (Irakere)
Jerry Gonzalez	

Percussion/Drums

Chano Pozo	Jack Costanzo
Tito Puente	Mongo Santamaria
Willie Bobo	Carlos Vidal
Candido	Armando Peraza
Potato Valdez	Ray Baretto
Poncho Sanchez	Ignacio Berroa
Giovanni Hidalgo	

Piano

Eddie Palmieri	Hilton Ruiz
Danilo Perez	Gonzalo Rubalcaba
Chucho Valdes	

Bass
Cachao
Alto/Clarinet
Paquito D'Rivera

Flute
Herbie Mann
Dave Valentin

Soprano
Jane Bunnett

Trumpet
Arturo Sandoval

Vibes
Cal Tjader

their performances. And given the growing Latino population in North America, one can expect the Latin influence in jazz to flourish and even broaden in the 21st century. — Richard S. Ginell

Ten recommended Latin jazz albums:

Machito, *Mucho Macho Machito and his Afro-Cuban Salseros* (Pablo)

Machito w. Charlie Parker, Flip Phillips; Dizzy Gillespie Big Band, *The Original Mambo Kings* (Verve)

Tito Puente, *50 Years Of Swing* (Ritmo Mundo Musical, 3-CD set)

Chico O'Farrill, *Cuban Blues* (Verve, 2-CD set)

Stan Kenton, *Cuban Fire!* (Capitol)

Mongo Santamaria, *Mongo's Greatest Hits* (Fantasy)

Cal Tjader, *Talkin' Verve* (Verve)

Irakere, *The Best Of Irakere* (Columbia)

Poncho Sanchez, *Baila Mi Gente—Salsa* (Concord Picante)

Ray Barretto and New World Spirit, *Ancestral Messages* (Concord Picante)

Important Events

1923 - Jelly Roll Morton uses a Latin rhythm (which he called a "Spanish tinge") on his solo piano recording of "New Orleans Joys."

1937 - Duke Ellington's valve trombonist Juan Tizol composes "Caravan."

1939 - Mario Bauza recommends Dizzy Gillespie to Cab Calloway.

1940 - Machito forms the "Afro-Cubans."

1941 - Mario Bauza joins Machito's band as musical director and begins hiring jazz arrangers for the influential group.

1943 - Mario Bauza writes "Tanga."

1947 - Afro-Cuban jazz is born as Chano Pozo joins the Dizzy Gillespie big band. Together they record "Manteca," Cubana Be" and "Cubana Bop."

Stan Kenton adds guitarist Laurindo Almeida and bongo player Jack Costanzo to his orchestra, using Machito on maraccas for recordings of "Cuban Carnival" and "The Peanut Vendor."

1948 - Chano Pozo is killed.

Charlie Parker, Flip Phillips and Buddy Rich record with Machito's Orchestra.

1949 - Jack Costanzo makes the Nat King Cole Trio a Quartet when he joins on bongos.

Chico O'Farrill contributes arrangements to both the Stan Kenton and Benny Goodman Orchestras.

1951 - Cal Tjader leaves the Dave Brubeck trio and records as a leader playing drums and bongos.

1954 - Cal Tjader makes his first full-fledged Latin jazz records.

1956 - Two of the most interesting records of the year are the Stan Kenton Orchestra's interpretations of Johnny Richards' *Cuban Fire* and Tito Puente's *Puente Goes Jazz.*

1958 - Cal Tjader cuts *Latin Concert* with his sextet featuring pianist Vince Guaraldi and both Willie Bobo and Mongo Santamaria on percussion.

1959 - Mongo Santamaria records his "Afro Blue" for the first time. Herbie Mann puts together a successful Afro-Cuban band.

1961 - Ray Barretto makes his first album as leader.

1963 - Mongo Santamaria has a hit with his version of Herbie Hancock's "Watermelon Man."

1974 - Chucho Valdes becomes the musical director of Irakere.

1976 - Cal Tjader's group includes Poncho Sanchez.

1978 - Irakere (with Arturo Sandoval and Paquito D'Rivera) performs and records at the Montreux Jazz Festival.

1982 - Cal Tjader dies.

Both Tito Puente and Poncho Sanchez begin recording regularly for the Concord Picante label.

Arturo Sandoval collaborates with Dizzy Gillespie on *To a Finland Station.*

Jerry Gonzalez's Fort Apache Band debuts on record.

1983 - Willie Bobo dies.

1984 - Dave Valetin makes his first record for GRP.

1988 - Jerry Gonzalez records *Rumba Para Monk*, a Latinized version of Thelonious Monk tunes.

1989 - Dizzy Gillespie tours and records with his United Nation Band.

1990 - Arturo Sandoval defects to the United States.

Gonzalo Rubalcaba plays at the Montreux Jazz Festival with Charlie Haden and Paul Motian.

1991 - Mario Bauza's Afro-Cuban Jazz orchestra records *Tanga.*

Jane Bunnett records *Spirits of Havana in Cuba.*

1992 - Tito Puente cuts his 100th album.

1993 - Dizzy Gillespie and Mario Bauza die.

Third Stream

Richard S. Ginell

This shorthand slogan describing mergers of jazz with classical music was coined in 1957 by composer/conductor Gunther Schuller, and in general it has been previously applied only to such music from the 1950s onward. But in fact, there have been so-called Third Stream experiments of one form or another throughout the 20th century.

The motivations behind these sometimes unwieldy, sometimes inspired shotgun marriages of idioms vary wildly. Some have done it, in Paul Whiteman's notorious words, out of the desire to "make a lady out of jazz," to remove the images of whorehouses and shady all-night joints from the public mind and make it acceptable to middle-class values. Some have done it perhaps out of envy, to gain the respect from the ivory towers of academia and taste that classical composers routinely enjoy. From the other side of the divide, classical composers have seen jazz as a way to spice up their music rhythmically, a few brave ones hoping to restore the improvisational element that had been missing in European classical music since J.S. Bach's time (a world-class improviser, by the way). Some juxtapose classical writing with jazz improvisation in separate but equal modules within their pieces, some have used classical writing to underscore jazz. More recently, younger musicians have shown that they don't give a damn about respectability or categories; having grown up with access to all kinds of music via the phonograph, tape deck and CD player, mixing classical writing with jazz influences comes as naturally to them as breathing.

Europeans were making use of the rhythmic elements of ragtime and/or jazz in classical pieces like Claude Debussy's "Golliwog's Cakewalk" (1908), Igor Stravinsky's *L'Histoire du Soldat* and *Ragtime for Eleven Instruments* (both 1918), and Darius Milhaud's *La creation du monde* (1923) well before the historic 1924 Paul Whiteman concert at New York's Aeolian Hall that introduced George Gershwin's *Rhapsody in Blue.* Indeed, one can hear Black influences as far back as the music of transplanted Creole composer/pianist Louis Moreau Gottschalk in the 1840s, and American iconoclast Charles Ives used ragtime exuberantly in *Central Park in the Dark* (1898-1907). However, *the Rhapsody*, along with an earlier Gershwin chamber opera *Blue Monday*, confirmed and launched an international trend, sometimes referred to as "symphonic jazz." They didn't call the 1920s the Jazz Age for nothing; jazz was in the air, and classical composers such as America's Aaron Copland and George Antheil, France's Maurice Ravel, Germany's Kurt Weill, even Czechoslovakia's Erwin Schulhoff and Russia's Dmitri Shostakovich couldn't help but use it. Conversely, back in America, jazzman Bix Beiderbecke toyed with Debussy's whole-tone scale on the piano and came up with a miniature classical/jazz masterpiece, "In A Mist," and pianist James P. Johnson wrote some orchestral works containing jazz colors.

The popular triumph that was the Swing Era did not satisfy the ambitions of some of its leaders who longed for acceptance in the classical world or tried to fuse their jazz artistry to it. Artie Shaw's first venture into bandleading in 1936 was a performance with a string quartet and rhythm section, followed by a big band that carefully integrated a string quartet into the sound in a swinging update of Whiteman's brand of symphonic jazz. The band was not commercially viable, but even in a conventional big band setting, Shaw never quite gave up, employing a classical composer William Grant Still on his arranging staff and even writing a Clarinet Concerto with a mostly improvised lead part. While Benny Goodman mostly stuck with straight classical pieces, he did commission classical works with strong jazz elements from Copland (Clarinet Concerto) and Morton Gould (Derivations). Duke Ellington tried to expand into long-form tone poems and suites, beginning with "Creole Rhapsody," but his music tended to avoid classical development procedures (not always so that of his classically-trained collaborator Billy Strayhorn). Woody Herman got into the act by commissioning the quirky Ebony Concerto from Stravinsky and Leonard Bernstein's wild and swinging *Prelude Fugue and Riffs* (which Herman, alas, never performed).

The use of jazz had fallen out of favor among classical composers (except in America) by the time World War II started; indeed the Nazis' classification of jazz as "entartete" (degenerate) music made the use of it life-threatening in much of Europe. Also the twelve-tone method of composition as championed by Arnold Schoenberg and refined by Anton Webern had come to vogue, to which improvisation and the pulse of jazz seemed quite alien. Yet there were a few brilliant fusions of dissonant or twelve-tone writing and jazz in the '50s—like Rolf Liebermann's *Concerto for Jazz Band and Orchestra,* (as performed by the surprisingly swinging combination of Fritz Reiner and the Chicago Symphony and the Sauter-Finegan Orchestra) or the "Cool" fugue from Bernstein's *West Side Story.*

The most significant classical/jazz fusions of the 1950s tended to originate from the jazz side of the fence. Stan Kenton began the decade by organizing the massive *Innovations in Modern Music Orchestra,* which featured bold, harmonically complex arrangements that crossed the line into the worlds of Hindemith and Stravinsky, sometimes with a jazz pulse, sometimes not. Dave Brubeck brought the polytonality of his teacher Milhaud and contrapuntal Bach to his small groups, adding an orchestra in works like his own *Elementals* and his brother Howard's *Dialogues for Jazz Combo and Orchestra.* The landmark Miles Davis/Gil Evans collaboration gradually turned toward a classical/jazz fusion when they attempted a translation of the slow movement of Joaquin Rodrigo's *Concierto de Aranjuez* on *Sketches of Spain.*

The formation of the Jazz and Classical Music Society by Gunther Schuller and the Modern Jazz Quartet's John Lewis in 1955 to promote concert music written by jazz composers led to full-blown formal attempts to integrate a jazz combo with an orchestra, as well as the birth of the term Third Stream to describe them. A number of pieces by Schuller, Lewis, William Russo, J.J. Johnson, Jimmy Giuffre and others emerged, not all of which were genuine classical/jazz fusions. But the MJQ, itself influenced by contrapuntal Baroque music, recorded an album called *Third*

Stream Music in which Lewis and Schuller successfully fused the cool jazz idiom and feeling with the classical Beaux Arts String Quartet. A perceived signal had been sent that jazz had finally grown up enough to merge with European music, and that would be the dominant wave of the future.

It didn't turn out that way. Few of the fusions proved to be commercially popular, and fewer still could get around the fact that most classical string, wind and brass players were not steeped in the fine art of swing and thus tended to bog down the jazz cats. The extroverted avant-garde movement spearheaded by Ornette Coleman and John Coltrane blunted the impact of the cooler, cerebral Third Stream in the 1960s. And some valuable figures like Andre Previn, who seemed ideally positioned to come up with a good classical/jazz fusion, chose to keep their hats in separate closets, so to speak.

But the idea of Third Stream refuses to die, and there have been plenty of worthwhile projects since its so-called heyday that have kept the dream of a fusion between two allegedly incompatible art forms alive. Stan Getz's scintillating collaboration with Eddie Sauter *Focus* was not only extremely fulfilling to Getz, it became one of his most revered albums. In 1965, Vince Guaraldi, Lalo Schifrin and Ellington started to fuse religious music with jazz, and three years later, Brubeck launched a series of distinctively stamped oratorios that juxtapose and mix jazz, classical, rock, ethnic and other genres and feature stretches of jazz improvisation. One very talented, almost forgotten Third Stream figure of the 1960s was composer/arranger William Fischer, who midwifed classical/jazz pieces for Cannonball Adderley and with Herbie Mann, recorded an unheralded masterpiece in Berlin, *Concerto Grosso in D Blues*. Roger Kellaway, through his Cello Quartet and orchestral pieces, has assembled lyrical, quirky fusions from the '70s onward; Eddie Daniels' album *Breakthrough* for clarinet and orchestra and *Memos from Paradise* (with Kellaway) for clarinet, string quartet and rhythm section are marvelously musical and well-balanced; and Schifrin's ongoing *Jazz Meets the Symphony* project of the 1990s continues to fuse tighter, more compatible mergers with each release. The idea of string quartets playing jazz caught fire in the 1980s—ignited by the Kronos Quartet, which played written-out arrangements of music by Thelonious Monk and Bill Evans, and taken further by the Turtle Island String Quartet, which could actually improvise. Other recent successful projects include Palle Mikkelborg's 1984 neo-Stravinsky/Gil Evans suite for Miles Davis, *Aura*; Jan Garbarek's improvising over *Early Music* backgrounds on *Officium* and Steven Mackey's miraculously well-integrated 1995 amalgam of jazz, rock and avant-garde classical music for guitarist Bill Frisell and the L.A. Philharmonic New Music Group, *Deal*.

As more universities, colleges and concert halls accept jazz as an art form on par with European classical music, and as long as musicians on both sides of the divide remain curious about other forms of music, the Third Stream should continue to flow into the next century. — *Richard S. Ginell*

Ten Recommended Third Stream albums

Leonard Bernstein, New York Philharmonic, *Gershwin: Rhapsody In Blue/An American In Paris, Bernstein: Symphonic Dances from West Side Story* (Sony Classical)

John Bruce Yeh, *DePaul University Wind and Jazz Ensembles, Ebony Concerto*, music by Stravinsky, Babin, Gould, Bernstein, Shaw (Reference Recordings)

Artie Shaw, *Best Of The Big Bands* (Columbia)

Stan Kenton, *City Of Glass* (Capitol)

Gunther Schuller, Jimmy Giuffre, etc., *The Birth of the Third Stream* (Columbia)

Modern Jazz Quartet, *Third Stream Music* (Atlantic, cassette only as of 1997)

Stan Getz, *Focus* (Verve)

Eddie Daniels, *Breakthrough* (GRP)

Dave Brubeck, *To Hope! A Celebration* (Telarc)

Lalo Schifrin, *Firebird* (Four Winds)

Avant-Garde/Free Jazz

Chris Kelsey

Of the many musical sub-species that have emerged and diverged from Jazz's evolutionary track, none has inspired such controversy as Free Jazz. Free Jazz represented a final break with the music's roots as a popular art form, casting it in an alternative role as an experimental art music, along the lines of the European "classical" avant-garde. The Free players were the first jazz musicians (early-beboppers and Duke Ellington notwithstanding) to focus almost exclusively on a furtherance of the music's creative possibilities, at the expense of being understood by a lay audience. Their emphasis on jazz's primarily expressive properties—and consequent de-emphasis of its harmonic and rhythmic customs-challenged listeners and disturbed mainstream players, who saw in Free Jazz an art form dominated by a totally unfamiliar set of musical values. Free Jazz was originally erected on a foundation of late '40s and early '50s bebop. The first Free Jazz recordings were made

---

Music Map

Third Stream

Pre-20th Century Jazz/Classical Fusion
Louis Moreau Gottschalk (1840s)
Charles Ives ("Central Park in the Dark," 1898-1907)

Early European Jazz/Classical Fusion
Claude Debussey ("Golliwog's Cakewalk," 1908)
Igor Stravinski ("L'Histoire du Soldat" and "Ragtime for Eleven Instruments," both 1918)
Darius Milhaud ("La creation du monde," 1923)

The Jazz Age
George Gershwin ("Blue Monday") • Paul Whiteman (introduces Gershwin's "Rhapsody in Blue," 1942) • Aaron Copeland • George Antheil • Maurice Ravel • Kurt Weill • Erwin Schulhoff • Dmitri Shostakovich • Bix Beiderbecke ("In a Mist") • James P. Johnson

The Swing Era
Artie Shaw • Benny Goodman • Duke Ellington • Billy Strayhorn • Woody Herman

Post-World War II Era
Rolf Liebermann ("Concerto for Jazz Band and Orchestra," performed by Fritz Reiner and the Chicago Symphony/Sauter-Finnegan Orchestra) • Leonard Berstein ("Cool" fugue from *West Side Story*)

The Late 1950s
Gunther Schuller (forms Jazz and Classical Music Society, 1955; coins phrase "Third Stream," 1957) • Stan Kenton (forms Innovations in Modern Music Orchestra) • Dave Brubeck • Howard Brubeck • Miles Davis/Gil Evans (*Sketches of Spain*) • John Lewis • William Russo • J.J. Johnson • Jimmy Giuffre

The 1960s
Stan Getz/Eddie Sauter • Vince Guaraldi • Lalo Schifrin • William Fischer • Cannonball Adderley • Herbie Mann

The 1970s Onward
Roger Kellaway • Eddie Daniels • Kronos Quartet • Turtle Island String Quartet • Palle Mikkelborg • Jan Garbarek • Steven Mackey

by the pianist Lennie Tristano for Capitol in 1949. Tristano was one of jazz's legion of unjustly-neglected geniuses; his heady, harmonically sophisticated and melodically intricate post loop extended the innovations of Charlie Parker. Tristano and his circle, which included most prominently the tenor saxophonist Warne Marsh and altoist Lee Konitz, paid great heed to the use of counterpoint in jazz composition and improvisation—a throwback, in a sense, to the earlybazz collectivism of New Orleans. A concern with jazz's contrapuntal properties distinguishes Tristano's first attempts at free-form improvisation. Those initial two Free Jazz sides—titled appropriately, *Intuition,* and *Digression*—were an outgrowth of experiments Tristano had conducted in private and, occasionally, in his nightclub sets. The free music recorded by Tristano's ensemble (Konitz, Marsh, guitarist Billy Bauer and bassist Arnold Fishkin) had no preordained themes or harmonies, no distinct formal structure or tonality. While tentative and somewhat unsatisfying to modern ears (due in part to a certain rhythmic stasis characteristic in general of Tristano), these tracks were without precedent in recorded jazz. Unfortunately, the music went unissued by Capitol for several years; it's uncertain just how influential Tristano was to the first wave of Free players. His music more directly affected the "cool school" of the 1950s. Certainly, freedom was "in the air," though it would be some time before it would spark a revolution.

That had to wait almost another decade. The years directly following Tristano's discoveries yielded intimations of the coming "New Thing," but it wasn't until 1958, when a young Texas-born and California-based alto saxophonist Ornette Coleman recorded his first album, "Something Else!," that the Free Jazz movement, as we know it, began. Coleman reached his first level of musical maturity in his home town of Fort Worth, playing alto in a style derived from Charlie Parker. In the early '50s, Coleman moved to Los Angeles and worked at a non-musical day job, studying music theory books and developing his own ideas of how jazz could be played. After suffering through repeated rejections by members of the local jazz elite, Coleman was befriended by the established bassist Red Mitchell, whose influence reportedly gained Coleman his first recording session for the Contemporary label. "Something Else!," the resulting LP, was a qualified success; the music was representative of his work mostly to the extent that it highlighted his compositions and the rapport he shared with Don Cherry. Coleman's next album, "Tomorrow is the Question," was more fully-realized, the band stripped of the piano that had cluttered up the first session. On 1959's "The Shape of Jazz to Come," his first album for the Atlantic label, Coleman brought together for the first time in the studio several of the musicians with whom he was to make his most enduring statements—Cherry, bassist Charlie Haden and drummer Billy Higgins. In the decade of the '60s, with this quartet and other groups featuring such soon-to-be Free Jazz icons as drummers Charles Moffett and Ed Blackwell, tenor saxophonist Dewey Redman, and bassists Scott LaFaro, Jimmy Garrison, and David Izenzon, Coleman would make a series of albums for Atlantic and Blue Note that permanently altered the face of jazz. These included such seminal documents as "Change of the Century," "At the Golden Circle, Volumes 1 and 2," and "Free Jazz"—the album that was to lend its name to the movement it epitomized.

Much of what Coleman did had ample precedent: his music swung in a relatively conventional sense; he used a traditional instrumentation (bard saxophonist Gerry Mulligan was only the most prominent of Coleman's predecessors to have recently dispensed with the piano); his lines—both improvised and composed—clearly reflected the rhythmic contours of bebop.

It was Coleman's manipulation of jazz's basic elements that was unusual. First and most obvious was the manner in which he dealt with tonality. Coleman's tunes were, essentially, very creative and quirky bebop "heads," melodically conceived, with simple harmonic underpinnings of secondary importance. Early Coleman tunes like "Chronology" or "Bird Food" were straight 4/4 swingers taken at a fast tempo, with tonal (or modal) harmonies implied in both the melody and the bass. The structures of these compositions were fairly ordinary; the way they were played was not. Coleman played bebop alto like a Rhythm & Blues shouter. His solos were vocalized to an extent unheard of in the self-possessed world of modern jazz. Drummer Shelly Manne said that when Coleman played, "he sounds like a person crying...or a person laughing." Coleman's phrases were chromatic in the extreme. The utter simplification of his harmonic accompaniment allowed for maximum freedom in his improvisations. Liberated from the need to "make the changes," Coleman's creative choices were unencumbered by the exigencies of functional harmony's consonant/dissonant relationship. His improvisational strategies were built, not on the composition's prescribed harmonies, but on its melody and the contingencies of performance. After the head was stated, his forms grew organically out of the interaction between the musicians. This shift in improvisational emphasis, from an adherence to a predetermined structure to the spontaneous interchange of ideas among the players, was the most revolutionary aspect of Coleman's music.

Following Coleman's innovations, a growing number of musicians turned to Free Jazz, excited by the seemingly unlimited possibilities of this new music. While

Coleman worked in the foreground of the public consciousness, most of these other players practiced their art in relative obscurity. Pianist Cecil Taylor studied classical music at the New England Conservatory in the early '50s, before devoting himself to jazz later in the decade. Initially influenced by straightahead pianists like Horace Silver and Thelonious Monk, Taylor eventually developed a concept that did away with tempo and functional harmony. Possessed of perhaps the most astounding technique of any jazz pianist ever, Taylor's mature music was a highly-energized tempest of freely improvised atonality. He continued to be a catalytic presence into the late '90s. Many of the players who passed through the early Taylor ensembles—soprano saxophonist Steve Lacy, drummer Sunny Murray, alto saxophonist Jimmy Lyons, and tenor saxophonist Archie Shepp—became forces on the scene. In 1964, Shepp's collaborator, the trumpeter Bill Dixon, organized a series of Free Jazz concerts at a New York cafe called "The October Revolution in Jazz," which presented many of the artists who would determine the direction of Free Jazz in the '60s and '70s—players like the trombonist Roswell Rudd, drummer Milford Graves, pianist/band-leader Sun Ra. The event went far in establishing Free Jazz as a movement, and led later that year to the founding of The Jazz Composers Guild, an ephemeral yet influential performance collective that counted Taylor, the pianist Paul They, and composer Carla They among its members. While these early Free players worked mostly underground, the music's second major figure carried out his experiments in full view of the jazz public. Unlike Ornette Coleman, John Coltrane came up through the ranks of the jazz mainstream, spending time in the bands of Dizzy Gillespie, Earl Bostic, and, most notably, Miles Davis, as a member of the latter's first great quintet. By the time Ornette had first attracted the jazz public's attention in the late '50s, Coltrane was already well-known as one of the most far-sighted hard-loop tenor saxophonists. Up to that point, Coltrane's greatest contribution had been his expansion of the jazz vocabulary; with each successive recording, one can hear him chafing at the bounds of tradition through the use of ever-more sophisticated harmonic, rhythmic, and melodic techniques in his improvisations. Where Coleman bypassed the theoretical implications of common jazz practice-largely by inventing his own system—Coltrane delved deeper into jazz's conventional harmony and rhythm than anyone before him. In the same year (1959) that Coleman defined his art by reducing jazz's tonal base to its bare essence, Coltrane increased the complexity of jazz harmony many times over with the recording of his epochal "Giant Steps." That album's and title cut remains the quintessence of jazz harmonic intricacy.

After "Giant Steps," Coltrane seemed to recognize the need for a greater contextual simplicity. Always an emotional player, Coltrane looked for ways in which he might obtain greater freedom to express his personal spirituality. In 1960, inspired by his experiences with Miles Davis, Coltrane began an extended exploration of modal jazz. The wealth of melodic choices given a soloist within such a system (a system somewhat like that which Ornette Coleman had simultaneously, yet independently, developed) appealed to Coltrane, and he began using it to his own ends. Over the next several years he recorded a series of modally-inclined albums that culminated in the late-1964 recording of his studio masterwork, "A Love Supreme," a heartfelt offering to God which featured the saxophonist's great quartet with pianist McCoy Tyner, bassist Jimmy Garrison, and drummer Elvin Jones.

It was at this point that Coltrane began to embrace Free Jazz in earnest. The year 1965 saw Coltrane recording a series of albums that became progressively more free in content, beginning with "John Coltrane Quartet Plays . . .," and including "Transition," "Kulu se Mama," "Om," "Meditations," and "Ascension"—Coltrane's large-group parallel to Ornette Coleman's "Free Jazz." Until his tragically premature death in 1967 at the age of 40, Coltrane continued to work in the realm of Free Jazz, experimenting with a variety of instrumentations and structures for improvisation. It's interesting that, over the years, Coltrane's saxophone playing did not change nearly as drastically as did the background provided by his accompanists. Though he did alternately expand and contract his phrasing a bit in his later work, Coltrane's manner of improvising remained essentially the same; his searing intensity and extraordinary facility never waned. What changed was his musical surroundings. A literal sense of swing was ever-present in Coltrane's early-'60s music; Elvin Jones played with a great deal of rhythmic flexibility, but was always grounded by a sense of pulse. Jones' successor, Rashied Ali, loosened time to a significant degree. While he still "swung," Ali's tempt fluctuated by design. His concept was altogether more coloristic; he would often drive the ensemble with waves of free rhythm. By 1966, Coltrane had replaced the explicit muscularity of pianist McCoy Tyner with the more ambiguous textures of his wife Alice Coltrane. Also added to the mix was the tenor saxophonist Pharoah Sanders, whose screaming multiphonic attack ignored the horn's basic tenets of sound production. This later music was raw and asymmetrical: intelligent, to be sure, but almost totally at the service of emotion and physicality. In his last years Coltrane transcended jazz, looking to create a more universal music by incorporating non-Western devices and instruments; no musician did more to expand the definition of jazz than he.

Music Map

Significant Avant-Garde/
Free Jazz Players

John Coltrane - tenor, soprano
Ornette Coleman - alto, composer
Cecil Taylor - piano
Eric Dolphy - alto, flute, bass clarinet
Sun Ra - keyboards, arranger, bandleader
Anthony Braxton - alto, clarinet, composer

Other Important Players

Alto Saxophone	
Roscoe Mitchell	Jimmy Lyons
Sonny Simmons	Joseph Jarman
Oliver Lake	Julius Hemphill
Henry Threadgill	Arthur Blythe
Tim Berne	John Zorn

Baritone Saxophone
Hamiett Bluiett

Bass

Charlie Haden	Gary Peacock
Reggie Workman	Jimmy Garrison
David Izenzon	Malachi Favors
Dave Holland	Cecil McBee
William Parker	Barry Guy

Bass Clarinet
David Murray

Clarinet
John Carter
Perry Robinson
Marty Ehrlich
Don Byron

Drums

Ed Blackwell	Elvin Jones
Rashied Ali	Charles Moffett
Andrew Cyrille	Sunny Murray
Don Moye	Beaver Harris
Barry Altschul	Paul Motian
Gerry Hemingway	Joey Baron
Han Bennink	

Flute
James Newton

Guitar
Sonny Sharrock
James "Blood" Ulmer
Derek Bailey

Piano

Paul Bley	Andrew Hill
Ran Blake	Mulah Richard Abrams
Don Pullen	Marilyn Crispell
Myra Melford	

Soprano Saxophone
Steve Lacy
Evan Parker

Tenor Saxophone

Archie Shepp	Pharoah Sanders
Albert Ayler	Sam Rivers
Evan Parker	David Murray
Peter Brotzmann	Charles Gayle
James Carter	

Trombone

Roswell Rudd	Grachan Moncur III
Albert Mangelsdorff	George Lewis
Craig Harris	Ray Anderson

Trumpet

Booker Little	Don Cherry
Lester Bowie	Bobby Bradford
Kenny Wheeler	Leo Smith

Violin
Leroy Jenkins
Billy Bang
Mark Feldman

Vocalists - Female
Betty Carter
Jeanne Lee
Jay Clayton
Kate Hammett-Vaughan

Coleman and Coltrane were of monolithic importance in the development of Free Jazz, but that's not to say that there weren't others who, in those formative times, made major contributions. Los Angeles born multi-reedist Eric Dolphy's first high profile gig came as a member of drummer Chico Hamilton's band in 1958. The next year he moved to New York and became a member of Charles Mingus' piano-less quartet, where he formed a front line with the trumpeter Ted Curson. His fleet and harmonically unpredictable style on flute, bass clarinet, and alto sax was, in it's way, as radical as Coleman's, only Dolphy worked—in the beginning, at least—within jazz's customary frameworks. Dolphy was briefly a member of Coltrane's classic band, before striking out on his own, recording a series of modal/free albums of an increasingly high quality that peaked with the remark-

able "Out to Lunch" in February 1964. Dolphy's untimely death four months later robbed the music of a dogged visionary.

Tenor saxophonist Albert Ayler fomented a revolution of sorts by virtue of his near-total indifference to the jazz that came before him. Ayler was born in Cleveland, where he was taught the basics of music by his saxophone-playing father. Some of his earliest performances took place in church; aspects of the African-American sanctified worship service characterized Ayler's mature style, with its ecstatic and cathartic whoops and screams. Reputedly, the young Ayler was conversant with bebop, though there is no convincing recorded evidence to support this thesis. Indeed, Ayler's music avoided the values of modern jazz; his art was, instead, a personal type of abstract expressionism made possible by the new aesthetic. His group concept was extremely free—Ayler used simple, hymn-like melodic materials played out-of-time and developed collectively. His saxophone technique was derived from the instrument's capacity for speed and tonal flexibility. Ayler's high-energy approach influenced Free Jazz saxophonists of his own time, and the generations to follow; John Coltrane took note of and was influenced by Ayler, who played at the former's funeral in 1967. Ayler himself died in 1970 at the age of 34—like so many of the greatest jazz musicians, well before his time.

The hyper-dense free improvisation of late-Coltrane and Ayler was the music's dominant strain in the late '60; at the same time, however, another group of players had begun working along very different lines. The musicians of the Coleman/Coltrane axis lived and worked mostly in New York City; this new movement was located in Chicago, and its priorities were considerably different.

The Association for the Advancement of Creative Musicians (AACM) was an outgrowth of the Chicago pianist/composer Muhal Richard Abrams' Experimental Band, an early '60s ensemble dedicated to finding new methods of jazz composition and performance. Members of the AACM included the saxophonists Anthony Braxton, Joseph Jarman, and Roscoe Mitchell, violinist Leroy Jenkins, drummer Steve McCall, and trumpeter Lester Bowie. Music of the various AACM players was characterized in the main by a concern for the use of textural contrast and compositional structure. Their early albums, such as Mitchell's "Sound" and Jarman's "Song For" defined a new, restrained concept that placed a premium on the use of unadorned space in the process of free improvisation. The Chicagoans' preoccupation with structure and silence was a logical reaction to the no-holds barred energy music preferred by the New York musicians.

By the end of the '70s, the AACM sensibility had gained ascendance. Members and associates like Braxton, saxophonist Henry Threadgill, and drummer Jack DeJohnette led important bands; Mitchell, Jarman, Bowie, bassist Malachi Favors, and drummer Don Moye formed the Art Ensemble of Chicago, the decade's preeminent Free Jazz group. In St. Louis, an AACM-like organization, the Black Artists Group (BAG), produced saxophonists Oliver Lake, Julius Hemphill, and Hamiet Bluiett—three-fourths of the World Saxophone Quartet, which in the '80s would become perhaps the most commercially-successful of all Free Jazz ensembles.

The '70s and '80s saw a greater awareness of Free Jazz in Europe; in England, the saxophonist Evan Parker developed an extraordinary method of improvisation that relied upon the technique known as circular-breathing. Parker was able to play the most complex lines without pause and at the most incredible speed. Also British, the guitarist Derek Bailey pioneered the use of alternative tunings and unusual effects; he also wrote a notable text on various aspects of musical improvisation. In the Soviet Union, the trio of pianist Vyacheslav Ganelin, percussionist Vladimir Tarasov, and saxophonist Vladimir Checkasin played a vital form of Free Jazz that combined elements of their own national musical tradition with the American high-energy aesthetic. In Norway, the saxophonist Jan Garbarek played a lyrical, folkish music reminiscent of Coltrane at his most tuneful. The German tenor saxophonist Peter Brotzman was a force of nature, playing a music reminiscent of Ayler, yet informed by the European art music continuum. In the '70s and '80s, Free Jazz truly became an international music, its many European practitioners by and large as accomplished and as critically acclaimed as their American counterparts.

The '80s and '90s were a period of both consolidation and fragmentation for Free Jazz. Innovation, where it existed, occurred in smaller increments. The older generation of musicians continued producing. Anthony Braxton continued his melding of jazz and contemporary classical music; Cecil Taylor refined his prodigious pianistic technique; Don Cherry, Charlie Haden, Dewey Redman and Ed Blackwell formed the quartet "Old and New Dreams," in tribute to their old boss, Ornette Coleman. As for Ornette, he reasserted his influence by adapting his concept of free polyphony (which he came to call "harmolodics") to funk music. Sun Ra, the mystic keyboardist/composer/philosopher, reached his greatest level of prominence. He led his long-lived "Arkestra" until his death in 1993; his group's highly theatrical performance style and the leader's eccentric personality drew attention away from a rather erratic and not always successful stylistic melange.

Younger musicians appeared, the most influential of whom was probably the tenor saxophonist David Murray. Murray came on the scene in the mid-'70s; he initially played tenor in a Free Expressionist style similar to that of Albert Ayler, except Murray displayed a greater interest in the whole of jazz's development. As the fourth member of the World Saxophone Quartet, Murray became that group's most volatile soloist and composer. With his own groups, Murray showed a consistent growth, bringing the opposing realms of mainstream and Free Jazz ever closer. By the late '90s, he had arguably become jazz's most conceptually well-rounded musician.

Other musicians who came on the scene in the '80s and '90s are too numerous to list; a few include the phenomenally dextrous pianist Borah Bergman, the timbrally-prescient saxophonist/trumpeter Joe McPhee, the powerful Free/Funk drummer Ronald Shannon Jackson, and the texturally inspired pianist Marilyn Crispell. In 1986, the Knitting Factory, a new night club on New York's Lower East Side,

opened, and quickly became the center of Free Jazz activity in the city. A great many of the most prominent Free players of the late '90s became inextricably linked to the club, including the influential conceptualist composer/alto saxophonist John Zorn, the jaggedly lyrical trumpeter Dave Douglas, and the explosively Ayler-esque tenor saxophonist Charles Gayle. Other players making their mark by the end of the decade included pianists Myra Melford and Matthew Shipp, guitarist Joe Morris, saxophonists Tim Berne, Thomas Chapin, Ken Vandermark, Joe Maneri, and David S. Ware, bassist William Parker, trumpeter Herb Robertson, and drummers Joey Baron and Bobby Previte.

The radical self-consciousness possessed by the Free players has led to the creation of some extraordinarily original and ultimately influential music. It sprung from the font of modern jazz, yet very quickly became quite a different thing, something very apart from the populist forms of the music that, even today, define jazz in the public's perception. Free Jazz is, however, a stubborn and resourceful art form, and while it will not (and probably should not) supplant the existing mainstream, it will certainly continue to thrive in its own iconoclastic way.

Twenty Essential Free Jazz Albums

Lennie Tristano, *Intuition* (Capitol)
Ornette Coleman, *The Shape of Jazz to Come* (Atlantic)
Ornette Coleman, *Free Jazz* (Atlantic)
Ornette Coleman, *Dancing in Your Head* (A&M)
John Coltrane, *Ascension* (Impulse),
John Coltrane, *Live in Japan* (Impulse)
Cecil Taylor, *Jazz Advance* (Blue Note)
Cecil Taylor, *For Olim* (A&M)
Eric Dolphy, *Out to Lunch* (Blue Note)
Archie Shepp, *Four For Trane* (Impulse)
Albert Ayler, *At Slug's Saloon, Vols. 1 and 2* (ESP)
Roscoe Mitchell, *Sound* (Delmark)
Art Ensemble of Chicago, *Full Force* (ECM)
Anthony Braxton, *The Complete Braxton* (Arista)
World Saxophone Quartet, *W.S.Q.* (Black Saint)
Ganelin Trio, *New Wine* (Leo)
David Murray, *Children* (Black Saint)
Borah Bergman and Evan Parker, *The Fire Tale* (Soul Note)
Ronald Shannon Jackson, *Barbeque Dog* (Antilles)
Dave Douglas, *Tiny Bell Trio* (Hat Art)

Nine Essential Books about Free Jazz

Four Lives in the Bebop Business, by A.B. Spellman (Limelight Editions, 1966)
The Freedom Principle: Jazz after 1958, by John Litweiler (Wm. Morrow, 1984)
Outcats, by Francis Davis (Oxford University Press, 1990)
Musical Improvisation: Its Nature and Practice in Music, by Derek Bailey (Prentice Hall, 1980)
Forces in Motion: The Music and Thoughts of Anthony Braxton, by Graham Lock
(DaCapo, 1988)
Ornette Coleman: A Harmolodic Life, by John Litweiler (Wm. Morrow, 1992)
Chasin' the Trane, by J.C. Thomas (DaCapo, 1975)
Free Jazz, by Ekkehard Jost (DaCapo,1974)
As Serious as Your Life: The Story of the New Jazz, by Valerie Wilmer (1977)

Important Events

1949 - Lennie Tristano and his sextet record "Intuition" and "Digression," the first jazz free improvisations.

1954 - Shelly Manne, Shorty Rogers and Jimmy Giuffre form an unusual trio at a recording session and perform a couple of free pieces.

1955 - Pianist Cecil Taylor makes his recording debut.
John Coltrane joins the Miles Davis Quintet.
Sun Ra makes first recordings as a bandleader.

1956 - Charles Mingus records "Pithecanthropus Erectus" and starts to greatly free up his music.

1957 - John Coltrane spends a few months with the Thelonious Monk Quartet.

1958 - Eric Dolphy joins the Chico Hamilton Quintet.

Ornette Coleman makes his recording debut for Contemporary.

1959 - Ornette Coleman's Quartet with cornetist Don Cherry, bassist Charlie Haden and drummer Billy Higgins records for Atlantic. Their stint at the Five Spot splits the jazz world.

1960 - John Coltrane forms his "classic quartet" with pianist McCoy Tyner, drummer Elvin Jones and eventually bassist Jimmy Garrison. Coltrane begins doubling on soprano and his recording of "My Favorite Things" becomes very influential.

Ornette Coleman records "Free Jazz."

Charles Mingus leads a quartet with Eric Dolphy, Ted Curson and Dannie Richmond.

Archie Shepp records with Cecil Taylor.

1961 - Jimmy Lyons joins the Cecil Taylor Unit.

Eric Dolphy spends a few months with the John Coltrane Quintet.

Richard Abrams forms the Experimental Band in Chicago.

1962 - Ornette Coleman retires for several years.

Albert Ayler makes his recording debut in Europe.

Sun Ra and his Arkestra resettle in New York.

1963 - Charles Mingus records "The Black Saint and the Sinner Lady."

1964 - Eric Dolphy tours Europe with Charles Mingus just months before his death.

John Coltrane records *A Love Supreme.*

Pharoah Sanders makes recording debut.

Albert Ayler records for ESP and Debut.

Bill Dixon stages four-day "October Revolution in Jazz" and 20 groups participate.

1965 - John Coltrane's music becomes atonal and he records the monumental "Ascension."

Ornette Coleman returns with a new trio featuring bassist

David Izenzon and drummer Charles Moffett.

Archie Shepp emerges as major force recording for Impulse. AACM formed in Chicago.

1966 - John Coltrane forms a new quintet with Alice Coltrane, Pharoah Sanders, Jimmy Garrison and Rashied Ali.

Roscoe Mitchell and his Art Ensemble (soon to be the Art Ensemble of Chicago) make first recordings.

1967 - John Coltrane dies.

1968 - Anthony Braxton makes first records as a leader.

1969 - Pharoah Sanders and Leon Thomas team up for surprising avant-garde pop hit "The Creator Has A Master Plan."

1971 - Albert Ayler dies.

Post-1971 - Too many events to list. The avant-garde has remained an important (if often underground) force in modern jazz.

Jazz-Fusion

Richard S. Ginell

The word "fusion," vague in itself (fusion of what?), has been turned into such a catch-all that it has trivialized what in the 1970s was a vigorous movement in American music. So one must ask two questions, the first of which is, what is fusion? Originally called jazz-rock, the term fusion has been erroneously expanded over the years to take in other forms that are more closely related to easy-listening pop or lightweight R&B—e.g. the Grover Washington Jr./Kenny G brand of instrumentals. Even the term jazz-rock was distorted to accomodate pop-rock groups in the late-1960s who added horns for flavoring (Blood, Sweat and Tears, Chicago, The Ides of March). Yet by the old definition, fusion was a mixture of jazz improvisation and the rhythms, timbres and energy of rock music that began to take hold in the wake of rock's Golden Era of the late-'60s, a much tougher, more driving and more abstract form than those that followed.

The second question is, who invented fusion? Some would point to guitarist Larry Coryell, who brought a rock-oriented tone and attack raw-edged instead of the smooth rounded tones that guitarists employed in jazz—to groups like Free Spirits in 1966 and Gary Burton's jazz group in 1967. Others would note the rock and blues sensibilities that drummer Jack DeJohnette and pianist Keith Jarrett brought to the Charles Lloyd Quartet, which became wildly popular among rock audiences in 1967 even though it used acoustic instruments. From England, jazz organist Brian Auger and the Trinity also developed a rock following in the late-

'60s, borrowing pop influences and clothing styles. One could even go back to 1959 and trace the development from Ray Charles' pioneering use of the Wurlitzer electric piano on his gospel/blues/jazz hit "What'd I Say," which was finally followed up by Joe Zawinul on the Cannonball Adderley Quintet's gospel-tinged hit "Mercy, Mercy, Mercy" in 1966. Or, if you want to get technical about it, maybe the first jazz/rock fusion was the truly bizarre mixture of Dixieland jazz and '50s rock on Elvis Presley's 1958 *King Creole* soundtrack! In other words, there is really no solid consensus on that point.

Music Map

Significant Fusion Players

Guitar

Larry Coryell	John McLaughlin
Al DiMeola	Steve Khan
Allan Holdsworth	Kazumi Watanabe
Hiram Bullock	Mike Stern
Frank Gambale	Scott Henderson

Keyboards

Joe Zawinul	Chick Corea
Herbie Hancock	Jan Hammer
Lyle Mays	Russell Ferrante
Jeff Lorber	

Electric Bass

Jaco Pastorius	Stanley Clarke
Marcus Miller	John Patitucci
Alphonso Johnson	Jamaaladeen Tacuma
Gerald Veasley	Mark Egan

Drums

Billy Cobham	Lenny White
Alphonse Mouzon	Steve Gadd
Jack DeJohnette	Tony Williams
Peter Erskine	Ronald Shannon Jackson
Dave Weckl	Bill Bruford

Composers

Joe Zawinul	Chick Corea
Herbie Hancock	Jaco Pastorius

Soprano

Wayne Shorter

Tenor

Michael Brecker

Trumpet

Miles Davis
Eddie Henderson
Randy Brecker

Vibes

Mike Mainieri

Violin

Jean Luc Ponty
Jerry Goodman
Didier Lockwood
Michael Urbaniak

Yet there seems to be little doubt as to who crystallized the fusion of jazz and rock, made it a vital, original force, and served as a guide and incubator for most of the future leaders of the movement. That would be Miles Davis, ever-curious, ever-restless, sensing the rock and R&B currents in the late-'60s and taking what he needed from them.

As jazz itself was in the Roaring '20s, rock and the parallel boom of soul music were in the air after the 1964 Beatles invasion—and sensitive artists in many fields could not ignore its vitality, nor its effect upon the culture. As the fading jazz scene became a pitched battle between the hard boppers and the angry avant-garde, many alienated or bored musicians began to look to rock, which after a rambunctious birth was rapidly developing into a multi-faceted, wildly-imaginative art form. The introduction of electronic keyboards such as the Wurlitzer and Fender-Rhodes electric pianos, the Hohner clavinet, synthesizers by ARP, Moog, Oberheim and others, plus sound effects devices like the Echoplex and ring modulator, presented pianists with a galaxy of new sounds to explore. The electric guitar became a loud, flashy focal point rather than just a demure solo instrument, and the acoustic bass gave way to the more portable guitar-shaped electric models. And drummers changed their styles, the dotted rhythms of bop giving way to a stiffer rock-oriented emphasis on every beat.

For Miles, fusing jazz and rock was an evolutionary process, taking the idea of using an electric piano from Zawinul, gradually adding more keyboards and electric guitars, getting first Tony Williams and then Jack DeJohnette to tighten up the beat, removing the old harmonic underpinnings, and lacing the solo horns throughout the turbulent texture. The evolution began in late 1967 (the results of which were not released until many years later), and gathered speed through *Miles In The Sky* and *Filles de Kilimanjaro* until the first electric masterpieces *In A Silent Way* and *Bitches Brew* alerted the world that Miles had met rock's challenge head-on. Dense and abstract despite the rock-influenced rhythms, *Bitches Brew* nevertheless turned out to be an unexpected hit upon release in 1970, achieving gold record status and launching the jazz-rock era.

The list of major fusionites who went in and out of Miles' incubator is staggering. There was Herbie Hancock, who left the band and eventually formed his own sextet that probed further into space electronics. Tony Williams split to form his own group Lifetime, a noisy high-energy trio heavily indebted to the fuzztone innovations of Jimi Hendrix. Zawinul and Wayne Shorter teamed up in 1970 to form Weather Report, which carried the jazz/rock banner into the mid-'80s with a flair for imaginative electronic textures, freewheeling improvisation, and a fondness for Third World influences. Guitarist John McLaughlin, first with Lifetime and then on his own with the Mahavishnu Orchestra, perfected a formula of high-volume, rapid-fire unison playing that gained a huge following among rock fans. Keyboardist Chick Corea at first lowered the volume with his Brazilian-influenced first edition of Return To Forever and then cranked it way up in the rock-minded second edition. Jarrett proved to be a combustible swordsman on electronic keyboards, as did Lifetime organist Larry Young.

Other veteran jazzmen began to try out the new form. Cannonball Adderley, of course, had been trading ideas with Miles from the get-go, and his records took on more of an electric jazz/rock flavor for a few years after 1970. Donald Byrd cautiously felt his way into the new field at first, then exploded with one great album *Electric Byrd* before abruptly moving off into jazz/funk, and soul/jazzman Les McCann switched to the Rhodes piano, took up synthesizers and produced some worthwhile fusion albums. Even Ornette Coleman converted, forming Prime Time and setting a funky, complex electric direction that he still follows. Adventurous rock guitarists like Frank Zappa, Jeff Beck and Carlos Santana entered fusion from the other direction; Santana added intense Latin heat to the mixture in his jazz period (1972-75). New fusion stars emerged from the big groups—keyboardist George Duke (Cannonball, Zappa), violinist Jean-Luc Ponty, drummer Billy Cobham and keyboardist Jan Hammer (Mahavishnu), bassist Jaco Pastorius (Weather Report), guitarist Al DiMeola, bassist Stanley Clarke and drummer Lenny White (Return To Forever).

It was a vigorous and heady time in jazz—on the electric side at least—and it seemed as if it would last forever. But well before the end of the '70s, a number of developments scattered the white heat of jazz/rock into diffuse forms that have yet to be sorted out. Miles put a wah-wah pedal on his horn and took the fusion further into a dense jungle of murky electronics that many thought incomprehensible, a direction that ended when he temporarily retired in 1975 for health reasons. Hancock disbanded the Sextet, formed a great best-selling jazz/funk band Headhunters but gradually scattered his energies in several idioms. Jarrett abruptedly renounced electric instruments in favor of his true love, the grand piano, and most keyboardists, including Corea and Hancock, eventually followed suit part or all of the way. McLaughlin pulled the plug on Mahavishnu to form the acoustic India-flavored Shakti and thereafter moved impulsively in and out of electric music. The next wave of electric-oriented groups—like Spyro Gyra and Yellowjackets—largely went into the milder forms of R&B/funk/pop-influenced jazz which ultimately

attracted wider audiences than the real fusion ever did. Moreover the inspiration behind rock itself was fading, co-opted and channeled by its corporate sponsors—and in the '80s, the renaissance of hard bop, accompanied by the widely publicized anti-electric polemics of Wynton Marsalis and his mentor Stanley Crouch, seemed to consign jazz-rock to the dustbin of history.

But not quite. A revived Miles Davis flourished from 1981 until his death with a heavily synthesized continuation of fusion where at last he seemed content to follow other leaders' directions. Zawinul continues to carry out the mission of Weather Report with his groove-oriented electric music, and Corea now and then tours and records with his jazz/rock Elektric Band. Guitarists John Scofield, Pat Metheny and Mike Stern have found their own personal roads to intelligent jazz/rock fusions and younger groups like Medeski, Martin and Wood have resurrected the fusion and funk of the '70s to push it into new directions in the '90s. Though buried underneath a confusing din of misleading labels, the true jazz-rock fusion is still very much with us. — *Richard S. Ginell*

Recommended Fusion Albums

Miles Davis, *In A Silent Way* (Columbia)

Miles Davis, *Bitches Brew* (Columbia, 2-CD set)

Herbie Hancock, *Mwandishi: The Complete Warner Bros. Recordings* (Warner Bros, 2-CD set.)

The Tony Williams Lifetime, *Spectrum: The Anthology* (Verve, 2-CD set)

Weather Report, *Weather Report* (Columbia)

Chick Corea w. Return To Forever, *Return To The Seventh Galaxy* (Verve, 2-CD set)

Carlos Santana and John McLaughlin, *Love, Devotion, Surrender* (Columbia)

Jaco Pastorius, *Jaco Pastorius* (Epic)

John Scofield, *Liquid Fire: The Best Of John Scofield* (Gramavision)

Medeski, Martin and Wood, *Friday Afternoon In The Universe* (Gramavision)

Jazz of the 1980s and '90s: Beyond Fusion

Scott Yanow

One of the most common questions that a newcomer makes when hearing a jazz performance is "What do you call it?" Since the mid-1970s it has become increasingly difficult to describe music as belonging to a certain set style, and one can say that the dominant style since that time has been "No Style!"

From 1915-75 the evolution of jazz moved remarkably fast as boundaries were broken and each style was a movement towards greater freedom and/or sophistication. From New Orleans jazz, classic jazz, Dixieland and swing to bop, cool jazz, hard bop, soul-jazz, free jazz and the avant-garde, the history moved quickly and logically. But after such intense and adventurous improvisers as pianist Cecil Taylor and tenor saxophonist Pharoah Sanders (in his early days) emerged, it became obvious that jazz could not get any freer. In fact, it could be said of tenor saxophonist Albert Ayler, whose music advanced from screaming sound explorations to early New Orleans-type marching bands, went so far ahead that he eventually came in at the beginning!

The rise of fusion in the late 1960s gave jazz a possible alternative future, borrowing aspects of creative rock (chiefly its sound, rhythms and volume) to revitalize improvised music. However not every jazz musician wanted to follow the newer trend and switch to electronics (nor should they have had to) and, with the decline of rock as a creative force in the mid-'70s, fusion became less significant within a few years.

Since that time detractors have complained that jazz is no longer advancing and that it has reached the end of its evolution. Although there is a little truth in that belief, the reality is much more complex. Since jazz had reached the "end" of its search for freedom, it was now up to younger players to develop their own sounds out of the innovations of the past rather than to merely break down new boundaries. "New" was no longer considered automatically superior to "old," so playing inventive swing or bop should not be thought of as old hat. In addition, because there was no longer any one dominant figure (on the level of a John Coltrane or Charlie Parker) whose every movement was being copied, jazz seemed to be aimless when in fact it was shooting out in a countless number of directions at the same time. Some artists stuck to playing in older styles, others mixed together different idioms or fused jazz with types of World Music. Acoustic instruments made a comeback while the electronic ones continued to be important. In the late 1990s, it seems as if every style of jazz (and all kinds of unique mixtures) was being played. Billboard Magazine did the jazz world a disservice by splitting its jazz sales chart into two: Traditional and Contemporary. While what it calls "Traditional" jazz (sometimes also mistakenly dubbed Mainstream) uses a 4/4 walking bass, "Contemporary Jazz" (which is often more conservative than what is listed as "Traditional") is an all-encompassing term that includes practically any music with funky rhythms including fusion, crossover, instrumental pop and R&B by jazz players.

Music Map

Jazz of the 1980s and 1990s: Beyond Fusion

The 1970s
The decline of fusion • The continued growth of avant-garde • The comeback of mainstream jazz

The Avant-Garde

Cecil Taylor
Ornette Coleman
Anthony Braxton
Sonny Simmons
Tim Berne
Henry Threadgill
Oliver Lake
Authur Blythe
John Zorn
Hamiet Bluiett
David Murray
Sam Rivers
Evan Parker
Charles Gayle
Albert Mangelsdorff
Craig Harris
Herb Robertson
Dave Douglas
Mark Feldman
Derek Bailey
James Newton
Ron Blake
Muhal Richard Abrams
Jon Jang
Myra Melford
Marilyn Crispell
Reggie Workman
William Parker
Barry Guy
Gerry Hemingway
Han Bennink
Joey Baron
Bill Frisell

Post-Bop
Based in hard bop, but also open to the influences of the Miles Davis Quintet of the mid-'60s and aspects of the avant-garde, as well as touches of funk and R&B.

Fusion to Crossover
In the tradition of Grover Washington, Jr., and David Sanborn (both jazz players improvising with heavy R&B inspiration), crossover is essentially instrumental pop with jazz and R&B flourishes.

Mainstream to Dixieland

New generation of swing players:

Scott Hamilton
Warren Vache
Dan Barrett
Ken Peplowski
Randy Sandke
Hal Smith
Howard Alden

Post-Bop Survivors

Chick Corea
Herbie Hancock
Joe Henderson
McCoy Tyner
Elvin Jones
Sonny Rollins
John Scofield
Pat Metheny
Michael Brecker
Joe Lovano
Kenny Garrett

Crossover Stars
Kenny G.
George Howard
Richard Elliot
Dave Koz

Latin Jazz
Tito Puente
Poncho Sanchez
Ray Barreto

The Young Lions
Wynton Marsalis
Terence Blanchard
Wallace Roney
Roy Hargrove
Philip Harper
Marlon Jordan
Nicholas Payton
Marcus Roberts
Benny Green
Donald Harrison
Christopher Hollyday
Branford Marsalis
Joshua Redman

New Age Influences
Keith Jarrett
Oregon
Paul Horn
Paul Winter

Modern Big Band Leaders
Rob McConnell
Gerald Wilson
Bill Holman
Bob Florence
Maria Schneider
Carla Bley

The Future of Jazz?
James Carter

Advertisers and publicists have followed suit in adopting these terms, leading to quite a bit of polarization and confusion. Pre-bop styles are ignored and the avant-garde (is Anthony Braxton "contemporary" or "traditional"?) is treated as if it does not exist.

In reality all styles of jazz have continued to exist in the 1980s and '90s and a more accurate division would be achieved by listing four general areas of music and realizing that these are only guides: Post Bop, the Avant-Garde, Fusion to Crossover and Mainstream to Dixieland. Post Bop has hard bop as its base while being open to the influences of the Miles Davis Quintet of the mid-1960s, aspects

of the avant-garde and touches of R&B and funk. Straightahead jazz was very overshadowed by fusion and rock throughout the 1970s but late in the decade the tide began to turn. Wynton Marsalis, a virtuosic 18-year old trumpeter, became a star soloist with Art Blakey's Jazz Messengers. His rise to fame as an articulate spokesman for jazz ended a decade in which few new trumpeters emerged. Because early on he played hard bop with a sound closely resembling Miles Davis in the mid-'60s and he was followed by other young players who started out in a similar spot, Marsalis soon became known as the leader of the Young Lions. Major labels went out of their way to sign and record these developing talents, some of whom were not quite mature yet. Most of the well-dressed musicians have since developed into strong voices but their early (and sometimes premature) prominence did result in a backlash by fans of more adventurous music, particularly after Marsalis made some provocative statements about the avant-garde and 1970s music in general. However the Young Lions (which also include trumpeters Terence Blanchard, Wallace Roney, Roy Hargrove, Philip Harper, Marlon Jordan and most recently Nicholas Payton, pianists Marcus Roberts and Benny Green, altoists Donald Harrison and Christopher Hollyday and tenor saxophonists Branford Marsalis and Joshua Redman along with quite a few others) have continued to improve year-by-year and now cover a much wider range of music than they had earlier on. Also their presence has greatly improved the image of jazz. No longer are jazz musicians portrayed in the media as social outcasts who are often drug addicts and incapable of playing other kinds of music or relating to the average human being. Since the Young Lions are generally classically-trained, clean-cut and highly intelligent in a conventional (as well as an intuitive) way, jazz itself has gained a great deal of additional respect.

In addition to the Young Lions, older survivors found more opportunities to record during the 1980s and '90s than they had in the 1970s. Straightahead music rose in popularity and whether it be fusion giants Chick Corea and Herbie Hancock (both of whom alternated between acoustic piano and synthesizers), masters from the 1960s such as tenor saxophonist Joe Henderson (who became surprisingly popular without changing his music in the slightest due to a very successful marketing campaign by Verve), pianist McCoy Tyner and drummer Elvin Jones or the immortal tenorman Sonny Rollins, jazz was finally showing its tradition proper respect.

The term Post Bop can also be applied to any style that is more advanced than bebop but not as free as the avant-garde. Falling into this area at times are guitarists John Scofield (whose distinctive distorted sound sometimes masks a bop-oriented sensibility), the versatile guitarist Pat Metheny, tenor saxophonists Michael Brecker (on his own projects) and Joe Lovano and altoist Kenny Garrett. In fact, the post bop field is quite overcrowded with major players and fresh voices.

Fusion started declining in the mid-1970s but it is still an exciting style when played with creativity. Chick Corea's Elektric Band, guitarist Kazumi Watanabe and Scott Henderson's Tribal Tech are examples of top fusion artists of the 1990s. However the offshoots of fusion are not always at the same level.

While fusion is the mixture of jazz improvisation with rock rhythms, jazz has also been mixed with other styles of music. The popular Spyro Gyra and saxophonists Grover Washington Jr. and David Sanborn infused their jazz improvising with heavy doses of R&B. Although guilty at times of making predictable records, these performers are capable of producing colorful music when playing live in concert.

During the 1980s and '90s scores of saxophonists did their best to imitate the sounds of Washington and Sanborn and, although their records generally sold well, from the jazz standpoint most of their efforts were rather dubious, essentially adding R&B-ish solos to what would otherwise be pop records. Dubbed "Contemporary Jazz" but more accurately called "Crossover" (the more jazz-oriented of the performances) or "Instrumental Pop" (outside of jazz), these artists were best-sellers but added less to jazz than one would hope. Kenny G., whose records made the pop charts, became the musician jazz fans loved to hate but he at least had his own attractive sound (based partly on Grover Washington). The music of saxophonists George Howard (a close imitation of Washington), Richard Elliot (a limited R&B player) and Dave Koz were generally irrelevant to jazz but still listed on the jazz charts (and they were sometimes booked at jazz festivals). With the rise in the 1990s of the "Smooth Jazz" format on radio, far too many musicians were tailoring their recordings specifically to satisfy indifferent radio programmers and be played on the air rather than creating music to satisfy their own musical soul.

Another trend but less significant in the long run was the popularity for a time of New Age music. Essentially relaxing background music that always stayed in the same soothing mood (serving as "healing music," presumably for those with too much exposure to heavy metal!), the idiom had its origin in some of Keith Jarrett's piano solos (a major influence on the New Age pacesetter George Winston), the folk/jazz/World Music group Oregon, the solo performances of Paul Horn and Paul Winter, classical guitar and some of the more introverted recordings on the ECM label. Championed by the Windham Hill company, New Age hit its peak in the late 1980s but eventually dropped greatly in popularity due to its limited emotional range. Because the blues are noticeably absent even when New Age players are improvising, New Age is outside of jazz and has since gone back to being strictly meditation music.

In contrast, the avant-garde has continued to thrive artistically even if it has a lower profile now than it did when it garnered headlines in the 1960s. The deaths of John Coltrane (1967) and Albert Ayler (1970) left unfillable gaps as did the decisions of Archie Shepp and Pharoah Sanders to eventually play more traditional music. However the gradual rise of a generation of players originally based in Chi-

cago and associated with the AACM (including the Art Ensemble Of Chicago, multi-reedist Anthony Braxton and trumpeter Leo Smith) gave the music new life. Rather than sticking to high-energy and unremittingly dense music, these musicians and their contemporaries added the use of silence, dynamics, variety and even melodies to the avant-garde.

In the 1970s many of the more advanced musicians played in small lofts in New York City for a time, a movement that almost escaped documentation. Artists began to record for their own private labels and, although it has remained difficult to make a living playing free music, openings in the education field (plus the proliferation of opportunities in Europe) have resulted in many of the avant-garde musicians enjoying a more stable lifestyle than their predecessors. With the opening of the Knitting Factory in New York City in the late 1980s (which has served as a homebase for dozens of artists) and the founding of many new record labels (including Black Saint/Soul Note in Italy), the music lives on. Among the more recent pacesetters are such veterans as pianist Cecil Taylor (who has not mellowed with age), altoist Ornette Coleman (whose fusion of avant-garde jazz with funk in the mid-'70s with his Prime Time group essentially founded free funk and helped to inspire altoists Steve Coleman and Greg Osby) and Anthony Braxton plus altoists Sonny Simmons (who made a comeback after two decades of obscurity in the mid-1990s), Tim Berne, Henry Threadgill, Oliver Lake, Arthur Blythe and John Zorn, baritonist Hamiet Bluiett, David Murray (on tenor and bass clarinet), tenors Sam Rivers, Evan Parker and the ferocious Charles Gayle, trombonists Albert Mangelsdorff and Craig Harris, trumpeters Herb Robertson and Dave Douglas, violinist Mark Feldman, guitarist Derek Bailey, flutist James Newton, pianists Ran Blake, Muhal Richard Abrams, Jon Jang (who mixes together jazz influenced by Charles Mingus with his Asian heritage), Myra Melford and Marilyn Crispell, bassists Reggie Workman, William Parker and Barry Guy and drummers Gerry Hemingway, Han Bennink and Joey Baron among many others. Guitarist Bill Frisell created colorful and eccentric music by combining his unpredictable flights and episodic ideas with a vast amount of unique sounds drawn from country music, intense rock and even Jim Hall.

Of more traditional styles, the overlapping Dixieland, classic jazz and New Orleans jazz genres continue to prosper in their own way through a countless number of weekend jazz festivals, documentation on such labels as Stomp Off, Jazzology, GHB and Arbors and in the worthy jazz monthly The Mississippi Rag. Mainstream jazz (modern small-group swing) was increasingly off records during the 1960s but by the mid-'70s was making a comeback thanks to such labels as Chiaroscuro and Norman Granz's Pablo company. The emergence of tenor saxophonist Scott Hamilton and cornetist Warren Vache in the late 1970s (preceding Wynton Marsalis by a few years) was a major shock for not only was this duo playing creatively within the prebop swing style, but they were both in their early '20s! Since that time a whole generation of younger swing players has emerged (including trombonist Dan Barrett, clarinetist-tenor Ken Peplowski, trumpeter Randy Sandke, drummer Hal Smith and guitarist Howard Alden) to join such veterans as guitarist-singer Marty Grosz, pianist Ralph Sutton and cornetist Ruby Braff in keeping the 1930s style alive and well. The Concord label has released a countless number of rewarding albums that show that mainstream jazz is very much alive and its Picante subsidiary documented the viable Latin jazz scene (including Tito Puente, Poncho Sanchez and Ray Barretto).

In addition to these styles, jazz of the 1990s has been played by many modern big bands. Unlike in earlier years when the jazz orchestras toured and were headed by colorful instrumentalists, very few large bands of the '90s leave their homebase except on rare occasions (the ghost bands such as Count Basie's are exceptions) and nearly all are headed by arranger-composers who provide their own material. Frequent recordings make many listeners think that groups led by Rob McConnell (his Boss Brass performs in public maybe ten days a year), Gerald Wilson, Bill Holman, Bob Florence, Maria Schneider and Carla Bley are full-time affairs but most of them do not work more often than the typical local stage band.

But jazz itself seems to be quite healthy as the 1990s draw to a close. Although it has not regained its place as America's popular music, there is more activity going on at this moment than ever before and never before have so many recordings been available. Possibly the best symbol for jazz in the 1990s is saxophonist James Carter, a gifted and young musician who has shown the ability to play creatively in nearly every style, from New Orleans jazz, swing and early R&B to bop and the avant-garde. His solos are both highly original and constantly borrowing from the tradition, sometimes being quite overcrowded, explosive (often changing directions without warning) and impatient but constantly taking chances and never taking it easy or relying on mere cliches. Jazz at its best! — *Scott Yanow*

Twenty-Five Essential Recordings of the 1980s and '90s (all styles)

Howard Alden/Dan Barrett, *ABQ Salutes Buck Clayton* (Concord Jazz)

Geri Allen, *In The Year Of The Dragon* (Verve)

Art Blakey, *Keystone 3* (Concord Jazz)

Ruby Braff, *A Sailboat In The Moonlight* (Concord Jazz)
Michael Brecker, *Michael Brecker* (MCA/Impulse)
James Carter, *Jurassic Classics* (DIW/Columbia)
Kenny Garrett, *Pursuance* (Warner Bros.)
Jerry Gonzalez, *Rhumba Para Monk* (Sunnyside)
George Gruntz Concert Jazz Band, *Fist Prize* (Enja)
Roy Hargrove, *Of Kindred Souls* (Novus)
Joe Henderson, *Lush Life* (Verve)
Keith Jarrett, *Bye Bye Blackbird* (ECM)
Joe Lovano, *Rush Hour* (Blue Note)
Branford Marsalis, *Trio Jeepy* (Columbia)
Wynton Marsalis, *Black Codes From The Underground* (Columbia)
Wynton Marsalis, *In This House, On This Morning* (Columbia)
Jackie McLean, *Dynasty* (Triloka)
Pat Metheny, *Letter From Home* (Geffen)
Mingus Big Band, *Nostalgia In Times Square* (Dreyfus)
David Murray, *Hope Scope* (Black Saint)
Buell Neidlinger, *Blue Chopsticks* (K2B2)
James Newton, *The African Flower* (Blue Note)
Tito Puente, *Goza Me Timbal* (Concord Picante)
John Scofield, *Hand Jive* (Blue Note)
Yellowjackets, *Four Corners* (MCA)

Five Essential Books About Jazz of the 1980s and '90s

Forces In Motion (Anthony Braxton) by Graham Lock (Da Capo Press, 1988)
Jazz—The 1980s Resurgence by Stuart Nicholson (Da Capo Press, 1990)
Outcats by Frances Davis (Oxford Univ. Press, 1990)
Rhythm-A-Ning by Gary Giddins (Oxford Univ. Press, 1985)
Talking Jazz by Ben Sidran (Da Capo Press, 1995)

Fusion, Crossover and Instrumental Pop

Important Events

1967 - Miles Davis uses electric piano (Herbie Hancock) in quintet for first time.
   Blues/rock guitarist Larry Coryell joins Gary Burton's quartet to form one of first fusion groups.
1968 - Chick Corea replaces Herbie Hancock with Miles Davis; plays electric piano for the first time.
   Blood, Sweat and Tears uses a horn section in a rock setting.
1969 - Miles Davis records early fusion classics *In a Silent Way* and *Bitches Brew* with expanded bands of young all stars.
   Tony Williams heads Lifetime, a trio with John McLaughlin and Larry Young.
1971 - Joe Zawinul and Wayne Shorter team up to form Weather Report.
   John McLaughlin forms Mahavishnu Orchestra.
1972 - The first edition of Chick Corea's Return to Forever records two albums.
1973 - Chick Corea teams up with Bill Connors, Stanley Clarke and Lenny White in Return to Forever; they record *Hymn of the Seventh Galaxy*.
   Herbie Hancock forms the Headhunters and has a big hit with "Chameleon."
   Ornette Coleman founds "free funk" with formation of Prime Time.
1974 - Al DiMeola replaces Bill Connors with Return To Forever. Grover Washington, Jr., a major influence in combining R&B with jazz, records "Mr. Magic."
1975 - Due to bad health Miles Davis retires for six years. David Sanborn records first album as leader.
   John McLaughlin switches to acoustic guitar and performs with World Music group Shakti.
   The Brecker Brothers record their first joint album.
1976 - Jaco Pastorius joins Weather Report.
   "Birdland" is a huge hit for Weather Report.
   Return To Forever breaks up. Al DiMeola begins his solo career.
   George Benson has pop vocal hit with "This Masquerade."
1977 - Spyro Gyra records first album.
   Jeff Lorber forms the Jeff Lorber Fusion, a group that would soon feature Kenny G. on saxophones.

Music Map

Significant Crossover/Instrumental Pop Players

Alto

David Sanborn	Sadao Watanabe
Jay Beckenstein	Brandon Fields
Marc Russo	

Tenor

Michael Brecker	Grover Washington, Jr.
Tom Scott	Ernie Watts
Bill Evans	John Klemmer
Wilton Felder	

Trumpet

Chuck Mangione
Tom Browne
Rick Braun

Soprano

Grover Washington, Jr.	George Howard
Kenny G.	Bill Evans

Guitar

Earl Klugh
Lee Ritenour
Larry Carlton

Keyboards

David Benoit	Joe Sample
George Winston	George Duke
Patrice Rushen	Bob James

Arranger

Don Sebesky
Bob James
Dave Grusin

Chuck Mangione has a big hit in "Feels So Good."
1978 - Pat Metheny makes his first recording with his Group.
1979 - Mike Mainieri forms Steps (later Steps Ahead).
   Ronald Shannon Jackson forms his Decoding Society.
1980 - Grover Washington, Jr. records his famous *Winelight* album.
1981 - Miles Davis returns to active playing.
   The Yellowjackets are formed.
1982 - New Age fad starts to catch on with release of George Winston piano solos.
1983 - Herbie Hancock scores with "Rockit."
1985 - Marc Russo is Robben Ford's replacement with the Yellowjackets.
1986 - Weather Report releases final album *This Is This* and then breaks up.
   Chick Corea teams up with bassist John Patitucci and soon forms his Elektric Band.
   Kenny G. becomes instrumental pop superstar with release of "Songbird."
1987 - Jaco Pastorius dies.
1991 - Miles Davis dies.
   Bob Mintzer joins the Yellowjackets in Marc Russo's place.
1995 - Spyro Gyra releases 17th album.

Jean-Luc Ponty, Al DiMeola and Stanley Clarke team up to form the Rite of Strings.

Fusion, crossover and instrumental pop are continually lumped together as contemporary jazz.

Jazz-Rap

John Bush

For a generation of hip-hop artists who remembered Charlie Parker or John Coltrane LPs resting on their parents' turntables, and who had ready access to sampling technology during the 1980s and '90s, jazz-rap worked simultaneously as a salute and connection point to the music of their youth and forebears, an alternative to the increasingly hardcore aspects of rap music as well as a way to introduce the somewhat alien aspects of hip-hop to inexperienced listeners (and critics). While rap's artistic vision and commercial sales grew during the late '80s and early '90s, the sampler was often replaced or expanded on by jazz instrumentalists, from Branford Marsalis, Donald Byrd and Herbie Hancock to Pharoah Sanders and Roy Ayers. For these jazz artists, the style functioned as an enjoyable holiday away from over-analytical critics and stuffy purists, as well as a chance to play to younger audiences unfamiliar with their vast bodies of work. For all involved, the style's shining moments reflected what each side could learn about another uniquely African-American cultural experience—the virtuoso playing and cerebral flair of jazz could add a new professionalism to the world of hip-hop, while the hard-hitting grooves and energetic free thought of rap's Young Lions could inject jazz with a renewed sense of purpose and vision.

The early pioneers of rap music were little concerned with jazz however, whether it was the DJs at South Bronx block parties of the mid-'70s, or the initial disco-inspired rap recording artists of the late '70s and early '80s. And when the use of samplers in rap became widespread during the mid-'80s, it was a heavy metal fanatic, Rick Rubin, who used the machine to push the singles of his artists (Run-D.M.C., LL Cool J and the Beastie Boys) by adding guitar riffs from AC/DC and others. (Rubin did play around just a bit with jazz, sampling Bob James for the Run-D.M.C. track "Peter Piper" in 1986). The first glimpses of serious rappers and producers wishing to pursue their roots in the field of jazz emerged a few years later. In 1988, the hip-hop band Stetsasonic sampled Lonnie Liston-Smith for a track called "Talkin' All That Jazz," and Gang Starr issued their debut single, "Words I Manifest," with a Charlie Parker line used as the main melody. The group's debut album *No More Mr. Nice Guy*, released one year later, caught the ear of filmmaker Spike Lee, who tapped the duo to appear on the soundtrack to 1990s *Mo' Better Blues*. Alongside Branford Marsalis, Terence Blanchard and Kenny Kirkland, the group appeared on the last cut, "Jazz Thing," with a spoken-word history of jazz (written by Lotis Eli) set to a hip-hop beat and rapping.

Enter the Native Tongue posse, an Afrocentric collective of groups formed in the late '80s by hip-hop pioneer Afrika Bambaataa. One of the first Native Tongue groups, the Jungle Brothers, released a debut album with several jazzy textures, 1988's *Straight Out the Jungle*. The following year, De La Soul released their own debut, *3 Feet High and Rising*. One of the most important albums in terms of rap's growing maturity in the 1980s, it was also the first to show the wide range of opportunities available to those with a large record collection and a sampler. The group's producer, Prince Paul, weaved the strains of whitebread pop groups like Hall & Oates, the Turtles and Steely Dan alongside the trio's intelligent raps.

Though De La Soul's follow-ups to *3 Feet High and Rising* were never half as interesting as their debut, one other Native Tongue group picked up the torch and took the artistic possibilities of jazz-rap to new heights. On their debut album, *People's Instinctive Travels and the Paths of Rhythm*, A Tribe Called Quest sounded much like their fellow Native Tongues, with an array of samples almost too eclectic for their own good, though their tough rapping style and ear for melody overcame many difficulties. A Tribe Called Quest's second album *The Low End Theory* was very nearly a perfect album, jazzy in mood and texture, though the only direct jazz ingredients were a Grant Green sample and a live appearance from bassist Ron Carter. No other group had made jazz-inspired hip-hop that actually enhanced the quality of the music, but on *The Low End Theory*, A Tribe Called Quest showed how smooth the style could sound.

The mellow innovations of De La Soul and A Tribe Called Quest proved quite influential and made them many fans (in the field of rap as well as alternative rock). Hence, the sound of jazz-rap gained significant exposure during 1992-93. Just before his death, Miles Davis cut an album called *Doo-Bop*, where he incorporated hip-hop rhythms and rapping for the first time, though Davis' weakened condition and the relative anonymity of the hip-hop partakers decreased its appeal. The trio known as Digable Planets made the first significant singles-chart success with their Top 20 debut single "Rebirth of Slick (Cool Like Dat)," and sampled Eddie Harris, Sonny Rollins, Art Blakey and the Crusaders (among others) on the accompanying album, *Reachin' (A New Refutation of Time and Space)*. A tour

with live musicians failed to advance the cause of jazz-rap very far—the players just repeated short lines instead of truly soloing—but the group branched out on their second, *Blowout Comb*, with several solos and more live playing than sampling. Up to this time, many samples by all but the most prominent groups had been obtained without permission, and both De La Soul and Biz Markie had lost notable cases over unauthorized sampling (significantly derailing their careers in the process). In mid-1993, however, Blue Note Records gave its stamp of approval to sampling by signing a British production duo named US3 and giving them exclusive license to plunder the vaults for any samples they wished. With a couple of New York rappers in tow, US3 hit the Top Ten in early 1994 with "Cantaloop (Flip Fantasia)," encompassing samples from Herbie Hancock's "Cantaloupe Island" and Pee Wee Marquette's introduction to an Art Blakey date at Birdland.

The most successful fusion of live jazz and rap, with little ground given to either, was a project begun by Gang Starr's lead vocalist, Guru. Named *Jazzmatazz* and released in mid-1993 (around the time of jazz-rap's greatest success on the charts), the album featured Roy Ayers, Courtney Pine and Lonnie Liston-Smith (among others), given much space to solo between the heady raps of Guru and others. In 1994, the AIDS benefit compilation series *Red Hot* introduced *Stolen Moments: Red Hot + Cool*, an album which paired jazz players with hip-hop acts, creating interesting combos like Me'Shell NdegeOcello with Herbie Hancock, Digable Planets with Lester Bowie and Wah Wah Watson, and the Roots with Roy Ayers. Standard groups which mixed live jazz playing with rapping and hip-hop beats included Branford Marsalis' Buckshot Lefonque project, an R&B group with equal inspirations from mainstream jazz and hip-hop, and the self-contained rap band the Roots. For the most part, though, by the late '90s most rap groups were less concerned with jazz-rap fusion, settling instead for occasional samples from the old masters. — *John Bush*

Recommended Listening:

The Jungle Brothers, *Straight Out the Jungle* (Warlock)
De La Soul, *3 Feet High and Rising* (Tommy Boy)
A Tribe Called Quest, *The Low End Theory* (Jive)
Gang Starr, *Daily Operation* (Chrysalis)
Guru, *Jazzmatazz, Vol. 1* (Chrysalis)
Digable Planets, *Reachin' (A New Refutation of Space and Time)* (Pendulum)
US3, *Hand on the Torch* (Blue Note)
V/A, *Stolen Moments: Red Hot + Cool* (GRP)
Buckshot Lefonque, *Buckshot Lefonque* (Sony)
The Roots, *Do You Want More?!!!??!* (DGC)

Acid Jazz

John Bush

An energetic, groove-centered variant of jazz for a generation of club-oriented youth, acid jazz as a style originated in London during the mid-'80s, fostered by rare-groove DJs who spun their favorite records, whether they were up-to-par from a jazz standpoint or not. In the clubs, the only thing that mattered was the groove, and these DJs were inspired in the main by the '70s fringe of jazz—fusion, jazz-funk and Afro-Cuban, with secondary elements of earlier soul-jazz. This exposure to a legion of previously unheard records influenced many in the British and American underground, which fed a pool of live musicians and studio-savvy producers working within the style by the early '90s. Though British chart success by Soul II Soul, the Brand New Heavies, and Stereo MC's created a glut of sub-par artists and compilations in the stores, players in the underground kept expanding the style, gradually building a global community of artists.

During the early '80s, ever-changing British pop-music trends had seen punk, new wave, and the mod revival come and go. By the mid-point of the decade, the hot music for club DJs was rare groove, a style which re-introduced listeners and dancers to the more obscure jazz-funk and soul records from the '70s. The style took as its cornerstones classics which jazz critics and purists had either neglected or dismissed: music from Miles Davis' electric period, commercial successes like Donald Byrd's *Black Byrd* and Herbie Hancock's *Headhunters*, and '70s Blue Note obscurities from the cutout bins of record stores. Of the many DJs around London, the one who became most identified with acid jazz was Gilles Peterson. (Various claims can be made as to his being the first to use the term as well.) Peterson originally started by spinning mammoth sets of jazz-fusion from his own personal pirate radio station, located in a garden shed near his home, and later made the move to broadcast on one of the hottest British pirate stations, Kiss-FM. He also maintained residencies at several London clubs during the late '80s. One of Peterson's buddies was Eddie Piller, the former head of Re-Elect the President Records, and the man who had released the debut album by a Hammond B-3 extraordinaire named James Taylor (not to be confused with either the singer-songwriter or the Kool & the Gang vocalist). When Taylor moved to Polydor in 1988, Piller received enough money to finance a new label, Acid Jazz Records, as a partnership with Peterson. The company's first releases were a series of compilations titled *Totally Wired*, each of which alternated jazz-funk obscurities from the 1970s with updated tracks from the new acid jazz.

Peterson later left Acid Jazz Records to form his own Talkin' Loud Records, which soon became one of the other top labels around; it also generated some commercial movement by signing former Acid Jazz artist Galliano as well as Young Disciples and Urban Species. In 1990, another British label, 4th & Broadway Records, began a compilation series titled *The Rebirth of Cool*, featuring an international cast of artists both young and old, including Pharoah Sanders, the Stereo MC's, French rapper MC Solaar, Courtney Pine and Japanese production team United Future Organization, among others. Acid jazz broke into the mainstream in 1991, led by the Brand New Heavies. The group had released one album through Acid Jazz Records, but then moved to Fffr Records for their greatest success, the singles "Never Stop" and "Dream Come True." After the initial British success of acid jazz groups inspired by the rare-groove revival, a spate of marginal compilations flooded the racks, leaving many consumers puzzled over what exactly acid jazz was, which artists played acid jazz, and how to identify the best recordings in the style.

The confusion grew no less clear in the 1990s, as vibrant acid jazz communities sprung up in the US as well, in San Francisco (Ubiquity Records), New York (the Giant Step collective) and Los Angeles (Solsonics). By that time, acid jazz could encompass anything from the spy-soundtrack soul-jazz of the James Taylor Quartet to Jamiroquai's pop-oriented Stevie Wonder imitations, from the globe-trotting musical eclecticism of Japanese producers United Future Organization to New York's Groove Collective, a ramshackle group of poets, players and hip-hoppers who shared club nights. The growth of interest in electronic club music during the mid- to late '90s appeared to quash much of the power of acid jazz with the buying public, though many communities around the world remained quite fresh and exciting. — *John Bush*

Essential Listening:

V/A, *Totally Wired* (Acid Jazz)

Brand New Heavies, *Brand New Heavies* (Delicious Vinyl)

Galliano, *What Colour Our Flag* (Talkin' Loud/Mercury)

United Future Organization, *No Sound Is Too Taboo* (Talkin' Loud/Verve)

Groove Collective, *Groove Collective* (Reprise)

James Taylor Quartet, *In the Hand of the Inevitable* (Hollywood)

Jamiroquai, *Return of the Space Cowboy* (Columbia)

Young Disciples, *Road to Freedom* (Talkin' Loud/Mercury)

Greyboy Allstars, *Town Called Earth* (Greyboy)

Medeski, Martin & Wood, *It's a Jungle in Here* (Gramavision)

Jazz-rock

Richie Unterberger

More than most such sub-genres, jazz-rock is a hybrid that has resisted true alchemy. The impulse to blend the basic drive of rock with the improvisational verve and rhythmic complexity of jazz is a challenge that has been taken up by many. Not only has it been successfully faced by few, but the results often prove more weighted toward either rock or jazz than a true fusion of the styles.

Half a century ago, rock and jazz were much more closely intertwined than they were today. In the big-band and swing era, jazz was a much more dance-oriented music; early R&B and jump blues acts that helped lay the foundation for rock 'n' roll drew much of their boogies, riffs, and rhythms (as well as instrumentalists) from jazz. Artists like Joe Turner and Jay McShann could have been classified as either jazz or R&B, but as rock 'n' roll grew into a full-grown giant and jazz evolved toward bebop, the styles took substantially divergent paths.

Jazz's influence on rock 'n' roll during the '50s and '60s wasn't negligible. Lots of R&B and soul bands, including those of Little Richard, Ray Charles, and James Brown, featured musicians from jazz backgrounds. Respected jazz musicians like Barney Kessel played on many rock 'n' roll sessions to help pay the rent, and drummer Cozy Cole crossed over to the rock 'n' roll market with his instrumental smash "Topsy. " In the mid-'60s, the Byrds openly credited John Coltrane as an influence on early psychedelic landmarks like "Eight Miles High," and used South African jazz trumpeter Hugh Masekela as a prominent sessionmen on a couple of their singles. Notable '60s groups like the Doors, Zombies, Blues Project, Paul Butterfield, Manfred Mann, Traffic, and Santana clearly displayed important secondary jazz influences. Jazz was also an important element in Van Morrison's late-'60s album *Astral Weeks*, which featured the rhythm section of noted jazz players Richard Davis on bass and Connie Kay of the Modern Jazz Quartet on drums.

Not to be overlooked, either, is '60s soul-jazz, a form which attracts little critical attention today, but was quite popular in its day—indeed, it might have been the

most popular form of jazz with urban, African-American audiences. Using organs, vocals, and R&B riffs with greater frequency than other jazz musicians, the most popular performers in this sub-genre would include Jimmy Smith, Jimmy McGriff, Big John Patton, and Jack McDuff. Ramsey Lewis and the spinoff combo Young-Holt Trio (later to become YoungHolt Unlimited) had a more pop-oriented take on soul-jazz that led to substantial Top 40 success.

"Jazz-rock" as a self-conscious label, however, didn't evolve until the late '60s. The first acts to be widely identified as jazz-rock bands (and, to this day, the most successful) weren't so much jazz-rockers as R&B-oriented White rock bands with jazzy horn sections. The Electric Flag, featuring Mike Bloomfield, Buddy Miles, and Nick Gravenites, were the first of these; Blood, Sweat & Tears and Chicago became huge stars, although the MOR nature of their hits led some critics to dub them as "wedding band" or "barmitzvah" soul.

A more ambitious, although extremely obscure, jazz-rock record that predates any of the bands in the above paragraph was the sole album by the New York-based Free Spirits, featuring the young Larry Coryell on guitar. This interesting but erratic effort came much closer to truly striking a midpoint between rock song forms and jazz instrumentation, although the songs remained in the neighborhood of three minutes, and the vocals were fairly weak. Concentrating more on the jazz and instrumental side of things, Coryell became one of the leading early jazz-rock and fusion performers as the leader of Eleventh House and as a solo artist.

Several British '60s bands featured players that emerged from a jazz background, most notably the Graham Bond Organization. Besides the leader, they featured Jack Bruce and Ginger Baker in their pre-Cream days, and, for a time, guitarist John McLaughlin, although they quickly gravitated toward the R&B and blues sounds of the day. Bruce and Baker have occasionally recorded respectable jazz albums right up to the present, and Bond-||||||">4860John Mayall spinoff-band Colosseum were probably the best jazz-oriented act to emerge from the British R&B-blues scene. The most successful British jazz-rock band of all, and indeed the one act that could be termed to have truly fused the two styles more than any other, were the Soft Machine. Starting as an underground psychedelic group (and a very good one), their late-'60s and early-'70s albums turned toward an increasingly improvisational and instrumental sound, retaining rock elements in Mike Ratledge's buzzing organ and Robert Wyatt's brilliant drumming and soulful vocals.

For most critics, though, the true peak of jazz-rock was reached by Miles Davis on his early-'70s recordings. Impressed by Jimi Hendrix and other late-'60s rock musicians, Davis brought electric guitars and keyboards into his band, culminating in the landmark 1970 LP *Bitches Brew*, roundly acclaimed as one of the most influential jazz recordings of all time. That record featured guitarist John McLaughlin, who would immediately become a leading jazz-rock figure himself, on his own, with Davis, with the Mahavishnu Orchestra, and in collaborations with ex-Davis drummer Tony Williams and Carlos Santana.

Other jazz musicians took the cue from Davis, always a leader and innovator, and added electric instruments and rock-influenced rhythms to their sound. Herbie Hancock, Chick Corea, and Weather Report were the best of these groups, although it's fair to say that, even more than Davis, they were really "rock-influenced jazz," not "jazz-rock." The compositions were usually instrumental, the melodic themes and improvisations clearly from the jazz tradition; the rock influence was felt in the electric instruments and the forceful funk of the arrangements.

Not unsurprisingly, jazz-rock quickly turned in a more commercial, watered-down direction that resulted in the style known as "fusion." As work became harder to find in the struggling jazz scene of the late '60s, notable jazzmen like Lou Donaldson, Herbie Mann, Les McCann, Hugh Masekela, and Grant Green had already been turning in a jazz-soul direction as a means of both broadening their horizons and survival. Many jazz players, usually for brief periods, brought electric instruments and funk rhythms into their arrangements during the 1970s, resulting by and large in unimpressive, at times embarrassing, results. Guitarist George Benson and trumpeter Donald Byrd, to name two of the most obvious examples, found much greater commercial success as pop-fusioneers than with their more critically-respected straight jazz efforts of the '60s.

Jazz-rock hasn't been a big critical or commercial deal since the mid-'70s, but occasional innovators have produced interesting efforts along the lines of the best jazz-rock pioneers. Frank Zappa couldn't properly be considered a jazz-rock musician, but several of his '70s recordings, most notably *Hot Rats*, rank among the most ambitious blends of rock and jazz principles. Guitarist James Blood Ulmer and drummer Ronald Shannon Jackson (whose band, the Decoding Society, featured future Living Colour guitarist Vernon Reid) were both students of the Ornette Coleman school of harmolodics. The best of their records have melded jazz improvisation, funk rhythms, and visceral electric drive as well as anyone. Coleman himself drew on jazz-rock innovations with his Prime Time band. Streetwise jazz poets Gil-Scott Heron and the Last Poets helped lay the foundation for rap music. Defunkt merged jazz and funk rhythms without, at least at the beginning, pandering to watered-down commercial fusion interests. And, most unpredictably, folk-rock star Joni Mitchell delved heavily into jazz improvisation in the late '70s with the help of sidemen Jaco Pastorius and Pat Metheny, and put lyrics to Charles Mingus' last compositions (at his request) on the 1979 album, Mingus.

The jazz-rock fusion continues to tempt musicians intermittently in the '90s. Several bands on the alternative rock label SST, most notably Alter Natives and Bazooka, played what was essentially improvisational jazz with fierce electric guitar-driven arrangements. The downtown New York avant-rock-whatchamacallit scene is too eclectic to be figured easily into the jazz-rock equation, but many of its performers are clearly strongly influenced by both worlds. Under the pseudonym Buckshot LeFonque, leading contemporary jazz musician Branford Marsalis took a stab at jazz-funk-R&B-soul-hip-hop. British act Us3 grafted hip-hop samples onto classic Blue Note jazz recordings, sparking some occasionally inspired jazz-hip-hop crossover recordings in the jazz community itself.

Recommended Recordings

Various Artists, *Blue Funk: The History of the Hammond Organ* (Blue Note). More quality soul-jazz was recorded on the Blue Note label than any other, and this compilation includes tracks by most of the biggest stars of the genre: Jimmy Smith, Jimmy McGriff, Jack McDuff, Grant Green, Big John Patton, Lou Donaldson.

The Free Spirits, ht, *Out of Sound* (ABC). Pretty hard to find these days, this stakes a strong claim as the first jazz-rock record.

The Electric Flag, *A Long Time Comin'* (Columbia). The best of the records by late-'60s White rock groups to be classified as "jazz-rock."

Miles Davis, Bitches Brew (Columbia). Still the most influential and respected jazz-rock recording.

The Soft Machine, *3rd* (Columbia). Their most successful pure jazz-rock outing, although their earlier, more psychedelic rock-flavored albums weren't too shabby either.

John McLaughlin, *Devotion* (Restless). It's really a matter of taste as to which early-'70s McLaughlin album stands as his best, but rock listeners might find this one of the more approachable ones, as it uses Jimi Hendrix's Band of Gypsies rhythm section.

Frank Zappa, *Hot Rats* (Rykodisc). One of his most jazz-rock-oriented recordings, this largely instrumental 1970 effort features some of his best guitar playing.

Herbie Hancock, *Headhunters* (Columbia). The album that broke fusion as a commercial force, though those looking for something a bit more adventurous in the jazz-rock vein might try the early-'70s LPs he released just prior to this effort.

Gil-Scott Heron, *The Revolution Will Not Be Televised* (Flying Dutchman). The leading jazz-R&B-rock poet.

Miles Davis, *Pangaea* (Columbia). Arguably the most recklessly electric of Davis' fusion sessions, featuring the guitar pyrotechnics of Pete Cosey. Those looking for something slightly less experimental should try Agharta, recorded on the same day.

Joni Mitchell, *Mingus* (Asylum). The central recording of Mitchell's jazz-rock phase, a period which inspired much debate among both fans and critics.

James Blood Ulmer, *Are You Glad to Be in America?* (Artists House). None of Ulmer's records could exactly be termed as accessible, but this strikes the best balance between funk-R&B grooves and harmolodics.

Ronald Shannon Jackson, *Decode Yourself* (Island). None of Jackson's albums particularly stands out as his most influential; this 1985 Bill Laswell-produced session is one of the more accessible.

Bazooka, *Blowhole* (SST). A group that, like others on the SST label, pursues the elusive goal of wedding Ornette Coleman to post-punk attitude and eclecticism. Various Artists, Stolen Moments: Red, Hot & Cool (GRP). The best jazz-hip-hop compilation, featuring some of the top talents from both worlds.

Jazz Recordings: A Beginner's Guide

Scott Yanow

For the beginner, going into a large record store and looking through the jazz section can be a bewildering experience. Jazz history is an endless series of names, most of them quite talented, and with a nonstop series of releases coming out on a daily basis, there is almost too much to absorb. Where does one start?

I have compiled this list of 455 recommended discs for listeners who are just beginning to collect jazz recordings. Rather than take the easy way out and simply include some of the huge and very complete sets that are currently available (such as Mosaic's 18-CD Nat King Cole trio box), many of which are limited-editions or beyond the budget of the beginner who wishes to simply get a taste of jazz, I have

instead concentrated on variety, giving the reader a sampling of the many styles and major players from all eras of jazz history. Not that many listeners will immediately enjoy every one of these records (the range of styles is quite vast) but by listening to all of this music with an open mind, its beauty and excitement will be gradually appreciated.

The emphasis is on smaller CD sets (with a few exceptions all are one or two CD's), domestic releases (also with a few exceptions) and music that is available as of this writing. Nearly every significant musician is represented somewhere on the list (for example Scott Hamilton is on Dave McKenna's *No Bass Hit*). Although we would never claim that these are the 455 "best" jazz recordings of all time, listeners should feel free to acquire as many of these releases as possible. On a whole this list will give collectors a very diverse sampling of virtually every jazz style. No two are identical and all are very good in their own way. — *Scott Yanow*

Cannonball Adderley /John Coltrane *Cannonball And Coltrane* (EmArcy)

Cannonball Adderley *Cannonball Adderley Quintet in San Francisco* (Original Jazz Classics [OJC])

Cannonball Adderley *Mercy, Mercy, Mercy* (Capitol)

Affinity *A Tribute To Ornette Coleman* (Music & Arts)

Air *Air Lore* (RCA/Bluebird)

Howard Alden/Dan Barrett Quintet *ABQ Salutes Buck Clayton* (Concord Jazz)

Geri Allen *In The Year Of The Dragon* (Verve)

Henry "Red" Allen *1929-1933* (Classics)

Henry "Red" Allen *World On A String* (Bluebird)

Mose Allison *I Don't Worry About A Thing* (Rhino/Atlantic)

Laurindo Almeida/Bud Shank *Brazilliance Vol.* (World Pacific)

Karrin Allyson *Collage* (Concord Jazz)

Franco Ambrosetti *Music For Symphony & Jazz Band* (Enja)

Albert Ammons *Meade Lux Lewis, The First Day* (Blue Note)

Gene Ammons *The Happy Blues* (OJC)

Gene Ammons/Sonny Stitt *Boss Tenors* (Verve)

Ray Anderson *Big Band Record* (Gramavision)

Louis Armstrong/ King Oliver *Louis Armstrong and King Oliver* (Milestone)

Louis Armstrong *Hot Fives, Vol. 1* (Columbia)

Louis Armstrong *Hot Fives & Sevens, Vol. 2* (Columbia)

Louis Armstrong *Hot Fives & Sevens, Vol. 3* (Columbia)

Louis Armstrong *Louis Armstrong and Earl Hines, Vol. 4* (Columbia)

Louis Armstrong *Pops: 1940s Small Band Sides* (RCA/Bluebird)

Louis Armstrong *Plays W.C. Handy* (Columbia/Legacy)

Art Ensemble of Chicago *Live* (Delmark)

Albert Ayler *Love Cry* (Impulse)

Chet Baker *Grey December* (Pacific Jazz)

Chet Baker *The Italian Sessions* (Bluebird)

Chet Baker *My Favorite Songs, Vols. 1 and 2: The Last Great Concert* (Enja)

Charlie Barnet *Clap Hands Here Comes Charlie* (Bluebird)

Charlie Barnet *Drop Me Off In Harlem* (Decca)

Count Basie *The Complete Decca Recordings (1937-1939)* (3CDs) (GRP)

Count Basie *April In Paris* (Verve)

Count Basie/Joe Williams *Count Basie Swings, Joe Williams Sings* (Verve)

Count Basie *Count Basie at Newport* (Verve)

Count Basie/Zoot Sims *Basie and Zoot* (OJC)

Sidney Bechet *Master Takes: Victor Sessions 1932-1943* (3CDs) (Bluebird)

Bix Beiderbecke *Vol. 1: Singin' The Blues* (Columbia)

Bix Beiderbecke *Vol. 2: At the Jazz Band Ball* (Columbia)

Bix Beiderbecke *Bix Lives* (RCA)

George Benson *Body Talk* (Columbia)

Bunny Berigan *The Pied Piper* (Bluebird)

Art Blakey *Moanin'* (Blue Note)

Art Blakey *A Night In Tunisia* (Blue Note)

Art Blakey *Keystone 3* (Concord Jazz)

Boswell Sisters *Vol. 1* (Collector's Classics)

Ruby Braff *A Sailboat in the Moonlight* (Concord Jazz)

Anthony Braxton *Dortmund (Quartet 1976)* (Hat Art)

Michael Brecker *Michael Brecker* (MCA/Impulse!)

Clifford Brown *Brown and Roach, Inc.* (EmArcy)
Clifford Brown *At Basin Street* (EmArcy)
Clifford Brown *The Beginning and the End* (Columbia)
Oscar Brown Jr. *Sin & Soul and then Some* (Columbia/Legacy)
Dave Brubeck *Jazz Goes To College* (Columbia)
Dave Brubeck *Time Out* (Columbia)
Jane Bunnett *Spirits Of Havana* (Denon)
Gary Burton *Artist's Choice* (Bluebird)
Don Byas *On Blue Star* (EmArcy)
Donald Byrd *Mustang* (Blue Note)
George Cables *Cables' Vision* (OJC)
Cab Calloway *1930-1931* (Classics)
Benny Carter *All Of Me* (Bluebird)
Benny Carter *Further Definitions* (Impulse!)
Benny Carter *Benny Carter 4: Montreux 1977* (OJC)
Betty Carter *Finally* (Roulette)
James Carter *Jurassic Classics* (DIW/Columbia)
Doc Cheatham *The Eighty-Seven Years Of Doc Cheatham* (Columbia)
The Cheathams *Basket Full Of Blues* (Concord Jazz)
Charlie Christian *The Genius Of The Electric Guitar* (Columbia)
June Christy *Something Cool* (Capitol)
Sonny Clark *Dial S For Sonny* (Blue Note)
Buck Clayton *The Essential* (Vanguard)
Clayton-Hamilton Jazz Orchestra *Heart And Soul* (Capri)
Clusone Trio *Soft Lights And Sweet Music* (Hat Art)
Arnett Cobb *Arnett Blows For 1300* (Delmark)
Al Cohn/Jimmy Rowles *Heavy Love* (Xanadu)
Nat King Cole *Jumpin' At Capitol* (Rhino)
Nat King Cole *Jazz Encounters* (Blue Note)
Ornette Coleman *The Shape Of Jazz To Come* (Atlantic)
Ornette Coleman *Free Jazz* (Atlantic)
Ornette Coleman *At The Golden Circle In Stockholm, Vol. 1* (Blue Note)
Steve Coleman *Rhythm People* (Novus)
John Coltrane *Blue Train* (Blue Note)
John Coltrane *Giant Steps* (Atlantic)
John Coltrane *John Coltrane and Johnny Hartman* (GRP/Impulse!)
John Coltrane *Live At Birdland* (Impulse!)
John Coltrane *Meditations* (MCA)
Eddie Condon *Dixieland All Stars* (GRP/Decca)
Bob Cooper *Coop! The Music Of Bob Cooper* (OJC)
Chick Corea *Now He Sings, Now He Sobs* (Blue Note)
Chick Corea *Return To The Seventh Galaxy* (2 CDs) (Verve)
Chick Corea *My Spanish Heart* (Polydor)
Marilyn Crispell *Live In San Francisco* (Music & Arts)
Sonny Criss *Crisscraft* (Muse)
Bob Crosby *Bob Crosby & His Orchestra* (GRP/Decca)
Eddie Daniels *Breakthrough* (GRP)
Eddie Lockjaw Davis *All Of Me* (Steeple Chase)
Miles Davis *Birth Of The Cool* (Capitol)
Miles Davis *Miles Ahead* (Columbia)
Miles Davis *Milestones* (Columbia)
Miles Davis *Kind Of Blue* (Columbia)
Miles Davis *The Complete Concert: 1964)My Funny Valentine) (2CDs)* (Columbia)
Miles Davis *Miles Smiles* (Columbia)
Miles Davis *Bitches Brew* (2 CDs) (Columbia)
Wild Bill Davison *The Commodore Master Takes* (Commodore)
Wild Bill Davison *Showcase* (Jazzology)
Jack DeJohnette *Special Edition* (ECM)
Paul Desmond/Gerry Mulligan *Two Of A Mind* (RCA)
Johnny Dodds *Blue Clarinet Stomp* (Bluebird)
Eric Dolphy *Outward Bound* (OJC)

Eric Dolphy *Out There* (OJC)
Eric Dolphy *Out To Lunch* (Blue Note)
Lou Donaldson *Blues Walk* (Blue Note)
Kenny Dorham *Jazz Contrasts* (OJC)
Kenny Dorham *Una Mas* (Blue Note)
Bob Dorough *Devil May Care* (Bethlehem)
Jimmy Dorsey *Contrasts* (GRP/Decca)
Tommy Dorsey *Yes Indeed* (Bluebird)
Dave Douglas *Five* (Soul Note)
Roy Eldridge *Little Jazz* (Columbia)
Roy Eldridge *Montreux, 1977* (OJC)
Kurt Elling *Close Your Eyes* (Blue Note)
Duke Ellington *Early Ellington (1927-1934)* (Bluebird)
Duke Ellington *Okeh Ellington* (2 CDs) (Columbia)
Duke Ellington *Blanton-Webster Band* (3 CDs) (Bluebird)
Duke Ellington *Fargo, ND, November 7, 1940* (2 CDs) (Vintage Jazz Classics)
Duke Ellington *The Carnegie Hall Concerts)January 1943), (2 CDs)* (Prestige)
Duke Ellington *The Far East Suite*)Bluebird)
Duke Ellington *Seventieth Birthday Concert* (2 CDs) (Blue Note)
Herb Ellis *Nothing But The Blues* (Verve)
Bill Evans *Portrait In Jazz* (OJC)
Bill Evans *Conversations With Myself* (Verve)
Gil Evans *New Bottle, Old Wine* (Blue Note)
Gil Evans *Blues In Orbit* (Enja)
Art Farmer *Meet The Jazztet* (MCA/Chess)
Maynard Ferguson *The Birdland Dream Band* (Bluebird)
Ella Fitzgerald *The War Years* (2 CDs) (GRP/Decca)
Ella Fitzgerald *Pure Ella* (GRP/Decca)
Ella Fitzgerald *The Complete Ella In Berlin* (Verve)
Bill Frisell *Have A Little Faith* (Elektra)
Dave Frishberg *Can't Take You Nowhere* (Fantasy)
Ganelin Trio *Encores* (Leo)
Erroll Garner *Concert By The Sea* (Columbia)
Kenny Garrett *Pursuance* (Warner Bros.)
Stan Getz *The Roost Quartet* (Roulette)
Stan Getz *Stan and J.J. Johnson At The Opera House* (Verve)
Stan Getz *Getz and Gilberto* (Verve)
Dizzy Gillespie *Shaw Nuff* (Musicraft)
Dizzy Gillespie *Complete RCA Victor Recordings 1947-1949*, (2CDs) (Bluebird)
Dizzy Gillespie/Roy Eldridge *Dizzy Gillespie with Roy Eldridge* (Verve)
Dizzy Gillespie *At Newport* (Verve)
Jerry Gonzalez *Rhumba Para Monk* (Sunnyside)
Benny Goodman *The Birth Of Swing* (3 CDs) (Bluebird)
Benny Goodman *Sing, Sing, Sing* (Bluebird)
Benny Goodman *Carnegie Hall Concert* (2 CDs) (Columbia)
Dexter Gordon *The Jumpin' Blues* (OJC)
Stephane Grappelli *Live In London* (Black Lion)
Stephane Grappelli *And David Grisman Live* (Warner Bros.)
Grant Green *The Latin Bit* (Blue Note)
Grant Green *Matador* (Blue Note)
Johnny Griffin *The Congregation* (Blue Note)
Marty Grosz *Extra! The Orphan Newsboys* (Jazzology)
George Gruntz Concert Jazz Band *First Prize* (Enja)
Vince Guaraldi *Jazz Impressions Of Black Orpheus* (OJC)
Barry Guy *London Jazz Composers Orchestra: Harmos* (Intakt)
Charlie Haden *Quartet West* (Verve)
Lionel Hampton *Midnight Sun* (GRP/Decca)
Herbie Hancock *Maiden Voyage* (Blue Note)
Herbie Hancock *The Complete Warner Bros. Recordings* (2 CDs) (Warner Archives)
Roy Hargrove *Of Kindred Souls* (Novus)
Eddie Harris *Exodus To Jazz* (Vee-Jay)

Coleman Hawkins *A Retrospective 1929-1963* (2 CDs) (Bluebird)
Coleman Hawkins *Rainbow Mist* (Delmark)
Erskine Hawkins *The Original Tuxedo Junction* (Bluebird)
Fletcher Henderson *A Study In Frustration* (3 CDs) (Columbia)
Joe Henderson *Page One* (Blue Note)
Joe Henderson *Lush Life* (Verve)
Woody Herman *Blues On Parade* (GRP)
Woody Herman *Thundering Herds* (Columbia)
Woody Herman *Keeper Of The Flame: Complete Capitol Recordings* (Capitol)
Andrew Hill *Point Of Departure* (Blue Note)
Earl Hines *Piano Man* (Bluebird)
Earl Hines *Spontaneous Explorations* (2 CDs) (Red Baron)
Milt Hinton *Old Man Time* (2 CDs) (Chiaroscuro)
Johnny Hodges *Everybody Knows Johnny Hodges* (Impulse!)
Billie Holiday *The Legacy* (3 CDs) (Columbia)
Billie Holiday *The Complete Decca Recordings* (2 CDs) (GRP/Decca)
Richard "Groove" Holmes *Groovin' With Jug* (Capitol/Pacific Jazz)
Shirley Horn *Close Enough For Love* (Verve)
Freddie Hubbard *Breaking Point* (Blue Note)
Freddie Hubbard *Straight Life* (CTI/Columbia)
Helen Humes *Songs I Like To Sing* (OJC)
Dick Hyman *Live From Toronto's Café Des Copains* (Music & Arts)
Milt Jackson *Bags' Opus* (Blue Note)
Willis Jackson *Bar Wars* (32 Jazz)
Illinois Jacquet *The Black Velvet Band* (Bluebird)
Ahmad Jamal *Jamal's Blues* (Chess)
Harry James *Snooty Fruity* (Columbia/Legacy)
Jon Jang *Two Flowers On A Stem* (Soul Note)
Keith Jarrett *Koln Concert* (ECM)
Keith Jarrett *My Song* (ECM)
Keith Jarrett *Mysteries* (4 CDs) (GRP/Impulse!)
Jazz At The Philharmonic *The First Concert* (Verve)
Jazz At The Philharmonic *Live At The Nichigeki Theatre 1953* (2 CDs) (Pablo)
Jazz At The Philharmonic *Stockholm '55—The Exciting Battle* (Pablo)
Jazz Crusaders *Live At The Lighthouse '66* (Pacific Jazz)
Eddie Jefferson *The Jazz Singer* (Evidence)
Bunk Johnson/Lu Watters *Bunk and Lu* (Good Time Jazz)
Bunk Johnson *Last Testament* (Delmark)
James P. Johnson *Snowy Morning Blues* (GRP)
Louis Jordan *The Best Of* (MCA)
Sheila Jordan *Portrait Of Sheila* (Blue Note)
Stan Kenton *Retrospective* (4 CDs) (Capitol)
Freddie Keppard *The Complete 1923/27* (King Jazz)
John Kirby *1938-1939* (Classics)
Andy Kirk *Mary's Idea* (GRP/Decca)
Rahsaan Roland Kirk *(Bright Moments* (2 CDs) (Rhino/Atlantic)
Lee Konitz *Subconscious-Lee* (OJC)
Gene Krupa *Uptown* (Columbia)
Steve Lacy *Evidence* (OJC)
Steve Lacy *Live At Sweet Basil* (Novus)
Bireli Lagrene *Routes To Django: Live* (Antilles)
Lambert, Hendricks & Ross *Sing A Song Of Basie* (GRP/Impulse!)
Lambert, Hendricks & Ross *The Hottest New Group In Jazz* (2 CDs) (Columbia/Legacy)
Pete LaRoca *Basra* (Blue Note)
George Lewis *Hot Creole Jazz, 1953* (DCC)
Lighthouse All-Stars *Music For Lighthousekeeping* (OJC)
Abbey Lincoln *Straight Ahead* (Candid)
Abbey Lincoln *Abbey Sings Billie* (Enja)
Booker Little *Booker Little 4 & Max Roach* (Blue Note)
Joe Lovano *Rush Hour* (Blue Note)
Jimmie Lunceford *Stomp It Off* (Decca)

Machito *Mucho Macho* (Pablo)
Manhattan Transfer *Vocalese* (Atlantic)
Shelly Manne *Vol. 1: The West Coast Sound* (OJC)
Shelly Manne *My Fair Lady* (OJC)
Joe Marsala *1936-1942* (Classics)
Branford Marsalis *Trio Jeepy* (2 CDs) (Columbia)
Wynton Marsalis *Black Codes (From The Underground)* (Columbia)
Wynton Marsalis *In This House, On This Morning* (2 CDs) (Columbia)
Les McCann *Les McCann Ltd. In New York* (Pacific Jazz)
Les McCann *Swiss Movement* (Rhino/Atlantic)
Susannah McCorkle *I'll Take Romance* (Concord Jazz)
Bobby McFerrin *Spontaneous Inventions* (Blue Note)
Dave McKenna *No Bass Hit* (Concord Jazz)
McKinney's Cotton Pickers *1928-1929* (Classics)
Jackie McLean *Let Freedom Ring* (Blue Note)
Jackie McLean *Dynasty* (Triloka)
Carmen McRae *Carmen Sings Monk* (Novus)
Jay McShann *Blues From Kansas City* (GRP)
Pat Metheny *80/81* (2 CDs) (ECM)
Pat Metheny *Letter From Home* (Geffen)
Glenn Miller *A Legendary Performer* (Bluebird)
Charles Mingus *New Tijuana Moods* (RCA)
Charles Mingus *Presents Charlie Mingus* (Candid)
Charles Mingus *Mingus At Antibes* (Atlantic)
Charles Mingus *Mingus, Mingus, Mingus, Mingus, Mingus* (Impulse!)
Charles Mingus *The Legendary Paris Concerts* (2 CDs) (Revenge)
Mingus Big Band *Nostalgia In Times Square* (Dreyfus)
Blue Mitchell *The Thing To Do* (Blue Note)
Roscoe Mitchell *Sound* (Delmark)
Hank Mobley *Workout* (Blue Note)
Modern Jazz Quartet *The Last Concert* (2 CDs) (Rhino/Atlantic)
Thelonious Monk *Brilliant Corners* (OJC)
Thelonious Monk *Big Band And Quartet In Concert* (2 CDs) (Columbia)
Wes Montgomery *The Incredible Jazz Guitar* (OJC)
Wes Montgomery *So Much Guitar* (OJC)
Lee Morgan *Candy* (Blue Note)
Lee Morgan *The Sidewinder* (Blue Note)
Jelly Roll Morton *Centennial: His Complete Victor Recordings* (5 CDs) (Bluebird)
Bennie Moten *South (1926-1929)* (Bluebird)
Bennie Moten *Basie Beginnings (1929-1932)* (Bluebird)
Gerry Mulligan *Best Of Mulligan Quartet With Chet Baker* (Pacific Jazz)
Gerry Mulligan *What Is There To Say* (Columbia)
Mark Murphy *Stolen . . . And Other Moments* (2 CDs) (32 Jazz)
Turk Murphy *Jazz Band Favorites* (Good Time Jazz)
David Murray *Hope Scope* (Black Saint)
Fats Navarro *And Tadd Dameron* (2 CDs) (Blue Note)
Buell Neidlinger *Blue Chopsticks* (K2B2)
Oliver Nelson *The Blues & The Abstract Truth* (Impulse!)
New Orleans Rhythm Kings *And Jelly Roll Morton* (Milestone)
James Newton *The African Flower* (Blue Note)
Jimmy Noone *Apex Blues* (GRP/Decca)
Red Norvo *Dance Of The Octopus* (Hep)
Anita O'Day *Anita Sings The Most* (Verve)
King Oliver *Sugar Foot Stomp* (GRP/Decca)
King Oliver *The New York Sessions* (Bluebird)
Original Dixieland Jazz Band *75th Anniversary* (Bluebird)
Kid Ory *Kid Ory's Creole Jazz Band (1954)* (Good Time Jazz)
Charlie Parker *The Ultimate* (2 CDs) (Rhino)
Charlie Parker *& Stars Of Modern Jazz At Carnegie Hall* (Jass)
Charlie Parker *At Massey Hall* (OJC)
Joe Pass *Virtuoso* (Pablo)

Art Pepper *Meets The Rhythm Section* (OJC)

Art Pepper *Landscape* (OJC)

Oscar Peterson *At The Stratford Shakespearean Festival* (Verve)

Oscar Peterson/Clark Terry *Oscar Peterson Trio + One* (Verve)

Oscar Peterson *My Favorite Instrument* (Verve)

Oscar Peterson *The Trio* (Pablo)

King Pleasure/Annie Ross *King Pleasure Sings With Annie Ross* (OJC)

Jean-Luc Ponty *Le Voyage* (2 CDs, (Rhino/Atlantic)

Bud Powell *The Complete Blue Note And Roost Recordings* (4 CDs) (Blue Note)

Louis Prima *Collectors Series* (Capitol)

Tito Puente *Goza Me Timbal* (Concord Picante)

Boyd Raeburn *Jubilee Broadcasts* (Hep)

Django Reinhardt *Django's Music* (Hep)

Django Reinhardt *Peche A La Mouche* (2 CDs) (Verve)

Buddy Rich *Mercy, Mercy* (Pacific Jazz)

Max Roach *Freedom Now Suite* (Columbia)

Max Roach *To The Max* (2 CDs) (Bluemoon)

Luckey Roberts *& Willie The Lion Smith* (Good Time Jazz)

Sonny Rollins *Saxophone Colossus And More* (OJC)

Sonny Rollins *Way Out West* (OJC)

Sonny Rollins *The Bridge* (RCA)

Annie Ross *Sings A Song With Mulligan* (EMI-Manhattan)

Rova *John Coltrane's Ascension* (Black Saint)

Gonzalo Rubalcaba *The Blessing* (Blue Note)

Poncho Sanchez *A Night At Kimball's East* (Concord Picante)

Pharoah Sanders *Karma* (Impulse)

Arturo Sandoval *Swingin'* (GRP)

Gunther Schuller *The Art Of Scott Joplin* (GM)

John Scofield *Hand Jive* (Blue Note)

Raymond Scott *Reckless Nights and Turkish Twilights* (Columbia)

Artie Shaw *Begin The Beguine* (Bluebird)

Artie Shaw *Blues In The Night* (Bluebird)

Woody Shaw *Last Of The Line* (2 CDs) (32 Jazz)

George Shearing *I Hear A Rhapsody* (Telarc)

Archie Shepp *Four For Trane* (Impulse)

Wayne Shorter *Speak No Evil* (Blue Note)

Horace Silver *Song For My Father* (Blue Note)

Sonny Simmons *Ancient Ritual* (Qwest/Reprise)

Zoot Sims *And the Gershwin Brothers* (OJC)

Bessie Smith *The Complete Recordings, Vol. 3* (2 CDs) (Columbia)

Jabbo Smith *1929-1938* (Retrieval)

Jimmy Smith *Back At The Chicken Shack* (Blue Note)

Jimmy Smith *The Sermon* (Blue Note)

Jimmy Smith/Wes Montgomery *The Dynamic Duo* (Verve)

Stuff Smith *1936-1939* (Classics)

Soprano Summit *Soprano Summit* (2 CDs) (Chiaroscuro)

Muggsy Spanier *The Ragtime Band Sessions* (Bluebird)

Sonny Stitt *Stitt Plays Bird* (Atlantic)

Sonny Stitt *Endgame Brilliance* (32 Jazz)

Supersax *Supersax Plays Bird* (Capitol)

Art Tatum *Piano Starts Here* (Columbia/Legacy)

Art Tatum *Classic Early Solos* (GRP/Decca)

Cecil Taylor *Jazz Advance* (Blue Note)

Cecil Taylor *Silent Tongues* (Freedom)

Jack Teagarden *The Indispensable* (2 CDs) (RCA)

Clark Terry *What A Wonderful World* (Red Baron)

Claude Thornhill *Best Of Big Bands* (Columbia)

Cal Tjader *Latin Concert* (OJC)

Mel Tormé *In Concert Tokyo* (Concord Jazz)

Lennie Tristano *The Complete Lennie Tristano On Keynote* (Mercury)

Lennie Tristano/Warne Marsh *Intuition* (Capitol)

Steve Turre *Steve Turre* (Verve)

Stanley Turrentine *Let It Go* (GRP/Impulse)

Stanley Turrentine *Sugar* (CTI)

McCoy Tyner *Enlightenment* (Milestone)

McCoy Tyner *Supertrios* (Milestone)

Sarah Vaughan *Complete: Live In Japan* (2 CDs) (Mobile Fidelity)

Joe Venuti *Fiddlesticks* (Conifer)

Bennie Wallace *Twilight Time* (Blue Note)

Fats Waller *And His Buddies* (Bluebird)

Dinah Washington *Dinah Jams* (EmArcy)

Grover Washington *Winelight* (Elektra)

Benny Waters *Live At 95* (Enja)

Lu Watters *Vol. 1: Dawn Club Favorites* (Good Time Jazz)

Weather Report *Heavy Weather* (Columbia)

Chick Webb *1929-1934* (Classics)

Ben Webster *Meet You At The Fair* (Impulse!)

Randy Weston *Uhuru Afrika/Highlife* (Roulette)

Kenny Wheeler *Gnu High* (ECM)

Clarence Williams *1926-1927* (Classics)

Mary Lou Williams *1927-1940* (Classics)

Tony Williams *Lifetime* (2 CDs) (Verve)

Cassandra Wilson *New Moon Daughter* (Blue Note)

Teddy Wilson *With Billie In Mind* (Chiaroscuro)

Phil Woods, *Rights Of Swing,* Candid

World's Greatest Jazz Band *Live At Roosevelt Grill* (Atlantic)

Yellowjackets *Four Corners* (MCA)

Larry Young *Unity* (Blue Note)

Lester Young *The Complete Aladdin Sessions* (2 CDs) (Blue Note)

Lester Young *The Jazz Giants '56* (Verve)

Various Artists *Esquire's All-American Hot Jazz Sessions* (Bluebird)

Various Artists *Jazz In The Thirties* (2 CDs) (Disques Swing)

Various Artists *Jumpin' Like Mad* (2 CD's) (Capitol)

Various Artists *Ridin' In Rhythm* (2 CDs) (Disques Swing)

Various Artists *The Jazz Scene* (2 CDs) (Verve)

Jazz on Film

Scott Yanow

An Overview

Although jazz is very much a visual as well as an audio art form (one can learn a great deal about an artist's music by seeing him or her live in concert as opposed to only hearing their records), jazz and the motion picture industry have had an odd and sometimes adversarial relationship through the decades. There have been many lost opportunities in documenting jazz because the motion picture studios have generally been primarily concerned with entertaining the largest possible audience and could care less about innovative music or personal expression. Jazz musicians have often been used by Hollywood as brief sideshows and their appearances in movies have been (until recent times) quite random. While Louis Armstrong and the swing big bandleaders (such as Benny Goodman, Tommy Dorsey, Glenn Miller and Artie Shaw) can be viewed today during their prime, Charlie Parker, Bix Beiderbecke, Art Tatum and Clifford Brown were barely caught on film and then in almost accidental circumstances. Their fate was still better than that of King Oliver, Jelly Roll Morton, Fletcher Henderson's Orchestra, Fats Navarro and Albert Ayler who were missed entirely and (barring future discoveries) will never be seen playing again.

On the brighter side, since the rise of the video recorder, hundreds of jazz videotapes have become available including filmed performances, documentaries and unusual cameo appearances in Hollywood films. So, if an artist from the past was lucky enough to be captured on film, the chances are better than even that the performance is now available to be played at will on one's TV set.

The 1920s

It is ironic that the first major sound film is titled *The Jazz Singer,* and that all three versions of that movie feature singers who were way outside of jazz: Al Jolson, Danny Thomas and Neil Diamond! Although jazz was not featured on film all that often in the 1920s, there are some major exceptions. The Original Dixieland Jazz Band made an appearance in a rare 1917 film titled *The Good For Nothing* but that was a silent movie so the ODJB could be seen but not heard. Pianist Eubie

Blake and singer Noble Sissle participated in some experimental short sound films in the early 1920s and in 1926 the virtuoso studio guitarist Roy Smeck demonstrated his technique on various string instruments. The remarkable video collection *At The Jazz Band Ball* (Yazoo Video) has some of the best clips of the 1925-1933 period including cornetist Bix Beiderbecke's only appearance on records (leading the ensemble with Paul Whiteman's Orchestra), a hot version of "Sweet Georgia Brown" by Ben Bernie's Big Band in 1925 and historic selections by Duke Ellington, Louis Armstrong, the Boswell Sisters and Bessie Smith (the majority of the short movie *St. Louis Blues* which was Bessie's only film appearance) among others. The most famous so-called jazz film of the period is Paul Whiteman's *The King Of Jazz* but, other than a spirited number by Bing Crosby with the Rhythm Boys and a wonderful 90 seconds from violinist Joe Venuti and guitarist Eddie Lang, the production is quite tedious and very dated. Also worth looking for is the pioneering 1929 Black movie *Hallelujah* which in one nightclub segment features Curtis Mosby's Blue Blowers on two numbers.

The Swing Era
Because swing (starting in 1935) captured the imagination of the mass public, big band leaders and their sidemen became regular props in Hollywood, helping to validate cliched storylines by performing a number or two before fading into the background. Many of the more interesting jazz-based films of the 1932-45 era show up regularly on television, although viewers may not be alerted to the music from reading the plot summary. Here are a few to look for: *The Big Broadcast* (a 1932 film with memorable numbers by Bing Crosby with guitarist Eddie Lang, the Boswell Sisters, Cab Calloway and the Mills Brothers), *Hollywood Hotel* (which is mostly unwatchable except for the Benny Goodman Quartet's rapid treatment of "I've Got A Heart Full Of Rhythm" and the full orchestra's "Sing, Sing, Sing"), *Sweet And Lowdown* (which has some stunning clarinet playing by Goodman on "The World Is Waiting For The Sunrise"), *Pennies From Heaven* (starring Bing Crosby and Louis Armstrong), *Best Foot Forward* (trumpeter Harry James at his prime), *Second Chorus* (clarinetist Artie Shaw performs "Concerto For Clarinet" while Fred Astaire and Burgess Meredith plot to land a spot in his trumpet section!), *Birth Of The Blues* (a fictional but Dixieland-filled movie with Crosby and trombonist Jack Teagarden), and the two Glenn Miller films *Orchestra Wives* and *Sun Valley Serenade* (the latter has some amazing dancing by the Nicholas Brothers on a definitive "Chattanooga Choo Choo").

During 1940-46 many orchestras recorded three-minute "soundies" for viewing on video jukeboxes. Generally they were low budget productions with the music obviously recorded separately from the performances, but these clips do give today's listeners an opportunity to see many entertainers from the era. Leonard Maltin's four-volume video series *Movie Memories* (BMG Video) has some of the best jazz soundies.

Black musicians had some notable opportunities to be documented outside of the standard White films. 1944's *Jammin' The Blues* is a classic three-song performance featuring tenors Lester Young and Illinois Jacquet and trumpeter Harry "Sweets" Edison; it can be seen completely intact at the end of *Song Of The Spirit*, a definitive Lester Young documentary. Feature-length films from Black-owned companies during the 1930s and '40s tend to be obscure and primitive (due to a lack of money) but quite a few have appearances by top jazzmen. *Five Guys Named Moe* (Vintage Jazz Classics) collects together some of the popular altoist-singer-entertainer Louis Jordan's better performances on film.

Two of the best all-Black musicals were made during 1942-43 for major studios. *Cabin In The Sky* stars Ethel Waters (who introduces "Takin' A Chance On Love") and Lena Horne while *Stormy Weather* has major parts for Horne, Bill "Bojangles" Robinson, Cab Calloway, Fats Waller (the best of his three film appearances) and the Nicholas Brothers who engage in an incredible dance number.

The 1940s and 1950s
Because bebop was not the popular commercial success that swing had been, film appearances by its innovators were a hit and miss affair. Neither Charlie Parker or Dizzy Gillespie were in demand by Hollywood. However *Things To Come* (Vintage Jazz Classics) does contain two of the most historical bop shorts, a strong performance by the 1946 Billy Eckstine Orchestra (which features tenor saxophonist Gene Ammons and drummer Art Blakey) and the musical numbers from *Jivin' In Bebop* by the 1947 Dizzy Gillespie big band.

The two best Hollywood jazz films of the 1945-50 era showcased earlier music. *A Song Is Born*, a Danny Kaye comedy, has contributions by Benny Goodman (who actually plays a role), Louis Armstrong and Lionel Hampton among others while New Orleans (which has yet to be released on video), even with its dumb storyline, contains a great deal of exciting music from Armstrong, Kid Ory and Billie Holiday (seen in her only Hollywood film).

In the 1950s several swing bandleaders became the subjects of nostalgic Hollywood biographies. Despite simplistic, inaccurate and overly sentimental storylines, most of these films have some worthwhile music. 1947's rather dull *The Fabulous*

Dorseys (in which Tommy and Jimmy Dorsey play themselves) is only notable for a jam session scene that features Art Tatum. *The Benny Goodman Story* (which stars Steve Allen) has lots of fine swing music even if the storyline focuses on a romance placed in the wrong time period and the plot totally neglects Goodman's successful fight against racism. *The Glenn Miller Story* is absurdly sweet although Jimmy Stewart (as Miller) is fine and the popular big bandleader's biggest hits are well played. *The Gene Krupa Story* portrays the great drummer as a "marijuana addict" and the worst of these films, 1972's *Lady Sings The Blues*, is offensive on all counts even if Diana Ross does her best to recreate Billie Holiday's singing style. Much more enjoyable is *The Five Pennies*, a very entertaining if fictional account of cornetist Red Nichols' life which stars Danny Kaye and Louis Armstrong. Other significant jazz films of the era include the much-maligned but actually fairly enjoyable *Young Man With A Horn*, *Pete Kelly's Blues* and *The Man With The Golden Arm*. The latter was one of the earlier films to feature jazz throughout the sound track, a trend started by Leith Stevens' use of Shorty Rogers' recordings in the 1953 Marlon Brando film *The Wild One*. Jazz soon gained a permanent spot in the scores of motion pictures, particularly as background music during crime scenes!

Jazz on Television
The first (and one of the few) regular jazz television series was *the Eddie Condon Floor Show* in 1949. As with Steve Allen's original *Tonight Show* a few years later, jazz was featured on a regular basis but most of the priceless kinescopes have been long since lost although some of the soundtracks have been issued on records.

Fortunately some other shows still survive and have even been released on videos. *The Sound Of Jazz* (Vintage Jazz Classics), which is arguably the greatest jazz film of all, is a 60-minute program that was originally a special on CBS. Featuring the Red Allen All-Stars, Count Basie, Pee Wee Russell, Coleman Hawkins, Ben Webster, Lester Young, Roy Eldridge, Thelonious Monk and many others, the spontaneity, mutual respect and competitiveness of the musicians really comes through. Billie Holiday's rendition of "Fine And Mellow" (the most famous of these performances) is quite touching. Also quite noteworthy are four videos put out by Shanachie of the legendary *Jazz Scene* shows of the early 1960s, featuring such notable groups as the Cannonball Adderley Sextet, Stan Kenton's Orchestra and combos led by Phineas Newborn and Jimmy Smith among others. And not to be missed is *The Coltrane Legacy* (Video Artists Int.) which has the innovative saxophonist's two half-hour television appearances with such sidemen as Eric Dolphy, McCoy Tyner and Elvin Jones.

Jazz Documentaries
Many jazz documentaries (most of which have been made since the 1960s) have the fault of not letting the music speak for itself, using annoying narrators who talk over the performances. However a few are special. *Jazz On A Summer's Day* (New Yorker Films), even with its wandering camera, documents several special moments (in color!) from the 1958 Newport Jazz Fetival. *Memories Of Duke* (A * Vision) has many clips from the Duke Ellington Orchestra's 1968 tour of Mexico. *David, Moffett and Ornette* (Rhapsody Films) is a fascinating look at the 1966 Ornette Coleman Trio as they work on recording a spontaneous film score. *Talmage Farlow* (Rhapsody Films) portrays the talented guitarist quite happy to be in musical semi-retirement and working as a sign painter! *The Jazz Messenger* (Rhapsody Films) follows drummer Art Blakey around during the period when trumpeter Terence Blanchard and altoist Donald Harrison were preparing to leave the Jazz Messengers. The outstanding *Straight No Chaser* (Rhapsody Films) gives one a complete picture of pianist Thelonious Monk (both privately and publicly) and has many clips from his 1967 European tour with an octet. Miles Davis' *Live At Montreux* (Warner Reprise) documents the trumpeter's revisit of Gil Evans' music shortly before his death. On the down side is Bruce Weber's *Let's Get Lost* (Little Bear Films) which inaccurately portrays Chet Baker as a washed-up singer rather than as a talented trumpeter.

Jazz Films of Recent Times
Starting with *'Round Midnight*, Hollywood has once again tried to depict the jazz life with mixed success. The dialogue and events run true in *'Round Midnight* even if the slightly downbeat story and the fact that tenor saxophonist Dexter Gordon (who gained an Oscar nomination for his work as the film's star) was past his prime are slightly disappointing. Clint Eastwood's *Bird* has its memorable moments even with its flaws (an emphasis on Charlie Parker's decline and an incomplete characterization of the complex altoist) while Spike Lee's *Mo' Better Blues*, although having an unlikely ending, does do a fine job of showing what the life of an up-and-coming local musician might very well be like. Both movies are certainly superior to Robert Altman's *Kansas City* which misuses its all-star band as a human jukebox that never speaks or does anything other than play in back of the obvious plot and a seemingly nonstop string of obscenities.

Music Map

Jazz on Film

The 1920s

The Good for Nothing (silent) • Eubie Blake and Noble Sissle (experimental short sound films) • Roy Smeck (instrument demonstration) • *At the Jazz Band Ball* • *The King of Jazz* • *Hallelujah*

The Swing Era

The Big Broadcast • *Hollywood Hotel* • *Sweet and Lowdown* • *Pennies from Heaven* • *Best Foot Forward* • *Birth of the Blues* • *Orchestra Wives* • *Sun Valley Serenade* • "Soundies" • *Jammin' the Blues* • *Five Guys Named Moe* • *Cabin in the Sky* • *Stormy Weather*

The 1940s and 1950s

Jivin' in Bebop • *A Song Is Born* • *New Orleans* • *The Fabulous Dorseys* • *The Benny Goodman Story* • *The Glenn Miller Story* • *The Gene Krupa Story* • *The Five Pennies* • *Young Man with a Horn* • *Pete Kelly's Blues* • *The Man with the Golden Arm*

Jazz on Television

The Eddie Condon Floor Show • *The Sound of Jazz* • *Jazz Scene* • *The Coltrane Legacy*

Jazz Documentaries

Jazz on a Summer's Day • *Memories of Duke* • *David, Moffett and Ornette* • *Talmage Farlow* • *The Jazz Messenger* • *Straight, No Chaser* • *Live at Montreux* • *Let's Get Lost*

Recent Jazz Films

'Round Midnight • *Bird* • *'Mo Better Blues* • *Kansas City*

But even if Hollywood lags far behind, there is no shortage of jazz performances on video and there are currently dozens of superior tapes to choose from. Although some of the early greats are lost to history, future generations will happily be able to not only hear but see the pacesetters of the 1980s and '90s at their best. -*Scott Yanow*

Twenty Essential Jazz Videos

After Hours (Rhapsody Films)
At The Jazz Band Ball (Yazoo Video)
Art Blakey—The Jazz Messenger (Rhapsody Films)
Buck Clayton All-Stars (Shanachie)
John Coltrane—The Coltrane Legacy (Video Artists Int.)
Talmage Farlow (Rhapsody Films)
Five Guys Named Moe (Vintage Jazz Classics)
Alberta Hunter—My Castle's Rockin' (View Video)

Jazz On A Summer's Day (New Yorker Video)
Jazz Scene USA—Cannonball Adderley/Teddy Edwards (Shanachie)
Gene Krupa—Jazz Legend (DCI Video)
Steve Lacy—Lift The Bandstand (Rhapsody Films)
Lady Day—The Man Faces Of Billie Holiday (Kulter)
Jackie McLean—Dynasty (Triloka Video)
Charles Mingus Sextet (Shanachie)
Thelonious Monk—Straight No Chaser (Warner Home Video)
The Sound Of Jazz (Vintage Jazz Classics)
Things To Come (Vintage Jazz Classics)
Vintage Collection Vol. 2 (A * Vision Entertainment)
Lester Young—Song Of The Spirit (Song Of The Spirit)

—*Scott Yanow*

Books

52nd Street, *Arnold Shaw* / 1971 / Da Capo Press ♦♦♦♦♦
52nd Street in New York during its prime (1935-47) was a truly remarkable place, an area where one club after another (which were sometimes next door to each other) featured the top names in jazz. It was possible in one night to see Coleman Hawkins, Art Tatum, Billie Holiday, Charlie Parker and Eddie Condon; every night was a jazz festival. Arnold Shaw, in this entertaining and very informative book, goes club-by-club through the Street. He interviewed musicians, singers, club owners and even a stripper to get a well-rounded picture of this very special (and never duplicated) center of jazz. *—Scott Yanow*

The 101 Best Jazz Albums, *Len Lyons* / 1980 / Morrow Quill ♦♦♦
Len Lyons had a great idea for this book, one that should be done again now that the CD era is in its prime. Lyons essentially related the history of jazz through 101 albums, not only extensively reviewing each release, but telling the story of the music and its style. In addition, he recommends quite a few related records. Now that all of the LPs are out of print, this consistently interesting book is quite dated, but for the time it was excellent, despite Lyons making the mistake of listing George Benson's *Weekend in L.A.* and *The Best of Chuck Mangione* among the 101! *—Scott Yanow*

Ain't Misbehavin', *Ed Kirkeby with Duncan P. Schiedt and Sinclair Traill* / 1966 / Da Capo Press ♦♦♦
Fats Waller was a legendary character of many parts: a brilliant stride pianist, a very likable vocalist, an often-hilarious speaker, a very talented composer and a pioneering jazz organist who accomplished everything while constantly partying! Ed Kirkeby was Waller's manager during his final eight years and this biography (put together with the assistance of two top English writers) recreates the unique genius' life and times quite lovingly. The first 14 chapters (dealing with Fats' earlier years) are in the third person; in the final four Kirkeby writes in the first person. There are many recreated conversations that may not always be completely accurate but the end results are informative and entertaining. This paperback edition is rounded out by a discography that was excellent for the time. *—Scott Yanow*

Alberta Hunter, *Frank Taylor & Gerald Cook* / 1987 / McGraw-Hill ♦♦♦♦
Alberta Hunter had a remarkable life. A talented blues performer in the 1920s who was quite successful as a stage actress and a cabaret performer in Europe during the 1930s, Hunter became a nurse while in her early sixties and worked until she was involuntarily retired at the age of 82; it was believed that she had just turned 70! At that point in time (1977), Alberta Hunter returned to singing and again became a hit until her death in 1984 at the age of 89. This biography (which was written by Frank Taylor with the assistance of Hunter's accompanist Gerald Cook) is a definitive and very readable work that not only details Hunter's public life but her well-hidden and sometimes difficult private life too. An excellent book which is rounded out by a good discography. *—Scott Yanow*

Alec Wilder in Spite of Himself, *Desmond Stone* / 1996 / Oxford University Press ♦♦♦♦

All What Jazz, *Philip Larkin* / 1985 / Farrar-Straus-Giroux ♦♦♦
Philip Larkin, a well-respected British poet and author, reviewed jazz on the side during 1961-71. This book collects virtually all of his reviews and since his taste leaned heavily towards prebop jazz and he had a strong and mischievous wit, some of the reviews of modern jazz (particularly the avant-garde) contain hilarious comments. The reviews are generally quite short (often only a sentence) and there is more opinion to these pieces than fact, but it does make for an entertaining read by veteran jazz collectors who do not take it all too seriously! *—Scott Yanow*

☆ **American Musicians**, *Whitney Balliett* / 1986 / Oxford University Press ♦♦♦♦♦
Whitney Balliett is the most picturesque of jazz writers, able to capture the joy and complexity of jazz, its creative process, the unique musicians and the music itself in words. This highly recommended book combines 49 of his best portraits, focusing on the life of 56 musicians in all. Although the majority of the stories deal with classic jazz, swing or mainstream players (as befits Balliett's taste),

there are intriguing articles on Ornette Coleman and Cecil Taylor. In nearly all cases, Balliett interviewed the subject and, even when it was impossible, associates were tracked down; trombonist Clyde Bernhardt's tales of life with King Oliver are utterly fascinating. Actually all of the chapters are of that level, giving readers a countless number of fresh anecdotes and insight into what drives these creative musicians. This is Whitney Balliett's most rewarding book. *—Scott Yanow*

☆ **American Musicians II**, *Whitney Balliett* / 1996 / Oxford University Press ♦♦♦♦♦

American Popular Song, *Alec Wilder* / 1972 / Oxford University Press ♦♦♦♦♦
This book has long been considered a classic of its kind. Alec Wilder discusses the songs written by the top American pop composers of 1920-50 including full chapters on six writers (Jerome Kern, Irving Berlin, George Gershwin, Richard Rodgers, Cole Porter and Harold Arlen) plus substantial space for the work of 17 others. He writes technically about how individual songs were constructed (sometimes using musical notation) and points out what was most unusual or colorful about most pieces. Although it helps to be able to read music, Wilder's writing is more accessible than expected and his book is never boring. An excellent scholarly work. *—Scott Yanow*

American Singers, *Whitney Balliett* / 1988 / Oxford University Press ♦♦♦♦
Whitney Balliett has the very rare ability to turn the experience of playing, living and creating jazz into words. His book *American Musicians* is highly recommended and *American Singers* (27 portraits in 25 chapters) is of the same quality. Not everyone covered in this book exclusively performed jazz (including Ray Charles, Tony Bennett, Mabel Mercer, Bobby Short, Hugh Shannon and Julie Wilson) and one (Alec Wilder) is not even a singer. However each chapter is well worth reading since Balliett does a definitive and colorful job of capturing his subjects. Some of these interviews are priceless. *—Scott Yanow*

The Art of Jazz, *edited by Martin Williams* / 1959 / Da Capo Press ♦♦♦♦♦
Martin Williams collected together 19 articles plus two of his own in this interesting book which is subtitled "Ragtime to Bebop." Covering different aspects and personalities from jazz history that range from blues harmonica Sonny Terry and Jelly Roll Morton, up to hard bop, this was a good all-round jazz book for 1959 although many of these topics have been discussed more definitively since then. Among the highlights are Ernest Ansermet's acclaimed and insightful assessment of Sidney Bechet in 1919, George Avakian's liner notes for Bix Beiderbecke and Bessie Smith reissues, William Russell's assessment of three boogie-woogie pianists, Andre Hodeir's provocative essay on Art Tatum and Ross Russell's discussion of bebop. *—Scott Yanow*

As Though I Had Wings, *Chet Baker* / 1997 / St. Martin's Press ♦♦♦

Avant-Garde Jazz Musicians Performing "Out There," *David Such* / 1993 / University of Iowa Press ♦♦♦

The Baby Dodds Story, *Baby Dodds & Larry Gara* / 1959 / Louisiana State University Press ♦♦♦
Until this book was republished (with a new introduction) in 1992, few jazz historians knew of its existence. Baby Dodds was one of the first significant jazz drummers; many would consider him the top drummer of the 1920s. In the 1950s he was extensively interviewed by Larry Gara and his tales about New Orleans in the teens, Chicago in the 1920s and his later experiences are often priceless. There are not too many people around anymore who can give firsthand accounts of playing with King Oliver, Fate Marable, Jelly Roll Morton and Johnny Dodds (Baby's brother)! Although the book is a bit short, there are a lot of memorable tales that should greatly interest fans of New Orleans jazz. *—Scott Yanow*

Back Beats and Rim Shots—The Johnny Blowers Story, *Warren Vache, Sr.* / 1997 / Scarecrow Press ♦♦♦♦

Barney, Bradley, and Max—16 Portraits in Jazz, *Whitney Balliett* / 1989 / Oxford University Press ♦♦♦♦
Whitney Balliett is one of the finest writers to ever tackle jazz. His portraits are

so picturesque and informative that one learns a great deal about his subjects in a short time and can almost hear their music without putting on a record. For this typically fascinating collection of pieces (eight of which had appeared in different forms in his earlier books) Balliett wrote about a fan (Jean Bach), three New York clubowners (Max Gordon, Barney Josephson and Bradley Cunningham), an obscure musician (Marie Marcus) and such favorites as Claude Thornhill, Jimmy Rowles, Mel Powell, George Shearing, Walter Norris, Harvey Philips, Benny Goodman (at the time of his 40th anniversary Carnegie Hall concert), Ruby Braff, Charlie Parker, Buddy DeFranco and Louie Bellson. The articles were composed during 1971-88 but none are dated and all add to one's understanding of these colorful and often-unique people. —*Scott Yanow*

☆ **Bass Line,** *Milt Hinton & David Berger* / 1988 / Temple University Press ✦✦✦✦✦
One of the most recorded jazz musicians of all time (who is possibly in first place), bassist Milt Hinton has been a fixture on the scene since the late 1920s. Little-known to most until the last decade was the fact that he has long been an equally talented photographer and has been snapping pictures constantly since the 1930s. This wonderful oversize book is really two in one. The very well-written text (essentially Hinton's autobiography) has many interesting stories about his life and the remarkable musicians he knew. But even if there were no anecdotes, this book would be highly recommended because the photos are consistently interesting, historic and sometimes quite moving. —*Scott Yanow*

Bassically Speaking—An Oral History of George Duvivier, *Edward Berger* / 1993 / Scarecrow Press ✦✦✦✦

Bebop—The Music and the Players, *Thomas Owens* / 1995 / Oxford University Press ✦✦✦

Bebop and Nothingness, *Francis Davis* / 1996 / Schirmer Books ✦✦✦
Francis Davis has long been one of the most articulate of all jazz journalists. In fact, the more educated and well-read one is, the more a reader can gain from absorbing his thought-provoking articles which often refer to novels and works from other fields. Davis' third collection of essays (following *Outcats* and *In the Moment*) has 36 pieces that mostly date from the 1990-93 period, the majority of which deal with jazz. As Davis frankly admits in the introduction, he has become somewhat jaded and disillusioned with the jazz scene. Although not as New Yorkcentric as some East Coast writers, Davis' view of the jazz world relies too much on what is occurring in New York City and the recordings that are released by the major labels. However, despite the moody nature of some of his pieces, most of the articles (which profile such individualists as Benny Carter, late-period Miles Davis, Art Blakey, Ruby Braff, Anthony Braxton, Charles Gayle, Don Byron and Grover Washington, Jr.) contain more than their share of fresh stories and original insights. In addition to the jazz pieces, there are profiles of Tony Bennett, Barbara Streisand, Stephen Sondheim's *Passion* and even Michael Jackson/Prince (in a piece called "Toons") and rap (which Davis enjoys although he is a bit besides himself in trying to explain why), showing that he is quite informed about most areas of current pop music. Even when one disagrees with Francis Davis, his articles are worth reading. —*Scott Yanow*

Benny Goodman—Listen to His Legacy, *D. Russell Connor* / 1988 / Scarecrow Press ✦✦✦✦✦
This is a massive book that every Benny Goodman fanatic can consider essential. D. Russell Connor had been BG's discographer for a couple of decades and this 1988 work was his final version. All of the clarinetist's recordings are listed in great detail along with radio appearances and unissued tapes of his live performances. It is possible to trace his whereabouts throughout every year of his long career and, when one considers the huge amount of recordings that Goodman made, it becomes clear that this oversized book (which has superb photos) is not only Benny Goodman's legacy but D. Russell Connor's too. —*Scott Yanow*

☆ **Bessie,** *Chris Albertson* / 1982 / Stein and Day ✦✦✦✦✦

The Best of Jazz, *Humphrey Lyttelton* / 1978 / Crescendo/Taplinger ✦✦✦✦
Humphrey Lyttelton, in addition to being a top trumpeter from Great Britain since the late 1940s, is a talented writer. In this first of two volumes (preceding *The Best of Jazz II*), Lyttelton contributes profiles on what he calls "Jazz Masters and Masterpieces, 1917-1930." His chapters (on the Original Dixieland Jazz Band, James P. Johnson, King Oliver, Sidney Bechet, Bessie Smith, Jelly Roll Morton, Fletcher Henderson, Louis Armstrong, Bix Beiderbecke, Duke Ellington, the Chicagoans, Johnny Dodds/Jimmy Noone, Louis Armstrong/Earl Hines, and Luis Russell) are filled with concise and easily understandable musical analysis of their styles and recordings. This book, which has more than its share of fresh ideas, will be most enjoyed by readers already a bit familiar with 1920s jazz. —*Scott Yanow*

The Best of Jazz II, *Humphrey Lyttelton* / 1981 / Taplinger Publications ✦✦✦✦
Trumpeter Humphrey Lyttelton, whose writing talents are on the same high level as his playing abilities, came out with this second book in 1981, three years after

The Best of Jazz. While the latter focused on musicians from the 1920s, this volume (subtitled "Enter the Giants, 1931-1944") has chapters on Louis Armstrong, Fats Waller, Coleman Hawkins, Jack Teagarden, Art Tatum, Johnny Hodges/Benny Carter, Dickie Wells, Lester Young, Billie Holiday and Roy Eldridge. Lyttelton concentrates on musical analysis of styles and recordings but his book is quite readable, avoids clichés and will be found quite thought-provoking by listeners who already have strong knowledge of the swing era. —*Scott Yanow*

☆ **The Big Bands,** *George T. Simon* / 1974 / Collier Books Editions ✦✦✦✦✦
First published in 1967 and enlarged a couple times since, this is considered the most comprehensive of all the reference books on the swing era. George T. Simon, who was on the staff of Metronome during much of the 1930s and '40s, witnessed virtually all of the big bands in action, and his summaries of the orchestras (which sometimes quote from his own reports of the time) are even-handed, consistent and quite informative. There are a variety of essays on aspects of the era (including chapters on the public, the vocalists, arrangers, businessmen, recordings, radio, movies and the press), chapters on 72 of the bands and a paragraph apiece on hundreds of others. The book concludes with interviews of surviving bandleaders Count Basie, Benny Goodman, Woody Herman, Harry James, Stan Kenton, Guy Lombardo and Artie Shaw conducted in 1971. Essential. —*Scott Yanow*

Bill Russell's American Music, *Mike Hazeldine* / 1993 / Jazzology Press ✦✦✦✦

Billie's Blues, *John Chilton* / 1975 / Da Capo Press ✦✦✦✦
This interesting book covers the life of Billie Holiday from the time of her first recording in 1933 up until her death in 1959. Not as detailed as John Chilton's magnificent Sidney Bechet book and purposely skipping Holiday's childhood, the narrative gives readers all of the usual details about the public life of Lady Day, what was known at the time of her distressing private affairs and in four chapters discusses her recordings. Although not as definitive as Donald Clarke's *Wishing on the Moon*, *Billie's Blues* is a useful introductory book to Billie Holiday and puts the emphasis where it belongs, on her music. —*Scott Yanow*

The Billie Holiday Companion, *Leslie Gourse, Editor* / 1997 / Schirmer Books ✦✦✦✦

☆ **Bird—The Legend of Charlie Parker,** *edited by Robert Reisner* / 1962 / Da Capo Press ✦✦✦✦✦
Even decades later, this is one of the better books on Charlie Parker. Robert Reisner, an acquaintance of the great altoist during his final two years, interviewed 81 people that knew Bird (including Miles Davis, Kenny Dorham, Dizzy Gillespie, Earl Hines, Charles Mingus, Anita O'Day, two of Parker's wives, Max Roach and Lennie Tristano) and their responses are full of interesting stories. Because the interviews are put in alphabetical order, this book jumps around chronologically quite a bit (although Reisner did contribute a 20-page introduction titled "I Remember Bird"). Taken as a whole the book gives one a good idea as to what Parker was like as a person; despite his excesses he comes across quite well. —*Scott Yanow*

☆ **Bird Lives,** *Ross Russell* / 1972 / Quartet Books ✦✦✦✦✦
Due to the fanciful (and sometimes inaccurate) nature of some of the stories told in this book, *Bird Lives* has often been put down as purely fiction. Actually it is one of the better books on Charlie Parker, written by Ross Russell who ran the Dial label. There are a few self-serving tales told but one gets a full picture of what Russell called "The High Life and Hard Times of Charlie 'Yardbird' Parker." The innovative altoist led an exciting if tumultuous life (actually several lives) before his death at age 34, and all aspects of this genius' crazy and self-destructive lifestyle are covered in this continually fascinating work. —*Scott Yanow*

The Birth of Bebop, *Scott DeVeaux* / 1997 / University of California Press ✦✦✦✦

☆ **Bix—Man and Legend,** *Richard Sudhalter and Philip Evans with William Dean Myatt* / 1974 / Schirmer Books ✦✦✦✦✦
This is the finest jazz biography written to date. Bix Beiderbecke was a legendary cornetist from the 1920s whose early death (at age 28 in 1931) led to him being considered one of jazz's first martyrs. Richard Sudhalter, Philip Evans and William Dean Myatt independently began research on Bix in 1957-58 and eventually joined forces, completing this remarkable work 16 years later. Beiderbecke's life is fully explored and discussed, many myths about him are disproved, a very complete chronology of his life (containing all kinds of trivial detail) is offered as one of the appendixes and there is a full discography. Due to the enormous amount of interviews conducted, the biography is full of fresh stories that explain many of the paradoxes of the legend's life. This is everything a jazz biography should be; it reads like a novel! —*Scott Yanow*

Black and Blue—The Life and Lyrics of Andy Razaf, *Barry Singer* / 1992 / Schirmer Books ✦✦✦✦

☆ **Black Beauty, White Heat,** *Frank Driggs & Harris Lewine* / 1982 / Morrow ♦♦♦♦♦

Frank Driggs owns what must be the largest jazz memorabilia collection in the world. This very impressive oversize book has over 1,500 rare photographs, advertisements and pictures of record labels dating from 1920-50. After a fine article by Paul Bacon about the joys of being a record collector in the 1940s and '50s, there are nine chapters that arrange the photos according to geography and time period, ranging from early New Orleans jazz to the bop era. A page or two of text introduces each chapter and the captions identify all of the musicians. *Black Beauty, White Heat* is the ultimate coffee table jazz book and will thrill early jazz collectors for dozens of hours. —*Scott Yanow*

Black Talk, *Ben Sidran* / 1971 / Da Capo Press ♦♦♦♦

Blue—The Murder of Jazz, *Eric Nisenson* / 1997 / St. Martin's Press ♦♦

Blue Flame—Woody Herman's Life in Music, *Robert Kriebel* / 1995 / Purdue University Press ♦♦♦

Blue Rhythms, *Chip Deffaa* / 1996 / University of Illinois Press ♦♦♦♦♦
This is really six books in one. Chip Deffaa's portraits of six rhythm and blues veterans (Ruth Brown, Little Jimmy Scott, Charles Brown, Floyd Dixon, LaVern Baker and Jimmy Witherspoon) are quite definitive. In most cases the stories of these artists are pretty similar. They came to fame fairly early (mostly during the 1945-55 era), made hit records for peanuts, signed away most of their royalties, worked constantly during their peak commercial years and then, when rock 'n' roll came in (except in the case of Baker who did not go into eclipse until the mid-1960s), they were soon forgotten. Years of neglect were followed by an eventual comeback in the 1980s. Each of the artists' careers overlapped at times with the jazz world (most notably in the case of Witherspoon but even Baker recorded a Bessie Smith tribute album) so their colorful stories should be of strong interest to jazz listeners. Deffaa conducted extensive interviews with each of the principals and some of their contemporaries and, most importantly, he displays a deep understanding of the artists' struggles and of their music. The narrative never bogs down and there is a great deal of fresh information in this highly recommended and important book. —*Scott Yanow*

Blues People, *LeRoi Jones* / 1963 / Morrow ♦♦♦♦
A bit of a classic although aspects of it are a little dated now, *Blues People* was the first important jazz book written by a black author. Dealing as much with the sociological aspects of being black in the United States of the 19th and 20th century as it is about jazz, this highly original book has a lot of valuable information about early pre-jazz black music and gives readers a different tilt towards aspects of jazz history and the struggle that black creative musicians have had through the decades, from Congo Square up to Ornette Coleman. —*Scott Yanow*

Blues Up and Down—Jazz in Our Time, *Tom Piazza* / 1997 / St. Martin's Press ♦♦♦

Boogie, Pete & the Senator, *Mark Miller* / 1987 / Nightwood Editions ♦♦♦♦
Through this book and *Jazz in Canada: Fourteen Lives*, Mark Miller has documented the often overlooked world of Canadian jazz. While the earlier book covered the history of jazz up North, this second effort concentrates on Canadian musicians who were active in the 1980s. Forty different musicians are portrayed including Ed Bickert, Paul Bley, Terry Clarke, Jim Galloway, Linton Garner, Sonny Greenwich, Oliver Jones, Fraser MacPherson, Rob McConnell, Phil Nimmons, Oscar Peterson, Paul Plimley, Bill Smith, Don Thompson and Kenny Wheeler along with lesser-known talents. This is a particularly valuable book for modern jazz followers who wish to expand their knowledge beyond knowing just the top American players. —*Scott Yanow*

Bouncing with Bud, *Carl Smith* / 1997 / Biddle Publishing Company ♦♦♦
Bud Powell changed the way that the piano is played in jazz, leading to the realignment of the entire rhythm section. By comping chords with his left hand rather than striding and playing long single-note runs with his right, Powell effectively transferred bebop to the piano. This book is not a biography of the troubled Powell (although an essay by Mark Gardner is included) but a discussion by Carl Smith of the many recordings that exist of Bud from his 20-year career (1944-64). The musical analysis is fairly basic but the book (an obvious labor of love) does have its value in sorting out Powell's LPs and CDs for collectors wondering which releases duplicate which. There are also many fine photos of Powell, various musicians and the pianist's albums, making this a worthwhile acquisition for fans of the innovative pianist. —*Scott Yanow*

Buck Clayton's Jazz World, *Buck Clayton and Nancy Miller Elliott* / 1986 / Oxford University Press ♦♦♦
Trumpeter Buck Clayton's memoirs start out so strong that its second half is anti-climatic and a bit disappointing. Clayton had a strong memory and his stories about his days before joining Count Basie are quite fresh and informative. But once he hits the 1950s and starts constantly touring around the world, far too

many pages are taken up by what is essentially a dull travelogue (those sections should be scanned and mostly skipped) before the story picks up again. It is always a rare treat to have a jazz autobiography by a major player and this book (even with its flaws) is well worth acquiring; it also contains a fine discography. —*Scott Yanow*

Buddy DeFranco: A Biographical Portrait and Discography, *John Kuehn and Arne Astrup* / 1993 / Scarecrow Press ♦♦♦
Buddy DeFranco has been the top clarinetist (along with Eddie Daniels) to emerge after 1940 yet has barely been recognized because his instrument went out of style after the swing era. This compact but nearly definitive book finally gives DeFranco some of the recognition he deserves. John Kuehn, a longtime fan, sums up the clarinetist's life in 38 pages and then devotes 62 to an extensive set of interviews with DeFranco in which he asks him every possible question (including his opinion of a couple dozen other clarinetists!). Arne Astrup's extensive discography takes up more than half of the book, making one wish that Kuehn's section was more than 100 pages. However until a better work comes along, this is the Buddy DeFranco book to get. —*Scott Yanow*

☆ **Bunny Berigan—Elusive Legend of Jazz,** *Robert Dupuis* / 1993 / Louisiana University Press ♦♦♦♦♦
The ill-fated Bunny Berigan was arguably the top trumpeter in jazz during 1935-39 and a dramatic soloist who had an adventurous spirit and full control over his horn. His alcoholism resulted in quite a few colorful episodes before his premature death in 1942 at age 33. Although this book was completed over a half-century after Bunny's passing, author Robert Dupuis was able to track down many of Berigan's surviving relatives, friends (including some from childhood) and musical associates to piece together a very compelling story. In addition to his musical career, one learns about Berigan's family life, friendships, personality and difficulties with alcohol. Many more descriptions of Berigan's recordings (particularly his obscure sessions) and a more detailed discography would have improved the results but this book is quite definitive and holds one's interest throughout. —*Scott Yanow*

Call Him George, *Ann Fairbairn* / 1969 / Bantam Books ♦♦♦

A Call to Assembly, *Willie Ruff* / 1991 / Viking Penguin ♦♦♦♦♦

Cats of Any Color, *Gene Lees* / 1994 / Oxford University Press ♦♦♦

☆ **Celebrating Bird,** *Gary Giddins* / 1987 / Beechtree Books ♦♦♦♦♦
This is a particularly attractive book on Charlie Parker. Gary Giddins' text is concise, colorful, accessible and filled with original ideas and stories, many gained by interviewing the great altoist's first wife Rebecca Parker Davis. In addition, this slightly oversized book has many rare (and some famous) photographs which by themselves would justify its purchase. Although it came out as a companion to a documentary film of the same title, the book is quite enjoyable independent of the movie. This is one that all Charlie Parker fans should get! —*Scott Yanow*

Celebrating the Duke, *Ralph Gleason* / 1975 / Da Capo Press ♦♦♦♦
Ralph Gleason's final book is one of his best. His portraits of the jazz artists who he called his "heroes" (Bessie Smith, Louis Armstrong, Jimmie Lunceford, Billie Holiday, Lester Young, Charlie Parker, Dizzy Gillespie, the Modern Jazz Quartet, Carmen McRae, John Coltrane, Miles Davis and Albert Ayler) are full of insight and open-minded ideas; the Louis Armstrong chapter in particular has plenty of surprises. Gleason, one of the very few writers to love both Dixieland and rock (some of the portraits originally appeared in Rolling Stone), finishes off this fine book with a 114-page discussion of Duke Ellington, tracing his experiences seeing and talking with the genius during 1952-74. Although now over 20 years old, many of the opinions expressed in *Celebrating the Duke* are still relevant. —*Scott Yanow*

Celebrating the Saxophone, *Paul Lindemeyer* / 1996 / Hearst Books ♦♦♦
Although a bit overpriced, this breezy book is quite colorful. It pays tribute to the saxophone with many unusual photos, commentary that accurately sums up the instrument's history and some surprising features. The giants of the idiom are saluted along with some lesser-known players and even veteran collectors will probably not have seen many of the pictures or read some of the humorous quotes. Purposely lightweight, this book is quite delightful. —*Scott Yanow*

Central Avenue—Its Rise and Fall, *Bette Yarbrough Cox* / 1996 / Beem Publications ♦♦♦♦

A Century of Jazz, *Roy Carr* / 1997 / Da Capo Press ♦♦♦♦♦
This very colorful book can serve both as a delightful introduction to jazz for novices and an eye-catching acquisition for veterans. A fun work filled with short breezy articles (that are often concise yet definitive) and hundreds of rare photos, the book covers everything from the beginnings of jazz and the swing era up to the Young Lions, Acid Jazz, Western swing and jazz in film. Nearly every page has some unusual information whether it be a list of every LP to make it onto

the pop charts (more than one would think), advertisements, rare album jackets or offbeat articles. Highly recommended. —*Scott Yanow*

Chasin' the Trane, *J.C. Thomas* / 1975 / Doubleday ✦✦✦

This book was an interesting first attempt to sum up the life and myth (or as its subtitle says "The Music and Mystique") of John Coltrane. J.C. Thomas uses quotes from many sources (although he seems to have conducted few new interviews) including the great saxophonist's friends, contemporaries and fans and put together a colorful if sometimes fanciful narrative of Coltrane's life. The book (which has its memorable sections) serves as a strong introduction to John Coltrane although it is far from definitive. —*Scott Yanow*

Chet—A Discography, *Thorbjorn Sjogren* / 1993 / Jazz Media ✦✦✦✦✦

Chicago Jazz, *William Howland Kenney* / 1993 / Oxford University Press ✦✦✦

Chris McGregor and the Brotherhood of Breath, *Maxine McGregor* / 1995 / Bamberger Books ✦✦✦✦

Chris McGregor was quite unique. A white South African pianist-composer who led interracial groups in his native land during the early days of apartheid, he emigrated to Europe in 1964 with the other members of his band, the Blue Notes (which included altoist Dudu Pukwana, trumpeter Mongezi Feza, bassist Johnny Dyani and drummer Louis Moholo). Later on McGregor led an unusual big band called the Brotherhood of Breath before his premature death in 1990. Chris McGregor had a strong respect for the jazz tradition along with the desire to combine together his South African folk heritage with aspects of avant-garde jazz. His wife Maxine McGregor's definitive book is at its most exciting when it discusses the remarkable amount of potential danger that the pianist and his musicians faced on a daily basis in South Africa in the early 1960s while trying to be apolitical and simply creating music. One breathes a sigh of relief when, after much red tape and some foulups, McGregor and his players were finally able to escape to Europe. However the general apathy that they faced from the European jazz community, coupled with the early deaths of all of the musicians except for Moholo, made the European years less of a success than they had hoped (despite the music). As the discography that closes the book shows, none of Chris McGregor's music has yet been made readily available in the US. Chris McGregor's important story, a potentially lost chapter in jazz history, is well worth reading. —*Scott Yanow*

Chuck Stewart's Jazz Files, *Charles Stewart and Paul Carter Harrison* / 1985 / Da Capo Press ✦✦✦✦

Chuck Stewart has been a top jazz photographer since the early 1950s so the release of his picture book was quite welcome in the mid-1980s. Paul Carter Harrison conducted an interview with Stewart about his life and craft in addition to contributing introductions to each of the sections. Stewart's work is divided by instruments with chapters titled Brass, Strings, Reeds, Keyboard, Percussion, Vocalists and Ensemble. Some of the photos are quite famous (and had been used on album jackets) while others are less familiar but generally quite memorable. Stewart's black and white photos include both candid photos and performance shots. Recommended. —*Scott Yanow*

Cool Blues, *Mark Miller* / 1989 / Nightwood Editions ✦✦✦✦

For this fairly slim paperback, Mark Miller fully documents Charlie Parker's two visits to Canada in 1953. One resulted in the famous Massey Hall concert with Dizzy Gillespie, Bud Powell, Charles Mingus and Max Roach while the other trip resulted in Bird being booked to play in Montreal and appear on a television show; Paul Bley made his recording debut during the latter. Both visits had more than their share of suspense (would Parker show up to play?) and the Massey Hall date involved so many difficult personalities that it is miraculous that it worked out. Miller's narrative is very informative and suspenseful, tracing Parker's adventures and leaving one with some sadness that there was so little time left; Bird would die two years later. Recommended. —*Scott Yanow*

Crazeology, *Bud Freeman and Robert Wolf* / 1989 / University of Illinois Press ✦✦✦

Tenor-saxophonist Bud Freeman, like altoist Paul Desmond of a later generation, was an excellent writer who wrote too little during his life. His autobiography has plenty of interesting stories (with a large dose of humor) and is quite colorful but it should have been three times as long! This is well worth picking up even though the slim volume (which also has a selective discography) leaves one wanting more. —*Scott Yanow*

Crazy Fingers—Claude Hopkins' Life in Jazz, *Warren Vache, Sr.* / 1992 / Smithsonian Institution ✦✦✦✦

The Creation of Jazz, *Burton Peretti* / University of Illinois Press ✦✦✦✦

The Dance Band Era, *Albert McCarthy* / 1991 / Chilton Book Co. ✦✦✦✦

Dancing in Your Head, *Gene Santoro* / 1994 / Oxford University Press ✦✦✦✦

Dialogues in Swing, *Fred Hall* / 1989 / Pathfinder Publishing ✦✦✦✦

Veteran disc jockey Fred Hall has a great love for the swing era. His book (which was followed by a second one, *More Dialogues in Swing*) features interviews that are recreated in a question and answer format. Hall asks intelligent questions and in most cases his subjects come up with some new stories and fresh information. The artists profiled are Bob Crosby, Dick Haymes, Jo Stafford & Paul Weston, Woody Herman, Mel Tormé, George Shearing, Wild Bill Davison, Peggy Lee, Artie Shaw, Jimmy Van Heusen, Maxene Andrews of the Andrews Sisters and several surviving alumni of the Glenn Miller Orchestra. When one considers that Crosby, Haymes, Herman, Davison, Van Heusen and Andrews have since passed on, the value of books such as this one continues to rise with time. —*Scott Yanow*

Different Drummers—Jazz in the Culture of Nazi Germany, *Michael Kater* / 1992 / Oxford University Press ✦✦✦✦✦

This is an utterly fascinating book that answers the question "What happened to Swing music and its musicians in Germany during the Nazi years?" Michael Kater has put together a very well detailed narrative that discusses jazz in Germany prior to the Nazis, the persecution that occurred as the Nazis gradually declared war on the decadent music (turning teenagers who liked to dance into potential criminals), the Germans' attempts to use Swing as propaganda during the War years and the rebirth of jazz in Germany after 1945. Even jazz historians will not have heard many of these tales before and Kater's extensive research (and ability to tie together many unrelated stories) makes this a very valuable book. —*Scott Yanow*

Dizzy, *edited by Lee Tanner* / 1992 / Pomegranate Artbooks ✦✦✦

To celebrate trumpeter Dizzy Gillespie's 75th (and, as it would sadly turn out, last) year, Lee Tanner edited and put out a collection of photographs that represent the work of 20 different photographers (including William Claxton, William Gottlieb, Milt Hinton, Herman Leonard and Tanner himself); most of these Gillespie shots are common but a few (especially the more recent ones) are quite a bit rarer. Put in chronological order and ranging from 1940-1992 (half are after 1976), the majority are placed next to a relevant quote. Also included in the book is Gene Lees' typically self-serving but interesting essay "Waiting for Dizzy." —*Scott Yanow*

Dizzy, Duke, the Count and Me, *Jimmy Lyons and Ira Kamin* / 1978 / California Living ✦✦✦✦

To celebrate the 20th anniversary of the Monterey Jazz Festival, its founder Jimmy Lyons put together this historical and colorful book. Filled with a countless number of photos, the collection has plenty of humorous anecdotes, Lyons' summary of each festival and a listing of each year's lineup. Happily, Monterey is currently celebrating its 40th year. This valuable book is well worth searching for. —*Scott Yanow*

Django Reinhardt, *Charles Delaunay* / 1961 / Da Capo Press ✦✦✦

Django Reinhardt was one of the all-time great jazz guitarists and a true original, both musically and in his very spontaneous personal life. French writer-producer Charles Delaunay did a fine job of summarizing Django's life; it helped that he knew both Reinhardt and violinist Stephane Grappelli. Although not definitive (the text is around 160 pages while a discography takes up 80 pages), this is still the only full-length Django Reinhardt biography to ever be published in English. —*Scott Yanow*

Downbeat: 60 Years of Jazz, *edited by Frank Alkyer* / 1995 / Hal Leonard ✦✦✦✦

☆ ### Drummin' Men, *Burt Korall* / 1990 / Schirmer Books ✦✦✦✦✦

This is one of the finest jazz books to be released in the 1990s. Burt Korall contributed full-length portrayals of seven of the top drummers of the swing era (Chick Webb, Gene Krupa, Ray McKinley, Jo Jones, Sid Catlett, Dave Tough and Buddy Rich) along with shorter sketches of about seven others (Sonny Greer, George Wettling, Cozy Cole, Jimmy Crawford, O'Neil Spencer, Cliff Leeman and Ray Bauduc). Not only does Korall cover these musicians' lives (complete with many interviews of their associates) but he intelligently discusses their styles in an accessible fashion that will be of great interest both to other drummers and to nonmusician jazz fans. Highly recommended. —*Scott Yanow*

Duke, *Derek Jewell* / 1977 / W.W. Norton & Co ✦✦✦

Derek Jewell's 1977 book, an excellent overview of Duke Ellington's musical career and life, was the first major biography written after the death of the remarkable bandleader-pianist-composer-arranger. Although more information on Ellington's personal life would surface in future years, this well-written and continually interesting volume is an excellent introduction to Duke's unique career. —*Scott Yanow*

Duke Ellington, *James Lincoln Collier* / 1987 / Oxford University Press ✦

James Collier seemingly wrote this book with the main purpose of proving that Duke Ellington was vastly overrated and never a genius. He tries his best to prove that nearly every one of Duke's compositions were actually stolen (or borrowed) from his sidemen and that Ellington was shrewd and expert at publicizing himself. Collier also asserts that little of Ellington's work after the mid-1950s is worth listening to; two of the chapters are titled "Decline and Fall" and "The Last Band" (which sums up Duke's 1956-74 work in ten pages!). Collier's amateur psychology and constant habit of repeatedly stating false assumptions that he eventually accepts as facts (without any proof) result in an erratic book that generally rings untrue. Pass! —*Scott Yanow*

Duke Ellington—Beyond Category, *John Edward Hasse* / 1993 / Simon & Schuster ✦✦✦✦✦
In 1988 the Smithsonian Institution acquired tens of thousands of pages of music, scrapbooks and documents from Mercer Ellington pertaining to his father Duke. John Edward Hasse drew liberally from this precious archive to put together a definitive biography that augments what was already known about the remarkable pianist-composer-arranger-bandleader with many new details. Combining stories about his musical career and personal life with concise reviews of his recordings, this is a superlative portrait of America's greatest composer. Although Duke Ellington's life cannot be fully covered in just one book, this one comes as close as any to summarizing his accomplishments. —*Scott Yanow*

☆ **Duke Ellington—Day By Day and Film By Film,** *Dr. Klaus Stratemann* / 1992 / Jazz Media ✦✦✦✦✦

Duke Ellington in Person, *Mercer Ellington and Stanley Dance* / 1977 / Da Capo Press ✦✦✦
Mercer Ellington had a love/hate relationship with his father Duke. Because Duke was constantly on the road during Mercer's formative years, sometimes used him without being considerate of his feelings and was such a genius that Mercer could never make a career for himself in music outside of his father's shadow, they were rarely close. Mercer does his best to be even-handed towards his father in this interesting biographical book but his resentment constantly shines through. —*Scott Yanow*

☆ **The Duke Ellington Reader,** *edited by Mark Tucker* / 1993 / Oxford University Press ✦✦✦✦✦
This is a book that all followers of Duke Ellington will have to have. Mark Tucker gathered 101 articles on the phenomenal pianist-composer-arranger-bandleader ranging from reviews (including one from 1923!), essays and interviews to analysis and pieces by Duke himself. Some of the articles are quite famous and historic while many are obscure and have been out of print since they were first published. Arranged more or less in chronological order, this large book has a huge amount of interesting information, sometimes-conflicting but always thought-provoking opinions and plenty of variety. —*Scott Yanow*

☆ **Early Jazz,** *Gunther Schuller* / 1968 / Oxford University Press ✦✦✦✦✦
The first of two massive works by the near-genius Gunther Schuller (the other is simply called *The Swing Era*) goes into great depth about jazz of the 1920s. The emphasis is on analysis of the music rather than historical anecdotes, yet always holds one's interest. Schuller has chapters on such topics as rhythm, form, harmony, melody, timbre and improvisation, the beginnings of the music, Louis Armstrong, Jelly Roll Morton, the virtuoso performers of the decade, the big bands (including territory bands) and early Duke Ellington. This important book will be most enjoyed by connoisseurs of the 1920s who may not agree with all of Schuller's opinions but will certainly find them stimulating. —*Scott Yanow*

Eddie Condon's Scarpbook of Jazz, *Eddie Condon and Hank O'Neal* / 1973 / St. Martin's Press ✦✦✦✦
Eddie Condon's third and final book is (as its title says) essentially a scrapbook filled with historic photos and memorabilia. Fortunately Condon's humorous comments are all throughout the book along with some longer essays and reviews. Fans of the Condon era (which featured freewheeling Chicago jazz played by all-star groups) will definitely want to search for this book; some of the photos are priceless. —*Scott Yanow*

Ella Fitzgerald, *Stuart Nicholson* / 1993 / Da Capo Press ✦✦✦✦
Ella Fitzgerald's life will never be the topic of a movie. After a short period of struggle she became a success at the age of 18 in 1935 singing with Chick Webb's Orchestra and she never looked back. Until the start of her decline 40 years later due to advancing age, she had one success after another. Also, despite giving a countless number of public performances, Ella was a very private person and a clean liver. Stuart Nicholson was unable to get an interview with the great singer for this book (the first biography of her), but he talked to practically everyone else including childhood friends and pieced together a very complete portrayal of "the First Lady of Song." There are only a few revelations (such as the fact that Ella is a year older than expected and that she was homeless before joining Webb) but the story is fairly interesting; Ella Fitzgerald comes across as a won-

derful (if somewhat lonely) human being. A lengthy discography concludes the well-conceived book. —*Scott Yanow*

Ellington—The Early Years, *Mark Tucker* / 1991 / University of Illinois Press ✦✦✦✦
Duke Ellington seemed to spring out of nowhere when he debuted at the Cotton Club in 1927, preceding over 46 years of remarkable musical accomplishments. Mark Tucker's well researched book ends with Ellington gaining the Cotton Club job! He fully explores Duke's beginnings in Washington D.C. and his struggles in New York during 1923-27, analyzes his first recordings and compositions, lists everything he could find about Ellington's early activities and tries (somewhat in vain) to explain where Duke got his musical genius from. Fans of Duke Ellington's music will find this definitive book about his beginnings quite interesting. —*Scott Yanow*

Emperor Norton's Hunch, *John Buchanan* / 1996 / Hambledon Productions ✦✦✦

The Encyclopedia of Jazz, *Leonard Feather* / 1960 / Da Capo Press ✦✦✦✦✦
Arguably Leonard Feather's greatest accomplishment, *The Encyclopedia of Jazz* (which was later followed by editions focusing on the 1960s and '70s) was the first book to fully cover jazz of the 1900-60 period. Although Feather had his weak points (not caring much for Dixieland and downgrading the piano playing of both Jelly Roll Morton and Thelonious Monk), most of the over 2,000 biographical entries are quite evenhanded and (even with a few inevitable errors) quite accurate. In addition to interesting but unnecessary "appreciations" by Duke Ellington, Benny Goodman and John Hammond, this book has an overview of the preceding 60 years, a chronology of important events, articles on the anatomy of jazz, jazz in American society (which is mostly about racism and drugs), jazz overseas, jazz and classical music (the latter written by Gunther Schuller), excerpts from Feather's famed "Blindfold Test" and a list of musicians' birthdays and birthplaces. However the bulk of the book is taken up by the invaluable entries, making this (over 35 years later) still a primary jazz reference book. —*Scott Yanow*

The Encyclopedia of Jazz in the Seventies, *Leonard Feather and Ira Gitler* / 1976 / Da Capo Press ✦✦✦✦
The third of Leonard Feather's *Encyclopedia of Jazz* books came out a decade after the second, so the focus in its 1,000 plus biographical entries is on events of the past ten years and musicians who have emerged since then. All three of the encyclopedias are quite valuable and this one stuffs a great deal of information (compiled by both Feather and Ira Gitler) into a short amount of space. Although Leonard Feather did not care for Dixieland, the avant-garde or fusion (and his prejudices are often felt throughout the book), most of the entries are quite even-handed and fair. In addition, there are humorous and interesting excerpts from Feather's "Blindfold Tests," lists of poll winners and articles on jazz education and jazz films (the latter by Leonard Maltin). —*Scott Yanow*

The Encyclopedia of Jazz in the Sixties, *Leonard Feather* / 1966 / Da Capo Press ✦✦✦✦
The second in Leonard Feather's monumental *Encyclopedia of Jazz* series appeared only six years after his revised first *Encyclopedia*. The 1,100 biographies focus on the participants' activities during the first half of the 1960s except in cases where the musician did not have an entry in the original book. In addition, there are excerpts from Feather's famous blindfold test, an article by Pete Welding on "The Blues and Folk Scene" and an overview of the important events of the past six years. Although not as essential as the original *Encyclopedia*, this book is quite valuable and very much reflects the time period from which it originated. —*Scott Yanow*

The Encyclopedia Yearbooks of Jazz, *Leonard Feather* / 1958 / Da Capo Press ✦✦✦✦
After completing the first *Encyclopedia of Jazz* in 1955, Leonard Feather decided to have yearly updates. *The Encyclopedia Yearbook of Jazz* (1956) and the *New Yearbook of Jazz* (1958) were the only yearbooks put out before Feather realized that it would be a better idea to rewrite the entire series (which resulted in 1960s *The New Encyclopedia of Jazz*). This reissue from Da Capo combines the two yearbooks. In addition to entries on the who's who of jazz (new entries plus updates on veterans), there are articles giving an overview of the period, a survey on the typical jazz fan, disc jockeys, polls of musicians about other musicians, reviews of the best records of the year, jazz overseas, jazz and classical music, entertaining blindfold tests and loads of valuable (and often-rare) photos. This book is an excellent time capsule which brings back the mid-1950s. —*Scott Yanow*

Eric Dolphy, *Vladimir Simosko and Barry Tepperman* / 1971 / Da Capo Press ✦✦✦
This was the first book written about the unique multireedist Eric Dolphy, who had a unique style on alto, bass clarinet (which he virtually introduced as a jazz

instrument) and flute. Vladimir Simosko wrote essays on Dolphy's musical development and his life story (corresponding with Eric's parents and a few fellow musicians) while Barry Tepperman put together a discography that, although ideal for the time, has become a bit out-of-date. Overall this is an excellent first effort but a new and more extensive Eric Dolphy biography is long overdue. —*Scott Yanow*

The Essential Jazz Records, Volume 1, *Max Harrison, Charles Fox and Eric Thacker* / 1984 / Greenwood Press ✦✦✦
The first of two planned volumes (the second has yet to appear) in this series has reviews of 250 LPs placed roughly in stylistic order from ragtime to early Charlie Parker. Although virtually all of the albums (with the emergence of the CD) are now out of print and many of the records reviewed were released by European labels (the three authors are British) most of the writing is still informative and should be of interest to fans of prebop jazz. The opinions expressed are generally quite even-handed and logical. But where is *Volume 2*? —*Scott Yanow*

Ethel Ennis—The Reluctant Jazz Star, *Sallie Kravetz* / 1984 / Gateway Press ✦✦✦✦

Every Day—The Story of Joe Williams, *Leslie Gourse* / 1985 / Da Capo Press ✦✦✦✦
Joe Williams, one of the top male jazz singers of the past forty years, is served well by Leslie Gourse's insightful biography. As is often true in Gourse's books, one gets a good feel for the subject as a human being and plenty of detail about Williams' private life in addition to the story of his musical career. Since this book (which has a now-dated discography) was written in 1985 and Williams had more than a full decade of accomplishments ahead of him, perhaps it is time for an updated version. Recommended. —*Scott Yanow*

The Face of Black Music, *Valerie Wilmer* / 1976 / Da Capo Press ✦✦✦✦
Valerie Wilmer is a very talented photographer and writer who brings out the humanity in her subjects. This collection emphasizes her photographs which range from Louis Armstrong and New Orleans jazz players to r&b, blues, soul and avant-garde jazz performers, reflecting Wilmer's diverse interests. Since the majority of the shots are jazz-related and there are several that would rate as classic, her book is worth searching for. —*Scott Yanow*

Faces in the Crowd, *Gary Giddins* / 1992 / Oxford University Press ✦✦✦✦

Fallen Heroes—A History of New Orleans Brass Bands, *Richard Knowles* / 1996 / Jazzology Press ✦✦✦✦

Father of the Blues, *W.C. Handy* / 1941 / Da Capo Press ✦✦✦✦

Fats Waller—His Life and Times, *Joel Vance* / 1977 / Berkley Publ. Co ✦✦✦
Subtitled "Ain't Misbehavin'" (the same title as Ed Kirkeby's slightly later Fats Waller book), this volume does a fine job of covering Fats Waller's rather remarkable career. The musical analysis is generally on the money, many funny stories are included and Joel Vance shows an obvious affection for his subject. Waller, whose life was a nonstop party, somehow found time to master the piano and organ, write a dozen standards and cut hundreds of enjoyable records. His definitive biography has yet to be written but this book and Kirkeby's are both worth getting. —*Scott Yanow*

First Lady of Song, Geoffrey *Mark Fidelman* / 1994 / Carol Publishing Group ✦✦✦

A Flat Tire on My Ass, *Errol Parker* / 1995 / Cadence Jazz Books ✦✦✦
This is definitely an eccentric book. Pianist-drummer-bandleader Errol Parker, whose use of bitonality and simulataneous solos in his groups has kept his music uncommercial and underrated, sought to gain some recognition with these unusual memoirs. In addition to stories about his musical development, he talks about picking up women (often unsuccessfully), his struggle to make a living, his erratic lifestyle and even includes a few recipes! Overall it makes for an entertaining read and hopefully resulted in more work for Errol Parker. —*Scott Yanow*

Forces in Motion, *Graham Lock* / 1988 / Da Capo Press ✦✦✦✦✦
Because his complex music is quite original and his liner notes tend to be very difficult to understand, multireedist Anthony Braxton's contributions to jazz are sometimes misunderstood, underrated and somewhat forbidding. Graham Lock has done the jazz world a major service with the release of this book, for it portrays Braxton as a likable, down-to-earth and sometimes humorous human being. Lock accompanied Braxton's quartet (which included the brilliant pianist Marilyn Crispell, bassist Mark Dresser and drummer Gerry Hemingway) on a tour in 1985 and conducted extensive and wide-ranging interviews with each of the musicians. Braxton not only talks with great detail about his music but about his history and any other topics that come up. Readers come away from this continually interesting book feeling that they have joined Lock, Braxton and the musicians on the journey and with a much deeper understanding as to what makes Anthony Braxton tick. —*Scott Yanow*

☆ **Four Lives in the Bebop Business,** *A.B. Spellman* / 1966 / Limelight ✦✦✦✦✦
This was an extraordinary book when it came out and it has retained its freshness and significance through the decades. A.B. Spellman's lengthy portraits of Cecil Taylor, Ornette Coleman, Herbie Nichols and Jackie McLean (each of whom he interviewed) are still definitive. All four musicians had to struggle to play the adventurous music they felt; Nichols did not make it but the other three are still major forces in modern jazz. There is a great deal of interesting information about the early days of Taylor and Coleman (both of whom did not record until their styles were almost fully formed) and Nichols has still not been fully discovered by much of the jazz world. This book is a gem. —*Scott Yanow*

Free Jazz, *Ekkehard Jost* / 1974 / Da Capo Press ✦✦✦✦
This is a pioneering work, the first full-length book to give an overview of the avant-garde jazz scene. The German author Ekkehard Jost does an excellent job of summing up and analyzing the music of John Coltrane, Charles Mingus, Ornette Coleman, Cecil Taylor, Archie Shepp, Albert Ayler, Don Cherry, Sun Ra and the AACM players. Although this book has been superseded to an extent by John Litweiler's *The Freedom Principle* (which was written a decade later) and its discography is out-of-date, Jost's comments and analysis are still relevant and accurate. —*Scott Yanow*

The Freedom Principle—Jazz After 1958, *John Litweiler* / 1984 / Da Capo Press ✦✦✦✦✦
There have been many books on jazz but relatively few dealing with an overview of the avant-garde movement of the 1960s. John Litweiler conducted a few interviews for this project (including the members of the Art Ensemble of Chicago, Derek Bailey, Ornette Coleman, Oliver Lake, Leo Smith and Charles Tyler) but most of the book consists of intelligent musical analysis that ably details the innovations and unusual aspects of the particular recordings. There are full chapters on Ornette Coleman, Eric Dolphy, John Coltrane, Sun Ra, Albert Ayler and Cecil Taylor, the beginnings of the avant-garde, modal jazz, and the players from Chicago and St. Louis. This is an excellent acquisition for free jazz collectors who wish to learn more about the music. —*Scott Yanow*

From Birdland to Broadway, *Bill Crow* / 1992 / Oxford University Press ✦✦✦✦✦

From Satchmo to Miles, *Leonard Feather* / 1972 / Da Capo Press ✦✦✦✦✦
Leonard Feather was unique among jazz critics in that, in addition to reporting on jazz history, he was a part of the history himself. *From Satchmo to Miles* profiles 13 important artists who Feather knew quite well: Louis Armstrong, Duke Ellington, Billie Holiday, Ella Fitzgerald, Count Basie, Lester Young, Charlie Parker, Dizzy Gillespie, producer Norman Granz, Oscar Peterson, Ray Charles (who arguably does not belong in a jazz book), Don Ellis and Miles Davis. Feather's stories are often quite personal and have much more to do with the artists' private lives than with mere musical analysis, making this the most accessible of all of Leonard Feather's books. Some of the stories are quite riveting. —*Scott Yanow*

Giants of Black Music, *Pauline Rivelli & Robert Levin* / 1979 / Da Capo Press ✦✦✦✦✦
Originally put out in 1970, this important book has interviews and essays about advanced jazz that originally appeared in the long-defunct *Jazz & Pop Magazine*. Such writers as Frank Kofsky, David Hunt, John Szwed, Will Smith and Nat Hentoff are represented in addition to Pauline Rivelli and Robert Levin. The interviews and articles on such then-contemporary players as John Coltrane, John Carter, Bobby Bradford, Pharoah Sanders, Elvin Jones, Sunny Murray, Oliver Nelson, Horace Tapscott, Gary Bartz, Ornette Coleman, Byard Lancaster, Leon Thomas, Archie Shepp, Alice Coltrane and Chicago's AACM were timely then and today give one a strong feel for the atmosphere of the 1960s. Recommended. —*Scott Yanow*

Glenn Miller & His Orchestra, *George Simon* / 1974 / Da Capo Press ✦✦✦✦✦
George Simon was uniquely qualified to write a biography on Glenn Miller for he was a top jazz journalist for Metronome during the swing era and knew Miller quite well. Although he was obviously a fan of Miller's, Simon is quite fair about evaluating aspects of the bandleader's career. He covers with great detail Miller's early life, his unsuccessful attempt to make it with his new big band of 1937, his eventual rise to fame and the glory years, and his years in the military heading his Army Air Force Band. This is the definitive work on Glenn Miller and even over 20 years later it remains irreplaceable. —*Scott Yanow*

The Golden Age of Jazz, *William Gottlieb* / 1995 / Da Capo Press ✦✦✦✦
This new edition of William Gottlieb's 1979 book revises and expands his original release. Gottlieb was a busy jazz photographer during 1939-48, taking classic photos of nearly every top jazz musician active during that era. This very attractive collection covers Dixieland and New Orleans jazz, swing, vocalists and the early days of bop with everyone from Leadbelly to Dizzy Gillespie being profiled. Some of the photos are quite famous while others (often equally as interesting)

are lesser-known. Gottlieb's excellent text gives backgrounds to the musicians and identifies the subjects. A delightful book that really captures the spirit and joy of the era. — *Scott Yanow*

Goin' to Kansas City, *Nathan Pearson* / 1987 / University of Illinois Press ✦✦✦

Good Morning Blues, *Count Basie and Albert Murray* / 1995 / DaCapo Press ✦✦

Goodbyes and Other Messages, *Whitney Balliett* / 1991 / Oxford University Press ✦✦✦✦

Gramophone Jazz Good CD Guide, *Keith Shadwick, Editor* / 1997 / Gramophone Publications Limited ✦✦✦✦

The Gramophone Jazz Good CD Guide, *Keith Shadwick* / 1995 / Gramaphone Publications Limited ✦✦✦

The premise behind this collection (which is subtitled *Reviews of the Best Jazz CDs You Can Buy*) is a bit flawed since not every one of the 1,600 records covered in the book is a classic, nor is every "good" jazz CD included. However, this is a volume that should certainly interest readers who enjoy consuming jazz reviews. Eighteen fine writers from Great Britain and the US (including Chuck Berg, Bob Blumenthal, Francis Davis, Art Lange, Barry McRae, Alun Morgan and Kevin Whitehead) contributed assessments of currently available releases, providing basic information, individual ratings of the music and the sound quality, and a paragraph or two about each recording. Although often written from the British point of view (with many European releases of American music being covered), US jazz record collectors should enjoy the contents which are generally open-minded and even-handed. — *Scott Yanow*

The Great Jazz Pianists, *Len Lyons* / 1983 / Quill ✦✦✦✦

For this book, Len Lyons interviewed 27 top pianists who were still active in the early 1980s: Teddy Wilson, Mary Lou Williams, John Lewis, Sun Ra, George Shearing, Dave Brubeck, Ahmad Jamal, Horace Silver, Oscar Peterson, Red Garland, Jimmy Rowles, Paul Bley, Marian McPartland, Billy Taylor, Jaki Byard, Ran Blake, Ramsey Lewis, Randy Weston, Bill Evans, Steve Kuhn, McCoy Tyner, Toshiko Akiyoshi, Chick Corea, Herbie Hancock, Joe Zawinul, Keith Jarrett and Cecil Taylor. In addition to an interview, each chapter has an introduction that sums up the pianist's career and concludes with a (now-dated) selected discography. In addition, Lyons contributed a 40-page summary of the history of the jazz piano that is well balanced and comprehensive. This book is worth searching for. — *Scott Yanow*

The Great Jazz Revival, *Jim Goggin & Pete Clute* / 1994 / Ewald Publishers ✦✦✦

This attractive book pays tribute to the New Orleans jazz revival that took place in the 1940s and still continues up to the present time. In what is essentially a picture book with many performance photos and shots of memorabilia from the era, the text is informative and nostalgic, giving readers a history of the movement. Highly recommended to fans of Lu Watters, Turk Murphy, Louis Armstrong and San Francisco-style Dixieland. — *Scott Yanow*

The Guitar in Jazz, *edited by James Sallis* / 1996 / University of Nebraska Press ✦✦

Not entirely without merit, this anthology (which was edited by James Sallis) is nevertheless a disappointment, particularly when one considers the subject matter. Although put together in 1995, very little of post-1970 jazz is covered except briefly; there is hardly any mention to be found of such giants of the 1990s as Pat Metheny, John Scofield or Bill Frisell. Another glaring omission is a strong article tracing the history of the jazz guitar. General pieces by Leonard Feather and Joachim Berendt (both taken from other easily available books) are badly dated, Bill Milkowski's joint Downbeat interview with Jim Hall and Mike Stern is only of modest interest and an article on Ralph Towner is from 1975! Better is an interview with the forgotten Nick Lucas about the 1920s, pieces on Eddie Lang and Charlie Christian and a 1980 discussion with Joe Pass. But the book certainly does not live up to its great potential. — *Scott Yanow*

Hard Bop, *David Rosenthal* / 1992 / Oxford University Press ✦✦✦✦

He Rambled!, *Jan Scobey* / 1976 / PAL Publishing ✦✦✦✦

Bob Scobey was a top trad jazz trumpeter who gained his initial fame with Lu Watters' influential Yerba Buena Jazz Band in the early '40s (helping to launch the revival of Dixieland). He had a fairly successful solo career and in 1958 met his second wife, the future Jan Scobey. They were married in late 1961 but cancer cut short the trumpeter's life in 1963. Years later his widow wrote *He Rambled 'Til Cancer Cut Him Down,* a well-detailed book full of historical photos and an intelligent summation of Scobey's career. While the first half deals with the trumpeter's life prior to 1958, the latter part discusses the Scobeys' personal relationship and his struggle against cancer. Although a loving story, Jan Scobey is honest about her husband's life and her own limitations, and very open about the immediate difficulties that she faced as a widow, concluding the narrative by giving advice to wives in danger of losing their spouse. Despite its depressing end-

ing, this is an informative book that New Orleans jazz fans will want. — *Scott Yanow*

☆ **Hear Me Talkin' to Ya,** *edited by Nat Hentoff & Nat Shapiro* / 1955 / Peter Davies ✦✦✦✦✦

This out-of-print book is the main one that needs to be reissued. In 1955 Nat Hentoff and Nat Shapiro conducted a series of interviews with active jazz musicians and also gathered significant quotes and anecdotes that had previously been printed. Through the words of the musicians (from Jelly Roll Morton to Dave Brubeck) the two editors essentially told the history of jazz. All of the classic and colorful stories are here, covering early New Orleans (including Buddy Bolden, Storyville, Bunk Johnson and King Oliver), the 1920s (the ODJB, Bix Beiderbecke, Louis Armstrong, the Chicago jazz scene), Harlem, the swing era, the Kansas City jam sessions, Minton's Playhouse, bop, West Coast jazz and the Dixieland revival. In all 150 musicians and important people in the jazz world are heard from, making this one of the great jazz history books. — *Scott Yanow*

Herman Chittison: A Bio-Discography, *James Doran* / 1993 / IAJRC ✦✦✦✦✦

Hidden in Plain Sight, *Martin Williams* / 1992 / Oxford University Press ✦✦✦

High Times, Hard Times, *Anita O'Day & George Ellis* / 1981 / G.E. Putnam & Sons ✦✦✦✦

In her very honest autobiography, singer Anita O'Day details her colorful up-and-down life. One learns what it was like to be a frequent contestant in marathon dances and walkathons, a successful singer with the Gene Krupa and Stan Kenton Orchestras, a star, and eventually a drug addict who almost died from her habits. The very frank memoirs contain many memorable episodes and the book concludes with O'Day making a successful comeback in the early 1980s. This is one of the best jazz autobiographies. — *Scott Yanow*

His Eye Is on the Sparrow, *Ethel Waters & Charles Samuels* / 1950 / Da Capo Press ✦✦✦✦

Ethel Waters' 1950 memoirs detail a difficult but mostly rewarding life. Growing up poor and in terrible conditions, Waters (through perserverance and talent) rose to become one of the top blues and jazz singers in the 1920s, a major pop vocalist and actress in the 1930s and the star of "Cabin in the Sky" in the early 1940s. Her autobiography contains some brutal and scary episodes along with tales of her success, and they help one to understand this complex women. A major plus of the 1992 Da Capo Press paperback reissue is the inclusion of an 11 page preface by Donald Bogle that tells of the events in Ethel Waters' life during the 26 years that followed the close of her autobiography. Recommended. — *Scott Yanow*

The History of Jazz, *Ted Gioia* / 1997 / Oxford University Press ✦✦✦✦✦

A History of Jazz in Britain 1919-50, *Jim Godbolt* / 1984 / Quartet Books ✦✦✦✦

Hot Jazz and Jazz Dance, *Roger Pryor Dodge* / 1995 / Oxford University Press ✦✦✦✦

Hot Man, *Art Hodes & Chadwick Hansen* / 1992 / University of Illinois Press ✦✦✦

Art Hodes was a talented pianist in the Dixieland/Chicago jazz style who was also a fine writer and a strong propagandist for the music. For his autobiography (published just a year before his death), Hodes brings back to life Chicago of the 1920s, Wingy Manone, the no-win moldy fig vs. bebop jazz wars of the '40s, 52nd Street, Eddie Condon, Bunk Johnson, Pee Wee Russell and many others. Chadwick Hansen, who transcribed Hodes' reminiscences, also added some historical background to each chapter while Howard Rye contributed a valuable (and very comprehensive) discography of the distinctive pianist. — *Scott Yanow*

I Guess I'll Get the Papers and Go Home, *Doc Cheatham with Alyn Shipton* / 1995 / Leicester University Press ✦✦

Trumpeter Doc Cheatham wrote his memoirs in 1995 when he was 90, but since the basic narrative of this book is only 87 pages, it is fair to say that the entire story is not here! What readers do get are some of the trumpeter's colorful tales about his early days, his tours with Sam Wooding and Cab Calloway and his more recent activities. There is also a discography by Howard Rye that lists all of Cheatham's recordings except for his work with Calloway. However the book has much less about Doc's personal life than one would hope (his first two marriages are covered in one paragraph!), nothing is said about his association in the 1960s with Herbie Mann and there is little about his feelings towards bebop and the avant-garde. What is here is fine but there should have been much more. — *Scott Yanow*

I Play As I Please, *Humphrey Lyttelton* / 1954 / Pan Books ✦✦✦

I Put a Spell on You, *Nina Simone and Stephen Cleary* / 1991 / Da Capo Press ✦✦✦✦

Nina Simone has always been a unique performer. Classically-trained on piano and often associated with jazz, Simone's singing ranges from folk music and traditional hymns to Black protest songs and pop. Her episodic memoirs read at times like both a novel and an adventure story. After discussing her early years and her beginnings in music, Simone's exploits overseas are somewhat remarkable and she reveals an extraordinary private life full of surprising moments. A fascinating book. —*Scott Yanow*

I Remember, *Clyde Bernhardt and Sheldon Harris* / 1986 / University of Pennsylvania Press ♦♦♦♦♦

Clyde Bernhardt was a talented trombonist and blues singer who, although he never became all that famous himself, had an extensive career reaching from the 1920s up until his death in 1986. Fortunately he also had a strong memory and the foresight to write his memoirs shortly before his death. His very fresh stories about his exploits with many forgotten territory bands in the '20s, King Oliver, Edgar Hayes, Jay McShann, Cecil Scott, Claude Hopkins, Luis Russell, Joe Garland, the Harlem Blues & Jazz Band and the Legends of Jazz (among many others) are quite colorful and informative. Bernhardt's chapter on King Oliver (who he played with in 1931) in particular is quite fascinating. Highly recommended to readers interested in Black prebop jazz. —*Scott Yanow*

The Illustrated Story of Jazz, *Keith Shadwick* / 1991 / Crescent Books ♦♦♦♦

Images of Jazz, *Lee Tanner* / 1996 / Friedman/Fairfax ♦♦♦♦

One of the most important of all jazz photographers, Lee Tanner has been a fixture on the jazz scene since the mid-1950s. He took his first jazz photo in 1953 and spent periods living in Pennsylvania, Boston and New Jersey before eventually settling in Northern California where he has often presented exhibits by a variety of photographers. In 1996 he finally came out with his first book, collecting much of his best work. Tanner, whose shots have been usually taken at or near performance areas, creatively uses the available light (often in dimly lit nightclubs) to capture the joy, ambiance, atmosphere and creativity of the music. Many of the top bop, hard bop and avant-garde greats are represented in this enjoyable book which also has a well-written historical overview by Tanner that introduces each chapter, along with a detailed introduction that tells his life story. Recommended. —*Scott Yanow*

The Imperfect Art, *Ted Gioia* / 1988 / Portable Stanford ♦♦♦♦

Subtitled "Reflections on Jazz and Modern Culture," Ted Gioia's slim but high-quality book is filled with original ideas and different angles in which to view jazz, its history and its future. The seven chapters (which have such provocative titles as "Louis Armstrong and Furniture Music," "Jazz and the Primitivist Myth" and "Boredom and Jazz") are accessible without being obvious, fresh without being radical and both educational and thought-provoking. Recommended. —*Scott Yanow*

Improvisation, *Derek Bailey* / 1992 / Da Capo Press ♦♦♦♦

In Search of Buddy Bolden, *Donald Marquis* / 1978 / Da Capo Press ♦♦♦♦♦

This is a remarkable book. Donald Marquis did everything he could to find out about cornetist Buddy Bolden, the very important jazz pioneer who played his last notes in 1907. Since Bolden had been a legend for 70 years, Marquis had to deal first with the myth and, through intense detective work, find out what was and what was not true about the man who in 1895 put together what could be considered the first jazz band. He uncovered a previously unknown drawing of Bolden (which is reproduced in the book) and enough fresh and accurate details to make this a definitive work, dispelling part of the legend (Bolden was never a barber nor an editor of a scandal sheet) and uncovering details that fill in the gaps. The finished product is perfectly done! —*Scott Yanow*

☆ **In the Mainstream,** *Chip Deffaa* / 1992 / Scarecrow Press ♦♦♦♦♦

Chip Deffaa's third book profiles 19 musicians (in 18 chapters) who had not been covered in his previous *Voices of the Jazz Age* and *Swing Legacy*. Focusing once again on artists who play music that could be considered pre-bop, Deffaa gives readers the colorful life stories of Doc Cheatham, Bill Challis, Andy Kirk, Ray McKinley, Bob Haggart, Erskine Hawkins, Bill Dillard, Johnny Mince, Buddy Morrow, George Kelly, Mahlon Clark, Sonny Igoe, Joe Wilder, Oliver Jackson, Buck and John Pizzarelli, Ken Peplowski, Dick Hyman and Jake Hanna. Several of these players have since passed on and Deffaa has done a major service to the jazz world (just as Stanley Dance had a couple decades earlier with his *World Of* series) by getting down on paper priceless anecdotes and details about the early days. Because Deffaa really knows his subjects well, these are not merely oral histories but definitive portraits. Highly recommended, as are his two previous books. —*Scott Yanow*

In the Moment, *Francis Davis* / 1996 / Da Capo Press ♦♦♦♦

First published in 1986, this collection of articles by Francis Davis (his first book) contains many thought-provoking ideas, mostly accurate predictions about jazz's future and interesting character studies. Davis generally concentrates on younger advanced musicians (although there are exceptions) and his stories act as a time capsule for a rather eclectic period in jazz's history. He profiles Anthony Davis, the Marsalises, David Murray, Bobby McFerrin, Craig Harris, John Blake, Billy

Bang, Mathias Ruegg, Scott Hamilton, Warren Vache, Sumi Tonooka, Stanley Jordan, Keshavan Maslak, Sonny Rollins, Ornette Coleman, Don Cherry, Warne Marsh, George Russell, Roscoe Mitchell, Arthur Blythe, Abbey Lincoln and producer Giovanni Bonandrini; in addition there are some recording reviews. Despite some dated passages, the articles hold up quite well. —*Scott Yanow*

In the Spirit of Jazz—The Otis Ferguson Reader, *Dorothy Chamberlain, Editor* / 1997 / Da Capo Press ♦♦♦♦

Inside Jazz, *Leonard Feather* / 1949 / Da Capo Press ♦♦♦♦

Originally titled "Inside Bebop," this important book (reissued by Da Capo Press in 1977 with a new introduction) was the first to intelligently discuss bop. Leonard Feather discusses the beginnings of the music, the lives of Dizzy Gillespie and Charlie Parker (at least up until 1949), explains in technical detail how bop differs from swing and, in a section that preceded the *Encyclopedia of Jazz*, gives biographical data about a variety of "modern" jazz players. Even over 45 years later, the book still reads quite well. —*Scott Yanow*

It's About Time—The Dave Brubeck Story, *Fred Hall* / 1996 / University of Arkansas Press ♦♦

The first full-length biography of Dave Brubeck is written by a long-time fan and broadcaster Fred Hall. Hall is unremitting in his praise of Brubeck, making this more of a lovefest than a serious biography although there are some fresh anecdotes. The discography (which lists albums in order of their labels rather than chronological) is of limited value. To Hall's credit, he did interview Brubeck and his many family members several times and put together a coherent narrative, but more critical opinion and musical analysis would have been a major plus. However, Brubeck biographers in the future should check this book out as a starting point. —*Scott Yanow*

Jack Teagarden, *Jay Smith & Len Guttridge* / 1960 / Da Capo Press ♦♦♦♦

This underrated book, written four years before trombonist Jack Teagarden's death and with his cooperation (a short preface by Martin Williams was added to the 1987 reissue) colorfully tells the Jack Teagarden story. From his early days in Texas with Peck Kelly and his discovery in the 1920s to his days with Paul Whiteman, leading his own unsuccessful big band and gigs with the Louis Armstrong All-Stars, the narrative never loses one's interest. The 1950s are sped through very quickly before the book concludes with details about Teagarden's extensive tour of the Orient. A fairly complete discography (which has become a bit dated) concludes this worthwhile book. —*Scott Yanow*

Jaco, *Bill Milkowski* / 1995 / Miller Freeman Books ♦♦♦♦♦

Jaco Pastorius was the world's top electric bassist, the first on his instrument to develop a truly distinctive voice. Writer Bill Milkowski was a friend of Jaco's during the later years of his life and in this superlative biography he not only gives readers the details of Pastorius' glory years with Weather Report, but the previously obscure details of his rise to fame plus an insightful look at Jaco's sad and fairly rapid decline (caused mostly by his untreated mental illness). The bassist definitely comes alive throughout this book for Milkowski contacted virtually all of Jaco's associates, friends and relatives, and adds some personal stories of his own to the legacy of Jaco Pastorius. —*Scott Yanow*

James P. Johnson—A Case of Mistaken Identity, *Scott E. Brown and Robert Hilbert* / 1986 / Scarecrow Press ♦♦♦

Although a bit dry, this bio-discography (which is really two books in one) does an excellent job of summing up the life and career of the pioneer stride pianist James P. Johnson. The first half is a well-researched biography by Scott E. Brown that quotes from the few interviews Johnson gave along with contemporary reports, giving one a fairly complete documentation of his life. The second part (after various indexes and appendixes) is a complete discography put together by Robert Hilbert that has James P.'s recordings (including piano rolls) from the 1917-50 period, listing all of the LPs (as of 1986) that contain his music. This is obviously a valuable book for James P. Johnson collectors. —*Scott Yanow*

Jazz, *edited by Nat Hentoff & Albert McCarthy* / 1959 / Da Capo Press ♦♦♦

Unlike most other jazz anthologies, this book's 14 articles (written by Ernest Borneman, Charles Edward Smith, Guy Waterman, Martin Williams, Paul Oliver, Max Harrison, John Steiner, Hsio Wen Shih, Frank Driggs, Gunther Schuller, Albert McCarthy and Nat Hentoff) were all commissioned specifically for the project. The essays, which cover all styles of jazz that were around at the time of the mid-1950s including New Orleans, ragtime, swing, boogie-woogie, bop and the revival of Dixieland, contains plenty of information, analysis and interesting opinions. Although now over 35 years old, most of the essays have not dated much and are still stimulating. —*Scott Yanow*

Jazz, *John Fordham* / 1993 / Dorling Kindersley ♦♦♦♦

This is one of the most colorful books to ever come out on jazz. John Fordham breezily discusses the history of jazz, the instruments used, the careers of 20 jazz giants and some of the classic recordings but it is the pictures (of album jackets, instruments and musicians) that are most appealing. Although published in England, this book is readily available domestically and serves as a very accessible (and rather informative) introduction to jazz. —*Scott Yanow*

Jazz, *David Spitzer* / 1994 / Woodford Press ✦✦✦✦

David Spitzer has taken photographs of jazz musicians since the 1970s and many of his best performance shots are in this attractive book. There are also quotations taken from interviews (mostly ones originally in *Cadence Magazine*) that generally fit the mood of the pictures. From Eddie "Cleanhead" Vinson to Anthony Braxton, Spitzer covers most jazz styles of the past 20 years, making this one of the better jazz picture books currently available. —*Scott Yanow*

Jazz, *William Claxton* / 1995 / Twelvetrees Press ✦✦✦✦

This handsome book features some of William Claxton's finest black and white photographs. Claxton, best-known for his shots of Chet Baker in the early to mid-1950s, fortunately took pictures of many other top jazzmen, many of which were colorfully posed. Dating from 1953-63, these often-memorable photos (which include many of Claxton's lesser-known pictures) range from Mahalia Jackson and Duke Ellington to John Coltrane and Ornette Coleman. —*Scott Yanow*

Jazz: America's Classical Music, *Grover Sales* / 1992 / Da Capo Press ✦✦✦✦

Jazz—A History of the New York Scene, *Samuel Charters & Leonard Kunstadt* / 1962 / Da Capo Press ✦✦✦

This book does an excellent job of summing up and documenting the many styles of jazz that were prominent in New York during 1900-60 Although there are chapters on Chick Webb, Count Basie, and Dizzy Gillespie, this book is at its strongest in covering the 1920s and earlier times with prominence given to Scott Joplin (shown trying unsuccessfully to produce his ragtime opera *Treemonisha*), Jim Europe, the blues craze and some of the lesser-known classic jazz bands. In fact, it might have made more sense for the authors to concentrate exclusively on the 1900-40 period since a lot less space is given to the 52nd Street nightly jazz festivals than one might hope. However, this book is continually interesting and well worth picking up for fans of early jazz. —*Scott Yanow*

Jazz—A History on Record, *Brian Priestley* / 1991 / Billboard Books ✦✦✦✦

English writer Brian Priestley explores in this book how the history of jazz was affected by the recording industry (and vice versa); a very different angle than is usual in most narratives and resulting in some fresh stories. He takes readers from jazz's beginnings with 78's up until the early years of the CD era, not neglecting fusion or the avant-garde. Priestley's open-minded approach is admirable as is the amount of research that went into this continually interesting work. —*Scott Yanow*

Jazz—Myth and Religion, *Neil Leonard* / 1987 / Oxford University Press ✦✦✦

This is definitely a thought-provoking book. Neil Leonard shows how jazz can be a religion to its followers and he draws many parallels in chapters entitled "Church," "Sect," "Prophets," "Gnosis," "Rituals," "Myths" and "Followers." Even if one does buy his premises, Leonard's well-researched work is quite intriguing and displays his wide knowledge of jazz past and present. Worth investigating. —*Scott Yanow*

Jazz—Photographs of the Masters, *Jacques Lowe, Bob Blumenthal and Cliff Preiss* / 1995 / Artisan ✦✦✦

This somewhat pricey picture book features the photography of Jacques Lowe which is accompanied by extensive text (usually giving the history of the artist) written by Bob Blumenthal, Cliff Preiss and Martin Johnson. The photos were all taken in recent times (mostly within the past five years) and are divided into five chapters ("Jazz Conquers America," "Jazz After Charlie Parker," "Waves of Change," "Breaking Boundaries" and 'The New Breed') that loosely result in the older veterans being at the front of the book and the younger players in the back. Although there are no new revelations in the text, it is fine for beginners while the posed black and white shots are generally appealing. —*Scott Yanow*

Jazz—The 1980s Resurgence, *Stuart Nicholson* / 1990 / Da Capo Press ✦✦✦✦

This is the type of jazz book that should be written for each decade. Stuart Nicholson essentially tells what nearly every top jazz musician (how could he miss Marian McPartland?) happened to be doing in the 1980s. Each chapter deals with a different style or aspect of the jazz field, from "Past Masters and Keepers of the Faith" and "Big Bands" to "Miles and the Fusion Junta" and "European Dreams and the Global Democracy." The narrative moves smoothly from one musician to another, from Wild Bill Davison to Steve Coleman, giving one a real feel for the decade. Highly recommended. —*Scott Yanow*

Jazz—The American Theme Song, *James Lincoln Collier* / 1993 / Oxford University Press ✦✦✦

Jazz—The Rough Guide, *Ian Carr, Digby Fairweather & Brian Priestley* / 1995 / Penguin Group ✦✦✦✦✦

This is the best of all the current jazz reference books (other than the one you are currently holding!). Co-written by three English musicians, there are over 1,600 (!) biographies of jazz musicians that, while giving the usual important information, also have enough space for color, stories and analysis; the writers are not shy to show their wit when it fits! The entries conclude by reviewing a few of the better available recordings by the artist and at the book's end there is an extensive glossary. More complete than the Grove *Dictionary of Jazz* and more up-to-date than Leonard Feather's *Encyclopedias of Jazz*, this is an essential book for all jazz collections. —*Scott Yanow*

Jazz Anecdotes, *Bill Crow* / 1990 / Oxford University Press ✦✦✦✦

For this book (which is as humorous as one might hope), bassist Bill Crow collected stories from previously printed material, unpublished oral histories and his own experiences. The tales, arranged by topics (such as teachers and students, hiring and firing, cutting contests, prejudice, nicknames and such musicians as Louis Armstrong, Benny Goodman, Joe Venuti and Charles Mingus) are sometimes hilarious, sometimes poignant and mostly quite fresh. This book is a perfect gift for jazz fans. —*Scott Yanow*

Jazz Band, *Max Kaminsky & V.E. Hughes* / 1963 / Da Capo Press ✦✦✦✦

This is a very successful and mostly entertaining autobiography. Max Kaminsky was a fine trumpeter often associated with Dixieland and Eddie Condon. A veteran of the 1920s, his stories about Bix Beiderbecke, Billie Holiday, Pee Wee Russell, Louis Armstrong, Artie Shaw, Condon and the many other musicians he played with are quite special and colorful. Kaminsky kept an open mind towards more modern styles of jazz (although it did not influence his playing) and his book is both valuable and enjoyable. —*Scott Yanow*

The Jazz Book, *Joachim Berendt* / 1992 / Lawrence Hill Books ✦✦✦✦

Ever since its first edition in 1953, Joachim Berendt's *The Jazz Book* has done an expert job of summing up all aspects of jazz history along with the current scene. Because the number of important names have multiplied several times since the '50s, the individual notations have become more and more brief, and in this information-packed volume, some musicians are only mentioned for a sentence or two. However, Berendt manages to still cover just about everyone and his book remains invaluable. There are overviews of the styles of jazz, some of the key musicians (including David Murray and Wynton Marsalis), the elements of jazz, the history of each instrument, vocalists, big bands and combos. Kevin Whitehead contributed an interesting if erratic selective discography. Recommended. —*Scott Yanow*

Jazz Changes, *Martin Williams* / 1992 / Oxford University Press ✦✦✦✦

Martin Williams was one of the most stimulating of all jazz writers, a journalist who somehow could make musical analysis seem colorful. This particular book (one of his last) is a collection of interviews, eye-witness accounts of recording sessions, and concert performances, and portraits dating from the 1950s to the late '80s. Among the many musicians featured are Earl Hines, Bob Wilber, Billie Holiday, Ruby Braff, producer Ross Russell, John Lewis, Thelonious Monk, Ornette Coleman and Pharoah Sanders. In addition there is an extensive reprint of Williams' liner notes for the Jelly Roll Morton Library of Congress recordings, a variety of other liner notes and some dated record reviews. In this, his third book, one gets a good all-round feel for Martin Williams' writing style and open-minded opinions. —*Scott Yanow*

Jazz Cooks—Portraits and Recipes of the Greats, *Bob Young, Al Stankus and Deborah Feingold* / 1992 / Stewart, Tabori & Chang ✦✦✦

The Jazz Crusade, *Big Bill Bissonnette* / 1992 / Special Request Books ✦✦✦✦

Big Bill Bissonnette crusaded for New Orleans jazz in the 1960s, running his own record label (Jazz Crusade), playing trombone with his Easy Riders Jazz Band and sponsoring dozens of tours by ancient New Orleans jazzmen. This frank and continually interesting book details his adventures with such musicians as George Lewis, Jim Robinson, Kid Thomas Valentine, Sammy Rimington and Capt. John Handy, among others. The stories (sometimes heartwarming, occasionally quite humorous) hold one's interest and add to the legacy of 1960s New Orleans jazz. The deluxe edition of this book includes a CD of music from the period including six previously unreleased selections. —*Scott Yanow*

The Jazz Exiles, *Bill Moody* / 1993 / University of Nevada Press ✦✦✦✦

Ever since the 1930s, many American jazz musicians have found Europe to be a welcome haven, a place where their music is much better appreciated than in the US. Drummer Bill Moody fully explores this phenomenon in his interesting book. He discusses the early jazz expatriates and has chapters on Garvin Bushell and Bud Freeman but mostly sticks to the "modern exiles" of the past 30 years. His portraits of Jay Cameron, Bob Dorough, Art Farmer, Mark Murphy, Eddie "Lockjaw" Davis, Phil Woods, Jon Hendricks, Nathan Davis, Red Mitchell and

Donald Bailey (all musicians who spent time overseas) are generally quite informative and give one hope for the future since many of the players eventually returned to the US (at least on a part-time basis) when the atmosphere improved. A fine book about an intriguing topic. —*Scott Yanow*

Jazz from the Beginning, *Garvin Bushell and Mark Tucker* / 1988 / University of Michigan Press ✦✦✦

Garvin Bushell was a very talented musician who began recording as a sideman with Mamie Smith back in 1920. A proficient player who could do an excellent job on clarinet, various saxophones, bassoon and oboe, Bushell was not a major jazz figure but he was associated with some of the greats through the years; he remained active as a studio player through the 1960s and as a teacher (one of his students was King Curtis) into the 1980s. For this sketchy but generally-fascinating autobiography, Bushell reminisces about his days with Ethel Waters, touring Europe with Sam Wooding in the 1920s, Fess Williams, Fats Waller, Cab Calloway, Chick Webb, Wilbur DeParis, and even Miles Davis and Eric Dolphy, among others. He is quite frank in his opinions, is sometimes a little gossipy about the old days and the result is a very interesting and colorful book, easily recommended to fans of early jazz. The discography (which includes comments by Bushell) is excellent too. —*Scott Yanow*

☆ **Jazz Giants,** *edited by K. Abe* / 1986 / Billboard Publications ✦✦✦✦✦

This large oversized book is one of the most attractive of the jazz photo books that have been released. In addition to K. Abe, the work of 13 other photographers (along with a few that are anonymous shots) are represented, including Ray Avery, trombonist Eddie Bert, William Claxton, William Gottlieb, Milt Hinton and Charles Stewart. Most of the photos are from the 1940s to the '60s although there are some of earlier and later vintage. Beautifully reproduced, this coffee table edition will give jazz fans many hours of enjoyment; Gottlieb's classic shot of 52nd Street at night is here in color and rightfully gets the centerfold position. Also check out the 1960 photo of Dizzy Gillespie sitting in with Ornette Coleman! —*Scott Yanow*

☆ **Jazz in Canada,** *Mark Miller* / 1982 / Nightwood Editions ✦✦✦✦✦

This is a very valuable book. Prior to its publication, relatively little was known about the history of jazz in Canada, particularly since few recordings were made prior to 1960. Mark Miller did what he could to correct the major oversight by portraying 14 important Canadian players: Trump & Teddy Davidson, Paul & P.J. Perry, Chris Gage, Herbie Spanier, Wray Downes, Larry Dubin, Nelson Symonds, Guy Nadon, Claude Ranger, Soony Greenwich, Brian Barley and Ron Park. Although a few of these players are reasonably well-known today (P.J. Perry, Spanier, Downes and Greenwich) most of the others are forgotten legends. Jazz followers who think they know all about jazz history are particularly advised to pick up this well written and important book. —*Scott Yanow*

Jazz in the Movies, *David Meeker* / 1981 / Da Capo Press ✦✦✦

This book is a very worthy project very much in need of being updated and rewritten. David Meeker lists 3,724 films and shorts that have some relevance to jazz. Quite often he spends too much time outlining the plot and not enough discussing what music is actually in the film. Also he should have segregated films where the jazz connection is very incidental (such as one using a number written by Quincy Jones) from more significant movies that have appearances by jazz musicians. In any case, this book was put together before the age of the video and it is now badly out of date, although still useful on a limited basis. —*Scott Yanow*

Jazz Is, *Nat Hentoff* / 1976 / Avon Books ✦✦✦

In this colorful but ultimately frivolous book, Nat Hentoff consolidates and recycles many of his pet ideas and stories. There are many interesting quotes from jazz greats in transitional segments between chapters called "Jazz Is:" that never really answer the question as to what jazz really is. There are sections on Duke Ellington, Billie Holiday, Louis Armstrong, Teddy Wilson, Gerry Mulligan, Miles Davis, Charles Mingus, Charlie Parker, John Coltrane, Cecil Taylor and Gato Barbieri that hold one's interest although Hentoff's *The Jazz Life* from 15 years earlier actually offered more information on several of these players. This book (which totally ignores fusion) is worth picking up but far from essential. —*Scott Yanow*

☆ **The Jazz Life,** *Nat Hentoff* / 1961 / Da Capo Press ✦✦✦✦✦

This is Nat Hentoff's most important book. Not only does Hentoff accurately portray what it was like to be a jazz musician in the 1950s (both the glory and the potential hazards) but his writings about Count Basie, John Lewis and particularly Charles Mingus, Miles Davis, Thelonious Monk and Ornette Coleman were among the first honest appraisals of these masterful musicians' lives. The Monk section contains all kinds of information previously unknown about the introverted genius. This book is one of the finest of the period. —*Scott Yanow*

The Jazz Makers, *edited by Nat Shapiro & Nat Hentoff* / 1957 / Da Capo Press ✦✦✦✦

This excellent work contains chapters on 21 top jazzmen; all but Charlie Parker and Dizzy Gillespie fall into the prebop era (including Jelly Roll Morton, Baby Dodds, Louis Armstrong, Bix Beiderbecke, Bessie Smith, Art Tatum, Benny Goodman, Duke Ellington, Lester Young and Billie Holiday). The writers (Orrin Keepnews, George Avakian, Charles Edward Smith, John S. Wilson, George Hoefer, Leonard Feather and Bill Simon in addition to Nat Shapiro and Nat Hentoff) were some of the finest of the time. The essays/biographies, although written from the standpoint of the 1950s, were generally definitive (especially Bill Simon's chapter on Charlie Christian) for the period and have been "borrowed" from often. —*Scott Yanow*

Jazz Masters in Transition 1957-1969, *Martin Williams* / 1970 / Da Capo Press ✦✦✦

The last release in the "Jazz Masters" series breaks the rules followed by the previous books (*Jazz Masters of New Orleans, Of the Twenties, The Thirties, The Forties* and *The Fifties*) in that, rather than covering the 1960s, it skips all over the place. The essays by Martin Williams were not written specifically for the book but were originally published in various magazines. Fortunately the articles are placed in roughly chronological order. They include essays, articles, reviews, liner notes and (best of all) detailed reports of recording sessions that Williams happened to attend. Since his musical tastes were wide, the subject matter ranges from Thelonious Monk, John Coltrane and Ornette Coleman to Art Tatum, Robert Johnson and Jack Teagarden. It is a pity that *Jazz Masters of the Sixties* was never really written but this book is a worthwhile entry in the "Jazz Masters" program. —*Scott Yanow*

Jazz Masters of New Orleans, *Martin Williams* / 1967 / Da Capo Press ✦✦✦✦

The first book chronologically in the valuable "Jazz Masters" series gave Martin Williams an opportunity to stretch out and examine (in a chapter apiece) the lives and music of Buddy Bolden, the Original Dixieland Jazz Band, Jelly Roll Morton, King Oliver, the New Orleans Rhythm Kings, Sidney Bechet, early Louis Armstrong, Zutty Singleton, Kid Ory, Bunk Johnson and Red Allen. Although some of the stories have become dated or been disproved (the Bolden chapter has been succeeded by the definitive book *In Search of Buddy Bolden*), the portrayals give today's readers a strong introduction into the creators of the joyous music called New Orleans Jazz. —*Scott Yanow*

Jazz Masters of the Fifties, *Joe Goldberg* / 1965 / Da Capo Press ✦✦✦✦

The fifth in the "Jazz Masters" series (following books on New Orleans Jazz, the Twenties, Thirties and Forties), Joe Goldberg's work has chapters on a wide variety of top artists: Gerry Mulligan, Thelonious Monk, Art Blakey, Miles Davis, Sonny Rollins, the Modern Jazz Quartet, Charles Mingus, Paul Desmond (but not Dave Brubeck!), Ray Charles, John Coltrane, Cecil Taylor and Ornette Coleman. What is here is excellent (the Cecil Taylor chapter is particularly interesting) but Goldberg ignores West Coast Jazz almost completely and in portraying Taylor, Ornette and Coltrane (the latter was still alive at the time), he slips into the early 1960s, so this book really covers 1955-65 rather than 1950-60. That reservation aside, the portrayals are well-written and informative, making this a recommended book along with the others in the valuable series. —*Scott Yanow*

☆ **Jazz Masters of the Forties,** *Ira Gitler* / 1966 / Da Capo Press ✦✦✦✦✦

This is one of the strongest books in the "Jazz Masters" series for not only does Ira Gitler (who really loves bebop) portray the leading players (Charlie Parker, Dizzy Gillespie, Bud Powell, J.J. Johnson, Oscar Pettiford, Kenny Clarke, Max Roach, Dexter Gordon, Lennie Tristano, Lee Konitz and Tadd Dameron) but each chapter also has shorter sketches on some of the other top bop stars to play the particular instruments (with chapters titled "J.J. Johnson and the Trombonists," "Oscar Pettiford and the Bassists," etc). This is strictly a bop book so the title (which implies that one would also get information on the second half of the swing era) is not completely accurate, but this collection (along with Gitler's later work *From Swing To Bop*) is highly recommended. —*Scott Yanow*

☆ **Jazz Masters of the Thirties,** *Rex Stewart* / 1972 / Da Capo Press ✦✦✦✦✦

One of the first jazz history books written by a musician that is not autobiographical, this entry in the valuable "Jazz Masters" series has particularly colorful chapters contributed by cornetist Rex Stewart. Although he does not cover all of the main innovators of the 1930s, since he largely wrote about musicians he knew, the stories are quite insightful. Stewart portrays the Jean Goldkette Orchestra, Fletcher Henderson, Louis Armstrong, Jimmy Harrison, Coleman Hawkins, Red Norvo, Duke Ellington, Tricky Sam Nanton, Barney Bigard, Ben Webster, Harry Carney, John Kirby, Sid Catlett, Benny Carter and Art Tatum. In addition there are appendixes by other writers on Count Basie and Rex Stewart himself. Since the book was published posthumously, there is not much on Benny Goodman, Lester Young and Roy Eldridge, but Stewart's picturesque and knowledgeable articles are consistently a joy to read. —*Scott Yanow*

Jazz Masters of the Twenties, *Richard Hadlock* / 1965 / Da Capo Press ✦✦✦✦✦
The second in the valuable "Jazz Masters" series focuses on the innovators of the 1920s. Richard Hadlock contributed a chapter apiece on Louis Armstrong (the 1924-31 period), Earl Hines, Bix Beiderbecke, the Chicagoans, Fats Waller and James P. Johnson, Jack Teagarden, Fletcher Henderson and Don Redman, Bessie Smith, and Eddie Lang (but not Joe Venuti!). One of the best books on these important early players (although full-length biographies on Bix and Bessie are obviously more definitive), Hadlock's analysis of the music of the Chicagoans and Fletcher Henderson in particular is quite rewarding. Recommended. —*Scott Yanow*

Jazz Matters, *Doug Ramsey* / 1989 / University of Arkansas Press ✦✦✦
Doug Ramsey, one of the better jazz writers of the past 20 years, collected a grab bag of reviews, liner notes, essays and articles for his first book. In most cases the material had been previously published, but it does give one a good overview of Ramsey's writing style, musical tastes and ideas. Among the musicians discussed are Clark Terry, Art Farmer, Miles Davis, John Coltrane, Bud Powell, Woody Herman, Thelonious Monk, Charles Mingus, Phil Woods, Gerry Mulligan, Chet Baker, Duke Ellington and (most memorably) Dave Brubeck and Paul Desmond. —*Scott Yanow*

The Jazz Musician, *edited by Mark Rowland & Tony Scherman* / 1994 / St. Martin's Press ✦✦✦✦

Jazz People, *Valerie Wilmer* / 1977 / Da Capo Press ✦✦✦✦
In sketches usually lasting a mere seven pages apiece, Valerie Wilmer colorfully portrays 14 top jazz musicians (Art Farmer, Cecil Taylor, Eddie "Lockjaw" Davis, Thelonious Monk, Billy Higgins, Jimmy Heath, Randy Weston, Babs Gonzales, Clark Terry, Jackie McLean, Buck Clayton, Howard McGhee, Big Joe Turner and Archie Shepp). Each interview tells at least several interesting stories and gives readers a good idea as to the personality of the artist, his philosophy, and his then-current situation in music and in life. This is a particularly memorable book, making one wish that Valerie Wilmer had written dozens more. —*Scott Yanow*

Jazz People, *Ole Brask and Dan Morgenstern* / 1993 / Da Capo Press ✦✦✦✦

Jazz Poetry, *Sascha Feinstein* / 1997 / Praeger Publishers ✦✦✦

Jazz Reader, *Dan Bied* / 1997 / Dan Bied ✦✦✦

The Jazz Scene, *Francis Newton* / 1961 / Weidenfeld & Nicolson ✦✦✦✦✦
This classic look at the sociology of the contemporary jazz scene of 1961 was actually written by British historian E.J. Hobsbawm under the pseudonym Francis Newton. In 1989 it was reprinted and happily Hobsbawm was present to write a new introduction that summarizes the changes in jazz during the prior three decades. Otherwise the text is the same as the original and it serves as a superb time capsule. With such chapters as "How to Recognize Jazz," "The Jazz Business," "The Public" and "Jazz as a Protest" (in addition to looks at jazz's history, instruments and musical qualities), this is a very intelligent book that discusses many rare topics pertaining to the jazz world. —*Scott Yanow*

The Jazz Scene, *W. Royal Stokes* / 1991 / Oxford University Press ✦✦✦✦
W. Royal Stokes during his career as a jazz journalist interviewed approximately 500 musicians from the 1970s up to 1990. He tied together many of the best stories to form what he accurately calls "An Informal History from New Orleans to 1990." By arranging the quotes and anecdotes into chapters ranging from "New Orleans," "The Big Bands" and "California" to "Post Bebop Developments" and "The Contemporary Scene," Stokes essentially gives readers a new history of jazz with fresh stories, some never previously published. This book is particularly recommended to readers who think they know everything about jazz history! The photos are great too. —*Scott Yanow*

☆ **Jazz Singing,** *Will Friedwald* / 1990 / Charles Scribner & Sons ✦✦✦✦✦
Will Friedwald's massive look at jazz singers is continually interesting, even when one disagrees him with him! A very inclusive critic, Friedwald stretches the meaning of jazz a bit (Sinatra, Bobby Darren, Doris Day?), but he also appreciates the undeservedly obscure talents such as Annette Hanshaw and the Boswell Sisters, and he clearly knows his stuff. This occasionally eccentric (and often witty) book will cause many listeners to rethink their positions and (due to its huge amount of information) it is essential for any serious jazz library. —*Scott Yanow*

Jazz Spoken Here, *Wayne Enstice & Paul Rubin* / 1992 / Louisiana State University Press ✦✦✦✦
This well-conceived book consists of 22 interviews that radio hosts Wayne Enstice and Paul Rubin conducted between 1975-81. Each chapter has a photo, an up-to-date introduction, the interview and a selected discography. Because the jazz greats represent a wide variety of idioms and are placed in alphabetical order

rather than stylistically, it is refreshing to have such different players next to each other (such as Ruby Braff and Anthony Braxton!). The questions are often quite original and the responses include fresh stories and some surprises. The subjects are Mose Allison, Art Blakey, Ruby Braff, Anthony Braxton, Bob Brookmeyer, Dave Brubeck, Ray Bryant, Larry Coryell, Mercer Ellington, Bill Evans, Gil Evans, Tommy Flanagan, Dizzy Gillespie, Chico Hamilton, Lee Konitz, Charles Mingus, Joe Pass, Sonny Stitt, Gabor Szabo, Clark Terry, Henry Threadgill and Bill Watrous; fans of any of these top musicians are advised to get this enjoyable book. —*Scott Yanow*

Jazz Style in Kansas City and the Southwest, *Ross Russell* / 1997 / Da Capo Press ✦✦✦✦✦

Jazz Titans, *Bob Reisner* / 1960 / Doubleday ✦✦✦

The Jazz Tradition, *Martin Williams* / 1982 / Oxford University Press ✦✦✦✦
The second edition of *The Jazz Tradition* (the first was published in 1970) includes some new essays by Martin Williams along with some major revisions. Williams' portraits of 21 top jazz musicians (ranging from King Oliver and Louis Armstrong to Horace Silver and Ornette Coleman) are analytical without being boring and are opinionated while being even-handed. Williams never cared all that much for John Coltrane but he gives him his due while stating his own personal reservations. Martin Williams always loved Jelly Roll Morton and Thelonious Monk so they have the longest chapters, but he actually covers each of the most significant pre-1970 musicians quite fairly, explaining and demonstrating why they were so important. A thought-provoking book; one of Williams' best. —*Scott Yanow*

Jazz Veterans: A Portrait Gallery, *Chip Deffaa, Nancy Miller Elliott and John & Andreas Johnsen* / 1996 / McNaughton & Gunn ✦✦✦

Jazz West Coast, *Robert Gordon* / 1986 / Quartet Books ✦✦
This is a book that needed to be written, but unfortunately Bob Gordon's narrative totally misses the mark. West Coast jazz has long been maligned by East Coast writers who unfairly call it "bloodless" and "over arranged" without naming names or seemingly ever hearing much of the music. Gordon attempted to give publicity to the Central Avenue scene of the late 1940s and the "cool jazz" movement of the 1950s but his book is, to be frank, quite boring. Rather than interviewing all of the key survivors that he could find, Gordon talked to six musicians and essentially wrote one long record review. He mostly recycles known facts and concentrates on the records rather than the club scene; the music deserves much better! —*Scott Yanow*

The Jazz Years, *Leonard Feather* / 1987 / Da Capo Press ✦✦✦✦
Of all of the jazz critics, Leonard Feather had the most remarkable life. A writer steadily from 1934 until his death sixty years later in 1994, Feather was the most famous of all jazz journalists, but was probably proudest of his ability as a songwriter. This particular book is a sort of autobiography, which he subtitled "Earwitness to an Era." Feather talks extensively about his life in jazz and, although he dishes some dirt and settles a few scores, he is honest about his own life and provides many new stories about the jazz greats he knew. Although there is little here that takes place after 1960 (when the former musical radical reluctantly became a defender of the status quo), this continually interesting book is recommended. —*Scott Yanow*

Jazz-Rock Fusion, *Julie Coryell and Laura Friedman* / 1978 / Delta ✦✦✦✦
This collector's item was one of the first books to take fusion seriously. The rare volume contains interviews with 58 top musicians active in the field in 1978: seven bassists, four trumpeters, two composers, seven drummers, 11 guitarists, 10 keyboardists, two percussionists, three vibraphonists, violinist Jean-Luc Ponty, two vocalists and nine saxophonists. Each of the subjects are seen in an appealing photo by Laura Friedman while Julie Coryell seems to have conducted most of the interviews. Some of the discussions are more informative than others but virtually every top pacesetter in the field (including Jaco Pastorius, Miles Davis, George Benson, John McLaughlin, Chick Corea, Herbie Hancock, Joe Zawinul, Grover Washington Jr. and even Keith Jarrett) is covered. This book will be difficult to find but is worth a search; it is both dated and strangely timeless. —*Scott Yanow*

Jazzmen, *edited by Frederic Ramsey & Charles Edward Smith* / 1939 / Harvest/ HBJ Books ✦✦✦✦✦
This 1967 reissue brought back the first great jazz book (since Hugues Panassie's slightly earlier *Le Jazz Hot* is greatly flawed). Most of the top jazz writers of the 1930s contributed historical articles, covering such topics as early New Orleans jazz, King Oliver, the blues, Louis Armstrong, Bix Beiderbecke, the Five Pennies, collecting jazz records and even reviews of the earlier jazz books. It was indirectly due to the focus that *Jazzmen* put on Bunk Johnson that the veteran trumpeter was able to come out of retirement. This is a classic work that still reads well today. —*Scott Yanow*

Jelly Roll, Bix and Hoagy, *Rick Kennedy* / 1994 / Indiana University Press ♦♦♦♦
In this very interesting book, Rick Kennedy relates the history of the Gennett record label, a company that in the 1920s recorded such important jazz as the New Orleans Rhythm Kings, King Oliver's Creole Jazz Band and Jelly Roll Morton, among many others. Most record companies deserve a book of this sort, for Kennedy did quite a bit of research in coming up with the story of the label's prehistory and the founding family, everything that is known about the company's recording sessions (which included early country music, some blues and pop along with the classic jazz), the decline of the label and its aftermath. It often reads like a novel! —*Scott Yanow*

☆ **John Coltrane—A Discography and Musical Biography**, *Yasuhiro Fujioka with Lewis Porter and Yoh-Ichi Hamada* / 1995 / Scarecrow Press ♦♦♦♦♦
This hardback book is the best John Coltrane discography compiled thus far. A major help to collectors in sorting out the many European CDs that document the great saxophonist's tours overseas (where his quartet frequently broadcast on the radio), this easy-to-use book not only lists both released and unreleased recordings but all the tapes known to exist; even the music played at Coltrane's funeral! Actually the book is much more than just a discography for there are around 110 photos (mostly unpublished) of Coltrane, 700 small photos of LP cover art and enough information to know where John Coltrane was at practically any night during his last 12 years. This is definitely an essential book for fans of John Coltrane. —*Scott Yanow*

The Journeyman Piano Player, *Bob Milne* / 1992 / Woodland Press ♦♦♦
Bob Milne is a fine ragtime-oriented piano player from the Midwest who has made his living for years playing at bars, restaurants and out-of-the-way establishments. He collected years of humorous stories about dealing with customers, playing practical jokes and the odd demands made on him by clubowners. The result is a very readable and likable book full of memorable (and sometimes oddly touching) episodes that are sure to provide some good laughs. —*Scott Yanow*

Keith Jarrett, *Ian Carr* / 1991 / Da Capo Press ♦♦♦♦

King of Ragtime, *Edward A. Berlin* / 1994 / Oxford University Press ♦♦♦♦♦
This is the most thorough biography of Scott Joplin written to date. Edward Berlin did a great deal of digging through old newspapers and came up with some gap-filling information that helps to give one a more complete picture of the innovative ragtime composer. Not only a biography but a summary of the ragtime era, this definitive book is highly recommended to anyone with an interest in the music of 1900-1920. —*Scott Yanow*

King of Swing, *edited by Stanley Baron* / 1979 / Da Capo Press ♦♦♦
This colorful paperback book is essentially a collection of pictures taken from Benny Goodman's library. Stanley Baron contributes a basic 57-page biography of BG that restates the usual facts but the bulk of the book is taken up by the photographs which are placed in roughly chronological order and cover the King of Swing's life from his childhood up until 1978. Many rarities are included. A perfect gift for the Benny Goodman fan. —*Scott Yanow*

Lady Sings the Blues, *Billie Holiday & William Dufty* / 1956 / Avon Books ♦♦♦
Much of this book (Billie Holiday's ghost-written memoirs) is a bit fanciful but the picturesque episodes are often quite memorable. Considered very frank (and a bit ground breaking) at the time, Lady Day's autobiography is half true, half semi-fictional but always colorful. Donald Clarke's more recent Holiday biography *Wishing on the Moon* analyzes this book in great detail. However, *Lady Sings the Blues* (which would have made a great movie if someone had had the wisdom to stick to reality!) is essential for it lets the reader inside Billie Holiday's mind late in her life. —*Scott Yanow*

Laughter from the Hip, *Leonard Feather & Jack Tracy* / 1963 / Da Capo Press ♦♦♦
This was the first jazz comedy book, preceding *Jazz Anecdotes* by 27 years. Leonard Feather and Jack Tracy put together a series of funny essays (including Feather's fantasy on what Hollywood would have come up with for *The Duke Ellington Story*), anecdotes about practical jokes (with extra space reserved for Joe Venuti stories!), tales about drunk musicians, etc. A few of the chapters are trivial, but it is good to have all of these humorous incidents (including those involving Benny Goodman, Dizzy Gillespie, Eddie Condon and Wingy Manone, among many others) available in one place. An enjoyable if purposely lightweight read. —*Scott Yanow*

Leader of the Band, *Gene Lees* / 1995 / Oxford University Press ♦♦♦♦

A Left Hand like God, *Peter J. Silvester* / 1988 / Da Capo Press ♦♦♦♦
Peter Silvester was moved to write this book, the history of boogie-woogie piano, because none existed. He expertly traces the roots of the music, its brief boom in Chicago in the 1920s, its near-disappearance (except as an influence) during the Depression, its prime period and its decline, rounding out the book with short

sketches of some of the younger pianists who were performing boogie-woogie in the late 1980s. There is also a list of available recordings along with short reviews. Silvester, who was able to integrate the unfinished manuscript of the late Denis Harbinson (who had been working on a similar project) into his book, does the music justice; the narrative stays interesting despite having to weave together many separate stories. —*Scott Yanow*

Les Paul, *Mary Alice Shaughnessy* / 1993 / William Morrow and Co. ♦♦♦♦

A Lester Young Reader, *edited by Louis Porter* / 1991 / Smithsonian Institution Press ♦♦♦♦♦
This very valuable book from the Smithsonian's *Reader* series has 14 articles on tenor-saxophonist Lester Young's life, nine interviews and 13 essays on his music; overall these are among the most rewarding articles ever written on the great tenor. The wide range of opinions (particularly about Young's playing during the 1950s) is contradictory but very interesting and the various critiques (which sometimes use different assumptions) on a whole present a fairly complete portrayal of Prez. Best are Young's interviews where he gets to speak for himself. Highly recommended to Lester Young fans. —*Scott Yanow*

Let the Good Times Roll—The Story of Louis Jordan, *John Chilton* / 1992 / University of Michigan Press ♦♦♦♦♦

A Life in Jazz, *Danny Barker & Alyn Shipton* / 1986 / Oxford University Press ♦♦♦♦
Danny Barker, a fine guitarist, banjoist, singer, jazz educator and humorist, put together his entertaining memoirs eight years before his death. Barker was always full of stories and he tells many of the best ones in his book, starting in his early days in New Orleans through his experiences with Jelly Roll Morton and Cab Calloway and then more skimpily through the 1960s and '70s and his return home. Barker's experiences in the classic jazz, swing and New Orleans revival worlds are well worth reading; his writing style is quite colorful and often laced with humor. A fine discography rounds out this recommended book. —*Scott Yanow*

A Life in Ragtime, *Reid Badger* / 1995 / Oxford University Press ♦♦♦♦♦
Although he was not active in jazz (and his murder in 1919 took away any chance he had of being a leader in the Jazz Age), James Reese Europe was important in the music of the teens. The first black bandleader to record, Europe's dance band and later military orchestra was influenced by ragtime and employed some future jazz musicians. This well-researched book is quite definitive with 75 pages of footnotes (!), a discography and a very readable text. This book is well worth getting by readers interested in the early days of jazz and ragtime. —*Scott Yanow*

Live at the Village Vanguard, *Max Gordon* / 1980 / Da Capo Press ♦♦♦
Although a bit dated in spots, clubowner Max Gordon's memoirs hold one's interest throughout. Gordon ran the Village Vanguard in New York from 1934 up until his death in the 1980s and for a period in the 1940s he also ran an upscale club called the Blue Angel. The Vanguard originally booked a variety of acts (including folk music, comedians and shows) before it became the most famous jazz club in the world. Gordon's breezy narrative is a bit sketchy in spots but it is full of priceless stories from the unusual vantage point of a clubowner. Covering everyone from Miles Davis and Rahsaan Roland Kirk to Judy Holiday and Lenny Bruce in conversational style, this is a unique book well worth searching for. —*Scott Yanow*

Louis, *Max Jones & John Chilton* / 1971 / Da Capo Press ♦♦♦♦
This excellent book (reissued on paperback by Da Capo in 1988) does a fine job of summarizing Louis Armstrong's colorful life, bringing out some information that was new at the time, along with some fresh angles, including an often-revealing interview with Armstrong that was conducted late in his life. Although the emphasis is on Louis' work in the 1920s and '30s, to the author's credit they do not write off his years with the All-Stars. A 40-page discussion of his recordings, a chronology and a film list round out this work which serves as a good introduction to the musical magic of the brilliant trumpeter-singer. —*Scott Yanow*

Louis Armstrong, *James Lincoln Collier* / 1983 / Oxford University Press ♦♦
Although subtitled "An American Genius," James Lincoln Collier's biography of Louis Armstrong is full of false assumptions which he repeatedly states in order to draw some unusual conclusions. Collier almost convinces readers (despite the lack of evidence) that Armstrong was really born in 1898 rather than 1900; later evidence showed that Louis was actually born in 1901! The endless psycho-analyzing is quite amateurish and ultimately destructive, and Collier virtually writes off all of Armstrong's post-1935 work. He does bring up some interesting points and new information along the way, so this book is not worthless, but it is generally disappointing. —*Scott Yanow*

Louis Armstrong, *Hugues Panassie* / 1971 / Charles Scribner's Books ◆◆◆
Hugues Panassie, an important early jazz writer, was a Louis Armstrong supporter since the 1930s. His last significant book was this loving tribute to Armstrong who had recently passed away. Although there are chapters on Louis Armstrong "The Man" and his style, the great majority of the book is an analysis of his recordings. Panassie is even-handed, fairly thorough, and although he naturally emphasizes Armstrong's earlier classic records, fair about his later output. Even with its lack of new revelations, this book is worth picking up. —*Scott Yanow*

Louis' Children, *Leslie Gourse* / 1984 / Morrow ◆◆◆◆
Although there is a chapter on Louis Armstrong, the main emphasis in this consistently interesting book (arguably Leslie Gourse's finest) is on the many jazz-oriented singers who were influenced by Satch. A writer who is able to bring out the personal side of each subject, Gourse portrays a wide variety of talents including Cousin Joe, Ethel Waters, Cab Calloway, Billie Holiday, Etta Jones, Helen Merrill, Billy Eckstine, Jon Hendricks, Mel Tormé, Nat King Cole, Joe Williams, Dinah Washington, Sarah Vaughan, Ella Fitzgerald, Carmen McRae, Annie Ross, Rosemary Clooney, Betty Carter, Janet Lawson and Tania Maria, among others. Although some of the singers that she predicted greatness for did not live up to their potential, this book holds one's interest and gives a bit of information about a lot of different vocalists. —*Scott Yanow*

☆ **Lush Life,** *David Hajdu* / 1996 / Farrar, Straus and Giroux ◆◆◆◆◆

Madame Jazz, *Leslie Gourse—Contemporary Women Instrumentalists* / 1995 / Oxford University Press ◆◆◆

☆ **The Man with the Green Shirt,** *Richard Williams* / 1993 / Henry Holt and Co. ◆◆◆◆◆
Although the most notable aspect to this attractive oversized book are the many photos (quite a few of which are rare), this portrait of Miles Davis also has an insightful narrative by Richard Williams. Other than dismissing Davis' work from the 1970s, Williams' writing is quite even-handed and does an excellent job of summarizing in concise fashion Miles Davis' productive and crowded life. However, it is the photos (many of which are in color) that really make this an essential acquisition for the trumpeter's fans. —*Scott Yanow*

Marshall Royal—Jazz Survivor, *Marshall Royal & Claire Gordon* / 1996 / Casell ◆◆◆
The title of this autobiography put together by Clarie Gordon is a bit ironic since altoist Marshall Royal passed away shortly before the book was published. Royal is best remembered for his many years with Count Basie's Orchestra and he talks about his stints with Basie and Lionel Hampton, but it is his stories about the jazz scene in 1930s Los Angeles (an era that has not been very well documented) that are most intriguing. The 134-page narrative is augmented by an extensive discography of all of Marshall Royal's non-Basie recordings. Gordon did a fine job of putting Royal's thoughts in coherent order, but additional chapters discussing his place in jazz history and his music would have made this book even more valuable. —*Scott Yanow*

The Melody Lingers On, *Jules & Jo Brooks Fox* / 1996 / Fithian Press ◆◆◆

Miles, *Miles Davis and Quincy Troupe* / 1989 / Simon & Schuster ◆◆◆◆
Miles Davis' somewhat infamous autobiography has far too many obscenities (especially in the first twenty pages), should have been more tightly edited (one-third could have been cut out) and was probably never read by the trumpeter himself. However, the many fresh stories, the honesty (Miles does not always come across too well) and the rare opportunity to get at least partly into his mind make this a unique and essential book. He comments on nearly all of his recording sessions, tells anecdotes about everyone from Charlie Parker to John Coltrane and constantly explains (but does not excuse) some of his unusual behavior. A must have. —*Scott Yanow*

Miles Davis, *Ian Carr* / 1982 / Quill ◆◆◆◆
This book, which traces Miles Davis' very productive and often stormy career up to his comeback in the early 1980s, is an excellent single volume that can be used as an introduction to the innovative trumpeter. Although Ian Carr (himself a fine trumpeter) did not get to interview Davis, he talked to many of his sidemen, put together the known facts of Miles' life in a coherent and easily readable fashion and does a fine job of analyzing his music. A few musical examples and a selective discography round out this fine book. —*Scott Yanow*

Miles Davis and David Liebman—Jazz Connections, *Larry Fisher & David Liebman* / 1996 / Edwin Mellon Press ◆◆◆

The Miles Davis Companion, *edited by Gary Carner* / 1996 / Schirmer Books ◆◆◆◆

A Miles Davis Reader, *Bill Kirchner, Editor* / 1997 / Smithsonian Institution Press ◆◆◆◆

Miles Davis: The Early Years, *Bill Cole* / 1974 / Da Capo Press ◆◆
This Miles Davis biography (which has been reissued by Da Capo in 1994) has always been a bit of a disappointment. Bill Cole, who dislikes all of Davis' output after 1968, also does not seem to appreciate or understand Davis' classic quintet of the 1960s. Rather than conducting interviews, his book is essentially a long essay about Miles Davis' biography and style; the inclusion of a lengthy discography (which cuts off in 1972), a long bibliography and many transcriptions means that the basic narrative is only 166 pages. Although Cole does have some interesting ideas about Davis' work of the 1950s, the lack of new interviews or much of anything about Miles' personal life makes this book of very limited value, especially compared to the superior (and more open-minded) Miles Davis biographies that have been released in more recent times. —*Scott Yanow*

Milestones 1, *Jack Chambers* / 1983 / Beech Tree Books ◆◆◆◆
In the first of his two comprehensive biographies of trumpeter Miles Davis, Jack Chambers covers Miles' career up to 1960. Although he did not interview Davis (or it seems anyone else), Jack Chambers does a superior job of organizing all of the known facts about Miles (the bibliography is quite extensive) and analyzing all of Davis' recordings (at least all of the ones released by 1983). The results are quite complete and very informative; the trumpeter's autobiography Miles (which came out six years later) helped fill in the remaining gaps. Recommended. —*Scott Yanow*

Milestones 2, *Jack Chambers* / 1985 / Beech Tree Books ◆◆◆◆
In the second of two books on the life of Miles Davis, Chambers expertly traces the events in the remarkable trumpeter's life and musical career during the 1960-85 period. Since he did not interview anyone, Chambers relies on previously printed material (which he expertly organized together) and concise musical analysis. Although much of his information and speculation about Davis' retirement (1975-81) was contradicted by Miles' autobiography of four years later, this book has dated quite well. Chambers gives the music of Miles Davis' "difficult" period (1969-75) an even-handed approach, and his two books are quite informative and educational. Recommended. —*Scott Yanow*

Mingus, *Brian Priestley* / 1982 / Da Capo Press ◆◆◆
The emphasis is on musical analysis during this interesting book on the great bassist-bandleader Charles Mingus. Until the definitive work on the volatile genius is written, this remains the top Mingus book; it discusses the usual biographical information but also goes into great detail about Mingus' music (including ten notated examples) and contains a complete discography of his work as both a leader and as a sideman. Recommended to his fans. —*Scott Yanow*

☆ **Mister Jelly Roll,** *Alan Lomax* / 1950 / Pantheon Books ◆◆◆◆◆
Alan Lomax's biography of Jelly Roll Morton, which is drawn from Morton's colorful interviews with Lomax for the Library of Congress in 1938 (and in reality the results are mostly autobiographical), is quite definitive. Reissued by Pantheon Books in 1993 with a new forward by Lomax (who rightfully blasts the hideous play *Jelly's Last Jam*), this classic book is full of fanciful but probably true stories by Morton about New Orleans, Storyville and Chicago in the 1920s. Lomax filled in some of the gaps with interludes and details about Morton's last years. In addition, there are appendixes that discuss Morton's tunes, records and discography. —*Scott Yanow*

Monterey Jazz Festival, *William Minor & Bill Wishner* / 1997 / Angel City Press ◆◆◆◆◆

More Dialogues in Swing, *Fred Hall* / 1991 / Pathfinder Publishing ◆◆◆◆
Fred Hall, a longtime disc jockey, had previously put out *Dialogues in Swing*. As with the first book, *More Dialogues in Swing* is a set of interviews with mostly swing-era personalities that appear in a question and answer format. Hall profiles Kay Starr, Count Basie (through a conversation with several of Basie's associates), Steve Allen, Teddy Wilson, Alvino Rey and the King Sisters, Herb Jeffries, Johnny Green, Les Brown, Helen Forrest, Helen O'Connell, Harry James and Tony Bennett. Both books are recommended since they contain fresh stories and allow one to learn a bit about each of the subjects. —*Scott Yanow*

Muggsy Spanier: The Lonesome Road, *Bert Whyatt* / 1995 / Jazzology Press ◆◆◆◆
The great Chicago cornetist Muggsy Spanier (a veteran of the 1920s who was active until his death in 1967) is given excellent treatment by Bert Whyatt in this book. Fortunately Whyatt was able to extensively interview Spanier's wife Ruth before her death and her memories help tie the Muggsy Spanier story together. In addition to the biography, Whyatt contributed an extensive discography and, as a bonus, there is an enclosed CD containing previously unreleased Spanier performances from 1941, 1948 and 1953 (with the sidemen including tenor-saxophonist Bud Freeman and pianist Jess Stacy). Recommended. —*Scott Yanow*

Music Is My Mistress, *Duke Ellington* / 1973 / Doubleday & Co. ♦♦♦

The problem with Duke Ellington's memoirs is that, because he was so diplomatic, he essentially praises everyone he has ever met. This large but rather episodic work is really a set of essays, some of which are philosophical while others merely relate incidents and adventures. Far from a complete survey into Duke's life (he would have had to have worked years on it!), the book gives the impression of being thrown together while Ellington was on the road. It is most valuable for his discussion of his early days and for the photos, but it is far from essential or definitive. —*Scott Yanow*

The Music of Anthony Braxton, *Mike Heffley* / 1996 / Greenwood ♦♦♦♦

Music on My Mind, *Willie "The Lion" Smith & George Hoefer* / 1964 / Da Capo Press ♦♦♦♦

Willie "The Lion" Smith was considered one of the "big three" of stride pianists in the 1920s. Unlike James P. Johnson and Fats Waller, he survived long enough to dictate his autobiography. Smith could be a bit of a braggart but most of his story (which is particularly valuable for describing the music heard on the East Coast during 1915-25) rings true. Smith mostly focuses on the pre-1950 era and there are a lot of colorful tales of life in the 1920s and '30s and of his contemporaries (from Jelly Roll Morton and Clarence Williams to Fats Waller and Sidney Bechet). Unfortunately he does not comment at all about bop or even much about swing but what is here is often quite fascinating, bringing attention to a lot of musicians who would otherwise be forgotten. —*Scott Yanow*

Music Universe, Music Mind, *Robert E. Sweet* / 1996 / Arborville Publishing ♦♦♦♦

Although underpublicized during its existence (1971-84), Karl Berger's Creative Music Studio in Woodstock, New York, must have been a wondrous place. This book's author, Robert E. Sweet, was one of many students who had the opportunity to interact informally in the open-ended setting with such masterful musicians as Don Cherry, Leo Smith, Anthony Braxton, Lee Konitz, Sam Rivers, Cecil Taylor, Oliver Lake, the Art Ensemble of Chicago and quite a few other giants. Important connections were made (pianist Marilyn Crispell met Braxton at Woodstock and soon joined his group) and it could be argued that many of the more creative aspects of World Music originated during the sessions. In colorful and informative fashion, Robert Sweet talks about the rise and fall of the Creative Music Studio (which expired when money finally ran out), casting light on a jazz utopia that should have been more fully supported by the music world. —*Scott Yanow*

Music Was Not Enough, *Bob Wilber & Derek Webster* / 1987 / Oxford University Press ♦♦♦♦

Bob Wilber, a talented clarinetist and soprano saxophonist, had an identity crisis throughout much of his career. A student of Sidney Bechet's, Wilber spent much of the 1950s and '60s doing his best to escape from Bechet's dominant influence and develop his own voice. His memoirs are primarily about his struggle to find himself both musically and personally. In this very honest autobiography, many top musicians (including Bechet, Louis Armstrong and Duke Ellington) make appearances and Wilber proves to be an expert story teller. His memoirs (which have a happy ending) are rounded out by a selective discography of the clarinetist's favorite sessions. —*Scott Yanow*

Musings, *Gunther Schuller* / 1986 / Oxford University Press ♦♦♦

My Life in New Orleans, *Louis Armstrong* / 1954 / Da Capo Press ♦♦♦♦

Louis Armstrong wrote two books and this effort was easily his best. The masterful trumpeter-vocalist discusses his early years very frankly, having the narrative end at the point when he first joined King Oliver's Creole Jazz Band in Chicago in 1922. His colorful stories about the characters to be found in New Orleans, his struggle against poverty and racism and his ultimate success make this a particularly memorable book. If only Armstrong had written a similar narrative about the next 40 years! —*Scott Yanow*

My Singing Teachers, *Mel Tormé* / 1994 / Oxford University Press ♦♦♦♦

The New Grove Dictionary of Jazz, *edited by Barry Kernfeld* / 1988 / St. Martin's Press ♦♦♦

Originally issued as two large books and then in 1994 combined into this one giant encyclopedia, the Grove Dictionary is quite impressive quantity-wise with over 4,500 entries and 1,800 discographies. Because so many different writers worked on it and the quality varies greatly, this book does have quite a few flaws with many major names (including Dorothy Donegan) being omitted altogether and some entries (such as Pete Fountain's whose biography essentially ends in 1959) being very incomplete. Still, this book (which has accurate birth and death dates) does have its value although it falls short of being truly definitive. —*Scott Yanow*

New York Notes, *Whitney Balliett* / 1976 / Da Capo Press ♦♦♦

In this book Whitney Balliett keeps track of the jazz activities that he witnessed and thought about during 1972-75. Although there is no table of contents and the chapters are merely named after the years, there are actually 35 portraits in this collection, including two apiece on Count Basie and Modern Jazz Quartet (which had just broken up), many on veterans who were still active during the period and a few who recently died, and some articles covering Balliett's favorites from the past. Ranging from Artie Shaw to Cecil Taylor, Balliett as usual brings the musicians' music to life on the written page but overall this is one of his less essential efforts. —*Scott Yanow*

The Night People, *Dicky Wells and Stanley Dance* / 1991 / Smithsonian Institution ♦♦

Dicky Wells was one of the more colorful trombonists of the swing era, most famous for his associations with Count Basie and Jimmy Rushing. With his many experiences from the 1920s into the early 1970s, this book should be a classic but instead it is a bit of a misfire. Wells' colorful language is a major plus and he does tell some funny stories, but as an autobiography, there is far too much missing, with little more than a few pages covering his post-1950 activity. In the appendixes, Andre Hodeir describes the style of Wells while Chris Sheridan contributes a discography; otherwise the book would be just 145 rather breezy pages. Although it does have its value, Dicky Wells' *The Night People* does not live up to its potential. —*Scott Yanow*

Notes and Tones, *Arthur Taylor* / 1993 / Da Capo Press ♦♦♦♦♦

Of Minnie the Moocher & Me, *Cab Calloway and Bryant Rollins* / 1976 / Thomas Y. Crowell Company ♦♦♦

Singer-entertainer Cab Calloway's memoirs have their interesting moments (particularly when he talks about the early days) but falls short of being definitive. Calloway is at his best when he talks about the 1930s and less interesting when discussing his love of horse racing and family life. Several people (bassist Milt Hinton, pianist Benny Payne and family members among others) uplift the book by contributing their own memories of Calloway. Although one gets the feeling that Cab never really understood why he was important, his book is entertaining and informative enough to search for. —*Scott Yanow*

Oh, Didn't He Ramble, *Lee Collins with Mary Collins* / 1974 / University of Illinois Press ♦♦♦♦

The legendary New Orleans trumpeter Lee Collins (who passed away in 1960) informally began writing his memoirs in 1943 and, with the assistance of his wife, his book was finally published in 1974. Collins was one of the few musicians around in the 1950s who could write with firsthand knowledge about such early players as Chris Kelly, Buddy Petit and Manuel Perez. His tales of the early days in New Orleans are very valuable as are his stories about New Orleans in the 1920s, Chicago in the '30s and his two European tours. In fact Collins even talks about what would be his final illness! A fascinating and rather unique book. —*Scott Yanow*

Oh, Jess!, *Keith Keller* / 1989 / Jazz Media ♦♦♦

On the Road with the Jimmy Dorsey Aggravation 1947-1949, *Gene Bockey* / 1996 / Gray Castle Press ♦♦

This thin book has the frequently amusing story of saxophonist Gene Bockey's two years spent touring with the Jimmy Dorsey Orchestra, with the emphasis on humorous anecdotes. A strong editor would have improved the book greatly since it has an excess of meaningless obscenities, asides and irrelevant remarks in addition to a few insults. However, the depiction of JD as a frequently drunk womanizer with a heart of gold and the general picture of life on the road make it worth picking up. —*Scott Yanow*

Ornette Coleman, *John Litweiler* / 1992 / Da Capo Press ♦♦♦♦

For the first biography ever written about one of jazz music's major innovators (nearly 40 years after his recording debut, some in the jazz audience still dismiss altoist Ornette Coleman's accomplishments), John Litweiler gathered all of the known information about Ornette, used a 1981 interview he had with Coleman, talked to most of Ornette's important sidemen and associates and added his own musical analysis. Although not quite definitive, this is an excellent effort that makes Coleman's unusual life and unique music more understandable; all future books on Ornette Coleman will have to deal with this one first. The discography, which goes up to 1991, is an added plus. —*Scott Yanow*

Oscar Peterson, *Gene Lees* / 1990 / Prima Publishing ♦♦♦♦

On first glance, pianist Oscar Peterson would seem to be a poor subject for a biography. A brilliant player with a quiet personal life, Peterson has been a very consistent performer throughout his productive career and he early on developed a style, that has changed very little during the past four decades. However as Gene Lees shows in this book (possibly his finest), Peterson's personal life and growth are more interesting than expected and even in Canada he had to battle racism. One gets a good idea as to what the Canadian jazz scene was like in the 1940s, the difference between each of Peterson's groups and what motivates and inspires the great pianist. Recommended. —*Scott Yanow*

☆ **Outcats,** *Francis Davis* / 1990 / Oxford University Press ♦♦♦♦♦
Francis Davis is one of the finest jazz writers of his generation. This entertaining and informative book has essays written in the 1980s on such artists as Duke Ellington, Sun Ra, Gil Evans, Cecil Taylor, Henry Threadgill, Doc Cheatham, Miles Davis (an often-humorous piece), Frank Morgan, Steve Lacy, Ran Blake, Susannah McCorkle, Harry Conick Jr., Steve Coleman and even Bobby Darin! No matter what style is being represented by his subject, Davis does justice to the artist and brings up some new points and fresh angles. This is a thought-provoking and highly recommended collection. —*Scott Yanow*

OverTime—The Jazz Photographs of Milt Hinton, *Milt Hinton, David Berger and Holly Maxson* / 1991 / Pomegranate ♦♦♦♦

Painting the Musical City, *Donna Cassidy* / 1997 / Smithsonian Press ♦♦♦

The Passion for Jazz, *Leonard Feather* / 1980 / Da Capo Press ♦♦♦
This particular book from Leonard Feather documents the music that interested him in the 1970s. The avant-garde and fusion get short shrift but he does a good job of discussing a variety of then-current affairs and controversies, some of which seemed more important at the time than they became. Feather's "Top Ten Jazz Artists" article is unfortunate since he leaves out Miles Davis and John Coltrane. Better are his pieces on the White House Jazz Festival, his travels and the deaths of Ethel Waters, Charles Mingus, Stan Kenton and Thad Jones. There are also articles on 16 artists and/or groups ranging from Donald Byrd (a classic interview), to Alberta Hunter, Benny Goodman to Urszula Dudziak plus other miscellaneous topics. Although an interesting time capsule, this book is not quite essential. —*Scott Yanow*

Pee Wee Russell, *Robert Hilbert* / 1993 / Oxford University Press ♦♦♦♦♦
Robert Hilbert, who would sadly pass away just a year after completing this book, put together a memorable portrait of the colorful (and utterly unique) clarinetist Pee Wee Russell, interviewing every possible person and tying together information from previously published sources to fill in the gaps. Russell emerges as likable if a bit self-destructive and one gets the full story of his early rise to fame, his successful flirtation with "modernism" in the early 1960s and his swift decline after his wife's death. Hilbert's *Pee Wee Speaks* (on Scarecrow Press) completes the picture with a full discography. —*Scott Yanow*

The Penguin Guide to Jazz on CD, Third Edition, *Richard Cook & Brian Morton* / 1996 / Penguin Books ♦♦♦♦

☆ **A Pictorial History of Jazz,** *Orrin Keepnews & Bill Grauer Jr.* / 1966 / Bonanza Books ♦♦♦♦♦
This wonderful book, reprinted in 1981, lives up to its title. Most of the more famous jazz photos are here along with many lesser-known shots. Although the emphasis is on jazz's early days (the first 12 of the 20 chapters stick primarily to the years before 1930), this book does reach up to Ornette Coleman and Archie Shepp. Orrin Keepnews' text is concise and insightful but it is the photos (compiled by Keepnews and his partner in running Riverside Records Bill Grauer, Jr.) that are especially memorable. This delightful book belongs in every jazz collection. —*Scott Yanow*

The Pleasures of Jazz, *Leonard Feather* / 1976 / Dell Publishing Co. ♦♦♦♦
For this somewhat obscure Leonard Feather book, the veteran writer interviewed and wrote about 43 different musicians and/or groups who were active in the 1970s, ranging from Freddie Hubbard and Herbie Hancock to Eubie Blake, Bob Crosby, Charles Lloyd and even Reb Spikes. Although Feather's biases are felt, he is generally quite sympathetic to his subjects and the results are quite informative and usually colorful. —*Scott Yanow*

The Poets of Tin Pin Alley, *Philip Furia* / 1990 / Oxford University Press ♦♦♦♦

Raise Up Off Me, *Hampton Hawes & Don Asher* / 1974 / Da Capo Press ♦♦♦♦
This was possibly the first important jazz autobiography from a member of the bebop generation. Pianist Hampton Hawes tells about the excitement of exploring new music and his problems with drugs. These very frank memoirs discuss many of Hawes' associates (including Charlie Parker, Miles Davis, Thelonious Monk and Billie Holiday), his time in jail, his pardon by President Kennedy and before ending optimistically. Hawes would pass away only two years later at the age of 49. Gary Giddins' fine introduction (written in 1979) fills in the gaps in the life of the talented pianist. —*Scott Yanow*

Reading Jazz, *David Meltzer* / 1993 / Mercury House ♦♦♦♦

Really the Blues, *Mezz Mezzrow & Bernard Wolfe* / 1946 / Doubleday ♦♦♦♦
Mezz Mezzrow had his heart in the right place, at least musically. An erratic clarinetist who was best on the blues, Mezzrow was a propagandist for New Orleans jazz who probably made more money from selling marijuana than he ever did

from music. His 1946 memoirs still are a bit sensational with many memorable tales of the jazz life including friendships with Sidney Bechet and Fats Waller, adventures with gangsters in Chicago, an opium addiction and eventual recovery, jail sentences and glorious jam sessions. Mezz might not have been much of a musician but he had a colorful story to tell! —*Scott Yanow*

The Real Jazz, *Hugues Panassie* / 1942 / Smith & Durrell, Inc. ♦♦♦

☆ **Red & Hot—The Fate of Jazz in the Soviet Union,** *S. Frederick Starr* / 1983 / Limelight Editions ♦♦♦♦♦
This is a consistently fascinating book, the type that should be written about each country's relationship with jazz. S. Frederick Starr's history of jazz in the Soviet Union often reads like a novel with plenty of scary (and sometimes tragic) adventures. Through extensive research, Starr is able to tell about the beginnings of jazz in Russia, the brief period in the 1920s when jazz was accepted, the repression felt under Stalin, the use of jazz as propaganda during World War II, a major backlash against jazz in the second half of the 1940s and the gradual acceptance of the music during the '60s and '70s. One learns about many obscure but important heroes who kept the music alive under Communism. —*Scott Yanow*

Red Head, *Stephen Stroff* / 1996 / Scarecrow Press ♦♦♦

The Red Nichols Story—After Intermission 1942-1965, *Philip Evans, Stanley Hester, Stephen Hester and Linda Evans* / 1997 / Scarecrow Press ♦♦♦♦

The Reluctant Art, *Benny Green* / 1976 / Da Capo Press ♦♦♦
Benny Green's thought-provoking essays on Bix Beiderbecke, Benny Goodman, Lester Young, Billie Holiday, Charlie Parker and Art Tatum (the latter was written as liner notes in 1976) have held up pretty well over the decades. Sometimes he puts a bit too much emphasis on the importance of recorded solos (which, after all, were generally improvised on the spot) and gets overly analytical but his ideas (such as Bix's happiness, not despair, at being in Paul Whiteman's Orchestra) were fresh at the time and have often become accepted. —*Scott Yanow*

Remembering Song, *Frederick Turner* / 1982 / Viking Press ♦♦♦
Frederick Turner's unusual book is essentially a backward look at the New Orleans jazz tradition, a nostalgic glance at the end of the past. He did extensive research into the prehistory of the music, interviewed clarinetist Willie Humphrey, guitarist Louis Keppard (Freddie's older brother!) and writer Bill Russell, wrote about Buddy Bolden and Bunk Johnson and attended trombonist Jim Robinson's somewhat out-of-control funeral (which symbolized the inevitable death of the original players). The overall effect of the book is both informative and bittersweet. —*Scott Yanow*

Reminiscing in Tempo, *Teddy Reig & Edward Berger* / 1990 / Scarecrow Press ♦♦♦
Teddy Reig was an insightful jazz record producer who worked extensively with Savoy (highlighted by the Charlie Parker sessions), Roost (his own label) and Roulette (including the Count Basie records). He was also a bit nuts, which helped him to deal with such characters as Herman Lubinsky of Savoy (a legendary cheapskate), uncaring executives and erratic but brilliant musicians. Reig was interviewed by Edward Berger but died before this project could be completed. The first 75 pages of the book are his memoirs (which are full of hilarious stories and revelations), Berger also interviewed ten people who knew Reig and wraps up the work with a selected discography of the albums Reig worked on. Despite its brevity, this book is recommended to fans of 1940s and '50s jazz. —*Scott Yanow*

Rhythm Man, *Steve Jordan and Tom Scanlan* / 1991 / University of Michigan Press ♦♦♦♦
Steve Jordan, a rhythm guitarist who emerged during the swing era, spent most of his career very much in the background as a nearly inaudible but important part of various rhythm sections. He completed his memoirs (which include a discography) shortly before he passed away. Throughout his lengthy career Jordan played with some of the best and his stories about such musicians as Ray McKinley, Freddie Slack, Artie Shaw, Glen Gray, Stan Kenton, Boyd Raeburn, Benny Goodman, Buck Clayton, Oscar Pettiford, Zoot Sims and many others are consistently colorful and sometimes quite humorous. Steve Jordan's tales of the jazz life (despite his lack of name recognition) are well worth enjoying. —*Scott Yanow*

☆ **Rhythm-A-Ning,** *Gary Giddins* / 1985 / Oxford University Press ♦♦♦♦♦
With the exception of fusion (which he has never accepted), Gary Giddins is one of the more open-minded and consistently talented jazz journalists of the past 20 years. This book (a bit of a time capsule) collects many of his best articles from the first half of the 1980s, 61 pieces in all. Among the subjects covered are Jaki Byard, Jack DeJohnette, Sarah Vaughan, comparisons of different versions of "Body and Soul," Teddy Wilson, Lester Young, Miles Davis, Arthur Blythe, obituaries on Art Pepper and Sonny Stitt, pieces on Woody Herman, Illinois Jacquet, Thelonious Monk and even Frank Sinatra, Tony Bennett and Jackie Wilson. In

general Giddin's articles (some of which are quite brief) will hold readers' interests and make one think. —*Scott Yanow*

Sassy, *Leslie Gourse* / 1993 / Charles Scribner & Sons ◆◆◆◆
The first full-length biography of the great singer Sarah Vaughan, Leslie Gourse's work does an admirable job of covering both her musical career and her personal life. Although one might think that Sassy's life did not contain much drama (she became a major success early on and never declined), the details of her marriages and relationships in addition to the musical challenges that she faced keep this narrative quite interesting. A discography (which unfortunately leaves out label numbers) rounds out the fine book. —*Scott Yanow*

Satchmo, *Gary Giddins* / 1988 / Anchor Books ◆◆◆◆◆
The many wonderful (beautifully reproduced) photos—many of which were formerly unpublished—tend to overshadow Giddins' enlightening text. Giddins punctuates the myths long surrounding Louis Armstrong because they are not needed; he was larger than life and a true hero anyway! This superb book will delight both beginners (who will get a strong introduction to the magic of Louis' life) and veteran collectors (who will find much to learn). Highly recommended to all. —*Scott Yanow*

Scott Joplin, *James Haskins & Kathleen Benson* / 1978 / Doubleday ◆◆◆◆
The best biography on Scott Joplin at the time (although somewhat eclipsed by 1994's *King of Ragtime*), this book gives one a definitive portrait of the most important ragtime composer. James Haskins begins logically with a prologue about the rediscovery of Joplin's music after decades of neglect, and then in eight well-written chapters covers his accomplishments and his eventual sad decline. This is a perfect introduction to the life of the innovative composer. —*Scott Yanow*

Selections From the Gutter, *edited by Art Hodes & Chadwick Hansen* / 1977 / University of California Press ◆◆◆◆◆
During 1943-47, pianist Art Hodes edited *The Jazz Record,* an extremely valuable jazz magazine that often told about the lives of jazz artists through the musician's own words. The emphasis is principally on vintage jazz. In addition to standard interviews and portraits, there are articles written by the likes of Cow Cow Davenport, Little Brother Montgomery, Big Bill Broonzy, Mezz Mezzrow, Zutty Singleton, Kaiser Marshall, Omer Simeon, Baby Dodds, Pops Foster, George Wettling, Doc Evans and many others. Hodes himself sets the stage by describing various aspects of the jazz scene of the mid-1940s. Overall the 79 articles included in this very enjoyable book are consistently colorful, informative and timeless. —*Scott Yanow*

Self-Portrait of a Jazz Artist, *David Liebman* / 1988 / Advance Music ◆◆◆
In this slim volume, soprano-saxophonist David Liebman does a masterful job of summing up his life's experiences, his musical evolution, how he creates music and why he plays jazz. He not only lists a discography of his recordings up to 1988 but a sampling of his personal favorite books and records. There is a lot of variety in this volume, making the book of great interest to anyone who collects Liebman's recordings. —*Scott Yanow*

Setting the Tempo—50 Years of Great Jazz Liner Notes, *edited by Tom Piazza* / 1996 / Bantam Doubleday Dell ◆◆◆

Showtime at the Apollo, *Ted Fox* / 1993 / Da Capo Press ◆◆◆◆

Sideman, *W.O. Smith* / 1991 / Rutledge Hill Press ◆◆◆
W.O. Smith was a fine bassist who, after being a respected sideman in the 1930s and '40s with such musicians as Coleman Hawkins and Dizzy Gillespie, became an important music educator in Tennessee. Although Smith never became famous himself, he experienced the jazz life for many years and his memoirs (completed a month before his death) are full of colorful and fresh stories about the latter years of the swing era and the prime years of bop, in addition to his later period as a teacher. —*Scott Yanow*

☆ **Sidney Bechet—The Wizard of Jazz,** *John Chilton* / 1987 / Oxford University Press ◆◆◆◆◆
This is an amazingly detailed biography, tracing the life of soprano-saxophonist Sidney Bechet nearly week-by-week throughout his busy career. Bechet, one of the masters of New Orleans jazz, had a fiery and occasionally erratic personality that was not absent of jealousy and pettiness. Through Chilton's very well-written narrative, the life of Bechet (from early New Orleans and his sometimes tumultuous tours overseas in the '20s through the Depression and his years in Paris in the 1950s when he was considered a national hero) is traced in colorful fashion. This book (which ranks second to *Bix—Man and Legend* as the best jazz biography ever written) would be worth getting if only to read about the up and mostly down relationship that Bechet had with Louis Armstrong. An essential acquisition for all jazz libraries. —*Scott Yanow*

Singing Jazz, *Bruce Crowther & Mike Pinfold* / 1996 / Miller Freeman Books ◆◆◆

The Song of the Hawk, *John Chilton* / 1990 / University of Michigan Press ◆◆◆◆
Although not quite at the same level as his remarkable Sidney Bechet biography, John Chilton's study of the great tenor Coleman Hawkins is very well researched and complete. Hawkins was not really all that interesting a personality (unlike the volatile Bechet) and was a very private person but Chilton did the best with what was available (although a discography would have been an asset). Even if his account of Hawk's childhood is a mere seven pages, the remainder of Hawkins' musical career, his evolution and what could be found about his private life is covered quite definitively. —*Scott Yanow*

The Sound of Miles Davis—The Discography, *Jan Lohmann* / 1992 / Jazz Media ◆◆◆◆

Space Is the Place, *John Szwed* / 1997 / Pantheon Books ◆◆◆◆◆
Of all the musicians who have played jazz during the past century, probably the most difficult to sum up in mere words is Sun Ra. An innovative keyboardist who used electronics as early as the mid-1950s, and a bandleader who influenced the avant-garde without actually being part of any movement, Ra considered his music a tool in which to communicate his complicated philosophy. Ra obscured the facts of his own life, stating that he was from Saturn and rarely talking about his family or his early years in Birmingham, Alabama. John Szwed clearly had his work cut out for him in tackling this very complex individual but in his superior book he gives readers a glimpse into Ra's remarkable mind. *Space Is the Place* is really three books in one, covering Ra's personal life, his music and his philosophy. The latter is difficult to comprehend and should just be skimmed through—even after a close reading, it will be almost impossible to grasp the logic of Ra's ideas. However, Szwed is very good at discussing the evolution of Sun Ra's music, recreating what his rehearsals were like and capturing Ra's personality and witty way with words. In making semi-coherent the mystery of Sun Ra, John Szwed comes close to making the impossible into reality. —*Scott Yanow*

Spirit Catcher—The Life and Art of John Coltrane, *John Fraim* / 1996 / Great-House ◆◆◆◆

Stan Getz—A Life in Jazz, *Donald L. Maggin* / 1996 / William Morrow & Co. ◆◆◆◆◆
Stan Getz was such a masterful tenor-saxophonist (and had such a beautiful tone) that it can be difficult to believe how erratic a personality he was offstage. Getz's life (both good and bad) is fully documented in this definitive biography. Most family members and many musicians, friends and associates were interviewed by Donald Maggin who did a superb job of tieing all of the stories and facts together in a very coherent narrative. However, this is not easy-reading because Getz, even when he was at the height of his commercial success, could be a terrible person and he frequently mistreated his family; his emotional difficulties went far beyond mere drug abuse. Although Maggin does his best, there really is no definite explanation as to why Stan Getz had such severe personal problems. —*Scott Yanow*

Stan Kenton—The Early Years, *Edward Gabel* / 1993 / Balboa Books ◆◆
Edward Gabel worked during 1941-47 for the Stan Kenton Orchestra in odd jobs ranging from setting up the band's instruments to giving Shirley Luster the name of June Christy! Gabel's storytelling generally holds one's interest and gives listeners an idea what it was like to be constantly travelling on the road with a major big band during the war years. But since he obviously worshipped Stan Kenton, the stories are not exactly even-handed and offer only a rather sketchy and breezy account of the early Kenton years; plus Gabel never says what he did with his life after 1947. This book is purely for Stan Kenton fanatics. —*Scott Yanow*

Stan Kenton—The Man and His Music, *Lillian Arganian* / 1989 / Artistry Press ◆◆◆◆◆
This work, a collection of interviews with Stan Kentonites and associates, was a labor of love for Lillian Arganian. Her interviews with 25 men and one woman (singer June Christy) associated with Kenton are quite valuable, particularly since several have since passed away. The discussions (reproduced in a question and answer format) are quite informative, intelligent and interesting enough to hold one's interest; among the subjects are Buddy Childers, Pete Rugolo, Milt Bernhart, Shelly Manne, Shorty Rogers, Bill Russo, Bud Shank and Hank Levy. Highly recommended for Stan Kenton fans. —*Scott Yanow*

Stan Kenton, *Carol Easton* / 1973 / Da Capo Press ◆◆◆◆
Rather than being a standard musical biography, Carol Easton in this book focuses on the unique personal life and personality of Stan Kenton, a man full of contradictions and accomplishments. Kenton's marriages and many bands are covered in detail and with honesty, giving readers an idea what it was like to travel constantly with his band. Kenton comes across (despite his flaws) as rather admirable and one imagines that after reading this book he gave Carol Easton

grudging respect. Recommended to all Stan Kenton fans, particularly those who feel he could do no wrong! —*Scott Yanow*

Stomp Off, Let's Go!—The Story of Bob Crosby, *John Chilton* / 1983 / Jazz Book Service ◆◆◆◆

Stormy Weather, *Linda Dahl* / 1984 / Limelight Editions ◆◆◆◆◆
This is the first truly definitive book on women in jazz. Linda Dahl divided her important work into five parts: "1890s-1920s," "Women Instrumentalists," "Women Vocalists," "1960s-1980s" and "Profiles" (the latter has chapters on Wilene Barton, Carla Bley, Clora Bryant, Dottie Dodgion, Helen Humes, Sheila Jordan, Helen Keane, Melba Liston, Mary Osborne and Ann Patterson). In addition, an appendix briefly discusses "More Women in Jazz" and there is a discography. Nearly every important female jazz singer and musician is discussed (although Annette Hanshaw is missing) and Dahl did a masterful job of putting together a unified narrative out of the many individual stories. Recommended. —*Scott Yanow*

The Story of Jazz, *Marshall Stearns* / 1956 / Oxford University Press ◆◆◆◆
This early jazz history book is most significant for logically discussing the pre-history of jazz (pre-1900) and where jazz probably came from. In addition, despite the lack of recordings, Stearns was able to cover with authority the music of early New Orleans, the work song, the early blues, minstrel shows, spirituals and ragtime. In fact, the book is nearly half finished before Stearns reaches 1920! After quickly covering the swing era, bop and Afro-Cuban jazz, Stearns makes a sincere attempt to explain what jazz is and to come up with a definition, although the latter is somewhat dated due to the rise of the avant-garde and fusion. But four decades later this book still reads quite well and is recommended for its discussion of jazz's roots. —*Scott Yanow*

The Story of the Original Dixieland Jazz Band, *H.O. Brunn* / 1960 / Louisiana State University Press ◆◆◆
This book is flawed since H.O. Brunn was a partisan for the Original Dixieland Jazz Band, but it is nevertheless still quite intriguing and informative. Brunn, who accepted without much question, all of cornetist Nick LaRocca's assertions as to the importance of the ODJB, effectively traces the evolution of the group, the events that occurred during its prime years (1917-23), the band's brief comeback in 1936 and the activities of the group's members up until 1960. Some of Brunn's opinions are offbase but this book reads quite well and does uncover a lot of information as to the lives of these jazz pioneers. —*Scott Yanow*

☆ **Straight Life,** *Art Pepper & Laurie Pepper* / 1979 / Da Capo Press ◆◆◆◆◆
This is one of the major jazz autobiographies. Art Pepper is extremely honest in his stories about life as both a great alto-saxophonist and a destructive drug addict. Some of the episodes are scary and Pepper is not shy to paint himself in a bad light. The early chapters about his days with the Stan Kenton Orchestra are fairly happy, in striking contrast to the tales of his years in prison. Laurie Pepper, who largely saved Art's life and made his successful comeback (before his death in 1982) possible, collaborated with him on the book and contributed in 1993 a 29-page "Afterword" that talks about Pepper's final three years and how the success of the book helped his career. The forward by Gary Giddins and a lengthy discography sandwich the fascinating narrative. —*Scott Yanow*

Straight, No Chaser, *Leslie Gourse* / 1997 / Schirmer Books ◆◆◆

Sweet Man, *Don George* / 1981 / G.P. Putnam & Sons ◆◆◆◆
This is a fun book. Don George, who wrote lyrics to several Duke Ellington songs in the 1940s (including "I'm Beginning to See the Light"), knew Duke fairly well during the era. He put together a saucy and often-humorous book filled with colorful (and sometimes outrageous) stories, most of which have turned out to be true. The emphasis is on the private lives of Ellington, his girlfriends and his sidemen; this gossipy book (which is quite good-natured) has many memorable anecdotes. —*Scott Yanow*

Sweet Swing Blues on the Road, *Wynton Marsalis & Frank Stewart* / 1994 / W.W. Norton ◆◆◆
Throughout this well-conceived and colorful book, trumpeter Wynton Marsalis talks about what it is like to go on the road (both the glamour and the drudgery), the joys of jazz and his personal philosophy. The many anecdotes are often quite humorous (Marsalis does not mind being the occasional butt of jokes) and he constantly shows the creative process in action. There are sketches of his band members and a few "heavy" discussions but most of the text is fairly breezy while remaining quite intelligent. The many photographs by Frank Stewart are a perfect complement to Wynton's text. —*Scott Yanow*

Swing City—Newark Nightlife 1925-50, *Barbara J. Kukla* / 1991 / Temple University Press ◆◆◆◆
Every major American city needs a book like this one, the history of jazz in Newark. Newark, New Jersey, was primarily used as a way station for musicians on their way to or from New York City but, as can be seen in this well-researched

narrative, Newark also had a jazz nightlife of its own. Barbara Kukla, who interviewed as many survivors of the era as she could find, recreates the Newark scene of 1925-50 with chapters featuring (among others) Willie "The Lion" Smith, Donald Lambert, Miss Rhapsody, Ike Quebec, Jabbo Smith and Sarah Vaughan, along with comedians, dancers and such popular local groups as the Savoy Sultans, the Savoy Dictators and the Barons of Rhythm. There are also many rare photos taken from private collections, a chapter on Savoy Records and appendixes that give a detailed "Who's Who of Newark Nightlife," bands and clubs. Although I wish that this recommended book also covered Newark of the past 45 years, it is quite comprehensive and full of fresh information. —*Scott Yanow*

☆ **The Swing Era,** *Gunther Schuller* / 1989 / Oxford University Press ◆◆◆◆◆
This is a massive work by the versatile near-genius Gunther Schuller. Focusing on the 1930-45 period, Schuller examines in depth the recordings of every major (and many minor) swing era musician and band in ten chapters: "Benny Goodman," "Duke Ellington," "Louis Armstrong," "Jimmie Lunceford/Count Basie," "The Great Black Bands," "The Great Soloists," "The White Bands," "The Territory Bands," "Small Groups" and "Things to Come." Although sometimes quite technical, Schuller's summaries are quite interesting, particularly since he is not afraid to criticize popular bands. The countless number of hours that he spent listening to swing era records is obvious and, even when one does not agree with him, his opinions are well worth reading. —*Scott Yanow*

Swing Era—New York, *W. Royal Stokes & Charles Peterson* / 1994 / Temple University Press ◆◆◆◆◆
The photos of the late Charles Peterson (many of which were previously unpublished) and the informative text of W. Royal Stokes are combined in this very attractive book. The candid photos (from 1935-42, 1945 and 1950-51) are often quite fascinating and worth close looks; in fact, in some of the shots one can almost hear the music! The photos are arranged into chapters entitled "Harlem," "52nd Street," "Jam Sessions," "The Recording Scene," "The Big Bands," "Nick's," "The Village Vanguard," "Cafe Society" and "Other Venues." The emphasis is generally on small group swing and the Eddie Condon-style of Dixieland, perfectly capturing the magic and joy of many of the classic musicians from the golden age of jazz. —*Scott Yanow*

☆ **Swing Legacy,** *Chip Deffaa* / 1989 / Scarecrow Press ◆◆◆◆◆
In this consistently interesting and well-written collection Chip Deffaa has interview/profiles with many of the top musicians who were helping to keep swing-styled jazz alive in the 1980s: Artie Shaw, Chris Griffin, Buck Clayton, Johnny Blowers, Maxine Sullivan, John Williams, Jr., Maurice Purtill, Lee Castle, Panama Francis, Stephane Grappelli, Mel Tormé, Harold Asby, Thad Jones, Frank Foster, Mercer Ellington, Warren Vache, Scott Hamilton and Woody Herman. Each of these musicians had an important story to tell and Deffaa draws out fresh anecdotes, insights and opinions from his subjects. Highly recommended, as are Deffaa's other important books. —*Scott Yanow*

Swing Out: Great Negro Dance Bands, *Gene Fernett* / 1970 / Da Capo Press ◆◆◆◆

Swing That Music, *Louis Armstrong and Horace Gerlach* / 1936 / Da Capo Press ◆◆
The first jazz autobiography, *Swing That Music* had good intentions when it was released but it is often quite inaccurate historically. Armstrong's breezy narrative was partly ghostwritten by Horace Gerlach and the overall story is often a bit confusing. Its greatest value is that it includes Armstrong's comments on events of 1922-35, the period that took place after the close of his later (and much more valuable) book *My Life in New Orleans*. But Louis' opinions on some matters (including the importance of the Original Dixieland Jazz Band) do not ring true, making this a book of limited value. —*Scott Yanow*

☆ **Swing to Bop,** *Ira Gitler* / 1985 / Oxford University Press ◆◆◆◆◆
This oral history is remarkable in that virtually all of the stories (dealing with the well documented transition of jazz in the 1940s) are new and fresh. Gitler, whose true love has long been bebop, interviewed 66 major figures who were around during the era (including many who have since passed on) about every aspect of the period from life in the big bands, the legendary sessions at Minton's and Monroe's, 52nd Street, the underrated scene in California, the bop era and the death of the brief "bop fad." Whether it be about drug abuse, life on the road, the public's indifference or the difficulty of older musicians to adjust to the new music, Ira Gitler (through the musicians' memories) does a superlative job of summing up the volatile time period. —*Scott Yanow*

☆ **Swing, Swing, Swing,** *Ross Firestone* / 1993 / W. W. Norton ◆◆◆◆◆
There has been a great deal written about clarinetist Benny Goodman through the decades but this biography is the definitive work. Rather than just focus on BG's glory years or his personal eccentricities, Ross Firestone gives readers the full story of Goodman's childhood, his unlikely rise to fame and his life after

1945 when Goodman suddenly found his music being considered old fashioned. There is plenty of fresh material in this book (which includes new interviews with Goodman's associates) and, even when Firestone recounts familiar stories, he gives the tales fresh angles and additional information. A perfectly done biography of the King of Swing. —*Scott Yanow*

Swinging' at the Savoy, *Norma Miller & Evette Jensen* / 1996 / Temple University Press ◆◆◆

Sylvester Ahola—The Gloucester Gabriel, / 1993 / Scarecrow Press ◆◆◆◆

Talking Jazz, *edited by Ben Sidran* / 1995 / Da Capo Press ◆◆◆◆
Ben Sidran for the National Public Radio show "Sidran on Record" interviewed over 100 jazz musicians. The 43 interviews included in this excellent book are taken from the 1984-90 period. Because Sidran is himself a musician, he was able to get these very interesting subjects to open up and discuss their music and their lives on a higher level than they might have if he were a typical journalist. Among the artists who interact with Sidran (reproduced in a question and answer format) are Miles Davis, Dizzy Gillespie, Max Roach, Betty Carter, Jackie McLean, Mose Allison, Sonny Rollins, Phil Woods, Archie Shepp, Keith Jarrett, Wynton Marsalis, Don Cherry, Bobby McFerrin and Bob James; each has an interesting story to tell and Sidran skillfully inspires them to express themselves in an intelligent and coherent fashion. —*Scott Yanow*

Tantalizing Tingles, *Ross Laird* / 1995 / Greenwood Press ◆◆◆
Of the many jazz discographies that have been put together, this is certainly one of the most unusual. Ross Laird compiled a list of every piano recording (mostly solos or piano duets) that relates to ragtime or jazz from the 1889-1934 period. A five-page introduction gives a concise summation of the history of ragtime and jazz piano (it is surprising how many piano records were cut back in 1889 and how piano ragtime was rarely documented on record before 1912) and the discography, although obviously for specialized tastes, is easy-to-use and perfectly done. —*Scott Yanow*

Thelonious Monk, *Thomas Fitterling* / 1997 / Berkley Hills Books ◆◆◆◆

There and Back, *Roy Porter and David Keller* / 1991 / Louisiana State University Press ◆◆◆
Roy Porter was an important bebop pioneer in Los Angeles of the mid- to late 1940s, recording with Charlie Parker and leading a big band that included a young Eric Dolphy. Unfortunately a heroin habit short-circuited his career by the early 1950s and Porter (who attempted a few comebacks) never regained his former stature. Porter tells his up-and-down story honestly (with some excuses) throughout this book which was expertly put together by writer David Keller. But it is difficult to know from reading the memoirs why Roy Porter made so few records after the mid-1950s and why he always stayed in Los Angeles; maybe he lacked the drive to try to make it big. Worth picking up. —*Scott Yanow*

They All Played Ragtime, *Rudi Blesh & Harriet Janis* / 1950 / Oak Publishers ◆◆◆◆◆
Although revised slightly (mostly the discography) upon its reissue in 1971, this is essentially the same magnificent book that came out in 1950. For what would be the first ever full-length book on ragtime (a style that had been neglected for 30 years at the time), Blesh and Janis interviewed scores of survivors (including Scott Joplin's widow and the great ragtime composer Joseph Lamb), consulted with musicians active in the revivalist movement and did an enormous amount of research. The results (which include 16 complete scores of rags) are still quite definitive 45 years later. All ragtime books written since 1950 have had to deal first with this admirable and accurate work, which essentially tells fans and scholars alike nearly everything they need to know about ragtime. *This Is Ragtime* by Terry Waldo (Da Capo Press, 1976, 244 pages, photos scattered throughout book) is valuable, but Rudi Blesh's *They All Played Ragtime* is the definitive book about this very likable music. In addition to covering most areas of classic ragtime, Waldo (himself a talented pianist) has separate chapters on novelty ragtime of the 1920s, and the ragtime revivals of the 1940s (in jazz groups), 1950s (honky tonk), 1960s and 1970s (the latter fueled by the release of *The Sting*). Waldo's even-handed account is colorful, entertaining and informative, bringing classic ragtime history's up to nearly the present day. A good selective discography concludes this fine work. —*Scott Yanow*

They're Playing Our Song, *Max Wilk* / 1997 / Da Capo Press ◆◆◆◆

Those Swinging Years, *Charlie Barnet and Stanley Dance* / 1984 / Louisiana State University Press ◆◆◆
This is a decent book that should have been a great one. Charlie Barnet, an important bandleader from the swing era, was famous for his many marriages (over a dozen) and his wild partying, in addition to heading a couple of superior jazz orchestras. Unfortunately his memoirs are quite sketchy in places and have a strong moralist tone in spots (contributed by Stanley Dance?). Known as a champion of bop in the late 1940s, in his book Barnet acts as if he regretted the whole

period! In general what is in this book is interesting (there are a fair number of humorous anecdotes) but the final result (which does not include a discography) is a slight disappointment considering its potential. —*Scott Yanow*

To Be or Not to Bop, *Dizzy Gillespie & Al Fraser* / 1979 / Doubleday ◆◆◆◆
Dizzy Gillespie's memoirs are extensive, educational and colorful although once it hits 1960 details become much more sparse; Jon Faddis is not mentioned once! This book is at its strongest when covering the innovative trumpeter's early years and the gradual formation of bebop. In addition to the 150 interviews that he conducted with Gillespie, Al Fraser gathered extensive quotes from dozens of Dizzy's associates (including relatives, Roy Eldridge, Kenny Clarke, Cab Calloway, Thelonious Monk, Mary Lou Williams, Billy Eckstine, Earl Hines, Sarah Vaughan, Max Roach, Ella Fitzgerald and even Miles Davis, among many others), including them in the relevant chapters (even when they occasionally contradict Gillespie's version of a story). This is a very valuable book as one might expect, highly recommended to fans of bop. —*Scott Yanow*

Too Marvelous for Words, *James Lester* / 1994 / Oxford University Press ◆◆◆◆
Art Tatum, one of the most remarkable musicians (not just in jazz) of all time, was a rather private person. As James Lester discovered in researching for his definitive book, Tatum rarely did any interviews and did not have much of a life outside of his music; although married twice, his women always played second fiddle to his piano. Lester did talk to everyone possible (including Art's childhood friends and many musicians) about Tatum and was able to piece together a fairly complete picture even though there are still some mysteries. This is a well-conceived book about one of the immortals, the only one ever written on Art Tatum. —*Scott Yanow*

Traditionalists & Revivalists in Jazz, *Chip Deffaa* / 1993 / Scarecrow Press ◆◆◆◆◆
For his fourth book, Chip Deffaa includes 14 portraits of musicians who play or sing vintage jazz in the 1990s. Unlike in his first three books, Deffaa sticks (with a couple of exceptions) to younger players rather than ancient veterans; only Marty Grosz had previously been profiled in a book. Each of the subjects (Vince Giordano, Terry Waldo, Eddy Davis, Peter Ecklund, Marty Grosz, Joe Muranyi, Richard Sudhalter, Dan Barrett, Ed Polcer, Stan Rubin, Carrie Smith, Sandra Reaves-Phillips, Orange Kellin and Vernel Bagneris) have interesting stories to tell with many previously unknown details and anecdotes about classic jazz, a truly underground form of jazz in the '90s. Recommended. —*Scott Yanow*

Tram—The Frank Trumbauer Story, *Philip Evans and Larry Kiner* / 1994 / Scarecrow Press ◆◆
On first glance this appears to be a huge book, but in reality a great many of the pages are wasted and the layout is greatly flawed. Frankie Trumbauer was the master of the C-melody saxophone in the 1920s (when he was a close associate of Bix Beiderbecke). He eventually gave up playing music in 1940 to become a pilot (other than a brief comeback attempt in 1946) but seems to have had a generally happy life; Philip Evans' 274-page biography is excellent and should have served as most of the book. Unfortunately, it is followed by a greatly stretched-out 275-page discography that makes the fatal error of listing recording sessions alphabetically by bandleader instead of in chronological order, making it almost unusable! After a valuable chronology of Trumbauer's life, 130 pages are wasted on a frivolous "song title index." This book could have been half as big with no loss of important information. —*Scott Yanow*

Traps—The Boy Wonder, *Mel Tormé* / 1991 / Oxford University Press ◆◆◆◆◆
Mel Tormé, a talented writer as well as singer, was a longtime friend of Buddy Rich and was asked by Rich back in 1975 to write his biography. This consistently fascinating book has a great deal of inside information about the amazing drummer along with many humorous stories. Rich, a true genius who was a top drummer in vaudeville by the time he was 18 months old (!), expected greatness at all times from his sidemen and was quite difficult to work for; Tormé is quite fair in evaluating Buddy's personality and temper. But when it came to drumming, Buddy Rich still ranks at the top and Tormé never shies away from the fact that Rich really was the world's greatest drummer. Highly recommended. —*Scott Yanow*

Treat It Gentle, *Sidney Bechet with Desmond Flower* / 1960 / Da Capo Press ◆◆◆◆
The great New Orleans pioneer Sidney Bechet's autobiography is one of the most picturesque in jazz history. Some of his stories are more legendary than fact (particularly the chapter on his grandfather), but there is a great deal of valuable information in these memoirs. Unfortunately, the masterful soprano-saxophonist died in 1959, a year before the book was published, and he had run out of time before saying much about his last decade when he was adopted as a national hero in France, but what is here is generally memorable. This book is recom-

mended as a complement to John Chilton's much more thorough Bechet biography *The Wizard of Jazz*. —*Scott Yanow*

The Trouble with Cinderella, *Artie Shaw* / 1952 / Da Capo Press ♦♦
Artie Shaw's memoirs are remarkably self-indulgent and tedious. Rather than discussing his career as a masterful clarinetist and bandleader or talking about his many wives and relationships, Shaw mostly focuses on his childhood and very early days in an endless search for his own identity; the amateur self-analysis drones on and on and is quite difficult to read. The definitive Artie Shaw biography has yet to be written; skip this misfire! —*Scott Yanow*

Trumpet Story, *Bill Coleman* / 1981 / Northeastern University Press ♦♦♦♦
Bill Coleman was an excellent swing trumpeter who emerged during the late 1920s, spent the latter half of the 1930s in France, came back to the US during World War II, and then spent the remainder of his life back in France. His memoirs (written without a collaborator) are remarkably detailed and are particularly valuable in casting light on some of the legendary territory bands of the 1920s and the European scene of the 1930s. Coleman's story gets sketchier once he reaches the 1960s but stays interesting until its conclusion in 1981. An excellent discography wraps up this recommended book. —*Scott Yanow*

Twenty Years on Wheels, *Andy Kirk and Amy Lee* / 1989 / University of Michigan Press ♦♦
The memoirs of Andy Kirk, an important bandleader during the swing era who lived to be 94, are a bit of a disappointment; he says almost nothing about his life after the early 1950s. Although often grouped with the Kansas City scene of the 1929-36 period, it is strange to realize how few of the fabled jam sessions and club dates Kirk actually saw. A stable happily-married family man, Kirk missed a great deal of important jazz history! Lester Young, Ben Webster, Charlie Parker are barely mentioned in his narrative, Coleman Hawkins is completely absent and even Count Basie hardly makes it into the book. The main reason to acquire this autobiography (which does have a discography) is for Kirk's stories about his own band which was in its commercial heyday during 1936-42. —*Scott Yanow*

Unfinished Dream, *Red Callender and Elaine Cohen* / 1985 / Quartet Jazz ♦♦♦♦
Red Callender, the only musician to turn down jobs with both the Louis Armstrong All-Stars and Duke Ellington's Orchestra (working in the studios of Los Angeles was more lucrative), was a versatile and talented bassist and tuba player who recorded extensively between 1937-84. Fortunately he had a very good memory and his interesting (if generally little-known) life story is full of intricate details, particularly up through the 1950s. This biography is easily recommended. —*Scott Yanow*

Unforgettable, *Leslie Gourse* / 1991 / St. Martin's Press ♦♦
Leslie Gourse's well-meaning biography of Nat King Cole is a bit of a disappointment. The definitive book on the pianist-singer (James Haskins' *Nat Cole: The Man and His Music*) had been published a couple years earlier and already contained the best Nat King Cole stories. Because Gourse did not want to directly copy the book, she reprised the anecdotes (which generally takes away from their power) and conducted original research of her own. Although her interviews added to the Nat King Cole story, one has to buy both biographies in order to get the full picture and Haskins' book is definitely the superior one. So Gourse's project (which contains too many repetitions in its narrative) is only recommended to readers who already have Haskins' biography and want to learn more. —*Scott Yanow*

Unzipped Souls, *Bill Minor* / 1995 / Temple University Press ♦♦♦♦
This very interesting book documents writer Bill Minor's visit to the Soviet Union in 1990, a moment in history when the country was beginning its transition from communism to capitalism. Minor's desire was to talk to Russian musicians about their lives and, after much struggle (he discusses all of the steps he had to go through in order to visit the USSR), he succeeded in meeting nearly every musician he desired. Part travelogue, part mystery drama, this narrative often reads like a novel. As well-informed as possible (Minor did his best to learn Russian beforehand and was quite familiar with much of the Russian jazz scene), the ambitious writer attended a jazz festival in Moscow and then visited many cities in search of the artists he admired. Although their names will be unfamiliar to most readers, Bill Minor makes each of the artists come alive with their hopes, dreams, accomplishments and frustrations. Well worth acquiring. —*Scott Yanow*

☆ Voices of the Jazz Age, *Chip Deffaa* / 1990 / University of Illinois Press ♦♦♦♦♦
Just as Stanley Dance in the early 1960s did the jazz world a major service by interviewing veteran jazzmen while they were still around, Chip Deffaa in his first book captured seven jazzmen before it was too late; only 96-year old Benny Waters is still around. Deffaa's portraits of Waters, Sam Wooding (who was on his deathbed!), Joe Tarto, Bud Freeman, Jimmy McPartland, Freddie Moore, Jabbo Smith and his tribute to Bix Beiderbecke are all pretty definitive with lots of new information. Deffaa brought to the interviews both enthusiasm and vast knowl-

edge, and the results are consistently memorable. This appealing book is highly recommended to fans of classic jazz. —*Scott Yanow*

☆ We Called It Music, *Eddie Condon and Thomas Sugrue* / 1947 / Da Capo Press ♦♦♦♦♦
This book (which was reissued in 1992 with a forward by Gary Giddins and a chapter added for the 1962 reprint) is a classic. Eddie Condon (bandleader, rhythm guitarist and propagandist for Chicago Dixieland) was one of the great wits of jazz. His colorful memoirs (which cover the first half of his career) are filled with memorable stories about the great early legends of jazz (including Bix Beiderbecke) and are augmented by Thomas Sugrue's "narration," which puts the anecdotes into historical perspective. One comes away from this entertaining book fully understanding why some jazzmen enjoy playing this freewheeling music and also with an appreciation for Eddie Condon's unique place in jazz history. —*Scott Yanow*

Wes Montgomery, *Adrian Ingram* / 1985 / Hal Leonard Publishing ♦♦
Adrian Ingram's tribute to Wes Montgomery is a reasonably enjoyable book that celebrates the life and career of the great guitarist. A jazz educator from England who also plays guitar, Ingram's love for Wes' music is obvious throughout the book which, in addition to a rather brief biography (just 40 pages), has rare pictures, an analysis of Montgomery's style, some comments from other musicians and a lengthy (if somewhat out-of-date) discography. Even if no new revelations are uncovered and Adrian Ingram cannot decide whether he loves or hates Montgomery's later commercial recordings (he criticizes both the music and the critics who cut down the records!), this breezy and well-intentioned book can serve as an effective (if lightweight) introduction to Wes Montgomery. —*Scott Yanow*

What a Wonderful World, *Bob Thiele and Bob Golden* / 1995 / Oxford University Press ♦♦
Bob Thiele was an important producer who worked on (and in some cases founded) such labels as Signature, Coral, Impulse, Dr. Jazz and Red Baron, among others. His memoirs, written less than a year before his death, should have been explosive and quite definitive (the stories he could have told!) but instead they are quite sketchy and often seem more intent on settling a few scores than giving readers a full understanding of the record business. Thiele does tell a few good tales (he worked with everyone from Duke Ellington to Buddy Holly) but there is an awful lot left unsaid and now lost to history; his collaborator Bob Golden should have gotten Thiele to really open up. —*Scott Yanow*

What Jazz Is, *Jonny King* / 1997 / Walker and Company ♦♦
Pianist Jonny King's book falls under the category of good intentions. In an easy-to-read and accessible style, King (a fine musician with recordings out on the Enja label) discusses the technical aspects of jazz, what beginners should listen for, the role of each instrument and some of his favorite recordings. The problem is that King concentrates almost exclusively on hard bop and post bop. There is no real mention of pop jazz, very little about music before bebop (he mistakenly places Bix Beiderbecke in the 1930s) and the avant-garde is only discussed in superficial fashion. According to King, jazz has to swing and hard bop is "modern jazz." Despite that major fault (which really limits the book's scope), his narrative has some value in introducing listeners to the type of jazz (personified by the Young Lions) that the pianist most loves. —*Scott Yanow*

☆ Who's Who of Jazz, *John Chilton* / 1978 / Chilton Book Co. ♦♦♦♦♦
This is one of the great jazz reference books. John Chilton has a biographical entry on virtually every important jazz musician (many of whom are little-known today) born before 1920. Although Dizzy Gillespie makes the book, the emphasis is on vintage and swing musicians. Chilton largely avoids commenting on the subject's musical significance, sticking to facts and providing a major service to historians and early jazz fans alike. There is a lot of information in this book that can not be found elsewhere. —*Scott Yanow*

☆ The Wildest One, *Hal Willard* / 1996 / Avondale Press ♦♦♦♦♦
Wild Bill Davison was the perfect Dixieland cornetist. His highly expressive solos were full of personality including growls, screams, whispers, sarcasm and sentimentality. Although Davison's playing tended to stay reasonably close to the melody, his timing was exquisite with perfectly placed high notes never failing to surprise listeners. Davison was also a legendary womanizer (he could not remember the name of his first wife who he only saw twice!), a hard drinker and an impulsive character who survived for 83 years despite it all. Hal Willard, a veteran of the *Washington Post*, spent over a decade putting together this colorful and utterly fascinating work. Willard was able to extensively interview Davison (who died in 1989), his fifth wife Ann Davison and every relative, friend, associate and significant musician he could find. Filled with hilarious stories about Davison's exploits (he earned the nickname "Wild Bill" many times), the narrative traces the cornetist's life quite thoroughly and will be entertaining and informative even to readers who are not that familiar with Davison's music. There are

two faults: next-to-nothing is said about Wild Bill's life in the 1980s (he was active up until the end) and no discography is included. But otherwise *The Wildest One* is a gem and highly recommended. —*Scott Yanow*

☆ **Wishing on the Moon,** *Donald Clarke* / 1994 / Viking ✦✦✦✦✦

Billie Holiday is one of the great jazz legends and has been written about steadily for the past four decades. Donald Clarke interviewed many of Lady Day's associates who had rarely been spoken to by biographers and he also had access to the files of Linda Kuehl (who had interviewed nearly 150 people before her death in the 1970s). The result is a truly definitive book that successfully separates facts from myths. Clarke disproves much of what was thought to be true about Holiday's early life (her *Lady Sings the Blues* memoirs are mostly fanciful) and shows that Billie brought a lot of her troubles on herself while still painting her as a largely sympathetic character. This is a masterful work that is a must for anyone wanting to know the true story of Billie Holiday. —*Scott Yanow*

With Louis and the Duke, *Barney Bigard and Barry Martyn* / 1985 / Oxford University Press ✦✦✦

The release of clarinetist Barney Bigard's memoirs in 1986 was a bit of a surprise since he had passed away in 1980. Barry Martyn fortunately had conducted quite a few interviews with the veteran clarinetist in the 1970s although he found it difficult at first since Bigard was not much of a talker and was modest about his own role in the music. But the results, although quite informal and chatty, are well worth reading. Bigard not only talks about his experiences playing with Duke Ellington and Louis Armstrong but of his early days in the 1920s and about King Oliver. Worth picking up by fans of early jazz. —*Scott Yanow*

Woody Herman—Chronicles of the Herds, *William Clancy & Audree Coke Kenton* / 1995 / Schirmer Books ✦✦✦✦

The Woodchopper's Ball, *Woody Herman and Stuart Troup* / 1990 / E.P. Dutton ✦✦

This book is a noble failure. Woody Herman simply started to put together his memoirs a bit too late and his health failed before his book could be completed. Herman's career is reasonably well documented up until the mid-1950s and then Herman's last 30 years are covered not very well in 47 pages! Stuart Troup should have done a great deal more research to fill in the gaps, and a discography would have been a major asset. As it is, this is very much an unfinished project that should probably not have released in this form. —*Scott Yanow*

The World of Count Basie, *Stanley Dance* / 1980 / Charles Scribner & Sons ✦✦✦✦✦

For the fourth book in his very valuable *World Of* series, Stanley Dance focused on Count Basie and his legacy. As with the prior books, Dance emphasizes oral histories from veteran players mostly taken in the 1960s and early '70s. The Lester Young chapter (an interview from a different source and a 1956 appreciation) is an exception. Heard from telling colorful stories in this enjoyable book are such Basie alumni as Jimmy Rushing, Buck Clayton, Jo Jones, Eddie Durham, Earle Warren, Dicky Wells, Harry "Sweets" Edison, Buddy Tate, Helen Humes, Snooky Young, Joe Newman, Preston Love, Marshall Royal, Eddie "Lockjaw" Davis, Frank Wess, Frank Foster, Joe Williams, Al Grey, Sonny Cohn, Eric Dixon, Bobby Plater, Richard Boone, Paul Quinichette and Basie himself. In addition there are interviews with such Basie associates as Nat Pierce, Jay McShann, Gene Ramey, Gus Johnson, Paul Quinichette, Jimmy Witherspoon, Eddie Barefield, Snub Mosley, Sir Charles Thompson and Melvin Moore. All four of Dance's books are well worth acquiring by fans of swing-oriented jazz. —*Scott Yanow*

The World of Duke Ellington, *Stanley Dance* / 1970 / Da Capo Press ✦✦✦✦✦

Stanley Dance's interviews with veteran swing musicians in his four *World Of* books are extremely valuable, saving stories and information for posterity that would otherwise be permanently lost. This important work starts off with a few interviews with Duke Ellington and then there are oral histories of many of his top associates including Billy Strayhorn, Mercer Ellington, Otto Hardwick, Sonny Greer, Harry Carney, Barney Bigard, Johnny Hodges, Cootie Williams, Juan Tizol, Lawrence Brown, Ben Webster, Ray Nance, Jimmy Hamilton, Cat Anderson, Russell Procope, Shorty Baker, Paul Gonsalves, Willie Cook, Clark Terry, Sam Woodyard, Booty Wood, Aaron Bell, Buster Cooper, Jimmy Jones, Jeff Castleman, Alice Babs, Harold Ashby and Wild Bill Davis. When one considers how few of these musicians are still around, it quickly become apparent just how valuable this project was. In addition Dance reports on some of the Ellington tours and festivals on which he was fortunate enough to attend. This book is not a standard biography nor is there much information on Duke's offstage life, but it is quite memorable anyway! —*Scott Yanow*

The World of Earl Hines, *Stanley Dance* / 1977 / Da Capo Press ✦✦✦✦✦

This entry in Stanley Dance's unique *World Of* series is the best book thus far written about pianist Earl "Fatha" Hines. In addition to extensive interviews with Hines that take up 100 pages, Dance includes oral histories of Hines' manager Charlie Carpenter plus 20 musicians including Lois Deppe (Hines' first boss), Walter Fuller, Teddy Wilson, Milt Hinton, Jimmy Mundy, Budd Johnson, Trummy Young, Billy Eckstine, Dizzy Gillespie and Dicky Wells, among others. In addition, there is a chapter on road stories, capsule biographies of Hines' 1946 band (taken from publicity material) and a chronology of his life. A superior effort. —*Scott Yanow*

World of Gene Krupa, *edited by Bruce Klauber* / 1990 / Pathfinder Publishing ✦✦✦

For this interesting book on Gene Krupa, Bruce Klauber supplied a brief retrospective of Krupa's life and some transitions. In addition he collected interviews with the influential drummer, reviews from his career and recollections of other musicians, splicing it all together to create a coherent and colorful tribute. There are no new revelations or inteviews but this is an easily recommended and colorful book that Gene Krupa collectors will enjoy. The work is rounded out by a chronology, a filmography and a list of available albums. —*Scott Yanow*

☆ **The World of Swing,** *Stanley Dance* / 1974 / Da Capo Press ✦✦✦✦✦

In the second of Stanley Dance's very valuable *World Of* series of books, rather than focusing on one individual (as in his Duke Ellington, Count Basie and Earl Hines books), Dance covers a wider spectrum. His profiles (most of which contain timeless interviews filled with valuable anecdotes) include pieces on Claude Hopkins, Sandy Williams, Taft Jordan, Willie Smith, Sy Oliver, Benny Carter, Coleman Hawkins, Roy Eldridge, Jonah Jones, Stuff Smith, Cozy Cole, Charlie Holmes, Benny Goodman, Lionel Hampton, Vic Dickenson, Doc Cheatham, Eddie Heywood, Al Casey, Tiny Grimes, Milt Hinton, Chick Webb, Mildred Bailey and Billie Holiday, among others. Fans of the swing era (particularly the many talented Black bands) are well advised to pick up this very interesting book. —*Scott Yanow*

You Just Fight for Your Life, *Frank Buchmann-Moller* / 1990 / Greenwood Press ✦✦✦✦

Lester Young was always a legendary figure with his own unusual personality, language and playing style. In this definitive book, Danish writer Frank Buchmann-Moller clears up some of the mysteries about the great tenor, he includes a great deal of previously unknown information that partly explains Young's eventual decline and he pieces together a very complete portrait. A valuable appendix lists all of Lester Young's known musical jobs. For readers who really want to study Young's playing, Buchmann-Moller's companion book *You Got to be Original, Man* has a discussion of all of Lester's solos, but more general collectors will be satisfied with this fine biography. —*Scott Yanow*

Venues

Jazz has been performed in all types of situations and settings through the years, from weddings and funerals to informal parties and concert halls. From before the 1920s into the 1990s, much of the most memorable music was created at night-clubs where musicians (particularly prior to the 1980s) had opportunities to play three or four sets a night and really develop their talents. With the rise of jazz festivals and the utilization of alternative spaces (including lofts, college campuses and prestigious settings formerly only used by classical orchestras), the nightclub has decreased a bit in importance. Today it is rare for any group to perform in the same club on a nightly basis for more than a week and many gigs are just one-night stands. However, there are exceptions and, despite the strong competition of other types of music and activities (including television), the jazz nightclub lives on. This section mentions some of the notable clubs and theatres of the past and lists some (but certainly not all) of the more significant nightclubs of today. This is by no means a complete list and listeners wishing to experience jazz in an intimate setting in person are advised to check their local newspapers and (if they are lucky enough to have one) jazz radio station. A recommended read for those traveling the U.S. in hopes of finding jazz is Christiane Bird's very detailed book *The Jazz and Blues Lover's Guide to the U.S.* (Addison-Wesley Publishing Co.). —Scott Yanow

Atlanta

Atlanta has had some jazz since the music's beginnings. On Decatur Street in the teens and '20s, blues and jazz musicians frequently found employment, and in the 1950s the Waluhaje thrived, but in general jazz has rarely been a major part of the city's culture.

Red Light Café - 553 Amsterdam Ave NE, Atlanta, GA 30306 (404) 874-7828

Café 290 - 290 Hilderbrand Rd., Atlanta, GA 30328 (404) 256-3942

Austin

In this Texas town, the main music area starting in the 1920s was found around East 11th Street. The blues has always been a more dominant force in Austin than jazz with the Victory Grill (which opened in 1945 and lasted into the '80s) and Antone's (a blues mecca since the mid-'70s) being the most famous local clubs.

Top of the Marc - 618 W. 6th St, Austin, TX 78701 (512) 472-9849

The Elephant Bar - 315 Congress, Austin, TX 78701 (512) 473-2279

The Ritz Theater - 320 E. 6th St, Austin, TX 78701 (512) 477-2123

Baltimore

Being on the East Coast, Baltimore has often acted as a training ground for up-and-coming musicians on their way to New York, but it has also generally had a strong local scene. For over three decades (the '20s through the '50s), Pennsylvania Avenue was Baltimore's equivalent of New York's 52nd Street with numerous clubs and a very musical environment. Also quite noteworthy was the Royal Theatre.

Buddies Pub & Jazz Club - 313 N. Charles St, Baltimore, MD 21201 (410) 332-4200

Benny's - 2701 N. Charles St., Baltimore, MD 21218 (410) 366-7779

The New Haven - 1552-1554 Havenwood Rd, Baltimore, MD 21218 (410) 366-7418

Boston

Although one might not think of Boston as being a major jazz town, in reality it has always ranked in the top ten. In addition to serving as home for the many young musicians who attend the Berklee College of Music, Boston has had its own strong local scene, particularly since the late '40s. Massachusetts and Columbus Avenues during the bebop era were the home for a half-dozen clubs including the Hi-Hat and the Savoy Café. George Wein's Storyville club in the 1950s imported major names from New York and two of the top venues during the latter half of the 1960s into the '70s were Lenny's on the Turnpike and the Jazz Workshop.

Regattabar - 1 Bennett St, Cambridge, MA 02138 (617) 876-8742

Scullers - 400 Soldiers Field Rd, Boston, MA (617) 595-5161

Willow Jazz Club - 699 Broadway, Somerville, MA 02144 (617) 262-6311

Chicago

Chicago has long had a rich jazz history. In fact, during the 1920-26 period, it could be safely argued that Chicago served as the center of jazz. King Oliver, Jelly Roll Morton, Louis Armstrong, Johnny Dodds, Jimmie Noone, Freddie Keppard, the New Orleans Rhythm Kings, the Austin High School Gang (the nucleus for Eddie Condon's future groups), Bix Beiderbecke, Hoagy Carmichael and Benny Goodman were regular residents. Such clubs as the Royal Gardens, the Lincoln Gardens (home of King Oliver's Creole Jazz Band), the Friar's Inn, Kelly's Stables, Midway Garden Ballroom, Sunset Café and the Vendome Theatre were quite significant. Even after many of the top players started relocating to New York in the mid-to-late '20s, the Apex Club (musical home of Jimmie Noone), the Club Alabam, the Cellar (later renamed the Three Deuces), the Grand Terrace Ballroom (where Earl Hines' big band regularly played), the Savoy Ballroom, the Dreamland Café, the Aragon Ballroom, the Regal Theatre and the Congress Hotel kept jazz alive in the Windy City. The Depression years found Chicago overshadowed by New York and soon jazz was subservient to the growing blues scene. During the bebop era, the Gate of Horn, the Sutherland Show Lounge, the Pershing Hotel, the New Regal Theatre, the Blue Note Club and the Bee Hive were important. Jazz Ltd. featured Dixieland, Oscar Peterson recorded extensively at the London House and Miles Davis made the Plugged Nickel immortal with his live recordings of late 1965. With the rise of the AACM and numerous advanced players in the late '60s, the musicians created many small alternative venues themselves so they would have a place to perform their explorative music. Chicago may today be best-known for the blues but its local jazz scene is actually one of the finest in the world although it remains underpublicized.

Joe Segal's Jazz Showcase - Blackstone Hotel, 636 S. Michigan Ave, Chicago, IL 60605 (312) 427-4300

Andy's Lounge - 11 E. Hubbard, Chicago, IL 60611 (312) 642-6805

The Green Mill - 4802 N. Broadway, Chicago, IL 60640 (312) 878-5552

The Green Orchid - Bismarck Hotel, 171 W. Randolph, Chicago, IL 60601 (312) 236-0123

Metropole/Fairmount Hotel, 200 N. Columbus Drive, Chicago, IL 60601 (312) 565-8000

The Bulls - 1916 N. Lincoln Park West, Chicago, IL 60614 (312) 337-3000

Cotton Club - 1710 S. Michigan Ave, Chicago, IL 60616 (312) 341-9787

Hot House - 1152 N. Milwaukee, Chicago, IL 60622 (312) 235-2334

The Bop Shop - 1807 Division St, Chicago, IL 60622 (312) 235-3232

Pops for Champagne - 2934 N. Sheffield Ave, Chicago, IL 60657 (312) 472-1000

Cincinnati

A minor city from the jazz standpoint, Cincinnati has had occasional brushes with jazz history. The Wolverines with Bix Beiderbecke played at Doyle's Dance Hall for a few months in 1924 and Lena Horne fronted the Noble Sissle Orchestra at the Moonlight Gardens Ballroom in 1936. In more recent times, the Blue Wisp Big Band helped make the club of the same name famous beyond the Cincinnati city limits.

The Blue Wisp - 19 Garfield Place, Cincinnati, OH 45202 (513) 721-9801

The Greenwich Tavern - 2442 Gilbert Ave, Cincinnati, OH 45206 (513) 221-6764

Dallas

Dallas' jazz heyday was in the 1920s when it was a stopping-off point for a variety of top territory bands that toured the South and the Midwest. The Adolphus Hotel (which at one point was the homebase for the Alphonse Trent Orchestra) was the best-known venue and the Tip Top Club was also a popular hangout. Unfortunately jazz has since declined in importance as part of Dallas' cultural life and in the 1990s, with the exception of Caravan of Dreams (which was located at 312 Houston in Fort Worth, 817-877-3000), which may no longer be open, there are no full-time jazz clubs in the area.

Detroit/Ann Arbor

Detroit was most significant in the 1920s as the homebase for the orchestras of Jean Goldkette including McKinney's Cotton Pickers. Its prime years in jazz, however, were during roughly the 1946-56 period when many young musicians called it home including Thad and Elvin Jones, Pepper Adams, Yusef Lateef, Donald Byrd, Billy Mitchell, Kenny Burrell, Charles McPherson and a piano tradition that included Hank Jones (who actually departed in 1945), Barry Harris, Tommy Flanagan and Roland Hanna. The Graystone Ballroom was the key venue in the 1920s, many big bands played at the Paradise Theatre in the 1940s, Baker's Keyboard Lounge was once famous and in the 1950s the Bluebird Inn and the World Stage were quite significant. The Detroit jazz scene has since declined although there are many local talents, many of whom have learned from trumpeter Marcus Belgrave.

Bird of Paradise - 207 S. Ashley, Ann Arbor, MI 48104 (313) 662-8310

Serengeti Ballroom - 2957 Woodward Ave, Detroit, MA 48202 (313) 832-3010

Kansas City

Kansas City will always be famous for its around-the-clock jazz activity during the 1920s and '30s. The Tom Pendergast political machine kept Prohibition out of the city and the many bars and dance halls gave employment to scores of musicians. Bennie Moten had the top Kansas City orchestra of the 1920s while his successor the following decade was Count Basie. Among the many other notable players who kept the local scene exciting (with classic jam sessions only hinted at in the rather poor mid-'90s film *Kansas City*) were tenors Lester Young, Ben Webster and Dick Wilson, trumpeter Hot Lips Page, pianists Mary Lou Williams, Julia Lee (who also sang) and Pete Johnson, the up-and-coming altoist Charlie Parker, singers Jimmy Rushing and Joe Turner and the orchestras of Andy Kirk and Jay McShann. During those prime years, the 18th and Vine intersection was at the center of Kansas City jazz with around 50 clubs in a six-block area (including the Reno Club, the Sunset, the Subway, the Hey Hay Club and the Cherry Blossom). After Pendergast was thrown in jail in 1938, many of the clubs were shut down and Kansas City became more of a minor-league jazz town, a place to briefly stop on the way to somewhere else. However the scene has improved during the past decade; the fine regional bimonthly JAM (which reports on such top local celebrities as Karrin Allyson, Claude Williams and Jay McShann) gives one the impression that Kansas City jazz is still very much alive.

The Drum Room - 1020 Westport Rd, Kansas City, MO 64111 (816) 756-3786

Club at Plaza III - 4749 Pennsylvania, Kansas City, MO 64112 (816) 444-6969

Club 427 - 427 Main St, Kansas City, MO 64112 (816) 421-2582

Los Angeles

Los Angeles has always had some memorable jazz, but it can be difficult to find! Quite a few New Orleans musicians came to Los Angeles in the early '20s before landing in Chicago, including Jelly Roll Morton, King Oliver and Kid Ory (who recorded in L.A. as early as 1922). In the 1920s Lionel Hampton played drums with Paul Howard's Quality Serenaders and Curtis Mosby's Blue Blowers were popular but quite a few other groups went largely undocumented, including many big bands during the swing era. During the mid- to late-'40s Los Angeles had its own version of New York's 52nd Street on Central Avenue, while the 1950s found cool jazz (also called West Coast jazz) for a few years dominating the jazz scene although it received little respect from the East Coast critics. Also virtually ignored were the beginnings of the avant-garde; Ornette Coleman and Eric Dolphy were barely documented while in L.A. and the contributions of Horace Tapscott and John Carter were greatly underrated. Many musicians settled in Los Angeles to work in the studios and became obscure for a time; even Benny Carter, J.J. Johnson, Benny Golson and Shorty Rogers gave up playing for much of the 1960s and into the '70s, choosing the more lucrative life of writing for motion pictures and television. A shortage of clubs in the 1980s and '90s have led to all but the most hardy jazz musicians choosing to relocate at least part of the time on the East Coast. But if one looks at Los Angeles' long jazz history, there have been many notable venues, including the Club Alabam, the Cocoanut Grove, the Palomar Ballroom, the Cotton Club, the Hangover Club, Billy Berg's in the 1940s, the Down Beat club, the legendary Lighthouse (which still operates as a part-time jazz club), the Haig, Shelly's Manne-Hole, Concerts by the Sea and Vine St. Bar & Grill.

Catalina Bar & Grill - 1640 N. Cahuenga Blvd, Hollywood, CA 90028 (213) 466-2210

The Jazz Bakery - 3233 Helms Ave, Los Angeles, CA 90034 (310) 271-9039

5th Street Dicks - 3347 1/2 W. 43rd Place, Los Angeles, CA 90008 (213) 296-3970

The World Stage - 4344 Degnan Blvd, Los Angeles, CA 90008 (213) 293-2451

Miami and Florida

Since Florida has long been a notable retirement and vacation resort, its jazz has tended to be on the conservative side through the years, ranging from Dixieland to Las Vegas-type entertainment. Overtown Square was once the main district for

Black performers with such clubs as the Lyric Theater, the Harlem Square Club and the Knight Beat Club. However, the opening of the Pleasure Island club at Disney World, the influence of Ira Sullivan (a resident of Florida since the 1960s) and the recent re-emergence of Sam Rivers has infused the jazz scene with some more adventurous music.

Pleasure Island Jazz Co. - 1675 Buena Vista Drive #450, Lake Buena Vista, FL 32830 (407) 828-5665

Sapphire Jazz & Blues Club - 54 N. Orange, Orlando, FL 32801 (407) 246-1419

Van Dykes Café - 846 Lincoln Rd, Miami Beach, FL 33139 (305) 534-3600

MoJazz Jazz Club - 928 671st St, Miami Beach, FL 33141 (305) 867-0950

Jazz Showcase - 424 24th St, West Palm Beach, FL 33407 (407) 833-4997

Minneapolis/St. Paul

Although the Minneapolis/St. Paul area has only played a small role in jazz history (both the Pettiford and Young family bands played there often in the 1920s and '30s), the scene has been having a minor boom in recent years.

Dakota Bar & Grill - Bandana Square, 1021 E. Bandana Blvd., St. Paul, MN 55108 (612) 642-1442

Café Luxeford - 1101 LaSalle Ave, Minneapolis, MN 55403 (612) 332-6800

O'Gara's - 164 N. Snelling, St. Paul, MN 55104 (612) 644-3333

The Times - 1036 Nicollet Mall, Minneapolis, MN 55403 (612) 333-2762

Jazzville - 9th & Robert, St. Paul, MN 55118 (612) 291-1767

New Orleans

Thought of as the symbolic birthplace of jazz, New Orleans has long been one of the most musical of all cities. During 1898-1917 the infamous red-light district Storyville gave employment to versatile pianists and some blues-oriented groups but much of the musical action took place in the streets (there were a countless number of brass bands), bars and social functions ranging from parties to funerals. New Orleans' music, although still healthy, declined a bit with the close of Storyville and the gradual exodus of many of its top players up North through the teens and 1920s; the Depression forced many of the local musicians to only play on a part-time basis. However, with the Dixieland revival of the 1940s, there was a greater demand to entertain tourists and some players (such as George Lewis and Pete Fountain) became major celebrities. Many of the more flexible younger musicians infused R&B in the 1950s with infectious parade rhythms. The opening of Preservation Hall in 1961 gave traditional jazz musicians a homebase, while the rise of Wynton Marsalis in the 1980s gave worldwide attention to the formerly underground New Orleans modern jazz scene. Among the more historic jazz clubs have been Economy Hall (from 1885 up until World War II), Funky Butt Hall (where Buddy Bolden played in the 1890s), Mahogany Hall, Pete Lala's, Tom Anderson's New Cabaret and Restaurant, Lincoln Park, Artisan Hall, the Cave (later the Blue Room), the Lyric Theater, the Astoria (in the 1920s and '30s), Bienville Roof Gardens, San Jacinto Hall, Paddock Lounge, the Famous Door (important in the 1940s and '50s), the Parisian Room, Preservation Hall, and the Blue Angel (which started in the 1970s).

Preservation Hall - 726 St. Peter, New Orleans, LA 70116 (504) 523-8939

Snug Harbor Jazz Bistro - 626 Frenchmen St, New Orleans, LA 70116 (504) 944-0696

Palm Court Jazz Café - 1204 Decatur St, New Orleans, LA 70116 (504) 525-0200

Maxwell's Toulouse Cabaret - 615 Toulouse St, New Orleans, LA 70130 (504) 523-4207

Pete Fountain's Nightclub - Hilton Hotel, 3rd Floor, New Orleans, LA 70140 (504) 523-4375

New York City

Ever since most of Chicago's top jazz musicians moved to New York in the mid-to-late '20s, New York City has been the most important of all jazz centers. Nearly every major jazz style of the past 70 years (with the exception of cool jazz) has been largely formed in the Big Apple. Although not every important jazz event occurs in New York, the huge number of major players who live in or near the area results in consistently stimulating and potentially limitless music. Probably the high point of New York's significance to jazz occurred during the 1935-47 era when 52nd Street had nearly a dozen important jazz clubs within a few blocks of each other, making for a nightly jazz festival. As one would expect, the number of significant jazz nightclubs that have been in New York through the years has been enormous. To name just a few of the most important ones by their most important decade: 1920s (Alhambra Theatre, the Band Box, Club Alabam, Connie's Inn, the Cotton Club, Kentucky Club, Lafayette Theatre, Lenox Club, Roseland Ballroom, Small's Paradise), 1930s (Adrian's Tap Room, the Apollo Theatre, Nick's, Onyx, Savoy Ballroom, Three Deuces), 1940s (Bop City, Café Society Uptown and Downtown, Eddie Condon's, Downbeat, the Famous Door, Hickory House, Jimmy Ryan's, Kelly's Stable, Minton's Playhouse, Monroe's Uptown House, Royal Roost, Spotlite, Stuyvesant Casino), 1950s (Birdland, Basin Street, Café Bohemia, Central Plaza, Count Basie's, Ember's, Half Note, Metropole), 1960s (Basin Street East, Jazz Gallery, Slug's, Village Gate), 1970s (Boomer's, Bradley's, the Cookery, Michael's Pub, Studio Rivbea) and 1980s (Fat Tuesday's, Hanratty's).

Birdland - 2745 Broadway, New York, NY 10025 (212) 749-2228

Blue Note - 131 W. 3rd St, New York, NY 10012 (212) 475-8592

Fez Under the Café, 380 Lafayette St, New York, NY 10003 (212) 533-7000

Five Spot, 4 W. 31st St, New York, NY 10001 (212) 631-0100

Iridium Room - 44 W. 63rd St, New York, NY 10023 (212) 582-2121

Knitting Factory, 74 Leonard St, New York, NY 10013 (212) 219-3006

Smalls, 183 W. 10th St, New York, NY 10014 (212) 929-7565

Sweet Basil, 88 7th Ave South, New York, NY 10014

Village Vanguard (open since 1935!), 178 7th Ave South, New York, NY 10014 (212) 255-4037

Visiones - 125 MacDougall St, New York, NY 10012 (212) 673-5576

Philadelphia

Although long thought of by New Yorkers as a minor-league city that trains musicians until they are strong enough to make it in NY, Philadelphia has had its own honorable jazz tradition; after all at various times Bessie Smith, Dizzy Gillespie, Jimmy Smith and John Coltrane have called Philadelphia home. Actually the list of Philadelphians is pretty endless (from Sun Ra to the Heath Brothers and Grover Washington, Jr.) but making a living in this city has always been difficult. Among the key venues through the years have been the Dunbar Theatre in the 1920s, the Pearl Theatre, the Lincoln Theatre, the Strand Ballroom, the Down Beat Club, Pep's Musical Bar, the Blue Note (in the 1950s), Showboat, Just Jazz, the Painted Bride, and Broad Street Tavern (in the '80s).

Ortlieb's Jazz Haus - 847 N. 3rd St., Philadelphia, PA 19123 (212) 922-1035

Morgan's - 17 E. Price St., Philadelphia, PA 19144 (215) 844-6067

JJ's Grotto - 27 South 21st, Philadelphia, PA 19103 (215) 988-9255

Zoot Bistro - 126 Chestnut St., Philadelphia, PA 19106 (215) 925-6220

Zanzibar Blue - 301-305 S. 11th St., Philadelphia, PA 19107 (215) 829-1990

Pittsburgh

Despite being famous for its many classic pianists (including Earl Hines, Mary Lou Williams, Erroll Garner, Ahmad Jamal and Billy Strayhorn) and many other homegrown talents (such as Roy Eldridge, Ray Brown, Art Blakey and George Benson), Pittsburgh was never a jazz center in its own right. Most of the city's earlier clubs are now forgotten (such as the Leader House in the 1920s and the Crawford Grill three decades later) and only a few venues in the 1990s show off the impressive local jazz talent.

Stolen Moments - 3239 Brighton Road, Pittsburgh, PA 15212 (412) 766-4770

The Shadyside Balcony - 5520 Walnut St, Pittsburgh, PA 15232 (412) 687-0110

San Francisco/Oakland/Bay Area

Except for bands passing through town, there was not all that much jazz in San Francisco prior to 1940. However, the rise of Lu Watters Yerba Buena Jazz Band resulted in the phenomenon of "San Francisco Jazz," revivalist Dixieland based in the 1920s music of King Oliver and Jelly Roll Morton that soon developed its own sound and repertoire. With the improved communications that developed in the '40s, San Francisco became less isolated from the rest of the country than it had been and it soon developed a viable modern jazz scene of its own that for a time made the city seem like a West Coast equivalent of New York. Rock dominated the local scene from the mid-'60s on but the general public in SF always seemed much more aware of jazz than did the audiences in most other cities. In the 1990s San Francisco was one of the few places where, in addition to avant-garde jazz, musicians started seriously exploring improvising within the R&Bish dance music called acid jazz. Among the key clubs through the years were the Dawn Club, Club Hangover, Earthquake McGoon's (Turk Murphy's homebase from 1960-78), Jimbo's Bop City, the Down Beat Club, the Jazz Workshop, the Hungry I, the Blackhawk, Both/And, Basin Street West and the legendary Keystone Korner.

Great American Music Hall - 859 O'Farrell St, San Francisco, CA 94109 (415) 885-0750

Rasselas Jazz Club - 2801 Divisadero, San Francisco, CA 94102 (415) 567-5010

DNA Lounge - 375 11th St, San Francisco, CA 94103 (415) 626-1409

Eleven Ristorante & Jazz Bar - 374 11th St, San Francisco, CA 94103 (415) 431-3337

Kimball's East - 5800 Shellmound St, Emeryville, CA 94608 (510) 658-2555

Yoshi's - 6030 Claremont Ave, Oakland, CA 94618 (510) 652-9200

Bach Dancing & Dynamite Society - P.O. Box 302, Miramar Beach, Half Moon Bay, El Granada, CA 94018 (415) 726-4143

Kuumbwa Jazz Center - 320-2 Cedar St, Santa Cruz, CA 95060 (408) 427-2227

Seattle

Although it has not been the home of any innovative new styles, Seattle has featured jazz at least on a part-time basis since the 1920s and the local scene in the 1990s is strong. And with the proliferation of the Canadian summer festivals, many top Canadian players gig in town, sometimes on their way to San Francisco.

Jazz Alley - 2033 6th Ave, Seattle, WA 98121 (206) 441-9729

Salute in Citta - 612 Stewart St, Seattle, WA 98101 (206) 728-1613

The Backstage - 2208 NW Market St, Seattle, WA 98107 (206) 789-1184

New Orleans Creole Restaurant - 114 First Ave South, Seattle, WA 98104 (206) 622-2563

Washington D.C.

Although it was the birthplace of Duke Ellington, Washington D.C. has mostly been a stopping-off point for jazz musicians who are touring the East Coast. For three decades starting in the mid-'20s, the U Street area was the main center of Black entertainment, including such venues as the Howard Theater, the Lincoln Theater, the Majestic Theater, the Crystal Caverns, the Jungle Club and the Club Bali. Things have declined since and although such players as Shirley Horn and Buck Hill were long part of the local scene, their obscurity during their years in the nation's capital serves as evidence that the residents of D.C.'s main area of interest is not jazz!

Blues Alley - 1073 Wisconsin Ave, NW, Washington, DC 20007 (202) 337-4141

Twins Lounge - 5516 Colorado Ave, NW, Washington, DC 20011 (202) 882-2523

Takoma Station Tavern - 6914 4th St, NW, Washington, DC 20012 (202) 829-1999

One Step Down - 2517 Pennsylvania Ave, NW, Washington, DC 20037 (202) 955-7141

Other Historic Clubs

Cedar Grove, NJ - Meadowbrook Inn - An important swing era ballroom

El Cerrito, CA - Hambone Kelly's - Lu Watters' Yerba Buena Jazz band performed here regularly during 1947-50.

New Rochelle, NY - Glen Island Casino - A breaking ground for swing bands in the 1930s including the Casa Loma Orchestra and Glenn Miller.

St. Louis, MO - Arcadia Ballroom - In the 1920s and early '30s it hosted the Arcadian Serenaders, Frankie Trumbauer's short-lived band and Charlie Creath among others.

Other Current Clubs

The Boarding House - 11311 Euclid Ave, Cleveland, OH 44106 (216) 421-8100

The Bop Stop - 1216 W. 6th St, Cleveland, OH 44113 (216) 664-6610

Wilbert's Bar & Grill - 1360 W. 9th, Cleveland, OH 44113 (216) 771-2583

Deer Head Inn - P.O. Box 277, 5 Main St, Delaware Water Gap, PA 18327 (717) 424-2000

El Chapultepec - 1962 Market, Denver, CO 80202 (303) 295-9126

Baich's Bar & Grille - 2016 Main, Houston, TX 77002 (713) 650-8830

Zena's Café - 122 W. Main St, Louisville, KY 40202 (502) 584-3074

The Pfister Hotel - 424 E. Wisconsin Ave, Milwaukee, WI 53202 (414) 273-8222

Christopher's Jazz Club - 1101 N. Old World Third St, Milwaukee, WI 53203 (414) 271-6368

The Estate - 2423 N. Murray Ave, Milwaukee, WI 53211 (414) 964-9923

Trumpets - 6 Depot Square, Montclair, NJ 07042 (201) 746-6100

All That Jazz - 333 E. Jefferson, Phoenix, AZ 85004 (602) 256-1437

Orbit Café - Central & Camelback, Phoenix, AZ 85012 (602) 265-2354

The Rhythm Room - 1019 E. Indian School Road, Phoenix, AZ 85014 (602) 256-4842

Timothy's - 6335 N. 16th St, Phoenix, AZ 85016 (602) 277-7634

Atwater's - 111 SW 5th Ave, Portland, OR 97204 (503) 275-3600

Jazz De Opus - 33 NW 2nd Ave, Portland, OR 97209 (503) 222-6077

Boulevard Café - 7958 SW Barbur Blvd., Portland, OR 97219 (503) 245-9954

Brasserie Montmartre - 626 SW Park St, Portland, OR 97223 (503) 224-5552

The Landing - Hyatt Regency Hotel, 123 Losoya (River Walk), San Antonio, TX (210) 222-1234

Rusty's Jazz Café - 220 Tedrow, Toledo, OH 43614 (419) 381-9194

After Hours/ 27 minutes / Rhapsody Films ♦♦♦♦
This 1959 pilot for a television series that never ran is supposed to show what it is like to attend an after-hours jam session. The narration is dated but the music (featuring tenor saxophonist Coleman Hawkins and trumpeter Roy Eldridge in a quintet) is often quite exciting. Highlights include Hawk's feature on "Lover Man" and a heated "Sunday." —*Scott Yanow*

Airto & Flora Purim—The Latin Jazz All-Stars / 60 minutes / View Video ♦♦♦

Alberta Hunter—My Castle's Rockin' / 60 minutes / View Video ♦♦♦♦
This documentary (narrated by Billy Taylor) traces the remarkable life of singer Alberta Hunter who had a major comeback (after 20 years out of the music business) when she was 82. There are some brief interviews but the bulk of the film features Hunter performing at the Cookery in the early 1980s. She is quite appealing and seemingly ageless on such tunes as "My Castle's Rockin'," "Downhearted Blues," "Handy Man" and "The Love I Have for You." —*Scott Yanow*

Art Blakey—The Jazz Messenger / 78 minutes / Rhapsody Films ♦♦♦♦
This 1987 film is quite fascinating, for a camera follows drummer-bandleader Art Blakey around for most of a year. Trumpeter Terence Blanchard and altoist Donald Harrison were on the verge of leaving the Jazz Messengers during this period so Blakey is seen auditioning various young musicians. In addition to lots of hard bop music, some of the alumni comment on the importance of their period with Blakey. Art jams with Courtney Pine, has sequences backing dance groups and gives the listeners quite a bit of his philosophy towards both jazz and life. If only a camera had followed Art Blakey for the 30 previous years too! —*Scott Yanow*

The Art Ensemble of Chicago—Live from the Jazz Showcase / 50 minutes / Rhapsody Films ♦♦♦♦♦
This enjoyable tape captures a lengthy performance by the Art Ensemble of Chicago from Nov. 1, 1981. During the set the Art Ensemble (featuring trumpeter Lester Bowie, Joseph Jarman and Roscoe Mitchell on reeds, bassist Malachi Favors and drummer Don Moye) cover a lot of ground from free jazz to bop and funk with a touch of New Orleans parade rhythms. This time capsule gives one a good idea as to how unique the adventurous group was in its prime. —*Scott Yanow*

☆ **At the Jazz Band Ball** / 60 minutes / Yazoo Video ♦♦♦♦♦
This essential tape has 16 clips of early jazz from the 1925-33 period, most of which were previously unavailable. The highlights include the Duke Ellington Orchestra in 1930 playing "Old Man Blues"; the Boswell Sisters in wonderful form on a 1931 rendition of "Heebie Jeebies"; the full 1933 clip of Louis Armstrong in Europe performing "I Cover the Waterfront," "Dinah" and "Tiger Rag"; a long excerpt from Bessie Smith's lone film *St. Louis Blues*, the superior 1928 dance band of Tommy Christian playing two songs; and Ben Bernie (in an extremely rare sound film from 1925) in hot form on "Sweet Georgia Brown." The most notable discovery, a newsreel excerpt that finds Bix Beiderbecke playing "My Ohio Home" with Paul Whiteman (!), is a bit of a disappointment since Bix does not solo but it is fascinating to watch. Other performers include the Dorsey Brothers (a brief but colorful song from 1929), Bill Robinson, Duke Ellington's band from 1929's *Black & Tan* and a few lesser singers and dancers. Overall, this video is a real collector's item; very highly recommended! —*Scott Yanow*

Barney Kessel—Rare Performances 1962-91 / 60 minutes / Vestapol ♦♦♦
The fine loop-based guitarist Barney Kessel is seen and heard on several different occasions during this well-rounded video. He is first interviewed in 1987, performs two songs on an episode of the 1962 TV show *Jazz Scene USA*, plays in Sweden in 1967 and 1973, in England in 1974, and in Switzerland five years later. In all circumstances he is featured performing with a trio except for three numbers jammed in 1979 with fellow guitarists Herb Ellis and Charlie Byrd in a quintet. This valuable tape concludes with him making a speech in 1991 at the Oklahoma Jazz Hall of Fame during which he speaks about the importance of improvised music; soon afterward Kessel's playing days would end when he suffered a serious stroke. Barney Kessel is in consistently fine form throughout these performances (it is interesting to observe the hair and clothes styles change!) and this video serves as a fine introduction to his music. —*Scott Yanow*

Benny Carter—Symphony in Riffs / 58 minutes / Rhapsody Films ♦♦♦♦

The Bill Evans Trio—Jazz at the Maintenance Shop / 59 minutes / Shanachie ♦♦♦♦♦
Pianist Bill Evans' last trio (a particularly strong one with bassist Marc Johnson and drummer Joe LaBarbera) is seen during a live performance from 1979 (only a year before the pianist's death) that was filmed for Iowa Public Television. The group performs eight numbers with the highlights including "The Peacocks," "The Theme From Mash," "In Your Own Sweet Way" and "My Romance." The musicians' close musical communication is as impressive as one would expect from a Bill Evans group. —*Scott Yanow*

Bird / 161 minutes / Warner Home Video ♦♦♦♦
Clint Eastwood's 1988 biography of Charlie Parker may be partly fictional, a bit downbeat (emphasizing his decline) and an incomplete picture of the genius, but it is one of the finest Hollywood films ever made about jazz. Forest Whitaker is excellent in the title role, his fingering during saxophone solos exactly fit the notes and Charlie Parker's own playing is heard throughout the film. A few scenes (the view of 52nd Street, Bird riding a horse and his relationship with Chan) ring true while some others (his crackup in 1946) are a little off the mark. Overall this well-intentioned film is a success. —*Scott Yanow*

Bix—An Interpretation of a Legend / 100 minutes / Rhapsody Films ♦♦

Blue Note—A Story In Modern Jazz / 60 minutes / Blue Note / ♦♦♦♦

Bob James—For the Record / 60 minutes / Warner Reprise Video ♦♦♦

The Bob Wilber Big Band—Bufadora Blow-Up / 65 minutes / Arbors ♦♦♦♦

☆ **Buck Clayton All-Stars** / 54 minutes / Shanachie ♦♦♦♦♦
Two half-hour Swiss television shows from 1961 feature trumpeter Buck Clayton with such swing all-stars as fellow trumpeter Emmett Berry, altoist Earle Warren, tenorman Buddy Tate, trombonist Dickie Wells, pianist Sir Charles Thompson, bassist Gene Ramey, drummer Oliver Jackson and singer Jimmy Witherspoon. There are 11 complete songs in all and each of the musicians space to stretch out during the series of informal but hard-swinging performances. —*Scott Yanow*

Buddy Rich, Part 1, 1917-1970 / 67 minutes / DCI Music Video ♦♦♦♦♦
This is the first of two videos that trace the career of the amazing Buddy Rich, who did deserve the title of the "world's greatest drummer." His formative years are traced through interviews, still pictures and lots of film clips; there is a wonderful example of him playing a four-bar drum break with Eddie Condon in the 1940s that is absolutely ferocious. Mel Tormé does the narration and sometimes there is talking over the music but there are quite a few stunning performances. Rich, who is seen with the bands of Artie Shaw, Tommy Dorsey (in one instance dueting with trumpeter Ziggy Elman) and Harry James (the latter in the 1960s) also has a drum battle with Gene Krupa (no contest!). The video (which also contains plenty of interesting and often-humorous stories) concludes with Rich leading his own big band in 1970. Highly recommended, as is the second volume. —*Scott Yanow*

Buddy Rich, Part 2 1970-1987 / 80 minutes / DCI Music Video ♦♦♦♦
The second of two full-length videos on the amazing drummer Buddy Rich mostly features him with his various big bands in live performances. Highlights include fairly incredible solos on "Channel One Suite" and "West Side Story." There is also a lot of storytelling from Rich, narrator Mel Tormé, Buddy's daughter Cathy and some fellow drummers. Although the first volume (due to the greater variety) gets the edge, both of these videos are easily recommended to viewers who love to see memorable drum solos. —*Scott Yanow*

Charles Mingus Sextet / 59 minutes / Shanachie ♦♦♦♦♦
For his European tour of 1964, bassist Charles Mingus led what was arguably his greatest band: a sextet with Eric Dolphy (tripling on alto, flute and bass clarinet), tenor-saxophonist Clifford Jordan, trumpeter Johnny Coles, pianist Jaki Byard and drummer Dannie Richmond. Miraculously this band was featured on a Norwegian television show and the results have survived and been released by Shanachie. The solos on "So Long Eric" are very exciting and the performances of "Orange Was the Color of Her Dress," and a medley of "Ow" and "Take the 'A' Train" are also

memorable. Just getting the opportunity to see Mingus and Richmond at work (their constant changing of grooves keeps the horns from ever getting too comfortable) and to observe Dolphy (who died a few months later) at the peak of his powers are reason enough to acquire this essential film. —*Scott Yanow*

Chester Zardis—The Spirit of New Orleans / 88 minutes / Rhapsody Films ✦✦✦

Count Basie—Whirly-Bird / 45 minutes / Vintage Jazz Classics ✦✦✦✦✦
The Count Basie Orchestra is in particularly fine form on ten numbers performed in London for a television show on Sept. 18, 1965. Although this edition of the Basie band mostly recorded commercial albums, live in concert it was as strong as ever. Highlights include "All of Me" (featuring the leader-pianist), the usual enthusiastic versions of the band's hits (such as "Jumpin' at the Woodside" with Eddie Lockjaw Davis' tough tenor, "April in Paris" and "Li'l Darlin'"), a showcase for altoist Marshall Royal (on "The Midnight Sun Never Sets") and occasional solo work from trumpeter Al Aarons, Eric Dixon on flute and tenor and (on "I Needs to be Bee'd With") trombonist Al Grey. But the most notable track is a very intense runthrough of "Whirly-Bird," which, after Lockjaw's solo, has a very powerful spot for the remarkable drummer Rufus "Speedy" Jones, who certainly lives up to his nickname! —*Scott Yanow*

Curlew—The Hardwood / 90 minutes / Cuneiform Records ✦✦✦

Dexter Gordon Quartet—Jazz at the Maintenance Shop / 58 minutes / Rhapsody Films ✦✦✦✦

Dingo / 90 minutes / Greycat Home Video ✦✦✦

Dizzy Gillespie—A Night in Chicago / 53 minutes / View Video ✦✦✦
Surprisingly trumpeter Dizzy Gillespie (who declined from the mid-1970s on) is in pretty good form on this undated club video which is probably from 1989. Dizzy is joined by baritonist Sayyad Abdul Al-Kahbyyr, pianist Walter Davis, Jr., (who passed away in 1990), electric bassist John Lee and drummer Nassyr Abdul Al-Kahbyyr. The music is spirited and often humorous, particularly the opening "Swing Low, Sweet Cadillac" which finds Gillespie trying out some of his dance steps over the funky rhythm. Diz is muted on most of his ballad feature "Embraceable You," Al-Kahbyyr takes a torrid yet rhythmic solo on "Nature Boy" (which is climaxed by an impressive cadenza) and Gillespie and Davis share "'Round Midnight." The catchy Dizzy original "Fiesta Mojo" (a funky calypso) has some screeching high notes from the baritonist and the whole band is featured on an extensive rendition of "A Night in Tunisia." A short excerpt of "Dizzy's Scat" (during which Gillespie shows off some of his virtuosic scatting) runs over the credits. Overall this video (which has good camerawork) holds one's interest. —*Scott Yanow*

Django—A Jazz Tribute / 26 minutes / View Video ✦✦✦

Duke Ellington / 25 minutes / Video Artists Int. ✦✦✦✦
In 1962 the Goodyear Tire Company sponsored several half-hour jazz films to be shown on television. This particular entry features the Duke Ellington Orchestra performing "Take the 'A' Train," "Satin Doll," "Blow by Blow" (a feature for tenorman Paul Gonsalves), "Things Ain't What They Used to Be" (altoist Johnny Hodges' showcase), "VIP Boogie/Jam with Sam" and a short workout for the rhythm section on "Kinda Dukish." Although nothing all that unusual occurs, it is enjoyable to see the Ellington band near their peak; the video reproduction of this color film is excellent. —*Scott Yanow*

Duke Ellington—Memories of Duke / 85 minutes / A-Vision Entertainment ✦✦✦✦✦
This is a particularly interesting film, for trumpeter Cootie Williams and clarinetist Russell Procope are seen in the mid-1970s watching and commenting on lengthy clips from Duke Ellington's 1968 tour of Mexico. There is quite a bit of strong music on this video with highlights including the medley of "Creole Love Call," "Black and Tan Fantasy" and "The Mooch," the obscure "Mexican Suite," "It Don't Mean a Thing" and "Mood Indigo." This is one of the best Duke Ellington videos currently available. —*Scott Yanow*

Eddie Jefferson—Live from the Jazz Showcase / 50 minutes / Rhapsody Films ✦✦✦✦✦
This performance by singer Eddie Jefferson (with a quartet that includes altoist Richie Cole and pianist John Campbell) was performed May 6, 1979, two days before he was shot to death! Ironically Jefferson is heard in top form doing a retrospective of his career with such pieces as "Moody's Mood for Love," his vocalese version of "I Cover the Waterfront," the humorous "Bennies from Heaven," "Jeannine," "Body and Soul" and "Freedom Jazz Dance"; 14 songs in all. If one can put the tragic and senseless tragedy of his murder out of their head, this definitive film is quite enjoyable. —*Scott Yanow*

Fiddlin' Man—The Life and Times of Bob Wills / 61 minutes / View Video ✦✦✦
Bob Wills, a good country-style violinist who was a fine singer and a colorful personality, was one of the major pioneers of Western swing. His Texas Playboys combined together country music with strong doses of 1930s jazz and blues (Wills' band by the late '30s even included some horn players along with the steel guitar

and violins) to create a diverse and very accessible style of music. This documentary by Gary Rhodes expertly uses valuable early clips, a coherent narration that covers Wills' productive life, many photos and short comments from sidemen, friends and associates. Best of the music are some selections taken from Wills' 1942 Hollywood B movies and television appearances from 1951 and 1962; "Sittin' on Top of the World," "Lone Star Rag" and "Take Me Back to Tulsa" are most memorable. One does wish that there were more performances along with additional details about Wills' personal life (his four wives are barely mentioned), but the film does give one a fine overview of Bob Wills life and music. —*Scott Yanow*

☆ **Five Guys Named Moe** / 55 minutes / Vintage Jazz Classics ✦✦✦✦✦
This enjoyable video is a must for fans of Louis Jordan and his Tympany Five. Jordan, a fine altoist, was a particularly talented singer and personality who appears "hip" forty years later. This video features him performing 21 songs, all but one from the 1942-46 period. The clips are taken from films, shorts and Soundies and they find Jordan doing most of his hits. Highlights include "Five Guys Named Moe," "Caldonia," "Let the Good Times Roll," "Beware," "Choo Choo Ch'Boogie," "Reef, Petite and Gone" and "Is You Is or Is You Ain't Ma Baby." —*Scott Yanow*

Flip Phillips' 80th Birthday Party / 118 minutes / Arbors ✦✦✦

Gene Krupa—Jazz Legend / 60 minutes / DCI Video ✦✦✦✦
Gene Krupa, a colorful figure who was the first drummer to become a national celebrity, is profiled throughout this well-done retrospective. Steve Allen narrates, there is an interview with Krupa and lots of footage including his Soundies from the 1940s and later television appearances. The results are quite fun and fairly definitive of the great legend. —*Scott Yanow*

Great Guitarists—Jazz at the Maintenance Shop / 58 minutes / Rhapsody Films ✦✦✦✦

Herbie Hancock—Hurricane / 60 minutes / View Video ✦✦✦✦
Herbie Hancock is so versatile that one never knows what he will do next. On this set (performed in Switzerland in 1984) the music is purely acoustic. With fine work from bassist Ron Carter and drummer Billy Cobham, Hancock performs seven selections including his "Eye of the Hurricane," "Dolphin Dance," the lengthy "Princess" and the blues "Walkin." Excellent modern straightahead (and sometimes impressionistic) jazz. —*Scott Yanow*

Jackie McLean—Dynasty / 58 minutes / Triloka Video ✦✦✦✦✦
This video is essentially a filmed version of a live recording from Nov. 5, 1988 released by Triloka on CD. Fortunately this is a very exciting session with altoist Jackie McLean (who is joined by his son Rene McLean on tenor, soprano, flute and alto, pianist Hotep Idris Galeta, bassist Nat Reeves and drummer Carl Allen) playing at his most intense and creative. Most of the selections are group originals, but Jackie's searing rendition of Burt Bacharach's "A House Is Not a Home" is one of the many highlights. The music bridges the gap between hard bop and the avant-garde and is consistently burning with passion. —*Scott Yanow*

☆ **Jackie McLean on Mars** / 31 minutes / Rhapsody Films ✦✦✦✦✦
Despite the odd title, this is a very coherent if overly brief portrait of Jackie McLean from the early 1980s. McLean talks with his students about jazz, drugs, the difficulties of surviving in the music business and the joys of the music itself. There is not enough playing by the great altoist but there are glimpses of his style (trumpeter Woody Shaw has a cameo) and this film increases one's understanding of his creativity and motivation; it certainly holds one's interest. —*Scott Yanow*

☆ **Jazz on a Summer's Day** / 84 minutes / New Yorker Video ✦✦✦✦✦
This is considered a classic. The beautifully photographed color film documents the 1958 Newport Jazz Festival and there are many musical highlights. The camerawork holds one's interest even though it occasionally wanders way from the music; Thelonious Monk's performance of "Blue Monk" becomes the background for an irrelevant if colorful America's Cup yacht race (one never learns who won!) and there are many distracting shots of the audience. Among the most memorable performers are Anita O'Day (her inventive rendition of "Tea For Two" was one of the high points of her career), Dinah Washington (quite strong and humorous on "All Of Me" with Terry Gibbs), the Jimmy Giuffre Three, Chico Hamilton's Quintet with Eric Dolphy, Sonny Stitt, Gerry Mulligan, Mahalia Jackson, Louis Armstrong (doing "Rockin' Chair" with Jack Teagarden) and an out-of-place but rocking number by Chuck Berry. Highly recommended. —*Scott Yanow*

Jazz Scene USA—Cannonball Adderley/Teddy Edwards / 60 minutes / Shanachie ✦✦✦✦✦
In 1962 *Jazz Scene USA* was a short-lived but imaginative half-hour jazz series shown on some syndicated television channels. Each week Oscar Brown, Jr., (as host) would introduce a major group or musician, conduct a short interview and provide segues between the performances. Eight of the shows (two per tape) have been made available by Shanachie on four videos; all are well worth acquiring. On this particular tape Cannonball Adderley is seen leading his finest group, the sextet with cornetist Nat Adderley, pianist Joe Zawinul and Yusef Lateef on tenor, flute

and oboe. They perform short but strong versions of "Jessica's Birthday," "Primitivo," "Jive Samba" and "Work Song." Tenor-saxophonist Teddy Edwards dominates his episode, leading a sextet that also has trumpeter Freddie Hill and trombonist Richard Boone on five of his originals including "Sunset Eyes." Overall, this tape is quite valuable, showing the state of hard bop in 1962. —*Scott Yanow*

Jazz Scene USA—Frank Rosolino/Stan Kenton / 60 minutes / Shanachie ✦✦✦✦✦

This is one of the most enjoyable of the four videos released to date by Shanachie in this important series. *Jazz Scene USA* was an attempt to intelligently feature jazz on television in 1962; naturally it only lasted a year! These legendary shows still look fine today with excellent camerawork, fine commentary by Oscar Brown, Jr., and well-played music. Trombonist Frank Rosolino performs a rapid "Yesterdays," "Mean to Me," "Lover Man," "Well You Needn't" and "Please Don't Bug Me," while accompanied by pianist Mike Melvoin, bassist Bob Bertaux and drummer Nick Martinis. The Stan Kenton Orchestra during their half hour mostly emphasizes ensemble work from the mellophonium band (highlights include "Limehouse Blues," "Malaguena" and "Maria") although there are short spots for trumpeter Marvin Stamm and Don Menza on tenor. Recommended. —*Scott Yanow*

Jazz Scene USA—Phineas Newborn/Jimmy Smith / 60 minutes / Shanachie ✦✦✦✦

Shanachie has thus far released four videos that contain two shows apiece from the legendary 1962 half-hour series *Jazz Scene USA*. One of the first attempts to feature jazz on television in an intelligent way (and with respect), these programs (hosted by Oscar Brown, Jr.) still communicate well today. This particular tape gives one a rare opportunity to see the great pianist Phineas Newborn, Jr. (in a trio with bassist Al McKibbon and drummer Kenny Dennis). He performs three originals (including "Blues Theme for Left Hand Only") and a pair of standards, showing off his ability to swing creatively at any tempo. Organist Jimmy Smith's set (with guitarist Quentin Warren and drummer Donald Bailey) is of lesser interest since he seems to be fooling around a lot but his versions of "Walk on the Wild Side," "Mack the Knife" and "The Champ" are reasonably enjoyable. All four videos in this valuable series are recommended. —*Scott Yanow*

Jazz Scene USA—Shelly Manne/Shorty Rogers / 60 minutes / Shanachie ✦✦✦✦

In 1962 half-hour episodes of *Jazz Scene USA* (an intelligent program hosted by Oscar Brown, Jr.) was shown on some television channels before passing into history as a legendary series. Shanachie has happily released eight of the shows on four video tapes. This particular one features two West Coast jazz groups at what was the tail-end of the cool jazz era. Drummer Shelly Manne's quintet was particularly strong since it comprised trumpeter Conte Candoli, Rickie Kamuca on tenor, pianist Russ Freeman and bassist Monty Budwig. Although the material it performs ("Speak Low," a Freeman original and two songs from the forgotten series *Checkmate*) is not all that memorable, it is fun to get to see these players perform together. Fluegelhornist Shorty Rogers, who would soon retire for a long time from active playing to concentrate on writing, heads a quintet with the tenor of Gary LeFebvre and a strong rhythm section (pianist Lou Levy, bassist Gary Peacock and drummer Larry Bunker). Their repertoire is more imaginative: "Greensleeves," "Time Was," LeFebvre's "The Outsider" and the near-classic "Martians Go Home." Recommended. —*Scott Yanow*

Joe Pass In Concert / 40 minutes / Vestapol ✦✦✦✦

Joe Pass revitalized and uplifted the art of playing unaccompanied jazz guitar. Unlike Stanley Jordan (who developed a radically new approach to playing guitar with his tapping technique), Pass' approach was conventional but at such a high level that it amazed fellow guitarists. On this video, the late guitarist is seen at a concert in Wales playing three Gershwin tunes, Dizzy Gillespie's "That's Earl Brother," "All the Things You Are" and his own "Joe's Blues." Pass, who played fast single-note lines in a bebop-oriented style yet always at least implied chords and baselines, was in his own category. —*Scott Yanow*

☆ John Coltrane—The Coltrane Legacy / 61 minutes / Video Artists Int. ✦✦✦✦✦

The bulk of John Coltrane's film appearances are on this essential video. First he is seen playing his solo from "So What" with Miles Davis in 1959 and then there are two complete half-hour television shows. Coltrane teams up with Eric Dolphy (who doubles on alto and flute), pianist McCoy Tyner, bassist Reggie Workman and drummer Elvin Jones on a 1961 West German show playing "Every Time We Say Goodbye," a burning version of "Impressions" and "My Favorite Things." The second half of the video is from 1964 (a PBS program produced by Ralph Gleason) that features Coltrane, Tyner, bassist Jimmy Garrison and Jones in prime form on intense renditions of "Afro Blue," "Impressions" and a melancholy "Alabama." This is a video that belongs in every jazz collection for the power of Coltrane's music really comes through. —*Scott Yanow*

Ken Peplowski Quintet—Live at Ambassador Auditorium / 67 minutes / Concord Jazz ✦✦✦✦

The Ladies Sing the Blues / 60 minutes / View Video ✦✦✦✦

A variety of historical clips (all featuring female singers) are included on this worthy video; 16 selections in all. Unfortunately there is little information included about dates but the quality of the music overrides any packaging faults. Bessie Smith performs "St. Louis Blues" from the film of the same name, Ethel Waters is on two lesser clips, Billie Holiday sings "Fine and Mellow" from *The Sound of Jazz* telecast, Ida Cox is seen in her only film appearance and there are generally memorable clips featuring Sister Rosetta Tharpe, Connee Boswell, Dinah Washington, Ruth Brown, Lena Horne, Sarah Vaughan, Helen Humes and Peggy Lee (her "I Cover the Waterfront" is haunting). —*Scott Yanow*

Lady Day—The Many Faces Of Billie Holiday / 60 minutes / Kultur ✦✦✦✦✦

This is a fine documentary that covers the difficult and erratic life of Billie Holiday. There are interviews with such associates as Carmen McRae, Annie Ross, Buck Clayton and Harry "Sweets" Edison, among others. Although Ruby Dee's readings from Lady Day's largely fictional memoirs are a bit frivolous, the clips (particularly the rare ones taken from 1958 and '59 television shows) are quite fascinating. Overall this interesting tribute is quite even-handed and worth acquiring by Billie Holiday collectors and admirers. —*Scott Yanow*

Last Date: Eric Dolphy / 92 minutes / Rhapsody Films ✦✦✦

Lee Konitz—Portrait of an Artist As Saxophonist / 83 minutes / Rhapsody Films ✦✦✦✦✦

From 1988, this documentary features six duets by altoist Lee Konitz and pianist Harold Danko (including "Struttin' with Some Barbecue," "Hi Beck" and "Subconscious-Lee") along with a great deal of talk. Konitz discusses his life and music at a workshop with students and is seen in several different settings. His wit and intelligence come across well and one learns a great deal about Lee Konitz's personality and attitudes. Elis fans will find this tape riveting at times. —*Scott Yanow*

Legends of Jazz Drumming, Part One / 63 minutes / DCI Music Video ✦✦✦✦
Legends of Jazz Drumming, Part Two / 73 minutes / DCI Music Video ✦✦✦✦
Legends of Jazz Guitar, Vol. 1 / 60 minutes / Vestapol ✦✦✦✦

The first of three samplers of the music of various bop-based guitarists put out by Vestapol is most notable for three performances ("Twisted Blues," "Jingles" and "Yesterdays") by Wes Montgomery in 1965, taken from an appearance on English television. In addition there are a pair of unaccompanied solos from Joe Pass, two selections apiece featuring Herb Ellis and Barney Kessel and a collaboration by the pair on 1979's "A Slow Burn." All of the performances are complete and worth seeing. —*Scott Yanow*

Legends of Jazz Guitar, Vol. 2 / 60 minutes / Vestapol ✦✦✦✦

The second of three videos in this valuable Vestapol series starts out with the most interesting performance, a blues ("Blue Mist") from 1969 featuring Barney Kessel, Kenny Burrell and Grant Green; the latter guitarist was hardly ever on film. Although the other tracks are to an extent anti-climatic, there are two numbers from Wes Montgomery in 1965 ("Full House" and "'Round Midnight") that are of great interest along with performances featuring Joe Pass, Burrell, Kessel and Charlie Byrd that make this well-rounded set a worthwhile purchase for fans of loop-based guitar. —*Scott Yanow*

Legends of Jazz Guitar, Vol. 3 / 60 minutes / Vestapol ✦✦✦✦

The third of three videos in this valuable Vestapol series has several intriguing selections by a variety of guitarists. Jim Hall in 1964 is featured on "I'm Getting Sentimental Over You" and shares the spotlight with fluegelhornist Art Farmer on "Valse Hot"; he also pops up in a lyrical 1986 duet with pianist Michel Petrucciani on "My Funny Valentine." In addition there are numbers featuring Tal Farlow, Pat Martino (in 1987) and Barney Kessel (the latter sometimes in collaborations with Herb Ellis and Charlie Byrd). All three entries in this program are worth picking up. —*Scott Yanow*

Legends of Western Swing Guitar / 60 minutes / Vestapol ✦✦✦

The 23 concise selections on this video (most of which clock in between two-three minutes) are jazz-oriented and mostly relaxed renditions of swing standards or Western swing tunes based on that style. Most prominent of the players is Eldon Shamblin (renowned as a masterful rhythm guitarist) who is on 15 of the 23 cuts (probably from the 1980s), including a trio featuring guitarists Billy Dozier and Bob Kiser, in a quartet with fellow guitarist Benny Garcia and on a few guitar duets with Tommy Morrell. Shamblin, who takes some solos along with offering expert accompaniment, sounds influenced by Charlie Christian and shows that he could have been a strong force in the jazz world if he had chosen that route. Also featured are veteran guitarist Zeke Campbell (both in recent times and in the 1930s with the Light Crust Doughboys), early Western swing guitarist Herb Boyd (in the mid-'30s) and, on clips from Bob Wills' 1940s films, guitarists Junior Barnard, Cameron Hill and Jimmy Wyble. It is a pity that the performances on this video are not given dates and personnel listings (other than the guitarists) and are not programmed in chronological order (they skip around quite a bit). However, the music does hold one's interest and shows how country and jazz guitar styles in the 1930s overlapped. —*Scott Yanow*

Les McCann Trio / 28 minutes / Rhapsody Films ✦✦✦✦
This valuable video features pianist-vocalist Les McCann and his trio (with bassist Jimmy Rowser and drummer Donald Dean) at the legendary Los Angeles club Shelly's Manne Hole sometime in the late 1960s/early '70s. McCann, at the top of his form, plays "Right On," "Sunny," "With These Hands" and his big hit "Compared to What" with spirit, power and soul. —*Scott Yanow*

Lester Young—Song of the Spirit / 110 minutes / Song of the Spirit ✦✦✦✦
Bruce Fredericksen's decision to make a documentary on the life of the great tenor Lester Young was a difficult decision because there is so little footage of Prez. However, by utilizing still photos and including a lot of interviews (by the likes of Norman Granz, John Hammond, Dizzy Gillespie, Count Basie, Harry "Sweets" Edison and Jo Jones among others), the Lester Young story is very capably told. A special bonus is the complete inclusion of the three-song 1944 short *Jammin' The Blues* (which features Young, Edison and Illinois Jacquet) at the end of this definitive video. —*Scott Yanow*

The Making of Burning for Buddy, Part One / 83 minutes / DCI Music Video ✦✦✦

The Making of Burning for Buddy, Part Two / 89 minutes / DCI Music Video ✦✦✦

Miles Davis—In Paris / 60 minutes / Warner/Reprise Video ✦✦✦✦
Caught at the Paris Jazz Festival on Nov. 3, 1989 (less than two years before his death), Miles Davis is in generally excellent form playing five songs with his septet of the time (comprising altoist Kenny Garrett, keyboardist Kei Akagi, Foley and Benjamin Rietveld on basses, drummer Ricky Wellman and percussionist John Bigham). There are a few brief interview segments and a bit too much stop-action photography, but in general this set gives one a good idea as to how the innovative trumpeter sounded during his final period. Best is "New Blues" and a brief "Mr. Pastorius." —*Scott Yanow*

Miles Davis—Live At Montreux / 75 minutes / Warner/Reprise Video ✦✦✦✦✦
In the summer of 1991 Miles Davis did what he said he would never do, revisit the past. Joined by a large orchestra conducted by Quincy Jones at that year's Montreux Jazz Festival (only a couple months before his death), Miles is seen performing Gil Evans arrangements from the Birth of the Cool band and the three famous albums *Miles Ahead*, *Porgy and Bess* and *Sketches of Spain*. Miles generally plays pretty well although his decision to allocate some of solo space to his chief imitator Wallace Roney and altoist Kenny Garrett was unfortunate. But overall this is a successful effort that ranks historically as Miles Davis' last hurrah. —*Scott Yanow*

The One Man Twins / 50 minutes / Rhino Video ✦✦✦✦
As remarkable as Rahsaan Roland Kirk was on record, one has to see him live to really get the full effect. How did he ever blow into three saxophones at once, get sounds out of both a flute and a nose recorder at the same time, and expertly juggle instruments on stage despite being blind? Very little footage was taken of the phenomenal performer, making this video (which partly answers all of the above questions) quite essential. Filmed on June 24, 1972 at the Montreux Jazz Festival, Kirk (who is joined by pianist Ron Burton, bassist Henry Pearson, drummer Robert Shy and percussionist Joe "Habao" Texidor) is seen very much in his element. On the opening "Improvisation" he harmonizes on two horns while backed by just Texidor's tambourine. "Balm In Gilead" (which is reminiscent of "Black and Tan Fantasy") has him alternating his New Orleans clarinet with some rollicking tenor. "Seasons" is a very expressive flute feature, Kirk combines together "Misty" and "I Want to Talk About You" on his tenor (the cadenza is remarkable) and "Blue Rol No. 2" features Rahsaan playing recorder with his nose while blowing through his mouth simultaneously on flute; isn't that supposed to be impossible? After concluding "Blue Rol No. 2" with some three-horn chording (watching Rahsaan finger his instruments with just two hands is rather fascinating), Kirk drives the audience to a frenzy on the lengthy "Volunteered Slavery" and at one point he goes out into the audience while playing. The tape concludes with brief versions of "Serenade to a Cuckoo" and "Never Can Say Goodbye." The One Man Twins has the video versions of some of the performances released for the first time on the CD *I, Eye, Aye*, but also contains some previously unreleased material. Well worth acquiring. —*Scott Yanow*

Ornette Coleman—David, Moffett & Ornette / 26 minutes / Rhapsody Films ✦✦✦✦
This is a rather unusual film. In 1966 the innovative Ornette Coleman (along with bassist David Izenzon and drummer Charles Moffett) was in Paris to improvise the soundtrack to a film titled *Who's Crazy?* The movie does appear to be a bit nuts and it is fascinating to see the trio (with Ornette switching between alto, trumpet and violin) performing while watching the film. The musicians' verbal comments about their lives at the time are also quite interesting and this video (which is

probably the earliest example of Ornette Coleman on film) has quite a few memorable moments. —*Scott Yanow*

Oscar Peterson—Music in the Key of Oscar / 106 minutes / View Video ✦✦✦✦✦

Pepper's Pow Wow / 57 minutes / Upstream Productions ✦✦✦✦

Phil Woods—In Concert / 67 minutes / View Video ✦✦✦
Altoist Phil Woods is in typically hard-swinging form on this video from the late 1980s. Woods, who is joined by baritonist Joe Sudler's Swing Machine (a 17-piece orchestra), is the main soloist throughout the date. Although the big band has obscure personnel (other than pianist Uri Caine and bassist Tyrone Brown, both of whom have their names misspelled on the back cover!), it has an appealing and unified sound. Woods alternates bop standards (such as "Groovin' High" and "Body and Soul") with swinging originals and the music should easily please collectors of straightahead jazz. —*Scott Yanow*

The Phil Woods Quartet—Jazz at the Maintenance Shop / 59 minutes / Rhapsody ✦✦✦✦
Phil Woods' group of the late 1970s (which includes pianist Mike Melillo, bassist Steve Gilmore and drummer Bill Goodwin) is featured in top form during an hour of music originally broadcast by Iowa Public Television. The boppish altoist rarely sounds uninspired and this set (which includes versions of "Song for Sisyphus," "A Little Piece," "Only When You're In My Arms," "Shaw Nuff" and "How's Your Mama") is an excellent example of his talents and is easily recommended to Phil Woods' many fans. —*Scott Yanow*

Piano Portraits: Jaki Byard, Cyrus Chesnut, Barry Harris / 63 minutes / Rhapsody Films ✦✦✦✦

Renee Rosnes—Jazz Pianist / 45 minutes / Rhapsody Films ✦✦✦✦

Rick Fay and Friends—Live at the State, April 5, 1992 / 98 minutes / Arbors Jazz ✦✦✦

Sarah Vaughan—The Divine One / 60 minutes / BMG Video ✦✦✦

Saxophone Colossus—Sonny Rollins / 101 minutes / Rhapsody Films ✦✦✦✦✦

Solo Flight: The Genius of Charlie Christian / 31 minutes / View Video ✦✦✦
Charlie Christian has to be one of the least likely subjects for a documentary since the innovative but short-lived guitarist never actually appeared on film and passed away back in 1942. However, Gary Rhodes for this video tracked down many of Christian's childhood friends and associates from Oklahoma who shed light on the pioneering electric guitarist's earlier and more obscure days. By using excerpts from the interviews (which also include comments from Jay McShann, Herb Ellis and briefly Lionel Hampton) and many rare photos, Rhodes was able to piece together Christian's truncated but significant life. Although one wishes he had talked more about Charlie Christian's musical accomplishments, this is a worthy project. —*Scott Yanow*

☆ **The Sound of Jazz** / 58 minutes / Vintage Jazz Classics ✦✦✦✦✦
It would not be an overstatement or an exaggeration to say chat *The Sound of Jazz* is the greatest of all jazz films. Many of the top swing stylists were featured in a variety of very informal settings, playing live for a large audience. This show was only broadcast once on CBS but it is so full of excitement, suspense and spontaneity that it rewards repeated viewings. The most famous performance is Billie Holiday's touching rendition of "Fine and Mellow" on which she is joined by trumpeter Roy Eldridge and tenors Lester Young (who takes a remarkably emotional one chorus solo), Coleman Hawkins and Ben Webster, but there is much more. On "Wild Man Blues" and "Rosetta" trumpeter Red Allen leads an extraordinary group that includes clarinetist Pee Wee Russell (who on the former song makes a squeak a logical part of his very speechlike solo) cornetist Rex Stewart (who satirizes Russell and challenges Allen with a high note), Hawkins and trombonist Vic Dickenson. When Thelonious Monk plays "Blue Monk," he gets very different facial expressions from Coleman Hawkins (pride at having discovered him 13 years earlier), Count Basie (who looks happily surprised) and Jimmy Rushing (he looks up to the heavens as if Monk is nuts!). In addition, Basie leads an all-star big band, Rushing gets to sing, the Jimmy Giuffre Three plays "The Train and the River" and Giuffre teams up with Russell for a closing blues. This video is truly essential. —*Scott Yanow*

Space is The Place—Sun Ra / 63 minutes / Rhapsody Films ✦✦

Stephane Grappelli—Live in San Francisco / 60 minutes / Rhapsody Films ✦✦✦✦
Already in his late '70s at the time of the two 1985 concerts that are on this video, violinist Stephane Grappelli proves to still be in prime form. Assisted by guitarist Diz Disley and bassist Jack Sewing, Grappelli swings hard on a variety of veteran standards including such old standbys as "Fascinating Rhythm," "Minor Swing," "Them There Eyes" and even Stevie Wonder's "You Are the Sunshine of My Life." Toward the end of this video, mandolinist David Grisman and his group join Grap-

pelli and the heat is turned up even more on "Sweet Georgia Brown" and "Honey-suckle Rose." —*Scott Yanow*

☆ **Steve Lacy—Lift the Bandstand** / 50 minutes / Rhapsody Films ✦✦✦✦✦
This is one of the better jazz documentaries. The virtuosic soprano saxophonist Steve Lacy talks about his entire career including his periods in Dixieland and his experiences with Cecil Taylor, exploring Thelonious Monk's music and forming his longtime sextet. Lacy also performs with his group and "Gay Paree Bop" is a high-point. Listeners new to Lacy's scalar music will learn a great deal about his history and his motivation by viewing this excellent video. —*Scott Yanow*

The String Trio of New York—Built By Hand / 30 minutes / Rhapsody Films ✦✦✦✦✦
Although only a half-hour long, this video has a lot of music and information about the avant-garde String Trio of New York. The trio at the time comprised violinist Charles Burnham, guitarist James Emery and bassist John Lindberg. Each of the musicians outline their hopes and goals and together they perform six originals, starting out with a fairly accessible blues and gradually evolving into the intense "Seven Vice." A thought-provoking and stimulating film. —*Scott Yanow*

Swiss Movement / 45 minutes / Rhino Video ✦✦✦✦✦
On June 21, 1969, pianist-vocalist Les McCann and his trio (with bassist Leroy Vinnegar and drummer Donald Dean) were scheduled to appear at the Montreux Jazz Festival. At almost the last minute it was decided to have tenor-saxophonist Eddie Harris and trumpeter Benny Bailey sit in with the group even though they were unfamiliar with most of the material. The unlikely result was the highpoint of Les McCann's career, a highlight of Eddie Harris' and a best-selling jazz record Swiss Movement. "Compared to What" (which has McCann's only vocal of the set) became a big hit and Harris' "Cold Duck Time" also caught on. More than a quarter-century later the actual performance was now been made available on this black and white video which is generally in good shape except for brief moments on "Compared to What." In addition to four of the six selections from the famous set, the film also features Eddie Harris on a version of "Listen Here" with an unidentified trio (including pianist Jodie Christian) from the same day, showing off his skills on an electronic sax. Seeing (rather than just hearing) this music leads to a few revelations. During Benny Bailey's spectacular solo on "Cold Duck Time" on the record the crowd seems to erupt in reaction to his playing, but on the film the truth comes out. The audience was actually excited by the sight of Ella Fitzgerald entering the hall and taking her seat! A highly recommended and rather historic video. —*Scott Yanow*

☆ **Talmage Farlow** / 58 minutes / Rhapsody Films ✦✦✦✦✦
This 1986 film is delightful. Guitarist Tal Farlow, one of the giants of bop, has long been semi-retired, preferring the easy-going life of a New England sign painter over having to constantly travel for gigs. This video expertly summarizes his career, shows what his day-to-day lifestyle is like, includes an exciting version of "Fascinatin' Rhythm" which features Farlow in a trio with pianist Tommy Flanagan and bassist Red Mitchell, and finds him preparing for (and playing at) a New York engagement. Director Lorenzo De Stefano, who put this labor of love together, certainly did an admirable job. —*Scott Yanow*

☆ **Tenor Legends—Coleman Hawkins/Dexter Gordon** / 57 minutes / Shanachie ✦✦✦✦✦
This video comprises two unrelated films. The great tenor Coleman Hawkins is featured in Brussels in 1962 with a group that includes pianist Georges Arvanitas, guitarist Mickey Baker, bassist Jimmy Woode and drummer Kansas Fields. Highlights include Hawkins' opening (and unaccompanied!) "Blowing for Adolphe Sax" and a heated "Disorder at the Border." The second half of this tape has the talented tenor Dexter Gordon at the Club Montmartre in 1969 with pianist Kenny Drew, bassist Niels Pedersen and drummer Makaya Ntshoko. Although the camerawork starts off an overly hyper, it eventually settles down and Dexter sounds in fine form, particularly on "Those Were the Days" and "Fried Bananas." But Hawkins takes honors on this recommended tape. —*Scott Yanow*

Texas Tenor—The Illinois Jacquet Story / 81 minutes / Rhapsody Films ✦✦✦✦

☆ **Thelonious Monk—Straight, No Chaser** / 90 minutes / Warner Home Video ✦✦✦✦✦
This is a remarkable film. In 1968 Michael and Christian Blackwood shot extensive footage of Thelonious Monk not only onstage but off. Twenty years later Bruce Ricker edited the priceless film and used other clips and new interviews to put together a pretty full portrait of the unique pianist-composer. In some of the more memorable scenes Monk is seen lying in bed ordering room service, arguing with producer Teo Macero at a recording session and appearing on stage with an under-rehearsed (and visibly struggling) octet; fortunately the latter group quickly improves after a rough start. Tenorman Charlie Rouse is often prominent but also seen are fluegelhornist Clark Terry, altoist Phil Woods and Johnny Griffin on tenor. However, the main focus is on Monk and there are many extraordinary moments.

This is a consistently intriguing and informative film that all bop and modern jazz followers should see! —*Scott Yanow*

Thelonious Monk In Oslo / 33 minutes / Rhapsody Films ✦✦✦✦
Taken from a Norwegian television show, this half-hour video features the Thelonious Monk Quartet which at the time (April 15, 1966) consisted of the pianist-leader, tenor-saxophonist Charlie Rouse, bassist Larry Gales and drummer Ben Riley. This straight performance film gives one an opportunity to see Monk in action on versions of "Lulu's Back in Town," "Blue Monk" and "Round Midnight." The musicians all play quite well although the lack of an applauding audience results in a few awkward pauses between songs! Recommended. —*Scott Yanow*

Things to Come / 55 minutes / Vintage Jazz Classics ✦✦✦✦
Two historical films from the bebop era are included on this valuable tape. Billy Eckstine's legendary big band is seen in 1946's *Rhythm In a Riff* performing ten numbers. The appealing singer, after largely getting rid of the plot, sings a few ballads and turns his band loose on such numbers as "Rhythm In a Riff," "Taps Miller" and "Our Delight." Among the prominent sidemen are tenor-saxophonist Gene Ammons, Frank Wess (also on tenor) and drummer Art Blakey who even back then was quite explosive. Also on this video is the classic Dizzy Gillespie short film *Jivin' In Bebop* which features his 1947 orchestra on such numbers as "Salt Peanuts," "Oop Bop Sh'Bam," "One Bass Hit" (a showcase for bassist Ray Brown) and the still-futuristic "Things to Come." Fortunately all of the dated comedy by other acts has been cut out although this print (and maybe all of the ones that exist) is not too clean and the sound is fuzzy. Still, the opportunity to see the leader-trumpeter when he was 30 (along with glimpses of James Moody, John Lewis, Milt Jackson, Ray Brown and singer Helen Humes) certainly compensates. —*Scott Yanow*

Toshiko Akiyoshi Jazz Orchestra—Strive for Jive / 48 minutes / View Video ✦✦✦✦
This video features the Toshiko Akiyoshi big band live in Chicago around 1992. Although there are short interview clips of pianist-arranger Akiyoshi and occasionally Lew Tabackin between the songs, except for a little bit of talking over the opening number, the music (five Akiyoshi compositions) is allowed to speak for itself. "Yellow Is Mellow" is a boppish piece with spots for Tabackin's high-powered tenor. "Strive for Jive" (based on the chord changes of "I Got Rhythm") has fiery solos by Tabackin, altoist Frank Wess, trombonist Hart Smith and trumpeter Brian Lynch. "Quadrille, Anyone?" is a modern jazz waltz with contributions by Walt Weiskopf on soprano and the tenor of Ed Xiques before becoming a charming European quadrille at its conclusion. The picturesque "Autumn Sea" is complex yet moving, serving eventually as a showcase for Tabackin's virtuosic Asian-sounding flute. "Warning, Success May Be Hazardous To Your Health" has a samba beat and brief spots for Lynch, altoist Jim Snidero and drummer Jeff Hirshfield. Strangely enough the video closes with a second version of "Strive for Jive" which is similar to the first. This fine all-round program is recommended to fans of modern big band jazz. —*Scott Yanow*

Trumpet Kings / 72 minutes / Video Artists Int. ✦✦✦✦
Wynton Marsalis hosts this series of clips featuring great trumpeters in loosely chronological order. Highlights include Louis Armstrong on two songs from 1933, Bunny Berigan in his only film appearance (1936's "Until Today"), Muggsy Spanier's "Someday Sweetheart," a trumpet battle by Charlie Shavers and Buck Clayton, Miles Davis on "So What," Lester Bowie in 1981 jamming freely over the chord changes of "I Got Rhythm" and the only joint appearance of Dizzy Gillespie and Louis Armstrong. Other trumpeters seen include Red Allen, Red Nichols, Freddie Jenkins, Cootie Williams, Harry James, Rex Stewart, Roy Eldridge, Lee Morgan, Art Farmer, Shorty Rogers, Clark Terry, Nat Adderley, Freddie Hubbard and Wynton himself. Some of the excerpts are more common than others but overall this video is well worth getting. —*Scott Yanow*

☆ **Vintage Collection, Vol. 2 1960-1961** / 45 minutes / A-Vision Entertainment ✦✦✦✦✦
While the first volume of A-Vision's *Vintage Collection* is largely a rip-off version of *The Sound of Jazz* (which is available in its complete form elsewhere), *Vol. 2* is much more valuable despite the inaccurate dates given on the cover. The Ahmad Jamal Trio (probably in 1959) with bassist Israel Crosby and drummer Vernel Fournier shows off their distinctive style and close interplay on "Darn That Dream" and "Ahmad's Blues." Tenor great Ben Webster (with pianist Hank Jones, bassist George Duvivier and drummer Jo Jones) follows up by being featured on the ballad "Chelsea Bridge" and he welcomes trumpeter Buck Clayton and trombonist Vic Dickenson to a stomping version of "Duke's Place." However, it is the second half of the tape that is most memorable, for it is Miles Davis' famous 1959 television half-hour special (his earliest appearance on film). Miles, tenor-saxophonist John Coltrane, pianist Wynton Kelly, bassist Paul Chambers and drummer Jimmy Cobb play a renowned version of "So What" before Davis (backed by the Gil Evans Orchestra) performs three lyrical numbers. This is classic music that was luckily captured for posterity. —*Scott Yanow*

Magazines

Cadence

Cadence is a monthly founded in 1976 that is edited and published by Bob Rusch. No other magazine in the world reviews as many jazz recordings and their coverage ranges from bop and the avant-garde to Dixieland, blues, reissues, imports and more commercial jazz-related genres. Its subtitle is "The Review of Jazz & Blues Creative Improvised Music" and *Cadence* lives up to the billing. No matter what label a recording comes out on, it receives equal consideration based purely on the quality of the music. In each issue, in addition to hundreds of reviews of CDs, books and videos, *Cadence* generally has two or three oral history interviews (some of them quite lengthy) with jazz and blues artists, both obscure and famous. The middle third of the approximately 112 pages has thousands of recordings for sale through *Cadence* at reasonable prices and fortunately there is no correlation between what is offered and whether a review is favorable or not. In fact *Cadence* is proud of its noncommercial status and even releases put out by Cadence Records have received negative reviews now and then. This magazine is essential for the true jazz record collector who wants to be informed as to what is available and its value from the jazz standpoint. Unfortunately *Cadence* is found on few newsstands so a subscription ($30 per year in the US, $35 outside) is essential. Its address is *Cadence*, Cadence Building, Redwood, NY 13679.

Coda

A consistent force in the jazz scene since 1958, *Coda* (which is co-run by John Norris and Bill Smith) has been Canada's top jazz magazine for decades. A bimonthly, *Coda* has an interesting (if sometimes out-of-date) news section, extensive coverage of the Canadian scene, many CD reviews (which are packaged together as articles) and interviews. Its coverage ranges from veteran bop and swing stars to the avant-garde with little notice taken of fusion or so-called contemporary jazz. Along with *Cadence*, *Coda* is the least commercial of all the jazz magazines and consistently makes for stimulating reading. Subscriptions are available for $24 annually in the U.S., $25.68 in Canada and $30 elsewhere. Its address is Coda Publications, Box 1002, Station 0, Toronto, Ontario M4A 2N4 CANADA.

Down Beat

Founded in 1934, *Down Beat* remains the most famous jazz magazine in the world. Its prime years were from about the mid-'40s up until the late '60s (some of its older articles and controversies are fascinating to read now) when its only competitor (at least up until 1960) was *Metronome*. However when it opened the door to covering rock in 1967, *Down Beat* alienated some of its audience who did not feel that the Beatles and the Rolling Stones should be covered in a jazz magazine. Even today its motto, "Jazz, Blues & Beyond" sometimes keeps it from being taken completely seriously in the jazz community. However *Down Beat*'s articles and interviews are consistently excellent and its CD reviews are generally quite informative if occasionally erratic. *Down Beat*'s jazz polls (both by the critics and its readers) are quite prestigious. There are also transcriptions and articles geared toward student musicians. *Down Beat* does not cover the jazz world with as much depth as *Jazz Times* (and virtually ignores the West Coast) but the two-thirds of each issue that deals with jazz is well worth reading. Subscription rates are $35 for one year, $46 for foreign subscribers. Its mailing address is *Down Beat*, P.O. Box 906, Elmhurst, IL 60126-0906.

Jazz Now

Founded in 1991 by its editor/publisher Haybert Houston, *Jazz Now* (originally called *California Jazz Now*) is based in the Bay Area and seems to be attempting to fill the gap caused by the demise of *Jazz Forum*. It calls itself "The Jazz World Magazine" and *Jazz Now* has correspondents and regular columns from Germany, the United Kingdom, Poland and New York but it remains primarily a West Coast publication. Published 11 times a year (every month but January), this interesting magazine features news and reviews from a variety of cities, emphasizes noncom-

merical jazz and generally has a few major interviews along with some CD and book reviews. An unusual innovation is a series of articles focusing on jazz fans who frequent Bay Area clubs. This magazine's progress during the next few years will be worth watching. Subscriptions are $21.65 in California and $20 for the rest of the U.S. Their mailing address is P.O. Box 19266, Oakland, CA 94619-0266.

The Jazz Report

Second to *Coda* among Canadian jazz magazines, the *Jazz Report* is a promising quarterly that was founded in 1988 by publisher Bill King and editor Greg Sutherland. Boasting slick paper and interesting photos, the *Jazz Report* generally has around three interviews per issue along with some CD and book reviews and news. Subscription rates are $20 in the U.S. and overseas and $18 in Canada for four issues. Its address is *The Jazz Report*, 14 London St, Toronto, Ontario M6G lM9 CANADA.

Jazz Times

Founded in 1970 by Ira Sabin as *Radio Free Jazz* and published ten times a year (every month but January and August), *Jazz Times* has become what is arguably the number one jazz magazine in the world. Certainly when it comes to its news section and keeping on top of the latest developments, *Jazz Times* has surpassed *Down Beat* and stayed ahead of *Jazziz*, retaining its credibility and becoming an influential force. Most issues have around 100 CD reviews (second to *Cadence*), six or seven major articles, up to ten shorter interviews and a few live reviews. *Jazz Times*'s weaknesses include a general neglect of the West Coast, an occasional tendency to copy *Down Beat* and an inconsistent coverage of fusion and so-called "contemporary" jazz, perhaps in reaction to *Jazziz*. All jazz followers can consider *Jazz Times* and *Cadence* to be the two essential monthly purchases. Yearly subscription rates are $23.95 in the U.S., $35.95 in Canada and $59.95 overseas. Its address is *Jazz Times*, P.O. Box 99050, Collingswood, NJ 08108-0613.

Jazziz

The most improved jazz magazine of the past few years, *Jazziz* still confuses many readers. Its coverage of the jazz scene through probing interviews, columns and individual CD reviews is quite impressive but because of a very diverse and large staff of writers, it can be inconsistent; it helps to know each writer's personal tastes! Because Michael and Lori Fagien (both of whom founded *Jazziz* in 1983) have always enjoyed pop music and crossover, its earlier issues tended to focus on the more commercial side of jazz. Under editor Larry Blumenfield's guidance in recent times, *Jazziz* has emphasized the New York scene and avant-garde jazz in general much more than in the past, while still often praising crossover. the monthly stretches in coverage from Henry Threadgill to Paul Simon, featuring profiles on world music and pop and ethnic music pacesetters in addition to current and historical jazz artists (most of whom have recent releases out). A very attractive-looking magazine with quite a few unusual and unique articles, *Jazziz* is both innovative and a bit controversial, a very useful tool in opening up one's musical horizons. *Jazziz*'s subscriptions are $69.95 per year (which includes a special CD compiliation each month). Its mailing address is 3620 N.W. 43rd Street, Gainesville, FL 32606.

The Mississippi Rag

Founded in 1973 by editor/publisher Leslie Johnson, the *Mississippi Rag* (which is actually located in Minnesota) has been the top classic jazz monthly ever since. Full of interesting interviews, CD reviews and news dealing with Dixieland, New Orleans jazz and swing, this newspaper is quite informative, even handed and both historical and up-to-date. Fans of early jazz will find lots of valuable information in this important paper. Subscriptions are $20 in the U.S., $22 elsewhere, and its mailing address is *The Mississippi Rag*, P.O. Box 19068, Minneapolis, MN 55419.

By Scott Yanow

Throughout jazz history, there have been hundreds of behind-the-scenes contributors who have helped keep jazz alive: record producers, jazz critics, publicists, propagandists, spouses and a countless number of fans. This section discusses 65 of the most important.

Chris Albertson

As an astute reviewer, Chris Albertson has long uplifted the field of jazz journalism. His main accomplishments are producing Riverside's The Living Legends series of the early 1960s that resulted in quite a few veterans of the 1920s and '30s returning to records before it was too late, and his writings on Bessie Smith. Albertson's extensive liner notes for Columbia's 1970 reissue of all of Bessie Smith's recordings were quite notable and served as a stepping-stone to his notable 1972 Smith biography *Bessie*.

George Avakian b. Mar. 15, 1919, Armarvir, Russia

George Avakian's contributions to jazz have been huge through the years. He was a jazz critic as early as 1937, wrote about jazz for *Mademoiselle* and *Pic* during 1946-48, helped revise Charles Delauney's famous *Hot Discography* when it was first published in the U.S. in 1948 and contributed to both *Down Beat* and *Metronome*. Avakian's greatest importance is as a producer. He put together one of the first jazz albums (Chicago Jazz) for Decca in 1940. Soon afterwards he began producing jazz records for Columbia, becoming quite influential in the 1950s when he also worked for the popular music department. Among the many artists who he worked closely with were Louis Armstrong, Dave Brubeck, Duke Ellington and Miles Davis, and he frequently penned insightful liner notes. After leaving Columbia in 1958, Avakian worked for World Pacific, Warner Bros. and RCA, freelanced with many other labels, was an important supporter of the Charles Lloyd Quartet and recently celebrated 60 years in the jazz business.

Steve Backer b. Brooklyn, NY

The founder of the Novus subsidiary, Steve Backer has managed to produce many adventurous jazz dates during periods when avant-garde jazz was in danger of disappearing from American labels. Although he had lessons on bass, Backer early on decided that it was best to help jazz from behind the scenes. He did promotional and A&R work for MGM/Verve and Elektra during 1969-71 and then in 1972 became ABC/Impulse's national promotion director. Within six months he was the general manager of Impulse and during the next two years he helped revive the dying label, recording and working with such artists as Keith Jarrett, Gato Barbieri, John Klemmer and Pharoah Sanders. In 1974 Backer moved over to Arista as their director of jazz A&R. For six years Backer was very busy at Arista, licensing music for the Arista Freedom label, reissuing vintage performances on Savoy and running Novus, which recorded new performances by many adventurous artists including most notably an extensive series by Anthony Braxton. He also helped out a bit with the up-and-coming subsidiary GRP. Since leaving Arista in 1980, Backer worked with Windham Hill during 1981-86 (where he formed the Magenta subsidiary) and then in the 1990s for RCA where he revitalized Bluebird and restarted Novus.

Whitney Balliett b. Apr. 17, 1926, New York, NY

One of the finest of all jazz writers, Whitney Balliett has the ability to bring his subjects to life and somehow transform the indescribable magic of jazz into words, which has long put him at the top of his field. Balliett graduated from Cornell University in 1951, had a short stint at *The New Yorker*, wrote for the *Saturday Review* during 1953-57 and since then has written regularly for *The New Yorker*. Along with Nat Hentoff, he was the musical advisor for the remarkable *Sound of Jazz* television special in 1957. Although his own tastes in jazz leans towards swing era veterans and mainstream, Balliett has also sympathetically and definitively portrayed most of the more modern giants. His articles have been collected in revised form in many books including *The Sound of Surprise* (a term that he coined to describe jazz at its best), *Dinosaurs in the Morning, Such Sweet Thunder, Ecstasy at the Onion, New York Notes, Improvising, Night Creature, Goodbyes*

and Other Messages, *American Singers, American Musicians* and *American Musicians II*, among others.

Amiri Baraka (Leroi Jones) b. Oct. 7, 1934, Newark, NJ

Amiria Baraka (also known as Leroi Jones) was one of the most important jazz writers of the 1960s. He had had strong musical training (on piano, drums and trumpet) and had already developed into both a playwright and a poet. A champion of the avant-garde, Baraka's writings for *Down Beat* in the 1960s were provocative and controversial but generally correct in hindsight. His 1963 book *Blues People* is an important sociological study of jazz and race relations (one of the first by a Black writer) while *Black Music* (1967) collects together some of his magazine articles. Since that era Baraka has written many plays, published a dozen volumes of poetry, championed David Murray and contributed some liner notes.

Joachim Berendt b. July 20, 1922, Berlin, Germany

One of the most significant forces in European jazz, Joachim Berendt has helped the music as an astute and very open-minded jazz critic (he has written more than 20 books), as an educator and as a producer of both concerts and records. In 1945 he founded the Sudwest Funk Baden-Baden, leading the jazz department until 1987. Among the events that Berendt produced were Jazztime Baden-Baden (1947), the Berliner Jazztage (1964-72) and the annual jazz concert at the Donaueschingen Festival for Contemporary Music (starting in 1954). He has long been a regular attraction on German radio and television, and his presentation of the John Coltrane Quintet (with Eric Dolphy) is available as part of the video *The Coltrane Legacy*. Berendt produced more than 250 recordings in jazz (including *Violin Summit*) and *World Music*, has been a skilled photographer and has long been a proponent both of the avant-garde and of various types of fusion. Perhaps Joachim Berendt's main legacy is *The Jazz Book*, an accessible yet very complete history of jazz survey that has been updated on a fairly regular basis since 1963.

Rudi Blesh b. Jan. 21, 1899, Guthrie, OK, d. Aug. 25, 1985, Gilmanton, NH

A supporter and propagandist for New Orleans jazz and ragtime, Rudi Blesh made an impact on the world of trad jazz. He attended Dartmouth College and then worked as a jazz critic for the *San Francisco Chronicle* in the early 1940s and for the *New York Herald Tribune* starting in 1944. Blesh, who promoted jazz concerts early on, hosted the important jazz radio series *This Is Jazz* in 1947 (the broadcasts are being reissued by the Jazzology label). Although his narration comes across as a bit wooden and is full of cliches, it is due to his work that top New Orleans jazz artists were featured on the air on a regular basis. Blesh's 1946 history of jazz book, *Shining Trumpets*, was flawed and biased if well intentioned, but his 1950 survey, *They All Played Ragtime*, is a classic. Written with Harriet Janis, *They All Played Ragtime* was the first thorough study of ragtime and it helped start a mini-revival of the music. Around that time Blesh formed the short-lived but valuable Circle label (whose music has since been acquired by Jazzology), which recorded new dates by vintage players and released Jelly Roll Morton's Library of Congress performances. Rudi Blesh, who in later years taught jazz history at various colleges, helped rediscover Joseph Lamb and Eubie Blake and contributed occasional liner notes into the 1980s.

Richard Bock b. 1927, d. 1988

Richard Bock was one of the most important producers of West Coast jazz. He founded Pacific Jazz (along with drummer Roy Harte) in 1952 and his first release was a classic set by the Gerry Mulligan Quartet with Chet Baker. Bock worked with many of the top artists of the next decade including Baker, Art Pepper, the Chico Hamilton Quintet, Jim Hall, Bud Shank, Wes Montgomery (who recorded "Bock to Bock" in tribute to the producer), Groove Holmes, Les McCann, Gerald Wilson and the Jazz Crusaders. In 1958 after recording Ravi Shankar, Bock started a subsidiary (World Pacific) to record a wider variety of music. Pacific Jazz remained quite active until Bock sold it to Liberty in 1965. He continued working on a part-time basis for the label through 1970. When Contemporary was reactivated in the early 1980s, Richard Bock assisted Lester Koenig as a producer up until his death.

Giovanni Bonandrini

In the 1970s when avant-garde jazz was becoming scarce on American labels, it was up to Italian producer Giovanni Bonandrini to give the music the documentation it deserved. The Black Saint label was formed in 1975 by Giacomo Pelliciotti. In 1978 Bonandrini took it over, he founded its sister label Soul Note the following year and since then has recorded hundreds of rewarding sessions. While Black Saint tends to focus more on the avant-garde side of jazz and Soul Note features more bop-oriented sessions, there has been a lot of overlapping. Among the scores of artists who have recorded some of their finest work for Bonandrini have been David Murray, the World Saxophone Quartet, Cecil Taylor, Anthony Braxton, Old And New Dreams, Steve Lacy and Muhal Richard Abrams among many others. Although Bonandrini has sometimes experienced difficulties with his American business associations (many of the parent labels have wished that he would release a lot few records so they could be marketed better), Giovanni Bonandrini has remained fiercely independent and stuck to his singular path, doing a major service for jazz.

Dr. George Butler

Dr. George Butler has been a controversial figure throughout his career. While working at Blue Note in the 1970s, he led the fabled label towards commercialism and, although there were major commercial successes with Donald Byrd, Bobbi Humphrey, Noel Pointer, Ronnie Laws and others, the music has since dated badly and the end result was the temporary end of Blue Note. Butler has run the jazz department at Columbia since the late 1970s. Some artists have fared much better at the label than others. Butler was wise enough to quickly sign up Wynton Marsalis, and many of the key "Young Lions" passed through the ranks (including Branford Marsalis, Terence Blanchard, Harry Connick and Marlon Jordan), some staying longer than others. Columbia has remained an important label during Butler's reign.

Ozzie Cadena

A lifelong friend of jazz, Ozzie Cadena was a key employee at Savoy during the second half of the 1950s, working as A&R head and producing many jazz sessions with some of the top hard bop players of the era. In addition to his work with Cannonball Adderley, Donald Byrd, Yusef Lateef and Milt Jackson (among others), Cadena in the 1960s produced many soul jazz organ dates for Prestige (including with Shirley Scott, Jack McDuff, Willis Jackson and Eddie "Lockjaw" Davis). In more recent times he has been based in Los Angeles, booking veterans for club dates.

John Chilton b. July 16, 1932, London, England

Although John Chilton has worked as a trumpeter with Dixieland, swing and mainstream groups, it is as an author that he is most significant. Chilton's *Who's Who of Jazz* contains many previously unknown details about jazz musicians born before 1920. His many other works include one of the great jazz biographies (*Sidney Bechet: The Wizard of Jazz*) and books on Louis Armstrong (*Salute to Satchmo*), Billie Holiday (*Billie's Blues*), Bob Crosby's Bob Cats (*Stomp Off, Let's Go*) and Coleman Hawkins.

Willis Conover b. 1920, d. 1996

Although rarely heard in the United States, Willis Conover was one of the most important radio broadcasters in jazz history. He worked in Washington D.C. and New York radio during the 1939-54 period but it was his association with Voice of America (starting in 1954) that was most significant. Conover's broadcasts introduced jazz to European (especially East European) listeners during the Cold War, paving the way for visits by American artists in the 1960s and '70s. Pianist Adam Makowicz was one of literally millions of listeners who first heard jazz on Conover's show. The broadcaster also served as emcee for the Newport Jazz Festival for over ten years, produced Duke Ellington's 70th birthday concert at the White House in 1969 and was the influential chairman of the jazz panel of the National Endowment for the Arts. Willis Conover's importance in spreading the jazz message worldwide cannot be overestimated.

Michael Cuscuna b. 1948

Michael Cuscuna has been one of the key figures in the reissue boom of the 1980s and '90s. When he produces a reissue, the emphasis is on coherent packaging, the reissuance of complete sessions and consistent high quality. Cuscuna played drums, saxophone and flute early on but his goal from the start was starting his own record label. He broadcast a jazz program on WXPN, worked for the ESP company in the late 1960s and wrote for *Jazz and Pop Magazine* and *Down Beat*. Cuscuna left radio in the early 1970s and became a producer for Atlantic (he had earlier produced a George Freeman date for Delmark), working with Dave Brubeck and the Art Ensemble of Chicago. Other jobs included a brief stint at Motown, reissuing Impulse! records for the ABC label, producing sets for Arista and Muse and working on the five-LP *Wildflowers* sessions for Alan Douglas. Cuscuna was involved in the Freedom and Novus labels with Steve Backer in the late

1970s. During 1975-81 he ran an extensive program in which he unearthed scores of important sessions for Blue Note. In 1983 Cuscuna and Charlie Lourie founded Mosaic, which has since been recognized as the No. 1 reissue label, reissuing complete sessions in lavish limited-edition box sets. In addition to Mosaic, Cuscuna has continued making major contributions to other reissue programs (including GRP's Impulse! series and Blue Note's ongoing program) and has often been voted Producer of the Year in *Down Beat's* Critics Poll.

Stanley Dance b. Sep. 15, 1910, Braintree, England

The oldest active jazz critic, Stanley Dance has done a great deal through the years to help swing and mainstream jazz musicians. In fact "mainstream" was his term, which he came up with in the 1950s to describe music played by musicians who were stylistically between dixieland and bebop. Dance first started writing about jazz for *Jazz Hot* in France back in 1935. He moved to the U.S. in 1937 and has since written for virtually every jazz periodical including *Down Beat, Metronome, Jazz Journal* (1948-76) and *Jazz Times* (starting in 1980) plus the *New York Herald Tribune* and *Saturday Review*. Dance has occasionally produced recording sessions through the years (most notably for Felsted in the 1950s but also for Columbia, Black Lion and RCA) and has in his own way influenced jazz history. For example, in 1964 he talked Earl Hines into appearing at a couple of concerts in New York that resulted in Hines being rediscovered. Dance's most important contributions to jazz have been his books, most notably *The World of Duke Ellington, The World of Swing, The World of Earl Hines* and *The World of Count Basie*; in addition he assisted on the autobiographies of Dicky Wells and Charlie Barnet. These valuable books contain many detailed interviews with important swing era veterans held just a few years before most of them passed away. Dance had a close relationship with Ellington (who he helped out with his memoirs) and he has contributed to a countless number of liner notes dealing with Ellington, Basie, Hines, Jimmy Lunceford and their sidemen. Stanley Dance's reviews in *Jazz Times* have often been controversial due to his distaste for bop but he has done a great deal to champion the styles that he does love. His wife, Helen Oakley Dance, who worked with Ellington's sidemen on their small group dates of the 1930s, has also contributed to many magazines and written a biography on T-Bone Walker.

Francis Davis

One of the most insightful jazz writers of the 1980s and '90s, Francis Davis has made regular contribtuions to the *Village Voice, Stereo Review* and the *Philadelphia Inquirer* in addition to being a contributing editor for *The Atlantic Monthly*. He has thus far written four books: *In the Moment, Outcats, The History of the Blues* and *Bebop and Nothingness*.

Chip Deffaa

Chip Deffaa can be thought of in some ways as being the Stanley Dance of the 1980s and '90s in that he has documented the thoughts and stories of many veteran jazz musicians before it was too late. Unlike Dance, Deffaa is also interested in later jazz styles although he has tended to emphasize prebop music. His main forum has been being the jazz critic of the *New York Post* and Deffa has contributed regularly to *Jazz Times*, the *Mississippi Rag*, England's *Crescendo* and *Entertainment Legacy*. But it is his books that will be his main significance in the long run. Thus far these include *Swing Legacy, Voices of the Jazz Age, In the Mainstream, Traditionalists and Revivalists in Jazz, Jazz Veterans* and *Blue Rhythms*

Charles Delauney b. Jan. 18, 1911, Paris, France, d. Feb. 16, 1988, Vineuil St. Firmin, France

One of the pioneer jazz writers and discographers, Delauney was, along with Hugues Panassie, the most important French nonmusician in early jazz. He helped found the Hot Club of France in 1933, an organization that would soon sponsor a quintet featuring Django Reinhardt and Stephane Grappelli. In 1935 Delauney started *Jazz Hot*, one of the first jazz magazines. In 1937 he formed the Swing label, which documented many important sessions. Delauney was active on radio from 1939 on, organized concerts and produced many record sessions; he was also an early jazz educator. Charles Delauney's *Hot Discography* in 1936 was the first important detailed listing of jazz recordings ("discography" was a term invented by him) and just one of his many important achievements. Panassie, formerly a good friend of Delauney, broke with him in the mid-1940s because of his openness to bebop. In 1949 Delaunay organized the Paris Jazz Festival (one of the world's first jazz festivals), which typically for him featured both Sidney Bechet and Charlie Parker. Charles Delauney, whose writings included a biography of Django Reinhardt, remained an important force in the European jazz world up until his death.

Joel Dorn

One of the most prominent producers in pop and jazz, Joel Dorn helmed records from some of the biggest names in music, among them Charles Mingus, Bette Midler and the Allman Brothers Band. He began his career in 1961 as a disc jockey with Philadelphia jazz station WHAT-FM; his radio success led to a meeting with Atlantic Records founder Nesuhi Ertegun, resulting in an offer allowing Dorn to produce the artist of his choice for the company's jazz imprint. He selected flutist Hubert Laws, and the resulting LP, 1964's *The Laws of Jazz*, proved so successful that by 1967 Dorn was employed at Atlantic full-time as Ertegun's assistant. Working not only as a producer but also in the A&R and marketing departments, he quickly rose to the position of vice president; the records he helmed were primarily jazz and R&B efforts, informed by a pop sensibility which became his signature. Among Dorn's hits as a producer were Roberta Flack's "The First Time Ever I Saw Your Face" and "Killing Me Softly," Keith Jarrett and Gary Burton, and Midler's debut *The Divine Miss M*; he left Atlantic in 1974, going on to work with a wide range of performers including the Neville Brothers, Leon Redbone, Mink DeVille, Lou Rawls and Asleep at the Wheel. During the mid-1980s Dorn formed Night Records, a label devoted to issuing previously unreleased live material from the likes of Rahsaan Roland Kirk, Cannonball Adderley and Les McCann; in 1995 he formed another reissue label, 32 Records.—*Jason Ankeny*

Manfred Eicher

In 1969 Manfred Eicher formed the ECM label and by the mid-1970s the label was well known for its atmospheric and sparse settings that made strong use of silence, brilliant recording quality and a sort of jazz minimalism. Some of its records are fairly free while others use folk melodies as the basis for their improvisations. Not all of the ECM sessions fit the stereotype (which was sometimes blamed for being the inspiration for the rise of New Age) such as dates by Old and New Dreams, Jack DeJohnette's Special Edition and Pat Metheny. Among the label's other top artists through the years have been Keith Jarrett, Gary Burton, Jan Garbarek, Terje Rypdal, Egberto Gismonti and Chick Corea. Producer Eicher has often been willing to stretch the boundaries of jazz into World Music, European folk songs and wholly composed classical music, admirably recording music that fit his taste without worrying about specific record sales.

Nesuhi Ertegun b. Nov. 27, 1917, Istanbul, Turkey, d. July 15, 1989, New York, NY

Throughout his career, Nesuhi Ertegun was responsible for many important jazz dates being recorded and, despite his rise in the record industry, he never lost his love for jazz. The older brother of Ahmet Ertegun, Nesuhi, the son of a Turkish diplomat, promoted jazz concerts in Washington D.C. during 1941-44. After moving to Los Angeles he helped organize Kid Ory's band, founded a trad jazz record company (Crescent) and then operated the Jazzman label (1946-51). Although his primary musical interest was initially New Orleans jazz (which he wrote about while serving as the editor of *Record Changer*), Ertegun was also open to more modern styles. During 1951-54 he taught at UCLA the first history of jazz course ever given at a college for credit. After working for the Good Time Jazz and Contemporary labels, Ertegun moved to New York to work as A&R chief for Atlantic, a label started by his brother Ahmet. It was largely due to Nesuhi that many rewarding jazz sessions were recorded for Atlantic (by such artists as the Modern Jazz Quartet, Charles Mingus, Ornette Coleman, Eddie Harris and Hank Crawford among others) during the next 15 years; he remained involved with the label up until his death.

Leonard Feather b. Sep. 13, 1914, London, England, d. Sep. 22, 1994, Sherman Oaks, CA

The most important jazz critic in the world during his lifetime (and virtually the only one known to the nonjazz public), Leonard Feather was both an important and a controversial figure. His contributions to jazz in a wide variety of areas were vast even though his lack of interest in New Orleans jazz, the avant-garde and fusion at times resulted in him sometimes unfairly criticizing various artists. Feather grew up in his native England, studied piano and clarinet and was self-taught as an arranger. Feather started writing about jazz in the mid-1930s and produced record sessions by Benny Carter and others while still in his early twenties. He moved to the U.S. shortly before World War II, did publicity work for Duke Ellington and very quickly became an important jazz critic. By 1945 he was championing bop (often at the expense of trad jazz) and participating in the self-destructive moldy fig vs. bebop jazz wars. Feather produced all-star sessions for Victor (connected with the *Esquire* jazz polls), wrote some hit songs (most notably "Evil Gal Blues" for Dinah Washington) and talked his friend George Shearing into forming a piano-vibes-guitar-bass-drums quintet. Feather's occasional contributions as a musician (he played basic piano) and more importantly as a composer are fully covered in his bio. As a writer, Feather's *Inside Bebop* in the late 1940s was the first book to fully deal with the new style. A prolific journalist who contributed at one time or another to virtually every jazz magazine (including *Metronome*, *Down Beat*, *Jazz Times* and *Jazziz*), Feather was also an in-demand emcee, an occasional record producer and a host of numerous radio and television programs on jazz. His *Encyclopedia of Jazz* in 1959 was the most famous of his dozen books and gave readers a definitive history of jazz up to that point. Other notable books included later *Encyclopedias of Jazz's* (*of the '60s* and *of the '70s*),

The Book of Jazz, From Satchmo to Miles, The Passion of Jazz and *The Jazz Years: Earwitness to an Era*. After moving to Los Angeles in the early 1960s, Feather became the jazz critic for the *Los Angeles Times* and found time to teach jazz classes. He wrote an estimated 2,000 liner notes in his career and was active up until months before his death.

Joe Fields

A longtime veteran of the record industry, Joe Fields joined together with Don Schlitten in 1972 to run Cobblestone (a jazz subsidiary of Buddah) and they soon founded the Muse label. For a time Muse and its sister label Onyx were run by the duo but a 1978 split found Fields taking control of Muse and Schlitten founding Xanadu. Up until 1996 when he sold the label to Joel Dorn (who has since reissued catalog items under the 32 Jazz banner), Fields ran Muse, turning it into one of the most significant hard bop labels of the era. From Houston Person, Pat Martino and Mark Murphy to Richie Cole, Eddie Jefferson and Sonny Stitt, Muse was a classic label. For a period Fields also owned the Savoy catalog (reissuing many classic sessions) and worked with the Landmark and Trix labels. After selling Muse, Fields and his son Barney Fields put together the HighNote label which has continued recording high- quality sessions in the same hard bop genre.

Milt Gabler

One of the top record producers of the 1940s and '50s, Milt Gabler will always be associated with his Commodore label. His father owned the Commodore Music Shop, which Milt (starting in 1926) helped turn into one of the top record stores in New York. At a time when reissues were unheard of, Gabler talked several labels into letting him lease items for his United Hot Clubs of America label and in 1935 these were the very first reissues. In 1938 Gabler started recording new music for his Commodore label and during the next eight years his company emphasized freewheeling small group jazz. Among the many artists recording for Commodore were Eddie Condon and his sidemen, Billie Holiday ("Strange Fruit" was made for Commodore when Columbia shied away from the controversial song), Coleman Hawkins, Lester Young and the Kansas City Six, Jelly Roll Morton and most of the who's who of swing and New Orleans jazz. After 1946 the label slowed down drastically although occasional material was recorded through 1957; all of the Commodore recordings were reissued on three massive limited-edition sets (totaling 67 LPs!) by Mosaic in the late 1980s. In addition to Commodore, Milt Gabler was quite active as a producer for Decca up until the late 1960s, working with both jazz and pop artists including Louis Armstrong, Ella Fitzgerald and Louis Jordan.

Gary Giddins b. Mar. 21, 1948, New York, NY

One of the top jazz writers of his generation, Gary Giddins is best known for his longtime work with the *Village Voice*, which he joined in 1973. In addition, he has written occasional pieces for jazz magazines, worked as a disc jockey, founded the short-lived American Jazz Orchestra in 1985 and written several books including *Ridin' on a Blue Note, Rhythm-A-Ning, Celebrating Bird* (also consulting on a documentary tied in with the Charlie Parker book), *Satchmo* and a biography of Bing Crosby.

Ira Gitler b. Dec. 18, 1928, New York, NY

One of the world's number one bebop fans, Ira Gitler's enthusiasm for the music has been a consistent feature of his prolific writing through the years. As a staff producer for Prestige during 1950-55, Gitler worked as a producer on many dates and generally wrote the colorful liner notes. He helped Leonard Feather out on his original *Encyclopedia of Jazz* and his role in subsequent *Encyclopedias* grew to the point where he received co-billing. Gitler was at one time an associate editor of *Down Beat*, he wrote for *Metronome* and has been a longtime contributor to *Jazz Times*. He has also taught jazz and written two classic books: *Jazz Masters of the Forties* and *From Swing to Bop*.

Ralph Gleason b. Mar. 1, 1917, New York, NY, d. June 3, 1975, Berkeley, CA

Ralph Gleason only lived to be 58 but he had a very productive career. After graduating from Columbia University in 1938, Gleason was the founder and editor of *Jazz Information*, one of the first jazz magazines. He was originally a partisan for Dixieland and New Orleans jazz but always kept an open mind. Gleason was a regular contributor to *Down Beat* (1948-61) and the *San Francisco Chronicle* (1950-75). He also wrote for a variety of magazines including *Stereo Review* and *Jazz*. Gleason was the editor of a 1958 book *Jam Session: An Anthology of Jazz*, helped found the Monterey Jazz Festival with Jimmy Lyons and was the host of the *Jazz Casual* television show (videos of which exist) in the 1960s. Gleason (who wrote many liner notes through the years) was always interested in popular music and he surprised many by not only founding *Rolling Stone* in 1967 but becoming its editor and embracing creative rock. However, his passion for jazz never lessened and Ralph Gleason (who was a vice president of Fantasy Records during 1970-75) came out with a jazz book (*Celebrating the Duke*) shortly before his premature death.

Norman Granz b. Aug. 6, 1918, Los Angeles, CA

At the height of his career, Norman Granz was one of the most powerful nonmusicians in jazz. He always fought for the music he believed in (having a love for freewheeling jam sessions), for his artists (who he accurately considered to be among the greatest in the world) and against racism, forcing many hotels and concert venues to become integrated in the 1940s and '50s. He studied at UCLA, served in the Army and then in 1944 began to make an impact on jazz. Granz supervised the award-winning film short *Jammin' the Blues* (which featured Lester Young) and put on a concert at the Philharmonic Auditorium in Los Angeles that he dubbed Jazz at the Philharmonic. The latter was such a big success that soon Granz was able to take the all-star jam sessions on domestic and eventually worldwide tours. The producer loved to team together top artists from the bop and swing worlds in "battles" and, although these rousing concerts were often criticized by conservative and somewhat humorless jazz critics, the jams resulted in a great deal of rewarding music. Not content with merely presenting concerts, Granz often recorded the performances even though, at 10-15 minutes, they were too long for a conventional three-minute "78." Granz founded Clef (1946) and Norgran (1953), eventually consolidating his music when he founded Verve in 1956. The rise of the LP in the early 1950s was perfect timing and Granz was able to release many JATP performances on records. In addition to his work as a record company head and a concert promoter, Granz managed Ella Fitzgerald and in 1956 he largely started Verve as a label to feature her recordings. Among the many other artists who prospered in the 1950s due to Granz were Oscar Peterson (who he discovered and managed), Lester Young, Roy Eldridge, Dizzy Gillespie, Art Tatum, Count Basie and Ben Webster. By the late 1950s JATP was drastically slowing down and in 1960 Granz sold Verve to MGM. He functioned mostly as a concert promoter and the manager of Ella and O.P. in the 1960s but in 1973 he returned full force to the record business, founding the very successful Pablo label. Many of Granz's favorite artists had had erratic recording careers in the 1960s (including Ella, Basie, Roy Eldridge and Dizzy Gillespie) but the rise of Pablo resulted in their discographies being uplifted and greatly expanded. Granz extensively recorded his artists (including Joe Pass who soon found fame, Zoot Sims, Sarah Vaughan, Eddie "Lockjaw" Davis and especially Oscar Peterson), emphasizing the spontaneity of jam sessions. The number of Pablo releases slowed down during the 1980s and in 1987 Granz sold the label to Fantasy where most of his sessions were eventually reissued on CD. Norman Granz has since retired to Switzerland, having greatly helped the music he loves.

Dave Grusin b. June 26, 1934, Denver, CO

Dave Grusin has had a multifaceted career, several in fact. As a pianist he was the musical director for pop singer Andy Williams (1959-66), recorded with Benny Goodman (1960) and had a stint as Sarah Vaughan's accompanist. As a composer and arranger he has written for a countless number of films (for which he has won Oscars) and television series. But it is as a producer that he has made his strongest impact in jazz. In 1974 he teamed up with former drummer Larry Rosen to form GRP, which started as an independent production firm. Grusin and Rosen gained early experience producing records under the GRP banner for Arista. In the late 1970s GRP became an independent label and soon Grusin and Rosen gained a reputation for producing a series of light and accessible jazz-oriented recordings with such musicians as Dave Valentin, David Benoit, Lee Ritenour, the Yellowjackets and Chick Corea in addition to Grusin's own projects. One can argue that much of what has been called "contemporary jazz" and later "smooth jazz" found its origins in GRP's blending of commercial and artistic elements which emphasized strong melody statements and catchy rhythms. As the 1980s progressed and GRP (one of the first companies to take full advantage of the rise of the CD) became a huge commercial success, the label opened itself up to more straightahead jazz including some special projects by Grusin (tributes to Duke Ellington and George Gershwin), Eddie Daniels and Arturo Sandoval. Eventually GRP was purchased by MCA but Grusin remained active in the company into the mid-1990s when Tommy LiPuma largely took over GRP's operations. Grusin has since worked for both the new N2K label (coming out with a *West Side Story* tribute set) and GRP (where he recorded a set of Henry Mancini tunes) while continuing to write memorable film scores for major films.

John Hammond b. Dec. 15, 1910, New York, NY, d. July 10, 1987, New York, NY

One of swing music's greatest propagandists, John Hammond was responsible for at least partly discovering a remarkable list of musicians through the years including Billie Holiday, Count Basie, Charlie Christian, George Benson, Aretha Franklin, Bob Dylan and Bruce Springsteen! Although these artists would certainly have made it on their own, Hammond's intervention made their rise to fame swifter. As a masterful talent scout, producer, promoter and an early fighter against racism, Hammond could be a bit dominant and overly forceful in his viewpoints, but time has found him to be have been generally right and well intentioned. Although born into a wealthy family and educated at Yale, John Hammond from nearly the

start had a great love for Black music. As early as 1933 (when he was 22), Hammond was active in the music business, discovering Billie Holiday and getting her into the recording studio, producing Bessie Smith's final sessions and becoming a friend of the young Benny Goodman (who would marry Hammond's sister). Hammond produced freewheeling American jazz sessions for the European market, worked with Fletcher Henderson and Benny Carter and encouraged Goodman to form his first big band. In 1935 he teamed up Lady Day with pianist Teddy Wilson for a series of classic recordings, the next year he discovered Count Basie's orchestra while randomly scanning the radio dial (he soon flew to Kansas City and encouraged Basie to come East) and in 1938 and '39 he organized the famous "Spirituals to Swing" all-star Carnegie Hall concerts. After hearing about Charlie Christian in 1939, Hammond took a plane to Oklahoma City, listened to the young guitarist for himself and flew him to Los Angeles where he had Christian audition for an initially reluctant Benny Goodman. In addition to his work as a promoter and a record producer (most notably for Columbia during 1937-43), Hammond also worked as a jazz critic where some of his very favorable pieces about artists he was working with can certainly be looked upon today as conflicts of interest! After serving in the military during World War II, Hammond felt out of sorts in the jazz scene of the mid-1940s; he never gained a taste for bebop. In the 1950s he produced a superior series of mainstream dates for Vanguard featuring swing era veterans, Hammond worked through the years for Keynote, Majestic and Mercury and during 1959-75 he was again a major force at Columbia where he helped the careers of Dylan, Franklin, Benson, Springsteen and Adam Makowicz among others. In 1967 he organized a new "Spirituals to Swing" concert and in 1977 his autobiography **John Hammond on Record** was published. His son John Hammond, Jr., has long been an impressive blues guitarist/singer. Although he could be a pain (Duke Ellington did not care for his dominant personality), John Hammond certainly made his mark on jazz and music history.

Nat Hentoff b. June 10, 1925, Boston, MA

One of the top jazz writers of the 1950s, Nat Hentoff wrote insightful chapters on Charles Mingus, Ornette Coleman and Thelonious Monk in his classic book *The Jazz Life*. Hentoff attended Northeastern University and Harvard in the 1940s, had a radio show on WMEX in Boston (1944-53) and was inspired by the local Boston area jazz scene. In addition to *The Jazz Life*, Hentoff co-edited *Hear Me Talkin' to Ya* with Nat Shapiro (the book told the history of jazz up to the mid-1950s through the words of jazz's greatest players), he co-edited *Jazz* with Albert McCarthy, wrote *The Jazz Makers*, during 1953-57 was the associate editor of *Down Beat* and was co-editor of the short-lived *Jazz Review* (1958-61). Hentoff founded and ran the Candid label during 1960-61. During the company's brief existence, Hentoff produced important sessions by quite a few artists including Charles Mingus, Phil Woods ("The Right of Swing"), Benny Bailey, Otis Spann, Buell Neidlinger (featuring Cecil Taylor) and Abbey Lincoln. After the early 1960s, Nat Hentoff largely drifted away from jazz, writing about social and political issues. He has on an occasional basis during the past three decades penned liner notes for such diverse artists as David Murray and Teresa Brewer!

Carl Jefferson

Carl Jefferson founded Concord Jazz, which he ran from 1972 until his death in 1995. A successful used car dealer, in 1969 he organized the Concord Summer Festival, which in a few years became the Concord Jazz Festival. A great fan of swinging mainstream jazz, Jefferson started the Concord label in 1972 because so few of the artists who he enjoyed were being recorded. At first its releases seemed to emphasize guitarists (including Herb Ellis, Charlie Byrd and Barney Kessel who recorded separately and together as Great Guitars) but soon its catalog gained more diversity. The young modern swing movement of Scott Hamilton, Warren Vache, Dan Barrett, Howard Alden and later Ken Peplowski were well documented, such veterans as Dave McKenna, Rosemary Clooney, Mel Tormé and George Shearing found a home, hard bop was well represented (including a few Art Blakey sets) and the subsidiary Concord Picante featured the best in Latin jazz (including Cal Tjader, Tito Puente, Mongo Santamaria and Poncho Sanchez). Prior to his death in March 1995, Jefferson produced over 500 sessions for his label.

Quincy Jones b. Mar. 14, 1933, Chicago, IL

Quincy Jones has long been a major force in the music business although his importance to the current jazz scene has diminished sharply since the 1960s. Jones was a decent section trumpeter who toured Europe with the Lionel Hampton big band in 1953 and a superior arranger who in the 1950s and '60s contributed charts to big bands (including Count Basie), orchestras, small group dates and vocalists. He led big bands on a few occasions, most notably during 1960-61. In 1957 Jones signed with Mercury Records and soon relocated to Paris, where the 24-year-old worked as producer for their Barclay subsidiary. In 1961 in New York he became the head of A&R for Mercury and in 1964 moved up to became the label's vice president. Jones, who by the late '60s was primarily writing for films and television and moving away from jazz, worked for A&M during 1969-81 and in 1980 founded Qwest. In the 1970s Jones begun shifting towards R&B and pop and in the '80s he became quite famous for his work as producer on Michael Jackson's *Thriller* recording. A household name, Quincy Jones in recent times has recorded some jazz artists for his Qwest label (including Sonny Simmons, Milt Jackson, Ernestine Anderson and the Clayton Brothers) and in 1993 he persuaded Miles Davis to perform Gil Evans charts at the Montreux Jazz Festival. But otherwise, Jones is primarily famous for his nonjazz work as a producer.

Orrin Keepnews b. Mar. 2, 1923, New York, NY
One of the most respected of all jazz producers, Orrin Keepnews has had a long and productive career. He graduated from Columbia University in 1943 and was originally primarily interested in Dixieland. Keepnews wrote for the *Record Changer* starting in 1948, which was started by his friend Bill Grauer. Four years later he helped reissue 1920s recordings with Grauer when they started RCA Victor's X label. Keepnews and Grauer founded the Riverside label in 1953 and soon Keepnews became interested in more modern jazz styles. The label scored a coup when they signed up Thelonious Monk in 1955 and other important artists produced by Keepnews for Riverside during the next decade included Wes Montgomery, Bill Evans and Cannonball Adderley, all of whom did some of their finest work under the producers' creative guidance. Riverside was a significant label during its life, which ended in 1964 shortly after Grauer's death with its bankruptcy. Keepnews continued producing records on a freelance basis. In 1966 he founded the Milestone label, running it until it was purchased by Fantasy in 1973. Since the Riverside catalog was also acquired by Fantasy (the year before), Keepnews had the opportunity to produce reissues of classic sessions that he had originally been involved in. He served as vice president of Fantasy throughout most of the 1970s, in 1985 founded yet another label (Landmark which was acquired by Muse in 1993) and through the years Orrin Keepnews has been involved in a countless number of important record dates, more recently producing reissues by the Bluebird and RCA labels. In addition to his work as a producer, Keepnews has written many liner notes and occasional articles through the years, working with Grauer to put out the wonderful *Pictorial History of Jazz* in 1956 and collecting together his articles for the semi-autobiographical *The View from Within* in the late 1980s.

Lester Koenig b. Dec. 3, 1918, New York, NY, d. Nov. 21, 1977, Los Angeles, CA
A very good friend of jazz, Lester Koenig was the founder and head of Contemporary Records. He started the company in 1951 and, along with Pacific Jazz, it was the top L.A.-based jazz label active during the cool era. A large number of Contemporary's releases became classic including numerous sets by Shorty Rogers, Shelly Manne, Art Pepper, Hampton Hawes, Chet Baker, the Lighthouse All-Stars, Benny Carter, Helen Humes, Phineas Newborn and Sonny Rollins. Koenig kept an open mind towards newer developments and in the late 1950s released recordings by Cecil Taylor and Ornette Coleman (the latter's first two dates). In addition, his love for Dixieland resulted in the Good Time Jazz subsidiary, a label most notable for the recordings of the Firehouse Five Plus Two, Kid Ory, Lu Watters' Yerba Buena Jazz Band (earlier sessions which were acquired), Bob Scobey and Turk Murphy among others. Although both labels became less active in the 1960s, Koenig helped keep the names of Art Pepper and Hampton Hawes alive during their prison sentences by gradually releasing "new" recordings stockpiled from the 1950s. In the 1970s, Koenig revived Contemporary, helped Art Pepper out during his comeback and recorded some newer classics before his death. The Contemporary and Good Time Jazz labels live on thanks to the extensive reissue policies of Fantasy (which eventually acquired the companies), keeping Lester Koenig's legacy quite relevant.

Bob Koester
The founder and chief of Delmark Records, Bob Koester has been recording and producing valuable jazz and blues records since he started the company in 1953. It was originally based in St. Louis and known as Delmar; Koester moved to Chicago in 1959 and permanently changed the name to Delmark. Delmark has had periods of great activity (including the mid-to-late 1990s) along with off times when it was almost inactive. Koester has primarily recorded music in four different genres: New Orleans jazz (including George Lewis and Albert Nicholas in the early days), blues, hard bop (such as Sonny Stitt, Jimmy Forrest and Lan Halliday) and the avant-garde jazz. Although Koester was never overly fond of the latter, he recognized its importance and released important early work from the Art Ensemble of Chicago, Muhal Richard Abrams, Anthony Braxton and Sun Ra. In addition, Koester (who runs the famous Jazz Record Mart in Chicago) acquired the United and Apollo catalogs, important sessions that Delmark has been reissuing on CDs.

Harry Lim b. Feb. 23, 1919, Batavia, Dutch East Indies, d. July 27, 1990, New York, NY
Although he was a lifelong fan of jazz, Harry Lim was primarily active in jazz during two different periods. He grew up in the Netherlands, where he became very fond of jazz, moving to the US in 1939. After working as a freelance record producer, during 1943-46 Lim was the Keystone label's jazz producer, putting together

scores of classic sessions. The emphasis was on small group jazz that ranged from Dixieland to bop but mostly focused on the top swing all-stars. The quality of the music under Lim's guidance was very high. Unfortunately in 1946 he was replaced by John Hammond and Keynote soon declined and became defunct. Lim had his own short-lived HL label in 1949, produced a few obscure sessions for Seeco and tried reviving Keynote in 1955 but ended up working at Sam Goody's New York record store (1956-73). Lim did return to producing in 1972 when he formed the Famous Door label, a top mainstream record company that recorded a variety of valuable (but now hard-to-find) sessions by Bill Watrous, Red Norvo, Zoot Sims and others up until the producer's death. Happily, Harry Lim was still around when Polygram reissued all of the Keynote jazz sessions on a huge LP-box set in 1986.

Alfred Lion b. Apr. 21, 1908, Berlin, Germany, d. Feb. 2, 1987, San Diego, CA
Alfred Lion was the founder of Blue Note and under his and Francis Wolff's leadership, Blue Note was for many years the top independent jazz label. Lion first discovered jazz when he saw Sam Wooding's Orchestra in Berlin in the 1920s. He emigrated to the United States in 1938 and started Blue Note with an Albert Ammons-Meade Lux Lewis session on Jan. 6, 1939. Wolff joined the label that October and would share artistic control of Blue Note with Lion until his death in 1971. At first Blue Note concentrated on small-group swing, Dixieland and boogie-woogie. However, in 1946 Lion and Wolff took time off to change the focus of the label. Inspired by Ike Quebec, who pointed out some of the greats of modern jazz, Lion soon signed up Thelonious Monk and Bud Powell. Although Blue Note had always been impressive, the company really came into its own in the mid-1950s when it started extensively recording hard bop including Art Blakey's Jazz Messengers, Horace Silver and the up-and-coming organist Jimmy Smith. Lion believed in each record being special so rehearsal often took place before sessions, an unheard-of practice for a small jazz label. The 1955-67 period is often thought of as Blue Note's prime when they had such major artists as Lee Morgan, Donald Byrd, Kenny Dorham, Curtis Fuller, Wayne Shorter, Hank Mobley, Jackie McLean and many others recording gems on a regular basis. In addition to hard bop and soul jazz, Lion was open to the sound of the avant-garde and Cecil Taylor and Ornette Coleman recorded major sets for Blue Note. In 1966 Lion and Wolff sold Blue Note to Liberty and the decline soon began. Alfred Lion retired altogether in 1967 but fortunately he lived long enough to see Blue Note being revived in the mid-1980s.

Herman Lubinsky b. Aug. 30, 1896, d. Mar. 16, 1974, Newark, NJ
Famous for being a rather profane cheapskate who had a low opinion of many of the musicians that he recorded, Herman Lubinsky was quite a character. He had been involved in radio (operating New Jersey's first station WNJ back in 1924) and with the United Radio Company. In 1942 he founded the Savoy label, which during the next two decades recorded sessions by Charlie Parker, Dexter Gordon, Fats Navarro, Errol Garner, Cannonball Adderley, Yusef Lateef and even Sun Ra among many others. Savoy gradually shifted its focus from swing and bop (it was one of the major bop labels) to R&B, blues, hard bop and finally (in the 1960s) gospel. Lubinsky primarily stuck to the business side and was best known for his desire to cut expenses at all costs! He is profiled in hilarious fashion in producer Teddy Reig's autobiography *Reminiscing in Tempo*.

Teo Macero b. Oct. 30, 1925, Glens Falls, NY
One of the best known of jazz producers, Teo Macero started out as a musician. After serving in the military, he moved to New York in 1948, attended Julliard and in 1953 became a member of Charles Mingus' Jazz Composers' Workshop. Macero played tenor and baritone with Mingus on a part-time basis and through the years was involved in various third-stream and avant-garde projects. However, his joining Columbia Records as a producer in 1957 was much more significant. For Columbia Macero produced many important sessions by Miles Davis, Thelonious Monk, Charles Mingus and Dave Brubeck plus many other jazz artists. After leaving Columbia in 1975, he became a freelancer although still working with Davis up until 1983.

Mark Miller
One of Canada's top jazz critics, Mark Miller has been writing for Toronto's *Globe and Mail* since 1978. He has freelanced for a variety of magazines (including *Down Beat*, *Jazz Forum* and *Coda*) and was associate editor for the *Encyclopedia of Music in Canada* in 1982. However, his main contributions thus far have been four books that have done a great deal to shed life on Canadian's well hidden jazz legacy: *Music in Canada—Fourteen Lives* (1982), *Boogie, Pete & the Senator* (1987), *Cool Blues—Charlie Parker in Canada 1953* (1989) and *Such Melodious Racket* (1997).

Dan Morgenstern b. Oct.24, 1929, Munich, Germany
When it comes to writing liner notes for reissues, few are in Dan Morgenstern's league. He moved to the United States in 1947, studied at Brandeis University

(1953-56) and was soon writing about jazz. Morgenstern wrote for *Jazz Journal* (1958-61) and was editor for *Metronome* (1961), *Jazz* (1962-63) and most notably *Down Beat* (1964-73). He has occasionally produced jazz concerts and lectured on jazz through the years in addition to writing the book *Jazz People*. In 1976 Morgenstern became the director of the Institute of Jazz Studies at Rutgers where he has helped put together one of the most remarkable of all jazz collections. It is in his role of establishing the important library along with his countless number of consistently informative liner notes that Dan Morgenstern has made his greatest contribution to jazz.

Chuck Nessa b. Michigan

Chuck Nessa was an important force in documenting many of the early AACM sessions. He started the Nessa label in 1967 and soon recorded Roscoe Mitchell and Lester Bowie about the time that the Art Ensemble of Chicago was being formed. In addition Nessa was involved as a producer in most of Delmark's more important free jazz dates of the era. Although the Nessa label was primarily avant-garde oriented (with sets by Bobby Bradford, Hal Smith, Charles Tyler and Fred Anderson among others), it also included sessions by such tenor saxophonists as Ben Webster, Warne Marsh, Lucky Thompson and Von Freeman. The Nessa label has been mostly inactive since the late 1970s but Chuck Nessa was involved in a 1993 Art Ensemble of Chicago box set.

Hank O'Neal

An important producer, Hank O'Neal helped keep mainstream jazz alive on records in the early 1970s when it was in danger of being forgotten. O'Neal formed Chiaroscuro in 1970 and until its sale to Audiophile in 1978 he consistently recorded swing-based veterans (including Earl Hines, Mary Lou Williams, Ruby Braff, Soprano Summit, Bobby Hackett and Joe Venuti) in peak form. During its last two years, Chiaroscuro also released more advanced dates by Abdullah Ibrahim, Hamiet Bluiett and others. After Chiaroscuro was sold, O'Neal maintained a low profile but in the late '80s he reacquired the catalog and (in addition to reissues) he has continued documenting mainstream jazz up to the present time.

Hugues Pannassie b. Feb. 27, 1912, Paris, France, d. Dec. 8, 1974, Montauban, France

Hugues Panassie's fiery comments and inability to recognize bebop as a logical step beyond swing made him appear to be quite reactionary by the late 1940s and hurt his longtime reputation. Panassie began writing about jazz around 1930 and in 1932 he helped found the Hot Club of France with his friend Charles Delauney. His pioneering work *Le Jazz Hot* in 1934 was among the first serious books on jazz although he amended many of his ideas (including the neglect of Duke Ellington) in 1942's *The Real Jazz*. Panassie was the editor of the magazine *Jazz Hot* and was a powerful force in European jazz during his prime. During visits to New York in 1938 and '39, he organized what would become knows as "The Panassie Sessions," small-group dates with Mezz Mezzrow (who became a close friend), James P. Johnson, Frankie Newton, Sidney Bechet and Tommy Ladnier. However in the mid-1940s he split with the more open-minded Delauney and became increasingly conservative and less significant to the jazz world. Late in life, Panassie wrote a Louis Armstrong biography (revised for its American edition in 1971).

Duke Pearson b. Aug. 17, 1932, Atlanta, GA, d. Aug. 4, 1980, Atlanta, GA

A major pianist and arranger, Duke Pearson was also important as a producer for Blue Note during 1963-71. The head of A&R during this period, Pearson oversaw many advanced hard bop dates as Blue Note, which continued recording hard bop and soul jazz dates, also documented early sessions by Herbie Hancock, McCoy Tyner, Andrew Hill, Joe Henderson, Bobby Hutcherson, Wayne Shorter and Tony Williams along with avant-garde dates by Sam Rivers, Cecil Taylor and Ornette Coleman. Pearson stayed with Blue Note until 1971 when, due to its sale and the death of Francis Wolff, it was heading toward instrumental pop and temporary oblivion.

Ike Quebec b. Aug. 17, 1918, Newark, NJ, d. Jan. 16, 1963, New York, NY

Ike Quebec was an important tenor saxophonist from the late swing era who made a brief comeback (after a decade mostly lost to drugs) in the early 1960s, only to be stricken from lung cancer. The reason he is included in this section is that he worked behind the scenes at Blue Note from the late 1940s until his death. Quebec persuaded Alfred Lion and Francis Wolff in the mid-1940s to check out the emerging bebop musicians including Thelonious Monk (which whom he recorded) and Bud Powell, convincing the owners to change Blue Note's musical direction. Quebec did A&R for the label, was one of their chief talent scouts and as an untitled producer helped Blue Note become a major force in hard bop.

Teddy Reig b. Nov. 23, 1918, New York, NY, d. Sep. 29, 1984

A colorful character and one of the most important jazz producers of all time, Teddy Reig was involved in many important sessions of the 1940s, '50s and '60s. He started producing in 1945 and was soon working regularly at Savoy on most of their most significant dates (including the Charlie Parker sessions), helping turn Savoy into a major jazz and R&B record company. Reig founded the Roost label in 1950 and in the mid-1950s switched over to Roulette where he extensively recorded Count Basie's Orchestra and other jazz musicians and singers. A skillful talent scout, Reig was a major force not only in jazz but in the R&B and Latin music worlds. Health problems forced his retirement in the 1970s.

Bob Rusch b. 1945, New York

Although Bob Rusch studied clarinet and drums early on and in the early 1970s wrote for a variety of jazz magazines (including *Down Beat* and *Jazz Journal*), his fame lies with *Cadence*, the monthly magazine that he founded in 1975. Through the years *Cadence* has reviewed nearly every jazz and blues release in addition to having extensive interviews with both the famous and the obscure. Rusch also started the Cadence label in 1980, a company that has released a variety of consistently strong performances, mostly from advanced players. In the mid-1990s the CIMP label was started and has come out with dozens of adventurous recordings in a short period of time. In addition, Rusch has run North Country Record Distribution (which handles hundreds of independent jazz labels) since he founded it in 1983. Bob Rusch is well known in the jazz world for his candor, honesty and musical open-mindedness.

Bill Russell b. Feb. 26, 1905, Canton, MO, d. Aug. 9, 1992, New Orleans, LA

One of the most important writers and historians involved in the New Orleans Revival of the 1940s, Bill Russell had many accomplishments behind the scenes. A violinist who had extensive study in both performance and composition, Russell was with the Red Gate Shadow Players during 1934-40. During that period he became enamoured with New Orleans jazz. He bought and sold records through the Hot Record Exchange, which he ran starting in 1935. Russell was a jazz journalist by the mid-1930s, contributing three chapters to the 1939 book *Jazzmen* and writing articles for *Jazz Hot*. Russell helped discover Bunk Johnson in 1942, recording the forgotten cornetist. For his American Music label during 1944-57, Russell documented a variety of famous and obscure New Orleans musicians; many of its sessions have since been reissued by GHB. Russell worked in New Orleans as the curator of the jazz archive at Tulane University from 1958-65 and his interviews helped document the early history of jazz. During his later years (starting in 1967) Bill Russell had opportunities to play violin with the New Orleans Ragtime Orchestra. His love for New Orleans jazz never wavered and throughout his life he did his best to save as many details of jazz's early history for posterity.

Ross Russell b. 1920, Los Angeles, CA

Ross Russell was a record store owner (the Tempo Music Shop) when he formed the Dial label in 1946, specifically to record Charlie Parker, who was staying in Los Angeles. Although Russell courted controversy by releasing Parker's infamous "Lover Man" session (feeling during Bird's resulting convalescence in Camarillo State Hospital that the altoist might never play again), he had other opportunities to document the great altoist and even acted as his manager for a year. Russell also recorded Dizzy Gillespie, Howard McGhee, Dodo Marmarosa, Dexter Gordon and Erroll Garner among others before Dial shut down in 1949. An unusual aspect to Dial's later reissues is that Russell saved the alternate takes, thereby multiplying the amount of music in the label's vaults, a fact that collectors in future years appreciated. Since the late 1940s, Russell often worked as a jazz journalist, contributing pieces to *Down Beat*, writing two books (*Jazz Style in Kansas City and the Southwest* and *Bird Lives*) and teaching jazz at colleges.

Brian Rust b. Mar. 19, 1922, London, England

Brian Rust's two-volume *Jazz Records 1897-1942* (first published in 1961 and revised and expanded several times since) is the definitive discography for early jazz. A record collector since the age of five, Rust worked for the BBC in the 1950s, has been a jazz journalist since 1948 (when he started reviewing records for the *Gramophone*) and has written many liner notes and reviews on early jazz ever since. In addition to the jazz discography, Brian Rust wrote a book on King Oliver with W.C. Allen in 1955 and has put together books on the recording output of a variety of labels plus compiling *The American Dance Band Discography* and *The Complete Entertainment Discography*.

Don Schlitten b. 1932

As a producer, Don Schlitten was involved in a countless number of sessions particularly with his main love, straightahead bop-oriented jazz. He cofounded the Signal label with Jules Colomby and Harold Goldberg in 1955, recording Duke Jordan, Gigi Gryce, Red Rodney and others. The label only lasted a couple years before being sold to Savoy. Schlitten worked as a producer on a freelance basis until the early 1970s when he joined Joe Fields in founding Cobblestone, a subsidiary of Buddah. Among Schlitten's major projects were a couple of Sonny Stitt's finest sessions (*Tune Up* and *Constellation*) and six records cut at the 1972 Newport in New York Jazz Festival. Later in 1972 Schlitten joined Fields at Muse and the two of them formed Onyx in 1973. A few years later the partners ended their collaborations, Fields ended up with Muse and Schlitten founded the Xanadu label. During the next decade Don Schlitten produced over 200 releases for Xanadu, both current bop dates for the likes of Barry Harris, Al Cohn, Charles McPherson and others plus historical reissues of bop sessions (mostly small label dates from the mid-to-late 1940s). Schlitten was not only the label head and producer but wrote many of the liner notes. His labor of love largely became inactive in the late 1980s with the rise of the CD although some the Xanadu dates have since been leased to European labels.

Nat Shapiro b. Sep. 27, 1922, New York, NY, d. Dec. 15, 1983, New York, NY

Nat Shariro is best known as a writer who with Nat Hentoff co-edited the classic books *Hear Me Talkin' to Ya* (1955) and *The Jazz Makers* (1957). However, he actually made his living working directly for record labels. Shapiro was Mercury's national promotional director (1948-50), was the head of public relations for BMI (1954-55) and as head of Columbia's A&R dept. during 1956-66 he produced scores of sessions. In all Shapiro produced around 100 albums for a variety of labels, a strong contribution although he will always be best remembered for his work on the two books.

George T. Simon b. May 9, 1912, New York, NY

Only Stanley Dance currently rivals George T. Simon's longevity as a jazz writer. Simon played drums early on and even performed briefly with Glenn Miller's struggling orchestra in 1937 but writing was his true talent. As associate editor (1935-39) and then editor-in-chief (1939-55) of *Metronome*, Simon was probably the most important jazz commentator during the swing era, reporting news and evaluating (usually with great accuracy) the talents of hundreds of big bands, musicians and singers. After leaving *Metronome*, he was involved with the Jazztone Society (1956-57), was a consultant for the Timex Jazz Shows and wrote about jazz for the *New York Herald Tribune* (1961-64) and the *New York Post* (1980-81). Simon produced recordings for several major labels, was open-minded enough to write the liner notes for Thelonious Monk's 1963 big band concert and has remained semi-active into the late 1990s. His books *The Big Bands* and *Glenn Miller* are essential; others include *The Feeling of Jazz, The Best of the Music Makers* and *Simon Says*.

John Snyder

One of the most important jazz record producers of the past 30 years, John Snyder on several occasions has succeeded in recording an extensive series of noncommercial music. He worked for CTI in the early 1970s, most notably on sessions by Jim Hall and Paul Desmond. For A&M in the mid-1970s, he created the Horizon subsidiary, which included a who's who of modern jazz including Hall, Desmond, Ornette Coleman, Dave Brubeck, the Thad Jones-Mel Lewis Orchestra and Charlie Haden. When that stint ran out, Snyder recorded many of the same musicians for his Artists House label, a company notable for its deluxe LP packaging and quality music during 1977-79. Since that time John Snyder has been an important behind-the-scenes player who has been responsible for many worthwhile dates being documented.

Marshall Stearns b. Oct. 18, 1908, Cambridge, MA, d. Dec. 18, 1966, Key West, FL

Marshall Stearns is today primarily known for his well-researched 1956 book *The Story of Jazz*, one with provocative yet usually insightful opinions. Stearns, who played drums in his college days, contributed articles to *Down Beat* starting in the 1940s and had a dual career as a jazz writer and an English literature professor. In 1952 he founded the Institute of Jazz Studies, which in 1966 after his death was transferred to Rutgers where Dan Morgenstern has been the director since 1976. During the 1950s Stearns was a consultant to Voice of America. His book *Jazz Dance* was published posthumously in 1968.

Creed Taylor b. 1929

Creed Taylor is best known for his CTI label of the 1970s but he has been important in the jazz recording industry for quite some time. He played trumpet early on before became a label executive in 1954 when he was hired as the head of A&R at Bethlehem Records. Taylor was at Bethlehem during its two most significant years, recording such artists as Chris Connor, Oscar Pettiford, Ruby Braff, Carmen McRae, Charles Mingus, Herbie Mann and the J.J. Johnson-Kai Winding Quintet. In 1956 Taylor switched to ABC-Paramount and in 1960 he founded its Impulse! subsidiary. Although he signed John Coltrane for Impulse! in 1960, Taylor soon left to accept a job with Verve. Among his successes as a producer during the next five years were the Stan Getz bossa nova records, sets by Jimmy Smith and work with Wes Montgomery. At A&M during 1967-69, Taylor's productions were often quite commercial (with the frequent use of strings and pop tunes) including Wes Montgomery's final three albums and some early efforts by George Benson. It was as if the producer were searching for the formula that was to come. In 1970 he founded CTI (Creed Taylor Inc.) and for much of the decade Taylor had great success in balancing the artistic with the commercial. Among the artists who

recorded some of their finest work for Taylor during this period were Freddie Hubbard, Stanley Turrentine, George Benson and Hubert Laws; the Kudu subsidiary had funkier but no less successful projects by Grover Washington Jr. and Hank Crawford among others. However by the mid-'70s, the larger labels were starting to lure Taylor's artists away and although he was able to record Chet Baker, Art Farmer and Yusef Lateef, financial problems eventually forced CTI to go bankrupt and to be acquired by Columbia. It is ironic that Creed Taylor has been blamed for the late 1970s/early '80s sellout efforts by Hubbard, Turrentine, Benson and Laws for other labels, which were quite inferior to their gems for CTI. After years off the scene, Taylor founded a new CTI in the 1990s which has had releases by Larry Coryell, Jim Hall and Donald Harrison (among others) but thus far failed to establish its own identity like its predecessor.

Bob Thiele b. July 27, 1922, Brooklyn, NY, d. Jan. 30, 1996, New York, NY

Bob Thiele was a major voice in the music industry for nearly six decades. Something of a child prodigy, Thiele started hosting a jazz radio show when he was 14. As a teenager he learned clarinet and led a big band locally in the New York area. During 1939-41 he was editor of *Jazz Magazine* and at the age of 17 in 1939 he founded the Signature label. As head of the label and its producer, Thiele recorded Art Hodes, Yank Lawson, Lester Young, Errol Garner, various Chicago jazz-style groups and most notably in 1943, a classic session by Coleman Hawkins. After Signature folded in 1948, Thiele freelanced and then in 1952 joined Decca where he produced sessions for their Coral and Brunswick labels. Although involved with some jazz, Thiele also worked with Teresa Brewer (his future wife), the McGuire Sisters, Lawrence Welk and several notables whose careers he helped launch: Buddy Holly (who Thiele largely discovered), Henry Mancini, Steve and Eydie and Jackie Wilson. He switched to Dot for a period in 1959, Thiele headed with Steve Allen the short-lived Hanover-Signature label (which had a big hit with Ray Bryant's "Little Susie") and he freelanced for other labels. Probably his proudest accomplishment was teaming up Duke Ellington and Louis Armstrong for a classic set on Roulette. During 1961-69, Bob Thiele was the main producer at ABC/Impulse. He gave John Coltrane permission to record as extensively as he wanted and Thiele also produced more than 100 other albums including sets by Charles Mingus, Oliver Nelson, Albert Ayler, Archie Shepp. Pharoah Sanders, Charlie Haden's Liberation Music Orchestra, Earl Hines, Johnny Hodges, Coleman Hawkins (including a date with Duke Ellington), Quincy Jones, Count Basie and many others. He started ABC's Bluesway subsidiary, which featured blues in the late 1960s (highlighted by dates from B.B. King, T-Bone Walker, Eddie "Cleanhead" Vinson and Big Joe Turner) and produced a variety of pop singers for ABC. After leaving ABC-Impulse, Thiele founded a series of short-term labels including Flying Dutchman, Blues Time, Dr. Jazz and finally Red Baron. Thiele wrote a lot of songs that his artists recorded through the years with "What a Wonderful World" being easily his biggest success. Among the many musicians who he produced during his last two decades were such favorites as Gato Barbieri, David Murray, Lonnie Liston Smith, Clark Terry and his wife, Teresa Brewer, who he teamed with Count Basie, Duke Ellington, Stephane Grappelli, Earl Hines, Ruby Braff and even Murray. As enthusiastic in his later years about music as he had been as a teenager, Bob Thiele was active up until his death. His 1995 memoirs, *What a Wonderful World*, are colorful if much too brief.

Rudy Van Gelder

The most famous engineer in jazz history, Rudy Van Gelder has captured on record many of the most significant jazz recordings of the past 45 years. No one has been able to figure out exactly why he is so successful but the large number of classic dates that are listed as being recorded in Englewood Cliffs, New Jersey, attest to his great success. The perfect balance and clean sound that are commonplace at the sessions he handles have uplifted many jazz performances. Originally Van Gelder began engineering dates for Blue Note in 1953 at his home in Hackensack, New Jersey. In 1959, when he ended his work as an optometrist to become a full-time engineer, he moved his studio to Englewood Cliffs. Virtually all of the post-1952 Blue Note studio albums were recorded by Van Gelder plus a countless number of sessions for other labels; dozens and dozens of hard bop and soul jazz classics. Rudy Van Gelder has remained quite active up to the present time, doing an occasional live date but mostly working at his fabled studio as a freelance engineer.

George Wein b. Oct. 3, 1925, Boston, MA

An excellent stride/swing pianist inspired by Earl Hines, George Wein is most significant as a concert promoter. After graduating from Boston University in 1950, he organized and presented groups at the Savoy in Boston and then opened his Storyville club. The next year he founded the Storyville label. Both the club and the label featured swing and Dixieland players (who were sometimes recorded live) including Ruby Braff, Pee Wee Russell, Lee Wiley and (in a slight departure) Lee Konitz. For a time Wein also had a second club, Mahogany Hall. But his main claim to fame occurred in 1954 when he founded the Newport Jazz Festival.

Despite riots in 1960 and 1971(the latter resulting in its move to New York), the transplanted Newport Jazz Festival (now known as the JVC Jazz Festival) is still flourishing. After its initial success, Wein became one of the country's top concert promoters and through the years he has worked with many other festivals (both in the US and in Europe) while occasionally touring as a pianist with the Newport All-Stars.

Bob Weinstock

During 1949-71, Bob Weinstock as the head of Prestige Records was very active in the jazz world. Prestige in the 1950s recorded most of the who's who of modern jazz, frequently in jam session settings. Although criticized for the lack of rehearsal time (as opposed to Blue Note's approach), most of the Prestige dates were reasonably well planned and still sound exciting today. Weinstock produced some of the sessions (including those by Miles Davis, Sonny Rollins and the Modern Jazz Quartet) and captured many artists in their early days (such as John Coltrane) before they were grabbed by larger labels. In the early 1960s Weinstock sought to stretch out a bit from the hard bop genre by forming three subsidiaries: Bluesville (featuring blues artists), Swingville (mainstream swing players) and Moodsville (emphasizing slow ballads); all of these ventures were short-lived although valuable in documenting some excellent sessions. During the 1960s Prestige leaned more toward soul jazz. Since selling Prestige to Fantasy in 1971, Bob Weinstock has been a freelance producer.

Martin Williams b. Aug. 9, 1924, Richmond, VA, d. Apr. 12, 1992, Alexandria, VA

One of the finest jazz journalists ever, Martin Williams had the rare ability to make musical analysis seem interesting and colorful. He studied at the University of Virginia, the University of Pennsylvania and Columbia University. Williams wrote early on for the *Saturday Review* and the *New York Times* and co-founded the *Jazz Review* with Nat Hentoff, serving as its editor during its brief existence (1958-61). Williams contributed articles during the next three decades to virtually every jazz magazine. In 1970 he became the director of the jazz program at the Smithsonian Institution and later the acquisitions editor at the Smithsonian Institution Press. In the former capacity he presented concerts and produced a variety of reissues (including the *Smithsonian Collection of Classic Jazz*). In addition, Williams wrote about jazz for the *Encyclopedia Britannica*, was an inspiration for Gary Giddins and came out with quite a few books including *The Art of Jazz*, *Jazz Panorama*, *Where's the Melody*, *Jazz Masters of New Orleans*, *Jazz Masters in Transition* and *The Jazz Tradition*.

Valerie Wilmer b. Dec. 7, 1941, Harrogate, England

A notable jazz photographer, Valerie Wilmer was one of the key jazz writers of the 1960s who embraced and wrote intelligently about avant-garde and free jazz. She started as a jazz journalist around 1960 and has since written for such magazines as *Melody Maker*, *Down Beat*, *Jazz Journal*, *Swing Journal* and *Jazz Forum* among many others. Her books include *Jazz People*, *The Face of Black Music*, *As Serious as Your Life* and her memoirs *Mama Said There'd Be Days Like This*.

Herb Wong

In the San Francisco Bay area, Herb Wong has long been thought of as the resident jazz expert. During his productive career he has hosted radio shows, taught jazz in schools and been an important early supporter of the Monterey Jazz Festival. In addition, Wong has had high positions with the International Association of Jazz Educators, been the main producer for the Blackhawk and Palo Alto labels and written a countless number of liner notes, articles and reviews.

A&M

Although one of its co-founders in the 1960s was a trumpeter (Herb Albert), A&M has released relatively little jazz through the years. In the late '60s arranger Creed Taylor (prior to forming CTI) and arranger Don Sebesky showcased some jazz stars with commercial string sections. Their most notable success saleswise was Wes Montgomery (who recorded three best sellers before his premature death) and there were dates by the likes of J.J. Johnson/Kai Winding, Nat Adderley and George Benson, among others, before Taylor departed. During 1975-77 producer John Snyder ran a jazz subsidiary (Horizon) that resulted in around 25 rewarding and often challenging releases (look under Horizon for more details) before the parent company lost interest. Snyder did some additional work for A&M during 1989-90 including dates led by Cecil Taylor, Sun Ra and Don Cherry (Art Deco), among others, and Herb Albert's friend Stan Getz was briefly on the label late in his career. But in general A&M has been mostly involved in pop music. —*Scott Yanow*

Accurate

In 1987 saxophonist Russ Gershon, the leader of the Either/Orchestra, founded the Accurate label in Cambridge, MA. During the years since, the company has not only documented quite a few brilliant sets by the Either/Orchestra, but many other adventurous jazz performers from New England including guitarist Garrison Fewell, Charlie Kohlhase (who doubles on alto and baritone), pianist Pandelis Karayorgis, singer Dominique Eade, the Ken Schaphorst Orchestra, the Mandala Octet and violinist Emery Davis, among others. —*Scott Yanow*

Aladdin

A major R&B label during the 1950s, Aladdin was formed in the mid-'40s by Jim and Edward Mesner as Philco, although the name was changed by 1947 to avoid being mixed up with the Philco company. Many jazz and blues dates were recorded along the way for this L.A.-based company featuring such top players as Lester Young, Billie Holiday (who had one four-song session in 1951), Louis Jordan, Illinois Jacquet, Art Pepper and Jay McShann. Aladdin also put out some dates by Erroll Garner and Howard McGhee that were originally cut for the Black and White label. By 1961 Aladdin was purchased by Imperial, two years later Minit had the masters and Liberty soon acquired the valuable music. In 1969 Liberty became part of United Artists which later was swallowed up by EMI. In more recent times some of the more significant jazz sessions have been put out on CD as part of a Blue Note reissue series including the Lester Young and Art Pepper dates. —*Scott Yanow*

American Music

New Orleans jazz historian Bill Russell founded and ran the American Music label on an irregular basis during 1942-57. The first to record cornetist Bunk Johnson, Russell also documented many of the most colorful veteran New Orleans jazzmen of the era including George Lewis, Jim Robinson, Wooden Joe Nicholas, Natty Dominique, Kid Shots Madison, Kid Thomas Valentine, Big Eye Louis Nelson and Baby Dodds (who played some pioneering unaccompanied drum solos). Storyville and the Japanese label Dan reissued some of the sessions on LP. George Buck's Jazzology has been repackaging and issuing virtually the entire catalog on CD in the 1990s. —*Scott Yanow*

Antilles

Affiliated with Island Records, Antilles by the early '90s (under the direction of its president Brian Bacchus) had releases by James Clay, Johnny Griffin, Frank Morgan, J.J. Johnson, Peter Apfelbaum, Randy Weston, Steve Turre, Teddy Edwards and Kenny Drew, Jr., among others. Antilles has become a particularly significant jazz label, doing a fine job of documenting the modern mainstream. —*Scott Yanow*

Apollo

Formed in 1944 by Hy Siegel and Ted Gottlieb, the Apollo label was sold a few years later to Ike and Bess Berman. An important postwar label, Apollo documented several styles of jazz and early R&B, in addition to plenty of gospel. Among the artists who recorded for Apollo were Coleman Hawkins, Charlie Parker (with Sir Charles Thompson's group), Dinah Washington, Illinois Jacquet, Arnett Cobb, Pete Johnson and Mahalia Jackson. In later years it emphasized rock 'n' roll and R&B, but continued recording jazz until it was sold in 1961 and soon became dormant (except for its gospel series). In the 1980s Bob Koester of Delmark purchased Apollo's jazz masters and has since initiated a rewarding CD reissue series. —*Scott Yanow*

Arabesque

Originally strictly a classical label, Arabesque released its first jazz CDs in 1992 including sets by Craig Handy and Ed Wilkerson's Eight Bold Souls. Since that time Arabesque has steadily come out with challenging modern mainstream dates including sets from Ray Drummond, Jane Ira Bloom, the String Trio of New York, Charles Sullivan and Charles McPherson. —*Scott Yanow*

Arbors

Founded in 1989 by Mat Domber, Arbors has quickly become one of the top Dixieland/swing labels around. At first many of its releases were built around the tenor, soprano and clarinet of Rick Fay, but over time Arbors has built up quite an impressive roster of regulars including trombonist/musical director Dan Barrett, cornetist Ruby Braff, fluegelhornist Jackie Coon, trumpeters Jon-Erik Kellso and Randy Sandke, clarinetists Chuck Hedges, Bobby Gordon and Kenny Davern, pianists Johnny Varro and Ray Sherman, bassist Bob Haggart, the reeds of Bob Wilber, the late drummer Gene Estes, and the Statesmen of Jazz. —*Scott Yanow*

Argo/Cadet

In 1955 the Chess label (the premiere blues company of the decade) established Argo, a separate jazz subsidiary. Although it changed its name to Cadet in 1965 due to the complaints of an English label also called Argo, this company issued jazz on a fairly regular basis until the death of Leonard Chess in 1971. Among the Chicago-based company's most popular artists were Ramsey Lewis, Ahmad Jamal and James Moody, and there were also valuable recordings by Ira Sullivan, Barry Harris, the Jazztet, Illinois Jacquet, Gene Ammons, Max Roach, Red Rodney, Lou Donaldson, John Klemmer and even Benny Goodman. The music was generally bop-oriented with strong touches of soul. After 1971 the label became inactive and went through several hands including GRT, All Platinum and Sugar Hill before being finally acquired by MCA. Some of the more classic sessions have been reissued on CD but many remain out of print. —*Scott Yanow*

Arista

During the mid- to late '70s, the pop-oriented Arista label was significant to jazz. Formed in 1974 by Clive Davis, Arista actually put out jazz on three different labels, all under the direction of producer Steve Backer. The parent company released an extensive series of works by Anthony Braxton along with more commercial recordings by the popular Brecker Brothers. The Arista-Novus label mostly stuck to avant-garde jazz with releases from such musicians as Muhal Richard Abrams, Henry Threadgill (both as a leader and with Air) and Oliver Lake, among others. The Arista-Freedom subsidiary contained reissues of music from the British Freedom label (including Albert Ayler, Cecil Taylor Randy Weston and Marion Brown) and some Black Lion records. In addition, in 1975 Arista gained control of the Savoy label and reissued most of the important sessions, quite often in two-LP sets. And the GRP label had its birth when Dave Grusin and Larry Rosen began producing crossover sets for Arista. But by the early '80s all of these jazz ventures ceased. Novus was discarded (although revived years later by RCA), Savoy was sold to Muse in 1985, the Black Lion and Freedom albums would eventually be reissued on CD by DA Music and GRP became a separate company. Arista, other than putting out lucrative Kenny G. records, has long discarded jazz altogether. — *Scott Yanow*

Artists House

It did not last long but the Artists House label made a strong impression. Producer John Snyder, whose association with A&M Horizon's label (1975-76) had ended, formed the label in 1977 but it was active for less than two years. Each of its LPs were treated as a prestige project with extensive liner notes, deluxe packaging and complete control over the music given to the players. Snyder recorded a gem by the Thad Jones-Mel Lewis Quartet, duet sessions by Charlie Haden/Hampton Hawes and Jim Hall/Red Mitchell, and sets by Ornette Coleman, Paul Desmond, David Liebman, Waymon Reed, Chet Baker, Andrew Hill and James Blood Ulmer among others. Only about a dozen albums were released during the two-year period although some of the sessions popped up on other labels in the 1980s; all still sound quite fresh two decades later. — *Scott Yanow*

Asian Improv

Pianist Jon Jang and saxophonist Francis Wong founded the nonprofit Asian Improv label in 1987 as a way not only to document their music but that of other Asian-Americans jazz musicians, many of whom perform in the San Francisco Bay area. Several of their releases have been quite political, often paying tribute to the Japanese-American internees who were held at American prison camps during World War II. In addition to Jang and Wong, bassist Mark Izu, pianist Glenn Horiuchi, bassist Tatsu Aoki, saxophonist Hafez Modirzadeh and (as a sideman) flutist James Newton have been important participants on the label along with others who play traditional Chinese and Japanese instruments. — *Scott Yanow*

Atlantic

Atlantic Records was founded in 1947 by Herb Abramson and Ahmet Ertegun. From the start it recorded a lot of jazz although Atlantic soon became well-known as one of the top R&B labels; major successes through the years in the latter area include Big Joe Turner, Ray Charles and Aretha Franklin. With the joining of Jerry Wexler in 1953 and Nesuhi Ertegun in 1955, Atlantic became a wide-ranging company with strengths in many areas. From the jazz standpoint, early sessions with Erroll Garner were followed by many important records from the Modern Jazz Quartet, Milt Jackson, Jimmy Yancey, Wilbur DeParis and his New New Orleans Band, Lennie Tristano, Lee Konitz, Charles Mingus, John Coltrane (1959-61), Ornette Coleman (1959-62), Rahsaan Roland Kirk, Eddie Harris, Les McCann, Mose Allison, Yusef Lateef, Keith Jarrett, Charles Lloyd, Gary Burton Jean-Luc Ponty and Herbie Mann among others. After being purchased by Warner Bros. in 1967, Atlantic's jazz activity slowed down, but on an irregular basis the label still shows interest in documenting jazz, including in recent times Cyrus Chestnut, Carl Allen, Gerald Albright and the MJQ. Starting in 1993, Rhino Records has been reissuing some of the highlights of the Atlantic jazz catalog on CD. — *Scott Yanow*

Audiophile

The Audiophile label has gone through three very different phases through the years. Founded in 1947 by E.D. Nunn (a recording engineer), Audiophile released Dixieland records with state-of-the-art sound in the 1950s and early '60s. In 1966 the company became owned by Jim Cullum who used the label to release records by his Happy Jazz Band along with some other local Dixieland bands. In the mid-'70s George Buck (of GHB and Jazzology) acquired the label (other than Cullum's records) and, in addition to repackaging reissues (including classic sessions by Lee Wiley), has recorded many new sets for Audiophile, emphasizing middle-of-the-road vocalists (such as Maxine Sullivan, Marlene Ver Planck, Polly Podewell, Chris Connor, Mike Campbell, Barbara Lea, Dick Haymes and many others) in addition to occasional Dixieland and swing dates. — *Scott Yanow*

AudioQuest

AudioQuest, an audio cable company, had their first venture in the recording business in the late '80s when they recorded bluesman Robert Lucas largely as a sort of demonstration record for their equipment. Since that time (under the direction of Joe Harley the label has come out with many advanced modern mainstream albums, some of which are a bit unique. Bennie Wallace made a ballad date, Larry Willis reorchestrated spiritual music and there have been albums by Jeff Palmer, Mokave, Bruce Katz, James Newton and an instrumental set from blues guitarist Ronnie Earl. — *Scott Yanow*

Bee Hive

Named after a popular Chicago jazz club, Bee Hive Records was founded in 1977 by Jim Neumann and during the next decade would release around 20 albums

with an emphasis on hard bop as played by underrated veterans. Nick Brignola and Pepper Adams were matched up in an exciting date (entitled *Baritone Madness*) and there were sessions led by Dizzy Reece, Sal Salvador, Clifford Jordan and Junior Mance. The label has been inactive since the late '80s and its valuable recordings have not yet appeared on CD. — *Scott Yanow*

Bethlehem

From 1953 until the early '60s, Bethlehem was one of the most consistently satisfying labels in jazz. Founded by Gus Wildi, the company documented East Coast hard bop, West Coast cool jazz, some Dixieland and many vocal sets. Chris Connor was on the first Bethlehem jazz album, Carmen McRae made her recording debut for the company, Duke Ellington cut two albums, and among the other artists were Charles Mingus, Dexter Gordon, Art Blakey (with John Coltrane), Zoot Sims, Ruby Braff, Jack Teagarden, Oscar Pettiford, Herbie Mann, Nina Simone, Johnny Hartman, Mel Tormé, Bob Dorough, Betty Roche, Booker Little and Herbie Nichols. However, after being sold to King Records in the early '60s, Bethlehem became inactive. There have been several reissue programs of Bethlehem's catalog through the years including a late '70s series on LP and recently Evidence has been putting out some of the music (often with previously unreleased performances added) on CD. — *Scott Yanow*

Big World

Neil Weiss, a big fan of Jaco Pastorius who (with the bassist's permission) recorded many of his live sessions, started the Big World label in 1990. Following years of listening to his tapes, Weiss used them as the nucleus of Big World's first few releases. After paying all of the musicians' royalties, Weiss used the remainder of the profits to expand his label, recording saxophonist Alex Foster, trombonist Tom Malone, drummer Kenwood Dennard and keyboardists Gil Goldstein, Michael Gerber and Charles Blenzig, among others. Although much of the music is funky, Big World's releases are not overly commercial, for the musicians are free to express themselves creatively without worrying about potential radio airplay. — *Scott Yanow*

Biograph

Founded in 1967 by Arnold Caplin, Biograph has mostly focused on early jazz and blues with an emphasis on recordings from the 1920s that the major labels have neglected. In addition to territory bands and blues singers, Biograph has reissued music by the likes of Jimmy O'Bryant, Clarence Williams, the California Ramblers, Ethel Waters, Earl Hines, Jack Teagarden, Benny Goodman, Ted Lewis, Ruth Etting, Bunny Berigan, Bing Crosby, Jabbo Smith and George Lewis. In 1970 Biograph gained the rights from the QRS Music Roll Company to put out recordings of their piano rolls (including Scott Joplin, Fats Waller and James P. Johnson), and since then the label has acquired Melodeon (1920s jazz) and the Dawn Record Company (1950s sessions by Stan Getz, Zoot Sims, Paul Quinichette and others). After a transitional period, starting in 1987 Biograph began reissuing some of their material on CD. — *Scott Yanow*

Black & Blue

During a period of time when mainstream and swing veterans were not being recorded, the French label Black & Blue gave them rare opportunities to jam on records. Founded in 1968 and active until the late '80s, Black & Blue starred such top players as Buddy Tate, Tiny Grimes, Milt Buckner, Sammy Price, Jay McShann, Illinois Jacquet, Ray Bryant and Panama Francis' Savoy Sultans on many stimulating sessions. Inner City in the 1970s leased many of the dates to be released domestically on its own Classic Jazz subsidiary. In the early '90s Evidence acquired the catalog and has thus far issued just a few of the dates on CD. — *Scott Yanow*

Black Jazz

This short-lived record company, one of the few Black-owned labels in the 1970s to be recording jazz, was run by Gene Russell during its brief existence (1971-late '70s). Among its artists were Harold Vick, Walter Bishop, Jr., and Doug and Jean Carn, but it failed to make much of an impression. — *Scott Yanow*

Black Lion

One of the top jazz labels in England, Black Lion was founded by Alan Bates in 1968. The majority of its releases have featured Americans including Thelonious Monk (his final sessions as a leader), Bud Freeman, Barney Kessel (with Stephane Grappelli), Dexter Gordon, Earl Hines and Teddy Wilson. Although Black Lion generally emphasizes mainstream jazz, Abdullah Ibrahim and Sun Ra have also appeared on the label and a subsidiary called Freedom features avant-garde sets by the likes of Albert Ayler, Julius Hemphill, Oliver Lake, Roswell Rudd and Cecil Taylor, among others. In addition, British players (including Humphrey Lyttelton,

Alex Welsh, Chris Barber and Freddy Randall) have recorded numerous sessions. Many of the Freedom releases were put out in the US by Arista in the mid- to late '70s and in the 1990s DA Music has reissued quite a few of the Black Lion and Freedom sets on CD. —*Scott Yanow*

Black Saint

From its formation in 1975, Black Saint and Soul Note have been among the most significant labels in jazz. As run by Giovanni Bonandrini since 1977, the large output by these companies has been consistently of the highest quality. Emphasizing highly original and advanced American players, Black Saint and Soul Note (the latter tends to concentrate a little more on hard bop-based players than the generally avant-garde Black Saint) have recorded practically all of the who's who of modern jazz, most notably David Murray, Max Roach, Anthony Braxton, Steve Lacy, Ran Blake, Mal Waldron, Art Farmer, the World Saxophone Quartet and many others. Although based in Italy, Black Saint and Soul Note have been generally available in the US (even with some distributor problems along the way); they are currently being handled by Sphere in New York. A perennial poll winner as jazz label of the year, Black Saint/Soul Note has done the jazz world a very valuable service by documenting a great deal of music that would otherwise have been lost. —*Scott Yanow*

Black Swan

The first Black-owned record label, Black Swan was run by Harry Pace, who had been a partner with W.C. Handy in the music publishing firm Pace & Handy. Opera singer Elizabeth Taylor Greenfield had been known as "the Black Swan," but classical music was only a small part of the company's catalogue, which also included early jazz, blues singers and dance music. Fletcher Henderson was the house pianist and Ethel Waters made her recording debut on the label. However, by July 1923 Black Swan was no longer making new recordings and the following year its records were being reissued by Paramount. A half-century later some of Black Swan's dates were put out on LPs by Biograph and Jazzology in the late '80s started an occasionally active Black Swan reissue series of CDs. —*Scott Yanow*

Blue Note

The most famous independent jazz label of all time (as opposed to Columbia and RCA for whom jazz is usually only a prestige item), Blue Note has gone through many phases. Most famous was the 1955-67 period when the "Blue Note sound" symbolized the finest in hard bop, but even by 1955, the label had already had a colorful history.

Alfred Lion, a jazz record collector who worked for an import-export firm in his native Germany, fled the Nazi regime for the United States in 1938. On January 6, 1939, he recorded boogie-woogie pianists Albert Ammons and Meade Lux Lewis (both of whom he had seen at the famed Spirituals to Spring concert two weeks earlier) and Blue Note was born. From the start Blue Note stood for uncompromising jazz as played by the top jazz musicians without regard to race or potential sales. By the end of 1939 Francis Wolff (Lion's childhood friend) had escaped from Germany and was a partner in the company. Before the label temporarily shut down in 1941 when Lion was drafted, there were already some classic Blue Note records available including sessions by Sidney Bechet (he had a hit with "Summertime"), the all-star Port of Harlem Jazzmen, Earl Hines and Edmond Hall's Celeste Quartet (with Charlie Christian on acoustic guitar).

By late 1943 Blue Note was active again and there were dates by Ike Quebec, Tiny Grimes, John Hardee, Jimmy Hamilton and Benny Morton that fell into the small-group swing genre, along with Dixieland by Art Hodes and Sidney DeParis. With the rise of bebop, Lion and Wolff took a year off to investigate the new music. Through Quebec, they met and soon were recording Thelonious Monk (an extensive and historic series), Bud Powell, Fats Navarro, Tadd Dameron, Art Blakey, J.J. Johnson, Miles Davis, Clifford Brown, Milt Jackson, Sonny Rollins and other modernists along with trad dates by Sidney Bechet and George Lewis.

By the mid-'50s, Blue Note was using nearly all of the top young modern jazz players in hard bop. Because the artistic far outweighed the commercial and musicians were given a chance to rehearse before they recorded, most of Blue Note's output still sounds fresh today. During 1955-68 many musicians were heard at their best on Blue Note including Art Blakey's Jazz Messengers, Horace Silver, Jimmy Smith, Jackie McLean, Kenny Dorham, Lee Morgan, Joe Henderson, Dexter Gordon, Herbie Hancock, Donald Byrd, Freddie Hubbard, Wayne Shorter, Hank Mobley, Herbie Nichols, Kenny Burrell, Grant Green and Stanley Turrentine. In addition, there were important avant-garde sessions by Cecil Taylor, Ornette Coleman, Eric Dolphy, Andrew Hill and Sam Rivers. Alfred Lion's decision to sell Blue Note to Liberty in 1966 was the beginning of the end. Lion worked at the company until he retired in 1967 and Frank Wolff was there until his death in 1971, but the quality of the label's output began to decline almost immediately.

Arranger/pianist Duke Pearson helped out for a while, but by the early '70s the label was shifting towards commercialism with Donald Byrd's *Black Byrd* and such mediocre artists as Bobbi Humphrey, Ronnie Laws, Noel Pointer and the pretty but vapid music of Earl Klugh. By the time Horace Silver left the label in 1980, Blue Note was essentially dead.

In 1980 EMI purchased Liberty and, although some older sessions were reissued, little was heard from Blue Note until its rebirth in 1985. Since that time, under the direction of Bruce Lundvall, there have been many new Blue Note recordings. Although not as consistent as the old Blue Note (there are occasional duds), the label has once again become prominent and significant during the past decade. Michael Cuscuna guides the reissues and there have been worthwhile new dates from a wide variety of artists including Stanley Jordan, Bobby McFerrin, Michel Petrucciani, Benny Green, James Newton, Bennie Wallace, Jimmy Smith and countless others. In fact, between the recent dates and the reissues, more Blue Note recordings are available as of this writing than ever before in its history! —*Scott Yanow*

Bluebird

Bluebird was a subsidiary of RCA Victor during 1932-50 and many valuable jazz and blues sessions (including those of Fats Waller, Earl Hines and Artie Shaw), along with reissues of earlier material, were issued on their 78s. In 1976 RCA began to use the Bluebird name for its swing-oriented reissue series (a notable series of two-LP sets) and, starting in the late '80s, many jazz CDs (including postswing material) have been repackaged under the legendary Bluebird name. —*Scott Yanow*

Broadway Intermission

This collector's label, run by Stanley Hester, released a series of LPs full of rare vintage jazz in the late '70s. Among its albums were sets featuring cornetist Red Nichols, Joe Tarto (who was humorously billed as "Titan of the Tuba"), two sets of "Hit of the Week Recordings," an album titled *It Sounds like Bix* which mostly featured trumpeters who did not sound all that much like Bix Beiderbecke (!), two Tommy Dorsey records full of rare material, territory band samplers and quite a few early Bing Crosby records (mostly taken from radio shows). These historic sets have not yet resurfaced on CD. —*Scott Yanow*

Brownstone

Founded in the mid-'90s, Brownstone Records under the direction of Jack Wertheimer has quickly become an important regional jazz label from Massachusetts. Many lesser-known talents who generally play straightahead jazz have recorded for the label including vibraphonist Cecilia Smith, clarinetist Harry Skoler, drummer Matt Gordy, altoist Greg Abate, guitarists Mitch Seidman and Rob Levit, singers Lisa Thorson and Paul Broadnax, trombonist Steve Davis and saxophonists Leonard Hochman and Dan Moretti. By 1996, Brownstone already had over 20 releases out. —*Scott Yanow*

CMP

A German company whose initials stand for "Creative Music Productions," CMP has since 1977 been recording adventurous jazz featuring Europeans and occasionally Americans. Among its releases have been dates headed by Charlie Mariano, Jeremy Steig, Philip Catherine, David Liebman, Richie Beirach and Joachim Kuhn. —*Scott Yanow*

CTI

CTI was one of the major labels of the 1970s, a brainchild of producer Creed Taylor that did a balancing act between the artistic and the commercial. Some critics complained about overproduction and the use of strings in many of Don Sebesky's arrangements, but such major artists as Freddie Hubbard (*Red Clay, Straight Life* and *First Light*), Stanley Turrentine (*Sugar*), George Benson (*White Rabbit* and *Body Talk*) and Hubert Laws recorded some of their finest work for the label. When they were gradually lured away to larger companies, their subsequent recordings were extremely commercial and sometimes unlistenable; somehow CTI got unfairly blamed for the sellouts.

Creed Taylor, who had previously worked with Bethlehem, Impulse (which he founded), Verve and A&M, struck gold for a period with CTI. Among his other artists were Ron Carter, Hank Crawford and Grover Washington, Jr. (the latter two on CTI's subsidiary Kudu). Taylor found able replacements at first when his artists defected later in the decade (including Art Farmer, Yusef Lateef, Chet Baker and Jim Hall) but problems with distribution forced CTI to go broke by the early '80s. However, a decade later, Creed Taylor returned with a new smaller CTI which has thus far released music by Jim Hall, Charles Fambrough, and Larry Coryell along with a few all-star projects. —*Scott Yanow*

Cadence

Bob Rusch, the editor of *Cadence* magazine, founded the Cadence label in 1980 and since then has released over 60 albums of noncommercial jazz from a wide variety of artists including Chet Baker, Marilyn Crispell, Frank Lowe, J.R. Monterose, Kim Parker, Bill Dixon and Ernie Krivda. In 1995 a related label, CIMP (Creative Improvised Music Productions), was started which has thus far included releases from Evan Parker, Krivda and Lowe, among others. —*Scott Yanow*

Candid

During 1960-61, Nat Hentoff owned and ran the Candid label. Each of its dozen or so releases were well-planned and definitive including sets led by Phil Woods, Charles Mingus, Buell Neidlinger (featuring Cecil Taylor), Benny Bailey, Clark Terry, Steve Lacy, Richard Williams, Don Ellis, Nancy Harrow, Booker Ervin, Abbey Lincoln, and bluesmen Otis Spann and Lightnin' Hopkins. Unfortunately the label did not last long and quickly went out of print. Years later the Barnaby label (which was owned by pop singer Andy Williams) reissued most of the Candid recordings on LPs. In the late '80s DA Music acquired the Candid catalog, released all of the music (including previously unheard sessions by Jaki Byard, Cal Massey and Don Ellis) and started recording new music from a variety of top players ranging from Ricky Ford, Dave Liebman and Gary Bartz to Art Hodes, Barry Harris and Shorty Rogers. —*Scott Yanow*

Capitol

Capitol was formed in 1942 by lyricist/vocalist Johnny Mercer, record-store executive Glenn Wallichs and Buddy de Sylva of Paramount Pictures. From the start Capitol recorded important jazz artists including Stan Kenton, Nat King Cole and later on George Shearing, who were with the label for decades. Dave Dexter, working in A&R, made sure that the company had a strong swing-based lineup in the mid-'40s, although by the end of the decade Capitol (as with the other large labels) experimented a bit by recording some bop sessions. Among the other significant jazz performers who were with the label were Benny Goodman (1947-49), Miles Davis (the *Birth of the Cool* sessions of 1949-50), Duke Ellington (1953-55), Peggy Lee and Jonah Jones. However Capitol switched almost totally towards pop and rock in the 1960s and, other than Cannonball Adderley (who recorded his most commercial dates for the company) and an occasional short-lived reissue series, there has been very little jazz released by Capitol during the past 30 years. —*Scott Yanow*

Capri

Founded in the 1980s by Tom Burns, Capri through its 40 or so releases has helped document some of the fine musicians found in Colorado, plus bigger names. Among the artists featured on Capri's LPs and CDs have been tenor-saxophonist Spike Robinson, pianist/vocalist Ellyn Rucker, flutist Holly Hoffman, the Clayton-Hamilton Jazz Orchestra, trombonist Phil Wilson, Ray Brown and Bud Shank. —*Scott Yanow*

Cexton

Guitarist John Anello, Jr., started the Cexton label in 1983 specifically to release his own album. Due to the success of his *For a Dancer*, he began recording other artists (including many based in Orange County, CA) and by 1990 had 19 albums out, ranging from guitarist Doug MacDonald and drummer Chiz Harris to the vocal group Beachfront Property, the Tom Kubis big band and his own projects. Although Cexton only releases CDs on an occasional basis, its quality has been quite impressive for a small label. —*Scott Yanow*

Challenge

This Dutch label is run by A&R Chief Hein Van De Geyn and Managing Director Anne de Jong. Founded in 1993 and available in the US since 1994, the label records both American and Dutch jazz artists and has releases by Clark Terry, Nat Adderley, Rick Margitza, Paul Bollenback, Spiegle Willcox, Dick Sudhalter, Bob Brookmeyer and Gary Bartz. —*Scott Yanow*

Charlie Parker

This small label was founded by Doris Parker (one of Charlie Parker's wives) and Aubrey Mayhew in 1961. In addition to releasing some live performances by Parker, Lester Young and Billie Holiday (many of which had erratic sound quality), Charlie Parker Records also documented some new dates by Cecil Payne, Duke Jordan, Teddy Wilson, Slide Hampton, Sadik Hakim and a few others before ceasing operation two years later. Audiofidelity Enterprises later purchased the masters and for a brief time reissued some of the music on LPs; none of the recordings have yet been issued on CD. —*Scott Yanow*

Chesky

Founded and run by the brothers David and Norman Chesky, this audiophile label has been releasing jazz and classical CDs since 1986. Although they have put a lot of effort into recording technically superb CDs, the quality of the music has not been neglected. Among Chesky's artists during the past decade have been Phil Woods, Clark Terry, Paquito D'Rivera, Johnny Frigo, Monty Alexander, Brazilian jazz artist Ana Caram, McCoy Tyner and Tom Harrell. —*Scott Yanow*

Chess

Chess was the premiere Chicago blues label of the 1950s but it also had a connection to jazz. Its jazz subsidiary Argo (later renamed Cadet) documented some important jazz sessions (look under Argo for more information) and Chess itself recorded Gene Ammons, Leo Parker and Al Hibbler in its early days before focusing almost entirely on the blues. MCA currently owns the Chess catalog and many of the more valuable blues and jazz dates have been reissued on CD. —*Scott Yanow*

Chiaroscuro

Hank O'Neal founded and ran the Chiaroscuro label during 1969-77, releasing nearly 100 records of mainstream jazz during an era when the music was being greatly neglected by nearly every other American label; Chiaroscuro predated both Concord and Pablo. Its artists included Earl Hines, Teddy Wilson, Joe Venuti, Ruby Braff, Bobby Hackett, Bob Wilber, Dick Wellstood, Soprano Summit, Eddie Condon and Jess Stacy; a few avant-garde players were also documented during the label's later years including Abdullah Ibrahim and Hamiet Bluiett. In 1978 O'Neal sold Chiaroscuro to Audiophile Enterprises and in time most of the records went out of print. In 1987 O'Neal reacquired the catalog, restarted Chiaroscuro and began recording new dates in addition to gradually reissuing his earlier sets on CD. Among the more impressive releases have been those featuring Dorothy Donegan, Al Grey, Louie Bellson, Milt Hinton, Jay McShann, Flip Phillips, Mel Powell, Clark Terry and Summit Reunion. —*Scott Yanow*

Choice

The Choice label only lasted from 1972-80 but nearly all of its 28 releases are well worth getting. Founded by Gerry MacDonald, Choice's albums include important dates led by Eddie Daniels, Joanne Brackeen, Lee Konitz, Adam Makowicz, Zoot Sims, Flip Phillips and Bruce Forman among others. In 1996 Koch Jazz acquired the catalog and hopefully Choice's fine output will be reissued on CD eventually. —*Scott Yanow*

Circle

Circle was founded in 1946 by Rudi Blesh and Harriet Janis and it documented the trad jazz scene of the period with recordings from Baby Dodds (historic unaccompanied drum solos), blues singer Chippie Hill, George Lewis, performances from Blesh's legendary *This Is Jazz* radio broadcasts (which featured all-star groups) and many others. Before it ceased operation in 1952, Circle also acquired Jelly Roll Morton's Library of Congress recordings and released them for the first time. During the 1950s some of the sessions from the Circle catalog were leased and reissued by Riverside. In the mid-'60s George Buck of Jazzology purchased the full catalog and a small sampling has since been reissued on CD. Buck has also used the Circle name for a series of swing-era big-band radio transcriptions. This Circle label is different than an identically titled German modern jazz company that has been active since 1976. —*Scott Yanow*

Columbia

Columbia has through the decades had a love/hate relationship with jazz, often recording important sessions but then treating them as a frivolity and allowing them to go out of print. The very first jazz recordings, "Darktown Strutters Ball" and "Indiana" by the Original Dixieland Jazz Band were made for Columbia in 1917 but not released (due to fear as to the reaction the innovative music would face) until Victor had a hit with their slightly later ODJB sides. Columbia recorded some early jazz-oriented groups (including W.C. Handy, Wilbur Sweatman and the very popular if corny Ted Lewis) and in 1923 it had sessions by both Bessie Smith and King Oliver. Throughout the 1920s Columbia documented some jazz, most notably Paul Whiteman and Clarence Williams, and with its acquisition in 1926 of OKeh (which became its subsidiary), Columbia became one of the most important holders of jazz recordings in the industry.

The Depression and bad business deals caused Columbia to go bankrupt in 1933 and disappear from US markets but it remained a force overseas and made a comeback by 1939. Among the artists in the swing era who signed with Columbia (thanks in large part to producer John Hammond) were Benny Goodman (starting in 1939), Billie Holiday, Teddy Wilson, Duke Ellington, Count Basie and Woody Herman. Columbia was slow to document bop and in the 1950s it established a pattern that has continued to the present day. In general Columbia waits for an artist to develop his or her skills elsewhere and then when they on the brink of success, the label signs them up, outbidding the competition. Columbia usually has a small and controllable jazz roster of steady sellers although, due to executive turnovers, there have been some notable purges of jazz players that have little to do with sales or artistic quality.

In the 1950s Columbia signed up Miles Davis, Dave Brubeck, Duke Ellington, Louis Armstrong, Charles Mingus, Eddie Condon and (for a notable series of jam sessions) Buck Clayton. The 1960s found new label-mate Thelonious Monk building on his past success (it took Blue Note to record Monk in the first place when his music was considered too dangerous) and in the 1970s with the rise of fusion (and spurred on by the success of Miles Davis' recordings), the Mahavishnu Orchestra, Weather Report and Herbie Hancock all recorded for Columbia. The 1980s found the label (under the direction of George Butler) signing up Wynton Marsalis (followed soon by both Branford and Ellis Marsalis) and jumping on the bandwagon in pushing the premature greatness of the "Young Lions." Avant-gardists Arthur Blythe and Tim Berne were also signed up with much fanfare, recorded a series of dates and then were dropped when sales did not live up to expectations; the quality of their music did not count for much.

Columbia, which is now owned by Sony, symbolizes what is both right and wrong about large record labels and their relationships to jazz. When Columbia gets behind a project or a reissue program, near-miracles can happen. But if a sympathetic executive leaves the label, then the bottom line takes precedent and jazz becomes a low priority again. The number of reissue programs that have started and stopped through the years stands as testament to Columbia's unfulfilled potential as a major jazz label. —*Scott Yanow*

Commodore

Commodore was one of the first independent jazz labels. Founded by Milt Gabler in 1938 (who ran the Commodore Music Shop), it was a company whose noncommercial music reflected the expert tastes of Gabler. There was a great deal of Chicago-type Dixieland by the likes of Eddie Condon and Wild Bill Davison but also high-quality small-group swing sessions from Coleman Hawkins, Hot Lips Page and Earl Hines. Commodore was one of the first labels to regularly release 12-inch (as opposed to the usual 10-inch) 78s which allowed performances to be four minutes rather than three. Its biggest hit was Billie Holiday's coupling of "Fine and Mellow" and "Strange Fruit," but Commodore was never about "hits" and was really a jazz lover's paradise. The label was at its prime during 1938-46 when it recorded nearly every significant name in jazz, but continued on an irregular basis for another decade. Some of its performances were reissued through the years by Mainstream, Atlantic and Columbia but it took the mighty Mosaic label in the late '80s to come out with every Commodore recording on three huge box sets which housed a total of 66 LPs. Some of these classic dates have since appeared on CD. —*Scott Yanow*

Concord

Founded by Carl Jefferson (a used-car dealer who had started the Concord Jazz Festival) in 1973, Concord quickly became the definitive mainstream jazz label. At first the label was a showcase for many top guitarists (including Herb Ellis, Barney Kessel, Charlie Byrd and George Barnes) but it soon expanded to encompass a wide variety of straightahead jazz performers. Tenor-saxophonist Scott Hamilton and cornetist Warren Vache (whose revival swing music preceded Wynton Marsalis' "Young Lions" by several years) found fame on the label, such groups as the Ruby Braff/George Barnes Quartet, the L.A. Four, Soprano Summit and Great Guitars were well showcased, pianist/vocalist/lyricist Dave Frishberg recorded some of his finest work and Rosemary Clooney had a renaissance with her jazz-oriented sets. Other highlights of the Concord catalog include Wynton Marsalis' playing with Art Blakey's Jazz Messengers, some top-notch Dave Brubeck dates and superior sets by pianist Dave McKenna, Stan Getz, Woody Herman's all-star small groups, the Capp/Pierce Juggernaut, Louie Bellson, Mel Tormé teaming up with George Shearing and several Concord "Super Bands." Concord Picante was formed to record Latin jazz bands (including Tito Puente and Poncho Sanchez), Concord Concerto recorded some classical music and Concord Crossover released some more poppish dates. In addition, Concord has a close association with Jazz Alliance which, in addition to reissues of some obscure sets for smaller labels, has documented a prestigious solo piano series held at Maybeck Recital Hall (which now numbers near 40 volumes) and a duet series (nearing ten). Although Carl Jefferson passed away in 1995, Concord has (if anything) accelerated the number of its releases without losing its direction. After 23 years, there are now over 700 Concord releases, most of which are currently available on CD! —*Scott Yanow*

Contemporary

Founded in 1951 by Lester Koenig, Contemporary was one of the top jazz labels of the 1950s. Based in Los Angeles, Contemporary did a superior job of documenting the West Coast jazz scene of the decade with many notable releases by such players as Shorty Rogers, Art Pepper, Shelly Manne, Barney Kessel, Hampton Hawes, the Lighthouse All-Stars, Andre Previn, Phineas Newborn, Harold Land, Teddy Edwards, Sonny Rollins, Benny Carter, Helen Humes, Benny Golson, Lennie Niehaus and others. In addition, Koenig kept an open mind towards the avant-garde and recorded Cecil Taylor and Ornette Coleman (his first two records) early on. After the early '60s the label was only active on a part-time basis (releasing music by Hawes and Pepper) until the early '70s when it was revived. Among its later releases were dates by George Cables, Woody Shaw, Art Farmer, Chico Freeman, Joe Henderson, Bobby Hutcherson, Frank Morgan and more from Art Pepper. After Koenig's death in 1977, Contemporary was run for a time by his son John Koenig before being sold to Fantasy. Nearly all of its releases (along with that of its subsidiary Good Time Jazz) have been reissued on CD in the *Original Jazz Classics* series. —*Scott Yanow*

Creative World

Organized by Stan Kenton in 1970, the Creative World label gave the bandleader an outlet with which to reissue his Capitol recordings (which he reacquired) plus put out new music. During the nine years until his death in 1979, Kenton was able to reissue the majority of his recordings, most of which had previously gone out of print. In addition there were big-band sets by Charlie Garnet, Billy May, Bill Holman, Johnny Richards and Les Hooper. After Kenton's death the label's 90 or so releases remained in print until the end of the LP era; Kenton's own dates have started to be reissued on CD by Capitol and Mosaic. —*Scott Yanow*

Criss Cross

A Dutch schoolteacher, Gerry Teekens founded Criss Cross in 1981 and has released over 100 albums ever since. Criss Cross has given both young and middle-aged players an opportunity to be heard and Teekens often teams unknowns with more famous musicians. Since Teekens' main interest is straightahead hard bop-oriented jazz, that is the main focus of his valuable label. Among the many artists who have led dates for Criss Cross have been Jimmy Raney, Warne Marsh, Chet Baker, Clifford Jordan, Kenny Garrett, Cedar Walton, Tom Harrell, Ralph Moore, Brian Lynch, Benny Green, Philip Catherine, Harold Ashby, Melvin Rhyne, Chris Potter, Don Braden, Gary Smulyan and Pete Christlieb, among many others. —*Scott Yanow*

DCC Compact Classics

Formed in 1986 as one of the first CD-only labels, DCC Compact Classics is strictly an audiophile reissue label, bringing back rock and jazz from the 1950-80 period on very well-recorded CDs. Among its releases have been the Ray Charles/Betty Carter duets, George Lewis, Maxine Sullivan, Wes Montgomery, Shelly Manne's *My Fair Lady*, Vince Guaraldi's *Jazz Impressions of Black Orpheus* and the four Miles Davis Prestige quintet albums of 1956. —*Scott Yanow*

DIW

One of the most consistently exciting of all the Japanese jazz labels, DIW has been recording both avant-garde stylists and piano trios since the early '80s. For a time during 1992-94 some of the releases were made available domestically through Columbia although that arrangement has since ended to the frustration of the jazz public; DIW's CDs are expensive! Among the American artists with releases on DIW are James Williams, Stanley Cowell, George Cables, Harold Mabern, David Murray (many!), Steve Grossman, the Art Ensemble of Chicago, Reggie Workman, John Hicks, Lester Bowie, Sun Ra, Phalanx and Steve Coleman. —*Scott Yanow*

DRG

Since the late '70s the DRG label has been releasing records that range from cabaret (there are a lot of singers on the roster) to swing and more modern jazz. For a time DRG leased and released many valuable LPs covering material from the pioneering French Swing label and later on Robert Parker's series of CDs that feature his "stereo" versions of early 78 recordings. Of DRG's own releases, there are interesting sets by Barbara Carroll, Anita O'Day, Maxine Sullivan, Babik Reinhardt, John Lewis, Gerry Mulligan, Django Reinhardt and others. —*Scott Yanow*

Debut

One of the very first artist-owned labels, Debut was run by Charles Mingus and Max Roach. Its main years were 1952-55 although a duo session that Mingus had with pianist Spaulding Givens in 1951 and a couple of obscure sessions from 1957 were also released on Debut. During its run, Debut documented more than its share of gems. Its catalog would later be acquired by Fantasy which in 1990 came out with a 12-CD box set that contains all of the Debut recordings that Mingus himself played on, featuring such artists as Jackie Paris, Lee Konitz, Paul Bley, Julius Watkins, Oscar Pettiford, Thad Jones, Hazel Scott, Miles Davis, Jimmy Knepper, an early session by Mingus' Jazz Workshop, the famous Massey Hall concert with Dizzy Gillespie, Charlie Parker and Bud Powell and a four-trombone date by J.J. Johnson, Kai Winding, Bennie Green and Willie Dennis. —*Scott Yanow*

Decca

Decca was one of the most significant labels of the swing era. Although started in England in 1929 by Edward Lewis, it was not until 1934 that Jack Kapp established an American branch. Among the artists who Kapp signed were Bing Crosby (who helped really make the label), Louis Armstrong, Chick Webb, Ella Fitzgerald, the Mills Brothers, Jimmy Lunceford, Count Basie, Woody Herman, Andy Kirk, Louis Jordan, Lionel Hampton, Billie Holiday and Art Tatum. Decca remained significant throughout the 1940s and '50s (mostly recording pop in the latter decade) before being purchased by MCA in 1959; there would be some more new sessions in the 1960s (including the Dukes of Dixieland) before Decca became completely inactive. Since then there have been several halfhearted and truncated reissue series of Decca's swing-era recordings with the most successful being the current CD programs undergone by GRP and the European Classics label. —*Scott Yanow*

Delmark

Bob Koester founded Delmark Records (as Delmar, after a street) in 1953 originally to record a Dixieland group in St. Louis. He leased some George Lewis recordings and in 1958 moved to Chicago where he opened the Jazz Record Mart and changed the label's name to Delmark. Since that time Delmark has documented Chicago blues, some Dixieland, bop, hard bop and (starting in 1966) important early music of the AACM (including Roscoe Mitchell, the Art Ensemble of Chicago and Anthony Braxton). Although Delmark was less active during part of the 1980s, it has since resumed a regular release schedule of new jazz and blues, reissues from its catalog and repackaging of material originally on the Apollo label in the 1940s. —*Scott Yanow*

Denon

The Japanese label Denon, one of the oldest in the world, started operating in the United States in 1983. Their jazz catalog includes interesting sessions by Eddie Gomez, Sonny Stitt, Bennie Wallace, Archie Shepp and Count Basie among others. In 1991 they purchased the Savoy label, a rich heritage whose most significant sessions had already been reissued by Arista in the 1970s and Muse in the 1980s. Denon has since released literally hundreds of reproductions of Savoy's '50s-era LPs on CD. The problem is that the scanty playing time and faults of the original releases have been duplicated, the liner notes are often microscopic or nearly nonexistent and the releases have been far from logical. There have been a few new recordings under Savoy's banner (including sets by Ralph Moore and Curtis Fuller) but thus far Denon's Savoy series has more than its share of problems. —*Scott Yanow*

Dial

Founded in 1946 by Ross Russell and only active until 1949, Dial was one of the most important of all the postwar bebop labels. Charlie Parker recorded seven classic sessions for Dial during 1946-47 and other modernists who made dates for the label included Dizzy Gillespie, Sonny Berman, Erroll Garner, Howard McGhee, Dodo Marmarosa, Dexter Gordon (including "The Chase"), Wardell Gray, and Fats Navarro (on a Don Lanphere set). In addition Dial had an unexpected hit with singer Earl Coleman's "Dark Shadows." Despite the many artistic successes, Russell stopped recording jazz after 1949. Through the years some of the Dial recordings (particularly Parker's dates) were reissued in piecemeal fashion. The British Spotlite label did a fine job in the late '60s/early '70s of reissuing the historic music on LPs and in recent times Stash has been bringing these classics back on CD. —*Scott Yanow*

Discovery

The Discovery label has had three lives. Founded by Albert Marx in 1948, Discovery was an important independent jazz label that had among its releases significant sessions by Art Pepper, George Shearing, Dizzy Gillespie (with strings), Hampton Hawes and others. However by the end of the 1950s the label was inactive and most of its catalog sold to Savoy (where it was included in later reissue programs). Albert Marx re-emerged in the 1970s, starting a new Discovery label and a subsidiary (Trend) that during the next 15 years documented many of the top bop-based musicians and jazz singers who were active at the time in the Los

Angeles area; among those artists were Bob Cooper, Bob Florence's Big Band, Milcho Leviev, Lorez Alexandria, Mike Wofford, Charlie Owens, Clare Fischer, Sue Raney, Ray Pizzi and Gerald Wilson. In addition Marx acquired the rights to the Musicraft catalog of the 1940s and reissued many of the historic sessions on Musicraft LPs, and he also leased some valuable sessions from the Warner Bros. catalog. After Marx's death in 1991, the Discovery label was temporarily defunct before being acquired by Jac Holzman (who had founded Elektra in 1950). Holzman reissued some of the better albums on CD and recorded a variety of his favorite performers (including James Dapogay, Sonya Jason, Bill Cunliffe and jazz performances of movie themes). However, Holzman has also begun taking Discovery in a different direction, recording pop and folk music, so the label's relevance to jazz may be declining in the future. —*Scott Yanow*

DMP

Tom Jung founded Digital Music Products (DMP) in 1982, a label that has put out a steady stream of well-recorded releases ever since. Among DMP's records have been sets by Bob Mintzer's big band, Dial and Oatts, Flim and the BB's, Warren Bernhardt, Joe Beck and the Dolphins. —*Scott Yanow*

Doctor Jazz

Producer Bob Thiele put together many short-lived labels during his career. Doctor Jazz, which was active in the 1980s before it was succeeded by Red Baron, had several notable Duke Ellington records, numerous examples of Thiele's wife singer Teresa Brewer being featured with jazz all-stars, releases by Gato Barbieri and Pharoah Sanders, and some reissues of classic performances originally made for his Signature label in the 1940s. —*Scott Yanow*

Double Time

Jamie Aebersold, the altoist and educator best-known for his Music Minus One jazz instructional records, took the plunge and started his own Double Time label in 1995. Within a year he had nine releases out, all fine examples of straightahead bop and hard bop. Among the artists represented are Bobby Shew, Conrad Herwig, Hal Galper, Steve Slagle and Dave Liebman; the latter is heard on a rare outing on tenor. —*Scott Yanow*

Dragon

Probably the premiere Swedish jazz label, Dragon has long had a huge catalog not only featuring Swedish jazz musicians such as Lars Gullin, Arne Domnerus, Bengt Hallberg and (from the 1940s) Stan Hasselgard but many examples of Americans playing in Europe (usually Sweden). Included among the latter are sets by Miles Davis (separate dates with John Coltrane and Sonny Stitt), Sonny Rollins, Lee Konitz, Chet Baker, Dizzy Gillespie, Stan Getz and many others. This is a straightahead jazz label well worth becoming acquainted with! —*Scott Yanow*

Dreamstreet

The Dreamstreet label was founded in the late '70s with Howard Kenyon serving as its president. The label only lasted a few years but came out with around ten worthy mainstream (small-group swing) releases. Among the highlights of its catalog were sessions headed by Warren Vache (*Blues Walk*, his first date as a leader), Lou Stein, Glenn Zottola, George Masso and Carmen Leggio. Dreamstreet's increasingly hard-to-find LPs have not yet been reissued on CD. —*Scott Yanow*

Dreyfus

Dreyfus was founded in France in 1991 by Francis Dreyfus, who had long been involved in the pop music world of Europe. Dreyfus started out with releases by Benny Golson, Marcus Miller and older unreleased tapes of Bill Evans, Bud Powell and Chet Baker. In 1994 Dreyfus made a strong impression in the US with sets by the Mingus Big Band, Roy Haynes, Steve Grossman, Michel Petrucciani and Bireli Lagrene and seems positioned to continue its success in the future. —*Scott Yanow*

Drive Archive

Founded by Don Grierson and Stephen Powers, Drive Archive is a huge reissue company that brings back vintage recordings from many styles of music. It has released dozens of swing-oriented CDs (many taken from radio broadcasts) along with some sessions from the 1950s; most are drawn from the catalogs of Everest, TKO, Ember and Real Time. —*Scott Yanow*

ECM

ECM was founded in Germany by Manfred Eicher in 1969. Eicher's vision has been felt on most of the releases ever since with an emphasis on space, silence, superb technical recording and thoughtful improvisations. Hundreds of ECM records have been released during the past 27 years by such artists as Pat Metheny (the label's biggest seller), Jan Garbarek, Keith Jarrett, Terje Rypdal, Gary Burton, Jack DeJohnette, Ralph Towner, Eberhard Weber, Chick Corea, Paul Motian, John Abercrombie, many European players and countless others. Although some may think of the ECM sound of the 1970s as being a forerunner of new age, Eicher's music usually had much more inner fire. In the 1990s, ECM (which, after a period as part of the Polygram family, is now distributed by RCA) remains a very important label. —*Scott Yanow*

Elektra

Since its formation in 1950 by Jac Holzman, Elektra has mostly been a pop label. However, in 1982 Bruce Lundvall established Elektra Musician as a creative jazz subsidiary and for the next three years a wide range of consistently significant records were released. Among the highlights of the Elektra Musician catalog were a live concert by the Young Lions, sets by Woody Shaw, Joe Albany, McCoy Tyner, Bobby McFerrin (including his classic *The Voice*), Sphere, Steps Ahead, Echoes of an Era, Charles Lloyd (with Michel Petruciani), and releases of early material by John McLaughlin, Bill Evans and Bud Powell. When Lundvall left Elektra Musician in 1985, the jazz subsidiary quickly became obsolete. Some of the recordings have been reissued on CD by Discovery in the 1990s. —*Scott Yanow*

EmArcy

EmArcy was formed in 1954 as a jazz subsidiary of Mercury; producers Bob Shad and Jack Tracy both had periods running the label. In the 1950s EmArcy recorded pany exciting sessions by the likes of Clifford Brown, Dinah Washington, Sarah Vaughan, Cannonball Adderley, Helen Merrill, Maynard Ferguson and Buddy Rich among others. In the 1960s Rahsaan Roland Kirk made some of his finest recordings for the label but by the latter half of the decade EmArcy (which was replaced by the short-lived Limelight label) was inactive. In the 1980s its owner Polygram revived EmArcy for both reissues and newer bop-oriented recordings including sessions by Merrill, Ray Bryant and CDs of previously unreleased material from Erroll Garner. —*Scott Yanow*

Enja

Enja, which is short for the European New Jazz Association, was founded in 1971 by Horst Weber and Matthias Winckelmann (who is still its president in the 1990s). Starting with a Mal Waldron live date, Enja has released literally hundreds of hard bop, post bop and avant-garde jazz dates through the years plus some blues sessions and even some crossover material. Among the many artists who have recorded for Enja are Tete Montoliu, Archie Shepp, Cecil Taylor, Abdullah Ibrahim, Bennie Wallace, John Scofield, Tommy Flanagan, Jerry Gonzalez, Jane Ira Bloom, Abbey Lincoln, Franco Ambrosetti, Ray Anderson, Clark Terry, Gary Thomas, George Gruntz's Concert Band, Leni Stern, Dizzy Gillespie, Barbara Dennerlein, McCoy Tyner, Max Roach, Michele Rosewoman, Maria Schneider's Jazz Orchestra and many more. —*Scott Yanow*

ESP

ESP was one of the most important free jazz labels of the 1960s. It consistently documented music that was even farther ahead than the output to be found on Impulse. Founded by Bernard Stollman in 1963, ESP's catalog included passionate recordings by Albert Ayler, Ornette Coleman (his *Town Hall Concert*), Pharoah Sanders (who made his recording debut on ESP), the New York Art Quartet, singer Patty Waters, Giuseppe Logan, Sun Ra, Marion Brown, Sonny Simmons, Paul Bley, Ran Blake, Charles Tyler, Willem Breuker, Perry Robinson and others. There were also incomplete series of live recordings by Charlie Parker, Bud Powell and Billie Holiday. ESP became inactive by the early '70s but nearly all of its brief but explosive releases have been reissued on CD. —*Scott Yanow*

Evidence

A collaboration between Jerry Gordon and Howard Rosen (former record-store owners), Evidence was founded in 1992. Since that time the small company has leased scores of sessions originally recorded for other labels (including King from Japan, Sweet Basil, Theresa, Black & Blue and Bethlehem). In addition to the many jazz and blues sets and a series of new recordings, Evidence has sorted through and organized many of Sun Ra's Saturn recordings which were originally issued in haphazard fashion. As of early 1996 Evidence had released over 150 jazz CDs and the number has grown since then, ranging in style from 1950s bop (in their Bethlehem sets) to hard bop, post bop and Sun Ra. The enormous quantity is fortunately matched by the consistent quality of Evidence's many important releases. —*Scott Yanow*

Famous Door

Harry Lim, who had headed the remarkable Keynote label during 1943-46, founded Famous Door in 1972. For the next decade, Lim recorded the music he most enjoyed: swing and straightahead bop. Among the artists who recorded for Famous Door were Bill Watrous, Zoot Sims, George Barnes, Red Norvo, Scott Hamilton (one of his earliest sessions), Dave McKenna, Butch Miles, Charlie Ventura, Danny Stiles, Eddie Miller and Milt Hinton. Famous Door became inactive by 1985 and, since Lim's death in 1990, its recordings (which have not yet appeared on CD) have been difficult to find. —*Scott Yanow*

Fantasy

Fantasy currently has in its gigantic catalog a large portion of the history of jazz. Founded by Max and Sol Weiss, Fantasy gained prominence in the 1950s for its recordings of Dave Brubeck, Gerry Mulligan and Cal Tjader among others. Although never a major label itself, Fantasy has had such artists in later years as Duke Ellington, Kenny Burrell, Flora Purim, Bill Evans and Ruth Brown (in addition to Creedence Clearwater and other rock and pop acts). More importantly, Fantasy has acquired through the years quite a few of its former competitors: Debut (1955), Prestige (1971), Riverside (1972), Milestone (1973), Contemporary/Good Time Jazz (early '80s) and Pablo (1987). Ambitious and very successful reissue programs included a series of around 200 double-LPs in the 1970s, and (starting in 1983 with the CD era) the *Original Jazz Classics* and *Original Blues Classics* programs which now number over 1000. Based on both quality and quantity, Fantasy owns the mightiest jazz catalog of all! —*Scott Yanow*

Fat Cat Jazz

Starting in the late '60s and continuing until his death in the early '90s, Johnson "Fat Cat" McRee released records on a steady basis on his Fat Cat Jazz Label. Dedicated to Dixieland, McRee started the label by recording sets at the annual Manassas Jazz Festival and many of those releases are undisciplined jam sessions that sometimes border on the chaotic. However, there were also quite a few more valuable (and coherent) releases and such players as Wild Bill Davison, Zutty Singleton, Eddie Condon, Don Ewell, Snoozer Quinn, Clancy Hayes, Cliff Jackson, Lou McGarity, Tony Parenti, Maxine Sullivan, Willie "The Lion" Smith, Art Hodes, Johnny Wiggs, Kenny Davern, Bob Wilber, Max Kaminsky, Doc Evans and Spencer Clark are heard in fine form. In addition, McRee put out a 12-LP series of broadcasts featuring Sidney Bechet (with either Bunk Johnson, Johnny Windhurst or Peter Bocage on cornet) from Boston in 1945. Shortly before Fat Cat McRee's death, he sold his label to George Buck of Jazzology; only a few dates have thus far appeared on CD. —*Scott Yanow*

Flying Dutchman

Flying Dutchman was one of the many labels that producer Bob Thiele headed during his very productive career. He founded the company in 1969 and during 1969-75 Thiele recorded many of his favorite artists including Oliver Nelson, Gato Barbieri (some of his finest records), Bobby Hackett, the World's Greatest Jazz Band, Bud Freeman, Leon Thomas, Ornette Coleman and Louis Armstrong, among others. Flying Dutchman was acquired by Atco (a subsidiary of Atlantic) in 1971 and in 1976 the label was taken over by RCA. Flying Dutchman continued releasing material until 1984 and would later be succeeded by Doctor Jazz and Red Baron. Most of its recordings are currently out of print. —*Scott Yanow*

Fmp

FMP (the Free Music Production) was formed in 1969 as a co-op that was directed by bassist Jost Gebers to promote and record exclusively free jazz music. The German label has since documented the who's who of the European avant-garde including Misha Mengelberg, Alex Von Schlippenbach, the Globe Unity Orchestra, Peter Brotzmann, Evan Parker, Lol Coxhill and such Americans as Cecil Taylor, Marilyn Crispell and Steve Lacy. —*Scott Yanow*

Folkways

Moses Asch, who had previously run the short-lived Asch and Disc labels, founded Folkways in 1947 with Marian Distler. During the next 40 years until his death in 1986, Asch recorded a vast variety of folk music and esoteric material. Jazz was only a small part of Folkways' huge catalog but Asch also released a series of ragtime recordings (many from the 1920s) plus sets featuring Zez Confrey, Roy Bargy, James P. Johnson, Joe Sullivan, Duke Ellington (a 1952 concert), Doc Evans, Art Tatum and Jelly Roll Morton (piano rolls in the latter's case), samplers of early jazz, some swing records and a valuable two-LP set of Mary Lou Williams' mid-'40s recordings. Shortly before his death, Moses Asch negotiated with the Smithsonian Institution to sell his catalog and Smithsonian/Folkways has since reissued some of the music on CDs; virtually every release is available in the meantime on cassette. —*Scott Yanow*

Fresh Sound

During the late '80's and '90s, the Spanish label Fresh Sound has reissued a countless number of otherwise forgotten sessions from the '50s, mostly focusing on bop and West Coast jazz. Among the artists who have had their releases reissued on CD (some of which were originally recorded for Bethlehem, Roulette, Roost, HiFi, Jubilee or Argo) are Herb Geller, Gerry Wiggins, Ruth Price, Gigi Gryce, Lou Levy and Lennie Niehaus. —*Scott Yanow*

GHB

In 1949 George Buck recorded Tony Parenti, Wild Bill Davison, and Art Hodes in a sextet and released it on his new Jazzology label. He did not make any further recordings until 1954 when Buck started the GHB label to specifically record New Orleans jazz. Since that time he has acquired many labels, releasing music under such subsidiaries as American Music, Black Swan, Circle, Solo Art, Audiophile, Southland and Progressive. GHB has stuck to its original goal and the music on this label ranges from the primitive to hot Dixieland. Among the artists with CDs on GHB are Burt Bales, George Lewis, Chris Barber, Turk Murphy, Lu Watters, Art Hodes, Louis Nelson, Sammy Rimington, Graeme Bell, Kid Thomas Valentine, Pete Fountain, Ernie Carson, Captain John Handy, Ken Colyer, Oscar Celestin and Percy Humphrey. —*Scott Yanow*

GM Recordings

Founded by Gunther Schuller in 1981, the GM label reflects his interests in classical music, ragtime and jazz. Of particular interest to jazz listeners are releases by the New England Ragtime Ensemble, Simon Nabatov, Orange Then Blue, George Schuller, Eric Dolphy (*Vintage Dolphy*), Ran Blake, Richard Todd, Joe Wilder, Ivo Perelman, Lee Konitz and Gunther Schuller himself. —*Scott Yanow*

GNP Crescendo

Gene Norman at one point promoted concerts, ran a nightclub (the Crescendo), was an important jazz disc jockey and headed his own record label GNP ("Gene Norman Presents"); he still does the latter. Norman founded the company in 1947, recording many of the live concerts that he presented including West Coast jam sessions and performances by Duke Ellington and Louis Armstrong. Other well-known GNP albums included Dizzy Gillespie's big band (1948), Charlie Ventura (1949), the Clifford Brown/Max Roach Quintet (1954), Lionel Hampton's classic version of "Stardust," Frank Morgan's recording debut, a few numbers by the Gerry Mulligan Quartet with Chet Baker and some Teddy Buckner Dixieland dates. After the 1950s, GNP spread out to cover other styles of music but on an occasional basis in the 1970s and '80s jazz artists were documented including Bobby Enriquez, Dave Pell's Prez conference (one of their records features Joe Williams), Anita O'Day and Bill Watrous. In addition, the Stan Kenton Creative World catalog was handled by GNP. Most of GNP Crescendo's output is currently available on CD. —*Scott Yanow*

GRP

Dave Grusin and Larry Rosen started producing projects together in 1976 and for a time organized some commercial jazz sessions for Arista. In 1982 they formed GRP Records, a label which soon had a reputation for melodic and lightly funky instrumental dates that fell into the new category of "contemporary jazz." Although many purists complained about the slickness of GRP's music, the label became so commercially successful that it was able to finance such projects as the GRP All-Star Big Band and Dave Grusin's tributes to George Gershwin and Duke Ellington. In 1990 MCA purchased GRP but the label has remained reasonably independent. In fact GRP essentially runs the Decca and Impulse reissue programs. Tommy LiPuma's arrival at GRP late in 1994 has resulted in the label cutting back its roster and dropping many of its more straightahead artists but its large catalog remains intact. Among the top GRP artists through the years have been Grusin, Chick Corea (both his Elektric and Akoustic Bands), Dave Valentin, David Benoit, Diane Schuur, Eddie Daniels, Arturo Sandoval, Don Grusin, John Patitucci, Gary Burton, Deborah Henson-Conant, Kevin Eubanks, Eric Marienthal, Tom Scott, Nelson Rangell, the Rippingtons, Lee Ritenour, Tom Scott and Special EFX. —*Scott Yanow*

Galaxy

The Galaxy name was first used in 1964 as a subsidiary of Fantasy and there were just a few releases, including early sides from late-'40s Detroit featuring Sonny Stitt, Russell Jacquet and Milt Jackson. After being unused during 1967-76, Galaxy was revived as a new label under the Fantasy banner. During the next decade

there were over 50 albums recorded including a dozen by Art Pepper (who recorded exclusively for Galaxy during his last years) and sets by Hank Jones, Red Garland, Tommy Flanagan, Dewey Redman, Chet Baker, Philly Joe Jones, Shelly Manne, Nat Adderley and others. But with the rise of the CD era, Galaxy became inactive although its releases (including the Art Peppers) have gradually been getting reissued in the *Original Jazz Classics* series. —*Scott Yanow*

Gazell

Gazell, which was founded by Dag Haeggqvist in 1950, has been directed by Sam Charters since the 1980s. Closely associated with Storyville and Silkheart, Gazell has some blues and zydeco in its catalog along with jazz ranging from swing to the avant-garde. Among the artists with CDs available are Chet Baker, the Paris Reunion Band, Benny Carter, Dizzy Gillespie, Stan Getz with Chet Baker, Vic Dickenson, Sonny Stitt, Joe Venuti, Dave Burrell, Oliver Lake and Byard Lancaster. —*Scott Yanow*

Gennett

One of the most important labels of the 1920s, Gennett was started in 1917 by the Starr Piano Co. in Richmond, IN. In the early days Gennett concentrated on dance music and it always documented a wide variety of stylists, but it also recorded Ladd's Black Aces (1921), the New Orleans Rhythm Kings (1922-23), King Oliver's Creole Jazz Band (1923), Jelly Roll Morton's first piano solos (1923), Bix Beiderbecke and the Wolverines (1924), Freddie Keppard with Doc Cook, Louis Armstrong with the Red Onion Jazz Babies and Hoagy Carmichael. Although the Gennett label released no further dates after 1930 (other than dance music on its subsidiaries Champion and Superior), its classic recordings have generally been in-print ever since. Many of the more famous sessions have been put out on CD by the Fantasy label. —*Scott Yanow*

Good Time Jazz

Lester Koenig founded the Good Time Jazz label in 1949 to record the Firehouse Five Plus Two. During the next decade, GTJ would be one of the top Dixieland record companies. Koenig, who also ran Contemporary, had perfect taste and his label (which also acquired some earlier performances) featured some of the best records by Bunk Johnson, Kid Ory, Lu Watters Yerba Buena Jazz Band, Turk Murphy and Bob Scobey. In addition, sessions by Jelly Roll Morton, Burt Bales, Paul Lingle, Luckey Roberts, Willie "The Lion" Smith, Wally Rose, the Banjo Kings, Jesse Fuller, George Lewis, Johnny Wiggs, Eddie Pierson, Santo Pecora, Armand Hug, Sharkey Bonano, Paul Barbarin, Bill Mathews, George Girard, the Bay City Jaz Band, Don Ewell, Clancy Hayes, Pete Daily and the Castle Jazz Band were released. Although most of the records came out by 1959, Good Time Jazz stayed active until the Firehouse Five's final date in 1969. Acquired by Fantasy in the early '80s, most of the albums have now been reissued on CD in the *Original Jazz Classics* series, a definitive four CD sampler was issued (*The Good Time Jazz Story*) and a few new sessions (by the Silver Leaf Jazz Band and Scott Black's Hot Horns along with a couple of previously unissued George Lewis dates) have been released. —*Scott Yanow*

Gramavision

Founded by Jonathan Rose in 1979, Gramavision has consistently released challenging music that is not afraid to avoid fitting into any specific category. Among the artists who have recorded stimulating sets for Gramavision are Anthony Davis, John Scofield, Bob Moses, James Newton, Oliver Lake and Jamaaladeen Tacuma. —*Scott Yanow*

Hat Hut/Hat Art

Founded in 1974 by Werner Uehlinger, the Swiss Hat Hut label (which in the 1980s changed its name to Hat Art) has documented quite a bit of challenging music during the past two decades that ranges from hard bop to free improvisations and modern classical music. Starting with a record by Joe McPhee, Hat Art has released numerous projects (most of which are available on CDs) by Steve Lacy, Cecil Taylor, Anthony Braxton, George Gruntz, John Zorn, Mike Westbrook, the Vienna Art Orchestra, Rova and many others plus a series of historic Max Roach duets with Braxton, Taylor and Archie Shepp. —*Scott Yanow*

Heads Up

In 1989 trumpeter David Love formed Heads Up, a small label based in Seattle. Although Dave Liebman and Richie Cole have appeared on some releases, most of Heads Up's artists are not quite as well known, including Kenny Blake, Joe McBride and violist Debbie Spring. The music featured by Heads Up ranges from poppish jazz to straightahead. —*Scott Yanow*

Heart

Under the direction of Tab Bartling, the Austin-based Heart label (and its related company Tafford) has released some fine music by pianist Joe LoCascio, guitarist Erich Avinger, tenorman Tony Campise, singer Carla Helmbrecht and saxophonist Elias Haslanger. —*Scott Yanow*

Hep

The top jazz label based in Scotland, Hep was founded by Alastair Robertson in 1976. Since that time Robertson has reissued classic studio recordings from the 1930s, put out for the first time many valuable radio performances by big bands from the 1940s (starting with a Boyd Raeburn set) and recorded new straighta-head jazz by the likes of Spike Robinson, Jessica Williams, Don Lanphere and Joe Temperley among others. Whether it be Slim Gaillard or Sam Donahue's Navy Band, Hep's releases feature both rare and rewarding music. —*Scott Yanow*

Hindsight

During the late '70s into the '80s the Hindsight label released over one hundred LPs filled with previously unreleased radio transcriptions by swing-era big bands. Among its more notable releases were five albums of Duke Ellington and numer-ous sets from Jimmy Dorsey (including his 1949 "Dorseyland" Band), Harry James (highlighted by his little-known bop orchestra of the late '40s), Artie Shaw, Stan Kenton (six volumes), Woody Herman, Mildred Bailey and some sweet bands. With the emergence of the CD era, Hindsight continued coming out with new material and also combined some of their former releases into box sets including packages featuring the orchestras of Duke Ellington, Harry James and Artie Shaw. —*Scott Yanow*

Horizon

The Horizon label, a jazz subsidiary of A&M run by John Snyder that was only active for two years (1975-77), made a big impression during its short life. The quality of its releases were high, the extensive liner notes and deluxe packaging were impressive and the playing (from such top musicians as Dave Brubeck, Paul Desmond, Jim Hall, the Thad Jones/Mel Lewis Orchestra, Ornette Coleman, Char-lie Haden and Hampton Hawes) was often inspired and memorable. When Snyder left A&M to form his own short-lived label Artists House (which was founded upon the same artistic principles), Horizon became inactive; many of its releases have not yet appeared on CD. —*Scott Yanow*

IAJRC

Short for the International Association of Jazz Educators, the IAJRC's record label came out with around 50 LPs before switching to CDs. Although most of the albums have not yet been reissued in the new format, there have been a dozen valuable CDs thus far. Most of the IAJRC releases deal with prebop music includ-ing historic sets by James Reese Europe, the Chicagoans of the 1920s and territory bands from North Carolina but there have also been CDs of rare material by Lucky Thompson and Oscar Pettiford among others. To acquire the releases of the IAJRC, one has to become a member. Information can be gained by sending an inquiry to P.O. Box 75155, Tampa, FL 33605. —*Scott Yanow*

Improvising Artists

Pianist Paul Bley and artist Carol Goss ran Improvising Artists from 1974 until it folded in the early '80s. Founded with the purpose of documenting music that emphasized improvisation, the label released 20 albums including dates that fea-tured Bley, Bill Connors (on acoustic guitar), Jimmy Giuffre, John Gilmore, Ran Blake, Sam Rivers, Dave Holland, Gary Peacock, Paul Motian, Barry Altschul, Lee Konitz, Jaco Pastorius, Pat Metheny (the latter two on their first recording), Steve Lacy, Sun Ra (two solo piano dates), Mike Nock, Bennie Maupin, Lester Bowie (in duets with Philip Wilson), Marion Brown (dueling with Gunter Hampel), Pete Rob-inson, Michael Gregory Jackson and Oliver Lake. After a period of being out of print, the IAI catalog was leased to Black Saint/Soul Note which has reissued vir-tually all of the music (in reproductions of the LPs) on CD. —*Scott Yanow*

Impulse!

The Impulse label has had several lives. It was founded in 1960 by producer Creed Taylor as a subsidiary of ABC-Paramount. Soon afterwards, Taylor was lured to Verve and Bob Thiele came in as his replacement. With the signing of John Col-trane (who recorded exclusively for the label during 1961-67), Impulse became famous for its avant-garde recordings of such major players as Archie Shepp, Mar-ion Brown, Pharoah Sanders and Albert Ayler. However, Bob Thiele always had wide taste in jazz so there were also sets cut by Art Blakey, Freddie Hubbard, Cole-man Hawkins, Benny Carter, Duke Ellington's sidemen, a Count Basie small

group, Yusef Lateef, Oliver Nelson and McCoy Tyner among others. The Impulse label gradually declined by the early '70s despite fine recordings from Pharoah Sanders, John Klemmer and Keith Jarrett. By the late '70s most of the catalog was out of print but, for a time in the mid-'80s, MCA-Impulse had some new record-ings (most notably by Michael Brecker and Jack DeJohnette) along with reissues. In the 1990s GRP has reissued many deluxe sets of Impulse material on CD in addition to gradually reactivating the label for new releases such as a meeting between McCoy Tyner and Michael Brecker. —*Scott Yanow*

Incus

This English avant-garde label was founded in 1970 by Derek Bailey, Evan Parker and Tony Oxley, three giants of the idiom. Oxley eventually dropped out but Bailey, Parker and their contemporaries documented their activities extensively on Incus during the past quarter-century. —*Scott Yanow*

India Navigation

Founded in the late '70s, India Navigation came out with around 70 releases of explorative music including sets by David Murray, Chico Freeman, Hamiet Bluiett, Arthur Blythe, Anthony Davis, James Newton, Clarinet Summit and Jay Hoggard. Although not that active after the mid-'80s, the label was revived in the 1990s as many of its earlier releases were reissued on CD. —*Scott Yanow*

Inner City

During the decade after it was formed in 1976 by Irv Kratka (as a subsidiary of the MMO Music Group), Inner City issued and repackaged a large amount of jazz LPs in the US. On its Classic Jazz division prebop music (much of it taken from the European Black & Blue label) was made available domestically, while the main Inner City label ranged from bop (including music licensed from Steeple Chase, Enja and East Wind) and the avant-garde to fusion and crossover. Inner City also distributed the Choice label. Overall Inner City was responsible for the release of around 200 records before it became inactive in the mid-'80s. While the Choice, Enja and Steeple Chase releases have been reissued on CD by the parent compa-nies, Inner City's own output remains out of print. —*Scott Yanow*

JVC

One of the top Japanese record labels, JVC licensed their jazz recordings to GRP during 1987-90. In 1991 they opened their own US offices and started making their releases available domestically. Among the more interesting artists in their jazz catalog are Ernie Watts, Frank Gambale, Special EFX, Jimmy Rowles, Gary Burton and Bill Holman. —*Scott Yanow*

Jazz Alliance

Started in the early '90s as a subsidiary label of Concord that would be involved primarily in reissuing worthy material from obscure small labels, within a few years Jazz Alliance became best-known for its *Piano Jazz* series of CDs that issue some of the best of Marian McPartland's famed radio shows. On each program McPartland interviews a jazz great (usually but not always a pianist) and plays duets with him or her. The Bill Evans show is best known but there have also been over 30 other releases to date and hundreds to choose from. —*Scott Yanow*

Jazz Crusade

Trombonist Big Bill Bissonnette, who ran the Jazz Crusade label in the 1960s in addition to booking tours for ancient New Orleans jazz veterans, returned to music in 1992 with the release of his memoirs and revival of his label (both titled "The Jazz Crusade"). Thus far Bissonnette has released music by a variety of recent New Orleans revival groups (including a series of British musicians) plus older performances from Kid Sheik Cola, Ken Colyer, Capt. John Handy, Wilbur DeParis and the Harlem Hamfats. —*Scott Yanow*

Jazz Focus

Started by Philip Barker in the early '90s, the Jazz Focus label's first ten releases include five by the brilliant pianist Jessica Williams and one apiece from Leroy Vinnegar, Kent Sangster, George Robert, Dado Moroni and Brian Buchanan. The emphasis on Jazz Focus is on advanced straightahead jazz and the Jessica Will-iams sets in particular are quite rewarding. —*Scott Yanow*

Jazz Inspiration

Founded in 1991 by Arnold Schwisberg, Jazz Inspiration out of Canada released 25 albums during its first five years. Its music ranges from the cool-toned bop of Lorne Lofsky and the Wes Montgomery-inspired guitarist Dawn Thomson to the fusion group 5 After 4, some crossover dates, sessions by the versatile Stan

Samole and work from pianist Brian Dickinson and swing violinist Lenny Solomon. — *Scott Yanow*

Jazzology

George Buck made his debut as a record producer by recording clarinetist Tony Parenti (with Wild Bill Davison) in 1949 for his new Jazzology label. Buck did not record his second album for another five years and at first concentrated on his New Orleans-oriented GHB label but eventually activated Jazzology as a Chicago jazz company (there was some overlapping with other subsidiaries). Its catalog contains many CDs from Wild Bill Davison and Art Hodes plus releases by the Original Salt City Six, the Lawson-Haggart Band, Kenny Davern, Jack Teagarden, Judy Carmichael, Marty Grosz, Randy Sandke, Bob Wilber and many others, in addition to all of the Eddie Condon Town Hall Concerts (on double-CDs). Jazzology Press has started to publish jazz books, sometimes (as with Muggsy Spanier's *The Lonesome Road*) with an enclosed CD included. — *Scott Yanow*

Justice

Founded by Randall Jamail in 1990, Justice Records made a strong impression during its first two years, particularly with its releases by Herb Ellis, Emily Remler, pianist Dave Catney, singer Nancy King and drummer Sebastian Whittaker. It has remained active but with a lower profile since that time. — *Scott Yanow*

Justin Time

Justin Time, which was founded by Jim West, started in 1983 with a release from Oliver Jones. The Canadian label now has over 75 CDs in its catalog including sets by Jeri Brown, Sonny Greenwich, John Abercrombie, the Denny Christiansen Big Band, Fraser MacPherson, Pat LaBarbera, Paul Bley, Diana Krall (her debut), Herbie Spanier and many from Oliver Jones. In addition, Justin Time has a "Just a Memory" subsidiary of live performances by jazz and blues artists taken from Montreal's Rising Sun club. — *Scott Yanow*

K2B2

This small Los Angeles-based company has documented some rather memorable sets by bassist Buell Neidlinger and tenor-saxophonist Marty Krystall since its formation in the 1980s. In addition to featuring such overlapping groups in its catalog as Krystall Klear and the Buells, Swingrass and Thelonious, the K2B2 label released an imaginative tribute to Herbie Nichols in 1995. — *Scott Yanow*

Keynote

Although Keynote (which was founded by Eric Bernay) was primarily a folk music label during 1940-42, when Harry Lim took it over, it became a very significant jazz record company. During 1943-46 Lim recorded an enormous amount of material, most of it with the who's who of small-group swing. Bad luck with pressing plants and bad business decisions resulted in the label being sold to Mercury in 1948. Other than a short revival in 1955, Keynote slipped into history. However, a massive 21-LP set was released by Polygram in 1986 that reissued every one of the Keynote recordings including 115 previously unreleased tracks. The box shows just how much Harry Lim knew his stuff for there are classic sessions by the likes of Lester Young, Dinah Washington, Roy Eldridge, Coleman Hawkins, Cozy Cole, the Kansas City Seven, Charlie Shavers, Rex Stewart, Red Norvo, Jonah Jones, Willie Smith, Chubby Jackson, Bill Harris, Bud Freeman, Benny Carter, Red Rodney and Lennie Tristano, among many others. Although the definitive LP box quickly went out of print, much of this timeless material has been repackaged in smaller CD packages by Polygram since then. — *Scott Yanow*

Knitting Factory Works

The Knitting Factory has been the Minton's Playhouse of the 1990s, a venue that has a very open-minded attitude and encourages adventurous musicians to stretch themselves and create previously unheard sounds. A *Live at the Knitting Factory* series on A&M was soon followed by the establishment of the Knitting Factory label in 1991 by Michael Dorf. Within two years Knitting Factory Works had released over 50 albums of avant-garde jazz and rock; by 1995 the number was over 100. Among the artists heard on the label are Charles Gayle, John Zorn, Thomas Chapin, Prima Materia, the Jazz Passengers, Anthony Braxton, Don Byron, Mark Dresser, Roscoe Mitchell, Marilyn Crispell and many others. — *Scott Yanow*

Koch Jazz

Koch, a major distributor whose jazz director is Donald Elfman, in 1995 began releasing jazz recordings of its own. Among its sets have been dates by tenor saxophonist Bruce Eskovitz, singer Trudy Desmond and tenorman Ernie Krivda. In addition, Koch has been reissuing long out-of-print dates including sessions from

the Columbia and Epic catalogs by Johnny Coles, Carol Sloane, John Handy and Dave McKenna. — *Scott Yanow*

Kokopelli

Founded by flutist Herbie Mann and Jim Geisler in 1994, Kokopelli made a strong impression from the start with releases by Jimmy Rowles, David Newman, the Dutch Jazz Orchestra (previously unknown Billy Strayhorn compositions), Trio Da Paz and from Mann himself. — *Scott Yanow*

Landmark

Landmark was founded by Orrin Keepnews in 1985. During its first few years it was distributed by Fantasy although later on its catalog has been handled by Muse. Landmark's releases reflect Keepnews' musical tastes with the emphasis on creative straightahead jazz and such artists are represented in Landmark's catalog as Bobby Hutcherson, Mulgrew Miller, Buddy Montgomery, Jimmy Heath, Vincent Herring, Elvin Jones and Ralph Moore. — *Scott Yanow*

LaserLight

LaserLight, which is part of Delta Music, has released quite a few budget-priced CDs of music dating from the 1930s up to the '70s and has occasionally recorded new music (including a Joe Pass Christmas jazz set). Unfortunately the label often does not furnish much recording data and its releases sometimes mix together rare and common performances. However, with a bit of research (and by using this guide!), one can figure out which CDs are of greatest interest. LaserLight's five-CD Nat King Cole set is a highlight of its large catalog. — *Scott Yanow*

Leo

Leo Feigin emigrated to England from the USSR in 1973 and in 1980 started Leo Records. Most important among Leo's early releases were sets smuggled out from the USSR of the Ganelin Trio, an innovative avant-garde group. Over time Leo has been one of the most significant labels in documenting adventurous musicians from Eastern Europe in addition to sets from better-known players such as Anthony Braxton, Marilyn Crispell and Cecil Taylor. In 1994 Leo started a subsidiary, Leo Lab, which showcases particularly obscure but talented avant-garde players. — *Scott Yanow*

Limelight

In the 1950s Mercury Records had EmArcy as its jazz subsidiary. In 1962 Limelight took EmArcy's place and its albums often featured expensive packaging. The label was only active for four years but in its time it had recordings from the likes of Dizzy Gillespie, Art Blakey, Rahsaan Roland Kirk, Gerry Mulligan and Oscar Peterson. Some of the releases were reissued in the 1970s by Trip and by Polygram on CD in the 1990s but many remain out of print. — *Scott Yanow*

MCA

Long an industry giant, MCA became significant in the jazz world when it purchased Decca in 1959. Since that time it has had several generally short-lived Decca reissue programs. In the 1980s MCA acquired both Impulse and GRP and has fortunately allowed its subsidiaries to both record new music and reissue many albums from its valuable catalogs. — *Scott Yanow*

Mainstream

Founded in the 1960s, the Mainstream label was run by its founder Bob Shad who had previously produced records for Savoy and Mercury/EmArcy. Although there were sessions leased from other labels, most of Mainstream's output consisted of new jazz dates. One classic (Sarah Vaughan *Live in Japan*) resulted along with many other albums (some of which were a bit commercial) including sessions by Blue Mitchell, Curtis Fuller, Carmen McRae, Harold Land, Maynard Ferguson, Frank Foster's Loud Minority and Leonard Feather' Night Blooming Jazzmen. The catalog went out of print by the late '70s but some of the titles were reissued on CD in the early '90s by Tamara Shad. — *Scott Yanow*

MAMA Foundation

Founded in 1992 by Gene Cerwinski, head of the Cerwin-Vega Corporation, the MAMA Foundation is a non-profit corporation dedicated to documenting jazz that might otherwise be lost forever. Its most ambitious effort was documenting highlights from the 50th anniversary Stan Kenton reunion billed as *Back to Balboa*. Other projects have included a Gerald Wilson spoken-word release and recordings from Wilson, Dave Mackay, Andy Simpkins, Bob Florence, Terry Trotter and the B Sharp Quartet. — *Scott Yanow*

Mapleshade

Pierre Sprey (starting in 1989) began recording jazz artists for his Mapleshade label at his studio in Upper Marlboro, Maryland. Since that time he has released significant albums by Walter Davis, Jr. (a solo set of Thelonious Monk tunes), Clifford Jordan, Sunnyland Slim, Leon Thomas, Eddie Gale, Norris Turney and Hamiet Bluiett, among others. —*Scott Yanow*

Maya Recordings

This English label has primarily been releasing very adventurous sets featuring bassist Barry Guy, sometimes in small groups with saxophonist Evan Parker, and on other occasions as leader of the London Composers' Orchestra. —*Scott Yanow*

Memphis Archives

Inside Sounds, a Memphis-based label that documents local music (particularly the blues), was founded in 1991 by Eddie Dattel. In 1994 Richard Hite started working with its subsidiary Memphis Archives in reissuing vintage jazz and blues from his valuable record collection. Most of the sets have been compilations but there have been CDs of Art Tatum's 1940 radio broadcasts, Jack Teagarden's historic performance at the 1963 Monterey Jazz Festival, a W.C. Handy album (dating from 1917-22) and a highly recommended two-CD set of a *Saturday Night Swing* club radio broadcast from the late '30s. —*Scott Yanow*

Mercury

Founded in 1945, Mercury was a major force in music for 25 years. In its early days it recorded such jazz artists as Erroll Garner, Gene Ammons, Albert Ammons, Eddie "Cleanhead" Vinson, Cootie Williams, Helen Humes and its biggest seller, Dinah Washington. By 1954 Mercury was releasing most of its jazz on its subsidiary EmArcy (which was succeeded by Limelight during 1962-66) but there was a certain amount of overlapping. Quincy Jones was an important executive at Mercury during 1956-66 and such artists as Cannonball Adderley, Buddy Rich, Sarah Vaughan and Ernestine Anderson had releases on the Mercury label. After being acquired by Polydor in the early '70s, Mercury's catalog was transferred to Polygram where some of the bigger name releases have since been reissued on CD. —*Scott Yanow*

Merry Makers

Run by Ted Shafer, the Merry Makers Record Company primarily features music from San Francisco-style trad bands including concert performances by Lu Watters' Yerba Buena Jazz Band, Turk Murphy, the South 'Frisco Jazz Band, Don Neely's Royal Society Jazz Orchestra and Ted Shafer's own Jelly Roll Jazz Band. —*Scott Yanow*

Messidor

Messidor is one of the top Latin labels in the world, particularly renowned for its Cuban jazz albums. Founded by Gotz Worner in Germany in 1980, the company has featured recordings by Astor Piazzolla, Paquito D'Rivera, Gonzalo Rubalcaba, Chucho Valdes of Irakere and Mario Bauza's Orchestra, among others. Messidor has been distributed domestically by Rounder since the early '90s. —*Scott Yanow*

Metronome

During the 1949-65 period, Metronome was among the most important of the Swedish jazz labels. Metronome did an excellent job of documenting such top Swedish players as Arne Domnerus, Lars Gullin, Bengt Hallberg, Rolf Ericson and singer Alice Babs in addition to such visitors as Zoot Sims and Toots Thielemans. —*Scott Yanow*

Milestone

Milestone has been such a familiar name in jazz that it is surprising to realize that it was only an independent label for six years. Founded in 1966 by Orrin Keepnews (former head of Riverside) and pianist Dick Katz, Milestone was acquired by Audio Fidelity in 1972 and Fantasy the following year but continued recording new sessions into the 1980s. Among the artists who have had significant dates for Milestone have been Lee Konitz, Joe Henderson (whose total output for the label has been reissued on an eight-CD box set), Sonny Rollins, McCoy Tyner and Flora Purim. In the late '70s with the start of Fantasy's reissue series of two-fers, both Milestone and Riverside sessions reappeared on Milestone two-LP sets. In the CD era many of the Milestone dates have been reissued in the *Original Jazz Classics* series. Milestone was reactivated in 1995 to record new Latin jazz-oriented sessions. —*Scott Yanow*

Minor Music

Although based in Koln, Germany, Stephan Meyner's Minor Music label has chiefly emphasized American jazzmen and women since the company's formation in the 1980s. Its CDs have deluxe gatefold covers (reminiscent of Impulse in the 1960s) and among his artists have been Maceo Parker, Fred Wesley, Pee Wee Ellis, Larry Goldings, Geri Allen, Cassandra Wilson (in the 1980s), Three of a Kind and German trumpeter Till Bronner. —*Scott Yanow*

Mobile Fidelity

Founded in 1977 and run since 1979 by Herb Belkin, Mobile Fidelity is an audiophile reissue label that has brought back gems from several idioms of music. Mobile Fidelity switched from LPs to CDs in 1984 although it still reissues music occasionally on LPs. Leasing music from other labels, it has reissued such classics as John Coltrane's *Blue Train* and *Giant Steps*, Cannonball Adderley's *Something Else* and *Getz/Gilberto*. —*Scott Yanow*

MoJazz

Motown, the most successful Black-owned record label, virtually ignored jazz until establishing its MoJazz subsidiary in 1994. Founded by Steve McKeever, the MoJazz label has had releases by Eric Reed, Norman Brown, Terre Sul and Foley, and a few reissues of rare material from the Crusaders, Monk Montgomery, Ahmad Jamal and Billy Eckstine, but thus far the label has been on the commercial side and has not lived up to its initial potential. —*Scott Yanow*

Monarch

In 1994 Steve and Ted Hall founded Monarch, a small San Francisco-based label which has since had releases from (among others) trumpeter Dmitri Matheny, pianists Cedar Walton, Mark Little and Patrick Polomo, a quartet co-led by trumpeter Tom Peron and drummer Bud Spangler and a date by guitarist Mimi Fox. —*Scott Yanow*

Mons

When drummer Thilo Berg could not find an outlet for his big-band recording, he started his own label in Germany in 1991. Mons has since averaged around eight records a year including sets by Clark Terry, tenorman Don Braden, trumpeter Bobby Shew, altoist George Robert, singer Barbara Morrison, trombonists Mark Nightingale and Jiggs Whigham and singer Allan Harris along with the Thilo Berg Big Band. —*Scott Yanow*

Mosaic

In 1983 Michael Cuscuna and Charles Laurie founded Mosaic as a mail order reissue label that would correct historical oversights, bringing back material (along with previously unissued recordings) and repackaging it in coherent fashion. In the years since, Mosaic's box sets (on both LP and CD) have set the standard in jazz and there is simply no other reissue label on their level. Virtually all of their releases (which are unfortunately limited-edition) are definitive and should be grabbed while they are in print. Among their most rewarding sets have been boxes dedicated to Gerry Mulligan/Chet Baker, Maynard Ferguson on Roulette, Tina Brooks, two on Chet Baker, T-Bone Walker, Charles Mingus, an 18-CD collection of the Nat King Cole Trio, Jimmy Smith, Art Blakey in 1960, Eddie Condon in the 1950s, the Thad Jones/Mel Lewis big band, Larry Young, Serge Chaloff, Louis Armstrong on Decca in the 1950s, two large Count Basie Roulette sets, two Stan Kenton boxes, the Buck Clayton Jam Sessions, Herbie Nichols, Buddy DeFranco, Sidney Bechet, Thelonious Monk, Shorty Rogers, Freddie Redd, George Lewis, Stan Getz/Jimmy Raney, Phil Woods, Andrew Hill, Illinois Jacquet, Lee Morgan and Duke Ellington on Capitol among others. The most remarkable series of all was the complete Commodore Jazz Recordings, three boxes totaling 66 LPs! All in all, Mosaic is a jazz collector's dream. —*Scott Yanow*

Muse

Founded in 1972 by Joe Fields, Muse has been one of the top independent jazz labels ever since, with a catalog that spans the full breadth of the modern mainstream, sometimes bordering on the avant-garde or fusion without losing its emphasis on the straightahead. Its large catalog is highlighted by releases from Pepper Adams, Cindy Blackman, Donald Brown, Richie Cole (some of his finest work), Larry Coryell, Sonny Criss, Charles Earland, Ricky Ford, Buck Hill, Jay Hoggard, Groove Holmes, Willis Jackson, Etta Jones, Sheila Jordan, Pat Martino, Jack McDuff, Mark Murphy, Houston Person, Wallace Roney, Woody Shaw, James Spaulding, Sonny Stitt, Jack Walrath and Cedar Walton. —*Scott Yanow*

Music & Arts

Founded in 1988, the Music & Arts label (under the direction of Fred Maroth) has very quietly been releasing some of the most interesting jazz CDs of the past decade. Not only does this label have stimulating works from such avant-gardists as Anthony Braxton, Marilyn Crispell, Reggie Workman, Andrew Cyrille, Paul Plimley, Julius Hemphill, Oliver Lake and Ran Blake but historically significant sets by Art Hodes, Duke Ellington, Nat King Cole, Stan Kenton, Count Basie and Art Tatum. —*Scott Yanow*

Music Masters

Music Masters started out in the early '80s as primarily a classical label but has shifted gradually towards jazz in the years since. Among its most impressive releases have been the Benny Goodman Yale Collection (taken from tapes left by the clarinetist to the Yale library and now numbering over ten CDs), and releases by Artie Shaw (of his 1954 Gramercy Five and late '40s boppish big band), Benny Carter, Duke Ellington (previously unreleased concert performances), Stanley Turrentine, Freddie Hubbard, Louis Bellson, Jim Hall and Dave Brubeck. —*Scott Yanow*

Musicraft

Founded in 1937, Musicraft was primarily a classical label until 1941 and recorded very little jazz until producer Albert Marx became the label's artistic director in 1944. During the next five years, Musicraft became an important independent jazz label, purchasing the Guild label and making it available in addition to recording significant work by Sarah Vaughan, Teddy Wilson, Georgie Auld, Artie Shaw, Duke Ellington and Dizzy Gillespie. After being sold in the early '50s, Musicraft became a lost label with its recordings being only erratically reissued for decades. However, Albert Marx in the late '70s revived Musicraft as a reissue subsidiary of Discovery and repackaged much of the material on LPs. In the 1990s some of the records were reissued on CDs. —*Scott Yanow*

NYC Records

Founded in 1992 by vibraphonist Mike Mainieri, NYC has not only given him an outlet for his records and for his group Steps Ahead, but has released recordings from other jazz-based musicians including Zachary Breaux, Rachel Z, Marc Antoine and Philip DeGruy. —*Scott Yanow*

Nessa

Started in 1967 by Chuck Nessa, this small label is primarily significant for its early documents of AACM players including the Art Ensemble of Chicago (a comprehensive five-CD set of its earliest performances was put out in the mid-'90s), Lester Bowie, Roscoe Mitchell, John Stevens and in the late '70s Warne Marsh and Von Freeman. It has been inactive (except for the Art Ensemble set) ever since. —*Scott Yanow*

New Artists

Formed in the late '70s by some of Lennie Tristano's former students, New Artists keeps the legacy of Tristano's music alive by documenting the playing of some musicians who learned from his example. Featured on the label's CDs (which tend to have brief playing time and very scanty liner notes) are pianists Connie Crothers, Liz Gorrill, and Michael Levy, altoist Richard Tabnik, guitarist Andy Fite, singer Bob Casanova and the tenors of Charley Krachy and Lenny Popkin. In addition, a set of Dick Twardzik performances from 1954 were released for the first time by New Artists. —*Scott Yanow*

New World

New World, a label with a diverse catalog that includes a wide variety of classical music, some opera and folk music, has long had a few jazz releases including dates by Roy Eldridge, Earl Hines, Steve Kuhn, Buddy Tate, Cecil Taylor and Jay McShann. In the early '90s a *CounterCurrents* series began that put the emphasis on avant-garde composer-oriented jazz. Recent releases (mostly in this series) include the New York Composer's Orchestra, Bob Nell, Mario Pavone, the Kamikaze Ground Crew, Richard Abrams, the Jazz Passengers, Tom Varner, Ned Rothenberg, Joey Baron, Robert Dick, Dave Douglas, Jerome Harris, Ed Jackson, George Lewis and Marty Ehrlich. In 1995 a ten-CD set of Butch Morris' "Conductions" was released. —*Scott Yanow*

Nine Winds

Started by Vinny Golia in 1977 and named after the number of woodwinds that he played at the time (a total that has more than doubled since), Nine Winds is an L.A.-based label that documents the local avant-garde jazz scene. Starting out with

a few Golia releases (in settings ranging from unaccompanied solos to his huge big band), the label has since expanded to include music by many top players including Wayne Peet, John Rapson, John Fumo, Bert Wilson, Kim Richmond, the New Orchestra Workshop, Paul Plimley, Joe Sellers, Brad Dutz, Big World, Dick Berk, Tadd Weed, Rob Blakeslee and many others. —*Scott Yanow*

OKeh

The OKeh label will always be best-remembered for issuing the classic Louis Armstrong Hot Five and Hot Seven records in the 1920s. Its first releases actually took place in 1918 (the New Orleans Jazz Band) and in 1920 the very first blues record (Mamie Smith's "Crazy Blues") appeared on OKeh. Within a couple years with Clarence Williams and Richard M. Jones as important talent scouts, OKeh had the top "race" catalog. King Oliver's Creole Jazz Band, Frankie Trumbauer (with Bix Beiderbecke) and Bennie Moten were only a few of the important jazz names who recorded for OKeh in the 1920s. Although acquired by Columbia in 1926, OKeh remained active until 1934. However, in 1938 OKeh was revived and a lot of swing (and in the 1950s, rhythm & blues) appeared on the label until the end of the 78 era when it was discontinued. —*Scott Yanow*

Original Jazz Classics

In the mid-'80s the Fantasy label began the Original Jazz Classics, reissuing a countless number of former LPs from the Prestige, Milestone, Riverside, Contemporary, Fantasy, Good Time Jazz, Galaxy, Debut, Moodsville, New Jazz, Swingville, Jazzland, Specialty and Pablo catalogs. The program (which also includes a subsidiary "limited edition" series) has accelerated since CDs took over and there are now around 1,000 reissues currently in print in what must be the world's largest jazz catalog. A similar Original Blues Classics series has also brought back many blues albums from these labels. —*Scott Yanow*

Owl

Founded in 1975 by Jean-Jacques Pussiau, this French jazz label has released quite a few fine albums during the past couple of decades including some from such players as Michel Petrucciani (some of his earliest recordings), Martial Solal and Stephane Grappelli. —*Scott Yanow*

PM

Founded by bassist Gene Perla in 1973, the PM label had a variety of fine releases during the last years of the LP era. Among the highlights of its catalog were dates featuring Elvin Jones, David Liebman, Steve Grossman, Bernie Senensky, Pat LaBarbera, Ed Bickert, Sonny Greenwich, Kathryn Moses, the fine vocal group Bug Alley and Perla himself. —*Scott Yanow*

Pablo

Norman Granz, who had run the Verve label until selling it in the late '50s, returned fulltime to recording the music he loved when he started the Pablo label (named after Pablo Picasso) in 1973. He signed up many of the alumni from the Verve days (including Ella Fitzgerald, Oscar Peterson, Count Basie, Dizzy Gillespie and Roy Eldridge) along with such swinging all-stars as Zoot Sims, Eddie "Lockjaw" Davis, Harry "Sweets" Edison, Milt Jackson, Benny Carter, Clark Terry and Joe Pass, recording them extensively in jam session-type settings. Among Granz's more ambitious projects were teaming Oscar Peterson on duet sessions with five different trumpeters, virtually taking over the 1977 and 1979 Montreux Jazz Festivals (recording and releasing nearly all of the music) and acquiring and reissuing all of his Art Tatum recordings of the 1950s; he also put out some historic concert recordings. By the early '80s the number of releases slowed down drastically due to Granz's erratic health and in 1987 he sold the Pablo label to Fantasy. Fortunately nearly all of the Pablo recordings have been reissued on CD, often in the *Original Jazz Classics* series. —*Scott Yanow*

Pacific Jazz

Pacific Jazz was founded in 1952 by Richard Bock and Roy Harte; Bock eventually became the sole owner. The label debuted with the first recordings of the Gerry Mulligan/Chet Baker pianoless quartet and soon was documenting the best in West Coast "cool" jazz. Among the musicians who were featured on the Pacific Jazz label were Chet Baker, the Chico Hamilton Quintet, Art Pepper, Wes Montgomery, Les McCann, Joe Pass, Richard "Groove" Holmes, Don Ellis and the Jazz Crusaders among many others. In 1958 Bock started the subsidiary World Pacific to record musicians such as sitarist Ravi Shankar who fell outside of jazz although some jazz was also released under that banner. In 1965 Bock sold Pacific Jazz to Liberty; its catalog was later acquired by Capitol which has reissued some of the music on CD in the 1990s. —*Scott Yanow*

Palmetto

Founded in 1991 by Matt Balitsaris, Palmetto has expanded from its fusion beginnings into more adventurous music. Its releases include music from C'Est What, Loose Shoes, organist Greg Hatza, pianist Steve Million and drummer Matt Wilson (with tenor great Dewey Redman). —*Scott Yanow*

Palo Alto

The Palo Alto label made a strong impression during its short existence. Founded in 1981 by Jim Benham, it operated in Palo Alto, California, under the direction of jazz educator Herb Wong; among its top sellers were Richie Cole (who had four fine albums) and there was an ambitious multi-artist tribute to pianist Bill Evans. But after Wong left the label in 1985, it essentially closed down. Most of its releases have not yet shown up on CD. —*Scott Yanow*

Parkwood

Started by Hugh Leal around 1983, the Parkwood label has had less than 20 releases to date but all are excellent examples of small-group swing. Among Parkwood's better sets are several featuring the great trumpeter Doc Cheatham, a duet date by Bob Wilber and Dick Welstood, records by Art Hodes and pianist Johnny O'Neal and a set of duets featuring Sammy Price. —*Scott Yanow*

Phontastic

The Phontastic label has long been one of the top Swedish jazz record companies with a huge catalog featuring such players as Arne Domnerus, Ove Lind, Ulf Johansson, Bengt Hallberg and Putte Wickman. In addition, Phontastic has put out an extensive series of Benny Goodman alternate takes from the 1940s, sets from Count Basie, Artie Shaw and Lester Young and appearances in Sweden by such Americans as Joe Newman, Tommy Flanagan, Bob Wilber, Ruby Braff and Scott Hamilton. —*Scott Yanow*

Postcards

Formed in May 1993, Postcards (under the direction of saxophonist Ralph Simon, who acts as its director of A&R and producer) has quickly emerged as a top post bop and avant-garde jazz label. Its early releases include an electric date by Paul Bley, duets by Gary Peacock and Bill Frisell, a Reggie Workman-led all-star session and albums by pianist Alan Pasqua, drummer Chip White and Simon. —*Scott Yanow*

Prestige

Founded by producer Bob Weinstock in 1949, Prestige in the 1950s recorded an extensive series of bop-oriented sessions, many of which were essentially jam sessions. Among Prestige's top artists were Miles Davis, John Coltrane, Gene Ammons, Sonny Stitt, Thelonious Monk, Stan Getz, Sonny Rollins, Mal Waldron, Jackie McLean, Donald Byrd, Lee Konitz, Wardell Gray, Elmo Hope, James Moody, Art Farmer, Phil Woods, Red Garland, Coleman Hawkins, Eddie "Lockjaw" Davis and Yusef Lateef. In the 1960s Prestige for a time had a mainstream label (Swingville), a mood music subsidiary (Moodsville) and recorded some blues artists on Bluesville. Later in the 1960s Prestige kept alive by releasing many soul jazz sets featuring organists such as Jack McDuff, Groove Holmes and Shirley Scott. In 1971 Prestige was acquired by Fantasy although it continued recording new music for most of the decade. Eventually the Prestige name was mostly used for a series of two-LP reissues and in the 1980s and '90s many of its sessions have been reissued on CD as part of Fantasy's *Original Jazz Classics* series. —*Scott Yanow*

Private Music

Although not exclusively a jazz label, Private Music in the 1990s released interesting sets by Toots Thielemans (two albums with his "Brazil Project") and singer Kenny Rankin (performing standards). —*Scott Yanow*

Progressive

The Progressive label has had three lives. Founded by Gus Statiras in 1950, Progressive had a few bop-oriented sessions in the early '50s (best-known were sets by Al Cohn and George Wallington) before becoming inactive. Its releases were acquired by Savoy and Prestige. In the late '70s Statiras brought back the label and recorded many new sessions including albums by Lee Konitz, Derek Smith, Hank Jones, Buddy DeFranco, Al Haig, Scott Hamilton, Roland Hanna, Arnett Cobb and Tommy Flanagan. The rise of CDs happened at the same time that Progressive ceased operations, but by the late '80s George Buck had acquired and added Progressive (still under Gus Statiras' direction) to its stable of labels along with G.H.B. and Jazzology, among others. Progressive has continued recording new sessions

(usually bop-oriented) on an occasional basis up until the present time in addition to making many of its earlier dates available on CD. —*Scott Yanow*

Pumpkin

Run by the late Robert Hilbert during the late '70s until the end of the LP era, the Pumpkin label released around a dozen mainstream and prebop albums of rare and often previously unreleased material. Among its albums were dates featuring Sidney Bechet, two records from pianist Donald Lambert, Coleman Hawkins with Earl Hines, Jack Teagarden, Roy Eldridge with Richie Kamuca, Zoot Sims and Wild Bill Davison. As of this writing these valuable collector's items remain out of print. —*Scott Yanow*

Qwest

Although Quincy Jones has not recorded any jazz of his own since the early '70s (being content to be a pop producer), his Qwest label (which became associated with Warner Bros. in the early '90s) has been responsible for important albums by several jazz artists including Milt Jackson, Ernestine Anderson and (best of all) Sonny Simmons. —*Scott Yanow*

RCA Victor

Known originally as Victor or the Victor Talking Machine Co. (until it was acquired by RCA in 1929), this veteran label was established by Eldridge Johnson in 1901. Victor pioneered jazz-oriented music by recording James Reese Europe during 1913-14 and releasing hit records by the Original Dixieland Jazz Band in 1917, but it was never strictly a jazz label. Victor did record a great deal of significant music during 1926-32 including sessions by Jelly Roll Morton, Duke Ellington, Bennie Moten, King Oliver and McKinney's Cotton Pickers. It was a potent force during the swing era (extensively recording Benny Goodman, Duke Ellington, Charlie Garnet, Glenn Miller, Fats Waller, Sidney Bechet, Artie Shaw and Tommy Dorsey among others) although a bit slow to document bop. Throughout the decades RCA has had brief jazz programs, which, usually due to lack of interest by the executives or lack of sales (or both), have been short-lived. The same goes for its many reissue programs, which include the highly-rated Vintage series in the 1960s and the two-fer Bluebirds of the '70s. In the 1990s under the direction of its Japanese owners at BMG, the Bluebird series was revived for CD reissues, the subsidiary Novus began to release challenging new music and the RCA name was used for both crossover releases and an "introduction to jazz" series. Also RCA was releasing music from the Vogue catalog (1950s jazz) and distributing ECM. —*Scott Yanow*

RAM

The Italian RAM label, founded in the early '90s, has thus far featured a variety of top modern postbop players, often in intimate settings. Guitarist Joe Diorio (who is otherwise under-recorded) is on many of the dates and other major improvisers include trumpeter Claudio Fasoli, guitarist Mick Goodrick and trombonist Hal Crook. —*Scott Yanow*

Red

The European Red label has documented many top American and European jazz musicians since the 1980s. Among the artists who have been featured on Red's releases (which now number over 200) are Steve Lacy, Julius Hemphill, Phil Woods, Woody Shaw, Steve Grossman, Bob Berg, Bobby Watson, Chet Baker, Sphere, Joe Henderson, Dave Liebman, Cedar Walton, Black Note, Jerry Bergonzi and many others. —*Scott Yanow*

Red Baron

From 1991 until his death in 1995, producer Bob Thiele ran Red Baron, the last of his many labels (and a direct successor to Flying Dutchman and Doctor Jazz). Among his releases on Red Baron were some unknown Duke Ellington performances, a McCoy Tyner set, a couple of albums from the Bob Thiele Collective (featuring players such as David Murray and Red Rodney) and several jazz projects for his wife, singer Teresa Brewer. —*Scott Yanow*

Reference

Run by its president J. Tamblyn Henderson since the 1980s, Reference is best-known as a classical label but it has had several notable jazz releases, especially by Dick Hyman and Mike Garson. —*Scott Yanow*

Reservoir

Founded in 1987 by Mark Feldman, Reservoir has become one of the top modern hard bop jazz labels around. Among the artists who have led dates for Reservoir have been Nick Brignola, Valery Ponomarev, Rob Schneiderman, Dick Berk, Peter Leitch, Ralph Moore, Kenny Barron, Claudio Roditi and Dick Katz. —*Scott Yanow*

Rhino

A major reissue label of a wide variety of musical styles since the 1970s, Rhino has worked closely with the Atlantic catalog since the late '80s, coming out with two-CD compilations of some of Atlantic's top jazz stars of the 1960s, remarkable box sets of John Coltrane and Ornette Coleman (reissuing their complete Atlantic output), some straight reproductions of earlier LPs and more general samplers drawn from many labels. —*Scott Yanow*

Riverside

During its decade (1953-63), Riverside was one of the top independent jazz labels. Co-founded by Bill Grauer and Orrin Keepnews, Riverside began by leasing vintage recordings from 1920s labels. In 1954 it started recording modern jazz and among the artists who benefited from the label's creative approach to documenting their musicians were Thelonious Monk, Bill Evans, Cannonball Adderley, Wes Montgomery (all four of whom recorded some of their very best material for the label), Sonny Rollins, Johnny Griffin, Jimmy Heath, Barry Harris, Bobby Timmons, Randy Weston, Coleman Hawkins, Abbey Lincoln, Benny Golson, Blue Mitchell, Nat Adderley, Clark Terry, Yusef Lateef, Sam Jones, George Russell and Milt Jackson. Riverside had a subsidiary (Jazzland) and a revival series (*The Living Legends*) but after Grauer's death in December 1963 the label went bankrupt. Acquired eventually by Fantasy, many of the top Riverside sessions were reissued on two-LP sets in the 1970s (usually by Milestone) and have been included in the *Original Jazz Classics* CD reissue series of the 1980s and '90s. —*Scott Yanow*

Rosetta

Rosetta Reitz founded the Rosetta label in 1980 as a way of putting the focus on the contributions of female jazz musicians who have been largely left out of history books. She released around 20 LPs of vintage jazz and blues, mostly compilations dealing with specific subject matter but also retrospectives of the International Sweethearts of Rhythm, trumpeter Valaida Snow, Dinah Washington and even Mae West. Very much a one-woman operation, these albums (none of which have been reissued on CD yet) have extensive liner notes written by Rosetta Reitz and are well worth searching for. —*Scott Yanow*

Roulette

Morris Levy was the head of a group of directors who founded Roulette in 1957. In addition to pop music and middle-of-the-road vocalists, Roulette had a pretty extensive jazz catalog, particularly in their *Birdland* series. Count Basie recorded for the label for five years and the roster also included Joe Williams, Maynard Ferguson, Sarah Vaughan, Dinah Washington and Randy Weston among others. Roulette became less active in the 1970s although there were new sessions by Art Blakey, Betty Carter and Lee Konitz. Its catalog has since been acquired by EMI and some of the highlights have been reissued on CD in a series headed by Michael Cuscuna. In addition, Mosaic leased all of the Count Basie studio and concert performances in the 1990s and put out two huge boxes that are unbeatable. —*Scott Yanow*

Sackville

John Norris and Bill Smith (the publisher and editor of *Coda*) founded Sackville in 1968 and have run it ever since. Sackville reflects the tastes of its founders in that there is both mainstream and the avant-garde to be found in its diverse catalog. Among its 100 or so releases (most of which have now been reissued on CD) are recordings by Teddy Wilson, Ralph Sutton, Jay McShann, Buck Clayton, Ben Webster, Doc Cheatham, Herb Hall, Leo Smith, Don Pullen, Ruby Braff, Archie Shepp, Joe McPhee, Abdullah Ibrahim, Bill Smith and many others. —*Scott Yanow*

Saturn

Saturn was the eccentric bandleader Sun Ra's main label from the mid-'50s until his death in 1993. Ra's releases were generally quite haphazard with incorrect dates and personnel often given and sometimes two unrelated sessions (recorded years apart) on the same LP. These cheaply made but sometimes historic releases were often offered for sale at Sun Ra concerts. Shortly before Ra's death, Jerry Gordon of Evidence negotiated successfully for the rights to reissue the music (in coherent fashion with correct information) on his CD label. Fifteen sets have thus far come out but there are dozens of additional sessions that have been only released as Saturn albums. —*Scott Yanow*

Savoy

Founded in 1942 by Herman Lubinsky, the Savoy label was one of the most significant of the many independent record companies to emerge during World War II. Producer Teddy Reig helped make Savoy one of the powerhouses of bop with historic sessions from Charlie Parker, J.J. Johnson, Dexter Gordon, Fats Navarro, Miles Davis, Erroll Garner and others during the 1945-49 period. In addition, many late-period swing records were made with the top Black veterans of the period but it was actually the rhythm & blues records that were the biggest sellers. Savoy also acquired quite a few small labels (including Regent, National, Discovery and Jewell). Although R&B kept Savoy in business during the 1950s, there were many modern jazz sessions held by Savoy during the decade (often directed by Ozzie Cadena) including dates featuring Cannonball Adderley, Yusef Lateef, Lee Morgan, Hank Mobley and Wilbur Harden (featuring John Coltrane). The 1960s found Savoy becoming primarily a major gospel label although there were some free jazz and avant-garde sessions held including sets led by Sun Ra, Bill Dixon, Archie Shepp, Marzette Watts, Paul Bley and Bill Barron. After Lubinsky died in 1974, the catalog was purchased by Arista who did a superb job of reissuing the music on single and double-LPs. In 1985 Muse acquired Savoy and largely finished the job. A few years later the Japanese label Denon took Savoy over but largely missed the point, reissuing so-called reproduction sets on CD that had the short playing time and the scanty (and sometimes inaccurate) information of Savoy's original LPs of the 1950s! —*Scott Yanow*

Schoolkids

Steve Bergman, who runs a large music store in Ann Arbor, Michigan, started the Schoolkids label in 1992, debuting with a record by boogie-woogie pianist Mr. B. Since then Schoolkids has had more than 50 releases, some of which have been jazz, including dates by singer Kathy Kosins, music from the early-'70s Ann Arbor Blues Festival and guitarists Steve Ferguson and George Bedard. —*Scott Yanow*

Sea Breeze

Since the late '70s, the Los Angeles-based Sea Breeze label has done an expert job of releasing modern mainstream jazz with an emphasis on big bands (including many college and high-school orchestras). Among the professionals who have recorded for the label have been Herbie Harper, Phil Woods, Bill Perkins, Nick Brignola, Al Haig, Frank Strazzeri, Walter Bishop, Jr., Roger Neumann, Rob McConnell's Boss Brass, Tom Talbert, Matt Catingub and Frank Mantooth. —*Scott Yanow*

Signal

Founded in 1955 by Jules Colomby, Harold Goldberg and Don Schlitten, Signal was unusual in its *Jazz Laboratory* series, on which one side of the LP would feature a quartet with a saxophone, while the other side had the exact same performance but without the horn (essentially a *Music Minus One* record). Phil Woods and Gigi Gryce sets were originally issued in this fashion. More conventional were sessions by Duke Jordan, Cecil Payne and a sextet caught live at a Charlie Parker tribute concert. Savoy ended up acquiring the bulk of this catalog by the late '50s and most of the Signal sets have been reissued several times through the years. —*Scott Yanow*

Signature

Signature, producer Bob Thiele's first label, was active during 1939-48 and among its very valuable sets were dates by Coleman Hawkins (the famous "The Man I Love" session with Eddie Heywood), Lester Young (with the Kansas City Six), Ben Webster, Johnny Hodges, Erroll Garner, Anita O'Day, Flip Phillips and Eddie "Lockjaw" Davis, among others. Somehow Thiele was able to reissue most of these sessions quite a few times through the years on his future labels Flying Dutchman, Dr. Jazz and Red Baron. —*Scott Yanow*

Silkheart

An avant-garde and free jazz subsidiary of Storyville, Silkheart has many stimulating sessions in its catalog including dates by Dennis Gonzales, Steve Lacy, Ahmed Abdullah, Charles Brackeen, David Ware, Charles Gayle, Rob Brown, Roscoe Mitchell and Hal Russell. —*Scott Yanow*

Silva Screen

In 1991 Yusuf Gandhi joined the London-based Silva Screen label, a record company that originally mostly specialized in movie soundtracks. In 1993 Gandhi started heading a jazz subsidiary called Hip Bop. Releases have included dates by Michael Urbaniak, Lenny White and Tom Browne, along with acoustic projects under the "Hip-Bop Essence" banner such as a Freddie Hubbard tribute, a Latin-jazz project, an organ summit, a 1960s Blue Note-type funk project and a showcase for Kenny Barron. —*Scott Yanow*

Sonet

Founded in 1956 by Sven Lindholm and Gunnar Bergstrom, Sonet was soon one of the top Danish jazz labels, eventually acquiring Storyville and Gazell. While Storyville has recorded much Dixieland, Sonet tends to focus on more bop-oriented (and generally American) players. Its catalog includes such top musicians as Al Cohn & Zoot Sims, Lee Konitz, Sonny Stitt, Red Rodney, Art Farmer, Buddy DeFranco, Joe Venuti, the New York Jazz Quartet, Bob Brookmeyer and Svend Asmussen. —*Scott Yanow*

Songlines

Formed in 1992 by Tony Reif, the Vancouver-based Canadian label Songlines has documented several avant-garde jazz sets including fine efforts from Francois Houle, Ellery Eskelin, Andy Laster, Ben Monder, Patrick Zimmerli and Paul Plimley. —*Scott Yanow*

Soul Note

In 1975 Giovanni Bonandrini founded the Black Saint label. Four years later he organized Soul Note as a slightly more conservative companion label that would focus on hard bop (as opposed to avant-garde) jazz performers. There has been a lot of overlap musically between the two pacesetting companies through the years and they are often thought of as one entry. Among the literally hundreds of artists who are represented in the Soul Note catalog (most of which has now been reissued on CD) are Billy Harper, George Russell, Ran Blake, Kim Parker, Steve Lacy, Kenny Drew, Paul Bley, Archie Shepp, Andrew Hill, Mal Waldron, Art Farmer, Cecil Taylor, Max Roach, Art Blakey, Joe Lovano, Arnett Cobb, Gil Evans, Lee Konitz, Chico Hamilton and Tim Berne. —*Scott Yanow*

Southport

Founded in 1980 by pianist Bradley Parker-Sparrow who was joined by singer Joanie Pallatto the following year, Southport has become one of the top jazz labels documenting music by Chicago artists. Its catalog includes albums not only by the co-owners but tenorman Von Freeman, pianist Don Bennett, trumpeter Bobby Lewis, pianist Corky McClerkin, singer April Aloisio, guitarist George Freeman, pianist Dave Gordon, flutist Michael Mason, vocalist Linda Tate and others. —*Scott Yanow*

Spotlite

Founded in 1968 by Tony Williams (obviously no relation to the drummer), this British company has done a splendid job of documenting both old and new bop. Spotlite is best-known for reissuing virtually the entire Dial catalog (including a great deal of Charlie Parker material) and broadcasts from the bop era, but from 1973 on, Spotlite has also made many new recordings of its own. In addition to such Americans as Al Haig, Red Rodney, Ben Webster, Pepper Adams and Joe Albany, Spotlite has recorded such top English players as Don Rendell, Kathy Stobart, John Stevens, Pete King, Brian Dee, Harry Beckett and Tubby Hayes. —*Scott Yanow*

Starline Productions

A successor to the Giants of Jazz label, the Los Angeles-based Starline (which is run by veteran Wayne Knight) has recorded a few excellent sets by pianist Page Cavanaugh and made available little-known sessions by guitarist Al Viola and pianist/composer Bobby Troup, among others. —*Scott Yanow*

Stash

Stash began in the 1970s with a bit of a gimmick. Its first dozen or so releases were collections filled with 1930s-era recordings that dealt with drugs and/or sex. After inevitably exhausting that topic, Stash (under the direction of Bernard Brightman) expanded to record new music (generally mainstream or bop-oriented) in addition to reissuing other vintage material. Stash has now been a fairly major jazz label for 20 years and its catalog includes releases by such players as Steve Turre, John Pizzarelli, Chris Connor, Buck Clayton's big band, Sal Salvador, Hilton Ruiz, Fats Waller, Eddie Condon, quite a few Charlie Parker sets (including his Dial recordings), Raymond Scott, the String Trio of New York, George Russell, Al Jolson, Randy Sandke and many others. In addition, Stash's subsidiary Jass contains many reissues. —*Scott Yanow*

Steeple Chase

Established by Nils Winther in 1972, this Copenhagen-based label has had hundreds of hard bop-oriented releases since that time. Although Danish players are represented, the majority of the valuable catalog features top American jazzmen. Dexter Gordon recorded some of his finest work for Steeple Chase and there are also many radio broadcasts of him playing overseas. Among the other stars of the label are Bud Powell, Jackie McLean, Clifford Jordan, Stan Getz, Chet Baker, Paul Bley, Eddie "Lockjaw" Davis, Kenny Drew, Johnny Dyani, Buck Hill, Shirley Horn, Clifford Jordan, Duke Jordan, Lee Konitz, Tete Montoliu, Horace Parlan, Doug Raney and Archie Shepp. —*Scott Yanow*

Stomp Off

In 1980 Bob Erdos founded Stomp Off, a trad jazz label that has had a major influence in the prebop jazz world. Because he has recorded literally hundreds of jazz groups (many of whom were little-known) and emphasized lesser-known songs in the classic jazz idiom, Erdos has drawn attention to the surprisingly strong artistic health of trad jazz both in the US and in Europe. Whether it be free-wheeling combos, big bands based in 1920s styles, solo pianists (both ragtime and stride) or ragtime orchestras, Stomp Off has done a superb job of documenting the "modern" traditional jazz scene through an enormous amount of high-quality releases. —*Scott Yanow*

Storyville

Founded in 1950 by Karl Emil Knudsen in the early '50s, Storyville (which was acquired by Sonet later in the decade) has been a major European jazz label for decades. Its emphasis has generally been prebop (including Dixieland and mainstream) although Storyville has also documented some more modern musicians. Among the players represented in its catalog are Benny Carter, Eddie "Lockjaw" Davis, Wild Bill Davison, Vic Dickenson, Duke Ellington, Stuff Smith, Jesper Thilo, Ben Webster, Teddy Wilson, Miles Davis, Niels Lan Doky, Stan Getz, Lee Konitz/Warne Marsh, Art Pepper, Louis Armstrong, Papa Bue Jensen and Chris Barber. In addition, Storyville has reissued the Mezz Mezzrow King Jazz records, has a blues series, handles the Collector's Classics reissues, come out with music from the *Dr. Jazz* radio programs of 1951-52 and compiled a *Masters of Jazz* series. —*Scott Yanow*

Strata-East

Strata-East was a nice try. Co-founded by trumpeter Charles Tolliver and pianist Stanley Cowell, Strata-East was one of the few labels of the era run by Black musicians, but it never really took off financially and by the end of the 1970s was essentially out of business. Tolliver's own recordings and the debut record by the Heath Brothers were the label's most notable releases (there were also dates by Cecil Payne, Charles Brackeen, Pharoah Sanders and the Piano Choir), but despite attempts at a revival in the late '80s, Strata-East's output largely remains out of print. —*Scott Yanow*

Sunbeam

Started in the 1970s, Sunbeam was a collector's label seemingly dedicated to reissuing as many broadcasts and rare recordings by Benny Goodman as possible. Over half of its catalog featured Goodman (often broadcasting during his prime years) although there were also other releases from swing-era bands and singers. Little has been heard from this interesting label since the replacement of LPs with CDs. —*Scott Yanow*

Sunnyside

Founded by Francois Zalacain and Christine Berthe in 1982, Sunnyside has been one of the more consistently satisfying small modern jazz labels around. Among its releases have been dates by Meredith d'Ambrosio, Harold Danko, Kirk Lightsey, Lee Konitz, James Williams, Billy Pierce, Geoff Keezer and Bob Belden. —*Scott Yanow*

Swaggie

Australia's top traditional jazz label, Swaggie was founded by pianist/bandleader Graeme Bell in 1949 and is managed by Nevill Sherburn. Swaggie has not only documented the strong Australia's Dixieland scene (with many releases by Bell and his associates) but Americans such as Earl Hines and Armand Hug. In addition, Swaggie's subsidiary Vintage Jazz Archives has reissued classic jazz performances dating from the 1920s through the '40s. —*Scott Yanow*

Telarc

Telarc earned its original reputation as a classical label. After a few false starts (including a 1979 Mel Lewis record) in 1989 Telarc officially launched its jazz division with an Andre Previn trio set. Since then the company has become a "label of champions" since it features so many veterans including George Shearing, Oscar Peterson, Dave Brubeck, Stephane Grappelli, Dizzy Gillespie (his last recordings), the Count Basie Orchestra, James Moody, Jon Hendricks, Jeannie Bryson (an exception to the veteran-dominated roster) and Lionel Hampton. *—Scott Yanow*

Timeless

Founded in 1975 by Wim Wigt, Timeless (which is based in the Netherlands) has stuck to its original vision in documenting primarily modern and swinging hard bop. Among the more significant artists heard in its 500 releases have been the Timeless All-Stars, the George Adams/Don Pullen Quartet, Art Blakey's Jazz Messengers, Cedar Walton, Tommy Flanagan, Pharoah Sanders, Chet Baker, Gary Bartz, Joanne Brackeen, Lionel Hampton, Curtis Fuller, Woody Shaw and Benny Golson plus many top European players. In addition, Timeless has a separate series for Dixieland-oriented groups such as Chris Barber. *—Scott Yanow*

United Artists

Established in 1958 as a subsidiary for United Artists Films, this record label for a decade recorded some worthwhile jazz including the only John Coltrane/Cecil Taylor collaboration, Duke Ellington's *Money Jungle*, and sessions by Count Basie, Art Blakey, Billie Holiday (live concerts), Art Farmer, Thad Jones, Gerry Mulligan, Ruby Braff, the MJQ, Kenny Dorham, Billy Strayhorn, Zoot Sims and others. In 1966 United Artists started a subsidiary, Solid State, that is best-known for Duke Ellington's *70th Birthday Concert* and a series by the Thad Jones/Mel Lewis Orchestra. For a period in the 1970s United Artists (as part of EMI) had a Blue Note reissue series but by then United Artists was no longer recording much new jazz. It has since become inactive although some of its sessions have been reissued on CD, usually under the Blue Note name. *—Scott Yanow*

Unity

Prior to 1960, very few Canadian jazz artists who chose to stay in their native country were documented on records. The Unity label, which has been active since the 1980s, has done a fine job of covering the current Canadian jazz scene. Among its over 50 releases are dates led by Mike Murley, Bernie Senensky, Alex Dean, Hugh Fraser, Brian Dickinson, P.J. Perry and the group Chelsea Bridge. *—Scott Yanow*

Uptown

Active since the mid-'80s, the small bop-oriented Uptown label has released historic recordings from Chet Baker, Charlie Parker, Serge Chaloff and Sonny Clark plus newer dates by Tommy Flanagan, Freddie Redd, Pepper Adams, Jimmy Gourley and Don Sickler among others. *—Scott Yanow*

VSOP

In the early '80s Peter Jacobson established the VSOP label and started reissuing obscure cool jazz and bop sessions from defunct companies (including Mode, Tampa, Andex, Interlude, Omega, Rave, Skylark and Ava); the music generally dates from the 1955-62 period. The valuable straightahead releases, which feature such players as Don Fagerquist, J.R. Monterose, Pepper Adams, Warne Marsh, Bob Enevoldsen, Frank Rosolino, Richie Kamuca, Oscar Moore, Bill Holman, Marty Paich, Art Pepper, Red Norvo, Conte Candoli, Pete Jolly and Clora Bryant, among others, has been augmented by some new sessions recorded by Jacobson. Of the latter, the releases by the Metropolitan Bopera House, Danny D'Imperio's Sextet, singer Stephanie Nakasian, Lanny Morgan, Herb Geller, Gabe Baltazar, George Wallington and the Bob Cooper-Conte Candoli Quintet are particularly noteworthy. *—Scott Yanow*

Vanguard

Founded in 1950 by Maynard and Seymour Solomon, Vanguard was initially a classical music label. However, during 1953-57 John Hammond produced a series of fine mainstream sessions featuring the likes of Vic Dickenson, Ruby Braff, Buck Clayton, Jo Jones, Mel Powell, Sir Charles Thompson and Mel Powell. In the late '60s Vanguard released several Larry Coryell records and in the 1970s it became the first label to record Oregon. Acquired by the Welk Music Group in 1986, much of Vanguard's catalog (which also contains blues, folk and ragtime) has been reissued on CD. *—Scott Yanow*

Vee-Jay

Founded in 1952 as a gospel label by Vivian and James Bracken and Calvin Carter, Vee-Jay also recorded R&B, blues and jazz during its relatively brief existence. Among its more important jazz albums were sets by Eddie Harris (his "Exodus" was a hit), Gene Ammons, Booker Little, Wynton Kelly, Lee Morgan, Wayne Shorter, Frank Strozier, Bill Henderson, Ira Sullivan, and Louis Hayes. The label ceased operations by the late '60s and some of its jazz dates have been reissued several times since then. In the early '90s an extensive CD reissue series brought back most of the better sessions and added unissued tracks when they could be found; in fact a full set of Frank Strozier performances from the early '60s was released for the first time in the 1990s. *—Scott Yanow*

Verve

Producer Norman Granz began recording in 1944 with his first Jazz at the Philharmonic concert. Granz's first labels were Norgran and Clef (his "Exodus") and then in 1956 he consolidated all of his holdings under the name of Verve. A great fan of all-star jam-session type performances, Granz had recorded many of the top veteran players during the 1950s and their releases became part of the Verve legacy; these include dates by Dizzy Gillespie, Roy Eldridge, Count Basie, Charlie Parker, Flip Phillips, Ben Webster, Lester Young, Coleman Hawkins, Benny Carter, Buddy Rich, Louie Bellson, Art Tatum, Louis Armstrong and especially Ella Fitzgerald and Oscar Peterson, among many others. In 1960 Granz sold Verve to MGM, but under Creed Taylor's direction during 1961-67, the label continued recording important jazz dates, particularly those led by Stan Getz (all of his bossa-nova hits), Jimmy Smith and Wes Montgomery. However, soon after Polydor bought Verve, the label stopped recording new music. There were several reissue programs (of various quality) through the years and now under the Polygram banner, many of the finest Verve dates are once again available. Also, Polygram revived Verve as an active label in the late '80s and it has been recording many new jazz sessions ever since, including important sets by Joe Henderson, Shirley Horn, Betty Carter, Abbey Lincoln, Nicholas Payton, Ahmad Jamal and others. *—Scott Yanow*

Victo

The Canadian Victo label, in conjunction with the Victoriaville Music Festival, has recorded some of the most adventurous jazz-based performers of the past few years. Its 40 releases (recommended to the open-eared) include several sets by Anthony Braxton (including duets with Derek Bailey), Fred Frith, Marilyn Crispell, Barre Phillips, Roscoe Mitchell, Zeena Parkins, Diedre Murray/Fred Hopkins, Paul Plimley, Charles Gayle, Rene Lussier & NOW Orchestra and the Far East Side Band. *—Scott Yanow*

Vocalion

One of the major labels of the 78 era, Vocalion began issuing records in 1916 including some selections by the Original Dixieland Jazz Band the following year. During the latter half of the 1920s, Vocalion documented performances by King Oliver, Duke Ellington and Jimmie Noone, among others. Vocalion, originally a division of Aeolian before being sold to Brunswick (1924), Warner Bros. (1930) and Consolidated Film Industries (1931), had its up and downs through the years but was active during the first half of the swing era with records by Billie Holiday and the small groups of Duke Ellington. CBS purchased Vocalion in 1938 and two years later the Vocalion name was no longer being used for new records although it has popped up in European reissue series on an infrequent basis ever since. Vocalion remains a legendary name to '78' collectors. *—Scott Yanow*

Vogue

Vogue was formed in France in 1948 with Charles Delaunay as an important force. During the next 14 years the label recorded many American jazzmen who were spending time overseas including Sidney Bechet, Clifford Brown, James Moody, Art Farmer, Dizzy Gillespie, Don Byas, Thelonious Monk, Gerry Mulligan and Buck Clayton, among others. Owned by British Decca from 1951, Vogue stopped recording new music in 1962 although its sessions have been reissued several times, most notably in the 1970s as a *Jazz Legacy* series by Inner City and in the 1990s by RCA. *—Scott Yanow*

Warner Bros.

A major label since the late '50s, Warner Bros. had only a peripheral association with jazz prior to the 1990s. In the late '50s Chico Hamilton's popular quintet recorded for WB as did Matty Matlock and some Dixieland groups, but little of importance was recorded in the jazz field by Warner Bros. in the 1960s or '70s (other than Bill Evans and just a few other projects such as a collaboration by

Warne Marsh and Pete Christlieb) while the '80s mostly found WB recording commercial acts such as George Benson, Al Jarreau, Earl Klugh and David Sanborn. However, in recent times Warner Bros. has done a great deal to help its reputation. Joshua Redman was signed to the label and somehow lived up to the tremendous hype he was given. Miles Davis was recorded at the Montreux Jazz Festival playing Gil Evans charts during what would be his farewell tour, and such talents as Wallace Roney, Kenny Garrett and Larry Goldings along with Fourplay, Kevin Mahogany, the Yellowjackets and Joe Sample were recorded and properly promoted. —*Scott Yanow*

Windham Hill

In the late '70s Windham Hill became a powerhouse as the nation's premiere new age label. For a time new age was being inaccurately grouped with jazz since it is instrumental music, however, its lack of mood variation and absence of blues elements mark it as a different idiom than jazz. There have been a few attempts through the years by the company to record jazz that does not fit into Windham Hill's format. Steel drummer Andy Narell ran the Hip Pocket label which for a time operated as a subsidiary of Windham Hill. There was Steve Backer's Magenta, an adventurous but short-lived jazz label that released two Anthony Braxton releases, among other sets. And on an occasional basis Windham Hall Jazz has recorded music of interest to jazz listeners. —*Scott Yanow*

Word of Mouth

This Canadian label (formed in the mid-'90s) features adventurous jazz vocalists. Among its releases thus far are sets by Jeanne Lee, Garbo's Hat and a sampler that includes Sheila Jordan and Jay Clayton. —*Scott Yanow*

World Jazz

In 1971 Barker Hickox, who was booking the World's Greatest Jazz Band, started the World Jazz label. The majority of the company's releases were by the WGJB (more than ten sets), but there were also LPs from Soprano Summit, Dick Hyman with the Perfect Jazz Quintet, a Jim Cullum Christmas jazz record, Peanuts Hucko, Lou Stein, George Masso, Bill Allred, Banu Gibson and the Phoenix Symphony Ragtime Ensemble. None of the releases have yet been reissued on CD. —*Scott Yanow*

Xanadu

Founded in 1975 by Don Schlitten, Xanadu became one of the top bebop labels of the 1970s and '80s, releasing over 200 albums. Xanadu recorded new dates by the likes of Al Cohn, Dexter Gordon, Sonny Criss, Barry Harris, Jimmy Raney, Sam Noto, Ronnie Cuber, Charles McPherson, Sam Most and others, while also reissuing obscure bop sessions, mostly from the 1945-65 period, including six LPs in its *Bebop Revisited* series. Unfortunately, Xanadu has been largely inactive since the rise of the CD in the mid- to late '80s. Some of its releases have reappeared on CD but no new music has been recorded in nearly a decade. —*Scott Yanow*

Yazoo

Since the 1970s, Yazoo has been one of the top blues reissue labels, coming up with dozens of LPs (some of which have reappeared on CD) of vintage prewar blues. In addition, Yazoo (founded by Nick Perls and now owned by Shenachie Entertainment) has had occasional releases of early jazz. In the latter category are *Kings of Ragtime Banjo* (featuring Vess Ossman and Fred Van Eps), separate sets by Ukulele Ike and Harry Reser, *Pioneers of the Jazz Guitar, Fun on the Frets* and albums headed by Eddie Lang and Joe Venuti. In addition, Shanachie has come up with the definitive early jazz video *At the Jazz Band Ball.* —*Scott Yanow*

it's what's inside that matters.

When you subscribe to JAZZIZ, we make sure that every issue is special with our monthly limited-edition collector's CDs (JAZZIZ ON DISC), in-depth articles on jazz culture and trends, artist interviews, critical commentaries, CD reviews, guides to clubs, festivals, radio programs, and websites.

JAZZIZ has earned the most prestigious awards in art, photography, design, and editorial, creating a special magazine for people who deserve much more. Each issue comes with a limited-edition collector's CD (JAZZIZ ON DISC) filled with new, classic, and exclusive music not available anywhere else!

Who has appeared on the JAZZIZ discs? Music legends like Ella Fitzgerald, Miles Davis, John Coltrane, David Sanborn, Pat Metheny, the Rippingtons, Ornette Coleman, Lee Ritenour, Herbie Hancock, Cassandra Wilson, and hundreds more! Don't miss an issue!

the world's most interesting jazz magazine.

Visit JAZZIZ Interactive on the World Wide Web at www.jazziz.com

diana krall, featured on the december 1997 cover, photographed exclusively for jazziz by tom legoff

  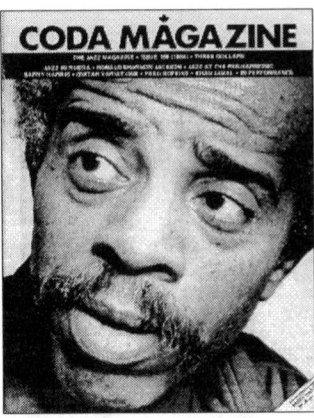